D1288383

THE
WOMAN'S
STUDY BIBLE

THIS BIBLE BELONGS TO:

....

....

DATE

THE
Ketubah Marriage Contract

NAME OF THE GROOM

NAME OF THE BRIDE

NAME OF THE GROOM'S FATHER

NAME OF THE BRIDE'S FATHER

LOCATION OF THE CEREMONY

CLOSEST BODY OF WATER

DATE OF THE WEDDING CEREMONY

THE FOCAL SCRIPTURE VERSE

THE WITNESSES

The *Ketubah* (Heb., lit. "her writing") is the Jewish marriage contract required from the groom and read aloud during the marriage ceremony. This one-sided contract was not an illusory obligation but a document prepared, according to the legal enactments of the Jewish sages, by the husband, detailing the responsibilities that he would have to his wife during their wedded life together (see Ex. 21:10; Lev. 18—21; Deut. 24:5). The rabbis extended the explicit Old Testament requirements of food, clothing, and conjugal rights to include the demand that a husband respect his wife and not make her cry. He must deny himself to provide for her needs. One groom wrote, "Be to me as wife according to the Law of Moses and Israel, and I will serve, honor, support, sustain, and clothe thee according to the customs of the Jewish husbands." The traditional order to these verbs expressing responsibility, beginning with "serve," indicates the spirit of the document. The wife has always had the happy responsibility of preserving this document!

Examples of the *Ketubah* have been found dating to the third century B.C. The use of the *Ketubah* began in an historical setting in which women were considered mere chattel in many societies, making the protection of the rights of a wife even more significant. For the Jewish community and for all the world, the *Ketubah* stands as a monumental example of the protection of the rights of women. God's plan for the woman in marriage is manifested beautifully in this one-sided document in which the groom makes his commitments to his bride. His signature, together with those who witness the docment, is required. The bride is not required to sign because she receives his commitment.

Marriage (Heb. *kiddushin*, lit. "sanctification") has always been greatly honored in the Jewish community. This holy ceremony sets apart one man and one woman from all others to accomplish the purposes for which they were created. In general terms, this could be understood as including companionship with one another, fellowship with the Creator, and continuation of generations (see Gen. 2, God's Plan for Marriage; The Creation of the Woman).

The *Ketubah* was designed primarily for women and often decorated in an aesthetically beautiful way. Jewish artists and scribes or calligraphers used their creativity and skill to create artistic masterpieces on high quality paper or parchment. The contract is still written in Aramaic, and popular artistic techniques include: micrography, the miniscule Hebrew writing painstakingly executed to shape interesting ornamental designs (usually with floral or geometric motif); paper cutting; figurative art depicting the bride and groom or biblical couples; and even signs of the zodiac conveying wishes for good luck. A suitable biblical quotation is often included. The documents are carefully preserved for their historical as well as artistic worth. Though required in the marriage ceremony, a commemorative *Ketubah* is also a favorite anniversary gift.

A *Ketubah* to commemorate your marriage may be prepared on the opposite page. It should contain the names of the bride and groom with the names of their fathers. For Jewish families, if either father is a Cohen or Levi, this should be indicated. The location of the wedding ceremony, including the city, state, and country and sometimes even the closest waterway (river, sea, lake) for a more exact location, is necessary. The date of the wedding ceremony is also important. In the Jewish tradition, the new day begins at sunset. If the wedding is on Friday night, Saturday's date would be used. The month and year are according to the Jewish sacred calendar (see chart, The Jewish Sacred Calendar).

The responsibilities of the bridegroom are carefully listed. The brideprice and the dowry, which is brought to the marriage and received by the bridegroom as a loan—to be repaid to the bride if the marriage is dissolved—are included (see 1 Kin. 9, Dowry). A customized *Ketubah* would include hobbies, professional occupations, family background, and personal interests. The document is then signed by the groom and witnesses who observed the solemn commitment ceremony.

Family History

Name

Birthday

Birthplace

Name

Birthday

Birthplace

Name

Birthday

Birthplace

Name

Birthday

Birthplace

MOTHER

Name

Birthday

Birthplace

FATHER

Name

Birthday

Birthplace

INTERESTING FAMILY HISTORY

MOTHER'S FAMILY

Her Mother

Grandmother   *Grandfather*

Her Father

Grandmother   *Grandfather*

Her Brothers

Her Sisters

INTERESTING FAMILY HISTORY

FATHER'S FAMILY

His Mother

Grandmother   *Grandfather*

His Father

Grandmother   *Grandfather*

His Brothers

His Sisters

INTERESTING FAMILY HISTORY

Special Family Memories

EVENT   DATE

EVENT   DATE

EVENT   DATE

EVENT   DATE

EVENT   DATE

EVENT   DATE

Special Family Memories

EVENT   DATE

EVENT   DATE

EVENT   DATE

EVENT   DATE

EVENT   DATE

EVENT   DATE

My Spiritual Mothers

Name

Godly Characteristic

Spiritual Gift

Special Verse

Name

Godly Characteristic

Spiritual Gift

Special Verse

Name

Godly Characteristic

Spiritual Gift

Special Verse

Name

Godly Characteristic

Spiritual Gift

Special Verse

Name

Godly Characteristic

Spiritual Gift

Special Verse

Name

Godly Characteristic

Spiritual Gift

Special Verse

The Woman's Study Bible

NEW KING JAMES VERSION

The Woman's Study Bible

NEW KING JAMES VERSION

EDITORIAL COMMITTEE

Dorothy Kelley Patterson
General Editor, First Edition

Rhonda Harrington Kelley
Managing Editor, First Edition

Jan Dargatz
Topical Notes; Contributing Editor, Second Edition

Helen Rhea Stumbo
History

Ann L. Bowman
Gospels, Acts

Jeanne Hendricks
Portraits

Constance N. Wieler
Poetry

Patty Comber
Pauline Epistles

Janice Meier
General Consultant

Paula Rinehart
Major Prophets

Mary Kassian
General Epistles, Revelation

Sharon Sterrenburg
Pentateuch

Karen H. Jobes
Minor Prophets

Carmen Leigh Howell
Index

THOMAS NELSON
Since 1798

NASHVILLE   DALLAS   MEXICO CITY   RIO DE JANEIRO

THE WOMAN'S STUDY BIBLE, SECOND EDITION

Copyright © 1995, 2006 by Thomas Nelson, Inc.

The Holy Bible, New King James Version

Copyright © 1982 by Thomas Nelson, Inc.

The text of the New King James Version® (NKJV®) may be quoted or reprinted without prior written permission with the following qualifications: (1) up to and including 1,000 verses may be quoted in printed form as long as the verses quoted amount to less than 50% of a complete book of the Bible and make up less than 50% of the total work in which they are quoted; (2) all NKJV quotations must conform accurately to the NKJV text.

Any use of the NKJV text must include a proper acknowledgement as follows:

> Scripture taken from the New King James Version®. Copyright © 1982 by Thomas Nelson, Inc. Used by permission. All rights reserved.

However, when quotations from the NKJV text are used in church bulletins, orders of service, Sunday school lessons, church newsletters, and similar works in the course of religious instruction or services at a place of worship or other religious assembly, the following notice may be used at the end of each quotation: NKJV.

For quotation requests not covered by the above guidelines, write to Thomas Nelson, Inc., Attention: Bible Rights and Permissions, P.O. Box 141000, Nashville, TN 37214-1000.

Bible map collection © 2008 by GeoNova.

*P*raise God for His Story as it is recorded in His Word. My sincere prayer is that this volume will become a tool to guide you in listening to the voice of God as He speaks through His Word.

The thrill of hearing Him speak today from this old Book, His Holy Word, has not left me. It has been life-changing. However, for many the Bible may be something of a closed door. Although its stories are all fairly familiar, there seems to be a great void of understanding exactly what these stories can mean for Christians living in the present day. Many people who read God's Word believe it; they just don't believe it works for them today. It does! You will find the factual information in introductory materials, annotations, topical notes, portraits, charts, and maps in *The Woman's Study Bible* to be helpful in showing you how it works.

Truth does not change (2 Tim. 3:16). While experts in science, technology, geology, and theology are constantly changing their findings and conclusions, God's Word has remained unchanged since it was written thousands of years ago. Various challenges may be made to the historical accounts found in the Bible, but you are going to be excited as you begin to read reasonable explanations for many of your questions. There will, of course, be some things, that is, the mysteries of God, for which there are no answers at this time, in this life. The challenge of these mysteries will lead you to worship a God whose ways are past finding out, whose thoughts are higher than our thoughts (Rom. 11:33; Is. 55:9).

Ask God to open your eyes that you might see Him in a fresh way and open your ears that you might hear His voice speaking to you as you read His Word, and let *The Woman's Study Bible* be your guide.

—*Anne Graham Lotz*

Foreword to the Second Edition

Dear Reader,

The Woman's Study Bible has blessed and touched countless women since it was first published over ten years ago, and we justly felt that a new, updated edition was long overdue. Our review of the features and study notes resulted in our keeping all of the same study helps, condensing a few articles and verse notes for a more effective and user-friendly layout. Next, we added an all-new set of articles called *Perspectives,* written by noted female authors, which touch on the importance of reading and studying God's word. Finally, we chose to give our Bible a beautiful new design—inside and out. Therefore, it is with great pleasure that we present to you *The Woman's Study Bible, Second Edition.* Our prayerful hope is that you will grow in a deeper knowledge and love for the Lord as He reveals Himself to you through these pages.

In Christ,
The Publishers

The Woman's Study Bible Contributors

FIRST EDITION

Aduke Akinola	Karen J. Hayter	Anne Ortlund
Myrna Alexander	Kristina Hemphill	Dorothy Kelley Patterson
Emilie Barnes	Jeanne Hendricks	Anabel Cantu Reimann
Shirley Cothran Barret	Kay Ho	Paula Rinehart
Susan Wise Bauer	Shari Lee Witt Hofstetter	Alice George Rogers
Judy Blue	Carmen Leigh Howell	Dale Evans Rogers
Mary Ellen Bork	June Hunt	Joyce Rogers
Ann L. Bowman	Susan Hunt	Kristi Sberna
Vonette Bright	Katherine Hyde	Edith Schaeffer
Jill Briscoe	Kay Coles James	Faye Short
Linda Buhler	Karen H. Jobes	Marsha A. Ellis Smith
Nancie Carmichael	Mary Kassian	Sharon Sneed
Annie Chapman	Rhonda Harrington Kelley	Gayle Somers
Grace Chavis	Grace Ketterman	Delores Steele
Debbie Church	Diane Knippers	Sharon Sterrenburg
Ann Coker	Beverly LaHaye	Helen Rhea Stumbo
Patty Comber	Tammi Ledbetter	Eleonore Stump
Dorian Coover Cox	Marilyn Lewis	Joni Eareckson Tada
Jan Dargatz	Eta Linnemann	Amanda Shao Tan
Melinda Delahoyde	Florence Littauer	Gigi Tchividjian
Beverly Demaurex	Karen Mains	Laverne Bell-Tolliver
Joy Griffin Dent	Hilary McFarlane	Noemi Vera
Linda Dillow	Linda McGinn	Diana Vermillion
Elisabeth Elliot	Janice Meier	Mary Whelchel
Denise George	Erika Moore	Constance N. Wieler
Sharon Gritz	Miriam Neff	Georgalyn Wilkinson
Margaret D. Hawley	Barbara O'Chester	Miltinnie Yih

SECOND EDITION

Emilie Barnes	Nancy Leigh DeMoss	Anne Graham Lotz
Dee Brestin	Linda Dillow	Stormie Omartian
Kimberly Daniels	Roberta Hromas	Kathy Troccoli

CONTENTS

THE OLD TESTAMENT

THE NEW TESTAMENT

The Woman's Study Bible is a unique tool for opening God's Word to women through a comprehensive study of Scripture prepared by women for women on subjects important to women. Recent history has awakened a growing awareness of and sensitivity to women and their concerns—their value in being made in the image of God, their innermost personal needs, and their challenging opportunities to serve the Lord. The Bible is one of the most important means by which a woman's identity and her place in society should be defined. The Creator presented His perfect plan, but Satan used his wiles through a woman to bring sin into the world. God countered this satanic attack by using a woman to give birth to the Savior who would provide redemption. A world distorted by the presence of sin and evil is full of suffering and pain, but God and His Holy Word are not responsible for creating the injustices and tragedies suffered by women or men.

Women in the ancient world did not have an easy or perfect life, but Israelite women were better off than their contemporaries. The Law of Israel was designed to protect women, their rights, and their freedom (Deut. 21:10–14; 22:13, 28). Israelite women did have certain rights as well as greater freedom, more varied pursuits, and better social status than the women from pagan nations. The vast majority of women primarily administered their households and cared for their husbands and children.

Jesus did not hesitate to teach women and to use them in parables and illustrations. Women were present at the Crucifixion (Luke 23:49); they prepared the Lord's body for burial (Luke 23:56); they were first at the tomb on Resurrection morning (Luke 24:1); they were the first to bear testimony to the Resurrection (Luke 24:9, 10); their faith and prayers were vital to the growth of the early church (Rom. 16:1). Everywhere Christianity has gone, the status of women has improved.

In 1895, Elizabeth Cady Stanton published *The Woman's Bible* with intent to achieve freedom from what she alleged to be the "oppression" of Scripture. She commented on passages of particular interest to women and removed verses she considered tainted with a male bias. She was motivated by an agenda based on her own experience and was grasping for a position that would place her *over* Scripture. This position helped lay the ideological foundation for a feministic theology that makes individual conscience and personal experience the ultimate basis for interpreting Scripture. A century later, the editorial committee of *The Woman's Study Bible* has chosen to line up *under* the authority of Scripture. We have followed an objective approach. We have sought to understand the message of the Bible, while committing ourselves to live out its principles in faith and practice. We are bound to the absolute veracity and uniqueness of God's Word. We do not need to twist or rewrite Scripture, to redefine its words, or to choose what we will accept as authoritative, which would exalt human reason. Rather we are committed to dig deep into Scripture in order to find a word from God about who we are and how we are to live.

More than eighty women from many different denominations, ethnic backgrounds, and occupations comprised the editorial team. Women have worked through every step of production—design and layout, typesetting, proofreading, marketing, and sales. Singles, wives, mothers, and grandmothers—all have combined their training and giftedness to expend the time, energy, and creativity to produce a timeless and Christ-honoring study tool uniquely designed to meet the needs of women whatever their situation in life—whether overwhelmed with family problems, frustrated from career injustices, burdened with the trials of everyday living, challenged with making life-changing decisions, or merely motivated to seek a word from God.

Before any research was begun or manuscript written, these guidelines were prayerfully adopted:

- *A distinctive exegesis* pulls out the meaning of the text instead of reading into the text personal whims.

- *Intuitive scholarship* combines the discernment of intuition with the disci-

pline of scholarship, bringing a new dimension to evangelical interpretation.

- *Nurturing sensitivity* brings new and exciting ways to encourage and inspire.
- *Mentoring friendships* undergird spiritual bonding, finding more common ground than polarity in a quest to understand and interpret Scripture.
- *Creative service* links mind and heart to present inspiration and guidance that is fresh and relevant.

The features of *The Woman's Study Bible* are skillfully woven together and easily accessed through an extensive referencing system. The *articles* provide thought-provoking scholarship, devotional meditation, and the practical development of faith.

Introductory material accompanies each book of the Bible with information about the author, date, setting, purpose, audience, literary characteristics, and themes. The outline will lead you through a study of the book in a systematic way. The *annotations* placed in sidebars are helpful in drawing out of the text necessary information to explain difficult passages, idiomatic phrases, or obscure words as well as in identifying places and people.

The *topical notes* on subjects of interest to women of all ages and in all stages of life have been prepared based upon principles found in Scripture, enabling and motivating you to make personal application of God's truth to your own problems.

More than one hundred *portraits* bring to life the women of the Bible, giving a brief glimpse of life in the ancient world, presenting their problems and how they solved them, showing both the good and the bad, sharing the results of doing something God's way in contrast to going your own way (Is. 53:6). We are awed by the faithfulness of many of these women to doing God's work, to obeying His Word, and to making significant contributions to the kingdom. Many of these Bible women will become your examples, your inspiration, your mentors, and your friends.

The twelve *Perspectives* articles shed light on the significance of the Bible and how to study God's word effectively. What's more, they are written by noted authors Emilie Barnes, Dee Brestin, Kimberly Daniels, Nancy Leigh DeMoss, Linda Dillow, Roberta Hromas, Anne Graham Lotz, Stormie Omartian, and Kathy Troccoli.

The *charts and maps* have been prepared for the unique focus of this volume. The travels of Ruth and Mary and the events in Christ's ministry are among the general subjects of maps that have been carefully designed to reflect the presence of women. Charts include the development of family trees and treatment of other subjects with special prominence given to women.

Inspirational quotations from women of many generations are found throughout, accompanied by planned space for preserving your own insights of application of the text to your own life. The most important part of studying God's Word is always a personal reading of the text of Scripture and a willingness to let its words speak to you and perhaps change your life.

Binding all these elements together is an index, an alphabetical *guide to the special features*—all the topical notes, portraits, charts, maps, and many of the subjects covered in annotations. In the extensive cross-referencing system, topical notes and portraits are noted by book and chapter at the point of reference; charts and maps can be easily located through the alphabetical guide. A brief *concordance* of important words in the Bible is also included.

This volume will provide rewarding study for the serious Bible student, while also offering a meaningful introduction to the study of God's Word for any woman who would come reverently to Scripture with an open heart. The inexhaustible Word of God will introduce you to the Father and His love; it will unveil and give understanding of His will; it will reveal His Law and principles for living; it will offer intellectual challenges for your mind, moral values for your will, and spiritual refreshment for your heart. For every woman who opens the Holy Word of God, *His/story* of redemption can become *her/story* of deliverance. Let *The Woman's Study Bible* become a catalyst for changing your life by helping you unlock God's Word, share His promises, and offer His challenges.

—Dorothy Kelley Patterson

A WORD FROM THE TRANSLATORS OF THE NEW KING JAMES VERSION

Purpose

In the preface to the 1611 edition of the Authorized Version, known popularly as the King James Bible, the translators state that it was not their purpose "to make a new translation . . . but to make a good one better." Indebted to the earlier work of William Tyndale and others, they saw their best contribution to consist in revising and enhancing the excellence of the English versions which had sprung from the Reformation of the sixteenth century. In harmony with the purpose of the King James scholars, the translators and editors of the present work have not pursued a goal of innovation. They have perceived the Holy Bible, New King James Version, as a continuation of the labors of the earlier translators, thus unlocking for today's readers the spiritual treasures found especially in the Authorized Version of the Holy Scriptures.

The King James translators were committed to producing an English Bible that would be a precise translation and by no means a paraphrase or a broadly approximate rendering. On the one hand, the scholars were almost as familiar with the original languages of the Bible as with their native English. On the other hand, their reverence for the divine Author and His Word assured a translation of Scripture in which only a principle of utmost accuracy could be accepted. Therefore, while seeking to unveil the excellent *form* of the traditional English Bible, special care has also been taken in the present edition to preserve the work of precision that is the legacy of the 1611 translators.

Complete Equivalence in Translation

Where new translation has been necessary in the New King James Version, the most complete representation of the original has been rendered by considering the history of usage and etymology of words in their contexts. This principle of *complete equivalence* seeks to preserve *all* of the information in the text, while presenting it in good literary form. *Dynamic equivalence*, a recent procedure in Bible translation, commonly results in paraphrasing where a more literal rendering is needed to reflect a specific and vital sense. For example, *complete equivalence* truly renders the original text in expressions such as "lifted her voice and wept" (Gen. 21:16) and "'Woman, what does your concern have to do with Me?'" (John 2:4). *Complete equivalence* translates fully, in order to provide an English text that is both accurate and readable.

In keeping with the principle of complete equivalence, it is the policy to translate interjections which are commonly omitted in modern language renderings of the Bible. As an example, the interjection *behold*, in the older King James editions, continues to have a place in English usage, especially in dramatically calling attention to a spectacular scene, or an event of profound importance such as the Immanuel prophecy of Isaiah 7:14. Consequently, *behold* is retained for these occasions in the present edition. However, the Hebrew and Greek originals for this word can be translated variously, depending on the circumstances in the passage. Therefore, in addition to *behold*, words such as *indeed, look, see*, and *surely* are also rendered to convey the appropriate sense suggested by the context in each case.

In faithfulness to God and to our readers, it was deemed appropriate that all participating scholars sign a statement affirming their belief in the verbal and plenary inspiration of Scripture, and in the inerrancy of the original autographs.

The Style

Students of the Bible applaud the timeless devotional character of our historic Bible. Yet it is also universally understood that the English language, like all living languages, has undergone profound change since 1611. Subsequent revisions of the King James Bible have sought to keep abreast of changes in English speech. The present work is a further step toward this objective. Where obsolescence and other reading difficulties exist, present-day vocabulary, punctuation, and grammar have been carefully

integrated. Words representing ancient objects, such as *chariot* and *phylactery*, have no modern substitutes and are therefore retained.

In the discipline of translating biblical and other ancient languages, a standard method of transliteration, that is, the English spelling of untranslated words, such as names of persons and places, has never been commonly adopted. In keeping with the design of the present work, the King James spelling of untranslated words is retained, although made uniform throughout. For example, instead of the spellings Isaiah and Elijah in the Old Testament, and Esaias and Elias in the New Testament, Isaiah and Elijah now appear in both Testaments.

King James doctrinal and theological terms, for example, *propitiation, justification,* and *sanctification,* are generally familiar to English-speaking peoples. Such terms have been retained except where the original language indicates need for a more precise translation.

Readers of the Authorized Version will immediately be struck by the absence of several pronouns: *thee, thou,* and *ye* are replaced by the simple *you,* while *your* and *yours* are substituted for *thy* and *thine* as applicable. *Thee, thou, thy,* and *thine* were once forms of address to express a special relationship to human as well as divine persons. These pronouns are no longer part of our language. However, reverence for God in the present work is preserved by capitalizing pronouns, including *You, Your,* and *Yours,* which refer to Him. Additionally, capitalization of these pronouns benefits the reader by clearly distinguishing divine and human persons referred to in a passage. Without such capitalization the distinction is often obscure, because the antecedent of a pronoun is not always clear in the English translation.

In addition to the pronoun usages of the seventeenth century, the *-eth* and *-est* verb endings are now obsolete. Contemporary English usage has been substituted for the previous verb endings.

The real character of the Authorized Version does not reside in its archaic pronouns or verbs or other grammatical forms of the seventeenth century, but rather in the care taken by its scholars to impart the letter and spirit of the original text in a majestic and reverent style.

The Format

The format of the New King James Version is designed to enhance the vividness and devotional quality of the Holy Scriptures:

- Subject headings assist the reader to identify topics and transitions in the biblical content.

- Words or phrases in *italics* indicate expressions in the original language which require clarification by additional English words, as also done throughout the history of the King James Bible.

- Oblique type in the New Testament indicates a quotation from the Old Testament.

- Verse numbers within a paragraph are easily distinguishable.

- Prose is divided into paragraphs to indicate the structure of thought.

- Poetry is structured as contemporary verse to reflect the poetic form and beauty of the passage in the original language.

- The covenant name of God was usually translated from the Hebrew as "Lord" or "God" (using capital letters as shown) in the King James Old Testament. This tradition is maintained. In the present edition the name is so capitalized whenever the covenant name is quoted in the New Testament from a passage in the Old Testament.

The Old Testament Text

The Hebrew Bible has come down to us through the scrupulous care of ancient scribes who copied the original text in successive generations. By the sixth century A.D. the scribes were succeeded by a group known as the Masoretes, who continued to preserve the sacred Scriptures for another five hundred years in a form known as the Masoretic Text. Babylonia, Palestine, and Tiberias were the main centers of Masoretic activity; but by the tenth century A.D. the Masoretes of Tiberias, led by the family of ben Asher, gained the

ascendancy. Through subsequent editions, the ben Asher text became in the twelfth century the only recognized form of the Hebrew Scriptures.

Daniel Bomberg printed the first Rabbinic Bible in 1516–17; that work was followed in 1524–25 by a second edition prepared by Jacob ben Chayyim and also published by Bomberg. The text of ben Chayyim was adopted in most subsequent Hebrew Bibles, including those used by the King James translators. The ben Chayyim text was also used for the first two editions of Rudolph Kittel's *Biblia Hebraica* of 1906 and 1912. In 1937 Paul Kahle published a third edition of *Biblia Hebraica*. This edition was based on the oldest dated manuscript of the ben Asher text, the Leningrad Manuscript B19a (A.D. 1008), which Kahle regarded as superior to that used by ben Chayyim.

For the New King James Version the text used was the 1967/1977 Stuttgart edition of the *Biblia Hebraica,* with frequent comparisons being made with the Bomberg edition of 1524–25. The Septuagint (Greek) Version of the Old Testament and the Latin Vulgate also were consulted. In addition to referring to a variety of ancient versions of the Hebrew Scriptures, the New King James Version draws on the resources of relevant manuscripts from the Dead Sea caves. In the few places where the Hebrew was so obscure that the 1611 King James was compelled to follow one of the versions, but where information is now available to resolve the problems, the New King James Version follows the Hebrew text. Significant variations are recorded in the textual footnotes.

The New Testament Text

There is more manuscript support for the New Testament than for any other body of ancient literature. Over five thousand Greek, eight thousand Latin, and many more manuscripts in other languages attest the integrity of the New Testament. There is only one basic New Testament used by Protestants, Roman Catholics, and Orthodox, by conservatives and liberals. Minor variations in hand copying have appeared through the centuries, before mechanical printing began about A.D. 1450.

Some variations exist in the spelling of Greek words, in word order, and in similar details. These ordinarily do not show up in translation and do not affect the sense of the text in any way.

Other manuscript differences such as omission or inclusion of a word or a clause, and two paragraphs in the gospels, should not overshadow the overwhelming degree of *agreement* which exists among the ancient records. Bible readers may be assured that the most important differences in English New Testaments of today are due, not to manuscript divergence, but to the way in which translators view the task of translation: How literally should the text be rendered? How does the translator view the matter of biblical inspiration? Does the translator adopt a paraphrase when a literal rendering would be quite clear and more to the point? The New King James Version follows the historic precedent of the Authorized Version in maintaining a literal approach to translation, except where the idiom of the original language cannot be translated directly into our tongue.

The King James New Testament was based on the traditional text of the Greek-speaking churches, first published in 1516, and later called the Textus Receptus or Received Text. Although based on the relatively few available manuscripts, these were representative of many more which existed at the time but only became known later. In the late nineteenth century, B. Wescott and F. Hort taught that this text had been officially edited by the fourth-century church, but a total lack of historical evidence for this event has forced a revision of the theory. It is now widely held that the Byzantine Text that largely supports the Textus Receptus has as much right as the Alexandrian or any other tradition to be weighed in determining the text of the New Testament. Those readings in the Textus Receptus which have weak support are indicated in the textual footnotes as being opposed by both Critical and Majority Texts.

Since the 1880s most contemporary translations of the New Testament have relied upon a relatively few manuscripts discovered chiefly in the late nineteenth and early twentieth centuries. Such translations depend primarily on two manuscripts, Codex Vaticanus and Codex Sinaiticus, because of their greater age. The Greek text obtained by using these sources and

the related papyri (our most ancient manuscripts) is known as the Alexandrian Text. However, some scholars have grounds for doubting the faithfulness of Vaticanus and Sinaiticus, since they often disagree with one another, and Sinaiticus exhibits excessive omission.

A third viewpoint of New Testament scholarship holds that the best text is based on the consensus of the majority of existing Greek manuscripts. This text is called the Majority Text. Most of these manuscripts are in substantial agreement. Even though many are late, and none is earlier than the fifth century, usually their readings are verified by papyri, ancient versions, quotations from the early church fathers, or a combination of these. The Majority Text is similar to the Textus Receptus, but it corrects those readings which have little or no support in the Greek manuscript tradition.

Today, scholars agree that the science of New Testament textual criticism is in a state of flux. Very few scholars still favor the Textus Receptus as such, and then often for its historical prestige as the text of Luther, Calvin, Tyndale, and the King James Version. For about a century most have followed a Critical Text (so called because it is edited according to specific principles of textual criticism) which depends heavily upon the Alexandrian type of text. More recently many have abandoned this Critical Text (which is quite similar to the one edited by Westcott and Hort) for one that is more eclectic. Finally, a small but growing number of scholars prefer the Majority Text, which is close to the traditional text except in the Revelation.

In light of these facts, and also because the New King James Version is the fifth revision of a historic document translated from specific Greek texts, the editors decided to retain the traditional text in the body of the New Testament and to indicate major Critical and Majority Text variant readings in the textual footnotes. Although these variations are duly indicated in the footnotes of the present edition, it is most important to emphasize that fully eighty-five percent of the New Testament text is the same in the Textus Receptus, the Alexandrian Text, and the Majority Text.

Textual Footnotes

Significant explanatory notes, alternate translations, and cross-references, as well as New Testament citations of Old Testament passages, are supplied in the textual footnotes.

Important textual variants in the Old Testament are identified in a standard form.

The textual notes in the present edition of the New Testament make no evaluation of readings, but do clearly indicate the manuscript sources of readings. They objectively present the facts without such tendentious remarks as "the best manuscripts omit" or "the most reliable manuscripts read." Such notes are value judgments that differ according to varying viewpoints on the text. By giving a clearly defined set of variants the New King James Version benefits readers of all textual persuasions.

Where significant variations occur in the New Testament Greek manuscripts, textual notes are classified as follows:

1. NU-Text

These variations from the traditional text generally represent the Alexandrian or Egyptian type of text described previously in "The New Testament Text." They are found in the Critical Text published in the twenty-sixth edition of the Nestlè-Aland Greek New Testament (N) and in the United Bible Societies' third edition (U), hence the acronym, "NU-Text."

2. M-Text

This symbol indicates points of variation in the Majority Text from the traditional text, as also previously discussed in "The New Testament Text." It should be noted that M stands for whatever reading is printed in the published Greek New Testament According to the Majority Text, whether supported by overwhelming, strong, or only a divided majority textual tradition.

The textual notes reflect the scholarship of the past 150 years and will assist the reader to observe the variations between the different manuscript traditions of the New Testament. Such information is generally not available in English translations of the New Testament.

Aram. Aramaic

Bomberg the 1524-35 edition of the Hebrew Old Testament, published by Daniel Bomberg (see article, The New King James Version)

ch., chs. chapter, chapters

DSS Dead Sea Scrolls

f, ff following verse, following verses

Gr., Gk. Greek

Heb. Hebrew

Kethib (Aram., lit. "written"). The written words of the Hebrew Old Testament preserved by the Masoretes.

Lat. Latin

lit. literally

LXX Septuagint—an ancient translation of the Old Testament into Greek

M-Text Majority Text (see article, The New King James Version)

MT-Text Masoretic Text—the traditional Hebrew Old Testament (see article, The New King James Version)

NU-Text The most promininent text of the Greek New Testament (see article, The New King James Version)

Qere (Aram., lit. "read"). Words read aloud that differ from the written words, in the Masoretic tradition of the Hebrew Old Testament (see *Kethib*)

Samaritan A variant Hebrew edition of the

Pentateuch books of Moses used by the Samaritan community

Targum An Aramaic paraphrase of the Old Testament

Textus "Received Text" (see article, The

Receptus New King James Version)

v., vv., verse, verses

Vulgate An ancient text of the Bible into Latin, translated and edited by Jerome

God Cares for Women
ETA LINNEMANN

In my pre-conversion life, I bitterly fought for women's equality in "spiritual office." The thorn of embitterment was ever driven into me anew by my so-called "brothers in ministry," especially by those who were my mental inferiors and possessed no other merit than the privilege of wearing trousers on the basis of their physical constitution. If my achievements had not been any better than theirs, I would not have made it even into the position in which I had to bear, of all things, the lifelong title of "lady curate" (assistant), while my male colleagues after one to two years exchanged the title of "curate" for that of "pastor."

At the general conventions, I was wounded with unkind regularity by such "brothers" in ministry in that at least one of them, or more likely an entire group, apprised me of the fact that the problem of women in ministry would indeed be solved if each of the women would marry a minister. That was the twofold wounding. Had I completed an entire course of theological study, including the two theological barrier examinations and even taken a doctor's degree, only to engage myself with children and kitchen as the wife of a minister? Even if I had wanted that—wouldn't I have only had the remotest possibility for it, now that a considerable portion of the men in my own age group had been killed during the Second World War on the battlefields of Europe?

My dear sisters, I felt that the fight for equal rights for women had been entrusted to me, along with the pain that these inequities caused. This *fight* was terminated with my preconversion life because now I am prepared to submit myself to God's Word—even to that which stands written therein concerning the woman. The *suffering,* however, was not yet ended thereby. It hurt just as badly when a "ministering brother" made it clear to the sisters, with arrogance and a pasha's behavior, that the assignment of all women was to work with their hands and to serve the brothers with their time and resources. Perhaps later the Lord would give women a prophetic office. That the "ministering brother" had made it up to cook in his former life, whereas the sister

had made it to a double doctorate in theology and a professorship was only marginally noted.

The reaction I faced was a rebellion, albeit resisted, against this God and a deep depression over my misfortune to have been created a woman. So it would have remained, had not God Himself taken up my case. I had begged Him to allow me to be done with this situation, which I could not resolve because I could find no acquiescence within myself to the role that He as Creator had assigned to me. Years later I grasped that this role was not simply identical with that which this "ministering brother" had ascribed to me. That God in the meantime had drastically interfered in the life of this brother should only be noted in passing, since it is not the most important thing.

God intervened. He healed me of my bitterness and the rebellion against being a woman. *Renewed by His grace,* I became a fulfilled woman—happy, contented, and full of thanksgiving. Perhaps this path is not reproducible for everyone. I am not at all saying that God has the same path in mind for others, but I do desire to share my testimony as a witness to His grace in my own life.

In my quiet time, I read Deuteronomy 21:10-14; through this often overlooked regulation concerning the treatment of women who had become spoils of war, God healed my heart. By means of these unlikely verses, His concern and love toward women became overpoweringly known to me.

Clearly, in my own heart, this regulation had been given in the midst of the raw reality of a fallen creation. The women of the vanquished became spoils to the victors. After a centuries-long Christian experience, indeed now this tragedy is no longer the usual thing, although even in this century, it became the gruesome experience of countless German women, who were delivered up defenseless to an incited, inflamed red beast called an "army."

Among all peoples it was self-evident that a woman who had become the spoils of war could come to be used at will as a slave of lust or labor. But God gave to His people totally differ-

ent regulations, which served to protect the human worth of such captive women.

> When you go out to war against your enemies, and the LORD your God delivers them into your hand, and you take them captive, and you see among the captives a beautiful woman, and desire her and would take her for your wife, then you shall bring her home to your house, and she shall shave her head and trim her nails. She shall put off the clothes of her captivity, remain in your house, and mourn her father and her mother a full month; after that you may go in to her and be her husband, and she shall be your wife. And it shall be, if you have no delight in her, then you shall set her free, but you certainly shall not sell her for money; you shall not treat her brutally, because you have humbled her.

> (Deut. 21:10–14)

What tenderness and sympathetic understanding call out from this admonition! The victor was not allowed to rush upon booty; he had to approach the prisoner of war with respect. He had to decide whether to retain her as worker or to take her as wife. Everything else was excluded. If he should take her as wife, he was henceforth not allowed to treat her as a prisoner. He must provide her with clothing because she was supposed to lay aside the clothing of her captivity. He was to allow her a full month of mourning, during which she was to be permitted to mourn and weep, according to proper decorum, for all of the relatives she lost in the war.

How God knows our feelings; how He respects them! With what love has He arranged the individual details that led to the restoration of the woman! She should be permitted to become whole again. She should have the opportunity to earn a positive attitude from her proprietor, who would perhaps then want to become her husband. The respect with which he had to treat this woman made marriage possible and even constituted the prerequisite for her success.

With what love and care had God personally taken precaution in the case of the failure of this marriage, which indeed stood beneath particular burdens because it took place across national and cultural lines! How He lovingly took up the woman Himself, guarded against her being reduced from the position of wife to that of bondslave, and also did not permit her to be treated as an object from which money could be earned at will. Her husband was allowed to put her away only by respecting her as a free person having full disposition over herself. Just as he himself was only allowed to approach her as a husband, with full respect for her personhood, so he was only allowed to dismiss her with full respect for her personhood.

How very much does God love women! How He respects us as persons of equal value to the man in that He has expended such care to decree these regulations concerning our protection! I can believe His disposition concerning me is that I should be a woman—together with what all that means according to God's Word—for my ultimate good. Once I began to accept His decree concerning me—to be a woman, then, little by little, I also have been made conscious of the good that He has thereby intended for me.

The Balanced Life: Reconciling Personal Faith with Practicing Dogma

HILARY McFARLANE

Dame Julian of Norwich said, "Prayer unites the soul to God." To know God is possible, and such knowledge is found through personal devotional life and spiritual practice. The private and personal dimension of spiritual life is important. It is woven throughout the Bible in the lives of different women of faith. Yet, at the same time, equally viable within Scripture is a very public dimension to the life of the believer and in the history of the church. The life of faith is not a purely subjective one; it is not allowed to follow its own private thoughts and opinions without restriction. Rather, the believer is instructed what she is to believe and how she is to live, sometimes very clearly and directly with little room for dissent and at other times more obliquely, with a wider horizon for personal input. The books of Leviticus or Deuteronomy or Paul's exhortations to the Christians living in Ephesus or Galatia identify the various rules and regulations given for living as the people of God. The Bible and subsequent Christian witness, then, make a clear distinction between private devotion and public testimony.

What is more problematic, however, is the way the two are combined. One can easily be dismissed in favor of the other, such as to insist that the personal is more important than the public, that private spirituality takes precedence over the teachings of the church, which may be defined as doctrine or dogma. Does God's revelation come first to the individual, then expand into wider dogma? Do words of doctrine or dogma only serve to express what we mean and make it possible for us to express what we already know and experience? This may well be true, but it is also true that without the boundaries of dogma and doctrine, we are prey to flights of fancy that, historically, have led groups of people into serious error. Without the guidelines of dogma, we are adrift on a sea of relativism and uncertainty. While each believer has a personal and unique testimony, each must be read against the backdrop of a whole history of testimonies that constitute what is believed.

Faith, then, clearly requires guidelines: Personal devotion and faith need public doctrine and dogma. If this is true, how do we reconcile dogma and doxology, faith and practice?

Perhaps this is best answered by first identifying what is meant by faith. Faith is identified as "the substance of things hoped for, the evidence of things not seen" (Heb. 11:1). This is clearly set within the context of *relationship,* the relationship between God and each individual who has dared to trust God despite what may be touched, seen, heard, or tasted—the criteria of materialism. For each of us, this assurance is based on things about which we have been told, that which has been handed to us (doctrine). This is not blind faith: It is intelligible and based on very specific content that we together can identify as our common belief.

Faith, then, can be identified as the actual relationship that exists between the believer and God and should be distinguished from three very specific issues that will be unpacked through the lives of women in the Bible:

1) **Legalism**—the relationship between faith and practice that rests on following rules and regulations;

2) **Propositionalism**—the belief that the content of faith is made up of statements that cannot change;

3) **Secularism**—what one believes must be correlated with the law of the land.

Legalism

One of the greatest dangers to faith is the temptation to believe that what can be seen is the real and that the unseen is less real. Paul makes the point that for the believer what cannot be seen is the most important, for *it* is what is *real* (2 Cor. 4:18). This sounds a bit strange until we realize that Paul is talking about the life of faith: Faith is the substance of things *unseen.* The life of faith is characterized by a constant and firm belief that something will happen. If we let go of this, then we begin to trust what we can see. When this occurs, we have taken a very small step toward legalism because we can *see* when people are

obeying rules and subscribing to regulations. In turn, we can also see when they are not! When this happens, we begin to judge such people by what can be *seen*. The dogmas of correct behavior cancel out the belief or faith that a person may change or that a person may *not* be as she appears.

One such example of the triumph of faith over dogma in this context can be seen in the way Jesus related to a Greek woman who had a demon-possessed daughter (Mark 7:24–30). Although according to Jewish laws Jesus did not need to relate to this woman, He chose to do so. He responded to someone who was unclean—a Greek, and a woman at that—but one who had a faithful heart. Here was someone who had faith even though Jewish dogma condemned her. She did not let the rules and regulations of the day stop her from receiving Jesus. She did not allow legalism to rob her of her desire to have her daughter healed.

Propositionalism

Those within religious circles have a tendency to want to control God. Dogmatic statements about the character of God and what He does offer little room for true faith in the unseen or the invisible. Belief in what is commonly held by the majority often is party to the tendency to legalism.

While it is very important to have *fundamentals,* that is, certain values and beliefs that remain constant, if these beliefs become rigid and fixed, then we often lose any meaningful space for faith. Once this space has disappeared, faith evaporates.

The triumph of faith over propositionalism is no clearer than in the story of Mary, the mother of Jesus Christ. In the example of Mary, we see a belief that God is higher than what is accepted as the norm. In Mary's case, God is higher than science.

A young woman, not yet married and thus with no sexual relationship with a man, is told that she will conceive and bear a son. Mary asks a natural question concerning the means by which this will happen, since she is not married. In addition, as an unwed woman, to become pregnant would have devastating social implications. However, she is told simply that, while humanly impossible, the birth of a child would not be impossible with God. The story of Mary has become so familiar that we can lose sight of the tremendous step of faith she took in saying, "Let it be to me according to your word" (Luke 1:38). In these words, we are confronted with the triumph of faith over propositions that would say God can only do one thing and not another. For Mary, faith was very much the substance of things unseen.

Secularism

Communicating the gospel in ways that are intelligible to the people around us is essential. Without such communication we would have nothing to say. What destroys the relationship between faith and dogma is that which radically alters what is believed to make it palatable to the surrounding culture. The "gospel of health and wealth" is a clear example of this. The Bible challenges this kind of approach again and again.

There is one example that resonates with tension and excitement as the story of faith over secularism unfolds. Rahab the prostitute refused to conform to the standards around her but took charge of her destiny in a remarkable way (Josh. 2:1–21). Perhaps a rather scheming woman and probably opportunistic enough to recognize her moment, Rahab tacitly acknowledged that the God of the Israelites was greater than her gods. She protected the Israelite spies, lying to her own people concerning the whereabouts of the spies in return for protection from the Israelites during their ensuing invasion.

What sets Rahab the prostitute apart is the fact that she, too, had faith in the unseen and marked her behavior accordingly, so much so that her story is recorded in Scripture, and she is commended for her faith. She did not demonstrate blind allegiance to the standards and norms of her society. Rather, she chose to believe what she had heard concerning the God of the Israelites. Turning her back on her own culture, Rahab found the true God. Despite her dubious profession, Rahab is marked as a woman who, in a rather circuitous way, stands as an outstanding example of one who opposed what was familiar and trusted in the unseen.

The intention of Scripture does not appear to reconcile absolutely faith and dogma. Rather, the two should be held in tension as the individual believer wrestles with the life of faith and appropriates the Word of God for herself.

See also notes on Access to God (Rom. 10); Priesthood of the Believer (1 Pet. 2)

The Old Testament

Genesis

Genesis (Heb. *Bere'shith,* lit. "in the beginning") is the first book of the Pentateuch or *Torah* (a designation for the first five books of the Old Testament). The title "Genesis" was first used in the Septuagint (a Greek translation of the Old Testament).

AUTHOR

Though Genesis has no explicit authorship statement, its inclusion in the Pentateuch suggests Mosaic authorship. Other books—Exodus, Numbers, and Deuteronomy—all assert Mosaic authorship (Ex. 17:14; 24:4–8; 34:27; Num. 33:1, 2; Deut. 31:9, 22). In the rest of the Old Testament, the Pentateuch is referred to collectively as "the Book of the Law of Moses" (Josh. 8:31; 2 Kin. 14:6; Neh. 13:1). The New Testament confirms this authorship (Matt. 19:8; Luke 24:27; John 5:45–47; Acts 3:22; Rom. 10:5; Rev. 15:3). The familiarity of the writer of Genesis with Egyptian geography (Gen. 45:10; 47:11) confirms that the author was well acquainted with Egyptian culture, as would have been Moses, who was reared in the household of Pharaoh. Some short sections of Genesis, such as the list of kings from the period of the Israelite monarchy, may have been added during the time of the divided kingdom (Gen. 36); in the same way, cities are often given the names they bore during the time of the monarchy rather than their patriarchal names. These scribal additions could well have been made in the process of copying manuscripts and do not affect the book's message other than to improve the clarity of Genesis for contemporary readers.

DATE

The book tells the story of mankind from creation to the death of Joseph. Dating the events which relate to the creation, the Flood, and the repopulation of the earth is impossible (Gen. 1—11), but the remainder of the book deals with the patriarchal age, which is roughly the same as the Middle Bronze Age (1950–1550 B.C.). The customs found in Genesis bear striking parallels to laws and customs recorded in other documents of the second millennium, most notably those found in tablets discovered at the Hurrian city of Nuzi in northeastern Mesopotamia.

The Pentateuch as a whole was written between the Exodus and the death of Moses (Deut. 34). The Exodus is variously dated, with 1445 B.C. as the earliest date. If this date is assumed, the death of Moses would fall around 1400 B.C. Genesis was thus produced sometime in the late fifteenth century B.C., several centuries after the patriarchs whose lives it describes.

BACKGROUND

SETTING: The setting is vast in scope since the book opens with the creation of the universe and closes with the small but growing number of the descendants of Jacob, now identified as Israel, who settled in the choice land of the Nile delta of Egypt. In between, the action focuses on the entire Fertile Crescent from the universal flood (which ended

on the mountains of Ararat) and the Tower of Babel (in the land of Shinar) to Abraham's journeys throughout Canaan.

PURPOSE: Genesis answers the question, "Who are we, and where did we come from?" God as the only Creator presented Himself to a people about to enter a land filled with false idols. God confirmed His selection and sovereign preservation of this nation facing hardships in a new land. Most importantly, Genesis reveals that Israel was set apart by God from the very beginning of creation. This knowledge provided a motivation for Israel to remain free from the idolatry and paganism surrounding the nation.

AUDIENCE: The Israelites were about to enter Canaan. Since the older generation (except Joshua and Caleb) had died in the desert, no others were left with a personal memory of God's miraculous deliverance from the Egyptians. The young nation entering the Promised Land would be faced with an immense temptation to assimilate the idolatry, intermarriage, and customs of the pagan nations around them. This same temptation faces God's people in every generation; Genesis reveals that God's plan for setting apart His people stretches back to creation.

LITERARY CHARACTERISTICS: Genesis is a carefully structured book; its literary structure reinforces its explicit message. The first section, the story of creation (Gen. 1:1—2:3), is set up in two segments of three days each. The creative works of the first and the fourth days are parallel, since during the first day God created light and darkness, while on the fourth day He created the sun and moon to govern the periods of light and darkness. On the second day, the firmament divided the waters; on the fifth day, the inhabitants of the sky and water were created. The third day dry land and vegetation appeared; the sixth day land-dwellers were created to consume the vegetation. The structure emphasizes God's plan and control over all aspects of creation.

After the introductory section, the book is divided by the recurrent phrase "These are the generations" (Heb. *toledoth*). Each occurrence of this phrase marks a new stage in God's development of a chosen people. The story of mankind is presented as a whole (Gen. 2:4—4:26). After the judgment of mankind, the phrase appears repeatedly as a reminder that God chooses one man from each family (for example, Seth, Noah, Shem, Abraham, Isaac, Jacob) to lead in preserving and carrying on the godly line. Also clear are the partnerships the patriarchs enjoyed with their wives—Abraham and Sarah, Isaac and Rebekah, and Jacob and Rachel were part of God's plan as well. The passing of God's covenant promises from one generation to the next is emphasized by the parallel structure of the stories themselves. Abraham, Isaac, and Jacob all traveled to Egypt; all three endured tests followed by covenant renewals. Sarah, Rebekah, and Rachel all suffered from barrenness, but each experienced God's grace in bearing children who would play a major role in the building of a nation.

THEMES

The primary theme of Genesis is God's formation of the nation and His providential protection of a special people for Himself. The methods God used to call out and shape this nation form the minor themes of the book.

God's Sovereignty—God appears first as sovereign Creator and Ruler; His power over history and the actions of His people reappears throughout the book in His preservation of His chosen ones.

God's Covenant—God uses the "covenant" (Heb. *berith*) continually to separate one man from the rest of mankind. The first covenant is made with Adam in the Garden of Eden (Gen. 2:16, 17; see chart, The Covenants of Genesis). After the Fall, God continues to make covenants with each subsequent generation, selecting one man from each family to continue godly seed for the next generation. Covenants are made with

Noah (Gen. 9:9), Abraham (Gen. 12:1–3), Isaac (Gen. 26:2–5), and Jacob (Gen. 28:13–15).

God's Redemption—The story of the formation of the chosen people is the story of redemption. The "seed of the woman," the godly line of those faithful to the Lord, will eventually crush the "seed of the serpent," the wicked who live in rebellion against God (Gen. 3:14, 15). This prophecy was ultimately fulfilled in the coming of Christ. Since Israel was God's chosen nation from whom the Messiah was to come, Israel's story reveals God's redemptive action in human history.

The Threat to God's Plan—The fourth theme of Genesis is the struggle of the serpent and his seed to destroy the chosen family. Sin, famine, war, and the threat of national assimilation into the surrounding Canaanite culture conspired to block the fulfillment of God's covenant promises. These threats are continually diverted by God's sovereign, preserving power.

OUTLINE

The History of Creation

1 In the beginning God created the heavens and the earth. ²The earth was without form, and void; and darkness *was*ᵃ on the face of the deep. And the Spirit of God was hovering over the face of the waters.

³Then God said, "Let there be light"; and there was light. ⁴And God saw the light, that *it was* good; and God divided the light from the darkness. ⁵God called the light Day, and the darkness He called Night. So the evening and the morning were the first day.

⁶Then God said, "Let there be a firmament in the midst of the waters, and let it divide the waters from the waters." ⁷Thus God made the firmament, and divided the waters which *were* under the firmament from the waters which *were* above the firmament; and it was so. ⁸And God called the firmament Heaven. So the evening and the morning were the second day.

⁹Then God said, "Let the waters under the heavens be gathered together into one place, and let the dry *land* appear"; and it was so. ¹⁰And God called the dry *land* Earth, and the gathering together of the waters He called Seas. And God saw that *it was* good.

¹¹Then God said, "Let the earth bring forth grass, the herb *that* yields seed, *and* the fruit tree *that* yields fruit according to its kind, whose seed *is* in itself, on the earth"; and it was so. ¹²And the earth brought forth grass, the herb *that* yields seed according to its kind, and the tree *that* yields fruit, whose seed *is* in itself according to its kind. And God saw that *it was* good. ¹³So the evening and the morning were the third day.

¹⁴Then God said, "Let there be lights in the firmament of the heavens to divide the day from the night; and let them be for signs and seasons, and for days and years; ¹⁵and let them be for lights in the firmament of the heavens to give light on the earth"; and it was so. ¹⁶Then God made two great lights: the greater light to rule the day, and the lesser light to rule the night. *He made* the stars also. ¹⁷God set them in the firmament of the heavens to give light on the earth, ¹⁸and to rule over the day and over the night, and to divide the light from the darkness. And God saw that *it was* good. ¹⁹So the evening and the morning were the fourth day.

²⁰Then God said, "Let the waters abound with an abundance of living creatures, and let birds fly above the earth across the face of the firmament of the heavens." ²¹So God created great sea creatures and every living thing that moves, with which the waters abounded, according to their kind, and every winged bird according to its kind. And God saw that *it was* good. ²²And God blessed them, saying, "Be fruitful and multiply, and fill the waters in the seas, and let birds multiply on the earth." ²³So the evening and the morning were the fifth day.

²⁴Then God said, "Let the earth bring forth the living creature according to its kind: cattle and creeping thing and beast of the earth, *each* according to its kind"; and it was so. ²⁵And God made the beast of the earth according to its kind, cattle according to its kind, and everything that creeps on the earth according to its kind. And God saw that *it was* good.

²⁶Then God said, "Let Us make man in Our im-

1:2 ᵃWords in italic type have been added for clarity. They are not found in the original Hebrew or Aramaic.

1:1 The first verse of Genesis reveals the book's vital underlying assumption: God is the ultimate Creator of everything. The verb "created" (Heb. *bara'*, lit. "to make from nothing," vv. 1, 21, 27; Gen. 2:4) is used almost exclusively of divine activity (see Is. 43:15). The other verbs used for God's creative activity are "made" (Heb. *'asah*, vv. 16, 25, 26; Gen. 2:18), "formed" (Heb. *yatsar*, Gen. 2:7, 19), and "made" (Heb. *banah*, lit. "built," Gen. 2:22). The first chapter of Genesis uses the Hebrew word *Elohim* for God, emphasizing God's character and power as the true and only God, the sole actor in creation. Though plural in form, the reference in number is to one and thus is used with a singular verb. This plural of majesty expresses honor and power.

1:2 This formlessness describes an earth wrecked by divine judgment (Is. 34:11; Jer. 4:23). Some have theorized that the creation of the heavens and earth described in verse 1 was destroyed in the judgment of Lucifer (see Is. 14; Ezek. 23). This "Gap Theory" assumes a stretch of time between verses 1 and 2; verse 2 then begins the story of the re-creation. More likely, Jeremiah and Ezekiel simply used the phrase as descriptive of utter desolation. According to this view, verse 1 describes God's first creative act, while verses 2–31 follow with a detailed description of His creative work with an interlude of unfinished business between verses 1 and 2. Here God is depicted as having a "Spirit" (Heb. *ruach*, lit. "wind" or "breath") who acts as His agent in creation, although the Spirit is not revealed as a separate member of the Trinity until the NT (see John 3:1–21; 14:16, 17, 26; 16:5–14; 20:22). "Hovering" implies "brooding" in the sense of a mother bird nurturing life.

1:5 The first day. The word "day" (Heb. *yom*) is somewhat ambiguous. It may refer to the 24-hour period of darkness and light (see Ex. 12:18) or simply to a specific period of time: for example, the "day of the LORD of hosts" is a time of judgment (Is. 2:12). "Day" is further defined as "evening and morning" (see Ps. 55:17).

1:11 The order of creation demanded that reproduction only occur within certain limits. Although it is impossible to determine the exact boundaries of "kind," divisions existed between types of vegetation (v. 12), types of sea creatures and birds (v. 21), and different species of earth animals (v. 25). Man is sharply separated from animals (v. 26).

1:26 The plurality used by God in reference to Himself does not detract from His unity (see v. 1, note). "Man" (Heb.

I could wish that all young persons might be exhorted to . . . read the great book of nature, wherein they may see the wisdom and power of the creator, in the order of the universe, and in the production and preservation of all things.

Anne Baynard, 1697

age, according to Our likeness; let them have dominion over the fish of the sea, over the birds of the air, and over the cattle, over all[a] the earth and over every creeping thing that creeps on the earth." 27So God created man in His *own* image; in the image of God He created him; male and female He created them. 28Then God blessed them, and God said to them, "Be fruitful and multiply; fill the earth and subdue it; have dominion over

the fish of the sea, over the birds of the air, and over every living thing that moves on the earth."

29And God said, "See, I have given you every herb *that* yields seed which *is* on the face of all the earth, and every tree whose fruit yields seed; to you it shall be for food. 30Also, to every beast of the earth, to every bird of the air, and to everything that creeps on the earth, in which *there is* life, *I have given* every green herb for food"; and it was so. 31Then God saw everything that He had made, and indeed *it was* very good. So the evening and the morning were the sixth day.

2Thus the heavens and the earth, and all the host of them, were finished. 2And on the seventh day God ended His work which He had done, and He rested on the seventh day from all His work which He had done. 3Then God blessed the seventh day and sanctified it, because in it He rested from all His work which God had created and made.

4This *is* the history[a] of the heavens and the earth when they were created, in the day that the LORD God made the earth and the heavens, 5before any plant of the field was in the earth and before any herb of the field had grown. For the LORD God had not caused it to rain on the earth, and *there was* no man to till the ground; 6but a mist went up from the earth and watered the whole face of the ground.

7And the LORD God formed man *of* the dust of the ground, and breathed into his nostrils the breath of life; and man became a living being.

THEOLOGICAL FOUNDATIONS FOR HEADSHIP

THEOLOGICAL TRUTH	REFERENCE
The priority of Adam's creation.	Gen. 2:7
The use of the name "Adam" for the entire race.	Gen. 2:20
The investiture of Adam with authority prior to Eve's creation.	Gen. 2:15
The assignment to the man of the responsibility for provision and protection.	Gen. 2:15–17
The responsibility of the man in naming the animals.	Gen. 2:20
The designation of the woman as the man's helper.	Gen. 2:18, 20
The naming of the woman by the man.	Gen. 2:23; 3:20
The recognition of the man as leader and spokesman.	Gen. 3:9, 11

1:26 [a]Syriac reads *all the wild animals of.*   **2:4** [a]Hebrew *toledoth,* literally *generations*

'Adam) is obviously a generic reference to both man and woman—mankind. The text of Scripture does not use gender-inclusive language and often lets the masculine serve for both masculine and feminine, as here (see also chart, Female Metaphors for God). The passage does not specify in what way mankind bears God's image. "Image" (representation) and "likeness" (similarity) are synonymous—both referring to something made after the pattern of something else.

2:2 The word "Sabbath" (Heb. *shabbath,* lit. "cease") is reserved for the seventh day, during which there is cessation from labor. God Himself modeled this pattern for rest (see Ex. 23, The Lord's Day; chart, The Principle of the Sabbath).

2:3 Sanctifying the Lord's Day is to separate it from the rest by dedicating it to God. Unlike the other six, the record of the seventh day is not recorded with the "evening and morning"

formula, perhaps suggesting the continuing observance of the Sabbath throughout the history of Israel.

2:4 The creation account. Some scholars have suggested that Genesis 1 and 2 are different creation stories placed side by side. The structure of chapter 2 does not support this theory. Verses 1–3 complete the recounting of the seven days of creation; verses 4–7 in Hebrew are one long sentence summarizing God's creative activity. A more detailed description follows of the creation of the man (vv. 7, 15–17), of the garden in which the man and woman would live (vv. 8–14), and of the woman who was to be his "helper" (vv. 18–25). The word "history" (lit. "generations") is elsewhere used to introduce genealogical lines (Gen. 5:1; 10:1). The name of the Creator (Heb. *Elohim*) is here joined to His covenant name (Heb. *Yahweh*) and translated "LORD God," making clear that the great Sovereign of the universe and the covenant God of Israel are one.

THE CREATION OF THE WOMAN

God identified Himself as a "Helper" (Heb. *'ezer*) to Israel (Ex. 18:4; Deut. 33:7). The word does not imply inferiority. It describes function rather than worth. No one loses value in humbly assuming the role of helper. As a "helper" to the man, the woman became his partner spiritually in the overwhelming task of obedience to God and dominion over the earth. She was also to be a vital part of extending the generations (Gen. 1:28). The woman, as ultimate friend to the man, would bring him comfort and fellowship (Gen. 2:23, 24). No one else could encourage and inspire him as she was created to do. The phrase "comparable to him" (Heb. *kenegdo,* lit. "corresponding to what is in front of him") occurs only in verses 18 and 20, emphasizing the commonality of the man and the woman. Designed as the perfect counterpart for the man, the woman was neither inferior nor superior, but she was alike and equal to the man in her personhood while different and unique in her function.

Man and woman were both created in God's image. Just as man was formed from earth, woman was formed from man. She corresponds perfectly to the man, the same flesh and blood, and in "the image of God" just as the man, equal to him in every way (Gen. 1:27). By the creative act itself, she is inseparably linked to the man. The unity of the race is assured (Gen. 1:27, 28); the woman's dignity and worth is affirmed (Gen. 2:22); the foundation for Christian marriage is set forth in a memorable way (v. 24).

The woman was not an afterthought. The man was designed and created physically, emotionally, socially, and spiritually with her coming creation planned and assured. In fact, God said that the man "alone" was not good; he needed the woman (v. 18). God made man from "the dust of the ground," but He made the woman from "the rib" (Heb. *tsela'*, lit. "side") of the man.

God uses Adam to express the uniqueness of the woman in a unique play on words. Even the language itself reflects the unity God planned between the man (Heb. *'ish*) and the woman (Heb. *'ishshah*). The expression "bone of my bones and flesh of my flesh" occurs elsewhere in the Old Testament as an expression of blood relationship. Though Adam's naming of the woman does not in itself require his authority over her, the act of assigning a name in the Oriental culture—even to now—is significant and in most cases does imply both authority and responsibility. Note, for example, the naming of the animals (vv. 19, 20), Pharaoh's renaming of Joseph (Gen. 41:45), the renaming of Mattaniah by Nebuchadnezzar (2 Kin. 24:17), and the renaming of Daniel and his friends by Nebuchadnezzar's eunuch (Dan. 1:6, 7). The woman's name is a recognition of her origins, in the same way that Adam's name acknowledges his creation from the earth (Gen. 2:19, note).

See also Gen. 1:27; 24:67; chart on God's Plan for Marriage; portrait of Eve (Gen. 3)

Life in God's Garden

[8]The LORD God planted a garden eastward in Eden, and there He put the man whom He had formed. [9]And out of the ground the LORD God made every tree grow that is pleasant to the sight and good for food. The tree of life *was* also in the midst of the garden, and the tree of the knowledge of good and evil.

[10]Now a river went out of Eden to water the garden, and from there it parted and became four riverheads. [11]The name of the first *is* Pishon; it *is* the one which skirts the whole land of Havilah, where *there is* gold. [12]And the gold of that land *is* good. Bdellium and the onyx stone *are* there. [13]The name of the second river *is* Gihon; it *is* the one which goes around the whole land of Cush. [14]The name of the third river *is* Hiddekel;[a] it *is* the one which goes toward the east of Assyria. The fourth river *is* the Euphrates.

[15]Then the LORD God took the man and put him in the garden of Eden to tend and keep it. [16]And the LORD God commanded the man, saying, "Of every tree of the garden you may freely eat; [17]but of the tree of the knowledge of good and evil you

2:14 [a]Or *Tigris*

2:8 The Garden of Eden (perhaps meaning "delight"). This original habitat (Heb. *gan,* lit. "a place hedged round" or "a protected place") was a delightful shelter, containing everything the man and woman needed: food (v. 9), beauty (v. 9), water (v. 10), fellowship with God (v. 16; see also Gen. 3:8), and human companionship (Gen. 2:22–25).

2:11–14 Two rivers may have connected the Tigris and Euphrates, which run parallel. The Pishon (v. 11) and the Gihon (v. 13) may also have been tributaries of the Nile. Havilah was probably in Armenia or Mesopotamia. The name is preceded by the definite article in this verse, distinguishing it from the territory mentioned in Genesis 25:18 and 1 Samuel 15:7. Cush is traditionally Ethiopia or Nubia but may also refer to Kassite territory east of the Tigris. Hiddekel is an ancient name for the Tigris. "Assyria" probably refers to the city of Asshur itself rather than the later empire.

2:15 Labor was instituted before the Fall, not as a result of the curse. "Tend" carries the idea of service; to "keep" (Heb. *shamar*) is to "guard" and "preserve" (a word used in reference to the cherubim who guard the tree of life, Gen. 3:24).

> *We can be confident that His desire to reveal will always be greater than our desire to know.*
>
> — Carrie Anna Pearce

shall not eat, for in the day that you eat of it you shall surely die."

¹⁸And the LORD God said, "*It is* not good that man should be alone; I will make him a helper comparable to him." ¹⁹Out of the ground the LORD God formed every beast of the field and every bird of the air, and brought *them* to Adam to see what he would call them. And whatever Adam called each living creature, that *was* its name. ²⁰So Adam gave names to all cattle, to the birds of the air, and to every beast of the field. But for Adam there was not found a helper comparable to him.

²¹And the LORD God caused a deep sleep to fall on Adam, and he slept; and He took one of his ribs, and closed up the flesh in its place. ²²Then the rib which the LORD God had taken from man He made into a woman, and He brought her to the man.

²³And Adam said:

"This *is* now bone of my bones
And flesh of my flesh;
She shall be called Woman,
Because she was taken out of Man."

²⁴Therefore a man shall leave his father and mother and be joined to his wife, and they shall become one flesh.

²⁵And they were both naked, the man and his wife, and were not ashamed.

The Temptation and Fall of Man

3 Now the serpent was more cunning than any beast of the field which the LORD God had made. And he said to the woman, "Has God indeed said, 'You shall not eat of every tree of the garden'?"

²And the woman said to the serpent, "We may eat the fruit of the trees of the garden; ³but of the fruit of the tree which *is* in the midst of the garden, God has said, 'You shall not eat it, nor shall you touch it, lest you die.'"

⁴Then the serpent said to the woman, "You will not surely die. ⁵For God knows that in the day you eat of it your eyes will be opened, and you will be like God, knowing good and evil."

⁶So when the woman saw that the tree *was* good for food, that it *was* pleasant to the eyes, and a tree desirable to make *one* wise, she took of its fruit and ate. She also gave to her husband with her, and he ate. ⁷Then the eyes of both of them were opened, and they knew that they *were* naked; and they sewed fig leaves together and made themselves coverings.

⁸And they heard the sound of the LORD God walking in the garden in the cool of the day, and Adam and his wife hid themselves from the presence of the LORD God among the trees of the garden.

⁹Then the LORD God called to Adam and said to him, "Where *are* you?"

¹⁰So he said, "I heard Your voice in the garden, and I was afraid because I was naked; and I hid myself."

¹¹And He said, "Who told you that you *were* naked? Have you eaten from the tree of which I commanded you that you should not eat?"

2:19 Adam is a name used for the first man and as a generic noun identifying the "man" and "woman" collectively and revealing their origin (v. 7, *'adamah*, Heb., lit. "ground" or "earth"; see Gen. 1—5).

2:24 The marriage covenant has three parts (see Gen. 4, God's Plan for Marriage):

1) to leave father and mother, a reference to the wedding ceremony or time of public commitment,

2) to "be joined," suggesting tender affection and faithful commitment in a permanent relationship of growing love, and

3) to "become one flesh" in physical union, which notes the deepest and most exclusive intimacy.

The verbs translated "leave" and "be joined to" are used elsewhere in Scripture to describe covenant relationships (see Deut. 4:4; Jer. 1:16).

3:1 Satan chose to disguise himself as a "cunning" (lit. "shrewd" or "clever") creature. The text does not comment on why the serpent approached the woman—perhaps because she, unlike Adam, did not receive this prohibition directly from God (see Gen. 2:16, 17).

3:3 Satan began his conversation with the woman by questioning God (v. 1). The woman distorted God's command by adding her own interpretation, "nor shall you touch it lest you die" (v. 3). Either she was exaggerating in hopes of making God's directive so restrictive as to appear unjust, or Adam did not properly convey the prohibition to her.

3:5 The serpent contradicted God, using the phrasing of the divine command (v. 4). The temptation to disobedience involved gaining knowledge without first learning obedience. Ultimately, every temptation is to go your own way instead of God's way (Prov. 14:12; 22:6, note).

3:6 The tree is attractive to the eye, appealing to the appetite, and enticing to ambition. Both the man and the woman sinned through listening to another created being rather than to God (see James 1:15; charts, The Results of Sin; Temptation: The Analysis of a Successful Trap).

MASCULINITY *THE NATURE OF A MAN*

God has gifted men with great capacities for responsible leadership. This can be channeled positively into the church and all walks of life through teaching, leading by moral example, and supporting righteous causes (1 Tim. 2:8). Masculine power when sanctified can be used in a positive way, such as in the lives of great men through whom God provides leadership. Abraham showed us the trait of "adventure" with God by taking steps of faith where no man had gone (Gen. 12—18). We see vision in Moses (Exodus) and faithfulness in Joshua, even when he was in the minority (Deut. 31:6–8). David showed courage to fight against incredible odds (1 Sam. 17), and Nehemiah had initiative as a builder, organizing men to rebuild a wall and a city (Neh. 1—8). By contrast, men like Nebuchadnezzar used their power for destruction and cruelty in war (2 Kin. 24:10–17).

How wonderful that God balances this image of dominant masculine strength and power with the example of the Lord Jesus who was moved by compassion (Matt. 20:34), loved little children (Mark 10:14), cried at the death of His friend (John 11:35), and gave His life so that others might live (John 3:16). The "man of integrity" (Job 31) finds a parallel in the "woman of strength" (Prov. 31:10–31).

See also Eph. 5:25–33; 6:4; chart on Biblical Manhood and Womanhood (Job 31); notes on Biblical Equality (Eph. 5); Fatherhood (Eph. 5); Femininity (Ps. 144); Husbands (Job 31; 2 Cor. 6)

---

¹²Then the man said, "The woman whom You gave *to be* with me, she gave me of the tree, and I ate."

¹³And the Lord God said to the woman, "What *is* this you have done?"

The woman said, "The serpent deceived me, and I ate."

¹⁴So the Lord God said to the serpent:

"Because you have done this,
  You *are* cursed more than all cattle,
  And more than every beast of the field;
  On your belly you shall go,
  And you shall eat dust
  All the days of your life.
¹⁵And I will put enmity
  Between you and the woman,
  And between your seed and her Seed;
  He shall bruise your head,
  And you shall bruise His heel."

¹⁶To the woman He said:

"I will greatly multiply your sorrow and your
    conception;
  In pain you shall bring forth children;
  Your desire *shall be* for your husband,
  And he shall rule over you."

¹⁷Then to Adam He said, "Because you have heeded the voice of your wife, and have eaten from the tree of which I commanded you, saying, 'You shall not eat of it':

"Cursed *is* the ground for your sake;
  In toil you shall eat *of* it
  All the days of your life.
¹⁸Both thorns and thistles it shall bring forth
    for you,
  And you shall eat the herb of the field.

3:12 Adam's response indicates his refusal to take responsibility for his own actions. The woman copied this typical response to sin (v. 13).

3:14 God's judgment on the serpent does not distinguish between the earthly creature and Satan, who is later revealed as the animal's motivating intelligence (Rev. 12:9). The serpent is charming but deadly (Num. 21:6; Eccl. 10:11) and represents opposition to God (Job 26:13; Is. 27:1).

3:15 The first prophecy of the coming of the Messiah is known as the "protevangelium" (Lat., lit. "the first preaching of the gospel"). In the OT, "seed" is used to refer both to individual offspring and to descendants in general. The woman plays a key role not only because she was approached and entrapped by Satan but also because she is "the mother of all living" (v. 20), for through her the Savior would come (Gal. 4:4). Whereas in human reproduction the sperm is delivered to the womb of the woman by the man; in the miraculous conception of Jesus the Messiah, the seed came to the woman as a result of the Holy Spirit's overshadowing her (Luke 1:35; see Is. 7, The

Virgin Birth). A messianic interpretation is justified since the bruising of the serpent's head implies a mortal wound. On the other hand, the bruising of the "heel" is not fatal, a reference ultimately to the Savior's sufferings, which were only preparatory to His victorious Resurrection (see Is. 53:5).

3:16 The woman's judgment. Unlike His words to the serpent and the man, God did not use the verb "cursed" (Heb. *'rur*) in passing judgment on the woman. The first part of the judgment can also be translated "your sorrow *in* conception"; the blessing of fertility still exists but has been distorted. The Hebrew word for "sorrow" is a form of the word translated "pain" in the next sentence, implying hard labor and appearing again as "toil" (v. 17). The word "desire" (Heb. *teshuqah*) appears only twice more in the OT (Gen. 4:7, where sin "longs" to have mastery over Cain; Song 7:10, where the man's longing for his beloved is described). The distortion of servant leadership, which was perfectly modeled in Christ, affected the relationship between husband and wife (see Job 31, Husbands).

¹⁹In the sweat of your face you shall eat bread
Till you return to the ground,
For out of it you were taken;
For dust you *are*,
And to dust you shall return."

²⁰And Adam called his wife's name Eve, because she was the mother of all living. ²¹Also for Adam and his wife the LORD God made tunics of skin, and clothed them.

²²Then the LORD God said, "Behold, the man has become like one of Us, to know good and evil. And now, lest he put out his hand and take also of the tree of life, and eat, and live forever"— ²³therefore the LORD God sent him out of the garden of Eden to till the ground from which he was taken. ²⁴So He drove out the man; and He placed cherubim at the east of the garden of Eden, and a flaming sword which turned every way, to guard the way to the tree of life.

Cain Murders Abel

4 Now Adam knew Eve his wife, and she conceived and bore Cain, and said, "I have acquired a man from the LORD." ²Then she bore again, this time his brother Abel. Now Abel was a keeper of sheep, but Cain was a tiller of the ground. ³And in the process of time it came to pass that Cain brought an offering of the fruit of the ground to the LORD. ⁴Abel also brought of the firstborn of his flock and of their fat. And the LORD respected Abel and his offering, ⁵but He did not respect Cain and his offering. And Cain was very angry, and his countenance fell.

⁶So the LORD said to Cain, "Why are you angry? And why has your countenance fallen? ⁷If you do well, will you not be accepted? And if you do not do well, sin lies at the door. And its desire *is* for you, but you should rule over it."

⁸Now Cain talked with Abel his brother;ᵃ and it came to pass, when they were in the field, that

THE RESULTS OF SIN	
VERSE	RESULT
3:7	• The experiential knowledge of evil. • The shame and guilt. • The search for clothing to cover.
3:8	• The desire for concealment. • The fear of God's presence. • The loss of fellowship with God.
3:12	• The refusal of personal responsibility. • The shifting of blame from self to others.

Cain rose up against Abel his brother and killed him.

⁹Then the LORD said to Cain, "Where *is* Abel your brother?"

He said, "I do not know. *Am* I my brother's keeper?"

¹⁰And He said, "What have you done? The voice of your brother's blood cries out to Me from the ground. ¹¹So now you *are* cursed from the earth, which has opened its mouth to receive your brother's blood from your hand. ¹²When you till the ground, it shall no longer yield its strength to you. A fugitive and a vagabond you shall be on the earth."

¹³And Cain said to the LORD, "My punishment *is* greater than I can bear! ¹⁴Surely You have driven me out this day from the face of the ground; I shall be hidden from Your face; I shall be a fugitive and a vagabond on the earth, and it will happen *that* anyone who finds me will kill me."

¹⁵And the LORD said to him, "Therefore,ᵃ whoever kills Cain, vengeance shall be taken on him

4:8 ᵃSamaritan Pentateuch, Septuagint, Syriac, and Vulgate add *"Let us go out to the field."* **4:15** ᵃFollowing Masoretic Text and Targum; Septuagint, Syriac, and Vulgate read *Not so.*

3:20 Adam's naming of Eve (Heb., lit. "life" or "living") was an act of faith in God's promise (v. 15). After the sentence of death, before any children are born, Adam affirmed the woman and her role in producing future generations, providing a counterbalance of hope.

3:21 Tunics of skin. The contrast is to the inadequate coverings of verse 7. God, not man, is able to cover shame and guilt. This reference is often seen as a prefiguration of Christ's atonement on the cross, which required the shedding of blood to cover guilt (Heb. 9:22) and pictured the death of the innocent for the guilty (2 Cor. 5:21; Rom. 5:6–11).

3:24 Expulsion from the garden. Adam and Eve were sent from the garden. Thus, God's action mingled justice and mercy, which had been central to their fellowship with God and a privilege the two were now unable to enjoy (v. 8). The gate to the garden, apparently in the east like the temple gate, would be guarded by cherubim, representing God's presence and His separation from unholy man (see 2 Kin. 19:15; Ps. 80:1).

4:1 Full knowledge ("knew," Heb. *yada'*) is often used in the OT to describe sexual intimacy.

4:4 Abel presented the firstborn of his flock—a lamb—as his offering to God, and in so doing he honored the Lord's Word (Heb. 11:4). God accepted that offering and commended Abel. Cain chose his own offering, which was rejected by God. Abel also included "fat" pieces, which, coupled with the reference to "firstborn," indicated that he gave God his best. Cain, on the other hand, presented his offering "in the process of time" or simply because it was time to give. God demands His requirements be met in His way. Ritual in itself never satisfies God and is an abomination to Him. Above all, Abel presented his sacrifice with the right heart, while Cain did not (vv. 4, 5).

4:15 The mark on Cain, like Adam and Eve's clothing, was for protection, an act of mercy even in the midst of judgment (Gen. 3:21). The "mark" (lit. "sign" or "pledge") was the concrete proof of God's promise.

MARRIAGE *GOD'S PLAN FOR MARRIAGE*

God's plan for marriage is introduced (Gen. 2:24) and repeated in the Gospels (Matt. 19:5) and in the Epistles (Eph. 5:31). Marriage was perfect in its establishment: one man and one woman in a lifetime commitment.

God never intended for man to be alone (Gen. 2:18). The very bone from which woman was crafted came from man (Gen. 2:23). Woman was taken out of man, then presented to man in order to complete him. God created the man and the woman in His image (Gen. 1:26) with physical and emotional needs that only another human being could meet (Gen. 2:18).

No parents were in Eden, but God's plan extended to the future with His formula for oneness in marriage. The partners are to "leave" their parents and "be joined" (KJV "cleave") in order to become one (Gen. 2:24). They are to be willing to lay aside all that pertains to their old loyalties and lifestyles of separate goals and plans and be joined to one another. This "joining" refers to a strong, enduring bond—making one unit bound together by unconditional commitment, love, and acceptance—resulting in a combined unit much stronger than either individual had been separately (Eccl. 4:9–12).

No other human relationship, not with parent or child, is to supersede the bond between husband and wife. Marriage is a covenant commitment—a vow made to God and the partner, not only to love but also to be faithful and to endure in this lifelong exclusive relationship (Matt. 19:6).

Marriage is a threefold miracle. It is a biological miracle by which two people actually become one flesh; it is a social miracle through which two families are grafted together; it is a spiritual miracle in that the marriage relationship pictures the union of Christ and His bride, the church (Eph. 5:23–27). God clearly intended transparency and openness as part of His plan for the marriage relationship—vulnerability without shame (Gen. 2:25).

See also notes on Biblical Equality (Eph. 5); Family (Gen. 32; 1 Sam. 3; Ps. 78; 127); Husbands (Job 31; 2 Cor. 6); Marriage (2 Sam. 6; Prov. 5; Hos. 2; Amos 3; 2 Cor. 13; Heb. 12); Wives (Prov. 31)

---

sevenfold." And the LORD set a mark on Cain, lest anyone finding him should kill him.

The Family of Cain

16Then Cain went out from the presence of the LORD and dwelt in the land of Nod on the east of Eden. 17And Cain knew his wife, and she conceived and bore Enoch. And he built a city, and called the name of the city after the name of his son—Enoch. 18To Enoch was born Irad; and Irad begot Mehujael, and Mehujael begot Methushael, and Methushael begot Lamech.

19Then Lamech took for himself two wives: the name of one *was* Adah, and the name of the second *was* Zillah. 20And Adah bore Jabal. He was the father of those who dwell in tents and have livestock. 21His brother's name *was* Jubal. He was the father of all those who play the harp and flute. 22And as for Zillah, she also bore Tubal-Cain, an instructor of every craftsman in bronze and iron. And the sister of Tubal-Cain *was* Naamah.

23Then Lamech said to his wives:

"Adah and Zillah, hear my voice;
Wives of Lamech, listen to my speech!
For I have killed a man for wounding me,
Even a young man for hurting me.
24If Cain shall be avenged sevenfold,
Then Lamech seventy-sevenfold."

A New Son

25And Adam knew his wife again, and she bore a son and named him Seth, "For God has appointed another seed for me instead of Abel, whom Cain killed." 26And as for Seth, to him also a son was born; and he named him Enosh.[a] Then *men* began to call on the name of the LORD.

The Family of Adam

5This is the book of the genealogy of Adam. In the day that God created man, He made him in the likeness of God. 2He created them male and female, and blessed them and called them Mankind

4:26 [a]Greek *Enos*

4:19 Two genealogical lines run in parallel—the line in rebellion against God, as Cain's was, and the godly chosen line (v. 26). The rebellious line may be related to the "seed of the serpent" (Gen. 3:15). Lamech, by taking two wives, illustrated the ungodliness of his family as the first to break the Creator's one-man, one-woman pattern for marriage (Gen. 2:24, note).

4:25 Christ's ancestry is traced back to Seth (Luke 3:38). Since Adam was 130 when Seth was born (Gen. 5:3), the narrative here skips back over the history in order to relate the emer-

gence of the godly line (Gen. 3:16–24). Seth (Heb., lit. "appointing" or "establishing") establishes the line of the seed of the woman (Gen. 3:15). This line is in opposition to Satan.

4:26 The LORD (Heb. *Yahweh*) is revealed to be the most detailed, personal, and powerful of God's names (Ex. 3:14; see chart, The Names of God). God introduced His covenant name in the detailed description of the creation of the man and woman and the outlining of their relationship to one another (see Gen. 2:4–22). Its use here is linked to the establishment of a godly, worshiping line.

in the day they were created. ³And Adam lived one hundred and thirty years, and begot *a son* in his own likeness, after his image, and named him Seth. ⁴After he begot Seth, the days of Adam were eight hundred years; and he had sons and daughters. ⁵So all the days that Adam lived were nine hundred and thirty years; and he died.

⁶Seth lived one hundred and five years, and begot Enosh. ⁷After he begot Enosh, Seth lived eight hundred and seven years, and had sons and daughters. ⁸So all the days of Seth were nine hundred and twelve years; and he died.

⁹Enosh lived ninety years, and begot Cainan.ᵃ ¹⁰After he begot Cainan, Enosh lived eight hundred and fifteen years, and had sons and daughters. ¹¹So all the days of Enosh were nine hundred and five years; and he died.

¹²Cainan lived seventy years, and begot Mahalalel. ¹³After he begot Mahalalel, Cainan lived eight hundred and forty years, and had sons and daughters. ¹⁴So all the days of Cainan were nine hundred and ten years; and he died.

¹⁵Mahalalel lived sixty-five years, and begot Jared. ¹⁶After he begot Jared, Mahalalel lived eight hundred and thirty years, and had sons and daughters. ¹⁷So all the days of Mahalalel were eight hundred and ninety-five years; and he died.

¹⁸Jared lived one hundred and sixty-two years, and begot Enoch. ¹⁹After he begot Enoch, Jared lived eight hundred years, and had sons and daughters. ²⁰So all the days of Jared were nine hundred and sixty-two years; and he died.

²¹Enoch lived sixty-five years, and begot Methuselah. ²²After he begot Methuselah, Enoch walked with God three hundred years, and had sons and daughters. ²³So all the days of Enoch

were three hundred and sixty-five years. ²⁴And Enoch walked with God; and he *was* not, for God took him.

²⁵Methuselah lived one hundred and eighty-seven years, and begot Lamech. ²⁶After he begot Lamech, Methuselah lived seven hundred and eighty-two years, and had sons and daughters. ²⁷So all the days of Methuselah were nine hundred and sixty-nine years; and he died.

²⁸Lamech lived one hundred and eighty-two years, and had a son. ²⁹And he called his name Noah, saying, "This *one* will comfort us concerning our work and the toil of our hands, because of the ground which the LORD has cursed." ³⁰After he begot Noah, Lamech lived five hundred and ninety-five years, and had sons and daughters. ³¹So all the days of Lamech were seven hundred and seventy-seven years; and he died.

³²And Noah was five hundred years old, and Noah begot Shem, Ham, and Japheth.

The Wickedness and Judgment of Man

6 Now it came to pass, when men began to multiply on the face of the earth, and daughters were born to them, ²that the sons of God saw the daughters of men, that they *were* beautiful; and they took wives for themselves of all whom they chose.

³And the LORD said, "My Spirit shall not striveᵃ with man forever, for he *is* indeed flesh; yet his days shall be one hundred and twenty years." ⁴There were giants on the earth in those days, and also afterward, when the sons of God came in to the daughters of men and they bore *children* to

5:9 ᵃHebrew *Qenan*   6:3 ᵃSeptuagint, Syriac, Targum, and Vulgate read *abide*.

5:3 Begot can refer to immediate descent (father to son) but can also be used as reference to grandsons or more distant descendants. The age of each patriarch at the birth of his first child, through whom the generations continue, as well as the number of years he lived after that birth and the entire length of his years is recorded (vv. 3–32; see chart, How Old Were the Patriarchs?).

5:18 Enoch occupies the seventh place in this genealogy, a place often reserved for particularly significant individuals. Lamech, seventh from Cain, shows the growing violence of the ungodly line (Gen. 4:23); Enoch, the seventh from Adam, is the most righteous of all men (v. 22). Only Enoch and Noah are recorded as having "walked with God" (v. 22; Gen. 6:9), describing the perfect fellowship of the Garden of Eden (Gen. 3:8).

5:24 God took him. Enoch's righteousness resulted in God's sparing him from physical death, affirming God's power over death (see Ps. 49:15; 73:24). Only the prophet Elijah shared this experience (2 Kin. 2:11).

5:29 A man of obedience. Noah (Heb., lit. "comfort") helped fulfill prophecy (see Gen. 3:15); God worked through Noah's obedience to prevent the complete corruption of humanity (Gen. 6:5, 9).

6:2 The sons of God. Three primary interpretations have been proposed for this phrase.

1) The "sons of God" were fallen angels who took human wives, a view based on the interpretation of this phrase as angels elsewhere in the OT (see Job 1:6; 38:7).

2) The "sons of God" were men from Cain's line who took wives descended from Seth. Although this interpretation fits the context (Gen. 1—11), "sons of God" does not elsewhere refer to men.

3) The "sons of God" were descendants of early pagan kings who, like Lamech, sinned through polygamy. This accounts for "all whom they chose" but is open to the same objection as the second view.

While there is no way of determining the precise meaning of the story, clearly humanity was so close to total, irredeemable corruption that God sent the Flood.

6:3 God's displeasure. God expressed His condemnation of the sin (vv. 5, 6). "Strive" can also be translated "abide with." God limited the time man could continue in sin. The 120 years refers either to the length of time before the Flood or to the shortened human lifespan after the Flood (see Gen. 11:10–26).

6:4 Giants on the earth appears only once more (Num. 13:33). However, the giants in Genesis (Heb. *Nephilim*) were

EVE   *The Mother of All Living*

Adam was given supervision over the creation, but God declared that for him to live his life alone was not good. From the man's rib God created a woman and presented her as a wife to Adam, climaxing His creative work (Gen. 2:18–24). Eve was not an afterthought or happenstance but an indispensable part of God's plan. Both Adam and Eve, made "in the image of God," stood as His representatives in the world to care for all He put under their dominion.

Purity and innocence were shattered, however, when the serpent entered the scene. Eve chose to believe Satan's lie. She was free to put her will above God's will, and she did. When she offered the fruit to her husband, he, too, disobeyed. In the New Testament, Paul clarified their actions, saying that Eve was deceived; whereas Adam ate with full knowledge of wrongdoing (2 Cor. 11:3; 1 Tim. 2:14). Then, filled with guilt, the couple hid from God, fashioning fig leaf coverings to hide their shame. Not only had they broken their relationship with God, but also they had broken their relationship with one another and with all the generations to come and even with the world and nature over which they were to rule.

God cursed the serpent and the ground for man's sake, and He prophesied sorrow, toil, and death for the first couple. Pain for the woman would come in giving birth and rearing children and in her relationship to her husband. She would resist his leadership just as his rule over her would be distorted (Gen. 3:16).

Evicted from her lovely home, Eve conceived and bore two sons, although her joy at their birth was changed by the heartache predicted by God. Cain murdered his brother in defiance of God's command concerning sacrifices, and God banished him. Eve was left childless until God's grace once again appeared in the form of another son, Seth, who became an ancestor of the Messiah.

Eve stands as an archetype of womanhood. Although created in God's image (Gen. 1:27), she exercised her will to disobey the Creator (Gen. 3:6), daring to challenge His authority. Disobedience was not in itself a motive but presupposed the motive. Her temptation was not merely to disobey but ultimately to have her own way or to get possession of what she wanted. As her daughter, every woman bears her likeness. Eve voices an early warning to every woman to follow the path of obedience and a resounding note of hope for women when they fail; she encountered God's justice, but she also experienced His grace (see Rom. 5:18, 19).

See also Gen. 2:18—4:25; 2 Cor. 11:3; 1 Tim. 2:13, 14; notes on Marriage (Gen. 2; 2 Sam. 6; Prov. 5; Hos. 2; Amos 3; 2 Cor. 13; Heb. 12); Motherhood (1 Sam. 1; Is. 49; Ezek. 16); Obedience (Philem.)

them. Those *were* the mighty men who *were* of old, men of renown.

[5]Then the Lord[a] saw that the wickedness of man *was* great in the earth, and *that* every intent of the thoughts of his heart *was* only evil continually. [6]And the Lord was sorry that He had made man on the earth, and He was grieved in His heart. [7]So the Lord said, "I will destroy man whom I have created from the face of the earth, both man and beast, creeping thing and birds of the air, for I am sorry that I have made them." [8]But Noah found grace in the eyes of the Lord.

Noah Pleases God

[9]This is the genealogy of Noah. Noah was a just man, perfect in his generations. Noah walked with God. [10]And Noah begot three sons: Shem, Ham, and Japheth.

[11]The earth also was corrupt before God, and the earth was filled with violence. [12]So God looked upon the earth, and indeed it was corrupt; for all flesh had corrupted their way on the earth.

The Ark Prepared

[13]And God said to Noah, "The end of all flesh has come before Me, for the earth is filled with violence through them; and behold, I will destroy them with the earth. [14]Make yourself an ark of gopherwood; make rooms in the ark, and cover it in-

····························

6:5 [a]Following Masoretic Text and Targum; Vulgate reads *God;* Septuagint reads Lord *God.*

destroyed in the Flood. They were not offspring of the unions of verse 2, since they existed both before and afterward. The word might possibly mean "fallen ones"; the verb is passive and conveys the meaning "those who were cast down." Thus the *Nephilim* appear to have been either giants or fallen angels. They are distinct from the "mighty men of old."

6:9 Noah's genealogy (Heb., *toledoth,* lit. "these are the generations of") marks the beginning of a new section in the book. The focus shifts from the history of humanity as a whole to that of the godly remnant miraculously preserved from judg-

ment (see chart, The Faithful Remnant). "Just" refers to Noah's actions toward other men. "Perfect" (Heb. *tamim,* lit. "sound, wholesome, having integrity") is later used to describe the perfection of sacrificial animals. Noah was "wholehearted" in his relationship to God.

6:14 The ark (Heb. *tebah,* lit. "box" or "chest") appears also in Exodus 2:3–5, where Moses is placed in an "ark" of bulrushes. The choice of words emphasizes the ark's character as a protection and hiding place. "Gopherwood" is unclear but may be cypress or another resinous wood.

Honour to Womankind! It needs must be that God loved Woman since He fashioned Thee.

Christine de Pisan, 1429

---

side and outside with pitch. [15]And this is how you shall make it: The length of the ark *shall be* three hundred cubits, its width fifty cubits, and its height thirty cubits. [16]You shall make a window for the ark, and you shall finish it to a cubit from above; and set the door of the ark in its side. You shall make it *with* lower, second, and third *decks.* [17]And behold, I Myself am bringing floodwaters on the earth, to destroy from under heaven all flesh in which *is* the breath of life; everything that *is* on the earth shall die. [18]But I will establish My covenant with you; and you shall go into the ark—you, your sons, your wife, and your sons' wives with you. [19]And of every living thing of all flesh you shall bring two of every *sort* into the ark, to keep *them* alive with you; they shall be male and female. [20]Of the birds after their kind, of animals after their kind, and of every creeping thing of the earth after its kind, two of every *kind* will come to you to keep *them* alive. [21]And you shall take for yourself of all food that is eaten, and you shall gather *it* to yourself; and it shall be food for you and for them."

[22]Thus Noah did; according to all that God commanded him, so he did.

The Great Flood

7 Then the LORD said to Noah, "Come into the ark, you and all your household, because I have seen *that* you *are* righteous before Me in this generation. [2]You shall take with you seven each of every clean animal, a male and his female; two each of animals that *are* unclean, a male and his female; [3]also seven each of birds of the air, male and female, to keep the species alive on the face of all the earth. [4]For after seven more days I will cause it to rain on the earth forty days and forty nights, and I will destroy from the face of the earth all living things that I have made." [5]And Noah did according to all that the LORD commanded him. [6]Noah *was* six hundred years old when the floodwaters were on the earth.

[7]So Noah, with his sons, his wife, and his sons' wives, went into the ark because of the waters of the flood. [8]Of clean animals, of animals that *are* unclean, of birds, and of everything that creeps on the earth, [9]two by two they went into the ark to Noah, male and female, as God had commanded Noah. [10]And it came to pass after seven days that the waters of the flood were on the earth. [11]In the six hundredth year of Noah's life, in the second month, the seventeenth day of the month, on that day all the fountains of the great deep were broken up, and the windows of heaven were opened. [12]And the rain was on the earth forty days and forty nights.

[13]On the very same day Noah and Noah's sons, Shem, Ham, and Japheth, and Noah's wife and the three wives of his sons with them, entered the ark— [14]they and every beast after its kind, all cattle after their kind, every creeping thing that creeps on the earth after its kind, and every bird after its kind, every bird of every sort. [15]And they went into the ark to Noah, two by two, of all flesh in which *is* the breath of life. [16]So those that entered, male and female of all flesh, went in as God had commanded him; and the LORD shut him in.

[17]Now the flood was on the earth forty days. The waters increased and lifted up the ark, and it rose high above the earth. [18]The waters prevailed and greatly increased on the earth, and the ark moved about on the surface of the waters. [19]And the waters prevailed exceedingly on the earth, and all the high hills under the whole heaven were covered. [20]The waters prevailed fifteen cubits upward, and the mountains were covered. [21]And all flesh died that moved on the earth: birds and cattle and beasts and every creeping thing that creeps on the earth, and every man. [22]All in whose nostrils *was* the breath of the spirit[a] of life, all that *was* on the dry *land,* died. [23]So He destroyed all living things which were on the face of the

---

7:22 [a]Septuagint and Vulgate omit *of the spirit.*

6:18 The covenant. This is the first biblical mention of covenant (Heb. *berith*). Covenants are made by God with man for the purpose of salvation. God declares His commitment and demands a response from man (see charts, The Covenants of Genesis).

7:1 The Lord. Genesis 6—9 alternates between use of God (*Elohim*) and the LORD (*Yahweh*). The more general name, *Elohim*, is used when the narrative relates the effect of the Flood on the entire world; *Yahweh*, the covenant name, is used to record the Lord's dealings with His people.

7:2 Rather than contradicting Genesis 6:19, this verse expands

upon God's previous command. Two of every animal were to be taken. In addition, extra pairs of clean animals were to be taken (see Lev. 10, Clean vs. Unclean). "Seven each" can also be translated "seven pairs."

7:11 The coming of the Flood, whether a natural catastrophe or miraculous event, was divinely directed. "The fountains of the great deep" refers to the invasion of the land by the sea, possibly with volcanic activity as part of the upheaval. "The windows of heaven were opened" is descriptive of torrential rain. The precise dating of the Flood confirms that this judgment occurred in human history (see chart, The Chronology of the Flood).

FALL OF CREATION · REJECTION OF THE CREATOR'S PLAN

The sentences passed on man and woman at the time of the Fall affected their relationships to God, nature, and each other. The judgment which followed is not necessarily related to the nature of the sin committed. However tragic and far-reaching the consequences, sin does not force the Creator to cancel His plan. Rather, sin perverts and hinders our response to His plan. As a result of the Fall, pain has been added to childbirth, tyranny to headship, rebellion to submission, and problems to work, as well as separation to the fellowship of union.

Of particular interest to women is the twofold judgment of Genesis 3:16. Women were assigned "pain in childbearing." Childbearing itself is not the judgment. Children are a heritage and reward from the Lord (Ps. 127:3), and giving birth is a woman's opportunity to link hands with the Creator to continue the generations (Gen. 1:28). Imagining a pain-free childbirth experience is difficult, but this is apparently the original plan of the Creator.

The second part of the judgment—"your desire will be for your husband, and he shall rule over you"— described the painful consequences of sin in the male-female relationship. Both the man and woman chose to ignore the Creator's plan and do things their own way. The complementary roles of man and woman, which had originally functioned to produce unity and harmony, would henceforth be a source of friction. God's plan did not change. However, woman would have a sin tendency to disrespect man's role of leadership, and man in his sinfulness would tend to abuse his authority and even crush the woman.

Christian men and women are given clear principles to counteract these effects of sin and are reminded of their equality as persons (1 Pet. 3:7) and of the complementary, harmonious relationship for which they were created (Eph. 5:21–33; Col. 3:18, 19).

See also notes on Biblical Equality (Eph. 5); Marriage (Gen. 2; 2 Sam. 6; Prov. 5; Hos. 2; Amos 3; 2 Cor. 13; Heb. 12); Submission (1 Pet. 3)

---

ground: both man and cattle, creeping thing and bird of the air. They were destroyed from the earth. Only Noah and those who *were* with him in the ark remained *alive*. ²⁴And the waters prevailed on the earth one hundred and fifty days.

Noah's Deliverance

8Then God remembered Noah, and every living thing, and all the animals that *were* with him in the ark. And God made a wind to pass over the earth, and the waters subsided. ²The fountains of the deep and the windows of heaven were also stopped, and the rain from heaven was restrained. ³And the waters receded continually from the earth. At the end of the hundred and fifty days the waters decreased. ⁴Then the ark rested in the seventh month, the seventeenth day of the month, on the mountains of Ararat. ⁵And the waters decreased continually until the tenth month. In the tenth *month,* on the first *day* of the month, the tops of the mountains were seen.

⁶So it came to pass, at the end of forty days, that Noah opened the window of the ark which he had made. ⁷Then he sent out a raven, which kept going to and fro until the waters had dried up from the earth. ⁸He also sent out from himself a dove, to see if the waters had receded from the face of the ground. ⁹But the dove found no resting place for the sole of her foot, and she returned into the ark to him, for the waters *were* on the face of the whole earth. So he put out his hand and took her, and drew her into the ark to himself. ¹⁰And he waited yet another seven days, and again he sent the dove out from the ark. ¹¹Then the dove came to him in the evening, and behold, a freshly plucked olive leaf *was* in her mouth; and Noah knew that the waters had receded from the earth. ¹²So he waited yet another seven days and sent out the dove, which did not return again to him anymore.

¹³And it came to pass in the six hundred and first year, in the first *month,* the first *day* of the month, that the waters were dried up from the earth; and Noah removed the covering of the ark and looked, and indeed the surface of the ground was dry. ¹⁴And in the second month, on the twenty-seventh day of the month, the earth was dried.

¹⁵Then God spoke to Noah, saying, ¹⁶"Go out of the ark, you and your wife, and your sons and your sons' wives with you. ¹⁷Bring out with you every living thing of all flesh that *is* with you: birds and cattle and every creeping thing that creeps on the earth, so that they may abound on the earth, and be fruitful and multiply on the earth." ¹⁸So Noah

---

8:1 God's remembrance in Scripture is a determined action rather than a mental process; when He remembers, He acts mercifully to save (see Gen. 30:22). God sends the wind (Heb. *ruach*), the same word used for the Spirit (Gen. 1:2). After destruction, God re-creates, just as He created from chaos.

8:4 Ararat, lying in modern eastern Armenia, was also known as Uratu in ancient times. The country itself is mountainous with a general elevation of 6,000 feet. Ararat is its highest peak at 17,000 feet, but this verse does not specify upon which mountain the ark finally rested.

THE CHRONOLOGY OF THE FLOOD

WHAT?	WHEN?	HOW LONG?
The rain began (Gen. 7:11).	Noah's 600th year, 2nd month, 17th day	*RAIN:* 40 days and 40 nights
The water remained (Gen. 7:24). The water decreased (Gen. 8:3). The ark rested (Gen. 8:4).	150 days At the end of 150 days Noah's 600th year, 7th month, 17th day	*LENGTH OF FLOOD:* 5 months of 30 days each
The tops of the mountains were visible (Gen. 8:5).	10th month, 1st day	*ARK IN PLACE:* 2 months, 13 days
Noah sent out the raven (Gen. 8:7).	40 days later	*ARK IN PLACE:* 3 months, 23 days
Noah sent out the dove (Gen. 8:10).	7 days later	*ARK IN PLACE:* 4 months
Noah sent out the dove again (Gen. 8:12).	7 days later	*ARK IN PLACE:* 4 months, 7 days
The waters dried up (Gen. 8:13). The earth was now dry (Gen. 8:14).	Noah's 601st year, 1st month, 1st day Noah's 601st year, 2nd month, 27th day	*TOTAL LENGTH OF FLOOD:* 365 days, 1 solar year

went out, and his sons and his wife and his sons' wives with him. ¹⁹Every animal, every creeping thing, every bird, *and* whatever creeps on the earth, according to their families, went out of the ark.

God's Covenant with Creation

²⁰Then Noah built an altar to the LORD, and took of every clean animal and of every clean bird, and offered burnt offerings on the altar. ²¹And the LORD smelled a soothing aroma. Then the LORD said in His heart, "I will never again curse the ground for man's sake, although the imagination of man's heart *is* evil from his youth; nor will I again destroy every living thing as I have done.

²²"While the earth remains,
　Seedtime and harvest,
　Cold and heat,
　Winter and summer,
　And day and night
　Shall not cease."

9 So God blessed Noah and his sons, and said to them: "Be fruitful and multiply, and fill the earth.ᵃ ²And the fear of you and the dread of you

shall be on every beast of the earth, on every bird of the air, on all that move *on* the earth, and on all the fish of the sea. They are given into your hand. ³Every moving thing that lives shall be food for you. I have given you all things, even as the green herbs. ⁴But you shall not eat flesh with its life, *that is,* its blood. ⁵Surely for your lifeblood I will demand *a reckoning;* from the hand of every beast I will require it, and from the hand of man. From the hand of every man's brother I will require the life of man.

⁶"Whoever sheds man's blood,
　By man his blood shall be shed;
　For in the image of God
　He made man.
⁷And as for you, be fruitful and multiply;
　Bring forth abundantly in the earth
　And multiply in it."

⁸Then God spoke to Noah and to his sons with him, saying: ⁹"And as for Me, behold, I establish My covenant with you and with your descendantsᵃ

9:1 ᵃCompare Genesis 1:28　　9:9 ᵃLiterally *seed*

8:20 Noah's altar is the first mentioned in Scripture. Noah, acting as did Adam, is given the task of repopulating a re-created earth. His first act is to worship God. Noah's sacrifice was a burnt offering in which the entire animal was consumed. In the covenant relationship between God and man, the primary purpose of this whole burnt offering was atonement (Lev. 1:4), symbolizing the complete consecration of the worshiper to God (see chart, The Offerings of the Lord).

8:21 An aroma pleasing to God is associated with burnt offerings (Lev. 1:9, 13) and indicates God's acceptance of the aton-

ing sacrifice. Although God recognized that the judgment of the Flood had not changed individual hearts, He promised to exercise mercy. Thus, this is the first example of the OT sacrifice as propitiation for sin (that is, satisfaction for the righteousness of God).

9:5 Because the man and woman are made in God's image (v. 6), their lives belong to God. The divine image was not destroyed by the Fall. God Himself instituted the penalty of death for murder (v. 5), and civil authorities are to execute that penalty (v. 6).

Perspective   by Anne Graham Lotz

GETTING TO KNOW THE AUTHOR (From *God's Story*)

Many people today have a knowledge that God is "up there somewhere." They may even be familiar with His Name, and they may know He is famous and important and powerful—but they haven't a clue as to Who He really is! The Bible is God's Story, and the best way to discover the author of the Bible, and our lives, is to read His story.

God's Story reveals God's eternal person, His infinite power, His unlimited love, and His matchless glory giving meaning to your life and joy to your heart and purpose to your step. The Bible reveals the God of glory Whose very Presence can give fulfillment to the empty . . . healing to the broken . . . forgiveness to the sinful . . . freedom to the bitter . . . purpose to the meaningless . . . help to the helpless . . . courage to the fearful . . . strength to the weak . . . reality to the religious . . . hope to the hopeless . . . and love to the loveless.

While God's Story gives no explanation or definition for God, the opening statement of Genesis makes it clear that God as Creator is eternal and therefore not bound by time. God created time, but He's not bound by or limited to it. The eternity of God can mean wonderful comfort in the face of something as final and frightening as death. When someone dies who belongs to Christ, that person is ushered into the Presence of Christ in eternity and enters a timeless state. God transcends time. For Him, all history—past, present, and future—is now. He sees everything at once. He doesn't see you *now,* then wait thirty years to see you *then.* He sees all of your life from the beginning to the end at one time.

Just as God is not bound by time, He is not bound by space. God can be everywhere at once.

God is greater than His Creation. There is nothing in your life—no circumstance or crisis, no organization or administration, no individual or alliance, no problem or pressure, no habit or heartache, no sickness or grief, no king or criminal, nothing visible or invisible—nothing is greater than God! He is the Creator Who is in authority over everything, fully able to control that which not only *seems* but is beyond our abilities to handle.

God is also separate from Creation. This means when something is wrong, He can right it. When something is broken, He can mend it. When something is lost, He can find it. When something doesn't work, He can fix it. When something is hurt, He can heal it. When someone is dead, He can raise him! Our failures, sins, mistakes, and shortcomings in no way dilute or deplete or weaken or harm *God*!

God is active as Creator. He is active in big ways . . . and small ways. He understands your big decision . . . big commitment . . . big problem. He notices your small tear . . . small kindness . . . small hurt feeling. God is active in unseen ways and initial ways. Even when we do not perceive that God is at work, He is actively present and involved. He takes the initiative in creation and in our lives. Your life and mine, both physical and spiritual, depend upon God's initiative.

God is personal and loving. God loves everyone on Planet Earth, and we can call God our Father when we come to Him in a personal relationship through faith in His Son. The glory of God the Father is made visible and accessible to us through God the Son, Jesus. And the glory of God the Son is made real and accessible to us through God the Spirit.

To have real, lasting and deep meaning for your life . . . know God.

To know God . . . read God's Story.

---

after you, ¹⁰and with every living creature that *is* with you: the birds, the cattle, and every beast of the earth with you, of all that go out of the ark, every beast of the earth. ¹¹Thus I establish My covenant with you: Never again shall all flesh be cut off by the waters of the flood; never again shall there be a flood to destroy the earth."

¹²And God said: "This *is* the sign of the covenant which I make between Me and you, and every living creature that *is* with you, for perpetual generations: ¹³I set My rainbow in the cloud, and it shall be for the sign of the covenant between Me and the earth. ¹⁴It shall be, when I bring a cloud over the earth, that the rainbow shall be seen in the cloud; ¹⁵and I will remember My covenant which *is* between Me and you and every living creature of all flesh; the waters shall never again become a flood to destroy all flesh. ¹⁶The rainbow shall be in the cloud, and I will look on it to remember the everlasting covenant between God and every living creature of all flesh that *is* on the earth." ¹⁷And God said to Noah, "This *is* the sign of the covenant which I have established between Me and all flesh that *is* on the earth."

Noah and His Sons

¹⁸Now the sons of Noah who went out of the ark were Shem, Ham, and Japheth. And Ham *was* the father of Canaan. ¹⁹These three *were* the sons of Noah, and from these the whole earth was populated.

²⁰And Noah began *to be* a farmer, and he planted a vineyard. ²¹Then he drank of the wine and was drunk, and became uncovered in his tent. ²²And Ham, the father of Canaan, saw the nakedness of his father, and told his two brothers outside. ²³But Shem and Japheth took a garment, laid *it* on both their shoulders, and went backward and covered the nakedness of their father. Their faces

THE FAITHFUL REMNANT

THE REMNANT	THE CIRCUMSTANCES	REFERENCE
Noah	The whole earth was wicked.	Gen. 6:5–8
Abram	His home country was given over to idolatry.	Gen. 12:1–4
Isaac	He lived among Canaanites, who worshiped false gods.	Gen. 24:3, 4
Jacob	He lived in a land filled with hostile Canaanites and Perizzites.	Gen. 34:30
Joseph	He was the only worshiper of God in the land of Egypt.	Gen. 41:16

were turned away, and they did not see their father's nakedness.

²⁴So Noah awoke from his wine, and knew what his younger son had done to him. ²⁵Then he said:

"Cursed *be* Canaan;
A servant of servants
He shall be to his brethren."

²⁶And he said:

"Blessed *be* the LORD,
The God of Shem,
And may Canaan be his servant.
²⁷May God enlarge Japheth,
And may he dwell in the tents of Shem;
And may Canaan be his servant."

²⁸And Noah lived after the flood three hundred and fifty years. ²⁹So all the days of Noah were nine hundred and fifty years; and he died.

Nations Descended from Noah

10 Now this *is* the genealogy of the sons of Noah: Shem, Ham, and Japheth. And sons were born to them after the flood.

²The sons of Japheth *were* Gomer, Magog, Madai, Javan, Tubal, Meshech, and Tiras. ³The sons of Gomer *were* Ashkenaz, Riphath,^a and Togarmah. ⁴The sons of Javan *were* Elishah, Tarshish, Kittim, and Dodanim.^a ⁵From these the coastland *peoples* of the Gentiles were separated into their lands, everyone according to his language, according to their families, into their nations.

⁶The sons of Ham *were* Cush, Mizraim, Put,^a and Canaan. ⁷The sons of Cush *were* Seba, Havilah, Sabtah, Raamah, and Sabtechah; and the sons of Raamah *were* Sheba and Dedan.

⁸Cush begot Nimrod; he began to be a mighty one on the earth. ⁹He was a mighty hunter before the LORD; therefore it is said, "Like Nimrod the mighty hunter before the LORD." ¹⁰And the beginning of his kingdom was Babel, Erech, Accad, and Calneh, in the land of Shinar. ¹¹From that land he went to Assyria and built Nineveh, Rehoboth Ir, Calah, ¹²and Resen between Nineveh and Calah (that *is* the principal city).

¹³Mizraim begot Ludim, Anamim, Lehabim,

10:3 ^aSpelled *Diphath* in 1 Chronicles 1:6   **10:4** ^aSpelled *Rodanim* in Samaritan Pentateuch and 1 Chronicles 1:7   **10:6** ^aOr *Phut*

9:25 Noah's curse. The verb tenses of this curse suggest an appeal to God. The cursing of Canaan, Ham's son, implies an early understanding of the principle that the iniquities of the fathers would be visited on the children (Ex. 34:7). The curse apparently is restricted to this single branch of Ham's descendants.

9:26 Abraham was a direct descendant of Shem. The descendants of Canaan, Ham's son, included the Jebusites (Gen. 10:6) and other Canaanite peoples later conquered by Israel. The curse was thus fulfilled in the taking of the Promised Land.

9:27 Japheth's descendants were Gentiles west and north of Israel. Often called the "Sea Peoples," the Japhethites, like the sons of Shem, took territory from the Canaanites. Peaceful relations between Japheth's descendants and those of Shem are predicted. Israel experienced times of peace with the Sea Peoples as well as occupation by the Greeks, who were descendants of Japheth.

10:8 Nimrod (from Heb. *marad*, lit. "revolt"), whose name itself points to his rebellion, founded four cities in Shinar at the tip of the Persian Gulf (v. 10). Babel became the capital of Babylonia; Erech was a Sumerian city; Accad was the capital of Sargon of Akkad, a prominent ruler of the 24th century B.C. Calneh may not be the name of a city, since it can also be translated "all of them." Nimrod is the first kingdom-builder, as Cain was the first city-builder. He evidently distinguished himself with bold and daring deeds as the "mighty one" (Heb. *gibor*, lit. "hero" or "tyrant"), though he seemed more concerned with furthering his own interests than serving the Lord. All this he did "before" or under the watchful eye of *Yahweh*. Again, an ungodly line, whose genealogy will be continued, is emerging (Gen. 11:1–9).

10:11 Assyria. The subject of this verse is unclear. Either Nimrod built Assyria and the other cities, or "Asshur," the ancestor of the Assyrians, built Nineveh, Rehoboth Ir, Calah, and Resen.

EUTHANASIA GOD'S TIMING IN DEATH

In a jealous rage, Cain killed his brother, Abel. God cursed Cain and sent him away. Fearing his own murder, Cain begged God for safety. God responded that whoever killed Cain would receive vengeance from Him. God then set a "mark" on Cain to protect his life and make a statement to all: life comes from God (Gen. 4:1–15). Not only does God prohibit vengeful killing, but He makes clear that life and death are solely in His domain. Life is sacred. God alone is responsible for the termination of life.

Euthanasia (Gk.) is defined as terminating life in order to achieve some concept of good, such as putting an end to physical suffering. It may include death by the individual's choice or by the choice of others. It also includes several other concepts, such as "death with dignity," "mercy killing," and even "death selection." Euthanasia covers a wide range and may be either active or passive. It may involve actions to produce death or could merely be the withholding of life-extending supports. Whereas extraordinary life-prolonging measures are praise-worthy and noble for those who can and choose to do so, there is no moral obligation to pursue this course. God has ordained a natural process for ending this life and beginning the next. However, in every case, euthanasia involves human decision to determine the manner and timing of death for some supposed good.

Christians should entrust mortality to God. Life is not something we own. Rather, the opportunity to experience life is a gift from our Creator, and the possession of life is a stewardship trust. God always remains the true "Owner" of life; so it is never ours to do with as we want. Death's timing is God's choice, not that of an individual or society. Life is valuable to the Lord, and even the life continuation of the murderer Cain was protected by the Creator of life.

See also Gen. 1:27; notes on Aging (Is. 46); Death (1 Cor. 15); Disabilities (Mark 2); Pain (Job 7; 2 Cor. 12); Sanctity of Life (Gen. 9); Suffering (Ps. 33; 113; Is. 43; 1 Pet. 5)

Naphtuhim, [14]Pathrusim, and Casluhim (from whom came the Philistines and Caphtorim).

[15]Canaan begot Sidon his firstborn, and Heth; [16]the Jebusite, the Amorite, and the Girgashite; [17]the Hivite, the Arkite, and the Sinite; [18]the Arvadite, the Zemarite, and the Hamathite. Afterward the families of the Canaanites were dispersed. [19]And the border of the Canaanites was from Sidon as you go toward Gerar, as far as Gaza; then as you go toward Sodom, Gomorrah, Admah, and Zeboiim, as far as Lasha. [20]These *were* the sons of Ham, according to their families, according to their languages, in their lands *and* in their nations.

[21]And *children* were born also to Shem, the father of all the children of Eber, the brother of Japheth the elder. [22]The sons of Shem *were* Elam, Asshur, Arphaxad, Lud, and Aram. [23]The sons of Aram *were* Uz, Hul, Gether, and Mash.[a] [24]Arphaxad begot Salah,[a] and Salah begot Eber. [25]To Eber were

born two sons: the name of one *was* Peleg, for in his days the earth was divided; and his brother's name *was* Joktan. [26]Joktan begot Almodad, Sheleph, Hazarmaveth, Jerah, [27]Hadoram, Uzal, Diklah, [28]Obal,[a] Abimael, Sheba, [29]Ophir, Havilah, and Jobab. All these *were* the sons of Joktan. [30]And their dwelling place was from Mesha as you go toward Sephar, the mountain of the east. [31]These *were* the sons of Shem, according to their families, according to their languages, in their lands, according to their nations.

[32]These *were* the families of the sons of Noah, according to their generations, in their nations; and from these the nations were divided on the earth after the flood.

10:23 [a]Called *Meshech* in Septuagint and 1 Chronicles 1:17   10:24 [a]Following Masoretic Text, Vulgate, and Targum; Septuagint reads *Arphaxad begot Cainan, and Cainan begot Salah* (compare Luke 3:35, 36).   10:28 [a]Spelled *Ebal* in 1 Chronicles 1:22

Nineveh, east of the Tigris, and Calah both served as capitals of Assyria. Rehoboth Ir is unknown but may refer to a section of Nineveh. Resen, "the principal city," cannot be located and may allude to the total area covered by the previous three cities (see v. 12; Jon. 1:2; 3:2, "great city").

10:19 The land of Canaan included not just the territory of Israel but also the land east of the Jordan. The inhabitants of Canaan are thought to have migrated from Arabia, where Ham had settled.

10:21 The sons of Shem were selected to be the godly seed that God would sovereignly protect. From Shem's descen-

dants came the three monotheistic religions—Islam, Judaism, and Christianity. Shem's great-grandson Eber (Heb.), transliterated to "Hebrew," the ancestor of Abraham, is singled out for special mention (see Gen. 11:10–26). Of Shem's five sons, Elam sired the Elamites, east of the Tigris; Lud is probably connected to the Lydians of Asia Minor; Aram founded the Syrian people known in the OT as Arameans. Asshur may have been involved with Nimrod in the building of Assyria, since both Hamitic and Semitic artifacts have been found in Assyrian ruins. The genealogy of Arphaxad, the ancestor of the Israelites, reappears (vv. 24–29; Gen. 11:10–26).

HOW OLD WERE THE PATRIARCHS?

ADAM 930 years (Gen. 5:5)

SETH 912 years (Gen. 5:8)

ENOSH 905 years (Gen. 5:11)

ENOCH 365 years (Gen. 5:23)

METHUSELAH 969 years (Gen. 5:27)

LAMECH 777 years (Gen. 5:31)

NOAH 950 years (Gen. 9:29)

The Flood 〰〰〰〰〰〰〰〰〰〰〰 The Flood

SHEM 600 years (Gen. 11:10, 11)

EBER 464 years (Gen. 11:16, 17)

TERAH 205 years (Gen. 11:32)

ABRAHAM 175 years (Gen. 25:7)

ISAAC 180 years (Gen. 35:28)

JACOB 147 years (Gen. 47:28)

JOSEPH 110 years (Gen. 50:26)

The patriarchs who lived before the Flood had an average lifespan of about 900 years (Gen. 5). The ages of post-Flood patriarchs dropped rapidly and gradually leveled off (Gen. 11). Some suggest that this was due to major environmental changes brought about by the Flood.

The Tower of Babel

11 Now the whole earth had one language and one speech. ²And it came to pass, as they journeyed from the east, that they found a plain in the land of Shinar, and they dwelt there. ³Then they said to one another, "Come, let us make bricks and bake *them* thoroughly." They had brick for stone, and they had asphalt for mortar. ⁴And they said, "Come, let us build ourselves a city, and a tower whose top *is* in the heavens; let us make a name for ourselves, lest we be scattered abroad over the face of the whole earth."

⁵But the LORD came down to see the city and the tower which the sons of men had built. ⁶And the LORD said, "Indeed the people *are* one and they all have one language, and this is what they begin to do; now nothing that they propose to do will be withheld from them. ⁷Come, let Us go down and there confuse their language, that they may not understand one another's speech." ⁸So the LORD scattered them abroad from there over the face of all the earth, and they ceased building the city. ⁹Therefore its name is called Babel, because there the LORD confused the language of all the earth; and from there the LORD scattered them abroad over the face of all the earth.

Shem's Descendants

¹⁰This *is* the genealogy of Shem: Shem *was* one hundred years old, and begot Arphaxad two years after the flood. ¹¹After he begot Arphaxad, Shem lived five hundred years, and begot sons and daughters.

11:1 Since mention of separate languages has already been made (Gen. 10:5, 20, 31), these events must occur soon after the Flood (vv. 1–9). Moses lists the table of nations before he tells the story of the events that divide them.

11:4 The city and tower. This is the first reference to city-building since Cain's project (Gen. 4:17). These settlers seemingly belonged to the ungodly, rebellious line. This is confirmed by the word for tower (Heb. *migdal*), appearing elsewhere in Scripture as a symbol of pride that displeased God (Is. 2:15–17). The purpose of the builders in remaining together and aspiring toward the heavens is in direct contrast to God's command to move throughout the earth and cultivate it (Gen. 1:28; 9:1). "Top in the heavens" is figuratively

suggesting great size and godless ambition (see Deut. 1:28; 9:1; Jer. 51:53).

11:6 Unbridled ambition. The Hebrew verbs translated "propose," "to do," and "be withheld" are used together elsewhere only when God describes His own purposes (Job 42:2). As in the Garden of Eden, mankind was attempting to usurp divine prerogatives and would thus suffer judgment (Gen. 3:1–6; see chart, The Results of Sin).

11:9 Babel (perhaps from Heb. *balal,* lit. "to confuse") is later associated with Babylon, used throughout Scripture as a symbol of pride and rebellion against God.

11:10 The genealogy of Shem is repeated after the story of Babel to emphasize God's preservation of a godly line in the

THE SANCTITY OF LIFE *CREATED IN HIS IMAGE*

God places special value on human life (Gen. 1:26, 27; Ps. 8:4–6). Human life is sacred because the man and woman alone were created in the image of God, and that life deserves protection. God commands His people to protect and defend innocent human life (Ezek. 16:20, 21, 36, 38). Under the Mosaic Law, the murder of another person deserved punishment by death because of the value of the life that was destroyed (Gen. 9:6; Ex. 20:13).

Scripture extends this special status and protection to human life in every stage of development and need (Is. 46:3, 4). The unborn child shares in God's image (Ps. 139:13-16) and is protected under Old Testament law (Ex. 21:22–25). Believers are exhorted to defend and care for the sick, the elderly, and the poor (Lev. 19:32; Deut. 15:7, 8). *No one* is excluded from protection and care.

Throughout history this biblical view of the sanctity of all human life has faced opposition—most notably from those who advocate a "quality of life" viewpoint, suggesting that human life must possess certain qualities and abilities before it can be considered truly valuable and worthy of life sustenance. According to this distorted humanistic view, if the unborn child, the handicapped infant, or the elderly person does not possess these qualities, that individual is not entitled to the protection which Scripture or the Law would give.

The Bible rejects this "quality of life" view. The value of human life does not depend upon the person's functional abilities or independent viability but is assured because of the image of God that is found in every human life. God does not measure the quality of a human being before He bestows His image. God calls upon us to extend our care and compassion to every life He has created, in every stage of development and in every need.

See also Matt. 18:3, note; notes on Abortion (Jer. 1); Childbirth (John 16); Children (2 Sam. 21; Ps. 128; Prov. 22; Luke 15); Disabilities (Mark 2); Image of God (Ps. 8); Pregnancy (Judg. 13)

---

[12]Arphaxad lived thirty-five years, and begot Salah. [13]After he begot Salah, Arphaxad lived four hundred and three years, and begot sons and daughters.

[14]Salah lived thirty years, and begot Eber. [15]After he begot Eber, Salah lived four hundred and three years, and begot sons and daughters.

[16]Eber lived thirty-four years, and begot Peleg. [17]After he begot Peleg, Eber lived four hundred and thirty years, and begot sons and daughters.

[18]Peleg lived thirty years, and begot Reu. [19]After he begot Reu, Peleg lived two hundred and nine years, and begot sons and daughters.

[20]Reu lived thirty-two years, and begot Serug. [21]After he begot Serug, Reu lived two hundred and seven years, and begot sons and daughters.

[22]Serug lived thirty years, and begot Nahor. [23]After he begot Nahor, Serug lived two hundred years, and begot sons and daughters.

[24]Nahor lived twenty-nine years, and begot Terah. [25]After he begot Terah, Nahor lived one hundred and nineteen years, and begot sons and daughters.

[26]Now Terah lived seventy years, and begot Abram, Nahor, and Haran.

Terah's Descendants

[27]This *is* the genealogy of Terah: Terah begot Abram, Nahor, and Haran. Haran begot Lot. [28]And Haran died before his father Terah in his native land, in Ur of the Chaldeans. [29]Then Abram and Nahor took wives: the name of Abram's wife *was* Sarai, and the name of Nahor's wife, Milcah, the daughter of Haran the father of Milcah and the father of Iscah. [30]But Sarai was barren; she had no child.

[31]And Terah took his son Abram and his grandson Lot, the son of Haran, and his daughter-in-law Sarai, his son Abram's wife, and they went out with them from Ur of the Chaldeans to go to the

---

midst of wickedness. The genealogy is presented in multiples of seven, with the seventh places occupied by men of particular importance. From Adam to Enoch are seven generations; from Enoch to Eber, ancestor of the Hebrews, are seven; and from Eber to Abram are seven generations.

11:28 Ur of the Chaldeans is almost overwhelmingly identified as the Sumerian city on the Euphrates in southern Mesopotamia.

11:29 Taking a wife. This expression is a Hebrew idiom for getting married. Abram and Nahor and the women they married are important for history in general and God's plan specifically. Abram married his half sister Sarai, the daughter of his father

but not his mother; Nahor married Milcah, the daughter of his brother Haran and therefore his niece (see chart, The Family Tree of Abraham). Though such relationships would later be forbidden as incestuous (see Lev. 18), God planned for the human race to descend from one couple, necessitating marriage between brothers and sisters for a time. Certainly, however, there was never a sanction for any such relationship outside of marriage (see Gen. 19:31–38; Lev. 18, Incest).

11:31 Haran is in northern Mesopotamia on an upper branch of the Euphrates, approximately 600 miles north of Ur (see v. 28, note).

THE COVENANTS OF GENESIS

COVENANT	REFERENCE	TERMS
Edenic	Gen. 2:15–17	*GOD:* Provides for all man's needs. *MANKIND:* Forbidden to eat from the tree of knowledge of good and evil.
Adamic	Gen. 3:14–21	*GOD:* Gives promise of the Messiah. *MANKIND:* No requirements, but mankind will suffer consequences of sin until coming of the Messiah.
Noahic	Gen. 9:1–19	*GOD:* Will never flood the earth again. *MANKIND:* No requirements. *SIGN:* Rainbow (vv. 12, 13)
Abrahamic	Gen. 15:3–21	*GOD:* Will make a mighty nation of Abraham's descendants and give them the land of Canaan. *ABRAHAM:* Will walk before God and be blameless (Gen. 17:1, 2). *SIGN:* Circumcision (Gen. 17:10–14).

land of Canaan; and they came to Haran and dwelt there. ³²So the days of Terah were two hundred and five years, and Terah died in Haran.

Promises to Abram

12Now the LORD had said to Abram:

"Get out of your country,
From your family
And from your father's house,
To a land that I will show you.
²I will make you a great nation;
I will bless you
And make your name great;
And you shall be a blessing.
³I will bless those who bless you,
And I will curse him who curses you;
And in you all the families of the earth shall be
    blessed."

⁴So Abram departed as the LORD had spoken to him, and Lot went with him. And Abram *was* seventy-five years old when he departed from Haran.

⁵Then Abram took Sarai his wife and Lot his brother's son, and all their possessions that they had gathered, and the people whom they had acquired in Haran, and they departed to go to the land of Canaan. So they came to the land of Canaan. ⁶Abram passed through the land to the place of Shechem, as far as the terebinth tree of Moreh.ᵃ And the Canaanites *were* then in the land.

⁷Then the LORD appeared to Abram and said, "To your descendants I will give this land." And there he built an altar to the LORD, who had appeared to him. ⁸And he moved from there to the mountain east of Bethel, and he pitched his tent *with* Bethel on the west and Ai on the east; there he built an altar to the LORD and called on the name of the LORD. ⁹So Abram journeyed, going on still toward the South.ᵃ

Abram in Egypt

¹⁰Now there was a famine in the land, and Abram went down to Egypt to dwell there, for

12:6 ᵃHebrew *Alon Moreh*   12:9 ᵃHebrew *Negev*

12:1 Abram's story, like Noah's, begins with a command and promise from *Yahweh,* the covenant God. The command is to separate himself from his countrymen, undoubtedly idolators. The promise includes seven clauses:
1) "I will make you a great nation" (Heb. *goy*), implying the giving of territory (v. 7).
2) "I will bless you."
3) "I will . . . make your name great." The promise to make Abram's name great is a deliberate contrast to the efforts of the tower builders (Gen. 11:4); this language is used of royalty elsewhere in the OT (2 Sam. 7:9; Ps. 72:17).
4) "You shall be a blessing." This imperative is related to the first imperative, "Get out," and is central and pivotal to the promise. Abram's separation will result in his bringing blessing to others. The next three clauses deal with those who will be blessed.
5) "I will bless those who bless you."
6) "I will curse him who curses you."
7) "And in you all the families of the earth shall be blessed"

(vv. 2, 3). This last clause of the promise emphasizes Abram's role in the fulfillment of the divine plan for all humanity.

12:6 Shechem, lying in a valley between Mt. Ebal and Mt. Gerizim, was in central Canaan, approximately 500 miles south of Haran. Whether or not this city was the present Nablus is not as important as the fact that here God appeared to Abram. The terebinth tree was associated with "Moreh," probably a Canaanite shrine for divining, before God chose to reveal His power here in a theophany (a visual appearance of the Lord, v. 7).

12:8 Bethel (Heb., lit. "house of God") was 12 miles north of the eventual site of Jerusalem. What happened to Abram also happened to Jacob (Gen. 28:10–22). The naming of the city Bethel occurred when Jacob slept there. At this time it was a Canaanite city called Luz. Ai (lit. "the ruin") was known by this name at the time of its destruction (Josh. 7; 8). Abram did not stay in Canaanite cities; he pitched a tent on the outskirts.

12:10 Abram had not been forbidden by *Yahweh* to travel to Egypt. During famine, it was common for Palestinian peoples

SARAI (SARAH)   *A Submissive Wife*

Sarah appears in the Bible as God's paragon of a married woman. Two notable characteristics mark her life: beauty and barrenness. Because of her beauty, even pagan rulers desired her; yet her infertility caused deep domestic humiliation and even marital dissension. Sarah undoubtedly had beauty, brilliance, and creativity, but the quality which implants her in our memories and sets her apart is her unique and unequivocal devotion toward her husband Abraham. She shared not only her husband's challenges and heart aches but also his dreams and blessings. She did not waver; she stood by his side through good choices and bad decisions, adversities and blessings, in youth and old age. She is a fine example of a woman who loved her husband unconditionally and tenaciously.

More space is devoted to Sarah than to any other woman of the Bible. An entire chapter discusses her death and burial (Gen. 23). Both her husband and son grieved deeply when she died (Gen. 23:2; 24:67).

Two New Testament citations commend Sarah (Heb. 11:11; 1 Peter 3:6); she is mentioned in Romans as well (Rom. 4:19; 9:9); and she is used to illustrate the differences between the bonded and free (Gal. 4:21–31). She is styled as one of "the holy women" of old because she entrusted to her husband her willing cooperation. From the narrative it is apparent that Sarah was strong willed; yet she chose to submit to Abraham, an attitude which God commended. She was consistently identified as Abraham's wife, reinforcing the fact that God viewed the pair as one flesh. Together they were asked to believe that God would give them a son.

Sarah is the only wife named in the heroes of the faith (Heb. 11:11). Sarah's mothering experience fluctuated from emotions of skepticism, embarrassment, envy, and cruel recrimination to intense exhilaration and joy. Even though Sarah fell into sin, God faithfully kept His promise that she would be "a mother of nations" (Gen. 17:16).

Perhaps more than any other biblical woman, Sarah stands to teach women two supreme characteristics of godly womanhood: humble submission to their husbands in marriage and fervent commitment to nurturing the next generation.

See also Gen. 11:29—23:20; Is. 51:2; Rom. 4:19; 9:9; Gal. 4:21–31; Heb. 11:11; 1 Pet. 3:5, 6; notes on Infertility (Gen. 11); Submission (1 Pet. 3); Wives (Prov. 31)

---

the famine *was* severe in the land. [11]And it came to pass, when he was close to entering Egypt, that he said to Sarai his wife, "Indeed I know that you *are* a woman of beautiful countenance. [12]Therefore it will happen, when the Egyptians see you, that they will say, 'This *is* his wife'; and they will kill me, but they will let you live. [13]Please say you *are* my sister, that it may be well with me for your sake, and that I[a] may live because of you."

[14]So it was, when Abram came into Egypt, that the Egyptians saw the woman, that she *was* very beautiful. [15]The princes of Pharaoh also saw her and commended her to Pharaoh. And the woman was taken to Pharaoh's house. [16]He treated Abram well for her sake. He had sheep, oxen, male donkeys, male and female servants, female donkeys, and camels.

[17]But the LORD plagued Pharaoh and his house with great plagues because of Sarai, Abram's wife. [18]And Pharaoh called Abram and said, "What *is* this you have done to me? Why did you not tell me that she *was* your wife? [19]Why did you say, 'She *is* my sister'? I might have taken her as my wife. Now therefore, here is your wife; take *her* and go your way." [20]So Pharaoh commanded *his* men concerning him; and they sent him away, with his wife and all that he had.

Abram Inherits Canaan

13 Then Abram went up from Egypt, he and his wife and all that he had, and Lot with him, to the South.[a] [2]Abram *was* very rich in livestock, in silver, and in gold. [3]And he went on his journey from the South as far as Bethel, to the place where his tent had been at the beginning, between Bethel and Ai, [4]to the place of the altar which he had made there at first. And there Abram called on the name of the LORD.

[5]Lot also, who went with Abram, had flocks and herds and tents. [6]Now the land was not able to support them, that they might dwell together, for their possessions were so great that they could not dwell together. [7]And there was strife between the herdsmen of Abram's livestock and the herdsmen of Lot's livestock. The Canaanites and the Perizzites then dwelt in the land.

[8]So Abram said to Lot, "Please let there be no strife between you and me, and between my herdsmen and your herdsmen; for we *are*

···················
12:13 [a]Literally *my soul*   13:1 [a]Hebrew *Negev*

---

to take refuge in Egypt, which was usually well watered by the seasonal flooding of the Nile.

12:13 Abram's sister. Sarai was his half sister (Gen. 11:29, note;

20:12). Sarai, now 65, was at the midpoint of the patriarchal life span, the equivalent of modern-day thirties or early forties.

To possess is the same thing as to know: the Bible is always right.

Marguerite Yourcenar, 1935

brethren. ⁹*Is* not the whole land before you? Please separate from me. If *you take* the left, then I will go to the right; or, if *you go* to the right, then I will go to the left."

¹⁰And Lot lifted his eyes and saw all the plain of Jordan, that it *was* well watered everywhere (before the Lᴏʀᴅ destroyed Sodom and Gomorrah) like the garden of the Lᴏʀᴅ, like the land of Egypt as you go toward Zoar. ¹¹Then Lot chose for himself all the plain of Jordan, and Lot journeyed east. And they separated from each other. ¹²Abram dwelt in the land of Canaan, and Lot dwelt in the cities of the plain and pitched *his* tent even as far as Sodom. ¹³But the men of Sodom *were* exceedingly wicked and sinful against the Lᴏʀᴅ.

¹⁴And the Lᴏʀᴅ said to Abram, after Lot had separated from him: "Lift your eyes now and look from the place where you are—northward, southward, eastward, and westward; ¹⁵for all the land which you see I give to you and your descendants[a] forever. ¹⁶And I will make your descendants as the dust of the earth; so that if a man could number the dust of the earth, *then* your descendants also could be numbered. ¹⁷Arise, walk in the land through its length and its width, for I give it to you."

¹⁸Then Abram moved *his* tent, and went and dwelt by the terebinth trees of Mamre,[a] which *are* in Hebron, and built an altar there to the Lᴏʀᴅ.

Lot's Captivity and Rescue

14 And it came to pass in the days of Amraphel king of Shinar, Arioch king of Ellasar, Chedorlaomer king of Elam, and Tidal king of nations,[a] ²*that* they made war with Bera king of Sodom, Birsha king of Gomorrah, Shinab king of Admah, Shemeber king of Zeboiim, and the king of Bela

(that is, Zoar). ³All these joined together in the Valley of Siddim (that is, the Salt Sea). ⁴Twelve years they served Chedorlaomer, and in the thirteenth year they rebelled.

⁵In the fourteenth year Chedorlaomer and the kings that *were* with him came and attacked the Rephaim in Ashteroth Karnaim, the Zuzim in Ham, the Emim in Shaveh Kiriathaim, ⁶and the Horites in their mountain of Seir, as far as El Paran, which *is* by the wilderness. ⁷Then they turned back and came to En Mishpat (that *is,* Kadesh), and attacked all the country of the Amalekites, and also the Amorites who dwelt in Hazezon Tamar.

⁸And the king of Sodom, the king of Gomorrah, the king of Admah, the king of Zeboiim, and the king of Bela (that *is,* Zoar) went out and joined together in battle in the Valley of Siddim ⁹against Chedorlaomer king of Elam, Tidal king of nations,[a] Amraphel king of Shinar, and Arioch king of Ellasar—four kings against five. ¹⁰Now the Valley of Siddim *was full of* asphalt pits; and the kings of Sodom and Gomorrah fled; *some* fell there, and the remainder fled to the mountains. ¹¹Then they took all the goods of Sodom and Gomorrah, and all their provisions, and went their way. ¹²They also took Lot, Abram's brother's son who dwelt in Sodom, and his goods, and departed.

¹³Then one who had escaped came and told Abram the Hebrew, for he dwelt by the terebinth trees of Mamre[a] the Amorite, brother of Eshcol and brother of Aner; and they *were* allies with Abram. ¹⁴Now when Abram heard that his brother was taken captive, he armed his three hundred

· · · · · · · · · · · · · · · ·

13:15 [a]Literally *seed,* and so throughout the book   **13:18; 14:13** [a]Hebrew *Alon Mamre*   **14:1** [a]Hebrew *goyim*   **14:9** [a]Hebrew *goyim*

13:9 Abram's concession. By allowing Lot first choice of land, Abram put aside his own right as head of the family. This appears to be an act of faith in God's promise and stands in contrast to his earlier actions based on fear (Gen. 12:7, 10–20).

13:13 Sodom, like Zoar, probably lay at the southern end of the Dead Sea and may now be underwater. Sodom was a center of homosexuality (Gen. 19:5), a sin directly against *Yahweh* (see Gen. 19:5; Lev. 18, Homosexuality).

13:18 Mamre is the modern site of Ramet el-Khalil, almost two miles north of Hebron in southcentral Canaan. Abram would probably have used the Negev for grazing land. Mamre was named after a prominent Amorite (Gen. 14:13).

14:5 Chedorlaomer and his allies formed a power complex which dominated territory all the way to the Jordan River. On its way down to the Dead Sea, the united army followed the

"King's Highway," which has been a major route of travel throughout history (Num. 20:17). The Rephaim, Zuzim, and Emim are described as "giants" (Deut. 2:10–12, 20–23). The path of conquest extended to the Wilderness of Paran, at the top of the Red Sea. The army then turned north to Kadesh, in the Negev south of Canaan, and ended up at Hazezon Tamar on the western shore of the Dead Sea. Archaeological evidence confirms great destruction in this area around 1900 B.C.

14:10 Asphalt pits. The Hebrew text repeats "pits" (lit. "pits of bitumen"), emphasizing the frequency and size of the depressions. Asphalt, or bitumen, is a mineral found in great deposits around the Dead Sea. A kind of pitch, this sticky substance was used on Noah's ark and for mortar (Gen. 6:14; 11:3). "Fall" can also mean "lower oneself," as in hiding, which explains the reappearance of the king of Sodom (v. 17).

B L E S S I N G S   GIFTS FROM A LOVING FATHER

The blessings of God are abundantly bestowed on all those who follow Him. God's blessings are not simply a reward for godly living but a gift from a loving Father. Life's blessings are not a measure of who we are but of who God is. God promises personal blessings to those who follow Him in obedience and exhorts His people to be a blessing to others (Gen. 12:2, 3).

Christians need only to reflect back over their own lives to discover blessings from God. While blessings are experienced in different ways, provision, protection, and salvation are among God's greatest blessings. The goodness of God is also apparent when Christians look around at present blessings.

Health, family, friends, and ministry are among God's choicest blessings. Christians can also look ahead to future blessings. God promises continual blessings on earth and eternal blessings in heaven.

The wonderful blessings of God should be remembered, not forgotten. The same gracious God who forgives sin, heals diseases, redeems lives, and bestows mercy, also promises abundant blessings (Ps. 103:2–5).

See also Num. 23:20; Is. 61:9; James 1:17; notes on Gratitude (Ps. 95); Promises of God (2 Pet. 1); Prosperity (Ps. 2); Providence (Eccl. 7); Spiritual Gifts (Rom. 12)

and eighteen trained *servants* who were born in his own house, and went in pursuit as far as Dan. [15]He divided his forces against them by night, and he and his servants attacked them and pursued them as far as Hobah, which *is* north of Damascus. [16]So he brought back all the goods, and also brought back his brother Lot and his goods, as well as the women and the people.

[17]And the king of Sodom went out to meet him at the Valley of Shaveh (that *is*, the King's Valley), after his return from the defeat of Chedorlaomer and the kings who *were* with him.

Abram and Melchizedek

[18]Then Melchizedek king of Salem brought out bread and wine; he *was* the priest of God Most High. [19]And he blessed him and said:

"Blessed be Abram of God Most High,
Possessor of heaven and earth;
[20]And blessed be God Most High,
Who has delivered your enemies into your
      hand."

And he gave him a tithe of all.
[21]Now the king of Sodom said to Abram, "Give me the persons, and take the goods for yourself."

[22]But Abram said to the king of Sodom, "I have raised my hand to the Lord, God Most High, the Possessor of heaven and earth, [23]that I *will take* nothing, from a thread to a sandal strap, and that I will not take anything that *is* yours, lest you should say, 'I have made Abram rich'— [24]except only what the young men have eaten, and the portion of the men who went with me: Aner, Eshcol, and Mamre; let them take their portion."

God's Covenant with Abram

15 After these things the word of the Lord came to Abram in a vision, saying, "Do not be afraid, Abram. I *am* your shield, your exceedingly great reward."

[2]But Abram said, "Lord God, what will You give me, seeing I go childless, and the heir of my house *is* Eliezer of Damascus?" [3]Then Abram said, "Look, You have given me no offspring; indeed one born in my house is my heir!"

[4]And behold, the word of the Lord *came* to him, saying, "This one shall not be your heir, but one who will come from your own body shall be your heir." [5]Then He brought him outside and said, "Look now toward heaven, and count the stars if you are able to number them." And He said to him, "So shall your descendants be."

[6]And he believed in the Lord, and He accounted it to him for righteousness.

[7]Then He said to him, "I *am* the Lord, who brought you out of Ur of the Chaldeans, to give you this land to inherit it."

14:18 Melchizedek, whose name means "my king is righteousness," is described as "king of Salem" or "king of peace." Some identify him as king of nearby Jerusalem (see Ps. 76:2). As both priest and king, Melchizedek foreshadowed Christ (Ps. 110:4). Like Abram, Melchizedek worshiped the true God. His description (v. 18), his blessing of Abram (vv. 19–20), and his acceptance of a tithe (v. 20) have prompted some to identify this as a Christophany, an appearance of the preincarnate Christ (see Heb. 7:1–10).

15:6 Abram's great faith took the words of God as proof enough (see Gen. 12:1–4). The word "believed" appears twice

more (Gen. 42:20; 45:26); both times it involves the presence of proof for the statement made. God placed Abram's faith on the scale of justice, causing it to tip toward righteousness (see Rom. 4:3).

15:7 Confirmation of the covenant. God makes the Abrahamic covenant with Abram (vv. 7–21). The confirmation of the covenant has five parts:

1) God reminded Abram of His faithfulness in the past (v. 7).

2) God gave a sign to confirm His promise (vv. 8–12).

3) God specified the provision of the covenant (vv. 13–16).

THE FAMILY TREE OF ABRAHAM

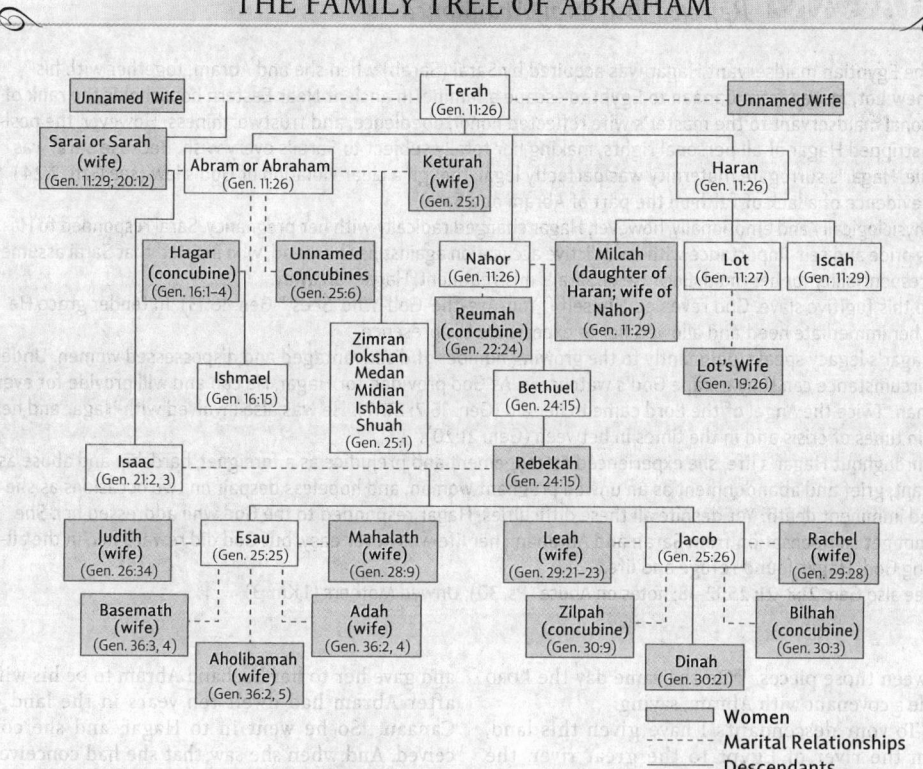

Terah (Gen. 11:26)

Unnamed Wife

Unnamed Wife

Sarai or Sarah (wife) (Gen. 11:29; 20:12)

Abram or Abraham (Gen. 11:26)

Keturah (wife) (Gen. 25:1)

Haran (Gen. 11:26)

Hagar (concubine) (Gen. 16:1–4)

Unnamed Concubines (Gen. 25:6)

Nahor (Gen. 11:26)

Milcah (daughter of Haran; wife of Nahor) (Gen. 11:29)

Lot (Gen. 11:27)

Iscah (Gen. 11:29)

Reumah (concubine) (Gen. 22:24)

Zimran Jokshan Medan Midian Ishbak Shuah (Gen. 25:1)

Ishmael (Gen. 16:15)

Bethuel (Gen. 24:15)

Lot's Wife (Gen. 19:26)

Isaac (Gen. 21:2, 3)

Rebekah (Gen. 24:15)

Judith (wife) (Gen. 26:34)

Esau (Gen. 25:25)

Mahalath (wife) (Gen. 28:9)

Leah (wife) (Gen. 29:21–23)

Jacob (Gen. 25:26)

Rachel (wife) (Gen. 29:28)

Basemath (wife) (Gen. 36:3, 4)

Adah (wife) (Gen. 36:2, 4)

Zilpah (concubine) (Gen. 30:9)

Bilhah (concubine) (Gen. 30:3)

Aholibamah (wife) (Gen. 36:2, 5)

Dinah (Gen. 30:21)

☐ Women
- - - - - Marital Relationships
——— Descendants

[8]And he said, "Lord GOD, how shall I know that I will inherit it?"

[9]So He said to him, "Bring Me a three-year-old heifer, a three-year-old female goat, a three-year-old ram, a turtledove, and a young pigeon." [10]Then he brought all these to Him and cut them in two, down the middle, and placed each piece opposite the other; but he did not cut the birds in two. [11]And when the vultures came down on the carcasses, Abram drove them away.

[12]Now when the sun was going down, a deep sleep fell upon Abram; and behold, horror *and* great darkness fell upon him. [13]Then He said to Abram: "Know certainly that your descendants will be strangers in a land *that is* not theirs, and will serve them, and they will afflict them four hundred years. [14]And also the nation whom they serve I will judge; afterward they shall come out with great possessions. [15]Now as for you, you shall go to your fathers in peace; you shall be buried at a good old age. [16]But in the fourth generation they shall return here, for the iniquity of the Amorites *is* not yet complete."

[17]And it came to pass, when the sun went down and it was dark, that behold, there appeared a smoking oven and a burning torch that passed

4) God ratified the covenant by a divine appearance (v. 17).

5) God concluded the covenant with an unconditional promise (v. 18).

15:9 The sign of the covenant. The animals have a double significance. They acted as the sacrifices which accompanied covenant-making in the OT. In addition, the party who passed through the animals bound himself to fulfill the covenant, lest a similar fate come upon him if the covenant were to be violated.

15:13 400 years is a rounded or approximate figure; 430 years is the exact duration of the exile (Ex. 12:40, 41).

15:16 The iniquity of the Amorites. Israel would only inherit the land after the Canaanite inhabitants had passed the point of divine tolerance. In His omniscient foreknowledge, God knew the timing of that ultimate judgment, which would give the Israelites their land.

15:17 Smoke and fire. Elsewhere in the Pentateuch, smoke and fire accompany manifestations of the divine presence (see Ex. 19:18). God passed between the cut halves of the animals. This was a strong method of covenant ratification (see v. 9, note). Abram was not required to perform this ritual; God chose to bind Himself to a unilateral obligation.

HAGAR *Rejected But Not Abandoned*

The Egyptian maidservant Hagar was acquired by Sarai (Sarah) when she and Abram, together with his nephew Lot, moved from Canaan to Egypt to escape a famine. In ancient Near Eastern households the rank of personal maidservant to the master's wife reflected honor, obedience, and trustworthiness. However, the position stripped Hagar of all personal rights, making her totally subject to Sarai's every wish. Because Sarai was sterile, Hagar's surrogate maternity was perfectly legal, though a clear violation of God's law (see Gen. 2:24) and evidence of a lack of faith on the part of Abram and Sarai.

Physiologically and emotionally, however, Hagar changed radically with her pregnancy. Sarai responded to Hagar's pride and self-importance with a vindictive accusation against her husband, who insisted that Sarai assume full responsibility for her maid. Because of Sarai's mistreatment, Hagar ran away.

To this fugitive slave, God revealed Himself ("You-Are-the-God-Who-Sees," Gen. 16:13). In tender grace He met her immediate need and allowed her to experience His presence.

Hagar's legacy speaks poignantly to the growing number of disadvantaged and dispossessed women. Under no circumstance can they escape God's watchcare. As God provided for Hagar, He can and will provide for every woman. Twice the Angel of the Lord came to her aid (Gen. 16:7; 21:17). He was also involved with Hagar and her son in times of crisis and in the times in between (Gen. 21:20).

Throughout Hagar's life, she experienced estrangement and prejudice as a foreigner, hardship and abuse as a servant, grief and abandonment as an unwed pregnant woman, and hopeless despair on two occasions as she faced imminent death. Yet despite all these difficulties, Hagar responded to the God who addressed her. She did not get compensation from Sarah and Abraham; her life was never easy, but God did reward her. In the all-seeing God, Hagar found refuge and life.

See also Gen. 21:8–21; 25:12–18; notes on Abuse (Ps. 30); Unwed Mothers (1 Kin. 3)

between those pieces. [18]On the same day the LORD made a covenant with Abram, saying:

"To your descendants I have given this land, from the river of Egypt to the great river, the River Euphrates— [19]the Kenites, the Kenezzites, the Kadmonites, [20]the Hittites, the Perizzites, the Rephaim, [21]the Amorites, the Canaanites, the Girgashites, and the Jebusites."

Hagar and Ishmael

16 Now Sarai, Abram's wife, had borne him no *children*. And she had an Egyptian maidservant whose name was Hagar. [2]So Sarai said to Abram, "See now, the LORD has restrained me from bearing *children*. Please, go in to my maid; perhaps I shall obtain children by her." And Abram heeded the voice of Sarai. [3]Then Sarai, Abram's wife, took Hagar her maid, the Egyptian, and gave her to her husband Abram to be his wife, after Abram had dwelt ten years in the land of Canaan. [4]So he went in to Hagar, and she conceived. And when she saw that she had conceived, her mistress became despised in her eyes.

[5]Then Sarai said to Abram, "My wrong *be* upon you! I gave my maid into your embrace; and when she saw that she had conceived, I became despised in her eyes. The LORD judge between you and me."

[6]So Abram said to Sarai, "Indeed your maid *is* in your hand; do to her as you please." And when Sarai dealt harshly with her, she fled from her presence.

[7]Now the Angel of the LORD found her by a spring of water in the wilderness, by the spring on the way to Shur. [8]And He said, "Hagar, Sarai's maid, where have you come from, and where are you going?"

15:18 The terms of the covenant promise are that God will give Abram's descendants the land belonging to the ten nations listed (vv. 19–21; see also chart, The Covenants of Genesis). The "river of Egypt" is the Wadi el-Arish, which divides Canaan and Egypt. The area across the Jordan was also promised. Israel reached these borders during the reign of David.

16:2 Sarai's plan. There is a parallel—both in the words used and in their respective actions—between Sarai, who "took Hagar . . . and gave her to her husband Abram," and Eve, who "took of its fruit and . . . also gave to her husband" (Gen. 3:6). In both cases, the woman willfully took the initiative, and the man was a willing recipient. Hagar became Abram's concubine and the mother of his child. The taking of a concubine to assure male heirs was both accepted and legal in the ancient

Near East. Nevertheless, Abram had been called out from his cultural surroundings (Gen. 12:1–3). Sarai's plan for securing an heir was in essence polygamy, and polygamy always has been in violation of the Creator's plan for marriage (Gen. 2:24; see 1 Tim. 3, Polygamy).

16:7 The Angel of the Lord is associated with the covenant God. The Angel is thought by many to be a theophany or an appearance of God Himself, as Hagar recognized (v. 13; see also chart, The Angel of the Lord). The Angel appears in Genesis to prevent the thwarting of God's plan for His chosen people (see Gen. 22:11). Because the Angel seems to distinguish Himself from *Yahweh* while still claiming deity (vv. 11–13), He has been identified by some as the preincarnate Christ.

16:8 Hagar was returning to her home country Egypt; Shur is

We can trust an unknown future to a known God.

Corrie Ten Boom

She said, "I am fleeing from the presence of my mistress Sarai."

⁹The Angel of the LORD said to her, "Return to your mistress, and submit yourself under her hand." ¹⁰Then the Angel of the LORD said to her, "I will multiply your descendants exceedingly, so that they shall not be counted for multitude." ¹¹And the Angel of the LORD said to her:

"Behold, you *are* with child,
And you shall bear a son.
You shall call his name Ishmael,
Because the LORD has heard your affliction.
¹²He shall be a wild man;
His hand *shall be* against every man,
And every man's hand against him.
And he shall dwell in the presence of all his
    brethren."

¹³Then she called the name of the LORD who spoke to her, You-Are-the-God-Who-Sees; for she said, "Have I also here seen Him who sees me?" ¹⁴Therefore the well was called Beer Lahai Roi;ᵃ observe, *it is* between Kadesh and Bered.

¹⁵So Hagar bore Abram a son; and Abram named his son, whom Hagar bore, Ishmael. ¹⁶Abram *was* eighty-six years old when Hagar bore Ishmael to Abram.

The Sign of the Covenant

17When Abram was ninety-nine years old, the LORD appeared to Abram and said to him, "I *am* Almighty God; walk before Me and be blame-less. ²And I will make My covenant between Me and you, and will multiply you exceedingly." ³Then Abram fell on his face, and God talked with him, saying: ⁴"As for Me, behold, My covenant is with you, and you shall be a father of many nations. ⁵No longer shall your name be called Abram, but your name shall be Abraham; for I have made you a father of many nations. ⁶I will make you exceedingly fruitful; and I will make nations of you, and kings shall come from you. ⁷And I will establish My covenant between Me and you and your descendants after you in their genera-tions, for an everlasting covenant, to be God to you and your descendants after you. ⁸Also I give to you and your descendants after you the land in which you are a stranger, all the land of Canaan, as an everlasting possession; and I will be their God."

⁹And God said to Abraham: "As for you, you shall keep My covenant, you and your descendants after you throughout their generations. ¹⁰This *is* My covenant which you shall keep, between Me and you and your descendants after you: Every male child among you shall be circumcised; ¹¹and you shall be circumcised in the flesh of your fore-skins, and it shall be a sign of the covenant be-tween Me and you. ¹²He who is eight days old among you shall be circumcised, every male child in your generations, he who is born in your house or bought with money from any foreigner who is

17:14 ᵃLiterally *Well of the One Who Lives and Sees Me*

at Canaan's southern border (v. 7). God's method of commu-nication often utilized questioning but never implied lack of omniscience (see Gen. 3:9–11; 4:6).

16:10 The Angel's promise. Hagar received directly from God a promise of descendants. Ishmael (Heb., lit. "God hears") was the father of 12 princes (v. 11; Gen. 25:13–16), paralleling the 12 tribes descended from Isaac's son Jacob. Still, Ishmael's de-scendants would not inherit the land. "In the presence of" also carries the sense of "against the face of" (v. 12), predict-ing the hostility between the descendants of Ishmael and Isaac. While God had compassion on Hagar, He did not allow Abram's attempt to secure an heir through his own means to defeat His plan.

16:14 The well (lit. "well of the living one who sees me") was between Kadesh and Bered on Canaan's southern border. Kadesh Barnea is the modern site of Ain Quedeis in the wilderness of the Negev.

17:1 The affirmation of the covenant. A second stage in the establishment of the Abrahamic covenant came 14 to 22 years after the events of chapter 15 (see chart, The Covenants of Genesis). This reaffirmation of the covenant, like its estab-lishment, involved God's revelation of Himself and a divine promise. In this chapter, reciprocal action is demanded from Abram (obedience, v. 1; circumcision, vv. 10–14). "Blameless" carries with it the idea of "unblemished" and possibly "trans-parent" or "candid." In Scripture, this is the first use of the name *El Shaddai* ("Almighty God"), which in Genesis appears in the context of resolving covenant difficulties, especially those involving the continuation of the covenant line (Gen. 28:3; 35:11).

17:5 The renaming of Abram (lit. "exalted father") is perhaps a reference to his own aristocratic family. The focus of this name change ("Abraham," lit. "father of many nations") is on his eventual progeny of kings and nations (v. 6), while earlier this focus was primarily concerned with Abram's immediate heir (Gen. 15).

17:10 Circumcision. The eternal covenant is accompanied by a permanent physical sign. Where earlier covenant signs merely commemorated the making of a covenant (Gen. 9:12, the rain-bow; 15:7, 8, the divine appearance), circumcision carried the additional function of separation (see Circumcision).

CIRCUMCISION   A SIGN OF THE COVENANT

Circumcision is the surgical removal of the foreskin of the penis. Baby boys are often circumcised for reasons of health and hygiene, but in biblical times and in modern Jewish communities, circumcision is a religious ritual, distinguishing the seed of Abraham or the Jew from the Gentile.

When God first made a covenant with Abraham, the father of all the faithful, God commanded circumcision as a sign of that faith relationship (Gen. 17:11). This act of obedience also represented the putting away of evil (Deut. 10:16; Jer. 4:4). Because God's covenant promises to Abraham were fully realized by Jesus Christ, the apostle Paul taught that every Christian, both male and female, is circumcised, not by human hands, but in Christ when the sinful nature is replaced by Christ's presence (Rom. 2:29; Col. 2:11).

See also Ex. 12:48; notes on Childbirth (John 16); Culture (Is. 51)

not your descendant. ¹³He who is born in your house and he who is bought with your money must be circumcised, and My covenant shall be in your flesh for an everlasting covenant. ¹⁴And the uncircumcised male child, who is not circumcised in the flesh of his foreskin, that person shall be cut off from his people; he has broken My covenant."

¹⁵Then God said to Abraham, "As for Sarai your wife, you shall not call her name Sarai, but Sarah *shall be* her name. ¹⁶And I will bless her and also give you a son by her; then I will bless her, and she shall be *a mother* of nations; kings of peoples shall be from her."

¹⁷Then Abraham fell on his face and laughed, and said in his heart, "Shall *a child* be born to a man who is one hundred years old? And shall Sarah, who is ninety years old, bear *a child?*" ¹⁸And Abraham said to God, "Oh, that Ishmael might live before You!"

¹⁹Then God said: "No, Sarah your wife shall bear you a son, and you shall call his name Isaac; I will establish My covenant with him for an everlasting covenant, *and* with his descendants after him. ²⁰And as for Ishmael, I have heard you. Behold, I have blessed him, and will make him fruitful, and will multiply him exceedingly. He shall beget twelve princes, and I will make him a great

nation. ²¹But My covenant I will establish with Isaac, whom Sarah shall bear to you at this set time next year." ²²Then He finished talking with him, and God went up from Abraham.

²³So Abraham took Ishmael his son, all who were born in his house and all who were bought with his money, every male among the men of Abraham's house, and circumcised the flesh of their foreskins that very same day, as God had said to him. ²⁴Abraham *was* ninety-nine years old when he was circumcised in the flesh of his foreskin. ²⁵And Ishmael his son *was* thirteen years old when he was circumcised in the flesh of his foreskin. ²⁶That very same day Abraham was circumcised, and his son Ishmael; ²⁷and all the men of his house, born in the house or bought with money from a foreigner, were circumcised with him.

The Son of Promise

18 Then the LORD appeared to him by the terebinth trees of Mamre,ª as he was sitting in the tent door in the heat of the day. ²So he lifted his eyes and looked, and behold, three men were standing by him; and when he saw *them,* he ran from the tent door to meet them, and bowed him-

····················
18:1 ªHebrew *Alon Mamre*

17:14 To be cut off can be interpreted either as excommunication from the nation (Ex. 12:19; Lev. 7:20, 21, 25; 17:9, 10) or as an untimely death by the congregation of Israel or by God Himself (Ex. 31:14).

17:15 Sarai's new name is obviously a part of the new covenant relationship, though the meaning of the change is not addressed as was the renaming of Abraham (v. 5). Clearly Sarah is an equal partner in the covenant (v. 16). Some have suggested "Sarai" as being from a root meaning "to contend" and "Sarah" as meaning "princess." The latter is definitely the prevalent meaning. In any case, the change added to the dignity of the occasion when God openly and publicly declared Sarah's part in the covenant.

17:17 Isaac's birth is connected with laughter. Isaac (Heb., lit. "he laughs," v. 19) not only alludes to the laughter of Abraham

and Sarah (Gen. 18:12; 21:6) but may also be an implied prayer that God will smile and show favor to this son.

17:20 Ishmael. The contrast with Isaac is clear; God does not make a covenant (Heb. *berith*) with Ishmael, although the promise to both sons is similar; the sons of each will form 12 tribes.

17:25 Ishmael's circumcision. Although Ishmael was not included in the covenant with Abraham, his circumcision marks his participation in God's grace towards Abraham's descendants (see Circumcision).

18:1 The appearance of the Lord. Abraham took the covenant-confirming step of circumcision. The three men could well have been God Himself, in a theophany or Christophany (vv. 13, 33), accompanied by two angels (Gen. 19:1).

self to the ground, ³and said, "My Lord, if I have now found favor in Your sight, do not pass on by Your servant. ⁴Please let a little water be brought, and wash your feet, and rest yourselves under the tree. ⁵And I will bring a morsel of bread, that you may refresh your hearts. After that you may pass by, inasmuch as you have come to your servant."

They said, "Do as you have said."

⁶So Abraham hurried into the tent to Sarah and said, "Quickly, make ready three measures of fine meal; knead *it* and make cakes." ⁷And Abraham ran to the herd, took a tender and good calf, gave *it* to a young man, and he hastened to prepare it. ⁸So he took butter and milk and the calf which he had prepared, and set *it* before them; and he stood by them under the tree as they ate.

⁹Then they said to him, "Where *is* Sarah your wife?"

So he said, "Here, in the tent."

¹⁰And He said, "I will certainly return to you according to the time of life, and behold, Sarah your wife shall have a son."

(Sarah was listening in the tent door which *was* behind him.) ¹¹Now Abraham and Sarah were old, well advanced in age; *and* Sarah had passed the age of childbearing.ᵃ ¹²Therefore Sarah laughed within herself, saying, "After I have grown old, shall I have pleasure, my lord being old also?"

¹³And the LORD said to Abraham, "Why did Sarah laugh, saying, 'Shall I surely bear *a child*, since I am old?' ¹⁴Is anything too hard for the LORD? At the appointed time I will return to you, according to the time of life, and Sarah shall have a son."

¹⁵But Sarah denied *it*, saying, "I did not laugh," for she was afraid.

And He said, "No, but you did laugh!"

Abraham Intercedes for Sodom

¹⁶Then the men rose from there and looked toward Sodom, and Abraham went with them to send them on the way. ¹⁷And the LORD said, "Shall I hide from Abraham what I am doing, ¹⁸since Abraham shall surely become a great and mighty nation, and all the nations of the earth shall be blessed in him? ¹⁹For I have known him, in order that he may command his children and his house-

hold after him, that they keep the way of the LORD, to do righteousness and justice, that the LORD may bring to Abraham what He has spoken to him." ²⁰And the LORD said, "Because the outcry against Sodom and Gomorrah is great, and because their sin is very grave, ²¹I will go down now and see whether they have done altogether according to the outcry against it that has come to Me; and if not, I will know."

²²Then the men turned away from there and went toward Sodom, but Abraham still stood before the LORD. ²³And Abraham came near and said, "Would You also destroy the righteous with the wicked? ²⁴Suppose there were fifty righteous within the city; would You also destroy the place and not spare *it* for the fifty righteous that were in it? ²⁵Far be it from You to do such a thing as this, to slay the righteous with the wicked, so that the righteous should be as the wicked; far be it from You! Shall not the Judge of all the earth do right?"

²⁶So the LORD said, "If I find in Sodom fifty righteous within the city, then I will spare all the place for their sakes."

²⁷Then Abraham answered and said, "Indeed now, I who *am but* dust and ashes have taken it upon myself to speak to the Lord: ²⁸Suppose there were five less than the fifty righteous; would You destroy all of the city for *lack of* five?"

So He said, "If I find there forty-five, I will not destroy *it*."

²⁹And he spoke to Him yet again and said, "Suppose there should be forty found there?"

So He said, "I will not do *it* for the sake of forty."

³⁰Then he said, "Let not the Lord be angry, and I will speak: Suppose thirty should be found there?"

So He said, "I will not do *it* if I find thirty there."

³¹And he said, "Indeed now, I have taken it upon myself to speak to the Lord: Suppose twenty should be found there?"

So He said, "I will not destroy *it* for the sake of twenty."

³²Then he said, "Let not the Lord be angry, and

18:11 ᵃLiterally *the manner of women had ceased to be with Sarah*

18:3 My Lord. The timing of Abraham's recognition of the identity of his visitors is not clear. *'Adonai* (Heb.), accompanied by the particle for polite request to a superior, could have also been used to address a distinguished earthly visitor. The lavishness of the feast—using approximately eight gallons of meal and an entire calf—may suggest a plan for later ritual offerings of meal and meat, hinting that Abraham does in fact recognize his visitor (v. 6).

18:9–12 God's question, "Where is?" continues His pattern of summoning His creation (v. 9; see Gen. 3:9; 4:9). The promise is a son for Sarah "according to the time of life" (lit. "the time

when it is reviving," v. 10). This phrase is commonly used for spring, meaning "at the same time next year," and emphasizing the contrast between Sarah's "I have grown old" (lit. "worn out" like a garment, v. 12) and God's promise of her renewed youth. This is apparently the first time Sarah has heard this promise applied specifically to her. Her response is identical to Abraham's (17:17).

18:23 Abraham's intercession is the first illustration of God's promise that Abraham will be a blessing to the entire world (Gen. 12:3).

MENOPAUSE *BEYOND FERTILITY*

Menopause—the cessation of a woman's monthly periods—announces the retirement of her ovaries from active duty and thus the end of her childbearing years. Aging and physical changes occurring after menopause are sometimes considered a negative issue. Indeed, there can be unpleasant physical repercussions. Yet God made clear that there is a season for all things (Eccl. 3:1–12). Events take place on heaven's timeline, but God encourages us to focus on today, to honor the wisdom that comes with aging (Job 12:12), and to serve Him in our own lifetime by doing good (Eccl. 3:12).

Three post-menopausal women stand out as key figures in the Bible. Naomi, who thought herself too old to be of any use in Ruth's life (Ruth 1:12), was essential in the courtship of Ruth and Boaz and contributed to the rearing of their son Obed (Ruth 4:16, 17). Both Sarah and Elizabeth in their old age conceived and bore sons who played important roles in the kingdom (Gen. 18:11; Luke 1:36). Each of these wise and godly women was instrumental in the familial lineage or events surrounding the birth of Jesus Christ.

Besides biblical encouragement, post-menopausal women also have medical help available. Enjoying of post-menopausal years in healthy activity is often a matter of personal choice and planning. The uncomfortable physical symptoms of menopause can often be avoided or minimized by working with a physician. God never meant for your value to be determined by age or constrained by hormone levels. Remember: God can use you at any age if your heart is faithful to Him.

See also Ruth 1:12; Eccl. 3:1; notes on Aging (Is. 46); Menstrual Cycle (Lev. 15); Premenstrual Syndrome (Prov. 21)

I will speak but once more: Suppose ten should be found there?"

And He said, "I will not destroy *it* for the sake of ten." ³³So the Lord went His way as soon as He had finished speaking with Abraham; and Abraham returned to his place.

Sodom's Depravity

19Now the two angels came to Sodom in the evening, and Lot was sitting in the gate of Sodom. When Lot saw *them,* he rose to meet them, and he bowed himself with his face toward the ground. ²And he said, "Here now, my lords, please turn in to your servant's house and spend the night, and wash your feet; then you may rise early and go on your way."

And they said, "No, but we will spend the night in the open square."

³But he insisted strongly; so they turned in to him and entered his house. Then he made them a feast, and baked unleavened bread, and they ate.

⁴Now before they lay down, the men of the city, the men of Sodom, both old and young, all the people from every quarter, surrounded the house. ⁵And they called to Lot and said to him, "Where are the men who came to you tonight? Bring them out to us that we may know them *carnally.*"

⁶So Lot went out to them through the doorway, shut the door behind him, ⁷and said, "Please, my brethren, do not do so wickedly! ⁸See now, I have two daughters who have not known a man; please, let me bring them out to you, and you may do to them as you wish; only do nothing to these men, since this is the reason they have come under the shadow of my roof."

⁹And they said, "Stand back!" Then they said, "This one came in to stay *here,* and he keeps acting as a judge; now we will deal worse with you than with them." So they pressed hard against the man Lot, and came near to break down the door. ¹⁰But the men reached out their hands and pulled Lot into the house with them, and shut the door. ¹¹And they struck the men who *were* at the doorway of the house with blindness, both small and great, so that they became weary *trying* to find the door.

Sodom and Gomorrah Destroyed

¹²Then the men said to Lot, "Have you anyone else here? Son-in-law, your sons, your daughters, and whomever you have in the city—take *them* out of this place! ¹³For we will destroy this place, because the outcry against them has grown great before the face of the Lord, and the Lord has sent us to destroy it."

19:1 The two angels. The three visitors to Abraham were a theophany of *Yahweh* (Gen. 18:13) and two heavenly companions. Lot's position "in the gate" demonstrates his social standing in Sodom as a man of importance; he no longer lives in a tent on the outskirts but has established himself in the heart of this wicked society (see Gen. 13:11, 12).

19:5 Lot's offer of his daughters leaves no doubt that this phrase refers to sexual intimacy (v. 8). Sexual perversions were common in Canaanite culture and religious rites. Lot re-

flects the effects of Sodom on his own morality. Sexual violence is condemned in Genesis 34 as well as in the rest of OT history (Judg. 19:22, 23; 2 Sam. 13). Lot is rescued not because of his own virtue but because of his relationship to Abraham (v. 29).

19:11 Blindness. This Hebrew word for blindness is unusual. It occurs again only in a divinely caused loss of sight (2 Kin. 6:18) and may carry the connotation of "dazzled," as in Saul's Damascus Road experience (Acts 9:3–8).

¹⁴So Lot went out and spoke to his sons-in-law, who had married his daughters, and said, "Get up, get out of this place; for the LORD will destroy this city!" But to his sons-in-law he seemed to be joking.

¹⁵When the morning dawned, the angels urged Lot to hurry, saying, "Arise, take your wife and your two daughters who are here, lest you be consumed in the punishment of the city." ¹⁶And while he lingered, the men took hold of his hand, his wife's hand, and the hands of his two daughters, the LORD being merciful to him, and they brought him out and set him outside the city. ¹⁷So it came to pass, when they had brought them outside, that heᵃ said, "Escape for your life! Do not look behind you nor stay anywhere in the plain. Escape to the mountains, lest you be destroyed."

¹⁸Then Lot said to them, "Please, no, my lords! ¹⁹Indeed now, your servant has found favor in your sight, and you have increased your mercy which you have shown me by saving my life; but I cannot escape to the mountains, lest some evil overtake me and I die. ²⁰See now, this city *is* near *enough* to flee to, and it *is* a little one; please let me escape there (*is* it not a little one?) and my soul shall live."

²¹And he said to him, "See, I have favored you concerning this thing also, in that I will not overthrow this city for which you have spoken. ²²Hurry, escape there. For I cannot do anything until you arrive there."

Therefore the name of the city was called Zoar. ²³The sun had risen upon the earth when Lot entered Zoar. ²⁴Then the LORD rained brimstone and fire on Sodom and Gomorrah, from the LORD out of the heavens. ²⁵So He overthrew those cities, all the plain, all the inhabitants of the cities, and what grew on the ground.

²⁶But his wife looked back behind him, and she became a pillar of salt.

²⁷And Abraham went early in the morning to the place where he had stood before the LORD. ²⁸Then he looked toward Sodom and Gomorrah, and toward all the land of the plain; and he saw, and behold, the smoke of the land which went up like the smoke of a furnace. ²⁹And it came to pass, when God destroyed the cities of the plain, that God remembered Abraham, and sent Lot out of the midst of the overthrow, when He overthrew the cities in which Lot had dwelt.

The Descendants of Lot

³⁰Then Lot went up out of Zoar and dwelt in the mountains, and his two daughters were with him; for he was afraid to dwell in Zoar. And he and his two daughters dwelt in a cave. ³¹Now the firstborn said to the younger, "Our father *is* old, and *there is* no man on the earth to come in to us as is the custom of all the earth. ³²Come, let us make our father drink wine, and we will lie with him, that we may preserve the lineage of our father." ³³So they made their father drink wine that night. And the firstborn went in and lay with her father, and he did not know when she lay down or when she arose.

³⁴It happened on the next day that the firstborn said to the younger, "Indeed I lay with my father last night; let us make him drink wine tonight also, and you go in *and* lie with him, that we may preserve the lineage of our father." ³⁵Then they made their father drink wine that night also. And the younger arose and lay with him, and he did not know when she lay down or when she arose.

³⁶Thus both the daughters of Lot were with child by their father. ³⁷The firstborn bore a son and called his name Moab; he *is* the father of the Moabites to this day. ³⁸And the younger, she also bore a son and called his name Ben-Ammi; he *is* the father of the people of Ammon to this day.

Abraham and Abimelech

20 And Abraham journeyed from there to the South, and dwelt between Kadesh and Shur, and stayed in Gerar. ²Now Abraham said of Sarah his wife, "She *is* my sister." And Abimelech king of Gerar sent and took Sarah.

³But God came to Abimelech in a dream by night, and said to him, "Indeed you *are* a dead man because of the woman whom you have taken, for she *is* a man's wife."

⁴But Abimelech had not come near her; and he said, "Lord, will You slay a righteous nation also? ⁵Did he not say to me, 'She *is* my sister'? And she,

19:17 ᵃSeptuagint, Syriac, and Vulgate read *they.*

19:14 Sons-in-law. Whether Lot had other married daughters who remained in the city with their husbands or whether these were Lot's prospective sons-in-law for his virgin daughters is unclear.

19:24 Brimstone and fire. The Dead Sea area abounds in petroleum, bitumen, salt, and sulphur. The Lord's use of these elements in destroying the city becomes an OT image for overwhelming judgment (Ps. 11:6; Ezek. 38:22).

19:31 Lot's daughters. The interposition of Lot's story between God's promise to Abraham (Gen. 18:10–14) and the birth of Isaac (Gen. 21:1–7) highlights God's preservation of a godly line. Even the descendants of Lot, Abraham's closest relative, had been corrupted. The defiling of this bloodline made the birth of Isaac imperative.

19:37 The children of Lot's daughters. Moab (Heb., lit. "from our father") and Ben-Ammi (Heb., lit. "son of my kinsman," v. 38) were the sons of Lot by his daughters. The Moabites and the Ammonites later introduced into Israel two of the most abhorrent false gods of the OT: the Moabite Baal of Peor, a sun god (Num. 25:1–3), and the Ammonite Molech (Lev. 18:21; 1 Kin. 11:7), who was worshiped with child sacrifice.

LOT'S DISOBEDIENT WIFE

Though Lot was a rich and influential man (Gen. 13:10, 11), the Scripture does not record his wife's name or any information concerning her race or family. From every indication, however, his wife was a worldly, materialistic woman. Certainly she failed in the spiritual nurturing of her children. Her daughters married men of Sodom, then initiated incest with their own father (Gen. 19:32–35).

Lot's wife did not have to die. She was offered a choice—obedience and life or disobedience and death in pursuit of the pleasures of the world. We do not know where Lot met his wife or when they were married, but we do know they had two daughters (Gen. 19:16). The kidnapping of Lot and his family (Gen. 14) would have included his wife, and she would have been among the company that was rescued by Abraham since Abraham "brought back his brother Lot and his goods, as well as the women and the people" (Gen. 14:16). This means she may well have heard Melchizedek's witness for God (Gen. 14:19, 20). In other words, she was well aware of the Lord and His dealings with Abraham. But the lifestyle of Sodom had a strong hold on her.

Sodom was a sophisticated town, offering a wide variety of cultural opportunities. The immorality had degenerated to the lowest point of sexual perversion so much that our term "sodomy" comes from the name of this city. Lot, though called a "righteous man," seemed also to be entangled in the grip of Sodom's influence (2 Pet. 2:7, 8). He chose to raise his family in Sodom, even though its reputation for depravity was well known. Still, the Lord sent messengers to rescue this family from their own destructive choices.

God wanted to save Lot's wife. He sent angels to warn, to escort, and finally physically to pull her out of harm's way. Whether she understood exactly what would happen to Sodom is uncertain, but being escorted by angels in this fashion surely alerted her to something supernatural.

The destruction most likely began with a violent earthquake, which set fire to the gases and sulphur. Firebrands were falling around her. Though she had followed her husband into the wilderness, she had the same problem the Israelites did in the wilderness as "in their hearts they turned back to Egypt" (Acts 7:39). Just like the Israelites, she was destroyed.

Lot's wife personifies the classic wisdom "for where your treasure is, there your heart will be also" (Matt. 6:21). Jesus used her as an example of someone who started the right way but looked back because she was not completely willing to give up her old ways to follow God in obedience (Luke 17:31–33).

See also Luke 17:29–33; notes on Decision Making (1 Cor. 8); Obedience (Philem.).

even she herself said, 'He *is* my brother.' In the integrity of my heart and innocence of my hands I have done this."

[6]And God said to him in a dream, "Yes, I know that you did this in the integrity of your heart. For I also withheld you from sinning against Me; therefore I did not let you touch her. [7]Now therefore, restore the man's wife; for he *is* a prophet, and he will pray for you and you shall live. But if you do not restore *her,* know that you shall surely die, you and all who *are* yours."

[8]So Abimelech rose early in the morning, called all his servants, and told all these things in their hearing; and the men were very much afraid. [9]And Abimelech called Abraham and said to him, "What have you done to us? How have I offended you, that you have brought on me and on my king-

dom a great sin? You have done deeds to me that ought not to be done." [10]Then Abimelech said to Abraham, "What did you have in view, that you have done this thing?"

[11]And Abraham said, "Because I thought, surely the fear of God *is* not in this place; and they will kill me on account of my wife. [12]But indeed *she is* truly my sister. She *is* the daughter of my father, but not the daughter of my mother; and she became my wife. [13]And it came to pass, when God caused me to wander from my father's house, that I said to her, 'This *is* your kindness that you should do for me: in every place, wherever we go, say of me, "He *is* my brother."' "

[14]Then Abimelech took sheep, oxen, and male and female servants, and gave *them* to Abraham; and he restored Sarah his wife to him. [15]And

20:7 In Canaanite religions, prophets were supposed to have the magical ability to intercede with the gods. The Israelite prophet functioned instead as a divine spokesman; but Abimelech, as a Canaanite, would have taken the former view. He rewarded Abraham, hoping that Abraham would intercede with his God for Abimelech's household (vv. 14–18).

20:11 Abraham's excuses. Like Adam, Abraham shifted the blame (Gen. 3:12). He excused himself on the basis of Abim-

elech's supposed lack of piety, an assumption disproved (vv. 3–7). Furthermore, Abraham blamed God for his own "wandering," using a Hebrew verb with a negative connotation and one frequently associated with mental error or intoxication (v. 13). Abraham excused Sarah. "Kindness" (Heb. *chesed*) is a reference to covenant obligation that Sarah owed her husband (v. 13).

Abimelech said, "See, my land *is* before you; dwell where it pleases you." [16]Then to Sarah he said, "Behold, I have given your brother a thousand *pieces* of silver; indeed this vindicates you[a] before all who *are* with you and before everybody." Thus she was rebuked.

[17]So Abraham prayed to God; and God healed Abimelech, his wife, and his female servants. Then they bore *children;* [18]for the LORD had closed up all the wombs of the house of Abimelech because of Sarah, Abraham's wife.

Isaac Is Born

21 And the LORD visited Sarah as He had said, and the LORD did for Sarah as He had spoken. [2]For Sarah conceived and bore Abraham a son in his old age, at the set time of which God had spoken to him. [3]And Abraham called the name of his son who was born to him—whom Sarah bore to him—Isaac. [4]Then Abraham circumcised his son Isaac when he was eight days old, as God had commanded him. [5]Now Abraham was one hundred years old when his son Isaac was born to him. [6]And Sarah said, "God has made me laugh, *and* all who hear will laugh with me." [7]She also said, "Who would have said to Abraham that Sarah would nurse children? For I have borne *him* a son in his old age."

Hagar and Ishmael Depart

[8]So the child grew and was weaned. And Abraham made a great feast on the same day that Isaac was weaned.

[9]And Sarah saw the son of Hagar the Egyptian, whom she had borne to Abraham, scoffing. [10]Therefore she said to Abraham, "Cast out this bondwoman and her son; for the son of this bondwoman shall not be heir with my son, *namely* with Isaac." [11]And the matter was very displeasing in Abraham's sight because of his son.

[12]But God said to Abraham, "Do not let it be displeasing in your sight because of the lad or because of your bondwoman. Whatever Sarah has said to you, listen to her voice; for in Isaac your seed shall be called. [13]Yet I will also make a nation of the son of the bondwoman, because he *is* your seed."

[14]So Abraham rose early in the morning, and took bread and a skin of water; and putting *it* on her shoulder, he gave *it* and the boy to Hagar, and sent her away. Then she departed and wandered in the Wilderness of Beersheba. [15]And the water in the skin was used up, and she placed the boy under one of the shrubs. [16]Then she went and sat down across from *him* at a distance of about a bowshot; for she said to herself, "Let me not see the death of the boy." So she sat opposite *him,* and lifted her voice and wept.

[17]And God heard the voice of the lad. Then the angel of God called to Hagar out of heaven, and said to her, "What ails you, Hagar? Fear not, for God has heard the voice of the lad where he *is.* [18]Arise, lift up the lad and hold him with your hand, for I will make him a great nation." [19]Then God opened her eyes, and she saw a well of water. And she went and filled the skin with water, and gave the lad a drink. [20]So God was with the lad; and he grew and dwelt in the wilderness, and became an archer. [21]He dwelt in the Wilderness of Paran; and his mother took a wife for him from the land of Egypt.

A Covenant with Abimelech

[22]And it came to pass at that time that Abimelech and Phichol, the commander of his army, spoke to Abraham, saying, "God *is* with you in all that you do. [23]Now therefore, swear to me by God that you will not deal falsely with me, with my offspring, or with my posterity; but that according to the kindness that I have done to you, you will do to me and to the land in which you have dwelt." [24]And Abraham said, "I will swear." [25]Then Abraham rebuked Abimelech because of a well of water which Abimelech's servants had seized. [26]And Abimelech said, "I do not know who has done this thing; you did not tell me, nor had I heard *of it* until today." [27]So Abraham took sheep and oxen and gave them to Abimelech, and the two of them made a covenant. [28]And Abraham set seven ewe lambs of the flock by themselves.

20:16 [a]Literally *it is a covering of the eyes for you*

20:16 Abraham's gift. OT law prescribed a money payment to a male relative in recompense for sexual wrong. Here the gift seemed to be Abimelech's acknowledgment that Sarah remained blameless throughout the incident. "Vindicate" (lit. "cover the eyes") is a legal term indicating innocence. "Rebuked" could also be translated as "justified" or "approved." The emphasis of the verse is on Sarah's vindication.

20:18 The Lord closed the wombs. The use of God's covenant name, *Yahweh*, emphasizes that God's action will prevent Sarah's child from being fathered by anyone but Abraham.

21:8 The weaning of children, in the ancient Near East, took

place around three or four years of age, occasionally even later (see Ex. 2, Breastfeeding).

21:14 Hagar was sent away. Mesopotamian law allowed a slave wife to claim freedom in return for waiving her children's rights to inheritance. Here Abraham initiated the exchange as a way of getting out of his difficulty. The Wilderness of Beersheba lay in the middle of the Negev, which would become southernmost Judah.

21:21 The wilderness of Paran lay between Canaan and Egypt. Hagar's choice of an Egyptian wife for Ishmael paralleled Abraham's efforts to find a wife of his own blood for Isaac (Gen. 24:1–4).

²⁹Then Abimelech asked Abraham, "What *is the meaning of* these seven ewe lambs which you have set by themselves?"

³⁰And he said, "You will take *these* seven ewe lambs from my hand, that they may be my witness that I have dug this well." ³¹Therefore he called that place Beersheba,ᵃ because the two of them swore an oath there.

³²Thus they made a covenant at Beersheba. So Abimelech rose with Phichol, the commander of his army, and they returned to the land of the Philistines. ³³Then *Abraham* planted a tamarisk tree in Beersheba, and there called on the name of the LORD, the Everlasting God. ³⁴And Abraham stayed in the land of the Philistines many days.

Abraham's Faith Confirmed

22 Now it came to pass after these things that God tested Abraham, and said to him, "Abraham!"

And he said, "Here I am."

²Then He said, "Take now your son, your only *son* Isaac, whom you love, and go to the land of Moriah, and offer him there as a burnt offering on one of the mountains of which I shall tell you."

³So Abraham rose early in the morning and saddled his donkey, and took two of his young men with him, and Isaac his son; and he split the wood for the burnt offering, and arose and went to the place of which God had told him. ⁴Then on the third day Abraham lifted his eyes and saw the place afar off. ⁵And Abraham said to his young men, "Stay here with the donkey; the ladᵃ and I will go yonder and worship, and we will come back to you."

⁶So Abraham took the wood of the burnt offering and laid *it* on Isaac his son; and he took the fire in his hand, and a knife, and the two of them went together. ⁷But Isaac spoke to Abraham his father and said, "My father!"

And he said, "Here I am, my son."

Then he said, "Look, the fire and the wood, but where *is* the lamb for a burnt offering?"

⁸And Abraham said, "My son, God will provide for Himself the lamb for a burnt offering." So the two of them went together.

⁹Then they came to the place of which God had told him. And Abraham built an altar there and placed the wood in order; and he bound Isaac his son and laid him on the altar, upon the wood. ¹⁰And Abraham stretched out his hand and took the knife to slay his son.

¹¹But the Angel of the LORD called to him from heaven and said, "Abraham, Abraham!"

So he said, "Here I am."

¹²And He said, "Do not lay your hand on the lad, or do anything to him; for now I know that you fear God, since you have not withheld your son, your only *son,* from Me."

¹³Then Abraham lifted his eyes and looked, and there behind *him was* a ram caught in a thicket by its horns. So Abraham went and took the ram, and offered it up for a burnt offering instead of his son. ¹⁴And Abraham called the name of the place, The-LORD-Will-Provide;ᵃ as it is said *to* this day, "In the Mount of the LORD it shall be provided."

¹⁵Then the Angel of the LORD called to Abraham a second time out of heaven, ¹⁶and said: "By Myself I have sworn, says the LORD, because you have done this thing, and have not withheld your son, your only *son*— ¹⁷blessing I will bless you, and multiplying I will multiply your descendants as the stars of the heaven and as the sand which *is* on the seashore; and your descendants shall possess the gate of their enemies. ¹⁸In your seed all the nations of the earth shall be blessed, because you have obeyed My voice." ¹⁹So Abraham returned to his young men, and they rose and went together to Beersheba; and Abraham dwelt at Beersheba.

The Family of Nahor

²⁰Now it came to pass after these things that it was told Abraham, saying, "Indeed Milcah also has

21:31 ᵃLiterally *Well of the Oath* or *Well of the Seven*   22:5 ᵃOr *young man*   22:14 ᵃHebrew *YHWH Yireh*

21:33 The tamarisk tree, an evergreen, could well represent God's eternal faithfulness; significantly, He is here called the Everlasting One. Trees and pillars served the patriarchs as memory aids, memorials to God's acts (see Gen. 28:18–22). God is witness to the treaty, which is expected to stand forever.

22:1 God's test. Abraham's trust and faith in God were tested and proven genuine and even stronger than his natural affections. The story of Abraham alternates reaffirmations of God's promise with the testing of that promise. This most severe test was followed by a strong restatement of the covenant (vv. 15–19).

22:2 Mount Moriah, in the territory later called Judah, would become the site of the temple (2 Chr. 3:1). In the NT, Calvary was identified with this site. This identification, along with the three days that Abraham traveled, suggests that this scene is a typology of God's sacrifice of His own Son.

22:5 We will come back. Abraham's use of the plural suggests that he was depending on God to resurrect Isaac (Heb. 11:17–19).

22:12 The fear of God suggests reverence and honor, demonstrated by Abraham's unquestioning obedience. God's repetition of "your son" highlights the severity of the test.

22:13 The substitutionary sacrifice. The ram in the thicket introduces substitutionary sacrifice (see Lev. 1).

22:14 This covenant name (Heb. *Yahweh Yir'eh,* lit. "the LORD will provide") expresses Abraham's confidence in the Lord. This name continued in use during the days of substitutionary sacrifice in the temple.

22:20 Nahor's family was still living in Haran. His sons were the ancestors of the Arameans who lived northeast of Israel. Abraham later sent to Nahor's family for a wife for Isaac (Gen. 24). Rebekah's genealogy appears here, after Isaac's

borne children to your brother Nahor: [21]Huz his firstborn, Buz his brother, Kemuel the father of Aram, [22]Chesed, Hazo, Pildash, Jidlaph, and Bethuel." [23]And Bethuel begot Rebekah.[a] These eight Milcah bore to Nahor, Abraham's brother. [24]His concubine, whose name was Reumah, also bore Tebah, Gaham, Thahash, and Maachah.

Sarah's Death and Burial

23Sarah lived one hundred and twenty-seven years; *these were* the years of the life of Sarah. [2]So Sarah died in Kirjath Arba (that *is,* Hebron) in the land of Canaan, and Abraham came to mourn for Sarah and to weep for her.

[3]Then Abraham stood up from before his dead, and spoke to the sons of Heth, saying, [4]"I *am* a foreigner and a visitor among you. Give me property for a burial place among you, that I may bury my dead out of my sight."

[5]And the sons of Heth answered Abraham, saying to him, [6]"Hear us, my lord: You *are* a mighty prince among us; bury your dead in the choicest of our burial places. None of us will withhold from you his burial place, that you may bury your dead."

[7]Then Abraham stood up and bowed himself to the people of the land, the sons of Heth. [8]And he spoke with them, saying, "If it is your wish that I bury my dead out of my sight, hear me, and meet with Ephron the son of Zohar for me, [9]that he may give me the cave of Machpelah which he has, which *is* at the end of his field. Let him give it to me at the full price, as property for a burial place among you."

[10]Now Ephron dwelt among the sons of Heth; and Ephron the Hittite answered Abraham in the presence of the sons of Heth, all who entered at the gate of his city, saying, [11]"No, my lord, hear me: I give you the field and the cave that *is* in it; I give it to you in the presence of the sons of my people. I give it to you. Bury your dead!"

[12]Then Abraham bowed himself down before the people of the land; [13]and he spoke to Ephron in the hearing of the people of the land, saying, "If you *will give it,* please hear me. I will give you money for the field; take *it* from me and I will bury my dead there."

[14]And Ephron answered Abraham, saying to him, [15]"My lord, listen to me; the land *is worth* four hundred shekels of silver. What *is* that between you and me? So bury your dead." [16]And Abraham listened to Ephron; and Abraham weighed out the silver for Ephron which he had named in the hearing of the sons of Heth, four hundred shekels of silver, currency of the merchants.

[17]So the field of Ephron which *was* in Machpelah, which *was* before Mamre, the field and the cave which *was* in it, and all the trees that *were* in the field, which *were* within all the surrounding borders, were deeded [18]to Abraham as a possession in the presence of the sons of Heth, before all who went in at the gate of his city.

[19]And after this, Abraham buried Sarah his wife in the cave of the field of Machpelah, before Mamre (that *is,* Hebron) in the land of Canaan. [20]So the field and the cave that *is* in it were deeded to Abraham by the sons of Heth as property for a burial place.

A Bride for Isaac

24Now Abraham was old, well advanced in age; and the LORD had blessed Abraham in all things. [2]So Abraham said to the oldest servant of his house, who ruled over all that he had, "Please, put your hand under my thigh, [3]and I will make you swear by the LORD, the God of heaven and the God of the earth, that you will not take a wife for my son from the daughters of the Canaanites, among whom I dwell; [4]but you shall go to my country and to my family, and take a wife for my son Isaac."

[5]And the servant said to him, "Perhaps the woman will not be willing to follow me to this land. Must I take your son back to the land from which you came?"

[6]But Abraham said to him, "Beware that you do not take my son back there. [7]The LORD God of heaven, who took me from my father's house and from the land of my family, and who spoke to me and swore to me, saying, 'To your descendants[a] I give this land,' He will send His angel before you,

---

22:23 [a]Spelled *Rebecca* in Romans 9:10   24:7 [a]Literally *seed*

---

deliverance from death, to indicate that God would now continue Abraham's line.

23:2 Hebron, 19 miles southwest of Jerusalem, served as David's first capital. Kirjath Arba was named after a hero of the gigantic Anakim. Caleb later captured the city and renamed it (Josh. 14:14, 15).

23:4 Abraham's negotiations. "Stranger" (Heb. *ger*) was a legal term for a resident alien with some rights but no land. Abraham's acquisition of land for Sarah is his first legal ownership within the promised territory. The Hittite offer may have been an attempt to prevent Abraham from acquiring the rights of a landholder within Canaan (v. 6).

23:9 The cave of Machpelah, a name which may indicate a

double cave, was located in the district near Mamre (v. 17). The burial place is traditionally thought to be located under a Moslem mosque in Hebron.

24:2 The servant's oath. The placing of the hand near the reproductive organs symbolized that the oath was sworn to Abraham's entire clan, to Isaac, and to all his descendants.

24:3 Abraham's command is the first appearance in the OT of the command not to marry outside the chosen people (Deut. 7:1–4). Abraham recognized that God's promise to build a nation would be fulfilled by Isaac. He did not ask Isaac to return to Haran (vv. 5–8) because this would undo Abraham's first covenant obligation to separate himself and come to the Land of Promise (Gen. 12:1–4).

REBEKAH *A Woman of Faltering Faith*

Rebekah would certainly rank among the most appealing of the young women in Scripture. She is pictured as chaste and beautiful (Gen. 24:16), courteous and helpful (v. 18), industrious (vv. 19, 20), hospitable (v. 25), as well as responsive and trusting (v. 58). She was chosen as the intended bride for Isaac.

Family ties were obviously close, for Rebekah's first response was to tell the women in her household all about her encounter at the well (v. 28). For a girl to be chosen for marriage to a wealthy relative was indeed considered a blessing of God. Her father and brother knew also that this was from God (v. 50), but the choice to leave home was hers to make, reflecting the autonomy that young women in her culture enjoyed (vv. 57, 58).

Rebekah volunteered a lowly service (v. 19), which opened to her a lofty destiny as God worked His plan for her life through her mundane daily responsibilities. Her courage and faith motivated her to venture from the known and familiar (family and friends) to the unknown (a new life in a strange land).

God rewarded Rebekah's faithfulness with a monogamous marriage, which began with romance and loving affection (v. 67; Gen. 26:8), and, in answer to Isaac's prayer for his wife's fertility, God removed her barrenness with the birth of twins, Esau and Jacob (Gen. 25:21).

In later years, Rebekah's weakness became clear at two points: the lack of reverence and respect for her husband and his leadership and the exhibition of favoritism concerning her sons, which brought into the home rivalry, deceit, and contention (Gen. 25:28; see Prov. 28, Favoritism). Rebekah's unwavering faith of her youth faltered, and she took into her own hands the direction of the future of her sons. Perhaps her own discernment of her sons—that is, recognizing Esau as worldly and adventuresome (Gen. 26:34, 35) and Jacob as having more potential for spiritual sensitivity (Gen. 25:31)—or her own affinity toward one son over the other (Gen. 25:28) or even a strong faith in God's revealed plan (Gen. 25:23) motivated her own deceitful acts.

In any case, the deceiving of her husband was without excuse and her poor example to her sons was a far-reaching tragedy (Gen. 27:12, 13). Even if her motive was pure, her action was wrong. She paid a bitter price in living out her final years in separation from the son whose presence she desired, in alienation from the son who would ever remember his mother's deception toward him, and in broken fellowship from a husband who had loved her devotedly.

See also Gen. 25:19—27:46; notes on Favoritism (Prov. 28); Marriage (2 Sam. 6)

and you shall take a wife for my son from there. [8]And if the woman is not willing to follow you, then you will be released from this oath; only do not take my son back there." [9]So the servant put his hand under the thigh of Abraham his master, and swore to him concerning this matter.

[10]Then the servant took ten of his master's camels and departed, for all his master's goods *were in* his hand. And he arose and went to Mesopotamia, to the city of Nahor. [11]And he made his camels kneel down outside the city by a well of water at evening time, the time when women go out to draw *water.* [12]Then he said, "O LORD God of my master Abraham, please give me success this day, and show kindness to my master Abraham. [13]Behold, *here* I stand by the well of water, and the daughters of the men of the city are coming out to draw water. [14]Now let it be that the young woman to whom I say, 'Please let down your pitcher that I may drink,' and she says, 'Drink, and I will also give your camels a drink'— *let* her *be the*

one You have appointed for Your servant Isaac. And by this I will know that You have shown kindness to my master."

[15]And it happened, before he had finished speaking, that behold, Rebekah, who was born to Bethuel, son of Milcah, the wife of Nahor, Abraham's brother, came out with her pitcher on her shoulder. [16]Now the young woman *was* very beautiful to behold, a virgin; no man had known her. And she went down to the well, filled her pitcher, and came up. [17]And the servant ran to meet her and said, "Please let me drink a little water from your pitcher."

[18]So she said, "Drink, my lord." Then she quickly let her pitcher down to her hand, and gave him a drink. [19]And when she had finished giving him a drink, she said, "I will draw *water* for your camels also, until they have finished drinking." [20]Then she quickly emptied her pitcher into the trough, ran back to the well to draw *water,* and drew for all his camels. [21]And the

---

24:10 Nahor, actually Haran, is so named after its most distinguished inhabitant, Abraham's brother (Gen. 22:20; see chart, The Family Tree of Abraham). "Mesopotamia" (Heb. *'Aram-Naharayim,* lit. "Aram between the two rivers") is the land between the Tigris and Euphrates.

24:15 Rebekah was Abraham's great-niece. The repetition of her grandmother's name, Milcah, shows that she was a descendant of Nahor's wife rather than his concubine (Gen. 22:20–24; see chart, The Family Tree of Abraham).

man, wondering at her, remained silent so as to know whether the LORD had made his journey prosperous or not.

²²So it was, when the camels had finished drinking, that the man took a golden nose ring weighing half a shekel, and two bracelets for her wrists weighing ten *shekels* of gold, ²³and said, "Whose daughter *are* you? Tell me, please, is there room *in* your father's house for us to lodge?"

²⁴So she said to him, "I *am* the daughter of Bethuel, Milcah's son, whom she bore to Nahor." ²⁵Moreover she said to him, "We have both straw and feed enough, and room to lodge."

²⁶Then the man bowed down his head and worshiped the LORD. ²⁷And he said, "Blessed *be* the LORD God of my master Abraham, who has not forsaken His mercy and His truth toward my master. As for me, being on the way, the LORD led me to the house of my master's brethren." ²⁸So the young woman ran and told her mother's household these things.

²⁹Now Rebekah had a brother whose name *was* Laban, and Laban ran out to the man by the well. ³⁰So it came to pass, when he saw the nose ring, and the bracelets on his sister's wrists, and when he heard the words of his sister Rebekah, saying, "Thus the man spoke to me," that he went to the man. And there he stood by the camels at the well. ³¹And he said, "Come in, O blessed of the LORD! Why do you stand outside? For I have prepared the house, and a place for the camels."

³²Then the man came to the house. And he unloaded the camels, and provided straw and feed for the camels, and water to wash his feet and the feet of the men who *were* with him. ³³*Food* was set before him to eat, but he said, "I will not eat until I have told about my errand."

And he said, "Speak on."

³⁴So he said, "I *am* Abraham's servant. ³⁵The LORD has blessed my master greatly, and he has become great; and He has given him flocks and herds, silver and gold, male and female servants, and camels and donkeys. ³⁶And Sarah my master's wife bore a son to my master when she was old; and to him he has given all that he has. ³⁷Now my master made me swear, saying, 'You shall not take a wife for my son from the daughters of the Canaanites, in whose land I dwell; ³⁸but you shall go to my father's house and to my family, and take a wife for my son.' ³⁹And I said to my master, 'Perhaps the woman will not follow me.' ⁴⁰But he said to me, 'The LORD, before whom I walk, will send His angel with you and prosper your way; and you shall take a wife for my son from my family and from my father's house. ⁴¹You will be clear from this oath when you arrive among my family; for if

they will not give *her* to you, then you will be released from my oath.'

⁴²"And this day I came to the well and said, 'O LORD God of my master Abraham, if You will now prosper the way in which I go, ⁴³behold, I stand by the well of water; and it shall come to pass that when the virgin comes out to draw *water,* and I say to her, "Please give me a little water from your pitcher to drink," ⁴⁴and she says to me, "Drink, and I will draw for your camels also,"—*let* her *be* the woman whom the LORD has appointed for my master's son.'

⁴⁵"But before I had finished speaking in my heart, there was Rebekah, coming out with her pitcher on her shoulder; and she went down to the well and drew *water.* And I said to her, 'Please let me drink.' ⁴⁶And she made haste and let her pitcher down from her *shoulder,* and said, 'Drink, and I will give your camels a drink also.' So I drank, and she gave the camels a drink also. ⁴⁷Then I asked her, and said, 'Whose daughter *are* you?' And she said, 'The daughter of Bethuel, Nahor's son, whom Milcah bore to him.' So I put the nose ring on her nose and the bracelets on her wrists. ⁴⁸And I bowed my head and worshiped the LORD, and blessed the LORD God of my master Abraham, who had led me in the way of truth to take the daughter of my master's brother for his son. ⁴⁹Now if you will deal kindly and truly with my master, tell me. And if not, tell me, that I may turn to the right hand or to the left."

⁵⁰Then Laban and Bethuel answered and said, "The thing comes from the LORD; we cannot speak to you either bad or good. ⁵¹Here *is* Rebekah before you; take *her* and go, and let her be your master's son's wife, as the LORD has spoken."

⁵²And it came to pass, when Abraham's servant heard their words, that he worshiped the LORD, *bowing himself* to the earth. ⁵³Then the servant brought out jewelry of silver, jewelry of gold, and clothing, and gave *them* to Rebekah. He also gave precious things to her brother and to her mother.

⁵⁴And he and the men who *were* with him ate and drank and stayed all night. Then they arose in the morning, and he said, "Send me away to my master."

⁵⁵But her brother and her mother said, "Let the young woman stay with us *a few* days, at least ten; after that she may go."

⁵⁶And he said to them, "Do not hinder me, since the LORD has prospered my way; send me away so that I may go to my master."

⁵⁷So they said, "We will call the young woman and ask her personally." ⁵⁸Then they called Rebekah and said to her, "Will you go with this man?"

24:49 Turn to the right hand. This Hebrew idiom means to look for another option.

24:58 Rebekah's consent. Although ancient Near Eastern marriages were arranged by the family, some contracts—

And she said, "I will go."

[59]So they sent away Rebekah their sister and her nurse, and Abraham's servant and his men. [60]And they blessed Rebekah and said to her:

"Our sister, *may* you *become*
The *mother of* thousands of ten thousands;
And may your descendants possess
The gates of those who hate them."

[61]Then Rebekah and her maids arose, and they rode on the camels and followed the man. So the servant took Rebekah and departed.

[62]Now Isaac came from the way of Beer Lahai Roi, for he dwelt in the South. [63]And Isaac went out to meditate in the field in the evening; and he lifted his eyes and looked, and there, the camels *were* coming. [64]Then Rebekah lifted her eyes, and when she saw Isaac she dismounted from her camel; [65]for she had said to the servant, "Who *is* this man walking in the field to meet us?"

The servant said, "It *is* my master." So she took a veil and covered herself.

[66]And the servant told Isaac all the things that he had done. [67]Then Isaac brought her into his mother Sarah's tent; and he took Rebekah and she became his wife, and he loved her. So Isaac was comforted after his mother's *death.*

Abraham and Keturah

25 Abraham again took a wife, and her name *was* Keturah. [2]And she bore him Zimran, Jokshan, Medan, Midian, Ishbak, and Shuah. [3]Jokshan begot Sheba and Dedan. And the sons of Dedan were Asshurim, Letushim, and Leummim. [4]And the sons of Midian *were* Ephah, Epher, Hanoch, Abidah, and Eldaah. All these *were* the children of Keturah.

[5]And Abraham gave all that he had to Isaac. [6]But Abraham gave gifts to the sons of the concubines which Abraham had; and while he was still living he sent them eastward, away from Isaac his son, to the country of the east.

Abraham's Death and Burial

[7]This *is* the sum of the years of Abraham's life which he lived: one hundred and seventy-five years. [8]Then Abraham breathed his last and died in a good old age, an old man and full *of years,* and was gathered to his people. [9]And his sons Isaac and Ishmael buried him in the cave of Machpelah, which *is* before Mamre, in the field of Ephron the son of Zohar the Hittite, [10]the field which Abraham purchased from the sons of Heth. There Abraham was buried, and Sarah his wife. [11]And it came to pass, after the death of Abraham, that God blessed his son Isaac. And Isaac dwelt at Beer Lahai Roi.

The Families of Ishmael and Isaac

[12]Now this *is* the genealogy of Ishmael, Abraham's son, whom Hagar the Egyptian, Sarah's maidservant, bore to Abraham. [13]And these *were* the names of the sons of Ishmael, by their names, according to their generations: The firstborn of Ishmael, Nebajoth; then Kedar, Adbeel, Mibsam, [14]Mishma, Dumah, Massa, [15]Hadar,[a] Tema, Jetur, Naphish, and Kedemah. [16]These *were* the sons of Ishmael and these *were* their names, by their towns and their settlements, twelve princes according to their nations. [17]These *were* the years of the life of Ishmael: one hundred and thirty-seven years; and he breathed his last and died, and was gathered to his people. [18](They dwelt from Havilah as far as Shur, which *is* east of Egypt as you go toward Assyria.) He died in the presence of all his brethren.

[19]This *is* the genealogy of Isaac, Abraham's son. Abraham begot Isaac. [20]Isaac was forty years old when he took Rebekah as wife, the daughter of Bethuel the Syrian of Padan Aram, the sister of Laban the Syrian. [21]Now Isaac pleaded with the

25:15 [a]Masoretic Text reads *Hadad.*

---

notably those of the Hurrians or Horites in Mesopotamia—required the consent of the bride, as Abraham himself recognized (v. 8).

24:60 The blessing on Rebekah echoes God's blessing on Abraham (Gen. 22:17), emphasizing God's covenant obligations from one generation to the next.

24:65 Veiling during the betrothal period was a Near Eastern custom. Unveiling came after marriage.

25:1 Abraham's second family. At what point in his life Abraham married Keturah is not explicitly stated. The narrative reads naturally as if Abraham married Keturah after the death of Sarah. The fact that Keturah is here called a "wife" would seem to eliminate the possibility of her being merely a concubine to Abraham during his marriage to Sarah. The nearly 40 years between Sarah's death and Abraham's allowed plenty of time for the development of a second family. Abraham's prolific second marriage reveals that God's mirac-

ulous working in the birth of Isaac centered on Sarah. The sons of Keturah eventually inhabited the lands south and southeast of Canaan, but only Isaac received the promised blessing (v. 5). Keturah, however, is also identified as a concubine in one place (1 Chr. 1:32; see also Gen. 25:6). Keturah may have been called a concubine because Abraham did not place her on the same footing with Sarah, the mother of Isaac. In any case, the fact that polygamy was outside of God's order would be demonstrated in the future; the descendants of Keturah, like those of Hagar, later proved troublesome to Israel (see chart, The Family Tree of Abraham). The Midianites oppressed Israel in the days of the judges and promoted Baal worship in Israel (v. 4; Judg. 6—8). The other sons are less known; Shuah was probably the tribe of Job's friend Bildad (Job 2:11), and Sheba and Dedan are mentioned as traders with Tyre (Ezek. 27:20–22).

25:21 Rebekah's children. The story has temporarily left Isaac to deal with his sons, demonstrating the certainty of the

LORD for his wife, because she *was* barren; and the LORD granted his plea, and Rebekah his wife conceived. ²²But the children struggled together within her; and she said, "If *all is* well, why *am I like* this?" So she went to inquire of the LORD.

²³And the LORD said to her:

"Two nations *are* in your womb,
Two peoples shall be separated from your
   body;
One people shall be stronger than the other,
And the older shall serve the younger."

²⁴So when her days were fulfilled *for her* to give birth, indeed *there were* twins in her womb. ²⁵And the first came out red. *He was* like a hairy garment all over; so they called his name Esau.^a ²⁶Afterward his brother came out, and his hand took hold of Esau's heel; so his name was called Jacob.^a Isaac *was* sixty years old when she bore them.

²⁷So the boys grew. And Esau was a skillful hunter, a man of the field; but Jacob was a mild man, dwelling in tents. ²⁸And Isaac loved Esau because he ate *of his* game, but Rebekah loved Jacob.

Esau Sells His Birthright

²⁹Now Jacob cooked a stew; and Esau came in from the field, and he *was* weary. ³⁰And Esau said to Jacob, "Please feed me with that same red *stew,* for I *am* weary." Therefore his name was called Edom.^a

³¹But Jacob said, "Sell me your birthright as of this day."

³²And Esau said, "Look, I *am* about to die; so what *is* this birthright to me?"

³³Then Jacob said, "Swear to me as of this day."

So he swore to him, and sold his birthright to Jacob. ³⁴And Jacob gave Esau bread and stew of lentils; then he ate and drank, arose, and went his way. Thus Esau despised *his* birthright.

Isaac and Abimelech

26 There was a famine in the land, besides the first famine that was in the days of Abraham. And Isaac went to Abimelech king of the Philistines, in Gerar.

²Then the LORD appeared to him and said: "Do not go down to Egypt; live in the land of which I shall tell you. ³Dwell in this land, and I will be with you and bless you; for to you and your descendants I give all these lands, and I will perform the oath which I swore to Abraham your father. ⁴And I will make your descendants multiply as the stars of heaven; I will give to your descendants all these lands; and in your seed all the nations of the earth shall be blessed; ⁵because Abraham obeyed My voice and kept My charge, My commandments, My statutes, and My laws."

⁶So Isaac dwelt in Gerar. ⁷And the men of the place asked about his wife. And he said, "She *is* my sister"; for he was afraid to say, "*She is* my wife," *because he thought*, "lest the men of the place kill me for Rebekah, because she *is* beautiful to behold." ⁸Now it came to pass, when he had been there a long time, that Abimelech king of the Philistines looked through a window, and saw, and there was Isaac, showing endearment to Rebekah his wife. ⁹Then Abimelech called Isaac and said, "Quite obviously she *is* your wife; so how could you say, 'She *is* my sister'?"

Isaac said to him, "Because I said, 'Lest I die on account of her.' "

¹⁰And Abimelech said, "What *is* this you have done to us? One of the people might soon have lain with your wife, and you would have brought guilt on us." ¹¹So Abimelech charged all *his* people,

25:25 ^aLiterally *Hairy*   **25:26** ^aLiterally *Supplanter*   **25:30** ^aLiterally *Red*

---

covenant fulfillment for the next generation. The barrenness of the matriarchs is a common theme in Genesis, revealing:

1) the effects of sin in the fallen world, which could have destroyed the godly line,

2) the need for God's miraculous intervention to protect His people, and

3) God's divine choice of both father and mother, which ran counter to the ancient Near Eastern practice of ascribing sole importance to the blood of the father.

25:23 Two nations. Jacob fathered the Israelites; Esau, the Edomites, who lived south of the Dead Sea (Gen. 36:9–43). The control of the Edomites by the Israelites reversed the ancient Near Eastern custom of giving preference to the older son (see Rom. 9:10–13). David conquered the Edomites, and they remained under Judean control for 130 years (2 Sam. 8:14).

25:26 The birth of Jacob. Rebekah had suffered 20 years of barrenness before the twins were born. Jacob's name (Heb., lit. "heeler," "heel-gripper," or "one who supplants") is a prophecy of the coming struggle between the two brothers.

25:31 The birthright guaranteed not only a larger part of the inheritance, but also headship of the family. Some ancient Near Eastern tribes allowed the selling of the birthright but invariably at a high price. The narrative emphasizes Esau's greed; "feed" is literally "to swallow greedily" or gulp (v. 30), and the story ends with a comment on the motives of Esau, not Jacob. Jacob did not earn the birthright through righteousness but received it through God's free favor.

26:4 God's covenant. The repetition of the covenant blessings to Abraham takes the form of covenant renewal (see chart, The Covenants of Genesis). God's part is to preserve Isaac in time of famine (vv. 2, 3). Isaac's part is to keep Abraham's fivefold obedience: to God's voice, His charge, His commandments, His statutes, and His Law (v. 5).

26:7 Isaac's deception copied his father's actions out of needless fear (see Gen. 12:10–20; 20:1–18). God had promised to preserve him (vv. 2–5). Rebekah, like Sarah, apparently cooperated with her husband's request, whether out of faith or indifference.

PATRIARCHY — A PATTERN FOR BIBLICAL SOCIETY

Patriarchy is a form of society in which the father functions as the authority figure of the family, tribe, or clan. In such an arrangement, descent is reckoned through the male line. The term "patriarch" is derived from a Latin word for "father" combined with a Greek word for "rule." Thus the patriarch was the "ruling father." He might also serve as the priest of his household.

The designation "patriarch" may refer to the fathers of the human race from Adam to Abraham. The three great fathers of the nation Israel (Abraham, Isaac, and Jacob) also are called "patriarchs." Finally, the term "patriarch" is applied to the heads of the twelve tribes of Israel who descended from Jacob.

Biblical society was patriarchal in contrast to matriarchal, which describes a form of community organization in which the mother functions as the head of the family, clan, or tribe. In biblical genealogies, lineage is traced through the male. For this reason, females are mentioned only rarely in tracing family lineage (Gen. 11:29; Num. 26:33).

This makes the mention of four women in addition to Mary in the genealogy of Jesus Christ very significant (Matt. 1:1–17). Tamar, the Canaanite daughter-in-law of Judah, bore him twins (Gen. 38:1–30; Matt. 1:3). Rahab of Jericho begat Boaz by Salmon (Josh. 2:1–24; 6:17, 22–25; Matt. 1:5). Ruth was the Moabitess through whom Boaz begot Obed (Ruth 4:13–17; Matt. 1:5). Finally, "the wife of Uriah," identified as the one by whom David begot Solomon, was Bathsheba (2 Sam. 11:1–4; 12:24–25; Matt. 1:6).

See also Gen. 22:1–19; 50:24; Ex. 3:6; notes on Authority (John 19); Fatherhood (Eph. 5); Fatherhood of God (Rom. 8); Feminism (Is. 5); Motherhood (1 Sam. 1; Is. 49; Ezek. 16)

---

saying, "He who touches this man or his wife shall surely be put to death."

¹²Then Isaac sowed in that land, and reaped in the same year a hundredfold; and the LORD blessed him. ¹³The man began to prosper, and continued prospering until he became very prosperous; ¹⁴for he had possessions of flocks and possessions of herds and a great number of servants. So the Philistines envied him. ¹⁵Now the Philistines had stopped up all the wells which his father's servants had dug in the days of Abraham his father, and they had filled them with earth. ¹⁶And Abimelech said to Isaac, "Go away from us, for you are much mightier than we."

¹⁷Then Isaac departed from there and pitched his tent in the Valley of Gerar, and dwelt there. ¹⁸And Isaac dug again the wells of water which they had dug in the days of Abraham his father, for the Philistines had stopped them up after the death of Abraham. He called them by the names which his father had called them.

¹⁹Also Isaac's servants dug in the valley, and found a well of running water there. ²⁰But the herdsmen of Gerar quarreled with Isaac's herdsmen, saying, "The water is ours." So he called the name of the well Esek,ᵃ because they quarreled with him. ²¹Then they dug another well, and they quarreled over that one also. So he called its name Sitnah.ᵃ ²²And he moved from there and dug another well, and they did not quarrel over it. So he called its name Rehoboth,ᵃ because he said, "For now the LORD has made room for us, and we shall be fruitful in the land."

²³Then he went up from there to Beersheba. ²⁴And the LORD appeared to him the same night and said, "I am the God of your father Abraham; do not fear, for I am with you. I will bless you and multiply your descendants for My servant Abraham's sake." ²⁵So he built an altar there and called on the name of the LORD, and he pitched his tent there; and there Isaac's servants dug a well.

²⁶Then Abimelech came to him from Gerar with Ahuzzath, one of his friends, and Phichol the commander of his army. ²⁷And Isaac said to them, "Why have you come to me, since you hate me and have sent me away from you?"

²⁸But they said, "We have certainly seen that the LORD is with you. So we said, 'Let there now be an oath between us, between you and us; and let us make a covenant with you, ²⁹that you will do us no harm, since we have not touched you, and since we have done nothing to you but good and have sent you away in peace. You are now the blessed of the LORD.'"

³⁰So he made them a feast, and they ate and drank. ³¹Then they arose early in the morning and swore an oath with one another; and Isaac sent them away, and they departed from him in peace.

³²It came to pass the same day that Isaac's ser-

•••••••••••••••••••••••

26:20 ᵃLiterally *Quarrel* **26:21** ᵃLiterally *Enmity* **26:22** ᵃLiterally *Spaciousness*

26:23 The covenant renewal is at Beersheba, at the southern border of Canaan, where Abraham made a treaty with Abimelech (Gen. 21:22–34). God's affirmation of the covenant here may indicate that this is the limit of the promised territory. The altar is Isaac's response to God's presence (v. 25).

vants came and told him about the well which they had dug, and said to him, "We have found water." ³³So he called it Shebah.^a Therefore the name of the city *is* Beersheba^b to this day.

³⁴When Esau was forty years old, he took as wives Judith the daughter of Beeri the Hittite, and Basemath the daughter of Elon the Hittite. ³⁵And they were a grief of mind to Isaac and Rebekah.

Isaac Blesses Jacob

27 Now it came to pass, when Isaac was old and his eyes were so dim that he could not see, that he called Esau his older son and said to him, "My son."

And he answered him, "Here I am."

²Then he said, "Behold now, I am old. I do not know the day of my death. ³Now therefore, please take your weapons, your quiver and your bow, and go out to the field and hunt game for me. ⁴And make me savory food, such as I love, and bring *it* to me that I may eat, that my soul may bless you before I die."

⁵Now Rebekah was listening when Isaac spoke to Esau his son. And Esau went to the field to hunt game and to bring *it.* ⁶So Rebekah spoke to Jacob her son, saying, "Indeed I heard your father speak to Esau your brother, saying, ⁷'Bring me game and make savory food for me, that I may eat it and bless you in the presence of the LORD before my death.' ⁸Now therefore, my son, obey my voice according to what I command you. ⁹Go now to the flock and bring me from there two choice kids of the goats, and I will make savory food from them for your father, such as he loves. ¹⁰Then you shall take *it* to your father, that he may eat *it,* and that he may bless you before his death."

¹¹And Jacob said to Rebekah his mother, "Look, Esau my brother *is* a hairy man, and I *am* a smooth-*skinned* man. ¹²Perhaps my father will feel me, and I shall seem to be a deceiver to him; and I shall bring a curse on myself and not a blessing."

¹³But his mother said to him, "*Let* your curse *be* on me, my son; only obey my voice, and go, get *them* for me." ¹⁴And he went and got *them* and brought *them* to his mother, and his mother made savory food, such as his father loved. ¹⁵Then Re-

bekah took the choice clothes of her elder son Esau, which *were* with her in the house, and put them on Jacob her younger son. ¹⁶And she put the skins of the kids of the goats on his hands and on the smooth part of his neck. ¹⁷Then she gave the savory food and the bread, which she had prepared, into the hand of her son Jacob.

¹⁸So he went to his father and said, "My father." And he said, "Here I am. Who *are* you, my son?"

¹⁹Jacob said to his father, "I *am* Esau your firstborn; I have done just as you told me; please arise, sit and eat of my game, that your soul may bless me."

²⁰But Isaac said to his son, "How *is it* that you have found *it* so quickly, my son?"

And he said, "Because the LORD your God brought *it* to me."

²¹Isaac said to Jacob, "Please come near, that I may feel you, my son, whether you *are* really my son Esau or not." ²²So Jacob went near to Isaac his father, and he felt him and said, "The voice *is* Jacob's voice, but the hands *are* the hands of Esau." ²³And he did not recognize him, because his hands were hairy like his brother Esau's hands; so he blessed him.

²⁴Then he said, "*Are* you really my son Esau?"

He said, "I *am.*"

²⁵He said, "Bring *it* near to me, and I will eat of my son's game, so that my soul may bless you." So he brought *it* near to him, and he ate; and he brought him wine, and he drank. ²⁶Then his father Isaac said to him, "Come near now and kiss me, my son." ²⁷And he came near and kissed him; and he smelled the smell of his clothing, and blessed him and said:

> "Surely, the smell of my son
> *Is* like the smell of a field
> Which the LORD has blessed.
> ²⁸Therefore may God give you
> Of the dew of heaven,
> Of the fatness of the earth,
> And plenty of grain and wine.
> ²⁹Let peoples serve you,

^{26:33} ^aLiterally *Oath* or *Seven* ^bLiterally *Well of the Oath* or *Well of the Seven*

26:34 Esau's foreign wives. The set-apart character of the covenant line was marred by Esau. Both Isaac and Jacob, the covenant keepers, married within the chosen clan. At this time the Hittites had settlements well into Canaan.

27:20 Jacob's lie. While it was God's will that Jacob be blessed, Jacob's deception was not sanctioned by God. In his lie Jacob used the phrase "the LORD *your* God" in recognition that the covenant blessing had not yet passed to him and that he had not yet committed himself totally to *Yahweh.*

27:27–29 The blessing. God overruled the sinfulness of all four participants—Isaac's stubborn partiality, Esau's reckless

determination to go his own way, Rebekah's deceit, and Jacob's ambition—to bring about His ends. The blessing has three elements:

1) the promise of plenty, which assumed possession of the land (see Gen. 17:8) and the blessing of fertility;

2) the promise of domination, echoing the promise to Abraham (Gen. 22:17), with the addition that the recipient will rule over the rest of his family as well;

3) the contrasting blessing and cursing, which repeated God's initial call to Abraham (Gen. 12:3).

MANIPULATION *CONTROL VS. TRUST*

Manipulation is rooted in pride and selfishness and involves viewing others as objects, not as individuals. It is an invasion of an individual's dignity because it seeks to limit freedom through control. The tools of manipulation are position, power, deception, and distortion. The results, even if perceived as successful, are always a denigration of God's best as the manipulative individual believes that she knows more than God.

Scripture has many vivid examples of manipulation of people and situations. Sarah manipulated her husband Abraham and her servant Hagar in order to influence what God had promised (Gen. 16:1–16). Rebekah manipulated her husband Isaac as well as her son Jacob in order to achieve her personal goal for her favorite son (Gen. 27:1–29). In these instances—and countless others—manipulation brought more sorrow than joy (Gen. 16:5; 27:42, 43).

Anytime a person focuses on self rather than God, the possibility of manipulation exists. Fundamentally, such an attitude shows a lack of trust in God and suggests the erroneous belief that since God is not doing the right thing, we must take matters into our own hands and attempt to control environment, circumstances, and people by whatever means available. Manipulation is ultimately rooted in a lack of trust in God and a negative self-image that manifests itself in a driving need to control.

See also Gen. 29:15–30; 38:1–30; 2 Sam. 11:1–17; Acts 5:1–11; notes on Codependency (Gen. 27); Conflict (Song 5; Matt. 18); Enabling (Mark 10); Family (1 Sam. 3); Favoritism (Prov. 28); portrait of Rebekah (Gen. 24)

And nations bow down to you.
Be master over your brethren,
And let your mother's sons bow down to you.
Cursed *be* everyone who curses you,
And blessed *be* those who bless you!"

Esau's Lost Hope

30Now it happened, as soon as Isaac had finished blessing Jacob, and Jacob had scarcely gone out from the presence of Isaac his father, that Esau his brother came in from his hunting. 31He also had made savory food, and brought it to his father, and said to his father, "Let my father arise and eat of his son's game, that your soul may bless me."

32And his father Isaac said to him, "Who *are* you?"

So he said, "I *am* your son, your firstborn, Esau."

33Then Isaac trembled exceedingly, and said, "Who? Where *is* the one who hunted game and brought *it* to me? I ate all *of it* before you came, and I have blessed him—*and* indeed he shall be blessed."

34When Esau heard the words of his father, he cried with an exceedingly great and bitter cry, and said to his father, "Bless me—me also, O my father!"

35But he said, "Your brother came with deceit and has taken away your blessing."

36And *Esau* said, "Is he not rightly named Jacob? For he has supplanted me these two times. He took away my birthright, and now look, he has taken away my blessing!" And he said, "Have you not reserved a blessing for me?"

37Then Isaac answered and said to Esau, "Indeed I have made him your master, and all his brethren I have given to him as servants; with grain and wine I have sustained him. What shall I do now for you, my son?"

38And Esau said to his father, "Have you only one blessing, my father? Bless me—me also, O my father!" And Esau lifted up his voice and wept.

39Then Isaac his father answered and said to him:

"Behold, your dwelling shall be of the fatness of the earth,
And of the dew of heaven from above.
40By your sword you shall live,
And you shall serve your brother;
And it shall come to pass, when you become restless,
That you shall break his yoke from your neck."

Jacob Escapes from Esau

41So Esau hated Jacob because of the blessing with which his father blessed him, and Esau said in his heart, "The days of mourning for my father are at hand; then I will kill my brother Jacob."

27:39–40. Esau's blessing. Esau would share in the fertility of the Land but would not reap its primary benefits. The Land later occupied by the Edomites, between the Dead Sea and the Gulf of Aqaba, is partially barren with areas of great fertility. Isaac predicted that Esau's descendants would live by war; his blessing was that the domination by Israel would have limited duration.

27:41 The result of the deception. The unrighteous method used to assure the carrying out of God's promise did not invalidate the promise, but it did result in family strife and separation.

⁴²And the words of Esau her older son were told to Rebekah. So she sent and called Jacob her younger son, and said to him, "Surely your brother Esau comforts himself concerning you *by intending* to kill you. ⁴³Now therefore, my son, obey my voice: arise, flee to my brother Laban in Haran. ⁴⁴And stay with him a few days, until your brother's fury turns away, ⁴⁵until your brother's anger turns away from you, and he forgets what you have done to him; then I will send and bring you from there. Why should I be bereaved also of you both in one day?"

⁴⁶And Rebekah said to Isaac, "I am weary of my life because of the daughters of Heth; if Jacob takes a wife of the daughters of Heth, like these *who are* the daughters of the land, what good will my life be to me?"

28 Then Isaac called Jacob and blessed him, and charged him, and said to him: "You shall not take a wife from the daughters of Canaan. ²Arise, go to Padan Aram, to the house of Bethuel your mother's father; and take yourself a wife from there of the daughters of Laban your mother's brother.

³"May God Almighty bless you,
And make you fruitful and multiply you,
That you may be an assembly of peoples;
⁴And give you the blessing of Abraham,
To you and your descendants with you,
That you may inherit the land
In which you are a stranger,
Which God gave to Abraham."

⁵So Isaac sent Jacob away, and he went to Padan Aram, to Laban the son of Bethuel the Syrian, the brother of Rebekah, the mother of Jacob and Esau.

Esau Marries Mahalath

⁶Esau saw that Isaac had blessed Jacob and sent him away to Padan Aram to take himself a wife from there, *and that* as he blessed him he gave him a charge, saying, "You shall not take a wife from the daughters of Canaan," ⁷and that Jacob had obeyed his father and his mother and had gone to Padan Aram. ⁸Also Esau saw that the daughters of Canaan did not please his father Isaac. ⁹So Esau went to Ishmael and took Mahalath the daughter of Ishmael, Abraham's son, the sister of Nebajoth, to be his wife in addition to the wives he had.

Jacob's Vow at Bethel

¹⁰Now Jacob went out from Beersheba and went toward Haran. ¹¹So he came to a certain place and stayed there all night, because the sun had set. And he took one of the stones of that place and put it at his head, and he lay down in that place to sleep. ¹²Then he dreamed, and behold, a ladder *was* set up on the earth, and its top reached to heaven; and there the angels of God were ascending and descending on it.

¹³And behold, the LORD stood above it and said: "I *am* the LORD God of Abraham your father and the God of Isaac; the land on which you lie I will give to you and your descendants. ¹⁴Also your descendants shall be as the dust of the earth; you shall spread abroad to the west and the east, to the north and the south; and in you and in your seed all the families of the earth shall be blessed. ¹⁵Behold, I *am* with you and will keep you wherever you go, and will bring you back to this land; for I will not leave you until I have done what I have spoken to you."

¹⁶Then Jacob awoke from his sleep and said, "Surely the LORD is in this place, and I did not know *it.*" ¹⁷And he was afraid and said, "How awesome *is* this place! This *is* none other than the house of God, and this *is* the gate of heaven!"

¹⁸Then Jacob rose early in the morning, and took the stone that he had put at his head, set it up as a pillar, and poured oil on top of it. ¹⁹And he called the name of that place Bethel;ᵃ but the name of that city had been Luz previously.

28:19 ᵃLiterally *House of God*

28:1–4 Jacob's blessing. Isaac confirmed the covenant blessing of Abraham in full knowledge of Jacob's identity. The name God Almighty (Heb. *El Shaddai*, v. 3), was also used by God in assigning the covenant sign of circumcision (Gen. 17, Circumcision). In the OT, the word "assembly" (Heb. *qahal*, v. 3) is used of God's congregation and later of the Jewish synagogue. This, along with Isaac's order not to marry a Canaanite wife, emphasizes the set-apart character of God's chosen people.

28:11–17 Jacob's dream. The phrase "a certain place" may indicate that Jacob was seeking an encounter with God. God's appearance to Jacob confirmed the covenant blessing already bestowed by Isaac. The encounter bears striking parallels to God's covenant appearances to Abraham (Gen. 12:7, 8; 13:3, 4).

28:12 Jacob's ladder. The ladder is better visualized as a stair

or ramp between heaven and earth. The word is unique in the OT, but other variations may mean "raised way" or "mound," as in the ramped earth cast up against the walls of a besieged city. The angels represent God's promised, constant, providential care over the earth (v. 15; see Zech. 1:10).

28:17 The gate of heaven may intentionally contrast Jacob, to whom God voluntarily and graciously came, to the builders of Babel (Gen. 11:1–9), seeking God in their own strength.

28:18 Jacob's pillar. Throughout the OT, raised objects—stones, trees, altars, pillars—serve as memory aids, reminders of God's covenant workings with His people (Gen. 21:33; Deut. 27:2, 3). Anointing with oil symbolized consecration to God.

28:19 Bethel (Heb., lit. "house of God"; see Gen. 12:8, note). The Canaanite name Luz applied both to this spot and to the general district where it was found (Josh. 16:2).

RACHEL *The Beloved Wife*

Rachel, whose name means "ewe," was caring for her father's sheep in Haran when she met an unexpected visitor, her cousin Jacob, who was looking for his family. After what seems to have been love at first sight (Gen. 29:11, 12), Jacob promised Rachel's father Laban that he would work seven years to earn the right to marry the beautiful shepherdess (Gen. 29:20). The wedding ceremony proceeded according to local tradition, allowing the men to celebrate, while keeping the bride out of sight until the groom entered her darkened tent.

Only after it was too late did Jacob realize that Laban had deceived him. He had actually married Laban's older daughter, Leah, whom he did not love. A week after his marriage to Leah, Jacob received Rachel as his wife. Rachel must have suffered agony. Seven years of anticipation were dashed by her father's trickery. The rivalry and jealousy between Rachel and Leah and perhaps a desire on Rachel's part for retaliation against her father for his deception must have greatly strained the family.

Furthermore, Rachel was unable to bear children (Gen. 29:31), increasing her jealousy of Leah. She blamed her husband, then allowed her maid to bear children for her. Finally, Rachel became pregnant and gave birth to Joseph, who became Jacob's favorite (Gen. 30:22–24). In due time Jacob decided to return to his homeland. After Jacob's departure, Laban found his household gods missing. Unknown to Jacob, Rachel had put the gods in her saddlebags, then seated herself on the camel. When Laban was given permission to search through their belongings, she pleaded weakness because of her menstrual cycle and did not dismount. Whatever a menstruating woman sat upon was later described as unclean (Lev. 15). These small images were customarily kept in homes. Likely the images were indispensible evidence for a claim to the family inheritance, though some believe Rachel was a secret believer in pagan superstitions. If this were true, she would have believed the images would give them safety in their journey and prosperity in their new home.

Rachel returned to her husband's homeland, but sometime later when they were moving again, she became pregnant for the second time. The travel in hilly country would have been difficult under any circumstance. Approaching Ephrath (Bethlehem), Rachel went into hard labor and died during the birth of Benjamin. She was buried there in Bethlehem (Gen. 35:19). Rachel, a woman greatly loved by her husband, gave the world outstanding sons; and despite her flaws, she stands as an honored daughter of *Yahweh*.

See also Gen. 29:26–30; 30:1–8, 22–26; 31:4, 14–19, 34, 35; 33:2, 7; 35:16–20; Weddings (John 2); chart on The Family Tree of Abraham

20Then Jacob made a vow, saying, "If God will be with me, and keep me in this way that I am going, and give me bread to eat and clothing to put on, 21so that I come back to my father's house in peace, then the LORD shall be my God. 22And this stone which I have set as a pillar shall be God's house, and of all that You give me I will surely give a tenth to You."

Jacob Meets Rachel

29 So Jacob went on his journey and came to the land of the people of the East. 2And he looked, and saw a well in the field; and behold, there were three flocks of sheep lying by it; for out of that well they watered the flocks. A large stone was on the well's mouth. 3Now all the flocks would be gathered there; and they would roll the stone from the well's mouth, water the sheep, and put the stone back in its place on the well's mouth.

4And Jacob said to them, "My brethren, where are you from?"

And they said, "We are from Haran."

5Then he said to them, "Do you know Laban the son of Nahor?"

And they said, "We know him."

6So he said to them, "Is he well?"

And they said, "*He is* well. And look, his daughter Rachel is coming with the sheep."

7Then he said, "Look, *it is* still high day; *it is* not time for the cattle to be gathered together. Water the sheep, and go and feed *them*."

8But they said, "We cannot until all the flocks are gathered together, and they have rolled the stone from the well's mouth; then we water the sheep."

9Now while he was still speaking with them, Rachel came with her father's sheep, for she was a shepherdess. 10And it came to pass, when Jacob

28:20, 22 Jacob's vow. Like Abraham, Jacob responded to God's presence with obedience (Gen. 17:23–27). He recognized that, in return for God's promised providential care, he was obligated to worship God alone (v. 15). He also followed the example of his grandfather in pledging a tithe as an act of worship (see Gen. 14:18, note).

29:3 The stone at the well. Ancient Near Eastern custom was to wait until all the local shepherds were present with their flocks before removing the stone seal on the well. This prevented any one herdsman from monopolizing the scarce water supply (v. 8).

saw Rachel the daughter of Laban his mother's brother, and the sheep of Laban his mother's brother, that Jacob went near and rolled the stone from the well's mouth, and watered the flock of Laban his mother's brother. [11]Then Jacob kissed Rachel, and lifted up his voice and wept. [12]And Jacob told Rachel that he *was* her father's relative and that he *was* Rebekah's son. So she ran and told her father.

[13]Then it came to pass, when Laban heard the report about Jacob his sister's son, that he ran to meet him, and embraced him and kissed him, and brought him to his house. So he told Laban all these things. [14]And Laban said to him, "Surely you *are* my bone and my flesh." And he stayed with him for a month.

Jacob Marries Leah and Rachel

[15]Then Laban said to Jacob, "Because you *are* my relative, should you therefore serve me for nothing? Tell me, what *should* your wages *be?*" [16]Now Laban had two daughters: the name of the elder *was* Leah, and the name of the younger *was* Rachel. [17]Leah's eyes *were* delicate, but Rachel was beautiful of form and appearance.

[18]Now Jacob loved Rachel; so he said, "I will serve you seven years for Rachel your younger daughter."

[19]And Laban said, "*It is* better that I give her to you than that I should give her to another man. Stay with me." [20]So Jacob served seven years for Rachel, and they seemed *only* a few days to him because of the love he had for her.

[21]Then Jacob said to Laban, "Give *me* my wife, for my days are fulfilled, that I may go in to her." [22]And Laban gathered together all the men of the place and made a feast. [23]Now it came to pass in the evening, that he took Leah his daughter and brought her to Jacob; and he went in to her. [24]And Laban gave his maid Zilpah to his daughter Leah *as* a maid. [25]So it came to pass in the morning, that behold, it *was* Leah. And he said to Laban, "What is this you have done to me? Was it not for Rachel that I served you? Why then have you deceived me?"

[26]And Laban said, "It must not be done so in our country, to give the younger before the first-born. [27]Fulfill her week, and we will give you this one also for the service which you will serve with me still another seven years."

[28]Then Jacob did so and fulfilled her week. So he gave him his daughter Rachel as wife also. [29]And Laban gave his maid Bilhah to his daughter Rachel as a maid. [30]Then *Jacob* also went in to Rachel, and he also loved Rachel more than Leah. And he served with Laban still another seven years.

The Children of Jacob

[31]When the LORD saw that Leah *was* unloved, He opened her womb; but Rachel *was* barren. [32]So Leah conceived and bore a son, and she called his name Reuben;[a] for she said, "The LORD has surely looked on my affliction. Now therefore, my husband will love me." [33]Then she conceived again and bore a son, and said, "Because the LORD has heard that I *am* unloved, He has therefore given me this *son* also." And she called his name Simeon.[a] [34]She conceived again and bore a son, and said, "Now this time my husband will become attached to me, because I have borne him three sons." Therefore his name was called Levi.[a] [35]And she conceived again and bore a son, and said, "Now I will praise the LORD." Therefore she called his name Judah.[a] Then she stopped bearing.

30 Now when Rachel saw that she bore Jacob no children, Rachel envied her sister, and said to Jacob, "Give me children, or else I die!"

[2]And Jacob's anger was aroused against Rachel, and he said, "*Am* I in the place of God, who has withheld from you the fruit of the womb?"

[3]So she said, "Here is my maid Bilhah; go in to her, and she will bear *a child* on my knees, that I also may have children by her." [4]Then she gave him Bilhah her maid as wife, and Jacob went in to her. [5]And Bilhah conceived and bore Jacob a son. [6]Then

---

29:32 [a]Literally *See, a Son*   **29:33** [a]Literally *Heard*   **29:34** [a]Literally *Attached*   **29:35** [a]Literally *Praise*

29:17 Delicate eyes may refer to lack of vision or physical unattractiveness. The former is more likely. The irony of the story lies in the deception of Jacob by his own eyes in the same way that the eyes of his blind father were deceived by Jacob's trickery (vv. 23–35; Gen. 27:18–29). Leah's own weak vision would strengthen the irony.

29:18 Jacob's service. Ancient Near Eastern custom demanded a bride-price (Heb. *mohar*) to be paid to the bride's parents (see 1 Kin. 9, Dowry). Syrian records indicate that it was common for a groom to work off the price in labor.

29:23 The trickery of Leah's substitution is an obvious judgment on Jacob for his own deceitfulness. Jacob, the younger brother, stole the older brother's blessing; later, he received the older sister rather than the younger. God, however, accomplished His purposes despite human failure. Leah became the mother of Levi and Judah, the tribes of Israel's priests and kings, and ultimately the ancestress of Christ.

29:30 Rachel's marriage. Jacob married both sisters the same week and served Laban for Rachel seven more years. Again, rupturing the Creator's design for the one-man, one-woman union leads to strife and conflict. Mosaic Law later forbade the taking of living sisters as wives (Lev. 18:18).

29:31 Leah's sons. "Unloved" (lit. "hated" or "rejected") reveals the immense contrast in Jacob's feelings for his two wives. It may also imply sexual avoidance. Nevertheless, God had chosen Leah as He chose Jacob (see v. 23, note).

30:3 Bilhah's children. Rachel followed the example of Sarah. The custom of laying a newborn child on his father's knees

LEAH *The Unwanted Wife*

Leah is described as having "delicate" or "weak" eyes (Gen. 29:17), which could allude to poor eyesight or merely to a lack of sparkle. Through subterfuge, Leah, instead of the promised Rachel, became the wife of Jacob. Although Leah may have been at least a willing participant in this deception, she could have been merely an obedient daughter. Nevertheless, she obviously loved Jacob and was devoted to him throughout their marriage, though surely Leah's soul must have shriveled to be the object of Jacob's disappointment and scorn as well as the tool of her conniving father.

Living with the constant comparison to her unusually beautiful sister, Leah was, nevertheless, not hidden from God's caring eyes. In His omniscience, God allowed her to conceive even though her sister's fertility was delayed. She had the honor of mothering Jacob's oldest son, but she wrongly assumed that it would earn love from her husband (Gen. 29:32). Leah faced her second childbirth realistically, but apparently deep desire gnawed at her (v. 33). When a third pregnancy came, she exclaimed, "Now this time my husband will become attached to me," revealing an intense longing for love (v. 34).

Leah began her marriage by focusing on what she lacked and being miserable, but she changed her heart and focus to what she had and determined to praise the Lord. Not until the birth of her fourth son, Judah, did this unwanted wife learn to trust *Yahweh* ("Now I will praise the Lord," Gen. 29:35). Tracing the messianic lineage, the world rejoices with Leah as her faithfulness was rewarded. "The Lion of the tribe of Judah," Jesus the Messiah, came through her offspring Judah and the priesthood through her son Levi (see Rev. 5:5). Leah personified for every woman the crucial need to live primarily for God and His glory. Though she may have been unattractive in appearance, unloved, unwanted, and even despised, God saw in her an inner beauty that equipped her to carry out His plan (Gen. 29:31). She could not change Jacob, but she could change herself and recognize God's hand in her life (Gen. 30:13). Leah, for her part, did not let the attitudes of others distract her from the task God had given to her.

See also Gen. 29:16, 17, 31–35; 34:1; 35:23; Ruth 4:11; notes on Bitterness (Heb. 12); Pain (Job 7)

Rachel said, "God has judged my case; and He has also heard my voice and given me a son." Therefore she called his name Dan.[a] [7]And Rachel's maid Bilhah conceived again and bore Jacob a second son. [8]Then Rachel said, "With great wrestlings I have wrestled with my sister, *and* indeed I have prevailed." So she called his name Naphtali.[a]

[9]When Leah saw that she had stopped bearing, she took Zilpah her maid and gave her to Jacob as wife. [10]And Leah's maid Zilpah bore Jacob a son. [11]Then Leah said, "A troop comes!"[a] So she called his name Gad.[b] [12]And Leah's maid Zilpah bore Jacob a second son. [13]Then Leah said, "I am happy, for the daughters will call me blessed." So she called his name Asher.[a]

[14]Now Reuben went in the days of wheat harvest and found mandrakes in the field, and brought them to his mother Leah. Then Rachel said to Leah, "Please give me *some* of your son's mandrakes."

[15]But she said to her, "*Is it* a small matter that you have taken away my husband? Would you take away my son's mandrakes also?"

And Rachel said, "Therefore he will lie with you tonight for your son's mandrakes."

[16]When Jacob came out of the field in the evening, Leah went out to meet him and said, "You must come in to me, for I have surely hired you with my son's mandrakes." And he lay with her that night.

[17]And God listened to Leah, and she conceived and bore Jacob a fifth son. [18]Leah said, "God has given me my wages, because I have given my maid to my husband." So she called his name Issachar.[a] [19]Then Leah conceived again and bore Jacob a sixth son. [20]And Leah said, "God has endowed me *with* a good endowment; now my husband will dwell with me, because I have borne him six sons." So she called his name Zebulun.[a] [21]Afterward she bore a daughter, and called her name Dinah.

[22]Then God remembered Rachel, and God listened to her and opened her womb. [23]And she con-

30:6 [a]Literally *Judge*   30:8 [a]Literally *My Wrestling*   30:11 [a]Following Qere, Syriac, and Targum; Kethib, Septuagint, and Vulgate read *in fortune.* [b]Literally *Troop* or *Fortune*   30:13 [a]Literally *Happy*   30:18 [a]Literally *Wages*   30:20 [a]Literally *Dwelling*

---

was a public acknowledgment of paternity. The laying of Bilhah's child on Rachel's knees would acknowledge that the child was legally Rachel's.

30:14 Reuben's mandrakes. The mandrake, related to the potato, was thought to be both an aphrodisiac and a fertility aid. The story reveals the continuing tendency of this family to resort to magic and trickery rather than to God. God had the

last word: Rachel remained barren; Leah gave up the mandrakes, but she conceived.

30:15 Leah's heartache. Two meanings are possible. Either Leah was accusing her sister of having usurped her position as firstborn and first wife—a wry reminder of Jacob's own past—or else Jacob was denying Leah her marital rights.

ceived and bore a son, and said, "God has taken away my reproach." [24]So she called his name Joseph,[a] and said, "The LORD shall add to me another son."

Jacob's Agreement with Laban

[25]And it came to pass, when Rachel had borne Joseph, that Jacob said to Laban, "Send me away, that I may go to my own place and to my country. [26]Give *me* my wives and my children for whom I have served you, and let me go; for you know my service which I have done for you." [27]And Laban said to him, "Please *stay,* if I have found favor in your eyes, *for* I have learned by experience that the LORD has blessed me for your sake." [28]Then he said, "Name me your wages, and I will give *it.*" [29]So *Jacob* said to him, "You know how I have served you and how your livestock has been with me. [30]For what you had before I *came was* little, and it has increased to a great amount; the LORD has blessed you since my coming. And now, when shall I also provide for my own house?" [31]So he said, "What shall I give you?"

And Jacob said, "You shall not give me anything. If you will do this thing for me, I will again feed and keep your flocks: [32]Let me pass through all your flock today, removing from there all the speckled and spotted sheep, and all the brown ones among the lambs, and the spotted and speckled among the goats; and *these* shall be my wages. [33]So my righteousness will answer for me in time to come, when the subject of my wages comes before you: every one that *is* not speckled and spotted among the goats, and brown among the lambs, will be considered stolen, if *it is* with me."

[34]And Laban said, "Oh, that it were according to your word!" [35]So he removed that day the male goats that were speckled and spotted, all the female goats that were speckled and spotted, every one that had *some* white in it, and all the brown ones among the lambs, and gave *them* into the hand of his sons. [36]Then he put three days' journey between himself and Jacob, and Jacob fed the rest of Laban's flocks.

[37]Now Jacob took for himself rods of green poplar and of the almond and chestnut trees, peeled white strips in them, and exposed the white which *was* in the rods. [38]And the rods which he had peeled, he set before the flocks in the gutters, in the watering troughs where the flocks came to drink, so that they should conceive when they came to drink. [39]So the flocks conceived before the rods, and the flocks brought forth streaked, speckled, and spotted. [40]Then Jacob separated the lambs, and made the flocks face toward the streaked and all the brown in the flock of Laban; but he put his own flocks by themselves and did not put them with Laban's flock.

[41]And it came to pass, whenever the stronger livestock conceived, that Jacob placed the rods before the eyes of the livestock in the gutters, that they might conceive among the rods. [42]But when the flocks were feeble, he did not put *them* in; so the feebler were Laban's and the stronger Jacob's. [43]Thus the man became exceedingly prosperous, and had large flocks, female and male servants, and camels and donkeys.

Jacob Flees from Laban

31 Now *Jacob* heard the words of Laban's sons, saying, "Jacob has taken away all that was our father's, and from what was our father's he has acquired all this wealth." [2]And Jacob saw the countenance of Laban, and indeed it *was* not *favorable* toward him as before. [3]Then the LORD said to Jacob, "Return to the land of your fathers and to your family, and I will be with you."

[4]So Jacob sent and called Rachel and Leah to the field, to his flock, [5]and said to them, "I see your father's countenance, that it *is* not *favorable* toward me as before; but the God of my father has been with me. [6]And you know that with all my might I have served your father. [7]Yet your father has deceived me and changed my wages ten times, but God did not allow him to hurt me. [8]If he said thus: 'The speckled shall be your wages,' then all the flocks bore speckled. And if he said thus: 'The streaked shall be your wages,' then all the flocks bore streaked. [9]So God has taken away the livestock of your father and given *them* to me.

[10]"And it happened, at the time when the flocks conceived, that I lifted my eyes and saw in a dream, and behold, the rams which leaped upon the flocks *were* streaked, speckled, and gray-spotted. [11]Then the Angel of God spoke to me in a dream, saying, 'Jacob.' And I said, 'Here I am.' [12]And He said, 'Lift your eyes now and see, all the rams which leap on the flocks *are* streaked, speckled, and gray-spotted; for I have seen all that Laban is doing to you. [13]I *am* the God of Bethel, where you anointed the pillar *and* where you made

---

30:24 [a]Literally *He Will Add*

30:22 God's gracious exercise of covenant faithfulness. Rachel displayed trust in this faithfulness when she named her son "Joseph" (lit. "He will add"), looking forward to the birth of more children.

30:43 Jacob's wealth. Over a six-year period Jacob built up a large flock (Gen. 31:14). Despite the trickery and manipulation used by all members of this family, God remained in control. God's blessing, not Jacob's scheming, was responsible for Jacob's prosperity (Gen. 31:9–13).

31:3 Jacob's flight. God continued to direct His chosen back to the Land of Promise. Isaac was driven back by conflicts over wells; Jacob, by Laban's resentment.

CODEPENDENCY A QUEST TO MEET NEEDS

The term codependency with its diverse definitions was coined in the context of treating alcoholism. However, it has evolved to mean a compulsion to rescue or control others by fixing their problems. Generally codependency emanates from unmet or blocked God-given needs, such as love, acceptance, and security in primary relationships, as with parent, spouse, or child.

More frequently codependency occurs in relationships with a dysfunctional person, resulting in a denial of the severity of the problem in the relationship, a heightened sense of responsibility, and an environment of controlling or being controlled by others. It nearly always produces a keen sense of guilt or shame, hurt, anger, and loneliness in a complex and desperate quest to avoid abandonment. Ultimately, this need for acceptance can be filled by God alone. His unconditional love prepares the codependent to move toward complete healing.

Healing from codependency requires confession to God that something or someone has been put in His place. You must then receive His forgiveness and grace (1 John 1:9, 10), establish effective and appropriate boundaries, and acquire new means of communicating and relating. Counseling may be appropriate and effective in finding complete healing (Prov. 11:14).

See also Matt. 20:20–28; notes on Alcoholism (Prov. 20); Counseling (Prov. 8); Family (1 Sam. 3); Guilt (2 Cor. 7); portrait of Rebekah (Gen. 24)

---

a vow to Me. Now arise, get out of this land, and return to the land of your family.' "

¹⁴Then Rachel and Leah answered and said to him, "Is there still any portion or inheritance for us in our father's house? ¹⁵Are we not considered strangers by him? For he has sold us, and also completely consumed our money. ¹⁶For all these riches which God has taken from our father are *really* ours and our children's; now then, whatever God has said to you, do it."

¹⁷Then Jacob rose and set his sons and his wives on camels. ¹⁸And he carried away all his livestock and all his possessions which he had gained, his acquired livestock which he had gained in Padan Aram, to go to his father Isaac in the land of Canaan. ¹⁹Now Laban had gone to shear his sheep, and Rachel had stolen the household idols that were her father's. ²⁰And Jacob stole away, unknown to Laban the Syrian, in that he did not tell him that he intended to flee. ²¹So he fled with all that he had. He arose and crossed the river, and headed toward the mountains of Gilead.

Laban Pursues Jacob

²²And Laban was told on the third day that Jacob had fled. ²³Then he took his brethren with him and pursued him for seven days' journey, and he overtook him in the mountains of Gilead. ²⁴But

God had come to Laban the Syrian in a dream by night, and said to him, "Be careful that you speak to Jacob neither good nor bad."

²⁵So Laban overtook Jacob. Now Jacob had pitched his tent in the mountains, and Laban with his brethren pitched in the mountains of Gilead. ²⁶And Laban said to Jacob: "What have you done, that you have stolen away unknown to me, and carried away my daughters like captives *taken* with the sword? ²⁷Why did you flee away secretly, and steal away from me, and not tell me; for I might have sent you away with joy and songs, with timbrel and harp? ²⁸And you did not allow me to kiss my sons and my daughters. Now you have done foolishly in *so* doing. ²⁹It is in my power to do you harm, but the God of your father spoke to me last night, saying, 'Be careful that you speak to Jacob neither good nor bad.' ³⁰And now you have surely gone because you greatly long for your father's house, *but* why did you steal my gods?"

³¹Then Jacob answered and said to Laban, "Because I was afraid, for I said, 'Perhaps you would take your daughters from me by force.' ³²With whomever you find your gods, do not let him live. In the presence of our brethren, identify what I have of yours and take *it* with you." For Jacob did not know that Rachel had stolen them.

31:14–16 Rachel and Leah respond. The response of Jacob's wives confirmed God's leading. An estrangement had developed because of Laban's greed (vv. 14–16). "Strangers" has a negative connotation, as in unwelcome foreigners (v. 15). "He has sold us" implies that Laban had given up any claim to fatherly respect and status by treating his daughters as a means of profit. "Riches" is a reference to the bride-price, part of which was often given back to the bride; Laban neglected to do this for his daughters (see 1 Kin. 9, Dowry).

31:19 Household idols. Laban was an idolater and not a worshiper of *Yahweh*. The idols are literally "teraphim," small household figurines possibly used for divination (Ezek. 21:21; Zech. 10:2). The Nuzi tablets, which record contemporary law for the Mesopotamian Hurrians, connect ownership of the household idols with inheritance rights; Rachel's motives may have been financial rather than religious (see Gen. 29, Rachel).

³³And Laban went into Jacob's tent, into Leah's tent, and into the two maids' tents, but he did not find *them.* Then he went out of Leah's tent and entered Rachel's tent. ³⁴Now Rachel had taken the household idols, put them in the camel's saddle, and sat on them. And Laban searched all about the tent but did not find *them.* ³⁵And she said to her father, "Let it not displease my lord that I cannot rise before you, for the manner of women *is* with me." And he searched but did not find the household idols.

³⁶Then Jacob was angry and rebuked Laban, and Jacob answered and said to Laban: "What *is* my trespass? What *is* my sin, that you have so hotly pursued me? ³⁷Although you have searched all my things, what part of your household things have you found? Set *it* here before my brethren and your brethren, that they may judge between us both! ³⁸These twenty years I *have been* with you; your ewes and your female goats have not miscarried their young, and I have not eaten the rams of your flock. ³⁹That which was torn *by beasts* I did not bring to you; I bore the loss of it. You required it from my hand, *whether* stolen by day or stolen by night. ⁴⁰*There* I was! In the day the drought consumed me, and the frost by night, and my sleep departed from my eyes. ⁴¹Thus I have been in your house twenty years; I served you fourteen years for your two daughters, and six years for your flock, and you have changed my wages ten times. ⁴²Unless the God of my father, the God of Abraham and the Fear of Isaac, had been with me, surely now you would have sent me away empty-handed. God has seen my affliction and the labor of my hands, and rebuked *you* last night."

Laban's Covenant with Jacob

⁴³And Laban answered and said to Jacob, "*These* daughters *are* my daughters, and *these* children *are* my children, and *this* flock *is* my flock; all that you see *is* mine. But what can I do this day to these my daughters or to their children whom they have borne? ⁴⁴Now therefore, come, let us make a covenant, you and I, and let it be a witness between you and me."

⁴⁵So Jacob took a stone and set it up *as* a pillar. ⁴⁶Then Jacob said to his brethren, "Gather stones." And they took stones and made a heap, and they ate there on the heap. ⁴⁷Laban called it Jegar Sahadutha,^a but Jacob called it Galeed.^b ⁴⁸And Laban said, "This heap *is* a witness between you and me this day." Therefore its name was called Galeed,

⁴⁹also Mizpah,^a because he said, "May the LORD watch between you and me when we are absent one from another. ⁵⁰If you afflict my daughters, or if you take *other* wives besides my daughters, *although* no man *is* with us— see, God *is* witness between you and me!"

⁵¹Then Laban said to Jacob, "Here is this heap and here is *this* pillar, which I have placed between you and me. ⁵²This heap *is* a witness, and *this* pillar *is* a witness, that I will not pass beyond this heap to you, and you will not pass beyond this heap and this pillar to me, for harm. ⁵³The God of Abraham, the God of Nahor, and the God of their father judge between us." And Jacob swore by the Fear of his father Isaac. ⁵⁴Then Jacob offered a sacrifice on the mountain, and called his brethren to eat bread. And they ate bread and stayed all night on the mountain. ⁵⁵And early in the morning Laban arose, and kissed his sons and daughters and blessed them. Then Laban departed and returned to his place.

Esau Comes to Meet Jacob

32 So Jacob went on his way, and the angels of God met him. ²When Jacob saw them, he said, "This *is* God's camp." And he called the name of that place Mahanaim.^a

³Then Jacob sent messengers before him to Esau his brother in the land of Seir, the country of Edom. ⁴And he commanded them, saying, "Speak thus to my lord Esau, 'Thus your servant Jacob says: "I have dwelt with Laban and stayed there until now. ⁵I have oxen, donkeys, flocks, and male and female servants; and I have sent to tell my lord, that I may find favor in your sight." ' "

⁶Then the messengers returned to Jacob, saying, "We came to your brother Esau, and he also is coming to meet you, and four hundred men *are* with him." ⁷So Jacob was greatly afraid and distressed; and he divided the people that *were* with him, and the flocks and herds and camels, into two companies. ⁸And he said, "If Esau comes to the one company and attacks it, then the other company which is left will escape."

⁹Then Jacob said, "O God of my father Abraham and God of my father Isaac, the LORD who said to me, 'Return to your country and to your family, and I will deal well with you': ¹⁰I am not

---

31:47 ^aLiterally, in Aramaic, *Heap of Witness* ^bLiterally, in Hebrew, *Heap of Witness* 31:49 ^aLiterally *Watch* 32:2 ^aLiterally *Double Camp*

31:45 The memorial. The pillar acts as a reminder of the covenant between the two men (see Gen. 28:18). The name "Heap of Witness" was given in Aramean by Laban and in Hebrew by Jacob. The name "Galeed" may be related to the designation "Gilead" later assigned to the district. This spot became known as Mizpah (Heb., lit. "watchtower"), which conveys the same idea (Josh. 11:3; Judg. 11:34).

32:2 Mahanaim (Heb., lit. "double camp"). This is a reference to Jacob's own caravan and the company of God. The angels demonstrated God's protection as Jacob advanced to meet Esau. Mahanaim later became an important fortress east of the Jordan River and probably north of the Jabbok River (2 Sam. 17:24–27).

BLENDED FAMILY BUILDING A NEW HOME

While the subject of blended families is not addressed specifically in Scripture, the Bible does give us some admonitions that seem relevant:

1) *Build your new family on Christ.* If mistakes were made in the past, seek the forgiveness of God and others and turn away from the past in order to move with joyful purpose to future opportunities. Recognize openly that each family member has a distinct and irreplaceable relationship with Christ and that together you are a "mini-version" of the body of Christ at work. Seek to understand and develop the unique spiritual gifts of each person in your new family. Pray together. Make Christ the focal point and supreme authority of your home.

2) *Clearly delineate the lines of authority and responsibility.* The more responsibility a parent has for a child, the greater the authority he or she must have. Discuss openly and candidly with your spouse the need for defining clearly the roles of both parents over each child in your blended family to maintain order in the household (1 Cor. 14:40).

3) *Foster communication.* Heartfelt harmony, peace, and order require clear, direct, and convincing communication. Provide a regular forum for airing grievances, sharing ideas and opinions, and making family decisions, showing appreciation for each person's contribution (Eph. 4:29–32).

4) *Recognize and value your individual differences*—even as you seek to blend together as a family. Allow each person the freedom to express his own personality, skills, and abilities within the constraints of family rules (Rom. 12:10–12).

5) *Find and pursue mutually satisfying activities* (Amos 3:3).

See also Gen. 29:15—33:17; notes on Divorce (Matt. 19); Family (1 Sam. 3; Ps. 78; 127); Marriage (Gen. 2; 2 Sam. 6; Prov. 5; Hos. 2; Amos 3; 2 Cor. 13; Heb. 12); Remarriage (Matt. 5); Siblings (Gen. 37); Step-parenthood (Gen. 35)

---

worthy of the least of all the mercies and of all the truth which You have shown Your servant; for I crossed over this Jordan with my staff, and now I have become two companies. ¹¹Deliver me, I pray, from the hand of my brother, from the hand of Esau; for I fear him, lest he come and attack me *and* the mother with the children. ¹²For You said, 'I will surely treat you well, and make your descendants as the sand of the sea, which cannot be numbered for multitude.' "

¹³So he lodged there that same night, and took what came to his hand as a present for Esau his brother: ¹⁴two hundred female goats and twenty male goats, two hundred ewes and twenty rams, ¹⁵thirty milk camels with their colts, forty cows and ten bulls, twenty female donkeys and ten foals. ¹⁶Then he delivered *them* to the hand of his servants, every drove by itself, and said to his servants, "Pass over before me, and put some distance between successive droves." ¹⁷And he commanded the first one, saying, "When Esau my brother meets you and asks you, saying, 'To whom do you belong, and where are you going? Whose *are* these in front of you?' ¹⁸then you shall say, 'They *are* your servant Jacob's. It *is* a present sent to my lord Esau; and behold, he also *is* behind us.' " ¹⁹So he

commanded the second, the third, and all who followed the droves, saying, "In this manner you shall speak to Esau when you find him; ²⁰and also say, 'Behold, your servant Jacob *is* behind us.' " For he said, "I will appease him with the present that goes before me, and afterward I will see his face; perhaps he will accept me." ²¹So the present went on over before him, but he himself lodged that night in the camp.

Wrestling with God

²²And he arose that night and took his two wives, his two female servants, and his eleven sons, and crossed over the ford of Jabbok. ²³He took them, sent them over the brook, and sent over what he had. ²⁴Then Jacob was left alone; and a Man wrestled with him until the breaking of day. ²⁵Now when He saw that He did not prevail against him, He touched the socket of his hip; and the socket of Jacob's hip was out of joint as He wrestled with him. ²⁶And He said, "Let Me go, for the day breaks."

But he said, "I will not let You go unless You bless me!"

²⁷So He said to him, "What *is* your name?"

He said, "Jacob."

32:22 The Jabbok River (Heb., lit. "wrestler"; see v. 24), modern Nahr ez Zerka, cuts through Gilead halfway between the Sea of Galilee and the Dead Sea and flows into the Jordan about 40 miles south of the Sea of Galilee.

32:24 Jacob's encounter with God. The wrestling match with

the One who revealed Himself as God (v. 28) sums up Jacob's lifelong attitude toward God. The ultimate power is confirmed as lying in God's hands, not in Jacob's strength or cunning (v. 25). Jacob's defeat resulted in his blessing (v. 29).

[28]And He said, "Your name shall no longer be called Jacob, but Israel;[a] for you have struggled with God and with men, and have prevailed."

[29]Then Jacob asked, saying, "Tell *me* Your name, I pray."

And He said, "Why *is* it *that* you ask about My name?" And He blessed him there.

[30]So Jacob called the name of the place Peniel:[a] "For I have seen God face to face, and my life is preserved." [31]Just as he crossed over Penuel[a] the sun rose on him, and he limped on his hip. [32]Therefore to this day the children of Israel do not eat the muscle that shrank, which *is* on the hip socket, because He touched the socket of Jacob's hip in the muscle that shrank.

Jacob and Esau Meet

33 Now Jacob lifted his eyes and looked, and there, Esau was coming, and with him were four hundred men. So he divided the children among Leah, Rachel, and the two maidservants. [2]And he put the maidservants and their children in front, Leah and her children behind, and Rachel and Joseph last. [3]Then he crossed over before them and bowed himself to the ground seven times, until he came near to his brother.

[4]But Esau ran to meet him, and embraced him, and fell on his neck and kissed him, and they wept. [5]And he lifted his eyes and saw the women and children, and said, "Who *are* these with you?"

So he said, "The children whom God has graciously given your servant." [6]Then the maidservants came near, they and their children, and bowed down. [7]And Leah also came near with her children, and they bowed down. Afterward Joseph and Rachel came near, and they bowed down.

[8]Then Esau said, "What *do* you *mean by* all this company which I met?"

And he said, "*These are* to find favor in the sight of my lord."

[9]But Esau said, "I have enough, my brother; keep what you have for yourself."

[10]And Jacob said, "No, please, if I have now found favor in your sight, then receive my present from my hand, inasmuch as I have seen your face as though I had seen the face of God, and you were pleased with me. [11]Please, take my blessing that is brought to you, because God has dealt graciously with me, and because I have enough." So he urged him, and he took *it*.

[12]Then Esau said, "Let us take our journey; let us go, and I will go before you."

[13]But Jacob said to him, "My lord knows that the children *are* weak, and the flocks and herds which *are* nursing *are* with me. And if the men should drive them hard one day, all the flock will die. [14]Please let my lord go on ahead before his servant. I will lead on slowly at a pace which the livestock that go before me, and the children, are able to endure, until I come to my lord in Seir."

[15]And Esau said, "Now let me leave with you *some* of the people who *are* with me."

But he said, "What need is there? Let me find favor in the sight of my lord." [16]So Esau returned that day on his way to Seir. [17]And Jacob journeyed to Succoth, built himself a house, and made booths for his livestock. Therefore the name of the place is called Succoth.[a]

Jacob Comes to Canaan

[18]Then Jacob came safely to the city of Shechem, which *is* in the land of Canaan, when he came from Padan Aram; and he pitched his tent before the city. [19]And he bought the parcel of land, where he had pitched his tent, from the children of Hamor, Shechem's father, for one hundred pieces of money. [20]Then he erected an altar there and called it El Elohe Israel.[a]

The Dinah Incident

34 Now Dinah the daughter of Leah, whom she had borne to Jacob, went out to see the daughters of the land. [2]And when Shechem the son of Hamor the Hivite, prince of the country, saw her, he took her and lay with her, and violated her. [3]His soul was strongly attracted to Dinah the daughter of Jacob, and he loved the young woman and spoke kindly to the young woman. [4]So Shechem spoke to his father Hamor, saying, "Get me this young woman as a wife."

32:28 [a]Literally *Prince with God* 32:30 [a]Literally *Face of God* 32:31 [a]Same as *Peniel*, verse 30 33:17 [a]Literally *Booths* 33:20 [a]Literally *God, the God of Israel*

32:28 Israel (Heb., lit. "he contends with God"). Once broken by God, Jacob ceased to become the supplanter and instead became the one for whom God Himself would strive.

32:30 Peniel (Heb., lit. "face of God"). God actually withdrew before dawn so that Jacob's vision was incomplete. A full vision of God was incompatible with mortal limitations (Ex. 33:20; Deut. 34:10).

33:19 The children of Hamor were the inhabitants of Shechem; "children of" or "sons of" indicates membership in the tribe that Hamor founded. "Shechem's father" may mean "the founder of Shechem." Since Shechem was the name of both the city and the son of its prince, it appears that "Shechem" and "Hamor" were either titles or hereditary names. This was the second acquisition of Canaanite land by a patriarch (see Gen. 23:4, note).

34:2 The rape of Dinah. The phrase "lay with her and violated her" conveys violence and should be interpreted as rape. Apparently, kidnapping was also involved (v. 26). Although Shechem appeared in a more kindly light in the rest of the story, the damage done by his violent act was irreversible (vv. 3, 19; see Rape; 2 Sam. 13, Date Rape). "Hivites," descendants of Canaan, were a loosely associated merchant tribe spread throughout Canaan (Gen. 10:17).

RAPE — *THE ULTIMATE VIOLATION*

A woman who is raped may experience the same type of terror the Levite's concubine must have felt (Judg. 19:23–26). Physical death is not inevitable in every case of rape, but almost any victim does feel as though a part of her has died. A rape victim may suffer for some time from nightmares, severe and lingering fears, and feelings of low self-worth.

The victim of rape should be encouraged to recognize God's promise never to leave or forsake her (Is. 41:10; Heb. 13:5, 6). A woman victimized by rape needs to seek comfort and healing from God, then from other believers (2 Cor. 1:3, 4). She must find a way of dealing with her anger toward her attacker. If she denies that anger, harbors it, or focuses on revenge, she is in danger of sinning herself (Heb. 12:14–16). On the other hand, as she forgives the one who has wronged her, she will open herself to recovery and growth (Matt. 6:14, 15).

The process of healing is not easy and takes time, but, as a rape victim learns to rely on God for strength as well as healing, she will also learn that her experience may be used for the Lord's glory and honor, perhaps even by sharing the healing she has received from God with other victims.

See also 2 Sam. 13:1–20; Mark 5:2, note; Gal. 5:19–21; Eph. 4:17–24; Col. 3:5; 1 Thess. 4:3–8; notes on Date Rape (2 Sam. 13); Healing (Ps. 13; 133; Eccl. 1; 2 Cor. 5; Gal. 6; James 5); Incest (Lev. 18); Sexual Purity (1 Cor. 7); portraits of Dinah (Gen. 34); The Levite's Defenseless Concubine (Judg. 19); Tamar (2 Sam. 13).

⁵And Jacob heard that he had defiled Dinah his daughter. Now his sons were with his livestock in the field; so Jacob held his peace until they came. ⁶Then Hamor the father of Shechem went out to Jacob to speak with him. ⁷And the sons of Jacob came in from the field when they heard *it;* and the men were grieved and very angry, because he had done a disgraceful thing in Israel by lying with Jacob's daughter, a thing which ought not to be done. ⁸But Hamor spoke with them, saying, "The soul of my son Shechem longs for your daughter. Please give her to him as a wife. ⁹And make marriages with us; give your daughters to us, and take our daughters to yourselves. ¹⁰So you shall dwell with us, and the land shall be before you. Dwell and trade in it, and acquire possessions for yourselves in it."

¹¹Then Shechem said to her father and her brothers, "Let me find favor in your eyes, and whatever you say to me I will give. ¹²Ask me ever so much dowry and gift, and I will give according to what you say to me; but give me the young woman as a wife."

¹³But the sons of Jacob answered Shechem and Hamor his father, and spoke deceitfully, because he had defiled Dinah their sister. ¹⁴And they said to them, "We cannot do this thing, to give our sister to one who is uncircumcised, for that *would be* a reproach to us. ¹⁵But on this *condition* we will

consent to you: If you will become as we *are,* if every male of you is circumcised, ¹⁶then we will give our daughters to you, and we will take your daughters to us; and we will dwell with you, and we will become one people. ¹⁷But if you will not heed us and be circumcised, then we will take our daughter and be gone."

¹⁸And their words pleased Hamor and Shechem, Hamor's son. ¹⁹So the young man did not delay to do the thing, because he delighted in Jacob's daughter. He *was* more honorable than all the household of his father.

²⁰And Hamor and Shechem his son came to the gate of their city, and spoke with the men of their city, saying: ²¹"These men *are* at peace with us. Therefore let them dwell in the land and trade in it. For indeed the land *is* large enough for them. Let us take their daughters to us as wives, and let us give them our daughters. ²²Only on this *condition* will the men consent to dwell with us, to be one people: if every male among us is circumcised as they *are* circumcised. ²³*Will* not their livestock, their property, and every animal of theirs *be* ours? Only let us consent to them, and they will dwell with us." ²⁴And all who went out of the gate of his city heeded Hamor and Shechem his son; every male was circumcised, all who went out of the gate of his city.

²⁵Now it came to pass on the third day, when

34:7 The reference to Jacob's family as Israel reveals an early nationalism. "Disgraceful thing" refers to outrageous acts of immorality often associated with Canaanite and non-Israelite practices (see 2 Sam. 13:12). The reaction of the brothers clearly shows that they were conscious of the family as a separate social unit.

34:17 Circumcision. The mere act would not have brought these Hivites into the line of promise. Hamor and Shechem presented it to the rest of the city as a commercial concession

(v. 23). This was not the original design for the covenant sign, which represented a special relationship to God (see Gen. 17, Circumcision).

34:25 The massacre. The revenge was carried out by Dinah's full brothers, the sons of Leah. The disabling pain of the operation would have been at its height on the third day, making it quite possible for Simeon and Levi to act alone. The other brothers appear to have joined only in the looting (v. 27).

they were in pain, that two of the sons of Jacob, Simeon and Levi, Dinah's brothers, each took his sword and came boldly upon the city and killed all the males. 26And they killed Hamor and Shechem his son with the edge of the sword, and took Dinah from Shechem's house, and went out. 27The sons of Jacob came upon the slain, and plundered the city, because their sister had been defiled. 28They took their sheep, their oxen, and their donkeys, what *was* in the city and what *was* in the field, 29and all their wealth. All their little ones and their wives they took captive; and they plundered even all that *was* in the houses.

30Then Jacob said to Simeon and Levi, "You have troubled me by making me obnoxious among the inhabitants of the land, among the Canaanites and the Perizzites; and since I *am* few in number, they will gather themselves together against me and kill me. I shall be destroyed, my household and I."

31But they said, "Should he treat our sister like a harlot?"

Jacob's Return to Bethel

35 Then God said to Jacob, "Arise, go up to Bethel and dwell there; and make an altar there to God, who appeared to you when you fled from the face of Esau your brother."

2And Jacob said to his household and to all who *were* with him, "Put away the foreign gods that *are* among you, purify yourselves, and change your garments. 3Then let us arise and go up to Bethel; and I will make an altar there to God, who answered me in the day of my distress and has been with me in the way which I have gone." 4So they gave Jacob all the foreign gods which *were* in their hands, and the earrings which *were* in their ears; and Jacob hid them under the terebinth tree which *was* by Shechem.

5And they journeyed, and the terror of God was upon the cities that *were* all around them, and they did not pursue the sons of Jacob. 6So Jacob came to Luz (that *is*, Bethel), which *is* in the land of Canaan, he and all the people who *were* with him. 7And he built an altar there and called the place El Bethel,a because there God appeared to him when he fled from the face of his brother.

8Now Deborah, Rebekah's nurse, died, and she was buried below Bethel under the terebinth tree. So the name of it was called Allon Bachuth.a

9Then God appeared to Jacob again, when he came from Padan Aram, and blessed him. 10And God said to him, "Your name *is* Jacob; your name shall not be called Jacob anymore, but Israel shall be your name." So He called his name Israel. 11Also God said to him: "I *am* God Almighty. Be fruitful and multiply; a nation and a company of nations shall proceed from you, and kings shall come from your body. 12The land which I gave Abraham and Isaac I give to you; and to your descendants after you I give this land." 13Then God went up from him in the place where He talked with him. 14So Jacob set up a pillar in the place where He talked with him, a pillar of stone; and he poured a drink offering on it, and he poured oil on it. 15And Jacob called the name of the place where God spoke with him, Bethel.

Death of Rachel

16Then they journeyed from Bethel. And when there was but a little distance to go to Ephrath, Rachel labored *in childbirth*, and she had hard labor. 17Now it came to pass, when she was in hard labor, that the midwife said to her, "Do not fear; you will have this son also." 18And so it was, as her soul was departing (for she died), that she called his name Ben-Oni;a but his father called him Benjamin.b 19So Rachel died and was buried on the way to Ephrath (that *is*, Bethlehem). 20And Jacob set a pillar on her grave, which *is* the pillar of Rachel's grave to this day.

21Then Israel journeyed and pitched his tent

35:7 aLiterally *God of the House of God*   35:8 aLiterally *Terebinth of Weeping*   35:18 aLiterally *Son of My Sorrow* bLiterally *Son of the Right Hand*

34:27 Plundering the city. Jacob's sons fell from their height of moral outrage and followed Canaanite custom themselves. Ancient Near Eastern military conquest typically included the claiming of the possessions and families of the defeated by the victors. In seizing the Hivite women, Jacob's sons put themselves on the same level as the violent Shechem.

34:30 Jacob's response centered not on his daughter's honor or the morality of his sons' revenge but on practical politics. Jacob's comment reveals that the position of God's chosen people within the Land of Promise was still precarious and that Jacob himself continued to be more concerned with pragmatic survival than with spiritual issues.

35:2 Covenant renewal. After the threat of assimilation by the Hivites, God called Jacob to Bethel to renew His covenant where the original covenant was confirmed (Gen. 28:13–22). In preparation, Jacob ordered his household to rid themselves of all traces of pagan influence, such as the idols Rachel had stolen and any other idols acquired in Mesopotamia (Gen. 31:19, note). The wearing of clean garments was symbolic of beginning a new way of life. Jacob buried these pagan objects to demonstrate the cleansing of his household (v. 4).

35:14 Jacob's pillar was set where a memorial stone and an altar already stood (Gen. 28:22; 35:7). The introduction of the drink offering transformed the location from a memorial to a place of worship (Gen. 28:20–22).

35:16 The death of Rachel. Jacob was traveling from Bethel, located to Jerusalem's north, to Ephrath or Bethlehem (v. 19), located south of Jerusalem. Rachel's death in childbirth was ironic, given her appeal to Jacob (Gen. 30:1). The fact that Jacob changed the name of Rachel's son was a reflection of the importance given a name in the ancient Near East; some thought that names helped to determine a child's future (see Is. 45, Naming of Children).

DINAH *An Innocent Victim*

Dinah was the only daughter among twelve sons of Jacob. When her father, Jacob, finally settled for a while near the city of Shechem, she decided to go exploring, perhaps to find friends. In her youthful exuberance Dinah ignored the dangers of the pagan lifestyle of the young people of Shechem, although it was in direct opposition to her family traditions. She may have felt confident that she could take care of herself even in a strange country.

What began as an excursion of curiosity ended in the tragedy of Dinah's rape by the young prince of Shechem (Gen. 34:2). Whatever the circumstances leading to this tragedy, Dinah surely did not expect or deserve this ultimate degradation. She would not only have to live with the trauma of rape, but she would have little chance for a happy marriage in the future.

Shechem's father Hamor approached Dinah's father to request a marriage, which was the custom of the day. The prince wanted her so much that Hamor told Jacob to name the brideprice (v. 12). Hamor also offered an alliance of their two peoples (something God had forbidden). Though Shechem's initial act of rape was deplorable, he showed more integrity in his attempt to rectify the situation than did Dinah's father and brothers. Through deceit they put the entire male population at a disadvantage, then slaughtered them.

The result of Dinah's visit to the city of Shechem was overwhelmingly tragic: she was raped; all the men of the town were murdered; wives and children of the townsmen were put in slavery; Jacob and his family were forced to flee their home; Dinah's chances for a good marriage were gone; God's name was dishonored among the idol worshipers. Even the most simple choices are often spiritual challenges in which our sisters and daughters must be cautioned that curiosity about the world can pull them into situations in which they suffer at the hands of the ungodly around them. Let parents as well be admonished to make their homes a shield and shelter for their children.

See also notes on Adversity (Acts 5); Date Rape (2 Sam. 13); Rape (Gen. 34); Siblings (Gen. 37)

beyond the tower of Eder. [22]And it happened, when Israel dwelt in that land, that Reuben went and lay with Bilhah his father's concubine; and Israel heard *about it.*

Jacob's Twelve Sons

Now the sons of Jacob were twelve: [23]the sons of Leah *were* Reuben, Jacob's firstborn, and Simeon, Levi, Judah, Issachar, and Zebulun; [24]the sons of Rachel *were* Joseph and Benjamin; [25]the sons of Bilhah, Rachel's maidservant, *were* Dan and Naphtali; [26]and the sons of Zilpah, Leah's maidservant, *were* Gad and Asher. These *were* the sons of Jacob who were born to him in Padan Aram.

Death of Isaac

[27]Then Jacob came to his father Isaac at Mamre, or Kirjath Arba[a] (that *is,* Hebron), where Abraham and Isaac had dwelt. [28]Now the days of Isaac were one hundred and eighty years. [29]So Isaac breathed his last and died, and was gathered to his people, *being* old and full of days. And his sons Esau and Jacob buried him.

The Family of Esau

36 Now this *is* the genealogy of Esau, who is Edom. [2]Esau took his wives from the daughters of Canaan: Adah the daughter of Elon the Hittite; Aholibamah the daughter of Anah, the daughter of Zibeon the Hivite; [3]and Basemath, Ishmael's daughter, sister of Nebajoth. [4]Now Adah bore Eliphaz to Esau, and Basemath bore Reuel. [5]And Aholibamah bore Jeush, Jaalam, and Korah. These *were* the sons of Esau who were born to him in the land of Canaan.

[6]Then Esau took his wives, his sons, his daughters, and all the persons of his household, his cattle and all his animals, and all his goods which he had gained in the land of Canaan, and went to a country away from the presence of his brother Jacob. [7]For their possessions were too great for them to dwell together, and the land where they were strangers could not support them because of their livestock. [8]So Esau dwelt in Mount Seir. Esau *is* Edom.

····························
35:27 [a]Literally *Town of Arba*

36:2 Esau's wives. Three wives are listed (vv. 2, 3): Adah, daughter of Elon the Hittite; Aholibamah, daughter of Anah; and Basemath, daughter of Ishmael. In another reference, Esau's wives are named as Judith, the daughter of Beeri the Hittite, and Basemath, the daughter of Elon the Hittite (Gen. 26:34). Esau also married Mahalath, daughter of Ishmael (Gen. 28:9). There are three possibilities for the differences in these accounts:

1) The wives have alternate names, as did Esau himself—"Edom" (Gen. 25:30).

2) Esau had more than three wives, but the descendants of only these three wives are listed (vv. 2, 3).

3) As the text has been passed from manuscript to manuscript over the years, there is also the possibility of an inadvertency in the process of copying.

⁹And this *is* the genealogy of Esau the father of the Edomites in Mount Seir. ¹⁰These *were* the names of Esau's sons: Eliphaz the son of Adah the wife of Esau, and Reuel the son of Basemath the wife of Esau. ¹¹And the sons of Eliphaz were Teman, Omar, Zepho,ª Gatam, and Kenaz.

¹²Now Timna was the concubine of Eliphaz, Esau's son, and she bore Amalek to Eliphaz. These *were* the sons of Adah, Esau's wife.

¹³These *were* the sons of Reuel: Nahath, Zerah, Shammah, and Mizzah. These were the sons of Basemath, Esau's wife.

¹⁴These were the sons of Aholibamah, Esau's wife, the daughter of Anah, the daughter of Zibeon. And she bore to Esau: Jeush, Jaalam, and Korah.

The Chiefs of Edom

¹⁵These *were* the chiefs of the sons of Esau. The sons of Eliphaz, the firstborn *son* of Esau, were Chief Teman, Chief Omar, Chief Zepho, Chief Kenaz, ¹⁶Chief Korah,ª Chief Gatam, *and* Chief Amalek. These *were* the chiefs of Eliphaz in the land of Edom. They *were* the sons of Adah.

¹⁷These *were* the sons of Reuel, Esau's son: Chief Nahath, Chief Zerah, Chief Shammah, and Chief Mizzah. These *were* the chiefs of Reuel in the land of Edom. These *were* the sons of Basemath, Esau's wife.

¹⁸And these *were* the sons of Aholibamah, Esau's wife: Chief Jeush, Chief Jaalam, and Chief Korah. These *were* the chiefs *who descended* from Aholibamah, Esau's wife, the daughter of Anah. ¹⁹These *were* the sons of Esau, who is Edom, and these *were* their chiefs.

The Sons of Seir

²⁰These *were* the sons of Seir the Horite who inhabited the land: Lotan, Shobal, Zibeon, Anah, ²¹Dishon, Ezer, and Dishan. These *were* the chiefs of the Horites, the sons of Seir, in the land of Edom.

²²And the sons of Lotan were Hori and Hemam.ª Lotan's sister *was* Timna.

²³These *were* the sons of Shobal: Alvan,ª Manahath, Ebal, Shepho,ᵇ and Onam.

²⁴These *were* the sons of Zibeon: both Ajah and Anah. This *was the* Anah who found the waterª in the wilderness as he pastured the donkeys of his father Zibeon. ²⁵These *were* the children of Anah: Dishon and Aholibamah the daughter of Anah.

²⁶These *were* the sons of Dishon:ª Hemdan,ᵇ Eshban, Ithran, and Cheran. ²⁷These *were* the sons of Ezer: Bilhan, Zaavan, and Akan.ª ²⁸These *were* the sons of Dishan: Uz and Aran.

²⁹These *were* the chiefs of the Horites: Chief Lotan, Chief Shobal, Chief Zibeon, Chief Anah, ³⁰Chief Dishon, Chief Ezer, and Chief Dishan. These *were* the chiefs of the Horites, according to their chiefs in the land of Seir.

The Kings of Edom

³¹Now these *were* the kings who reigned in the land of Edom before any king reigned over the children of Israel: ³²Bela the son of Beor reigned in Edom, and the name of his city *was* Dinhabah. ³³And when Bela died, Jobab the son of Zerah of Bozrah reigned in his place. ³⁴When Jobab died, Husham of the land of the Temanites reigned in his place. ³⁵And when Husham died, Hadad the son of Bedad, who attacked Midian in the field of Moab, reigned in his place. And the name of his city *was* Avith. ³⁶When Hadad died, Samlah of Masrekah reigned in his place. ³⁷And when Samlah died, Saul of Rehoboth-*by*-the-River reigned in his place. ³⁸When Saul died, Baal-Hanan the son of Achbor reigned in his place. ³⁹And when Baal-Hanan the son of Achbor died, Hadarª reigned in his place; and the name of his city *was* Pau.ᵇ His wife's name *was* Mehetabel, the daughter of Matred, the daughter of Mezahab.

The Chiefs of Esau

⁴⁰And these *were* the names of the chiefs of Esau, according to their families and their places, by their names: Chief Timnah, Chief Alvah,ª Chief Jetheth, ⁴¹Chief Aholibamah, Chief Elah, Chief Pinon, ⁴²Chief Kenaz, Chief Teman, Chief Mibzar, ⁴³Chief Magdiel, and Chief Iram. These *were* the chiefs of Edom, according to their dwelling places in the land of their possession. Esau *was* the father of the Edomites.

Joseph Dreams of Greatness

37 Now Jacob dwelt in the land where his father was a stranger, in the land of Canaan. ²This *is* the history of Jacob.

Joseph, *being* seventeen years old, was feeding the flock with his brothers. And the lad *was* with the sons of Bilhah and the sons of Zilpah, his

36:11 ªSpelled *Zephi* in 1 Chronicles 1:36   **36:16** ªSamaritan Pentateuch omits *Chief Korah.*   **36:22** ªSpelled *Homam* in 1 Chronicles 1:39   **36:23** ªSpelled *Alian* in 1 Chronicles 1:40   ᵇSpelled *Shephi* in 1 Chronicles 1:40   **36:24** ªFollowing Masoretic Text and Vulgate (*hot springs*); Septuagint reads *Jamin;* Targum reads *mighty men;* Talmud interprets as *mules.*   **36:26** ªHebrew *Dishan*   ᵇSpelled *Hamran* in 1 Chronicles 1:41   **36:27** ªSpelled *Jaakan* in 1 Chronicles 1:42   **36:39** ªSpelled *Hadad* in Samaritan Pentateuch, Syriac, and 1 Chronicles 1:50   ᵇSpelled *Pai* in 1 Chronicles 1:50   **36:40** ªSpelled *Aliah* in 1 Chronicles 1:51

36:39 Baal-Hanan, meaning "Baal is gracious," indicates worship of the Canaanite deity Baal among the Edomites.

37:2 The history of Jacob. This final genealogy (Heb. *toledoth*) introduces the last section of Genesis, the story of Joseph, and takes the godly line from its existence in a single family to its existence as a nation (Gen. 47:27) in fulfillment of the first part of God's promise to Abraham (Gen. 12:1–3).

TAMAR *A Deceitful Widow*

The men in Tamar's life had failed her. Her place should have been secure as the matriarch of this prominent tribe. Instead, because of the sins of her husband, she was both childless and a widow. God had prepared for such situations by instituting the laws of levirate marriages (Deut. 25:5, 6, note), which assured a man's lineage by having the brother of the deceased take the widow for his wife and produce children for his brother's name. Judah, Tamar's father-in-law, was responsible to see that this was done. He did attempt to accomplish this with Onan, but when this second son died because of deliberate sin (Gen. 38:9, 10), Judah seemed to have lost heart for the whole matter.

Tamar was at her father-in-law's mercy since she could not marry without his arranging it. In other words, she had no place inside the family and no place outside it. In addition, without heirs, the tribe of Judah now faced extinction. Unknown at the time was the importance of continuing Judah's lineage. King David would come from this tribe, as well as Mary, the mother of Jesus, and Joseph, the husband of Mary (Matt. 1:3; Luke 3:33).

The lot of a widow in ancient times was a precarious one. Taking matters in her own hands, Tamar set out to right the wrong the men in her family had caused. During the festive time of sheep shearing, sympathetic magic was practiced by the Canaanites. When they wanted the gods to do something, they would enact the deed themselves, encouraging the gods to come through. Prostitution was their attempt to encourage the gods to give them a fertile year. Tamar knew Judah would be participating in this celebration. Disguising herself as a temple prostitute, heavily veiled as was customary of such women, she intercepted her father-in-law and became impregnated by him. The risk was great. For a widow to become pregnant usually meant the death sentence (see Gen. 38:24).

Scripture does not comment on her actions, but it does give her a prominent place in the genealogy of Christ. In Matthew 1, she is the first of only five women mentioned. Tamar's actions were not only deceitful but a direct violation of God's Law. Nevertheless, God is able to bring about His purposes and execute His plans even when we fail. Tamar had a worthy goal, that is, to continue the line of Judah; but she did not trust God to fulfill His promises and decided to move ahead with her own plans. Even if our motivation is pure and our goal worthy, we do not please God by disobedience.

See also Deut. 25:5; Matt 1:3; notes on Inheritance (Prov. 13); Widowhood (Ps. 68; Jer. 29; 1 Cor. 2)

father's wives; and Joseph brought a bad report of them to his father.

3Now Israel loved Joseph more than all his children, because he *was* the son of his old age. Also he made him a tunic of *many* colors. 4But when his brothers saw that their father loved him more than all his brothers, they hated him and could not speak peaceably to him.

5Now Joseph had a dream, and he told *it* to his brothers; and they hated him even more. 6So he said to them, "Please hear this dream which I have dreamed: 7There we were, binding sheaves in the field. Then behold, my sheaf arose and also stood upright; and indeed your sheaves stood all around and bowed down to my sheaf."

8And his brothers said to him, "Shall you indeed reign over us? Or shall you indeed have dominion over us?" So they hated him even more for his dreams and for his words.

9Then he dreamed still another dream and told it to his brothers, and said, "Look, I have dreamed another dream. And this time, the sun, the moon, and the eleven stars bowed down to me."

10So he told *it* to his father and his brothers; and his father rebuked him and said to him, "What *is* this dream that you have dreamed? Shall your mother and I and your brothers indeed come to bow down to the earth before you?" 11And his brothers envied him, but his father kept the matter *in mind.*

Joseph Sold by His Brothers

12Then his brothers went to feed their father's flock in Shechem. 13And Israel said to Joseph, "Are not your brothers feeding *the flock* in Shechem? Come, I will send you to them."

So he said to him, "Here I am."

14Then he said to him, "Please go and see if it is well with your brothers and well with the flocks, and bring back word to me." So he sent him out of the Valley of Hebron, and he went to Shechem.

15Now a certain man found him, and there he

37:6 Joseph's dreams. Throughout Genesis, dreams often reveal God's plans (see 15:1, 12; 28:12). Joseph's dreams placed him in the line of those chosen by God to receive blessing.

37:11 The response of the brothers. Although all of Jacob's

children are included in the covenant, Joseph was chosen for a special role. The hostility of his brothers is comparable to the hostility of Ishmael (Gen. 21:8, 9) and Esau (Gen. 27:41).

was, wandering in the field. And the man asked him, saying, "What are you seeking?"

[16]So he said, "I am seeking my brothers. Please tell me where they are feeding *their flocks.*"

[17]And the man said, "They have departed from here, for I heard them say, 'Let us go to Dothan.'" So Joseph went after his brothers and found them in Dothan.

[18]Now when they saw him afar off, even before he came near them, they conspired against him to kill him. [19]Then they said to one another, "Look, this dreamer is coming! [20]Come therefore, let us now kill him and cast him into some pit; and we shall say, 'Some wild beast has devoured him.' We shall see what will become of his dreams!"

[21]But Reuben heard *it,* and he delivered him out of their hands, and said, "Let us not kill him." [22]And Reuben said to them, "Shed no blood, *but* cast him into this pit which *is* in the wilderness, and do not lay a hand on him"— that he might deliver him out of their hands, and bring him back to his father.

[23]So it came to pass, when Joseph had come to his brothers, that they stripped Joseph *of* his tunic, the tunic of *many* colors that *was* on him. [24]Then they took him and cast him into a pit. And the pit *was* empty; *there was* no water in it.

[25]And they sat down to eat a meal. Then they lifted their eyes and looked, and there was a company of Ishmaelites, coming from Gilead with their camels, bearing spices, balm, and myrrh, on their way to carry *them* down to Egypt. [26]So Judah said to his brothers, "What profit *is there* if we kill our brother and conceal his blood? [27]Come and let us sell him to the Ishmaelites, and let not our hand be upon him, for he *is* our brother *and* our flesh." And his brothers listened. [28]Then Midianite traders passed by; so *the brothers* pulled Joseph up and lifted him out of the pit, and sold him to the Ishmaelites for twenty *shekels* of silver. And they took Joseph to Egypt.

[29]Then Reuben returned to the pit, and indeed Joseph *was* not in the pit; and he tore his clothes. [30]And he returned to his brothers and said, "The lad *is* no *more;* and I, where shall I go?"

[31]So they took Joseph's tunic, killed a kid of the goats, and dipped the tunic in the blood. [32]Then they sent the tunic of *many* colors, and they brought *it* to their father and said, "We have found this. Do you know whether it *is* your son's tunic or not?"

[33]And he recognized it and said, "*It is* my son's tunic. A wild beast has devoured him. Without doubt Joseph is torn to pieces." [34]Then Jacob tore his clothes, put sackcloth on his waist, and mourned for his son many days. [35]And all his sons and all his daughters arose to comfort him; but he refused to be comforted, and he said, "For I shall go down into the grave to my son in mourning." Thus his father wept for him.

[36]Now the Midianites[a] had sold him in Egypt to Potiphar, an officer of Pharaoh *and* captain of the guard.

Judah and Tamar

38It came to pass at that time that Judah departed from his brothers, and visited a certain Adullamite whose name *was* Hirah. [2]And Judah saw there a daughter of a certain Canaanite whose name *was* Shua, and he married her and went in to her. [3]So she conceived and bore a son, and he called his name Er. [4]She conceived again and bore a son, and she called his name Onan. [5]And she conceived yet again and bore a son, and called his name Shelah. He was at Chezib when she bore him.

[6]Then Judah took a wife for Er his firstborn, and her name *was* Tamar. [7]But Er, Judah's firstborn, was wicked in the sight of the LORD, and the LORD killed him. [8]And Judah said to Onan, "Go in to your brother's wife and marry her, and raise up an heir to your brother." [9]But Onan knew that the heir would not be his; and it came to pass, when he went in to his brother's wife, that he emitted on the ground, lest he should give an heir to his brother. [10]And the thing which he did displeased the LORD; therefore He killed him also.

[11]Then Judah said to Tamar his daughter-in-law, "Remain a widow in your father's house till my son Shelah is grown." For he said, "Lest he also die like his brothers." And Tamar went and dwelt in her father's house.

[12]Now in the process of time the daughter of Shua, Judah's wife, died; and Judah was comforted,

---

37:36 [a]Masoretic Text reads *Medanites.*

37:28 Midianites is an overlapping term for Ishmaelites, who were the offspring of Ishmael. Midianites occupied land east of the Jordan, down into the Sinai peninsula. Twenty shekels of silver was two-thirds the value of an ordinary slave (Ex. 21:32).

38:6 Tamar appears to have been a Canaanite as well. However, she, like the Moabitess Ruth, was an ancestress of Christ (Matt. 1:3). God preserved His godly line despite Judah's sin.

38:8 Onan's duty. The custom of levirate marriage, later regulated, guaranteed the continuance of the older brother's line

(Deut. 25:5, 6, note). Onan's children would have inherited Er's name and property, perpetuating the name of his brother instead of his own, and thus displeasing Onan. Clearly, Onan's *coitus interruptus* was a habitual practice; his sin lay not in the act itself but in his refusal to perform his brotherly duty (v. 9).

38:11 Judah had no intention of fulfilling his promise; he sent Tamar to her father's house, though usually a widow remained with the family of her husband.

STEP-PARENTHOOD AN IMPORTANT INFLUENCE

Although the Bible does not address step-parenting directly, sound biblical principles that will ultimately bring blessings can be applied toward responsible and godly step-parenting. A woman's character is not determined by her circumstances. Rather the character of a woman will affect how she will
respond within her circumstances—which may include step-parenting. A stepmother should begin
preparation for her parenting task with the continuation of prayerful development of her own godly
character.

Clear examples of step-parenting as we experience it today are not found in the Bible. Most families
in Bible times were what we today would call extended families—families in which several generations
lived together, and the families of aunts and uncles were frequently as close as the next tent.

In the New Testament, Joseph might be considered a stepparent as the legal father of Jesus, although his circumstances were quite unique. We can learn from Joseph three important qualities for godly stepparents:

- He did what the Lord asked him to do (Matt. 1:24);
- He allowed others to give good things to the child in his care (Matt. 2:11); and
- He acted quickly to protect his child (Matt. 2:14, 15).

Stepmothers today are wise to follow his example—seeking the Lord's direction always in the relationship
the Lord desires for them to have with their stepchildren, allowing others to provide blessings for the children,
and providing protection from evil for the children.

A stepmother can be an important influence for Christ in a child's life by:

- Praying for her stepchild daily;
- Sharing the Word of God with her stepchild; and
- Including her stepchild in the fellowship of her church family.

Above all, a stepmother is called upon to show "love in action" to her stepchildren—to give freely and generously to them. In order for that to be possible, a stepmother needs to ask the Holy Spirit to work in and through
her, so that she might have the patience, tolerance, fortitude, and courage it takes to give to a child who very often does not want to receive.

A stepmother needs to remember always to allow the child's affection for her own mother to flourish, being
respectful of the relationship the child has with her mother if she is living or the memories of her life if she is
dead.

See also Gen. 29—35; Prov. 12:4; Matt. 18:3, note; Eph. 5:22, 24, 33; notes on Children (2 Sam. 21; Ps. 128; Prov.
22; Luke 15); Divorce (Matt. 19); Family (Gen. 32); Motherhood (1 Sam. 1; Is. 49; Ezek. 16); Parenthood (Prov. 10);
Remarriage (Matt. 5)

---

and went up to his sheepshearers at Timnah, he
and his friend Hirah the Adullamite. [13]And it was
told Tamar, saying, "Look, your father-in-law is going up to Timnah to shear his sheep." [14]So she
took off her widow's garments, covered *herself*
with a veil and wrapped herself, and sat in an
open place which *was* on the way to Timnah; for
she saw that Shelah was grown, and she was not
given to him as a wife. [15]When Judah saw her, he
thought she *was* a harlot, because she had covered
her face. [16]Then he turned to her by the way, and
said, "Please let me come in to you"; for he did not
know that she *was* his daughter-in-law.

So she said, "What will you give me, that you
may come in to me?"

[17]And he said, "I will send a young goat from
the flock."

So she said, "Will you give *me* a pledge till you
send *it?*"

[18]Then he said, "What pledge shall I give you?"

So she said, "Your signet and cord, and your
staff that *is* in your hand." Then he gave *them* to
her, and went in to her, and she conceived by
him. [19]So she arose and went away, and laid aside
her veil and put on the garments of her widowhood.

[20]And Judah sent the young goat by the hand
of his friend the Adullamite, to receive *his* pledge
from the woman's hand, but he did not find her.
[21]Then he asked the men of that place, saying,

38:14 Tamar's strategy. Tamar put on the dress of a cultic
prostitute. Canaanite sheep-shearing festivals involved cultic
worship and ritual prostitution as a magic aid to fertility. The
word "harlot" is often synonymous with "sacred prostitute"
(vv. 21, 22).

38:18 Judah's pledge. The signet was a cylindrical seal hung
by a cord around the neck; its impression was the equivalent
of a personal signature. Staffs were elaborately carved by
their owners. Both items were instantly recognizable (vv. 25,
26).

"Where is the harlot who *was* openly by the roadside?"

And they said, "There was no harlot in this *place.*"

²²So he returned to Judah and said, "I cannot find her. Also, the men of the place said there was no harlot in this *place.*"

²³Then Judah said, "Let her take *them* for herself, lest we be shamed; for I sent this young goat and you have not found her."

²⁴And it came to pass, about three months after, that Judah was told, saying, "Tamar your daughter-in-law has played the harlot; furthermore she *is* with child by harlotry."

So Judah said, "Bring her out and let her be burned!"

²⁵When she *was* brought out, she sent to her father-in-law, saying, "By the man to whom these belong, I *am* with child." And she said, "Please determine whose these *are*—the signet and cord, and staff."

²⁶So Judah acknowledged *them* and said, "She has been more righteous than I, because I did not give her to Shelah my son." And he never knew her again.

²⁷Now it came to pass, at the time for giving birth, that behold, twins *were* in her womb. ²⁸And so it was, when she was giving birth, that *the one* put out *his* hand; and the midwife took a scarlet *thread* and bound it on his hand, saying, "This one came out first." ²⁹Then it happened, as he drew back his hand, that his brother came out unexpectedly; and she said, "How did you break through? *This* breach *be* upon you!" Therefore his name was called Perez.ᵃ ³⁰Afterward his brother came out who had the scarlet *thread* on his hand. And his name was called Zerah.

Joseph a Slave in Egypt

39 Now Joseph had been taken down to Egypt. And Potiphar, an officer of Pharaoh, captain of the guard, an Egyptian, bought him from the Ishmaelites who had taken him down there. ²The LORD was with Joseph, and he was a successful man; and he was in the house of his master the Egyptian. ³And his master saw that the LORD *was* with him and that the LORD made all he did to prosper in his hand. ⁴So Joseph found favor in his sight, and served him. Then he made him overseer of his house, and all *that* he had he put under his authority. ⁵So it was, from the time *that* he had made him overseer of his house and all that he had, that the LORD blessed the Egyptian's house for Joseph's sake; and the blessing of the LORD was on all that he had in the house and in the field. ⁶Thus he left all that he had in Joseph's hand, and he did not know what he had except for the bread which he ate.

Now Joseph was handsome in form and appearance.

⁷And it came to pass after these things that his master's wife cast longing eyes on Joseph, and she said, "Lie with me."

⁸But he refused and said to his master's wife, "Look, my master does not know what *is* with me in the house, and he has committed all that he has to my hand. ⁹*There is* no one greater in this house than I, nor has he kept back anything from me but you, because you *are* his wife. How then can I do this great wickedness, and sin against God?"

¹⁰So it was, as she spoke to Joseph day by day, that he did not heed her, to lie with her *or* to be with her.

¹¹But it happened about this time, when Joseph went into the house to do his work, and none of the men of the house *was* inside, ¹²that she caught him by his garment, saying, "Lie with me." But he left his garment in her hand, and fled and ran outside. ¹³And so it was, when she saw that he had left his garment in her hand and fled outside, ¹⁴that she called to the men of her house and spoke to them, saying, "See, he has brought in to us a Hebrew to mock us. He came in to me to lie with me, and I cried out with a loud voice. ¹⁵And it happened, when he heard that I lifted my voice and cried out, that he left his garment with me, and fled and went outside."

¹⁶So she kept his garment with her until his master came home. ¹⁷Then she spoke to him with words like these, saying, "The Hebrew servant whom you brought to us came in to me to mock me; ¹⁸so it happened, as I lifted my voice and cried out, that he left his garment with me and fled outside."

¹⁹So it was, when his master heard the words which his wife spoke to him, saying, "Your servant did to me after this manner," that his anger was aroused. ²⁰Then Joseph's master took him and put

38:29 ᵃLiterally *Breach* or *Breakthrough*

39:4 Overseer. Joseph became the superintendent of Potiphar's estate, a position common in large Egyptian households. Potiphar concerned himself with nothing but his meals. Egyptians typically did not eat with Hebrews, probably for religious reasons (see Gen. 43:32).

39:7 The temptation of Potiphar's wife. Joseph's reaction to the temptation of a foreign woman is presented in clear contrast to Judah's conduct in the preceding chapter. Joseph, the chosen one through whom Israel would be saved, held up God's standards in the face of constant temptation ("day by day," v. 10).

39:20 Imprisonment. The Egyptian penalty for attempted rape of a married woman was death. Joseph was only imprisoned, testifying to God's sovereign plan. His rise further confirmed God's watchful care (vv. 22, 23).

him into the prison, a place where the king's prisoners *were* confined. And he was there in the prison. 21But the Lord was with Joseph and showed him mercy, and He gave him favor in the sight of the keeper of the prison. 22And the keeper of the prison committed to Joseph's hand all the prisoners who *were* in the prison; whatever they did there, it was his doing. 23The keeper of the prison did not look into anything *that was* under *Joseph's* authority,a because the Lord was with him; and whatever he did, the Lord made *it* prosper.

The Prisoners' Dreams

40It came to pass after these things *that* the butler and the baker of the king of Egypt offended their lord, the king of Egypt. 2And Pharaoh was angry with his two officers, the chief butler and the chief baker. 3So he put them in custody in the house of the captain of the guard, in the prison, the place where Joseph *was* confined. 4And the captain of the guard charged Joseph with them, and he served them; so they were in custody for a while.

5Then the butler and the baker of the king of Egypt, who *were* confined in the prison, had a dream, both of them, each man's dream in one night *and* each man's dream with its *own* interpretation. 6And Joseph came in to them in the morning and looked at them, and saw that they *were* sad. 7So he asked Pharaoh's officers who *were* with him in the custody of his lord's house, saying, "Why do you look *so* sad today?"

8And they said to him, "We each have had a dream, and *there is* no interpreter of it."

So Joseph said to them, "Do not interpretations belong to God? Tell *them* to me, please."

9Then the chief butler told his dream to Joseph, and said to him, "Behold, in my dream a vine *was* before me, 10and in the vine *were* three branches; it *was* as though it budded, its blossoms shot forth, and its clusters brought forth ripe grapes. 11Then Pharaoh's cup *was* in my hand; and I took the grapes and pressed them into Pharaoh's cup, and placed the cup in Pharaoh's hand."

12And Joseph said to him, "This *is* the interpretation of it: The three branches *are* three days. 13Now within three days Pharaoh will lift up your head and restore you to your place, and you will put Pharaoh's cup in his hand according to the former manner, when you were his butler. 14But

remember me when it is well with you, and please show kindness to me; make mention of me to Pharaoh, and get me out of this house. 15For indeed I was stolen away from the land of the Hebrews; and also I have done nothing here that they should put me into the dungeon."

16When the chief baker saw that the interpretation was good, he said to Joseph, "I also *was* in my dream, and there *were* three white baskets on my head. 17In the uppermost basket *were* all kinds of baked goods for Pharaoh, and the birds ate them out of the basket on my head."

18So Joseph answered and said, "This *is* the interpretation of it: The three baskets *are* three days. 19Within three days Pharaoh will lift off your head from you and hang you on a tree; and the birds will eat your flesh from you."

20Now it came to pass on the third day, *which was* Pharaoh's birthday, that he made a feast for all his servants; and he lifted up the head of the chief butler and of the chief baker among his servants. 21Then he restored the chief butler to his butlership again, and he placed the cup in Pharaoh's hand. 22But he hanged the chief baker, as Joseph had interpreted to them. 23Yet the chief butler did not remember Joseph, but forgot him.

Pharaoh's Dreams

41 Then it came to pass, at the end of two full years, that Pharaoh had a dream; and behold, he stood by the river. 2Suddenly there came up out of the river seven cows, fine looking and fat; and they fed in the meadow. 3Then behold, seven other cows came up after them out of the river, ugly and gaunt, and stood by the *other* cows on the bank of the river. 4And the ugly and gaunt cows ate up the seven fine looking and fat cows. So Pharaoh awoke. 5He slept and dreamed a second time; and suddenly seven heads of grain came up on one stalk, plump and good. 6Then behold, seven thin heads, blighted by the east wind, sprang up after them. 7And the seven thin heads devoured the seven plump and full heads. So Pharaoh awoke, and indeed, *it was* a dream. 8Now it came to pass in the morning that his spirit was troubled, and he sent and called for all the magicians of Egypt and all its wise men. And Pharaoh told them his dreams, but *there was* no one who could interpret them for Pharaoh.

••••••••••••••••••••••••••••••

39:23 aLiterally *his hand*

40:1 Butler and baker. "Butler" is more accurately "cupbearer," the same position Nehemiah held under Artaxerxes (Neh. 2:1). "Baker" is the "superintendent of the bakery." Both were prestigious and responsible court positions.

40:5 These dreams reveal true events (Gen. 37:7–9). The interpretation of dreams was an important part of Egyptian culture, and interpreters held a high position socially. Joseph's re-

sponse placed his God above the gods of the land who gave dream interpretations to their devotees (v. 8). The accuracy of Joseph's interpretations confirmed the superiority of his God.

40:19 To be hanged on a tree was reprehensible both in Hebrew and Egyptian cultures (Deut. 21:22, 23). The Egyptian rite of mummification arose from the immense importance of the dead body in the Egyptian religion.

9Then the chief butler spoke to Pharaoh, saying: "I remember my faults this day. 10When Pharaoh was angry with his servants, and put me in custody in the house of the captain of the guard, *both* me and the chief baker, 11we each had a dream in one night, he and I. Each of us dreamed according to the interpretation of his *own* dream. 12Now there *was* a young Hebrew man with us there, a servant of the captain of the guard. And we told him, and he interpreted our dreams for us; to each man he interpreted according to his *own* dream. 13And it came to pass, just as he interpreted for us, so it happened. He restored me to my office, and he hanged him."

14Then Pharaoh sent and called Joseph, and they brought him quickly out of the dungeon; and he shaved, changed his clothing, and came to Pharaoh. 15And Pharaoh said to Joseph, "I have had a dream, and *there is* no one who can interpret it. But I have heard it said of you *that* you can understand a dream, to interpret it."

16So Joseph answered Pharaoh, saying, "*It is* not in me; God will give Pharaoh an answer of peace."

17Then Pharaoh said to Joseph: "Behold, in my dream I stood on the bank of the river. 18Suddenly seven cows came up out of the river, fine looking and fat; and they fed in the meadow. 19Then behold, seven other cows came up after them, poor and very ugly and gaunt, such ugliness as I have never seen in all the land of Egypt. 20And the gaunt and ugly cows ate up the first seven, the fat cows. 21When they had eaten them up, no one would have known that they had eaten them, for they *were* just as ugly as at the beginning. So I awoke. 22Also I saw in my dream, and suddenly seven heads came up on one stalk, full and good. 23Then behold, seven heads, withered, thin, *and* blighted by the east wind, sprang up after them. 24And the thin heads devoured the seven good heads. So I told *this* to the magicians, but *there was* no one who could explain *it* to me."

25Then Joseph said to Pharaoh, "The dreams of Pharaoh *are* one; God has shown Pharaoh what He *is* about to do: 26The seven good cows *are* seven years, and the seven good heads *are* seven years; the dreams *are* one. 27And the seven thin and ugly cows which came up after them *are* seven years, and the seven empty heads blighted by the east wind are seven years of famine. 28This *is* the thing which I have spoken to Pharaoh. God has shown Pharaoh what He *is* about to do. 29Indeed seven years of great plenty will come throughout all the land of Egypt; 30but after them seven years of famine will arise, and all the plenty will be forgotten in the land of Egypt; and the famine will deplete the land. 31So the plenty will not be known in the land because of the famine following, for it *will be* very severe. 32And the dream was repeated to Pharaoh twice because the thing *is* established by God, and God will shortly bring it to pass.

33"Now therefore, let Pharaoh select a discerning and wise man, and set him over the land of Egypt. 34Let Pharaoh do *this*, and let him appoint officers over the land, to collect one-fifth *of the produce* of the land of Egypt in the seven plentiful years. 35And let them gather all the food of those good years that are coming, and store up grain under the authority of Pharaoh, and let them keep food in the cities. 36Then that food shall be as a reserve for the land for the seven years of famine which shall be in the land of Egypt, that the land may not perish during the famine."

Joseph's Rise to Power

37So the advice was good in the eyes of Pharaoh and in the eyes of all his servants. 38And Pharaoh said to his servants, "Can we find *such a one* as this, a man in whom *is* the Spirit of God?"

39Then Pharaoh said to Joseph, "Inasmuch as God has shown you all this, *there is* no one as discerning and wise as you. 40You shall be over my house, and all my people shall be ruled according to your word; only in regard to the throne will I be greater than you." 41And Pharaoh said to Joseph, "See, I have set you over all the land of Egypt." 42Then Pharaoh took his signet ring off his hand and put it on Joseph's hand; and he clothed him in garments of fine linen and put a gold chain around his neck. 43And he had him ride in the second chariot which he had; and they cried out before him, "Bow the knee!" So he set him over all the land of Egypt. 44Pharaoh also said to Joseph, "I *am* Pharaoh, and without your consent no man may lift his hand or foot in all the land of Egypt." 45And Pharaoh called Joseph's name Zaphnath-Paaneah. And he gave him as a wife Asenath, the

---

41:16 God's answer. Joseph's interpretation showed the superiority of his God over the gods of the magicians and wise men. Such a showdown was repeated by Moses and Aaron (Ex. 7—10). "Peace" (Heb. *shalom*) is used as an idiom meaning "the correct answer."

41:33 Joseph's advice. Egyptian cities contained granaries for the storing of grain-taxes and the provision of the army. The supervisor of these granaries held one of the highest ranks in Egypt. Joseph recommended that an already-existing position be filled by a capable man endowed with emergency powers.

41:42 Joseph's position. Joseph appeared to have been appointed vizier or governor. The signet ring carried Pharaoh's deputized authority. "Fine linen" is an Egyptian loan-word for court dress. The gold chain was a reward for services already rendered, that is, the interpretation of the dream. The "second chariot" confirmed that Joseph was subordinate only to Pharaoh (v. 43).

41:45 Joseph's new name indicated that Pharaoh had made him an Egyptian citizen. The meaning of the name is uncertain, but a likely translation is "the god speaks and he lives."

daughter of Poti-Pherah priest of On. So Joseph went out over *all* the land of Egypt.

[46]Joseph was thirty years old when he stood before Pharaoh king of Egypt. And Joseph went out from the presence of Pharaoh, and went throughout all the land of Egypt. [47]Now in the seven plentiful years the ground brought forth abundantly. [48]So he gathered up all the food of the seven years which were in the land of Egypt, and laid up the food in the cities; he laid up in every city the food of the fields which surrounded them. [49]Joseph gathered very much grain, as the sand of the sea, until he stopped counting, for *it was* immeasurable.

[50]And to Joseph were born two sons before the years of famine came, whom Asenath, the daughter of Poti-Pherah priest of On, bore to him. [51]Joseph called the name of the firstborn Manasseh:[a] "For God has made me forget all my toil and all my father's house." [52]And the name of the second he called Ephraim:[a] "For God has caused me to be fruitful in the land of my affliction."

[53]Then the seven years of plenty which were in the land of Egypt ended, [54]and the seven years of famine began to come, as Joseph had said. The famine was in all lands, but in all the land of Egypt there was bread. [55]So when all the land of Egypt was famished, the people cried to Pharaoh for bread. Then Pharaoh said to all the Egyptians, "Go to Joseph; whatever he says to you, do." [56]The famine was over all the face of the earth, and Joseph opened all the storehouses[a] and sold to the Egyptians. And the famine became severe in the land of Egypt. [57]So all countries came to Joseph in Egypt to buy *grain,* because the famine was severe in all lands.

Joseph's Brothers Go to Egypt

42 When Jacob saw that there was grain in Egypt, Jacob said to his sons, "Why do you look at one another?" [2]And he said, "Indeed I have heard that there is grain in Egypt; go down to that place and buy for us there, that we may live and not die."

[3]So Joseph's ten brothers went down to buy grain in Egypt. [4]But Jacob did not send Joseph's brother Benjamin with his brothers, for he said, "Lest some calamity befall him." [5]And the sons of Israel went to buy *grain* among those who journeyed, for the famine was in the land of Canaan.

[6]Now Joseph *was* governor over the land; and it was he who sold to all the people of the land. And Joseph's brothers came and bowed down before him with *their* faces to the earth. [7]Joseph saw his brothers and recognized them, but he acted as a stranger to them and spoke roughly to them. Then he said to them, "Where do you come from?"

And they said, "From the land of Canaan to buy food."

[8]So Joseph recognized his brothers, but they did not recognize him. [9]Then Joseph remembered the dreams which he had dreamed about them, and said to them, "You *are* spies! You have come to see the nakedness of the land!"

[10]And they said to him, "No, my lord, but your servants have come to buy food. [11]We *are* all one man's sons; we *are* honest *men;* your servants are not spies."

[12]But he said to them, "No, but you have come to see the nakedness of the land."

[13]And they said, "Your servants *are* twelve brothers, the sons of one man in the land of Canaan; and in fact, the youngest *is* with our father today, and one *is* no more."

[14]But Joseph said to them, "It *is* as I spoke to you, saying, 'You *are* spies!' [15]In this *manner* you shall be tested: By the life of Pharaoh, you shall not leave this place unless your youngest brother comes here. [16]Send one of you, and let him bring your brother; and you shall be kept in prison, that your words may be tested to see whether *there is* any truth in you; or else, by the life of Pharaoh, surely you *are* spies!" [17]So he put them all together in prison three days.

[18]Then Joseph said to them the third day, "Do this and live, *for* I fear God: [19]If you *are* honest *men,* let one of your brothers be confined to your prison house; but you, go and carry grain for the famine of your houses. [20]And bring your youngest brother to me; so your words will be verified, and you shall not die."

And they did so. [21]Then they said to one another, "We *are* truly guilty concerning our brother, for we saw the anguish of his soul when he pleaded with us, and we would not hear; therefore this distress has come upon us."

[22]And Reuben answered them, saying, "Did I not speak to you, saying, 'Do not sin against the boy'; and you would not listen? Therefore behold,

---

41:51 [a]Literally *Making Forgetful*   41:52 [a]Literally *Fruitfulness*
41:56 [a]Literally *all that was in them*

41:50 Joseph's sons. Joseph's marriage to an Egyptian is presented without comment; the names of Joseph's sons are Hebrew, suggesting that his wife may have taken his faith.

42:7 Joseph's greeting. Joseph's actions toward his brothers were intended to determine whether their characters had changed (Gen. 42—45).

42:9 Spies. Egypt was prone to invasion from Canaan, and its

northeastern borders were heavily fortified. "Nakedness of the land" is an idiom meaning "to pry into private affairs."

42:16 By the life of Pharaoh. This oath was the Egyptian equivalent to the Hebrew "As God lives" (1 Kin. 17:1).

42:18 For I fear God. This was Joseph's assurance that, even as an Egyptian, he would not act with complete injustice due to his respect for higher powers.

his blood is now required of us." ²³But they did not know that Joseph understood *them*, for he spoke to them through an interpreter. ²⁴And he turned himself away from them and wept. Then he returned to them again, and talked with them. And he took Simeon from them and bound him before their eyes.

The Brothers Return to Canaan

²⁵Then Joseph gave a command to fill their sacks with grain, to restore every man's money to his sack, and to give them provisions for the journey. Thus he did for them. ²⁶So they loaded their donkeys with the grain and departed from there. ²⁷But as one *of them* opened his sack to give his donkey feed at the encampment, he saw his money; and there it was, in the mouth of his sack. ²⁸So he said to his brothers, "My money has been restored, and there it is, in my sack!" Then their hearts failed *them* and they were afraid, saying to one another, "What *is* this *that* God has done to us?"

²⁹Then they went to Jacob their father in the land of Canaan and told him all that had happened to them, saying: ³⁰"The man *who is* lord of the land spoke roughly to us, and took us for spies of the country. ³¹But we said to him, 'We *are* honest *men;* we are not spies. ³²We *are* twelve brothers, sons of our father; one *is* no *more,* and the youngest *is* with our father this day in the land of Canaan.' ³³Then the man, the lord of the country, said to us, 'By this I will know that you *are* honest *men:* Leave one of your brothers *here* with me, take *food for* the famine of your households, and be gone. ³⁴And bring your youngest brother to me; so I shall know that you *are* not spies, but *that* you *are* honest *men.* I will grant your brother to you, and you may trade in the land.' "

³⁵Then it happened as they emptied their sacks, that surprisingly each man's bundle of money *was* in his sack; and when they and their father saw the bundles of money, they were afraid. ³⁶And Jacob their father said to them, "You have bereaved me: Joseph is no *more,* Simeon is no *more,* and you want to take Benjamin. All these things are against me."

³⁷Then Reuben spoke to his father, saying, "Kill my two sons if I do not bring him *back* to you; put him in my hands, and I will bring him back to you." ³⁸But he said, "My son shall not go down with you, for his brother is dead, and he is left alone. If any calamity should befall him along the way in which you go, then you would bring down my gray hair with sorrow to the grave."

Joseph's Brothers Return with Benjamin

43 Now the famine *was* severe in the land. ²And it came to pass, when they had eaten up the grain which they had brought from Egypt, that their father said to them, "Go back, buy us a little food."

³But Judah spoke to him, saying, "The man solemnly warned us, saying, 'You shall not see my face unless your brother *is* with you.' ⁴If you send our brother with us, we will go down and buy you food. ⁵But if you will not send *him,* we will not go down; for the man said to us, 'You shall not see my face unless your brother *is* with you.' "

⁶And Israel said, "Why did you deal *so* wrongfully with me *as* to tell the man whether you had still *another* brother?"

⁷But they said, "The man asked us pointedly about ourselves and our family, saying, '*Is* your father still alive? Have you *another* brother?' And we told him according to these words. Could we possibly have known that he would say, 'Bring your brother down'?"

⁸Then Judah said to Israel his father, "Send the lad with me, and we will arise and go, that we may live and not die, both we and you *and* also our little ones. ⁹I myself will be surety for him; from my hand you shall require him. If I do not bring him *back* to you and set him before you, then let me bear the blame forever. ¹⁰For if we had not lingered, surely by now we would have returned this second time."

¹¹And their father Israel said to them, "If *it must be* so, then do this: Take some of the best fruits of the land in your vessels and carry down a present for the man—a little balm and a little honey, spices and myrrh, pistachio nuts and almonds. ¹²Take double money in your hand, and take back in your hand the money that was returned in the mouth of your sacks; perhaps it was an oversight. ¹³Take your brother also, and arise, go back to the man. ¹⁴And may God Almighty give you mercy before the man, that he may release your other brother and Benjamin. If I am bereaved, I am bereaved!"

¹⁵So the men took that present and Benjamin, and they took double money in their hand, and arose and went down to Egypt; and they stood before Joseph. ¹⁶When Joseph saw Benjamin with them, he said to the steward of his house, "Take *these* men to my home, and slaughter an animal and make ready; for *these* men will dine with me at noon." ¹⁷Then the man did as Joseph ordered, and the man brought the men into Joseph's house.

43:11 The giving of a present was an ancient Near Eastern custom for approaching someone of rank. Balm, a resin used for healing wounds, was extracted from a tree that grew in Gilead. "Honey" is probably grape juice boiled down to a syrup, a delicacy like the nuts. "Myrrh" was prized in Egypt for its use in embalming (see chart, The Herbs of the Bible).

43:14 God Almighty (Heb. *El Shaddai*) is the name used for God as He resolves difficulties or dangers for His covenant people (see Gen. 17:1, note).

SIBLINGS — UNITY AND DIVERSITY

The world is made up of the interweaving and intersecting between individuals and groups, which we call human relationships. Society exists as a result of these relationships. They provide companionship and communication, and through them we give and receive love and understanding. Through relationships we develop, grow, and learn, and from them we obtain self-esteem, identity, and significance. All of Scripture involves relationships, both with God and with our fellow human beings. Some of the most challenging relationships are those within the family circle, especially among siblings. The Lord's plan from the beginning has been for the family to be the foremost arena in which each of us develops identity, self-esteem, self-worth, and a relationship with God. Our siblings play an important role in helping determine not only who we are but also who we become.

Siblings provide one another with a unique opportunity to give and receive love as well as to develop tolerance, an appreciation for others, communication skills, an ability to forgive others, and an understanding of genuine companionship.

Scripture offers these principles about sibling relationships:

1) We must allow a sibling freedom to develop his or her own traits and abilities and to pursue the unique call of God in life. Martha and Mary were very different in personality; yet each had a unique relationship with the Lord (Luke 10:38–42; John 11:20–44).

2) We are not to criticize our siblings in public, but we are to resolve our differences in the privacy of the family circle. Miriam paid a high price for publicly criticizing her brother's choice of a wife (Num. 12:1–15).

3) We are to rejoice without jealousy or ill will when good things happen to our siblings (Luke 15:11–32).

4) We are to do our best always to introduce our brothers and sisters to the Lord and build up their faith, just as Andrew introduced Simon Peter to Jesus (John 1:40–42).

Because the way siblings relate to one another is largely based on the way they perceive their parents' regard for them, a special burden rests on parents to treat all their children with equal love and value, just as our heavenly Father does. Yet, at the same time, each child must be nurtured according to his or her unique capabilities and attributes.

Unity and diversity must be linked to togetherness and individuality and all within the framework of the family's unified goals and direction.

See also Gen. 4:1–12; 21:8–14; 27:1–46; notes on Adolescence (Luke 2); Bitterness (Heb. 12); Conflict: Resolution (Matt. 18); Family (Gen. 32; 1 Sam. 3; Ps. 78; 127); Favoritism (Prov. 28); Girlhood (Prov. 1); Inheritance (Prov. 13); Jealousy (Song 8)

18Now the men were afraid because they were brought into Joseph's house; and they said, "*It is* because of the money, which was returned in our sacks the first time, that we are brought in, so that he may make a case against us and seize us, to take us as slaves with our donkeys."

19When they drew near to the steward of Joseph's house, they talked with him at the door of the house, 20and said, "O sir, we indeed came down the first time to buy food; 21but it happened, when we came to the encampment, that we opened our sacks, and there, *each* man's money *was* in the mouth of his sack, our money in full weight; so we have brought it back in our hand. 22And we have brought down other money in our hands to buy food. We do not know who put our money in our sacks."

23But he said, "Peace *be* with you, do not be afraid. Your God and the God of your father has given you treasure in your sacks; I had your money." Then he brought Simeon out to them.

24So the man brought the men into Joseph's house and gave *them* water, and they washed their feet; and he gave their donkeys feed. 25Then they made the present ready for Joseph's coming at noon, for they heard that they would eat bread there.

26And when Joseph came home, they brought him the present which *was* in their hand into the house, and bowed down before him to the earth. 27Then he asked them about *their* well-being, and said, "*Is* your father well, the old man of whom you spoke? *Is* he still alive?"

28And they answered, "Your servant our father *is* in good health; he *is* still alive." And they bowed their heads down and prostrated themselves.

29Then he lifted his eyes and saw his brother Benjamin, his mother's son, and said, "*Is* this your younger brother of whom you spoke to me?" And he said, "God be gracious to you, my son." 30Now his heart yearned for his brother; so Joseph made haste and sought *somewhere* to weep. And he went into *his* chamber and wept there. 31Then he washed his face and came out; and he restrained himself, and said, "Serve the bread."

³²So they set him a place by himself, and them by themselves, and the Egyptians who ate with him by themselves; because the Egyptians could not eat food with the Hebrews, for that *is* an abomination to the Egyptians. ³³And they sat before him, the firstborn according to his birthright and the youngest according to his youth; and the men looked in astonishment at one another. ³⁴Then he took servings to them from before him, but Benjamin's serving was five times as much as any of theirs. So they drank and were merry with him.

Joseph's Cup

44 And he commanded the steward of his house, saying, "Fill the men's sacks with food, as much as they can carry, and put each man's money in the mouth of his sack. ²Also put my cup, the silver cup, in the mouth of the sack of the youngest, and his grain money." So he did according to the word that Joseph had spoken. ³As soon as the morning dawned, the men were sent away, they and their donkeys. ⁴When they had gone out of the city, *and* were not *yet* far off, Joseph said to his steward, "Get up, follow the men; and when you overtake them, say to them, 'Why have you repaid evil for good? ⁵*Is* not this *the one* from which my lord drinks, and with which he indeed practices divination? You have done evil in so doing.'"

⁶So he overtook them, and he spoke to them these same words. ⁷And they said to him, "Why does my lord say these words? Far be it from us that your servants should do such a thing. ⁸Look, we brought back to you from the land of Canaan the money which we found in the mouth of our sacks. How then could we steal silver or gold from your lord's house? ⁹With whomever of your servants it is found, let him die, and we also will be my lord's slaves."

¹⁰And he said, "Now also *let* it *be* according to your words; he with whom it is found shall be my slave, and you shall be blameless." ¹¹Then each man speedily let down his sack to the ground, and each opened his sack. ¹²So he searched. He began with the oldest and left off with the youngest; and the cup was found in Benjamin's sack. ¹³Then they tore their clothes, and each man loaded his donkey and returned to the city.

¹⁴So Judah and his brothers came to Joseph's house, and he *was* still there; and they fell before him on the ground. ¹⁵And Joseph said to them, "What deed *is* this you have done? Did you not know that such a man as I can certainly practice divination?"

¹⁶Then Judah said, "What shall we say to my lord? What shall we speak? Or how shall we clear ourselves? God has found out the iniquity of your servants; here we are, my lord's slaves, both we and *he* also with whom the cup was found."

¹⁷But he said, "Far be it from me that I should do so; the man in whose hand the cup was found, he shall be my slave. And as for you, go up in peace to your father."

Judah Intercedes for Benjamin

¹⁸Then Judah came near to him and said: "O my lord, please let your servant speak a word in my lord's hearing, and do not let your anger burn against your servant; for you *are* even like Pharaoh. ¹⁹My lord asked his servants, saying, 'Have you a father or a brother?' ²⁰And we said to my lord, 'We have a father, an old man, and a child of *his* old age, *who is* young; his brother is dead, and he alone is left of his mother's children, and his father loves him.' ²¹Then you said to your servants, 'Bring him down to me, that I may set my eyes on him.' ²²And we said to my lord, 'The lad cannot leave his father, for *if* he should leave his father, *his father* would die.' ²³But you said to your servants, 'Unless your youngest brother comes down with you, you shall see my face no more.'

²⁴"So it was, when we went up to your servant my father, that we told him the words of my lord. ²⁵And our father said, 'Go back *and* buy us a little food.' ²⁶But we said, 'We cannot go down; if our youngest brother is with us, then we will go down; for we may not see the man's face unless our youngest brother *is* with us.' ²⁷Then your servant my father said to us, 'You know that my wife bore me two sons; ²⁸and the one went out from me, and I said, "Surely he is torn to pieces"; and I have not seen him since. ²⁹But if you take this one

---

43:32 A place apart. Egyptians did not eat with Hebrews for cultic reasons. Presence of the foreigners would defile the food ritually. The word "abomination" often implies something forbidden on religious grounds.

43:34 Benjamin's portion. The double portion was an ancient Near Eastern custom for honoring a particular guest.

44:2 The silver cup. Divination with a cup was widely practiced in Egypt (v. 5). The water was disturbed by a small coin or a drop of oil, and the resulting patterns were read and interpreted. The penalty for the theft of an object of divination was death (v. 9). The placement of the cup in Benjamin's sack was designed to test the brothers' attitude toward Benjamin as the child of Rachel.

44:16 Judah's answer. Judah attributed the finding of the cup, like the money, to a divine force he could not understand. The word "iniquity," meaning "guilt," is ironic, considering the greater guilt of the sin against Joseph. Judah's plea revealed a change in character from the greed and callousness displayed earlier (vv. 18–34; see also Gen. 37).

also from me, and calamity befalls him, you shall bring down my gray hair with sorrow to the grave.'

³⁰"Now therefore, when I come to your servant my father, and the lad *is* not with us, since his life is bound up in the lad's life, ³¹it will happen, when he sees that the lad *is* not *with us,* that he will die. So your servants will bring down the gray hair of your servant our father with sorrow to the grave. ³²For your servant became surety for the lad to my father, saying, 'If I do not bring him *back* to you, then I shall bear the blame before my father forever.' ³³Now therefore, please let your servant remain instead of the lad as a slave to my lord, and let the lad go up with his brothers. ³⁴For how shall I go up to my father if the lad *is* not with me, lest perhaps I see the evil that would come upon my father?"

Joseph Revealed to His Brothers

45 Then Joseph could not restrain himself before all those who stood by him, and he cried out, "Make everyone go out from me!" So no one stood with him while Joseph made himself known to his brothers. ²And he wept aloud, and the Egyptians and the house of Pharaoh heard *it.*

³Then Joseph said to his brothers, "I *am* Joseph; does my father still live?" But his brothers could not answer him, for they were dismayed in his presence. ⁴And Joseph said to his brothers, "Please come near to me." So they came near. Then he said: "I *am* Joseph your brother, whom you sold into Egypt. ⁵But now, do not therefore be grieved or angry with yourselves because you sold me here; for God sent me before you to preserve life. ⁶For these two years the famine *has been* in the land, and *there are* still five years in which *there will be* neither plowing nor harvesting. ⁷And God sent me before you to preserve a posterity for you in the earth, and to save your lives by a great deliverance. ⁸So now *it was* not you *who* sent me here, but God; and He has made me a father to Pharaoh, and lord of all his house, and a ruler throughout all the land of Egypt.

⁹"Hurry and go up to my father, and say to him, 'Thus says your son Joseph: "God has made me lord of all Egypt; come down to me, do not tarry. ¹⁰You shall dwell in the land of Goshen, and you shall be near to me, you and your children, your children's children, your flocks and your herds, and all that you have. ¹¹There I will provide for you, lest you and your household, and all that you have, come to poverty; for *there are* still five years of famine."'

¹²"And behold, your eyes and the eyes of my brother Benjamin see that *it is* my mouth that speaks to you. ¹³So you shall tell my father of all my glory in Egypt, and of all that you have seen; and you shall hurry and bring my father down here."

¹⁴Then he fell on his brother Benjamin's neck and wept, and Benjamin wept on his neck. ¹⁵Moreover he kissed all his brothers and wept over them, and after that his brothers talked with him.

¹⁶Now the report of it was heard in Pharaoh's house, saying, "Joseph's brothers have come." So it pleased Pharaoh and his servants well. ¹⁷And Pharaoh said to Joseph, "Say to your brothers, 'Do this: Load your animals and depart; go to the land of Canaan. ¹⁸Bring your father and your households and come to me; I will give you the best of the land of Egypt, and you will eat the fat of the land. ¹⁹Now you are commanded—do this: Take carts out of the land of Egypt for your little ones and your wives; bring your father and come. ²⁰Also do not be concerned about your goods, for the best of all the land of Egypt *is* yours.' "

²¹Then the sons of Israel did so; and Joseph gave them carts, according to the command of Pharaoh, and he gave them provisions for the journey. ²²He gave to all of them, to each man, changes of garments; but to Benjamin he gave three hundred *pieces* of silver and five changes of garments. ²³And he sent to his father these *things:* ten donkeys loaded with the good things of Egypt, and ten female donkeys loaded with grain, bread, and food for his father for the journey. ²⁴So he sent his brothers away, and they departed; and he said to them, "See that you do not become troubled along the way."

²⁵Then they went up out of Egypt, and came to the land of Canaan to Jacob their father. ²⁶And they told him, saying, "Joseph *is* still alive, and he *is* governor over all the land of Egypt." And Jacob's heart stood still, because he did not believe them. ²⁷But when they told him all the words which Joseph had said to them, and when he saw the carts which Joseph had sent to carry him, the spirit of Jacob their father revived. ²⁸Then Israel said, "*It is* enough. Joseph my son *is* still alive. I will go and see him before I die."

45:5 God's overruling sovereignty was recognized by Joseph. Despite the sins of His people, the God of the covenant sovereignly acted to carry out His plan. Joseph's slavery was used for the preservation of the covenant line (v. 7).

45:8 Father to Pharaoh. The Egyptian title meant "advisor" or

"administrator" and was regularly given to the vizier or governor.

45:10 Goshen, later known as the "land of Rameses," occupied the northeastern portion of the Nile delta (Gen. 47:11). It was choice, well-irrigated land. "Near to me" alludes to proximity to Tanis, the royal seat.

Jacob's Journey to Egypt

46 So Israel took his journey with all that he had, and came to Beersheba, and offered sacrifices to the God of his father Isaac. [2]Then God spoke to Israel in the visions of the night, and said, "Jacob, Jacob!"

And he said, "Here I am."

[3]So He said, "I *am* God, the God of your father; do not fear to go down to Egypt, for I will make of you a great nation there. [4]I will go down with you to Egypt, and I will also surely bring you up *again;* and Joseph will put his hand on your eyes."

[5]Then Jacob arose from Beersheba; and the sons of Israel carried their father Jacob, their little ones, and their wives, in the carts which Pharaoh had sent to carry him. [6]So they took their livestock and their goods, which they had acquired in the land of Canaan, and went to Egypt, Jacob and all his descendants with him. [7]His sons and his sons' sons, his daughters and his sons' daughters, and all his descendants he brought with him to Egypt.

[8]Now these *were* the names of the children of Israel, Jacob and his sons, who went to Egypt: Reuben *was* Jacob's firstborn. [9]The sons of Reuben *were* Hanoch, Pallu, Hezron, and Carmi. [10]The sons of Simeon *were* Jemuel,[a] Jamin, Ohad, Jachin,[b] Zohar,[c] and Shaul, the son of a Canaanite woman. [11]The sons of Levi *were* Gershon, Kohath, and Merari. [12]The sons of Judah *were* Er, Onan, Shelah, Perez, and Zerah (but Er and Onan died in the land of Canaan). The sons of Perez were Hezron and Hamul. [13]The sons of Issachar *were* Tola, Puvah,[a] Job,[b] and Shimron. [14]The sons of Zebulun *were* Sered, Elon, and Jahleel. [15]These *were* the sons of Leah, whom she bore to Jacob in Padan Aram, with his daughter Dinah. All the persons, his sons and his daughters, *were* thirty-three.

[16]The sons of Gad *were* Ziphion,[a] Haggi, Shuni, Ezbon,[b] Eri, Arodi,[c] and Areli. [17]The sons of Asher *were* Jimnah, Ishuah, Isui, Beriah, and Serah, their sister. And the sons of Beriah *were* Heber and Malchiel. [18]These *were* the sons of Zilpah, whom Laban gave to Leah his daughter; and these she bore to Jacob: sixteen persons.

[19]The sons of Rachel, Jacob's wife, *were* Joseph and Benjamin. [20]And to Joseph in the land of Egypt were born Manasseh and Ephraim, whom Asenath, the daughter of Poti-Pherah priest of On, bore to him. [21]The sons of Benjamin *were* Belah, Becher, Ashbel, Gera, Naaman, Ehi, Rosh, Muppim, Huppim,[a] and Ard. [22]These *were* the sons of Rachel, who were born to Jacob: fourteen persons in all.

[23]The son of Dan *was* Hushim.[a] [24]The sons of Naphtali *were* Jahzeel,[a] Guni, Jezer, and Shillem.[b] [25]These *were* the sons of Bilhah, whom Laban gave to Rachel his daughter, and she bore these to Jacob: seven persons in all.

[26]All the persons who went with Jacob to Egypt, who came from his body, besides Jacob's sons' wives, *were* sixty-six persons in all. [27]And the sons of Joseph who were born to him in Egypt *were* two persons. All the persons of the house of Jacob who went to Egypt were seventy.

Jacob Settles in Goshen

[28]Then he sent Judah before him to Joseph, to point out before him *the way* to Goshen. And they came to the land of Goshen. [29]So Joseph made ready his chariot and went up to Goshen to meet his father Israel; and he presented himself to him, and fell on his neck and wept on his neck a good while.

[30]And Israel said to Joseph, "Now let me die, since I have seen your face, because you *are* still alive."

46:10 [a]Spelled *Nemuel* in 1 Chronicles 4:24 [b]Called *Jarib* in 1 Chronicles 4:24 [c]Called *Zerah* in 1 Chronicles 4:24 **46:13** [a]Spelled *Puah* in 1 Chronicles 7:1 [b]Same as *Jashub* in Numbers 26:24 and 1 Chronicles 7:1 **46:16** [a]Spelled *Zephon* in Samaritan Pentateuch, Septuagint, and Numbers 26:15 [b]Called *Ozni* in Numbers 26:16 [c]Spelled *Arod* in Numbers 26:17 **46:21** [a]Called *Hupham* in Numbers 26:39 **46:23** [a]Called *Shuham* in Numbers 26:42 **46:24** [a]Spelled *Jahziel* in 1 Chronicles 7:13 [b]Spelled *Shallum* in 1 Chronicles 7:13

46:1 Jacob's journey began at Hebron and continued south about 20 miles to Beersheba. God had confirmed the covenant to Isaac at Beersheba, making it an important place of worship (Gen. 26:23–25). Jacob's sacrifices were a request for divine guidance.

46:3 God guided Jacob into Egypt. Earlier, God had forbidden Isaac to enter that country (Gen. 26:1–5) during a similar famine. God now planned to build a nation by isolating the Israelites within Egypt, among people who would not approve of intermarriage. In Canaan, Israel was in danger of being assimilated by the native Canaanites (Gen. 34:8–10). The promise shifted from the nation ("I will also surely bring you up again") to Jacob himself (v. 4). The last phrase confirmed that Joseph would be the one to close Jacob's eyes after death; that is, there would be no more separation between them.

46:8 The household of Jacob. The list of those who accompanied Jacob to Egypt is grouped into 70, probably for mnemonic reasons (v. 27). The total count of persons listed is 71, including Dinah, who is not included in the count of 33 (v. 15). Er and Onan were buried in Canaan (v. 12); Joseph, Manasseh, and Ephraim were already in Egypt. This reduces the number to 66 (v. 26). The narrator then re-adds Jacob, Joseph, Manasseh, and Ephraim to make 70. Rather than the actual number in Jacob's household, this number reflects only those who are actual legal ancestors of the nation of Israel. The number 70 also signified that the complete tribe had journeyed to Egypt and served as a reminder that God had done a complete work in preparing Israel for their task as God's people.

46:21 Benjamin had ten sons, confirming his mature age. Comparison with Numbers 26:38–40 and 1 Chronicles 7:6–12 suggests that grandsons have been added.

COOKING WHAT'S FOR SUPPER?

A wide assortment of clay pots was used for various cooking purposes—storage of water or food, meal preparation, or serving. Some women had the luxury of cooking on clay stoves—a fire burned within the plaster-covered "bricks," and two or three openings on top of the oven provided "burners" on which to place pots.

Bread, stew—generally made with vegetables, and sometimes seasoned with meat (Gen. 25:29–34; 2 Kin. 4:38–41)—and drink were considered a complete meal. As one of the oldest "menus" provided in the Bible, Sarah served cakes made of fine meal, a "tender and good calf," butter, and milk (Gen. 18:6–8) to the divine messengers who visited her home. Family and guests generally dipped into large serving dishes with their fingers or with pieces of flat bread. Grinding grains and baking bread was a daily ritual. The dough was formed into flat cakes and baked on heated stones or in rounded, hive-shaped ovens located just outside a home or tent.

In what is perhaps the world's oldest cookbook—three clay tablets dating back some 4,000 years—a recipe for beef stew was found:

Take some meat. Prepare water, throw fat into it, then add . . . . leek and garlic, all crushed together, and some plain *shuhutinnu* [probably onion].

One of the tablets has twenty-five recipes, including four vegetable dishes and twenty-one meat dishes (featuring deer, gazelle, lamb, pigeon, and wild dove).

See also notes on Hospitality (1 Pet. 4); Mealtime (Ps. 104); Nutrition (Lev. 11)

31Then Joseph said to his brothers and to his father's household, "I will go up and tell Pharaoh, and say to him, 'My brothers and those of my father's house, who *were* in the land of Canaan, have come to me. 32And the men *are* shepherds, for their occupation has been to feed livestock; and they have brought their flocks, their herds, and all that they have.' 33So it shall be, when Pharaoh calls you and says, 'What is your occupation?' 34that you shall say, 'Your servants' occupation has been with livestock from our youth even till now, both we *and* also our fathers,' that you may dwell in the land of Goshen; for every shepherd *is* an abomination to the Egyptians."

47 Then Joseph went and told Pharaoh, and said, "My father and my brothers, their flocks and their herds and all that they possess, have come from the land of Canaan; and indeed they *are* in the land of Goshen." 2And he took five men from among his brothers and presented them to Pharaoh. 3Then Pharaoh said to his brothers, "What *is* your occupation?"

And they said to Pharaoh, "Your servants *are* shepherds, both we *and* also our fathers." 4And they said to Pharaoh, "We have come to dwell in the land, because your servants have no pasture for their flocks, for the famine *is* severe in the land of Canaan. Now therefore, please let your servants dwell in the land of Goshen."

5Then Pharaoh spoke to Joseph, saying, "Your father and your brothers have come to you. 6The land of Egypt *is* before you. Have your father and brothers dwell in the best of the land; let them dwell in the land of Goshen. And if you know *any* competent men among them, then make them chief herdsmen over my livestock."

7Then Joseph brought in his father Jacob and set him before Pharaoh; and Jacob blessed Pharaoh. 8Pharaoh said to Jacob, "How old *are* you?"

9And Jacob said to Pharaoh, "The days of the years of my pilgrimage *are* one hundred and thirty years; few and evil have been the days of the years of my life, and they have not attained to the days of the years of the life of my fathers in the days of their pilgrimage." 10So Jacob blessed Pharaoh, and went out from before Pharaoh.

11And Joseph situated his father and his brothers, and gave them a possession in the land of Egypt, in the best of the land, in the land of Rameses, as Pharaoh had commanded. 12Then Joseph provided his father, his brothers, and all his father's household with bread, according to the number in *their* families.

Joseph Deals with the Famine

13Now *there was* no bread in all the land; for the famine *was* very severe, so that the land of Egypt and the land of Canaan languished because of the famine. 14And Joseph gathered up all the money

---

46:34 An abomination. The Egyptians had an aversion to the occupation of shepherding. Joseph wanted to emphasize their nationality and profession so that Pharaoh would not keep them in the city; he implied that their presence there would be disturbing to Egyptians. Goshen was both fertile and politically sensitive, being located close to the border. Joseph's maneuver guaranteed that Pharaoh would not object to his family's settling there (Gen. 47:6; see also Gen. 43:32, note).

that was found in the land of Egypt and in the land of Canaan, for the grain which they bought; and Joseph brought the money into Pharaoh's house.

¹⁵So when the money failed in the land of Egypt and in the land of Canaan, all the Egyptians came to Joseph and said, "Give us bread, for why should we die in your presence? For the money has failed."

¹⁶Then Joseph said, "Give your livestock, and I will give you *bread* for your livestock, if the money is gone." ¹⁷So they brought their livestock to Joseph, and Joseph gave them bread *in exchange* for the horses, the flocks, the cattle of the herds, and for the donkeys. Thus he fed them with bread *in exchange* for all their livestock that year.

¹⁸When that year had ended, they came to him the next year and said, "We will not hide from my lord that our money is gone; my lord also has our herds of livestock. There is nothing left in the sight of my lord but our bodies and our lands. ¹⁹Why should we die before your eyes, both we and our land? Buy us and our land for bread, and we and our land will be servants of Pharaoh; give *us* seed, that we may live and not die, that the land may not be desolate."

²⁰Then Joseph bought all the land of Egypt for Pharaoh; for every man of the Egyptians sold his field, because the famine was severe upon them. So the land became Pharaoh's. ²¹And as for the people, he moved them into the cities,ᵃ from *one* end of the borders of Egypt to the *other* end. ²²Only the land of the priests he did not buy; for the priests had rations *allotted to them* by Pharaoh, and they ate their rations which Pharaoh gave them; therefore they did not sell their lands.

²³Then Joseph said to the people, "Indeed I have bought you and your land this day for Pharaoh. Look, *here is* seed for you, and you shall sow the land. ²⁴And it shall come to pass in the harvest that you shall give one-fifth to Pharaoh. Four-fifths shall be your own, as seed for the field and for your food, for those of your households and as food for your little ones."

²⁵So they said, "You have saved our lives; let us find favor in the sight of my lord, and we will be Pharaoh's servants." ²⁶And Joseph made it a law over the land of Egypt to this day, *that* Pharaoh should have one-fifth, except for the land of the priests only, *which* did not become Pharaoh's.

Joseph's Vow to Jacob

²⁷So Israel dwelt in the land of Egypt, in the country of Goshen; and they had possessions there and grew and multiplied exceedingly. ²⁸And Jacob lived in the land of Egypt seventeen years. So the length of Jacob's life was one hundred and forty-seven years. ²⁹When the time drew near that Israel must die, he called his son Joseph and said to him, "Now if I have found favor in your sight, please put your hand under my thigh, and deal kindly and truly with me. Please do not bury me in Egypt, ³⁰but let me lie with my fathers; you shall carry me out of Egypt and bury me in their burial place."

And he said, "I will do as you have said."

³¹Then he said, "Swear to me." And he swore to him. So Israel bowed himself on the head of the bed.

Jacob Blesses Joseph's Sons

48 Now it came to pass after these things that Joseph was told, "Indeed your father *is* sick"; and he took with him his two sons, Manasseh and Ephraim. ²And Jacob was told, "Look, your son Joseph is coming to you"; and Israel strengthened himself and sat up on the bed. ³Then Jacob said to Joseph: "God Almighty appeared to me at Luz in the land of Canaan and blessed me, ⁴and said to me, 'Behold, I will make you fruitful and multiply you, and I will make of you a multitude of people, and give this land to your descendants after you *as* an everlasting possession.' ⁵And now your two sons, Ephraim and Manasseh, who were born to you in the land of Egypt before I came to you in Egypt, *are* mine; as Reuben and Simeon, they shall be mine. ⁶Your offspring whom you beget after them shall be yours; they will be called by the name of their brothers in their inheritance. ⁷But as for me, when I came from Padan, Rachel died beside me in the land of Canaan on the way, when *there was* but a little distance to go to Ephrath; and I buried her there on the way to Ephrath (that is, Bethlehem)."

⁸Then Israel saw Joseph's sons, and said, "Who *are* these?"

⁹Joseph said to his father, "They *are* my sons, whom God has given me in this *place*."

47:21ᵃFollowing Masoretic Text and Targum; Samaritan Pentateuch, Septuagint, and Vulgate read *made the people virtual slaves.*

47:20 Result of the famine. In order to buy grain, Pharaoh's people, with the exception of the priestly class, became serfs of the crown (v. 22). Relocation of the population to urban areas would make food distribution easier (v. 21). After the famine, farmers were required to hand over one-fifth of their crops. This was not exorbitant by ancient standards; eastern kings often demanded from one-third to three-fourths of the crops of peasants.

47:29 Jacob's request to be buried in Canaan reflected his faith in God's promise that Canaan would one day belong to Israel. Like Abraham, he asked Joseph to swear an oath (Gen. 24:1–9). The form of the oath emphasized that the promise would affect Jacob's descendants (see Gen. 24:2, note).

And he said, "Please bring them to me, and I will bless them." ¹⁰Now the eyes of Israel were dim with age, *so that* he could not see. Then Joseph brought them near him, and he kissed them and embraced them. ¹¹And Israel said to Joseph, "I had not thought to see your face; but in fact, God has also shown me your offspring!"

¹²So Joseph brought them from beside his knees, and he bowed down with his face to the earth. ¹³And Joseph took them both, Ephraim with his right hand toward Israel's left hand, and Manasseh with his left hand toward Israel's right hand, and brought *them* near him. ¹⁴Then Israel stretched out his right hand and laid *it* on Ephraim's head, who *was* the younger, and his left hand on Manasseh's head, guiding his hands knowingly, for Manasseh *was* the firstborn. ¹⁵And he blessed Joseph, and said:

"God, before whom my fathers Abraham and
    Isaac walked,
The God who has fed me all my life long to this
    day,
¹⁶The Angel who has redeemed me from all evil,
    Bless the lads;
Let my name be named upon them,
And the name of my fathers Abraham and
    Isaac;
And let them grow into a multitude in the
    midst of the earth."

¹⁷Now when Joseph saw that his father laid his right hand on the head of Ephraim, it displeased him; so he took hold of his father's hand to remove it from Ephraim's head to Manasseh's head. ¹⁸And Joseph said to his father, "Not so, my father, for this *one is* the firstborn; put your right hand on his head." ¹⁹But his father refused and said, "I know, my son, I know. He also shall become a people, and he also shall be great; but truly his younger brother shall be greater than he, and his descendants shall become a multitude of nations." ²⁰So he blessed them that day, saying, "By you

Israel will bless, saying, 'May God make you as Ephraim and as Manasseh!' " And thus he set Ephraim before Manasseh.

²¹Then Israel said to Joseph, "Behold, I am dying, but God will be with you and bring you back to the land of your fathers. ²²Moreover I have given to you one portion above your brothers, which I took from the hand of the Amorite with my sword and my bow."

Jacob's Last Words to His Sons

49 And Jacob called his sons and said, "Gather together, that I may tell you what shall befall you in the last days:

²"Gather together and hear, you sons of Jacob,
    And listen to Israel your father.

³"Reuben, you are my firstborn,
    My might and the beginning of my strength,
    The excellency of dignity and the excellency of
        power.
⁴Unstable as water, you shall not excel,
    Because you went up to your father's bed;
    Then you defiled *it*—
    He went up to my couch.

⁵"Simeon and Levi *are* brothers;
    Instruments of cruelty *are in* their dwelling
        place.
⁶Let not my soul enter their council;
    Let not my honor be united to their assembly;
    For in their anger they slew a man,
    And in their self-will they hamstrung an ox.
⁷Cursed *be* their anger, for *it is* fierce;
    And their wrath, for it is cruel!
    I will divide them in Jacob
    And scatter them in Israel.

⁸"Judah, you *are he* whom your brothers shall
        praise;
    Your hand *shall be* on the neck of your enemies;
    Your father's children shall bow down before
        you.

48:22 Joseph's portion. This verse is obscure in meaning. "Portion" (lit. "shoulder" or "mountain ridge") seems to refer to some specific area Jacob is deeding to Joseph—possibly Shechem (Heb., lit. "shoulder"). However, Jacob did not participate in the taking of Shechem (Gen. 34). Either he is speaking of the actions of his sons, or this refers to an unrecorded incident in Canaan.

49:1 Jacob's last oracles. Genesis ends as it began, with blessings, curses, and predictions for the future of the chosen seed (see Gen. 3:16–19). Jacob's last words are echoed by Moses (see Deut. 33). "The last days" is a general phrase meaning "days to come"—that is, the time for occupation of the Promised Land.

49:3 The land allotted to Reuben east of the Dead Sea came

under continual encroachment from Moab. The tribe of Reuben never gained real power or influence in the tribal confederacy and was condemned by Deborah as weak and irresolute during times of crisis (Judg. 5:15, 16).

49:5 Simeon and Levi were condemned for the massacre of Shechem (Gen. 34:25–31). Jacob's words recall the actions of Lamech (Gen. 4:23, 24), emphasizing the violence and wickedness of the action. While the tribe of Simeon was later swallowed by Judah (Josh. 19:2–9), Levi experienced reprieve and was given priestly duties because the people demonstrated their faithfulness to God (Ex. 32:25–29).

49:9, 10 Judah is given pre-eminence among his brothers until the coming of the Messiah (v. 10). "Lawgiver" or "statutemaker" can also be rendered "commander." "From between

⁹Judah *is* a lion's whelp;
  From the prey, my son, you have gone up.
  He bows down, he lies down as a lion;
  And as a lion, who shall rouse him?
¹⁰The scepter shall not depart from Judah,
  Nor a lawgiver from between his feet,
  Until Shiloh comes;
  And to Him *shall be* the obedience of the
      people.
¹¹Binding his donkey to the vine,
  And his donkey's colt to the choice vine,
  He washed his garments in wine,
  And his clothes in the blood of grapes.
¹²His eyes *are* darker than wine,
  And his teeth whiter than milk.

¹³"Zebulun shall dwell by the haven of the sea;
  He *shall become* a haven for ships,
  And his border shall adjoin Sidon.

¹⁴"Issachar is a strong donkey,
  Lying down between two burdens;
¹⁵He saw that rest *was* good,
  And that the land *was* pleasant;
  He bowed his shoulder to bear *a burden*,
  And became a band of slaves.

¹⁶"Dan shall judge his people
  As one of the tribes of Israel.
¹⁷Dan shall be a serpent by the way,
  A viper by the path,
  That bites the horse's heels
  So that its rider shall fall backward.
¹⁸I have waited for your salvation, O LORD!

¹⁹"Gad, a troop shall tramp upon him,
  But he shall triumph at last.

²⁰"Bread from Asher *shall be* rich,
  And he shall yield royal dainties.

²¹"Naphtali *is* a deer let loose;
  He uses beautiful words.

²²"Joseph *is* a fruitful bough,
  A fruitful bough by a well;
  His branches run over the wall.
²³The archers have bitterly grieved him,

Shot *at him* and hated him.
²⁴But his bow remained in strength,
  And the arms of his hands were made strong
  By the hands of the Mighty *God* of Jacob
  (From there *is* the Shepherd, the Stone of
      Israel),
²⁵By the God of your father who will help you,
  And by the Almighty who will bless you
  With blessings of heaven above,
  Blessings of the deep that lies beneath,
  Blessings of the breasts and of the womb.
²⁶The blessings of your father
  Have excelled the blessings of my ancestors,
  Up to the utmost bound of the everlasting
      hills.
  They shall be on the head of Joseph,
  And on the crown of the head of him who was
      separate from his brothers.

²⁷"Benjamin is a ravenous wolf;
  In the morning he shall devour the prey,
  And at night he shall divide the spoil."

²⁸All these *are* the twelve tribes of Israel, and this *is* what their father spoke to them. And he blessed them; he blessed each one according to his own blessing.

Jacob's Death and Burial

²⁹Then he charged them and said to them: "I am to be gathered to my people; bury me with my fathers in the cave that *is* in the field of Ephron the Hittite, ³⁰in the cave that *is* in the field of Machpelah, which *is* before Mamre in the land of Canaan, which Abraham bought with the field of Ephron the Hittite as a possession for a burial place. ³¹There they buried Abraham and Sarah his wife, there they buried Isaac and Rebekah his wife, and there I buried Leah. ³²The field and the cave that *is* there *were* purchased from the sons of Heth." ³³And when Jacob had finished commanding his sons, he drew his feet up into the bed and breathed his last, and was gathered to his people.

50 Then Joseph fell on his father's face and wept over him, and kissed him. ²And Joseph commanded his servants the physicians to

---

his feet" refers to procreation; Judah would continually produce leaders. "Shiloh," a difficult word, is not elsewhere a title of the Messiah. It has been interpreted both as a reference to the place Shiloh (although the city has no particular messianic function) and as a verb form meaning "until he comes to whom it [namely, the scepter] belongs."

49:16, 17 Dan. The comparison with the snake pictures Dan's force and strength in contrast to its small size. The imagery is negative; Dan was treacherous and idolatrous (Judg. 18).

49:22 Joseph's blessings fell upon his sons, Ephraim and Ma-

nasseh (Gen. 48:13). The blessing recognized the faithfulness of the covenant God by using the name *Shaddai* (Heb., lit. "Mighty One," v. 24; see Gen. 17:1, note). "From there" is better translated "in the name of." The emphasis on nature reveals God's superiority over the nature gods of Egypt and Canaan (vv. 25, 26).

49:27 Benjamin. Although a small tribe, Benjamin gave Israel its first king, Saul (1 Sam. 9:1, 2). Benjamites were fierce fighters (Judg. 19—21).

embalm his father. So the physicians embalmed Israel. [3]Forty days were required for him, for such are the days required for those who are embalmed; and the Egyptians mourned for him seventy days.

[4]Now when the days of his mourning were past, Joseph spoke to the household of Pharaoh, saying, "If now I have found favor in your eyes, please speak in the hearing of Pharaoh, saying, [5]'My father made me swear, saying, 'Behold, I am dying; in my grave which I dug for myself in the land of Canaan, there you shall bury me.' Now therefore, please let me go up and bury my father, and I will come back.'"

[6]And Pharaoh said, "Go up and bury your father, as he made you swear."

[7]So Joseph went up to bury his father; and with him went up all the servants of Pharaoh, the elders of his house, and all the elders of the land of Egypt, [8]as well as all the house of Joseph, his brothers, and his father's house. Only their little ones, their flocks, and their herds they left in the land of Goshen. [9]And there went up with him both chariots and horsemen, and it was a very great gathering.

[10]Then they came to the threshing floor of Atad, which is beyond the Jordan, and they mourned there with a great and very solemn lamentation. He observed seven days of mourning for his father. [11]And when the inhabitants of the land, the Canaanites, saw the mourning at the threshing floor of Atad, they said, "This is a deep mourning of the Egyptians." Therefore its name was called Abel Mizraim,[a] which is beyond the Jordan.

[12]So his sons did for him just as he had commanded them. [13]For his sons carried him to the land of Canaan, and buried him in the cave of the field of Machpelah, before Mamre, which Abraham bought with the field from Ephron the Hittite as property for a burial place. [14]And after he had buried his father, Joseph returned to Egypt, he and his brothers and all who went up with him to bury his father.

Joseph Reassures His Brothers

[15]When Joseph's brothers saw that their father was dead, they said, "Perhaps Joseph will hate us, and may actually repay us for all the evil which we did to him." [16]So they sent messengers to Joseph, saying, "Before your father died he commanded, saying, [17]'Thus you shall say to Joseph: "I beg you, please forgive the trespass of your brothers and their sin; for they did evil to you." ' Now, please, forgive the trespass of the servants of the God of your father." And Joseph wept when they spoke to him.

[18]Then his brothers also went and fell down before his face, and they said, "Behold, we are your servants."

[19]Joseph said to them, "Do not be afraid, for am I in the place of God? [20]But as for you, you meant evil against me; but God meant it for good, in order to bring it about as it is this day, to save many people alive. [21]Now therefore, do not be afraid; I will provide for you and your little ones." And he comforted them and spoke kindly to them.

Death of Joseph

[22]So Joseph dwelt in Egypt, he and his father's household. And Joseph lived one hundred and ten years. [23]Joseph saw Ephraim's children to the third generation. The children of Machir, the son of Manasseh, were also brought up on Joseph's knees.

[24]And Joseph said to his brethren, "I am dying; but God will surely visit you, and bring you out of this land to the land of which He swore to Abraham, to Isaac, and to Jacob." [25]Then Joseph took an oath from the children of Israel, saying, "God will surely visit you, and you shall carry up my bones from here." [26]So Joseph died, being one hundred and ten years old; and they embalmed him, and he was put in a coffin in Egypt.

····················
50:11 [a]Literally Mourning of Egypt

50:3 Seventy days is only two days short of the mourning period for a pharaoh and probably was done out of respect for Joseph.

50:25 Joseph's request. Genesis ends with Israel's isolation in Egypt, where God could purify and build up His people.

Joseph's request indicated his faith that Israel would eventually occupy the Land of Promise. The request was fulfilled by Moses (Ex. 13:19).

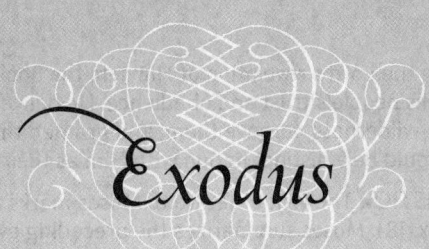

Exodus

Although the Book of Exodus does not declare the name of its author, strong and ancient tradition attributes it, along with the other books of the Pentateuch, to Moses. The Pentateuch, or the first five books of the Old Testament, also is called the Law of Moses, the Law, or the *Torah* (Heb., lit. "law" or "instruction"). Numerous Old and New Testament references to the Law of Moses support the attributing of Exodus to Moses as part of the Pentateuch (Josh. 8:31–35; 1 Kin. 2:1–3; 1 Chr. 6:49; 15:15; Luke 24:27, 44; Acts 28:23). Christ referred to the account of the burning bush (Ex. 3:1–6) as written "in the book of Moses" (Mark 12:26). Meanwhile, Exodus itself tells of Moses composing written records of important events, as was customary in the ancient Near East (Ex. 17:14; 24:4, 7; 34:27, 28).

DATE

Exodus briefly mentions earlier events (Jacob and Joseph in Egypt, Ex. 1:5, 6) and the Israelites' later travels (Ex. 16:35; 40:36–38). It also describes the oppression of the Israelites in Egypt (Ex. 1). But most of the book concerns the period from the birth of Moses (about 1526 B.C.) through the dedication of the tabernacle (1445 B.C.), a span of eighty-one years. Moses could have begun writing Exodus while the Israelites camped at Mt. Sinai (about 1445 B.C.) and completed his work on it before his death in 1406 B.C.

This explanation accepts 1445 B.C. as the most likely date for Israel's Exodus from Egypt. It coincides with information in Exodus about the dates when various events took place and with chronological statements elsewhere in the Old Testament (Ex. 7:7; 12:40; Judg. 11:26; 1 Kin. 6:1).

BACKGROUND

SETTING: When Moses was born in Egypt, an era now called the New Kingdom or Empire Period had begun with the start of Egypt's Eighteenth Dynasty of kings. Symbolic of Egypt's long national and cultural existence, the pyramids at Giza (or Gizeh) were around one thousand years old. Egyptian military might have extended north through Canaan and Syria to the Euphrates River. Taxation and trade brought in valuables from Nubia to the south, as well as from Canaan and Mesopotamia. Egyptian sciences, literature, art, religion, and customs were long established.

AUDIENCE: The first audience for Exodus was composed of Israelites who had grown up in the wilderness and stood on the verge of entering the Promised Land of Canaan. Their parents and grandparents were the adults who had experienced life in Egypt, the parting of the Red Sea, the first appearance of manna, the giving of the Law at Sinai, and the other events recorded in Exodus. However, following generations were also in view as is shown by the institution of ceremonies commemorating important events, by the provisions given for corporate worship, and by the emphasis in the Pentateuch and throughout the Old Testament on preserving what Moses wrote.

PURPOSE: By presenting the Lord's revelation of Himself, the Book of Exodus shows that the Lord deserves His people's trust and obedience. He delivered Israel from Egypt, provided for them in the wilderness, forgave them, and granted them a covenant relationship in which they would be a distinct nation with Him as their God.

LITERARY CHARACTERISTICS: The visit of Jethro to Moses marks a turning point in the structure of the book (Ex. 18). Moses summarizes the preceding events, and Jethro's response shows that the Lord's actions are having their intended effect. Jethro's offering of sacrifices prepares the reader for the subsequent chapters about worship and the building of the tabernacle. Jethro's observation of the need for laws and community organization prepares for the legal material found in the book. In other words, the account of Jethro's visit serves as a skillful thematic transition.

THEMES

The Lord's revelation of Himself is the foremost unifying theme in the Book of Exodus. The confrontations with Pharaoh and deliverance of Israel from Egypt, the preservation of Israel in the wilderness, and the giving of laws for everyday life and for worship all serve to reveal the Lord's essential character. In the process of identifying Himself, the Lord also gave the Israelites a distinctive identity as His people. Because of what the Lord did for them, Israel's identity, privileges, and responsibilities as a nation are built on Israel's association with the Lord Himself. Similarly, questions about who Moses is and about his abilities are answered in terms of who the Lord is.

OUTLINE

I. The Lord's Deliverance and Provision (1:1—18:27)
   A. Deliverance from Egypt (1:1—15:21)
      1. The people's need for deliverance (1:1—4:31)
      2. The Lord's revelation of Himself (5:1—7:7)
      3. The display of the Lord's power (7:8—11:10)
      4. The departure of the people (12:1—13:16)
      5. The path of escape (13:17—14:31)
      6. The celebration of deliverance (15:1—21)
   B. Provision in the wilderness (15:22—17:16)
      1. Sweet water to drink (15:22–27)
      2. Manna to eat (16:1–36)
      3. Water from a rock (17:1–7)
      4. Victory in battle (17:8–16)
   C. The visit of Jethro (18:1–27)
      1. Jethro's response to all the Lord had done (18:1–12)
      2. Jethro's advice for administering God's laws (18:13–27)

II. The Lord's Covenant Provisions for a Continuing Relationship with His People (19:1—40:38)
   A. The making of a covenant (19:1—24:18)
      1. Preparation for the covenant (19:1–25)
      2. The requirements of the covenant (20:1—23:33)
      3. Ratifying the covenant (24:1–18)
   B. The instructions for building the tabernacle (25:1—31:18)
   C. The breaking and renewing of the covenant (32:1—34:35)
      1. The worship of the golden calf by the people (32:1–35)
      2. The desire of Moses to know the Lord (33:1–23)
      3. The restoration of the covenant (34:1–35)
   D. The construction of the tabernacle (35:1—40:38)

Israel's Suffering in Egypt

1 Now these *are* the names of the children of Israel who came to Egypt; each man and his household came with Jacob: [2]Reuben, Simeon, Levi, and Judah; [3]Issachar, Zebulun, and Benjamin; [4]Dan, Naphtali, Gad, and Asher. [5]All those who were descendants[a] of Jacob were seventy[b] persons (for Joseph was in Egypt *already*). [6]And Joseph died, all his brothers, and all that generation. [7]But the children of Israel were fruitful and increased abundantly, multiplied and grew exceedingly mighty; and the land was filled with them.

[8]Now there arose a new king over Egypt, who did not know Joseph. [9]And he said to his people, "Look, the people of the children of Israel *are* more and mightier than we; [10]come, let us deal shrewdly with them, lest they multiply, and it happen, in the event of war, that they also join our enemies and fight against us, and *so* go up out of the land." [11]Therefore they set taskmasters over them to afflict them with their burdens. And they built for Pharaoh supply cities, Pithom and Raamses. [12]But the more they afflicted them, the more they multiplied and grew. And they were in dread of the children of Israel. [13]So the Egyptians made the children of Israel serve with rigor. [14]And they made their lives bitter with hard bondage—in mortar, in brick, and in all manner of service in the field. All their service in which they made them serve *was* with rigor.

[15]Then the king of Egypt spoke to the Hebrew midwives, of whom the name of one *was* Shiphrah and the name of the other Puah; [16]and he said, "When you do the duties of a midwife for the Hebrew women, and see *them* on the birthstools, if it *is* a son, then you shall kill him; but if it *is* a daughter, then she shall live." [17]But the midwives feared God, and did not do as the king of Egypt commanded them, but saved the male children alive. [18]So the king of Egypt called for the midwives and said to them, "Why have you done this thing, and saved the male children alive?"

[19]And the midwives said to Pharaoh, "Because the Hebrew women *are* not like the Egyptian women; for they *are* lively and give birth before the midwives come to them."

[20]Therefore God dealt well with the midwives, and the people multiplied and grew very mighty. [21]And so it was, because the midwives feared God, that He provided households for them. [22]So Pharaoh commanded all his people, saying, "Every son who is born[a] you shall cast into the river, and every daughter you shall save alive."

Moses Is Born

2 And a man of the house of Levi went and took *as wife* a daughter of Levi. [2]So the woman conceived and bore a son. And when she saw that he *was* a beautiful *child,* she hid him three months. [3]But when she could no longer hide him, she took an ark of bulrushes for him, daubed it with asphalt and pitch, put the child in it, and laid *it* in the reeds by the river's bank. [4]And his sister stood afar off, to know what would be done to him.

[5]Then the daughter of Pharaoh came down to bathe at the river. And her maidens walked along the riverside; and when she saw the ark among the reeds, she sent her maid to get it. [6]And when she opened *it,* she saw the child, and behold, the

1:5 [a]Literally *who came from the loins of* [b]Dead Sea Scrolls and Septuagint read *seventy-five* (compare Acts 7:14).   **1:22** [a]Samaritan Pentateuch, Septuagint, and Targum add *to the Hebrews*.

1:7 Emphasis on the growing number of Israelites (vv. 7, 9, 10, 12, 20) recalls God's blessings and instructions—"Be fruitful and multiply"—given at creation (Gen. 1:28), after the Flood (Gen. 9:1, 7), and to Jacob (Gen. 35:11). "The land" of Goshen, in the eastern Nile River delta of northern Egypt, was an area deemed suitable for shepherds and flocks (Gen. 46:34—47:6).

1:8, 9 The new Egyptian king may have been Ahmosis (1570–1546 B.C.) or perhaps Amenhotep I, his successor. Ahmosis reunited Egypt by defeating the Hyksos, a Semitic people who had invaded and dominated Egypt for about 150 years. He did not personally "know Joseph," who had died many years earlier, nor did he have any reason to perpetuate the memory of Joseph. The oppression also may have begun earlier under a Hyksos ruler, who was part of an ethnic minority without historical ties of gratitude to Joseph.

1:15–22 The killing of Israelite sons would have eliminated the perceived military threat; daughters could be assimilated into Egyptian society as servants and wives. Unknown to the king, the success of his plans would have wiped out the Israelites as a distinct people with whom God could keep His covenant promises. Shiphrah and Puah may have been leaders representing the large number of midwives that the Israelites would have needed. In a culture in which the naming of people and preservation of a person's name were important, the midwives are named, but the king of Egypt is not. These women were faithful to play a vital part in God's plan.

1:17 The midwives feared God. The first mention of God in Exodus presents Him as superior to the king, whom Egyptian religion honored as a god. Out of reverence for the true God, the midwives risked their own security and refused to kill infants.

1:19–21 The midwives' explanation reflects favorably on Hebrew women. The text does not comment on whether or not the explanation was true, but it must have been plausible. The midwives were rewarded with "households," that is, families (as in v. 1), not because of their explanation but because they "feared God."

2:2–4 The king of Egypt thought it safe to let Hebrew daughters live (Ex. 1:16, 22). But Jochebed, a resourceful "daughter of Levi" (v. 1; Ex. 6:20), and her daughter Miriam circumvented the king's plans (as had the midwives). Among women coming to wash or draw water at a well-chosen spot along the river, a mother leaving a basket and a sister standing watch could escape attention, and they might reasonably hope that the baby would be found.

BREASTFEEDING   A NATURAL SOURCE OF NOURISHMENT

Breast milk is God's way of providing a natural source of nourishment for the newborn child: Until this century it was the only method available for feeding infants.

Two complementary functions take place after the birth of a child: the mother's mammary glands fill up with milk and need to be emptied, and a baby displays sucking behavior. Children with mothers who were unable or unwilling to nurse them were given to "wet nurses"—women capable of breast-feeding them (as in the case of Pharaoh's daughter using a nurse for Moses, Ex. 2:7).

In Scripture, four aspects of breastfeeding are worth special note:

1) Breastfeeding is regarded as a satisfying bonding period between mother and child (Is. 66:11).

2) Breastfeeding requires a special commitment on the part of a mother to her child (Is. 49:15). While her husband and household made their annual trip to make sacrifices to the Lord, Hannah stayed behind to nurse her son Samuel (1 Sam. 1:22–24).

3) Weaning of the child—usually by the age of three—was an occasion for great celebration, a milestone in the child's life (Gen. 21:8). It was after weaning that a child was expected to receive the teaching of knowledge and doctrine (Is. 28:9).

4) Breastfeeding was believed by many to be a natural, though not absolute, method of birth control (see Gomer, Hos. 2) since during the postpartum period, nursing tends to suppress a woman's ovulation.

See also notes on Childbirth (John 16); Child Care (John 15); Motherhood (1 Sam. 1; Is. 49; Ezek. 16); Pregnancy (Judg. 13).

baby wept. So she had compassion on him, and said, "This is one of the Hebrews' children."

⁷Then his sister said to Pharaoh's daughter, "Shall I go and call a nurse for you from the Hebrew women, that she may nurse the child for you?"

⁸And Pharaoh's daughter said to her, "Go." So the maiden went and called the child's mother. ⁹Then Pharaoh's daughter said to her, "Take this child away and nurse him for me, and I will give *you* your wages." So the woman took the child and nursed him. ¹⁰And the child grew, and she brought him to Pharaoh's daughter, and he became her son. So she called his name Moses,ᵃ saying, "Because I drew him out of the water."

Moses Flees to Midian

¹¹Now it came to pass in those days, when Moses was grown, that he went out to his brethren and looked at their burdens. And he saw an Egyptian beating a Hebrew, one of his brethren. ¹²So he looked this way and that way, and when he saw no one, he killed the Egyptian and hid him in the sand. ¹³And when he went out the second day, behold, two Hebrew men were

fighting, and he said to the one who did the wrong, "Why are you striking your companion?"

¹⁴Then he said, "Who made you a prince and a judge over us? Do you intend to kill me as you killed the Egyptian?"

So Moses feared and said, "Surely this thing is known!" ¹⁵When Pharaoh heard of this matter, he sought to kill Moses. But Moses fled from the face of Pharaoh and dwelt in the land of Midian; and he sat down by a well.

¹⁶Now the priest of Midian had seven daughters. And they came and drew water, and they filled the troughs to water their father's flock. ¹⁷Then the shepherds came and drove them away; but Moses stood up and helped them, and watered their flock.

¹⁸When they came to Reuel their father, he said, "How *is it that* you have come so soon today?"

¹⁹And they said, "An Egyptian delivered us from the hand of the shepherds, and he also drew enough water for us and watered the flock."

²⁰So he said to his daughters, "And where *is* he?

· ·

2:10 ᵃLiterally *Drawn Out*

2:10 The name Moses appears in the Egyptian names Ahmose and Thutmose. It was also appropriate because it sounded like the Hebrew verb *mashah*, "to draw out," recalling the circumstances of Moses' discovery.

2:11 Moses was about 40 years old when he observed an injustice and acted to rescue one of his people from oppression (Acts 7:23, 24).

2:15 The current pharaoh was Thutmose III. His first 20 years of reign were dominated by Hatshepsut, who was his mother-in-law as well as his father's widow and half-sister.

After her death, he showed his hatred for her by defacing her monuments and attempting to remove all record of her name and accomplishments. He may well have viewed Moses as a personal threat, since Moses, as the adopted son of a pharaoh's daughter, may have been the son of Hatshepsut herself. The Midianites were descendants of Midian, a son borne by Keturah, who became Abraham's wife after the death of Sarah (Gen. 25:1–6; see the Family Tree of Abraham). They were nomadic people who lived in the Sinai peninsula east of the Gulf of Aqaba.

Why *is* it *that* you have left the man? Call him, that he may eat bread."

[21]Then Moses was content to live with the man, and he gave Zipporah his daughter to Moses. [22]And she bore *him* a son. He called his name Gershom,[a] for he said, "I have been a stranger in a foreign land."

[23]Now it happened in the process of time that the king of Egypt died. Then the children of Israel groaned because of the bondage, and they cried out; and their cry came up to God because of the bondage. [24]So God heard their groaning, and God remembered His covenant with Abraham, with Isaac, and with Jacob. [25]And God looked upon the children of Israel, and God acknowledged *them.*

Moses at the Burning Bush

3 Now Moses was tending the flock of Jethro his father-in-law, the priest of Midian. And he led the flock to the back of the desert, and came to Horeb, the mountain of God. [2]And the Angel of the LORD appeared to him in a flame of fire from the midst of a bush. So he looked, and behold, the bush was burning with fire, but the bush *was* not consumed. [3]Then Moses said, "I will now turn aside and see this great sight, why the bush does not burn."

[4]So when the LORD saw that he turned aside to look, God called to him from the midst of the bush and said, "Moses, Moses!"

And he said, "Here I am."

[5]Then He said, "Do not draw near this place. Take your sandals off your feet, for the place where you stand *is* holy ground." [6]Moreover He said, "I *am* the God of your father—the God of Abraham, the God of Isaac, and the God of Jacob." And Moses hid his face, for he was afraid to look upon God.

[7]And the LORD said: "I have surely seen the oppression of My people who *are* in Egypt, and have heard their cry because of their taskmasters, for I know their sorrows. [8]So I have come down to deliver them out of the hand of the Egyptians, and to bring them up from that land to a good and large land, to a land flowing with milk and honey, to the place of the Canaanites and the Hittites and the Amorites and the Perizzites and the Hivites and the Jebusites. [9]Now therefore, behold, the cry of the children of Israel has come to Me, and I have also seen the oppression with which the Egyptians oppress them. [10]Come now, therefore, and I will send you to Pharaoh that you may bring My people, the children of Israel, out of Egypt."

[11]But Moses said to God, "Who *am* I that I should go to Pharaoh, and that I should bring the children of Israel out of Egypt?"

[12]So He said, "I will certainly be with you. And this *shall be* a sign to you that I have sent you: When you have brought the people out of Egypt, you shall serve God on this mountain."

[13]Then Moses said to God, "Indeed, *when* I come to the children of Israel and say to them, 'The God of your fathers has sent me to you,' and they say to me, 'What *is* His name?' what shall I say to them?"

[14]And God said to Moses, "I AM WHO I AM." And He said, "Thus you shall say to the children of Israel, 'I AM has sent me to you.' " [15]Moreover God said to Moses, "Thus you shall say to the children of Israel: 'The LORD God of your fathers, the God of Abraham, the God of Isaac, and the God of Jacob, has sent me to you. This *is* My name forever, and this *is* My memorial to all generations.' [16]Go and gather the elders of Israel together, and say to them, 'The LORD God of your fathers, the God of

2:22 [a]Literally *Stranger There*

2:22 Gershom has the consonants *g-r-sh-m*, of the verb "drove them away" (see v. 17). It also sounds like "stranger" (Heb. *ger*) "there" (Heb. *sham*). Moses chose the name to commemorate his experience as a "stranger in a foreign land." Egypt was not his true home, nor was Midian, away from his people (Gen. 15:13; Ex. 22:21; Acts 7:29).

2:24 God remembered His covenant. God had promised that the descendants of Abraham, Isaac, and Jacob would become a nation and possess the land of Canaan. He "remembered" the covenant in the sense that He acted upon it (see Ex. 20:8; Lev. 26:42; Num. 15:39). Verses 23–25 provide the background for the encounter that begins in chapter 3.

3:1 Also called Mount Sinai, the exact location of Horeb in the Sinai peninsula is uncertain. It is called "the mountain of God" in view of the later events that distinguished it. The "back" of the desert is its western portion, since directions were given as if facing east.

3:11, 12 Questions about Moses' identity highlight the central issue of the Lord's identity (see also Ex. 2:14; 4:10; 16:8). Moses asked a question about himself and his ability (v. 11).

and received an answer about God (v. 12). God was sending him and would provide divine enablement. The sign, given as a pledge of certitude, introduces the important theme of worship. The last "you" in verse 12 is plural, referring not just to Moses. The Israelites would "serve" the Lord instead of Pharaoh. The sign was fulfilled (Ex. 18:5–12; 24:1–11; 34:1–8).

3:13–15 The declaration I AM is preceded by wordplay connecting God's name with the verb "to be" (Heb. *hayah*). "I will be with you" (or "I AM with you," v. 12) ties the promise of His effective presence to His very being. The same form is used to declare, "I AM WHO I AM" (v. 14). And Moses was to use this verb in place of God's name to tell the Israelites, "I AM has sent me" (v. 14). In a later pronouncement of judgment, the Lord used this verb form to say literally, "You are not My people, and I am not I AM to you" (Hos. 1:9—2:1). God's beneficial presence in sending and aiding Moses is tied to God's essential being as independent and self-existent and therefore fully able to keep promises and be so known forever. This section begins a pattern prominent in the book of associating what God does with His name.

JOCHEBED   *A Resourceful Mother*

Moses introduced his mother as "a daughter of Levi" (Ex. 2:1). As he penned his nation's early history, he was careful to identify her family heritage. Jochebed's husband was placed into a mental slot that the Hebrew mind later labeled "priestly," but until the lifetime of Amram and Jochebed, the name Levi connoted violence and revenge (see Gen. 34:25–31; 49:3–7).

Often Hebrew thinking equated wealth with sons and daughters, the promise of God to Abraham (Gen. 12:2). Note the initiatives of this Levite mother. She "conceived . . . bore a son . . . saw that he was . . . beautiful . . . took an ark . . . put the child in it" (Ex. 2:2, 3). These actions denote a fearless and focused woman of faith. Her motivation and its results are clarified by the writer to the Hebrews (see Heb. 11:23–27). She circumvented the edict to destroy her baby: to place him in the Nile River was the law (Ex. 1:22); to surround him with protection, including a watchful sister, was faith (Ex. 2:3, 4).

Western minds cannot comprehend the terror tactics of ancient pharaohs. Idolatrous and corrupt, they held nothing but contempt for the mysterious *Yahweh* of their Israelite underdogs. Hatred, hostility, and hard labor were facts of life. Yet one woman, acting as a caring and resourceful mother, soared above the evil around her. God saw her heart, heard her prayers, and intervened in her behalf. Her fame lives on through the lives of her remarkable children (Num. 26:59). God honored her steadfast purpose by using one of her sons to deliver the Hebrews from Egyptian servitude and by appointing her other son, Aaron, as High Priest. Her daughter Miriam became the leader of the Hebrew women, and Jochebed's entire tribal family was selected by God to lead the rituals of worship for His people.

Jochebed models for contemporary women an infectious courage to fear God instead of people and a firm faith in His promises and providences. The author of Hebrews records that Moses left Egypt, "not fearing the wrath of the king" (Heb. 11:27), and that his parents before him were "not afraid of the king's command" (v. 23). The important thing is not so much who you are but what you do to meet the challenges and responsibilities that come. Jochebed took her motherhood very seriously, nurturing her children in the Lord with conscientious devotion. Surely she must have been the chief influence unto God in the preparation of these children for the great tasks God gave to each in leading His people out of bondage.

See also Ex. 2:1–10; Num. 26:59; Heb. 11:23–29; notes on Motherhood (1 Sam. 1); Sanctity of Life (Gen. 9)

Abraham, of Isaac, and of Jacob, appeared to me, saying, "I have surely visited you and *seen* what is done to you in Egypt; [17]and I have said I will bring you up out of the affliction of Egypt to the land of the Canaanites and the Hittites and the Amorites and the Perizzites and the Hivites and the Jebusites, to a land flowing with milk and honey." '
[18]Then they will heed your voice; and you shall come, you and the elders of Israel, to the king of Egypt; and you shall say to him, 'The LORD God of the Hebrews has met with us; and now, please, let us go three days' journey into the wilderness, that we may sacrifice to the LORD our God.' [19]But I am sure that the king of Egypt will not let you go, no, not even by a mighty hand. [20]So I will stretch out My hand and strike Egypt with all My wonders which I will do in its midst; and after that he will let you go. [21]And I will give this people favor in the sight of the Egyptians; and it shall be, when

you go, that you shall not go empty-handed. [22]But every woman shall ask of her neighbor, namely, of her who dwells near her house, articles of silver, articles of gold, and clothing; and you shall put *them* on your sons and on your daughters. So you shall plunder the Egyptians."

Miraculous Signs for Pharaoh

4 Then Moses answered and said, "But suppose they will not believe me or listen to my voice; suppose they say, 'The LORD has not appeared to you.' "
[2]So the LORD said to him, "What *is* that in your hand?"

He said, "A rod."

[3]And He said, "Cast it on the ground." So he cast it on the ground, and it became a serpent; and Moses fled from it. [4]Then the LORD said to Moses, "Reach out your hand and take *it* by the tail" (and he reached out his hand and caught it,

---

3:18 Because the Lord had identified the Israelites as His people (vv. 7, 10) and had begun to act on their behalf, they could call Him "our God" and identify Him to Pharaoh as the God of the despised Hebrews. They were to be let go for the purpose of worshiping the Lord, in keeping with the sign given in verse 12 and contrary to Egyptian religion, in which the king, and not the Lord, was worshiped as a most important god. Subsequent bargaining between Pharaoh and

Moses may indicate that from the start they both understood the request to go "three days' journey" and "sacrifice to the LORD our God" as leading to complete departure and an end to Pharaoh's rule over the Israelites (Ex. 5:3, note; 8:25–28; 10:7–11, 24–26).

4:3, 4 To grasp the serpent by the tail, rather than immediately behind the head to avoid being bitten, required an exercise of faith (see Ex. 7:9–12, note).

and it became a rod in his hand), [5]"that they may believe that the LORD God of their fathers, the God of Abraham, the God of Isaac, and the God of Jacob, has appeared to you."

[6]Furthermore the LORD said to him, "Now put your hand in your bosom." And he put his hand in his bosom, and when he took it out, behold, his hand *was* leprous, like snow. [7]And He said, "Put your hand in your bosom again." So he put his hand in his bosom again, and drew it out of his bosom, and behold, it was restored like his *other* flesh. [8]"Then it will be, if they do not believe you, nor heed the message of the first sign, that they may believe the message of the latter sign. [9]And it shall be, if they do not believe even these two signs, or listen to your voice, that you shall take water from the river[a] and pour *it* on the dry *land.* The water which you take from the river will become blood on the dry *land.*"

[10]Then Moses said to the LORD, "O my Lord, I *am* not eloquent, neither before nor since You have spoken to Your servant; but I *am* slow of speech and slow of tongue."

[11]So the LORD said to him, "Who has made man's mouth? Or who makes the mute, the deaf, the seeing, or the blind? *Have* not I, the LORD? [12]Now therefore, go, and I will be with your mouth and teach you what you shall say."

[13]But he said, "O my Lord, please send by the hand of whomever *else* You may send."

[14]So the anger of the LORD was kindled against Moses, and He said: "Is not Aaron the Levite your brother? I know that he can speak well. And look, he is also coming out to meet you. When he sees you, he will be glad in his heart. [15]Now you shall speak to him and put the words in his mouth. And I will be with your mouth and with his mouth, and I will teach you what you shall do. [16]So he shall be your spokesman to the people. And he himself shall be as a mouth for you, and you shall be to him as God. [17]And you shall take this rod in your hand, with which you shall do the signs."

Moses Goes to Egypt

[18]So Moses went and returned to Jethro his father-in-law, and said to him, "Please let me go and return to my brethren who *are* in Egypt, and see whether they are still alive."

And Jethro said to Moses, "Go in peace."

[19]Now the LORD said to Moses in Midian, "Go, return to Egypt; for all the men who sought your life are dead." [20]Then Moses took his wife and his sons and set them on a donkey, and he returned to the land of Egypt. And Moses took the rod of God in his hand.

[21]And the LORD said to Moses, "When you go back to Egypt, see that you do all those wonders before Pharaoh which I have put in your hand. But I will harden his heart, so that he will not let the people go. [22]Then you shall say to Pharaoh, 'Thus says the LORD: "Israel *is* My son, My firstborn. [23]So I say to you, let My son go that he may serve Me. But if you refuse to let him go, indeed I will kill your son, your firstborn." ' "

[24]And it came to pass on the way, at the encampment, that the LORD met him and sought to kill him. [25]Then Zipporah took a sharp stone and cut off the foreskin of her son and cast *it* at Moses'[a] feet, and said, "Surely you *are* a husband of blood to me!" [26]So He let him go. Then she said, "*You are* a husband of blood!"—because of the circumcision.

[27]And the LORD said to Aaron, "Go into the wilderness to meet Moses." So he went and met him on the mountain of God, and kissed him. [28]So

---

4:9 [a]That is, the Nile   4:25 [a]Literally *his*

4:6 The sudden appearance and disappearance of disease would show the Lord's power over human life as well as animal life (see vv. 3, 4, serpent) and inanimate things (see v. 9, water).

4:9 The Nile was central to Egypt, with desert on both sides. The Nile provided transportation, as well as water for drinking, washing, and irrigating crops; and its regular floods deposited fertile soil on fields. To alter it indicated the power to destroy all Egyptian life.

4:10–12 Moses raised an objection focused on himself and received an answer focused on the Lord.

4:21 The heart is the center of internal life—involving intellect, emotion, and will—where moral choices are made, according to Hebrew (and Egyptian) symbolism (Gen. 6:5; Prov. 6:18; 18:15). Despite signs and wonders and Moses' attempts to persuade, Pharaoh rejected the Lord's sovereignty. The issue here is not Pharaoh's salvation but his continued rejection of the Lord. God chose to use this self-hardened, pagan monarch as a means to show His power. After each of the first five and the seventh miraculous signs, Pharaoh's heart is described as growing "hard" (Ex. 7:22; 8:15, 19, 32; 9:7, 34). After the sixth, eighth, ninth, and tenth plagues, the Lord hardened his heart (Ex. 9:12; 10:20, 27). Later the Philistines profited from Pharaoh's example (1 Sam. 6:6; 2 Chr. 34:27; see also Ex. 14, Justice).

4:22, 23 God's interest in the welfare of the Israelites is parallel to Pharaoh's interest in the welfare of his own privileged firstborn. Pharaoh saw the Israelites as slaves, but the Lord called Israel His son, calling to mind their covenant relationship. In ancient Near Eastern suzerain-vassal treaties, the sovereign overlord referred to his subordinate as his son, whom he promised to defend and whom he expected to serve him (see also 2 Sam. 7:12–16; John 1:12; Gal. 4:4–7; Eph. 1:5; 5:1; Rev. 21:7).

4:24–26 Circumcision had been commanded for Abraham's descendants as the sign of the covenant between God and Abraham (Gen. 17:9–14), the covenant God was now acting to fulfill (see chart, The Covenants of Genesis). Moses, who was being sent to represent God, had neglected an important part of that covenant.

ZIPPORAH *A Resistive Wife*

This daughter of Jethro, the Midianite priest, is mentioned because of her marriage to Moses. When Pharaoh sought to kill Moses, he retreated through the desert across what is now the Sinai peninsula into exile. He met Zipporah along the caravan route when he defended her and her sisters from ruffians at a well near her home.

Jethro extended hospitality to Moses and subsequently offered his daughter in marriage. Their first son was named Gershom, which contains a word for "alien," "stranger," commemorating Moses' status as a foreigner. Their second son was Eliezer, whose name means "my God is help," in memory of God's preserving Moses' life (Ex. 18:3, 4).

When Moses was confronted by the Lord with his disobedience in failing to circumcise his son (Gen. 17:14), his very life was in danger. Zipporah, therefore, had to circumcise her son, perhaps Eliezer, the second one, in order to save her husband's life (Ex. 4:24–26). She did so with evident disgust. The exact meaning of the incident and her words has long been debated.

At some point, Moses sent Zipporah and their sons back to stay with her father (Ex. 18:2, 3). Many months passed before she saw her husband again. The deliverance from Egypt had been accomplished, and as leader of his people, Moses brought them to Mount Horeb, in keeping with God's promise at the burning bush (see Ex. 3:12). There Jethro visited him, and the family was reunited. Zipporah may have died en route after she joined the procession toward the Promised Land, since nothing further is reported of her. The later reference to Moses' Ethiopian wife (see Num. 12:1) lends credence to this supposition. This wife was of Hamite descent, perhaps an Egyptian believer.

Zipporah remains an enigmatic woman. Her example reminds us that a wife resisting God's will not only endangers God's divine purposes but also places her family in spiritual jeopardy. Nevertheless, her quick and decisive action seemingly saved Moses' life.

See also Ex. 4:20–26; 18:2–6: notes on Husbands (Job 31); Motherhood (1 Sam. 1)

Moses told Aaron all the words of the LORD who had sent him, and all the signs which He had commanded him. ²⁹Then Moses and Aaron went and gathered together all the elders of the children of Israel. ³⁰And Aaron spoke all the words which the LORD had spoken to Moses. Then he did the signs in the sight of the people. ³¹So the people believed; and when they heard that the LORD had visited the children of Israel and that He had looked on their affliction, then they bowed their heads and worshiped.

First Encounter with Pharaoh

5 Afterward Moses and Aaron went in and told Pharaoh, "Thus says the LORD God of Israel: 'Let My people go, that they may hold a feast to Me in the wilderness.'"

²And Pharaoh said, "Who *is* the LORD, that I should obey His voice to let Israel go? I do not know the LORD, nor will I let Israel go."

³So they said, "The God of the Hebrews has met with us. Please, let us go three days' journey into the desert and sacrifice to the LORD our God, lest He fall upon us with pestilence or with the sword."

⁴Then the king of Egypt said to them, "Moses and Aaron, why do you take the people from their work? Get *back* to your labor." ⁵And Pharaoh said,

"Look, the people of the land *are* many now, and you make them rest from their labor!"

⁶So the same day Pharaoh commanded the taskmasters of the people and their officers, saying, "'You shall no longer give the people straw to make brick as before. Let them go and gather straw for themselves. ⁸And you shall lay on them the quota of bricks which they made before. You shall not reduce it. For they are idle; therefore they cry out, saying, 'Let us go *and* sacrifice to our God.' ⁹Let more work be laid on the men, that they may labor in it, and let them not regard false words."

¹⁰And the taskmasters of the people and their officers went out and spoke to the people, saying, "Thus says Pharaoh: 'I will not give you straw. ¹¹Go, get yourselves straw where you can find it; yet none of your work will be reduced.'" ¹²So the people were scattered abroad throughout all the land of Egypt to gather stubble instead of straw. ¹³And the taskmasters forced *them* to hurry, saying, "Fulfill your work, *your* daily quota, as when there was straw." ¹⁴Also the officers of the children of Israel, whom Pharaoh's taskmasters had set over them, were beaten *and* were asked, "Why have you not fulfilled your task in making brick both yesterday and today, as before?"

5:3 Let us go and sacrifice. Egyptian records indicate that Moses' request may have been unusual. Other workers made such pilgrimages. Pharaoh's refusal shows that he intended no easing of Israelite servitude, and worse, that he had no regard for the Lord. "Pestilence" and "sword" speak of divine judgment, such as Egypt experienced in the ten plagues and such as Israel received at various times (Deut. 28:15–68).

Worry is most often a prideful way of thinking that you have more control over life and its circumstances than you actually do.

June Hunt

---

¹⁵Then the officers of the children of Israel came and cried out to Pharaoh, saying, "Why are you dealing thus with your servants? ¹⁶There is no straw given to your servants, and they say to us, 'Make brick!' And indeed your servants *are* beaten, but the fault *is* in your *own* people."

¹⁷But he said, "You *are* idle! Idle! Therefore you say, 'Let us go *and* sacrifice to the LORD.' ¹⁸Therefore go now *and* work; for no straw shall be given you, yet you shall deliver the quota of bricks." ¹⁹And the officers of the children of Israel saw *that* they *were* in trouble after it was said, "You shall not reduce *any* bricks from your daily quota."

²⁰Then, as they came out from Pharaoh, they met Moses and Aaron who stood there to meet them. ²¹And they said to them, "Let the LORD look on you and judge, because you have made us abhorrent in the sight of Pharaoh and in the sight of his servants, to put a sword in their hand to kill us."

Israel's Deliverance Assured

²²So Moses returned to the LORD and said, "Lord, why have You brought trouble on this people? Why *is* it You have sent me? ²³For since I came to Pharaoh to speak in Your name, he has done evil to this people; neither have You delivered Your people at all."

6 Then the LORD said to Moses, "Now you shall see what I will do to Pharaoh. For with a strong hand he will let them go, and with a strong hand he will drive them out of his land."

²And God spoke to Moses and said to him: "I *am* the LORD. ³I appeared to Abraham, to Isaac, and to Jacob, as God Almighty, but *by* My name LORDª I was not known to them. ⁴I have also established My covenant with them, to give them the land of Canaan, the land of their pilgrimage, in which they were strangers. ⁵And I have also heard the groaning of the children of Israel whom the Egyptians keep in bondage, and I have remembered My covenant. ⁶Therefore say to the children of Israel: 'I *am* the LORD; I will bring you out from under the burdens of the Egyptians, I will rescue you from their bondage, and I will redeem you with an outstretched arm and with great judgments. ⁷I will take you as My people, and I will be your God. Then you shall know that I *am* the LORD your God who brings you out from under the burdens of the Egyptians. ⁸And I will bring you into the land which I swore to give to Abraham, Isaac, and Jacob; and I will give it to you *as* a heritage: I *am* the

· · · · · · · · · · · · · · · ·

6:3 ªHebrew *YHWH*, traditionally *Jehovah*

5:23 For Moses to speak in the Lord's name meant that the Lord's authority and reputation were at stake. The mention of His name continues to highlight the theme of the Lord's identity (see Ex. 3:6, 13–15; 4:11; 5:2; 6:2–8).

6:2–8 I am the LORD. Again when Moses raised a problem, the Lord answered with statements about Himself. The declaration "I am the LORD" is in a form used by ancient Near Eastern kings. It brackets the section (vv. 2, 8) and appears in verses 6 and 7 as its central subject. When God promised Abraham that his descendants would come out of Egypt, He used this declaration (Gen. 15:7). It stands at the start of the covenant Law (Ex. 20:2) and frequently is found in Leviticus as the fundamental reason for the stipulations and for obedience to them. Here again the name *Yahweh* is associated with the character of God as one who keeps promises (as in Ex. 3:15–17). His covenant-keeping actions and His laws are grounded in His essence, who He is. The name *El Shaddai*, usually rendered God Almighty, is tied etymologically by some to an Akkadian word for "mountain." More importantly, it is tied by usage to promises of fruitfulness (Gen. 17:1–2; 28:3; 35:11; 48:3–4; 49:25). This was an important aspect of God's dealings with the patriarchs. In verse 3 God was not saying that His name *Yahweh*, or LORD, was previously unknown or unused (Gen. 4:26; 14:22; 15:2–7; 28:13). The Lord explained that the Israelites would know Him as *Yahweh* by means of what He would do (Ex. 6:6–8). The word translated "know"

carries here the idea of "know by experience and personal involvement" (see Gen. 4:1; Ex. 33:12, 17; Ps. 9:10; Jer. 16:21). The events in the Book of Exodus gave new meaning to the name *Yahweh*. By contrast Moses referred to other gods as gods that the Israelites had not known (Deut. 13:2, 6, 13).

6:6 I will redeem you. The actions of a kinsman-redeemer in Israel illustrate what God would do (see Ruth 2:20, note). The human redeemer was a close relative who paid to free a destitute man from slavery and restore his inheritance (his means of making a living) or who perpetuated his name by marrying his widow and having a son for him (Lev. 25:25, 47–49; Deut. 25:5–10; Ruth 3—4). The Lord would similarly free from slavery, give land, and guarantee the perpetuation of Israel (see also Ps. 77:14, 15; Is. 43:1–7; Eph. 1:7, 14).

6:7 I will take you as My people. Beginning here and frequently in Exodus, God announced that He would act so that someone (the Israelites, the Egyptians, Pharaoh, later generations) would know that He is the LORD (see vv. 6, 7; Ex. 7:5, 17; 10:2; 16:6, 12; 29:45, 46). By His actions, the LORD was making known His personal character and His relationship with Israel. The Israelites would know who He is, and they themselves would acquire an identity as His people. Christians similarly find their identity as God's people because of what the Lord has done for them (see Acts 15:14; 2 Cor. 6:16; 1 Pet. 2:10).

LORD.'" [9]So Moses spoke thus to the children of Israel; but they did not heed Moses, because of anguish of spirit and cruel bondage.

[10]And the LORD spoke to Moses, saying, [11]"Go in, tell Pharaoh king of Egypt to let the children of Israel go out of his land."

[12]And Moses spoke before the LORD, saying, "The children of Israel have not heeded me. How then shall Pharaoh heed me, for I *am* of uncircumcised lips?"

[13]Then the LORD spoke to Moses and Aaron, and gave them a command for the children of Israel and for Pharaoh king of Egypt, to bring the children of Israel out of the land of Egypt.

The Family of Moses and Aaron

[14]These *are* the heads of their fathers' houses: The sons of Reuben, the firstborn of Israel, *were* Hanoch, Pallu, Hezron, and Carmi. These are the families of Reuben. [15]And the sons of Simeon *were* Jemuel,[a] Jamin, Ohad, Jachin, Zohar, and Shaul the son of a Canaanite woman. These *are* the families of Simeon. [16]These *are* the names of the sons of Levi according to their generations: Gershon, Kohath, and Merari. And the years of the life of Levi *were* one hundred and thirty-seven. [17]The sons of Gershon *were* Libni and Shimi according to their families. [18]And the sons of Kohath *were* Amram, Izhar, Hebron, and Uzziel. And the years of the life of Kohath *were* one hundred and thirty-three. [19]The sons of Merari *were* Mahli and Mushi. These *are* the families of Levi according to their generations.

[20]Now Amram took for himself Jochebed, his father's sister, as wife; and she bore him Aaron and Moses. And the years of the life of Amram *were* one hundred and thirty-seven. [21]The sons of Izhar *were* Korah, Nepheg, and Zichri. [22]And the sons of Uzziel *were* Mishael, Elzaphan, and Zithri. [23]Aaron took to himself Elisheba, daughter of Amminadab, sister of Nahshon, as wife; and she bore him Nadab, Abihu, Elemazar, and Ithamar. [24]And the sons of Korah *were* Assir, Elkanah, and Abiasaph. These are the families of the Korahites.

[25]Eleazar, Aaron's son, took for himself one of the daughters of Putiel as wife; and she bore him Phinehas. These *are* the heads of the fathers' houses of the Levites according to their families.

[26]These *are the same* Aaron and Moses to whom the LORD said, "Bring out the children of Israel from the land of Egypt according to their armies." [27]These *are* the ones who spoke to Pharaoh king of Egypt, to bring out the children of Israel from Egypt. These *are the same* Moses and Aaron.

Aaron Is Moses' Spokesman

[28]And it came to pass, on the day the LORD spoke to Moses in the land of Egypt, [29]that the LORD spoke to Moses, saying, "I *am* the LORD. Speak to Pharaoh king of Egypt all that I say to you."

[30]But Moses said before the LORD, "Behold, I *am* of uncircumcised lips, and how shall Pharaoh heed me?"

7 So the LORD said to Moses: "See, I have made you *as* God to Pharaoh, and Aaron your brother shall be your prophet. [2]You shall speak all that I command you. And Aaron your brother shall tell Pharaoh to send the children of Israel out of his land. [3]And I will harden Pharaoh's heart, and multiply My signs and My wonders in the land of Egypt. [4]But Pharaoh will not heed you, so that I may lay My hand on Egypt and bring My armies *and* My people, the children of Israel, out of the land of Egypt by great judgments. [5]And the Egyptians shall know that I *am* the LORD, when I stretch out My hand on Egypt and bring out the children of Israel from among them."

[6]Then Moses and Aaron did *so;* just as the LORD commanded them, so they did. [7]And Moses *was* eighty years old and Aaron eighty-three years old when they spoke to Pharaoh.

Aaron's Miraculous Rod

[8]Then the LORD spoke to Moses and Aaron, saying, [9]"When Pharaoh speaks to you, saying, 'Show

••••••••••••••••••
6:15 [a]Spelled *Nemuel* in Numbers 26:12

6:9 They did not heed. Events in the first 17 chapters of Exodus demonstrate repeatedly that obedience to the Lord does not necessarily lead to immediate ease. The Israelites had been and were still miserable. Their unbelief and rejection of Moses were based on their feelings in the present circumstances rather than on the facts of who the Lord is and what He would do (see also 2 Pet. 3:3–13).

6:14–27 A selective genealogy comes in the middle of the account of God's renewed command to Moses. It focuses on the tribe of Levi (vv. 16–25), mentioning three important generations before Moses and Aaron, and ends with attention on Aaron's son Eleazar and grandson Phinehas (v. 25), all well known to the first audience of the book (see Ex. 28:1; Num. 3—4; 25:6–15; 26:9–11). The section prepares for the following events by formally identifying Moses and Aaron, remind-

ing readers of who they were and what came of them in Israel. It especially authenticates Aaron, earlier identified only as Moses' brother (Ex. 4:14), which could otherwise have meant merely kinsman (as in Ex. 4:18) rather than brother. As verses 26 and 27 stress, God sent to Pharaoh these men who were hesitant and badly received by Pharaoh and often by the Israelites, and through them God permanently altered Israel's history.

7:6 Many similar statements stress complete obedience to the Lord's command (for example, vv. 10, 20; Ex. 12:28, 50; 16:34; 39:1, 5). Obedience is of primary concern rather than the skill of the messenger or the response of the recipient.

7:9–12 Serpents were feared and worshiped in Egypt. Since the image of a cobra was a royal symbol, appearing on the

THE GODDESSES OF EGYPT

NAME	RESPONSIBILITY	FORM ASSUMED
Edjo	Goddess of Delta/Lower Egypt	Serpent
Hathor	Theban deity; Goddess of love, beauty, and joy	Cow-headed human figure; cow horns
Heket	Goddess of fertility; Primordial goddess	Frog
Heqt	Wife of Khnum; Symbol of resurrection and fertility	Serpent-headed
Isis	Daughter of Geb; Mother of Horus; Consort and sister of Osiris; Goddess of life and healing	Human
Maat	Daughter of Ra; Goddess of Justice	Human
Meskhenet	Goddess protector of newborns and of destiny	Vulture or human
Mut	Consort of Amon-Re; Mother of Khons	
Nekhbet	Goddess of Upper Egypt	
Nut	Consort of Geb; Mother of Osiris and Seth; Mother of heavenly bodies; Sky goddess	
Sekhmet	Goddess of war and sickness	Lion-headed
Seshat	Goddess of writing and books	
Thermuthis	Goddess of fate; Goddess of fertility and harvest	Serpent
Thoueris	Goddess of fertility and women in labor	Hippopotamus

a miracle for yourselves,' then you shall say to Aaron, 'Take your rod and cast *it* before Pharaoh, *and* let it become a serpent.'" [10]So Moses and Aaron went in to Pharaoh, and they did so, just as the LORD commanded. And Aaron cast down his rod before Pharaoh and before his servants, and it became a serpent.

[11]But Pharaoh also called the wise men and the sorcerers; so the magicians of Egypt, they also did in like manner with their enchantments. [12]For

---

front of the headdress of the pharaohs, the use of a serpent as a first sign was sure to attract the king's close attention. His men controlled serpents, which people ordinarily feared. This symbolized his power. But the Lord and His men were greater; Aaron's rod ate the rods of the magicians. Magic, fortune-telling, astrology, reading of omens, witchcraft, and necromancy were prevalent throughout the ancient Near East as people attempted to influence events and gods, whose dispositions were uncertain (see Deut. 18, The Occult; 1 Sam. 15, Witchcraft). Here and elsewhere God taught His people the folly of such practices in view of His proven and dependable concern for them.

7:11 Professional wise men served in the king's court to provide advice. Egypt's international reputation for having outstanding wise men is preserved both by extrabiblical collections of Egyptian proverbs and instructions and by biblical references (1 Kin. 4:30; Is. 19:11, 12). The wise men and sorcerers are referred to as a group by the word translated "magicians," which refers to a variety of religious functionaries who were skilled readers and copyists expected to work wonders and interpret dreams (Gen. 41:8, 24). They used "enchantments"—elaborate incantations and secret spells—to produce their results. Moses and Aaron did not work this way.

every man threw down his rod, and they became serpents. But Aaron's rod swallowed up their rods. [13]And Pharaoh's heart grew hard, and he did not heed them, as the LORD had said.

The First Plague: Waters Become Blood

[14]So the LORD said to Moses: "Pharaoh's heart *is* hard; he refuses to let the people go. [15]Go to Pharaoh in the morning, when he goes out to the water, and you shall stand by the river's bank to meet him; and the rod which was turned to a serpent you shall take in your hand. [16]And you shall say to him, 'The LORD God of the Hebrews has sent me to you, saying, "Let My people go, that they may serve Me in the wilderness"; but indeed, until now you would not hear! [17]Thus says the LORD: "By this you shall know that I *am* the LORD. Behold, I will strike the waters which *are* in the river with the rod that *is* in my hand, and they shall be turned to blood. [18]And the fish that *are* in the river shall die, the river shall stink, and the Egyptians will loathe to drink the water of the river." ' "

[19]Then the LORD spoke to Moses, "Say to Aaron, 'Take your rod and stretch out your hand over the waters of Egypt, over their streams, over their rivers, over their ponds, and over all their pools of water, that they may become blood. And there shall be blood throughout all the land of Egypt, both in *buckets of* wood and *pitchers of* stone.' " [20]And Moses and Aaron did so, just as the LORD commanded. So he lifted up the rod and struck the waters that *were* in the river, in the sight of Pharaoh and in the sight of his servants. And all the waters that *were* in the river were turned to blood. [21]The fish that *were* in the river died, the river stank, and the Egyptians could not drink the water of the river. So there was blood throughout all the land of Egypt.

[22]Then the magicians of Egypt did so with their enchantments; and Pharaoh's heart grew hard, and he did not heed them, as the LORD had said. [23]And Pharaoh turned and went into his house. Neither was his heart moved by this. [24]So all the Egyptians dug all around the river for water to drink, because they could not drink the water of the river. [25]And seven days passed after the LORD had struck the river.

The Second Plague: Frogs

8 And the LORD spoke to Moses, "Go to Pharaoh and say to him, 'Thus says the LORD: "Let My people go, that they may serve Me. [2]But if you refuse to let *them* go, behold, I will smite all your territory with frogs. [3]So the river shall bring forth frogs abundantly, which shall go up and come into your house, into your bedroom, on your bed, into the houses of your servants, on your people, into your ovens, and into your kneading bowls. [4]And the frogs shall come up on you, on your people, and on all your servants." ' "

[5]Then the LORD spoke to Moses, "Say to Aaron, 'Stretch out your hand with your rod over the streams, over the rivers, and over the ponds, and cause frogs to come up on the land of Egypt.' " [6]So Aaron stretched out his hand over the waters of Egypt, and the frogs came up and covered the land of Egypt. [7]And the magicians did so with their enchantments, and brought up frogs on the land of Egypt.

[8]Then Pharaoh called for Moses and Aaron, and said, "Entreat the LORD that He may take away the frogs from me and from my people; and I will let the people go, that they may sacrifice to the LORD." [9]And Moses said to Pharaoh, "Accept the honor of saying when I shall intercede for you, for your servants, and for your people, to destroy the frogs from you and your houses, *that* they may remain in the river only." [10]So he said, "Tomorrow." And he said, "*Let it be* according to your word, that you may know that

7:14 The supernatural source of these plagues is apparent (see chart, The Ten Plagues on Egypt). The plagues were controlled with regard to:

• timing, with an announcement of the start and finish;
• extent, with the sparing of the Israelite region; and
• intensity, with the gradual increase in severity.

Pharaoh's servants and even Pharaoh himself, at times, recognized and confessed that the Lord had acted. In addition, the plagues not only attacked Egyptian polytheism but also explicitly demonstrated that the Lord was sovereign over Egypt and personally involved in delivering His people.

7:14–25 The first plague: blood. This plague, like the following ones, attacked the Egyptian gods. The Nile was central to Egyptian life (see Ex. 4:9, note). Numerous Egyptian gods were associated with the river, including the pharaohs, who were thought to control the Nile. The Lord, however, ruled the Nile and all water connected to it. What the Egyptians regarded as their source of life the Lord turned into a river of

death. The Egyptian magicians might imitate the plague, but neither they nor Pharaoh could reverse it in order to protect their people. They just made the plague worse. Turning the Nile to blood served also as a punishment for its use in killing Israelite babies.

8:1–13 The second plague: frogs. Frogs were venerated in Egypt because they were associated with fertility. But the Lord, the true giver of fruitfulness (see Gen. 1:20; Ex. 1:7), turned what had been revered into a cause for disgust. This plague may also be an ironic punishment directed at Egyptian attempts to prevent the increase of God's people (see chart, The Ten Plagues on Egypt). In each statement of Moses, the pronoun "you" or "your" is prominent, emphasizing the impact of the plague on Pharaoh, who was unable to protect his person, property, or people. Again the magicians made the plague worse by their imitation. As further evidence of the Lord's uniqueness, Moses permitted Pharaoh to say when he would like the plague to end (v. 10; Ex. 7:14, note).

THE TEN PLAGUES ON EGYPT

THE PLAGUE ON THE PEOPLE	THE EFFECT ON PHARAOH
1. The waters of the Nile were turned to blood (Ex. 7:14–25).	1. His heart "grew hard" (Ex. 7:22).
2. Frogs spread through the land of Egypt (Ex. 8:1–15).	2. He asked for relief, promised freedom (Ex. 8:8), then "hardened his heart" (Ex. 8:15).
3. Lice infested the land (Ex. 8:16–19).	3. His heart "grew hard" (Ex. 8:19).
4. Flies swarmed throughout the land (Ex. 8:20–32).	4. He bargained (Ex. 8:28), then "hardened his heart" (Ex. 8:32).
5. The livestock were stricken with disease (Ex. 9:1–7).	5. His heart "became hard" (Ex. 9:7).
6. Boils infected the Egyptians (Ex. 9:8–12).	6. The Lord "hardened" Pharaoh's heart (Ex. 9:12).
7. A hail storm destroyed the Egyptian fields but did not touch the land of Goshen (Ex. 9:13–35).	7. He begged for relief (Ex. 9:27), promised freedom (Ex. 9:28), but his heart "was hard" (Ex. 9:35).
8. Hordes of locusts infested the land (Ex. 10:1–20).	8. He bargained (Ex. 10:11), begged relief (Ex. 10:17), but "the Lord hardened Pharaoh's heart" (Ex. 10:20).
9. Darkness covered the land (Ex. 10:21–29).	9. He bargained (Ex. 10:24), but "the Lord hardened Pharaoh's heart" (Ex. 10:27).
10. The firstborn in every Egyptian family died (Ex. 12:29, 30).	10. Pharaoh and the Egyptians begged Israel to leave Egypt (Ex. 12:31–33).

See also note on Justice (Ex. 14).

there is no one like the Lord our God. ¹¹And the frogs shall depart from you, from your houses, from your servants, and from your people. They shall remain in the river only."

¹²Then Moses and Aaron went out from Pharaoh. And Moses cried out to the Lord concerning the frogs which He had brought against Pharaoh. ¹³So the Lord did according to the word of Moses. And the frogs died out of the houses, out of the courtyards, and out of the fields. ¹⁴They gathered them together in heaps, and the land stank. ¹⁵But when Pharaoh saw that there was relief, he hardened his heart and did not heed them, as the Lord had said.

The Third Plague: Lice

¹⁶So the Lord said to Moses, "Say to Aaron, 'Stretch out your rod, and strike the dust of the land, so that it may become lice throughout all the land of Egypt.'" ¹⁷And they did so. For Aaron stretched out his hand with his rod and struck the dust of the earth, and it became lice on man and beast. All the dust of the land became lice throughout all the land of Egypt.

¹⁸Now the magicians so worked with their enchantments to bring forth lice, but they could not. So there were lice on man and beast. ¹⁹Then the magicians said to Pharaoh, "This *is* the finger of

8:16–19 The third plague: lice. Translators have long debated the exact meaning of the term translated "lice," and some ancient renderings understood it to mean stinging "gnats." For this third plague, as with the sixth and ninth, Pharaoh received no warning (see chart, The Ten Plagues on Egypt). His magicians were unable to imitate it, and they correctly understood that God had sent it. Now Pharaoh rejected the warning of his own advisers.

God." But Pharaoh's heart grew hard, and he did not heed them, just as the LORD had said.

The Fourth Plague: Flies

²⁰And the LORD said to Moses, "Rise early in the morning and stand before Pharaoh as he comes out to the water. Then say to him, 'Thus says the LORD: "Let My people go, that they may serve Me. ²¹Or else, if you will not let My people go, behold, I will send swarms *of flies* on you and your servants, on your people and into your houses. The houses of the Egyptians shall be full of swarms *of flies*, and also the ground on which they *stand.* ²²And in that day I will set apart the land of Goshen, in which My people dwell, that no swarms *of flies* shall be there, in order that you may know that I *am* the LORD in the midst of the land. ²³I will make a difference[a] between My people and your people. Tomorrow this sign shall be." ' " ²⁴And the LORD did so. Thick swarms *of flies* came into the house of Pharaoh, *into* his servants' houses, and into all the land of Egypt. The land was corrupted because of the swarms *of flies.*

²⁵Then Pharaoh called for Moses and Aaron, and said, "Go, sacrifice to your God in the land."

²⁶And Moses said, "It is not right to do so, for we would be sacrificing the abomination of the Egyptians to the LORD our God. If we sacrifice the abomination of the Egyptians before their eyes, then will they not stone us? ²⁷We will go three days' journey into the wilderness and sacrifice to the LORD our God as He will command us."

²⁸So Pharaoh said, "I will let you go, that you may sacrifice to the LORD your God in the wilderness; only you shall not go very far away. Intercede for me."

²⁹Then Moses said, "Indeed I am going out from you, and I will entreat the LORD, that the swarms *of flies* may depart tomorrow from Pharaoh, from his servants, and from his people.

But let Pharaoh not deal deceitfully anymore in not letting the people go to sacrifice to the LORD."

³⁰So Moses went out from Pharaoh and entreated the LORD. ³¹And the LORD did according to the word of Moses; He removed the swarms *of flies* from Pharaoh, from his servants, and from his people. Not one remained. ³²But Pharaoh hardened his heart at this time also; neither would he let the people go.

The Fifth Plague: Livestock Diseased

9 Then the Lord said to Moses, "Go in to Pharaoh and tell him, 'Thus says the LORD God of the Hebrews: "Let My people go, that they may serve Me. ²For if you refuse to let *them* go, and still hold them, ³behold, the hand of the LORD will be on your cattle in the field, on the horses, on the donkeys, on the camels, on the oxen, and on the sheep—a very severe pestilence. ⁴And the LORD will make a difference between the livestock of Israel and the livestock of Egypt. So nothing shall die of all *that* belongs to the children of Israel." ' " ⁵Then the LORD appointed a set time, saying, "Tomorrow the LORD will do this thing in the land."

⁶So the LORD did this thing on the next day, and all the livestock of Egypt died; but of the livestock of the children of Israel, not one died. ⁷Then Pharaoh sent, and indeed, not even one of the livestock of the Israelites was dead. But the heart of Pharaoh became hard, and he did not let the people go.

The Sixth Plague: Boils

⁸So the LORD said to Moses and Aaron, "Take for yourselves handfuls of ashes from a furnace, and let Moses scatter it toward the heavens in the sight of Pharaoh. ⁹And it will become fine dust in all the land of Egypt, and it will cause boils that break out in sores on man and beast throughout all the land

8:23 ªLiterally *set a ransom* (compare Exodus 9:4 and 11:7)

8:20–32 The fourth plague: swarms of flies. This time as a sign that the Lord is sovereign even in Egypt, He would distinguish His people. The flies would not afflict their region (Ex. 7:14, note; chart, The Ten Plagues on Egypt). Pharaoh bargained with Moses, telling him first that the Israelites could sacrifice within the land, then in the wilderness but not far away. Again, the end of the plague came in response to intercession by Moses.

9:1–7 The fifth plague: disease. In the preceding negotiations (Ex. 8:25–29) the word "sacrifice" is prominent, and again Pharaoh failed to permit the Israelites to go and sacrifice to the Lord. As a result disease struck Egyptian livestock at the appointed time, while Israelite animals were preserved (mentioned three times). Previous plagues were noisome and painful; this was the first that caused loss of personal property (see chart, The Ten Plagues on Egypt). Valuable animals used in transportation and farming, as well as animals the Egyptians considered sacred, died.

9:6 If all the livestock of Egypt were killed by disease, how is it that Egyptian livestock were there to be killed by the later plague of hail (vv. 19–25) and horses were available to pull the chariots (Ex. 14:9)? It may be that the disease struck only animals "in the field" (v. 3). The passage of time between plagues may also have allowed the Egyptians to acquire new animals. It may also be that "all the livestock" (v. 6) is to be understood similarly to "all the dust of the land" (Ex. 8:17), the force of the expression being that the effect was thorough and pervasive.

9:8–12 The sixth plague: boils. Now the Egyptians, including the magicians, had firsthand experience with the Lord's power over the physical health of both people and animals. Like the third plague, no verbal announcement or warning preceded this plague, but, as on other occasions, a dramatic enactment marked its start (see chart, The Ten Plagues on Egypt).

You are she who is not, and I am Who is.

St. Catherine of Siena

of Egypt." [10]Then they took ashes from the furnace and stood before Pharaoh, and Moses scattered *them* toward heaven. And *they* caused boils that break out in sores on man and beast. [11]And the magicians could not stand before Moses because of the boils, for the boils were on the magicians and on all the Egyptians. [12]But the LORD hardened the heart of Pharaoh; and he did not heed them, just as the LORD had spoken to Moses.

The Seventh Plague: Hail

[13]Then the LORD said to Moses, "Rise early in the morning and stand before Pharaoh, and say to him, 'Thus says the LORD God of the Hebrews: "Let My people go, that they may serve Me, [14]for at this time I will send all My plagues to your very heart, and on your servants and on your people, that you may know that *there is* none like Me in all the earth. [15]Now if I had stretched out My hand and struck you and your people with pestilence, then you would have been cut off from the earth. [16]But indeed for this *purpose* I have raised you up, that I may show My power *in* you, and that My name may be declared in all the earth. [17]As yet you exalt yourself against My people in that you will not let them go. [18]Behold, tomorrow about this time I will cause very heavy hail to rain down, such as has not been in Egypt since its founding until now. [19]Therefore send now *and* gather your livestock and all that you have in the field, for the hail shall come down on every man and every animal which is found in the field and is not brought home; and they shall die." ' "

[20]He who feared the word of the LORD among the servants of Pharaoh made his servants and his livestock flee to the houses. [21]But he who did not regard the word of the LORD left his servants and his livestock in the field.

[22]Then the LORD said to Moses, "Stretch out your hand toward heaven, that there may be hail in all the land of Egypt— on man, on beast, and on every herb of the field, throughout the land of Egypt." [23]And Moses stretched out his rod toward heaven; and the LORD sent thunder and hail, and fire darted to the ground. And the LORD rained hail on the land of Egypt. [24]So there was hail, and fire mingled with the hail, so very heavy that there was none like it in all the land of Egypt since it became a nation. [25]And the hail struck throughout the whole land of Egypt, all that *was* in the field, both man and beast; and the hail struck every herb of the field and broke every tree of the field. [26]Only in the land of Goshen, where the children of Israel *were,* there was no hail.

[27]And Pharaoh sent and called for Moses and Aaron, and said to them, "I have sinned this time. The LORD *is* righteous, and my people and I *are* wicked. [28]Entreat the LORD, that there may be no *more* mighty thundering and hail, for *it is* enough. I will let you go, and you shall stay no longer."

[29]So Moses said to him, "As soon as I have gone out of the city, I will spread out my hands to the LORD; the thunder will cease, and there will be no more hail, that you may know that the earth *is* the LORD's. [30]But as for you and your servants, I know that you will not yet fear the LORD God."

[31]Now the flax and the barley were struck, for the barley *was* in the head and the flax *was* in bud. [32]But the wheat and the spelt were not struck, for they *are* late crops.

[33]So Moses went out of the city from Pharaoh and spread out his hands to the LORD; then the thunder and the hail ceased, and the rain was not poured on the earth. [34]And when Pharaoh saw that the rain, the hail, and the thunder had ceased, he sinned yet more; and he hardened his heart, he

9:13–35 The seventh plague: hail. As the series of plagues intensified, now for the first time human life was at stake. The Lord warned the Egyptians to protect their servants and animals. God did not owe Pharaoh anything and could have destroyed him at any time (v. 15). Pharaoh's continued existence was an opportunity for the Lord to show His uniqueness and His power (v. 14), so that His name (character and reputation) would be declared (v. 16). The God whom Pharaoh had said he did not know and would not obey would be recognized worldwide (Ex. 5:2). As a further result of the plague of hail, Pharaoh should understand that the earth belongs to the Lord to rule (v. 29; see chart, The Ten Plagues on Egypt). Certainly none of the Egyptians' many gods protected them (see chart, The Goddesses of Egypt). For the first time, Pharaoh admitted he was wrong and promised without reservation to

let the Israelites go to serve the Lord (vv. 27, 28), but Moses knew Pharaoh did not yet intend to obey the Lord (v. 30; see also Ex. 14, Justice). Again Pharaoh rebelled as soon as the storm ended (vv. 34, 35).

9:19–21 The plagues were having their proper effect in the lives of some Egyptians. They respected the Lord's command and brought their servants and animals under cover. The phrase "did not regard the word of the LORD" can be literally rendered "did not put his heart to the word of the LORD." For these people, the plagues directed toward their hearts met resistance rather than obedience (see vv. 14, 34). This experience of warning and response needed to be a lesson for the Israelites when they received instructions before the tenth plague, as well as anytime the Lord later spoke.

CELEBRATIONS AND HOLIDAYS *SET APART TO REMEMBER*

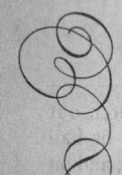 One of the problems with a finite created being having a relationship with the infinite Creator God is the tendency for the one created to lose perspective on her life, forgetting what God has done for her in the past. Knowing this, God reminds us in His Word to remember who He is and what He has done. Thus, throughout the Old Testament, feasts and festivals were established, accompanied by carefully planned rituals—as well as authorized memorials of stones and altars to be built across the wilderness of Bible lands.

In the New Testament, Jesus instructed His disciples to eat and drink the Lord's Supper in remembrance of Him (Luke 22:19). Thus, a key characteristic of celebrations and holy days is that they be times set apart to remember specific works of the Lord God.

Often, modern holidays are little more than occasions for family gatherings or days off work. As Christians, we can bring the Lord back into these holidays and celebrations by focusing on Him in unique ways:

- New Year's may be set aside as a time for spiritual renewal.
- Valentine's Day might be a time to focus on the unconditional love of our Savior Jesus Christ.
- Easter can be a time to share a personal testimony about the difference the risen Christ has made in your life.
- Spring can be a time to reflect on fruitfulness and growth in the Christian life.
- Thanksgiving is a time to thank the Lord in special ways for His blessings.
- Christmas is the season to focus on the meaning of Jesus' coming into the world.

Holidays or "holy days" were originally times to bring God back into our everyday lives. Special thought and care is needed to do this, but putting the Lord into the holidays can build a rich Christian heritage of traditions and memories. The rhythm of celebrating holidays for the Lord can truly change your ordinary days into holy days for Him.

See also Ex. 12:1–51; Lev. 23:1–44; Josh. 4:1–24; Matt. 6:16–18, note; 1 Cor. 11:24–26; chart on Feasts of Israel; notes on Family (Gen. 32; 1 Sam. 3; Ps. 78; 127); Leisure (Mark 6); Mealtime (Ps. 104); Traditions (1 Sam. 7)

---

and his servants. [35]So the heart of Pharaoh was hard; neither would he let the children of Israel go, as the LORD had spoken by Moses.

The Eighth Plague: Locusts

10Now the LORD said to Moses, "Go in to Pharaoh; for I have hardened his heart and the hearts of his servants, that I may show these signs of Mine before him, [2]and that you may tell in the hearing of your son and your son's son the mighty things I have done in Egypt, and My signs which I have done among them, that you may know that I *am* the LORD."

[3]So Moses and Aaron came in to Pharaoh and said to him, "Thus says the LORD God of the Hebrews: 'How long will you refuse to humble yourself before Me? Let My people go, that they may serve Me. [4]Or else, if you refuse to let My people go, behold, tomorrow I will bring locusts into your territory. [5]And they shall cover the face of the earth, so that no one will be able to see the earth; and they shall eat the residue of what is left, which remains to you from the hail, and they shall eat every tree which grows up for you out of the field. [6]They shall fill your houses, the houses of all your servants, and the houses of all the Egyptians—which neither your fathers nor your fathers' fathers have seen, since the day that they were on the earth to this day.' " And he turned and went out from Pharaoh.

[7]Then Pharaoh's servants said to him, "How long shall this man be a snare to us? Let the men go, that they may serve the LORD their God. Do you not yet know that Egypt is destroyed?"

[8]So Moses and Aaron were brought again to Pharaoh, and he said to them, "Go, serve the LORD your God. Who *are* the ones that are going?"

[9]And Moses said, "We will go with our young and our old; with our sons and our daughters, with our flocks and our herds we will go, for we must hold a feast to the LORD."

[10]Then he said to them, "The LORD had better

10:1–20 The eighth plague: locusts. With this plague, the food Egyptians needed was consumed. Locusts ate whatever had grown or recovered since the hail storm (see chart, The Ten Plagues on Egypt). The plagues had undermined Pharaoh's strength at court; his servants now told him to let the Israelites go and serve the Lord (v. 7). For the first time he tried to forestall an announced disaster, but he failed because he insisted on maintaining control of the Israelites, allowing only the men to go (v. 11).

10:8–11 Serving the Lord must involve all the Israelites, not just the men. Pharaoh's refusal to let everyone go was a refusal to humble himself before the Lord (v. 3). By imposing conditions, Pharaoh attempted to preserve the illusion that he was in control and could give orders without actually submitting to the Lord. He wanted to avoid trouble yet not truly recognize the Lord's authority in his life. His lack of regard for the Lord's presence with the Israelites is apparent (v. 10).

be with you when I let you and your little ones go! Beware, for evil is ahead of you. [11]Not so! Go now, you *who are* men, and serve the LORD, for that is what you desired." And they were driven out from Pharaoh's presence.

[12]Then the LORD said to Moses, "Stretch out your hand over the land of Egypt for the locusts, that they may come upon the land of Egypt, and eat every herb of the land—all that the hail has left." [13]So Moses stretched out his rod over the land of Egypt, and the LORD brought an east wind on the land all that day and all *that* night. When it was morning, the east wind brought the locusts. [14]And the locusts went up over all the land of Egypt and rested on all the territory of Egypt. *They were* very severe; previously there had been no such locusts as they, nor shall there be such after them. [15]For they covered the face of the whole earth, so that the land was darkened; and they ate every herb of the land and all the fruit of the trees which the hail had left. So there remained nothing green on the trees or on the plants of the field throughout all the land of Egypt.

[16]Then Pharaoh called for Moses and Aaron in haste, and said, "I have sinned against the LORD your God and against you. [17]Now therefore, please forgive my sin only this once, and entreat the LORD your God, that He may take away from me this death only." [18]So he went out from Pharaoh and entreated the LORD. [19]And the LORD turned a very strong west wind, which took the locusts away and blew them into the Red Sea. There remained not one locust in all the territory of Egypt. [20]But the LORD hardened Pharaoh's heart, and he did not let the children of Israel go.

The Ninth Plague: Darkness

[21]Then the LORD said to Moses, "Stretch out your hand toward heaven, that there may be darkness over the land of Egypt, darkness *which* may even be felt." [22]So Moses stretched out his hand toward heaven, and there was thick darkness in all the land of Egypt three days. [23]They did not see one another; nor did anyone rise from his place for three days. But all the children of Israel had light in their dwellings.

[24]Then Pharaoh called to Moses and said, "Go, serve the LORD; only let your flocks and your herds be kept back. Let your little ones also go with you."

[25]But Moses said, "You must also give us sacrifices and burnt offerings, that we may sacrifice to the LORD our God. [26]Our livestock also shall go with us; not a hoof shall be left behind. For we must take some of them to serve the LORD our God, and even we do not know with what we must serve the LORD until we arrive there."

[27]But the LORD hardened Pharaoh's heart, and he would not let them go. [28]Then Pharaoh said to him, "Get away from me! Take heed to yourself and see my face no more! For in the day you see my face you shall die!"

[29]So Moses said, "You have spoken well. I will never see your face again."

Death of the Firstborn Announced

11 And the LORD said to Moses, "I will bring one more plague on Pharaoh and on Egypt. Afterward he will let you go from here. When he lets *you* go, he will surely drive you out of here altogether. [2]Speak now in the hearing of the people, and let every man ask from his neighbor and every woman from her neighbor, articles of silver and articles of gold." [3]And the LORD gave the people favor in the sight of the Egyptians. Moreover the man Moses *was* very great in the land of Egypt, in the sight of Pharaoh's servants and in the sight of the people.

[4]Then Moses said, "Thus says the LORD: 'About midnight I will go out into the midst of Egypt; [5]and all the firstborn in the land of Egypt shall die, from the firstborn of Pharaoh who sits on his throne, even to the firstborn of the female servant who *is* behind the handmill, and all the firstborn of the animals. [6]Then there shall be a great cry throughout all the land of Egypt, such as was not like it *before*, nor shall be like it again. [7]But against none of the children of Israel shall a dog move its tongue, against man or beast, that you may know that the LORD does make a difference between the Egyptians and Israel.' [8]And all these your servants shall come down to me and bow down to me, saying, 'Get out, and all the people who follow you!' After that I will go out." Then he went out from Pharaoh in great anger.

[9]But the LORD said to Moses, "Pharaoh will not heed you, so that My wonders may be multiplied in the land of Egypt." [10]So Moses and Aaron did all these wonders before Pharaoh; and the LORD hardened Pharaoh's heart, and he did not let the children of Israel go out of his land.

The Passover Instituted

12 Now the LORD spoke to Moses and Aaron in the land of Egypt, saying, [2]"This month *shall be* your beginning of months; it *shall be* the first month of the year to you. [3]Speak to all the congregation of Israel, saying: 'On the tenth of

---

10:21–29 The ninth plague: darkness. Like the third and sixth plagues, number nine came unannounced (see chart, The Ten Plagues on Egypt). Now the supreme Egyptian deity, the sun god Ra, was shown powerless to help the Egyptians. Pharaoh did not need to be told who was responsible; yet he still attempted to retain control by requiring the Israelites to leave their livestock behind.

this month every man shall take for himself a lamb, according to the house of *his* father, a lamb for a household. ⁴And if the household is too small for the lamb, let him and his neighbor next to his house take *it* according to the number of the persons; according to each man's need you shall make your count for the lamb. ⁵Your lamb shall be without blemish, a male of the first year. You may take *it* from the sheep or from the goats. ⁶Now you shall keep it until the fourteenth day of the same month. Then the whole assembly of the congregation of Israel shall kill it at twilight. ⁷And they shall take *some* of the blood and put *it* on the two doorposts and on the lintel of the houses where they eat it. ⁸Then they shall eat the flesh on that night; roasted in fire, with unleavened bread *and* with bitter *herbs* they shall eat it. ⁹Do not eat it raw, nor boiled at all with water, but roasted in fire—its head with its legs and its entrails. ¹⁰You shall let none of it remain until morning, and what remains of it until morning you shall burn with fire. ¹¹And thus you shall eat it: *with* a belt on your waist, your sandals on your feet, and your staff in your hand. So you shall eat it in haste. It *is* the LORD's Passover.

¹²For I will pass through the land of Egypt on that night, and will strike all the firstborn in the land of Egypt, both man and beast; and against all the gods of Egypt I will execute judgment: I *am* the LORD. ¹³Now the blood shall be a sign for you on the houses where you *are*. And when I see the blood, I will pass over you; and the plague shall not be on you to destroy *you* when I strike the land of Egypt.

¹⁴'So this day shall be to you a memorial; and you shall keep it as a feast to the LORD throughout your generations. You shall keep it as a feast by an everlasting ordinance. ¹⁵Seven days you shall eat unleavened bread. On the first day you shall remove leaven from your houses. For whoever eats leavened bread from the first day until the seventh day, that person shall be cut off from Israel. ¹⁶On the first day *there shall be* a holy convocation, and on the seventh day there shall be a holy convocation for you. No manner of work shall be done on them; but *that* which everyone must eat—that only may be prepared by you. ¹⁷So you shall ob-

serve *the Feast of* Unleavened Bread, for on this same day I will have brought your armies out of the land of Egypt. Therefore you shall observe this day throughout your generations as an everlasting ordinance. ¹⁸In the first *month*, on the fourteenth day of the month at evening, you shall eat unleavened bread, until the twenty-first day of the month at evening. ¹⁹For seven days no leaven shall be found in your houses, since whoever eats what is leavened, that same person shall be cut off from the congregation of Israel, whether *he is* a stranger or a native of the land. ²⁰You shall eat nothing leavened; in all your dwellings you shall eat unleavened bread.' "

²¹Then Moses called for all the elders of Israel and said to them, "Pick out and take lambs for yourselves according to your families, and kill the Passover *lamb*. ²²And you shall take a bunch of hyssop, dip *it* in the blood that *is* in the basin, and strike the lintel and the two doorposts with the blood that *is* in the basin. And none of you shall go out of the door of his house until morning. ²³For the LORD will pass through to strike the Egyptians; and when He sees the blood on the lintel and on the two doorposts, the LORD will pass over the door and not allow the destroyer to come into your houses to strike *you*. ²⁴And you shall observe this thing as an ordinance for you and your sons forever. ²⁵It will come to pass when you come to the land which the LORD will give you, just as He promised, that you shall keep this service. ²⁶And it shall be, when your children say to you, 'What do you mean by this service?' ²⁷that you shall say, 'It *is* the Passover sacrifice of the LORD, who passed over the houses of the children of Israel in Egypt when He struck the Egyptians and delivered our households.' " So the people bowed their heads and worshiped. ²⁸Then the children of Israel went away and did *so;* just as the LORD had commanded Moses and Aaron, so they did.

The Tenth Plague: Death of the Firstborn

²⁹And it came to pass at midnight that the LORD struck all the firstborn in the land of Egypt, from the firstborn of Pharaoh who sat on his throne to the firstborn of the captive who *was* in the dungeon, and all the firstborn of livestock.

12:6 The meaning of twilight is debated. Since a new day began at sundown, the lamb was killed on the 14th and the meal eaten at the beginning of the 15th, the day the Israelites left Egypt. By the time of Christ, the custom was to kill the lamb between 3:00 and 5:00 P.M.

12:15 A week of eating unleavened bread would accompany the Passover. This commemorated the haste in which Israel left Egypt (vv. 11, 34, 39; Deut. 16:3). Perhaps because leaven pervades dough and involves fermentation, a kind of decay, leaven was (or later became) symbolic of corruption and sin, which needed to be removed (see Matt. 16:6; 1 Cor. 5:1–8). A

person who disobediently ate leavened bread indicated willful rejection of the Lord's covenant with Israel (see Gen. 17:14). Such a person would be cut off from Israel, certainly in the sense of not enjoying covenant benefits; "cut off" may also refer to premature death by the Lord or by execution (see Ex. 31:14–15; Lev. 7:20; 20:1–6; 22:9; Num. 15:30–36).

12:25, 26 The word translated service is the same one used earlier in Exodus for the Israelites' service to Pharaoh (Ex. 1:13–14). Because the Lord was delivering them, they would have a new overlord (who loved them) and a new service that

THE EXODUS FROM EGYPT

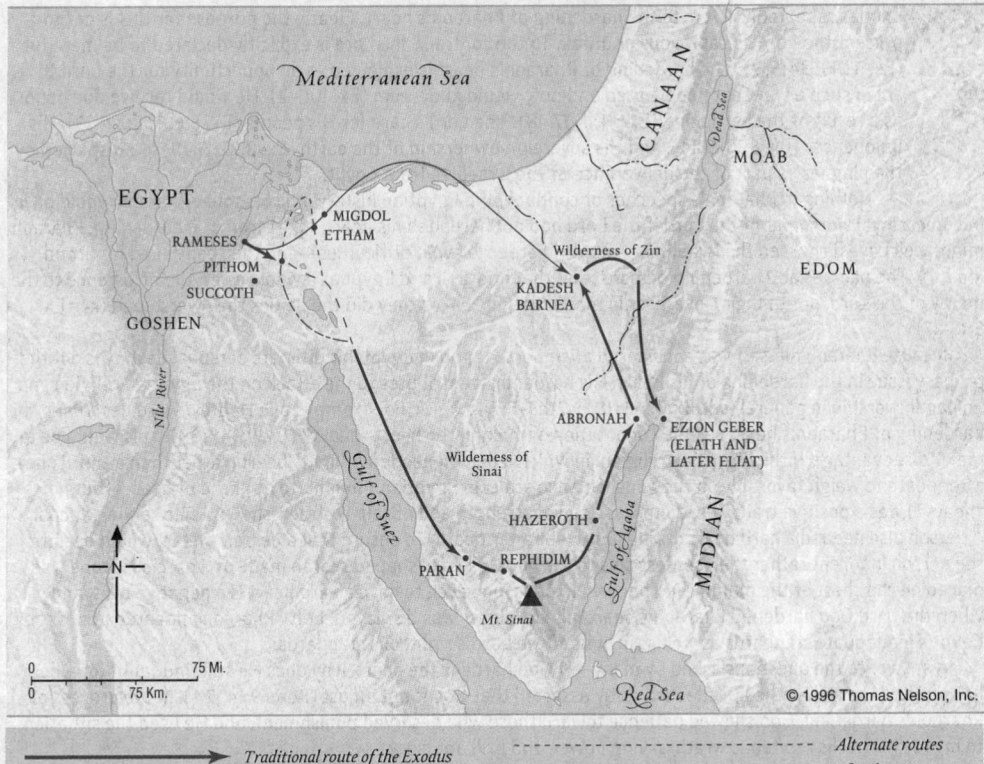

Traditional route of the Exodus
Alternate route of the Exodus

Alternate routes
of Red Sea
crossing

© 1996 Thomas Nelson, Inc.

Though the precise route of the Exodus is uncertain, the southern route is more likely. The journey to Sinai took about two months. They encamped at Sinai for about ten months to receive God's revelation.

---

³⁰So Pharaoh rose in the night, he, all his servants, and all the Egyptians; and there was a great cry in Egypt, for *there was* not a house where *there was* not one dead.

The Exodus

³¹Then he called for Moses and Aaron by night, and said, "Rise, go out from among my people, both you and the children of Israel. And go, serve the LORD as you have said. ³²Also take your flocks and your herds, as you have said, and be gone; and bless me also."

³³And the Egyptians urged the people, that they might send them out of the land in haste. For they said, "We *shall* all *be* dead." ³⁴So the people took their dough before it was leavened, having their kneading bowls bound up in their clothes on their shoulders. ³⁵Now the children of Israel had done according to the word of Moses, and they had asked from the Egyptians articles of silver, articles of gold, and clothing. ³⁶And the LORD had given the people favor in the sight of the Egyptians, so that they granted them *what they requested.* Thus they plundered the Egyptians.

---

recalled and was based on what He had done for them (see similarly 2 Cor. 5:15).

12:28 For the Israelites to obey the instructions for this meal was an expression of faith, both before and after the initial Passover event.

12:34, 35 The Lord was behind the Egyptians' surprising re-sponse, in that He gave the Israelites favor with them (see Ex. 3:21; 11:2, 3; 12:35, 36). What the Israelites received from the Egyptians and their own animals (v. 38) fulfilled the prophecy that Abraham's descendants would come out of slavery "with great possessions" (Gen. 15:14; see also Deut. 15:12–15).

JUSTICE *IS GOD FAIR?*

Exodus repeatedly refers to the hardening of Pharaoh's heart. Clearly the purpose for this is not to present the Lord as capricious or unfair. To the contrary, the Lord is explicitly declared to be merciful (Ex. 33:19; 34:6, 7). The hardening of Pharaoh's heart is explained as an opportunity for the Lord to act in such a way that people then and now would know Him (Ex. 10:1–2). He would receive due honor as a result of the hardening (Ex. 14:4, 17, 18). The Lord's care for His people (Ex. 6:6, 7; 8:22, 23), His uniqueness (Ex. 8:10; 9:14), and His sovereign ownership of the earth (Ex. 8:22; 9:29) are displayed by the plagues as part of the deliverance of the Israelites from Egypt.

Nothing in Pharaoh's speeches or conduct or in Egyptian history indicates that Pharaoh would have become a loyal worshiper of the Lord if the Lord had not hardened his heart. Apart from the hardening, Pharaoh might well have dismissed the Israelites—simply in order to avoid difficulties—and then continued his proud idolatry. The plagues and hardening demonstrate that Pharaoh and Egypt as a whole owed their existence to the mercy of the Lord, not to their cleverness in manipulating Him as they did the deities they worshiped (see Ex. 9:15–17).

Because Pharaoh himself was considered an important god in Egypt, his ultimate personal destiny is not the primary issue in the hardening of his heart. His hardening contributes to the attack on the Egyptian religion and on pagan worship in general (see Ex. 12:12; 18:11; 20:3–5; 34:10–17). For example, one Hebrew word describing the hardening of Pharaoh's heart has the connotation of making the heart "heavy" (Ex. 9:34; 10:1). This would be a major disadvantage within Egyptian religion, in which a person needed a "light" heart (rather than a sinful one) after death to weigh favorably on the gods' balance scale. In Egyptian thought, to be "hard of heart" (but not "heavy") was a positive trait. The idiom was used of strength and of self-restraint shown while serving at court. A person also needed a hard heart during judgment after death. To ensure that a person's heart would declare the person innocent rather than confess sins to the gods, a heart-shaped scarab made of a precious stone was placed on the chest of the mummified body. In Exodus, however, to have a hard heart is a negative trait, and when the Lord God hardened Pharaoh's heart, his sinfulness was displayed. Lofty Pharaoh appeared at a loss by Egypt's inadequate standards as well as in light of the Lord's righteous standards.

In answer to the questions asked by many—If God hardens the heart, why does He still find fault, for who has resisted His will?—the apostle Paul flatly asserted that God is not unjust (Rom. 9:14–24). In the process of Pharaoh's hardening, God showed patience toward those who deserved punishment, and He used the situation to make known His righteous wrath, saving power, and brilliant glory.

See also Ex. 4:21; notes on Attributes of God (Deut. 32; 2 Chr. 19); Freedom (Rom. 6)

---

[37]Then the children of Israel journeyed from Rameses to Succoth, about six hundred thousand men on foot, besides children. [38]A mixed multitude went up with them also, and flocks and herds—a great deal of livestock. [39]And they baked unleavened cakes of the dough which they had brought out of Egypt; for it was not leavened, because they were driven out of Egypt and could not wait, nor had they prepared provisions for themselves.

[40]Now the sojourn of the children of Israel who lived in Egypt[a] *was* four hundred and thirty years. [41]And it came to pass at the end of the four hundred and thirty years—on that very same day—it came to pass that all the armies of the LORD went out from the land of Egypt. [42]It *is* a night of solemn observance to the LORD for bringing them out of the land of Egypt. This *is* that night of the LORD, a solemn observance for all the children of Israel throughout their generations.

Passover Regulations

[43]And the LORD said to Moses and Aaron, "This *is* the ordinance of the Passover: No foreigner shall eat it. [44]But every man's servant who is bought for money, when you have circumcised him, then he may eat it. [45]A sojourner and a hired

12:40 [a]Samaritan Pentateuch and Septuagint read *Egypt and Canaan.*

12:37 The word translated men has military connotations—not a reference to men in general but to potential fighting men. The word translated "children" (Heb. *taph*, lit. "little ones") is used to reference only children when women are also mentioned (Gen. 34:29; 45:19; 46:5), but the term is used in a broader sense for women and children (Gen. 43:8; 47:12; Ex. 10:10, 24; Num. 32:16, 24). The women and children were military dependents.

12:38 Apparently other disaffected people took the opportunity to leave Egypt. The instructions in verses 43–49 show that they could become part of the worshiping community.

12:39 Following God's instructions, the Israelites had Egyptian treasures but not provisions of food for themselves. God would provide food, and the treasures would be useful in building the tabernacle.

servant shall not eat it. ⁴⁶In one house it shall be eaten; you shall not carry any of the flesh outside the house, nor shall you break one of its bones. ⁴⁷All the congregation of Israel shall keep it. ⁴⁸And when a stranger dwells with you *and wants* to keep the Passover to the LORD, let all his males be circumcised, and then let him come near and keep it; and he shall be as a native of the land. For no uncircumcised person shall eat it. ⁴⁹One law shall be for the native-born and for the stranger who dwells among you."

⁵⁰Thus all the children of Israel did; as the LORD commanded Moses and Aaron, so they did. ⁵¹And it came to pass, on that very same day, that the LORD brought the children of Israel out of the land of Egypt according to their armies.

The Firstborn Consecrated

13 Then the LORD spoke to Moses, saying, ²"Consecrate to Me all the firstborn, whatever opens the womb among the children of Israel, *both* of man and beast; it is Mine."

The Feast of Unleavened Bread

³And Moses said to the people: "Remember this day in which you went out of Egypt, out of the house of bondage; for by strength of hand the LORD brought you out of this *place.* No leavened bread shall be eaten. ⁴On this day you are going out, in the month Abib. ⁵And it shall be, when the LORD brings you into the land of the Canaanites and the Hittites and the Amorites and the Hivites and the Jebusites, which He swore to your fathers to give you, a land flowing with milk and honey, that you shall keep this service in this month. ⁶Seven days you shall eat unleavened bread, and on the seventh day *there shall be* a feast to the LORD. ⁷Unleavened bread shall be eaten seven days. And no leavened bread shall be seen among you, nor shall leaven be seen among you in all your quarters. ⁸And you shall tell your son in that day, saying, '*This is done* because of what the LORD did for me when I came up from Egypt.' ⁹It shall be as a sign to you on your hand and as a memorial between your eyes, that the LORD's law may be in your mouth; for with a strong hand the LORD has brought you out of Egypt. ¹⁰You shall therefore keep this ordinance in its season from year to year.

The Law of the Firstborn

¹¹"And it shall be, when the LORD brings you into the land of the Canaanites, as He swore to you and your fathers, and gives it to you, ¹²that you shall set apart to the LORD all that open the womb, that is, every firstborn that comes from an animal which you have; the males *shall be* the LORD's. ¹³But every firstborn of a donkey you shall redeem with a lamb; and if you will not redeem *it,* then you shall break its neck. And all the firstborn of man among your sons you shall redeem. ¹⁴So it shall be, when your son asks you in time to come, saying, 'What *is* this?' that you shall say to him, 'By strength of hand the LORD brought us out of Egypt, out of the house of bondage. ¹⁵And it came to pass, when Pharaoh was stubborn about letting us go, that the LORD killed all the firstborn in the land of Egypt, both the firstborn of man and the firstborn of beast. Therefore I sacrifice to the LORD all males that open the womb, but all the firstborn of my sons I redeem.' ¹⁶It shall be as a sign on your hand and as frontlets between your eyes, for by strength of hand the LORD brought us out of Egypt."

The Wilderness Way

¹⁷Then it came to pass, when Pharaoh had let the people go, that God did not lead them *by* way of the land of the Philistines, although that *was* near; for God said, "Lest perhaps the people change their minds when they see war, and

---

12:49 Passover was to be more than just an ethnic or national festival (v. 48; see chart, The Feasts of Israel). All those willing to participate in a covenant relationship with the Lord, signified by circumcision in the case of males (Gen. 17:10–14), could rightfully celebrate the Passover and consider themselves beneficiaries of the Israelites' deliverance from Egypt (see Ruth 2:10–12).

13:2 To sanctify, consecrate, or treat as holy is to set apart from the common a person or thing for a special purpose (see Ex. 3:5; 28:1–4; 29:43–46). Verses 12–15 record how the Israelites were to sanctify the firstborn. The word "man" (Heb. *'adam*) clearly refers to mankind, male and female, as it does in Genesis 1:26 and 27. For the Israelites, viewing all firstborn males as the Lord's was tied to the events of the first Passover night and the Lord's decree, not to anything inherently superior about the firstborn (Ex. 13:2, 15). This was in contrast to widespread pagan beliefs.

13:8, 9 The yearly Passover feast and week of unleavened bread, along with the sacrifice and redemption of the first-

born (vv. 13–15; Num. 3:13), would preserve the memory of the Lord's actions for the sake of later generations (see chart, The Feasts of Israel). As a result, His Law would be in their mouths; that is, they would obey Him.

13:13–15 The donkey, as an unclean animal, could not be offered as a sacrifice (Lev. 11:26). But to spare its life, an owner could "redeem" or buy it back with a lamb offered in sacrifice in its place. As the Lord had redeemed His firstborn son Israel, so the Israelites must redeem their firstborn as a reminder of what God had done for them (Ex. 4:22; 2 Sam. 7:23, 24). Redemption of the firstborn sons involved the dedication of the tribe of Levi and payment of five shekels of silver (Num. 3:40–51; 8:14–18; 18:15–17).

13:16 Exactly what ancient headwear or ornament is described by "frontlets" is uncertain (Deut. 6:8, 9, note; see also Matt. 23:5, "phylacteries"). Obeying the instructions in verses 1–15 would recall God's mighty actions to the individual (like a mark on the hand) and to others (like something displayed on the forehead).

return to Egypt." [18]So God led the people around *by* way of the wilderness of the Red Sea. And the children of Israel went up in orderly ranks out of the land of Egypt.

[19]And Moses took the bones of Joseph with him, for he had placed the children of Israel under solemn oath, saying, "God will surely visit you, and you shall carry up my bones from here with you."[a]

[20]So they took their journey from Succoth and camped in Etham at the edge of the wilderness. [21]And the LORD went before them by day in a pillar of cloud to lead the way, and by night in a pillar of fire to give them light, so as to go by day and night. [22]He did not take away the pillar of cloud by day or the pillar of fire by night *from* before the people.

The Red Sea Crossing

14 Now the LORD spoke to Moses, saying: [2]"Speak to the children of Israel, that they turn and camp before Pi Hahiroth, between Migdol and the sea, opposite Baal Zemphon; you shall camp before it by the sea. [3]For Pharaoh will say of the children of Israel, 'They *are* bewildered by the land; the wilderness has closed them in.' [4]Then I will harden Pharaoh's heart, so that he will pursue them; and I will gain honor over Pharaoh and over all his army, that the Egyptians may know that I *am* the LORD." And they did so.

[5]Now it was told the king of Egypt that the people had fled; and the heart of Pharaoh and his servants was turned against the people; and they said, "Why have we done this, that we have let Israel go from serving us?" [6]So he made ready his chariot and took his people with him. [7]Also, he took six hundred choice chariots, and all the chariots of Egypt with captains over every one of them. [8]And the LORD hardened the heart of Pharaoh king of Egypt, and he pursued the children of Israel; and the children of Israel went out with boldness. [9]So the Egyptians pursued them, all the horses *and* chariots of Pharaoh, his horsemen and his army, and overtook them camping by the sea beside Pi Hahiroth, before Baal Zephon.

[10]And when Pharaoh drew near, the children of Israel lifted their eyes, and behold, the Egyptians marched after them. So they were very afraid, and the children of Israel cried out to the LORD.

[11]Then they said to Moses, "Because *there were* no graves in Egypt, have you taken us away to die in the wilderness? Why have you so dealt with us, to bring us up out of Egypt? [12]*Is* this not the word that we told you in Egypt, saying, 'Let us alone that we may serve the Egyptians'? For *it would have been* better for us to serve the Egyptians than that we should die in the wilderness."

[13]And Moses said to the people, "Do not be afraid. Stand still, and see the salvation of the LORD, which He will accomplish for you today. For the Egyptians whom you see today, you shall see again no more forever. [14]The LORD will fight for you, and you shall hold your peace."

[15]And the LORD said to Moses, "Why do you cry to Me? Tell the children of Israel to go forward. [16]But lift up your rod, and stretch out your hand over the sea and divide it. And the children of Israel shall go on dry *ground* through the midst of the sea. [17]And I indeed will harden the hearts of the Egyptians, and they shall follow them. So I will gain honor over Pharaoh and over all his army, his chariots, and his horsemen. [18]Then the Egyptians shall know that I *am* the LORD, when I have gained honor for Myself over Pharaoh, his chariots, and his horsemen."

[19]And the Angel of God, who went before the camp of Israel, moved and went behind them; and the pillar of cloud went from before them and stood behind them. [20]So it came between the camp of the Egyptians and the camp of Israel. Thus it was a cloud and darkness *to the one,* and it gave light by night *to the other,* so that the one did not come near the other all that night.

[21]Then Moses stretched out his hand over the sea; and the LORD caused the sea to go *back* by a strong east wind all that night, and made the sea into dry *land,* and the waters were divided. [22]So the children of Israel went into the midst of the sea on the dry *ground,* and the waters *were* a wall to them on their right hand and on their left. [23]And the Egyptians pursued and went after them into the midst of the sea, all Pharaoh's horses, his chariots, and his horsemen.

[24]Now it came to pass, in the morning watch, that the LORD looked down upon the army of the

•••••••••••••••••
13:19 [a]Genesis 50:25

13:18 The Red Sea (Heb. *Yam. Suph,* lit. "Reed Sea") goes back to the ancient Greek translation of the OT (LXX) made prior to the time of Christ. The name for the lower sea included branches now called the Gulf of Suez and the Gulf of Aqaba. The area north of the Gulf of Suez had numerous lakes and marsh land that were later dug out to build the Suez Canal. The exact location of the Israelite crossing is still debated (see map, The Exodus from Egypt).

14:8 The LORD hardened the heart of Pharaoh (see Ex. 4:21, note; Ex. 14, Justice).

14:12 When facing difficulty, the Israelites quickly forgot the oppression they had left and assumed it would be better to serve the Egyptians than to serve the Lord. The apostle Paul wanted Christians to avoid any similar mistake (Rom. 6:21–23).

14:17, 18 Those who learn to recognize the Lord, the One deserving above all others to be honored, receive benefit. Illusions are dispelled as people become aware of the ultimate reality of who He is and who they are in dealing with Him (see Josh. 2:9–14 and Ps. 100 in contrast with Rom. 1:21–23).

Fear is a fact of life. Some fear is positive—the holy fear we feel for our awesome God and the self-preserving fear that makes us run from danger.

Carol Kent

Egyptians through the pillar of fire and cloud, and He troubled the army of the Egyptians. [25]And He took off[a] their chariot wheels, so that they drove them with difficulty; and the Egyptians said, "Let us flee from the face of Israel, for the LORD fights for them against the Egyptians."

[26]Then the LORD said to Moses, "Stretch out your hand over the sea, that the waters may come back upon the Egyptians, on their chariots, and on their horsemen." [27]And Moses stretched out his hand over the sea; and when the morning appeared, the sea returned to its full depth, while the Egyptians were fleeing into it. So the LORD overthrew the Egyptians in the midst of the sea. [28]Then the waters returned and covered the chariots, the horsemen, *and* all the army of Pharaoh that came into the sea after them. Not so much as one of them remained. [29]But the children of Israel had walked on dry *land* in the midst of the sea, and the waters *were* a wall to them on their right hand and on their left.

[30]So the LORD saved Israel that day out of the hand of the Egyptians, and Israel saw the Egyptians dead on the seashore. [31]Thus Israel saw the great work which the LORD had done in Egypt; so the people feared the LORD, and believed the LORD and His servant Moses.

The Song of Moses

15 Then Moses and the children of Israel sang this song to the LORD, and spoke, saying:

"I will sing to the LORD,
  For He has triumphed gloriously!
  The horse and its rider
  He has thrown into the sea!
[2]The LORD *is* my strength and song,
  And He has become my salvation;
  He *is* my God, and I will praise Him;
  My father's God, and I will exalt Him.
[3]The LORD *is* a man of war;
  The LORD *is* His name.
[4]Pharaoh's chariots and his army He has cast
  into the sea;

His chosen captains also are drowned in the
  Red Sea.
[5]The depths have covered them;
  They sank to the bottom like a stone.

[6]"Your right hand, O LORD, has become glorious
  in power;
  Your right hand, O LORD, has dashed the
  enemy in pieces.
[7]And in the greatness of Your excellence
  You have overthrown those who rose against
  You;
  You sent forth Your wrath;
  It consumed them like stubble.
[8]And with the blast of Your nostrils
  The waters were gathered together;
  The floods stood upright like a heap;
  The depths congealed in the heart of the sea.
[9]The enemy said, 'I will pursue,
  I will overtake,
  I will divide the spoil;
  My desire shall be satisfied on them.
  I will draw my sword,
  My hand shall destroy them.'
[10]You blew with Your wind,
  The sea covered them;
  They sank like lead in the mighty waters.

[11]"Who *is* like You, O LORD, among the gods?
  Who *is* like You, glorious in holiness,
  Fearful in praises, doing wonders?
[12]You stretched out Your right hand;
  The earth swallowed them.
[13]You in Your mercy have led forth
  The people whom You have redeemed;
  You have guided *them* in Your strength
  To Your holy habitation.
[14]"The people will hear *and* be afraid;
  Sorrow will take hold of the inhabitants of
  Philistia.
[15]Then the chiefs of Edom will be dismayed;
  The mighty men of Moab,
  Trembling will take hold of them;

14:25 [a]Samaritan Pentateuch, Septuagint, and Syriac read *bound*.

15:2, 3 My father's God presents the Red Sea crossing as part of God's keeping His covenant promises to the ancestors. The metaphor "a man of war" likens God to an accomplished warrior who fights for His people (Ex. 14:14, 25; Deut. 1:30; Ps. 35:1–10; Rev. 19:11–15). At Ai Israel learned what happened when God did not fight for them (Josh. 7:1–12).

15:14–17 News of God's actions spread and had the expected effect on future enemies (Num. 22:2–6; Josh. 2:9–11; 5:1;

9:3–11; 1 Sam. 6:1–6). Knowledge of the Lord's superior character and actions (vv. 11–13) leads to confidence regarding the fulfillment of promises for the future (vv. 14–18). The Lord would certainly bring the Israelites to the Land He had promised, where He would dwell among them in a unique way. Believers in every generation can have the same confidence (see John 14:1–3; 1 Thess. 4:14–18).

DANCING A CELEBRATION BEFORE THE LORD

In primitive and civilized cultures alike, dance has been an important means of expressing the deepest feelings of the human soul. Like any art form, dance has the power not only to express emotion but to stir it up, in both participants and observers. As the story of Herodias' daughter shows (Mark 6:17–28), dance can easily be abused when used as a tool of sensual power in which the chief end is selfish pleasure or the lustful arousal of others. Job warned about people who were so busy dancing and playing that they rejected serving the Lord (Job 21:11–14).

In Scripture, dance was used to express joy and praise to the Lord (2 Sam. 6:14; Ps. 149:3; 150:4; Jer. 31:4, 13). Dancing was a part of the celebration of the prodigal son's return to his father in Jesus' parable of the Lost Son (Luke 15:25). The Hebrew people used dance to celebrate the glory of God and His marvelous works. David danced before the Lord in joyous celebration of the return of the ark to Jerusalem. Such exuberant dancing, when described in the text of Scripture, was generally done by women (Ex. 15:20, 21; Judg. 21:19–21), singly or in groups, but not by a man and woman together; it was often spontaneous and unchoreographed (1 Sam. 18:6)—a genuine expression of spiritual delight (Ps. 30:11, 12).

In any case, every believer is responsible before God for living a holy life without moral compromise (Rom. 14:21; 1 Cor. 6:19, 20; Gal. 5:16; 1 Thess. 4:3–8) and with diligence to glorify God in every sphere of life (1 Cor. 10:31).

See also notes on Celebrations and Holidays (Ex. 12); Creativity (Col. 1); Fruit of the Spirit: Joy (Rom. 15); Sexual Purity (1 Cor. 7)

All the inhabitants of Canaan will melt away.
16Fear and dread will fall on them;
By the greatness of Your arm
They will be *as* still as a stone,
Till Your people pass over, O LORD,
Till the people pass over
Whom You have purchased.
17You will bring them in and plant them
In the mountain of Your inheritance,
In the place, O LORD, *which* You have made
For Your own dwelling,
The sanctuary, O Lord, *which* Your hands have
established.

18"The LORD shall reign forever and ever."

19For the horses of Pharaoh went with his chariots and his horsemen into the sea, and the LORD brought back the waters of the sea upon them. But the children of Israel went on dry *land* in the midst of the sea.

The Song of Miriam

20Then Miriam the prophetess, the sister of Aaron, took the timbrel in her hand; and all the women went out after her with timbrels and with dances. 21And Miriam answered them:

"Sing to the LORD,
For He has triumphed gloriously!
The horse and its rider
He has thrown into the sea!"

Bitter Waters Made Sweet

22So Moses brought Israel from the Red Sea; then they went out into the Wilderness of Shur. And they went three days in the wilderness and found no water. 23Now when they came to Marah, they could not drink the waters of Marah, for they *were* bitter. Therefore the name of it was called Marah.a 24And the people complained against Moses, saying, "What shall we drink?" 25So he cried out to the LORD, and the LORD showed him a tree. When he cast *it* into the waters, the waters were made sweet.

There He made a statute and an ordinance for them, and there He tested them, 26and said, "If you diligently heed the voice of the LORD your

•••••••••••••••
15:23 aLiterally *Bitter*

15:22—17:16 The description of how the Lord provided water, food, and protection from enemies continues the theme of knowing the Lord based on His actions (Ex. 15:26; 16:6, 12). The Lord led the Israelites to places where their needs would teach them to trust Him.

15:22 The Wilderness of Shur in the Sinai peninsula east of Egypt was known to Hagar (Gen. 16:7–14) and Abraham (Gen. 20:1). Moses had talked of going three days' journey into the wilderness to worship the Lord (Ex. 3:18; 5:3; 8:27), but after

three days of wilderness travel, the Israelites seemingly have had no thought of worship.

15:24 The people complained against Moses. This is the most frequent description of the Israelites in the wilderness. Their faithless rebellion against Moses was not merely dissatisfaction or honest questioning but ultimately rejection of the Lord (see Ex. 16:7, 8; 17:2–4; Num. 14:2–4, 27, 28).

15:26 To avoid the plagues inflicted on Egypt, the Israelites must obey the Lord (see chart, The Ten Plagues on Egypt). In

God and do what is right in His sight, give ear to His commandments and keep all His statutes, I will put none of the diseases on you which I have brought on the Egyptians. For I *am* the LORD who heals you."

27Then they came to Elim, where there *were* twelve wells of water and seventy palm trees; so they camped there by the waters.

Bread from Heaven

16 And they journeyed from Elim, and all the congregation of the children of Israel came to the Wilderness of Sin, which is between Elim and Sinai, on the fifteenth day of the second month after they departed from the land of Egypt. 2Then the whole congregation of the children of Israel complained against Moses and Aaron in the wilderness. 3And the children of Israel said to them, "Oh, that we had died by the hand of the LORD in the land of Egypt, when we sat by the pots of meat *and* when we ate bread to the full! For you have brought us out into this wilderness to kill this whole assembly with hunger."

4Then the LORD said to Moses, "Behold, I will rain bread from heaven for you. And the people shall go out and gather a certain quota every day, that I may test them, whether they will walk in My law or not. 5And it shall be on the sixth day that they shall prepare what they bring in, and it shall be twice as much as they gather daily."

6Then Moses and Aaron said to all the children of Israel, "At evening you shall know that the LORD has brought you out of the land of Egypt. 7And in the morning you shall see the glory of the LORD; for He hears your complaints against the LORD. But what *are* we, that you complain against us?" 8Also Moses said, "*This shall be seen* when the LORD gives you meat to eat in the evening, and in the morning bread to the full; for the LORD hears your complaints which you make against Him. And what *are* we? Your complaints *are* not against us but against the LORD."

9Then Moses spoke to Aaron, "Say to all the congregation of the children of Israel, 'Come near before the LORD, for He has heard your complaints.' " 10Now it came to pass, as Aaron spoke to the whole congregation of the children of Israel, that they looked toward the wilderness, and behold, the glory of the LORD appeared in the cloud.

11And the LORD spoke to Moses, saying, 12"I have heard the complaints of the children of Israel. Speak to them, saying, 'At twilight you shall eat meat, and in the morning you shall be filled with bread. And you shall know that I *am* the LORD your God.' "

13So it was that quails came up at evening and covered the camp, and in the morning the dew lay all around the camp. 14And when the layer of dew lifted, there, on the surface of the wilderness, was a small round substance, *as* fine as frost on the ground. 15So when the children of Israel saw *it*, they said to one another, "What is it?" For they did not know what it *was*.

And Moses said to them, "This *is* the bread which the LORD has given you to eat. 16This is the thing which the LORD has commanded: 'Let every man gather it according to each one's need, one omer for each person, *according to the* number of persons; let every man take for *those* who *are* in his tent.' "

17Then the children of Israel did so and gathered, some more, some less. 18So when they measured *it* by omers, he who gathered much had nothing left over, and he who gathered little had no lack. Every man had gathered according to each one's need. 19And Moses said, "Let no one leave any of it till morning." 20Notwithstanding they did not heed Moses. But some of them left part of it until morning, and it bred worms and stank. And Moses was angry with them. 21So they gathered it every morning, every man according to his need. And when the sun became hot, it melted.

22And so it was, on the sixth day, *that* they gathered twice as much bread, two omers for each

---

their complaining, they were like the bitter water and needed the Lord's healing for themselves (see also Deut. 32:39; Ps. 41:4). One day Egypt will likewise know Him as Healer (Is. 19:21, 22).

16:3 Death "by the hand of the LORD" may refer to "natural causes" or even to death as punishment for riot leaving Egypt to worship (Ex. 5:3). In this case they were claiming that early death would have come whether or not they obeyed the Lord. Such a claim was especially fatalistic and unfair to the Lord. They imagined the past as better than it was (slaves in Egypt did not eat meat in abundance). Their unbelief distorted their perception of reality. They did not believe God would keep His promises.

16:6, 7 God would give meat and bread, and they would learn from the experience (v. 12). The knowing and the seeing are

the results of receiving God's miraculous provision. This provision would help the people recognize that the Lord was their splendid deliverer. This message needed to be assimilated so as to influence how they viewed life and made decisions.

16:15 Provision of manna meant the Israelites could travel without concern for obtaining food. Since manna (Heb. *man hu'*, lit. "What is it?") was not the product of strenuous labor, its gracious provision in a sense reversed a result of the Fall (see Gen. 3:17–19).

16:20 Since each had what was needed for a day (vv. 17, 18), to attempt to save part for a second day meant going hungry and failing to enjoy properly what God had given for that day. This disobedience grew out of refusing to trust God (v. 19).

MIRIAM   *A Natural Leader*

Miriam, an intelligent child, became, with her brothers Aaron and Moses, a leader of the people of Israel. Her first appearance, babysitting her little brother beside the Nile River, demonstrates her keen mind. She volunteered to find a wet nurse for the baby when the Egyptian princess expressed her intention to adopt the child, thus allowing Moses' mother, Jochebed, to nurture him.

More than eighty years later, God delivered His people from the bondage of Egypt; and after the miracle of crossing the Red Sea on dry land, Miriam led the women in dancing and singing as a celebration to God. She was clearly gifted as a natural leader and was considered the foremost of all the Hebrew women, being also gifted as a musician and prophetess (Ex. 15:20). She undoubtedly was included at the council table with her brothers, and Miriam, as his older sister, may even have acted as a surrogate mother to Moses. There is no evidence in the text that she ever married. As a single woman, she committed herself to building the nation of Israel. Her career appears to be outside the home.

During the tumultuous days journeying across the desert, Moses' wife became a concern to Miriam. Whether this "Ethiopian woman" who had joined the group was Zipporah or a second wife is not known (see Num. 12:1). But her presence was cause for criticism and jealousy from Miriam and Aaron. They were not concerned because of her color but because she was from a foreign land. They apparently discussed their feelings, concluding together that they as leaders were being slighted. Miriam's mistake was her sarcastic rejection of her brother's leadership.

In anger the Lord disciplined Miriam with instant leprosy, thus banning her from the camp (Num. 12:10, 14). Because of the fervent prayers of her brothers, God restored her, but there is no evidence that her influence was again blessed of God. She died before reaching the Promised Land (Num. 20:1).

This gifted woman left a caution for every female leader. God alone gives and removes both talent and importance. Miriam incurred God's displeasure when she allowed herself to challenge the authority God had given Moses. She allowed jealousy and spitefulness to rob her of fulfillment in her later years.

See also Ex. 2:4–10; Num. 12:1–16; 20:1; 26:59; Deut. 24:9; Micah 6:4; notes on Bitterness (Heb. 12); Feminine Leadership (1 Sam. 25); Sanctity of Life (Gen. 9).

---

one. And all the rulers of the congregation came and told Moses. ²³Then he said to them, "This *is what* the LORD has said: 'Tomorrow *is* a Sabbath rest, a holy Sabbath to the LORD. Bake what you will bake *today,* and boil what you will boil; and lay up for yourselves all that remains, to be kept until morning.' " ²⁴So they laid it up till morning, as Moses commanded; and it did not stink, nor were there any worms in it. ²⁵Then Moses said, "Eat that today, for today *is* a Sabbath to the LORD; today you will not find it in the field. ²⁶Six days you shall gather it, but on the seventh day, the Sabbath, there will be none."

²⁷Now it happened *that some* of the people went out on the seventh day to gather, but they found none. ²⁸And the LORD said to Moses, "How long do you refuse to keep My commandments and My laws? ²⁹See! For the LORD has given you the Sabbath; therefore He gives you on the sixth day bread for two days. Let every man remain in his place; let no man go out of his place on the seventh day." ³⁰So the people rested on the seventh day.

³¹And the house of Israel called its name Manna.ᵃ And it *was* like white coriander seed, and the taste of it *was* like wafers *made* with honey.

³²Then Moses said, "This *is* the thing which the LORD has commanded: 'Fill an omer with it, to be kept for your generations, that they may see the bread with which I fed you in the wilderness, when I brought you out of the land of Egypt.' " ³³And Moses said to Aaron, "Take a pot and put an omer of manna in it, and lay it up before the LORD, to be kept for your generations." ³⁴As the LORD commanded Moses, so Aaron laid it up before the Testimony, to be kept. ³⁵And the children of Israel ate manna forty years, until they came to an inhabited land; they ate manna until they came to

••••••••••••••••••

16:31 ᵃLiterally *What?* (compare Exodus 16:15)

16:29, 30 The Lord's provision made rest possible. The people could stop working and rest on the seventh day because the Lord had given what they needed. Pharaoh would not have done this for them.

16:31–36 The name manna, its description, the record of its duration, the mention of the measure used for it, and, most important, the command to save some of it would be a memorial of God's provision to share with future generations (see v. 15, note). God's people must remember His provision in order to trust His love and ability to meet future needs (see also Deut. 8; John 6:1–13). "The Testimony" refers to the tablets of stone that God gave Moses and to the "ark of the Testimony," in which the tablets were deposited (v. 34; Ex. 25:16, 21, 22; 30:36; 31:18).

the border of the land of Canaan. ³⁶Now an omer *is* one-tenth of an ephah.

Water from the Rock

17 Then all the congregation of the children of Israel set out on their journey from the Wilderness of Sin, according to the commandment of the LORD, and camped in Rephidim; but *there was* no water for the people to drink. ²Therefore the people contended with Moses, and said, "Give us water, that we may drink."

So Moses said to them, "Why do you contend with me? Why do you tempt the LORD?"

³And the people thirsted there for water, and the people complained against Moses, and said, "Why *is* it you have brought us up out of Egypt, to kill us and our children and our livestock with thirst?"

⁴So Moses cried out to the LORD, saying, "What shall I do with this people? They are almost ready to stone me!"

⁵And the LORD said to Moses, "Go on before the people, and take with you some of the elders of Israel. Also take in your hand your rod with which you struck the river, and go. ⁶Behold, I will stand before you there on the rock in Horeb; and you shall strike the rock, and water will come out of it, that the people may drink."

And Moses did so in the sight of the elders of Israel. ⁷So he called the name of the place Massah[a] and Meribah,[b] because of the contention of the children of Israel, and because they tempted the LORD, saying, "Is the LORD among us or not?"

Victory over the Amalekites

⁸Now Amalek came and fought with Israel in Rephidim. ⁹And Moses said to Joshua, "Choose us some men and go out, fight with Amalek. Tomorrow I will stand on the top of the hill with the rod of God in my hand." ¹⁰So Joshua did as Moses said to him, and fought with Amalek. And Moses, Aaron, and Hur went up to the top of the hill. ¹¹And so it was, when Moses held up his hand, that Israel prevailed; and when he let down his hand, Amalek prevailed. ¹²But Moses' hands *became* heavy; so they took a stone and put *it* under him, and he sat on it. And Aaron and Hur supported his hands, one on one side, and the other on the other side; and his hands were steady until the going down of the sun. ¹³So Joshua defeated Amalek and his people with the edge of the sword.

¹⁴Then the LORD said to Moses, "Write this *for* a memorial in the book and recount it in the hearing of Joshua, that I will utterly blot out the remembrance of Amalek from under heaven." ¹⁵And Moses built an altar and called its name, The-LORD-Is-My-Banner;[a] ¹⁶for he said, "Because the LORD has sworn: the LORD *will have* war with Amalek from generation to generation."

Jethro's Advice

18 And Jethro, the priest of Midian, Moses' father-in-law, heard of all that God had done for Moses and for Israel His people—that the LORD had brought Israel out of Egypt. ²Then Jethro, Moses' father-in-law, took Zipporah, Moses' wife, after he had sent her back, ³with her two sons, of whom the name of one *was* Gershom (for he said, "I have been a stranger in a foreign land")[a] ⁴and the name of the other *was* Eliezer[a] (for *he said,* "The God of my father *was* my help, and delivered me from the sword of Pharaoh"); ⁵and Jethro, Moses' father-in-law, came with his sons and his wife to Moses in the wilderness, where he was encamped at the mountain of God. ⁶Now he had said to Moses, "I, your father-in-law Jethro, am coming to you with your wife and her two sons with her."

⁷So Moses went out to meet his father-in-law, bowed down, and kissed him. And they asked each other about *their* well-being, and they went into the tent. ⁸And Moses told his father-in-law all that the LORD had done to Pharaoh and to the Egyptians

---

17:7 [a]Literally *Tempted* [b]Literally *Contention*   17:15 [a]Hebrew *YHWH Nissi*   18:3 [a]Compare Exodus 2:22   18:4 [a]Literally *My God Is Help*

17:7 Massah and Meribah recall the Israelites' behavior in Rephidim. The name Massah is related to the verb translated "tempt" (vv. 2, 7) and "test" (Ex. 15:25; 16:4; Deut. 8:2, 16). The name Meribah is related to the verb translated "contend" (Ex. 17:2) and the noun "contention" (v. 7). This second family of words was frequently used of legal disputes (Ex. 23:2, 3, 6). The Israelites had "brought charges" against the Lord, not Moses, accusing the Lord of not properly taking care of them. The question about His presence among them summarizes their accusation that He was not acting on their behalf as they thought He should.

17:11 The lifting of Moses' hands symbolized dependence on the Lord, especially since Moses held the rod that God had instructed him to use in the past (vv. 5–7, 9; Ex. 4:17; 7:10–12; 9:23; 10:13; 14:16). There was no victory apart from God's intervention.

17:15 For the purpose of worship in gratitude for deliverance, Moses built a commemorative altar (see similarly Gen. 8:18–20; 12:7, 8; 33:18–20; 35:1–7). Aside from drought and famine, war was the greatest threat to Israel's physical existence and prosperity. In ancient and modern warfare, banners and flags symbolize unity and strength of purpose. The name Moses gave the altar reminded the people that the Lord was responsible for their victories.

18:1 Jethro. See Ex. 2:16, note.

18:3 Gershom. See Ex. 2:22, note.

18:4 Eliezer (Heb.), containing the elements *'eli* ("my God") and *'ezer* ("help") gave praise to God for Moses' safe escape from Pharaoh (see Ex. 2:11–15).

18:5 The mountain of God (see Ex. 3:1, note; 3:12; 4:27; 19:2, 3, 11; 24:13).

for Israel's sake, all the hardship that had come upon them on the way, and *how* the LORD had delivered them. [9]Then Jethro rejoiced for all the good which the LORD had done for Israel, whom He had delivered out of the hand of the Egyptians. [10]And Jethro said, "Blessed *be* the LORD, who has delivered you out of the hand of the Egyptians and out of the hand of Pharaoh, *and* who has delivered the people from under the hand of the Egyptians. [11]Now I know that the LORD *is* greater than all the gods; for in the very thing in which they behaved proudly, *He was* above them." [12]Then Jethro, Moses' father-in-law, took[a] a burnt offering and *other* sacrifices *to offer* to God. And Aaron came with all the elders of Israel to eat bread with Moses' father-in-law before God.

[13]And so it was, on the next day, that Moses sat to judge the people; and the people stood before Moses from morning until evening. [14]So when Moses' father-in-law saw all that he did for the people, he said, "What *is* this thing that you are doing for the people? Why do you alone sit, and all the people stand before you from morning until evening?"

[15]And Moses said to his father-in-law, "Because the people come to me to inquire of God. [16]When they have a difficulty, they come to me, and I judge between one and another; and I make known the statutes of God and His laws."

[17]So Moses' father-in-law said to him, "The thing that you do *is* not good. [18]Both you and these people who *are* with you will surely wear yourselves out. For this thing *is* too much for you; you are not able to perform it by yourself. [19]Listen now to my voice; I will give you counsel, and God will be with you: Stand before God for the people, so that you may bring the difficulties to God. [20]And you shall teach them the statutes and the laws, and show them the way in which they must walk and the work they must do. [21]Moreover you shall select from all the people able men, such as fear God, men of truth, hating covetousness; and place *such* over them *to be* rulers of thousands, rulers of hundreds, rulers of fifties, and rulers of

tens. [22]And let them judge the people at all times. Then it will be *that* every great matter they shall bring to you, but every small matter they themselves shall judge. So it will be easier for you, for they will bear *the burden* with you. [23]If you do this thing, and God *so* commands you, then you will be able to endure, and all this people will also go to their place in peace."

[24]So Moses heeded the voice of his father-in-law and did all that he had said. [25]And Moses chose able men out of all Israel, and made them heads over the people: rulers of thousands, rulers of hundreds, rulers of fifties, and rulers of tens. [26]So they judged the people at all times; the hard cases they brought to Moses, but they judged every small case themselves.

[27]Then Moses let his father-in-law depart, and he went his way to his own land.

Israel at Mount Sinai

19In the third month after the children of Israel had gone out of the land of Egypt, on the same day, they came *to* the Wilderness of Sinai. [2]For they had departed from Rephidim, had come *to* the Wilderness of Sinai, and camped in the wilderness. So Israel camped there before the mountain.

[3]And Moses went up to God, and the LORD called to him from the mountain, saying, "Thus you shall say to the house of Jacob, and tell the children of Israel: [4]'You have seen what I did to the Egyptians, and *how* I bore you on eagles' wings and brought you to Myself. [5]Now therefore, if you will indeed obey My voice and keep My covenant, then you shall be a special treasure to Me above all people; for all the earth *is* Mine. [6]And you shall be to Me a kingdom of priests and a holy nation.' These *are* the words which you shall speak to the children of Israel."

[7]So Moses came and called for the elders of the people, and laid before them all these words which

---

18:12 [a]Following Masoretic Text and Septuagint; Syriac, Targum, and Vulgate read *offered.*

19:1, 2 This mountain, Mount Sinai, is traditionally identified with Jebel Musa in the south-central Sinai peninsula (v. 11). "Wilderness" and "desert" translate a term that refers to uninhabited land with enough grass for grazing at certain times.

19:5 Covenants of two kinds regulated relations between individuals and between nations in the ancient Near East. Parity covenants were negotiated between equals. In suzerain-vassal covenants, a powerful king set out his terms that were to be obeyed by an underling. The covenant between the Lord and Israel described in Exodus 19–24 and in Deuteronomy has features of a suzerain-vassal treaty, a legal instrument that the Israelites would readily have understood. Such features visible in Exodus include a preamble that identifies the giver of the treaty (Ex. 20:2), a historical prologue stating benefi-

cial actions by the king (v. 4; Ex. 20:2; and in a sense Ex. 1–17), covenant stipulations (Ex. 20–23), requirement of absolute allegiance (Ex. 20:3, 23; 23:13, 24, 25; 34:11–17), formal sealing of the covenant (Ex. 24:9–11), and provisions for preserving the covenant document (Ex. 24:4, 7, 12; 25:16; 34:27, 28). No other ancient Near East treaty exists between a god and people.

19:6 As the priests were to the other Israelites, so Israel should be to the nations. Priests represented God to the people, and they represented the people to God. They were to aid people bringing sacrifices and offerings in worship that acknowledged dependence on God for forgiveness and the necessities of physical life. They were also responsible to teach the Law of God and to act as impartial judges (see Mal. 2:4–9).

Worry is a choice that displeases God. When you worry, you reveal that you don't really trust God to provide all that you need.

June Hunt

the LORD commanded him. [8]Then all the people answered together and said, "All that the LORD has spoken we will do." So Moses brought back the words of the people to the LORD. [9]And the LORD said to Moses, "Behold, I come to you in the thick cloud, that the people may hear when I speak with you, and believe you forever."

So Moses told the words of the people to the LORD.

[10]Then the LORD said to Moses, "Go to the people and consecrate them today and tomorrow, and let them wash their clothes. [11]And let them be ready for the third day. For on the third day the LORD will come down upon Mount Sinai in the sight of all the people. [12]You shall set bounds for the people all around, saying, 'Take heed to yourselves *that* you do *not* go up to the mountain or touch its base. Whoever touches the mountain shall surely be put to death. [13]Not a hand shall touch him, but he shall surely be stoned or shot *with an arrow;* whether man or beast, he shall not live.' When the trumpet sounds long, they shall come near the mountain."

[14]So Moses went down from the mountain to the people and sanctified the people, and they washed their clothes. [15]And he said to the people, "Be ready for the third day; do not come near *your* wives."

[16]Then it came to pass on the third day, in the morning, that there were thunderings and lightnings, and a thick cloud on the mountain; and the sound of the trumpet was very loud, so that all the people who *were* in the camp trembled. [17]And Moses brought the people out of the camp to meet with God, and they stood at the foot of the mountain. [18]Now Mount Sinai *was* completely in smoke, because the LORD descended upon it in fire. Its smoke ascended like the smoke of a furnace, and the whole mountain[a] quaked greatly. [19]And when the blast of the trumpet sounded long and became louder and louder, Moses spoke, and God answered him by voice. [20]Then the LORD came down upon Mount Sinai, on the top of the mountain. And the LORD called Moses to the top of the mountain, and Moses went up.

[21]And the LORD said to Moses, "Go down and warn the people, lest they break through to gaze at the LORD, and many of them perish. [22]Also let the priests who come near the LORD consecrate themselves, lest the LORD break out against them."

[23]But Moses said to the LORD, "The people cannot come up to Mount Sinai; for You warned us, saying, 'Set bounds around the mountain and consecrate it.'"

[24]Then the LORD said to him, "Away! Get down and then come up, you and Aaron with you. But do not let the priests and the people break through to come up to the LORD, lest He break out against them." [25]So Moses went down to the people and spoke to them.

The Ten Commandments

20 And God spoke all these words, saying:

[2]"I *am* the LORD your God, who brought you out of the land of Egypt, out of the house of bondage.

[3]"You shall have no other gods before Me.

[4]"You shall not make for yourself a carved image— any likeness *of anything* that *is* in

19:18 [a]Septuagint reads *all the people.*

19:15 The Israelites needed to be consecrated or sanctified (that is, set apart from what was ordinary and everyday) in recognition of the presence of the Lord (vv. 10, 14). The concept of holiness and sanctification requires the making of distinctions (see Lev. 19, Clean vs. Unclean; Lev. 20, Holiness). To set off the coming event, the Israelites were to wash their clothes and stay off the mountain (v. 12; see also Ex. 3:5). Prohibiting sexual intercourse reflected the need to be clean ritually (see Lev. 15:16–18, 31) and would also have distinguished this event from pagan worship, which often included sexual rites. The span of time (three days) and the special instructions gave an opportunity for thoughtful assent to the covenant.

19:16–19 This display of God's power had purpose (v. 9; Ex. 20:20). The thunder, lightning, trumpet, thick cloud, smoke, fire, trembling mountain, and audible voice called all the senses to attention so as to inspire awe at the special presence of the Lord. Yet they provided no fixed appearance that could be used to make an image to worship.

20:1–17 The Ten Commandments (lit. "words" or "pronouncements"; see Ex. 34:28; Deut. 4:13; 10:4; chart, The Ten Commandments Throughout Scripture). Also called the Decalogue (Gk. *deka,* "ten," and *logoi,* "words"), these statements are the basic principles of the Lord's covenant with Israel (Ex. 20:23—23:19). Reasons for obedience are prominently tied to who the Lord is and what He does (vv. 2, 5–7, 11, 12). The statements address each person individually (using "you" singular), with verses 2–11 centering on the individual's relationship with the Lord, while verses 12–17 discuss dealings with others.

20:3 No other gods before Me (lit. "in the presence of") does not imply that other gods could be worshiped secondarily or along with the Lord (see v. 5).

heaven above, or that *is* in the earth beneath, or that *is* in the water under the earth; [5]you shall not bow down to them nor serve them. For I, the LORD your God, *am* a jealous God, visiting the iniquity of the fathers upon the children to the third and fourth *generations* of those who hate Me, [6]but showing mercy to thousands, to those who love Me and keep My commandments.

[7]"You shall not take the name of the LORD your God in vain, for the LORD will not hold *him* guiltless who takes His name in vain.

[8]"Remember the Sabbath day, to keep it holy. [9]Six days you shall labor and do all your work, [10]but the seventh day *is* the Sabbath of the LORD your God. *In it* you shall do no work: you, nor your son, nor your daughter, nor your male servant, nor your female servant, nor your cattle, nor your stranger who *is* within your gates. [11]For *in* six days the LORD made the heavens and the earth, the sea, and all that *is* in them, and rested the seventh day. Therefore the LORD blessed the Sabbath day and hallowed it.

[12]"Honor your father and your mother, that your days may be long upon the land which the LORD your God is giving you.

[13]"You shall not murder.

[14]"You shall not commit adultery.

[15]"You shall not steal.

[16]"You shall not bear false witness against your neighbor.

[17]"You shall not covet your neighbor's house; you shall not covet your neighbor's wife, nor his male servant, nor his female servant, nor his ox, nor his donkey, nor anything that *is* your neighbor's."

The People Afraid of God's Presence

[18]Now all the people witnessed the thunderings, the lightning flashes, the sound of the trumpet, and the mountain smoking; and when the people saw *it*, they trembled and stood afar off. [19]Then they said to Moses, "You speak with us, and we will hear; but let not God speak with us, lest we die."

[20]And Moses said to the people, "Do not fear; for God has come to test you, and that His fear may be before you, so that you may not sin." [21]So the people stood afar off, but Moses drew near the thick darkness where God *was*.

The Law of the Altar

[22]Then the LORD said to Moses, "Thus you shall say to the children of Israel: 'You have seen that I have talked with you from heaven. [23]You shall not make *anything to be* with Me—gods of silver or gods of gold you shall not make for yourselves. [24]An altar of earth you shall make for Me, and you shall sacrifice on it your burnt offerings and your peace offerings, your sheep and your oxen. In every place where I record My name I will come to you, and I will bless you. [25]And if you make Me an altar of stone, you shall not build it of hewn stone; for if you use your tool on it, you have profaned it. [26]Nor shall you go up by steps to My altar, that your nakedness may not be exposed on it.'

The Law Concerning Servants

21 "Now these *are* the judgments which you shall set before them: [2]If you buy a Hebrew

---

20:5, 6 The word translated jealous does not mean "suspicious" or "envious." Rather, God is zealous to protect what properly belongs to Him. The right understanding of His nature and deeds leads to exclusive worship. That understanding and worship are both lost when anything He created becomes an object of devotion (see Deut. 4, Attributes of God). The clause "those who hate Me" may apply to parents or children or both. For children to experience the consequences of the sins of their parents does not imply that God neglected to punish the parents (see Deut. 7:9, 10; Ezek. 18:19–23, 30–32) or that the Israelites inflicted punishment on children for the crimes of their parents (see Deut. 24:16; 2 Kin. 14:6). The word translated "mercy" (Heb. *chesed*, lit. "loyal love" or "lovingkindness") has to do with keeping covenantal bonds and promises, as illustrated by David and Jonathan (1 Sam. 18:1–4; 20:12–17; 2 Sam. 9:1–7).

20:7 In vain has the idea of "for nothing, uselessly, falsely" (Ex. 23:1). One use of the Lord's name was in taking oaths, in which the speaker affirmed a statement by saying, "As the LORD lives" (that is, witnesses my words and will hold me accountable; see Lev. 19:12; 2 Sam. 2:27; Jer. 4:2). The Lord's name includes His nature and reputation, which the Israelites were to guard, so as not to associate Him with any lie, pagan cursing, magic incantations, fortune-telling, or any other empty or insincere purpose. To take the Lord's name "in vain" amounted to denying the reality of His existence or moral character. More than verbal profanity is prohibited here (see also Matt. 6:9; John 17:6; 2 Tim. 2:19).

20:8–11 No connection has been established between the Israelite Sabbath and observances in any other ancient culture. Nor does it derive from movements of the sun, moon, or stars, as do other units of time. It reflects the fact that the governing of time and activity belongs to the Lord (see Ex. 23, The Lord's Day; chart, The Principle of the Sabbath).

20:24 Burnt offerings are sacrifices that were totally burned on the altar (see chart, The Offerings of the Lord). This signified the complete dedication of the one offering the sacrifice. "Peace offerings" pointed to the covenant relationship and communion between individuals and God. Part of the sacrifice was burned and part was eaten. Hospitality in a communal meal was made possible because of God's actions on behalf of the one who offered the sacrifice.

20:25 To cut the stones with tools would "profane" the stone, in other words, make it common and ordinary the opposite of holy, sanctified, consecrated, set apart.

21:1 The judgments, a collection of case studies or judicial rulings, are introduced (Ex. 21:2—22:17). Beginning with an

THE TEN COMMANDMENTS THROUGHOUT SCRIPTURE

	COMMANDMENTS	PRACTICAL APPLICATION	OLD TESTAMENT REFERENCES	NEW TESTAMENT REFERENCES
1	You shall have no other gods before Me (Ex. 20:3, 23; 34:14).	Show respect to God and to those He has placed in authority over you.	Deut. 5:7; 6:4, 14; 13:6–10; 2 Kin. 17:35; Ps. 81:9; Jer. 25:6; 35:15	Matt. 4:10; 22:37, 38; Mark 12:29, 30; Luke 4:8
2	You shall not make for yourself a carved image (Ex. 20:4–6; 34:17).	Live your life in whole-hearted devotion to God.	Lev. 19:4; 26:1; Deut. 4:15–20; 5:8–10; 7:25; Ps. 115:4–8; Is. 44:9–20	Rom. 1:22, 23; 1 John 5:21; Rev. 14:9–11
3	You shall not take the name of the LORD your God in vain (Ex. 20:7).	Guard your speech and strive to communicate effectively and respectfully.	Lev. 18:21; 19:12; 22:2; 24:16; Deut. 5:11; 6:13; Ezek. 39:7	Matt. 5:33–37; James 5:12
4	Remember the Sabbath day, to keep it holy (Ex 20:8–11; 16:23–30; 31:13–16; 35:2, 3).	Allow time for meditation with proper rest and relaxation.	Gen. 2:3; Lev. 19:3, 30; Deut. 5:12–15; Jer. 17:21–27; Ezek. 20:12	Mark 2:27, 28
5	Honor your father and your mother (Ex. 20:12; 21:17).	Treat parents with respect.	Lev. 19:3; Deut. 5:16; 27:16; Prov. 6:20–22	Matt. 15:4–9; 19:19; Mark 7:10–13; 10:19; Luke 18:20; Eph. 6:1–3; Col. 3:20
6	You shall not murder (Ex. 20:13).	Recognize God's control over life and death.	Gen. 9:5, 6; Lev. 24:17; Deut. 5:17	Matt. 5:21, 22; 19:18; Mark 10:19; Luke 18:20; Rom. 13:9
7	You shall not commit adultery (Ex. 20:14).	Honor the vow of faithfulness to spouse and God.	Lev. 18:20; 20:10; Deut. 5:18; 22:22; Prov. 6:29, 32	Matt. 5:27, 28; Mark 10:19; Luke 18:20; Rom. 13:9; James 2:11
8	You shall not steal (Ex. 20:15; 21:16).	Guard against taking what is not yours.	Lev. 19:11, 13; Deut. 5:19	Matt. 19:18; Rom. 13:9; Eph. 4:28
9	You shall not bear false witness against your neighbor (Ex. 20:16; 23:1, 7).	Respond to others in integrity and respect.	Deut. 5:20; Ps. 101:5; Prov. 6:16–19; 19:5; Zech. 8:16	Matt. 19:18; Mark 10:19; Luke 18:20; Rom. 13:9; Eph. 4:25; Col. 3:9
10	You shall not covet (Ex. 20:17).	Be satisfied with your own possessions and resources.	Deut. 5:21; 7:25; Prov. 28:16	Luke 12:15; Rom. 7:7; 13:9; Eph. 5:3, 5; Heb. 13:5

"if" clause, these "case laws" set forth a particular situation, followed by a conclusion. In contrast to the Ten Commandments, they deal with specific situations requiring decisions concerning disputes and conflicting rights and wishes. Unlike other ancient Near Eastern collections of laws, which are presented as coming from human kings, these judgments, along with the Ten Commandments, came from God as part of His provision for His people to live distinctively as a "holy nation" with Him in their midst (Ex. 19:6; see Deut. 4:5–8).

21:2 Poverty-stricken Israelites, whether male or female, could discharge debts and secure food and shelter by selling

GODDESS RELIGION *OPPOSED TO GOD*

Goddess worshipers believe that deity is immanent in all things. They view "God" as an internal, universal feminine *force* rather than an external, autonomous Being, and they consider the female body as the direct incarnation of the waxing and waning life and death cycle in nature. They use idols of ancient female deities such as Artemis, Asherah, or Isis to represent universal female (and thus their own) power.

Goddess worshipers seek to create justice as well as ecological and social balance through ritual magic, spellcasting, and the generation of energy. They purport that the New Age will appear when all people come to recognize their oneness with the universe and respect the deity of others and of nature.

Goddess religion stands in direct opposition to the monotheistic worship of *Yahweh* God. God's wrath is against those who change His glory into images of humans and animals and who worship and serve the creation rather than the Creator (Rom. 1:22–26).

See also Rom. 1:22–26; notes on Fatherhood of God (Rom. 8); Heresies (1 Cor. 1); Idolatry (Is. 42); Witchcraft (1 Sam. 15)

servant, he shall serve six years; and in the seventh he shall go out free and pay nothing. ³If he comes in by himself, he shall go out by himself; if he *comes in* married, then his wife shall go out with him. ⁴If his master has given him a wife, and she has borne him sons or daughters, the wife and her children shall be her master's, and he shall go out by himself. ⁵But if the servant plainly says, 'I love my master, my wife, and my children; I will not go out free,' ⁶then his master shall bring him to the judges. He shall also bring him to the door, or to the doorpost, and his master shall pierce his ear with an awl; and he shall serve him forever.

⁷And if a man sells his daughter to be a female slave, she shall not go out as the male slaves do. ⁸If she does not please her master, who has betrothed her to himself, then he shall let her be redeemed. He shall have no right to sell her to a foreign people, since he has dealt deceitfully with her. ⁹And if he has betrothed her to his son, he shall deal with her according to the custom of daughters. ¹⁰If he takes another *wife*, he shall not diminish her food, her clothing, and her marriage rights. ¹¹And if he does not do these three for her, then she shall go out free, without *paying* money.

The Law Concerning Violence

¹²"He who strikes a man so that he dies shall surely be put to death. ¹³However, if he did not lie in wait, but God delivered *him* into his hand, then I will appoint for you a place where he may flee. ¹⁴But if a man acts with premeditation against his neighbor, to kill him by treachery, you shall take him from My altar, that he may die.

¹⁵"And he who strikes his father or his mother shall surely be put to death.

¹⁶"He who kidnaps a man and sells him, or if he is found in his hand, shall surely be put to death.

¹⁷"And he who curses his father or his mother shall surely be put to death.

¹⁸"If men contend with each other, and one strikes the other with a stone or with *his* fist, and he does not die but is confined to *his* bed, ¹⁹if he rises again and walks about outside with his staff, then he who struck *him* shall be acquitted. He shall only pay *for* the loss of his time, and shall provide *for him* to be thoroughly healed.

²⁰"And if a man beats his male or female servant with a rod, so that he dies under his hand, he shall surely be punished. ²¹Notwithstanding, if he remains alive a day or two, he shall not be punished; for he *is* his property.

²²"If men fight, and hurt a woman with child, so that she gives birth prematurely, yet no harm follows, he shall surely be punished accordingly as the woman's husband imposes on him; and he shall pay as the judges *determine*. ²³But if *any* harm follows, then you shall give life for life, ²⁴eye for

themselves as servants, to be freed after six years (Deut. 15:12–18; see Luke 9, the Homeless; Luke 16, Poverty).

21:7–11 The situation of a girl sold by her father was different from that of the servants (vv. 2–6). Her father sold her with the expectation that she would in due time marry the household's master or his son. If designated for the son, she must be protected like a daughter (v. 9). This presupposes not a loveless relationship but one of loving concern. The meaning of the word translated "marriage rights" is disputed (v. 10). Some scholars connect it to words meaning "dwelling" and "shelter." In any case, the master of the house was to provide for her, even if there were another wife (see also Deut. 21:15–17). The regulations governing any exceptions seem to

have the interest of the slave rather than the master in mind (see also article, Renewed by His Grace).

21:22, 23 Though in recent decades both proponents and opponents of abortion have cited these verses for support, several observations prohibit using these verses to support abortion.

- They appear in the context of the Book of Exodus with its concern for preserving infant life (Ex. 1; 2).
- The fact of pregnancy as part of the case must imply concern for the unborn child, or the situation could involve another bystander and be covered by other verses (vv. 12–14, 18, 19).
- Even if it is asserted that a fine was assessed for the death

eye, tooth for tooth, hand for hand, foot for foot, [25]burn for burn, wound for wound, stripe for stripe.

[26]"If a man strikes the eye of his male or female servant, and destroys it, he shall let him go free for the sake of his eye. [27]And if he knocks out the tooth of his male or female servant, he shall let him go free for the sake of his tooth.

Animal Control Laws

[28]"If an ox gores a man or a woman to death, then the ox shall surely be stoned, and its flesh shall not be eaten; but the owner of the ox *shall be* acquitted. [29]But if the ox tended to thrust with its horn in times past, and it has been made known to his owner, and he has not kept it confined, so that it has killed a man or a woman, the ox shall be stoned and its owner also shall be put to death. [30]If there is imposed on him a sum of money, then he shall pay to redeem his life, whatever is imposed on him. [31]Whether it has gored a son or gored a daughter, according to this judgment it shall be done to him. [32]If the ox gores a male or female servant, he shall give to their master thirty shekels of silver, and the ox shall be stoned.

[33]"And if a man opens a pit, or if a man digs a pit and does not cover it, and an ox or a donkey falls in it, [34]the owner of the pit shall make *it* good; he shall give money to their owner, but the dead *animal* shall be his.

[35]"If one man's ox hurts another's, so that it dies, then they shall sell the live ox and divide the money from it; and the dead *ox* they shall also divide. [36]Or if it was known that the ox tended to thrust in time past, and its owner has not kept it confined, he shall surely pay ox for ox, and the dead animal shall be his own.

Responsibility for Property

22 "If a man steals an ox or a sheep, and slaughters it or sells it, he shall restore five oxen for an ox and four sheep for a sheep. [2]If the thief is found breaking in, and he is struck so that he dies, *there shall be* no guilt for his bloodshed. [3]If the sun has risen on him, *there shall be* guilt for his bloodshed. He should make full restitution; if he has nothing, then he shall be sold for his theft. [4]If the theft is certainly found alive in his hand, whether it is an ox or donkey or sheep, he shall restore double.

[5]"If a man causes a field or vineyard to be grazed, and lets loose his animal, and it feeds in another man's field, he shall make restitution from the best of his own field and the best of his own vineyard.

[6]"If fire breaks out and catches in thorns, so that stacked grain, standing grain, or the field is consumed, he who kindled the fire shall surely make restitution.

[7]"If a man delivers to his neighbor money or articles to keep, and it is stolen out of the man's house, if the thief is found, he shall pay double. [8]If the thief is not found, then the master of the house shall be brought to the judges *to see* whether he has put his hand into his neighbor's goods.

[9]"For any kind of trespass, *whether it concerns* an ox, a donkey, a sheep, or clothing, *or* for any kind of lost thing which *another* claims to be his, the cause of both parties shall come before the judges; *and* whomever the judges condemn shall pay double to his neighbor. [10]If a man delivers to his neighbor a donkey, an ox, a sheep, or any animal to keep, and it dies, is hurt, or driven away, no one seeing *it,* [11]then an oath of the LORD shall be between them both, that he has not put his hand into his neighbor's goods; and the owner of it shall accept *that,* and he shall not make *it* good. [12]But if, in fact, it is stolen from him, he shall make restitution to the owner of it. [13]If it is torn to pieces *by a beast, then* he shall bring it as evidence, *and* he shall not make good what was torn.

[14]"And if a man borrows *anything* from his neighbor, and it becomes injured or dies, the owner of it not *being* with it, he shall surely make *it* good. [15]If its owner *was* with it, he shall not make *it* good; if it *was* hired, it came for its hire.

Moral and Ceremonial Principles

[16]"If a man entices a virgin who is not betrothed, and lies with her, he shall surely pay the bride-price for her *to be* his wife. [17]If her father utterly refuses to give her to him, he shall pay money according to the bride-price of virgins.

[18]"You shall not permit a sorceress to live.

[19]"Whoever lies with an animal shall surely be put to death.

[20]"He who sacrifices to *any* god, except to the LORD only, he shall be utterly destroyed.

[21]"You shall neither mistreat a stranger nor oppress him, for you were strangers in the land of Egypt.

---

of the child rather than the death penalty, that does not indicate that unborn life is valueless or can be extinguished without penalty but just the opposite (see differing penalties involving adults, children, and slaves, vv. 30–32).

• The case in Exodus describes unintentional injury.

22:18 Numerous OT passages condemn the practices and practitioners of sorcery and related activities (Lev. 19:26, 31; 20:6, 27; Deut. 18:9–14; Is. 47:9–14; Mic. 5:12; Mal. 3:5; see Acts 13:8–10; 19:19). To attempt to exercise power by means of knowledge or control of spirits could never combine with allegiance to the one true and living Lord God (see Deut. 18, The Occult; 1 Sam. 15, Witchcraft). All such practices in essence deny the Lord's power and goodness.

MISCARRIAGE AN EXPERIENCE OF BEREAVEMENT

Though the experience of miscarriage is described in the Bible, the word "miscarriage" is seldom used in the Old Testament and never used in the New Testament. The Hebrew word *shakol* is translated as "miscarriage" or "miscarrying" (Ex. 23:26; Hos. 9:14). Other forms are translated "bereavement" in relationship to children. To be pregnant is to be "with child" (Ex. 21:22). To miscarry, an experience of bereavement, is to miss the opportunity to carry a child from conception until the child can live outside the womb.

As a child develops in the womb, an emotional bond between mother and child is established and grows in strength. The unborn child responds to things in the internal and external environment (Luke 1:41). The depth of grief following miscarriage varies according to the degree of bonding that has taken place between the parents and the child in the womb (Prov. 13:12). The miscarriage of a pregnant bystander (owing to a fight between men) carried a severe penalty (Ex. 21:22). The fine, proposed by the father and imposed by judges, may have been determined by the development of the child.

Hosea proposed "miscarrying wombs" as one of the consequences of Israel's longstanding, deliberate disobedience to the covenant the Lord had made with Israel (Hos. 9:13–16). Miscarriage, however, was not viewed as judgment on selected women for personal sin. It is rather a consequence of living in a fallen world (Rom. 5:12, 14).

Both parents share in the loss of their child and need to be comforted by Christian friends (Eccl. 3:4; Rom. 12:15; Phil. 2:1, 2). The parents may need to be reminded that God's love encompasses the preborn and that He is involved in the development of the child in the womb (Ps. 139:13, 14). The "infants who never saw light" of day are at rest (Job 3:16, 17). Children, though lost to earthly life, are special to God (Mark 10:14), and Christian parents will one day be reunited with them (2 Sam. 12:23).

See also notes on Abortion (Jer. 1); Childbirth (John 16); Children (2 Sam. 21); Grief (Is. 53); Pain (Job 7; 2 Cor. 12); Pregnancy (Judg. 13); Sanctity of Life (Gen. 9)

22"You shall not afflict any widow or fatherless child. 23If you afflict them in any way, *and* they cry at all to Me, I will surely hear their cry; 24and My wrath will become hot, and I will kill you with the sword; your wives shall be widows, and your children fatherless.

25"If you lend money to *any of* My people *who are* poor among you, you shall not be like a moneylender to him; you shall not charge him interest. 26If you ever take your neighbor's garment as a pledge, you shall return it to him before the sun goes down. 27For that *is* his only covering, it *is* his garment for his skin. What will he sleep in? And it will be that when he cries to Me, I will hear, for I *am* gracious.

28"You shall not revile God, nor curse a ruler of your people.

29"You shall not delay *to offer* the first of your ripe produce and your juices. The firstborn of your sons you shall give to Me. 30Likewise you shall do with your oxen *and* your sheep. It shall be with its mother seven days; on the eighth day you shall give it to Me.

31"And you shall be holy men to Me: you shall not eat meat torn *by beasts* in the field; you shall throw it to the dogs.

Justice for All

23 "You shall not circulate a false report. Do not put your hand with the wicked to be an unrighteous witness. 2You shall not follow a crowd to do evil; nor shall you testify in a dispute so as to turn aside after many to pervert *justice.* 3You shall not show partiality to a poor man in his dispute.

4"If you meet your enemy's ox or his donkey going astray, you shall surely bring it back to him again. 5If you see the donkey of one who hates you lying under its burden, and you would refrain from helping it, you shall surely help him with it.

6"You shall not pervert the judgment of your poor in his dispute. 7Keep yourself far from a false matter; do not kill the innocent and righteous. For I will not justify the wicked. 8And you shall take no bribe, for a bribe blinds the discerning and perverts the words of the righteous.

9"Also you shall not oppress a stranger, for you know the heart of a stranger, because you were strangers in the land of Egypt.

The Law of Sabbaths

10"Six years you shall sow your land and gather in its produce, 11but the seventh *year* you shall let it rest and lie fallow, that the poor of your people may eat; and what they leave, the beasts of the field may eat. In like manner you shall do with your vineyard *and* your olive grove. 12Six days you shall do your work, and on the seventh day you shall rest, that your ox and your donkey may rest, and the son of your female servant and the stranger may be refreshed.

13"And in all that I have said to you, be circum-

spect and make no mention of the name of other gods, nor let it be heard from your mouth.

Three Annual Feasts

14"Three times you shall keep a feast to Me in the year: 15You shall keep the Feast of Unleavened Bread (you shall eat unleavened bread seven days, as I commanded you, at the time appointed in the month of Abib, for in it you came out of Egypt; none shall appear before Me empty); 16and the Feast of Harvest, the firstfruits of your labors which you have sown in the field; and the Feast of Ingathering at the end of the year, when you have gathered in *the fruit of* your labors from the field.

17"Three times in the year all your males shall appear before the Lord GOD.a

18"You shall not offer the blood of My sacrifice with leavened bread; nor shall the fat of My sacrifice remain until morning. 19The first of the firstfruits of your land you shall bring into the house of the LORD your God. You shall not boil a young goat in its mother's milk.

The Angel and the Promises

20"Behold, I send an Angel before you to keep you in the way and to bring you into the place which I have prepared. 21Beware of Him and obey His voice; do not provoke Him, for He will not pardon your transgressions; for My name *is* in Him. 22But if you indeed obey His voice and do all that I speak, then I will be an enemy to your enemies and an adversary to your adversaries. 23For My Angel will go before you and bring you in to the Amorites and the Hittites and the Perizzites and the Canaanites and the Hivites and the Jebusites; and I will cut them off. 24You shall not bow down to their gods, nor serve them, nor do according to their works; but you shall utterly overthrow them and completely break down their *sacred* pillars.

25"So you shall serve the LORD your God, and He will bless your bread and your water. And I will take sickness away from the midst of you. 26No one shall suffer miscarriage or be barren in your land; I will fulfill the number of your days.

27"I will send My fear before you, I will cause confusion among all the people to whom you come, and will make all your enemies turn *their* backs to you. 28And I will send hornets before you, which shall drive out the Hivite, the Canaanite, and the Hittite from before you. 29I will not drive them out from before you in one year, lest the land become desolate and the beasts of the field become too numerous for you. 30Little by little I will drive them out from before you, until you have increased, and you inherit the land. 31And I will set your bounds from the Red Sea to the sea, Philistia, and from the desert to the River.a For I will deliver the inhabitants of the land into your hand, and you shall drive them out before you. 32You shall make no covenant with them, nor with their gods. 33They shall not dwell in your land, lest they make you sin against Me. For *if* you serve their gods, it will surely be a snare to you."

Israel Affirms the Covenant

24 Now He said to Moses, "Come up to the LORD, you and Aaron, Nadab and Abihu, and seventy of the elders of Israel, and worship from afar. 2And Moses alone shall come near the LORD, but they shall not come near; nor shall the people go up with him."

3So Moses came and told the people all the words of the LORD and all the judgments. And all the people answered with one voice and said, "All the words which the LORD has said we will do." 4And Moses wrote all the words of the LORD. And he rose early in the morning, and built an altar at the foot of the mountain, and twelve pillars according to the twelve tribes of Israel. 5Then he sent young men of the children of Israel, who offered burnt offerings and sacrificed peace

23:17 aHebrew YHWH, usually translated LORD   23:31 aHebrew Na-har, the Euphrates

23:16 The Feast of Harvest—also called the Feast of Weeks (Heb. *shavu'ot*, lit. "weeks"), Pentecost, "the day of the firstfruits" (Num. 28:26), and "the firstfruits of wheat harvest" (Ex. 34:22)—fell during the wheat harvest, seven weeks after the Feast of Unleavened Bread (see chart, The Feasts of Israel). The Feast of Ingathering or Tabernacles (Heb. *sukkot*, lit. "booths"), during which the people lived in temporary shelters, came at the end of the agricultural year when olives, grapes, and other fruits were picked.

23:17 Women also came to the three great celebrations but were not required to do so (Deut. 16:11, 14; 1 Sam. 1; Luke 2:41–44).

23:18, 19 The prohibition against boiling a young goat (v. 19) has received no entirely satisfactory explanation. Perhaps it attacked a pagan fertility rite, had a humane basis, or was connected with the Feast of Harvest. Since the statute prohibits cooking a kid in the milk of its own mother, its symbolism could have been focused on those who looked contemptuously on the relationship ordained of God between mother and child or on those who placed so low a value on life as to cook a young kid in what should have given it life (see Deut. 14:21, note). Later Judaism extended this to prohibit eating meat with any dairy product in the same meal, going beyond the directive in the text.

23:20–23 This section continues the Lord's revelation of Himself, inasmuch as His name—highly important in Exodus—was "in Him (the Angel)" (v. 21). Among the character traits revealed are leadership (He would have the task of guarding the people and bringing them to Canaan, v. 20), authority (He must be obeyed, v. 21), and righteousness (He would not pardon rebellion—violation of covenant obligations, v. 21). What He said is closely identified with what the Lord said (v. 22; see also Ex. 3:2, 11, 12, 13–15, notes).

THE LORD'S DAY   A TIME FOR REST AND WORSHIP

The Sabbath—which means "rest"—is the seventh day of the Hebrew week (Gen. 2:2, 3). The Israelites were commanded to keep this day as a holy day of rest, reflection, and re-creation in honor of the Lord (Ex. 20:8–11).

The Sabbath served to remind the Israelites of their identity as God's covenant people and of their deliverance from Egypt (Ex. 31:12–17; Deut. 5:15; Is. 58:13, 14). It was a day that offered refreshment from work, both spiritually and physically (Ex. 23:10–12). Traditionally, Jews spend three days each week in eager anticipation of the Sabbath, then after it has passed, three days reflecting on its joy. The Old Testament has very sharp reminders to keep the Sabbath day (Is. 56:2; Jer. 17:19–27; Ezek. 44:24), as well as harsh punishment for a person who broke the Sabbath (Num. 15:32–36).

The Lord's Day, by comparison, was considered to be the "first day" of the week. A sign of the new beginning marked by the Resurrection of Jesus from the tomb, the Lord's Day quickly became the day on which the early church met for weekly worship (Acts 20:7; 1 Cor. 16:2). Yet rest remains an important part of the Lord's Day.

The Lord's Day is not to be filled with legalism, for that is what Christ frequently rebuked in His day. It should be the joyful focal point of the week, a day eagerly anticipated by the believer. We should approach it physically rested and attitudinally ready for the Lord to reveal Himself to us (Ps. 118:24).

See also Ex. 20:8–11; notes on Celebrations and Holidays (Ex. 12); Leisure (Mark 6); Praise (Ps. 149); Priorities (Matt. 6)

---

offerings of oxen to the LORD. ⁶And Moses took half the blood and put *it* in basins, and half the blood he sprinkled on the altar. ⁷Then he took the Book of the Covenant and read in the hearing of the people. And they said, "All that the LORD has said we will do, and be obedient." ⁸And Moses took the blood, sprinkled *it* on the people, and said, "This is the blood of the covenant which the LORD has made with you according to all these words."

On the Mountain with God

⁹Then Moses went up, also Aaron, Nadab, and Abihu, and seventy of the elders of Israel, ¹⁰and they saw the God of Israel. And *there was* under His feet as it were a paved work of sapphire stone, and it was like the very heavens in *its* clarity. ¹¹But on the nobles of the children of Israel He did not lay His hand. So they saw God, and they ate and drank.

¹²Then the LORD said to Moses, "Come up to Me on the mountain and be there; and I will give you tablets of stone, and the law and commandments which I have written, that you may teach them."

¹³So Moses arose with his assistant Joshua, and Moses went up to the mountain of God. ¹⁴And he said to the elders, "Wait here for us until we come back to you. Indeed, Aaron and Hur *are* with you. If any man has a difficulty, let him go to them." ¹⁵Then Moses went up into the mountain, and a cloud covered the mountain.

¹⁶Now the glory of the LORD rested on Mount Sinai, and the cloud covered it six days. And on the seventh day He called to Moses out of the midst of the cloud. ¹⁷The sight of the glory of the LORD *was* like a consuming fire on the top of the mountain in the eyes of the children of Israel. ¹⁸So Moses went into the midst of the cloud and went up into the mountain. And Moses was on the mountain forty days and forty nights.

Offerings for the Sanctuary

25 Then the LORD spoke to Moses, saying: ²"Speak to the children of Israel, that they bring Me an offering. From everyone who gives it willingly with his heart you shall take My offering. ³And this *is* the offering which you shall take from them: gold, silver, and bronze; ⁴blue, purple, and scarlet *thread,* fine linen, and goats' *hair;* ⁵ram skins dyed red, badger skins, and acacia wood; ⁶oil for the light, and spices for the anointing oil and for the sweet incense; ⁷onyx stones, and stones to be set in the ephod and in the breastplate. ⁸And let them make Me a sanctuary,

---

25:1–31:18 The Lord had announced that He would bring the Israelites out of Egypt so that they would be able to worship and serve Him by means that included sacrifices (Ex. 8:20–29). Exodus 25—31 records directions for constructing a place of worship and its furnishings and for making the clothing and conducting the dedication of the priests and Levites, who would tend the tabernacle and lead the nation in worship (see charts, The Furniture of the Tabernacle; The Plan of the Tabernacle).

25:8, 9 Let them make Me a sanctuary. The word translated "sanctuary" is closely related to words translated "holy, holiness, consecrate, sanctify." This was appropriate to God's holy character; He is separate from defilement. The tabernacle would be devoted to a special purpose, separated from everything profane or mundane, a holy place, so that it would be clear that God, though living among the Israelites, was separate from them (see Lev. 20, Holiness; Is. 6, Attributes of God).

THE FEASTS OF ISRAEL

NAME OF FEAST	REFERENCES	JEWISH MONTH (MODERN EQUIVALENT) AND DAY	PURPOSE	PROPHETIC SIGNIFICANCE
1. Passover (Heb. *pesah*)	Ex. 12:1–28, 43–49; Lev. 23:5; Num. 28:16; Deut. 16:1–8; Matt. 26:17–20	Nisan or Abib (March/April), 14	To commemorate Israel's deliverance from Egypt; To remind the children of Israel that God spared their firstborn (Ex. 12:27)	Christ as our Passover (John 1:29; 19:36; 1 Cor. 5:7; 1 Pet. 1:18, 19) Passover as the foundation for the Lord's Supper (Matt. 26:17–30; Mark 14:12–25; Luke 22:1–20) Passover as foreshadowing the marriage supper of the Lamb (Matt. 26:29; Mark 14:25; Luke 22:16–18)
2. Feast of Unleavened Bread* (Heb. *matsot*)	Ex. 12:15–20; 13:3–10; Lev. 23:6–8; Num. 28:17–25; Deut. 16:3–8	Nisan (March/April), 15–21	To commemorate the hardships of Israel's flight from Egypt (Ex. 12:39); To symbolize consecration and devotion to God	Unleavened bread as: a type of Christ (John 6:30–59; 1 Cor. 11:24); a type of the true church (1 Cor. 5:7, 8)
3. Day of Firstfruits (Heb. *bikkurim*)	Lev. 23:9–14	Nisan (March/April), 16	To dedicate and consecrate the firstfruits of the barley harvest	Firstfruits as: a type of the bodily resurrection of Christ (1 Cor. 15:20–23); a guarantee of the bodily resurrection of all believers (1 Cor. 15:20–23; 1 Thess. 4:13–18); a type of the consecration of the church
4. Feast of Pentecost* (Harvest or Weeks; Heb. *shabuot*)	Ex. 23:16; Lev. 23:15–22; Num. 28:26–31; Deut. 16:9–12; Acts 2:1	Sivan (May/June), 6	To dedicate and consecrate the firstfruits of the wheat harvest	The outpouring of the Holy Spirit on the church on the Day of Pentecost
5. Day of Trumpets (Heb. *rosh hashanah*)	Lev. 23:23–25; Num. 10:10; 29:1–6	Tishri (September/October), 1, 2	To consecrate the seventh month as the sabbatical month	In the NT, association of the blowing of the trumpet with the return of the Lord (Matt. 24:31; 1 Cor. 15:52; 1 Thess. 4:16)
6. Day of Atonement (Heb. *yom kippur*)	Lev. 16:1–34; 23:26–32; Num. 29:7–11; Heb. 9:7	Tishri (September/October), 10	To make atonement for the sins of the priest and the people annually; To make atonement for the tabernacle of meeting	Ultimate fulfillment in the crucifixion of Christ, representing His redeeming work more adequately than any other OT type.
7. Feast of Tabernacles* (Booths or Ingathering; Heb. *sukkot*)	Lev. 23:33–43; Num. 29:12–38; Deut. 16:13–17; Neh. 8:13–18; John 7:2	Tishri (September/October), 15–22	To commemorate God's deliverance and protection during the wilderness wandering (Lev. 23:43); To rejoice in the completion of harvest (Lev. 23:39)	Foreshadowing the peace and prosperity of the millennial reign of Christ (Zech. 14:16)

The three major feasts for which all males of Israel were required to travel to the temple in Jerusalem (Ex. 23:14–19).

that I may dwell among them. ⁹According to all that I show you, *that is,* the pattern of the tabernacle and the pattern of all its furnishings, just so you shall make *it.*

The Ark of the Testimony

¹⁰"And they shall make an ark of acacia wood; two and a half cubits *shall be* its length, a cubit and a half its width, and a cubit and a half its height. ¹¹And you shall overlay it with pure gold, inside and out you shall overlay it, and shall make on it a molding of gold all around. ¹²You shall cast four rings of gold for it, and put *them* in its four corners; two rings *shall be* on one side, and two rings on the other side. ¹³And you shall make poles *of* acacia wood, and overlay them with gold. ¹⁴You shall put the poles into the rings on the sides of the ark, that the ark may be carried by them. ¹⁵The poles shall be in the rings of the ark; they shall not be taken from it. ¹⁶And you shall put into the ark the Testimony which I will give you.

¹⁷"You shall make a mercy seat of pure gold; two and a half cubits *shall be* its length and a cubit and a half its width. ¹⁸And you shall make two cherubim of gold; of hammered work you shall make them at the two ends of the mercy seat. ¹⁹Make one cherub at one end, and the other cherub at the other end; you shall make the cherubim at the two ends of it *of one piece* with the mercy seat. ²⁰And the cherubim shall stretch out *their* wings above, covering the mercy seat with their wings, and they shall face one another; the faces of the cherubim *shall be* toward the mercy seat. ²¹You shall put the mercy seat on top of the ark, and in the ark you shall put the Testimony that I will give you. ²²And there I will meet with you, and I will speak with you from above the mercy seat, from between the two cherubim which *are* on the ark of the Testimony, about everything which I will give you in commandment to the children of Israel.

The Table for the Showbread

²³"You shall also make a table of acacia wood; two cubits *shall be* its length, a cubit its width, and a cubit and a half its height. ²⁴And you shall overlay it with pure gold, and make a molding of gold all around. ²⁵You shall make for it a frame of a handbreadth all around, and you shall make a gold molding for the frame all around. ²⁶And you shall make for it four rings of gold, and put the rings on the four corners that *are* at its four legs. ²⁷The rings shall be close to the frame, as holders for the poles to bear the table. ²⁸And you shall make the poles of acacia wood, and overlay them with gold, that the table may be carried with them. ²⁹You shall make its dishes, its pans, its pitchers, and its bowls for pouring. You shall make them of pure gold. ³⁰And you shall set the showbread on the table before Me always.

The Gold Lampstand

³¹"You shall also make a lampstand of pure gold; the lampstand shall be of hammered work. Its shaft, its branches, its bowls, its *ornamental* knobs, and flowers shall be *of one piece.* ³²And six branches shall come out of its sides: three branches of the lampstand out of one side, and three branches of the lampstand out of the other side. ³³Three bowls *shall be* made like almond *blossoms* on one branch, *with* an *ornamental* knob and a flower, and three bowls made like almond *blossoms* on the other branch, *with* an *ornamental* knob and a flower—and so for the six branches that come

---

25:10 The ark of the Testimony, a repository of the Law of God (v. 16), symbolized the covenant between God and His people and reminded the people of God's will and their duty. The tablets of Law, called "the Testimony" (v. 21) were to be a constant—though silent—witness, unfolding the people's responsibility to obey the Lord. They also were a witness in the sense of revealing how the people had failed. Yet the top of the ark, "the mercy seat" (v. 21), was between the witness and the presence of the Lord. The blood sprinkled on it once a year (Lev. 16:2, 14–16) made possible forgiveness and the continuation of communion between the holy God and His sinful people (see chart, The Furniture of the Tabernacle).

25:17 The word translated mercy seat is closely related to the word translated "atonement" (Ex. 30:10), referring to propitiation or the satisfaction of God's wrath against sin. This was to be accomplished by the means He provided in the sacrificial system (see Lev. 17:11; chart, The Offerings of the Lord).

25:18 The cherubim, as guardians of the Lord's presence, are like the attendants of a great king. The cherubim are associated with fire and judgment (see Gen. 3:24; Ezek. 10:1–22).

25:22 God said He would be between the two cherubim; nothing made by man as an idol would contain or represent Him. By divine appointment the high priest would sprinkle blood on the ark between God's righteous presence and the record of the Law, which contained His righteous demands for His people. The arrangement of the ark indicated each person's need for forgiveness and cleansing in order to enjoy fellowship with the holy God. The Lord honored His people by His special presence with them to communicate with them and not just judge them or arbitrarily dictate what would happen to them.

25:30 The showbread is also called "the bread of the presence." Each Sabbath day 12 fresh loaves of bread (representing the 12 tribes of Israel) were to be placed in two rows on the table, which stood in the holy place outside the enclosure containing the ark (see chart, The Plan of the Tabernacle). The priests would eat the bread that was removed (Lev. 24:5–9). What had been placed before God ultimately became sustenance for the people.

25:31 The Lord instructed Moses to make a large and highly decorated lampstand (Heb. *menorah*) that would give light for access to the Lord's presence and would be kept always alight (Ex. 27:20; see chart, The Furniture of the Tabernacle).

out of the lampstand. [34]On the lampstand itself four bowls *shall be* made like almond *blossoms, each with* its *ornamental* knob and flower. [35]And *there shall be* a knob under the *first* two branches of the same, a knob under the *second* two branches of the same, and a knob under the *third* two branches of the same, according to the six branches that extend from the lampstand. [36]Their knobs and their branches *shall be of one piece;* all of it *shall be* one hammered piece of pure gold. [37]You shall make seven lamps for it, and they shall arrange its lamps so that they give light in front of it. [38]And its wick-trimmers and their trays *shall be* of pure gold. [39]It shall be made of a talent of pure gold, with all these utensils. [40]And see to it that you make *them* according to the pattern which was shown you on the mountain.

The Tabernacle

26 "Moreover you shall make the tabernacle *with* ten curtains *of* fine woven linen and blue, purple, and scarlet *thread;* with artistic designs of cherubim you shall weave them. [2]The length of each curtain *shall be* twenty-eight cubits, and the width of each curtain four cubits. And every one of the curtains shall have the same measurements. [3]Five curtains shall be coupled to one another, and *the other* five curtains *shall be* coupled to one another. [4]And you shall make loops of blue *yarn* on the edge of the curtain on the selvedge of *one* set, and likewise you shall do on the outer edge of *the other* curtain of the second set. [5]Fifty loops you shall make in the one curtain, and fifty loops you shall make on the edge of the curtain that *is* on the end of the second set, that the loops may be clasped to one another. [6]And you shall make fifty clasps of gold, and couple the curtains together with the clasps, so that it may be one tabernacle.

[7]"You shall also make curtains of goats' *hair,* to be a tent over the tabernacle. You shall make eleven curtains. [8]The length of each curtain *shall be* thirty cubits, and the width of each curtain four cubits; and the eleven curtains shall all have the same measurements. [9]And you shall couple five curtains by themselves and six curtains by themselves, and you shall double over the sixth curtain at the forefront of the tent. [10]You shall make fifty loops on the edge of the curtain that is

outermost in *one* set, and fifty loops on the edge of the curtain of the second set. [11]And you shall make fifty bronze clasps, put the clasps into the loops, and couple the tent together, that it may be one. [12]The remnant that remains of the curtains of the tent, the half curtain that remains, shall hang over the back of the tabernacle. [13]And a cubit on one side and a cubit on the other side, of what remains of the length of the curtains of the tent, shall hang over the sides of the tabernacle, on this side and on that side, to cover it.

[14]"You shall also make a covering of ram skins dyed red for the tent, and a covering of badger skins above that.

[15]"And for the tabernacle you shall make the boards of acacia wood, standing upright. [16]Ten cubits *shall be* the length of a board, and a cubit and a half *shall be* the width of each board. [17]Two tenons *shall be* in each board for binding one to another. Thus you shall make for all the boards of the tabernacle. [18]And you shall make the boards for the tabernacle, twenty boards for the south side. [19]You shall make forty sockets of silver under the twenty boards: two sockets under each of the boards for its two tenons. [20]And for the second side of the tabernacle, the north side, *there shall be* twenty boards [21]and their forty sockets of silver: two sockets under each of the boards. [22]For the far side of the tabernacle, westward, you shall make six boards. [23]And you shall also make two boards for the two back corners of the tabernacle. [24]They shall be coupled together at the bottom and they shall be coupled together at the top by one ring. Thus it shall be for both of them. They shall be for the two corners. [25]So there shall be eight boards with their sockets of silver— sixteen sockets—two sockets under each of the boards.

[26]"And you shall make bars of acacia wood: five for the boards on one side of the tabernacle, [27]five bars for the boards on the other side of the tabernacle, and five bars for the boards of the side of the tabernacle, for the far side westward. [28]The middle bar shall pass through the midst of the boards from end to end. [29]You shall overlay the boards with gold, make their rings of gold *as* holders for the bars, and overlay the bars with gold. [30]And you shall raise up the tabernacle according to its pattern which you were shown on the mountain.

25:39 A talent, by one system of calculation, weighed about 75 pounds. All calculations make the talent a large amount of gold.

26:1 The tabernacle, mentioned in verses 1–7, is not the entire tabernacle complex but the portable structure that housed the items described in Exodus 25—the ark, table, and lampstand (see chart, The Furniture of the Tabernacle). The colorful first and innermost layer was to be made of linen woven with a cherubim design. Then came a goat hair layer (the

"tent over the tabernacle," v. 7), a ram skin layer ("a covering . . . for the tent"), and finally "a covering of badger skins" (v. 14). The last layer may have been for use in transporting the tabernacle curtains, in view of the use of "badger skins" when moving other items (see Num. 4:8–14).

26:15 A system of gilded boards and crossbars was to support the four layers of curtains that made up the tabernacle.

26:17 The tenons (lit., "hands") on the boards fit into silver sockets, or pedestals.

[31]"You shall make a veil woven of blue, purple, and scarlet *thread*, and fine woven linen. It shall be woven with an artistic design of cherubim. [32]You shall hang it upon the four pillars of acacia *wood* overlaid with gold. Their hooks *shall be* gold, upon four sockets of silver. [33]And you shall hang the veil from the clasps. Then you shall bring the ark of the Testimony in there, behind the veil. The veil shall be a divider for you between the holy *place* and the Most Holy. [34]You shall put the mercy seat upon the ark of the Testimony in the Most Holy. [35]You shall set the table outside the veil, and the lampstand across from the table on the side of the tabernacle toward the south; and you shall put the table on the north side.

[36]"You shall make a screen for the door of the tabernacle, *woven of* blue, purple, and scarlet *thread*, and fine woven linen, made by a weaver. [37]And you shall make for the screen five pillars of acacia *wood*, and overlay them with gold; their hooks *shall be* gold, and you shall cast five sockets of bronze for them.

The Altar of Burnt Offering

27 "You shall make an altar of acacia wood, five cubits long and five cubits wide—the altar shall be square—and its height *shall be* three cubits. [2]You shall make its horns on its four corners; its horns shall be of one piece with it. And you shall overlay it with bronze. [3]Also you shall make its pans to receive its ashes, and its shovels and its basins and its forks and its firepans; you shall make all its utensils of bronze. [4]You shall make a grate for it, a network of bronze; and on the network you shall make four bronze rings at its four corners. [5]You shall put it under the rim of the altar beneath, that the network may be midway up the altar. [6]And you shall make poles for the altar, poles of acacia wood, and overlay them with bronze. [7]The poles shall be put in the rings, and the poles shall be on the two sides of the altar to bear it. [8]You shall make it hollow with boards; as it was shown you on the mountain, so shall they make *it*.

The Court of the Tabernacle

[9]"You shall also make the court of the tabernacle. For the south side *there shall be* hangings for the court *made of* fine woven linen, one hundred cubits long for one side. [10]And its twenty pillars and their twenty sockets *shall be* bronze. The hooks of the pillars and their bands *shall be* silver. [11]Likewise along the length of the north side *there shall be* hangings one hundred *cubits* long, with its twenty pillars and their twenty sockets of bronze, and the hooks of the pillars and their bands of silver.

[12]"And along the width of the court on the west side *shall be* hangings of fifty cubits, with their ten pillars and their ten sockets. [13]The width of the court on the east side *shall be* fifty cubits. [14]The hangings on *one* side *of the gate shall be* fifteen cubits, *with* their three pillars and their three sockets. [15]And on the other side *shall be* hangings of fifteen *cubits, with* their three pillars and their three sockets.

[16]"For the gate of the court *there shall be* a screen twenty cubits long, *woven of* blue, purple, and scarlet *thread*, and fine woven linen, made by a weaver. It *shall have* four pillars and four sockets. [17]All the pillars around the court shall have bands of silver; their hooks *shall be* of silver and their sockets of bronze. [18]The length of the court *shall be* one hundred cubits, the width fifty throughout, and the height five cubits, *made of* fine woven linen, and its sockets of bronze. [19]All the utensils of the tabernacle for all its service, all its pegs, and all the pegs of the court, *shall be* of bronze.

The Care of the Lampstand

[20]"And you shall command the children of Israel that they bring you pure oil of pressed

---

26:31–35 The veil, a colorful curtain with the cherubim design, was to make two rooms inside the tabernacle (see chart, The Plan of the Tabernacle). The smaller, interior room (the "Most Holy Place" or "Holy of Holies") would house the ark, while the table and lampstand would stand in the outer room (the holy place). The presence of the glory of the Lord among His people would be hidden from sight by the tabernacle and the veil. Later the temple in Jerusalem had a similar veil, which was torn from top to bottom when the Lord Jesus died (Matt. 27:51). The writer of Hebrews saw the body of Christ as a kind of veil through which access to God is offered (Heb. 4:16; 10:19, 20). As with the tabernacle, God dwelled among His people in the Person of the Lord Jesus (Matt. 1:23; John 1:14) and provided forgiveness of sins and access to worship and fellowship in His presence.

27:1 Altars were a familiar part of Israelite history and worship (see Ex. 17:15; 20:24). Now the Israelites must build the altar that would stand outside the tabernacle (see chart, The

Furniture of the Tabernacle). On the altar would be placed sacrifices burned in worship (see Ps. 118:27). The altar also was a place of refuge. A person might grasp its horns in hopes that he would be seen as belonging to God and thus under protection (Ex. 21:13, 14: 1 Kin. 1:50–53; 2:28–32).

27:9 Surrounding the tabernacle and the altar would be a rectangular courtyard of about 150 by 75 feet outlined by bronze pillars and linen fabric that made a fence about 7.5 feet high. Moving symbolically away from the special presence of the Lord, items outside the tabernacle itself were made with silver and bronze, which were less costly than gold (see chart, The Plan of the Tabernacle).

27:20 The refined grade of olive oil described would give the best light and least smoke when used in the lampstand (Ex. 25:31–40). Mention of the responsibility of Aaron and his sons leads into the descriptions of their clothing and consecration ceremonies (Ex. 28; 29).

THE FURNITURE OF THE TABERNACLE

Ark of the Covenant or Ark of the Testimony (Ex. 25:10–22)
The ark was most sacred of all the furniture in the tabernacle. Here the Hebrews kept a copy of the Ten Commandments, which summarized the covenant requirements.

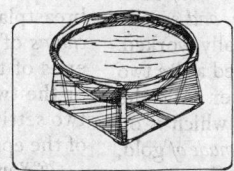

Bronze Laver (Ex. 30:17–21)
The priests would come to the laver of bronze for cleansing. They must be pure to enter the presence of God.

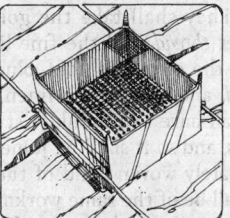

Altar of Burnt Offering (Ex. 27:1–8)
Animal sacrifices were offered on this altar, located in the court in front of the tabernacle. The blood of the sacrifice was sprinkled on the four horns of the altar.

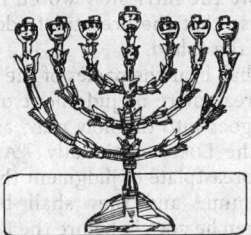

Gold Lampstand or Menorah (Ex. 25:31–40)
The gold lampstand stood in the holy place, opposite the table of showbread. It held seven lamps, flat bowls in which a wick lay with one end in the oil of the bowl and the lighted end hanging out.

Table of Showbread (Ex. 25:23–30)
Always in God's presence was the table with twelve loaves of bread representing the twelve tribes of Israel.

Altar of Incense (Ex. 30:1–10)
The altar of incense inside the tabernacle was much smaller than the altar of burnt offering outside. The incense burned on the altar made a sweet-smelling aroma.

---

olives for the light, to cause the lamp to burn continually. 21In the tabernacle of meeting, outside the veil which *is* before the Testimony, Aaron and his sons shall tend it from evening until morning before the LORD. *It shall be* a statute forever to their generations on behalf of the children of Israel.

Garments for the Priesthood

28 "Now take Aaron your brother, and his sons with him, from among the children of Israel, that he may minister to Me as priest, Aaron

and Aaron's sons: Nadab, Abihu, Eleazar, and Ithamar. 2And you shall make holy garments for Aaron your brother, for glory and for beauty. 3So you shall speak to all *who are* gifted artisans, whom I have filled with the spirit of wisdom, that they may make Aaron's garments, to consecrate him, that he may minister to Me as priest. 4And these *are* the garments which they shall make: a breastplate, an ephod,[a] a robe, a skillfully woven tunic, a turban, and a sash. So they shall make

28:4 [a] That is, an ornamented vest

28:2 These beautiful and skillfully made garments would mark Aaron and his sons as set apart for service to the Lord at the tabernacle (see chart, The High Priest's Clothing). Articles are described for Aaron as high priest and his successors (vv. 5–43). Clothing for the priests in general is also pre-

scribed (vv. 40–42; see 1 Chr. 23:13; Mal. 2:5–7 for summaries of a priest's duties). All Christians have a position like that of the OT priests; the apostle Peter spoke of Christians as "a holy priesthood" responsible to offer "spiritual sacrifices" (see Rom. 10, Access to God; 1 Pet. 2, Priesthood of the Believer).

holy garments for Aaron your brother and his sons, that he may minister to Me as priest.

The Ephod

⁵"They shall take the gold, blue, purple, and scarlet *thread,* and the fine linen, ⁶and they shall make the ephod of gold, blue, purple, *and* scarlet *thread,* and fine woven linen, artistically worked. ⁷It shall have two shoulder straps joined at its two edges, and *so* it shall be joined together. ⁸And the intricately woven band of the ephod, which *is* on it, shall be of the same workmanship, *made of* gold, blue, purple, and scarlet *thread,* and fine woven linen.

⁹"Then you shall take two onyx stones and engrave on them the names of the sons of Israel: ¹⁰six of their names on one stone and six names on the other stone, in order of their birth. ¹¹With the work of an engraver in stone, *like* the engravings of a signet, you shall engrave the two stones with the names of the sons of Israel. You shall set them in settings of gold. ¹²And you shall put the two stones on the shoulders of the ephod *as* memorial stones for the sons of Israel. So Aaron shall bear their names before the LORD on his two shoulders as a memorial. ¹³You shall also make settings of gold, ¹⁴and you shall make two chains of pure gold like braided cords, and fasten the braided chains to the settings.

The Breastplate

¹⁵"You shall make the breastplate of judgment. Artistically woven according to the workmanship of the ephod you shall make it: of gold, blue, purple, and scarlet *thread,* and fine woven linen, you shall make it. ¹⁶It shall be doubled into a square: a span *shall be* its length, and a span *shall be* its width. ¹⁷And you shall put settings of stones in it, four rows of stones: *The first* row *shall be* a sardius, a topaz, and an emerald; *this shall be* the first row; ¹⁸the second row *shall be* a turquoise, a sapphire, and a diamond; ¹⁹the third row, a jacinth, an agate, and an amethyst; ²⁰and the fourth row, a beryl, an onyx, and a jasper. They shall be set in gold settings. ²¹And the stones shall have the names of the sons of Israel, twelve according to their names, *like*

the engravings of a signet, each one with its own name; they shall be according to the twelve tribes. ²²"You shall make chains for the breastplate at the end, like braided cords of pure gold. ²³And you shall make two rings of gold for the breastplate, and put the two rings on the two ends of the breastplate. ²⁴Then you shall put the two braided *chains* of gold in the two rings which are on the ends of the breastplate; ²⁵and the *other* two ends of the two braided *chains* you shall fasten to the two settings, and put them on the shoulder straps of the ephod in the front.

²⁶"You shall make two rings of gold, and put them on the two ends of the breastplate, on the edge of it, which is on the inner side of the ephod. ²⁷And two *other* rings of gold you shall make, and put them on the two shoulder straps, underneath the ephod toward its front, right at the seam above the intricately woven band of the ephod. ²⁸They shall bind the breastplate by means of its rings to the rings of the ephod, using a blue cord, so that it is above the intricately woven band of the ephod, and so that the breastplate does not come loose from the ephod.

²⁹"So Aaron shall bear the names of the sons of Israel on the breastplate of judgment over his heart, when he goes into the holy *place,* as a memorial before the LORD continually. ³⁰And you shall put in the breastplate of judgment the Urim and the Thummim,ᵃ and they shall be over Aaron's heart when he goes in before the LORD. So Aaron shall bear the judgment of the children of Israel over his heart before the LORD continually.

Other Priestly Garments

³¹"You shall make the robe of the ephod all of blue. ³²There shall be an opening for his head in the middle of it; it shall have a woven binding all around its opening, like the opening in a coat of mail, so that it does not tear. ³³And upon its hem you shall make pomegranates of blue, purple, and scarlet, all around its hem, and bells of gold between them all around: ³⁴a golden bell and a pomegranate, a golden bell and a pomegranate, upon the

28:30 ᵃLiterally *the Lights and the Perfections* (compare Leviticus 8:8)

28:6 The word ephod is a transliteration of the Hebrew name, which refers to an item of clothing that is no longer familiar. Based on a description from near the time of Christ, the ephod may have been a kind of waistcoat with sleeves and shoulder straps (see chart, The High Priest's Clothing). One might also envision a kind of pinafore with sleeves. In any case, it was richly woven with the colors of the tabernacle curtains, plus gold threads. Its description focuses on the two stones set on the shoulders and engraved with the names of the 12 tribes (vv. 9–12). The high priest would wear these as he represented the people and interceded for them before the Lord.

28:15 The breastplate of judgment, a square, pouchlike item,

was woven of the same materials as the ephod (see chart, The Breastplate of the High Priest). On it were set 12 stones, each engraved with the name of one of the tribes of Israel. It was attached to the top of the ephod so that the high priest wore these names over his heart (vv. 21, 29). It is called the breastplate, or breastpiece, of "judgment" because it contained the Urim and Thummim (v. 30), which were used for receiving decisions from God, somewhat like casting lots (see Num. 27:21; Deut. 33:8, note; 1 Sam. 28:6; Ezra 2:63). The Bible does not describe the appearance of the Urim and Thummim, but they fit inside the breastpiece, which was "a span" (about nine inches) long and wide (v. 16).

THE PLAN OF THE TABERNACLE

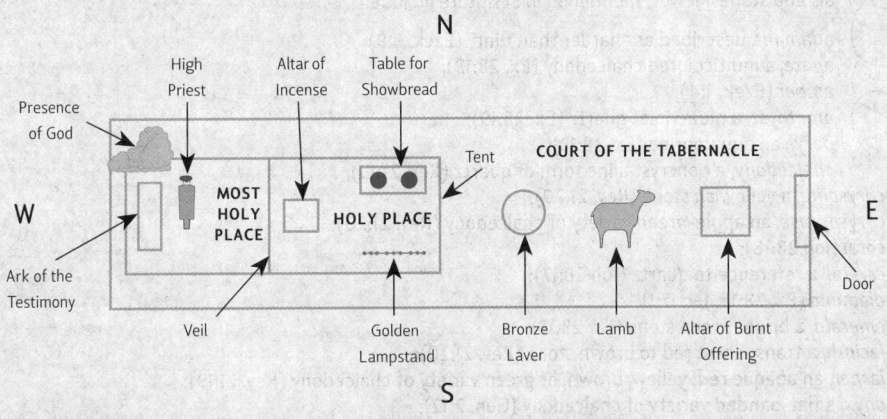

N

Presence of God — High Priest — Altar of Incense — Table for Showbread — Tent — **COURT OF THE TABERNACLE**

W — Ark of the Testimony — **MOST HOLY PLACE** — Veil — **HOLY PLACE** — Golden Lampstand — Bronze Laver — Lamb — Altar of Burnt Offering — Door — **E**

S

THE SYMBOLISM IN THE TABERNACLE

OLD TESTAMENT	DIVISION WITHIN THE TABERNACLE	NEW TESTAMENT
The people tried to reach God at the tabernacle (Ex. 25:8).		People reached God through Jesus Christ (Eph. 2:19, 22).
COURT		
Ex. 29:4, 11, 42; 33:9	Door	John 10:1, 9; 14:6
Ex. 27:1–8; 38:1–7	Altar of Burnt Offering	Matt. 26:28; Heb. 9:12, 22
Lev. 1:1–10	Lamb	John 1:29, 36; 2 Cor. 5:21; 1 Pet. 1:19
Ex. 30:17–20; 38:8	Bronze Laver	Titus 3:5; Heb. 10:22; 1 John 1:7
HOLY PLACE		
Ex. 26:1–37	Tent of Meeting	Eph. 2:13, 19
Ex. 25:23–30; 37:10–16	Table for Showbread	John 6:32, 35
Ex. 25:31–40; 27:20, 21; 37:17–24	Golden Lampstand	John 8:12
Ex. 30:1–10; 37:25–28; Ps. 141:1, 2	Altar of Incense	Eph. 5:2
Ex. 26:31	Veil	Heb. 10:19, 20
MOST HOLY PLACE		
Ex. 28:1–43	High Priest	Heb. 6:20; 8:1; 9:11, 12
Ex. 25:10–22; 37:1–9;	Ark of the Testimony	Mark 16:19; Eph. 1:20;
Num. 7:89	and the Mercy Seat	Heb. 4:14, 16; 9:24, 25
Ex. 29:45, 46; Ps. 78:14; 91:1	Presence of God	Matt. 17:5; Luke 21:27

hem of the robe all around. ³⁵And it shall be upon Aaron when he ministers, and its sound will be heard when he goes into the holy *place* before the LORD and when he comes out, that he may not die.

³⁶"You shall also make a plate of pure gold and engrave on it, *like* the engraving of a signet:

HOLINESS TO THE LORD.

³⁷And you shall put it on a blue cord, that it may be on the turban; it shall be on the front of the turban. ³⁸So it shall be on Aaron's forehead, that Aaron may bear the iniquity of the holy things

---

28:36–38 To make the meaning of the high priest's position clear, along with the special garments already described, the high priest would wear an inscription attached to his turban (see chart, The High Priest's Clothing). The phrase translated

JEWELRY   ADORNED AS A BRIDE

From ancient times, women and men have adorned themselves with precious and semi-precious metals and stones. Jewels mentioned in Scripture include:

adamant, described as "harder than flint" (Ezek. 3:9);
agate, a multicolored chalcedony (Ex. 28:19);
amber (Ezek. 1:4);
amethyst, a blue-violet quartz (Ex. 28:19);
beryl, an aquamarine (Ex. 39:13);
chalcedony, a noncrystalline form of quartz (Rev. 21:19);
chrysolite, a yellowish stone (Rev. 21:20);
chrysoprase, an apple-green variety of chalcedony (Rev. 21:20);
coral (Job 28:18);
crystal, a reference to quartz (Job 28:17);
diamond (Ex. 28:18; Jer. 17:1);
emerald, a bright green stone (Ex. 28:17);
jacinth, a transparent red to brown stone (Rev. 21:20);
jasper, an opaque red, yellow, brown, or green variety of chalcedony (Rev. 21:19);
onyx, a flat-banded variety of chalcedony (Gen. 2:12);
quartz (Job 28:18);
ruby (Job 28:18);
sapphire, a blue variety of corundum (Ex. 24:10);
sardius, a brownish red variety of chalcedony (Rev. 21:20);
sardonyx, which includes layers of carnelian (Rev. 21:20);
topaz, a yellow, reddish, or pink transparent stone that is quite hard (Job 28:19); and
pearl, a whitish, glossy stone formed around foreign matter in some shellfish (Rev. 17:4).

Women wore bracelets (Gen. 24:47), necklaces (Song 1:10), earrings (Gen. 35:4), nose rings (24:30), and rings. When the Israelites left Egypt, they received articles of gold and silver from the Egyptians (Ex. 12:35). A significant portion of this jewelry apparently was given as an offering toward the adornment of the tabernacle (Ex. 35:21, 22).

The Lord described Israel as a beautiful bride (Ezek. 16:11, 12). In His parable of the lost coin, Jesus referred to one of the most prized pieces of jewelry worn by a bride—her dowry headpiece, often adorned with gold coins or jewels. Accordingly, the married woman diligently searched for the coin lost from her headdress (Luke 15:8–10).

See also chart on Gems and Minerals (Song); notes on Appearance (2 Cor. 3); Beauty (Prov. 4); Clothing (Ezek. 16); Dowry (1 Kin. 9); Femininity (Ps. 144)

---

which the children of Israel hallow in all their holy gifts; and it shall always be on his forehead, that they may be accepted before the LORD.

39"You shall skillfully weave the tunic of fine linen *thread,* you shall make the turban of fine linen, and you shall make the sash of woven work. 40"For Aaron's sons you shall make tunics, and you shall make sashes for them. And you shall make hats for them, for glory and beauty. 41So you shall put them on Aaron your brother and on his sons with him. You shall anoint them, consecrate them, and sanctify them, that they may minister to Me as priests. 42And you shall make for them

linen trousers to cover their nakedness; they shall reach from the waist to the thighs. 43They shall be on Aaron and on his sons when they come into the tabernacle of meeting, or when they come near the altar to minister in the holy *place,* that they do not incur iniquity and die. *It shall be* a statute forever to him and his descendants after him.

Aaron and His Sons Consecrated

29 "And this is what you shall do to them to hallow them for ministering to Me as priests: Take one young bull and two rams without blemish, 2and unleavened bread, unleavened

---

HOLINESS TO THE LORD (v. 36) also characterizes the Sabbath day as "holy to the LORD" (Ex. 31:15). Even as the Sabbath was set apart because of the Lord and for the Lord, so the high priest was dedicated and given the responsibility of presenting what the Israelites brought to Him (see Lev. 21:6, 8; 23, The Principle of the Sabbath; Jer. 2:2, 3; Heb. 12:10, 14, 28).

29:1 Obedience to the commands of this chapter are recorded in Leviticus 8 and 9. As Moses received the directions for building the tabernacle and also recorded the doing of it, so the directions for consecrating the priests are matched by the doing (Ex. 35—40).

cakes mixed with oil, and unleavened wafers anointed with oil (you shall make them of wheat flour). [3]You shall put them in one basket and bring them in the basket, with the bull and the two rams.

[4]"And Aaron and his sons you shall bring to the door of the tabernacle of meeting, and you shall wash them with water. [5]Then you shall take the garments, put the tunic on Aaron, and the robe of the ephod, the ephod, and the breastplate, and gird him with the intricately woven band of the ephod. [6]You shall put the turban on his head, and put the holy crown on the turban. [7]And you shall take the anointing oil, pour it on his head, and anoint him. [8]Then you shall bring his sons and put tunics on them. [9]And you shall gird them with sashes, Aaron and his sons, and put the hats on them. The priesthood shall be theirs for a perpetual statute. So you shall consecrate Aaron and his sons.

[10]"You shall also have the bull brought before the tabernacle of meeting, and Aaron and his sons shall put their hands on the head of the bull. [11]Then you shall kill the bull before the LORD, by the door of the tabernacle of meeting. [12]You shall take some of the blood of the bull and put it on the horns of the altar with your finger, and pour all the blood beside the base of the altar. [13]And you shall take all the fat that covers the entrails, the fatty lobe attached to the liver, and the two kidneys and the fat that is on them, and burn them on the altar. [14]But the flesh of the bull, with its skin and its offal, you shall burn with fire outside the camp. It is a sin offering.

[15]"You shall also take one ram, and Aaron and his sons shall put their hands on the head of the ram; [16]and you shall kill the ram, and you shall take its blood and sprinkle it all around on the altar. [17]Then you shall cut the ram in pieces, wash its entrails and its legs, and put them with its pieces and with its head. [18]And you shall burn the whole ram on the altar. It is a burnt offering to the LORD; it is a sweet aroma, an offering made by fire to the LORD.

[19]"You shall also take the other ram, and Aaron and his sons shall put their hands on the head of the ram. [20]Then you shall kill the ram, and take some of its blood and put it on the tip of the right ear of Aaron and on the tip of the right ear of his sons, on the thumb of their right hand and on the big toe of their right foot, and sprinkle the blood all around on the altar. [21]And you shall take some of the blood that is on the altar, and some of the anointing oil, and sprinkle it on Aaron and on his garments, on his sons and on the garments of his sons with him; and he and his garments shall be hallowed, and his sons and his sons' garments with him.

[22]"Also you shall take the fat of the ram, the fat tail, the fat that covers the entrails, the fatty lobe attached to the liver, the two kidneys and the fat on them, the right thigh (for it is a ram of consecration), [23]one loaf of bread, one cake made with oil, and one wafer from the basket of the unleavened bread that is before the LORD; [24]and you shall put all these in the hands of Aaron and in the hands of his sons, and you shall wave them as a wave offering before the LORD. [25]You shall receive them back from their hands and burn them on the altar as a burnt offering, as a sweet aroma before the LORD. It is an offering made by fire to the LORD.

[26]"Then you shall take the breast of the ram of Aaron's consecration and wave it as a wave offering before the LORD; and it shall be your portion. [27]And from the ram of the consecration you shall consecrate the breast of the wave offering which is waved, and the thigh of the heave offering which is raised, of that which is for Aaron and of that which is for his sons. [28]It shall be from the children of Israel for Aaron and his sons by a statute forever. For it is a heave offering; it shall be a heave offering from the children of Israel from the sacrifices of their peace offerings, that is, their heave offering to the LORD.

[29]"And the holy garments of Aaron shall be his sons' after him, to be anointed in them and to be consecrated in them. [30]That son who becomes priest in his place shall put them on for seven days, when he enters the tabernacle of meeting to minister in the holy place.

[31]"And you shall take the ram of the consecration and boil its flesh in the holy place. [32]Then Aaron and his sons shall eat the flesh of the ram, and the bread that is in the basket, by the door of the tabernacle of meeting. [33]They shall eat those things with which the atonement was made, to consecrate and to sanctify them; but an outsider shall not eat them, because they are holy. [34]And if any of the flesh of the consecration offerings, or of the bread, remains until the morning, then you

---

29:6 The holy crown is the plate inscribed with "HOLINESS TO THE LORD" (Ex. 28:36, 37).

29:7 Specially formulated anointing oil was used to designate persons and items meant for particular service to the Lord (see Ex. 30:22–30; 1 Sam. 10:1; 16:1, 12, 13; 1 Kin. 19:16; Acts 10:38; 2 Cor. 1:21).

29:10 Aaron and his sons are instructed to put their hands on the head of the animal to be sacrificed (vv. 10, 15, 19). This ac-

tion associated the person with the animal, which became the person's representative or substitute (see Lev. 16:21).

29:18 The burnt offering was not a sin offering (described in vv. 10–14; see also chart, The Offerings of the Lord). That the "offering made by fire" made a "sweet aroma" means it was pleasing to God, who accepted the worshiper's self-surrender indicated by the sacrifice.

NEEDLEWORK *AN EXPRESSION OF CREATIVITY*

Ornamental needlework was certainly a part of the Old Testament culture. It was used in decorating the screen for the tabernacle door (Ex. 26:36; 36:37), the screen for the court gate (Ex. 27:16; 38:18), and the priestly garments (Ex. 28:39; 39:29). Embroidery was a sign of royal luxury (Ezek. 16:10, 13, 18; 26:16), a valuable product in commerce (Ezek. 27:16), and a prized spoil of battle (Judg. 5:30).

Garments were marked by original designs (Ex. 28:6), innovative applique (Ex. 39:24), and even skillfully woven work that could be akin to our needlepoint (Ex. 28:4), Joseph's "tunic of many colors" was likely just such a treasured, embroidered heirloom garment (see Gen. 37:3).

This expression of creativity, which transforms simple materials into works of art, is a way to share yourself with your family, as did the "woman of strength" in Proverbs (31:13, 19, 22, 24), and with others, as did Dorcas (Acts 9:36–42) and those who prepared textiles for the tabernacle. As the ordinary becomes the extraordinary, an inheritance is left for generations to come through a woman's investment of herself in such projects.

See also notes on Clothing (Ezek. 16); Creativity (Col. 1); Homemaking (Prov. 24); portrait of Dorcas (Acts 9)

shall burn the remainder with fire. It shall not be eaten, because it *is* holy.

[35]"Thus you shall do to Aaron and his sons, according to all that I have commanded you. Seven days you shall consecrate them. [36]And you shall offer a bull every day *as* a sin offering for atonement. You shall cleanse the altar when you make atonement for it, and you shall anoint it to sanctify it. [37]Seven days you shall make atonement for the altar and sanctify it. And the altar shall be most holy. Whatever touches the altar must be holy.[a]

The Daily Offerings

[38]"Now this *is* what you shall offer on the altar: two lambs of the first year, day by day continually. [39]One lamb you shall offer in the morning, and the other lamb you shall offer at twilight. [40]With the one lamb shall be one-tenth *of an ephah* of flour mixed with one-fourth of a hin of pressed oil, and one-fourth of a hin of wine *as* a drink offering. [41]And the other lamb you shall offer at twilight; and you shall offer with it the grain offering and the drink offering, as in the morning, for a sweet aroma, an offering made by fire to the LORD. [42]*This shall be* a continual burnt offering throughout your generations *at* the door of the tabernacle of meeting before the LORD, where I will meet you to speak with you. [43]And there I will meet with the children of Israel, and *the tabernacle* shall be sanctified by My glory. [44]So I will conse-

crate the tabernacle of meeting and the altar. I will also consecrate both Aaron and his sons to minister to Me as priests. [45]I will dwell among the children of Israel and will be their God. [46]And they shall know that I *am* the LORD their God, who brought them up out of the land of Egypt, that I may dwell among them. I *am* the LORD their God.

The Altar of Incense

30 "You shall make an altar to burn incense on; you shall make it of acacia wood. [2]A cubit *shall be* its length and a cubit its width—it shall be square—and two cubits *shall be* its height. Its horns *shall be* of one piece with it. [3]And you shall overlay its top, its sides all around, and its horns with pure gold; and you shall make for it a molding of gold all around. [4]Two gold rings you shall make for it, under the molding on both its sides. You shall place *them* on its two sides, and they will be holders for the poles with which to bear it. [5]You shall make the poles of acacia wood, and overlay them with gold. [6]And you shall put it before the veil that *is* before the ark of the Testimony, before the mercy seat that *is* over the Testimony, where I will meet with you.

[7]"Aaron shall burn on it sweet incense every morning; when he tends the lamps, he shall burn incense on it. [8]And when Aaron lights the lamps at twilight, he shall burn incense on it, a perpet-

···············
29:37 [a]Compare Numbers 4:15 and Haggai 2:11–13

29:40 The word "hin" has an Egyptian derivation (as does *'ephah*). It refers to a pot whose capacity is not known with certainty but has been estimated to contain one gallon.

29:42–46 The significance of building and worshiping at the tabernacle is summarized. The Lord had brought the Israelites out of Egypt in order to dwell among them, acting on their behalf as their God, and in order that they might serve Him (Ex. 6:6, 7; 7:16, 17; 10:2; 16:12; 25:8, 22). As they had learned to know Him through the rescue from Egypt and preservation in the wilderness, now they would also know

Him through His presence with them and His provision for worship and communion with Him at the tabernacle.

30:1–10 The incense altar would stand inside the tabernacle, in the room with the lampstand and table of bread (see chart, The Plan of the Tabernacle). No "strange incense" could be offered on it (v. 9), only the specially formulated "sweet incense" (v. 7; see vv. 34–38). No other offerings could be made on this altar; the other offerings were to be made outside the tabernacle and should already have been made before the priest entered the tabernacle to tend or light the lamps. Else-

ual incense before the LORD throughout your generations. ⁹You shall not offer strange incense on it, or a burnt offering, or a grain offering; nor shall you pour a drink offering on it. ¹⁰And Aaron shall make atonement upon its horns once a year with the blood of the sin offering of atonement; once a year he shall make atonement upon it throughout your generations. It *is* most holy to the LORD."

The Ransom Money

¹¹Then the LORD spoke to Moses, saying: ¹²"When you take the census of the children of Israel for their number, then every man shall give a ransom for himself to the LORD, when you number them, that there may be no plague among them when *you* number them. ¹³This is what everyone among those who are numbered shall give: half a shekel according to the shekel of the sanctuary (a shekel *is* twenty gerahs). The half-shekel *shall be* an offering to the LORD. ¹⁴Everyone included among those who are numbered, from twenty years old and above, shall give an offering to the LORD. ¹⁵The rich shall not give more and the poor shall not give less than half a shekel, when *you* give an offering to the LORD, to make atonement for yourselves. ¹⁶And you shall take the atonement money of the children of Israel, and shall appoint it for the service of the tabernacle of meeting, that it may be a memorial for the children of Israel before the LORD, to make atonement for yourselves."

The Bronze Laver

¹⁷Then the LORD spoke to Moses, saying: ¹⁸"You shall also make a laver of bronze, with its base also of bronze, for washing. You shall put it between the tabernacle of meeting and the altar. And you shall put water in it, ¹⁹for Aaron and his sons shall wash their hands and their feet in water from it. ²⁰When they go into the tabernacle of meeting, or when they come near the altar to minister, to burn an offering made by fire to the LORD, they shall wash with water, lest they die. ²¹So they shall wash their hands and their feet, lest they die. And it shall be a statute forever to them—to him and his descendants throughout their generations."

The Holy Anointing Oil

²²Moreover the LORD spoke to Moses, saying: ²³"Also take for yourself quality spices—five hundred *shekels* of liquid myrrh, half as much sweet-smelling cinnamon (two hundred and fifty *shekels*), two hundred and fifty *shekels* of sweet-smelling cane, ²⁴five hundred *shekels* of cassia, according to the shekel of the sanctuary, and a hin of olive oil. ²⁵And you shall make from these a holy anointing oil, an ointment compounded according to the art of the perfumer. It shall be a holy anointing oil. ²⁶With it you shall anoint the tabernacle of meeting and the ark of the Testimony; ²⁷the table and all its utensils, the lampstand and its utensils, and the altar of incense; ²⁸the altar of burnt offering with all its utensils, and the laver and its base. ²⁹You shall consecrate them, that they may be most holy; whatever touches them must be holy.ᵃ ³⁰And you shall anoint Aaron and his sons, and consecrate them, that *they* may minister to Me as priests.

³¹"And you shall speak to the children of Israel, saying: 'This shall be a holy anointing oil to Me throughout your generations. ³²It shall not be poured on man's flesh; nor shall you make *any other* like it, according to its composition. It *is* holy, *and* it shall be holy to you. ³³Whoever compounds *any* like it, or whoever puts *any* of it on an outsider, shall be cut off from his people.'"

The Incense

³⁴And the LORD said to Moses: "Take sweet spices, stacte and onycha and galbanum, and pure frankincense with *these* sweet spices; there shall be equal amounts of each. ³⁵You shall make of these an incense, a compound according to the art of the perfumer, salted, pure, *and* holy. ³⁶And you shall beat *some* of it very fine, and put some of it before the Testimony in the tabernacle of meeting where I will meet with you. It shall be most holy to you. ³⁷But *as for* the incense which you shall make, you shall not make any for yourselves, according

30:29 ᵃCompare Numbers 4:15 and Haggai 2:11–13

where the burning of incense is associated with prayer (Ps. 141:1–4; Luke 1:8–13; Rev. 8:3, 4).

30:11–16 Numbering the men of Israel was usually associated with military service and warfare (see Num. 1:2, 3, 19–46; Judg. 20:2, 15–17; 1 Sam. 11:8; 15:4). At the age of twenty a man could begin to serve as a soldier (v. 14; Num. 1:3). The silver collected was used in building the tabernacle (Ex. 38:25–28). The numbering and ransom reflected the equality of rich and poor in standing before God (v. 15) and reminded the people of their dependence on the Lord rather than upon numerical strength, and of their responsibility to care for the house of God.

30:18–21 The priests needed to wash for physical cleanliness, due to the blood of sacrifices and dust from the tabernacle court. Washing was also symbolic of spiritual cleansing (see Ps. 26:6). Washing was enforced by the threat of death because of the prominent role and position of the priests and because of its theological significance. God is holy, and the priests must prepare to serve Him by being as pure as possible themselves. The repeated washings reinforce the seriousness of approaching God (see also Ps. 51:2; Is. 1:16; Eph. 5:25–27).

30:35 Salt in the incense enhanced its burning as well as perhaps acting as a preservative. It may also have had symbolic significance as an element in sacrifices and as a reminder of a secure covenant (see Lev. 2:13; Num. 18:19; 2 Chr. 13:5).

THE BREASTPLATE OF THE HIGH PRIEST

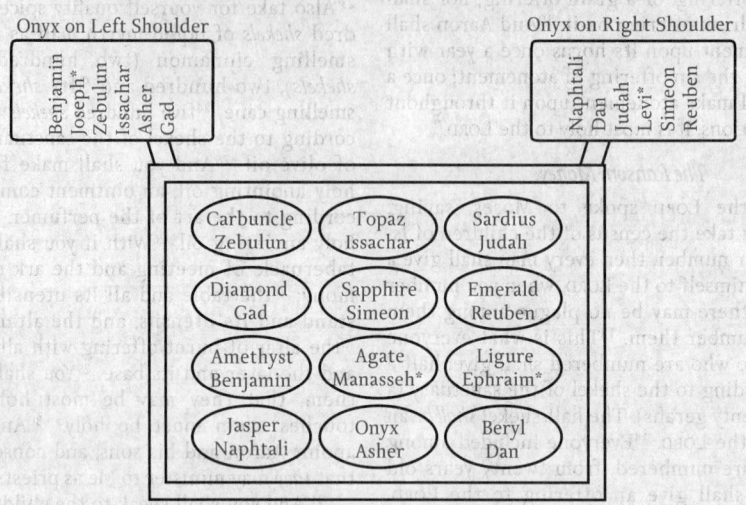

Onyx on Left Shoulder

Benjamin
Joseph*
Zebulun
Issachar
Asher
Gad

Onyx on Right Shoulder

Naphtali
Dan
Judah
Levi*
Simeon
Reuben

Carbuncle Zebulun	Topaz Issachar	Sardius Judah
Diamond Gad	Sapphire Simeon	Emerald Reuben
Amethyst Benjamin	Agate Manasseh*	Ligure Ephraim*
Jasper Naphtali	Onyx Asher	Beryl Dan

NAME	HEBREW	DESCRIPTION OF STONE	MODERN EQUIVALENT
1. Sardius	odem	red quartz stone	carnelian
2. Topaz	pitdah	rich yellow stone	topaz
3. Carbuncle	bareketh	flashing red stone	garnet
4. Emerald	nophech	green stone	emerald
5. Sapphire	sappeer	pure, deep blue stone	sapphire
6. Diamond	yah ghalohm	very hard colorless stone	diamond
7. Ligure	leh-sham	orange or yellow zircon stone	
8. Agate	shvoo	gray, brown colored layered quartz stone	agate
9. Amethyst	agh-lah-mah	purple or violet quartz stone of great hardness and beauty	amethyst
10. Beryl	tarshish	light green stone	beryl
11. Onyx	shoh-ham	black quartz stone	onyx
12. Jasper	jahsh-peh	variegated quartz stone of brilliant hues	jasper

The shoulderpieces were onyx stones on which the names of the twelve tribes were engraved according to their birth order (Ex. 28:10). Note that Hebrew is read right to left, which explains the order found on the shoulderpieces and breastplate.

Sometimes the listing of the tribes differed (as Joseph and Levi or Ephraim and Manasseh), but there were always twelve.

THE HIGH PRIEST'S CLOTHING

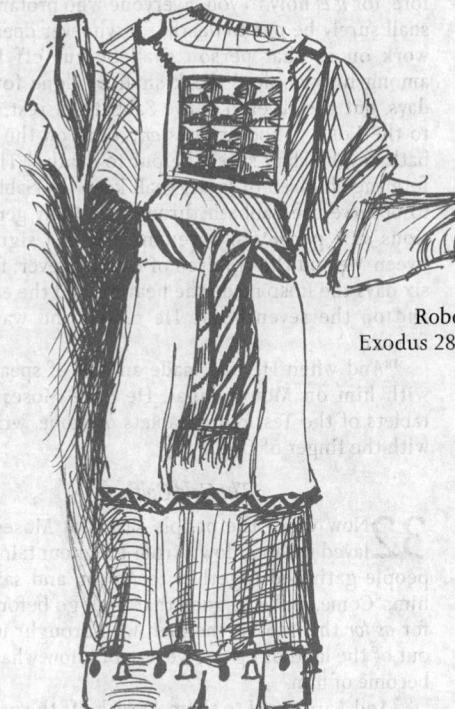

Turban
Exodus 28:36–38

Robe
Exodus 28:31–34

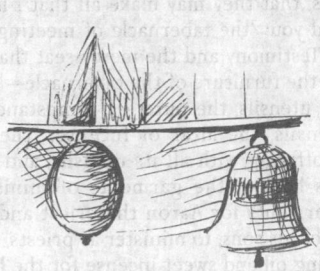

**Scarlet Pomegranate
Golden Bell Ornaments**
Exodus 28:33–35

Sash
Exodus 28:4, 39, 40

Ephod
Exodus 28:5–15, 31

to its composition. It shall be to you holy for the LORD. [38]Whoever makes *any* like it, to smell it, he shall be cut off from his people."

Artisans for Building the Tabernacle

31 Then the LORD spoke to Moses, saying: [2]"See, I have called by name Bezalel the son of Uri, the son of Hur, of the tribe of Judah. [3]And I have filled him with the Spirit of God, in wisdom, in understanding, in knowledge, and in all *manner of* workmanship, [4]to design artistic works, to work in gold, in silver, in bronze, [5]in cutting jewels for setting, in carving wood, and to work in all *manner of* workmanship.

[6]"And I, indeed I, have appointed with him Aholiab the son of Ahisamach, of the tribe of Dan; and I have put wisdom in the hearts of all the gifted artisans, that they may make all that I have commanded you: [7]the tabernacle of meeting, the ark of the Testimony and the mercy seat that *is* on it, and all the furniture of the tabernacle— [8]the table and its utensils, the pure *gold* lampstand with all its utensils, the altar of incense, [9]the altar of burnt offering with all its utensils, and the laver and its base— [10]the garments of ministry,[a] the holy garments for Aaron the priest and the garments of his sons, to minister as priests, [11]and the anointing oil and sweet incense for the holy *place.* According to all that I have commanded you they shall do."

The Sabbath Law

[12]And the LORD spoke to Moses, saying, [13]"Speak also to the children of Israel, saying: 'Surely My Sabbaths you shall keep, for it *is* a sign between Me and you throughout your generations, that *you* may know that I *am* the LORD who sanctifies you. [14]You shall keep the Sabbath, therefore, for *it is* holy to you. Everyone who profanes it shall surely be put to death; for whoever does *any* work on it, that person shall be cut off from among his people. [15]Work shall be done for six days, but the seventh *is* the Sabbath of rest, holy to the LORD. Whoever does *any* work on the Sabbath day, he shall surely be put to death. [16]Therefore the children of Israel shall keep the Sabbath, to observe the Sabbath throughout their generations *as* a perpetual covenant. [17]It *is* a sign between Me and the children of Israel forever; for *in* six days the LORD made the heavens and the earth, and on the seventh day He rested and was refreshed.'"

[18]And when He had made an end of speaking with him on Mount Sinai, He gave Moses two tablets of the Testimony, tablets of stone, written with the finger of God.

The Gold Calf

32 Now when the people saw that Moses delayed coming down from the mountain, the people gathered together to Aaron, and said to him, "Come, make us gods that shall go before us; for *as for* this Moses, the man who brought us up out of the land of Egypt, we do not know what has become of him."

[2]And Aaron said to them, "Break off the golden earrings which *are* in the ears of your wives, your sons, and your daughters, and bring *them* to me."

···················

31:10 [a]Or *woven garments*

31:3 By His Spirit God enabled people for tasks needed to accomplish what He commanded the nation to do—build the tabernacle. In this case enablement involved the ability to make a variety of needed items, to make them with excellence and beauty, and to teach others these skills (Ex. 35:34; see also Ex. 28, Needlework). The abilities were diversified according to the particular job. The use of terms related to "wisdom" (Heb. *chokmah*) in this passage and later (vv. 3, 6; Ex. 35:10, 25, 26, 31, 35; 36:1, 2, 4) presents wisdom as the skill for doing what needed to be done in a way pleasing to God. Those with wisdom made things that were useful in serving God. In broader application the Book of Proverbs presents wisdom as the skill for living (see Prov. 1:1–7; 2:6; 3:13–26). "Understanding" involves discernment, leading to the ability to recognize correct choices in solving problems (see John 5, Problem Solving; 1 Cor, 8, Decision Making). "Knowledge" involves know-how resulting from a store of experience.

31:13 Previously in Exodus the Lord explained that He was acting in a particular way so that He would be known (for example, Ex. 8:10; 9:14; 16:6, 7; 29:43–46). Now the Israelites must act in order to know. Even while building the tabernacle, they must keep the Sabbath for the sake of knowing the Lord as the one who set them apart ("the LORD who sanctifies you") and as the one who created the world in six days (v. 17). Observing the Sabbath as a "sign" would remind the Israelites of

the Lord's identity as the Creator, who made it possible for them to cease from work as He had done (see chart, The Principle of the Sabbath). In revealing His own identity to them, He gave them an identity as His people. God's instructions for making the tabernacle and its furnishings and designating priests, all set apart for God's service, exemplified what it meant for the people themselves to be sanctified (see Ex. 19:4–6; Lev. 20:26; 22:32, 33; 1 Thess. 4:1–8).

32:1 Shortly after the Israelites had agreed to be the Lord's covenant people, they began to worship an idol. Their demand to Aaron directly contradicted what the Lord had said at the start of the Ten Commandments (v. 1; Ex. 20:2–4). According to the Lord, *the Lord* their God had brought the Israelites out of Egypt, and He told them, "You shall have *no other* gods before Me" (Ex. 20:3), and they must *not make* for themselves any image. But according to the Israelites, Moses—a *man,* not the Lord—had brought them from Egypt. Therefore, they told Aaron, "*Make us gods* that shall go before us" (v. 1).

32:2–4 The description of making the calf contrasts with the description of preparing for the tabernacle (Ex. 35:21–35). Aaron commanded the people to bring gold by taking it from family members. In preparation for building the tabernacle, the emphasis is on each individual's willing and spontaneous

*The woman who wants to make a difference must seek
inner strength instead of self-sufficiency.*

Joy P. Gage

³So all the people broke off the golden earrings which *were* in their ears, and brought *them* to Aaron. ⁴And he received *the gold* from their hand, and he fashioned it with an engraving tool, and made a molded calf.

Then they said, "This *is* your god, O Israel, that brought you out of the land of Egypt!"

⁵So when Aaron saw *it,* he built an altar before it. And Aaron made a proclamation and said, "Tomorrow *is* a feast to the LORD." ⁶Then they rose early on the next day, offered burnt offerings, and brought peace offerings; and the people sat down to eat and drink, and rose up to play.

⁷And the LORD said to Moses, "Go, get down! For your people whom you brought out of the land of Egypt have corrupted *themselves.* ⁸They have turned aside quickly out of the way which I commanded them. They have made themselves a molded calf, and worshiped it and sacrificed to it, and said, 'This *is* your god, O Israel, that brought you out of the land of Egypt!' " ⁹And the LORD said to Moses, "I have seen this people, and indeed it *is* a stiff-necked people! ¹⁰Now therefore, let Me alone, that My wrath may burn hot against them and I may consume them. And I will make of you a great nation."

¹¹Then Moses pleaded with the LORD his God, and said: "LORD, why does Your wrath burn hot against Your people whom You have brought out of the land of Egypt with great power and with a mighty hand? ¹²Why should the Egyptians speak, and say, 'He brought them out to harm them, to kill them in the mountains, and to consume them from the face of the earth'? Turn from Your fierce wrath,

and relent from this harm to Your people. ¹³Remember Abraham, Isaac, and Israel, Your servants, to whom You swore by Your own self, and said to them, 'I will multiply your descendants as the stars of heaven; and all this land that I have spoken of I give to your descendants, and they shall inherit *it* forever.' "ᵃ ¹⁴So the LORD relented from the harm which He said He would do to His people.

¹⁵And Moses turned and went down from the mountain, and the two tablets of the Testimony *were* in his hand. The tablets *were* written on both sides; on the one *side* and on the other they were written. ¹⁶Now the tablets *were* the work of God, and the writing *was* the writing of God engraved on the tablets.

¹⁷And when Joshua heard the noise of the people as they shouted, he said to Moses, "*There is* a noise of war in the camp."

¹⁸But he said:

"*It is* not the noise of the shout of victory,
   Nor the noise of the cry of defeat,
   But the sound of singing I hear."

¹⁹So it was, as soon as he came near the camp, that he saw the calf *and* the dancing. So Moses' anger became hot, and he cast the tablets out of his hands and broke them at the foot of the mountain. ²⁰Then he took the calf which they had made, burned *it* in the fire, and ground *it* to powder; and he scattered *it* on the water and made the children of Israel drink *it.* ²¹And Moses said to Aaron,

32:13 ᵃGenesis 13:15 and 22:17

---

giving (Ex. 35:21–35). Aaron made the calf, but in Exodus 35 skilled workers made things of far superior quality because of enablement from God. In ancient Near Eastern cultures a young bull or ox was associated with strength, lordship, fertility, and morally degrading rituals.

32:5 Aaron's proclamation appears to have been a cover-up of sorts. The following verses make it clear that the celebration was in no way acceptable to the Lord.

32:6 In this setting the word translated "play" (Heb. *tsachaq*) is not innocent fun. It implies sexual immorality such as is connected with pagan rituals (see Gen. 26:8; 39:14, 17).

32:7 The Lord's statement ironically echoes the people, who said that Moses had brought them out of Egypt (v. 1). The word translated "have corrupted themselves" is used of the destruction of Sodom and Gomorrah (Gen. 19:13, 29) and of a trampled and ruined vineyard (Jer. 12:10). The Israelites had become the opposite of the holy, set apart nation that God intended them to be.

32:10 Let Me alone introduces the possibility of the opposite; that is, Moses may intercede for the Israelites. The Lord proposed that He start over again with Moses to fulfill promises to the patriarchs concerning making a "great nation" (see Gen. 12:2; 18:18; 46:3).

32:11–14 As mediator for the nation, Moses pleaded with the Lord because of His past action in delivering the people who belong to Him, because of His reputation (referring to one of God's stated purposes, Ex. 14:4), and because of His promises to His servants Abraham, Isaac, and Jacob. In response, the Lord did not destroy all the people and begin again with Moses (see also Ezek. 33:13–19).

32:19 Breaking the tablets of Testimony, like tearing up a modern contract, pictured the destruction of the covenant to which the tablets bore witness. Israel's relationship with *Yahweh* as their covenant overlord was in jeopardy.

32:21 Ugaritic and Egyptian equivalents to the expression translated "so great a sin" and "great sin" (vv. 30 and 31) are

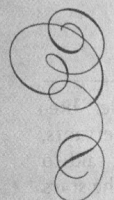

COSMETICS ENHANCING PHYSICAL BEAUTY

Perfumes. In the unsanitary and odor-laden ancient world, perfumes were highly prized. Perfume making, which included the preparation of both cosmetics and medical ointments, is an ancient and noble profession (Ex. 30:25, 35; 1 Sam. 8:13; Neh. 3:8).

Perfume ingredients mentioned in Scripture include aloes, bdellium, calumus, cassia, cinnamon, frankincense, myrrh, nard, onycha, and saffron. Perfume came in the form of powders, liquids, incense, or ointments. Sachets of dried spices were worn under clothing (Song 1:13), and liquids and ointments were contained in flasks and jars (Mark 14:3; Luke 7:37). Perfumed oils were used in these ways:

- to soften the skin and mask unpleasant odors (see Ruth 3:3; Ps. 45:8; Luke 7:38)
- as a moisturizer in the dry desert climate (see Ps. 133:2; Song 1:13)
- as an enticement to lovemaking (see Esth. 2:12; Prov. 7:17)
- as a symbol of honor and hospitality to be poured over the feet or heads of banquet guests (see Matt. 26:7).

Cosmetics. Some suggest that henna (bright orange in color) was mixed with oil and applied to the palms of the hands, feet, nails, and sometimes the hair (see Song 4:13). Dark black kohl was used to outline eyes (2 Kin. 9:30; Jer. 4:30; Ezek. 23:40), and rouge and various colored powders were made by grinding minerals and mixing them with water or gum. Cosmetic dyes were mixed with oil and kept in small jars.

Mirrors. An important beauty aid since ancient times, mirrors were frequently made of highly polished bronze, since glass was not introduced until the first century A.D. Paul used the analogy of a mirror to describe the "poor reflection" we have of a true spiritual reality (1 Cor. 13:12).

See also notes Appearance (2 Cor. 3); Beauty (Prov. 4); Clothing (Ezek. 16); Femininity (Ps. 144)

"What did this people do to you that you have brought *so* great a sin upon them?" ²²So Aaron said, "Do not let the anger of my lord become hot. You know the people, that they *are set* on evil. ²³For they said to me, 'Make us gods that shall go before us; *as for* this Moses, the man who brought us out of the land of Egypt, we do not know what has become of him.' ²⁴And I said to them, 'Whoever has any gold, let them break *it* off.' So they gave *it* to me, and I cast it into the fire, and this calf came out."

²⁵Now when Moses saw that the people *were* unrestrained (for Aaron had not restrained them, to *their* shame among their enemies, ²⁶then Moses stood in the entrance of the camp, and said, "Whoever *is* on the LORD's side—*come* to me!" And all the sons of Levi gathered themselves together to him. ²⁷And he said to them, "Thus says the LORD God of Israel: 'Let every man put his sword on his side, and go in and out from entrance to entrance throughout the camp, and let every man kill his brother, every man his companion, and every man his neighbor.' " ²⁸So the sons of Levi did according to the word of Moses. And about three thousand men of the people fell that day. ²⁹Then Moses said, "Consecrate yourselves today to the LORD, that He may bestow on you a blessing this day, for every man has opposed his son and his brother."

³⁰Now it came to pass on the next day that Moses said to the people, "You have committed a great sin. So now I will go up to the LORD; perhaps I can make atonement for your sin." ³¹Then Moses returned to the LORD and said, "Oh, these people have committed a great sin, and have made for themselves a god of gold! ³²Yet now, if You will forgive their sin—but if not, I pray, blot me out of Your book which You have written."

³³And the LORD said to Moses, "Whoever has sinned against Me, I will blot him out of My book. ³⁴Now therefore, go, lead the people to *the place* of which I have spoken to you. Behold, My Angel shall go before you. Nevertheless, in the day when I visit for punishment, I will visit punishment upon them for their sin."

³⁵So the LORD plagued the people because of what they did with the calf which Aaron made.

The Command to Leave Sinai

33 Then the LORD said to Moses, "Depart *and* go up from here, you and the people whom you have brought out of the land of Egypt, to the land of which I swore to Abraham, Isaac, and Jacob, saying, 'To your descendants I will give it.'

---

found in marriage contracts, as legal terms for adultery (see also Gen. 20:9; 39:9). Israel's unfaithfulness to the Lord was a breaking of the covenant just as adultery breaks the covenant of marriage. For the Israelites to drink the water (Ex. 32:20) paralleled the trial of a wife accused of adultery (Num. 5:14–28). God's intervention would show who was guilty.

32:22–24 Aaron's explanation, regrettably, resembled that of Adam and Eve after they had sinned (Gen. 3:11–13); he quickly blamed the people and took little responsibility himself— "this calf came out" (Ex. 32:24; compare vv. 2–5). However, Aaron was responsible because he had failed to restrain the people (v. 25; see also Deut. 9:20).

²And I will send *My* Angel before you, and I will drive out the Canaanite and the Amorite and the Hittite and the Perizzite and the Hivite and the Jebusite. ³*Go up* to a land flowing with milk and honey; for I will not go up in your midst, lest I consume you on the way, for you *are* a stiff-necked people."

⁴And when the people heard this bad news, they mourned, and no one put on his ornaments. ⁵For the LORD had said to Moses, "Say to the children of Israel, 'You *are* a stiff-necked people. I could come up into your midst in one moment and consume you. Now therefore, take off your ornaments, that I may know what to do to you.' " ⁶So the children of Israel stripped themselves of their ornaments by Mount Horeb.

Moses Meets with the LORD

⁷Moses took his tent and pitched it outside the camp, far from the camp, and called it the tabernacle of meeting. And it came to pass *that* everyone who sought the LORD went out to the tabernacle of meeting which *was* outside the camp. ⁸So it was, whenever Moses went out to the tabernacle, *that* all the people rose, and each man stood *at* his tent door and watched Moses until he had gone into the tabernacle. ⁹And it came to pass, when Moses entered the tabernacle, that the pillar of cloud descended and stood *at* the door of the tabernacle, and *the LORD* talked with Moses. ¹⁰All the people saw the pillar of cloud standing *at* the tabernacle door, and all the people rose and worshiped, each man *in* his tent door. ¹¹So the LORD spoke to Moses face to face, as a man speaks to his friend. And he would return to the camp, but his servant Joshua the son of Nun, a young man, did not depart from the tabernacle.

The Promise of God's Presence

¹²Then Moses said to the LORD, "See, You say to me, 'Bring up this people.' But You have not let me know whom You will send with me. Yet You have said, 'I know you by name, and you have also found grace in My sight.' ¹³Now therefore, I pray, if I have found grace in Your sight, show me now Your way, that I may know You and that I may find grace in Your sight. And consider that this nation *is* Your people."

¹⁴And He said, "My Presence will go *with you,* and I will give you rest."

¹⁵Then he said to Him, "If Your Presence does not go *with us,* do not bring us up from here. ¹⁶For how then will it be known that Your people and I have found grace in Your sight, except You go with us? So we shall be separate, Your people and I, from all the people who *are* upon the face of the earth."

¹⁷So the LORD said to Moses, "I will also do this thing that you have spoken; for you have found grace in My sight, and I know you by name."

¹⁸And he said, "Please, show me Your glory."

¹⁹Then He said, "I will make all My goodness pass before you, and I will proclaim the name of the LORD before you. I will be gracious to whom I will be gracious, and I will have compassion on whom I will have compassion." ²⁰But He said, "You cannot see My face; for no man shall see Me, and live." ²¹And the LORD said, "Here is a place by Me, and you shall stand on the rock. ²²So it shall be, while My glory passes by, that I will put you in the cleft of the rock, and will cover you with My hand while I pass by. ²³Then I will take away My hand, and you shall see My back; but My face shall not be seen."

33:3 I will not go up in your midst. This statement shows that the relationship between the Lord and the Israelites was not yet settled and at peace, even though the land promises were renewed (see also v. 5). The people recognized their loss and mourned when they heard that the Lord would not go among them. That He would not now go among them implied that they should not build the tabernacle, the place where He had said He would dwell among them (Ex. 25:8; 29:44-46). It would have been pointless to build an ark and a tabernacle in which to place the covenant record, a tabernacle designated as a dwelling for the Lord, where He would meet His people—if there were no covenant and if the Lord would not dwell among the Israelites.

33:7-11 The word translated tabernacle (Heb. *'ohel*) *is* the usual one for "tent," not the word used in Exodus 26 to describe the structure that would contain "the holy place and the Most Holy Place" (Ex. 26:33). These verses explain that Moses customarily talked with God in a tent outside the camp (see also Ex. 34:29-35; Deut. 34:10-12; chart, The Plan of the Tabernacle).

33:14 My presence (lit. "My face") is used as a way of saying "I

Myself." The same idiom is used concerning the Lord (vv. 20, 23) and Moses (v. 19). That the Lord would give rest may indicate security He would give in the Land (see Deut. 12:9, 10; 25:19; Josh. 23:1). If, however, Moses took it as rest for himself personally, he did not accept it as sufficient but pressed for the Lord's presence with the people as a whole (v. 16; Ex. 34:9).

33:15, 16 For the Lord to have given Israel land as promised would not have distinguished them as unique, since He had given land to others (Ex. 32:34—33:3; see Deut. 2:5, 9, 19-22). Only by the Lord's special presence among the Israelites would anyone know that He had shown them favor and given them a distinct identity.

33:18 Asking to see the Lord's glory repeats in other terms the request in verse 13. Moses wanted a full disclosure of the Lord's essential character (see Heb. 1:1-3). The answer to these requests is first of all the proclamation of the Lord's name, which lists qualities central to His dealings with the Israelites in the Book of Exodus, and then also the display of the Lord's presence in the finished tabernacle (Ex. 34:5-7; 40:34, 35).

ATTRIBUTES OF GOD *HE IS PERSONAL*

God is the Ultimate Being. He is a living, speaking, loving, feeling, and seeking God. Though He is spirit (John 4:24), He has intellect (1 Cor. 2:10, 11), will (Dan. 4:35), and emotions (Deut. 4:21, 24), and He communicates with us (Job 22:21, 22; Prov. 2:6). One of the pervading themes in Scripture is God's desire for a personal relationship with the man and woman whom He created in His image.

God has used nearly every relationship of personal commitment we know to reveal Himself to us: husband (Jer. 31:32), father (Gal. 4:6, 7), mother (Is. 49:15), brother (Prov. 18:24), lover (Song), bridegroom (Rev. 19:7–9), shepherd (Ps. 23), creator and designer (Ps. 139:13–16), king (Ps. 10:16), provider (Matt. 6:25–33), protector (Jer. 20:11), teacher (Ps. 25:8–12), counselor (Is. 9:6), friend (John 15:14, 15), physician (Matt. 9:12, 13), master (Luke 16:13), servant (Mark 10:45), and military commander (Eph. 6:11–18).

The ultimate communication of God to us is Jesus (John 1:18; 10:30; 12:45; 14:9). Only the God of the Bible is the living God. He was not made by human hands (Is. 45:5–7; Col. 1:15–17; Rev. 1:8), but He made and fashioned the world and all that is in it (Ps. 100:3; 115:15; Eccl. 3:11). His greatest glory is found in His creation with whom He is personally and intimately involved and of whom Christ is the crowning expression.

See also Is. 45:4; Lam. 3:22, note; Matt. 11:28–30; Heb. 1:1–4; notes on Attributes of God (Deut. 4; 32; 2 Chr. 19; Job 23; 42; Ps. 25; 90; 102; 119; Is. 6; 65; Jer. 23; Rom. 2; Eph. 1; 1 John 5); Access to God (Rom. 10); Communication (Prov. 15); God's Will (Eph. 5); Prayer (Jer. 33; Heb. 4; 1 John 5; 3 John)

Moses Makes New Tablets

34 And the LORD said to Moses, "Cut two tablets of stone like the first *ones,* and I will write on *these* tablets the words that were on the first tablets which you broke. ²So be ready in the morning, and come up in the morning to Mount Sinai, and present yourself to Me there on the top of the mountain. ³And no man shall come up with you, and let no man be seen throughout all the mountain; let neither flocks nor herds feed before that mountain."

⁴So he cut two tablets of stone like the first *ones.* Then Moses rose early in the morning and went up Mount Sinai, as the LORD had commanded him; and he took in his hand the two tablets of stone.

⁵Now the LORD descended in the cloud and stood with him there, and proclaimed the name of the LORD. ⁶And the LORD passed before him and proclaimed, "The LORD, the LORD God, merciful and gracious, longsuffering, and abounding in goodness and truth, ⁷keeping mercy for thousands, forgiving iniquity and transgression and sin, by no means clearing *the guilty,* visiting the iniquity of the fathers upon the children and the children's children to the third and the fourth generation."

⁸So Moses made haste and bowed his head toward the earth, and worshiped. ⁹Then he said, "If now I have found grace in Your sight, O Lord, let my Lord, I pray, go among us, even though we *are* a stiff-necked people; and pardon our iniquity and our sin, and take us as Your inheritance."

The Covenant Renewed

¹⁰And He said: "Behold, I make a covenant. Before all your people I will do marvels such as have not been done in all the earth, nor in any nation; and all the people among whom you *are* shall see the work of the LORD. For it *is* an awesome thing that I will do with you. ¹¹Observe what I command you this day. Behold, I am driving out from before you the Amorite and the Canaanite and the Hittite and the Perizzite and the Hivite and the Jebusite. ¹²Take heed to yourself, lest you make a covenant with the inhabitants of the land where you are going, lest it be a snare in your midst. ¹³But you shall destroy their altars, break their *sacred* pillars, and cut down their wooden images ¹⁴(for you shall worship no other god, for the LORD, whose name *is* Jealous, *is* a jealous God), ¹⁵lest you make a covenant with the inhabitants of

34:8 In responding to the Lord's revelation of Himself, Moses bowed in worship. This stands as a climactic personal fulfillment of the sign given to Moses (Ex. 3:12); verse 8 is the only place in Exodus that the verb translated "worshiped" is used of Moses separately.

34:10 I make a covenant. Throughout this chapter parallels to earlier events and instructions confirm that the Lord was reinstating the covenant relationship formalized in Exodus 19—24. Renewal of the covenant meant that the Lord was agreeing to Moses' requests on behalf of the Israelites (v. 9). It provided for a continuing relationship in which the Israelites would know the Lord as their God, doing "marvels" in such a

way that surrounding peoples would "see the work of the LORD" (v. 10). Restoration following the Israelites' worship of the golden calf seems to have had three stages:

1) the Lord's decision not to destroy all the people,
2) a proposed arrangement that would have given the Israelites a land but no distinctive identity, and
3) pardon and full restoration of ongoing presence and covenant involvement.

34:15, 16 Worshiping idols by both pagans and Israelites is characterized as harlotry. Pagan worship is not neutral and is never directed toward the Lord (see Is. 42, Idolatry; Jer. 7, Paganism).

the land, and they play the harlot with their gods and make sacrifice to their gods, and *one of them* invites you and you eat of his sacrifice, ¹⁶and you take of his daughters for your sons, and his daughters play the harlot with their gods and make your sons play the harlot with their gods.

¹⁷"You shall make no molded gods for yourselves.

¹⁸"The Feast of Unleavened Bread you shall keep. Seven days you shall eat unleavened bread, as I commanded you, in the appointed time of the month of Abib; for in the month of Abib you came out from Egypt.

¹⁹"All that open the womb *are* Mine, and every male firstborn among your livestock, *whether* ox or sheep. ²⁰But the firstborn of a donkey you shall redeem with a lamb. And if you will not redeem *him,* then you shall break his neck. All the firstborn of your sons you shall redeem.

"And none shall appear before Me empty-handed.

²¹"Six days you shall work, but on the seventh day you shall rest; in plowing time and in harvest you shall rest.

²²"And you shall observe the Feast of Weeks, of the firstfruits of wheat harvest, and the Feast of Ingathering at the year's end.

²³"Three times in the year all your men shall appear before the Lord, the LORD God of Israel. ²⁴For I will cast out the nations before you and enlarge your borders; neither will any man covet your land when you go up to appear before the LORD your God three times in the year.

²⁵"You shall not offer the blood of My sacrifice with leaven, nor shall the sacrifice of the Feast of the Passover be left until morning.

²⁶"The first of the firstfruits of your land you shall bring to the house of the LORD your God. You shall not boil a young goat in its mother's milk."

²⁷Then the LORD said to Moses, "Write these words, for according to the tenor of these words I have made a covenant with you and with Israel." ²⁸So he was there with the LORD forty days and forty nights; he neither ate bread nor drank water. And He wrote on the tablets the words of the covenant, the Ten Commandments.^a

The Shining Face of Moses

²⁹Now it was so, when Moses came down from Mount Sinai (and the two tablets of the Testimony *were* in Moses' hand when he came down from the mountain), that Moses did not know that the skin of his face shone while he talked with Him. ³⁰So when Aaron and all the children of Israel saw Moses, behold, the skin of his face shone, and they were afraid to come near him. ³¹Then Moses called to them, and Aaron and all the rulers of the congregation returned to him; and Moses talked with them. ³²Afterward all the children of Israel came near, and he gave them as commandments all that the LORD had spoken with him on Mount Sinai. ³³And when Moses had finished speaking with them, he put a veil on his face. ³⁴But whenever Moses went in before the LORD to speak with Him, he would take the veil off until he came out; and he would come out and speak to the children of Israel whatever he had been commanded. ³⁵And whenever the children of Israel saw the face of Moses, that the skin of Moses' face shone, then Moses would put the veil on his face again, until he went in to speak with Him.

Sabbath Regulations

35 Then Moses gathered all the congregation of the children of Israel together, and said to them, "These *are* the words which the LORD has commanded *you* to do: ²Work shall be done for six days, but the seventh day shall be a holy day for you, a Sabbath of rest to the LORD. Whoever does any work on it shall be put to death. ³You shall kindle no fire throughout your dwellings on the Sabbath day."

Offerings for the Tabernacle

⁴And Moses spoke to all the congregation of the children of Israel, saying, "This *is* the thing which the LORD commanded, saying: ⁵Take from among you an offering to the LORD. Whoever *is* of a willing heart, let him bring it as an offering to the LORD: gold, silver, and bronze; ⁶blue, purple, and scarlet *thread,* fine linen, and goats' *hair;* ⁷ram skins dyed red, badger skins, and acacia wood; ⁸oil for the light, and spices for the anointing oil and for the sweet incense; ⁹onyx stones, and stones to be set in the ephod and in the breastplate.

Articles of the Tabernacle

¹⁰All *who are* gifted artisans among you shall come and make all that the LORD has commanded:

34:28 ^aLiterally *Ten Words*

34:20–24 References to appearing before the Lord (vv. 20, 23, 24) and to His house (v. 26) reflect the fact that the Lord would indeed dwell among the Israelites, as Moses had asked. To appear before the Lord was an act of recognizing Him as the great King who could institute a covenant with a vassal people. They, in turn, would affirm their loyalty and bring Him tribute at regular intervals.

34:26 See Ex. 23:18, 19, note.

35:1 Making the tabernacle. Exodus 35—39 records the Israelites' obedience in following the instructions for the tabernacle, as given to Moses during his first 40 days on Mount Sinai (Ex. 25:1—31:18). Repeating the specifications and repeating the phrase "as the Lord had commanded" and its parallels emphasize the exactness of the obedience (Ex. 36:1; 38:22; 39:1, and throughout Ex. 39; 40; chart, The Plan of the Tabernacle).

¹¹the tabernacle, its tent, its covering, its clasps, its boards, its bars, its pillars, and its sockets; ¹²the ark and its poles, *with* the mercy seat, and the veil of the covering; ¹³the table and its poles, all its utensils, and the showbread; ¹⁴also the lampstand for the light, its utensils, its lamps, and the oil for the light; ¹⁵the incense altar, its poles, the anointing oil, the sweet incense, and the screen for the door at the entrance of the tabernacle; ¹⁶the altar of burnt offering with its bronze grating, its poles, all its utensils, *and* the laver and its base; ¹⁷the hangings of the court, its pillars, their sockets, and the screen for the gate of the court; ¹⁸the pegs of the tabernacle, the pegs of the court, and their cords; ¹⁹the garments of ministry,ᵃ for ministering in the holy *place*—the holy garments for Aaron the priest and the garments of his sons, to minister as priests.' "

The Tabernacle Offerings Presented

²⁰And all the congregation of the children of Israel departed from the presence of Moses. ²¹Then everyone came whose heart was stirred, and everyone whose spirit was willing, *and* they brought the LORD's offering for the work of the tabernacle of meeting, for all its service, and for the holy garments. ²²They came, both men and women, as many as had a willing heart, *and* brought earrings and nose rings, rings and necklaces, all jewelry of gold, that is, every man who *made* an offering of gold to the LORD. ²³And every man, with whom was found blue, purple, and scarlet *thread,* fine linen, goats' *hair,* red skins of rams, and badger skins, brought *them.* ²⁴Everyone who offered an offering of silver or bronze brought the LORD's offering. And everyone with whom was found acacia wood for any work of the service, brought *it.* ²⁵All the women *who were* gifted artisans spun yarn with their hands, and brought what they had spun, of blue, purple, *and* scarlet, and fine linen. ²⁶And all the women whose hearts stirred with wisdom spun yarn of goats' *hair.* ²⁷The rulers brought onyx stones, and the stones to be set in the ephod and in the breastplate, ²⁸and spices and oil for the light, for the anointing oil, and for the sweet incense. ²⁹The children of Israel brought a freewill offering to the LORD, all the men and women whose hearts were willing to bring *material* for all kinds of work which the LORD, by the hand of Moses, had commanded to be done.

The Artisans Called by God

³⁰And Moses said to the children of Israel, "See, the LORD has called by name Bezalel the son of Uri, the son of Hur, of the tribe of Judah; ³¹and He has filled him with the Spirit of God, in wisdom and understanding, in knowledge and all manner of workmanship, ³²to design artistic works, to work in gold and silver and bronze, ³³in cutting jewels for setting, in carving wood, and to work in all manner of artistic workmanship.

³⁴"And He has put in his heart the ability to teach, *in* him and Aholiab the son of Ahisamach, of the tribe of Dan. ³⁵He has filled them with skill to do all manner of work of the engraver and the designer and the tapestry maker, in blue, purple, and scarlet *thread,* and fine linen, and of the weaver—those who do every work and those who design artistic works.

36 "And Bezalel and Aholiab, and every gifted artisan in whom the LORD has put wisdom and understanding, to know how to do all manner of work for the service of the sanctuary, shall do according to all that the LORD has commanded."

The People Give More than Enough

²Then Moses called Bezalel and Aholiab, and every gifted artisan in whose heart the LORD had put wisdom, everyone whose heart was stirred, to come and do the work. ³And they received from Moses all the offering which the children of Israel had brought for the work of the service of making the sanctuary. So they continued bringing to him freewill offerings every morning. ⁴Then all the craftsmen who were doing all the work of the sanctuary came, each from the work he was doing, ⁵and they spoke to Moses, saying, "The people bring much more than enough for the service of the work which the LORD commanded *us* to do."

⁶So Moses gave a commandment, and they caused it to be proclaimed throughout the camp, saying, "Let neither man nor woman do any more work for the offering of the sanctuary." And the people were restrained from bringing, ⁷for the material they had was sufficient for all the work to be done—indeed too much.

Building the Tabernacle

⁸Then all the gifted artisans among them who worked on the tabernacle made ten curtains woven of fine linen, and of blue, purple, and scarlet *thread; with* artistic designs of cherubim they made them. ⁹The length of each curtain *was* twenty-eight cubits, and the width of each curtain four cubits; the curtains *were* all the same size. ¹⁰And he coupled five curtains to one another, and

· · · · · · · · · · · · · · · · · · · ·

35:19 ᵃOr *woven garments*

35:12 The veil of the covering was the curtain that divided the tabernacle into two rooms; it kept the ark of the covenant from being seen.

36:8–38 See Ex. 26:1, note.

the other five curtains he coupled to one another. [11]He made loops of blue *yarn* on the edge of the curtain on the selvedge of one set; likewise he did on the outer edge of *the other* curtain of the second set. [12]Fifty loops he made on one curtain, and fifty loops he made on the edge of the curtain on the end of the second set; the loops held one *curtain* to another. [13]And he made fifty clasps of gold, and coupled the curtains to one another with the clasps, that it might be one tabernacle.

[14]He made curtains of goats' *hair* for the tent over the tabernacle; he made eleven curtains. [15]The length of each curtain *was* thirty cubits, and the width of each curtain four cubits; the eleven curtains *were* the same size. [16]He coupled five curtains by themselves and six curtains by themselves. [17]And he made fifty loops on the edge of the curtain that is outermost in one set, and fifty loops he made on the edge of the curtain of the second set. [18]He also made fifty bronze clasps to couple the tent together, that it might be one. [19]Then he made a covering for the tent of ram skins dyed red, and a covering of badger skins above *that.*

[20]For the tabernacle he made boards of acacia wood, standing upright. [21]The length of each board *was* ten cubits, and the width of each board a cubit and a half. [22]Each board had two tenons for binding one to another. Thus he made for all the boards of the tabernacle. [23]And he made boards for the tabernacle, twenty boards for the south side. [24]Forty sockets of silver he made to go under the twenty boards: two sockets under each of the boards for its two tenons. [25]And for the other side of the tabernacle, the north side, he made twenty boards [26]and their forty sockets of silver: two sockets under each of the boards. [27]For the west side of the tabernacle he made six boards. [28]He also made two boards for the two back corners of the tabernacle. [29]And they were coupled at the bottom and coupled together at the top by one ring. Thus he made both of them for the two corners. [30]So there were eight boards and their sockets— sixteen sockets of silver— two sockets under each of the boards.

[31]And he made bars of acacia wood: five for the boards on one side of the tabernacle, [32]five bars for the boards on the other side of the tabernacle, and five bars for the boards of the tabernacle on the far side westward. [33]And he made the middle bar to pass through the boards from one end to the other. [34]He overlaid the boards with gold, made their rings of gold *to be* holders for the bars, and overlaid the bars with gold.

[35]And he made a veil of blue, purple, and scarlet *thread,* and fine woven linen; it was worked *with* an artistic design of cherubim. [36]He made for it four pillars of acacia *wood,* and overlaid them with gold, with their hooks of gold; and he cast four sockets of silver for them.

[37]He also made a screen for the tabernacle door, of blue, purple, and scarlet *thread,* and fine woven linen, made by a weaver, [38]and its five pillars with their hooks. And he overlaid their capitals and their rings with gold, but their five sockets *were* bronze.

Making the Ark of the Testimony

37Then Bezalel made the ark of acacia wood; two and a half cubits *was* its length, a cubit and a half its width, and a cubit and a half its height. [2]He overlaid it with pure gold inside and outside, and made a molding of gold all around it. [3]And he cast for it four rings of gold *to be set* in its four corners: two rings on one side, and two rings on the other side of it. [4]He made poles of acacia wood, and overlaid them with gold. [5]And he put the poles into the rings at the sides of the ark, to bear the ark. [6]He also made the mercy seat of pure gold; two and a half cubits *was* its length and a cubit and a half its width. [7]He made two cherubim of beaten gold; he made them of one piece at the two ends of the mercy seat: [8]one cherub at one end on this side, and the other cherub at the *other* end on that side. He made the cherubim at the two ends *of one piece* with the mercy seat. [9]The cherubim spread out *their* wings above, *and* covered the mercy seat with their wings. They faced one another; the faces of the cherubim were toward the mercy seat.

Making the Table for the Showbread

[10]He made the table of acacia wood; two cubits *was* its length, a cubit its width, and a cubit and a half its height. [11]And he overlaid it with pure gold, and made a molding of gold all around it. [12]Also he made a frame of a handbreadth all around it, and made a molding of gold for the frame all around it. [13]And he cast for it four rings of gold, and put the rings on the four corners that *were* at its four legs. [14]The rings were close to the frame, as holders for the poles to bear the table. [15]And he made the poles of acacia wood to bear the table, and overlaid them with gold. [16]He made of pure gold the utensils which were on the table: its dishes, its cups, its bowls, and its pitchers for pouring.

Making the Gold Lampstand

[17]He also made the lampstand of pure gold; of hammered work he made the lampstand. Its shaft, its branches, its bowls, its *ornamental* knobs, and

---

37:1–9 See Ex. 25:10, note.
37:10–16 See Ex. 25:30, note.

37:17–24 See Ex. 25:31, note.

its flowers were of the same piece. ¹⁸And six branches came out of its sides: three branches of the lampstand out of one side, and three branches of the lampstand out of the other side. ¹⁹There were three bowls made like almond *blossoms* on one branch, with an *ornamental* knob and a flower, and three bowls made like almond *blossoms* on the other branch, with an *ornamental* knob and a flower— and so for the six branches coming out of the lampstand. ²⁰And on the lampstand itself *were* four bowls made like almond *blossoms, each with* its *ornamental* knob and flower. ²¹*There was* a knob under the *first* two branches of the same, a knob under the *second* two branches of the same, and a knob under the *third* two branches of the same, according to the six branches extending from it. ²²Their knobs and their branches were of one piece; all of it *was* one hammered piece of pure gold. ²³And he made its seven lamps, its wicktrimmers, and its trays of pure gold. ²⁴Of a talent of pure gold he made it, with all its utensils.

Making the Altar of Incense

²⁵He made the incense altar of acacia wood. Its length *was* a cubit and its width a cubit— *it was* square—and two cubits *was* its height. Its horns were *of one piece* with it. ²⁶And he overlaid it with pure gold: its top, its sides all around, and its horns. He also made for it a molding of gold all around it. ²⁷He made two rings of gold for it under its molding, by its two corners on both sides, as holders for the poles with which to bear it. ²⁸And he made the poles of acacia wood, and overlaid them with gold.

Making the Anointing Oil and the Incense

²⁹He also made the holy anointing oil and the pure incense of sweet spices, according to the work of the perfumer.

Making the Altar of Burnt Offering

38 He made the altar of burnt offering of acacia wood; five cubits *was* its length and five cubits its width— *it was* square— and its height *was* three cubits. ²He made its horns on its four corners; the horns were *of one piece* with it. And he overlaid it with bronze. ³He made all the utensils for the altar: the pans, the shovels, the basins, the forks, and the firepans; all its utensils he made of bronze. ⁴And he made a grate of bronze network

for the altar, under its rim, midway from the bottom. ⁵He cast four rings for the four corners of the bronze grating, *as* holders for the poles. ⁶And he made the poles of acacia wood, and overlaid them with bronze. ⁷Then he put the poles into the rings on the sides of the altar, with which to bear it. He made the altar hollow with boards.

Making the Bronze Laver

⁸He made the laver of bronze and its base of bronze, from the bronze mirrors of the serving women who assembled at the door of the tabernacle of meeting.

Making the Court of the Tabernacle

⁹Then he made the court on the south side; the hangings of the court *were of* fine woven linen, one hundred cubits long. ¹⁰There *were* twenty pillars for them, with twenty bronze sockets. The hooks of the pillars and their bands *were* silver. ¹¹On the north side *the hangings were* one hundred cubits *long,* with twenty pillars and their twenty bronze sockets. The hooks of the pillars and their bands *were* silver. ¹²And on the west side *there were* hangings of fifty cubits, with ten pillars and their ten sockets. The hooks of the pillars and their bands *were* silver. ¹³For the east side *the hangings were* fifty cubits. ¹⁴The hangings of one side *of the gate were* fifteen cubits *long, with* their three pillars and their three sockets, ¹⁵and the same for the other side of the court gate; on this side and that *were* hangings of fifteen cubits, *with* their three pillars and their three sockets. ¹⁶All the hangings of the court all around *were of* fine woven linen. ¹⁷The sockets for the pillars *were* bronze, the hooks of the pillars and their bands *were* silver, and the overlay of their capitals *was* silver; and all the pillars of the court had bands of silver. ¹⁸The screen for the gate of the court *was* woven of blue, purple, and scarlet *thread,* and *of* fine woven linen. The length *was* twenty cubits, and the height along its width *was* five cubits, corresponding to the hangings of the court. ¹⁹And *there were* four pillars *with* their four sockets of bronze; their hooks *were* silver, and the overlay of their capitals and their bands *was* silver. ²⁰All the pegs of the tabernacle, and of the court all around, *were* bronze.

Materials of the Tabernacle

²¹This is the inventory of the tabernacle, the tabernacle of the Testimony, which was counted

---

38:1–7 See Ex. 27:1, note.

38:8 The laver of bronze and its base were made from melted down mirrors brought by "serving" women. Little is known about them (see 1 Sam. 2:22). The term used to describe them is used also of Levites (Num. 4:23; 6:24), some of whom were responsible for carrying tabernacle curtains and cords and who took orders from the priests. Except for the tribal leaders who gave stones to be inscribed with the names of the tribes

(Ex. 35:27) and the men required to give a half-shekel of silver (Ex. 30:12–16; 38:25, 26), this group of women is the only group or class singled out for mention as having made a specific donation used for certain items. Bronze mirrors, which are known to have been made in Egypt, might not have been easy to replace in the wilderness (see Ex. 30, Cosmetics; article, What They Left Behind).

according to the commandment of Moses, for the service of the Levites, by the hand of Ithamar, son of Aaron the priest.

22Bezalel the son of Uri, the son of Hur, of the tribe of Judah, made all that the LORD had commanded Moses. 23And with him *was* Aholiab the son of Ahisamach, of the tribe of Dan, an engraver and designer, a weaver of blue, purple, and scarlet *thread,* and of fine linen.

24All the gold that was used in all the work of the holy *place,* that is, the gold of the offering, was twenty-nine talents and seven hundred and thirty shekels, according to the shekel of the sanctuary. 25And the silver from those who were numbered of the congregation *was* one hundred talents and one thousand seven hundred and seventy-five shekels, according to the shekel of the sanctuary: 26a bekah for each man (*that is,* half a shekel, according to the shekel of the sanctuary), for everyone included in the numbering from twenty years old and above, for six hundred and three thousand, five hundred and fifty *men.* 27And from the hundred talents of silver were cast the sockets of the sanctuary and the bases of the veil: one hundred sockets from the hundred talents, one talent for each socket. 28Then from the one thousand seven hundred and seventy-five *shekels* he made hooks for the pillars, overlaid their capitals, and made bands for them.

29The offering of bronze *was* seventy talents and two thousand four hundred shekels. 30And with it he made the sockets for the door of the tabernacle of meeting, the bronze altar, the bronze grating for it, and all the utensils for the altar, 31the sockets for the court all around, the bases for the court gate, all the pegs for the tabernacle, and all the pegs for the court all around.

Making the Garments of the Priesthood

39 Of the blue, purple, and scarlet *thread* they made garments of ministry,[a] for ministering in the holy *place,* and made the holy garments for Aaron, as the LORD had commanded Moses.

Making the Ephod

2He made the ephod of gold, blue, purple, and scarlet *thread,* and of fine woven linen. 3And they beat the gold into thin sheets and cut *it into* threads, to work *it* in *with* the blue, purple, and scarlet *thread,* and the fine linen, *into* artistic designs. 4They made shoulder straps for it to couple *it* together; it was coupled together at its two edges. 5And the intricately woven band of his ephod that *was* on it *was* of the same workmanship, *woven of* gold, blue, purple, and scarlet *thread,* and of fine woven linen, as the LORD had commanded Moses.

6And they set onyx stones, enclosed in settings of gold; they were engraved, as signets are engraved, with the names of the sons of Israel. 7He put them on the shoulders of the ephod *as* memorial stones for the sons of Israel, as the LORD had commanded Moses.

Making the Breastplate

8And he made the breastplate, artistically woven like the workmanship of the ephod, of gold, blue, purple, and scarlet *thread,* and of fine woven linen. 9They made the breastplate square by doubling it; a span *was* its length and a span its width when doubled. 10And they set in it four rows of stones: a row with a sardius, a topaz, and an emerald *was* the first row; 11the second row, a turquoise, a sapphire, and a diamond; 12the third row, a jacinth, an agate, and an amethyst; 13the fourth row, a beryl, an onyx, and a jasper. *They were* enclosed in settings of gold in their mountings. 14*There were* twelve stones according to the names of the sons of Israel: according to their names, *engraved like* a signet, each one with its own name according to the twelve tribes. 15And they made chains for the breastplate at the ends, like braided cords of pure gold. 16They also made two settings of gold and two gold rings, and put the two rings on the two ends of the breastplate. 17And they put the two braided *chains* of gold in the two rings on the ends of the breastplate. 18The two ends of the two braided *chains* they fastened in the two settings, and put them on the shoulder straps of the ephod in the front. 19And they made two rings of gold and put *them* on the two ends of the breastplate, on the edge of it, which *was* on the inward side of the ephod. 20They made two *other* gold rings and put them on the two shoulder straps, underneath the ephod toward its front, right at the seam above the intricately woven band of the ephod. 21And they bound the breastplate by means of its rings to the rings of the ephod with a blue cord, so that it would be above the intricately woven band of the ephod, and that the breastplate would not come loose from the ephod, as the LORD had commanded Moses.

Making the Other Priestly Garments

22He made the robe of the ephod of woven work, all of blue. 23And *there was* an opening in the middle of the robe, like the opening in a coat of mail, *with* a woven binding all around the opening, so that it would not tear. 24They made on the hem of the robe pomegranates of blue, purple, and scarlet, and of fine woven *linen.* 25And they made bells of pure gold, and put the bells between the pomegranates on the hem of the robe all around between the pomegranates: 26a bell and a pomegranate, a bell and a pomegranate, all around the

39:1 [a]Or *woven garments*

hem of the robe to minister in, as the LORD had commanded Moses.

[27]They made tunics, artistically woven of fine linen, for Aaron and his sons, [28]a turban of fine linen, exquisite hats of fine linen, short trousers of fine woven linen, [29]and a sash of fine woven linen with blue, purple, and scarlet *thread,* made by a weaver, as the LORD had commanded Moses.

[30]Then they made the plate of the holy crown of pure gold, and wrote on it an inscription *like* the engraving of a signet:

HOLINESS TO THE LORD.

[31]And they tied to it a blue cord, to fasten *it* above on the turban, as the LORD had commanded Moses.

The Work Completed

[32]Thus all the work of the tabernacle of the tent of meeting was finished. And the children of Israel did according to all that the LORD had commanded Moses; so they did. [33]And they brought the tabernacle to Moses, the tent and all its furnishings: its clasps, its boards, its bars, its pillars, and its sockets; [34]the covering of ram skins dyed red, the covering of badger skins, and the veil of the covering; [35]the ark of the Testimony with its poles, and the mercy seat; [36]the table, all its utensils, and the showbread; [37]the pure *gold* lampstand with its lamps (the lamps set in order), all its utensils, and the oil for light; [38]the gold altar, the anointing oil, and the sweet incense; the screen for the tabernacle door; [39]the bronze altar, its grate of bronze, its poles, and all its utensils; the laver with its base; [40]the hangings of the court, its pillars and its sockets, the screen for the court gate, its cords, and its pegs; all the utensils for the service of the tabernacle, for the tent of meeting; [41]and the garments of ministry,[a] to minister in the holy *place:* the holy garments for Aaron the priest, and his sons' garments, to minister as priests.

[42]According to all that the LORD had commanded Moses, so the children of Israel did all the work. [43]Then Moses looked over all the work, and indeed they had done it; as the LORD had commanded, just so they had done it. And Moses blessed them.

The Tabernacle Erected and Arranged

40 Then the LORD spoke to Moses, saying: [2]"On the first day of the first month you shall set up the tabernacle of the tent of meeting. [3]You shall put in it the ark of the Testimony, and parti-

tion off the ark with the veil. [4]You shall bring in the table and arrange the things that are to be set in order on it; and you shall bring in the lampstand and light its lamps. [5]You shall also set the altar of gold for the incense before the ark of the Testimony, and put up the screen for the door of the tabernacle. [6]Then you shall set the altar of the burnt offering before the door of the tabernacle of the tent of meeting. [7]And you shall set the laver between the tabernacle of meeting and the altar, and put water in it. [8]You shall set up the court all around, and hang up the screen at the court gate.

[9]"And you shall take the anointing oil, and anoint the tabernacle and all that *is* in it; and you shall hallow it and all its utensils, and it shall be holy. [10]You shall anoint the altar of the burnt offering and all its utensils, and consecrate the altar. The altar shall be most holy. [11]And you shall anoint the laver and its base, and consecrate it.

[12]"Then you shall bring Aaron and his sons to the door of the tabernacle of meeting and wash them with water. [13]You shall put the holy garments on Aaron, and anoint him and consecrate him, that he may minister to Me as priest. [14]And you shall bring his sons and clothe them with tunics. [15]You shall anoint them, as you anointed their father, that they may minister to Me as priests; for their anointing shall surely be an everlasting priesthood throughout their generations."

[16]Thus Moses did; according to all that the LORD had commanded him, so he did.

[17]And it came to pass in the first month of the second year, on the first *day* of the month, *that* the tabernacle was raised up. [18]So Moses raised up the tabernacle, fastened its sockets, set up its boards, put in its bars, and raised up its pillars. [19]And he spread out the tent over the tabernacle and put the covering of the tent on top of it, as the LORD had commanded Moses. [20]He took the Testimony and put *it* into the ark, inserted the poles through the rings of the ark, and put the mercy seat on top of the ark. [21]And he brought the ark into the tabernacle, hung up the veil of the covering, and partitioned off the ark of the Testimony, as the LORD had commanded Moses.

[22]He put the table in the tabernacle of meeting, on the north side of the tabernacle, outside the veil; [23]and he set the bread in order upon it before the LORD, as the LORD had commanded Moses. [24]He put the lampstand in the tabernacle

39:41 [a]Or *woven garments*

39:43 In a fashion reminiscent of the Lord's inspecting what He had made, approving it, and then blessing it (Gen. 1:21, 22, 25, 28, 31), Moses inspected what the Israelites had made at the Lord's command and blessed them. A new creation was being completed. In blessing the workers, Moses declared what was already an established fact. As a result of and in the process of their obedience, the people were experiencing God's beneficence.

40:17 The tabernacle was raised. This took place on New Year's day, at the start of the second year after the Israelites' departure from Egypt (Ex. 12:2–6, 15–17) and nine months after their arrival at Mount Sinai (Ex. 19:1).

of meeting, across from the table, on the south side of the tabernacle; [25]and he lit the lamps before the LORD, as the LORD had commanded Moses. [26]He put the gold altar in the tabernacle of meeting in front of the veil; [27]and he burned sweet incense on it, as the LORD had commanded Moses. [28]He hung up the screen *at* the door of the tabernacle. [29]And he put the altar of burnt offering *before* the door of the tabernacle of the tent of meeting, and offered upon it the burnt offering and the grain offering, as the LORD had commanded Moses. [30]He set the laver between the tabernacle of meeting and the altar, and put water there for washing; [31]and Moses, Aaron, and his sons would wash their hands and their feet *with water* from it. [32]Whenever they went into the tabernacle of meeting, and when they came near the altar, they washed, as the LORD had commanded Moses. [33]And he raised up the court all around the tabernacle and the altar, and hung up the screen of the court gate. So Moses finished the work.

The Cloud and the Glory

[34]Then the cloud covered the tabernacle of meeting, and the glory of the LORD filled the tabernacle. [35]And Moses was not able to enter the tabernacle of meeting, because the cloud rested above it, and the glory of the LORD filled the tabernacle. [36]Whenever the cloud was taken up from above the tabernacle, the children of Israel would go onward in all their journeys. [37]But if the cloud was not taken up, then they did not journey till the day that it was taken up. [38]For the cloud of the LORD *was* above the tabernacle by day, and fire was over it by night, in the sight of all the house of Israel, throughout all their journeys.

40:34–38 The glory of the LORD filled the tabernacle. This section marks the fulfillment of the Lord's intention to hallow the tabernacle by His presence and to dwell among the Israelites in such a way that they would know Him as their God, who had rescued them from Egypt for that purpose (see similarly 1 Kin. 8:10–13, 22–30, 56–60; Ezek. 43:2–7; 44:4; and in fuller measure, John 1:14; 14:1–3 , 16–21; 17:24–26; 1 Cor. 6:19, 20; Eph. 2:19–22; 1 Thess. 5:9–11, 23; Rev. 21:1–3). The central goal of the Exodus had been achieved, and the book ends with a forward emphasis in the description of journeying with the guidance of the Lord.

Leviticus

EXODUS 10:38

of meeting, across from the Table on the...by prayers on the court all around the tabernacle side of the tabernacle, and he...and...up the screen of the court before the Lord, as the Lord had...on of the work.

TITLE

The first word in Leviticus became its title in the Hebrew text (*wayyiqra*, lit. "and He called"). In the Septuagint, an ancient Greek translation of the Old Testament, Leviticus received the title *Leuitikon* (Gk.), meaning "pertaining to the Levites." The English title "Leviticus" was derived from the title *Leviticus* or *Leviticum* appearing in the Latin Vulgate. The book emphasizes covenant matters of specifically Levitical or priestly interest with a focus on holiness and worship.

AUTHOR

Although the author's name is not identified within the book, this third book of the Pentateuch has traditionally been ascribed to Moses, Israel's great lawgiver. The Book of Leviticus consists primarily of laws and regulations governing the daily life of the Lord's people. Twenty of the 27 chapters of Leviticus begin with the notation that the Lord spoke to Moses, emphasizing that the book reveals guidance for worship from the Lord Himself. The introductory and concluding verses of Leviticus (Lev. 1:1; 27:34) indicate that these laws were revealed to Israel through Moses. The laws set forth in the Book of Leviticus belong to the covenant relationship established at Mount Sinai between God and Israel. With such internal evidence, Moses' authorship is strongly affirmed. Jesus also affirmed Mosaic authorship in His reference to the law concerning cleansing from leprosy (Matt. 8:4; see Lev. 14:2–32).

DATE

Leviticus was written during the third month after the people of Israel had departed from Egypt (Ex. 19:1; see Introduction: Setting). Traditionally, the Exodus from Egypt has been dated around 1445 B.C.

BACKGROUND

SETTING: The setting is the base of Mount Sinai, where the people of Israel camped for an extensive period following the Exodus from Egypt (Ex. 19:1; Num. 10:11, 12).

PURPOSE: The Book of Leviticus is an extensive guidebook showing God's people how to live daily in relationship to Him and one another. God desired fellowship with His people, and the Book of Leviticus taught the people how to maintain that fellowship by experiencing the Lord's presence and dedicating their lives to Him. They were to be holy, for the Lord Himself is holy (Lev. 11:44; 19:2; 20:7). God's people were to separate themselves from evil and impurity and unto righteousness and obedience. Through the sacrificial system described in Leviticus, the worshiping community learned about the nature of God and how to enjoy a right relationship with Him. Reading Leviticus alongside the Psalms provides an even more complete picture of the nature of Israel's worship.

AUDIENCE: God spoke through Moses to the people of Israel camped at Mount Sinai (Lev. 1:2). Leviticus, as part of the canon of Scripture, also has impacted the chosen people throughout their history and carries a tremendous message for believers in every generation.

LITERARY CHARACTERISTICS: Leviticus is an ordered collection of regulations governing the offering of sacrifices, the organization of the priesthood, and various other matters concerning Israel's relationship with the Lord and their interaction with other nations. The book divides naturally into two major sections. The first section addresses the worship of and relationship with a holy God (Lev. 1—16). The second section deals with the daily life before a holy God and other people. The phrase "the Lord spoke" appears more than thirty times in the book and emphasizes the fact that the book is the Lord's Word.

THEMES

Holiness (lit. "separateness") is a major theme. Some form of the word appears more than 100 times in Leviticus. The worshiper is called to be holy as the Lord is holy (Lev. 11:44; 19:2). The concept of the Lord's holiness involves His uniqueness and His separateness from all that is evil. The concept of the worshiper's holiness indicates that the believer should live an obedient life of purity. God's people are called to commit every aspect of their lives to Him. Another theme is that of atonement or covering for sins. The central chapter of the book deals with the Day of Atonement (Heb. *Yom Kippur*, lit. "day of covering"; see Lev. 16). By forgiving sin, God enables us to enjoy fellowship with Him. The book deals with a proper response to the Lord and especially with the concept of worship. The book affirms that all people can know God and that God has revealed the way by which all can approach Him. It reveals forms and principles of worship that reach their full significance in the Person and work of Christ. The writer of the Book of Hebrews helps Christians draw parallels between the regulations of Leviticus and the work of Christ. The laws of Leviticus point to the Cross of Christ.

OUTLINE

I. Regulations on Holiness for Approaching the Holy God (1:1—16:34)
   A. Instructions concerning offerings (1:1—7:38)
   B. Instructions concerning the priests (8:1—10:20)
   C. Instructions concerning cleanness and uncleanness (11:1—15:33)
   D. Instructions concerning the Day of Atonement (16:1—34)

II. Regulations on Holiness for Fellowshiping with the Holy God (17:1—27:34)
   A. Instructions concerning separation (17:1—22:33)
   B. Instructions concerning holy days (23:1—25:55)
   C. Instructions concerning blessings and curses (26:1—46)
   D. Instructions concerning vows (27:1—34)

The Burnt Offering

1 Now the LORD called to Moses, and spoke to him from the tabernacle of meeting, saying, [2]"Speak to the children of Israel, and say to them: 'When any one of you brings an offering to the LORD, you shall bring your offering of the livestock— of the herd and of the flock.

[3]'If his offering is a burnt sacrifice of the herd, let him offer a male without blemish; he shall offer it of his own free will at the door of the tabernacle of meeting before the LORD. [4]Then he shall put his hand on the head of the burnt offering, and it will be accepted on his behalf to make atonement for him. [5]He shall kill the bull before the LORD; and the priests, Aaron's sons, shall bring the blood and sprinkle the blood all around on the altar that is by the door of the tabernacle of meeting. [6]And he shall skin the burnt offering and cut it into its pieces. [7]The sons of Aaron the priest shall put fire on the altar, and lay the wood in order on the fire. [8]Then the priests, Aaron's sons, shall lay the parts, the head, and the fat in order on the wood that is on the fire upon the altar; [9]but he shall wash its entrails and its legs with water. And the priest shall burn all on the altar as a burnt sacrifice, an offering made by fire, a sweet aroma to the LORD.

[10]'If his offering is of the flocks— of the sheep or of the goats— as a burnt sacrifice, he shall bring a male without blemish. [11]He shall kill it on the north side of the altar before the LORD; and the priests, Aaron's sons, shall sprinkle its blood all around on the altar. [12]And he shall cut it into its pieces, with its head and its fat; and the priest shall lay them in order on the wood that is on the fire upon the altar; [13]but he shall wash the entrails and the legs with water. Then the priest shall bring it all and burn it on the altar; it is a burnt sacrifice, an offering made by fire, a sweet aroma to the LORD.

[14]'And if the burnt sacrifice of his offering to the LORD is of birds, then he shall bring his offering of turtledoves or young pigeons. [15]The priest shall bring it to the altar, wring off its head, and burn it on the altar; its blood shall be drained out at the side of the altar. [16]And he shall remove its crop with its feathers and cast it beside the altar on the east side, into the place for ashes. [17]Then he shall split it at its wings, but shall not divide it completely; and the priest shall burn it on the altar, on the wood that is on the fire. It is a burnt sacrifice, an offering made by fire, a sweet aroma to the LORD.

The Grain Offering

2 'When anyone offers a grain offering to the LORD, his offering shall be of fine flour. And he shall pour oil on it, and put frankincense on it. [2]He shall

---

1:1 God takes the initiative to establish fellowship with His people. The tabernacle or tent of meeting, a portable sanctuary, represented the Lord's presence among the people of Israel. The Lord's instructions to Moses for building the tabernacle and its furnishings are recorded (Ex. 25—31). A manual on the proper procedures for sacrifice follows (Lev. 1:1—7:38).

1:3–17 The burnt offering (Heb. 'olah) is mentioned first, as the oldest and most important type of sacrifice (Gen. 8:20; see chart, The Offerings of the Lord). Sacrificial animals could not be carnivorous; they must be domesticated and without blemish. God in His mercy provided a way to restore to Himself a relationship that had been broken by sin. The offering was burned completely (except the skin), symbolizing total commitment to God. In placing (lit. "leaning") his hand on the head of the burnt offering (v. 4), the worshiper identified himself with the offering. Provision was made for the poor to offer a common bird as a burnt offering (vv. 14–17). The appointment of representative male leaders from the tribe of Levi to be priests was to be done with consistency throughout the history of Israel (Ex. 28:1–3). The selection of priests was not just along gender lines, for all blemished males were also refused (Lev. 21:17–21). Spiritual leadership in any Israelite family was vested in a male head of the family. For example, Noah offered the sacrifice for his family (Gen. 8:20); Abraham, as did the other patriarchs and Job, built altars for his family (Gen. 12:7; 13:18). Wives and children were covered through the sacrifice made by the male head of the household. This male role in public worship never negated any woman's direct access to God on the personal level, nor did it deter women from having personal appearances from God (Judg. 13:2–6; 1 Sam. 1:9–18). There is no intrinsic inferiority of

the woman suggested; rather the man was created first (1 Gen. 11:8) and given an assignment from God Himself for leadership of his family (Eph. 5:22–24; see 1 Pet. 3, Submission; chart, Theological Foundations for Headship). This was not a statement on worth or value but a directive concerning order, roles, and responsibilities.

1:5 Blood, mentioned more than 80 times in Leviticus, represents the life force of a living being (Lev. 17:11).

1:9 The burnt offering is described as a sweet (lit. "soothing" or "pleasing") aroma to the Lord. Clearly the sacrifice was not regarded as a means of appeasing an angry, capricious deity, but of illustrating the need for atonement between the holy God and sinful man.

1:11 Killing the animal was a religious act. Generally, the worshiper participated by bringing the animal, identifying with the animal through laying hands on its head (illustrating the concept of substitution), by confession of sin, and by assisting the priest in slaying the animal. Such acts as pouring out the blood, maintaining the fire, placing the pieces on the altar, cleansing portions of the animal, and burning the sacrifice were designated as priestly functions as the priest did his work as mediator between sinful man and a holy God.

2:1–16 The Hebrew name for the grain or cereal offering simply means "gift." This offering expressed the worshiper's spontaneous gratitude to God (see chart, The Offerings of the Lord). No specific requirements regarding its time and frequency were given. The gift involved the product of a woman's daily activities in the home: flour or baked cakes. Dedication of life expresses itself in the simplicity of everyday activity. This offering also produced a "sweet aroma" to the

bring it to Aaron's sons, the priests, one of whom shall take from it his handful of fine flour and oil with all the frankincense. And the priest shall burn *it as* a memorial on the altar, an offering made by fire, a sweet aroma to the LORD. ³The rest of the grain offering *shall be* Aaron's and his sons'. *It is* most holy of the offerings to the LORD made by fire.

⁴And if you bring as an offering a grain offering baked in the oven, *it shall be* unleavened cakes of fine flour mixed with oil, or unleavened wafers anointed with oil. ⁵But if your offering *is* a grain offering *baked* in a pan, *it shall be of* fine flour, unleavened, mixed with oil. ⁶You shall break it in pieces and pour oil on it; it *is* a grain offering.

⁷If your offering *is* a grain offering *baked* in a covered pan, it shall be made *of* fine flour with oil. ⁸You shall bring the grain offering that is made of these things to the LORD. And when it is presented to the priest, he shall bring it to the altar. ⁹Then the priest shall take from the grain offering a memorial portion, and burn *it* on the altar. *It is* an offering made by fire, a sweet aroma to the LORD. ¹⁰And what is left of the grain offering *shall be* Aaron's and his sons'. *It is* most holy of the offerings to the LORD made by fire.

¹¹No grain offering which you bring to the LORD shall be made with leaven, for you shall burn no leaven nor any honey in any offering to the LORD made by fire. ¹²As for the offering of the firstfruits, you shall offer them to the LORD, but they shall not be burned on the altar for a sweet aroma. ¹³And every offering of your grain offering you shall season with salt; you shall not allow the salt of the covenant of your God to be lacking from your grain offering. With all your offerings you shall offer salt.

¹⁴If you offer a grain offering of your firstfruits to the LORD, you shall offer for the grain offering of your firstfruits green heads of grain roasted on the fire, grain beaten from full heads. ¹⁵And you shall put oil on it, and lay frankincense on it. It *is* a grain offering. ¹⁶Then the priest shall burn the memorial portion: *part* of its beaten grain and *part* of its oil, with all the frankincense, as an offering made by fire to the LORD.

The Peace Offering

3 ¹When his offering *is* a sacrifice of a peace offering, if he offers *it* of the herd, whether male or female, he shall offer it without blemish before the LORD. ²And he shall lay his hand on the head of his offering, and kill it *at* the door of the tabernacle of meeting; and Aaron's sons, the priests, shall sprinkle the blood all around on the altar. ³Then he shall offer from the sacrifice of the peace offering an offering made by fire to the LORD. The fat that covers the entrails and all the fat that *is* on the entrails, ⁴the two kidneys and the fat that *is* on them by the flanks, and the fatty lobe *attached* to the liver above the kidneys, he shall remove; ⁵and Aaron's sons shall burn it on the altar upon the burnt sacrifice, which *is* on the wood that *is* on the fire, *as* an offering made by fire, a sweet aroma to the LORD.

⁶If his offering as a sacrifice of a peace offering to the LORD *is* of the flock, *whether* male or female, he shall offer it without blemish. ⁷If he offers a lamb as his offering, then he shall offer it before the LORD. ⁸And he shall lay his hand on the head of his offering, and kill it before the tabernacle of meeting; and Aaron's sons shall sprinkle its blood all around on the altar.

⁹Then he shall offer from the sacrifice of the peace offering, as an offering made by fire to the LORD, its fat *and* the whole fat tail which he shall remove close to the backbone. And the fat that covers the entrails and all the fat that *is* on the entrails, ¹⁰the two kidneys and the fat that *is* on them by the flanks, and the fatty lobe *attached* to the liver above the kidneys, he shall remove; ¹¹and the priest shall burn *them* on the altar *as* food, an offering made by fire to the LORD.

¹²And if his offering *is* a goat, then he shall offer it before the LORD. ¹³He shall lay his hand on its head and kill it before the tabernacle of meeting; and the sons of Aaron shall sprinkle its blood all around on the altar. ¹⁴Then he shall offer from it his offering, as an offering made by fire to the LORD. The fat that covers the entrails and all the fat that *is* on the entrails, ¹⁵the two kidneys and

---

Lord (vv. 2, 9, 12; Lev. 1:9, note). Only a small portion of the grain offering was consumed by fire. The remainder was given to the priests and considered part of their income (v. 3; Lev. 6:16). While leaven and honey (probably due to the fermentation of fruit-honey) were forbidden as part of the grain offering (v. 11), salt was to be included (v. 13). Leaven symbolized that which was unacceptable to God, while salt symbolized friendship and communion with Him. Both leavened bread and honey could be brought as offerings for the priests to consume but could not be burned on the altar (v. 11).

3:1 The peace offering, the last of the basic prescribed sacrifices, constituted the third type of "sweet aroma" offering. The peace offering expressed love and gratitude to God and promoted communion with Him. The offering of this sacrifice was an occasion for joy and thanksgiving. The distinctive element of the peace offering was that it ended with a communal meal shared by the worshiper with family and friends. Women had a unique opportunity to be involved in the preparation of this special meal. Peace offerings consisted of thank offerings, votive offerings, and freewill offerings. "Peace" (Heb. *shelem,* lit. "benefit") conveys the ideas of wholeness and completeness. Such ideas as wholeness and health and peace are found in the traditional Jewish greeting "Shalom," which is still used. The fat of the animal was considered the choicest part, and, therefore, it belonged to the Lord (vv. 3-5). Peace offerings might be given voluntarily or in fulfillment of a vow (see chart, The Offerings of the Lord).

THE OFFERINGS OF THE LORD

NAME	SCRIPTURE REFERENCE	PURPOSE	CONTENT
1. Burnt Offering (Heb. *Olah*) Sweet aroma; Voluntary	Lev. 1:3–17; 6:8–13.	Propitiation for sin in general (Lev. 1:4); Expression of complete dedication and consecration to God; hence, the "whole burnt offering"	According to wealth: 1. Bull without blemish (Lev. 1:3–9); 2. Male sheep or goat without blemish (Lev. 1:10–13); 3. Turtledoves or young pigeons (Lev. 1:14–17)
2. Grain Offering (Heb. *minhah*) Sweet aroma; Voluntary	Lev. 2:1–16; 6:14–18; 7:12, 13.	An accompaniment to all the burnt offerings, signifying homage and thanksgiving to God	1. Fine flour mixed with oil and frankincense (Lev. 2:1–3); 2. Cakes made of fine flour, cooked with oil, and baked in oven (Lev. 2:4), pan (Lev. 2:5), or covered pan (Lev. 2:7); 3. Green heads of roasted grain mixed with oil and frankincense (Lev. 2:14, 15)
3. Peace Offering (Heb. *shelem*) Sweet aroma; Voluntary	Lev. 3:1–17; 7:11–21, 28–34.	Generally an expression of peace and fellowship between the offerer and God, culminating in a communal meal *Thank Offering* to express gratitude for an unexpected blessing or deliverance *Votive Offering* to express gratitude for a blessing or deliverance granted when a vow had accompanied the petition *Freewill Offering* to express gratitude to God without regard to any specific blessing or deliverance	According to wealth: 1. From the herd, a male or female without blemish (Lev. 3:1–5); 2. From the flock, a male or female without blemish (Lev. 3:6–11); 3. From the goats (Lev. 3:12–17) *Note:* Minor imperfections were permitted when the peace offering was a freewill offering of a bull or a lamb (Lev. 22:23)
4. Sin Offering (Heb. *hattat*) Non-sweet aroma; Compulsory	Lev. 4:1— 5:13; 6:24–30.	An atonement for sins committed unknowingly, especially where no restitution was possible The sin offering not acceptable in cases of defiant rebellion against God (Num. 15:30, 31)	1. For the high priest, a bull without blemish (Lev. 4:3–12) 2. For the congregation, a bull without blemish (Lev. 4:13–21) 3. For a ruler, a male goat without blemish (Lev. 4:22–26) 4. For a commoner, a female goat or female lamb without blemish (Lev. 4:27–35) 5. In cases of poverty, two turtledoves or two young pigeons (one for a sin offering, the other for a burnt offering; Lev. 5:7–10) 6. In cases of extreme poverty, fine flour as a substitute (Lev. 5:11–13; see Heb. 9:22)
5. Trespass Offering (Heb. *'asham*) Non-sweet aroma; Compulsory	Lev. 5:14— 6:7; 7:1–7.	An atonement for sins committed unknowingly, especially where restitution was possible	1. If the offense were against the Lord (tithes, offerings, etc.), a ram without blemish was to be brought; with restitution reckoned according to the priest's estimate of the value of the trespass, plus one-fifth (Lev. 5:15, 16) 2. If the offense were against man, a ram without blemish with restitution reckoned according to the value plus one-fifth (Lev. 6:4–6)

THE OFFERINGS OF THE LORD (cont.)

GOD'S PORTION	PRIESTS' PORTION	OFFERER'S PORTION	PROPHETIC SIGNIFICANCE
Entirety burned on the altar of burnt offering (Lev. 1:9), except the skin (Lev. 7:8)	Skin only (Lev. 7:8)	None	Signifying complete dedication of life to God: On the part of Christ (Matt. 26:39–44; Mark 14:36; Luke 22:42; Phil. 2:5–11) On the part of the believer (Rom. 12:1, 2; Heb. 13:15)
Memorial portion burned on the altar of burnt offering (Lev. 2:2, 9, 16)	Remainder eaten in the court of the tabernacle (Lev. 2:3, 10; 6:16–18; 7:14, 15)	None	Signifying the perfect humanity of Christ: The absence of leaven typifies the sinlessness of Christ (Heb. 4:15; 1 John 3:5) The presence of oil is emblematic of the Holy Spirit (Luke 4:18; 1 John 2:20, 27)
Fatty portions burned on the altar of burnt offering (Lev. 3:3–5)	Breast or wave offering and right thigh or heave offering (Lev. 7:30–34)	Remainder eaten in the court by the offerer and his family: *Thank offering*—to be eaten the same day (Lev. 7:15) *Votive and freewill offerings*—to be eaten the first and second day (Lev. 7:16–18) *Note:* This is the only offering in which the offerer shared	Foreshadowing the peace that the believer has with God through Jesus Christ (Rom. 5:1; Col. 1:20)
1. Fatty portions to be burned on the altar of burnt offering (Lev. 4:8–10, 19, 26, 31, 35). 2. The remainder of the bull to be burned outside the camp when the sin offering was for the high priest or congregation (Lev. 4:11, 12, 20, 21)	Remainder of the goat or lamb eaten in the tabernacle court when the sin offering was for a ruler or commoner (Lev. 6:26)	None	Prefiguring His death: Christ was made sin for us (2 Cor. 5:21); Christ suffered outside the gates of Jerusalem (Heb. 13:11–13)
Fatty portions to be burned on the altar of burnt offering (Lev. 7:3–5)	Remainder eaten in a holy place (Lev. 7:6, 7)	None	Foreshadowing Christ as our trespass offering (Col. 2:13)

the fat that *is* on them by the flanks, and the fatty lobe *attached* to the liver above the kidneys, he shall remove; [16]and the priest shall burn them on the altar *as* food, an offering made by fire for a sweet aroma; all the fat *is* the LORD's.

[17]'*This shall be* a perpetual statute throughout your generations in all your dwellings: you shall eat neither fat nor blood.'"

The Sin Offering

4 Now the LORD spoke to Moses, saying, [2]"Speak to the children of Israel, saying: 'If a person sins unintentionally against any of the commandments of the LORD *in anything* which ought not to be done, and does any of them, [3]if the anointed priest sins, bringing guilt on the people, then let him offer to the LORD for his sin which he has sinned a young bull without blemish as a sin offering. [4]He shall bring the bull to the door of the tabernacle of meeting before the LORD, lay his hand on the bull's head, and kill the bull before the LORD. [5]Then the anointed priest shall take some of the bull's blood and bring it to the tabernacle of meeting. [6]The priest shall dip his finger in the blood and sprinkle some of the blood seven times before the LORD, in front of the veil of the sanctuary. [7]And the priest shall put some of the blood on the horns of the altar of sweet incense before the LORD, which is in the tabernacle of meeting; and he shall pour the remaining blood of the bull at the base of the altar of the burnt offering, which is at the door of the tabernacle of meeting. [8]He shall take from it all the fat of the bull as the sin offering. The fat that covers the entrails and all the fat which *is* on the entrails, [9]the two kidneys and the fat that *is* on them by the flanks, and the fatty lobe *attached* to the liver above the kidneys, he shall remove, [10]as it was taken from the bull of the sacrifice of the peace offering; and the priest shall burn them on the altar of the burnt offering. [11]But the bull's hide

and all its flesh, with its head and legs, its entrails and offal— [12]the whole bull he shall carry outside the camp to a clean place, where the ashes are poured out, and burn it on wood with fire; where the ashes are poured out it shall be burned.

[13]'Now if the whole congregation of Israel sins unintentionally, and the thing is hidden from the eyes of the assembly, and they have done *something against* any of the commandments of the LORD *in anything* which should not be done, and are guilty; [14]when the sin which they have committed becomes known, then the assembly shall offer a young bull for the sin, and bring it before the tabernacle of meeting. [15]And the elders of the congregation shall lay their hands on the head of the bull before the LORD. Then the bull shall be killed before the LORD. [16]The anointed priest shall bring some of the bull's blood to the tabernacle of meeting. [17]Then the priest shall dip his finger in the blood and sprinkle *it* seven times before the LORD, in front of the veil. [18]And he shall put *some* of the blood on the horns of the altar which *is* before the LORD, which *is* in the tabernacle of meeting; and he shall pour the remaining blood at the base of the altar of burnt offering, which is at the door of the tabernacle of meeting. [19]He shall take all the fat from it and burn *it* on the altar. [20]And he shall do with the bull as he did with the bull as a sin offering; thus he shall do with it. So the priest shall make atonement for them, and it shall be forgiven them. [21]Then he shall carry the bull outside the camp, and burn it as he burned the first bull. It *is* a sin offering for the assembly.

[22]'When a ruler has sinned, and done *something* unintentionally *against* any of the commandments of the LORD his God *in anything* which should not be done, and is guilty, [23]or if his sin which he has committed comes to his knowledge, he shall bring as his offering a kid of the goats, a male without blemish. [24]And he shall lay his hand on the head of

---

3:17 Neither the fat nor the blood of any sacrifice should be consumed by the worshiper. These parts were dedicated to the Lord. Blood was treated in this special way because it is the essence of life (see Lev. 17:11), and life is the gift of God. Shed blood was the basis for atonement and was not to be profaned. Also, heathen religions used the drinking of blood in their rituals, and the people of Israel were to be holy or set apart. The fatty parts of the animal were viewed as places where the life force of the animal was located. The fatty portions were to be given back to the Lord in recognition that the Lord is the source of all life.

4:1 The offenses requiring a sin offering or a guilt offering are described (Lev. 4:1—6:7; see chart, The Offerings of the Lord). The original distinction between these two kinds of sacrifices has been lost. Leviticus 4 focuses on sins committed unknowingly and unintentionally. The Hebrew word for sin employed here means "to miss the mark." Unintentional sin might involve unknown violations of ritual regulations. This designation also included unpremeditated sins committed. Uninten-

tional sin is distinguished from presumptuous sin—a deliberate revolt against God (Num. 15:30, 31), for which no sin offering was prescribed. The worshiper could only cast himself on the mercy of God. An example of the confession of deliberate sin is found in David's plea for forgiveness following his adultery with Bathsheba and his murder of Uriah (Ps. 51).

4:3 The anointed priest most likely refers to the high priest, who had special responsibility for the people's relationship with the Lord. Worship leaders must be in right relationship with the Lord before they can minister effectively to the people. The sin offering consisted of a bull in cases where the high priest or the congregation sinned. If the offender was a ruler (a king or tribal representative, v. 22) or a common person, a goat or lamb was offered. In other words, God had a plan enabling all levels of society (from the poorest peasant to the wealthiest ruler) to worship Him (see chart, The Offerings of the Lord).

the goat, and kill it at the place where they kill the burnt offering before the LORD. It *is* a sin offering. ²⁵The priest shall take some of the blood of the sin offering with his finger, put *it* on the horns of the altar of burnt offering, and pour its blood at the base of the altar of burnt offering. ²⁶And he shall burn all its fat on the altar, like the fat of the sacrifice of the peace offering. So the priest shall make atonement for him concerning his sin, and it shall be forgiven him.

²⁷"If anyone of the common people sins unintentionally by doing *something against* any of the commandments of the LORD *in anything* which ought not to be done, and is guilty, ²⁸or if his sin which he has committed comes to his knowledge, then he shall bring as his offering a kid of the goats, a female without blemish, for his sin which he has committed. ²⁹And he shall lay his hand on the head of the sin offering, and kill the sin offering at the place of the burnt offering. ³⁰Then the priest shall take *some* of its blood with his finger, put *it* on the horns of the altar of burnt offering, and pour all *the remaining* blood at the base of the altar. ³¹He shall remove all its fat, as fat is removed from the sacrifice of the peace offering; and the priest shall burn it on the altar for a sweet aroma to the LORD. So the priest shall make atonement for him, and it shall be forgiven him.

³²"If he brings a lamb as his sin offering, he shall bring a female without blemish. ³³Then he shall lay his hand on the head of the sin offering, and kill it as a sin offering at the place where they kill the burnt offering. ³⁴The priest shall take *some* of the blood of the sin offering with his finger, put *it* on the horns of the altar of burnt offering, and pour all *the remaining* blood at the base of the altar. ³⁵He shall remove all its fat, as the fat of the lamb is removed from the sacrifice of the peace offering. Then the priest shall burn it on the altar, according to the offerings made by fire to the LORD. So the priest shall make atonement for his sin that he has committed, and it shall be forgiven him.

The Trespass Offering

5 "If a person sins in hearing the utterance of an oath, and *is* a witness, whether he has seen or known *of the matter*—if he does not tell *it*, he bears guilt.

²Or if a person touches any unclean thing, whether *it is* the carcass of an unclean beast, or the carcass of unclean livestock, or the carcass of unclean creeping things, and he is unaware of it, he also shall be unclean and guilty. ³Or if he touches human uncleanness—whatever uncleanness with which a man may be defiled, and he is unaware of it—when he realizes *it*, then he shall be guilty.

⁴Or if a person swears, speaking thoughtlessly with *his* lips to do evil or to do good, whatever *it is* that a man may pronounce by an oath, and he is unaware of it—when he realizes *it*, then he shall be guilty in any of these *matters*.

⁵And it shall be, when he is guilty in any of these *matters*, that he shall confess that he has sinned in that *thing*; ⁶and he shall bring his trespass offering to the LORD for his sin which he has committed, a female from the flock, a lamb or a kid of the goats as a sin offering. So the priest shall make atonement for him concerning his sin.

⁷"If he is not able to bring a lamb, then he shall bring to the LORD, for his trespass which he has committed, two turtledoves or two young pigeons: one as a sin offering and the other as a burnt offering. ⁸And he shall bring them to the priest, who shall offer *that* which *is* for the sin offering first, and wring off its head from its neck, but shall not divide *it* completely. ⁹Then he shall sprinkle *some* of the blood of the sin offering on the side of the altar, and the rest of the blood shall be drained out at the base of the altar. It *is* a sin offering. ¹⁰And he shall offer the second *as* a burnt offering according to the prescribed manner. So the priest shall make atonement on his behalf for his sin which he has committed, and it shall be forgiven him.

¹¹"But if he is not able to bring two turtledoves or two young pigeons, then he who sinned shall bring for his offering one-tenth of an ephah of fine flour as a sin offering. He shall put no oil on it, nor shall he put frankincense on it, for it *is* a sin offering. ¹²Then he shall bring it to the priest, and the priest shall take his handful of it as a memorial portion, and burn *it* on the altar according to the offerings made by fire to the LORD. It *is* a sin offering. ¹³The priest shall make atonement for him, for his sin that he has committed in any of these matters; and it shall be forgiven him. *The rest* shall be the priest's as a grain offering.' "

Offerings with Restitution

¹⁴Then the LORD spoke to Moses, saying: ¹⁵"If a person commits a trespass, and sins unintentionally

---

5:2, 3 In the ancient world everything belonged either to a clean or an unclean category. Uncleanness referred to contamination by a physical, ritual, or moral impurity (see Lev. 10, Clean vs. Unclean). Laws of clean and unclean applied to people, food, places, and objects in the OT. People became unclean by contact with a dead body, by discharge of bodily fluids, by eating forbidden foods, or by leprosy. When a person became unclean, purification rituals were necessary. Such rituals accompanied birth, for example. Purification rituals involved a waiting period; called for the use of water, fire, or another cleansing agent; and often required a sacrificial sin offering.

5:14–19 Both an offering to God and restitution to others were required in certain situations in which the rights of both God and man had been violated. Three types of violations required such a guilt offering:

in regard to the holy things of the LORD, then he shall bring to the LORD as his trespass offering a ram without blemish from the flocks, with your valuation in shekels of silver according to the shekel of the sanctuary, as a trespass offering. [16]And he shall make restitution for the harm that he has done in regard to the holy thing, and shall add one-fifth to it and give it to the priest. So the priest shall make atonement for him with the ram of the trespass offering, and it shall be forgiven him.

[17]"If a person sins, and commits any of these things which are forbidden to be done by the commandments of the LORD, though he does not know *it,* yet he is guilty and shall bear his iniquity. [18]And he shall bring to the priest a ram without blemish from the flock, with your valuation, as a trespass offering. So the priest shall make atonement for him regarding his ignorance in which he erred and did not know *it,* and it shall be forgiven him. [19]It is a trespass offering; he has certainly trespassed against the LORD."

6 And the LORD spoke to Moses, saying: [2]"If a person sins and commits a trespass against the LORD by lying to his neighbor about what was delivered to him for safekeeping, or about a pledge, or about a robbery, or if he has extorted from his neighbor, [3]or if he has found what was lost and lies concerning it, and swears falsely— in any one of these things that a man may do in which he sins: [4]then it shall be, because he has sinned and is guilty, that he shall restore what he has stolen, or the thing which he has extorted, or what was delivered to him for safekeeping, or the lost thing which he found, [5]or all that about which he has sworn falsely. He shall restore its full value, add one-fifth more to it, *and* give it to whomever it belongs, on the day of his trespass offering. [6]And he shall bring his trespass offering to the LORD, a ram without blemish from the flock, with your valuation, as a trespass offering, to the priest. [7]So the priest shall make atonement for him before the LORD, and he shall be forgiven for any one of these things that he may have done in which he trespasses."

The Law of the Burnt Offering

[8]Then the LORD spoke to Moses, saying, [9]"Command Aaron and his sons, saying, 'This *is* the law of the burnt offering: The burnt offering *shall be* on the hearth upon the altar all night until morning, and the fire of the altar shall be kept burning on it. [10]And the priest shall put on his linen garment, and his linen trousers he shall put on his body, and take up the ashes of the burnt offering which the fire has consumed on the altar, and he shall put them beside the altar. [11]Then he shall take off his garments, put on other garments, and carry the ashes outside the camp to a clean place. [12]And the fire on the altar shall be kept burning on it; it shall not be put out. And the priest shall burn wood on it every morning, and lay the burnt offering in order on it; and he shall burn on it the fat of the peace offerings. [13]A fire shall always be burning on the altar; it shall never go out.

The Law of the Grain Offering

[14]"This *is* the law of the grain offering: The sons of Aaron shall offer it on the altar before the LORD. [15]He shall take from it his handful of the fine flour of the grain offering, with its oil, and all the frankincense which *is* on the grain offering, and shall burn *it* on the altar *for* a sweet aroma, as a memorial to the LORD. [16]And the remainder of it Aaron and his sons shall eat; with unleavened bread it shall be eaten in a holy place; in the court of the tabernacle of meeting they shall eat it. [17]It shall not be baked with leaven. I have given it *as* their portion of My offerings made by fire; it *is* most holy, like the sin offering and the trespass offering. [18]All the males among the children of Aaron may eat it. *It shall be* a statute forever in your generations concerning the offerings made by fire to the LORD. Everyone who touches them must be holy.' "[a]

[19]And the LORD spoke to Moses, saying, [20]"This *is* the offering of Aaron and his sons, which they shall offer to the LORD, *beginning* on the day when he is anointed: one-tenth of an ephah of fine flour

··················

6:18 [a]Compare Numbers 4:15 and Haggai 2:11–13

---

1) sinning against the Lord concerning holy things (vv. 15, 16),

2) disregarding the commandments of the Lord through ignorance (vv. 17–19), and

3) dealing falsely with a neighbor (Lev. 6:1–7).

Verses 14–16 deal with an unintentional sin concerning holy things. The priest levied an assessed value on the sacrificial ram (v. 15). The offender also was required to make restitution as well as an added fifth for the priest (v. 16). While some aspects of Israel's sacrificial system remain unclear, one thing is certain: different sacrifices are not required for different sins. Nor do believers have to fear that some sins remain uncovered. Christ atoned for all sins. He fulfilled the OT

requirement for sacrifice as the way to forgiveness and a right relationship with God (1 John 1:7).

6:8–13 Priestly regulations for burnt offerings (see Lev. 1:3–17). The daily or continual burnt offering required two lambs, one sacrificed in the morning and the other at twilight (Ex. 29:38–42). Additional burnt offerings were sacrificed on Sabbaths, New Moons, and at the times of religious feasts. The fire was to be kept burning. The continual burning of the offering signified the dedication of the people to God. Certain instructions in this passage relate specifically to the priests, such as the specifications concerning garments to be worn. The ordinary individual was not permitted to perform any function involving direct contact with the altar.

as a daily grain offering, half of it in the morning and half of it at night. ²¹It shall be made in a pan with oil. *When it is* mixed, you shall bring it in. The baked pieces of the grain offering you shall offer *for* a sweet aroma to the LORD. ²²The priest from among his sons, who is anointed in his place, shall offer it. *It is* a statute forever to the LORD. It shall be wholly burned. ²³For every grain offering for the priest shall be wholly burned. It shall not be eaten."

The Law of the Sin Offering

²⁴Also the LORD spoke to Moses, saying, ²⁵"Speak to Aaron and to his sons, saying, 'This *is* the law of the sin offering: In the place where the burnt offering is killed, the sin offering shall be killed before the LORD. It *is* most holy. ²⁶The priest who offers it for sin shall eat it. In a holy place it shall be eaten, in the court of the tabernacle of meeting. ²⁷Everyone who touches its flesh must be holy.ᵃ And when its blood is sprinkled on any garment, you shall wash that on which it was sprinkled, in a holy place. ²⁸But the earthen vessel in which it is boiled shall be broken. And if it is boiled in a bronze pot, it shall be both scoured and rinsed in water. ²⁹All the males among the priests may eat it. It *is* most holy. ³⁰But no sin offering from which *any* of the blood is brought into the tabernacle of meeting, to make atonement in the holy *place*,ᵃ shall be eaten. It shall be burned in the fire.

The Law of the Trespass Offering

7 'Likewise this *is* the law of the trespass offering (it *is* most holy): ²In the place where they kill the burnt offering they shall kill the trespass offering. And its blood he shall sprinkle all around on the altar. ³And he shall offer from it all its fat. The fat tail and the fat that covers the entrails, ⁴the two kidneys and the fat that *is* on them by the flanks, and the fatty lobe *attached* to the liver above the kidneys, he shall remove; ⁵and the priest shall burn them on the altar *as* an offering made by fire

to the LORD. It *is* a trespass offering. ⁶Every male among the priests may eat it. It shall be eaten in a holy place. It *is* most holy. ⁷The trespass offering *is* like the sin offering; *there is* one law for them both: the priest who makes atonement with it shall have it. ⁸And the priest who offers anyone's burnt offering, that priest shall have for himself the skin of the burnt offering which he has offered. ⁹Also every grain offering that is baked in the oven and all that is prepared in the covered pan, or in a pan, shall be the priest's who offers it. ¹⁰Every grain offering, *whether* mixed with oil or dry, shall belong to all the sons of Aaron, to one *as much* as the other.

The Law of Peace Offerings

¹¹'This *is* the law of the sacrifice of peace offerings which he shall offer to the LORD: ¹²If he offers it for a thanksgiving, then he shall offer, with the sacrifice of thanksgiving, unleavened cakes mixed with oil, unleavened wafers anointed with oil, or cakes of blended flour mixed with oil. ¹³Besides the cakes, *as* his offering he shall offer leavened bread with the sacrifice of thanksgiving of his peace offering. ¹⁴And from it he shall offer one cake from each offering *as* a heave offering to the LORD. It shall belong to the priest who sprinkles the blood of the peace offering.

¹⁵'The flesh of the sacrifice of his peace offering for thanksgiving shall be eaten the same day it is offered. He shall not leave any of it until morning. ¹⁶But if the sacrifice of his offering *is* a vow or a voluntary offering, it shall be eaten the same day that he offers his sacrifice; but on the next day the remainder of it also may be eaten; ¹⁷the remainder of the flesh of the sacrifice on the third day must be burned with fire. ¹⁸And if *any* of the flesh of the sacrifice of his peace offering is eaten at all on the third day, it shall not be accepted, nor shall it be imputed to him; it shall be

· · · · · · · · · · · · · · · · ·

6:27 ᵃCompare Numbers 4:15 and Haggai 2:11–13   6:30 ᵃThe Most Holy Place when capitalized

---

6:24–30 Priestly regulations for sin offerings. The priests evidently were permitted to eat the flesh of the sin offering only under certain conditions (see vv. 26, 29, 30). Both holiness and uncleanness were thought to be transferred through contact. Thus, clothing stained with sacrificial blood had to be washed according to the law (v. 27). Vessels involved in the sacrificial process had to be cleansed (v. 28). The holiness and purity of God are contrasted with the sinfulness of the people.

7:11 Priestly regulations for peace offerings. The occasion for the offering described is the giving of thanks (v. 12), a vow, or a voluntary offering (v. 16). Previous regulations for the peace offering concerned whether the animal sacrifice came from the herd or from the flock (see Lev. 3:1–17). In this passage other stipulations are made. If the reason for the offering was thanksgiving, apparently the peace offering (see Lev. 3:1–17) was combined with a grain or cereal offering (see Lev. 2:1–16).

A prohibition is given against consuming blood and fat (vv. 22–27). The fat of the animal was regarded as the choicest part, while the blood represented the animal's life force (Lev. 17:11). Thus, both the fat and the blood belonged to the Lord and were not to be eaten (see Lev. 3:17, note). While Leviticus reveals the proper outward form of worship, the psalms reveal the inner attitude that should accompany the outward observance. Worship is costly and requires discipline (Lev. 1:1—7:38). Genuine sacrifices were those accompanied by the obedience of the worshiper.

7:14 The heave offering (Heb. *terumah*, lit. "lift up"), in which the "breast" was to be "heaved" or lifted heavenward, is understood to be symbolic of dependence on God for supplying needs. The up and down motion before the Lord is indicative of that vertical relationship in which all comes from the Lord and all is returned to Him.

an abomination *to* him who offers it, and the person who eats of it shall bear guilt.

¹⁹'The flesh that touches any unclean thing shall not be eaten. It shall be burned with fire. And as for the *clean* flesh, all who are clean may eat of it. ²⁰But the person who eats the flesh of the sacrifice of the peace offering that *belongs* to the LORD, while he is unclean, that person shall be cut off from his people. ²¹Moreover the person who touches any unclean thing, *such as* human uncleanness, *an* unclean animal, or any abominable unclean thing,ª and who eats the flesh of the sacrifice of the peace offering that *belongs* to the LORD, that person shall be cut off from his people.' "

Fat and Blood May Not Be Eaten

²²And the LORD spoke to Moses, saying, ²³"Speak to the children of Israel, saying: 'You shall not eat any fat, of ox or sheep or goat. ²⁴And the fat of an animal that dies *naturally,* and the fat of what is torn by wild beasts, may be used in any other way; but you shall by no means eat it. ²⁵For whoever eats the fat of the animal of which men offer an offering made by fire to the LORD, the person who eats *it* shall be cut off from his people. ²⁶Moreover you shall not eat any blood in any of your dwellings, *whether* of bird or beast. ²⁷Whoever eats any blood, that person shall be cut off from his people.' "

The Portion of Aaron and His Sons

²⁸Then the LORD spoke to Moses, saying, ²⁹"Speak to the children of Israel, saying: 'He who offers the sacrifice of his peace offering to the LORD shall bring his offering to the LORD from the sacrifice of his peace offering. ³⁰His own hands shall bring the offerings made by fire to the LORD. The fat with the breast he shall bring, that the breast may be waved *as* a wave offering before the LORD. ³¹And the priest shall burn the fat on the al-

tar, but the breast shall be Aaron's and his sons'. ³²Also the right thigh you shall give to the priest *as* a heave offering from the sacrifices of your peace offerings. ³³He among the sons of Aaron, who offers the blood of the peace offering and the fat, shall have the right thigh for *his* part. ³⁴For the breast of the wave offering and the thigh of the heave offering I have taken from the children of Israel, from the sacrifices of their peace offerings, and I have given them to Aaron the priest and to his sons from the children of Israel by a statute forever.' "

³⁵This *is* the consecrated portion for Aaron and his sons, from the offerings made by fire to the LORD, on the day when *Moses* presented them to minister to the LORD as priests. ³⁶The LORD commanded this to be given to them by the children of Israel, on the day that He anointed them, *by* a statute forever throughout their generations.

³⁷This *is* the law of the burnt offering, the grain offering, the sin offering, the trespass offering, the consecrations, and the sacrifice of the peace offering, ³⁸which the LORD commanded Moses on Mount Sinai, on the day when He commanded the children of Israel to offer their offerings to the LORD in the Wilderness of Sinai.

Aaron and His Sons Consecrated

8 And the LORD spoke to Moses, saying: ²"Take Aaron and his sons with him, and the garments, the anointing oil, a bull as the sin offering, two rams, and a basket of unleavened bread; ³and gather all the congregation together at the door of the tabernacle of meeting."

⁴So Moses did as the LORD commanded him. And the congregation was gathered together at the door of the tabernacle of meeting. ⁵And Moses

---

7:21 ªFollowing Masoretic Text, Septuagint, and Vulgate; Samaritan Pentateuch, Syriac, and Targum read *swarming thing* (compare 5:2).

7:28–36 Compensation for ministry. These verses stipulate that the priests should receive their portion of the sacrifice. The principle expressed in these latter verses is that those who minister should receive compensation for their ministry (1 Cor. 9:13, 14).

7:30–32 The wave offering (Heb. *tenuphah,* lit. "brandishing") is a reference to the "thigh" as being "waved" before the Lord. Like the "heaving," the "waving" was symbolic of consecration to God. This sideways or back and forth motion acknowledged God as provider and sustainer. This movement toward the altar was symbolic of transferring the sacrifice to God and back again as a sign of the receiving of the sacrifice by the priests as a gift from God (see chart, The Offerings of the Lord).

8:1–4 Note the repetition of the phrase affirming that the Lord directed Moses (v. 1), which authenticates the following instructions as the Lord's words. Leviticus 8 details the consecration or ordination of Aaron and his sons as priests (see Ex. 29:1–46). The elements essential for the ordination proce-

dure are listed (v. 2). The priestly ministry was limited to Aaron and his descendants. No one could appoint himself to the priesthood. God set these men apart through Moses. Such duties required specialized knowledge that could be passed on most easily within one family. Both the ritual of ordination and the priestly garments carried symbolic meaning. The priesthood in Israel preshadowed the priesthood of Christ. In the NT, every believer becomes a priest (see 1 Pet. 2, The Priesthood of the Believer).

8:5–9 Clothing the high priest in his specialized garments was preceded by a ritual washing, symbolizing the need to be clean or pure in the presence of the Lord. The symbolic meaning of the priestly garments is more apparent in Exodus 28 (see Ex. 28:15, note; see chart, The High Priest's Clothing). The Urim and the Thummim (Ex. 28:30) were two stones used for discerning the will of God. The high priest's garments emphasized the two main functions of the priest: to bring the people to God by interceding for them and to bring God to the people by helping them know His will.

said to the congregation, "This *is* what the LORD commanded to be done."

⁶Then Moses brought Aaron and his sons and washed them with water. ⁷And he put the tunic on him, girded him with the sash, clothed him with the robe, and put the ephod on him; and he girded him with the intricately woven band of the ephod, and with it tied *the ephod* on him. ⁸Then he put the breastplate on him, and he put the Urim and the Thummimª in the breastplate. ⁹And he put the turban on his head. Also on the turban, on its front, he put the golden plate, the holy crown, as the LORD had commanded Moses.

¹⁰Also Moses took the anointing oil, and anointed the tabernacle and all that *was* in it, and consecrated them. ¹¹He sprinkled some of it on the altar seven times, anointed the altar and all its utensils, and the laver and its base, to consecrate them. ¹²And he poured some of the anointing oil on Aaron's head and anointed him, to consecrate him.

¹³Then Moses brought Aaron's sons and put tunics on them, girded them with sashes, and put hats on them, as the LORD had commanded Moses.

¹⁴And he brought the bull for the sin offering. Then Aaron and his sons laid their hands on the head of the bull for the sin offering, ¹⁵and Moses killed *it*. Then he took the blood, and put *some* on the horns of the altar all around with his finger, and purified the altar. And he poured the blood at the base of the altar, and consecrated it, to make atonement for it. ¹⁶Then he took all the fat that *was* on the entrails, the fatty lobe *attached to* the liver, and the two kidneys with their fat, and Moses burned *them* on the altar. ¹⁷But the bull, its hide, its flesh, and its offal, he burned with fire outside the camp, as the LORD had commanded Moses.

¹⁸Then he brought the ram as the burnt offering. And Aaron and his sons laid their hands on the head of the ram, ¹⁹and Moses killed *it*. Then he sprinkled the blood all around on the altar. ²⁰And he cut the ram into pieces; and Moses burned the head, the pieces, and the fat. ²¹Then he washed the entrails and the legs in water. And Moses burned the whole ram on the altar. It *was* a burnt sacrifice for a sweet aroma, an offering made by fire to the LORD, as the LORD had commanded Moses.

²²And he brought the second ram, the ram of consecration. Then Aaron and his sons laid their hands on the head of the ram, ²³and Moses killed *it*. Also he took *some* of its blood and put it on the tip of Aaron's right ear, on the thumb of his right hand, and on the big toe of his right foot. ²⁴Then he brought Aaron's sons. And Moses put *some* of the blood on the tips of their right ears, on the thumbs of their right hands, and on the big toes of their right feet. And Moses sprinkled the blood all around on the altar. ²⁵Then he took the fat and the fat tail, all the fat that *was* on the entrails, the fatty lobe *attached to* the liver, the two kidneys and their fat, and the right thigh; ²⁶and from the basket of unleavened bread that was before the LORD he took one unleavened cake, a cake of bread *anointed with* oil, and one wafer, and put *them* on the fat and on the right thigh; ²⁷and he put all *these* in Aaron's hands and in his sons' hands, and waved them *as* a wave offering before the LORD. ²⁸Then Moses took them from their hands and burned *them* on the altar, on the burnt offering. They *were* consecration offerings for a sweet aroma. That *was* an offering made by fire to the LORD. ²⁹And Moses took the breast and waved it *as* a wave offering before the LORD. It was Moses' part of the ram of consecration, as the LORD had commanded Moses.

³⁰Then Moses took some of the anointing oil

8:8 ªLiterally *the Lights and the Perfections* (compare Exodus 28:30)

8:10–13 The anointing oil was poured on the high priest. Anointing with oil signified consecration to the Lord. Olive oil was used in such ceremonies. Objects, including the tabernacle, the altar, and the utensils, also were anointed (vv. 10, 11; see also chart, The Furniture of the Tabernacle). The people of Israel also anointed their kings (see 1 Sam. 16:1–13).

8:14–17 Sin offering for Aaron and his sons (see Lev. 4:1, 3, notes). Atonement was to be made for the altar itself (v. 15). This action suggests that atonement involves consecration. Aaron and his sons placed their hands on the head of the bull to signify their identification with the bull. Through the sin offering, Aaron and his sons experienced the Lord's forgiveness. Those who serve the Lord must first experience His gift of forgiveness.

8:18–21 The burnt offering for Aaron and his sons symbolized the complete dedication of the priests to God. The entire sacrificial ram was burned on the altar, symbolizing that the worship leaders totally gave themselves to the Lord in ministry (Ex. 29:15–18; Lev. 1:3–17, note).

8:22–30 The consecration offering appears almost identical to the peace offering (see Lev. 7:11–38). "Consecrate" or "ordain" (lit. "fill the hand"; see Ex. 32:29) may refer to the responsibilities committed to the priests. The person was to be brought under the power and protection of the blood (vv. 23, 24). This ritual of consecration involved total obedience and willing service in the tabernacle. This dedication to God came in a unique ceremony in which the placement of blood was significant:

1) on the right ear lobe, to hear and obey the Word of God;

2) on the thumb of the right hand, to perform the service and commands of God; and

3) on the right big toe, to walk in the ways of God in an exemplary manner.

The whole person, along with his garments, was therefore dedicated and consecrated to God (v. 30).

CLEAN AND UNCLEAN *A DIVINE DISTINCTION*

The biblical distinction between "clean" and "unclean" has nothing to do with hygiene. Rather, it is the way God designated the difference between what He could receive into His presence and what must remain apart from Him. Only people, animals, and objects designated as clean could enter the tabernacle, and later the temple, as part of the worship of God. Specific rituals were instituted by God for making an "unclean" person or object "clean" (see Lev. 14; Is. 1:16).

The designation of "clean" and "unclean" also implies a distinction between ethical character and behavior that is acceptable to God ("holy") from that which is unacceptable ("unholy"). Jesus clearly taught that it is a person's character ("heart") which determines whether or not she is "clean" and can be received into God's presence (Mark 7:15). Because of the spiritual nature of human character, external rituals cannot make anyone admissible to the Lord's presence. Only the blood of Jesus Christ can make us "clean" and only through Him are we welcomed into the presence of God the Father (1 John 1:9).

See also Mark 7:15; Rom. 3:23, note; 2 Cor. 6:17; notes on Access to God (Rom. 10); Holiness (Lev. 20); Purity (1 John 3)

and some of the blood which *was* on the altar, and sprinkled *it* on Aaron, on his garments, on his sons, and on the garments of his sons with him; and he consecrated Aaron, his garments, his sons, and the garments of his sons with him.

31And Moses said to Aaron and his sons, "Boil the flesh *at* the door of the tabernacle of meeting, and eat it there with the bread that *is* in the basket of consecration offerings, as I commanded, saying, 'Aaron and his sons shall eat it.' 32What remains of the flesh and of the bread you shall burn with fire. 33And you shall not go outside the door of the tabernacle of meeting *for* seven days, until the days of your consecration are ended. For seven days he shall consecrate you. 34As he has done this day, *so* the LORD has commanded to do, to make atonement for you. 35Therefore you shall stay *at* the door of the tabernacle of meeting day and night for seven days, and keep the charge of the LORD, so that you may not die; for so I have been commanded." 36So Aaron and his sons did all the things that the LORD had commanded by the hand of Moses.

The Priestly Ministry Begins

9 It came to pass on the eighth day that Moses called Aaron and his sons and the elders of Israel. 2And he said to Aaron, "Take for yourself a young bull as a sin offering and a ram as a burnt offering, without blemish, and offer *them* before the LORD. 3And to the children of Israel you shall speak, saying, 'Take a kid of the goats as a sin offering, and a calf and a lamb, *both* of the first year, without blemish, as a burnt offering, 4also a bull and a ram as peace offerings, to sacrifice before the LORD, and a grain offering mixed with oil; for today the LORD will appear to you.' "

5So they brought what Moses commanded before the tabernacle of meeting. And all the congregation drew near and stood before the LORD. 6Then Moses said, "This *is* the thing which the LORD commanded you to do, and the glory of the LORD will appear to you." 7And Moses said to Aaron, "Go to the altar, offer your sin offering and your burnt offering, and make atonement for yourself and for the people. Offer the offering of the people, and make atonement for them, as the LORD commanded."

8Aaron therefore went to the altar and killed the calf of the sin offering, which *was* for himself. 9Then the sons of Aaron brought the blood to him. And he dipped his finger in the blood, put *it* on the horns of the altar, and poured the blood at the base of the altar. 10But the fat, the kidneys, and the fatty lobe from the liver of the sin offering he burned on the altar, as the LORD had com-

---

8:31–36 Like the peace offering, the ordination procedure also included a communal meal (see Lev. 7:11–38). Altogether the ordination ceremonies lasted seven days. The priests were reminded of their tremendous responsibility and of the awesome consequences of failure in their God-given position (v. 35). Although those who minister for the Lord no longer undergo the ritual procedures described for priests in Leviticus, some of the basic concepts remain applicable for anyone who wants to serve the Lord effectively. For example, a woman who would serve the Lord must experience forgiveness and cleansing, consecrating and dedicating herself both to the Lord and to the task.

9:1 Experiencing God's glory. Leviticus 9 describes the beginnings of the priestly ministry, an extremely significant event for Israel as Aaron and his sons performed their priestly duties for the first time. Through a series of four sacrifices, the people experienced the glory of God. The word translated "glory" (Heb. *kabod* means literally "to be heavy"). The Lord's glory is the overwhelming heaviness of His presence. The glory of the Lord was the visible, supernatural manifestation of His presence (Ex. 33:18; see Ps. 19:1, note). Women can bring glory to God as they seek to extend His influence in the world by their lifestyles and actions. The only adequate response to the revelation of the glory of God is worship expressed in words and actions.

manded Moses. [11]The flesh and the hide he burned with fire outside the camp.

[12]And he killed the burnt offering; and Aaron's sons presented to him the blood, which he sprinkled all around on the altar. [13]Then they presented the burnt offering to him, with its pieces and head, and he burned *them* on the altar. [14]And he washed the entrails and the legs, and burned *them* with the burnt offering on the altar.

[15]Then he brought the people's offering, and took the goat, which *was* the sin offering for the people, and killed it and offered it for sin, like the first one. [16]And he brought the burnt offering and offered it according to the prescribed manner. [17]Then he brought the grain offering, took a handful of it, and burned *it* on the altar, besides the burnt sacrifice of the morning.

[18]He also killed the bull and the ram *as* sacrifices of peace offerings, which *were* for the people. And Aaron's sons presented to him the blood, which he sprinkled all around on the altar, [19]and the fat from the bull and the ram—the fatty tail, what covers *the entrails* and the kidneys, and the fatty lobe *attached to* the liver; [20]and they put the fat on the breasts. Then he burned the fat on the altar; [21]but the breasts and the right thigh Aaron waved *as* a wave offering before the LORD, as Moses had commanded.

[22]Then Aaron lifted his hand toward the people, blessed them, and came down from offering the sin offering, the burnt offering, and peace offerings. [23]And Moses and Aaron went into the tabernacle of meeting, and came out and blessed the people. Then the glory of the LORD appeared to all the people, [24]and fire came out from before the LORD and consumed the burnt offering and the fat on the altar. When all the people saw *it*, they shouted and fell on their faces.

The Profane Fire of Nadab and Abihu

10Then Nadab and Abihu, the sons of Aaron, each took his censer and put fire in it, put incense on it, and offered profane fire before the LORD, which He had not commanded them. [2]So fire went out from the LORD and devoured them,

and they died before the LORD. [3]And Moses said to Aaron, "This is what the LORD spoke, saying:

'By those who come near Me
I must be regarded as holy;
And before all the people
I must be glorified.' "

So Aaron held his peace.

[4]Then Moses called Mishael and Elzaphan, the sons of Uzziel the uncle of Aaron, and said to them, "Come near, carry your brethren from before the sanctuary out of the camp." [5]So they went near and carried them by their tunics out of the camp, as Moses had said.

[6]And Moses said to Aaron, and to Eleazar and Ithamar, his sons, "Do not uncover your heads nor tear your clothes, lest you die, and wrath come upon all the people. But let your brethren, the whole house of Israel, bewail the burning which the LORD has kindled. [7]You shall not go out from the door of the tabernacle of meeting, lest you die, for the anointing oil of the LORD *is* upon you." And they did according to the word of Moses.

Conduct Prescribed for Priests

[8]Then the LORD spoke to Aaron, saying: [9]"Do not drink wine or intoxicating drink, you, nor your sons with you, when you go into the tabernacle of meeting, lest you die. *It shall be* a statute forever throughout your generations, [10]that you may distinguish between holy and unholy, and between unclean and clean, [11]and that you may teach the children of Israel all the statutes which the LORD has spoken to them by the hand of Moses."

[12]And Moses spoke to Aaron, and to Eleazar and Ithamar, his sons who were left: "Take the grain offering that remains of the offerings made by fire to the LORD, and eat it without leaven beside the altar; for it *is* most holy. [13]You shall eat it in a holy place, because it *is* your due and your sons' due, of the sacrifices made by fire to the LORD; for so I have been commanded. [14]The breast of the wave offering and the thigh of the heave offering you shall eat in a clean place, you, your

---

10:1–7 Nadab and Abihu, the two older sons of Aaron, took unfair advantage of their priestly position and allowed pride and arrogance to dominate. The nature of the "profane fire" is unclear. Though the fire for their censers should have been taken from the brazen altar in the court, instead it probably had been taken from a convenient fireplace. They may have entered the Most Holy Place, which was reserved for the high priest alone. The brothers may have forgotten that their responsibility was to serve; they may have viewed themselves as above the people and the law; or they may have been drunk (see v. 9). Whether they did not trust the authorities God had placed over them, had no fear of God, or simply acted out of defiance, the actions of Nadab and Abihu constituted deliberate disobedience to the Lord (v. 1), and they experienced the

Lord's judgment. Leadership brings not only privileges but also responsibilities. God has consistently judged His leaders. The actions forbidden in verse 6 were associated with mourning.

10:8–20 When officiating before the Lord, the priests were to abstain from wine and intoxicating drink (v. 9). The priests had the responsibility of instructing the people in the Law of God (see Deut. 17; 18). Effectiveness in their duties required a clear mind. The reference to "women" indicates that a part of the offering was to be used in feeding their families (v. 14). This admonition affirms the responsibility of a priest for meeting the needs of his family (see also 1 Tim. 5:8). The remainder of this chapter resumes a discussion of the offering of sacrifices (see Lev. 9; see chart, The Offerings of the Lord).

DIETARY LAWS *OBEDIENCE OF A NATION SET APART*

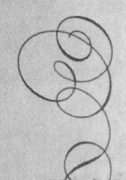

Food, nutrition, and dietary laws are a pervasive biblical theme beginning with God's creation of plants for Adam's food (Gen. 1:29). At Satan's urging, Eve ate the only forbidden food (Gen. 3:6), bringing about the Fall of mankind. After the flood, "every moving thing" became potential food for Noah (Gen. 9:2, 3).

Levitical dietary law (Lev. 11) carefully outlined what God wanted the Hebrews to eat (clean foods) and not eat (unclean foods). Food categorization thus became a part of the Hebrew religion, law, and culture. Adherence to these laws and others symbolized the obedience to and love of God on the part of His people.

Even in captivity these rules helped God's people to cling together as a nation set apart. Daniel's obedience to God in eating only "clean" foods, despite the lavish variety provided from the king's table, is admirable (Dan. 1:8). In Old Testament times, obedience to God's laws as presented by Moses was essential in order to receive God's blessings (Ex. 20:12; Deut. 28:1–68).

Under the New Covenant in Christ, we receive God's blessings by grace and not by works (Rom. 4:13; Gal. 5:22, 23). Therefore, following Mosaic or Old Testament laws concerning food consumption is not necessary for Christians today. However, "self-control" is important and is one fruit of the Spirit (Gal. 5:23). In addition, we are wise to recognize that many of the "unclean" foods noted in Leviticus are not considered healthful foods by nutritionists today for a wide variety of reasons. We should enjoy food as we need it, making healthy selections and appropriate portion sizes, remembering that in so doing we honor Him who has chosen our bodies to be His temple (1 Cor. 6:19).

See also 1 Cor. 9:25; notes on Eating Disorders (Lev. 26); Fitness (Phil. 1); Gluttony (Prov. 23); Mealtime (Ps. 104); Weight Control (1 Cor. 11)

---

sons, and your daughters with you; for *they are* your due and your sons' due, *which* are given from the sacrifices of peace offerings of the children of Israel. [15]The thigh of the heave offering and the breast of the wave offering they shall bring with the offerings of fat made by fire, to offer *as* a wave offering before the LORD. And it shall be yours and your sons' with you, by a statute forever, as the LORD has commanded."

[16]Then Moses made careful inquiry about the goat of the sin offering, and there it was—burned up. And he was angry with Eleazar and Ithamar, the sons of Aaron *who were* left, saying, [17]"Why have you not eaten the sin offering in a holy place, since it *is* most holy, and *God* has given it to you to bear the guilt of the congregation, to make atonement for them before the LORD? [18]See! Its blood was not brought inside the holy *place;*[a] indeed you should have eaten it in a holy *place,* as I commanded."

[19]And Aaron said to Moses, "Look, this day they have offered their sin offering and their burnt offering before the LORD, and such things have befallen me! *If* I had eaten the sin offering today, would it have been accepted in the sight of the LORD?" [20]So when Moses heard *that,* he was content.

Foods Permitted and Forbidden

11 Now the LORD spoke to Moses and Aaron, saying to them, [2]"Speak to the children of Israel, saying, 'These *are* the animals which you may eat among all the animals that *are* on the earth: [3]Among the animals, whatever divides the hoof, having cloven hooves *and* chewing the cud—that you may eat. [4]Nevertheless these you shall not eat among those that chew the cud or those that have cloven hooves: the camel, because it chews the cud but does not have cloven hooves, is unclean to you; [5]the rock hyrax, because it chews

• • • • • • • • • • • • • • • •
10:18 [a]The Most Holy Place when capitalized

11:1–3 Clean and unclean animals. Leviticus 11—15 deal with instructions regarding what is clean and unclean (see Lev. 10, Clean vs. Unclean). The four fundamental areas of concern were clean and unclean animals, purification of women, leprosy, and bodily discharges. No single rationale existed for classification of animals as clean or unclean outside of divine decree. Possible suggestions are as follows. Hygienic principles were involved in the prohibition of eating certain animals. These instructions from the Lord may reveal God's concern about the well-being of the whole person. His laws demonstrate concern for physical as well as spiritual wholeness. Also certain animals may have been regarded as unclean because of their usage in pagan rituals of worship. For example, the pig was used in Canaanite sacrifice (see vv. 7, 8). The fact that some animals were regarded as unclean may relate to the OT concept of the life residing in the blood. Since life came from the Lord, in ritual the blood was returned to Him. Thus, certain animals and birds that ate flesh were forbidden (v. 13). Although the explicit rationale for practices related to clean and unclean cannot be identified, through these rituals God's people testified to the concept of His purity. Also through these distinctive practices, God's people identified themselves to the world as uniquely belonging to Him (2 Pet. 3:11; 1 John 4:4–6).

The key to maintaining a disciplined life is a lifetime of perseverance.

Rhonda Kelley

the cud but does not have cloven hooves, *is* unclean to you; ⁶the hare, because it chews the cud but does not have cloven hooves, *is* unclean to you; ⁷and the swine, though it divides the hoof, having cloven hooves, yet does not chew the cud, *is* unclean to you. ⁸Their flesh you shall not eat, and their carcasses you shall not touch. They *are* unclean to you.

⁹"These you may eat of all that *are* in the water: whatever in the water has fins and scales, whether in the seas or in the rivers—that you may eat. ¹⁰But all in the seas or in the rivers that do not have fins and scales, all that move in the water or any living thing which *is* in the water, they *are* an abomination to you. ¹¹They shall be an abomination to you; you shall not eat their flesh, but you shall regard their carcasses as an abomination. ¹²Whatever in the water does not have fins or scales—that *shall be* an abomination to you.

¹³"And these you shall regard as an abomination among the birds; they shall not be eaten, they *are* an abomination: the eagle, the vulture, the buzzard, ¹⁴the kite, and the falcon after its kind; ¹⁵every raven after its kind, ¹⁶the ostrich, the short-eared owl, the sea gull, and the hawk after its kind; ¹⁷the little owl, the fisher owl, and the screech owl; ¹⁸the white owl, the jackdaw, and the carrion vulture; ¹⁹the stork, the heron after its kind, the hoopoe, and the bat.

²⁰All flying insects that creep on *all* fours *shall be* an abomination to you. ²¹Yet these you may eat of every flying insect that creeps on *all* fours: those which have jointed legs above their feet with which to leap on the earth. ²²These you may eat: the locust after its kind, the destroying locust after its kind, the cricket after its kind, and the grasshopper after its kind. ²³But all *other* flying insects which have four feet *shall be* an abomination to you.

Unclean Animals

²⁴"By these you shall become unclean; whoever touches the carcass of any of them shall be unclean until evening; ²⁵whoever carries part of the carcass of any of them shall wash his clothes and be unclean until evening: ²⁶*The carcass* of any animal which divides the foot, but is not cloven-hoofed or does not chew the cud, *is* unclean to you. Everyone who touches it shall be unclean. ²⁷And whatever goes on its paws, among all kinds of animals that go on *all* fours, those *are* unclean to you. Whoever touches any such carcass shall be

unclean until evening. ²⁸Whoever carries *any such* carcass shall wash his clothes and be unclean until evening. It *is* unclean to you.

²⁹"These also *shall be* unclean to you among the creeping things that creep on the earth: the mole, the mouse, and the large lizard after its kind; ³⁰the gecko, the monitor lizard, the sand reptile, the sand lizard, and the chameleon. ³¹These *are* unclean to you among all that creep. Whoever touches them when they are dead shall be unclean until evening. ³²Anything on which *any* of them falls, when they are dead shall be unclean, whether *it is* any item of wood or clothing or skin or sack, whatever item *it is*, in which *any* work is done, it must be put in water. And it shall be unclean until evening; then it shall be clean. ³³Any earthen vessel into which *any* of them falls you shall break; and whatever *is* in it shall be unclean: ³⁴in such a vessel, any edible food upon which water falls becomes unclean, and any drink that may be drunk from it becomes unclean. ³⁵And everything on which *a part* of *any such* carcass falls shall be unclean; *whether it is* an oven or cooking stove, it shall be broken down; *for* they *are* unclean, and shall be unclean to you. ³⁶Nevertheless a spring or a cistern, *in which there is* plenty of water, shall be clean, but whatever touches any such carcass becomes unclean. ³⁷And if a part of *any such* carcass falls on any planting seed which is to be sown, it *remains* clean. ³⁸But if water is put on the seed, and if *a part* of *any such* carcass falls on it, it *becomes* unclean to you.

³⁹"And if any animal which you may eat dies, he who touches its carcass shall be unclean until evening. ⁴⁰He who eats of its carcass shall wash his clothes and be unclean until evening. He also who carries its carcass shall wash his clothes and be unclean until evening.

⁴¹"And every creeping thing that creeps on the earth *shall be* an abomination. It shall not be eaten. ⁴²Whatever crawls on its belly, whatever goes on *all* fours, or whatever has many feet among all creeping things that creep on the earth—these you shall not eat, for they *are* an abomination. ⁴³You shall not make yourselves abominable with any creeping thing that creeps; nor shall you make yourselves unclean with them, lest you be defiled by them. ⁴⁴For I *am* the LORD your God. You shall therefore consecrate yourselves, and you shall be holy; for I *am* holy. Neither shall you defile yourselves with any creeping thing that creeps on the earth. ⁴⁵For I *am* the LORD who brings you up out

of the land of Egypt, to be your God. You shall therefore be holy, for I *am* holy.

⁴⁶"This *is* the law of the animals and the birds and every living creature that moves in the waters, and of every creature that creeps on the earth, ⁴⁷to distinguish between the unclean and the clean, and between the animal that may be eaten and the animal that may not be eaten.'"

The Ritual After Childbirth

12Then the LORD spoke to Moses, saying, ²"Speak to the children of Israel, saying: 'If a woman has conceived, and borne a male child, then she shall be unclean seven days; as in the days of her customary impurity she shall be unclean. ³And on the eighth day the flesh of his foreskin shall be circumcised. ⁴She shall then continue in the blood of *her* purification thirty-three days. She shall not touch any hallowed thing, nor come into the sanctuary until the days of her purification are fulfilled.

⁵"But if she bears a female child, then she shall be unclean two weeks, as in her customary impurity, and she shall continue in the blood of *her* purification sixty-six days.

⁶"When the days of her purification are fulfilled, whether for a son or a daughter, she shall bring to the priest a lamb of the first year as a burnt offering, and a young pigeon or a turtledove as a sin offering, to the door of the tabernacle of meeting. ⁷Then he shall offer it before the LORD, and make atonement for her. And she shall be clean from the flow of her blood. This *is* the law for her who has borne a male or a female.

⁸'And if she is not able to bring a lamb, then she may bring two turtledoves or two young pigeons—one as a burnt offering and the other as a sin offering. So the priest shall make atonement for her, and she will be clean.'"

The Law Concerning Leprosy

13And the LORD spoke to Moses and Aaron, saying: ²"When a man has on the skin of his body a swelling, a scab, or a bright spot, and it becomes on the skin of his body *like* a leprous[a] sore, then he shall be brought to Aaron the priest or to one of his sons the priests. ³The priest shall examine the sore on the skin of the body; and if the hair on the sore has turned white, and the sore appears *to be* deeper than the skin of his body, it *is* a leprous sore. Then the priest shall examine him, and pronounce him unclean. ⁴But if the bright spot *is* white on the skin of his body, and does not appear *to be* deeper than the skin, and its hair has not turned white, then the priest shall isolate *the one who has* the sore seven days. ⁵And the priest shall examine him on the seventh day; and indeed *if* the sore appears to be as it was, *and* the sore has not spread on the skin, then the priest shall isolate him another seven days. ⁶Then the priest shall examine him again on the seventh day; and indeed *if* the sore has faded, *and* the sore has not spread on the skin, then the priest shall pronounce him clean; it *is only* a scab, and he shall wash his clothes and be clean. ⁷But if the scab should at all spread over the skin, after he has been seen by the priest for his cleansing, he shall be seen by the priest again. ⁸And *if* the priest sees that the scab has indeed spread on the skin, then the priest shall pronounce him unclean. It *is* leprosy.

⁹"When the leprous sore is on a person, then he shall be brought to the priest. ¹⁰And the priest shall examine *him;* and indeed *if* the swelling on the skin *is* white, and it has turned the hair white, and *there is* a spot of raw flesh in the swelling, ¹¹it *is* an old leprosy on the skin of his body. The priest

13:2 ªHebrew *saraath,* disfiguring skin diseases, including leprosy, and so in verses 2–46 and 14:1–32

12:1–8 Purification following childbirth (see John 16, Childbirth). The birth of a male rendered the mother unclean for 40 days, while the birth of a female made the mother unclean for 80 days (40 days to purify the mother and 40 days to purify the female child). Various theories have been advanced to explain this distinction. The difference may relate to the male's more favored status in ancient times. The difference also could indicate that circumcision of the male child incorporated the concept of cleansing for the male child, meeting the requirements for his cleansing, while the 80 days were necessary to cleanse both the mother and the female child (see Gen. 17, Circumcision). The time of purification, in any case, physiologically benefited the mother. It provided her time to regain her strength—since she could neither cook nor keep the house during this period—and to recover from the challenge, and sometimes trauma, of childbirth. This freed the mother to bond and to establish a schedule with her newborn baby in relative isolation. The sacrifice for the burnt offering and the sin offering was the same, regardless of the sex of the child. Two turtledoves or two young pigeons were designated as the entire offering for the poor who could not af-

ford a lamb for the burnt offering. Mary brought the offering of the poor when her time of purification was complete following the birth of Jesus (Luke 2:22–24). Even though she was the mother of the Messiah, she did not describe herself as sinless.

13:1 Regulations regarding leprosy. Leviticus 13 and 14 deal with laws concerning leprosy and the cleansing of leprous persons and objects. Leprosy referred to any scaly or eruptive skin condition. The term was used to designate a number of diseases, perhaps including ringworm, fungus, and psoriasis. The priests were responsible for diagnosing leprosy and determining whether an individual was healed. An individual diagnosed as leprous by the priest was pronounced unclean and was forced to live in isolation. The isolated leper engaged in mourning rituals, such as wearing torn clothing (Lev. 10:6), since his illness was viewed as being linked with the power of death. Inanimate objects, including garments (vv. 47–59) and houses (Lev. 14:33–57), also might be diagnosed as leprous. Leprosy of inanimate objects might also be identified as fungus or mildew.

shall pronounce him unclean, and shall not isolate him, for he *is* unclean.

12"And if leprosy breaks out all over the skin, and the leprosy covers all the skin of *the one who has* the sore, from his head to his foot, wherever the priest looks, 13then the priest shall consider; and indeed *if* the leprosy has covered all his body, he shall pronounce *him* clean *who has* the sore. It has all turned white. He *is* clean. 14But when raw flesh appears on him, he shall be unclean. 15And the priest shall examine the raw flesh and pronounce him to be unclean; *for* the raw flesh *is* unclean. It *is* leprosy. 16Or if the raw flesh changes and turns white again, he shall come to the priest. 17And the priest shall examine him; and indeed *if* the sore has turned white, then the priest shall pronounce *him* clean *who has* the sore. He *is* clean.

18"If the body develops a boil in the skin, and it is healed, 19and in the place of the boil there comes a white swelling or a bright spot, reddish-white, then it shall be shown to the priest; 20and *if,* when the priest sees it, it indeed appears deeper than the skin, and its hair has turned white, the priest shall pronounce him unclean. It *is* a leprous sore which has broken out of the boil. 21But if the priest examines it, and indeed *there are* no white hairs in it, and it *is* not deeper than the skin, but has faded, then the priest shall isolate him seven days; 22and if it should at all spread over the skin, then the priest shall pronounce him unclean. It *is* a leprous sore. 23But if the bright spot stays in one place, *and* has not spread, it *is* the scar of the boil; and the priest shall pronounce him clean.

24"Or if the body receives a burn on its skin by fire, and the raw *flesh* of the burn becomes a bright spot, reddish-white or white, 25then the priest shall examine it; and indeed *if* the hair of the bright spot has turned white, and it appears deeper than the skin, it *is* leprosy broken out in the burn. Therefore the priest shall pronounce him unclean. It *is* a leprous sore. 26But if the priest examines it, and indeed *there are* no white hairs in the bright spot, and it *is* not deeper than the skin, but has faded, then the priest shall isolate him seven days. 27And the priest shall examine him on the seventh day. If it has at all spread over the skin, then the priest shall pronounce him unclean. It *is* a leprous sore. 28But if the bright spot stays in one place, *and* has not spread on the skin, but has faded, it *is* a swelling from the burn. The priest shall pronounce him clean, for it *is* the scar from the burn.

29"If a man or woman has a sore on the head or the beard, 30then the priest shall examine the sore; and indeed if it appears deeper than the skin, *and there is* in it thin yellow hair, then the priest shall pronounce him unclean. It *is* a scaly leprosy of the head or beard. 31But if the priest examines the scaly sore, and indeed it does not appear deeper than the skin, and *there is* no black hair in it, then the priest shall isolate *the one who has* the scale seven days. 32And on the seventh day the priest shall examine the sore; and indeed *if* the scale has not spread, and there is no yellow hair in it, and the scale does not appear deeper than the skin, 33he shall shave himself, but the scale he shall not shave. And the priest shall isolate *the one who has* the scale another seven days. 34On the seventh day the priest shall examine the scale; and indeed *if* the scale has not spread over the skin, and does not appear deeper than the skin, then the priest shall pronounce him clean. He shall wash his clothes and be clean. 35But if the scale should at all spread over the skin after his cleansing, 36then the priest shall examine him; and indeed *if* the scale has spread over the skin, the priest need not seek for yellow hair. He *is* unclean. 37But if the scale appears to be at a standstill, and there is black hair grown up in it, the scale has healed. He *is* clean, and the priest shall pronounce him clean.

38"If a man or a woman has bright spots on the skin of the body, *specifically* white bright spots, 39then the priest shall look; and indeed *if* the bright spots on the skin of the body *are* dull white, it *is* a white spot *that* grows on the skin. He *is* clean.

40"As for the man whose hair has fallen from his head, he *is* bald, *but* he *is* clean. 41He whose hair has fallen from his forehead, he *is* bald on the forehead, *but* he *is* clean. 42And if there is on the bald head or bald forehead a reddish-white sore, it *is* leprosy breaking out on his bald head or his bald forehead. 43Then the priest shall examine it; and indeed *if* the swelling of the sore *is* reddish-white on his bald head or on his bald forehead, as the appearance of leprosy on the skin of the body, 44he is a leprous man. He *is* unclean. The priest shall surely pronounce him unclean; his sore *is* on his head.

45"Now the leper on whom the sore *is,* his clothes shall be torn and his head bare; and he shall cover his mustache, and cry, 'Unclean! Unclean!' 46He shall be unclean. All the days he has the sore he shall be unclean. He *is* unclean, and he shall dwell alone; his dwelling *shall be* outside the camp.

The Law Concerning Leprous Garments

47"Also, if a garment has a leprous plague[a] in it, *whether it is* a woolen garment or a linen garment, 48whether *it is* in the warp or woof of linen or wool, whether in leather or in anything made of leather, 49and if the plague is greenish or reddish in the garment or in the leather, whether in the warp or in the woof, or in anything made of

13:47 [a] A mold, fungus, or similar infestation, and so in verses 47–59

leather, it *is* a leprous plague and shall be shown to the priest. [50]The priest shall examine the plague and isolate *that which has* the plague seven days. [51]And he shall examine the plague on the seventh day. If the plague has spread in the garment, either in the warp or in the woof, in the leather *or* in anything made of leather, the plague *is* an active leprosy. It *is* unclean. [52]He shall therefore burn that garment in which is the plague, whether warp or woof, in wool or in linen, or anything of leather, for it *is* an active leprosy; *the garment* shall be burned in the fire.

[53]"But if the priest examines *it,* and indeed the plague has not spread in the garment, either in the warp or in the woof, or in anything made of leather, [54]then the priest shall command that they wash *the thing* in which *is* the plague; and he shall isolate it another seven days. [55]Then the priest shall examine the plague after it has been washed; and indeed *if* the plague has not changed its color, though the plague has not spread, it *is* unclean, and you shall burn it in the fire; it continues eating away, *whether* the damage *is* outside or inside. [56]If the priest examines *it,* and indeed the plague has faded after washing it, then he shall tear it out of the garment, whether out of the warp or out of the woof, or out of the leather. [57]But if it appears again in the garment, either in the warp or in the woof, or in anything made of leather, it *is* a spreading *plague;* you shall burn with fire that in which is the plague. [58]And if you wash the garment, either warp or woof, or whatever is made of leather, if the plague has disappeared from it, then it shall be washed a second time, and shall be clean.

[59]"This *is* the law of the leprous plague in a garment of wool or linen, either in the warp or woof, or in anything made of leather, to pronounce it clean or to pronounce it unclean."

The Ritual for Cleansing Healed Lepers

14 Then the LORD spoke to Moses, saying, [2]"This shall be the law of the leper for the day of his cleansing: He shall be brought to the priest. [3]And the priest shall go out of the camp, and the priest shall examine *him;* and indeed, *if* the leprosy is healed in the leper, [4]then the priest shall command to take for him who is to be cleansed two living *and* clean birds, cedar wood, scarlet, and hyssop. [5]And the priest shall command that one of the birds be killed in an earthen vessel over running water. [6]As for the living bird, he shall take it, the cedar wood and the scarlet and the hyssop, and dip them and the living bird in the blood of the bird *that was* killed over the running water. [7]And he shall sprinkle it seven times on him who is to be cleansed from the leprosy, and shall pronounce him clean, and shall let the living bird loose in the open field. [8]He who is to be cleansed shall wash his clothes, shave off all his hair, and wash himself in water, that he may be clean. After that he shall come into the camp, and shall stay outside his tent seven days. [9]But on the seventh day he shall shave all the hair off his head and his beard and his eyebrows— all his hair he shall shave off. He shall wash his clothes and wash his body in water, and he shall be clean.

[10]"And on the eighth day he shall take two male lambs without blemish, one ewe lamb of the first year without blemish, three-tenths *of an ephah* of fine flour mixed with oil as a grain offering, and one log of oil. [11]Then the priest who makes *him* clean shall present the man who is to be made clean, and those things, before the LORD, *at* the door of the tabernacle of meeting. [12]And the priest shall take one male lamb and offer it as a trespass offering, and the log of oil, and wave them *as* a wave offering before the LORD. [13]Then he shall kill the lamb in the place where he kills the sin offering and the burnt offering, in a holy place; for as the sin offering *is* the priest's, so *is* the trespass offering. It *is* most holy. [14]The priest shall take *some* of the blood of the trespass offering, and the priest shall put *it* on the tip of the right ear of him who is to be cleansed, on the thumb of his right hand, and on the big toe of his right foot. [15]And the priest shall take *some* of the log of oil, and pour *it* into the palm of his own left hand. [16]Then the priest shall dip his right finger in the oil that *is* in his left hand, and shall sprinkle some of the oil with his finger seven times before the LORD. [17]And of the rest of the oil in his hand, the priest shall put *some* on the tip of the right ear of him who is to be cleansed, on the thumb of his right hand, and on the big toe of his right foot, on the blood of the trespass offering. [18]The

---

14:1 Purification rituals for lepers were for ceremonial, not healing, purposes. The priest had the responsibility for examining the leper and pronouncing him healed. The ruling that the priest should go outside the camp to examine the leper probably was introduced to prevent the spread of the disease (v. 3). Two purification ceremonies for healed lepers are described (vv. 1–32). The first ritual consisted of bringing two living birds to the priest (vv. 4–7). One bird was killed over a jar of spring water. Cedarwood, scarlet material, and hyssop were placed in the dead bird's blood. The living bird then was dipped into this liquid and permitted to fly away, while the liquid was sprinkled on the healed leper. Setting the live bird free symbolically pictured the carrying away of the healed leper's uncleanness. After this procedure, the leper shaved and washed himself and his garments. He was permitted to reenter his tent after seven days. On the eighth day the cleansed leper offered the sacrifices described (vv. 10–20). This second purification ritual involved a guilt or trespass offering, a sin offering, and a burnt offering. Observe the emphasis on the right side of the body (v. 17; see Lev. 8:22–30, note). Purification rituals for the poor are also described (Lev. 14:21–32).

Women should do less, not more. Less of what we want, more of what God wants.

Cindy Lewis Dake

rest of the oil that *is* in the priest's hand he shall put on the head of him who is to be cleansed. So the priest shall make atonement for him before the LORD.

19"Then the priest shall offer the sin offering, and make atonement for him who is to be cleansed from his uncleanness. Afterward he shall kill the burnt offering. 20And the priest shall offer the burnt offering and the grain offering on the altar. So the priest shall make atonement for him, and he shall be clean.

21"But if he *is* poor and cannot afford it, then he shall take one male lamb *as* a trespass offering to be waved, to make atonement for him, one-tenth *of an ephah* of fine flour mixed with oil as a grain offering, a log of oil, 22and two turtledoves or two young pigeons, such as he is able to afford: one shall be a sin offering and the other a burnt offering. 23He shall bring them to the priest on the eighth day for his cleansing, to the door of the tabernacle of meeting, before the LORD. 24And the priest shall take the lamb of the trespass offering and the log of oil, and the priest shall wave them *as* a wave offering before the LORD. 25Then he shall kill the lamb of the trespass offering, and the priest shall take *some* of the blood of the trespass offering and put *it* on the tip of the right ear of him who is to be cleansed, on the thumb of his right hand, and on the big toe of his right foot. 26And the priest shall pour some of the oil into the palm of his own left hand. 27Then the priest shall sprinkle with his right finger *some* of the oil that *is* in his left hand seven times before the LORD. 28And the priest shall put *some* of the oil that *is* in his hand on the tip of the right ear of him who is to be cleansed, on the thumb of the right hand, and on the big toe of his right foot, on the place of the blood of the trespass offering. 29The rest of the oil that *is* in the priest's hand he shall put on the head of him who is to be cleansed, to make atonement for him before the LORD. 30And he shall offer one of the turtledoves or young pigeons, such as he can afford— 31such as

he is able to afford, the one *as* a sin offering and the other *as* a burnt offering, with the grain offering. So the priest shall make atonement for him who is to be cleansed before the LORD. 32This *is* the law *for one* who had a leprous sore, who cannot afford the usual cleansing."

The Law Concerning Leprous Houses

33And the LORD spoke to Moses and Aaron, saying: 34"When you have come into the land of Canaan, which I give you as a possession, and I put the leprous plague[a] in a house in the land of your possession, 35and he who owns the house comes and tells the priest, saying, 'It seems to me that *there is* some plague in the house,' 36then the priest shall command that they empty the house, before the priest goes *into it* to examine the plague, that all that *is* in the house may not be made unclean; and afterward the priest shall go in to examine the house. 37And he shall examine the plague; and indeed *if* the plague *is* on the walls of the house with ingrained streaks, greenish or reddish, which appear to be deep in the wall, 38then the priest shall go out of the house, to the door of the house, and shut up the house seven days. 39And the priest shall come again on the seventh day and look; and indeed *if* the plague has spread on the walls of the house, 40then the priest shall command that they take away the stones in which *is* the plague, and they shall cast them into an unclean place outside the city. 41And he shall cause the house to be scraped inside, all around, and the dust that they scrape off they shall pour out in an unclean place outside the city. 42Then they shall take other stones and put *them* in the place of *those* stones, and he shall take other mortar and plaster the house.

43"Now if the plague comes back and breaks out in the house, after he has taken away the stones, after he has scraped the house, and after it

14:34 [a]Decomposition by mildew, mold, dry rot, etc., and so in verses 34–53

14:33 The house of a leper required cleansing. The leprous condition of the house could refer to infection by leprosy or to the existence of such plagues as mildew and fungus. If the house could not be completely cleansed, then the building was to be totally destroyed (v. 45). These regulations regarding health and hygiene related to public safety. Although a fungus or mildew might be quite harmless in itself, the damp conditions which encouraged such growth were unhealthy. This regulation reminds women of the Lord's concern for

health and hygiene for all. Housing and living conditions contributing to the spread of disease should not be tolerated. The statement identifying the Lord as the source of the leprous plague reveals the limited perspective of people in early Israel (vv. 33, 34). According to their viewpoint, no secondary causes were evident. They did not consider the interaction of people with the environment. Everything, both pleasant and unpleasant, came from the Lord.

THE MENSTRUAL CYCLE — A NATURAL FLOW

Menstruation, which begins at puberty and ends with menopause, is a woman's monthly discharge of blood and tissue that has built up during the previous month in the uterus. This tissue lined the womb in preparation for the growth of a baby and is discharged when conception does not take place. This gives opportunity for the development of a new lining and the possibility of pregnancy in the coming month.

Mosaic Law is explicit concerning the bodily discharge of women—both normal (Lev. 15:19–24) and abnormal (vv. 25–30) menstruation. The Old Testament describes menstruous women as being unclean, and men are told not to have sexual relations with them during this time of menstruation. All references to the actual menstrual flow are in the Old Testament; none appear in the New Testament. However, from this passage in Leviticus describing an abnormal menstrual period, we can better understand the loneliness and isolation of the woman with "a flow of blood" who came to Jesus for healing (Lev. 15:25–30; Matt. 9:20–22; Mark 5:25–34; Luke 8:43–48).

Though this natural physiological function is often viewed as a burden for a woman, in reality menstruation affords her the opportunity to link hands with the Creator in forming another life within her own body (Gen. 4:1). The closeness between a woman and her offspring is a miracle that would not be possible without menstruation.

See also notes on Childbirth (John 16); Menopause (Gen. 18); Premenstrual Syndrome (Prov. 21)

is plastered, ⁴⁴then the priest shall come and look; and indeed *if* the plague has spread in the house, it *is* an active leprosy in the house. It *is* unclean. ⁴⁵And he shall break down the house, its stones, its timber, and all the plaster of the house, and he shall carry *them* outside the city to an unclean place. ⁴⁶Moreover he who goes into the house at all while it is shut up shall be unclean until evening. ⁴⁷And he who lies down in the house shall wash his clothes, and he who eats in the house shall wash his clothes.

⁴⁸"But if the priest comes in and examines *it,* and indeed the plague has not spread in the house after the house was plastered, then the priest shall pronounce the house clean, because the plague is healed. ⁴⁹And he shall take, to cleanse the house, two birds, cedar wood, scarlet, and hyssop. ⁵⁰Then he shall kill one of the birds in an earthen vessel over running water; ⁵¹and he shall take the cedar wood, the hyssop, the scarlet, and the living bird, and dip them in the blood of the slain bird and in the running water, and sprinkle the house seven times. ⁵²And he shall cleanse the house with the blood of the bird and the running water, and the living bird, with the cedar wood, the hyssop, and the scarlet. ⁵³Then he shall let the living bird loose outside the city in the open field, and make atonement for the house, and it shall be clean.

⁵⁴"This *is* the law for any leprous sore and scale, ⁵⁵for the leprosy of a garment and of a house, ⁵⁶for a swelling and a scab and a bright spot, ⁵⁷to teach when *it is* unclean and when *it is* clean. This *is* the law of leprosy."

The Law Concerning Bodily Discharges

15 And the LORD spoke to Moses and Aaron, saying, ²"Speak to the children of Israel, and say to them: 'When any man has a discharge from his body, his discharge *is* unclean. ³And this shall be his uncleanness in regard to his discharge— whether his body runs with his discharge, or his body is stopped up by his discharge, it *is* his uncleanness. ⁴Every bed is unclean on which he who

---

15:1 Regulations regarding bodily discharges delineated what rendered an individual unclean. God's concern for matters such as life, blood, sexual relations, and bodily discharges emphasized His desire for His people to be holy unto Him. Verses 1–15 deal with a man who had a bodily discharge, presumably related to illness. Verses 16–18 concern the discharge of semen. Bodily discharges related to the generative organs may have been particularly loathsome to the male because they indicated contamination and pollution in the area of the covenant seal of circumcision. The remainder of the chapter concerns female bodily discharges. A woman was considered unclean both during her menstrual period and for seven days afterward (see Menstrual Cycle). This may have been required to protect a woman with cramps and discomfort from unwelcome advances of an insensitive husband. Intercourse with her during the seven-day period rendered the male un-

clean for seven days (vv. 19–24). This in no way suggests that sexual intimacy between husband and wife is anything but wonderful and holy and a vital part of the marital union (Heb. 13:4). Discharges of blood in women also could indicate illness (vv. 25–30). Any quarantine for this reason would prevent the passing of contagious disease and give the woman rest from family responsibilities, including marital intimacy, until she could regain her strength and her physical health. Verses 31–33 summarize the section on uncleanness through bodily discharges. No offering is prescribed in the cases of menstruation and discharge of semen, probably because these were regular occurrences and regarded as normal. Some connection may have been made between holiness and good health (see Phil. 1, Fitness). Note also that the offering prescribed for a woman with bodily discharge was the same as for a man with a discharge (vv. 13–15, 28–30).

has the discharge lies, and everything on which he sits shall be unclean. ⁵And whoever touches his bed shall wash his clothes and bathe in water, and be unclean until evening. ⁶He who sits on anything on which he who has the discharge sat shall wash his clothes and bathe in water, and be unclean until evening. ⁷And he who touches the body of him who has the discharge shall wash his clothes and bathe in water, and be unclean until evening. ⁸If he who has the discharge spits on him who is clean, then he shall wash his clothes and bathe in water, and be unclean until evening. ⁹Any saddle on which he who has the discharge rides shall be unclean. ¹⁰Whoever touches anything that was under him shall be unclean until evening. He who carries *any of* those things shall wash his clothes and bathe in water, and be unclean until evening. ¹¹And whomever the one who has the discharge touches, and has not rinsed his hands in water, he shall wash his clothes and bathe in water, and be unclean until evening. ¹²The vessel of earth that he who has the discharge touches shall be broken, and every vessel of wood shall be rinsed in water.

¹³And when he who has a discharge is cleansed of his discharge, then he shall count for himself seven days for his cleansing, wash his clothes, and bathe his body in running water; then he shall be clean. ¹⁴On the eighth day he shall take for himself two turtledoves or two young pigeons, and come before the LORD, to the door of the tabernacle of meeting, and give them to the priest. ¹⁵Then the priest shall offer them, the one *as* a sin offering and the other *as* a burnt offering. So the priest shall make atonement for him before the LORD because of his discharge.

¹⁶'If any man has an emission of semen, then he shall wash all his body in water, and be unclean until evening. ¹⁷And any garment and any leather on which there is semen, it shall be washed with water, and be unclean until evening. ¹⁸Also, when a woman lies with a man, and *there is* an emission of semen, they shall bathe in water, and be unclean until evening.

¹⁹'If a woman has a discharge, *and* the discharge from her body is blood, she shall be set apart seven days; and whoever touches her shall be unclean until evening. ²⁰Everything that she lies on during her impurity shall be unclean; also everything that she sits on shall be unclean. ²¹Whoever touches her bed shall wash his clothes and bathe in water, and be unclean until evening. ²²And whoever touches anything that she sat on shall wash his clothes and bathe in water, and be unclean until evening. ²³If *anything* is on *her* bed or on anything on which she sits, when he touches it, he shall be unclean until evening. ²⁴And if any man lies with her at all, so that her impurity is on him, he shall be unclean seven days; and every bed on which he lies shall be unclean.

²⁵'If a woman has a discharge of blood for many days, other than at the time of her *customary* impurity, or if it runs beyond her *usual time of* impurity, all the days of her unclean discharge shall be as the days of her *customary* impurity. She *shall be* unclean. ²⁶Every bed on which she lies all the days of her discharge shall be to her as the bed of her impurity; and whatever she sits on shall be unclean, as the uncleanness of her impurity. ²⁷Whoever touches those things shall be unclean; he shall wash his clothes and bathe in water, and be unclean until evening.

²⁸'But if she is cleansed of her discharge, then she shall count for herself seven days, and after that she shall be clean. ²⁹And on the eighth day she shall take for herself two turtledoves or two young pigeons, and bring them to the priest, to the door of the tabernacle of meeting. ³⁰Then the priest shall offer the one *as* a sin offering and the other *as* a burnt offering, and the priest shall make atonement for her before the LORD for the discharge of her uncleanness.

³¹'Thus you shall separate the children of Israel from their uncleanness, lest they die in their uncleanness when they defile My tabernacle that *is* among them. ³²This *is* the law for one who has a discharge, and *for him* who emits semen and is unclean thereby, ³³and for her who is indisposed because of her *customary* impurity, and for one who has a discharge, either man or woman, and for him who lies with her who is unclean.' "

The Day of Atonement

16 Now the LORD spoke to Moses after the death of the two sons of Aaron, when they offered *profane fire* before the LORD, and died; ²and

---

16:1 The Day of Atonement (Heb. *Yom Kippur*) was celebrated annually among the people of Israel on the tenth day of the seventh month, probably October (Lev. 23:27; see chart, The Feasts of Israel). Leviticus 16 is the central chapter of the book both in terms of its placement and its importance. The Hebrew word translated "atonement" comes from a root meaning "to cover over." The ritual pictured the covering of sins (v. 34). The high priest was allowed to enter the Most Holy Place (Holy of Holies) only once each year, on the Day of Atonement. Aaron as high priest brought a sin offering and a burnt offering to atone for the sins of himself and his house,

first making himself right with the Lord before he could minister to others. When Aaron approached the LORD within the Most Holy Place, he did not wear his elaborate high priestly garments. Instead he wore special garments of linen for the occasion, which symbolized his humility before God (vv. 4, 23, 24). Later when he stood before the people, he wore the high priestly garments (v. 14; see chart, The High Priest's Clothing). Aaron cast lots on the two goats. The goat on which the Lord's lot fell was offered as a sin offering for the people. The other goat, designated as the scapegoat, was sent away into the wilderness (vv. 7-10). The writer of the Book of Hebrews

the LORD said to Moses: "Tell Aaron your brother not to come at *just* any time into the Holy *Place* inside the veil, before the mercy seat which *is* on the ark, lest he die; for I will appear in the cloud above the mercy seat.

³"Thus Aaron shall come into the Holy *Place:* with *the blood of* a young bull as a sin offering, and *of* a ram as a burnt offering. ⁴He shall put the holy linen tunic and the linen trousers on his body; he shall be girded with a linen sash, and with the linen turban he shall be attired. These *are* holy garments. Therefore he shall wash his body in water, and put them on. ⁵And he shall take from the congregation of the children of Israel two kids of the goats as a sin offering, and one ram as a burnt offering.

⁶"Aaron shall offer the bull as a sin offering, which *is* for himself, and make atonement for himself and for his house. ⁷He shall take the two goats and present them before the LORD *at* the door of the tabernacle of meeting. ⁸Then Aaron shall cast lots for the two goats: one lot for the LORD and the other lot for the scapegoat. ⁹And Aaron shall bring the goat on which the LORD's lot fell, and offer it *as* a sin offering. ¹⁰But the goat on which the lot fell to be the scapegoat shall be presented alive before the LORD, to make atonement upon it, *and* to let it go as the scapegoat into the wilderness.

¹¹"And Aaron shall bring the bull of the sin offering, which is for himself, and make atonement for himself and for his house, and shall kill the bull as the sin offering which *is* for himself. ¹²Then he shall take a censer full of burning coals of fire from the altar before the LORD, with his hands full of sweet incense beaten fine, and bring *it* inside the veil. ¹³And he shall put the incense on the fire before the LORD, that the cloud of incense may cover the mercy seat that *is* on the Testimony,

lest he die. ¹⁴He shall take some of the blood of the bull and sprinkle *it* with his finger on the mercy seat on the east *side;* and before the mercy seat he shall sprinkle some of the blood with his finger seven times.

¹⁵"Then he shall kill the goat of the sin offering, which *is* for the people, bring its blood inside the veil, do with that blood as he did with the blood of the bull, and sprinkle it on the mercy seat and before the mercy seat. ¹⁶So he shall make atonement for the Holy *Place,* because of the uncleanness of the children of Israel, and because of their transgressions, for all their sins; and so he shall do for the tabernacle of meeting which remains among them in the midst of their uncleanness. ¹⁷There shall be no man in the tabernacle of meeting when he goes in to make atonement in the Holy *Place,* until he comes out, that he may make atonement for himself, for his household, and for all the assembly of Israel. ¹⁸And he shall go out to the altar that *is* before the LORD, and make atonement for it, and shall take some of the blood of the bull and some of the blood of the goat, and put it on the horns of the altar all around. ¹⁹Then he shall sprinkle some of the blood on it with his finger seven times, cleanse it, and consecrate it from the uncleanness of the children of Israel.

²⁰"And when he has made an end of atoning for the Holy *Place,* the tabernacle of meeting, and the altar, he shall bring the live goat. ²¹Aaron shall lay both his hands on the head of the live goat, confess over it all the iniquities of the children of Israel, and all their transgressions, concerning all their sins, putting them on the head of the goat, and shall send *it* away into the wilderness by the hand of a suitable man. ²²The goat shall bear on itself all their iniquities to an uninhabited land; and he shall release the goat in the wilderness.

---

noted the significance of the Day of Atonement for Christians (Heb. 10:4). The procedure on the Day of Atonement pointed toward Christ as the perfect High Priest who had no need to make atonement for His own sins because He is sinless (Heb. 7:26–28; see chart, The Plan of the Tabernacle). Christ is not only the perfect High Priest; He is also the sin offering. He offered Himself for our sins (Heb. 9:11–15). Christ also fulfilled the function of the scapegoat in the ritual on the Day of Atonement. He has carried sins away (see Is. 53:6; Ps. 103:12). Finally, Christ offered Himself once for all to secure an eternal redemption. No longer do sacrifices need to be offered year by year. Christ as the perfect High Priest and the perfect sacrifice has offered His own blood once for all time (Heb. 9:23–28). Christ's redemptive act was the perfect completion of atonement (Heb. 7:27; 10:10).

16:11–28 Special cleansing procedures were carried out for the tabernacle and the altar (vv. 16–19). Aaron entered the Most Holy Place three times on the Day of Atonement:

1) He carried into the Most Holy Place a censer of hot coals with incense, which was to shield him from God's awesome presence (vv. 12, 13).

2) Aaron also carried into this most sacred area a bull to make a sin offering for himself and his family (vv. 11, 14).

3) Finally, he carried into the Most Holy Place a sin offering for all Israel (v. 15).

Both the goat sacrificed and the scapegoat sent away were part of the sin offering. The goat sacrificed symbolized propitiation for sins, and the scapegoat pictured the complete removal of the sins for which atonement had been made. The scapegoat was sent away into the wilderness (vv. 20–22). In laying his hands on the head of the goat, the high priest symbolically transferred all the confessed sins of the people to the animal. The high priest bathed and changed his garments after the scapegoat was sent away (vv. 23, 24). The burnt offering and the fat of the sin offering were consumed on the altar (vv. 24, 25). The individual selected to release the scapegoat bathed and washed his clothing (v. 26). The one who burned the prescribed parts of the sin offering outside the camp bathed and washed his garments (vv. 27, 28).

Never utter in your neighbour's absence what you would not say in their presence.

St. Mary Magdalene dei Pazzi

---

²³"Then Aaron shall come into the tabernacle of meeting, shall take off the linen garments which he put on when he went into the Holy *Place,* and shall leave them there. ²⁴And he shall wash his body with water in a holy place, put on his garments, come out and offer his burnt offering and the burnt offering of the people, and make atonement for himself and for the people. ²⁵The fat of the sin offering he shall burn on the altar. ²⁶And he who released the goat as the scapegoat shall wash his clothes and bathe his body in water, and afterward he may come into the camp. ²⁷The bull *for* the sin offering and the goat *for* the sin offering, whose blood was brought in to make atonement in the Holy *Place,* shall be carried outside the camp. And they shall burn in the fire their skins, their flesh, and their offal. ²⁸Then he who burns them shall wash his clothes and bathe his body in water, and afterward he may come into the camp.

²⁹"*This* shall be a statute forever for you: In the seventh month, on the tenth *day* of the month, you shall afflict your souls, and do no work at all, *whether* a native of your own country or a stranger who dwells among you. ³⁰For on that day *the priest* shall make atonement for you, to cleanse you, *that* you may be clean from all your sins before the LORD. ³¹It *is* a sabbath of solemn rest for you, and you shall afflict your souls. *It is* a statute forever. ³²And the priest, who is anointed and consecrated to minister as priest in his father's place, shall make atonement, and put on the linen clothes, the holy garments; ³³then he shall make atonement for the Holy Sanctuary,ᵃ and he shall make atonement for the tabernacle of meeting and for the altar, and he shall make atonement for the priests and for all the people of the assembly. ³⁴This shall

be an everlasting statute for you, to make atonement for the children of Israel, for all their sins, once a year." And he did as the LORD commanded Moses.

The Sanctity of Blood

17 And the LORD spoke to Moses, saying, ²"Speak to Aaron, to his sons, and to all the children of Israel, and say to them, 'This *is* the thing which the LORD has commanded, saying: ³"Whatever man of the house of Israel who kills an ox or lamb or goat in the camp, or who kills *it* outside the camp, ⁴and does not bring it to the door of the tabernacle of meeting to offer an offering to the LORD before the tabernacle of the LORD, the guilt of bloodshed shall be imputed to that man. He has shed blood; and that man shall be cut off from among his people, ⁵to the end that the children of Israel may bring their sacrifices which they offer in the open field, that they may bring them to the LORD at the door of the tabernacle of meeting, to the priest, and offer them *as* peace offerings to the LORD. ⁶And the priest shall sprinkle the blood on the altar of the LORD *at* the door of the tabernacle of meeting, and burn the fat for a sweet aroma to the LORD. ⁷They shall no more offer their sacrifices to demons, after whom they have played the harlot. This shall be a statute forever for them throughout their generations."

⁸"Also you shall say to them: 'Whatever man of the house of Israel, or of the strangers who dwell among you, who offers a burnt offering or sacrifice, ⁹and does not bring it to the door of the

16:33 ᵃThat is, the Most Holy Place

16:29–34 The Day of Atonement was established as an annual occurrence because God's people needed continual forgiveness. The Day of Atonement involved humility and confession of sin, affirming that only the Lord could take away sin (see chart, The Feasts of Israel).

17:1 Regulations for fellowship with God include the "Holiness Code" (Lev. 17—26). Holiness or separateness was to be a way of life, involving commitment to the Lord in every aspect. Instructions concerning separation are included (Lev. 17:1–22:33). God's people were to commit themselves uniquely to Him and to separate themselves from the pagan practices of their neighbors. Leviticus 17 deals with the sacredness of life represented by the blood. Life is sacred because it is the gift of God. The ancient Israelite viewed life as residing in the blood (v. 14). Regulations regarding the sanctity of life are outlined in this chapter (see Gen. 9, Sanctity of Life). Any domestic animal slain either within or without the camp had to

be brought to the tabernacle as a peace offering to the Lord (vv. 1–7). The rationale behind this command is the sanctity of the blood. The blood represented the creature's life, and all life belongs to the Lord. Anyone who violated this command brought bloodguilt on himself and was considered guilty of murder. No sacrifice was to be offered at any place except the tabernacle (vv. 8, 9). The command to worship at one central sanctuary is an emphasis in Deuteronomy (see Deut. 12:10–14). Worship at other places, sometimes designated as high places, was considered sinful. Blood was never to be eaten (vv. 10–14). This prohibition may be traced back to the time of Noah (Gen. 9:4). Any animal that died of itself, whether it experienced a natural death or was torn by beasts, should not be eaten (vv. 15, 16). At the basis of these commands is a reverence for life (see v. 11, the book's key verse). The shedding of the blood of sacrificial animals foreshadows the coming of Christ, who gave His life to atone for sin.

INCEST *THE ULTIMATE BETRAYAL*

The Bible does not use the word "incest," but it strongly advocates the purity of the most intimate family circle (Lev. 18:6–18) and speaks against sexual relationships between close family members. Incest describes the abuse and distortion of God-ordained relationships.

Sexual intimacy between closely related persons was strictly prohibited, and the punishment was death, childlessness, or being "cut off" from the community (Lev. 20:11–21). The person who committed such acts was cursed of God (Deut. 27:20–23).

In Scripture, incest is addressed as the defilement of the recognized relationships of parent and child, brother and sister, half-brother and half-sister, grandparent and grandchild, aunts and uncles, father and daughter-in-law, and father and children from polygamous unions. Laws of family fidelity set believers apart from the heathen; preserved emotional, physical, spiritual, and psychological health; and guarded against unhealthy genetic mutation.

God has always been interested in the wholeness of the individual, and His laws are given to establish and maintain wholeness—physically, emotionally, and spiritually.

Perhaps the foremost incident of incest in the Bible is the one in which Lot's daughters encouraged their father to get drunk; then each became pregnant by him. These acts of incest produced two tribes with whom the Israelites struggled frequently and bitterly: the Moabites and the Ammonites (Gen. 19:30–38).

See also Gen. 38:6–30; Rom. 3:23, note; notes on Abuse (Ps. 31); Codependency (Gen. 27); Family (1 Sam. 3); Rape (Gen. 34); Sexual Immorality (Prov. 6); portrait of Tamar (2 Sam. 13)

tabernacle of meeting, to offer it to the LORD, that man shall be cut off from among his people.

10"And whatever man of the house of Israel, or of the strangers who dwell among you, who eats any blood, I will set My face against that person who eats blood, and will cut him off from among his people. 11For the life of the flesh *is* in the blood, and I have given it to you upon the altar to make atonement for your souls; for it *is* the blood *that* makes atonement for the soul.' 12Therefore I said to the children of Israel, 'No one among you shall eat blood, nor shall any stranger who dwells among you eat blood.'

13"Whatever man of the children of Israel, or of the strangers who dwell among you, who hunts and catches any animal or bird that may be eaten, he shall pour out its blood and cover it with dust; 14for *it is* the life of all flesh. Its blood sustains its life. Therefore I said to the children of Israel, 'You shall not eat the blood of any flesh, for the life of all flesh is its blood. Whoever eats it shall be cut off.'

15"And every person who eats what died *naturally* or what was torn *by beasts, whether he is* a native of your own country or a stranger, he shall both wash his clothes and bathe in water, and be unclean until evening. Then he shall be clean. 16But if he does not wash *them* or bathe his body, then he shall bear his guilt."

Laws of Sexual Morality

18 Then the LORD spoke to Moses, saying, 2"Speak to the children of Israel, and say to them: 'I am the LORD your God. 3According to the doings of the land of Egypt, where you dwelt, you shall not do; and according to the doings of the land of Canaan, where I am bringing you, you shall not do; nor shall you walk in their ordinances. 4You shall observe My judgments and keep My ordinances, to walk in them: I *am* the LORD your God. 5You shall therefore keep My statutes and My judgments, which if a man does, he shall live by them: I *am* the LORD.

6'None of you shall approach anyone who is near of kin to him, to uncover his nakedness: I *am* the LORD. 7The nakedness of your father or the nakedness of your mother you shall not uncover. She *is* your mother; you shall not uncover her

---

18:1 A general call to obedience commands the people of Israel not to follow the practices of the Egyptians or the Canaanites but rather to keep the Lord's statutes (vv. 1–5). In Leviticus 20, the prohibitions are given before the punishments, underscoring the idea that warnings are given prior to consequences. The basis for this command is the covenant relationship: "I am the LORD your God" (v. 4). In some forms of kinship, marriage and sexual relations are prohibited (vv. 6–18). Further rules are provided regarding sexual and parental relationships (vv. 19–23). A further warning against violating the Lord's standards for sexual morality is given

(vv. 24–30). Sexual activity was sacred because it resulted in procreation of life, the gift of God.

18:4, 5 Some judgments, ordinances, statutes, decrees, and laws are unfathomable by human intelligence and logic. The words "I am the LORD" convey the idea that we are not to decide whether or not to obey, but rather we are to trust God's faithful intention to do what is best for His children (v. 5; Rom. 8:28; see Eccl. 7, Providence).

18:6–18 Incest is forbidden. Uncovering nakedness refers to sexual relationships or cohabitation. In the patriarchal society

nakedness. [8]The nakedness of your father's wife you shall not uncover; it *is* your father's nakedness. [9]The nakedness of your sister, the daughter of your father, or the daughter of your mother, *whether* born at home or elsewhere, their nakedness you shall not uncover. [10]The nakedness of your son's daughter or your daughter's daughter, their nakedness you shall not uncover; for theirs *is* your own nakedness. [11]The nakedness of your father's wife's daughter, begotten by your father—she *is* your sister—you shall not uncover her nakedness. [12]You shall not uncover the nakedness of your father's sister; she *is* near of kin to your father. [13]You shall not uncover the nakedness of your mother's sister, for she *is* near of kin to your mother. [14]You shall not uncover the nakedness of your father's brother. You shall not approach his wife; she *is* your aunt. [15]You shall not uncover the nakedness of your daughter-in-law—she *is* your son's wife—you shall not uncover her nakedness. [16]You shall not uncover the nakedness of your brother's wife; it *is* your brother's nakedness. [17]You shall not uncover the nakedness of a woman and her daughter, nor shall you take her son's daughter or her daughter's daughter, to uncover her nakedness. They *are* near of kin to her. It *is* wickedness. [18]Nor shall you take a woman as a rival to her sister, to uncover her nakedness while the other is alive.

[19]Also you shall not approach a woman to uncover her nakedness as long as she is in her *customary* impurity. [20]Moreover you shall not lie carnally with your neighbor's wife, to defile yourself with her. [21]And you shall not let any of your descendants pass through *the fire* to Molech, nor shall you profane the name of your God: I *am* the LORD. [22]You shall not lie with a male as with a woman. It *is* an abomination. [23]Nor shall you mate with any animal, to defile yourself with it. Nor shall any woman stand before an animal to mate with it. It *is* perversion.

[24]Do not defile yourselves with any of these things; for by all these the nations are defiled, which I am casting out before you. [25]For the land is defiled; therefore I visit the punishment of its iniquity upon it, and the land vomits out its inhabitants. [26]You shall therefore keep My statutes and My judgments, and shall not commit *any* of these abominations, *either* any of your own nation or any stranger who dwells among you [27](for all these abominations the men of the land have done, who *were* before you, and thus the land is defiled), [28]lest the land vomit you out also when you defile it, as it vomited out the nations that *were* before you. [29]For whoever commits any of these abominations, the persons who commit *them* shall be cut off from among their people.

[30]Therefore you shall keep My ordinance, so that *you* do not commit *any* of these abominable customs which were committed before you, and that you do not defile yourselves by them: I *am* the LORD your God.' "

Moral and Ceremonial Laws

19 And the LORD spoke to Moses, saying, [2]"Speak to all the congregation of the children of Israel, and say to them: 'You shall be holy, for I the LORD your God *am* holy.

[3]Every one of you shall revere his mother and his father, and keep My Sabbaths: I *am* the LORD your God.

[4]Do not turn to idols, nor make for yourselves molded gods: I *am* the LORD your God.

[5]And if you offer a sacrifice of a peace offering to the LORD, you shall offer it of your own free will. [6]It shall be eaten the same day you offer *it*,

---

of ancient Israel, families lived together in clans or large groups. Incestuous relationships were forbidden among the people of Israel (see Incest). Although the law stipulated that one should not have sexual relations with his brother's wife (v. 16), this law did not contradict that of levirate marriage, since in the latter instance the brother would be dead (see Deut. 25:5–10). The prohibitions contained in this chapter uphold the sanctity of the marriage bond (Heb. 13:4). The sexual act is not viewed as sinful but rather as a part of God's plan within the proper setting (see Gen. 2:24).

18:19–23 At times a woman was not to be approached by her own husband (v. 19). Sexual activity was prohibited during the period a woman was unclean because of her menstrual cycle (v. 19; see Lev. 15:1, note). This underscored the importance of subjugating even the most legitimate sexual expression to the Lord's directive (Ezek. 22:10; see Lev. 11:1–3, note; 15, Menstrual Cycle). Adultery was prohibited, thus protecting the sanctity of marriage and the home (see v. 20; Ex. 20:14). Child sacrifice was forbidden (v. 21; see Lev. 20:2–5). Molech was generally identified as an Ammonite god. The context of verse 21 suggests that the offering of a child to Molech was associated in some way with sexual abuse. Homosexuality is prohibited (v. 22; see Homosexuality), and bestiality or sexual relations with animals is condemned (v. 23; Deut. 27:21).

18:24–30 A strong warning against perverted sexual behavior concludes this chapter. Such violations had resulted in casting the Canaanites out of the land (v. 24). In addition to spiritual and social ramifications associated with sin, the entire land is contaminated by the debauchery. Elsewhere Scripture also pictures nature as suffering because of the sins of mankind (see Hos. 4:1–3). Likewise nature is presented as sharing in the glorious peace of the messianic age (Is. 11:6–9). The Hebrew word translated "iniquity" refers to moral crookedness or perversion (v. 25). The basis for the Lord's prohibitions is made clear in this chapter: "I am the LORD your God" (v. 30). The covenant people were expected to meet the ethical demands of the covenant relationship. Any nation that persists in such abominable practices as those described in this chapter is doomed for destruction (v. 28).

19:1 Leviticus 19 contains a variety of commandments or expressions of God's will for appropriate behavior toward God and with others. The basis for these commands is an individual's relationship with God: "You shall be holy, for I the LORD

HOMOSEXUALITY   *UNNATURAL AFFECTION*

Scripture states that homosexual behavior is an abomination to God. Such perversion of God's plan for marriage (Gen. 2:24) mars the image of God (Gen. 1:27), distorts the oneness God intended in the sexual union between a woman and man, and defies childbirth, thereby eventually terminating the generations.

In the Old Testament, homosexual behavior, which includes lesbianism, was forbidden, considered unclean, and was punishable by death (Lev. 18:22; 20:13). Paul states that this deviant behavior, which is the antithesis of God's design, falls under the judgment of God (Rom. 1:18–32).

God offers the individual who has participated in this sinful lifestyle mercy and forgiveness (1 Cor. 6:9, 11), but homosexual acts are an abomination and cannot be tolerated by a holy God. Although some have claimed that homosexuality has roots in a genetic mutation, there is no substantiated proof of this. God will not create a person predestined to condemnation (Ps. 139; John 3:16).

Both the Old Testament and the New Testament eliminate the possibility of excusing homosexual behavior for biological reasons. In the Old Testament, the Creator of all life charges that no one caught in an act of homosexuality can blame anyone other than himself (Lev. 20:13). He cannot blame the Creator. In the New Testament, God indicates that homosexuals can change and are not trapped by their genetic makeup (1 Cor. 6:11).

Even if a case could be made for some sort of genetic predisposition toward an aberrant behavior, this cannot remove moral responsibility nor make such behavior right. All human action is subject to the individual's will. If you make your own will subject to God's plan for your life, any type of behavior can be changed. For anyone who has engaged in homosexual behavior, God's forgiveness, grace, and mercy are always available.

See also Gen 19:1–11; 1 Kin. 14:24; 1 Cor. 6:9; 1 Tim. 1:8–11; notes on Image of God (Ps. 8); Masculinity (Gen. 2); Sexual Immorality (Prov. 6); Sin (Rom. 3)

---

and on the next day. And if any remains until the third day, it shall be burned in the fire. [7]And if it is eaten at all on the third day, it *is* an abomination. It shall not be accepted. [8]Therefore *everyone* who eats it shall bear his iniquity, because he has profaned the hallowed *offering* of the LORD; and that person shall be cut off from his people.

[9]"When you reap the harvest of your land, you shall not wholly reap the corners of your field, nor shall you gather the gleanings of your harvest. [10]And you shall not glean your vineyard, nor shall you gather *every* grape of your vineyard; you shall leave them for the poor and the stranger: I *am* the LORD your God.

[11]"You shall not steal, nor deal falsely, nor lie to one another. [12]And you shall not swear by My name falsely, nor shall you profane the name of your God: I *am* the LORD.

[13]"You shall not cheat your neighbor, nor rob *him.* The wages of him who is hired shall not remain with you all night until morning. [14]You shall not curse the deaf, nor put a stumbling block before the blind, but shall fear your God: I *am* the LORD.

[15]"You shall do no injustice in judgment. You shall not be partial to the poor, nor honor the person of the mighty. In righteousness you shall judge your neighbor. [16]You shall not go about *as a*

---

your God am holy" (v. 2). Holiness conveys the concept of being set apart from evil and for good. Verse 2 is one of the key verses related to holiness, a major theme of Leviticus (see Introduction: Purpose and Theme). The contents of this chapter can be summarized under the same two basic themes as the Ten Commandments: love for God and love for your neighbor (see Ex. 20:1–17; Matt. 22:35–40). Note direct parallels to the Ten Commandments (see Ex. 20:1–17; see chart, The Ten Commandments Throughout Scripture): honoring father and mother (v. 3), keeping the Sabbath (vv. 3, 30; see also chart, The Principle of the Sabbath), rejecting idol worship (v. 4; see Is. 42, Idolatry; Jer. 7, Paganism), not stealing (vv. 11, 35, 36), and not taking the Lord's name in vain (v. 12). The latter directive incorporates the idea that a person can "profane" God's name by a lifestyle that is contradictory to holiness as well as by verbal profanity. In addition, the poor of the land were to receive provisions (vv. 9, 10; see also Luke 9, The Homeless; 14, Poverty); employees and handicapped people were to receive right treatment (vv. 13, 14; see also

Mark 2; Acts 20, Disabilities); and strangers were to be treated properly (vv. 33, 34; see 1 Pet. 4, Hospitality). Proper sexual relationships (vv. 20–22; see Song 4, Sexuality; 1 Cor. 7, Sexual Purity), as well as showing respect toward your elders (v. 32), were emphasized. The basis for appropriate conduct is the covenant relationship with the Lord (v. 36). Obedience is a proper response to God's grace (see Philem., Obedience). Holiness or separateness is emphasized in these regulations (see Lev. 20, Holiness). In each generation believers reveal the level of their commitment by the quality of their behavior.

19:3 Mention of the mother first in this command is unusual (see Ex. 20:12; Eph. 6:2). This statement may reflect a situation in which the mother's place was considered in danger, such as in a polygamous household; it may be a deference to her; or there may be no particular reason. In any case, holiness must begin at home. Through parents a child should be able to learn what God is like and what He requires (see Ps. 127, Family).

talebearer among your people; nor shall you take a stand against the life of your neighbor: I *am* the LORD.

¹⁷'You shall not hate your brother in your heart. You shall surely rebuke your neighbor, and not bear sin because of him. ¹⁸You shall not take vengeance, nor bear any grudge against the children of your people, but you shall love your neighbor as yourself: I *am* the LORD.

¹⁹'You shall keep My statutes. You shall not let your livestock breed with another kind. You shall not sow your field with mixed seed. Nor shall a garment of mixed linen and wool come upon you.

²⁰'Whoever lies carnally with a woman who *is* betrothed to a man as a concubine, and who has not at all been redeemed nor given her freedom, for this there shall be scourging; *but* they shall not be put to death, because she was not free. ²¹And he shall bring his trespass offering to the LORD, to the door of the tabernacle of meeting, a ram as a trespass offering. ²²The priest shall make atonement for him with the ram of the trespass offering before the LORD for his sin which he has committed. And the sin which he has committed shall be forgiven him.

²³'When you come into the land, and have planted all kinds of trees for food, then you shall count their fruit as uncircumcised. Three years it shall be as uncircumcised to you. *It* shall not be eaten. ²⁴But in the fourth year all its fruit shall be holy, a praise to the LORD. ²⁵And in the fifth year you may eat its fruit, that it may yield to you its increase: I *am* the LORD your God.

²⁶'You shall not eat *anything* with the blood, nor shall you practice divination or soothsaying. ²⁷You shall not shave around the sides of your head, nor shall you disfigure the edges of your beard. ²⁸You shall not make any cuttings in your flesh for the dead, nor tattoo any marks on you: I *am* the LORD.

²⁹'Do not prostitute your daughter, to cause her to be a harlot, lest the land fall into harlotry, and the land become full of wickedness.

³⁰'You shall keep My Sabbaths and reverence My sanctuary: I *am* the LORD.

³¹'Give no regard to mediums and familiar spirits; do not seek after them, to be defiled by them: I *am* the LORD your God.

³²'You shall rise before the gray headed and honor the presence of an old man, and fear your God: I *am* the LORD.

³³'And if a stranger dwells with you in your land, you shall not mistreat him. ³⁴The stranger who dwells among you shall be to you as one born among you, and you shall love him as yourself; for you were strangers in the land of Egypt: I *am* the LORD your God.

³⁵'You shall do no injustice in judgment, in measurement of length, weight, or volume. ³⁶You shall have honest scales, honest weights, an honest ephah, and an honest hin: I *am* the LORD your God, who brought you out of the land of Egypt.

³⁷'Therefore you shall observe all My statutes and all My judgments, and perform them: I *am* the LORD.' "

Penalties for Breaking the Law

20 Then the LORD spoke to Moses, saying, ²"Again, you shall say to the children of Israel: 'Whoever of the children of Israel, or of the strangers who dwell in Israel, who gives *any* of his descendants to Molech, he shall surely be put to death. The people of the land shall stone him with stones. ³I will set My face against that man, and will cut him off from his people, because he has given *some* of his descendants to Molech, to defile My sanctuary and profane My holy name. ⁴And if the people of the land should in any way hide their eyes from the man, when he gives *some* of his descendants to Molech, and they do not kill him, ⁵then I will set My face against that man and against his family; and I will cut him off from his people, and all who prostitute themselves with him to commit harlotry with Molech.

⁶'And the person who turns to mediums and familiar spirits, to prostitute himself with them, I will set My face against that person and cut him off from his people. ⁷Consecrate yourselves therefore, and be holy, for I *am* the LORD your God. ⁸And you shall keep My statutes, and perform them: I *am* the LORD who sanctifies you.

⁹'For everyone who curses his father or his mother shall surely be put to death. He has cursed his father or his mother. His blood *shall be* upon him.

¹⁰'The man who commits adultery with *another*

20:1–27 This entire chapter reinforces unswerving obedience to God as an indication of a holy life or a life set apart to God. It bears essential similarity to Leviticus 18. However, while Leviticus 18 does not make immediate reference to punishment, Leviticus 20 regards covenant breaking from the perspective of the death penalty.

20:1–9 A strong warning against the worship of Molech, the idol of the Ammonites, appears in these verses. Those who worshiped Molech participated in child sacrifice. The death penalty is imposed on any of the people of Israel who sacrificed to Molech (v. 2). False sources of guidance and revelation also were condemned (v. 6; see Lev. 19:31). Cursing father and mother also merited the severe penalty of death (v. 9). The reference is not merely to an angry outburst from a child in a fit of temper. The word used in Hebrew can include bitterness and venom and even blaspheming the name of God (Lev. 24:11–16). Such cursing would be equivalent to putting a hex on someone, often including an appeal to a pagan deity. Failure in family relationships merits maximum punishment.

20:10–21 Adultery, incest, homosexuality, and bestiality were subject to the death penalty. The laws of the Israelites took the sacredness of marriage very seriously (see Gen. 2:24).

HOLINESS *SET APART UNTO THE LORD*

Holiness describes the character of God and the code for Christian conduct. Scripture reveals the holiness of God and expresses God's desire for His children to develop a similar holiness (Ex. 19:6; Lev. 11:44, 45; 19:2; 1 Pet. 1:15).

The word "holiness" has several different meanings. In terms of an individual's relationship to God, it means "set apart." God is the "wholly other" or totally different One, unlike any other. Holiness also describes a way to live. Christians are called to live according to a different set of principles and standards than the ungodly world—to lead a pure life in accordance with God's call, commandments, and consequences. This "set apart" life of righteousness is of God and from God (1 Cor. 1:2; 3:16, 17). A holy life is a life that always chooses to do what God desires.

Obedient believers are instructed no longer to be conformed to their old desires and patterns of thinking and behaving (1 Pet. 1:13–16). The conforming to a life of holiness, however, requires more than the will of a person to "change." It is the work of the Holy Spirit made possible through Christ's death on the Cross.

True holiness is exemplified only in God, though the Holy Spirit empowers His children to pursue holiness (1 Thess. 4:7, 8). The good news is that as we seek to be holy and invite the Holy Spirit to do His work in us, the Lord responds by cleansing us, leading us into His righteous and holy paths, and strengthening us to withstand the temptation to return to our former ungodly lives.

We cannot make ourselves holy; but, if we desire to become holy and set our wills toward following the Lord, He will make us so. The Lord never commands us to do something that He does not enable us to do (Rom. 4:21).

See also Rom. 12:1; Eph. 1:3–6; notes on Attributes of God (Is. 6); Clean vs. Unclean (Lev. 10); Fruit of the Spirit (Ps. 86; Rom. 5; 15; 1 Cor. 10; 13; Gal. 5; Eph. 4; Col. 3; 2 Thess. 1; Rev. 2); Purity (1 John 3)

---

man's wife, *he* who commits adultery with his neighbor's wife, the adulterer and the adulteress, shall surely be put to death. ¹¹The man who lies with his father's wife has uncovered his father's nakedness; both of them shall surely be put to death. Their blood *shall be* upon them. ¹²If a man lies with his daughter-in-law, both of them shall surely be put to death. They have committed perversion. Their blood *shall be* upon them. ¹³If a man lies with a male as he lies with a woman, both of them have committed an abomination. They shall surely be put to death. Their blood *shall be* upon them. ¹⁴If a man marries a woman and her mother, it *is* wickedness. They shall be burned with fire, both he and they, that there may be no wickedness among you. ¹⁵If a man mates with an animal, he shall surely be put to death, and you shall kill the animal. ¹⁶If a woman approaches any animal and mates with it, you shall kill the woman and the animal. They shall surely be put to death. Their blood *is* upon them.

¹⁷If a man takes his sister, his father's daughter or his mother's daughter, and sees her nakedness and she sees his nakedness, it *is* a wicked thing. And they shall be cut off in the sight of their people. He has uncovered his sister's nakedness. He shall bear his guilt. ¹⁸If a man lies with a woman during her sickness and uncovers her nakedness, he has exposed her flow, and she has uncovered the flow of her blood. Both of them shall be cut off from their people.

¹⁹You shall not uncover the nakedness of your mother's sister nor of your father's sister, for that would uncover his near of kin. They shall bear their guilt. ²⁰If a man lies with his uncle's wife, he has uncovered his uncle's nakedness. They shall bear their sin; they shall die childless. ²¹If a man takes his brother's wife, it *is* an unclean thing. He has uncovered his brother's nakedness. They shall be childless.

²²You shall therefore keep all My statutes and all My judgments, and perform them, that the land where I am bringing you to dwell may not vomit you out. ²³And you shall not walk in the statutes of the nation which I am casting out before you; for they commit all these things, and therefore I abhor them. ²⁴But I have said to you, "You shall inherit their land, and I will give it to you to possess, a land flowing with milk and honey." I *am* the LORD your God, who has separated you from the peoples. ²⁵You shall therefore distinguish between clean animals and unclean, between unclean birds and clean, and you shall not make yourselves abominable by beast or by bird, or by any kind of living thing that creeps on the ground, which I have separated from you as unclean. ²⁶And you shall be holy to Me, for I the LORD *am* holy, and have separated you from the peoples, that you should be Mine.

²⁷A man or a woman who is a medium, or who has familiar spirits, shall surely be put to death;

20:22–27 Summary exhortation (see Lev. 18:24–30, note). Any nation persisting in the abominable practices forbidden in this chapter ultimately will experience destruction.

they shall stone them with stones. Their blood *shall be* upon them.' "

Regulations for Conduct of Priests

21 And the LORD said to Moses, "Speak to the priests, the sons of Aaron, and say to them: 'None shall defile himself for the dead among his people, [2]except for his relatives who are nearest to him: his mother, his father, his son, his daughter, and his brother; [3]also his virgin sister who is near to him, who has had no husband, for her he may defile himself. [4]*Otherwise* he shall not defile himself, *being* a chief man among his people, to profane himself.

[5]'They shall not make any bald *place* on their heads, nor shall they shave the edges of their beards nor make any cuttings in their flesh. [6]They shall be holy to their God and not profane the name of their God, for they offer the offerings of the LORD made by fire, *and* the bread of their God; therefore they shall be holy. [7]They shall not take a wife *who is* a harlot or a defiled woman, nor shall they take a woman divorced from her husband; for *the priest*[a] is holy to his God. [8]Therefore you shall consecrate him, for he offers the bread of your God. He shall be holy to you, for I the LORD, who sanctify you, *am* holy. [9]The daughter of any priest, if she profanes herself by playing the harlot, she profanes her father. She shall be burned with fire.

[10]*He who is* the high priest among his brethren, on whose head the anointing oil was poured and who is consecrated to wear the garments, shall not uncover his head nor tear his clothes; [11]nor shall he go near any dead body, nor defile himself for his father or his mother; [12]nor shall he go out of the sanctuary, nor profane the sanctuary of his God; for the consecration of the anointing oil of his God *is* upon him: I *am* the LORD. [13]And he shall take a wife in her virginity. [14]A widow or a divorced woman or a defiled woman *or* a harlot— these he shall not marry; but he shall take a virgin of his own people as wife. [15]Nor shall he profane his posterity among his people, for I the LORD sanctify him.' "

[16]And the LORD spoke to Moses, saying, [17]"Speak to Aaron, saying: 'No man of your descendants in *succeeding* generations, who has *any* defect, may approach to offer the bread of his God. [18]For any man who has a defect shall not approach: a man blind or lame, who has a marred *face* or any *limb* too long, [19]a man who has a broken foot or broken hand, [20]or is a hunchback or a dwarf, or *a man* who has a defect in his eye, or eczema or scab, or is a eunuch. [21]No man of the descendants of Aaron the priest, who has a defect, shall come near to offer the offerings made by fire to the LORD. He has a defect; he shall not come near to offer the bread of his God. [22]He may eat the bread of his God, *both* the most holy and the holy; [23]only he shall not go near the veil or approach the altar, because he has a defect, lest he profane My sanctuaries; for I the LORD sanctify them.' "

[24]And Moses told *it* to Aaron and his sons, and to all the children of Israel.

22 Then the LORD spoke to Moses, saying, [2]"Speak to Aaron and his sons, that they separate themselves from the holy things of the children of Israel, and that they do not profane My holy name *by* what they dedicate to Me: I *am* the LORD. [3]Say to them: 'Whoever of all your descendants throughout your generations, who goes near the holy things which the children of Israel dedicate to the LORD, while he has uncleanness upon him, that person shall be cut off from My presence: I *am* the LORD.

[4]'Whatever man of the descendants of Aaron, who *is* a leper or has a discharge, shall not eat the holy offerings until he is clean. And whoever touches anything made unclean *by* a corpse, or a man who has had an emission of semen, [5]or whoever touches any creeping thing by which he would be made unclean, or any person by whom he would become unclean, whatever his uncleanness may be— [6]the person who has touched any such thing shall be unclean until evening, and shall not eat the holy *offerings* unless he washes his body with water. [7]And when the sun goes down he shall be clean; and afterward he may eat the holy

21:7 [a]Literally *he*

21:1 The priest functioned as a mediator between man and God. Such a role required holiness of life. A strict code of conduct was required for the priests. Verses 1–15 deal with the conduct of priests who currently were serving, while verses 16–23 concern the conduct of those who one day would inherit the office. Those with certain physical defects were forbidden to serve as priests. Demands requiring greater self-discipline were made on a high priest than on other priests (vv. 10–15). Greater privilege always carries greater responsibility. Jesus is the perfect High Priest (see Heb. 4:15; 7:26).

21:10 The high priest was forbidden to tear his garments. Caiaphas violated this law at the trial of Jesus (Matt. 26:65; Mark 14:63).

22:1 The various guidelines indicate that all offerings consecrated to the Lord were holy in a unique sense and thus must be protected from uncleanness. The regulations given here indicate the seriousness of worship. Reverence for the majesty of God required a proper approach to Him. Only an individual's best should be offered to the Lord (vv. 20–25). A freewill offering was a voluntary contribution. A votive offering was given in fulfillment of a previous vow. If the animal intended for the votive offering became blemished prior to sacrifice, it must be replaced (v. 23). A person could not give less than what he had promised to give (see Num. 30, Vows). To the Hebrew, a name denoted character and personality (v. 32; see Is. 45, Naming of Children).

THE PASTOR'S WIFE *THE SHEPHERDESS*

"Shepherding God's people" is a role that varies widely according to time and place, but biblical principles regarding leadership remain constant. In the Bible, "priests," "prophets," and "deacons" may refer to similar leadership positions, and many were unmarried because of difficult conditions and circumstances. Women who married these men were inevitably linked to a twofold requirement: a life denouncing worldly gain and behavior modeling the highest spiritual standards of integrity.

Often testing is required to develop total faith in God for everyday sustenance. Elisha's advice to the newly widowed wife of one prophet illustrates the faithful provision of the Lord for His servants (2 Kin. 4:1–7). Paul taught that the laborer is worthy of his hire (1 Tim. 5:18), but God's people frequently failed or were too poor to furnish sufficient upkeep.

The Mosaic Law assigned Aaron, the High Priest of Israel, and his tribe of Levi the oversight and care of all aspects of corporate worship. The Levitical priests were to represent God to the people until the Law was fulfilled in Christ. This demanded a life of holiness. Their wives were hand-picked virgins (Lev. 21:7, 13). The Law from Sinai adequately provided for support of the priests and their families (Num. 18:8–20), but in later years poverty and spiritual defection were recorded. Malachi strongly denounced divorce and personal decay in the priesthood (Mal. 2:11). In writing to Timothy, his young pastor protégé, Paul delineated qualities of reverence and self-control needed in the wives of spiritual leaders (1 Tim. 3:11, 12).

Modern church life still calls for women with a high level of commitment to serve as wives of pastors. To balance marriage, home, and family with exemplary devotion and dedication to the ministry requires unselfish teamwork and zealous compassion for the cause of Christ.

See also 1 Tim. 3:1–7; Titus 1:5–9; notes on Fruit of the Spirit (Ps. 86; Rom. 5; 15; 1 Cor. 10; 13; Gal. 5; Eph. 4; Col. 3; 2 Thess. 1; Rev. 2); Holiness (Lev. 20); Marriage (Gen. 2; 2 Sam. 6; Prov. 5; Hos. 2; Amos 3; 2 Cor. 13; Heb. 12); Wives (Prov. 31); Women's Ministries (John 4; Acts 2; 1 Cor. 11; Eph. 2; 1 Tim. 3; Titus 2)

---

offerings, because it *is* his food. ⁸Whatever dies *naturally* or is torn *by beasts* he shall not eat, to defile himself with it: I *am* the LORD.

⁹'They shall therefore keep My ordinance, lest they bear sin for it and die thereby, if they profane it: I the LORD sanctify them.

¹⁰'No outsider shall eat the holy *offering;* one who dwells with the priest, or a hired servant, shall not eat the holy thing. ¹¹But if the priest buys a person with his money, he may eat it; and one who is born in his house may eat his food. ¹²If the priest's daughter is married to an outsider, she may not eat of the holy offerings. ¹³But if the priest's daughter is a widow or divorced, and has no child, and has returned to her father's house as in her youth, she may eat her father's food; but no outsider shall eat it.

¹⁴'And if a man eats the holy *offering* unintentionally, then he shall restore a holy *offering* to the priest, and add one-fifth to it. ¹⁵They shall not profane the holy *offerings* of the children of Israel, which they offer to the LORD, ¹⁶or allow them to bear the guilt of trespass when they eat their holy *offerings;* for I the LORD sanctify them.'"

Offerings Accepted and Not Accepted

¹⁷And the LORD spoke to Moses, saying, ¹⁸"Speak to Aaron and his sons, and to all the children of Israel, and say to them: 'Whatever man of the house of Israel, or of the strangers in Israel, who offers his sacrifice for any of his vows or for any of his freewill offerings, which they offer to the LORD as a

burnt offering— ¹⁹*you shall offer* of your own free will a male without blemish from the cattle, from the sheep, or from the goats. ²⁰Whatever has a defect, you shall not offer, for it shall not be acceptable on your behalf. ²¹And whoever offers a sacrifice of a peace offering to the LORD, to fulfill *his* vow, or a freewill offering from the cattle or the sheep, it must be perfect to be accepted; there shall be no defect in it. ²²Those *that are* blind or broken or maimed, or have an ulcer or eczema or scabs, you shall not offer to the LORD, nor make an offering by fire of them on the altar to the LORD. ²³Either a bull or a lamb that has any limb too long or too short you may offer *as* a freewill offering, but for a vow it shall not be accepted.

²⁴'You shall not offer to the LORD what is bruised or crushed, or torn or cut; nor shall you make *any offering of them* in your land. ²⁵Nor from a foreigner's hand shall you offer any of these as the bread of your God, because their corruption *is* in them, *and* defects *are* in them. They shall not be accepted on your behalf.'"

²⁶And the LORD spoke to Moses, saying: ²⁷"When a bull or a sheep or a goat is born, it shall be seven days with its mother; and from the eighth day and thereafter it shall be accepted as an offering made by fire to the LORD. ²⁸*Whether it is* a cow or ewe, do not kill both her and her young on the same day. ²⁹And when you offer a sacrifice of thanksgiving to the LORD, offer *it* of your own free will. ³⁰On the same day it shall be eaten; you shall leave none of it until morning: I *am* the LORD.

[31]"Therefore you shall keep My commandments, and perform them: I *am* the LORD. [32]You shall not profane My holy name, but I will be hallowed among the children of Israel. I *am* the LORD who sanctifies you, [33]who brought you out of the land of Egypt, to be your God: I *am* the LORD."

Feasts of the LORD

23 And the LORD spoke to Moses, saying, [2]"Speak to the children of Israel, and say to them: 'The feasts of the LORD, which you shall proclaim *to be* holy convocations, these *are* My feasts.

The Sabbath

[3]'Six days shall work be done, but the seventh day *is* a Sabbath of solemn rest, a holy convocation. You shall do no work *on it;* it *is* the Sabbath of the LORD in all your dwellings.

The Passover and Unleavened Bread

[4]'These *are* the feasts of the LORD, holy convocations which you shall proclaim at their appointed times. [5]On the fourteenth *day* of the first month at twilight *is* the LORD's Passover. [6]And on the fifteenth day of the same month *is* the Feast of Unleavened Bread to the LORD; seven days you must eat unleavened bread. [7]On the first day you shall have a holy convocation; you shall do no customary work on it. [8]But you shall offer an offering made by fire to the LORD for seven days. The seventh day *shall be* a holy convocation; you shall do no customary work *on it.*' "

The Feast of Firstfruits

[9]And the LORD spoke to Moses, saying, [10]"Speak to the children of Israel, and say to them: 'When you come into the land which I give to you, and reap its harvest, then you shall bring a sheaf of the firstfruits of your harvest to the priest. [11]He shall wave the sheaf before the LORD, to be accepted on your behalf; on the day after the Sabbath the priest shall wave it. [12]And you shall offer on that day, when you wave the sheaf, a male lamb of the first year, without blemish, as a burnt offering to the LORD. [13]Its grain offering *shall be* two-tenths *of an ephah* of fine flour mixed with oil, an offering made by fire to the LORD, for a sweet aroma; and its drink offering *shall be* of wine, one-fourth of a hin. [14]You shall eat neither bread nor parched grain nor fresh grain until the same day that you have brought an offering to your God; *it shall be* a statute forever throughout your generations in all your dwellings.

The Feast of Weeks

[15]'And you shall count for yourselves from the day after the Sabbath, from the day that you brought the sheaf of the wave offering: seven Sabbaths shall be completed. [16]Count fifty days to the day after the seventh Sabbath; then you shall offer a new grain offering to the LORD. [17]You shall bring from your dwellings two wave *loaves* of two-tenths *of an ephah.* They shall be of fine flour; they shall be baked with leaven. *They are* the firstfruits to the LORD. [18]And you shall offer with the bread seven lambs of the first year, without blemish, one young bull, and two rams. They shall be *as* a burnt offering to the LORD, with their grain offering and their drink offerings, an offering made by fire for a sweet aroma to the LORD. [19]Then you shall sacrifice one kid of the goats as a sin offering, and two male lambs of the first year as a sacrifice of a peace offering. [20]The priest shall wave them with the bread of the firstfruits *as* a wave offering before the LORD, with the two lambs. They shall be holy to the LORD for the priest. [21]And you shall

---

23:1 The holy observances of Israel were times of rest, public worship, celebration, and praise (see chart, The Jewish Sacred Calendar). All adult males were to observe three annual feasts (Ex. 23:14–19; Passover or the Feast of Unleavened Bread, Pentecost or the Feast of Harvest or Firstfruits, and the Feast of Ingathering or Tabernacles). In Leviticus 23, the three major festivals are retained, but two of the feasts are expanded greatly. The celebration of the feasts indicated the symbolic dedication of all time to the Lord (see chart, The Feasts of Israel). The Sabbath also is given a place in the annual calendar of feasts (see chart, The Principle of the Sabbath). Israel observed a lunar month of 29$\frac{1}{2}$ days. The Hebrew term translated "month" literally refers to the "new moon." For the people of Israel, the day began at sundown (Gen. 1:5, 8, 13; see Ps. 55:17).

23:5–8 Passover was held in the spring on the 14th day of the first month (Abib or Nisan; see Ex. 12:2, 18; 13:3, 4; 23:15; Neh. 2:1; see chart, The Jewish Sacred Calendar). The Feast of Unleavened Bread was a week-long celebration beginning on the 15th day of the first month. Passover commemorated the release from bondage in Egypt, so named because the LORD "passed over" the Hebrew homes where the blood of the

lamb was sprinkled. The Feast of Unleavened Bread reminded the people of the food of affliction eaten in Egypt as well as of the hardships at their hurried departure from Egypt. This festival reminds Christians of Christ's deliverance of His people from the bondage of sin. In Scripture, leaven generally symbolizes evil or sin (Matt. 16:6, 11, 12; Mark 8:15; Luke 12:1; see also chart, The Feasts of Israel).

23:9–14 The Feast of Firstfruits occurred on the day after the Sabbath of Passover week. It provided an opportunity to consecrate the barley harvest to the Lord (see chart, The Feasts of Israel). The first sheaf of the grain was offered to God as a token of gratitude. After the firstfruits had been presented to the Lord, the people could enjoy the benefits of the harvest. Jesus' bodily resurrection became the firstfruits and the promise of the resurrection for Christians (1 Cor. 15:20–23).

23:15–22 The Feast of Weeks, also called Pentecost, meaning "fiftieth," fell 50 days after Passover. This harvest feast was also a firstfruits celebration because its purpose was to dedicate the firstfruits of the wheat harvest to the Lord (see chart, The Feasts of Israel). The Holy Spirit was poured out at the celebration of Pentecost (Acts 2:1–4).

proclaim on the same day *that* it is a holy convocation to you. You shall do no customary work *on it. It shall be* a statute forever in all your dwellings throughout your generations.

22'When you reap the harvest of your land, you shall not wholly reap the corners of your field when you reap, nor shall you gather any gleaning from your harvest. You shall leave them for the poor and for the stranger: I *am* the LORD your God.'"

The Feast of Trumpets

23Then the LORD spoke to Moses, saying, 24"Speak to the children of Israel, saying: 'In the seventh month, on the first *day* of the month, you shall have a sabbath-*rest*, a memorial of blowing of trumpets, a holy convocation. 25You shall do no customary work *on it;* and you shall offer an offering made by fire to the LORD.'"

The Day of Atonement

26And the LORD spoke to Moses, saying: 27"Also the tenth *day* of this seventh month *shall be* the Day of Atonement. It shall be a holy convocation for you; you shall afflict your souls, and offer an offering made by fire to the LORD. 28And you shall do no work on that same day, for it *is* the Day of Atonement, to make atonement for you before the LORD your God. 29For any person who is not afflicted *in soul* on that same day shall be cut off from his people. 30And any person who does any work on that same day, that person I will destroy from among his people. 31You shall do no manner of work; *it shall be* a statute forever throughout your generations in all your dwellings. 32It *shall be* to you a sabbath of *solemn* rest, and you shall afflict your souls; on the ninth *day* of the month at evening, from evening to evening, you shall celebrate your sabbath."

The Feast of Tabernacles

33Then the LORD spoke to Moses, saying, 34"Speak to the children of Israel, saying: 'The fifteenth day of this seventh month *shall be* the Feast of Tabernacles *for* seven days to the LORD. 35On the first day *there shall be* a holy convocation. You shall do no customary work *on it.* 36For seven days you shall offer an offering made by fire to the LORD. On the eighth day you shall have a holy convocation, and you shall offer an offering made by fire to the LORD. It *is* a sacred assembly, *and* you shall do no customary work *on it.*

37'These *are* the feasts of the LORD which you shall proclaim *to be* holy convocations, to offer an offering made by fire to the LORD, a burnt offering and a grain offering, a sacrifice and drink offerings, everything on its day— 38besides the Sabbaths of the LORD, besides your gifts, besides all your vows, and besides all your freewill offerings which you give to the LORD.

39'Also on the fifteenth day of the seventh month, when you have gathered in the fruit of the land, you shall keep the feast of the LORD *for* seven days; on the first day *there shall be* a sabbath-*rest*, and on the eighth day a sabbath-*rest*. 40And you shall take for yourselves on the first day the fruit of beautiful trees, branches of palm trees, the boughs of leafy trees, and willows of the brook; and you shall rejoice before the LORD your God for seven days. 41You shall keep it as a feast to the LORD for seven days in the year. *It shall be* a statute forever in your generations. You shall celebrate it in the seventh month. 42You shall dwell in booths for seven days. All who are native Israelites shall dwell in booths, 43that your generations may know that I made the children of Israel dwell in booths when I brought them out of the land of Egypt: I *am* the LORD your God.'"

44So Moses declared to the children of Israel the feasts of the LORD.

Care of the Tabernacle Lamps

24 Then the LORD spoke to Moses, saying: 2"Command the children of Israel that they bring to you pure oil of pressed olives for the light, to make the lamps burn continually. 3Outside the veil of the Testimony, in the tabernacle of meeting, Aaron shall be in charge of it

---

23:23–25 The Feast of Trumpets occurred on the first day of the seventh month (see chart, The Feasts of Israel). Trumpets typically were blown at the beginning of every month (Num. 10:10). The first day of the seventh month (Tishri) was especially sacred since the Day of Atonement fell during that month.

23:33–44 The Feast of Tabernacles, also known as Booths, began on the 15th day of the seventh month and lasted a week. It celebrated the end of the grape and olive harvests and also commemorated the time the people lived in tents in the wilderness. To celebrate this joyous festival, the people constructed simple outdoor huts, hence the designation "Booths." Through the celebration of these regularly appointed festivals, the people of Israel reaffirmed that the entire year belonged to the Lord (see chart, The Feasts of Israel).

24:1 Ritual and ethical stipulations included care for the tabernacle lamps and bread (vv. 1–9). The light of the lamps symbolized the presence of God, while the bread, eaten only by the priests, represented His sustenance for His people. Ethical stipulations involved the death penalty for blasphemy, as well as stipulations regarding injury and murder (vv. 10–23). Compare the Ten Commandments (Ex. 20:1–17; see chart, The Ten Commandments) and the Book of the Covenant (Ex. 20:22—23:33). Note that the Israelite mother is mentioned by name (vv. 10–16, especially v. 11); the father was an Egyptian and is unnamed. Even though resident foreigners were to keep Israelite laws (vv. 10–16), the child's heritage passed through the mother, who was an Israelite.

THE PRINCIPLE OF THE SABBATH

NAME	REFERENCE	TIME	PURPOSE	PROPHETIC SIGNIFICANCE
Sabbath (Heb. *Shabbat*)	Ex. 20:8–11; 31:12–17; Lev. 23:3; Deut. 5:12–15	The evening of the sixth day to the evening of the next day	1. To rest from work, to honor God, and to reflect on God's covenant with Israel. 2. To commemorate God's completion of creation (Gen. 2:2, 3).	Jesus is Lord of the Sabbath (Mark 2:23–28).
Sabbath Year	Ex. 23:10, 11; Lev. 25:1–7, 20–22; Deut. 15:1–18	Every seventh year	1. To allow the land to rest or lie fallow. 2. To forgive debts. 3. To release Hebrews bound to servitude because of debt.	God through Jesus Christ has given rest, forgiven us, and set us free (Matt. 11:28; John 8:36; Eph. 1:7).
Year of Jubilee, (lit."Year of the Blowing the Ram's Horn")	Lev. 25:8–55; 27:17–24; Ezek. 46:17	The fiftieth year following seven Sabbath years	1. To proclaim liberty to those who were slaves because of debt. 2. To return land to the former owners. 3. To rejoice and celebrate— with no crops to be planted.	This observance pictures the deliverance from the bondage and slavery of sin that comes in Christ (John 8:36; Gal. 5:1).

from evening until morning before the LORD continually; *it shall be* a statute forever in your generations. ⁴He shall be in charge of the lamps on the pure *gold* lampstand before the LORD continually.

The Bread of the Tabernacle

⁵"And you shall take fine flour and bake twelve cakes with it. Two-tenths *of an ephah* shall be in each cake. ⁶You shall set them in two rows, six in a row, on the pure *gold* table before the LORD. ⁷And you shall put pure frankincense on *each* row, that it may be on the bread for a memorial, an offering made by fire to the LORD. ⁸Every Sabbath he shall set it in order before the LORD continually, *being taken* from the children of Israel by an everlasting covenant. ⁹And it shall be for Aaron and his sons, and they shall eat it in a holy place; for it *is* most holy to him from the offerings of the LORD made by fire, by a perpetual statute."

The Penalty for Blasphemy

¹⁰Now the son of an Israelite woman, whose father *was* an Egyptian, went out among the children of Israel; and this Israelite *woman's* son and a man of Israel fought each other in the camp. ¹¹And the Israelite woman's son blasphemed the name *of the LORD* and cursed; and so they brought him to Moses. (His mother's name *was* Shelomith the daughter of Dibri, of the tribe of Dan.) ¹²Then

they put him in custody, that the mind of the LORD might be shown to them.

¹³And the LORD spoke to Moses, saying, ¹⁴"Take outside the camp him who has cursed; then let all who heard *him* lay their hands on his head, and let all the congregation stone him. ¹⁵"Then you shall speak to the children of Israel, saying: 'Whoever curses his God shall bear his sin. ¹⁶And whoever blasphemes the name of the LORD shall surely be put to death. All the congregation shall certainly stone him, the stranger as well as him who is born in the land. When he blasphemes the name *of the LORD*, he shall be put to death.

¹⁷'Whoever kills any man shall surely be put to death. ¹⁸Whoever kills an animal shall make it good, animal for animal.

¹⁹'If a man causes disfigurement of his neighbor, as he has done, so shall it be done to him— ²⁰fracture for fracture, eye for eye, tooth for tooth; as he has caused disfigurement of a man, so shall it be done to him. ²¹And whoever kills an animal shall restore it; but whoever kills a man shall be put to death. ²²You shall have the same law for the stranger and for one from your own country; for I *am* the LORD your God.'"

²³Then Moses spoke to the children of Israel; and they took outside the camp him who had cursed, and stoned him with stones. So the children of Israel did as the LORD commanded Moses.

The Sabbath of the Seventh Year

25 And the LORD spoke to Moses on Mount Sinai, saying, [2] "Speak to the children of Israel, and say to them: 'When you come into the land which I give you, then the land shall keep a sabbath to the LORD. [3] Six years you shall sow your field, and six years you shall prune your vineyard, and gather its fruit; [4] but in the seventh year there shall be a sabbath of solemn rest for the land, a sabbath to the LORD. You shall neither sow your field nor prune your vineyard. [5] What grows of its own accord of your harvest you shall not reap, nor gather the grapes of your untended vine, *for* it is a year of rest for the land. [6] And the sabbath *produce* of the land shall be food for you: for you, your male and female servants, your hired man, and the stranger who dwells with you, [7] for your livestock and the beasts that *are* in your land—all its produce shall be for food.

The Year of Jubilee

[8] And you shall count seven sabbaths of years for yourself, seven times seven years; and the time of the seven sabbaths of years shall be to you forty-nine years. [9] Then you shall cause the trumpet of the Jubilee to sound on the tenth *day* of the seventh month; on the Day of Atonement you shall make the trumpet to sound throughout all your land. [10] And you shall consecrate the fiftieth year, and proclaim liberty throughout *all* the land to all its inhabitants. It shall be a Jubilee for you; and each of you shall return to his possession, and each of you shall return to his family. [11] That fiftieth year shall be a Jubilee to you; in it you shall neither sow nor reap what grows of its own accord, nor gather *the grapes* of your untended vine. [12] For it *is* the Jubilee; it shall be holy to you; you shall eat its produce from the field.

[13] In this Year of Jubilee, each of you shall return to his possession. [14] And if you sell anything to your neighbor or buy from your neighbor's hand, you shall not oppress one another. [15] According to the number of years after the Jubilee you shall buy from your neighbor, and according to the number of years of crops he shall sell to you. [16] According to the multitude of years you shall increase its price, and according to the fewer number of years you shall diminish its price; for he sells to you *according* to the number *of the years* of the crops. [17] Therefore you shall not oppress one another, but you shall fear your God; for I *am* the LORD your God.

Provisions for the Seventh Year

[18] So you shall observe My statutes and keep My judgments, and perform them; and you will dwell in the land in safety. [19] Then the land will yield its fruit, and you will eat your fill, and dwell there in safety.

[20] And if you say, "What shall we eat in the seventh year, since we shall not sow nor gather in our produce?" [21] Then I will command My blessing on you in the sixth year, and it will bring forth produce enough for three years. [22] And you shall sow in the eighth year, and eat old produce until the ninth year; until its produce comes in, you shall eat *of* the old *harvest.*

Redemption of Property

[23] "The land shall not be sold permanently, for the land *is* Mine; for you *are* strangers and sojourners with Me. [24] And in all the land of your possession you shall grant redemption of the land.

[25] "If one of your brethren becomes poor, and has sold *some* of his possession, and if his redeeming relative comes to redeem it, then he may redeem what his brother sold. [26] Or if the man has no one to redeem it, but he himself becomes able to redeem it, [27] then let him count the years since its sale, and restore the remainder to the man to whom he sold it, that he may return to his possession. [28] But if he is not able to have *it* restored to himself, then what was sold shall remain in the hand of him who bought it until the Year of Jubilee; and in the Jubilee it shall be released, and he shall return to his possession.

[29] "If a man sells a house in a walled city, then he may redeem it within a whole year after it is sold; *within* a full year he may redeem it. [30] But if it is not redeemed within the space of a full year, then the house in the walled city shall belong permanently to him who bought it, throughout his generations. It shall not be released in the Jubilee. [31] However the houses of villages which have no

---

25:1–7 The Sabbath year. The land was to be allowed to lie fallow in the seventh year. By allowing the land to rest, this regulation guarded against covetousness, as well as being sound agricultural stewardship. Through this observance the people of Israel acknowledged that the land belonged to the Lord and was His gift to them. The Babylonian captivity resulted, in part, from the people's failure to observe the Sabbath years (2 Chr. 36:15–21; see chart, The Principle of the Sabbath).

25:8–17 The Year of Jubilee. Every 50th year was designated the Year of Jubilee. In this year slaves were to be freed and

properties were to revert to the families of their original owners. The basic principle is that everything belongs to the Lord (Lev. 25). Freeing both land and slaves served as reminders that God's people are stewards of His gifts (see Luke 16, Stewardship; chart, The Principle of the Sabbath).

25:25 Kinsman-redeemer (Heb. *go'el*) or redeeming relative was the nearest of kin in ancient Israel (see Ruth 2:20; 4:7, notes). His responsibilities included redeeming property in danger of being sold outside the family, providing an heir for the deceased, and avenging the blood of the deceased. Christ is the Kinsman-Redeemer of His people.

For perfection does not consist in lacerating or killing the body,
but in killing our perverse self-will.

St. Catherine of Siena

wall around them shall be counted as the fields of the country. They may be redeemed, and they shall be released in the Jubilee. ³²Nevertheless the cities of the Levites, *and* the houses in the cities of their possession, the Levites may redeem at any time. ³³And if a man purchases a house from the Levites, then the house that was sold in the city of his possession shall be released in the Jubilee; for the houses in the cities of the Levites *are* their possession among the children of Israel. ³⁴But the field of the common-land of their cities may not be sold, for it *is* their perpetual possession.

Lending to the Poor

³⁵'If one of your brethren becomes poor, and falls into poverty among you, then you shall help him, like a stranger or a sojourner, that he may live with you. ³⁶Take no usury or interest from him; but fear your God, that your brother may live with you. ³⁷You shall not lend him your money for usury, nor lend him your food at a profit. ³⁸I *am* the LORD your God, who brought you out of the land of Egypt, to give you the land of Canaan *and* to be your God.

The Law Concerning Slavery

³⁹'And if *one of* your brethren *who dwells* by you becomes poor, and sells himself to you, you shall not compel him to serve as a slave. ⁴⁰As a hired servant *and* a sojourner he shall be with you, *and* shall serve you until the Year of Jubilee. ⁴¹And *then* he shall depart from you— he and his children with him— and shall return to his own family. He shall return to the possession of his fathers. ⁴²For they *are* My servants, whom I brought out of the land of Egypt; they shall not be sold as slaves. ⁴³You shall not rule over him with rigor, but you shall fear your God. ⁴⁴And as for your male and female slaves whom you may have—from the nations that are around you, from them you may buy male and female slaves. ⁴⁵Moreover you may buy the children of the strangers who dwell among you, and their families who are with you, which they beget in your land; and they shall become your property. ⁴⁶And you may take them as an inheritance for your children after you, to inherit *them as* a possession; they shall be your permanent slaves. But regarding your brethren, the children of Israel, you shall not rule over one another with rigor.

⁴⁷'Now if a sojourner or stranger close to you becomes rich, and *one of* your brethren *who dwells* by him becomes poor, and sells himself to the stranger *or* sojourner close to you, or to a member of the stranger's family, ⁴⁸after he is sold he may be redeemed again. One of his brothers may redeem him; ⁴⁹or his uncle or his uncle's son may redeem him; or *anyone* who is near of kin to him in his family may redeem him; or if he is able he may redeem himself. ⁵⁰Thus he shall reckon with him who bought him: The price of his release shall be according to the number of years, from the year that he was sold to him until the Year of Jubilee; *it shall be* according to the time of a hired servant for him. ⁵¹If *there are* still many years *remaining,* according to them he shall repay the price of his redemption from the money with which he was bought. ⁵²And if there remain but a few years until the Year of Jubilee, then he shall reckon with him, *and* according to his years he shall repay him the price of his redemption. ⁵³He shall be with him as a yearly hired servant, and he shall not rule with rigor over him in your sight. ⁵⁴And if he is not redeemed in these *years,* then he shall be released in the Year of Jubilee— he and his children with him. ⁵⁵For the children of Israel *are* servants to Me; they *are* My servants whom I brought out of the land of Egypt: I *am* the LORD your God.

Promise of Blessing and Retribution

26 'You shall not make idols for yourselves; neither a carved image nor a *sacred* pillar shall you rear up for yourselves;
nor shall you set up an engraved stone in your land, to bow down to it;
for I *am* the LORD your God.
²You shall keep My Sabbaths and reverence My sanctuary:
I *am* the LORD.

³'If you walk in My statutes and keep My commandments, and perform them,
⁴then I will give you rain in its season, the land shall yield its produce, and the trees of the field shall yield their fruit.
⁵Your threshing shall last till the time of vintage, and the vintage shall last till the time of sowing;

26:1 Blessings and curses. This chapter records the requirements for blessings in the land (vv. 1–13) and the punishment for disobedience (vv. 14–46). Each woman must choose the way she will go. Compare also Deuteronomy 28.

EATING DISORDERS *FOOD THAT DOES NOT SATISFY*

God recognizes our intimate need and desire for food. Scripture assures us that God desires to feed us, both physically and emotionally (Matt. 6:25; 25:35). Jesus called Himself "the bread of life" and said that all who come to Him will never hunger or thirst (John 4:14; 6:35).

Yet even Moses noticed that some "shall eat and not be satisfied" (Lev. 26:26). This dissatisfaction is usually an emotional one and can manifest itself in bulimia, anorexia, or compulsive overeating. Satan can find these weak links and use them to "sift you as wheat" (Luke 22:31, 32).

Often we do not understand why we succumb to eating disorders. Even the apostle Paul struggled with repeatedly doing things he did not really want to do (Rom. 7:15–25). When seeking recovery from an eating disorder, first ask yourself, "Do I want to be made well? Am I ready to give up this frailty of character and even sin in my life?" (see John 5:6).

To find willpower against eating disorders, you must first desire to be made well, righteous, and free of your addiction. Then God is faithful and true to help you battle these problems. You provide the will, others provide encouragement, and God provides the power.

See also notes on Fitness (Phil. 1); Gluttony (Prov. 23); Nutrition (Lev. 11); Weight Control (1 Cor. 11)

---

you shall eat your bread to the full, and dwell
 in your land safely.
6I will give peace in the land, and you shall lie
 down, and none will make *you* afraid;
I will rid the land of evil beasts,
and the sword will not go through your land.
7You will chase your enemies, and they shall fall
 by the sword before you.
8Five of you shall chase a hundred, and a
 hundred of you shall put ten thousand to
 flight;
your enemies shall fall by the sword before you.
9'For I will look on you favorably and make you
 fruitful, multiply you and confirm My
 covenant with you.
10You shall eat the old harvest, and clear out the
 old because of the new.
11I will set My tabernacle among you, and My
 soul shall not abhor you.
12I will walk among you and be your God, and
 you shall be My people.
13I *am* the LORD your God, who brought you out
 of the land of Egypt, that *you* should not
 be their slaves;
I have broken the bands of your yoke and made
 you walk upright.

14'But if you do not obey Me, and do not observe
 all these commandments,
15and if you despise My statutes, or if your soul
 abhors My judgments, so that you do not
 perform all My commandments, *but* break
 My covenant,
16I also will do this to you:
I will even appoint terror over you, wasting
 disease and fever which shall consume the
 eyes and cause sorrow of heart.

And you shall sow your seed in vain, for your
 enemies shall eat it.
17I will set My face against you, and you shall be
 defeated by your enemies.
Those who hate you shall reign over you, and
 you shall flee when no one pursues you.

18'And after all this, if you do not obey Me, then I
 will punish you seven times more for your
 sins.
19I will break the pride of your power;
I will make your heavens like iron and your
 earth like bronze.
20And your strength shall be spent in vain;
for your land shall not yield its produce,
 nor shall the trees of the land yield
 their fruit.
21'Then, if you walk contrary to Me, and are not
 willing to obey Me, I will bring on you
 seven times more plagues, according to
 your sins.
22I will also send wild beasts among you, which
 shall rob you of your children, destroy
 your livestock, and make you few in
 number;
and your highways shall be desolate.

23'And if by these things you are not reformed by
 Me, but walk contrary to Me,
24then I also will walk contrary to you, and I will
 punish you yet seven times for your sins.
25And I will bring a sword against you that will
 execute the vengeance of the covenant;
when you are gathered together within your
 cities I will send pestilence among you;
and you shall be delivered into the hand of the
 enemy.

26:26 See Leviticus 26, Eating Disorders.

²⁶When I have cut off your supply of bread, ten women shall bake your bread in one oven, and they shall bring back your bread by weight, and you shall eat and not be satisfied.

²⁷'And after all this, if you do not obey Me, but walk contrary to Me,
²⁸then I also will walk contrary to you in fury; and I, even I, will chastise you seven times for your sins.
²⁹You shall eat the flesh of your sons, and you shall eat the flesh of your daughters.
³⁰I will destroy your high places, cut down your incense altars, and cast your carcasses on the lifeless forms of your idols; and My soul shall abhor you.
³¹I will lay your cities waste and bring your sanctuaries to desolation, and I will not smell the fragrance of your sweet aromas.
³²I will bring the land to desolation, and your enemies who dwell in it shall be astonished at it.
³³I will scatter you among the nations and draw out a sword after you; your land shall be desolate and your cities waste.
³⁴Then the land shall enjoy its sabbaths as long as it lies desolate and you *are* in your enemies' land; then the land shall rest and enjoy its sabbaths.
³⁵As long as *it* lies desolate it shall rest— for the time it did not rest on your sabbaths when you dwelt in it.

³⁶'And as for those of you who are left, I will send faintness into their hearts in the lands of their enemies; the sound of a shaken leaf shall cause them to flee; they shall flee as though fleeing from a sword, and they shall fall when no one pursues.
³⁷They shall stumble over one another, as it were before a sword, when no one pursues; and you shall have no *power* to stand before your enemies.
³⁸You shall perish among the nations, and the land of your enemies shall eat you up.
³⁹And those of you who are left shall waste away in their iniquity in your enemies' lands; also in their fathers' iniquities, which are with them, they shall waste away.

⁴⁰'*But* if they confess their iniquity and the iniquity of their fathers, with their unfaithfulness in which they were unfaithful to Me, and that they also have walked contrary to Me,
⁴¹and *that* I also have walked contrary to them and have brought them into the land of their enemies; if their uncircumcised hearts are humbled, and they accept their guilt—
⁴²then I will remember My covenant with Jacob, and My covenant with Isaac and My covenant with Abraham I will remember; I will remember the land.
⁴³The land also shall be left empty by them, and will enjoy its sabbaths while it lies desolate without them; they will accept their guilt, because they despised My judgments and because their soul abhorred My statutes.
⁴⁴Yet for all that, when they are in the land of their enemies, I will not cast them away, nor shall I abhor them, to utterly destroy them and break My covenant with them; for I *am* the Lᴏʀᴅ their God.
⁴⁵But for their sake I will remember the covenant of their ancestors, whom I brought out of the land of Egypt in the sight of the nations, that I might be their God: I *am* the Lᴏʀᴅ.' "

⁴⁶These *are* the statutes and judgments and laws which the Lᴏʀᴅ made between Himself and the children of Israel on Mount Sinai by the hand of Moses.

Redeeming Persons and Property Dedicated to God

27 Now the Lᴏʀᴅ spoke to Moses, saying, ²"Speak to the children of Israel, and say to them: 'When a man consecrates by a vow certain persons to the Lᴏʀᴅ, according to your valuation, ³if your valuation is of a male from twenty years old up to sixty years old, then your valuation shall be fifty shekels of silver, according to the shekel of the sanctuary. ⁴If it *is* a female, then your valuation shall be thirty shekels; ⁵and if from five years old up to twenty years old, then your valuation for a male shall be twenty shekels, and for a female ten shekels; ⁶and if from a month old up to five years old, then your valuation for a male shall be

---

27:1–34 Dedication to the Lord through vows and tithes. Everything an individual possesses, including life itself, is a gift from God. God has required that a portion of all be dedicated and consecrated to Him (see Luke 16, Stewardship; 2 Cor. 9, Giving). Vows and tithes were a means of expressing devotion to the Lord and were regarded as binding commit-ments (see Num. 30, Vows). The tithe or tenth was considered holy to the Lord. The giving of the tenth symbolized the recognition that all belonged to the Lord. This chapter consti-tutes the final section of the Holiness Code (vv. 1–46; see Lev. 17:1, note).

five shekels of silver, and for a female your valuation shall be three shekels of silver; [7]and if from sixty years old and above, if *it is* a male, then your valuation shall be fifteen shekels, and for a female ten shekels.

[8]'But if he is too poor to pay your valuation, then he shall present himself before the priest, and the priest shall set a value for him; according to the ability of him who vowed, the priest shall value him.

[9]'If *it is* an animal that men may bring as an offering to the LORD, all that *anyone* gives to the LORD shall be holy. [10]He shall not substitute it or exchange it, good for bad or bad for good; and if he at all exchanges animal for animal, then both it and the one exchanged for it shall be holy. [11]If *it is* an unclean animal which they do not offer as a sacrifice to the LORD, then he shall present the animal before the priest; [12]and the priest shall set a value for it, whether it is good or bad; as you, the priest, value it, so it shall be. [13]But if he *wants* at all *to* redeem it, then he must add one-fifth to your valuation.

[14]'And when a man dedicates his house *to be* holy to the LORD, then the priest shall set a value for it, whether it is good or bad; as the priest values it, so it shall stand. [15]If he who dedicated it *wants to* redeem his house, then he must add one-fifth of the money of your valuation to it, and it shall be his.

[16]'If a man dedicates to the LORD *part* of a field of his possession, then your valuation shall be according to the seed for it. A homer of barley seed *shall be valued* at fifty shekels of silver. [17]If he dedicates his field from the Year of Jubilee, according to your valuation it shall stand. [18]But if he dedicates his field after the Jubilee, then the priest shall reckon to him the money due according to the years that remain till the Year of Jubilee, and it shall be deducted from your valuation. [19]And if he who dedicates the field ever wishes to redeem it, then he must add one-fifth of the money of your valuation to it, and it shall belong to him. [20]But if he does not want to redeem the field, or if he has sold the field to another man, it shall not be redeemed anymore; [21]but the field, when it is released in the Jubilee, shall be holy to the LORD, as a devoted field; it shall be the possession of the priest.

[22]'And if a man dedicates to the LORD a field which he has bought, which is not the field of his possession, [23]then the priest shall reckon to him the worth of your valuation, up to the Year of Jubilee, and he shall give your valuation on that day *as* a holy *offering* to the LORD. [24]In the Year of Jubilee the field shall return to him from whom it was bought, to the one who *owned* the land as a possession. [25]And all your valuations shall be according to the shekel of the sanctuary: twenty gerahs to the shekel.

[26]'But the firstborn of the animals, which should be the LORD's firstborn, no man shall dedicate; whether *it is* an ox or sheep, it *is* the LORD's. [27]And if *it is* an unclean animal, then he shall redeem *it* according to your valuation, and shall add one-fifth to it; or if it is not redeemed, then it shall be sold according to your valuation.

[28]'Nevertheless no devoted *offering* that a man may devote to the LORD of all that he has, *both* man and beast, or the field of his possession, shall be sold or redeemed; every devoted *offering is* most holy to the LORD. [29]No person under the ban, who may become doomed to destruction among men, shall be redeemed, *but* shall surely be put to death. [30]And all the tithe of the land, *whether* of the seed of the land *or* of the fruit of the tree, *is* the LORD's. It *is* holy to the LORD. [31]If a man wants at all to redeem *any* of his tithes, he shall add one-fifth to it. [32]And concerning the tithe of the herd or the flock, of whatever passes under the rod, the tenth one shall be holy to the LORD. [33]He shall not inquire whether it is good or bad, nor shall he exchange it; and if he exchanges it at all, then both it and the one exchanged for it shall be holy; it shall not be redeemed.' "

[34]These *are* the commandments which the LORD commanded Moses for the children of Israel on Mount Sinai.

Numbers

The English title for the Book of Numbers comes from the Latin Vulgate (*Liber Numeri*) and the Greek Septuagint (*Arithmoi*). These names developed because of the two censuses (Num. 1; 26). The Hebrew Masoretic texts use the name *Bemidbar* (lit. "in the wilderness"), which is closer to a description of the book's overall content. The Hebrews also called the book *Wayyedabber* (lit. "and He said"), following their custom of using the first word of the text as a title.

AUTHOR

Although the book may have undergone editing from later scribes, Moses is the logical author because of his firsthand experience with both Israelite and Egyptian cultures. More than forty years of his life were recorded in this book. Those who dispute Mosaic authorship cite two main objections: Numbers was written as third person narrative, and Moses affirmed his own meekness (Num. 12:3). Both are easily explained. The first is a matter of style; the second was Moses' defense against unfounded accusations.

Numbers must be studied with Exodus, Leviticus, and Deuteronomy. These four books of the Pentateuch contain the same theme of revelation: God spoke to His people Israel through His prophet Moses.

DATE

The fourth book in the Pentateuch was written during Israel's wilderness experience, approximately 1445–1405 B.C.

BACKGROUND

SETTING: The Book of Numbers starts at Mt. Sinai and ends on the plains of Moab. Its narrative picks up where Exodus left off (Ex. 40:34–38; Num. 9:15–23) and connects with Deuteronomy "on this side of the Jordan in the wilderness" (Deut. 1:1).

PURPOSE: Numbers is probably the last book most people would choose for devotional reading. We could also wish for better chronology, more thorough explanations, faster-paced narrative, and less repetition. In addition, the book lacks answers to questions like these: Was the census exact and realistic or expanded to include Israel as the seed for fulfilling God's promise? Why is the climactic wilderness experience the shortest recorded section when it is the longest time period (Num. 14:34—20:21)? Why was Israel so disobedient and their murmuring so incessant when they were being led by a mighty God who had proven His provision and protection time and again? Nevertheless, for any reader willing to put forth some effort in study, Numbers is far from dull.

The apostle Paul gave two reasons that prompt a study of the Book of Numbers: "Now all these things happened to them as examples, and they were written for our admonition" (1 Cor. 10:11); "For whatever things were written before were written for our learning, that we through the patience and comfort of the Scriptures might have hope" (Rom. 15:4).

LITERARY CHARACTERISTICS: Numbers is unusual in its arrangement. The events of organization described in the first six chapters actually took place after the events described later in the book (Num. 7:1—10:10). This arrangement was probably done for emphasis so that the reader would be reminded of the completeness of God's provision as shown again and again during Israel's conquest of the Promised Land.

THEMES

Many contrasting themes are woven throughout Numbers: God's faithfulness and human failures; God's guidance and human stubbornness; God's purpose and human disobedience; God's provision and human complaints; God's holiness and human sinfulness. These themes reflect God's choice to reveal Himself to His people, to show forth His glory. God's twofold plan was *to reveal* His faithfulness through provision and deliverance and *to relate* His Law, which prepared Israel to maintain covenant relationship with the Lord and to fulfill the task of being God's people in the midst of an ungodly world.

A key thematic verse is: "Truly, as I live, all the earth shall be filled with the glory of the Lord" (Num. 14:21). God *shall* be glorified through His creation, for His purpose is to make and bring unto Himself a holy people. Making Israel a holy people was more difficult than bringing them out of Egypt and into the Promised Land because God had given man and woman the power to choose His way or their way (Gen. 2:16, 17; 3:6). Time and again His people chose disobedience rather than obedience, even though God clearly had revealed Himself and His way (see chart, Models of Obedience and Disobedience). This repetitive disobedience is counterbalanced only by God's constant mercy and faithfulness.

OUTLINE

I. Preparing to Leave Sinai (1:1—10:10)
  A. Taking the first census (1:1—4:49)
    1. The numbering "by families" (1:1—2:34)
    2. The duties of the Levites (3:1—4:49)
  B. Receiving cleansing and blessing (5:1—10:10)
    1. Purity and vows (5:1—6:21)
    2. Blessing and offerings (6:22—8:4)
    3. The cleansing of the Levites (8:5–26)
    4. The observance of Passover (9:1–14)
    5. The movement of the camp (9:15—10:10)
II. Wandering in the Wilderness (10:11—20:21)
  A. Order and opposition (10:11—12:16)
    1. Order of the march (10:11–36)
    2. Opposition within the camp (11:1–35)
    3. Opposition within the family (12:1–16)
  B. Rebellion and retribution (13:1—20:21)
    1. The provoking of rebellion (13:1–33)
    2. The requirements of holiness (14:1—16:50)
    3. The vindication of Aaron's house (17:1—18:32)
    4. The provision for purification (19:1–22)
    5. Moses' sin and God's punishment (20:1–21)
III. Making the Journey: Oppositions and Regulations (20:22—36:13)
  A. The route from Kadesh to Moab (20:22—21:35)
    1. Aaron's funeral (20:22–29)
    2. Sin: its consequence and remedy (21:1–9)
    3. Deliverance in battle (21:10–35)
  B. The encounter with Balaam the diviner (22:1—25:18)
    1. A diviner used of God (22:1—24:25)
    2. Judgment because of idolatry (25:1–18)
  C. The preparations to possess the land (26:1—36:13)
    1. The second census (26:1–65)
    2. Daughters and inheritance laws (27:1–11)
    3. Leaders, offerings, and feasts (27:12—29:40)
    4. Vows made by women (30:1–16)
    5. God's vengeance on the Midianites (31:1–54)
    6. Reviewing the journey (32:1—33:56)
    7. Boundaries and cities of refuge (34:1—36:13)

The First Census of Israel

1 Now the LORD spoke to Moses in the Wilderness of Sinai, in the tabernacle of meeting, on the first *day* of the second month, in the second year after they had come out of the land of Egypt, saying: ²"Take a census of all the congregation of the children of Israel, by their families, by their fathers' houses, according to the number of names, every male individually, ³from twenty years old and above— all who *are able to* go to war in Israel. You and Aaron shall number them by their armies. ⁴And with you there shall be a man from every tribe, each one the head of his father's house.

⁵"These are the names of the men who shall stand with you: from Reuben, Elizur the son of Shedeur; ⁶from Simeon, Shelumiel the son of Zurishaddai; ⁷from Judah, Nahshon the son of Amminadab; ⁸from Issachar, Nethanel the son of Zuar; ⁹from Zebulun, Eliab the son of Helon; ¹⁰from the sons of Joseph: from Ephraim, Elishama the son of Ammihud; from Manasseh, Gamaliel the son of Pedahzur; ¹¹from Benjamin, Abidan the son of Gideoni; ¹²from Dan, Ahiezer the son of Ammishaddai; ¹³from Asher, Pagiel the son of Ocran; ¹⁴from Gad, Eliasaph the son of Deuel;ᵃ ¹⁵from Naphtali, Ahira the son of Enan." ¹⁶These *were* chosen from the congregation, leaders of their fathers' tribes, heads of the divisions in Israel.

¹⁷Then Moses and Aaron took these men who had been mentioned by name, ¹⁸and they assembled all the congregation together on the first *day* of the second month; and they recited their ancestry by families, by their fathers' houses, according to the number of names, from twenty years old and above, each one individually. ¹⁹As the LORD commanded Moses, so he numbered them in the Wilderness of Sinai.

²⁰Now the children of Reuben, Israel's oldest son, their genealogies by their families, by their fathers' house, according to the number of names, every male individually, from twenty years old and above, all who *were able to* go to war: ²¹those who were numbered of the tribe of Reuben *were* forty-six thousand five hundred.

²²From the children of Simeon, their genealogies by their families, by their fathers' house, of those who were numbered, according to the number of names, every male individually, from twenty years old and above, all who *were able to* go to war: ²³those who were numbered of the tribe of Simeon *were* fifty-nine thousand three hundred.

²⁴From the children of Gad, their genealogies by their families, by their fathers' house, according to the number of names, from twenty years old and above, all who *were able to* go to war: ²⁵those who were numbered of the tribe of Gad *were* forty-five thousand six hundred and fifty.

²⁶From the children of Judah, their genealogies by their families, by their fathers' house, according to the number of names, from twenty years old and above, all who *were able to* go to war: ²⁷those who were numbered of the tribe of Judah *were* seventy-four thousand six hundred.

²⁸From the children of Issachar, their genealogies by their families, by their fathers' house, according to the number of names, from twenty years old and above, all who *were able to* go to war: ²⁹those who were numbered of the tribe of Issachar *were* fifty-four thousand four hundred.

³⁰From the children of Zebulun, their genealogies by their families, by their fathers' house, according to the number of names, from twenty years old and above, all who *were able to* go to war: ³¹those who were numbered of the tribe of Zebulun *were* fifty-seven thousand four hundred.

³²From the sons of Joseph, the children of Ephraim, their genealogies by their families, by their fathers' house, according to the number of names, from twenty years old and above, all who *were able to* go to war: ³³those who were numbered of the tribe of Ephraim *were* forty thousand five hundred.

³⁴From the children of Manasseh, their genealogies by their families, by their fathers' house, according to the number of names, from twenty years old and above, all who *were able to* go

---

1:14 ᵃSpelled *Reuel* in 2:14

1:1 The setting and time are announced; the main characters are introduced. God spoke to an individual, Moses, in an established place of meeting—the tabernacle—erected one month prior (see Ex. 29:42; 40:17). The Israelites had not left Sinai, but God's place of revelation had moved from the mount to "the wilderness."

1:2 The census was to be done in an orderly manner by family units, not by economic or political groupings. "Fathers' houses" were subdivisions within the tribes. This enrollment was to determine military strength (v. 3). God's purpose for an army was the defense of His people and the future conquest of Canaan.

1:4–17 Each household head was "mentioned by name." This

tribal prince would assist in the census. Tribal lineage was through the father.

1:20 The order by which the tribes were listed varies slightly (Num. 1; 2). Reuben, the eldest, was listed first here, but Judah heads the list in the next chapter because his division camped east of the tabernacle and led the march (see Num. 10:14; charts, The Encampment of the Tribes of Israel; Marching Order of the Tribes of Israel). Numbering was done by thousands, hundreds, and fifties as military units. Figures in this census can be compared with an earlier one (Ex. 30:11–16; 38:26) and a later one (Num. 26:1–56). Their purposes differ: The Exodus census was to determine their atonement offering; the first census in Numbers, military strength; the second, land grants.

to war: ³⁵those who were numbered of the tribe of Manasseh *were* thirty-two thousand two hundred.

³⁶From the children of Benjamin, their genealogies by their families, by their fathers' house, according to the number of names, from twenty years old and above, all who *were able to* go to war: ³⁷those who were numbered of the tribe of Benjamin *were* thirty-five thousand four hundred.

³⁸From the children of Dan, their genealogies by their families, by their fathers' house, according to the number of names, from twenty years old and above, all who *were able to* go to war: ³⁹those who were numbered of the tribe of Dan *were* sixty-two thousand seven hundred.

⁴⁰From the children of Asher, their genealogies by their families, by their fathers' house, according to the number of names, from twenty years old and above, all who *were able to* go to war: ⁴¹those who were numbered of the tribe of Asher *were* forty-one thousand five hundred.

⁴²From the children of Naphtali, their genealogies by their families, by their fathers' house, according to the number of names, from twenty years old and above, all who *were able to* go to war: ⁴³those who were numbered of the tribe of Naphtali *were* fifty-three thousand four hundred.

⁴⁴These are the ones who were numbered, whom Moses and Aaron numbered, with the leaders of Israel, twelve men, each one representing his father's house. ⁴⁵So all who were numbered of the children of Israel, by their fathers' houses, from twenty years old and above, all who *were able to* go to war in Israel— ⁴⁶all who were numbered were six hundred and three thousand five hundred and fifty.

⁴⁷But the Levites were not numbered among them by their fathers' tribe; ⁴⁸for the LORD had spoken to Moses, saying: ⁴⁹"Only the tribe of Levi you shall not number, nor take a census of them among the children of Israel; ⁵⁰but you shall appoint the Levites over the tabernacle of the Testimony, over all its furnishings, and over all things

that belong to it; they shall carry the tabernacle and all its furnishings; they shall attend to it and camp around the tabernacle. ⁵¹And when the tabernacle is to go forward, the Levites shall take it down; and when the tabernacle is to be set up, the Levites shall set it up. The outsider who comes near shall be put to death. ⁵²The children of Israel shall pitch their tents, everyone by his own camp, everyone by his own standard, according to their armies; ⁵³but the Levites shall camp around the tabernacle of the Testimony, that there may be no wrath on the congregation of the children of Israel; and the Levites shall keep charge of the tabernacle of the Testimony."

⁵⁴Thus the children of Israel did; according to all that the LORD commanded Moses, so they did.

The Tribes and Leaders by Armies

2And the LORD spoke to Moses and Aaron, saying: ²"Everyone of the children of Israel shall camp by his own standard, beside the emblems of his father's house; they shall camp some distance from the tabernacle of meeting. ³On the east side, toward the rising of the sun, those of the standard of the forces with Judah shall camp according to their armies; and Nahshon the son of Amminadab *shall be* the leader of the children of Judah." ⁴And his army was numbered at seventy-four thousand six hundred.

⁵"Those who camp next to him *shall be* the tribe of Issachar, and Nethanel the son of Zuar *shall be* the leader of the children of Issachar." ⁶And his army was numbered at fifty-four thousand four hundred.

⁷"Then *comes* the tribe of Zebulun, and Eliab the son of Helon *shall be* the leader of the children of Zebulun." ⁸And his army was numbered at fifty-seven thousand four hundred. ⁹All who were numbered according to their armies of the forces with Judah, one hundred and eighty-six thousand four hundred—these shall break camp first.

¹⁰"On the south side *shall be* the standard of the

1:46 The Bible records that Jacob entered Egypt with 70 members of his family (Ex. 1:5). According to statistics, if there were 600,000 males, 20 years and older, there would be one million males total and about one million females. Though some question these numbers as unrealistic, such phenomenal growth among the Israelites is not impossible, especially when the miraculous blessing of God upon the people is considered (see Num. 11:21). Though many efforts have been made to explain away the figures, the best approach is to accept the numbers as given.

1:47–54 Exempt from military duty, the Levites would "attend to" the tabernacle diligently as their own possession (v. 50). They camped "around the tabernacle" to prevent desecration of the place that God's glory sanctified (Ex. 29:43; see chart, The Encampment of the Tribes of Israel). Disobedience would incur God's "wrath" (Num. 1:53).

2:2 God organized Israel's encampment with military preci-

sion: the 12 tribes formed four large divisions of an army preparing for war against the nations of Canaan. Each tribe knew its position under the unit's "standard" (a large field sign), and all camped in reference to the tabernacle (see chart, The Encampment of the Tribes of Israel). "Some distance" may be one mile (2,000 cubits, Josh. 3:4). The emphasis is that the ark and tabernacle were representations of God's revelation of Himself and thus treated as holy. Jesus Christ is the literal fulfillment of the ark and the tabernacle (John 1:14; see chart, The Plan of the Tabernacle).

2:9 Judah's forces would "break camp first" (see chart, Marching Order of the Tribes of Israel). Although Reuben was the eldest son, Judah had the responsibility for leadership. This position may relate to the blessing given earlier by Jacob (Gen. 49:10) and repeated in Balaam's fourth oracle, which refers to the kings and ultimately to the King of Kings who will come from the tribe of Judah (Num. 24:17).

THE ENCAMPMENT OF THE TRIBES OF ISRAEL

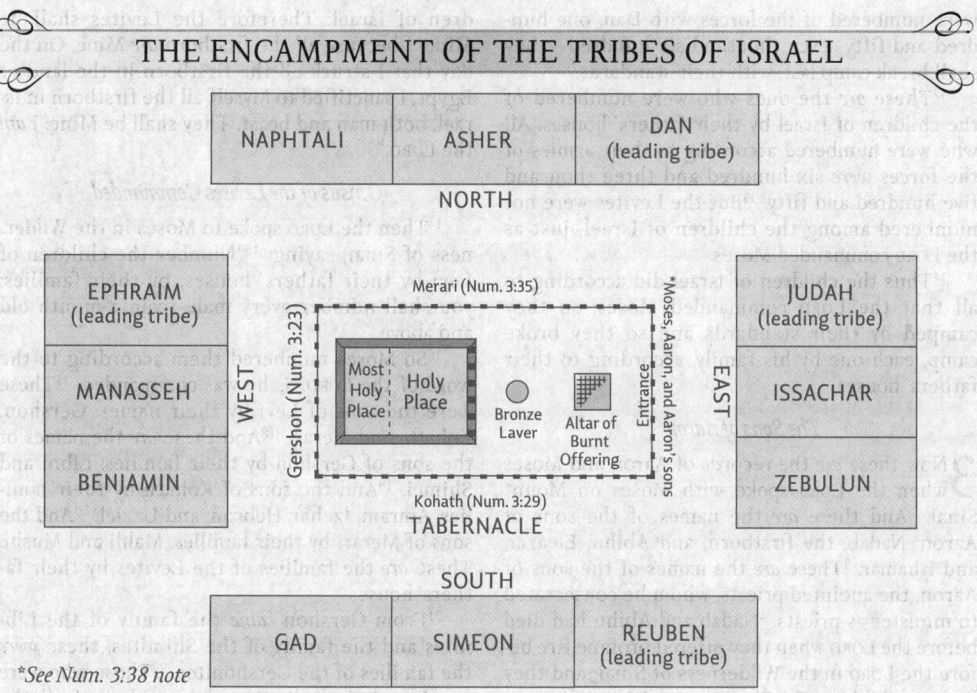

NAPHTALI ASHER DAN (leading tribe)

NORTH

EPHRAIM (leading tribe)

MANASSEH

BENJAMIN

WEST Gershon (Num. 3:23)

Merari (Num. 3:35)

Most Holy Place | Holy Place

Bronze Laver

Altar of Burnt Offering

Entrance

Kohath (Num. 3:29)

TABERNACLE

*Moses, Aaron, and Aaron's sons

EAST

JUDAH (leading tribe)

ISSACHAR

ZEBULUN

SOUTH

*See Num. 3:38 note

GAD SIMEON REUBEN (leading tribe)

forces with Reuben according to their armies, and the leader of the children of Reuben *shall be* Elizur the son of Shedeur." [11]And his army was numbered at forty-six thousand five hundred.

[12]"Those who camp next to him *shall be* the tribe of Simeon, and the leader of the children of Simeon *shall be* Shelumiel the son of Zurishaddai." [13]And his army was numbered at fifty-nine thousand three hundred.

[14]"Then *comes* the tribe of Gad, and the leader of the children of Gad *shall be* Eliasaph the son of Reuel."[a] [15]And his army was numbered at forty-five thousand six hundred and fifty. [16]"All who were numbered according to their armies of the forces with Reuben, one hundred and fifty-one thousand four hundred and fifty—they shall be the second to break camp.

[17]"And the tabernacle of meeting shall move out with the camp of the Levites in the middle of the camps; as they camp, so they shall move out, everyone in his place, by their standards.

[18]"On the west side *shall be* the standard of the forces with Ephraim according to their armies, and the leader of the children of Ephraim *shall be* Elishama the son of Ammihud." [19]And his army was numbered at forty thousand five hundred.

[20]"Next to him *comes* the tribe of Manasseh,

and the leader of the children of Manasseh *shall be* Gamaliel the son of Pedahzur." [21]And his army was numbered at thirty-two thousand two hundred.

[22]"Then *comes* the tribe of Benjamin, and the leader of the children of Benjamin *shall be* Abidan the son of Gideoni." [23]And his army was numbered at thirty-five thousand four hundred. [24]"All who were numbered according to their armies of the forces with Ephraim, one hundred and eight thousand one hundred—they shall be the third to break camp.

[25]"The standard of the forces with Dan *shall be* on the north side according to their armies, and the leader of the children of Dan *shall be* Ahiezer the son of Ammishaddai." [26]And his army was numbered at sixty-two thousand seven hundred.

[27]"Those who camp next to him *shall be* the tribe of Asher, and the leader of the children of Asher *shall be* Pagiel the son of Ocran." [28]And his army was numbered at forty-one thousand five hundred.

[29]"Then *comes* the tribe of Naphtali, and the leader of the children of Naphtali *shall be* Ahira the son of Enan." [30]And his army was numbered at fifty-three thousand four hundred. [31]"All who

2:14 [a]Spelled *Deuel* in 1:14 and 7:42

2:17 Whether the Israelites were camping or marching, the tabernacle was centrally located, symbolic of God's presence

in their midst (see Ps. 46:4, 5; charts, The Encampment of the Tribes of Israel, Marching Order of the Tribes of Israel).

were numbered of the forces with Dan, one hundred and fifty-seven thousand six hundred—they shall break camp last, with their standards."

³²These *are* the ones who were numbered of the children of Israel by their fathers' houses. All who were numbered according to their armies of the forces *were* six hundred and three thousand five hundred and fifty. ³³But the Levites were not numbered among the children of Israel, just as the LORD commanded Moses.

³⁴Thus the children of Israel did according to all that the LORD commanded Moses; so they camped by their standards and so they broke camp, each one by his family, according to their fathers' houses.

The Sons of Aaron

3 Now these *are* the records of Aaron and Moses when the LORD spoke with Moses on Mount Sinai. ²And these *are* the names of the sons of Aaron: Nadab, the firstborn, and Abihu, Eleazar, and Ithamar. ³These *are* the names of the sons of Aaron, the anointed priests, whom he consecrated to minister as priests. ⁴Nadab and Abihu had died before the LORD when they offered profane fire before the LORD in the Wilderness of Sinai; and they had no children. So Eleazar and Ithamar ministered as priests in the presence of Aaron their father.

The Levites Serve in the Tabernacle

⁵And the LORD spoke to Moses, saying: ⁶"Bring the tribe of Levi near, and present them before Aaron the priest, that they may serve him. ⁷And they shall attend to his needs and the needs of the whole congregation before the tabernacle of meeting, to do the work of the tabernacle. ⁸Also they shall attend to all the furnishings of the tabernacle of meeting, and to the needs of the children of Israel, to do the work of the tabernacle. ⁹And you shall give the Levites to Aaron and his sons; they *are* given entirely to himᵃ from among the children of Israel. ¹⁰So you shall appoint Aaron and his sons, and they shall attend to their priesthood; but the outsider who comes near shall be put to death."

¹¹Then the LORD spoke to Moses, saying: ¹²"Now behold, I Myself have taken the Levites from among the children of Israel instead of every firstborn who opens the womb among the children of Israel. Therefore the Levites shall be Mine, ¹³because all the firstborn *are* Mine. On the day that I struck all the firstborn in the land of Egypt, I sanctified to Myself all the firstborn in Israel, both man and beast. They shall be Mine: I *am* the LORD."

Census of the Levites Commanded

¹⁴Then the LORD spoke to Moses in the Wilderness of Sinai, saying: ¹⁵"Number the children of Levi by their fathers' houses, by their families; you shall number every male from a month old and above."

¹⁶So Moses numbered them according to the word of the LORD, as he was commanded. ¹⁷These were the sons of Levi by their names: Gershon, Kohath, and Merari. ¹⁸And these *are* the names of the sons of Gershon by their families: Libni and Shimei. ¹⁹And the sons of Kohath by their families: Amram, Izehar, Hebron, and Uzziel. ²⁰And the sons of Merari by their families: Mahli and Mushi. These *are* the families of the Levites by their fathers' houses.

²¹From Gershon *came* the family of the Libnites and the family of the Shimites; these *were* the families of the Gershonites. ²²Those who were numbered, according to the number of all the males from a month old and above—of those who were numbered *there were* seven thousand five hundred. ²³The families of the Gershonites were to camp behind the tabernacle westward. ²⁴And the leader of the father's house of the Gershonites *was* Eliasaph the son of Lael. ²⁵The duties of the children of Gershon in the tabernacle of meeting *included* the tabernacle, the tent with its covering, the screen for the door of the tabernacle of meeting, ²⁶the screen for the door of the court, the hangings of the court which *are* around the tabernacle and the altar, and their cords, according to all the work relating to them.

²⁷From Kohath *came* the family of the Amramites, the family of the Izharites, the family of the Hebronites, and the family of the Uzzielites; these *were* the families of the Kohathites. ²⁸According to the number of all the males, from a month old and above, *there were* eight thousand sixᵃ hundred keeping charge of the sanctuary.

···················
3:9 ᵃSamaritan Pentateuch and Septuagint read *Me.*   3:28 ᵃSome manuscripts of the Septuagint read *three.*

3:1–4 These records established the line of priests, explaining why Eleazar and Ithamar, and not their older brothers, were ordained for priesthood. This was no casual appointment: God had an order for worship. When Nadab and Abihu offered alien or unauthorized fire, God smote them with fire, leaving them without heirs (see Ex. 30:9). To be barren was a reproach to women, and to die childless was a judgment upon these two men whose sons would have succeeded them as priests (see 1 Sam. 1:6, note).

3:11–13 God adopted the whole tribe of Levi as His own; they belonged to Him. The "firstborn in Israel" were to be consecrated to the Lord. Here He is putting the entire tribe of Levi in that place (see v. 41).

3:14, 15 A separate census was taken among the Levites, beginning the count at "a month old," the age at which the firstborn was to be given to the Lord or "redeemed" (vv. 15, 40, 43; Num. 18:16).

²⁹The families of the children of Kohath were to camp on the south side of the tabernacle. ³⁰And the leader of the fathers' house of the families of the Kohathites *was* Elizaphan the son of Uzziel. ³¹Their duty *included* the ark, the table, the lampstand, the altars, the utensils of the sanctuary with which they ministered, the screen, and all the work relating to them.

³²And Eleazar the son of Aaron the priest *was to be* chief over the leaders of the Levites, *with* oversight of those who kept charge of the sanctuary.

³³From Merari *came* the family of the Mahlites and the family of the Mushites; these *were* the families of Merari. ³⁴And those who were numbered, according to the number of all the males from a month old and above, *were* six thousand two hundred. ³⁵The leader of the fathers' house of the families of Merari *was* Zuriel the son of Abihail. These *were* to camp on the north side of the tabernacle. ³⁶And the appointed duty of the children of Merari *included* the boards of the tabernacle, its bars, its pillars, its sockets, its utensils, all the work relating to them, ³⁷and the pillars of the court all around, with their sockets, their pegs, and their cords.

³⁸Moreover those who were to camp before the tabernacle on the east, before the tabernacle of meeting, *were* Moses, Aaron, and his sons, keeping charge of the sanctuary, to meet the needs of the children of Israel; but the outsider who came near was to be put to death. ³⁹All who were numbered of the Levites, whom Moses and Aaron numbered at the commandment of the LORD, by their families, all the males from a month old and above, *were* twenty-two thousand.

Levites Dedicated Instead of the Firstborn

⁴⁰Then the LORD said to Moses: "Number all the firstborn males of the children of Israel from a month old and above, and take the number of their names. ⁴¹And you shall take the Levites for Me—I *am* the LORD—instead of all the firstborn among the children of Israel, and the livestock of the Levites instead of all the firstborn among livestock of the children of Israel." ⁴²So Moses numbered all the firstborn among the children of Israel, as the LORD commanded him. ⁴³And all the firstborn males, according to the number of names from a month old and above, of those who were numbered of them, were twenty-two thousand two hundred and seventy-three.

⁴⁴Then the LORD spoke to Moses, saying: ⁴⁵"Take the Levites instead of all the firstborn among the children of Israel, and the livestock of the Levites instead of their livestock. The Levites shall be Mine: I *am* the LORD. ⁴⁶And for the redemption of the two hundred and seventy-three of the firstborn of the children of Israel, who are more than the number of the Levites, ⁴⁷you shall take five shekels for each one individually; you shall take *them* in the currency of the shekel of the sanctuary, the shekel of twenty gerahs. ⁴⁸And you shall give the money, with which the excess number of them is redeemed, to Aaron and his sons."

⁴⁹So Moses took the redemption money from those who were over and above those who were redeemed by the Levites. ⁵⁰From the firstborn of the children of Israel he took the money, one thousand three hundred and sixty-five *shekels*, according to the shekel of the sanctuary. ⁵¹And Moses gave their redemption money to Aaron and his sons, according to the word of the LORD, as the LORD commanded Moses.

Duties of the Sons of Kohath

4 Then the LORD spoke to Moses and Aaron, saying: ²"Take a census of the sons of Kohath from among the children of Levi, by their families, by their fathers' house, ³from thirty years old and above, even to fifty years old, all who enter the service to do the work in the tabernacle of meeting.

⁴"This *is* the service of the sons of Kohath in the tabernacle of meeting, *relating to* the most holy things: ⁵When the camp prepares to journey, Aaron and his sons shall come, and they shall take down the covering veil and cover the ark of the Testimony with it. ⁶Then they shall put on it a covering of badger skins, and spread over *that* a cloth entirely of blue; and they shall insert its poles.

⁷"On the table of showbread they shall spread a blue cloth, and put on it the dishes, the pans, the bowls, and the pitchers for pouring; and the showbread[a] shall be on it. ⁸They shall spread over them a scarlet cloth, and cover the same with a covering of badger skins; and they shall insert its poles. ⁹And they shall take a blue cloth and cover the lampstand of the light, with its lamps, its wick-trimmers, its trays, and all its oil vessels, with

4:7 [a]Literally *the continual bread*

3:46–51 The sanctuary shekel, mentioned first in Exodus 30:13, was used to redeem or buy back each Israelite firstborn after the number of firstborn exceeded the number of Levites. The amount of "five shekels" probably represented about six months of salary for the average worker (see chart, Money and Measurements in the Bible). For women, the story of Ruth and Boaz gives special meaning to redemption (see

Ruth 4). Ultimately, Christ is the only satisfactory redemption price for every person.

4:7 Whether the Israelites were camped or marching, the "showbread" was never moved from the table until it was renewed every Sabbath (Lev. 24:8; see chart, The Furniture of the Tabernacle).

which they service it. ¹⁰Then they shall put it with all its utensils in a covering of badger skins, and put *it* on a carrying beam.

¹¹"Over the golden altar they shall spread a blue cloth, and cover it with a covering of badger skins; and they shall insert its poles. ¹²Then they shall take all the utensils of service with which they minister in the sanctuary, put *them* in a blue cloth, cover them with a covering of badger skins, and put *them* on a carrying beam. ¹³Also they shall take away the ashes from the altar, and spread a purple cloth over it. ¹⁴They shall put on it all its implements with which they minister there—the firepans, the forks, the shovels, the basins, and all the utensils of the altar—and they shall spread on it a covering of badger skins, and insert its poles. ¹⁵And when Aaron and his sons have finished covering the sanctuary and all the furnishings of the sanctuary, when the camp is set to go, then the sons of Kohath shall come to carry *them;* but they shall not touch any holy thing, lest they die.

"These *are* the things in the tabernacle of meeting which the sons of Kohath are to carry.

¹⁶"The appointed duty of Eleazar the son of Aaron the priest *is* the oil for the light, the sweet incense, the daily grain offering, the anointing oil, the oversight of all the tabernacle, of all that *is* in it, with the sanctuary and its furnishings."

¹⁷Then the LORD spoke to Moses and Aaron, saying: ¹⁸"Do not cut off the tribe of the families of the Kohathites from among the Levites; ¹⁹but do this in regard to them, that they may live and not die when they approach the most holy things: Aaron and his sons shall go in and appoint each of them to his service and his task. ²⁰But they shall not go in to watch while the holy things are being covered, lest they die."

Duties of the Sons of Gershon

²¹Then the LORD spoke to Moses, saying: ²²"Also take a census of the sons of Gershon, by their fathers' house, by their families. ²³From thirty years old and above, even to fifty years old, you shall number them, all who enter to perform the service, to do the work in the tabernacle of meeting. ²⁴This *is* the service of the families of the Gershonites, in serving and carrying: ²⁵They shall carry the curtains of the tabernacle and the tabernacle of meeting *with* its covering, the covering of badger skins that *is* on it, the screen for the door of the tabernacle of meeting, ²⁶the screen for the door of the gate of the court, the hangings of the court which *are* around the tabernacle and altar, and their cords, all the furnishings for their service and all that is made for these things: so shall they serve.

²⁷"Aaron and his sons shall assign all the service of the sons of the Gershonites, all their tasks and all their service. And you shall appoint to

them all their tasks as their duty. ²⁸This *is* the service of the families of the sons of Gershon in the tabernacle of meeting. And their duties *shall be* under the authorityᵃ of Ithamar the son of Aaron the priest.

Duties of the Sons of Merari

²⁹"*As for* the sons of Merari, you shall number them by their families and by their fathers' house. ³⁰From thirty years old and above, even to fifty years old, you shall number them, everyone who enters the service to do the work of the tabernacle of meeting. ³¹And this *is* what they must carry as all their service for the tabernacle of meeting: the boards of the tabernacle, its bars, its pillars, its sockets, ³²and the pillars around the court with their sockets, pegs, and cords, with all their furnishings and all their service; and you shall assign *to each man* by name the items he must carry. ³³This *is* the service of the families of the sons of Merari, as all their service for the tabernacle of meeting, under the authorityᵃ of Ithamar the son of Aaron the priest."

Census of the Levites

³⁴And Moses, Aaron, and the leaders of the congregation numbered the sons of the Kohathites by their families and by their fathers' house, ³⁵from thirty years old and above, even to fifty years old, everyone who entered the service for work in the tabernacle of meeting; ³⁶and those who were numbered by their families were two thousand seven hundred and fifty. ³⁷These *were* the ones who were numbered of the families of the Kohathites, all who might serve in the tabernacle of meeting, whom Moses and Aaron numbered according to the commandment of the LORD by the hand of Moses.

³⁸And those who were numbered of the sons of Gershon, by their families and by their fathers' house, ³⁹from thirty years old and above, even to fifty years old, everyone who entered the service for work in the tabernacle of meeting— ⁴⁰those who were numbered by their families, by their fathers' house, were two thousand six hundred and thirty. ⁴¹These *are* the ones who were numbered of the families of the sons of Gershon, of all who might serve in the tabernacle of meeting, whom Moses and Aaron numbered according to the commandment of the LORD.

⁴²Those of the families of the sons of Merari who were numbered, by their families, by their fathers' house, ⁴³from thirty years old and above, even to fifty years old, everyone who entered the service for work in the tabernacle of meeting— ⁴⁴those who were numbered by their families were three thousand two hundred. ⁴⁵These *are* the ones

4:28; 33 ᵃLiterally *hand*

Numbers is neither dull nor boring, but has great truths for our Christian walk.

Ann L. Coker

who were numbered of the families of the sons of Merari, whom Moses and Aaron numbered according to the word of the LORD by the hand of Moses.

⁴⁶All who were numbered of the Levites, whom Moses, Aaron, and the leaders of Israel numbered, by their families and by their fathers' houses, ⁴⁷from thirty years old and above, even to fifty years old, everyone who came to do the work of service and the work of bearing burdens in the tabernacle of meeting— ⁴⁸those who were numbered were eight thousand five hundred and eighty.

⁴⁹According to the commandment of the LORD they were numbered by the hand of Moses, each according to his service and according to his task; thus were they numbered by him, as the LORD commanded Moses.

Ceremonially Unclean Persons Isolated

5 And the LORD spoke to Moses, saying: ²"Command the children of Israel that they put out of the camp every leper, everyone who has a discharge, and whoever becomes defiled by a corpse. ³You shall put out both male and female; you shall put them outside the camp, that they may not defile their camps in the midst of which I dwell." ⁴And the children of Israel did so, and put them outside the camp; as the LORD spoke to Moses, so the children of Israel did.

Confession and Restitution

⁵Then the LORD spoke to Moses, saying, ⁶"Speak to the children of Israel: 'When a man or woman commits any sin that men commit in unfaithfulness against the LORD, and that person is guilty, ⁷then he shall confess the sin which he has committed. He shall make restitution for his tres-

pass in full, plus one-fifth of it, and give *it* to the one he has wronged. ⁸But if the man has no relative to whom restitution may be made for the wrong, the restitution for the wrong *must go* to the LORD for the priest, in addition to the ram of the atonement with which atonement is made for him. ⁹Every offering of all the holy things of the children of Israel, which they bring to the priest, shall be his. ¹⁰And every man's holy things shall be his; whatever any man gives the priest shall be his.'"

Concerning Unfaithful Wives

¹¹And the LORD spoke to Moses, saying, ¹²"Speak to the children of Israel, and say to them: 'If any man's wife goes astray and behaves unfaithfully toward him, ¹³and a man lies with her carnally, and it is hidden from the eyes of her husband, and it is concealed that she has defiled herself, and *there was* no witness against her, nor was she caught— ¹⁴if the spirit of jealousy comes upon him and he becomes jealous of his wife, who has defiled herself; or if the spirit of jealousy comes upon him and he becomes jealous of his wife, although she has not defiled herself— ¹⁵then the man shall bring his wife to the priest. He shall bring the offering required for her, one-tenth of an ephah of barley meal; he shall pour no oil on it and put no frankincense on it, because it *is* a grain offering of jealousy, an offering for remembering, for bringing iniquity to remembrance.

¹⁶'And the priest shall bring her near, and set her before the LORD. ¹⁷The priest shall take holy water in an earthen vessel, and take some of the dust that is on the floor of the tabernacle and put *it* into the water. ¹⁸Then the priest shall stand the woman before the LORD, uncover the woman's

---

4:49 Each closing verse of chapters 1—4 refers to God's command and Israel's obedience. God assigned tasks for assembling and dismantling the tabernacle both to family groups and to individuals, each doing his assignment for the effectiveness of the whole. This concept is seen in Paul's analogy of the body and the church (1 Cor. 12:12–31).

5:5–10 The sin of theft or vandalism required full restitution of what was taken plus 20 percent for the wronged party or relative (v. 7). When no relatives existed, payment along with atonement went to the priests, God's representatives, as a step in restoring broken fellowship with the Lord (v. 8).

5:15 Various interpretations have been given for the use of barley meal rather than the usual meal-offering of fine wheat flour. While barley was fodder for animals, the wife was not associated with a beast. The sacrifice was only for suspicion

of a violation since her guilt had not been proven. Barley meal was used more often by the poor without oil or frankincense mixed with it. The latter was commonly associated with God and prayer. The object of the procedure was to confirm or disprove grounds for the husband's jealousy.

5:18 Bitter water was described as "holy water" (v. 17) because it had been dedicated to God. The water probably was taken from the bronze laver, which held water for ritual cleansing in the tabernacle (see chart, The Furniture of the Tabernacle), and then it was mixed with dust from the tabernacle floor (v. 17), which was also considered holy because it had been in God's presence. The mixture was not done in a special vessel used in worship but in a common earthen vessel (v. 17). The emphasis is not on the taste of the water but on its potential to bear a bitter curse. The exact meaning of uncovering the

head, and put the offering for remembering in her hands, which *is* the grain offering of jealousy. And the priest shall have in his hand the bitter water that brings a curse. ¹⁹And the priest shall put her under oath, and say to the woman, "If no man has lain with you, and if you have not gone astray to uncleanness *while* under your husband's *authority*, be free from this bitter water that brings a curse. ²⁰But if you have gone astray *while* under your husband's *authority*, and if you have defiled yourself and some man other than your husband has lain with you"— ²¹then the priest shall put the woman under the oath of the curse, and he shall say to the woman— "the LORD make you a curse and an oath among your people, when the LORD makes your thigh rot and your belly swell; ²²and may this water that causes the curse go into your stomach, and make *your* belly swell and *your* thigh rot."

'Then the woman shall say, "Amen, so be it."

²³'Then the priest shall write these curses in a book, and he shall scrape *them* off into the bitter water. ²⁴And he shall make the woman drink the bitter water that brings a curse, and the water that brings the curse shall enter her *to become* bitter. ²⁵Then the priest shall take the grain offering of jealousy from the woman's hand, shall wave the offering before the LORD, and bring it to the altar; ²⁶and the priest shall take a handful of the offering, as its memorial portion, burn *it* on the altar, and afterward make the woman drink the water. ²⁷When he has made her drink the water, then it shall be, if she has defiled herself and behaved unfaithfully toward her husband, that the water that brings a curse will enter her *and become* bitter, and her belly will swell, her thigh will rot, and the woman will become a curse among her people. ²⁸But if the woman has not defiled herself, and is clean, then she shall be free and may conceive children.

²⁹'This *is* the law of jealousy, when a wife, *while* under her husband's *authority*, goes astray and defiles herself, ³⁰or when the spirit of jealousy comes upon a man, and he becomes jealous of his wife; then he shall stand the woman before the LORD, and the priest shall execute all this law upon her. ³¹Then the man shall be free from iniquity, but that woman shall bear her guilt.' "

The Law of the Nazirite

6 Then the LORD spoke to Moses, saying, ²"Speak to the children of Israel, and say to them: 'When either a man or woman consecrates an offering to take the vow of a Nazirite, to separate himself to the LORD, ³he shall separate himself from wine and *similar* drink; he shall drink neither vinegar made from wine nor vinegar made from *similar* drink; neither shall he drink any grape juice, nor eat fresh grapes or raisins. ⁴All the days of his separation he shall eat nothing that is produced by the grapevine, from seed to skin.

⁵'All the days of the vow of his separation no razor shall come upon his head; until the days are fulfilled for which he separated himself to the LORD, he shall be holy. *Then* he shall let the locks of the hair of his head grow. ⁶All the days that he separates himself to the LORD he shall not go near a dead body. ⁷He shall not make himself unclean even for his father or his mother, for his brother or his sister, when they die, because his separation to God *is* on his head. ⁸All the days of his separation he shall be holy to the LORD.

⁹'And if anyone dies very suddenly beside him, and he defiles his consecrated head, then he shall shave his head on the day of his cleansing; on the

---

woman's head is not clear (see chart, Head Coverings for Women). The unbinding of hair could merely be a sign of openness on her part before the Lord and the people, or more likely the loosely hanging hair was a sign of mourning, meaning here that, if guilty, she would be in mourning (Lev. 10:6; 13:45; 21:10). The unbound hair could also be a sign of uncleanness or a sign of shame. This "bitter water" would act as poison to bring harm to the guilty; or again, if guilty, the woman's life would be made bitter by the "holy water."

5:19, 20 The phrase under her husband refers to their mutual commitment. This "law of jealousy" (v. 29) was important because of its association with the covenant relationship between God and His people and the faithfulness required of both relationships.

5:27, 28 Punishment for guilt, when taken in context, was probably related to sterility or miscarriage and the blessing of innocence to conception and fruitfulness.

5:30, 31 The woman suffered, whether guilty or innocent, because of the stigma of any trial.

6:1, 2 In biblical usage, vows were only made to a deity. This passage is one of only two references in which a person is dedicated to the Lord by a vow (see Lev. 27:1–8; Num. 30, Vows). The Nazirite vow was a dedication of the individual to God and could be made voluntarily by a man or woman. The terms could be for a limited time or for life, with positive and negative aspects of separation. First, the positive is stated: separation "to the Lord," a phrase repeated nine times in this chapter.

6:3–8 Restrictions were also part of the Nazirite's separation:

1) not eating or drinking the fruit of the vine, whether wine, vinegar, or juice (a greater restriction than for priests; see Lev. 10:9);

2) not cutting the hair, which was recognized as an outward sign of consecration;

3) not touching a corpse, even of a family member.

6:9–12 Although God did not require the vow, He did not take it lightly when a vow was broken. Therefore, if a Nazirite accidently had contact with death, cleansing through atonement must be made with proper offerings.

seventh day he shall shave it. [10]Then on the eighth day he shall bring two turtledoves or two young pigeons to the priest, to the door of the tabernacle of meeting; [11]and the priest shall offer one as a sin offering and *the* other as a burnt offering, and make atonement for him, because he sinned in regard to the corpse; and he shall sanctify his head that same day. [12]He shall consecrate to the LORD the days of his separation, and bring a male lamb in its first year as a trespass offering; but the former days shall be lost, because his separation was defiled.

[13]'Now this *is* the law of the Nazirite: When the days of his separation are fulfilled, he shall be brought to the door of the tabernacle of meeting. [14]And he shall present his offering to the LORD: one male lamb in its first year without blemish as a burnt offering, one ewe lamb in its first year without blemish as a sin offering, one ram without blemish as a peace offering, [15]a basket of unleavened bread, cakes of fine flour mixed with oil, unleavened wafers anointed with oil, and their grain offering with their drink offerings.

[16]'Then the priest shall bring *them* before the LORD and offer his sin offering and his burnt offering; [17]and he shall offer the ram as a sacrifice of a peace offering to the LORD, with the basket of unleavened bread; the priest shall also offer its grain offering and its drink offering. [18]Then the Nazirite shall shave his consecrated head *at* the door of the tabernacle of meeting, and shall take the hair from his consecrated head and put *it* on the fire which is under the sacrifice of the peace offering.

[19]And the priest shall take the boiled shoulder of the ram, one unleavened cake from the basket, and one unleavened wafer, and put *them* upon the hands of the Nazirite after he has shaved his consecrated *hair,* [20]and the priest shall wave them as a wave offering before the LORD; they *are* holy for the priest, together with the breast of the wave offering and the thigh of the heave offering. After that the Nazirite may drink wine.'

[21]"This is the law of the Nazirite who vows to the LORD the offering for his separation, and besides that, whatever else his hand is able to provide; according to the vow which he takes, so he must do according to the law of his separation."

The Priestly Blessing

[22]And the LORD spoke to Moses, saying: [23]"Speak to Aaron and his sons, saying, 'This is the way you shall bless the children of Israel. Say to them:

[24]"The LORD bless you and keep you;
[25]The LORD make His face shine upon you,
And be gracious to you;
[26]The LORD lift up His countenance upon you,
And give you peace." '

[27]"So they shall put My name on the children of Israel, and I will bless them."

Offerings of the Leaders

7 Now it came to pass, when Moses had finished setting up the tabernacle, that he anointed it and consecrated it and all its furnishings, and the altar and all its utensils; so he anointed them and consecrated them. [2]Then the leaders of Israel, the heads of their fathers' houses, who *were* the leaders of the tribes and over those who were numbered, made an offering. [3]And they brought their offering before the LORD, six covered carts and twelve oxen, a cart for *every* two of the leaders, and for each one an ox; and they presented them before the tabernacle.

[4]Then the LORD spoke to Moses, saying, [5]"Accept *these* from them, that they may be used in doing the work of the tabernacle of meeting; and you shall give them to the Levites, *to* every man according to his service." [6]So Moses took the carts and the oxen, and gave them to the Levites. [7]Two carts and four oxen he gave to the sons of Gershon, according to their service; [8]and four carts and eight oxen he gave to the sons of Merari, according to their service, under the authority[a] of Ithamar the son of Aaron the priest. [9]But to the sons of Kohath he gave none, because theirs *was* the service of the holy things, *which* they carried on their shoulders.

[10]Now the leaders offered the dedication *offering* for the altar when it was anointed; so the leaders offered their offering before the altar. [11]For

7:8 [a]Literally *hand*

6:18 Shaving the head meant the Nazirite was released from his vow, free to resume former practices or to make another vow (vv. 19, 20).

6:22–27 Only when the camp was in order and they were prepared for the march did God give His blessing of protection, presence, and peace through this benediction that was pronounced by the priests. By this blessing, God linked His name—that is, His character—with the people of Israel (vv. 24–26).

7:1 Anointing to signify separation unto God was given to the

"furnishings" as well as to the priests who performed the tabernacle service. These objects of worship were no longer for "common" use, but were "holy" and set apart for God (see Ex. 40:9, 10).

7:10 Offerings (vv. 10–83). The 12 tribal leaders, each listed by name, presented 12 identical offerings, each recorded separately, each of equal value, given on 12 successive days (v. 11). God was pleased with these gifts as expressions of worship from their glad hearts.

the LORD said to Moses, "They shall offer their offering, one leader each day, for the dedication of the altar."

12And the one who offered his offering on the first day *was* Nahshon the son of Amminadab, from the tribe of Judah. 13His offering *was* one silver platter, the weight of which *was* one hundred and thirty *shekels,* and one silver bowl of seventy shekels, according to the shekel of the sanctuary, both of them full of fine flour mixed with oil as a grain offering; 14one gold pan of ten *shekels,* full of incense; 15one young bull, one ram, and one male lamb in its first year, as a burnt offering; 16one kid of the goats as a sin offering; 17and for the sacrifice of peace offerings: two oxen, five rams, five male goats, and five male lambs in their first year. This *was* the offering of Nahshon the son of Amminadab.

18On the second day Nethanel the son of Zuar, leader of Issachar, presented *an offering.* 19For his offering he offered one silver platter, the weight of which *was* one hundred and thirty *shekels,* and one silver bowl of seventy shekels, according to the shekel of the sanctuary, both of them full of fine flour mixed with oil as a grain offering; 20one gold pan of ten *shekels,* full of incense; 21one young bull, one ram, and one male lamb in its first year, as a burnt offering; 22one kid of the goats as a sin offering; 23and as the sacrifice of peace offerings: two oxen, five rams, five male goats, and five male lambs in their first year. This *was* the offering of Nethanel the son of Zuar.

24On the third day Eliab the son of Helon, leader of the children of Zebulun, *presented an offering.* 25His offering *was* one silver platter, the weight of which *was* one hundred and thirty *shekels,* and one silver bowl of seventy shekels, according to the shekel of the sanctuary, both of them full of fine flour mixed with oil as a grain offering; 26one gold pan of ten *shekels,* full of incense; 27one young bull, one ram, and one male lamb in its first year, as a burnt offering; 28one kid of the goats as a sin offering; 29and for the sacrifice of peace offerings: two oxen, five rams, five male goats, and five male lambs in their first year. This *was* the offering of Eliab the son of Helon.

30On the fourth day Elizur the son of Shedeur, leader of the children of Reuben, *presented an offering.* 31His offering *was* one silver platter, the weight of which *was* one hundred and thirty *shekels,* and one silver bowl of seventy shekels, according to the shekel of the sanctuary, both of them full of fine flour mixed with oil as a grain offering; 32one gold pan of ten *shekels,* full of incense; 33one young bull, one ram, and one male

lamb in its first year, as a burnt offering; 34one kid of the goats as a sin offering; 35and as the sacrifice of peace offerings: two oxen, five rams, five male goats, and five male lambs in their first year. This *was* the offering of Elizur the son of Shedeur.

36On the fifth day Shelumiel the son of Zurishaddai, leader of the children of Simeon, *presented an offering.* 37His offering *was* one silver platter, the weight of which *was* one hundred and thirty *shekels,* and one silver bowl of seventy shekels, according to the shekel of the sanctuary, both of them full of fine flour mixed with oil as a grain offering; 38one gold pan of ten *shekels,* full of incense; 39one young bull, one ram, and one male lamb in its first year, as a burnt offering; 40one kid of the goats as a sin offering; 41and as the sacrifice of peace offerings: two oxen, five rams, five male goats, and five male lambs in their first year. This *was* the offering of Shelumiel the son of Zurishaddai.

42On the sixth day Eliasaph the son of Deuel,[a] leader of the children of Gad, *presented an offering.* 43His offering *was* one silver platter, the weight of which *was* one hundred and thirty *shekels,* and one silver bowl of seventy shekels, according to the shekel of the sanctuary, both of them full of fine flour mixed with oil as a grain offering; 44one gold pan of ten *shekels,* full of incense; 45one young bull, one ram, and one male lamb in its first year, as a burnt offering; 46one kid of the goats as a sin offering; 47and as the sacrifice of peace offerings: two oxen, five rams, five male goats, and five male lambs in their first year. This *was* the offering of Eliasaph the son of Deuel.

48On the seventh day Elishama the son of Ammihud, leader of the children of Ephraim, *presented an offering.* 49His offering *was* one silver platter, the weight of which *was* one hundred and thirty *shekels,* and one silver bowl of seventy shekels, according to the shekel of the sanctuary, both of them full of fine flour mixed with oil as a grain offering; 50one gold pan of ten *shekels,* full of incense; 51one young bull, one ram, and one male lamb in its first year, as a burnt offering; 52one kid of the goats as a sin offering; 53and as the sacrifice of peace offerings: two oxen, five rams, five male goats, and five male lambs in their first year. This *was* the offering of Elishama the son of Ammihud.

54On the eighth day Gamaliel the son of Pedahzur, leader of the children of Manasseh, *presented an offering.* 55His offering *was* one silver platter, the weight of which *was* one hundred and

7:42 aSpelled *Reuel* in 2:14

7:13 Purpose in worship. Bowls were necessary to hold grain offerings, an indication that each gift had purpose, and all gifts were set apart for God's purposes in worship.

What a tragedy when high hopes are defeated by low efforts!

Rhonda Kelley

thirty *shekels*, and one silver bowl of seventy shekels, according to the shekel of the sanctuary, both of them full of fine flour mixed with oil as a grain offering; [56]one gold pan of ten *shekels*, full of incense; [57]one young bull, one ram, and one male lamb in its first year, as a burnt offering; [58]one kid of the goats as a sin offering; [59]and as the sacrifice of peace offerings: two oxen, five rams, five male goats, and five male lambs in their first year. This *was* the offering of Gamaliel the son of Pedahzur.

[60]On the ninth day Abidan the son of Gideoni, leader of the children of Benjamin, *presented an offering.* [61]His offering *was* one silver platter, the weight of which *was* one hundred and thirty *shekels*, and one silver bowl of seventy shekels, according to the shekel of the sanctuary, both of them full of fine flour mixed with oil as a grain offering; [62]one gold pan of ten *shekels*, full of incense; [63]one young bull, one ram, and one male lamb in its first year, as a burnt offering; [64]one kid of the goats as a sin offering; [65]and as the sacrifice of peace offerings: two oxen, five rams, five male goats, and five male lambs in their first year. This *was* the offering of Abidan the son of Gideoni.

[66]On the tenth day Ahiezer the son of Ammishaddai, leader of the children of Dan, *presented an offering.* [67]His offering *was* one silver platter, the weight of which *was* one hundred and thirty *shekels*, and one silver bowl of seventy shekels, according to the shekel of the sanctuary, both of them full of fine flour mixed with oil as a grain offering; [68]one gold pan of ten *shekels*, full of incense; [69]one young bull, one ram, and one male lamb in its first year, as a burnt offering; [70]one kid of the goats as a sin offering; [71]and as the sacrifice of peace offerings: two oxen, five rams, five male goats, and five male lambs in their first year. This *was* the offering of Ahiezer the son of Ammishaddai.

[72]On the eleventh day Pagiel the son of Ocran, leader of the children of Asher, *presented an offering.* [73]His offering *was* one silver platter, the weight of which *was* one hundred and thirty *shekels*, and one silver bowl of seventy shekels, according to the shekel of the sanctuary, both of them full of fine flour mixed with oil as a grain offering; [74]one gold pan of ten *shekels*, full of incense; [75]one young bull, one ram, and one male lamb in its first year, as a burnt offering; [76]one kid

of the goats as a sin offering; [77]and as the sacrifice of peace offerings: two oxen, five rams, five male goats, and five male lambs in their first year. This *was* the offering of Pagiel the son of Ocran.

[78]On the twelfth day Ahira the son of Enan, leader of the children of Naphtali, *presented an offering.* [79]His offering *was* one silver platter, the weight of which *was* one hundred and thirty *shekels*, and one silver bowl of seventy shekels, according to the shekel of the sanctuary, both of them full of fine flour mixed with oil as a grain offering; [80]one gold pan of ten *shekels*, full of incense; [81]one young bull, one ram, and one male lamb in its first year, as a burnt offering; [82]one kid of the goats as a sin offering; [83]and as the sacrifice of peace offerings: two oxen, five rams, five male goats, and five male lambs in their first year. This *was* the offering of Ahira the son of Enan.

[84]This *was* the dedication *offering* for the altar from the leaders of Israel, when it was anointed: twelve silver platters, twelve silver bowls, and twelve gold pans. [85]Each silver platter *weighed* one hundred and thirty *shekels* and each bowl seventy *shekels.* All the silver of the vessels *weighed* two thousand four hundred *shekels,* according to the shekel of the sanctuary. [86]The twelve gold pans full of incense *weighed* ten *shekels* apiece, according to the shekel of the sanctuary; all the gold of the pans *weighed* one hundred and twenty *shekels.* [87]All the oxen for the burnt offering *were* twelve young bulls, the rams twelve, the male lambs in their first year twelve, with their grain offering, and the kids of the goats as a sin offering twelve. [88]And all the oxen for the sacrifice of peace offerings were twenty-four bulls, the rams sixty, the male goats sixty, and the lambs in their first year sixty. This *was* the dedication *offering* for the altar after it was anointed.

[89]Now when Moses went into the tabernacle of meeting to speak with Him, he heard the voice of One speaking to him from above the mercy seat that *was* on the ark of the Testimony, from between the two cherubim; thus He spoke to him.

Arrangement of the Lamps

8 And the LORD spoke to Moses, saying: [2]"Speak to Aaron, and say to him, 'When you arrange the lamps, the seven lamps shall give light in front of the lampstand.'" [3]And Aaron did so; he arranged the lamps to face toward the front of the lampstand, as

---

7:89 God spoke. God was heard, not seen. Fellowship with God followed worship and sacrificial offerings (see Mal. 3:10).

8:1–4 Lampstand (see chart, The Furniture of the Tabernacle).

the LORD commanded Moses. [4]Now this workmanship of the lampstand *was* hammered gold; from its shaft to its flowers it *was* hammered work. According to the pattern which the LORD had shown Moses, so he made the lampstand.

Cleansing and Dedication of the Levites

[5]Then the LORD spoke to Moses, saying: [6]"Take the Levites from among the children of Israel and cleanse them *ceremonially.* [7]Thus you shall do to them to cleanse them: Sprinkle water of purification on them, and let them shave all their body, and let them wash their clothes, and *so* make themselves clean. [8]Then let them take a young bull with its grain offering of fine flour mixed with oil, and you shall take another young bull as a sin offering. [9]And you shall bring the Levites before the tabernacle of meeting, and you shall gather together the whole congregation of the children of Israel. [10]So you shall bring the Levites before the LORD, and the children of Israel shall lay their hands on the Levites; [11]and Aaron shall offer the Levites before the LORD *like* a wave offering from the children of Israel, that they may perform the work of the LORD. [12]Then the Levites shall lay their hands on the heads of the young bulls, and you shall offer one as a sin offering and the other as a burnt offering to the LORD, to make atonement for the Levites.

[13]"And you shall stand the Levites before Aaron and his sons, and then offer them *like* a wave offering to the LORD. [14]Thus you shall separate the Levites from among the children of Israel, and the Levites shall be Mine. [15]After that the Levites shall go in to service the tabernacle of meeting. So you shall cleanse them and offer them *like* a wave offering. [16]For they *are* wholly given to Me from among the children of Israel; I have taken them for Myself instead of all who open the womb, the firstborn of all the children of Israel. [17]For all the firstborn among the children of Israel *are* Mine, *both* man and beast; on the day that I struck all the firstborn in the land of Egypt I sanctified them to Myself. [18]I have taken the Levites instead of all the firstborn of the children of Israel. [19]And I have given the Levites as a gift to Aaron and his sons from among the children of Israel, to do the work for the children of Israel in the tabernacle of meeting, and to make atonement for the children of Israel, that there be no plague among the children of Israel when the children of Israel come near the sanctuary."

[20]Thus Moses and Aaron and all the congregation of the children of Israel did to the Levites; according to all that the LORD commanded Moses concerning the Levites, so the children of Israel did to them. [21]And the Levites purified themselves and washed their clothes; then Aaron presented them *like* a wave offering before the LORD, and Aaron made atonement for them to cleanse them. [22]After that the Levites went in to do their work in the tabernacle of meeting before Aaron and his sons; as the LORD commanded Moses concerning the Levites, so they did to them.

[23]Then the LORD spoke to Moses, saying, [24]"This *is* what *pertains* to the Levites: From twenty-five years old and above one may enter to perform service in the work of the tabernacle of meeting; [25]and at the age of fifty years they must cease performing this work, and shall work no more. [26]They may minister with their brethren in the tabernacle of meeting, to attend to needs, but they *themselves* shall do no work. Thus you shall do to the Levites regarding their duties."

The Second Passover

9 Now the LORD spoke to Moses in the Wilderness of Sinai, in the first month of the second year after they had come out of the land of Egypt, saying: [2]"Let the children of Israel keep the Passover at its appointed time. [3]On the fourteenth day of this month, at twilight, you shall keep it at its appointed time. According to all its rites and ceremonies you shall keep it." [4]So Moses told the children of Israel that they should keep the Passover. [5]And they kept the Passover on the fourteenth day of the first month, at twilight, in the Wilderness of Sinai; according to all that the LORD commanded Moses, so the children of Israel did.

[6]Now there were *certain* men who were defiled

8:7 Preparation for worship was customary in order to prepare the Levites to come close to holy objects and God Himself. There were three steps: sprinkling with "water of purification," shaving themselves completely, and washing their clothes. This procedure was similar to the cleansing required by lepers (see Ex. 19:10, 11; Lev. 14:8, 9; 2 Chr. 30:13–27).

8:11 The Levites were symbolically offered to the Lord with thanksgiving and praise. The Israelites had every reason to thank God for the Levites who would make possible their access to God by making atonement for them in the tabernacle (v. 19).

8:16 Firstborn is generally restricted in the Pentateuch to identify the firstborn son (Ex. 13:13). If "all who open the womb" and "firstborn" were meant to be equivalent, then daughters would be included. In any case, the Levites have been chosen by God to be substitutes for the firstborn of Israel (Num. 8:17, 18).

8:24 The work of the tabernacle required vigor. Here age 25 is the starting point; whereas elsewhere it is set at 30 (Num. 4:3) and later by David at 20 (1 Chr. 23:27).

9:1 God appointed a time for observance of the Passover in order to remember their deliverance from Egypt through the blood of the slain lamb, the mark of God's covenant with His people. Christ is the door of the New Covenant, marked with His own blood, which was shed for our deliverance from sin (John 10:9).

9:6–14 Although these men knew that they could not participate in the Passover observance, they asked why they could

by a human corpse, so that they could not keep the Passover on that day; and they came before Moses and Aaron that day. [7]And those men said to him, "We *became* defiled by a human corpse. Why are we kept from presenting the offering of the LORD at its appointed time among the children of Israel?"

[8]And Moses said to them, "Stand still, that I may hear what the LORD will command concerning you."

[9]Then the LORD spoke to Moses, saying, [10]"Speak to the children of Israel, saying: 'If anyone of you or your posterity is unclean because of a corpse, or *is* far away on a journey, he may still keep the LORD's Passover. [11]On the fourteenth day of the second month, at twilight, they may keep it. They shall eat it with unleavened bread and bitter herbs. [12]They shall leave none of it until morning, nor break one of its bones. According to all the ordinances of the Passover they shall keep it. [13]But the man who *is* clean and is not on a journey, and ceases to keep the Passover, that same person shall be cut off from among his people, because he did not bring the offering of the LORD at its appointed time; that man shall bear his sin.

[14]And if a stranger dwells among you, and would keep the LORD's Passover, he must do so according to the rite of the Passover and according to its ceremony; you shall have one ordinance, both for the stranger and the native of the land.' "

The Cloud and the Fire

[15]Now on the day that the tabernacle was raised up, the cloud covered the tabernacle, the tent of the Testimony; from evening until morning it was above the tabernacle like the appearance of fire. [16]So it was always: the cloud covered it *by day,* and the appearance of fire by night. [17]Whenever the cloud was taken up from above the tabernacle, after that the children of Israel would journey; and in the place where the cloud settled, there the children of Israel would pitch their tents. [18]At the command of the LORD the children of Israel would journey, and at the command of the LORD they would camp; as long as the cloud stayed above the tabernacle they remained encamped. [19]Even when the cloud continued long, many days above the tabernacle, the children of Israel kept the charge of the LORD and did not journey. [20]So it was, when the cloud was above the tabernacle a few days: according to the command of the LORD they would remain encamped, and according to the command of the LORD they would journey. [21]So it was, when the cloud remained only from evening until morning: when the cloud was taken up in the morning, then they would journey; whether by day or by night, whenever the cloud was taken up, they would journey. [22]*Whether it was* two days, a month, or a year that the cloud remained above the tabernacle, the children of Israel would remain encamped and not journey; but when it was taken up, they would journey. [23]At the command of the LORD they remained encamped, and at the command of the LORD they journeyed; they kept the charge of the LORD, at the command of the LORD by the hand of Moses.

Two Silver Trumpets

10 And the LORD spoke to Moses, saying: [2]"Make two silver trumpets for yourself; you shall make them of hammered work; you shall use them for calling the congregation and for directing the movement of the camps. [3]When they blow both of them, all the congregation shall gather before you at the door of the tabernacle of meeting. [4]But if they blow *only* one, then the leaders, the heads of the divisions of Israel, shall gather to you. [5]When you sound the advance, the camps that lie on the east side shall then begin their journey. [6]When you sound the advance the second time, then the camps that lie on the south side shall begin their journey; they shall sound the call for them to begin their journeys. [7]And when the assembly is to be gathered together, you shall blow, but not sound the advance. [8]The sons of Aaron, the priests, shall blow the trumpets; and these shall be to you as an ordinance forever throughout your generations.

[9]"When you go to war in your land against the enemy who oppresses you, then you shall sound an alarm with the trumpets, and you will be remembered before the LORD your God, and you will be saved from your enemies. [10]Also in the day of your gladness, in your appointed feasts, and at the beginning of your months, you shall blow the trumpets over your burnt offerings and over the sacrifices of your peace offerings; and they shall be a memorial for you before your God: I *am* the LORD your God."

---

not. Moses brought the matter to the Lord. The solution was to allow the men to celebrate the Passover one month later, giving time for their purification. The solution made no provision for those who failed to celebrate the Passover without cause, but it did make provision for circumcised strangers to participate (v. 13; see also Ex. 12:48, 49).

9:15 The day here is the same as in Exodus 40:17. "Above the tabernacle" is repeated six times (vv. 15–22). The cloud, which at night had "the appearance of fire," was the visible manifestation of God's presence. No other nation could boast the presence of God in their midst (see Rom. 9:4).

9:23 The moving and settling of the cloud signified God's interaction with His people, giving direction ("encamped" or "journeyed"), revelation ("at the command of the Lord"), and communion ("by the hand of Moses").

10:11, 12 Nineteen days after the census date, God commanded Israel to "set out" (Num. 1:1). These verses summarize the wilderness journey (see Num. 10:13—12:16).

Departure from Sinai

11Now it came to pass on the twentieth *day* of the second month, in the second year, that the cloud was taken up from above the tabernacle of the Testimony. 12And the children of Israel set out from the Wilderness of Sinai on their journeys; then the cloud settled down in the Wilderness of Paran. 13So they started out for the first time according to the command of the LORD by the hand of Moses.

14The standard of the camp of the children of Judah set out first according to their armies; over their army was Nahshon the son of Amminadab. 15Over the army of the tribe of the children of Issachar *was* Nethanel the son of Zuar. 16And over the army of the tribe of the children of Zebulun *was* Eliab the son of Helon.

17Then the tabernacle was taken down; and the sons of Gershon and the sons of Merari set out, carrying the tabernacle.

18And the standard of the camp of Reuben set out according to their armies; over their army *was* Elizur the son of Shedeur. 19Over the army of the tribe of the children of Simeon *was* Shelumiel the son of Zurishaddai. 20And over the army of the tribe of the children of Gad *was* Eliasaph the son of Deuel.

21Then the Kohathites set out, carrying the holy things. (The tabernacle would be prepared for their arrival.)

22And the standard of the camp of the children of Ephraim set out according to their armies; over their army *was* Elishama the son of Ammihud. 23Over the army of the tribe of the children of Manasseh *was* Gamaliel the son of Pedahzur. 24And over the army of the tribe of the children of Benjamin *was* Abidan the son of Gideoni.

25Then the standard of the camp of the children of Dan (the rear guard of all the camps) set out according to their armies; over their army *was* Ahiezer the son of Ammishaddai. 26Over the army of the tribe of the children of Asher *was* Pagiel the son of Ocran. 27And over the army of the tribe of the children of Naphtali *was* Ahira the son of Enan.

28Thus *was* the order of march of the children of Israel, according to their armies, when they began their journey.

29Now Moses said to Hobab the son of Reuel[a] the Midianite, Moses' father-in-law, "We are setting out for the place of which the LORD said, 'I will give it to you.' Come with us, and we will treat you well; for the LORD has promised good things to Israel."

30And he said to him, "I will not go, but I will depart to my *own* land and to my relatives."

31So *Moses* said, "Please do not leave, inasmuch as you know how we are to camp in the wilderness, and you can be our eyes. 32And it shall be, if you go with us—indeed it shall be—that whatever good the LORD will do to us, the same we will do to you."

33So they departed from the mountain of the LORD on a journey of three days; and the ark of the covenant of the LORD went before them for the three days' journey, to search out a resting place for them. 34And the cloud of the LORD *was* above them by day when they went out from the camp.

35So it was, whenever the ark set out, that Moses said:

"Rise up, O LORD!
Let Your enemies be scattered,
And let those who hate You flee before You."

36And when it rested, he said:

"Return, O LORD,
To the many thousands of Israel."

The People Complain

11 Now *when* the people complained, it displeased the LORD; for the LORD heard *it,* and His anger was aroused. So the fire of the LORD burned among them, and consumed *some* in the outskirts of the camp. 2Then the people cried out to Moses, and when Moses prayed to the LORD, the fire was quenched. 3So he called the name of the place Taberah,[a] because the fire of the LORD had burned among them.

4Now the mixed multitude who were among them yielded to intense craving; so the children of Israel also wept again and said: "Who will give us

---

10:29 [a]Septuagint reads *Raguel* (compare Exodus 2:18).　11:3 [a]Literally *Burning*

10:13 Following the census the Lord organized the march—orderly, as an army on the move (Num. 2:9–31; see chart, Marching Order of the Tribes of Israel). One addition was made at the time of setting out: The three families of Levites were given their positions in order to have the tabernacle readied for camp (Num. 10:17, 21).

10:29–32 Moses insisted his brother-in-law stay and be their guide, attesting to his firsthand knowledge of the wilderness terrain. While God led the army with His presence, He also provided human leaders for Israel. Moses pledged a share of

God's promised bounty to Hobab. Later records show that Hobab's descendants lived in Canaan (Judg. 1:16; 4:11).

11:4 The mixed multitude were probably children of mixed marriages (Hebrew and Egyptian). Considered a rabble of camp followers, they probably lived on the "outskirts" of camp, for they did not belong to the true Israel (v. 1).

11:1–6 The murmuring of the people had now become a contagious habit, an attitude mirroring distrust. They "wept again," indicating earlier complaints, which are here likened to mourning the death of a loved one (vv. 4, 10). Their "craving"

MARCHING ORDER OF THE TRIBES OF ISRAEL

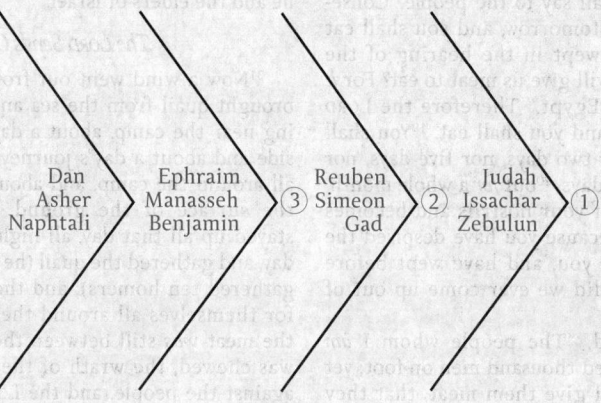

Dan
Asher
Naphtali

③ Ephraim
Manasseh
Benjamin

③ Reuben
Simeon
Gad

② Judah
Issachar
Zebulun

①

① Levites carry the ark (Josh. 3:3, 4).

② Gershonites and Merarites carry the tabernacle (Num. 10:17).

③ Kohathites carry the tabernacle furnishings (Num. 10:21).

meat to eat? ⁵We remember the fish which we ate freely in Egypt, the cucumbers, the melons, the leeks, the onions, and the garlic; ⁶but now our whole being *is* dried up; *there is* nothing at all except this manna *before* our eyes!"

⁷Now the manna *was* like coriander seed, and its color like the color of bdellium. ⁸The people went about and gathered *it*, ground *it* on millstones or beat *it* in the mortar, cooked *it* in pans, and made cakes of it; and its taste was like the taste of pastry prepared with oil. ⁹And when the dew fell on the camp in the night, the manna fell on it.

¹⁰Then Moses heard the people weeping throughout their families, everyone at the door of his tent; and the anger of the LORD was greatly aroused; Moses also was displeased. ¹¹So Moses said to the LORD, "Why have You afflicted Your servant? And why have I not found favor in Your sight, that You have laid the burden of all these

people on me? ¹²Did I conceive all these people? Did I beget them, that You should say to me, 'Carry them in your bosom, as a guardian carries a nursing child,' to the land which You swore to their fathers? ¹³Where am I to get meat to give to all these people? For they weep all over me, saying, 'Give us meat, that we may eat.' ¹⁴I am not able to bear all these people alone, because the burden *is* too heavy for me. ¹⁵If You treat me like this, please kill me here and now— if I have found favor in Your sight— and do not let me see my wretchedness!"

The Seventy Elders

¹⁶So the LORD said to Moses: "Gather to Me seventy men of the elders of Israel, whom you know to be the elders of the people and officers over them; bring them to the tabernacle of meeting, that they may stand there with you. ¹⁷Then I will come down and talk with you there. I will take of

is associated with gluttony, lusting for anything other than a one-food diet (v. 6; see Prov. 23, Gluttony). Their selective memory recalled the meats but not the miseries of Egypt (Num. 11:5). Their cattle would not have been sufficient supply for sacrifices and food.

11:7 Coriander, of the carrot family, is an aromatic and sweet herb still used today in preparing oriental pastries and fruit dishes. "Bdellium" is similar to myrrh (see chart, The Herbs of the Bible).

11:12 The word "guardian" comes from a root meaning "truth" or "trust," referring to men and women entrusted with the

care of a child. Here the masculine form is used, as of Mordecai (Esth. 2:7), while the feminine form is used of Naomi (Ruth 4:16; see also Gen. 1:26, note). Moses, discontent under the burden of a rebellious people, declared that he was not a guardian for the people—thus implying that God was. The Lord conceived this people, and thus He must be their nurse, mother, "guardian" (see chart, Female Metaphors for God).

11:16 To assist Moses, God anointed 70 men with the "same" Spirit given to Moses (v. 17). Nothing was taken from Moses— as light is not diminished from a lamp when used to light another.

the Spirit that *is* upon you and will put *the same* upon them; and they shall bear the burden of the people with you, that you may not bear *it* yourself alone. [18]Then you shall say to the people, 'Consecrate yourselves for tomorrow, and you shall eat meat; for you have wept in the hearing of the LORD, saying, "Who will give us meat to eat? For *it was* well with us in Egypt." Therefore the LORD will give you meat, and you shall eat. [19]You shall eat, not one day, nor two days, nor five days, nor ten days, nor twenty days, [20]but *for* a whole month, until it comes out of your nostrils and becomes loathsome to you, because you have despised the LORD who is among you, and have wept before Him, saying, "Why did we ever come up out of Egypt?" ' "

[21]And Moses said, "The people whom I *am* among *are* six hundred thousand men on foot; yet You have said, 'I will give them meat, that they may eat *for* a whole month.' [22]Shall flocks and herds be slaughtered for them, to provide enough for them? Or shall all the fish of the sea be gathered together for them, to provide enough for them?"

[23]And the LORD said to Moses, "Has the LORD's arm been shortened? Now you shall see whether what I say will happen to you or not."

[24]So Moses went out and told the people the words of the LORD, and he gathered the seventy men of the elders of the people and placed them around the tabernacle. [25]Then the LORD came down in the cloud, and spoke to him, and took of the Spirit that *was* upon him, and placed *the same* upon the seventy elders; and it happened, when the Spirit rested upon them, that they prophesied, although they never did *so* again.[a]

[26]But two men had remained in the camp: the name of one *was* Eldad, and the name of the other Medad. And the Spirit rested upon them. Now they *were* among those listed, but who had not gone out to the tabernacle; yet they prophesied in the camp. [27]And a young man ran and told Moses, and said, "Eldad and Medad are prophesying in the camp."

[28]So Joshua the son of Nun, Moses' assistant, *one* of his choice men, answered and said, "Moses my lord, forbid them!"

[29]Then Moses said to him, "Are you zealous for my sake? Oh, that all the LORD's people were prophets *and* that the LORD would put His Spirit upon them!" [30]And Moses returned to the camp, he and the elders of Israel.

The LORD Sends Quail

[31]Now a wind went out from the LORD, and it brought quail from the sea and left *them* fluttering near the camp, about a day's journey on this side and about a day's journey on the other side, all around the camp, and about two cubits above the surface of the ground. [32]And the people stayed up all that day, all night, and all the next day, and gathered the quail (he who gathered least gathered ten homers); and they spread *them* out for themselves all around the camp. [33]But while the meat *was* still between their teeth, before it was chewed, the wrath of the LORD was aroused against the people, and the LORD struck the people with a very great plague. [34]So he called the name of that place Kibroth Hattaavah,[a] because there they buried the people who had yielded to craving.

[35]From Kibroth Hattaavah the people moved to Hazeroth, and camped at Hazeroth.

Dissension of Aaron and Miriam

12 Then Miriam and Aaron spoke against Moses because of the Ethiopian woman whom he had married; for he had married an Ethiopian woman. [2]So they said, "Has the LORD indeed spoken only through Moses? Has He not spoken through us also?" And the LORD heard *it.* [3](Now the man Moses *was* very humble, more than all men who *were* on the face of the earth.)

[4]Suddenly the LORD said to Moses, Aaron, and Miriam, "Come out, you three, to the tabernacle of meeting!" So the three came out. [5]Then the LORD came down in the pillar of cloud and stood *in* the door of the tabernacle, and called Aaron and Miriam. And they both went forward. [6]Then He said,

"Hear now My words:
If there is a prophet among you,

11:25 [a]Targum and Vulgate read *did not cease.* **11:34** [a]Literally *Graves of Craving*

11:31, 32 The quail flew three feet above the ground and could easily be caught. "Ten homers" would equal about 110 bushels or 1,000 gallons (see chart, Money and Measurements in the Bible).

11:33 Rejection of God's provision, exhibited in their lustful cravings, brought fulfillment of God's judgment (vv. 18–20). The noun "plague" is akin to the verb "smote." This natural sickness from overeating was predicted by God.

12:1, 2 Rebellion hit closer to home. The real issue of contention from the sister and brother of Moses was not the ancestry of Moses' wife but their coveting the authority of Moses and thereby questioning God's authority (see Song 8, Jealousy; 1 Cor. 3, Competition). God "heard" their resentment even before it was uttered.

12:3 Some scholars use this verse to explain away Moses' authorship of Numbers, but Moses was only acting in his own defense. After all, humility is recognition of being "under the mighty hand of God" (1 Pet. 5:5, 6). Jesus also stated His own meekness (Matt. 11:29; see Phil. 2, Humility).

FEMALE METAPHORS FOR GOD

A PICTURE OF GOD AS:	SCRIPTURE REFERENCE
Conceiving, carrying life in His womb, laboring, and giving birth	Job 38:8; Is. 42:14; John 3:6
Nursing mother	Num. 11:12; Ps. 131:1, 2; Is. 49:15; 1 Pet. 2:2, 3
Nurturing mother	Job 10:10–12; Is. 46:3, 4; Hos. 11:3, 4
Midwife	Ps. 22:9, 10; Is. 66:9
Mistress of the house	Ps. 123:2
Mother bear	Hos. 13:8
Mother eagle	Deut. 32:11, 12
Mother hen	Luke 13:34

Many rich female metaphors for God are found in Scripture. A metaphor is a figure of speech in which a term or phrase implies a comparison between something essentially unlike another in order to suggest a resemblance. Therefore, although female metaphors for God can be found, the literary devices do not imply that the masculine pronouns God chose to use for Himself can be altered or cast aside. However, they do indicate that the character of God encompasses and supersedes both masculinity and femininity. God is neither female nor male, although He may choose to liken His role to that of a mother when He conceives, bears, nurses, nurtures, and cares for His children. The umbilical metaphor is a useful tool to reveal God's nature and to communicate His love and concern through simple examples easily understood by all people.

See also notes on Attributes of God (Ex. 33; Deut. 4; 32; 2 Chr. 19; Job 23; 42; Ps. 25; 90; 102; 119; Is. 6; 65; Jer. 23; Rom. 2; Eph. 1; 1 John 5); Fatherhood of God (Rom. 8); Goddess Religion (Ex. 20)

I, the LORD, make Myself known to him in a
vision;
I speak to him in a dream.
[7]Not so with My servant Moses;
He *is* faithful in all My house.
[8]I speak with him face to face,
Even plainly, and not in dark sayings;
And he sees the form of the LORD.
Why then were you not afraid
To speak against My servant Moses?"

[9]So the anger of the LORD was aroused against them, and He departed. [10]And when the cloud departed from above the tabernacle, suddenly Miriam *became* leprous, as *white as* snow. Then Aaron turned toward Miriam, and there she was, a leper. [11]So Aaron said to Moses, "Oh, my lord! Please do not lay *this* sin on us, in which we have done foolishly and in which we have sinned. [12]Please do not let her be as one dead, whose flesh

is half consumed when he comes out of his mother's womb!"
[13]So Moses cried out to the LORD, saying, "Please heal her, O God, I pray!"
[14]Then the LORD said to Moses, "If her father had but spit in her face, would she not be shamed seven days? Let her be shut out of the camp seven days, and afterward she may be received *again*." [15]So Miriam was shut out of the camp seven days, and the people did not journey till Miriam was brought in *again*. [16]And afterward the people moved from Hazeroth and camped in the Wilderness of Paran.

Spies Sent into Canaan

13 And the LORD spoke to Moses, saying, [2]"Send men to spy out the land of Canaan, which I am giving to the children of Israel; from each tribe of their fathers you shall send a man, every one a leader among them."

12:14, 15 God likened Miriam's shame to having her father spit on her, a practice especially abhorred by people in the ancient Near East. The seven-day exile was normal for purification and restoration (see also Ex. 15, Miriam).

12:16 Kadesh "in the Wilderness of Paran" is well established as Kadesh Barnea (now *Kudes*), described by Moses as "that great and terrible wilderness" (Deut. 1:19). An area well adequate to accommodate the Israelite encampment, the borders of Kadesh were Canaan to the north, the valley of

Arabah to the east, the desert of Sinai to the south, and the river or brook *Wadi el Arish* to the west.

13:1, 2 Procedural details for this passage are found elsewhere (Deut. 1:19–25). The people requested that spies be sent into the land before they would enter. A note of fear and discouragement was sounded. These tribal representatives were not the same leaders listed in Numbers 1:5–15. In both incidents, the tribe of Levi is not included in negotiations about the Land. The number of representatives in both chapters is

³So Moses sent them from the Wilderness of Paran according to the command of the LORD, all of them men who *were* heads of the children of Israel. ⁴Now these *were* their names: from the tribe of Reuben, Shammua the son of Zaccur; ⁵from the tribe of Simeon, Shaphat the son of Hori; ⁶from the tribe of Judah, Caleb the son of Jephunneh; ⁷from the tribe of Issachar, Igal the son of Joseph; ⁸from the tribe of Ephraim, Hosheaª the son of Nun; ⁹from the tribe of Benjamin, Palti the son of Raphu; ¹⁰from the tribe of Zebulun, Gaddiel the son of Sodi; ¹¹from the tribe of Joseph, *that is,* from the tribe of Manasseh, Gaddi the son of Susi; ¹²from the tribe of Dan, Ammiel the son of Gemalli; ¹³from the tribe of Asher, Sethur the son of Michael; ¹⁴from the tribe of Naphtali, Nahbi the son of Vophsi; ¹⁵from the tribe of Gad, Geuel the son of Machi.

¹⁶These *are* the names of the men whom Moses sent to spy out the land. And Moses called Hosheaª the son of Nun, Joshua.

¹⁷Then Moses sent them to spy out the land of Canaan, and said to them, "Go up this *way* into the South, and go up to the mountains, ¹⁸and see what the land is like: whether the people who dwell in it *are* strong or weak, few or many; ¹⁹whether the land they dwell in *is* good or bad; whether the cities they inhabit *are* like camps or strongholds; ²⁰whether the land *is* rich or poor; and whether there are forests there or not. Be of good courage. And bring some of the fruit of the land." Now the time *was* the season of the first ripe grapes.

²¹So they went up and spied out the land from the Wilderness of Zin as far as Rehob, near the entrance of Hamath. ²²And they went up through the South and came to Hebron; Ahiman, Sheshai, and Talmai, the descendants of Anak, *were* there. (Now Hebron was built seven years before Zoan in Egypt.) ²³Then they came to the Valley of Eshcol, and there cut down a branch with one cluster of grapes; they carried it between two of them on a pole. *They* also *brought* some of the pomegranates and figs. ²⁴The place was called the Valley of Eshcol,ª because of the cluster which the men of Israel cut down there. ²⁵And they returned from spying out the land after forty days.

²⁶Now they departed and came back to Moses and Aaron and all the congregation of the children of Israel in the Wilderness of Paran, at Kadesh; they brought back word to them and to all the congregation, and showed them the fruit of the land. ²⁷Then they told him, and said: "We went to the land where you sent us. It truly flows with milk and honey, and this *is* its fruit. ²⁸Nevertheless the people who dwell in the land *are* strong; the cities *are* fortified *and* very large; moreover we saw the descendants of Anak there. ²⁹The Amalekites dwell in the land of the South; the Hittites, the Jebusites, and the Amorites dwell in the mountains; and the Canaanites dwell by the sea and along the banks of the Jordan."

³⁰Then Caleb quieted the people before Moses, and said, "Let us go up at once and take possession, for we are well able to overcome it."

³¹But the men who had gone up with him said, "We are not able to go up against the people, for they *are* stronger than we." ³²And they gave the children of Israel a bad report of the land which they had spied out, saying, "The land through which we have gone as spies *is* a land that devours its inhabitants, and all the people whom we saw in it *are* men of *great* stature. ³³There we saw the giantsª (the descendants of Anak came from the giants); and we were like grasshoppers in our own sight, and so we were in their sight."

Israel Refuses to Enter Canaan

14 So all the congregation lifted up their voices and cried, and the people wept that night. ²And all the children of Israel complained against Moses and Aaron, and the whole congregation said to them, "If only we had died in the land of Egypt! Or if only we had died in this wilderness! ³Why has the LORD brought us to this land to fall by the sword, that our wives and children should become victims? Would it not be better for us to return to Egypt?" ⁴So they said to one another, "Let us select a leader and return to Egypt."

13:8, 16 ªSeptuagint and Vulgate read *Oshea*.   **13:24** ªLiterally *Cluster*   **13:33** ªHebrew *nephilim*

---

12 because of dividing the tribe of Joseph to accommodate his two sons Ephraim and Manasseh (Gen. 48:12–22).

13:16 Jesus is the Greek form of Joshua (Heb. *Hoshea*, lit. "The Lord is Salvation"; see Matt. 1:21).

14:2 In the wilderness, the Israelites "complained" about being without meal, water, and the comforts of Egypt. Although the wilderness lacked many things, it was never without the Lord's presence (Ex. 33:14). Wilderness life was bearable only because of God and His provision. Again and again, people have found God's sufficient supply in wilderness experiences: from the Israelites' "forty years in the wilderness" (Deut. 29:5) to Christ's temptation "in the wilderness forty days" (Mark 1:13) to the woman with child who "fled into the wilder-

ness, where she has a place prepared by God, that they should feed her there one thousand two hundred and sixty days" (Rev. 12:6).

14:3 The men spoke of their wives and children as "victims" and actually blamed God for abusing their children when God, in fact, spared their "little ones" (v. 31). There is no evidence in the text that the men did anything to express concern beyond their verbal complaints.

14:4 Rebellion broke out, and they were ready to return to Egypt under a new leader. Unbelief was at the base of Israel's fear of entering the Land God had promised. Crucial to understanding the book is this pivotal chapter depicting both Israel's rebellion and God's glory (ch. 14).

⁵Then Moses and Aaron fell on their faces before all the assembly of the congregation of the children of Israel.

⁶But Joshua the son of Nun and Caleb the son of Jephunneh, *who were* among those who had spied out the land, tore their clothes; ⁷and they spoke to all the congregation of the children of Israel, saying: "The land we passed through to spy out *is* an exceedingly good land. ⁸If the LORD delights in us, then He will bring us into this land and give it to us, 'a land which flows with milk and honey.'ᵃ ⁹Only do not rebel against the LORD, nor fear the people of the land, for they *are* our bread; their protection has departed from them, and the LORD *is* with us. Do not fear them."

¹⁰And all the congregation said to stone them with stones. Now the glory of the LORD appeared in the tabernacle of meeting before all the children of Israel.

Moses Intercedes for the People

¹¹Then the LORD said to Moses: "How long will these people reject Me? And how long will they not believe Me, with all the signs which I have performed among them? ¹²I will strike them with the pestilence and disinherit them, and I will make of you a nation greater and mightier than they."

¹³And Moses said to the LORD: "Then the Egyptians will hear *it*, for by Your might You brought these people up from among them, ¹⁴and they will tell *it* to the inhabitants of this land. They have heard that You, LORD, *are* among these people; that You, LORD, are seen face to face and Your cloud stands above them, and You go before them in a pillar of cloud by day and in a pillar of fire by night. ¹⁵Now *if* You kill these people as one man, then the nations which have heard of Your fame will speak, saying, ¹⁶'Because the LORD was not able to bring this people to the land which He swore to give them, therefore He killed them in the wilderness.' ¹⁷And now, I pray, let the power of my Lord be great, just as You have spoken, saying, ¹⁸'The LORD is longsuffering and abundant in mercy, forgiving iniquity and transgression; but

He by no means clears *the guilty*, visiting the iniquity of the fathers on the children to the third and fourth *generation.*'ᵃ ¹⁹Pardon the iniquity of this people, I pray, according to the greatness of Your mercy, just as You have forgiven this people, from Egypt even until now."

²⁰Then the LORD said: "I have pardoned, according to your word; ²¹but truly, as I live, all the earth shall be filled with the glory of the LORD— ²²because all these men who have seen My glory and the signs which I did in Egypt and in the wilderness, and have put Me to the test now these ten times, and have not heeded My voice, ²³they certainly shall not see the land of which I swore to their fathers, nor shall any of those who rejected Me see it. ²⁴But My servant Caleb, because he has a different spirit in him and has followed Me fully, I will bring into the land where he went, and his descendants shall inherit it. ²⁵Now the Amalekites and the Canaanites dwell in the valley; tomorrow turn and move out into the wilderness by the Way of the Red Sea."

Death Sentence on the Rebels

²⁶And the LORD spoke to Moses and Aaron, saying, ²⁷"How long *shall I bear with* this evil congregation who complain against Me? I have heard the complaints which the children of Israel make against Me. ²⁸Say to them, 'As I live,' says the LORD, 'just as you have spoken in My hearing, so I will do to you: ²⁹The carcasses of you who have complained against Me shall fall in this wilderness, all of you who were numbered, according to your entire number, from twenty years old and above. ³⁰Except for Caleb the son of Jephunneh and Joshua the son of Nun, you shall by no means enter the land which I swore I would make you dwell in. ³¹But your little ones, whom you said would be victims, I will bring in, and they shall know the land which you have despised. ³²But *as for* you, your carcasses shall fall in this wilderness. ³³And your sons shall be shepherds in the wilderness

14:8 ᵃExodus 3:8   14:18 ᵃExodus 34:6, 7

14:5–9 Two positive reactions followed Israel's revolt: Moses and Aaron humbled themselves before the Lord; Joshua and Caleb exhorted the people about the Lord's plan of provision and protection.

14:9–12 In the way that God gave them "bread," He would deliver these defenseless "giants" into their hands (Num. 13:33). Instead of trusting God, the people turned on God's spokesmen. Stoning, the customary punishment for some crimes under Levitical law (Lev. 24:16), was also practiced in Egypt (Ex. 8:26). Like a bolt of lightning visible to all, God's glory "appeared in the tabernacle" to confront their unbelief (see Num. 14:21; 16:19; 20:6). A time will come, not unlike this scene, when God's glory will fill the holy New Jerusalem—but the "unbelieving" will have no inheritance there (Rev. 21:1–11).

14:19, 20 Moses' request to pardon this people once again was honored by God immediately (see John 14:14). Moses knew he could meet with God at the "mercy seat" (Ex. 25:17–22). Daniel also pleaded for pardon on the merits of God's mercy (Dan. 9:3–19). Likewise, believers are bid to "come boldly to the throne of grace, that we may obtain mercy" (Heb. 4:16).

14:22 The idea of full measure is seen in the expression "ten times," although ten references to Israel's rejection could be cited if the figure is taken literally. Unbelief was comprehensive, evident in such words as "all" and "whole" (vv. 1, 2, 7, 10).

14:30, 31 Because of their trust in God (v. 24), Joshua and Caleb were spared God's wrath and would be among the children who would inhabit the Promised Land. The word "swore" is literally "lifted up My hand" (see Ex. 6:8).

SECOND CHANCES   *BEGINNING ANEW*

God gives love and forgiveness over and over again (2 Chr. 7:14). Often, the believer who accepts His free gift by faith fails to follow Him completely or consistently. Even so, God graciously makes available again and again a new beginning, an "extended opportunity."

Beyond the realm of forgiveness, Scripture presents numerous accounts in which the Lord reversed certain conditions or circumstances and gave a chance to His people to begin anew. The mother of Moses was given a second chance to rear her son (Ex. 2:7–9). Miriam was given a second chance when God forgave her rebellious spirit and healed her leprosy (Num. 12:10–15). Hannah's barrenness was overruled so that she might bear Samuel and dedicate him to the Lord (1 Sam. 1:2–28).

Women are offered a new beginning in many New Testament accounts. Elizabeth conceived a child in her later years and gave birth to John the Baptist (Luke 1:5–25). The widow of Nain was given another chance when her son was raised from the dead (Luke 7:11–17). The woman caught in the act of adultery was given another opportunity to live a God-fearing life (John 8:3–11). Dorcas was raised from the dead by Peter and given additional years in which to serve the Lord (Acts 9:36–42).

The Bible also presents stories of lives in which women did not accept the second chance offered to them by God. Jezebel rejected her second chance and deliberately disobeyed God (2 Kin. 9:30–37). Bernice heard the gospel message as preached by Paul; yet, we have no indication she accepted it (Acts 25:23; 26:30–32).

God's mercy and justice are balanced. Though a believer may still experience some temporal consequences for her disobedience, she can receive forgiveness and assurance of life because her sins are covered by the blood of Christ. Another opportunity does not necessarily mean an absence of consequences. God's justice often allows consequences for past sinful behavior even after a person has turned to Him in obedience, but His mercy continues to offer the protection of a gracious and forgiving heavenly Father (Luke 15:20; John 10:28, 29).

See also Ex. 2:7–9; 1 Sam. 1:2–28; Luke 1:5–25; 24:47, note; Acts 9:36–42; notes on Forgiveness (Ps. 51; Luke 17); Renewal (Hab. 3); portraits of Naomi (Ruth 1); Ruth (Ruth 2)

---

forty years, and bear the brunt of your infidelity, until your carcasses are consumed in the wilderness. ³⁴According to the number of the days in which you spied out the land, forty days, for each day you shall bear your guilt one year, *namely* forty years, and you shall know My rejection. ³⁵I the LORD have spoken this. I will surely do so to all this evil congregation who are gathered together against Me. In this wilderness they shall be consumed, and there they shall die.' "

³⁶Now the men whom Moses sent to spy out the land, who returned and made all the congregation complain against him by bringing a bad report of the land, ³⁷those very men who brought the evil report about the land, died by the plague before the LORD. ³⁸But Joshua the son of Nun and Caleb the son of Jephunneh remained alive, of the men who went to spy out the land.

A Futile Invasion Attempt

³⁹Then Moses told these words to all the children of Israel, and the people mourned greatly. ⁴⁰And they rose early in the morning and went up to the top of the mountain, saying, "Here we are, and we will go up to the place which the LORD has promised, for we have sinned!"

⁴¹And Moses said, "Now why do you transgress

the command of the LORD? For this will not succeed. ⁴²Do not go up, lest you be defeated by your enemies, for the LORD *is* not among you. ⁴³For the Amalekites and the Canaanites *are* there before you, and you shall fall by the sword; because you have turned away from the LORD, the LORD will not be with you."

⁴⁴But they presumed to go up to the mountaintop. Nevertheless, neither the ark of the covenant of the LORD nor Moses departed from the camp. ⁴⁵Then the Amalekites and the Canaanites who dwelt in that mountain came down and attacked them, and drove them back as far as Hormah.

Laws of Grain and Drink Offerings

15 And the LORD spoke to Moses, saying, ²"Speak to the children of Israel, and say to them: 'When you have come into the land you are to inhabit, which I am giving to you, ³and you make an offering by fire to the LORD, a burnt offering or a sacrifice, to fulfill a vow or as a freewill offering or in your appointed feasts, to make a sweet aroma to the LORD, from the herd or the flock, ⁴then he who presents his offering to the LORD shall bring a grain offering of one-tenth *of an ephah* of fine flour mixed with one-fourth of a hin of oil; ⁵and one-fourth of a hin of wine as a

---

14:34 Rejection works both ways: the people rejected God, and consequently they knew His "rejection" (vv. 11, 23; see also Job 3:10).

drink offering you shall prepare with the burnt offering or the sacrifice, for each lamb. 6Or for a ram you shall prepare as a grain offering two-tenths *of an ephah* of fine flour mixed with one-third of a hin of oil; 7and as a drink offering you shall offer one-third of a hin of wine as a sweet aroma to the LORD. 8And when you prepare a young bull as a burnt offering, or as a sacrifice to fulfill a vow, or as a peace offering to the LORD, 9then shall be offered with the young bull a grain offering of three-tenths *of an ephah* of fine flour mixed with half a hin of oil; 10and you shall bring as the drink offering half a hin of wine as an of-fering made by fire, a sweet aroma to the LORD.

11"Thus it shall be done for each young bull, for each ram, or for each lamb or young goat. 12Ac-cording to the number that you prepare, so you shall do with everyone according to their number. 13All who are native-born shall do these things in this manner, in presenting an offering made by fire, a sweet aroma to the LORD. 14And if a stranger dwells with you, or whoever *is* among you throughout your generations, and would present an offering made by fire, a sweet aroma to the LORD, just as you do, so shall he do. 15One ordi-nance *shall be* for you of the assembly and for the stranger who dwells *with you,* an ordinance forever throughout your generations; as you are, so shall the stranger be before the LORD. 16One law and one custom shall be for you and for the stranger who dwells with you.' "a

17Again the LORD spoke to Moses, saying, 18"Speak to the children of Israel, and say to them: 'When you come into the land to which I bring you, 19then it will be, when you eat of the bread of the land, that you shall offer up a heave offering to the LORD. 20You shall offer up a cake of the first of your ground meal *as* a heave offering; as a heave offering of the threshing floor, so shall you offer it up. 21Of the first of your ground meal you shall give to the LORD a heave offering throughout your generations.

Laws Concerning Unintentional Sin

22'If you sin unintentionally, and do not observe all these commandments which the LORD has spo-ken to Moses— 23all that the LORD has com-manded you by the hand of Moses, from the day the LORD gave commandment and onward throughout your generations— 24then it will be, if

it is unintentionally committed, without the knowledge of the congregation, that the whole congregation shall offer one young bull as a burnt offering, as a sweet aroma to the LORD, with its grain offering and its drink offering, according to the ordinance, and one kid of the goats as a sin of-fering. 25So the priest shall make atonement for the whole congregation of the children of Israel, and it shall be forgiven them, for it was uninten-tional; they shall bring their offering, an offering made by fire to the LORD, and their sin offering before the LORD, for their unintended sin. 26It shall be forgiven the whole congregation of the children of Israel and the stranger who dwells among them, because all the people *did it* uninten-tionally.

27'And if a person sins unintentionally, then he shall bring a female goat in its first year as a sin offering. 28So the priest shall make atonement for the person who sins unintentionally, when he sins unintentionally before the LORD, to make atone-ment for him; and it shall be forgiven him. 29You shall have one law for him who sins unintention-ally, *for* him who is native-born among the chil-dren of Israel and for the stranger who dwells among them.

Law Concerning Presumptuous Sin

30'But the person who does *anything* presump-tuously, *whether he is* native-born or a stranger, that one brings reproach on the LORD, and he shall be cut off from among his people. 31Because he has despised the word of the LORD, and has broken His commandment, that person shall be com-pletely cut off; his guilt *shall be* upon him.' "

Penalty for Violating the Sabbath

32Now while the children of Israel were in the wilderness, they found a man gathering sticks on the Sabbath day. 33And those who found him gath-ering sticks brought him to Moses and Aaron, and to all the congregation. 34They put him under guard, because it had not been explained what should be done to him.

35Then the LORD said to Moses, "The man must surely be put to death; all the congregation shall stone him with stones outside the camp." 36So, as the LORD commanded Moses, all the congregation

---

15:16 aCompare Exodus 12:49

15:20, 21 Firstfruits were introduced here and discussed more fully in Numbers 18. Such rituals were meant to hallow family life in such common practices as baking bread and cakes (Ezek. 44:30). "A heave offering" suggests the idea of lifting up thanks.

15:22 Sins of ignorance and defiance. Immediately following Is-rael's rebellion at Kadesh, God instructed them about the sig-nificant difference between sinning "unintentionally" and sin-

ning "presumptuously" (vv. 30–36). In the case of sins commit-ted in ignorance, unwittingly done in error, pardon and restora-tion were provided through "their sin offering" (v. 25). However, sins of defiance, made with full knowledge of the Law, were met only with punishment, exclusion, and even death, as illus-trated by the incident of Sabbath breaking (vv. 32–36). With David's prayer in their hearts (Ps. 19:13), Christians are admon-ished to avoid intentional sin (1 John 3:4–9).

brought him outside the camp and stoned him with stones, and he died.

Tassels on Garments

37Again the LORD spoke to Moses, saying, 38"Speak to the children of Israel: Tell them to make tassels on the corners of their garments throughout their generations, and to put a blue thread in the tassels of the corners. 39And you shall have the tassel, that you may look upon it and remember all the commandments of the LORD and do them, and that you *may* not follow the harlotry to which your own heart and your own eyes are inclined, 40and that you may remember and do all My commandments, and be holy for your God. 41I *am* the LORD your God, who brought you out of the land of Egypt, to be your God: I *am* the LORD your God."

Rebellion Against Moses and Aaron

16Now Korah the son of Izhar, the son of Kohath, the son of Levi, with Dathan and Abiram the sons of Eliab, and On the son of Peleth, sons of Reuben, took *men;* 2and they rose up before Moses with some of the children of Israel, two hundred and fifty leaders of the congregation, representatives of the congregation, men of renown. 3They gathered together against Moses and Aaron, and said to them, *"You take* too much upon yourselves, for all the congregation *is* holy, every one of them, and the LORD *is* among them. Why then do you exalt yourselves above the assembly of the LORD?"

4So when Moses heard *it,* he fell on his face; 5and he spoke to Korah and all his company, saying, "Tomorrow morning the LORD will show who *is* His and *who is* holy, and will cause *him* to come near to Him. That one whom He chooses He will cause to come near to Him. 6Do this: Take censers, Korah and all your company; 7put fire in them and put incense in them before the LORD tomorrow, and it shall be *that* the man whom the LORD chooses *is* the holy one. *You take* too much upon yourselves, you sons of Levi!"

8Then Moses said to Korah, "Hear now, you sons of Levi: 9*Is it* a small thing to you that the God of Israel has separated you from the congregation of Israel, to bring you near to Himself, to do the work of the tabernacle of the LORD, and to stand before the congregation to serve them; 10and that He has brought you near *to Himself,* you and all your brethren, the sons of Levi, with you? And are you seeking the priesthood also? 11Therefore you and all your company *are* gathered together against the LORD. And what *is* Aaron that you complain against him?"

12And Moses sent to call Dathan and Abiram the sons of Eliab, but they said, "We will not come up! 13*Is it* a small thing that you have brought us up out of a land flowing with milk and honey, to kill us in the wilderness, that you should keep acting like a prince over us? 14Moreover you have not brought us into a land flowing with milk and honey, nor given us inheritance of fields and vineyards. Will you put out the eyes of these men? We will not come up!"

15Then Moses was very angry, and said to the LORD, "Do not respect their offering. I have not taken one donkey from them, nor have I hurt one of them."

16And Moses said to Korah, "Tomorrow, you and all your company be present before the LORD—you and they, as well as Aaron. 17Let each take his censer and put incense in it, and each of you bring his censer before the LORD, two hundred and fifty censers; both you and Aaron, each *with* his censer." 18So every man took his censer, put fire in it, laid incense on it, and stood at the door of the tabernacle of meeting with Moses and Aaron. 19And Korah gathered all the congregation against them at the door of the tabernacle of meeting. Then the glory of the LORD appeared to all the congregation.

20And the LORD spoke to Moses and Aaron, saying, 21"Separate yourselves from among this congregation, that I may consume them in a moment."

15:38 As a reminder to obey the Commandments, the people wore "tassels on the corners of their garments." A "blue cord" was used on the turbans worn by the priests (Ex. 28:37; see chart, The High Priest's Clothing). In Jesus' day, the Pharisees enlarged these tassels or fringes to make much of their strict observance of the Law (Matt. 23:5). The woman, who needed healing from a persistent flow of blood, touched the "hem" of the Savior's garment (Gk. *kraspedon,* lit. "tassel" or "edge"; Matt. 9:20).

16:1–3 Whether this incident of rebellion followed soon after God's instruction regarding presumptuous sin or much later (Num. 15:30–36), it illustrates the depth of sin and its consequences. Korah, a Levite with important responsibilities, joined forces with Dathan and Abiram in a common protest (Num. 10:21; see also Rebellion). Their accusation against the authority of Moses and Aaron was turned back on them

when Moses said in essence, "You have gone too far" (Num. 16:7).

16:5 God's choice. Both Moses and Korah acted with confidence: Moses affirmed God's command and left the decision up to Him (vv. 16, 17); Korah assumed vindication (vv. 18, 19).

16:8–11 The real issue. Moses got to the heart of the matter—contempt for assigned duties and desire for another's glory. The real contention was with God, for God had assigned the specialized duties (vv. 30, 38; Num. 4; 10). Paul used this concept when comparing the church with a physical body, having varying parts and functions but all working together (1 Cor. 12).

16:13 The natural progression of sin. With the assertion that Egypt is "a land flowing with milk and honey," these men called good what was evil and evil what was good (Is. 5:20–25).

²²Then they fell on their faces, and said, "O God, the God of the spirits of all flesh, shall one man sin, and You be angry with all the congregation?"

²³So the LORD spoke to Moses, saying, ²⁴"Speak to the congregation, saying, 'Get away from the tents of Korah, Dathan, and Abiram.' "

²⁵Then Moses rose and went to Dathan and Abiram, and the elders of Israel followed him. ²⁶And he spoke to the congregation, saying, "Depart now from the tents of these wicked men! Touch nothing of theirs, lest you be consumed in all their sins." ²⁷So they got away from around the tents of Korah, Dathan, and Abiram; and Dathan and Abiram came out and stood at the door of their tents, with their wives, their sons, and their little children.

²⁸And Moses said: "By this you shall know that the LORD has sent me to do all these works, for *I* have not *done them* of my own will. ²⁹If these men die naturally like all men, or if they are visited by the common fate of all men, *then* the LORD has not sent me. ³⁰But if the LORD creates a new thing, and the earth opens its mouth and swallows them up with all that belongs to them, and they go down alive into the pit, then you will understand that these men have rejected the LORD."

³¹Now it came to pass, as he finished speaking all these words, that the ground split apart under them, ³²and the earth opened its mouth and swallowed them up, with their households and all the men with Korah, with all *their* goods. ³³So they and all those with them went down alive into the pit; the earth closed over them, and they perished from among the assembly. ³⁴Then all Israel who *were* around them fled at their cry, for they said, "Lest the earth swallow us up *also!*"

³⁵And a fire came out from the LORD and consumed the two hundred and fifty men who were offering incense.

³⁶Then the LORD spoke to Moses, saying: ³⁷"Tell Eleazar, the son of Aaron the priest, to pick up the censers out of the blaze, for they are holy, and scatter the fire some distance away. ³⁸The censers of these men who sinned against their own souls, let them be made into hammered plates as a covering for the altar. Because they presented them before the LORD, therefore they are holy; and they shall be a sign to the children of Israel." ³⁹So Eleazar the priest took the bronze censers, which those who were burned up had presented, and they were hammered out as a covering on the al-

tar, ⁴⁰*to be* a memorial to the children of Israel that no outsider, who *is* not a descendant of Aaron, should come near to offer incense before the LORD, that he might not become like Korah and his companions, just as the LORD had said to him through Moses.

Complaints of the People

⁴¹On the next day all the congregation of the children of Israel complained against Moses and Aaron, saying, "You have killed the people of the LORD." ⁴²Now it happened, when the congregation had gathered against Moses and Aaron, that they turned toward the tabernacle of meeting; and suddenly the cloud covered it, and the glory of the LORD appeared. ⁴³Then Moses and Aaron came before the tabernacle of meeting.

⁴⁴And the LORD spoke to Moses, saying, ⁴⁵"Get away from among this congregation, that I may consume them in a moment."

And they fell on their faces.

⁴⁶So Moses said to Aaron, "Take a censer and put fire in it from the altar, put incense *on it,* and take it quickly to the congregation and make atonement for them; for wrath has gone out from the LORD. The plague has begun." ⁴⁷Then Aaron took *it* as Moses commanded, and ran into the midst of the assembly; and already the plague had begun among the people. So he put in the incense and made atonement for the people. ⁴⁸And he stood between the dead and the living; so the plague was stopped. ⁴⁹Now those who died in the plague were fourteen thousand seven hundred, besides those who died in the Korah incident. ⁵⁰So Aaron returned to Moses at the door of the tabernacle of meeting, for the plague had stopped.

The Budding of Aaron's Rod

17 And the LORD spoke to Moses, saying: ²"Speak to the children of Israel, and get from them a rod from each father's house, all their leaders according to their fathers' houses— twelve rods. Write each man's name on his rod. ³And you shall write Aaron's name on the rod of Levi. For there shall be one rod for the head of *each* father's house. ⁴Then you shall place them in the tabernacle of meeting before the Testimony, where I meet with you. ⁵And it shall be *that* the rod of the man whom I choose will blossom; thus I will rid Myself of the complaints of the children of Israel, which they make against you."

⁶So Moses spoke to the children of Israel, and

16:48 The accused became the savior: Moses "stood between" the condemned and God. Jesus Christ "stood between" heaven and hell; He was crucified to redeem the world (Titus 2:14).

17:5 Aaron and his descendants proved to be God's unmistakable choice and were thus vindicated from all the "com-

plaints" levied against the priesthood. The "rod" had been a symbol of God's authority (Ex. 4:1–5); that Aaron's rod bore fruit was symbolic of present and future life and blessing for God's people through His priestly order (Num. 17:8). Christ is our High Priest, "a Rod from the stem of Jesse" (Is. 11:1).

REBELLION *WILLFUL DISOBEDIENCE*

Rebellion takes many different forms and has widely divergent results and consequences. The root of rebellion, however, remains the same: sin or willful disobedience. A rebellious spirit is one that does not please God. Moses notes this in describing Korah's turning from the Lord. Korah and other sons of Levi took "too much upon [themselves]" (Num. 16:7). Rather than trust the Lord and rely upon His sovereignty and justice, they sought to operate solely according to their own desires. They believed more in themselves and their own strength than in God.

Rebellion can be directly against God, parents, the law, the church. Ultimately, however, all rebellion is against God in that it violates His established patterns of authority. Korah and his "company" were not only in rebellion against Moses and Aaron but against the Lord God (Num. 16:11, 30).

Rebellion always involves envy of someone or something—perhaps envy of a position, a salary, a friend or relative, or even of a spouse. Korah was envious of the authority which God had given Moses and Aaron (Num. 16:3). This drove Korah to his rebellion and ultimately to his death (Num. 16:32). We must carefully guard our hearts and minds in each decision we make and in each goal we attempt to achieve, asking ourselves if we are honoring God or striving to exalt and please ourselves.

See also Luke 15:11–32; notes on Authority (John 19); Discipline (Prov. 22); Obedience (Philem.); Submission (1 Pet. 3); Surrender (James 4)

each of their leaders gave him a rod apiece, for each leader according to their fathers' houses, twelve rods; and the rod of Aaron *was* among their rods. [7]And Moses placed the rods before the LORD in the tabernacle of witness.

[8]Now it came to pass on the next day that Moses went into the tabernacle of witness, and behold, the rod of Aaron, of the house of Levi, had sprouted and put forth buds, had produced blossoms and yielded ripe almonds. [9]Then Moses brought out all the rods from before the LORD to all the children of Israel; and they looked, and each man took his rod.

[10]And the LORD said to Moses, "Bring Aaron's rod back before the Testimony, to be kept as a sign against the rebels, that you may put their complaints away from Me, lest they die." [11]Thus did Moses; just as the LORD had commanded him, so he did.

[12]So the children of Israel spoke to Moses, saying, "Surely we die, we perish, we all perish! [13]Whoever even comes near the tabernacle of the LORD must die. Shall we all utterly die?"

Duties of Priests and Levites

18 Then the LORD said to Aaron: "You and your sons and your father's house with you shall bear the iniquity *related to* the sanctuary, and you and your sons with you shall bear the iniquity *associated with* your priesthood. [2]Also bring with you your brethren of the tribe of Levi, the tribe of your father, that they may be joined with you and serve you while you and your sons *are* with you before the tabernacle of witness. [3]They shall attend

to your needs and all the needs of the tabernacle; but they shall not come near the articles of the sanctuary and the altar, lest they die—they and you also. [4]They shall be joined with you and attend to the needs of the tabernacle of meeting, for all the work of the tabernacle; but an outsider shall not come near you. [5]And you shall attend to the duties of the sanctuary and the duties of the altar, that there *may* be no more wrath on the children of Israel. [6]Behold, I Myself have taken your brethren the Levites from among the children of Israel; *they are* a gift to you, given by the LORD, to do the work of the tabernacle of meeting. [7]Therefore you and your sons with you shall attend to your priesthood for everything at the altar and behind the veil; and you shall serve. I give your priesthood *to you* as a gift for service, but the outsider who comes near shall be put to death."

Offerings for Support of the Priests

[8]And the LORD spoke to Aaron: "Here, I Myself have also given you charge of My heave offerings, all the holy gifts of the children of Israel; I have given them as a portion to you and your sons, as an ordinance forever. [9]This shall be yours of the most holy things *reserved* from the fire: every offering of theirs, every grain offering and every sin offering and every trespass offering which they render to Me, *shall be* most holy for you and your sons. [10]In a most holy *place* you shall eat it; every male shall eat it. It shall be holy to you.

[11]"This also *is* yours: the heave offering of their gift, with all the wave offerings of the children of Israel; I have given them to you, and your sons and

---

18:1 The Levites were divinely selected for both privileged position and heavy responsibility (Num. 1:53). They not only bore the care of the "sanctuary," but they also bore "the iniq- uity," the defilement of their own offerings (Lev. 16:11) and those of the people "that they may be accepted before the Lord" (Ex. 28:38; see also Heb. 7:26, 27).

daughters with you, as an ordinance forever. Everyone who is clean in your house may eat it.

[12]"All the best of the oil, all the best of the new wine and the grain, their firstfruits which they offer to the LORD, I have given them to you. [13]Whatever first ripe fruit is in their land, which they bring to the LORD, shall be yours. Everyone who is clean in your house may eat it.

[14]"Every devoted thing in Israel shall be yours.

[15]"Everything that first opens the womb of all flesh, which they bring to the LORD, whether man or beast, shall be yours; nevertheless the firstborn of man you shall surely redeem, and the firstborn of unclean animals you shall redeem. [16]And those redeemed of the devoted things you shall redeem when one month old, according to your valuation, for five shekels of silver, according to the shekel of the sanctuary, which is twenty gerahs. [17]But the firstborn of a cow, the firstborn of a sheep, or the firstborn of a goat you shall not redeem; they are holy. You shall sprinkle their blood on the altar, and burn their fat as an offering made by fire for a sweet aroma to the LORD. [18]And their flesh shall be yours, just as the wave breast and the right thigh are yours.

[19]"All the heave offerings of the holy things, which the children of Israel offer to the LORD, I have given to you and your sons and daughters with you as an ordinance forever; it is a covenant of salt forever before the LORD with you and your descendants with you."

[20]Then the LORD said to Aaron: "You shall have no inheritance in their land, nor shall you have any portion among them; I am your portion and your inheritance among the children of Israel.

Tithes for Support of the Levites

[21]"Behold, I have given the children of Levi all the tithes in Israel as an inheritance in return for the work which they perform, the work of the tabernacle of meeting. [22]Hereafter the children of Israel shall not come near the tabernacle of meeting, lest they bear sin and die. [23]But the Levites shall perform the work of the tabernacle of meeting, and they shall bear their iniquity; it shall be a statute forever, throughout your generations, that among the children of Israel they shall have no inheritance. [24]For the tithes of the children of Israel, which they offer up as a heave offering to the LORD, I have given to the Levites as an inheritance; therefore I have said to them, 'Among the children of Israel they shall have no inheritance.' "

The Tithe of the Levites

[25]Then the LORD spoke to Moses, saying, [26]"Speak thus to the Levites, and say to them: 'When you take from the children of Israel the tithes which I have given you from them as your inheritance, then you shall offer up a heave offering of it to the LORD, a tenth of the tithe. [27]And your heave offering shall be reckoned to you as though it were the grain of the threshing floor and as the fullness of the winepress. [28]Thus you shall also offer a heave offering to the LORD from all your tithes which you receive from the children of Israel, and you shall give the LORD's heave offering from it to Aaron the priest. [29]Of all your gifts you shall offer up every heave offering due to the LORD, from all the best of them, the consecrated part of them.' [30]Therefore you shall say to them: 'When you have lifted up the best of it, then the rest shall be accounted to the Levites as the produce of the threshing floor and as the produce of the winepress. [31]You may eat it in any place, you and your households, for it is your reward for your work in the tabernacle of meeting. [32]And you shall bear no sin because of it, when you have lifted up the best of it. But you shall not profane the holy gifts of the children of Israel, lest you die.' "

Laws of Purification

19 Now the LORD spoke to Moses and Aaron, saying, [2]"This is the ordinance of the law which the LORD has commanded, saying: 'Speak to the children of Israel, that they bring you a red heifer without blemish, in which there is no defect and on which a yoke has never come. [3]You shall give it to Eleazar the priest, that he may take it outside the camp, and it shall be slaughtered before him; [4]and Eleazar the priest shall take some of its blood with his finger, and sprinkle some of its blood seven times directly in front of the tabernacle of meeting. [5]Then the heifer shall be burned in his sight: its hide, its flesh, its blood, and its offal shall be burned. [6]And the priest shall take cedar wood and hyssop and scarlet, and cast them into the midst of the fire burning the heifer. [7]Then the priest shall wash his clothes, he shall

---

18:12–14 Offering firstfruits is giving your best to the Lord. It is associated with living off "the fat of the land" (Gen. 45:18). These offerings were brought "to the Lord" by way of the priests who, having no land, received these offerings as compensation for their services (Num. 3:44–48).

18:26 While the Levites received tithes from the people, they were not exempt. They were expected to give "a tenth of the tithe" back "to the Lord" (see Luke 16, Stewardship). Sacrificial living was just as essential for the priests as for the people (see Mic. 7, Sacrificial Living).

19:1, 2 The unique ritual of the "red heifer" is found only here in the OT. Unlike other sacrificial animals, the heifer was totally consumed in fire "outside the camp." Its ashes were saved for the purpose of "purification" (v. 9). Dying to sin, which is symbolized in this ritual, is characteristic of holy living (Rom. 12:1, 2).

19:5 Offal, the viscera and trimmings of a butchered animal, is different from the "fat" of offerings used by priests (Gen. 45:18).

bathe in water, and afterward he shall come into the camp; the priest shall be unclean until evening. [8]And the one who burns it shall wash his clothes in water, bathe in water, and shall be unclean until evening. [9]Then a man *who is* clean shall gather up the ashes of the heifer, and store *them* outside the camp in a clean place; and they shall be kept for the congregation of the children of Israel for the water of purification;[a] it *is* for purifying from sin. [10]And the one who gathers the ashes of the heifer shall wash his clothes, and be unclean until evening. It shall be a statute forever to the children of Israel and to the stranger who dwells among them.

[11]"He who touches the dead body of anyone shall be unclean seven days. [12]He shall purify himself with the water on the third day and on the seventh day; *then* he will be clean. But if he does not purify himself on the third day and on the seventh day, he will not be clean. [13]Whoever touches the body of anyone who has died, and does not purify himself, defiles the tabernacle of the LORD. That person shall be cut off from Israel. He shall be unclean, because the water of purification was not sprinkled on him; his uncleanness *is* still on him.

[14]"This *is* the law when a man dies in a tent: All who come into the tent and all who *are* in the tent shall be unclean seven days; [15]and every open vessel, which has no cover fastened on it, *is* unclean. [16]Whoever in the open field touches one who is slain by a sword or who has died, or a bone of a man, or a grave, shall be unclean seven days.

[17]"And for an unclean *person* they shall take some of the ashes of the heifer burnt for purification from sin, and running water shall be put on them in a vessel. [18]A clean person shall take hyssop and dip *it* in the water, sprinkle *it* on the tent, on all the vessels, on the persons who were there, or on the one who touched a bone, the slain, the dead, or a grave. [19]The clean *person* shall sprinkle the unclean on the third day and on the seventh day; and on the seventh day he shall purify himself, wash his clothes, and bathe in water; and at evening he shall be clean.

[20]"But the man who is unclean and does not purify himself, that person shall be cut off from among the assembly, because he has defiled the sanctuary of the LORD. The water of purification has not been sprinkled on him; he *is* unclean. [21]It shall be a perpetual statute for them. He who sprinkles the water of purification shall wash his clothes; and he who touches the water of purification shall be unclean until evening. [22]Whatever the unclean *person* touches shall be unclean; and the person who touches *it* shall be unclean until evening.' "

Moses' Error at Kadesh

20Then the children of Israel, the whole congregation, came into the Wilderness of Zin in the first month, and the people stayed in Kadesh; and Miriam died there and was buried there.

[2]Now there was no water for the congregation; so they gathered together against Moses and Aaron. [3]And the people contended with Moses and spoke, saying: "If only we had died when our brethren died before the LORD! [4]Why have you brought up the assembly of the LORD into this wilderness, that we and our animals should die here? [5]And why have you made us come up out of Egypt, to bring us to this evil place? It *is* not a place of grain or figs or vines or pomegranates; nor *is* there any water to drink." [6]So Moses and Aaron went from the presence of the assembly to the door of the tabernacle of meeting, and they fell on their faces. And the glory of the LORD appeared to them.

[7]Then the LORD spoke to Moses, saying, [8]"Take the rod; you and your brother Aaron gather the congregation together. Speak to the rock before their eyes, and it will yield its water; thus you shall bring water for them out of the rock, and give drink to the congregation and their animals." [9]So Moses took the rod from before the LORD as He commanded him.

[10]And Moses and Aaron gathered the assembly together before the rock; and he said to them, "Hear now, you rebels! Must we bring water for you out of this rock?" [11]Then Moses lifted his hand and struck the rock twice with his rod; and water came out abundantly, and the congregation and their animals drank.

[12]Then the LORD spoke to Moses and Aaron, "Because you did not believe Me, to hallow Me in the eyes of the children of Israel, therefore you shall not bring this assembly into the land which I have given them."

[13]This *was* the water of Meribah,[a] because the children of Israel contended with the LORD, and He was hallowed among them.

19:9 [a]Literally *impurity* 20:13 [a]Literally *Contention*

20:1–3 At a time of personal sorrow over the death of Miriam, Moses also had to endure again the "contention" (Heb, *Meribah*, v. 13) of an insensitive people. Again and again Moses and Aaron were scapegoats receiving from the people assaults hurled at God, even after all the Lord had done for His people (Deut. 8:1–5; see Num. 16, Rebellion).

20:10–12 With a dramatic flare, Moses demonstrated God's answer to the complaints of the people. However, he "struck the rock twice with his rod," when God had instructed him in simple trust only to "speak" to this symbol of His authority (v. 8). Moses' sin was in the fact that he tried to share the credit line (note the usage of "we" in v. 10). God's holiness was at stake (v. 12). Moses was silenced by God's punishment.

Passage Through Edom Refused

14Now Moses sent messengers from Kadesh to the king of Edom. "Thus says your brother Israel: 'You know all the hardship that has befallen us, 15how our fathers went down to Egypt, and we dwelt in Egypt a long time, and the Egyptians afflicted us and our fathers. 16When we cried out to the LORD, He heard our voice and sent the Angel and brought us up out of Egypt; now here we are in Kadesh, a city on the edge of your border. 17Please let us pass through your country. We will not pass through fields or vineyards, nor will we drink water from wells; we will go along the King's Highway; we will not turn aside to the right hand or to the left until we have passed through your territory.'"

18Then Edom said to him, "You shall not pass through my *land*, lest I come out against you with the sword."

19So the children of Israel said to him, "We will go by the Highway, and if I or my livestock drink any of your water, then I will pay for it; let me only pass through on foot, nothing *more.*"

20Then he said, "You shall not pass through." So Edom came out against them with many men and with a strong hand. 21Thus Edom refused to give Israel passage through his territory; so Israel turned away from him.

Death of Aaron

22Now the children of Israel, the whole congregation, journeyed from Kadesh and came to Mount Hor. 23And the LORD spoke to Moses and Aaron in Mount Hor by the border of the land of Edom, saying: 24"Aaron shall be gathered to his people, for he shall not enter the land which I have given to the children of Israel, because you rebelled against My word at the water of Meribah. 25Take Aaron and Eleazar his son, and bring them up to Mount Hor; 26and strip Aaron of his garments and put them on Eleazar his son; for Aaron shall be gathered *to his people* and die there." 27So Moses did just as the LORD commanded, and they went up to Mount Hor in the sight of all the congregation. 28Moses stripped Aaron of his garments and put them on Eleazar his son; and Aaron died there on the top of the mountain. Then Moses and Eleazar came down from the mountain. 29Now when all the congregation saw that Aaron was dead, all the house of Israel mourned for Aaron thirty days.

Canaanites Defeated at Hormah

21 The king of Arad, the Canaanite, who dwelt in the South, heard that Israel was coming on the road to Atharim. Then he fought against Israel and took *some* of them prisoners. 2So Israel made a vow to the LORD, and said, "If You will indeed deliver this people into my hand, then I will utterly destroy their cities." 3And the LORD listened to the voice of Israel and delivered up the Canaanites, and they utterly destroyed them and their cities. So the name of that place was called Hormah.a

The Bronze Serpent

4Then they journeyed from Mount Hor by the Way of the Red Sea, to go around the land of Edom; and the soul of the people became very discouraged on the way. 5And the people spoke against God and against Moses: "Why have you brought us up out of Egypt to die in the wilderness? For *there is* no food and no water, and our soul loathes this worthless bread." 6So the LORD sent fiery serpents among the people, and they bit the people; and many of the people of Israel died.

7Therefore the people came to Moses, and said, "We have sinned, for we have spoken against the LORD and against you; pray to the LORD that He take away the serpents from us." So Moses prayed for the people.

8Then the LORD said to Moses, "Make a fiery *serpent,* and set it on a pole; and it shall be that everyone who is bitten, when he looks at it, shall live." 9So Moses made a bronze serpent, and put it on a pole; and so it was, if a serpent had bitten anyone, when he looked at the bronze serpent, he lived.

From Mount Hor to Moab

10Now the children of Israel moved on and camped in Oboth. 11And they journeyed from

---

21:3 aLiterally *Utter Destruction*

20:17 The King's Highway, the broad road on which the Israelite army traveled, was probably the Wadi el Ghuweir, a military road built by a king. It was known for its good pastures and spring "wells" and is still a major thoroughfare (see also Num. 21:22).

20:22 Mount Hor, present-day *Harun,* was only 30 miles northeast of Kadesh Barnea, which gives credibility to the phrase "wanderings in the wilderness." "All the congregation" could easily have seen Aaron's funeral conducted upon the mountain in Hor (v. 27; Num. 14:29, 30).

21:6 Before Moses could intercede, God sent judgment from venomous snakes. "Fiery" (Heb. *seraphim,* lit. "burning") is the same word used to describe the creatures in Isaiah's vision in the temple (Is. 6:1–7). The glory of the Lord caused Isaiah to cry out "Woe is me" (Is. 6:5) and the Israelites to lament "We have sinned" (Num. 21:7), an indication of a change of heart.

21:8 God sent the remedy, in the form of a brass serpent, instead of taking away the punishment. The people must look upon the serpent to be healed. Jesus explained this to Nicodemus (see John 3:14, 15).

Oboth and camped at Ije Abarim, in the wilderness which *is* east of Moab, toward the sunrise. [12]From there they moved and camped in the Valley of Zered. [13]From there they moved and camped on the other side of the Arnon, which *is* in the wilderness that extends from the border of the Amorites; for the Arnon *is* the border of Moab, between Moab and the Amorites. [14]Therefore it is said in the Book of the Wars of the LORD:

"Waheb in Suphah,[a]
The brooks of the Arnon,
[15]And the slope of the brooks
That reaches to the dwelling of Ar,
And lies on the border of Moab."

[16]From there *they went* to Beer, which *is* the well where the LORD said to Moses, "Gather the people together, and I will give them water." [17]Then Israel sang this song:

"Spring up, O well!
All of you sing to it—
[18]The well the leaders sank,
Dug by the nation's nobles,
By the lawgiver, with their staves."

And from the wilderness *they went* to Mattanah, [19]from Mattanah to Nahaliel, from Nahaliel to Bamoth, [20]and from Bamoth, *in* the valley that *is* in the country of Moab, to the top of Pisgah which looks down on the wasteland.[a]

King Sihon Defeated

[21]Then Israel sent messengers to Sihon king of the Amorites, saying, [22]"Let me pass through your land. We will not turn aside into fields or vineyards; we will not drink water from wells. We will go by the King's Highway until we have passed through your territory." [23]But Sihon would not allow Israel to pass through his territory. So Sihon gathered all his people together and went out against Israel in the wilderness, and he came to Jahaz and fought against Israel. [24]Then Israel defeated him with the edge of the sword, and took

possession of his land from the Arnon to the Jabbok, as far as the people of Ammon; for the border of the people of Ammon *was* fortified. [25]So Israel took all these cities, and Israel dwelt in all the cities of the Amorites, in Heshbon and in all its villages. [26]For Heshbon *was* the city of Sihon king of the Amorites, who had fought against the former king of Moab, and had taken all his land from his hand as far as the Arnon. [27]Therefore those who speak in proverbs say:

"Come to Heshbon, let it be built;
Let the city of Sihon be repaired.

[28]"For fire went out from Heshbon,
A flame from the city of Sihon;
It consumed Ar of Moab,
The lords of the heights of the Arnon.
[29]Woe to you, Moab!
You have perished, O people of Chemosh!
He has given his sons as fugitives,
And his daughters into captivity,
To Sihon king of the Amorites.

[30]"But we have shot at them;
Heshbon has perished as far as Dibon.
Then we laid waste as far as Nophah,
Which *reaches* to Medeba."

[31]Thus Israel dwelt in the land of the Amorites. [32]Then Moses sent to spy out Jazer; and they took its villages and drove out the Amorites who *were* there.

King Og Defeated

[33]And they turned and went up by the way to Bashan. So Og king of Bashan went out against them, he and all his people, to battle at Edrei. [34]Then the LORD said to Moses, "Do not fear him, for I have delivered him into your hand, with all his people and his land; and you shall do to him as you did to Sihon king of the Amorites, who dwelt

---

21:14 [a]Ancient unknown places; Vulgate reads *What He did in the Red Sea.*   21:20 [a]Hebrew *Jeshimon*

21:14, 15 The Book of the Wars of the Lord is cited only here in Scripture. The quotation has neither subject nor verb, unless the opening place name "Waheb" (Heb.) is understood to mean "God gave."

21:17, 18 The Well Song is to be used by those digging a well or by the people in dedication or celebration of completion of a well or perhaps even by women going to the well to draw water. This song may be the closest thing in Scripture to a "popular" song of the people (see Ps. 147, Music; Chart, Hymns and Songs Associated with Women). Certainly there is an element of joy due to their anticipation of crossing into the Promised Land. A NT parallel may be drawn from the account of Jesus offering Himself as "living water" to the woman who came to "draw water" at the well in Samaria (John 4:7–15).

22:8, 9 Balaam was solicited as a diviner (v. 7), and though he knew the Lord's revealed name, he certainly suffered from divided loyalty (see 2 Pet. 2:15). Nonetheless, God constrained him to bless, not curse, Israel (Num. 23:11, 20).

22:20 After the persuasive tactics of Balak, Balaam received God's permission to accept the invitation—but to speak "only the word" of God. Disobedience is often punished by God's permitting transgressions to produce their natural consequences (see Prov. 1:29–31).

22:28–31 Consistency requires us to believe all, not just part, of the Balaam narrative, which would include the speech delivered in a supernatural way from the mouth of his donkey. "The Lord opened the mouth of the donkey" in order to open the eyes of its master Balaam (vv. 28, 31).

THE JOURNEY TO CANAAN

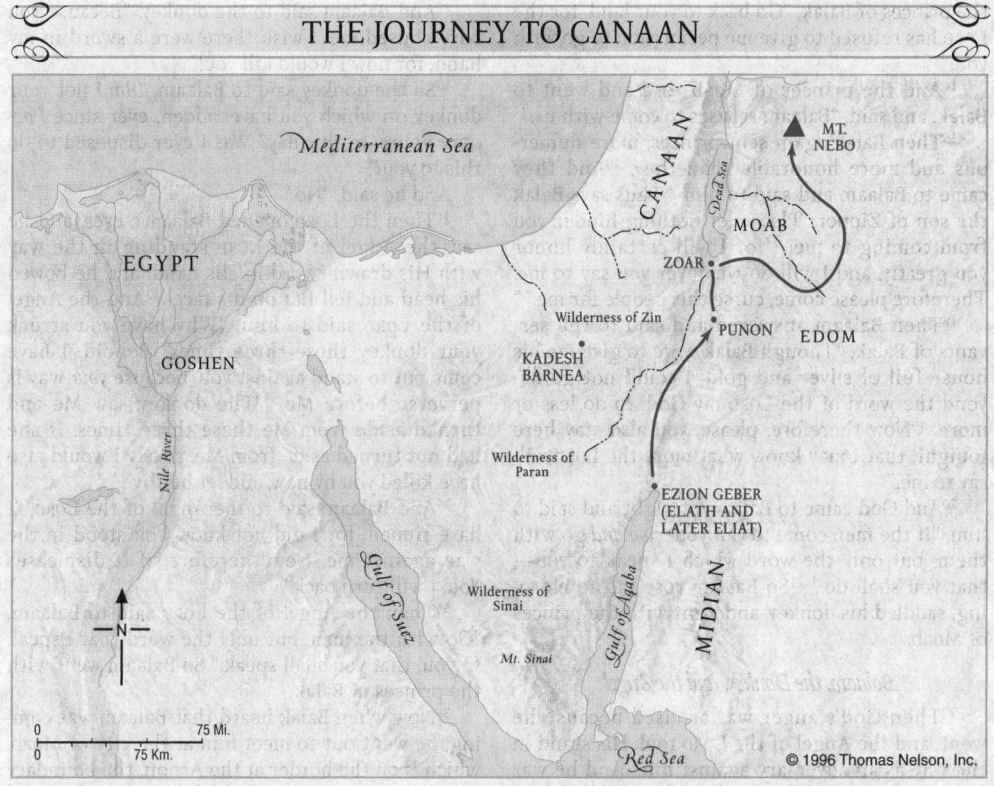

The itinerary of travel from the Wilderness to Canaan is not given in Scripture, but this route is suggested.

at Heshbon." ³⁵So they defeated him, his sons, and all his people, until there was no survivor left him; and they took possession of his land.

Balak Sends for Balaam

22 Then the children of Israel moved, and camped in the plains of Moab on the side of the Jordan *across from* Jericho.

²Now Balak the son of Zippor saw all that Israel had done to the Amorites. ³And Moab was exceedingly afraid of the people because they *were* many, and Moab was sick with dread because of the children of Israel. ⁴So Moab said to the elders of Midian, "Now this company will lick up everything around us, as an ox licks up the grass of the field." And Balak the son of Zippor *was* king of the Moabites at that time. ⁵Then he sent messengers to Balaam the son of Beor at Pethor, which *is* near the River[a] in the land of the sons of his people,[b] to call him, saying: "Look, a people has come from Egypt. See, they cover the face of the earth, and are settling next to me! ⁶Therefore please come at once, curse this people for me, for they *are* too mighty for me. Perhaps I shall be able to defeat

them and drive them out of the land, for I know that he whom you bless *is* blessed, and he whom you curse is cursed."

⁷So the elders of Moab and the elders of Midian departed with the diviner's fee in their hand, and they came to Balaam and spoke to him the words of Balak. ⁸And he said to them, "Lodge here tonight, and I will bring back word to you, as the LORD speaks to me." So the princes of Moab stayed with Balaam.

⁹Then God came to Balaam and said, "Who *are* these men with you?"

¹⁰So Balaam said to God, "Balak the son of Zippor, king of Moab, has sent to me, *saying,* ¹¹'Look, a people has come out of Egypt, and they cover the face of the earth. Come now, curse them for me; perhaps I shall be able to overpower them and drive them out.' "

¹²And God said to Balaam, "You shall not go with them; you shall not curse the people, for they *are* blessed."

¹³So Balaam rose in the morning and said to

· ·

22:5 ᵃThat is, the Euphrates ᵇOr *the people of Amau*

the princes of Balak, "Go back to your land, for the LORD has refused to give me permission to go with you."

[14]And the princes of Moab rose and went to Balak, and said, "Balaam refuses to come with us."

[15]Then Balak again sent princes, more numerous and more honorable than they. [16]And they came to Balaam and said to him, "Thus says Balak the son of Zippor: 'Please let nothing hinder you from coming to me; [17]for I will certainly honor you greatly, and I will do whatever you say to me. Therefore please come, curse this people for me.' "

[18]Then Balaam answered and said to the servants of Balak, "Though Balak were to give me his house full of silver and gold, I could not go beyond the word of the LORD my God, to do less or more. [19]Now therefore, please, you also stay here tonight, that I may know what more the LORD will say to me."

[20]And God came to Balaam at night and said to him, "If the men come to call you, rise *and* go with them; but only the word which I speak to you—that you shall do." [21]So Balaam rose in the morning, saddled his donkey, and went with the princes of Moab.

Balaam, the Donkey, and the Angel

[22]Then God's anger was aroused because he went, and the Angel of the LORD took His stand in the way as an adversary against him. And he was riding on his donkey, and his two servants *were* with him. [23]Now the donkey saw the Angel of the LORD standing in the way with His drawn sword in His hand, and the donkey turned aside out of the way and went into the field. So Balaam struck the donkey to turn her back onto the road. [24]Then the Angel of the LORD stood in a narrow path between the vineyards, *with* a wall on this side and a wall on that side. [25]And when the donkey saw the Angel of the LORD, she pushed herself against the wall and crushed Balaam's foot against the wall; so he struck her again. [26]Then the Angel of the LORD went further, and stood in a narrow place where there *was* no way to turn either to the right hand or to the left. [27]And when the donkey saw the Angel of the LORD, she lay down under Balaam; so Balaam's anger was aroused, and he struck the donkey with his staff. [28]Then the LORD opened the mouth of the donkey, and she said to Balaam, "What have I done to you, that you have struck me these three times?"

[29]And Balaam said to the donkey, "Because you have abused me. I wish there were a sword in my hand, for now I would kill you!"

[30]So the donkey said to Balaam, "*Am* I not your donkey on which you have ridden, ever since *I became* yours, to this day? Was I ever disposed to do this to you?"

And he said, "No."

[31]Then the LORD opened Balaam's eyes, and he saw the Angel of the LORD standing in the way with His drawn sword in His hand; and he bowed his head and fell flat on his face. [32]And the Angel of the LORD said to him, "Why have you struck your donkey these three times? Behold, I have come out to stand against you, because *your* way is perverse before Me. [33]The donkey saw Me and turned aside from Me these three times. If she had not turned aside from Me, surely I would also have killed you by now, and let her live."

[34]And Balaam said to the Angel of the LORD, "I have sinned, for I did not know You stood in the way against me. Now therefore, if it displeases You, I will turn back."

[35]Then the Angel of the LORD said to Balaam, "Go with the men, but only the word that I speak to you, that you shall speak." So Balaam went with the princes of Balak.

[36]Now when Balak heard that Balaam was coming, he went out to meet him at the city of Moab, which *is* on the border at the Arnon, the boundary of the territory. [37]Then Balak said to Balaam, "Did I not earnestly send to you, calling for you? Why did you not come to me? Am I not able to honor you?"

[38]And Balaam said to Balak, "Look, I have come to you! Now, have I any power at all to say anything? The word that God puts in my mouth, that I must speak." [39]So Balaam went with Balak, and they came to Kirjath Huzoth. [40]Then Balak offered oxen and sheep, and he sent *some* to Balaam and to the princes who *were* with him.

Balaam's First Prophecy

[41]So it was, the next day, that Balak took Balaam and brought him up to the high places of Baal, that from there he might observe the extent of the people.

23 Then Balaam said to Balak, "Build seven altars for me here, and prepare for me here seven bulls and seven rams."

22:41 Balak brought Balaam up to three "high places": the worship site of Baal, Pisgah (Num. 23:14), and Peor (Num. 23:28). Each was probably higher than the last, mounting along with Balak's desperation to impress Balaam with the vast Israelite camp and the "extent" of his problem.

23:1 Traditionally, a monarch might also act as priest, and "seven" would have been a significant number of altars. For Israel, multiple altars meant idolatry. Later Balaam told God about these altars, but God ignored that and emphasized His Word (vv. 4, 5). In all of Balaam's "seven" oracles, he employed the Hebrew poetic use of synonymous parallelism, in which the second line repeats the thought of the first (Num. 22—24).

[2]And Balak did just as Balaam had spoken, and Balak and Balaam offered a bull and a ram on *each* altar. [3]Then Balaam said to Balak, "Stand by your burnt offering, and I will go; perhaps the LORD will come to meet me, and whatever He shows me I will tell you." So he went to a desolate height. [4]And God met Balaam, and he said to Him, "I have prepared the seven altars, and I have offered on *each* altar a bull and a ram."

[5]Then the LORD put a word in Balaam's mouth, and said, "Return to Balak, and thus you shall speak." [6]So he returned to him, and there he was, standing by his burnt offering, he and all the princes of Moab.

[7]And he took up his oracle and said:

"Balak the king of Moab has brought me from Aram,
From the mountains of the east.
'Come, curse Jacob for me,
And come, denounce Israel!'

[8]"How shall I curse whom God has not cursed?
And how shall I denounce *whom* the LORD has not denounced?
[9]For from the top of the rocks I see him,
And from the hills I behold him;
There! A people dwelling alone,
Not reckoning itself among the nations.

[10]"Who can count the dust[a] of Jacob,
Or number one-fourth of Israel?
Let me die the death of the righteous,
And let my end be like his!"

[11]Then Balak said to Balaam, "What have you done to me? I took you to curse my enemies, and look, you have blessed *them* bountifully!"

[12]So he answered and said, "Must I not take heed to speak what the LORD has put in my mouth?"

Balaam's Second Prophecy

[13]Then Balak said to him, "Please come with me to another place from which you may see them; you shall see only the outer part of them, and shall not see them all; curse them for me from there." [14]So he brought him to the field of Zophim, to the top of Pisgah, and built seven altars, and offered a bull and a ram on *each* altar.

[15]And he said to Balak, "Stand here by your burnt offering while I meet[a] *the LORD* over there."

[16]Then the LORD met Balaam, and put a word in his mouth, and said, "Go back to Balak, and thus you shall speak." [17]So he came to him, and there he was, standing by his burnt offering, and the princes of Moab were with him. And Balak said to him, "What has the LORD spoken?"

[18]Then he took up his oracle and said:

"Rise up, Balak, and hear!
Listen to me, son of Zippor!

[19]"God *is* not a man, that He should lie,
Nor a son of man, that He should repent.
Has He said, and will He not do?
Or has He spoken, and will He not make it good?
[20]Behold, I have received *a command* to bless;
He has blessed, and I cannot reverse it.

[21]"He has not observed iniquity in Jacob,
Nor has He seen wickedness in Israel.
The LORD his God *is* with him,
And the shout of a King *is* among them.
[22]God brings them out of Egypt;
He has strength like a wild ox.

[23]"For *there is* no sorcery against Jacob,
Nor any divination against Israel.
It now must be said of Jacob
And of Israel, 'Oh, what God has done!'
[24]Look, a people rises like a lioness,
And lifts itself up like a lion;
It shall not lie down until it devours the prey,
And drinks the blood of the slain."

[25]Then Balak said to Balaam, "Neither curse them at all, nor bless them at all!"

[26]So Balaam answered and said to Balak, "Did I not tell you, saying, 'All that the LORD speaks, that I must do'?"

Balaam's Third Prophecy

[27]Then Balak said to Balaam, "Please come, I will take you to another place; perhaps it will please God that you may curse them for me from there." [28]So Balak took Balaam to the top of Peor,

---

23:10 [a]Or *dust cloud*   **23:15** [a]Following Masoretic Text, Targum, and Vulgate; Syriac reads *call*; Septuagint reads *go and ask God.*

23:9 Under the constraint of God, Balaam spoke an important truth about Israel: The separateness of Israel from other nations in a physical and spiritual sense was absolutely essential (Deut. 7:6). Throughout history God has proven that those who belong to Him are powerful.

23:10, 11 Balak was displeased that Balaam's oracle turned out to be a blessing on his enemy. As God had promised blessing to

Abraham (Gen. 12:2), so He informed Balaam earlier that "they are blessed" (Num. 22:12). Balaam would have counted it a privilege to be as blessed as the people of God (Num. 23:10).

23:21 God neither ignores nor excuses "iniquity" and "wickedness," but His enduring mercy and love is intent on keeping His covenant relationship. While God cannot abide sin, He does abide with His people.

that overlooks the wasteland.[a] 29Then Balaam said to Balak, "Build for me here seven altars, and prepare for me here seven bulls and seven rams." 30And Balak did as Balaam had said, and offered a bull and a ram on *every* altar.

24 Now when Balaam saw that it pleased the LORD to bless Israel, he did not go as at other times, to seek to use sorcery, but he set his face toward the wilderness. 2And Balaam raised his eyes, and saw Israel encamped according to their tribes; and the Spirit of God came upon him. 3Then he took up his oracle and said:

"The utterance of Balaam the son of Beor,
The utterance of the man whose eyes are
    opened,
4The utterance of him who hears the words of
    God,
Who sees the vision of the Almighty,
Who falls down, with eyes wide open:

5"How lovely are your tents, O Jacob!
Your dwellings, O Israel!
6Like valleys that stretch out,
Like gardens by the riverside,
Like aloes planted by the LORD,
Like cedars beside the waters.
7He shall pour water from his buckets,
And his seed *shall be* in many waters.

"His king shall be higher than Agag,
And his kingdom shall be exalted.

8"God brings him out of Egypt;
He has strength like a wild ox;
He shall consume the nations, his enemies;
He shall break their bones
And pierce *them* with his arrows.
9"He bows down, he lies down as a lion;
And as a lion, who shall rouse him?'[a]

"Blessed *is* he who blesses you,
And cursed *is* he who curses you."

10Then Balak's anger was aroused against Balaam, and he struck his hands together; and Balak said to Balaam, "I called you to curse my enemies, and look, you have bountifully blessed *them* these three times! 11Now therefore, flee to your place. I said I would greatly honor you, but in fact, the LORD has kept you back from honor."

12So Balaam said to Balak, "Did I not also speak to your messengers whom you sent to me, saying, 13'If Balak were to give me his house full of silver and gold, I could not go beyond the word of the LORD, to do good or bad of my own will. What the LORD says, that I must speak'? 14And now, indeed, I am going to my people. Come, I will advise you what this people will do to your people in the latter days."

Balaam's Fourth Prophecy

15So he took up his oracle and said:

"The utterance of Balaam the son of Beor,
And the utterance of the man whose eyes are
    opened;
16The utterance of him who hears the words of
    God,
And has the knowledge of the Most High,
Who sees the vision of the Almighty,
Who falls down, with eyes wide open:

17"I see Him, but not now;
I behold Him, but not near;
A Star shall come out of Jacob;
A Scepter shall rise out of Israel,
And batter the brow of Moab,
And destroy all the sons of tumult.[a]

18"And Edom shall be a possession;
Seir also, his enemies, shall be a possession,
While Israel does valiantly.
19Out of Jacob One shall have dominion,
And destroy the remains of the city."

20Then he looked on Amalek, and he took up his oracle and said:

"Amalek *was* first among the nations,
But *shall be* last until he perishes."

21Then he looked on the Kenites, and he took up his oracle and said:

"Firm is your dwelling place,
And your nest is set in the rock;
22Nevertheless Kain shall be burned.
How long until Asshur carries you away
    captive?"

23:28 [a]Hebrew *Jeshimon*   **24:9** [a]Genesis 49:9   **24:17** [a]Hebrew *Sheth* (compare Jeremiah 48:45)

24:2 The Spirit of God came upon Balaam when from Mt. Peor he saw the broad expanse of the Israelite encampment (Num. 23:28). Under inspiration he uttered an accurate and amazing prophecy describing the future of God's people. Balaam was enabled for a particular time to accomplish God's purpose. However, in no sense is this equal to the anointing of God's Spirit (Is. 61:1) or the gift of the Holy Spirit at Pentecost

(Acts 2:1–4). In similar fashion, God used an unlikely person in Caiaphas to declare His Purposes (see John 11:49–52).

24:17 While the content of this verse was realized in King David, who conquered the Moabites, it also may be related to David's greater Son, born "King of the Jews," whose kingdom is everlasting (Matt. 1:17; 2:2). Jude later wrote of a similar prophecy of judgment by Enoch (Jude 14, 15).

²³Then he took up his oracle and said:

"Alas! Who shall live when God does this?
²⁴But ships *shall come* from the coasts of Cyprus,ᵃ
And they shall afflict Asshur and afflict Eber,
And so shall *Amalek*,ᵇ until he perishes."

²⁵So Balaam rose and departed and returned to his place; Balak also went his way.

Israel's Harlotry in Moab

25 Now Israel remained in Acacia Grove,ᵃ and the people began to commit harlotry with the women of Moab. ²They invited the people to the sacrifices of their gods, and the people ate and bowed down to their gods. ³So Israel was joined to Baal of Peor, and the anger of the LORD was aroused against Israel.

⁴Then the LORD said to Moses, "Take all the leaders of the people and hang the offenders before the LORD, out in the sun, that the fierce anger of the LORD may turn away from Israel."

⁵So Moses said to the judges of Israel, "Every one of you kill his men who were joined to Baal of Peor."

⁶And indeed, one of the children of Israel came and presented to his brethren a Midianite woman in the sight of Moses and in the sight of all the congregation of the children of Israel, who *were* weeping at the door of the tabernacle of meeting. ⁷Now when Phinehas the son of Eleazar, the son of Aaron the priest, saw *it*, he rose from among the congregation and took a javelin in his hand; ⁸and he went after the man of Israel into the tent and thrust both of them through, the man of Israel,

and the woman through her body. So the plague was stopped among the children of Israel. ⁹And those who died in the plague were twenty-four thousand.

¹⁰Then the LORD spoke to Moses, saying: ¹¹"Phinehas the son of Eleazar, the son of Aaron the priest, has turned back My wrath from the children of Israel, because he was zealous with My zeal among them, so that I did not consume the children of Israel in My zeal. ¹²Therefore say, 'Behold, I give to him My covenant of peace; ¹³and it shall be to him and his descendants after him a covenant of an everlasting priesthood, because he was zealous for his God, and made atonement for the children of Israel.'"

¹⁴Now the name of the Israelite who was killed, who was killed with the Midianite woman, *was* Zimri the son of Salu, a leader of a father's house among the Simeonites. ¹⁵And the name of the Midianite woman who was killed *was* Cozbi the daughter of Zur; he *was* head of the people of a father's house in Midian.

¹⁶Then the LORD spoke to Moses, saying: ¹⁷"Harass the Midianites, and attack them; ¹⁸for they harassed you with their schemes by which they seduced you in the matter of Peor and in the matter of Cozbi, the daughter of a leader of Midian, their sister, who was killed in the day of the plague because of Peor."

The Second Census of Israel

26 And it came to pass, after the plague, that the LORD spoke to Moses and Eleazar the

24:24 ᵃHebrew *Kittim* ᵇLiterally *he* or *that one*   25:1 ᵃHebrew *Shittim*

24:25 After all that had been spoken about the Lord and His purposes for Israel, Balaam and Balak, seemingly unmoved, returned to their previous ways. No further reference to Balak appears in Scripture; Balaam was later killed in a battle between the Midianites and Israel (Num. 31:8).

25:1–3 What Balak could not achieve with sorcery was almost accomplished by subversion (Num. 22—24). Through the counsel of Balaam (Num. 31:16), "the women of Moab . . . invited" the men of Israel to eat and sleep with them (Num. 26:1, 2). Succumbing to harlotry led to idolatry, and God's people began worshiping Moab's god Baal of Peor. The Hebrew word *Ba'al* means "master, possessor, husband"; hence the word "joined" is used when referring to the result of Israel's unholy alliance with harlots. No wonder God was enraged (Num. 25:3).

25:10–13 God's anger over Israel's sin resulted in an execution (v. 4), a plague (v. 9), and a battle (v. 17). One man, Phinehas, grandson of Aaron, exacted judgment upon two specific offenders who shamelessly continued in immorality, even while the congregation showed signs of contrition (v. 6). God vindicated Phinehas as "zealous" and counted his action as atonement for His people.

25:14, 15 The names of the two slain people and their families are given. Cozbi (lit. "my lie" or "deception") is identified only

as the daughter of Zur, a Midianite king (Num. 31:8). Her claim to fame is as an example of the tragic deception found in pagan worship (Num. 25:15, 18). She may have been a pagan priestess. Some interpret the presentation of the Midianite woman to be a reference to her involvement with the Israelite in immoral intimacy, as in Baal worship, at the very entrance to the tabernacle (v. 6). Both Zimri, a prince in the house of Simeon, and Cozbi were from prominent noble families and had promising futures.

26:2 A second census was required to determine Israel's military strength for further battles and to ascertain their numerical size before land grants in Canaan could be issued. Two significant differences appear between the first census (Num. 1) and the second (Num. 26). The term "the family of" (v. 5) is used more often in the second census than "the son of" (Num. 1:5). Also the total size of some tribes had changed drastically. For example, the tribe of Reuben had decreased by 2,770, while the tribe of Benjamin had increased by 10,200. Within the account of the second census are several other items of interest (Num. 26). The children of Korah were spared death in the earthquake of judgment (v. 32). Zelophehad, from the tribe of Manasseh, "had no sons" (v. 33), and his daughters requested attention later (see Num. 26, Daughters of Zelophehad). Serah, daughter of Asher, was listed among her brothers (Num. 26:46; see also Gen. 46:17; 1 Chr. 7:30).

THE DAUGHTERS OF ZELOPHEHAD

God's law-and-order training for His formerly enslaved people included careful directions about the passing of property rights from one generation to the next. Under Israel's patriarchal system, the land and related responsibilities were distributed to each tribe descending from the sons of Jacob. But what about the inheritance when there was no son?

Gilead was the great-grandson of Joseph through Manasseh (see Gen. 48:14–20). Generations later, one of Gilead's grandsons had five daughters, and the legacy of land did not fit the prescribed legal pattern. Moses' leadership here reveals God's careful concern for women. First, they were given the right to choose their own husbands. Even though families gave (or withheld) consent, the bride made the final decision. Her choice was to be within the tribe, which would retain her inheritance within the extended family. The record shows that the daughters of Zelophehad complied.

Each daughter is named (Mahlah, Noah, Hoglah, Milcah, and Tirzah; see Num. 26:33; 27:1; 36:11), emphasizing that God sees each as an individual and holds each responsible for the privilege of living and contributing to her community. Moreover, the women initiated the request for their inheritance through prescribed channels, with a review of their family history (Num. 27:1–8). They were not just asking for property previously held by their father but for what had been promised. Thus their request was an act of faith. As their divinely appointed leader, Moses affirmed them (Num. 27:5–7) and elevated them to equality with their male cousins in terms of family wealth.

The orderliness of God's economy is always based on sound reasoning. The space devoted to these heirs demonstrates that God does not accord secondary status to women; but neither does He elevate women over men. His balance of power is perfect and His expectations purposeful. Daughters were to marry and bear children; owners were to guard their estates with serious stewardship so that all might benefit (see Num. 36:3, 4, 8). From what may appear as a trivial legal matter, the daughters of Zelophehad speak to us about God's priorities for community welfare and personal security.

See also Num. 27:7; 36:2–11; notes on Children (Luke 15); Inheritance (Prov. 13)

son of Aaron the priest, saying: [2]"Take a census of all the congregation of the children of Israel from twenty years old and above, by their fathers' houses, all who are able to go to war in Israel." [3]So Moses and Eleazar the priest spoke with them in the plains of Moab by the Jordan, *across from* Jericho, saying: [4]*"Take a census of the people* from twenty years old and above, just as the LORD commanded Moses and the children of Israel who came out of the land of Egypt."

[5]Reuben *was* the firstborn of Israel. The children of Reuben *were: of* Hanoch, the family of the Hanochites; *of* Pallu, the family of the Palluites; [6]*of* Hezron, the family of the Hezronites; *of* Carmi, the family of the Carmites. [7]These *are* the families of the Reubenites: those who were numbered of them were forty-three thousand seven hundred and thirty. [8]And the son of Pallu *was* Eliab. [9]The sons of Eliab *were* Nemuel, Dathan, and Abiram. These *are* the Dathan and Abiram, representatives of the congregation, who contended against Moses and Aaron in the company of Korah, when they contended against the LORD; [10]and the earth opened its mouth and swallowed them up together with Korah when that company died, when the fire devoured two hundred and fifty men; and they became a sign. [11]Nevertheless the children of Korah did not die.

[12]The sons of Simeon according to their families *were: of* Nemuel,[a] the family of the Nemuelites; *of* Jamin, the family of the Jaminites; *of* Jachin,[b] the family of the Jachinites; [13]*of* Zerah,[a] the family of the Zarhites; *of* Shaul, the family of the Shaulites. [14]These *are* the families of the Simeonites: twenty-two thousand two hundred.

[15]The sons of Gad according to their families *were: of* Zephon,[a] the family of the Zephonites; *of* Haggi, the family of the Haggites; *of* Shuni, the family of the Shunites; [16]*of* Ozni,[a] the family of the Oznites; *of* Eri, the family of the Erites; [17]*of* Arod,[a] the family of the Arodites; *of* Areli, the family of the Arelites. [18]These *are* the families of the sons of Gad according to those who were numbered of them: forty thousand five hundred.

[19]The sons of Judah *were* Er and Onan; and Er and Onan died in the land of Canaan. [20]And the sons of Judah according to their families were: *of* Shelah, the family of the Shelanites; *of* Perez, the family of the Parzites; *of* Zerah, the family of the Zarhites. [21]And the sons of Perez were: *of* Hezron, the family of the Hezronites; *of* Hamul, the family of the Hamulites. [22]These *are* the families of Judah

26:12 [a]Spelled *Jemuel* in Genesis 46:10 and Exodus 6:15 [b]Called *Jarib* in 1 Chronicles 4:24 26:13 [a]Called *Zohar* in Genesis 46:10 26:15 [a]Called *Ziphion* in Genesis 46:16 26:16 [a]Called *Ezbon* in Genesis 46:16 26:17 [a]Spelled *Arodi* in Samaritan Pentateuch, Syriac, and Genesis 46:16

In his earliest dealings with the people of Israel, God asked obedience and they disobeyed. God gave them promises, dependent on their willingness to do what he asked, and they did not do it. But he did not give them up. It was the glory of his own name that was at stake. . . . In countless ways he bore with them, corrected them, punished them, goaded them, and brought them to the Promised Land. His love for them was inexorable.

Elisabeth Elliot

according to those who were numbered of them: seventy-six thousand five hundred.

²³The sons of Issachar according to their families *were: of* Tola, the family of the Tolaites; of Puah,[a] the family of the Punites;[b] ²⁴of Jashub, the family of the Jashubites; of Shimron, the family of the Shimronites. ²⁵These *are* the families of Issachar according to those who were numbered of them: sixty-four thousand three hundred.

²⁶The sons of Zebulun according to their families *were:* of Sered, the family of the Sardites; of Elon, the family of the Elonites; of Jahleel, the family of the Jahleelites. ²⁷These *are* the families of the Zebulunites according to those who were numbered of them: sixty thousand five hundred.

²⁸The sons of Joseph according to their families, by Manasseh and Ephraim, *were:* ²⁹The sons of Manasseh: of Machir, the family of the Machirites; and Machir begot Gilead; of Gilead, the family of the Gileadites. ³⁰These *are* the sons of Gilead: *of* Jeezer,[a] the family of the Jeezerites; of Helek, the family of the Helekites; ³¹*of* Asriel, the family of the Asrielites; *of* Shechem, the family of the Shechemites; ³²*of* Shemida, the family of the Shemidaites; *of* Hepher, the family of the Hepherites. ³³Now Zelophehad the son of Hepher had no sons, but daughters; and the names of the daughters of Zelophehad *were* Mahlah, Noah, Hoglah, Milcah, and Tirzah. ³⁴These *are* the families of Manasseh; and those who were numbered of them *were* fifty-two thousand seven hundred.

³⁵These *are* the sons of Ephraim according to their families: of Shuthelah, the family of the Shuthalhites; of Becher,[a] the family of the Bachrites; of Tahan, the family of the Tahanites. ³⁶And these *are* the sons of Shuthelah: of Eran, the family of the Eranites. ³⁷These *are* the families of the sons of Ephraim according to those who were numbered of them: thirty-two thousand five hundred.

These *are* the sons of Joseph according to their families.

³⁸The sons of Benjamin according to their families were: of Bela, the family of the Belaites; of Ashbel, the family of the Ashbelites; of Ahiram, the family of the Ahiramites; ³⁹of Shupham,[a] the family of the Shuphamites; of Hupham,[b] the fam-

ily of the Huphamites. ⁴⁰And the sons of Bela were Ard[a] and Naaman: *of Ard,* the family of the Ardites; of Naaman, the family of the Naamites. ⁴¹These *are* the sons of Benjamin according to their families; and those who were numbered of them *were* forty-five thousand six hundred.

⁴²These *are* the sons of Dan according to their families: of Shuham,[a] the family of the Shuhamites. These *are* the families of Dan according to their families. ⁴³All the families of the Shuhamites, according to those who were numbered of them, *were* sixty-four thousand four hundred.

⁴⁴The sons of Asher according to their families *were:* of Jimna, the family of the Jimnites; of Jesui, the family of the Jesuites; of Beriah, the family of the Beriites. ⁴⁵Of the sons of Beriah: of Heber, the family of the Heberites; of Malchiel, the family of the Malchielites. ⁴⁶And the name of the daughter of Asher *was* Serah. ⁴⁷These *are* the families of the sons of Asher according to those who were numbered of them: fifty-three thousand four hundred.

⁴⁸The sons of Naphtali according to their families *were:* of Jahzeel,[a] the family of the Jahzeelites; of Guni, the family of the Gunites; ⁴⁹of Jezer, the family of the Jezerites; of Shillem, the family of the Shillemites. ⁵⁰These *are* the families of Naphtali according to their families; and those who were numbered of them *were* forty-five thousand four hundred.

⁵¹These *are* those who were numbered of the children of Israel: six hundred and one thousand seven hundred and thirty.

⁵²Then the LORD spoke to Moses, saying: ⁵³"To these the land shall be divided as an inheritance, according to the number of names. ⁵⁴To a large *tribe* you shall give a larger inheritance, and to a small *tribe* you shall give a smaller inheritance. Each shall be given its inheritance according to

26:23 ᵃHebrew *Puvah* (compare Genesis 46:13 and 1 Chronicles 7:1); Samaritan Pentateuch, Septuagint, Syriac, and Vulgate read *Puah.* ᵇSamaritan Pentateuch, Septuagint, Syriac, and Vulgate read *Puaites.* 26:30 ᵃCalled *Abiezer* in Joshua 17:2 26:35 ᵃCalled *Bered* in 1 Chronicles 7:20 26:39 ᵃMasoretic Text reads *Shephupham,* spelled *Shephuphan* in 1 Chronicles 8:5. ᵇCalled *Huppim* in Genesis 46:21 26:40 ᵃCalled *Addar* in 1 Chronicles 8:3 26:42 ᵃCalled *Hushim* in Genesis 46:23 26:48 ᵃSpelled *Jahziel* in 1 Chronicles 7:13

those who were numbered of them. ⁵⁵But the land shall be divided by lot; they shall inherit according to the names of the tribes of their fathers. ⁵⁶According to the lot their inheritance shall be divided between the larger and the smaller."

⁵⁷And these *are* those who were numbered of the Levites according to their families: of Gershon, the family of the Gershonites; of Kohath, the family of the Kohathites; of Merari, the family of the Merarites. ⁵⁸These *are* the families of the Levites: the family of the Libnites, the family of the Hebronites, the family of the Mahlites, the family of the Mushites, and the family of the Korathites. And Kohath begot Amram. ⁵⁹The name of Amram's wife *was* Jochebed the daughter of Levi, who was born to Levi in Egypt; and to Amram she bore Aaron and Moses and their sister Miriam. ⁶⁰To Aaron were born Nadab and Abihu, Eleazar and Ithamar. ⁶¹And Nadab and Abihu died when they offered profane fire before the LORD.

⁶²Now those who were numbered of them were twenty-three thousand, every male from a month old and above; for they were not numbered among the other children of Israel, because there was no inheritance given to them among the children of Israel.

⁶³These *are* those who were numbered by Moses and Eleazar the priest, who numbered the children of Israel in the plains of Moab by the Jordan, *across from* Jericho. ⁶⁴But among these there was not a man of those who were numbered by Moses and Aaron the priest when they numbered the children of Israel in the Wilderness of Sinai. ⁶⁵For the LORD had said of them, "They shall surely die in the wilderness." So there was not left a man of them, except Caleb the son of Jephunneh and Joshua the son of Nun.

Inheritance Laws

27 Then came the daughters of Zelophehad the son of Hepher, the son of Gilead, the son of Machir, the son of Manasseh, from the families of Manasseh the son of Joseph; and these *were* the names of his daughters: Mahlah, Noah, Hoglah, Milcah, and Tirzah. ²And they stood before Moses, before Eleazar the priest, and before the leaders and all the congregation, *by* the doorway of the tabernacle of meeting, saying: ³"Our father died in the wilderness; but he was not in the company of those who gathered together against the LORD, in company with Korah, but he died in his own sin; and he had no sons. ⁴Why should the name of our father be removed from among his family because he had no son? Give us a possession among our father's brothers."

⁵So Moses brought their case before the LORD. ⁶And the LORD spoke to Moses, saying: ⁷"The daughters of Zelophehad speak *what is* right; you shall surely give them a possession of inheritance among their father's brothers, and cause the inheritance of their father to pass to them. ⁸And you shall speak to the children of Israel, saying: 'If a man dies and has no son, then you shall cause his inheritance to pass to his daughter. ⁹If he has no daughter, then you shall give his inheritance to his brothers. ¹⁰If he has no brothers, then you shall give his inheritance to his father's brothers. ¹¹And if his father has no brothers, then you shall give his inheritance to the relative closest to him in his family, and he shall possess it.' " And it shall be to the children of Israel a statute of judgment, just as the LORD commanded Moses.

Joshua the Next Leader of Israel

¹²Now the LORD said to Moses: "Go up into this Mount Abarim, and see the land which I have

---

26:62–65 The second generation needed counting because God's judgment was fulfilled: The first generation of Israelites had died in the wilderness due to unbelief (Num. 14:29). Only Caleb and Joshua were spared because of their confidence in God's faithfulness to bring them into the Land (Num. 14:30). Moses and Eleazar, also of the first generation census, were Levites and therefore "not numbered . . . because there was no inheritance" (Num. 26:62).

27:1–4 Other families without male heirs surely existed before this incident, but it is evident here that no precedent had been established for daughters to receive territorial inheritance. The request of Mahlah, Noah, Hoglah, Milcah, and Tirzah is indeed bold because land was bequeathed to sons and because they challenged the existing Hebrew law given by God's command (see Num. 26, Daughters of Zelophehad). Their challenge differs from that of Miriam because of motive (Num. 12:2; 27:4). Standing in the most public assembly before the tabernacle and before the male leaders, these five disadvantaged women also stood on their personal belief in God's promise of land not yet allocated (v. 2). Their concern was twofold: their father's land and his name. Without these

they lacked hope of property or posterity under the present statutes (see Num. 36).

27:5–7 God declared the request of these five sisters to be right and allocated their due inheritance. The Hebrew word for "them" is masculine gender with two possibilities (v. 7): These daughters were either viewed the same as sons according to the law, or this reference was made to their future sons (see article, Renewed By His Grace).

27:11 A precedent was set. The new regulation was generalized and expanded to include situations similar to that presented by the daughters of Zelophehad. This "statute of judgment" was in regard to territorial inheritance.

27:12–14 Because Moses had rebelled, he could only view the Land of Promise but not enter it. This brings up a factor involved in biblical study—that of spiritualizing biblical narrative. The case in question is making the Exodus journey represent our spiritual pilgrimage and Canaan a type of heaven. While there are evident parallels, all "types" break down at some point. Thus, this form of study must be approached with great caution.

given to the children of Israel. ¹³And when you have seen it, you also shall be gathered to your people, as Aaron your brother was gathered. ¹⁴For in the Wilderness of Zin, during the strife of the congregation, you rebelled against My command to hallow Me at the waters before their eyes." (These *are* the waters of Meribah, at Kadesh in the Wilderness of Zin.)

¹⁵Then Moses spoke to the Lord, saying: ¹⁶"Let the Lord, the God of the spirits of all flesh, set a man over the congregation, ¹⁷who may go out before them and go in before them, who may lead them out and bring them in, that the congregation of the Lord may not be like sheep which have no shepherd."

¹⁸And the Lord said to Moses: "Take Joshua the son of Nun with you, a man in whom *is* the Spirit, and lay your hand on him; ¹⁹set him before Eleazar the priest and before all the congregation, and inaugurate him in their sight. ²⁰And you shall give *some* of your authority to him, that all the congregation of the children of Israel may be obedient. ²¹He shall stand before Eleazar the priest, who shall inquire before the Lord for him by the judgment of the Urim. At his word they shall go out, and at his word they shall come in, he and all the children of Israel with him— all the congregation."

²²So Moses did as the Lord commanded him. He took Joshua and set him before Eleazar the priest and before all the congregation. ²³And he laid his hands on him and inaugurated him, just as the Lord commanded by the hand of Moses.

Daily Offerings

28 Now the Lord spoke to Moses, saying, ²"Command the children of Israel, and say to them, 'My offering, My food for My offerings made by fire as a sweet aroma to Me, you shall be careful to offer to Me at their appointed time.'

³"And you shall say to them, 'This *is* the offering made by fire which you shall offer to the Lord: two male lambs in their first year without blemish, day by day, as a regular burnt offering. ⁴The one lamb you shall offer in the morning, the other lamb you shall offer in the evening, ⁵and one-tenth of an ephah of fine flour as a grain offering mixed with one-fourth of a hin of pressed oil. ⁶*It is* a regular burnt offering which was ordained at Mount Sinai for a sweet aroma, an offering made by fire to the Lord. ⁷And its drink offering *shall be* one-fourth of a hin for each lamb; in a holy *place* you shall pour out the drink to the Lord as an offering. ⁸The other lamb you shall offer in the evening; as the morning grain offering and its drink offering, you shall offer *it* as an offering made by fire, a sweet aroma to the Lord.

Sabbath Offerings

⁹And on the Sabbath day two lambs in their first year, without blemish, and two-tenths *of an ephah* of fine flour as a grain offering, mixed with oil, with its drink offering— ¹⁰*this is* the burnt offering for every Sabbath, besides the regular burnt offering with its drink offering.

Monthly Offerings

¹¹'At the beginnings of your months you shall present a burnt offering to the Lord: two young bulls, one ram, and seven lambs in their first year, without blemish; ¹²three-tenths *of an ephah* of fine flour as a grain offering, mixed with oil, for each bull; two-tenths *of an ephah* of fine flour as a grain offering, mixed with oil, for the one ram; ¹³and one-tenth *of an ephah* of fine flour, mixed with oil, as a grain offering for each lamb, as a burnt offering of sweet aroma, an offering made by fire to the Lord. ¹⁴Their drink offering shall be half a hin of wine for a bull, one-third of a hin for a ram, and one-fourth of a hin for a lamb; this *is* the burnt offering for each month throughout the months of the year. ¹⁵Also one kid of the goats as a sin offering to the Lord shall be offered, besides the regular burnt offering and its drink offering.

28:1–3 Personal possessive pronouns in these verses emphasize God's ownership of all that is offered to Him. All the silver and gold (Hag. 2:8), all the beasts and cattle belong to God; believers return or "offer" them to Him (Ps. 50:10). Focusing on the regularity of these sacrifices in the community of the redeemed reveals how they were naturally and spontaneously interwoven into the fabric of life itself—morning and evening and special sacrifices on the Sabbath and on the first of the month (Num. 28:2; Ps. 55:17; see Dan. 2:23, note; charts, The Offerings of the Lord; The Principle of the Sabbath). Actually the worship of God apart from sacrifice cannot be imagined, and an act cannot be identified as sacrifice without obedience (see 1 Sam. 15:22; Philem., Obedience). Any woman considering this overwhelming emphasis on sacrifice will be convicted of the importance of recognizing the holiness of God in contrast to her own sinfulness. Believers are challenged to establish a regular and "appointed time" to focus upon the

Lord. A worthy investment of time and energies—an acceptable gift and not merely leftovers—must be given (see Lev. 22:17–33; 2 Sam. 24:24). These timely and acceptable sacrifices are "a sweet aroma to the Lord" (Num. 28:2, 6, 7), and our obedience—not the sacrificing itself—brings God pleasure (Ps. 40:6–8; Mic. 6:6–8; Rom. 12:1, 2). "Regular burnt offerings" were not made for atonement but expressed praise and thanks. Animals sacrificed for this purpose outnumbered those sacrificed for sin offerings on nearly a 40 to 1 ratio, indicating the importance of praise in Hebrew worship (see Ps. 150, Praise).

28:9 Sabbath offerings, mentioned here for the first time, are in addition to regular offerings. God commands observance of the Sabbath (Ex. 20:8–11; see chart, The Principle of the Sabbath), which He established at the time of creation (Gen. 2:3). The latter passage is the first reference to holiness or "setting apart."

Offerings at Passover

16'On the fourteenth day of the first month *is* the Passover of the LORD. 17And on the fifteenth day of this month *is* the feast; unleavened bread shall be eaten for seven days. 18On the first day *you shall have* a holy convocation. You shall do no customary work. 19And you shall present an offering made by fire as a burnt offering to the LORD: two young bulls, one ram, and seven lambs in their first year. Be sure they are without blemish. 20Their grain offering shall be of fine flour mixed with oil: three-tenths *of an ephah* you shall offer for a bull, and two-tenths for a ram; 21you shall offer one-tenth *of an ephah* for each of the seven lambs; 22also one goat *as* a sin offering, to make atonement for you. 23You shall offer these besides the burnt offering of the morning, which *is* for a regular burnt offering. 24In this manner you shall offer the food of the offering made by fire daily for seven days, as a sweet aroma to the LORD; it shall be offered besides the regular burnt offering and its drink offering. 25And on the seventh day you shall have a holy convocation. You shall do no customary work.

Offerings at the Feast of Weeks

26'Also on the day of the firstfruits, when you bring a new grain offering to the LORD at your *Feast of* Weeks, you shall have a holy convocation. You shall do no customary work. 27You shall present a burnt offering as a sweet aroma to the LORD: two young bulls, one ram, and seven lambs in their first year, 28with their grain offering of fine flour mixed with oil: three-tenths *of an ephah* for each bull, two-tenths for the one ram, 29and one-tenth for each of the seven lambs; 30*also* one kid of the goats, to make atonement for you. 31Be sure they are without blemish. You shall present *them* with their drink offerings, besides the regular burnt offering with its grain offering.

Offerings at the Feast of Trumpets

29'And in the seventh month, on the first *day* of the month, you shall have a holy convo-

cation. You shall do no customary work. For you it is a day of blowing the trumpets. 2You shall offer a burnt offering as a sweet aroma to the LORD: one young bull, one ram, *and* seven lambs in their first year, without blemish. 3Their grain offering *shall be* fine flour mixed with oil: three-tenths *of an ephah* for the bull, two-tenths for the ram, 4and one-tenth for each of the seven lambs; 5also one kid of the goats *as* a sin offering, to make atonement for you; 6besides the burnt offering with its grain offering for the New Moon, the regular burnt offering with its grain offering, and their drink offerings, according to their ordinance, as a sweet aroma, an offering made by fire to the LORD.

Offerings on the Day of Atonement

7'On the tenth *day* of this seventh month you shall have a holy convocation. You shall afflict your souls; you shall not do any work. 8You shall present a burnt offering to the LORD *as* a sweet aroma: one young bull, one ram, *and* seven lambs in their first year. Be sure they are without blemish. 9Their grain offering *shall be of* fine flour mixed with oil: three-tenths *of an ephah* for the bull, two-tenths for the one ram, 10and one-tenth for each of the seven lambs; 11also one kid of the goats *as* a sin offering, besides the sin offering for atonement, the regular burnt offering with its grain offering, and their drink offerings.

Offerings at the Feast of Tabernacles

12'On the fifteenth day of the seventh month you shall have a holy convocation. You shall do no customary work, and you shall keep a feast to the LORD seven days. 13You shall present a burnt offering, an offering made by fire as a sweet aroma to the LORD: thirteen young bulls, two rams, *and* fourteen lambs in their first year. They shall be without blemish. 14Their grain offering *shall be of* fine flour mixed with oil: three-tenths *of an ephah* for each of the thirteen bulls, two-tenths for each

28:16 Passover, along with other rituals, had not been kept by Israel during their wilderness wanderings. With their coming entry into the Promised Land, Israel was again instructed concerning the Passover ceremony. In the NT, Christ is often called the Passover Lamb, for He completed what had been given in part in the OT (1 Cor. 5:7).

28:26 The Feast of Weeks, celebrated at the time of barley harvest, is known in the NT as Pentecost because it came 50 days after Passover (or the Feast of Unleavened Bread; see chart, The Feasts of Israel).

29:1 The seventh or sabbatical month in the Hebrew calendar had more rituals than any other month (see chart, The Jewish Sacred Calendar). Ushered in with "a memorial of blowing of trumpets" (Lev. 23:24), it was known as the "Feast of Trumpets," the first of three holy days of the "sev-

enth month" (see chart, The Feasts of Israel). The trumpets of verse 1 and Leviticus 23:24 were probably not the "silver trumpets" in Numbers 10:2 but the ram's horn (Heb. *shophar*) used for the Jubilee (see Lev. 25:9; see chart, The Principle of the Sabbath).

29:7–11 The Day of Atonement is the most sacred of all the Hebrew religious rites (see Lev. 16). Referenced as "the Fast" (Acts 27:9), it was accompanied by humiliation (Num. 29:7). God's moral Law was capable of revealing sin and bringing condemnation and accusation, but the Law was incomplete in that it was not capable of offering relief or salvation. Hence, the Israelites needed a system of sacrifices—"the sin offering for atonement" (v. 11; see chart, The Offerings of the Lord). Christ is the completed sacrifice, offered "once for all" (see Heb. 10:1–10).

of the two rams, [15]and one-tenth for each of the fourteen lambs; [16]also one kid of the goats *as* a sin offering, besides the regular burnt offering, its grain offering, and its drink offering.

[17]"On the second day *present* twelve young bulls, two rams, fourteen lambs in their first year without blemish, [18]and their grain offering and their drink offerings for the bulls, for the rams, and for the lambs, by their number, according to the ordinance; [19]also one kid of the goats *as* a sin offering, besides the regular burnt offering with its grain offering, and their drink offerings.

[20]"On the third day *present* eleven bulls, two rams, fourteen lambs in their first year without blemish, [21]and their grain offering and their drink offerings for the bulls, for the rams, and for the lambs, by their number, according to the ordinance; [22]also one goat *as* a sin offering, besides the regular burnt offering, its grain offering, and its drink offering.

[23]"On the fourth day *present* ten bulls, two rams, *and* fourteen lambs in their first year, without blemish, [24]and their grain offering and their drink offerings for the bulls, for the rams, and for the lambs, by their number, according to the ordinance; [25]also one kid of the goats *as* a sin offering, besides the regular burnt offering, its grain offering, and its drink offering.

[26]"On the fifth day *present* nine bulls, two rams, *and* fourteen lambs in their first year without blemish, [27]and their grain offering and their drink offerings for the bulls, for the rams, and for the lambs, by their number, according to the ordinance; [28]also one goat *as* a sin offering, besides the regular burnt offering, its grain offering, and its drink offering.

[29]"On the sixth day *present* eight bulls, two rams, *and* fourteen lambs in their first year without blemish, [30]and their grain offering and their drink offerings for the bulls, for the rams, and for the lambs, by their number, according to the ordinance; [31]also one goat *as* a sin offering, besides the regular burnt offering, its grain offering, and its drink offering.

[32]"On the seventh day *present* seven bulls, two rams, *and* fourteen lambs in their first year without blemish, [33]and their grain offering and their drink offerings for the bulls, for the rams, and for the lambs, by their number, according to the ordinance; [34]also one goat *as* a sin offering, besides the regular burnt offering, its grain offering, and its drink offering.

[35]"On the eighth day you shall have a sacred assembly. You shall do no customary work. [36]You shall present a burnt offering, an offering made by fire as a sweet aroma to the LORD: one bull, one ram, seven lambs in their first year without blemish, [37]and their grain offering and their drink offerings for the bull, for the ram, and for the lambs, by their number, according to the ordinance; [38]also one goat *as* a sin offering, besides the regular burnt offering, its grain offering, and its drink offering.

[39]"These you shall present to the LORD at your appointed feasts (besides your vowed offerings and your freewill offerings) as your burnt offerings and your grain offerings, as your drink offerings and your peace offerings.'"

[40]So Moses told the children of Israel everything, just as the LORD commanded Moses.

The Law Concerning Vows

30Then Moses spoke to the heads of the tribes concerning the children of Israel, saying, "This *is* the thing which the LORD has commanded: [2]If a man makes a vow to the LORD, or swears an oath to bind himself by some agreement, he shall not break his word; he shall do according to all that proceeds out of his mouth.

[3]"Or if a woman makes a vow to the LORD, and binds *herself* by some agreement while in her father's house in her youth, [4]and her father hears her vow and the agreement by which she has bound herself, and her father holds his peace, then all her vows shall stand, and every agreement with which she has bound herself shall stand. [5]But if her father overrules her on the day that he hears, then none of her vows nor her agreements by which she has bound herself shall stand; and the LORD will release her, because her father overruled her.

[6]"If indeed she takes a husband, while bound by her vows or by a rash utterance from her lips by which she bound herself, [7]and her husband hears *it,* and makes no response to her on the day that he hears, then her vows shall stand, and her agreements by which she bound herself shall stand. [8]But if her husband overrules her on the day that he hears *it,* he shall make void her vow which she took and what she uttered with her lips, by which she bound herself, and the LORD will release her.

[9]"Also any vow of a widow or a divorced woman, by which she has bound herself, shall stand against her.

[10]"If she vowed in her husband's house, or

30:13 When either a vow of performance or abstinence was made "to afflict her soul," a woman's motive was spiritual worship and involved humbling herself before the Lord. Hannah's vow is representative, for she asked the Lord, "Look on the affliction of Your maidservant," repeating "maidservant" three times in her vow (1 Sam. 1, Hannah, especially v. 11). It is also possible that the phrase is a way of indicating those cases in which a husband or father negated a vow because of its potential harm to the woman involved (see Vows).

bound herself by an agreement with an oath, [11]and her husband heard *it*, and made no response to her *and* did not overrule her, then all her vows shall stand, and every agreement by which she bound herself shall stand. [12]But if her husband truly made them void on the day he heard *them*, then whatever proceeded from her lips concerning her vows or concerning the agreement binding her, it shall not stand; her husband has made them void, and the LORD will release her. [13]Every vow and every binding oath to afflict her soul, her husband may confirm it, or her husband may make it void. [14]Now if her husband makes no response whatever to her from day to day, then he confirms all her vows or all the agreements that bind her; he confirms them, because he made no response to her on the day that he heard *them*. [15]But if he does make them void after he has heard *them*, then he shall bear her guilt."

[16]These *are* the statutes which the LORD commanded Moses, between a man and his wife, and between a father and his daughter in her youth in her father's house.

Vengeance on the Midianites

31 And the LORD spoke to Moses, saying: [2]"Take vengeance on the Midianites for the children of Israel. Afterward you shall be gathered to your people."

[3]So Moses spoke to the people, saying, "Arm some of yourselves for war, and let them go against the Midianites to take vengeance for the LORD on Midian. [4]A thousand from each tribe of all the tribes of Israel you shall send to the war."

[5]So there were recruited from the divisions of Israel one thousand from *each* tribe, twelve thousand armed for war. [6]Then Moses sent them to the war, one thousand from *each* tribe; he sent them to the war with Phinehas the son of Eleazar the priest, with the holy articles and the signal trumpets in his hand. [7]And they warred against the Midianites, just as the LORD commanded Moses,

and they killed all the males. [8]They killed the kings of Midian with *the rest of* those who were killed—Evi, Rekem, Zur, Hur, and Reba, the five kings of Midian. Balaam the son of Beor they also killed with the sword.

[9]And the children of Israel took the women of Midian captive, with their little ones, and took as spoil all their cattle, all their flocks, and all their goods. [10]They also burned with fire all the cities where they dwelt, and all their forts. [11]And they took all the spoil and all the booty—of man and beast.

Return from the War

[12]Then they brought the captives, the booty, and the spoil to Moses, to Eleazar the priest, and to the congregation of the children of Israel, to the camp in the plains of Moab by the Jordan, *across from* Jericho. [13]And Moses, Eleazar the priest, and all the leaders of the congregation, went to meet them outside the camp. [14]But Moses was angry with the officers of the army, *with* the captains over thousands and captains over hundreds, who had come from the battle.

[15]And Moses said to them: "Have you kept all the women alive? [16]Look, these *women* caused the children of Israel, through the counsel of Balaam, to trespass against the LORD in the incident of Peor, and there was a plague among the congregation of the LORD. [17]Now therefore, kill every male among the little ones, and kill every woman who has known a man intimately. [18]But keep alive for yourselves all the young girls who have not known a man intimately. [19]And as for you, remain outside the camp seven days; whoever has killed any person, and whoever has touched any slain, purify yourselves and your captives on the third day and on the seventh day. [20]Purify every garment, everything made of leather, everything woven of goats' *hair*, and everything made of wood."

[21]Then Eleazar the priest said to the men of war who had gone to the battle, "This *is* the ordi-

---

31:1–5 When God's authority is challenged, He will legitimately "take vengeance," which is different than human revenge. After 40 years of wilderness training, some of these second-generation campers became foot soldiers in a holy war (v. 6), commanded by God in fulfillment of His judgment against the Midianites and "their schemes" (Num. 25:16–18).

31:6 Because Phinehas was not the high priest, these "holy articles" probably did not include the ark of the covenant, although this was not a presumptuous conflict (see Num. 14:44). After the war, the soldiers and their booty went through ritual cleansing (Num. 31:19-24), and offerings were made for atonement (v. 50).

31:7, 8 All the kings of Midian and all their male subjects were slain by the small squad of Israelite soldiers. The record of the conquest is brief, but the battle was crucial. Only with God's anointing could these Israelite soldiers have been so mighty in battle against these five monarchs. Among the kings was Zur,

father of Cozbi, the only woman named in the shameless act of harlotry within the Israelite camp (Num. 25:14, 15, note). "Also killed with the sword" was Balaam, the false prophet who incited the idolatrous event with the Midianites (Num. 31:16; Rev. 2:14).

31:11, 12 Captives referred to women and children; "booty" included cattle; "spoil" was all the rest, the prizes due the conquerors (see v. 50 for examples).

31:14–18 Women and children of Midian were spared and this angered Moses. "These women caused" the "incident of Peor" that provoked God's judgment. So Moses commanded that only virgins be spared in the killings. That male children should be slain was reasonable because they would be future Midianites, posing a threat to the Israelites in their Land. God's passion for righteousness is not partial but calls for spiritual separation from all unrighteousness (see Josh. 6:17, note; Ezra 10:11; Rom. 1:18).

nance of the law which the LORD commanded Moses: [22]"Only the gold, the silver, the bronze, the iron, the tin, and the lead, [23]everything that can endure fire, you shall put through the fire, and it shall be clean; and it shall be purified with the water of purification. But all that cannot endure fire you shall put through water. [24]And you shall wash your clothes on the seventh day and be clean, and afterward you may come into the camp."

Division of the Plunder

[25]Now the LORD spoke to Moses, saying: [26]"Count up the plunder that was taken—of man and beast—you and Eleazar the priest and the chief fathers of the congregation; [27]and divide the plunder into two parts, between those who took part in the war, who went out to battle, and all the congregation. [28]And levy a tribute for the LORD on the men of war who went out to battle: one of every five hundred of the persons, the cattle, the donkeys, and the sheep; [29]take it from their half, and give it to Eleazar the priest as a heave offering to the LORD. [30]And from the children of Israel's half you shall take one of every fifty, drawn from the persons, the cattle, the donkeys, and the sheep, from all the livestock, and give them to the Levites who keep charge of the tabernacle of the LORD." [31]So Moses and Eleazar the priest did as the LORD commanded Moses.

[32]The booty remaining from the plunder, which the men of war had taken, was six hundred and seventy-five thousand sheep, [33]seventy-two thousand cattle, [34]sixty-one thousand donkeys, [35]and thirty-two thousand persons in all, of women who had not known a man intimately. [36]And the half, the portion for those who had gone out to war, was in number three hundred and thirty-seven thousand five hundred sheep; [37]and the LORD's tribute of the sheep was six hundred and seventy-five. [38]The cattle were thirty-six thousand, of which the LORD's tribute was seventy-two. [39]The donkeys were thirty thousand five hundred, of which the LORD's tribute was sixty-one. [40]The persons were sixteen thousand, of which the LORD's tribute was thirty-two persons. [41]So Moses gave the tribute which was the LORD's heave offering to Eleazar the priest, as the LORD commanded Moses.

[42]And from the children of Israel's half, which Moses separated from the men who fought— [43]now the half belonging to the congregation was three hundred and thirty-seven thousand five hundred sheep, [44]thirty-six thousand cattle, [45]thirty thousand five hundred donkeys, [46]and sixteen thousand persons— [47]and from the children of Israel's half Moses took one of every fifty, drawn from man and beast, and gave them to the Levites, who kept charge of the tabernacle of the LORD, as the LORD commanded Moses.

[48]Then the officers who were over thousands of the army, the captains of thousands and captains of hundreds, came near to Moses; [49]and they said to Moses, "Your servants have taken a count of the men of war who are under our command, and not a man of us is missing. [50]Therefore we have brought an offering for the LORD, what every man found of ornaments of gold: armlets and bracelets and signet rings and earrings and necklaces, to make atonement for ourselves before the LORD." [51]So Moses and Eleazar the priest received the gold from them, all the fashioned ornaments. [52]And all the gold of the offering that they offered to the LORD, from the captains of thousands and captains of hundreds, was sixteen thousand seven hundred and fifty shekels. [53](The men of war had taken spoil, every man for himself.) [54]And Moses and Eleazar the priest received the gold from the captains of thousands and of hundreds, and brought it into the tabernacle of meeting as a memorial for the children of Israel before the LORD.

The Tribes Settling East of the Jordan

32 Now the children of Reuben and the children of Gad had a very great multitude of livestock; and when they saw the land of Jazer and the land of Gilead, that indeed the region was a place for livestock, [2]the children of Gad and the children of Reuben came and spoke to Moses, to Eleazar the priest, and to the leaders of the congregation, saying, [3]"Ataroth, Dibon, Jazer, Nimrah, Heshbon, Elealeh, Shebam, Nebo, and Beon, [4]the country which the LORD defeated before the congregation of Israel, is a land for livestock, and your servants have livestock." [5]Therefore they said, "If we have found favor in your sight, let this land be given to your servants as a possession. Do not take us over the Jordan."

[6]And Moses said to the children of Gad and to the children of Reuben: "Shall your brethren go to war while you sit here? [7]Now why will you discourage the heart of the children of Israel from going over into the land which the LORD has given them? [8]Thus your fathers did when I sent them away from Kadesh Barnea to see the land. [9]For when they went up to the Valley of Eshcol and saw the

---

31:25–31 The plunder was divided between those who went to war and those who stayed in camp. Both divisions were to "levy" (lit. "lift up") a "tribute for the Lord," a "heave offering." The soldiers contributed half of 0.2 percent to the priests, and the congregation 2 percent to the Levites. It was God who set the equitable portions. Over and above the Lord's request, a thank offering was made by the "captains" because all the troops had been spared (vv. 48–54; see chart, The Offerings of the Lord).

VOWS — EXPRESSIONS OF DEVOTION

In Scripture, vows were voluntary expressions of devotion and could be made by both women and men. At the same time, once spoken aloud, a vow became a sacred duty (Deut. 23:21–23), which could be

- positive—a promise to give something (Heb. *neder*, lit. "vow") or
- negative—a promise to abstain from something (Heb. *issar*, lit. "bond").

In the Old Testament, vows were often conditional promises made to God, which hinged upon His doing something to promote an act of devotion. Such was the case of Hannah who promised God that if He gave her a son, she would return him to the Lord (1 Sam. 1:11). On the other hand, some vows were made purely out of personal devotion with no conditions, such as Ruth's vow to Naomi (Ruth 1:16, 17). Almost anything might be promised to God by a vow and could be redeemed by money—the value ascribed to the item or person, plus one-fifth (see Lev. 27). These vows were made in the context of worship. Numbers 30 follows the discussion of offerings and feasts. In gratitude "for all His benefits," the psalmist paid vows "to the Lord" (Ps. 116:12–14).

Vows in Numbers 30 cover four classifications of women: unmarried girls living with their fathers (vv. 3–5); women unmarried when they made a vow but married before the vow was fulfilled (vv. 6–8); widows or divorced women (v. 9); and married women (vv. 10–15). A husband could veto his wife's vow and a father the vow of his daughter, but the veto had to be uttered when the husband or father first heard the vow made. The underlying principle of this veto is the protection due women by those responsible for them—a father for his daughter (v. 5), a husband for his wife (v. 13). When vetoed, a broken vow incurred neither guilt nor punishment upon the woman (vv. 5, 8). The heavier liability rested with the one responsible for her protection (see v. 15). Neither the wife nor daughter is bound, even by a spiritual vow, if her husband or father in some way prohibits her keeping that vow (Num. 30:8). Widows and divorced women were not affected by a veto (v. 9).

The most sacred promise made in Scripture—a vow that cannot be broken—is the covenant God made with His people. God repeated several times His vow to keep the promises He made to Abraham and Israel (Gen. 22:16–18; Ps. 89:35; Is. 45:23; Jer. 44:26; Amos 6:8). The New Testament confirms that God's promises are a "binding oath" (Luke 1:73–75; Acts 2:30; Heb. 7:20–25).

Jesus taught that a person's word, or promise, is as binding as a sacred oath, regardless of the cleverness by which a promise might be phrased (Matt. 5:33–37). Whether conditional or not, vows are made to be kept, and an unfulfilled vow is worse than no vow at all (Eccl. 5:4, 5).

See also Lam. 3:22, note; notes on Commitment (Matt. 16); Marriage (Gen. 2; 2 Sam. 6; Prov. 5; Hos. 2; Amos 3; 2 Cor. 13; Heb. 12); Weddings (John 2); portrait of Jepthah's Obedient Daughter (Judg. 11)

---

land, they discouraged the heart of the children of Israel, so that they did not go into the land which the LORD had given them. [10]So the LORD's anger was aroused on that day, and He swore an oath, saying, [11]'Surely none of the men who came up from Egypt, from twenty years old and above, shall see the land of which I swore to Abraham, Isaac, and Jacob, because they have not wholly followed Me, [12]except Caleb the son of Jephunneh, the Kenizzite, and Joshua the son of Nun, for they have wholly followed the LORD.' [13]So the LORD's anger was aroused against Israel, and He made them wander in the wilderness forty years, until all the generation that had done evil in the sight of the LORD was gone. [14]And look! You have risen in your fathers' place, a brood of sinful men, to increase still more the fierce anger of the LORD against Israel. [15]For if you turn away from following Him, He will once again leave them in the wilderness, and you will destroy all these people."

[16]Then they came near to him and said: "We will build sheepfolds here for our livestock, and cities for our little ones, [17]but we ourselves will be armed, ready *to go* before the children of Israel until we have brought them to their place; and our little ones will dwell in the fortified cities because of the inhabitants of the land. [18]We will not return to our homes until every one of the children of Israel has received his inheritance. [19]For we will not inherit with them on the other side of the Jordan and beyond, because our inheritance has fallen to us on this eastern side of the Jordan."

[20]Then Moses said to them: "If you do this thing, if you arm yourselves before the LORD for the war, [21]and all your armed men cross over the Jordan before the LORD until He has driven out His enemies from before Him, [22]and the land is subdued before the LORD, then afterward you may return and be blameless before the LORD and before Israel; and this land shall be your possession

---

32:22 God's plan was for all Israel to enter Canaan, west of the Jordan River, but when the tribes of Reuben and Gad (and the half tribe of Manasseh, v. 33) saw the fertile lands east of the Jordan, they requested this land "as a possession" (v. 5).

before the LORD. 23But if you do not do so, then take note, you have sinned against the LORD; and be sure your sin will find you out. 24Build cities for your little ones and folds for your sheep, and do what has proceeded out of your mouth."

25And the children of Gad and the children of Reuben spoke to Moses, saying: "Your servants will do as my lord commands. 26Our little ones, our wives, our flocks, and all our livestock will be there in the cities of Gilead; 27but your servants will cross over, every man armed for war, before the LORD to battle, just as my lord says."

28So Moses gave command concerning them to Eleazar the priest, to Joshua the son of Nun, and to the chief fathers of the tribes of the children of Israel. 29And Moses said to them: "If the children of Gad and the children of Reuben cross over the Jordan with you, every man armed for battle before the LORD, and the land is subdued before you, then you shall give them the land of Gilead as a possession. 30But if they do not cross over armed with you, they shall have possessions among you in the land of Canaan."

31Then the children of Gad and the children of Reuben answered, saying: "As the LORD has said to your servants, so we will do. 32We will cross over armed before the LORD into the land of Canaan, but the possession of our inheritance *shall remain* with us on this side of the Jordan."

33So Moses gave to the children of Gad, to the children of Reuben, and to half the tribe of Manasseh the son of Joseph, the kingdom of Sihon king of the Amorites and the kingdom of Og king of Bashan, the land with its cities within the borders, the cities of the surrounding country. 34And the children of Gad built Dibon and Ataroth and Aroer, 35Atroth and Shophan and Jazer and Jogbehah, 36Beth Nimrah and Beth Haran, fortified cities, and folds for sheep. 37And the children of Reuben built Heshbon and Elealeh and Kirjathaim, 38Nebo and Baal Meon (*their* names being changed) and Shibmah; and they gave *other* names to the cities which they built.

39And the children of Machir the son of Manasseh went to Gilead and took it, and dispossessed the Amorites who *were* in it. 40So Moses gave Gilead to Machir the son of Manasseh, and

he dwelt in it. 41Also Jair the son of Manasseh went and took its small towns, and called them Havoth Jair.a 42Then Nobah went and took Kenath and its villages, and he called it Nobah, after his own name.

Israel's Journey from Egypt Reviewed

33 These *are* the journeys of the children of Israel, who went out of the land of Egypt by their armies under the hand of Moses and Aaron. 2Now Moses wrote down the starting points of their journeys at the command of the LORD. And these *are* their journeys according to their starting points:

3They departed from Rameses in the first month, on the fifteenth day of the first month; on the day after the Passover the children of Israel went out with boldness in the sight of all the Egyptians. 4For the Egyptians were burying all *their* firstborn, whom the LORD had killed among them. Also on their gods the LORD had executed judgments.

5Then the children of Israel moved from Rameses and camped at Succoth. 6They departed from Succoth and camped at Etham, which *is* on the edge of the wilderness. 7They moved from Etham and turned back to Pi Hahiroth, which *is* east of Baal Zephon; and they camped near Migdol. 8They departed from before Hahirotha and passed through the midst of the sea into the wilderness, went three days' journey in the Wilderness of Etham, and camped at Marah. 9They moved from Marah and came to Elim. At Elim *were* twelve springs of water and seventy palm trees; so they camped there.

10They moved from Elim and camped by the Red Sea. 11They moved from the Red Sea and camped in the Wilderness of Sin. 12They journeyed from the Wilderness of Sin and camped at Dophkah. 13They departed from Dophkah and camped at Alush. 14They moved from Alush and camped at Rephidim, where there was no water for the people to drink.

32:41 aLiterally *Towns of Jair* 33:8 aMany Hebrew manuscripts, Samaritan Pentateuch, Syriac, Targum, and Vulgate read *from Pi Hahiroth* (compare verse 7).

Their first reason was "for livestock" (v. 4); then they shifted their cause "for our little ones" (v. 16). When Moses accused them of alienation (lit. "discouragement," vv. 7, 9), the tribal leaders revised their request with a promise to assist their brethren in the conquest of Canaan (v. 17), a promise they kept (see Josh. 12—16). The heart of the matter is found in the word "wholly" (Num. 32:11, 12), for God must have total commitment from His people. A look into the future reveals that the Gadarenes, the swine herders, were descendants of the tribe of Gad (Mark 5).

33:1 Moses shared what had already happened (a common

theme of the Lord: "remember") in preparation for what was to come. In summary fashion this is the basic content of such psalms (Ps. 105; 106). The Passover appropriately begins the account (Num. 33:3). The journeys are divided in two sections: from Rameses to Mt. Hor (Num. 33:3–37) and Mt. Hor to the plains of Moab (Num. 33:41–49). Whenever they "moved," wherever they "camped," the Lord was ever with them (Heb. 13:5). Between these two sections are two events: Aaron's death "in the fortieth year" of their journey and the time a Canaanite king "heard of the coming" of God's people through his territory (Num. 33:38–40).

15They departed from Rephidim and camped in the Wilderness of Sinai. 16They moved from the Wilderness of Sinai and camped at Kibroth Hattaavah. 17They departed from Kibroth Hattaavah and camped at Hazeroth. 18They departed from Hazeroth and camped at Rithmah. 19They departed from Rithmah and camped at Rimmon Perez. 20They departed from Rimmon Perez and camped at Libnah. 21They moved from Libnah and camped at Rissah. 22They journeyed from Rissah and camped at Kehelathah. 23They went from Kehelathah and camped at Mount Shepher. 24They moved from Mount Shepher and camped at Haradah. 25They moved from Haradah and camped at Makheloth. 26They moved from Makheloth and camped at Tahath. 27They departed from Tahath and camped at Terah. 28They moved from Terah and camped at Mithkah. 29They went from Mithkah and camped at Hashmonah. 30They departed from Hashmonah and camped at Moseroth. 31They departed from Moseroth and camped at Bene Jaakan. 32They moved from Bene Jaakan and camped at Hor Hagidgad. 33They went from Hor Hagidgad and camped at Jotbathah. 34They moved from Jotbathah and camped at Abronah. 35They departed from Abronah and camped at Ezion Geber. 36They moved from Ezion Geber and camped in the Wilderness of Zin, which is Kadesh. 37They moved from Kadesh and camped at Mount Hor, on the boundary of the land of Edom.

38Then Aaron the priest went up to Mount Hor at the command of the LORD, and died there in the fortieth year after the children of Israel had come out of the land of Egypt, on the first day of the fifth month. 39Aaron was one hundred and twenty-three years old when he died on Mount Hor.

40Now the king of Arad, the Canaanite, who dwelt in the South in the land of Canaan, heard of the coming of the children of Israel.

41So they departed from Mount Hor and camped at Zalmonah. 42They departed from Zalmonah and camped at Punon. 43They departed from Punon and camped at Oboth. 44They departed from Oboth and camped at Ije Abarim, at the border of Moab. 45They departed from Ijima and camped at Dibon Gad. 46They moved from Dibon Gad and camped at Almon Diblathaim. 47They moved from Almon Diblathaim and camped in the mountains of Abarim, before Nebo. 48They departed from the mountains of Abarim and camped in the plains of Moab by the Jordan, across from Jericho. 49They camped by the Jordan, from Beth Jesimoth as far as the Abel Acacia Grovea in the plains of Moab.

Instructions for the Conquest of Canaan

50Now the LORD spoke to Moses in the plains of Moab by the Jordan, across from Jericho, saying, 51"Speak to the children of Israel, and say to them: 'When you have crossed the Jordan into the land of Canaan, 52then you shall drive out all the inhabitants of the land from before you, destroy all their engraved stones, destroy all their molded images, and demolish all their high places; 53you shall dispossess the inhabitants of the land and dwell in it, for I have given you the land to possess. 54And you shall divide the land by lot as an inheritance among your families; to the larger you shall give a larger inheritance, and to the smaller you shall give a smaller inheritance; there everyone's inheritance shall be whatever falls to him by lot. You shall inherit according to the tribes of your fathers. 55But if you do not drive out the inhabitants of the land from before you, then it shall be that those whom you let remain shall be irritants in your eyes and thorns in your sides, and they shall harass you in the land where you dwell. 56Moreover it shall be that I will do to you as I thought to do to them.' "

The Appointed Boundaries of Canaan

34 Then the LORD spoke to Moses, saying, 2"Command the children of Israel, and say to them: 'When you come into the land of Canaan, this is the land that shall fall to you as an inheritance—the land of Canaan to its boundaries. 3Your southern border shall be from the Wilderness of Zin along the border of Edom; then your southern border shall extend eastward to the end of the Salt Sea; 4your border shall turn from the southern side of the Ascent of Akrabbim, continue to Zin, and be on the south of Kadesh Barnea; then it shall go on to Hazar Addar, and continue to Azmon; 5the border shall turn from Azmon to the Brook of Egypt, and it shall end at the Sea.

6As for the western border, you shall have the Great Sea for a border; this shall be your western border.

7And this shall be your northern border: From the Great Sea you shall mark out your border line

33:45 aSame as Ije Abarim, verse 44   33:49 aHebrew Abel Shittim

---

33:51 Following a recital of the past (vv. 1–49), God prepared the people for the future (see also Num. 15:2). His expectation remained the same: Obedience is the only way to absolute victory. The people must destroy all forms of idolatry for their own good—physically, economically, and spiritually. Because Israel allowed a remnant of the Canaanites and their "high places" within their borders, the Lord fulfilled prophecy with the Assyrian and Babylonian exiles (see Num. 33:56). Archaeological evidence of the "molded images" they kept has remained (v. 52); and the Bible records the history of sexual sins through which Israel imitated Canaanite life and worship.

to Mount Hor; [8]from Mount Hor you shall mark out *your border* to the entrance of Hamath; then the direction of the border shall be toward Zedad; [9]the border shall proceed to Ziphron, and it shall end at Hazar Enan. This shall be your northern border.

[10]'You shall mark out your eastern border from Hazar Enan to Shepham; [11]the border shall go down from Shepham to Riblah on the east side of Ain; the border shall go down and reach to the eastern side of the Sea of Chinnereth; [12]the border shall go down along the Jordan, and it shall end at the Salt Sea. This shall be your land with its surrounding boundaries.' "

[13]Then Moses commanded the children of Israel, saying: "This *is* the land which you shall inherit by lot, which the LORD has commanded to give to the nine tribes and to the half-tribe. [14]For the tribe of the children of Reuben according to the house of their fathers, and the tribe of the children of Gad according to the house of their fathers, have received *their inheritance;* and the half-tribe of Manasseh has received its inheritance. [15]The two tribes and the half-tribe have received their inheritance on this side of the Jordan, *across from* Jericho eastward, toward the sunrise."

The Leaders Appointed to Divide the Land

[16]And the LORD spoke to Moses, saying, [17]"These *are* the names of the men who shall divide the land among you as an inheritance: Eleazar the priest and Joshua the son of Nun. [18]And you shall take one leader of every tribe to divide the land for the inheritance. [19]These *are* the names of the men: from the tribe of Judah, Caleb the son of Jephunneh; [20]from the tribe of the children of Simeon, Shemuel the son of Ammihud; [21]from the tribe of Benjamin, Elidad the son of Chislon; [22]a leader from the tribe of the children of Dan, Bukki the son of Jogli; [23]from the sons of Joseph: a leader from the tribe of the children of Manasseh, Hanniel the son of Ephod, [24]and a leader from the tribe of the children of Ephraim, Kemuel the son of Shiphtan; [25]a leader from the tribe of the children of Zebulun, Elizaphan the son of Parnach; [26]a leader from the tribe of the children of Issachar, Paltiel the son of Azzan; [27]a leader from the tribe of the children of Asher, Ahihud the son of Shelomi; [28]and a leader from the tribe of the children of Naphtali, Pedahel the son of Ammihud."

[29]These *are* the ones the LORD commanded to divide the inheritance among the children of Israel in the land of Canaan.

Cities for the Levites

35 And the LORD spoke to Moses in the plains of Moab by the Jordan *across from* Jericho, saying: [2]"Command the children of Israel that they give the Levites cities to dwell in from the inheritance of their possession, and you shall *also* give the Levites common-land around the cities. [3]They shall have the cities to dwell in; and their common-land shall be for their cattle, for their herds, and for all their animals. [4]The common-land of the cities which you will give the Levites *shall extend* from the wall of the city outward a thousand cubits all around. [5]And you shall measure outside the city on the east side two thousand cubits, on the south side two thousand cubits, on the west side two thousand cubits, and on the north side two thousand cubits. The city *shall be* in the middle. This shall belong to them as common-land for the cities.

[6]"Now among the cities which you will give to the Levites *you shall appoint* six cities of refuge, to which a manslayer may flee. And to these you shall add forty-two cities. [7]So all the cities you will give to the Levites *shall be* forty-eight; these *you shall give* with their common-land. [8]And the cities which you will give *shall be* from the possession of the children of Israel; from the larger *tribe* you shall give many, from the smaller you shall give few. Each shall give some of its cities to the Levites, in proportion to the inheritance that each receives."

Cities of Refuge

[9]Then the LORD spoke to Moses, saying, [10]"Speak to the children of Israel, and say to them: 'When you cross the Jordan into the land of Canaan, [11]then you shall appoint cities to be cities of refuge for you, that the manslayer who kills any person accidentally may flee there. [12]They shall be cities of refuge for you from the avenger, that the manslayer may not die until he stands before the congregation in judgment. [13]And of the cities which you give, you shall have six cities of refuge. [14]You shall appoint three cities on this side of the Jordan, and three cities you shall appoint in the land of Canaan, *which* will be cities of refuge. [15]These six cities shall be for refuge for the children of Israel, for the stranger, and for the sojourner among them, that anyone who kills a person accidentally may flee there.

[16]'But if he strikes him with an iron implement, so that he dies, he *is* a murderer; the murderer shall surely be put to death. [17]And if he strikes him with a stone in the hand, by which one

---

35:1–3 Because the Levites were not one of the 12 tribes, they were allotted special cities in which to live and have pasture land for the cattle they used for both food and sacrifices. Establishing the cities for the Levites throughout the whole of the tribal lands was done for the purpose of providing instruction in the Law for all the people (see Deut. 33:10).

could die, and he does die, he *is* a murderer; the murderer shall surely be put to death. ¹⁸Or *if* he strikes him with a wooden hand weapon, by which one could die, and he does die, he *is* a murderer; the murderer shall surely be put to death. ¹⁹The avenger of blood himself shall put the murderer to death; when he meets him, he shall put him to death. ²⁰If he pushes him out of hatred or, while lying in wait, hurls something at him so that he dies, ²¹or in enmity he strikes him with his hand so that he dies, the one who struck *him* shall surely be put to death. He *is* a murderer. The avenger of blood shall put the murderer to death when he meets him.

²²However, if he pushes him suddenly without enmity, or throws anything at him without lying in wait, ²³or uses a stone, by which a man could die, throwing *it* at him without seeing *him,* so that he dies, while he was not his enemy or seeking his harm, ²⁴then the congregation shall judge between the manslayer and the avenger of blood according to these judgments. ²⁵So the congregation shall deliver the manslayer from the hand of the avenger of blood, and the congregation shall return him to the city of refuge where he had fled, and he shall remain there until the death of the high priest who was anointed with the holy oil. ²⁶But if the manslayer at any time goes outside the limits of the city of refuge where he fled, ²⁷and the avenger of blood finds him outside the limits of his city of refuge, and the avenger of blood kills the manslayer, he shall not be guilty of blood, ²⁸because he should have remained in his city of refuge until the death of the high priest. But after the death of the high priest the manslayer may return to the land of his possession.

²⁹And these *things* shall be a statute of judgment to you throughout your generations in all your dwellings. ³⁰Whoever kills a person, the murderer shall be put to death on the testimony of witnesses; but one witness is not *sufficient* testimony against a person for the death *penalty.* ³¹Moreover you shall take no ransom for the life of a murderer who *is* guilty of death, but he shall surely be put to death. ³²And you shall take no ransom for him who has fled to his city of refuge, that he may return to dwell in the land before the death of the priest. ³³So you shall not pollute the land where you *are;* for blood defiles the land, and no atonement can be made for the land, for the blood that is shed on it, except by the blood of him who shed it. ³⁴Therefore do not defile the land which you inhabit, in the midst of which I dwell; for I the LORD dwell among the children of Israel.' "

Marriage of Female Heirs

36 Now the chief fathers of the families of the children of Gilead the son of Machir, the son of Manasseh, of the families of the sons of Joseph, came near and spoke before Moses and before the leaders, the chief fathers of the children of Israel. ²And they said: "The LORD commanded my lord *Moses* to give the land as an inheritance by lot to the children of Israel, and my lord was commanded by the LORD to give the inheritance of our brother Zelophehad to his daughters. ³Now if they are married to any of the sons of the *other* tribes of the children of Israel, then their inheritance will be taken from the inheritance of our fathers, and it will be added to the inheritance of the tribe into which they marry; so it will be taken from the lot of our inheritance. ⁴And when the Jubilee of the children of Israel comes, then their inheritance will be added to the inheritance of the tribe into which they marry; so their inheritance will be taken away from the inheritance of the tribe of our fathers."

⁵Then Moses commanded the children of Israel according to the word of the LORD, saying: "What the tribe of the sons of Joseph speaks is right. ⁶This *is* what the LORD commands concerning the daughters of Zelophehad, saying, 'Let them marry whom they think best, but they may marry only within the family of their father's tribe.' ⁷So the inheritance of the children of Israel shall not change hands from tribe to tribe, for every one of the children of Israel shall keep the inheritance of the tribe of his fathers. ⁸And every daughter who possesses an inheritance in any tribe of the children of Israel shall be the wife of one of the family of her father's tribe, so that the children of Israel each may possess the inheritance of his fathers. ⁹Thus no inheritance shall change hands from *one* tribe to another, but every tribe of the children of Israel shall keep its own inheritance."

35:25 Manslayers received only temporary retreat until a fair trial was arranged. Only the death of another could atone for killing an individual, whether it was murder or manslaughter (vv. 21, 25). "The death of the high priest who was anointed with the holy oil" may have been understood as a means of cleansing the Land by being the satisfaction for the blood that had been shed. God demands a "reckoning" when "lifeblood" is shed, for we are made in His image (Gen. 9:5, 6). Christ offered Himself as sufficient atonement, for "without shedding of blood there is no remission" (Heb. 9:22–28).

36:1–4 While the five daughters of Zelophehad were noticeably absent here, their uncles represented them when they presented a potential problem concerning property rights to Moses (see Num. 26, Daughters of Zelophehad).

36:10–13 The Book of Numbers closes on the practical note of obedience, individual and corporate (see Philem. Obedience). Mahlah, Tirzah, Hoglah, Milcah, and Noah—the daughters of Zelophehad—obeyed God's command by marrying within the tribe. Harmony within marriage is symbolic here of harmony with God through obedience to all His commandments.

¹⁰Just as the LORD commanded Moses, so did the daughters of Zelophehad; ¹¹for Mahlah, Tirzah, Hoglah, Milcah, and Noah, the daughters of Zelophehad, were married to the sons of their father's brothers. ¹²They were married into the families of the children of Manasseh the son of Joseph, and their inheritance remained in the tribe of their father's family.

¹³These *are* the commandments and the judgments which the LORD commanded the children of Israel by the hand of Moses in the plains of Moab by the Jordan, *across from* Jericho.

Deuteronomy

AUTHOR

Besides being Israel's great lawgiver, Moses is also known as the founder of Israel's religion. Though he was reluctant at first, he became the greatest leader the nation of Israel ever had—the first prophet of the nation of Israel and the example by which all succeeding prophets were measured. Moses knew God intimately and talked to Him face to face (Deut. 34:10). But more importantly, God knew Moses and entrusted him with leadership (Ps. 103:7). The Mosaic authorship of Deuteronomy, held within Judaism and Christianity alike, was not challenged until the late eighteenth and early nineteenth centuries. Mosaic authorship is indicated by texts within the book itself (Deut. 1:5; 31:9, 22, 24, 30), by other passages within the Old Testament (1 Kin. 2:3; 8:53; 2 Kin. 14:6; 18:6, 12), by the words of Jesus Himself (Matt. 19:7, 8; Mark 10:3–5; John 5:46, 47), and by other New Testament references (Acts 3:22; 7:37, 38; Rom. 10:19). The account of Moses' death was probably added to the text after the death of Moses (Deut. 34).

DATE

Mosaic authorship requires dating the book in the fifteenth century B.C. The structure of Deuteronomy resembles the Near Eastern vassal treaties common during the second millennium B.C. Often a conquering ruler would make a treaty with the defeated ruler and allow him to rule his own people in a subservient role. In exchange, the vassal state would pay homage to the conquering ruler and would pledge tribute and allegiance. Israel was to be a vassal state, but not to any earthly kingdom. Her allegiance was to be to God alone.

BACKGROUND

SETTING: After forty years of wandering, the nation of Israel was poised at the southeastern entrance to Canaan ready to enter and occupy the Land that had been promised to them (Deut. 1:8). Moses knew that he would not enter the Land with Israel and that his death was imminent (Deut. 1:37; 3:23–29; 31:2; 32:49–52); therefore, Moses restated the covenant with the nation and used the occasion to stress the importance of obedience to the Lord.

PURPOSE: Deuteronomy is not just a review of the Law. It is the explanation of the Law that would make the demands of God clear to the people (Deut. 1:5). Moses was calling the nation of Israel to remember their covenant with God and to renew their allegiance to Him so that their conquest of Canaan would be successful. Deuteronomy emphasizes that the Law given to a specific generation is to be binding on all subsequent generations (Deut. 6:7–9).

AUDIENCE: Because of unbelief most of the generation of Israelites that left Egypt with Moses had died in the desert (Deut. 1:34–40). Their children stood before Moses to receive his message of obedience to the Lord.

LITERARY CHARACTERISTICS: The structure of Deuteronomy is closely associated with that of a typical Near Eastern vassal treaty of the Mosaic age. The treaty usually included the following elements: a preamble (Deut. 1:1–5), a historical prologue (Deut. 1:6—4:49), main provisions (Deut. 5—11), specific provisions (Deut. 12—26), curses and blessings (Deut. 27—28), and divine witnesses (Deut. 30:19; 31:19; 32:1–43). Each of these elements appears in the structure of Deuteronomy as indicated by the references cited.

THEMES

The main theme—obedience to God—can be found in every exhortation of Moses in the Book of Deuteronomy. The history of Israel, the laws of God, the blessings, the curses, and the Song of Moses all point the people of Israel to obedience. The very existence of the nation of Israel hinged on the people's obedience (Deut. 6:24; 8:20; 11:17; 30:19, 20; 32:46, 47). Phrases such as "Hear, O Israel . . ." and "Be careful to do . . ." all precede a call to obedience and allegiance to the Lord (Deut. 5:32; 6:4). The people's motivation for obedience was not merely their fear of judgment but also their understanding of the mercy and goodness of God (Deut. 4:31; 7:12–16; 30:3; 32:36).

OUTLINE

The Previous Command to Enter Canaan

1 These *are* the words which Moses spoke to all Israel on this side of the Jordan in the wilderness, in the plain[a] opposite Suph,[b] between Paran, Tophel, Laban, Hazeroth, and Dizahab. [2]*It is* eleven days' *journey* from Horeb by way of Mount Seir to Kadesh Barnea. [3]Now it came to pass in the fortieth year, in the eleventh month, on the first *day* of the month, *that* Moses spoke to the children of Israel according to all that the LORD had given him as commandments to them, [4]after he had killed Sihon king of the Amorites, who dwelt in Heshbon, and Og king of Bashan, who dwelt at Ashtaroth in[a] Edrei.

[5]On this side of the Jordan in the land of Moab, Moses began to explain this law, saying, [6]"The LORD our God spoke to us in Horeb, saying: 'You have dwelt long enough at this mountain. [7]Turn and take your journey, and go to the mountains of the Amorites, to all the neighboring *places* in the plain,[a] in the mountains and in the lowland, in the South and on the seacoast, to the land of the Canaanites and to Lebanon, as far as the great river, the River Euphrates. [8]See, I have set the land before you; go in and possess the land which the LORD swore to your fathers— to Abraham, Isaac, and Jacob— to give to them and their descendants after them.'

Tribal Leaders Appointed

[9]"And I spoke to you at that time, saying: 'I alone am not able to bear you. [10]The LORD your God has multiplied you, and here you *are* today, as the stars of heaven in multitude. [11]May the LORD God of your fathers make you a thousand times more numerous than you are, and bless you as He has promised you! [12]How can I alone bear your problems and your burdens and your complaints?

[13]Choose wise, understanding, and knowledgeable men from among your tribes, and I will make them heads over you.' [14]And you answered me and said, 'The thing which you have told *us* to do *is* good.' [15]So I took the heads of your tribes, wise and knowledgeable men, and made them heads over you, leaders of thousands, leaders of hundreds, leaders of fifties, leaders of tens, and officers for your tribes.

[16]"Then I commanded your judges at that time, saying, 'Hear *the cases* between your brethren, and judge righteously between a man and his brother or the stranger who is with him. [17]You shall not show partiality in judgment; you shall hear the small as well as the great; you shall not be afraid in any man's presence, for the judgment *is* God's. The case that is too hard for you, bring to me, and I will hear it.' [18]And I commanded you at that time all the things which you should do.

Israel's Refusal to Enter the Land

[19]"So we departed from Horeb, and went through all that great and terrible wilderness which you saw on the way to the mountains of the Amorites, as the LORD our God had commanded us. Then we came to Kadesh Barnea. [20]And I said to you, 'You have come to the mountains of the Amorites, which the LORD our God is giving us. [21]Look, the LORD your God has set the land before you; go up *and* possess *it*, as the LORD God of your fathers has spoken to you; do not fear or be discouraged.'

[22]"And every one of you came near to me and said, 'Let us send men before us, and let them search out the land for us, and bring back word to

1:1 [a]Hebrew *arabah* [b]One manuscript of the Septuagint, also Targum and Vulgate, read *Red Sea.*   **1:4** [a]Septuagint, Syriac, and Vulgate read *and* (compare Joshua 12:4).   **1:7** [a]Hebrew *arabah*

1:1 Moses delivered a series of sermons to prepare the children of Israel to take possession of the Land that God had promised them (Gen. 12:7). They are camped "on this side of the Jordan," that is, the Transjordan region, "in the plain opposite Suph" or Arabah. This area was characterized by a great rift valley extending from the Sea of Tiberias in the north to the Gulf of Aqaba in the south.

1:2 Moses reminded the children of Israel of their disobedience by mentioning that the initial journey from Horeb to Kadesh Barnea should have taken only 11 days. However, their refusal to believe the good report of Joshua and Caleb transformed an 11-day journey into a 40-year wandering (Num. 14:7–21). In Deuteronomy, Horeb is used interchangeably with Mt. Sinai, where God established His covenant with Israel. Kadesh Barnea, located about 50 miles southwest of Beersheba, was 150 miles from Horeb and was to be their point of entrance into Canaan.

1:5 Moses explained (Heb. *be'er*, lit. "to make absolutely plain or clear") the Law to the people with the intent of making it unmistakably understood, which is the purpose of all good biblical exposition.

1:10 When Moses described Israel as having become as "the stars of heaven in multitude," the people were reminded of one aspect of the promise of God to Abraham. Having experienced the fulfillment of this promise of increase, the nation could trust God's ability to fulfill the whole of the Abrahamic covenant (Gen. 15:5; 22:17; see chart, The Covenants of Genesis).

1:12–15 Moses delegated responsibilities. The nation had grown to the point that it was not possible for Moses to govern alone. Moses recognized the need to have politicial and judicial leaders to assist him. The people selected their own leaders to represent the respective tribes; Moses assigned tasks to these leaders (v. 13). The division of thousands, hundreds, and fifties implies a military grouping, which would be necessary for the upcoming conquests as well as for administrative purposes.

1:22 The Lord directed Moses to send out the spies (Num. 13:1, 2). However, that request was initiated by the people, then agreed upon by the Lord (see chart, The Tale of Two Committees). He directed Moses accordingly. The initial purpose of the spies' infiltration was to determine a point of entry as well as a plan for possession of the land of Canaan.

us of the way by which we should go up, and of the cities into which we shall come.'

²³"The plan pleased me well; so I took twelve of your men, one man from *each* tribe. ²⁴And they departed and went up into the mountains, and came to the Valley of Eshcol, and spied it out. ²⁵They also took *some* of the fruit of the land in their hands and brought *it* down to us; and they brought back word to us, saying, '*It is* a good land which the LORD our God is giving us.'

²⁶"Nevertheless you would not go up, but rebelled against the command of the LORD your God; ²⁷and you complained in your tents, and said, 'Because the LORD hates us, He has brought us out of the land of Egypt to deliver us into the hand of the Amorites, to destroy us. ²⁸Where can we go up? Our brethren have discouraged our hearts, saying, "The people *are* greater and taller than we; the cities *are* great and fortified up to heaven; moreover we have seen the sons of the Anakim there." '

²⁹"Then I said to you, 'Do not be terrified, or afraid of them. ³⁰The LORD your God, who goes before you, He will fight for you, according to all He did for you in Egypt before your eyes, ³¹and in the wilderness where you saw how the LORD your God carried you, as a man carries his son, in all the way that you went until you came to this place.' ³²Yet, for all that, you did not believe the LORD your God, ³³who went in the way before you to search out a place for you to pitch your tents, to show you the way you should go, in the fire by night and in the cloud by day.

The Penalty for Israel's Rebellion

³⁴"And the LORD heard the sound of your words, and was angry, and took an oath, saying, ³⁵'Surely not one of these men of this evil generation shall see that good land of which I swore to give to your fathers, ³⁶except Caleb the son of Jephunneh; he shall see it, and to him and his children I am giv-

ing the land on which he walked, because he wholly followed the LORD.' ³⁷The LORD was also angry with me for your sakes, saying, 'Even you shall not go in there. ³⁸Joshua the son of Nun, who stands before you, he shall go in there. Encourage him, for he shall cause Israel to inherit it.

³⁹'Moreover your little ones and your children, who you say will be victims, who today have no knowledge of good and evil, they shall go in there; to them I will give it, and they shall possess it. ⁴⁰But *as for* you, turn and take your journey into the wilderness by the Way of the Red Sea.'

⁴¹"Then you answered and said to me, 'We have sinned against the LORD; we will go up and fight, just as the LORD our God commanded us.' And when everyone of you had girded on his weapons of war, you were ready to go up into the mountain.

⁴²"And the LORD said to me, 'Tell them, "Do not go up nor fight, for I *am* not among you; lest you be defeated before your enemies." ' ⁴³So I spoke to you; yet you would not listen, but rebelled against the command of the LORD, and presumptuously went up into the mountain. ⁴⁴And the Amorites who dwelt in that mountain came out against you and chased you as bees do, and drove you back from Seir to Hormah. ⁴⁵Then you returned and wept before the LORD, but the LORD would not listen to your voice nor give ear to you.

⁴⁶"So you remained in Kadesh many days, according to the days that you spent *there.*

The Desert Years

2 "Then we turned and journeyed into the wilderness of the Way of the Red Sea, as the LORD spoke to me, and we skirted Mount Seir for many days.

²"And the LORD spoke to me, saying: ³'You have skirted this mountain long enough; turn northward. ⁴And command the people, saying, "You *are about to* pass through the territory of your brethren, the descendants of Esau, who live in

---

1:26, 27 The sin of unbelief manifested itself in the people's refusal to take possession of the good land that the Lord had already promised them. Their unbelief caused them to complain and question the motives and the leading of the Lord.

1:28 Their fears were based on the size of their enemies as well as the fortification of the cities to be conquered. As formidable as these may seem, however, neither would be able to stand against the hand of *Yahweh* if only the people had trusted Him. "The sons of Anakim" were traditionally identified as a tribe or clan of giants towering seven to nine feet tall.

1:39 The people rationalized their unbelief by using the safety of their children as an excuse for not entering the Land at the Lord's command. However, God was more concerned for the children than they were; therefore, He promised that the children would enter the Land. "Having no knowledge of good and evil" is a Hebrew idiom that means "not knowing any-

thing." The fact that the children 20 years and younger would escape judgment incurred by their parents teaches that God does not hold children accountable for sins their parents commit or for sins into which they are led but over which they have no control (Num. 14:29). Apparently God does not hold accountable those who are unable to discern the difference between good and evil.

1:41–43 This rash action came when the people realized the magnitude of God's judgment because of their lack of faith. They did not enter the Land of Canaan when first commanded to do so because of their fear of the enemy and their lack of trust in God's ability to deliver them. Then because of the fear of dying in the wilderness, they presumed to go to battle without the Lord's direction, believing they could win in their own strength. Their motivation to fight was not faith but fear, and unfortunately, the opportunity once afforded them was gone.

Seir; and they will be afraid of you. Therefore watch yourselves carefully. [5]Do not meddle with them, for I will not give you *any* of their land, no, not so much as one footstep, because I have given Mount Seir to Esau *as* a possession. [6]You shall buy food from them with money, that you may eat; and you shall also buy water from them with money, that you may drink.

[7]"For the LORD your God has blessed you in all the work of your hand. He knows your trudging through this great wilderness. These forty years the LORD your God *has been* with you; you have lacked nothing." '

[8]"And when we passed beyond our brethren, the descendants of Esau who dwell in Seir, away from the road of the plain, away from Elath and Ezion Geber, we turned and passed by way of the Wilderness of Moab. [9]Then the LORD said to me, 'Do not harass Moab, nor contend with them in battle, for I will not give you *any* of their land *as* a possession, because I have given Ar to the descendants of Lot *as* a possession.' "

[10](The Emim had dwelt there in times past, a people as great and numerous and tall as the Anakim. [11]They were also regarded as giants,[a] like the Anakim, but the Moabites call them Emim. [12]The Horites formerly dwelt in Seir, but the descendants of Esau dispossessed them and destroyed them from before them, and dwelt in their place, just as Israel did to the land of their possession which the LORD gave them.)

[13]" 'Now rise and cross over the Valley of the Zered.' So we crossed over the Valley of the Zered. [14]And the time we took to come from Kadesh Barnea until we crossed over the Valley of the Zered *was* thirty-eight years, until all the generation of the men of war was consumed from the midst of the camp, just as the LORD had sworn to them. [15]For indeed the hand of the LORD was against them, to destroy them from the midst of the camp until they were consumed.

[16]"So it was, when all the men of war had finally perished from among the people, [17]that the LORD spoke to me, saying: [18]'This day you are to cross over at Ar, the boundary of Moab. [19]And *when* you come near the people of Ammon, do not harass them or meddle with them, for I will not give you *any* of the land of the people of Ammon *as* a possession, because I have given it to the descendants of Lot *as* a possession.' "

[20](That was also regarded as a land of giants;[a] giants formerly dwelt there. But the Ammonites call them Zamzummim, [21]a people as great and numerous and tall as the Anakim. But the LORD destroyed them before them, and they dispossessed them and dwelt in their place, [22]just as He had done for the descendants of Esau, who dwelt in Seir, when He destroyed the Horites from before them. They dispossessed them and dwelt in their place, even to this day. [23]And the Avim, who dwelt in villages as far as Gaza—the Caphtorim, who came from Caphtor, destroyed them and dwelt in their place.)

[24]" 'Rise, take your journey, and cross over the River Arnon. Look, I have given into your hand Sihon the Amorite, king of Heshbon, and his land. Begin to possess *it,* and engage him in battle. [25]This day I will begin to put the dread and fear of you upon the nations under the whole heaven, who shall hear the report of you, and shall tremble and be in anguish because of you.'

King Sihon Defeated

[26]"And I sent messengers from the Wilderness of Kedemoth to Sihon king of Heshbon, with words of peace, saying, [27]'Let me pass through your land; I will keep strictly to the road, and I will turn neither to the right nor to the left. [28]You shall sell me food for money, that I may eat, and give me water for money, that I may drink; only let me pass through on foot, [29]just as the descendants of Esau who dwell in Seir and the Moabites who dwell in Ar did for me, until I cross the Jordan to the land which the LORD our God is giving us.'

[30]"But Sihon king of Heshbon would not let us pass through, for the LORD your God hardened his spirit and made his heart obstinate, that He might deliver him into your hand, as *it is* this day.

[31]"And the LORD said to me, 'See, I have begun to give Sihon and his land over to you. Begin to possess *it,* that you may inherit his land.' [32]Then Sihon and all his people came out against us to fight at Jahaz. [33]And the LORD our God delivered him over to us; so we defeated him, his sons, and all his people. [34]We took all his cities at that time, and we utterly destroyed the men, women, and little ones of every city; we left none remaining.

2:11, 20 [a]Hebrew *rephaim*

2:10–12 **These parenthetical verses** are an explanatory note. The author and date for insertions such as this one are uncertain. "Emim" were a people characterized as "terrible or frightful ones." "Giants" (Heb. *rephaim*) can also refer to an area's early inhabitants that are no longer in existence.

2:30 **Sihon's heart is hardened.** Moses could see God's plan in Sihon's rejection of the offer of the Israelites. By hardening

Sihon's heart, the Lord was only confirming what was already there (Num. 21:21–23; see also Ex. 14, Justice).

2:34 **The practice of complete destruction** (Heb. *cherem*, lit. "devoted to destruction") is an ancient one. The purpose was to dispose of anyone or anything that opposed the holiness of God. Not only was this destruction an expression of God's judgment on wicked nations, but it also kept Israel isolated from the false gods and wicked practices of their enemies.

35We took only the livestock as plunder for ourselves, with the spoil of the cities which we took. 36From Aroer, which *is* on the bank of the River Arnon, and *from* the city that *is* in the ravine, as far as Gilead, there was not one city too strong for us; the LORD our God delivered all to us. 37Only you did not go near the land of the people of Ammon—anywhere along the River Jabbok, or to the cities of the mountains, or wherever the LORD our God had forbidden us.

King Og Defeated

3 "Then we turned and went up the road to Bashan; and Og king of Bashan came out against us, he and all his people, to battle at Edrei. 2And the LORD said to me, 'Do not fear him, for I have delivered him and all his people and his land into your hand; you shall do to him as you did to Sihon king of the Amorites, who dwelt at Heshbon.'

3"So the LORD our God also delivered into our hands Og king of Bashan, with all his people, and we attacked him until he had no survivors remaining. 4And we took all his cities at that time; there was not a city which we did not take from them: sixty cities, all the region of Argob, the kingdom of Og in Bashan. 5All these cities *were* fortified with high walls, gates, and bars, besides a great many rural towns. 6And we utterly destroyed them, as we did to Sihon king of Heshbon, utterly destroying the men, women, and children of every city. 7But all the livestock and the spoil of the cities we took as booty for ourselves.

8"And at that time we took the land from the hand of the two kings of the Amorites who *were* on this side of the Jordan, from the River Arnon to Mount Hermon 9(the Sidonians call Hermon Sirion, and the Amorites call it Senir), 10all the cities of the plain, all Gilead, and all Bashan, as far as Salcah and Edrei, cities of the kingdom of Og in Bashan.

11"For only Og king of Bashan remained of the remnant of the giants.a Indeed his bedstead *was* an iron bedstead. (*Is* it not in Rabbah of the people of Ammon?) Nine cubits *is* its length and four cubits its width, according to the standard cubit.

The Land East of the Jordan Divided

12"And this land, *which* we possessed at that time, from Aroer, which *is* by the River Arnon, and half the mountains of Gilead and its cities, I gave to the Reubenites and the Gadites. 13The rest of Gilead, and all Bashan, the kingdom of Og, I gave to half the tribe of Manasseh. (All the region of Argob, with all Bashan, was called the land of the giants.a 14Jair the son of Manasseh took all the region of Argob, as far as the border of the Geshurites and the Maachathites, and called Bashan after his own name, Havoth Jair,a to this day.)

15"Also I gave Gilead to Machir. 16And to the Reubenites and the Gadites I gave from Gilead as far as the River Arnon, the middle of the river as *the* border, as far as the River Jabbok, the border of the people of Ammon; 17the plain also, with the Jordan as *the* border, from Chinnereth as far as the east side of the Sea of the Arabah (the Salt Sea), below the slopes of Pisgah.

18"Then I commanded you at that time, saying: 'The LORD your God has given you this land to possess. All you men of valor shall cross over armed before your brethren, the children of Israel. 19But your wives, your little ones, and your livestock (I know that you have much livestock) shall stay in your cities which I have given you, 20until the LORD has given rest to your brethren as to you, and they also possess the land which the LORD your God is giving them beyond the Jordan. Then each of you may return to his possession which I have given you.'

21"And I commanded Joshua at that time, saying, 'Your eyes have seen all that the LORD your God has done to these two kings; so will the LORD do to all the kingdoms through which you pass. 22You must not fear them, for the LORD your God Himself fights for you.'

Moses Forbidden to Enter the Land

23"Then I pleaded with the LORD at that time, saying: 24'O Lord GOD, You have begun to show Your servant Your greatness and Your mighty

3:11, 13 aHebrew *rephaim*   3:14 aLiterally *Towns of Jair*

3:11 The bedstead of Og, which may have been a reference to his "last couch," that is, his coffin or sarcophagus, was made of an ironlike mineral called basalt. The cubit was reportedly the distance from the elbow to the tip of the middle finger or approximately 18 inches. From these dimensions, 13½ feet by 6 feet, this was indeed a king-sized bed! By recalling the great stature of Og, the people were reminded of the great victory the Lord provided for them.

3:18 Although Reubenites, Gadites, and the half-tribe of Manasseh were laying claim to their allotment in the Transjordan, they were still required to fight alongside their fellow Israelites in the continuing conquest of Canaan (see Num. 32:17).

3:19 Women did not participate in the military. However, the wives and the children who were left behind would not be defenseless. No doubt some men who did not meet requirements for battle would stay and protect the families and possessions of the warriors (see Deut. 20:5–8). They would also be protected by the Lord.

3:24, 25 Having seen the greatness of the Lord in the deliverance of Sihon and Og, Moses pleaded earnestly with the Lord to rescind His judgment and allow him to see the good Land. The intense passion of Moses is seen in this supplication.

ATTRIBUTES OF GOD HE IS JEALOUS

Jealousy (Heb. *qin'ah*) denotes "zeal, passion, single-mindedness." God's jealousy does not covet something that belongs to another but rather preserves something that belongs to Himself. Just as the relationship between a husband and wife in marriage is designed to be exclusive, so is the relationship between God and His people (Ex. 34:27).

God pledged Himself to the Israelites (Ex. 19:4–6); they responded with their vows (Ex. 19:8, 9; 24:3, 7), and the ceremony was complete (Ex. 24:12, 18). Then the issue became faithfulness. God's faithfulness is sure, though His people may waver.

To be intertwined in heart and life with the world is the worst kind of adultery (James 4:4, 5). God considers it hatred of Himself (Ex. 20:5) and prostitution with the Evil One (1 Cor. 10:21, 22). The consequence of spiritual adultery is a severed relationship with God (Ps. 78:56–60).

The teachings of God's jealousy are given in the context of worship. He alone is God; to worship another is betrayal. God takes His relationship with His people seriously, and so must they take theirs with Him (Ex. 34:10–16).

See also Deut. 6:14, 15; 29:20; 32:16, 21; Josh. 24:18, 19; Ps. 79:5; Lam. 3:22, note; Ezek. 8:3–5; 16:38, 42; 39:25; notes on Attributes of God (Ex. 33; Deut. 4; 32; 2 Chr. 19; Job 23; 42; Ps. 25; 90; 102; 119; Is. 6; 65; Jer. 23; Rom. 2; Eph. 1; 1 John 5); Fear of the Lord (Prov. 2); Holiness (Lev. 20); Jealousy (Song 8).

hand, for what god *is there* in heaven or on earth who can do *anything* like Your works and Your mighty *deeds?* ²⁵I pray, let me cross over and see the good land beyond the Jordan, those pleasant mountains, and Lebanon.'

²⁶But the LORD was angry with me on your account, and would not listen to me. So the LORD said to me: 'Enough of that! Speak no more to Me of this matter. ²⁷Go up to the top of Pisgah, and lift your eyes toward the west, the north, the south, and the east; behold *it* with your eyes, for you shall not cross over this Jordan. ²⁸But command Joshua, and encourage him and strengthen him; for he shall go over before this people, and he shall cause them to inherit the land which you will see.'

²⁹"So we stayed in the valley opposite Beth Peor.

Moses Commands Obedience

4 "Now, O Israel, listen to the statutes and the judgments which I teach you to observe, that you may live, and go in and possess the land which the LORD God of your fathers is giving you. ²You shall not add to the word which I command you, nor take from it, that you may keep the commandments of the LORD your God which I command you. ³Your eyes have seen what the LORD did at Baal Peor; for the LORD your God has destroyed from

among you all the men who followed Baal of Peor. ⁴But you who held fast to the LORD your God *are* alive today, every one of you.

⁵"Surely I have taught you statutes and judgments, just as the LORD my God commanded me, that you should act according *to them* in the land which you go to possess. ⁶Therefore be careful to observe *them;* for this *is* your wisdom and your understanding in the sight of the peoples who will hear all these statutes, and say, 'Surely this great nation *is* a wise and understanding people.'

⁷"For what great nation *is there* that has God so near to it, as the LORD our God *is* to us, for whatever *reason* we may call upon Him? ⁸And what great nation *is there* that has *such* statutes and righteous judgments as are in all this law which I set before you this day? ⁹Only take heed to yourself, and diligently keep yourself, lest you forget the things your eyes have seen, and lest they depart from your heart all the days of your life. And teach them to your children and your grandchildren, ¹⁰*especially concerning* the day you stood before the LORD your God in Horeb, when the LORD said to me, 'Gather the people to Me, and I will let them hear My words, that they may learn to fear Me all the days they live on the earth, and *that* they may teach their children.'

¹¹"Then you came near and stood at the foot of the mountain, and the mountain burned with fire

4:1 Having seen the deliverance of the Lord, obedience to His commands is expected. Listening involves hearing with the intent to obey. Obedience to the Lord would result in life. This theme is dominant in Deuteronomy.

4:6–8 Obedience to the Law brought the blessings of the Lord and provided a witness to the pagan nations. The wisdom of the Law and the obedience of the people to the Law would illustrate the uniqueness of Israel and her God.

4:9, 10 Though the Israelites did not have a tangible representation of the Lord, they had seen His power and received His words. They were to remember these events and teach them to their children. Moses' concern for the children and their knowledge of God is seen often (Deut. 6:7, 20; 11:19; 31:13; 32:46). If the covenant is not taught to the children, the failure of the nation is assured.

to the midst of heaven, with darkness, cloud, and thick darkness. [12]And the LORD spoke to you out of the midst of the fire. You heard the sound of the words, but saw no form; *you* only *heard* a voice. [13]So He declared to you His covenant which He commanded you to perform, the Ten Commandments; and He wrote them on two tablets of stone. [14]And the LORD commanded me at that time to teach you statutes and judgments, that you might observe them in the land which you cross over to possess.

Beware of Idolatry

[15]"Take careful heed to yourselves, for you saw no form when the LORD spoke to you at Horeb out of the midst of the fire, [16]lest you act corruptly and make for yourselves a carved image in the form of any figure: the likeness of male or female, [17]the likeness of any animal that *is* on the earth or the likeness of any winged bird that flies in the air, [18]the likeness of anything that creeps on the ground or the likeness of any fish that *is* in the water beneath the earth. [19]And *take heed,* lest you lift your eyes to heaven, and *when* you see the sun, the moon, and the stars, all the host of heaven, you feel driven to worship them and serve them, which the LORD your God has given to all the peoples under the whole heaven as a heritage. [20]But the LORD has taken you and brought you out of the iron furnace, out of Egypt, to be His people, an inheritance, as you are this day. [21]Furthermore the LORD was angry with me for your sakes, and swore that I would not cross over the Jordan, and that I would not enter the good land which the LORD your God is giving you as an inheritance. [22]But I must die in this land, I must not cross over the Jordan; but you shall cross over and possess that good land. [23]Take heed to yourselves, lest you forget the covenant of the LORD your God which He made with you, and make for yourselves a carved image in the form of anything which the LORD your God has forbidden you. [24]For the LORD your God *is* a consuming fire, a jealous God.

[25]"When you beget children and grandchildren and have grown old in the land, and act corruptly and make a carved image in the form of anything, and do evil in the sight of the LORD your God to provoke Him to anger, [26]I call heaven and earth to witness against you this day, that you will soon utterly perish from the land which you cross over the Jordan to possess; you will not prolong *your* days in it, but will be utterly destroyed. [27]And the LORD will scatter you among the peoples, and you will be left few in number among the nations where the LORD will drive you. [28]And there you will serve gods, the work of men's hands, wood and stone, which neither see nor hear nor eat nor smell. [29]But from there you will seek the LORD your God, and you will find *Him* if you seek Him with all your heart and with all your soul. [30]When you are in distress, and all these things come upon you in the latter days, when you turn to the LORD your God and obey His voice [31](for the LORD your God *is* a merciful God), He will not forsake you nor destroy you, nor forget the covenant of your fathers which He swore to them.

[32]"For ask now concerning the days that are past, which were before you, since the day that God created man on the earth, and *ask* from one end of heaven to the other, whether *any* great *thing* like this has happened, or *anything* like it has been heard. [33]Did *any* people *ever* hear the voice of God speaking out of the midst of the fire, as you have heard, and live? [34]Or did God *ever* try to go *and* take for Himself a nation from the midst of *another* nation, by trials, by signs, by wonders, by war, by a mighty hand and an outstretched arm, and by great terrors, according to all that the LORD your God did for you in Egypt before your eyes? [35]To you it was shown, that you might know that the LORD Himself *is* God; *there is* none other besides Him. [36]Out of heaven He let you hear His voice, that He might instruct you; on earth He showed you His great fire, and you heard His words out of the midst of the fire. [37]And because He loved your fathers, therefore He chose their descendants after them; and He brought you out of Egypt with His Presence, with His mighty power, [38]driving out from before you nations greater and mightier than you, to bring you in, to give you their land *as* an inheritance, as *it is* this day. [39]Therefore know this day, and consider *it* in your heart, that the LORD Himself *is* God in heaven above and on the earth beneath; *there is* no other. [40]You shall therefore keep His statutes and His commandments which I command you today, that it may go well with you and with your children after you, and that you may prolong *your* days

---

4:15 The fact that God took no form at Horeb enforces the command against idolatry, a pagan practice (see Is. 42, Idolatry). To try to limit God to a form or object made by a human hand would be denying the transcendence of God.

4:26 The calling of heaven and earth, or the entire created universe, as a witness was characteristic of Near Eastern treaties. They were personified as living witnesses with a permanent and unchanging quality, standing in direct contrast to the uselessness and ineffectiveness of idols.

4:29 The mercy of God in His covenant relationship with Israel is seen in this verse. Although they had sinned, He would always remember His covenant with them and receive and forgive the rebel who repents.

4:37 God's choice of the nation of Israel was based solely on His love for their forefathers and mercy toward all His people (see Ps. 89; 1 John 4, Attributes of God).

Perspective by Nancy Leigh DeMoss

A BALANCED SPIRITUAL DIET (From *A Place of Quiet Rest*, 168–172)

As I was writing this afternoon, I took a break to go make myself a sandwich. Can you imagine if I had opened the refrigerator, closed my eyes, and grabbed whatever items my hand happened to reach first? Instead of peanut butter and jelly sandwich, I might have ended up with a plate of onions, mustard, and whipped cream—not especially appetizing or nourishing. Yet that is a picture of the way many people approach the Word of God. They blindly "grab" whatever passage they come to first, in no particular sequence or order. When passages are separated from their context, their meaning is changed and well-meaning believers can easily be misled.

Others read the Bible much like a teenager whose preferred diet consists of pizza, chips, pop, and ice cream. Our bodies require a nutritionally balanced diet in order to stay healthy. Likewise, our spirits need the balance that comes from taking in the "whole counsel of God," not limiting ourselves to those passages that seem particularly appetizing. The spiritual growth of some believers has been stunted due to a diet that consists primarily of the Psalms with perhaps a smidgen of the New Testament Epistles.

It is true that not all parts of the Bible are equally easy to digest. This week I have been reading in 1 Chronicles and Ezekiel. Unlike the "succulent" passages we might discover in 1 Peter or the gospel of John, there are some passages in those books that seem particularly tedious and even unnecessary. Even the great Puritan pastor John Bunyan admitted, "I have sometimes seen more in a line of the Bible than I could well tell how to stand under, and yet at another time the whole Bible hath been to me as dry as a stick."

But Paul reminded Timothy that "*all* Scripture is given by inspiration of God, and is profitable for doctrine, for reproof, for correction, for instruction in righteousness" (2 Tim. 3:16, emphasis added). That means that we need a diet that includes *all* of God's Word. Yes, we need the Psalms and the Epistles. But we also need the Books of the Law, the Historical Books, the Prophets, and the Gospels. We need the whole of God's Word. And we need to read in such a way that we get a sense of the flow of the Word.

The fact that the Bible is a whole doesn't mean it can only be read straight through, from Genesis to Revelation, although many believers find great blessing in doing this on a regular basis. It does mean that context and flow are important. Individual verses need to be read in the context of the paragraph and chapter in which they appear. Chapters should be studied in light of the entire book where they are found. And the various books make more sense if we understand how they fit into the scheme and flow of the Bible and God's eternal, redemptive plan. If you want to get a balanced spiritual diet as well as an understanding of the whole plan of God, make sure that you are not overlooking or bypassing certain portions of the Word.

There are many different ways to read the Bible systematically. There are numerous Bible reading plans available today, some designed to help you read through the entire Bible in a year, others in a longer time span. Personally, I generally prefer to read in both the Old and New Testaments at the same time. There are several reasons for this: First, the Old Testament sheds light on the New and vice versa. Those connections are easier to see when I am reading in both Testaments. Second, I don't like to go for long periods of time without reading in the Gospels. That is where we get the clearest picture of the Lord Jesus. If the goal of our devotional life is to know Him and to be conformed to His image, then we will want to go back to the Gospels over and over again. Third, by reading in both Testaments, the more difficult Old Testament passages are balanced out with other portions that are easier to "digest."

Some time ago, a dear, older servant of the Lord recommended an approach to Bible reading that I have found to be a great blessing. He suggested dividing the Bible into six major sections, beginning in Genesis, Joshua, Job, Isaiah, Matthew, and Romans. Each day, read one or more chapters consecutively in each of those sections. Mark where you end up in each section so you can pick up at that location the next day.

This has been one of the most exciting ways I have discovered to read the Word. Though penned by many different authors over a period of fifteen hundred years, there is a unity and coherence in the Scripture that can only be supernatural. Invariably, I find that what I am reading in one portion dovetails precisely with what I am reading in another.

At times you may feel the need to take a particular book or section of the Bible and "place it under a microscope." One way of doing that is to take a specific book of the Bible and read through it every day for thirty days. This is a good way to gain deeper insight into the heart and message of an individual book.

You will probably find that your devotional life stays fresher if you vary your approach to Bible reading from time to time. At times, you may want to read just a small portion each day, meditating on each word and phrase. During other seasons, you may choose to cover more ground more quickly, looking for the broader, overarching themes. Occasionally, you may wish to take a break from reading consecutively in order to focus on a particular topic, word, or character from the Bible. However, it is not wise to neglect systematic reading of the Scripture for any length of time.

in the land which the LORD your God is giving you for all time."

Cities of Refuge East of the Jordan

⁴¹Then Moses set apart three cities on this side of the Jordan, toward the rising of the sun, ⁴²that the manslayer might flee there, who kills his neighbor unintentionally, without having hated him in time past, and that by fleeing to one of these cities he might live: ⁴³Bezer in the wilderness on the plateau for the Reubenites, Ramoth in Gilead for the Gadites, and Golan in Bashan for the Manassites.

Introduction to God's Law

⁴⁴Now this *is* the law which Moses set before the children of Israel. ⁴⁵These *are* the testimonies, the statutes, and the judgments which Moses spoke to the children of Israel after they came out of Egypt, ⁴⁶on this side of the Jordan, in the valley opposite Beth Peor, in the land of Sihon king of the Amorites, who dwelt at Heshbon, whom Moses and the children of Israel defeated after they came out of Egypt. ⁴⁷And they took possession of his land and the land of Og king of Bashan, two kings of the Amorites, who *were* on this side of the Jordan, toward the rising of the sun, ⁴⁸from Aroer, which *is* on the bank of the River Arnon, even to Mount Sionᵃ (that is, Hermon), ⁴⁹and all the plain on the east side of the Jordan as far as the Sea of the Arabah, below the slopes of Pisgah.

The Ten Commandments Reviewed

5 And Moses called all Israel, and said to them: "Hear, O Israel, the statutes and judgments which I speak in your hearing today, that you may learn them and be careful to observe them. ²The LORD our God made a covenant with us in Horeb. ³The LORD did not make this covenant with our fathers, but with us, those who *are* here today, all of us who *are* alive. ⁴The LORD talked with you face to face on the mountain from the midst of the fire. ⁵I stood between the LORD and you at that time, to declare to you the word of the LORD; for you were afraid because of the fire, and you did not go up the mountain. *He* said:

⁶'I *am* the LORD your God who brought you out of the land of Egypt, out of the house of bondage. ⁷'You shall have no other gods before Me. ⁸'You shall not make for yourself a carved image—any likeness *of anything* that *is* in heaven above, or that *is* in the earth beneath, or that *is* in the water under the earth; ⁹you shall not bow down to them nor serve them. For I, the LORD your God, *am* a jealous God, visiting the iniquity of the fathers upon the children to the third and fourth *generations* of those who hate Me, ¹⁰but showing mercy to thousands, to those who love Me and keep My commandments.

¹¹'You shall not take the name of the LORD your God in vain, for the LORD will not hold *him* guiltless who takes His name in vain.

¹²'Observe the Sabbath day, to keep it holy, as the LORD your God commanded you. ¹³Six days you shall labor and do all your work, ¹⁴but the seventh day *is* the Sabbath of the LORD your God. *In it* you shall do no work: you, nor your son, nor your daughter, nor your male servant, nor your female servant, nor your ox, nor your donkey, nor any of your cattle, nor your stranger who *is* within your gates, that your male servant and your female servant may rest as well as you. ¹⁵And remember that you were a slave in the land of Egypt, and the LORD your God brought you out from there by a mighty hand and by an outstretched arm; therefore the LORD your God commanded you to keep the Sabbath day.

¹⁶'Honor your father and your mother, as the LORD your God has commanded you, that your days may be long, and that it may be well with you in the land which the LORD your God is giving you.

¹⁷'You shall not murder.
¹⁸'You shall not commit adultery.
¹⁹'You shall not steal.
²⁰'You shall not bear false witness against your neighbor.

4:48 ᵃSyriac reads *Sirion* (compare 3:9).

4:41–43 After Moses' address, he set aside three cities in Transjordan to serve as asylums for anyone who committed involuntary manslaughter. This system provided safety from revenge until legal procedures could be undertaken (Deut. 19:1–13).

5:9, 10 The Lord will not tolerate any violation of His holiness and sovereignty, for such would affect all the generations to come. Parents who act as if they hate God teach their children to do the same by their actions as well as their words. Therefore, the children are not punished for the parent's rebellion but rather because the children rebel in the same manner. The life of the parent will be reflected in the children who have watched the lives of their parents and, in turn, will pass that lifestyle on to their own children. Notice the contrast between judgment that extends to the third and fourth generation and mercy that is shown to thousands.

5:12–15 The reason for keeping the Sabbath holy is different here than that stated in Exodus 20:11 (see chart, The Principle of the Sabbath). In the Exodus accounting, the rest on the Sabbath coincides with the rest of God after completing His creative activity. However, here the Sabbath rest is in remembrance of their deliverance from Egypt (see also Ex. 23, The Lord's Day).

HOME SCHOOLING A PLACE OF LEARNING

God has given to His people commands that are to be passed along to their children so they "may fear the Lord" and keep His commandments that their "days may be prolonged."

As the children of Israel trekked from Egypt to the Promised Land, the teaching of children was not an activity isolated to a particular location or a limited time of day. Rather, it was instruction interwoven with all the activities of life. The teaching was to be while they were sitting, walking, lying down, and rising up (Deut. 6:1–7).

Home schooling is one way many families are fulfilling this command to pass on godly values and to instruct their children about life from a godly perspective. Even though they want their children to be exposed to other people and other ideas, most home schooling parents feel that they have the primary responsibility for influencing the lives of their children. Home schooling allows them the opportunity to present information in the context of values.

Home schooling families have many reasons for educating their children at home:

- Children are encouraged to grow in all areas at their own pace—emotionally, spiritually, socially, and mentally. This education accommodates the uniqueness of each child, including physiological and neurological differences.
- Many of the negative effects of peer pressure are minimized.
- An opportunity for children to pursue their respective interests in particular subjects is provided. In a relaxed home atmosphere, the child's natural curiosity can lead to learning experiences.
- A unique family bond is created since parents and children are together many hours each day. Much of home schooling involves a one-to-one tutorial approach, considered the finest method ever devised for formal instruction.
- Domestic skills, hobbies, earning and managing money, responding to the needs of others, and other practical areas of life are included in the training.

Home schooling is a big responsibility, but many parents are discovering the enriching rewards of teaching their own children, and they take it seriously enough to make the investment of time it requires. Home schoolers have a great deal in common with the early Hebrews, as well as with the many parents who have instructed their children at home throughout history.

See also Deut. 11:18–20; Prov. 22:6; Matt. 18:3, note; Eph. 6:4; notes on Children (2 Sam. 21; Ps. 128; Prov. 22; Luke 15); Creativity (Col. 1); Education (Deut 6; Prov. 12; 2 Tim. 3); Family (Gen. 32; 1 Sam. 3; Ps. 78; 127); Flexibility (Deut. 10)

21"You shall not covet your neighbor's wife; and you shall not desire your neighbor's house, his field, his male servant, his female servant, his ox, his donkey, or anything that *is* your neighbor's.'

22"These words the Lord spoke to all your assembly, in the mountain from the midst of the fire, the cloud, and the thick darkness, with a loud voice; and He added no more. And He wrote them on two tablets of stone and gave them to me.

The People Afraid of God's Presence

23"So it was, when you heard the voice from the midst of the darkness, while the mountain was burning with fire, that you came near to me, all the heads of your tribes and your elders. 24And you said: 'Surely the LORD our God has shown us His glory and His greatness, and we have heard

His voice from the midst of the fire. We have seen this day that God speaks with man; yet he *still* lives. 25Now therefore, why should we die? For this great fire will consume us; if we hear the voice of the LORD our God anymore, then we shall die. 26For who *is there* of all flesh who has heard the voice of the living God speaking from the midst of the fire, as we *have,* and lived? 27You go near and hear all that the LORD our God may say, and tell us all that the LORD our God says to you, and we will hear and do *it.'*

28"Then the LORD heard the voice of your words when you spoke to me, and the LORD said to me: 'I have heard the voice of the words of this people which they have spoken to you. They are right *in* all that they have spoken. 29Oh, that they had such a heart in them that they would fear Me and always keep all My commandments, that it might be well with them and with their children

---

5:21 This last commandment is concerned mostly with a condition of the heart that would manifest itself in actions listed in the previous four commandments.

forever! [30]Go and say to them, "Return to your tents." [31]But as for you, stand here by Me, and I will speak to you all the commandments, the statutes, and the judgments which you shall teach them, that they may observe *them* in the land which I am giving them to possess.'

[32]"Therefore you shall be careful to do as the LORD your God has commanded you; you shall not turn aside to the right hand or to the left. [33]You shall walk in all the ways which the LORD your God has commanded you, that you may live and *that it may be* well with you, and *that* you may prolong *your* days in the land which you shall possess.

The Greatest Commandment

6 "Now this *is* the commandment, *and these are* the statutes and judgments which the LORD your God has commanded to teach you, that you may observe *them* in the land which you are crossing over to possess, [2]that you may fear the LORD your God, to keep all His statutes and His commandments which I command you, you and your son and your grandson, all the days of your life, and that your days may be prolonged. [3]Therefore hear, O Israel, and be careful to observe *it*, that it may be well with you, and that you may multiply greatly as the LORD God of your fathers has promised you—'a land flowing with milk and honey.'[a]

[4]"Hear, O Israel: The LORD our God, the LORD *is* one![a] [5]You shall love the LORD your God with all your heart, with all your soul, and with all your strength.

[6]"And these words which I command you today shall be in your heart. [7]You shall teach them diligently to your children, and shall talk of them when you sit in your house, when you walk by the way, when you lie down, and when you rise up. [8]You shall bind them as a sign on your hand, and they shall be as frontlets between your eyes. [9]You shall write them on the doorposts of your house and on your gates.

Caution Against Disobedience

[10]"So it shall be, when the LORD your God brings you into the land of which He swore to your fathers, to Abraham, Isaac, and Jacob, to give you large and beautiful cities which you did not build, [11]houses full of all good things, which you did not fill, hewn-out wells which you did not dig, vineyards and olive trees which you did not plant—when you have eaten and are full— [12]then beware, lest you forget the LORD who brought you out of the land of Egypt, from the house of bondage. [13]You shall fear the LORD your God and serve Him, and shall take oaths in His name. [14]You shall not go after other gods, the gods of the peoples who *are* all around you [15](for the LORD your God *is* a jealous God among you), lest the anger of the LORD your God be aroused against you and destroy you from the face of the earth.

[16]"You shall not tempt the LORD your God as you tempted *Him* in Massah. [17]You shall diligently keep the commandments of the LORD your God, His testimonies, and His statutes which He has commanded you. [18]And you shall do *what is* right and good in the sight of the LORD, that it may be well with you, and that you may go in and possess

6:3 [a]Exodus 3:8 6:4 [a]Or *The LORD is our God, the LORD alone* (that is, the only one)

6:1 The commandment, the statutes, and the judgments. "The commandments" (Heb. *mitsvah;* see Deut. 4:2) is a reference to the sum and substance of the Law—the Ten Commandments or perhaps encompassing all the *Torah.* "The statutes" (Heb. *chuqim*) may refer to the ceremonial laws dealing with how to approach God or that which was prescribed as moral or ritual or civil code. "The judgments" (Heb. *mishpatim,* lit. "right") could allude to the narrative passages that express what happens when a person keeps or violates the Law.

6:4, 5 The *Shema* (Heb., lit. "hear"), as this passage is often called, expresses the uniqueness as well as the unity of God. The *Shema* was fundamental to the Jewish faith and was to be recited morning and night. The word "one" (Heb. *'ekad*) implies unity made up of several parts, and this oneness is seen in the Christian doctrine of the Trinity. By believing this confession, the people of Israel would guard themselves against idolatry. *Yahweh* was affirmed as the one true God, and He was identified as Israel's God.

6:6, 7 So important were the commands of the Lord that Moses directed the nation to do everything possible to remember these commands and to incorporate them into everyday life. The spiritual education of the children was the responsibility of the parent. The teaching would take place daily through the example of the parents as well as through the repetition of the Law. The importance of this command is seen by the extent to which parents were to go in order to teach their children. This was more than teaching the facts of the Law; it was to be the demonstration of a lifestyle woven into the tapestry of everyday life. Creativity was needed to teach the precepts of God while involved in mundane chores of the household.

6:8, 9 The binding of God's Word as symbols on their hands and on their foreheads and the enclosing of these written verses in attachments for doorframes could well be intended to be metaphorical, but in later times the Jews treated these admonitions as literal commands. They would copy several verses of Scripture on a parchment and place it in a small container called a "frontlet" (see Ex. 13:16, note; Matt. 23:5, "phylacteries," small leather containers worn around the head and around the left arm near the heart). The wearing of these was especially important whenever the *Shema* (Heb.) was recited. They would also put the same verses in a small container called a *mezuzah* (Heb.), which they would attach to the doorposts or gateposts of their homes, a custom still observed today.

6:12 The danger of prosperity lay in becoming satisfied and forgetting the deliverance of the Lord (Prov. 30:7–9).

EDUCATION *TEACHING OUR CHILDREN*

The family, throughout Scripture, is considered to be the basic channel for the moral and practical teaching of children (Deut. 6:6, 7). Within the home, children are to learn the praises of the Lord and His strengths and works (Ps. 78:1–4), daily self-discipline (Prov. 13:24; 22:15; 29:15), and the history of God's people (Deut. 6:20–25).

Historically, the instruction of children was to be in three basic areas:

- *Religious education.* Children were expected to learn the Law in order to become a kingdom of priests and a holy people (Ex. 19:6).
- *Occupational skills.* Children learned trades in an apprentice environment and took on such responsibilities at an early age (1 Sam. 16:11).
- *Military strategy and skills.* Agility and courage were emphasized (2 Sam. 22:34).

Oral instruction was prevalent, with an emphasis on recitation of historical exploits, proverbs, and the Torah (the first five books of the Bible). Instruction was to be daily—highly repetitive and behavior-oriented—so that lessons might be committed to memory and result in action (Deut. 11:18–21; Prov. 22:6; Is. 28:9, 10).

Women were a vital link in teaching their own children (2 Tim. 1:5) and mentoring younger women (Titus 2:3–5). They were also trained in professional skills such as midwifery (Ex. 1:15–21), cooking (1 Sam. 8:13), professional mourning (Jer. 9:17–19), singing in the royal court (Eccl. 2:8), poetic expression and prophecy (Ex. 15:20, 21).

The first mention of education in a public setting is one in which the people of God are commanded to read the covenant publicly once every seven years in the presence of all the people (Deut. 31:10–13). Parents are admonished to teach with love and responsibility (Eph. 6:4–7) and children to learn with an attitude of respect (Ex. 20:12; Lev. 19:3).

See also Matt. 18:3, note; notes on Children (2 Sam. 21; Ps. 128; Prov. 22; Luke 15); Education (Prov. 12; 2 Tim. 3); Home Schooling (Deut. 6); Parenthood (Prov. 10)

the good land of which the LORD swore to your fathers, [19]to cast out all your enemies from before you, as the LORD has spoken.

[20]"When your son asks you in time to come, saying, 'What *is the meaning of* the testimonies, the statutes, and the judgments which the LORD our God has commanded you?' [21]then you shall say to your son: 'We were slaves of Pharaoh in Egypt, and the LORD brought us out of Egypt with a mighty hand; [22]and the LORD showed signs and wonders before our eyes, great and severe, against Egypt, Pharaoh, and all his household. [23]Then He brought us out from there, that He might bring us in, to give us the land of which He swore to our fathers. [24]And the LORD commanded us to observe all these statutes, to fear the LORD our God, for our good always, that He might preserve us alive, as *it is* this day. [25]Then it will be righteousness for us, if we are careful to observe all these commandments before the LORD our God, as He has commanded us.'

A Chosen People

7 "When the LORD your God brings you into the land which you go to possess, and has cast out many nations before you, the Hittites and the Girgashites and the Amorites and the Canaanites and the Perizzites and the Hivites and the Jebusites, seven nations greater and mightier than you, [2]and when the LORD your God delivers them over to you, you shall conquer them *and* utterly destroy them. You shall make no covenant with them nor show mercy to them. [3]Nor shall you make marriages with them. You shall not give your daughter to their son, nor take their daughter for your son. [4]For they will turn your sons away from following Me, to serve other gods; so the anger of the LORD will be aroused against you and destroy you suddenly. [5]But thus you shall deal with them: you shall destroy their altars, and break down their *sacred* pillars, and cut down their wooden images,[a] and burn their carved images with fire.

[6]"For you *are* a holy people to the LORD your God; the LORD your God has chosen you to be a people for Himself, a special treasure above all the peoples on the face of the earth. [7]The LORD did not set His love on you nor choose you because

7:5 [a]Hebrew *Asherim,* Canaanite deities

6:20 **If the parents were keeping the commands of the Lord,** then questions of this nature would arise out of the curiosity characteristic of children. This kind of question would not be asked in a home where the statutes were not observed.

6:21–25 **The children were not to be ignored** but rather answered in a complete manner. The response was to be a comprehensive testimony of their bondage, deliverance, protection, provision, and submission to *Yahweh.*

7:3, 4 See Neh. 10, Interfaith Marriage.

INSTRUCTIONS TO ISRAEL

DO NOT . . .	CONSEQUENCE	DO . . .	REWARD
Forget the Lord (Deut. 6:12).	The anger of God will be aroused against you (Deut. 6:15).	Fear God and keep His statutes and commandments—both you and your children (Deut. 6:2).	All your days will be prosperous. It will be well with you; you will multiply greatly and inherit a Land flowing with milk and honey (Deut. 6:3).
Go after other gods (Deut. 6:14).		Be careful to observe these (Deut. 6:3).	
Tempt the Lord (Deut. 6:16).		Love the Lord with all your heart, soul, and strength (Deut. 6:5).	
Make marriages with those in the Land (Deut. 7:3).	They will turn your children from the Lord (Deut. 7:4).	Keep these words in your heart (Deut. 6:6).	
Be afraid of them (Deut. 7:18).	The Lord will do to them what He did to the Egyptians (Deut. 7:18, 19).	Teach them diligently to your children (Deut. 6:7).	The Lord will give you large and beautiful cities, houses full of good things, wells you did not dig, trees you did not plant (Deut. 6:10, 11).
Be terrified of them (Deut. 7:21).		Bind them as a sign on your hand and as frontlets between your eyes (Deut. 6:8).	
Covet their silver and gold (Deut. 7:25).	You will be snared (Deut. 7:25).	Write them on your doorposts (Deut. 6:9).	
Bring abomination into your house (Deut. 7:26).	You will be doomed to destruction (Deut. 7:26).	Do what is right and good in the sight of the Lord (Deut. 6:18).	It will be well with you, and you will possess the Land (Deut. 6:18).
		Utterly destroy them; make no covenant with them; show them no mercy (Deut. 7:2).	Your enemies will be cast out (Deut. 6:19).
		Destroy their altars, break their sacred pillars, cut down wooden images (Deut. 7:5).	God will love, bless, and multiply you (Deut. 7:13).
		Burn their idols (Deut. 7:5).	You will be blessed above all people, not barren (Deut. 7:14).
		Listen and keep His judgments (Deut. 7:12).	He will take away all sickness (Deut. 7:15).

*Note—Commandments, statutes, and judgments are all important. Though each has its own precise meaning, they are often used interchangeably to refer to that for which God's people are responsible.

you were more in number than any other people, for you were the least of all peoples; [8]but because the LORD loves you, and because He would keep the oath which He swore to your fathers, the LORD has brought you out with a mighty hand, and re-deemed you from the house of bondage, from the hand of Pharaoh king of Egypt.

[9]"Therefore know that the LORD your God, He is God, the faithful God who keeps covenant and mercy for a thousand generations with those who

love Him and keep His commandments; [10]and He repays those who hate Him to their face, to destroy them. He will not be slack with him who hates Him; He will repay him to his face. [11]Therefore you shall keep the commandment, the statutes, and the judgments which I command you today, to observe them.

Blessings of Obedience

[12]"Then it shall come to pass, because you listen to these judgments, and keep and do them, that the LORD your God will keep with you the covenant and the mercy which He swore to your fathers. [13]And He will love you and bless you and multiply you; He will also bless the fruit of your womb and the fruit of your land, your grain and your new wine and your oil, the increase of your cattle and the offspring of your flock, in the land of which He swore to your fathers to give you. [14]You shall be blessed above all peoples; there shall not be a male or female barren among you or among your livestock. [15]And the LORD will take away from you all sickness, and will afflict you with none of the terrible diseases of Egypt which you have known, but will lay them on all those who hate you. [16]Also you shall destroy all the peoples whom the LORD your God delivers over to you; your eye shall have no pity on them; nor shall you serve their gods, for that will be a snare to you.

[17]"If you should say in your heart, 'These nations are greater than I; how can I dispossess them?'— [18]you shall not be afraid of them, but you shall remember well what the LORD your God did to Pharaoh and to all Egypt: [19]the great trials which your eyes saw, the signs and the wonders, the mighty hand and the outstretched arm, by which the LORD your God brought you out. So shall the LORD your God do to all the peoples of whom you are afraid. [20]Moreover the LORD your God will send the hornet among them until those who are left, who hide themselves from you, are destroyed. [21]You shall not be terrified of them; for the LORD your God, the great and awesome God, is among you. [22]And the LORD your God will drive out those nations before you little by little; you will be unable to destroy them at once, lest the beasts of the field become too numerous for you. [23]But the LORD your God will deliver them over to you, and will inflict defeat upon them until they are destroyed. [24]And He will deliver their kings into your hand, and you will destroy their name from under heaven; no one shall be able to stand against you until you have destroyed them. [25]You

shall burn the carved images of their gods with fire; you shall not covet the silver or gold that is on them, nor take it for yourselves, lest you be snared by it; for it is an abomination to the LORD your God. [26]Nor shall you bring an abomination into your house, lest you be doomed to destruction like it. You shall utterly detest it and utterly abhor it, for it is an accursed thing.

Remember the LORD Your God

8 "Every commandment which I command you today you must be careful to observe, that you may live and multiply, and go in and possess the land of which the LORD swore to your fathers. [2]And you shall remember that the LORD your God led you all the way these forty years in the wilderness, to humble you and test you, to know what was in your heart, whether you would keep His commandments or not. [3]So He humbled you, allowed you to hunger, and fed you with manna which you did not know nor did your fathers know, that He might make you know that man shall not live by bread alone; but man lives by every word that proceeds from the mouth of the LORD. [4]Your garments did not wear out on you, nor did your foot swell these forty years. [5]You should know in your heart that as a man chastens his son, so the LORD your God chastens you.

[6]"Therefore you shall keep the commandments of the LORD your God, to walk in His ways and to fear Him. [7]For the LORD your God is bringing you into a good land, a land of brooks of water, of fountains and springs, that flow out of valleys and hills; [8]a land of wheat and barley, of vines and fig trees and pomegranates, a land of olive oil and honey; [9]a land in which you will eat bread without scarcity, in which you will lack nothing; a land whose stones are iron and out of whose hills you can dig copper. [10]When you have eaten and are full, then you shall bless the LORD your God for the good land which He has given you.

[11]"Beware that you do not forget the LORD your God by not keeping His commandments, His judgments, and His statutes which I command you today, [12]lest—when you have eaten and are full, and have built beautiful houses and dwell in them; [13]and when your herds and your flocks multiply, and your silver and your gold are multiplied, and all that you have is multiplied; [14]when your heart is lifted up, and you forget the LORD your God who brought you out of the land of Egypt, from the house of bondage; [15]who led you through that great and terrible wilderness, in which were fiery serpents and scorpions and thirsty land where

---

7:12–15 The blessings of God, including good health, were contingent on the obedience of Israel (Ex. 15:26; 23:25). The terrible diseases they had observed in Egypt would not afflict them.

8:2 Since God already knew what was in their hearts, the testing allowed the Israelites to see themselves as they really

were. The wilderness wandering taught the people dependence on God, which would be of utmost importance in the conquest of Canaan. By being humbled, they were able to see their insufficiency and their constant need for Yahweh.

there was no water; who brought water for you out of the flinty rock; [16]who fed you in the wilderness with manna, which your fathers did not know, that He might humble you and that He might test you, to do you good in the end— [17]then you say in your heart, 'My power and the might of my hand have gained me this wealth.'

[18]"And you shall remember the LORD your God, for *it is* He who gives you power to get wealth, that He may establish His covenant which He swore to your fathers, as *it is* this day. [19]Then it shall be, if you by any means forget the LORD your God, and follow other gods, and serve them and worship them, I testify against you this day that you shall surely perish. [20]As the nations which the LORD destroys before you, so you shall perish, because you would not be obedient to the voice of the LORD your God.

Israel's Rebellions Reviewed

9 "Hear, O Israel: You *are* to cross over the Jordan today, and go in to dispossess nations greater and mightier than yourself, cities great and fortified up to heaven, [2]a people great and tall, the descendants of the Anakim, whom you know, and *of whom* you heard *it said,* 'Who can stand before the descendants of Anak?' [3]Therefore understand today that the LORD your God *is* He who goes over before you *as* a consuming fire. He will destroy them and bring them down before you; so you shall drive them out and destroy them quickly, as the LORD has said to you.

[4]"Do not think in your heart, after the LORD your God has cast them out before you, saying, 'Because of my righteousness the LORD has brought me in to possess this land'; but *it is* because of the wickedness of these nations *that* the LORD is driving them out from before you. [5]*It is* not because of your righteousness or the uprightness of your heart *that* you go in to possess their land, but because of the wickedness of these nations *that* the LORD your God drives them out from before you, and that He may fulfill the word which the LORD swore to your fathers, to Abraham, Isaac, and Jacob. [6]Therefore understand that the LORD your God is not giving you this good

land to possess because of your righteousness, for you *are* a stiff-necked people.

[7]"Remember! Do not forget how you provoked the LORD your God to wrath in the wilderness. From the day that you departed from the land of Egypt until you came to this place, you have been rebellious against the LORD. [8]Also in Horeb you provoked the LORD to wrath, so that the LORD was angry *enough* with you to have destroyed you. [9]When I went up into the mountain to receive the tablets of stone, the tablets of the covenant which the LORD made with you, then I stayed on the mountain forty days and forty nights. I neither ate bread nor drank water. [10]Then the LORD delivered to me two tablets of stone written with the finger of God, and on them *were* all the words which the LORD had spoken to you on the mountain from the midst of the fire in the day of the assembly. [11]And it came to pass, at the end of forty days and forty nights, *that* the LORD gave me the two tablets of stone, the tablets of the covenant.

[12]"Then the LORD said to me, 'Arise, go down quickly from here, for your people whom you brought out of Egypt have acted corruptly; they have quickly turned aside from the way which I commanded them; they have made themselves a molded image.'

[13]"Furthermore the LORD spoke to me, saying, 'I have seen this people, and indeed they are a stiff-necked people. [14]Let Me alone, that I may destroy them and blot out their name from under heaven; and I will make of you a nation mightier and greater than they.'

[15]"So I turned and came down from the mountain, and the mountain burned with fire; and the two tablets of the covenant *were* in my two hands. [16]And I looked, and behold, you had sinned against the LORD your God—had made for yourselves a molded calf! You had turned aside quickly from the way which the LORD had commanded you. [17]Then I took the two tablets and threw them out of my two hands and broke them before your eyes. [18]And I fell down before the LORD, as at the first, forty days and forty nights; I neither ate bread nor drank water, because of all your sin which you committed in doing wickedly in the sight of the LORD, to provoke

---

8:18 In the desert, the Israelites depended on God for their food, clothing, and shelter. Once they had settled in the Land it would be easy for them to attribute their gains to their own abilities. Moses warned against this, stating that even the ability to produce their own shelter, food, and clothing would be a gift from God. In the desert they ate manna directly from the hand of God. In their new Land they would plant their own food, but the increase of it would be from the Lord. Every provision in life is a result of the grace of God (James 1:17).

9:3 Destruction of the Anakim, giants that descended from the *Nephilim* (Heb.), was assured because the Lord would destroy them. The Israelites were merely participants; the victory belonged to the Lord.

9:4–6 Moses warned against spiritual pride. The Israelites could become proud if they thought their own righteousness had led the Lord to dispossess the Canaanites. The reason for the destruction of their enemies was twofold. These wicked enemies were under the judgment of God, and the Lord would always be faithful to the covenant that He swore to the patriarchs.

9:17 The breaking of the tablets symbolized what the people had already done to the covenant agreement. Before Moses had even returned from Mt. Horeb (Sinai) where he received the covenant, the people had already violated their agreement with God. Their apostasy was confirmed in the breaking of the tablets.

YIELDING EXPECTATIONS

The flexible are those who yield themselves to the Lord and serve Him (Ex. 24:7; 2 Chr. 30:8), who submit to the Father's will even when it goes against what they personally desire to do (Matt. 26:42), and who choose to be obedient to Christ—in their behavior and in their "thought lives" (2 Cor. 10:4–6).

The opposite of flexibility in Scripture is to have a "hard heart" and a "stiff neck"—which includes resisting the Holy Spirit (Acts 7:51), being impudent and stubborn against the Lord (Ezek. 2:2–4), and worshiping false gods (Ex. 32:8, 9)—all of which point toward a rebellious spirit. The person with a hard heart and stiff neck is subject to calamity and God's wrath (Prov. 28:14).

In your relationships with others, you are to submit your will to those in authority (Heb. 13:17), "giving preference" to others rather than demanding your own way (Rom. 12:10); yet, at the same time, abhor evil and stand up for what is good (Rom. 12:9). Above all, you are to be ready to present the Good News of the gospel in any setting to everyone God sends to you.

See also Eccl. 9:10; Phil. 2:14; 4:11, 13; Col. 3:23, 24; notes on Creativity (Col. 1); Organization (John 9); Priorities (Matt. 6); Time Management (Ps. 31)

Him to anger. ¹⁹For I was afraid of the anger and hot displeasure with which the LORD was angry with you, to destroy you. But the LORD listened to me at that time also. ²⁰And the LORD was very angry with Aaron *and* would have destroyed him; so I prayed for Aaron also at the same time. ²¹Then I took your sin, the calf which you had made, and burned it with fire and crushed it *and* ground *it* very small, until it was as fine as dust; and I threw its dust into the brook that descended from the mountain.

²²"Also at Taberah and Massah and Kibroth Hattaavah you provoked the LORD to wrath. ²³Likewise, when the LORD sent you from Kadesh Barnea, saying, 'Go up and possess the land which I have given you,' then you rebelled against the commandment of the LORD your God, and you did not believe Him nor obey His voice. ²⁴You have been rebellious against the LORD from the day that I knew you.

²⁵"Thus I prostrated myself before the LORD; forty days and forty nights I kept prostrating myself, because the LORD had said He would destroy you. ²⁶Therefore I prayed to the LORD, and said: 'O Lord GOD, do not destroy Your people and Your inheritance whom You have redeemed through Your greatness, whom You have brought out of Egypt with a mighty hand. ²⁷Remember Your servants, Abraham, Isaac, and Jacob; do not look on the stubbornness of this people, or on their wickedness or their sin, ²⁸lest the land from which You brought us should say, "Because

the LORD was not able to bring them to the land which He promised them, and because He hated them, He has brought them out to kill them in the wilderness." ²⁹Yet they *are* Your people and Your inheritance, whom You brought out by Your mighty power and by Your outstretched arm.'

The Second Pair of Tablets

10 "At that time the LORD said to me, 'Hew for yourself two tablets of stone like the first, and come up to Me on the mountain and make yourself an ark of wood. ²And I will write on the tablets the words that were on the first tablets, which you broke; and you shall put them in the ark.'

³"So I made an ark of acacia wood, hewed two tablets of stone like the first, and went up the mountain, having the two tablets in my hand. ⁴And He wrote on the tablets according to the first writing, the Ten Commandments, which the LORD had spoken to you in the mountain from the midst of the fire in the day of the assembly; and the LORD gave them to me. ⁵Then I turned and came down from the mountain, and put the tablets in the ark which I had made; and there they are, just as the LORD commanded me."

⁶(Now the children of Israel journeyed from the wells of Bene Jaakan to Moserah, where Aaron died, and where he was buried; and Eleazar his son ministered as priest in his stead. ⁷From there they journeyed to Gudgodah, and from Gudgodah to

9:22 At each of these places the people complained and murmured. Their complaining showed lack of faith in God.

9:24 The continued rebellion of the people kept Moses in constant intercession for them. However, his pleas were not based on their merit but on God's promise to the patriarchs. The destruction of Israel would cause the pagan nations to question His faithfulness. The mercy God showed Israel is linked to the intercession of Moses.

10:1 At that time is a reference to the time of Moses' prayer for grace for the nation (Deut. 9:25–29). "Like the first" indicates that the covenant was to be renewed according to God's great mercy on a rebellious people.

10:3 Though Moses himself did not build the ark, he gave the instructions for its building according to what the Lord had told him (Ex. 25:10–22; see chart, The Furniture of the Tabernacle). The carpenter was Bezalel (Ex. 37:1–9).

Jotbathah, a land of rivers of water. [8]At that time the LORD separated the tribe of Levi to bear the ark of the covenant of the LORD, to stand before the LORD to minister to Him and to bless in His name, to this day. [9]Therefore Levi has no portion nor inheritance with his brethren; the LORD *is* his inheritance, just as the LORD your God promised him.)

[10]"As at the first time, I stayed in the mountain forty days and forty nights; the LORD also heard me at that time, *and* the LORD chose not to destroy you. [11]Then the LORD said to me, 'Arise, begin *your* journey before the people, that they may go in and possess the land which I swore to their fathers to give them.'

The Essence of the Law

[12]"And now, Israel, what does the LORD your God require of you, but to fear the LORD your God, to walk in all His ways and to love Him, to serve the LORD your God with all your heart and with all your soul, [13]and to keep the commandments of the LORD and His statutes which I command you today for your good? [14]Indeed heaven and the highest heavens belong to the LORD your God, *also* the earth with all that *is* in it. [15]The LORD delighted only in your fathers, to love them; and He chose their descendants after them, you above all peoples, as *it is* this day. [16]Therefore circumcise the foreskin of your heart, and be stiff-necked no longer. [17]For the LORD your God *is* God of gods and Lord of lords, the great God, mighty and awesome, who shows no partiality nor takes a bribe. [18]He administers justice for the fatherless and the widow, and loves the stranger, giving him food and clothing. [19]Therefore love the stranger, for you were strangers in the land of Egypt. [20]You shall fear the LORD your God; you shall serve Him, and to Him you shall hold fast, and take oaths in His name. [21]He *is* your praise, and He *is* your God, who has done for you these great and awesome things which your eyes have seen. [22]Your fathers went down to Egypt with seventy persons, and now the LORD your God has made you as the stars of heaven in multitude.

Love and Obedience Rewarded

11 "Therefore you shall love the LORD your God, and keep His charge, His statutes, His judgments, and His commandments always. [2]Know today that *I do* not *speak* with your children, who have not known and who have not seen the chastening of the LORD your God, His greatness and His mighty hand and His outstretched arm— [3]His signs and His acts which He did in the midst of Egypt, to Pharaoh king of Egypt, and to all his land; [4]what He did to the army of Egypt, to their horses and their chariots: how He made the waters of the Red Sea overflow them as they pursued you, and *how* the LORD has destroyed them to this day; [5]what He did for you in the wilderness until you came to this place; [6]and what He did to Dathan and Abiram the sons of Eliab, the son of Reuben: how the earth opened its mouth and swallowed them up, their households, their tents, and all the substance that *was* in their possession, in the midst of all Israel— [7]but your eyes have seen every great act of the LORD which He did.

[8]"Therefore you shall keep every commandment which I command you today, that you may be strong, and go in and possess the land which you cross over to possess, [9]and that you may prolong *your* days in the land which the LORD swore to give your fathers, to them and their descendants, 'a land flowing with milk and honey.'ᵃ [10]For the land which you go to possess *is* not like the land of Egypt from which you have come, where you sowed your seed and watered *it* by foot, as a vegetable garden; [11]but the land which you cross over to possess *is* a land of hills and valleys, which drinks water from the rain of heaven, [12]a land for which the LORD your God cares; the eyes of the LORD your God *are* always on it, from the beginning of the year to the very end of the year.

[13]"And it shall be that if you earnestly obey My commandments which I command you today, to love the LORD your God and serve Him with all your heart and with all your soul, [14]then Iᵃ will

11:9 ᵃExodus 3:8   11:14 ᵃFollowing Masoretic Text and Targum; Samaritan Pentateuch, Septuagint, and Vulgate read *He*.

10:8, 9 The tribe of Levi was set apart for the priesthood. They were not allotted land in Canaan; therefore, they received their sustenance from the offerings of the people (Deut. 18:1–8).

10:16 Circumcision is used metaphorically to stress the need to cut away any affections that would interrupt complete obedience to the Lord. Circumcision of the heart would not be an outward sign but an inward attitude that would manifest itself outwardly in the actions of the people. A circumcised heart is open and responsive to the commands of the Lord.

11:2 The chastening of the Lord was discipline for the purpose of educating the people. Whether by grace or punishment, the Lord's dealings with the nation were always designed to teach them about His holiness and prepare them for future events.

11:9 Dathan and Abiram had referred to Egypt as a land flowing with milk and honey (v. 6). Moses drew the contrast between Egypt and the Land of Promise, which would be so productive that the Land was described metaphorically as flowing with milk and honey.

11:10 The only source for water in Egypt was the Nile River, from which water had to be distributed to the fields through irrigation.

11:13–17 The early rain and the latter rain refers to Canaan's rainy season between October and April, during which the rain would come in torrents (v. 14). These rains would be contingent on Israel's obedience.

WORSHIP *GLORIFYING GOD*

All of the great religions of the world claim to worship God. In our society, any form of worship, when sincerely practiced, is commonly thought to be legitimate. The Bible tells us otherwise. It teaches that God Himself commands how He is to be worshiped.

God called His people Israel to forsake other religions. He commanded them from the beginning not to worship the Lord as other peoples worship their "gods" (Deut. 12:4, 31). The Lord instructed that His people were to worship only in the place He chooses to make His name abide and that they must come with blood sacrifices (Deut. 12:5, 11, 14, 18, 26).

Worshiping God in any way we may choose is still not legitimate. God must be worshiped where He chooses to make His name abide. God still requires an atoning sacrifice for sin. As God's work in history progressed, He revealed Jesus Christ, "the name which is above every name" (Phil. 2:9), as the final atoning Sacrifice for sin (Heb. 9:12). Though there are many competing religions in the world, Jesus Christ came to reveal that He is the one and only way to the Father (John 14:6).

Although the style of Christian worship may vary from congregation to congregation, Christians can be confident that worship centered around Christ will glorify and please God (Luke 19:28–38; Eph. 1:6).

See also Ps. 95:6; Rom. 1:25; Rev. 22:9; notes on Access to God (Rom. 10); The Lord's Day (Ex. 23); Music (Ps. 147); Paganism (Jer. 7); Praise (Ps. 149)

give *you* the rain for your land in its season, the early rain and the latter rain, that you may gather in your grain, your new wine, and your oil. [15]And I will send grass in your fields for your livestock, that you may eat and be filled.' [16]Take heed to yourselves, lest your heart be deceived, and you turn aside and serve other gods and worship them, [17]lest the LORD's anger be aroused against you, and He shut up the heavens so that there be no rain, and the land yield no produce, and you perish quickly from the good land which the LORD is giving you.

[18]"Therefore you shall lay up these words of mine in your heart and in your soul, and bind them as a sign on your hand, and they shall be as frontlets between your eyes. [19]You shall teach them to your children, speaking of them when you sit in your house, when you walk by the way, when you lie down, and when you rise up. [20]And you shall write them on the doorposts of your house and on your gates, [21]that your days and the days of your children may be multiplied in the land of which the LORD swore to your fathers to give them, like the days of the heavens above the earth.

[22]"For if you carefully keep all these commandments which I command you to do— to love the LORD your God, to walk in all His ways, and to hold fast to Him— [23]then the LORD will drive out all these nations from before you, and you will dispossess greater and mightier nations than yourselves. [24]Every place on which the sole of your foot treads shall be yours: from the wilderness and Lebanon, from the river, the River Euphrates, even to the Western Sea,[a] shall be your territory. [25]No man shall be able to stand against you; the LORD your God will put the dread of you and the fear of you upon all the land where you tread, just as He has said to you.

[26]"Behold, I set before you today a blessing and a curse: [27]the blessing, if you obey the commandments of the LORD your God which I command you today; [28]and the curse, if you do not obey the commandments of the LORD your God, but turn aside from the way which I command you today, to go after other gods which you have not known. [29]Now it shall be, when the LORD your God has brought you into the land which you go to possess, that you shall put the blessing on Mount Gerizim and the curse on Mount Ebal. [30]*Are* they not on the other side of the Jordan, toward the setting sun, in the land of the Canaanites who dwell in the plain opposite Gilgal, beside the terebinth trees of Moreh? [31]For you will cross over the Jordan and go in to possess the land which the LORD your God is giving you, and you will possess it and dwell in it. [32]And you shall be careful to observe all the statutes and judgments which I set before you today.

A Prescribed Place of Worship

12 "These *are* the statutes and judgments which you shall be careful to observe in the

11:24 [a]That is, the Mediterranean

11:18–21 Teaching the precepts of the Lord to their children was vital in order to ensure blessing and prosperity to each generation. Obedience in each generation was the key to continued blessing (Deut. 6:6–9).

11:29 The blessings and curses, which were to be announced from these two mountains, are listed in Deuteronomy 27 and 28.

land which the LORD God of your fathers is giving you to possess, all the days that you live on the earth. ²You shall utterly destroy all the places where the nations which you shall dispossess served their gods, on the high mountains and on the hills and under every green tree. ³And you shall destroy their altars, break their *sacred* pillars, and burn their wooden images with fire; you shall cut down the carved images of their gods and destroy their names from that place. ⁴You shall not worship the LORD your God *with* such *things.*

⁵"But you shall seek the place where the LORD your God chooses, out of all your tribes, to put His name for His dwelling place; and there you shall go. ⁶There you shall take your burnt offerings, your sacrifices, your tithes, the heave offerings of your hand, your vowed offerings, your freewill offerings, and the firstborn of your herds and flocks. ⁷And there you shall eat before the LORD your God, and you shall rejoice in all to which you have put your hand, you and your households, in which the LORD your God has blessed you.

⁸"You shall not at all do as we are doing here today— every man doing whatever *is* right in his own eyes— ⁹for as yet you have not come to the rest and the inheritance which the LORD your God is giving you. ¹⁰But *when* you cross over the Jordan and dwell in the land which the LORD your God is giving you to inherit, and He gives you rest from all your enemies round about, so that you dwell in safety, ¹¹then there will be the place where the LORD your God chooses to make His name abide. There you shall bring all that I command you: your burnt offerings, your sacrifices, your tithes, the heave offerings of your hand, and all your choice offerings which you vow to the LORD. ¹²And you shall rejoice before the LORD your God, you and your sons and your daughters, your male and female servants, and the Levite who *is* within your gates, since he has no portion nor inheritance with you. ¹³Take heed to yourself that you do not offer your burnt offerings in every place that you see; ¹⁴but in the place which the LORD chooses, in one of your tribes, there you shall offer your burnt offerings, and there you shall do all that I command you.

¹⁵"However, you may slaughter and eat meat within all your gates, whatever your heart desires, according to the blessing of the LORD your God which He has given you; the unclean and the clean may eat of it, of the gazelle and the deer alike. ¹⁶Only you

shall not eat the blood; you shall pour it on the earth like water. ¹⁷You may not eat within your gates the tithe of your grain or your new wine or your oil, of the firstborn of your herd or your flock, of any of your offerings which you vow, of your freewill offerings, or of the heave offering of your hand. ¹⁸But you must eat them before the LORD your God in the place which the LORD your God chooses, you and your son and your daughter, your male servant and your female servant, and the Levite who *is* within your gates; and you shall rejoice before the LORD your God in all to which you put your hands. ¹⁹Take heed to yourself that you do not forsake the Levite as long as you live in your land.

²⁰"When the LORD your God enlarges your border as He has promised you, and you say, 'Let me eat meat,' because you long to eat meat, you may eat as much meat as your heart desires. ²¹If the place where the LORD your God chooses to put His name is too far from you, then you may slaughter from your herd and from your flock which the LORD has given you, just as I have commanded you, and you may eat within your gates as much as your heart desires. ²²Just as the gazelle and the deer are eaten, so you may eat them; the unclean and the clean alike may eat them. ²³Only be sure that you do not eat the blood, for the blood *is* the life; you may not eat the life with the meat. ²⁴You shall not eat it; you shall pour it on the earth like water. ²⁵You shall not eat it, that it may go well with you and your children after you, when you do *what is* right in the sight of the LORD. ²⁶Only the holy things which you have, and your vowed offerings, you shall take and go to the place which the LORD chooses. ²⁷And you shall offer your burnt offerings, the meat and the blood, on the altar of the LORD your God; and the blood of your sacrifices shall be poured out on the altar of the LORD your God, and you shall eat the meat. ²⁸Observe and obey all these words which I command you, that it may go well with you and your children after you forever, when you do *what is* good and right in the sight of the LORD your God.

Beware of False Gods

²⁹"When the LORD your God cuts off from before you the nations which you go to dispossess, and you displace them and dwell in their land, ³⁰take heed to yourself that you are not ensnared

---

12:5 Unlike the heathen religion of the Canaanites, whose worship centers were on every high hill and under every luxuriant tree (v. 2), the Israelites were to have only one central sanctuary chosen by God Himself.

12:8 While in the desert, the religious life of the Israelites was dictated by their circumstances. In the Promised Land, however, their worship would be in a central sanctuary, promoting structure and order, according to the Lord's direction.

12:15, 16 A diet of respect. The Israelites were not required to bring the meat they ate for their daily meals to the central sanctuary. They were, however, restricted from the blood of the meat. The blood symbolized life and was treated with respect because God is the Creator of life (v. 23). By pouring out the blood, an Israelite was acknowledging the sacredness of life and was symbolically giving the life back to God.

to follow them, after they are destroyed from before you, and that you do not inquire after their gods, saying, 'How did these nations serve their gods? I also will do likewise.' ³¹You shall not worship the LORD your God in that way; for every abomination to the LORD which He hates they have done to their gods; for they burn even their sons and daughters in the fire to their gods.

³²"Whatever I command you, be careful to observe it; you shall not add to it nor take away from it.

Punishment of Apostates

13 "If there arises among you a prophet or a dreamer of dreams, and he gives you a sign or a wonder, ²and the sign or the wonder comes to pass, of which he spoke to you, saying, 'Let us go after other gods'—which you have not known—'and let us serve them,' ³you shall not listen to the words of that prophet or that dreamer of dreams, for the LORD your God is testing you to know whether you love the LORD your God with all your heart and with all your soul. ⁴You shall walk after the LORD your God and fear Him, and keep His commandments and obey His voice; you shall serve Him and hold fast to Him. ⁵But that prophet or that dreamer of dreams shall be put to death, because he has spoken in order to turn you away from the LORD your God, who brought you out of the land of Egypt and redeemed you from the house of bondage, to entice you from the way in which the LORD your God commanded you to walk. So you shall put away the evil from your midst.

⁶"If your brother, the son of your mother, your son or your daughter, the wife of your bosom, or your friend who is as your own soul, secretly entices you, saying, 'Let us go and serve other gods,' which you have not known, neither you nor your fathers, ⁷of the gods of the people which are all around you, near to you or far off from you, from one end of the earth to the other end of the earth, ⁸you shall not consent to him or listen to him, nor shall your eye pity him, nor shall you spare him or conceal him; ⁹but you shall surely kill him; your hand shall be first against him to put him to death, and afterward the hand of all the people. ¹⁰And you shall stone him with stones until he dies, because he sought to entice you away from the LORD your God, who brought you out of the land of Egypt, from the house of bondage. ¹¹So all Israel shall hear and fear, and not again do such wickedness as this among you.

¹²"If you hear someone in one of your cities, which the LORD your God gives you to dwell in, saying, ¹³'Corrupt men have gone out from among you and enticed the inhabitants of their city, saying, "Let us go and serve other gods" '—which you have not known— ¹⁴then you shall inquire, search out, and ask diligently. And if it is indeed true and certain that such an abomination was committed among you, ¹⁵you shall surely strike the inhabitants of that city with the edge of the sword, utterly destroying it, all that is in it and its livestock—with the edge of the sword. ¹⁶And you shall gather all its plunder into the middle of the street, and completely burn with fire the city and all its plunder, for the LORD your God. It shall be a heap forever; it shall not be built again. ¹⁷So none of the accursed things shall remain in your hand, that the LORD may turn from the fierceness of His anger and show you mercy, have compassion on you and multiply you, just as He swore to your fathers, ¹⁸because you have listened to the voice of the LORD your God, to keep all His commandments which I command you today, to do what is right in the eyes of the LORD your God.

12:31 Child sacrifice, one of the most abominable sins to the Lord, was most often associated with the worship of Molech, the pagan god of the Ammonites. In ceremonial fashion, children would be shoved into a furnace as a sacrifice to appease and invoke the blessing of Molech. The Canaanites were described as merciless murderers of their defenseless children. The God of Israel, by contrast, required the death penalty for such an act (Lev. 20:2–4). Both Manasseh and Ahaz were guilty of child sacrifice (2 Kin. 21:6; 2 Chr. 28:3).

13:1 The true test of a prophet of God is not in the miracles but in his message. The prophet of God performed signs and wonders to attest to the power of God and to teach the commands of God. A false prophet could often duplicate the signs and wonders by power given to him by Satan. Moses emphasized here that the fulfillment of a certain prediction could not be the sole means of testing a prophet's authenticity. The standard for truth was the message he preached. If anyone advocated a false worship or anything contrary to the Word of God, then he would be labeled as a false prophet. The danger of such deception demanded death (v. 5).

13:3 The Lord permitted false prophets in order to test the Israelites. Although God always knew the disposition of their hearts, the testing allowed the people to see themselves in the same light. It also allowed them to exercise their faith (1 Cor. 10:13). By resisting the temptation to follow false gods, they would strengthen their faith and increase their love for God.

13:6–9 Each of these relationships stresses intimacy. However, because of the seriousness of the sin, there could be no security or tolerance for such a person, regardless of the relationship. Such sin was to be reported and punished with execution by stoning. The most tragic nature of this sin would be that the trusted friend would have to be the one to expose the sin, and his hand would throw the first stone in the execution. To those who witnessed such a death, the memory of the pain to both parties would not soon fade. Hopefully, the event would serve as a deterrent to others who would consider idolatry (Lev. 24:14). The people were strongly warned not to yield to, listen to, show pity to, or shield an enticer for a false religion.

Improper Mourning

14 "You *are* the children of the LORD your God; you shall not cut yourselves nor shave the front of your head for the dead. [2]For you *are* a holy people to the LORD your God, and the LORD has chosen you to be a people for Himself, a special treasure above all the peoples who *are* on the face of the earth.

Clean and Unclean Meat

[3]"You shall not eat any detestable thing. [4]These *are* the animals which you may eat: the ox, the sheep, the goat, [5]the deer, the gazelle, the roe deer, the wild goat, the mountain goat,[a] the antelope, and the mountain sheep. [6]And you may eat every animal with cloven hooves, having the hoof split into two parts, *and that* chews the cud, among the animals. [7]Nevertheless, of those that chew the cud or have cloven hooves, you shall not eat, *such as* these: the camel, the hare, and the rock hyrax; for they chew the cud but do not have cloven hooves; they *are* unclean for you. [8]Also the swine is unclean for you, because it has cloven hooves, yet *does* not *chew* the cud; you shall not eat their flesh or touch their dead carcasses.

[9]"These you may eat of all that *are* in the waters: you may eat all that have fins and scales. [10]And whatever does not have fins and scales you shall not eat; it *is* unclean for you.

[11]"All clean birds you may eat. [12]But these you shall not eat: the eagle, the vulture, the buzzard, [13]the red kite, the falcon, and the kite after their kinds; [14]every raven after its kind; [15]the ostrich, the short-eared owl, the sea gull, and the hawk after their kinds; [16]the little owl, the screech owl, the white owl, [17]the jackdaw, the carrion vulture, the fisher owl, [18]the stork, the heron after its kind, and the hoopoe and the bat.

[19]"Also every creeping thing that flies is unclean for you; they shall not be eaten. [20]"You may eat all clean birds.

[21]"You shall not eat anything that dies *of itself;* you may give it to the alien who *is* within your gates, that he may eat it, or you may sell it to a foreigner; for you *are* a holy people to the LORD your God.

"You shall not boil a young goat in its mother's milk.

Tithing Principles

[22]"You shall truly tithe all the increase of your grain that the field produces year by year. [23]And you shall eat before the LORD your God, in the place where He chooses to make His name abide, the tithe of your grain and your new wine and your oil, of the firstborn of your herds and your flocks, that you may learn to fear the LORD your God always. [24]But if the journey is too long for you, so that you are not able to carry *the tithe, or* if the place where the LORD your God chooses to put His name is too far from you, when the LORD your God has blessed you, [25]then you shall exchange *it* for money, take the money in your hand, and go to the place which the LORD your God chooses. [26]And you shall spend that money for whatever your heart desires: for oxen or sheep, for wine or similar drink, for whatever your heart desires; you shall eat there before the LORD your God, and you shall rejoice, you and your household. [27]You shall not forsake the Levite who *is* within your gates, for he has no part nor inheritance with you.

[28]"At the end of *every* third year you shall bring out the tithe of your produce of that year and store *it* up within your gates. [29]And the Levite,

14:5 [a]Or *addax*

14:1 A holy lifestyle. As "children of the Lord" the Israelites were to differentiate themselves from the pagan Canaanite religions. The Canaanites shaved their heads and cut themselves in a ritual to mourn the dead. Israel, as a holy nation, was not to identify with any pagan practices.

14:3 The system behind distinguishing between clean and unclean foods is uncertain. Hygiene may be one criterion. Some meats were more toxic than others and would be unhealthy for the nation to consume. Some animals listed as unclean were predators that ate the blood of their prey. To eat the meat of these predators would defile the Israelite. Another criterion for the distinction between clean and unclean may be based on the pagan religions. Some animals, such as the serpent and the pig, were sacred among foreign religions. This association with idolatry made them unclean to the Israelite. Another explanation is that the distinctions could be based solely on the random choice of God for the purpose of presenting Israel as unique and holy in every area of life. Whatever the principle behind the distinctions, the observance of these food laws would serve as a testimony to separate Israel from other nations. A more comprehensive listing of the meats is given (Lev. 11:9–30, 41–43; see also Lev. 10, Clean vs. Unclean).

14:21 Anything that dies of itself would not have had its blood properly drained as commanded (Deut. 12:16, 23, 24). A common practice among the Canaanites' fertility cult was to cook a young goat in the milk from its mother. The Israelites were to abstain from this practice not only because of its association with the pagan ritual, but also because it was profaning that which gives life (the mother's milk). Instead of being used to sustain the life of the young goat, it would be the medium of its death (Ex. 23:18, 19, note; 34:26).

14:22 The giving of the tithe (lit. "a tenth") was an act of worship acknowledging God as the Creator of the produce as well as the Sustainer and Provider of the nation (see Luke 16, Stewardship).

14:28 In God's economy, provision was always made for those less fortunate (see Luke 9, the Homeless; 14, Poverty). Every third year the tithe was kept within their own community to provide for those who were poor as well as for the Levite. By obeying God's command to provide for these, Israel would enjoy the blessing of God on their labor. As long as this cycle was unbroken, both the rich and the poor would enjoy the provision of the Lord.

The most important filter your child can have in any decision-making process is the Word of God.

Susan Alexander Yates

because he has no portion nor inheritance with you, and the stranger and the fatherless and the widow who *are* within your gates, may come and eat and be satisfied, that the LORD your God may bless you in all the work of your hand which you do.

Debts Canceled Every Seven Years

15 "At the end of *every* seven years you shall grant a release *of debts.* [2]And this *is* the form of the release: Every creditor who has lent *anything* to his neighbor shall release *it;* he shall not require *it* of his neighbor or his brother, because it is called the LORD's release. [3]Of a foreigner you may require *it;* but you shall give up your claim to what is owed by your brother, [4]except when there may be no poor among you; for the LORD will greatly bless you in the land which the LORD your God is giving you to possess *as* an inheritance— [5]only if you carefully obey the voice of the LORD your God, to observe with care all these commandments which I command you today. [6]For the LORD your God will bless you just as He promised you; you shall lend to many nations, but you shall not borrow; you shall reign over many nations, but they shall not reign over you.

Generosity to the Poor

[7]"If there is among you a poor man of your brethren, within any of the gates in your land which the LORD your God is giving you, you shall not harden your heart nor shut your hand from your poor brother, [8]but you shall open your hand wide to him and willingly lend him sufficient for his need, whatever he needs. [9]Beware lest there be a wicked thought in your heart, saying, 'The seventh year, the year of release, is at hand,' and your eye be evil against your poor brother and you give him nothing, and he cry out to the LORD against you, and it become sin among you. [10]You shall surely give to him, and your heart should not be grieved when you give to him, because for this

thing the LORD your God will bless you in all your works and in all to which you put your hand. [11]For the poor will never cease from the land; therefore I command you, saying, 'You shall open your hand wide to your brother, to your poor and your needy, in your land.'

The Law Concerning Bondservants

[12]"If your brother, a Hebrew man, or a Hebrew woman, is sold to you and serves you six years, then in the seventh year you shall let him go free from you. [13]And when you send him away free from you, you shall not let him go away empty-handed; [14]you shall supply him liberally from your flock, from your threshing floor, and from your winepress. *From what* the LORD your God has blessed you with, you shall give to him. [15]You shall remember that you were a slave in the land of Egypt, and the LORD your God redeemed you; therefore I command you this thing today. [16]And if it happens that he says to you, 'I will not go away from you,' because he loves you and your house, since he prospers with you, [17]then you shall take an awl and thrust *it* through his ear to the door, and he shall be your servant forever. Also to your female servant you shall do likewise. [18]It shall not seem hard to you when you send him away free from you; for he has been worth a double hired servant in serving you six years. Then the LORD your God will bless you in all that you do.

The Law Concerning Firstborn Animals

[19]"All the firstborn males that come from your herd and your flock you shall sanctify to the LORD your God; you shall do no work with the firstborn of your herd, nor shear the firstborn of your flock. [20]You and your household shall eat *it* before the LORD your God year by year in the place which the LORD chooses. [21]But if there is a defect in it, *if it is* lame or blind *or has* any serious defect, you shall not sacrifice it to the LORD your God. [22]You may

---

15:1–4 As an antidote to poverty, a provision was made every seven years to cancel outstanding debts. The release of debt in the seventh year would help to rid the nation of poverty and to promote brotherhood within the community. The elimination of poverty from the nation could become a reality only if the people were careful to obey the commands of God (see Luke 9, The Homeless; 14, Poverty).

15:7–10 As the year of release approached, some would withhold their generosity because the debt would be canceled soon and the payback would be minimal if any. Moses warned

against this attitude. To be generous at all times, regardless of the year or possibility of collection, would invoke God's blessing of prosperity.

15:16, 17 After six years of serving his employer, a close relationship might have developed so that the slave would not wish to leave. If that were the case, the owner was to push a piercing tool through the slave's ear lobe and into the doorpost of the home. This action symbolically joined the slave to the master's household, marking him as a slave for life (Ex. 21:5, 6).

eat it within your gates; the unclean and the clean *person* alike *may eat it,* as *if it were* a gazelle or a deer. [23]Only you shall not eat its blood; you shall pour it on the ground like water.

The Passover Reviewed

16 "Observe the month of Abib, and keep the Passover to the LORD your God, for in the month of Abib the LORD your God brought you out of Egypt by night. [2]Therefore you shall sacrifice the Passover to the LORD your God, from the flock and the herd, in the place where the LORD chooses to put His name. [3]You shall eat no leavened bread with it; seven days you shall eat unleavened bread with it, *that is,* the bread of affliction (for you came out of the land of Egypt in haste), that you may remember the day in which you came out of the land of Egypt all the days of your life. [4]And no leaven shall be seen among you in all your territory for seven days, nor shall *any* of the meat which you sacrifice the first day at twilight remain overnight until morning.

[5]"You may not sacrifice the Passover within any of your gates which the LORD your God gives you; [6]but at the place where the LORD your God chooses to make His name abide, there you shall sacrifice the Passover at twilight, at the going down of the sun, at the time you came out of Egypt. [7]And you shall roast and eat *it* in the place which the LORD your God chooses, and in the morning you shall turn and go to your tents. [8]Six days you shall eat unleavened bread, and on the seventh day there *shall be* a sacred assembly to the LORD your God. You shall do no work *on it.*

The Feast of Weeks Reviewed

[9]"You shall count seven weeks for yourself; begin to count the seven weeks from *the time* you begin *to put* the sickle to the grain. [10]Then you shall keep the Feast of Weeks to the LORD your God with the tribute of a freewill offering from your hand, which you shall give as the LORD your God

blesses you. [11]You shall rejoice before the LORD your God, you and your son and your daughter, your male servant and your female servant, the Levite who *is* within your gates, the stranger and the fatherless and the widow who *are* among you, at the place where the LORD your God chooses to make His name abide. [12]And you shall remember that you were a slave in Egypt, and you shall be careful to observe these statutes.

The Feast of Tabernacles Reviewed

[13]"You shall observe the Feast of Tabernacles seven days, when you have gathered from your threshing floor and from your winepress. [14]And you shall rejoice in your feast, you and your son and your daughter, your male servant and your female servant and the Levite, the stranger and the fatherless and the widow, who *are* within your gates. [15]Seven days you shall keep a sacred feast to the LORD your God in the place which the LORD chooses, because the LORD your God will bless you in all your produce and in all the work of your hands, so that you surely rejoice.

[16]"Three times a year all your males shall appear before the LORD your God in the place which He chooses: at the Feast of Unleavened Bread, at the Feast of Weeks, and at the Feast of Tabernacles; and they shall not appear before the LORD empty-handed. [17]Every man *shall give* as he is able, according to the blessing of the LORD your God which He has given you.

Justice Must Be Administered

[18]"You shall appoint judges and officers in all your gates, which the LORD your God gives you, according to your tribes, and they shall judge the people with just judgment. [19]You shall not pervert justice; you shall not show partiality, nor take a bribe, for a bribe blinds the eyes of the wise and twists the words of the righteous. [20]You shall follow what is altogether just, that you may live and inherit the land which the LORD your God is giving you.

16:1 On the 14th day of Abib, in the spring month corresponding to March-April, the people were to celebrate the night the Lord "passed over" the homes of the Israelites that had been sprinkled with the blood of a lamb (see charts, The Feasts of Israel; The Feasts of Israel). The firstborn of the Israelite was spared death (Ex. 12:1–28; see also 1 Cor. 5:7 in which Christ is pictured as our passover).

16:3, 4 The Feast of Passover and the Feast of Unleavened Bread were closely linked. The Passover was observed on the 14th of the month, and the Unleavened Bread Feast began on the 15th and lasted seven days (Ex. 23:15; see chart, The Feasts of Israel).

16:9–12 The Feast of Weeks or Feast of Harvest, later called Pentecost, is also mentioned (Ex. 23:16; 34:22). This feast to celebrate the blessing of God on the harvest began on the day

following the Sabbath of the Feast of Passover (Lev. 23:15, 16; see also chart, The Feasts of Israel).

16:13–17 The Feast of Tabernacles, Booths, or Ingathering lasted from the 15th day to the 21st day of Tishri which corresponds to September-October (see chart, The Jewish Sacred Calendar). During this feast the people were to live in booths and rejoice in the goodness of God (Lev. 23:34–39, 42; Num. 29:12; see also chart, The Feasts of Israel).

16:16 Only the men, as representatives of their families, were required to make these three pilgrimages. Although women at times did accompany them (v. 11, 14), they were not required to do so—probably because of domestic obligations and the monthly occurrence of their menstrual cycle, during which they were considered unclean (see Lev. 15, Menstrual Cycle).

²¹"You shall not plant for yourself any tree, as a wooden image, near the altar which you build for yourself to the LORD your God. ²²You shall not set up a *sacred* pillar, which the LORD your God hates.

17 "You shall not sacrifice to the LORD your God a bull or sheep which has any blemish *or* defect, for that *is* an abomination to the LORD your God.

²"If there is found among you, within any of your gates which the LORD your God gives you, a man or a woman who has been wicked in the sight of the LORD your God, in transgressing His covenant, ³who has gone and served other gods and worshiped them, either the sun or moon or any of the host of heaven, which I have not commanded, ⁴and it is told you, and you hear *of it,* then you shall inquire diligently. And if *it is* indeed true *and* certain that such an abomination has been committed in Israel, ⁵then you shall bring out to your gates that man or woman who has committed that wicked thing, and shall stone to death that man or woman with stones. ⁶Whoever is deserving of death shall be put to death on the testimony of two or three witnesses; he shall not be put to death on the testimony of one witness. ⁷The hands of the witnesses shall be the first against him to put him to death, and afterward the hands of all the people. So you shall put away the evil from among you.

⁸"If a matter arises which is too hard for you to judge, between degrees of guilt for bloodshed, between one judgment or another, or between one punishment or another, matters of controversy within your gates, then you shall arise and go up to the place which the LORD your God chooses. ⁹And you shall come to the priests, the Levites, and to the judge *there* in those days, and inquire *of them;* they shall pronounce upon you the sentence of judgment. ¹⁰You shall do according to the sentence which they pronounce upon you in that place which the LORD chooses. And you shall be careful to do according to all that they order you. ¹¹According to the sentence of the law in which they instruct you, according to the judgment which they tell you, you shall do; you shall not turn aside *to* the right hand or *to* the left from the sentence which they pronounce upon you. ¹²Now the man who acts presumptuously and will not heed the priest who stands to minister there before the LORD your God, or the judge, that man shall die. So you shall put away the evil from Israel. ¹³And all the people shall hear and fear, and no longer act presumptuously.

Principles Governing Kings

¹⁴"When you come to the land which the LORD your God is giving you, and possess it and dwell in it, and say, 'I will set a king over me like all the nations that *are* around me,' ¹⁵you shall surely set a king over you whom the LORD your God chooses; *one* from among your brethren you shall set as king over you; you may not set a foreigner over you, who *is* not your brother. ¹⁶But he shall not multiply horses for himself, nor cause the people to return to Egypt to multiply horses, for the LORD has said to you, 'You shall not return that way again.' ¹⁷Neither shall he multiply wives for himself, lest his heart turn away; nor shall he greatly multiply silver and gold for himself.

¹⁸"Also it shall be, when he sits on the throne of his kingdom, that he shall write for himself a copy of this law in a book, from *the one* before the priests, the Levites. ¹⁹And it shall be with him, and he shall read it all the days of his life, that he may learn to fear the LORD his God and be careful to observe all the words of this law and these statutes, ²⁰that his heart may not be lifted above

---

16:21, 22 The wooden image and the "sacred pillar" were symbolic of the pagan goddess, Asherah, and the pagan god, Baal, respectively (see Is. 42, Idolatry; Jer. 7, Paganism; chart, The Goddesses of Egypt).

17:5 The gates designated the place where judges assembled to hear the disputes of the people.

17:6, 7 One witness was not sufficient to convict a person because of the inability to substantiate his testimony. The one who brought the accusation would throw the first stone in the execution. If later his testimony proved to be false, the accuser would suffer the same execution as his penalty for murdering the innocent one he had accused (Deut. 13:6–9, note; 19:15–21).

17:12, 13 Authority was to be respected and obeyed. Disobedience was punishable by death. The Law was strict at this point in order to deter others from committing the same sin.

17:14, 15 The prophecy of Moses was fulfilled (1 Sam. 8:5). Moses envisaged a time when the nation would call for an earthly king in the manner of the other nations. Knowing this, Moses set forth requirements for a king: the man must be chosen by God (Deut. 17:15); he must be an Israelite (v. 15); his heart was to be wholly dependent on and devoted to God (vv. 16–20).

17:16 Horses were synonymous with military power. To amass an army of horses and chariots, rather than the usual infantry, would cause the people to rely on their own resources in battle. Israel's strength was her God.

17:17 Often, for political reasons, kings would marry foreign women, a practice Moses had already forbidden (Deut. 7:3–5). The religious influence of these pagan wives would corrupt the king, and ultimately the nation, with idolatry (1 Kin. 11, Solomon's Pagan Wives). Affluence also could cause a king's heart to turn away from the Lord.

17:20 The king was to possess a copy of the covenant-treaty as his sole source of wisdom. By learning and studying the Law, the king would display his devotion to God and would rule wisely.

his brethren, that he may not turn aside from the commandment *to* the right hand or *to* the left, and that he may prolong *his* days in his kingdom, he and his children in the midst of Israel.

The Portion of the Priests and Levites

18 "The priests, the Levites— all the tribe of Levi— shall have no part nor inheritance with Israel; they shall eat the offerings of the LORD made by fire, and His portion. ²Therefore they shall have no inheritance among their brethren; the LORD is their inheritance, as He said to them.

³"And this shall be the priest's due from the people, from those who offer a sacrifice, whether *it is* bull or sheep: they shall give to the priest the shoulder, the cheeks, and the stomach. ⁴The first-fruits of your grain and your new wine and your oil, and the first of the fleece of your sheep, you shall give him. ⁵For the LORD your God has chosen him out of all your tribes to stand to minister in the name of the LORD, him and his sons forever.

⁶"So if a Levite comes from any of your gates, from where he dwells among all Israel, and comes with all the desire of his mind to the place which the LORD chooses, ⁷then he may serve in the name of the LORD his God as all his brethren the Levites *do,* who stand there before the LORD. ⁸They shall have equal portions to eat, besides what comes from the sale of his inheritance.

Avoid Wicked Customs

⁹"When you come into the land which the LORD your God is giving you, you shall not learn to follow the abominations of those nations. ¹⁰There shall not be found among you *anyone* who makes his son or his daughter pass through the fire, *or one* who practices witchcraft, *or* a soothsayer, or one who interprets omens, or a sorcerer, ¹¹or one who conjures spells, or a medium, or a spiritist, or one who calls up the dead. ¹²For all who do these things *are* an abomination to the LORD, and because of these abominations the LORD your God

drives them out from before you. ¹³You shall be blameless before the LORD your God. ¹⁴For these nations which you will dispossess listened to soothsayers and diviners; but as for you, the LORD your God has not appointed such for you.

A New Prophet Like Moses

¹⁵"The LORD your God will raise up for you a Prophet like me from your midst, from your brethren. Him you shall hear, ¹⁶according to all you desired of the LORD your God in Horeb in the day of the assembly, saying, 'Let me not hear again the voice of the LORD my God, nor let me see this great fire anymore, lest I die.'

¹⁷"And the LORD said to me: 'What they have spoken is good. ¹⁸I will raise up for them a Prophet like you from among their brethren, and will put My words in His mouth, and He shall speak to them all that I command Him. ¹⁹And it shall be *that* whoever will not hear My words, which He speaks in My name, I will require *it* of him. ²⁰But the prophet who presumes to speak a word in My name, which I have not commanded him to speak, or who speaks in the name of other gods, that prophet shall die.' ²¹And if you say in your heart, 'How shall we know the word which the LORD has not spoken?'— ²²when a prophet speaks in the name of the LORD, if the thing does not happen or come to pass, that *is* the thing which the LORD has not spoken; the prophet has spoken it presumptuously; you shall not be afraid of him.

Three Cities of Refuge

19 "When the LORD your God has cut off the nations whose land the LORD your God is giving you, and you dispossess them and dwell in their cities and in their houses, ²you shall separate three cities for yourself in the midst of your land which the LORD your God is giving you to possess. ³You shall prepare roads for yourself, and divide into three parts the territory of your land which the LORD your God is giving you to inherit, that any manslayer may flee there.

18:1–4 The Levites were to serve as priests, ministers, and teachers of the Law. Only the Levites in the line of Aaron were allowed to serve as priests. The rest of the Levites served in various assisting roles. Since the Levites did not receive a portion of the Land, the nation was responsible for their sustenance.

18:10 All the practices listed here were common among the Canaanite religions. These exercises were dangerous not only because they identified the participant with pagan cults but also because wisdom was sought through magical and spiritualistic means rather than from God. A "soothsayer" was someone who received magical powers by incantations. A "sorcerer" would brew herbs to make magical potions to control circumstances as well as people. One who "conjures spells" (lit. "one who ties knots") sought to bind people by the use of magic spells and incantations. Cultic practices were

used as an attempt to communicate with evil and departed spirits (see also The Occult; 1 Sam. 15, Witchcraft).

18:15 By way of contrast, Moses directed the people away from magic and to the true prophets of God, who would deliver the truth from the heart of God. This prophecy was ultimately fulfilled in the Lord Jesus Christ (John 6:14; Acts 3:22, 23).

19:1–4 Three cities on the east side of the Jordan had already been set aside as cities of refuge (Deut. 4:41–43). Moses instructed the people to do the same on the west side of the Jordan. These cities provided a safe haven for anyone guilty of involuntary manslaughter. The "avenger of blood" was the nearest male relative to the deceased (Deut. 19:6). One of his responsibilities was to vindicate the death of a relative (see also Num. 35:19–28).

THE OCCULT   *EXTRAORDINARY MANIPULATION*

The word "occult" is derived from the Latin *occultus*, which means something "hidden" or "concealed," referring to that which is inner, secret, mysterious, and beyond the range of ordinary human knowledge. Occultism involves various types of secret techniques directed at altering human consciousness and manipulating the supernatural in order to attain psycho-spiritual power. White and black magic, spiritism (spirit contact), and fortune telling are common forms.

Occultists distinguish between white and black magic. White magic is considered by its practitioners to be beneficent—helpful for the good of others. It ceremonially evokes spirits and seeks to control them with such ritual tools as wands, daggers, robes, and belts. White magic is associated with the contemporary practice of feminist goddess worship and witchcraft. Black magic refers to the practice of sorcery and necromancy (1 Sam. 28:7–25). In contrast to white magic, it is used against others or for the purpose of personal and material gain.

Other occultic practices include:

- Spiritism—making contact with deceased or invisible personalities through spirit mediums (1 Sam. 28:3–20) or through trance channeling, a form of voluntary possession.
- Fortune telling (divination)—using a wide variety of methods and objects to give advice (Acts 16:16–18).
- Astrology—the ancient method of mapping celestial events by means of horoscopes (Is. 47:13–15; Dan. 2:2; 5:7).
- Numerology—which attaches special significance to numbers and uses those numbers to analyze character and to predict the future (Gen. 41:1–36).
- Palmistry—which interprets the future by analyzing the lines on the palms of the hands.
- Tarot cards—which use special occultic symbols to predict the future.
- Automatic writing—in which the participant writes in a trance-like state without conscious control.

All these occultic practices are demonic in origin and prohibited by Scripture (Deut. 18:10, 11).

See also 2 Kin. 21:5, 6; Is. 3:2, 3; Ezek. 21:21; Jon. 1:7, 8; notes on Goddess Religion (Ex. 20); Paganism (Jer. 7); Witchcraft (1 Sam. 15).

4"And this *is* the case of the manslayer who flees there, that he may live: Whoever kills his neighbor unintentionally, not having hated him in time past— 5as when *a man* goes to the woods with his neighbor to cut timber, and his hand swings a stroke with the ax to cut down the tree, and the head slips from the handle and strikes his neighbor so that he dies— he shall flee to one of these cities and live; 6lest the avenger of blood, while his anger is hot, pursue the manslayer and overtake him, because the way is long, and kill him, though he *was* not deserving of death, since he had not hated the victim in time past. 7Therefore I command you, saying, 'You shall separate three cities for yourself.'

8"Now if the LORD your God enlarges your territory, as He swore to your fathers, and gives you the land which He promised to give to your fathers, 9and if you keep all these commandments and do them, which I command you today, to love the LORD your God and to walk always in His ways, then you shall add three more cities for yourself besides these three, 10lest innocent blood be shed in the midst of your land which the LORD your God is giving you *as* an inheritance, and *thus* guilt of bloodshed be upon you.

11"But if anyone hates his neighbor, lies in wait for him, rises against him and strikes him mortally, so that he dies, and he flees to one of these cities, 12then the elders of his city shall send and bring him from there, and deliver him over to the hand of the avenger of blood, that he may die. 13Your eye shall not pity him, but you shall put away *the guilt of* innocent blood from Israel, that it may go well with you.

Property Boundaries

14"You shall not remove your neighbor's landmark, which the men of old have set, in your inheritance which you will inherit in the land that the LORD your God is giving you to possess.

The Law Concerning Witnesses

15"One witness shall not rise against a man concerning any iniquity or any sin that he commits; by the mouth of two or three witnesses the matter shall be established. 16If a false witness rises against any man to testify against him of wrongdoing, 17then both men in the controversy shall stand before the LORD, before the priests and the judges who serve in those days. 18And the judges shall make careful inquiry, and indeed, *if* the witness *is* a false witness, who has testified falsely against his brother, 19then you shall do to him as he thought to have done to his brother; so you shall put away the evil from among you. 20And

those who remain shall hear and fear, and hereafter they shall not again commit such evil among you. [21]Your eye shall not pity: life *shall be* for life, eye for eye, tooth for tooth, hand for hand, foot for foot.

Principles Governing Warfare

20 "When you go out to battle against your enemies, and see horses and chariots *and* people more numerous than you, do not be afraid of them; for the LORD your God *is* with you, who brought you up from the land of Egypt. [2]So it shall be, when you are on the verge of battle, that the priest shall approach and speak to the people. [3]And he shall say to them, 'Hear, O Israel: Today you are on the verge of battle with your enemies. Do not let your heart faint, do not be afraid, and do not tremble or be terrified because of them; [4]for the LORD your God *is* He who goes with you, to fight for you against your enemies, to save you.'

[5]"Then the officers shall speak to the people, saying: 'What man *is there* who has built a new house and has not dedicated it? Let him go and return to his house, lest he die in the battle and another man dedicate it. [6]Also what man *is there* who has planted a vineyard and has not eaten of it? Let him go and return to his house, lest he die in the battle and another man eat of it. [7]And what man *is there* who is betrothed to a woman and has not married her? Let him go and return to his house, lest he die in the battle and another man marry her.'

[8]"The officers shall speak further to the people, and say, 'What man *is there who is* fearful and fainthearted? Let him go and return to his house, lest the heart of his brethren faint[a] like his heart.' [9]And so it shall be, when the officers have finished speaking to the people, that they shall make captains of the armies to lead the people.

[10]"When you go near a city to fight against it, then proclaim an offer of peace to it. [11]And it shall be that if they accept your offer of peace, and open to you, then all the people *who are* found in it shall be placed under tribute to you, and serve you. [12]Now if *the city* will not make peace with you, but war against you, then you shall besiege it. [13]And when the LORD your God delivers it into your hands, you shall strike every male in it with the edge of the sword. [14]But the women, the little ones, the livestock, and all that is in the city, all its spoil, you shall plunder for yourself; and you shall eat the enemies' plunder which the LORD your God gives you. [15]Thus you shall do to all the cities *which are* very far from you, which *are* not of the cities of these nations.

[16]"But of the cities of these peoples which the LORD your God gives you *as* an inheritance, you shall let nothing that breathes remain alive, [17]but you shall utterly destroy them: the Hittite and the Amorite and the Canaanite and the Perizzite and the Hivite and the Jebusite, just as the LORD your God has commanded you, [18]lest they teach you to do according to all their abominations which they have done for their gods, and you sin against the LORD your God.

[19]"When you besiege a city for a long time, while making war against it to take it, you shall not destroy its trees by wielding an ax against them; if you can eat of them, do not cut them down to use in the siege, for the tree of the field *is* man's *food.* [20]Only the trees which you know *are* not trees for food you may destroy and cut down, to build siegeworks against the city that makes war with you, until it is subdued.

The Law Concerning Unsolved Murder

21 "If *anyone* is found slain, lying in the field in the land which the LORD your God is giving you to possess, *and* it is not known who killed him, [2]then your elders and your judges shall go out and

---

20:8 [a]Following Masoretic Text and Targum; Samaritan Pentateuch, Septuagint, Syriac, and Vulgate read *lest he make his brother's heart faint.*

19:21 The law of retribution was not license for vengeance. It was used to set boundaries for punishment to guard against leniency as well as excessiveness and to ensure justice (Ex. 21:23–25; Lev. 24:17–20).

20:5 The first three exemptions were not based on a person's moral opposition to war but his moral responsibility to domestic affairs.

20:6 The fruit of the vineyard was not eaten during the first three years. In the fourth year, the fruit was consecrated to the Lord. Personal enjoyment of the fruit did not come until the fifth year.

20:7 Exemption from military service for the newlywed was for one year (Deut. 24:5). Even in the case of war, the sanctity of the family was a priority to God.

20:8 The last exemption was for the coward. To remove the fainthearted from the battle ranks would protect the morale of the other soldiers. The fearful were those whose faith in God was weak and who did not receive the encouragement from the priests (vv. 3, 4).

20:15 The cities which are very far from you were cities beyond Transjordan and Canaan. They were not subject to total destruction as were the Canaanite nations.

20:16–18 Canaanite cities had to be completely destroyed to dispel the influence of their pagan religions and to execute the judgment of God on their wicked, degenerate practices (Deut. 2:34; 7:1–2).

21:1–9 When a murderer was not apprehended and escaped judgment, even though the people of the city were innocent, they incurred the guilt of the unknown murderer. Atonement for justice had to be made. A procedure is provided to satisfy the Lord's justice and remove corporate guilt. An unworked heifer would be substituted for the murderer. It would be

measure *the distance* from the slain man to the surrounding cities. ³And it shall be *that* the elders of the city nearest to the slain man will take a heifer which has not been worked *and* which has not pulled with a yoke. ⁴The elders of that city shall bring the heifer down to a valley with flowing water, which is neither plowed nor sown, and they shall break the heifer's neck there in the valley. ⁵Then the priests, the sons of Levi, shall come near, for the LORD your God has chosen them to minister to Him and to bless in the name of the LORD; by their word every controversy and every assault shall be *settled.* ⁶And all the elders of that city nearest to the slain *man* shall wash their hands over the heifer whose neck was broken in the valley. ⁷Then they shall answer and say, 'Our hands have not shed this blood, nor have our eyes seen *it.* ⁸Provide atonement, O LORD, for Your people Israel, whom You have redeemed, and do not lay innocent blood to the charge of Your people Israel.' And atonement shall be provided on their behalf for the blood. ⁹So you shall put away the *guilt of* innocent blood from among you when you do *what is* right in the sight of the LORD.

Female Captives

¹⁰"When you go out to war against your enemies, and the LORD your God delivers them into your hand, and you take them captive, ¹¹and you see among the captives a beautiful woman, and desire her and would take her for your wife, ¹²then you shall bring her home to your house, and she shall shave her head and trim her nails.

¹³She shall put off the clothes of her captivity, remain in your house, and mourn her father and her mother a full month; after that you may go in to her and be her husband, and she shall be your wife. ¹⁴And it shall be, if you have no delight in her, then you shall set her free, but you certainly shall not sell her for money; you shall not treat her brutally, because you have humbled her.

Firstborn Inheritance Rights

¹⁵"If a man has two wives, one loved and the other unloved, and they have borne him children, *both* the loved and the unloved, and *if* the firstborn son is of her who is unloved, ¹⁶then it shall be, on the day he bequeaths his possessions to his sons, *that* he must not bestow firstborn status on the son of the loved wife in preference to the son of the unloved, the *true* firstborn. ¹⁷But he shall acknowledge the son of the unloved wife *as* the firstborn by giving him a double portion of all that he has, for he *is* the beginning of his strength; the right of the firstborn *is* his.

The Rebellious Son

¹⁸"If a man has a stubborn and rebellious son who will not obey the voice of his father or the voice of his mother, and *who,* when they have chastened him, will not heed them, ¹⁹then his father and his mother shall take hold of him and bring him out to the elders of his city, to the gate of his city. ²⁰And they shall say to the elders of his city, 'This son of ours is stubborn and rebellious; he will not obey our voice; he is a glutton and a

---

taken to an unworked valley with a flowing brook and there its neck would be broken. The flowing water would carry away the blood, and the ground would drink the rest. By breaking the neck of the heifer, the elders symbolized the fact that the unknown murderer deserved the death penalty. The heifer, by its death, cleared the land of the guilt of bloodshed. The elders symbolized that they were free of the guilt of bloodshed by washing their hands, although they accepted responsibility for it. Atonement for the crime was effected only when the elders kept this charge.

21:12, 13 As a symbol of purification and initiation into the Israelite nation, the captured woman would shave her head and cut her nails (Lev. 14:8; Num. 8:7)—actions that indicated mourning. She would exchange the clothes of her former life for the clothing of an Israelite woman, thus depicting a change in status. Out of sensitivity to the natural grieving that would occur, the woman was allowed a full month to lament. The time spent in her prospective husband's home would also allow her to disassociate herself from her former life and to grow accustomed to her new family and lifestyle. Men would be restrained from rape, and women would have time to adjust to a new environment (see article, Renewed by His Grace).

21:14 No perimeters were set for the husband's motivation for divorce from a former captive. Most likely, the grounds for divorce were based on some type of incompatibility, probably from the husband's point of view. Nevertheless, the woman

was entitled to certain rights. She retained her social status and was not to be sold as a slave or exchanged for another woman or material goods.

21:15 Whether the two wives are successive or concurrent is unclear. If concurrent, the dangers and problems of polygamy are illustrated. Polygamy was a very old practice (Gen. 4:19), but it was not the design God intended for marriage (see Gen. 2; 2 Sam. 6; Prov. 5; Hos. 2; Amos 3; 2 Cor. 13; Heb. 12, Marriage; Gen. 4, God's Plan for Marriage). Whenever practiced, polygamy produced a variety of problems, such as the one mentioned in this passage. The families of both Jacob and Solomon illustrate how a polygamous situation creates a problem of primogeniture or lineage. Normally birth order and not the favoritism of the father governed succession. The "unloved" wife was not necessarily a hated wife; she was sometimes simply loved or desired less than the other wife. Such was the case in Jacob's treatment of Leah (Gen. 29:30; see also Prov. 28, Favoritism; 1 Tim. 3, Polygamy).

21:17 Regardless of the father's feelings for the son's mother, the oldest son as successor to his father was entitled to a double portion of the father's estate according to Israelite law.

21:18–21 A rebellious society is an extension of rebellious families. For this reason, disobedience in the home was not to be tolerated (Deut. 5:16). If the child would not obey the authority of his parents, his rebellion against the elders and ultimately against God would lead to his death. In cases of per-

drunkard.' ²¹Then all the men of his city shall stone him to death with stones; so you shall put away the evil from among you, and all Israel shall hear and fear.

Miscellaneous Laws

²²"If a man has committed a sin deserving of death, and he is put to death, and you hang him on a tree, ²³his body shall not remain overnight on the tree, but you shall surely bury him that day, so that you do not defile the land which the Lord your God is giving you *as* an inheritance; for he who is hanged *is* accursed of God.

22 "You shall not see your brother's ox or his sheep going astray, and hide yourself from them; you shall certainly bring them back to your brother. ²And if your brother *is* not near you, or if you do not know him, then you shall bring it to your own house, and it shall remain with you until your brother seeks it; then you shall restore it to him. ³You shall do the same with his donkey, and so shall you do with his garment; with any lost thing of your brother's, which he has lost and you have found, you shall do likewise; you must not hide yourself.

⁴"You shall not see your brother's donkey or his ox fall down along the road, and hide yourself from them; you shall surely help him lift *them* up again.

⁵"A woman shall not wear anything that pertains to a man, nor shall a man put on a woman's garment, for all who do so *are* an abomination to the Lord your God.

⁶"If a bird's nest happens to be before you along the way, in any tree or on the ground, with young ones or eggs, with the mother sitting on the young or on the eggs, you shall not take the mother with the young; ⁷you shall surely let the mother go, and take the young for yourself, that it may be well with you and *that* you may prolong *your* days.

⁸"When you build a new house, then you shall make a parapet for your roof, that you may not bring guilt of bloodshed on your household if anyone falls from it.

⁹"You shall not sow your vineyard with different kinds of seed, lest the yield of the seed which you have sown and the fruit of your vineyard be defiled.

¹⁰"You shall not plow with an ox and a donkey together.

¹¹"You shall not wear a garment of different sorts, *such as* wool and linen mixed together.

¹²"You shall make tassels on the four corners of the clothing with which you cover *yourself.*

Laws of Sexual Morality

¹³"If any man takes a wife, and goes in to her, and detests her, ¹⁴and charges her with shameful conduct, and brings a bad name on her, and says, 'I took this woman, and when I came to her I found she *was* not a virgin,' ¹⁵then the father and mother of the young woman shall take and bring out *the evidence of* the young woman's virginity to the elders of the city at the gate. ¹⁶And the young woman's father shall say to the elders, 'I gave my daughter to this man as wife, and he detests her.

---

sistent rebellion against parental authority and chastisement, the child was to be subject to the judgment of the elders. The parents could not bring the child to the elders unless he had been disciplined and subsequently had rejected that discipline. Both parents were to be in agreement in their decision to set the boy before the elders. If the parents' claims were found true, then the child was to be stoned to death by the men of the city. No examples of parents going to this extreme are found in the OT. This warning against rebellion was a deterrent as well as a strong incentive for parents to disciple their children in the Law of God (Deut. 6:6–9; see also Prov. 22, Children).

21:22, 23 After a criminal was executed, his body would be hanged on a tree for display to remind the people of the sure judgment that would follow such crimes. The body was accursed of God, not because it was hanging on a tree, but because the individual had incurred the wrath of God. Christ became accursed and incurred the divine wrath for us (Gal. 3:13).

22:5 The wearing of clothing of the opposite sex could suggest a role reversal and blur the distinction of the sexes God had designed (Gen. 1:27). It especially refers to the practice of transvestism (the adoption of dress and behavior unnatural to one's own sex), which was associated with some forms of homosexuality as well as some pagan cults. "Abomination" is also used in reference to homosexuality (Lev. 18:22; 20:13).

22:6, 7 This law esteemed motherhood and protected the food supply. If the mother had been taken with the young, the future food supply would be jeopardized. Even if the mother had been taken alone, the young would not survive. Therefore, the mother is left to reproduce and supply more food while the young bird or the eggs are taken for sustenance. This seemingly insignificant law demonstrates the wisdom of God in every area of life.

22:8 A parapet was a retaining wall built around the roof of the house to serve as a safeguard against falling. Without a parapet, the owner of the home could be guilty of involuntary manslaughter (Deut. 19:4–7).

22:15 Evidence of the young woman's virginity was a bloodstained article of clothing or bedsheet from the woman's wedding night, indicating her first intercourse (v. 17). Knowing that the life of the girl hinged on proof of virginity, the parents would keep these sheets to present as proof. A young woman was often engaged to be married soon after she entered puberty. Proof of a regular menstruation cycle would confirm that the woman was not pregnant at the time of marriage and thus had not been unfaithful during her engagement (see Lev. 15, Menstrual Cycle). The Law protected an innocent bride from an unreasonable husband who might seek to put her away on a whim, and it discouraged premarital infidelity among young women. Other laws addressed a husband who had previously been unfaithful (Deut. 22:22–29).

BATTERED WIVES *A TREASURE UNPROTECTED*

To batter means to hit or beat repeatedly with heavy blows so as to bruise, shatter, demolish, or kill. The Hebrews frowned on wife-battering. The Jewish ideal was that a wife was a man's crown, the queen of her home, and a treasure to be defended at all costs (Prov. 12:4; 31:10–31). Nonetheless, although Scripture records no particular example of wife-beating in the home, some men doubtless regarded women as their "property" and as a result treated them as socially inferior.

Under the Levitical Law, if a new bride could not produce evidence of her virginity (a blood-stained bedsheet after initial intercourse), by law she could be stoned (or battered) to death (Deut. 22:13–21).

Since the Law forbade adultery (Deut. 22:22), a wife accused of having intercourse with another man faced embarrassing "tests" (Num. 5:16–31). If the tests proved her guilty, she faced death by stoning.

In the New Testament, even as wives are encouraged to submit to the leadership of their husbands (Eph. 5:22), those husbands are admonished to love their wives unconditionally and sacrificially (Eph. 5:25) as they would their own bodies (Eph. 5:28, 29). This would certainly preclude abuse of any kind!

For a woman who has experienced abuse, the Lord, as the "God of all comfort," offers His love and acceptance. She should reach out to Him to meet her innermost needs. She should also turn to family, the household of faith, and civil authorities for protection.

See also Num. 5:16–31; notes on Abuse (Ps. 31); Conflict (Song 5; Matt. 18); Pain (Job 7; 2 Cor. 12); Suffering (Ps. 33; 113; Is. 43; 1 Pet. 5)

[17]Now he has charged her with shameful conduct, saying, "I found your daughter *was* not a virgin," and yet these *are the evidences of* my daughter's virginity.' And they shall spread the cloth before the elders of the city. [18]Then the elders of that city shall take that man and punish him; [19]and they shall fine him one hundred *shekels* of silver and give *them* to the father of the young woman, because he has brought a bad name on a virgin of Israel. And she shall be his wife; he cannot divorce her all his days.

[20]"But if the thing is true, *and evidences of* virginity are not found for the young woman, [21]then they shall bring out the young woman to the door of her father's house, and the men of her city shall stone her to death with stones, because she has done a disgraceful thing in Israel, to play the harlot in her father's house. So you shall put away the evil from among you.

[22]"If a man is found lying with a woman married to a husband, then both of them shall die— the man that lay with the woman, and the woman; so you shall put away the evil from Israel.

[23]"If a young woman *who is* a virgin is betrothed to a husband, and a man finds her in the city and lies with her, [24]then you shall bring them both out to the gate of that city, and you shall stone them to death with stones, the young woman because she did not cry out in the city, and the man because he humbled his neighbor's wife; so you shall put away the evil from among you.

[25]"But if a man finds a betrothed young woman in the countryside, and the man forces her and lies with her, then only the man who lay with her shall die. [26]But you shall do nothing to the young woman; *there is* in the young woman no sin *deserving* of death, for just as when a man rises against his neighbor and kills him, even so *is* this matter. [27]For he found her in the countryside, *and* the betrothed young woman cried out, but *there was* no one to save her.

[28]"If a man finds a young woman *who is* a virgin, who is not betrothed, and he seizes her and lies with her, and they are found out, [29]then the man who lay with her shall give to the young woman's father fifty *shekels* of silver, and she shall be his wife because he has humbled her; he shall not be permitted to divorce her all his days.

22:19 Because of his false accusation, the husband was not allowed to divorce the woman. She was protected from the further humiliation of divorce and was guaranteed support the rest of her life.

22:21 If the young wife was judged guilty, then she was stoned in front of her father's home. This action served as a deterrent to fornication and also showed the partial responsibility the father had in the conduct of his daughter. "In her father's house" does not necessarily imply that the sin took place in that locality but rather that she was under the care of her father when the sin was committed.

22:24 Engagement was considered as legally binding as marriage. The fact that the woman did not cry out implied that

she consented to the act, making both guilty of adultery and subject to the death penalty (see Gen. 34, Rape; 2 Sam. 13, Date Rape).

22:25–27 The young woman who was raped in a secluded area, such as the countryside, would not suffer death because her cries would have been unheard. Rape is likened to murder in this passage (see Gen. 34, Rape).

22:28 The man who raped an unbetrothed virgin did not receive the death penalty, for this act was not considered adultery as in verses 22–27. However, he must pay a fine to her father and marry the girl with no chance of divorce. This law protected the girl and any child that might be born as a result of the rape (see Gen. 34, Rape).

³⁰"A man shall not take his father's wife, nor uncover his father's bed.

Those Excluded from the Congregation

23 "He who is emasculated by crushing or mutilation shall not enter the assembly of the LORD.

²"One of illegitimate birth shall not enter the assembly of the LORD; even to the tenth generation none of his *descendants* shall enter the assembly of the LORD.

³"An Ammonite or Moabite shall not enter the assembly of the LORD; even to the tenth generation none of his *descendants* shall enter the assembly of the LORD forever, ⁴because they did not meet you with bread and water on the road when you came out of Egypt, and because they hired against you Balaam the son of Beor from Pethor of Mesopotamia,ᵃ to curse you. ⁵Nevertheless the LORD your God would not listen to Balaam, but the LORD your God turned the curse into a blessing for you, because the LORD your God loves you. ⁶You shall not seek their peace nor their prosperity all your days forever.

⁷"You shall not abhor an Edomite, for he *is* your brother. You shall not abhor an Egyptian, because you were an alien in his land. ⁸The children of the third generation born to them may enter the assembly of the LORD.

Cleanliness of the Campsite

⁹"When the army goes out against your enemies, then keep yourself from every wicked thing. ¹⁰If there is any man among you who becomes unclean by some occurrence in the night, then he shall go outside the camp; he shall not come inside the camp. ¹¹But it shall be, when evening comes, that he shall wash with water; and when the sun sets, he may come into the camp.

¹²"Also you shall have a place outside the camp, where you may go out; ¹³and you shall have an implement among your equipment, and when you sit down outside, you shall dig with it and turn and cover your refuse. ¹⁴For the LORD your God walks in the midst of your camp, to deliver you and give your enemies over to you; therefore your camp shall be holy, that He may see no unclean thing among you, and turn away from you.

Miscellaneous Laws

¹⁵"You shall not give back to his master the slave who has escaped from his master to you. ¹⁶He may dwell with you in your midst, in the place which he chooses within one of your gates, where it seems best to him; you shall not oppress him.

¹⁷"There shall be no *ritual* harlotᵃ of the daughters of Israel, or a pervertedᵇ one of the sons of Israel. ¹⁸You shall not bring the wages of a harlot or the price of a dog to the house of the LORD your God for any vowed offering, for both of these *are* an abomination to the LORD your God.

¹⁹"You shall not charge interest to your brother—interest on money *or* food *or* anything that is lent out at interest. ²⁰To a foreigner you may charge interest, but to your brother you shall not charge interest, that the LORD your God may bless you in all to which you set your hand in the land which you are entering to possess.

²¹"When you make a vow to the LORD your God, you shall not delay to pay it; for the LORD your God will surely require it of you, and it would be sin to you. ²²But if you abstain from vowing, it shall not be sin to you. ²³That which has gone from your lips you shall keep and perform, for you voluntarily vowed to the LORD your God what you have promised with your mouth.

²⁴"When you come into your neighbor's vineyard, you may eat your fill of grapes at your pleasure, but you shall not put *any* in your container. ²⁵When you come into your neighbor's standing grain, you may pluck the heads with your hand,

····················

23:4 ᵃHebrew *Aram Naharaim*   23:17 ᵃHebrew *qedeshah*, feminine of *qadesh* (see note b)   ᵇHebrew *qadesh*, that is, one practicing sodomy and prostitution in religious rituals

---

23:1–3 The assembly of the LORD refers to a gathering of the people of Israel at feasts, wars, and religious activities. Different groups of people were excluded from this assembly. Eunuchs were excluded because of their castration, which was often a sign of their involvement in a pagan cult. To God, such deliberate mutilations were an abomination for His holy people. Those who had been castrated by accident or illness would not be included in this category (Is. 56:3–5). Those "of illegitimate birth," who were born as a result of incest or cultic prostitution, were likewise prohibited from the assembly. The Ammonites and the Moabites were excluded from the assembly also based on their treatment of Israel in the wilderness and because they were descended from the incestuous relationship of Lot and his daughters (Gen. 19:30–38). The Moabitess Ruth, who was an ancestor of both King David and the Lord Jesus, is a reminder of God's lovingkindness and re-

demptive work (Matt. 1:5). "To the tenth generation" indicates forever. "Ten" is a number of completeness (see chart, The Significance of Numbers in Scripture). Therefore, these three groups were to be excluded from the assembly of the Lord as long as the nation existed.

23:9–14 Cleanliness in the camp was not only for hygiene but also was a symbol of purity, for the Lord Himself walked in their midst.

23:18 The term dog refers to a male cultic prostitute. Money that had been procured through evil practices was not to be presented to the Lord.

23:24, 25 Hospitality to neighbors was common in the Near East. Someone passing by could quench his appetite in the field of his fellow Israelite. However, to carry any sustenance with him would be stealing (see 1 Pet. 4, Hospitality).

but you shall not use a sickle on your neighbor's standing grain.

Law Concerning Divorce

24 "When a man takes a wife and marries her, and it happens that she finds no favor in his eyes because he has found some uncleanness in her, and he writes her a certificate of divorce, puts *it* in her hand, and sends her out of his house, ²when she has departed from his house, and goes and becomes another man's *wife*, ³*if* the latter husband detests her and writes her a certificate of divorce, puts *it* in her hand, and sends her out of his house, or if the latter husband dies who took her as his wife, ⁴*then* her former husband who divorced her must not take her back to be his wife after she has been defiled; for that *is* an abomination before the LORD, and you shall not bring sin on the land which the LORD your God is giving you *as* an inheritance.

Miscellaneous Laws

⁵"When a man has taken a new wife, he shall not go out to war or be charged with any business; he shall be free at home one year, and bring happiness to his wife whom he has taken.

⁶"No man shall take the lower or the upper millstone in pledge, for he takes *one's* living in pledge.

⁷"If a man is found kidnapping any of his brethren of the children of Israel, and mistreats him or sells him, then that kidnapper shall die; and you shall put away the evil from among you.

⁸"Take heed in an outbreak of leprosy, that you carefully observe and do according to all that the priests, the Levites, shall teach you; just as I commanded them, *so* you shall be careful to do. ⁹Remember what the LORD your God did to Miriam on the way when you came out of Egypt!

¹⁰"When you lend your brother anything, you shall not go into his house to get his pledge. ¹¹You shall stand outside, and the man to whom you lend shall bring the pledge out to you. ¹²And if the man *is* poor, you shall not keep his pledge overnight. ¹³You shall in any case return the pledge to him again when the sun goes down, that he may sleep in his own garment and bless you; and it shall be righteousness to you before the LORD your God.

¹⁴"You shall not oppress a hired servant *who is* poor and needy, *whether* one of your brethren or one of the aliens who *is* in your land within your gates. ¹⁵Each day you shall give *him* his wages, and not let the sun go down on it, for he *is* poor and has set his heart on it; lest he cry out against you to the LORD, and it be sin to you.

¹⁶"Fathers shall not be put to death for *their* children, nor shall children be put to death for *their* fathers; a person shall be put to death for his own sin.

¹⁷"You shall not pervert justice due the stranger or the fatherless, nor take a widow's garment as a pledge. ¹⁸But you shall remember that you were a slave in Egypt, and the LORD your God redeemed you from there; therefore I command you to do this thing.

¹⁹"When you reap your harvest in your field, and forget a sheaf in the field, you shall not go back to get it; it shall be for the stranger, the fatherless, and the widow, that the LORD your God

---

24:1–4 This passage contains information about divorce and remarriage but does not legislate these matters. Although divorce, even at this time, was widespread (Lev. 21:7, 14; 22:13; Num. 30:9), it was never encouraged by God (Mal. 2:16). This case concerns remarriage after divorce with the impetus found in the phrase "some uncleanness in her." This "uncleanness" cannot refer to adultery, for the penalty for adultery was death (Deut. 22:22). It must refer to some indecent exposure or unwomanly conduct. The husband in such a case might choose to divorce his wife. Divorce was initiated by men, not by women. If the woman was remarried and divorced again, her first husband could not remarry her because her remarriage after the first divorce would be considered equivalent to adultery in the sense that she had then lived with another man. This strictness on divorce would also stop the practice of wife swapping and loaning for procreation or merely on a whim (see Matt. 5, Remarriage; Matt. 19, Divorce).

24:5 A newly married man was exempted from military service as well as any public service that might be required. This guarded against the untimely death of the husband and prohibited his prolonged absence from the home immediately after the wedding. The sanctity of marriage and the home is seen in this legislation. God directed a man to fortify his marriage and home with unique devotion to his wife during their first year of marriage.

24:6 Each Israelite home was equipped with a small milling machine. The top stone would rotate over the bottom stone to grind the grain. This grain was used to prepare the bread. To take either the whole mill, or even a part of it, was to take away life itself since it would deprive a family of their daily bread.

24:10–13 A borrower's home was protected from intrusion by the lender. The creditor could only stand outside the home and wait for the borrower to bring his pledge. The very poor could only offer some piece of clothing, called a "garment" (v. 13). This "garment" would be used as a coat during the daytime but as a blanket at night. If the "garment" was taken as a pledge, it must be returned by nightfall for the protection of its poor owner against the elements.

24:17–22 Moses is concerned with the protection of the rights of those who were often subjects of oppression, such as the stranger, the fatherless, and the widow. The nation is compelled to show mercy and kindness to the needy in light of their oppression by Pharaoh (see Luke 9, The Homeless; Luke 14, Poverty). Those who were needy were supposed to be able to glean during the harvest and not have to beg or borrow (Lev. 23:22; Ruth 2:7, note).

may bless you in all the work of your hands. [20]When you beat your olive trees, you shall not go over the boughs again; it shall be for the stranger, the fatherless, and the widow. [21]When you gather the grapes of your vineyard, you shall not glean *it* afterward; it shall be for the stranger, the fatherless, and the widow. [22]And you shall remember that you were a slave in the land of Egypt; therefore I command you to do this thing.

25 "If there is a dispute between men, and they come to court, that *the judges* may judge them, and they justify the righteous and condemn the wicked, [2]then it shall be, if the wicked man deserves to be beaten, that the judge will cause him to lie down and be beaten in his presence, according to his guilt, with a certain number of blows. [3]Forty blows he may give him *and* no more, lest he should exceed this and beat him with many blows above these, and your brother be humiliated in your sight.

[4]"You shall not muzzle an ox while it treads out *the grain.*

Marriage Duty of the Surviving Brother

[5]"If brothers dwell together, and one of them dies and has no son, the widow of the dead man shall not be *married* to a stranger outside *the family;* her husband's brother shall go in to her, take her as his wife, and perform the duty of a husband's brother to her. [6]And it shall be *that* the firstborn son which she bears will succeed to the name of his dead brother, that his name may not be blotted out of Israel. [7]But if the man does not want to take his brother's wife, then let his brother's wife go up to the gate to the elders, and say, 'My husband's brother refuses to raise up a name to his brother in Israel; he will not perform the duty of my husband's brother.' [8]Then the elders of his city shall call him and speak to him. But *if* he stands firm and says, 'I do not want to take her,' [9]then his brother's wife shall come to him in the presence of the elders, remove his sandal from his foot, spit in his face, and answer and say, 'So shall it be done to the man who will not build up his brother's house.' [10]And his name shall be called in Israel, 'The house of him who had his sandal removed.'

Miscellaneous Laws

[11]"If *two* men fight together, and the wife of one draws near to rescue her husband from the hand of the one attacking him, and puts out her hand and seizes him by the genitals, [12]then you shall cut off her hand; your eye shall not pity *her.*

[13]"You shall not have in your bag differing weights, a heavy and a light. [14]You shall not have in your house differing measures, a large and a small. [15]You shall have a perfect and just weight, a perfect and just measure, that your days may be lengthened in the land which the LORD your God is giving you. [16]For all who do such things, all who behave unrighteously, *are* an abomination to the LORD your God.

Destroy the Amalekites

[17]"Remember what Amalek did to you on the way as you were coming out of Egypt, [18]how he met you on the way and attacked your rear ranks, all the stragglers at your rear, when you *were* tired and weary; and he did not fear God. [19]Therefore it shall be, when the LORD your God has given you rest from your enemies all around, in the land which the LORD your God is giving you to possess

---

25:3 The maximum number of lashes with the rod was set at 40. To go over that would humiliate a man and be inhumane, perhaps endangering health and life. By NT times, the Jews set the maximum at 39 in fear of exceeding 40 (2 Cor. 11:24).

25:4 The ox was used to pull a threshing sledge over the grain. To muzzle him would prevent him from eating as he worked. The apostle Paul quoted this verse to defend the laborer's right to his wage (1 Cor. 9:9; 1 Tim. 5:18).

25:5, 6 Levirate marriage (from the Latin *levir,* "brother-in-law" or husband's brother) was to assure the continuity of the family and the rightful land distribution to that family through a legal heir. Prerequisites vary, perhaps due to historical development or from trying to interpret the passages too rigidly (see Gen. 38; Ruth 3:3–9, note; Deut. 5—10). The two brothers had to be living together and sharing the responsibilities of that family unit. Another requirement was that a son had not been born to the deceased man. Without a son, there was not a legal inheritor of the father's property. If these prerequisites were met, the brother-in-law of the widow would take her as a wife, and legally the firstborn son of this new union would be considered the son of the deceased and would inherit the property of his father.

25:7–10 The brother-in-law reserved the right to refuse to marry the widow. If that was the case, he would be subjected to public humiliation. The removing of the sandal symbolized the fact that the brother had rejected his responsibility, and spitting in his face brought disgrace upon him. If there were not a male child as a legal heir to the deceased brother's inheritance, then the brother-in-law would become the heir. Selfishness, therefore, could be the motive behind not marrying his sister-in-law.

25:11, 12 This legislation is the only occurrence in the Law where maiming served as judgment against a crime. The purpose of such legislation was to emphasize the need for modesty of women and to protect the man's ability to reproduce.

25:13–16 The Israelites were to be characterized as honest and just in their business practices. The stones were used to measure. A large stone in buying would allow the Israelite more than his portion, and a small stone when selling would cheat the buyer of his portion. Dishonesty in business was another way of showing lack of faith in God's ability to provide (see Ps. 26, Integrity).

as an inheritance, *that* you will blot out the remembrance of Amalek from under heaven. You shall not forget.

Offerings of Firstfruits and Tithes

26 "And it shall be, when you come into the land which the LORD your God is giving you *as* an inheritance, and you possess it and dwell in it, ²that you shall take some of the first of all the produce of the ground, which you shall bring from your land that the LORD your God is giving you, and put *it* in a basket and go to the place where the LORD your God chooses to make His name abide. ³And you shall go to the one who is priest in those days, and say to him, 'I declare today to the LORD your[a] God that I have come to the country which the LORD swore to our fathers to give us.'

⁴"Then the priest shall take the basket out of your hand and set it down before the altar of the LORD your God. ⁵And you shall answer and say before the LORD your God: 'My father *was* a Syrian,[a] about to perish, and he went down to Egypt and dwelt there, few in number; and there he became a nation, great, mighty, and populous. ⁶But the Egyptians mistreated us, afflicted us, and laid hard bondage on us. ⁷Then we cried out to the LORD God of our fathers, and the LORD heard our voice and looked on our affliction and our labor and our oppression. ⁸So the LORD brought us out of Egypt with a mighty hand and with an outstretched arm, with great terror and with signs and wonders. ⁹He has brought us to this place and has given us this land, "a land flowing with milk and honey";[a] ¹⁰and now, behold, I have brought the firstfruits of the land which you, O LORD, have given me.'

"Then you shall set it before the LORD your God, and worship before the LORD your God. ¹¹So you shall rejoice in every good *thing* which the LORD your God has given to you and your house, you and the Levite and the stranger who *is* among you.

¹²"When you have finished laying aside all the tithe of your increase in the third year—the year of tithing—and have given *it* to the Levite, the stranger, the fatherless, and the widow, so that they may eat within your gates and be filled, ¹³then you shall say before the LORD your God: 'I have removed the holy *tithe* from *my* house, and also have given them to the Levite, the stranger, the fatherless, and the widow, according to all Your commandments which You have commanded me; I have not transgressed Your commandments, nor have I forgotten *them.* ¹⁴I have not eaten any of it when in mourning, nor have I removed *any* of it for an unclean *use,* nor given *any* of it for the dead. I have obeyed the voice of the LORD my God, and have done according to all that You have commanded me. ¹⁵Look down from Your holy habitation, from heaven, and bless Your people Israel and the land which You have given us, just as You swore to our fathers, "a land flowing with milk and honey." '[a]

A Special People of God

¹⁶"This day the LORD your God commands you to observe these statutes and judgments; therefore you shall be careful to observe them with all your heart and with all your soul. ¹⁷Today you have proclaimed the LORD to be your God, and that you will walk in His ways and keep His statutes, His commandments, and His judgments, and that you will obey His voice. ¹⁸Also today the LORD has proclaimed you to be His special people, just as He promised you, that *you* should keep all His commandments, ¹⁹and that He will set you high above all nations which He has made, in praise, in name, and in honor, and that you may be a holy people to the LORD your God, just as He has spoken."

The Law Inscribed on Stones

27 Now Moses, with the elders of Israel, commanded the people, saying: "Keep all the commandments which I command you today. ²And it shall be, on the day when you cross over the Jordan to the land which the LORD your God is giving you, that you shall set up for yourselves large stones, and whitewash them with lime. ³You shall write on them all the words of this law, when you

••••••••••••••••••

26:3 ᵃSeptuagint reads *my.* 26:5 ᵃOr *Aramean* 26:9, 15 ᵃExodus 3:8

25:19 The Amalekites were the offspring of Esau's son Eliphaz. They were finally wiped out during the days of Hezekiah (1 Chr. 4:41–43).

26:18 Israel was special (Heb. *segullah,* lit. "treasured possession") to God. This position in God's heart was not given because of the merit of the people but because God graciously conferred it.

27:2 Upon entering the Promised Land, one of the nation's first tasks would be to erect large stones upon which the Law would be written. At that time, a common practice in the Near East, especially in Egypt, was to write laws upon whitewashed

boulders. The whitewashing was produced by roasting gypsum producing lime. Gypsum was readily available in the Dead Sea valley as well as the Jordan valley. This white background made the Law easier to read.

27:4 Mount Ebal was located about 35 miles north of Jerusalem. At its base was the city of Shechem. Here the Lord first appeared to Abraham and gave him the promise of a nation and a land, and Abraham built his first altar to the Lord (Gen. 12:1–7). Mount Ebal would serve as a reminder of the covenant and of Israel's commitment to the Lord.

have crossed over, that you may enter the land which the LORD your God is giving you, 'a land flowing with milk and honey,'ᵃ just as the LORD God of your fathers promised you. ⁴Therefore it shall be, when you have crossed over the Jordan, *that* on Mount Ebal you shall set up these stones, which I command you today, and you shall white-wash them with lime. ⁵And there you shall build an altar to the LORD your God, an altar of stones; you shall not use an iron *tool* on them. ⁶You shall build with whole stones the altar of the LORD your God, and offer burnt offerings on it to the LORD your God. ⁷You shall offer peace offerings, and shall eat there, and rejoice before the LORD your God. ⁸And you shall write very plainly on the stones all the words of this law."

⁹Then Moses and the priests, the Levites, spoke to all Israel, saying, "Take heed and listen, O Israel: This day you have become the people of the LORD your God. ¹⁰Therefore you shall obey the voice of the LORD your God, and observe His commandments and His statutes which I command you today."

Curses Pronounced from Mount Ebal

¹¹And Moses commanded the people on the same day, saying, ¹²"These shall stand on Mount Gerizim to bless the people, when you have crossed over the Jordan: Simeon, Levi, Judah, Issachar, Joseph, and Benjamin; ¹³and these shall stand on Mount Ebal to curse: Reuben, Gad, Asher, Zebulun, Dan, and Naphtali.

¹⁴"And the Levites shall speak with a loud voice and say to all the men of Israel: ¹⁵'Cursed *is* the one who makes a carved or molded image, an abomination to the LORD, the work of the hands of the craftsman, and sets *it* up in secret.'

"And all the people shall answer and say, 'Amen!'

¹⁶'Cursed *is* the one who treats his father or his mother with contempt.'

"And all the people shall say, 'Amen!'

¹⁷'Cursed *is* the one who moves his neighbor's landmark.'

"And all the people shall say, 'Amen!'

¹⁸'Cursed *is* the one who makes the blind to wander off the road.'

"And all the people shall say, 'Amen!'

¹⁹'Cursed *is* the one who perverts the justice due the stranger, the fatherless, and widow.'

"And all the people shall say, 'Amen!'

²⁰'Cursed *is* the one who lies with his father's wife, because he has uncovered his father's bed.'

"And all the people shall say, 'Amen!'

²¹'Cursed *is* the one who lies with any kind of animal.'

"And all the people shall say, 'Amen!'

²²'Cursed *is* the one who lies with his sister, the daughter of his father or the daughter of his mother.'

"And all the people shall say, 'Amen!'

²³'Cursed *is* the one who lies with his mother-in-law.'

"And all the people shall say, 'Amen!'

²⁴'Cursed *is* the one who attacks his neighbor secretly.'

"And all the people shall say, 'Amen!'

²⁵'Cursed *is* the one who takes a bribe to slay an innocent person.'

"And all the people shall say, 'Amen!'

²⁶'Cursed *is* the one who does not confirm *all* the words of this law by observing them.'

"And all the people shall say, 'Amen!' "

Blessings on Obedience

28 "Now it shall come to pass, if you diligently obey the voice of the LORD your God, to observe carefully all His commandments which I command you today, that the LORD your God will set you high above all nations of the earth. ²And all these blessings shall come upon you and over-

27:3 ᵃExodus 3:8

27:5, 6 The Israelites did not possess iron. Acquiring iron tools meant going to a foreign people to buy them. This action would create a dependency on foreign nations and their metalsmiths (1 Sam. 13:19–23).

27:11–13 Curses or blessings? The six tribes that pronounced the blessings from Mount Gerizim descended from Leah and Rachel. These were the legitimate wives of Jacob. The six remaining tribes stood on Mount Ebal to pronounce the curses. Four of these tribes—Gad, Asher, Dan, and Naphtali—were descended from Jacob's concubines Bilhah and Zilpah. Reuben and Zebulun also stood to pronounce curses. Reuben was the firstborn of Leah, who lost his birthright because of incest (Gen. 35:22; 49:3–4), and Zebulun was the youngest son of Leah. The Levites stood in the valley between the two mountains and recited the blessings and the curses (Josh. 8:30–35). "Curse" (Heb. *qelalah*) is sometimes translated "humiliated" (Deut. 25:3). The reference is to shame or disgrace

by the lowering of a person's social status. If Israel did not keep her commitment to the covenant of God, she would surely be humiliated, disgraced, and lowered in her social status in the eyes of the nations around her.

27:26 By replying amen, the people were agreeing with and assenting to the proclamation. They were affirming the legitimacy of the curses and agreeing to the judgment incurred by breaking the covenant.

28:1–14 The blessings of God were contingent on Israel's obedience as a nation. Just as disobedience would bring the humiliation of Israel among the nations (see Deut. 27:11–13, note), so obedience would bring national exaltation (v. 1). The blessings of God encompassed every area of life.

28:2 The blessings of God will "overtake" (Heb. *nasag*, lit. "to reach") or seek and find those who are obedient. The same Hebrew word is used of the avenger of blood (Deut. 19:6).

take you, because you obey the voice of the LORD your God:

³"Blessed *shall* you *be* in the city, and blessed *shall* you *be* in the country.

⁴"Blessed *shall be* the fruit of your body, the produce of your ground and the increase of your herds, the increase of your cattle and the offspring of your flocks.

⁵"Blessed *shall be* your basket and your kneading bowl.

⁶"Blessed *shall* you *be* when you come in, and blessed *shall* you *be* when you go out.

⁷"The LORD will cause your enemies who rise against you to be defeated before your face; they shall come out against you one way and flee before you seven ways.

⁸"The LORD will command the blessing on you in your storehouses and in all to which you set your hand, and He will bless you in the land which the LORD your God is giving you.

⁹"The LORD will establish you as a holy people to Himself, just as He has sworn to you, if you keep the commandments of the LORD your God and walk in His ways. ¹⁰Then all peoples of the earth shall see that you are called by the name of the LORD, and they shall be afraid of you. ¹¹And the LORD will grant you plenty of goods, in the fruit of your body, in the increase of your livestock, and in the produce of your ground, in the land of which the LORD swore to your fathers to give you. ¹²The LORD will open to you His good treasure, the heavens, to give the rain to your land in its season, and to bless all the work of your hand. You shall lend to many nations, but you shall not borrow. ¹³And the LORD will make you the head and not the tail; you shall be above only, and not be beneath, if you heed the commandments of the LORD your God, which I command you today, and are careful to observe *them.* ¹⁴So you shall not turn aside from any of the words which I command you this day, *to* the right or the left, to go after other gods to serve them.

Curses on Disobedience

¹⁵"But it shall come to pass, if you do not obey the voice of the LORD your God, to observe carefully all His commandments and His statutes which I command you today, that all these curses will come upon you and overtake you:

¹⁶"Cursed *shall* you *be* in the city, and cursed *shall* you *be* in the country.

¹⁷"Cursed *shall be* your basket and your kneading bowl.

¹⁸"Cursed *shall be* the fruit of your body and the produce of your land, the increase of your cattle and the offspring of your flocks.

¹⁹"Cursed *shall* you *be* when you come in, and cursed *shall* you *be* when you go out.

²⁰"The LORD will send on you cursing, confusion, and rebuke in all that you set your hand to do, until you are destroyed and until you perish quickly, because of the wickedness of your doings in which you have forsaken Me. ²¹The LORD will make the plague cling to you until He has consumed you from the land which you are going to possess. ²²The LORD will strike you with consumption, with fever, with inflammation, with severe burning fever, with the sword, with scorching, and with mildew; they shall pursue you until you perish. ²³And your heavens which *are* over your head shall be bronze, and the earth which is under you *shall be* iron. ²⁴The LORD will change the rain of your land to powder and dust; from the heaven it shall come down on you until you are destroyed.

²⁵"The LORD will cause you to be defeated before your enemies; you shall go out one way against them and flee seven ways before them; and you shall become troublesome to all the kingdoms of the earth. ²⁶Your carcasses shall be food for all the birds of the air and the beasts of the earth, and no one shall frighten *them* away. ²⁷The LORD will strike you with the boils of Egypt, with tumors, with the scab, and with the itch, from which you cannot be healed. ²⁸The LORD will strike you with madness and blindness and confusion of heart. ²⁹And you shall grope at noonday, as a blind man gropes in darkness; you shall not prosper in your ways; you shall be only oppressed and plundered continually, and no one shall save *you.*

³⁰"You shall betroth a wife, but another man shall lie with her; you shall build a house, but you shall not dwell in it; you shall plant a vineyard, but shall not gather its grapes. ³¹Your ox *shall be* slaughtered before your eyes, but you shall not eat of it; your donkey *shall be* violently taken away from before you, and shall not be restored to you; your sheep *shall be* given to your enemies, and you shall have no one to rescue *them.* ³²Your sons and your daughters *shall be* given to another people, and your eyes shall look and fail *with longing* for them all day long; and *there shall be* no strength in

---

28:5 The basket and "kneading bowl" blessing refers to provision of daily food. The basket was used to gather and keep food. The kneading bowl was used to prepare the daily bread.

28:10 The blessings of God were not an end in themselves. They were the outcome of obedience for the purpose of glorifying God among the nations (see Gen. 12, Blessings).

28:23 The bronze heavens indicate that the sun would be hot

and never darkened by rain clouds. The drought would make the earth as hard as "iron" so that crops could not grow.

28:32, 33 Disobedience to the Lord would result in the taking of the sons and daughters of Israel into captivity as slaves to foreign nations. The parents would be unable to save their children. Their only recourse would be to wait endlessly for them to return.

your hand. [33]A nation whom you have not known shall eat the fruit of your land and the produce of your labor, and you shall be only oppressed and crushed continually. [34]So you shall be driven mad because of the sight which your eyes see. [35]The LORD will strike you in the knees and on the legs with severe boils which cannot be healed, and from the sole of your foot to the top of your head.

[36]"The LORD will bring you and the king whom you set over you to a nation which neither you nor your fathers have known, and there you shall serve other gods—wood and stone. [37]And you shall become an astonishment, a proverb, and a byword among all nations where the LORD will drive you.

[38]"You shall carry much seed out to the field but gather little in, for the locust shall consume it. [39]You shall plant vineyards and tend *them,* but you shall neither drink *of* the wine nor gather the *grapes;* for the worms shall eat them. [40]You shall have olive trees throughout all your territory, but you shall not anoint *yourself* with the oil; for your olives shall drop off. [41]You shall beget sons and daughters, but they shall not be yours; for they shall go into captivity. [42]Locusts shall consume all your trees and the produce of your land.

[43]"The alien who *is* among you shall rise higher and higher above you, and you shall come down lower and lower. [44]He shall lend to you, but you shall not lend to him; he shall be the head, and you shall be the tail.

[45]"Moreover all these curses shall come upon you and pursue and overtake you, until you are destroyed, because you did not obey the voice of the LORD your God, to keep His commandments and His statutes which He commanded you. [46]And they shall be upon you for a sign and a wonder, and on your descendants forever.

[47]"Because you did not serve the LORD your God with joy and gladness of heart, for the abundance of everything, [48]therefore you shall serve your enemies, whom the LORD will send against you, in hunger, in thirst, in nakedness, and in need of everything; and He will put a yoke of iron on your neck until He has destroyed you. [49]The LORD will bring a nation against you from afar, from the end of the earth, *as swift* as the eagle flies, a nation whose language you will not understand, [50]a nation of fierce countenance, which does not respect the elderly nor show favor to the young. [51]And they shall eat the increase of your livestock and the produce of your land, until you are destroyed; they shall not leave you grain or new wine or oil, *or* the increase of your cattle or the offspring of your flocks, until they have destroyed you.

[52]"They shall besiege you at all your gates until your high and fortified walls, in which you trust, come down throughout all your land; and they shall besiege you at all your gates throughout all your land which the LORD your God has given you. [53]You shall eat the fruit of your own body, the flesh of your sons and your daughters whom the LORD your God has given you, in the siege and desperate straits in which your enemy shall distress you. [54]The sensitive and very refined man among you will be hostile toward his brother, toward the wife of his bosom, and toward the rest of his children whom he leaves behind, [55]so that he will not give any of them the flesh of his children whom he will eat, because he has nothing left in the siege and desperate straits in which your enemy shall distress you at all your gates. [56]The tender and delicate woman among you, who would not venture to set the sole of her foot on the ground because of her delicateness and sensitivity, will refuse[a] to the husband of her bosom, and to her son and her daughter, [57]her placenta which comes out from between her feet and her children whom she bears; for she will eat them secretly for lack of everything in the siege and desperate straits in which your enemy shall distress you at all your gates.

[58]"If you do not carefully observe all the words of this law that are written in this book, that you may fear this glorious and awesome name, THE LORD YOUR GOD, [59]then the LORD will bring upon you and your descendants extraordinary plagues— great and prolonged plagues— and serious and prolonged sicknesses. [60]Moreover He will bring back on you all the diseases of Egypt, of which you were afraid, and they shall cling to you. [61]Also every sickness and every plague, which *is* not written in this Book of the Law, will the LORD bring upon you until you are destroyed. [62]You shall be left few in number, whereas you were as the stars of heaven in multitude, because you would not obey the voice of the LORD your God. [63]And it shall be, *that* just as the LORD rejoiced over you to do you good and multiply you, so the

---

28:56 [a]Literally *her eye shall be evil toward*

28:46 The curses upon a rebellious nation would attest to the holiness of a righteous God (see Is. 6, Attributes of God). They would serve to educate future generations and pagan nations. Just as the blessings of God were not an end in themselves (see v. 10, note), neither are the curses.

28:53–57 Israel, by virtue of her own disobedience to God, would be reduced to a nation enveloped in perversity and de-

pravity to the extent that parents would eat their own children while their enemies received the produce of the land (v. 51). A woman would become anesthetized to the suffering of her own family and would devour her own newborn infant. The natural selflessness of motherhood would be obliterated by hunger and hopelessness. Such is the nature of disobedience to God.

LORD will rejoice over you to destroy you and bring you to nothing; and you shall be plucked from off the land which you go to possess. [64]"Then the LORD will scatter you among all peoples, from one end of the earth to the other, and there you shall serve other gods, which neither you nor your fathers have known—wood and stone. [65]And among those nations you shall find no rest, nor shall the sole of your foot have a resting place; but there the LORD will give you a trembling heart, failing eyes, and anguish of soul. [66]Your life shall hang in doubt before you; you shall fear day and night, and have no assurance of life. [67]In the morning you shall say, 'Oh, that it were evening!' And at evening you shall say, 'Oh, that it were morning!' because of the fear which terrifies your heart, and because of the sight which your eyes see.

[68]"And the LORD will take you back to Egypt in ships, by the way of which I said to you, 'You shall never see it again.' And there you shall be offered for sale to your enemies as male and female slaves, but no one will buy *you.*"

The Covenant Renewed in Moab

29 These *are* the words of the covenant which the LORD commanded Moses to make with the children of Israel in the land of Moab, besides the covenant which He made with them in Horeb. [2]Now Moses called all Israel and said to them: "You have seen all that the LORD did before your eyes in the land of Egypt, to Pharaoh and to all his servants and to all his land— [3]the great trials which your eyes have seen, the signs, and those great wonders. [4]Yet the LORD has not given you a heart to perceive and eyes to see and ears to hear, to this *very* day. [5]And I have led you forty years in the wilderness. Your clothes have not worn out on you, and your sandals have not worn out on your feet. [6]You have not eaten bread, nor have you drunk wine or *similar* drink, that you may know that I *am* the LORD your God. [7]And when you came to this place, Sihon king of Heshbon and Og king of Bashan came out against us to battle, and we conquered them. [8]We took their land and gave it as an inheritance to the Reubenites, to the Gadites, and to half the tribe of Manasseh. [9]Therefore keep the words of this covenant, and do them, that you may prosper in all that you do.

[10]"All of you stand today before the LORD your God: your leaders and your tribes and your elders and your officers, all the men of Israel, [11]your little ones and your wives—also the stranger who *is* in your camp, from the one who cuts your wood to the one who draws your water— [12]that you may enter into covenant with the LORD your God, and into His oath, which the LORD your God makes with you today, [13]that He may establish you today as a people for Himself, and *that* He may be God to you, just as He has spoken to you, and just as He has sworn to your fathers, to Abraham, Isaac, and Jacob.

[14]"I make this covenant and this oath, not with you alone, [15]but with *him* who stands here with us today before the LORD our God, as well as with *him* who *is* not here with us today [16](for you know that we dwelt in the land of Egypt and that we came through the nations which you passed by, [17]and you saw their abominations and their idols which *were* among them—wood and stone and silver and gold); [18]so that there may not be among you man or woman or family or tribe, whose heart turns away today from the LORD our God, to go *and* serve the gods of these nations, and that there may not be among you a root bearing bitterness or wormwood; [19]and so it may not happen, when he hears the words of this curse, that he blesses himself in his heart, saying, 'I shall have peace, even though I follow the dictates[a] of my heart'— as though the drunkard could be included with the sober. [20]"The LORD would not spare him; for then the anger of the LORD and His jealousy would burn against that man, and every curse that is written in this book would settle on him, and the LORD would blot out his name from under heaven. [21]And the LORD would separate him from all the tribes of Israel for adversity, according to all the curses of the covenant that are written in this Book of the Law, [22]so that the coming generation of your children who rise up after you, and the foreigner who comes from a far land, would say, when they see the plagues of that land and the sicknesses which the LORD has laid on it: [23]'The whole land *is* brimstone, salt, and burning; it is not sown, nor does it bear, nor

·······················

29:19 [a]Or *stubbornness*

29:2–4 The people of Israel had seen all that the Lord had done on their behalf, yet they had not fully realized all the implications of the working of God among their nation. When they were in the midst of such difficulties and trials, often their focus was on their circumstances and not on the direction of God. With time and wisdom, they would be able to look back and see the hand of God in their experiences, but even then it would require faith to receive the insight.

29:18–20 The sin of one affects a nation. Israel was a covenant community. As such, it would experience national blessing or cursing (Deut. 27:14—28:68). The individual who sinned could not expect to find anonymity within the community as a whole and escape the judgment of God. The metaphor of the "root bearing bitterness or wormwood" refers to a tree that is no longer bearing good fruit because of one branch that bears poisonous fruit. The sin of the single individual or family would affect the nation as a whole.

does any grass grow there, like the overthrow of Sodom and Gomorrah, Admah, and Zeboiim, which the LORD overthrew in His anger and His wrath.' ²⁴All nations would say, 'Why has the LORD done so to this land? What does the heat of this great anger mean?' ²⁵Then *people* would say: 'Because they have forsaken the covenant of the LORD God of their fathers, which He made with them when He brought them out of the land of Egypt; ²⁶for they went and served other gods and worshiped them, gods that they did not know and that He had not given to them. ²⁷Then the anger of the LORD was aroused against this land, to bring on it every curse that is written in this book. ²⁸And the LORD uprooted them from their land in anger, in wrath, and in great indignation, and cast them into another land, as *it is* this day.'

²⁹"The secret *things belong* to the LORD our God, but those *things which are* revealed *belong* to us and to our children forever, that *we* may do all the words of this law.

The Blessing of Returning to God

30 "Now it shall come to pass, when all these things come upon you, the blessing and the curse which I have set before you, and you call *them* to mind among all the nations where the LORD your God drives you, ²and you return to the LORD your God and obey His voice, according to all that I command you today, you and your children, with all your heart and with all your soul, ³that the LORD your God will bring you back from captivity, and have compassion on you, and gather you again from all the nations where the LORD your God has scattered you. ⁴If *any* of you are driven out to the farthest *parts* under heaven, from there the LORD your God will gather you, and from there He will bring you. ⁵Then the LORD your God will bring you to the land which your fathers possessed, and you shall possess it. He will prosper you and multiply you more than your fathers. ⁶And the LORD your God will circumcise your heart and the heart of your descendants, to love the LORD your God with all your heart and with all your soul, that you may live.

⁷Also the LORD your God will put all these curses on your enemies and on those who hate you, who persecuted you. ⁸And you will again obey the voice of the LORD and do all His commandments which I command you today. ⁹The LORD your God will make you abound in all the work of your hand, in the fruit of your body, in the increase of your livestock, and in the produce of your land for good. For the LORD will again rejoice over you for good as He rejoiced over your fathers, ¹⁰if you obey the voice of the LORD your God, to keep His commandments and His statutes which are written in this Book of the Law, *and* if you turn to the LORD your God with all your heart and with all your soul.

The Choice of Life or Death

¹¹"For this commandment which I command you today *is* not *too* mysterious for you, nor *is* it far off. ¹²It *is* not in heaven, that you should say, 'Who will ascend into heaven for us and bring it to us, that we may hear it and do it?' ¹³Nor *is* it beyond the sea, that you should say, 'Who will go over the sea for us and bring it to us, that we may hear it and do it?' ¹⁴But the word *is* very near you, in your mouth and in your heart, that you may do it.

¹⁵"See, I have set before you today life and good, death and evil, ¹⁶in that I command you today to love the LORD your God, to walk in His ways, and to keep His commandments, His statutes, and His judgments, that you may live and multiply; and the LORD your God will bless you in the land which you go to possess. ¹⁷But if your heart turns away so that you do not hear, and are drawn away, and worship other gods and serve them, ¹⁸I announce to you today that you shall surely perish; you shall not prolong *your* days in the land which you cross over the Jordan to go in and possess. ¹⁹I call heaven and earth as witnesses today against you, *that* I have set before you life and death, blessing and cursing; therefore choose life, that both you and your descendants may live; ²⁰that you may love the LORD your God, that you may obey His voice, and that you may cling to Him, for He *is* your life and the length of your days; and that you may dwell in the land which the LORD swore to your fathers, to Abraham, Isaac, and Jacob, to give them."

29:29 The secret things refer to future events or motives of God that are not disclosed to man. The "revealed" things, such as the Law of God and His will according to the Law, are sufficient to lead the people into obedience. Being acquainted with the secret things of God is not necessary to know Him and to pledge allegiance to Him.

30:1–3 Because of the grace of God, a promise of restoration is offered to the nation of Israel if the people will return wholeheartedly to the Lord.

30:6 This verse refers to the New Covenant of which Jeremiah and Ezekiel prophesied (Jer. 31:31–34; Ezek. 36:24–32). Israel will no longer be characterized by her stubbornness but by her love for her God (Deut. 9:27).

30:11–14 A special interpreter or envoy was not needed to bring the will of God to the people. Because of God's great love for His people, His commands were within reach. Indeed, the commands were in their mouths so that they were able to teach them to their children, and they were in their own hearts to be obeyed.

Joshua the New Leader of Israel

31 Then Moses went and spoke these words to all Israel. ²And he said to them: "I *am* one hundred and twenty years old today. I can no longer go out and come in. Also the LORD has said to me, 'You shall not cross over this Jordan.' ³The LORD your God Himself crosses over before you; He will destroy these nations from before you, and you shall dispossess them. Joshua himself crosses over before you, just as the LORD has said. ⁴And the LORD will do to them as He did to Sihon and Og, the kings of the Amorites and their land, when He destroyed them. ⁵The LORD will give them over to you, that you may do to them according to every commandment which I have commanded you. ⁶Be strong and of good courage, do not fear nor be afraid of them; for the LORD your God, He *is* the One who goes with you. He will not leave you nor forsake you."

⁷Then Moses called Joshua and said to him in the sight of all Israel, "Be strong and of good courage, for you must go with this people to the land which the LORD has sworn to their fathers to give them, and you shall cause them to inherit it. ⁸And the LORD, He *is* the One who goes before you. He will be with you, He will not leave you nor forsake you; do not fear nor be dismayed."

The Law to Be Read Every Seven Years

⁹So Moses wrote this law and delivered it to the priests, the sons of Levi, who bore the ark of the covenant of the LORD, and to all the elders of Israel. ¹⁰And Moses commanded them, saying: "At the end of *every* seven years, at the appointed time in the year of release, at the Feast of Tabernacles, ¹¹when all Israel comes to appear before the LORD your God in the place which He chooses, you shall read this law before all Israel in their hearing. ¹²Gather the people together, men and women and little ones, and the stranger who *is* within your gates, that they may hear and that they may learn to fear the LORD your God and carefully observe all the words of this law, ¹³and *that* their children, who have not known it, may hear and learn to fear the LORD your God as long as you live in the land which you cross the Jordan to possess."

Prediction of Israel's Rebellion

¹⁴Then the LORD said to Moses, "Behold, the days approach when you must die; call Joshua, and present yourselves in the tabernacle of meeting, that I may inaugurate him."

So Moses and Joshua went and presented themselves in the tabernacle of meeting. ¹⁵Now the LORD appeared at the tabernacle in a pillar of cloud, and the pillar of cloud stood above the door of the tabernacle.

¹⁶And the LORD said to Moses: "Behold, you will rest with your fathers; and this people will rise and play the harlot with the gods of the foreigners of the land, where they go *to be* among them, and they will forsake Me and break My covenant which I have made with them. ¹⁷Then My anger shall be aroused against them in that day, and I will forsake them, and I will hide My face from them, and they shall be devoured. And many evils and troubles shall befall them, so that they will say in that day, 'Have not these evils come upon us because our God *is* not among us?' ¹⁸And I will surely hide My face in that day because of all the evil which they have done, in that they have turned to other gods.

¹⁹"Now therefore, write down this song for yourselves, and teach it to the children of Israel; put it in their mouths, that this song may be a witness for Me against the children of Israel. ²⁰When I have brought them to the land flowing with milk and honey, of which I swore to their fathers, and they have eaten and filled themselves and grown fat, then they will turn to other gods and serve them; and they will provoke Me and break My covenant. ²¹Then it shall be, when many evils and troubles have come upon them, that this song will testify against them as a witness; for it will not be forgotten in the mouths of their descendants, for I know the inclination of their behavior today, even before I have brought them to the land of which I swore *to give them.*"

²²Therefore Moses wrote this song the same day, and taught it to the children of Israel. ²³Then He inaugurated Joshua the son of Nun, and said, "Be strong and of good courage; for you shall bring the children of Israel into the land of which I swore to them, and I will be with you."

31:2 I can no longer go out and come in is a Hebrew idiom for engaging in a day's work (Deut. 28:6). Because Moses would not be allowed to enter the Land of Promise with the nation, he would not be able to fulfill his normal daily affairs.

31:9–13 The written Law was entrusted to the Levitical priests and the elders. It was such a treasure to the people that every seven years, during the year of canceling debt, the priests were to read the entire Law at the Feast of Tabernacles (see chart, The Feasts of Israel). Traveling to the central sanctuary for the public reading of the Law reminded Israel that they were a covenant community with covenant obligations. This event was not the only time they heard the Law. If parents were obeying God's command, the Law was being repeated and taught daily (Deut. 6:6, 7, note).

31:19 Moses is instructed to write a song and to teach it to the nation. Words that are set to a melody settle deeply into the mind and are more easily recalled than just a spoken word (see Ps. 147, Music). The unforgettable song would testify to Israel's unfaithfulness to a holy God.

²⁴So it was, when Moses had completed writing the words of this law in a book, when they were finished, ²⁵that Moses commanded the Levites, who bore the ark of the covenant of the LORD, saying: ²⁶"Take this Book of the Law, and put it beside the ark of the covenant of the LORD your God, that it may be there as a witness against you; ²⁷for I know your rebellion and your stiff neck. *If* today, while I am yet alive with you, you have been rebellious against the LORD, then how much more after my death? ²⁸Gather to me all the elders of your tribes, and your officers, that I may speak these words in their hearing and call heaven and earth to witness against them. ²⁹For I know that after my death you will become utterly corrupt, and turn aside from the way which I have commanded you. And evil will befall you in the latter days, because you will do evil in the sight of the LORD, to provoke Him to anger through the work of your hands."

The Song of Moses

³⁰Then Moses spoke in the hearing of all the assembly of Israel the words of this song until they were ended:

32 "Give ear, O heavens, and I will speak;
And hear, O earth, the words of my mouth.
²Let my teaching drop as the rain,
My speech distill as the dew,
As raindrops on the tender herb,
And as showers on the grass.
³For I proclaim the name of the LORD:
Ascribe greatness to our God.
⁴*He is* the Rock, His work *is* perfect;
For all His ways *are* justice,
A God of truth and without injustice;
Righteous and upright *is* He.

⁵"They have corrupted themselves;
They are not His children,
Because of their blemish:
A perverse and crooked generation.
⁶Do you thus deal with the LORD,
O foolish and unwise people?
Is He not your Father, *who* bought you?
Has He not made you and established you?

⁷"Remember the days of old,
Consider the years of many generations.

Ask your father, and he will show you;
Your elders, and they will tell you:
⁸When the Most High divided their inheritance to the nations,
When He separated the sons of Adam,
He set the boundaries of the peoples
According to the number of the children of Israel.
⁹For the LORD's portion *is* His people;
Jacob *is* the place of His inheritance.

¹⁰"He found him in a desert land
And in the wasteland, a howling wilderness;
He encircled him, He instructed him,
He kept him as the apple of His eye.
¹¹As an eagle stirs up its nest,
Hovers over its young,
Spreading out its wings, taking them up,
Carrying them on its wings,
¹²*So* the LORD alone led him,
And *there was* no foreign god with him.

¹³"He made him ride in the heights of the earth,
That he might eat the produce of the fields;
He made him draw honey from the rock,
And oil from the flinty rock;
¹⁴Curds from the cattle, and milk of the flock,
With fat of lambs;
And rams of the breed of Bashan, and goats,
With the choicest wheat;
And you drank wine, the blood of the grapes.

¹⁵"But Jeshurun grew fat and kicked;
You grew fat, you grew thick,
You are obese!
Then he forsook God *who* made him,
And scornfully esteemed the Rock of his salvation.
¹⁶They provoked Him to jealousy with foreign *gods;*
With abominations they provoked Him to anger.
¹⁷They sacrificed to demons, not to God,
To gods they did not know,
To new *gods,* new arrivals
That your fathers did not fear.
¹⁸Of the Rock *who* begot you, you are unmindful,
And have forgotten the God who fathered you.

31:26 The Book of the Law was to be beside the ark of the covenant, which was housed in the tabernacle (see chart, The Furniture of the Tabernacle). Only the Decalogue, along with a pot of manna and Aaron's rod, was placed in the ark (Ex. 16:33; 25:16; Num. 17:10; 1 Kin. 8:9).

32:11, 12 A loving God. Moses compared the loving care of God for His people to that of an eagle for her young. An eagle teaches her young to fly by pushing them out of the nest so that they may try their wings (see chart, Female Metaphors for God). She does not leave them to fend for themselves,

however. She swoops down below and allows them to drop onto her wings, then carries them safely to the nest. The Lord, in the same manner, took Israel from captivity in Egypt and thrust them into the desert but did not leave them there to fend for themselves. He remained with the nation to give them protection, strength, and guidance.

32:15 Jeshurun (lit. "the upright one") is an ironic reference to Israel. The term reminded Israel of her calling and of her ingratitude.

¹⁹"And when the LORD saw *it*, He spurned *them*,
Because of the provocation of His sons and His daughters.
²⁰And He said: 'I will hide My face from them,
I will see what their end *will be*,
For they *are* a perverse generation,
Children in whom *is* no faith.
²¹They have provoked Me to jealousy by *what* is not God;
They have moved Me to anger by their foolish idols.
But I will provoke them to jealousy by *those who are* not a nation;
I will move them to anger by a foolish nation.
²²For a fire is kindled in My anger,
And shall burn to the lowest hell;
It shall consume the earth with her increase,
And set on fire the foundations of the mountains.

²³'I will heap disasters on them;
I will spend My arrows on them.
²⁴*They shall be* wasted with hunger,
Devoured by pestilence and bitter destruction;
I will also send against them the teeth of beasts,
With the poison of serpents of the dust.
²⁵The sword shall destroy outside;
There shall be terror within
For the young man and virgin,
The nursing child with the man of gray hairs.
²⁶I would have said, "I will dash them in pieces,
I will make the memory of them to cease from among men,"
²⁷Had I not feared the wrath of the enemy,
Lest their adversaries should misunderstand,
Lest they should say, "Our hand *is* high;
And it is not the LORD who has done all this." '

²⁸"For they *are* a nation void of counsel,
Nor *is there any* understanding in them.
²⁹Oh, that they were wise, *that* they understood this,
That they would consider their latter end!
³⁰How could one chase a thousand,
And two put ten thousand to flight,
Unless their Rock had sold them,
And the LORD had surrendered them?
³¹For their rock *is* not like our Rock,
Even our enemies themselves *being* judges.
³²For their vine *is* of the vine of Sodom
And of the fields of Gomorrah;
Their grapes *are* grapes of gall,
Their clusters *are* bitter.

³³Their wine *is* the poison of serpents,
And the cruel venom of cobras.

³⁴*Is* this not laid up in store with Me,
Sealed up among My treasures?
³⁵Vengeance is Mine, and recompense;
Their foot shall slip in *due* time;
For the day of their calamity *is* at hand,
And the things to come hasten upon them.'

³⁶"For the LORD will judge His people
And have compassion on His servants,
When He sees that *their* power is gone,
And *there is* no one *remaining,* bond or free.
³⁷He will say: 'Where *are* their gods,
The rock in which they sought refuge?
³⁸Who ate the fat of their sacrifices,
And drank the wine of their drink offering?
Let them rise and help you,
And be your refuge.

³⁹'Now see that I, *even* I, *am* He,
And *there is* no God besides Me;
I kill and I make alive;
I wound and I heal;
Nor *is there any* who can deliver from My hand.
⁴⁰For I raise My hand to heaven,
And say, "*As* I live forever,
⁴¹If I whet My glittering sword,
And My hand takes hold on judgment,
I will render vengeance to My enemies,
And repay those who hate Me.
⁴²I will make My arrows drunk with blood,
And My sword shall devour flesh,
With the blood of the slain and the captives,
From the heads of the leaders of the enemy." '

⁴³"Rejoice, O Gentiles, *with* His people;^a
For He will avenge the blood of His servants,
And render vengeance to His adversaries;
He will provide atonement for His land *and* His people."

⁴⁴So Moses came with Joshua^a the son of Nun and spoke all the words of this song in the hearing of the people. ⁴⁵Moses finished speaking all these words to all Israel, ⁴⁶and he said to them: "Set your hearts on all the words which I testify among you today, which you shall command your

· · · · · · · · · · · · · · · · · · · ·

32:43 ^aA Dead Sea Scroll fragment adds *And let all the gods (angels) worship Him* (compare Septuagint and Hebrews 1:6).   **32:44** ^aHebrew *Hoshea* (compare Numbers 13:8, 16)

32:40 Raising the hand symbolized making an oath. Normally an oath was initiated by the statement, "As the Lord lives, I will . . ." However, here the Lord swears by His own name and authenticates the oath.

32:46, 47 The words of the Lord were to be the desire and life of the people of Israel. The Law was not to be considered insignificant or secondary, for it was the essence of life. Their obedience to the Law would determine their quality of life.

children to be careful to observe— all the words of this law. ⁴⁷For it *is* not a futile thing for you, because it *is* your life, and by this word you shall prolong *your* days in the land which you cross over the Jordan to possess."

Moses to Die on Mount Nebo

⁴⁸Then the LORD spoke to Moses that very same day, saying: ⁴⁹"Go up this mountain of the Abarim, Mount Nebo, which *is* in the land of Moab, across from Jericho; view the land of Canaan, which I give to the children of Israel as a possession; ⁵⁰and die on the mountain which you ascend, and be gathered to your people, just as Aaron your brother died on Mount Hor and was gathered to his people; ⁵¹because you trespassed against Me among the children of Israel at the waters of Meribah Kadesh, in the Wilderness of Zin, because you did not hallow Me in the midst of the children of Israel. ⁵²Yet you shall see the land before *you*, though you shall not go there, into the land which I am giving to the children of Israel."

Moses' Final Blessing on Israel

33 Now this *is* the blessing with which Moses the man of God blessed the children of Israel before his death. ²And he said:

"The LORD came from Sinai,
  And dawned on them from Seir;
  He shone forth from Mount Paran,
  And He came with ten thousands of saints;
  From His right hand
  Came a fiery law for them.
³Yes, He loves the people;
  All His saints *are* in Your hand;
  They sit down at Your feet;
  Everyone receives Your words.
⁴Moses commanded a law for us,
  A heritage of the congregation of Jacob.
⁵And He was King in Jeshurun,
  When the leaders of the people were
    gathered,
  All the tribes of Israel together.

⁶"Let Reuben live, and not die,
  Nor let his men be few."

⁷And this he said of Judah:

"Hear, LORD, the voice of Judah,
  And bring him to his people;
  Let his hands be sufficient for him,
  And may You be a help against his enemies."

⁸And of Levi he said:

"*Let* Your Thummim and Your Urim *be* with Your
    holy one,
  Whom You tested at Massah,
  And with whom You contended at the waters
    of Meribah,
⁹Who says of his father and mother,
  'I have not seen them';
  Nor did he acknowledge his brothers,
  Or know his own children;
  For they have observed Your word
  And kept Your covenant.
¹⁰They shall teach Jacob Your judgments,
  And Israel Your law.
  They shall put incense before You,
  And a whole burnt sacrifice on Your altar.
¹¹Bless his substance, LORD,
  And accept the work of his hands;
  Strike the loins of those who rise against him,
  And of those who hate him, that they rise not
    again."

¹²Of Benjamin he said:

"The beloved of the LORD shall dwell in safety by
    Him,
  Who shelters him all the day long;
  And he shall dwell between His shoulders."

¹³And of Joseph he said:

"Blessed of the LORD *is* his land,
  With the precious things of heaven, with the dew,

32:49 Mt. Nebo is a peak in the Abarim mountain range, overlooking the northern coast of the Dead Sea. Moses forfeited his right to enter the Promised Land because of disobedience (Num. 20:1–13), but by God's grace, he was permitted to see the Land.

33:1 Moses, acting as a father to the nation of Israel, invoked a blessing upon Israel before his death. In a similar passage, Jacob blessed his sons (Gen. 49).

33:7 Judah marched at the head of the army of Israel. In this position, the tribe would be most vulnerable to attack. Moses prayed for Judah to have military success by God's help.

33:8 The blessing of Levi was for strength and protection to perform duties of education and worship. The "Thummim" (Heb., lit. "perfections") and the "Urim" (Heb., lit. "lights"),

the two stones kept in the high priest's breastplate, were used to determine the will of God in matters where the decision was difficult. The method for accomplishing this task is uncertain, however. The stones were apparently inscribed with the words "Urim" and "Thummim." The "Urim" may have symbolized a negative answer and the "Thummim" a positive answer, though there is no absolute certainty how they were used. When the stones were tossed by the high priest, if both stones showed Urim, the answer was a negative one. If Thummim was shown on both stones, then the answer was a positive one (see Ex. 28:15, note). Perhaps more than anything else, the stones represented the faithfulness of the Lord in giving wisdom to the high priest as he led the people and represented them before the Lord.

ATTRIBUTES OF GOD · HE IS RIGHTEOUS

As the ultimate standard for right, God always does the right thing (Ps. 18:30). The idea of righteousness (Heb. *tsedeq*) is "to be straight." It denotes a right behavior, conforming to an ethical or moral standard.

God is the standard of "right"—His ways are right because He is right (Ps. 145:17). He loves His standards (Ps. 45:7) and never deviates from them (1 John 1:5). His only limitation is what He chooses to place on Himself.

God's righteousness is immovable (Ps. 36:5, 6). In other words, His standards are nonnegotiable. Often His righteousness is coupled with judgment (Ps. 36:6; 50:1–6). He is the perfect Judge—fair, just, and consistent. He does wrong to no one—ever!

Setting your own standards about what is right and wrong is an attempt at being God and as such is doomed to failure (Rom. 3:10). Though you cannot determine righteousness (Rom. 10:3), you can become righteous in Christ (2 Cor. 5:21) and be led in the paths of righteousness through His presence within (Ps. 23:3).

One day you will be clothed and crowned in righteousness (Rev. 19:8). In other words, a day will come when you will always want to live and be able to live the right way.

See also Ps. 11:7; 116:5; Lam. 3:22, note; Rev. 19:11; notes on Attributes of God (Ex. 33; Deut. 4; 2 Chr. 19; Job 23; 42; Ps. 25; 90; 102; 119; Is. 6; 65; Jer. 23; Rom. 2; Eph. 1; 1 John 5); Holiness (Lev. 20); Fear of the Lord (Prov. 2); Worship (Deut. 12)

And the deep lying beneath,
14 With the precious fruits of the sun,
With the precious produce of the months,
15 With the best things of the ancient mountains,
With the precious things of the everlasting hills,
16 With the precious things of the earth and its fullness,
And the favor of Him who dwelt in the bush.
Let *the blessing* come 'on the head of Joseph,
And on the crown of the head of him *who was* separate from his brothers.'[a]
17 His glory *is like* a firstborn bull,
And his horns *like* the horns of the wild ox;
Together with them
He shall push the peoples
To the ends of the earth;
They *are* the ten thousands of Ephraim,
And they *are* the thousands of Manasseh."

18 And of Zebulun he said:

"Rejoice, Zebulun, in your going out,
And Issachar in your tents!
19 They shall call the peoples *to* the mountain;
There they shall offer sacrifices of righteousness;
For they shall partake *of* the abundance of the seas
And *of* treasures hidden in the sand."

20 And of Gad he said:

"Blessed *is* he who enlarges Gad;
He dwells as a lion,
And tears the arm and the crown of his head.

21 He provided the first *part* for himself,
Because a lawgiver's portion was reserved there.
He came *with* the heads of the people;
He administered the justice of the Lord,
And His judgments with Israel."

22 And of Dan he said:

"Dan *is* a lion's whelp;
He shall leap from Bashan."

23 And of Naphtali he said:

"O Naphtali, satisfied with favor,
And full of the blessing of the Lord,
Possess the west and the south."

24 And of Asher he said:

"Asher *is* most blessed of sons;
Let him be favored by his brothers,
And let him dip his foot in oil.
25 Your sandals *shall be* iron and bronze;
As your days, *so shall* your strength *be.*

26 "*There is* no one like the God of Jeshurun,
Who rides the heavens to help you,
And in His excellency on the clouds.
27 The eternal God *is your* refuge,
And underneath *are* the everlasting arms;
He will thrust out the enemy from before you,
And will say, 'Destroy!'
28 Then Israel shall dwell in safety,

33:16 [a]Genesis 49:26

33:18, 19 **These two tribes** would find their prosperity from the sea through fishing and commerce (Gen. 49:13–15).

The fountain of Jacob alone,
In a land of grain and new wine;
His heavens shall also drop dew.
²⁹Happy *are* you, O Israel!
Who *is* like you, a people saved by the LORD,
The shield of your help
And the sword of your majesty!
Your enemies shall submit to you,
And you shall tread down their high places."

Moses Dies on Mount Nebo

34 Then Moses went up from the plains of Moab to Mount Nebo, to the top of Pisgah, which is across from Jericho. And the LORD showed him all the land of Gilead as far as Dan, ²all Naphtali and the land of Ephraim and Manasseh, all the land of Judah as far as the Western Sea,ᵃ ³the South, and the plain of the Valley of Jericho, the city of palm trees, as far as Zoar. ⁴Then the LORD said to him, "This *is* the land of which I swore to give Abraham, Isaac, and Jacob, saying, 'I will give it to your descendants.' I have caused you to see *it* with your eyes, but you shall not cross over there."

⁵So Moses the servant of the LORD died there in the land of Moab, according to the word of the LORD. ⁶And He buried him in a valley in the land of Moab, opposite Beth Peor; but no one knows his grave to this day. ⁷Moses *was* one hundred and twenty years old when he died. His eyes were not dim nor his natural vigor diminished. ⁸And the children of Israel wept for Moses in the plains of Moab thirty days. So the days of weeping *and* mourning for Moses ended.

⁹Now Joshua the son of Nun was full of the spirit of wisdom, for Moses had laid his hands on him; so the children of Israel heeded him, and did as the LORD had commanded Moses.

¹⁰But since then there has not arisen in Israel a prophet like Moses, whom the LORD knew face to face, ¹¹in all the signs and wonders which the LORD sent him to do in the land of Egypt, before Pharaoh, before all his servants, and in all his land, ¹²and by all that mighty power and all the great terror which Moses performed in the sight of all Israel.

34:2 ᵃThat is, the Mediterranean

34:6 The people of Israel no doubt watched as Moses ascended Mt. Nebo until he was no longer in their sight. Jewish tradition states that God took away the soul of Moses with a kiss. No one knows the manner in which Moses died, only that he died according to the word of the Lord and was buried by God Himself. So special was Moses to the heart of God that his death was not a public matter but a private communion between two good friends.

34:10–12 Moses was the greatest of all the prophets, and the signs and wonders performed through him were unequaled throughout Israel's history. However, nothing Moses experienced can surpass the greatness of being known intimately by God (1 Cor. 8:3).

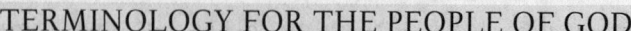

TERMINOLOGY FOR THE PEOPLE OF GOD

HEBREWS

The term "Hebrews," an alternate designation for the Israelites, often is applied by foreigners (Gen. 39:14; Ex. 1:16), although on occasion the term "Hebrew" is applied also by the Israelites to themselves (Ex. 1:15–19; Jon. 1:9). In such cases the terms Hebrew and Israelite are interchangeable. The ancestor of the Hebrews is identified as Eber, son of Shem (Gen. 10:21–32). Abraham, Nahor, and Lot are included among his descendants (Gen. 11:10–32). Abraham is the ancestor of the Hebrews, Nahor of the Arameans, and Lot of the Moabites and Ammonites. Abraham is called "the Hebrew" (Gen. 14:13). Generally the term "Hebrew" is an ethnic term.

JEWS

In the postexilic period, the designation "Jew" referred to a member of the Babylonian or Persian province of Judah (Neh. 4:1; Esth. 9:15–19; Zech. 8:23). In Esther 8:17, the term refers to a proselyte to the Jewish faith. The designation "Jew" also appears in Jeremiah, whose ministry is dated in the late seventh and early sixth centuries B.C. (Jer. 32:12; 40:11). Thus, the usage of the term "Jew" was somewhat fluid in biblical times. A person may be characterized as a Jew by religion and/or by ethnic origin.

ISRAEL

The name "Israel" first is applied to the patriarch Jacob after his encounter with God at Peniel (Gen. 32:28). Israel also functions in the Old Testament as a designation for God's people as a whole. Israel, the children of Israel, and the twelve tribes of Israel designate God's people during the times of their sojourn in Egypt, the Exodus from Egypt, their journey in the wilderness, their entry into Canaan under Joshua, and during the time of the judges and Samuel (Gen. 49:28; Deut. 33:5, 10, 28).

ZION

Zion appears in the Old Testament as a designation for the people of Jerusalem as a community (Joel 2:23; Is. 3:16; Jer. 4:31).

TERMINOLOGY FOR THE LAND

PALESTINE

The term "Palestine" originated from the name of the *Pelishtim* or Philistines (1 Sam. 4:1), one of the tribes of Sea Peoples who invaded the area early in the twelfth century B.C. Since these Sea Peoples dominated the Canaanites and also took possession of the most accessible part of the land, their name was applied by strangers to the whole land. In the Old Testament, the designation "Philistia" is used, not for the whole land, but only for the southern seacoast plain, Philistia proper (see Ex. 15:14; Is. 14:29–31; Joel 3:4). In modern usage the designation "Palestine" is applied to the whole territory allotted to the Twelve Tribes, located both east and west of the Jordan River.

CANAAN

In the Old Testament, "Canaan" designated the whole territory west of the Jordan inhabited by the Canaanites (Gen. 12:5; Num. 33:51). In other passages the Canaanites appear to be occupants of a limited area along the coast or in the plain (Num. 13:29; 14:25; Josh. 11:3). Thus, in the Old Testament, the designation "Canaan" may refer to a limited area or to the whole area west of the Jordan.

ISRAEL

References to both God's people and the Promised Land as "Israel" appear in the time of the early monarchy during the reigns of Saul, David, and Solomon. Saul was anointed king over Israel (1 Sam. 9:16, 17). David also was anointed by Samuel as king over Israel in place of Saul (1 Sam. 16:1, 13). In reality, David reigned first as king of Judah, establishing his capital at Hebron (2 Sam. 2:4, 11). Ishbosheth, son of Saul, reigned over Israel (2 Sam. 2:8–10). Eventually David ruled over all Israel, including Judah, establishing his capital at Jerusalem (2 Sam. 5:1–5). Solomon inherited the kingdom of his father David (1 Kin. 2:11, 12; 4:1).

Following Solomon's reign and the division of the kingdom in 931 B.C., Israel became the designation for the northern kingdom, consisting essentially of ten tribes (1 Kin. 11:30, 31). The northern kingdom also is termed the "house of Israel" (Hos. 5:1; Amos 5:1; Mic. 1:5). "Israel" is used to designate the southern kingdom, after the fall of the northern kingdom in 722 B.C. (Ezra 1:3; 4:3).

TERMINOLOGY FOR THE DIVIDED KINGDOM

NORTHERN KINGDOM	SOUTHERN KINGDOM
This designation was applied to the northern ten tribes following the division of the kingdom (931 B.C.). Alternate designations for the northern kingdom include Israel, Ephraim, and Samaria (Hos. 4:16, 17; 7:1).	The southern kingdom is an alternate designation for Judah applied after the division of the kingdom in 931 B.C. The tribe of Simeon (and/or Benjamin) was included in this terminology.

EPHRAIM	JUDAH
The basis for the designation of Israel as Ephraim resulted from the outcome of the Syro-Ephraimitic War (734 B.C.) in which Israel lost its peripheral territories and was reduced to the area originally occupied by the tribes of Ephraim and Manasseh. Because Ephraim, the most influential tribe in the north, overshadowed Manasseh, the title "Ephraim" became associated with the area.	Judah was the designation for the southern kingdom following the division of the kingdom in 931 B.C. When Jeroboam I led the northern tribes to revolt, the southern tribe of Judah remained loyal to Rehoboam and stayed faithful to the Davidic dynasty until its fall in 586 B.C. Basically this area consisted of territory belonging to the tribes of Judah and Simeon. The chronicler designated the inhabitants of the south as "Judah and Benjamin" (1 Chr. 12:16; 2 Chr. 11:1). After the fall of the northern kingdom, Judah sometimes was designated as Israel (Ezra 1:3; 4:3).

SAMARIA	ZION
This is an alternate designation for Ephraim, the northern kingdom, and Israel. This northern area did not become so designated until Samaria became its capital under Omri in the ninth century B.C. After the fall of the northern kingdom (722 B.C.) and the deportation of its inhabitants, the Assyrians settled captives from other areas in the cities of Samaria (2 Kin. 17:24-26). The Assyrians called the territory the province of Samerena and ruled it until the late seventh century B.C. King Josiah of Judah (640-609 B.C.) was able to destroy the high places in the cities of Samaria (2 Kin. 23:19). With the fall of Nineveh, the capital of Assyria, in 612 B.C., the territory of Samaria became a Babylonian province. After the southern kingdom fell in 586 B.C., the northern hill country of Judah, including Jerusalem, became a part of the province of Samaria. With the conquest of the Persians in 539 B.C., the territory became a province or satrapy of the Persian Empire. In the period of Ezra (about 450 B.C.) and Nehemiah (about 445-424 B.C.), the governors of Samaria attempted to prevent the exiles from rebuilding the temple and the walls (Ezra 4:4-24; Neh. 2:9-20). In Nehemiah's time, the hill country of northern Judah was made a separate province, and the southern border of Samaria was established approximately in its pre-Babylonian location. This area became the center of the Samaritans, following the split between Jews and Samaritans in the time of Ezra and Nehemiah.	The name "Zion" first appeared (2 Sam. 5:6-10; 1 Chr. 11:4-9) in connection with David's conquest of Jerusalem. "Zion" there referred to a specific fortified hill. The term "Zion" later was extended to the temple area itself (Ps. 2:6; 132:13). Zion became an equivalent of Jerusalem (Is. 28:16; 40:9; Joel 3:16; Mic. 3:10). Zion also became equivalent to the heavenly Jerusalem in the New Testament (Rev. 14:1).

Joshua

TERMINOLOGY FOR THE DIVIDED KINGDOM
NORTHERN KINGDOM
JUDAH

TITLE

Joshua's birth name was *Hoshea* (Heb., lit. "salvation," Num. 13:8), but Moses called him "Joshua" (Heb. *yehoshua,* lit. "the Lord saves"; Num. 13:16). "Jesus" is the Greek form of the Hebrew "Joshua." While parts of the book appear to be written after Joshua's death (Josh. 10:12, 13; 24:29–33), tradition identifies Joshua as the primary author of the work. Assuming that Joshua and his fellow spy Caleb were of similar age when they were part of the original spy mission to Canaan forty years earlier, Joshua would have been about eighty years old when the Israelites entered the Promised Land.

AUTHOR

Joshua was divinely prepared to lead the Israelites (see chart, Preparation for Leadership). He had been a slave, a free man, a man without a country, the general of an ill-equipped nomadic army, a conqueror against incredible odds, a land agent, a statesman, and a settler. He witnessed extraordinary miracles: the ten plagues of Egypt, the parting of the Red Sea and the Jordan River, the miraculous provision of food for forty years in the wilderness, water flowing from rocks, city walls falling down, the sun standing still, and army after army falling away at his approach.

DATE

The Book of Joshua covers approximately thirty years during what is now called the Late Bronze Age (1500–1200 B.C.). The actual invasion probably occurred about 1405 B.C. during the reign of Amenhotep III in Egypt (see Deut. 1:3–8; 1 Kin. 6:1).

BACKGROUND

SETTING: The first five books of the Bible (the Pentateuch) provide background for the Book of Joshua. The people's preparation began in Genesis with the promise of the Land to Abraham, Isaac, and Jacob (Gen. 12:1–3, 7; 13:15; 15:7, 18; 17:8; 26:3; 28:13). Preparation continued as for two centuries Abraham's descendants lived in the Land but never fully controlled it.

For the next four centuries the Israelites lived in Egypt. The Book of Exodus records their escape from slavery and the giving of the Law. Leviticus prepares them for worship. Numbers and Deuteronomy provide for them a civic structure. Even the language in Joshua's account detailing Israel's entry into the Land is similar to the Deuteronomy description of Israel's preparation for entry into the Promised Land. The Book of Joshua refers to the Pentateuch as a completed entity normative for that generation (Josh. 1:7, 8).

Although the Law and Israel's special covenant relationship with God defined the nation's identity, God also had promised the Israelites a Land of their own. The Book of Joshua is the record of their conquest of that Land under God's leadership.

Canaan, the strategic land bridge connecting Africa with Asia and ultimately with Europe, is a unique land (see chart, Terminology for the Land). It links the Indian Ocean

(via the Red Sea) with the Atlantic Ocean (via the Mediterranean). It claims more military occupations, battles, and blood baths than any country on the globe; at least thirty world powers have trampled its soil. People living in this land need a special relationship with their defender.

The Promised Land was a pagan land. Though God had placed a witness to Himself in the land with the election of Abraham and his descendants as His chosen people, the people of Canaan persisted in the worship of numerous gods and goddesses. By the time of the conquest, the religious climate of Canaan had grown so decadent that a variety of detestable practices expressly forbidden to the Israelites, including cult prostitution and child sacrifice, had evolved (Lev. 18:21; Deut. 12:31; 23:17).

Egypt, the political Goliath of the day, showed little concern. Other political powers had waned, and Canaan's own native inhabitants lacked unity. The timing for the Israelite invasion was perfect.

PURPOSE: The book is a reminder to the Israelites, including future generations, that their Land was a gift from God and that their possession of the Land was the fulfillment of His promise. What began as a promise to Abraham, Isaac, and Jacob, and continued through Moses now would be fulfilled under Joshua.

The faithfulness of Joshua's generation would be tested in battle. Greater tests would come, however, as future generations changed from the nomadic life of herdsmen to a new life as permanent settlers.

THEMES

Though Joshua is a history book, its primary theme is the faithfulness of God as exhibited repeatedly through His presence, power, protection, provision, and fulfilled promises. A secondary theme is the faithfulness of God's people. The Israelites were about to enter an advanced culture of experienced farmers whose life was tied elaborately to the worship of pagan gods of nature; those gods would be a constant temptation to the Israelites. Their willingness to obey God would be tested, and many times they failed the test. Yet God's faithfulness never ceased.

OUTLINE

God's Commission to Joshua

1 After the death of Moses the servant of the LORD, it came to pass that the LORD spoke to Joshua the son of Nun, Moses' assistant, saying: [2]"Moses My servant is dead. Now therefore, arise, go over this Jordan, you and all this people, to the land which I am giving to them—the children of Israel. [3]Every place that the sole of your foot will tread upon I have given you, as I said to Moses. [4]From the wilderness and this Lebanon as far as the great river, the River Euphrates, all the land of the Hittites, and to the Great Sea toward the going down of the sun, shall be your territory. [5]No man shall *be able to* stand before you all the days of your life; as I was with Moses, *so* I will be with you. I will not leave you nor forsake you. [6]Be strong and of good courage, for to this people you shall divide as an inheritance the land which I swore to their fathers to give them. [7]Only be strong and very courageous, that you may observe to do according to all the law which Moses My servant commanded you; do not turn from it to the right hand or to the left, that you may prosper wherever you go. [8]This Book of the Law shall not depart from your mouth, but you shall meditate in it day and night, that you may observe to do according to all that is written in it. For then you will make your way prosperous, and then you will have good success. [9]Have I not commanded you? Be strong and of good courage; do not be afraid, nor be dismayed, for the LORD your God *is* with you wherever you go."

The Order to Cross the Jordan

[10]Then Joshua commanded the officers of the people, saying, [11]"Pass through the camp and command the people, saying, 'Prepare provisions for yourselves, for within three days you will cross over this Jordan, to go in to possess the land which the LORD your God is giving you to possess.'"

[12]And to the Reubenites, the Gadites, and half the tribe of Manasseh Joshua spoke, saying, [13]"Remember the word which Moses the servant of the LORD commanded you, saying, 'The LORD your God is giving you rest and is giving you this land.' [14]Your wives, your little ones, and your livestock shall remain in the land which Moses gave you on this side of the Jordan. But you shall pass before your brethren armed, all your mighty men of valor, and help them, [15]until the LORD has given your brethren rest, as He *gave* you, and they also have taken possession of the land which the LORD your God is giving them. Then you shall return to the land of your possession and enjoy it, which Moses the LORD's servant gave you on this side of the Jordan toward the sunrise."

[16]So they answered Joshua, saying, "All that you command us we will do, and wherever you send us we will go. [17]Just as we heeded Moses in all things, so we will heed you. Only the LORD your God be with you, as He was with Moses. [18]Whoever rebels against your command and does not heed your words, in all that you command him, shall be put to death. Only be strong and of good courage."

Rahab Hides the Spies

2 Now Joshua the son of Nun sent out two men from Acacia Grove[a] to spy secretly, saying, "Go, view the land, especially Jericho."

So they went, and came to the house of a har-

••••••••••••••••••

2:1 [a]Hebrew *Shittim*

1:1 The Israelites had been at the border of the Promised Land 40 years earlier (Num. 13:1—14:45), at which time the people had doubted that God could accomplish His promises. They refused to enter Canaan, and their disobedience resulted in God's judgment (see chart, Tale of Two Committees). None of the adults except Joshua and Caleb were allowed to enter the Land (Josh. 5:6; see chart, Caleb: Portrait of a Hero). The death of Moses completed this judgment. God was ready to lead the Israelites into the Land as He had promised. Joshua's position as "assistant" indicates a unique position of personal service, and thus the new leader of Israel began with a direct communication from the Lord (see chart, Preparation for Leadership).

1:2 The crossing of the Jordan was considered the first step of the campaign (Deut. 32:47; Josh. 3:10–13). Although normally not very wide this close to Jericho, at flood stage the river could have been a mile wide.

1:3 Treading upon the soil symbolized acceptance of property ownership (Deut. 11:24; Josh. 14:9); handing your shoe to another symbolized the transfer of land (Ruth 4:7, note). The transaction bound the new owners to the law, the land, and the god of that region. God used the same formula (Law, Josh. 1:7, 8; Land, v. 2; Himself, vv. 5, 9).

1:6 Repetition was typically used by the Hebrews for emphasis, with the threefold repetition as the highest degree (vv. 6, 7, 9; see also Is. 6:3; John 21:15–17). God's renewed promise to guide Joshua not only through the conquest but also through the distribution of the Land followed (Josh. 13—21; see map, The Division of the Land).

1:8 The command to meditate on God's Law (the Torah) included incorporating its teachings into one's lifestyle as the basis of true success in life.

1:12–15 The Reubenites, the Gadites, and half the tribe of Manasseh already had claimed and settled the Land east of the Jordan with the understanding that they would fight alongside their brothers until the rest of the Land was conquered. This commitment was important for the unity of the nation and demonstrated the faith of these tribes that God would provide for and protect those left behind while the fighting men were away (Num. 34:14, 15).

2:1 Ancient Jericho (Heb., lit. "moon" and thus "moon city") may be the oldest city in the world and likely was dedicated to the worship of a moon god. Located about five miles west of the Jordan River, Jericho was an oasis in the Dead Sea area. This fortress city controlled the entrance to the Land. The

lot named Rahab, and lodged there. ²And it was told the king of Jericho, saying, "Behold, men have come here tonight from the children of Israel to search out the country."

³So the king of Jericho sent to Rahab, saying, "Bring out the men who have come to you, who have entered your house, for they have come to search out all the country."

⁴Then the woman took the two men and hid them. So she said, "Yes, the men came to me, but I did not know where they *were* from. ⁵And it happened as the gate was being shut, when it was dark, that the men went out. Where the men went I do not know; pursue them quickly, for you may overtake them." ⁶(But she had brought them up to the roof and hidden them with the stalks of flax, which she had laid in order on the roof.) ⁷Then the men pursued them by the road to the Jordan, to the fords. And as soon as those who pursued them had gone out, they shut the gate.

⁸Now before they lay down, she came up to them on the roof, ⁹and said to the men: "I know that the LORD has given you the land, that the terror of you has fallen on us, and that all the inhabitants of the land are fainthearted because of you. ¹⁰For we have heard how the LORD dried up the water of the Red Sea for you when you came out of Egypt, and what you did to the two kings of the Amorites who *were* on the other side of the Jordan, Sihon and Og, whom you utterly destroyed. ¹¹And as soon as we heard *these things*, our hearts melted; neither did there remain any more courage in anyone because of you, for the LORD your God, He *is* God in heaven above and on earth beneath. ¹²Now therefore, I beg you, swear to me by the LORD, since I have shown you kindness, that you also will show kindness to my father's house,

and give me a true token, ¹³and spare my father, my mother, my brothers, my sisters, and all that they have, and deliver our lives from death."

¹⁴So the men answered her, "Our lives for yours, if none of you tell this business of ours. And it shall be, when the LORD has given us the land, that we will deal kindly and truly with you."

¹⁵Then she let them down by a rope through the window, for her house *was* on the city wall; she dwelt on the wall. ¹⁶And she said to them, "Get to the mountain, lest the pursuers meet you. Hide there three days, until the pursuers have returned. Afterward you may go your way."

¹⁷So the men said to her: "We *will be* blameless of this oath of yours which you have made us swear, ¹⁸unless, *when* we come into the land, you bind this line of scarlet cord in the window through which you let us down, and unless you bring your father, your mother, your brothers, and all your father's household to your own home. ¹⁹So it shall be *that* whoever goes outside the doors of your house into the street, his blood *shall be* on his own head, and we *will be* guiltless. And whoever is with you in the house, his blood *shall be* on our head if a hand is laid on him. ²⁰And if you tell this business of ours, then we will be free from your oath which you made us swear."

²¹Then she said, "According to your words, so *be* it." And she sent them away, and they departed. And she bound the scarlet cord in the window.

²²They departed and went to the mountain, and stayed there three days until the pursuers returned. The pursuers sought *them* all along the way, but did not find *them.* ²³So the two men returned, descended from the mountain, and crossed over; and they came to Joshua the son of Nun, and told him all that had befallen them.

conquest of Jericho formed the initial stage of Joshua's military strategy of "divide and conquer." Rahab's house was probably built over the gap between the two walls, 12 to 15 feet apart, a common practice in that day (v. 15). Rahab is described as a "harlot" (Heb. *zanah*). There is no evidence that she was a sacred prostitute in the service of her pagan gods (see Rahab). Prostitution was practiced commonly in the Canaanite culture. Lodging in the house of a prostitute may have been a way for the spies to avoid detection when entering and leaving the city.

2:9 The spies needed help, and Rahab needed protection. Apparently of all the inhabitants of Jericho, Rahab alone believed in Israel's God. Her words are an indictment of the Israelites whose unbelief caused them to lose 40 years in the wilderness. In effect, she told them the battle had been won when God delivered them from Egypt (vv. 10, 11). Rahab did lie to protect the spies (vv. 4, 5), for deception and espionage are part of warfare. Scripture unequivocally forbids lying, and nowhere does God condone Rahab's lying (Prov. 12:22). However, we must affirm Rahab's great faith and leave any judgment of her to God. Extenuating circumstances challenged the new faith of this resourceful woman, and God honored

her faith by giving her a place in the lineage of the Messiah (Matt. 1:5).

2:11 Our hearts melted indicated physical and emotional distress resulting in the inability to act (Ps. 97:5). Rahab's words confirm the fulfillment of Moses' song of victory after crossing the Red Sea (Ex. 15:14–16). Rahab drew a contrast between the one God of Israel and the many gods of the Canaanites. Unlike the Canaanite gods, *Yahweh* is not a god of a particular place and function; rather He is supreme everywhere. He is actively involved in the lives and events of His people (Josh. 2:9–11). In contrast, the Canaanite gods competed for rule, were limited to particular areas and functions, and were involved with their own lusts, murders, and intrigues.

2:12–21 Middle Eastern culture centered around the family and clan. The faith and actions of one member could affect the whole family (see Josh. 7:24, 25; chart, Temptation: The Analysis of a Successful Trap). The agreement between Rahab and the spies required faithfulness on both sides (Josh. 2:14). Rahab was to keep secret the activities of the spies, bring all her family into her house, and display the scarlet cord (vv. 14, 17, 18). The spies were to see that all Israel spared her house and everyone in it.

Perspective by Roberta Hromas

BEGINNING TO READ AND STUDY THE BIBLE (From *Passport to the Bible*)

The Bible tells us how to know God . . . how to find eternal life . . . and how to experience genuine life in our inner person. It gives health to our souls and tells us how to heal broken relationships. The answers to life's questions are found in the Bible. But where does a person begin in reading and studying the Bible. Here's an approach that has been effective in the lives of many people around the world:

Start By Reading Ten Minutes a Day. The truth of the Bible is like food for your soul. The Bible will literally become a part of you, and your hunger for God's Word will increase if you begin reading God's Word daily. If you find that ten minutes a day isn't enough to satisfy your spiritual hunger for the Word, try ten minutes in the morning and ten minutes in the evening. You may need several ten-minute feedings throughout the day.

Make sure you have a small, readable copy of the Bible that you can carry with you. Ask God to guide your reading. If you have difficulty concentrating as your read, read the Bible out loud.

Read as if God Is Speaking Directly to You. Always look for the personal application. God knows the number of hairs on your head, and he desires to make his Word come alive to you in practical, personal ways. This does not mean that you are the sole source of interpreting the Bible or that you can bend the Bible's message to fit your own life and your own ideas. Bible truths are eternal and absolute. The Bible spans all cultures, history, social levels, and occupations, all ages, races, and nationalities. But the way in which a particular passage of the Bible applies to your circumstances and your experience is unique to you each day. If a verse stands out to you in a particular way, write it down on a card and carry it with you all day. Read it over and over. Think about why the verse stood out to you.

Five Ways to Study the Bible. In addition to your daily reading of the Bible, discipline yourself to engage periodically in a more in-depth study of the Bible. Here are five approaches to Bible study:

- *Word and Subject Studies.* This approach to study begins with the question, "I wonder what the Bible has to say about . . . ?" The word or topic you choose is the subject of your study! Use a concordance to look up various references from Genesis to Revelation. With pencil and paper in hand, begin to look up references, and as you read each one, write down a few words that summarize what you believe to be a practical meaning or application of the verse to your life. Be sure to look up a number of verses or passages in both the Old Testament and New Testament—perhaps a dozen or more verses or passages. You may also want to look up synonyms (similar words) and antonyms (opposite words).

  Word and subject studies make great devotional studies to share with others. They reveal the nature of God and God's "opinion" on a wide variety of problems and issues.

- *Journey Studies.* The Bible tells the story of many journeys—both journeys of individuals and the journey of the children of God. A study of these journeys can help us see that life happens in stages . . . situations do change . . . and that no circumstance lasts forever. Life has good times and bad times. You may want to study the journeys of these men and women: Joseph, the Children of Israel as they left Egypt, Abraham and Sarah, David, Paul, and most certainly, Jesus. Journey studies lead us to an understanding that life is in constant motion and that natural life has a *progression* to it.

- *Progression Studies.* In progression studies we are concerned with progress in our *spiritual* lives. The Christian life must have an *upward* trend so that we are always growing more into the likeness of Christ, closer to God, and upward in spirit. Some very familiar passages may be read in a progressive way that reveals growth toward spiritual maturity, including the Beatitude portion of the Sermon on the Mount (Matt. 5:3–12), Psalm 22–24 (which gives insight into Jesus as our Shepherd), Galatians 5:22–23 (one character trait gives rise to the next as we bear the fruit of the Spirit), Ephesians 3:14–19 (a spiritual progression for those who pray with boldness and confidence), 1 Thessalonians 5:16–18 (for those who are living in the day of the Lord's return). As you engage in a progression study, read the whole before dissecting the parts. Look for a strong relationship among the verses—don't contrive a relationship that doesn't exist; check your progression with other Scriptures; keep in mind that the last verse or last passage must bring you closer to Jesus than the first.

- *Type and Shadow Studies.* A rewarding way to study the Old Testament is to look for the people, objects, and events that cast spiritual shadows. These studies reflect "types" of experiences and events that happen to us on a spiritual level today. In themselves, the stories are about Old Testament people and events. The *shadows* of these stories tell us more about God, outlining for us the nature and working of God on the spiritual level. As such, they tell us a great deal about our spiritual selves and help us understand our spiritual purpose. Type and shadow studies reveal the interplay of the Holy Spirit and Jesus in our lives as we make the steps.

  How do these studies differ from Journey and Progression studies?

- Journey studies show how God works in our natural lives; type and shadow studies, in contrast, show us the master plan for our lives in the context of eternity.

- Progression studies make us aware of the steps that occur in spiritual growth. A type and shadow study, in contrast, tells us how these steps occur and why.

  The story of Ruth (Book of Ruth) is a good story for type and shadow studies. (Ask: who is Ruth? Who is Boaz? Who is Naomi?) The way in which God dealt with the Children of Israel in the Book of Deuteronomy makes a good type-and-shadow study, as do the stories of Esther, Jonah, and Job.

- *Symbol Studies.* The Bible has many symbols, including numbers, colors, and tangible objects used as symbols in various places. In many cases, understanding a symbol is the key to understanding an entire story or teaching. Symbols indicate eternal value, eternal meaning, and eternal reasons. For an object to be a genuine symbol, the meaning associated with that symbol must run from cover to cover in the Bible. Among the symbols that make great studies are: gold and silver, wood, crown, seals, stone vs. dust. Objects that are filled with symbols make good studies, including the Ark of the Covenant, Noah's ark, Nehemiah's wall, and Daniel's den of lions. Ask the Holy Spirit to make the meanings of the symbols known to you and be sure to check and cross-check your interpretation of a symbol to make certain that your interpretation is valid. A true symbol does not mean one thing in one place and another thing in another place—it must have a consistent meaning throughout the Bible.

The more you read and study your Bible, the more you will *want* to read and study it. Its spiritual riches cannot be fully mined in any one lifetime . . . that's all the more reason to begin today and continue reading and studying every day for the rest of your life!

²⁴And they said to Joshua, "Truly the LORD has delivered all the land into our hands, for indeed all the inhabitants of the country are fainthearted because of us."

Israel Crosses the Jordan

3 Then Joshua rose early in the morning; and they set out from Acacia Grove[a] and came to the Jordan, he and all the children of Israel, and lodged there before they crossed over. ²So it was, after three days, that the officers went through the camp; ³and they commanded the people, saying, "When you see the ark of the covenant of the LORD your God, and the priests, the Levites, bearing it, then you shall set out from your place and go after it. ⁴Yet there shall be a space between you and it, about two thousand cubits by measure. Do not come near it, that you may know the way by which you must go, for you have not passed *this* way before."

⁵And Joshua said to the people, "Sanctify yourselves, for tomorrow the LORD will do wonders among you." ⁶Then Joshua spoke to the priests,

saying, "Take up the ark of the covenant and cross over before the people."

So they took up the ark of the covenant and went before the people.

⁷And the LORD said to Joshua, "This day I will begin to exalt you in the sight of all Israel, that they may know that, as I was with Moses, *so* I will be with you. ⁸You shall command the priests who bear the ark of the covenant, saying, 'When you have come to the edge of the water of the Jordan, you shall stand in the Jordan.'"

⁹So Joshua said to the children of Israel, "Come here, and hear the words of the LORD your God." ¹⁰And Joshua said, "By this you shall know that the living God *is* among you, and *that* He will without fail drive out from before you the Canaanites and the Hittites and the Hivites and the Perizzites and the Girgashites and the Amorites and the Jebusites: ¹¹Behold, the ark of the covenant of the Lord of all the earth is crossing over before you into the Jordan. ¹²Now therefore, take for yourselves twelve

3:1 [a] Hebrew *Shittim*

2:24 The report of the spies reflected Rahab's words (vv. 9–11). Unlike the report of the spies who returned to Moses 40 years earlier with a report emphasizing the weakness of the Israelites and the strength of the inhabitants of the Land, this report emphasized God's strength and faithfulness to deliver the Land into the hands of His people (see Num. 13:26–33; see chart, Tale of Two Committees).

3:3 The ark of the covenant (a wooden box overlaid with gold, approximately 45″ long × 27″ wide by 27″ high) was the centerpiece of the tabernacle (see chart, The Plan of the Tabernacle). The ark contained the tablets God gave Moses on Mt. Sinai, a jar of manna, and Aaron's rod (Ex. 25:10–16; Heb. 9:4, 5; see chart, The Furniture of the Tabernacle). The "mercy

seat" symbolized the presence of God and rested on top of the ark (Ex. 25:17–22). Here the priests sprinkled the sacrificial blood for the sins of the people and met God (Lev. 16:14). The bringing of the ark, which represented God's presence, before the people meant that they were about to move. As the people prepared to enter the Land, they were to follow the ark of the covenant.

3:4 Two thousand cubits was about 3,000 feet or 925 meters (one cubit equals approximately 18 inches; see chart, Money and Measurements in the Bible). The ark still functioned as a guide. The distance required emphasized the sacred nature of the ark of the covenant and also affirmed the inappropriateness of irreverent familiarity.

RAHAB *A Discerning Deliverer*

Rahab was obviously an intelligent woman. She showed a remarkable knowledge of the recent history of Israel as well as of what God was doing for the Israelites when they approached her country. In fact, she seemed more aware of God's intervention for Israel than Israel was (notice the similarity of her words in Josh. 2:9–11 with Josh. 1:2, 11, 13). In addition, she obtained an agreement for protection from the spies, hid them, and outsmarted her own people when they came looking for them.

Rahab also showed initiative in arranging for the deliverance of her entire family. She was a woman of great courage. Siding with the Israelites was treason, punishable by death, not only for herself but also for all her family. Once she made her decision, there was no turning back.

Finally, Rahab was a woman with spiritual insight. She recognized the disparity between Israel's God and the gods she and her people served. Israel's God was supreme—He did not share the rule in the heavens and the earth the way their gods reportedly did (Josh. 2:11). Rahab's initial confession of faith is seen in the use of the name *Yahweh*. Without any support or input from her world or Israel's, she claimed the covenant name God gave to Moses when the Israelites first left Egypt (Ex. 3:14). Then, again without any encouragement from others, she acted on her commitment by hiding the spies. This kind of faith was not often seen in God's people in the Old Testament, let alone from a Gentile harlot.

Rahab is a role model for making the right decisions and standing firm, even when it means going against your own peers. No wonder God wanted to honor her faith and courage by placing such a woman in the line of the Messiah. Boaz, one of the most gentle and godly men in the Old Testament, was her offspring (see Matt. 1:5 and the Book of Ruth; see chart, The Family Tree of Jesus). God honored Rahab's faith and courage by placing her in the lineage not only of Israel's great King David (Matt. 1:6) but also of Jesus, the King of Kings (Matt. 1:1).

See also Matt. 1:5; Heb. 11:31; James 2:25; notes on Decision Making (1 Cor. 8); Heroines (Heb. 11)

---

men from the tribes of Israel, one man from every tribe. [13]And it shall come to pass, as soon as the soles of the feet of the priests who bear the ark of the LORD, the Lord of all the earth, shall rest in the waters of the Jordan, *that* the waters of the Jordan shall be cut off, the waters that come down from upstream, and they shall stand as a heap."

[14]So it was, when the people set out from their camp to cross over the Jordan, with the priests bearing the ark of the covenant before the people, [15]and as those who bore the ark came to the Jordan, and the feet of the priests who bore the ark dipped in the edge of the water (for the Jordan overflows all its banks during the whole time of harvest), [16]that the waters which came down from upstream stood *still, and* rose in a heap very far away at Adam, the city that *is* beside Zaretan. So the waters that went down into the Sea of the Arabah, the Salt Sea, failed, *and* were cut off; and the people crossed over opposite Jericho. [17]Then the priests who bore the ark of the covenant of the LORD stood firm on dry ground in the midst of the Jordan; and all Israel crossed over on dry ground, until all the people had crossed completely over the Jordan.

The Memorial Stones

4 And it came to pass, when all the people had completely crossed over the Jordan, that the LORD spoke to Joshua, saying: [2]"Take for yourselves twelve men from the people, one man from every tribe, [3]and command them, saying, 'Take for yourselves twelve stones from here, out of the midst of the Jordan, from the place where the priests' feet stood firm. You shall carry them over with you and leave them in the lodging place where you lodge tonight.' "

[4]Then Joshua called the twelve men whom he had appointed from the children of Israel, one man from every tribe; [5]and Joshua said to them: "Cross over before the ark of the LORD your God into the midst of the Jordan, and each one of you take up a stone on his shoulder, according to the number of the tribes of the children of Israel, [6]that this may be a sign among you when your children ask in time to come, saying, 'What do these stones *mean* to you?' [7]Then you shall answer

---

3:14–17 Only the priests (the spiritual leaders) had to get their feet wet. Seeing the priests obey God through their obedience to Joshua was important for the people.

4:3–9 As a reminder of His miraculous provision, the Lord instructed the people to build a monument with stones taken

from the riverbed they had crossed. The Hebrew text itself, according to some scholars, suggests a second monument in the river itself (v. 9). In any event, the monument was to serve as a witness of God's faithfulness to His children for future generations.

TALE OF TWO COMMITTEES

	SPIES OF MOSES (NUM. 13)	SPIES OF JOSHUA (JOSH. 2)
NUMBER:	Twelve men were chosen.	Two men were helped and perhaps inspired by a woman–Rahab.
IDENTIFICATION:	The spies were named by Moses.	The spies were chosen by Joshua.
DEBRIEFING PROCEDURE:	The spies reported directly to the people.	The spies reported directly to Joshua.
REPORT:	The enemy is "bigger than we are."	"God is bigger" than any enemy.
COMMITTEE VOTE:	Ten out of twelve agreed with the report.	100% supported the report.
DEBRIEFING REPORT:	Mission impossible!	Go for it!
ACTION TAKEN:	The people voted.	The people acted.
RESULTS:	The people wandered 40 more years.	The people settled in the Land of Promise.

them that the waters of the Jordan were cut off before the ark of the covenant of the LORD; when it crossed over the Jordan, the waters of the Jordan were cut off. And these stones shall be for a memorial to the children of Israel forever."

⁸And the children of Israel did so, just as Joshua commanded, and took up twelve stones from the midst of the Jordan, as the LORD had spoken to Joshua, according to the number of the tribes of the children of Israel, and carried them over with them to the place where they lodged, and laid them down there. ⁹Then Joshua set up twelve stones in the midst of the Jordan, in the place where the feet of the priests who bore the ark of the covenant stood; and they are there to this day.

¹⁰So the priests who bore the ark stood in the midst of the Jordan until everything was finished that the LORD had commanded Joshua to speak to the people, according to all that Moses had commanded Joshua; and the people hurried and crossed over. ¹¹Then it came to pass, when all the people had completely crossed over, that the ark of the LORD and the priests crossed over in the presence of the people. ¹²And the men of Reuben, the men of Gad, and half the tribe of Manasseh crossed over armed before the children of Israel, as Moses had spoken to them. ¹³About forty thousand prepared for war crossed over before the LORD for battle, to the plains of Jericho. ¹⁴On that

day the LORD exalted Joshua in the sight of all Israel; and they feared him, as they had feared Moses, all the days of his life.

¹⁵Then the LORD spoke to Joshua, saying, ¹⁶"Command the priests who bear the ark of the Testimony to come up from the Jordan." ¹⁷Joshua therefore commanded the priests, saying, "Come up from the Jordan." ¹⁸And it came to pass, when the priests who bore the ark of the covenant of the LORD had come from the midst of the Jordan, and the soles of the priests' feet touched the dry land, that the waters of the Jordan returned to their place and overflowed all its banks as before.

¹⁹Now the people came up from the Jordan on the tenth day of the first month, and they camped in Gilgal on the east border of Jericho. ²⁰And those twelve stones which they took out of the Jordan, Joshua set up in Gilgal. ²¹Then he spoke to the children of Israel, saying: "When your children ask their fathers in time to come, saying, 'What are these stones?' ²²then you shall let your children know, saying, 'Israel crossed over this Jordan on dry land'; ²³for the LORD your God dried up the waters of the Jordan before you until you had crossed over, as the LORD your God did to the Red Sea, which He dried up before us until we had crossed over, ²⁴that all the peoples of the earth may know the hand of the LORD, that it is mighty, that you may fear the LORD your God forever."

JUSTICE THE DESTRUCTION OF INNOCENTS

God's command to destroy everyone in these cities often troubles modern readers (Deut. 7:1–6). Two basic reasons are given for this command:

1) the inhabitants had reached the point of no return in their depravity (see Gen. 6:5, 6), and

2) if the Israelites lived beside these pagan people, they, too, would be infected with their wickedness (Ex. 34:12–16; Deut. 7:4).

In any case, Joshua was obeying a specific directive from God just as in the devastation of the Flood (Gen. 7:23) and the destruction of Sodom and Gomorrah (Gen. 19:24, 25). While the loss of innocent life is always a tragedy, at times only radical action can save, as would be true with a deadly cancer in the body. We living on this side of the Cross are much more fortunate and have the promise of ultimate victory (Rom. 8:31–39).

Even secular scholars acknowledge that the practices of these Canaanite religions are some of the most perverse recorded in history. The goddess Asherah is noted for love of murder and war. When the people wanted their gods to do something, they would sometimes enact the deed themselves. They lived in an agricultural society. To insure that Baal (the fertility god) would provide the rain (which they believed to be his semen), they practiced every imaginable sexual perversion with both male and female prostitutes as well as with animals (Ex. 22:19, 20). They did everything God hated (Lev. 18:20–24). They even threw their children into the fire as sacrifices (Lev. 18:21; Deut. 12:31). This act is a measure of their depravity, for no mother worthy of the name would willingly participate in the murder of her own child. God identified the abominations as so detestable that the land itself was defiled (Lev. 18:25).

These people had known about God (see Josh. 2:8–14). God had given them hundreds of years to change (Gen. 15:16). The destruction of the Canaanites was not ordered merely to secure the Land for Israel. God was not unjust to other nations in order to reward Israel. The pagan nations were to be destroyed because of their own wickedness. God is a God of patience and mercy, but He is also a just God (Gen. 18:25). He does what is right, however it may appear to our finite minds and limited judgment. He will judge sin because He is holy (Deut. 7:10; 9:3–5; see also Ex. 14, Justice). Some of these perplexities await final understanding from God Himself.

The Second Generation Circumcised

5 So it was, when all the kings of the Amorites who *were* on the west side of the Jordan, and all the kings of the Canaanites who *were* by the sea, heard that the LORD had dried up the waters of the Jordan from before the children of Israel until we[a] had crossed over, that their heart melted; and there was no spirit in them any longer because of the children of Israel.

[2]At that time the LORD said to Joshua, "Make flint knives for yourself, and circumcise the sons of Israel again the second time." [3]So Joshua made flint knives for himself, and circumcised the sons of Israel at the hill of the foreskins.[a] [4]And this *is* the reason why Joshua circumcised them: All the people who came out of Egypt *who were* males, all the men of war, had died in the wilderness on the way, after they had come out of Egypt. [5]For all the people who came out had been circumcised, but all the people born in the wilderness, on the way as they came out of Egypt, had not been circum-

cised. [6]For the children of Israel walked forty years in the wilderness, till all the people *who were* men of war, who came out of Egypt, were consumed, because they did not obey the voice of the LORD— to whom the LORD swore that He would not show them the land which the LORD had sworn to their fathers that He would give us, "a land flowing with milk and honey."[a] [7]Then Joshua circumcised their sons *whom* He raised up in their place; for they were uncircumcised, because they had not been circumcised on the way.

[8]So it was, when they had finished circumcising all the people, that they stayed in their places in the camp till they were healed. [9]Then the LORD said to Joshua, "This day I have rolled away the reproach of Egypt from you." Therefore the name of the place is called Gilgal[a] to this day.

[10]Now the children of Israel camped in Gilgal,

· · · · · · · · · · · · · · · · · · · ·

5:1 [a]Following Kethib; Qere, some Hebrew manuscripts and editions, Septuagint, Syriac, Targum, and Vulgate read *they*. 5:3 [a]Hebrew *Gibeath Haaraloth* 5:6 [a]Exodus 3:8 5:9 [a]Literally *Rolling*

5:5 Circumcision had been a covenant requirement since the time of Abraham (Gen. 17:9–14). The reason Hebrew males were not circumcised during the 40 years in the wilderness is not known, though the answer may be in the phrase "on the way," indicating that during the years of constant wandering it was not feasible. For whatever reason, clearly God intended this time as another reminder to the Israelites of their special relationship with Him (see Gen. 17, Circumcision).

5:6 The land flowing with milk and honey was not a tropical garden but rather one that was hospitable to flocks and meadows (the milk of goats and the honey of bees).

5:10–12 The reminders of God's faithfulness became apparent to the Israelites after they completed their wilderness wanderings, crossed the Jordan River, and prepared to take the city of Jericho. The "Passover" was celebrated in remem-

PREPARATION FOR LEADERSHIP

The relationship between Moses and Joshua shows a mentoring pattern for developing leadership qualities.

EARLY YEARS	• Joshua was born in slavery and oppression (Ex. 1:13). • He was among those who cried out to God for deliverance (Ex. 2:23).
THE EXODUS	• Joshua observed the plagues (Ex. 7:14—12:29). • He saw the impotency of Egypt's gods (Ex. 7:10–13). • He observed Pharaoh's humiliation (Ex. 8:8–10). • He witnessed the miraculous provision of God (Num. 11:31–33).
LEADERSHIP TRAINING	• Joshua was the leader of a tribe (Num. 13:2, 8, 16). • He stood for God at the risk of his own life (Num. 14:6–10). • Though in the minority, he wholly followed God (Num. 32:11, 12). • He co-led the people (Num. 27:18–23). • He led battles (Ex. 17:9, 10).
OBSERVATION OF MOSES	• Moses delegated authority (Ex.18:17–26). • He encountered God on Mt. Sinai (Ex. 24:12, 13). • He experienced the rebellion of the people (Num. 12:1–15; 16:1–50). • He responded to complaining (Ex. 17:1–7). • He experienced frustration at the disobedience of the people (Ex. 16:25–30). • He obeyed God (Ex. 40:16–19).
TEACHING BY MOSES	• Joshua received the book written by Moses (Ex. 17:14). • He shared authority with Moses (Num. 27:18–23). • Moses gave instructions to Joshua (Josh. 1:7).
OBSERVATIONS OF JOSHUA'S PREPARATION	• Joshua learned patience (40 years waiting to get into the Land). • He learned to seek God (Num. 27:15–18). • He learned to obey only God (Num. 14:8, 9). • He learned to lead (Num. 27:18–23).
GOD'S CALL	• God told Moses that Joshua was the new leader (Num. 27:15–23). • God told Joshua that he was the new leader (Josh 1:1–9). • God showed the people Joshua was the leader (Josh. 3:7). • God personally appeared to Joshua (Josh. 5:13–15).
GOD'S SPECIFIC PROMISES	• Joshua would possess every place his foot would tread (Josh. 1:3). • God would be with Joshua as He was with Moses (Josh. 1:5, 9). • No one would be able to usurp Joshua's position (Josh. 1:5). • Joshua would prosper (Josh. 1:7).
GOD'S INSTRUCTIONS	• Be strong and courageous (Josh. 1:6, 9). • Observe all Moses' commands (Josh. 1:7, 13). • Meditate on the Book day and night (Josh. 1:8). • Do not be afraid (Josh. 1:9).
PUBLIC AFFIRMATION	• The people accepted him as Moses' replacement (Josh. 1:16, 17). • They gave him their allegiance (Josh. 1:18). • Leaders (priests) responded to him (Josh. 3:8–17; 4:16–18).
JOSHUA'S LEADERSHIP	• Joshua acted quickly (Josh. 3:1). • He sent only two spies, and they reported to him (Josh. 2:1, 23). • He relayed God's promises to the people (Josh. 3:5, 8). • He set up memorials (Josh. 4:1–9). • He recognized and worshiped the real Commander (Josh. 5:13–15). • He made mistakes (Josh. 7:1–9). • He experienced God's direct involvement (Josh. 10:14). • He administered the division of Land (Josh. 13—19).
EVALUATIONS OF JOSHUA'S LEADERSHIP	• Joshua practiced immediate obedience (Josh. 11:23). • He learned from the past (Josh. 10:25). • He held to God's Word (Josh. 8:34, 35). • He taught the people the importance of God's Word (Josh. 23:6). • He read God's Word to the people (Josh. 8:35). • In victory, he praised God (Josh. 8:30). • He recognized that God fulfilled every need (Josh. 23:14). • He continually gave God the credit (Josh. 3:5, 10; 4:23, 24; 23:3). • He made a life-long commitment (Josh. 24:15).

and kept the Passover on the fourteenth day of the month at twilight on the plains of Jericho. [11]And they ate of the produce of the land on the day after the Passover, unleavened bread and parched grain, on the very same day. [12]Then the manna ceased on the day after they had eaten the produce of the land; and the children of Israel no longer had manna, but they ate the food of the land of Canaan that year.

The Commander of the Army of the LORD

[13]And it came to pass, when Joshua was by Jericho, that he lifted his eyes and looked, and behold, a Man stood opposite him with His sword drawn in His hand. And Joshua went to Him and said to Him, "*Are* You for us or for our adversaries?"

[14]So He said, "No, but *as* Commander of the army of the LORD I have now come."

And Joshua fell on his face to the earth and worshiped, and said to Him, "What does my Lord say to His servant?"

[15]Then the Commander of the LORD's army said to Joshua, "Take your sandal off your foot, for the place where you stand *is* holy." And Joshua did so.

The Destruction of Jericho

6 Now Jericho was securely shut up because of the children of Israel; none went out, and none came in. [2]And the LORD said to Joshua: "See! I have given Jericho into your hand, its king, *and* the mighty men of valor. [3]You shall march around the city, all *you* men of war; you shall go all around the city once. This you shall do six days. [4]And seven priests shall bear seven trumpets of rams' horns before the ark. But the seventh day you shall march around the city seven times, and the priests shall blow the trumpets. [5]It shall come to pass, when they make a long *blast* with the ram's horn, *and* when you hear the sound of the trumpet, that all the people shall shout with a great shout; then the wall of the city will fall down flat. And the people shall go up every man straight before him."

[6]Then Joshua the son of Nun called the priests and said to them, "Take up the ark of the covenant, and let seven priests bear seven trumpets of rams' horns before the ark of the LORD." [7]And he said to the people, "Proceed, and march around the city, and let him who is armed advance before the ark of the LORD."

[8]So it was, when Joshua had spoken to the people, that the seven priests bearing the seven trumpets of rams' horns before the LORD advanced and blew the trumpets, and the ark of the covenant of the LORD followed them. [9]The armed men went before the priests who blew the trumpets, and the rear guard came after the ark, while *the priests* continued blowing the trumpets. [10]Now Joshua had commanded the people, saying, "You shall not shout or make any noise with your voice, nor shall a word proceed out of your mouth, until the day I say to you, 'Shout!' Then you shall shout." [11]So he had the ark of the LORD circle the city, going around *it* once. Then they came into the camp and lodged in the camp.

[12]And Joshua rose early in the morning, and the priests took up the ark of the LORD. [13]Then seven priests bearing seven trumpets of rams' horns before the ark of the LORD went on continually and blew with the trumpets. And the armed men went before them. But the rear guard came after the ark of the LORD, while *the priests* continued blowing the trumpets. [14]And the second day they marched around the city once and returned to the camp. So they did six days.

[15]But it came to pass on the seventh day that they rose early, about the dawning of the day, and marched around the city seven times in the same manner. On that day only they marched around the city seven times. [16]And the seventh time it happened, when the priests blew the trumpets, that Joshua said to the people: "Shout, for the LORD has given you the city! [17]Now the city shall be doomed by the LORD to destruction, it and all who *are* in it. Only Rahab the harlot shall live, she and all who *are* with her in the house, because she hid the messengers that we sent. [18]And you, by all means abstain from the accursed things, lest you

---

brance of their deliverance from slavery in Egypt (see chart, The Feasts of Israel). As they ate the "produce of the land," surely they must have marveled that God timed their arrival in Canaan during a season when the Land would support them. As they ate of the Land's abundance, the "manna ceased." This miraculous provision of food, gathered each morning, had been a daily reminder that God fulfilled His promises.

5:13–15 The visitation to Joshua is similar to Moses' experience at the burning bush (Ex. 3:2–8). In the appearances to both men, the Lord pronounced the ground "holy" and instructed them to remove their sandals (Josh. 5:15). Joshua would have recognized the scenario immediately and understood this theophany (a visible appearance of God in bodily form) as another affirmation of his appointment as Moses' successor. The presence of this divine Commander had been promised 40 years earlier (Ex. 23:20; Josh. 1:9).

6:5 Conquering a walled city usually required breaching the walls or laying siege until the inhabitants exhausted their food and water supplies (a process often taking months). But God displayed His power to the Israelites by leveling the walls that had frightened their fathers 40 years earlier (Num. 13:28).

6:8–16 The psychological warfare is ingenious. The residents of Jericho already were paralyzed with fear. In addition, for six days they watched this fearsome people, led by the ark, symbolizing God's presence, march daily around their city with only trumpet blasts piercing the silence. Imagine how they felt on the seventh day when the process was repeated over and over!

6:18 Destroying the spoils of war was a recognized method of

TEMPTATION: THE ANALYSIS OF A SUCCESSFUL TRAP

SATAN	EVE	ACHAN	DAVID
A perfect, anointed cherub (Ezek. 28:12, 13)	The perfect creation of God (Gen. 2:18, 22, 23)	A member of the tribe of Judah (Josh. 7:1)	The king of Israel (2 Sam. 12:7)
↓	↓	↓	↓
Saw God's glory (Ezek. 28:13)	Saw the fruit (Gen. 3:6)	Saw the treasures (Josh. 7:21)	Saw a woman (2 Sam. 11:2)
↓	↓	↓	↓
Desired to be like Him (Is. 14:13, 14)	Desired to be like God (Gen. 3:6)	Coveted what God had specified as His (Josh. 7:21)	Desired the wife of another man (2 Sam. 11:2)
↓	↓	↓	↓
Took what he wanted (Is. 14:14; Ezek. 28:6)	Took the fruit (Gen. 3:6)	Took the spoils of battle (Josh. 7:1, 21)	Took her for himself (2 Sam. 11:2–5, 26, 27)
↓	↓	↓	↓
	Gave it to Adam (Gen. 3:6)	Hid the valuable objects (Josh. 7:21)	Lied and created a web of deception (2 Sam. 11:6–15)
↓	↓	↓	↓
Became the enemy of God (Is. 14:15; Ezek. 28:9)	Ushered sin into the world (Gen. 3:7, 11–13, 16)	Caused the defeat of a nation (Josh. 7:12)	Caused the death of Uriah (2 Sam. 11:16, 17, 21)
	↓	↓	↓
	Was expelled from the Garden of Eden (Gen. 3:23, 24)	Destroyed himself and his family (Josh. 7:11, 15, 24, 25)	Broke fellowship with God (Gen. 12: 7–12)

become accursed when you take of the accursed things, and make the camp of Israel a curse, and trouble it. ¹⁹But all the silver and gold, and vessels of bronze and iron, *are* consecrated to the LORD; they shall come into the treasury of the LORD."

²⁰So the people shouted when *the priests* blew the trumpets. And it happened when the people heard the sound of the trumpet, and the people shouted with a great shout, that the wall fell down flat. Then the people went up into the city, every man straight before him, and they took the city. ²¹And they utterly destroyed all that *was* in the city, both man and woman, young and old, ox and sheep and donkey, with the edge of the sword.

²²But Joshua had said to the two men who had spied out the country, "Go into the harlot's house, and from there bring out the woman and all that she has, as you swore to her." ²³And the young men who had been spies went in and brought out Rahab, her father, her mother, her brothers, and all that she had. So they brought out all her relatives and left them outside the camp of Israel. ²⁴But they burned the city and all that *was* in it with fire. Only the silver and gold, and the vessels of bronze and iron, they put into the treasury of the house of the LORD. ²⁵And Joshua spared Rahab the harlot, her father's household, and all that she had. So she dwells in Israel to this day, because she hid the messengers whom Joshua sent to spy out Jericho.

devoting these spoils to a deity. To covet and take what had been devoted to God was sin and would have far-reaching consequences. A consistent OT theme is the effect of an individual's sin on the family, the community, and even an entire nation (see Josh. 7:10–26; chart, Temptation: The Analysis of a Successful Trap). When a nation comes under judgment and even innocents are destroyed, its people have themselves to blame and not God (Amos 2:4). The booty was not important

to God but rather the obedience of His people. He did not demand the spoils from all the cities (Josh. 8:2). But the booty of Jericho, the first victory, was considered the firstfruits. The firstfruits were to be given to Him in acknowledgment that all comes from Him (Ex. 23:19; 34:19, 26).

6:23 Rahab was willing to give up her pagan gods and turn to the one true God. She is listed among the heroes of faith (Heb. 11:31; see Josh. 2, Rahab).

[26]Then Joshua charged *them* at that time, saying, "Cursed *be* the man before the LORD who rises up and builds this city Jericho; he shall lay its foundation with his firstborn, and with his youngest he shall set up its gates."

[27]So the LORD was with Joshua, and his fame spread throughout all the country.

Defeat at Ai

7 But the children of Israel committed a trespass regarding the accursed things, for Achan the son of Carmi, the son of Zabdi,[a] the son of Zerah, of the tribe of Judah, took of the accursed things; so the anger of the LORD burned against the children of Israel.

[2]Now Joshua sent men from Jericho to Ai, which *is* beside Beth Aven, on the east side of Bethel, and spoke to them, saying, "Go up and spy out the country." So the men went up and spied out Ai. [3]And they returned to Joshua and said to him, "Do not let all the people go up, but let about two or three thousand men go up and attack Ai. Do not weary all the people there, for *the people of Ai are* few." [4]So about three thousand men went up there from the people, but they fled before the men of Ai. [5]And the men of Ai struck down about thirty-six men, for they chased them *from* before the gate as far as Shebarim, and struck them down on the descent; therefore the hearts of the people melted and became like water.

[6]Then Joshua tore his clothes, and fell to the earth on his face before the ark of the LORD until evening, he and the elders of Israel; and they put dust on their heads. [7]And Joshua said, "Alas, Lord GOD, why have You brought this people over the Jordan at all—to deliver us into the hand of the Amorites, to destroy us? Oh, that we had been content, and dwelt on the other side of the Jordan! [8]O Lord, what shall I say when Israel turns its back before its enemies? [9]For the Canaanites and all the inhabitants of the land will hear *it,* and surround us, and cut off our name from the earth. Then what will You do for Your great name?"

The Sin of Achan

[10]So the LORD said to Joshua: "Get up! Why do you lie thus on your face? [11]Israel has sinned, and they have also transgressed My covenant which I commanded them. For they have even taken some of the accursed things, and have both stolen and deceived; and they have also put *it* among their own stuff. [12]Therefore the children of Israel could not stand before their enemies, *but* turned *their* backs before their enemies, because they have become doomed to destruction. Neither will I be with you anymore, unless you destroy the accursed from among you. [13]Get up, sanctify the people, and say, 'Sanctify yourselves for tomorrow, because thus says the LORD God of Israel: "*There is* an accursed thing in your midst, O Israel; you cannot stand before your enemies until you take away the accursed thing from among you." [14]In the morning therefore you shall be brought according to your tribes. And it shall be *that* the tribe which the LORD takes shall come according to families; and the family which the LORD takes shall come by households; and the household which the LORD takes shall come man by man. [15]Then it shall be *that* he who is taken with the accursed thing shall be burned with fire, he and all that he has, because he has transgressed the covenant of the LORD, and because he has done a disgraceful thing in Israel.' "

[16]So Joshua rose early in the morning and brought Israel by their tribes, and the tribe of Judah was taken. [17]He brought the clan of Judah, and he took the family of the Zarhites; and he brought the family of the Zarhites man by man, and Zabdi was taken. [18]Then he brought his household man by man, and Achan the son of Carmi, the son of Zabdi, the son of Zerah, of the tribe of Judah, was taken.

[19]Now Joshua said to Achan, "My son, I beg you, give glory to the LORD God of Israel, and make confession to Him, and tell me now what you have done; do not hide *it* from me."

•••••••••••••••••

7:1 [a]Called *Zimri* in 1 Chronicles 2:6

6:26 To sacrifice a firstborn child at the founding of a city was not uncommon for ancient pagans. Joshua's prediction came true in the time of Ahab, one of Israel's most evil kings (see 1 Kin. 16:34, note).

7:1 Accursed things. When taking Jericho, the Israelites were commanded to spare Rahab and her family and to abstain from the things "accursed" (Heb. *cherem*, lit. "devoted"). The term has evolved to describe the enclosed, private apartments for women. This curse applied to Jericho was the most severe, meaning that someone and/or something was absolutely and irrevocably consecrated to destruction with no possibility of redemption (Lev. 27:28, 29). The experience of Achan illustrates how the sin of an individual has consequences for the family and community. However unfair it may seem, the wrongdoing of one does indeed affect others ad-

versely (Deut. 5:9; Josh. 6:17–19). Individual responsibility and corporate guilt often go hand in hand (see chart, Temptation: The Analysis of a Successful Trap).

7:4–7 The path to depression is clear in this experience of Joshua at Ai (see also 1 Sam. 16, Depression). It begins with overwhelming defeat (v. 4). Defeat brought discouragement (v. 5), followed by depression (v. 6) and loss of vision (v. 7). God offered recovery: Sanctify or set yourself apart (v. 13) and do what the Lord directs you to do (Josh. 8:1).

7:19 Personal confession. Though God pointed the finger at Achan, Achan himself needed to confess his sin before the people. The expression "give glory to the LORD God of Israel" is used here and elsewhere to call for an honest confession (1 Sam. 6:5; Jer. 13:16; John 9:24).

faith is being in advance of what only makes sense in reverse.

Jo Ann Leavell

---

²⁰And Achan answered Joshua and said, "Indeed I have sinned against the LORD God of Israel, and this is what I have done: ²¹When I saw among the spoils a beautiful Babylonian garment, two hundred shekels of silver, and a wedge of gold weighing fifty shekels, I coveted them and took them. And there they are, hidden in the earth in the midst of my tent, with the silver under it."

²²So Joshua sent messengers, and they ran to the tent; and there it was, hidden in his tent, with the silver under it. ²³And they took them from the midst of the tent, brought them to Joshua and to all the children of Israel, and laid them out before the LORD. ²⁴Then Joshua, and all Israel with him, took Achan the son of Zerah, the silver, the garment, the wedge of gold, his sons, his daughters, his oxen, his donkeys, his sheep, his tent, and all that he had, and they brought them to the Valley of Achor. ²⁵And Joshua said, "Why have you troubled us? The LORD will trouble you this day." So all Israel stoned him with stones; and they burned them with fire after they had stoned them with stones.

²⁶Then they raised over him a great heap of stones, still there to this day. So the LORD turned from the fierceness of His anger. Therefore the name of that place has been called the Valley of Achor[a] to this day.

The Fall of Ai

8 Now the LORD said to Joshua: "Do not be afraid, nor be dismayed; take all the people of war with you, and arise, go up to Ai. See, I have given into your hand the king of Ai, his people, his city, and his land. ²And you shall do to Ai and its king as you did to Jericho and its king. Only its spoil and its cattle you shall take as booty for yourselves. Lay an ambush for the city behind it."

³So Joshua arose, and all the people of war, to go up against Ai; and Joshua chose thirty thousand mighty men of valor and sent them away by night. ⁴And he commanded them, saying: "Behold, you shall lie in ambush against the city, behind the city. Do not go very far from the city, but all of you be ready. ⁵Then I and all the people who *are* with me will approach the city; and it will come about, when they come out against us as at the first, that we shall flee before them. ⁶For they will come out after us till we have drawn them from the city, for they will say, '*They are* fleeing before us as at the first.' Therefore we will flee before them. ⁷Then you shall rise from the ambush and seize the city, for the LORD your God will deliver it into your hand. ⁸And it will be, when you have taken the city, *that* you shall set the city on fire. According to the commandment of the LORD you shall do. See, I have commanded you."

⁹Joshua therefore sent them out; and they went to lie in ambush, and stayed between Bethel and Ai, on the west side of Ai; but Joshua lodged that night among the people. ¹⁰Then Joshua rose up early in the morning and mustered the people, and went up, he and the elders of Israel, before the people to Ai. ¹¹And all the people of war who *were* with him went up and drew near; and they came before the city and camped on the north side of Ai. Now a valley *lay* between them and Ai. ¹²So he took about five thousand men and set them in ambush between Bethel and Ai, on the west side of the city. ¹³And when they had set the people, all the army that *was* on the north of the city, and its rear guard on the west of the city, Joshua went that night into the midst of the valley.

¹⁴Now it happened, when the king of Ai saw *it*, that the men of the city hurried and rose early and went out against Israel to battle, he and all his people, at an appointed place before the plain. But he did not know that *there was* an ambush against him behind the city. ¹⁵And Joshua and all Israel made as if they were beaten before them, and fled by the way of the wilderness. ¹⁶So all the people who *were* in Ai were called together to pursue them. And they pursued Joshua and were drawn away from the city. ¹⁷There was not a man left in Ai or Bethel who did not go out after Israel. So they left the city open and pursued Israel.

¹⁸Then the LORD said to Joshua, "Stretch out the spear that *is* in your hand toward Ai, for I will give it into your hand." And Joshua stretched out the spear that *was* in his hand toward the city. ¹⁹So *those in* ambush arose quickly out of their place; they ran as soon as he had stretched out his hand, and they entered the city and took it, and hurried

7:26 [a]Literally *Trouble*

7:24 The Valley of Achor (Heb., lit. "trouble") is so named because of Achan's sin and the consequences it brought on the Israelites. Later through the prophet Hosea, God promised to make the Valley of Achor "a door of hope" (Hos. 2:15).

8:2 The booty of Ai was not the firstfruits as in the case of Jericho (see Josh. 6:18, note); so Israel was allowed to take the booty specified. Consulting the Lord concerning each battle was important because the Lord seldom used the same method twice. He led the Israelites in psychological warfare at Jericho but used military strategy at Ai.

to set the city on fire. [20]And when the men of Ai looked behind them, they saw, and behold, the smoke of the city ascended to heaven. So they had no power to flee this way or that way, and the people who had fled to the wilderness turned back on the pursuers.

[21]Now when Joshua and all Israel saw that the ambush had taken the city and that the smoke of the city ascended, they turned back and struck down the men of Ai. [22]Then the others came out of the city against them; so they were *caught* in the midst of Israel, some on this side and some on that side. And they struck them down, so that they let none of them remain or escape. [23]But the king of Ai they took alive, and brought him to Joshua.

[24]And it came to pass when Israel had made an end of slaying all the inhabitants of Ai in the field, in the wilderness where they pursued them, and when they all had fallen by the edge of the sword until they were consumed, that all the Israelites returned to Ai and struck it with the edge of the sword. [25]So it was *that* all who fell that day, both men and women, *were* twelve thousand—all the people of Ai. [26]For Joshua did not draw back his hand, with which he stretched out the spear, until he had utterly destroyed all the inhabitants of Ai. [27]Only the livestock and the spoil of that city Israel took as booty for themselves, according to the word of the LORD which He had commanded Joshua. [28]So Joshua burned Ai and made it a heap forever, a desolation to this day. [29]And the king of Ai he hanged on a tree until evening. And as soon as the sun was down, Joshua commanded that they should take his corpse down from the tree, cast it at the entrance of the gate of the city, and raise over it a great heap of stones *that remains* to this day.

Joshua Renews the Covenant

[30]Now Joshua built an altar to the LORD God of Israel in Mount Ebal, [31]as Moses the servant of the LORD had commanded the children of Israel, as it is written in the Book of the Law of Moses: "an altar of whole stones over which no man has wielded an iron *tool.*"[a] And they offered on it burnt offerings to the LORD, and sacrificed peace offerings. [32]And there, in the presence of the children of Israel, he wrote on the stones a copy of the law of Moses, which he had written. [33]Then all Israel, with their elders and officers and judges, stood on either side of the ark before the priests, the Levites, who bore the ark of the covenant of the LORD, the stranger as well as he who was born among them. Half of them *were* in front of Mount Gerizim and half of them in front of Mount Ebal, as Moses the servant of the LORD had commanded before, that they should bless the people of Israel. [34]And afterward he read all the words of the law, the blessings and the cursings, according to all that is written in the Book of the Law. [35]There was not a word of all that Moses had commanded which Joshua did not read before all the assembly of Israel, with the women, the little ones, and the strangers who were living among them.

The Treaty with the Gibeonites

9 And it came to pass when all the kings who *were* on this side of the Jordan, in the hills and in the lowland and in all the coasts of the Great Sea toward Lebanon—the Hittite, the Amorite, the Canaanite, the Perizzite, the Hivite, and the Jebusite—heard *about it,* [2]that they gathered together to fight with Joshua and Israel with one accord.

[3]But when the inhabitants of Gibeon heard what Joshua had done to Jericho and Ai, [4]they worked craftily, and went and pretended to be ambassadors. And they took old sacks on their donkeys, old wineskins torn and mended, [5]old and patched sandals on their feet, and old garments on themselves; and all the bread of their provision was dry *and* moldy. [6]And they went to Joshua, to the camp at Gilgal, and said to him and to the men of Israel, "We have come from a far country; now therefore, make a covenant with us."

[7]Then the men of Israel said to the Hivites, "Perhaps you dwell among us; so how can we make a covenant with you?"

[8]But they said to Joshua, "We *are* your servants."

8:31 [a]Deuteronomy 27:5, 6

8:33 The stranger in this verse may refer to non-Israelites who had accepted Israel's God and therefore had been accepted into the Hebrew community (see also v. 35). Aliens or strangers who embraced *Yahweh* as God and chose to live among God's people were assimilated into the nation (1 Kin. 8:41–43).

8:34 The blessings and curses are outlined in Deuteronomy 27:1—28:68.

8:35 Two requirements were fulfilled by Joshua: the altar and its sacrifices were a visual reaffirmation of Moses' covenant (vv. 30, 31; Ex. 24:3–8), and the reading was a fulfillment of Moses' written memorial (Ex. 17:14; Josh. 1:8).

9:1, 2 The reputation of Israel's conquering army under the leadership of Joshua provided the impetus needed to unite these traditionally independent cities. From this point, Israel faced a coalition of united forces rather than one city at a time.

9:1–15 The inhabitants of Gibeon were identified as the Hivites, one of the seven nations God had promised to drive out of the Land before Israel (v. 7; Josh. 3:10; see also Deut. 7:1–2; map, The Division of the Land). The testimony of the Gibeonites provides additional evidence that the people of Canaan were not totally ignorant of God's truth (v. 9). They knew Israel was allowed to make treaties with cities that accepted peace and became Israel's servants, except for the seven nations named (Deut. 20:10, 11); so they concealed their identity to deceive Joshua and save themselves.

Goals are a joint effort process: getting in touch with our heart and setting a course; then depending on and being willing for God to direct us one step at a time.

Sheila West

And Joshua said to them, "Who *are* you, and where do you come from?"

9So they said to him: "From a very far country your servants have come, because of the name of the LORD your God; for we have heard of His fame, and all that He did in Egypt, 10and all that He did to the two kings of the Amorites who *were* beyond the Jordan—to Sihon king of Heshbon, and Og king of Bashan, who was at Ashtaroth. 11Therefore our elders and all the inhabitants of our country spoke to us, saying, 'Take provisions with you for the journey, and go to meet them, and say to them, "We *are* your servants; now therefore, make a covenant with us." ' 12This bread of ours we took hot *for* our provision from our houses on the day we departed to come to you. But now look, it is dry and moldy. 13And these wineskins which we filled *were* new, and see, they are torn; and these our garments and our sandals have become old because of the very long journey."

14Then the men of Israel took some of their provisions; but they did not ask counsel of the LORD. 15So Joshua made peace with them, and made a covenant with them to let them live; and the rulers of the congregation swore to them.

16And it happened at the end of three days, after they had made a covenant with them, that they heard that they *were* their neighbors who dwelt near them. 17Then the children of Israel journeyed and came to their cities on the third day. Now their cities *were* Gibeon, Chephirah, Beeroth, and Kirjath Jearim. 18But the children of Israel did not attack them, because the rulers of the congregation had sworn to them by the LORD God of Israel. And all the congregation complained against the rulers.

19Then all the rulers said to all the congregation, "We have sworn to them by the LORD God of Israel; now therefore, we may not touch them. 20This we will do to them: We will let them live, lest wrath be upon us because of the oath which we swore to them." 21And the rulers said to them, "Let them live, but let them be woodcutters and water carriers for all the congregation, as the rulers had promised them."

22Then Joshua called for them, and he spoke to them, saying, "Why have you deceived us, saying, 'We *are* very far from you,' when you dwell near us? 23Now therefore, you *are* cursed, and none of you shall be freed from being slaves—woodcutters and water carriers for the house of my God."

24So they answered Joshua and said, "Because your servants were clearly told that the LORD your God commanded His servant Moses to give you all the land, and to destroy all the inhabitants of the land from before you; therefore we were very much afraid for our lives because of you, and have done this thing. 25And now, here we are, in your hands; do with us as it seems good and right to do to us." 26So he did to them, and delivered them out of the hand of the children of Israel, so that they did not kill them. 27And that day Joshua made them woodcutters and water carriers for the congregation and for the altar of the LORD, in the place which He would choose, even to this day.

The Sun Stands Still

10Now it came to pass when Adoni-Zedek king of Jerusalem heard how Joshua had taken Ai and had utterly destroyed it—as he had done to Jericho and its king, so he had done to Ai and its king—and how the inhabitants of Gibeon had made peace with Israel and were among them, 2that they feared greatly, because Gibeon *was* a great city, like one of the royal cities, and because it *was* greater than Ai, and all its men *were* mighty. 3Therefore Adoni-Zedek king of Jerusalem sent to Hoham king of Hebron, Piram king of Jarmuth, Japhia king of Lachish, and Debir king of Eglon, saying, 4"Come up to me and help me, that we may attack Gibeon, for it has made peace with Joshua and with the children of Israel." 5Therefore the five kings of the Amorites, the king of Jerusalem, the king of Hebron, the king of Jarmuth, the king of Lachish, *and* the king of Eglon, gathered together and went up, they and all their armies, and camped before Gibeon and made war against it.

6And the men of Gibeon sent to Joshua at the camp at Gilgal, saying, "Do not forsake your servants; come up to us quickly, save us and help us,

9:19–20 Even though the treaty was based on deceit, the leaders of Israel were obligated to honor it since they had sworn by the Lord God of Israel. The commitment of the oath was to the Lord, not to the Gibeonites (vv. 18–20).

10:1 The five kings of the Amorites. As a result of their previous victories and the surrender of the Gibeonites, the Is-

raelites were entrenched in the central highlands close to Jerusalem. The coalition's strategy was to recapture Gibeon because of its strategic location.

10:6–11 Gibeon's treaty with Israel required Israel to come to the aid of the Gibeonites (Josh. 9:15). God gave His people victory.

for all the kings of the Amorites who dwell in the mountains have gathered together against us."

7So Joshua ascended from Gilgal, he and all the people of war with him, and all the mighty men of valor. 8And the LORD said to Joshua, "Do not fear them, for I have delivered them into your hand; not a man of them shall stand before you." 9Joshua therefore came upon them suddenly, having marched all night from Gilgal. 10So the LORD routed them before Israel, killed them with a great slaughter at Gibeon, chased them along the road that goes to Beth Horon, and struck them down as far as Azekah and Makkedah. 11And it happened, as they fled before Israel *and* were on the descent of Beth Horon, that the LORD cast down large hailstones from heaven on them as far as Azekah, and they died. *There were* more who died from the hailstones than the children of Israel killed with the sword.

12Then Joshua spoke to the LORD in the day when the LORD delivered up the Amorites before the children of Israel, and he said in the sight of Israel:

"Sun, stand still over Gibeon;
  And Moon, in the Valley of Aijalon."
13So the sun stood still,
  And the moon stopped,
  Till the people had revenge
  Upon their enemies.

Is this not written in the Book of Jasher? So the sun stood still in the midst of heaven, and did not hasten to go *down* for about a whole day. 14And there has been no day like that, before it or after it, that the LORD heeded the voice of a man; for the LORD fought for Israel.

15Then Joshua returned, and all Israel with him, to the camp at Gilgal.

The Amorite Kings Executed

16But these five kings had fled and hidden themselves in a cave at Makkedah. 17And it was told Joshua, saying, "The five kings have been found hidden in the cave at Makkedah."

18So Joshua said, "Roll large stones against the mouth of the cave, and set men by it to guard them. 19And do not stay *there* yourselves, *but* pursue your enemies, and attack their rear *guard*. Do not allow them to enter their cities, for the LORD your God has delivered them into your hand."

20Then it happened, while Joshua and the children of Israel made an end of slaying them with a very great slaughter, till they had finished, that those who escaped entered fortified cities. 21And all the people returned to the camp, to Joshua at Makkedah, in peace.

No one moved his tongue against any of the children of Israel.

22Then Joshua said, "Open the mouth of the cave, and bring out those five kings to me from the cave." 23And they did so, and brought out those five kings to him from the cave: the king of Jerusalem, the king of Hebron, the king of Jarmuth, the king of Lachish, *and* the king of Eglon.

24So it was, when they brought out those kings to Joshua, that Joshua called for all the men of Israel, and said to the captains of the men of war who went with him, "Come near, put your feet on the necks of these kings." And they drew near and put their feet on their necks. 25Then Joshua said to them, "Do not be afraid, nor be dismayed; be strong and of good courage, for thus the LORD will do to all your enemies against whom you fight." 26And afterward Joshua struck them and killed them, and hanged them on five trees; and they were hanging on the trees until evening. 27So it was at the time of the going down of the sun *that* Joshua commanded, and they took them down from the trees, cast them into the cave where they had been hidden, and laid large stones against the cave's mouth, *which remain* until this very day.

Conquest of the Southland

28On that day Joshua took Makkedah, and struck it and its king with the edge of the sword. He utterly destroyed them[a]— all the people who *were* in it. He let none remain. He also did to the king of Makkedah as he had done to the king of Jericho.

29Then Joshua passed from Makkedah, and all Israel with him, to Libnah; and they fought against Libnah. 30And the LORD also delivered it and its king into the hand of Israel; he struck it and all the people who *were* in it with the edge of the sword. He let none remain in it, but did to its king as he had done to the king of Jericho.

10:28 [a]Following Masoretic Text and most authorities; many Hebrew manuscripts, some manuscripts of the Septuagint, and some manuscripts of the Targum read *it.*

10:12–14 Joshua's longest day. One of God's most miracles is cited also in the Book of Jasher, a piece of Hebrew poetic literature chronicling Israel's victories that is now lost (see 2 Sam. 1:18). Subsequent verses give strategic and military details of the battle. Exact details on the inner workings of the miracle are not recorded. Perhaps the earth tilted so that Israel would experience a northern-type long day, or the rotation of the earth may have slowed. Numerous details

about the battle are noted: the extent of Israel's march, their attack and pursuit, the names of battle sites, the names of kings, a description of the hailstorm. The supplying of such details shows that this is not mere legend but an actual military debriefing. We do know these three things about the miracle of the sun standing still: nothing like this ever happened before or after; God was responsible for whatever transpired; and He acted because Joshua called upon Him for help.

We are not interested in the possibilities of defeat.

Queen Victoria

31Then Joshua passed from Libnah, and all Israel with him, to Lachish; and they encamped against it and fought against it. 32And the LORD delivered Lachish into the hand of Israel, who took it on the second day, and struck it and all the people who *were* in it with the edge of the sword, according to all that he had done to Libnah. 33Then Horam king of Gezer came up to help Lachish; and Joshua struck him and his people, until he left him none remaining.

34From Lachish Joshua passed to Eglon, and all Israel with him; and they encamped against it and fought against it. 35They took it on that day and struck it with the edge of the sword; all the people who *were* in it he utterly destroyed that day, according to all that he had done to Lachish.

36So Joshua went up from Eglon, and all Israel with him, to Hebron; and they fought against it. 37And they took it and struck it with the edge of the sword—its king, all its cities, and all the people who *were* in it; he left none remaining, according to all that he had done to Eglon, but utterly destroyed it and all the people who *were* in it.

38Then Joshua returned, and all Israel with him, to Debir; and they fought against it. 39And he took it and its king and all its cities; they struck them with the edge of the sword and utterly destroyed all the people who *were* in it. He left none remaining; as he had done to Hebron, so he did to Debir and its king, as he had done also to Libnah and its king.

40So Joshua conquered all the land: the mountain country and the Southa and the lowland and the wilderness slopes, and all their kings; he left none remaining, but utterly destroyed all that breathed, as the LORD God of Israel had commanded. 41And Joshua conquered them from Kadesh Barnea as far as Gaza, and all the country of Goshen, even as far as Gibeon. 42All these kings and their land Joshua took at one time, because the LORD God of Israel fought for Israel. 43Then Joshua returned, and all Israel with him, to the camp at Gilgal.

The Northern Conquest

11 And it came to pass, when Jabin king of Hazor heard *these things*, that he sent to Jobab king of Madon, to the king of Shimron, to the king of Achshaph, 2and to the kings who *were* from the north, in the mountains, in the plain south of Chinneroth, in the lowland, and in the heights of Dor on the west, 3to the Canaanites in the east and in the west, the Amorite, the Hittite, the Perizzite, the Jebusite in the mountains, and the Hivite below Hermon in the land of Mizpah. 4So they went out, they and all their armies with them, *as* many people *as* the sand that *is* on the seashore in multitude, with very many horses and chariots. 5And when all these kings had met together, they came and camped together at the waters of Merom to fight against Israel.

6But the LORD said to Joshua, "Do not be afraid because of them, for tomorrow about this time I will deliver all of them slain before Israel. You shall hamstring their horses and burn their chariots with fire." 7So Joshua and all the people of war with him came against them suddenly by the waters of Merom, and they attacked them. 8And the LORD delivered them into the hand of Israel, who defeated them and chased them to Greater Sidon, to the Brook Misrephoth,a and to the Valley of Mizpah eastward; they attacked them until they left none of them remaining. 9So Joshua did to them as the LORD had told him: he hamstrung their horses and burned their chariots with fire.

10Joshua turned back at that time and took Hazor, and struck its king with the sword; for Hazor was formerly the head of all those kingdoms. 11And they struck all the people who *were* in it with the edge of the sword, utterly destroying *them.* There was none left breathing. Then he burned Hazor with fire.

12So all the cities of those kings, and all their kings, Joshua took and struck with the edge of the sword. He utterly destroyed them, as Moses the servant of the LORD had commanded. 13But *as for*

10:40 aHebrew *Negev,* and so throughout this book   **11:8** aHebrew *Misrephoth Maim*

10:40 Joshua conquered all the Land. This summary statement indicated that by the taking of certain strategically located cities, Israel gained a measure of control over the southern region. Full political control would take place much later under King David.

11:1 Hazor was much more formidable than any of the previous cities (see map, The Division of Land). Located ten miles north of the Sea of Chinnereth (later Sea of Galilee), Hazor covered at least 200 acres (compared with Jericho's approximately seven acres). It had massive walls and was surrounded by a fortified ditch. Conquering Hazor was essential to the conquest of the northern portion of the country. Recent archaeological excavations at Hazor have uncovered a wide variety of Canaanite structures.

the cities that stood on their mounds,[a] Israel burned none of them, except Hazor only, *which* Joshua burned. [14]And all the spoil of these cities and the livestock, the children of Israel took as booty for themselves; but they struck every man with the edge of the sword until they had destroyed them, and they left none breathing. [15]As the LORD had commanded Moses his servant, so Moses commanded Joshua, and so Joshua did. He left nothing undone of all that the LORD had commanded Moses.

Summary of Joshua's Conquests

[16]Thus Joshua took all this land: the mountain country, all the South, all the land of Goshen, the lowland, and the Jordan plain[a]—the mountains of Israel and its lowlands, [17]from Mount Halak and the ascent to Seir, even as far as Baal Gad in the Valley of Lebanon below Mount Hermon. He captured all their kings, and struck them down and killed them. [18]Joshua made war a long time with all those kings. [19]There was not a city that made peace with the children of Israel, except the Hivites, the inhabitants of Gibeon. All *the others* they took in battle. [20]For it was of the LORD to harden their hearts, that they should come against Israel in battle, that He might utterly destroy them, *and* that they might receive no mercy, but that He might destroy them, as the LORD had commanded Moses.

[21]And at that time Joshua came and cut off the Anakim from the mountains: from Hebron, from Debir, from Anab, from all the mountains of Judah, and from all the mountains of Israel; Joshua utterly destroyed them with their cities. [22]None of the Anakim were left in the land of the children of Israel; they remained only in Gaza, in Gath, and in Ashdod.

[23]So Joshua took the whole land, according to all that the LORD had said to Moses; and Joshua gave it as an inheritance to Israel according to their divisions by their tribes. Then the land rested from war.

The Kings Conquered by Moses

12 These *are* the kings of the land whom the children of Israel defeated, and whose land they possessed on the other side of the Jordan toward the rising of the sun, from the River Arnon

to Mount Hermon, and all the eastern Jordan plain: [2]One king was Sihon king of the Amorites, who dwelt in Heshbon *and* ruled half of Gilead, from Aroer, which is on the bank of the River Arnon, from the middle of that river, even as far as the River Jabbok, *which is* the border of the Ammonites, [3]and the eastern Jordan plain from the Sea of Chinneroth as far as the Sea of the Arabah (the Salt Sea), the road to Beth Jeshimoth, and southward below the slopes of Pisgah. [4]*The other king was* Og king of Bashan and his territory, *who was* of the remnant of the giants, who dwelt at Ashtaroth and at Edrei, [5]and reigned over Mount Hermon, over Salcah, over all Bashan, as far as the border of the Geshurites and the Maachathites, and over half of Gilead *to* the border of Sihon king of Heshbon.

[6]These Moses the servant of the LORD and the children of Israel had conquered; and Moses the servant of the LORD had given it *as* a possession to the Reubenites, the Gadites, and half the tribe of Manasseh.

The Kings Conquered by Joshua

[7]And these *are* the kings of the country which Joshua and the children of Israel conquered on this side of the Jordan, on the west, from Baal Gad in the Valley of Lebanon as far as Mount Halak and the ascent to Seir, which Joshua gave to the tribes of Israel *as* a possession according to their divisions, [8]in the mountain country, in the lowlands, in the *Jordan* plain, in the slopes, in the wilderness, and in the South—the Hittites, the Amorites, the Canaanites, the Perizzites, the Hivites, and the Jebusites: [9]the king of Jericho, one; the king of Ai, which *is* beside Bethel, one; [10]the king of Jerusalem, one; the king of Hebron, one; [11]the king of Jarmuth, one; the king of Lachish, one; [12]the king of Eglon, one; the king of Gezer, one; [13]the king of Debir, one; the king of Geder, one; [14]the king of Hormah, one; the king of Arad, one; [15]the king of Libnah, one; the king of Adullam, one; [16]the king of Makkedah, one; the king of Bethel, one; [17]the king of Tappuah, one; the king of Hepher, one; [18]the king of Aphek, one; the king of Lasharon, one; [19]the king of Madon, one; the

---

11:13 [a]Hebrew *tel*, a heap of successive city ruins   11:16 [a]Hebrew *arabah*

11:19, 20 Instruments of judgment. When God promised the Land to Abraham, He did not instruct him to drive out or destroy the inhabitants of the Land because at that time the iniquity of the Amorites was "not yet complete" (Gen. 15:16). God was patient with the inhabitants of Canaan for hundreds of years, giving them many opportunities to repent. Yet despite the witness of God's people to the one true God and such warnings as the destruction of Sodom and Gomorrah, the sin, rebellion, and depravity of the Canaanites continued until the day came when God's judgment fell on them. God

uses many instruments of judgment. In the case of the Canaanites, the instrument was the Israelite army (see Josh. 6, Justice).

11:22 The Anakim were the "giants" who frightened the Israelites 40 years earlier (Num. 13:33).

12:1–24 The leadership of Moses and Joshua (vv. 1–24) displayed the continuity of God's mission. A list of the defeated kings would be a permanent record and reminder of the reality of the conquest.

THE DIVISION OF LAND

Asher– Daughter Serah
(Num. 26:46)

Benjamin–Women of
Benjamin (Judg. 21:1-23)

Dan– Bilhah, mother of
Dan (Gen. 30:5, 6)

Ephraim– Deborah, judge
of Israel (Judg. 4:5)

Gad– Leah, mother of
Zebulun (Gen. 30:11)

Issachar– Leah, mother of
Zebulun (Gen. 30:20)

Judah–Tamar, wife of
Judah (Gen. 38:6)

Manasseh– Daughter of Manasseh
received inheritance (Josh. 17:6)

Naphtali–Hiram's mother
widowed (1 Kin. 7:14)

Reuben– Bilhah, victim of
Reuben's incest (Gen. 35:22)

Simeon– Dinah, sister of
Simeon (Gen. 34:25)

Zebulun– Leah, mother of
Zebulun (Gen. 30:20)

Women are mentioned from respective tribes.

ASHER
NAPHTALI
BASHAN
ZEBULUN
ISSACHAR
Sea of
Chinnereth
(Galilee)
MANASSEH
GREAT SEA
(MEDITERRANEAN)
EPHRAIM
GILEAD
Jordan River
GAD
DAN
AMMON
BENJAMIN
REUBEN
JUDAH
Dead Sea
N
SIMEON
MOAB

0 ———— 300 Mi.
0 ———— 300 Km.

king of Hazor, one; 20the king of Shimron Meron, one; 21the king of Achshaph, one; 21the king of Taanach, one; 21the king of Megiddo, one; 22the king of Kedesh, one; the king of Jokneam in Carmel, one; 23the king of Dor in the heights of Dor, one; the king of the people of Gilgal, one; 24the king of Tirzah, one— all the kings, thirty-one.

Remaining Land to Be Conquered

13 Now Joshua was old, advanced in years. And the LORD said to him: "You are old, advanced in years, and there remains very much land yet to be possessed. 2This is the land that yet remains: all the territory of the Philistines and all that of the Geshurites, 3from Sihor, which is east of Egypt, as far as the border of Ekron northward (which is

counted as Canaanite); the five lords of the Philistines—the Gazites, the Ashdodites, the Ashkelonites, the Gittites, and the Ekronites; also the Avites; [4]from the south, all the land of the Canaanites, and Mearah that belongs to the Sidonians as far as Aphek, to the border of the Amorites; [5]the land of the Gebalites,[a] and all Lebanon, toward the sunrise, from Baal Gad below Mount Hermon as far as the entrance to Hamath; [6]all the inhabitants of the mountains from Lebanon as far as the Brook Misrephoth,[a] *and* all the Sidonians—them I will drive out from before the children of Israel; only divide it by lot to Israel as an inheritance, as I have commanded you. [7]Now therefore, divide this land as an inheritance to the nine tribes and half the tribe of Manasseh."

The Land Divided East of the Jordan

[8]With the other half-tribe the Reubenites and the Gadites received their inheritance, which Moses had given them, beyond the Jordan eastward, as Moses the servant of the LORD had given them: [9]from Aroer which *is* on the bank of the River Arnon, and the town that *is* in the midst of the ravine, and all the plain of Medeba as far as Dibon; [10]all the cities of Sihon king of the Amorites, who reigned in Heshbon, as far as the border of the children of Ammon; [11]Gilead, and the border of the Geshurites and Maachathites, all Mount Hermon, and all Bashan as far as Salcah; [12]all the kingdom of Og in Bashan, who reigned in Ashtaroth and Edrei, who remained of the remnant of the giants; for Moses had defeated and cast out these.

[13]Nevertheless the children of Israel did not drive out the Geshurites or the Maachathites, but the Geshurites and the Maachathites dwell among the Israelites until this day.

[14]Only to the tribe of Levi he had given no inheritance; the sacrifices of the LORD God of Israel made by fire *are* their inheritance, as He said to them.

The Land of Reuben

[15]And Moses had given to the tribe of the children of Reuben *an inheritance* according to their families. [16]Their territory was from Aroer, which *is* on the bank of the River Arnon, and the city that *is* in the midst of the ravine, and all the plain by Medeba; [17]Heshbon and all its cities that *are* in the plain: Dibon, Bamoth Baal, Beth Baal Meon, [18]Jahaza, Kedemoth, Mephaath, [19]Kirjathaim,

Sibmah, Zereth Shahar on the mountain of the valley, [20]Beth Peor, the slopes of Pisgah, and Beth Jeshimoth— [21]all the cities of the plain and all the kingdom of Sihon king of the Amorites, who reigned in Heshbon, whom Moses had struck with the princes of Midian: Evi, Rekem, Zur, Hur, and Reba, who *were* princes of Sihon dwelling in the country. [22]The children of Israel also killed with the sword Balaam the son of Beor, the soothsayer, among those who were killed by them. [23]And the border of the children of Reuben was the bank of the Jordan. This *was* the inheritance of the children of Reuben according to their families, the cities and their villages.

The Land of Gad

[24]Moses also had given *an inheritance* to the tribe of Gad, to the children of Gad according to their families. [25]Their territory was Jazer, and all the cities of Gilead, and half the land of the Ammonites as far as Aroer, which *is* before Rabbah, [26]and from Heshbon to Ramath Mizpah and Betonim, and from Mahanaim to the border of Debir, [27]and in the valley Beth Haram, Beth Nimrah, Succoth, and Zaphon, the rest of the kingdom of Sihon king of Heshbon, with the Jordan as *its* border, as far as the edge of the Sea of Chinnereth, on the other side of the Jordan eastward. [28]This *is* the inheritance of the children of Gad according to their families, the cities and their villages.

Half the Tribe of Manasseh (East)

[29]Moses also had given *an inheritance* to half the tribe of Manasseh; it was for half the tribe of the children of Manasseh according to their families: [30]Their territory was from Mahanaim, all Bashan, all the kingdom of Og king of Bashan, and all the towns of Jair which are in Bashan, sixty cities; [31]half of Gilead, and Ashtaroth and Edrei, cities of the kingdom of Og in Bashan, *were* for the children of Machir the son of Manasseh, for half of the children of Machir according to their families.

[32]These *are the areas* which Moses had distributed as an inheritance in the plains of Moab on the other side of the Jordan, by Jericho eastward. [33]But to the tribe of Levi Moses had given no inheritance; the LORD God of Israel *was* their inheritance, as He had said to them.

····················

13:5 [a]Or *Giblites* 13:6 [a]Hebrew *Misrephoth Maim*

13:2 **The designation Palestine** comes from the name "Philistines" (see chart, Terminology for the Land).

13:7 **The land not yet conquered** was to be allotted to the various tribes (see Josh. 13—21). From this point, the conquest would be carried out by the respective tribes in the allotted area of each.

13:14 **The tribe of Levi** was to be scattered among the people

with the assignment of performing the sacrifices and teaching the Law (Deut. 33:8–10). Therefore, this tribe would not be counted among the 12 in the land division. The inheritance of Joseph was divided between two tribes named after Joseph's sons Ephraim and Manasseh, bringing the count again to 12 tribes (see chart, The Breastplate of the High Priest's Clothing).

CALEB: PORTRAIT OF A HERO

CALEB'S ACTIONS	GOD'S EVALUATION	GOD'S REWARDS
1. He sided with the Lord (Num. 14:6–10).	1. You have "a different spirit" (Num. 14:24).	1. God named Caleb as one of only two adults who left Egypt and were allowed to enter the Land of Promise (Num. 14:29, 30).
2. He was not afraid of God's enemies, even though others were (Num. 13:30–33).	2. "You have wholly followed the LORD my God" (Josh. 14:8, 9).	2. He kept Caleb alive forty more years (Josh. 14:10).
3. He risked his life rather than forsake the Lord (Num. 14:6–10).	3. You are "My servant" (Num. 14:24).	3. He preserved his energy and strength (Josh. 14:11).
4. He suffered in the wilderness because of the lack of faith of others (Num. 14:20–24, 30–38).		4. He gave Caleb victory over the Canaanites in his own territory (Josh. 15:13, 14).
5. He kept his faith and enthusiasm for God through the wilderness wandering (Josh. 14:7, 8).		5. He gave Caleb and his descendants the promised inheritance (Josh. 14:13, 14).
6. He was ready to move against God's enemies (the Anakim) forty years later (Josh. 15:14–16).		
CALEB IS FAITHFUL	GOD IS PLEASED	GOD REWARDS

The Land Divided West of the Jordan

14 These *are the areas* which the children of Israel inherited in the land of Canaan, which Eleazar the priest, Joshua the son of Nun, and the heads of the fathers of the tribes of the children of Israel distributed as an inheritance to them. ²Their inheritance *was* by lot, as the LORD had commanded by the hand of Moses, for the nine tribes and the half-tribe. ³For Moses had given the inheritance of the two tribes and the half-tribe on the other side of the Jordan; but to the Levites he had given no inheritance among them. ⁴For the children of Joseph were two tribes: Manasseh and Ephraim. And they gave no part to the Levites in the land, except cities to dwell *in,* with their common-lands for their livestock and their property. ⁵As the LORD had commanded Moses, so the children of Israel did; and they divided the land.

Caleb Inherits Hebron

⁶Then the children of Judah came to Joshua in Gilgal. And Caleb the son of Jephunneh the Kenizzite said to him: "You know the word which the LORD said to Moses the man of God concerning you and me in Kadesh Barnea. ⁷I *was* forty years old when Moses the servant of the LORD sent me from Kadesh Barnea to spy out the land, and I brought back word to him as *it was* in my heart. ⁸Nevertheless my brethren who went up with me made the heart of the people melt, but I wholly followed the LORD my God. ⁹So Moses swore on that day, saying, 'Surely the land where your foot has trodden shall be your inheritance and your children's forever, because you have wholly followed the LORD my God.' ¹⁰And now, behold, the LORD has kept me alive, as He said, these forty-five years, ever since the LORD spoke this word to Moses while Israel wandered in the wilderness; and now, here I am this day, eighty-five years old. ¹¹As yet I *am as* strong this day as on the day that Moses sent me; just as my strength *was* then, so now *is* my strength for war, both for going out and for coming in. ¹²Now therefore, give me this mountain of which the LORD spoke in that day; for you heard in that day how the Anakim *were* there,

---

14:1 Eleazar is named first because he, as priest, would have the ephod with the Urim and Thummim (see Ex. 28:15; Deut. 33:8, notes). Though the exact procedure is not clear, the Urim and Thummim apparently were sacred lots used to determine God's direction. The Israelites considered the use of lots as a way to leave the choice completely in God's hands.

ACHSAH   *The Clever Daughter of Caleb*

Achsah, Caleb's daughter, appeared on the scene when her father offered a marriage between her and whomever was able to conquer the town Kirjath Sepher. The primary interest for everyone at that time was the land. Everything depended on it—their worship, home, food, financial and political security, and the ability to raise a family. Since it was the custom of the day for parents to arrange marriages, the offer Caleb made was not unusual.

Caleb's nephew Othniel accepted the challenge, took the Canaanite town, and won both Achsah and the portion of land promised. Yet Achsah knew their land would only be productive with a water source. Seeing the solution in the nearby springs, Achsah discussed the situation with her husband and convinced him that they needed to approach her father for help. Her approach to her father for a blessing was likely a request for a wedding present and was consistent with the blessings for weddings and families (Deut. 28:1–14).

Achsah showed interest and involvement in her inheritance, her marriage, and her future. She was not greedy, but neither was she hesitant to pursue what was needed just as the industrious woman pictured in Proverbs 31:27.

See also notes on Decision Making (1 Cor. 8); Feminine Leadership (1 Sam. 25); Wives (Prov. 31)

and *that* the cities *were* great *and* fortified. It may be that the LORD *will be* with me, and I shall be able to drive them out as the LORD said."

[13]And Joshua blessed him, and gave Hebron to Caleb the son of Jephunneh as an inheritance. [14]Hebron therefore became the inheritance of Caleb the son of Jephunneh the Kenizzite to this day, because he wholly followed the LORD God of Israel. [15]And the name of Hebron formerly was Kirjath Arba (*Arba was* the greatest man among the Anakim).

Then the land had rest from war.

The Land of Judah

15 So *this* was the lot of the tribe of the children of Judah according to their families:

The border of Edom at the Wilderness of Zin southward *was* the extreme southern boundary. [2]And their southern border began at the shore of the Salt Sea, from the bay that faces southward. [3]Then it went out to the southern side of the Ascent of Akrabbim, passed along to Zin, ascended on the south side of Kadesh Barnea, passed along to Hezron, went up to Adar, and went around to Karkaa. [4]*From there* it passed toward Azmon and went out to the Brook of Egypt; and the border ended at the sea. This shall be your southern border.

[5]The east border *was* the Salt Sea as far as the mouth of the Jordan.

And the border on the northern quarter *began* at the bay of the sea at the mouth of the Jordan. [6]The border went up to Beth Hoglah and passed north of Beth Arabah; and the border went up to the stone of Bohan the son of Reuben. [7]Then the border went up toward Debir from the Valley of Achor, and it turned northward toward Gilgal, which *is* before the Ascent of Adummim, which *is* on the south side of the valley. The border continued toward the waters of En Shemesh and ended at En Rogel. [8]And the border went up by the Valley of the Son of Hinnom to the southern slope of the Jebusite *city* (which *is* Jerusalem). The border went up to the top of the mountain that *lies* before the Valley of Hinnom westward, which *is* at the end of the Valley of Rephaim[a] northward. [9]Then the border went around from the top of the hill to the fountain of the water of Nephtoah, and extended to the cities of Mount Ephron. And the border went around to Baalah (which *is* Kirjath Jearim). [10]Then the border turned westward from Baalah to Mount Seir, passed along to the side of Mount Jearim on the north (which *is* Chesalon), went down to Beth Shemesh, and passed on to Timnah. [11]And the border went out to the side of Ekron northward. Then the border went around to Shicron, passed along to Mount Baalah, and extended to Jabneel; and the border ended at the sea.

[12]The west border *was* the coastline of the Great Sea. This *is* the boundary of the children of Judah all around according to their families.

Caleb Occupies Hebron and Debir

[13]Now to Caleb the son of Jephunneh he gave a share among the children of Judah, according to

•••••••••••••••••••

15:8 [a]Literally *Giants*

15:1 The tribe of Judah was not the largest, nor was Judah the eldest son of Jacob. However, a line of kings, beginning with David and ending with Christ, the King of Kings, came from this tribe (Gen. 49:10).

15:4 The Brook of Egypt was a stream that ran into the Mediterranean and served as the southern boundary between Judah's inheritance and Egypt. The sea (or Great Sea, v. 12) is the Mediterranean (see map, The Division of Land).

the commandment of the LORD to Joshua, *namely,* Kirjath Arba, which *is* Hebron (*Arba was* the father of Anak). [14]Caleb drove out the three sons of Anak from there: Sheshai, Ahiman, and Talmai, the children of Anak. [15]Then he went up from there to the inhabitants of Debir (formerly the name of Debir *was* Kirjath Sepher).

[16]And Caleb said, "He who attacks Kirjath Sepher and takes it, to him I will give Achsah my daughter as wife." [17]So Othniel the son of Kenaz, the brother of Caleb, took it; and he gave him Achsah his daughter as wife. [18]Now it was so, when she came *to him,* that she persuaded him to ask her father for a field. So she dismounted from *her* donkey, and Caleb said to her, "What do you wish?" [19]She answered, "Give me a blessing; since you have given me land in the South, give me also springs of water." So he gave her the upper springs and the lower springs.

The Cities of Judah

[20]This *was* the inheritance of the tribe of the children of Judah according to their families:

[21]The cities at the limits of the tribe of the children of Judah, toward the border of Edom in the South, were Kabzeel, Eder, Jagur, [22]Kinah, Dimonah, Adadah, [23]Kedesh, Hazor, Ithnan, [24]Ziph, Telem, Bealoth, [25]Hazor, Hadattah, Kerioth, Hezron (which *is* Hazor), [26]Amam, Shema, Moladah, [27]Hazar Gaddah, Heshmon, Beth Pelet, [28]Hazar Shual, Beersheba, Bizjothjah, [29]Baalah, Ijim, Ezem, [30]Eltolad, Chesil, Hormah, [31]Ziklag, Madmannah, Sansannah, [32]Lebaoth, Shilhim, Ain, and Rimmon: all the cities *are* twenty-nine, with their villages.

[33]In the lowland: Eshtaol, Zorah, Ashnah, [34]Zanoah, En Gannim, Tappuah, Enam, [35]Jarmuth, Adullam, Socoh, Azekah, [36]Sharaim, Adithaim, Gederah, and Gederothaim: fourteen cities with their villages; [37]Zenan, Hadashah, Migdal Gad, [38]Dilean, Mizpah, Joktheel, [39]Lachish, Bozkath, Eglon, [40]Cabbon, Lahmas,[a] Kithlish, [41]Gederoth, Beth Dagon, Naamah, and Makkedah: sixteen cities with their villages; [42]Libnah, Ether, Ashan, [43]Jiphtah, Ashnah, Nezib, [44]Keilah, Achzib, and Mareshah: nine cities with their villages; [45]Ekron, with its towns and villages; [46]from Ekron to the sea, all that *lay* near Ashdod, with their villages; [47]Ashdod with its towns and villages, Gaza with its

towns and villages—as far as the Brook of Egypt and the Great Sea with *its* coastline.

[48]And in the mountain country: Shamir, Jattir, Sochoh, [49]Dannah, Kirjath Sannah (which *is* Debir), [50]Anab, Eshtemoh, Anim, [51]Goshen, Holon, and Giloh: eleven cities with their villages; [52]Arab, Dumah, Eshean, [53]Janum, Beth Tappuah, Aphekah, [54]Humtah, Kirjath Arba (which *is* Hebron), and Zior: nine cities with their villages; [55]Maon, Carmel, Ziph, Juttah, [56]Jezreel, Jokdeam, Zanoah, [57]Kain, Gibeah, and Timnah: ten cities with their villages; [58]Halhul, Beth Zur, Gedor, [59]Maarath, Beth Anoth, and Eltekon: six cities with their villages; [60]Kirjath Baal (which *is* Kirjath Jearim) and Rabbah: two cities with their villages.

[61]In the wilderness: Beth Arabah, Middin, Secacah, [62]Nibshan, the City of Salt, and En Gedi: six cities with their villages.

[63]As for the Jebusites, the inhabitants of Jerusalem, the children of Judah could not drive them out; but the Jebusites dwell with the children of Judah at Jerusalem to this day.

Ephraim and West Manasseh

16 The lot fell to the children of Joseph from the Jordan, by Jericho, to the waters of Jericho on the east, to the wilderness that goes up from Jericho through the mountains to Bethel, [2]then went out from Bethel to Luz,[a] passed along to the border of the Archites at Ataroth, [3]and went down westward to the boundary of the Japhletites, as far as the boundary of Lower Beth Horon to Gezer; and it ended at the sea.

[4]So the children of Joseph, Manasseh and Ephraim, took their inheritance.

The Land of Ephraim

[5]The border of the children of Ephraim, according to their families, was *thus:* The border of their inheritance on the east side was Ataroth Addar as far as Upper Beth Horon.

[6]And the border went out toward the sea on the north side of Michmethath; then the border went around eastward to Taanath Shiloh, and passed by it on the east of Janohah. [7]Then it went

15:40 [a]Or *Lahmam*   16:2 [a]Septuagint reads *Bethel* (that is, Luz).

15:18, 19 Caleb apparently reared his family well (see chart, Caleb: Portrait of a Hero). His daughter Achsah was not afraid to speak up, and her forthrightness was rewarded (see Achsah). Othniel, Caleb's nephew, became Achsah's husband, and later was one of the judges of Israel (Judg. 1:12–15; 3:9–11; see chart, The Period of the Judges).

15:63 The final conquest of Jerusalem occurred under King David, several hundred years later (see 2 Sam. 5:6, 7). The Book of Joshua combines victories and failures in a natural

way. The rewards of obedience and penalties for disobedience are clear (see chart, Models of Obedience and Disobedience). God responds to the cries of His people, but He is not subject to them.

16:1 The descendants of Joseph drew one lot, but the land was divided between the tribes of Joseph's two sons, Ephraim and Manasseh. Jacob, Joseph's father, had regarded the two sons of Joseph as his own (Gen. 48:5), bringing the count of the territories to 12, since the Levites did not inherit a specific area (see Josh. 13:14, note).

down from Janohah to Ataroth and Naarah,[a] reached to Jericho, and came out at the Jordan.

[8]The border went out from Tappuah westward to the Brook Kanah, and it ended at the sea. This was the inheritance of the tribe of the children of Ephraim according to their families. [9]The separate cities for the children of Ephraim were among the inheritance of the children of Manasseh, all the cities with their villages.

[10]And they did not drive out the Canaanites who dwelt in Gezer; but the Canaanites dwell among the Ephraimites to this day and have become forced laborers.

The Other Half-Tribe of Manasseh (West)

17 There was also a lot for the tribe of Manasseh, for he was the firstborn of Joseph: namely for Machir the firstborn of Manasseh, the father of Gilead, because he was a man of war; therefore he was given Gilead and Bashan. [2]And there was a lot for the rest of the children of Manasseh according to their families: for the children of Abiezer,[a] the children of Helek, the children of Asriel, the children of Shechem, the children of Hepher, and the children of Shemida; these were the male children of Manasseh the son of Joseph according to their families.

[3]But Zelophehad the son of Hepher, the son of Gilead, the son of Machir, the son of Manasseh, had no sons, but only daughters. And these are the names of his daughters: Mahlah, Noah, Hoglah, Milcah, and Tirzah. [4]And they came near before Eleazar the priest, before Joshua the son of Nun, and before the rulers, saying, "The LORD commanded Moses to give us an inheritance among our brothers." Therefore, according to the commandment of the LORD, he gave them an inheritance among their father's brothers. [5]Ten shares fell to Manasseh, besides the land of Gilead and Bashan, which were on the other side of the Jordan, [6]because the daughters of Manasseh received an inheritance among his sons; and the rest of Manasseh's sons had the land of Gilead.

[7]And the territory of Manasseh was from Asher to Michmethath, that lies east of Shechem; and the border went along south to the inhabitants of En Tappuah. [8]Manasseh had the land of Tappuah, but Tappuah on the border of Manasseh belonged to the children of Ephraim. [9]And the border descended to the Brook Kanah, southward to the brook. These

cities of Ephraim are among the cities of Manasseh. The border of Manasseh was on the north side of the brook; and it ended at the sea.

[10]Southward it was Ephraim's, northward it was Manasseh's, and the sea was its border. Manasseh's territory was adjoining Asher on the north and Issachar on the east. [11]And in Issachar and in Asher, Manasseh had Beth Shean and its towns, Ibleam and its towns, the inhabitants of Dor and its towns, the inhabitants of En Dor and its towns, the inhabitants of Taanach and its towns, and the inhabitants of Megiddo and its towns—three hilly regions. [12]Yet the children of Manasseh could not drive out the inhabitants of those cities, but the Canaanites were determined to dwell in that land. [13]And it happened, when the children of Israel grew strong, that they put the Canaanites to forced labor, but did not utterly drive them out.

More Land for Ephraim and Manasseh

[14]Then the children of Joseph spoke to Joshua, saying, "Why have you given us only one lot and one share to inherit, since we are a great people, inasmuch as the LORD has blessed us until now?"

[15]So Joshua answered them, "If you are a great people, then go up to the forest country and clear a place for yourself there in the land of the Perizzites and the giants, since the mountains of Ephraim are too confined for you."

[16]But the children of Joseph said, "The mountain country is not enough for us; and all the Canaanites who dwell in the land of the valley have chariots of iron, both those who are of Beth Shean and its towns and those who are of the Valley of Jezreel."

[17]And Joshua spoke to the house of Joseph—to Ephraim and Manasseh—saying, "You are a great people and have great power; you shall not have only one lot, [18]but the mountain country shall be yours. Although it is wooded, you shall cut it down, and its farthest extent shall be yours; for you shall drive out the Canaanites, though they have iron chariots and are strong."

The Remainder of the Land Divided

18 Now the whole congregation of the children of Israel assembled together at Shiloh, and

16:7 [a]Or Naaran (compare 1 Chronicles 7:28)   17:2 [a]Called Jeezer in Numbers 26:30

17:3, 4 See Num. 26, Daughters of Zelophehad; 27:1–4, 5–7; 36:1–12, notes.

17:14–18 **The descendants of Joseph** approached Joshua with two problems: They faced the iron chariots of the Canaanites, and they expressed the need for more land because of their size. Their allotment was already one of the largest as well as being in one of the most fertile regions, but it did include a large mountain range. Joshua turned their argument around and suggested that they could best drive out the Canaanites

and clear the mountain ranges precisely because their tribe was so large.

18:1 **The camp was moved from Gilgal** on the fringe of the inheritance to the center at Shiloh (modern Khirbet Seilun about 12 miles south of Shechem). Moving the ark of the covenant and setting up the tabernacle of meeting indicated the certainty of conquest and symbolized unification under God's presence as the tribes began settling the Land.

Even Christians struggle with negative fear, but I believe it's possible to turn fear into faith, renewed confidence, and positive action.

Carol Kent

set up the tabernacle of meeting there. And the land was subdued before them. [2]But there remained among the children of Israel seven tribes which had not yet received their inheritance.

[3]Then Joshua said to the children of Israel: "How long will you neglect to go and possess the land which the LORD God of your fathers has given you? [4]Pick out from among you three men for *each* tribe, and I will send them; they shall rise and go through the land, survey it according to their inheritance, and come *back* to me. [5]And they shall divide it into seven parts. Judah shall remain in their territory on the south, and the house of Joseph shall remain in their territory on the north. [6]You shall therefore survey the land in seven parts and bring *the survey* here to me, that I may cast lots for you here before the LORD our God. [7]But the Levites have no part among you, for the priesthood of the LORD *is* their inheritance. And Gad, Reuben, and half the tribe of Manasseh have received their inheritance beyond the Jordan on the east, which Moses the servant of the LORD gave them."

[8]Then the men arose to go away; and Joshua charged those who went to survey the land, saying, "Go, walk through the land, survey it, and come back to me, that I may cast lots for you here before the LORD in Shiloh." [9]So the men went, passed through the land, and wrote the survey in a book in seven parts by cities; and they came to Joshua at the camp in Shiloh. [10]Then Joshua cast lots for them in Shiloh before the LORD, and there Joshua divided the land to the children of Israel according to their divisions.

The Land of Benjamin

[11]Now the lot of the tribe of the children of Benjamin came up according to their families, and the territory of their lot came out between the children of Judah and the children of Joseph. [12]Their border on the north side began at the Jordan, and the border went up to the side of Jericho on the north, and went up through the mountains westward; it ended at the Wilderness of Beth Aven. [13]The border went over from there toward Luz, to the side of Luz (which *is* Bethel) southward; and the border descended to Ataroth Addar, near the hill that *lies* on the south side of Lower Beth Horon.

[14]Then the border extended around the west side to the south, from the hill that *lies* before Beth Horon southward; and it ended at Kirjath Baal (which *is* Kirjath Jearim), a city of the children of Judah. This *was* the west side.

[15]The south side *began* at the end of Kirjath Jearim, and the border extended on the west and went out to the spring of the waters of Nephtoah. [16]Then the border came down to the end of the mountain that *lies* before the Valley of the Son of Hinnom, which *is* in the Valley of the Rephaim[a] on the north, descended to the Valley of Hinnom, to the side of the Jebusite *city* on the south, and descended to En Rogel. [17]And it went around from the north, went out to En Shemesh, and extended toward Geliloth, which is before the Ascent of Adummim, and descended to the stone of Bohan the son of Reuben. [18]Then it passed along toward the north side of Arabah,[a] and went down to Arabah. [19]And the border passed along to the north side of Beth Hoglah; then the border ended at the north bay at the Salt Sea, at the south end of the Jordan. This *was* the southern boundary.

[20]The Jordan was its border on the east side. This *was* the inheritance of the children of Benjamin, according to its boundaries all around, according to their families.

[21]Now the cities of the tribe of the children of Benjamin, according to their families, were Jericho, Beth Hoglah, Emek Keziz, [22]Beth Arabah, Zemaraim, Bethel, [23]Avim, Parah, Ophrah, [24]Chephar Haammoni, Ophni, and Gaba: twelve cities with their villages; [25]Gibeon, Ramah, Beeroth, [26]Mizpah, Chephirah, Mozah, [27]Rekem, Irpeel, Taralah, [28]Zelah, Eleph, Jebus (which *is* Jerusalem), Gibeath, *and* Kirjath: fourteen cities with their villages. This was the inheritance of the children of Benjamin according to their families.

Simeon's Inheritance with Judah

19 The second lot came out for Simeon, for the tribe of the children of Simeon according to their families. And their inheritance was within

18:16 [a]Literally *Giants*   18:18 [a]Or *Beth Arabah* (compare 15:6 and 18:22)

18:6 The casting of lots would have been done by Eleazar the priest in the presence of the ark of the covenant, establishing the results as God's choice (see Deut. 33:8, note).

18:11–28 The inheritance of Benjamin is described at length. Though Judah was the tribe of the promised line of kings, Saul, the first king of Israel, came from the tribe of Benjamin. Jerusalem, which eventually would be captured by King David and become the capital of the nation, was near the border between the territories of Benjamin and Judah.

the inheritance of the children of Judah. [2]They had in their inheritance Beersheba (Sheba), Moladah, [3]Hazar Shual, Balah, Ezem, [4]Eltolad, Bethul, Hormah, [5]Ziklag, Beth Marcaboth, Hazar Susah, [6]Beth Lebaoth, and Sharuhen: thirteen cities and their villages; [7]Ain, Rimmon, Ether, and Ashan: four cities and their villages; [8]and all the villages that *were* all around these cities as far as Baalath Beer, Ramah of the South. This *was* the inheritance of the tribe of the children of Simeon according to their families.

[9]The inheritance of the children of Simeon *was included* in the share of the children of Judah, for the share of the children of Judah was too much for them. Therefore the children of Simeon had *their* inheritance within the inheritance of that people.

The Land of Zebulun

[10]The third lot came out for the children of Zebulun according to their families, and the border of their inheritance was as far as Sarid. [11]Their border went toward the west and to Maralah, went to Dabbasheth, and extended along the brook that is east of Jokneam. [12]Then from Sarid it went eastward toward the sunrise along the border of Chisloth Tabor, and went out toward Daberath, bypassing Japhia. [13]And from there it passed along on the east of Gath Hepher, toward Eth Kazin, and extended to Rimmon, which borders on Neah. [14]Then the border went around it on the north side of Hannathon, and it ended in the Valley of Jiphthah El. [15]Included were Kattath, Nahallal, Shimron, Idalah, and Bethlehem: twelve cities with their villages. [16]This *was* the inheritance of the children of Zebulun according to their families, these cities with their villages.

The Land of Issachar

[17]The fourth lot came out to Issachar, for the children of Issachar according to their families. [18]And their territory went to Jezreel, and *included* Chesulloth, Shunem, [19]Haphraim, Shion, Anaharath, [20]Rabbith, Kishion, Abez, [21]Remeth, En Gannim, En Haddah, and Beth Pazzez. [22]And the border reached to Tabor, Shahazimah, and Beth Shemesh; their border ended at the Jordan: sixteen cities with their villages. [23]This *was* the inheritance of the tribe of the children of Issachar according to their families, the cities and their villages.

The Land of Asher

[24]The fifth lot came out for the tribe of the children of Asher according to their families. [25]And their territory included Helkath, Hali, Beten, Achshaph, [26]Alammelech, Amad, and Mishal; it reached to Mount Carmel westward, along *the Brook* Shihor Libnath. [27]It turned toward the sunrise to Beth Dagon; and it reached to Zebulun and to the Valley of Jiphthah El, then northward beyond Beth Emek and Neiel, bypassing Cabul *which was* on the left, [28]including Ebron,[a] Rehob, Hammon, and Kanah, as far as Greater Sidon. [29]And the border turned to Ramah and to the fortified city of Tyre; then the border turned to Hosah, and ended at the sea by the region of Achzib. [30]Also Ummah, Aphek, and Rehob *were included:* twenty-two cities with their villages. [31]This *was* the inheritance of the tribe of the children of Asher according to their families, these cities with their villages.

The Land of Naphtali

[32]The sixth lot came out to the children of Naphtali, for the children of Naphtali according to their families. [33]And their border began at Heleph, enclosing the territory from the terebinth tree in Zaanannim, Adami Nekeb, and Jabneel, as far as Lakkum; it ended at the Jordan. [34]From Heleph the border extended westward to Aznoth Tabor, and went out from there toward Hukkok; it adjoined Zebulun on the south side and Asher on the west side, and ended at Judah by the Jordan toward the sunrise. [35]And the fortified cities *are* Ziddim, Zer, Hammath, Rakkath, Chinnereth, [36]Adamah, Ramah, Hazor, [37]Kedesh, Edrei, En Hazor, [38]Iron, Migdal El, Horem, Beth Anath, and Beth Shemesh: nineteen cities with their villages. [39]This *was* the inheritance of the tribe of the children of Naphtali according to their families, the cities and their villages.

The Land of Dan

[40]The seventh lot came out for the tribe of the children of Dan according to their families. [41]And the territory of their inheritance was Zorah, Eshtaol, Ir Shemesh, [42]Shaalabbin, Aijalon, Jethlah, [43]Elon, Timnah, Ekron, [44]Eltekeh, Gibbethon, Baalath, [45]Jehud, Bene Berak, Gath Rimmon, [46]Me Jarkon, and Rakkon, with the region near Joppa. [47]And the border of the children of Dan went beyond these, because the children of Dan went up to fight against Leshem and took it; and they struck it with the edge of the sword, took possession of it, and dwelt in it. They called Leshem, Dan, after the name of Dan their father. [48]This *is* the inheritance of the tribe of the children of Dan according to their families, these cities with their villages.

19:28 [a]Following Masoretic Text, Targum, and Vulgate; a few Hebrew manuscripts read *Abdon* (compare 21:30 and 1 Chronicles 6:74).

19:15 Bethlehem was the site east of Mount Carmel, not the Bethlehem in Judah where Jesus was born.

Joshua's Inheritance

[49]When they had made an end of dividing the land as an inheritance according to their borders, the children of Israel gave an inheritance among them to Joshua the son of Nun. [50]According to the word of the LORD they gave him the city which he asked for, Timnath Serah in the mountains of Ephraim; and he built the city and dwelt in it.

[51]These were the inheritances which Eleazar the priest, Joshua the son of Nun, and the heads of the fathers of the tribes of the children of Israel divided as an inheritance by lot in Shiloh before the LORD, at the door of the tabernacle of meeting. So they made an end of dividing the country.

The Cities of Refuge

20 The LORD also spoke to Joshua, saying, [2]"Speak to the children of Israel, saying: 'Appoint for yourselves cities of refuge, of which I spoke to you through Moses, [3]that the slayer who kills a person accidentally or unintentionally may flee there; and they shall be your refuge from the avenger of blood. [4]And when he flees to one of those cities, and stands at the entrance of the gate of the city, and declares his case in the hearing of the elders of that city, they shall take him into the city as one of them, and give him a place, that he may dwell among them. [5]Then if the avenger of blood pursues him, they shall not deliver the slayer into his hand, because he struck his neighbor unintentionally, but did not hate him beforehand. [6]And he shall dwell in that city until he stands before the congregation for judgment, and until the death of the one who is high priest in those days. Then the slayer may return and come to his own city and his own house, to the city from which he fled.'"

[7]So they appointed Kedesh in Galilee, in the mountains of Naphtali, Shechem in the mountains of Ephraim, and Kirjath Arba (which is Hebron) in the mountains of Judah. [8]And on the other side of the Jordan, by Jericho eastward, they assigned Bezer in the wilderness on the plain, from the tribe of Reuben, Ramoth in Gilead, from the tribe of Gad, and Golan in Bashan, from the tribe of Manasseh. [9]These were the cities appointed for all the children of Israel and for the stranger who dwelt among them, that whoever killed a person accidentally might flee there, and not die by the hand of the avenger of blood until he stood before the congregation.

Cities of the Levites

21 Then the heads of the fathers' houses of the Levites came near to Eleazar the priest, to Joshua the son of Nun, and to the heads of the fathers' houses of the tribes of the children of Israel. [2]And they spoke to them at Shiloh in the land of Canaan, saying, "The LORD commanded through Moses to give us cities to dwell in, with their common-lands for our livestock." [3]So the children of Israel gave to the Levites from their inheritance, at the commandment of the LORD, these cities and their common-lands:

[4]Now the lot came out for the families of the Kohathites. And the children of Aaron the priest, who were of the Levites, had thirteen cities by lot from the tribe of Judah, from the tribe of Simeon, and from the tribe of Benjamin. [5]The rest of the children of Kohath had ten cities by lot from the families of the tribe of Ephraim, from the tribe of Dan, and from the half-tribe of Manasseh.

[6]And the children of Gershon had thirteen cities by lot from the families of the tribe of Issachar, from the tribe of Asher, from the tribe of Naphtali, and from the half-tribe of Manasseh in Bashan.

[7]The children of Merari according to their families had twelve cities from the tribe of Reuben, from the tribe of Gad, and from the tribe of Zebulun.

[8]And the children of Israel gave these cities with their common-lands by lot to the Levites, as the LORD had commanded by the hand of Moses.

[9]So they gave from the tribe of the children of Judah and from the tribe of the children of Simeon these cities which are designated by name, [10]which were for the children of Aaron, one of the families of the Kohathites, who were of the children of Levi; for the lot was theirs first. [11]And they gave them Kirjath Arba (Arba was the father of Anak), which is Hebron, in the mountains of Judah, with the common-land surrounding it. [12]But the fields of the city and its villages they gave to Caleb the son of Jephunneh as his possession.

[13]Thus to the children of Aaron the priest they gave Hebron with its common-land (a city of refuge for the slayer), Libnah with its common-land, [14]Jattir with its common-land, Eshtemoa with its common-land, [15]Holon with its common-land,

---

19:49 The allotments began with Caleb's (Josh. 14:13) and ended with Joshua's. These were the only two men who experienced the entire saga of leaving Egypt, wandering in the wilderness, and participating in the conquest.

20:1–9 Cities of refuge were established to provide asylum for an individual who accidentally killed another (Ex. 21:12, 13; Num. 35:6–34). A distinction was to be made between willful murder and accidental killing or manslaughter (Num. 35:6–34; Deut. 19:1–13). The practice of blood revenge (often leading to long-lasting feuds) was customary in OT times.

21:1–42 The 48 cities of the Levites were scattered among all the territories because a major part of the role of the priests was to teach all the people God's Law (see Josh. 13:14, note).

Debir with its common-land, [16]Ain with its common-land, Juttah with its common-land, and Beth Shemesh with its common-land: nine cities from those two tribes; [17]and from the tribe of Benjamin, Gibeon with its common-land, Geba with its common-land, [18]Anathoth with its common-land, and Almon with its common-land: four cities. [19]All the cities of the children of Aaron, the priests, *were* thirteen cities with their common-lands.

[20]And the families of the children of Kohath, the Levites, the rest of the children of Kohath, even they had the cities of their lot from the tribe of Ephraim. [21]For they gave them Shechem with its common-land in the mountains of Ephraim (a city of refuge for the slayer), Gezer with its common-land, [22]Kibzaim with its common-land, and Beth Horon with its common-land: four cities; [23]and from the tribe of Dan, Eltekeh with its common-land, Gibbethon with its common-land, [24]Aijalon with its common-land, *and* Gath Rimmon with its common-land: four cities; [25]and from the half-tribe of Manasseh, Tanach with its common-land and Gath Rimmon with its common-land: two cities. [26]All the ten cities with their common-lands were for the rest of the families of the children of Kohath.

[27]Also to the children of Gershon, of the families of the Levites, from the *other* half-tribe of Manasseh, *they gave* Golan in Bashan with its common-land (a city of refuge for the slayer), and Be Eshterah with its common-land: two cities; [28]and from the tribe of Issachar, Kishion with its common-land, Daberath with its common-land, [29]Jarmuth with its common-land, *and* En Gannim with its common-land: four cities; [30]and from the tribe of Asher, Mishal with its common-land, Abdon with its common-land, [31]Helkath with its common-land, and Rehob with its common-land: four cities; [32]and from the tribe of Naphtali, Kedesh in Galilee with its common-land (a city of refuge for the slayer), Hammoth Dor with its common-land, and Kartan with its common-land: three cities. [33]All the cities of the Gershonites according to their families *were* thirteen cities with their common-lands.

[34]And to the families of the children of Merari, the rest of the Levites, from the tribe of Zebulun, Jokneam with its common-land, Kartah with its common-land, [35]Dimnah with its common-land, *and* Nahalal with its common-land: four cities; [36]and from the tribe of Reuben, Bezer with its common-land, Jahaz with its common-land, [37]Kedemoth with its common-land, and Mephaath with its common-land: four cities;[a] [38]and from the tribe of Gad, Ramoth in Gilead with its common-land (a city of refuge for the slayer), Mahanaim with its common-land, [39]Heshbon with its common-land, *and* Jazer with its common-land: four cities in all. [40]So all the cities for the children of Merari according to their families, the rest of the families of the Levites, were *by* their lot twelve cities.

[41]All the cities of the Levites within the possession of the children of Israel *were* forty-eight cities with their common-lands. [42]Every one of these cities had its common-land surrounding it; thus *were* all these cities.

The Promise Fulfilled

[43]So the LORD gave to Israel all the land of which He had sworn to give to their fathers, and they took possession of it and dwelt in it. [44]The LORD gave them rest all around, according to all that He had sworn to their fathers. And not a man of all their enemies stood against them; the LORD delivered all their enemies into their hand. [45]Not a word failed of any good thing which the LORD had spoken to the house of Israel. All came to pass.

Eastern Tribes Return to Their Lands

22Then Joshua called the Reubenites, the Gadites, and half the tribe of Manasseh, [2]and said to them: "You have kept all that Moses the servant of the LORD commanded you, and have obeyed my voice in all that I commanded you. [3]You have not left your brethren these many days, up to this day, but have kept the charge of the commandment of the LORD your God. [4]And now the LORD your God has given rest to your brethren, as He promised them; now therefore, return and go to your tents *and* to the land of your possession, which Moses the servant of the LORD gave you on the other side of the Jordan. [5]But take careful heed to do the commandment and the law which Moses the servant of the LORD commanded you, to love the LORD your God, to walk in all His ways, to keep His commandments, to hold fast to Him, and to serve Him with all your heart and with all your soul." [6]So Joshua blessed them and sent them away, and they went to their tents.

21:37 aFollowing Septuagint and Vulgate (compare 1 Chronicles 6:78, 79); Masoretic Text, Bomberg, and Targum omit verses 36 and 37.

22:10–34 The move to Shiloh for the two and a half eastern tribes made immediate access to the tabernacle of meeting impossible (see Josh. 18:1, note). The Jordan River divided them from the rest of Israel (Josh. 22:25). To avoid becoming a separated people, they built an altar before God as a "witness" to their unity with the tribes on the western side of the river (v. 34). This action was misinterpreted by those on the western side. Thinking the group had already regressed into worshiping other gods, they feared God's judgment would come upon all of them again as it had when they sinned at Peor by falling into Baal worship (v. 17). Their zeal might have meant disaster if they had not followed God's plan for dealing with conflict or misunderstanding. Their action was postponed until the facts were clear (see Deut. 13:13–15).

[7]Now to half the tribe of Manasseh Moses had given a possession in Bashan, but to the *other* half of it Joshua gave *a possession* among their brethren on this side of the Jordan, westward. And indeed, when Joshua sent them away to their tents, he blessed them, [8]and spoke to them, saying, "Return with much riches to your tents, with very much livestock, with silver, with gold, with bronze, with iron, and with very much clothing. Divide the spoil of your enemies with your brethren."

[9]So the children of Reuben, the children of Gad, and half the tribe of Manasseh returned, and departed from the children of Israel at Shiloh, which *is* in the land of Canaan, to go to the country of Gilead, to the land of their possession, which they had obtained according to the word of the LORD by the hand of Moses.

An Altar by the Jordan

[10]And when they came to the region of the Jordan which *is* in the land of Canaan, the children of Reuben, the children of Gad, and half the tribe of Manasseh built an altar there by the Jordan—a great, impressive altar. [11]Now the children of Israel heard *someone* say, "Behold, the children of Reuben, the children of Gad, and half the tribe of Manasseh have built an altar on the frontier of the land of Canaan, in the region of the Jordan—on the children of Israel's side." [12]And when the children of Israel heard *of it*, the whole congregation of the children of Israel gathered together at Shiloh to go to war against them.

[13]Then the children of Israel sent Phinehas the son of Eleazar the priest to the children of Reuben, to the children of Gad, and to half the tribe of Manasseh, into the land of Gilead, [14]and with him ten rulers, one ruler each from the chief house of every tribe of Israel; and each one *was* the head of the house of his father among the divisions[a] of Israel. [15]Then they came to the children of Reuben, to the children of Gad, and to half the tribe of Manasseh, to the land of Gilead, and they spoke with them, saying, [16]"Thus says the whole congregation of the LORD: 'What treachery *is* this that you have committed against the God of Israel, to turn away this day from following the LORD, in that you have built for yourselves an altar, that you might rebel this day against the LORD? [17]*Is* the iniquity of Peor not enough for us, from which we are not cleansed till this day, although there was a plague in the congregation of the LORD, [18]but that you must turn away this day from following the LORD? And it shall be, if you rebel today against the LORD, that tomorrow He will be angry with the whole congregation of Israel. [19]Nevertheless, if the land of your possession *is* unclean, *then* cross over to the land of the possession of the LORD, where the LORD's tabernacle stands, and take possession

among us; but do not rebel against the LORD, nor rebel against us, by building yourselves an altar besides the altar of the LORD our God. [20]Did not Achan the son of Zerah commit a trespass in the accursed thing, and wrath fell on all the congregation of Israel? And that man did not perish alone in his iniquity.' "

[21]Then the children of Reuben, the children of Gad, and half the tribe of Manasseh answered and said to the heads of the divisions[a] of Israel: [22]"The LORD God of gods, the LORD God of gods, He knows, and let Israel itself know—if *it is* in rebellion, or if in treachery against the LORD, do not save us this day. [23]If we have built ourselves an altar to turn from following the LORD, or if to offer on it burnt offerings or grain offerings, or if to offer peace offerings on it, let the LORD Himself require *an account.* [24]But in fact we have done it for fear, for a reason, saying, 'In time to come your descendants may speak to our descendants, saying, "What have you to do with the LORD God of Israel? [25]For the LORD has made the Jordan a border between you and us, *you* children of Reuben and children of Gad. You have no part in the LORD." So your descendants would make our descendants cease fearing the LORD.' [26]Therefore we said, 'Let us now prepare to build ourselves an altar, not for burnt offering nor for sacrifice, [27]but *that* it *may be* a witness between you and us and our generations after us, that we may perform the service of the LORD before Him with our burnt offerings, with our sacrifices, and with our peace offerings; that your descendants may not say to our descendants in time to come, "You have no part in the LORD." ' [28]Therefore we said that it will be, when they say *this* to us or to our generations in time to come, that we may say, 'Here is the replica of the altar of the LORD which our fathers made, though not for burnt offerings nor for sacrifices; but it *is* a witness between you and us.' [29]Far be it from us that we should rebel against the LORD, and turn from following the LORD this day, to build an altar for burnt offerings, for grain offerings, or for sacrifices, besides the altar of the LORD our God which *is* before His tabernacle."

[30]Now when Phinehas the priest and the rulers of the congregation, the heads of the divisions[a] of Israel who *were* with him, heard the words that the children of Reuben, the children of Gad, and the children of Manasseh spoke, it pleased them. [31]Then Phinehas the son of Eleazar the priest said to the children of Reuben, the children of Gad, and the children of Manasseh, "This day we perceive that the LORD *is* among us, because you have not committed this treachery against the LORD. Now you have delivered the children of Israel out of the hand of the LORD."

22:14, 21, 30 [a]Literally *thousands*

[32]And Phinehas the son of Eleazar the priest, and the rulers, returned from the children of Reuben and the children of Gad, from the land of Gilead to the land of Canaan, to the children of Israel, and brought back word to them. [33]So the thing pleased the children of Israel, and the children of Israel blessed God; they spoke no more of going against them in battle, to destroy the land where the children of Reuben and Gad dwelt.

[34]The children of Reuben and the children of Gad[a] called the altar, *Witness*, "For *it is* a witness between us that the LORD *is* God."

Joshua's Farewell Address

23 Now it came to pass, a long time after the LORD had given rest to Israel from all their enemies round about, that Joshua was old, advanced in age. [2]And Joshua called for all Israel, for their elders, for their heads, for their judges, and for their officers, and said to them:

"I am old, advanced in age. [3]You have seen all that the LORD your God has done to all these nations because of you, for the LORD your God *is* He who has fought for you. [4]See, I have divided to you by lot these nations that remain, to be an inheritance for your tribes, from the Jordan, with all the nations that I have cut off, as far as the Great Sea westward. [5]And the LORD your God will expel them from before you and drive them out of your sight. So you shall possess their land, as the LORD your God promised you. [6]Therefore be very courageous to keep and to do all that is written in the Book of the Law of Moses, lest you turn aside from it to the right hand or to the left, [7]*and* lest you go among these nations, these who remain among you. You shall not make mention of the name of their gods, nor cause *anyone* to swear *by them;* you shall not serve them nor bow down to them, [8]but you shall hold fast to the LORD your God, as you have done to this day. [9]For the LORD has driven out from before you great and strong nations; but *as*

for you, no one has been able to stand against you to this day. [10]One man of you shall chase a thousand, for the LORD your God *is* He who fights for you, as He promised you. [11]Therefore take careful heed to yourselves, that you love the LORD your God. [12]Or else, if indeed you do go back, and cling to the remnant of these nations—these that remain among you—and make marriages with them, and go in to them and they to you, [13]know for certain that the LORD your God will no longer drive out these nations from before you. But they shall be snares and traps to you, and scourges on your sides and thorns in your eyes, until you perish from this good land which the LORD your God has given you.

[14]"Behold, this day I *am* going the way of all the earth. And you know in all your hearts and in all your souls that not one thing has failed of all the good things which the LORD your God spoke concerning you. All have come to pass for you; not one word of them has failed. [15]Therefore it shall come to pass, that as all the good things have come upon you which the LORD your God promised you, so the LORD will bring upon you all harmful things, until He has destroyed you from this good land which the LORD your God has given you. [16]When you have transgressed the covenant of the LORD your God, which He commanded you, and have gone and served other gods, and bowed down to them, then the anger of the LORD will burn against you, and you shall perish quickly from the good land which He has given you."

The Covenant at Shechem

24 Then Joshua gathered all the tribes of Israel to Shechem and called for the elders of Israel, for their heads, for their judges, and for their officers; and they presented themselves before God. [2]And Joshua said to all the people, "Thus says

---

22:34 [a]Septuagint adds *and half the tribe of Manasseh*.

23:2 The farewell addresses of Joshua are recorded (Josh. 23; 24). Chapter 23 may have been addressed to the leaders (v. 2), while chapter 24 was addressed to all the people (Josh. 23:2).

23:3 The secret of Joshua's success was his acknowledgment of the Lord as the great Defender of Israel. He pointed out an important principle: Faith in the Lord is rooted in historical realities. The NT teaches the same principle (John 20:30, 31).

23:6 The command to demonstrate courage in obedience has not lost its importance (Josh. 1:6, 7, 9, 18). It would require as much courage for the Israelites to stay true to the Lord in peace as it did for them to march for the Lord in war. Joshua gave the people, almost verbatim, the same instructions the Lord gave him (Josh. 1:7).

23:8 Joshua's personal commitment to the Lord is described by the words "hold fast" (Heb. *davaq*). The same Hebrew word appears in Genesis 2:24 where a man is instructed to leave his father and mother and to "be joined to" or "cling" to

his wife in the most binding, intimate human relationship. It also describes a uniquely close relationship with the Lord (Deut. 4:4; 10:20; 11:22; 13:4).

23:14, 15 God's faithfulness is the constant theme in Joshua (Josh. 1:3; 2:24; 3:10; 10:42; 11:8; 21:43–45). Israel had seen God's faithfulness in keeping His promises; they needed to be reminded that He is also faithful in His judgment against sin.

23:16 The word covenant does not occur often in the Book of Joshua, but the idea of covenant is at the heart of all that Joshua and the Israelites experienced. Marks of the covenant are clearly recognized: the ark (Josh. 3:8–17), circumcision (Josh. 5:2–7), the Passover (Josh. 5:10), the altar, the rereading of the Law of Moses with the blessings and curses (Josh. 8:30–35), and a recitation of the Lord's faithfulness (Josh. 24:2–13).

24:1 At Shechem, located in the hill country of Ephraim, Joshua presented covenant renewal. Joshua's first message, in abbreviated form, was to the two and a half tribes who were

the LORD God of Israel: 'Your fathers, *including* Terah, the father of Abraham and the father of Nahor, dwelt on the other side of the River[a] in old times; and they served other gods. ³Then I took your father Abraham from the other side of the River, led him throughout all the land of Canaan, and multiplied his descendants and gave him Isaac. ⁴To Isaac I gave Jacob and Esau. To Esau I gave the mountains of Seir to possess, but Jacob and his children went down to Egypt. ⁵Also I sent Moses and Aaron, and I plagued Egypt, according to what I did among them. Afterward I brought you out.

⁶'Then I brought your fathers out of Egypt, and you came to the sea; and the Egyptians pursued your fathers with chariots and horsemen to the Red Sea. ⁷So they cried out to the LORD; and He put darkness between you and the Egyptians, brought the sea upon them, and covered them. And your eyes saw what I did in Egypt. Then you dwelt in the wilderness a long time. ⁸And I brought you into the land of the Amorites, who dwelt on the other side of the Jordan, and they fought with you. But I gave them into your hand, that you might possess their land, and I destroyed them from before you. ⁹Then Balak the son of Zippor, king of Moab, arose to make war against Israel, and sent and called Balaam the son of Beor to curse you. ¹⁰But I would not listen to Balaam; therefore he continued to bless you. So I delivered you out of his hand. ¹¹Then you went over the Jordan and came to Jericho. And the men of Jericho fought against you—*also* the Amorites, the Perizzites, the Canaanites, the Hittites, the Girgashites, the Hivites, and the Jebusites. But I delivered them into your hand. ¹²I sent the hornet before you which drove them out from before you, *also* the two kings of the Amorites, *but* not with your sword or with your bow. ¹³I have given you a land for which you did not labor, and cities which you did not build, and you dwell in them; you eat of the vineyards and olive groves which you did not plant.'

¹⁴"Now therefore, fear the LORD, serve Him in sincerity and in truth, and put away the gods which your fathers served on the other side of the River and in Egypt. Serve the LORD! ¹⁵And if it seems evil to you to serve the LORD, choose for yourselves this day whom you will serve, whether the gods which your fathers served that *were* on the other side of the River, or the gods of the Amorites, in whose land you dwell. But as for me and my house, we will serve the LORD."

¹⁶So the people answered and said: "Far be it from us that we should forsake the LORD to serve other gods; ¹⁷for the LORD our God *is* He who brought us and our fathers up out of the land of Egypt, from the house of bondage, who did those great signs in our sight, and preserved us in all the way that we went and among all the people through whom we passed. ¹⁸And the LORD drove out from before us all the people, including the Amorites who dwelt in the land. We also will serve the LORD, for He *is* our God."

¹⁹But Joshua said to the people, "You cannot serve the LORD, for He *is* a holy God. He *is* a jealous God; He will not forgive your transgressions nor your sins. ²⁰If you forsake the LORD and serve foreign gods, then He will turn and do you harm and consume you, after He has done you good."

²¹And the people said to Joshua, "No, but we will serve the LORD!"

²²So Joshua said to the people, "You *are* witnesses against yourselves that you have chosen the LORD for yourselves, to serve Him."

And they said, "*We are* witnesses!"

²³"Now therefore," *he said*, "put away the foreign gods which *are* among you, and incline your heart to the LORD God of Israel."

²⁴And the people said to Joshua, "The LORD our God we will serve, and His voice we will obey!"

²⁵So Joshua made a covenant with the people

24:2 [a]Hebrew *Nahar*, the Euphrates, and so in verses 3, 14, and 15

---

returning to their land on the east side of the Jordan (Josh. 22:1–5). The second was possibly to a group of the nation's leaders (Josh. 23). At Shechem, where God previously promised the Land of Canaan to Abraham and his descendants (Gen. 12:6, 7), Joshua renewed the covenant for the last time (see Josh. 8:30–35).

24:3 Joshua began with Abraham, whose decision to separate himself from the safety and community of his clan in Ur and to walk away from the religion of his fathers was a mighty act of faith. Throughout Scripture Abraham is presented as the prime example of faith (Acts 7:2–8; Rom. 4:1–4; Gal. 3:6, 7; Heb. 11:8–12, 17–19; James 2:23).

24:6, 7 The safe passage through the Red Sea often is used by God as a reference pointing to His faithfulness and power (Deut. 11:4; Josh. 2:10; 4:23; Neh. 9:9–11; Ps. 106:8–11, 22; 136:13–15; Is. 51:10; Acts 7:36; Heb. 11:29).

24:15 God's faithfulness is a constant theme in Joshua (see

Josh. 23:14, 15, note). The question is: Will His people respond faithfully in return? Joshua presented only two choices: Serve the Lord God or serve foreign gods. They could not serve both (see Josh. 24:19, 20, note). Such a challenge might seem more appropriate at the beginning of the book rather than at the end because at this stage the people had won the wars, obtained their land, and begun settling it. But Joshua understood that the challenge of choice—faithfulness and obedience, or unfaithfulness and disobedience—would be continually faced in the daily routines of life. He called the people to declare their loyalty and allegiance to God.

24:19, 20 The Lord stands alone. Other religions cannot be incorporated with devotion to the Lord. The first commandment makes this clear (Ex. 20:3). Apostasy seldom starts with an outright denial of the Lord, but rather with small compromises of His teachings. God will not tolerate unfaithfulness and idolatry.

that day, and made for them a statute and an ordinance in Shechem.

26Then Joshua wrote these words in the Book of the Law of God. And he took a large stone, and set it up there under the oak that *was* by the sanctuary of the LORD. 27And Joshua said to all the people, "Behold, this stone shall be a witness to us, for it has heard all the words of the LORD which He spoke to us. It shall therefore be a witness to you, lest you deny your God." 28So Joshua let the people depart, each to his own inheritance.

Death of Joshua and Eleazar

29Now it came to pass after these things that Joshua the son of Nun, the servant of the LORD, died, *being* one hundred and ten years old. 30And they buried him within the border of his inheri-

tance at Timnath Serah, which *is* in the mountains of Ephraim, on the north side of Mount Gaash.

31Israel served the LORD all the days of Joshua, and all the days of the elders who outlived Joshua, who had known all the works of the LORD which He had done for Israel.

32The bones of Joseph, which the children of Israel had brought up out of Egypt, they buried at Shechem, in the plot of ground which Jacob had bought from the sons of Hamor the father of Shechem for one hundred pieces of silver, and which had become an inheritance of the children of Joseph.

33And Eleazar the son of Aaron died. They buried him in a hill *belonging to* Phinehas his son, which was given to him in the mountains of Ephraim.

24:31 The testimony to the effectiveness of Joshua's leadership is that not only he but also those he trained were faithful to the Lord (Josh. 11:15; 24:15; see chart, Preparation for Leadership).

24:32 The bones of Joseph were to be buried in the Land which God had promised to give to Abraham, Isaac, and Jacob—the Land in which the Israelites now lived (Gen. 50:24,

25). Following Joseph's instructions symbolized the completion of this stage of Israel's national life and testified to God's faithfulness in fulfilling His promises to Abraham, Isaac, and Jacob.

24:33 The death of a servant of God begins and ends this book (Josh. 1:1; 24:29-33). However, God's work continues, and His faithfulness to His children never ends.

Judges

TITLE

The title of the Book of Judges (Heb. *shophetim,* Gk. *kritai* in LXX; lit. "judges") is the same in the Vulgate as well (Lat. *Liber Judicum*). The book introduces the military leaders known as judges, whom God raised up to deliver Israel from oppression. Divinely appointed and empowered, they did not rule by heredity.

AUTHOR

Although containing no explicit claim to authorship, traditionally the Book of Judges has been ascribed to Samuel.

DATE

Some scholars view the Book of Judges as a series of stories compiled by anonymous individuals during the Exile, sometime after 586 B.C. Most evangelical scholars believe the Book of Judges was written during the early period of the monarchy, beginning around 1050 B.C. Evidence for this earlier date is stronger:

1) The reference to the Jebusites in Jerusalem, indicating a time before David's capture of the city (Judg. 1:21; 2 Sam. 5:6, 7).

2) The mention of the Canaanites in Gezer, which suggests a date prior to Pharaoh's gift of this city to his daughter as a dowry on the occasion of her marriage to Solomon (Judg. 1:29; see 1 Kin. 9, Dowry).

3) The prominence of Sidon over Tyre, which was only true prior to the twelfth century (Judg. 3:3).

BACKGROUND

SETTING: During this time of decadence and weakness in the Egyptian, Hittite, and Assyrian empires, a vacuum of power existed. In Canaan, Israel was a tiny, emerging nation (actually still a league of tribes). Canaan, an extremely important land at the crossroads of three empires, was inhabited by an incredible mix of peoples and religions. It was regarded as the linking highway of the ancient world. The Book of Judges records the history of Israel from Joshua's death to Samuel's leadership and the beginning of the monarchy around 1050 B.C. If the terms of all the judges were added together, the total span of time recorded in the Book of Judges would exceed four hundred years, presenting a chronological difficulty. A solution to this challenge lies in the observation that most likely the judges were local deliverers whose terms overlapped except for some, like Deborah, who were national leaders.

PURPOSE: The Book of Judges describes the history of Israel from a theological or spiritual viewpoint. The book records one of the darkest periods in Israel's history. This history is recorded honestly, with no apparent attempt to gloss over the repeated failures of God's people. Israel's unfaithfulness to God began with the nation's failure to possess

the Promised Land as God commanded. After Joshua's death, an adulterous generation of Israelites failed to love and obey God and His Law. They reaped the painful consequences of their disobedience. God disciplined His people by allowing neighboring nations to enslave and oppress them. Yet God proved faithful, and, with the testing, He provided leaders for deliverance.

A recurring cycle appears in the stories of the six major judges.

1) At the first stage in the cycle, God's people sinned against Him by rebellion and disobedience, turning away from the Lord.

2) As a consequence, God allowed His people to be oppressed by their enemies.

3) Eventually the people would cry out to the Lord for deliverance.

4) Then God would raise up a military deliverer or judge to rescue His people.

The Book of Judges reveals that obedience to the Lord results in blessing, while disobedience brings punishment. The Lord Himself is identified as the sovereign Judge of His people (Judg. 11:27).

AUDIENCE: Because the book was written in the early period of the monarchy, Judges could have helped Israel see the advantages of a faithful king over the local and temporary leadership of a judge. Presumably a king would provide central leadership and guide the nation as a whole in obedient and righteous ways, a development much preferred over the turbulent and immoral times they had experienced. Eventually, however, their own history would demonstrate the inability of an earthly king to provide peace or righteousness without the commitment of the people to walk obediently before God.

The Book of Judges reminds Christians of the serious nature of sin. As in the times of the judges, Christians wage war continually against the temptation to be unfaithful to God and His Word. Through judgment or discipline, the Lord draws His children closer to Himself, seeking to conform them to His image. Finally, the Book of Judges reveals the need for a true King who will bring the peace and rest that can be found only in Christ, the Prince of Peace and King of Kings.

LITERARY CHARACTERISTICS: The Book of Judges is a collection of material that records the history of Israel in short episodes and cycles. The book consists of the introduction (Judg. 1:1—3:6), the history of the judges (Judg. 3:7—16:31), and examples of the moral depravity of the Land (Judg. 17:1—21:25). Judges contains colorful stories, word riddles, old songs, ironic sayings, and vivid descriptions of brutal events. Deborah's song is an ancient piece of Hebrew poetry (Judg. 5). Jotham's parable of the trees (Judg. 9:7–15) and Samson's ancient riddles (Judg. 14:14, 18; 15:16) are other literary forms appearing in the book.

THEMES

In the Book of Judges, God's faithfulness to His covenant and His people prevailed despite Israel's unfaithfulness. God's love for His people was revealed in His patient discipline.

Failure to obtain rest in the Promised Land was the result of disobedience to the covenant (Deut. 12:9; 28:65). The failure of the generations after Joshua to teach God's covenant to their children brought devastating spiritual, political, social, and economic consequences. A lack of godly leadership caused chaos and a breakdown of justice in the Land.

God uses those people who willingly offer themselves to serve Him regardless of their background. The divinely appointed leaders were not always those expected: a woman

like Deborah, who came out of a family setting, a repentant idolater like Gideon, a foreigner like Shamgar, an illegitimate son like Jephthah. Leaders like these challenged cultural and political expectations and traditions. As the sovereign God, the Lord is in control of history, and He is a reality in the daily lives of His people.

OUTLINE

The Continuing Conquest of Canaan

1 Now after the death of Joshua it came to pass that the children of Israel asked the LORD, saying, "Who shall be first to go up for us against the Canaanites to fight against them?"

[2]And the LORD said, "Judah shall go up. Indeed I have delivered the land into his hand."

[3]So Judah said to Simeon his brother, "Come up with me to my allotted territory, that we may fight against the Canaanites; and I will likewise go with you to your allotted territory." And Simeon went with him. [4]Then Judah went up, and the LORD delivered the Canaanites and the Perizzites into their hand; and they killed ten thousand men at Bezek. [5]And they found Adoni-Bezek in Bezek, and fought against him; and they defeated the Canaanites and the Perizzites. [6]Then Adoni-Bezek fled, and they pursued him and caught him and cut off his thumbs and big toes. [7]And Adoni-Bezek said, "Seventy kings with their thumbs and big toes cut off used to gather *scraps* under my table; as I have done, so God has repaid me." Then they brought him to Jerusalem, and there he died.

[8]Now the children of Judah fought against Jerusalem and took it; they struck it with the edge of the sword and set the city on fire. [9]And afterward the children of Judah went down to fight against the Canaanites who dwelt in the mountains, in the South,[a] and in the lowland. [10]Then Judah went against the Canaanites who dwelt in Hebron. (Now the name of Hebron *was* formerly Kirjath Arba.) And they killed Sheshai, Ahiman, and Talmai.

[11]From there they went against the inhabitants of Debir. (The name of Debir *was* formerly Kirjath Sepher.)

[12]Then Caleb said, "Whoever attacks Kirjath Sepher and takes it, to him I will give my daughter Achsah as wife." [13]And Othniel the son of Kenaz, Caleb's younger brother, took it; so he gave him his daughter Achsah as wife. [14]Now it happened, when she came *to him,* that she urged him[a] to ask her father for a field. And she dismounted from *her* donkey, and Caleb said to her, "What do you wish?" [15]So she said to him, "Give me a blessing; since you have given me land in the South, give me also springs of water."

And Caleb gave her the upper springs and the lower springs.

[16]Now the children of the Kenite, Moses' father-in-law, went up from the City of Palms with the children of Judah into the Wilderness of Judah, which *lies* in the South *near* Arad; and they went and dwelt among the people. [17]And Judah went with his brother Simeon, and they attacked the Canaanites who inhabited Zephath, and utterly destroyed it. So the name of the city was called Hormah. [18]Also Judah took Gaza with its territory, Ashkelon with its territory, and Ekron with its territory. [19]So the LORD was with Judah. And they drove out the mountaineers, but they could not drive out the inhabitants of the lowland, because they had chariots of iron. [20]And they

•••••••••••••••••

1:9 [a]Hebrew *Negev,* and so throughout this book   1:14 [a]Septuagint and Vulgate read *he urged her.*

1:1 The death of a leader. Like the Book of Joshua, the Book of Judges begins by recording the death of a great leader. Later in the book the writer gives more details about Joshua's death (see Judg. 2:7–9). Here the notation serves as a general introduction to the book, giving a framework for events that took place during the latter part of Joshua's life and after his death. The introduction, like the two appendices at the end of the book, is arranged in thematic rather than chronological order. The ark of the covenant (Num. 10:35), the rod of Moses, and the sacred lots served as symbols for Israel. Israel customarily inquired concerning the Lord's will before a military campaign. The method of casting lots through the Urim and Thummim was believed to be controlled by God (Ex. 28:15, note). The main encampment of the Israelites was probably at Gilgal, near Jericho. The Canaanites lived mostly in cities in the hill country.

1:2, 3 Judah played a crucial role in leading Israel to war against external and internal enemies at the beginning and at the end of Judges (Judg. 20:18). The writer is aware that the righteous leadership Israel needed will come from the tribe of Judah. Because its inheritance lay within Judah's borders, Simeon assisted Judah and gradually lost its own tribal identity, while Judah became powerful in the southern part of Canaan.

1:4–6 The Canaanites were already living in Canaan, mainly along the coastline (Deut. 1:7). However, the term here gener-

ally refers to all the inhabitants of the Land at the time of the conquest (see Judg. 3:3, 6, notes). What the Israelites did to Adoni-Bezek was a common practice with prisoners of war in the ancient Near East. Mutilation prevented men from fighting again because they could not hold and use a weapon. Since Adoni-Bezek had admitted to mutilating others (v. 7), this could be an example of the law of retaliation (*lex talionis,* Lat.; Ex. 21:24).

1:8 Jerusalem, in the period of the judges, was occupied by the Jebusites (see Judg. 3:3, note). Despite this successful attack on Jerusalem, the Israelites did not occupy the city until David's reign (2 Sam. 5:6, 7).

1:13–15 Achsah. In ancient Near Eastern cultures, the groom commonly gave a dowry or bride price for a wife (Gen. 34:11, 12; see also 1 Kin. 9, Dowry), and, in this case, victory in battle was an adequate payment (see 1 Sam. 18:25). Achsah's bold petition had tremendous advantages for her husband's clan (see Josh. 15, Achsah; chart, The Period of the Judges). The Kenizzites could establish themselves in the well-watered lands of southern Palestine.

1:19–21 The conquest of Canaan was a long-term endeavor that started under Joshua's leadership (see also vv. 27–36). In the time of David, portions of the Land remained under enemy control. David went to war repeatedly against the Philistines. Joshua had led the major conquest, but it remained for each tribe to drive out the Canaanites and settle in

THE PERIOD OF THE JUDGES
1375–1050 B.C.

JUDGE (TRIBE)	SCRIPTURE REFERENCE	OPPRESSOR	LENGTH OF OPPRESSION	PERIOD OF REST/JUDGESHIP
1. Othniel (Judah)	Josh. 15:16–19; Judg. 1:11–15; 3:7–11; 1 Chr. 4:13	Mesopotamians (Judg. 3:8)	8 yrs. (Judg. 3:8)	40 yrs. (Judg. 3:11)
2. Ehud (Benjamin)	Judg. 3:12–30; 4:1	Moabites Ammonites Amalekites (Judg. 3:12, 13)	18 yrs. (Judg. 3:14)	80 yrs. (Judg. 3:30)
3. Shamgar (Unknown— perhaps foreigner)	Judg. 3:31; 5:6	Philistines (Judg. 3:31)		
4. Deborah (Ephraim)	Judg. 4:1—5:31	Canaanites (Judg. 4:2)	20 yrs. (Judg. 4:3)	40 yrs. (Judg. 5:31)
5. Gideon (Manasseh)— Also called Jerubbaal or Jerubbesheth	Judg. 6:1—8:32; Heb. 11:32	Midianites Amalekites "People of the East" (Judg. 6:1, 3, 33; 7:12)	7 yrs. (Judg. 6:1)	40 yrs. (Judg. 8:28)
6. Abimelech (Manasseh)	Judg. 8:33—9:57; 2 Sam. 11:21	Civil War		Rule of 3 yrs. (Judg. 9:22)
7. Tola (Issachar)	Judg. 10:1, 2			23 yrs. (Judg. 10:2)
8. Jair (Manasseh)	Judg. 10:3–5		18 yrs. (Judg. 10:8)	22 yrs. (Judg. 10:3)
9. Jephthah (Manasseh)	Judg. 10:6—12:7; Heb. 11:32	Philistines Ammonites Civil War with Ephraimites (Judg. 10:7; 12:4)		6 yrs. (Judg. 12:7)
10. Ibzan (Judah or Zebulun)	Judg. 12:8–10			7 yrs. (Judg. 12:9)
11. Elon (Zebulun)	Judg. 12:11, 12			10 yrs. (Judg. 12:11)
12. Abdon (Ephraim)	Judg. 12:13–15			8 yrs. (Judg. 12:14)
13. Samson (Dan)	Judg. 13:1—16:31; Heb. 11:32	Philistines (Judg. 13:1)	40 yrs. (Judg. 13:1)	20 yrs. (Judg. 15:20; 16:31)

its allotted section. The Israelites doubted their ability to occupy the coastal plains because of the Canaanites' superior weapons (v. 19). In some instances, the people of God decided to make treaties with their enemies. In other cases, some tribes decided to impose tribute on the conquered peoples,

eventually mixing with them (vv. 28, 30, 33, 35). Israel failed by disobeying God's command to reject covenants with the inhabitants of the Land, to avoid intermarriage, and to have nothing to do with Canaanite religions.

gave Hebron to Caleb, as Moses had said. Then he expelled from there the three sons of Anak. [21]But the children of Benjamin did not drive out the Jebusites who inhabited Jerusalem; so the Jebusites dwell with the children of Benjamin in Jerusalem to this day.

[22]And the house of Joseph also went up against Bethel, and the LORD *was* with them. [23]So the house of Joseph sent men to spy out Bethel. (The name of the city *was* formerly Luz.) [24]And when the spies saw a man coming out of the city, they said to him, "Please show us the entrance to the city, and we will show you mercy." [25]So he showed them the entrance to the city, and they struck the city with the edge of the sword; but they let the man and all his family go. [26]And the man went to the land of the Hittites, built a city, and called its name Luz, which *is* its name to this day.

Incomplete Conquest of the Land

[27]However, Manasseh did not drive out *the inhabitants of* Beth Shean and its villages, or Taanach and its villages, or the inhabitants of Dor and its villages, or the inhabitants of Ibleam and its villages, or the inhabitants of Megiddo and its villages; for the Canaanites were determined to dwell in that land. [28]And it came to pass, when Israel was strong, that they put the Canaanites under tribute, but did not completely drive them out.

[29]Nor did Ephraim drive out the Canaanites who dwelt in Gezer; so the Canaanites dwelt in Gezer among them.

[30]Nor did Zebulun drive out the inhabitants of Kitron or the inhabitants of Nahalol; so the Canaanites dwelt among them, and were put under tribute.

[31]Nor did Asher drive out the inhabitants of Acco or the inhabitants of Sidon, or of Ahlab, Achzib, Helbah, Aphik, or Rehob. [32]So the Asherites dwelt among the Canaanites, the inhabitants of the land; for they did not drive them out.

[33]Nor did Naphtali drive out the inhabitants of Beth Shemesh or the inhabitants of Beth Anath; but they dwelt among the Canaanites, the inhabitants of the land. Nevertheless the inhabitants of Beth Shemesh and Beth Anath were put under tribute to them.

[34]And the Amorites forced the children of Dan into the mountains, for they would not allow them to come down to the valley; [35]and the Amorites were determined to dwell in Mount Heres, in Aijalon, and in Shaalbim;[a] yet when the strength of the house of Joseph became greater, they were put under tribute.

[36]Now the boundary of the Amorites *was* from the Ascent of Akrabbim, from Sela, and upward.

Israel's Disobedience

2 Then the Angel of the LORD came up from Gilgal to Bochim, and said: "I led you up from Egypt and brought you to the land of which I swore to your fathers; and I said, 'I will never break My covenant with you. [2]And you shall make no covenant with the inhabitants of this land; you shall tear down their altars.' But you have not obeyed My voice. Why have you done this? [3]Therefore I also said, 'I will not drive them out before you; but they shall be *thorns* in your side,[a] and their gods shall be a snare to you.' " [4]So it was, when the Angel of the LORD spoke these words to all the children of Israel, that the people lifted up their voices and wept.

[5]Then they called the name of that place Bochim;[a] and they sacrificed there to the LORD. [6]And when Joshua had dismissed the people, the children of Israel went each to his own inheritance to possess the land.

Death of Joshua

[7]So the people served the LORD all the days of Joshua, and all the days of the elders who outlived Joshua, who had seen all the great works of the LORD which He had done for Israel. [8]Now Joshua the son of Nun, the servant of the LORD, died *when he was* one hundred and ten years old. [9]And they buried him within the border of his inheritance at Timnath Heres, in the mountains of Ephraim, on the north side of Mount Gaash. [10]When all that generation had been gathered to their fathers, another generation arose after them who did not know the LORD nor the work which He had done for Israel.

· · · · · · · · · · · · · · · · · ·

1:35 [a]Spelled *Shaalabbin* in Joshua 19:42   2:3 [a]Septuagint, Targum, and Vulgate read *enemies to you.*   2:5 [a]Literally *Weeping*

2:1–5 The Angel of the Lord is a mysterious emissary from God who appeared to the people, bringing deliverance, revelation, or judgment (see chart, The Angel of the Lord). Some scholars believe these visits were theophanies (visible appearances of God in bodily form). The Angel (lit. "messenger") announced the consequences of Israel's disobedience. The Israelites had doubted God's ability to provide victory in the face of superior weapons. They had disobeyed clear instructions with regard to intermarriage and pagan religions. To cleanse and prepare them to be a holy nation, God's judgment would come in the form of oppression by neighboring countries. "Bochim" (Heb., lit. "weepers") was an adequate name to describe their new painful relationship with God. God, however, still loved His people and did not abandon them to their sufferings. Repeatedly He provided them with deliverers (see v. 16, note).

2:10 A tragic and inevitable consequence of sin is that it always affects others. Because of the failure of the previous generation to teach their children about the Lord, an unfaithful generation of Israelites who were ignorant of God's char-

ISRAEL'S UNFAITHFULNESS TO GOD

ISRAEL'S GOD	PAGAN GODS
– is over nature	– are in nature
– is a personal God who reveals Himself in His Law	– are usually impersonal forces
– shows His power in the supernatural events in history	– are called upon to show their powers in the cyclic repetition of the seasons in nature
– calls His people out of slavery and spiritual darkness to lead them to a life of faith and rest	– maintain the system of paganism centered around the repetition of the seasons, with no purpose or goal in history

WORSHIPERS	
OF ISRAEL'S GOD	OF PAGAN GODS
– cannot manipulate God's will by human techniques	– are supposedly stimulated by imitating and re-enacting fertility on earth
– are called to obey God's will as revealed in His Law	– practice sacred prostitution in the temples to guarantee fertility for people, animals, and the land
– are promised blessings and prosperity when obeying the Law	– are promised prosperity in exchange for participating in the cult

Israel's Unfaithfulness

[11]Then the children of Israel did evil in the sight of the LORD, and served the Baals; [12]and they forsook the LORD God of their fathers, who had brought them out of the land of Egypt; and they followed other gods from *among* the gods of the people who *were* all around them, and they bowed down to them; and they provoked the LORD to anger. [13]They forsook the LORD and served Baal and the Ashtoreths.[a] [14]And the anger of the LORD was hot against Israel. So He delivered them into the hands of plunderers who despoiled them; and He sold them into the hands of their enemies all around, so that they could no longer stand before their enemies. [15]Wherever they went out, the hand of the LORD was against them for calamity, as the LORD had said, and as the LORD had sworn to them. And they were greatly distressed.

[16]Nevertheless, the LORD raised up judges who delivered them out of the hand of those who plun-

dered them. [17]Yet they would not listen to their judges, but they played the harlot with other gods, and bowed down to them. They turned quickly from the way in which their fathers walked, in obeying the commandments of the LORD; they did not do so. [18]And when the LORD raised up judges for them, the LORD was with the judge and delivered them out of the hand of their enemies all the days of the judge; for the LORD was moved to pity by their groaning because of those who oppressed them and harassed them. [19]And it came to pass, when the judge was dead, that they reverted and behaved more corruptly than their fathers, by following other gods, to serve them and bow down to them. They did not cease from their own doings nor from their stubborn way.

[20]Then the anger of the LORD was hot against

2:13 [a]Canaanite goddesses

acter and His Law arose (see chart, Israel's Unfaithfulness to God).

2:11–23 Among the Canaanite gods, an inactive father-god named El was followed by a court of deities who represented the masculine and feminine aspects of the fertility cult. *Ba'al* (Heb., lit. "lord") was associated with the storm god Hadad. Anat (in other places in the Bible known as "Beth-anath") was his consort. Asherah and Astarte were other goddesses associated with wooden cult objects representing provocative sacred courtesans, pregnant mothers, or bloodthirsty women of war. According to this pagan belief, Ba'al's annual death and resurrection provided the power behind fertility in nature. In Baalism, men and women participated in sexual immorality in

order to convince the gods to bring fertility to the land, to animals, and to people. Thus, this religion was totally devoid of social and moral concerns. In following this nature religion, Israel was abandoning its unique place in God's purpose and calling in history (see chart, Israel's Unfaithfulness to God).

2:16 The judges (Heb. *shophetim*) were primarily military leaders, though some, like Deborah (Judg. 4:4, 5), were also administrators and judges. These judges were also empowered by God to lead the Israelites against their oppressors. Some judges are mentioned only briefly (Judg. 3:31; 10:1, 3; 12:8, 11, 13). The judges were primarily local deliverers. In some cases, several judges ruled in different parts of the Land at the same time.

Israel; and He said, "Because this nation has transgressed My covenant which I commanded their fathers, and has not heeded My voice, [21]I also will no longer drive out before them any of the nations which Joshua left when he died, [22]so that through them I may test Israel, whether they will keep the ways of the LORD, to walk in them as their fathers kept *them*, or not." [23]Therefore the LORD left those nations, without driving them out immediately; nor did He deliver them into the hand of Joshua.

The Nations Remaining in the Land

3 Now these *are* the nations which the LORD left, that He might test Israel by them, *that is,* all who had not known any of the wars in Canaan [2](*this was* only so that the generations of the children of Israel might be taught to know war, at least those who had not formerly known it), [3]*namely,* five lords of the Philistines, all the Canaanites, the Sidonians, and the Hivites who dwelt in Mount Lebanon, from Mount Baal Hermon to the entrance of Hamath. [4]And they were *left, that He might* test Israel by them, to know whether they would obey the commandments of the LORD, which He had commanded their fathers by the hand of Moses.

[5]Thus the children of Israel dwelt among the Canaanites, the Hittites, the Amorites, the Perizzites, the Hivites, and the Jebusites. [6]And they took their daughters to be their wives, and gave their daughters to their sons; and they served their gods.

Othniel

[7]So the children of Israel did evil in the sight of the LORD. They forgot the LORD their God, and served the Baals and Asherahs.[a] [8]Therefore the anger of the LORD was hot against Israel, and He sold them into the hand of Cushan-Rishathaim king of Mesopotamia; and the children of Israel served Cushan-Rishathaim eight years. [9]When the children of Israel cried out to the LORD, the LORD raised up a deliverer for the children of Israel, who delivered them: Othniel the son of Kenaz, Caleb's younger brother. [10]The Spirit of the LORD came upon him, and he judged Israel. He went out to war, and the LORD delivered Cushan-Rishathaim king of Mesopotamia into his hand; and his hand prevailed over Cushan-Rishathaim. [11]So the land had rest for forty years. Then Othniel the son of Kenaz died.

Ehud

[12]And the children of Israel again did evil in the sight of the LORD. So the LORD strengthened Eglon king of Moab against Israel, because they had done evil in the sight of the LORD. [13]Then he gathered to himself the people of Ammon and Amalek, went and defeated Israel, and took possession of the City of Palms. [14]So the children of Israel served Eglon king of Moab eighteen years.

[15]But when the children of Israel cried out to the LORD, the LORD raised up a deliverer for them:

••••••••••••••••••••
3:7 [a]Name or symbol for Canaanite goddesses

3:1, 2, 4 God tested Israel by leaving enemies in the Land. Yet His providence was active even in the darkest times of Israel's history. God wanted His people to remain faithful to His commandments when they faced the alternative of disobedience. God's people would reveal their love for Him by choosing to obey Him. Compare Judges 2:20–23, where the writer noted that God allowed other nations to remain in the Land to chasten or discipline His people. Human history is not a series of chance events or the result of impersonal forces. The history of Israel is the history of God's providence and guidance. God's people could choose their response to His covenant of love. Obedience to His law would bring blessing, while disobedience would result in suffering the curses of the covenant (Lev. 26:25; Deut. 28:15). Even in the times of discipline and testing, God is present with His people (Ps. 23:4, 5).

3:3 Canaan, the land bridge of the ancient world, linked Egypt and Mesopotamia. Thus this region became an incredible melting pot of peoples and religions. The Canaanites were culturally united but without any political identity. They were already in the Land at the time of the occupation of Israel under Joshua. They lived mainly along the coastline (Deut. 1:7). The Amorites occupied the hill country and had arrived in the Land during the time of Abram, around 2090 B.C. The Hittites usually represented the non-Semitic elements in the population. The Perizzites and the Hivites (which also included the Girgashites and the Jebusites) were the descendants of an old Hurrian immigration which had arrived in Canaan between 1700 and 1500 B.C. The Sidonians were the forefathers of the Phoenicians and lived along the coastline (see Introduction).

Finally, the Philistines were "the peoples of the sea" who arrived in Palestine following the dissolution of the Greek Mycenaen Empire after the Trojan War. They brought with them superior weapons and a more sophisticated culture.

3:6 Intermarriage in the Land. An important way of insuring peace among the different groups of the Land was through marriage alliances (1 Kin. 11, Solomon's Pagan Wives; Neh. 10, Interfaith Marriage). The graphic imagery of the Bible in describing Israel's unfaithfulness to *Yahweh* as "playing the harlot" with other gods had striking connections with reality. Idolatry in Israel started in an intimate, domestic setting.

3:7 Israel's apostasy followed a cycle of oppression, repentance, and deliverance. The cycle always began with the people doing "evil in the sight of the LORD."

3:8 Mesopotamia refers to modern eastern Syria and northern Iraq, a region around the city of Haran (Gen. 24:10). The kings mentioned in Judges, for the most part, ruled over small states as a hereditary noble class with semi-free peasantry and numerous slaves. An approximate date for this incident is 1360 B.C.

3:15 Ehud killed Eglon, king of Moab, with his dagger. He was successful in his mission because he was left-handed. His dagger was fastened on his right thigh, which evidently was not checked. He gained entrance to the king's presence with his dagger and killed the king. Ehud was a Benjamite. Ironically, here was a member of the tribe of Benjamin, which means "son of the right hand," who was left-handed or ambidextrous (see chart, The Period of the Judges).

THE JUDGES OF ISRAEL

Othniel defeated the Canaanites (Judg. 1:11–13; 3:7–11).

Jephthah, a harlot's son, delivered Israel from the Ammonites (Judg. 11:1—12:7).

Gideon defeated the Midianites (Judg. 6—8).

Sea of Chinnereth (Galilee)

Deborah, wife of Lapidoth, mother of Israel, judge, and prophetess, led in subduing the Canaanites (Judg. 4:1–24).

Shamgar delivered Israel from the Philistines (Judg. 3:31; 5:6).

GREAT SEA (MEDITERRANEAN)

Jordan River

AMMON

Samson was a man of great physical strength but moral weakness (Judg. 13—16).

Jerusalem

Debir

Ehud delivered Israel from Moab (Judg. 3:12–30).

Gaza

Dead Sea

MOAB

0 — 300 Mi.

0 — 300 Km.

Ehud the son of Gera, the Benjamite, a left-handed man. By him the children of Israel sent tribute to Eglon king of Moab. ¹⁶Now Ehud made himself a dagger (it was double-edged and a cubit in length) and fastened it under his clothes on his right thigh. ¹⁷So he brought the tribute to Eglon king of Moab. (Now Eglon *was* a very fat man.) ¹⁸And when he had finished presenting the tribute, he sent away the people who had carried the tribute. ¹⁹But he himself turned back from the stone images that *were* at Gilgal, and said, "I have a secret message for you, O king."

He said, "Keep silence!" And all who attended him went out from him.

²⁰So Ehud came to him (now he was sitting upstairs in his cool private chamber). Then Ehud said, "I have a message from God for you." So he arose from *his* seat. ²¹Then Ehud reached with his left hand, took the dagger from his right thigh, and thrust it into his belly. ²²Even the hilt went in after the blade, and the fat closed over the blade, for he did not draw the dagger out of his belly; and his entrails came out. ²³Then Ehud went out through the porch and shut the doors of the upper room behind him and locked them.

²⁴When he had gone out, *Eglon's*[a] servants came

3:24 [a]Literally *his*

DEBORAH *A Distinguished Judge*

Deborah (Heb. "bee") appears to have been a homemaker at the time she is selected for service to her country. Having no aristocratic lineage, she is identified simply as "the wife of Lapidoth." Yet Deborah was the only woman in Scripture elevated to high political power by the common consent of her peers. Though her homemaking responsibilities well may have taken a backseat during her service to her country, she described herself as "a mother in Israel" (Judg. 5:7) before she became a judge. Whether this is a reference to her own off-spring or an expression of her spiritual motherhood toward every son and daughter of Israel is immaterial.

In spiritually parched Israel, characterized by rejection of God and by a determination among the people for each to do things her own way (Judg. 17:6; 21:25), Deborah was first a counselor, as she displayed her leadership under a large palm tree near her home by discussing and suggesting solutions to people with problems. The civil court system was inept; the military was too weak to defend national borders; the priesthood of what had been a theocracy was impotent and ineffective. Normal life was no longer possible, and thus Deborah became a judge and finally a deliverer of her people in time of war.

In this area the despised King Jabin was harassing the Israelites. Deborah summoned Barak, from the tribe of Naphtali on the northern border, and ordered him to recruit an army of ten thousand men from his own tribe and the neighboring tribe Zebulun.

Barak wavered, insisting that Deborah accompany him for the task (Judg. 4:8). She not only joined the drive to raise an army but also suggested their strategy. God had spoken in the past through His leaders Moses and Joshua, and now He was speaking through Deborah. *Yahweh* came to her aid with a violent thunderstorm (Judg. 5:4). In a mini-replay of the crossing of the Red Sea, the horse-drawn chariots of the enemy floundered.

The destruction of the Canaanite power was immortalized in one of the finest specimens of Hebrew poetry by Deborah and Barak, as they picture in a song of praise the events which led to victory for the people (see Judg. 5). Long before Deborah exercised her uncommon leadership and decision-making skills to save her nation in a time of trouble, she was a homemaker—a wife and mother in Israel. Her compassion had been awakened by the atrocities suffered by her people. She arose to make herself available, and she was victorious as she herself trusted God, then inspired others within her sphere of influence with that same trust.

See also Judg. 5; notes on Feminine Leadership (1 Sam. 25); Government and Citizenship (Rom. 13); Heroines (Heb. 11).

---

to look, and *to their* surprise, the doors of the upper room were locked. So they said, "He is probably attending to his needs in the cool chamber." ²⁵So they waited till they were embarrassed, and still he had not opened the doors of the upper room. Therefore they took the key and opened *them.* And there was their master, fallen dead on the floor.

²⁶But Ehud had escaped while they delayed, and passed beyond the stone images and escaped to Seirah. ²⁷And it happened, when he arrived, that he blew the trumpet in the mountains of Ephraim, and the children of Israel went down with him from the mountains; and he led them. ²⁸Then he said to them, "Follow *me,* for the LORD has delivered your enemies the Moabites into your hand." So they went down after him, seized the fords of the Jordan leading to Moab, and did not allow anyone to cross over. ²⁹And at that time they killed about ten thousand men of Moab, all stout men of valor; not a man escaped. ³⁰So Moab was subdued that day under the hand of Israel. And the land had rest for eighty years.

Shamgar

³¹After him was Shamgar the son of Anath, who killed six hundred men of the Philistines with an ox goad; and he also delivered Israel.

Deborah

4 When Ehud was dead, the children of Israel again did evil in the sight of the LORD. ²So the LORD sold them into the hand of Jabin king of Canaan, who reigned in Hazor. The commander of

---

4:1–24 The Canaanite oppression probably resulted from a coalition of Canaanite cities in the north of Palestine which sought to restore Canaanite power in the Land (a more serious threat than simple plunder). Moreover, with the introduction of iron, military strategy was revolutionized, forcing the Israelites to build and seek refuge in fortress towns like Megiddo. Sisera, the commander of King Jabin's army, wanted to take advantage of the Israelites by fighting in the valley of Jezreel where he could utilize his chariots of iron. Deborah's call to the tribes in the south of Ephraim is evidence of the unity of the tribes at this time. Deborah, a judge in the south, heard the plight of the northern tribes and chose Barak, a military commander from the north.

4:3 Chariots of iron normally would mean an army was nearly invincible, but in the providence of God a storm turned the

his army *was* Sisera, who dwelt in Harosheth Hagoyim. ³And the children of Israel cried out to the LORD; for Jabin had nine hundred chariots of iron, and for twenty years he had harshly oppressed the children of Israel.

⁴Now Deborah, a prophetess, the wife of Lapidoth, was judging Israel at that time. ⁵And she would sit under the palm tree of Deborah between Ramah and Bethel in the mountains of Ephraim. And the children of Israel came up to her for judgment. ⁶Then she sent and called for Barak the son of Abinoam from Kedesh in Naphtali, and said to him, "Has not the LORD God of Israel commanded, 'Go and deploy *troops* at Mount Tabor; take with you ten thousand men of the sons of Naphtali and of the sons of Zebulun; ⁷and against you I will deploy Sisera, the commander of Jabin's army, with his chariots and his multitude at the River Kishon; and I will deliver him into your hand'?"

⁸And Barak said to her, "If you will go with me, then I will go; but if you will not go with me, I will not go!"

⁹So she said, "I will surely go with you; nevertheless there will be no glory for you in the journey you are taking, for the LORD will sell Sisera into the hand of a woman." Then Deborah arose and went with Barak to Kedesh. ¹⁰And Barak called Zebulun and Naphtali to Kedesh; he went up with ten thousand men under his command,ᵃ and Deborah went up with him.

¹¹Now Heber the Kenite, of the children of Hobab the father-in-law of Moses, had separated himself from the Kenites and pitched his tent near the terebinth tree at Zaanaim, which *is* beside Kedesh.

¹²And they reported to Sisera that Barak the son of Abinoam had gone up to Mount Tabor. ¹³So Sisera gathered together all his chariots, nine hundred chariots of iron, and all the people who *were* with him, from Harosheth Hagoyim to the River Kishon.

¹⁴Then Deborah said to Barak, "Up! For this *is* the day in which the LORD has delivered Sisera into your hand. Has not the LORD gone out before you?" So Barak went down from Mount Tabor with ten thousand men following him. ¹⁵And the LORD routed Sisera and all *his* chariots and all *his* army with the edge of the sword before Barak; and Sisera alighted from *his* chariot and fled away on foot. ¹⁶But Barak pursued the chariots and the army as far as Harosheth Hagoyim, and all the army of Sisera fell by the edge of the sword; not a man was left.

¹⁷However, Sisera had fled away on foot to the tent of Jael, the wife of Heber the Kenite; for *there was* peace between Jabin king of Hazor and the house of Heber the Kenite. ¹⁸And Jael went out to meet Sisera, and said to him, "Turn aside, my lord, turn aside to me; do not fear." And when he had turned aside with her into the tent, she covered him with a blanket.

¹⁹Then he said to her, "Please give me a little water to drink, for I am thirsty." So she opened a jug of milk, gave him a drink, and covered him. ²⁰And he said to her, "Stand at the door of the tent, and if any man comes and inquires of you, and says, 'Is there any man here?' you shall say, 'No.'"

²¹Then Jael, Heber's wife, took a tent peg and took a hammer in her hand, and went softly to him and drove the peg into his temple, and it went down into the ground; for he was fast asleep and weary. So he died. ²²And then, as Barak pursued Sisera, Jael came out to meet him, and said to him, "Come, I will show you the man whom you seek." And when he went into her *tent,* there lay Sisera, dead with the peg in his temple.

²³So on that day God subdued Jabin king of Canaan in the presence of the children of Israel. ²⁴And the hand of the children of Israel grew stronger and stronger against Jabin king of Canaan, until they had destroyed Jabin king of Canaan.

4:10 ᵃLiterally *at his feet*

Kishon River into a mud hole in which chariots were useless (see Judg. 4:6, 7; 5:19–21).

4:4 Deborah (Heb., lit. "bee") is the only woman judge (see chart, The Period of the Judges). She has been described as "a bee in peace and a wasp in war." She was also a prophetess and military leader. Other prophetesses in the Bible included Miriam (Ex. 15:20), Huldah (2 Kin. 22:14), Noadiah (Neh. 6:14), and Anna (Luke 2:36; see also Acts 21:9). Through the generations God has chosen women to serve in leadership roles (see charts, Deborah: A Leader of Israel; Esther: A Leader of the Jews).

4:9 For a man to die at the hands of a woman was considered a disgrace in the ancient Near East (Judg. 9:54). Ironically, the victory over the Canaanites is an example of God's warfare

strategy: God's power (the flood) overturned the strength of the enemies (great numbers of warriors with chariots of iron) and built upon the weaknesses of His faithful people (a few warriors and a woman).

4:11 Jael was in a difficult position of conflicting loyalties. Her husband Heber the Kenite had made an alliance with the enemies of Israel. The Israelites were distant relatives of the Kenites, who are identified as "children of Hobab the father-in-law of Moses" (v. 11). They had been associated closely with the Israelites since earlier times. This clan of metalworkers in the Sinai peninsula was semi-nomadic, living in tents and engaging partly in agriculture. Jael's decision and actions proved her loyalty to the Israelites and their God.

JAEL *A Cunning Bedouin*

Jael, Heber's wife, belonged to the semi-nomadic desert tribe of the Kenites, who since the time of Moses were in close contact with the Israelites. They were farmers and metalworkers who had possibly learned their skills in the Egyptian copper mines of the Sinai peninsula.

Heber (which means "ally") had left his own people, the Kenites, and had pitched his tent far north, close to Hazor. He had become an ally of Jabin, possibly helping him to develop his powerful chariots. Thus Jael's decision to side with the Israelites and not with the Canaanites, her husband's allies, was highly significant. Such action suggests that she placed her heart's commitment to God above that to her own husband.

Clearly, Jael called to Sisera and granted him refuge in her tent. She gave him goat's milk or yogurt (still a precious drink for Bedouins) and cunningly helped him to sleep. Then, using her own working tools, a peg and a hammer with which she erected her tents, Jael killed her guest, the enemy of Israel and of *Yahweh*.

The fact that Sisera sought safety in the tent of a friend and found death is ironic, as is the fact that he fearfully hid from the mighty warriors who pursued him, while fearlessly trusting himself for shelter to the hands of an humble woman. Sisera, the great warrior, suffered the ultimate in humiliation in dying at the hands of a woman; Jael received consummate praise for her heroic act in Deborah's song (Judg. 5:24).

Yahweh again showed Himself as the one true God through fulfilled prophecy (Judg. 4:9, 21) and glorious victory (vv. 23, 24). Womanhood was honored as Deborah and Jael were used of God to accomplish His purpose of delivering His people from their enemies.

See also Judg. 5:17–27; notes on Providence (Eccl. 7); Decision Making (1 Cor. 8)

The Song of Deborah

5 Then Deborah and Barak the son of Abinoam sang on that day, saying:

2 "When leaders lead in Israel,
   When the people willingly offer themselves,
   Bless the LORD!

3 "Hear, O kings! Give ear, O princes!
   I, *even* I, will sing to the LORD;
   I will sing praise to the LORD God of Israel.

4 "LORD, when You went out from Seir,
   When You marched from the field of Edom,
   The earth trembled and the heavens poured,
   The clouds also poured water;
5 The mountains gushed before the LORD,
   This Sinai, before the LORD God of Israel.

6 "In the days of Shamgar, son of Anath,
   In the days of Jael,
   The highways were deserted,
   And the travelers walked along the byways.

7 Village life ceased, it ceased in Israel,
   Until I, Deborah, arose,
   Arose a mother in Israel.
8 They chose new gods;
   Then *there was* war in the gates;
   Not a shield or spear was seen among forty
      thousand in Israel.
9 My heart *is* with the rulers of Israel
   Who offered themselves willingly with the
      people.
   Bless the LORD!

10 "Speak, you who ride on white donkeys,
   Who sit in judges' attire,
   And who walk along the road.
11 Far from the noise of the archers, among the
      watering places,
   There they shall recount the righteous acts of
      the LORD,
   The righteous acts *for* His villagers in
      Israel;
   Then the people of the LORD shall go down to
      the gates.

5:1 Deborah's song, an ancient piece of Hebrew poetry, was probably written by Deborah. A common practice among the Israelites was to commemorate a national victory in song (see Num. 21:14, 15, note; chart, Hymns and Songs Associated with Women). One of the oldest poems of the Bible, Deborah's song builds on central themes of the OT, such as God's covenant with His people.

The poem can be divided as follows: purpose (Judg. 5:2), the call of witnesses (v. 3), God's past deliverances (vv. 4, 5), oppression in Israel before God's deliverance (vv. 6–9), an accounting of God's righteous acts (vv. 10, 11), Deborah's call (v. 12), a remembrance of the response of the tribes of Israel (vv. 13–18), the battle (vv. 19–23), Jael's triumph (vv. 24–27), the anxiety of Sisera's mother (vv. 28–30), and the conclusion (v. 31). This song also illustrates a type of Hebrew poetic parallelism in which themes or concepts are repeated in different words (vv. 26, 27). The same words are repeated also to make the poem flow like a song. The poem or song ends with irony in which Jael's killing is contrasted with the anxious waiting of Sisera's mother (vv. 28–30). Finally, this song is one of the earliest sources describing life and conditions in Israel at that time.

DEBORAH: A LEADER OF ISRAEL

EARLY YEARS	There is no information on Deborah's early years.
FAMILY STATUS	She was a homemaker, the wife of Lapidoth (Judg. 4:4). She is called "a mother in Israel" (Judg. 5:7) though children are not named.
LEADERSHIP TRAINING	She judged Israel during the oppression by Jabin (Judg. 4:3, 4).
GOD'S CALL	She was a prophetess when God chose her to judge Israel (Judg. 4:4).
GOD'S PROMISES	God promised to deliver Israel from Sisera (Judg. 4:7).
GOD'S INSTRUCTION	The Lord commanded her to send the troops out to destroy Sisera (Judg. 4:6, 7).
THE PEOPLE'S AFFIRMATION	Barak and the people followed the leadership of Deborah (Judg. 4:8).
DEBORAH'S LEADERSHIP	She inspired Barak to pursue God's plan, leading him into battle (Judg. 4:9).
OBSERVATIONS	She listened to God (Judg. 4:5). She had a servant's heart (Judg. 4:9). She delegated tasks (Judg. 4:6, 7). She offered praise (Judg. 5:2). She led with authority from God (Judg. 4:4). She motivated the people (Judg. 4:9, 14). She was a respected leader (Judg. 4:8).

12"Awake, awake, Deborah!
Awake, awake, sing a song!
Arise, Barak, and lead your captives away,
O son of Abinoam!

13"Then the survivors came down, the people
against the nobles;
The Lord came down for me against the
mighty.
14From Ephraim *were* those whose roots were in
Amalek.
After you, Benjamin, with your peoples,
From Machir rulers came down,
And from Zebulun those who bear the
recruiter's staff.
15And the princes of Issachar[a] *were* with
Deborah;
As Issachar, so *was* Barak
Sent into the valley under his command;[b]
Among the divisions of Reuben
There were great resolves of heart.
16Why did you sit among the sheepfolds,
To hear the pipings for the flocks?
The divisions of Reuben have great searchings
of heart.
17Gilead stayed beyond the Jordan,
And why did Dan remain on ships?[a]
Asher continued at the seashore,
And stayed by his inlets.

18Zebulun *is* a people *who* jeopardized their lives
to the point of death,
Naphtali also, on the heights of the battlefield.

19"The kings came *and* fought,
Then the kings of Canaan fought
In Taanach, by the waters of Megiddo;
They took no spoils of silver.
20They fought from the heavens;
The stars from their courses fought against
Sisera.
21The torrent of Kishon swept them away,
That ancient torrent, the torrent of Kishon.
O my soul, march on in strength!
22Then the horses' hooves pounded,
The galloping, galloping of his steeds.
23'Curse Meroz,' said the angel[a] of the Lord,
'Curse its inhabitants bitterly,
Because they did not come to the help of the
Lord,
To the help of the Lord against the mighty.'

24"Most blessed among women is Jael,
The wife of Heber the Kenite;
Blessed is she among women in tents.

5:15 [a]Following Septuagint, Syriac, Targum, and Vulgate; Masoretic
Text reads *And my princes in Issachar.* [b]Literally *at his feet* 5:17 [a]Or
at ease 5:23 [a]Or *Angel*

25He asked for water, she gave milk;
  She brought out cream in a lordly bowl.
26She stretched her hand to the tent peg,
  Her right hand to the workmen's hammer;
  She pounded Sisera, she pierced his head,
  She split and struck through his temple.
27At her feet he sank, he fell, he lay still;
  At her feet he sank, he fell;
  Where he sank, there he fell dead.

28"The mother of Sisera looked through the
    window,
  And cried out through the lattice,
  'Why is his chariot *so* long in coming?
  Why tarries the clatter of his chariots?'
29Her wisest ladies answered her,
  Yes, she answered herself,
30"Are they not finding and dividing the spoil:
  To every man a girl *or* two;
  For Sisera, plunder of dyed garments,
  Plunder of garments embroidered and dyed,
  Two pieces of dyed embroidery for the neck of
    the looter?'

31"Thus let all Your enemies perish, O LORD!
  But *let* those who love Him *be* like the sun
  When it comes out in full strength."

So the land had rest for forty years.

Midianites Oppress Israel

6 Then the children of Israel did evil in the sight
  of the LORD. So the LORD delivered them into
the hand of Midian for seven years, 2and the hand
of Midian prevailed against Israel. Because of the
Midianites, the children of Israel made for themselves the dens, the caves, and the strongholds
which *are* in the mountains. 3So it was, whenever Israel had sown, Midianites would come up; also
Amalekites and the people of the East would come
up against them. 4Then they would encamp
against them and destroy the produce of the earth
as far as Gaza, and leave no sustenance for Israel,
neither sheep nor ox nor donkey. 5For they would
come up with their livestock and their tents, coming in as numerous as locusts; both they and their
camels were without number; and they would en-

ter the land to destroy it. 6So Israel was greatly impoverished because of the Midianites, and the children of Israel cried out to the LORD.

7And it came to pass, when the children of Israel cried out to the LORD because of the Midianites, 8that the LORD sent a prophet to the children
of Israel, who said to them, "Thus says the LORD
God of Israel: 'I brought you up from Egypt and
brought you out of the house of bondage; 9and I
delivered you out of the hand of the Egyptians
and out of the hand of all who oppressed you, and
drove them out before you and gave you their
land. 10Also I said to you, "I *am* the LORD your God;
do not fear the gods of the Amorites, in whose
land you dwell." But you have not obeyed My
voice.' "

Gideon

11Now the Angel of the LORD came and sat under the terebinth tree which *was* in Ophrah,
which *belonged* to Joash the Abiezrite, while his
son Gideon threshed wheat in the winepress, in
order to hide *it* from the Midianites. 12And the Angel of the LORD appeared to him, and said to him,
"The LORD *is* with you, you mighty man of valor!"

13Gideon said to Him, "O my lord,[a] if the LORD is
with us, why then has all this happened to us? And
where *are* all His miracles which our fathers told us
about, saying, 'Did not the LORD bring us up from
Egypt?' But now the LORD has forsaken us and delivered us into the hands of the Midianites."

14Then the LORD turned to him and said, "Go in
this might of yours, and you shall save Israel from
the hand of the Midianites. Have I not sent you?"

15So he said to Him, "O my Lord,[a] how can I
save Israel? Indeed my clan *is* the weakest in Manasseh, and I *am* the least in my father's house."

16And the LORD said to him, "Surely I will be
with you, and you shall defeat the Midianites as
one man."

17Then he said to Him, "If now I have found favor in Your sight, then show me a sign that it is
You who talk with me. 18Do not depart from here,
I pray, until I come to You and bring out my offering and set *it* before You."

6:13 [a]Hebrew *adoni*, used of man   6:15 [a]Hebrew *Adonai*, used of God

---

6:1–10. The Midianite and Amalekite oppression. The first reference to semi-nomadic, camel-riding Bedouins who infiltrated Israel occurs here (v. 5). The Midianites lived in the
south of Edom (close to the Gulf of Aqaba) and were joined in
their raids by the Amalekites who lived in the wasteland of
the Sinai peninsula and by the "people of the East" who were
a nomadic group from the Syrian desert. The speed and mo-
bility of the camel made raids possible even from long distances, causing great terror and destruction for the Israelites.
Moreover, these nomads with their tents and livestock inevitably clashed with the sedentary Israelite farmers, reducing them almost to servitude.

6:11–27 Gideon was the youngest in his father's house and
came from the weakest clan in the tribe of Manasseh (see
charts, The Period of the Judges; The Angel of the Lord). He
did not have impressive credentials for leadership. But Gideon
obeyed the Lord by cleansing his father's household of idols.
Despite Gideon's need of reassurance (see vv. 36–40, note),
he was willing to die for others in the battle against the enemy. Leadership requires personal sacrifice (see chart, Esther: A Leader of the Jews).

And He said, "I will wait until you come back."

[19]So Gideon went in and prepared a young goat, and unleavened bread from an ephah of flour. The meat he put in a basket, and he put the broth in a pot; and he brought *them* out to Him under the terebinth tree and presented *them.* [20]The Angel of God said to him, "Take the meat and the unleavened bread and lay *them* on this rock, and pour out the broth." And he did so. [21]Then the Angel of the LORD put out the end of the staff that *was* in His hand, and touched the meat and the unleavened bread; and fire rose out of the rock and consumed the meat and the unleavened bread. And the Angel of the LORD departed out of his sight.

[22]Now Gideon perceived that He *was* the Angel of the LORD. So Gideon said, "Alas, O Lord GOD! For I have seen the Angel of the LORD face to face."

[23]Then the LORD said to him, "Peace *be* with you; do not fear, you shall not die." [24]So Gideon built an altar there to the LORD, and called it The-LORD-*Is*-Peace.[a] To this day it *is* still in Ophrah of the Abiezrites.

[25]Now it came to pass the same night that the LORD said to him, "Take your father's young bull, the second bull of seven years old, and tear down the altar of Baal that your father has, and cut down the wooden image[a] that *is* beside it; [26]and build an altar to the LORD your God on top of this rock in the proper arrangement, and take the second bull and offer a burnt sacrifice with the wood of the image which you shall cut down." [27]So Gideon took ten men from among his servants and did as the LORD had said to him. But because he feared his father's household and the men of the city too much to do *it* by day, he did *it* by night.

Gideon Destroys the Altar of Baal

[28]And when the men of the city arose early in the morning, there was the altar of Baal, torn down; and the wooden image that *was* beside it was cut down, and the second bull was being offered on the altar *which had been* built. [29]So they said to one another, "Who has done this thing?" And when they had inquired and asked, they said, "Gideon the son of Joash has done this thing." [30]Then the men of the city said to Joash, "Bring out your son, that he may die, because he has torn down the altar of Baal, and because he has cut down the wooden image that *was* beside it."

[31]But Joash said to all who stood against him, "Would you plead for Baal? Would you save him? Let the one who would plead for him be put to death by morning! If he *is* a god, let him plead for himself, because his altar has been torn down!" [32]Therefore on that day he called him Jerubbaal,[a] saying, "Let Baal plead against him, because he has torn down his altar."

[33]Then all the Midianites and Amalekites, the people of the East, gathered together; and they crossed over and encamped in the Valley of Jezreel. [34]But the Spirit of the LORD came upon Gideon; then he blew the trumpet, and the Abiezrites gathered behind him. [35]And he sent messengers throughout all Manasseh, who also gathered behind him. He also sent messengers to Asher, Zebulun, and Naphtali; and they came up to meet them.

The Sign of the Fleece

[36]So Gideon said to God, "If You will save Israel by my hand as You have said— [37]look, I shall put a fleece of wool on the threshing floor; if there is dew on the fleece only, and *it is* dry on all the ground, then I shall know that You will save Israel by my hand, as You have said." [38]And it was so. When he rose early the next morning and squeezed the fleece together, he wrung the dew out of the fleece, a bowlful of water. [39]Then Gideon said to God, "Do not be angry with me, but let me speak just once more: Let me test, I pray, just once more with the fleece; let it now be dry only on the fleece, but on all the ground let there be dew." [40]And God did so that night. It was dry on the fleece only, but there was dew on all the ground.

Gideon's Valiant Three Hundred

7 Then Jerubbaal (that *is,* Gideon) and all the people who *were* with him rose early and encamped beside the well of Harod, so that the camp of the Midianites was on the north side of them by the hill of Moreh in the valley.

[2]And the LORD said to Gideon, "The people who *are* with you *are* too many for Me to give the Midianites into their hands, lest Israel claim glory for itself against Me, saying, 'My own hand has saved me.' [3]Now therefore, proclaim in the hearing of

---

6:24 [a]Hebrew *YHWH Shalom*　**6:25** [a]Hebrew *Asherah,* a Canaanite goddess　**6:32** [a]Literally *Let Baal Plead*

6:36–40 In the incident with the fleece, Gideon, who already had obeyed the Lord by destroying idolatry in his father's household, was not necessarily trying to guess God's will. Rather, he was asking boldly for reassurance of God's help in the military campaign, in the style of Jacob's clinging to God (Gen. 32:22–32). God was patient and gracious to Gideon and obviously responded to his request.

7:2–7 No conclusive evidence demonstrates something special or better about those warriors who knelt down and scooped up the water, while remaining alert (vv. 5–7). Rather this limitation in the number of troops reaffirmed that the battle was God's. God's power, not human power, would destroy the enemies of His people.

the people, saying, 'Whoever *is* fearful and afraid, let him turn and depart at once from Mount Gilead.' " And twenty-two thousand of the people returned, and ten thousand remained.

4But the Lord said to Gideon, "The people *are* still *too* many; bring them down to the water, and I will test them for you there. Then it will be, *that* of whom I say to you, 'This one shall go with you,' the same shall go with you; and of whomever I say to you, 'This one shall not go with you,' the same shall not go." 5So he brought the people down to the water. And the Lord said to Gideon, "Everyone who laps from the water with his tongue, as a dog laps, you shall set apart by himself; likewise everyone who gets down on his knees to drink." 6And the number of those who lapped, *putting* their hand to their mouth, was three hundred men; but all the rest of the people got down on their knees to drink water. 7Then the Lord said to Gideon, "By the three hundred men who lapped I will save you, and deliver the Midianites into your hand. Let all the *other* people go, every man to his place." 8So the people took provisions and their trumpets in their hands. And he sent away all *the rest of* Israel, every man to his tent, and retained those three hundred men. Now the camp of Midian was below him in the valley.

9It happened on the same night that the Lord said to him, "Arise, go down against the camp, for I have delivered it into your hand. 10But if you are afraid to go down, go down to the camp with Purah your servant, 11and you shall hear what they say; and afterward your hands shall be strengthened to go down against the camp." Then he went down with Purah his servant to the outpost of the armed men who *were* in the camp. 12Now the Midianites and Amalekites, all the people of the East, were lying in the valley as numerous as locusts; and their camels *were* without number, as the sand by the seashore in multitude.

13And when Gideon had come, there was a man telling a dream to his companion. He said, "I have had a dream: *To my* surprise, a loaf of barley bread tumbled into the camp of Midian; it came to a tent and struck it so that it fell and overturned, and the tent collapsed."

14Then his companion answered and said, "This *is* nothing else but the sword of Gideon the son of Joash, a man of Israel! Into his hand God has delivered Midian and the whole camp."

15And so it was, when Gideon heard the telling of the dream and its interpretation, that he worshiped. He returned to the camp of Israel, and said, "Arise, for the Lord has delivered the camp of Midian into your hand." 16Then he divided the three hundred men *into* three companies, and he put a trumpet into every man's hand, with empty pitchers, and torches inside the pitchers. 17And he said to them, "Look at me and do likewise; watch, and when I come to the edge of the camp you shall do as I do: 18When I blow the trumpet, I and all who *are* with me, then you also blow the trumpets on every side of the whole camp, and say, '*The sword of* the Lord and of Gideon!' "

19So Gideon and the hundred men who *were* with him came to the outpost of the camp at the beginning of the middle watch, just as they had posted the watch; and they blew the trumpets and broke the pitchers that *were* in their hands. 20Then the three companies blew the trumpets and broke the pitchers—they held the torches in their left hands and the trumpets in their right hands for blowing—and they cried, "The sword of the Lord and of Gideon!" 21And every man stood in his place all around the camp; and the whole army ran and cried out and fled. 22When the three hundred blew the trumpets, the Lord set every man's sword against his companion throughout the whole camp; and the army fled to Beth Acacia,a toward Zererah, as far as the border of Abel Meholah, by Tabbath.

23And the men of Israel gathered together from Naphtali, Asher, and all Manasseh, and pursued the Midianites.

24Then Gideon sent messengers throughout all the mountains of Ephraim, saying, "Come down against the Midianites, and seize from them the watering places as far as Beth Barah and the Jordan." Then all the men of Ephraim gathered together and seized the watering places as far as Beth Barah and the Jordan. 25And they captured two princes of the Midianites, Oreb and Zeeb. They killed Oreb at the rock of Oreb, and Zeeb they killed at the winepress of Zeeb. They pursued Midian and brought the heads of Oreb and Zeeb to Gideon on the other side of the Jordan.

Gideon Subdues the Midianites

8Now the men of Ephraim said to him, "Why have you done this to us by not calling us when

7:22 aHebrew *Beth Shittah*

7:13–15 God revealed the future in dreams in the OT on several occasions (Gen. 40:1–22; 41:1–36; Dan. 2:1–45; 4:4–27). In this case, both dreamer and interpreter are not Israelites, reassuring Gideon that God is in control of everything: of the battle, the enemies, and Israel. The loaf of barley (bread made from an inferior grain grown by many poor Israelite farmers) symbolized a weak Israel fighting against a strong

Midian (symbolized by a nomadic tent). Like Rahab and the inhabitants of Jericho, the enemy was afraid and knew that Israel's powerful God would give the victory to Israel. God not only provided Gideon with encouragement; He did it through the mouths of his enemies. A suitable response to such encouragement was not further speculation or fear but worship.

8:1–3 This tribal dispute gives evidence of early tensions

What if I am a woman? Is not the God of ancient times the God of these modern days? Did he not raise up Deborah, to be a mother, and a judge in Israel? Did not queen Esther save the lives of the Jews?

Maria W. Stewart, 1835

you went to fight with the Midianites?" And they reprimanded him sharply.

²So he said to them, "What have I done now in comparison with you? *Is* not the gleaning *of the grapes* of Ephraim better than the vintage of Abiezer? ³God has delivered into your hands the princes of Midian, Oreb and Zeeb. And what was I able to do in comparison with you?" Then their anger toward him subsided when he said that.

⁴When Gideon came to the Jordan, he and the three hundred men who *were* with him crossed over, exhausted but still in pursuit. ⁵Then he said to the men of Succoth, "Please give loaves of bread to the people who follow me, for they are exhausted, and I am pursuing Zebah and Zalmunna, kings of Midian."

⁶And the leaders of Succoth said, "*Are* the hands of Zebah and Zalmunna now in your hand, that we should give bread to your army?"

⁷So Gideon said, "For this cause, when the LORD has delivered Zebah and Zalmunna into my hand, then I will tear your flesh with the thorns of the wilderness and with briers!" ⁸Then he went up from there to Penuel and spoke to them in the same way. And the men of Penuel answered him as the men of Succoth had answered. ⁹So he also spoke to the men of Penuel, saying, "When I come back in peace, I will tear down this tower!"

¹⁰Now Zebah and Zalmunna *were* at Karkor, and their armies with them, about fifteen thousand, all who were left of all the army of the people of the East; for one hundred and twenty thousand men who drew the sword had fallen. ¹¹Then Gideon went up by the road of those who dwell in tents on the east of Nobah and Jogbehah; and he attacked the army while the camp felt secure.

¹²When Zebah and Zalmunna fled, he pursued them; and he took the two kings of Midian, Zebah and Zalmunna, and routed the whole army.

¹³Then Gideon the son of Joash returned from battle, from the Ascent of Heres. ¹⁴And he caught a young man of the men of Succoth and interrogated him; and he wrote down for him the leaders of Succoth and its elders, seventy-seven men. ¹⁵Then he came to the men of Succoth and said, "Here are Zebah and Zalmunna, about whom you ridiculed me, saying, '*Are* the hands of Zebah and Zalmunna now in your hand, that we should give bread to your weary men?' " ¹⁶And he took the elders of the city, and thorns of the wilderness and briers, and with them he taught the men of Succoth. ¹⁷Then he tore down the tower of Penuel and killed the men of the city.

¹⁸And he said to Zebah and Zalmunna, "What kind of men *were they* whom you killed at Tabor?"

So they answered, "As you *are*, so *were* they; each one resembled the son of a king."

¹⁹Then he said, "They *were* my brothers, the sons of my mother. *As* the LORD lives, if you had let them live, I would not kill you." ²⁰And he said to Jether his firstborn, "Rise, kill them!" But the youth would not draw his sword; for he was afraid, because he *was* still a youth.

²¹So Zebah and Zalmunna said, "Rise yourself, and kill us; for as a man *is, so is* his strength." So Gideon arose and killed Zebah and Zalmunna, and took the crescent ornaments that *were* on their camels' necks.

Gideon's Ephod

²²Then the men of Israel said to Gideon, "Rule over us, both you and your son, and your grandson

---

among the tribes of Israel, eventually leading to the division of Israel after Solomon's death. However, in this case, Gideon chose to maintain peace by telling the Ephraimites that even the gleanings (the worst) of Ephraim were better than the entire harvest (the best) of Abiezer, Gideon's clan. Gideon's statement appears to be an ancient proverb reflecting the superiority of Ephraim.

8:19 Men frequently had several wives and concubines in the ancient Near East. Thus, it was necessary to distinguish between full and half-brothers, especially when disputes over inheritance occurred. Polygamy entered history when Lamech (the seventh in Cain's line starting with Adam) wanted to appropriate God's original blessings (fruitfulness

and multiplication) on his own terms (Gen. 4:19; see also 1 Tim. 3, Polygamy). However, in the beginning God had established monogamy (see Gen. 2, God's Plan for Marriage; Judg. 8:31, note; 19:1, 2).

8:22, 23 Gideon's rejection of the monarchy was a recognition that God was Israel's king. Two motivations can be found in this petition. First, the people longed for a lasting security that would not die with the death of the judge. Second, perhaps the people sought to imitate the Canaanite kingdoms. They thought deliverance and power would come from a human king. Gideon's answer seemed to criticize this second motivation. He encouraged the people to depend on the Lord for security.

also; for you have delivered us from the hand of Midian."

²³But Gideon said to them, "I will not rule over you, nor shall my son rule over you; the LORD shall rule over you." ²⁴Then Gideon said to them, "I would like to make a request of you, that each of you would give me the earrings from his plunder." For they had golden earrings, because they *were* Ishmaelites.

²⁵So they answered, "We will gladly give *them.*" And they spread out a garment, and each man threw into it the earrings from his plunder. ²⁶Now the weight of the gold earrings that he requested was one thousand seven hundred *shekels* of gold, besides the crescent ornaments, pendants, and purple robes which *were* on the kings of Midian, and besides the chains that *were* around their camels' necks. ²⁷Then Gideon made it into an ephod and set it up in his city, Ophrah. And all Israel played the harlot with it there. It became a snare to Gideon and to his house.

²⁸Thus Midian was subdued before the children of Israel, so that they lifted their heads no more. And the country was quiet for forty years in the days of Gideon.

Death of Gideon

²⁹Then Jerubbaal the son of Joash went and dwelt in his own house. ³⁰Gideon had seventy sons who were his own offspring, for he had many wives. ³¹And his concubine who *was* in Shechem also bore him a son, whose name he called Abimelech. ³²Now Gideon the son of Joash died at a good old age, and was buried in the tomb of Joash his father, in Ophrah of the Abiezrites.

³³So it was, as soon as Gideon was dead, that the children of Israel again played the harlot with the Baals, and made Baal-Berith their god. ³⁴Thus the children of Israel did not remember the LORD their God, who had delivered them from the hands of all their enemies on every side; ³⁵nor did they show kindness to the house of Jerubbaal (Gideon) in accordance with the good he had done for Israel.

Abimelech's Conspiracy

9Then Abimelech the son of Jerubbaal went to Shechem, to his mother's brothers, and spoke with them and with all the family of the house of his mother's father, saying, ²"Please speak in the hearing of all the men of Shechem: 'Which is better for you, that all seventy of the sons of Jerubbaal reign over you, or that one reign over you?' Remember that I *am* your own flesh and bone."

³And his mother's brothers spoke all these words concerning him in the hearing of all the men of Shechem; and their heart was inclined to follow Abimelech, for they said, "He is our brother." ⁴So they gave him seventy *shekels* of silver from the temple of Baal-Berith, with which Abimelech hired worthless and reckless men; and they followed him. ⁵Then he went to his father's house at Ophrah and killed his brothers, the seventy sons of Jerubbaal, on one stone. But Jotham the youngest son of Jerubbaal was left, because he hid himself. ⁶And all the men of Shechem gathered together, all of Beth Millo, and they went and made Abimelech king beside the terebinth tree at the pillar that *was* in Shechem.

The Parable of the Trees

⁷Now when they told Jotham, he went and stood on top of Mount Gerizim, and lifted his voice and cried out. And he said to them:

"Listen to me, you men of Shechem,
That God may listen to you!

⁸"The trees once went forth to anoint a king over them.

8:27 The ephod is described as a colorful vest worn by the priest and used to discern God's will (see Ex. 28, The High Priest's Clothing). However, this object also became associated with idolatry (as a free standing image) in the final chapters of Judges (see Judg. 17:5, 6, note). The tragic words, "all Israel played the harlot with it there," indicate that Gideon's intentions, as well as the Israelites' response, were highly influenced by the surrounding Canaanite idol worship.

8:31 Abimelech and his origins (see chart, The Period of the Judges). Gideon had many wives and concubines, a common sign of wealth or royalty in the ancient Near East. But the disastrous effects of this custom in Israel can be traced back at least as early as the case of Sarah and Hagar (Gen. 16:2), where the violation of marriage occurred because of basic disbelief in God's promises. The passage clearly distinguishes between the 70 sons of Gideon who "were his own offspring" (Judg. 8:30) and Abimelech who was the son of Gideon's concubine in Shechem. That concubine may well have remained in her family's home (see Judg. 14:10, 11, note). The children of these illegitimate relationships generally belonged to the wife's family, thus undermining even further Abimelech's subsequent unlawful claim to a monarchy which his father Gideon had rejected!

8:33 Baal-Berith is described as the god of Shechem, orginally a Canaanite city located about 40 miles north of Jerusalem between Mt. Ebal and Mt. Gerizim (Judg. 9:46). The city later became an important religious and political center in Israel. The form of worship at Shechem, at best, was a blending of Canaanite and Israelite elements. Ironically, Shechem had been the place where Joshua had renewed two crucial covenants between God and Israel (Josh. 8:30–35; 24:25–27; see also Gen. 12:6, 7; 33:18–20).

9:7–15 Mount Gerizim, located near Shechem, where Joshua fulfilled Moses' command to renew the covenant between God and Israel, was the place chosen by Jotham to relate his parable. He preached against the lawlessness of Abimelech and the Shechemites and prophesied against the disastrous

And they said to the olive tree,
'Reign over us!'
⁹But the olive tree said to them,
'Should I cease giving my oil,
With which they honor God and men,
And go to sway over trees?'

¹⁰"Then the trees said to the fig tree,
'You come *and* reign over us!'
¹¹But the fig tree said to them,
'Should I cease my sweetness and my good
fruit,
And go to sway over trees?'

¹²"Then the trees said to the vine,
'You come *and* reign over us!'
¹³But the vine said to them,
'Should I cease my new wine,
Which cheers *both* God and men,
And go to sway over trees?'

¹⁴"Then all the trees said to the bramble,
'You come *and* reign over us!'
¹⁵And the bramble said to the trees,
'If in truth you anoint me as king over you,
Then come *and* take shelter in my shade;
But if not, let fire come out of the bramble
And devour the cedars of Lebanon!'

¹⁶"Now therefore, if you have acted in truth and sincerity in making Abimelech king, and if you have dealt well with Jerubbaal and his house, and have done to him as he deserves— ¹⁷for my father fought for you, risked his life, and delivered you out of the hand of Midian; ¹⁸but you have risen up against my father's house this day, and killed his seventy sons on one stone, and made Abimelech, the son of his female servant, king over the men of Shechem, because he is your brother— ¹⁹if then you have acted in truth and sincerity with Jerubbaal and with his house this day, *then* rejoice in Abimelech, and let him also rejoice in you. ²⁰But if not, let fire come from Abimelech and devour the men of Shechem and Beth Millo; and let fire come from the men of Shechem and from Beth Millo and devour Abimelech!" ²¹And Jotham ran away and fled; and he went to Beer and dwelt there, for fear of Abimelech his brother.

Downfall of Abimelech

²²After Abimelech had reigned over Israel three years, ²³God sent a spirit of ill will between Abimelech and the men of Shechem; and the men of Shechem dealt treacherously with Abimelech, ²⁴that the crime *done* to the seventy sons of Jerubbaal might be settled and their blood be laid on Abimelech their brother, who killed them, and on the men of Shechem, who aided him in the killing of his brothers. ²⁵And the men of Shechem set men in ambush against him on the tops of the mountains, and they robbed all who passed by them along that way; and it was told Abimelech.

²⁶Now Gaal the son of Ebed came with his brothers and went over to Shechem; and the men of Shechem put their confidence in him. ²⁷So they went out into the fields, and gathered *grapes* from their vineyards and trod *them,* and made merry. And they went into the house of their god, and ate and drank, and cursed Abimelech. ²⁸Then Gaal the son of Ebed said, "Who *is* Abimelech, and who *is* Shechem, that we should serve him? *Is he* not the son of Jerubbaal, and *is not* Zebul his officer? Serve the men of Hamor the father of Shechem; but why should we serve him? ²⁹If only this people were under my authority!ᵃ Then I would remove Abimelech." So heᵇ said to Abimelech, "Increase your army and come out!"

³⁰When Zebul, the ruler of the city, heard the words of Gaal the son of Ebed, his anger was aroused. ³¹And he sent messengers to Abimelech secretly, saying, "Take note! Gaal the son of Ebed and his brothers have come to Shechem; and here they are, fortifying the city against you. ³²Now therefore, get up by night, you and the people who *are* with you, and lie in wait in the field. ³³And it shall be, as soon as the sun is up in the morning, *that* you shall rise early and rush upon the city; and *when* he and the people who are with him come out against you, you may then do to them as you find opportunity."

³⁴So Abimelech and all the people who *were* with him rose by night, and lay in wait against Shechem in four companies. ³⁵When Gaal the son of Ebed went out and stood in the entrance to the city gate, Abimelech and the people who *were* with him rose from lying in wait. ³⁶And when Gaal saw the people, he said to Zebul, "Look, people are coming down from the tops of the mountains!"

But Zebul said to him, "You see the shadows of the mountains as *if they were* men."

³⁷So Gaal spoke again and said, "See, people are coming down from the center of the land, and

---

9:29 ᵃLiterally *hand* ᵇFollowing Masoretic Text and Targum; Dead Sea Scrolls read *they;* Septuagint reads *I.*

---

rule of Abimelech in Shechem. The ironic tone of the story is obvious. The trees of the forest invited the valued olive, fig, and vine to rule over them. Each refused. The worthless bramble representing Abimelech (a menace to farmers and fit only to be burned) accepted the invitation. The bramble's offer to provide the trees with shade was a false promise because the bramble lies too close to the earth to provide shade. The ominous threat of fire was a true prophecy of the Shechemites' future death (vv. 45–49).

ABIMELECH'S KILLER

The unnamed woman was in a desperate situation. Abimelech, an impostor king, had already burned to death a thousand men and women in the tower of Shechem and intended to do the same to this humble woman and her people in the tower of Thebez, ten miles northeast of Shechem. She had located whatever she could find for defending herself, namely, a simple millstone (typically 2 or 3 inches thick and 18 inches in diameter with a hole in the center) with which she usually did the grinding of the corn.

Like Abimelech, people still forget that God uses the weak, the poor, and the lowly to make and change history. "Thus God repaid the wickedness of Abimelech," and in so doing memorialized this unnamed heroine, a patriot who used her simple millstone to do what she could to save her people.

See also 2 Samuel 11:21; notes on Providence (Eccl. 7); Heroines (Heb. 11)

another company is coming from the Diviners'ª Terebinth Tree."

³⁸Then Zebul said to him, "Where indeed *is* your mouth now, with which you said, 'Who *is* Abimelech, that we should serve him?' *Are* not these the people whom you despised? Go out, if you will, and fight with them now."

³⁹So Gaal went out, leading the men of Shechem, and fought with Abimelech. ⁴⁰And Abimelech chased him, and he fled from him; and many fell wounded, to the *very* entrance of the gate. ⁴¹Then Abimelech dwelt at Arumah, and Zebul drove out Gaal and his brothers, so that they would not dwell in Shechem.

⁴²And it came about on the next day that the people went out into the field, and they told Abimelech. ⁴³So he took his people, divided them into three companies, and lay in wait in the field. And he looked, and there were the people, coming out of the city; and he rose against them and attacked them. ⁴⁴Then Abimelech and the company that *was* with him rushed forward and stood at the entrance of the gate of the city; and the *other* two companies rushed upon all who *were* in the fields and killed them. ⁴⁵So Abimelech fought against the city all that day; he took the city and killed the people who *were* in it; and he demolished the city and sowed it with salt.

⁴⁶Now when all the men of the tower of Shechem had heard *that,* they entered the stronghold of the temple of the god Berith. ⁴⁷And it was told Abimelech that all the men of the tower of Shechem were gathered together. ⁴⁸Then Abimelech went up to Mount Zalmon, he and all the people who *were* with him. And Abimelech took an ax in his hand and cut down a bough from the trees, and took it and laid *it* on his shoulder; then he said to the people who were with him, "What you have seen me do, make haste *and* do as I *have*

done." ⁴⁹So each of the people likewise cut down his own bough and followed Abimelech, put *them* against the stronghold, and set the stronghold on fire above them, so that all the people of the tower of Shechem died, about a thousand men and women.

⁵⁰Then Abimelech went to Thebez, and he encamped against Thebez and took it. ⁵¹But there was a strong tower in the city, and all the men and women—all the people of the city—fled there and shut themselves in; then they went up to the top of the tower. ⁵²So Abimelech came as far as the tower and fought against it; and he drew near the door of the tower to burn it with fire. ⁵³But a certain woman dropped an upper millstone on Abimelech's head and crushed his skull. ⁵⁴Then he called quickly to the young man, his armorbearer, and said to him, "Draw your sword and kill me, lest men say of me, 'A woman killed him.' " So his young man thrust him through, and he died. ⁵⁵And when the men of Israel saw that Abimelech was dead, they departed, every man to his place.

⁵⁶Thus God repaid the wickedness of Abimelech, which he had done to his father by killing his seventy brothers. ⁵⁷And all the evil of the men of Shechem God returned on their own heads, and on them came the curse of Jotham the son of Jerubbaal.

Tola

10 After Abimelech there arose to save Israel Tola the son of Puah, the son of Dodo, a man of Issachar; and he dwelt in Shamir in the mountains of Ephraim. ²He judged Israel twenty-three years; and he died and was buried in Shamir.

9:37 ªHebrew *Meonenim*

9:53, 54 In fulfillment of Jotham's parable, the Shechemites and the rebels found fire instead of shade under Abimelech's rule (see vv. 7–15, note). While the men defended the tower with their weapons (arrows and spears), women helped by dropping stones that were normally used for domestic purposes. God is in control of history. Abimelech reaped the results of his wickedness through the actions of a woman (see Judg. 4:9, note; Abimelech's Killer).

*I am only one; but still I am one. I cannot do everything,
but still I can do something.*

Helen Keller

Jair

³After him arose Jair, a Gileadite; and he judged Israel twenty-two years. ⁴Now he had thirty sons who rode on thirty donkeys; they also had thirty towns, which are called "Havoth Jair"ᵃ to this day, which *are* in the land of Gilead. ⁵And Jair died and was buried in Camon.

Israel Oppressed Again

⁶Then the children of Israel again did evil in the sight of the LORD, and served the Baals and the Ashtoreths, the gods of Syria, the gods of Sidon, the gods of Moab, the gods of the people of Ammon, and the gods of the Philistines; and they forsook the LORD and did not serve Him. ⁷So the anger of the LORD was hot against Israel; and He sold them into the hands of the Philistines and into the hands of the people of Ammon. ⁸From that year they harassed and oppressed the children of Israel for eighteen years— all the children of Israel who *were* on the other side of the Jordan in the land of the Amorites, in Gilead. ⁹Moreover the people of Ammon crossed over the Jordan to fight against Judah also, against Benjamin, and against the house of Ephraim, so that Israel was severely distressed.

¹⁰And the children of Israel cried out to the LORD, saying, "We have sinned against You, because we have both forsaken our God and served the Baals!"

¹¹So the LORD said to the children of Israel, "*Did I* not *deliver you* from the Egyptians and from the Amorites and from the people of Ammon and from the Philistines? ¹²Also the Sidonians and Amalekites and Maonitesᵃ oppressed you; and you cried out to Me, and I delivered you from their hand. ¹³Yet you have forsaken Me and served other gods. Therefore I will deliver you no more. ¹⁴Go and cry out to the gods which you have chosen; let them deliver you in your time of distress."

¹⁵And the children of Israel said to the LORD, "We have sinned! Do to us whatever seems best to You; only deliver us this day, we pray." ¹⁶So they put away the foreign gods from among them and served the LORD. And His soul could no longer endure the misery of Israel.

¹⁷Then the people of Ammon gathered together and encamped in Gilead. And the children of Israel assembled together and encamped in Mizpah. ¹⁸And the people, the leaders of Gilead, said to one another, "Who *is* the man who will begin the fight against the people of Ammon? He shall be head over all the inhabitants of Gilead."

Jephthah

11 Now Jephthah the Gileadite was a mighty man of valor, but he *was* the son of a harlot; and Gilead begot Jephthah. ²Gilead's wife bore sons; and when his wife's sons grew up, they drove Jephthah out, and said to him, "You shall have no inheritance in our father's house, for you *are* the son of another woman." ³Then Jephthah fled from his brothers and dwelt in the land of Tob; and worthless men banded together with Jephthah and went out *raiding* with him.

⁴It came to pass after a time that the people of Ammon made war against Israel. ⁵And so it was, when the people of Ammon made war against Israel, that the elders of Gilead went to get Jephthah from the land of Tob. ⁶Then they said to Jephthah, "Come and be our commander, that we may fight against the people of Ammon."

⁷So Jephthah said to the elders of Gilead, "Did you not hate me, and expel me from my father's house? Why have you come to me now when you are in distress?"

⁸And the elders of Gilead said to Jephthah, "That is why we have turned again to you now, that you may go with us and fight against the people of Ammon, and be our head over all the inhabitants of Gilead."

⁹So Jephthah said to the elders of Gilead, "If you take me back home to fight against the people of Ammon, and the LORD delivers them to me, shall I be your head?"

¹⁰And the elders of Gilead said to Jephthah, "The LORD will be a witness between us, if we do not do according to your words." ¹¹Then Jephthah went with the elders of Gilead, and the people made him head and commander over them; and

· · · · · · · · · · · · · · · · ·

10:4 ᵃLiterally *Towns of Jair* (compare Numbers 32:41 and Deuteronomy 3:14)   **10:12** ᵃSome Septuagint manuscripts read *Midianites*.

11:1–10 Jephthah's credentials for leadership, like many of Israel's judges, were not impressive. The son of a prostitute, he had been expelled from his father's house and had become a bandit, a social outcast. Unlike Gideon, Jephthah's initial answer to the elders of Gilead seems to have been motivated by his own self-interest rather than by a desire to serve the Lord. At the end, however, his decision to lead Israel also was motivated by loyalty to the same people who had first rejected him because of his origins (see chart, The Period of the Judges).

JEPHTHAH'S OBEDIENT DAUGHTER

Jephthah's daughter illuminates the hard realities of daily life during the period of the judges. This period of Israel's history was a time of widespread defection from and disobedience toward God. Judges were generally political or military leaders whom, imperfect as they were, God was able to use to deliver His people.

Nothing is known about this young woman except what is captured in these verses, but they express a significant teaching. Obviously, even though the Spirit of the Lord had come upon him (Judg. 11:29), Jephthah evidently still felt the need to do something further to win assurance of God's favor in battle. Making a vow before battle was common, and Jephthah lived in a society where human sacrifices to pagan gods were routine. The original language indicates that Jephthah intentionally made a vow which could well include human sacrifice, although God had specifically prohibited such (Lev. 18:21; 20:1-5). This vow signifies Jephthah's incomplete knowledge of or blatant insensitivity to the law of Moses.

What do we learn about this young girl in these few verses? When her father returned after the battle with the Ammonites, she ran to greet him with timbrels and dancing, the customary greeting of women for their men who were returning victoriously from battle. No doubt she was as horrified as he was when she learned that she was to be the fulfillment of her father's vow. Rather than grieving over the tragedy that she would never marry and have children, the supreme fulfillment of Hebrew women, or even the tragedy of her impending death, as Josephus and most commentators understand the passage to mean, she submitted to the very limited understanding she had of her father's fatal vow (Judg. 11:36). This young girl exhibited total commitment, albeit to a misguided understanding of God's expectations.

What can Jephthah's daughter teach women today? Certainly she is a sterling example of a daughter's willing obedience to her father and total commitment to God. However, with the entire witness of Scripture as guidance for life, there is little excuse for such gross misinterpretation of God's requirements. Today, as in the time of Jephthah's daughter, children often bear the consequences of their parents' decisions. Parents need to be exceedingly wise as well as deliberate in making decisions that affect their children's lives (see Eph. 6:4).

See also notes on Fatherhood (Eph. 5); Girlhood (Prov. 1); Vows (Num. 30)

Jephthah spoke all his words before the LORD in Mizpah.

¹²Now Jephthah sent messengers to the king of the people of Ammon, saying, "What do you have against me, that you have come to fight against me in my land?"

¹³And the king of the people of Ammon answered the messengers of Jephthah, "Because Israel took away my land when they came up out of Egypt, from the Arnon as far as the Jabbok, and to the Jordan. Now therefore, restore those *lands* peaceably."

¹⁴So Jephthah again sent messengers to the king of the people of Ammon, ¹⁵and said to him, "Thus says Jephthah: 'Israel did not take away the land of Moab, nor the land of the people of Ammon; ¹⁶for when Israel came up from Egypt, they walked through the wilderness as far as the Red Sea and came to Kadesh. ¹⁷Then Israel sent messengers to the king of Edom, saying, "Please let me pass through your land." But the king of Edom would not heed. And in like manner they sent to the king of Moab, but he would not con-

sent. So Israel remained in Kadesh. ¹⁸And they went along through the wilderness and bypassed the land of Edom and the land of Moab, came to the east side of the land of Moab, and encamped on the other side of the Arnon. But they did not enter the border of Moab, for the Arnon *was* the border of Moab. ¹⁹Then Israel sent messengers to Sihon king of the Amorites, king of Heshbon; and Israel said to him, "Please let us pass through your land into our place." ²⁰But Sihon did not trust Israel to pass through his territory. So Sihon gathered all his people together, encamped in Jahaz, and fought against Israel. ²¹And the LORD God of Israel delivered Sihon and all his people into the hand of Israel, and they defeated them. Thus Israel gained possession of all the land of the Amorites, who inhabited that country. ²²They took possession of all the territory of the Amorites, from the Arnon to the Jabbok and from the wilderness to the Jordan.

²³And now the LORD God of Israel has dispossessed the Amorites from before His people Israel; should you then possess it? ²⁴Will you not possess

---

11:14–28 Jephthah's response to the Ammonite menace was an example of contemporary international diplomacy. Often appeals were made to the gods (in this case, the one true God, v. 27) to establish and protect territorial frontiers. Jephthah's ironic reply goes back to when Israel began the conquest of the Land by battling against the Amorites and *not* against the

Ammonites (Num. 21:21-32). God had long ago given the Promised Land to Israel. It was ridiculous for the Ammonites to try to claim a territory that previously belonged to the Amorites and now belonged to Israel! If the Ammonites had some claim to the Land, why did they wait 300 years to press it (v. 26)?

whatever Chemosh your god gives you to possess? So whatever the LORD our God takes possession of before us, we will possess. [25]And now, *are* you any better than Balak the son of Zippor, king of Moab? Did he ever strive against Israel? Did he ever fight against them? [26]While Israel dwelt in Heshbon and its villages, in Aroer and its villages, and in all the cities along the banks of the Arnon, for three hundred years, why did you not recover *them* within that time? [27]Therefore I have not sinned against you, but you wronged me by fighting against me. May the LORD, the Judge, render judgment this day between the children of Israel and the people of Ammon.' " [28]However, the king of the people of Ammon did not heed the words which Jephthah sent him.

Jephthah's Vow and Victory

[29]Then the Spirit of the LORD came upon Jephthah, and he passed through Gilead and Manasseh, and passed through Mizpah of Gilead; and from Mizpah of Gilead he advanced *toward* the people of Ammon. [30]And Jephthah made a vow to the LORD, and said, "If You will indeed deliver the people of Ammon into my hands, [31]then it will be that whatever comes out of the doors of my house to meet me, when I return in peace from the people of Ammon, shall surely be the LORD's, and I will offer it up as a burnt offering."

[32]So Jephthah advanced toward the people of Ammon to fight against them, and the LORD delivered them into his hands. [33]And he defeated them from Aroer as far as Minnith—twenty cities—and to Abel Keramim,[a] with a very great slaughter. Thus the people of Ammon were subdued before the children of Israel.

Jephthah's Daughter

[34]When Jephthah came to his house at Mizpah, there was his daughter, coming out to meet him with timbrels and dancing; and she *was his* only child. Besides her he had neither son nor daughter. [35]And it came to pass, when he saw her, that he tore his clothes, and said, "Alas, my daughter! You have brought me very low! You are among those who trouble me! For I have given my word to the LORD, and I cannot go back on it."

[36]So she said to him, "My father, *if* you have given your word to the LORD, do to me according to what has gone out of your mouth, because the LORD has avenged you of your enemies, the people of Ammon." [37]Then she said to her father, "Let this thing be done for me: let me alone for two months, that I may go and wander on the mountains and bewail my virginity, my friends and I."

[38]So he said, "Go." And he sent her away *for* two months; and she went with her friends, and bewailed her virginity on the mountains. [39]And it was so at the end of two months that she returned to her father, and he carried out his vow with her which he had vowed. She knew no man.

And it became a custom in Israel [40]*that* the daughters of Israel went four days each year to lament the daughter of Jephthah the Gileadite.

Jephthah's Conflict with Ephraim

12 Then the men of Ephraim gathered together, crossed over toward Zaphon, and said to Jephthah, "Why did you cross over to fight against the people of Ammon, and did not call us to go with you? We will burn your house down on you with fire!"

[2]And Jephthah said to them, "My people and I were in a great struggle with the people of Ammon; and when I called you, you did not deliver me out of their hands. [3]So when I saw that you would not deliver *me,* I took my life in my hands and crossed over against the people of Ammon; and the LORD delivered them into my hand. Why then have you come up to me this day to fight against me?" [4]Now Jephthah gathered together all the men of Gilead and fought against Ephraim. And

11:33 [a]Literally *Plain of Vineyards*

11:27 The Lord alone receives the designation "Judge" in the Book of Judges, although others are described as exercising the function of a judge.

11:30, 31 In the midst of the battle, Jephthah sought to bargain with God by offering the Lord a private sacrifice to ensure his own victory (see Jephthah's Obedient Daughter). God's use of Jephthah to deliver the Israelites was not in response to Jephthah's vow. God had rejected human sacrifice and had given specific prohibitions against it (Lev. 18:21; 20:1–5; Deut. 12:29–32; 18:9–12). Parents were not allowed to sacrifice their children. But here Jephthah, influenced no doubt by the customs of the pagan cultures around him, tried to get what he wanted in his own way, without knowing the outcome of his foolish vow. Ironically, as Jephthah suffered for the sins of his parents, his daughter was to suffer because of her father's foolish vow. The unnamed girl responded with courage and accepted the consequences of her father's vow (Judg. 11:39,

40). Jephthah's line came to an end—even if Jephthah merely devoted his daughter to perpetual virginity, as some scholars believe happened. Other references are made to unlawful human sacrifices (2 Kin. 16:3; 17:17; 21:6; 2 Chr. 33:6; Jer. 7:31; 19:5; 32:35; Ezek. 16:20, 21).

12:1–7 Jephthah, unlike Gideon, did not seek to appease the Ephraimites (Judg. 8:1–3). Apparently the Israelites who lived east of the Jordan pronounced the first letter of "Shibboleth" (Heb., lit. "flowing stream" or "ear of grain") with a "sh" sound, while those living in Canaan pronounced it with an "s" sound, giving evidence of the growing separation between eastern and western tribes. Thus, the Ephraimites were identified by their speech. Jephthah, though vindicated as a leader of Gilead, responded to the insults of Ephraim with force. This intertribal war was costly in that 42,000 Ephraimites were slain.

PREGNANCY *THE ULTIMATE CREATIVE ACTIVITY*

The biblical description of pregnancy is not comforting. From the time of Eve's disobedience God stated clearly, "I will greatly multiply your sorrow and your conception; In pain you shall bring forth children" (Gen. 3:16).

Anyone who has endured the nausea or vomiting of the first trimester or the seemingly endless misery of the last trimester clearly knows what God meant. The trials of pregnancy, however, produce results that are highly positive.

First, this condition can produce in the mother patience that will be of crucial importance after her child is born. A mother's patience, in turn, can both calm and strengthen her children. On the other hand, a woman who becomes angry and self-pitying during pregnancy can produce damage in both herself and her child. Second, the pain and discomfort of pregnancy only serves to heighten the joy associated with birth.

Instead of considering Genesis 1:28 as a commandment, look at these words as the unveiling of a divine blessing. Such is certainly consistent with the whole of Scripture. Procreation is not something we must do to please God so much as what God allows us to do with Him. All babies are created with unique purpose by Him (Ps. 139:13–16). Of course, the possibility of morning sickness, weight gain, and the awkwardness of body and schedule changes may overshadow this potentially delightful and joyous experience. Nevertheless, as we share in the ultimate creative activity, we have God's promise that children are a rewarding gift from Him (Ps. 127:3–5).

See also Ex. 21:22; notes on Childbirth (John 16); Fruit of the Spirit (Ps. 86; Rom. 5; 15; 1 Cor. 10; 13; Gal. 5; Eph. 4; Col. 3; 2 Thess. 1; Rev. 2); Motherhood (1 Sam. 1; Is. 49; Ezek. 16); Parenthood (Prov. 10); Sanctity of Life (Gen. 9); portraits of Mary of Nazareth (Luke 1); Elizabeth (Luke 1)

---

the men of Gilead defeated Ephraim, because they said, "You Gileadites *are* fugitives of Ephraim among the Ephraimites *and* among the Manassites." ⁵The Gileadites seized the fords of the Jordan before the Ephraimites *arrived.* And when *any* Ephraimite who escaped said, "Let me cross over," the men of Gilead would say to him, "*Are* you an Ephraimite?" If he said, "No," ⁶then they would say to him, "Then say, 'Shibboleth'!" And he would say, "Sibboleth," for he could not pronounce *it* right. Then they would take him and kill him at the fords of the Jordan. There fell at that time forty-two thousand Ephraimites.

⁷And Jephthah judged Israel six years. Then Jephthah the Gileadite died and was buried among the cities of Gilead.

Ibzan, Elon, and Abdon

⁸After him, Ibzan of Bethlehem judged Israel. ⁹He had thirty sons. And he gave away thirty daughters in marriage, and brought in thirty daughters from elsewhere for his sons. He judged Israel seven years. ¹⁰Then Ibzan died and was buried at Bethlehem.

¹¹After him, Elon the Zebulunite judged Israel. He judged Israel ten years. ¹²And Elon the Zebulun-

ite died and was buried at Aijalon in the country of Zebulun.

¹³After him, Abdon the son of Hillel the Pirathonite judged Israel. ¹⁴He had forty sons and thirty grandsons, who rode on seventy young donkeys. He judged Israel eight years. ¹⁵Then Abdon the son of Hillel the Pirathonite died and was buried in Pirathon in the land of Ephraim, in the mountains of the Amalekites.

The Birth of Samson

13Again the children of Israel did evil in the sight of the LORD, and the LORD delivered them into the hand of the Philistines for forty years.

²Now there was a certain man from Zorah, of the family of the Danites, whose name *was* Manoah; and his wife *was* barren and had no children. ³And the Angel of the LORD appeared to the woman and said to her, "Indeed now, you are barren and have borne no children, but you shall conceive and bear a son. ⁴Now therefore, please be careful not to drink wine or *similar* drink, and not to eat anything unclean. ⁵For behold, you shall conceive and bear a son. And no razor shall come upon his head, for the child shall be a

---

13:1 The final oppression recorded in Judges lasted 40 years and involved Samson, a Danite judge. He probably judged western Israel around the time of Jephthah's judgeship. Eventually, the Philistine threat led Israel to seek the stronger and more permanent leadership of a king.

13:2–5 Samson's mother, childless, as were Sarah (Gen. 11:30; 16:1), Rebekah (Gen. 25:21), Hannah (1 Sam. 1:2), and Eliza-

beth (Luke 1:7), received two visits from the Angel of the Lord (see chart, The Angel of the Lord). God's announcement to her must have seemed an incredible gift. She had been humiliated, bearing the reproach of a woman who would soon be forgotten because she had no children to keep her memory alive (see Samson's Confident Mother).

THE ANGEL OF THE LORD

THE ANGEL OF THE LORD APPEARED	THE ANGEL OF THE LORD ACTED	THE ANGEL OF THE LORD EXPRESSED GOD'S CONCERN
To Hagar	By telling Hagar to return to Sarah (Gen. 16:9).	For a mistreated WOMAN by promising her many descendants (Gen. 16:10).
To the Israelites	By announcing judgment against God's people because of their disobedience (Judg. 2:1–3).	For a fledgling NATION by bringing them to repentance (Judg. 2:4, 5).
To Gideon	By commissioning Gideon to destroy idolatry in his father's house and to wage war against the Midianites (Judg. 6:11–25).	For FAMILIES by cleansing Gideon's family from idolatry (Judg. 6:26–28).
To Samson's mother	By announcing Samson's birth (Judg. 13:3–5).	For a barren WOMAN by blessing her with the birth of a special child (Judg. 13:24).
To Samson's parents	By announcing Samson's ministry (Judg. 13:5–21).	For a COUPLE by helping them with godly parenting (Judg. 13:11–14).
To Elizabeth's husband	By announcing the birth of John the Baptist (Luke 1:13–17).	For a MAN of God and his WIFE by giving them a son and heir in their old age (Luke 1:24, 25, 57, 58).

Note: The Angel of the Lord is shrouded in mystery. Clearly He is a messenger of the Lord appearing according to divine assignment to deliver God's Word concerning revelation, deliverance, or judgment. Many consider this heavenly messenger to be a Christophany or an appearance of the pre-incarnate Christ to human beings who otherwise would not have been able to look upon God and live (see Ex. 33:20).

Nazirite to God from the womb; and he shall begin to deliver Israel out of the hand of the Philistines."

⁶So the woman came and told her husband, saying, "A Man of God came to me, and His countenance *was* like the countenance of the Angel of God, very awesome; but I did not ask Him where He *was* from, and He did not tell me His name. ⁷And He said to me, 'Behold, you shall conceive and bear a son. Now drink no wine or *similar* drink, nor eat anything unclean, for the child shall be a Nazirite to God from the womb to the day of his death.'"

⁸Then Manoah prayed to the LORD, and said, "O my Lord, please let the Man of God whom You sent come to us again and teach us what we shall do for the child who will be born."

⁹And God listened to the voice of Manoah, and the Angel of God came to the woman again as she was sitting in the field; but Manoah her husband *was* not with her. ¹⁰Then the woman ran in haste and told her husband, and said to him, "Look, the Man who came to me the *other* day has just now appeared to me!"

¹¹So Manoah arose and followed his wife. When he came to the Man, he said to Him, "Are You the Man who spoke to this woman?"

And He said, "I *am*."

¹²Manoah said, "Now let Your words come to *pass!* What will be the boy's rule of life, and his work?"

¹³So the Angel of the LORD said to Manoah, "Of all that I said to the woman let her be careful. ¹⁴She may not eat anything that comes from the

SAMSON'S CONFIDENT MOTHER

An humble and childless woman was accosted in the field by an Angel of the Lord who prophesied that she would bear a son who would deliver Israel from the heavy-handed Philistines. This unnamed woman was married to Manoah of the tribe of Dan. They lived in Zorah, west of Jerusalem.

Manoah and his wife were apparently devout believers, but the Angel's prophecy seemed almost too good to be true. The wife told her husband all that had happened, and Manoah prayed that the Man of God would return in order to "teach us what we shall do for the child who will be born" (Judg. 13:8). They did not hesitate to believe. The Angel returned for the third time to repeat the rules of the Nazirite vow: no wine or fruit, no razor on the head, no touching of anything unclean.

Although this woman may have been illiterate and dependent upon her husband, as a believer and an expectant mother she had no trouble complying with the instruction of the heavenly messenger. Manoah made an offering to God on the spot, and as the flame ascended, the Angel went with it. Terrified, the two fell on their faces (vv. 19, 20).

The revelation of the supernatural was required for a depraved society such as theirs, and the dramatic display confirmed God's supernatural intervention, no doubt answering their prayers. When Manoah expressed his fear that they themselves would die because they had seen God, his wife demonstrated confidence in God: "If the Lord had desired to kill us, He would not have accepted [an offering]" (v. 23).

The promised son, Samson (meaning "sunlike" or "splendor"), chose a lifestyle reflecting the fallen nature of his world; nevertheless, God used him to restrain the Philistines. As a result, his name is found with the heroes of faith in Hebrews (Judg. 11:32).

The disappointment of barrenness was transformed into the joy of motherhood. Though grateful for a son of such unusual strength, this humble mother must also have grieved over Samson's selfishness and disobedience to God. Certainly his mother's prayers and nurturing played a part in the contribution Samson made as a deliverer of his people. This unnamed woman will be remembered as a believing woman who left her testimony: Every woman must not only listen for God's direction but also obey Him even in the minutest details (Judg. 13:14). God's holy angels are poised to bring about His will even when least expected.

See also Judges 14:2–5; Motherhood (1 Sam. 1)

---

vine, nor may she drink wine or *similar* drink, nor eat anything unclean. All that I commanded her let her observe."

¹⁵Then Manoah said to the Angel of the LORD, "Please let us detain You, and we will prepare a young goat for You."

¹⁶And the Angel of the LORD said to Manoah, "Though you detain Me, I will not eat your food. But if you offer a burnt offering, you must offer it to the LORD." (For Manoah did not know He *was* the Angel of the LORD.)

¹⁷Then Manoah said to the Angel of the LORD, "What *is* Your name, that when Your words come *to pass* we may honor You?"

¹⁸And the Angel of the LORD said to him, "Why do you ask My name, seeing it *is* wonderful?"

¹⁹So Manoah took the young goat with the grain offering, and offered it upon the rock to the LORD. And He did a wondrous thing while Manoah and his wife looked on— ²⁰it happened as the flame went up toward heaven from the altar—the

Angel of the LORD ascended in the flame of the altar! When Manoah and his wife saw *this,* they fell on their faces to the ground. ²¹When the Angel of the LORD appeared no more to Manoah and his wife, then Manoah knew that He *was* the Angel of the LORD.

²²And Manoah said to his wife, "We shall surely die, because we have seen God!"

²³But his wife said to him, "If the LORD had desired to kill us, He would not have accepted a burnt offering and a grain offering from our hands, nor would He have shown us all these *things,* nor would He have told us *such things* as these at this time."

²⁴So the woman bore a son and called his name Samson; and the child grew, and the LORD blessed him. ²⁵And the Spirit of the LORD began to move upon him at Mahaneh Danª between Zorah and Eshtaol.

· · · · · · · · · · · · · · · · · · ·
13:25 ªLiterally *Camp of Dan* (compare 18:12)

13:24 Samson was to be a Nazirite from birth (see v. 5), serving the Lord all his life. As a Nazirite, he was to abstain from wine or strong drink, to avoid the razor, and to avoid defilement by contact with anything dead (Num. 6:1, 2, 3–8, notes). Samson (Heb., lit. "sun" or "brightness"), like the nation of Israel, had been chosen to be holy to God. But just as Samson

was attracted to foreign women, Israel was attracted to the pagan practices of the Canaanites. Finally, just as a defeated and blind Samson ended his life grinding corn in chains, Israel also succumbed to a long period of Philistine oppression (see chart, The Period of the Judges).

Samson's Philistine Wife

14 Now Samson went down to Timnah, and saw a woman in Timnah of the daughters of the Philistines. ²So he went up and told his father and mother, saying, "I have seen a woman in Timnah of the daughters of the Philistines; now therefore, get her for me as a wife."

³Then his father and mother said to him, "*Is there* no woman among the daughters of your brethren, or among all my people, that you must go and get a wife from the uncircumcised Philistines?"

And Samson said to his father, "Get her for me, for she pleases me well."

⁴But his father and mother did not know that it was of the LORD— that He was seeking an occasion to move against the Philistines. For at that time the Philistines had dominion over Israel.

⁵So Samson went down to Timnah with his father and mother, and came to the vineyards of Timnah.

Now *to his* surprise, a young lion *came* roaring against him. ⁶And the Spirit of the LORD came mightily upon him, and he tore the lion apart as one would have torn apart a young goat, though *he had* nothing in his hand. But he did not tell his father or his mother what he had done.

⁷Then he went down and talked with the woman; and she pleased Samson well. ⁸After some time, when he returned to get her, he turned aside to see the carcass of the lion. And behold, a swarm of bees and honey *were* in the carcass of the lion. ⁹He took some of it in his hands and went along, eating. When he came to his father and mother, he gave *some* to them, and they also ate. But he did not tell them that he had taken the honey out of the carcass of the lion.

¹⁰So his father went down to the woman. And Samson gave a feast there, for young men used to do so. ¹¹And it happened, when they saw him, that they brought thirty companions to be with him.

¹²Then Samson said to them, "Let me pose a riddle to you. If you can correctly solve and explain it to me within the seven days of the feast, then I will give you thirty linen garments and thirty changes of clothing. ¹³But if you cannot explain *it* to me, then you shall give me thirty linen garments and thirty changes of clothing."

And they said to him, "Pose your riddle, that we may hear it."

¹⁴So he said to them:

"Out of the eater came something to eat,
And out of the strong came something sweet."

Now for three days they could not explain the riddle.

¹⁵But it came to pass on the seventh[a] day that they said to Samson's wife, "Entice your husband, that he may explain the riddle to us, or else we will burn you and your father's house with fire. Have you invited us in order to take what is ours? *Is that* not *so?*"

¹⁶Then Samson's wife wept on him, and said, "You only hate me! You do not love me! You have

---

14:15 [a]Following Masoretic Text, Targum, and Vulgate; Septuagint and Syriac read *fourth*.

14:1–3 Timnah was a Philistine town in the Sorek valley approximately four miles southwest of Zorah (Judg. 13:25). The Philistines (or "sea peoples") already had mastered the use of iron (see Judg. 3:3, note). Marrying someone from a stronger and more prestigious culture may have seemed attractive and beneficial by human standards. Samson's decision to marry the unnamed woman of Timnah, however, was a conscious choice to neglect his special ministry and disobey God's explicit command not to intermarry with the Canaanites (Ex. 34:11–16; Deut. 7:1–3; see also Samson's Pagan Bride). Samson's parents were rightly upset. In Hebrew society, the father was expected to choose a wife for his son. Samson's parents were in a difficult position because they remembered what the Angel of the Lord had required of their son (see Judg. 14:4, note; chart, The Angel of the Lord).

14:4 God is in control of history, but people are also fully responsible and accountable for their actions. This tension exists in the daily lives of God's people. The Book of Judges correctly records the history of Israel from this theological viewpoint. Samson was fully responsible for his disobedience, but God in His providence, despite Samson's failure, used him to bring deliverance to the Israelites.

14:10, 11 Samson's feast was held to celebrate a marriage commitment in which the bride did not join her husband's family but stayed with her own family and received occa-

sional visits from her husband. In metronymic marriage, the husband was viewed as joining his wife's family and in theory was subservient to his wife's father, and any children of such a marriage were considered members of the mother's family. Samson's marriage feast lasted seven days. The marriage could be physically consummated at the end of the feast. The 30 companions served as protectors of the wedding party. How ironic that the usually joyful occasion of a wedding became the tragic cause of Samson's breaking two of his Nazirite vows—the prohibitions against drinking wine and having contact with a dead body.

14:15–17 A disgraced bride. Unhappy at the possibility of having to come up with payment to Samson if they could not solve his riddle, the 30 companions, who were supposedly wedding protectors, threatened physical violence against the bride and her family if she did not learn the riddle's answer for them. They even implied that she was involved in an attempt to relieve them of their wedding finery. Linen garments and changes of clothing, frequently taken as spoils of war by triumphant forces, were costly items and used for special events. A person might possess only one such garment in an entire lifetime. This young Timnite woman, in seeking to save herself, lost everything. In his anger, Samson never entered the bridal chamber; thus she became a disgraced bride (see Judg. 15:1, 2).

SAMSON'S PAGAN BRIDE

This impressive woman from Timnah captured Samson's affection with her beauty and charm, and she, too, must have been infatuated with his strength and wit. They married hurriedly and despite parental opposition. The marriage was doomed from its beginning because of competing loyalties which pulled at the young couple as well as selfishness and immaturity on the part of both.

The Timnite, who had remained in her parents' home after her wedding, was most concerned with her own self-preservation. Just as Samson, she was accustomed to getting her own way, if by no other means, through her tears and whining (Judg. 14:2, 3, 16, 17). She used all her manipulative skills, including a week of tears, to meet the demands of her countrymen, knowing all the while that they planned evil against her husband. When Samson finally trusted her with his secret, she blatantly, and seemingly without remorse, betrayed him. She was under threat for the lives of herself and her family, but in the end, perhaps because of her own wrong choices, all their lives were lost (Judg. 15:6). Who knows what protection Samson might have afforded the family if only his wife had communicated her fears to him.

The Timnite and Samson erred when they rushed into the serious commitment of marriage based upon initial infatuation and physical attraction (Judg. 14:2, 3). Neither had left father and mother in order to give primary loyalty to the other (see Gen. 2:24). Neither reached beyond self to be concerned about the best interest of the other (see Eph. 5:33). Neither had considered the ramifications of being linked to another who did not have the same spiritual commitments (see Amos 3:3). Marriage to a foreign woman who was not committed to the God of Israel was strictly forbidden because intermarriage was a definite factor in the destruction of the nation (see Deut. 7:1–4; Judg. 3:5, 6). Not only was Samson an Israelite and thus committed to *Yahweh,* but he was also a Nazirite and thus set apart by God in a special way (Judg. 13:4, 5). For a judge to fail in this area shows the far-reaching result of spiritual apathy. This marriage put Samson on the road to estrangement from *Yahweh;* yet only the Lord could have given wisdom and channeled the love needed to overcome the overwhelming obstacles that faced Samson and the Timnite in their challenging marriage.

See also notes on Interfaith Marriage (Neh. 10); Rebellion (Num. 16)

---

posed a riddle to the sons of my people, but you have not explained *it* to me."

And he said to her, "Look, I have not explained *it* to my father or my mother; so should I explain *it* to you?" [17]Now she had wept on him the seven days while their feast lasted. And it happened on the seventh day that he told her, because she pressed him so much. Then she explained the riddle to the sons of her people. [18]So the men of the city said to him on the seventh day before the sun went down:

"What *is* sweeter than honey?
And what *is* stronger than a lion?"

And he said to them:

"If you had not plowed with my heifer,
You would not have solved my riddle!"

[19]Then the Spirit of the LORD came upon him mightily, and he went down to Ashkelon and killed thirty of their men, took their apparel, and gave the changes *of clothing* to those who had explained the riddle. So his anger was aroused, and he went back up to his father's house. [20]And Samson's wife was *given* to his companion, who had been his best man.

Samson Defeats the Philistines

15 After a while, in the time of wheat harvest, it happened that Samson visited his wife with a young goat. And he said, "Let me go in to my wife, into *her* room." But her father would not permit him to go in.

[2]Her father said, "I really thought that you thoroughly hated her; therefore I gave her to your companion. *Is* not her younger sister better than she? Please, take her instead."

[3]And Samson said to them, "This time I shall be blameless regarding the Philistines if I harm them!" [4]Then Samson went and caught three hundred foxes; and he took torches, turned *the foxes* tail to tail, and put a torch between each pair of tails. [5]When he had set the torches on fire, he let *the foxes* go into the standing grain of the Philistines, and burned up both the shocks and the standing grain, as well as the vineyards *and* olive groves.

[6]Then the Philistines said, "Who has done this?"

And they answered, "Samson, the son-in-law of the Timnite, because he has taken his wife and given her to his companion." So the Philistines came up and burned her and her father with fire.

[7]Samson said to them, "Since you would do a

thing like this, I will surely take revenge on you, and after that I will cease." [8]So he attacked them hip and thigh with a great slaughter; then he went down and dwelt in the cleft of the rock of Etam.

[9]Now the Philistines went up, encamped in Judah, and deployed themselves against Lehi. [10]And the men of Judah said, "Why have you come up against us?"

So they answered, "We have come up to arrest Samson, to do to him as he has done to us."

[11]Then three thousand men of Judah went down to the cleft of the rock of Etam, and said to Samson, "Do you not know that the Philistines rule over us? What *is* this you have done to us?"

And he said to them, "As they did to me, so I have done to them."

[12]But they said to him, "We have come down to arrest you, that we may deliver you into the hand of the Philistines."

Then Samson said to them, "Swear to me that you will not kill me yourselves."

[13]So they spoke to him, saying, "No, but we will tie you securely and deliver you into their hand; but we will surely not kill you." And they bound him with two new ropes and brought him up from the rock.

[14]When he came to Lehi, the Philistines came shouting against him. Then the Spirit of the LORD came mightily upon him; and the ropes that *were* on his arms became like flax that is burned with fire, and his bonds broke loose from his hands. [15]He found a fresh jawbone of a donkey, reached out his hand and took it, and killed a thousand men with it. [16]Then Samson said:

> "With the jawbone of a donkey,
> Heaps upon heaps,
> With the jawbone of a donkey
> I have slain a thousand men!"

[17]And so it was, when he had finished speaking, that he threw the jawbone from his hand, and called that place Ramath Lehi.[a]

[18]Then he became very thirsty; so he cried out to the LORD and said, "You have given this great deliverance by the hand of Your servant; and now shall I die of thirst and fall into the hand of the uncircumcised?" [19]So God split the hollow place that *is* in Lehi,[a] and water came out, and he drank; and his spirit returned, and he revived. Therefore he called its name En Hakkore,[b] which is in Lehi to this day. [20]And he judged Israel twenty years in the days of the Philistines.

Samson and Delilah

16Now Samson went to Gaza and saw a harlot there, and went in to her. [2]*When* the Gazites *were told,* "Samson has come here!" they surrounded *the place* and lay in wait for him all night at the gate of the city. They were quiet all night, saying, "In the morning, when it is daylight, we will kill him." [3]And Samson lay *low* till midnight; then he arose at midnight, took hold of the doors of the gate of the city and the two gateposts, pulled them up, bar and all, put *them* on his shoulders, and carried them to the top of the hill that faces Hebron.

[4]Afterward it happened that he loved a woman in the Valley of Sorek, whose name *was* Delilah. [5]And the lords of the Philistines came up to her and said to her, "Entice him, and find out where his great strength *lies,* and by what *means* we may overpower him, that we may bind him to afflict him; and every one of us will give you eleven hundred *pieces* of silver."

[6]So Delilah said to Samson, "Please tell me where your great strength *lies,* and with what you may be bound to afflict you."

[7]And Samson said to her, "If they bind me with seven fresh bowstrings, not yet dried, then I shall become weak, and be like any *other* man."

[8]So the lords of the Philistines brought up to her seven fresh bowstrings, not yet dried, and she bound him with them. [9]Now *men were* lying in

---

15:17 [a]Literally *Jawbone Height*   15:19 [a]Literally *Jawbone* (compare verse 14) [b]Literally *Spring of the Caller*

15:11 The great fear of the Israelites for the Philistines is evidenced in their lack of loyalty to one of their own countrymen. The men of Judah clearly were willing to deliver Samson over to the Philistines in return for their own safety.

15:19 Though Samson had disobeyed his Nazirite vows and though clearly he was controlled by his sensual nature, he was used by God as an agent of deliverance for God's people. God's grace in Samson's life was evidenced by the supernatural provision of water when Samson was exhausted and discouraged.

16:1 Gaza, an important Philistine city, was southwest of Zorah, a few miles inland from the Mediterranean Sea, along the trade routes between Egypt and western Asia. The man whom God had blessed with supernatural strength again showed himself to be morally and spiritually weak.

16:4 Delilah lived in the Valley of Sorek, close to Zorah. Much intermarriage had occurred between the Philistines and those whom they conquered. Most likely Delilah was a Philistine (see Delilah; Seduction). Her relationship with Samson must have been a lengthy and important one for the Philistine leaders to have noticed it. Regardless of the depth of their relationship, she was heartless when given the choice between her lover Samson and a large sum of money.

16:5 The amount of money offered by the Philistine lords for Samson's betrayal and capture indicates their great fear of Samson. Each Philistine lord offered Delilah 1,100 shekels of silver. The payment to a Levite for an entire year of service was about ten shekels (Judg. 17:10; see chart, Money and Measurements in the Bible).

DELILAH *The Teasing Temptress*

Samson and Delilah are among the most well-known couples in the Bible. Samson is known for his strength; Delilah is known for her seductive manipulation.

Delilah lived in a small village near Samson's hometown. She was possibly a Philistine, although her name is Semitic. She may have been a temple prostitute. Apparently Samson had been visiting her frequently, and their relationship became known to the Philistine leaders. They went to Delilah with an offer she could not refuse.

Samson's background, his upbringing, and his own experience should have taught him to stay away from foreign entanglements, but the record is clear that Samson felt an emotional attachment to Delilah. No evidence exists that she felt personal admiration or affection for him. To the contrary, clearly she was motivated by greed; she was perfectly willing to use all her charming seductiveness (which apparently was considerable) to earn a large cash bonus.

The ingredients for disaster were in place: a morally weak man with uncontrollable sexual passions; a seductive temptress motivated by greed; a group of foreign leaders with unlimited funds and the strong conviction that their national security, perhaps even their national survival, was at stake.

Her methods were simple, and though it took time, they eventually worked. She was playful and teasing. She was coquettish and provocative. She was alluring and enticing. She coaxed and cajoled. She pouted and demanded. There was a fortune waiting for her if she could discover the secret of his strength. She was determined, and she ultimately succeeded in prying Samson's secret from him.

Convinced that he had finally told her the truth, she sent for the Philistine leaders. She lulled her lover to sleep and had his hair cut off. With utter heartlessness she watched as he struggled out of a deep sleep, thinking he would fend off his attackers as easily as before, only to discover to his horror that his strength was gone. No doubt she was counting her money as they led him out.

Delilah personifies the immoral woman of Proverbs 5. "In the end she is bitter as wormwood" (see Prov. 5:4–6).

See also note on Temptation (Heb. 2)

---

wait, staying with her in the room. And she said to him, "The Philistines *are* upon you, Samson!" But he broke the bowstrings as a strand of yarn breaks when it touches fire. So the secret of his strength was not known.

¹⁰Then Delilah said to Samson, "Look, you have mocked me and told me lies. Now, please tell me what you may be bound with."

¹¹So he said to her, "If they bind me securely with new ropes that have never been used, then I shall become weak, and be like any *other* man."

¹²Therefore Delilah took new ropes and bound him with them, and said to him, "The Philistines *are* upon you, Samson!" And *men were* lying in wait, staying in the room. But he broke them off his arms like a thread.

¹³Delilah said to Samson, "Until now you have mocked me and told me lies. Tell me what you may be bound with."

And he said to her, "If you weave the seven locks of my head into the web of the loom"—

¹⁴So she wove *it* tightly with the batten of the loom, and said to him, "The Philistines *are* upon

you, Samson!" But he awoke from his sleep, and pulled out the batten and the web from the loom.

¹⁵Then she said to him, "How can you say, 'I love you,' when your heart *is* not with me? You have mocked me these three times, and have not told me where your great strength *lies*." ¹⁶And it came to pass, when she pestered him daily with her words and pressed him, *so* that his soul was vexed to death, ¹⁷that he told her all his heart, and said to her, "No razor has ever come upon my head, for I *have been* a Nazirite to God from my mother's womb. If I am shaven, then my strength will leave me, and I shall become weak, and be like any *other* man."

¹⁸When Delilah saw that he had told her all his heart, she sent and called for the lords of the Philistines, saying, "Come up once more, for he has told me all his heart." So the lords of the Philistines came up to her and brought the money in their hand. ¹⁹Then she lulled him to sleep on her knees, and called for a man and had him shave off the seven locks of his head. Then she began to tor-

---

16:19–21 Samson found himself in the most tragic situation when the third of his Nazirite vows was broken by the cutting of his hair. God had left him. Samson's source of strength was not in his long hair but in the Lord's power, which was available to him only as long as he faithfully kept the Nazirite vow.

Samson was completely at the mercy of his captors, who blinded him and assigned him to the menial task of grinding grain in a prison near Gaza, the scene of some of his previous great exploits.

ment him,[a] and his strength left him. [20]And she said, "The Philistines *are* upon you, Samson!" So he awoke from his sleep, and said, "I will go out as before, at other times, and shake myself free!" But he did not know that the LORD had departed from him.

[21]Then the Philistines took him and put out his eyes, and brought him down to Gaza. They bound him with bronze fetters, and he became a grinder in the prison. [22]However, the hair of his head began to grow again after it had been shaven.

Samson Dies with the Philistines

[23]Now the lords of the Philistines gathered together to offer a great sacrifice to Dagon their god, and to rejoice. And they said:

"Our god has delivered into our hands
  Samson our enemy!"

[24]When the people saw him, they praised their god; for they said:

"Our god has delivered into our hands our
    enemy,
The destroyer of our land,
And the one who multiplied our dead."

[25]So it happened, when their hearts were merry, that they said, "Call for Samson, that he may perform for us." So they called for Samson from the prison, and he performed for them. And they stationed him between the pillars. [26]Then Samson said to the lad who held him by the hand, "Let me feel the pillars which support the temple, so that I can lean on them." [27]Now the temple was full of men and women. All the lords of the Philistines *were* there—about three thousand men and women on the roof watching while Samson performed.

[28]Then Samson called to the LORD, saying, "O Lord GOD, remember me, I pray! Strengthen me, I pray, just this once, O God, that I may with one *blow* take vengeance on the Philistines for my two eyes!" [29]And Samson took hold of the two middle pillars which supported the temple, and he braced himself against them, one on his right and the other on his left. [30]Then Samson said, "Let me die with the Philistines!" And he pushed with *all his* might, and the temple fell on the lords and all the people who *were* in it. So the dead that he killed at his death were more than he had killed in his life.

[31]And his brothers and all his father's household came down and took him, and brought *him* up and buried him between Zorah and Eshtaol in the tomb of his father Manoah. He had judged Israel twenty years.

Micah's Idolatry

17 Now there was a man from the mountains of Ephraim, whose name *was* Micah. [2]And he said to his mother, "The eleven hundred *shekels* of silver that were taken from you, and on which you put a curse, even saying it in my ears—here *is* the silver with me; I took it."

And his mother said, "*May you be* blessed by the LORD, my son!" [3]So when he had returned the eleven hundred *shekels* of silver to his mother, his mother said, "I had wholly dedicated the silver from my hand to the LORD for my son, to make a carved image and a molded image; now therefore, I will return it to you." [4]Thus he returned the silver to his mother. Then his mother took two hundred *shekels* of silver and gave them to the silversmith, and he made it into a carved image and a

---

16:19 [a]Following Masoretic Text, Targum, and Vulgate; Septuagint reads *he began to be weak.*

16:23 Dagon (Heb., lit. "grain") was a god of vegetation adopted by the Philistines as their principal deity upon their arrival in Canaan. The size of the crowd indicated a nationally organized observance honoring Dagon because of Samson's capture.

16:24–30 Samson's final act occurred in an open court, where Samson was humiliated and forced to perform publicly. Ancient Near Eastern temples had similar constructions in which a covered portion overlooked the court. The roof was supported by wooden pillars placed on stone foundations. Some 3,000 spectators were on the roof (v. 27). One final burst of strength enabled Samson to push the large columns off their foundations, and the roof collapsed, killing those below. God responded to Samson's prayer (v. 28).

17:1—21:25 Two examples of the moral depravity in the land contained in this final section (Judg. 17—21) do not follow the previous chapter chronologically but rather serve as examples of the moral and religious chaos which resulted when "everyone did what was right in his own eyes" (Judg. 21:25). The be-

havior recorded in these two stories was not condoned by God. Instead, these accounts, written under the guidance of the Holy Spirit, are honest portrayals of one of the bleakest periods in Israel's history.

17:1, 2 The unnamed mother of Micah pronounced a curse on the large amount of money that someone had stolen from her (see Micah's Unfaithful Mother). Because curses were taken seriously in the superstitious pagan cultures of the ancient Near East, no doubt she was hoping to increase her chances of recovering the money. The text does not indicate whether she knew that her son had taken the money. There is reason, however, to question her genuineness in dedicating the money to the Lord. Only about one fifth of the total was actually given. To make matters worse, for her, dedicating the money to the Lord meant having the money made into idols, which is indicative of her ignorance of God's Law. Such total ignorance of the true worship of the Lord exemplifies an entire generation in Israel, who, following Joshua's death, uncritically adopted Canaanite practices, bringing moral and religious decay to the Land (see Judg. 2:10, note).

SEDUCTION *ROOTED IN A LIE*

Seduction extends far beyond sexual misconduct, although that is certainly included among its manifestations (see Rev. 2:20). Seducers, "imposters" who present evil as good, include those who have "spoken nonsense", and those who have presented falsehood as truth (Ezek. 13:10; 2 Tim. 3:13).

The seducer acts consciously and willfully to put another person into a position of vulnerability or weakness with the ultimate intent to dominate completely or destroy. Delilah purposefully set herself to bring about Samson's destruction (Judg. 16:15–17). Her seduction was unrelenting as she "pestered" and "pressed" Samson daily (v. 16). She aimed ultimately at Samson's spirit so that his soul was "vexed to death" (v. 16). Her seduction was rooted in a lie that everything would be all right, even to the point of believing that the Lord is unconcerned about and approves of wrong behavior (v. 20).

The ultimate seduction—whether in Samson's life, in the life of Israel, or in your life today—is to be led astray from God's presence and power and not even realize what is happening.

See also notes on Adultery (Hos. 3); Manipulation (Gen. 27); Sexual Immorality (Prov. 6); Sexual Purity (1 Cor. 6); Temptation (Heb. 2); portraits of the Adulteress of Proverbs (Prov. 5); Bathsheba (2 Sam. 11); Delilah (Judg. 16); Herodias and Salome (Matt. 14); Tamar (Gen. 38).

molded image; and they were in the house of Micah.

⁵The man Micah had a shrine, and made an ephod and household idols;ᵃ and he consecrated one of his sons, who became his priest. ⁶In those days *there was* no king in Israel; everyone did *what was* right in his own eyes.

⁷Now there was a young man from Bethlehem in Judah, of the family of Judah; he *was* a Levite, and was staying there. ⁸The man departed from the city of Bethlehem in Judah to stay wherever he could find *a place.* Then he came to the mountains of Ephraim, to the house of Micah, as he journeyed. ⁹And Micah said to him, "Where do you come from?"

So he said to him, "I *am* a Levite from Bethlehem in Judah, and I am on my way to find *a place* to stay."

¹⁰Micah said to him, "Dwell with me, and be a father and a priest to me, and I will give you ten *shekels* of silver per year, a suit of clothes, and your sustenance." So the Levite went in. ¹¹Then the Levite was content to dwell with the man; and the young man became like one of his sons to him. ¹²So Micah consecrated the Levite, and the young man became his priest, and lived in the house of Micah. ¹³Then Micah said, "Now I know that the LORD will be good to me, since I have a Levite as priest!"

The Danites Adopt Micah's Idolatry

18 In those days *there was* no king in Israel. And in those days the tribe of the Danites was seeking an inheritance for itself to dwell in; for until that day *their* inheritance among the tribes of Israel had not fallen to them. ²So the children of Dan sent five men of their family from their territory, men of valor from Zorah and Eshtaol, to spy out the land and search it. They said to them, "Go, search the land." So they went to the mountains of Ephraim, to the house of Micah, and lodged there. ³While they *were* at the house of Micah, they recognized the voice of the young Levite. They turned aside and said to him, "Who brought you here? What are you doing in this *place?* What do you have here?"

⁴He said to them, "Thus and so Micah did for me. He has hired me, and I have become his priest."

⁵So they said to him, "Please inquire of God, that we may know whether the journey on which we go will be prosperous."

⁶And the priest said to them, "Go in peace. The presence of the LORD *be* with you on your way."

⁷So the five men departed and went to Laish. They saw the people who *were* there, how they dwelt safely, in the manner of the Sidonians, quiet

17:5 ᵃHebrew *teraphim*

17:5, 6 The paganized worship of God that the Danites later adopted started in a simple household. A disobedient mother had shaped her son's worldview to the point that he carried out concretely what he had been taught and had viewed as "normal" in his house. In this case, the shrine and the ephod were used for divination, seeking to control the deity (see Judg. 8:27, note).

18:1 The territory of the tribe of Dan originally consisted of a western part of Canaan between the territories of Judah and Ephraim. This land, however, was attacked and settled by the Philistines and the Amorites, thus forcing the Danites to move

north. Confined in an area too small for them and unable to drive out the Amorites and Philistines, the Danites were trying to find a more suitable situation.

18:5, 6 A pagan inquiry of God. God had already revealed His will by giving each tribe its own original territory. But the Danites were unfaithful to this covenant and decided to search for new territory through their own methods. Their cynical inquiry of the Lord was matched by an equally cynical priest who reassured them in their unjust exploits and who proved to be more interested in money than in true worship of the Lord (see vv. 18–20, note).

and secure. *There were* no rulers in the land who might put *them* to shame for anything. They *were* far from the Sidonians, and they had no ties with anyone.[a]

[8]Then *the spies* came back to their brethren at Zorah and Eshtaol, and their brethren said to them, "What *is* your *report?*"

[9]So they said, "Arise, let us go up against them. For we have seen the land, and indeed it *is* very good. *Would* you *do* nothing? Do not hesitate to go, *and* enter to possess the land. [10]When you go, you will come to a secure people and a large land. For God has given it into your hands, a place where *there is* no lack of anything that *is* on the earth."

[11]And six hundred men of the family of the Danites went from there, from Zorah and Eshtaol, armed with weapons of war. [12]Then they went up and encamped in Kirjath Jearim in Judah. (Therefore they call that place Mahaneh Dan[a] to this day. There *it is*, west of Kirjath Jearim.) [13]And they passed from there to the mountains of Ephraim, and came to the house of Micah.

[14]Then the five men who had gone to spy out the country of Laish answered and said to their brethren, "Do you know that there are in these houses an ephod, household idols, a carved image, and a molded image? Now therefore, consider what you should do." [15]So they turned aside there, and came to the house of the young Levite man—to the house of Micah—and greeted him. [16]The six hundred men armed with their weapons of war, who *were* of the children of Dan, stood by the entrance of the gate. [17]Then the five men who had gone to spy out the land went up. Entering there, they took the carved image, the ephod, the household idols, and the molded image. The priest stood at the entrance of the gate with the six hundred men *who were* armed with weapons of war.

[18]When these went into Micah's house and took the carved image, the ephod, the household idols, and the molded image, the priest said to them, "What are you doing?"

[19]And they said to him, "Be quiet, put your hand over your mouth, and come with us; be a father and a priest to us. *Is it* better for you to be a priest to the household of one man, or that you be a priest to a tribe and a family in Israel?" [20]So the priest's heart was glad; and he took the ephod, the household idols, and the carved image, and took his place among the people.

[21]Then they turned and departed, and put the little ones, the livestock, and the goods in front of them. [22]When they were a good way from the house of Micah, the men who *were* in the houses near Micah's house gathered together and overtook the children of Dan. [23]And they called out to the children of Dan. So they turned around and said to Micah, "What ails you, that you have gathered such a company?"

[24]So he said, "You have taken away my gods which I made, and the priest, and you have gone away. Now what more do I have? How can you say to me, 'What ails you?' "

[25]And the children of Dan said to him, "Do not let your voice be heard among us, lest angry men fall upon you, and you lose your life, with the lives of your household!" [26]Then the children of Dan went their way. And when Micah saw that they *were* too strong for him, he turned and went back to his house.

Danites Settle in Laish

[27]So they took *the things* Micah had made, and the priest who had belonged to him, and went to Laish, to a people quiet and secure; and they struck them with the edge of the sword and burned the city with fire. [28]*There was* no deliverer, because it *was* far from Sidon, and they had no ties with anyone. It was in the valley that belongs to Beth Rehob. So they rebuilt the city and dwelt there. [29]And they called the name of the city Dan, after the name of Dan their father, who was born to Israel. However, the name of the city formerly *was* Laish.

[30]Then the children of Dan set up for themselves the carved image; and Jonathan the son of Gershom, the son of Manasseh,[a] and his sons were priests to the tribe of Dan until the day of the captivity of the land. [31]So they set up for themselves Micah's carved image which he made, all the time that the house of God was in Shiloh.

The Levite's Concubine

19And it came to pass in those days, when *there was* no king in Israel, that there was a certain Levite staying in the remote mountains of Ephraim. He took for himself a concubine from Bethlehem in Judah. [2]But his concubine played the harlot against him, and went away from him to her father's house at Bethlehem in Judah, and was

18:7 [a]Following Masoretic Text, Targum, and Vulgate; Septuagint reads *with Syria*. **18:12** [a]Literally *Camp of Dan* **18:30** [a]Septuagint and Vulgate read *Moses*.

18:18–20 Cynicism and distortion of true worship of the Lord are clearly evident in the mercenary Levite's obvious intent and willingness to promote himself.

19:1, 2 This second appendix is another reflection of the religious, political, and social chaos of the period. Having concubines had become an accepted custom, originating with childless couples who sought to produce heirs. Later, the custom evolved into relationships with free women who did not have the full status of a wife. This custom was not pleasing to God, though He had regulated its potential problems in the Law (Ex. 21:7–11; Deut. 21:10–14; see The Levite's Defenseless Concubine; article, Renewed by His Grace).

MICAH'S UNFAITHFUL MOTHER

Someone had stolen 1,100 pieces of silver from Micah's mother. Thus she pronounced a curse on the money, a really fearful threat for ancient Near Eastern cultures. Whether or not she knew that her own son was the thief is not clear, but, curiously enough, she made sure to tell her son that the stolen money had become taboo because she had not only cursed it but also dedicated it to *Yahweh*. She believed the curse and the dedication would enhance the seriousness of the theft and increase the possibilities of recovering it.

The mother's tactic worked: Micah confessed, and she reversed the curse by blessing him. Then, as an offering of thanksgiving, she gave a fifth of the total originally promised to *Yahweh* to a local silversmith to make idols for her son. She apparently wanted to worship God but was ignorant of the one true God.

This mother characterized a whole generation in Israel who did not know the Lord and who had already brought up their children in superstition. She thought that God could be manipulated by techniques of magic to fulfill human wishes of fertility and security, that God could be reduced to pottery, and that He could be carried around like a talisman of good luck. This unnamed mother, by ignoring God and His law, not only failed to obey the Lord but, more tragically, led her own son to his spiritual death.

See also notes on Idolatry (Is. 42); Motherhood (1 Sam. 1)

there four whole months. ³Then her husband arose and went after her, to speak kindly to her *and* bring her back, having his servant and a couple of donkeys with him. So she brought him into her father's house; and when the father of the young woman saw him, he was glad to meet him. ⁴Now his father-in-law, the young woman's father, detained him; and he stayed with him three days. So they ate and drank and lodged there.

⁵Then it came to pass on the fourth day that they arose early in the morning, and he stood to depart; but the young woman's father said to his son-in-law, "Refresh your heart with a morsel of bread, and afterward go your way."

⁶So they sat down, and the two of them ate and drank together. Then the young woman's father said to the man, "Please be content to stay all night, and let your heart be merry." ⁷And when the man stood to depart, his father-in-law urged him; so he lodged there again. ⁸Then he arose early in the morning on the fifth day to depart, but the young woman's father said, "Please refresh your heart." So they delayed until afternoon; and both of them ate.

⁹And when the man stood to depart—he and his concubine and his servant—his father-in-law, the young woman's father, said to him, "Look, the day is now drawing toward evening; please spend the night. See, the day is coming to an end; lodge here, that your heart may be merry. Tomorrow go your way early, so that you may get home."

¹⁰However, the man was not willing to spend that night; so he rose and departed, and came opposite Jebus (that *is*, Jerusalem). With him were the two saddled donkeys; his concubine *was* also with him. ¹¹They *were* near Jebus, and the day was far spent; and the servant said to his master, "Come, please, and let us turn aside into this city of the Jebusites and lodge in it."

¹²But his master said to him, "We will not turn aside here into a city of foreigners, who *are* not of the children of Israel; we will go on to Gibeah." ¹³So he said to his servant, "Come, let us draw near to one of these places, and spend the night in Gibeah or in Ramah." ¹⁴And they passed by and went their way; and the sun went down on them near Gibeah, which belongs to Benjamin. ¹⁵They turned aside there to go in to lodge in Gibeah. And when he went in, he sat down in the open square of the city, for no one would take them into *his* house to spend the night.

¹⁶Just then an old man came in from his work in the field at evening, who also *was* from the mountains of Ephraim; he was staying in Gibeah, whereas the men of the place *were* Benjamites. ¹⁷And when he raised his eyes, he saw the traveler in the open square of the city; and the old man said, "Where are you going, and where do you come from?"

¹⁸So he said to him, "We *are* passing from Bethlehem in Judah toward the remote mountains of Ephraim; I *am* from there. I went to Bethlehem in Judah; *now* I am going to the house of the LORD. But there *is* no one who will take me into his house, ¹⁹although we have both straw and fodder for our donkeys, and bread and wine for myself, for your female servant, and for the young man *who is* with your servant; *there is* no lack of anything."

²⁰And the old man said, "Peace *be* with you!

19:11–21 The Levite and his servant consciously avoided Jebus (or Jerusalem, a city of foreigners at that time; see Judg. 1:8, note), seeking hospitality instead from the Benjamites in Gibeah. Ironically enough, another foreigner, who was also an Ephraimite, opened his house to them.

However, *let* all your needs *be* my responsibility; only do not spend the night in the open square." ²¹So he brought him into his house, and gave fodder to the donkeys. And they washed their feet, and ate and drank.

Gibeah's Crime

²²As they were enjoying themselves, suddenly certain men of the city, perverted men,ᵃ surrounded the house *and* beat on the door. They spoke to the master of the house, the old man, saying, "Bring out the man who came to your house, that we may know him *carnally!*"

²³But the man, the master of the house, went out to them and said to them, "No, my brethren! I beg you, do not act *so* wickedly! Seeing this man has come into my house, do not commit this outrage. ²⁴Look, *here is* my virgin daughter and *the man'sᵃ* concubine; let me bring them out now. Humble them, and do with them as you please; but to this man do not do such a vile thing!" ²⁵But the men would not heed him. So the man took his concubine and brought *her* out to them. And they knew her and abused her all night until morning; and when the day began to break, they let her go.

²⁶Then the woman came as the day was dawning, and fell down at the door of the man's house where her master *was,* till it was light.

²⁷When her master arose in the morning, and opened the doors of the house and went out to go his way, there was his concubine, fallen *at* the door of the house with her hands on the threshold. ²⁸And he said to her, "Get up and let us be going." But there was no answer. So the man lifted her onto the donkey; and the man got up and went to his place.

²⁹When he entered his house he took a knife, laid hold of his concubine, and divided her into twelve pieces, limb by limb,ᵃ and sent her throughout all the territory of Israel. ³⁰And so it was that all who saw it said, "No such deed has been done or seen from the day that the children of Israel came up from the land of Egypt until this day. Consider it, confer, and speak up!"

Israel's War with the Benjamites

20So all the children of Israel came out, from Dan to Beersheba, as well as from the land of Gilead, and the congregation gathered together as one man before the LORD at Mizpah. ²And the leaders of all the people, all the tribes of Israel, presented themselves in the assembly of the people of God, four hundred thousand foot soldiers who drew the sword. ³(Now the children of Benjamin heard that the children of Israel had gone up to Mizpah.)

Then the children of Israel said, "Tell *us,* how did this wicked deed happen?"

⁴So the Levite, the husband of the woman who was murdered, answered and said, "My concubine and I went into Gibeah, which belongs to Benjamin, to spend the night. ⁵And the men of Gibeah rose against me, and surrounded the house at night because of me. They intended to kill me, but instead they ravished my concubine so that she died. ⁶So I took hold of my concubine, cut her in pieces, and sent her throughout all the territory of the inheritance of Israel, because they committed lewdness and outrage in Israel. ⁷Look! All of you *are* children of Israel; give your advice and counsel here and now!"

⁸So all the people arose as one man, saying, "None *of us* will go to his tent, nor will any turn back to his house; ⁹but now this *is* the thing which we will do to Gibeah: *We will go up* against it by lot. ¹⁰We will take ten men out of *every* hundred throughout all the tribes of Israel, a hundred out of *every* thousand, and a thousand out of *every* ten thousand, to make provisions for the people, that when they come to Gibeah in Benjamin, they may repay all the vileness that they have done in Israel." ¹¹So all the men of Israel were gathered against the city, united together as one man.

¹²Then the tribes of Israel sent men through all the tribe of Benjamin, saying, "What *is* this wickedness that has occurred among you? ¹³Now

19:22 ᵃLiterally *sons of Belial*   19:24 ᵃLiterally *his*   19:29 ᵃLiterally with her bones

---

19:22–28 The peaceful domestic scene in Gibeah became a nightmare of violence, depravity, and injustice similar to Lot's situation in Sodom (Gen. 19:1–29). The Levite's disregard for his concubine reflected a total breakdown of justice in the Land, a lack of loyalty to God, and the absence of concern for others. Furthermore, his apparent disinterest toward his abused concubine highlights his scandalous lack of spiritual leadership (Judg. 20:4–6).

19:29, 30 The dismemberment of the concubine's body was an outrageous action. Its significance has received varied interpretations. Some scholars interpret this action as a ritual sacrifice, which served as a call to redress this grievance or be struck with the sword themselves. Other scholars view it as a way to incite horror and indignation (see 1 Sam. 11:1–8 where Saul performed a similar action with oxen).

20:1–48 In this second example, a domestic event again evolves into a tribal problem. The irony in this final section of Judges is that the tribe of Judah, who led the Israelites against the Canaanites at the beginning of Judges, was leading the Israelites against their own countrymen, the Benjamites, who chose to defend the actions of the men of Gibeah. Judah represented righteous leadership against an overt case of immorality and disobedience.

20:4–6 The Levite's incomplete account of the events in Gibeah revealed the lack of justice and the violence experienced by the weaker members of this society. Furthermore, the Levite sought justice because of the tribal system's emphasis on loyalty; yet he himself failed to show loyalty to his closest neighbor, his concubine.

THE LEVITE'S DEFENSELESS CONCUBINE

The concubine had been unfaithful to the Levite and left him (Judg. 19:2). The Levite had gone after her (v. 3). They had come from the house of the concubine's father in Bethlehem when they stopped in Gibeah for the night. As darkness came, apparently nobody in Gibeah wanted to extend hospitality to the Levite, his servant, and his concubine (one privileged over slaves but not a full legal wife).

Having intentionally passed by the pagan city Jebus (renamed Jerusalem after David's conquest), they had sought a better place of rest among the Israelites. Finally, an old man, a foreigner himself in that unfriendly town, opened his home, ominously begging them not to spend the night outside in the marketplace. Then, while they were eating and resting, men who were willing sodomites surrounded the house, seeking to rape the Levite guest. The Levite, supposedly a spiritual leader, sacrificed his defenseless concubine to a night of brutality to save his own life. This incident occurred during the darkest period of Israel's history, during which everyone was a law unto himself (see Judg. 21:25). Israel as a community was repulsed by this heinous crime and accordingly took serious steps to hold the guilty accountable (Judg. 20:6, 13, 23).

The concubine was betrayed by her lover and his host. She was raped, tortured, and murdered. She lived in an unjust world where violence permeated even the closest of relationships and where moral decay extended even to the spiritual leaders.

See also Gen. 19:8; Sexual Immorality (Prov. 6); Suffering (Ps. 33; 113; Is. 43; 1 Pet. 5)

therefore, deliver up the men, the perverted men[a] who *are* in Gibeah, that we may put them to death and remove the evil from Israel!" But the children of Benjamin would not listen to the voice of their brethren, the children of Israel. [14]Instead, the children of Benjamin gathered together from their cities to Gibeah, to go to battle against the children of Israel. [15]And from their cities at that time the children of Benjamin numbered twenty-six thousand men who drew the sword, besides the inhabitants of Gibeah, who numbered seven hundred select men. [16]Among all this people *were* seven hundred select men *who were* left-handed; every one could sling a stone at a hair's *breadth* and not miss. [17]Now besides Benjamin, the men of Israel numbered four hundred thousand men who drew the sword; all of these *were* men of war.

[18]Then the children of Israel arose and went up to the house of God[a] to inquire of God. They said, "Which of us shall go up first to battle against the children of Benjamin?"

The LORD said, "Judah first!"

[19]So the children of Israel rose in the morning and encamped against Gibeah. [20]And the men of Israel went out to battle against Benjamin, and the men of Israel put themselves in battle array to fight against them at Gibeah. [21]Then the children of Benjamin came out of Gibeah, and on that day cut down to the ground twenty-two thousand men of the Israelites. [22]And the people, that is, the men of Israel, encouraged themselves and again formed the battle line at the place where they had

put themselves in array on the first day. [23]Then the children of Israel went up and wept before the LORD until evening, and asked counsel of the LORD, saying, "Shall I again draw near for battle against the children of my brother Benjamin?"

And the LORD said, "Go up against him."

[24]So the children of Israel approached the children of Benjamin on the second day. [25]And Benjamin went out against them from Gibeah on the second day, and cut down to the ground eighteen thousand more of the children of Israel; all these drew the sword.

[26]Then all the children of Israel, that is, all the people, went up and came to the house of God[a] and wept. They sat there before the LORD and fasted that day until evening; and they offered burnt offerings and peace offerings before the LORD. [27]So the children of Israel inquired of the LORD (the ark of the covenant of God *was* there in those days, [28]and Phinehas the son of Eleazar, the son of Aaron, stood before it in those days), saying, "Shall I yet again go out to battle against the children of my brother Benjamin, or shall I cease?"

And the LORD said, "Go up, for tomorrow I will deliver them into your hand."

[29]Then Israel set men in ambush all around Gibeah. [30]And the children of Israel went up against the children of Benjamin on the third day, and put themselves in battle array against Gibeah as at the other times. [31]So the children of Ben-

20:13 [a]Literally *sons of Belial*   20:18, 26 [a]Or *Bethel*

20:27, 28 **The only mention of the ark of the covenant in Judges** occurs in verse 27. Since Phinehas, the grandson of Aaron, was mentioned as the priest in the tabernacle during Joshua's time (Num. 25:9; Josh. 22:13), the events of this second incident must have occurred in the early period of the judges.

jamin went out against the people, *and* were drawn away from the city. They began to strike down *and* kill some of the people, as at the other times, in the highways (one of which goes up to Bethel and the other to Gibeah) and in the field, about thirty men of Israel. ³²And the children of Benjamin said, "They *are* defeated before us, as at first."

But the children of Israel said, "Let us flee and draw them away from the city to the highways." ³³So all the men of Israel rose from their place and put themselves in battle array at Baal Tamar. Then Israel's men in ambush burst forth from their position in the plain of Geba. ³⁴And ten thousand select men from all Israel came against Gibeah, and the battle was fierce. But *the Benjamites*ᵃ did not know that disaster *was* upon them. ³⁵The LORD defeated Benjamin before Israel. And the children of Israel destroyed that day twenty-five thousand one hundred Benjamites; all these drew the sword.

³⁶So the children of Benjamin saw that they were defeated. The men of Israel had given ground to the Benjamites, because they relied on the men in ambush whom they had set against Gibeah. ³⁷And the men in ambush quickly rushed upon Gibeah; the men in ambush spread out and struck the whole city with the edge of the sword. ³⁸Now the appointed signal between the men of Israel and the men in ambush was that they would make a great cloud of smoke rise up from the city, ³⁹whereupon the men of Israel would turn in battle. Now Benjamin had begun to strike *and* kill about thirty of the men of Israel. For they said, "Surely they are defeated before us, as *in* the first battle." ⁴⁰But when the cloud began to rise from the city in a column of smoke, the Benjamites looked behind them, and there was the whole city going up *in smoke* to heaven. ⁴¹And when the men of Israel turned back, the men of Benjamin panicked, for they saw that disaster had come upon them. ⁴²Therefore they turned *their backs* before the men of Israel in the direction of the wilderness; but the battle overtook them, and whoever *came* out of the cities they destroyed in their midst. ⁴³They surrounded the Benjamites, chased them, *and* easily trampled them down as far as the front of Gibeah toward the east. ⁴⁴And eighteen thousand men of Benjamin fell; all these *were* men

of valor. ⁴⁵Then theyᵃ turned and fled toward the wilderness to the rock of Rimmon; and they cut down five thousand of them on the highways. Then they pursued them relentlessly up to Gidom, and killed two thousand of them. ⁴⁶So all who fell of Benjamin that day were twenty-five thousand men who drew the sword; all these *were* men of valor.

⁴⁷But six hundred men turned and fled toward the wilderness to the rock of Rimmon, and they stayed at the rock of Rimmon for four months. ⁴⁸And the men of Israel turned back against the children of Benjamin, and struck them down with the edge of the sword—from *every* city, men and beasts, all who were found. They also set fire to all the cities they came to.

Wives Provided for the Benjamites

21 Now the men of Israel had sworn an oath at Mizpah, saying, "None of us shall give his daughter to Benjamin as a wife." ²Then the people came to the house of God,ᵃ and remained there before God till evening. They lifted up their voices and wept bitterly, ³and said, "O LORD God of Israel, why has this come to pass in Israel, that today there should be one tribe *missing* in Israel?"

⁴So it was, on the next morning, that the people rose early and built an altar there, and offered burnt offerings and peace offerings. ⁵The children of Israel said, "Who *is there* among all the tribes of Israel who did not come up with the assembly to the LORD?" For they had made a great oath concerning anyone who had not come up to the LORD at Mizpah, saying, "He shall surely be put to death." ⁶And the children of Israel grieved for Benjamin their brother, and said, "One tribe is cut off from Israel today. ⁷What shall we do for wives for those who remain, seeing we have sworn by the LORD that we will not give them our daughters as wives?"

⁸And they said, "What one *is there* from the tribes of Israel who did not come up to Mizpah to the LORD?" And, in fact, no one had come to the camp from Jabesh Gilead to the assembly. ⁹For when the people were counted, indeed, not one of the inhabitants of Jabesh Gilead *was* there. ¹⁰So

20:34 ᵃLiterally *they* **20:45** ᵃSeptuagint reads *the rest.* **21:2** ᵃOr *Bethel*

21:1–25 The wives of Benjamin. Against a sordid background of violence and immorality the record of the Israelite judges closes with lawlessness as "everyone did what was right in his own eyes" (v. 25). Sexual perversion and family erosion had left many women as pawns or booty.

A hideous murder (see Judg. 19:25–29) provoked a bloody civil war from which only 600 unmarried men of the tribe of Benjamin survived (see Judg. 20:47). The question then was how to save this tribe from extinction. In the wake of this crime, the opposing tribes swore an oath not to allow their

daughters to marry Benjamites; however, to preserve Benjamin's future, the men could choose wives from Jabesh Gilead from among the 400 young virgins who had survived the onslaught (Judg. 21:10–12). From Shiloh were gathered 200 additional virgins who could become wives of the remaining Benjamites (vv. 19–23). Because the people of this city had not participated in the oath, these women would be chosen as they danced in a religious feast (v. 23). The men then returned to their homes to rebuild. Their wives had opportunity to influence their husbands away from evil.

THE WIVES OF BENJAMIN

The hideous murder of the Levite's concubine (see Judg. 19:29) provoked a bloody civil war in which only six hundred unmarried men of the tribe of Benjamin survived (see Judg. 20:47). In the wake of this retaliatory crime of passion, the opposing tribes swore an unwise oath not to allow their daughters to marry Benjamites (Judg. 21:1, 18). The elders of Israel, instead of consulting the Lord, again tried by their own means to correct the wrong perpetrated. Every wrong was answered with another wrong, which is certainly not God's way.

The question then arose concerning how to preserve the future of the tribe of Benjamin. The Israelite leaders continued their own problem-solving with their proposed abduction of the innocent women of Jabesh Gilead and Shiloh. The men of Benjamin were instructed to choose wives from the surviving four hundred young virgins of Jabesh Gilead (vv. 10–12).

The remaining two hundred Benjamites without spouses were to capture the "daughters of Shiloh" for wives (vv. 14, 19–23). The local unmarried women from the Shiloh area were merely celebrating the festival (likely the Feast of Tabernacles) by dancing in the vineyards. As unmarried women, they were viewed as potential wives for the Benjamites. The senseless and cruel plan was to ambush the young virgins, seize the number required, and carry them off. This highly unorthodox method of obtaining a wife must have disturbed the relatives of the victims. Though there is no explicit recorded complaint from the fathers or brothers of these innocent young women, the elders were certain enough that such would be forthcoming that they prepared an answer (v. 22).

Against a sordid background of violence and immorality the record of the Israelite judges closes with a reminder of the lawlessness that prevailed as "everyone did what was right in his own eyes" (v. 25). Sexual perversion and family erosion left women as pawns in the power brokering of the tribes. In the midst of sin and tragedy, these women married, bore children, and reared another generation. God in His grace used the victims of this tragedy to accomplish His own purpose in selecting Saul, a member of the tribe of Benjamin, as the first king of Israel (1 Sam. 9:1, 2).

See also Judg. 19; 20; notes on Family (Ps. 127); Wives (Prov. 31).

---

the congregation sent out there twelve thousand of their most valiant men, and commanded them, saying, "Go and strike the inhabitants of Jabesh Gilead with the edge of the sword, including the women and children. [11]And this *is* the thing that you shall do: You shall utterly destroy every male, and every woman who has known a man intimately." [12]So they found among the inhabitants of Jabesh Gilead four hundred young virgins who had not known a man intimately; and they brought them to the camp at Shiloh, which is in the land of Canaan.

[13]Then the whole congregation sent *word* to the children of Benjamin who *were* at the rock of Rimmon, and announced peace to them. [14]So Benjamin came back at that time, and they gave them the women whom they had saved alive of the women of Jabesh Gilead; and yet they had not found enough for them.

[15]And the people grieved for Benjamin, because the LORD had made a void in the tribes of Israel.

[16]Then the elders of the congregation said, "What shall we do for wives for those who remain, since the women of Benjamin have been

destroyed?" [17]And they said, "There *must be* an inheritance for the survivors of Benjamin, that a tribe may not be destroyed from Israel. [18]However, we cannot give them wives from our daughters, for the children of Israel have sworn an oath, saying, 'Cursed *be* the one who gives a wife to Benjamin.'" [19]Then they said, "In fact, *there is* a yearly feast of the LORD in Shiloh, which *is* north of Bethel, on the east side of the highway that goes up from Bethel to Shechem, and south of Lebonah."

[20]Therefore they instructed the children of Benjamin, saying, "Go, lie in wait in the vineyards, [21]and watch; and just when the daughters of Shiloh come out to perform their dances, then come out from the vineyards, and every man catch a wife for himself from the daughters of Shiloh; then go to the land of Benjamin. [22]Then it shall be, when their fathers or their brothers come to us to complain, that we will say to them, 'Be kind to them for our sakes, because we did not take a wife for any of them in the war; for *it is* not *as though* you have given the *women* to them at this time, making yourselves guilty of your oath.'"

21:18–23 The children of Israel had vowed not to give their daughters as wives for the Benjamites. Their vow could not be broken. Practically speaking, however, they achieved a technical compliance with their vow while arranging a method whereby the Benjamites could "steal" wives from a feast.

²³And the children of Benjamin did so; they took enough wives for their number from those who danced, whom they caught. Then they went and returned to their inheritance, and they rebuilt the cities and dwelt in them. ²⁴So the children of Israel departed from there at that time, every man to his tribe and family; they went out from there, every man to his inheritance.

²⁵In those days *there was* no king in Israel; everyone did *what was* right in his own eyes.

21:25 This single verse is a sad and revealing commentary on the period of the judges. Because the children of Israel did not serve the one true God as their King, they fell prey to the moral and political chaos that is the inevitable result of spiritual decay. Though later in their history they would establish a monarchy over the nation, that monarchy would serve only to illustrate the necessity of obedience to the divine King if they were to experience peace and blessing.

Ruth

AUTHOR

The author is not identified in the text. Samuel is suggested by the Talmud and Jewish tradition because of the similarity of language within the books of Ruth, Judges, and Samuel. Hezekiah and David also have been suggested as possible authors. However, the textual evidence does not confirm any of these theories.

DATE

According to the text, the story is set during the period of the judges, probably the latter part of that era (Ruth 1:1; 4:18–22), but the date of authorship is generally understood to be during the reign of David (1010–970 B.C.). The book must not have been completed before the time of David (Ruth 4:22); yet surely it was not completed after the time of Solomon, or Solomon would have been included.

BACKGROUND

SETTING: The setting for Ruth begins and ends in the Judahite village of Bethlehem with a Moab sojourn in between. Moab was the pagan nation that began with the incestuous relationship between Lot and his elder daughter (Gen. 19:36, 37). The Moabites, as perpetual enemies of Israel, were the recipients of consistent pronouncements of judgment from the prophets (see Is. 15:1–9).

PURPOSE: With its sad beginning and happy ending, the Book of Ruth portrays the village life of a family faithfully honoring *Yahweh* and pictures divine providence even in the midst of adversities and sorrows. God uses simple people and ordinary events to accomplish His great purposes.

AUDIENCE: The Book of Ruth is a primer on family relationships with a message for all. However, women must have been especially interested in this narrative in which the virtues of womanhood are abundantly clear. Also, those interested in history must have found the account of David's genealogy helpful. The book makes clear David's faithful ancestry, though he was also of Moabite descent.

LITERARY CHARACTERISTICS: The author uses chiastic structure, a device which consists of repeating a series of elements in reverse order through the restating or paralleling of words, ideas, actions, or characters that meet in the center. Especially common in the Old Testament, this device organizes extensive narratives like the Book of Ruth, in which the turning point is found at the end of chapter 2. Note this expression of chiastic structure:

    1:1–5 The Family of Elimelech
        1:6–22 The Faithfulness of Ruth
            2:1–23 The Kinsman-Redeemer in the Barley Field
            3:1–18 The Kinsman-Redeemer at the Threshing Floor
        4:1–17 The Faithfulness of Boaz
    4:18–22 The Family of David

Some distinct themes appear in the Book of Ruth:

Divine Providence—God's undergirding hand is seen and felt throughout the book. God brought comfort to Naomi in her greatest hurt, following the deaths of her husband and sons, through Ruth's tender and loving care (Ruth 1:16, 17). God provided sustenance in the days of poverty for Ruth and Naomi, through the generous "close relative" Boaz, who became the kinsman-redeemer (Ruth 2:7, 8; 4:10). God replaced Naomi's root of bitterness with a fountain of joy, through the birth of her grandson Obed (Ruth 4:15, 16). God used the brokenness of two women who, though seeming to lose all, found the highest honor in becoming part of the ancestry of the Messiah (Ruth 4:17; see also Matt. 1:3–6; Luke 3:31–33).

Commitment in Relationships—The Book of Ruth clearly establishes commitment as the key to all interpersonal relationships (see Ruth 1; Matt. 16, Commitment). The following elements of commitment are clearly illustrated in Ruth herself (Ruth 1:16, 17): a willingness to give up home and family; a determination to follow the living God; an acceptance of different people, a strange land, and a new faith; an awareness of the exclusiveness of a new faith; a testimony to the permanency of her pledge; and a consistent example of perseverance even in the midst of adversities. Ruth's commitment was tested repeatedly, beginning with the departure from her birth family, her native land, and her secure environment, and continuing as she experienced the opportunities and trials of a new life and faith. The routine cycles of life—up and down, good and bad, hope and despair (see chart, The Cycle of Life)—typically challenge all commitments.

Friendship Between Women—The remarkable friendship between Ruth and Naomi—women from diverse backgrounds (one a Gentile and the other a Hebrew) and different generations (one young and in the prime of life and the other old and beyond childbearing age)—illustrates the unique joys found in the caring relationships women have with one another as their lives and hearts are knit together in mutual affection and reciprocal commitment (see Luke 1, Friendship). They are carried through difficult times not only by God's providential care but also by their extraordinary devotion to one another and creative initiative to care for one another.

Romantic Love—This book also describes the growing relationship between a man and a woman, as the romance of Ruth and Boaz unfolds in a charming way (see Song 2, Romance). Gentile and Hebrew are ultimately united in marriage to become a link in the chain of redemption.

Redemption and Reconciliation—The Moabitess Ruth experienced spiritual reconciliation as she was drawn into the family of God. She chose the godly Hebrew family; then God adopted Ruth into His family. As Ruth remained committed even in the midst of sorrow and poverty, God in His providence rewarded her with the security of a husband's protective care, the joy of a mother's nurturing task, and the legacy of her own place in the ancestry of Messiah.

COMMITMENT   *THE BEDROCK OF A RELATIONSHIP*

Commitment is the foundation for every relationship, whether earthly or heavenly. The Book of Ruth brings the heavenly concept of covenant into vital contact with earthly life. Ruth's statement of commitment (Ruth 1:16, 17) concerned events, situations, and relationships that would permanently bind the two women. She willingly accepted an unsettled future and bound herself by solemn oath not only to Naomi but also to the God of Israel. Only here did Ruth use the covenant name *Yahweh* instead of the impersonal *Elohim*, though Naomi, Boaz, and others used *Yahweh* frequently for blessing or complaint. Ruth officially joined the people whose God was *Yahweh*. He had become her God as well as Naomi's and was the present witness to and future judge of all subsequent activities. A commitment described by permanent bonding of hearts and pervasive linking of lives extends beyond a passing companionship.

Ruth "clung" to Naomi (Ruth 1:14; see 2:8, 21, where the same word is translated "stayed close"). This covenant language is also used to describe the intimate relationship between husband and wife (Gen. 2:24) and to picture the faithfulness of God to His covenant people (Deut. 10:20). The word describes friendship more binding than brotherhood.

A foundation of purposeful love and the outworking of devoted deeds set Ruth's commitment apart from verbal cliches and the whim of momentary emotions. Abram left home after being commanded to do so (Gen. 12:1); Ruth left her pagan homeland on her own initiative, despite the protest of her mother-in-law, in order to come under the "wings" of God (Ruth 2:12). Ruth offered herself first to Naomi and ultimately to God.

See also note on Commitment (Matt. 16)

Elimelech's Family Goes to Moab

1 Now it came to pass, in the days when the judges ruled, that there was a famine in the land. And a certain man of Bethlehem, Judah, went to dwell in the country of Moab, he and his wife and his two sons. ²The name of the man *was* Elimelech, the name of his wife *was* Naomi, and the names of his two sons *were* Mahlon and Chilion— Ephrathites of Bethlehem, Judah. And they went to the country of Moab and remained there. ³Then Elimelech, Naomi's husband, died; and she was left, and her two sons. ⁴Now they took wives of the women of Moab: the name of the one *was* Orpah, and the name of the other Ruth. And they dwelt there about ten years. ⁵Then both Mahlon and Chilion also died; so the woman survived her two sons and her husband.

Naomi Returns with Ruth

⁶Then she arose with her daughters-in-law that she might return from the country of Moab, for she had heard in the country of Moab that the LORD had visited His people by giving them bread. ⁷Therefore she went out from the place where she was, and her two daughters-in-law with her; and they went on the way to return to the land of Judah. ⁸And Naomi said to her two daughters-in-law, "Go, return each to her mother's house. The LORD deal kindly with you, as you have dealt with the dead and with me. ⁹The LORD grant that you may find rest, each in the house of her husband."

So she kissed them, and they lifted up their voices and wept. ¹⁰And they said to her, "Surely we will return with you to your people."

¹¹But Naomi said, "Turn back, my daughters;

1:1 The text gives no evidence that God directed Elimelech (Heb., lit. "my God is king") to leave Bethlehem (contrast Abraham's exodus from his homeland, Gen. 12:1). Fertility of soil and abundance in harvest have never been ultimate security against famine. Neither is changing location necessarily God's way of dealing with a crisis (see Rom. 8:37–39). Elimelech's departure from Bethlehem (Heb., lit. "house of bread") did not keep him and his two sons from dying in a foreign land, leaving his wife Naomi perhaps more destitute and isolated than if she had remained among friends and relatives.

1:5 The plight of a widow in biblical days was especially precarious. Young widows were allowed lodging in their father's home (Gen. 38:11; see also 2 Kin. 4; Ps. 68; Jer. 29; 1 Cor. 2, Widowhood), but an older widow whose parents were dead was dependent upon her children for support. Seemingly, God had snatched away her family's usefulness and productivity.

1:8 God's dealings with His children are described theologically as "kindly" (Heb. *chesed;* see Ex. 20:5, 6, note; 34:5–7; Ruth 3:10). No ingredient is more essential in an intimate relationship because such an attitude precludes bitterness, retaliation, negative criticism, or other destructive behavior. *Chesed* is love joined to loyalty and integrated with mutual commitment (see Jer. 31:3); it is action and feeling combined. What is received is returned. The mixture of divine will and human activity joins the warmth of God's fellowship with the security of His faithfulness.

1:9 Rest is more than the cessation of work and the absence of anxiety. Certainly this "rest" implied much more than a marriage ceremony, and included security, provision, and blessing (see Josh. 21:44). The same word is translated "security" in Ruth 3:1.

THE CYCLE OF LIFE

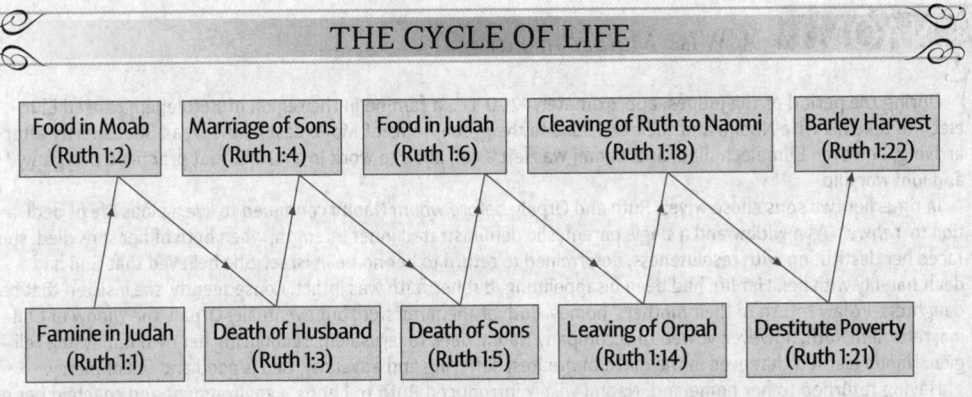

| Food in Moab (Ruth 1:2) | Marriage of Sons (Ruth 1:4) | Food in Judah (Ruth 1:6) | Cleaving of Ruth to Naomi (Ruth 1:18) | Barley Harvest (Ruth 1:22) |

| Famine in Judah (Ruth 1:1) | Death of Husband (Ruth 1:3) | Death of Sons (Ruth 1:5) | Leaving of Orpah (Ruth 1:14) | Destitute Poverty (Ruth 1:21) |

why will you go with me? *Are* there still sons in my womb, that they may be your husbands? [12]Turn back, my daughters, go— for I am too old to have a husband. If I should say I have hope, *if* I should have a husband tonight and should also bear sons, [13]would you wait for them till they were grown? Would you restrain yourselves from having husbands? No, my daughters; for it grieves me very much for your sakes that the hand of the LORD has gone out against me!"

[14]Then they lifted up their voices and wept again; and Orpah kissed her mother-in-law, but Ruth clung to her.

[15]And she said, "Look, your sister-in-law has gone back to her people and to her gods; return after your sister-in-law."

[16]But Ruth said:

"Entreat me not to leave you,
Or to turn back from following after you;
For wherever you go, I will go;
And wherever you lodge, I will lodge;
Your people *shall be* my people,
And your God, my God.

[17]Where you die, I will die,
And there will I be buried.
The LORD do so to me, and more also,
If *anything but* death parts you and me."

[18]When she saw that she was determined to go with her, she stopped speaking to her.

[19]Now the two of them went until they came to Bethlehem. And it happened, when they had come to Bethlehem, that all the city was excited because of them; and the women said, "*Is* this Naomi?"

[20]But she said to them, "Do not call me Naomi;[a] call me Mara,[b] for the Almighty has dealt very bitterly with me. [21]I went out full, and the LORD has brought me home again empty. Why do you call me Naomi, since the LORD has testified against me, and the Almighty has afflicted me?"

[22]So Naomi returned, and Ruth the Moabitess her daughter-in-law with her, who returned from the country of Moab. Now they came to Bethlehem at the beginning of barley harvest.

···················

1:20 [a]Literally *Pleasant* [b]Literally *Bitter*

1:13 For anyone who accepts full sovereignty of a just and merciful God, the existence of evil by divine permission (theodicy) is a natural dilemma. Naomi implied an indictment of unfaithfulness against God, whose relationship to His people had always been based squarely upon the presupposition of His faithfulness. Naomi determined, because of her personal losses, that God had turned away from her, and she decided to reciprocate by turning away from Him. She asked to be called "Mara" (Heb., lit. "bitter"; see v. 20). Nevertheless, a glimmer of hope existed for Naomi because she, by her reference to the LORD (Heb. *Yahweh*), placed these tragic experiences of losing her husband, sons, and earthly belongings in the setting of the covenant promise. This use of the Lord's personal covenant name reminded Naomi and her daughters-in-law of God's ultimate faithfulness.

1:20, 21 The Almighty has dealt bitterly with me. What a natural reaction to blame God for any misfortune (see Heb.12, Bitterness). Naomi was conscious of her own wrong-doing and viewed her suffering as God's punishment for her own sins (see Ruth 1:13, 20, 21). On the other hand, God views affliction as a necessary part of His sovereign and loving purpose (Eccl. 7:14; 2 Cor. 12:7–10; see also Ps. 33; Is. 43; 1 Pet. 5, Suffering). A believer going through the fire can produce a beautiful and pleasant aroma to the Lord (Num. 29:6; 2 Cor. 2:15).

In contrast to the verse 1 reference to the devastation of famine, Naomi testified, "I went out full," realizing that her husband and sons were worth far more than land and wealth (a restoration of her own sense of values). She had been genuinely blessed in Bethlehem, even in the midst of famine and poverty. Naomi chose to assign the blame for her tragedies to the Lord. Contrasting her own weakness, she referred to His power by calling Him *Shaddai* (Heb.), here translated "Almighty" and understood by some to mean "all-sufficiency." God must be trusted "for better or worse" (see Prov. 24:10).

NAOMI *A Wise Mother-in-Law*

During the period of the judges, approximately 1200 B.C., a famine in the region of Bethlehem caused Elimelech to take his wife Naomi and their two sons to the green fields of Moab east of the Dead Sea. Shortly after arriving, however, Elimelech died, and Naomi was left as an alien to work in a nation that practiced polygamy and idol worship.

In time, her two sons chose wives, Ruth and Orpah, before whom Naomi continued to live a pious life of dedication to *Yahweh*. As a widow and a single parent, she demonstrated inner strength; when both of her sons died, she faced her destitution with resoluteness, determined to return to her home in Israel. She believed that God had dealt harshly with her. Her life had been disappointing, but her faith was intact. Consequently, she insisted that her daughters-in-law return to their mothers' homes. Both of them resisted, but eventually Orpah, the widow of Chilion, returned. Ruth, however, vowed to accompany Naomi back to Jerusalem, renouncing her own family and religion. Naomi learned that even in the midst of greatest suffering and adversity, God is good and full of mercy.

Having returned to her homeland, Naomi wisely introduced Ruth to her new environment and coached her on proper behavior, masterminding Ruth's contacts with Boaz, a relative of Elimelech. Naomi models the way God works through a woman who moves forward, even in the midst of tragedy and trial, actively seizing every opportunity God provides rather than waiting passively for events to happen. In the providential care of God, eventually Boaz agreed to act as the *goel* (Heb.) or kinsman-redeemer provided in Jewish law, buying the estate of Naomi and taking Ruth as his wife. The blessing of God on their home produced a son, Obed, who became an ancestor of King David and of Jesus Christ.

Naomi had not always responded appropriately in her time of affliction. Though she acknowledged God's working in her life, she misjudged God, for example, when she said that she left Bethlehem full. Actually it had been the emptiness of famine that had driven her family away from their homeland. She continued her analogy by accusing God of bringing her back empty, and indeed she had lost her husband and sons, but in their place God had given her Ruth, a devoted daughter-in-law (Ruth 4:15). By focusing on the negative, Naomi became so bitter (Ruth 1:20) that she could not see the good and positive plans God was working.

Naomi lives as a true heroine. Her stalwart faith during years of adversity and her careful tutoring of her young protégé Ruth under difficult circumstances exemplify a woman of deep spiritual understanding. The result of her wisdom shines throughout Scripture.

See also chart on In-Law or In-Love (Ruth 4); notes on Widowhood (Ps. 68; Jer. 29; 1 Cor. 2)

Ruth Meets Boaz

2 There was a relative of Naomi's husband, a man of great wealth, of the family of Elimelech. His name *was* Boaz. ²So Ruth the Moabitess said to Naomi, "Please let me go to the field, and glean heads of grain after *him* in whose sight I may find favor."

And she said to her, "Go, my daughter."

³Then she left, and went and gleaned in the field after the reapers. And she happened to come to the part of the field *belonging* to Boaz, who *was* of the family of Elimelech.

⁴Now behold, Boaz came from Bethlehem, and said to the reapers, "The LORD *be* with you!"

And they answered him, "The LORD bless you!"

⁵Then Boaz said to his servant who was in charge of the reapers, "Whose young woman *is* this?"

⁶So the servant who was in charge of the reapers answered and said, "It *is* the young Moabite woman who came back with Naomi from the country of Moab. ⁷And she said, 'Please let me glean and gather after the reapers among the sheaves.' So she came and has continued from morning until now, though she rested a little in the house."

⁸Then Boaz said to Ruth, "You will listen, my daughter, will you not? Do not go to glean in another field, nor go from here, but stay close by my young women. ⁹Let your eyes *be* on the field which

---

2:1 Boaz was rich and influential (v. 1), a landowner (v. 3), a kind and considerate employer (v. 4), a gentleman who showed respect and courtesy to Ruth and others (vv. 8, 9), a sensitive leader who complimented Ruth with genuine praise (v. 12), a generous benefactor (v. 14; Ruth 3:15), a spiritual leader (Ruth 2:12), a man who chose to be a channel for happiness (vv. 15, 16), and a man of high moral character (Ruth 3:7–13; see also Gen. 2, Masculinity; chart, Biblical Manhood and Womanhood).

2:3 The bringing together of Ruth and Boaz cannot be attributed to chance, especially when God begins with provision of

food in famine (Ruth 1:6) and ends with the gift of a child to an empty womb (Ruth 4:13). Chance ("happened") simply means that no *human* intent was involved; the fact that Ruth chose the field of her close relative in which to glean was unplanned and unforeseen on her part.

2:7 The ancient custom of gleaning as codified in the Law gave the widow, or even a resident alien, the right to gather grain anywhere she pleased (Lev. 19:9; 23:22; Deut. 24:19). In OT Law, a landowner was instructed not to reap completely the corners of his fields, leaving the gleanings for the

A COMPARISON BETWEEN RUTH AND THE "VIRTUOUS WOMAN"

DESCRIPTION	REFERENCE IN RUTH	REFERENCE IN PROVERBS
Her family commitment is noted by others	2:11, 12	31:11, 12
She provided sustenance for her household	2:14, 18	31:15
She gave attention to her appearance	3:3, 5	31:22
Her selfless lifestyle drew praise from others	2:11; 3:10; 4:15	31:28
She committed herself to *Yahweh* as God	1:16	31:30

See chart on Biblical Manhood and Womanhood

they reap, and go after them. Have I not commanded the young men not to touch you? And when you are thirsty, go to the vessels and drink from what the young men have drawn."

[10]So she fell on her face, bowed down to the ground, and said to him, "Why have I found favor in your eyes, that you should take notice of me, since I *am* a foreigner?"

[11]And Boaz answered and said to her, "It has been fully reported to me, all that you have done for your mother-in-law since the death of your husband, and *how* you have left your father and your mother and the land of your birth, and have come to a people whom you did not know before. [12]The LORD repay your work, and a full reward be given you by the LORD God of Israel, under whose wings you have come for refuge."

[13]Then she said, "Let me find favor in your sight, my lord; for you have comforted me, and have spoken kindly to your maidservant, though I am not like one of your maidservants."

[14]Now Boaz said to her at mealtime, "Come here, and eat of the bread, and dip your piece of bread in the vinegar." So she sat beside the reapers, and he passed parched *grain* to her; and she ate and was satisfied, and kept some back. [15]And when she rose up to glean, Boaz commanded his young men, saying, "Let her glean even among the sheaves, and do not reproach her. [16]Also let *grain* from the bundles fall purposely for her; leave *it* that she may glean, and do not rebuke her."

[17]So she gleaned in the field until evening, and beat out what she had gleaned, and it was about an ephah of barley. [18]Then she took *it* up and went into the city, and her mother-in-law saw what she had gleaned. So she brought out and gave to her what she had kept back after she had been satisfied.

[19]And her mother-in-law said to her, "Where have you gleaned today? And where did you work? Blessed be the one who took notice of you."

So she told her mother-in-law with whom she had worked, and said, "The man's name with whom I worked today *is* Boaz."

[20]Then Naomi said to her daughter-in-law, "Blessed *be* he of the LORD, who has not forsaken His kindness to the living and the dead!" And Naomi said to her, "This man *is* a relation of ours, one of our close relatives."

[21]Ruth the Moabitess said, "He also said to me, 'You shall stay close by my young men until they have finished all my harvest.'"

---

strangers and the poor. God's welfare plan has always made provision for the poor (Lev. 19:9, 10; 23:22; see Luke 9, the Homeless; 14, Poverty), but the needy, as they were able, also willingly worked for what they received (2 Thess. 3:10). This generous provision in the Law is understood to be an act of grace freely given and not a mandate for personal rights forcibly demanded. Those who receive are to *accept* whatever care God provides, including food and shelter, with an humble spirit and grateful heart (Ruth 2:17–19; see Eph. 5:20). Those who can *share* from abundance are to express spiritual concern, exemplifying the character of God that prompts such generosity to others (Ruth 2:11, 12; see Matt. 10:8; Luke 6:38).

2:20 Two important Hebrew concepts were motivated by commitment to family and a determination to cooperate in continuing the family line: the function of the *qo'el* (Heb., lit. "kinsman-redeemer" or "close relative"; see Ruth 3:1–18) and the practice of levirate marriage (see also Deut. 25:5–10). Only in the Book of Ruth are these two concepts linked. The "close relative" (Heb. *go'el*) or "kinsman-redeemer" functioned in behalf of another person and his property within the family circle in times of crisis. These are his functions:

1) He redeems property by purchasing what has been lost and returning it to the one who was forced to sell (Lev. 25:25–28).

2) He redeems persons, that is, a relative who was forced to sell himself into slavery (Lev. 25:47–55).

ORPAH · *The Daughter-in-Law With a Wavering Faith*

Orpah is a name with root meanings as diverse as "fawn or young doe," "double-minded," or even "nape of the neck"—suggesting the meaning of "stubborn" or "stiff-necked." She wavered in her commitment to Naomi and chose to return to her life in Moab instead of clinging to *Yahweh* (Ruth 1:4–14; 4:9, 10).

Orpah was not a bad woman and, in fact, showed deep affection for the mother of her deceased husband Chilion. However, although Orpah loved and respected her mother-in-law Naomi, she did not have the depth of loyalty and spirit of selflessness for a permanent lifestyle commitment to Naomi and the God of Israel.

Naomi's persuasive words painted a vivid picture of the uncertainties to come, and Orpah seemingly turned her thoughts to her own devices for happiness. With her return to Moab, she vanished from the pages of biblical history.

See also chart on In-Law or In-Love (Ruth 4)

²²And Naomi said to Ruth her daughter-in-law, "*It is* good, my daughter, that you go out with his young women, and that people do not meet you in any other field." ²³So she stayed close by the young women of Boaz, to glean until the end of barley harvest and wheat harvest; and she dwelt with her mother-in-law.

Ruth's Redemption Assured

3 Then Naomi her mother-in-law said to her, "My daughter, shall I not seek security for you, that it may be well with you? ²Now Boaz, whose young women you were with, *is he* not our relative? In fact, he is winnowing barley tonight at the threshing floor. ³Therefore wash yourself and anoint yourself, put on your *best* garment and go down to the threshing floor; *but* do not make yourself known to the man until he has finished eating and drinking. ⁴Then it shall be, when he lies down, that you shall notice the place where he lies; and you

shall go in, uncover his feet, and lie down; and he will tell you what you should do."

⁵And she said to her, "All that you say to me I will do."

⁶So she went down to the threshing floor and did according to all that her mother-in-law instructed her. ⁷And after Boaz had eaten and drunk, and his heart was cheerful, he went to lie down at the end of the heap of grain; and she came softly, uncovered his feet, and lay down.

⁸Now it happened at midnight that the man was startled, and turned himself; and there, a woman was lying at his feet. ⁹And he said, "Who *are* you?"

So she answered, "I *am* Ruth, your maidservant. Take your maidservant under your wing,ᵃ for you are a close relative."

¹⁰Then he said, "Blessed *are* you of the LORD, my daughter! For you have shown more kindness

••••••••••••••••••

3:9 ᵃOr *Spread the corner of your garment over your maidservant*

---

3) He redeems blood; that is, he avenges the death of a relative who has been murdered (Num. 35:16–21, 31).

Because Boaz (Heb., lit. "in him is strength") was a relative of Elimelech, he was eligible to be the *go'el* or "kinsman-redeemer" with the right and responsibility to redeem the forfeited inheritance of the family so that the property of the dead man remained within the family. This responsibility usually included care for the widow (see Deut. 25:5–10). Boaz functioned as Ruth's "kinsman-redeemer" and in so doing prefigured Christ as the ultimate *go'el*. Three requirements of the *go'el* have been fulfilled in Christ: He must be related by blood (Phil. 2:5–8); He must be able to pay the price (1 Pet. 1:18, 19); and He must be willing to redeem (Matt. 20:28).

3:3–9 Naomi's daring plan. Love culminating in a desire for the highest good in the person loved, even to the point of self-sacrifice, is illustrated in Naomi. Sensing that Boaz and Ruth were already genuinely attracted to one another and understanding well the law of the "kinsman-redeemer," Naomi devised a strategy based upon knowledge of levirate marriage (see Deut. 25:5–10). By this practice a widow became the wife of her husband's brother or another close relative in order to produce a child who would inherit her first husband's estate and preserve his name. Some scholars debate whether levirate marriage is fully applicable in the story of Ruth. In any case, the producing of a male child to continue the "name" of

the deceased was at stake in Ruth. Ruth's loyalty to the tradition of her husband's people and her desire to care for Naomi by marrying someone within the family was a tribute to her commitment to the family of her deceased husband. Without any effort to trap Boaz or put him in a compromising situation, Ruth made a straightforward, yet delicate and beautiful, appeal to inspire Boaz to do the duty of a "close relative." The "kinsman" duty was one performed, not for personal gain but as an act of pure love. The *go'el* was motivated to marry not by the force of law but by the influence of custom prompted by the intent expressed in Deuteronomy 25.

Ruth's request, "Take your maidservant under your wing," is a metaphor suggesting her need for protection just as young birds would run under the wings of their mothers to escape birds of prey. *Yahweh's* "wing" is Boaz's "wing"! A Jewish husband covers his bride with the end of his prayer shawl (Heb. *tallith*) as a symbolic gesture that she is under his protection (see Ezek. 16:8). Ruth's humble request to Boaz is for his protection as a "close relative." Any argument for sexual consummation goes beyond what the text states and runs counter to the characterization of Ruth and Boaz as a virtuous couple who would not have yielded to the temptation to consummate their relationship before the proper time. The risk to spoil God's plan is certainly there. The Hebrew text uses words that are commonly used for sexual relationships ("lie down" and "uncover," vv. 4, 7), implying that Ruth and Boaz

RUTH'S SPIRITUAL JOURNEY: FROM FOREIGNER TO FAMILY

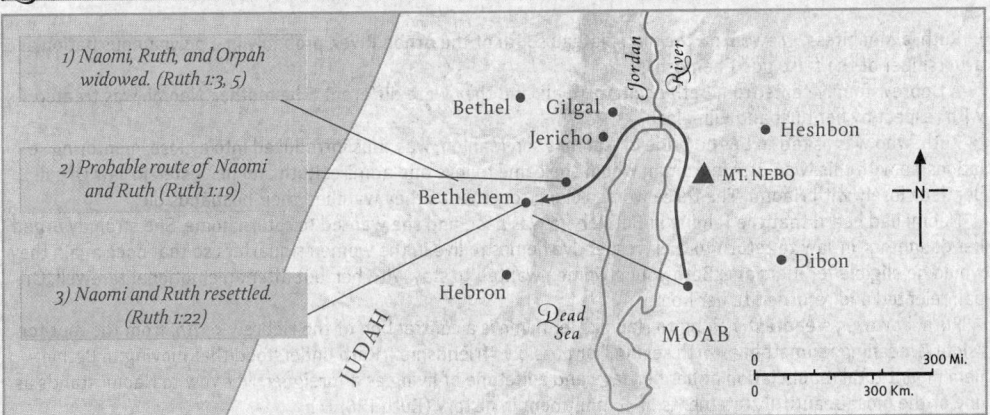

1) Naomi, Ruth, and Orpah widowed. (Ruth 1:3, 5)

2) Probable route of Naomi and Ruth (Ruth 1:19)

3) Naomi and Ruth resettled. (Ruth 1:22)

at the end than at the beginning, in that you did not go after young men, whether poor or rich. ¹¹And now, my daughter, do not fear. I will do for you all that you request, for all the people of my town know that you *are* a virtuous woman. ¹²Now it is true that I *am* a close relative; however, there is a relative closer than I. ¹³Stay this night, and in the morning it shall be *that* if he will perform the duty of a close relative for you— good; let him do it. But if he does not want to perform the duty for you, then I will perform the duty for you, *as* the LORD lives! Lie down until morning."

¹⁴So she lay at his feet until morning, and she arose before one could recognize another. Then he said, "Do not let it be known that the woman came to the threshing floor." ¹⁵Also he said, "Bring the shawl that *is* on you and hold it." And when she held it, he measured six *ephahs* of barley, and laid *it* on her. Then she[a] went into the city.

RUTH AND ORPAH: A CONTRAST IN WOMEN

RUTH	ORPAH
An intelligent love of choice	An emotional love of feeling
Quiet fidelity	Passionate affection
Love that bore testing	Love that failed in adversity
Genuine spiritual base for her conduct and decisions	Selfish basis for decision making
A resolute exercise of the will	An easy change of emotions

had opportunity but rightly refused to disobey God's Law. Compare and contrast Ruth, who did the honorable thing,

¹⁶When she came to her mother-in-law, she said, "*Is* that you, my daughter?"

Then she told her all that the man had done for her. ¹⁷And she said, "These six *ephahs* of barley he gave me; for he said to me, 'Do not go empty-handed to your mother-in-law.'"

¹⁸Then she said, "Sit still, my daughter, until you know how the matter will turn out; for the man will not rest until he has concluded the matter this day."

Boaz Redeems Ruth

4 Now Boaz went up to the gate and sat down there; and behold, the close relative of whom Boaz had spoken came by. So Boaz said, "Come aside, friend,[a] sit down here." So he came aside and sat down. ²And he took ten men of the elders of the city, and said, "Sit down here." So they sat down. ³Then he said to the close relative, "Naomi, who has come back from the country of Moab, sold the piece of land which *belonged* to our brother Elimelech. ⁴And I thought to inform you, saying, 'Buy *it* back in the presence of the inhabitants and the elders of my people. If you will redeem *it,* redeem *it;* but if you[a] will not redeem *it, then* tell me, that I may know; for *there is* no one but you to redeem *it,* and I *am* next after you.'"

And he said, "I will redeem *it.*"

⁵Then Boaz said, "On the day you buy the field from the hand of Naomi, you must also buy *it* from Ruth the Moabitess, the wife of the dead, to

3:15 [a]Many Hebrew manuscripts, Syriac, and Vulgate read *she;* Masoretic Text, Septuagint, and Targum read *he.* 4:1 [a]Hebrew *peloni almoni;* literally *so and so* 4:4 [a]Following many Hebrew manuscripts, Septuagint, Syriac, Targum, and Vulgate; Masoretic Text reads *he.*

with Tamar, who played the harlot (see Gen. 38, Tamar). Ruth trusted God; Tamar took matters into her own hands.

RUTH   *A Faithful Moabitess*

Ruth, a Moabitess, grew up on the high plateau south of the Arnon River, probably in a polygamous nation as a worshiper of the false god Chemosh.

A Hebrew family came from Bethlehem to Moab, and they were different. The mother, Naomi, was treated with respect by her husband Elimelech.

Ruth, who was asked to be the bride of Naomi's son Mahlon, was thus introduced into a close, mentoring relationship with this wise, stable woman whom she came to love and admire. Ruth and her sister-in-law Orpah bonded closely with Naomi. The three women clung together as they watched their husbands die.

Naomi had heard that the famine in Bethlehem was past, and she wanted to return home. She strongly urged her daughters-in-law to return to their respective homes to live in the women's quarters so that once again they would be eligible for marriage. Both young women wanted to stay with her, but after an emotional farewell, Orpah relented and returned to her home.

Ruth, however, steadfastly clung to Naomi. Her name is a contraction of the Hebrew *reuth,* from the root for "sight," meaning "something worth seeing," or possibly "friendship." Ruth understood that moving to Bethlehem meant total renunciation of her heritage and a lifetime of living as a foreigner. Her vow to Naomi stands as one of the most beautiful statements of commitment in history (Ruth 1:16, 17).

The arrival of the two women in Bethlehem marked the beginning of a new life for Ruth. She worked in the barley fields of Naomi's relative, Boaz, gleaning the edges left for the poor people. The stalks of grain were collected and threshed with a heavy wooden hand tool; then with a large fork the grain was lifted into the air to allow the wind to blow away the chaff. Many of the poor women flirted with the reapers and tried to steal grain, but Ruth soon gained a reputation for such honesty and integrity that the owner commended her.

Following the wise counsel of her mother-in-law, humble Ruth won the respect and eventually the love of Naomi's kinsman Boaz, who bought the estate of Naomi and took Ruth as his wife. In so doing he became a kinsman-redeemer (see Lev. 25:25).

Ruth lives in history as a model of womanhood, willing in joy and confidence to break with her past on the basis of God's revelation taught to her by a loving mother-in-law. God uses the faithfulness of ordinary women to accomplish His extraordinary plans: He provided bread for two widows through Ruth's gleaning; He provided security for the young widow Ruth through her marriage to Boaz; He provided posterity for Naomi through Obed, the son born to Ruth and Boaz; God provided a great king for Israel and even the Messiah through this Gentile woman.

See also Lev. 25:25; Is. 59:20; Matt. 1:5; note on Vows (Num. 30); chart on In-Law or In-Love (Ruth 4)

perpetuate[a] the name of the dead through his inheritance."

6And the close relative said, "I cannot redeem *it* for myself, lest I ruin my own inheritance. You redeem my right of redemption for yourself, for I cannot redeem *it.*"

7Now this *was the custom* in former times in Israel concerning redeeming and exchanging, to confirm anything: one man took off his sandal and gave *it* to the other, and this *was* a confirmation in Israel.

8Therefore the close relative said to Boaz, "Buy *it* for yourself." So he took off his sandal. 9And Boaz said to the elders and all the people, "You *are* witnesses this day that I have bought all that was Elimelech's, and all that *was* Chilion's and Mahlon's,

from the hand of Naomi. 10Moreover, Ruth the Moabitess, the widow of Mahlon, I have acquired as my wife, to perpetuate the name of the dead through his inheritance, that the name of the dead may not be cut off from among his brethren and from his position at the gate.[a] You *are* witnesses this day."

11And all the people who *were* at the gate, and the elders, said, "*We are* witnesses. The LORD make the woman who is coming to your house like Rachel and Leah, the two who built the house of Israel; and may you prosper in Ephrathah and be famous in Bethlehem. 12May your house be like the house of Perez, whom Tamar bore to Judah,

•••••••••••••••••••
4:5 [a]Literally *raise up*   4:10 [a]Probably his civic office

---

4:7 The nearest kinsman could refuse to act as *qo'el* (see Ruth 2:20, note), thereby losing the right to the inheritance and perhaps even experiencing the indignity of the contemptuous spitting in the face. In this case, the next kinsman could then come forward. Since treading upon the soil signified taking possession of fixed property, taking off the sandal and giving it to another would symbolize the transfer of property or possession.

4:11 This wedding prayer suggests a blessing which might have customarily been recited on the occasion of betrothals in Bethlehem. Ruth was like Rachel in being blessed with children after a long period of barrenness.

THE FAMILY TREE OF RUTH

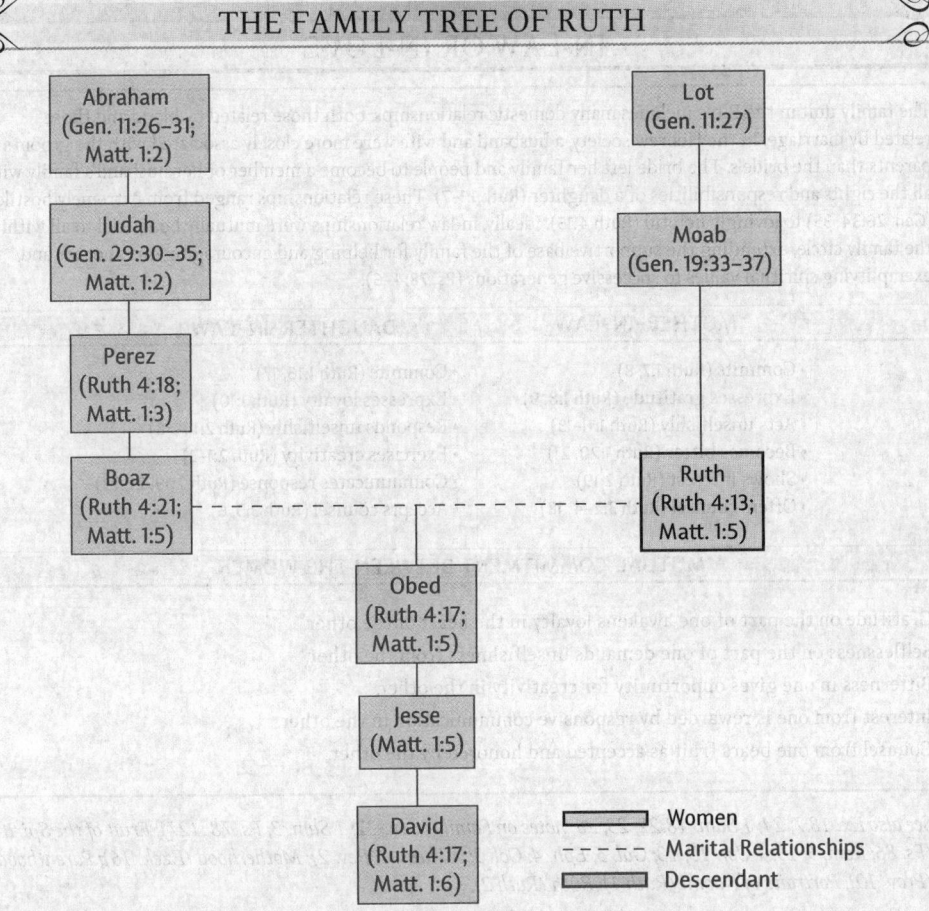

Abraham
(Gen. 11:26–31;
Matt. 1:2)

Judah
(Gen. 29:30–35;
Matt. 1:2)

Perez
(Ruth 4:18;
Matt. 1:3)

Boaz
(Ruth 4:21;
Matt. 1:5)

Lot
(Gen. 11:27)

Moab
(Gen. 19:33–37)

Ruth
(Ruth 4:13;
Matt. 1:5)

Obed
(Ruth 4:17;
Matt. 1:5)

Jesse
(Matt. 1:5)

David
(Ruth 4:17;
Matt. 1:6)

☐☐☐ Women
– – – – Marital Relationships
☐☐☐ Descendant

because of the offspring which the LORD will give you from this young woman."

Descendants of Boaz and Ruth

¹³So Boaz took Ruth and she became his wife; and when he went in to her, the LORD gave her conception, and she bore a son. ¹⁴Then the women said to Naomi, "Blessed *be* the LORD, who has not left you this day without a close relative; and may his name be famous in Israel! ¹⁵And may he be to you a restorer of life and a nourisher of your old age; for your daughter-in-law, who loves you, who is better to you than seven sons, has borne him." ¹⁶Then Naomi took the child and laid him on her bosom, and became a nurse to him. ¹⁷Also the neighbor women gave him a name, saying, "There is a son

4:15 To be described as better than seven sons, in a culture in which sons were so highly esteemed, is a supreme compliment. This commendation of Ruth as an extraordinary woman also bears testimony to the loving ministries she performed in Naomi's behalf above what would have been expected of any daughter or son. The relationship between mother and daughter-in-law is described by many as the most troublesome in the human family. Yet the lives of Ruth and Naomi portray an example of the joy found when divine principles are followed even in that most difficult relationship. The result is loving commitment, mutual comfort, and consistent edification (see chart, In-Law or In-Love).

Decisions to follow God's way are always honored and blessed by God. Ruth determined to respond to Naomi in a loving and godly way. Her decision to care for the aged, impoverished, and embittered Naomi is rewarded both by the security of a wealthy and devoted husband and by the joy and blessing of motherhood in bearing a son, who, in turn, gave her a place in the ancestry of the Messiah. The commitment between these two is a pattern for mutual benefit and a doorway for the blessings of heaven to be showered upon them both (Ruth 1:7, 8, 16, 17).

4:17 The book ends with an outline of the lineage of the Messiah as a reminder of redemption. The focus falls upon the vital link in which the Hebrew (Boaz) and the Gentile (Ruth) unite to share in the ancestry of David, through whom would come Jesus Christ.

IN-LAW OR IN-LOVE

The family unit in the Bible includes many domestic relationships: both those related by blood and those related by marriage. In the Hebrew society, a husband and wife were more closely associated with the groom's parents than the bride's. The bride left her family and people to become a member of her husband's family with all the rights and responsibilities of a daughter (Ruth 1:1–7). These relationships ranged from extremely hostile (Gen. 26:34, 35) to lovingly helpful (Ruth 4:15). Ideally, in-law relationships were mutually beneficial to all within the family circle, extending the supportive base of the family for helping and encouraging one another and exemplifying spiritual values to successive generations (Ps. 78:4–6).

MOTHER-IN-LAW	DAUGHTER-IN-LAW
• Commits (Ruth 1:7, 8)	• Commits (Ruth 1:16, 17)
• Expresses gratitude (Ruth 1:8, 9)	• Expresses loyalty (Ruth 1:10)
• Acts unselfishly (Ruth 1:11–13)	• Responds unselfishly (Ruth 2:14–18)
• Becomes bitter (Ruth 1:20, 21)	• Exercises creativity (Ruth 2:1–3)
• Shows interest (Ruth 2:19)	• Communicates response (Ruth 2:19, 21, 23)
• Offers counsel (Ruth 3:2–4, 18)	• Accepts counsel (Ruth 3:5, 6)

MUTUAL COMMITMENT BETWEEN THE WOMEN

Gratitude on the part of one awakens loyalty in the heart of the other.

Selflessness on the part of one demands unselfishness from the other.

Bitterness in one gives opportunity for creativity in the other.

Interest from one is rewarded by responsive communication in the other.

Counsel from one bears fruit as accepted and honored by the other.

See also Ex. 18:7, 24; 1 Sam. 18:22, 23, 26; notes on Family (Gen. 32; 1 Sam. 3; Ps. 78; 127); Fruit of the Spirit (Ps. 86; Rom. 5; 15; 1 Cor. 10; 13; Gal. 5; Eph. 4; Col. 3; 2 Thess. 1; Rev. 2); Motherhood (Ezek. 16); Parenthood (Prov. 10); Portraits of Naomi (Ruth 1); Ruth (Ruth 2).

born to Naomi." And they called his name Obed. He *is* the father of Jesse, the father of David.

[18]Now this *is* the genealogy of Perez: Perez begot Hezron; [19]Hezron begot Ram, and Ram begot Amminadab; [20]Amminadab begot Nahshon, and Nahshon begot Salmon;[a] [21]Salmon begot Boaz, and Boaz begot Obed; [22]Obed begot Jesse, and Jesse begot David.

4:20 [a]Hebrew *Salmah*

1 Samuel

TITLE

First and 2 Samuel are one book in Hebrew tradition. Though there is no reference to an author in the biblical text, Samuel made some written records (1 Sam. 10:25); and the prophets Samuel, Nathan, and Gad recorded many of the acts of David (1 Chr. 29:29). This has led Jewish tradition to claim that Samuel wrote the first part of the book, while others supplied supplementary information after Samuel died (see 2 Sam. 1:18). Most likely an ancient historian or editor compiled the books, making use of records such as those of Samuel, Nathan, and Gad.

DATE

First Samuel records the history of Israel from the end of the age of the judges to the death of Saul, the first king of Israel's monarchy. This period covers approximately 110 years (about 1120–1010 B.C.). Since the "last words of David" are recorded, the Samuel books could not have been completed before David's death in about 970 B.C. (2 Sam. 23:1). The majority of scholars place the date of the composition of the books of Samuel somewhere between the death of David and the Assyrian captivity (722 B.C.).

BACKGROUND

SETTING: The Book of 1 Samuel begins with Israel at one of the lowest points in her history. During the conquest of Canaan, the tribes of Israel had not fully carried out God's command to drive out the Canaanites (Josh. 17:12, 13). Moral and spiritual failures resulted. Thus God brought discipline through foreign nations. A tragic cycle began in which Israel would briefly return to God under the leadership of a divinely appointed judge/deliverer, only to lapse again into disobedience. At the beginning of 1 Samuel, Israel's priest Eli was weak and his family corrupt. Disrespect for God and His ways permeated the culture. At this point in time Israel constituted a group of twelve tribes loosely held together by worship, gathered around a central sanctuary, the tabernacle, where *Yahweh* was to dwell among them. They had no central leader and frequently fell prey to other nations because of their failure to trust and obey their God. But tremendous changes—politically, socially, and religiously—were about to take place. At the end of 1 Samuel this same nation was ready to anoint its second king, David, whose appointment would usher in the period recognized as the zenith of the kingdom of Israel in the Old Testament world.

PURPOSE: The Book of 1 Samuel was written to show the rise and development of the monarchy in Israel and the need for its leadership to reverence and obey God.

AUDIENCE: First and 2 Samuel were originally one book in the Hebrew Bible, recording Israel's history from the end of the period of the judges through the rise of the monarchy. The historical narrative was compiled for the people of Israel at the end of David's reign, or at least no later than the Assyrian captivity of 722 B.C., which would probably have been mentioned in the text if the date were after that major event.

LITERARY CHARACTERISTICS: First Samuel contains historical prose narratives, with the exception of Hannah's prayer in the form of a poetic hymn, and a few proverbial statements.

THEMES

Within the historical narrative of 1 Samuel, key themes are found. The rise of the monarchy in Israel is described. Clearly this period of history affirms that leaders must be led by God, not by their desires, culture, religious tradition, or situation.

Reverence for God is demonstrated by obedience to His commands (see chart, Models of Obedience and Disobedience). God must be the object of faith; patience and trust are necessary to allow Him to work in His time and way. The sovereignty of God is specifically seen in Hannah's life and in the choosing of Samuel (1 Sam. 1:1, 20), Saul (1 Sam. 10:20–24), and David (1 Sam. 16:6–13).

OUTLINE

I. Transition—From Judges to Monarchy (1:1—7:17)
  A. Samuel's birth and childhood (1:1—2:11)
    1. Samuel's family members (1:1–3)
    2. Hannah's barrenness and prayer for a child (1:4–18)
    3. God's gift of a child and Hannah's obedience in dedicating the child (1:19–28)
    4. Hannah's praise (2:1–10)
    5. Samuel's apprenticeship (2:11)
  B. The corrupt priesthood (2:12–36)
    1. The sins of the priesthood (2:12–17)
    2. The blessing of children (2:18–21)
    3. The judgment upon the priesthood (2:22–36)
  C. Samuel's call (3:1—4:1)
    1. God's call to Samuel (3:1–14)
    2. Samuel's obedience to God's call (3:15–18)
    3. Samuel as a prophet (3:19—4:1)
  D. The ark of the covenant (4:1—7:17)
    1. The capture of the ark by the Philistines (4:1–22)
    2. The Lord's judgment on the Philistines (5:1–12)
    3. The ark's return (6:1—7:1)
    4. Samuel the judge (7:2–17)
II. The Beginning of Israel's Monarchy (8:1—15:35)
  A. The rise of Saul as the first king (8:1—12:25)
    1. The demand of Israel for a king (8:1–22)
    2. The anointing of Saul and his presentation as king (9:1—10:27)
    3. Saul's first victory (11:1–15)
    4. The pitfalls of the monarchy (12:1–25)
  B. The decline of Saul (13:1—15:35)
    1. Samuel's rebuke of Saul (13:1–23)
    2. Saul's rash vows (14:1–52)
    3. Saul's rejection (15:1–35)
III. The Rise of David (16:1—31:13)
  A. Samuel's anointing of David, the shepherd (16:1–23)
  B. David's killing of Goliath (17:1–58)
  C. David's escape from Saul's jealous rage (18:1—19:24)
  D. Jonathan's friendship (20:1–42)
  E. David as a fugitive (21:1—28:2)
    1. Saul's pursuit of David (21:1—23:29)
    2. The sparing of Saul's life by David (24:1–22)
    3. David and Abigail (25:1–44)
    4. The second sparing of Saul's life (26:1–25)
    5. David with the Philistines (27:1—28:2)
  F. Saul's death (28:3—31:13)
    1. Saul and the medium of En Dor (28:3–25)
    2. David's return to Ziklag (29:1—30:31)
    3. Saul's death on Mount Gilboa (31:1–13)

The Family of Elkanah

1 Now there was a certain man of Ramathaim Zophim, of the mountains of Ephraim, and his name *was* Elkanah the son of Jeroham, the son of Elihu,[a] the son of Tohu,[b] the son of Zuph, an Ephraimite. ²And he had two wives: the name of one *was* Hannah, and the name of the other Peninnah. Peninnah had children, but Hannah had no children. ³This man went up from his city yearly to worship and sacrifice to the LORD of hosts in Shiloh. Also the two sons of Eli, Hophni and Phinehas, the priests of the LORD, *were* there. ⁴And whenever the time came for Elkanah to make an offering, he would give portions to Peninnah his wife and to all her sons and daughters. ⁵But to Hannah he would give a double portion, for he loved Hannah, although the LORD had closed her womb. ⁶And her rival also provoked her severely, to make her miserable, because the LORD had closed her womb. ⁷So it was, year by year, when she went up to the house of the LORD, that she provoked her; therefore she wept and did not eat.

Hannah's Vow

⁸Then Elkanah her husband said to her, "Hannah, why do you weep? Why do you not eat? And why is your heart grieved? *Am* I not better to you than ten sons?"

⁹So Hannah arose after they had finished eating and drinking in Shiloh. Now Eli the priest was sitting on the seat by the doorpost of the tabernacle[a] of the LORD. ¹⁰And she *was* in bitterness of soul, and prayed to the LORD and wept in anguish. ¹¹Then she made a vow and said, "O LORD of hosts, if You will indeed look on the affliction of Your maidservant and remember me, and not forget Your maidservant, but will give Your maidservant a male child, then I will give him to the LORD all the days of his life, and no razor shall come upon his head."

¹²And it happened, as she continued praying before the LORD, that Eli watched her mouth. ¹³Now Hannah spoke in her heart; only her lips moved, but her voice was not heard. Therefore Eli thought she was drunk. ¹⁴So Eli said to her, "How long will you be drunk? Put your wine away from you!"

¹⁵But Hannah answered and said, "No, my lord, I *am* a woman of sorrowful spirit. I have drunk neither wine nor intoxicating drink, but have poured out my soul before the LORD. ¹⁶Do not consider your maidservant a wicked woman,[a] for out of the abundance of my complaint and grief I have spoken until now."

¹⁷Then Eli answered and said, "Go in peace, and the God of Israel grant your petition which you have asked of Him."

¹⁸And she said, "Let your maidservant find favor in your sight." So the woman went her way and ate, and her face was no longer *sad*.

Samuel Is Born and Dedicated

¹⁹Then they rose early in the morning and worshiped before the LORD, and returned and came to their house at Ramah. And Elkanah knew Hannah

1:1 [a]Spelled *Eliel* in 1 Chronicles 6:34 [b]Spelled *Toah* in 1 Chronicles 6:34 1:9 [a]Hebrew *heykal*, palace or temple 1:16 [a]Literally *daughter of Belial*

1:1 Birthplace and lineage of Samuel. "Ramathaim Zophim" (also "Ramah," v. 19) was a city located in the hill country of Ephraim, five and a half miles north of Jerusalem. This was the home of Elkanah and Hannah and the birthplace of their son, Samuel (see Hannah). Both Elkanah (Heb., lit. "God created") and his son Samuel were Levites by lineage (1 Chr. 6:33–38). Therefore, the young boy Samuel was qualified to serve in the tabernacle and later as a priest for the nation (1 Sam. 7:9; 9:13; 10:8; 11:15; 16:5). Following the instructions of the Law, Elkanah took his two wives to the tabernacle at Shiloh to worship and sacrifice to the Lord (1 Sam. 1:3; Ex. 34:23; Deut. 16:16) despite religious corruption at Shiloh (1 Sam. 2:12–17).

1:2 Polygamy was culturally acceptable in Samuel's day. High priority was placed on having numerous descendants to carry on the family name and inheritance as well as to work the fields. However, whenever God discusses, arranges, or illustrates marriage in Scripture, it is always in a context of monogamy (see Gen. 2:24, note; 1 Tim. 3, Polygamy). God gave Adam one wife (Gen. 2:18); God's concept of oneness in marriage implies one spouse (Gen. 2:22–24); God designed marriage as a complementary relationship of two people (Gen. 2:18, 21, 22); the king of Israel was specifically commanded not to take many wives (Deut. 17:15–17; see also 1 Kin. 11, Solomon's Pagan Wives).

1:6 Barrenness was a disgrace in OT times (see Ps. 113, Suffering). However, it is clear from the text that the sovereign God was responsible for Hannah's barrenness (1 Sam. 1:5, 6; see also Gen. 16:2; 20:18; 30:2). In addition to her sorrow, Hannah repeatedly experienced the cruelty of Elkanah's other wife, Peninnah (1 Sam. 1:2, 6, 7). This prolific childbearer ("all her sons and daughters," v. 4) made Hannah miserable, provoking her to the point of grief and pain (v. 6). Yet in the midst of Hannah's suffering, she became a woman of prayer and praise (v. 10; 1 Sam. 2:1–10). When the situation was unbearable, Hannah turned in prayer to God, not to someone or something else. In spite of her bitterness of soul, Hannah in fervent prayer focused on the Person of God as Lord of the hosts of heaven and earth (v. 11). Her perspective is significant since Israel was at one of the lowest points in her history, with a small and weak army, surrounded by powerful enemies. Hannah also was content to trust God to avenge Peninnah's cruelty (see Deut. 32:35; and David's words in 2 Sam. 3:39).

1:11 Devout Israelite parents were expected to commit their firstborn son to the Lord, a requirement of the Mosaic Law (Ex. 22:29). Hannah went further in her prayer (see Phil. 1, Prayers for Your Children). Though she did not use the word "Nazirite," Hannah clearly was dedicating the entire life of her anticipated son for service to the Lord. Though the Nazirite vow was seldom taken for a lifetime, no other incidents of the taking of this vow in behalf of someone else are found (Num. 6:2–7).

HANNAH *A Devoted Mother*

Out of the materialism and ruthlessness of Israel during the period of the judges, Hannah emerged as a woman of faith. From her home in the hills north of Jerusalem, she had traveled to Shiloh, the national place of worship. Her sadness of heart and persistence in prayer contrasted sharply with the prevalent corruption in worship led by Eli's sons (1 Sam. 2:12–17).

Hannah's personal life was one of despair in her childlessness as she recoiled from Peninnah's pestering reproach. Her prayer exhibits selflessness as she pleads for a son whom she might present to God for His use (1 Sam. 1:11). Clearly, Hannah was loved and valued for herself by her husband, Elkanah, but even the intensity of a devoted husband's love could not penetrate her inner disquiet nor overcome her yearning for a child (v. 8). The throbbing emotions of her despair were so evident in Hannah's prayers that the aged Eli accused her of drunkenness. But beyond her prayers and tears, a vow erupts. Hannah, in effect, makes a pact with God; she pledges to give back to Him the precious life He might give to her. God honored her bold and decisive act.

Hannah's faith is rewarded, and her son is named Samuel (Heb. *shemu'el,* "Heard by God") because she "asked for him from the LORD" (1 Sam. 1:20). According to custom, she probably nursed him several years, giving time for her to convey to Samuel her own spirit of deep reverence and piety and also to knit her heart with his through maternal bonding. Nonetheless, she kept her word to the Lord. Into the defiled worship center she placed her very young, impressionable son. Although humanly it seemed to border on foolishness, this was an act of saintly sacrifice. Her commitment was to God; her gift was pre-arranged with Him. With prophetic insight she planted the next generation just as promised.

Samuel grew up to become the last judge, an outstanding and gifted prophet, and the one who would anoint the first two kings of Israel. Samuel was the pivotal spiritual leader who turned the nation toward *Yahweh.* His mother Hannah played her part in this spiritual awakening as she trusted God, leaving for all posterity an example of determined devotion in her motherhood.

See also notes on Motherhood (1 Sam. 1); Naming of Children (Is. 45); Vows (Num. 30).

---

his wife, and the LORD remembered her. [20]So it came to pass in the process of time that Hannah conceived and bore a son, and called his name Samuel,[a] saying, "Because I have asked for him from the LORD."

[21]Now the man Elkanah and all his house went up to offer to the LORD the yearly sacrifice and his vow. [22]But Hannah did not go up, for she said to her husband, "*Not* until the child is weaned; then I will take him, that he may appear before the LORD and remain there forever."

[23]So Elkanah her husband said to her, "Do what seems best to you; wait until you have weaned him. Only let the LORD establish His[a] word." Then the woman stayed and nursed her son until she had weaned him.

[24]Now when she had weaned him, she took him up with her, with three bulls,[a] one ephah of flour, and a skin of wine, and brought him to the house of the LORD in Shiloh. And the child *was* young. [25]Then they slaughtered a bull, and brought the child to Eli. [26]And she said, "O my lord! As your soul lives, my lord, I *am* the woman who stood by you here, praying to the LORD. [27]For this child I prayed, and the LORD has granted me my petition which I asked of Him. [28]Therefore I also have lent him to the LORD; as long as he lives he shall be lent to the LORD." So they worshiped the LORD there.

1:20 [a]Literally *Heard by God*   **1:23** [a]Following Masoretic Text, Targum, and Vulgate; Dead Sea Scrolls, Septuagint, and Syriac read *your.*   **1:24** [a]Dead Sea Scrolls, Septuagint, and Syriac read a *three-year-old bull.*

1:24 The normal time for weaning a child among the Israelite mothers of this period was about three years of age (see Ex. 2, Breastfeeding).

1:24 Hannah was faithful to her vow as she brought Samuel to the house of the Lord. At the birth of the monarchy in Israel, God focused on one family and in particular one woman in that family, Hannah, who modeled reverence for God and obedience to Him (vv. 7, 11, 24–28; 1 Sam. 2:19; see also Hannah; Prov. 31, The Virtuous Wife of Proverbs). Such an attitude is a key theme as 1 Samuel records the rise of the monarchy in Israel. Though leadership that reverenced and obeyed God was practically non-existent at this time in Israel's history, both reverence and obedience to God were modeled by Han-

nah for her son Samuel, who in turn modeled them for a nation (see chart, Models of Obedience and Disobedience). The example of Samuel's life also was observed by Israel's first two kings, Saul and David (1 Sam.10:1; 16:13). The influence of one life can never be underestimated.

1:28 Samuel (Heb., lit. "God heard") was presented to Eli the priest at the tabernacle (v. 24), but in actuality he had already been dedicated to the Lord and belonged to Him (v. 28; see also Is. 45, Naming of Children). First, Samuel's father worshiped the Lord (1 Sam. 1:28); then his mother worshiped in a song of praise that focuses on the One who heard her prayer (1 Sam. 2:1–10). Samuel personified the response of God to the prayerful intercession of His people.

MODELS OF OBEDIENCE AND DISOBEDIENCE

THE MODELING OF OBEDIENCE	THE MODELING OF DISOBEDIENCE
The Obedience of Samuel's Parents 1. They were obedient in worship (1 Sam. 1:3, 7, 19; 2:19, 21). 2. They were obedient to a vow (1 Sam. 1:11, 24, 27, 28).	The Disobedience of Eli 1. Eli disobeyed the Lord's commands concerning His sacrifices and offerings (1 Sam. 2:13–17, 29). 2. Eli put his sons before the Lord (1 Sam. 2:29). 3. Eli did not discipline his sons (1 Sam. 3:13).
The Obedience of Samuel 1. As a child, Samuel ministered to the Lord (1 Sam. 2:11, 18; 3:1). 2. Samuel was obedient to Eli (1 Sam. 3:4–9). 3. Samuel was obedient to God (1 Sam. 3:10).	The Disobedience of Eli's Sons 1. Eli's sons despised the Lord's sacrifices and offerings (1 Sam. 2:13–17). 2. Eli's sons disobeyed the Lord's moral commands (1 Sam. 2:22). 3. Eli's sons did not obey their father (1 Sam. 2:25).
The Result of Obedience 1. Samuel saw the blessing of the Lord on his parents (1 Sam. 2:20, 21). 2. Samuel grew before the Lord (1 Sam. 2:21). 3. Samuel "grew in stature, and in favor both with the Lord and men" (1 Sam. 2:26). 4. Samuel was established and sustained as the Lord's prophet by God's presence (1 Sam. 3:19, 20). 5. Samuel became God's spokesman to the people (1 Sam. 3:21–4:1).	The Result of Disobedience 1. Eli's sons were corrupt; they did not know the Lord (1 Sam. 2:12). 2. The disobedient model of Eli's sons caused the Lord's people to sin (1 Sam. 2:17, 24). 3. The house of Eli was judged by God (1 Sam. 2:27–36; 3:11–14). 4. The death of Hophni and Phinehas occurred on the same day (1 Sam. 2:34; 4:11).

Hannah's Prayer

2 And Hannah prayed and said:

"My heart rejoices in the LORD;
My horn[a] is exalted in the LORD.
I smile at my enemies,
Because I rejoice in Your salvation.

[2] "No one is holy like the LORD,
For *there is* none besides You,
Nor *is there* any rock like our God.

[3] "Talk no more so very proudly;
Let no arrogance come from your mouth,
For the LORD *is* the God of knowledge;
And by Him actions are weighed.

[4] "The bows of the mighty men *are* broken,
And those who stumbled are girded with strength.
[5] *Those who were* full have hired themselves out for bread,

2:1 [a] That is, strength

2:1 Hannah's praise, like the psalms, is in the poetic hymnic form of Hebrew poetry. Hers is the fruit of an intimate relationship with God developed in the midst of trial and the declaration of who God is and what He does (vv. 1–10; see Deut. 10:21). Hannah, led by the Spirit of God, spoke prophetically of the future king the Lord would give His people (1 Sam. 2:10). Significantly, Hannah's words were similar to the praise of Mary, the mother of Jesus, in the *Magnificat* (Luke 1:46–55) and of Zacharias, the father of John the Baptist (Luke 1:68–79). Hannah not only focused her praise on the Person of God but also on what He had done for her. "Horn" was used as a symbol of strength in the OT (see Ps. 89:17, 24). Hannah rejoiced that "my horn is lifted high" because the Lord had strengthened her to have a child.

2:2 Declaring the unique holiness of God, Hannah used "rock" imagery to highlight God's divine strength, refuge, and stability (see Deut. 32:4). She joyously testified to God's powerful intervention in her personal life, using the strongest of terms to express her deliverance and salvation. In light of God's character, Hannah warned all, including Peninnah, how foolish it is to be arrogant. God knows our pride and will evaluate it by His standards. The Lord also will "thunder against" all who oppose Him (1 Sam. 2:10).

2:4–8 God's sovereignty is emphasized through a series of vivid life reversals (for example, the strong are broken, while the weak are strengthened, vv. 4–8). This section of contrasts

M O T H E R H O O D   MOTHERS AND SONS

Mothers have a unique relationship with their sons. The understanding and forgiveness is usually free-flowing, as is the affection; yet for some sons a good mother also needs to be firm, expecting and demanding appropriate respect. Mothers must regulate the atmosphere in order to receive its blessings. If they are too busy or overloaded, they will not be in the mood for receiving.

Never is it too early or too late to begin ministering to your children. Jochebed and Hannah are two women in the Bible who have often been sources of encouragement and example. Both of these godly women had their little boys only until they were weaned, which in those days meant perhaps three to four years (Ex. 2:9, 10; 1 Sam. 1:22). Then Moses was sent to the immoral and affluent Egyptian court (Ex. 2:10), and Samuel was sent to the temple to be trained and raised by an elderly priest who had not been able to train his own sons (1 Sam. 1:27, 28; 3:13). Yet both Moses and Samuel grew to become powerful men of God (Ex. 9:16; 1 Sam. 3:19). The influence of a mother on her son can be significant just as the early influence of Jochebed and Hannah no doubt played a vital role in the later success of their sons.

See also Gen. 27:1–29, 41–46; Ex. 2:1–10; 1 Sam. 1:19–28; 2 Kin. 12:1–3; 22:1, 2; Luke 2:43–52; notes on Adolescence (Luke 2); Family (Gen. 32; 1 Sam. 3; Ps. 78; 127); Masculinity (Gen. 2); Motherhood (Is. 49; Ezek. 16); Parenthood (Prov. 10); Siblings (Gen. 37); portraits of Hannah (1 Sam. 1); Lois and Eunice (2 Tim. 1); Rebekah (Gen. 24)

And the hungry have ceased *to hunger.*
Even the barren has borne seven,
And she who has many children has become
    feeble.
⁶"The LORD kills and makes alive;
He brings down to the grave and brings up.
⁷The LORD makes poor and makes rich;
He brings low and lifts up.
⁸He raises the poor from the dust
And lifts the beggar from the ash heap,
To set *them* among princes
And make them inherit the throne of
    glory.

"For the pillars of the earth *are* the LORD's,
And He has set the world upon them.
⁹He will guard the feet of His saints,
But the wicked shall be silent in darkness.

"For by strength no man shall prevail.
¹⁰The adversaries of the LORD shall be broken in
    pieces;
From heaven He will thunder against them.
The LORD will judge the ends of the earth.

"He will give strength to His king,
And exalt the horn of His anointed."

¹¹Then Elkanah went to his house at Ramah. But the child ministered to the LORD before Eli the priest.

The Wicked Sons of Eli

¹²Now the sons of Eli *were* corrupt;[a] they did not know the LORD. ¹³And the priests' custom with the people *was that* when any man offered a sacrifice, the priest's servant would come with a three-pronged fleshhook in his hand while the meat was boiling. ¹⁴Then he would thrust *it* into the pan, or kettle, or caldron, or pot; and the priest would take for himself all that the fleshhook brought up. So they did in Shiloh to all the Israelites who came there. ¹⁵Also, before they burned the fat, the priest's servant would come and say to the man who sacrificed, "Give meat for roasting to the priest, for he will not take boiled meat from you, but raw." ¹⁶And *if* the man said to him, "They should really burn the fat first; *then* you may take *as much* as your heart desires," he would then answer him, "*No,* but you must give *it* now; and if not, I will take *it* by force." ¹⁷Therefore the sin of the young men was very

··········
2:12 ªLiterally *sons of Belial*

climaxes in declaring God's power over life and death (v. 6). Hannah illustrates that a sovereign God can, and in her situation did, reverse human circumstances (1 Sam. 1:20; 2:5; see also Eccl. 7, Providence).

2:8 The "pillars of the earth" pictures the stability and firmness of God's creation under His sovereign control. Along with upholding His creation, God protects and sustains the righteous (1 Sam. 2:8, 9; see Job 38:4; Ps. 75:3, 10).

2:10 Even before the establishment of the monarchy, Hannah spoke prophetically of Israel's coming king whose kingdom

would culminate in the Messiah (see also Gen. 49:10; Deut. 17:14–20).

2:14 God had provided for specified portions of the sacrificial offering to go to the priests after the fat had been burned on the altar (Lev. 7:30–36), but Eli's sons, Hophni and Phinehas, took unlawful portions even before the Lord received what was His (1 Sam. 2:16, 17), treating the Lord's offering with contempt (v. 17). Worst of all, they caused the Lord's people to sin (v. 24).

Being busy is not a satisfactory substitute for being holy.

Jo Ann Leavell

great before the LORD, for men abhorred the offering of the LORD.

Samuel's Childhood Ministry

[18]But Samuel ministered before the LORD, *even as* a child, wearing a linen ephod. [19]Moreover his mother used to make him a little robe, and bring *it* to him year by year when she came up with her husband to offer the yearly sacrifice. [20]And Eli would bless Elkanah and his wife, and say, "The LORD give you descendants from this woman for the loan that was given to the LORD." Then they would go to their own home.

[21]And the LORD visited Hannah, so that she conceived and bore three sons and two daughters. Meanwhile the child Samuel grew before the LORD.

Prophecy Against Eli's Household

[22]Now Eli was very old; and he heard everything his sons did to all Israel,[a] and how they lay with the women who assembled at the door of the tabernacle of meeting. [23]So he said to them, "Why do you do such things? For I hear of your evil dealings from all the people. [24]No, my sons! For *it is* not a good report that I hear. You make the LORD's people transgress. [25]If one man sins against another, God will judge him. But if a man sins against the LORD, who will intercede for him?" Nevertheless they did not heed the voice of their father, because the LORD desired to kill them.

[26]And the child Samuel grew in stature, and in favor both with the LORD and men.

[27]Then a man of God came to Eli and said to him, "Thus says the LORD: 'Did I not clearly reveal Myself to the house of your father when they were in Egypt in Pharaoh's house? [28]Did I not choose him out of all the tribes of Israel *to be* My priest, to offer upon My altar, to burn incense, and to wear an ephod before Me? And did I not give to the house of your father all the offerings of the children of Israel made by fire? [29]Why do you kick at My sacrifice and My offering which I have commanded *in My* dwelling place, and honor your sons more than Me, to make yourselves fat with the best of all the offerings of Israel My people?' [30]Therefore the LORD God of Israel says: 'I said indeed *that* your house and the house of your father would walk before Me forever.' But now the LORD says: 'Far be it from Me; for those who honor Me I will honor, and those who despise Me shall be lightly esteemed. [31]Behold, the days are coming that I will cut off your arm and the arm of your father's house, so that there will not be an old man in your house. [32]And you will see an enemy *in My* dwelling place, *despite* all the good which God does for Israel. And there shall not be an old man in your house forever. [33]But any of your men *whom* I do not cut off from My altar shall consume your

2:22 [a]Following Masoretic Text, Targum, and Vulgate; Dead Sea Scrolls and Septuagint omit the rest of this verse.

2:19 Samuel ministered unto the Lord as he grew up under the oversight of Eli, participating in the duties performed by priests in connection with the worship of God. He wore the white linen ephod, the priest's short sleeveless tunic with a belt (v. 18). Each year when Hannah came to worship at Shiloh, bringing a handmade robe, probably resembling the "robe of the ephod" described but without the symbolical ornaments of the official garment (see Ex. 28:31–34; see 1 Sam. 1, Motherhood; chart, The High Priest's Clothing). Hannah's annual gift to her son may have been a visual reminder to Samuel that he had been set apart to lifelong service to the Lord.

2:22 Though the Israelites conquered the Promised Land, they did not fulfill the Lord's command to drive out the Canaanites, whose influence permeated Israel, especially in the religious realm. "Sacred prostitution" was practiced by the Canaanites and may have influenced Eli's immoral sons, who slept with women at the door of the tabernacle (see Ex. 38:8), thus desecrating the sanctuary. Such behavior was specifically forbidden to the people of God (Deut. 23:17). The sin of Hophni and Phinehas was against the Lord (1 Sam. 2:12–17, 22, 25). Eli's mild rebuke had no effect on his wicked

sons, who had neither reverence for God nor respect for their father (see 1 Sam. 3, Family). A person who disobeys authority does not grow properly (1 Sam. 2:11–3:18). The ultimate authority for Eli's sons was self, not God (see Prov. 22, Children). The ultimate penalty for showing contempt for the priesthood (Deut. 17:12, 13), as well as for constant, blatant rebellion against one's parents, was death (Deut. 21:18–21).

2:27 As high priest, Eli was to illustrate reverence for God. But Eli did not model this reverence to his sons when he honored them more than God (v. 29) and with them was a part in choosing the best of all the offerings of God's people (vv. 13–16). Eli knew the evil actions of his sons and did not discipline them (1 Sam. 3:13). For God's leaders in particular, continuing disrespect for God and His ways brings discipline and judgment (1 Sam. 2:17, 27–34; 3:11–14). Scripture records the fulfillment of God's prophecy against the house of Eli (1 Sam. 4:11, 18; 22:17–20; 1 Kin. 2:26, 27), illustrating the truth in Psalm 119:89. The predicted "enemy in My dwelling place" (1 Sam. 2:32, the tabernacle) implies the Philistines' capture of the ark (1 Sam. 4:11) and the subsequent destruction of Shiloh (see 1 Sam. 4:22).

THE DYSFUNCTIONAL FAMILY FAILURE TO MEET NEEDS

In a fallen world, there is no such thing as a perfect family. Children have many needs: physical needs (food, shelter, clothing); emotional needs (love, acceptance, affirmation); intellectual needs (the opportunity to learn daily living skills and to develop intellectually); and spiritual needs (guidance in how to know God personally and to mature in that relationship). However, a dysfunctional family is one which is consistently inadequate in meeting some or all of these needs. Notable dysfunctional families in the Bible include those of Isaac (Gen. 25:19—28:9), Jacob (Gen. 29:14—35:26; 37:1—38:30), Eli (1 Sam. 2:12–36; 3:11–14), and David (2 Sam. 11:1—19:8).

Dysfunctional families have common patterns: they do not talk, keeping the family secrets; they do not see, ignoring inappropriate behavior as well as altered perceptions of reality; they do not feel, disregarding legitimate emotions; they do not trust, living in isolation and fearing more broken promises; the children strive desperately to be perfect, trying to meet all parental expectations.

Such families are shaped by impaired parents who consistently distort or deny reality to conceal their own problems, such as workaholism or abusive behavior (addictive, sexual, physical, emotional). The result in their children's lives is shame, a deep sense of inadequacy and worthlessness, and the burden of unmet, unrealistic parental expectations. The good news is that the Lord desires to be the "Repairer of the Breach" for families in which children have been maligned or afflicted (Is. 58:9–12).

See also Mark 5:2, note; notes on Family (Gen. 32; Ps. 78; 127); Healing (Ps. 13; 133; Eccl. 1; 2 Cor. 5; Gal. 6; James 5); Mental Health (John 10)

---

eyes and grieve your heart. And all the descendants of your house shall die in the flower of their age. ³⁴Now this *shall be* a sign to you that will come upon your two sons, on Hophni and Phinehas: in one day they shall die, both of them. ³⁵Then I will raise up for Myself a faithful priest *who* shall do according to what *is* in My heart and in My mind. I will build him a sure house, and he shall walk before My anointed forever. ³⁶And it shall come to pass that everyone who is left in your house will come *and* bow down to him for a piece of silver and a morsel of bread, and say, "Please, put me in one of the priestly positions, that I may eat a piece of bread." ' "

Samuel's First Prophecy

3 Now the boy Samuel ministered to the LORD before Eli. And the word of the LORD was rare in those days; *there was* no widespread revelation. ²And it came to pass at that time, while Eli *was* lying down in his place, and when his eyes had begun to grow so dim that he could not see, ³and before the lamp of God went out in the tabernacleᵃ of the LORD where the ark of God *was,* and while

Samuel was lying down, ⁴that the LORD called Samuel. And he answered, "Here I am!" ⁵So he ran to Eli and said, "Here I am, for you called me."

And he said, "I did not call; lie down again." And he went and lay down.

⁶Then the LORD called yet again, "Samuel!"

So Samuel arose and went to Eli, and said, "Here I am, for you called me." He answered, "I did not call, my son; lie down again." ⁷(Now Samuel did not yet know the LORD, nor was the word of the LORD yet revealed to him.)

⁸And the LORD called Samuel again the third time. So he arose and went to Eli, and said, "Here I am, for you did call me."

Then Eli perceived that the LORD had called the boy. ⁹Therefore Eli said to Samuel, "Go, lie down; and it shall be, if He calls you, that you must say, 'Speak, LORD, for Your servant hears.' " So Samuel went and lay down in his place.

¹⁰Now the LORD came and stood and called as at other times, "Samuel! Samuel!"

··················

3:3 ᵃHebrew *heykal,* palace or temple

3:3 Samuel's encounter with the Lord most likely took place at night as evidenced by the fact that lamps on the seven-branched lampstand in the tabernacle, filled with olive oil and lit at twilight, burned until morning (v. 3; Ex. 25:31–40; 30:8).

3:4 Samuel's heart of obedience is demonstrated by his response to what he perceived as calls from Eli as well as by his following Eli's instructions explicitly (vv. 4–10, 16, 18). However difficult it may have been for Samuel to tell Eli the Lord's word of judgment on his house, the boy was obedient (see Philem., Obedience). He hid nothing from Eli (v. 18). Such a heart attitude soon would enable Samuel to know the Lord

(vv. 7, 11). The young boy had seen the obedience of his parents and the result of blessing in their lives (1 Sam. 1:28; 2:19–21). Samuel, the apprentice priest, was about to become the spokesman of God—Samuel, the prophet (1 Sam. 3:19–21), at a time when a word from God was rare (v. 1). Becoming a prophet was based solely upon a divine call and the empowerment of God's Spirit. Samuel's faithfulness to speak God's word indicated that he was fit to be God's voice in Israel (v. 18). When Samuel spoke, people listened (v. 20; 1 Sam. 4:1). God caused Samuel's words to come true (vv. 19, 21).

And Samuel answered, "Speak, for Your servant hears."

[11]Then the LORD said to Samuel: "Behold, I will do something in Israel at which both ears of everyone who hears it will tingle. [12]In that day I will perform against Eli all that I have spoken concerning his house, from beginning to end. [13]For I have told him that I will judge his house forever for the iniquity which he knows, because his sons made themselves vile, and he did not restrain them. [14]And therefore I have sworn to the house of Eli that the iniquity of Eli's house shall not be atoned for by sacrifice or offering forever."

[15]So Samuel lay down until morning,[a] and opened the doors of the house of the LORD. And Samuel was afraid to tell Eli the vision. [16]Then Eli called Samuel and said, "Samuel, my son!"

He answered, "Here I am."

[17]And he said, "What is the word that the LORD spoke to you? Please do not hide it from me. God do so to you, and more also, if you hide anything from me of all the things that He said to you." [18]Then Samuel told him everything, and hid nothing from him. And he said, "It is the LORD. Let Him do what seems good to Him."

[19]So Samuel grew, and the LORD was with him and let none of his words fall to the ground. [20]And all Israel from Dan to Beersheba knew that Samuel had been established as a prophet of the LORD. [21]Then the LORD appeared again in Shiloh. For the LORD revealed Himself to Samuel in Shiloh by the word of the LORD.

4 And the word of Samuel came to all Israel.[a]

The Ark of God Captured

Now Israel went out to battle against the Philistines, and encamped beside Ebenezer; and the Philistines encamped in Aphek. [2]Then the Philistines put themselves in battle array against Israel. And when they joined battle, Israel was defeated by the Philistines, who killed about four thousand men of the army in the field. [3]And when the people had come into the camp, the elders of Israel said, "Why has the LORD defeated us today before the Philistines? Let us bring the ark of the covenant of the LORD from Shiloh to us, that when it comes among us it may save us from the hand of our enemies." [4]So the people sent to Shiloh, that they might bring from there the ark of the covenant of the LORD of hosts, who dwells between the cherubim. And the two sons of Eli, Hophni and Phinehas, were there with the ark of the covenant of God.

[5]And when the ark of the covenant of the LORD came into the camp, all Israel shouted so loudly that the earth shook. [6]Now when the Philistines heard the noise of the shout, they said, "What does the sound of this great shout in the camp of the Hebrews mean?" Then they understood that the ark of the LORD had come into the camp. [7]So the Philistines were afraid, for they said, "God has come into the camp!" And they said, "Woe to us! For such a thing has never happened before. [8]Woe to us! Who will deliver us from the hand of these mighty gods? These are the gods who struck the Egyptians with all the plagues in the wilderness. [9]Be strong and conduct yourselves like men, you Philistines, that you do not become servants of the Hebrews, as they have been to you. Conduct yourselves like men, and fight!"

[10]So the Philistines fought, and Israel was defeated, and every man fled to his tent. There was a very great slaughter, and there fell of Israel thirty thousand foot soldiers. [11]Also the ark of God was captured; and the two sons of Eli, Hophni and Phinehas, died.

Death of Eli

[12]Then a man of Benjamin ran from the battle line the same day, and came to Shiloh with his clothes torn and dirt on his head. [13]Now when he came, there was Eli, sitting on a seat by the wayside watching,[a] for his heart trembled for the ark of God. And when the man came into the city and told it, all the city cried out. [14]When Eli heard the

---

3:15 [a]Following Masoretic Text, Targum, and Vulgate; Septuagint adds and he arose in the morning.   4:1 [a]Following Masoretic Text and Targum; Septuagint and Vulgate add And it came to pass in those days that the Philistines gathered themselves together to fight; Septuagint adds further against Israel.   4:13 [a]Following Masoretic Text and Vulgate; Septuagint reads beside the gate watching the road.

4:3 Israel experienced a terrible defeat at Aphek (v. 2). Instead of engaging in sober reflection as to why God had allowed the Philistine victory (v. 3), the Israelites brought the ark of the covenant into the camp (v. 5). Their quick solution is a tragic example of misplaced confidence. Israel confused a sacred, but material, object with God Himself, demonstrating their lack of understanding of God's omnipotence and omnipresence. They superstitiously believed that divine power resided in the ark itself (see Josh. 6). In this, Israel may have been influenced by her pagan neighbors, who believed their gods inhabited their idols of wood and stone. To the Philistines, the arrival of the ark on the battle site meant Israel's God had come (1 Sam. 4:6–8). Israel also expectantly believed her God would perform (v. 5). But Israel's sovereign God could not be manipulated (1 Sam. 4—7). Israel's Almighty God was present, however, faithfully performing His prophetic word (1 Sam. 4:10, 11, 16–22; see 1 Sam. 2:31-36), but the outcome was not what the people expected. Israel learned the battle's tragic outcome when the messenger arrived with clothes torn and dust on his head, the sign of extreme anguish. God is not mocked, nor can He be manipulated by man. Twenty years later at this same site, the Israelites, led by Samuel, would learn that victory is preceded by repentance and a return to God and His ways.

noise of the outcry, he said, "What *does* the sound of this tumult *mean?*" And the man came quickly and told Eli. [15]Eli was ninety-eight years old, and his eyes were so dim that he could not see.

[16]Then the man said to Eli, "I *am* he who came from the battle. And I fled today from the battle line."

And he said, "What happened, my son?"

[17]So the messenger answered and said, "Israel has fled before the Philistines, and there has been a great slaughter among the people. Also your two sons, Hophni and Phinehas, are dead; and the ark of God has been captured."

[18]Then it happened, when he made mention of the ark of God, that Eli fell off the seat backward by the side of the gate; and his neck was broken and he died, for the man was old and heavy. And he had judged Israel forty years.

Ichabod

[19]Now his daughter-in-law, Phinehas's wife, was with child, *due* to be delivered; and when she heard the news that the ark of God was captured, and that her father-in-law and her husband were dead, she bowed herself and gave birth, for her labor pains came upon her. [20]And about the time of her death the women who stood by her said to her, "Do not fear, for you have borne a son." But she did not answer, nor did she regard it. [21]Then she named the child Ichabod,[a] saying, "The glory has departed from Israel!" because the ark of God had been captured and because of her father-in-law and her husband. [22]And she said, "The glory has departed from Israel, for the ark of God has been captured."

The Philistines and the Ark

5 Then the Philistines took the ark of God and brought it from Ebenezer to Ashdod. [2]When the Philistines took the ark of God, they brought it into the house of Dagon[a] and set it by Dagon. [3]And when the people of Ashdod arose early in the morning, there was Dagon, fallen on its face to the earth before the ark of the LORD. So they took Dagon and set it in its place again. [4]And when they arose early the next morning, there was Dagon, fallen on its face to the ground before the ark of the LORD. The head of Dagon and both the palms of its hands *were* broken off on the threshold; only Dagon's *torso*[a] was left of it. [5]Therefore neither the priests of Dagon nor any who come into Dagon's

house tread on the threshold of Dagon in Ashdod to this day.

[6]But the hand of the LORD was heavy on the people of Ashdod, and He ravaged them and struck them with tumors,[a] *both* Ashdod and its territory. [7]And when the men of Ashdod saw how *it was*, they said, "The ark of the God of Israel must not remain with us, for His hand is harsh toward us and Dagon our god." [8]Therefore they sent and gathered to themselves all the lords of the Philistines, and said, "What shall we do with the ark of the God of Israel?"

And they answered, "Let the ark of the God of Israel be carried away to Gath." So they carried the ark of the God of Israel away. [9]So it was, after they had carried it away, that the hand of the LORD was against the city with a very great destruction; and He struck the men of the city, both small and great, and tumors broke out on them.

[10]Therefore they sent the ark of God to Ekron. So it was, as the ark of God came to Ekron, that the Ekronites cried out, saying, "They have brought the ark of the God of Israel to us, to kill us and our people!" [11]So they sent and gathered together all the lords of the Philistines, and said, "Send away the ark of the God of Israel, and let it go back to its own place, so that it does not kill us and our people." For there was a deadly destruction throughout all the city; the hand of God was very heavy there. [12]And the men who did not die were stricken with the tumors, and the cry of the city went up to heaven.

The Ark Returned to Israel

6 Now the ark of the LORD was in the country of the Philistines seven months. [2]And the Philistines called for the priests and the diviners, saying, "What shall we do with the ark of the LORD? Tell us how we should send it to its place."

[3]So they said, "If you send away the ark of the God of Israel, do not send it empty; but by all means return *it* to Him *with* a trespass offering. Then you will be healed, and it will be known to you why His hand is not removed from you."

[4]Then they said, "What *is* the trespass offering which we shall return to Him?"

•••••••••••••••••••••••••••••••

4:21 [a]Literally *Inglorious*   5:2 [a]A Philistine idol   5:4 [a]Following Septuagint, Syriac, Targum, and Vulgate; Masoretic Text reads *Dagon.*   5:6 [a]Probably bubonic plague. Septuagint and Vulgate add here *And in the midst of their land rats sprang up, and there was a great death panic in the city.*

4:21 Phinehas's wife went into premature labor when she heard her father-in-law (the high priest), as well as her husband and his brother (the high priest's successors), were all dead (v. 19). She viewed it as an even greater tragedy that the ark of the covenant had been captured by pagans (evidenced by her repetition of this fact, vv. 21, 22). Even in the agony of dying in childbirth, she recognized these events as the judgment of God. She interpreted the situation accurately when she named her newborn child Ichabod (Heb., lit. "no glory")

because the ark of the covenant had departed. In the OT the departure of the Lord's glory is always a sign of God's judgment (see Ezek. 1; 9—11). God's glory had left Israel because of the sins of the people, in particular the sins of Israel's leadership. There is archaeological evidence that Shiloh was burned during this time period. This destruction likely was caused by the Philistine invasion (compare Jer. 7:12–14; 26:6–9).

They answered, "Five golden tumors and five golden rats, *according to* the number of the lords of the Philistines. For the same plague *was* on all of you and on your lords. ⁵Therefore you shall make images of your tumors and images of your rats that ravage the land, and you shall give glory to the God of Israel; perhaps He will lighten His hand from you, from your gods, and from your land. ⁶Why then do you harden your hearts as the Egyptians and Pharaoh hardened their hearts? When He did mighty things among them, did they not let the people go, that they might depart? ⁷Now therefore, make a new cart, take two milk cows which have never been yoked, and hitch the cows to the cart; and take their calves home, away from them. ⁸Then take the ark of the LORD and set it on the cart; and put the articles of gold which you are returning to Him *as* a trespass offering in a chest by its side. Then send it away, and let it go. ⁹And watch: if it goes up the road to its own territory, to Beth Shemesh, *then* He has done us this great evil. But if not, then we shall know that *it is* not His hand *that* struck us—it happened to us by chance."

¹⁰Then the men did so; they took two milk cows and hitched them to the cart, and shut up their calves at home. ¹¹And they set the ark of the LORD on the cart, and the chest with the gold rats and the images of their tumors. ¹²Then the cows headed straight for the road to Beth Shemesh, *and* went along the highway, lowing as they went, and did not turn aside to the right hand or the left. And the lords of the Philistines went after them to the border of Beth Shemesh.

¹³Now *the people of* Beth Shemesh *were* reaping their wheat harvest in the valley; and they lifted their eyes and saw the ark, and rejoiced to see *it.* ¹⁴Then the cart came into the field of Joshua of Beth Shemesh, and stood there; a large stone *was* there. So they split the wood of the cart and offered the cows as a burnt offering to the LORD. ¹⁵The Levites took down the ark of the LORD and the chest that *was* with it, in which *were* the articles of gold, and put *them* on the large stone. Then the men of Beth Shemesh offered burnt offerings and made sacrifices the same day to the LORD. ¹⁶So when the five lords of the Philistines had seen *it,* they returned to Ekron the same day.

¹⁷These *are* the golden tumors which the Philistines returned *as* a trespass offering to the LORD: one for Ashdod, one for Gaza, one for Ashkelon, one for Gath, one for Ekron; ¹⁸and the golden rats, *according to* the number of all the cities of the Philistines *belonging* to the five lords, *both* fortified cities and country villages, even as far as the large *stone of* Abel on which they set the ark of the LORD, *which stone remains* to this day in the field of Joshua of Beth Shemesh.

¹⁹Then He struck the men of Beth Shemesh, because they had looked into the ark of the LORD. He struck fifty thousand and seventy menᵃ of the people, and the people lamented because the LORD had struck the people with a great slaughter.

The Ark at Kirjath Jearim

²⁰And the men of Beth Shemesh said, "Who is able to stand before this holy LORD God? And to whom shall it go up from us?" ²¹So they sent messengers to the inhabitants of Kirjath Jearim, saying, "The Philistines have brought back the ark of the LORD; come down *and* take it up with you."

7 Then the men of Kirjath Jearim came and took the ark of the LORD, and brought it into the house of Abinadab on the hill, and consecrated Eleazar his son to keep the ark of the LORD.

Samuel Judges Israel

²So it was that the ark remained in Kirjath Jearim a long time; it was there twenty years. And all the house of Israel lamented after the LORD.

6:19 ᵃOr *He struck seventy men of the people and fifty oxen of a man*

6:13 The Philistines set up an impossible test (vv. 6–9) but to no avail. Against animal instinct, the cows had not returned to their newborn calves but had gone in the opposite direction, drawing the cart carrying the ark back to Israel (v. 12). Without realizing it the Philistines had set up a test that provided an opportunity for the living God to demonstrate His power and glory before those who did not know Him (vv. 12–16). The Philistines had learned they could neither mock nor defy God, but Israel still needed to understand this principle. The Israelites of Beth Shemesh were jubilant when they saw the ark of the covenant (v. 13). They praised God and consecrated themselves unto the Lord (vv. 14, 15). Some, however, were grossly disrespectful because they still had the same perspective as when the ark had left (v. 19). God had allowed the ark to be taken because of the lack of faithfulness and the disobedience of Israel's leadership. The leadership had not modeled obedience, nor had they taught the people reverence for God's ways (1 Sam. 2:17, 26; see chart, Models for Obedience and Disobedience). The irreverence for a holy God, demonstrated by some of the men of Beth Shemesh when they casually looked into the ark, is illustrative of this permissive disrespect (v. 19). Whether foolish curiosity resulting from ignorance of God's Word, lack of enforcement of God's ways, or just lustful pleasure, these men played with the things of God. Their action was incompatible with the holiness of the ark of God. The Law strictly prohibited any Israelite from having contact with the ark of God (Num. 4:5, 15, 20). Now, as the ark returned to Israel, the necessity of reverence for God had to be reemphasized.

6:19 The number of men put to death is problematic. Some scholars eliminate the 50,000 because a few manuscripts do not include this phrase. Though these scholars maintain that the reference to 50,000 is scarce in extant texts, this number is found in all major ancient versions. Josephus interestingly recorded the number as seventy. What we do know clearly is that there was a great smiting by the Lord at Beth Shemesh (v. 19).

TRADITIONS PRESERVING YOUR HERITAGE

Many cultures create and practice traditions to commemorate and preserve a piece of significant history (Ex. 12:1–28). The Bible itself is a source for many traditions. One of those involves the concept of God's covenant with His people to protect and sustain them (Ex. 31:12, 13; Deut. 6:2–13).

Much of the Law is related to personal, family, and social customs or traditions (Deut. 6:8, for example, is a reference to phylacteries, or small containers holding Scripture, worn by the Jews). The Old Testament prophet Samuel called for the Israelites to put away their false gods and serve the Lord God alone. They complied, and, in anticipation of an attack by the Philistines, they asked Samuel to pray to God for protection. To honor God's provision, they established a tradition in honor of God's protection against an enemy attack. Samuel named a stone "Ebenezer," literally "stone of help," reminding the Israelites then and throughout the generations of what God had done for His people after they repented and returned to Him (1 Sam. 7:1–13).

The entire liturgical calendar, which varies among the various denominations—with its holy days and seasons of Advent, Christmas, Epiphany, Lent, Easter, and Pentecost—represents a sequence of traditions established by the early church as a means of relating faith in God to daily life and activities. Many families, communities, and churches, of course, have developed their own traditions over time to commemorate special events—such as anniversaries and birthdays. Scripture does not speak against such traditions—as long as they do not detract in any way from the covenant relationship that the Lord seeks to have with His people.

Traditions provide a reminder to us of who God is and where He is taking us (Luke 22:14–20). They are an integral part of the Judeo-Christian faith; and when we keep them, we come closer to understanding what God has done for us and desires to do through us (Deut. 27:1–8).

See also Josh. 4:1–24; chart on The Feasts of Israel; notes on Celebrations and Holidays (Ex. 12); Family (Gen. 32; 1 Sam. 3; Ps. 78; 127); The Lord's Day (Ex. 23)

---

³Then Samuel spoke to all the house of Israel, saying, "If you return to the LORD with all your hearts, *then* put away the foreign gods and the Ashtoreths[a] from among you, and prepare your hearts for the LORD, and serve Him only; and He will deliver you from the hand of the Philistines." ⁴So the children of Israel put away the Baals and the Ashtoreths,[a] and served the LORD only.

⁵And Samuel said, "Gather all Israel to Mizpah, and I will pray to the LORD for you." ⁶So they gathered together at Mizpah, drew water, and poured *it* out before the LORD. And they fasted that day, and said there, "We have sinned against the LORD." And Samuel judged the children of Israel at Mizpah.

⁷Now when the Philistines heard that the children of Israel had gathered together at Mizpah, the lords of the Philistines went up against Israel. And when the children of Israel heard *of it,* they were afraid of the Philistines. ⁸So the children of Israel said to Samuel, "Do not cease to cry out to the LORD our God for us, that He may save us from the hand of the Philistines."

⁹And Samuel took a suckling lamb and offered *it as* a whole burnt offering to the LORD. Then Samuel cried out to the LORD for Israel, and the LORD answered him. ¹⁰Now as Samuel was offering up the burnt offering, the Philistines drew near to battle against Israel. But the LORD thundered with a loud thunder upon the Philistines that day, and so confused them that they were overcome before Israel. ¹¹And the men of Israel went out of Mizpah and pursued the Philistines, and drove them back as far as below Beth Car. ¹²Then Samuel took a stone and set *it* up between Mizpah and Shen, and called its name Ebenezer,[a] saying, "Thus far the LORD has helped us."

....

7:3 [a]Canaanite goddesses 7:4 [a]Canaanite goddesses 7:12 [a]Literally *Stone of Help*

7:4 Reverence and obedience. Finally Israel began to understand reverential awe for the Lord (vv. 3–6; 1 Sam. 6:20), which in turn produced a heart of repentance (1 Sam. 7:6). Such a return to the Lord preceded their deliverance from enemy domination (vv. 10–14; see 1 Sam. 4:3, note).

7:9 When the Israelites were afraid of the Philistines, Samuel modeled a response of prayer (v. 9; see also chart, Solomon's Prayer). The people knew Samuel prayed (vv. 8, 9). As his mother before him (1 Sam. 1:10–12; 2:1–10), Samuel was deeply committed to prayer (1 Sam. 7:8, 9; 8:6; 12:19, 23; 15:11; Ps. 99:6). Scripture repeatedly records that Samuel prayed when

he was troubled (1 Sam. 8:6; 15:11), as did his mother (1 Sam. 1:15; see also chart, Prayers for Your Children).

God heard Samuel's prayers (1 Sam. 7:9; see Ps. 99:6), and the people knew it (1 Sam. 7:8; 12:19). The event recorded in 1 Sam. 7:10 is illustrative of God's response to Samuel's prayer. Before the Israelites even began to fight, the Lord thundered against the Philistines, and they were routed before the Israelites (see 1 Sam. 2:10; 2 Sam. 22:14, 15). To wait on God is not a waste of time. Samuel took time to intercede for the people (1 Sam. 8:6, 21, 22). He did not stop praying for the people (1 Sam. 12:23), even after they rejected him (1 Sam. 8:5).

[13]So the Philistines were subdued, and they did not come anymore into the territory of Israel. And the hand of the LORD was against the Philistines all the days of Samuel. [14]Then the cities which the Philistines had taken from Israel were restored to Israel, from Ekron to Gath; and Israel recovered its territory from the hands of the Philistines. Also there was peace between Israel and the Amorites.

[15]And Samuel judged Israel all the days of his life. [16]He went from year to year on a circuit to Bethel, Gilgal, and Mizpah, and judged Israel in all those places. [17]But he always returned to Ramah, for his home was there. There he judged Israel, and there he built an altar to the LORD.

Israel Demands a King

[8]Now it came to pass when Samuel was old that he made his sons judges over Israel. [2]The name of his firstborn was Joel, and the name of his second, Abijah; they were judges in Beersheba. [3]But his sons did not walk in his ways; they turned aside after dishonest gain, took bribes, and perverted justice.

[4]Then all the elders of Israel gathered together and came to Samuel at Ramah, [5]and said to him, "Look, you are old, and your sons do not walk in your ways. Now make us a king to judge us like all the nations."

[6]But the thing displeased Samuel when they said, "Give us a king to judge us." So Samuel prayed to the LORD. [7]And the LORD said to Samuel, "Heed the voice of the people in all that they say to you; for they have not rejected you, but they have rejected Me, that I should not reign over them. [8]According to all the works which they have done since the day that I brought them up out of Egypt, even to this day— with which they have forsaken Me and served other gods— so they are doing to you also. [9]Now therefore, heed their voice. However, you shall solemnly forewarn them, and show them the behavior of the king who will reign over them."

[10]So Samuel told all the words of the LORD to the people who asked him for a king. [11]And he said, "This will be the behavior of the king who will reign over you: He will take your sons and appoint them for his own chariots and to be his horsemen, and some will run before his chariots. [12]He will appoint captains over his thousands and captains over his fifties, will set some to plow his ground and reap his harvest, and some to make his weapons of war and equipment for his chariots. [13]He will take your daughters to be perfumers, cooks, and bakers. [14]And he will take the best of your fields, your vineyards, and your olive groves, and give them to his servants. [15]He will take a tenth of your grain and your vintage, and give it to his officers and servants. [16]And he will take your male servants, your female servants, your finest young men,[a] and your donkeys, and put them to his work. [17]He will take a tenth of your sheep. And you will be his servants. [18]And you will cry out in that day because of your king whom you have chosen for yourselves, and the LORD will not hear you in that day."

[19]Nevertheless the people refused to obey the voice of Samuel; and they said, "No, but we will have a king over us, [20]that we also may be like all the nations, and that our king may judge us and go out before us and fight our battles."

[21]And Samuel heard all the words of the people, and he repeated them in the hearing of the LORD. [22]So the LORD said to Samuel, "Heed their voice, and make them a king."

And Samuel said to the men of Israel, "Every man go to his city."

Saul Chosen to Be King

[9]There was a man of Benjamin whose name was Kish the son of Abiel, the son of Zeror, the son of Bechorath, the son of Aphiah, a Benjamite, a mighty man of power. [2]And he had a choice and

8:16 [a]Septuagint reads cattle.

8:5 God was Israel's king, guiding, protecting, and caring for her (v. 7; Ex. 19:5, 6), but God's people went their own way, disobeying Him. God disciplined His children through the oppression of other nations (Deut. 29:14—30:1). However, they thought they were being overtaken by other armies because they did not have a visible human king. Samuel, as prophet and priest, had repeatedly pointed the people to God, their king (1 Sam. 7:3); and at the same time, Samuel modeled a life of reverence and obedience to God (see chart, Models of Obedience and Disobedience). When Samuel was old, he appointed his sons as judges over Israel, but they chose not to follow in his godly ways (1 Sam. 8:5). Having a king was not inherently wrong, since God had already promised a king (Gen. 49:10) and had given guidelines through Moses for a king's behavior (Deut. 17:14–20). Even Samuel's godly mother prophesied that the Lord "will give strength to his king" (1 Sam. 2:10). But the people's motive was wrong in asking for a king (1 Sam. 8:20). They desired to be like other nations, having a king to fight their battles for them, even after Samuel warned the people how a king would treat them (vv. 11–18, taxation, forced labor, military service). The paradox was that Israel's true King desired to do just what their hearts desired (v. 7; see 1 Sam. 10:19). The people would soon learn their mistake when their difficulties increased.

8:6 Samuel's prayer relationship with God is demonstrated. Samuel was concerned with Israel's demand for a king, and he spoke to the Lord. When the Lord responded to Samuel (vv. 7–9), Samuel knew what to say to the people (vv. 10–18). The people's refusal to listen and their insistent demand for a king saddened Samuel (vv. 19, 20); as a result, he talked to the Lord again (v. 21). The Lord's response enabled Samuel to guide the people (v. 22). Samuel constantly modeled that prayer is the key for effective ministry (1 Sam. 7:5; see 1 Thess. 5:17; James 5:16; see also chart, Solomon's Prayer).

handsome son whose name *was* Saul. *There was* not a more handsome person than he among the children of Israel. From his shoulders upward *he was* taller than any of the people.

³Now the donkeys of Kish, Saul's father, were lost. And Kish said to his son Saul, "Please take one of the servants with you, and arise, go and look for the donkeys." ⁴So he passed through the mountains of Ephraim and through the land of Shalisha, but they did not find *them.* Then they passed through the land of Shaalim, and *they were* not *there.* Then he passed through the land of the Benjamites, but they did not find *them.*

⁵When they had come to the land of Zuph, Saul said to his servant who *was* with him, "Come, let us return, lest my father cease *caring* about the donkeys and become worried about us."

⁶And he said to him, "Look now, *there is* in this city a man of God, and *he is* an honorable man; all that he says surely comes to pass. So let us go there; perhaps he can show us the way that we should go."

⁷Then Saul said to his servant, "But look, *if* we go, what shall we bring the man? For the bread in our vessels is all gone, and *there is* no present to bring to the man of God. What do we have?"

⁸And the servant answered Saul again and said, "Look, I have here at hand one-fourth of a shekel of silver. I will give *that* to the man of God, to tell us our way." ⁹(Formerly in Israel, when a man went to inquire of God, he spoke thus: "Come, let us go to the seer"; for *he who is* now *called* a prophet was formerly called a seer.)

¹⁰Then Saul said to his servant, "Well said; come, let us go." So they went to the city where the man of God *was.*

¹¹As they went up the hill to the city, they met some young women going out to draw water, and said to them, "Is the seer here?"

¹²And they answered them and said, "Yes, there he is, just ahead of you. Hurry now; for today he came to this city, because there is a sacrifice of the people today on the high place. ¹³As soon as you come into the city, you will surely find him before he goes up to the high place to eat. For the people will not eat until he comes, because he must bless the sacrifice; afterward those who are invited will eat. Now therefore, go up, for about this time you will find him." ¹⁴So they went up to the city. As they were coming into the city, there was Samuel, coming out toward them on his way up to the high place.

¹⁵Now the LORD had told Samuel in his ear the day before Saul came, saying, ¹⁶"Tomorrow about this time I will send you a man from the land of Benjamin, and you shall anoint him commander over My people Israel, that he may save My people from the hand of the Philistines; for I have looked upon My people, because their cry has come to Me."

¹⁷So when Samuel saw Saul, the LORD said to him, "There he is, the man of whom I spoke to you. This one shall reign over My people." ¹⁸Then Saul drew near to Samuel in the gate, and said, "Please tell me, where *is* the seer's house?"

¹⁹Samuel answered Saul and said, "I *am* the seer. Go up before me to the high place, for you shall eat with me today; and tomorrow I will let you go and will tell you all that *is* in your heart. ²⁰But as for your donkeys that were lost three days ago, do not be anxious about them, for they have been found. And on whom *is* all the desire of Israel? *Is it* not on you and on all your father's house?"

²¹And Saul answered and said, "*Am* I not a Benjamite, of the smallest of the tribes of Israel, and my family the least of all the families of the tribeª of Benjamin? Why then do you speak like this to me?"

²²Now Samuel took Saul and his servant and brought them into the hall, and had them sit in the place of honor among those who were invited; there *were* about thirty persons. ²³And Samuel said to the cook, "Bring the portion which I gave you, of which I said to you, 'Set it apart.'" ²⁴So the cook took up the thigh with its upper part and set *it* before Saul. And *Samuel* said, "Here it is, what was kept back. *It* was set apart for you. Eat; for until this time it has been kept for you, since I said I invited the people." So Saul ate with Samuel that day.

²⁵When they had come down from the high place into the city, *Samuel* spoke with Saul on the top of the house.ª ²⁶They arose early; and it was about the dawning of the day that Samuel called to Saul on the top of the house, saying, "Get up, that I may send you on your way." And Saul arose, and both of them went outside, he and Samuel.

Saul Anointed King

²⁷As they were going down to the outskirts of the city, Samuel said to Saul, "Tell the servant to

---

9:21 ªLiterally *tribes*   **9:25** ªFollowing Masoretic Text and Targum; Septuagint omits *He spoke with Saul on the top of the house;* Septuagint and Vulgate add *And he prepared a bed for Saul on the top of the house, and he slept.*

9:3 The establishment of Israel's monarchy in chapters 9 and 10 illustrated the sovereignty of God as Israel's true King. Saul, Israel's future king, was brought into contact with Samuel, the kingmaker (1 Sam. 9:14–18), through the human circumstance of the lost donkeys (vv. 3–6). The sovereignty of God was demonstrated through the manner in which God confirmed to Saul that he was to be Israel's first king (1 Sam. 10:2–7). God revealed to Israel that Saul was their new chosen king (1 Sam. 10:20–22, 24).

*. . . It is enough to know I am only called to obedience, to see
with clear eyes of faith that the harvest will come later.*

Nancie Carmichael

go on ahead of us." And he went on. "But you stand here awhile, that I may announce to you the word of God."

10 Then Samuel took a flask of oil and poured *it* on his head, and kissed him and said: *"Is it* not because the LORD has anointed you commander over His inheritance?ª ²When you have departed from me today, you will find two men by Rachel's tomb in the territory of Benjamin at Zelzah; and they will say to you, 'The donkeys which you went to look for have been found. And now your father has ceased caring about the donkeys and is worrying about you, saying, "What shall I do about my son?" ' ³Then you shall go on forward from there and come to the terebinth tree of Tabor. There three men going up to God at Bethel will meet you, one carrying three young goats, another carrying three loaves of bread, and another carrying a skin of wine. ⁴And they will greet you and give you two *loaves* of bread, which you shall receive from their hands. ⁵After that you shall come to the hill of God where the Philistine garrison *is*. And it will happen, when you have come there to the city, that you will meet a group of prophets coming down from the high place with a stringed instrument, a tambourine, a flute, and a harp before them; and they will be prophesying. ⁶Then the Spirit of the LORD will come upon you, and you will prophesy with them and be turned into another man. ⁷And let it be, when these signs come to you, *that* you do as the occasion demands; for God *is* with you. ⁸You shall go down before me to Gilgal; and surely I will come down to you to offer burnt offerings *and* make sacrifices of peace offerings. Seven days you shall wait, till I come to you and show you what you should do."

⁹So it was, when he had turned his back to go from Samuel, that God gave him another heart; and all those signs came to pass that day. ¹⁰When they came there to the hill, there was a group of prophets to meet him; then the Spirit of God came upon him, and he prophesied among them. ¹¹And it happened, when all who knew him formerly saw that he indeed prophesied among the prophets, that the people said to one another, "What *is* this *that* has come upon the son of Kish?

Is Saul also among the prophets?" ¹²Then a man from there answered and said, "But who *is* their father?" Therefore it became a proverb: "*Is* Saul also among the prophets?" ¹³And when he had finished prophesying, he went to the high place.

¹⁴Then Saul's uncle said to him and his servant, "Where did you go?"

So he said, "To look for the donkeys. When we saw that *they were* nowhere *to be found,* we went to Samuel."

¹⁵And Saul's uncle said, "Tell me, please, what Samuel said to you."

¹⁶So Saul said to his uncle, "He told us plainly that the donkeys had been found." But about the matter of the kingdom, he did not tell him what Samuel had said.

Saul Proclaimed King

¹⁷Then Samuel called the people together to the LORD at Mizpah, ¹⁸and said to the children of Israel, "Thus says the LORD God of Israel: 'I brought up Israel out of Egypt, and delivered you from the hand of the Egyptians *and* from the hand of all kingdoms and from those who oppressed you.' ¹⁹But you have today rejected your God, who Himself saved you from all your adversities and your tribulations; and you have said to Him, 'No, set a king over us!' Now therefore, present yourselves before the LORD by your tribes and by your clans."ª

²⁰And when Samuel had caused all the tribes of Israel to come near, the tribe of Benjamin was chosen. ²¹When he had caused the tribe of Benjamin to come near by their families, the family of Matri was chosen. And Saul the son of Kish was chosen. But when they sought him, he could not be found. ²²Therefore they inquired of the LORD further, "Has the man come here yet?"

And the LORD answered, "There he is, hidden among the equipment."

²³So they ran and brought him from there; and when he stood among the people, he was taller

---

10:1 ªFollowing Masoretic Text, Targum, and Vulgate; Septuagint reads *His people Israel; and you shall rule the people of the Lord;* Septuagint and Vulgate add *And you shall deliver His people from the hands of their enemies all around them. And this shall be a sign to you, that God has anointed you to be a prince.* **10:19** ªLiterally *thousands*

10:1 The anointing ceremony was a public expression of divine consecration to office. It recognized God's choice of an individual and the empowerment of the Holy Spirit for accomplishing the God-appointed job (Ex. 28:41; 40:13–15; 1 Sam. 9:16). NT believers are also anointed and empowered by the Spirit who indwells each one (2 Cor. 1:21; 1 John 2:20, 21).

than any of the people from his shoulders upward. [24]And Samuel said to all the people, "Do you see him whom the LORD has chosen, that *there is* no one like him among all the people?"

So all the people shouted and said, "Long live the king!"

[25]Then Samuel explained to the people the behavior of royalty, and wrote *it* in a book and laid *it* up before the LORD. And Samuel sent all the people away, every man to his house. [26]And Saul also went home to Gibeah; and valiant *men* went with him, whose hearts God had touched. [27]But some rebels said, "How can this man save us?" So they despised him, and brought him no presents. But he held his peace.

Saul Saves Jabesh Gilead

11 Then Nahash the Ammonite came up and encamped against Jabesh Gilead; and all the men of Jabesh said to Nahash, "Make a covenant with us, and we will serve you."

[2]And Nahash the Ammonite answered them, "On this *condition* I will make *a covenant* with you, that I may put out all your right eyes, and bring reproach on all Israel."

[3]Then the elders of Jabesh said to him, "Hold off for seven days, that we may send messengers to all the territory of Israel. And then, if *there is* no one to save us, we will come out to you."

[4]So the messengers came to Gibeah of Saul and told the news in the hearing of the people. And all the people lifted up their voices and wept. [5]Now there was Saul, coming behind the herd from the field; and Saul said, "What *troubles* the people, that they weep?" And they told him the words of the men of Jabesh. [6]Then the Spirit of God came upon Saul when he heard this news, and his anger was greatly aroused. [7]So he took a yoke of oxen and cut *them* in pieces, and sent *them* throughout all the territory of Israel by the hands of messengers, saying, "Whoever does not go out with Saul and Samuel to battle, so it shall be done to his oxen."

And the fear of the LORD fell on the people, and they came out with one consent. [8]When he numbered them in Bezek, the children of Israel were three hundred thousand, and the men of Judah thirty thousand. [9]And they said to the messengers who came, "Thus you shall say to the men of Jabesh Gilead: 'Tomorrow, by *the time* the sun is hot, you shall have help.' " Then the messengers came and reported *it* to the men of Jabesh, and they were glad. [10]Therefore the men of Jabesh said, "Tomorrow we will come out to you, and you may do with us whatever seems good to you."

[11]So it was, on the next day, that Saul put the people in three companies; and they came into the midst of the camp in the morning watch, and killed Ammonites until the heat of the day. And it happened that those who survived were scattered, so that no two of them were left together.

[12]Then the people said to Samuel, "Who *is* he who said, 'Shall Saul reign over us?' Bring the men, that we may put them to death."

[13]But Saul said, "Not a man shall be put to death this day, for today the LORD has accomplished salvation in Israel."

[14]Then Samuel said to the people, "Come, let us go to Gilgal and renew the kingdom there." [15]So all the people went to Gilgal, and there they made Saul king before the LORD in Gilgal. There they made sacrifices of peace offerings before the LORD, and there Saul and all the men of Israel rejoiced greatly.

Samuel's Address at Saul's Coronation

12 Now Samuel said to all Israel: "Indeed I have heeded your voice in all that you said to me, and have made a king over you. [2]And now here is the king, walking before you; and I am old and grayheaded, and look, my sons *are* with you. I have walked before you from my childhood to this day. [3]Here I am. Witness against me before the LORD and before His anointed: Whose ox have I taken, or whose donkey have I taken, or whom have I cheated? Whom have I oppressed, or from whose hand have I received *any* bribe with which to blind my eyes? I will restore *it* to you."

[4]And they said, "You have not cheated us or op-

10:24 Israel had been ruled as a theocracy. Now the establishment of an earthly monarchy was bringing Israel to a strategic point in her history. The only way Israel's monarchy could work was for her king to submit to divine leadership and dominion as he ruled over Israel. The king's authority was to be carried out in the name of the Lord. Israel's ruler was to be God's instrument for accomplishing God's will. God raised up prophets to work alongside the king, making known God's purposes. Israel as a nation would be blessed when the heart of the king followed this pattern. Tragically, however, Israel's kings seldom had such a heart attitude. All too often they opposed God's will, lacking personal discipline and causing the nation ultimately to go into captivity under God's judgment.

11:13 At the beginning of Saul's reign, his attitude was one of humility (1 Sam. 10:16, 21–23) and graciousness (1 Sam. 10:26,

27). He was valiant (1 Sam. 11:7, 11), giving honor due to the Lord (v. 13). The "Spirit of the Lord" had come upon Saul to enable him to rule God's people Israel (1 Sam. 10:6; see Judg. 3:10; 6:34; 1 Sam. 16:13; see Ezek. 11:5).

12:1 Samuel—the priest, prophet, and judge of Israel—combined his farewell warning (vv. 14, 15) and challenge to Israel (vv. 20, 21, 24, 25) with a covenant renewal ceremony. Here Samuel again modeled commitment to God's will. At God's command, Samuel listened to the people asking for a king (1 Sam. 8:7, 9, 22). Though personally reluctant, Samuel officially transferred the leadership from himself to Saul (1 Sam. 8:6; 12:2, 13). At this point the period of the monarchy formally began. Saul was now the official leader of Israel, although Samuel continued in his role as priest and prophet (1 Sam. 12:23; 13:8–12; 15:30, 31; 16:13). The monarchy had

DAVID: HOW GOOD PEOPLE GET INTO TROUBLE

PERSON AND CHARACTER	PROBLEMS AND FAILURES	PARABLE AND CONVICTION	PUNISHMENT AND CONSEQUENCES	PSALM AND PRAYER
1. God's choice (1 Sam. 13:14; 16:7; Acts 13:22)	1. Disobedience (2 Sam. 11:1–4)	1. Nathan's divinely inspired story (2 Sam. 12:1–4)	1. Disgracing of wives (2 Sam. 12:11, 12; 20:3)	1. Plea for mercy (Ps. 51:1–6)
2. Anointed with the Spirit (1 Sam. 16:13, 18)	2. Compromise (2 Sam. 11:2, 3)	2. David's spontaneous reaction (2 Sam. 12:5, 6)	2. Death of baby (2 Sam. 12:14–19)	2. Request for pardon (Ps. 51:7–12)
3. Musician (1 Sam. 16:17–23)	3. Immorality (2 Sam. 11:4, 5)	3. God's clear condemnation (2 Sam. 12:7–9)	3. Rape and incest in his family (2 Sam. 12:11–14)	3. Acceptance of God's promise (Ps. 51:10–13)
4. Hero in battle (1 Sam. 17:49–58; 18:7–11)	4. Cover-up *Deception of self* Plan A (2 Sam. 11:6–11); Plan B (2 Sam. 11:12, 13); Plan C (2 Sam. 11:14–17) *Deception of others* (2 Sam. 11:26, 27)		4. Murder of his son Amnon (2 Sam. 13:32)	4. Outpouring of penitence (Ps. 51:16, 17)
5. Victim of jealousy (1 Sam. 18:29)			5. Rebellion of his son Absalom (2 Sam. 15:1–37)	5. Utterance of praise (Ps. 51:18, 19)
6. Bridegroom (1 Sam. 18:27)			6. Death of his son Absalom (2 Sam. 18:9–15)	
7. King (2 Sam. 5:3, 4)				
8. Godly man (2 Sam. 5:10)				

pressed us, nor have you taken anything from any man's hand."

⁵Then he said to them, "The LORD *is* witness against you, and His anointed *is* witness this day, that you have not found anything in my hand."

And they answered, "*He is* witness."

⁶Then Samuel said to the people, "*It is* the LORD who raised up Moses and Aaron, and who brought your fathers up from the land of Egypt. ⁷Now therefore, stand still, that I may reason with you before the LORD concerning all the righteous acts of the LORD which He did to you and your fathers:

been preceded by the development of the prophetic office (1 Sam. 3:19—4:1). Israel's first king, Saul, had been anointed and presented to the people by Samuel (1 Sam. 10:1, 24), the official head of the prophetic line (1 Sam. 9:6–10, 19; Acts 3:24; Heb. 11:32). The offices of king and prophet were to work together. The king was to administer the Lord's covenant; the prophet was to give spiritual counsel as well as

divine instruction, exhortation, and rebuke. This working relationship made it necessary for the king to respect and be sensitive to the prophets. The prophet's responsibility in this regard was to be above reproach. Samuel's godly behavior and determination never to use his prophetic office for selfish gain is set in contrast to his previous warnings of oppressive kingship (1 Sam. 8:11–17).

[8]When Jacob had gone into Egypt,[a] and your fathers cried out to the LORD, then the LORD sent Moses and Aaron, who brought your fathers out of Egypt and made them dwell in this place. [9]And when they forgot the LORD their God, He sold them into the hand of Sisera, commander of the army of Hazor, into the hand of the Philistines, and into the hand of the king of Moab; and they fought against them. [10]Then they cried out to the LORD, and said, 'We have sinned, because we have forsaken the LORD and served the Baals and Ashtoreths;[a] but now deliver us from the hand of our enemies, and we will serve You.' [11]And the LORD sent Jerubbaal,[a] Bedan,[b] Jephthah, and Samuel,[c] and delivered you out of the hand of your enemies on every side; and you dwelt in safety. [12]And when you saw that Nahash king of the Ammonites came against you, you said to me, 'No, but a king shall reign over us,' when the LORD your God *was* your king.

[13]"Now therefore, here is the king whom you have chosen *and* whom you have desired. And take note, the LORD has set a king over you. [14]If you fear the LORD and serve Him and obey His voice, and do not rebel against the commandment of the LORD, then both you and the king who reigns over you will continue following the LORD your God. [15]However, if you do not obey the voice of the LORD, but rebel against the commandment of the LORD, then the hand of the LORD will be against you, as *it was* against your fathers.

[16]"Now therefore, stand and see this great thing which the LORD will do before your eyes: [17]*Is* today not the wheat harvest? I will call to the LORD, and He will send thunder and rain, that you may perceive and see that your wickedness *is* great, which you have done in the sight of the LORD, in asking a king for yourselves."

[18]So Samuel called to the LORD, and the LORD sent thunder and rain that day; and all the people greatly feared the LORD and Samuel.

[19]And all the people said to Samuel, "Pray for your servants to the LORD your God, that we may not die; for we have added to all our sins the evil of asking a king for ourselves."

[20]Then Samuel said to the people, "Do not fear. You have done all this wickedness; yet do not turn aside from following the LORD, but serve the LORD with all your heart. [21]And do not turn aside; for *then you would go* after empty things which cannot profit or deliver, for they *are* nothing. [22]For the LORD will not forsake His people, for His great name's sake, because it has pleased the LORD to make you His people. [23]Moreover, as for me, far be it from me that I should sin against the LORD in ceasing to pray for you; but I will teach you the good and the right way. [24]Only fear the LORD, and serve Him in truth with all your heart; for consider what great things He has done for you. [25]But if you still do wickedly, you shall be swept away, both you and your king."

Saul's Unlawful Sacrifice

13 Saul reigned one year; and when he had reigned two years over Israel,[a] [2]Saul chose for himself three thousand *men* of Israel. Two thousand were with Saul in Michmash and in the mountains of Bethel, and a thousand were with Jonathan in Gibeah of Benjamin. The rest of the people he sent away, every man to his tent.

[3]And Jonathan attacked the garrison of the Philistines that *was* in Geba, and the Philistines heard *of it*. Then Saul blew the trumpet throughout all the land, saying, "Let the Hebrews hear!" [4]Now all Israel heard it said *that* Saul had attacked a garrison of the Philistines, and *that* Israel had also become an abomination to the Philistines. And the people were called together to Saul at Gilgal.

[5]Then the Philistines gathered together to fight with Israel, thirty[a] thousand chariots and six thousand horsemen, and people as the sand which *is* on the seashore in multitude. And they came up and encamped in Michmash, to the east of Beth Aven. [6]When the men of Israel saw that they were in danger (for the people were distressed), then the people hid in caves, in thickets, in rocks, in holes, and in pits. [7]And *some of* the Hebrews crossed over the Jordan to the land of Gad and Gilead.

As for Saul, he *was* still in Gilgal, and all the people followed him trembling. [8]Then he waited seven days, according to the time set by Samuel. But Samuel did not come to Gilgal; and the people were scattered from him. [9]So Saul said, "Bring a burnt offering and peace offerings here to me." And he offered the burnt offering. [10]Now it happened, as soon as he had finished presenting the burnt offering, that Samuel came; and Saul went out to meet him, that he might greet him.

••••••••••••••••••

12:8 [a]Following Masoretic Text, Targum, and Vulgate; Septuagint adds *and the Egyptians afflicted them.* **12:10** [a]Canaanite goddesses **12:11** [a]Syriac reads *Deborah;* Targum reads *Gideon.* [b]Septuagint and Syriac read *Barak;* Targum reads *Simson.* [c]Syriac reads *Simson.* **13:1** [a]The Hebrew is difficult (compare 2 Samuel 5:4; 2 Kings 14:2; see also 2 Samuel 2:10; Acts 13:21). **13:5** [a]Following Masoretic Text, Septuagint, Targum, and Vulgate; Syriac and some manuscripts of the Septuagint read *three.*

12:14 Samuel's exhortation to Israel emphasized reverence for God ("fear the Lord" v. 14; see Prov. 1:7; Ps. 111:10). The fear of the Lord is evidenced by departing from evil (1 Sam. 12:14; see Job 28:28) and obeying God's commands (1 Sam. 12:14; see Eccl. 12:13). A strong warning was given to the people about impending consequences if they did not heed the exhortation (1 Sam. 12:15). Samuel concluded with the encouraging promise that God "will not forsake His people" (v. 22); and he, Samuel, would not cease to pray for them (v. 23).

[11]And Samuel said, "What have you done?"

Saul said, "When I saw that the people were scattered from me, and *that* you did not come within the days appointed, and *that* the Philistines gathered together at Michmash, [12]then I said, 'The Philistines will now come down on me at Gilgal, and I have not made supplication to the LORD.' Therefore I felt compelled, and offered a burnt offering."

[13]And Samuel said to Saul, "You have done foolishly. You have not kept the commandment of the LORD your God, which He commanded you. For now the LORD would have established your kingdom over Israel forever. [14]But now your kingdom shall not continue. The LORD has sought for Himself a man after His own heart, and the LORD has commanded him *to be* commander over His people, because you have not kept what the LORD commanded you."

[15]Then Samuel arose and went up from Gilgal to Gibeah of Benjamin.[a] And Saul numbered the people present with him, about six hundred men.

No Weapons for the Army

[16]Saul, Jonathan his son, and the people present with them remained in Gibeah of Benjamin. But the Philistines encamped in Michmash. [17]Then raiders came out of the camp of the Philistines in three companies. One company turned onto the road to Ophrah, to the land of Shual, [18]another company turned to the road *to* Beth Horon, and another company turned *to* the road of the border that overlooks the Valley of Zeboim toward the wilderness.

[19]Now there was no blacksmith to be found throughout all the land of Israel, for the Philistines said, "Lest the Hebrews make swords or spears." [20]But all the Israelites would go down to the Philistines to sharpen each man's plowshare, his mattock, his ax, and his sickle; [21]and the charge for a sharpening was a pim[a] for the plowshares, the mattocks, the forks, and the axes, and to set the points of the goads. [22]So it came about, on the day of battle, that there was neither sword nor spear found in the hand of any of the people who *were* with Saul and Jonathan. But they were found with Saul and Jonathan his son.

[23]And the garrison of the Philistines went out to the pass of Michmash.

Jonathan Defeats the Philistines

14 Now it happened one day that Jonathan the son of Saul said to the young man who bore his armor, "Come, let us go over to the Philistines' garrison that *is* on the other side." But he did not tell his father. [2]And Saul was sitting in the outskirts of Gibeah under a pomegranate tree which *is* in Migron. The people who *were* with him *were* about six hundred men. [3]Ahijah the son of Ahitub, Ichabod's brother, the son of Phinehas, the son of Eli, the LORD's priest in Shiloh, was wearing an ephod. But the people did not know that Jonathan had gone.

[4]Between the passes, by which Jonathan sought to go over to the Philistines' garrison, *there was* a sharp rock on one side and a sharp rock on the other side. And the name of one *was* Bozez, and the name of the other Seneh. [5]The front of one faced northward opposite Michmash, and the other southward opposite Gibeah.

[6]Then Jonathan said to the young man who bore his armor, "Come, let us go over to the garrison of these uncircumcised; it may be that the LORD will work for us. For nothing restrains the LORD from saving by many or by few."

[7]So his armorbearer said to him, "Do all that is in your heart. Go then; here I am with you, according to your heart."

[8]Then Jonathan said, "Very well, let us cross over to *these* men, and we will show ourselves to them. [9]If they say thus to us, 'Wait until we come to you,' then we will stand still in our place and not go up to them. [10]But if they say thus, 'Come up to us,' then we will go up. For the LORD has delivered them into our hand, and this *will be* a sign to us."

[11]So both of them showed themselves to the garrison of the Philistines. And the Philistines said, "Look, the Hebrews are coming out of the holes where they have hidden." [12]Then the men of the garrison called to Jonathan and his armorbearer, and said, "Come up to us, and we will show you something."

Jonathan said to his armorbearer, "Come after me, for the LORD has delivered them into the hand of Israel." [13]And Jonathan climbed up on his hands and knees with his armorbearer after him; and they fell before Jonathan. And as he came after him, his armorbearer killed them. [14]That first slaughter which Jonathan and his armorbearer made was about twenty men within about half an acre of land.[a]

13:15 [a]Following Masoretic Text and Targum; Septuagint and Vulgate add *And the rest of the people went up after Saul to meet the people who fought against them, going from Gilgal to Gibeah in the hill of Benjamin.*   **13:21** [a]About two-thirds shekel weight   **14:14** [a]Literally half the area plowed by a yoke (of oxen in a day)

13:13 As king of Israel, Saul was to submit to divine leadership (see 1 Sam. 10:24, note). God's specific command had been given to Saul through Samuel the prophet (1 Sam. 10:8). During the pressure of military crisis, Saul did not follow God's instructions (1 Sam. 13:5, 6). He chose his own way as the best plan (vv. 11, 12). He disobeyed God's word and thus sinned (v. 9). Saul also failed to give godly leadership to his dwindling army and to put his trust in the Lord (contrast Jonathan, 1 Sam. 14:6–23; see 1 Sam. 15:22–23; 17:8, note).

[15]And there was trembling in the camp, in the field, and among all the people. The garrison and the raiders also trembled; and the earth quaked, so that it was a very great trembling. [16]Now the watchmen of Saul in Gibeah of Benjamin looked, and *there* was the multitude, melting away; and they went here and there. [17]Then Saul said to the people who *were* with him, "Now call the roll and see who has gone from us." And when they had called the roll, surprisingly, Jonathan and his armorbearer *were* not *there*. [18]And Saul said to Ahijah, "Bring the ark[a] of God here" (for at that time the ark[b] of God was with the children of Israel). [19]Now it happened, while Saul talked to the priest, that the noise which *was* in the camp of the Philistines continued to increase; so Saul said to the priest, "Withdraw your hand." [20]Then Saul and all the people who *were* with him assembled, and they went to the battle; and indeed every man's sword was against his neighbor, *and there was* very great confusion. [21]Moreover the Hebrews *who* were with the Philistines before that time, who went up with them into the camp *from the* surrounding *country,* they also joined the Israelites who *were* with Saul and Jonathan. [22]Likewise all the men of Israel who had hidden in the mountains of Ephraim, *when* they heard that the Philistines fled, they also followed hard after them in the battle. [23]So the LORD saved Israel that day, and the battle shifted to Beth Aven.

Saul's Rash Oath

[24]And the men of Israel were distressed that day, for Saul had placed the people under oath, saying, "Cursed *is* the man who eats *any* food until evening, before I have taken vengeance on my enemies." So none of the people tasted food. [25]Now all *the people* of the land came to a forest; and there was honey on the ground. [26]And when the people had come into the woods, there was the honey, dripping; but no one put his hand to his mouth, for the people feared the oath. [27]But Jonathan had not heard his father charge the people with the oath; therefore he stretched out the end of the rod that *was* in his hand and dipped it in a honeycomb, and put his hand to his mouth; and his countenance brightened. [28]Then one of the people said, "Your father strictly charged the people with an oath, saying, 'Cursed *is* the man who eats food this day.'" And the people were faint.

[29]But Jonathan said, "My father has troubled the land. Look now, how my countenance has brightened because I tasted a little of this honey. [30]How much better if the people had eaten freely today of the spoil of their enemies which they found! For now would there not have been a much greater slaughter among the Philistines?"

[31]Now they had driven back the Philistines that day from Michmash to Aijalon. So the people were very faint. [32]And the people rushed on the spoil, and took sheep, oxen, and calves, and slaughtered *them* on the ground; and the people ate *them* with the blood. [33]Then they told Saul, saying, "Look, the people are sinning against the LORD by eating with the blood!"

14:18 [a]Following Masoretic Text, Targum, and Vulgate; Septuagint reads *ephod.* [b]Following Masoretic Text, Targum, and Vulgate; Septuagint reads *ephod.*

14:18 Knowing God's will. The Septuagint's use here of the word "ephod" instead of the term "ark" may be the better reading. The ark had already been deposited at Kirjath Jearim (1 Sam. 7:1). The ark remained there (1 Sam. 7:2) until David moved it to Jerusalem (2 Sam. 6:1–17). Bringing it to Saul's camp seems unlikely since the ark was not an object casually carried about (see Num. 4:15, 20). Since Saul is speaking to a priest, it would seem more logical that he would be seeking to know God's will rather than to have the ark present.

In the OT era, the priest wore a special garment, the "ephod," upon which were fastened the Urim and Thummim (see Ex. 28:15, note). This "ephod" was also used to consult God (Ex. 28:8–14; 1 Sam. 2:28; 14:3; 23:9–12). The Urim and Thummim of the ephod served as a means of knowing God's will (Ex. 28:30; Lev. 8:8). Scripture is not clear as to what these objects looked like or how they were used. One theory is that the priests used the stones in a type of lot-casting manner, answering "yes" or "no" questions (1 Sam. 14:41).

14:19 The heart of Saul, characterized by religious performance without genuine commitment to God, is revealed (1 Sam. 13—15). Saul offered the burnt offering to the Lord before the Philistine battle, disobeying God's specific commands given through Samuel (1 Sam. 13:9, 13). When Jonathan's courageous attack on the Philistines created tumult in their camp, Saul called for the "ark of God" (LXX reads "ephod") to inquire of the Lord as to what to do (1 Sam. 14:18). But Saul canceled the inquiry when it appeared more

expedient to go quickly to the battle (vv. 19, 20). Neglecting the needs of his men, Saul foolishly placed them under oath not to eat until the battle was over (v. 24). His foolish oath encouraged them to sin. Their hunger and battle fatigue caused them to break the Lord's command (v. 32; see Lev. 3:17; 17:10–14). Properly, Saul stopped the people and dealt with their offense (1 Sam. 14:34, 35). When Saul did inquire of the Lord and He was silent, Saul initiated an investigation, assuming God's silence was the result of the violation of the fasting vow (vv. 24, 37). Piously, Saul declared the death penalty for the offender, making his second rash vow (vv. 39, 44). Saul was shown to be a fool when the people overruled him to save their innocent hero (v. 45). Distracted by his hasty vow, Saul lost his best opportunity to rid Israel of the Philistines (v. 46). God gave a specific "ban" instruction to Saul (see 1 Sam. 15:3, note). But Saul disobeyed the Lord's command ("unwilling" to destroy, a verb linked elsewhere with the sin of rebellion, Deut. 1:26), finding something good in what the Lord had condemned (1 Sam. 14:9). Saul gave in to the people (lit. "obeyed them") when he should have been obeying God (vv. 19, 22). Being a people pleaser, Saul seemed more afraid of the people than God (the paradox of such behavior is seen in Prov. 29:25; Is. 51:12, 13). Arrogantly, Saul set up a monument for himself (v. 12). When confronted by Samuel, Saul rationalized his sinful actions, passing blame onto the people (vv. 18–21). The opinions of people were more important to Saul than genuine repentance (vv. 25, 30).

THE FAMILY TREE OF SAUL

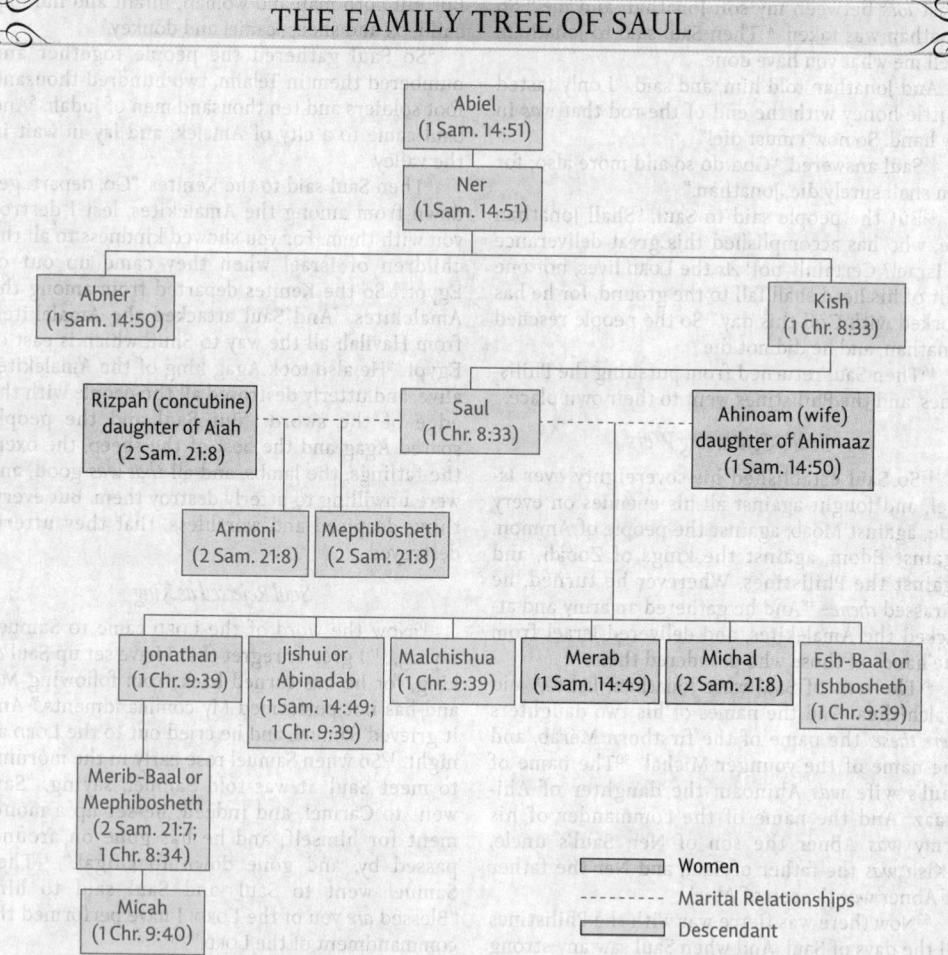

Abiel
(1 Sam. 14:51)

Ner
(1 Sam. 14:51)

Abner
(1 Sam. 14:50)

Kish
(1 Chr. 8:33)

Rizpah (concubine)
daughter of Aiah
(2 Sam. 21:8)

Saul
(1 Chr. 8:33)

Ahinoam (wife)
daughter of Ahimaaz
(1 Sam. 14:50)

Armoni
(2 Sam. 21:8)

Mephibosheth
(2 Sam. 21:8)

Jonathan
(1 Chr. 9:39)

Jishui or
Abinadab
(1 Sam. 14:49;
1 Chr. 9:39)

Malchishua
(1 Chr. 9:39)

Merab
(1 Sam. 14:49)

Michal
(2 Sam. 21:8)

Esh-Baal or
Ishbosheth
(1 Chr. 9:39)

Merib-Baal or
Mephibosheth
(2 Sam. 21:7;
1 Chr. 8:34)

Micah
(1 Chr. 9:40)

```
▭  Women
---  Marital Relationships
▭  Descendant
```

So he said, "You have dealt treacherously; roll a large stone to me this day." [34]Then Saul said, "Disperse yourselves among the people, and say to them, 'Bring me here every man's ox and every man's sheep, slaughter *them* here, and eat; and do not sin against the LORD by eating with the blood.'" So every one of the people brought his ox with him that night, and slaughtered *it* there. [35]Then Saul built an altar to the LORD. This was the first altar that he built to the LORD.

[36]Now Saul said, "Let us go down after the Philistines by night, and plunder them until the morning light; and let us not leave a man of them."

And they said, "Do whatever seems good to you."

Then the priest said, "Let us draw near to God here."

[37]So Saul asked counsel of God, "Shall I go down after the Philistines? Will You deliver them into the hand of Israel?" But He did not answer him that day. [38]And Saul said, "Come over here, all you chiefs of the people, and know and see what this sin was today. [39]For *as* the LORD lives, who saves Israel, though it be in Jonathan my son, he shall surely die." But not a man among all the people answered him. [40]Then he said to all Israel, "You be on one side, and my son Jonathan and I will be on the other side."

And the people said to Saul, "Do what seems good to you."

[41]Therefore Saul said to the LORD God of Israel, "Give a perfect *lot*."a So Saul and Jonathan were taken, but the people escaped. [42]And Saul said,

14:41aFollowing Masoretic Text and Targum; Septuagint and Vulgate read *Why do You not answer Your servant today? If the injustice is with me or Jonathan my son, O LORD God of Israel, give proof; and if You say it is with Your people Israel, give holiness.*

"Cast *lots* between my son Jonathan and me." So Jonathan was taken. 43Then Saul said to Jonathan, "Tell me what you have done."

And Jonathan told him, and said, "I only tasted a little honey with the end of the rod that *was* in my hand. So now I must die!"

44Saul answered, "God do so and more also; for you shall surely die, Jonathan."

45But the people said to Saul, "Shall Jonathan die, who has accomplished this great deliverance in Israel? Certainly not! *As* the LORD lives, not one hair of his head shall fall to the ground, for he has worked with God this day." So the people rescued Jonathan, and he did not die.

46Then Saul returned from pursuing the Philistines, and the Philistines went to their own place.

Saul's Continuing Wars

47So Saul established his sovereignty over Israel, and fought against all his enemies on every side, against Moab, against the people of Ammon, against Edom, against the kings of Zobah, and against the Philistines. Wherever he turned, he harassed *them*.ᵃ 48And he gathered an army and attacked the Amalekites, and delivered Israel from the hands of those who plundered them.

49The sons of Saul were Jonathan, Jishui,ᵃ and Malchishua. And the names of his two daughters *were these:* the name of the firstborn Merab, and the name of the younger Michal. 50The name of Saul's wife *was* Ahinoam the daughter of Ahimaaz. And the name of the commander of his army *was* Abner the son of Ner, Saul's uncle. 51Kish *was* the father of Saul, and Ner the father of Abner *was* the son of Abiel.

52Now there was fierce war with the Philistines all the days of Saul. And when Saul saw any strong man or any valiant man, he took him for himself.

Saul Spares King Agag

15 Samuel also said to Saul, "The LORD sent me to anoint you king over His people, over Israel. Now therefore, heed the voice of the words of the LORD. 2Thus says the LORD of hosts: 'I will punish Amalek *for* what he did to Israel, how he ambushed him on the way when he came up from Egypt. 3Now go and attack Amalek, and utterly destroy all that they have, and do not spare them.

But kill both man and woman, infant and nursing child, ox and sheep, camel and donkey.' "

4So Saul gathered the people together and numbered them in Telaim, two hundred thousand foot soldiers and ten thousand men of Judah. 5And Saul came to a city of Amalek, and lay in wait in the valley.

6Then Saul said to the Kenites, "Go, depart, get down from among the Amalekites, lest I destroy you with them. For you showed kindness to all the children of Israel when they came up out of Egypt." So the Kenites departed from among the Amalekites. 7And Saul attacked the Amalekites, from Havilah all the way to Shur, which is east of Egypt. 8He also took Agag king of the Amalekites alive, and utterly destroyed all the people with the edge of the sword. 9But Saul and the people spared Agag and the best of the sheep, the oxen, the fatlings, the lambs, and all *that was* good, and were unwilling to utterly destroy them. But everything despised and worthless, that they utterly destroyed.

Saul Rejected as King

10Now the word of the LORD came to Samuel, saying, 11"I greatly regret that I have set up Saul *as* king, for he has turned back from following Me, and has not performed My commandments." And it grieved Samuel, and he cried out to the LORD all night. 12So when Samuel rose early in the morning to meet Saul, it was told Samuel, saying, "Saul went to Carmel, and indeed, he set up a monument for himself; and he has gone on around, passed by, and gone down to Gilgal." 13Then Samuel went to Saul, and Saul said to him, "Blessed *are* you of the LORD! I have performed the commandment of the LORD."

14But Samuel said, "What then *is* this bleating of the sheep in my ears, and the lowing of the oxen which I hear?"

15And Saul said, "They have brought them from the Amalekites; for the people spared the best of the sheep and the oxen, to sacrifice to the LORD your God; and the rest we have utterly destroyed."

14:47 ªSeptuagint and Vulgate read *prospered.* **14:49** ªCalled *Abinadab* in 1 Chronicles 8:33 and 9:39

15:3 The Amalekites, descendants of Esau (Gen. 36:12), were put under divine judgment by God after they attacked Israel at Rephidim during the time of the Exodus (Ex. 17:8–16). Saul was commanded to carry out this judgment, putting the Amalekites under the ban (Heb. *cherem*). Such action meant that the city, people, animals, and possessions were devoted to the Lord for destruction (see Deut. 7:2–6; 12:2, 3; 20:16–18). The destruction of all people and goods removed any financial motivation for the war, making it solely a "holy war" divinely planned and executed. Some are troubled that a loving God could give such a command. But to be consistent with Scripture it must be remembered that God, while graciously longsuffering, is also just and judges sin (1 Sam. 15:2, 18). Furthermore, the total circumstances surrounding this judgment are unknown. For example, consider the extent of evil among the Amalekites. They were responsible for the contamination of surrounding peoples, especially Israel, and they threatened painful losses of, if not extermination for, the nation of Israel. Since religious aspects were a part of almost all wars in the ancient Near East, the battlefield was often viewed as a place of divine retribution (see also Rom. 9:15–24).

[16]Then Samuel said to Saul, "Be quiet! And I will tell you what the LORD said to me last night." And he said to him, "Speak on."

[17]So Samuel said, "When you *were* little in your own eyes, *were* you not head of the tribes of Israel? And did not the LORD anoint you king over Israel? [18]Now the LORD sent you on a mission, and said, 'Go, and utterly destroy the sinners, the Amalekites, and fight against them until they are consumed.' [19]Why then did you not obey the voice of the LORD? Why did you swoop down on the spoil, and do evil in the sight of the LORD?"

[20]And Saul said to Samuel, "But I have obeyed the voice of the LORD, and gone on the mission on which the LORD sent me, and brought back Agag king of Amalek; I have utterly destroyed the Amalekites. [21]But the people took of the plunder, sheep and oxen, the best of the things which should have been utterly destroyed, to sacrifice to the LORD your God in Gilgal."

[22]So Samuel said:

"Has the LORD *as great* delight in burnt offerings
    and sacrifices,
As in obeying the voice of the LORD?
Behold, to obey is better than sacrifice,
And to heed than the fat of rams.
[23]For rebellion *is as* the sin of witchcraft,
    And stubbornness *is as* iniquity and idolatry.
Because you have rejected the word of the
    LORD,
He also has rejected you from *being* king."

[24]Then Saul said to Samuel, "I have sinned, for I have transgressed the commandment of the LORD and your words, because I feared the people and obeyed their voice. [25]Now therefore, please pardon my sin, and return with me, that I may worship the LORD."

[26]But Samuel said to Saul, "I will not return with you, for you have rejected the word of the LORD, and the LORD has rejected you from being king over Israel."

[27]And as Samuel turned around to go away, *Saul* seized the edge of his robe, and it tore. [28]So Samuel said to him, "The LORD has torn the kingdom of Israel from you today, and has given it to a neighbor of yours, *who is* better than you. [29]And also the Strength of Israel will not lie nor relent. For He *is* not a man, that He should relent."

[30]Then he said, "I have sinned; *yet* honor me now, please, before the elders of my people and before Israel, and return with me, that I may worship the LORD your God." [31]So Samuel turned back after Saul, and Saul worshiped the LORD.

[32]Then Samuel said, "Bring Agag king of the Amalekites here to me." So Agag came to him cautiously.

And Agag said, "Surely the bitterness of death is past."

[33]But Samuel said, "As your sword has made women childless, so shall your mother be childless among women." And Samuel hacked Agag in pieces before the LORD in Gilgal.

[34]Then Samuel went to Ramah, and Saul went up to his house at Gibeah of Saul. [35]And Samuel went no more to see Saul until the day of his death. Nevertheless Samuel mourned for Saul, and the LORD regretted that He had made Saul king over Israel.

David Anointed King

16 Now the LORD said to Samuel, "How long will you mourn for Saul, seeing I have rejected him from reigning over Israel? Fill your horn with oil, and go; I am sending you to Jesse the Bethlehemite. For I have provided Myself a king among his sons."

[2]And Samuel said, "How can I go? If Saul hears *it*, he will kill me."

But the LORD said, "Take a heifer with you, and say, 'I have come to sacrifice to the LORD.' [3]Then invite Jesse to the sacrifice, and I will show you what you shall do; you shall anoint for Me the one I name to you."

[4]So Samuel did what the LORD said, and went to Bethlehem. And the elders of the town trembled at his coming, and said, "Do you come peaceably?"

[5]And he said, "Peaceably; I have come to sacrifice to the LORD. Sanctify yourselves, and come with me to the sacrifice." Then he consecrated Jesse and his sons, and invited them to the sacrifice.

[6]So it was, when they came, that he looked at Eliab and said, "Surely the LORD's anointed *is* before Him!"

[7]But the LORD said to Samuel, "Do not look at his appearance or at his physical stature, because I have refused him. For *the LORD does* not *see* as man sees;[a] for man looks at the outward appearance, but the LORD looks at the heart."

16:7 [a]Septuagint reads *For God does not see as man sees;* Targum reads *It is not by the appearance of a man;* Vulgate reads *Nor do I judge according to the looks of a man.*

16:2 Saul's actions had been erratic (1 Sam. 14:24–26), and Samuel's concern over the danger involved in anointing Saul's successor is realistic. The Lord promised to lead Samuel through the difficult situation (1 Sam. 16:3, 12, 17). The Lord gave Samuel another legitimate reason for going to Bethlehem so that the prophet would not attract attention when he anointed David (vv. 2, 3). Sacrifices were offered at different places after the ark had been removed from the tabernacle. Despite Samuel's sadness over Saul's disobedience and rejection by God and his fear of what Saul would do to him, Samuel still obeyed God's command (vv. 2–4; see Philem. Obedience).

WITCHCRAFT — SORCERY AND MAGIC

Witchcraft is closely associated with goddess worship and radical feminism. Witches claim the "goddess" as a model for the stages of a woman's life. They maintain that the feminine life-force of the universe, the goddess, appears in three forms: the maiden, the mother, and the crone. This triple aspect of the goddess is supposedly intertwined with the cycle of the moon. The waxing moon is the maiden, the full moon is the mother, and the waning moon is the crone. Witches draw meaning from the fact that the moon's twenty-eight day cycle is mirrored by the twenty-eight day menstrual cycle.

Witches characteristically belong to a coven—a small group of no more than thirteen members who meet to cast spells, conduct rituals, or raise a cone of healing energy at the full moon or solstice when the lunar or solar energies are considered to be at their high points.

"White" magic is somewhat related to but contrasted with "black" magic and blatant Satanism. Black magic attempts to produce evil results through such methods as curses, spells, and alliance with evil spirits. White magic tries to undo curses and spells and to use occult means (gods, demons, spirits, or "forces") for what the coven perceives to be the good of themselves or others. Rituals are used in both black and white magic to bend psychic force to the will of those in a coven.

Witchcraft, sorcery, and magic are always condemned in Scripture (see Lev. 19:26; 20:27; Deut. 18:10–14; Judg. 8:21, 26; 2 Kin. 9:22; Is. 3:18–23; Ezek. 13:17–23; Mic. 5:12).

See also Gal. 5:20; notes on Goddess Religion (Ex. 20); The Occult (Deut. 18); portrait of the Medium of En Dor (1 Sam. 28).

8So Jesse called Abinadab, and made him pass before Samuel. And he said, "Neither has the LORD chosen this one." 9Then Jesse made Shammah pass by. And he said, "Neither has the LORD chosen this one." 10Thus Jesse made seven of his sons pass before Samuel. And Samuel said to Jesse, "The LORD has not chosen these." 11And Samuel said to Jesse, "Are all the young men here?" Then he said, "There remains yet the youngest, and there he is, keeping the sheep."

And Samuel said to Jesse, "Send and bring him. For we will not sit down[a] till he comes here." 12So he sent and brought him in. Now he *was* ruddy, with bright eyes, and good-looking. And the LORD said, "Arise, anoint him; for this *is* the one!" 13Then Samuel took the horn of oil and anointed him in the midst of his brothers; and the Spirit of the LORD came upon David from that day forward. So Samuel arose and went to Ramah.

A Distressing Spirit Troubles Saul

14But the Spirit of the LORD departed from Saul, and a distressing spirit from the LORD troubled him. 15And Saul's servants said to him, "Surely, a distressing spirit from God is troubling you. 16Let our master now command your servants, *who are* before you, to seek out a man *who is* a skillful player on the harp. And it shall be that he will play it with his hand when the distressing spirit from God is upon you, and you shall be well."

17So Saul said to his servants, "Provide me now a man who can play well, and bring *him* to me." 18Then one of the servants answered and said, "Look, I have seen a son of Jesse the Bethlehemite, *who is* skillful in playing, a mighty man of valor, a

••••••••••••••••••
16:11 aFollowing Septuagint and Vulgate; Masoretic Text reads *turn around*; Targum and Syriac read *turn away*.

16:11 David is introduced as a shepherd tending his father's flock. In the ancient world, "shepherd" was often used as a metaphor for a ruler. In the OT and NT, God's people are by analogy described as a flock, while God's representatives are called shepherds (2 Sam. 5:2; 7:7, 8; Ps. 23:1; 78:71, 72; Ezek. 34:1–31; John 10:1–18). David reflected on the model of God Himself as a Shepherd (Ps. 23). The shepherd/flock image is a recurring theme associated with David, as it is with the Lord Himself (see 1 Sam. 17:15, 20, 28, 34, 40; 2 Sam. 5:2; 7:8; Ezek. 34:23).

16:12 God sought out a man after his own heart for Israel's next king (1 Sam. 13:14). Above all else this description meant reverencing and obeying God (see 1 Sam. 2:30; 15:22). The uniqueness of God's perspective was stressed in Samuel's process of reflection as he met the sons of Jesse. Initially, Samuel assumed the new king would look like his predecessor (1 Sam. 16:6). On the contrary, God's concern was the heart.

He "saw" into the heart of the brothers (v. 7; see 1 Kin. 8:39; 1 Chr. 28:9; Luke 16:15). Jesse's son David, was chosen because he was a man after God's own heart. Though chosen, David did not receive the Spirit of the Lord in power until he was officially anointed (1 Sam. 16:13).

16:14 God's judgment upon Saul for his sin and lack of repentance was twofold. God's Spirit departed (v. 14), leaving Saul to rule in his own strength. Saul had already chosen his own way when he rebelled against God's word (vv. 13–15). Instead of God's Spirit, a troubling (lit., a "distressing," "injurious," or "evil") spirit from the Lord came to Saul, causing him to be severely miserable and depressed, even to the point of madness (vv. 14, 23; see Depression; Ps. 18, Distress). That God used evil spirits to serve Him is seen in the OT (1 Chr. 21:1). This spirit may have been sent to humble Saul so he would turn and seek the Lord's help.

man of war, prudent in speech, and a handsome person; and the LORD is with him."

[19]Therefore Saul sent messengers to Jesse, and said, "Send me your son David, who is with the sheep." [20]And Jesse took a donkey loaded with bread, a skin of wine, and a young goat, and sent them by his son David to Saul. [21]So David came to Saul and stood before him. And he loved him greatly, and he became his armorbearer. [22]Then Saul sent to Jesse, saying, "Please let David stand before me, for he has found favor in my sight." [23]And so it was, whenever the spirit from God was upon Saul, that David would take a harp and play it with his hand. Then Saul would become refreshed and well, and the distressing spirit would depart from him.

David and Goliath

17Now the Philistines gathered their armies together to battle, and were gathered at Sochoh, which belongs to Judah; they encamped between Sochoh and Azekah, in Ephes Dammim. [2]And Saul and the men of Israel were gathered together, and they encamped in the Valley of Elah, and drew up in battle array against the Philistines. [3]The Philistines stood on a mountain on one side, and Israel stood on a mountain on the other side, with a valley between them.

[4]And a champion went out from the camp of the Philistines, named Goliath, from Gath, whose height was six cubits and a span. [5]He had a bronze helmet on his head, and he was armed with a coat of mail, and the weight of the coat was five thousand shekels of bronze. [6]And he had bronze armor on his legs and a bronze javelin between his shoulders. [7]Now the staff of his spear was like a weaver's beam, and his iron spearhead weighed six hundred shekels; and a shield-bearer went before him. [8]Then he stood and cried out to the armies of Israel, and said to them, "Why have you come out to line up for battle? Am I not a Philistine, and you the servants of Saul? Choose a man for yourselves, and let him come down to me. [9]If he is able to fight with me and kill me, then we will be your servants. But if I prevail against him and kill him, then you shall be our servants and serve us." [10]And the Philistine said, "I defy the armies of Israel this day; give me a man, that we may fight together." [11]When Saul and all Israel heard these words of the Philistine, they were dismayed and greatly afraid.

[12]Now David was the son of that Ephrathite of Bethlehem Judah, whose name was Jesse, and who had eight sons. And the man was old, advanced in years, in the days of Saul. [13]The three oldest sons of Jesse had gone to follow Saul to the battle. The names of his three sons who went to the battle were Eliab the firstborn, next to him Abinadab, and the third Shammah. [14]David was the youngest. And the three oldest followed Saul. [15]But David occasionally went and returned from Saul to feed his father's sheep at Bethlehem.

[16]And the Philistine drew near and presented himself forty days, morning and evening.

[17]Then Jesse said to his son David, "Take now for your brothers an ephah of this dried grain and these ten loaves, and run to your brothers at the camp. [18]And carry these ten cheeses to the captain of their thousand, and see how your brothers fare, and bring back news of them." [19]Now Saul and they and all the men of Israel were in the Valley of Elah, fighting with the Philistines.

[20]So David rose early in the morning, left the sheep with a keeper, and took the things and went as Jesse had commanded him. And he came to the camp as the army was going out to the fight and shouting for the battle. [21]For Israel and the Philistines had drawn up in battle array, army against army. [22]And David left his supplies in the hand of the supply keeper, ran to the army, and came and greeted his brothers. [23]Then as he talked with them, there was the champion, the Philistine of Gath, Goliath by name, coming up from the armies of the Philistines; and he spoke according to the same words. So David heard them. [24]And all the men of Israel, when they saw the man, fled from him and were dreadfully afraid. [25]So the men of Israel said, "Have you seen this man who has come up? Surely he has come up to defy Israel; and it shall be that the man who kills him the king will enrich with great riches, will give him his daughter, and give his father's house exemption from taxes in Israel."

[26]Then David spoke to the men who stood by him, saying, "What shall be done for the man who kills this Philistine and takes away the reproach from Israel? For who is this uncircumcised Philistine, that he should defy the armies of the living God?"

[27]And the people answered him in this manner, saying, "So shall it be done for the man who kills him."

17:8 One form of warfare between nations during this period was to select a warrior from one nation who would "duel" with the champion of the other nation. The loser's nation was to submit to that of the winner. Often, the champion was the king of the nation since he was the chief of the army and normally a strong warrior. In the battle between the Israelites and Philistines, Saul himself might have been expected to confront Goliath. But once again Saul forfeited an opportunity to achieve victory by relying upon himself instead of God (compare 1 Sam. 13; 14, especially 13:13, note). David, the shepherd, accepted the blasphemous challenge of the more than nine-foot-tall giant, Goliath (1 Sam. 17:32). The success of David was not his own. Like Jonathan before him (1 Sam. 14:6), David put his faith in God (1 Sam. 17:45-47; see 1 Sam. 14:6, 45). God was the source of David's accomplishment (1 Sam. 17:50).

DEPRESSION · *THE ULTIMATE DESPAIR*

The word "depressed" literally means "pressed down," that is, not up to your usual bounce. Saul was depressed because he felt rejected. He had been chosen to be king and pledged to obey God's Word; but he made his own rules, did not follow the Lord, and when caught, he blamed the people (1 Sam. 15:24).

Samuel, under divine direction, anointed David to be king (1 Sam. 16:13) and even as the Spirit of the Lord came upon David, "the Spirit of the Lord departed from Saul, and a distressing spirit from the Lord troubled him" (1 Sam. 16:14). Such a "distressing spirit" would be understood as depression.

Saul's depression was rooted in the fact that he had disobeyed God's clear direction for his life. David, on the other hand, was rejected by his own family as well as by some of his best friends for following God's leading. When this happened, he cried out to the Lord (Ps. 6:2, 3).

When a woman is troubled with depression, God has a plan for her healing:

1) Long for Him (Ps. 42:1, 2)
2) Call out to Him (Ps. 3:4)
3) Rest in Him (Ps. 3:5; 23:2)
4) Know that He hears (Ps. 6:8; 31:22)
5) Recognize that He sees (Ps. 10:14; 34:15)
6) Acknowledge that He will keep you (Ps. 17:8; 34:18)
7) Praise God (Ps. 35:17, 18; 109:30)
8) Seek restoration and witness to others (Ps. 51:12, 13)
9) Keep praying (Ps. 55:16, 17, 22)

See also Ps. 13:1–6; 69:1–20; 88:4, 6, 15; 102:2; notes on Death (1 Cor. 15); Emotions (Ps. 42); Grief (Is. 53); Mental Health (John 10); Prayer (Jer. 33; Heb. 4; 1 John 5; 3 John); Suffering (Ps. 33; 113; Is. 43; 1 Pet. 5); Tears (Ps. 56)

28Now Eliab his oldest brother heard when he spoke to the men; and Eliab's anger was aroused against David, and he said, "Why did you come down here? And with whom have you left those few sheep in the wilderness? I know your pride and the insolence of your heart, for you have come down to see the battle."

29And David said, "What have I done now? *Is there* not a cause?" 30Then he turned from him toward another and said the same thing; and these people answered him as the first ones *did.*

31Now when the words which David spoke were heard, they reported *them* to Saul; and he sent for him. 32Then David said to Saul, "Let no man's heart fail because of him; your servant will go and fight with this Philistine."

33And Saul said to David, "You are not able to go against this Philistine to fight with him; for you *are* a youth, and he a man of war from his youth."

34But David said to Saul, "Your servant used to keep his father's sheep, and when a lion or a bear came and took a lamb out of the flock, 35I went out after it and struck it, and delivered *the lamb* from its mouth; and when it arose against me, I caught *it* by its beard, and struck and killed it. 36Your servant has killed both lion and bear; and this uncircumcised Philistine will be like one of them, seeing he has defied the armies of the living God."

37Moreover David said, "The LORD, who delivered me from the paw of the lion and from the paw of the bear, He will deliver me from the hand of this Philistine."

And Saul said to David, "Go, and the LORD be with you!"

38So Saul clothed David with his armor, and he put a bronze helmet on his head; he also clothed him with a coat of mail. 39David fastened his sword to his armor and tried to walk, for he had not tested *them.* And David said to Saul, "I cannot walk with these, for I have not tested *them.*" So David took them off.

40Then he took his staff in his hand; and he chose for himself five smooth stones from the brook, and put them in a shepherd's bag, in a pouch which he had, and his sling was in his hand. And he drew near to the Philistine. 41So the Philistine came, and began drawing near to David, and the man who bore the shield *went* before him. 42And when the Philistine looked about and saw David, he disdained him; for he was *only* a youth, ruddy and good-looking. 43So the Philistine said to David, "*Am* I a dog, that you come to me with sticks?" And the Philistine cursed David by his gods. 44And the Philistine said to David, "Come to me, and I will give your flesh to the birds of the air and the beasts of the field!"

⁴⁵Then David said to the Philistine, "You come to me with a sword, with a spear, and with a javelin. But I come to you in the name of the LORD of hosts, the God of the armies of Israel, whom you have defied. ⁴⁶This day the LORD will deliver you into my hand, and I will strike you and take your head from you. And this day I will give the carcasses of the camp of the Philistines to the birds of the air and the wild beasts of the earth, that all the earth may know that there is a God in Israel. ⁴⁷Then all this assembly shall know that the LORD does not save with sword and spear; for the battle *is* the LORD's, and He will give you into our hands."

⁴⁸So it was, when the Philistine arose and came and drew near to meet David, that David hurried and ran toward the army to meet the Philistine. ⁴⁹Then David put his hand in his bag and took out a stone; and he slung *it* and struck the Philistine in his forehead, so that the stone sank into his forehead, and he fell on his face to the earth. ⁵⁰So David prevailed over the Philistine with a sling and a stone, and struck the Philistine and killed him. But *there was* no sword in the hand of David. ⁵¹Therefore David ran and stood over the Philistine, took his sword and drew it out of its sheath and killed him, and cut off his head with it.

And when the Philistines saw that their champion was dead, they fled. ⁵²Now the men of Israel and Judah arose and shouted, and pursued the Philistines as far as the entrance of the valleyᵃ and to the gates of Ekron. And the wounded of the Philistines fell along the road to Shaaraim, even as far as Gath and Ekron. ⁵³Then the children of Israel returned from chasing the Philistines, and they plundered their tents. ⁵⁴And David took the head of the Philistine and brought it to Jerusalem, but he put his armor in his tent.

⁵⁵When Saul saw David going out against the Philistine, he said to Abner, the commander of the army, "Abner, whose son *is* this youth?"

And Abner said, "As your soul lives, O king, I do not know."

⁵⁶So the king said, "Inquire whose son this young man *is*."

⁵⁷Then, as David returned from the slaughter of the Philistine, Abner took him and brought him before Saul with the head of the Philistine in his hand. ⁵⁸And Saul said to him, "Whose son *are* you, young man?"

So David answered, "*I am* the son of your servant Jesse the Bethlehemite."

Saul Resents David

18 Now when he had finished speaking to Saul, the soul of Jonathan was knit to the soul of David, and Jonathan loved him as his own

17:45 The Lord of Hosts (see 1 Sam. 1:11; 4:4; 15:2). This majestic title for God is used in the book which records the beginnings of Israel's monarchy. This is a fitting name for Israel's true King, whose sovereignty could never be overshadowed by an earthly ruler (Josh. 5:14, 15; 2 Sam. 5:10; 7:26; 1 Chr. 17:24; Ps. 24:8–10; Is. 5:7; 6:3, 5; 24:23; Mal. 1:14). Since "hosts" can mean celestial bodies or the armies of heaven or earth, this term describes all the powers under God's command throughout creation, as well as identifying His military role as chief of the armies of Israel.

17:46 David maintained a perspective focused on the Person of God rather than upon the nine-foot-tall giant before him. Though Goliath was carrying an impressive sword, spear, and javelin, David was armed "in the name of the LORD of Hosts" (v. 45). In OT times, the name of a person represented the totality of his being. To David, the Almighty God dwarfed the giant (vv. 26, 36). By claiming the Lord of Hosts as his strength, David declared that Goliath was confronting God Himself (v. 47).

17:55 Saul's ignorance of David's father was not unreasonable, though it appears to conflict with 1 Samuel 16:14–23. Saul was first introduced to David as a shepherd harpist whose music soothed Saul's troubled soul (1 Sam. 16:16–23). At that time, Saul's only interest in David may have been in one who met his need. Now in a different context Saul was very curious about David, the warrior (three times Saul states his desire to know the identity of this "young man," 1 Sam. 17:55, 56, 58; see Saul's policy in 1 Sam. 14:52). Saul was interested in David's family and perhaps his social standing. Also Saul may have forgotten David's father's name in the period between 1 Samuel 16 and 17. Perhaps Saul was eager to learn more of David's background after his victory over Goliath. The conversation between Saul and David was longer than a mere answer to Saul's question would require (1 Sam. 18:1).

18:1 The close bond of friendship between David and Jonathan is described in the phrase, "the soul of Jonathan was knit to the soul of David" (v. 1, Heb. *nephesh*, lit. "soul bound with soul"). The word for "love" here (Heb. *'ahab*) is a term used in political, commercial, and friendship covenants (see 1 Kin. 5:1 for *'ahab* in a treaty/covenant). It bound together the two parties in loyalty and reciprocal responsibility—a relationship in which both parties could depend upon each other. The word is fitting in this context where Jonathan made a covenant of friendship with David (1 Sam. 18:3). The characteristics of commitment, loyalty (1 Sam. 19:1, 4, 5, 7), affection, self-sacrifice, and responsibility understood in such covenants were evidenced in their purest form through the lives of Jonathan and David (see Luke 1, Friendship). The sober sincerity of this relationship was demonstrated by its being stated, then reaffirmed four times (1 Sam. 18:3; 20:16, 42; 23:18). Though the covenant was mutually binding, the circumstances put a heavier burden on Jonathan (see Jonathan's sober vow, 1 Sam. 20:13). As a covenant pledge, Jonathan gave his robe (a symbol of the kingdom, see 1 Sam. 15:27, 28), along with his weapons, to David. This relatively common practice in antiquity indicated transfer of position. Jonathan was likely signifying acknowledgment and acceptance of God's choice of David as king by transferring, with complete disregard of self, his place as heir to the throne to David.

MICHAL *A Scornful Wife*

Michal (lit. "Who is like God?"), the younger daughter of Saul, was in love with David. Saul sought to use this as a snare to lure David to his death (1 Sam. 18:21). David accepted her love to better his position before Saul (1 Sam. 18:26).

Saul feared David, but when he sent soldiers to David's house to kill him, Michal lied and schemed in order to save him. However, by helping David to escape, she lost him. Later, Michal was given away by her father to another man as wife.

During the years of their separation, there is no record of David's concern for Michal or of any attempt on his part to contact her. Fourteen years later and seven years after the death of Saul, David was still not king over all of Israel. As a condition of a treaty with Abner, David demanded the return of Michal in order to stabilize his position over the kingdom. Once again, Michal was used for political advantage. Her brother, Ishbosheth, took Michal from her sobbing husband, Paltiel, and gave her back to David.

In Michal's final encounter with David, she accused him of acting unlike a king when the ark was returned to Jerusalem (2 Sam. 6:20). Her scorn for her husband, who also happened to be God's chosen king, resulted in the loss of her ability to bear children, the ultimate curse for any Hebrew woman (2 Sam. 6:23).

See also 1 Sam. 14:49; 19:8–18; 25:43, 44; 2 Sam. 3:12–16; 6:12–23; notes on Bitterness (Heb. 12); Marriage (2 Sam. 6); Wives (Prov. 31).

soul. ²Saul took him that day, and would not let him go home to his father's house anymore. ³Then Jonathan and David made a covenant, because he loved him as his own soul. ⁴And Jonathan took off the robe that *was* on him and gave it to David, with his armor, even to his sword and his bow and his belt.

⁵So David went out wherever Saul sent him, *and* behaved wisely. And Saul set him over the men of war, and he was accepted in the sight of all the people and also in the sight of Saul's servants. ⁶Now it had happened as they were coming *home,* when David was returning from the slaughter of the Philistine, that the women had come out of all the cities of Israel, singing and dancing, to meet King Saul, with tambourines, with joy, and with musical instruments. ⁷So the women sang as they danced, and said:

"Saul has slain his thousands,
And David his ten thousands."

⁸Then Saul was very angry, and the saying displeased him; and he said, "They have ascribed to David ten thousands, and to me they have ascribed only thousands. Now what more can he have but the kingdom?" ⁹So Saul eyed David from that day forward.

¹⁰And it happened on the next day that the distressing spirit from God came upon Saul, and he prophesied inside the house. So David played *music* with his hand, as at other times; but *there was* a spear in Saul's hand. ¹¹And Saul cast the spear, for he said, "I will pin David to the wall!" But David escaped his presence twice.

¹²Now Saul was afraid of David, because the LORD was with him, but had departed from Saul. ¹³Therefore Saul removed him from his presence, and made him his captain over a thousand; and he went out and came in before the people. ¹⁴And David behaved wisely in all his ways, and the LORD *was* with him. ¹⁵Therefore, when Saul saw that he behaved very wisely, he was afraid of him. ¹⁶But all Israel and Judah loved David, because he went out and came in before them.

David Marries Michal

¹⁷Then Saul said to David, "Here is my older daughter Merab; I will give her to you as a wife. Only be valiant for me, and fight the LORD's battles." For Saul thought, "Let my hand not be against him, but let the hand of the Philistines be against him."

¹⁸So David said to Saul, "Who *am* I, and what *is* my life *or* my father's family in Israel, that I should be son-in-law to the king?" ¹⁹But it happened at the time when Merab, Saul's daughter, should have been given to David, that she was given to Adriel the Meholathite as a wife.

18:5 This significant summary statement obviously postdates the arrival home of the army from the battlefield where David killed Goliath (vv. 6–9). David's increasing popularity and military success is recorded as Saul's schizophrenic behavior is revealed. Saul's attitude toward David had changed from one of love (1 Sam. 16:21) to one of hate (1 Sam. 18:11). Chapter 18 presents Saul as jealous and afraid of David, even desiring to destroy him at times (vv. 8, 9, 11, 12, 15). But this verse indicates there were times when Saul appreciated David enough to reward his service. David's continued triumphs as a warrior are summarized using the root that combines the virtues of success and wisdom (Heb. *skl;* see vv. 14, 15, 30) as characteristic aspects of David's victories.

18:10 See 1 Samuel 16:14, note.

20Now Michal, Saul's daughter, loved David. And they told Saul, and the thing pleased him. 21So Saul said, "I will give her to him, that she may be a snare to him, and that the hand of the Philistines may be against him." Therefore Saul said to David a second time, "You shall be my son-in-law today."

22And Saul commanded his servants, "Communicate with David secretly, and say, 'Look, the king has delight in you, and all his servants love you. Now therefore, become the king's son-in-law.' "

23So Saul's servants spoke those words in the hearing of David. And David said, "Does it seem to you a light thing to be a king's son-in-law, seeing I am a poor and lightly esteemed man?" 24And the servants of Saul told him, saying, "In this manner David spoke."

25Then Saul said, "Thus you shall say to David: 'The king does not desire any dowry but one hundred foreskins of the Philistines, to take vengeance on the king's enemies.' " But Saul thought to make David fall by the hand of the Philistines. 26So when his servants told David these words, it pleased David well to become the king's son-in-law. Now the days had not expired; 27therefore David arose and went, he and his men, and killed two hundred men of the Philistines. And David brought their foreskins, and they gave them in full count to the king, that he might become the king's son-in-law. Then Saul gave him Michal his daughter as a wife.

28Thus Saul saw and knew that the LORD was with David, and that Michal, Saul's daughter, loved him; 29and Saul was still more afraid of David. So Saul became David's enemy continually. 30Then the princes of the Philistines went out to war. And so it was, whenever they went out, that David behaved more wisely than all the servants of Saul, so that his name became highly esteemed.

Saul Persecutes David

19 Now Saul spoke to Jonathan his son and to all his servants, that they should kill David; but Jonathan, Saul's son, delighted greatly in David. 2So Jonathan told David, saying, "My father Saul seeks to kill you. Therefore please be on your guard until morning, and stay in a secret place and hide. 3And I will go out and stand beside my father in the field where you are, and I will speak with my father about you. Then what I observe, I will tell you."

4Thus Jonathan spoke well of David to Saul his father, and said to him, "Let not the king sin against his servant, against David, because he has not sinned against you, and because his works have been very good toward you. 5For he took his life in his hands and killed the Philistine, and the LORD brought about a great deliverance for all Israel. You saw it and rejoiced. Why then will you sin against innocent blood, to kill David without a cause?"

6So Saul heeded the voice of Jonathan, and Saul swore, "As the LORD lives, he shall not be killed." 7Then Jonathan called David, and Jonathan told him all these things. So Jonathan brought David to Saul, and he was in his presence as in times past.

8And there was war again; and David went out and fought with the Philistines, and struck them with a mighty blow, and they fled from him.

9Now the distressing spirit from the LORD came upon Saul as he sat in his house with his spear in his hand. And David was playing music with his hand. 10Then Saul sought to pin David to the wall with the spear, but he slipped away from Saul's presence; and he drove the spear into the wall. So David fled and escaped that night.

11Saul also sent messengers to David's house to watch him and to kill him in the morning. And Michal, David's wife, told him, saying, "If you do not save your life tonight, tomorrow you will be killed." 12So Michal let David down through a window. And he went and fled and escaped. 13And Michal took an image and laid it in the bed, put a cover of goats' hair for his head, and covered it with clothes. 14So when Saul sent messengers to take David, she said, "He is sick."

15Then Saul sent the messengers back to see David, saying, "Bring him up to me in the bed, that I may kill him." 16And when the messengers had come in, there was the image in the bed, with a cover of goats' hair for his head. 17Then Saul said to Michal, "Why have you deceived me like this, and sent my enemy away, so that he has escaped?"

And Michal answered Saul, "He said to me, 'Let me go! Why should I kill you?' "

18So David fled and escaped, and went to Samuel at Ramah, and told him all that Saul had done to him. And he and Samuel went and stayed in Naioth. 19Now it was told Saul, saying, "Take note, David is at Naioth in Ramah!" 20Then Saul

---

18:25 A snare turns to an advantage. Saul offered his daughter at a bride price intended to cost David his life (vv. 21, 25; see Michal). Yet God protected David (v. 27; see also 2 Chr. 16:9), turning Saul's evil plot (1 Sam. 18:25) into an advantage through which David's prestige grew (vv. 27, 28, 30). The event also illustrates the contrast between Saul's malicious pride (vv. 17, 19, 21, 25) and David's humility (vv. 18, 23; see also Prov. 29:23). A tragic aspect of David's success is that it sealed Saul's hatred and fear of David (a fear with deep psychological

roots stemming from Saul's awareness that the Lord had departed from him and was with David, 1 Sam. 18:12, 29).

19:18–24 Saul's prophesying. The passage demonstrates God's power over the hearts of individuals to guide them at will. Thus, not only were Saul's messengers (vv. 20, 21), and finally Saul himself (vv. 22, 23), unable to capture David, but their evil purpose was reversed to bring praise to God. The events demonstrated to Saul that David was God's choice to

sent messengers to take David. And when they saw the group of prophets prophesying, and Samuel standing *as* leader over them, the Spirit of God came upon the messengers of Saul, and they also prophesied. ²¹And when Saul was told, he sent other messengers, and they prophesied likewise. Then Saul sent messengers again the third time, and they prophesied also. ²²Then he also went to Ramah, and came to the great well that *is* at Sechu. So he asked, and said, "Where *are* Samuel and David?"

And *someone* said, "Indeed *they are* at Naioth in Ramah." ²³So he went there to Naioth in Ramah. Then the Spirit of God was upon him also, and he went on and prophesied until he came to Naioth in Ramah. ²⁴And he also stripped off his clothes and prophesied before Samuel in like manner, and lay down naked all that day and all that night. Therefore they say, "*Is* Saul also among the prophets?"ª

Jonathan's Loyalty to David

20 Then David fled from Naioth in Ramah, and went and said to Jonathan, "What have I done? What *is* my iniquity, and what *is* my sin before your father, that he seeks my life?"

²So Jonathan said to him, "By no means! You shall not die! Indeed, my father will do nothing either great or small without first telling me. And why should my father hide this thing from me? It *is* not *so!*"

³Then David took an oath again, and said, "Your father certainly knows that I have found favor in your eyes, and he has said, 'Do not let Jonathan know this, lest he be grieved.' But truly, *as* the LORD lives and *as* your soul lives, *there is* but a step between me and death."

⁴So Jonathan said to David, "Whatever you yourself desire, I will do *it* for you."

⁵And David said to Jonathan, "Indeed tomorrow *is* the New Moon, and I should not fail to sit with the king to eat. But let me go, that I may hide in the field until the third *day* at evening. ⁶If your father misses me at all, then say, 'David earnestly asked *permission* of me that he might run over to Bethlehem, his city, for *there is* a yearly sacrifice there for all the family.' ⁷If he says thus: '*It is* well,' your servant will be safe. But if he is very angry, be sure that evil is determined by him. ⁸Therefore you shall deal kindly with your servant, for you have brought your servant into a covenant of the LORD with you. Nevertheless, if there is iniquity in me, kill me yourself, for why should you bring me to your father?"

⁹But Jonathan said, "Far be it from you! For if I knew certainly that evil was determined by my father to come upon you, then would I not tell you?"

¹⁰Then David said to Jonathan, "Who will tell me, or what *if* your father answers you roughly?"

¹¹And Jonathan said to David, "Come, let us go out into the field." So both of them went out into the field. ¹²Then Jonathan said to David: "The LORD God of Israel *is witness!* When I have sounded out my father sometime tomorrow, *or* the third *day*, and indeed *there is* good toward David, and I do not send to you and tell you, ¹³may the LORD do so and much more to Jonathan. But if it pleases my father *to do* you evil, then I will report it to you and send you away, that you may go in safety. And the LORD be with you as He has been with my father. ¹⁴And you shall not only

19:24 ªCompare 1 Samuel 10:12

---

be king. David's future was indicated not just by Samuel's word or by David's popularity with the people but by the expressed will and purpose of God. Before the call of Samuel as prophet, God's word was rare in Israel (1 Sam. 3:1). The passage also suggests that a group of prophets under the leadership of Samuel may have resided in Naioth (a common building or a town, though Samuel had his own house at Ramah, 1 Sam. 7:17). This is the initial hint of an association or School of Prophets, which possibly continued into the days of Elijah and Elisha as the "sons of the prophets" (see 1 Kin. 20:35, 41; 2 Kin. 2:3–15; 4:1, 38; 5:22; 6:1–7; 9:1; Amos 7:14). This group apparently existed to disciple men called of God (some for the prophetic office). The times of Samuel and those of the prophets Elijah and Elisha were both characterized by rampant sin and idolatry.

20:5 A joyous celebration took place at the appearance of the new moon (Num. 10:10). Burnt offerings were offered in the midst of the feast as a monthly reminder that the Lord was their God (Num. 28:14). When Samuel was a boy, the normal place of the feast was Shiloh, the place of the tabernacle (1 Sam. 1:3). But in David's day, since Shiloh had been destroyed, the sacrifices were offered in the home towns of the celebrants.

20:13 The close relationship between Jonathan and David was underscored when the stark reality that Saul was seeking to take David's life became evident to David (vv. 1–17; 1 Sam. 19:10, 11) but not to Jonathan (1 Sam. 20:2). Even so Jonathan promised to be loyal. His dependence upon the sovereignty of God in terms of the immediate danger facing David was evident (v. 22). Agreeing with others that the Lord was with David (1 Sam. 16:18; 17:37; 18:12, 14, 28), Jonathan prayed, "the LORD be with you as He has been with my father." This indicates Jonathan's recognition that David, not Jonathan, would be the next king, making Jonathan's love for and protection of David even more remarkable. Reminding David twice of their everlasting covenant of friendship (1 Sam. 20:17, 23; see 1 Sam. 18:3), Jonathan asked that it be extended to include that David would never cut off his kindness to Jonathan's line (1 Sam. 20:15; 24:21; 2 Sam. 9:3). Since mutual responsibilities were involved in such covenants, Jonathan asked David to vow agreement. For both men the Lord was "between you and me forever" as witness and judge should one of them break this covenant (see v. 23; Gen. 31:48–50). David kept his vow of kindness in his treatment of Jonathan's son, Mephibosheth (2 Sam. 9:3–7; 21:7).

show me the kindness of the LORD while I still live, that I may not die; [15]but you shall not cut off your kindness from my house forever, no, not when the LORD has cut off every one of the enemies of David from the face of the earth." [16]So Jonathan made *a covenant* with the house of David, *saying*, "Let the LORD require *it* at the hand of David's enemies."

[17]Now Jonathan again caused David to vow, because he loved him; for he loved him as he loved his own soul. [18]Then Jonathan said to David, "Tomorrow *is* the New Moon; and you will be missed, because your seat will be empty. [19]And *when* you have stayed three days, go down quickly and come to the place where you hid on the day of the deed; and remain by the stone Ezel. [20]Then I will shoot three arrows to the side, as though I shot at a target; [21]and there I will send a lad, *saying*, 'Go, find the arrows.' If I expressly say to the lad, 'Look, the arrows *are* on this side of you; get them and come'— then, as the LORD lives, *there is* safety for you and no harm. [22]But if I say thus to the young man, 'Look, the arrows *are* beyond you'— go your way, for the LORD has sent you away. [23]And as for the matter which you and I have spoken of, indeed the LORD *be* between you and me forever."

[24]Then David hid in the field. And when the New Moon had come, the king sat down to eat the feast. [25]Now the king sat on his seat, as at other times, on a seat by the wall. And Jonathan arose,[a] and Abner sat by Saul's side, but David's place was empty. [26]Nevertheless Saul did not say anything that day, for he thought, "Something has happened to him; he *is* unclean, surely he *is* unclean." [27]And it happened the next day, the second *day* of the month, that David's place was empty. And Saul said to Jonathan his son, "Why has the son of Jesse not come to eat, either yesterday or today?"

[28]So Jonathan answered Saul, "David earnestly asked *permission* of me *to go* to Bethlehem. [29]And he said, 'Please let me go, for our family has a sacrifice in the city, and my brother has commanded me *to be there.* And now, if I have found favor in your eyes, please let me get away and see my brothers.' Therefore he has not come to the king's table."

[30]Then Saul's anger was aroused against Jonathan, and he said to him, "You son of a perverse, rebellious *woman!* Do I not know that you have chosen the son of Jesse to your own shame and to the shame of your mother's nakedness? [31]For as long as the son of Jesse lives on the earth, you shall not be established, nor your kingdom. Now therefore, send and bring him to me, for he shall surely die."

[32]And Jonathan answered Saul his father, and said to him, "Why should he be killed? What has he done?" [33]Then Saul cast a spear at him to kill him, by which Jonathan knew that it was determined by his father to kill David.

[34]So Jonathan arose from the table in fierce anger, and ate no food the second day of the month, for he was grieved for David, because his father had treated him shamefully.

[35]And so it was, in the morning, that Jonathan went out into the field at the time appointed with David, and a little lad *was* with him. [36]Then he said to his lad, "Now run, find the arrows which I shoot." As the lad ran, he shot an arrow beyond him. [37]When the lad had come to the place where the arrow was which Jonathan had shot, Jonathan cried out after the lad and said, "*Is* not the arrow beyond you?" [38]And Jonathan cried out after the lad, "Make haste, hurry, do not delay!" So Jonathan's lad gathered up the arrows and came back to his master. [39]But the lad did not know anything. Only Jonathan and David knew of the matter. [40]Then Jonathan gave his weapons to his lad, and said to him, "Go, carry *them* to the city."

[41]As soon as the lad had gone, David arose from *a place* toward the south, fell on his face to the ground, and bowed down three times. And they kissed one another; and they wept together, but David more so. [42]Then Jonathan said to David, "Go in peace, since we have both sworn in the name of the LORD, saying, 'May the LORD be between you and me, and between your descendants and my descendants, forever.' " So he arose and departed, and Jonathan went into the city.

David and the Holy Bread

21 Now David came to Nob, to Ahimelech the priest. And Ahimelech was afraid when he met David, and said to him, "Why *are* you alone, and no one is with you?"

21:1 Nob, a city of priests (1 Sam. 22:19), may have been the location of the tabernacle, though not the ark of the covenant (see 1 Sam. 7:2), and the site of legal worship after the destruction of Shiloh (see 1 Sam. 4:22). When David fled from Saul and came to Nob, Ahimelech the priest was fearful and made anxious inquiry of David because he recognized David's authority. Why David resorted to deception at this point is not clear. He may have responded in panic either to get Ahimelech to supply his needs and/or to protect the priest from later accusations concerning knowledge of David's flight. The brief

mention of Doeg anticipated his future merciless role (1 Sam. 22:18, 19). In the twisted mind of the rejected king the presence of David at Nob and the help Ahimelech gave David seemed a conspiracy (1 Sam. 22:8, 13, 16, 17). With total contempt for the priesthood, Saul called for death of the priests (1 Sam. 22:16–18). His Israelite servants refused such a heinous order, but there was no hesitancy on the part of the Edomite Doeg (1 Sam. 20:18), who extended the massacre to all Nob as a city under the ban (see 1 Sam. 15:3, note). This was a further fulfillment of the prophecy against Eli's house

²So David said to Ahimelech the priest, "The king has ordered me on some business, and said to me, 'Do not let anyone know anything about the business on which I send you, or what I have commanded you.' And I have directed *my* young men to such and such a place. ³Now therefore, what have you on hand? Give *me* five *loaves of* bread in my hand, or whatever can be found."

⁴And the priest answered David and said, "*There is* no common bread on hand; but there is holy bread, if the young men have at least kept themselves from women."

⁵Then David answered the priest, and said to him, "Truly, women *have been* kept from us about three days since I came out. And the vessels of the young men are holy, and *the bread is* in effect common, even though it was consecrated in the vessel this day."

⁶So the priest gave him holy *bread;* for there was no bread there but the showbread which had been taken from before the LORD, in order to put hot bread *in its place* on the day when it was taken away.

⁷Now a certain man of the servants of Saul *was* there that day, detained before the LORD. And his name *was* Doeg, an Edomite, the chief of the herdsmen who *belonged* to Saul.

⁸And David said to Ahimelech, "Is there not here on hand a spear or a sword? For I have brought neither my sword nor my weapons with me, because the king's business required haste."

⁹So the priest said, "The sword of Goliath the Philistine, whom you killed in the Valley of Elah, there it is, wrapped in a cloth behind the ephod. If you will take that, take *it.* For *there is* no other except that one here."

And David said, "*There is* none like it; give it to me."

David Flees to Gath

¹⁰Then David arose and fled that day from before Saul, and went to Achish the king of Gath. ¹¹And the servants of Achish said to him, "*Is* this not David the king of the land? Did they not sing of him to one another in dances, saying:

'Saul has slain his thousands,
And David his ten thousands'?"[a]

¹²Now David took these words to heart, and was very much afraid of Achish the king of Gath. ¹³So he changed his behavior before them, pretended madness in their hands, scratched on the doors of the gate, and let his saliva fall down on his beard. ¹⁴Then Achish said to his servants, "Look, you see the man is insane. Why have you brought him to me? ¹⁵Have I need of madmen, that you have brought this *fellow* to play the madman in my presence? Shall this *fellow* come into my house?"

David's Four Hundred Men

22David therefore departed from there and escaped to the cave of Adullam. So when his brothers and all his father's house heard *it,* they went down there to him. ²And everyone *who was* in distress, everyone who *was* in debt, and everyone *who was* discontented gathered to him. So he became captain over them. And there were about four hundred men with him.

³Then David went from there to Mizpah of Moab; and he said to the king of Moab, "Please let my father and mother come here with you, till I know what God will do for me." ⁴So he brought them before the king of Moab, and they dwelt with him all the time that David was in the stronghold.

⁵Now the prophet Gad said to David, "Do not stay in the stronghold; depart, and go to the land of Judah." So David departed and went into the forest of Hereth.

Saul Murders the Priests

⁶When Saul heard that David and the men who *were* with him had been discovered— now Saul was staying in Gibeah under a tamarisk tree in Ramah, with his spear in his hand, and all his servants standing about him— ⁷then Saul said to his servants who stood about him, "Hear now, you Benjamites! Will the son of Jesse give every one of you fields and vineyards, *and* make you all captains of thousands and captains of hundreds? ⁸All of you have conspired against me, and *there is* no one who reveals to me that my son has made a covenant

·····················

21:11 ªCompare 1 Samuel 18:7

(1 Sam. 2:31–33; 4:11, 18; 1 Kin. 2:26, 27). When David learned of the disaster through Abiathar, he confessed that he was ultimately responsible for it. This is a tragic example of how sin affects others. David assured Abiathar safety because David was sure of divine protection (1 Sam. 22:23).

21:4 The holy bread or "consecrated bread" was set apart for use in the tabernacle and was only to be eaten by the priests (Ex. 25:30; Lev. 24:5–9). Ahimelech apparently realized that moral obligation to preserve David's life superseded the ceremonial regulation concerning the bread, a conclusion Jesus honored in the NT (Matt. 12:3, 4; Mark 2:25, 26). The issue

here does not involve God's moral law, which is immutable. After David's men were ceremonially clean (see Lev. 15:16), Ahimelech offered David the "consecrated bread."

22:2 The early band of men drawn to David were united by all types of adverse circumstances. God later brought an army of valiant warriors to David (see 1 Chr. 12:8).

22:3 David's journey to Moab and his request of the Moabite king to care for his father and mother are of special interest in light of the fact that his great grandmother Ruth was from Moab, meaning that David probably had family ties there.

Make many acts of love, for they set the soul on fire and make it gentle.

Ronda De Sola Chervin

with the son of Jesse; and *there is* not one of you who is sorry for me or reveals to me that my son has stirred up my servant against me, to lie in wait, as *it is* this day."

[9]Then answered Doeg the Edomite, who was set over the servants of Saul, and said, "I saw the son of Jesse going to Nob, to Ahimelech the son of Ahitub. [10]And he inquired of the LORD for him, gave him provisions, and gave him the sword of Goliath the Philistine."

[11]So the king sent to call Ahimelech the priest, the son of Ahitub, and all his father's house, the priests who *were* in Nob. And they all came to the king. [12]And Saul said, "Hear now, son of Ahitub!"

He answered, "Here I am, my lord."

[13]Then Saul said to him, "Why have you conspired against me, you and the son of Jesse, in that you have given him bread and a sword, and have inquired of God for him, that he should rise against me, to lie in wait, as it is this day?"

[14]So Ahimelech answered the king and said, "And who among all your servants *is as* faithful as David, who is the king's son-in-law, who goes at your bidding, and is honorable in your house? [15]Did I then begin to inquire of God for him? Far be it from me! Let not the king impute anything to his servant, *or* to any in the house of my father. For your servant knew nothing of all this, little or much."

[16]And the king said, "You shall surely die, Ahimelech, you and all your father's house!" [17]Then the king said to the guards who stood about him, "Turn and kill the priests of the LORD, because their hand also *is* with David, and because they knew when he fled and did not tell it to me." But the servants of the king would not lift their hands to strike the priests of the LORD. [18]And the king said to Doeg, "You turn and kill the priests!" So Doeg the Edomite turned and struck the priests, and killed on that day eighty-five men who wore a linen ephod. [19]Also Nob, the city of the priests, he struck with the edge of the sword, both men and women, children and nursing infants, oxen and donkeys and sheep—with the edge of the sword.

[20]Now one of the sons of Ahimelech the son of Ahitub, named Abiathar, escaped and fled after David. [21]And Abiathar told David that Saul had killed the LORD's priests. [22]So David said to Abiathar, "I knew that day, when Doeg the Edomite *was* there, that he would surely tell Saul. I have caused *the death* of all the persons of your father's house. [23]Stay with me; do not fear. For he who seeks my life seeks your life, but with me you *shall be* safe."

David Saves the City of Keilah

23 Then they told David, saying, "Look, the Philistines are fighting against Keilah, and they are robbing the threshing floors."

[2]Therefore David inquired of the LORD, saying, "Shall I go and attack these Philistines?"

And the LORD said to David, "Go and attack the Philistines, and save Keilah."

[3]But David's men said to him, "Look, we are afraid here in Judah. How much more then if we go to Keilah against the armies of the Philistines?" [4]Then David inquired of the LORD once again.

And the LORD answered him and said, "Arise, go down to Keilah. For I will deliver the Philistines into your hand." [5]And David and his men went to Keilah and fought with the Philistines, struck them with a mighty blow, and took away their livestock. So David saved the inhabitants of Keilah.

[6]Now it happened, when Abiathar the son of Ahimelech fled to David at Keilah, *that* he went down *with* an ephod in his hand.

[7]And Saul was told that David had gone to Keilah. So Saul said, "God has delivered him into my hand, for he has shut himself in by entering a town that has gates and bars." [8]Then Saul called all the people together for war, to go down to Keilah to besiege David and his men.

[9]When David knew that Saul plotted evil against him, he said to Abiathar the priest, "Bring the ephod here." [10]Then David said, "O LORD God of Israel, Your servant has certainly heard that Saul seeks to come to Keilah to destroy the city for my sake. [11]Will the men of Keilah deliver me into his hand? Will Saul come down, as Your servant has heard? O LORD God of Israel, I pray, tell Your servant."

And the LORD said, "He will come down."

[12]Then David said, "Will the men of Keilah deliver me and my men into the hand of Saul?"

And the LORD said, "They will deliver *you*."

23:9 The use of the ephod helped David realize his dangerous situation. The "yes" or "no" questions assume the use of the Urim and Thummim (see Ex. 28:15; Deut. 33:8, notes). This shows that God knows all the alternatives and is able to reveal them.

¹³So David and his men, about six hundred, arose and departed from Keilah and went wherever they could go. Then it was told Saul that David had escaped from Keilah; so he halted the expedition.

David in Wilderness Strongholds

¹⁴And David stayed in strongholds in the wilderness, and remained in the mountains in the Wilderness of Ziph. Saul sought him every day, but God did not deliver him into his hand. ¹⁵So David saw that Saul had come out to seek his life. And David *was* in the Wilderness of Ziph in a forest.ª ¹⁶Then Jonathan, Saul's son, arose and went to David in the woods and strengthened his hand in God. ¹⁷And he said to him, "Do not fear, for the hand of Saul my father shall not find you. You shall be king over Israel, and I shall be next to you. Even my father Saul knows that." ¹⁸So the two of them made a covenant before the LORD. And David stayed in the woods, and Jonathan went to his own house.

¹⁹Then the Ziphites came up to Saul at Gibeah, saying, "Is David not hiding with us in strongholds in the woods, in the hill of Hachilah, which *is* on the south of Jeshimon? ²⁰Now therefore, O king, come down according to all the desire of your soul to come down; and our part *shall be* to deliver him into the king's hand."

²¹And Saul said, "Blessed *are* you of the LORD, for you have compassion on me. ²²Please go and find out for sure, and see the place where his hideout is, *and* who has seen him there. For I am told he is very crafty. ²³See therefore, and take knowledge of all the lurking places where he hides; and come back to me with certainty, and I will go with you. And it shall be, if he is in the land, that I will search for him throughout all the clansª of Judah."

²⁴So they arose and went to Ziph before Saul. But David and his men *were* in the Wilderness of Maon, in the plain on the south of Jeshimon. ²⁵When Saul and his men went to seek *him,* they told David. Therefore he went down to the rock, and stayed in the Wilderness of Maon. And when Saul heard *that,* he pursued David in the Wilderness of Maon. ²⁶Then Saul went on one side of the mountain, and David and his men on the other side of the mountain. So David made haste to get away from Saul, for Saul and his men were encircling David and his men to take them.

²⁷But a messenger came to Saul, saying, "Hurry and come, for the Philistines have invaded the land!" ²⁸Therefore Saul returned from pursuing David, and went against the Philistines; so they called that place the Rock of Escape.ª ²⁹Then David went up from there and dwelt in strongholds at En Gedi.

David Spares Saul

24 Now it happened, when Saul had returned from following the Philistines, that it was told him, saying, "Take note! David *is* in the Wilderness of En Gedi." ²Then Saul took three thousand chosen men from all Israel, and went to seek David and his men on the Rocks of the Wild Goats. ³So he came to the sheepfolds by the road, where there *was* a cave; and Saul went in to attend to his needs. (David and his men were staying in the recesses of the cave.) ⁴Then the men of David said to him, "This is the day of which the LORD said to you, 'Behold, I will deliver your enemy into your hand, that you may do to him as it seems good to you.' " And David arose and secretly cut off a corner of Saul's robe. ⁵Now it happened afterward that David's heart troubled him because he had cut Saul's *robe.* ⁶And he said to his men, "The LORD forbid that I should do this thing to my master, the LORD's anointed, to stretch out my hand against him, seeing he *is* the anointed of the LORD." ⁷So David restrained his servants with *these* words, and did not allow them to rise against Saul. And Saul got up from the cave and went on *his* way.

⁸David also arose afterward, went out of the cave, and called out to Saul, saying, "My lord the king!" And when Saul looked behind him, David stooped with his face to the earth, and bowed down. ⁹And David said to Saul: "Why do you listen to the words of men who say, 'Indeed David seeks your harm'? ¹⁰Look, this day your eyes have seen that the LORD delivered you today into my hand in the cave, and *someone* urged *me* to kill you. But *my eye* spared you, and I said, 'I will not stretch out my hand against my lord, for he *is* the LORD's anointed.' ¹¹Moreover, my father, see! Yes, see the corner of your robe in my hand! For in that I cut off the corner of your robe, and did not kill you, know and see that *there is* neither evil nor rebellion in my hand, and I have not sinned against you. Yet you hunt my life to take it. ¹²Let the LORD judge between you and me, and let the LORD avenge me on you. But my hand shall not be against you. ¹³As the proverb of the ancients says, 'Wickedness proceeds from the wicked.' But my hand shall not be against you. ¹⁴After whom has the king of Israel come out? Whom do you pursue? A dead dog? A flea? ¹⁵Therefore let the LORD be judge, and judge between you and me, and see and plead my case, and deliver me out of your hand."

23:15 ªOr *in Horesh* **23:23** ªLiterally *thousands* **23:28** ªHebrew *Sela Hammahlekoth*

23:15 Jonathan encouraged David. Jonathan came to David in the wilderness of Ziph in a forest at a time when David was in great need of encouragement that God's will concerning him would be fulfilled (v. 17). Jonathan strengthened David by the

16So it was, when David had finished speaking these words to Saul, that Saul said, "*Is* this your voice, my son David?" And Saul lifted up his voice and wept. 17Then he said to David: "You *are* more righteous than I; for you have rewarded me with good, whereas I have rewarded you with evil. 18And you have shown this day how you have dealt well with me; for when the LORD delivered me into your hand, you did not kill me. 19For if a man finds his enemy, will he let him get away safely? Therefore may the LORD reward you with good for what you have done to me this day. 20And now I know indeed that you shall surely be king, and that the kingdom of Israel shall be established in your hand. 21Therefore swear now to me by the LORD that you will not cut off my descendants after me, and that you will not destroy my name from my father's house."

22So David swore to Saul. And Saul went home, but David and his men went up to the stronghold.

Death of Samuel

25 Then Samuel died; and the Israelites gathered together and lamented for him, and buried him at his home in Ramah. And David arose and went down to the Wilderness of Paran.[a]

David and the Wife of Nabal

2Now *there was* a man in Maon whose business *was* in Carmel, and the man *was* very rich. He had three thousand sheep and a thousand goats. And he was shearing his sheep in Carmel. 3The name of the man *was* Nabal, and the name of his wife Abigail. And *she was* a woman of good understanding and beautiful appearance; but the man *was* harsh and evil in *his* doings. He *was of the house of Caleb.*

4When David heard in the wilderness that Nabal was shearing his sheep, 5David sent ten young men; and David said to the young men, "Go up to Carmel, go to Nabal, and greet him in my name. 6And thus you shall say to him who lives *in prosperity:* 'Peace *be* to you, peace to your house, and peace to all that you have! 7Now I have heard that you have shearers. Your shepherds were with us, and we did not hurt them, nor was there anything missing from them all the while they were in Carmel. 8Ask your young men, and they will tell you. Therefore let *my* young men find favor in your eyes, for we come on a feast day. Please give whatever comes to your hand to your servants and to your son David.' "

9So when David's young men came, they spoke to Nabal according to all these words in the name of David, and waited.

10Then Nabal answered David's servants, and said, "Who *is* David, and who *is* the son of Jesse? There are many servants nowadays who break away each one from his master. 11Shall I then take my bread and my water and my meat that I have killed for my shearers, and give *it* to men when I do not know where they *are* from?"

12So David's young men turned on their heels and went back; and they came and told him all these words. 13Then David said to his men, "Every man gird on his sword." So every man girded on his sword, and David also girded on his sword.

25:1 [a]Following Masoretic Text, Syriac, Targum, and Vulgate; Septuagint reads *Maon.*

---

promises of God, reminding David of the Lord's concern that Saul would not find him, and of the fact that he, David, would be king over Israel (see 2 Pet. 1, The Promises of God). Jonathan's selfless perspective is an OT example of Philippians 2:2–4, and his friendship for David embodies the concept of Proverbs 18:24. After making a covenant together, they parted, perhaps never to see each other again since no other meetings are recorded. They modeled a friendship to be emulated by all generations (see Luke 1, Friendship).

24:1 En Gedi was a lovely oasis with a freshwater spring above the bleak shores of the Dead Sea. The area around the spring stands in stark contrast to the surrounding desert. The limestone rock in the region is permeated with caves, providing good places to hide.

24:6 David's reverence for God and His sovereignty over the affairs of mankind and history influenced his actions even in the midst of severe persecution (see 1 Sam. 24; 26). To David's men, Saul's presence inside the same cave in which they were hiding was a door of opportunity from the Lord to get rid of their enemy (1 Sam. 24:4); but to David, Saul was the Lord's anointed, both by divine appointment and human proclamation (v. 6; see also 1 Sam. 9:16; 10:1, 24; 11:15). Thus David felt he had no right to lay a hand against "the LORD's anointed," a phrase used repeatedly (1 Sam. 24:6, 10; 26:9, 11, 16, 23). "David's heart troubled him" after he cut off a corner

of Saul's robe (1 Sam. 24:5), for David considered this act as harm done to the king himself, and therefore sin on David's part. Restraining his men, David solemnly vowed he would never do harm to his master, for in no way should he harm one whom God had placed in authority (v. 7). In no way did this attitude toward Saul condone the wretched sinfulness of Saul's life. Rather, out of respect for God, David refused to take matters into his own hands (vv. 12, 15; 1 Sam. 26:9); instead he trusted God to bring about justice (Deut. 32:35; Rom. 12:17–21).

25:13 David's impassioned desire to take immediate vengeance upon Nabal for his insult and cruelty to David and his men, if carried out, would have caused David to sin against the Lord and His people. God preserved David from shedding innocent blood (a major theme in 1 Sam. 24—26 but perhaps most obvious in 1 Sam. 25) through the swift and wise intervention of Nabal's wife Abigail, a woman described as "beautiful" (lit. "lovely in form," the same phrase describing Rachel in Gen. 29:17 and Esther in Esth. 2:7) and good in understanding (2 Chr. 30:22; Ps. 111:10; Prov. 13:15; see also Abigail). Sensing the impending disaster that would come after Nabal repaid David's good with evil (1 Sam. 25:10, 11), a young man in Nabal's household came to Abigail explaining the praiseworthy behavior of David and his men (vv. 15, 16) and imploring her to right the wrong of her husband (vv. 14,

ABIGAIL *An Intelligent Beauty*

Abigail was the intelligent and beautiful wife (1 Sam. 25:3) of Nabal, a wealthy, foolish scoundrel who was harsh and overbearing (1 Sam. 25:3, 17). Although many women are in unhappy marriages by their own choices, Abigail probably entered this union with such a difficult man through no choice of her own, since most marriages in her day were arranged by parents. This woman of faith acted humbly and wisely in giving David and his men food to save the lives of all his household.

After Nabal rudely insulted the future king of Israel and his men, David reacted swiftly, intent on hotheaded vengeance. Forewarned by a servant, Abigail moved with perception and precision to try to avert the extermination of the entire household. She intercepted David with humility and warm hospitality. Her voice was a call to reason, and her manner was altogether disarming. She used all her creativity to minimize the damage done by her foolish husband. In going against Nabal's wishes, she acted to save his life.

How did she dissuade David and his men? She could have been a resentful wife, looking for ways to blame her husband, but her speech was artfully persuasive and honest. She showed deference for her husband by claiming that it was her own oversight that David's men saw Nabal instead of her, perhaps suggesting that she was not available for hospitality (1 Sam. 25:25). Her words were not a betrayal but rather a tactful confession that defused David's anger. She made no effort to deceive her husband but chose wisely the time to give him a full account of what she had done (1 Sam. 25:36, 37). Her conversation with David showed respect for his position and knowledge of his character and actions, resulting in the future king's pronouncement of a threefold blessing: praise to God, gratitude for her advice, and thanksgiving for Abigail herself (1 Sam. 25:32, 33).

When David heard that Nabal had died, he was greatly relieved that he had allowed God to take the vengeance. He also wasted no time in asking Abigail to continue to bless his life as his own wife. She was the one to whom David said, "I . . . respected your person" (1 Sam. 25:35). She had earned from him respect, and she illustrates for wives today vital principles of restraint and proper priorities, as well as the determination to make the best out of a difficult situation.

See also 2 Sam. 3:3; notes on Change Points in Life (Eccl. 3); Decision Making (1 Cor. 8)

And about four hundred men went with David, and two hundred stayed with the supplies.

¹⁴Now one of the young men told Abigail, Nabal's wife, saying, "Look, David sent messengers from the wilderness to greet our master; and he reviled them. ¹⁵But the men *were* very good to us, and we were not hurt, nor did we miss anything as long as we accompanied them, when we were in the fields. ¹⁶They were a wall to us both by night and day, all the time we were with them keeping the sheep. ¹⁷Now therefore, know and consider what you will do, for harm is determined against our master and against all his household. For he *is* such a scoundrel[a] that *one* cannot speak to him."

¹⁸Then Abigail made haste and took two hundred *loaves* of bread, two skins of wine, five sheep already dressed, five seahs of roasted *grain,* one hundred clusters of raisins, and two hundred cakes of figs, and loaded *them* on donkeys. ¹⁹And she said to her servants, "Go on before me; see, I

am coming after you." But she did not tell her husband Nabal.

²⁰So it was, *as* she rode on the donkey, that she went down under cover of the hill; and there were David and his men, coming down toward her, and she met them. ²¹Now David had said, "Surely in vain I have protected all that this *fellow* has in the wilderness, so that nothing was missed of all that *belongs* to him. And he has repaid me evil for good. ²²May God do so, and more also, to the enemies of David, if I leave one male of all who *belong* to him by morning light."

²³Now when Abigail saw David, she dismounted quickly from the donkey, fell on her face before David, and bowed down to the ground. ²⁴So she fell at his feet and said: "On me, my lord, *on me let* this iniquity *be!* And please let your maidservant speak in your ears, and hear the words of

25:17 [a]Literally *son of Belial*

17). As a godly wife, Abigail was first responsible to God, then to her husband. Thus she acted with speed to prepare generous supplies for David and his men with the hope of intercepting them enroute. Encountering the angry army of 400 men, Abigail courageously demonstrated wisdom, respect, and submissiveness as she admonished David not to avenge himself and blot his career with blood guilt (vv. 26, 28, 30, 31). She reminded David that he was the Lord's anointed, fighting the Lord's battles, and thus under God's protection

(vv. 28, 29). David's teachable spirit, illustrated both by his listening to Abigail's words as well as his heeding her advice, is admirable here. David honored Abigail by stating that she had been sent by the Lord to keep him from sin (vv. 32–34). As a responsible wife, Abigail returned to her husband and at an appropriate time told him all she had done, willing to accept any possible consequences. God demonstrated to David that He is faithful to avenge wrong in striking Nabal dead (v. 38).

your maidservant. [25]Please, let not my lord regard this scoundrel Nabal. For as his name *is*, so *is* he: Nabal[a] *is* his name, and folly *is* with him! But I, your maidservant, did not see the young men of my lord whom you sent. [26]Now therefore, my lord, *as* the LORD lives and *as* your soul lives, since the LORD has held you back from coming to bloodshed and from avenging yourself with your own hand, now then, let your enemies and those who seek harm for my lord be as Nabal. [27]And now this present which your maidservant has brought to my lord, let it be given to the young men who follow my lord. [28]Please forgive the trespass of your maidservant. For the LORD will certainly make for my lord an enduring house, because my lord fights the battles of the LORD, and evil is not found in you throughout your days. [29]Yet a man has risen to pursue you and seek your life, but the life of my lord shall be bound in the bundle of the living with the LORD your God; and the lives of your enemies He shall sling out, *as from* the pocket of a sling. [30]And it shall come to pass, when the LORD has done for my lord according to all the good that He has spoken concerning you, and has appointed you ruler over Israel, [31]that this will be no grief to you, nor offense of heart to my lord, either that you have shed blood without cause, or that my lord has avenged himself. But when the LORD has dealt well with my lord, then remember your maidservant."

[32]Then David said to Abigail: "Blessed *is* the LORD God of Israel, who sent you this day to meet me! [33]And blessed *is* your advice and blessed *are* you, because you have kept me this day from coming to bloodshed and from avenging myself with my own hand. [34]For indeed, *as* the LORD God of Israel lives, who has kept me back from hurting you, unless you had hurried and come to meet me, surely by morning light no males would have been left to Nabal!" [35]So David received from her hand what she had brought him, and said to her, "Go up in peace to your house. See, I have heeded your voice and respected your person."

[36]Now Abigail went to Nabal, and there he was, holding a feast in his house, like the feast of a king. And Nabal's heart *was* merry within him, for he *was* very drunk; therefore she told him nothing, little or much, until morning light. [37]So it was, in the morning, when the wine had gone from Nabal, and his wife had told him these things, that his heart died within him, and he became *like* a stone. [38]Then it happened, *after* about ten days, that the LORD struck Nabal, and he died.

[39]So when David heard that Nabal was dead, he said, "Blessed *be* the LORD, who has pleaded the cause of my reproach from the hand of Nabal, and has kept His servant from evil! For the LORD has returned the wickedness of Nabal on his own head."

And David sent and proposed to Abigail, to take her as his wife. [40]When the servants of David had come to Abigail at Carmel, they spoke to her saying, "David sent us to you, to ask you to become his wife."

[41]Then she arose, bowed her face to the earth, and said, "Here is your maidservant, a servant to wash the feet of the servants of my lord." [42]So Abigail rose in haste and rode on a donkey, attended by five of her maidens; and she followed the messengers of David, and became his wife. [43]David also took Ahinoam of Jezreel, and so both of them were his wives.

[44]But Saul had given Michal his daughter, David's wife, to Palti[a] the son of Laish, who *was* from Gallim.

David Spares Saul a Second Time

26 Now the Ziphites came to Saul at Gibeah, saying, "Is David not hiding in the hill of Hachilah, opposite Jeshimon?" [2]Then Saul arose and went down to the Wilderness of Ziph, having three thousand chosen men of Israel with him, to seek David in the Wilderness of Ziph. [3]And Saul encamped in the hill of Hachilah, which *is* opposite Jeshimon, by the road. But David stayed in the wilderness, and he saw that Saul came after him into the wilderness. [4]David therefore sent out spies, and understood that Saul had indeed come.

[5]So David arose and came to the place where Saul had encamped. And David saw the place where Saul lay, and Abner the son of Ner, the commander of his army. Now Saul lay within the camp, with the people encamped all around him. [6]Then David answered, and said to Ahimelech the Hittite and to Abishai the son of Zeruiah, brother of Joab, saying, "Who will go down with me to Saul in the camp?"

And Abishai said, "I will go down with you."

25:25 [a]Literally *Fool*   **25:44** [a]Spelled *Paltiel* in 2 Samuel 3:15

25:27 In the wilderness of Paran, where David fled after Samuel died, roving bands of robbers were very common. Even to the present day, groups of men protect the life and property of wilderness dwellers in return for gifts. Even during David's most difficult times, he took upon himself the care and protection of his countrymen (vv. 7, 8, 15, 16).

25:29 Bound in the bundle of the living is a graphic Hebrew saying used by Abigail to picture the Lord's care for David. This phrase is often found on Jewish tombstones referring to life beyond the grave. The image comes from the custom of bundling valuable possessions to keep them from being broken or damaged. The picture is one of a precious jewel, carefully tied up in a bundle in order to keep it secure and safe. Abigail is saying that David is in God's bundle and is securely protected.

THE MEDIUM OF EN DOR *An Accomplice to Disobedience*

Saul's desperate attempt to learn the future on the eve of battle introduces the medium of En Dor in Scripture. The medium, a mere prop on history's stage, set the scene for Saul's final disobedience to God, which ended in judgment (1 Chr. 10:13, 14). There was a tragic submissiveness in her repeated compliance to Saul's evil request.

The medium lived in eleventh-century B.C. En Dor, a Canaanite city three miles southwest of Mt. Tabor and within the territory of Manasseh's tribe. She practiced divination, a common occupation among ancient Near Eastern women. During Saul's time, the term "medium" meant one who consulted the dead on behalf of the living. Witchcraft had flourished in the nations Israel had been commanded to expel during the conquest of the Promised Land. Manasseh, however, had not driven the Canaanites from En Dor (Josh. 17:12, 13).

Though the medium likely was pagan, she knew her craft was forbidden. All forms of witchcraft had been condemned by God (Ex. 22:18; Lev. 19:31; 20:6, 27; Deut. 18:10–12, 14); Saul himself had exercised civil authority and driven mediums from the land (1 Sam. 28:3). Yet this medium was still in Israel, and her presence was known (1 Sam. 28:7)!

The woman was cautious and suspicious of a trap when asked to bring up Samuel (1 Sam. 28:9). But she quickly complied to Saul's request after being assured of personal safety. God's word was not her authority. Her fearful shock at the sight of Samuel implied that she had never experienced the appearance of such a figure. With sudden clairvoyance, she recognized Saul and boldly challenged the king with own deception (v. 12). Again Saul assured her safety, and she responded to his request.

When Saul fell to the ground in despair, the woman showed natural sympathy as she prepared food to try to revive his strength (v. 22). As she coaxed Saul to respond, she twice referred to herself with the submissive phrase "your maidservant" (vv. 21, 22). Then she put forth her best hospitality in preparing a royal meal.

The medium of En Dor stands, however, as an example of one who, while doing good in practicing human kindness, did evil in disobeying God and sinned in so doing. She will be remembered as one who chose to be an accomplice to King Saul in his personal disobedience to God.

See also 1 Chr. 10:13, 14; notes on The Occult (Deut. 18); Witchcraft (1 Sam. 15)

---

⁷So David and Abishai came to the people by night; and there Saul lay sleeping within the camp, with his spear stuck in the ground by his head. And Abner and the people lay all around him. ⁸Then Abishai said to David, "God has delivered your enemy into your hand this day. Now therefore, please, let me strike him at once with the spear, right to the earth; and I will not *have to strike* him a second time!"

⁹But David said to Abishai, "Do not destroy him; for who can stretch out his hand against the LORD's anointed, and be guiltless?" ¹⁰David said furthermore, "*As* the LORD lives, the LORD shall strike him, or his day shall come to die, or he shall go out to battle and perish. ¹¹The LORD forbid that I should stretch out my hand against the LORD's anointed. But please, take now the spear and the jug of water that *are* by his head, and let us go." ¹²So David took the spear and the jug of water *by* Saul's head, and they got away; and no man saw or knew *it* or awoke. For they *were* all asleep, because a deep sleep from the LORD had fallen on them.

¹³Now David went over to the other side, and stood on the top of a hill afar off, a great distance *being* between them. ¹⁴And David called out to the people and to Abner the son of Ner, saying, "Do you not answer, Abner?"

Then Abner answered and said, "Who *are* you, calling out to the king?"

¹⁵So David said to Abner, "*Are* you not a man? And who *is* like you in Israel? Why then have you not guarded your lord the king? For one of the people came in to destroy your lord the king. ¹⁶This thing that you have done *is* not good. *As* the LORD lives, you deserve to die, because you have not guarded your master, the LORD's anointed. And now see where the king's spear *is,* and the jug of water that *was* by his head."

¹⁷Then Saul knew David's voice, and said, "*Is* that your voice, my son David?"

David said, "*It is* my voice, my lord, O king." ¹⁸And he said, "Why does my lord thus pursue his servant? For what have I done, or what evil *is* in my hand? ¹⁹Now therefore, please, let my lord the king hear the words of his servant: If the LORD has stirred you up against me, let Him accept an offering. But if *it is* the children of men, *may* they *be* cursed before the LORD, for they have driven me out this day from sharing in the inheritance of the LORD, saying, 'Go, serve other gods.' ²⁰So now, do not let my blood fall to the earth before the face of the LORD. For the king of Israel has come out to seek a flea, as when one hunts a partridge in the mountains."

²¹Then Saul said, "I have sinned. Return, my

son David. For I will harm you no more, because my life was precious in your eyes this day. Indeed I have played the fool and erred exceedingly."

²²And David answered and said, "Here is the king's spear. Let one of the young men come over and get it. ²³May the LORD repay every man *for* his righteousness and his faithfulness; for the LORD delivered you into *my* hand today, but I would not stretch out my hand against the LORD's anointed. ²⁴And indeed, as your life was valued much this day in my eyes, so let my life be valued much in the eyes of the LORD, and let Him deliver me out of all tribulation."

²⁵Then Saul said to David, "*May* you *be* blessed, my son David! You shall both do great things and also still prevail."

So David went on his way, and Saul returned to his place.

David Allied with the Philistines

27 And David said in his heart, "Now I shall perish someday by the hand of Saul. *There is* nothing better for me than that I should speedily escape to the land of the Philistines; and Saul will despair of me, to seek me anymore in any part of Israel. So I shall escape out of his hand." ²Then David arose and went over with the six hundred men who *were* with him to Achish the son of Maoch, king of Gath. ³So David dwelt with Achish at Gath, he and his men, each man with his household, *and* David with his two wives, Ahinoam the Jezreelitess, and Abigail the Carmelitess, Nabal's widow. ⁴And it was told Saul that David had fled to Gath; so he sought him no more.

⁵Then David said to Achish, "If I have now found favor in your eyes, let them give me a place in some town in the country, that I may dwell there. For why should your servant dwell in the royal city with you?" ⁶So Achish gave him Ziklag that day. Therefore Ziklag has belonged to the kings of Judah to this day. ⁷Now the time that David dwelt in the country of the Philistines was one full year and four months.

⁸And David and his men went up and raided the Geshurites, the Girzites,ᵃ and the Amalekites. For those *nations were* the inhabitants of the land from of old, as you go to Shur, even as far as the land of Egypt. ⁹Whenever David attacked the land, he left neither man nor woman alive, but took away the sheep, the oxen, the donkeys, the camels, and the apparel, and returned and came to Achish. ¹⁰Then Achish would say, "Where have you made a raid today?" And David would say, "Against the southern *area* of Judah, or against the southern *area* of the Jerahmeelites, or against the southern *area* of the Kenites." ¹¹David would save neither man nor woman alive, to bring *news* to Gath, saying, "Lest they should inform on us, saying, 'Thus David did.' " And thus *was* his behavior all the time he dwelt in the country of the Philistines. ¹²So Achish believed David, saying, "He has made his people Israel utterly abhor him; therefore he will be my servant forever."

28 Now it happened in those days that the Philistines gathered their armies together for war, to fight with Israel. And Achish said to David, "You assuredly know that you will go out with me to battle, you and your men."

²So David said to Achish, "Surely you know what your servant can do."

And Achish said to David, "Therefore I will make you one of my chief guardians forever."

Saul Consults a Medium

³Now Samuel had died, and all Israel had lamented for him and buried him in Ramah, in his own city. And Saul had put the mediums and the spiritists out of the land.

⁴Then the Philistines gathered together, and came and encamped at Shunem. So Saul gathered all Israel together, and they encamped at Gilboa. ⁵When Saul saw the army of the Philistines, he was afraid, and his heart trembled greatly. ⁶And when Saul inquired of the LORD, the LORD did not answer him, either by dreams or by Urim or by the prophets.

⁷Then Saul said to his servants, "Find me a woman who is a medium, that I may go to her and inquire of her."

And his servants said to him, "In fact, *there is* a woman who is a medium at En Dor."

⁸So Saul disguised himself and put on other clothes, and he went, and two men with him; and they came to the woman by night. And he said, "Please conduct a séance for me, and bring up for me the one I shall name to you."

27:8 ᵃOr *Gezrites*

27:6 Ziklag, originally assigned to the tribe of Simeon (Josh. 19:1–5) but later incorporated into the Negev province of Judah (Josh. 15:20–31), was located about 15 miles southeast of Gath. During the reign of Saul, Ziklag was under Philistine control. When David despaired after running from Saul for a long time, he concluded that Saul would kill him. So David left Israel and went to the land of the Philistines (1 Sam. 27:1).

Achish, the king of Gath, knowing the hostility between Saul and David, brought David under his protection as a vassal (v. 5). Achish gave the unoccupied Philistine city of Ziklag to David as a gift for David's presumed loyalty (v. 6). The city became the base from which David and his men successfully attacked various groups who threatened Judah's southern borders (vv. 8, 9, 11).

LEADERSHIP AN AWESOME RESPONSIBILITY

Jewish culture accepted women in positions of leadership. Though highly valued and given a new dignity by Christ, the roles of women were different from those of the men Christ selected for leadership positions. No woman was called, commissioned, or named as one of the twelve apostles. Yet women gave to Christ, served Him, fellowshiped with Him, learned from Him, prayed for Him, and testified of Him as the Savior. They provided leadership through their service.

Leadership is an awesome responsibility, demanding spiritual preparation grounded in consistent personal devotional time (Matt. 6:33). Leaders must also seek godly counsel (Prov. 15:22). They must work willingly and energetically (Eccl. 9:10). Essential ingredients in leadership include creativity, encouragement of others (Prov. 15:23; 25:11), inspiration (Prov. 16:24; 17:22), expressions of gratitude (Ps. 13:6; 69:30; Eph. 5:20), and a servant's heart (Prov. 3:27; Matt. 23:11).

Abigail's unique leadership of her household staff included a servant's heart and boldness, which was tempered with restraint and discretion (1 Sam. 25:23–33). Abigail exerted great influence over David when she persuaded him not to kill Nabal. In fact, David later recognized that Abigail changed the direction of his life.

People must consistently be more important than tasks. Self-sacrifice, gentleness, service without expected reward, patience, kindness, nurturing of relationships, mercy—all these qualities are a part of the Lord's leadership. We see exemplified in the Lord Himself those qualities which are necessary in all godly leaders.

See also Ex. 15:20, 21; charts on Deborah: A Leader is Israel; Esther: A Leader of the Jews; Spiritual Gifts of Women in the Bible (1 Cor. 12); notes on Boldness (Prov. 28); Encouragement (Eph. 4); Spiritual Gifts (Rom. 12); Women's Ministries series (John 4; Acts 2; 1 Cor. 11; Eph. 2; 1 Tim. 3; Titus 2); portraits of Athaliah (2 Kin. 11); Deborah (Judg. 4); Miriam (Ex. 15)

9Then the woman said to him, "Look, you know what Saul has done, how he has cut off the mediums and the spiritists from the land. Why then do you lay a snare for my life, to cause me to die?"

10And Saul swore to her by the LORD, saying, "*As* the LORD lives, no punishment shall come upon you for this thing."

11Then the woman said, "Whom shall I bring up for you?"

And he said, "Bring up Samuel for me."

12When the woman saw Samuel, she cried out with a loud voice. And the woman spoke to Saul, saying, "Why have you deceived me? For you *are* Saul!"

13And the king said to her, "Do not be afraid. What did you see?"

And the woman said to Saul, "I saw a spirit[a] ascending out of the earth."

14So he said to her, "What *is* his form?"

And she said, "An old man is coming up, and he *is* covered with a mantle." And Saul perceived that it *was* Samuel, and he stooped with *his* face to the ground and bowed down.

15Now Samuel said to Saul, "Why have you disturbed me by bringing me up?"

And Saul answered, "I am deeply distressed; for the Philistines make war against me, and God has departed from me and does not answer me anymore, neither by prophets nor by dreams. Therefore I have called you, that you may reveal to me what I should do."

16Then Samuel said: "So why do you ask me, seeing the LORD has departed from you and has become your enemy? 17And the LORD has done for Himself[a] as He spoke by me. For the LORD has torn the kingdom out of your hand and given it to your neighbor, David. 18Because you did not obey the voice of the LORD nor execute His fierce wrath upon Amalek, therefore the LORD has done this thing to you this day. 19Moreover the LORD will also deliver Israel with you into the hand of the Philistines. And tomorrow you and your sons *will be* with me. The LORD will also deliver the army of Israel into the hand of the Philistines."

20Immediately Saul fell full length on the ground, and was dreadfully afraid because of the words of Samuel. And there was no strength in him, for he had eaten no food all day or all night.

21And the woman came to Saul and saw that he was severely troubled, and said to him, "Look, your maidservant has obeyed your voice, and I have put my life in my hands and heeded the words which you spoke to me. 22Now therefore, please, heed also the voice of your maidservant, and let me set a piece of bread before you; and eat, that you may have strength when you go on *your* way."

23But he refused and said, "I will not eat."

So his servants, together with the woman, urged him; and he heeded their voice. Then he arose from the ground and sat on the bed. 24Now the woman had a fatted calf in the house, and she hastened to kill it. And she took flour and kneaded *it*, and baked unleavened bread from it. 25So she brought *it* before Saul and his servants, and they ate. Then they rose and went away that night.

28:13 [a]Hebrew *elohim*   28:17 [a]Or *him*, that is, David

The Philistines Reject David

29 Then the Philistines gathered together all their armies at Aphek, and the Israelites encamped by a fountain which *is* in Jezreel. ²And the lords of the Philistines passed in review by hundreds and by thousands, but David and his men passed in review at the rear with Achish. ³Then the princes of the Philistines said, "What *are* these Hebrews *doing here?*"

And Achish said to the princes of the Philistines, "*Is* this not David, the servant of Saul king of Israel, who has been with me these days, or these years? And to this day I have found no fault in him since he defected *to me.*"

⁴But the princes of the Philistines were angry with him; so the princes of the Philistines said to him, "Make this fellow return, that he may go back to the place which you have appointed for him, and do not let him go down with us to battle, lest in the battle he become our adversary. For with what could he reconcile himself to his master, if not with the heads of these men? ⁵*Is* this not David, of whom they sang to one another in dances, saying:

'Saul has slain his thousands,
And David his ten thousands'?"ᵃ

⁶Then Achish called David and said to him, "Surely, *as* the LORD lives, you have been upright, and your going out and your coming in with me in the army *is* good in my sight. For to this day I have not found evil in you since the day of your coming to me. Nevertheless the lords do not favor you. ⁷Therefore return now, and go in peace, that you may not displease the lords of the Philistines."

⁸So David said to Achish, "But what have I done? And to this day what have you found in your servant as long as I have been with you, that I may not go and fight against the enemies of my lord the king?"

⁹Then Achish answered and said to David, "I know that you *are* as good in my sight as an angel of God; nevertheless the princes of the Philistines have said, 'He shall not go up with us to the battle.' ¹⁰Now therefore, rise early in the morning with your master's servants who have come with you.ᵃ And as soon as you are up early in the morning and have light, depart."

¹¹So David and his men rose early to depart in the morning, to return to the land of the Philistines. And the Philistines went up to Jezreel.

David's Conflict with the Amalekites

30 Now it happened, when David and his men came to Ziklag, on the third day, that the Amalekites had invaded the South and Ziklag, attacked Ziklag and burned it with fire, ²and had taken captive the women and those who *were* there, from small to great; they did not kill anyone, but carried *them* away and went their way. ³So David and his men came to the city, and there it was, burned with fire; and their wives, their sons, and their daughters had been taken captive. ⁴Then David and the people who *were* with him lifted up their voices and wept, until they had no more power to weep. ⁵And David's two wives, Ahinoam the Jezreelitess, and Abigail the widow of Nabal the Carmelite, had been taken captive. ⁶Now David was greatly distressed, for the people spoke of stoning him, because the soul of all the people was grieved, every man for his sons and his daughters. But David strengthened himself in the LORD his God.

⁷Then David said to Abiathar the priest, Ahimelech's son, "Please bring the ephod here to me." And Abiathar brought the ephod to David. ⁸So David inquired of the LORD, saying, "Shall I pursue this troop? Shall I overtake them?"

And He answered him, "Pursue, for you shall surely overtake *them* and without fail recover *all.*"

⁹So David went, he and the six hundred men who *were* with him, and came to the Brook Besor, where those stayed who were left behind. ¹⁰But David pursued, he and four hundred men; for two hundred stayed *behind*, who were so weary that they could not cross the Brook Besor.

¹¹Then they found an Egyptian in the field, and brought him to David; and they gave him bread and he ate, and they let him drink water. ¹²And they gave him a piece of a cake of figs and two clusters of raisins. So when he had eaten, his strength came back to him; for he had eaten no bread nor drunk water for three days and three nights. ¹³Then David said to him, "To whom do you *belong*, and where *are* you from?"

And he said, "I *am* a young man from Egypt, servant of an Amalekite; and my master left me behind, because three days ago I fell sick. ¹⁴We made an invasion of the southern *area* of the Cherethites, in the *territory* which *belongs* to Judah,

---

29:5 ᵃCompare 1 Samuel 18:7   29:10 ᵃFollowing Masoretic Text, Targum, and Vulgate; Septuagint adds *and go to the place which I have selected for you there; and set no bothersome word in your heart, for you are good before me. And rise on your way.*

30:6 With the devastating scene of nothing but their burned city before them and with the loss of their families, the grief of David's men was so overwhelming that they wanted to stone David. David had faced countless trials before. There was a purpose for David's trials in that they made real what David believed (see Ps. 11, Testing). David had learned that in the midst of trials God is trustworthy (1 Sam. 23:27, 28; 25:39). David had developed within himself a pattern for strength because he had come to know God (see Ps. 34; 54; 56; 59). Knowledge of God makes no difference in a life unless it is lived out. Now in this ultimate crisis, "David strengthened himself in the LORD his God."

and of the southern *area* of Caleb; and we burned Ziklag with fire."

[15]And David said to him, "Can you take me down to this troop?"

So he said, "Swear to me by God that you will neither kill me nor deliver me into the hands of my master, and I will take you down to this troop."

[16]And when he had brought him down, there they were, spread out over all the land, eating and drinking and dancing, because of all the great spoil which they had taken from the land of the Philistines and from the land of Judah. [17]Then David attacked them from twilight until the evening of the next day. Not a man of them escaped, except four hundred young men who rode on camels and fled. [18]So David recovered all that the Amalekites had carried away, and David rescued his two wives. [19]And nothing of theirs was lacking, either small or great, sons or daughters, spoil or anything which they had taken from them; David recovered all. [20]Then David took all the flocks and herds they had driven before those *other* livestock, and said, "This *is* David's spoil."

[21]Now David came to the two hundred men who had been so weary that they could not follow David, whom they also had made to stay at the Brook Besor. So they went out to meet David and to meet the people who *were* with him. And when David came near the people, he greeted them. [22]Then all the wicked and worthless men[a] of those who went with David answered and said, "Because they did not go with us, we will not give them *any* of the spoil that we have recovered, except for every man's wife and children, that they may lead *them* away and depart."

[23]But David said, "My brethren, you shall not do so with what the LORD has given us, who has preserved us and delivered into our hand the troop that came against us. [24]For who will heed you in this matter? But as his part *is* who goes down to the battle, so *shall* his part *be* who stays by the supplies; they shall share alike." [25]So it was, from that day forward; he made it a statute and an ordinance for Israel to this day.

[26]Now when David came to Ziklag, he sent *some* of the spoil to the elders of Judah, to his friends, saying, "Here is a present for you from the spoil of the enemies of the LORD"— [27]to *those* who *were* in Bethel, *those* who *were* in Ramoth of the South, *those* who *were* in Jattir, [28]*those* who *were* in Aroer, *those* who *were* in Siphmoth, *those* who *were* in Eshtemoa, [29]*those* who *were* in Rachal, *those* who *were* in the cities of the Jerahmeelites, *those* who *were* in the cities of the Kenites, [30]*those* who *were* in Hormah, *those* who *were* in Chorashan,[a] *those* who *were* in Athach, [31]*those* who *were* in Hebron, and to all the places where David himself and his men were accustomed to rove.

The Tragic End of Saul and His Sons

31 Now the Philistines fought against Israel; and the men of Israel fled from before the Philistines, and fell slain on Mount Gilboa. [2]Then the Philistines followed hard after Saul and his sons. And the Philistines killed Jonathan, Abinadab, and Malchishua, Saul's sons. [3]The battle became fierce against Saul. The archers hit him, and he was severely wounded by the archers.

[4]Then Saul said to his armorbearer, "Draw your sword, and thrust me through with it, lest these uncircumcised men come and thrust me through and abuse me."

But his armorbearer would not, for he was greatly afraid. Therefore Saul took a sword and fell on it. [5]And when his armorbearer saw that Saul was dead, he also fell on his sword, and died with him. [6]So Saul, his three sons, his armorbearer, and all his men died together that same day.

[7]And when the men of Israel who *were* on the other side of the valley, and *those* who *were* on the other side of the Jordan, saw that the men of Israel had fled and that Saul and his sons were dead, they forsook the cities and fled; and the Philistines came and dwelt in them. [8]So it happened the next day, when the Philistines came to strip the slain, that they found Saul and his three sons fallen on Mount Gilboa. [9]And they cut off his head and stripped off his armor, and sent *word* throughout the land of the Philistines, to proclaim *it in* the temple of their idols and among the people. [10]Then they put his armor in the temple of the Ashtoreths, and they fastened his body to the wall of Beth Shan.[a]

[11]Now when the inhabitants of Jabesh Gilead heard what the Philistines had done to Saul, [12]all the valiant men arose and traveled all night, and took the body of Saul and the bodies of his sons from the wall of Beth Shan; and they came to Jabesh and burned them there. [13]Then they took their bones and buried *them* under the tamarisk tree at Jabesh, and fasted seven days.

••••••••••••••••••••

30:22 [a]Literally *men of Belial* **30:30** [a]Or *Borashan* **31:10** [a]Spelled *Beth Shean* in Joshua 17:11 and elsewhere

2 Samuel

TITLE

In the Hebrew text, 1 and 2 Samuel originally made up one volume. Though its author is not named, tradition assigns both 1 and 2 Samuel to the prophet Samuel and credits the prophets Nathan and Gad with the completion of the volume after Samuel's death (1 Sam. 25:1; see 1 Sam., Introduction).

DATE

The Book of 2 Samuel covers the forty years of David's reign (1010 B.C. to 970 B.C.).

BACKGROUND

SETTING: As one of the historical books of the Old Testament, 2 Samuel was written primarily to give the Hebrew people the facts as well as the implications of King David's reign. The book focuses on the effects of David's reign on the nation from a spiritual perspective.

After the death of Saul, David first ruled over Judah in Hebron for seven and one-half years. He then united Judah with Israel and established Jerusalem as his capital city. Through military conquest and political alliances, he extended his control from the Gulf of Aqaba to the Phoenician coast. As his empire grew, David set up an efficient administration and developed trade and international relations. He also organized the nation's religious life and encouraged musical expression. Despite domestic and political problems, which this book describes in detail, David left his son Solomon a strong, pacified kingdom.

THEMES

Second Samuel is part of the larger story of God's relationship with the people of Israel. This book focuses on King David, one of the nation's greatest leaders. David was concerned above all with God's approval and humbly recognized that all his victories came from the Lord. God promised to establish from David's line a dynasty of kings that would rule forever. This covenant looks forward to the Messiah, the Son of David, and His eternal reign. David was called a man after God's own heart; yet his sins, including adultery and murder, led to disaster in David's family and in the nation.

Second Samuel shows how God deals with His children in sin. When they repent, their relationship with Him is fully restored, and they again can experience peace and hope. There are painful consequences to their actions that cannot be avoided, but in the midst of correction, God also reveals His grace. The people of God suffer when a leader sins; yet hope exists, even in the worst situations. God is with His people to deliver and to provide a better way.

Finally, the life of King David illustrates the danger of multiple marriages. Even when such polygamous unions are culturally acceptable, they undermine moral character and weaken parental authority. An additional consequence of polgamy is that children often suffer from jealousy, strife, and abuse (see Gen. 32, Blended Family; Prov. 28, Favoritism; 1 Tim. 3., Polygamy).

OUTLINE

I. David's Reign from Hebron (1:1—4:12)
  A. The death of Saul and Jonathan (1:1–27)
  B. The war between David's house and Saul's house (2:1—3:39)
    1. David and Abner (2:1—3:1)
    2. The birth of David's sons in Hebron (3:2–5)
    3. The defection of Abner from the house of Saul (3:6–21)
    4. Joab's murder of Abner (3:22–39)
  C. The murder of Ish-bosheth (4:1–12)
II. David's Reign in Jerusalem (5:1—10:19)
  A. The conquest of Jerusalem (5:1–25)
  B. The moving of the ark to Jerusalem (6:1–23)
  C. God's covenant with David (7:1–29)
  D. The conquests of David (8:1–18)
  E. David and Mephibosheth (9:1–13)
  F. David's triumph over Ammon and Syria (10:1–19)
III. David's Sin and Its Consequences (11:1—20:26)

A. David's sin against Bathsheba and Uriah (11:1–27)
  B. Nathan's rebuke and David's repentance (12:1–31)
  C. Amnon's sin against Tamar and Absalom's revenge (13:1–39)
  D. Absalom's return from exile (14:1–33)
  E. Absalom's rebellion (15:1—19:8)
    1. David's escape (15:1–37)
    2. David's friends and foes (16:1–14)
    3. Ahithophel's advice (16:15—17:29)
    4. Absalom's death (18:1—19:8)
  F. David's restoration to the throne (19:9–43)
  G. Sheba's revolt (20:1–26)
IV. A Commentary on David's Reign (21:1—24:25)
  A. The execution of Saul's descendants (21:1–22)
  B. David's song of praise (22:1–51)
  C. David's heroes (23:1–39)
  D. The census and plague (24:1–25)

The Report of Saul's Death

1 Now it came to pass after the death of Saul, when David had returned from the slaughter of the Amalekites, and David had stayed two days in Ziklag, ²on the third day, behold, it happened that a man came from Saul's camp with his clothes torn and dust on his head. So it was, when he came to David, that he fell to the ground and prostrated himself.

³And David said to him, "Where have you come from?"

So he said to him, "I have escaped from the camp of Israel."

⁴Then David said to him, "How did the matter go? Please tell me."

And he answered, "The people have fled from the battle, many of the people are fallen and dead, and Saul and Jonathan his son are dead also."

⁵So David said to the young man who told him, "How do you know that Saul and Jonathan his son are dead?"

⁶Then the young man who told him said, "As I happened by chance *to be* on Mount Gilboa, there was Saul, leaning on his spear; and indeed the chariots and horsemen followed hard after him. ⁷Now when he looked behind him, he saw me and called to me. And I answered, 'Here I am.' ⁸And he said to me, 'Who *are* you?' So I answered him, 'I *am* an Amalekite.' ⁹He said to me again, 'Please stand over me and kill me, for anguish has come upon me, but my life still *remains* in me.' ¹⁰So I stood over him and killed him, because I was sure that he could not live after he had fallen. And I took the crown that *was* on his head and the bracelet that *was* on his arm, and have brought them here to my lord."

¹¹Therefore David took hold of his own clothes and tore them, and *so did* all the men who *were* with him. ¹²And they mourned and wept and fasted until evening for Saul and for Jonathan his son, for the people of the LORD and for the house of Israel, because they had fallen by the sword.

¹³Then David said to the young man who told him, "Where *are* you from?"

And he answered, "I *am* the son of an alien, an Amalekite."

¹⁴So David said to him, "How was it you were not afraid to put forth your hand to destroy the LORD's anointed?" ¹⁵Then David called one of the young men and said, "Go near, *and* execute him!" And he struck him so that he died. ¹⁶So David said to him, "Your blood *is* on your own head, for your own mouth has testified against you, saying, 'I have killed the LORD's anointed.'"

The Song of the Bow

¹⁷Then David lamented with this lamentation over Saul and over Jonathan his son, ¹⁸and he told *them* to teach the children of Judah *the Song of* the Bow; indeed *it is* written in the Book of Jasher:

¹⁹"The beauty of Israel is slain on your high
    places!
  How the mighty have fallen!
²⁰Tell *it* not in Gath,
  Proclaim *it* not in the streets of Ashkelon—
  Lest the daughters of the Philistines rejoice,
  Lest the daughters of the uncircumcised
    triumph.

²¹"O mountains of Gilboa,
  Let there be no dew nor rain upon you,
  Nor fields of offerings.
  For the shield of the mighty is cast away
    there!
  The shield of Saul, not anointed with oil.
²²From the blood of the slain,
  From the fat of the mighty,
  The bow of Jonathan did not turn back,
  And the sword of Saul did not return empty.

²³"Saul and Jonathan *were* beloved and pleasant in
    their lives,
  And in their death they were not divided;
  They were swifter than eagles,
  They were stronger than lions.

²⁴"O daughters of Israel, weep over Saul,
  Who clothed you in scarlet, with luxury;
  Who put ornaments of gold on your apparel.

²⁵"How the mighty have fallen in the midst of the
    battle!
  Jonathan *was* slain in your high places.

1:2 Torn clothes and dust on the head indicated that a person was in mourning. Also common was the expression of grief by loud weeping, fasting, and wearing sackcloth. This behavior was expected at a time of death or major disaster.

1:16 Saul had committed suicide, but the Amalekite claimed he had helped Saul take his life (1 Sam. 31:4). He probably fabricated this story, hoping to gain a reward from David. Whether the tale was true or not, David refused any part in the death of Saul. Only God should take the life of His anointed king. The Amalekite was judged on his own words and executed for murder and treason.

1:18 The book of Jasher is a lost collection of ancient songs that praise the heroes of Israel.

1:21 Anointing a shield with oil is a poetic image in which David recognized Saul's valor as a warrior. When in use, a wooden or leather shield was oiled to keep it from drying out or cracking, but Saul's shield had been abandoned on the battlefield where he died on Mount Gilboa. Although Saul had been his enemy, David was sincere in expressing grief at Saul's tragic end.

RIZPAH *A Silent Witness*

Rizpah, having little or no control over her own life, still managed to maintain a sense of the dignity of life. As a concubine of King Saul, she bore him two sons, Armoni and Mephibosheth (apparently a namesake of the son of David's beloved friend Jonathan).

Concubines in the ancient world were considered property, though they were not slaves. Though afforded some protection by Mosaic Law, they could be divorced more easily than wives. To sleep with the concubine of a king was considered an act of usurpation against the throne.

Rizpah, one of King Saul's concubines, was caught in the middle of the political intrigue surrounding the king's death. Although Saul's army commander Abner remained the real power behind the throne, he named Saul's son Ishbosheth king. When Ishbosheth later accused Abner of sleeping with a royal concubine, the charge amounted to treason, since a king's harem usually passed to his heir. Abner was so angry that he determined to work to "transfer the kingdom from the house of Saul, and set up the throne of David" (see 2 Sam. 3:10).

Over the ensuing months, with Abner's help, David consolidated his power over all of Israel and was crowned king. Later in the midst of a dreadful famine, David searched for a reason for what he interpreted as God's judgment on the land. Because it was due to King Saul's killing of the Gibeonites in violation of their ancient covenant with the Israelites, David inquired as to what would avenge their loss. Their reply was this: the death of seven of Saul's descendants.

Rizpah watched helplessly as her beloved sons were hanged because they were descendants of Saul. She paid a terrible price for the sins of Saul and his family. The grief of a mother's heart took the form of a fierce determination to watch over the bodies. Spreading her sackcloth (a sign of mourning), she protected the unburied bodies from the birds during the day and from beasts during the night.

When King David heard of Rizpah's long and lonely vigil over the corpses of her loved ones, he was moved to provide a proper burial for the bodies that Rizpah had shielded, as well as for King Saul and Jonathan, in the tomb of Saul's father Kish. Though she was helpless to save them in life, Rizpah's courage in protecting those she loved in death was rewarded with the knowledge that her profound witness to decency and the dignity of the human body provided a proper burial for those over whom she had watched.

Rizpah's reverence for life and respect for the bodies of her sons who had been executed contributed to God's favorable response to the nation, hearing and answering prayer (see 2 Sam. 21:14).

See also 2 Sam. 21:8–11; notes on Children (2 Sam. 21); Motherhood (1 Sam. 1); Grandparenthood (Ps. 71)

---

[26]I am distressed for you, my brother Jonathan;
You have been very pleasant to me;
Your love to me was wonderful,
Surpassing the love of women.

[27]"How the mighty have fallen,
And the weapons of war perished!"

David Anointed King of Judah

2 It happened after this that David inquired of the LORD, saying, "Shall I go up to any of the cities of Judah?"

And the LORD said to him, "Go up."

David said, "Where shall I go up?"

And He said, "To Hebron."

[2]So David went up there, and his two wives also, Ahinoam the Jezreelitess, and Abigail the widow of Nabal the Carmelite. [3]And David brought up the men who *were* with him, every man with his household. So they dwelt in the cities of Hebron.

[4]Then the men of Judah came, and there they anointed David king over the house of Judah. And they told David, saying, "The men of Jabesh Gilead *were the ones* who buried Saul." [5]So David sent messengers to the men of Jabesh Gilead, and said to them, "You *are* blessed of the LORD, for you have shown this kindness to your lord, to Saul, and have buried him. [6]And now may the LORD show kindness and truth to you. I also will repay you this kindness, because you have done this thing. [7]Now therefore, let your hands be strengthened, and be valiant; for your master Saul is dead, and also the house of Judah has anointed me king over them."

Ishbosheth Made King of Israel

[8]But Abner the son of Ner, commander of Saul's army, took Ishbosheth[a] the son of Saul and brought him over to Mahanaim; [9]and he made him

2:8 [a]Called *Esh-Baal* in 1 Chronicles 8:33 and 9:39

1:26 Jonathan's love for David in no way implies a homosexual relationship. The word "love" is used in this poetic statement to describe the quality of friendship between David and Jonathan. Homosexuality was clearly forbidden in the OT (see Lev. 18, Homosexuality). Jonathan loved David as his own soul (1 Sam. 18:1). There was a selfless quality in his friendship. Between the two men grew a deep bond of brotherhood.

king over Gilead, over the Ashurites, over Jezreel, over Ephraim, over Benjamin, and over all Israel. [10]Ishbosheth, Saul's son, *was* forty years old when he began to reign over Israel, and he reigned two years. Only the house of Judah followed David. [11]And the time that David was king in Hebron over the house of Judah was seven years and six months.

Israel and Judah at War

[12]Now Abner the son of Ner, and the servants of Ishbosheth the son of Saul, went out from Mahanaim to Gibeon. [13]And Joab the son of Zeruiah, and the servants of David, went out and met them by the pool of Gibeon. So they sat down, one on one side of the pool and the other on the other side of the pool. [14]Then Abner said to Joab, "Let the young men now arise and compete before us."

And Joab said, "Let them arise."

[15]So they arose and went over by number, twelve from Benjamin, *followers* of Ishbosheth the son of Saul, and twelve from the servants of David. [16]And each one grasped his opponent by the head and *thrust* his sword in his opponent's side; so they fell down together. Therefore that place was called the Field of Sharp Swords,[a] which *is* in Gibeon. [17]So there was a very fierce battle that day, and Abner and the men of Israel were beaten before the servants of David.

[18]Now the three sons of Zeruiah were there: Joab and Abishai and Asahel. And Asahel *was as* fleet of foot as a wild gazelle. [19]So Asahel pursued Abner, and in going he did not turn to the right hand or to the left from following Abner.

[20]Then Abner looked behind him and said, "*Are* you Asahel?"

He answered, "I *am*."

[21]And Abner said to him, "Turn aside to your right hand or to your left, and lay hold on one of the young men and take his armor for yourself." But Asahel would not turn aside from following him. [22]So Abner said again to Asahel, "Turn aside from following me. Why should I strike you to the ground? How then could I face your brother Joab?" [23]However, he refused to turn aside. Therefore Abner struck him in the stomach with the blunt end of the spear, so that the spear came out

of his back; and he fell down there and died on the spot. So it was *that* as many as came to the place where Asahel fell down and died, stood still.

[24]Joab and Abishai also pursued Abner. And the sun was going down when they came to the hill of Ammah, which *is* before Giah by the road to the Wilderness of Gibeon. [25]Now the children of Benjamin gathered together behind Abner and became a unit, and took their stand on top of a hill. [26]Then Abner called to Joab and said, "Shall the sword devour forever? Do you not know that it will be bitter in the latter end? How long will it be then until you tell the people to return from pursuing their brethren?"

[27]And Joab said, "*As* God lives, unless you had spoken, surely then by morning all the people would have given up pursuing their brethren." [28]So Joab blew a trumpet; and all the people stood still and did not pursue Israel anymore, nor did they fight anymore. [29]Then Abner and his men went on all that night through the plain, crossed over the Jordan, and went through all Bithron; and they came to Mahanaim.

[30]So Joab returned from pursuing Abner. And when he had gathered all the people together, there were missing of David's servants nineteen men and Asahel. [31]But the servants of David had struck down, of Benjamin and Abner's men, three hundred and sixty men who died. [32]Then they took up Asahel and buried him in his father's tomb, which *was in* Bethlehem. And Joab and his men went all night, and they came to Hebron at daybreak.

3 Now there was a long war between the house of Saul and the house of David. But David grew stronger and stronger, and the house of Saul grew weaker and weaker.

Sons of David

[2]Sons were born to David in Hebron: His firstborn was Amnon by Ahinoam the Jezreelitess; [3]his second, Chileab, by Abigail the widow of Nabal the Carmelite; the third, Absalom the son of

---

2:16 [a]Hebrew *Helkath Hazzurim*

2:13 The pool of Gibeon has been discovered by archaeologists. It is an impressive pit, approximately 36 feet in diameter and 30 feet deep, dug into solid rock and used in connection with the local wine-making industry.

2:14 In the battle by the pool of Gibeon, 24 young men had been selected by Joab and Abner to fight in representative combat, according to the rules of that day. The hope was that one side would come out ahead so that further hatred and bloodshed would be avoided. However, the opponents were so well matched that they killed each other, and a fierce general battle ensued.

2:23 Abner wanted to avoid a blood feud with Joab, and he did not necessarily intend to kill Asahel with this blow. Perhaps he only tried to stop the young man from pursuing him. However, the butt of the spear was sharp and hit him in the stomach with such force that he was not only wounded but killed instantly.

3:2–5 Polygamy was widely practiced by the nations surrounding Israel. Although the Law warned against multiple wives, the custom was tolerated in OT times (Deut. 17:17; see also 1 Tim. 3, Polygamy). Some of David's marriages amounted to a political alliance, as with Maacah, princess of

Maacah, the daughter of Talmai, king of Geshur; [4]the fourth, Adonijah the son of Haggith; the fifth, Shephatiah the son of Abital; [5]and the sixth, Ithream, by David's wife Eglah. These were born to David in Hebron.

Abner Joins Forces with David

[6]Now it was so, while there was war between the house of Saul and the house of David, that Abner was strengthening *his hold* on the house of Saul.

[7]And Saul had a concubine, whose name *was* Rizpah, the daughter of Aiah. So *Ishbosheth* said to Abner, "Why have you gone in to my father's concubine?"

[8]Then Abner became very angry at the words of Ishbosheth, and said, "*Am* I a dog's head that belongs to Judah? Today I show loyalty to the house of Saul your father, to his brothers, and to his friends, and have not delivered you into the hand of David; and you charge me today with a fault concerning this woman? [9]May God do so to Abner, and more also, if I do not do for David as the LORD has sworn to him— [10]to transfer the kingdom from the house of Saul, and set up the throne of David over Israel and over Judah, from Dan to Beersheba." [11]And he could not answer Abner another word, because he feared him.

[12]Then Abner sent messengers on his behalf to David, saying, "Whose *is* the land?" saying *also,* "Make your covenant with me, and indeed my hand *shall be* with you to bring all Israel to you."

[13]And *David* said, "Good, I will make a covenant with you. But one thing I require of you: you shall not see my face unless you first bring Michal, Saul's daughter, when you come to see my face."

[14]So David sent messengers to Ishbosheth, Saul's son, saying, "Give *me* my wife Michal, whom I be-

trothed to myself for a hundred foreskins of the Philistines." [15]And Ishbosheth sent and took her from *her* husband, from Paltiel[a] the son of Laish. [16]Then her husband went along with her to Bahurim, weeping behind her. So Abner said to him, "Go, return!" And he returned.

[17]Now Abner had communicated with the elders of Israel, saying, "In time past you were seeking for David *to be* king over you. [18]Now then, do *it!* For the LORD has spoken of David, saying, 'By the hand of My servant David, I[a] will save My people Israel from the hand of the Philistines and the hand of all their enemies.' " [19]And Abner also spoke in the hearing of Benjamin. Then Abner also went to speak in the hearing of David in Hebron all that seemed good to Israel and the whole house of Benjamin.

[20]So Abner and twenty men with him came to David at Hebron. And David made a feast for Abner and the men who *were* with him. [21]Then Abner said to David, "I will arise and go, and gather all Israel to my lord the king, that they may make a covenant with you, and that you may reign over all that your heart desires." So David sent Abner away, and he went in peace.

Joab Murders Abner

[22]At that moment the servants of David and Joab came from a raid and brought much spoil with them. But Abner *was* not with David in Hebron, for he had sent him away, and he had gone in peace. [23]When Joab and all the troops that *were* with him had come, they told Joab, saying, "Abner

---

3:15 [a]Spelled *Palti* in 1 Samuel 25:44   3:18 [a]Following many Hebrew manuscripts, Septuagint, Syriac, and Targum; Masoretic Text reads *he.*

Geshur. While the list of sons born to David in Hebron would seem to show his growing strength, none of these men are later mentioned in a favorable way (Amnon will commit incest; Absalom, murder and revolution). The wives David chose did not necessarily instill godly values in his children (see chart, The Family Tree of David). In addition, the atmosphere of the harem was more conducive to gossip, jealousy, and strife than to wise and peaceful living. David himself did not always set a good example for his own family. After the years of hardship he spent fleeing from Saul and conquering the kingdom, David's moral character was weakened by a life of ease and sensual indulgence, which led to adultery and murder.

3:7 **When a king died,** customarily his harem was passed to his successor. To approach a royal concubine was a serious offense. Abner was infringing on royal rights, perhaps even initiating a claim to the throne (see 2 Sam. 16:21; 1 Kin. 2:13–25).

3:8 **Dogs** were not viewed with much affection in Palestine. Usually untamed, they roamed in packs and fed on refuse. Calling someone a dog was a serious insult. "A dog's head that belongs to Judah" indicates a contemptible traitor (see 2 Sam. 9:8; 16:9).

3:14 **Michal** was David's first and rightful wife. Although she was the daughter of his enemy Saul, she had proven her affection and loyalty to him (1 Sam. 18:20; 19:11–17; see also 1 Sam. 18, Michal; chart, The Family Tree of David). Saul had forced the couple's separation and was thus responsible for Michal's second marriage to Paltiel and its unhappy end (1 Sam. 25:44). David was anxious to redress the injustice done to him by Saul (note David's words "my wife") and to strengthen his claim to Saul's throne (note David's reference to Michal as "Saul's daughter," 2 Sam. 3:13). In regaining his wife Michal, he won additional political support and strengthened his claim to the throne of all Israel. David's reclaiming of Michal as his wife is not a violation of Deuteronomy 24:1–4 because his separation from her had been involuntary. We are not told how Michal reacted to her marriage to Paltiel, whether or not she still loved David, and how attached she had become to her new, devoted husband. Although women of her day did not expect much freedom of choice, her forced return to David may have caused bitterness in her heart (see 2 Sam. 6:16). On the other hand, she may have been flattered to be the king's wife and seen this as an opportunity for status.

*Resolve to keep happy, and your joy and you shall form
an invincible host against difficulties.*

Helen Keller

the son of Ner came to the king, and he sent him away, and he has gone in peace." [24]Then Joab came to the king and said, "What have you done? Look, Abner came to you; why *is it that* you sent him away, and he has already gone? [25]Surely you realize that Abner the son of Ner came to deceive you, to know your going out and your coming in, and to know all that you are doing."

[26]And when Joab had gone from David's presence, he sent messengers after Abner, who brought him back from the well of Sirah. But David did not know *it*. [27]Now when Abner had returned to Hebron, Joab took him aside in the gate to speak with him privately, and there stabbed him in the stomach, so that he died for the blood of Asahel his brother.

[28]Afterward, when David heard *it*, he said, "My kingdom and I *are* guiltless before the LORD forever of the blood of Abner the son of Ner. [29]Let it rest on the head of Joab and on all his father's house; and let there never fail to be in the house of Joab one who has a discharge or is a leper, who leans on a staff or falls by the sword, or who lacks bread." [30]So Joab and Abishai his brother killed Abner, because he had killed their brother Asahel at Gibeon in the battle.

David's Mourning for Abner

[31]Then David said to Joab and to all the people who were with him, "Tear your clothes, gird yourselves with sackcloth, and mourn for Abner." And King David followed the coffin. [32]So they buried Abner in Hebron; and the king lifted up his voice and wept at the grave of Abner, and all the people wept. [33]And the king sang *a lament* over Abner and said:

"Should Abner die as a fool dies?
[34]Your hands were not bound
Nor your feet put into fetters;
As a man falls before wicked men, *so* you fell."

Then all the people wept over him again.

[35]And when all the people came to persuade David to eat food while it was still day, David took an oath, saying, "God do so to me, and more also, if I taste bread or anything else till the sun goes down!" [36]Now all the people took note *of it,* and it pleased them, since whatever the king did pleased all the people. [37]For all the people and all Israel understood that day that it had not been the king's *intent* to kill Abner the son of Ner. [38]Then the king said to his servants, "Do you not know that a prince and a great man has fallen this day in Israel? [39]And I *am* weak today, though anointed king; and these men, the sons of Zeruiah, *are* too harsh for me. The LORD shall repay the evildoer according to his wickedness."

Ishbosheth Is Murdered

4 When Saul's son[a] heard that Abner had died in Hebron, he lost heart, and all Israel was troubled. [2]Now Saul's son *had* two men *who were* captains of troops. The name of one *was* Baanah and the name of the other Rechab, the sons of Rimmon the Beerothite, of the children of Benjamin. (For Beeroth also was *part* of Benjamin, [3]because the Beerothites fled to Gittaim and have been sojourners there until this day.)

[4]Jonathan, Saul's son, had a son *who was* lame in *his* feet. He was five years old when the news about Saul and Jonathan came from Jezreel; and his nurse took him up and fled. And it happened, as she made haste to flee, that he fell and became lame. His name *was* Mephibosheth.[a]

[5]Then the sons of Rimmon the Beerothite, Rechab and Baanah, set out and came at about the heat of the day to the house of Ishbosheth, who was lying on his bed at noon. [6]And they came there, all the way into the house, *as though* to get wheat,

---

4:1 [a]That is, Ishbosheth   4:4 [a]Called *Merib-Baal* in 1 Chronicles 8:34 and 9:40

3:29 To have a discharge made a person impure and unfit for religious service (see Lev. 15:1, note). "Who leans on a staff" can be a reference to a "crutch" or a "spindle." In the latter case, the reference would be to an effeminate male, one who is only fit for what was considered to be the work of women.

3:39 There are several possible reasons why Joab murdered Abner. He may have feared for his own position as captain of David's troops. Perhaps he really believed David had been deceived by Abner. He certainly wanted to avenge his brother Asahel (2 Sam. 2:23). Whatever the reasons, David wanted no

part in this murder, which threatened the peace of the newly established kingdom. But Joab was a powerful figure, and David felt unable to punish his crime at this point. However, he believed that, in the justice of God, there would be consequences for Joab and for his family after him.

4:5, 6 Ishbosheth's murder. It may have been the custom for Rechab and Baanah to get wheat for their men in Ishbosheth's granary. Their presence in the house then would not have seemed suspicious. Also, as it was a rest time, the guards were not sufficiently alert in protecting the king.

THE FAMILY TREE OF DAVID

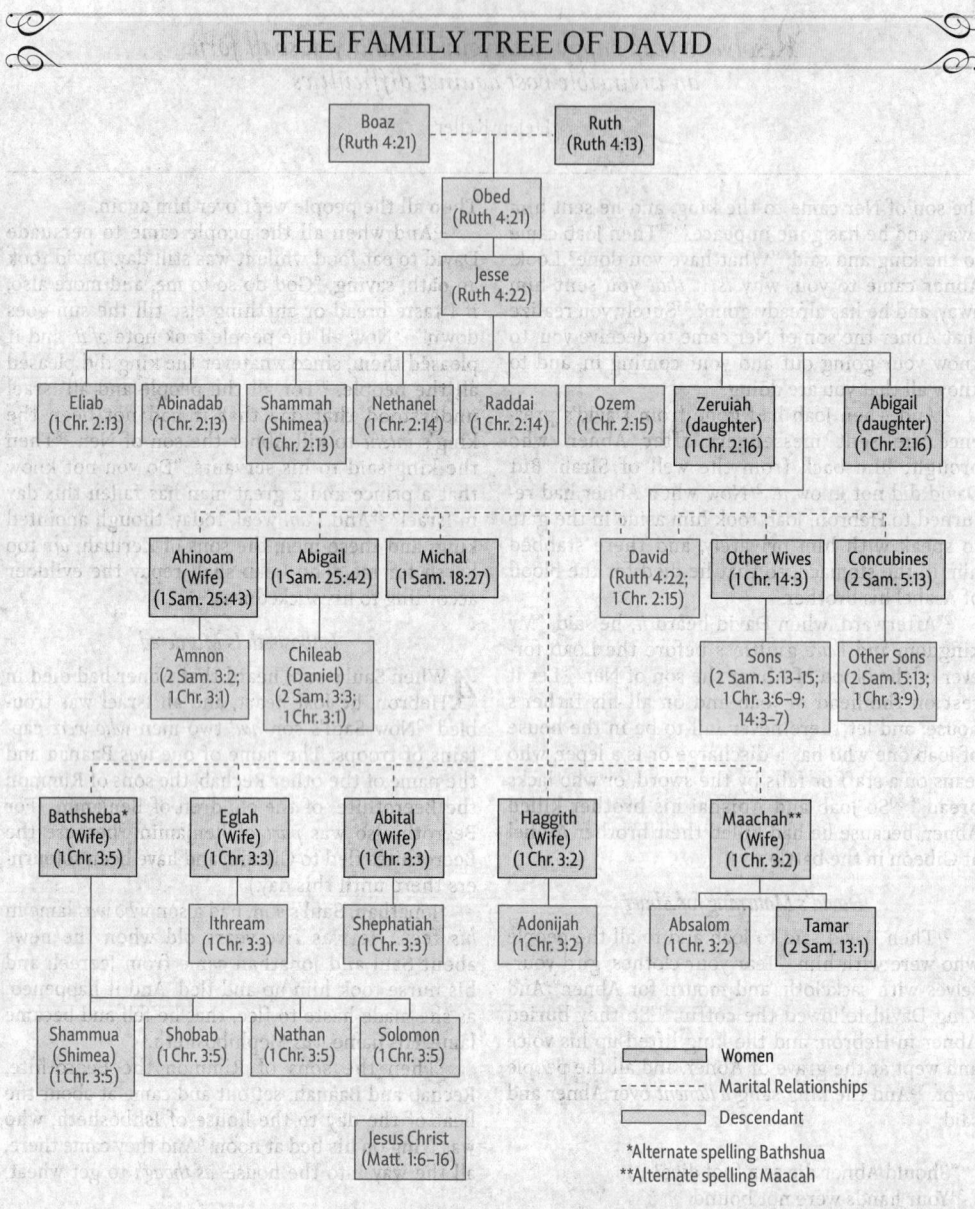

and they stabbed him in the stomach. Then Rechab and Baanah his brother escaped. [7]For when they came into the house, he was lying on his bed in his bedroom; then they struck him and killed him, beheaded him and took his head, and were all night escaping through the plain. [8]And they brought the head of Ishbosheth to David at Hebron, and said to the king, "Here is the head of Ishbosheth, the son of Saul your enemy, who sought your life; and the

LORD has avenged my lord the king this day of Saul and his descendants."

[9]But David answered Rechab and Baanah his brother, the sons of Rimmon the Beerothite, and said to them, "As the LORD lives, who has redeemed my life from all adversity, [10]when someone told me, saying, 'Look, Saul is dead,' thinking to have brought good news, I arrested him and had him executed in Ziklag—the one who *thought* I would give

him a reward for *his* news. [11]How much more, when wicked men have killed a righteous person in his own house on his bed? Therefore, shall I not now require his blood at your hand and remove you from the earth?" [12]So David commanded his young men, and they executed them, cut off their hands and feet, and hanged *them* by the pool in Hebron. But they took the head of Ishbosheth and buried *it* in the tomb of Abner in Hebron.

David Reigns over All Israel

5 Then all the tribes of Israel came to David at Hebron and spoke, saying, "Indeed we *are* your bone and your flesh. [2]Also, in time past, when Saul was king over us, you were the one who led Israel out and brought them in; and the LORD said to you, 'You shall shepherd My people Israel, and be ruler over Israel.' " [3]Therefore all the elders of Israel came to the king at Hebron, and King David made a covenant with them at Hebron before the LORD. And they anointed David king over Israel. [4]David *was* thirty years old when he began to reign, *and* he reigned forty years. [5]In Hebron he reigned over Judah seven years and six months, and in Jerusalem he reigned thirty-three years over all Israel and Judah.

The Conquest of Jerusalem

[6]And the king and his men went to Jerusalem against the Jebusites, the inhabitants of the land, who spoke to David, saying, "You shall not come in here; but the blind and the lame will repel you," thinking, "David cannot come in here." [7]Nevertheless David took the stronghold of Zion (that *is*, the City of David).

[8]Now David said on that day, "Whoever climbs up by way of the water shaft and defeats the Jebusites (the lame and the blind, *who are* hated by David's soul), *he shall be chief and captain*."[a] Therefore they say, "The blind and the lame shall not come into the house."

[9]Then David dwelt in the stronghold, and called it the City of David. And David built all around from the Millo[a] and inward. [10]So David went on and became great, and the LORD God of hosts *was* with him.

[11]Then Hiram king of Tyre sent messengers to David, and cedar trees, and carpenters and masons. And they built David a house. [12]So David knew that the LORD had established him as king

over Israel, and that He had exalted His kingdom for the sake of His people Israel.

[13]And David took more concubines and wives from Jerusalem, after he had come from Hebron. Also more sons and daughters were born to David. [14]Now these *are* the names of those who were born to him in Jerusalem: Shammua,[a] Shobab, Nathan, Solomon, [15]Ibhar, Elishua,[a] Nepheg, Japhia, [16]Elishama, Eliada, and Eliphelet.

The Philistines Defeated

[17]Now when the Philistines heard that they had anointed David king over Israel, all the Philistines went up to search for David. And David heard *of it* and went down to the stronghold. [18]The Philistines also went and deployed themselves in the Valley of Rephaim. [19]So David inquired of the LORD, saying, "Shall I go up against the Philistines? Will You deliver them into my hand?"

And the LORD said to David, "Go up, for I will doubtless deliver the Philistines into your hand."

[20]So David went to Baal Perazim, and David defeated them there; and he said, "The LORD has broken through my enemies before me, like a breakthrough of water." Therefore he called the name of that place Baal Perazim.[a] [21]And they left their images there, and David and his men carried them away.

[22]Then the Philistines went up once again and deployed themselves in the Valley of Rephaim. [23]Therefore David inquired of the LORD, and He said, "You shall not go up; circle around behind them, and come upon them in front of the mulberry trees. [24]And it shall be, when you hear the sound of marching in the tops of the mulberry trees, then you shall advance quickly. For then the LORD will go out before you to strike the camp of the Philistines." [25]And David did so, as the LORD commanded him; and he drove back the Philistines from Geba[a] as far as Gezer.

The Ark Brought to Jerusalem

6 Again David gathered all *the* choice *men* of Israel, thirty thousand. [2]And David arose and went with all the people who *were* with him from

5:8 [a]Compare 1 Chronicles 11:6   **5:9** [a]Literally *The Landfill*   **5:14** [a]Spelled *Shimea* in 1 Chronicles 3:5   **5:15** [a]Spelled *Elishama* in 1 Chronicles 3:6   **5:20** [a]Literally *Master of Breakthroughs*   **5:25** [a]Following Masoretic Text, Targum, and Vulgate; Septuagint reads *Gibeon*.

5:6, 8 Jerusalem's strategic strength was such that a garrison of blind and lame may indeed have been enough to protect it. In answer to their boasting, David referred to all Jebusites as "blind and lame," using this as a pre-battle verbal taunt (see also 2 Kin. 18:19–27).

5:7 Jerusalem, a Caananite fortress occupied by the Jebusites until David conquered it, was considered impregnable because of the valleys protecting it on three sides, as well as

the remarkable Jebusite walls, which now have been excavated. The city made an excellent choice for a capital because it was centrally positioned in the kingdom and was located on the border between Judah and the rest of Israel, which David was bringing together. Jerusalem would remain the capital until Nebuchadnezzar destroyed the city 400 years later.

5:13 See 2 Samuel 3:2–5, note.

MARRIAGE *PROBLEM SOLVING*

One of the more distressing facts of life is that every marriage must face problems. These cannot be sidestepped but must be faced and resolved:

- Children can be a great source of enjoyment, but they can also add stress to a marriage. The mothering instinct is so strong in many women that they tend to neglect their husbands as they care for their children (see 1 Sam. 1:8). At times, a wife will even deceive her husband in favor of her child (Gen. 27:1–29). A wife must remember that her union with her husband is second only to her relationship with God.
- Financial problems can also put undue stress on a relationship, especially if the couple bickers over who is going to make what sacrifices. If a couple will seek God's direction in financial matters, He will be faithful to meet their needs (Matt. 6:33; Phil. 4:19).
- Unresolved anger can build into resentment and bitterness so that meaningful communication ceases (Heb. 12:15; Eph. 4:26).
- The temptation and the opportunity to be unfaithful is ever present (Prov. 7:6–23). An intimate and vibrant fellowship with God will undergird the relationship between the husband and wife and provide strength and vitality to the marriage.
- Isolation, the state of being excluded, is one of the more subtle maladies of marriage. Marriage can easily slip out of priority. People take their mates for granted, give their attention to other "urgent" matters, and soon warmth and communication have diminished. The remedy for isolation is to guard the marriage relationship tenderly and to give priority to your spouse, being open and honest and not keeping secrets from one another.

Problems can be a negative weapon in a marriage, dividing hearts and destroying unity, or they can be a positive catalyst for recommitment and renewal.

See also Song 5:1–16; Matt. 6:33; Phil. 4:19; notes on Conflict (Song 5; Matt. 18); Debt (Ps. 37); Forgiveness (Ps. 51; Luke 17); Marriage (Gen. 2; Prov. 5; Hos. 2; Amos 3; 2 Cor. 13; Heb. 12); Problem Solving (John 5); portraits of Leah (Gen. 30); Rachel (Gen. 29)

Baale Judah to bring up from there the ark of God, whose name is called by the Name,[a] the LORD of Hosts, who dwells *between* the cherubim. ³So they set the ark of God on a new cart, and brought it out of the house of Abinadab, which *was* on the hill; and Uzzah and Ahio, the sons of Abinadab, drove the new cart.[a] ⁴And they brought it out of the house of Abinadab, which *was* on the hill, accompanying the ark of God; and Ahio went before the ark. ⁵Then David and all the house of Israel played *music* before the LORD on all kinds of *instruments of* fir wood, on harps, on stringed instruments, on tambourines, on sistrums, and on cymbals.

⁶And when they came to Nachon's threshing floor, Uzzah put out *his hand* to the ark of God and took hold of it, for the oxen stumbled. ⁷Then the anger of the LORD was aroused against Uzzah, and God struck him there for *his* error; and he died there by the ark of God. ⁸And David became angry

because of the LORD's outbreak against Uzzah; and he called the name of the place Perez Uzzah[a] to this day.

⁹David was afraid of the LORD that day; and he said, "How can the ark of the LORD come to me?" ¹⁰So David would not move the ark of the LORD with him into the City of David; but David took it aside into the house of Obed-Edom the Gittite. ¹¹The ark of the LORD remained in the house of Obed-Edom the Gittite three months. And the LORD blessed Obed-Edom and all his household.

¹²Now it was told King David, saying, "The LORD has blessed the house of Obed-Edom and all that *belongs* to him, because of the ark of God." So David went and brought up the ark of God from the house of Obed-Edom to the City of

• • • • • • • • • • • • • • • • • •

6:2 ᵃSeptuagint, Targum, and Vulgate omit *by the Name;* many Hebrew manuscripts and Syriac read *there.* **6:3** ᵃSeptuagint adds *with the ark.* **6:8** ᵃLiterally *Outburst Against Uzzah*

6:7 According to the instructions given, the ark was to be carried by priests, not set on a cart (Num. 4:15; 1 Chr. 15:11–15). However, in moving the ark to Jerusalem, God's Law was not consulted so that the entire party was guilty of irreverence. But Uzzah, whose family had been especially appointed to keep the ark (1 Sam. 7:1), showed great presumption in reaching out to touch the ark. He was aware of God's punishment

on the Philistines for keeping the ark and the care they took to return it properly. He knew that a great number of men from Beth Shemesh had died because they looked inside the ark (1 Sam. 5:6). Uzzah's careless gesture showed that he did not truly recognize the majesty and holiness of God, which were symbolized by the ark.

David with gladness. ¹³And so it was, when those bearing the ark of the LORD had gone six paces, that he sacrificed oxen and fatted sheep. ¹⁴Then David danced before the LORD with all *his* might; and David *was* wearing a linen ephod. ¹⁵So David and all the house of Israel brought up the ark of the LORD with shouting and with the sound of the trumpet.

¹⁶Now as the ark of the LORD came into the City of David, Michal, Saul's daughter, looked through a window and saw King David leaping and whirling before the LORD; and she despised him in her heart. ¹⁷So they brought the ark of the LORD, and set it in its place in the midst of the tabernacle that David had erected for it. Then David offered burnt offerings and peace offerings before the LORD. ¹⁸And when David had finished offering burnt offerings and peace offerings, he blessed the people in the name of the LORD of hosts. ¹⁹Then he distributed among all the people, among the whole multitude of Israel, both the women and the men, to everyone a loaf of bread, a piece *of meat*, and a cake of raisins. So all the people departed, everyone to his house.

²⁰Then David returned to bless his household. And Michal the daughter of Saul came out to meet David, and said, "How glorious was the king of Israel today, uncovering himself today in the eyes of the maids of his servants, as one of the base fellows shamelessly uncovers himself!"

²¹So David said to Michal, "*It was* before the LORD, who chose me instead of your father and all his house, to appoint me ruler over the people of the LORD, over Israel. Therefore I will play *music* before the LORD. ²²And I will be even more undignified than this, and will be humble in my own sight. But as for the maidservants of whom you have spoken, by them I will be held in honor."

²³Therefore Michal the daughter of Saul had no children to the day of her death.

God's Covenant with David

7Now it came to pass when the king was dwelling in his house, and the LORD had given him rest from all his enemies all around, ²that the king said to Nathan the prophet, "See now, I dwell in a house of cedar, but the ark of God dwells inside tent curtains."

³Then Nathan said to the king, "Go, do all that *is* in your heart, for the LORD *is* with you."

⁴But it happened that night that the word of the LORD came to Nathan, saying, ⁵"Go and tell My servant David, 'Thus says the LORD: "Would you build a house for Me to dwell in? ⁶For I have not dwelt in a house since the time that I brought the children of Israel up from Egypt, even to this day, but have moved about in a tent and in a tabernacle. ⁷Wherever I have moved about with all the children of Israel, have I ever spoken a word to anyone from the tribes of Israel, whom I commanded to shepherd My people Israel, saying, 'Why have you not built Me a house of cedar?' " ' ⁸Now therefore, thus shall you say to My servant David, 'Thus says the LORD of hosts: "I took you from the sheepfold, from following the sheep, to be ruler over My people, over Israel. ⁹And I have been with you wherever you have gone, and have cut off all your enemies from before you, and have made you a great name, like the name of the great men who *are* on the earth. ¹⁰Moreover I will appoint a place for My people Israel, and will plant them, that they may dwell in a place of their own and move no more; nor shall the sons of wickedness oppress them anymore, as previously, ¹¹since the time that I commanded judges *to be* over My people Israel, and have caused you to rest from all your

---

6:14 Dancing among the Jews was an act of worship celebrating a joyous occasion. The body moved rhythmically to the sound of tambourines and other musical instruments. Women danced most often, singly or in groups. When both sexes participated in a celebration, they usually danced separately (see Ex. 15, Dancing). Dancing as sensual entertainment is a Greek, not Hebrew, tradition. The "ephod" was a linen vest, worn by the priest over his robe and associated with service in the temple. It was much shorter than the usual outer garment, which made it convenient for dancing. This was probably not the distinctive ephod worn by the high priest (see chart, The High Priest's Clothing).

6:16 Michal, the daughter of Saul, was concerned with royal dignity. She therefore accused David of behavior unfitting his position when he danced in public before the Lord. She obviously did not share in David's enthusiasm when the ark arrived in Jerusalem. Perhaps she was bitter against her husband for personal reasons (see 2 Sam. 3:14, note), but her devotion to God also seemed superficial, and her main concern was the opinion of others. In this she was truly Saul's daughter. The childlessness that followed does not necessarily mean that

David withdrew from her. It did insure, however, that no descendant of Saul would become heir to the throne of David (see 1 Sam. 18, Michal; chart, The Family Tree of David).

7:7 At a time in his life when David enjoyed peace and prosperity, he wished to honor God by building Him a permanent house of cedar, the finest material for construction in that day. A tent, on the other hand, was a temporary shelter with a plain interior used by nomads. David did not feel a tent was worthy lodging for God's ark in Jerusalem.

7:11–15 The Lord will make you a house. Although David wanted to honor God, he was not the one chosen to build God's house, nor was the time right for the construction of the temple (see 1 Chr. 22:7–10). However, God Himself promised a house to David, meaning a dynasty of kings who would lead Israel. God would have a special relationship with these descendants of David, treating them as a father does his sons. He would correct them when necessary but not reject them altogether. Second Samuel 7:12, 13 refer specifically to David's first successor, Solomon, who built the temple.

enemies. Also the LORD tells you that He will make you a house.[a]

12"When your days are fulfilled and you rest with your fathers, I will set up your seed after you, who will come from your body, and I will establish his kingdom. 13He shall build a house for My name, and I will establish the throne of his kingdom forever. 14I will be his Father, and he shall be My son. If he commits iniquity, I will chasten him with the rod of men and with the blows of the sons of men. 15But My mercy shall not depart from him, as I took it from Saul, whom I removed from before you. 16And your house and your kingdom shall be established forever before you.[a] Your throne shall be established forever." ' "

17According to all these words and according to all this vision, so Nathan spoke to David.

David's Thanksgiving to God

18Then King David went in and sat before the LORD; and he said: "Who am I, O Lord GOD? And what is my house, that You have brought me this far? 19And yet this was a small thing in Your sight, O Lord GOD; and You have also spoken of Your servant's house for a great while to come. Is this the manner of man, O Lord GOD? 20Now what more can David say to You? For You, Lord GOD, know Your servant. 21For Your word's sake, and according to Your own heart, You have done all these great things, to make Your servant know them. 22Therefore You are great, O Lord GOD.[a] For there is none like You, nor is there any God besides You, according to all that we have heard with our ears. 23And who is like Your people, like Israel, the one nation on the earth whom God went to redeem for Himself as a people, to make for Himself a name— and to do for Yourself great and awesome deeds for Your land— before Your people whom You redeemed for Yourself from Egypt, the nations, and their gods? 24For You have made Your people Israel Your very own people forever; and You, LORD, have become their God.

25"Now, O LORD God, the word which You have spoken concerning Your servant and concerning his house, establish it forever and do as You have said. 26So let Your name be magnified forever, saying, 'The LORD of hosts is the God over Israel.' And let the house of Your servant David be established before You. 27For You, O LORD of hosts, God of Israel, have revealed this to Your servant, saying, 'I will build you a house.' Therefore Your servant has found it in his heart to pray this prayer to You.

28"And now, O Lord GOD, You are God, and Your words are true, and You have promised this goodness to Your servant. 29Now therefore, let it please You to bless the house of Your servant, that it may continue before You forever; for You, O Lord GOD, have spoken it, and with Your blessing let the house of Your servant be blessed forever."

David's Further Conquests

8 After this it came to pass that David attacked the Philistines and subdued them. And David took Metheg Ammah from the hand of the Philistines.

2Then he defeated Moab. Forcing them down to the ground, he measured them off with a line. With two lines he measured off those to be put to death, and with one full line those to be kept alive. So the Moabites became David's servants, and brought tribute.

3David also defeated Hadadezer the son of Rehob, king of Zobah, as he went to recover his territory at the River Euphrates. 4David took from him one thousand chariots, seven hundred[a] horsemen, and twenty thousand foot soldiers. Also David hamstrung all the chariot horses, except that he spared enough of them for one hundred chariots.

5When the Syrians of Damascus came to help Hadadezer king of Zobah, David killed twenty-two thousand of the Syrians. 6Then David put garrisons in Syria of Damascus; and the Syrians became David's servants, and brought tribute. So the LORD preserved David wherever he went. 7And David took the shields of gold that had belonged to the servants of Hadadezer, and brought them to Jerusalem. 8Also from Betah[a] and from Berothai, cities of Hadadezer, King David took a large amount of bronze.

9When Toi[a] king of Hamath heard that David had defeated all the army of Hadadezer, 10then Toi sent Joram[a] his son to King David, to greet him and bless him, because he had fought against Hadadezer and defeated him (for Hadadezer had been at war with Toi); and Joram brought with him articles of silver, articles of gold, and articles of

---

7:11 [a]That is, a royal dynasty   7:16 [a]Septuagint reads Me.   7:22 [a]Targum and Syriac read O LORD God.   8:4 [a]Or seven thousand (compare 1 Chronicles 18:4)   8:8 [a]Spelled Tibhath in 1 Chronicles 18:8   8:9 [a]Spelled Tou in 1 Chronicles 18:9   8:10 [a]Spelled Hadoram in 1 Chronicles 18:10

7:16 Your throne shall be established forever. This promise of an eternal throne for David's line was a major factor in developing the hope of a Messiah among the people of Israel. In the later years of captivity, occupation, and exile, the people longed for the king who would restore to Israel the glory of David's reign. This prophecy would only be fulfilled when Jesus Christ, the Son of David, established His eternal kingdom on earth (Matt. 25:31).

8:2 He measured them off with a line. Two-thirds of the Moabite men were put to death, while a full third had their lives spared. This severe form of punishment was actually more humane than some of David's earlier attacks on other areas (1 Sam. 27:9, 11). David had previously asked the king of Moab to watch over his parents (1 Sam. 22:3), and Ruth the Moabitess was his ancestress (Ruth 4:17).

Never do anything that you cannot do in the presence of all.
Never assert anything without first being assured of it.

St. Teresa of Avila

bronze. [11]King David also dedicated these to the LORD, along with the silver and gold that he had dedicated from all the nations which he had subdued— [12]from Syria,[a] from Moab, from the people of Ammon, from the Philistines, from Amalek, and from the spoil of Hadadezer the son of Rehob, king of Zobah.

[13]And David made *himself* a name when he returned from killing eighteen thousand Syrians[a] in the Valley of Salt. [14]He also put garrisons in Edom; throughout all Edom he put garrisons, and all the Edomites became David's servants. And the LORD preserved David wherever he went.

David's Administration

[15]So David reigned over all Israel; and David administered judgment and justice to all his people. [16]Joab the son of Zeruiah *was* over the army; Jehoshaphat the son of Ahilud *was* recorder; [17]Zadok the son of Ahitub and Ahimelech the son of Abiathar *were* the priests; Seraiah[a] *was* the scribe; [18]Benaiah the son of Jehoiada *was over* both the Cherethites and the Pelethites; and David's sons were chief ministers.

David's Kindness to Mephibosheth

9 Now David said, "Is there still anyone who is left of the house of Saul, that I may show him kindness for Jonathan's sake?"

[2]And *there was* a servant of the house of Saul whose name *was* Ziba. So when they had called him to David, the king said to him, "*Are* you Ziba?"

He said, "At your service!"

[3]Then the king said, "*Is* there not still someone of the house of Saul, to whom I may show the kindness of God?"

And Ziba said to the king, "There is still a son of Jonathan *who is* lame in *his* feet."

[4]So the king said to him, "Where *is* he?"

And Ziba said to the king, "Indeed he *is* in the house of Machir the son of Ammiel, in Lo Debar."

[5]Then King David sent and brought him out of the house of Machir the son of Ammiel, from Lo Debar.

[6]Now when Mephibosheth the son of Jonathan, the son of Saul, had come to David, he fell on his face and prostrated himself. Then David said, "Mephibosheth?"

And he answered, "Here is your servant!"

[7]So David said to him, "Do not fear, for I will surely show you kindness for Jonathan your father's sake, and will restore to you all the land of Saul your grandfather; and you shall eat bread at my table continually."

[8]Then he bowed himself, and said, "What *is* your servant, that you should look upon such a dead dog as I?"

[9]And the king called to Ziba, Saul's servant, and said to him, "I have given to your master's son all that belonged to Saul and to all his house. [10]You therefore, and your sons and your servants, shall work the land for him, and you shall bring in *the harvest*, that your master's son may have food to eat. But Mephibosheth your master's son shall eat bread at my table always." Now Ziba had fifteen sons and twenty servants.

[11]Then Ziba said to the king, "According to all that my lord the king has commanded his servant, so will your servant do."

"As for Mephibosheth," *said the king,* "he shall eat at my table[a] like one of the king's sons." [12]Mephibosheth had a young son whose name *was* Micha. And all who dwelt in the house of Ziba *were* servants of Mephibosheth. [13]So Mephibosheth dwelt in Jerusalem, for he ate continually at the king's table. And he was lame in both his feet.

The Ammonites and Syrians Defeated

10 It happened after this that the king of the people of Ammon died, and Hanun his son

- - - - - - - - - - - - - - - - - -
8:12 [a]Septuagint, Syriac, and some Hebrew manuscripts read *Edom*. **8:13** [a]Septuagint, Syriac, and some Hebrew manuscripts read *Edomites* (compare 1 Chronicles 18:12). **8:17** [a]Spelled *Shavsha* in 1 Chronicles 18:16 **9:11** [a]Septuagint reads *David's table.*

8:15–18 David's conquests placed him at the head of a large territory that needed a well-organized administration. David himself was the supreme administration of justice. The recorder informed and advised the king on state business, while the scribe acted as secretary. The Cherethites and Pelethites were foreign mercenaries with special responsibility for the person of the king.

9:7 Do not fear. In the ancient world, kings customarily exterminated all members of the previous dynasty as potential rivals. So Mephibosheth had good reason to fear David. However, the king was not one to forget his promises (1 Sam. 20:15). He went beyond what was required by his covenant with Jonathan. He returned Saul's personal estates in the area assigned to the tribe of Benjamin to Mephibosheth and invited him to eat at the king's table, a special mark of honor.

reigned in his place. ²Then David said, "I will show kindness to Hanun the son of Nahash, as his father showed kindness to me."

So David sent by the hand of his servants to comfort him concerning his father. And David's servants came into the land of the people of Ammon. ³And the princes of the people of Ammon said to Hanun their lord, "Do you think that David really honors your father because he has sent comforters to you? Has David not *rather* sent his servants to you to search the city, to spy it out, and to overthrow it?"

⁴Therefore Hanun took David's servants, shaved off half of their beards, cut off their garments in the middle, at their buttocks, and sent them away. ⁵When they told David, he sent to meet them, because the men were greatly ashamed. And the king said, "Wait at Jericho until your beards have grown, and *then* return."

⁶When the people of Ammon saw that they had made themselves repulsive to David, the people of Ammon sent and hired the Syrians of Beth Rehob and the Syrians of Zoba, twenty thousand foot soldiers; and from the king of Maacah one thousand men, and from Ish-Tob twelve thousand men. ⁷Now when David heard *of it*, he sent Joab and all the army of the mighty men. ⁸Then the people of Ammon came out and put themselves in battle array at the entrance of the gate. And the Syrians of Zoba, Beth Rehob, Ish-Tob, and Maacah *were* by themselves in the field.

⁹When Joab saw that the battle line was against him before and behind, he chose some of Israel's best and put *them* in battle array against the Syrians. ¹⁰And the rest of the people he put under the command of Abishai his brother, that he might set *them* in battle array against the people of Ammon. ¹¹Then he said, "If the Syrians are too strong for me, then you shall help me; but if the people of Ammon are too strong for you, then I will come and help you. ¹²Be of good courage, and let us be strong for our people and for the cities of our God. And may the LORD do *what is* good in His sight."

¹³So Joab and the people who *were* with him drew near for the battle against the Syrians, and they fled before him. ¹⁴When the people of Ammon saw that the Syrians were fleeing, they also fled before Abishai, and entered the city. So Joab returned from the people of Ammon and went to Jerusalem.

¹⁵When the Syrians saw that they had been defeated by Israel, they gathered together. ¹⁶Then Hadadezer[a] sent and brought out the Syrians who *were* beyond the River,[b] and they came to Helam. And Shobach the commander of Hadadezer's army *went* before them. ¹⁷When it was told David, he gathered all Israel, crossed over the Jordan, and came to Helam. And the Syrians set themselves in battle array against David and fought with him. ¹⁸Then the Syrians fled before Israel; and David killed seven hundred charioteers and forty thousand horsemen of the Syrians, and struck Shobach the commander of their army, who died there. ¹⁹And when all the kings *who were* servants to Hadadezer[a] saw that they were defeated by Israel, they made peace with Israel and served them. So the Syrians were afraid to help the people of Ammon anymore.

David, Bathsheba, and Uriah

11 It happened in the spring of the year, at the time when kings go out *to battle,* that David sent Joab and his servants with him, and all Israel; and they destroyed the people of Ammon and besieged Rabbah. But David remained at Jerusalem.

²Then it happened one evening that David arose from his bed and walked on the roof of the king's house. And from the roof he saw a woman bathing, and the woman *was* very beautiful to behold. ³So David sent and inquired about the woman. And *someone* said, "Is this not Bathsheba, the daughter of Eliam, the wife of Uriah the Hittite?" ⁴Then David sent messengers, and took her; and she came to him, and he lay with her, for she was cleansed from her impurity; and she returned to her house. ⁵And the woman conceived; so she sent and told David, and said, "I *am* with child."

⁶Then David sent to Joab, *saying,* "Send me Uriah the Hittite." And Joab sent Uriah to David. ⁷When Uriah had come to him, David asked how Joab was doing, and how the people were doing, and how the war prospered. ⁸And David said to

••••••••••••••••

10:16 ªHebrew *Hadarezer* ᵇThat is, the Euphrates 10:19 ªHebrew *Hadarezer*

10:4 Most Hebrew men wore full beards, which they kept and oiled with pride. To shave off half the beard of David's servants, as well as to cut their clothing to an indecent length, was a grave insult. This action was especially provocative because these men, as ambassadors of a king, should have been granted the usual diplomatic immunity. The whole incident was a deliberate affront to David.

11:2 David saw a woman bathing. Instead of leading his army to battle, David chose to remain in the comfort of his palace. After resting in the heat of the day, he went out to enjoy the cooler evening breezes on the flat roof, which functioned as a terrace of his house. Apparently, the king's palace rose above most other buildings so that David was in a good position to gaze into the closely connected courtyards and terraces of Jerusalem. In this way, he happened to see a woman bathing in the privacy of her home (see Bathsheba). Therefore, Bathsheba should not be accused of seeking the king's attention. The text does not indicate that she resisted his advances, but nowhere is she mentioned as a guilty party. In Nathan's parable, she even seems to be a victim, as she could be likened to the stolen lamb (2 Sam. 12:3, 4).

11:8 Wash your feet is a phrase that meant "make yourself comfortable in your house." Some interpret this as a euphemism for the male genitals, thereby suggesting directly sex-

Uriah, "Go down to your house and wash your feet." So Uriah departed from the king's house, and a gift *of food* from the king followed him. ⁹But Uriah slept at the door of the king's house with all the servants of his lord, and did not go down to his house. ¹⁰So when they told David, saying, "Uriah did not go down to his house," David said to Uriah, "Did you not come from a journey? Why did you not go down to your house?"

¹¹And Uriah said to David, "The ark and Israel and Judah are dwelling in tents, and my lord Joab and the servants of my lord are encamped in the open fields. Shall I then go to my house to eat and drink, and to lie with my wife? *As* you live, and *as* your soul lives, I will not do this thing."

¹²Then David said to Uriah, "Wait here today also, and tomorrow I will let you depart." So Uriah remained in Jerusalem that day and the next. ¹³Now when David called him, he ate and drank before him; and he made him drunk. And at evening he went out to lie on his bed with the servants of his lord, but he did not go down to his house.

¹⁴In the morning it happened that David wrote a letter to Joab and sent *it* by the hand of Uriah. ¹⁵And he wrote in the letter, saying, "Set Uriah in the forefront of the hottest battle, and retreat from him, that he may be struck down and die." ¹⁶So it was, while Joab besieged the city, that he assigned Uriah to a place where he knew there *were* valiant men. ¹⁷Then the men of the city came out and fought with Joab. And *some* of the people of the servants of David fell; and Uriah the Hittite died also.

¹⁸Then Joab sent and told David all the things concerning the war, ¹⁹and charged the messenger, saying, "When you have finished telling the matters of the war to the king, ²⁰if it happens that the king's wrath rises, and he says to you: 'Why did you approach so near to the city when you fought? Did you not know that they would shoot from the wall? ²¹Who struck Abimelech the son of Jerubbesheth?[a] Was it not a woman who cast a piece of a millstone on him from the wall, so that he died in Thebez? Why did you go near the

wall?'— then you shall say, 'Your servant Uriah the Hittite is dead also.' "

²²So the messenger went, and came and told David all that Joab had sent by him. ²³And the messenger said to David, "Surely the men prevailed against us and came out to us in the field; then we drove them back as far as the entrance of the gate. ²⁴The archers shot from the wall at your servants; and *some* of the king's servants are dead, and your servant Uriah the Hittite is dead also."

²⁵Then David said to the messenger, "Thus you shall say to Joab: 'Do not let this thing displease you, for the sword devours one as well as another. Strengthen your attack against the city, and overthrow it.' So encourage him."

²⁶When the wife of Uriah heard that Uriah her husband was dead, she mourned for her husband. ²⁷And when her mourning was over, David sent and brought her to his house, and she became his wife and bore him a son. But the thing that David had done displeased the LORD.

Nathan's Parable and David's Confession

12 Then the LORD sent Nathan to David. And he came to him, and said to him: "There were two men in one city, one rich and the other poor. ²The rich *man* had exceedingly many flocks and herds. ³But the poor *man* had nothing, except one little ewe lamb which he had bought and nourished; and it grew up together with him and with his children. It ate of his own food and drank from his own cup and lay in his bosom; and it was like a daughter to him. ⁴And a traveler came to the rich man, who refused to take from his own flock and from his own herd to prepare one for the wayfaring man who had come to him; but he took the poor man's lamb and prepared it for the man who had come to him."

⁵So David's anger was greatly aroused against the man, and he said to Nathan, "*As* the LORD lives, the man who has done this shall surely die! ⁶And he shall restore fourfold for the lamb, because he did this thing and because he had no pity."

11:21 ᵃSame as *Jerubbaal* (Gideon), Judges 6:32ff

---

ual coitus. With these words, David was suggesting that Uriah go home and lie with his wife, as is made clear (v. 11). However, a soldier in ancient times was expected to refrain from sexual activity during a military campaign. Uriah the Hittite was a man of principle. His name meant *"Yahweh* is my light," indicating that he worshiped God, although he was not of Hebrew origin. He was a loyal mercenary in the king's personal guard, listed among David's mighty men (2 Sam. 23:39). Perhaps, due to gossip, Uriah suspected the king's relationship with his wife. But his strong resolve, even in a drunken state, is in clear contrast to the king's self-indulgence. To cover up his sin of adultery, David was ready to murder an innocent, valiant, and trustworthy man.

11:15 David and Bathsheba should both have been sentenced to death, if they had been found lying together, because she was already married to Uriah (Deut. 22:22). Bathsheba's pregnancy would have revealed their adultery as her husband had been away from her the whole spring season. If Uriah had spent one night with his wife when he was called back to Jerusalem, the matter could have remained hidden. But since Uriah refused to do so, the only way David could protect his own name was to have Uriah killed immediately. He could then quickly marry Bathsheba, and her pregnancy would cause no further difficulty. So David plotted an "accidental" death for Uriah in order to protect himself.

BATHSHEBA *Forgiven and Restored*

Bathsheba was the beautiful wife of Uriah the Hittite, who was a trusted and loyal commander in the king's army. When Bathsheba knew she was pregnant by the adulterous encounter with King David, she sent word to the king. David brought her husband home from battle, hoping Uriah would enjoy intimacy with Bathsheba and thereby perceive himself as the father of her unborn child. When this plan went awry, David arranged for Uriah's death on the battlefield, then sent his messengers and brought Bathsheba to his palace. Though perhaps she could have rejected the king's initial overtures, by this point she obviously had no choice in the matter.

Did she realize that her husband's death was the result of deliberate orders by the king? What went through her mind on hearing the prophet Nathan's words of judgment on the king? When David came to comfort her after the death of their child (2 Sam. 12:24), did she recoil from the man whose lust for her had caused the death of a loyal and trusting husband and brought judgment on her child? She mourned for her husband (2 Sam. 11:26), and her heart must have broken as she held her dying baby, watching helplessly as life slipped out of the tiny body. In spite of her love and even the king's fasting and pleading before God for his son's life, the little one died. However, in due time, another son, Solomon, was born to her.

As queen, she must have been aware of the various intrigues which occurred when David's sons rose up against him and vied with each other to take power from the king. When David was near the end of his life, Bathsheba heard rumblings that another of David's sons, Adonijah, had set himself up as king. Politically astute enough to realize that her own son's succession was in danger, she must have been grateful when the prophet Nathan presented a plan for insuring the fulfillment of David's promise that Solomon would sit on his throne.

Realizing he must act quickly to establish Solomon as the successor to the throne in the eyes of the people, David gave instructions for the high priest to anoint Solomon as king. Solomon then served as a co-regent until David's death. As Queen Mother, Bathsheba enjoyed additional respect and exercised authority over the women of the king's house.

Bathsheba lived long. She had been a victim of a king's lust, a grieving mother, a political schemer, and a revered Queen Mother. Her experiences encompassed the worst and the best, the heights and the depths of human circumstance and emotion. But perhaps the notoriety of her scandalous adultery is ultimately overshadowed by her legacy as mother of the wisest of Israel's kings.

See also 2 Sam. 12:15–24; 1 Kin. 1:11–31; 2:13–22; charts on David: How Good People Get Into Trouble; The Family Tree of David; notes on Adultery (Hos. 3); Children (2 Sam. 21)

---

⁷Then Nathan said to David, "You *are* the man! Thus says the Lord God of Israel: 'I anointed you king over Israel, and I delivered you from the hand of Saul. ⁸I gave you your master's house and your master's wives into your keeping, and gave you the house of Israel and Judah. And if *that had been* too little, I also would have given you much more! ⁹Why have you despised the commandment of the Lord, to do evil in His sight? You have killed Uriah the Hittite with the sword; you have taken his wife *to be* your wife, and have killed him with the sword of the people of Ammon. ¹⁰Now therefore, the sword shall never depart from your house, because you have despised Me, and have taken the wife of Uriah the Hittite to be your wife.' ¹¹Thus says the Lord: 'Behold, I will raise up adversity against you from your own house; and I will take your wives before your eyes and give *them* to your neighbor, and he shall lie with your wives in the sight of this sun. ¹²For you did *it* secretly, but I will do this thing before all Israel, before the sun.' "

¹³So David said to Nathan, "I have sinned against the Lord."

And Nathan said to David, "The Lord also has put away your sin; you shall not die. ¹⁴However, because by this deed you have given great occasion to the enemies of the Lord to blaspheme, the

---

12:7–14 Nathan appealed to David as supreme judge of the land. With his clever story, he made David condemn himself with his own mouth. Nathan then boldly delivered God's message to the king: "You are the man" who deserves to die (v. 7). David's main problem was his heart attitude. In the midst of power and prosperity, he had lost a proper reverence for God's Law. He used his position as king to avoid getting caught (see 2 Sam. 11:15, note). His sin was first against God (see David's words, Ps. 51). When David acknowledged this, his death sentence was annulled and his relationship with God was fully restored. This restored relationship can be seen in the attitude of trust and hope he later displayed, even when he was suffering under God's correction (2 Sam. 12:22; 16:10–12). Although David's sin was forgiven, the consequences of his actions could not be avoided. First of all, his sons followed his example, which led to violent deaths for Amnon and Absalom as well as to further trauma in his dynasty. Then, because David had brought shame to God's cause, his actions were publicly condemned. Absalom led a revolution against his father and took the wives of his father for all to see.

child also *who is* born to you shall surely die." [15]Then Nathan departed to his house.

The Death of David's Son

And the LORD struck the child that Uriah's wife bore to David, and it became ill. [16]David therefore pleaded with God for the child, and David fasted and went in and lay all night on the ground. [17]So the elders of his house arose *and went* to him, to raise him up from the ground. But he would not, nor did he eat food with them. [18]Then on the seventh day it came to pass that the child died. And the servants of David were afraid to tell him that the child was dead. For they said, "Indeed, while the child was alive, we spoke to him, and he would not heed our voice. How can we tell him that the child is dead? He may do some harm!"

[19]When David saw that his servants were whispering, David perceived that the child was dead. Therefore David said to his servants, "Is the child dead?"

And they said, "He is dead."

[20]So David arose from the ground, washed and anointed himself, and changed his clothes; and he went into the house of the LORD and worshiped. Then he went to his own house; and when he requested, they set food before him, and he ate. [21]Then his servants said to him, "What *is* this that you have done? You fasted and wept for the child *while he was* alive, but when the child died, you arose and ate food."

[22]And he said, "While the child was alive, I fasted and wept; for I said, 'Who can tell *whether* the LORD[a] will be gracious to me, that the child may live?' [23]But now he is dead; why should I fast? Can I bring him back again? I shall go to him, but he shall not return to me."

Solomon Is Born

[24]Then David comforted Bathsheba his wife, and went in to her and lay with her. So she bore a son, and he[a] called his name Solomon. Now the LORD loved him, [25]and He sent *word* by the hand of Nathan the prophet: So he[a] called his name Jedidiah,[b] because of the LORD.

Rabbah Is Captured

[26]Now Joab fought against Rabbah of the people of Ammon, and took the royal city. [27]And Joab sent messengers to David, and said, "I have fought against Rabbah, and I have taken the city's water *supply.* [28]Now therefore, gather the rest of the people together and encamp against the city and take it, lest I take the city and it be called after my name." [29]So David gathered all the people together and went to Rabbah, fought against it, and took it. [30]Then he took their king's crown from his head. Its weight *was* a talent of gold, with precious stones. And it was *set* on David's head. Also he brought out the spoil of the city in great abundance. [31]And he brought out the people who *were* in it, and put *them to work* with saws and iron picks and iron axes, and made them cross over to the brick works. So he did to all the cities of the people of Ammon. Then David and all the people returned to Jerusalem.

Amnon and Tamar

13 After this Absalom the son of David had a lovely sister, whose name *was* Tamar; and Amnon the son of David loved her. [2]Amnon was so distressed over his sister Tamar that he became sick; for she *was* a virgin. And it was improper for Amnon to do anything to her. [3]But Amnon had a friend whose name *was* Jonadab the son of Shimeah, David's brother. Now Jonadab *was* a very crafty man. [4]And he said to him, "Why *are* you, the king's son, becoming thinner day after day? Will you not tell me?"

Amnon said to him, "I love Tamar, my brother Absalom's sister."

[5]So Jonadab said to him, "Lie down on your bed and pretend to be ill. And when your father comes to see you, say to him, 'Please let my sister Tamar come and give me food, and prepare the food in my sight, that I may see *it* and eat it from her hand.' " [6]Then Amnon lay down and pretended to be ill; and when the king came to see him, Amnon said to the king, "Please let Tamar my sister come and make a couple of cakes for me in my sight, that I may eat from her hand."

[7]And David sent home to Tamar, saying, "Now

12:22 [a]A few Hebrew manuscripts and Syriac read *God.* **12:24** [a]Following Kethib, Septuagint, and Vulgate; Qere, a few Hebrew manuscripts, Syriac, and Targum read *she.* **12:25** [a]Qere, some Hebrew manuscripts, Syriac, and Targum read *she.* [b]Literally *Beloved of the LORD*

12:23 David was not following the usual custom of mourning after the death of his child (see 2 Sam. 1:2, note). He had fasted and remained lying on the ground for a week during the child's illness. This was the sign of a spiritual struggle, an humble pleading with God to negate the consequence of his sin. When the child died, however, David showed his acceptance of God's correction by resuming a normal life. He recognized that though the child would not return, he himself would join the child someday. Exactly how much David understood of the afterlife is not clear, but this thought seems to have brought him comfort (2 Sam. 13:23, 24).

13:1–5 Tamar was Absalom's sister but only a half-sister to Amnon. Because she was of marriageable age, she was kept under close surveillance. However, Jonadab suggested a way for Amnon to gain the king's permission to see her alone. Customarily a special meal was prepared for the person who was ill. The cooking was usually done in a side-chamber, as the sick person watched from his bed. The dish was then carried to him by a servant. Amnon's request to have Tamar herself feed him was interpreted as the whim of a spoiled prince. The servants were sent away out of consideration for his illness as well as his high position.

DATE RAPE A TRAGIC ENCOUNTER

The pain of being raped while on a date evokes strong emotions such as shock, denial, shame, guilt, anger, and depression. The woman may ask herself how she could have allowed such a situation to occur, why her judgment of character was not better, or what she did that might have caused the man to rape her. She may feel dirty or sinful as a result of the abuse she has experienced. She may also feel hostility and anger, wanting the individual to suffer as she has suffered.

The victim of a date rape needs the comfort of believers (2 Cor. 1:3, 4) during the initial period of shock as she begins to accept what has happened to her. The victim *must not* take upon herself responsibility for the perpetrator's behavior.

The emotional healing process nearly always includes:

1) Asking God's cleansing for the guilt she feels, even as the innocent party (Ps. 51:10–13).
2) Forgiving the rapist for his actions lest she harbor anger that might lead to bitterness or some other destructive behavior (Gal. 5:19–21; 1 Thess. 5:15; Heb. 12:15).
3) Renewing her commitment to the Lord, knowing that He does not *will* evil upon her and that when He *allows* a tragedy, He is ever working to bring restoration and growth (Rom. 8:28).
4) Moving forward with her life with a determination to grow through this experience, allowing God to guide her as she develops relationships with other believers.

See also Gen. 34:1–4; Ex. 22:16, 17; Matt. 5:27–30; 15:19; 1 Thess. 4:3–8; notes on Dating (1 Tim. 4); Incest (Lev. 18); Rape (Gen. 34); Seduction (Judg. 16); Sexual Purity (1 Cor. 6); Suffering (Ps. 33; 113; Is. 43; 1 Pet. 5); portraits of Dinah (Gen. 34); Tamar (2 Sam. 13)

go to your brother Amnon's house, and prepare food for him." ⁸So Tamar went to her brother Amnon's house; and he was lying down. Then she took flour and kneaded *it,* made cakes in his sight, and baked the cakes. ⁹And she took the pan and placed *them* out before him, but he refused to eat. Then Amnon said, "Have everyone go out from me." And they all went out from him. ¹⁰Then Amnon said to Tamar, "Bring the food into the bedroom, that I may eat from your hand." And Tamar took the cakes which she had made, and brought *them* to Amnon her brother in the bedroom. ¹¹Now when she had brought *them* to him to eat, he took hold of her and said to her, "Come, lie with me, my sister."

¹²But she answered him, "No, my brother, do not force me, for no such thing should be done in Israel. Do not do this disgraceful thing! ¹³And I, where could I take my shame? And as for you, you would be like one of the fools in Israel. Now therefore, please speak to the king; for he will not withhold me from you." ¹⁴However, he would not heed

her voice; and being stronger than she, he forced her and lay with her.

¹⁵Then Amnon hated her exceedingly, so that the hatred with which he hated her *was* greater than the love with which he had loved her. And Amnon said to her, "Arise, be gone!"

¹⁶So she said to him, "No, indeed! This evil of sending me away *is* worse than the other that you did to me."

But he would not listen to her. ¹⁷Then he called his servant who attended him, and said, "Here! Put this *woman* out, away from me, and bolt the door behind her." ¹⁸Now she had on a robe of many colors, for the king's virgin daughters wore such apparel. And his servant put her out and bolted the door behind her.

¹⁹Then Tamar put ashes on her head, and tore her robe of many colors that *was* on her, and laid her hand on her head and went away crying bitterly. ²⁰And Absalom her brother said to her, "Has Amnon your brother been with you? But now hold your peace, my sister. He *is* your brother; do not

13:13 Tamar's response to Amnon's advances was gentle and reasonable (see Tamar). In a touching way she suggested they might be allowed to marry. Though the marriage of half-brothers and sisters was forbidden, this commandment may not have been strictly observed at that time (Lev. 18:11). However, mad with passion, Amnon would not listen to reason. He was intent on satisfying his lust, regardless of the consequences. His attraction then quickly turned to disgust (see Date Rape; Gen. 34, Rape). This lack of restraint seems characteristic of his behavior (2 Sam. 13:20) and indicates the lack of discipline he received while growing up. In addition, David had not set a good example for his son when he took the wife

of another (2 Sam. 11). Finally, the presence in the same family of half-brothers and sisters, the children of David's many wives, increased the potential for abuse and incest.

13:20 Tamar's reaction to rape was natural and healthy, showing proper self-respect. She mourned openly, tearing her clothes and weeping loudly. Absalom's attitude was typical of some family members who are confronted with incest. Absalom asked her to keep silent in order to protect the family name. He also minimized the offense because her half-brother was involved. However, Tamar was deeply affected by this violence and rejection. Not only did it leave her with a

take this thing to heart." So Tamar remained desolate in her brother Absalom's house.

²¹But when King David heard of all these things, he was very angry. ²²And Absalom spoke to his brother Amnon neither good nor bad. For Absalom hated Amnon, because he had forced his sister Tamar.

Absalom Murders Amnon

²³And it came to pass, after two full years, that Absalom had sheepshearers in Baal Hazor, which *is* near Ephraim; so Absalom invited all the king's sons. ²⁴Then Absalom came to the king and said, "Kindly note, your servant has sheepshearers; please, let the king and his servants go with your servant."

²⁵But the king said to Absalom, "No, my son, let us not all go now, lest we be a burden to you." Then he urged him, but he would not go; and he blessed him.

²⁶Then Absalom said, "If not, please let my brother Amnon go with us."

And the king said to him, "Why should he go with you?" ²⁷But Absalom urged him; so he let Amnon and all the king's sons go with him.

²⁸Now Absalom had commanded his servants, saying, "Watch now, when Amnon's heart is merry with wine, and when I say to you, 'Strike Amnon!' then kill him. Do not be afraid. Have I not commanded you? Be courageous and valiant." ²⁹So the servants of Absalom did to Amnon as Absalom had commanded. Then all the king's sons arose, and each one got on his mule and fled.

³⁰And it came to pass, while they were on the way, that news came to David, saying, "Absalom has killed all the king's sons, and not one of them is left!" ³¹So the king arose and tore his garments and lay on the ground, and all his servants stood by with their clothes torn. ³²Then Jonadab the son of Shimeah, David's brother, answered and said, "Let not my lord suppose they have killed all the young men, the king's sons, for only Amnon is dead. For by the command of Absalom this has been determined from the day that he forced his sister Tamar. ³³Now therefore, let not my lord the king take the thing to his heart, to think that all the king's sons are dead. For only Amnon is dead."

Absalom Flees to Geshur

³⁴Then Absalom fled. And the young man who was keeping watch lifted his eyes and looked, and there, many people were coming from the road on the hillside behind him.ᵃ ³⁵And Jonadab said to the king, "Look, the king's sons are coming; as your servant said, so it is." ³⁶So it was, as soon as he had finished speaking, that the king's sons indeed came, and they lifted up their voice and wept. Also the king and all his servants wept very bitterly.

³⁷But Absalom fled and went to Talmai the son of Ammihud, king of Geshur. And *David* mourned for his son every day. ³⁸So Absalom fled and went to Geshur, and was there three years. ³⁹And King Davidᵃ longed to go toᵇ Absalom. For he had been comforted concerning Amnon, because he was dead.

Absalom Returns to Jerusalem

14 So Joab the son of Zeruiah perceived that the king's heart *was* concerned about Absalom. ²And Joab sent to Tekoa and brought from there a wise woman, and said to her, "Please pretend to be a mourner, and put on mourning apparel; do not anoint yourself with oil, but act like a woman who has been mourning a long time for the dead. ³Go to the king and speak to him in this manner." So Joab put the words in her mouth.

⁴And when the woman of Tekoa spokeᵃ to the king, she fell on her face to the ground and prostrated herself, and said, "Help, O king!"

⁵Then the king said to her, "What troubles you?"

And she answered, "Indeed I *am* a widow, my husband is dead. ⁶Now your maidservant had two sons; and the two fought with each other in the field, and *there was* no one to part them, but the one struck the other and killed him. ⁷And now the whole family has risen up against your maidservant, and they

---

13:34 ᵃSeptuagint adds *And the watchman went and told the king, and said, "I see men from the way of Horonaim, from the regions of the mountains."* 13:39 ᵃFollowing Masoretic Text, Syriac, and Vulgate; Septuagint reads *the spirit of the king;* Targum reads *the soul of King David.* ᵇFollowing Masoretic Text and Targum; Septuagint and Vulgate read *ceased to pursue after.* 14:4 ᵃMany Hebrew manuscripts, Septuagint, Syriac, and Vulgate read *came.*

permanent social stigma, which meant she would probably never marry, but the wrong done to her had not been addressed. David had rushed to Amnon's bedside when he was ill (v. 6), but he did nothing, it seems, to help his daughter. He was angry, but weak, when it came to punishing his eldest son. When David did not take action, Absalom also chose to remain silent. Instead of resolving the issue, he let his anger grow and plotted revenge. If he had dealt with Amnon justly, David might have avoided the murder and rebellion of which Absalom later became guilty (see 2 Sam. 14:27, note).

13:38 Absalom fled to Geshur. Absalom's mother, Maacah, was the daughter of King Talmai (see chart, The Family Tree of David). David's marriage to her was based on a political alliance, not a common faith in the God of Israel. In spite of his education in the palace of Jerusalem, Absalom was no doubt influenced by the pagan values of his mother's family. He returned from exile in Geshur with a proud, rebellious spirit.

14:7 When a man was murdered, the nearest of kin was bound by sacred duty to seek vengeance (Num. 35; Deut. 19). In this case, the woman's family, in avenging the death of one son, would be taking the life of the other. Their main interest was not in seeking justice but in taking over her husband's possessions by eliminating his remaining heir. The king, as supreme judge, had the power to override the custom of blood vengeance.

TAMAR *A Violated Princess*

Many women, though not members of a royal family, can identify with Tamar. What they have in common with her is the horrifying experience of having been raped by someone they assumed could be trusted, whether a family member, a friend, or an acquaintance.

Tamar should have had little reason to fear for her personal safety. She was the daughter of King David and Princess Maacah (see 2 Sam. 3:3) and the beautiful sister of Absalom. She wore the richly colored robes of a princess and no doubt lived a secluded, pampered life.

Her half brother Amnon, overcome by her beauty and his own lust, with the help of his crafty friend and cousin, concocted a foolproof method by which he could spend time alone with her. Pretending to be sick, he requested of his father King David that Tamar be the one to come and prepare a meal for him and feed him in his illness.

Having no reason to be suspicious or fearful of her own half brother, Tamar obliged by going to Amnon's house to make breadlike cakes for him. When she offered the cakes to Amnon, however, he refused to eat them. Sending all the servants from the room, he asked that Tamar bring the cakes and feed him in the bedroom.

There, to her horror and despair, he raped her. She protested; she resisted; she begged him not to disgrace her by this shameful act. She tried persuasion; she even suggested that a request for permission to marry her would probably be granted by the king (Abraham had married his half sister Sarah; see Gen. 20:12), but she could not escape his violence.

After his lust was satisfied, Amnon's feelings changed from "love" to utter hatred and contempt. Compounding his sinful act, he had the servants throw Tamar out as if she were a piece of trash to be discarded after use.

Tamar's grief was such that she tore her beautiful robes and put ashes on her head in grief and humiliation. Understanding the emotional damage involved in rape and the consequent necessity for strong support of its victims, we can imagine how she must have felt. Her own brother Absalom callously brushed off her experience, "Hold your peace . . . do not take this thing to heart" (2 Sam. 13:20). Even King David, her own father, though he was angry, did nothing. While Absalom eventually had Amnon killed in retribution (2 Sam. 13:32), Tamar suffered the lifelong emotional trauma. Even though she was a princess, her royal status could neither protect her from an act of sexual violence nor provide the emotional support she needed to begin the process of healing. Countless women like Tamar have known the fear, pain, and shame of being raped by someone they trusted; and, like her, they need love, understanding, and compassion, which ultimately can be found only in the Lord, who is the "God of all comfort" (2 Cor 1:3; see also 2 Cor. 5:17; Heb. 4:16).

See also notes on Date Rape (2 Sam. 13); Rape (Gen. 34)

---

said, 'Deliver him who struck his brother, that we may execute him for the life of his brother whom he killed; and we will destroy the heir also.' So they would extinguish my ember that is left, and leave to my husband *neither* name nor remnant on the earth."

[8]Then the king said to the woman, "Go to your house, and I will give orders concerning you."

[9]And the woman of Tekoa said to the king, "My lord, O king, *let* the iniquity *be* on me and on my father's house, and the king and his throne *be* guiltless."

[10]So the king said, "Whoever says *anything* to you, bring him to me, and he shall not touch you anymore."

[11]Then she said, "Please let the king remember the LORD your God, and do not permit the avenger of blood to destroy anymore, lest they destroy my son."

And he said, "*As* the LORD lives, not one hair of your son shall fall to the ground."

[12]Therefore the woman said, "Please, let your maidservant speak *another* word to my lord the king."

And he said, "Say on."

[13]So the woman said: "Why then have you schemed such a thing against the people of God? For the king speaks this thing as one who is guilty, *in that* the king does not bring his banished one home again. [14]For we will surely die and *become* like water spilled on the ground, which cannot be gathered up again. Yet God does not take away a life; but He devises means, so that His banished ones are not expelled from Him. [15]Now

---

14:14 The woman of Tekoa compared the passing of our days to water that is poured out on the ground and cannot be recaptured (see The Wise Woman of Tekoa). This applied to David's own life and his need for a successor and emphasized how little time may have been left for a reconciliation with Absalom. The woman then reminded David of the mercy God

shows to sinners. He had provided cities of refuge for murderers (Num. 35:15). She may also have meant that David himself had deserved to die but was granted forgiveness (2 Sam. 12:13). With this striking image, she encouraged the king to pardon his son while there was still time.

therefore, I have come to speak of this thing to my lord the king because the people have made me afraid. And your maidservant said, 'I will now speak to the king; it may be that the king will perform the request of his maidservant. [16]For the king will hear and deliver his maidservant from the hand of the man *who would* destroy me and my son together from the inheritance of God.' [17]Your maidservant said, 'The word of my lord the king will now be comforting; for as the angel of God, so *is* my lord the king in discerning good and evil. And may the LORD your God be with you.'"

[18]Then the king answered and said to the woman, "Please do not hide from me anything that I ask you."

And the woman said, "Please, let my lord the king speak."

[19]So the king said, "*Is* the hand of Joab with you in all this?" And the woman answered and said, "*As* you live, my lord the king, no one can turn to the right hand or to the left from anything that my lord the king has spoken. For your servant Joab commanded me, and he put all these words in the mouth of your maidservant. [20]To bring about this change of affairs your servant Joab has done this thing; but my lord *is* wise, according to the wisdom of the angel of God, to know everything that *is* in the earth."

[21]And the king said to Joab, "All right, I have granted this thing. Go therefore, bring back the young man Absalom."

[22]Then Joab fell to the ground on his face and bowed himself, and thanked the king. And Joab said, "Today your servant knows that I have found favor in your sight, my lord, O king, in that the king has fulfilled the request of his servant." [23]So Joab arose and went to Geshur, and brought Absalom to Jerusalem. [24]And the king said, "Let him return to his own house, but do not let him see my face." So Absalom returned to his own house, but did not see the king's face.

David Forgives Absalom

[25]Now in all Israel there was no one who was praised as much as Absalom for his good looks. From the sole of his foot to the crown of his head there was no blemish in him. [26]And when he cut the hair of his head—at the end of every year he cut *it* because it was heavy on him—when he cut it, he weighed the hair of his head at two hundred shekels according to the king's standard. [27]To Absalom were born three sons, and one daughter whose name *was* Tamar. She was a woman of beautiful appearance.

[28]And Absalom dwelt two full years in Jerusalem, but did not see the king's face. [29]Therefore Absalom sent for Joab, to send him to the king, but he would not come to him. And when he sent again the second time, he would not come. [30]So he said to his servants, "See, Joab's field is near mine, and he has barley there; go and set it on fire." And Absalom's servants set the field on fire.

[31]Then Joab arose and came to Absalom's house, and said to him, "Why have your servants set my field on fire?"

[32]And Absalom answered Joab, "Look, I sent to you, saying, 'Come here, so that I may send you to the king, to say, "Why have I come from Geshur? *It would be* better for me *to be* there still."' Now therefore, let me see the king's face; but if there is iniquity in me, let him execute me."

[33]So Joab went to the king and told him. And when he had called for Absalom, he came to the king and bowed himself on his face to the ground before the king. Then the king kissed Absalom.

Absalom's Treason

15 After this it happened that Absalom provided himself with chariots and horses, and fifty men to run before him. [2]Now Absalom would rise early and stand beside the way to the gate. *So* it was, whenever anyone who had a lawsuit came to the king for a decision, that Absalom would call to him and say, "What city *are* you from?" And he would say, "Your servant *is* from such and such a tribe of Israel." [3]Then Absalom would say to him, "Look, your case *is* good and right; but *there is* no deputy of the king to hear you." [4]Moreover Absalom would say, "Oh, that I were made judge in the land, and everyone who has any suit or cause would come to me; then I would give him justice." [5]And *so* it was, whenever anyone came near to bow

---

14:26 Absalom's hair probably weighed between 4 and 5 pounds. The king's standard weight was recognized both in Israel and Babylon. Absalom was admired by the people as an attractive and refined prince, the likely successor to David's throne after the death of his brother Amnon.

14:27 Absalom's sister Tamar, who had been raped by their half-brother Amnon, had found refuge in Absalom's house, where she lived as a widow (see 2 Sam. 13, Tamar). In giving her name to a little niece, the family showed the love and consideration with which she was treated, thus ending her tragic story on a comforting note (see 2 Sam. 13, notes).

15:2 The gate of the city was the place where commercial and legal transactions took place. Absalom intercepted those who were coming to the king for justice and expressed great sympathy for whatever grievances they might have felt against David's administration. Perhaps the king had become slow and complacent; perhaps he was unequal to his tremendous task as supreme judge. Absalom was patient and methodical in planning his rebellion. He impressed the people with pomp and ceremony, as well as a feigned interest in their problems. As the eldest living prince, Absalom could have merely waited to succeed his father. He may have feared being passed over because of their forced reconciliation. He was angered by the indecisive way David had dealt with him in the past and was motivated by arrogance and ruthless ambition (2 Sam. 14:32).

THE WISE WOMAN OF TEKOA

David faced a major dilemma: Was he first a father or a king? His beloved son Absalom had been in exile for three years after killing his brother Amnon. David longed for his son but could not justify the return of a murderer.

Joab sensed the king's inner conflict and believed Absalom would be a good successor to the throne. To change David's mind, he sought out a woman of unusual ability, a good actress, quick-witted and subtle. The wise woman of Tekoa was well known for her talent with oratory and intrigue. She agreed to dress as a widow in deep mourning and approach the king with the story Joab gave her. According to this story, one of her sons had killed the other and was now being pursued by her clan for murder. If he died, she would be left alone, without resource or heir to the family name. Tekoa was far enough from Jerusalem that her story could not easily be verified.

Her presentation was brilliant, with vivid imagery (see 2 Sam. 14:14, note), moving David to compassion. She was insisting that he commit himself in her favor without giving away the real purpose of her mission. With tact and respect, she prompted David to follow his own inclination and call Absalom back to Jerusalem.

This woman's charm and eloquence make her speech one of the finest recorded in the Bible, but perhaps, by pleading Absalom's case, she did not use her wisdom in a worthy cause. A woman's influence, like all God-given resources, should be exercised with responsible stewardship.

See also notes on Influence (Esth. 4); Rebellion (Num. 16)

down to him, that he would put out his hand and take him and kiss him. [6]In this manner Absalom acted toward all Israel who came to the king for judgment. So Absalom stole the hearts of the men of Israel.

[7]Now it came to pass after forty[a] years that Absalom said to the king, "Please, let me go to Hebron and pay the vow which I made to the LORD. [8]For your servant took a vow while I dwelt at Geshur in Syria, saying, 'If the LORD indeed brings me back to Jerusalem, then I will serve the LORD.' "

[9]And the king said to him, "Go in peace." So he arose and went to Hebron.

[10]Then Absalom sent spies throughout all the tribes of Israel, saying, "As soon as you hear the sound of the trumpet, then you shall say, 'Absalom reigns in Hebron!' " [11]And with Absalom went two hundred men invited from Jerusalem, and they went along innocently and did not know anything. [12]Then Absalom sent for Ahithophel the Gilonite, David's counselor, from his city—from Giloh—while he offered sacrifices. And the conspiracy grew strong, for the people with Absalom continually increased in number.

David Escapes from Jerusalem

[13]Now a messenger came to David, saying, "The hearts of the men of Israel are with Absalom."

[14]So David said to all his servants who were with him at Jerusalem, "Arise, and let us flee, or we shall not escape from Absalom. Make haste to depart, lest he overtake us suddenly and bring disaster upon us, and strike the city with the edge of the sword."

[15]And the king's servants said to the king, "We are your servants, ready to do whatever my lord the king commands." [16]Then the king went out with all his household after him. But the king left ten women, concubines, to keep the house. [17]And the king went out with all the people after him, and stopped at the outskirts. [18]Then all his servants passed before him; and all the Cherethites, all the Pelethites, and all the Gittites, six hundred men who had followed him from Gath, passed before the king.

[19]Then the king said to Ittai the Gittite, "Why are you also going with us? Return and remain with the king. For you are a foreigner and also an exile from your own place. [20]In fact, you came only yesterday. Should I make you wander up and down with us today, since I go I know not where? Return, and take your brethren back. Mercy and truth be with you."

[21]But Ittai answered the king and said, "As the LORD lives, and as my lord the king lives, surely in whatever place my lord the king shall be, whether in death or life, even there also your servant will be."

[22]So David said to Ittai, "Go, and cross over." Then Ittai the Gittite and all his men and all the little ones who were with him crossed over. [23]And all the country wept with a loud voice, and all the people crossed over. The king himself also crossed over the Brook Kidron, and all the people crossed over toward the way of the wilderness.

[24]There was Zadok also, and all the Levites with him, bearing the ark of the covenant of God. And they set down the ark of God, and Abiathar went up until all the people had finished crossing over from the city. [25]Then the king said to Zadok,

15:7 [a]Septuagint manuscripts, Syriac, and Josephus read four.

"Carry the ark of God back into the city. If I find favor in the eyes of the LORD, He will bring me back and show me *both* it and His dwelling place. ²⁶But if He says thus: 'I have no delight in you,' here I am, let Him do to me as seems good to Him." ²⁷The king also said to Zadok the priest, "*Are* you *not* a seer? Return to the city in peace, and your two sons with you, Ahimaaz your son, and Jonathan the son of Abiathar. ²⁸See, I will wait in the plains of the wilderness until word comes from you to inform me." ²⁹Therefore Zadok and Abiathar carried the ark of God back to Jerusalem. And they remained there.

³⁰So David went up by the Ascent of the *Mount of* Olives, and wept as he went up; and he had his head covered and went barefoot. And all the people who *were* with him covered their heads and went up, weeping as they went up. ³¹Then *someone* told David, saying, "Ahithophel *is* among the conspirators with Absalom." And David said, "O LORD, I pray, turn the counsel of Ahithophel into foolishness!"

³²Now it happened when David had come to the top *of the mountain,* where he worshiped God— there was Hushai the Archite coming to meet him with his robe torn and dust on his head. ³³David said to him, "If you go on with me, then you will become a burden to me. ³⁴But if you return to the city, and say to Absalom, 'I will be your servant, O king; *as* I *was* your father's servant previously, so I *will* now also *be* your servant,' then you may defeat the counsel of Ahithophel for me. ³⁵And *do* you not *have* Zadok and Abiathar the priests with you there? Therefore it will be *that* whatever you hear from the king's house, you shall tell to Zadok and Abiathar the priests. ³⁶Indeed *they have* there with them their two sons, Ahimaaz, Zadok's *son,* and Jonathan, Abiathar's *son;* and by them you shall send me everything you hear."

³⁷So Hushai, David's friend, went into the city. And Absalom came into Jerusalem.

Mephibosheth's Servant

16When David was a little past the top *of the mountain,* there was Ziba the servant of Mephibosheth, who met him with a couple of saddled donkeys, and on them two hundred *loaves* of bread, one hundred clusters of raisins, one hundred summer fruits, and a skin of wine. ²And the king said to Ziba, "What do you mean to do with these?"

So Ziba said, "The donkeys *are* for the king's household to ride on, the bread and summer fruit for the young men to eat, and the wine for those who are faint in the wilderness to drink."

³Then the king said, "And where *is* your master's son?"

And Ziba said to the king, "Indeed he is staying in Jerusalem, for he said, 'Today the house of Israel will restore the kingdom of my father to me.'"

⁴So the king said to Ziba, "Here, all that *belongs* to Mephibosheth *is* yours."

And Ziba said, "I humbly bow before you, *that* I may find favor in your sight, my lord, O king!"

Shimei Curses David

⁵Now when King David came to Bahurim, there was a man from the family of the house of Saul, whose name *was* Shimei the son of Gera, coming from there. He came out, cursing continuously as he came. ⁶And he threw stones at David and at all the servants of King David. And all the people and all the mighty men *were* on his right hand and on his left. ⁷Also Shimei said thus when he cursed: "Come out! Come out! You bloodthirsty man, you rogue! ⁸The LORD has brought upon you all the blood of the house of Saul, in whose place you have reigned; and the LORD has delivered the kingdom into the hand of Absalom your son. So now you *are caught* in your own evil, because you are a bloodthirsty man!"

⁹Then Abishai the son of Zeruiah said to the king, "Why should this dead dog curse my lord the king? Please, let me go over and take off his head!"

¹⁰But the king said, "What have I to do with you, you sons of Zeruiah? So let him curse, because the LORD has said to him, 'Curse David.' Who then shall say, 'Why have you done so?'"

¹¹And David said to Abishai and all his servants, "See how my son who came from my own body seeks my life. How much more now *may this* Benjamite? Let him alone, and let him curse; for so the LORD has ordered him. ¹²It may be that the LORD will look on my affliction,[a] and that the LORD

16:12 [a]Following Kethib, Septuagint, Syriac, and Vulgate; Qere reads *my eyes;* Targum reads *tears of my eyes.*

16:3 Ziba saw David's escape as an opportunity to prove his loyalty and to gain an advantage over his master Mephibosheth. The gifts he carried were appreciated at this time of need. When David heard that Mephibosheth had remained in Jerusalem, he readily accepted Ziba's explanation as true. The other side of the story will be given (see 2 Sam. 19:26). It seems difficult to believe that Absalom's rebellion could have benefited Mephibosheth in any way, especially since he was crippled. However, David's reaction shows that, in spite of his previous kindness to Mephibosheth, he remained suspicious of anyone who belonged to Saul's house.

16:8–12 Shimei, who was related to Saul, obviously found pleasure in the fall of a king who had taken the place of his family on the throne. In calling David a bloodthirsty man, he made him responsible for the murder of Abner (2 Sam. 3:27) and Ishbosheth (2 Sam. 4:7). This accusation would apply more justly to the death of Uriah (2 Sam. 11:15). David recognized that beyond the curse of an angry man, he was perhaps hearing the voice of God. He submitted to the correction he deserved, yet hoped in the mercy and goodness of God for the future.

will repay me with good for his cursing this day." [13]And as David and his men went along the road, Shimei went along the hillside opposite him and cursed as he went, threw stones at him and kicked up dust. [14]Now the king and all the people who *were* with him became weary; so they refreshed themselves there.

The Advice of Ahithophel

[15]Meanwhile Absalom and all the people, the men of Israel, came to Jerusalem; and Ahithophel *was* with him. [16]And so it was, when Hushai the Archite, David's friend, came to Absalom, that Hushai said to Absalom, "*Long* live the king! *Long* live the king!"

[17]So Absalom said to Hushai, "*Is* this your loyalty to your friend? Why did you not go with your friend?"

[18]And Hushai said to Absalom, "No, but whom the LORD and this people and all the men of Israel choose, his I will be, and with him I will remain. [19]"Furthermore, whom should I serve? *Should I* not *serve* in the presence of his son? As I have served in your father's presence, so will I be in your presence."

[20]Then Absalom said to Ahithophel, "Give advice as to what we should do."

[21]And Ahithophel said to Absalom, "Go in to your father's concubines, whom he has left to keep the house; and all Israel will hear that you are abhorred by your father. Then the hands of all who are with you will be strong." [22]So they pitched a tent for Absalom on the top of the house, and Absalom went in to his father's concubines in the sight of all Israel.

[23]Now the advice of Ahithophel, which he gave in those days, *was* as if one had inquired at the oracle of God. So *was* all the advice of Ahithophel both with David and with Absalom.

17 Moreover Ahithophel said to Absalom, "Now let me choose twelve thousand men, and I will arise and pursue David tonight. [2]I will come upon him while he *is* weary and weak, and make him afraid. And all the people who *are* with him will flee, and I will strike only the king. [3]Then I will bring back all the people to you. When all return except the man whom you seek, all the people will be at peace." [4]And the saying pleased Absalom and all the elders of Israel.

The Advice of Hushai

[5]Then Absalom said, "Now call Hushai the Archite also, and let us hear what he says too." [6]And when Hushai came to Absalom, Absalom spoke to him, saying, "Ahithophel has spoken in this manner. Shall we do as he says? If not, speak up."

[7]So Hushai said to Absalom: "The advice that Ahithophel has given *is* not good at this time. [8]For," said Hushai, "you know your father and his men, that they *are* mighty men, and they *are* enraged in their minds, like a bear robbed of her cubs in the field; and your father *is* a man of war, and will not camp with the people. [9]Surely by now he is hidden in some pit, or in some *other* place. And it will be, when some of them are overthrown at the first, that whoever hears *it* will say, 'There is a slaughter among the people who follow Absalom.' [10]And even he *who is* valiant, whose heart *is* like the heart of a lion, will melt completely. For all Israel knows that your father *is* a mighty man, and *those* who *are* with him *are* valiant men. [11]Therefore I advise that all Israel be fully gathered to you, from Dan to Beersheba, like the sand that *is* by the sea for multitude, and that you go to battle in person. [12]So we will come upon him in some place where he may be found, and we will fall on him as the dew falls on the ground. And of him and all the men who *are* with him there shall not be left so much as one. [13]Moreover, if he has withdrawn into a city, then all Israel shall bring ropes to that city; and we will pull it into the river, until there is not one small stone found there."

[14]So Absalom and all the men of Israel said, "The advice of Hushai the Archite *is* better than the advice of Ahithophel." For the LORD had purposed to defeat the good advice of Ahithophel, to the intent that the LORD might bring disaster on Absalom.

Hushai Warns David to Escape

[15]Then Hushai said to Zadok and Abiathar the priests, "Thus and so Ahithophel advised Absalom and the elders of Israel, and thus and so I have advised. [16]Now therefore, send quickly and tell David, saying, 'Do not spend this night in the plains of the wilderness, but speedily cross over, lest the king and all the people who *are* with him be swallowed up.' " [17]Now Jonathan and Ahimaaz stayed at En Rogel, for they dared not be seen coming into the city; so a female servant would come and tell

---

16:21 If Absalom took David's concubines, a reconciliation would be impossible, as it was the worst public insult to a king, declaring in effect that he was dead. The action was all the more serious because Absalom was David's son, and therefore Absalom deserved a curse for taking his father's concubines (Gen. 49:4).

17:17 The valleys of Hinnom and Kidron meet at En Rogel, a watering place. A female servant would not have aroused suspicion walking back and forth between the city and En Rogel, as young women were frequently sent for the water needed in the household. This alert and trustworthy woman played an important role in securing intelligence from Jerusalem for King David. In a dangerous setting, she discreetly relayed exact information from Zadok and Abiathar the priests to their sons Jonathan and Ahimaaz.

them, and they would go and tell King David. [18]Nevertheless a lad saw them, and told Absalom. But both of them went away quickly and came to a man's house in Bahurim, who had a well in his court; and they went down into it. [19]Then the woman took and spread a covering over the well's mouth, and spread ground grain on it; and the thing was not known. [20]And when Absalom's servants came to the woman at the house, they said, "Where are Ahimaaz and Jonathan?"

So the woman said to them, "They have gone over the water brook."

And when they had searched and could not find them, they returned to Jerusalem. [21]Now it came to pass, after they had departed, that they came up out of the well and went and told King David, and said to David, "Arise and cross over the water quickly. For thus has Ahithophel advised against you." [22]So David and all the people who were with him arose and crossed over the Jordan. By morning light not one of them was left who had not gone over the Jordan.

[23]Now when Ahithophel saw that his advice was not followed, he saddled a donkey, and arose and went home to his house, to his city. Then he put his household in order, and hanged himself, and died; and he was buried in his father's tomb.

[24]Then David went to Mahanaim. And Absalom crossed over the Jordan, he and all the men of Israel with him. [25]And Absalom made Amasa captain of the army instead of Joab. This Amasa was the son of a man whose name was Jithra,[a] an Israelite,[b] who had gone in to Abigail the daughter of Nahash, sister of Zeruiah, Joab's mother. [26]So Israel and Absalom encamped in the land of Gilead.

[27]Now it happened, when David had come to Mahanaim, that Shobi the son of Nahash from Rabbah of the people of Ammon, Machir the son of Ammiel from Lo Debar, and Barzillai the Gileadite from Rogelim, [28]brought beds and basins, earthen vessels and wheat, barley and flour, parched grain and beans, lentils and parched seeds, [29]honey and curds, sheep and cheese of the herd, for David and the people who were with him to eat.

For they said, "The people are hungry and weary and thirsty in the wilderness."

Absalom's Defeat and Death

18And David numbered the people who were with him, and set captains of thousands and captains of hundreds over them. [2]Then David sent out one third of the people under the hand of Joab, one third under the hand of Abishai the son of Zeruiah, Joab's brother, and one third under the hand of Ittai the Gittite. And the king said to the people, "I also will surely go out with you myself."

[3]But the people answered, "You shall not go out! For if we flee away, they will not care about us; nor if half of us die, will they care about us. But you are worth ten thousand of us now. For you are now more help to us in the city."

[4]Then the king said to them, "Whatever seems best to you I will do." So the king stood beside the gate, and all the people went out by hundreds and by thousands. [5]Now the king had commanded Joab, Abishai, and Ittai, saying, "Deal gently for my sake with the young man Absalom." And all the people heard when the king gave all the captains orders concerning Absalom.

[6]So the people went out into the field of battle against Israel. And the battle was in the woods of Ephraim. [7]The people of Israel were overthrown there before the servants of David, and a great slaughter of twenty thousand took place there that day. [8]For the battle there was scattered over the face of the whole countryside, and the woods devoured more people that day than the sword devoured.

[9]Then Absalom met the servants of David. Absalom rode on a mule. The mule went under the thick boughs of a great terebinth tree, and his head caught in the terebinth; so he was left hanging between heaven and earth. And the mule which was under him went on. [10]Now a certain

17:25 [a]Spelled Jether in 1 Chronicles 2:17 and elsewhere [b]Following Masoretic Text, some manuscripts of the Septuagint, and Targum; some manuscripts of the Septuagint read Ishmaelite (compare 1 Chronicles 2:17); Vulgate reads of Jezrael.

17:19 David's spies hid down in a well, which was probably an empty cistern used to collect rain water. The woman of the house, who must have known the young men, appraised the situation quickly and was resourceful in concealing the opening of her well. When Absalom's servants arrived in pursuit of the spies, she sent them off in the wrong direction. Her words cannot be condoned, as God does not need lies to defend his people. There was little time to ponder the issue, however. Her lively response allowed the men to escape and give David information vital to his safety.

18:5 David spoke here as a father, not as a king. He was ready to forgive his son, but lost sight of the fact that this was more than a domestic quarrel. Absalom's revolt had jeopardized

the stability and future of the kingdom and caused great loss of life. Joab totally disregarded David's orders (v. 14), as he rightly discerned that only Absalom's death could put an end to the conflict. Although Joab had saved his throne, David would never forgive him for the ruthless killing of his son (1 Kin. 2:5, 6).

18:8 The woods devoured people. The forest of Ephraim was a treacherous area. A large variety of trees flourished amidst thick undergrowth, concealing rocks, pits, and crevices. The land itself claimed many victims, but David's experienced men also used this difficult terrain to their advantage.

HAIR — A MARK OF DISTINCTION

In Old Testament times, both men and women let their hair grow long. Hair was an important physical trait for a number of Bible men—such as Absalom, whose much-admired, long, thick hair was cut annually because it was so heavy (2 Sam. 14:26). Elisha, on the other hand, was ridiculed for his baldness (2 Kin. 2:23).

In New Testament times, however, length of hair was considered a mark of distinction between men and women (1 Cor. 11:14, 15). Braided hair for women was addressed by both Peter and Paul (1 Tim. 2:9; 1 Pet. 3:3).

Mention of gray hair in Scripture nearly always includes respect shown to age, wisdom, and experience (see 1 Sam. 12:2; Job 15:10). To give a guest ointment for his head was a mark of hospitality (Luke 7:46).

A number of biblical references to hair have become everyday phrases, such as "not one hair of his head shall fall to the ground," referring to Jonathan's personal safety (1 Sam. 14:45); "more than the hairs of my head," meaning an unspecified but great number (Ps. 40:12); and "the very hairs of your head are all numbered," referring to God's great concern for each individual (Matt. 10:30).

See also Song 4:1; John 11:2; notes on Appearance (2 Cor. 3); Beauty (Prov. 4); Clothing (Ezek. 16); Cosmetics (Ex. 30); Femininity (Ps. 144)

man saw *it* and told Joab, and said, "I just saw Absalom hanging in a terebinth tree!"

[11]So Joab said to the man who told him, "You just saw *him!* And why did you not strike him there to the ground? I would have given you ten *shekels* of silver and a belt."

[12]But the man said to Joab, "Though I were to receive a thousand *shekels* of silver in my hand, I would not raise my hand against the king's son. For in our hearing the king commanded you and Abishai and Ittai, saying, 'Beware lest anyone *touch* the young man Absalom!'ᵃ [13]Otherwise I would have dealt falsely against my own life. For there is nothing hidden from the king, and you yourself would have set yourself against *me.*"

[14]Then Joab said, "I cannot linger with you." And he took three spears in his hand and thrust them through Absalom's heart, while he was *still* alive in the midst of the terebinth tree. [15]And ten young men who bore Joab's armor surrounded Absalom, and struck and killed him.

[16]So Joab blew the trumpet, and the people returned from pursuing Israel. For Joab held back the people. [17]And they took Absalom and cast him into a large pit in the woods, and laid a very large heap of stones over him. Then all Israel fled, everyone to his tent.

[18]Now Absalom in his lifetime had taken and set up a pillar for himself, which *is* in the King's Valley. For he said, "I have no son to keep my name in remembrance." He called the pillar after his own name. And to this day it is called Absalom's Monument.

David Hears of Absalom's Death

[19]Then Ahimaaz the son of Zadok said, "Let me run now and take the news to the king, how the LORD has avenged him of his enemies."

[20]And Joab said to him, "You shall not take the news this day, for you shall take the news another day. But today you shall take no news, because the king's son is dead." [21]Then Joab said to the Cushite, "Go, tell the king what you have seen." So the Cushite bowed himself to Joab and ran.

[22]And Ahimaaz the son of Zadok said again to Joab, "But whatever happens, please let me also run after the Cushite."

So Joab said, "Why will you run, my son, since you have no news ready?"

[23]"But whatever happens," *he said,* "let me run."

So he said to him, "Run." Then Ahimaaz ran by way of the plain, and outran the Cushite.

[24]Now David was sitting between the two gates. And the watchman went up to the roof over the gate, to the wall, lifted his eyes and looked, and there was a man, running alone. [25]Then the watchman cried out and told the king. And the king said, "If he *is* alone, *there is* news in his mouth." And he came rapidly and drew near.

[26]Then the watchman saw *another* man running, and the watchman called to the gatekeeper and said, "There is *another* man, running alone!"

And the king said, "He also brings news."

[27]So the watchman said, "I think the running

••••••••••••••••••
18:12 ᵃThe ancient versions read *'Protect the young man Absalom for me!'*

18:18 Three sons were born to Absalom (2 Sam. 14:27). He probably built this pillar near Jerusalem after their early deaths. It can no longer be seen today, but there is another monument named after Absalom in the Kidron valley.

18:20 Ahimaaz was bursting with pride at the victory over the rebellious forces, but he had not realized that David might consider Absalom's death to be tragic. Joab would not allow the young man to run with the news. Perhaps he feared a violent reaction against the messenger, and thus he used a slave to deliver the message (2 Sam. 4:10).

of the first is like the running of Ahimaaz the son of Zadok."

And the king said, "He *is* a good man, and comes with good news."

²⁸So Ahimaaz called out and said to the king, "All is well!" Then he bowed down with his face to the earth before the king, and said, "Blessed *be* the LORD your God, who has delivered up the men who raised their hand against my lord the king!"

²⁹The king said, "Is the young man Absalom safe?"

Ahimaaz answered, "When Joab sent the king's servant and *me* your servant, I saw a great tumult, but I did not know what *it was about.*"

³⁰And the king said, "Turn aside *and* stand here." So he turned aside and stood still.

³¹Just then the Cushite came, and the Cushite said, "There is good news, my lord the king! For the LORD has avenged you this day of all those who rose against you."

³²And the king said to the Cushite, "Is the young man Absalom safe?"

So the Cushite answered, "May the enemies of my lord the king, and all who rise against you to do harm, be like *that* young man!"

David's Mourning for Absalom

³³Then the king was deeply moved, and went up to the chamber over the gate, and wept. And as he went, he said thus: "O my son Absalom— my son, my son Absalom— if only I had died in your place! O Absalom my son, my son!"

19 And Joab was told, "Behold, the king is weeping and mourning for Absalom." ²So the victory that day was *turned* into mourning for all the people. For the people heard it said that day, "The king is grieved for his son." ³And the people stole back into the city that day, as people who are ashamed steal away when they flee in battle. ⁴But the king covered his face, and the king cried out with a loud voice, "O my son Absalom! O Absalom, my son, my son!"

⁵Then Joab came into the house to the king, and said, "Today you have disgraced all your servants who today have saved your life, the lives of your sons and daughters, the lives of your wives and the lives of your concubines, ⁶in that you love your enemies and hate your friends. For you have declared today that you regard neither princes nor servants; for today I perceive that if Absalom had lived and all of us had died today, then it would have pleased you well. ⁷Now therefore, arise, go out and speak comfort to your servants. For I swear by the LORD, if you do not go out, not one will stay with you this night. And that will be worse for you than all the evil that has befallen you from your youth until now." ⁸Then the king arose and sat in the gate. And they told all the people, saying, "There is the king, sitting in the gate." So all the people came before the king.

For everyone of Israel had fled to his tent.

David Returns to Jerusalem

⁹Now all the people were in a dispute throughout all the tribes of Israel, saying, "The king saved us from the hand of our enemies, he delivered us from the hand of the Philistines, and now he has fled from the land because of Absalom. ¹⁰But Absalom, whom we anointed over us, has died in battle. Now therefore, why do you say nothing about bringing back the king?"

¹¹So King David sent to Zadok and Abiathar the priests, saying, "Speak to the elders of Judah, saying, 'Why are you the last to bring the king back to his house, since the words of all Israel have come to the king, to his *very* house? ¹²You *are* my brethren, you *are* my bone and my flesh. Why then are you the last to bring back the king?' ¹³And say to Amasa, '*Are* you not my bone and my flesh? God do so to me, and more also, if you are not commander of the army before me continually in place of Joab.' " ¹⁴So he swayed the hearts of all the men of Judah, just as *the heart of* one man, so that they sent *this word* to the king: "Return, you and all your servants!"

¹⁵Then the king returned and came to the Jordan. And Judah came to Gilgal, to go to meet the king, to escort the king across the Jordan. ¹⁶And Shimei the son of Gera, a Benjamite, who *was* from Bahurim, hurried and came down with the men of Judah to meet King David. ¹⁷*There were* a

---

19:7 Speak comfort to your servants. David was overwhelmed with sorrow at the death of his rebellious son. Any chance of reconciliation was now lost. With remorse he must have remembered the words of Nathan, predicting violence in the royal family as a result of his own sin (2 Sam. 12:10, 11). He was so preoccupied with his personal loss that he did not even consider the effect his behavior was having on the people. But Joab was quick to see the danger in the king's deep mourning. His followers needed proper recognition of their sacrifice for him. With brutal words, he roused David from his grief and reminded him of his duty. Joab's heart was loyal but unfeeling, and his manner was harsh. Nevertheless, David followed his advice and went to the gate, where he officially expressed gratitude to his loyal supporters (see 2 Sam. 15:2, note).

19:13 In naming Amasa, who had been Absalom's captain, instead of Joab to be commander-in-chief of his own army, David hoped to win back those who had joined his son's rebellion, especially in the ranks of Judah. He also revealed his lasting resentment against Joab for disregarding his wishes and killing his son Absalom (2 Sam. 18:14). In rewarding a rebel above the loyal Joab, David allowed grief to impair his good judgment. This hasty action increased the jealousy between Judah and Israel and opened the way for Amasa's rebellion (2 Sam. 19:40–43).

thousand men of Benjamin with him, and Ziba the servant of the house of Saul, and his fifteen sons and his twenty servants with him; and they went over the Jordan before the king. [18]Then a ferryboat went across to carry over the king's household, and to do what he thought good.

David's Mercy to Shimei

Now Shimei the son of Gera fell down before the king when he had crossed the Jordan. [19]Then he said to the king, "Do not let my lord impute iniquity to me, or remember what wrong your servant did on the day that my lord the king left Jerusalem, that the king should take *it* to heart. [20]For I, your servant, know that I have sinned. Therefore here I am, the first to come today of all the house of Joseph to go down to meet my lord the king."

[21]But Abishai the son of Zeruiah answered and said, "Shall not Shimei be put to death for this, because he cursed the LORD's anointed?"

[22]And David said, "What have I to do with you, you sons of Zeruiah, that you should be adversaries to me today? Shall any man be put to death today in Israel? For do I not know that today I *am* king over Israel?" [23]Therefore the king said to Shimei, "You shall not die." And the king swore to him.

David and Mephibosheth Meet

[24]Now Mephibosheth the son of Saul came down to meet the king. And he had not cared for his feet, nor trimmed his mustache, nor washed his clothes, from the day the king departed until the day he returned in peace. [25]So it was, when he had come to Jerusalem to meet the king, that the king said to him, "Why did you not go with me, Mephibosheth?"

[26]And he answered, "My lord, O king, my servant deceived me. For your servant said, 'I will saddle a donkey for myself, that I may ride on it and go to the king,' because your servant *is* lame. [27]And he has slandered your servant to my lord the king, but my lord the king *is* like the angel of God. Therefore do *what is* good in your eyes. [28]For all my father's house were but dead men before my lord the king. Yet you set your servant among those who eat at your own table. Therefore what right have I still to cry out anymore to the king?"

[29]So the king said to him, "Why do you speak anymore of your matters? I have said, 'You and Ziba divide the land.' "

[30]Then Mephibosheth said to the king, "Rather, let him take it all, inasmuch as my lord the king has come back in peace to his own house."

David's Kindness to Barzillai

[31]And Barzillai the Gileadite came down from Rogelim and went across the Jordan with the king, to escort him across the Jordan. [32]Now Barzillai was a very aged man, eighty years old. And he had provided the king with supplies while he stayed at Mahanaim, for he *was* a very rich man. [33]And the king said to Barzillai, "Come across with me, and I will provide for you while you are with me in Jerusalem."

[34]But Barzillai said to the king, "How long have I to live, that I should go up with the king to Jerusalem? [35]I *am* today eighty years old. Can I discern between the good and bad? Can your servant taste what I eat or what I drink? Can I hear any longer the voice of singing men and singing women? Why then should your servant be a further burden to my lord the king? [36]Your servant will go a little way across the Jordan with the king. And why should the king repay me *with* such a reward? [37]Please let your servant turn back again, that I may die in my own city, near the grave of my father and mother. But here is your servant Chimham; let him cross over with my lord the king, and do for him what seems good to you."

[38]And the king answered, "Chimham shall cross over with me, and I will do for him what seems good to you. Now whatever you request of me, I will do for you." [39]Then all the people went over the Jordan. And when the king had crossed over, the king kissed Barzillai and blessed him, and he returned to his own place.

The Quarrel About the King

[40]Now the king went on to Gilgal, and Chimham[a] went on with him. And all the people of Judah escorted the king, and also half the people of Israel. [41]Just then all the men of Israel came to the king, and said to the king, "Why have our brethren, the men of Judah, stolen you away and brought the king, his household, and all David's men with him across the Jordan?"

•••••••••••••••••••••••••••••••

19:40 [a]Masoretic Text reads *Chimhan*.

19:26 I will saddle a donkey for myself. As Mephibosheth was lame, this meant "I will have a donkey saddled." He had been given orders to leave Jerusalem and join the king, but his servant Ziba had taken advantage of his infirmity. Ziba may have saddled the donkey, loaded it with provisions and set off after David, leaving his master behind; or he may have used some other means to prevent Mephibosheth from leaving the city before Absalom arrived. Mephibosheth's unkempt appearance when he came to meet David was evidence that he had been mourning since the king had left Jerusalem. Although he seemed innocent, David did not decide between the two men. He refused to deal out punishment on this day of rejoicing. Instead, he divided Saul's estate between them. Even half of this fortune was evidence of his continued kindness to Mephibosheth (see 2 Sam. 16:3, note).

⁴²So all the men of Judah answered the men of Israel, "Because the king *is* a close relative of ours. Why then are you angry over this matter? Have we ever eaten at the king's *expense?* Or has he given us any gift?"

⁴³And the men of Israel answered the men of Judah, and said, "We have ten shares in the king; therefore we also have more *right* to David than you. Why then do you despise us—were we not the first to advise bringing back our king?"

Yet the words of the men of Judah were fiercer than the words of the men of Israel.

The Rebellion of Sheba

20 And there happened to be there a rebel,ᵃ whose name *was* Sheba the son of Bichri, a Benjamite. And he blew a trumpet, and said:

"We have no share in David,
Nor do we have inheritance in the son of Jesse;
Every man to his tents, O Israel!"

²So every man of Israel deserted David, *and* followed Sheba the son of Bichri. But the men of Judah, from the Jordan as far as Jerusalem, remained loyal to their king.

³Now David came to his house at Jerusalem. And the king took the ten women, his concubines whom he had left to keep the house, and put them in seclusion and supported them, but did not go in to them. So they were shut up to the day of their death, living in widowhood.

⁴And the king said to Amasa, "Assemble the men of Judah for me within three days, and be present here yourself." ⁵So Amasa went to assemble *the men of* Judah. But he delayed longer than the set time which David had appointed him. ⁶And David said to Abishai, "Now Sheba the son of Bichri will do us more harm than Absalom. Take your lord's servants and pursue him, lest he find for himself fortified cities, and escape us." ⁷So

Joab's men, with the Cherethites, the Pelethites, and all the mighty men, went out after him. And they went out of Jerusalem to pursue Sheba the son of Bichri. ⁸When they *were* at the large stone which *is* in Gibeon, Amasa came before them. Now Joab was dressed in battle armor; on it was a belt *with* a sword fastened in its sheath at his hips; and as he was going forward, it fell out. ⁹Then Joab said to Amasa, "*Are* you in health, my brother?" And Joab took Amasa by the beard with his right hand to kiss him. ¹⁰But Amasa did not notice the sword that *was* in Joab's hand. And he struck him with it in the stomach, and his entrails poured out on the ground; and he did not *strike* him again. Thus he died.

Then Joab and Abishai his brother pursued Sheba the son of Bichri. ¹¹Meanwhile one of Joab's men stood near Amasa, and said, "Whoever favors Joab and whoever *is* for David—follow Joab!" ¹²But Amasa wallowed in *his* blood in the middle of the highway. And when the man saw that all the people stood still, he moved Amasa from the highway to the field and threw a garment over him, when he saw that everyone who came upon him halted. ¹³When he was removed from the highway, all the people went on after Joab to pursue Sheba the son of Bichri.

¹⁴And he went through all the tribes of Israel to Abel and Beth Maachah and all the Berites. So they were gathered together and also went after *Sheba.*ᵃ ¹⁵Then they came and besieged him in Abel of Beth Maachah; and they cast up a siege mound against the city, and it stood by the rampart. And all the people who *were* with Joab battered the wall to throw it down.

¹⁶Then a wise woman cried out from the city, "Hear, hear! Please say to Joab, 'Come nearby, that I may speak with you.' " ¹⁷When he had come near to her, the woman said, "*Are* you Joab?"

20:1 ᵃLiterally *man of Belial*   20:14 ᵃLiterally *him*

20:3 These ten concubines had been left behind to keep David's house when he escaped from Jerusalem during Absalom's rebellion (see chart, The Family Tree of David). On entering the city, Absalom had publicly insulted his father by lying with these women (see 2 Sam. 16:21, note). Although they were not responsible for what had happened, David's concubines had become unclean to him. Their appearence in public would have caused him shame. They were not free to marry other men because they had belonged to the king. Within the context of his day, David was kind and just in caring for these women. Their personal tragedy was caused by Absalom's arrogant and lawless behavior. But in a broader sense, it resulted from the custom of multiple wives, to which David conformed in spite of the instructions given in God's Law (see 2 Sam. 3:2–5, note).

20:4–14 Thus Amasa died. Amasa, who had been captain of Absalom's rebellious troops, had been named commander of David's army as punishment to Joab (see 2 Sam. 19:13, note).

When Sheba's revolt broke out, David quickly became aware of his mistake. Amasa was slow and inefficient in gathering the men of Judah to fight. Still holding a grudge, David called on Joab's brother Abishai to lead the famous royal bodyguard against the rebels. When Joab met Amasa with the troops he had finally managed to rally, he had no qualms in dealing with Amasa. Joab hid his sword from Amasa while they embraced, then ruthlessly stabbed him. As with Abner, he used treachery to deal with the one who threatened his position, even though he was a relative (2 Sam. 3:27). But Joab, despite his sins, always remained loyal to David and was used to bring prosperity to Israel.

20:16 A wise woman cried out. Perhaps for the first time, Joab was dealing with a woman in war. The wise woman of Abel had the boldness and insight to avert disaster for her city. She appealed directly to Joab as commander-in-chief of the attacking army, pointing out the good reputation of the town he was about to destroy. The inhabitants of Abel were faithful

He answered, "I *am*."

Then she said to him, "Hear the words of your maidservant."

And he answered, "I am listening."

[18]So she spoke, saying, "They used to talk in former times, saying, 'They shall surely seek *guidance* at Abel,' and so they would end *disputes*. [19]I *am among the* peaceable *and* faithful in Israel. You seek to destroy a city and a mother in Israel. Why would you swallow up the inheritance of the LORD?"

[20]And Joab answered and said, "Far be it, far be it from me, that I should swallow up or destroy! [21]That *is* not so. But a man from the mountains of Ephraim, Sheba the son of Bichri by name, has raised his hand against the king, against David. Deliver him only, and I will depart from the city."

So the woman said to Joab, "Watch, his head will be thrown to you over the wall." [22]Then the woman in her wisdom went to all the people. And they cut off the head of Sheba the son of Bichri, and threw *it* out to Joab. Then he blew a trumpet, and they withdrew from the city, every man to his tent. So Joab returned to the king at Jerusalem.

David's Government Officers

[23]And Joab *was* over all the army of Israel; Benaiah the son of Jehoiada *was* over the Cherethites and the Pelethites; [24]Adoram *was* in charge of revenue; Jehoshaphat the son of Ahilud *was* recorder; [25]Sheva *was* scribe; Zadok and Abiathar *were* the priests; [26]and Ira the Jairite was a chief minister under David.

David Avenges the Gibeonites

21 Now there was a famine in the days of David for three years, year after year; and David inquired of the LORD. And the LORD answered, "*It is* because of Saul and *his* bloodthirsty house, because he killed the Gibeonites." [2]So the king called the Gibeonites and spoke to them. Now the Gibeonites *were* not of the children of Israel, but of the remnant of the Amorites; the chil-

dren of Israel had sworn protection to them, but Saul had sought to kill them in his zeal for the children of Israel and Judah.

[3]Therefore David said to the Gibeonites, "What shall I do for you? And with what shall I make atonement, that you may bless the inheritance of the LORD?"

[4]And the Gibeonites said to him, "We will have no silver or gold from Saul or from his house, nor shall you kill any man in Israel for us."

So he said, "Whatever you say, I will do for you."

[5]Then they answered the king, "As for the man who consumed us and plotted against us, *that* we should be destroyed from remaining in any of the territories of Israel, [6]let seven men of his descendants be delivered to us, and we will hang them before the LORD in Gibeah of Saul, *whom* the LORD chose."

And the king said, "I will give *them*."

[7]But the king spared Mephibosheth the son of Jonathan, the son of Saul, because of the LORD's oath that *was* between them, between David and Jonathan the son of Saul. [8]So the king took Armoni and Mephibosheth, the two sons of Rizpah the daughter of Aiah, whom she bore to Saul, and the five sons of Michal[a] the daughter of Saul, whom she brought up for Adriel the son of Barzillai the Meholathite; [9]and he delivered them into the hands of the Gibeonites, and they hanged them on the hill before the LORD. So they fell, *all* seven together, and were put to death in the days of harvest, in the first *days,* in the beginning of barley harvest.

[10]Now Rizpah the daughter of Aiah took sackcloth and spread it for herself on the rock, from the beginning of harvest until the late rains poured on them from heaven. And she did not allow the birds of the air to rest on them by day nor the beasts of the field by night.

21:8 [a]Or *Merab* (compare 1 Samuel 18:19 and 25:44; 2 Samuel 3:14 and 6:23)

---

men and women of Israel, the city acted as a "mother" to the villages around and was a place where disputes were known to be settled peacefully. This daring woman also commanded the respect of her own people. When she had come to an agreement with Joab, she also persuaded the people to sacrifice Sheba in order to save the town.

21:1–6 The Gibeonites were foreigners who were allowed to live in Israel but were restricted to menial labor, following a special treaty with Joshua (Josh. 9:3–27). Though the Gibeonites had obtained this treaty by deceiving the Israelites, Saul was wrong to break the promise made to them. In trying to destroy them, he had been guilty of murder. When a crime goes unpunished, the land is polluted (Num. 35:33). God brought this injustice to David's attention by sending three years of famine. Under normal circumstances, Saul's children should not have been punished for their father's

crime (Deut. 24:16). However, men were not the judges here. God Himself had intervened, calling Saul's entire house bloodthirsty. Seemingly Saul's children had followed in his footsteps and also deserved punishment (1 Sam. 21:1). This episode shows God's concern that justice be done to every man, even citizens like the Gibeonites.

21:10 When a man was put to death, his body was to be buried the same day (Deut. 21:22, 23). However, no one assumed this responsibility when Saul's seven sons were hung by the Gibeonites. Rizpah, Saul's concubine, made a tent of sackcloth to protect their corpses from wild animals (see 2 Sam. 3, Rizpah). She watched over them from April or early May, when barley was harvested, until rain fell again. Perhaps this refers to the autumn showers, which normally occur in October or November, but her vigil may have been much shorter if God sent rain out of season. Rain indicated that the curse on

[11]And David was told what Rizpah the daughter of Aiah, the concubine of Saul, had done. [12]Then David went and took the bones of Saul, and the bones of Jonathan his son, from the men of Jabesh Gilead who had stolen them from the street of Beth Shan,[a] where the Philistines had hung them up, after the Philistines had struck down Saul in Gilboa. [13]So he brought up the bones of Saul and the bones of Jonathan his son from there; and they gathered the bones of those who had been hanged. [14]They buried the bones of Saul and Jonathan his son in the country of Benjamin in Zelah, in the tomb of Kish his father. So they performed all that the king commanded. And after that God heeded the prayer for the land.

Philistine Giants Destroyed

[15]When the Philistines were at war again with Israel, David and his servants with him went down and fought against the Philistines; and David grew faint. [16]Then Ishbi-Benob, who *was* one of the sons of the giant, the weight of whose bronze spear *was* three hundred *shekels,* who was bearing a new *sword,* thought he could kill David. [17]But Abishai the son of Zeruiah came to his aid, and struck the Philistine and killed him. Then the men of David swore to him, saying, "You shall go out no more with us to battle, lest you quench the lamp of Israel."

[18]Now it happened afterward that there was again a battle with the Philistines at Gob. Then Sibbechai the Hushathite killed Saph,[a] who *was* one of the sons of the giant. [19]Again there was war at Gob with the Philistines, where Elhanan the son of Jaare-Oregim[a] the Bethlehemite killed *the brother of* Goliath the Gittite, the shaft of whose spear *was* like a weaver's beam.

[20]Yet again there was war at Gath, where there was a man of *great* stature, who had six fingers on each hand and six toes on each foot, twenty-four in number; and he also was born to the giant. [21]So when he defied Israel, Jonathan the son of Shimea,[a] David's brother, killed him.

[22]These four were born to the giant in Gath, and fell by the hand of David and by the hand of his servants.

Praise for God's Deliverance

22 Then David spoke to the LORD the words of this song, on the day when the LORD had delivered him from the hand of all his enemies, and from the hand of Saul. [2]And he said:[a]

"The LORD *is* my rock and my fortress and my
  deliverer;
[3]The God of my strength, in whom I will trust;
My shield and the horn of my salvation,
My stronghold and my refuge;
My Savior, You save me from violence.
[4]I will call upon the LORD, *who is worthy* to be
  praised;
So shall I be saved from my enemies.

[5]"When the waves of death surrounded me,
The floods of ungodliness made me afraid.
[6]The sorrows of Sheol surrounded me;
The snares of death confronted me.
[7]In my distress I called upon the LORD,
And cried out to my God;
He heard my voice from His temple,
And my cry *entered* His ears.

[8]"Then the earth shook and trembled;
The foundations of heaven[a] quaked and were
  shaken,
Because He was angry.
[9]Smoke went up from His nostrils,
And devouring fire from His mouth;
Coals were kindled by it.
[10]He bowed the heavens also, and came down
With darkness under His feet.
[11]He rode upon a cherub, and flew;
And He was seen[a] upon the wings of the wind.
[12]He made darkness canopies around Him,
Dark waters *and* thick clouds of the skies.

21:12 [a]Spelled *Beth Shean* in Joshua 17:11 and elsewhere **21:18** [a]Spelled *Sippai* in 1 Chronicles 20:4 **21:19** [a]Spelled *Jair* in 1 Chronicles 20:5 **21:21** [a]Spelled *Shammah* in 1 Samuel 16:9 and elsewhere **22:2** [a]Compare Psalm 18 **22:8** [a]Following Masoretic Text, Septuagint, and Targum; Syriac and Vulgate read *hills* (compare Psalm 18:7). **22:11** [a]Following Masoretic Text and Septuagint; many Hebrew manuscripts, Syriac, and Vulgate read *He flew* (compare Psalm 18:10); Targum reads *He spoke with power.*

---

the land was lifted and crops would begin to grow again. David honored the memory of Saul and Jonathan by taking their remains along with the bones of Saul's seven descendants, to their family tomb (see chart, The Family Tree of Saul). In this way, he was also showing that the execution of these men had not been dictated by revenge.

22:1 The psalm of deliverance recorded in this chapter is nearly identical to a psalm probably composed by David after his victories (see 2 Sam. 8; Ps. 18), at a time in his life where he enjoyed almost unbroken success. This psalm was placed at the end of the book for a definite purpose—to show that the period of instability and rebellion in the kingdom was over. David could look forward to the future with confidence,

resting on God's promises to him and his descendants. This psalm also describes David's personal relationship with God and gives meaning to the entire history recorded in 1 and 2 Samuel.

22:9 David used bold poetic imagery to describe God's activity. These human features do not indicate that God is in the image of man but rather that he has personality. His coming is pictured as a major cataclysm (vv. 8–16). When God intervenes in the spiritual or natural realm, all the forces of heaven and earth are at His disposal. Smoke, fire, and coals could be connected with a volcanic eruption, showing God's anger. This whole section reveals God's majesty, His righteousness, and His power to save His people.

CHILDREN *DEATH OF A CHILD*

The death of a child is a heartbreak to the parents, engulfing them in a flood of grief and blame. Only someone who has had this experience can fully understand the anguish of losing a child. The bereaved mother may well hold her dying child, crying in disbelief, feeling that somehow this death is her fault, just as Hagar moved away from her dying son's side (Gen. 21:16).

Rizpah's sons were killed because of the sins of Saul and the evil he brought on his entire family. Even after the seven were sacrificed, Rizpah spread a sackcloth on a rock beside their bodies to protect them from being ravaged by birds and wild animals (2 Sam. 21:9, 10). Surely she must have wondered what she had done to deserve such tragedy!

When Jesus, the prophesied son of God, was born of Mary, she became his devoted mother. Imagine the anguish Mary felt as she stood by the cruel Cross and saw her son crucified (John 19:25, 26). Only a parent in pain can know her grief; yet we all can have her hope (Rev. 21:4). The woman who has lost a child or is facing the death of a loved one has the eternal hope that her child's life is not over. She has the assurance that for those who die in the Lord or those who have not yet reached the age of accountability the Lord transforms "our lowly body that it may be conformed to His glorious body" (Phil. 3:21). A woman can go through this experience triumphantly with the God of all comfort (2 Cor. 1:3, 4).

See also 2 Kin. 4:8–37; Matt. 18:3, note; notes on Children (2 Sam. 21; Ps. 128; Prov. 22; Luke 15); Grief (Is. 53); Motherhood (1 Sam. 1; Is. 49; Ezek. 16); Providence (Eccl. 7); Suffering (Ps. 33; 113; Is. 43; 1 Pet. 5); portraits of Jairus' Resurrected Daughter (Mark 5); Rizpah (2 Sam. 3); Shunammite Woman (2 Kin. 4)

---

¹³From the brightness before Him
 Coals of fire were kindled.

¹⁴"The Lord thundered from heaven,
 And the Most High uttered His voice.
¹⁵He sent out arrows and scattered them;
 Lightning bolts, and He vanquished them.
¹⁶Then the channels of the sea were seen,
 The foundations of the world were uncovered,
 At the rebuke of the Lord,
 At the blast of the breath of His nostrils.

¹⁷"He sent from above, He took me,
 He drew me out of many waters.
¹⁸He delivered me from my strong enemy,
 From those who hated me;
 For they were too strong for me.
¹⁹They confronted me in the day of my calamity,
 But the Lord was my support.
²⁰He also brought me out into a broad place;
 He delivered me because He delighted in me.

²¹"The Lord rewarded me according to my righteousness;
 According to the cleanness of my hands
 He has recompensed me.
²²For I have kept the ways of the Lord,
 And have not wickedly departed from my God.

²³For all His judgments *were* before me;
 And *as for* His statutes, I did not depart from them.
²⁴I was also blameless before Him,
 And I kept myself from my iniquity.
²⁵Therefore the Lord has recompensed me according to my righteousness,
 According to my cleanness in His eyes.[a]

²⁶"With the merciful You will show Yourself merciful;
 With a blameless man You will show Yourself blameless;
²⁷With the pure You will show Yourself pure;
 And with the devious You will show Yourself shrewd.
²⁸You will save the humble people;
 But Your eyes *are* on the haughty, *that* You may bring *them* down.

²⁹"For You *are* my lamp, O Lord;
 The Lord shall enlighten my darkness.
³⁰For by You I can run against a troop;
 By my God I can leap over a wall.
³¹*As for* God, His way *is* perfect;

· ·

22:25 [a]Septuagint, Syriac, and Vulgate read *the cleanness of my hands in His sight* (compare Psalm 18:24); Targum reads *my cleanness before His word.*

22:24 When David stated that he was blameless, he did not mean that he was without sin. The wrong he had done had been confessed and forgiven so that all was now in order between him and the Lord (2 Sam. 12:13). In spite of his weaknesses, David had made the Law his rule and had never turned to other gods. He was afraid of sin and lived humbly before the Lord. Because of this attitude, God delighted in David and delivered him, even after his sin against Uriah. David's triumphant return to Jerusalem after Absalom's rebellion was the sign of God's continued favor on his life (see 2 Sam. 15:25, 26).

The word of the LORD *is* proven;
He *is* a shield to all who trust in Him.

[32]"For who *is* God, except the LORD?
And who *is* a rock, except our God?
[33]God *is* my strength *and* power,[a]
And He makes my[b] way perfect.
[34]He makes my[a] feet like the *feet* of deer,
And sets me on my high places.
[35]He teaches my hands to make war,
So that my arms can bend a bow of bronze.

[36]"You have also given me the shield of Your
salvation;
Your gentleness has made me great.
[37]You enlarged my path under me;
So my feet did not slip.

[38]"I have pursued my enemies and destroyed
them;
Neither did I turn back again till they were
destroyed.
[39]And I have destroyed them and wounded them,
So that they could not rise;
They have fallen under my feet.
[40]For You have armed me with strength for the
battle;
You have subdued under me those who rose
against me.
[41]You have also given me the necks of my
enemies,
So that I destroyed those who hated me.
[42]They looked, but *there was* none to save,
Even to the LORD, but He did not answer them.
[43]Then I beat them as fine as the dust of the
earth;
I trod them like dirt in the streets,
And I spread them out.

[44]"You have also delivered me from the strivings
of my people;
You have kept me as the head of the nations.
A people I have not known shall serve me.
[45]The foreigners submit to me;
As soon as they hear, they obey me.
[46]The foreigners fade away,
And come frightened[a] from their hideouts.

[47]"The LORD lives!
Blessed *be* my Rock!

Let God be exalted,
The Rock of my salvation!
[48]*It is* God who avenges me,
And subdues the peoples under me;
[49]He delivers me from my enemies.
You also lift me up above those who rise
against me;
You have delivered me from the violent man.
[50]Therefore I will give thanks to You, O LORD,
among the Gentiles,
And sing praises to Your name.

[51]*He is* the tower of salvation to His king,
And shows mercy to His anointed,
To David and his descendants forevermore."

David's Last Words

23 Now these *are* the last words of David.

Thus says David the son of Jesse;
Thus says the man raised up on high,
The anointed of the God of Jacob,
And the sweet psalmist of Israel:

[2]"The Spirit of the LORD spoke by me,
And His word *was* on my tongue.
[3]The God of Israel said,
The Rock of Israel spoke to me:
'He who rules over men *must be* just,
Ruling in the fear of God.
[4]And *he shall be* like the light of the morning
when the sun rises,
A morning without clouds,
Like the tender grass *springing* out of the
earth,
By clear shining after rain.'

[5]"Although my house *is* not so with God,
Yet He has made with me an everlasting
covenant,
Ordered in all *things* and secure.
For *this is* all my salvation and all *my* desire;
Will He not make *it* increase?

22:33 [a]Dead Sea Scrolls, Septuagint, Syriac, and Vulgate read *It is God who arms me with strength* (compare Psalm 18:32); Targum reads *It is God who sustains me with strength.* [b]Following Qere, Septuagint, Syriac, Targum, and Vulgate (compare Psalm 18:32); Kethib reads *His.* 22:34 [a]Following Qere, Septuagint, Syriac, Targum, and Vulgate (compare Psalm 18:33); Kethib reads *His.* 22:46 [a]Following Septuagint, Targum, and Vulgate (compare Psalm 18:45); Masoretic Text reads *gird themselves.*

23:1–7 David's last words were probably composed in the closing years of his life and may have represented his final words as a poet inspired by God. David gave his last instructions to Solomon, but this psalm was his spiritual testament to Israel (see 1 Kin. 2). He described his own relationship with God, indicated what made a good leader, and recalled God's promise of a dynasty after him. This truly is a fitting conclusion to the life of a man after God's own heart.

23:5 Although my house is not so with God is alternately translated "So lives my house with God, for He has made with me an everlasting covenant." Neither David himself nor his sons lived up to the ideal of a king (vv. 3, 4), but David's life provides an inkling of what a perfect leader could achieve. God had promised David a dynasty (2 Sam. 7). This covenant did not rest on the merits of David and his sons but on the grace of God and His presence in their lives.

⁶But *the sons* of rebellion *shall* all *be* as thorns
   thrust away,
Because they cannot be taken with hands.
⁷But the man *who* touches them
Must be armed with iron and the shaft of a
   spear,
And they shall be utterly burned with fire in
   their place."

David's Mighty Men

⁸These *are* the names of the mighty men whom
David had: Josheb-Basshebeth[a] the Tachmonite,
chief among the captains.[b] He was called Adino
the Eznite, because he had killed eight hundred
men at one time. ⁹And after him *was* Eleazar the
son of Dodo,[a] the Ahohite, *one* of the three mighty
men with David when they defied the Philistines
who were gathered there for battle, and the men
of Israel had retreated. ¹⁰He arose and attacked
the Philistines until his hand was weary, and his
hand stuck to the sword. The LORD brought about
a great victory that day; and the people returned
after him only to plunder. ¹¹And after him *was*
Shammah the son of Agee the Hararite. The
Philistines had gathered together into a troop
where there was a piece of ground full of lentils.
So the people fled from the Philistines. ¹²But he
stationed himself in the middle of the field, defended it, and killed the Philistines. So the LORD
brought about a great victory.

¹³Then three of the thirty chief men went
down at harvest time and came to David at the
cave of Adullam. And the troop of Philistines encamped in the Valley of Rephaim. ¹⁴David *was* then
in the stronghold, and the garrison of the Philistines *was* then *in* Bethlehem. ¹⁵And David said
with longing, "Oh, that someone would give me a
drink of the water from the well of Bethlehem,
which *is* by the gate!" ¹⁶So the three mighty men
broke through the camp of the Philistines, drew
water from the well of Bethlehem that *was* by the
gate, and took it and brought *it* to David. Nevertheless he would not drink it, but poured it out to
the LORD. ¹⁷And he said, "Far be it from me, O
LORD, that I should do this! Is *this not* the blood of
the men who went in *jeopardy of* their lives?"
Therefore he would not drink it.
   These things were done by the three mighty
men.

¹⁸Now Abishai the brother of Joab, the son of
Zeruiah, was chief of *another* three.[a] He lifted his
spear against three hundred *men*, killed *them*, and

won a name among *these* three. ¹⁹Was he not the
most honored of three? Therefore he became
their captain. However, he did not attain to the
first three.
   ²⁰Benaiah *was* the son of Jehoiada, the son of a
valiant man from Kabzeel, who had done many
deeds. He had killed two lion-like heroes of Moab.
He also had gone down and killed a lion in the
midst of a pit on a snowy day. ²¹And he killed an
Egyptian, a spectacular man. The Egyptian *had* a
spear in his hand; so he went down to him with a
staff, wrested the spear out of the Egyptian's
hand, and killed him with his own spear. ²²These
things Benaiah the son of Jehoiada did, and won a
name among three mighty men. ²³He was more
honored than the thirty, but he did not attain to
the *first* three. And David appointed him over his
guard.
   ²⁴Asahel the brother of Joab *was* one of the
thirty; Elhanan the son of Dodo of Bethlehem,
²⁵Shammah the Harodite, Elika the Harodite,
²⁶Helez the Paltite, Ira the son of Ikkesh the
Tekoite, ²⁷Abiezer the Anathothite, Mebunnai the
Hushathite, ²⁸Zalmon the Ahohite, Maharai the Netophathite, ²⁹Heleb the son of Baanah (the
Netophathite), Ittai the son of Ribai from Gibeah
of the children of Benjamin, ³⁰Benaiah a Pirathonite, Hiddai from the brooks of Gaash, ³¹Abi-
Albon the Arbathite, Azmaveth the Barhumite,
³²Eliahba the Shaalbonite (of the sons of Jashen),
Jonathan, ³³Shammah the Hararite, Ahiam the son
of Sharar the Hararite, ³⁴Eliphelet the son of Ahas-
bai, the son of the Maachathite, Eliam the son of
Ahithophel the Gilonite, ³⁵Hezrai[a] the Carmelite,
Paarai the Arbite, ³⁶Igal the son of Nathan of
Zobah, Bani the Gadite, ³⁷Zelek the Ammonite, Naharai the Beerothite (armorbearer of Joab the son
of Zeruiah), ³⁸Ira the Ithrite, Gareb the Ithrite,
³⁹*and* Uriah the Hittite: thirty-seven in all.

David's Census of Israel and Judah

24 Again the anger of the LORD was aroused
against Israel, and He moved David against
them to say, "Go, number Israel and Judah."
   ²So the king said to Joab the commander of the
army who *was* with him, "Now go throughout all

23:8 [a]Literally *One Who Sits in the Seat* (compare 1 Chronicles 11:11)
[b]Following Masoretic Text and Targum; Septuagint and Vulgate read
the three. 23:9 [a]Spelled *Dodai* in 1 Chronicles 27:4 23:18
[a]Following Masoretic Text, Septuagint, and Vulgate; some Hebrew
manuscripts and Syriac read *thirty*; Targum reads *the mighty men.*
23:35 [a]Spelled *Hezro* in 1 Chronicles 11:37

23:8–39 David's mighty men were professional soldiers who
stood beside David throughout his life. They are divided into
groups: The first three stood apart for their outstanding
feats; but among the others, leaders such as Abishai and Benaiah were also famous for their valor. The last soldier mentioned was Uriah the Hittite, a subtle tribute to the man
whom David had betrayed (2 Sam. 11:15).

24:1 The Lord moved David against Israel. For reasons not
given, God was angry with the people of Israel. The chronicler
records that Satan incited David to number the people (1 Chr.
21:1). Here it is said that God was the instigator. No contradiction exists. As in all situations, God is in control, and there is a
difference between what God causes and what He allows. He
did not prevent David from carrying out the evil action that

Genuine giving releases a part of yourself—your own creativity, energies, time, things are merely a foretaste or afterthought of you.

Florence Littauer

the tribes of Israel, from Dan to Beersheba, and count the people, that I may know the number of the people."

³And Joab said to the king, "Now may the LORD your God add to the people a hundred times more than there are, and may the eyes of my lord the king see *it.* But why does my lord the king desire this thing?" ⁴Nevertheless the king's word prevailed against Joab and against the captains of the army. Therefore Joab and the captains of the army went out from the presence of the king to count the people of Israel.

⁵And they crossed over the Jordan and camped in Aroer, on the right side of the town which *is* in the midst of the ravine of Gad, and toward Jazer. ⁶Then they came to Gilead and to the land of Tahtim Hodshi; they came to Dan Jaan and around to Sidon; ⁷and they came to the stronghold of Tyre and to all the cities of the Hivites and the Canaanites. Then they went out to South Judah *as far as* Beersheba. ⁸So when they had gone through all the land, they came to Jerusalem at the end of nine months and twenty days. ⁹Then Joab gave the sum of the number of the people to the king. And there were in Israel eight hundred thousand valiant men who drew the sword, and the men of Judah were five hundred thousand men.

The Judgment on David's Sin

¹⁰And David's heart condemned him after he had numbered the people. So David said to the LORD, "I have sinned greatly in what I have done; but now, I pray, O LORD, take away the iniquity of Your servant, for I have done very foolishly."

¹¹Now when David arose in the morning, the word of the LORD came to the prophet Gad, David's seer, saying, ¹²"Go and tell David, 'Thus

says the LORD: "I offer you three *things;* choose one of them for yourself, that I may do *it* to you." ' " ¹³So Gad came to David and told him; and he said to him, "Shall sevenª years of famine come to you in your land? Or shall you flee three months before your enemies, while they pursue you? Or shall there be three days' plague in your land? Now consider and see what answer I should take back to Him who sent me."

¹⁴And David said to Gad, "I am in great distress. Please let us fall into the hand of the LORD, for His mercies *are* great; but do not let me fall into the hand of man."

¹⁵So the LORD sent a plague upon Israel from the morning till the appointed time. From Dan to Beersheba seventy thousand men of the people died. ¹⁶And when the angelª stretched out His hand over Jerusalem to destroy it, the LORD relented from the destruction, and said to the angel who was destroying the people, "It is enough; now restrain your hand." And the angel of the LORD was by the threshing floor of Araunahᵇ the Jebusite.

¹⁷Then David spoke to the LORD when he saw the angel who was striking the people, and said, "Surely I have sinned, and I have done wickedly; but these sheep, what have they done? Let Your hand, I pray, be against me and against my father's house."

The Altar on the Threshing Floor

¹⁸And Gad came that day to David and said to him, "Go up, erect an altar to the LORD on the

---

24:13 ªFollowing Masoretic Text, Syriac, Targum, and Vulgate; Septuagint reads *three* (compare 1 Chronicles 21:12).   24:16 ªOr *Angel* ᵇSpelled *Ornan* in 1 Chronicles 21:15

Satan had suggested. In this whole chapter, the taking of a census seems wrong. Numbering the people also led to a plague (Ex. 30:12). Other men of the ancient world held similar views. Joab and the captains of the army recognized the dangers in such an undertaking (2 Sam. 24:4). The census may have been connected with David's plans for building the temple, his main project at the end of his life. David may have wished to reorganize the systems of taxation, military service, and forced labor throughout the kingdom. However, numbering the people showed a proud spirit, a desire to measure his own greatness. It also indicated an attitude of self-sufficiency. David was putting his trust in human means, and forgetting that victories and achievements come from the Lord.

24:14 Let us fall into the hand of the Lord. The people of Israel had displeased the Lord, and David their king had also

sinned by taking the census. Quickly David sensed in his heart that he had done wrong, and he repented before the Lord. He did not seek to justify his actions, although there were perhaps good reasons for taking the census (see v. 1, note). God forgave David, yet sent correction to him and his people (2 Sam. 12:13, 14). When presented with a choice among three evils for the land, David's answer is remarkable. Even when God is about to strike him, he shows an intimate trust in God's goodness and mercy. He believes that even in the consequences of sin, the Lord will be gracious. Indeed, God stopped the plague before the appointed time and chose this moment in history to reveal the location of the future temple (2 Chr. 3:1).

24:18 The threshing floor of Araunah was located north of Jerusalem on Mt. Moriah, the same mountain on which

threshing floor of Araunah the Jebusite." [19]So David, according to the word of Gad, went up as the LORD commanded. [20]Now Araunah looked, and saw the king and his servants coming toward him. So Araunah went out and bowed before the king with his face to the ground.

[21]Then Araunah said, "Why has my lord the king come to his servant?"

And David said, "To buy the threshing floor from you, to build an altar to the LORD, that the plague may be withdrawn from the people."

[22]Now Araunah said to David, "Let my lord the king take and offer up whatever *seems* good to him. Look, *here are* oxen for burnt sacrifice, and threshing implements and the yokes of the oxen for wood. [23]All these, O king, Araunah has given to the king."

And Araunah said to the king, "May the LORD your God accept you."

[24]Then the king said to Araunah, "No, but I will surely buy *it* from you for a price; nor will I offer burnt offerings to the LORD my God with that which costs me nothing." So David bought the threshing floor and the oxen for fifty shekels of silver. [25]And David built there an altar to the LORD, and offered burnt offerings and peace offerings. So the LORD heeded the prayers for the land, and the plague was withdrawn from Israel.

Abraham had offered his son Isaac and received God's promises (Gen. 22:2). Here God, in grace, restrained His angel from destroying the people of Israel with the plague. When David saw the angel of the Lord on the threshing floor, he repented of his sin in taking the census (see 2 Chr. 3:1). Offering Israel reconciliation and peace, God instructed him to build an altar there. Refusing to offer God that which cost him nothing,

David purchased the site. He understood that this was the place chosen for the temple that his son Solomon would build. Although 2 Samuel does not give this information, early readers immediately understood that the threshing floor of Araunah referred to the site of the temple. This book ends not with a plague but with a story of deliverance and the promise of future blessing.

1 Kings

AUTHOR

First Kings contains no explicit authorship claim. The unknown author knew the writings of Moses well, since he constantly measured the kings of Israel and Judah against the Lord's commands, especially those recorded in Deuteronomy. The writer drew from several sources, including the "book of the acts of Solomon" (1 Kin. 11:41), the "book of the chronicles of the kings of Israel" (1 Kin. 14:19), and the "book of the chronicles of the kings of Judah" (1 Kin. 14:29). The books of 1 and 2 Kings have the same author and were originally one book.

DATE

The date of 1 and 2 Kings is around 560 B.C. Second Kings ends with the release of Jehoiachin, sometime during the reign of Evil-Merodach between 562 and 560 B.C. The style of the Hebrew is consistent with this date. By 560 B.C., Israel had been conquered and dispersed by Assyria (around 722 B.C.), and Judah had been taken into captivity by the Babylonians (around 586 B.C.).

BACKGROUND

SETTING: The chosen people had been conquered and were in exile; Babylon was in control of the Promised Land; Jerusalem lay in ruins; the temple had been destroyed; and Jehoiachin, David's descendant, was a captive. In this time of disruption, the exiles wondered what had happened to God's promises to His people.

PURPOSE: Kings reveals that God did not forget His people. Rather, God fulfilled His covenant promises. Idolatry and lawbreaking brought the covenant curses upon Israel (Deut. 28:15–68). First and 2 Kings do not record God's neglect of His people but present His faithfulness to His Word. The books end on a note of hope. Second Kings ends with Jehoiachin, the last king of Judah, still alive. God's covenant people still have hope if they turn and obey.

AUDIENCE: Both 1 and 2 Kings record the history of Israel and Judah for the Jewish people scattered by the exile. These books remind believers of all generations that God blesses obedience and judges disobedience by documenting His workings with His chosen people in the past.

LITERARY CHARACTERISTICS: The books of 1 and 2 Kings are not a simple recounting of kings and wars. The writer records history through the lens of the standards of the Law. The kings are evaluated by their adherence to or disregard for God's commands rather than by their building programs and conquests. The writer utilizes those sources in order to make theological commentary. The literary structure of Kings is built on an accounting of kings' reigns, each summed up by a simple formula. The formula includes the king's name and his burial place; it may also record the length of his reign, sources used to document his life, and his successors.

The chronology of 1 and 2 Kings is an ongoing problem for scholars. Each king's reign is dated by the reign of his counterpart in Israel or Judah (see chart, The Kings of Israel and Judah). Some historical events can also be dated from extrabiblical sources. When these events are recorded in a particular year of a king's reign, they provide a firm reference point for dating. The dating may be affected by several factors:

1) Coregencies. In many cases, father and son may have ruled jointly for some years, making it almost impossible to date their reigns without overlapping.
2) Accession and non-accession-year dating. In accession-year dating, the reckoning of the new king's reign does not begin officially until the new year. In non-accession-year dating, the last months of the preceding king's reign are reckoned as one year, while the remaining months are also reckoned as a full year for the new ruler. To further complicate matters, Israel used non-accession-year dating until about 900 B.C., then changed to accession-year dating. Judah used accession-year dating until about 850 B.C., then adopted the other method.
3) Religious and civil new years (see chart, The Jewish Sacred Calendar). Years were reckoned both from Tishri to Tishri (the seventh month) and from Nisan to Nisan (the first month).

Some see the chronologies found in Kings as contradictory and inconsistent. However, over the years these problems and seeming inconsistencies are being resolved so that God's Word is clearly trustworthy.

THEMES

Since God's blessing or judgment depends on the obedience of the people to the Law, these books focus on the requirements of the Law and how they were broken or obeyed. Most important were the prohibitions against foreign alliances and marriages (Deut. 7:3, 4; 17:17; 1 Kin. 11:2), the tests for true and false prophets (Deut. 18:21, 22; 1 Kin. 17:1–7), and the commands against idol worship (Deut. 12:3, 4; 1 Kin. 12:26–30). The books also show that God did not break His promise to David that his line would endure (2 Sam. 7:15–16).

OUTLINE

I. The Succession of Solomon (1:1—2:12)
  A. Adonijah's rebellion (1:1–53)
  B. David's charge to Solomon (2:1–9)
  C. The death of David (2:10–12)
II. The Reign of Solomon (2:13—11:43)
  A. Solomon's securing of the kingdom (2:13–46)
  B. The wisdom of Solomon (3:1–28)
  C. The greatness of Solomon's kingdom (4:1—10:29)
    1. Solomon's government (4:1–34)
    2. Solomon's building programs (5:1—7:51)
    3. Solomon's dedication of the temple (8:1—9:9)
    4. Solomon's additional accomplishments (9:10—10:29)
  D. God's judgment of Solomon (11:1–40)
    1. Solomon and his foreign wives (11:1–8)
    2. God's rebuke of Solomon (11:9–40)
  E. The death of Solomon (11:41–43)
III. The Division of the Kingdom (12:1—22:53)
  A. The reign of Jeroboam in Israel (12:1—14:20)

  B. The reign of Rehoboam in Judah (14:21–31)
  C. The reign of Abijam in Judah (15:1–8)
  D. The reign of Asa in Judah (15:9–24)
  E. The reign of Nadab in Israel (15:25–32)
  F. The reign of Baasha in Israel (15:33—16:7)
  G. The reign of Elah in Israel (16:8–14)
  H. The reign of Zimri in Israel (16:15–20)
  I. The reign of Omri in Israel (16:21–28)
  J. The reign of Ahab in Israel (16:29—22:40)
    1. Ahab's evil (16:29–34)
    2. God's sending of Elijah to Israel (17:1—19:21)
    3. Ahab's battle with the Syrians (20:1–34)
    4. The condemnation of Ahab for his evil (20:35—21:29)
    5. The death of Ahab in battle (22:1–40)
  K. The reign of Jehoshaphat in Judah (22:41–50)
  L. The reign of Ahaziah in Israel (22:51–53)

Adonijah Presumes to Be King

1 Now King David was old, advanced in years; and they put covers on him, but he could not get warm. [2]Therefore his servants said to him, "Let a young woman, a virgin, be sought for our lord the king, and let her stand before the king, and let her care for him; and let her lie in your bosom, that our lord the king may be warm." [3]So they sought for a lovely young woman throughout all the territory of Israel, and found Abishag the Shunammite, and brought her to the king. [4]The young woman *was* very lovely; and she cared for the king, and served him; but the king did not know her.

[5]Then Adonijah the son of Haggith exalted himself, saying, "I will be king"; and he prepared for himself chariots and horsemen, and fifty men to run before him. [6](And his father had not rebuked him at any time by saying, "Why have you done so?" He *was* also very good-looking. *His mother* had borne him after Absalom.) [7]Then he conferred with Joab the son of Zeruiah and with Abiathar the priest, and they followed and helped Adonijah. [8]But Zadok the priest, Benaiah the son of Jehoiada, Nathan the prophet, Shimei, Rei, and the mighty men who *belonged* to David were not with Adonijah.

[9]And Adonijah sacrificed sheep and oxen and fattened cattle by the stone of Zoheleth, which *is* by En Rogel; he also invited all his brothers, the king's sons, and all the men of Judah, the king's servants. [10]But he did not invite Nathan the prophet, Benaiah, the mighty men, or Solomon his brother.

[11]So Nathan spoke to Bathsheba the mother of Solomon, saying, "Have you not heard that Adonijah the son of Haggith has become king, and David our lord does not know *it*? [12]Come, please, let me now give you advice, that you may save your own life and the life of your son Solomon. [13]Go im-

mediately to King David and say to him, 'Did you not, my lord, O king, swear to your maidservant, saying, "Assuredly your son Solomon shall reign after me, and he shall sit on my throne"? Why then has Adonijah become king?' [14]Then, while you are still talking there with the king, I also will come in after you and confirm your words."

[15]So Bathsheba went into the chamber to the king. (Now the king was very old, and Abishag the Shunammite was serving the king.) [16]And Bathsheba bowed and did homage to the king. Then the king said, "What is your wish?"

[17]Then she said to him, "My lord, you swore by the LORD your God to your maidservant, *saying,* 'Assuredly Solomon your son shall reign after me, and he shall sit on my throne.' [18]So now, look! Adonijah has become king; and now, my lord the king, you do not know about *it.* [19]He has sacrificed oxen and fattened cattle and sheep in abundance, and has invited all the sons of the king, Abiathar the priest, and Joab the commander of the army; but Solomon your servant he has not invited. [20]And as for you, my lord, O king, the eyes of all Israel *are* on you, that you should tell them who will sit on the throne of my lord the king after him. [21]Otherwise it will happen, when my lord the king rests with his fathers, that I and my son Solomon will be counted as offenders."

[22]And just then, while she was still talking with the king, Nathan the prophet also came in. [23]So they told the king, saying, "Here is Nathan the prophet." And when he came in before the king, he bowed down before the king with his face to the ground. [24]And Nathan said, "My lord, O king, have you said, 'Adonijah shall reign after me, and he shall sit on my throne'? [25]For he has gone down today, and has sacrificed oxen and fattened cattle and sheep in abundance, and has invited all the king's sons, and the commanders of the army, and Abiathar the priest; and look! They are eating

---

1:2 Abishag was from Shunem, in the Plain of Esdraelon just south of the Sea of Chinnereth (or Sea of Galilee). She served as a nurse to King David. Although David had no marital relations with her, this young virgin had the status of a concubine for the rest of her life. Josephus described this ancient treatment for hypothermia, in which the body heat of a healthy person warms the body of the one who is afflicted.

1:5, 6 Adonijah was Absalom's younger brother (v. 6). He may have been the oldest of David's living sons. His bid for the throne was similar to that of Absalom (see 2 Sam. 15:1–12). Adonijah, though willful and self-centered like his brother Absalom, exhibited leadership skills and charisma. As a parent, David, just as Eli and Samuel before him, had failed miserably by not restraining or disciplining his children (v. 6; 1 Sam. 3:13; 8:1–3).

1:9 En Rogel was located near Jerusalem where the Kidron and Hinnom valleys met. Its modern name is Bir Ayyub. Since En Rogel lies on the border between the tribal territories of Judah (Josh. 15:7) and Benjamin (Josh. 18:16), Adonijah's loca-

tion would have appealed to both sides. "Zoheleth" (Heb., lit. "crawling thing" or "serpent") suggests the possibility that this rock had been used for pagan worship in the past. The use of foreign altars and high places was forbidden (Deut. 7:5).

1:15 Bathsheba's son Solomon was far from the oldest of David's sons, since, when Bathsheba became David's wife, he already had six children (2 Sam. 3:2–5). However, Bathsheba seems to have been David's favorite wife. Her approach to him indicates the dignity and influence of a queen in Israelite society (see chart, The Queens of the Old Testament). Bathsheba had the king's ear, but no real power. She approached her husband like any suppliant asking for favor.

1:24 The true place of a prophet is demonstrated in Kings. God's plan for Israel's government had three offices: A king to govern, a priest to approach God for the people, and a prophet to approach the people from God. Nathan exercised his proper function of reproving and guiding the king (see chart, The Prophets Who Spoke to Kings).

THE PROPHETS WHO SPOKE TO KINGS

CHAPTER	KING	PROPHET	TRUE OR FALSE	MESSAGE
1 Kin. 1	David	Nathan	True	Solomon's place on the throne was assured.
1 Kin. 11	Solomon	Ahijah	True	Jeroboam would become king.
1 Kin. 12	Rehoboam	Shemaiah	True	Israel would be released without a battle.
1 Kin. 13	Jeroboam	Man of God	True	Josiah would defile the altar.
1 Kin. 14	Jeroboam	Ahijah	True	Jeroboam's son would die, and his dynasty would end.
1 Kin. 16	Baasha	Jehu	True	Baasha's dynasty would end.
1 Kin. 17	Ahab	Elijah	True	Ahab and Israel must repent of idolatry.
1 Kin. 18	Ahab	Obadiah	True	God's prophets would be protected.
1 Kin. 20	Ahab	"Certain Prophet"	True	Because Ahab released Ben-Hadad, Ahab would die.
1 Kin. 22	Ahab	"Court prophets"	False	Syria would be attacked.
1 Kin. 22	Ahab	"Micaiah"	True	If Ahab attacked Syria, he would die.

and drinking before him; and they say, '*Long* live King Adonijah!' [26]But he has not invited me—me your servant—nor Zadok the priest, nor Benaiah the son of Jehoiada, nor your servant Solomon. [27]Has this thing been done by my lord the king, and you have not told your servant who should sit on the throne of my lord the king after him?"

David Proclaims Solomon King

[28]Then King David answered and said, "Call Bathsheba to me." So she came into the king's presence and stood before the king. [29]And the king took an oath and said, "*As* the LORD lives, who has redeemed my life from every distress, [30]just as I swore to you by the LORD God of Israel, saying, 'Assuredly Solomon your son shall be king after me, and he shall sit on my throne in my place,' so I certainly will do this day."

[31]Then Bathsheba bowed with *her* face to the earth, and paid homage to the king, and said, "Let my lord King David live forever!"

[32]And King David said, "Call to me Zadok the priest, Nathan the prophet, and Benaiah the son of Jehoiada." So they came before the king. [33]The king also said to them, "Take with you the servants of your lord, and have Solomon my son ride on my own mule, and take him down to Gihon. [34]There let Zadok the priest and Nathan the prophet anoint him king over Israel; and blow the horn, and say, '*Long* live King Solomon!' [35]Then you shall come up after him, and he shall come and sit on my throne, and he shall be king in my place. For I have appointed him to be ruler over Israel and Judah."

[36]Benaiah the son of Jehoiada answered the king and said, "Amen! May the LORD God of my lord the king say so *too.* [37]As the LORD has been with my lord the king, even so may He be with Solomon, and make his throne greater than the throne of my lord King David."

[38]So Zadok the priest, Nathan the prophet, Benaiah the son of Jehoiada, the Cherethites, and

---

1:33 Gihon spring, the primary source of water for Jerusalem, is located in the Kidron valley. Solomon's coronation procession would have been invisible but clearly audible to Adonijah's party.

1:38 Solomon was proclaimed king. There was no accepted method of succession in Israel. David was only the country's second king, and he had received the crown through prophetic anointing and conquest rather than through blood

the Pelethites went down and had Solomon ride on King David's mule, and took him to Gihon. [39]Then Zadok the priest took a horn of oil from the tabernacle and anointed Solomon. And they blew the horn, and all the people said, *"Long* live King Solomon!" [40]And all the people went up after him; and the people played the flutes and rejoiced with great joy, so that the earth *seemed to* split with their sound.

[41]Now Adonijah and all the guests who *were* with him heard *it* as they finished eating. And when Joab heard the sound of the horn, he said, "Why *is* the city in such a noisy uproar?" [42]While he was still speaking, there came Jonathan, the son of Abiathar the priest. And Adonijah said to him, "Come in, for you *are* a prominent man, and bring good news."

[43]Then Jonathan answered and said to Adonijah, "No! Our lord King David has made Solomon king. [44]The king has sent with him Zadok the priest, Nathan the prophet, Benaiah the son of Jehoiada, the Cherethites, and the Pelethites; and they have made him ride on the king's mule. [45]So Zadok the priest and Nathan the prophet have anointed him king at Gihon; and they have gone up from there rejoicing, so that the city is in an uproar. This *is* the noise that you have heard. [46]Also Solomon sits on the throne of the kingdom. [47]And moreover the king's servants have gone to bless our lord King David, saying, 'May God make the name of Solomon better than your name, and may He make his throne greater than your throne.' Then the king bowed himself on the bed. [48]Also the king said thus, 'Blessed *be* the LORD God of Israel, who has given *one* to sit on my throne this day, while my eyes see *it!*'"

[49]So all the guests who were with Adonijah were afraid, and arose, and each one went his way. [50]Now Adonijah was afraid of Solomon; so he arose, and went and took hold of the horns of the altar. [51]And it was told Solomon, saying, "Indeed Adonijah is afraid of King Solomon; for look, he has taken hold of the horns of the altar, saying,

'Let King Solomon swear to me today that he will not put his servant to death with the sword.'"

[52]Then Solomon said, "If he proves himself a worthy man, not one hair of him shall fall to the earth; but if wickedness is found in him, he shall die." [53]So King Solomon sent them to bring him down from the altar. And he came and fell down before King Solomon; and Solomon said to him, "Go to your house."

David's Instructions to Solomon

2 Now the days of David drew near that he should die, and he charged Solomon his son, saying: [2]"I go the way of all the earth; be strong, therefore, and prove yourself a man. [3]And keep the charge of the LORD your God: to walk in His ways, to keep His statutes, His commandments, His judgments, and His testimonies, as it is written in the Law of Moses, that you may prosper in all that you do and wherever you turn; [4]that the LORD may fulfill His word which He spoke concerning me, saying, 'If your sons take heed to their way, to walk before Me in truth with all their heart and with all their soul,' He said, 'you shall not lack a man on the throne of Israel.'

[5]"Moreover you know also what Joab the son of Zeruiah did to me, *and* what he did to the two commanders of the armies of Israel, to Abner the son of Ner and Amasa the son of Jether, whom he killed. And he shed the blood of war in peacetime, and put the blood of war on his belt that *was* around his waist, and on his sandals that *were* on his feet. [6]Therefore do according to your wisdom, and do not let his gray hair go down to the grave in peace.

[7]"But show kindness to the sons of Barzillai the Gileadite, and let them be among those who eat at your table, for so they came to me when I fled from Absalom your brother.

[8]"And see, *you have* with you Shimei the son of Gera, a Benjamite from Bahurim, who cursed me with a malicious curse in the day when I went to Mahanaim. But he came down to meet me at the

UNWED MOTHERS   *TRUSTING GOD*

In Bible times, to bear a child outside the union of marriage was cause for a woman to be disowned by her family. Unwed mothers often turned to prostitution to support themselves and their children.

One of the best-known stories in the Bible is about two harlots, unwed mothers, who came to Solomon for a judgment regarding one child they both claimed as their own (1 Kin. 3:16–27). In the story, we find two principles that can relate to all unwed mothers:

• Although unwed, a woman can be a loving mother (1 Kin. 3:26).
• Sometimes being a loving mother means giving up the child so that others might care for him.

The mother in this story was willing to give her child to another in order for her child to live (1 Kin. 3:26). An unwed mother who cannot support her child financially or emotionally may choose to make her child available for adoption. This does not mean that she is unloving, for her "giving" her child to another may be the greatest act of love she can express toward her child.

An unwed mother can also trust God to bless her child. The circumstances of a child's birth do not limit that child's capabilities or potential in God's eyes.

See also Gen. 16:1–16; 21:8–21; Is. 49:15; notes on Child Care (John 14); Date Rape (2 Sam. 13); Motherhood (1 Sam. 1; Is. 49; Ezek. 16); Rape (Gen. 34); Sexual Immorality (Prov. 6)

Jordan, and I swore to him by the LORD, saying, 'I will not put you to death with the sword.' ⁹Now therefore, do not hold him guiltless, for you *are* a wise man and know what you ought to do to him; but bring his gray hair down to the grave with blood."

Death of David

¹⁰So David rested with his fathers, and was buried in the City of David. ¹¹The period that David reigned over Israel *was* forty years; seven years he reigned in Hebron, and in Jerusalem he reigned thirty-three years. ¹²Then Solomon sat on the throne of his father David; and his kingdom was firmly established.

Solomon Executes Adonijah

¹³Now Adonijah the son of Haggith came to Bathsheba the mother of Solomon. So she said, "Do you come peaceably?"

And he said, "Peaceably." ¹⁴Moreover he said, "I have something *to say* to you."

And she said, "Say it."

¹⁵Then he said, "You know that the kingdom was mine, and all Israel had set their expectations on me, that I should reign. However, the kingdom has been turned over, and has become my brother's; for it was his from the LORD. ¹⁶Now I ask one petition of you; do not deny me."

And she said to him, "Say it."

¹⁷Then he said, "Please speak to King Solomon,

for he will not refuse you, that he may give me Abishag the Shunammite as wife."

¹⁸So Bathsheba said, "Very well, I will speak for you to the king."

¹⁹Bathsheba therefore went to King Solomon, to speak to him for Adonijah. And the king rose up to meet her and bowed down to her, and sat down on his throne and had a throne set for the king's mother; so she sat at his right hand. ²⁰Then she said, "I desire one small petition of you; do not refuse me."

And the king said to her, "Ask it, my mother, for I will not refuse you."

²¹So she said, "Let Abishag the Shunammite be given to Adonijah your brother as wife."

²²And King Solomon answered and said to his mother, "Now why do you ask Abishag the Shunammite for Adonijah? Ask for him the kingdom also— for he *is* my older brother— for him, and for Abiathar the priest, and for Joab the son of Zeruiah." ²³Then King Solomon swore by the LORD, saying, "May God do so to me, and more also, if Adonijah has not spoken this word against his own life! ²⁴Now therefore, *as* the LORD lives, who has confirmed me and set me on the throne of David my father, and who has established a houseᵃ for me, as He promised, Adonijah shall be put to death today!"

²⁵So King Solomon sent by the hand of Benaiah

· · · · · · · · · · · · · · · · · · ·
2:24 ᵃThat is, a royal dynasty

2:10–12 This statement is an example of the formula used in Kings to summarize a king's reign. The formula begins with the king's death and burial, continues with the length of his reign and other information, and concludes with the accession of the next king.

2:19 Queen mother was a position similar to that of queen: In-

fluence, but no power (see chart, The Queens of the Old Testament).

2:22 Adonijah's request. In the ancient Near East, a king normally laid claim to the harem of his predecessor (2 Sam. 16:21, 22). Adonijah's request was treasonous and demonstrates that Abishag was legally David's concubine.

the son of Jehoiada; and he struck him down, and he died.

Abiathar Exiled, Joab Executed

26And to Abiathar the priest the king said, "Go to Anathoth, to your own fields, for you *are* deserving of death; but I will not put you to death at this time, because you carried the ark of the Lord GOD before my father David, and because you were afflicted every time my father was afflicted." 27So Solomon removed Abiathar from being priest to the LORD, that he might fulfill the word of the LORD which He spoke concerning the house of Eli at Shiloh.

28Then news came to Joab, for Joab had defected to Adonijah, though he had not defected to Absalom. So Joab fled to the tabernacle of the LORD, and took hold of the horns of the altar. 29And King Solomon was told, "Joab has fled to the tabernacle of the LORD; there *he is*, by the altar." Then Solomon sent Benaiah the son of Jehoiada, saying, "Go, strike him down." 30So Benaiah went to the tabernacle of the LORD, and said to him, "Thus says the king, 'Come out!'"

And he said, "No, but I will die here." And Benaiah brought back word to the king, saying, "Thus said Joab, and thus he answered me."

31Then the king said to him, "Do as he has said, and strike him down and bury him, that you may take away from me and from the house of my father the innocent blood which Joab shed. 32So the LORD will return his blood on his head, because he struck down two men more righteous and better than he, and killed them with the sword—Abner the son of Ner, the commander of the army of Israel, and Amasa the son of Jether, the commander of the army of Judah—though my father David did not know *it.* 33Their blood shall therefore return upon the head of Joab and upon the head of his descendants forever. But upon David and his descendants, upon his house and his throne, there shall be peace forever from the LORD."

34So Benaiah the son of Jehoiada went up and struck and killed him; and he was buried in his own house in the wilderness. 35The king put Benaiah the son of Jehoiada in his place over the army, and the king put Zadok the priest in the place of Abiathar.

Shimei Executed

36Then the king sent and called for Shimei, and said to him, "Build yourself a house in Jerusalem and dwell there, and do not go out from there anywhere. 37For it shall be, on the day you go out and cross the Brook Kidron, know for certain you shall surely die; your blood shall be on your own head."

38And Shimei said to the king, "The saying *is* good. As my lord the king has said, so your servant will do." So Shimei dwelt in Jerusalem many days.

39Now it happened at the end of three years, that two slaves of Shimei ran away to Achish the son of Maachah, king of Gath. And they told Shimei, saying, "Look, your slaves *are* in Gath!" 40So Shimei arose, saddled his donkey, and went to Achish at Gath to seek his slaves. And Shimei went and brought his slaves from Gath. 41And Solomon was told that Shimei had gone from Jerusalem to Gath and had come back. 42Then the king sent and called for Shimei, and said to him, "Did I not make you swear by the LORD, and warn you, saying, 'Know for certain that on the day you go out and travel anywhere, you shall surely die'? And you said to me, 'The word I have heard *is* good.' 43Why then have you not kept the oath of the LORD and the commandment that I gave you?" 44The king said moreover to Shimei, "You know, as your heart acknowledges, all the wickedness that you did to my father David; therefore the LORD will return your wickedness on your own head. 45But King Solomon *shall be* blessed, and the throne of David shall be established before the LORD forever."

46So the king commanded Benaiah the son of Jehoiada; and he went out and struck him down, and he died. Thus the kingdom was established in the hand of Solomon.

Solomon Requests Wisdom

3 Now Solomon made a treaty with Pharaoh king of Egypt, and married Pharaoh's daughter; then he brought her to the City of David until he had finished building his own house, and the house of the LORD, and the wall all around Jerusalem. 2Meanwhile the people sacrificed at the high places, because there was no house built for the name of the LORD until those days. 3And Solomon loved the LORD, walking in the statutes of his father David, except that he sacrificed and burned incense at the high places.

2:26 Solomon merely exiled Abiathar because of his priestly status and because he had served his father David faithfully (2 Sam. 15:24, 29; 1 Chr. 15:11–15). Solomon followed David's instructions concerning Joab and Shimei (1 Kin. 2:5, 6, 8, 9; see also vv. 31, 34, 42–46).

3:1 Solomon's aim as king was to maintain the large kingdom David had conquered. Thus, his foreign policy primarily involved treaty-making rather than war. This marriage with an Egyptian princess shows the level of importance that Israel

had reached. In addition, Egypt was weakening. This princess was probably the daughter of Siamun, of the weak 21st dynasty. The marriage was profitable for Solomon, resulting in a treaty and territory gained (1 Kin. 9:16). It also violated God's prohibition of marriage with pagans (Deut. 7:3; see Kin. 11, Solomon's Pagan Wives).

3:3 Idolatry was Solomon's first breach of the law against idolatry (Deut. 12:3).

⁴Now the king went to Gibeon to sacrifice there, for that *was* the great high place: Solomon offered a thousand burnt offerings on that altar. ⁵At Gibeon the LORD appeared to Solomon in a dream by night; and God said, "Ask! What shall I give you?"

⁶And Solomon said: "You have shown great mercy to Your servant David my father, because he walked before You in truth, in righteousness, and in uprightness of heart with You; You have continued this great kindness for him, and You have given him a son to sit on his throne, as *it is* this day. ⁷Now, O LORD my God, You have made Your servant king instead of my father David, but I *am* a little child; I do not know *how* to go out or come in. ⁸And Your servant *is* in the midst of Your people whom You have chosen, a great people, too numerous to be numbered or counted. ⁹Therefore give to Your servant an understanding heart to judge Your people, that I may discern between good and evil. For who is able to judge this great people of Yours?"

¹⁰The speech pleased the LORD, that Solomon had asked this thing. ¹¹Then God said to him: "Because you have asked this thing, and have not asked long life for yourself, nor have asked riches for yourself, nor have asked the life of your enemies, but have asked for yourself understanding to discern justice, ¹²behold, I have done according to your words; see, I have given you a wise and understanding heart, so that there has not been anyone like you before you, nor shall any like you arise after you. ¹³And I have also given you what you have not asked: both riches and honor, so that there shall not be anyone like you among the kings all your days. ¹⁴So if you walk in My ways, to keep My statutes and My commandments, as your father David walked, then I will lengthen your days."

¹⁵Then Solomon awoke; and indeed it had been a dream. And he came to Jerusalem and stood before the ark of the covenant of the LORD, offered up burnt offerings, offered peace offerings, and made a feast for all his servants.

Solomon's Wise Judgment

¹⁶Now two women *who were* harlots came to the king, and stood before him. ¹⁷And one woman said, "O my lord, this woman and I dwell in the same house; and I gave birth while she *was* in the house. ¹⁸Then it happened, the third day after I had given birth, that this woman also gave birth. And we *were* together; no one *was* with us in the house, except the two of us in the house. ¹⁹And this woman's son died in the night, because she lay on him. ²⁰So she arose in the middle of the night and took my son from my side, while your maidservant slept, and laid him in her bosom, and laid her dead child in my bosom. ²¹And when I rose in the morning to nurse my son, there he was, dead. But when I had examined him in the morning, indeed, he was not my son whom I had borne."

²²Then the other woman said, "No! But the living one *is* my son, and the dead one *is* your son."

And the first woman said, "No! But the dead one *is* your son, and the living one *is* my son."

Thus they spoke before the king.

²³And the king said, "The one says, 'This *is* my son, who lives, and your son *is* the dead one'; and the other says, 'No! But your son *is* the dead one, and my son *is* the living one.' " ²⁴Then the king said, "Bring me a sword." So they brought a sword before the king. ²⁵And the king said, "Divide the living child in two, and give half to one, and half to the other."

²⁶Then the woman whose son *was* living spoke to the king, for she yearned with compassion for her son; and she said, "O my lord, give her the living child, and by no means kill him!"

But the other said, "Let him be neither mine nor yours, *but* divide *him*."

²⁷So the king answered and said, "Give the first woman the living child, and by no means kill him; she *is* his mother."

²⁸And all Israel heard of the judgment which the king had rendered; and they feared the king, for they saw that the wisdom of God *was* in him to administer justice.

Solomon's Administration

4 So King Solomon was king over all Israel. ²And these *were* his officials: Azariah the son of Zadok, the priest; ³Elihoreph and Ahijah, the sons of Shisha, scribes; Jehoshaphat the son of Ahilud, the recorder; ⁴Benaiah the son of Jehoiada, over the army; Zadok and Abiathar, the priests; ⁵Azariah the son of Nathan, over the officers; Zabud the son of Nathan, a priest *and* the king's friend; ⁶Ahishar, over the household; and Adoniram the son of Abda, over the labor force.

3:4 Gibeon was a Canaanite city slightly northwest of Jerusalem. The tabernacle was there (2 Chr. 1:3). It was also the location of a great pagan shrine.

3:14 Obedience. Although Solomon was given supernatural wisdom, obedience to the covenant Law was still necessary for him to take advantage of that gift.

3:16 Solomon's wisdom in dealing with the harlots shows the extent of his justice. Women employed as prostitutes were considered the lowest and most powerless members of Israelite society; yet even they received a fair hearing before the king (see Unwed Mothers). This was the height of the monarchy. From this point, the administration of justice by the successive kings sinks slowly to the level of King Ahab, who ordered the murder of a poor man for his vineyard (1 Kin. 21).

THE PLAN OF SOLOMON'S TEMPLE

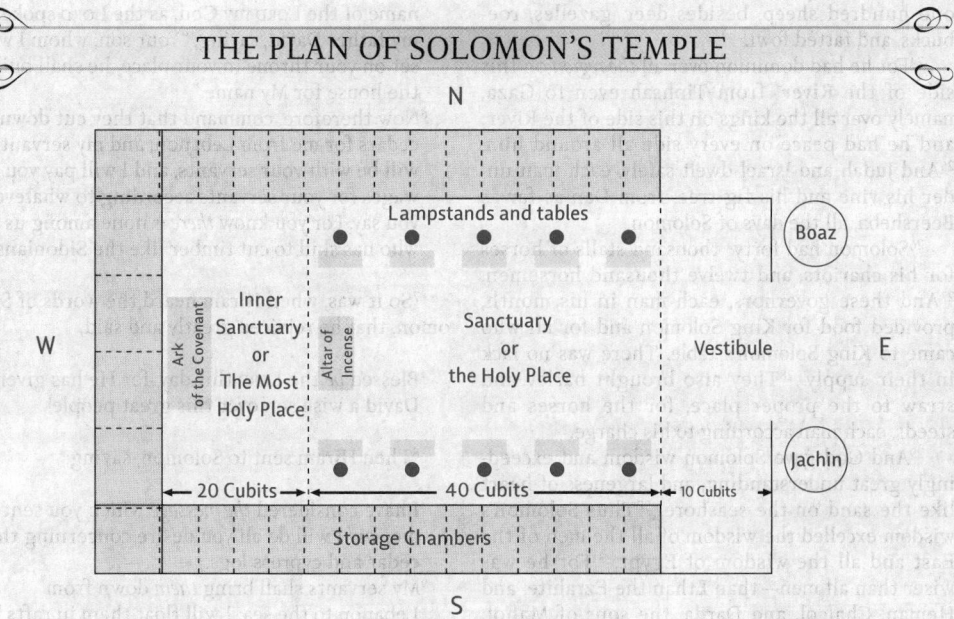

N

Lampstands and tables

Boaz

Inner
Sanctuary
or
The Most
Holy Place

Ark of the Covenant

Altar of Incense

Sanctuary
or
the Holy Place

Vestibule

W

E

Jachin

←— 20 Cubits —→ ←———— 40 Cubits ————→ ←10 Cubits→

Storage Chambers

S

Solomon constructed the temple on Mt. Moriah, north of the ancient City of David, based on the plans his father David received from the Lord (1 Chr. 28:11–13, 19). The plan is similar to that of the tabernacle but on a grander scale.

7And Solomon had twelve governors over all Israel, who provided food for the king and his household; each one made provision for one month of the year. 8These *are* their names: Ben-Hur,ᵃ in the mountains of Ephraim; 9Ben-Deker,ᵃ in Makaz, Shaalbim, Beth Shemesh, and Elon Beth Hanan; 10Ben-Hesed,ᵃ in Arubboth; to him *belonged* Sochoh and all the land of Hepher; 11Ben-Abinadab,ᵃ *in* all the regions of Dor; he had Taphath the daughter of Solomon as wife; 12Baana the son of Ahilud, *in* Taanach, Megiddo, and all Beth Shean, which *is* beside Zaretan below Jezreel, from Beth Shean to Abel Meholah, as far as the other side of Jokneam; 13Ben-Geber,ᵃ in Ramoth Gilead; to him *belonged* the towns of Jair the son of Manasseh, in Gilead; to him *also belonged* the region of Argob in Bashan—sixty large cities with walls and bronze gate-bars; 14Ahinadab the son of Iddo, *in* Mahanaim; 15Ahimaaz, in Naphtali; he also took Basemath the daughter of Solomon as wife; 16Baanah the son of Hushai, in Asher and Aloth;

17Jehoshaphat the son of Paruah, in Issachar; 18Shimei the son of Elah, in Benjamin; 19Geber the son of Uri, in the land of Gilead, *in* the country of Sihon king of the Amorites, and of Og king of Bashan. *He was* the only governor who *was* in the land.

Prosperity and Wisdom of Solomon's Reign

20Judah and Israel *were* as numerous as the sand by the sea in multitude, eating and drinking and rejoicing. 21So Solomon reigned over all kingdoms from the Riverᵃ *to* the land of the Philistines, as far as the border of Egypt. *They* brought tribute and served Solomon all the days of his life.

22Now Solomon's provision for one day was thirty kors of fine flour, sixty kors of meal, 23ten fatted oxen, twenty oxen from the pastures, and

4:8 ᵃLiterally *Son of Hur*   **4:9** ᵃLiterally *Son of Deker*   **4:10** ᵃLiterally *Son of Hesed*   **4:11** ᵃLiterally *Son of Abinadab*   **4:13** ᵃLiterally *Son of Geber*   **4:21** ᵃThat is, the Euphrates

4:7 The 12 districts for administration and taxation formed by Solomon did not follow tribal boundaries. Each district probably contained around 100,000 people and was expected to supply Solomon's immense court with provisions for one month—a severe tax burden. Administrative officers Ben-Abinadab and Ahimaaz were Solomon's sons-in-law (vv. 11, 15).

4:20 Sand by the sea alluded to God's promise to Abraham. God had fulfilled His side of the covenant. He had multiplied Abraham's seed, brought them into a Land of their own, subdued the nations, and put David's line on the throne. Whether or not Israel would live up to its part in the covenant was uncertain, but God's faithfulness to His part of the covenant was absolutely certain.

one hundred sheep, besides deer, gazelles, roe-bucks, and fatted fowl.

[24] For he had dominion over all *the region* on this side of the River[a] from Tiphsah even to Gaza, namely over all the kings on this side of the River; and he had peace on every side all around him. [25] And Judah and Israel dwelt safely, each man under his vine and his fig tree, from Dan as far as Beersheba, all the days of Solomon.

[26] Solomon had forty[a] thousand stalls of horses for his chariots, and twelve thousand horsemen. [27] And these governors, each man in his month, provided food for King Solomon and for all who came to King Solomon's table. There was no lack in their supply. [28] They also brought barley and straw to the proper place, for the horses and steeds, each man according to his charge.

[29] And God gave Solomon wisdom and exceedingly great understanding, and largeness of heart like the sand on the seashore. [30] Thus Solomon's wisdom excelled the wisdom of all the men of the East and all the wisdom of Egypt. [31] For he was wiser than all men—than Ethan the Ezrahite, and Heman, Chalcol, and Darda, the sons of Mahol; and his fame was in all the surrounding nations. [32] He spoke three thousand proverbs, and his songs were one thousand and five. [33] Also he spoke of trees, from the cedar tree of Lebanon even to the hyssop that springs out of the wall; he spoke also of animals, of birds, of creeping things, and of fish. [34] And men of all nations, from all the kings of the earth who had heard of his wisdom, came to hear the wisdom of Solomon.

Solomon Prepares to Build the Temple

5 Now Hiram king of Tyre sent his servants to Solomon, because he heard that they had anointed him king in place of his father, for Hiram had always loved David. [2] Then Solomon sent to Hiram, saying:

[3] You know how my father David could not build a house for the name of the LORD his God because of the wars which were fought against him on every side, until the LORD put *his foes*[a] under the soles of his feet.
[4] But now the LORD my God has given me rest on every side; *there is* neither adversary nor evil occurrence.
[5] And behold, I propose to build a house for the name of the LORD my God, as the LORD spoke to my father David, saying, "Your son, whom I will set on your throne in your place, he shall build the house for My name."
[6] Now therefore, command that they cut down cedars for me from Lebanon; and my servants will be with your servants, and I will pay you wages for your servants according to whatever you say. For you know *there is* none among us who has skill to cut timber like the Sidonians.

[7] So it was, when Hiram heard the words of Solomon, that he rejoiced greatly and said,

Blessed *be* the LORD this day, for He has given David a wise son over this great people!

[8] Then Hiram sent to Solomon, saying:

I have considered *the message* which you sent me, *and* I will do all you desire concerning the cedar and cypress logs.
[9] My servants shall bring *them* down from Lebanon to the sea; I will float them in rafts by sea to the place you indicate to me, and will have them broken apart there; then you can take *them* away. And you shall fulfill my desire by giving food for my household.

[10] Then Hiram gave Solomon cedar and cypress logs *according to* all his desire. [11] And Solomon gave Hiram twenty thousand kors of wheat *as* food for his household, and twenty[a] kors of pressed oil. Thus Solomon gave to Hiram year by year. [12] So the LORD gave Solomon wisdom, as He had promised him; and there was peace between Hiram and Solomon, and the two of them made a treaty together.

[13] Then King Solomon raised up a labor force out of all Israel; and the labor force was thirty thousand men. [14] And he sent them to Lebanon, ten thousand a month in shifts: they were one month in Lebanon *and* two months at home; Adoniram *was* in charge of the labor force. [15] Solomon had seventy thousand who carried burdens,

4:24 [a]That is, the Euphrates 4:26 [a]Following Masoretic Text and most other authorities; some manuscripts of the Septuagint read *four* (compare 2 Chronicles 9:25). 5:3 [a]Literally *them* 5:11 [a]Following Masoretic Text, Targum, and Vulgate; Septuagint and Syriac read *twenty thousand.*

4:27 While David supported himself through his personal income and taxes on his foreign subjects, Solomon's more lavish court put an ever-increasing tax burden on native Israelites, creating resentment (1 Kin. 12:4).

5:1 King Hiram of Tyre aided David's construction of the royal palace and had a longstanding treaty with Israel (2 Sam. 5:11).

5:9 The logs probably came ashore on the Mediterranean coast north of Joppa, about 35 miles northwest of Jerusalem; they had to be hauled the remaining distance.

5:13 In order to build the temple, Solomon resorted to forced labor. David had demanded forced labor only from conquered peoples, but Solomon extended this policy to native Israelites. Able-bodied men were required to spend four months of the year working without pay for the king. This requirement was greatly resented by the people.

and eighty thousand who quarried *stone* in the mountains, [16]besides three thousand three hundred[a] from the chiefs of Solomon's deputies, who supervised the people who labored in the work. [17]And the king commanded them to quarry large stones, costly stones, *and* hewn stones, to lay the foundation of the temple.[a] [18]So Solomon's builders, Hiram's builders, and the Gebalites quarried *them;* and they prepared timber and stones to build the temple.

Solomon Builds the Temple

6 And it came to pass in the four hundred and eightieth[a] year after the children of Israel had come out of the land of Egypt, in the fourth year of Solomon's reign over Israel, in the month of Ziv, which *is* the second month, that he began to build the house of the LORD. [2]Now the house which King Solomon built for the LORD, its length *was* sixty cubits, its width twenty, and its height thirty cubits. [3]The vestibule in front of the sanctuary[a] of the house *was* twenty cubits long across the width of the house, *and* the width of *the vestibule*[b] *extended* ten cubits from the front of the house. [4]And he made for the house windows with beveled frames.

[5]Against the wall of the temple he built chambers all around, *against* the walls of the temple, all around the sanctuary and the inner sanctuary.[a] Thus he made side chambers all around it. [6]The lowest chamber *was* five cubits wide, the middle *was* six cubits wide, and the third *was* seven cubits wide; for he made narrow ledges around the outside of the temple, so that *the support beams* would not be fastened into the walls of the temple. [7]And the temple, when it was being built, was built with stone finished at the quarry, so that no hammer or chisel *or* any iron tool was heard in the temple while it was being built. [8]The doorway for the middle story[a] *was* on the right side of the temple. They went up by stairs to the middle *story,* and from the middle to the third.

[9]So he built the temple and finished it, and he paneled the temple with beams and boards of cedar. [10]And he built side chambers against the entire temple, each five cubits high; they were attached to the temple with cedar beams.

[11]Then the word of the LORD came to Solomon, saying: [12]"*Concerning* this temple which you are building, if you walk in My statutes, execute My judgments, keep all My commandments, and walk in them, then I will perform My word with you, which I spoke to your father David. [13]And I will

dwell among the children of Israel, and will not forsake My people Israel."

[14]So Solomon built the temple and finished it. [15]And he built the inside walls of the temple with cedar boards; from the floor of the temple to the ceiling he paneled the inside with wood; and he covered the floor of the temple with planks of cypress. [16]Then he built the twenty-cubit room at the rear of the temple, from floor to ceiling, with cedar boards; he built *it* inside as the inner sanctuary, as the Most Holy *Place.* [17]And in front of it the temple sanctuary was forty cubits *long.* [18]The inside of the temple was cedar, carved with ornamental buds and open flowers. All *was* cedar; there was no stone *to be* seen.

[19]And he prepared the inner sanctuary inside the temple, to set the ark of the covenant of the LORD there. [20]The inner sanctuary *was* twenty cubits long, twenty cubits wide, and twenty cubits high. He overlaid it with pure gold, and overlaid the altar of cedar. [21]So Solomon overlaid the inside of the temple with pure gold. He stretched gold chains across the front of the inner sanctuary, and overlaid it with gold. [22]The whole temple he overlaid with gold, until he had finished all the temple; also he overlaid with gold the entire altar that *was* by the inner sanctuary.

[23]Inside the inner sanctuary he made two cherubim *of* olive wood, *each* ten cubits high. [24]One wing of the cherub *was* five cubits, and the other wing of the cherub five cubits: ten cubits from the tip of one wing to the tip of the other. [25]And the other cherub *was* ten cubits; both cherubim *were* of the same size and shape. [26]The height of one cherub *was* ten cubits, and so *was* the other cherub. [27]Then he set the cherubim inside the inner room;[a] and they stretched out the wings of the cherubim so that the wing of the one touched *one* wall, and the wing of the other cherub touched the other wall. And their wings touched each other in the middle of the room. [28]Also he overlaid the cherubim with gold.

[29]Then he carved all the walls of the temple all

5:16 [a]Following Masoretic Text, Targum, and Vulgate; Septuagint reads *three thousand six hundred.*   **5:17** [a]Literally *house,* and so frequently throughout this book   **6:1** [a]Following Masoretic Text, Targum, and Vulgate; Septuagint reads *fortieth.*   **6:3** [a]Hebrew *heykal;* here the main room of the temple, elsewhere called the holy place (compare Exodus 26:33 and Ezekiel 41:1)   [b]Literally *it*   **6:5** [a]Hebrew *debir;* here the inner room of the temple, elsewhere called the Most Holy Place (compare verse 16)   **6:8** [a]Following Masoretic Text and Vulgate; Septuagint reads *upper story;* Targum reads *ground story.*   **6:27** [a]Literally *house*

6:1 The temple was the fulfillment of the prophecy in which God promised to make a place for His name to dwell and the evidence of God's promise to give Israel her own country (Deut. 12:5). The settlement was not complete until Israel had a permanent place to worship God. The temple construction probably began in 966 B.C.

6:23 The cherubim were angels whose specific function was to stand in the presence of God and reflect His glory. When Ezekiel saw God departing from the temple, the cherubim left as well (Ezek. 10). They were located in the inner sanctuary, the Most Holy Place, because God's presence dwelt there (see chart, The Plan of Solomon's Temple).

around, both the inner and outer *sanctuaries*, with carved figures of cherubim, palm trees, and open flowers. [30]And the floor of the temple he overlaid with gold, both the inner and outer *sanctuaries*.

[31]For the entrance of the inner sanctuary he made doors *of* olive wood; the lintel *and* doorposts *were* one-fifth *of the wall.* [32]The two doors *were of* olive wood; and he carved on them figures of cherubim, palm trees, and open flowers, and overlaid *them* with gold; and he spread gold on the cherubim and on the palm trees. [33]So for the door of the sanctuary he also made doorposts *of* olive wood, one-fourth *of the wall.* [34]And the two doors *were of* cypress wood; two panels *comprised* one folding door, and two panels *comprised* the other folding door. [35]Then he carved cherubim, palm trees, and open flowers *on them,* and overlaid *them* with gold applied evenly on the carved work.

[36]And he built the inner court with three rows of hewn stone and a row of cedar beams.

[37]In the fourth year the foundation of the house of the LORD was laid, in the month of Ziv. [38]And in the eleventh year, in the month of Bul, which is the eighth month, the house was finished in all its details and according to all its plans. So he was seven years in building it.

Solomon's Other Buildings

7 But Solomon took thirteen years to build his own house; so he finished all his house.

[2]He also built the House of the Forest of Lebanon; its length *was* one hundred cubits, its width fifty cubits, and its height thirty cubits, with four rows of cedar pillars, and cedar beams on the pillars. [3]And *it was* paneled with cedar above the beams that *were* on forty-five pillars, fifteen *to* a row. [4]*There were* windows *with beveled frames* in three rows, and window *was* opposite window *in* three tiers. [5]And all the doorways and doorposts *had* rectangular frames; and window *was* opposite window *in* three tiers.

[6]He also made the Hall of Pillars: its length *was* fifty cubits, and its width thirty cubits; and in front of them *was* a portico with pillars, and a canopy *was* in front of them.

[7]Then he made a hall for the throne, the Hall of Judgment, where he might judge; and *it was* paneled with cedar from floor to ceiling.[a]

[8]And the house where he dwelt *had* another court inside the hall, of like workmanship. Solomon also made a house like this hall for Pharaoh's daughter, whom he had taken *as wife.*

[9]All these *were of* costly stones cut to size, trimmed with saws, inside and out, from the foundation to the eaves, and also on the outside to the great court. [10]The foundation *was of* costly stones, large stones, some ten cubits and some eight cubits. [11]And above *were* costly stones, hewn to size, and cedar wood. [12]The great court *was* enclosed with three rows of hewn stones and a row of cedar beams. So were the inner court of the house of the LORD and the vestibule of the temple.

Hiram the Craftsman

[13]Now King Solomon sent and brought Huram[a] from Tyre. [14]He *was* the son of a widow from the tribe of Naphtali, and his father *was* a man of Tyre, a bronze worker; he was filled with wisdom and understanding and skill in working with all kinds of bronze work. So he came to King Solomon and did all his work.

The Bronze Pillars for the Temple

[15]And he cast two pillars of bronze, each one eighteen cubits high, and a line of twelve cubits measured the circumference of each. [16]Then he made two capitals *of* cast bronze, to set on the tops of the pillars. The height of one capital *was* five cubits, and the height of the other capital *was* five cubits. [17]*He made* a lattice network, with wreaths of chainwork, for the capitals which *were* on top of the pillars: seven chains for one capital and seven for the other capital. [18]So he made the pillars, and two rows of pomegranates above the network all around to cover the capitals that *were* on top; and thus he did for the other capital. [19]The capitals which *were* on top of the pillars in the hall *were* in the shape of lilies, four cubits. [20]The capitals on the two pillars also *had pomegranates* above, by the convex surface which *was* next to the network; and there *were* two hundred such pomegranates in rows on each of the capitals all around.

••

7:7 [a]Literally *floor,* that is, of the upper level   7:13 [a]Hebrew *Hiram* (compare 2 Chronicles 2:13, 14)

6:38 The temple was probably completed in 959 B.C.

7:1 Solomon's building program was a measure of his secular success and prosperity. Solomon built extensively, especially in Jerusalem, and later found himself in financial difficulty from his massive spending.

7:8 Pharaoh's daughter, as the symbol of Israel's most important foreign alliance, rated a palace of her own (1 Kin. 3:1, note; see also 1 Kin. 11, Solomon's Pagan Wives).

7:13 Solomon's trade agreement with Phoenicia allowed him to exploit the greater technical skill of the Phoenicians for his building projects. The phrase "filled with wisdom and understanding" implies that Huram (also Hiram) of Tyre may have had an empowering from the Spirit of God to do his work.

7:21 The purpose of the pillars of bronze is unclear. However, such monuments were often built as memory aids, reminders of events in Israel's history. Jacob erected such a pillar in memory of his covenant with God (Gen. 28:10–19). The names of the pillars suggest that they were to remind the Israelites of God's strength and sovereignty in establishing His people.

*Prayer reveals to souls the vanity of earthly goods and pleasures.
It fills them with light, strength and consolation, and gives them a foretaste
of the calm bliss of our heavenly home.*

St. Rose of Viterbo

21Then he set up the pillars by the vestibule of the temple; he set up the pillar on the right and called its name Jachin, and he set up the pillar on the left and called its name Boaz. 22The tops of the pillars were in the shape of lilies. So the work of the pillars was finished.

The Sea and the Oxen

23And he made the Sea of cast bronze, ten cubits from one brim to the other; *it was* completely round. Its height *was* five cubits, and a line of thirty cubits measured its circumference. 24Below its brim *were* ornamental buds encircling it all around, ten to a cubit, all the way around the Sea. The ornamental buds *were* cast in two rows when it was cast. 25It stood on twelve oxen: three looking toward the north, three looking toward the west, three looking toward the south, and three looking toward the east; the Sea *was set* upon them, and all their back parts *pointed* inward. 26It *was* a handbreadth thick; and its brim was shaped like the brim of a cup, *like* a lily blossom. It contained two thousand[a] baths.

The Carts and the Lavers

27He also made ten carts of bronze; four cubits *was* the length of each cart, four cubits its width, and three cubits its height. 28And this *was* the design of the carts: They had panels, and the panels *were* between frames; 29on the panels that *were* between the frames *were* lions, oxen, and cherubim. And on the frames *was* a pedestal on top. Below the lions and oxen *were* wreaths of plaited work. 30Every cart had four bronze wheels and axles of bronze, and its four feet had supports. Under the laver *were* supports of cast *bronze* beside each wreath. 31Its opening inside the crown at the top *was* one cubit in diameter; and the opening *was* round, shaped *like* a pedestal, one and a half cubits in outside diameter; and also on the opening *were* engravings, but the panels were square, not round. 32Under the panels *were* the four wheels, and the axles of the wheels *were joined* to the cart. The height of a wheel *was* one and a half cubits. 33The workmanship of the wheels *was* like the workmanship of a chariot wheel; their axle pins, their rims, their spokes, and their hubs *were* all of cast *bronze*. 34And *there were* four supports at the four corners of each cart; its supports *were* part of

the cart itself. 35On the top of the cart, at the height of half a cubit, *it was* perfectly round. And on the top of the cart, its flanges and its panels *were* of the same casting. 36On the plates of its flanges and on its panels he engraved cherubim, lions, and palm trees, wherever there was a clear space on each, with wreaths all around. 37Thus he made the ten carts. All of them were of the same mold, one measure, *and* one shape.

38Then he made ten lavers of bronze; each laver contained forty baths, *and* each laver *was* four cubits. On each of the ten carts *was* a laver. 39And he put five carts on the right side of the house, and five on the left side of the house. He set the Sea on the right side of the house, toward the southeast.

Furnishings of the Temple

40Huram[a] made the lavers and the shovels and the bowls. So Huram finished doing all the work that he was to do for King Solomon *for* the house of the LORD: 41the two pillars, the *two* bowl-shaped capitals that *were* on top of the two pillars; the two networks covering the two bowl-shaped capitals which *were* on top of the pillars; 42four hundred pomegranates for the two networks (two rows of pomegranates for each network, to cover the two bowl-shaped capitals that *were* on top of the pillars); 43the ten carts, and ten lavers on the carts; 44one Sea, and twelve oxen under the Sea; 45the pots, the shovels, and the bowls.

All these articles which Huram[a] made for King Solomon *for* the house of the LORD *were of* burnished bronze. 46In the plain of Jordan the king had them cast in clay molds, between Succoth and Zaretan. 47And Solomon did not weigh all the articles, because *there were* so many; the weight of the bronze was not determined.

48Thus Solomon had all the furnishings made for the house of the LORD: the altar of gold, and the table of gold on which *was* the showbread; 49the lampstands of pure gold, five on the right *side* and five on the left in front of the inner sanctuary, with the flowers and the lamps and the wick-trimmers of gold; 50the basins, the trimmers,

---

7:26 [a]Or *three thousand* (compare 2 Chronicles 4:5) 7:40 [a]Hebrew *Hiram* (compare 2 Chronicles 2:13, 14) 7:45 [a]Hebrew *Hiram* (compare 2 Chronicles 2:13, 14)

the bowls, the ladles, and the censers of pure gold; and the hinges of gold, *both* for the doors of the inner room (the Most Holy *Place*) *and* for the doors of the main hall of the temple. [51]So all the work that King Solomon had done for the house of the LORD was finished; and Solomon brought in the things which his father David had dedicated: the silver and the gold and the furnishings. He put them in the treasuries of the house of the LORD.

The Ark Brought into the Temple

8 Now Solomon assembled the elders of Israel and all the heads of the tribes, the chief fathers of the children of Israel, to King Solomon in Jerusalem, that they might bring up the ark of the covenant of the LORD from the City of David, which *is* Zion. [2]Therefore all the men of Israel assembled with King Solomon at the feast in the month of Ethanim, which *is* the seventh month. [3]So all the elders of Israel came, and the priests took up the ark. [4]Then they brought up the ark of the LORD, the tabernacle of meeting, and all the holy furnishings that *were* in the tabernacle. The priests and the Levites brought them up. [5]Also King Solomon, and all the congregation of Israel who were assembled with him, *were* with him before the ark, sacrificing sheep and oxen that could not be counted or numbered for multitude. [6]Then the priests brought in the ark of the covenant of the LORD to its place, into the inner sanctuary of the temple, to the Most Holy *Place,* under the wings of the cherubim. [7]For the cherubim spread *their* two wings over the place of the ark, and the cherubim overshadowed the ark and its poles. [8]The poles extended so that the ends of the poles could be seen from the holy *place,* in front of the inner sanctuary; but they could not be seen from outside. And they are there to this day. [9]Nothing *was* in the ark except the two tablets of stone which Moses put there at Horeb, when the LORD made *a covenant* with the children of Israel, when they came out of the land of Egypt.

[10]And it came to pass, when the priests came out of the holy *place,* that the cloud filled the house of the LORD, [11]so that the priests could not continue ministering because of the cloud; for the glory of the LORD filled the house of the LORD. [12]Then Solomon spoke:

"The LORD said He would dwell in the dark cloud.
[13]I have surely built You an exalted house, And a place for You to dwell in forever."

Solomon's Speech at Completion of the Work

[14]Then the king turned around and blessed the whole assembly of Israel, while all the assembly of Israel was standing. [15]And he said: "Blessed *be* the LORD God of Israel, who spoke with His mouth to my father David, and with His hand has fulfilled *it,* saying, [16]'Since the day that I brought My people Israel out of Egypt, I have chosen no city from any tribe of Israel *in which* to build a house, that My name might be there; but I chose David to be over My people Israel.' [17]Now it was in the heart of my father David to build a temple[a] for the name of the LORD God of Israel. [18]But the LORD said to my father David, 'Whereas it was in your heart to build a temple for My name, you did well that it was in your heart. [19]Nevertheless you shall not build the temple, but your son who will come from your body, he shall build the temple for My name.' [20]So the LORD has fulfilled His word which He spoke; and I have filled the position of my father David, and sit on the throne of Israel, as the LORD promised; and I have built a temple for the name of the LORD God of Israel. [21]And there I have made a place for the ark, in which *is* the covenant of the LORD which He made with our fathers, when He brought them out of the land of Egypt."

Solomon's Prayer of Dedication

[22]Then Solomon stood before the altar of the LORD in the presence of all the assembly of Israel, and spread out his hands toward heaven; [23]and he said: "LORD God of Israel, *there is* no God in heaven above or on earth below like You, who keep *Your* covenant and mercy with Your servants who walk before You with all their hearts. [24]You have kept what You promised Your servant David my father; You have both spoken with Your mouth and fulfilled *it* with Your hand, as *it* is this day. [25]Therefore, LORD God of Israel, now keep what You promised Your servant David my father, saying, 'You shall not fail to have a man sit before Me on the throne of Israel, only if your sons take heed to

---

8:17 [a]Literally *house,* and so in verses 18–20

8:1 The ark carried through the wilderness by the children of Israel following the Exodus had been at Gibeon awaiting a permanent residence (1 Kin. 3:4).

8:2 The Feast of Tabernacles is a time for Israel to remember God's faithfulness in bringing them out of Egypt (Lev. 23:34; see chart, The Feasts of Israel).

8:10 God selected a place for His name and a place where His people could come into His presence (Deut. 12:5; see chart,

The Plan of the Tabernacle). The cloud, signifying God's presence, had formerly rested on the tabernacle of meeting, where the ark had been kept during the Exodus (Ex. 40:34–38).

8:25 In Solomon's prayer of dedication, he realized the conditions of God's promise (see chart, Solomon's Prayer). Obedience brings blessing (Deut. 28:1–14) and the perpetuity of David's line (2 Sam. 7:12–16); sin brings the covenant curses (Deut. 28:15–68). Solomon's later actions stand condemned by his own words.

their way, that they walk before Me as you have walked before Me.' [26]And now I pray, O God of Israel, let Your word come true, which You have spoken to Your servant David my father.

[27]"But will God indeed dwell on the earth? Behold, heaven and the heaven of heavens cannot contain You. How much less this temple which I have built! [28]Yet regard the prayer of Your servant and his supplication, O Lord my God, and listen to the cry and the prayer which Your servant is praying before You today: [29]that Your eyes may be open toward this temple night and day, toward the place of which You said, 'My name shall be there,' that You may hear the prayer which Your servant makes toward this place. [30]And may You hear the supplication of Your servant and of Your people Israel, when they pray toward this place. Hear in heaven Your dwelling place; and when You hear, forgive.

[31]"When anyone sins against his neighbor, and is forced to take an oath, and comes *and* takes an oath before Your altar in this temple, [32]then hear in heaven, and act, and judge Your servants, condemning the wicked, bringing his way on his head, and justifying the righteous by giving him according to his righteousness.

[33]"When Your people Israel are defeated before an enemy because they have sinned against You, and when they turn back to You and confess Your name, and pray and make supplication to You in this temple, [34]then hear in heaven, and forgive the sin of Your people Israel, and bring them back to the land which You gave to their fathers.

[35]"When the heavens are shut up and there is no rain because they have sinned against You, when they pray toward this place and confess Your name, and turn from their sin because You afflict them, [36]then hear in heaven, and forgive the sin of Your servants, Your people Israel, that You may teach them the good way in which they should walk; and send rain on Your land which You have given to Your people as an inheritance.

[37]"When there is famine in the land, pestilence *or* blight *or* mildew, locusts *or* grasshoppers; when their enemy besieges them in the land of their cities; whatever plague or whatever sickness *there is;* [38]whatever prayer, whatever supplication is made by anyone, *or* by all Your people Israel, when each one knows the plague of his own heart, and spreads out his hands toward this temple: [39]then hear in heaven Your dwelling place, and forgive, and act, and give to everyone according to all his ways, whose heart You know (for You alone know the hearts of all the sons of men), [40]that they may fear You all the days that they live in the land which You gave to our fathers.

[41]"Moreover, concerning a foreigner, who *is* not of Your people Israel, but has come from a far country for Your name's sake [42](for they will hear of Your great name and Your strong hand and Your outstretched arm), when he comes and prays toward this temple, [43]hear in heaven Your dwelling place, and do according to all for which the foreigner calls to You, that all peoples of the earth may know Your name and fear You, as *do* Your people Israel, and that they may know that this temple which I have built is called by Your name.

[44]"When Your people go out to battle against their enemy, wherever You send them, and when they pray to the Lord toward the city which You have chosen and the temple which I have built for Your name, [45]then hear in heaven their prayer and their supplication, and maintain their cause.

[46]"When they sin against You (for *there is* no one who does not sin), and You become angry with them and deliver them to the enemy, and they take them captive to the land of the enemy, far or near; [47]*yet* when they come to themselves in the land where they were carried captive, and repent, and make supplication to You in the land of those who took them captive, saying, 'We have sinned and done wrong, we have committed wickedness'; [48]and *when* they return to You with all their heart and with all their soul in the land of their enemies who led them away captive, and pray to You toward their land which You gave to their fathers, the city which You have chosen and the temple which I have built for Your name: [49]then hear in heaven Your dwelling place their prayer and their supplication, and maintain their cause, [50]and forgive Your people who have sinned against You, and all their transgressions which they have transgressed against You; and grant them compassion before those who took them captive, that they may have compassion on them [51](for they *are* Your people and Your inheritance, whom You brought out of Egypt, out of the iron furnace), [52]that Your eyes may be open to the supplication of Your servant and the supplication of Your people Israel, to listen to them whenever they call to You. [53]For You separated them from among all the peoples of the earth *to be* Your inheritance, as You spoke by Your servant Moses, when You brought our fathers out of Egypt, O Lord God."

Solomon Blesses the Assembly

[54]And so it was, when Solomon had finished praying all this prayer and supplication to the Lord, that he arose from before the altar of the Lord, from kneeling on his knees with his hands spread up to heaven. [55]Then he stood and blessed all the assembly of Israel with a loud voice, saying: [56]"Blessed *be* the Lord, who has given rest to His people Israel, according to all that He promised. There has not failed one word of all His good promise, which He promised through His servant

DOWRY   SEALING THE BETROTHAL

The dowry was an essential ingredient in Hebrew marriages except in very poor families. It sealed the betrothal, making the marriage legal even before the official ceremony or physical consummation of the marriage.

The dowry could assume several different forms: the "bride-price" (Heb. *mohar*) paid to the father or brothers of the bride to compensate for the economic loss to the bride's family by her departure (Gen. 34:12), gifts from the bridegroom to the bride, gifts to members of the bride's family (Heb. *mattan,* Gen. 24:53), or gifts from the bride's father to the bride (Judg. 1:15; 1 Kin. 9:16). All gifts to the bride herself helped to ensure her financial security in case of the untimely death of her husband or his departure, since theoretically she remained the owner of her dowry.

In most cases, the dowry was fashioned according to the wealth and position of the bride and her family, even though it was a voluntary gift (1 Sam. 18:23–25). This property was assigned to the bride and brought into her husband's house upon marriage to help the young couple establish their household. Some have suggested that the dowry was an advance inheritance, meaning that the daughter received her share of the father's estate upon marriage, while her brothers had to wait until their father's death to receive their shares.

The contents of the dowry were usually "portables" such as money, jewelry, or other valuables (Gen. 24:22). The lost silver coin in Jesus' parable (Luke 15:8) likely referred to a dowry headpiece of silver coins, popular in Jesus' day. A dowry could also include work rendered (Gen. 29:18), workers to help in her work (Gen. 29:24, 29), or even deeds of bravery (Josh. 15:16), and in very rare cases land (Judg. 1:13–15).

This beautiful Old Testament tradition has continued over the centuries as family and friends join together to give brides both useful and aesthetically beautiful gifts and to provide loving service in helping a newly married couple to establish their household.

See also notes on Engagement (Matt. 1); Family (Gen. 32; 1 Sam. 3; Ps. 78; 127); Inheritance (Prov. 13); Marriage (Gen. 2; 2 Sam. 6; Prov. 5; Hos. 2; Amos 3; 2 Cor. 13; Heb. 12); Weddings (John 2); Wives (Prov. 31); portrait of Rebekah (Gen. 24)

Moses. 57May the LORD our God be with us, as He was with our fathers. May He not leave us nor forsake us, 58that He may incline our hearts to Himself, to walk in all His ways, and to keep His commandments and His statutes and His judgments, which He commanded our fathers. 59And may these words of mine, with which I have made supplication before the LORD, be near the LORD our God day and night, that He may maintain the cause of His servant and the cause of His people Israel, as each day may require, 60that all the peoples of the earth may know that the LORD *is* God; *there is* no other. 61Let your heart therefore be loyal to the LORD our God, to walk in His statutes and keep His commandments, as at this day."

Solomon Dedicates the Temple

62Then the king and all Israel with him offered sacrifices before the LORD. 63And Solomon offered a sacrifice of peace offerings, which he offered to the LORD, twenty-two thousand bulls and one hundred and twenty thousand sheep. So the king and all the children of Israel dedicated the house of the LORD. 64On the same day the king consecrated the middle of the court that *was* in front of the house of the LORD; for there he offered burnt offerings, grain offerings, and the fat of the peace offerings, because the bronze altar that *was* before the LORD *was* too small to receive the burnt offerings, the grain offerings, and the fat of the peace offerings.

65At that time Solomon held a feast, and all Israel with him, a great assembly from the entrance of Hamath to the Brook of Egypt, before the LORD our God, seven days and seven *more* days—fourteen days. 66On the eighth day he sent the people away; and they blessed the king, and went to their tents joyful and glad of heart for all the good that the LORD had done for His servant David, and for Israel His people.

God's Second Appearance to Solomon

9 And it came to pass, when Solomon had finished building the house of the LORD and the king's house, and all Solomon's desire which he wanted to do, 2that the LORD appeared to Solomon the second time, as He had appeared to him at Gibeon. 3And the LORD said to him: "I have heard your prayer and your supplication that you have made before Me; I have consecrated this house which you have built to put My name there forever, and My eyes and My heart will be there perpetually.

8:65 The Feast of Tabernacles was mandatory for all Israelite males (Deut. 16:16; see chart, The Feasts of Israel).

9:3 God appeared again to Solomon with instructions (see 1 Kin. 3:14). The writer of Kings is emphasizing that Solomon knew the conditions and requirements of the Law.

⁴Now if you walk before Me as your father David walked, in integrity of heart and in uprightness, to do according to all that I have commanded you, *and* if you keep My statutes and My judgments, ⁵then I will establish the throne of your kingdom over Israel forever, as I promised David your father, saying, 'You shall not fail to have a man on the throne of Israel.' ⁶*But* if you or your sons at all turn from following Me, and do not keep My commandments *and* My statutes which I have set before you, but go and serve other gods and worship them, ⁷then I will cut off Israel from the land which I have given them; and this house which I have consecrated for My name I will cast out of My sight. Israel will be a proverb and a byword among all peoples. ⁸And *as for* this house, *which* is exalted, everyone who passes by it will be astonished and will hiss, and say, 'Why has the LORD done thus to this land and to this house?' ⁹Then they will answer, 'Because they forsook the LORD their God, who brought their fathers out of the land of Egypt, and have embraced other gods, and worshiped them and served them; therefore the LORD has brought all this calamity on them.' "

Solomon and Hiram Exchange Gifts

¹⁰Now it happened at the end of twenty years, when Solomon had built the two houses, the house of the LORD and the king's house ¹¹(Hiram the king of Tyre had supplied Solomon with cedar and cypress and gold, as much as he desired), *that* King Solomon then gave Hiram twenty cities in the land of Galilee. ¹²Then Hiram went from Tyre to see the cities which Solomon had given him, but they did not please him. ¹³So he said, "What *kind of* cities *are* these which you have given me, my brother?" And he called them the land of Cabul,ª as they are to this day. ¹⁴Then Hiram sent the king one hundred and twenty talents of gold.

Solomon's Additional Achievements

¹⁵And this *is* the reason for the labor force which King Solomon raised: to build the house of the LORD, his own house, the Millo,ª the wall of Je-

rusalem, Hazor, Megiddo, and Gezer. ¹⁶(Pharaoh king of Egypt had gone up and taken Gezer and burned it with fire, had killed the Canaanites who dwelt in the city, and had given it *as* a dowry to his daughter, Solomon's wife.) ¹⁷And Solomon built Gezer, Lower Beth Horon, ¹⁸Baalath, and Tadmor in the wilderness, in the land *of Judah*, ¹⁹all the storage cities that Solomon had, cities for his chariots and cities for his cavalry, and whatever Solomon desired to build in Jerusalem, in Lebanon, and in all the land of his dominion.

²⁰All the people *who were* left of the Amorites, Hittites, Perizzites, Hivites, and Jebusites, who *were* not of the children of Israel— ²¹that is, their descendants who were left in the land after them, whom the children of Israel had not been able to destroy completely— from these Solomon raised forced labor, as it is to this day. ²²But of the children of Israel Solomon made no forced laborers, because they *were* men of war and his servants: his officers, his captains, commanders of his chariots, and his cavalry.

²³Others *were* chiefs of the officials who *were* over Solomon's work: five hundred and fifty, who ruled over the people who did the work.

²⁴But Pharaoh's daughter came up from the City of David to her house which *Solomon*ª had built for her. Then he built the Millo.

²⁵Now three times a year Solomon offered burnt offerings and peace offerings on the altar which he had built for the LORD, and he burned incense with them *on the altar* that *was* before the LORD. So he finished the temple.

²⁶King Solomon also built a fleet of ships at Ezion Geber, which *is* near Elathª on the shore of the Red Sea, in the land of Edom. ²⁷Then Hiram sent his servants with the fleet, seamen who knew the sea, to work with the servants of Solomon. ²⁸And they went to Ophir, and acquired four hundred and twenty talents of gold from there, and brought *it* to King Solomon.

9:13 ªLiterally *Good for Nothing* **9:15** ªLiterally *The Landfill* **9:24** ªLiterally *he* (compare 2 Chronicles 8:11) **9:26** ªHebrew *Eloth* (compare 2 Kings 14:22)

9:11 Solomon's vast expenditure forced him to sell territory to Hiram in order to raise money (v. 14). This action probably occasioned some hostility among Solomon's northern subjects. The relinquishment of northern territory by the Judean king would have been highly unpopular in Israel.

9:15 Military fortifications were built by Solomon in addition to building the temple and his own palace. Solomon strengthened the walls of Jerusalem and built the Millo, probably a series of terraces upon which houses were built. He also turned strategically located cities into military bases. Hazor was in Galilee, near the newly conquered Arameans. Megiddo, one of the most strategic cities of Canaan, guarded the main pass through the Carmel mountain range. Gezer, along with Beth Horon (v. 17) and Baalath (v. 18), faced west across the plain

on the Mediterranean's shores. Tadmor's location, though still disputed, is usually identified as modern Palmyra in the Syrian desert (v. 18). Each of these cities housed a sizable military force, including horses and chariots.

9:22 Solomon's conscription of the Israelites was for temporary labor, not permanent enslavement (see 1 Kin. 5:13, note).

9:26–28 The seaport of Ezion Geber lay at the northern end of the Gulf of Aqaba. Archaeological research has revealed both copper and iron refineries at the site, now known as Tell el-Kheleifeh. The tell is two and one-half miles west of ancient Elath, now modern Aqaba. Solomon enlisted Phoenician help to construct a merchant fleet, which carried on an active trade with southern Arabia. Ophir may be the same as modern Somaliland.

THE QUEEN OF SHEBA

The Queen of Sheba possessed not only great position and influence but also enormous wealth and possessions. Not willing to rely on the reports about Solomon's wisdom and wealth from others, she was eager to see him for herself. Accompanied by a great retinue, she made her exhausting trip through hundreds of miles of desert to Jerusalem. Finally, she was face to face with the wise Solomon. There she opened before him all that was in her heart. Sheba, about 1,400 miles south of Jerusalem, was a land with influence extending throughout the ancient world. Since Sheba's considerable economy was dependent on worldwide, overland spice trade, Israel's activities, power, and location must have been of particular interest to the queen and her caravans. Solomon, with the assistance of Hiram, king of Tyre, had begun to undertake sailing expeditions to Ophir from the newly established seaport of Ezion Geber (1 Kin. 9:26–28; 10:11). This newly created trade alliance may have been the cause of some concern to the Queen of Sheba. The queen's visit was not based merely on curiosity about or admiration for the king of Israel. The exchange of gifts is evidence that negotiations were probably a part of her agenda with Solomon (1 Kin. 10:10, 13).

The Queen of Sheba is significant, however, not for her economic or political accomplishments but for her reaction to the king of Israel. This woman, with enormous wealth and wisdom of her own, was overwhelmed by the magnificence of Solomon's wisdom and wealth. In response she broke forth in highest praise to Solomon's God.

Perhaps the greatest tribute to the Queen of Sheba came from the mouth of Jesus (Matt. 12:42). A godless queen came from the "ends of the earth to hear the wisdom of Solomon," and she praised God. The "godly" (better described as "religious") Pharisees needed only to look upon the One already standing before them to see the wisdom of God. But they would not see Him. The queen's example stands as a sharp rebuke against the Pharisees.

See also 2 Chr. 9:1–12; Matt. 12:42; Luke 11:31; notes on Feminine Leadership (1 Sam. 25); Government and Citizenship (Rom. 13); map of The Land of Sheba.

The Queen of Sheba's Praise of Solomon

10 Now when the queen of Sheba heard of the fame of Solomon concerning the name of the LORD, she came to test him with hard questions. ²She came to Jerusalem with a very great retinue, with camels that bore spices, very much gold, and precious stones; and when she came to Solomon, she spoke with him about all that was in her heart. ³So Solomon answered all her questions; there was nothing so difficult for the king that he could not explain *it* to her. ⁴And when the queen of Sheba had seen all the wisdom of Solomon, the house that he had built, ⁵the food on his table, the seating of his servants, the service of his waiters and their apparel, his cupbearers, and his entryway by which he went up to the house of the LORD, there was no more spirit in her. ⁶Then she said to the king: "It was a true report which I heard in my own land about your words and your wisdom. ⁷However I did not believe the words until I came and saw with my own eyes; and indeed the half was not told me. Your wisdom and prosperity exceed the fame of which I heard. ⁸Happy *are* your men and happy *are* these your servants, who stand continually

before you *and* hear your wisdom! ⁹Blessed be the LORD your God, who delighted in you, setting you on the throne of Israel! Because the LORD has loved Israel forever, therefore He made you king, to do justice and righteousness."

¹⁰Then she gave the king one hundred and twenty talents of gold, spices in great quantity, and precious stones. There never again came such abundance of spices as the queen of Sheba gave to King Solomon. ¹¹Also, the ships of Hiram, which brought gold from Ophir, brought great quantities of almug[a] wood and precious stones from Ophir. ¹²And the king made steps of the almug wood for the house of the LORD and for the king's house, also harps and stringed instruments for singers. There never again came such almug wood, nor has the like been seen to this day.

¹³Now King Solomon gave the queen of Sheba all she desired, whatever she asked, besides what Solomon had given her according to the royal generosity. So she turned and went to her own country, she and her servants.

••••••••••••••••••••

10:11 [a]Or *algum* (compare 2 Chronicles 9:10, 11)

10:1 The queen of Sheba was probably Sabean, ruling the area that is now eastern Yemen (see map, The Land of Sheba). This position allowed the Sabeans to control the trade routes stretching from southwestern Arabia northward into Pales-

tine. The queen of Sheba intended to negotiate a trade agreement with Solomon; she was successful, since the listing of Solomon's wealth includes merchandise "from all the kings of Arabia" (v. 15; see also The Queen of Sheba).

Solomon's Great Wealth

[14]The weight of gold that came to Solomon yearly was six hundred and sixty-six talents of gold, [15]besides *that* from the traveling merchants, from the income of traders, from all the kings of Arabia, and from the governors of the country.

[16]And King Solomon made two hundred large shields *of* hammered gold; six hundred *shekels* of gold went into each shield. [17]He also *made* three hundred shields *of* hammered gold; three minas of gold went into each shield. The king put them in the House of the Forest of Lebanon.

[18]Moreover the king made a great throne of ivory, and overlaid it with pure gold. [19]The throne had six steps, and the top of the throne *was* round at the back; *there were* armrests on either side of the place of the seat, and two lions stood beside the armrests. [20]Twelve lions stood there, one on each side of the six steps; nothing like *this* had been made for any *other* kingdom.

[21]All King Solomon's drinking vessels *were* gold, and all the vessels of the House of the Forest of Lebanon *were* pure gold. Not *one was* silver, for this was accounted as nothing in the days of Solomon. [22]For the king had merchant ships[a] at sea with the fleet of Hiram. Once every three years the merchant ships came bringing gold, silver, ivory, apes, and monkeys.[b] [23]So King Solomon surpassed all the kings of the earth in riches and wisdom.

[24]Now all the earth sought the presence of Solomon to hear his wisdom, which God had put in his heart. [25]Each man brought his present: articles of silver and gold, garments, armor, spices, horses, and mules, at a set rate year by year.

[26]And Solomon gathered chariots and horsemen; he had one thousand four hundred chariots and twelve thousand horsemen, whom he stationed[a] in the chariot cities and with the king at Jerusalem. [27]The king made silver *as common* in Jerusalem as stones, and he made cedar trees as abundant as the sycamores which *are* in the lowland.

[28]Also Solomon had horses imported from Egypt and Keveh; the king's merchants bought them in Keveh at the *current* price. [29]Now a chariot that was imported from Egypt cost six hundred

shekels of silver, and a horse one hundred and fifty; and thus, through their agents,[a] they exported *them* to all the kings of the Hittites and the kings of Syria.

Solomon's Heart Turns from the LORD

11 But King Solomon loved many foreign women, as well as the daughter of Pharaoh: women of the Moabites, Ammonites, Edomites, Sidonians, *and* Hittites— [2]from the nations of whom the LORD had said to the children of Israel, "You shall not intermarry with them, nor they with you. Surely they will turn away your hearts after their gods." Solomon clung to these in love. [3]And he had seven hundred wives, princesses, and three hundred concubines; and his wives turned away his heart. [4]For it was so, when Solomon was old, that his wives turned his heart after other gods; and his heart was not loyal to the LORD his God, as *was* the heart of his father David. [5]For Solomon went after Ashtoreth the goddess of the Sidonians, and after Milcom the abomination of the Ammonites. [6]Solomon did evil in the sight of the LORD, and did not fully follow the LORD, as *did* his father David. [7]Then Solomon built a high place for Chemosh the abomination of Moab, on the hill that *is* east of Jerusalem, and for Molech the abomination of the people of Ammon. [8]And he did likewise for all his foreign wives, who burned incense and sacrificed to their gods.

[9]So the LORD became angry with Solomon, because his heart had turned from the LORD God of Israel, who had appeared to him twice, [10]and had commanded him concerning this thing, that he should not go after other gods; but he did not keep what the LORD had commanded. [11]Therefore the LORD said to Solomon, "Because you have done this, and have not kept My covenant and My statutes, which I have commanded you, I will surely tear the kingdom away from you and give it to your servant. [12]Nevertheless I will not do it in your days, for the sake of your father David; I will tear it out of the hand of your son. [13]However I

10:22 [a]Literally *ships of Tarshish,* deep-sea vessels [b]Or *peacocks*
10:26 [a]Following Septuagint, Syriac, Targum, and Vulgate (compare 2 Chronicles 9:25); Masoretic Text reads *led.* 10:29 [a]Literally *by their hands*

10:22 **Merchant ships** carried goods through the Mediterranean Sea to supplement the goods brought by ships operating on the Red Sea, later the Gulf of Aqaba (1 Kin. 9:26).

10:28 **Chariots were state-of-the-art weapons of war** in the ancient Near East. Since Israel did not manufacture chariots, Solomon imported them from Egypt. He also used his monopoly on trade routes to profit from the chariot trade between Egypt and the Hittites and Syrians to Israel's north.

11:1 **Solomon broke God's Law** by mingling with the pagans around him (Deut. 7:1–5). Rather than leading the Israelites in maintaining separateness from the other nations, the king

married foreign women, worshiped foreign gods (1 Kin. 11:5), made alliances with pagan kings, and even built pagan places of worship. From this point, Solomon began to experience the covenant curses (Deut. 28:15–68). The writer of Kings indicates in the first two chapters that David was also guilty of these infractions on a smaller scale. David married foreign women, resulting in a household in disarray (see chart, The Family Tree of David), and he included pagan mercenaries in his troops (1 Kin. 1:38, note).

11:13 **Even in the face of Solomon's disobedience,** God remained loyal to His promise to David (2 Sam. 7:15, 16).

THE LAND OF SHEBA

The Queen of Sheba visited Solomon (1 Kin. 10:1–13; Luke 11:31).

will not tear away the whole kingdom; I will give one tribe to your son for the sake of My servant David, and for the sake of Jerusalem which I have chosen."

Adversaries of Solomon

[14]Now the LORD raised up an adversary against Solomon, Hadad the Edomite; he *was* a descendant of the king in Edom. [15]For it happened, when David was in Edom, and Joab the commander of the army had gone up to bury the slain, after he had killed every male in Edom [16](because for six months Joab remained there with all Israel, until he had cut down every male in Edom), [17]that Hadad fled to go to Egypt, he and certain Edomites of his father's servants with him. Hadad *was* still a little child. [18]Then they arose from Midian and came to Paran; and they took men with them from Paran and came to Egypt, to Pharaoh king of Egypt, who gave him a house, apportioned food for him, and gave him land. [19]And Hadad

found great favor in the sight of Pharaoh, so that he gave him as wife the sister of his own wife, that is, the sister of Queen Tahpenes. [20]Then the sister of Tahpenes bore him Genubath his son, whom Tahpenes weaned in Pharaoh's house. And Genubath was in Pharaoh's household among the sons of Pharaoh.

[21]So when Hadad heard in Egypt that David rested with his fathers, and that Joab the commander of the army was dead, Hadad said to Pharaoh, "Let me depart, that I may go to my own country."

[22]Then Pharaoh said to him, "But what have you lacked with me, that suddenly you seek to go to your own country?"

So he answered, "Nothing, but do let me go anyway."

[23]And God raised up *another* adversary against him, Rezon the son of Eliadah, who had fled from his lord, Hadadezer king of Zobah. [24]So he gathered men to him and became captain over a band

---

11:14 The southern land of Edom had added to David's kingdom early in his reign (2 Sam. 8:14). In God's act of judgment on Solomon, these conquered people found favor with the

Pharaoh of Egypt, Sheshonq I. Solomon had previously held this alliance.

of raiders, when David killed those *of Zobah.* And they went to Damascus and dwelt there, and reigned in Damascus. ²⁵He was an adversary of Israel all the days of Solomon (besides the trouble that Hadad *caused*); and he abhorred Israel, and reigned over Syria.

Jeroboam's Rebellion

²⁶Then Solomon's servant, Jeroboam the son of Nebat, an Ephraimite from Zereda, whose mother's name *was* Zeruah, a widow, also rebelled against the king.

²⁷And this *is* what caused him to rebel against the king: Solomon had built the Millo *and* repaired the damages to the City of David his father. ²⁸The man Jeroboam *was* a mighty man of valor; and Solomon, seeing that the young man was industrious, made him the officer over all the labor force of the house of Joseph.

²⁹Now it happened at that time, when Jeroboam went out of Jerusalem, that the prophet Ahijah the Shilonite met him on the way; and he had clothed himself with a new garment, and the two *were* alone in the field. ³⁰Then Ahijah took hold of the new garment that *was* on him, and tore it *into* twelve pieces. ³¹And he said to Jeroboam, "Take for yourself ten pieces, for thus says the LORD, the God of Israel: 'Behold, I will tear the kingdom out of the hand of Solomon and will give ten tribes to you ³²(but he shall have one tribe for the sake of My servant David, and for the sake of Jerusalem, the city which I have chosen out of all the tribes of Israel), ³³because they have[a] forsaken Me, and worshiped Ashtoreth the goddess of the Sidonians, Chemosh the god of the Moabites, and Milcom the god of the people of Ammon, and have not walked in My ways to do *what is* right in My eyes and *keep* My statutes and My judgments, as *did* his father David. ³⁴However I will not take the whole kingdom out of his hand, because I have made him ruler all the days of his life for the sake of My servant David, whom I chose because he kept My commandments and My statutes. ³⁵But I will take the kingdom out of his son's hand and give it to you— ten tribes. ³⁶And to his son I will give one tribe, that My servant David may always have a lamp before Me in Jerusalem, the city which I have chosen for Myself, to put My name there. ³⁷So I will take you, and you shall reign over all your heart desires, and you shall be king over Israel. ³⁸Then it shall be, if you heed all that I command you, walk in My ways, and do *what is* right in My sight, to keep My statutes and My commandments, as My servant David did, then I will be with you and build for you an enduring house, as I built for David, and will give Israel to you. ³⁹And I will afflict the descendants of David because of this, but not forever.' "

⁴⁰Solomon therefore sought to kill Jeroboam. But Jeroboam arose and fled to Egypt, to Shishak king of Egypt, and was in Egypt until the death of Solomon.

Death of Solomon

⁴¹Now the rest of the acts of Solomon, all that he did, and his wisdom, *are* they not written in the book of the acts of Solomon? ⁴²And the period that Solomon reigned in Jerusalem over all Israel *was* forty years. ⁴³Then Solomon rested with his fathers, and was buried in the City of David his father. And Rehoboam his son reigned in his place.

The Revolt Against Rehoboam

12 And Rehoboam went to Shechem, for all Israel had gone to Shechem to make him king. ²So it happened, when Jeroboam the son of Nebat heard *it* (he was still in Egypt, for he had fled from the presence of King Solomon and had been dwelling in Egypt), ³that they sent and called him. Then Jeroboam and the whole assembly of Israel came and spoke to Rehoboam, saying, ⁴"Your father made our yoke heavy; now therefore, lighten the burdensome service of your father, and his heavy yoke which he put on us, and we will serve you."

⁵So he said to them, "Depart *for* three days, then come back to me." And the people departed.

⁶Then King Rehoboam consulted the elders who stood before his father Solomon while he still lived, and he said, "How do you advise *me* to answer these people?"

⁷And they spoke to him, saying, "If you will be a servant to these people today, and serve them, and answer them, and speak good words to them, then they will be your servants forever."

11:33 [a]Following Masoretic Text and Targum; Septuagint, Syriac, and Vulgate read *he has.*

11:25 David had conquered Zobah and Damascus, adding Syrian territory to his own kingdom (v. 24; 2 Sam. 8:3–6). Solomon lost this northern area when Rezon began a new Syrian dynasty (see chart, The Kings of Syria).

11:26 Jeroboam was the head of forced labor for the tribes of Ephraim and Manasseh. These northern tribes became part of Israel when the kingdom divided. The widespread support for Jeroboam's rebellion showed the level of discontent in Israel over Solomon's reign. Years of heavy taxation and forced labor, along with preferential treatment of Judah, had completely alienated the northern tribes from the government in Jerusalem. While Solomon himself did not lose the kingdom, he lived to see the beginning of the schism; Jeroboam later became king of Israel (see chart, The Prophets Who Spoke to Kings).

11:40 Again Egypt helped Solomon's enemies, reversing the country's earlier treaties with Solomon. Shishak is usually identified as Sheshonq I.

SOLOMON'S PAGAN WIVES

Women influenced and dramatically altered the life and career of Israel's King Solomon. He ascended the throne when the nation was at its peak of power, free from external threats and well organized internally. His great wealth, extraordinary wisdom, and unparalleled understanding of life catapulted him to the peak of international prominence. During Solomon's reign, however, Israel began to unravel because of his disobedience primarily in one area—his multiple marriages to foreign women. The use of the conjunction *but* (see 1 Kin. 11:1) highlights his folly and shows his disregard of the Mosaic warning from God against marriage to idolaters (see Deut. 7:1–4; 17:17).

In the royal harem appeared seven hundred wives and three hundred concubines. Solomon's callousness toward the Lord seems to have grown in proportion to his addiction to women (see 1 Kin. 11:9). Some of Solomon's marriages were political moves; the king was forming alliances with neighboring countries. He married Pharaoh's daughter (1 Kin. 3:1) and built a palace for her; he received the city of Gezer as her dowry (1 Kin. 9:16), guaranteeing Egypt's friendship. However, he continued to marry foreign wives long after the political need was past. These women were idolaters, worshiping Ashtoreth, the fertility goddess (whose worship included sacred prostitution), and Molech (whose worship sometimes involved child sacrifice).

Solomon himself penned the wisdom of monogamy (see Eccl. 9:9). The writer of Proverbs warned vigorously against adultery (see Prov. 5). Yet Solomon allowed these very violations of God's law to be his undoing. His wives encouraged Solomon to build shrines to their foreign gods in Israel (see Deut. 4:15–20), eventually destroying and dispersing the nation. Not only was Solomon led astray personally, but also his entire family was corrupted because his children were not taught to follow God's laws.

See also Deut. 4:15–20; 1 Kin. 3:1; 9:16; notes on Influence (Esth. 4); Interfaith Marriage (Neh. 10)

---

[8]But he rejected the advice which the elders had given him, and consulted the young men who had grown up with him, who stood before him. [9]And he said to them, "What advice do you give? How should we answer this people who have spoken to me, saying, 'Lighten the yoke which your father put on us'?"

[10]Then the young men who had grown up with him spoke to him, saying, "Thus you should speak to this people who have spoken to you, saying, 'Your father made our yoke heavy, but you make *it* lighter on us'—thus you shall say to them: 'My little *finger* shall be thicker than my father's waist! [11]And now, whereas my father put a heavy yoke on you, I will add to your yoke; my father chastised you with whips, but I will chastise you with scourges!' "a

[12]So Jeroboam and all the people came to Rehoboam the third day, as the king had directed, saying, "Come back to me the third day." [13]Then the king answered the people roughly, and rejected the advice which the elders had given him; [14]and he spoke to them according to the advice of the young men, saying, "My father made your yoke heavy, but I will add to your yoke; my father chastised you with whips, but I will chastise you with scourges!"a [15]So the king did not listen to the people; for the turn *of events* was from the LORD, that He might fulfill His word, which the LORD had spoken by Ahijah the Shilonite to Jeroboam the son of Nebat.

[16]Now when all Israel saw that the king did not listen to them, the people answered the king, saying:

"What share have we in David?
We have no inheritance in the son of Jesse.
To your tents, O Israel!
Now, see to your own house, O David!"

So Israel departed to their tents. [17]But Rehoboam reigned over the children of Israel who dwelt in the cities of Judah.

[18]Then King Rehoboam sent Adoram, who *was* in charge of the revenue; but all Israel stoned him with stones, and he died. Therefore King Rehoboam mounted his chariot in haste to flee to Jerusalem. [19]So Israel has been in rebellion against the house of David to this day.

[20]Now it came to pass when all Israel heard that Jeroboam had come back, they sent for him and called him to the congregation, and made him king over all Israel. There was none who followed the house of David, but the tribe of Judah only.

[21]And when Rehoboam came to Jerusalem, he

· ·

12:11, 14 aLiterally *scorpions*

12:18 Adoram's unsuccessful mission. Rehoboam, in an act of incredible stupidity, sent his chief of forced labor to Israel. Israel, still seething over Solomon's imposition of forced labor, murdered Adoram, and the split in the kingdom was final. Ten tribes rebelled; the tribes of Judah and eventually Benjamin were loyal to Rehoboam.

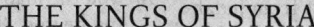

THE KINGS OF SYRIA

KING OF SYRIA	*DATE	KING OF ISRAEL/JUDAH	REFERENCE
Hezion (Rezon)	990–930 B.C.	Solomon	1 Kin. 11:23–25; 15:18
Ben-Hadad I	885–860 B.C.	Asa of Judah	1 Kin. 15:18–20
Ben-Hadad II	860–841 B.C.	Ahab of Israel	1 Kin. 20; 2 Kin. 6:24; 8:7, 9, 15
Hazael	841–801 B.C.	Jehu of Israel	1 Kin. 19:15, 17; 2 Kin. 8:7–15; 9:14, 15; 10:32; 12:17, 18; 13:3, 22, 24, 25
Ben-Hadad III	807–780 B.C.	Jehoahaz of Israel	2 Kin. 13:3, 24, 25
Rezin	780–732 B.C.	Jotham of Judah	2 Kin. 15:37; 16:5, 6, 9

All dates are approximate.

assembled all the house of Judah with the tribe of Benjamin, one hundred and eighty thousand chosen *men* who were warriors, to fight against the house of Israel, that he might restore the kingdom to Rehoboam the son of Solomon. ²²But the word of God came to Shemaiah the man of God, saying, ²³"Speak to Rehoboam the son of Solomon, king of Judah, to all the house of Judah and Benjamin, and to the rest of the people, saying, ²⁴'Thus says the LORD: "You shall not go up nor fight against your brethren the children of Israel. Let every man return to his house, for this thing is from Me." ' " Therefore they obeyed the word of the LORD, and turned back, according to the word of the LORD.

Jeroboam's Gold Calves

²⁵Then Jeroboam built Shechem in the mountains of Ephraim, and dwelt there. Also he went out from there and built Penuel. ²⁶And Jeroboam said in his heart, "Now the kingdom may return to the house of David: ²⁷If these people go up to offer sacrifices in the house of the LORD at Jerusalem, then the heart of this people will turn back to their lord, Rehoboam king of Judah, and they

will kill me and go back to Rehoboam king of Judah."

²⁸Therefore the king asked advice, made two calves of gold, and said to the people, "It is too much for you to go up to Jerusalem. Here are your gods, O Israel, which brought you up from the land of Egypt!" ²⁹And he set up one in Bethel, and the other he put in Dan. ³⁰Now this thing became a sin, for the people went *to worship* before the one as far as Dan. ³¹He made shrines^a on the high places, and made priests from every class of people, who were not of the sons of Levi.

³²Jeroboam ordained a feast on the fifteenth day of the eighth month, like the feast that *was* in Judah, and offered sacrifices on the altar. So he did at Bethel, sacrificing to the calves that he had made. And at Bethel he installed the priests of the high places which he had made. ³³So he made offerings on the altar which he had made at Bethel on the fifteenth day of the eighth month, in the month which he had devised in his own heart. And he ordained a feast for the children of Israel, and offered sacrifices on the altar and burned incense.

12:31^aLiterally *a house*

12:24 The final schism. Rehoboam did not attempt to reconquer Israel (see charts, The Prophets Who Spoke to Kings; The Kings of Israel and Judah). The effort would have been bloody and probably unsuccessful; much of Solomon's carefully assembled military force was garrisoned in northern cities!

12:25 Jeroboam turned Shechem into his capital city. "Built" has the additional meaning of "fortified." Israel had no central government and no administrative structure at the time of the schism. Shechem would have pleased both the ten tribes and non-Israelites, since the city was not strongly associated with any one tribe. Jeroboam shrewdly also associated

himself with Penuel (also Peniel), located on the site of Jacob's struggle with the angel of God (Gen. 32:30); the new king thus places himself in the line of great patriarchs.

12:28 Jeroboam moved from improper worship to idolatry. He did not feel that he could maintain his throne and allow the people to worship in Jerusalem. This change was in direct violation of God's express command. Jeroboam also violated God's laws by installing non-Levite priests (v. 31) and by changing the dates of Israel's sacred feasts (v. 33; see chart, The Feasts of Israel).

The Message of the Man of God

13 And behold, a man of God went from Judah to Bethel by the word of the LORD, and Jeroboam stood by the altar to burn incense. ²Then he cried out against the altar by the word of the LORD, and said, "O altar, altar! Thus says the LORD: 'Behold, a child, Josiah by name, shall be born to the house of David; and on you he shall sacrifice the priests of the high places who burn incense on you, and men's bones shall be burned on you.' " ³And he gave a sign the same day, saying, "This *is* the sign which the LORD has spoken: Surely the altar shall split apart, and the ashes on it shall be poured out."

⁴So it came to pass when King Jeroboam heard the saying of the man of God, who cried out against the altar in Bethel, that he stretched out his hand from the altar, saying, "Arrest him!" Then his hand, which he stretched out toward him, withered, so that he could not pull it back to himself. ⁵The altar also was split apart, and the ashes poured out from the altar, according to the sign which the man of God had given by the word of the LORD. ⁶Then the king answered and said to the man of God, "Please entreat the favor of the LORD your God, and pray for me, that my hand may be restored to me."

So the man of God entreated the LORD, and the king's hand was restored to him, and became as before. ⁷Then the king said to the man of God, "Come home with me and refresh yourself, and I will give you a reward."

⁸But the man of God said to the king, "If you were to give me half your house, I would not go in with you; nor would I eat bread nor drink water in this place. ⁹For so it was commanded me by the word of the LORD, saying, 'You shall not eat bread, nor drink water, nor return by the same way you came.' " ¹⁰So he went another way and did not return by the way he came to Bethel.

Death of the Man of God

¹¹Now an old prophet dwelt in Bethel, and his sons came and told him all the works that the man of God had done that day in Bethel; they also told their father the words which he had spoken to the king. ¹²And their father said to them, "Which way did he go?" For his sons had seen[a] which way the man of God went who came from Judah. ¹³Then he said to his sons, "Saddle the donkey for me." So they saddled the donkey for him; and he rode on it, ¹⁴and went after the man of God, and found him sitting under an oak. Then he said to him, "*Are* you the man of God who came from Judah?"

And he said, "I *am.*"

¹⁵Then he said to him, "Come home with me and eat bread."

¹⁶And he said, "I cannot return with you nor go in with you; neither can I eat bread nor drink water with you in this place. ¹⁷For I have been told by the word of the LORD, 'You shall not eat bread nor drink water there, nor return by going the way you came.' "

¹⁸He said to him, "I too *am* a prophet as you *are*, and an angel spoke to me by the word of the LORD, saying, 'Bring him back with you to your house, that he may eat bread and drink water.' " (He was lying to him.)

¹⁹So he went back with him, and ate bread in his house, and drank water.

²⁰Now it happened, as they sat at the table, that the word of the LORD came to the prophet who had brought him back; ²¹and he cried out to the man of God who came from Judah, saying, "Thus says the LORD: 'Because you have disobeyed the word of the LORD, and have not kept the commandment which the LORD your God commanded you, ²²but you came back, ate bread, and drank water in the place of which *the LORD* said to you, "Eat no bread and drink no water," your corpse shall not come to the tomb of your fathers.' "

²³So it was, after he had eaten bread and after he had drunk, that he saddled the donkey for him, the prophet whom he had brought back. ²⁴When he was gone, a lion met him on the road and killed him. And his corpse was thrown on the road, and the donkey stood by it. The lion also stood by the corpse. ²⁵And there, men passed by and saw the corpse thrown on the road, and the lion standing by the corpse. Then they went and told *it* in the city where the old prophet dwelt.

²⁶Now when the prophet who had brought him back from the way heard *it,* he said, "It *is* the man of God who was disobedient to the word of the LORD. Therefore the LORD has delivered him to the lion, which has torn him and killed him, according to the word of the LORD which He spoke to him." ²⁷And he spoke to his sons, saying, "Saddle the donkey for me." So they saddled *it.* ²⁸Then he went and found his corpse thrown on the road, and the donkey and the lion standing by the corpse. The lion had not eaten the corpse nor torn the donkey. ²⁹And the prophet took up the corpse of the man

---

13:12 [a]Septuagint, Syriac, Targum, and Vulgate read *showed him.*

13:2 The appearance of a prophet. Since no prophet in the north was found to deliver God's Word, a prophet was sent to Jeroboam from Judah (see chart, The Prophets Who Spoke to Kings). He went right to the pagan altar where Jeroboam led in worship of false gods. There the "man of God" prophesied that a king from the lineage of David would come to cleanse the altar of its pagan sacrifices. This prophecy was fulfilled by King Josiah nearly three centuries later. The splitting of the altar signified that God invalidated the pagan sacrifices (v. 3).

13:18 Any prophet who commands disobedience, no matter how powerful, is a false prophet (Deut. 13:1–5).

THE KINGS OF ISRAEL AND JUDAH

KINGS OF JUDAH	DATES OF REIGN	KINGS OF ISRAEL	DATES OF REIGN
Rehoboam	931–913 B.C.	Jeroboam I	931–910 B.C.
Abijam	913–911 B.C.		
Asa	911–870 B.C.		
		Nadab	910–909 B.C.
		Baasha	909–886 B.C.
		Elah	886–885 B.C.
		Zimri	885 B.C.
		Omri	885–874 B.C.
		Ahab	874–853 B.C.
Jehoshaphat	870–848 B.C.		
Jehoram	848–841 B.C.	Ahaziah	853–852 B.C.

of God, laid it on the donkey, and brought it back. So the old prophet came to the city to mourn, and to bury him. ³⁰Then he laid the corpse in his own tomb; and they mourned over him, *saying,* "Alas, my brother!" ³¹So it was, after he had buried him, that he spoke to his sons, saying, "When I am dead, then bury me in the tomb where the man of God *is* buried; lay my bones beside his bones. ³²For the saying which he cried out by the word of the LORD against the altar in Bethel, and against all the shrines[a] on the high places which *are* in the cities of Samaria, will surely come to pass."

³³After this event Jeroboam did not turn from his evil way, but again he made priests from every class of people for the high places; whoever wished, he consecrated him, and he became *one* of the priests of the high places. ³⁴And this thing was the sin of the house of Jeroboam, so as to exterminate and destroy *it* from the face of the earth.

Judgment on the House of Jeroboam

14 At that time Abijah the son of Jeroboam became sick. ²And Jeroboam said to his wife, "Please arise, and disguise yourself, that they may not recognize you as the wife of Jeroboam, and go to Shiloh. Indeed, Ahijah the prophet *is* there, who told me that *I would be* king over this people. ³Also take with you ten loaves, *some* cakes, and a jar of honey, and go to him; he will tell you what will become of the child." ⁴And Jeroboam's wife did so; she arose and went to Shiloh, and came to the house of Ahijah. But Ahijah could not see, for his eyes were glazed by reason of his age.

⁵Now the LORD had said to Ahijah, "Here is the wife of Jeroboam, coming to ask you something about her son, for he *is* sick. Thus and thus you shall say to her; for it will be, when she comes in, that she will pretend *to be* another *woman.*"

⁶And so it was, when Ahijah heard the sound of her footsteps as she came through the door, he said, "Come in, wife of Jeroboam. Why do you pretend *to be* another *person?* For I *have been* sent to you *with* bad *news.* ⁷Go, tell Jeroboam, 'Thus says the LORD God of Israel: "Because I exalted you from among the people, and made you ruler over My people Israel, ⁸and tore the kingdom away from the house of David, and gave it to you; and

13:32 [a]Literally *houses*

14:2 Shiloh had a long prophetic tradition. Located in Ephraim, north of Bethel, it was the site of the tabernacle during the time of Samuel.

14:4 The wife of Jeroboam may have been Egyptian, although the author of Kings does not describe her. The Septuagint, the oldest Greek translation of the OT, identified her as Ano, the daughter of Pharaoh Shishak.

yet you have not been as My servant David, who kept My commandments and who followed Me with all his heart, to do only *what was* right in My eyes; [9]but you have done more evil than all who were before you, for you have gone and made for yourself other gods and molded images to provoke Me to anger, and have cast Me behind your back— [10]therefore behold! I will bring disaster on the house of Jeroboam, and will cut off from Jeroboam every male in Israel, bond and free; I will take away the remnant of the house of Jeroboam, as one takes away refuse until it is all gone. [11]The dogs shall eat whoever belongs to Jeroboam and dies in the city, and the birds of the air shall eat whoever dies in the field; for the LORD has spoken!" ' [12]Arise therefore, go to your own house. When your feet enter the city, the child shall die. [13]And all Israel shall mourn for him and bury him, for he is the only one of Jeroboam who shall come to the grave, because in him there is found something good toward the LORD God of Israel in the house of Jeroboam.

[14]"Moreover the LORD will raise up for Himself a king over Israel who shall cut off the house of Jeroboam; this is the day. What? Even now! [15]For the LORD will strike Israel, as a reed is shaken in the water. He will uproot Israel from this good land which He gave to their fathers, and will scatter them beyond the River,[a] because they have made their wooden images,[b] provoking the LORD to anger. [16]And He will give Israel up because of the sins of Jeroboam, who sinned and who made Israel sin."

[17]Then Jeroboam's wife arose and departed, and came to Tirzah. When she came to the threshold of the house, the child died. [18]And they buried him; and all Israel mourned for him, according to the word of the LORD which He spoke through His servant Ahijah the prophet.

Death of Jeroboam

[19]Now the rest of the acts of Jeroboam, how he made war and how he reigned, indeed they *are* written in the book of the chronicles of the kings of Israel. [20]The period that Jeroboam reigned *was* twenty-two years. So he rested with his fathers. Then Nadab his son reigned in his place.

Rehoboam Reigns in Judah

[21]And Rehoboam the son of Solomon reigned in Judah. Rehoboam *was* forty-one years old when he became king. He reigned seventeen years in Jerusalem, the city which the LORD had chosen out of all the tribes of Israel, to put His name there. His mother's name *was* Naamah, an Ammonitess. [22]Now Judah did evil in the sight of the LORD, and they provoked Him to jealousy with their sins which they committed, more than all that their fathers had done. [23]For they also built for themselves high places, *sacred* pillars, and wooden images on every high hill and under every green tree. [24]And there were also perverted persons[a] in the land. They did according to all the abominations of the nations which the LORD had cast out before the children of Israel.

[25]It happened in the fifth year of King Rehoboam *that* Shishak king of Egypt came up against Jerusalem. [26]And he took away the treasures of the house of the LORD and the treasures of the king's house; he took away everything. He also took away all the gold shields which Solomon had made. [27]Then King Rehoboam made bronze shields in their place, and committed *them* to the hands of the captains of the guard, who guarded the doorway of the king's house. [28]And whenever the king entered the house of the LORD, the guards carried them, then brought them back into the guardroom.

[29]Now the rest of the acts of Rehoboam, and all that he did, *are* they not written in the book of the chronicles of the kings of Judah? [30]And there was war between Rehoboam and Jeroboam all *their*

14:15 [a]That is, the Euphrates [b]Hebrew *Asherim*, Canaanite deities
14:24 [a]Hebrew *qadesh*, that is, one practicing sodomy and prostitution in religious rituals

---

14:9 Since Jeroboam had violated the Law, his dynasty would not survive (see chart, The Prophets Who Spoke to Kings). Israel's monarchy went through nine different dynasties before the country was conquered by Assyria. Jeroboam's dynasty, the first, lasted only through the brief reign of his son Nadab (see chart, The Kings of Israel and Judah).

14:17 Tirzah, the Canaanite city to which Jeroboam had shifted the capital, like Shechem, was not associated with any one tribe. Modern Tell el-Farah, about seven miles northeast of Shechem, has been tentatively identified with Tirzah.

14:21 David's descendants ruled Judah until the Exile (see chart, The Kings of Israel and Judah). Judah's royal family, although dynastically stable, alternated between kings who tolerated pagan practices and reforming kings who attempted to wipe out pagan worship.

14:24 Perverted persons in the land is a reference to sacred prostitution, including male prostitutes.

14:25 Divided, the empire rapidly dwindled. Damascus and the Philistine cities were lost; Moab probably declared independence at this time; and the Egyptians invaded Judah. Shishak (probably Sheshonq I), the first ruler of the 22nd dynasty, had earlier weakened Israel's monarchy by sheltering Jeroboam (see 1 Kin. 11:40, note). Egyptian inscriptions reveal that Sheshonq leveled cities throughout Palestine. The invasion from the south extended eastward past the Jordan and northward all the way to Megiddo, 50 miles north of Jerusalem. The war so weakened Israel and Judah that neither had the military force to attack the other.

days. 31So Rehoboam rested with his fathers, and was buried with his fathers in the City of David. His mother's name *was* Naamah, an Ammonitess. Then Abijam[a] his son reigned in his place.

Abijam Reigns in Judah

15In the eighteenth year of King Jeroboam the son of Nebat, Abijam became king over Judah. 2He reigned three years in Jerusalem. His mother's name *was* Maachah the granddaughter of Abishalom. 3And he walked in all the sins of his father, which he had done before him; his heart was not loyal to the LORD his God, as was the heart of his father David. 4Nevertheless for David's sake the LORD his God gave him a lamp in Jerusalem, by setting up his son after him and by establishing Jerusalem; 5because David did *what was* right in the eyes of the LORD, and had not turned aside from anything that He commanded him all the days of his life, except in the matter of Uriah the Hittite. 6And there was war between Rehoboam[a] and Jeroboam all the days of his life. 7Now the rest of the acts of Abijam, and all that he did, *are* they not written in the book of the chronicles of the kings of Judah? And there was war between Abijam and Jeroboam.

8So Abijam rested with his fathers, and they buried him in the City of David. Then Asa his son reigned in his place.

Asa Reigns in Judah

9In the twentieth year of Jeroboam king of Israel, Asa became king over Judah. 10And he reigned forty-one years in Jerusalem. His grandmother's name *was* Maachah the granddaughter of Abishalom. 11Asa did *what was* right in the eyes of the LORD, as *did* his father David. 12And he banished the perverted persons[a] from the land, and removed all the idols that his fathers had made. 13Also he removed Maachah his grandmother from *being* queen mother, because she had made an obscene image of Asherah.[a] And Asa cut down her obscene image and burned *it* by the Brook Kidron. 14But the high places were not removed. Nevertheless Asa's heart was loyal to the LORD all

his days. 15He also brought into the house of the LORD the things which his father had dedicated, and the things which he himself had dedicated: silver and gold and utensils.

16Now there was war between Asa and Baasha king of Israel all their days. 17And Baasha king of Israel came up against Judah, and built Ramah, that he might let none go out or come in to Asa king of Judah. 18Then Asa took all the silver and gold *that was* left in the treasuries of the house of the LORD and the treasuries of the king's house, and delivered them into the hand of his servants. And King Asa sent them to Ben-Hadad the son of Tabrimmon, the son of Hezion, king of Syria, who dwelt in Damascus, saying, 19"*Let there be* a treaty between you and me, as there was between my father and your father. See, I have sent you a present of silver and gold. Come and break your treaty with Baasha king of Israel, so that he will withdraw from me."

20So Ben-Hadad heeded King Asa, and sent the captains of his armies against the cities of Israel. He attacked Ijon, Dan, Abel Beth Maachah, and all Chinneroth, with all the land of Naphtali. 21Now it happened, when Baasha heard *it*, that he stopped building Ramah, and remained in Tirzah. 22Then King Asa made a proclamation throughout all Judah; none *was* exempted. And they took away the stones and timber of Ramah, which Baasha had used for building; and with them King Asa built Geba of Benjamin, and Mizpah.

23The rest of all the acts of Asa, all his might, all that he did, and the cities which he built, *are* they not written in the book of the chronicles of the kings of Judah? But in the time of his old age he was diseased in his feet. 24So Asa rested with his fathers, and was buried with his fathers in the City of David his father. Then Jehoshaphat his son reigned in his place.

14:31 [a]Spelled *Abijah* in 2 Chronicles 12:16ff **15:6** [a]Following Masoretic Text, Septuagint, Targum, and Vulgate; some Hebrew manuscripts and Syriac read *Abijam*. **15:12** [a]Hebrew *qedeshim*, that is, those practicing sodomy and prostitution in religious rituals **15:13** [a]A Canaanite goddess

---

14:31 Abijam is probably a popular designation or alternate name for Abijah (Heb., lit. "my father is *Yahweh*"; 2 Chr. 12:16; see chart, The Prophets Who Spoke to Kings).

15:2 Maachah was apparently the daughter of Uriel of Gibeah and Tamar and the granddaughter of Absalom, but her name suggests foreign blood (2 Sam. 14:27; 2 Chr. 13:2). She worshiped Asherah, a Canaanite fertility goddess (1 Kin. 15:13); the rites involved sacred prostitution. As the favorite of Rehoboam's 18 wives, she was the mother of Abijah and the grandmother of Asa (vv. 9, 10; see chart, The Queens of the Old Testament). Maachah apparently served as regent during Asa's younger years, so that Judah suffered pagan rule for some years. She continued to hold a semi-official position at court until removed by Asa (v. 13).

15:13 The Brook Kidron runs through the valley between Jerusalem and the Mount of Olives. The Garden of Gethsemane was located near Kidron (John 18:1).

15:17 Ramah, now known as el-Ram, was located in Benjamin, about five miles north of Jerusalem. The city was Baasha's frontier hold against Judah.

15:18 Ben-Hadad's grandfather Hezion is called Rezon (1 Kin. 11:23; see chart, The Kings of Syria). Asa made an illegitimate alliance with the Syrians (see Deut. 7:2). The Syrians then threatened Israel's northeast border, distracting Baasha from the Judah-Israel boundary.

Nadab Reigns in Israel

25Now Nadab the son of Jeroboam became king over Israel in the second year of Asa king of Judah, and he reigned over Israel two years. 26And he did evil in the sight of the LORD, and walked in the way of his father, and in his sin by which he had made Israel sin.

27Then Baasha the son of Ahijah, of the house of Issachar, conspired against him. And Baasha killed him at Gibbethon, which *belonged* to the Philistines, while Nadab and all Israel laid siege to Gibbethon. 28Baasha killed him in the third year of Asa king of Judah, and reigned in his place. 29And it was so, when he became king, *that* he killed all the house of Jeroboam. He did not leave to Jeroboam anyone that breathed, until he had destroyed him, according to the word of the LORD which He had spoken by His servant Ahijah the Shilonite, 30because of the sins of Jeroboam, which he had sinned and by which he had made Israel sin, because of his provocation with which he had provoked the LORD God of Israel to anger.

31Now the rest of the acts of Nadab, and all that he did, *are* they not written in the book of the chronicles of the kings of Israel? 32And there was war between Asa and Baasha king of Israel all their days.

Baasha Reigns in Israel

33In the third year of Asa king of Judah, Baasha the son of Ahijah became king over all Israel in Tirzah, and *reigned* twenty-four years. 34He did evil in the sight of the LORD, and walked in the way of Jeroboam, and in his sin by which he had made Israel sin.

16Then the word of the LORD came to Jehu the son of Hanani, against Baasha, saying: 2"Inasmuch as I lifted you out of the dust and made you ruler over My people Israel, and you have walked in the way of Jeroboam, and have made My people Israel sin, to provoke Me to anger with their sins, 3surely I will take away the posterity of Baasha and the posterity of his house, and I will make your house like the house of Jeroboam the son of Nebat. 4The dogs shall eat whoever belongs to Baasha and dies in the city, and the birds of the air shall eat whoever dies in the fields."

5Now the rest of the acts of Baasha, what he did, and his might, *are* they not written in the book of the chronicles of the kings of Israel? 6So Baasha rested with his fathers and was buried in Tirzah. Then Elah his son reigned in his place.

7And also the word of the LORD came by the prophet Jehu the son of Hanani against Baasha and his house, because of all the evil that he did in the sight of the LORD in provoking Him to anger with the work of his hands, in being like the house of Jeroboam, and because he killed them.

Elah Reigns in Israel

8In the twenty-sixth year of Asa king of Judah, Elah the son of Baasha became king over Israel, *and reigned* two years in Tirzah. 9Now his servant Zimri, commander of half *his* chariots, conspired against him as he was in Tirzah drinking himself drunk in the house of Arza, steward of *his* house in Tirzah. 10And Zimri went in and struck him and killed him in the twenty-seventh year of Asa king of Judah, and reigned in his place.

11Then it came to pass, when he began to reign, as soon as he was seated on his throne, *that* he killed all the household of Baasha; he did not leave him one male, neither of his relatives nor of his friends. 12Thus Zimri destroyed all the household of Baasha, according to the word of the LORD, which He spoke against Baasha by Jehu the prophet, 13for all the sins of Baasha and the sins of Elah his son, by which they had sinned and by which they had made Israel sin, in provoking the LORD God of Israel to anger with their idols.

14Now the rest of the acts of Elah, and all that he did, *are* they not written in the book of the chronicles of the kings of Israel?

Zimri Reigns in Israel

15In the twenty-seventh year of Asa king of Judah, Zimri had reigned in Tirzah seven days. And the people *were* encamped against Gibbethon, which *belonged* to the Philistines. 16Now the people *who were* encamped heard it said, "Zimri has conspired and also has killed the king." So all Israel made Omri, the commander of the army, king over Israel that day in the camp. 17Then Omri and all Israel with him went up from Gibbethon, and they besieged Tirzah. 18And it happened, when Zimri saw that the city was taken, that he went into the

---

15:27 The succession in Israel. Israel's throne was unstable because it lacked a divinely appointed royal line (see chart, The Kings of Israel and Judah). Anyone of high birth, possessing military power, or receiving prophetic anointing had a chance of claiming the crown (see charts, The Dynasties of Israel—Parts I and II). When Jeroboam's family dishonored God, Baasha assassinated Nadab during a battle against the Philistines. Baasha, although a commoner, had apparently been recognized by a prophet (see chart, The Prophets Who Spoke to Kings); he is called "ruler" (Heb. *nagid*).

15:33 The dynasty of Baasha lasted only one year after his death (1 Kin. 16:8–10; see chart, The Dynasties of Israel—Part 2).

16:9 Zimri had neither prophetic support nor charismatic appeal. His dynasty lasted seven days (see chart, The Dynasties of Israel—Part 1). Zimri's sole function as king was to bring upon Baasha's family the same fate that Baasha had inflicted upon Jeroboam's family. The massacre also fulfilled the prophecy of Jehu, establishing him as a true prophet (see chart, The Prophets Who Spoke to Kings).

citadel of the king's house and burned the king's house down upon himself with fire, and died, [19]because of the sins which he had committed in doing evil in the sight of the LORD, in walking in the way of Jeroboam, and in his sin which he had committed to make Israel sin.

[20]Now the rest of the acts of Zimri, and the treason he committed, *are* they not written in the book of the chronicles of the kings of Israel?

Omri Reigns in Israel

[21]Then the people of Israel were divided into two parts: half of the people followed Tibni the son of Ginath, to make him king, and half followed Omri. [22]But the people who followed Omri prevailed over the people who followed Tibni the son of Ginath. So Tibni died and Omri reigned. [23]In the thirty-first year of Asa king of Judah, Omri became king over Israel, *and reigned* twelve years. Six years he reigned in Tirzah. [24]And he bought the hill of Samaria from Shemer for two talents of silver; then he built on the hill, and called the name of the city which he built, Samaria, after the name of Shemer, owner of the hill. [25]Omri did evil in the eyes of the LORD, and did worse than all who *were* before him. [26]For he walked in all the ways of Jeroboam the son of Nebat, and in his sin by which he had made Israel sin, provoking the LORD God of Israel to anger with their idols.

[27]Now the rest of the acts of Omri which he did, and the might that he showed, *are* they not written in the book of the chronicles of the kings of Israel?

[28]So Omri rested with his fathers and was buried in Samaria. Then Ahab his son reigned in his place.

Ahab Reigns in Israel

[29]In the thirty-eighth year of Asa king of Judah, Ahab the son of Omri became king over Israel; and Ahab the son of Omri reigned over Israel

THE DYNASTIES OF ISRAEL— PART 1		
DYNASTY	SUCCESSORS	REFERENCE
Dynasty of Jeroboam	Jeroboam I Nadab	1 Kin. 12:20 1 Kin. 15:25
Dynasty of Baasha	Baasha Elah	1 Kin. 15:33 1 Kin. 16:8
Dynasty of Zimri	Zimri	1 Kin. 16:15
Dynasty of Omri	Omri Ahab Ahaziah	1 Kin. 16:23 1 Kin. 16:29 1 Kin. 22:51

in Samaria twenty-two years. [30]Now Ahab the son of Omri did evil in the sight of the LORD, more than all who *were* before him. [31]And it came to pass, as though it had been a trivial thing for him to walk in the sins of Jeroboam the son of Nebat, that he took as wife Jezebel the daughter of Ethbaal, king of the Sidonians; and he went and served Baal and worshiped him. [32]Then he set up an altar for Baal in the temple of Baal, which he had built in Samaria. [33]And Ahab made a wooden image.[a] Ahab did more to provoke the LORD God of Israel to anger than all the kings of Israel who were before him. [34]In his days Hiel of Bethel built Jericho. He laid its foundation with Abiram his firstborn, and with his youngest *son* Segub he set up its gates, according to the word of the LORD, which He had spoken through Joshua the son of Nun.[a]

Elijah Proclaims a Drought

17 And Elijah the Tishbite, of the inhabitants of Gilead, said to Ahab, "*As* the LORD God of

16:33 [a]Hebrew *Asherah*, a Canaanite goddess 16:34 [a]Compare Joshua 6:26

16:23 The family of Omri held the throne for four generations (see chart, The Dynasties of Israel—Part 1). Omri was an able politician who brought stability to an Israel suffering from internal conflict. Israel had lost territory to Syria, and Assyria was a growing threat. Omri married his son Ahab to Jezebel of Tyre (v. 31) and also matched his daughter Athaliah to Jehoram of Judah, creating two important alliances for Israel (see chart, The Queens of the Old Testament). He also conquered Moab. Despite these achievements, Omri is dismissed in six verses as an evil king; the historian is giving God's point of view on Omri's success.

16:24 Omri bought Samaria, a high hill, ideal for defense, proving that Israel's prosperity had improved under his reign.

16:31 Violations of God's Law under Ahab reached new heights. Ahab's pagan wife, Jezebel of Tyre, attempted to make the worship of Baal Melqart and Asherah official at court (see 1 Kin. 18, Jezebel). Ahab built a temple for Baal and worshiped him, and prophets of Baal were given official status (1 Kin. 18:19).

16:34 Jericho is in southern Israel between Jerusalem and Amman. Child sacrifice is specifically listed as an abomination to God (Deut. 12:31). Joshua had earlier prophesied that Jericho would not be rebuilt without child sacrifice (Josh. 6:26). As long as Israel obeyed God, Jericho would never be rebuilt; the rebuilt city stood as proof of Israel's immense distance from God, and Hiel lost his eldest and youngest sons whether as a deliberate sacrifice or through an accident during the rebuilding process.

17:1 Elijah the Tishbite. Gilead was Israelite territory just east of the Jordan; the exact location of Tishbe is unknown. Elijah (Heb., lit. *"Yahweh* is my God") upheld the claims of *Yahweh* against pagan gods. His first appearance established him as a true prophet; his first prophecy was immediately fulfilled (see Deut. 18:22; chart, The Prophets Who Spoke to Kings).

WIDOW OF ZAREPHATH

After one of his many confrontations with King Ahab and Queen Jezebel of Israel, Elijah was sent by God to hide by the Brook Cherith, where the ravens fed him during the drought he had predicted. When the brook dried up, God instructed Elijah to go to the town of Zarephath, a small town seven miles south of Sidon on the Mediterranean coast, to stay with a widow whom He had commanded to take care of the prophet.

Among the poorest members in the society, this widow apparently had no kinsman to take care of her, and she in turn had to provide for a young son. She was facing either the wrenching heartbreak of watching her child die before her eyes or of knowing that her son would be left without love and care if she died first. As a Phoenician, she had no claim upon Israel's God. Notice her words, "the LORD your God" (1 Kin. 17:12).

In spite of her despair, she still was able to feel some compassion for Elijah as she moved to get him some water. But when he also asked for a small morsel of bread, she revealed to the prophet the seriousness of her own plight: she had only a handful (not even a cup) of flour and a little bit of oil.

Elijah's request that she make him a small cake before she prepared food for her son and herself called for a tremendous exercise of faith on the part of this Gentile woman. What elicited from her this response of faith in Elijah's God? Was there something compelling in the tone of Elijah's voice? Was it the desperation that she had little to lose, since one small meal was all that stood between them and starvation? Clearly she believed Elijah, did what he asked, and was rewarded for her obedience by the constant provision of flour and oil from the Lord as Elijah had promised.

This widow learned to trust God during those days. What must she have felt when her son fell ill and died, after all that miraculous provision? Why had Elijah allowed such tragedy to happen? Had she committed some sin for which her son's death was punishment (a common belief)?

The days of trusting God for daily provision surely must have made it a bit easier to follow the prophet's instructions. Her joy at seeing her son restored to life was crowned by a deeper degree of faith in Israel's God, the Provider for all who trust Him (see Luke 4:25, 26).

See also notes on Providence (Eccl. 7); Widowhood (Ps. 68; Jer. 29)

Israel lives, before whom I stand, there shall not be dew nor rain these years, except at my word."

²Then the word of the LORD came to him, saying, ³"Get away from here and turn eastward, and hide by the Brook Cherith, which flows into the Jordan. ⁴And it will be *that* you shall drink from the brook, and I have commanded the ravens to feed you there."

⁵So he went and did according to the word of the LORD, for he went and stayed by the Brook Cherith, which flows into the Jordan. ⁶The ravens brought him bread and meat in the morning, and bread and meat in the evening; and he drank from the brook. ⁷And it happened after a while that the brook dried up, because there had been no rain in the land.

Elijah and the Widow

⁸Then the word of the LORD came to him, saying, ⁹"Arise, go to Zarephath, which *belongs to* Sidon, and dwell there. See, I have commanded a widow there to provide for you." ¹⁰So he arose and went to Zarephath. And when he came to the gate of the city, indeed a widow *was* there gathering sticks. And he called to her and said, "Please bring me a little water in a cup, that I may drink." ¹¹And as she was going to get *it,* he called to her and said, "Please bring me a morsel of bread in your hand."

¹²So she said, "As the LORD your God lives, I do not have bread, only a handful of flour in a bin, and a little oil in a jar; and see, I *am* gathering a couple of sticks that I may go in and prepare it for myself and my son, that we may eat it, and die."

¹³And Elijah said to her, "Do not fear; go *and* do as you have said, but make me a small cake from it first, and bring *it* to me; and afterward make *some* for yourself and your son. ¹⁴For thus says the LORD God of Israel: 'The bin of flour shall not be used up, nor shall the jar of oil run dry, until the day the LORD sends rain on the earth.'"

¹⁵So she went away and did according to the word of Elijah; and she and he and her household ate for *many* days. ¹⁶The bin of flour was not used up, nor did the jar of oil run dry, according to the word of the LORD which He spoke by Elijah.

17:9 Elijah's flight. Sidon was in Phoenician territory on the coast north of Tyre. Zarephath was near this large city. Because Elijah's identification with *Yahweh* put him out of favor with the Baal-dominated court, God showed Elijah that His divine providence would care for His prophet outside of the structure of Israelite society. When the drought became so se-vere that even the tributaries of the Jordan dried up, God provided for Elijah in a foreign country. He used the widow of Zarephath, a humble, poor woman without a husband and a native of Jezebel's home country (see The Widow of Zarephath). God demonstrated to Elijah that the prophet's well-being depended not on human society but on God alone.

Elijah Revives the Widow's Son

[17]Now it happened after these things *that* the son of the woman who owned the house became sick. And his sickness was so serious that there was no breath left in him. [18]So she said to Elijah, "What have I to do with you, O man of God? Have you come to me to bring my sin to remembrance, and to kill my son?"

[19]And he said to her, "Give me your son." So he took him out of her arms and carried him to the upper room where he was staying, and laid him on his own bed. [20]Then he cried out to the LORD and said, "O LORD my God, have You also brought tragedy on the widow with whom I lodge, by killing her son?" [21]And he stretched himself out on the child three times, and cried out to the LORD and said, "O LORD my God, I pray, let this child's soul come back to him." [22]Then the LORD heard the voice of Elijah; and the soul of the child came back to him, and he revived.

[23]And Elijah took the child and brought him down from the upper room into the house, and gave him to his mother. And Elijah said, "See, your son lives!"

[24]Then the woman said to Elijah, "Now by this I know that you *are* a man of God, *and* that the word of the LORD in your mouth *is* the truth."

Elijah's Message to Ahab

18 And it came to pass *after* many days that the word of the LORD came to Elijah, in the third year, saying, "Go, present yourself to Ahab, and I will send rain on the earth."

[2]So Elijah went to present himself to Ahab; and *there was* a severe famine in Samaria. [3]And Ahab had called Obadiah, who *was* in charge of *his* house. (Now Obadiah feared the LORD greatly. [4]For so it was, while Jezebel massacred the prophets of the LORD, that Obadiah had taken one hundred prophets and hidden them, fifty to a cave, and had fed them with bread and water.) [5]And Ahab had said to Obadiah, "Go into the land to all the springs of water and to all the brooks; perhaps we may find grass to keep the horses and mules alive, so that we will not have to kill any livestock." [6]So they divided the land between them to explore it; Ahab went one way by himself, and Obadiah went another way by himself.

[7]Now as Obadiah was on his way, suddenly Elijah met him; and he recognized him, and fell on his face, and said, "*Is* that you, my lord Elijah?"

[8]And he answered him, "*It is* I. Go, tell your master, 'Elijah *is here.*' "

[9]So he said, "How have I sinned, that you are delivering your servant into the hand of Ahab, to kill me? [10]*As* the LORD your God lives, there is no nation or kingdom where my master has not sent someone to hunt for you; and when they said, '*He is* not *here*,' he took an oath from the kingdom or nation that they could not find you. [11]And now you say, 'Go, tell your master, "Elijah *is here*" '! [12]And it shall come to pass, *as soon as* I am gone from you, that the Spirit of the LORD will carry you to a place I do not know; so when I go and tell Ahab, and he cannot find you, he will kill me. But I your servant have feared the LORD from my youth. [13]Was it not reported to my lord what I did when Jezebel killed the prophets of the LORD, how I hid one hundred men of the LORD's prophets, fifty to a cave, and fed them with bread and water? [14]And now you say, 'Go, tell your master, "Elijah *is here*." ' He will kill me!"

[15]Then Elijah said, "*As* the LORD of hosts lives, before whom I stand, I will surely present myself to him today."

[16]So Obadiah went to meet Ahab, and told him; and Ahab went to meet Elijah.

[17]Then it happened, when Ahab saw Elijah, that Ahab said to him, "*Is that* you, O troubler of Israel?"

[18]And he answered, "I have not troubled Israel, but you and your father's house *have*, in that you have forsaken the commandments of the LORD and have followed the Baals. [19]Now therefore, send *and* gather all Israel to me on Mount Carmel, the four hundred and fifty prophets of Baal, and the four hundred prophets of Asherah,[a] who eat at Jezebel's table."

Elijah's Mount Carmel Victory

[20]So Ahab sent for all the children of Israel, and gathered the prophets together on Mount Carmel. [21]And Elijah came to all the people, and said, "How long will you falter between two opinions? If the

18:19 [a]A Canaanite goddess

18:3 Obadiah, from the northern kingdom, is probably not the same as the author of the biblical book Obadiah. The book is generally thought to have been authored by a native of Judah.

18:4 Massacre of the prophets. Jezebel apparently possessed more power than most Israelite queens (see Jezebel). She exercised it by promoting the cause of Baal with missionary zeal. The writer of Kings contrasted the evil that this foreign woman did to the godly people of Israel by recording the righteous acts of the foreign widow of Zarephath (see 1 Kin. 17, The Widow of Zarephath).

18:17 Troubler of Israel. Ahab suggested that Elijah was seeking to do Israel harm. Elijah immediately reversed the charge: It was Ahab who had harmed Israel by his worship of evil spirits, Baal and Asherah.

18:20 Mount Carmel is near the coast, close to Phoenician territory. The confrontation reveals the true conflict within Israel. It was not between Elijah and Ahab but between Elijah and the prophets of Baal, between the true God and false gods. The prophets of Baal failed the test of true prophecy when their pleas were not answered; Elijah's prayers were heard.

JEZEBEL *An Evil Queen*

Jezebel was the daughter of Ethbaal, the king of Sidon and Tyre (Phoenicia), an ardent worshiper of Melquart, the Baal of Tyre. In a political marriage designed to cement an alliance between Israel and Tyre, she became the wife of Israel's evil king Ahab (1 Kin. 16:31).

Jezebel's domineering influence on Ahab allowed her to bring a fanatical form of Baal worship with her—into her home, into the nation, and even into the temple itself. Four hundred fifty prophets of Baal joined her retinue, along with a similar number of prophets of Asherah, the female consort of Baal. Corrupt, sensual practices involved in the worship of Baal were observed throughout the country, as Jezebel demanded that her god be considered equal to Israel's God (Yahweh). Her insistence on the equality of Baal with God brought her into direct conflict with Elijah, the prophet of God.

Repeatedly, Jezebel had opportunity to see that Yahweh was the true God. Baal was powerless to provide life-giving rains during the drought which occurred as Elijah had prophesied. In a dramatic contest on Mount Carmel, the prophets of Baal were unable to call down fire to their altar, though they danced and chanted, even slashing their own bodies while Elijah taunted them. After Elijah's simple prayer to God for a demonstration of His power to His people, the fire fell on the altar built by Elijah and consumed the sacrifice (1 Kin. 18:23–38). Elijah instructed the people to seek out and destroy the prophets of Baal (v. 40). In raging fury, Jezebel sent word to Elijah that she would do the same to him.

Jezebel also focused her royal power to a willful and wicked advantage. She arranged for the murder of Naboth and the greedy confiscation of his vineyard which Ahab had coveted (1 Kin. 21:15).

Elijah finally delivered the pronouncement of God's judgment on the royal pair. After Ahab's death, Jezebel wielded her evil power as Queen Mother during the reigns of her sons. She never repented. Defiant and decadent to the end, she applied facial make-up and mocked the newly anointed king who had killed her sons. The eunuchs of her own household threw her to a gruesome death in the field whose owner she had murdered. Elijah's prophecy that her body would be torn apart by dogs came true (2 Kin. 9:10).

Jezebel personifies the principle of reaping what is sown (see Gal 6:7). She also demonstrates that the power and influence of evil, although allowed by God for a limited time in chastisement of His own people when they are disobedient, ultimately never triumphs.

See also 1 Kin. 16:31; 19:1, 2; 21:5–16; 2 Kin. 9:10, 22, 30–37; notes on Idolatry (Is. 42); Influence (Esth. 4); Wives (Prov. 31); chart on The Queens of the Old Testament.

LORD *is* God, follow Him; but if Baal, follow him." But the people answered him not a word. ²²Then Elijah said to the people, "I alone am left a prophet of the LORD; but Baal's prophets *are* four hundred and fifty men. ²³Therefore let them give us two bulls; and let them choose one bull for themselves, cut it in pieces, and lay *it* on the wood, but put no fire *under it;* and I will prepare the other bull, and lay *it* on the wood, but put no fire *under it.* ²⁴Then you call on the name of your gods, and I will call on the name of the LORD; and the God who answers by fire, He is God."

So all the people answered and said, "It is well spoken."

²⁵Now Elijah said to the prophets of Baal, "Choose one bull for yourselves and prepare *it* first, for you *are* many; and call on the name of your god, but put no fire *under it.*"

²⁶So they took the bull which was given them, and they prepared *it,* and called on the name of Baal from morning even till noon, saying, "O Baal, hear us!" But *there was* no voice; no one answered. Then they leaped about the altar which they had made.

²⁷And so it was, at noon, that Elijah mocked them and said, "Cry aloud, for he *is* a god; either he is meditating, or he is busy, or he is on a journey, *or* perhaps he is sleeping and must be awakened." ²⁸So they cried aloud, and cut themselves, as was their custom, with knives and lances, until the blood gushed out on them. ²⁹And when midday was past, they prophesied until the *time* of the offering of the *evening* sacrifice. But *there was* no voice; no one answered, no one paid attention.

³⁰Then Elijah said to all the people, "Come near to me." So all the people came near to him. And he repaired the altar of the LORD *that was* broken down. ³¹And Elijah took twelve stones, according to the number of the tribes of the sons of Jacob, to whom the word of the LORD had come, saying, "Israel shall be your name."ᵃ ³²Then with the stones he built an altar in the name of the LORD; and he made a trench around the altar large enough to hold two seahs of seed. ³³And he put the wood in order, cut the bull in pieces, and laid *it* on the wood, and said, "Fill four waterpots with water, and pour *it* on the burnt sacrifice and on the wood." ³⁴Then he said, "Do *it* a second time," and

18:31 ᵃGenesis 32:28

they did *it* a second time; and he said, "Do *it* a third time," and they did *it* a third time. ³⁵So the water ran all around the altar; and he also filled the trench with water.

³⁶And it came to pass, at *the time of* the offering of the *evening* sacrifice, that Elijah the prophet came near and said, "LORD God of Abraham, Isaac, and Israel, let it be known this day that You *are* God in Israel and I *am* Your servant, and *that* I have done all these things at Your word. ³⁷Hear me, O LORD, hear me, that this people may know that You *are* the LORD God, and *that* You have turned their hearts back *to You* again."

³⁸Then the fire of the LORD fell and consumed the burnt sacrifice, and the wood and the stones and the dust, and it licked up the water that *was* in the trench. ³⁹Now when all the people saw *it*, they fell on their faces; and they said, "The LORD, He *is* God! The LORD, He *is* God!"

⁴⁰And Elijah said to them, "Seize the prophets of Baal! Do not let one of them escape!" So they seized them; and Elijah brought them down to the Brook Kishon and executed them there.

The Drought Ends

⁴¹Then Elijah said to Ahab, "Go up, eat and drink; for *there is* the sound of abundance of rain." ⁴²So Ahab went up to eat and drink. And Elijah went up to the top of Carmel; then he bowed down on the ground, and put his face between his knees, ⁴³and said to his servant, "Go up now, look toward the sea."

So he went up and looked, and said, "*There is* nothing." And seven times he said, "Go again." ⁴⁴Then it came to pass the seventh *time*, that he said, "There is a cloud, as small as a man's hand, rising out of the sea!" So he said, "Go up, say to Ahab, 'Prepare *your chariot*, and go down before the rain stops you.'"

⁴⁵Now it happened in the meantime that the sky became black with clouds and wind, and there was a heavy rain. So Ahab rode away and went to Jezreel. ⁴⁶Then the hand of the LORD came upon Elijah; and he girded up his loins and ran ahead of Ahab to the entrance of Jezreel.

Elijah Escapes from Jezebel

19 And Ahab told Jezebel all that Elijah had done, also how he had executed all the prophets with the sword. ²Then Jezebel sent a messenger to Elijah, saying, "So let the gods do *to me*, and more also, if I do not make your life as the life of one of them by tomorrow about this time." ³And when he saw *that*, he arose and ran for his life, and went to Beersheba, which *belongs* to Judah, and left his servant there.

⁴But he himself went a day's journey into the wilderness, and came and sat down under a broom tree. And he prayed that he might die, and said, "It is enough! Now, LORD, take my life, for I *am* no better than my fathers!"

⁵Then as he lay and slept under a broom tree, suddenly an angelᵃ touched him, and said to him, "Arise *and* eat." ⁶Then he looked, and there by his head *was* a cake baked on coals, and a jar of water. So he ate and drank, and lay down again. ⁷And the angelᵃ of the LORD came back the second time, and touched him, and said, "Arise *and* eat, because the journey *is* too great for you." ⁸So he arose, and ate and drank; and he went in the strength of that food forty days and forty nights as far as Horeb, the mountain of God.

⁹And there he went into a cave, and spent the night in that place; and behold, the word of the LORD *came* to him, and He said to him, "What are you doing here, Elijah?"

¹⁰So he said, "I have been very zealous for the LORD God of hosts; for the children of Israel have forsaken Your covenant, torn down Your altars, and killed Your prophets with the sword. I alone am left; and they seek to take my life."

God's Revelation to Elijah

¹¹Then He said, "Go out, and stand on the mountain before the LORD." And behold, the LORD passed by, and a great and strong wind tore into the mountains and broke the rocks in pieces before the LORD, *but* the LORD *was* not in the wind; and after the wind an earthquake, *but* the LORD *was* not in the earthquake; ¹²and after the earthquake a fire, *but* the LORD *was* not in the fire; and after the fire a still small voice.

¹³So it was, when Elijah heard *it*, that he wrapped his face in his mantle and went out and stood in the entrance of the cave. Suddenly a voice

---

19:5, 7 ᵃOr *Angel*

18:46 Jezreel was the second residence of Omri's dynasty and is the modern Arab village of Zerin at the foot of Mount Gilboa and southeast of Nazareth midway between Megiddo and Beth Shan (or Beth Shean). This strategic valley divides Galilee from Samaria. It has been an important battle site throughout the centuries (see Judg. 4—7; 2 Sam. 4; 2 Kin. 9;10; 2 Kin. 22).

19:3 Elijah's second flight. Beersheba is far into Judah, about 40 miles south of Jerusalem and nearly 100 miles from north-

ern Jezreel. Again God provided supernaturally for Elijah's needs (v. 5).

19:8 Horeb, another name for Mount Sinai, is located in the south central part of a peninsula in northwestern Arabia. The modern name for the traditional site is Jebel Musa.

19:9–13 Elijah's experience with God on Mount Horeb is similar to Moses' experience with God (see Ex. 33). Elijah spent 40 days and nights traveling, apparently without food. Moses fasted during the 40 days and nights he spent on the same

came to him, and said, "What are you doing here, Elijah?"

[14]And he said, "I have been very zealous for the LORD God of hosts; because the children of Israel have forsaken Your covenant, torn down Your altars, and killed Your prophets with the sword. I alone am left; and they seek to take my life."

[15]Then the LORD said to him: "Go, return on your way to the Wilderness of Damascus; and when you arrive, anoint Hazael as king over Syria. [16]Also you shall anoint Jehu the son of Nimshi as king over Israel. And Elisha the son of Shaphat of Abel Meholah you shall anoint as prophet in your place. [17]It shall be that whoever escapes the sword of Hazael, Jehu will kill; and whoever escapes the sword of Jehu, Elisha will kill. [18]Yet I have reserved seven thousand in Israel, all whose knees have not bowed to Baal, and every mouth that has not kissed him."

Elisha Follows Elijah

[19]So he departed from there, and found Elisha the son of Shaphat, who was plowing with twelve yoke of oxen before him, and he was with the twelfth. Then Elijah passed by him and threw his mantle on him. [20]And he left the oxen and ran after Elijah, and said, "Please let me kiss my father and my mother, and then I will follow you."

And he said to him, "Go back again, for what have I done to you?"

[21]So Elisha turned back from him, and took a yoke of oxen and slaughtered them and boiled their flesh, using the oxen's equipment, and gave it to the people, and they ate. Then he arose and followed Elijah, and became his servant.

Ahab Defeats the Syrians

20 Now Ben-Hadad the king of Syria gathered all his forces together; thirty-two kings were with him, with horses and chariots. And he went up and besieged Samaria, and made war against it. [2]Then he sent messengers into the city to Ahab king of Israel, and said to him, "Thus says Ben-Hadad: [3]'Your silver and your gold are mine; your loveliest wives and children are mine.'"

[4]And the king of Israel answered and said, "My lord, O king, just as you say, I and all that I have are yours."

[5]Then the messengers came back and said, "Thus speaks Ben-Hadad, saying, 'Indeed I have sent to you, saying, "You shall deliver to me your silver and your gold, your wives and your children"; [6]but I will send my servants to you tomorrow about this time, and they shall search your house and the houses of your servants. And it shall be, that whatever is pleasant in your eyes, they will put it in their hands and take it.'"

[7]So the king of Israel called all the elders of the land, and said, "Notice, please, and see how this man seeks trouble, for he sent to me for my wives, my children, my silver, and my gold; and I did not deny him."

[8]And all the elders and all the people said to him, "Do not listen or consent."

[9]Therefore he said to the messengers of Ben-Hadad, "Tell my lord the king, 'All that you sent for to your servant the first time I will do, but this thing I cannot do.'"

And the messengers departed and brought back word to him.

[10]Then Ben-Hadad sent to him and said, "The gods do so to me, and more also, if enough dust is left of Samaria for a handful for each of the people who follow me."

[11]So the king of Israel answered and said, "Tell him, 'Let not the one who puts on his armor boast like the one who takes it off.'"

[12]And it happened when Ben-Hadad heard this message, as he and the kings were drinking at the command post, that he said to his servants, "Get ready." And they got ready to attack the city.

[13]Suddenly a prophet approached Ahab king of Israel, saying, "Thus says the LORD: 'Have you seen all this great multitude? Behold, I will deliver it into your hand today, and you shall know that I am the LORD.'"

[14]So Ahab said, "By whom?"

And he said, "Thus says the LORD: 'By the young leaders of the provinces.'"

---

mountain. Elijah hid in a cave as Moses hid in the rocky cleft. In both situations, Israel had deserted God for pagan idols. Both men finally experienced God's presence and were given a message from God.

19:15 Ben-Hadad, the king of Syria at this time, had already allied himself with Asa of Judah against Israel during the reign of Baasha. Syria had taken land in the north away from Israel and apparently continued to raid Israel during Ahab's reign. God used Elijah to predict not only the end of Omri's dynasty but the supplanting of Ben-Hadad by his general Hazael. Neither coup would occur for some years.

19:19 Elisha was the son of a well-to-do farmer; Abel Meholah has not been positively identified but probably lay in the fer-

tile land around the Jordan in eastern Israel (v. 16). The passing of the mantle suggested anointing, just as anointing with oil indicated the appointment of a king. Although anointed, Elisha still had to undergo a discipleship. Jesus echoed the words of Elijah when he explained the cost of discipleship (Luke 9:61, 62).

20:1 Because Ben-Hadad's alliance with Asa against Israel took place some 30 years earlier, most scholars assume that this is his son, Ben-Hadad II (see chart, The Kings of Syria). Syria continued its raids into Israelite territory, and Ben-Hadad's strength was so great that he could already address Ahab as a servant.

Then he said, "Who will set the battle in order?"

And he answered, "You."

¹⁵Then he mustered the young leaders of the provinces, and there were two hundred and thirty-two; and after them he mustered all the people, all the children of Israel— seven thousand.

¹⁶So they went out at noon. Meanwhile Ben-Hadad and the thirty-two kings helping him were getting drunk at the command post. ¹⁷The young leaders of the provinces went out first. And Ben-Hadad sent out *a patrol,* and they told him, saying, "Men are coming out of Samaria!" ¹⁸So he said, "If they have come out for peace, take them alive; and if they have come out for war, take them alive."

¹⁹Then these young leaders of the provinces went out of the city with the army which followed them. ²⁰And each one killed his man; so the Syrians fled, and Israel pursued them; and Ben-Hadad the king of Syria escaped on a horse with the cavalry. ²¹Then the king of Israel went out and attacked the horses and chariots, and killed the Syrians with a great slaughter.

²²And the prophet came to the king of Israel and said to him, "Go, strengthen yourself; take note, and see what you should do, for in the spring of the year the king of Syria will come up against you."

The Syrians Again Defeated

²³Then the servants of the king of Syria said to him, "Their gods *are* gods of the hills. Therefore they were stronger than we; but if we fight against them in the plain, surely we will be stronger than they. ²⁴So do this thing: Dismiss the kings, each from his position, and put captains in their places; ²⁵and you shall muster an army like the army that you have lost, horse for horse and chariot for chariot. Then we will fight against them in the plain; surely we will be stronger than they."

And he listened to their voice and did so.

²⁶So it was, in the spring of the year, that Ben-Hadad mustered the Syrians and went up to Aphek to fight against Israel. ²⁷And the children of Israel were mustered and given provisions, and they went against them. Now the children of Israel encamped before them like two little flocks of goats, while the Syrians filled the countryside.

²⁸Then a man of God came and spoke to the king of Israel, and said, "Thus says the LORD: 'Because the Syrians have said, "The LORD *is* God of the hills, but He *is* not God of the valleys," therefore I will deliver all this great multitude into your hand, and you shall know that I *am* the LORD.' "

²⁹And they encamped opposite each other for seven days. So it was that on the seventh day the battle was joined; and the children of Israel killed one hundred thousand foot soldiers *of* the Syrians in one day. ³⁰But the rest fled to Aphek, into the city; then a wall fell on twenty-seven thousand of the men *who were* left.

And Ben-Hadad fled and went into the city, into an inner chamber.

Ahab's Treaty with Ben-Hadad

³¹Then his servants said to him, "Look now, we have heard that the kings of the house of Israel *are* merciful kings. Please, let us put sackcloth around our waists and ropes around our heads, and go out to the king of Israel; perhaps he will spare your life." ³²So they wore sackcloth around their waists and *put* ropes around their heads, and came to the king of Israel and said, "Your servant Ben-Hadad says, 'Please let me live.' "

And he said, "*Is* he still alive? He *is* my brother."

³³Now the men were watching closely to see whether *any sign of mercy would come* from him; and they quickly grasped *at this word* and said, "Your brother Ben-Hadad."

So he said, "Go, bring him." Then Ben-Hadad came out to him; and he had him come up into the chariot.

³⁴So *Ben-Hadad* said to him, "The cities which my father took from your father I will restore; and you may set up marketplaces for yourself in Damascus, as my father did in Samaria."

Then *Ahab said,* "I will send you away with this treaty." So he made a treaty with him and sent him away.

20:23 The Syrians recognized that divine intervention was responsible for their defeat; Ben-Hadad had gathered his numerous allies against Israel's tiny army! They attributed Ahab's success to the strength of Israel's regional gods. Whether Syria thought God or Baal was responsible is not clear; God had triumphed on Mount Carmel, but Baal and Asherah were also worshiped on high places.

20:26 Aphek was probably just east of the Sea of Chinnereth (or Sea of Galilee), at the head of the Jordan. The city lay on a plain on the Syria-Israel border.

20:31 The use of sackcloth and ropes indicated more than simple surrender. Ben-Hadad's men were acknowledging Ahab as master, a reversal of their earlier threats (vv. 1–6).

20:34 The treaty with Ben-Hadad was a move of desperation. Ahab did not think he could afford to lose Ben-Hadad's help. Assyria was growing in strength. Under David and Solomon, Assyria had been confined to its own land. At the time of Ahab, the Assyrian king was Shalmaneser III. His father Ashur-nasir-pal had conquered westward into Philistine territory as well as northward into Babylonia. Shalmaneser III continued the expansion, fighting southward to the Persian Gulf and attempting to conquer all of western Asia. All western kingdoms were threatened, and none was strong enough to stand alone against Assyria. Ahab, by pardoning Ben-Hadad, supplied himself with an extra defense against Shalmaneser's invasion. Ben-Hadad relinquished the territory lost to Syria by Baasha and opened trade routes for Israel.

Ahab Condemned

³⁵Now a certain man of the sons of the prophets said to his neighbor by the word of the LORD, "Strike me, please." And the man refused to strike him. ³⁶Then he said to him, "Because you have not obeyed the voice of the LORD, surely, as soon as you depart from me, a lion shall kill you." And as soon as he left him, a lion found him and killed him.

³⁷And he found another man, and said, "Strike me, please." So the man struck him, inflicting a wound. ³⁸Then the prophet departed and waited for the king by the road, and disguised himself with a bandage over his eyes. ³⁹Now as the king passed by, he cried out to the king and said, "Your servant went out into the midst of the battle; and there, a man came over and brought a man to me, and said, 'Guard this man; if by any means he is missing, your life shall be for his life, or else you shall pay a talent of silver.' ⁴⁰While your servant was busy here and there, he was gone."

Then the king of Israel said to him, "So *shall* your judgment *be;* you yourself have decided *it.*"

⁴¹And he hastened to take the bandage away from his eyes; and the king of Israel recognized him as one of the prophets. ⁴²Then he said to him, "Thus says the LORD: 'Because you have let slip out of *your* hand a man whom I appointed to utter destruction, therefore your life shall go for his life, and your people for his people.' "

⁴³So the king of Israel went to his house sullen and displeased, and came to Samaria.

Naboth Is Murdered for His Vineyard

21 And it came to pass after these things *that* Naboth the Jezreelite had a vineyard which *was* in Jezreel, next to the palace of Ahab king of Samaria. ²So Ahab spoke to Naboth, saying, "Give me your vineyard, that I may have it for a vegetable garden, because it *is* near, next to my house; and for it I will give you a vineyard better than it. *Or,* if it seems good to you, I will give you its worth in money."

³But Naboth said to Ahab, "The LORD forbid that I should give the inheritance of my fathers to you!"

⁴So Ahab went into his house sullen and displeased because of the word which Naboth the Jezreelite had spoken to him; for he had said, "I will not give you the inheritance of my fathers." And he lay down on his bed, and turned away his face, and would eat no food. ⁵But Jezebel his wife came to him, and said to him, "Why is your spirit so sullen that you eat no food?"

⁶He said to her, "Because I spoke to Naboth the Jezreelite, and said to him, 'Give me your vineyard for money; or else, if it pleases you, I will give you *another* vineyard for it.' And he answered, 'I will not give you my vineyard.' "

⁷Then Jezebel his wife said to him, "You now exercise authority over Israel! Arise, eat food, and let your heart be cheerful; I will give you the vineyard of Naboth the Jezreelite."

⁸And she wrote letters in Ahab's name, sealed *them* with his seal, and sent the letters to the elders and the nobles who *were* dwelling in the city with Naboth. ⁹She wrote in the letters, saying,

Proclaim a fast, and seat Naboth with high honor among the people; ¹⁰and seat two men, scoundrels, before him to bear witness against him, saying, "You have blasphemed God and the king." *Then* take him out, and stone him, that he may die.

¹¹So the men of his city, the elders and nobles who were inhabitants of his city, did as Jezebel had sent to them, as it *was* written in the letters which she had sent to them. ¹²They proclaimed a fast, and seated Naboth with high honor among the people. ¹³And two men, scoundrels, came in and sat before him; and the scoundrels witnessed against him, against Naboth, in the presence of the people, saying, "Naboth has blasphemed God and the king!" Then they took him outside the city and stoned him with stones, so that he died. ¹⁴Then they sent to Jezebel, saying, "Naboth has been stoned and is dead."

¹⁵And it came to pass, when Jezebel heard that Naboth had been stoned and was dead, that Jezebel said to Ahab, "Arise, take possession of the vineyard of Naboth the Jezreelite, which he refused to give you for money; for Naboth is not alive, but dead." ¹⁶So it was, when Ahab heard that Naboth was dead, that Ahab got up and went

---

20:35 The prophet and the lion. The "sons of the prophets" were a community of prophets living together. In this brief incident, disobedience brought death; Ahab's death was only delayed (see vv. 35–43; chart, The Prophets Who Spoke to Kings).

20:42 Alliances. Part of God's condition in the conquering of the Promised Land was that pagan nations were to be destroyed (Deut. 7:2). Foreign alliances, like foreign marriages, drew Israel away from reliance on *Yahweh.*

21:10 Jezebel had learned enough Jewish law to abide by the stipulation that no man could be put to death without two or three witnesses to his crime (Deut. 17:6). She used this knowledge to break covenant Law, not to abide by it. In Ahab's reign, the oppression of the poor by the rich began, although it was later condemned by Amos. Jezebel's marriage to Ahab is a worst-case example of violating the prohibition warning that foreign wives would turn Israel to other gods (Deut. 7:4; see 1 Kin. 18, Jezebel).

down to take possession of the vineyard of Naboth the Jezreelite.

The Lord Condemns Ahab

[17]Then the word of the Lord came to Elijah the Tishbite, saying, [18]"Arise, go down to meet Ahab king of Israel, who *lives* in Samaria. There *he is*, in the vineyard of Naboth, where he has gone down to take possession of it. [19]You shall speak to him, saying, 'Thus says the Lord: "Have you murdered and also taken possession?" ' And you shall speak to him, saying, 'Thus says the Lord: "In the place where dogs licked the blood of Naboth, dogs shall lick your blood, even yours." ' "

[20]So Ahab said to Elijah, "Have you found me, O my enemy?"

And he answered, "I have found *you,* because you have sold yourself to do evil in the sight of the Lord: [21]Behold, I will bring calamity on you. I will take away your posterity, and will cut off from Ahab every male in Israel, both bond and free. [22]I will make your house like the house of Jeroboam the son of Nebat, and like the house of Baasha the son of Ahijah, because of the provocation with which you have provoked *Me* to anger, and made Israel sin.' [23]And concerning Jezebel the Lord also spoke, saying, 'The dogs shall eat Jezebel by the wall[a] of Jezreel.' [24]The dogs shall eat whoever belongs to Ahab and dies in the city, and the birds of the air shall eat whoever dies in the field."

[25]But there was no one like Ahab who sold himself to do wickedness in the sight of the Lord, because Jezebel his wife stirred him up. [26]And he behaved very abominably in following idols, according to all *that* the Amorites had done, whom the Lord had cast out before the children of Israel.

[27]So it was, when Ahab heard those words, that he tore his clothes and put sackcloth on his body, and fasted and lay in sackcloth, and went about mourning.

[28]And the word of the Lord came to Elijah the Tishbite, saying, [29]"See how Ahab has humbled himself before Me? Because he has humbled himself before Me, I will not bring the calamity in his days. In the days of his son I will bring the calamity on his house."

Micaiah Warns Ahab

22Now three years passed without war between Syria and Israel. [2]Then it came to pass, in the third year, that Jehoshaphat the king of Judah went down to *visit* the king of Israel.

[3]And the king of Israel said to his servants, "Do you know that Ramoth in Gilead *is* ours, but we hesitate to take it out of the hand of the king of Syria?" [4]So he said to Jehoshaphat, "Will you go with me to fight at Ramoth Gilead?"

Jehoshaphat said to the king of Israel, "I *am* as you *are,* my people as your people, my horses as your horses." [5]Also Jehoshaphat said to the king of Israel, "Please inquire for the word of the Lord today."

[6]Then the king of Israel gathered the prophets together, about four hundred men, and said to them, "Shall I go against Ramoth Gilead to fight, or shall I refrain?"

So they said, "Go up, for the Lord will deliver *it* into the hand of the king."

[7]And Jehoshaphat said, "*Is there* not still a prophet of the Lord here, that we may inquire of Him?"[a]

[8]So the king of Israel said to Jehoshaphat, "*There is* still one man, Micaiah the son of Imlah, by whom we may inquire of the Lord; but I hate him, because he does not prophesy good concerning me, but evil."

And Jehoshaphat said, "Let not the king say such things!"

21:23 [a]Following Masoretic Text and Septuagint; some Hebrew manuscripts, Syriac, Targum, and Vulgate read *plot of ground* (compare 2 Kings 9:36). 22:7 [a]Or *him*

21:19–26 Omri's dynasty would meet the same fate as the dynasties of Jeroboam and Baasha (see charts, The Dynasties of Israel—Parts 1 and 2). Jezebel is specifically included in the curse due to her unusually prominent evil activity during Ahab's reign (see 1 Kin. 18, Jezebel). The comparison to the Amorites puts Ahab in the same class with the Canaanites who inhabited the Promised Land before the Exodus. Ahab, like those pagans, will be destroyed by God.

21:29 Ahab's repentance. The end of the dynasty and Jezebel's death were postponed until the reign of Joram, Ahab's second son (2 Kin. 9).

22:1 War with Assyria. The biblical account does not record the results of the Syrian-Israelite alliance. In 853 B.C., the year of Ahab's death, Shalmaneser III of Assyria invaded. The western armies, led by Ahab, Ben-Hadad, and the king of Hamath, and including some Egyptian forces, faced the Assyrians at Qarqar on the Orontes River. In official Assyrian inscriptions, Shalmaneser claimed a decisive victory, but the Assyrians apparently were checked; Shalmaneser stayed out of Syria for several years.

22:3 Ramoth-Gilead, east of the Jordan River, had belonged to Israel under Solomon (1 Kin. 4:13). Ahab apparently felt that the Syrian alliance had served its purpose.

22:5 The Davidic king of Judah upheld the true faith, removing idols and teaching the Law to his people (2 Chr. 17:3–9). However, Jehoshaphat allied himself to the wicked house of Ahab by arranging for the marriage of his son Jehoram to Ahab and Jezebel's daughter Athaliah (see 2 Kin. 11, Athaliah; chart, Relationships Between the Royal Families).

22:6 Ahab had no more prophets of the Lord in his court; the prophets in his court simply told him what he wanted to hear (see chart, The Prophets Who Spoke to Kings). Micaiah was one of the few prophets who still fulfilled the task of a true prophet in Israel, reminding Israel's kings of covenant Law and *Yahweh*'s true sovereignty.

THE QUEENS OF THE OLD TESTAMENT

NAME	GENERAL INFORMATION
Abi (Abijah)	Daughter of Zechariah; Mother of King Hezekiah of Judah (2 Kin. 18:2).
Athaliah	Daughter of Jezebel and Ahab (2 Kin. 8:18, 26); Granddaughter of King Omri (2 Chr. 22:2, 3); Mother of King Ahaziah of Judah (2 Kin. 11:1–3, 13–16; 2 Chr. 22:10).
Azubah	Daughter of Shilhi; Mother of King Jehoshaphat of Judah (1 Kin. 22:42).
Bathsheba	Daughter of Eliam (Ammiel, 1 Chr. 3:5); Wife of Uriah the Hittite (2 Sam. 11:3). Wife of King David (2 Sam. 11:27); Mother of King Solomon (2 Sam. 12:24; 1 Kin. 1:11).
Esther	Daughter of Abihail (Esth. 2:15); Wife of King Ahasuerus of Persia (Esth. 2:16, 17).
Hamutal	Daughter of Jeremiah of Libnah (2 Kin. 23:31); Mother of King Jehoahaz and King Zedekiah of Judah (2 Kin. 24:18).
Hephzibah	Mother of King Manasseh of Judah (2 Kin. 21:1).
Jecholiah	Resident of Jerusalem; Mother of King Azariah of Judah (2 Kin. 15:2).
Jedidah	Daughter of Adaiah of Bozkath; Mother of King Josiah of Judah (2 Kin. 22:1).
Jehoaddan	Resident of Jerusalem; Mother of King Amaziah of Judah (2 Kin. 14:2).
Jezebel	Daughter of King Ethbaal of Sidon (1 Kin. 16:31); Wife of King Ahab of Israel (1 Kin. 18:13, 19; 19:1, 2; 21:1–25; 2 Kin. 9:30–37); Mother of Queen Athaliah.
Maachah (Michaiah)	Granddaughter of Abishalom (1 Kin. 15:1, 2, 10); Mother of King Abijam (Abijah); Grandmother of King Asa of Judah (1 Kin. 15:10; 2 Chr. 13:2; 15:16).
Meshullemeth	Daughter of Haruz of Jotbah; Mother of King Amon of Judah (2 Kin. 21:19).
Michal	Daughter of King Saul (1 Sam. 18:20–28); Wife of King David (2 Sam. 3:13–16; 6:20–23).
Naamah	An Ammonitess; Mother of King Rehoboam of Judah (1 Kin. 14:21, 31).
Nehushta	Daughter of Elnathan of Jerusalem; Mother of King Jehoiachin (Jeconiah) of Judah (2 Kin. 24:8; Jer. 29:2).
Queen of Sheba	Visitor to the court of King Solomon (1 Kin. 10:1–13). Identified as Nikauli by the Jewish historian Josephus.
Tahpenes	Wife of a weak pharaoh of 21st dynasty who ruled at the end of David's reign and the beginning of Solomon's reign (1 Kin. 11:19, 20). Foster mother to Hadad, a son of the king of Edom.
Vashti	Wife of King Ahasuerus of Persia (Esth. 1:9, 16, 19).
Zebudah	Daughter of Pedaiah of Rumah; Mother of King Jehoiakim of Judah (2 Kin. 23:36).

Although the term "king" appears more than 2,000 times in the Bible, its parallel "queen" is used only about 50 times. Most biblical queens are unnamed and are noted only incidentally. With the exception of the usurper Athaliah, no queen in Jewish or Old Testament history is "queen" in the sense of one who reigns. Queens in this setting were recognized more in their roles as queen-mothers than as the wives of ruling monarchs. This chart is not intended to be exhaustive or comprehensive. It includes both those who had some ruling capacity or influence and those who were called queens only because they were the wives of kings.

[9]Then the king of Israel called an officer and said, "Bring Micaiah the son of Imlah quickly!"

[10]The king of Israel and Jehoshaphat the king of Judah, having put on *their* robes, sat each on his throne, at a threshing floor at the entrance of the gate of Samaria; and all the prophets prophesied before them. [11]Now Zedekiah the son of Chenaanah had made horns of iron for himself; and he said, "Thus says the LORD: 'With these you shall gore the Syrians until they are destroyed.' " [12]And all the prophets prophesied so, saying, "Go up to Ramoth Gilead and prosper, for the LORD will deliver *it* into the king's hand."

[13]Then the messenger who had gone to call Micaiah spoke to him, saying, "Now listen, the words of the prophets with one accord encourage the king. Please, let your word be like the word of one of them, and speak encouragement."

[14]And Micaiah said, "*As* the LORD lives, whatever the LORD says to me, that I will speak."

[15]Then he came to the king; and the king said to him, "Micaiah, shall we go to war against Ramoth Gilead, or shall we refrain?"

And he answered him, "Go and prosper, for the LORD will deliver *it* into the hand of the king!"

[16]So the king said to him, "How many times shall I make you swear that you tell me nothing but the truth in the name of the LORD?"

[17]Then he said, "I saw all Israel scattered on the mountains, as sheep that have no shepherd. And the LORD said, 'These have no master. Let each return to his house in peace.' "

[18]And the king of Israel said to Jehoshaphat, "Did I not tell you he would not prophesy good concerning me, but evil?"

[19]Then *Micaiah* said, "Therefore hear the word of the LORD: I saw the LORD sitting on His throne, and all the host of heaven standing by, on His right hand and on His left. [20]And the LORD said, 'Who will persuade Ahab to go up, that he may fall at Ramoth Gilead?' So one spoke in this manner, and another spoke in that manner. [21]Then a spirit came forward and stood before the LORD, and said, 'I will persuade him.' [22]The LORD said to him, 'In what way?' So he said, 'I will go out and be a lying spirit in the mouth of all his prophets.' And the LORD said, 'You shall persuade *him,* and also prevail. Go out and do so.' [23]Therefore look! The LORD has put a lying spirit in the mouth of all these prophets of yours, and the LORD has declared disaster against you."

[24]Now Zedekiah the son of Chenaanah went near and struck Micaiah on the cheek, and said, "Which way did the spirit from the LORD go from me to speak to you?"

[25]And Micaiah said, "Indeed, you shall see on that day when you go into an inner chamber to hide!"

[26]So the king of Israel said, "Take Micaiah, and return him to Amon the governor of the city and to Joash the king's son; [27]and say, 'Thus says the king: "Put this *fellow* in prison, and feed him with bread of affliction and water of affliction, until I come in peace." ' "

[28]But Micaiah said, "If you ever return in peace, the LORD has not spoken by me." And he said, "Take heed, all you people!"

Ahab Dies in Battle

[29]So the king of Israel and Jehoshaphat the king of Judah went up to Ramoth Gilead. [30]And the king of Israel said to Jehoshaphat, "I will disguise myself and go into battle; but you put on your robes." So the king of Israel disguised himself and went into battle.

[31]Now the king of Syria had commanded the thirty-two captains of his chariots, saying, "Fight with no one small or great, but only with the king of Israel." [32]So it was, when the captains of the chariots saw Jehoshaphat, that they said, "Surely it *is* the king of Israel!" Therefore they turned aside to fight against him, and Jehoshaphat cried out. [33]And it happened, when the captains of the chariots saw that it *was* not the king of Israel, that they turned back from pursuing him. [34]Now a *certain* man drew a bow at random, and struck the king of Israel between the joints of his armor. So he said to the driver of his chariot, "Turn around and take me out of the battle, for I am wounded."

[35]The battle increased that day; and the king was propped up in his chariot, facing the Syrians, and died at evening. The blood ran out from the wound onto the floor of the chariot. [36]Then, as the sun was going down, a shout went throughout the army, saying, "Every man to his city, and every man to his own country!"

[37]So the king died, and was brought to Samaria. And they buried the king in Samaria. [38]Then *someone* washed the chariot at a pool in Samaria, and the dogs licked up his blood while the harlots bathed,[a] according to the word of the LORD which He had spoken.

22:38 [a]Syriac and Targum read *they washed his armor.*

22:11 Horns of iron. Moses promised the tribes of Ephraim and Manasseh dominion over the earth in terms of a bull's horns pushing back the pagan nations (Deut. 33:17). The incongruity of Zedekiah claiming this blessing for a king who had shattered the Law is unmistakable.

22:26 This Joash is not the boy king of Judah, who would not be born for another ten years, but probably a younger son of Ahab. The two families, related by marriage, shared several names (see chart, Relationships Between the Royal Families).

22:34 Ahab's death. In light of the theme of Kings, God's unfailing sovereignty in His dealings with His people, the phrase "at random" is a shining example of irony.

³⁹Now the rest of the acts of Ahab, and all that he did, the ivory house which he built and all the cities that he built, *are* they not written in the book of the chronicles of the kings of Israel? ⁴⁰So Ahab rested with his fathers. Then Ahaziah his son reigned in his place.

Jehoshaphat Reigns in Judah

⁴¹Jehoshaphat the son of Asa had become king over Judah in the fourth year of Ahab king of Israel. ⁴²Jehoshaphat *was* thirty-five years old when he became king, and he reigned twenty-five years in Jerusalem. His mother's name *was* Azubah the daughter of Shilhi. ⁴³And he walked in all the ways of his father Asa. He did not turn aside from them, doing *what was* right in the eyes of the LORD. Nevertheless the high places were not taken away, *for* the people offered sacrifices and burned incense on the high places. ⁴⁴Also Jehoshaphat made peace with the king of Israel.

⁴⁵Now the rest of the acts of Jehoshaphat, the might that he showed, and how he made war, *are* they not written in the book of the chronicles of the kings of Judah? ⁴⁶And the rest of the perverted persons,ᵃ who remained in the days of his father Asa, he banished from the land. ⁴⁷There *was* then no king in Edom, only a deputy of the king.

⁴⁸Jehoshaphat made merchant shipsᵃ to go to Ophir for gold; but they never sailed, for the ships were wrecked at Ezion Geber. ⁴⁹Then Ahaziah the son of Ahab said to Jehoshaphat, "Let my servants go with your servants in the ships." But Jehoshaphat would not.

⁵⁰And Jehoshaphat rested with his fathers, and was buried with his fathers in the City of David his father. Then Jehoram his son reigned in his place.

Ahaziah Reigns in Israel

⁵¹Ahaziah the son of Ahab became king over Israel in Samaria in the seventeenth year of Jehoshaphat king of Judah, and reigned two years over Israel. ⁵²He did evil in the sight of the LORD, and walked in the way of his father and in the way of his mother and in the way of Jeroboam the son of Nebat, who had made Israel sin; ⁵³for he served Baal and worshiped him, and provoked the LORD God of Israel to anger, according to all that his father had done.

·······················

22:46 ᵃHebrew *qadesh*, that is, one practicing sodomy and prostitution in religious rituals   22:48 ᵃOr *ships of Tarshish*

22:39 Ahab's achievements included one of the most extensive building programs of any king in Israel. The "ivory house" or palace was probably at the capital, Samaria, where ivory has been found in excavations. Ahab's foreign policy was highly successful as well. He recaptured Syrian territory, held off Assyria, and allied himself with Judah. The account of his reign in Kings focuses little attention on these secular accomplishments. In God's eyes, Ahab was the worst of the kings of Israel because of his complete rejection of covenant Law and his embracement of idolatry (1 Kin. 16:30).

22:47 The territory of Edom, southeast of Judah, had been a province of Judah since the time of David. The deputy in charge answered to Jehoshaphat.

22:48 Merchant ships. This effort to duplicate Solomon's fleet by opening a trade route to Ophir was doomed; Judah could not recapture the golden days of the empire. Incidentally, Jehoshaphat refused Israel's help in the venture, apparently having learned his lesson in the war against Syria. The prophets of the Lord in Judah advised Jehoshaphat against the alliance (2 Chr. 20:37).

2 Kings

AUTHOR

Both 1 and 2 Kings have the same author. Originally one book, they were first divided in the Septuagint (the oldest Greek version of the Old Testament). See 1 Kings, Introduction: Author.

DATE

The chronology of 2 Kings ends around 560 B.C. with a notation regarding the release of Jehoiachin during the reign of the Babylonian king Evil-Merodach (Amel-Marduk), between 562 and 560 B.C. Second Kings was written during the Babylonian Exile. The language and style of the book is consistent with this date. By 560 B.C., the northern kingdom of Israel had long been dispersed by Assyria (around 722 B.C.), and the southern kingdom of Judah had been taken into captivity by the Babylonians (586 B.C.).

BACKGROUND

SETTING: See 1 Kings, Introduction: Setting.

PURPOSE: Second Kings reveals that God remained faithful to His covenant. The writer outlined the disobedience of Israel and Judah. Second Kings recorded the penalties that must be carried out for disobedience of the Law of His covenant (Deut. 28:15–68; 2 Kin. 17:5–23; 24:20). But 2 Kings ends with Jehoiachin, the last king of Judah and a descendant of King David, released from prison, offering hope for God's covenant people if they repented and obeyed.

AUDIENCE: See 1 Kings, Introduction: Audience.

LITERARY CHARACTERISTICS: See 1 Kings, Introduction: Literary Characteristics.

THEMES

The overall theme of Kings is God's faithfulness to His covenant people (see 1 Kings, Introduction: Themes). The reigns of Hezekiah (2 Kin. 18) and Josiah (2 Kin. 22:1—23:25) were both times when godly Davidic kings led the people in righteousness. During these times, Judah enjoyed blessings of covenant obedience (Deut. 7:12–26). However, because Judah consistently failed to repent and obey, God's judgment was inevitable (2 Kin. 23:26, 27).

OUTLINE

God Judges Ahaziah

1 Moab rebelled against Israel after the death of Ahab.

²Now Ahaziah fell through the lattice of his upper room in Samaria, and was injured; so he sent messengers and said to them, "Go, inquire of Baal-Zebub, the god of Ekron, whether I shall recover from this injury." ³But the angel[a] of the LORD said to Elijah the Tishbite, "Arise, go up to meet the messengers of the king of Samaria, and say to them, '*Is it* because *there is* no God in Israel *that* you are going to inquire of Baal-Zebub, the god of Ekron?' ⁴Now therefore, thus says the LORD: 'You shall not come down from the bed to which you have gone up, but you shall surely die.'" So Elijah departed.

⁵And when the messengers returned to him, he said to them, "Why have you come back?"

⁶So they said to him, "A man came up to meet us, and said to us, 'Go, return to the king who sent you, and say to him, "Thus says the LORD: '*Is it* because *there is* no God in Israel *that* you are sending to inquire of Baal-Zebub, the god of Ekron? Therefore you shall not come down from the bed to which you have gone up, but you shall surely die.'"'"

1:3 ªOr *Angel*

1:1 Moab's rebellion. Ahab's son, Ahaziah, continued the wickedness of his father and accordingly received divine judgment. Moab had been a vassal state of Israel for two generations before seizing the opportunity to rebel against Jehoram at the time of Ahab's death (2 Kin. 3:4–27). An account of this successful rebellion is inscribed on the Moabite Stone (discovered in 1868 near ancient Dibon and known also as the Mesha Inscription).

1:2 Baal-Zebub (Heb., lit. "lord of flies") was a native Canaanite god (see also Matt. 12:24). Ekron was a Philistine city near Israel's southwestern border with Judah and Philistia and was conquered by Israel during David's rule. The "upper room" is a reference to the typical Syrian balcony, usually enclosed with fragile lattice work, which gave an appearance of privacy.

1:3 The angel of the Lord sometimes refers to the pre-incarnate Christ. This instance is not clear. The phrase may merely refer to a messenger of *Yahweh*. God's messengers operated in contradistinction to the messengers of the ungodly king.

RELATIONSHIPS BETWEEN THE ROYAL FAMILIES

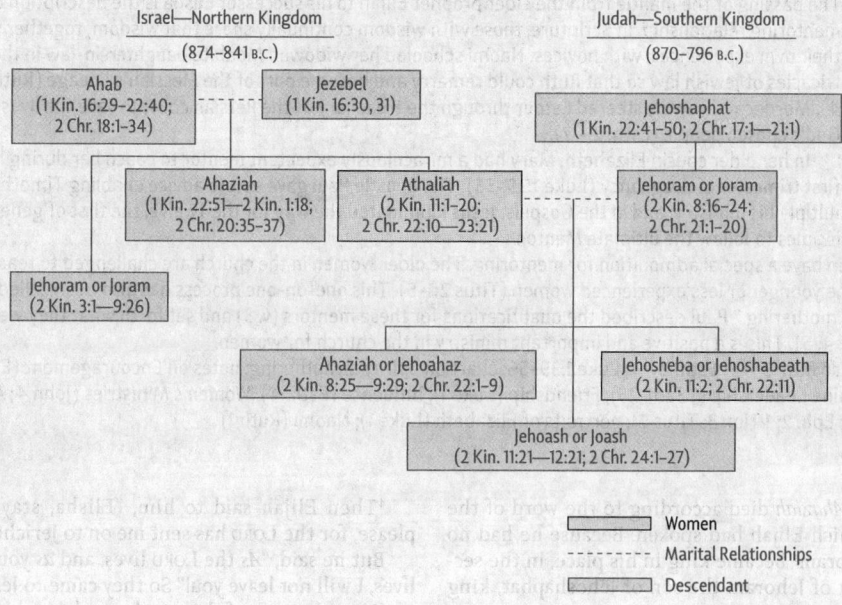

Israel—Northern Kingdom
(874–841 B.C.)

Judah—Southern Kingdom
(870–796 B.C.)

Ahab
(1 Kin. 16:29–22:40;
2 Chr. 18:1–34)

Jezebel
(1 Kin. 16:30, 31)

Jehoshaphat
(1 Kin. 22:41–50; 2 Chr. 17:1—21:1)

Ahaziah
(1 Kin. 22:51—2 Kin. 1:18;
2 Chr. 20:35–37)

Athaliah
(2 Kin. 11:1–20;
2 Chr. 22:10—23:21)

Jehoram or Joram
(2 Kin. 8:16–24;
2 Chr. 21:1–20)

Jehoram or Joram
(2 Kin. 3:1—9:26)

Ahaziah or Jehoahaz
(2 Kin. 8:25—9:29; 2 Chr. 22:1–9)

Jehosheba or Jehoshabeath
(2 Kin. 11:2; 2 Chr. 22:11)

Jehoash or Joash
(2 Kin. 11:21—12:21; 2 Chr. 24:1–27)

Women
Marital Relationships
Descendant

7Then he said to them, "What kind of man *was it* who came up to meet you and told you these words?"

8So they answered him, "A hairy man wearing a leather belt around his waist."

And he said, "It *is* Elijah the Tishbite."

9Then the king sent to him a captain of fifty with his fifty men. So he went up to him; and there he was, sitting on the top of a hill. And he spoke to him: "Man of God, the king has said, 'Come down!' "

10So Elijah answered and said to the captain of fifty, "If I *am* a man of God, then let fire come down from heaven and consume you and your fifty men." And fire came down from heaven and consumed him and his fifty. 11Then he sent to him another captain of fifty with his fifty men.

And he answered and said to him: "Man of God, thus has the king said, 'Come down quickly!' "

12So Elijah answered and said to them, "If I *am* a man of God, let fire come down from heaven and consume you and your fifty men." And the fire of God came down from heaven and consumed him and his fifty.

13Again, he sent a third captain of fifty with his fifty men. And the third captain of fifty went up, and came and fell on his knees before Elijah, and pleaded with him, and said to him: "Man of God, please let my life and the life of these fifty servants of yours be precious in your sight. 14Look, fire has come down from heaven and burned up the first two captains of fifties with their fifties. But let my life now be precious in your sight."

15And the angel[a] of the LORD said to Elijah, "Go down with him; do not be afraid of him." So he arose and went down with him to the king. 16Then he said to him, "Thus says the LORD: 'Because you have sent messengers to inquire of Baal-Zebub, the god of Ekron, *is it* because *there is* no God in Israel to inquire of His word? Therefore you shall not come down from the bed to which you have gone up, but you shall surely die.' "

· · · · · · · · · · · · · · · · · · · ·

1:15 [a]Or *Angel*

1:8 **The hairy man** (lit. "possessor of hair") is an obvious parallel with Elisha. The hair on Elijah would have distinguished him from the bald Elisha (see 2 Kin. 2:23). Some interpret this as a reference to a "garment of hair," pointing to the similarity between Elijah and John the Baptist (see Matt. 3:4). Elijah

fulfilled the same task for *Yahweh* that John did for Jesus—calling the people to repentance (Matt. 17:11–13; Luke 1:17).

1:10 **The immediate fulfillment of Elijah's word** was another affirmation of his status as a true prophet (Deut. 18:21, 22; 1 Kin. 17:1, note).

MENTORING SPIRITUAL MOTHERING

The passing of the mantle from the elder prophet Elijah to his successor Elisha is the description of a mentoring relationship. In Scripture, those with wisdom continually share that wisdom, together with their own experiences, with novices. Naomi schooled her widowed Moabite daughter-in-law in the intricacies of Jewish law so that Ruth could remarry and become part of the Messiah's lineage (Ruth 3—4). Mordecai shrewdly steered Esther through the treachery of the Persian court to save the lives of God's chosen people (Esth. 2—7).

In her older cousin Elizabeth, Mary had a miraculously expectant mentor to coach her during her first trimester of pregnancy (Luke 1:39–56). The apostle Paul gave astute advice enabling Timothy and Titus to multiply his ministry; and in the Gospels, Jesus illuminated the way for the Twelve, the first of generations of disciples to follow the ultimate Mentor.

Women have a special admonition for mentoring. The older women in the church are challenged to teach or mentor the younger or less experienced women (Titus 2:1–5). This one-on-one process has also been called "spiritual mothering." Paul described the qualifications for these mentors (v. 3) and set forth what they were to teach (vv. 4, 5). This is a positive and important ministry in the church for women.

See also Ruth 3—4; Esth. 2—7; Luke 1:39–56; chart on Spiritual Mothering; notes on Encouragement (Eph. 4); Feminine Leadership (1 Sam. 25); Friendship (Luke 1); Influence (Esth. 4); Women's Ministries (John 4; Acts 2;1 Cor. 11; Eph. 2; 1 Tim. 3; Titus 2); portraits of Elizabeth (Luke 1); Naomi (Ruth 1)

---

[17]So *Ahaziah* died according to the word of the LORD which Elijah had spoken. Because he had no son, Jehoram[a] became king in his place, in the second year of Jehoram the son of Jehoshaphat, king of Judah.

[18]Now the rest of the acts of Ahaziah which he did, *are* they not written in the book of the chronicles of the kings of Israel?

Elijah Ascends to Heaven

2 And it came to pass, when the LORD was about to take up Elijah into heaven by a whirlwind, that Elijah went with Elisha from Gilgal. [2]Then Elijah said to Elisha, "Stay here, please, for the LORD has sent me on to Bethel."

But Elisha said, "*As* the LORD lives, and *as* your soul lives, I will not leave you!" So they went down to Bethel.

[3]Now the sons of the prophets who *were* at Bethel came out to Elisha, and said to him, "Do you know that the LORD will take away your master from over you today?"

And he said, "Yes, I know; keep silent!"

[4]Then Elijah said to him, "Elisha, stay here, please, for the LORD has sent me on to Jericho."

But he said, "*As* the LORD lives, and *as* your soul lives, I will not leave you!" So they came to Jericho.

[5]Now the sons of the prophets who *were* at Jericho came to Elisha and said to him, "Do you know that the LORD will take away your master from over you today?"

So he answered, "Yes, I know; keep silent!"

[6]Then Elijah said to him, "Stay here, please, for the LORD has sent me on to the Jordan."

But he said, "*As* the LORD lives, and *as* your soul lives, I will not leave you!" So the two of them went on. [7]And fifty men of the sons of the prophets went and stood facing *them* at a distance, while the two of them stood by the Jordan. [8]Now Elijah took his mantle, rolled *it* up, and struck the water; and it was divided this way and that, so that the two of them crossed over on dry ground.

[9]And so it was, when they had crossed over,

1:17 [a]The son of Ahab king of Israel (compare 3:1)

1:17 The accession of Jehoram, Ahaziah's younger brother. Due to the alliance between Israel and Judah (Jehoram's sister Athaliah married Jehoram of Judah), the royal families shared several names (see chart, Relationships Between the Royal Families).

2:1 Gilgal was near the Jordan just north of the Israel-Judah border. The men of Israel who came out of the wilderness were circumcised (Josh. 5:4–9), and Saul was made king there (1 Sam. 11:15), suggesting that the worship of *Yahweh* may have been a strong tradition in the city.

2:3 The sons of the prophets is a reference to the prophets loyal to *Yahweh*. They were located at Jericho and Bethel.

Bethel was established by Jeroboam as an alternate place of worship for Israel (1 Kin. 12:32). The sons of the prophets lived in communities, perhaps wandering from city to city, supported by gifts from true worshipers and upholding the worship of *Yahweh* (2 Kin. 4:38–44).

2:9 Elijah was mightily endowed with the Holy Spirit. Elisha realized he could never follow in Elijah's steps in his own strength. The humble Elisha asked for a "double portion" of Elijah's spirit—for spiritual power beyond his own capabilities. This request could be a reference to the standard inheritance of the firstborn (see Ex. 13:2, note; Deut. 21:17). In any case, Elisha was seeking spiritual heirship because he realized the enormous task before him.

that Elijah said to Elisha, "Ask! What may I do for you, before I am taken away from you?"

Elisha said, "Please let a double portion of your spirit be upon me."

[10]So he said, "You have asked a hard thing. *Nevertheless,* if you see me *when I am* taken from you, it shall be so for you; but if not, it shall not be *so.*" [11]Then it happened, as they continued on and talked, that suddenly a chariot of fire *appeared* with horses of fire, and separated the two of them; and Elijah went up by a whirlwind into heaven.

[12]And Elisha saw *it,* and he cried out, "My father, my father, the chariot of Israel and its horsemen!" So he saw him no more. And he took hold of his own clothes and tore them into two pieces. [13]He also took up the mantle of Elijah that had fallen from him, and went back and stood by the bank of the Jordan. [14]Then he took the mantle of Elijah that had fallen from him, and struck the water, and said, "Where *is* the LORD God of Elijah?" And when he also had struck the water, it was divided this way and that; and Elisha crossed over.

[15]Now when the sons of the prophets who *were* from Jericho saw him, they said, "The spirit of Elijah rests on Elisha." And they came to meet him, and bowed to the ground before him. [16]Then they said to him, "Look now, there are fifty strong men with your servants. Please let them go and search for your master, lest perhaps the Spirit of the LORD has taken him up and cast him upon some mountain or into some valley."

And he said, "You shall not send anyone." [17]But when they urged him till he was ashamed, he said, "Send *them!*" Therefore they sent fifty men, and they searched for three days but did not find him. [18]And when they came back to him, for he had stayed in Jericho, he said to them, "Did I not say to you, 'Do not go'?"

Elisha Performs Miracles

[19]Then the men of the city said to Elisha, "Please notice, the situation of this city *is* pleasant, as my lord sees; but the water *is* bad, and the ground barren."

[20]And he said, "Bring me a new bowl, and put salt in it." So they brought *it* to him. [21]Then he went out to the source of the water, and cast in the salt there, and said, "Thus says the LORD: 'I have healed this water; from it there shall be no more death or barrenness.' " [22]So the water remains healed to this day, according to the word of Elisha which he spoke.

[23]Then he went up from there to Bethel; and as he was going up the road, some youths came from the city and mocked him, and said to him, "Go up, you baldhead! Go up, you baldhead!"

[24]So he turned around and looked at them, and pronounced a curse on them in the name of the LORD. And two female bears came out of the woods and mauled forty-two of the youths.

[25]Then he went from there to Mount Carmel, and from there he returned to Samaria.

Moab Rebels Against Israel

3 Now Jehoram the son of Ahab became king over Israel at Samaria in the eighteenth year of Jehoshaphat king of Judah, and reigned twelve years. [2]And he did evil in the sight of the LORD, but not like his father and mother; for he put away the *sacred* pillar of Baal that his father had made. [3]Nevertheless he persisted in the sins of Jeroboam the son of Nebat, who had made Israel sin; he did not depart from them.

[4]Now Mesha king of Moab was a sheepbreeder, and he regularly paid the king of Israel one hundred thousand lambs and the wool of one hundred thousand rams. [5]But it happened, when Ahab died, that the king of Moab rebelled against the king of Israel.

[6]So King Jehoram went out of Samaria at that time and mustered all Israel. [7]Then he went and sent to Jehoshaphat king of Judah, saying, "The king of Moab has rebelled against me. Will you go with me to fight against Moab?"

And he said, "I will go up; I *am* as you *are,* my people as your people, my horses as your horses." [8]Then he said, "Which way shall we go up?"

And he answered, "By way of the Wilderness of Edom."

[9]So the king of Israel went with the king of Judah and the king of Edom, and they marched on that roundabout route seven days; and there was no water for the army, nor for the animals that followed them. [10]And the king of Israel said, "Alas! For the LORD has called these three kings together to deliver them into the hand of Moab."

2:11 Elijah and Enoch never experienced death (see also Gen. 5:24). The fiery chariot could have been part of some type of theophany. In any case, Elijah was translated immediately into the Lord's presence.

2:18 Jericho, just north of the Israel-Judah border, was in the fertile Jordan plain. Joshua had pronounced a curse on the rebuilding of Jericho (Josh. 6). Evidently, Elisha's miracle reversed the judgment and gave new fertility to the region (2 Kin. 3:20–22). Salt was used in rituals of purification (see Lev. 2:13; Num. 18:19).

3:4 The rebellion of Moab against Israel is recorded on the Moabite Stone (see 2 Kin. 1:1, note). Jehoram allied himself with Jehoshaphat of Judah and marched south through Judah, around the southern end of the Dead Sea, through Edom. Edom was at this time a province of Judah (1 Kin. 22:47). Although the war apparently ended in victory for Israel (2 Kin. 3:24–26), Moab's loyalty to Jehoram was short-lived. The Moabite Stone reveals that Mesha later invaded eastern Israel, killing Israelites and settling Moabites.

THE PROPHET'S WIDOW

The unnamed widow for whom the prophet Elisha performed a miracle was a believer in *Yahweh*, as evidenced by her strict obedience to the prophet's instructions. Her experience is the first in this series of five miracles demonstrating the power and goodness of *Yahweh* during this period in the northern kingdom of Israel when there was no functioning priesthood. God raised up prophets, such as Elisha, who traveled and taught at a group of schools, training young men in the ancient Law, and who existed as a force for righteousness in the nation. Students were called "sons of the prophets," and in this instance, one of them died, leaving his wife and two sons without adequate provision.

At this time in Israel, a child could be sold into slavery (see Lev. 25:39–41; Deut. 15:2; Jer. 34:9). This woman, who had lost her husband and her livelihood and who now faced the prospect of losing her sons, exercised faith by coming to the man of God for advice. Willingly, she stepped out to do what she had been told to do, even though her actions appeared to be futile. When she started to pour the oil in the privacy of her home, under the watchful eyes of her sons, she witnessed a miraculous display of God's abundant supply. Not only could she pay her debts and protect her family, but she had the means to support her sons until they could become wage earners.

This widow exemplifies God's concern for women, even in an apostate nation. There is also the expectation for financial responsibility even in poverty. Her faith was coupled with obedient action. This truly helpless woman was required only to "trust and obey."

See also notes on Children (2 Kin. 4); Motherhood (1 Sam. 1); Widowhood (Ps. 68; Jer. 29; 1 Cor. 2)

[11]But Jehoshaphat said, "*Is there* no prophet of the LORD here, that we may inquire of the LORD by him?"

So one of the servants of the king of Israel answered and said, "Elisha the son of Shaphat *is* here, who poured water on the hands of Elijah."

[12]And Jehoshaphat said, "The word of the LORD is with him." So the king of Israel and Jehoshaphat and the king of Edom went down to him.

[13]Then Elisha said to the king of Israel, "What have I to do with you? Go to the prophets of your father and the prophets of your mother."

But the king of Israel said to him, "No, for the LORD has called these three kings *together* to deliver them into the hand of Moab."

[14]And Elisha said, "*As* the LORD of hosts lives, before whom I stand, surely were it not that I regard the presence of Jehoshaphat king of Judah, I would not look at you, nor see you. [15]But now bring me a musician."

Then it happened, when the musician played, that the hand of the LORD came upon him. [16]And he said, "Thus says the LORD: 'Make this valley full of ditches.' [17]For thus says the LORD: 'You shall not see wind, nor shall you see rain; yet that valley shall be filled with water, so that you, your cattle, and your animals may drink.' [18]And this is a simple matter in the sight of the LORD; He will also deliver the Moabites into your hand. [19]Also you shall attack every fortified city and every choice city, and shall cut down every good tree, and stop up

every spring of water, and ruin every good piece of land with stones."

[20]Now it happened in the morning, when the grain offering was offered, that suddenly water came by way of Edom, and the land was filled with water.

[21]And when all the Moabites heard that the kings had come up to fight against them, all who were able to bear arms and older were gathered; and they stood at the border. [22]Then they rose up early in the morning, and the sun was shining on the water; and the Moabites saw the water on the other side *as* red as blood. [23]And they said, "This is blood; the kings have surely struck swords and have killed one another; now therefore, Moab, to the spoil!"

[24]So when they came to the camp of Israel, Israel rose up and attacked the Moabites, so that they fled before them; and they entered *their* land, killing the Moabites. [25]Then they destroyed the cities, and each man threw a stone on every good piece of land and filled it; and they stopped up all the springs of water and cut down all the good trees. But they left the stones of Kir Haraseth *intact.* However the slingers surrounded and attacked it.

[26]And when the king of Moab saw that the battle was too fierce for him, he took with him seven hundred men who drew swords, to break through to the king of Edom, but they could not. [27]Then he took his eldest son who would have reigned in

---

3:25 Kir Haraseth, in southern Moab near the Dead Sea, was probably the largest city in Moab and may have been the capital.

3:27 Child sacrifice. Israel's indignation and revulsion over this act may well have hindered them from carrying out God's command to destroy Moab completely, just as the act may

his place, and offered him *as* a burnt offering upon the wall; and there was great indignation against Israel. So they departed from him and returned to *their own* land.

Elisha and the Widow's Oil

4 A certain woman of the wives of the sons of the prophets cried out to Elisha, saying, "Your servant my husband is dead, and you know that your servant feared the LORD. And the creditor is coming to take my two sons to be his slaves."

2So Elisha said to her, "What shall I do for you? Tell me, what do you have in the house?" And she said, "Your maidservant has nothing in the house but a jar of oil."

3Then he said, "Go, borrow vessels from everywhere, from all your neighbors— empty vessels; do not gather just a few. 4And when you have come in, you shall shut the door behind you and your sons; then pour it into all those vessels, and set aside the full ones."

5So she went from him and shut the door behind her and her sons, who brought *the vessels* to her; and she poured *it* out. 6Now it came to pass, when the vessels were full, that she said to her son, "Bring me another vessel."

And he said to her, "*There is* not another vessel." So the oil ceased. 7Then she came and told the man of God. And he said, "Go, sell the oil and pay your debt; and you *and* your sons live on the rest."

Elisha Raises the Shunammite's Son

8Now it happened one day that Elisha went to Shunem, where there *was* a notable woman, and she persuaded him to eat some food. So it was, as often as he passed by, he would turn in there to eat some food. 9And she said to her husband, "Look now, I know that this *is* a holy man of God, who passes by us regularly. 10Please, let us make a small upper room on the wall; and let us put a bed for him there, and a table and a chair and a lampstand; so it will be, whenever he comes to us, he can turn in there."

11And it happened one day that he came there, and he turned in to the upper room and lay down there. 12Then he said to Gehazi his servant, "Call this Shunammite woman." When he had called her, she stood before him. 13And he said to him, "Say now to her, 'Look, you have been concerned for us with all this care. What *can* I do for you? Do you want me to speak on your behalf to the king or to the commander of the army?'"

She answered, "I dwell among my own people."

14So he said, "What then *is* to be done for her?"

And Gehazi answered, "Actually, she has no son, and her husband is old."

15So he said, "Call her." When he had called her, she stood in the doorway. 16Then he said, "About this time next year you shall embrace a son."

And she said, "No, my lord. Man of God, do not lie to your maidservant!"

17But the woman conceived, and bore a son when the appointed time had come, of which Elisha had told her.

18And the child grew. Now it happened one day that he went out to his father, to the reapers. 19And he said to his father, "My head, my head!"

So he said to a servant, "Carry him to his mother." 20When he had taken him and brought him to his mother, he sat on her knees till noon, and *then* died. 21And she went up and laid him on the bed of the man of God, shut *the door* upon him, and went out. 22Then she called to her husband, and said, "Please send me one of the young men and one of the donkeys, that I may run to the man of God and come back."

23So he said, "Why are you going to him today? *It is* neither the New Moon nor the Sabbath."

And she said, "*It is* well." 24Then she saddled a donkey, and said to her servant, "Drive, and go forward; do not slacken the pace for me unless I tell you." 25And so she departed, and went to the man of God at Mount Carmel.

So it was, when the man of God saw her afar off, that he said to his servant Gehazi, "Look, the Shunammite woman! 26Please run now to meet her, and say to her, '*Is it* well with you? *Is it* well with your husband? *Is it* well with the child?'"

And she answered, "*It is* well." 27Now when she came to the man of God at the hill, she caught him by the feet, but Gehazi came near to push her away. But the man of God said, "Let her alone; for her soul *is* in deep distress, and the LORD has hidden *it* from me, and has not told me."

28So she said, "Did I ask a son of my lord? Did I not say, 'Do not deceive me'?"

29Then he said to Gehazi, "Get yourself ready, and take my staff in your hand, and be on your way. If you meet anyone, do not greet him; and if anyone greets you, do not answer him; but lay my staff on the face of the child."

30And the mother of the child said, "*As the* LORD lives, and *as* your soul lives, I will not leave you." So he arose and followed her. 31Now Gehazi

---

have rallied the troops of Moab. The Israelites lifted the siege and returned to their homes. Moab, though its power was momentarily broken, later invaded Israel as a direct result of Israel's disobedience.

4:1 Under the dynasty of Omri, many poor Israelites were

forced into debt and slavery, increasing among the people the rising resentment against the royal family.

4:8 Shunem, a city in central Israel, was apparently located on a main thoroughfare from north to south. This woman was part of a minority in Israel faithful to God and still observing some of the old festivals (v. 23).

A SHUNAMMITE WOMAN

A "notable woman" and her elderly husband lived in the town of Shunem in southern Galilee southeast of Mt. Carmel. Their gracious home became a frequent way station for the prophet Elisha during his journeys throughout the countryside. Such hospitality to strangers in both Old and New Testaments was not optional (Gen. 18:1–8; Deut. 10:17–19; Matt. 25:35; Heb. 13:2).

Eventually, the Shunammite woman decided to provide a more comfortable place for the prophet, a permanent, enclosed structure accessible by an outer stairway. Such accommodations were invaluable in a day when public lodging was very poor, if available at all.

Elisha wished to do something in return for her gracious hospitality, though she had asked nothing. The observant servant Gehazi reminded Elisha that the Shunammite had no children, and infertility was a personal tragedy for an Israelite woman. Elisha announced to her that next year she would hold a son in her arms. She must have been stunned because she and her husband were old (see Luke 18:27). In later years, the child fell ill while working with his father in the fields; he died in his mother's lap.

In silent grief the mother laid the boy on Elisha's bed and closed the door. With urgent determination she sought the prophet. Did she question why God had given her a child, only to take him away from her? Was her swift determination to find Elisha the response of faith that the God who used His prophet to promise her a child could also use His prophet to restore the child's life?

She found Elisha and fell at his feet. Seeing her anguish, Elisha quickly ascertained that something was the matter with the boy. He asked Gehazi to go and lay his prophet's staff on the boy's face, but the Shunammite refused to leave Elisha; together they began the journey back to Shunem. The mother waited anxiously outside the prophet's room—hoping, fearing, wondering. Meanwhile, Elisha prayed and the boy revived.

Imagine the woman's elation at seeing her son, the child of promise, restored to life. While her actions clearly indicated she knew such a miracle was possible, the overwhelming joy at holding her child once again was indescribable.

The woman's gracious provision for the Lord's prophet resulted in the coming of a precious son into her life (see Prov. 11:25). Though some consider namelessness as merely the absence of power, in this unnamed woman is the reward for a servant's heart—power with God and gratitude from His prophet. Her inward beauty (servant's heart) prompted outward duty (hospitality); Elisha's inward virtue (gratitude) unfolded in outward deeds (gift of a son). The Shunammite's unsolicited hospitality awakened Elisha's thoughtful gratitude. Her pro-active faith and confident determination in the midst of grief resulted in the restoration of her son's life.

See also 2 Kin. 8:1–6; notes on Children (2 Sam. 21); Hospitality (1 Pet. 4)

went on ahead of them, and laid the staff on the face of the child; but *there was* neither voice nor hearing. Therefore he went back to meet him, and told him, saying, "The child has not awakened."

³²When Elisha came into the house, there was the child, lying dead on his bed. ³³He went in therefore, shut the door behind the two of them, and prayed to the LORD. ³⁴And he went up and lay on the child, and put his mouth on his mouth, his eyes on his eyes, and his hands on his hands; and he stretched himself out on the child, and the flesh of the child became warm. ³⁵He returned and walked back and forth in the house, and again went up and stretched himself out on him; then the child sneezed seven times, and the child opened his eyes. ³⁶And he called Gehazi and said, "Call this Shunammite woman." So he called her. And when she came in to him, he said, "Pick up your son." ³⁷So she went in, fell at his feet, and

bowed to the ground; then she picked up her son and went out.

Elisha Purifies the Pot of Stew

³⁸And Elisha returned to Gilgal, and *there was* a famine in the land. Now the sons of the prophets *were* sitting before him; and he said to his servant, "Put on the large pot, and boil stew for the sons of the prophets." ³⁹So one went out into the field to gather herbs, and found a wild vine, and gathered from it a lapful of wild gourds, and came and sliced *them* into the pot of stew, though they did not know *what they were.* ⁴⁰Then they served it to the men to eat. Now it happened, as they were eating the stew, that they cried out and said, "Man of God, *there is* death in the pot!" And they could not eat *it.*

⁴¹So he said, "Then bring some flour." And he put *it* into the pot, and said, "Serve *it* to the peo-

---

4:34 The resurrection of the Shunammite's son parallels Elijah's resurrection of the widow's son (1 Kin. 17:17–24). This miracle established Elisha as Elijah's true successor.

4:38 The famine in Israel lasted seven years and was a judgment from God (2 Kin. 8:1). That it lasted more than twice as long as the famine during Elijah's ministry suggests that Israel's wickedness had increased (1 Kin. 18:1).

ple, that they may eat." And there was nothing harmful in the pot.

Elisha Feeds One Hundred Men

42Then a man came from Baal Shalisha, and brought the man of God bread of the firstfruits, twenty loaves of barley bread, and newly ripened grain in his knapsack. And he said, "Give *it* to the people, that they may eat."

43But his servant said, "What? Shall I set this before one hundred men?"

He said again, "Give it to the people, that they may eat; for thus says the LORD: 'They shall eat and have *some* left over.' " 44So he set *it* before them; and they ate and had *some* left over, according to the word of the LORD.

Naaman's Leprosy Healed

5Now Naaman, commander of the army of the king of Syria, was a great and honorable man in the eyes of his master, because by him the LORD had given victory to Syria. He was also a mighty man of valor, *but* a leper. 2And the Syrians had gone out on raids, and had brought back captive a young girl from the land of Israel. She waited on Naaman's wife. 3Then she said to her mistress, "If only my master *were* with the prophet who *is* in Samaria! For he would heal him of his leprosy." 4And *Naaman* went in and told his master, saying, "Thus and thus said the girl who *is* from the land of Israel."

5Then the king of Syria said, "Go now, and I will send a letter to the king of Israel."

So he departed and took with him ten talents of silver, six thousand *shekels* of gold, and ten changes of clothing. 6Then he brought the letter to the king of Israel, which said,

Now be advised, when this letter comes to you, that I have sent Naaman my servant to you, that you may heal him of his leprosy.

7And it happened, when the king of Israel read the letter, that he tore his clothes and said, "*Am* I God,

to kill and make alive, that this man sends a man to me to heal him of his leprosy? Therefore please consider, and see how he seeks a quarrel with me."

8So it was, when Elisha the man of God heard that the king of Israel had torn his clothes, that he sent to the king, saying, "Why have you torn your clothes? Please let him come to me, and he shall know that there is a prophet in Israel."

9Then Naaman went with his horses and chariot, and he stood at the door of Elisha's house. 10And Elisha sent a messenger to him, saying, "Go and wash in the Jordan seven times, and your flesh shall be restored to you, and *you shall* be clean." 11But Naaman became furious, and went away and said, "Indeed, I said to myself, 'He will surely come out *to me,* and stand and call on the name of the LORD his God, and wave his hand over the place, and heal the leprosy.' 12*Are* not the Abanah[a] and the Pharpar, the rivers of Damascus, better than all the waters of Israel? Could I not wash in them and be clean?" So he turned and went away in a rage. 13And his servants came near and spoke to him, and said, "My father, *if* the prophet had told you *to do* something great, would you not have done *it?* How much more then, when he says to you, 'Wash, and be clean'?" 14So he went down and dipped seven times in the Jordan, according to the saying of the man of God; and his flesh was restored like the flesh of a little child, and he was clean.

15And he returned to the man of God, he and all his aides, and came and stood before him; and he said, "Indeed, now I know that *there is* no God in all the earth, except in Israel; now therefore, please take a gift from your servant."

16But he said, "*As* the LORD lives, before whom I stand, I will receive nothing." And he urged him to take *it,* but he refused.

17So Naaman said, "Then, if not, please let your servant be given two mule-loads of earth; for your servant will no longer offer either burnt offering

5:12 [a]Following Kethib, Septuagint, and Vulgate; Qere, Syriac, and Targum read *Amanah.*

4:42 Shalisha is located between Ephraim and Benjamin, near the Israel-Judah border (1 Sam. 9:4). "Baal" suggests that the town was named after the Canaanite deity who served as its protector. However, some Israelites still remembered the firstfruits offering (Lev. 23:10–14). These offerings should have been presented to the priests (see Deut. 18:1–6). This man brought the offering to the sons of the prophets, suggesting that the prophetic community had unofficially assumed some of the duties of the priesthood, which was now totally corrupt (see 1 Kin. 12:25–31).

5:1 Syria, a large country northeast of Israel, had an unstable relationship with Israel (see chart, The Kings and Their Conflicts). The king during Naaman's time was Ben-Hadad II (about 860–841 B.C.), who had been Ahab's ally against the Assyrian threat (1 Kin. 20:31–34). The two countries still

fought over the border cities (1 Kin. 22:1–3) and raided each other's territory (v. 2). During Jehoram's weak administration, Syria grew more antagonistic. The battle over Ramoth-Gilead, in which Ahab died, was in progress eight years later (2 Kin. 9:14). Still, the kings of Israel and Syria maintained some diplomatic relationship (2 Kin. 5:5, 6).

5:17 Naaman requested soil from Israel so that he could worship *Yahweh* on *Yahweh*'s own ground or perhaps to use to build an altar in Syria. This suggests that although he was convinced that *Yahweh* was the one true God, he still viewed *Yahweh* as a limited local deity like his own gods. Naaman wanted land that belonged to the Lord in order to worship Him. He showed his lack of understanding of *Yahweh,* yet a sincere desire to worship *Yahweh.*

CHILDREN ONLY ONE PARENT IN THE HOUSE

God has a special place in His heart for mothers and their children. Throughout Scripture He insists they be defended and given appropriate care (Is. 1:17; 1 Tim. 5:16).

Children tend to mirror the behavior and to "defend" the parent with whom they live, whether single parenting is the result of widowhood, divorce, or a prolonged separation (as in the case of women whose husbands are away for long periods owing to war or business travel). Where children have a parent modeling trust in the Lord and attentiveness to God's Word, the bond between parent and child can be very strong (1 Tim. 5:4). God is aware of the awesome responsibility a single parent faces, and He is more than able to meet all the needs of the child and parent—even employing what may seem to be miraculous means.

Single parents are encouraged to:

- Spend time in the Word each day to receive the divine direction needed, especially during stress-filled times (Ps. 119:11).
- Schedule regular times for family worship, recreation, and communication (Ps. 78:5, 6).
- Be consistent in church attendance and active in service so that both parent and child can be nurtured spiritually and emotionally through fellowship with other believers (Heb. 10:25).

See also Gen. 21:8–21; 2 Kin. 4:1–7; Matt. 18:3; Luke 7:11–17, notes on Brokenheartedness (Ps. 34); Children (2 Sam. 21; Ps. 128; Prov. 22; Luke 15); Death (1 Cor. 15); Family (Gen. 32; 1 Sam. 3; Ps. 78; 127); Grief (Is. 53); Motherhood (1 Sam. 1; Is. 49; Ezek. 16); Widowhood (Ps. 68; Jer. 29; 1 Cor. 2); portraits of The Prophet's Widow (2 Kin. 4) and The widow of Zarephath (1 Kin. 17:7–24). In addition, see notes on Divorce (Matt. 19); Family (Gen. 32; 1 Sam. 3; Ps. 78; 127); Family Worship (Ps. 78); Motherhood (1 Sam. 1; Is. 49; Ezek. 16); Parenthood (Prov. 10); Singleness (Ps. 62; 1 Cor. 7)

or sacrifice to other gods, but to the LORD. ¹⁸Yet in this thing may the LORD pardon your servant: when my master goes into the temple of Rimmon to worship there, and he leans on my hand, and I bow down in the temple of Rimmon—when I bow down in the temple of Rimmon, may the LORD please pardon your servant in this thing."

¹⁹Then he said to him, "Go in peace." So he departed from him a short distance.

Gehazi's Greed

²⁰But Gehazi, the servant of Elisha the man of God, said, "Look, my master has spared Naaman this Syrian, while not receiving from his hands what he brought; but as the LORD lives, I will run after him and take something from him." ²¹So Gehazi pursued Naaman. When Naaman saw him running after him, he got down from the chariot to meet him, and said, "Is all well?"

²²And he said, "All is well. My master has sent me, saying, 'Indeed, just now two young men of the sons of the prophets have come to me from the mountains of Ephraim. Please give them a talent of silver and two changes of garments.'"

²³So Naaman said, "Please, take two talents." And he urged him, and bound two talents of silver in two bags, with two changes of garments, and handed them to two of his servants; and they carried them on ahead of him. ²⁴When he came to the citadel, he took them from their hand, and stored them away in the house; then he let the men go, and they departed. ²⁵Now he went in and stood before his master. Elisha said to him, "Where did you go, Gehazi?"

And he said, "Your servant did not go anywhere."

²⁶Then he said to him, "Did not my heart go with you when the man turned back from his chariot to meet you? Is it time to receive money and to receive clothing, olive groves and vineyards, sheep and oxen, male and female servants? ²⁷Therefore the leprosy of Naaman shall cling to you and your descendants forever." And he went out from his presence leprous, as white as snow.

The Floating Ax Head

6 And the sons of the prophets said to Elisha, "See now, the place where we dwell with you is too small for us. ²Please, let us go to the Jordan, and let every man take a beam from there, and let us make there a place where we may dwell."

5:18 Rimmon was the Syrian king's chief god. The name (perhaps meaning "thunder") suggests that Rimmon was a god of wind, rain, and storms (see Zech. 12:11).

5:20 Prophets were traditionally paid for their services. Ahab's court prophets were supported by the crown.

Saul expected to pay Samuel for his help (1 Sam. 9:7, 8). True prophets often declined the fee (1 Kin. 13:7, 8).

6:1 Godly prophets. Apparently, the number of those loyal to Yahweh was growing, since the community needed new quarters. Popular dissatisfaction with the idolatrous dynasty of

THE KINGS AND THEIR CONFLICTS

KING OF SYRIA	KING OF ISRAEL/JUDAH	CONFLICT
Ben-Hadad II	Jehoram (I)	Territorial: Samaria (2 Kin. 6:8—7:20)
Hazael	Ahaziah (J) Jehoram (Joram) (I)	Territorial: Ramoth Gilead (2 Kin. 8:28, 29)
	Jehu (I)	Territorial: From the Jordan eastward (2 Kin. 10:32, 33)
	Joash (Jehoash) (J)	Territorial: Gath (2 Kin. 12:17, 18)
	Jehoahaz (I)	Territorial: Israel (2 Kin. 13:3–7)
Ben-Hadad III	Jehoash (I)	Territorial: Israel (2 Kin. 13:22–25)
	Jeroboam II (I)	Territorial: Syria (2 Kin. 14:25–28)
Rezin	Jotham (J)	Territorial: Judah (2 Kin. 15:37)
	Ahaz (J)	Territorial: Elath, Jerusalem (2 Kin. 16:5–9)

SYRIA DESTROYED BY ASSYRIA IN 732 B.C.

Syrian forces serving Babylon under Nebuchadnezzar	Jehoiakim (J)	Rebellion against Babylon (2 Kin. 24:2)

I = Israel   J = Judah

So he answered, "Go."

³Then one said, "Please consent to go with your servants."

And he answered, "I will go." ⁴So he went with them. And when they came to the Jordan, they cut down trees. ⁵But as one was cutting down a tree, the iron *ax head* fell into the water; and he cried out and said, "Alas, master! For it was borrowed."

⁶So the man of God said, "Where did it fall?" And he showed him the place. So he cut off a stick, and threw *it* in there; and he made the iron float. ⁷Therefore he said, "Pick *it* up for yourself." So he reached out his hand and took it.

The Blinded Syrians Captured

⁸Now the king of Syria was making war against Israel; and he consulted with his servants, saying, "My camp *will be* in such and such a place." ⁹And the man of God sent to the king of Israel, saying, "Beware that you do not pass this place, for the Syrians are coming down there." ¹⁰Then

---

Omri was increasing, as evidenced by the support given to Jehu's rebellion (2 Kin. 9; 10).

6:8 Syria's attack. Clearly Israel's relationship with Syria had

deteriorated since the time that Namaan had traveled into Israelite territory. Jehoram had turned the army against him (2 Kin. 9:14–26; see chart, The Kings and Their Conflicts).

NAAMAN'S MAIDSERVANT · *A Channel for Blessing*

Naaman's maidservant, probably not yet in her teens, was captured and taken to Syria during the reign of Ahab's son Joram, a time when Israel was constantly invaded by surrounding nations. Although living in a foreign land and serving people who may have killed her family, she demonstrated a sincere desire to serve her master well (Matt. 5:44), offering her service "as to the Lord, and not to men" (Eph. 6:5–8).

This Hebrew child had obviously been taught that God's hand was on her life. Though in the midst of a pagan setting, she was securely committed to Yahweh as a God of mercy. This young girl determined to reveal the superiority of Israel's God over the pagan gods of Syria, even in an atmosphere of war and oppression. She exercised her own simple faith and testified to God's power to heal leprosy, which resulted not only in the saving of her master's life but also in his introduction to the power of the God of Israel. Her persevering testimony led Naaman to submerge his pride and make the decision to put his faith in the God of Israel.

This young captive maid shows the capacity of even a young child to remember and obey wholeheartedly God's commands in difficult circumstances (see Dan. 1:3–20). Though seemingly a minor character in Israel's history, she became an effective channel for one of the most significant miracles in the Old Testament.

See also notes on Decision Making (1 Cor. 8); Evangelism (1 Pet. 4)

the king of Israel sent *someone* to the place of which the man of God had told him. Thus he warned him, and he was watchful there, not just once or twice.

¹¹Therefore the heart of the king of Syria was greatly troubled by this thing; and he called his servants and said to them, "Will you not show me which of us *is* for the king of Israel?"

¹²And one of his servants said, "None, my lord, O king; but Elisha, the prophet who *is* in Israel, tells the king of Israel the words that you speak in your bedroom."

¹³So he said, "Go and see where he *is,* that I may send and get him."

And it was told him, saying, "Surely *he is* in Dothan."

¹⁴Therefore he sent horses and chariots and a great army there, and they came by night and surrounded the city. ¹⁵And when the servant of the man of God arose early and went out, there was an army, surrounding the city with horses and chariots. And his servant said to him, "Alas, my master! What shall we do?"

¹⁶So he answered, "Do not fear, for those who *are* with us *are* more than those who *are* with them." ¹⁷And Elisha prayed, and said, "LORD, I pray, open his eyes that he may see." Then the LORD opened the eyes of the young man, and he saw. And behold, the mountain *was* full of horses and chariots of fire all around Elisha. ¹⁸So when *the Syrians* came down to him, Elisha prayed to the LORD, and said, "Strike this people, I pray, with

blindness." And He struck them with blindness according to the word of Elisha.

¹⁹Now Elisha said to them, "This *is* not the way, nor *is* this the city. Follow me, and I will bring you to the man whom you seek." But he led them to Samaria.

²⁰So it was, when they had come to Samaria, that Elisha said, "LORD, open the eyes of these *men,* that they may see." And the LORD opened their eyes, and they saw; and there *they were,* inside Samaria!

²¹Now when the king of Israel saw them, he said to Elisha, "My father, shall I kill *them?* Shall I kill *them?*"

²²But he answered, "You shall not kill *them.* Would you kill those whom you have taken captive with your sword and your bow? Set food and water before them, that they may eat and drink and go to their master." ²³Then he prepared a great feast for them; and after they ate and drank, he sent them away and they went to their master. So the bands of Syrian *raiders* came no more into the land of Israel.

Syria Besieges Samaria in Famine

²⁴And it happened after this that Ben-Hadad king of Syria gathered all his army, and went up and besieged Samaria. ²⁵And there was a great famine in Samaria; and indeed they besieged it until a donkey's head was *sold* for eighty *shekels* of silver, and one-fourth of a kab of dove droppings for five *shekels* of silver.

6:13 Dothan was in the region of central Israel later known as Samaria after its largest city. The city was on a well-traveled, north-south trade route. Israel's army must have been in a weakened and disorganized state for Syria secretly to penetrate so far into Israelite territory. The temporary peace that resulted from this incident was due entirely to Elisha's intervention, not Jehoram's policies (vv. 21–23).

6:24 Ben-Hadad's siege. Samaria was a large city near Dothan. At this time, it served as the capital of Israel (1 Kin. 16:24), and the royal family had a temple to Baal there (1 Kin. 16:32). The famine, coinciding with the Syrian siege, was a judgment on this idolatry.

²⁶Then, as the king of Israel was passing by on the wall, a woman cried out to him, saying, "Help, my lord, O king!"

²⁷And he said, "If the LORD does not help you, where can I find help for you? From the threshing floor or from the winepress?" ²⁸Then the king said to her, "What is troubling you?"

And she answered, "This woman said to me, 'Give your son, that we may eat him today, and we will eat my son tomorrow.' ²⁹So we boiled my son, and ate him. And I said to her on the next day, 'Give your son, that we may eat him'; but she has hidden her son."

³⁰Now it happened, when the king heard the words of the woman, that he tore his clothes; and as he passed by on the wall, the people looked, and there underneath *he had* sackcloth on his body. ³¹Then he said, "God do so to me and more also, if the head of Elisha the son of Shaphat remains on him today!"

³²But Elisha was sitting in his house, and the elders were sitting with him. And *the king* sent a man ahead of him, but before the messenger came to him, he said to the elders, "Do you see how this son of a murderer has sent someone to take away my head? Look, when the messenger comes, shut the door, and hold him fast at the door. *Is* not the sound of his master's feet behind him?" ³³And while he was still talking with them, there was the messenger, coming down to him; and then *the king* said, "Surely this calamity *is* from the LORD; why should I wait for the LORD any longer?"

7 Then Elisha said, "Hear the word of the LORD. Thus says the LORD: 'Tomorrow about this time a seah of fine flour *shall be sold* for a shekel, and two seahs of barley for a shekel, at the gate of Samaria.'"

²So an officer on whose hand the king leaned answered the man of God and said, "Look, *if* the LORD would make windows in heaven, could this thing be?"

And he said, "In fact, you shall see *it* with your eyes, but you shall not eat of it."

The Syrians Flee

³Now there were four leprous men at the entrance of the gate; and they said to one another, "Why are we sitting here until we die? ⁴If we say, 'We will enter the city,' the famine *is* in the city, and we shall die there. And if we sit here, we die also. Now therefore, come, let us surrender to the army of the Syrians. If they keep us alive, we shall live; and if they kill us, we shall only die." ⁵And they rose at twilight to go to the camp of the Syrians; and when they had come to the outskirts of the Syrian camp, to their surprise no one *was* there. ⁶For the LORD had caused the army of the Syrians to hear the noise of chariots and the noise of horses—the noise of a great army; so they said to one another, "Look, the king of Israel has hired against us the kings of the Hittites and the kings of the Egyptians to attack us!" ⁷Therefore they arose and fled at twilight, and left the camp intact—their tents, their horses, and their donkeys—and they fled for their lives. ⁸And when these lepers came to the outskirts of the camp, they went into one tent and ate and drank, and carried from it silver and gold and clothing, and went and hid *them;* then they came back and entered another tent, and carried *some* from there *also,* and went and hid *it.*

⁹Then they said to one another, "We are not doing right. This day *is* a day of good news, and we remain silent. If we wait until morning light, some punishment will come upon us. Now therefore, come, let us go and tell the king's household." ¹⁰So they went and called to the gatekeepers of the city, and told them, saying, "We went to the Syrian camp, and surprisingly no one *was* there, not a human sound—only horses and donkeys tied, and the tents intact." ¹¹And the gatekeepers called out, and they told *it* to the king's household inside.

¹²So the king arose in the night and said to his servants, "Let me now tell you what the Syrians have done to us. They know that we *are* hungry; therefore they have gone out of the camp to hide themselves in the field, saying, 'When they come out of the city, we shall catch them alive, and get into the city.'"

¹³And one of his servants answered and said, "Please, let several *men* take five of the remaining horses which are left in the city. Look, they *may either become* like all the multitude of Israel that are left in it; or indeed, *I say,* they *may become* like all the multitude of Israel left from those who are consumed; so let us send them and see." ¹⁴Therefore

---

6:30 Jehoram's repentance. Sackcloth was the traditional sign of grief for sin, but clearly Jehoram blamed Elisha for the siege, not recognizing the siege as punishment for his own idolatry (v. 31).

6:33 The identity of the speaker is unclear. If the speaker is in fact Jehoram, whether or not he ever repented is not made clear elsewhere in the story. In addition, although Samaria is delivered, the judgment of famine remains during Jehoram's reign (2 Kin. 8:1), suggesting that he continued unrepentant.

7:2 The officer was probably the commander of the army, if Israel's military organization was similar to Syria's. Namaan occupied this position for Ben-Hadad.

7:6 Hittites and Egyptians were rumored to have come to the aid of Israel as mercenaries. Such a threat from former allies must have heightened the fear of the Syrians, who immediately abandoned their camp and possessions.

they took two chariots with horses; and the king sent them in the direction of the Syrian army, saying, "Go and see." [15]And they went after them to the Jordan; and indeed all the road *was* full of garments and weapons which the Syrians had thrown away in their haste. So the messengers returned and told the king. [16]Then the people went out and plundered the tents of the Syrians. So a seah of fine flour was *sold* for a shekel, and two seahs of barley for a shekel, according to the word of the Lord.

[17]Now the king had appointed the officer on whose hand he leaned to have charge of the gate. But the people trampled him in the gate, and he died, just as the man of God had said, who spoke when the king came down to him. [18]So it happened just as the man of God had spoken to the king, saying, "Two seahs of barley for a shekel, and a seah of fine flour for a shekel, shall be *sold* tomorrow about this time in the gate of Samaria."

[19]Then that officer had answered the man of God, and said, "Now look, *if* the Lord would make windows in heaven, could such a thing be?"

And he had said, "In fact, you shall see *it* with your eyes, but you shall not eat of it." [20]And so it happened to him, for the people trampled him in the gate, and he died.

The King Restores the Shunammite's Land

8 Then Elisha spoke to the woman whose son he had restored to life, saying, "Arise and go, you and your household, and stay wherever you can; for the Lord has called for a famine, and furthermore, it will come upon the land for seven years." [2]So the woman arose and did according to the saying of the man of God, and she went with her household and dwelt in the land of the Philistines seven years.

[3]It came to pass, at the end of seven years, that the woman returned from the land of the Philistines; and she went to make an appeal to the king for her house and for her land. [4]Then the king talked with Gehazi, the servant of the man of God, saying, "Tell me, please, all the great things Elisha has done." [5]Now it happened, as he was telling the king how he had restored the dead to life, that there was the woman whose son he had restored to life, appealing to the king for her house and for her land. And Gehazi said, "My lord, O king, this *is* the woman, and this *is* her son

whom Elisha restored to life." [6]And when the king asked the woman, she told him.

So the king appointed a certain officer for her, saying, "Restore all that *was* hers, and all the proceeds of the field from the day that she left the land until now."

Death of Ben-Hadad

[7]Then Elisha went to Damascus, and Ben-Hadad king of Syria was sick; and it was told him, saying, "The man of God has come here." [8]And the king said to Hazael, "Take a present in your hand, and go to meet the man of God, and inquire of the Lord by him, saying, 'Shall I recover from this disease?' " [9]So Hazael went to meet him and took a present with him, of every good thing of Damascus, forty camel-loads; and he came and stood before him, and said, "Your son Ben-Hadad king of Syria has sent me to you, saying, 'Shall I recover from this disease?' "

[10]And Elisha said to him, "Go, say to him, 'You shall certainly recover.' However the Lord has shown me that he will really die." [11]Then he set his countenance in a stare until he was ashamed; and the man of God wept. [12]And Hazael said, "Why is my lord weeping?"

He answered, "Because I know the evil that you will do to the children of Israel: Their strongholds you will set on fire, and their young men you will kill with the sword; and you will dash their children, and rip open their women with child."

[13]So Hazael said, "But what *is* your servant—a dog, that he should do this gross thing?"

And Elisha answered, "The Lord has shown me that you *will become* king over Syria." [14]Then he departed from Elisha, and came to his master, who said to him, "What did Elisha say to you?" And he answered, "He told me you would surely recover." [15]But it happened on the next day that he took a thick cloth and dipped *it* in water, and spread *it* over his face so that he died; and Hazael reigned in his place.

Jehoram Reigns in Judah

[16]Now in the fifth year of Joram the son of Ahab, king of Israel, Jehoshaphat *having been* king of Judah, Jehoram the son of Jehoshaphat began to reign as king of Judah. [17]He was thirty-two years old when he became king, and he reigned eight

---

8:3 The judgment of the famine led some Israelites to abandon their homes. Apparently, the famine was localized; Philistia is just south of Israel, between Judah and the coast. The royal family had claimed all deserted land, adding greatly to the crown's wealth.

8:7, 8 Hazael. God had given Elijah the command to anoint Hazael as king of Syria (1 Kin. 19:15; see chart, The Kings on the family of Syria). This was to be part of the judgment on the family of Ahab. Hazael, who became king about 841 B.C., would attack

Israel from the north before he was besieged by the Assyrians (see chart, The Kings and Their Conflicts).

8:16 Joram of Israel, Ahab's son, is also called Jehoram (2 Kin. 1:17; see chart, The Kings With Two Names); Jehoram of Judah is also known as Joram (2 Kin. 8:21). Verses 16–24 refer to the activities of the king of Judah. The two kings were brothers-in-law (see chart, Relationships Between the Royal Families).

To relieve leadership, you make committees and boards;
but to reproduce leadership, you make disciples.

Anne Ortlund

---

years in Jerusalem. [18]And he walked in the way of the kings of Israel, just as the house of Ahab had done, for the daughter of Ahab was his wife; and he did evil in the sight of the LORD. [19]Yet the LORD would not destroy Judah, for the sake of His servant David, as He promised him to give a lamp to him *and* his sons forever.

[20]In his days Edom revolted against Judah's authority, and made a king over themselves. [21]So Joram[a] went to Zair, and all his chariots with him. Then he rose by night and attacked the Edomites who had surrounded him and the captains of the chariots; and the troops fled to their tents. [22]Thus Edom has been in revolt against Judah's authority to this day. And Libnah revolted at that time.

[23]Now the rest of the acts of Joram, and all that he did, *are* they not written in the book of the chronicles of the kings of Judah? [24]So Joram rested with his fathers, and was buried with his fathers in the City of David. Then Ahaziah his son reigned in his place.

Ahaziah Reigns in Judah

[25]In the twelfth year of Joram the son of Ahab, king of Israel, Ahaziah the son of Jehoram, king of Judah, began to reign. [26]Ahaziah *was* twenty-two years old when he became king, and he reigned one year in Jerusalem. His mother's name *was* Athaliah the granddaughter of Omri, king of Israel. [27]And he walked in the way of the house of Ahab, and did evil in the sight of the LORD, like the house of Ahab, for he *was* the son-in-law of the house of Ahab.

[28]Now he went with Joram the son of Ahab to war against Hazael king of Syria at Ramoth Gilead; and the Syrians wounded Joram. [29]Then King Joram went back to Jezreel to recover from the wounds which the Syrians had inflicted on him at Ramah, when he fought against Hazael king of Syria. And Ahaziah the son of Jehoram, king of Judah, went down to see Joram the son of Ahab in Jezreel, because he was sick.

Jehu Anointed King of Israel

9 And Elisha the prophet called one of the sons of the prophets, and said to him, "Get yourself ready, take this flask of oil in your hand, and go to Ramoth Gilead. [2]Now when you arrive at that place, look there for Jehu the son of Jehoshaphat, the son of Nimshi, and go in and make him rise up from among his associates, and take him to an inner room. [3]Then take the flask of oil, and pour *it* on his head, and say, 'Thus says the LORD: "I have anointed you king over Israel." ' Then open the door and flee, and do not delay."

[4]So the young man, the servant of the prophet, went to Ramoth Gilead. [5]And when he arrived, there *were* the captains of the army sitting; and he said, "I have a message for you, Commander."

Jehu said, "For which *one* of us?"

And he said, "For you, Commander." [6]Then he arose and went into the house. And he poured the oil on his head, and said to him, "Thus says the LORD God of Israel: 'I have anointed you king over the people of the LORD, over Israel. [7]You shall strike down the house of Ahab your master, that I may avenge the blood of My servants the prophets, and the blood of all the servants of the LORD, at the hand of Jezebel. [8]For the whole house of Ahab shall perish; and I will cut off from Ahab all the males in Israel, both bond and free. [9]So I will make the house of Ahab like the house of Jeroboam the

---

8:21 [a]Spelled *Jehoram* in verse 16

8:18 The wife of Jehoram of Judah is Athaliah, who seized the throne after her son's death (see 2 Kin. 11, Athaliah).

8:20 Edom, located southeast of Judah, had been conquered by David and had paid tribute to Israel (2 Sam. 8:14). Jehoram of Judah lost this territory. The loss meant that Ezion-Geber (the fortified seaport at the head of the Red Sea, known later as the Gulf of Aqaba) and the trade routes southward into Arabia were both unavailable to Israel. The lost trade opportunities brought severe economic consequences.

8:23 Joram of Judah may have reigned as coregent with his father Jehoshaphat for six years. His personal reign would then have lasted only two unsuccessful years (see chart, Relationships Between the Royal Families).

8:27 Ahaziah of Judah was also married to an Israelite princess.

This unidentified woman was probably a daughter of Jehoram of Israel. Ahaziah also allied himself with the Israelite king against Hazael (see chart, The Kings and Their Conflicts).

8:28 Ramoth Gilead was on the Syria-Israel border. The Israel-Judah alliance against Syria had previously besieged Ramoth Gilead under Jehoshaphat and Ahab. Here the city is in Israelite hands, and the new king of Syria is attempting to recapture it (2 Kin. 9:14).

9:9 The dynasties of Israel since the schism were those of Jeroboam I, Baasha, and Omri (see chart, The Dynasties of Israel's Kings—Part 1). Each dynasty proved unfaithful to God. Jehu was anointed not by Elisha, but by a lesser prophet; his role proved to be solely one of vengeance, since his own dynasty was also idolatrous (2 Kin. 10:29–31).

THE KINGS WITH TWO NAMES

ISRAEL	JUDAH
Jehoram, son of Ahab, also known as Joram (2 Kin. 3:1; 8:16–29)	Jehoram, son of Jehoshaphat, also known as Joram (2 Kin 8:16, 21–24)
Jehoash, son of Jehoahaz, also known as Joash (2 Kin. 13:10, 12, 13)	Ahaziah, son of Jehoram, also known as Azariah (2 Kin. 8:25–27; 2 Chr. 22:6)
	Joash, son of Ahaziah, also known as Jehoash (2 Kin. 12:1–3, 19)
	Uzziah, son of Amaziah, also known as Azariah (2 Kin. 15:1–7; 2 Chr. 26:1–4)
	Eliakim, son of Josiah; name changed to Jehoiakim (2 Kin. 23:34)
	Mattaniah, uncle of Jehoiachin; name changed to Zedekiah (2 Kin. 24:17)

son of Nebat, and like the house of Baasha the son of Ahijah. ¹⁰The dogs shall eat Jezebel on the plot *of ground* at Jezreel, and *there shall be* none to bury her.'" And he opened the door and fled.

¹¹Then Jehu came out to the servants of his master, and *one* said to him, "*Is* all well? Why did this madman come to you?"

And he said to them, "You know the man and his babble."

¹²And they said, "A lie! Tell us now."

So he said, "Thus and thus he spoke to me, saying, 'Thus says the LORD: "I have anointed you king over Israel."'"

¹³Then each man hastened to take his garment and put *it* under him on the top of the steps; and they blew trumpets, saying, "Jehu is king!"

Joram of Israel Killed

¹⁴So Jehu the son of Jehoshaphat, the son of Nimshi, conspired against Joram. (Now Joram had been defending Ramoth Gilead, he and all Israel, against Hazael king of Syria. ¹⁵But King Joram had returned to Jezreel to recover from the wounds which the Syrians had inflicted on him when he fought with Hazael king of Syria.) And Jehu said, "If you are so minded, let no one leave *or* escape

from the city to go and tell *it* in Jezreel." ¹⁶So Jehu rode in a chariot and went to Jezreel, for Joram was laid up there; and Ahaziah king of Judah had come down to see Joram.

¹⁷Now a watchman stood on the tower in Jezreel, and he saw the company of Jehu as he came, and said, "I see a company of men."

And Joram said, "Get a horseman and send him to meet them, and let him say, '*Is it* peace?'"

¹⁸So the horseman went to meet him, and said, "Thus says the king: '*Is it* peace?'"

And Jehu said, "What have you to do with peace? Turn around and follow me."

So the watchman reported, saying, "The messenger went to them, but is not coming back."

¹⁹Then he sent out a second horseman who came to them, and said, "Thus says the king: '*Is it* peace?'"

And Jehu answered, "What have you to do with peace? Turn around and follow me."

²⁰So the watchman reported, saying, "He went up to them and is not coming back; and the driving *is* like the driving of Jehu the son of Nimshi, for he drives furiously!"

²¹Then Joram said, "Make ready." And his chariot was made ready. Then Joram king of Israel and Ahaziah king of Judah went out, each in his chariot; and they went out to meet Jehu, and met him on the property of Naboth the Jezreelite. ²²Now it happened, when Joram saw Jehu, that he said, "*Is it* peace, Jehu?"

So he answered, "What peace, as long as the harlotries of your mother Jezebel and her witchcraft *are so* many?"

²³Then Joram turned around and fled, and said to Ahaziah, "Treachery, Ahaziah!" ²⁴Now Jehu drew his bow with full strength and shot Jehoram between his arms; and the arrow came out at his heart, and he sank down in his chariot. ²⁵Then *Jehu* said to Bidkar his captain, "Pick *him* up, *and* throw him into the tract of the field of Naboth the Jezreelite; for remember, when you and I were riding together behind Ahab his father, that the LORD laid this burden upon him: ²⁶'Surely I saw yesterday the blood of Naboth and the blood of his sons,' says the LORD, 'and I will repay you in this plot,' says the LORD. Now therefore, take *and* throw him on the plot *of ground,* according to the word of the LORD."

Ahaziah of Judah Killed

²⁷But when Ahaziah king of Judah saw *this,* he fled by the road to Beth Haggan.ᵃ So Jehu pursued

9:27 ᵃLiterally *The Garden House*

9:13 Jehu's recognition. Because there was no stable dynasty in Israel, anyone with charisma, prophetic anointing, or popular support could seize the throne. Jehu apparently possessed all three. The military ineptness of Jehoram and Ahaziah had produced discontent in the army, and the widening gap between rich and poor in Israel, along with the worsening idolatry of the royal family, fueled popular discontent as well.

9:14 Joram or Jehoram of Israel was the son of Ahab (see chart, The Kings With Two Names). At this time he was at Ahab's old capital, Jezreel (v. 15).

9:27 Ahaziah fled south but was overtaken by Jehu's men at Ibleam, seven miles from Jezreel. When wounded, he turned north and finally died in Megiddo, ten miles north of Ibleam and almost 50 miles north of Judah.

him, and said, "Shoot him also in the chariot." *And they shot him* at the Ascent of Gur, which is by Ibleam. Then he fled to Megiddo, and died there. [28]And his servants carried him in the chariot to Jerusalem, and buried him in his tomb with his fathers in the City of David. [29]In the eleventh year of Joram the son of Ahab, Ahaziah had become king over Judah.

Jezebel's Violent Death

[30]Now when Jehu had come to Jezreel, Jezebel heard *of it;* and she put paint on her eyes and adorned her head, and looked through a window. [31]Then, as Jehu entered at the gate, she said, *"Is it peace, Zimri, murderer of your master?"*

[32]And he looked up at the window, and said, "Who *is* on my side? Who?" So two *or* three eunuchs looked out at him. [33]Then he said, "Throw her down." So they threw her down, and *some* of her blood spattered on the wall and on the horses; and he trampled her underfoot. [34]And when he had gone in, he ate and drank. Then he said, "Go now, see to this accursed *woman,* and bury her, for she was a king's daughter." [35]So they went to bury her, but they found no more of her than the skull and the feet and the palms of *her* hands. [36]Therefore they came back and told him. And he said, "This *is* the word of the LORD, which He spoke by His servant Elijah the Tishbite, saying, 'On the plot *of ground* at Jezreel dogs shall eat the flesh of Jezebel;[a] [37]and the corpse of Jezebel shall be as refuse on the surface of the field, in the plot at Jezreel, so that they shall not say, "Here *lies* Jezebel." '"

Ahab's Seventy Sons Killed

10 Now Ahab had seventy sons in Samaria. And Jehu wrote and sent letters to Samaria, to the rulers of Jezreel,[a] to the elders, and to those who reared Ahab's *sons,* saying:

[2]Now as soon as this letter comes to you, since your master's sons *are* with you, and you have chariots and horses, a fortified city also, and weapons, [3]choose the best qualified of your master's sons, set *him* on his father's throne, and fight for your master's house.

[4]But they were exceedingly afraid, and said, "Look, two kings could not stand up to him; how then can we stand?" [5]And he who *was* in charge of the house, and he who *was* in charge of the city, the elders also, and those who reared *the sons,* sent to Jehu, saying, "We *are* your servants, we will do all you tell us; but we will not make anyone king. Do *what is* good in your sight." [6]Then he wrote a second letter to them, saying:

If you *are* for me and will obey my voice, take the heads of the men, your master's sons, and come to me at Jezreel by this time tomorrow.

Now the king's sons, seventy persons, *were* with the great men of the city, *who* were rearing them. [7]So it was, when the letter came to them, that they took the king's sons and slaughtered seventy persons, put their heads in baskets and sent *them* to him at Jezreel.

[8]Then a messenger came and told him, saying, "They have brought the heads of the king's sons."

And he said, "Lay them in two heaps at the entrance of the gate until morning."

[9]So it was, in the morning, that he went out and stood, and said to all the people, "You *are* righteous. Indeed I conspired against my master and killed him; but who killed all these? [10]Know now that nothing shall fall to the earth of the word of the LORD which the LORD spoke concerning the house of Ahab; for the LORD has done what He spoke by His servant Elijah." [11]So Jehu killed all who remained of the house of Ahab in Jezreel, and all his great men and his close acquaintances and his priests, until he left him none remaining.

Ahaziah's Forty-two Brothers Killed

[12]And he arose and departed and went to Samaria. On the way, at Beth Eked[a] of the Shepherds, [13]Jehu met with the brothers of Ahaziah king of Judah, and said, "Who *are* you?"

So they answered, "We *are* the brothers of Ahaziah; we have come down to greet the sons of the king and the sons of the queen mother."

[14]And he said, "Take them alive!" So they took them alive, and killed them at the well of Beth Eked, forty-two men; and he left none of them.

9:36 [a]1 Kings 21:23   10:1 [a]Following Masoretic Text, Syriac, and Targum; Septuagint reads *Samaria;* Vulgate reads *city.*   10:12 [a]Or *The Shearing House*

9:30 **Jezebel's dress** may refer to a style related to idol worship, or it may be a reference to royal adornment fitting a queen (see also Ex. 30, Cosmetics; Ezek. 16, Clothing). Jezebel was Tyrian and worshiped Baal Melqart (see 1 Kin. 18, Jezebel).

9:31 **Zimri** had commanded part of the army during the reign of Elah of Israel. He had murdered Elah and all his household, which was a fulfillment of prophecy (1 Kin. 16:8-13). Zimri reigned only seven days before being replaced by Omri, another army commander (see chart, The Dynasties of Israel's Kings—Part 1).

10:14 **Jehu,** anointed to carry out God's judgment on Israel's royal house, extended the purge to Judah. The Davidic line was in danger of being corrupted and finally wiped out through its intermarriage with Ahab's family (2 Kin. 11:1-3). Jehu's execution of Ahaziah and his brothers prevented David's family line from ultimate destruction.

ATHALIAH · *A Wicked Queen*

Athaliah, the daughter of King Ahab and Queen Jezebel and the granddaughter of Omri (2 Kings 8:18, 26), was born into an atmosphere that completely denied the one true God. She married Jehoram, the firstborn of Judah's godly king Jehoshaphat. Jehoram had allied himself with Israel for political reasons (2 Chr. 22:5). Just as her mother had done, Athaliah promoted Baal worship and led both the people of Judah and her husband away from the Lord (see 2 Chr. 21:6). Jehoram died prematurely at age forty (see 2 Chr. 21:18–20).

Ahaziah, the son of Jehoram and Athaliah, became king, and his mother continued her evil influence (2 Chr. 22:3). Following the deaths of her sons at the hands of the Philistines and the Arabians, Athaliah murdered even her own grandsons, who were the legitimate heirs to the throne (see 2 Chr. 21:17). Gaining the throne for herself, Athaliah then reigned for six years as an illegitimate occupant of the royal seat, since she had not been born into the Davidic lineage. She carried on the idolatrous traditions in which she was reared.

Judah had never had a ruler who was not a descendant of David. The Levite priests supported Davidic kingship. When they led a rebellion against this northern usurper, the people followed willingly (see 2 Kin. 11:13–20). Athaliah was killed dishonorably, like the other members of Ahab's family, at the Horse's Gate. Her wickedness stains the pages of Israel's history, and this queen stands as a sobering reminder of the escalation of evil influence that can work in the heart of a rebellious woman who determines to go her own way, rejecting God and grasping for her own power (2 Chr. 22:3, 10; 24:7).

See also 2 Kin. 8:26; 2 Chr. 22:10–12; 23:12–15; 24:7; notes on Feminine Leadership (1 Sam. 25); Influence (Esth. 4)

The Rest of Ahab's Family Killed

¹⁵Now when he departed from there, he met Jehonadab the son of Rechab, *coming* to meet him; and he greeted him and said to him, "Is your heart right, as my heart *is* toward your heart?"

And Jehonadab answered, "It is."

Jehu said, "If it is, give *me* your hand." So he gave *him* his hand, and he took him up to him into the chariot. ¹⁶Then he said, "Come with me, and see my zeal for the LORD." So they had him ride in his chariot. ¹⁷And when he came to Samaria, he killed all who remained to Ahab in Samaria, till he had destroyed them, according to the word of the LORD which He spoke to Elijah.

Worshipers of Baal Killed

¹⁸Then Jehu gathered all the people together, and said to them, "Ahab served Baal a little, Jehu will serve him much. ¹⁹Now therefore, call to me all the prophets of Baal, all his servants, and all his priests. Let no one be missing, for I have a great sacrifice for Baal. Whoever is missing shall not live." But Jehu acted deceptively, with the intent of destroying the worshipers of Baal. ²⁰And Jehu said, "Proclaim a solemn assembly for Baal." So they proclaimed *it*. ²¹Then Jehu sent throughout all Israel; and all the worshipers of Baal came, so that there was not a man left who did not come. So they came into the temple[a] of Baal, and the temple of Baal was full from one end to the other. ²²And he said to the one in charge of the wardrobe, "Bring out vestments for all the worshipers of Baal." So he brought out vestments for them. ²³Then Jehu and Jehonadab the son of Rechab went into the temple of Baal, and said to the worshipers of Baal, "Search and see that no servants of the LORD are here with you, but only the worshipers of Baal." ²⁴So they went in to offer sacrifices and burnt offerings. Now Jehu had appointed for himself eighty men on the outside, and had said, "*If* any of the men whom I have brought into your hands escapes, *whoever lets him escape, it shall be* his life for the life of the other."

²⁵Now it happened, as soon as he had made an end of offering the burnt offering, that Jehu said to the guard and to the captains, "Go in *and* kill them; let no one come out!" And they killed them with the edge of the sword; then the guards and the officers threw *them* out, and went into the inner room of the temple of Baal. ²⁶And they brought the *sacred* pillars out of the temple of Baal and burned them. ²⁷Then they broke down the *sacred* pillar of Baal, and tore down the temple of Baal and made it a refuse dump to this day. ²⁸Thus Jehu destroyed Baal from Israel.

²⁹However Jehu did not turn away from the

10:21 ᵃLiterally *house*, and so elsewhere in this chapter

10:15 Jehonadab's father Rechab probably founded the Israelite group known as Rechabites. These men lived in tents and drank no wine. They were loyal to *Yahweh*. Jehonadab was mentioned as upholding the laws that were rapidly being forgotten in Israel (Jer. 35:6–16).

10:25 Jehu was commended for destroying Baal worship. Nevertheless, a later word of the Lord to Hosea made clear that Jehu's bloodshed was excessive (Hos. 1:4).

sins of Jeroboam the son of Nebat, who had made Israel sin, *that is*, from the golden calves that *were* at Bethel and Dan. [30]And the LORD said to Jehu, "Because you have done well in doing *what is* right in My sight, *and* have done to the house of Ahab all that *was* in My heart, your sons shall sit on the throne of Israel to the fourth *generation*." [31]But Jehu took no heed to walk in the law of the LORD God of Israel with all his heart; for he did not depart from the sins of Jeroboam, who had made Israel sin.

Death of Jehu

[32]In those days the LORD began to cut off *parts* of Israel; and Hazael conquered them in all the territory of Israel [33]from the Jordan eastward: all the land of Gilead—Gad, Reuben, and Manasseh—from Aroer, which *is* by the River Arnon, including Gilead and Bashan.

[34]Now the rest of the acts of Jehu, all that he did, and all his might, *are* they not written in the book of the chronicles of the kings of Israel? [35]So Jehu rested with his fathers, and they buried him in Samaria. Then Jehoahaz his son reigned in his place. [36]And the period that Jehu reigned over Israel in Samaria *was* twenty-eight years.

Athaliah Reigns in Judah

11 When Athaliah the mother of Ahaziah saw that her son was dead, she arose and destroyed all the royal heirs. [2]But Jehosheba, the daughter of King Joram, sister of Ahaziah, took Joash the son of Ahaziah, and stole him away from among the king's sons *who were* being murdered; and they hid him and his nurse in the bedroom, from Athaliah, so that he was not killed. [3]So he was hidden with her in the house of the LORD for six years, while Athaliah reigned over the land.

Joash Crowned King of Judah

[4]In the seventh year Jehoiada sent and brought the captains of hundreds—of the bodyguards and the escorts—and brought them into the house of the LORD to him. And he made a covenant with them and took an oath from them in the house of the LORD, and showed them the king's son. [5]Then he commanded them, saying, "This *is* what you shall do: One-third of you who come on duty on the Sabbath shall be keeping watch over the king's house, [6]one-third *shall be* at the gate of Sur, and

THE DYNASTIES OF ISRAEL— PART 2		
DYNASTY	**SUCCESSORS**	**REFERENCE**
Dynasty of Omri	Omri	1 Kin. 16:23
	Ahab	1 Kin. 16:29
	Ahaziah	1 Kin. 22:51
	Jehoram	2 Kin. 3:1
Dynasty of Jehu	Jehu	2 Kin. 9:1–13
	Jehoahaz	2 Kin. 13:1
	Jehoash	2 Kin. 13:10
	Jeroboam II	2 Kin. 14:23
	Zechariah	2 Kin. 15:8
Dynasty of Shallum	Shallum	2 Kin. 15:13
Dynasty of Menahem	Menahem	2 Kin. 15:17
	Pekahiah	2 Kin. 15:23
Dynasty of Pekah	Pekah	2 Kin. 15:27
Dynasty of Hoshea	Hoshea	2 Kin. 17:1

one-third at the gate behind the escorts. You shall keep the watch of the house, lest it be broken down. [7]The two contingents of you who go off duty on the Sabbath shall keep the watch of the house of the LORD for the king. [8]But you shall surround the king on all sides, every man with his weapons in his hand; and whoever comes within range, let him be put to death. You are to be with the king as he goes out and as he comes in."

[9]So the captains of the hundreds did according to all that Jehoiada the priest commanded. Each of them took his men who were to be on duty on the Sabbath, with those who were going off duty on the Sabbath, and came to Jehoiada the priest. [10]And the priest gave the captains of hundreds the spears and shields which *had belonged* to King David, that were in the temple of the LORD. [11]Then the escorts stood, every man with his weapons in his hand, all around the king, from the right side of the temple to the left side of the temple, by the altar and the house. [12]And he brought out the king's son, put the crown on him, and *gave him* the Testimony;[a] they made him king and anointed

11:12 [a]That is, the Law (compare Exodus 25:16, 21 and Deuteronomy 31:9)

10:35 Jehu carried out God's judgment on Ahab and founded a new dynasty in Israel (see chart, The Dynasties of Israel—Part 2). However, Israel continued to shrink in size. The purge had alienated Phoenicia, Jezebel's home country, and Judah. Without allies, Israel was too weak to fight off Syrian invasion (see chart, The Kings and Their Conflicts). Jehu lost all the land east of the Jordan down to the border of Moab. Extrabiblical sources confirm that during Jehu's reign Shalmaneser III of Assyria made Israel a subject country (see chart,

The Kings of Assyria). The Black Obelisk (discovered in 1846) shows that Jehu brought tribute to Shalmaneser.

11:1 Athaliah, the daughter of Ahab and Jezebel, attempted to wipe out David's line (see Athaliah). However, as an Israelite she had no popular support in Judah; and as a non-Davidic ruler, who was also half Phoenician, she had no support from the Levitic priesthood.

11:12 The crowning of Joash was a turning point in Judah's

him, and they clapped their hands and said, "Long live the king!"

Death of Athaliah

13Now when Athaliah heard the noise of the escorts *and* the people, she came to the people *in* the temple of the LORD. 14When she looked, there was the king standing by a pillar according to custom; and the leaders and the trumpeters were by the king. All the people of the land were rejoicing and blowing trumpets. So Athaliah tore her clothes and cried out, "Treason! Treason!"

15And Jehoiada the priest commanded the captains of the hundreds, the officers of the army, and said to them, "Take her outside under guard, and slay with the sword whoever follows her." For the priest had said, "Do not let her be killed in the house of the LORD." 16So they seized her; and she went by way of the horses' entrance *into* the king's house, and there she was killed.

17Then Jehoiada made a covenant between the LORD, the king, and the people, that they should be the LORD's people, and *also* between the king and the people. 18And all the people of the land went to the temple of Baal, and tore it down. They thoroughly broke in pieces its altars and images, and killed Mattan the priest of Baal before the altars. And the priest appointed officers over the house of the LORD. 19Then he took the captains of hundreds, the bodyguards, the escorts, and all the people of the land; and they brought the king down from the house of the LORD, and went by way of the gate of the escorts to the king's house. Then he sat on the throne of the kings. 20So all the people of the land rejoiced; and the city was quiet, for they had slain Athaliah with the sword *in* the king's house. 21Jehoash *was* seven years old when he became king.

Jehoash Repairs the Temple

12In the seventh year of Jehu, Jehoasha became king, and he reigned forty years in Jerusalem. His mother's name *was* Zibiah of Beersheba. 2Jehoash did *what was* right in the sight of the LORD all the days in which Jehoiada the priest instructed him. 3But the high places were not taken away; the people still sacrificed and burned incense on the high places.

4And Jehoash said to the priests, "All the money of the dedicated gifts that are brought into the house of the LORD—each man's census money,

each man's assessment moneya—*and* all the money that a man purposes in his heart to bring into the house of the LORD, 5let the priests take *it* themselves, each from his constituency; and let them repair the damages of the temple, wherever any dilapidation is found."

6Now it was so, by the twenty-third year of King Jehoash, *that* the priests had not repaired the damages of the temple. 7So King Jehoash called Jehoiada the priest and the *other* priests, and said to them, "Why have you not repaired the damages of the temple? Now therefore, do not take *more* money from your constituency, but deliver it for repairing the damages of the temple." 8And the priests agreed that they would neither receive *more* money from the people, nor repair the damages of the temple.

9Then Jehoiada the priest took a chest, bored a hole in its lid, and set it beside the altar, on the right side as one comes into the house of the LORD; and the priests who kept the door put there all the money brought into the house of the LORD. 10So it was, whenever they saw that *there was* much money in the chest, that the king's scribe and the high priest came up and put it in bags, and counted the money that was found in the house of the LORD. 11Then they gave the money, which had been apportioned, into the hands of those who did the work, who had the oversight of the house of the LORD; and they paid it out to the carpenters and builders who worked on the house of the LORD, 12and to masons and stonecutters, and for buying timber and hewn stone, to repair the damage of the house of the LORD, and for all that was paid out to repair the temple. 13However there were not made for the house of the LORD basins of silver, trimmers, sprinkling-bowls, trumpets, any articles of gold or articles of silver, from the money brought into the house of the LORD. 14But they gave that to the workmen, and they repaired the house of the LORD with it. 15Moreover they did not require an account from the men into whose hand they delivered the money to be paid to workmen, for they dealt faithfully. 16The money from the trespass offerings and the money from the sin offerings was not brought into the house of the LORD. It belonged to the priests.

· ·

12:1 aSpelled *Joash* in 11:2ff   12:4 aCompare Leviticus 27:2ff

---

history. This Davidic king had a loyal priesthood and possessed the Testimony, the written Law (see Deut. 31:9–26; see chart, The Kings of Israel and Judah).

11:14 The pillar, if in the temple, was a testimony to God's faithfulness and sovereignty (1 Kin. 7:15–22).

11:16 Athaliah's death. Like the rest of Ahab's family, Athaliah died ignominiously as prophesied (1 Kin. 21:24).

12:4 The temple, during the influence of Athaliah, had been looted and its treasure offered to Baal (2 Chr. 24:7). Under Mosaic Law, the priests were supported by food and guilt offerings, but the census and atonement money was to go for upkeep of the tabernacle (Ex. 30:11–16). Before Joash, the priests had taken all the offerings. During his reign the proper balance was restored (2 Kin. 12:16).

Hazael Threatens Jerusalem

[17]Hazael king of Syria went up and fought against Gath, and took it; then Hazael set his face to go up to Jerusalem. [18]And Jehoash king of Judah took all the sacred things that his fathers, Jehoshaphat and Jehoram and Ahaziah, kings of Judah, had dedicated, and his own sacred things, and all the gold found in the treasuries of the house of the LORD and in the king's house, and sent *them* to Hazael king of Syria. Then he went away from Jerusalem.

Death of Joash

[19]Now the rest of the acts of Joash,[a] and all that he did, *are* they not written in the book of the chronicles of the kings of Judah?

[20]And his servants arose and formed a conspiracy, and killed Joash in the house of the Millo,[a] which goes down to Silla. [21]For Jozachar[a] the son of Shimeath and Jehozabad the son of Shomer,[b] his servants, struck him. So he died, and they buried him with his fathers in the City of David. Then Amaziah his son reigned in his place.

Jehoahaz Reigns in Israel

13 In the twenty-third year of Joash[a] the son of Ahaziah, king of Judah, Jehoahaz the son of Jehu became king over Israel in Samaria, *and reigned* seventeen years. [2]And he did evil in the sight of the LORD, and followed the sins of Jeroboam the son of Nebat, who had made Israel sin. He did not depart from them.

[3]Then the anger of the LORD was aroused against Israel, and He delivered them into the hand of Hazael king of Syria, and into the hand of Ben-Hadad the son of Hazael, all *their* days. [4]So Jehoahaz pleaded with the LORD, and the LORD listened to him; for He saw the oppression of Israel, because the king of Syria oppressed them. [5]Then the LORD gave Israel a deliverer, so that they escaped from under the hand of the Syrians; and the children of Israel dwelt in their tents as before. [6]Nevertheless they did not depart from the sins of

the house of Jeroboam, who had made Israel sin, *but* walked in them; and the wooden image[a] also remained in Samaria. [7]For He left of the army of Jehoahaz only fifty horsemen, ten chariots, and ten thousand foot soldiers; for the king of Syria had destroyed them and made them like the dust at threshing.

[8]Now the rest of the acts of Jehoahaz, all that he did, and his might, *are* they not written in the book of the chronicles of the kings of Israel? [9]So Jehoahaz rested with his fathers, and they buried him in Samaria. Then Joash his son reigned in his place.

Jehoash Reigns in Israel

[10]In the thirty-seventh year of Joash king of Judah, Jehoash[a] the son of Jehoahaz became king over Israel in Samaria, *and reigned* sixteen years. [11]And he did evil in the sight of the LORD. He did not depart from all the sins of Jeroboam the son of Nebat, who made Israel sin, *but* walked in them.

[12]Now the rest of the acts of Joash, all that he did, and his might with which he fought against Amaziah king of Judah, *are* they not written in the book of the chronicles of the kings of Israel? [13]So Joash rested with his fathers. Then Jeroboam sat on his throne. And Joash was buried in Samaria with the kings of Israel.

Death of Elisha

[14]Elisha had become sick with the illness of which he would die. Then Joash the king of Israel came down to him, and wept over his face, and said, "O my father, my father, the chariots of Israel and their horsemen!"

[15]And Elisha said to him, "Take a bow and some arrows." So he took himself a bow and some arrows. [16]Then he said to the king of Israel, "Put your hand on the bow." So he put his hand *on it*, and Elisha put his hands on the king's hands.

12:19; 13:1 [a]Spelled *Jehoash* in 12:1ff **12:20** [a]Literally *The Landfill* **12:21** [a]Called *Zabad* in 2 Chronicles 24:26 [b]Called *Shimrith* in 2 Chronicles 24:26 **13:6** [a]Hebrew *Asherah*, a Canaanite goddess **13:10** [a]Spelled *Joash* in verse 9

12:17, 18 Syria and Judah. After taking Israel's land east of the Jordan, Hazael was strong enough to attack Judah (2 Kin. 10:32, 33; see chart, The Kings and Their Conflicts). His southern border was now just north of Moab, giving him an easy route into Judah. By conquering Gath, a city on the Judah-Philistia border, Hazael was able to open a double-front war against Judah. Rather than fight as Jehu of Israel had, Jehoash (Joash; see chart, The Kings With Two Names) protected Judah by sending Hazael an enormous tribute.

12:20 Joash (Jehoash; see chart, The Kings With Two Names) is given no summary evaluation in Kings. He seemingly followed God only while Jehoiada continued as high priest (2 Kin. 12:2; 2 Chr. 24).

13:5 Deliverance from the Syrians. About 805 B.C., the Assyrians, under their king Adad-nirari III, attacked Syria again (see

chart, The Kings and Their Conflicts). By 802 B.C., Hazael was a vassal of Assyria. By the time of Hazael's son Ben-Hadad III, Syria no longer had the strength to keep Israel in subjection (see chart, The Kings of Syria).

13:6 The wooden image. Jehoahaz was a worshiper of Asherah, a Canaanite goddess. God delivered him, not because He was pleased with Jehoahaz, but rather in accordance with His promise to Jehu (2 Kin. 10:30).

13:7 The reign of Jehoahaz. The small number of men and horses indicates that Jehoahaz was now a vassal of the Syrian king (see chart, The Kings and Their Conflicts).

13:14 Joash of Israel. The phrase "the chariots of Israel and their horsemen" also occurs at the time of Elijah's ascension (2 Kin. 2:12), indicating that the prophet spoke the words of *Yahweh*.

[17]And he said, "Open the east window"; and he opened it. Then Elisha said, "Shoot"; and he shot. And he said, "The arrow of the LORD's deliverance and the arrow of deliverance from Syria; for you must strike the Syrians at Aphek till you have destroyed them." [18]Then he said, "Take the arrows"; so he took them. And he said to the king of Israel, "Strike the ground"; so he struck three times, and stopped. [19]And the man of God was angry with him, and said, "You should have struck five or six times; then you would have struck Syria till you had destroyed it! But now you will strike Syria only three times."

[20]Then Elisha died, and they buried him. And the raiding bands from Moab invaded the land in the spring of the year. [21]So it was, as they were burying a man, that suddenly they spied a band of raiders; and they put the man in the tomb of Elisha; and when the man was let down and touched the bones of Elisha, he revived and stood on his feet.

Israel Recaptures Cities from Syria

[22]And Hazael king of Syria oppressed Israel all the days of Jehoahaz. [23]But the LORD was gracious to them, had compassion on them, and regarded them, because of His covenant with Abraham, Isaac, and Jacob, and would not yet destroy them or cast them from His presence.

[24]Now Hazael king of Syria died. Then Ben-Hadad his son reigned in his place. [25]And Jehoash[a] the son of Jehoahaz recaptured from the hand of Ben-Hadad, the son of Hazael, the cities which he had taken out of the hand of Jehoahaz his father by war. Three times Joash defeated him and recaptured the cities of Israel.

Amaziah Reigns in Judah

14 In the second year of Joash the son of Jehoahaz, king of Israel, Amaziah the son of Joash, king of Judah, became king. [2]He was twenty-five years old when he became king, and he reigned twenty-nine years in Jerusalem. His mother's name was Jehoaddan of Jerusalem. [3]And he did what was right in the sight of the LORD, yet not like his father David; he did everything as his father Joash had done. [4]However the high places

were not taken away, and the people still sacrificed and burned incense on the high places.

[5]Now it happened, as soon as the kingdom was established in his hand, that he executed his servants who had murdered his father the king. [6]But the children of the murderers he did not execute, according to what is written in the Book of the Law of Moses, in which the LORD commanded, saying, "Fathers shall not be put to death for their children, nor shall children be put to death for their fathers; but a person shall be put to death for his own sin."[a]

[7]He killed ten thousand Edomites in the Valley of Salt, and took Sela by war, and called its name Joktheel to this day.

[8]Then Amaziah sent messengers to Jehoash[a] the son of Jehoahaz, the son of Jehu, king of Israel, saying, "Come, let us face one another in battle." [9]Jehoash king of Israel sent to Amaziah king of Judah, saying, "The thistle that was in Lebanon sent to the cedar that was in Lebanon, saying, 'Give your daughter to my son as wife'; and a wild beast that was in Lebanon passed by and trampled the thistle. [10]You have indeed defeated Edom, and your heart has lifted you up. Glory in that, and stay at home; for why should you meddle with trouble so that you fall—you and Judah with you?"

[11]But Amaziah would not heed. Therefore Jehoash king of Israel went out; so he and Amaziah king of Judah faced one another at Beth Shemesh, which belongs to Judah. [12]And Judah was defeated by Israel, and every man fled to his tent. [13]Then Jehoash king of Israel captured Amaziah king of Judah, the son of Jehoash, the son of Ahaziah, at Beth Shemesh; and he went to Jerusalem, and broke down the wall of Jerusalem from the Gate of Ephraim to the Corner Gate—four hundred cubits. [14]And he took all the gold and silver, all the articles that were found in the house of the LORD and in the treasuries of the king's house, and hostages, and returned to Samaria.

[15]Now the rest of the acts of Jehoash which he did—his might, and how he fought with Amaziah king of Judah—are they not written in the book of

---

13:25 [a]Spelled *Joash* in verses 12–14, 25 14:6 [a]Deuteronomy 24:16
14:8 [a]Spelled *Joash* in 13:12ff and 2 Chronicles 25:17ff

13:17 Aphek was a city in the Plain of Sharon southwest of the Sea of Chinnereth (or Sea of Galilee; see 1 Kin. 20:26, note).

13:20 Israel's preoccupation with the northern Syrian threat left the country vulnerable to raiders from Philistia to the west and Moab to the east.

13:21 Elisha's body. The physical bodies of Christ and His three great prophetic predecessors are given special attention in Scripture. Moses' body was buried by God (Deut. 34:5, 6). Elijah's body ascended into heaven (2 Kin. 2:11). Elisha's body retained power after death (2 Kin. 13:21); and Christ's glorified body was physical, yet heavenly (Luke 24:30, 31).

13:25 Jehoash's victory. Ben-Hadad III, preoccupied by Assyrian pressure, was not able to send his full force against Israel.

Jehoash was thus able to regain some of the territory lost to Syria.

14:7 Amaziah reconquered Edom, lost by Jehoram. Sela has been tentatively identified with the famous ancient city of Petra, 50 miles south of the Dead Sea.

14:8 Amaziah fought Israel. The quarrel is explained (2 Chr. 25:5–24). Amaziah had hired Israelite soldiers to help him against Edom. When a prophet of God warned him not to employ Israelites, Amaziah sent them home. Insulted, they looted Judean towns on their return north.

14:12 Judah's defeat under the godly Amaziah and the judgment on his righteous son Uzziah are linked with their incomplete purge of idolatry in Judah (2 Chr. 25:2).

the chronicles of the kings of Israel? [16]So Jehoash rested with his fathers, and was buried in Samaria with the kings of Israel. Then Jeroboam his son reigned in his place.

[17]Amaziah the son of Joash, king of Judah, lived fifteen years after the death of Jehoash the son of Jehoahaz, king of Israel. [18]Now the rest of the acts of Amaziah, *are* they not written in the book of the chronicles of the kings of Judah? [19]And they formed a conspiracy against him in Jerusalem, and he fled to Lachish; but they sent after him to Lachish and killed him there. [20]Then they brought him on horses, and he was buried at Jerusalem with his fathers in the City of David.

[21]And all the people of Judah took Azariah,[a] who *was* sixteen years old, and made him king instead of his father Amaziah. [22]He built Elath and restored it to Judah, after the king rested with his fathers.

Jeroboam II Reigns in Israel

[23]In the fifteenth year of Amaziah the son of Joash, king of Judah, Jeroboam the son of Joash, king of Israel, became king in Samaria, *and reigned* forty-one years. [24]And he did evil in the sight of the Lord; he did not depart from all the sins of Jeroboam the son of Nebat, who had made Israel sin. [25]He restored the territory of Israel from the entrance of Hamath to the Sea of the Arabah, according to the word of the Lord God of Israel, which He had spoken through His servant Jonah the son of Amittai, the prophet who *was* from Gath Hepher. [26]For the Lord saw *that* the affliction of Israel *was* very bitter; and whether bond or free, there was no helper for Israel. [27]And the Lord did not say that He would blot out the name of Israel from under heaven; but He saved them by the hand of Jeroboam the son of Joash.

[28]Now the rest of the acts of Jeroboam, and all that he did—his might, how he made war, and how he recaptured for Israel, from Damascus and Hamath, *what had belonged* to Judah—*are* they not written in the book of the chronicles of the kings of Israel? [29]So Jeroboam rested with his fathers, the kings of Israel. Then Zechariah his son reigned in his place.

Azariah Reigns in Judah

15 In the twenty-seventh year of Jeroboam king of Israel, Azariah the son of Amaziah, king of Judah, became king. [2]He was sixteen years old when he became king, and he reigned fifty-two years in Jerusalem. His mother's name *was* Jecholiah of Jerusalem. [3]And he did *what was* right in the sight of the Lord, according to all that his father Amaziah had done, [4]except that the high places were not removed; the people still sacrificed and burned incense on the high places. [5]Then the Lord struck the king, so that he was a leper until the day of his death; so he dwelt in an isolated house. And Jotham the king's son *was* over the *royal* house, judging the people of the land.

[6]Now the rest of the acts of Azariah, and all that he did, *are* they not written in the book of the chronicles of the kings of Judah? [7]So Azariah rested with his fathers, and they buried him with his fathers in the City of David. Then Jotham his son reigned in his place.

Zechariah Reigns in Israel

[8]In the thirty-eighth year of Azariah king of Judah, Zechariah the son of Jeroboam reigned over Israel in Samaria six months. [9]And he did evil

14:21 [a]Called *Uzziah* in 2 Chronicles 26:1ff, Isaiah 6:1, and elsewhere

---

14:22 Elath was located at the tip of the Red Sea (later the Gulf of Aqaba) on Edom's southern border. Through this port city, Azariah (also known as Uzziah; see chart, The Kings With Two Names) was able to reopen trade routes to the south. Judah retained her hold on Edom during the conflict with Israel.

14:25 Jeroboam II was a highly successful politician and fighter (see chart, The Kings and Their Conflicts). Under him, Israel's northern border returned to Hamath, where Solomon's had been (1 Kin. 8:65). The southern border lay at the Dead Sea, implying conquest of Moab. Jeroboam may also have captured much Syrian territory (1 Kin. 14:28). Due to peace with Judah, trade to the south resumed. Archaeological evidence has revealed great prosperity and population increase during this time.

14:26 The condition of Israel. Despite its great prosperity, Israel was sick. The Book of Amos reveals great oppression of the poor by the rich during Jeroboam II's reign (Amos 8:4–6), and paganism flourished (Amos 2:7, 8). The prophet Hosea painted a vivid picture of Israel's unfaithfulness to God's covenant during this time.

15:1 Azariah, also known as Uzziah, was as successful as his

contemporary in Israel (see chart, The Kings with Two Names). He refortified Jerusalem and took territory from the Philistines (2 Chr. 26:6–10). He inherited control over Edom and built forts far into the southern deserts to protect Judah's trade routes. Under Azariah and Jeroboam II, Judah and Israel together came close to reestablishing the borders of Solomon's kingdom.

15:4 Despite Judah's prosperity and peace, internal corruption reigned here as well as in Israel. The condemnatory oracles of the prophets Amos and Hosea were directed against Judah as well as Israel, and idolatry continued.

15:5 Azariah's leprosy. Chronicles links Azariah's leprosy to presumption; the king usurped priestly duties (2 Chr. 26). The writer of Kings ascribed it to a more general sin, a laxity in observing and enforcing God's commands.

15:8 Israel after Jeroboam II. After the death of its strong leader, Israel fell apart. The country had already disintegrated socially (Hos. 4:1–3; 7:1–7). Now it disintegrated politically as well. Zechariah reigned six months; his usurper lasted only one month (2 Kin. 15:13; see chart, The Kings of Israel and Judah). In approximately 25 years, Israel would be obliterated.

in the sight of the LORD, as his fathers had done; he did not depart from the sins of Jeroboam the son of Nebat, who had made Israel sin. [10]Then Shallum the son of Jabesh conspired against him, and struck and killed him in front of the people; and he reigned in his place.

[11]Now the rest of the acts of Zechariah, indeed they *are* written in the book of the chronicles of the kings of Israel.

[12]This *was* the word of the LORD which He spoke to Jehu, saying, "Your sons shall sit on the throne of Israel to the fourth *generation.*"[a] And so it was.

Shallum Reigns in Israel

[13]Shallum the son of Jabesh became king in the thirty-ninth year of Uzziah[a] king of Judah; and he reigned a full month in Samaria. [14]For Menahem the son of Gadi went up from Tirzah, came to Samaria, and struck Shallum the son of Jabesh in Samaria and killed him; and he reigned in his place.

[15]Now the rest of the acts of Shallum, and the conspiracy which he led, indeed they *are* written in the book of the chronicles of the kings of Israel. [16]Then from Tirzah, Menahem attacked Tiphsah, all who *were* there, and its territory. Because they did not surrender, therefore he attacked *it.* All the women there who were with child he ripped open.

Menahem Reigns in Israel

[17]In the thirty-ninth year of Azariah king of Judah, Menahem the son of Gadi became king over Israel, *and reigned* ten years in Samaria. [18]And he did evil in the sight of the LORD; he did not depart all his days from the sins of Jeroboam the son of Nebat, who had made Israel sin. [19]Pul[a] king of Assyria came against the land; and Menahem gave Pul a thousand talents of silver, that his hand might be with him to strengthen the kingdom under his control. [20]And Menahem exacted the money from Israel, from all the very wealthy, from each man fifty shekels of silver, to give to the king of Assyria. So the king of Assyria turned back, and did not stay there in the land.

[21]Now the rest of the acts of Menahem, and all that he did, *are* they not written in the book of the chronicles of the kings of Israel? [22]So Menahem rested with his fathers. Then Pekahiah his son reigned in his place.

Pekahiah Reigns in Israel

[23]In the fiftieth year of Azariah king of Judah, Pekahiah the son of Menahem became king over Israel in Samaria, *and reigned* two years. [24]And he did evil in the sight of the LORD; he did not depart from the sins of Jeroboam the son of Nebat, who had made Israel sin. [25]Then Pekah the son of Remaliah, an officer of his, conspired against him and killed him in Samaria, in the citadel of the king's house, along with Argob and Arieh; and with him were fifty men of Gilead. He killed him and reigned in his place.

[26]Now the rest of the acts of Pekahiah, and all that he did, indeed they *are* written in the book of the chronicles of the kings of Israel.

Pekah Reigns in Israel

[27]In the fifty-second year of Azariah king of Judah, Pekah the son of Remaliah became king over Israel in Samaria, *and reigned* twenty years. [28]And he did evil in the sight of the LORD; he did not depart from the sins of Jeroboam the son of Nebat, who had made Israel sin. [29]In the days of Pekah king of Israel, Tiglath-Pileser king of Assyria came and took Ijon, Abel Beth Maachah, Janoah, Kedesh, Hazor, Gilead, and Galilee, all the land of Naphtali; and he carried them captive to Assyria. [30]Then Hoshea the son of Elah led a conspiracy against Pekah the son of Remaliah, and struck and killed him; so he reigned in his place in the twentieth year of Jotham the son of Uzziah.

[31]Now the rest of the acts of Pekah, and all that

15:12 [a]2 Kings 10:30 15:13 [a]Called *Azariah* in 14:21ff and 15:1ff 15:19 [a]That is, Tiglath-Pileser III (compare verse 29)

15:14 Menahem declared Tirzah, an ancient and beautiful Canaanite city strategically located along the trade route (see Song 6:4), to be Israel's capital, as it had been until the days of Omri (see 1 Kin. 16:8, 9). If Tiphsah, whose location is uncertain, is the same as Thapscus, on the Euphrates far north of Israel, Menahem's attack was not against the Israelites (2 Kin. 15:16). Many scholars believe that the city in question is Tappuah, 15 miles north of Bethel in central Israel. In this case, Menahem began a savage civil war.

15:19 Pul, king of Assyria. Although this is the first time a king of Assyria is directly mentioned in the text, Assyrian attacks had already been weathered by Ahab and Jehu. Pul is Tiglath-Pileser III, an ambitious ruler who turned his attention to Assyria's western frontier (see chart, The Kings of Assyria). Menahem of Israel paid tribute rather than resisting. This campaign probably occurred between 743–740 B.C.

15:20 Ransom for Israel. Fifty shekels was the Assyrian price for a slave. Israelites had to pay this price to the Assyrians, or they would have been sold into slavery.

15:25 The presence of men of Gilead in Pekah's band indicates that Israel once again was on friendly terms with Syria. Gilead lay between Israel and Syria, near Ramoth-Gilead.

15:29 Pekah's revolt may have been supported by those who resented Menahem's tribute to Assyria. Pekah adopted an aggressive attitude toward Assyria and was badly beaten. Israel lost all territory west of the Jordan, all Galilee to the far north, and Naphtali between the Sea of Chinnereth (or the Sea of Galilee) and the coast. The destruction extended to approximately 30 miles north of Samaria.

15:30 Tiglath-Pileser III probably refrained from completely destroying Israel due to the change in Israel's leadership.

he did, indeed they *are* written in the book of the chronicles of the kings of Israel.

Jotham Reigns in Judah

32In the second year of Pekah the son of Remaliah, king of Israel, Jotham the son of Uzziah, king of Judah, began to reign. 33He was twenty-five years old when he became king, and he reigned sixteen years in Jerusalem. His mother's name *was* Jerusha[a] the daughter of Zadok. 34And he did *what was* right in the sight of the LORD; he did according to all that his father Uzziah had done. 35However the high places were not removed; the people still sacrificed and burned incense on the high places. He built the Upper Gate of the house of the LORD.

36Now the rest of the acts of Jotham, and all that he did, *are* they not written in the book of the chronicles of the kings of Judah? 37In those days the LORD began to send Rezin king of Syria and Pekah the son of Remaliah against Judah. 38So Jotham rested with his fathers, and was buried with his fathers in the City of David his father. Then Ahaz his son reigned in his place.

Ahaz Reigns in Judah

16 In the seventeenth year of Pekah the son of Remaliah, Ahaz the son of Jotham, king of Judah, began to reign. 2Ahaz *was* twenty years old when he became king, and he reigned sixteen years in Jerusalem; and he did not do *what was* right in the sight of the LORD his God, as his father David *had done.* 3But he walked in the way of the kings of Israel; indeed he made his son pass through the fire, according to the abominations of the nations whom the LORD had cast out from before the children of Israel. 4And he sacrificed and burned incense on the high places, on the hills, and under every green tree.

5Then Rezin king of Syria and Pekah the son of Remaliah, king of Israel, came up to Jerusalem to *make* war; and they besieged Ahaz but could not overcome *him.* 6At that time Rezin king of Syria captured Elath for Syria, and drove the men of Judah from Elath. Then the Edomites[a] went to Elath, and dwell there to this day.

7So Ahaz sent messengers to Tiglath-Pileser king of Assyria, saying, "I *am* your servant and your son. Come up and save me from the hand of the king of Syria and from the hand of the king of Israel, who rise up against me." 8And Ahaz took the silver and gold that was found in the house of the LORD, and in the treasuries of the king's house, and sent *it as* a present to the king of Assyria. 9So the king of Assyria heeded him; for the king of Assyria went up against Damascus and took it, carried *its people* captive to Kir, and killed Rezin.

10Now King Ahaz went to Damascus to meet Tiglath-Pileser king of Assyria, and saw an altar that *was* at Damascus; and King Ahaz sent to Urijah the priest the design of the altar and its pattern, according to all its workmanship. 11Then Urijah the priest built an altar according to all that King Ahaz had sent from Damascus. So Urijah the priest made *it* before King Ahaz came back from Damascus. 12And when the king came back from Damascus, the king saw the altar; and the king approached the altar and made offerings on it. 13So he burned his burnt offering and his grain offering; and he poured his drink offering and sprinkled the blood of his peace offerings on the altar. 14He also brought the bronze altar which *was* before the LORD, from the front of the temple—from between the *new* altar and the house of the LORD—and put it on the north side of the *new* altar. 15Then King Ahaz commanded Urijah the priest, saying, "On the great *new* altar burn the morning burnt offering, the evening grain offering, the king's burnt sacrifice, and his grain offering, with the burnt offering of all the people of the land, their grain offering, and their drink offerings; and sprinkle on it all the blood of the burnt offering and all the blood of the sacrifice. And the bronze altar shall be for me to inquire *by.*" 16Thus did Urijah the priest, according to all that King Ahaz commanded.

17And King Ahaz cut off the panels of the carts, and removed the lavers from them; and he took down the Sea from the bronze oxen that *were* under it, and put it on a pavement of stones.

15:33 [a]Spelled *Jerushah* in 2 Chronicles 27:1　16:6 [a]Some ancient authorities read *Syrians.*

16:3 Ahaz of Judah violated the Law (Deut. 12:29–32). Child sacrifice to Molech was the most evil pagan practice.

16:5 The attack of Pekah on Judah was brought on by Ahaz's refusal to join Israel and Syria in alliance against Assyria. The alliance, not wishing to have hostile fronts to both north and south, attempted to conquer Ahaz before attacking Assyria. This event is identified as the Syro-Israelite crisis (735/734 B.C.; see Is. 7).

16:6 The loss of Elath as a seaport on the Red Sea (later the Gulf of Aqaba) meant the loss of a southern trade route and subsequent economic distress for Israel.

16:7, 8 Ahaz not only allied himself with Assyria against Israel and Syria but also gave the temple treasure as tribute. The alliance made Judah a vassal of Assyria (see Deut. 7:1, 2).

16:9 Assyria and Damascus. Tiglath-Pileser III destroyed Syria in 732 B.C. and formed it into four Assyrian provinces.

16:10 The Assyrian religion in Judah. As a vassal of Assyria, Ahaz wanted to demonstrate his loyalty. He chose to worship Ashur, Assyria's national god, in disobedience to God (Deut. 4:15–40). He also used the altar of the Lord for divination (2 Kin. 16:15).

THE KINGS OF ASSYRIA

KING	SCRIPTURE	DATE OF REIGN
Ashur-nasirpal II		883–859 B.C.
Shalmaneser III		858–824 B.C.
Shamshi-Adad V		823–811 B.C.
Adad-nirari III		810–783 B.C.
Shalmaneser IV		782–773 B.C.
Ashur-dan III		772–755 B.C.
Ashur-nirari V		754–745 B.C.
Tiglath-Pileser III (Pul)	2 Kin. 15:19, 29; 16:7–10; 1 Chr. 5:26; 2 Chr. 28:20	745–727 B.C.
Shalmaneser V	2 Kin. 17:1–6; 18:9	727–722 B.C.
Sargon II	Is. 20:1	722–705 B.C.
Sennacherib	2 Kin. 18—19	705–681 B.C.
Esarhaddon	2 Kin. 19:37; Ezra 4:2; Is. 37:38	681–669 B.C.
Ashurbanipal		668–627 B.C.

¹⁸Also he removed the Sabbath pavilion which they had built in the temple, and he removed the king's outer entrance from the house of the LORD, on account of the king of Assyria.

¹⁹Now the rest of the acts of Ahaz which he did, *are* they not written in the book of the chronicles of the kings of Judah? ²⁰So Ahaz rested with his fathers, and was buried with his fathers in the City of David. Then Hezekiah his son reigned in his place.

Hoshea Reigns in Israel

17 In the twelfth year of Ahaz king of Judah, Hoshea the son of Elah became king of Israel in Samaria, *and he reigned* nine years. ²And he did evil in the sight of the LORD, but not as the kings of Israel who were before him. ³Shalmaneser king of Assyria came up against him; and Hoshea became his vassal, and paid him tribute money.

⁴And the king of Assyria uncovered a conspiracy by Hoshea; for he had sent messengers to So, king of Egypt, and brought no tribute to the king of Assyria, as *he had done* year by year. Therefore the king of Assyria shut him up, and bound him in prison.

Israel Carried Captive to Assyria

⁵Now the king of Assyria went throughout all the land, and went up to Samaria and besieged it for three years. ⁶In the ninth year of Hoshea, the king of Assyria took Samaria and carried Israel away to Assyria, and placed them in Halah and by the Habor, the River of Gozan, and in the cities of the Medes.

⁷For so it was that the children of Israel had sinned against the LORD their God, who had brought them up out of the land of Egypt, from under the hand of Pharaoh king of Egypt; and they had feared other gods, ⁸and had walked in the statutes of the nations whom the LORD had cast out from before the children of Israel, and of the kings of Israel, which they had made. ⁹Also the children of Israel secretly did against the LORD their God things that *were* not right, and they built for themselves high places in all their cities, from watchtower to fortified city. ¹⁰They set up for themselves *sacred* pillars and wooden imagesᵃ on every high hill and under every green tree. ¹¹There they burned incense on all the high places, like the nations whom the LORD had carried away before them; and they did wicked things to provoke the LORD to anger, ¹²for they served idols, of which the LORD had said to them, "You shall not do this thing."

¹³Yet the LORD testified against Israel and against Judah, by all of His prophets, every seer, saying, "Turn from your evil ways, and keep My commandments *and* My statutes, according to all the law which I commanded your fathers, and which I sent to you by My servants the prophets." ¹⁴Nevertheless they would not hear, but stiffened their necks, like the necks of their fathers, who did not believe in the LORD their God. ¹⁵And they rejected His statutes and His covenant that He

17:10 ᵃHebrew *Asherim*, Canaanite deities

16:18 The king's outer entrance. Tiglath-Pileser III forced Ahaz to close his private entrance into the temple, demonstrating that Ahaz was no longer Judah's official spiritual leader.

17:3 Shalmaneser V. Tiglath-Pileser III, who had spared Hoshea, died in 727 B.C. (2 Kin. 15:29, 30; see chart, The Kings of Assyria). Shalmaneser, his son and successor, continued to collect tribute from Israel.

17:4 Hoshea attempted to break away from Assyria with the help of Egypt. Egypt, however, was weak and in no condition to fight against Assyria.

17:6 Deportation. Sargon II, Shalmaneser V's successor, took credit for Samaria's ultimate downfall (see chart, The Kings of Assyria). He records in his annals that he carried away 27,290 inhabitants. He then rebuilt and resettled the territory (v. 24). Israelites were deported to Assyrian cities.

17:7–23 Israel's sin. The writer of Kings reviewed Israel's violation of the Law: intermarriage and alliances with pagan peoples (Deut. 7:1–11), improper worship of God (Deut. 12:1–11), and the worship of idols (Deut 18:9–14).

had made with their fathers, and His testimonies which He had testified against them; they followed idols, became idolaters, and *went* after the nations who *were* all around them, *concerning* whom the LORD had charged them that they should not do like them. [16]So they left all the commandments of the LORD their God, made for themselves a molded image *and* two calves, made a wooden image and worshiped all the host of heaven, and served Baal. [17]And they caused their sons and daughters to pass through the fire, practiced witchcraft and soothsaying, and sold themselves to do evil in the sight of the LORD, to provoke Him to anger. [18]Therefore the LORD was very angry with Israel, and removed them from His sight; there was none left but the tribe of Judah alone.

[19]Also Judah did not keep the commandments of the LORD their God, but walked in the statutes of Israel which they made. [20]And the LORD rejected all the descendants of Israel, afflicted them, and delivered them into the hand of plunderers, until He had cast them from His sight. [21]For He tore Israel from the house of David, and they made Jeroboam the son of Nebat king. Then Jeroboam drove Israel from following the LORD, and made them commit a great sin. [22]For the children of Israel walked in all the sins of Jeroboam which he did; they did not depart from them, [23]until the LORD removed Israel out of His sight, as He had said by all His servants the prophets. So Israel was carried away from their own land to Assyria, *as it is* to this day.

Assyria Resettles Samaria

[24]Then the king of Assyria brought *people* from Babylon, Cuthah, Ava, Hamath, and from Sepharvaim, and placed *them* in the cities of Samaria instead of the children of Israel; and they took possession of Samaria and dwelt in its cities. [25]And it was so, at the beginning of their dwelling there, *that* they did not fear the LORD; therefore the LORD sent lions among them, which killed *some* of them. [26]So they spoke to the king of Assyria, saying, "The nations whom you have removed and placed in the cities of Samaria do not know the rituals of the God of the land; therefore He has sent lions among them, and indeed, they are killing them because they do not know the rituals of the God of the land." [27]Then the king of Assyria commanded, saying, "Send there one of the priests whom you brought from there; let him go and dwell there, and let him teach them the ritu-

als of the God of the land." [28]Then one of the priests whom they had carried away from Samaria came and dwelt in Bethel, and taught them how they should fear the LORD.

[29]However every nation continued to make gods of its own, and put *them* in the shrines on the high places which the Samaritans had made, *every* nation in the cities where they dwelt. [30]The men of Babylon made Succoth Benoth, the men of Cuth made Nergal, the men of Hamath made Ashima, [31]and the Avites made Nibhaz and Tartak; and the Sepharvites burned their children in fire to Adrammelech and Anammelech, the gods of Sepharvaim. [32]So they feared the LORD, and from every class they appointed for themselves priests of the high places, who sacrificed for them in the shrines of the high places. [33]They feared the LORD, yet served their own gods—according to the rituals of the nations from among whom they were carried away.

[34]To this day they continue practicing the former rituals; they do not fear the LORD, nor do they follow their statutes or their ordinances, or the law and commandment which the LORD had commanded the children of Jacob, whom He named Israel, [35]with whom the LORD had made a covenant and charged them, saying: "You shall not fear other gods, nor bow down to them nor serve them nor sacrifice to them; [36]but the LORD, who brought you up from the land of Egypt with great power and an outstretched arm, Him you shall fear, Him you shall worship, and to Him you shall offer sacrifice. [37]And the statutes, the ordinances, the law, and the commandment which He wrote for you, you shall be careful to observe forever; you shall not fear other gods. [38]And the covenant that I have made with you, you shall not forget, nor shall you fear other gods. [39]But the LORD your God you shall fear; and He will deliver you from the hand of all your enemies." [40]However they did not obey, but they followed their former rituals. [41]So these nations feared the LORD, yet served their carved images; also their children and their children's children have continued doing as their fathers did, even to this day.

Hezekiah Reigns in Judah

18Now it came to pass in the third year of Hoshea the son of Elah, king of Israel, *that* Hezekiah the son of Ahaz, king of Judah, began to reign. [2]He was twenty-five years old when he became king, and he reigned twenty-nine years in

---

17:24 Sargon II's policy was to destroy national ties by moving conquered peoples into different lands. The foreigners resettled in Israelite territory became the ancestors of the people called Samaritans.

17:28 Religion in Israel. In a short time, Israel became popu-

lated with people of different religions (v. 41). Along with Babylonian and Mesopotamian gods, *Yahweh* was probably still worshiped by a few Israelites left in the Land (v. 32). However, more Israelites followed the pagan practices of the new inhabitants (vv. 34–40).

Jerusalem. His mother's name *was* Abi[a] the daughter of Zechariah. [3]And he did *what was* right in the sight of the LORD, according to all that his father David had done.

[4]He removed the high places and broke the *sacred* pillars, cut down the wooden image[a] and broke in pieces the bronze serpent that Moses had made; for until those days the children of Israel burned incense to it, and called it Nehushtan.[b] [5]He trusted in the LORD God of Israel, so that after him was none like him among all the kings of Judah, nor who were before him. [6]For he held fast to the LORD; he did not depart from following Him, but kept His commandments, which the LORD had commanded Moses. [7]The LORD was with him; he prospered wherever he went. And he rebelled against the king of Assyria and did not serve him. [8]He subdued the Philistines, as far as Gaza and its territory, from watchtower to fortified city.

[9]Now it came to pass in the fourth year of King Hezekiah, which *was* the seventh year of Hoshea the son of Elah, king of Israel, *that* Shalmaneser king of Assyria came up against Samaria and besieged it. [10]And at the end of three years they took it. In the sixth year of Hezekiah, that *is,* the ninth year of Hoshea king of Israel, Samaria was taken. [11]Then the king of Assyria carried Israel away captive to Assyria, and put them in Halah and by the Habor, the River of Gozan, and in the cities of the Medes, [12]because they did not obey the voice of the LORD their God, but transgressed His covenant *and* all that Moses the servant of the LORD had commanded; and they would neither hear nor do *them.*

[13]And in the fourteenth year of King Hezekiah, Sennacherib king of Assyria came up against all the fortified cities of Judah and took them. [14]Then Hezekiah king of Judah sent to the king of Assyria at Lachish, saying, "I have done wrong; turn away from me; whatever you impose on me I will pay."

And the king of Assyria assessed Hezekiah king of Judah three hundred talents of silver and thirty talents of gold. [15]So Hezekiah gave *him* all the silver that was found in the house of the LORD and in the treasuries of the king's house. [16]At that time Hezekiah stripped *the gold from* the doors of the temple of the LORD, and *from* the pillars which Hezekiah king of Judah had overlaid, and gave it to the king of Assyria.

Sennacherib Boasts Against the LORD

[17]Then the king of Assyria sent *the* Tartan,[a] *the* Rabsaris,[b] *and the* Rabshakeh[c] from Lachish, with a great army against Jerusalem, to King Hezekiah. And they went up and came to Jerusalem. When they had come up, they went and stood by the aqueduct from the upper pool, which *was* on the highway to the Fuller's Field. [18]And when they had called to the king, Eliakim the son of Hilkiah, who *was* over the household, Shebna the scribe, and Joah the son of Asaph, the recorder, came out to them. [19]Then *the* Rabshakeh said to them, "Say now to Hezekiah, 'Thus says the great king, the king of Assyria: "What confidence *is* this in which you trust? [20]You speak of *having* plans and power for war; but *they are* mere words. And in whom do you trust, that you rebel against me? [21]Now look! You are trusting in the staff of this broken reed, Egypt, on which if a man leans, it will go into his hand and pierce it. So *is* Pharaoh king of Egypt to all who trust in him. [22]But if you say to me, 'We trust in the LORD our God,' *is* it not He whose high places and whose altars Hezekiah has taken away, and said to Judah and Jerusalem, 'You shall worship before this altar in Jerusalem'?" ' [23]Now therefore, I urge you, give a pledge to my master

---

18:2 [a]Called *Abijah* in 2 Chronicles 29:1ff 18:4 [a]Hebrew *Asherah,* a Canaanite goddess [b]Literally *Bronze Thing* 18:17 [a]A title, probably *Commander in Chief* [b]A title, probably *Chief Officer* [c]A title, probably *Chief of Staff* or *Governor*

18:3 Hezekiah was the most godly king of Judah since David. His purge of paganism was complete (v. 4).

18:7 The blessings of obedience were praised in the covenant Law. Victory was promised to the nation that obeyed (Deut. 7:16–24).

18:13 Assyria attacked Judah. Assyria had been involved elsewhere for some years; Sargon II, Sennacherib's father, had led campaigns against Babylon, Carchemish, and Egypt. Sennacherib himself faced a rebellious alliance that included Babylon, Egypt, and parts of Phoenicia and Philistia. Hezekiah joined the revolt against the advice of Isaiah, who pointed out that an alliance with Egypt was against God's command to avoid foreign alliances (Is. 30:1–5). In 701 B.C., Sennacherib conquered Tyre and the Philistine cities in the alliance. According to Assyrian records, he then destroyed 46 of Judah's own cities and captured 200,150 people. Archaeological excavations at Lachish, one of the cities conquered, have confirmed a conflict with many casualties.

18:15 Hezekiah's tribute. Sennacherib divided Judah's terri-

tory among his loyal vassals. He also demanded a huge tribute and took several of Hezekiah's daughters as concubines. These punishments had been predicted (Deut. 28:32–36).

18:17 The siege of Jerusalem. These verses may describe a second attack on Judah after a lapse of time. In this case, Hezekiah would have again attempted to rebel, taking advantage of unrest in Babylon and a new ally in Egypt (vv. 20, 21).

18:18 Siege negotiations are described in more detail by Isaiah (Is. 36; 37). Earlier in Isaiah, Shebna is condemned as unfaithful and Eliakim commended as worthy to supervise the house of David (Is. 22:15–25).

18:21 A broken reed. The image of Egypt as a broken reed is repeated (Ezek. 29:6, 7). Judah could not resist turning to Egypt, God's enemy, for help, but Egypt never gave true aid to Judah. Part of the covenant curse for disobedience is a return to Egypt in slavery (Deut. 28:68). In Scripture, Egypt often occurs as a figure for various enemy nations. In this case, considering the domination of Egypt by the Babylonian Empire, the curse comes true literally (see 2 Kin. 24:7; 25:11).

the king of Assyria, and I will give you two thousand horses—if you are able on your part to put riders on them! ²⁴How then will you repel one captain of the least of my master's servants, and put your trust in Egypt for chariots and horsemen? ²⁵Have I now come up without the Lord against this place to destroy it? The Lord said to me, 'Go up against this land, and destroy it.'"

²⁶Then Eliakim the son of Hilkiah, Shebna, and Joah said to the Rabshakeh, "Please speak to your servants in Aramaic, for we understand it; and do not speak to us in Hebrew[a] in the hearing of the people who are on the wall."

²⁷But the Rabshakeh said to them, "Has my master sent me to your master and to you to speak these words, and not to the men who sit on the wall, who will eat and drink their own waste with you?"

²⁸Then the Rabshakeh stood and called out with a loud voice in Hebrew, and spoke, saying, "Hear the word of the great king, the king of Assyria! ²⁹Thus says the king: 'Do not let Hezekiah deceive you, for he shall not be able to deliver you from his hand; ³⁰nor let Hezekiah make you trust in the Lord, saying, "The Lord will surely deliver us; this city shall not be given into the hand of the king of Assyria." ' ³¹Do not listen to Hezekiah; for thus says the king of Assyria: 'Make peace with me by a present and come out to me; and every one of you eat from his own vine and every one from his own fig tree, and every one of you drink the waters of his own cistern; ³²until I come and take you away to a land like your own land, a land of grain and new wine, a land of bread and vineyards, a land of olive groves and honey, that you may live and not die. But do not listen to Hezekiah, lest he persuade you, saying, "The Lord will deliver us." ³³Has any of the gods of the nations at all delivered its land from the hand of the king of Assyria? ³⁴Where are the gods of Hamath and Arpad? Where are the gods of Sepharvaim and Hena and Ivah? Indeed, have they delivered Samaria from my hand? ³⁵Who among all the gods of the lands have delivered their countries from my hand, that the Lord should deliver Jerusalem from my hand?' "

³⁶But the people held their peace and answered him not a word; for the king's commandment was, "Do not answer him." ³⁷Then Eliakim the son of Hilkiah, who was over the household, Shebna the scribe, and Joah the son of Asaph, the recorder, came to Hezekiah with their clothes torn, and told him the words of the Rabshakeh.

Isaiah Assures Deliverance

19And so it was, when King Hezekiah heard it, that he tore his clothes, covered himself with sackcloth, and went into the house of the Lord. ²Then he sent Eliakim, who was over the household, Shebna the scribe, and the elders of the priests, covered with sackcloth, to Isaiah the prophet, the son of Amoz. ³And they said to him, "Thus says Hezekiah: 'This day is a day of trouble, and rebuke, and blasphemy; for the children have come to birth, but there is no strength to bring them forth. ⁴It may be that the Lord your God will hear all the words of the Rabshakeh, whom his master the king of Assyria has sent to reproach the living God, and will rebuke the words which the Lord your God has heard. Therefore lift up your prayer for the remnant that is left.' "

⁵So the servants of King Hezekiah came to Isaiah. ⁶And Isaiah said to them, "Thus you shall say to your master, 'Thus says the Lord: "Do not be afraid of the words which you have heard, with which the servants of the king of Assyria have blasphemed Me. ⁷Surely I will send a spirit upon him, and he shall hear a rumor and return to his own land; and I will cause him to fall by the sword in his own land." ' "

Sennacherib's Threat and Hezekiah's Prayer

⁸Then the Rabshakeh returned and found the king of Assyria warring against Libnah, for he heard that he had departed from Lachish. ⁹And the king heard concerning Tirhakah king of Ethiopia, "Look, he has come out to make war with you." So he again sent messengers to Hezekiah, saying, ¹⁰"Thus you shall speak to Hezekiah king of Judah, saying: 'Do not let your God in whom you trust deceive you, saying, "Jerusalem shall not be given into the hand of the king of Assyria." ¹¹Look! You have heard what the kings of Assyria have done to all lands by utterly destroying them; and shall you be delivered? ¹²Have the gods of the nations delivered those whom my fathers have destroyed, Gozan and Haran and Rezeph, and the people of Eden who were in Telassar? ¹³Where is the king of Hamath, the king of Arpad, and the king of the city of Sepharvaim, Hena, and Ivah?' "

¹⁴And Hezekiah received the letter from the hand of the messengers, and read it; and Hezekiah

18:26 [a]Literally Judean

18:25–35 **A common tactic of warfare** in the ancient Near East was to claim the favor of an opponent's god.

18:8 **Libnah and Lachish** were Judah's fortified frontier cities. The fact that Sennacherib was reconquering them has led some scholars to believe that the siege of Jerusalem took place in a second campaign against Judah (see 2 Kin. 18:17, note).

19:9 **Egyptian pharaohs** were Ethiopian in lineage at this time. The pharaoh Tirhakah took the throne in 690/689 B.C. and immediately set out to fight the Assyrian threat. Sennacherib then marched south against Egypt, giving Jerusalem a temporary reprieve.

went up to the house of the LORD, and spread it before the LORD. [15]Then Hezekiah prayed before the LORD, and said: "O LORD God of Israel, *the One* who dwells *between* the cherubim, You are God, You alone, of all the kingdoms of the earth. You have made heaven and earth. [16]Incline Your ear, O LORD, and hear; open Your eyes, O LORD, and see; and hear the words of Sennacherib, which he has sent to reproach the living God. [17]Truly, LORD, the kings of Assyria have laid waste the nations and their lands, [18]and have cast their gods into the fire; for they *were* not gods, but the work of men's hands—wood and stone. Therefore they destroyed them. [19]Now therefore, O LORD our God, I pray, save us from his hand, that all the kingdoms of the earth may know that You *are* the LORD God, You alone."

The Word of the LORD Concerning Sennacherib

[20]Then Isaiah the son of Amoz sent to Hezekiah, saying, "Thus says the LORD God of Israel: 'Because you have prayed to Me against Sennacherib king of Assyria, I have heard.' [21]This *is* the word which the LORD has spoken concerning him:

'The virgin, the daughter of Zion,
Has despised you, laughed you to scorn;
The daughter of Jerusalem
Has shaken *her* head behind your back!

[22]'Whom have you reproached and blasphemed?
Against whom have you raised *your* voice,
And lifted up your eyes on high?
Against the Holy *One* of Israel.
[23]By your messengers you have reproached the Lord,
And said: "By the multitude of my chariots
I have come up to the height of the mountains,
To the limits of Lebanon;
I will cut down its tall cedars
And its choice cypress trees;
I will enter the extremity of its borders,
To its fruitful forest.
[24]I have dug and drunk strange water,
And with the soles of my feet I have dried up
All the brooks of defense."

[25]'Did you not hear long ago
How I made it,
From ancient times that I formed it?
Now I have brought it to pass,
That you should be

For crushing fortified cities *into* heaps of ruins.
[26]Therefore their inhabitants had little power;
They were dismayed and confounded;
They were *as* the grass of the field
And the green herb,
As the grass on the housetops
And *grain* blighted before it is grown.

[27]'But I know your dwelling place,
Your going out and your coming in,
And your rage against Me.
[28]Because your rage against Me and your tumult
Have come up to My ears,
Therefore I will put My hook in your nose
And My bridle in your lips,
And I will turn you back
By the way which you came.

[29]'This *shall be* a sign to you:

You shall eat this year such as grows of itself,
And in the second year what springs from the same;
Also in the third year sow and reap,
Plant vineyards and eat the fruit of them.
[30]And the remnant who have escaped of the house of Judah
Shall again take root downward,
And bear fruit upward.
[31]For out of Jerusalem shall go a remnant,
And those who escape from Mount Zion.
The zeal of the LORD of hosts[a] will do this.'

[32]"Therefore thus says the LORD concerning the king of Assyria:

'He shall not come into this city,
Nor shoot an arrow there,
Nor come before it with shield,
Nor build a siege mound against it.
[33]By the way that he came,
By the same shall he return;
And he shall not come into this city,'
Says the LORD.
[34]'For I will defend this city, to save it
For My own sake and for My servant David's sake.' "

19:31 [a]Following many Hebrew manuscripts and ancient versions (compare Isaiah 37:32); Masoretic Text omits *of hosts*.

19:15 The mercy seat of the ark, God's dwelling place on earth, was made with a cherub on either side.

19:28 Assyrian conquerors often led captives by means of hooks in their noses.

19:29 Isaiah's prophecy appears to be that, although Assyria would occupy the land and reap its crops, Judah would not be entirely destroyed (see Deut. 28:51). Like a plant that lies dormant, Judah would appear conquered but would again bear fruit (see Is. 11:1–11).

Sennacherib's Defeat and Death

[35]And it came to pass on a certain night that the angel[a] of the LORD went out, and killed in the camp of the Assyrians one hundred and eighty-five thousand; and when *people* arose early in the morning, there were the corpses—all dead. [36]So Sennacherib king of Assyria departed and went away, returned *home,* and remained at Nineveh. [37]Now it came to pass, as he was worshiping in the temple of Nisroch his god, that his sons Adrammelech and Sharezer struck him down with the sword; and they escaped into the land of Ararat. Then Esarhaddon his son reigned in his place.

Hezekiah's Life Extended

20 In those days Hezekiah was sick and near death. And Isaiah the prophet, the son of Amoz, went to him and said to him, "Thus says the LORD: 'Set your house in order, for you shall die, and not live.' "

[2]Then he turned his face toward the wall, and prayed to the LORD, saying, [3]"Remember now, O LORD, I pray, how I have walked before You in truth and with a loyal heart, and have done *what was* good in Your sight." And Hezekiah wept bitterly.

[4]And it happened, before Isaiah had gone out into the middle court, that the word of the LORD came to him, saying, [5]"Return and tell Hezekiah the leader of My people, 'Thus says the LORD, the God of David your father: "I have heard your prayer, I have seen your tears; surely I will heal you. On the third day you shall go up to the house of the LORD. [6]And I will add to your days fifteen years. I will deliver you and this city from the hand of the king of Assyria; and I will defend this city for My own sake, and for the sake of My servant David." ' "

[7]Then Isaiah said, "Take a lump of figs." So they took and laid *it* on the boil, and he recovered.

[8]And Hezekiah said to Isaiah, "What *is* the sign that the LORD will heal me, and that I shall go up to the house of the LORD the third day?"

[9]Then Isaiah said, "This is the sign to you from the LORD, that the LORD will do the thing which He has spoken: *shall* the shadow go forward ten degrees or go backward ten degrees?"

[10]And Hezekiah answered, "It is an easy thing for the shadow to go down ten degrees; no, but let the shadow go backward ten degrees."

[11]So Isaiah the prophet cried out to the LORD, and He brought the shadow ten degrees backward, by which it had gone down on the sundial of Ahaz.

The Babylonian Envoys

[12]At that time Berodach-Baladan[a] the son of Baladan, king of Babylon, sent letters and a present to Hezekiah, for he heard that Hezekiah had been sick. [13]And Hezekiah was attentive to them, and showed them all the house of his treasures—the silver and gold, the spices and precious ointment, and all[a] his armory—all that was found among his treasures. There was nothing in his house or in all his dominion that Hezekiah did not show them.

[14]Then Isaiah the prophet went to King Hezekiah, and said to him, "What did these men say, and from where did they come to you?"

So Hezekiah said, "They came from a far country, from Babylon."

[15]And he said, "What have they seen in your house?"

So Hezekiah answered, "They have seen all that *is* in my house; there is nothing among my treasures that I have not shown them."

[16]Then Isaiah said to Hezekiah, "Hear the word of the LORD: [17]'Behold, the days are coming when all that *is* in your house, and what your fathers have accumulated until this day, shall be carried to Babylon; nothing shall be left,' says the LORD. [18]And they shall take away some of your sons who will descend from you, whom you will beget; and

19:35 [a]Or *Angel* 20:12 [a]Spelled *Merodach-Baladan* in Isaiah 39:1 20:13 [a]Following many Hebrew manuscripts, Syriac, and Targum; Masoretic Text omits *all.*

19:35 Assyria's defeat. Sennacherib's records make no mention of this event, but the Assyrians typically recorded only their victories. The ancient historian Herodotus recorded that the Assyrian camp was overrun by mice, driving the army away from Jerusalem and suggesting that the Assyrians attributed the deaths to a plague associated with rats. Sennacherib fought another five campaigns but never returned to Judah.

19:36 Nineveh, on the River Tigris far to Israel's northeast, had been a Babylonian city until incorporated into the Assyrian Empire. Sargon II, Sennacherib's father, made Nineveh his capital. Excavations at Nineveh have uncovered bas reliefs portraying Sennacherib's siege of Judah.

19:37 Sennacherib's death is a fulfillment of prophecy (v. 7).

20:11 The miracle of the sundial. Isaiah proved his trustworthiness as a prophet of God when the sign for which he asked came to pass (see Deut. 18:22). No explanation has satisfactorily explained this phenomenon. Seemingly, its effect was confined to Judah. The incident was clearly an answer from God to confirm His mercy toward Hezekiah.

20:12 Babylon had also rebelled against the Assyrian overlords. Sennacherib had put down their rebellion in 689 B.C., but Babylon and Elam again revolted against Esarhaddon. Hezekiah would have been sorely tempted to ally himself once more with a rebellion against Assyria.

20:17 Judgment on Hezekiah. Although a righteous man, Hezekiah persisted in making forbidden foreign alliances.

they shall be eunuchs in the palace of the king of Babylon.' "

[19]So Hezekiah said to Isaiah, "The word of the LORD which you have spoken *is* good!" For he said, "Will there not be peace and truth at least in my days?"

Death of Hezekiah

[20]Now the rest of the acts of Hezekiah—all his might, and how he made a pool and a tunnel and brought water into the city—*are* they not written in the book of the chronicles of the kings of Judah? [21]So Hezekiah rested with his fathers. Then Manasseh his son reigned in his place.

Manasseh Reigns in Judah

21 Manasseh *was* twelve years old when he became king, and he reigned fifty-five years in Jerusalem. His mother's name *was* Hephzibah. [2]And he did evil in the sight of the LORD, according to the abominations of the nations whom the LORD had cast out before the children of Israel. [3]For he rebuilt the high places which Hezekiah his father had destroyed; he raised up altars for Baal, and made a wooden image,[a] as Ahab king of Israel had done; and he worshiped all the host of heaven[b] and served them. [4]He also built altars in the house of the LORD, of which the LORD had said, "In Jerusalem I will put My name." [5]And he built altars for all the host of heaven in the two courts of the house of the LORD. [6]Also he made his son pass through the fire, practiced soothsaying, used witchcraft, and consulted spiritists and mediums. He did much evil in the sight of the LORD, to provoke *Him* to anger. [7]He even set a carved image of Asherah[a] that he had made, in the house of which the LORD had said to David and to Solomon his son, "In this house and in Jerusalem, which I have chosen out of all the tribes of Israel, I will put My name forever; [8]and I will not make the feet of Israel wander anymore from the land which I gave their fathers—only if they are careful to do according to all that I have commanded them, and according to all the law that My servant Moses commanded them." [9]But they paid no attention,

and Manasseh seduced them to do more evil than the nations whom the LORD had destroyed before the children of Israel.

[10]And the LORD spoke by His servants the prophets, saying, [11]"Because Manasseh king of Judah has done these abominations (he has acted more wickedly than all the Amorites who *were* before him, and has also made Judah sin with his idols), [12]therefore thus says the LORD God of Israel: 'Behold, *I* am bringing *such* calamity upon Jerusalem and Judah, that whoever hears of it, both his ears will tingle. [13]And I will stretch over Jerusalem the measuring line of Samaria and the plummet of the house of Ahab; I will wipe Jerusalem as *one* wipes a dish, wiping *it* and turning *it* upside down. [14]So I will forsake the remnant of My inheritance and deliver them into the hand of their enemies; and they shall become victims of plunder to all their enemies, [15]because they have done evil in My sight, and have provoked Me to anger since the day their fathers came out of Egypt, even to this day.' "

[16]Moreover Manasseh shed very much innocent blood, till he had filled Jerusalem from one end to another, besides his sin by which he made Judah sin, in doing evil in the sight of the LORD.

[17]Now the rest of the acts of Manasseh—all that he did, and the sin that he committed—*are* they not written in the book of the chronicles of the kings of Judah? [18]So Manasseh rested with his fathers, and was buried in the garden of his own house, in the garden of Uzza. Then his son Amon reigned in his place.

Amon's Reign and Death

[19]Amon *was* twenty-two years old when he became king, and he reigned two years in Jerusalem. His mother's name *was* Meshullemeth the daughter of Haruz of Jotbah. [20]And he did evil in the sight of the LORD, as his father Manasseh had done. [21]So he walked in all the ways that his father had walked; and he served the idols that his father had served, and worshiped them. [22]He forsook the

---

21:3 [a]Hebrew *Asherah*, a Canaanite goddess [b]The gods of the Assryians   21:7 [a]A Canaanite goddess

---

20:20 Hezekiah's building program. The pool, connected to the spring of Gihon by the Siloam tunnel, was built by Hezekiah in preparation for Sennacherib's siege of Jerusalem. Two teams worked with hand tools from opposite ends, directed by someone from above, until they met in the center. This tunnel runs through solid rock almost 600 yards. It was uncovered in 1880, and people continue to wade through its narrow and circuitous route.

21:3 Manasseh broke every law against idol worship. He built high places and Baal altars, dealt with spiritualists, and sacrificed his son to Molech. Further, he played the part of a loyal

vassal by worshiping Assyrian gods and defiling the temple (vv. 3, 5).

21:5 Worship in Judah. At this time, Judah was in danger of polytheism, worshiping a whole array of gods, with *Yahweh* at their head. God's heavenly host could easily be confused with the Assyrian pantheon. Manasseh's evil brought negative consequences (see 2 Kin. 24:3).

21:18 Manasseh's death. Assyria spared Judah during Manasseh's life because he willingly subjected Judah to Esarhaddon. Assyrian records reveal that Manasseh contributed to Esarhaddon's building campaigns. He also allied himself with Esarhaddon's successor, Ashurbanipal, to fight against Egypt.

LORD God of his fathers, and did not walk in the way of the LORD.

²³Then the servants of Amon conspired against him, and killed the king in his own house. ²⁴But the people of the land executed all those who had conspired against King Amon. Then the people of the land made his son Josiah king in his place.

²⁵Now the rest of the acts of Amon which he did, *are* they not written in the book of the chronicles of the kings of Judah? ²⁶And he was buried in his tomb in the garden of Uzza. Then Josiah his son reigned in his place.

Josiah Reigns in Judah

22 Josiah *was* eight years old when he became king, and he reigned thirty-one years in Jerusalem. His mother's name *was* Jedidah the daughter of Adaiah of Bozkath. ²And he did *what was* right in the sight of the LORD, and walked in all the ways of his father David; he did not turn aside to the right hand or to the left.

Hilkiah Finds the Book of the Law

³Now it came to pass, in the eighteenth year of King Josiah, *that* the king sent Shaphan the scribe, the son of Azaliah, the son of Meshullam, to the house of the LORD, saying: ⁴"Go up to Hilkiah the high priest, that he may count the money which has been brought into the house of the LORD, which the doorkeepers have gathered from the people. ⁵And let them deliver it into the hand of those doing the work, who are the overseers in the house of the LORD; let them give it to those who *are* in the house of the LORD doing the work, to repair the damages of the house— ⁶to carpenters and builders and masons—and to buy timber and hewn stone to repair the house. ⁷However there need be no accounting made with them of the money delivered into their hand, because they deal faithfully."

⁸Then Hilkiah the high priest said to Shaphan the scribe, "I have found the Book of the Law in the house of the LORD." And Hilkiah gave the book to Shaphan, and he read it. ⁹So Shaphan the scribe went to the king, bringing the king word, saying, "Your servants have gathered the money that was found in the house, and have delivered it into the hand of those who do the work, who oversee the house of the LORD." ¹⁰Then Shaphan the scribe showed the king, saying, "Hilkiah the priest has given me a book." And Shaphan read it before the king.

¹¹Now it happened, when the king heard the words of the Book of the Law, that he tore his clothes. ¹²Then the king commanded Hilkiah the priest, Ahikam the son of Shaphan, Achbor[a] the son of Michaiah, Shaphan the scribe, and Asaiah a servant of the king, saying, ¹³"Go, inquire of the LORD for me, for the people and for all Judah, concerning the words of this book that has been found; for great *is* the wrath of the LORD that is aroused against us, because our fathers have not obeyed the words of this book, to do according to all that is written concerning us."

¹⁴So Hilkiah the priest, Ahikam, Achbor, Shaphan, and Asaiah went to Huldah the prophetess, the wife of Shallum the son of Tikvah, the son of Harhas, keeper of the wardrobe. (She dwelt in Jerusalem in the Second Quarter.) And they spoke with her. ¹⁵Then she said to them, "Thus says the LORD God of Israel, 'Tell the man who sent you to Me, ¹⁶"Thus says the LORD: 'Behold, I will bring calamity on this place and on its inhabitants—all the words of the book which the king of Judah has read— ¹⁷because they have forsaken Me and burned incense to other gods, that they might provoke Me to anger with all the works of their hands. Therefore My wrath shall be aroused against this place and shall not be quenched.' " ' ¹⁸But as for the king of Judah, who sent you to inquire of the LORD, in this manner you shall speak to him, 'Thus says the LORD God of Israel: *"Concerning* the words which you have heard— ¹⁹because your heart was tender, and you humbled yourself before the LORD when you heard what I spoke against this place and against its inhabitants, that they would become a desolation and a curse, and you tore your clothes and wept before Me, I also have heard *you,*" says the LORD. ²⁰"Surely, therefore, I will gather you to your fathers, and you shall be gathered to your grave in peace; and your eyes shall not see all the calamity which I will bring on this place." ' " So they brought back word to the king.

22:12 ªAbdon the son of Micah in 2 Chronicles 34:20

22:1 Josiah's accession. During the days of Josiah, Judah was a free country. The Assyrian ruler was Ashurbanipal. Babylon, always restless under Assyrian rule, had once again revolted. While Assyria managed temporarily to subdue Babylon in 648 B.C., the war, plus the pressures of invading Scythians and the growing power of the Medes in the east, left Assyria no resources to deal with Judah.

22:3-7 Josiah took advantage of Assyrian absence to cleanse the country of Manasseh's foreign idols. The official Assyrian cult was rejected, and Manasseh's damage to the temple was repaired (2 Kin. 21:5, 7).

22:8 The Book of the Law is probably the entire Pentateuch. This would have been the official copy, deposited in the temple and somehow covered over or hidden during changes made there by idolatrous kings. The time of the Law's disappearance is unknown. Presumably one of Judah's wicked kings destroyed all the copies that were not hidden.

22:14-20 Huldah was probably an official member of the royal court. Her faithful prophecy confirms God's Word: Idolatry brings judgment (v. 17; see also Deut. 28:15). Huldah's husband Shallum (son of Tokhath, 2 Chr. 34:22) has the same name as Jeremiah's uncle (Jer. 32:7); the two men may be the same.

HULDAH *The Prophetess Who Changed a Nation*

Huldah played a significant part in the history of Israel, although she appeared only once on the stage of the nation's history, during a time of religious defection.

In Jerusalem, King Josiah of Judah initiated renewed interest in the Book of the Law, and Huldah participated in the subsequent spiritual revival. She was the wife of Shallum, who was "keeper of the wardrobe" (possibly either royal robes and attire or priestly garments and vestments). They lived in the Second Quarter, a newer section of Jerusalem which developed as a westward or northern expansion of the old city (perhaps somewhat like a modern-day suburb).

Huldah, and not Jeremiah or Zephaniah, both of whom were active as prophets during this time, was consulted when the king instructed the priests to "inquire of the Lord" as to the meaning of the Book of the Law, a scroll that had been found during the work of restoration and cleaning in the temple. It was significant that with the number of prophets living in Jerusalem at that time, the priest Hilkiah and the rest of the king's advisors turned to a woman for a word from God. This nullifies the reasoning some use to suggest that God only uses women for such ministry when no men are available. Obviously, whether in a private audience or in the presence of the congregation, God used Huldah to bear testimony and deliver a message from Him to the High Priest and to the king (2 Kin. 22:14–20).

The tradition of female prophets is mentioned only sporadically in the Old Testament, but Huldah is not the only one highlighted. She is in good company with Deborah and Miriam; however, another female prophet, Noadiah (see Neh. 6:14), was a false prophet and worked against the people of God.

The regard for Huldah's own integrity and authority as a woman of God made her validation of the recently discovered Book of the Law all that was required for immediate action on the part of the king. Her message was not her own, but from the Lord. The fact that the phrase "Thus says the Lord . . ." is repeated four times in her short prophecy emphasizes that Huldah understood her responsibility and opportunity to be a channel through whom God delivered His Word (2 Kin. 22:15–17, 19).

All the reforms set forth by King Josiah were based on the Word of God as given to this woman. Huldah was apparently so well known as a woman of God and so highly trusted with regard to her understanding of God's Law that for a time her nation's whole religious consciousness and practice was re-ignited in faithfulness to God. Huldah, a deeply devout woman, made her God-given spiritual gifts available to God, and she was obedient and faithful to deliver the Word from God to her people.

See also 2 Chronicles 34:22–28; notes on Government and Citizenship (Rom. 13); Feminine Leadership (1 Sam. 25); Women's Ministries (1 Cor. 11)

Josiah Restores True Worship

23 Now the king sent them to gather all the elders of Judah and Jerusalem to him. [2]The king went up to the house of the LORD with all the men of Judah, and with him all the inhabitants of Jerusalem—the priests and the prophets and all the people, both small and great. And he read in their hearing all the words of the Book of the Covenant which had been found in the house of the LORD.

[3]Then the king stood by a pillar and made a covenant before the LORD, to follow the LORD and to keep His commandments and His testimonies and His statutes, with all *his* heart and all *his* soul, to perform the words of this covenant that were written in this book. And all the people took a stand for the covenant. [4]And the king commanded Hilkiah the high priest, the priests of the second order, and the doorkeepers, to bring out of the temple of the LORD all the articles that were made for Baal, for Asherah,[a] and for all the host of heaven;[b] and he burned them outside Jerusalem in the fields of Kidron, and carried their ashes to Bethel. [5]Then he removed the idolatrous priests whom the kings of Judah had ordained to burn incense on the high places in the cities of Judah and in the places all around Jerusalem, and those who burned incense to Baal, to the sun, to the moon, to the constellations, and to all the host of heaven. [6]And he brought out the wooden image[a] from the house of the LORD, to the Brook Kidron outside Jerusalem, burned it at the Brook Kidron and ground *it* to ashes, and threw its ashes on the graves of the common people. [7]Then he tore down the *ritual* booths of the perverted persons[a] that *were* in the house of the LORD, where the women wove hangings for the wooden image. [8]And he brought all the priests from the cities of Judah, and defiled the high places where the priests had

···
23:4 [a]A Canaanite goddess [b]The gods of the Assyrians **23:6** [a]Hebrew *Asherah*, a Canaanite goddess **23:7** [a]Hebrew *qedeshim*, that is, those practicing sodomy and prostitution in religious rituals

---

23:7 Perverted persons is a reference to prostitutes attached to various Canaanite cults (see 1 Kin 14:24, note).

burned incense, from Geba to Beersheba; also he broke down the high places at the gates which *were* at the entrance of the Gate of Joshua the governor of the city, which *were* to the left of the city gate. [9]Nevertheless the priests of the high places did not come up to the altar of the LORD in Jerusalem, but they ate unleavened bread among their brethren.

[10]And he defiled Topheth, which *is* in the Valley of the Son[a] of Hinnom, that no man might make his son or his daughter pass through the fire to Molech. [11]Then he removed the horses that the kings of Judah had dedicated to the sun, at the entrance to the house of the LORD, by the chamber of Nathan-Melech, the officer who *was* in the court; and he burned the chariots of the sun with fire. [12]The altars that *were* on the roof, the upper chamber of Ahaz, which the kings of Judah had made, and the altars which Manasseh had made in the two courts of the house of the LORD, the king broke down and pulverized there, and threw their dust into the Brook Kidron. [13]Then the king defiled the high places that *were* east of Jerusalem, which *were* on the south of the Mount of Corruption, which Solomon king of Israel had built for Ashtoreth the abomination of the Sidonians, for Chemosh the abomination of the Moabites, and for Milcom the abomination of the people of Ammon. [14]And he broke in pieces the *sacred* pillars and cut down the wooden images, and filled their places with the bones of men.

[15]Moreover the altar that *was* at Bethel, *and* the high place which Jeroboam the son of Nebat, who made Israel sin, had made, both that altar and the high place he broke down; and he burned the high place *and* crushed *it* to powder, and burned the wooden image. [16]As Josiah turned, he saw the tombs that *were* there on the mountain. And he sent and took the bones out of the tombs and burned *them* on the altar, and defiled it according to the word of the LORD which the man of God proclaimed, who proclaimed these words. [17]Then he said, "What gravestone *is* this that I see?"

So the men of the city told him, "*It is* the tomb of the man of God who came from Judah and proclaimed these things which you have done against the altar of Bethel."

[18]And he said, "Let him alone; let no one move his bones." So they let his bones alone, with the bones of the prophet who came from Samaria.

[19]Now Josiah also took away all the shrines of the high places that *were* in the cities of Samaria, which the kings of Israel had made to provoke the LORD[a] to anger; and he did to them according to all the deeds he had done in Bethel. [20]He executed all the priests of the high places who *were* there, on the altars, and burned men's bones on them; and he returned to Jerusalem.

[21]Then the king commanded all the people, saying, "Keep the Passover to the LORD your God, as *it is* written in this Book of the Covenant." [22]Such a Passover surely had never been held since the days of the judges who judged Israel, nor in all the days of the kings of Israel and the kings of Judah. [23]But in the eighteenth year of King Josiah this Passover was held before the LORD in Jerusalem. [24]Moreover Josiah put away those who consulted mediums and spiritists, the household gods and idols, all the abominations that were seen in the land of Judah and in Jerusalem, that he might perform the words of the law which were written in the book that Hilkiah the priest found in the house of the LORD. [25]Now before him there was no king like him, who turned to the LORD with all his heart, with all his soul, and with all his might, according to all the Law of Moses; nor after him did *any* arise like him.

Impending Judgment on Judah

[26]Nevertheless the LORD did not turn from the fierceness of His great wrath, with which His anger was aroused against Judah, because of all the provocations with which Manasseh had provoked Him. [27]And the LORD said, "I will also remove Judah from My sight, as I have removed Israel, and will cast off this city Jerusalem which I have chosen, and the house of which I said, 'My name shall be there.' "[a]

Josiah Dies in Battle

[28]Now the rest of the acts of Josiah, and all that he did, *are* they not written in the book of the chronicles of the kings of Judah? [29]In his days

---

23:10 [a]Kethib reads *Sons.*   23:19 [a]Following Septuagint, Syriac, and Vulgate; Masoretic Text and Targum omit *the LORD.*   23:27 [a]1 Kings 8:29

23:10 Topheth. Solomon had built an altar to Molech in Topheth (Heb., lit. "the burning place"), which is in the valley of Hinnom below the hill of Zion. There human sacrifices were offered to Molech (1 Kin. 11:7). Presumably, Ahaz and Manasseh made use of the place when they sacrificed their sons to that god (2 Kin. 16:3; 21:6).

23:11 Worship of the sun god Shemesh may have been related to worship of the "host of heaven." It was conducted on rooftops (v. 12; Jer. 19:13).

23:13 The Mount of Corruption or Mount of Olives is here used as a high place. It is on the east side of Jerusalem, separated from the city by the Kidron Valley. The gods being worshiped there were Canaanite; Chemosh is Shemesh the sun god, and Milcom is Molech.

23:19 Reform in Samaria. While Assyria was occupied with Babylon, Josiah reconquered much of Israel's territory and added it to Judah. He also retook some Philistine land. He was killed at Megiddo in northern Israel, indicating that he was moving into Galilee as well.

THE KINGS OF BABYLON

KING	SCRIPTURE	DATE OF REIGN*
Merodach-Baladan II	2 Kin. 20:12; Is. 39:1	721–689 B.C.
Nabopolassar		626–605 B.C.
Nebuchadnezzar II	2 Kin. 24—25; Dan. 1—4	605–562 B.C.
Evil-Merodach	2 Kin. 25:27–30; Jer. 52:31–34	562–560 B.C.
Neriglissar		560–556 B.C.
Labashi-Marduk		556 B.C.
Nabonidus		556–539 B.C.
Belshazzar (co-regent with Nabonidus)		556–539 B.C.

*There is some difference among scholars on the dates of these reigns.

Pharaoh Necho king of Egypt went to the aid of the king of Assyria, to the River Euphrates; and King Josiah went against him. And *Pharaoh Necho* killed him at Megiddo when he confronted him. ³⁰Then his servants moved his body in a chariot from Megiddo, brought him to Jerusalem, and buried him in his own tomb. And the people of the land took Jehoahaz the son of Josiah, anointed him, and made him king in his father's place.

The Reign and Captivity of Jehoahaz

³¹Jehoahaz *was* twenty-three years old when he became king, and he reigned three months in Jerusalem. His mother's name *was* Hamutal the daughter of Jeremiah of Libnah. ³²And he did evil in the sight of the LORD, according to all that his fathers had done. ³³Now Pharaoh Necho put him in prison at Riblah in the land of Hamath, that he might not reign in Jerusalem; and he imposed on the land a tribute of one hundred talents of silver and a talent of gold. ³⁴Then Pharaoh Necho made Eliakim the son of Josiah king in place of his fa-

ther Josiah, and changed his name to Jehoiakim. And *Pharaoh* took Jehoahaz and went to Egypt, and he[a] died there.

Jehoiakim Reigns in Judah

³⁵So Jehoiakim gave the silver and gold to Pharaoh; but he taxed the land to give money according to the command of Pharaoh; he exacted the silver and gold from the people of the land, from every one according to his assessment, to give *it* to Pharaoh Necho. ³⁶Jehoiakim *was* twenty-five years old when he became king, and he reigned eleven years in Jerusalem. His mother's name *was* Zebudah the daughter of Pedaiah of Rumah. ³⁷And he did evil in the sight of the LORD, according to all that his fathers had done.

Judah Overrun by Enemies

24 In his days Nebuchadnezzar king of Babylon came up, and Jehoiakim became his vassal *for* three years. Then he turned and rebelled against him. ²And the LORD sent against him *raiding* bands of Chaldeans, bands of Syrians, bands of Moabites, and bands of the people of Ammon; He sent them against Judah to destroy it, according to the word of the LORD which He had spoken by His servants the prophets. ³Surely at the commandment of the LORD *this* came upon Judah, to remove *them* from His sight because of the sins of Manasseh, according to all that he had done, ⁴and also because of the innocent blood that he had shed; for he had filled Jerusalem with innocent blood, which the LORD would not pardon.

⁵Now the rest of the acts of Jehoiakim, and all that he did, *are* they not written in the book of the chronicles of the kings of Judah? ⁶So Jehoiakim rested with his fathers. Then Jehoiachin his son reigned in his place.

⁷And the king of Egypt did not come out of his land anymore, for the king of Babylon had taken all that belonged to the king of Egypt from the Brook of Egypt to the River Euphrates.

....

23:34 [a]That is, Jehoahaz

23:29 Josiah ruled until about 609 B.C. Assyria had been driven out of Babylon in 612 B.C. The Assyrian capital then moved to Haran, which was likewise attacked by the Babylonians in 610 B.C. Egypt, seeing Babylon about to take possession of Israel and Judah, marched north to fight on Assyria's side. Josiah hoped to keep Judah's independence from all three kingdoms. He intercepted Pharaoh Necho on his way to Haran but was killed. However, the delay of Egyptian reinforcements allowed the Babylonian king Nabopolassar finally to destroy the remains of the Assyrian Empire. Judah now lay between a hostile Babylon to the north and a strong Egypt to the south.

23:33 During the reign of Jehoahaz, Egypt claimed ownership of Judah. The country was never free again.

23:34 The renaming of Eliakim (Jehoiakim) indicates mastery. Jehoiakim paid a vassal's tribute to Egypt.

24:1 The rise of Babylon. In 605 B.C., the Egyptians and the Babylonians fought at the River Euphrates. The Babylonian army, under Nabopolassar's son and coregent Nebuchadnezzar II, crushed the Egyptians at Carchemish, far to Judah's north, and drove south. By 604 B.C., Babylon was in Philistia. By 603 B.C., Jehoiakim paid tribute to Babylon.

24:1, 2 Jehoiakim rebelled against Nebuchadnezzar around 598 B.C. The Chaldeans, Syrians, Moabites, and Ammonites were mercenaries of Nebuchadnezzar (see also 2 Kin. 25:4, 5). In the meantime, Nebuchadnezzar began to march south toward Jerusalem.

The Reign and Captivity of Jehoiachin

[8]Jehoiachin *was* eighteen years old when he became king, and he reigned in Jerusalem three months. His mother's name *was* Nehushta the daughter of Elnathan of Jerusalem. [9]And he did evil in the sight of the LORD, according to all that his father had done.

[10]At that time the servants of Nebuchadnezzar king of Babylon came up against Jerusalem, and the city was besieged. [11]And Nebuchadnezzar king of Babylon came against the city, as his servants were besieging it. [12]Then Jehoiachin king of Judah, his mother, his servants, his princes, and his officers went out to the king of Babylon; and the king of Babylon, in the eighth year of his reign, took him prisoner.

The Captivity of Jerusalem

[13]And he carried out from there all the treasures of the house of the LORD and the treasures of the king's house, and he cut in pieces all the articles of gold which Solomon king of Israel had made in the temple of the LORD, as the LORD had said. [14]Also he carried into captivity all Jerusalem: all the captains and all the mighty men of valor, ten thousand captives, and all the craftsmen and smiths. None remained except the poorest people of the land. [15]And he carried Jehoiachin captive to Babylon. The king's mother, the king's wives, his officers, and the mighty of the land he carried into captivity from Jerusalem to Babylon. [16]All the valiant men, seven thousand, and craftsmen and smiths, one thousand, all *who were* strong *and* fit for war, these the king of Babylon brought captive to Babylon.

Zedekiah Reigns in Judah

[17]Then the king of Babylon made Mattaniah, *Jehoiachin's*[a] uncle, king in his place, and changed his name to Zedekiah.

[18]Zedekiah *was* twenty-one years old when he became king, and he reigned eleven years in Jerusalem. His mother's name *was* Hamutal the daughter of Jeremiah of Libnah. [19]He also did evil in the sight of the LORD, according to all that Jehoiakim had done. [20]For because of the anger of the LORD *this* happened in Jerusalem and Judah, that He finally cast them out from His presence. Then Zedekiah rebelled against the king of Babylon.

The Fall and Captivity of Judah

25Now it came to pass in the ninth year of his reign, in the tenth month, on the tenth *day* of the month, *that* Nebuchadnezzar king of Babylon and all his army came against Jerusalem and encamped against it; and they built a siege wall against it all around. [2]So the city was besieged until the eleventh year of King Zedekiah. [3]By the ninth *day* of the *fourth* month the famine had become so severe in the city that there was no food for the people of the land.

[4]Then the city wall was broken through, and all the men of war *fled* at night by way of the gate between two walls, which was by the king's garden, even though the Chaldeans *were* still encamped all around against the city. And *the king*[a] went by way of the plain.[b] [5]But the army of the Chaldeans pursued the king, and they overtook him in the plains of Jericho. All his army was scattered from him. [6]So they took the king and brought him up to the king of Babylon at Riblah, and they pronounced judgment on him. [7]Then they killed the sons of Zedekiah before his eyes, put out the eyes of Zedekiah, bound him with bronze fetters, and took him to Babylon.

[8]And in the fifth month, on the seventh *day* of the month (which *was* the nineteenth year of King Nebuchadnezzar king of Babylon), Nebuzaradan the captain of the guard, a servant of the king of Babylon, came to Jerusalem. [9]He burned the house of the LORD and the king's house; all the houses of Jerusalem, that is, all the houses of the great, he burned with fire. [10]And all the army of the Chaldeans who *were with* the captain of the guard broke down the walls of Jerusalem all around.

[11]Then Nebuzaradan the captain of the guard carried away captive the rest of the people *who* remained in the city and the defectors who had deserted to the king of Babylon, with the rest of the multitude. [12]But the captain of the guard left *some* of the poor of the land as vinedressers and farmers. [13]The bronze pillars that *were* in the house of the LORD, and the carts and the bronze Sea that *were* in the house of the LORD, the Chaldeans broke in pieces, and carried their bronze to Babylon. [14]They also took away the pots, the shovels, the trimmers, the spoons, and all the bronze utensils with which the priests ministered. [15]The

24:17 [a]Literally *his*   **25:4** [a]Literally *he* [b]Or *Arabah,* that is, the Jordan Valley

---

24:10 The siege of Jerusalem. During the rebellion, Jehoiakim died and was succeeded by Jehoiachin (v. 6). No Egyptian help came, and Jerusalem was captured in 597 B.C. (v. 7).

24:12 The first deportation. Nebuchadnezzar took the cream of Judah's society captive, while raiding Jerusalem for treasure. Daniel was taken into captivity around this time.

25:6 Riblah, located on the Orontes River, was along a major

trade route. Nebuchadnezzar used the site for his military operations.

25:9 The destruction of the temple. Since God's people did not honor the place where He had set His name, God allowed it to be destroyed (Deut. 12:5). He also allowed the bronze pillars that commemorated His establishment of Israel to be taken away (2 Kin. 25:13, 17; see also 1 Kin. 7:21).

firepans and the basins, the things of solid gold and solid silver, the captain of the guard took away. [16]The two pillars, one Sea, and the carts, which Solomon had made for the house of the LORD, the bronze of all these articles was beyond measure. [17]The height of one pillar *was* eighteen cubits, and the capital on it *was* of bronze. The height of the capital was three cubits, and the network and pomegranates all around the capital were all of bronze. The second pillar was the same, with a network.

[18]And the captain of the guard took Seraiah the chief priest, Zephaniah the second priest, and the three doorkeepers. [19]He also took out of the city an officer who had charge of the men of war, five men of the king's close associates who were found in the city, the chief recruiting officer of the army, who mustered the people of the land, and sixty men of the people of the land *who were* found in the city. [20]So Nebuzaradan, captain of the guard, took these and brought them to the king of Babylon at Riblah. [21]Then the king of Babylon struck them and put them to death at Riblah in the land of Hamath. Thus Judah was carried away captive from its own land.

Gedaliah Made Governor of Judah

[22]Then he made Gedaliah the son of Ahikam, the son of Shaphan, governor over the people who remained in the land of Judah, whom Nebuchadnezzar king of Babylon had left. [23]Now when all the captains of the armies, they and *their* men, heard that the king of Babylon had made Gedaliah governor, they came to Gedaliah at Mizpah—Ishmael the son of Nethaniah, Johanan the son of Careah, Seraiah the son of Tanhumeth the Netophathite, and Jaazaniah[a] the son of a Maachathite, they and their men. [24]And Gedaliah took an oath before them and their men, and said to them, "Do not be afraid of the servants of the Chaldeans. Dwell in the land and serve the king of Babylon, and it shall be well with you."

[25]But it happened in the seventh month that Ishmael the son of Nethaniah, the son of Elishama, of the royal family, came with ten men and struck and killed Gedaliah, the Jews, as well as the Chaldeans who were with him at Mizpah. [26]And all the people, small and great, and the captains of the armies, arose and went to Egypt; for they were afraid of the Chaldeans.

Jehoiachin Released from Prison

[27]Now it came to pass in the thirty-seventh year of the captivity of Jehoiachin king of Judah, in the twelfth month, on the twenty-seventh *day* of the month, *that* Evil-Merodach[a] king of Babylon, in the year that he began to reign, released Jehoiachin king of Judah from prison. [28]He spoke kindly to him, and gave him a more prominent seat than those of the kings who *were* with him in Babylon. [29]So Jehoiachin changed from his prison garments, and he ate bread regularly before the king all the days of his life. [30]And as for his provisions, *there was* a regular ration given him by the king, a portion for each day, all the days of his life.

•••••••••••••••••••

25:23 [a]Spelled *Jezaniah* in Jeremiah 40:8   25:27 [a]Literally *Man of Marduk*

25:22 Judah became part of Babylon's provincial system. An inscription found at Lachish identified Gedaliah as the former prime minister under Zedekiah; he was made governor under Nebuchadnezzar.

25:23 Mizpah. Because Jerusalem was uninhabitable, the government was moved to Mizpah, where Saul had been proclaimed king (1 Sam. 10:17–19).

25:24 The Chaldeans were the dominant ethnic group within the Babylonian Empire.

25:25, 26 Gedaliah's appointment had probably been Nebuchadnezzar's gesture of goodwill toward those still living in Judah. However, Gedaliah was hated by the people as a traitor because of his official status. He was assassinated, along with a Babylonian garrison, in Mizpah. Many of Judah's inhabitants, afraid of reprisal, then fled to Egypt (Jer. 42; 43). After the Exile, which began in 586 B.C., Judah was probably incorporated into the province of Samaria. All fortified cities had been completely destroyed. The population of Judah, which had reached a high of about 250,000 in the eighth century, fell below 20,000. Meanwhile, Israelite-Canaanite descendants in the north practiced a mixture of paganism and Yahwehism.

25:27 Jehoiachin's release. Although God's people disobeyed Him and brought exile upon themselves, a descendant of David remained alive. Evil-Merodach, the son of Nebuchadnezzar, gave Jehoiachin a semi-official position at court. The book ends with hope even in the midst of despair. God's judgment had to come, but even in judgment, God's mercy was abundant as a foretaste of the nation's future deliverance according to God's promise (Jer. 31:18; Lam. 5:21).

1 Chronicles

TITLE

In the Hebrew Bible, the title given to 1 and 2 Chronicles is translated "The Events of the Days," and the books are placed at the end of the volume. With the Septuagint title, "The Things Left Out," Chronicles was placed after Kings since it was thought to be a repetition, for the most part, of the books of Samuel and Kings, with additional material regarding the priests and Levites. This perspective ignored the unique contribution of the purpose and theology of Chronicles. Jerome referred to these books as the "chronicles of the whole of sacred history," beginning with Adam (1 Chr. 1:1) and ending with Cyrus, king of Persia (2 Chr. 36:22, 23). Thus, the title "Chronicles" was given. Jesus was familiar with 1 and 2 Chronicles and demonstrated that He considered the books to be authoritative when He referred to passages from Chronicles (compare 2 Chr. 24:20–22 with Matt. 23:35).

AUTHOR

The author, whom scholars identify as the chronicler, is unnamed. It is certain, however, that the same person wrote 1 and 2 Chronicles. The two books originally formed one united whole and therefore should not be assigned separate authors. Comparing and relating Chronicles with the Book of Ezra has been helpful in determining dates and authorship. For this reason, many have identified Ezra as the author.

DATE

Chronicles was written after the Jews returned from Exile in Babylon. The most probable date for the completed form of Chronicles is fifth century B.C.

BACKGROUND

SETTING: The return of the Jews to Jerusalem from Exile is dated from the decree of Cyrus, king of Persia, which authorized the return (538 B.C.). Those who wished to do so were allowed to return to the land to rebuild the temple and the city. The temple was completed in 516 B.C., and the walls of the city were rebuilt around 445 B.C. The returned Jewish community needed encouragement as they structured their civil and religious life. Chronicles establishes continuity between the preexilic Israel of the past and the postexilic present, thus legitimizing the order of this new community.

PURPOSE: The returned Jewish community was concerned with the status of their relationship to God after the Exile. In order to demonstrate the continuity of the present with the past, the chronicler centered his focus around the preexilic history of Samuel and Kings, especially as it referred to David's throne and the temple. Chronicles is not a mere repetition of the history of Israel to the time of the Exile. Rather it is a record of that history emphasizing the necessity for all Israel to live in obedience in temple worship and in loyalty to David's throne. The chronicler's interest was in a true Israel living in Jerusalem (not an ethnic Israel but a pure, faithful remnant) with life centered around

the joyful worship of God at the temple and with the unanimous support of the throne of David. A united Israel (referred to as "all Israel"), the unique role of the temple, and the significance of David's throne are inseparable themes in Chronicles. The religious and political structure of the returned community is shown to be rooted in the past and thus is legitimate for the present. God's covenant relation with Israel has not changed.

LITERARY CHARACTERISTICS: The chronicler makes deliberate use of the history of Samuel and Kings for much of his work. He assumes his reader is already familiar with this history of Israel's kingdom. Therefore, critical to the understanding of the chronicler's interpretation of this history are those passages which are unique to the chronicler and not found in Samuel and Kings. In the same way, changes in vocabulary and the omission of phrases from Samuel and Kings provide clues to the chronicler's purpose.

THEMES

The major themes in Chronicles include these:

1) the notion of "all Israel;"
2) the centrality of the temple and Jerusalem in the life of Israel;
3) the idealized and interdependent reigns of David and Solomon; and
4) the theology of retribution.

"All Israel" is defined theologically as the people of God who are faithful in temple worship and loyal to David's throne. "All Israel" accepts David and Solomon as king without opposition, brings the ark back to Jerusalem in a joyful procession, and contributes generously to the building of the temple. They are "all Israel" by virtue of their identification with the tribe of Judah, whose capital is Jerusalem. Contrary to the suggestion by some that Chronicles is negative in its estimation of the north, Chronicles is positive in its identification of "all Israel." The northern kingdom is drawn together with Judah as one collective, united, true Israel centered around Jerusalem. Distinctions between north and south are not valid within the chronicler's concept of "all Israel."

Jerusalem and the temple have a unique position in the life of Israel. The abundant preparations for the temple made by David, the willingness of all Israel to contribute to the temple, the building of the temple by Solomon, and the joy and celebration of temple worship are critical to the chronicler's purposes.

Another dominant theme is to show an ideal king over "all Israel" whose goal is building the house of the Lord. The combined reigns of David and Solomon form an interdependent kingship within the context of temple building. David is the temple planner; Solomon is the temple builder. Threats and blemishes against each king are largely omitted by the chronicler—perhaps because these weaknesses are covered in other materials (David in 2 Sam. 1—4; 6:20–23; 11–21; Solomon in 1 Kin. 1:28–53; 11:1–13). Each king is chosen by God, enjoys the unanimous support of all Israel, acts first in regard to the temple, and reigns forty years with complete devotion to God.

The chronicler's concept of retribution is fundamental to the interpretation and understanding of Chronicles. Simply stated, obedience is always rewarded with blessing, while disobedience results in God's judgment. Faithfulness characterized by devotion and commitment to God and to the temple brings prosperity, rest, honor and fame, a victorious army, building projects, and tribute from foreign kings. Faithlessness or the worship of foreign gods and the failure to observe the Law results in war, defeat, conspiracy from within and without Israel, and disease. Nevertheless, God always provides an opportunity for repentance.

The Family of Adam—Seth to Abraham

1 Adam, Seth, Enosh, [2]Cainan,[a] Mahalalel, Jared, [3]Enoch, Methuselah, Lamech, [4]Noah,[a] Shem, Ham, and Japheth.

[5]The sons of Japheth were Gomer, Magog, Madai, Javan, Tubal, Meshech, and Tiras. [6]The sons of Gomer were Ashkenaz, Diphath,[a] and Togarmah. [7]The sons of Javan were Elishah, Tarshishah,[a] Kittim, and Rodanim.[b]

[8]The sons of Ham were Cush, Mizraim, Put, and Canaan. [9]The sons of Cush were Seba, Havilah, Sabta,[a] Raama,[b] and Sabtecha. The sons of Raama were Sheba and Dedan. [10]Cush begot Nimrod; he began to be a mighty one on the earth. [11]Mizraim begot Ludim, Anamim, Lehabim, Naphtuhim, [12]Pathrusim, Casluhim (from whom came the Philistines and the Caphtorim). [13]Canaan begot Sidon, his firstborn, and Heth; [14]the Jebusite, the Amorite, and the Girgashite; [15]the Hivite, the Arkite, and the Sinite; [16]the Arvadite, the Zemarite, and the Hamathite.

[17]The sons of Shem were Elam, Asshur, Arphaxad, Lud, Aram, Uz, Hul, Gether, and Meshech.[a] [18]Arphaxad begot Shelah, and Shelah begot Eber. [19]To Eber were born two sons: the name of one was Peleg,[a] for in his days the earth was divided; and his brother's name was Joktan. [20]Joktan begot Almodad, Sheleph, Hazarmaveth, Jerah, [21]Hadoram, Uzal, Diklah, [22]Ebal,[a] Abimael, Sheba, [23]Ophir, Havilah, and Jobab. All these were the sons of Joktan.

[24]Shem, Arphaxad, Shelah, [25]Eber, Peleg, Reu, [26]Serug, Nahor, Terah, [27]and Abram, who is Abraham. [28]The sons of Abraham were Isaac and Ishmael.

The Family of Ishmael

[29]These are their genealogies: The firstborn of Ishmael was Nebajoth; then Kedar, Adbeel, Mibsam, [30]Mishma, Dumah, Massa, Hadad,[a] Tema,

. . . .

1:2 [a]Hebrew Qenan 1:4 [a]Following Masoretic Text and Vulgate; Septuagint adds the sons of Noah. 1:6 [a]Spelled Riphath in Genesis 10:3 1:7 [a]Spelled Tarshish in Genesis 10:4 [b]Spelled Dodanim in Genesis 10:4 1:9 [a]Spelled Sabtah in Genesis 10:7 [b]Spelled Raamah in Genesis 10:7 1:17 [a]Spelled Mash in Genesis 10:23 1:19 [a]Literally Division 1:22 [a]Spelled Obal in Genesis 10:28 1:30 [a]Spelled Hadar in Genesis 25:15

1:1–4 Genealogies of the ancient Near East were fluid in nature. The relationship between names might change: Names might be added, or names might be omitted (see chart, The Kings with Two Names). Genealogies were used to legitimize a person's position by showing his relationship to a recognized and accepted ancestor (linear genealogy). They also demonstrated the relationships among members or segments of the same family (segmented or mixed genealogy; see 1 Chr. 23:6, note). The genealogies of 1 Chronicles provide evidence that God is sovereign over history from creation. Names within genealogies are reminders of what God has done in the past and often embody hope for the future as well (see Is. 45, Naming of Children). Continuity with the past is also demon-strated in God's hand at work in establishing and preserving Israel. The chronicler's interest is in God's choice—whether of an individual (Abraham), a nation (Israel), a tribe (Judah), or a king (David and Solomon).

1:8 Geographical areas and genealogies. Genealogies of the ancient Near East commonly treated a geographical area or a people group as an individual person with descendants. The sons of Ham included Mizraim (Egypt) and Canaan (see also vv. 11, 12, 13–16). This practice illustrates the relationship of Israel to the surrounding nations, with whom they sometimes had a degree of kinship, and further emphasizes God's election of Israel from the nations of the earth.

³¹Jetur, Naphish, and Kedemah. These *were* the sons of Ishmael.

The Family of Keturah

³²Now the sons born to Keturah, Abraham's concubine, *were* Zimran, Jokshan, Medan, Midian, Ishbak, and Shuah. The sons of Jokshan *were* Sheba and Dedan. ³³The sons of Midian *were* Ephah, Epher, Hanoch, Abida, and Eldaah. All these were the children of Keturah.

The Family of Isaac

³⁴And Abraham begot Isaac. The sons of Isaac *were* Esau and Israel. ³⁵The sons of Esau *were* Eliphaz, Reuel, Jeush, Jaalam, and Korah. ³⁶And the sons of Eliphaz *were* Teman, Omar, Zephi,ᵃ Gatam, *and* Kenaz; and *by* Timna,ᵇ Amalek. ³⁷The sons of Reuel *were* Nahath, Zerah, Shammah, and Mizzah.

The Family of Seir

³⁸The sons of Seir *were* Lotan, Shobal, Zibeon, Anah, Dishon, Ezer, and Dishan. ³⁹And the sons of Lotan *were* Hori and Homam; Lotan's sister *was* Timna. ⁴⁰The sons of Shobal *were* Alian,ᵃ Manahath, Ebal, Shephi,ᵇ and Onam. The sons of Zibeon *were* Ajah and Anah. ⁴¹The son of Anah *was* Dishon. The sons of Dishon *were* Hamran,ᵃ Eshban, Ithran, and Cheran. ⁴²The sons of Ezer *were* Bilhan, Zaavan, *and* Jaakan.ᵃ The sons of Dishan *were* Uz and Aran.

The Kings of Edom

⁴³Now these *were* the kings who reigned in the land of Edom before a king reigned over the children of Israel: Bela the son of Beor, and the name of his city was Dinhabah. ⁴⁴And when Bela died, Jobab the son of Zerah of Bozrah reigned in his place. ⁴⁵When Jobab died, Husham of the land of the Temanites reigned in his place. ⁴⁶And when Husham died, Hadad the son of Bedad, who attacked Midian in the field of Moab, reigned in his place. The name of his city *was* Avith. ⁴⁷When Hadad died, Samlah of Masrekah reigned in his place. ⁴⁸And when Samlah died, Saul of Rehoboth-by-the-River reigned in his place. ⁴⁹When Saul died, Baal-Hanan the son of Achbor reigned in his place. ⁵⁰And when Baal-Hanan died, Hadadᵃ reigned in his place; and the name of his city was Pai.ᵇ His wife's name was Mehetabel the daughter of Matred, the daughter of Mezahab. ⁵¹Hadad died also. And the chiefs of Edom were Chief Timnah, Chief Aliah,ᵃ Chief Jetheth, ⁵²Chief Aholibamah, Chief Elah, Chief Pinon, ⁵³Chief Kenaz, Chief Teman, Chief Mibzar, ⁵⁴Chief Magdiel, and Chief Iram. These *were* the chiefs of Edom.

The Family of Israel

2 These *were* the sons of Israel: Reuben, Simeon, Levi, Judah, Issachar, Zebulun, ²Dan, Joseph, Benjamin, Naphtali, Gad, and Asher.

From Judah to David

³The sons of Judah *were* Er, Onan, and Shelah. *These* three were born to him by the daughter of Shua, the Canaanitess. Er, the firstborn of Judah, was wicked in the sight of the LORD; so He killed him. ⁴And Tamar, his daughter-in-law, bore him Perez and Zerah. All the sons of Judah *were* five. ⁵The sons of Perez *were* Hezron and Hamul.

••••••••••••••••••

1:36 ᵃSpelled *Zepho* in Genesis 36:11 ᵇCompare Genesis 36:12 **1:40** ᵃSpelled *Alvan* in Genesis 36:23 ᵇSpelled *Shepho* in Genesis 36:23 **1:41** ᵃSpelled *Hemdan* in Genesis 36:26 **1:42** ᵃSpelled *Akan* in Genesis 36:27 **1:50** ᵃSpelled *Hadar* in Genesis 36:39 ᵇSpelled *Pau* in Genesis 36:39 **1:51** ᵃSpelled *Alvah* in Genesis 36:40

1:28 The genealogies of the first chapter are taken from the Book of Genesis and assume the historicity of the early chapters of Genesis (Gen. 5; 10; 11; 25; 36). The fact that Israel's history is rooted in creation is shown by an ancestry that extends back to Adam. Israel did not become a nation by accident but according to the purposes of God from creation.

1:32, 33 Keturah, Abraham's second wife, bore him many children (Gen. 25:1–4; see chart, The Family Tree of Abraham). Even so, Abraham gave Isaac all that he had, thereby granting to Isaac the position of privilege among all his children (Gen. 25:5).

1:34 The chronicler preferred the name Israel rather than Jacob for the second son of Isaac (Gen. 32:28). This preference is true throughout Chronicles with one exception (1 Chr. 16:8–36; see also Ps. 105). The chronicler's purpose was to focus attention on all Israel; thus the choice of this name is appropriate. The record of Israel's early history follows the pattern of Genesis, separating the genealogies with the flood. Chapter 1 introduces the sons of Israel (Jacob), the true interest of the chronicler.

1:36 Timna, as a daughter of Seir and sister of Lotan (vv. 38, 39), was the concubine of Eliphaz (son of Esau, Gen. 36:12). Her name was assigned to an Edomite chieftan and adopted by his district (Gen. 36:40; 1 Chr. 1:51). The reason she was so honored is not given.

1:38 Sons of Seir (vv. 38–42; Gen. 36:20–28). Seir is associated with Edom and is used as an alternate designation for Edom (Gen. 32:3; Ezek. 35). Edom is the name assigned to Esau (Gen. 25:30; 36:43).

2:3—4:23 The chronicler begins with the prominent tribe of Judah and its descendants (Gen. 49:8–12; 1 Chr. 28:4). The order of the sons in this genealogical section (Judah, 1 Chr. 2:3–3:24; 4:1–23; Simeon, 4:24–43; Reuben, Gad, half Manasseh, 5:1–26; Levi, 6:1–81; Issachar, Benjamin, Naphtali, half Manasseh, Ephraim, Asher, 7:1–40) illustrates the fluidity of ancient genealogies (see 1 Chr. 1:1–4, note). The chronicler does not use Joseph as a tribal name, referring instead to his sons, Ephraim and Manasseh (see 1 Chr. 5:23, 24 note; 6:28, 29). Genealogies for Zebulun and Dan are absent. Nevertheless, 12 tribes are listed, giving a sense of completeness and reinforcing the chronicler's notion of "all Israel" (see 1 Chr. 6:54; 12:23–37; 27:1, notes).

⁶The sons of Zerah *were* Zimri, Ethan, Heman, Calcol, and Dara—five of them in all.

⁷The son of Carmi *was* Achar,ᵃ the troubler of Israel, who transgressed in the accursed thing.

⁸The son of Ethan *was* Azariah.

⁹Also the sons of Hezron who were born to him *were* Jerahmeel, Ram, and Chelubai.ᵃ ¹⁰Ram begot Amminadab, and Amminadab begot Nahshon, leader of the children of Judah; ¹¹Nahshon begot Salma,ᵃ and Salma begot Boaz; ¹²Boaz begot Obed, and Obed begot Jesse; ¹³Jesse begot Eliab his firstborn, Abinadab the second, Shimeaᵃ the third, ¹⁴Nethanel the fourth, Raddai the fifth, ¹⁵Ozem the sixth, *and* David the seventh.

¹⁶Now their sisters *were* Zeruiah and Abigail. And the sons of Zeruiah *were* Abishai, Joab, and Asahel—three. ¹⁷Abigail bore Amasa; and the father of Amasa *was* Jether the Ishmaelite.ᵃ

The Family of Hezron

¹⁸Caleb the son of Hezron had children by Azubah, *his* wife, and by Jerioth. Now these were her sons: Jesher, Shobab, and Ardon. ¹⁹When Azubah died, Caleb took Ephrathᵃ as his wife, who bore him Hur. ²⁰And Hur begot Uri, and Uri begot Bezalel.

²¹Now afterward Hezron went in to the daughter of Machir the father of Gilead, whom he married when he *was* sixty years old; and she bore him Segub. ²²Segub begot Jair, who had twenty-three cities in the land of Gilead. ²³(Geshur and Syria took from them the towns of Jair, with Kenath and its towns—sixty towns.) All these *belonged to* the sons of Machir the father of Gilead. ²⁴After Hezron died in Caleb Ephrathah, Hezron's wife Abijah bore him Ashhur the father of Tekoa.

The Family of Jerahmeel

²⁵The sons of Jerahmeel, the firstborn of Hezron, *were* Ram, the firstborn, and Bunah, Oren, Ozem, *and* Ahijah. ²⁶Jerahmeel had another wife, whose name was Atarah; she was the mother of Onam. ²⁷The sons of Ram, the firstborn of Jerahmeel, were Maaz, Jamin, and Eker. ²⁸The sons of Onam were Shammai and Jada. The sons of Shammai *were* Nadab and Abishur.

²⁹And the name of the wife of Abishur *was* Abihail, and she bore him Ahban and Molid. ³⁰The sons of Nadab *were* Seled and Appaim; Seled died without children. ³¹The son of Appaim *was* Ishi, the son of Ishi *was* Sheshan, and Sheshan's son *was* Ahlai. ³²The sons of Jada, the brother of Shammai, *were* Jether and Jonathan; Jether died without children. ³³The sons of Jonathan *were* Peleth and Zaza. These were the sons of Jerahmeel.

³⁴Now Sheshan had no sons, only daughters. And Sheshan had an Egyptian servant whose name *was* Jarha. ³⁵Sheshan gave his daughter to Jarha his servant as wife, and she bore him Attai. ³⁶Attai begot Nathan, and Nathan begot Zabad; ³⁷Zabad begot Ephlal, and Ephlal begot Obed; ³⁸Obed begot Jehu, and Jehu begot Azariah; ³⁹Azariah begot Helez, and Helez begot Eleasah; ⁴⁰Eleasah begot Sismai, and Sismai begot Shallum; ⁴¹Shallum begot Jekamiah, and Jekamiah begot Elishama.

The Family of Caleb

⁴²The descendants of Caleb the brother of Jerahmeel *were* Mesha, his firstborn, who was the father of Ziph, and the sons of Mareshah the father of Hebron. ⁴³The sons of Hebron *were* Korah, Tappuah, Rekem, and Shema. ⁴⁴Shema begot Raham the father of Jorkoam, and Rekem begot Shammai.

···················

2:7 ᵃSpelled *Achan* in Joshua 7:1 and elsewhere **2:9** ᵃSpelled *Caleb* in 2:18, 42 **2:11** ᵃSpelled *Salmon* in Ruth 4:21 and Luke 3:32 **2:13** ᵃSpelled *Shammah* in 1 Samuel 16:9 and elsewhere **2:17** ᵃCompare 2 Samuel 17:25 **2:19** ᵃSpelled *Ephrathah* elsewhere

---

2:6–8 The sons of Zerah probably span the generations and are mentioned in relation to the temple musicians (Heman and Ethan in the titles of Ps. 88; 89) and to Solomon (1 Kin. 4:30, 31). These men from the tribe of Judah are not to be confused with the Levites Heman, Asaph, and Ethan who were David's musicians (1 Chr. 15:19). Achar, elsewhere Achan (Josh. 7:1, 18, 19, 24), is a deliberate word play in Hebrew. "Trouble" (Heb. *'akar*) comes from the "troubler" (Heb. *oker*). The story of Achar is an example of the chronicler's theology of retribution (see also Josh. 7:1–26).

2:9 This genealogy legitimizes David's position as king over Israel by tracing his lineage back to Judah (Gen. 49:8–12). David is identified as Jesse's seventh son here but as the eighth son elsewhere (v. 15; see 1 Sam. 16:1–13; 17:12). This additional unnamed son may have died at an early age, or this could be an example of the fluid character of ancient genealogies. The sisters presumably were stepdaughters of Jesse (Zeruiah and Abigail), born to David's mother probably in an earlier marriage to Nahash (2 Sam. 17:25; see chart, The

Family Tree of David). Women played an important role in the history of Israel, and the sons of these women were key individuals during the reign of David.

2:18–20 Bezalel is a key figure ending the genealogy of Caleb. Men bearing this name played a significant role in both the building of the tabernacle and the building of the temple (Ex. 31:2–5; 2 Chr. 1:5).

2:22 Jair's descent is traced through Segub's mother, the daughter of Machir rather than through his father Hezron and thus from Manasseh (vv. 21, 23; Num. 32:41; Deut. 3:14; Judg. 10:3; 1 Chr. 7:14). An association by marriage apparently exists between Judah through Hezron and Manasseh through Machir. These descendants of Hezron are then rightfully considered a part of Manasseh.

2:42–55 Many of the place names and sites are close to the city of Hebron (vv. 42–49). David was king of Judah at Hebron for seven years before becoming king over all Israel. Kirjath Jearim is located in the northern part of Judah along the

45And the son of Shammai *was* Maon, and Maon *was* the father of Beth Zur.

46Ephah, Caleb's concubine, bore Haran, Moza, and Gazez; and Haran begot Gazez. 47And the sons of Jahdai *were* Regem, Jotham, Geshan, Pelet, Ephah, and Shaaph.

48Maachah, Caleb's concubine, bore Sheber and Tirhanah. 49She also bore Shaaph the father of Madmannah, Sheva the father of Machbenah and the father of Gibea. And the daughter of Caleb *was* Achsah.

50These were the descendants of Caleb: The sons of Hur, the firstborn of Ephrathah, *were* Shobal the father of Kirjath Jearim, 51Salma the father of Bethlehem, *and* Hareph the father of Beth Gader.

52And Shobal the father of Kirjath Jearim had descendants: Haroeh, *and* half of the *families of* Manuhoth.a 53The families of Kirjath Jearim *were* the Ithrites, the Puthites, the Shumathites, and the Mishraites. From these came the Zorathites and the Eshtaolites.

54The sons of Salma *were* Bethlehem, the Netophathites, Atroth Beth Joab, half of the Manahethites, and the Zorites.

55And the families of the scribes who dwelt at Jabez *were* the Tirathites, the Shimeathites, *and* the Suchathites. These *were* the Kenites who came from Hammath, the father of the house of Rechab.

The Family of David

3 Now these were the sons of David who were born to him in Hebron: The firstborn *was* Amnon, by Ahinoam the Jezreelitess; the second, Daniel,a by Abigail the Carmelitess; 2the third, Absalom the son of Maacah, the daughter of Talmai, king of Geshur; the fourth, Adonijah the

son of Haggith; 3the fifth, Shephatiah, by Abital; the sixth, Ithream, by his wife Eglah.

4*These* six were born to him in Hebron. There he reigned seven years and six months, and in Jerusalem he reigned thirty-three years. 5And these were born to him in Jerusalem: Shimea,a Shobab, Nathan, and Solomon—four by Bathshuab the daughter of Ammiel.c 6Also *there* were Ibhar, Elishama,a Eliphelet,b 7Nogah, Nepheg, Japhia, 8Elishama, Eliada,a and Eliphelet—nine *in all.* 9*These were* all the sons of David, besides the sons of the concubines, and Tamar their sister.

The Family of Solomon

10Solomon's son *was* Rehoboam; Abijaha *was* his son, Asa his son, Jehoshaphat his son, 11Jorama his son, Ahaziah his son, Joashb his son, 12Amaziah his son, Azariaha his son, Jotham his son, 13Ahaz his son, Hezekiah his son, Manasseh his son, 14Amon his son, *and* Josiah his son. 15The sons of Josiah *were* Johanan the firstborn, the second Jehoiakim, the third Zedekiah, and the fourth Shallum.a 16The sons of Jehoiakim *were* Jeconiah his son *and* Zedekiaha his son.

The Family of Jeconiah

17And the sons of Jeconiaha *were* Assir,b Shealtiel his son, 18*and* Malchiram, Pedaiah, Shenazzar, Jecamiah, Hoshama, and Nedabiah.

••••••••••••••••••••

2:52 aSame as *the Manahethites,* verse 54   3:1 aCalled *Chileab* in 2 Samuel 3:3   3:5 aSpelled *Shammua* in 14:4 and 2 Samuel 5:14 bSpelled *Bathsheba* in 2 Samuel 11:3 cCalled *Eliam* in 2 Samuel 11:3   3:6 aSpelled *Elishua* in 14:5 and 2 Samuel 5:15 bSpelled *Elpelet* in 14:5   3:8 aSpelled *Beeliada* in 14:7   3:10 aSpelled *Abijam* in 1 Kings 15:1   3:11 aSpelled *Jehoram* in 2 Kings 1:17 and 8:16 bSpelled *Jehoash* in 2 Kings 12:1   3:12 aCalled *Uzziah* in Isaiah 6:1   3:15 aCalled *Jehoahaz* in 2 Kings 23:31   3:16 aCompare 2 Kings 24:17   3:17 aAlso called *Coniah* in Jeremiah 22:24 and *Jehoiachin* in 2 Kings 24:8 bOr *Jeconiah the captive were*

---

border with Dan and Benjamin (v. 50; Josh. 15:60; 18:14, 15). Since the early days of Samuel, the ark of the covenant was kept at Kirjath Jearim (1 Sam. 6:20–7:2). David attempted to bring the ark from there to Jerusalem but failed. He instead took it to Obed-Edom (2 Sam. 6:1–11; 1 Chr. 13:1–14). Bethlehem was the hometown of David (1 Chr. 2:51; 1 Sam. 16:1).

2:49 Achsah was the daughter of Caleb, the faithful companion of Joshua (1 Chr. 4:15). She married Caleb's nephew Othniel, who later became a judge of Israel (Josh. 15:16, 17; Judg. 1:12, 13; 3:9–11; see also Josh. 15, Achsah).

3:1 The chronicler focused attention on David as the central figure of all the descendants of Judah (see chart, The Family Tree of David). A previous genealogy showed the ancestry of David back to Judah (1 Chr. 2:3–17). Now David's line is extended to the generations that followed him. This genealogy divides into three historical sections: The reigns of David and Solomon, the preexilic kings of the southern kingdom, and the postexilic descendants of David. The sons of David during the reign of David (1 Chr. 3:1–9, with the reign of Solomon implied) were followed by the sons of Solomon, who ruled over the southern kingdom before the Exile (vv. 10–16). Zedekiah

(v. 16) was placed on the throne by Nebuchadnezzar of Babylon after Jeconiah (Jehoiachin) had been put in prison in Babylon (2 Kin. 24:13–20; 2 Chr. 36:9, 10). Since Jeconiah was the legitimate king, the royal line after the Exile continued through him (1 Chr. 3:17, note).

3:9 Adonijah tried to usurp the throne before the death of David (v. 2; 1 Kin. 1). Luke traced Jesus' genealogy from David through Nathan (1 Chr. 3:5; Luke 3:31); Matthew, from David through Solomon (Matt. 1:6).

3:10–16 The descendants listed ruled as kings over Judah during the divided kingdom (2 Chr. 10—36; see also 1 Kin. 12—2 Kin. 25). Two omissions are significant. Adonijah illegitimately proclaimed himself king (1 Chr. 3:2), but Solomon was made king instead (1 Kin. 1). Athaliah, the daughter of Jezebel, reigned over the southern kingdom after the death of her son Ahaziah (2 Kin. 11:1; 2 Chr. 22:10). She was not from the house of David and is not included here.

3:17 This reference may be to Jeconiah (see chart, The Kings with Two Names) during his time in a Babylonian prison (2 Kin. 24:15; 25:27–30; 2 Chr. 36:9, 10) rather than a reference to a son named "Assir" (Heb., lit. "prisoner").

[19]The sons of Pedaiah *were* Zerubbabel and Shimei. The sons of Zerubbabel *were* Meshullam, Hananiah, Shelomith their sister, [20]and Hashubah, Ohel, Berechiah, Hasadiah, and Jushab-Hesed— five *in all*.

[21]The sons of Hananiah *were* Pelatiah and Jeshaiah, the sons of Rephaiah, the sons of Arnan, the sons of Obadiah, and the sons of Shechaniah. [22]The son of Shechaniah was Shemaiah. The sons of Shemaiah *were* Hattush, Igal, Bariah, Neariah, and Shaphat— six *in all*. [23]The sons of Neariah *were* Elioenai, Hezekiah, and Azrikam— three *in all*. [24]The sons of Elioenai *were* Hodaviah, Eliashib, Pelaiah, Akkub, Johanan, Delaiah, and Anani— seven *in all*.

The Family of Judah

4 The sons of Judah *were* Perez, Hezron, Carmi, Hur, and Shobal. [2]And Reaiah the son of Shobal begot Jahath, and Jahath begot Ahumai and Lahad. These *were* the families of the Zorathites. [3]These *were* the sons *of the father* of Etam: Jezreel, Ishma, and Idbash; and the name of their sister *was* Hazelelponi; [4]and Penuel *was* the father of Gedor, and Ezer *was the* father of Hushah.

These *were* the sons of Hur, the firstborn of Ephrathah the father of Bethlehem.

[5]And Ashhur the father of Tekoa had two wives, Helah and Naarah. [6]Naarah bore him Ahuzzam, Hepher, Temeni, and Haahashtari. These *were* the sons of Naarah. [7]The sons of Helah *were* Zereth, Zohar, and Ethnan; [8]and Koz begot Anub, Zobebah, and the families of Aharhel the son of Harum.

[9]Now Jabez was more honorable than his brothers, and his mother called his name Jabez,[a] saying, "Because I bore *him* in pain." [10]And Jabez called on the God of Israel saying, "Oh, that You would bless me indeed, and enlarge my territory, that Your hand would be with me, and that You would keep *me* from evil, that I may not cause pain!" So God granted him what he requested.

[11]Chelub the brother of Shuhah begot Mehir, who *was* the father of Eshton. [12]And Eshton begot Beth-Rapha, Paseah, and Tehinnah the father of Ir-Nahash. These *were* the men of Rechah.

[13]The sons of Kenaz *were* Othniel and Seraiah. The sons of Othniel *were* Hathath,[a] [14]and Me-

onothai *who* begot Ophrah. Seraiah begot Joab the father of Ge Harashim,[a] for they were craftsmen. [15]The sons of Caleb the son of Jephunneh *were* Iru, Elah, and Naam. The son of Elah *was* Kenaz. [16]The sons of Jehallelel *were* Ziph, Ziphah, Tiria, and Asarel. [17]The sons of Ezrah *were* Jether, Mered, Epher, and Jalon. And *Mered's wife*[a] bore Miriam, Shammai, and Ishbah the father of Eshtemoa. [18](His wife Jehudijah[a] bore Jered the father of Gedor, Heber the father of Sochoh, and Jekuthiel the father of Zanoah.) And these were the sons of Bithiah the daughter of Pharaoh, whom Mered took.

[19]The sons of Hodiah's wife, the sister of Naham, *were* the fathers of Keilah the Garmite and of Eshtemoa the Maachathite. [20]And the sons of Shimon *were* Amnon, Rinnah, Ben-Hanan, and Tilon. And the sons of Ishi *were* Zoheth and Ben-Zoheth.

[21]The sons of Shelah the son of Judah *were* Er the father of Lecah, Laadah the father of Mareshah, and the families of the house of the linen workers of the house of Ashbea; [22]also Jokim, the men of Chozeba, and Joash; Saraph, who ruled in Moab, and Jashubi-Lehem. Now the records are ancient. [23]These *were* the potters and those who dwell at Netaim[a] and Gederah;[b] there they dwelt with the king for his work.

The Family of Simeon

[24]The sons of Simeon *were* Nemuel, Jamin, Jarib,[a] Zerah,[b] *and* Shaul, [25]Shallum his son, Mibsam his son, and Mishma his son. [26]And the sons of Mishma *were* Hamuel his son, Zacchur his son, and Shimei his son. [27]Shimei had sixteen sons and six daughters; but his brothers did not have many children, nor did any of their families multiply as much as the children of Judah.

[28]They dwelt at Beersheba, Moladah, Hazar Shual, [29]Bilhah, Ezem, Tolad, [30]Bethuel, Hormah, Ziklag, [31]Beth Marcaboth, Hazar Susim, Beth Biri, and at Shaaraim. These *were* their cities until the reign of David. [32]And their villages *were* Etam, Ain, Rimmon, Tochen, and Ashan— five cities—

4:9 [a]Literally *He Will Cause Pain*   **4:13** [a]Septuagint and Vulgate add *and Meonothai.*   **4:14** [a]Literally *Valley of Craftsmen*   **4:17** [a]Literally *she*   **4:18** [a]Or *His Judean wife*   **4:23** [a]Literally *Plants* [b]Literally *Hedges*   **4:24** [a]Called *Jachin* in Genesis 46:10 [b]Called *Zohar* in Genesis 46:10

3:19 Zerubbabel was the civil leader of the returned Jewish community in Jerusalem. He is a key figure in the books of Haggai, Zechariah, and Ezra. Although he never became king over Israel, he was the representative of David's eternal throne for the returned Jewish community (see Hag. 2:20–23; Zech. 4:8–10) and was included in the genealogies of Jesus (Matt. 1:12, 13; Luke 3:27).

4:17 The wife of Mered is identified as Bithiah, the daughter of a pharaoh (v. 18). For a Hebrew to marry into the Egyptian royal family may have been possible because of Joseph's prominence.

4:24 The inheritance of Simeon was located within the inheritance of Judah (Num. 26:12, 13; Josh. 19:1). Simeon never outgrew Judah and was probably incorporated within Judah early in Israel's history. This genealogy includes the sons of Simeon (1 Chr. 4:24–27), their dwelling places (vv. 28–33), and their leaders and victories (vv. 34–40). The dwelling places were in southern Judah, and some were resettled by those returning from Exile. The battles recorded here are unknown elsewhere in the OT (vv. 41–43).

[33]and all the villages that *were* around these cities as far as Baal.[a] These *were* their dwelling places, and they maintained their genealogy: [34]Meshobab, Jamlech, and Joshah the son of Amaziah; [35]Joel, and Jehu the son of Joshibiah, the son of Seraiah, the son of Asiel; [36]Elioenai, Jaakobah, Jeshohaiah, Asaiah, Adiel, Jesimiel, and Benaiah; [37]Ziza the son of Shiphi, the son of Allon, the son of Jedaiah, the son of Shimri, the son of Shemaiah— [38]these mentioned by name *were* leaders in their families, and their father's house increased greatly.

[39]So they went to the entrance of Gedor, as far as the east side of the valley, to seek pasture for their flocks. [40]And they found rich, good pasture, and the land *was* broad, quiet, and peaceful; for some Hamites formerly lived there.

[41]These recorded by name came in the days of Hezekiah king of Judah; and they attacked their tents and the Meunites who were found there, and utterly destroyed them, as it is to this day. So they dwelt in their place, because *there was* pasture for their flocks there. [42]Now *some* of them, five hundred men of the sons of Simeon, went to Mount Seir, having as their captains Pelatiah, Neariah, Rephaiah, and Uzziel, the sons of Ishi. [43]And they defeated the rest of the Amalekites who had escaped. They have dwelt there to this day.

The Family of Reuben

5 Now the sons of Reuben the firstborn of Israel—he *was* indeed the firstborn, but because he defiled his father's bed, his birthright was given to the sons of Joseph, the son of Israel, so that the genealogy is not listed according to the birthright; [2]yet Judah prevailed over his brothers, and from him *came* a ruler, although the birthright was Joseph's— [3]the sons of Reuben the firstborn of Israel were Hanoch, Pallu, Hezron, and Carmi.

[4]The sons of Joel *were* Shemaiah his son, Gog his son, Shimei his son, [5]Micah his son, Reaiah his son, Baal his son, [6]and Beerah his son, whom Tiglath-Pileser[a] king of Assyria carried into captivity. He *was* leader of the Reubenites. [7]And his brethren by their families, when the genealogy of their generations was registered: the chief, Jeiel, and Zechariah, [8]and Bela the son of Azaz, the son of Shema, the son of Joel, who dwelt in Aroer, as far as Nebo and Baal Meon. [9]Eastward they settled as far as the entrance of the wilderness this side of the River Euphrates, because their cattle had multiplied in the land of Gilead.

[10]Now in the days of Saul they made war with the Hagrites, who fell by their hand; and they dwelt in their tents throughout the entire *area* east of Gilead.

The Family of Gad

[11]And the children of Gad dwelt next to them in the land of Bashan as far as Salcah: [12]Joel *was* the chief, Shapham the next, then Jaanai and Shaphat in Bashan, [13]and their brethren of their father's house: Michael, Meshullam, Sheba, Jorai, Jachan, Zia, and Eber—seven *in all*. [14]These *were* the children of Abihail the son of Huri, the son of Jaroah, the son of Gilead, the son of Michael, the son of Jeshishai, the son of Jahdo, the son of Buz; [15]Ahi the son of Abdiel, the son of Guni, *was* chief of their father's house. [16]And *the Gadites* dwelt in Gilead, in Bashan and in its villages, and in all the common-lands of Sharon within their borders. [17]All these were registered by genealogies in the days of Jotham king of Judah, and in the days of Jeroboam king of Israel.

[18]The sons of Reuben, the Gadites, and half the tribe of Manasseh *had* forty-four thousand seven hundred and sixty valiant men, men able to bear shield and sword, to shoot with the bow, and skillful in war, who went to war. [19]They made war with the Hagrites, Jetur, Naphish, and Nodab. [20]And they were helped against them, and the Hagrites were delivered into their hand, and all who *were* with them, for they cried out to God in the battle. He heeded their prayer, because they put their trust in Him. [21]Then they took away their livestock—fifty thousand of their camels, two hundred and fifty thousand of their sheep, and two thousand of their donkeys—also one hundred thousand of their men; [22]for many fell dead, because the war *was* God's. And they dwelt in their place until the captivity.

4:33 [a]Or *Baalath Beer* (compare Joshua 19:8) **5:6** [a]Hebrew *Tilgath-Pilneser*

5:1 Reuben lost his firstborn rights, including a double portion of inheritance (Deut. 21:17) because he committed incest with his father's concubine Bilhah (Gen. 35:22).

5:6 Tiglath-Pileser III, king of Assyria from 745–727 B.C., was also known as Pul in the OT (v. 26, see chart, The Kings of Assyria). After stabilizing his kingdom, he began military campaigns against smaller realms such as Palestine. Kings of the northern kingdom paid monetary tribute to Tiglath-Pileser for his protection (2 Kin. 15:19, 20). Ahaz, king of Judah, made an alliance with him against the king of Israel and the king of Syria (2 Kin. 16:5–9; see chart, The Kings and Their Conflicts).

This episode may be Tiglath-Pileser's conquering of the Transjordan region and carrying the people into exile in 733 B.C. (2 Kin. 15:29). Although the date given to the captivity of the northern kingdom by Assyria is 722 B.C., the deportation of Israel to other parts of the Assyrian Empire occurred in stages. This episode is consistent with the chronicler's theme of retribution.

5:10 The Hagrites, descendants of Hagar, the Egyptian mother of Ishmael, were traditional enemies of the Transjordan tribes (vv. 19, 20; Ps. 83:5–8).

The Family of Manasseh (East)

23So the children of the half-tribe of Manasseh dwelt in the land. Their *numbers* increased from Bashan to Baal Hermon, that is, to Senir, or Mount Hermon. 24These *were* the heads of their fathers' houses: Epher, Ishi, Eliel, Azriel, Jeremiah, Hodaviah, and Jahdiel. They were mighty men of valor, famous men, *and* heads of their fathers' houses.

25And they were unfaithful to the God of their fathers, and played the harlot after the gods of the peoples of the land, whom God had destroyed before them. 26So the God of Israel stirred up the spirit of Pul king of Assyria, that is, Tiglath-Pileser[a] king of Assyria. He carried the Reubenites, the Gadites, and the half-tribe of Manasseh into captivity. He took them to Halah, Habor, Hara, and the river of Gozan to this day.

The Family of Levi

6 The sons of Levi *were* Gershon, Kohath, and Merari. 2The sons of Kohath *were* Amram, Izhar, Hebron, and Uzziel. 3The children of Amram *were* Aaron, Moses, and Miriam. And the sons of Aaron *were* Nadab, Abihu, Eleazar, and Ithamar. 4Eleazar begot Phinehas, *and* Phinehas begot Abishua; 5Abishua begot Bukki, and Bukki begot Uzzi; 6Uzzi begot Zerahiah, and Zerahiah begot Meraioth; 7Meraioth begot Amariah, and Amariah begot Ahitub; 8Ahitub begot Zadok, and Zadok begot Ahimaaz; 9Ahimaaz begot Azariah, and Azariah

begot Johanan; 10Johanan begot Azariah (it was he who ministered as priest in the temple that Solomon built in Jerusalem); 11Azariah begot Amariah, and Amariah begot Ahitub; 12Ahitub begot Zadok, and Zadok begot Shallum; 13Shallum begot Hilkiah, and Hilkiah begot Azariah; 14Azariah begot Seraiah, and Seraiah begot Jehozadak. 15Jehozadak went *into captivity* when the LORD carried Judah and Jerusalem into captivity by the hand of Nebuchadnezzar.

16The sons of Levi *were* Gershon,[a] Kohath, and Merari. 17These are the names of the sons of Gershon: Libni and Shimei. 18The sons of Kohath *were* Amram, Izhar, Hebron, and Uzziel. 19The sons of Merari *were* Mahli and Mushi. Now these *are* the families of the Levites according to their fathers: 20Of Gershon *were* Libni his son, Jahath his son, Zimmah his son, 21Joah his son, Iddo his son, Zerah his son, *and* Jeatherai his son. 22The sons of Kohath *were* Amminadab his son, Korah his son, Assir his son, 23Elkanah his son, Ebiasaph his son, Assir his son, 24Tahath his son, Uriel his son, Uzziah his son, and Shaul his son. 25The sons of Elkanah *were* Amasai and Ahimoth. 26*As for* Elkanah,[a] the sons of Elkanah *were* Zophai[b] his son, Nahath[c] his son, 27Eliab[a] his son, Jeroham his son, *and* Elkanah his

5:26 [a]Hebrew *Tilgath-Pileser* 6:16 [a]Hebrew *Gershom* (alternate spelling of *Gershon*, as in verses 1, 17, 20, 43, 62, and 71) 6:26 [a]Compare verse 35 [b]Spelled *Zuph* in verse 35 and 1 Samuel 1:1 [c]Compare verse 34 6:27 [a]Compare verse 34

5:23, 24 The inheritance for Joseph had been split between his two sons, Ephraim and Manasseh, on either side of the Jordan River (Gen. 48:1–22; Josh. 16:1–17:18; see 1 Chr. 7:28, 29, note). The "half-tribe of Manasseh" settled east of the Jordan in the Transjordan.

5:25, 26 Israel continually acted unfaithfully before God (2 Kin. 17:7–18). The metaphor of a harlot is used often to describe Israel's unfaithfulness (see the Book of Hosea). General unfaithfulness is a characteristic of Israel when the nation worshiped other gods (2 Kin. 5:25). Thus, the king of Assyria rose up against them (see 1 Chr. 5:6, note). In accord with the concept of retribution in Chronicles, unfaithfulness was punished. The Transjordan tribes were placed in captivity by the hand of God. The lands mentioned are those to which the northern kingdom was exiled in 722 B.C. by Shalmaneser V (727–722 B.C.), the son of Tiglath-Pileser III (see v. 6, note; 2 Kin. 17:6; see chart, The Kings of Assyria). The Assyrian method of dealing with conquered nations was to scatter them throughout the Assyrian Empire. Other conquered nations were then placed in Palestine (Samaria) in their stead (2 Kin. 17:24).

6:1 The sons of Levi are listed in this longest part of the genealogy of Israel (1 Chr. 4:1—7:40; compare with Judah's sole position in 1 Chr. 2:3—3:24). This emphasis on Levi and Judah is consistent with the chronicler's focus on David's throne and the temple. The genealogy of Levi is divided into four parts. The genealogy of the high priestly line of Aaron is given first (1 Chr. 6:1–15). Next, the sons of Levi are divided into three groups, each headed by a son: Gershon, Kohath, Merari (1 Chr. 6:16–30). The temple musicians were appointed by David, and

other Levites were shown to be subordinate to the line of Aaron (vv. 31–53). Finally, the dwelling places of the Levites throughout Israel are given (vv. 54–81).

6:3 The genealogy of the high priestly line, which followed from Levi through Kohath to Aaron and Eleazar is noted (vv. 1–4). Aaron's sons Nadab and Abihu were put to death by the Lord because of their sin (Lev. 10:1–3; Num. 3:4). The dominant line of the high priest descending through Eleazar is extended to the time of Solomon and ends with the Exile (1 Chr. 6:10–15). Focus is placed on the temple with the explanation regarding Azariah (v. 10). Hilkiah was high priest during the reforms of Josiah (v. 13; 2 Chr. 34; 35). Seraiah was killed at the time of the Exile (1 Chr. 6:14; 2 Kin. 25:18–21). Some were omitted from this genealogy, such as Jehoiada (2 Chr. 22:11), Azariah (2 Chr. 31:10), Urijah (2 Kin. 16:11), and others.

6:16 The Levites (vv. 33–47; see Ex. 6:16–19) descended from the three sons of Levi: Gershon (1 Chr. 6:17, 20, 21); Kohath (v. 18, 22–24); Merari (vv. 19, 29, 30). The previous verses listed the high priestly line through Kohath's son Amram (vv. 1–15). Kohath's line through Amminadab is listed here (v. 22). Levitical tradition says that Kohath is the dominant line of Levi (vv. 18, 19). "Amminadab" may be an alternate for Izhar (v. 2; Num. 16:1) or may be a genealogical addition (see 1 Chr. 1:1–4, note). The use of the name by the chronicler is deliberate in order to establish a connection between the Levites and David. Aaron married the daughter of Amminadab from the tribe of Judah (Ex. 6:23; Ruth 4:19; 1 Chr. 2:10). Samuel, elsewhere called an Ephraimite (1 Chr. 6:28; 1 Sam. 1:1), exercised Levitical duties (1 Sam. 2:11, 18; 10:8).

son. [28]The sons of Samuel were Joel[a] the firstborn, and Abijah the second.[b] [29]The sons of Merari were Mahli, Libni his son, Shimei his son, Uzzah his son, [30]Shimea his son, Haggiah his son, and Asaiah his son.

Musicians in the House of the LORD

[31]Now these are the men whom David appointed over the service of song in the house of the LORD, after the ark came to rest. [32]They were ministering with music before the dwelling place of the tabernacle of meeting, until Solomon had built the house of the LORD in Jerusalem, and they served in their office according to their order.

[33]And these are the ones who ministered with their sons: Of the sons of the Kohathites were Heman the singer, the son of Joel, the son of Samuel, [34]the son of Elkanah, the son of Jeroham, the son of Eliel,[a] the son of Toah,[b] [35]the son of Zuph, the son of Elkanah, the son of Mahath, the son of Amasai, [36]the son of Elkanah, the son of Joel, the son of Azariah, the son of Zephaniah, [37]the son of Tahath, the son of Assir, the son of Ebiasaph, the son of Korah, [38]the son of Izhar, the son of Kohath, the son of Levi, the son of Israel. [39]And his brother Asaph, who stood at his right hand, was Asaph the son of Berachiah, the son of Shimea, [40]the son of Michael, the son of Baaseiah, the son of Malchijah, [41]the son of Ethni, the son of Zerah, the son of Adaiah, [42]the son of Ethan, the son of Zimmah, the son of Shimei, [43]the son of Jahath, the son of Gershon, the son of Levi.

[44]Their brethren, the sons of Merari, on the left hand, were Ethan the son of Kishi, the son of Abdi, the son of Malluch, [45]the son of Hashabiah, the son of Amaziah, the son of Hilkiah, [46]the son of Amzi, the son of Bani, the son of Shamer, [47]the son of Mahli, the son of Mushi, the son of Merari, the son of Levi.

[48]And their brethren, the Levites, were appointed to every kind of service of the tabernacle of the house of God.

The Family of Aaron

[49]But Aaron and his sons offered sacrifices on the altar of burnt offering and on the altar of incense, for all the work of the Most Holy Place, and to make atonement for Israel, according to all that Moses the servant of God had commanded. [50]Now these are the sons of Aaron: Eleazar his son, Phinehas his son, Abishua his son, [51]Bukki his son, Uzzi

his son, Zerahiah his son, [52]Meraioth his son, Amariah his son, Ahitub his son, [53]Zadok his son, and Ahimaaz his son.

Dwelling Places of the Levites

[54]Now these are their dwelling places throughout their settlements in their territory, for they were given by lot to the sons of Aaron, of the family of the Kohathites: [55]They gave them Hebron in the land of Judah, with its surrounding commonlands. [56]But the fields of the city and its villages they gave to Caleb the son of Jephunneh. [57]And to the sons of Aaron they gave one of the cities of refuge, Hebron; also Libnah with its commonlands, Jattir, Eshtemoa with its common-lands, [58]Hilen[a] with its common-lands, Debir with its common-lands, [59]Ashan[a] with its common-lands, and Beth Shemesh with its common-lands. [60]And from the tribe of Benjamin: Geba with its common-lands, Alemeth[a] with its common-lands, and Anathoth with its common-lands. All their cities among their families were thirteen.

[61]To the rest of the family of the tribe of the Kohathites they gave by lot ten cities from half the tribe of Manasseh. [62]And to the sons of Gershon, throughout their families, they gave thirteen cities from the tribe of Issachar, from the tribe of Asher, from the tribe of Naphtali, and from the tribe of Manasseh in Bashan. [63]To the sons of Merari, throughout their families, they gave twelve cities from the tribe of Reuben, from the tribe of Gad, and from the tribe of Zebulun. [64]So the children of Israel gave these cities with their common-lands to the Levites. [65]And they gave by lot from the tribe of the children of Judah, from the tribe of the children of Simeon, and from the tribe of the children of Benjamin these cities which are called by their names.

[66]Now some of the families of the sons of Kohath were given cities as their territory from the tribe of Ephraim. [67]And they gave them one of the cities of refuge, Shechem with its common-lands, in the mountains of Ephraim, also Gezer with its common-lands, [68]Jokmeam with its common-lands, Beth Horon with its common-lands, [69]Aijalon with its common-lands, and Gath Rimmon with its

---

6:28 [a]Following Septuagint, Syriac, and Arabic (compare verse 33 and 1 Samuel 8:2) [b]Hebrew Vasheni   6:34 [a]Spelled Elihu in 1 Samuel 1:1 [b]Spelled Tohu in 1 Samuel 1:1   6:58 [a]Spelled Holon in Joshua 21:15 6:59 [a]Spelled Ain in Joshua 21:16   6:60 [a]Spelled Almon in Joshua 21:18

6:31 The temple musicians (vv. 16–30; 1 Chr. 15:17–19) descended from the sons of Levi: Heman from Kohath (1 Chr. 6: 33–38); Asaph from Gershon (vv. 39–43); Ethan from Merari (vv. 44–47). Although the musicians were appointed by David, tracing their lineage back to Levi legitimized their appointment according to the will of God (vv. 31, 32; 1 Chr. 15).

6:54 The Levites were not given a specific inheritance within the Promised Land but were scattered throughout Israel to areas donated by the other tribes (Josh. 21:1–42). The central cities of Hebron (of Judah, 1 Chr. 6:55) and Shechem (of Ephraim, v. 67) also head each summary. Judah and Ephraim, when appearing together, stand for all Israel. All other tribes contributed to the Levites.

common-lands. [70]And from the half-tribe of Manasseh: Aner with its common-lands and Bileam with its common-lands, for the rest of the family of the sons of Kohath.

[71]From the family of the half-tribe of Manasseh the sons of Gershon *were given* Golan in Bashan with its common-lands and Ashtaroth with its common-lands. [72]And from the tribe of Issachar: Kedesh with its common-lands, Daberath with its common-lands, [73]Ramoth with its common-lands, and Anem with its common-lands. [74]And from the tribe of Asher: Mashal with its common-lands, Abdon with its common-lands, [75]Hukok with its common-lands, and Rehob with its common-lands. [76]And from the tribe of Naphtali: Kedesh in Galilee with its common-lands, Hammon with its common-lands, and Kirjathaim with its common-lands.

[77]From the tribe of Zebulun the rest of the children of Merari *were given* Rimmon[a] with its common-lands and Tabor with its common-lands. [78]And on the other side of the Jordan, across from Jericho, on the east side of the Jordan, *they were given* from the tribe of Reuben: Bezer in the wilderness with its common-lands, Jahzah with its common-lands, [79]Kedemoth with its common-lands, and Mephaath with its common-lands. [80]And from the tribe of Gad: Ramoth in Gilead with its common-lands, Mahanaim with its common-lands, [81]Heshbon with its common-lands, and Jazer with its common-lands.

The Family of Issachar

7The sons of Issachar *were* Tola, Puah,[a] Jashub, and Shimron— four *in all.* [2]The sons of Tola *were* Uzzi, Rephaiah, Jeriel, Jahmai, Jibsam, and Shemuel, heads of their father's house. *The sons of* Tola *were* mighty men of valor in their generations; their number in the days of David *was* twenty-two thousand six hundred. [3]The son of Uzzi *was* Izrahiah, and the sons of Izrahiah *were* Michael, Obadiah, Joel, and Ishiah. All five of them *were* chief men. [4]And with them, by their generations, according to their fathers' houses, *were* thirty-six thousand troops ready for war; for they had many wives and sons.

[5]Now their brethren among all the families of Issachar *were* mighty men of valor, listed by their genealogies, eighty-seven thousand in all.

The Family of Benjamin

[6]*The sons* of Benjamin *were* Bela, Becher, and Jediael— three *in all.* [7]The sons of Bela were Ezbon, Uzzi, Uzziel, Jerimoth, and Iri— five *in all.* They *were* heads of *their* fathers' houses, and they were listed by their genealogies, twenty-two thousand and thirty-four mighty men of valor.

[8]The sons of Becher *were* Zemirah, Joash, Eliezer, Elioenai, Omri, Jerimoth, Abijah, Anathoth, and Alemeth. All these *are* the sons of Becher. [9]And they were recorded by genealogy according to their generations, heads of their fathers' houses, twenty thousand two hundred mighty men of valor. [10]The son of Jediael *was* Bilhan, and the sons of Bilhan *were* Jeush, Benjamin, Ehud, Chenaanah, Zethan, Tharshish, and Ahishahar.

[11]All these sons of Jediael *were* heads of their fathers' houses; *there were* seventeen thousand two hundred mighty men of valor fit to go out for war *and* battle. [12]Shuppim and Huppim[a] *were* the sons of Ir, *and* Hushim *was* the son of Aher.

The Family of Naphtali

[13]The sons of Naphtali *were* Jahziel,[a] Guni, Jezer, and Shallum,[b] the sons of Bilhah.

The Family of Manasseh (West)

[14]The descendants of Manasseh: his Syrian concubine bore him Machir the father of Gilead, the father of Asriel.[a] [15]Machir took as his wife *the sister* of Huppim and Shuppim,[a] whose name *was* Maachah. The name of *Gilead's* grandson[b] *was* Zelophehad,[c] but Zelophehad begot only daughters. [16](Maachah the wife of Machir bore a son, and she called his name Peresh. The name of his brother *was* Sheresh, and his sons *were* Ulam and Rakem. [17]The son of Ulam *was* Bedan.) These *were* the descendants of Gilead the son of Machir, the son of Manasseh.

[18]His sister Hammoleketh bore Ishhod, Abiezer, and Mahlah.

[19]And the sons of Shemida were Ahian, Shechem, Likhi, and Aniam.

The Family of Ephraim

[20]The sons of Ephraim *were* Shuthelah, Bered his son, Tahath his son, Eladah his son, Tahath his son, [21]Zabad his son, Shuthelah his son, and Ezer and Elead. The men of Gath who were born in *that* land killed *them* because they came down to take away their cattle. [22]Then Ephraim their father mourned many days, and his brethren came to comfort him.

6:77 [a]Hebrew *Rimmono,* alternate spelling of *Rimmon;* see 4:32   **7:1** [a]Spelled *Puvah* in Genesis 46:13   **7:12** [a]Called *Hupham* in Numbers 26:39   **7:13** [a]Spelled *Jahzeel* in Genesis 46:24   [b]Spelled *Shillem* in Genesis 46:24   **7:14** [a]The son of Gilead (compare Numbers 26:30, 31)   **7:15** [a]Compare verse 12   [b]Literally *the second*   [c]Compare Numbers 26:30–33

7:20–27 The genealogy of Ephraim culminated with Joshua, the successor to Moses and the conqueror of the Promised Land (v. 27). The story of Ezer and Elead is otherwise unknown in Scripture but is placed here solely to explain the naming of Beriah, the ancestor of Joshua.

²³And when he went in to his wife, she conceived and bore a son; and he called his name Beriah,ᵃ because tragedy had come upon his house. ²⁴Now his daughter *was* Sheerah, who built Lower and Upper Beth Horon and Uzzen Sheerah; ²⁵and Rephah *was* his son, *as well as* Resheph, and Telah his son, Tahan his son, ²⁶Laadan his son, Ammihud his son, Elishama his son, ²⁷Nunᵃ his son, and Joshua his son.

²⁸Now their possessions and dwelling places *were* Bethel and its towns: to the east Naaran, to the west Gezer and its towns, and Shechem and its towns, as far as Ayyahᵃ and its towns; ²⁹and by the borders of the children of Manasseh *were* Beth Shean and its towns, Taanach and its towns, Megiddo and its towns, Dor and its towns. In these dwelt the children of Joseph, the son of Israel.

The Family of Asher

³⁰The sons of Asher *were* Imnah, Ishvah, Ishvi, Beriah, and their sister Serah. ³¹The sons of Beriah *were* Heber and Malchiel, who was the father of Birzaith.ᵃ ³²And Heber begot Japhlet, Shomer,ᵃ Hotham,ᵇ and their sister Shua. ³³The sons of Japhlet *were* Pasach, Bimhal, and Ashvath. These *were* the children of Japhlet. ³⁴The sons of Shemer *were* Ahi, Rohgah, Jehubbah, and Aram. ³⁵And the sons of his brother Helem *were* Zophah, Imna, Shelesh, and Amal. ³⁶The sons of Zophah *were* Suah, Harnepher, Shual, Beri, Imrah, ³⁷Bezer, Hod, Shamma, Shilshah, Jithran,ᵃ and Beera. ³⁸The sons of Jether *were* Jephunneh, Pispah, and Ara. ³⁹The sons of Ulla *were* Arah, Haniel, and Rizia.

⁴⁰All these *were* the children of Asher, heads of *their* fathers' houses, choice men, mighty men of valor, chief leaders. And they were recorded by genealogies among the army fit for battle; their number *was* twenty-six thousand.

The Family Tree of King Saul of Benjamin

8 Now Benjamin begot Bela his firstborn, Ashbel the second, Aharahᵃ the third, ²Nohah the fourth, and Rapha the fifth. ³The sons of Bela *were* Addar,ᵃ Gera, Abihud, ⁴Abishua, Naaman, Ahoah, ⁵Gera, Shephuphan, and Huram.

⁶These *are* the sons of Ehud, who were the heads of the fathers' *houses* of the inhabitants of Geba, and who forced them to move to Manahath: ⁷Naaman, Ahijah, and Gera who forced them to move. He begot Uzza and Ahihud.

⁸Also Shaharaim had children in the country of Moab, after he had sent away Hushim and Baara his wives. ⁹By Hodesh his wife he begot Jobab, Zibia, Mesha, Malcam, ¹⁰Jeuz, Sachiah, and Mirmah. These *were* his sons, heads of their fathers' *houses*.

¹¹And by Hushim he begot Abitub and Elpaal. ¹²The sons of Elpaal *were* Eber, Misham, and Shemed, who built Ono and Lod with its towns; ¹³and Beriah and Shema, who *were* heads of their fathers' *houses* of the inhabitants of Aijalon, who drove out the inhabitants of Gath. ¹⁴Ahio, Shashak, Jeremoth, ¹⁵Zebadiah, Arad, Eder, ¹⁶Michael, Ispah, and Joha *were* the sons of Beriah. ¹⁷Zebadiah, Meshullam, Hizki, Heber, ¹⁸Ishmerai, Jizliah, and Jobab *were* the sons of Elpaal. ¹⁹Jakim, Zichri, Zabdi, ²⁰Elienai, Zillethai, Eliel, ²¹Adaiah, Beraiah, and Shimrath *were* the sons of Shimei. ²²Ishpan, Eber, Eliel, ²³Abdon, Zichri, Hanan, ²⁴Hananiah, Elam, Antothijah, ²⁵Iphdeiah, and Penuel *were* the sons of Shashak. ²⁶Shamsherai, Shehariah, Athaliah, ²⁷Jaareshiah, Elijah, and Zichri *were* the sons of Jeroham.

²⁸These *were* heads of the fathers' *houses* by their generations, chief men. These dwelt in Jerusalem.

²⁹Now the father of Gibeon, whose wife's name *was* Maacah, dwelt at Gibeon. ³⁰And his firstborn son *was* Abdon, then Zur, Kish, Baal, Nadab, ³¹Gedor, Ahio, Zecher, ³²and Mikloth, *who* begot Shimeah.ᵃ They also dwelt alongside their relatives in Jerusalem, with their brethren. ³³Nerᵃ begot Kish, Kish begot Saul, and Saul begot Jonathan, Malchishua, Abinadab,ᵇ and Esh-Baal.ᶜ ³⁴The son of Jonathan *was* Merib-Baal,ᵃ and Merib-Baal begot Micah. ³⁵The sons of Micah *were* Pithon, Melech, Tarea, and Ahaz. ³⁶And Ahaz begot Jehoaddah;ᵃ Jehoaddah begot Alemeth, Azmaveth, and Zimri; and Zimri begot Moza. ³⁷Moza begot Binea, Raphahᵃ his son, Eleasah his son, *and* Azel his son.

³⁸Azel had six sons whose names *were* these: Azrikam, Bocheru, Ishmael, Sheariah, Obadiah,

···················

7:23 ᵃLiterally *In Tragedy*   **7:27** ᵃHebrew *Non*   **7:28** ᵃMany Hebrew manuscripts, Bomberg, Septuagint, Targum, and Vulgate read *Gazza.*   **7:31** ᵃOr *Birzavith* or *Birzoth*   **7:32** ᵃSpelled *Shemer* in verse 34   ᵇSpelled *Helem* in verse 35   **7:37** ᵃSpelled *Jether* in verse 38   **8:1** ᵃSpelled *Ahiram* in Numbers 26:38   **8:3** ᵃCalled *Ard* in Numbers 26:40   **8:32** ᵃSpelled *Shimeam* in 9:38   **8:33** ᵃAlso the son of Gibeon (compare 9:36, 39)   ᵇCalled *Jishui* in 1 Samuel 14:49   ᶜCalled *Ishbosheth* in 2 Samuel 2:8 and elsewhere   **8:34** ᵃCalled *Mephibosheth* in 2 Samuel 4:4   **8:36** ᵃSpelled *Jarah* in 9:42   **8:37** ᵃSpelled *Rephaiah* in 9:43

7:28, 29 Joseph's inheritance is not named for him but rather for his two sons Manasseh and Ephraim. Ephraim was the chosen son and therefore the dominant tribe (Gen. 48:11–20). The land occupied by the sons of Joseph was divided between Manasseh and Ephraim. Ephraim is a name equivalent to Israel and the northern kingdom (see chart, Terminology for the Land).

8:1 The genealogy of Benjamin is longer than any except those of Judah and Levi. This link may reflect the tradition that Benjamin remained loyal to Judah and to David's throne after the split of the kingdom. This is not a repetition of a previous genealogy (1 Chr. 7:6–12) but lists additional descendants with Saul as the central figure (1 Chr. 8:29–38, repeated in 1 Chr. 9:35–44).

and Hanan. All these *were* the sons of Azel. ³⁹And the sons of Eshek his brother *were* Ulam his first-born, Jeush the second, and Eliphelet the third.

⁴⁰The sons of Ulam were mighty men of valor—archers. *They* had many sons and grand-sons, one hundred and fifty *in all*. These *were* all sons of Benjamin.

9 So all Israel was recorded by genealogies, and indeed, they *were* inscribed in the book of the kings of Israel. But Judah was carried away captive to Babylon because of their unfaithfulness. ²And the first inhabitants who *dwelt* in their possessions in their cities *were* Israelites, priests, Levites, and the Nethinim.

Dwellers in Jerusalem

³Now in Jerusalem the children of Judah dwelt, and some of the children of Benjamin, and of the children of Ephraim and Manasseh: ⁴Uthai the son of Ammihud, the son of Omri, the son of Imri, the son of Bani, of the descendants of Perez, the son of Judah. ⁵Of the Shilonites: Asaiah the firstborn and his sons. ⁶Of the sons of Zerah: Jeuel, and their brethren—six hundred and ninety. ⁷Of the sons of Benjamin: Sallu the son of Meshullam, the son of Hodaviah, the son of Hassenuah; ⁸Ibneiah the son of Jeroham; Elah the son of Uzzi, the son of Michri; Meshullam the son of Shephatiah, the son of Reuel, the son of Ibnijah; ⁹and their brethren, according to their generations— nine hundred and fifty-six. All these men *were* heads of a father's *house* in their fathers' houses.

The Priests at Jerusalem

¹⁰Of the priests: Jedaiah, Jehoiarib, and Jachin; ¹¹Azariah the son of Hilkiah, the son of Meshullam, the son of Zadok, the son of Meraioth, the son of Ahitub, the officer over the house of God; ¹²Adaiah the son of Jeroham, the son of Pashur, the son of Malchijah; Maasai the son of Adiel, the son of Jahzerah, the son of Meshullam, the son of Meshillemith, the son of Immer; ¹³and their brethren, heads of their fathers' houses— one thousand seven hundred and sixty. *They were* very able men for the work of the service of the house of God.

The Levites at Jerusalem

¹⁴Of the Levites: Shemaiah the son of Hasshub, the son of Azrikam, the son of Hashabiah, of the sons of Merari; ¹⁵Bakbakkar, Heresh, Galal, and Mattaniah the son of Micah, the son of Zichri, the son of Asaph; ¹⁶Obadiah the son of Shemaiah, the son of Galal, the son of Jeduthun; and Berechiah the son of Asa, the son of Elkanah, who lived in the villages of the Netophathites.

The Levite Gatekeepers

¹⁷And the gatekeepers *were* Shallum, Akkub, Talmon, Ahiman, and their brethren. Shallum *was* the chief. ¹⁸Until then *they had been* gatekeepers for the camps of the children of Levi at the King's Gate on the east. ¹⁹Shallum the son of Kore, the son of Ebiasaph, the son of Korah, and his brethren, from his father's house, the Korahites, *were* in charge of the work of the service, gatekeepers of the tabernacle. Their fathers had been keepers of the entrance to the camp of the LORD. ²⁰And Phinehas the son of Eleazar had been the officer over them in time past; the LORD *was* with him. ²¹Zechariah the son of Meshelemiah *was* keeper of the door of the tabernacle of meeting.

²²All those chosen as gatekeepers *were* two hundred and twelve. They were recorded by their genealogy, in their villages. David and Samuel the seer had appointed them to their trusted office. ²³So they and their children *were* in charge of the gates of the house of the LORD, the house of the tabernacle, by assignment. ²⁴The gatekeepers were assigned to the four directions: the east, west, north, and south. ²⁵And their brethren in their villages *had* to come with them from time to time for seven days. ²⁶For in this trusted office *were* four chief gatekeepers; they were Levites. And they had charge over the chambers and treasuries of the house of God. ²⁷And they lodged *all* around the house of God because they *had* the responsibility, and they *were* in charge of opening *it* every morning.

Other Levite Responsibilities

²⁸Now *some* of them were in charge of the serving vessels, for they brought them in and took

---

9:1 The book of the kings of Israel, otherwise unknown, was probably used as a source for the chronicler's work. Judah's captivity is mentioned since the chronicler is interested only in the return to Judah, and specifically the return to Jerusalem. Judah was punished for unfaithfulness, but now the true inhabitants of Jerusalem must live in faithfulness. Only the faithful in Jerusalem can be called "all Israel" (see Introduction: Themes).

9:2 Postexilic Jerusalem. The focus is on groups who returned from exile to Jerusalem (Neh. 11). The Israelites were from the tribes of Judah, Benjamin, Ephraim, and Manasseh (1 Chr. 9:3–9). These designations for the southern and northern

kingdoms, respectively, picture all Israel as having returned and now living in Jerusalem. The priests (vv. 10–13) were to serve in the tabernacle/temple (see 1 Chr. 28:1, note), and the Levites returned to be available for service as well (1 Chr. 9:14–16). The "Nethinim" (Heb. *natan,* lit. "to give," v. 2), probably refers to those who were given to the service of the house of the Lord (see 1 Chr. 23:24, note). They acted as gatekeepers (1 Chr. 9:17–27; 1 Chr. 15:18, 23, 24; 23:5; 26:1–19). They were also in charge of serving vessels (1 Chr. 9:28) and cared for the furnishings and the implements of the sanctuary—the incense and ointment (vv. 29, 30) and the showbread (vv. 31, 32; 1 Chr. 23:29). They were also singers (1 Chr. 6:31–47; 25).

them out by count. [29]*Some* of them *were* appointed over the furnishings and over all the implements of the sanctuary, and over the fine flour and the wine and the oil and the incense and the spices. [30]And *some* of the sons of the priests made the ointment of the spices.

[31]Mattithiah of the Levites, the firstborn of Shallum the Korahite, had the trusted office over the things that were baked in the pans. [32]And some of their brethren of the sons of the Kohathites *were* in charge of preparing the showbread for every Sabbath.

[33]These are the singers, heads of the fathers' *houses* of the Levites, *who lodged* in the chambers, *and were* free *from other duties;* for they were employed in *that* work day and night. [34]These heads of the fathers' *houses* of the Levites *were* heads throughout their generations. They dwelt at Jerusalem.

The Family of King Saul

[35]Jeiel the father of Gibeon, whose wife's name *was* Maacah, dwelt at Gibeon. [36]His firstborn son *was* Abdon, then Zur, Kish, Baal, Ner, Nadab, [37]Gedor, Ahio, Zechariah,[a] and Mikloth. [38]And Mikloth begot Shimeam.[a] They also dwelt alongside their relatives in Jerusalem, with their brethren. [39]Ner begot Kish, Kish begot Saul, and Saul begot Jonathan, Malchishua, Abinadab, and Esh-Baal. [40]The son of Jonathan *was* Merib-Baal, and Merib-Baal begot Micah. [41]The sons of Micah *were* Pithon, Melech, Tahrea,[a] and Ahaz.[b] [42]And Ahaz begot Jarah;[a] Jarah begot Alemeth, Azmaveth, and Zimri; and Zimri begot Moza; [43]Moza begot Binea, Rephaiah[a] his son, Eleasah his son, and Azel his son.

[44]And Azel had six sons whose names *were* these: Azrikam, Bocheru, Ishmael, Sheariah, Obadiah, and Hanan; these *were* the sons of Azel.

Tragic End of Saul and His Sons

10 Now the Philistines fought against Israel; and the men of Israel fled from before the Philistines, and fell slain on Mount Gilboa. [2]Then the Philistines followed hard after Saul and his sons. And the Philistines killed Jonathan, Abinadab, and Malchishua, Saul's sons. [3]The battle became fierce against Saul. The archers hit him, and he was wounded by the archers. [4]Then Saul said to his armorbearer, "Draw your sword, and thrust me

through with it, lest these uncircumcised men come and abuse me." But his armorbearer would not, for he was greatly afraid. Therefore Saul took a sword and fell on it. [5]And when his armorbearer saw that Saul was dead, he also fell on his sword and died. [6]So Saul and his three sons died, and all his house died together. [7]And when all the men of Israel who *were* in the valley saw that they had fled and that Saul and his sons were dead, they forsook their cities and fled; then the Philistines came and dwelt in them.

[8]So it happened the next day, when the Philistines came to strip the slain, that they found Saul and his sons fallen on Mount Gilboa. [9]And they stripped him and took his head and his armor, and sent word throughout the land of the Philistines to proclaim the news *in the temple* of their idols and among the people. [10]Then they put his armor in the temple of their gods, and fastened his head in the temple of Dagon.

[11]And when all Jabesh Gilead heard all that the Philistines had done to Saul, [12]all the valiant men arose and took the body of Saul and the bodies of his sons; and they brought them to Jabesh, and buried their bones under the tamarisk tree at Jabesh, and fasted seven days.

[13]So Saul died for his unfaithfulness which he had committed against the LORD, because he did not keep the word of the LORD, and also because he consulted a medium for guidance. [14]But *he* did not inquire of the LORD; therefore He killed him, and turned the kingdom over to David the son of Jesse.

David Made King over All Israel

11 Then all Israel came together to David at Hebron, saying, "Indeed we *are* your bone and your flesh. [2]Also, in time past, even when Saul was king, you *were* the one who led Israel out and brought them in; and the LORD your God said to you, 'You shall shepherd My people Israel, and be ruler over My people Israel.' " [3]Therefore all the elders of Israel came to the king at Hebron, and David made a covenant with them at Hebron before the LORD. And they anointed David king over Israel, according to the word of the LORD by Samuel.

· · · · · · · · · · · · · · · · ·

9:37 [a]Called *Zecher* in 8:31 9:38 [a]Spelled *Shimeah* in 8:32 9:41 [a]Spelled *Tarea* in 8:35 [b]Following Arabic, Syriac, Targum, and Vulgate (compare 8:35); Masoretic Text and Septuagint omit *and Ahaz.* 9:42 [a]Spelled *Jehoaddah* in 8:36 9:43 [a]Spelled *Raphah* in 8:37

9:35–44 A genealogical introduction of Saul takes the reader to the time before the Exile (see 1 Chr. 8:29–38). It introduces Saul, whose reign is seen as merely a prelude to David (1 Chr. 10:1–14; chart, The Family Tree of Saul).

10:4 The death of Saul is interpreted by the chronicler as the destruction of Saul's entire family (v. 6), thereby eliminating all threats to David's throne (see 1 Sam. 31). The treatment of Saul's body emphasizes the total destruction of his dynasty

(1 Chr. 9:8–10; 1 Sam. 31:9, 10). Saul's house was destroyed, but David's house would flourish (1 Chr. 17:9–12).

10:13, 14 Saul's death is explained as God's punishment for sin. These verses are unique to the chronicler. Saul did not look to the Lord but sought the advice of a medium for guidance (1 Sam. 28:3–25). In general, Saul's life was characterized by unfaithfulness. Thus, the kingdom was taken from Saul and given to David—the ideal and faithful king.

The City of David

4And David and all Israel went to Jerusalem, which is Jebus, where the Jebusites *were*, the inhabitants of the land. 5But the inhabitants of Jebus said to David, "You shall not come in here!" Nevertheless David took the stronghold of Zion (that is, the City of David). 6Now David said, "Whoever attacks the Jebusites first shall be chief and captain." And Joab the son of Zeruiah went up first, and became chief. 7Then David dwelt in the stronghold; therefore they called it the City of David. 8And he built the city around it, from the Millo[a] to the surrounding area. Joab repaired the rest of the city. 9So David went on and became great, and the LORD of hosts *was* with him.

The Mighty Men of David

10Now these *were* the heads of the mighty men whom David had, who strengthened themselves with him in his kingdom, with all Israel, to make him king, according to the word of the LORD concerning Israel.

11And this *is* the number of the mighty men whom David had: Jashobeam the son of a Hachmonite, chief of the captains;[a] he had lifted up his spear against three hundred, killed *by him* at one time.

12After him *was* Eleazar the son of Dodo, the Ahohite, who *was one* of the three mighty men. 13He was with David at Pasdammim. Now there the Philistines were gathered for battle, and there was a piece of ground full of barley. So the people fled from the Philistines. 14But they stationed themselves in the middle of *that* field, defended it, and killed the Philistines. So the LORD brought about a great victory.

15Now three of the thirty chief men went down to the rock to David, into the cave of Adullam; and the army of the Philistines encamped in the Valley of Rephaim. 16David *was* then in the stronghold, and the garrison of the Philistines *was* then in Bethlehem. 17And David said with longing, "Oh, that someone would give me a drink of water from the well of Bethlehem, which is by the gate!" 18So the three broke through the camp of the Philistines, drew water from the well of Bethlehem that *was* by the gate, and took *it* and brought *it* to David. Nevertheless David would not drink it, but poured it out to the LORD. 19And he said, "Far be it from me, O my God, that I should do this! Shall I drink the blood of these men *who have put their lives in jeopardy?* For at the risk of their lives they brought it." Therefore he would not drink it. These things were done by the three mighty men.

20Abishai the brother of Joab was chief of *an-other* three.[a] He had lifted up his spear against three hundred *men,* killed *them,* and won a name among *these* three. 21Of the three he was more honored than the other two men. Therefore he became their captain. However he did not attain to the *first* three.

22Benaiah was the son of Jehoiada, the son of a valiant man from Kabzeel, who had done many deeds. He had killed two lion-like heroes of Moab. He also had gone down and killed a lion in the midst of a pit on a snowy day. 23And he killed an Egyptian, a man of *great* height, five cubits tall. In the Egyptian's hand *there was* a spear like a weaver's beam; and he went down to him with a staff, wrested the spear out of the Egyptian's hand, and killed him with his own spear. 24These *things* Benaiah the son of Jehoiada did, and won a name among three mighty men. 25Indeed he was more honored than the thirty, but he did not attain to the *first* three. And David appointed him over his guard.

26Also the mighty warriors *were* Asahel the brother of Joab, Elhanan the son of Dodo of Bethlehem, 27Shammoth the Harorite,[a] Helez the Pelonite,[b] 28Ira the son of Ikkesh the Tekoite, Abiezer the Anathothite, 29Sibbechai the Hushathite, Ilai the Ahohite, 30Maharai the Netophathite, Heled[a] the son of Baanah the Netophathite, 31Ithai[a] the son of Ribai of Gibeah, of the sons of Benjamin, Benaiah the Pirathonite, 32Hurai[a] of the brooks of Gaash, Abiel[b] the Arbathite, 33Azmaveth the Baharumite,[a] Eliahba the Shaalbonite, 34the sons of Hashem the Gizonite, Jonathan the son of Shageh the Hararite, 35Ahiam the son of Sacar the Hararite, Eliphal the son of Ur, 36Hepher the Mecherathite, Ahijah the Pelonite, 37Hezro the Carmelite, Naarai the son of Ezbai, 38Joel the brother of Nathan, Mibhar the son of Hagri, 39Zelek the Ammonite, Naharai the Berothite[a] (the armorbearer of Joab the son of Zeruiah), 40Ira the Ithrite, Gareb the Ithrite, 41Uriah the Hittite, Zabad the son of Ahlai, 42Adina the son of Shiza the Reubenite (a chief of the Reubenites) and thirty with him, 43Hanan the son of Maachah, Joshaphat the Mithnite, 44Uzzia the Ashterathite, Shama and Jeiel the sons of Hotham the Aroerite, 45Jediael the son of Shimri, and Joha

11:8 [a]Literally *The Landfill* 11:11 [a]Following Qere; Kethib, Septuagint, and Vulgate read *the thirty* (compare 2 Samuel 23:8). 11:20 [a]Following Masoretic Text, Septuagint, and Vulgate; Syriac reads *thirty.* 11:27 [a]Spelled *Harodite* in 2 Samuel 23:25 [b]Called *Paltite* in 2 Samuel 23:26 11:30 [a]Spelled *Heleb* in 2 Samuel 23:29 and *Heldai* in 1 Chronicles 27:15 11:31 [a]Spelled *Ittai* in 2 Samuel 23:29 11:32 [a]Spelled *Hiddai* in 2 Samuel 23:30 [b]Spelled *Abi-Albon* in 2 Samuel 23:31 11:33 [a]Spelled *Barhumite* in 2 Samuel 23:31 11:39 [a]Spelled *Beerothite* in 2 Samuel 23:37

11:4-9 **Joab was David's nephew** and the general of David's army (1 Chr. 27:34). He was not mentioned in the 2 Samuel 5 account. Jebus is the former name of Jerusalem, and the Jebusites were the Canaanites living in that city (Josh. 15:8). The Millo is the steep slope to the east of the city.

his brother, the Tizite, ⁴⁶Eliel the Mahavite, Jeribai and Joshaviah the sons of Elnaam, Ithmah the Moabite, ⁴⁷Eliel, Obed, and Jaasiel the Mezobaite.

The Growth of David's Army

12Now these *were* the men who came to David at Ziklag while he was still a fugitive from Saul the son of Kish; and they *were* among the mighty men, helpers in the war, ²armed with bows, using both the right hand and the left in *hurling* stones and *shooting* arrows with the bow. *They were* of Benjamin, Saul's brethren.

³The chief *was* Ahiezer, then Joash, the sons of Shemaah the Gibeathite; Jeziel and Pelet the sons of Azmaveth; Berachah, and Jehu the Anathothite; ⁴Ishmaiah the Gibeonite, a mighty man among the thirty, and over the thirty; Jeremiah, Jahaziel, Johanan, and Jozabad the Gederathite; ⁵Eluzai, Jerimoth, Bealiah, Shemariah, and Shephatiah the Haruphite; ⁶Elkanah, Jisshiah, Azarel, Joezer, and Jashobeam, the Korahites; ⁷and Joelah and Zebadiah the sons of Jeroham of Gedor.

⁸Some Gadites joined David at the stronghold in the wilderness, mighty men of valor, men trained for battle, who could handle shield and spear, whose faces *were like* the faces of lions, and *were* as swift as gazelles on the mountains: ⁹Ezer the first, Obadiah the second, Eliab the third, ¹⁰Mishmannah the fourth, Jeremiah the fifth, ¹¹Attai the sixth, Eliel the seventh, ¹²Johanan the eighth, Elzabad the ninth, ¹³Jeremiah the tenth, and Machbanai the eleventh. ¹⁴These *were* from the sons of Gad, captains of the army; the least was over a hundred, and the greatest was over a thousand. ¹⁵These *are* the ones who crossed the Jordan in the first month, when it had overflowed all its banks; and they put to flight all *those* in the valleys, to the east and to the west.

¹⁶Then some of the sons of Benjamin and Judah came to David at the stronghold. ¹⁷And David went out to meet them, and answered and said to them, "If you have come peaceably to me to help me, my heart will be united with you; but if to betray me to my enemies, since *there is* no wrong in my hands, may the God of our fathers look and bring judgment." ¹⁸Then the Spirit came upon Amasai, chief of the captains, *and he said:*

"*We are* yours, O David;
  We *are* on your side, O son of Jesse!
  Peace, peace to you,
  And peace to your helpers!
  For your God helps you."

So David received them, and made them captains of the troop.

¹⁹And *some* from Manasseh defected to David when he was going with the Philistines to battle against Saul; but they did not help them, for the lords of the Philistines sent him away by agreement, saying, "He may defect to his master Saul *and endanger* our heads." ²⁰When he went to Ziklag, those of Manasseh who defected to him were Adnah, Jozabad, Jediael, Michael, Jozabad, Elihu, and Zillethai, captains of the thousands who *were* from Manasseh. ²¹And they helped David against the bands *of raiders,* for they *were* all mighty men of valor, and they were captains in the army. ²²For at *that* time they came to David day by day to help him, until *it was* a great army, like the army of God.

David's Army at Hebron

²³Now these *were* the numbers of the divisions *that were* equipped for war, *and* came to David at Hebron to turn *over* the kingdom of Saul to him, according to the word of the LORD: ²⁴of the sons of Judah bearing shield and spear, six thousand eight hundred armed for war; ²⁵of the sons of Simeon, mighty men of valor fit for war, seven thousand one hundred; ²⁶of the sons of Levi four thousand six hundred; ²⁷Jehoiada, the leader of the Aaronites, and with him three thousand seven hundred; ²⁸Zadok, a young man, a valiant warrior, and from his father's house twenty-two captains; ²⁹of

---

12:1 The mighty men of Benjamin and Gad. Support for David was such that men from Saul's own tribe of Benjamin, even while he was king, pledged their allegiance to David. The emphasis here is not on Saul's opposition to David but on the loyalty of Benjamin to David.

12:16–18 Amasai was the chief of the captains in David's army. He is significant for the manner in which his words align with the chronicler's presentation of the complete support of all Israel for David from the beginning. The name "Amasai" may allude to Amasa, the head of Absalom's army (2 Sam. 17:25). The disloyalty of Amasa to David, by contrast, serves to magnify the loyalty of Amasai and of all Israel to David.

12:19 The men of Manasseh joined David at Ziklag (see vv. 19–22). Manasseh is probably used here as a representative of the northern tribes (see 1 Chr. 9:3). The tribes closest to Judah had supported Judah, and now those farthest away would lend their support as well. All Israel was loyal to David.

12:22 David's army was the army of God, just as David's victories were God's victories. The army of God is comprised only of those devoted to Him. In the same way, David's army would lend complete devotion to its king.

12:23–37 Twelve divisions of David's army at Hebron are listed (1 Chr. 11:1–3). With Reuben, Gad, and the half-tribe of Manasseh forming one Transjordan division (1 Chr. 12:37), there were 12 divisions representing all Israel (see 1 Chr. 2:3—7:40). Explanations continue concerning the exceedingly large numbers of each division. Such numbers may not be intended as actual totals but may be used to identify military leaders—as "six [commanders of] thousands, eight [commanders of] hundreds." The numbers in Chronicles do demonstrate the complete and full support of all Israel for David.

the sons of Benjamin, relatives of Saul, three thousand (until then the greatest part of them had remained loyal to the house of Saul); [30]of the sons of Ephraim twenty thousand eight hundred, mighty men of valor, famous men throughout their father's house; [31]of the half-tribe of Manasseh eighteen thousand, who were designated by name to come and make David king; [32]of the sons of Issachar who had understanding of the times, to know what Israel ought to do, their chiefs were two hundred; and all their brethren were at their command; [33]of Zebulun there were fifty thousand who went out to battle, expert in war with all weapons of war, stouthearted men who could keep ranks; [34]of Naphtali one thousand captains, and with them thirty-seven thousand with shield and spear; [35]of the Danites who could keep battle formation, twenty-eight thousand six hundred; [36]of Asher, those who could go out to war, able to keep battle formation, forty thousand; [37]of the Reubenites and the Gadites and the half-tribe of Manasseh, from the other side of the Jordan, one hundred and twenty thousand armed for battle with every *kind* of weapon of war.

[38]All these men of war, who could keep ranks, came to Hebron with a loyal heart, to make David king over all Israel; and all the rest of Israel *were* of one mind to make David king. [39]And they were there with David three days, eating and drinking, for their brethren had prepared for them. [40]Moreover those who were near to them, from as far away as Issachar and Zebulun and Naphtali, were bringing food on donkeys and camels, on mules and oxen— provisions of flour and cakes of figs and cakes of raisins, wine and oil and oxen and sheep abundantly, for *there was* joy in Israel.

The Ark Brought from Kirjath Jearim

13 Then David consulted with the captains of thousands and hundreds, *and* with every leader. [2]And David said to all the assembly of Israel, "If *it seems* good to you, and if it is of the LORD our God, let us send out to our brethren everywhere *who are* left in all the land of Israel, and with them to the priests and Levites *who are* in their cities *and* their common-lands, that they

may gather together to us; [3]and let us bring the ark of our God back to us, for we have not inquired at it since the days of Saul." [4]Then all the assembly said that they would do so, for the thing was right in the eyes of all the people.

[5]So David gathered all Israel together, from Shihor in Egypt to as far as the entrance of Hamath, to bring the ark of God from Kirjath Jearim. [6]And David and all Israel went up to Baalah,[a] to Kirjath Jearim, which belonged to Judah, to bring up from there the ark of God the LORD, who dwells *between* the cherubim, where *His* name is proclaimed. [7]So they carried the ark of God on a new cart from the house of Abinadab, and Uzza and Ahio drove the cart. [8]Then David and all Israel played *music* before God with all *their* might, with singing, on harps, on stringed instruments, on tambourines, on cymbals, and with trumpets.

[9]And when they came to Chidon's[a] threshing floor, Uzza put out his hand to hold the ark, for the oxen stumbled. [10]Then the anger of the LORD was aroused against Uzza, and He struck him because he put his hand to the ark; and he died there before God. [11]And David became angry because of the LORD's outbreak against Uzza; therefore that place is called Perez Uzza[a] to this day. [12]David was afraid of God that day, saying, "How can I bring the ark of God to me?"

[13]So David would not move the ark with him into the City of David, but took it aside into the house of Obed-Edom the Gittite. [14]The ark of God remained with the family of Obed-Edom in his house three months. And the LORD blessed the house of Obed-Edom and all that he had.

David Established at Jerusalem

14 Now Hiram king of Tyre sent messengers to David, and cedar trees, with masons and carpenters, to build him a house. [2]So David knew that the LORD had established him as king over Israel, for his kingdom was highly exalted for the sake of His people Israel.

13:6 [a]Called *Baale Judah* in 2 Samuel 6:2   **13:9** [a]Called *Nachon* in 2 Samuel 6:6   **13:11**[a]Literally *Outburst Against Uzza*

13:1 The chronicler's arrangement of events. In the Book of 2 Samuel, the order is: The conquest of Jerusalem, the defeat of the Philistines, the moving of the ark to Obed-Edom, and the transfer of the ark to Jerusalem (2 Sam. 5; 6). These events are deliberately rearranged by the chronicler: The movement of the ark to Obed-Edom, the establishment of Jerusalem as the capital, the defeat of the Philistines, the moving of the ark to Jerusalem. David's first major act as king has to do with the ark (a temple-related action). The chronicler presented David as the recipient of blessings because of his faithfulness, as evidenced by the tribute from Hiram (see 1 Chr. 14:1), the increase in his family (1 Chr. 14:3-7), David's victory over the Philistines

(1 Chr. 14:8-16), and David's widespread fame (1 Chr. 14:17). The ark was returned to Jerusalem in complete obedience and with joyful celebration (1 Chr. 15:1—16:43).

13:1-4 The ark of the covenant traveled wherever Israel went, signifying the presence of God with His people (Ex. 25:17-22; 40:34-38; Num. 9:15-23; 1 Chr. 28:2). The ark had been captured by the Philistines and returned to Israel (1 Sam. 4:1-11; 5:1—7:1). It remained at Kirjath Jearim for 20 years (1 Sam. 7:2; 1 Chr. 13:3-6). David and the people together decided to return the ark to Jerusalem.

³Then David took more wives in Jerusalem, and David begot more sons and daughters. ⁴And these are the names of his children whom he had in Jerusalem: Shammua,ᵃ Shobab, Nathan, Solomon, ⁵Ibhar, Elishua,ᵃ Elpelet,ᵇ ⁶Nogah, Nepheg, Japhia, ⁷Elishama, Beeliada,ᵃ and Eliphelet.

The Philistines Defeated

⁸Now when the Philistines heard that David had been anointed king over all Israel, all the Philistines went up to search for David. And David heard *of it* and went out against them. ⁹Then the Philistines went and made a raid on the Valley of Rephaim. ¹⁰And David inquired of God, saying, "Shall I go up against the Philistines? Will You deliver them into my hand?"

The LORD said to him, "Go up, for I will deliver them into your hand."

¹¹So they went up to Baal Perazim, and David defeated them there. Then David said, "God has broken through my enemies by my hand like a breakthrough of water." Therefore they called the name of that place Baal Perazim.ᵃ ¹²And when they left their gods there, David gave a commandment, and they were burned with fire.

¹³Then the Philistines once again made a raid on the valley. ¹⁴Therefore David inquired again of God, and God said to him, "You shall not go up after them; circle around them, and come upon them in front of the mulberry trees. ¹⁵And it shall be, when you hear a sound of marching in the tops of the mulberry trees, then you shall go out to battle, for God has gone out before you to strike the camp of the Philistines." ¹⁶So David did as God commanded him, and they drove back the army of the Philistines from Gibeon as far as Gezer. ¹⁷Then the fame of David went out into all lands, and the LORD brought the fear of him upon all nations.

The Ark Brought to Jerusalem

15 *David* built houses for himself in the City of David; and he prepared a place for the ark of God, and pitched a tent for it. ²Then David said, "No one may carry the ark of God but the Levites, for the LORD has chosen them to carry the ark of God and to minister before Him forever." ³And David gathered all Israel together at Jerusalem, to bring up the ark of the LORD to its place, which he

had prepared for it. ⁴Then David assembled the children of Aaron and the Levites: ⁵of the sons of Kohath, Uriel the chief, and one hundred and twenty of his brethren; ⁶of the sons of Merari, Asaiah the chief, and two hundred and twenty of his brethren; ⁷of the sons of Gershom, Joel the chief, and one hundred and thirty of his brethren; ⁸of the sons of Elizaphan, Shemaiah the chief, and two hundred of his brethren; ⁹of the sons of Hebron, Eliel the chief, and eighty of his brethren; ¹⁰of the sons of Uzziel, Amminadab the chief, and one hundred and twelve of his brethren.

¹¹And David called for Zadok and Abiathar the priests, and for the Levites: for Uriel, Asaiah, Joel, Shemaiah, Eliel, and Amminadab. ¹²He said to them, "You *are* the heads of the fathers' *houses* of the Levites; sanctify yourselves, you and your brethren, that you may bring up the ark of the LORD God of Israel to *the place* I have prepared for it. ¹³For because you *did* not *do it* the first *time*, the LORD our God broke out against us, because we did not consult Him about the proper order."

¹⁴So the priests and the Levites sanctified themselves to bring up the ark of the LORD God of Israel. ¹⁵And the children of the Levites bore the ark of God on their shoulders, by its poles, as Moses had commanded according to the word of the LORD.

¹⁶Then David spoke to the leaders of the Levites to appoint their brethren *to be* the singers accompanied by instruments of music, stringed instruments, harps, and cymbals, by raising the voice with resounding joy. ¹⁷So the Levites appointed Heman the son of Joel; and of his brethren, Asaph the son of Berechiah; and of their brethren, the sons of Merari, Ethan the son of Kushaiah; ¹⁸and with them their brethren of the second *rank:* Zechariah, Ben,ᵃ Jaaziel, Shemiramoth, Jehiel, Unni, Eliab, Benaiah, Maaseiah, Mattithiah, Elipheleh, Mikneiah, Obed-Edom, and Jeiel, the gatekeepers; ¹⁹the singers, Heman, Asaph, and Ethan, *were* to sound the cymbals of bronze; ²⁰Zechariah, Aziel, Shemiramoth, Jehiel, Unni, Eliab, Maaseiah, and Benaiah, with strings according to Alamoth; ²¹Mattithiah, Elipheleh,

14:4 ᵃSpelled *Shimea* in 3:5   14:5 ᵃSpelled *Elishama* in 3:6 ᵇSpelled *Eliphelet* in 3:6   14:7 ᵃSpelled *Eliada* in 3:8   14:11 ᵃLiterally *Master of Breakthroughs*   15:18 ᵃFollowing Masoretic Text and Vulgate; Septuagint omits *Ben*.

14:3 David and his wives (see chart, The Family Tree of David; 1 Sam. 18, Michal; 25, Abigail; 2 Sam. 11, Bathsheba). Though David's polygamy was a historical reality, certainly it represented a moral failure on his part (Deut. 17:17; 1 Tim. 3, Polygamy). David's sin led to his own heartache and to tragedy within his family (see 2 Sam. 12:7–14, note; chart, David: How Good People Get into Trouble).

15:4 The Levites were instructed to bring up the ark to Jerusalem according to the proper order. They were to sanctify themselves (Ex. 29:1–35; 40:12–15), and carry the ark on poles

(Ex. 25:10–15). This obedience to the Law resulted in joyful celebration (1 Chr. 15:16—16:43).

15:11 Zadok and Abiathar served as high priests for David. Zadok was descended from Aaron; he remained loyal to David (1 Kin. 1:8). He anointed Solomon as king and served as priest to Solomon (1 Kin. 1:34; 2:35). Abiathar, a descendant of Eli (1 Sam. 1—4), escaped the slaughter of Saul (1 Sam. 22:20–23). He chose to side with Adonijah and was deposed by Solomon (1 Kin. 1; 2:27).

Mikneiah, Obed-Edom, Jeiel, and Azaziah, to direct with harps on the Sheminith; ²²Chenaniah, leader of the Levites, was instructor *in charge of* the music, because he *was* skillful; ²³Berechiah and Elkanah *were* doorkeepers for the ark; ²⁴Shebaniah, Joshaphat, Nethanel, Amasai, Zechariah, Benaiah, and Eliezer, the priests, were to blow the trumpets before the ark of God; and Obed-Edom and Jehiah, doorkeepers for the ark.

²⁵So David, the elders of Israel, and the captains over thousands went to bring up the ark of the covenant of the LORD from the house of Obed-Edom with joy. ²⁶And so it was, when God helped the Levites who bore the ark of the covenant of the LORD, that they offered seven bulls and seven rams. ²⁷David was clothed with a robe of fine linen, as were all the Levites who bore the ark, the singers, and Chenaniah the music master *with* the singers. David also wore a linen ephod. ²⁸Thus all Israel brought up the ark of the covenant of the LORD with shouting and with the sound of the horn, with trumpets and with cymbals, making music with stringed instruments and harps.

²⁹And it happened, *as* the ark of the covenant of the LORD came to the City of David, that Michal, Saul's daughter, looked through a window and saw King David whirling and playing music; and she despised him in her heart.

The Ark Placed in the Tabernacle

16 So they brought the ark of God, and set it in the midst of the tabernacle that David had erected for it. Then they offered burnt offerings and peace offerings before God. ²And when David had finished offering the burnt offerings and the peace offerings, he blessed the people in the name of the LORD. ³Then he distributed to everyone of Israel, both man and woman, to everyone a loaf of bread, a piece *of meat,* and a cake of raisins.

⁴And he appointed some of the Levites to minister before the ark of the LORD, to commemorate, to thank, and to praise the LORD God of Israel: ⁵Asaph the chief, and next to him Zechariah, *then* Jeiel, Shemiramoth, Jehiel, Mattithiah, Eliab, Benaiah, and Obed-Edom: Jeiel with stringed instruments and harps, but Asaph made music with cymbals; ⁶Benaiah and Jahaziel the priests regularly *blew* the trumpets before the ark of the covenant of God.

David's Song of Thanksgiving

⁷On that day David first delivered *this psalm* into the hand of Asaph and his brethren, to thank the LORD:

⁸Oh, give thanks to the LORD!
  Call upon His name;
  Make known His deeds among the peoples!
⁹Sing to Him, sing psalms to Him;
  Talk of all His wondrous works!
¹⁰Glory in His holy name;
  Let the hearts of those rejoice who seek the
    LORD!
¹¹Seek the LORD and His strength;
  Seek His face evermore!
¹²Remember His marvelous works which He has
    done,
  His wonders, and the judgments of His
    mouth,
¹³O seed of Israel His servant,
  You children of Jacob, His chosen ones!

¹⁴He *is* the LORD our God;
  His judgments *are* in all the earth.
¹⁵Remember His covenant forever,
  The word which He commanded, for a
    thousand generations,
¹⁶*The covenant which* He made with Abraham,
  And His oath to Isaac,
¹⁷And confirmed it to Jacob for a statute,
  To Israel *for* an everlasting covenant,
¹⁸Saying, "To you I will give the land of Canaan
  As the allotment of your inheritance,"
¹⁹When you were few in number,
  Indeed very few, and strangers in it.

²⁰When they went from one nation to another,
  And from *one* kingdom to another people,
²¹He permitted no man to do them wrong;
  Yes, He rebuked kings for their sakes,
²²Saying, "Do not touch My anointed ones,
  And do My prophets no harm."ᵃ

²³Sing to the LORD, all the earth;
  Proclaim the good news of His salvation from
    day to day.
²⁴Declare His glory among the nations,
  His wonders among all peoples.

²⁵For the LORD *is* great and greatly to be praised;
  He *is* also to be feared above all gods.
²⁶For all the gods of the peoples *are* idols,
  But the LORD made the heavens.
²⁷Honor and majesty *are* before Him;
  Strength and gladness are in His place.

²⁸Give to the LORD, O families of the peoples,
  Give to the LORD glory and strength.

16:22 ᵃCompare verses 8–22 with Psalm 105:1–15

16:7 Three psalms in the Book of Psalms contain most of the elements of this psalm: Giving thanks for the covenant faithfulness of the Lord (vv. 8–22; Ps. 105:1–15), calling the people to worship before the Lord (1 Chr. 16:23–33; Ps. 96:1–13), and praising God for the forgiveness of sin (1 Chr. 16:34–36; Ps. 106:1, 47, 48).

²⁹Give to the LORD the glory *due* His name;
Bring an offering, and come before Him.
Oh, worship the LORD in the beauty of holiness!
³⁰Tremble before Him, all the earth.
The world also is firmly established,
It shall not be moved.

³¹Let the heavens rejoice, and let the earth be glad;
And let them say among the nations, "The LORD reigns."
³²Let the sea roar, and all its fullness;
Let the field rejoice, and all that *is* in it.
³³Then the trees of the woods shall rejoice before the LORD,
For He is coming to judge the earth.ᵃ

³⁴Oh, give thanks to the LORD, for *He is* good!
For His mercy *endures* forever.ᵃ
³⁵And say, "Save us, O God of our salvation;
Gather us together, and deliver us from the Gentiles,
To give thanks to Your holy name,
To triumph in Your praise."

³⁶Blessed *be* the LORD God of Israel
From everlasting to everlasting!ᵃ

And all the people said, "Amen!" and praised the LORD.

Regular Worship Maintained

³⁷So he left Asaph and his brothers there before the ark of the covenant of the LORD to minister before the ark regularly, as every day's work required; ³⁸and Obed-Edom with his sixty-eight brethren, including Obed-Edom the son of Jeduthun, and Hosah, *to be* gatekeepers; ³⁹and Zadok the priest and his brethren the priests, before the tabernacle of the LORD at the high place that *was* at Gibeon, ⁴⁰to offer burnt offerings to the LORD on the altar of burnt offering regularly morning and evening, and *to do* according to all that is written in the Law of the LORD which He commanded Israel; ⁴¹and with them Heman and Jeduthun and the rest who were chosen, who were designated by name, to give thanks to the LORD, because His mercy *endures* forever; ⁴²and with them Heman and Jeduthun, to sound aloud with trumpets and cymbals and the musical instruments of God. Now the sons of Jeduthun *were* gatekeepers.

⁴³Then all the people departed, every man to his house; and David returned to bless his house.

God's Covenant with David

17Now it came to pass, when David was dwelling in his house, that David said to Nathan the prophet, "See now, I dwell in a house of cedar, but the ark of the covenant of the LORD *is* under tent curtains."

²Then Nathan said to David, "Do all that *is* in your heart, for God *is* with you."

³But it happened that night that the word of God came to Nathan, saying, ⁴"Go and tell My servant David, 'Thus says the LORD: "You shall not build Me a house to dwell in. ⁵For I have not dwelt in a house since the time that I brought up Israel, even to this day, but have gone from tent to tent, and from *one* tabernacle *to another.* ⁶Wherever I have moved about with all Israel, have I ever spoken a word to any of the judges of Israel, whom I commanded to shepherd My people, saying, 'Why have you not built Me a house of cedar?' " ' ⁷Now therefore, thus shall you say to My servant David, 'Thus says the LORD of hosts: "I took you from the sheepfold, from following the sheep, to be ruler over My people Israel. ⁸And I have been with you wherever you have gone, and have cut off all your enemies from before you, and have made you a name like the name of the great men who *are* on the earth. ⁹Moreover I will appoint a place for My people Israel, and will plant them, that they may dwell in a place of their own and move no more; nor shall the sons of wickedness oppress them anymore, as previously, ¹⁰since the time that I commanded judges *to be* over My people Israel. Also I will subdue all your enemies. Furthermore I tell you that the LORD will build you a house.ᵃ ¹¹And it shall be, when your days are fulfilled, when you must go *to be* with your fathers, that I will set up your seed after you, who will be of your sons; and I will establish his kingdom. ¹²He shall build Me a house, and I will establish his throne forever. ¹³I will be his Father, and he shall be My son; and I will not take My mercy away from him, as I took *it* from *him* who was before you. ¹⁴And I will establish him in My house and in My kingdom

---

16:33 ᵃCompare verses 23–33 with Psalm 96:1–13   16:34 ᵃCompare verse 34 with Psalm 106:1   16:36 ᵃCompare verses 35, 36 with Psalm 106:47, 48   17:10 ᵃThat is, a royal dynasty

---

17:1 David, the temple planner. The chronicler's understanding of the temple establishes the interdependence of David and Solomon. David did not "rest from all his enemies" (2 Sam. 7:1–12) but was instead a man of war (1 Chr. 22:8; 28:3). His enemies were only subdued (1 Chr. 17:10). As a man of war, he would not be allowed to build the house of the Lord. Instead, the Lord would build David a house or dynasty (1 Chr. 17:10). This action was the pinnacle of all the Lord had done for David (vv. 16–27). David would make preparations for his son Solomon to build the house of the Lord (1 Chr. 18–29). Nathan was the prophet of the Lord during the reigns of David and Solomon. He was consulted regarding David's desire to build the temple; he exposed David's sin with Bathsheba (2 Sam. 12:1–15); and he anointed Solomon as king (1 Kin. 1:32–40).

forever; and his throne shall be established forever." ' "

¹⁵According to all these words and according to all this vision, so Nathan spoke to David.

¹⁶Then King David went in and sat before the LORD; and he said: "Who *am* I, O LORD God? And what is my house, that You have brought me this far? ¹⁷And *yet* this was a small thing in Your sight, O God; and You have *also* spoken of Your servant's house for a great while to come, and have regarded me according to the rank of a man of high degree, O LORD God. ¹⁸What more can David *say* to You for the honor of Your servant? For You know Your servant. ¹⁹O LORD, for Your servant's sake, and according to Your own heart, You have done all this greatness, in making known all these great things. ²⁰O LORD, *there is* none like You, nor *is there any* God besides You, according to all that we have heard with our ears. ²¹And who *is* like Your people Israel, the one nation on the earth whom God went to redeem for Himself *as* a people—to make for Yourself a name by great and awesome deeds, by driving out nations from before Your people whom You redeemed from Egypt? ²²For You have made Your people Israel Your very own people forever; and You, LORD, have become their God.

²³"And now, O LORD, the word which You have spoken concerning Your servant and concerning his house, *let it* be established forever, and do as You have said. ²⁴So let it be established, that Your name may be magnified forever, saying, 'The LORD of hosts, the God of Israel, *is* Israel's God.' And let the house of Your servant David be established before You. ²⁵For You, O my God, have revealed to Your servant that You will build him a house. Therefore Your servant has found it *in his heart* to pray before You. ²⁶And now, LORD, You are God, and have promised this goodness to Your servant. ²⁷Now You have been pleased to bless the house of Your servant, that it may continue before You forever; for You have blessed it, O LORD, and *it shall be* blessed forever."

David's Further Conquests

18 After this it came to pass that David attacked the Philistines, subdued them, and took Gath and its towns from the hand of the Philistines. ²Then he defeated Moab, and the Moabites became David's servants, *and* brought tribute.

³And David defeated Hadadezerᵃ king of Zobah *as far as* Hamath, as he went to establish his power by the River Euphrates. ⁴David took from him one thousand chariots, seven thousandᵃ horsemen, and twenty thousand foot soldiers. Also David hamstrung all the chariot *horses*, except that he spared enough of them for one hundred chariots.

⁵When the Syrians of Damascus came to help Hadadezer king of Zobah, David killed twenty-two thousand of the Syrians. ⁶Then David put *garrisons* in Syria of Damascus; and the Syrians became David's servants, *and* brought tribute. So the LORD preserved David wherever he went. ⁷And David took the shields of gold that were on the servants of Hadadezer, and brought them to Jerusalem. ⁸Also from Tibhathᵃ and from Chun, cities of Hadadezer, David brought a large amount of bronze, with which Solomon made the bronze Sea, the pillars, and the articles of bronze.

⁹Now when Touᵃ king of Hamath heard that David had defeated all the army of Hadadezer king of Zobah, ¹⁰he sent Hadoramᵃ his son to King David, to greet him and bless him, because he had fought against Hadadezer and defeated him (for Hadadezer had been at war with Tou); and *Hadoram brought with him* all kinds of articles of gold, silver, and bronze. ¹¹King David also dedicated these to the LORD, along with the silver and gold that he had brought from all *these* nations—from Edom, from Moab, from the people of Ammon, from the Philistines, and from Amalek.

¹²Moreover Abishai the son of Zeruiah killed eighteen thousand Edomitesᵃ in the Valley of Salt. ¹³He also put garrisons in Edom, and all the Edomites became David's servants. And the LORD preserved David wherever he went.

David's Administration

¹⁴So David reigned over all Israel, and administered judgment and justice to all his people. ¹⁵Joab the son of Zeruiah *was* over the army; Jehoshaphat the son of Ahilud *was* recorder; ¹⁶Zadok the son of Ahitub and Abimelech the son of Abiathar *were* the priests; Shavshaᵃ *was* the scribe; ¹⁷Benaiah the son of Jehoiada *was* over the Cherethites and the Pelethites; and David's sons *were* chief ministers at the king's side.

18:3 ᵃHebrew *Hadarezer*, and so throughout chapters 18 and 19 **18:4** ᵃOr *seven hundred* (compare 2 Samuel 8:4) **18:8** ᵃSpelled *Betah* in 2 Samuel 8:8 **18:9** ᵃSpelled *Toi* in 2 Samuel 8:9, 10 **18:10** ᵃSpelled *Joram* in 2 Samuel 8:10 **18:12** ᵃOr *Syrians* (compare 2 Samuel 8:13) **18:16** ᵃSpelled *Seraiah* in 2 Samuel 8:17

17:16 David's prayer. The contexts of the two accounts of this prayer differ markedly. In 2 Samuel, the focus is on the establishment of David's kingdom, emphasizing the political and military aspects of his reign (2 Sam. 7:18–29). In Chronicles, the focus is on the religious aspects of David's reign. This prayer introduces David's role as temple planner (see also chart, Solomon's Prayer). With enthusiastic obedience, David would begin to prepare for the temple (1 Chr. 18—29).

18:1 David, the man of war (see also 2 Sam. 8—10). The mention of these wars reinforces the fact that David was a man of war (see 1 Chr. 17:1, note). David's victories were evidence of his obedience. Also, David began his preparations for building the temple with the materials and money from the spoils of these wars (1 Chr. 18:8; 22:2–4; 28:11–19; 29:1–5).

The Ammonites and Syrians Defeated

19 It happened after this that Nahash the king of the people of Ammon died, and his son reigned in his place. [2]Then David said, "I will show kindness to Hanun the son of Nahash, because his father showed kindness to me." So David sent messengers to comfort him concerning his father. And David's servants came to Hanun in the land of the people of Ammon to comfort him.

[3]And the princes of the people of Ammon said to Hanun, "Do you think that David really honors your father because he has sent comforters to you? Did his servants not come to you to search and to overthrow and to spy out the land?"

[4]Therefore Hanun took David's servants, shaved them, and cut off their garments in the middle, at their buttocks, and sent them away. [5]Then *some* went and told David about the men; and he sent to meet them, because the men were greatly ashamed. And the king said, "Wait at Jericho until your beards have grown, and *then* return."

[6]When the people of Ammon saw that they had made themselves repulsive to David, Hanun and the people of Ammon sent a thousand talents of silver to hire for themselves chariots and horsemen from Mesopotamia,[a] from Syrian Maacah, and from Zobah.[b] [7]So they hired for themselves thirty-two thousand chariots, with the king of Maacah and his people, who came and encamped before Medeba. Also the people of Ammon gathered together from their cities, and came to battle.

[8]Now when David heard *of it*, he sent Joab and all the army of the mighty men. [9]Then the people of Ammon came out and put themselves in battle array before the gate of the city, and the kings who had come *were* by themselves in the field.

[10]When Joab saw that the battle line was against him before and behind, he chose some of Israel's best, and put *them* in battle array against the Syrians. [11]And the rest of the people he put under the command of Abishai his brother, and they set *themselves* in battle array against the people of Ammon. [12]Then he said, "If the Syrians are too strong for me, then you shall help me; but if the people of Ammon are too strong for you, then I will help you. [13]Be of good courage, and let us be strong for our people and for the cities of our God. And may the LORD do *what is* good in His sight."

[14]So Joab and the people who *were* with him drew near for the battle against the Syrians, and they fled before him. [15]When the people of Ammon saw that the Syrians were fleeing, they also fled before Abishai his brother, and entered the city. So Joab went to Jerusalem.

[16]Now when the Syrians saw that they had been defeated by Israel, they sent messengers and brought the Syrians who were beyond the River,[a] and Shophach[b] the commander of Hadadezer's army *went* before them. [17]When it was told David, he gathered all Israel, crossed over the Jordan and came upon them, and set up in *battle* array against them. So when David had set up in battle array against the Syrians, they fought with him. [18]Then the Syrians fled before Israel; and David killed seven thousand[a] charioteers and forty thousand foot soldiers[b] of the Syrians, and killed Shophach the commander of the army. [19]And when the servants of Hadadezer saw that they were defeated by Israel, they made peace with David and became his servants. So the Syrians were not willing to help the people of Ammon anymore.

Rabbah Is Conquered

20 It happened in the spring of the year, at the time kings go out *to battle*, that Joab led out the armed forces and ravaged the country of the people of Ammon, and came and besieged Rabbah. But David stayed at Jerusalem. And Joab defeated Rabbah and overthrew it. [2]Then David took their king's crown from his head, and found it to weigh a talent of gold, and *there were* precious stones in it. And it was set on David's head. Also he brought out the spoil of the city in great abundance. [3]And he brought out the people who *were* in it, and put *them* to work[a] with saws, with iron picks, and with axes. So David did to all the cities of the people of Ammon. Then David and all the people returned *to* Jerusalem.

Philistine Giants Destroyed

[4]Now it happened afterward that war broke out at Gezer with the Philistines, at which time Sibbechai the Hushathite killed Sippai,[a] *who was* one of the sons of the giant. And they were subdued.

[5]Again there was war with the Philistines, and Elhanan the son of Jair[a] killed Lahmi the brother of Goliath the Gittite, the shaft of whose spear *was* like a weaver's beam.

[6]Yet again there was war at Gath, where there was a man of *great* stature, with twenty-four fingers and toes, six *on each hand* and six *on each foot;* and he also was born to the giant. [7]So when he defied Israel, Jonathan the son of Shimea,[a] David's brother, killed him.

[8]These were born to the giant in Gath, and they fell by the hand of David and by the hand of his servants.

· · · · · · · · · · · · · · · · · · ·

19:6 [a]Hebrew *Aram Naharaim* [b]Spelled *Zoba* in 2 Samuel 10:6   **19:16** [a]That is, the Euphrates [b]Spelled *Shobach* in 2 Samuel 10:16   **19:18** [a]Or *seven hundred* (compare 2 Samuel 10:18) [b]Or *horsemen* (compare 2 Samuel 10:18)   **20:3** [a]Septuagint reads *cut them.*   **20:4** [a]Spelled *Saph* in 2 Samuel 21:18   **20:5** [a]Spelled *Jaare-Oregim* in 2 Samuel 21:19   **20:7** [a]Spelled *Shimeah* in 2 Samuel 21:21 and *Shammah* in 1 Samuel 16:9

The Census of Israel and Judah

21 Now Satan stood up against Israel, and moved David to number Israel. ²So David said to Joab and to the leaders of the people, "Go, number Israel from Beersheba to Dan, and bring the number of them to me that I may know *it.*"

³And Joab answered, "May the LORD make His people a hundred times more than they are. But, my lord the king, *are* they not all my lord's servants? Why then does my lord require this thing? Why should he be a cause of guilt in Israel?"

⁴Nevertheless the king's word prevailed against Joab. Therefore Joab departed and went throughout all Israel and came to Jerusalem. ⁵Then Joab gave the sum of the number of the people to David. All Israel *had* one million one hundred thousand men who drew the sword, and Judah *had* four hundred and seventy thousand men who drew the sword. ⁶But he did not count Levi and Benjamin among them, for the king's word was abominable to Joab.

⁷And God was displeased with this thing; therefore He struck Israel. ⁸So David said to God, "I have sinned greatly, because I have done this thing; but now, I pray, take away the iniquity of Your servant, for I have done very foolishly."

⁹Then the LORD spoke to Gad, David's seer, saying, ¹⁰"Go and tell David, saying, 'Thus says the LORD: "I offer you three *things;* choose one of them for yourself, that I may do *it* to you." ' "

¹¹So Gad came to David and said to him, "Thus says the LORD: 'Choose for yourself, ¹²either three[a] years of famine, or three months to be defeated by your foes with the sword of your enemies overtaking *you,* or else for three days the sword of the LORD—the plague in the land, with the angel[b] of the LORD destroying throughout all the territory of Israel.' Now consider what answer I should take back to Him who sent me."

¹³And David said to Gad, "I am in great distress. Please let me fall into the hand of the LORD, for His mercies *are* very great; but do not let me fall into the hand of man."

¹⁴So the LORD sent a plague upon Israel, and seventy thousand men of Israel fell. ¹⁵And God sent an angel to Jerusalem to destroy it. As he[a] was destroying, the LORD looked and relented of the disaster, and said to the angel who was destroying, "It is enough; now restrain your[b] hand." And the angel of the LORD stood by the threshing floor of Ornan[c] the Jebusite.

¹⁶Then David lifted his eyes and saw the angel of the LORD standing between earth and heaven, having in his hand a drawn sword stretched out over Jerusalem. So David and the elders, clothed in sackcloth, fell on their faces. ¹⁷And David said to God, "Was it not I who commanded the people to be numbered? I am the one who has sinned and done evil indeed; but these sheep, what have they done? Let Your hand, I pray, O LORD my God, be against me and my father's house, but not against Your people that they should be plagued."

¹⁸Therefore, the angel of the LORD commanded Gad to say to David that David should go and erect an altar to the LORD on the threshing floor of Ornan the Jebusite. ¹⁹So David went up at the word of Gad, which he had spoken in the name of the LORD. ²⁰Now Ornan turned and saw the angel; and his four sons *who were* with him hid themselves, but Ornan continued threshing wheat. ²¹So David came to Ornan, and Ornan looked and saw David. And he went out from the threshing floor, and bowed before David with *his* face to the ground. ²²Then David said to Ornan, "Grant me the place of *this* threshing floor, that I may build an altar on it to the LORD. You shall grant it to me at the full price, that the plague may be withdrawn from the people."

²³But Ornan said to David, "Take *it* to yourself, and let my lord the king do *what is* good in his eyes. Look, I *also* give *you* the oxen for burnt offerings, the threshing implements for wood, and the wheat for the grain offering; I give *it* all."

²⁴Then King David said to Ornan, "No, but I will surely buy *it* for the full price, for I will not take what is yours for the LORD, nor offer burnt offerings with *that which* costs *me* nothing." ²⁵So David gave Ornan six hundred shekels of gold by weight for the place. ²⁶And David built there an altar to the LORD, and offered burnt offerings and peace offerings, and called on the LORD; and He answered him from heaven by fire on the altar of burnt offering.

²⁷So the LORD commanded the angel, and he returned his sword to its sheath.

21:12 [a]Or *seven* (compare 2 Samuel 24:13) [b]Or *Angel,* and so elsewhere in this chapter   **21:15** [a]Or *He* [b]Or *Your* [c]Spelled *Araunah* in 2 Samuel 24:16

21:1 The numbering of Israel. Details not vital to the numbering are omitted by the chronicler (see 2 Sam. 24:5–8). No reason for the census is given. Most often a census was used as the basis for levying taxes (Ex. 30:12; Num. 3:40–51) or as a means for registration for military service (Num. 26:1–4). This could have been a census to conscript laborers for a vast project like building the temple (1 Kin. 5:13, note). Satan instigates the numbering (1 Kin. 21:1; contrast with 2 Sam. 24:1). The words chosen by the chronicler place greater emphasis on David's guilt. The action of the angel is more vivid (1 Chr. 21:16; see 2 Sam. 24:16) and more central to the chronicler's account than the plague (1 Chr. 21:14, 15, 27; see 2 Sam. 24:15, 16). The concern of the chronicler is for the people of God (all Israel) in Jerusalem.

21:27–30 The temple site. These verses are unique to the chronicler. David's disobedience in numbering the people led to the purchase of Araunah's threshing floor, which later

²⁸At that time, when David saw that the LORD had answered him on the threshing floor of Ornan the Jebusite, he sacrificed there. ²⁹For the tabernacle of the LORD and the altar of the burnt offering, which Moses had made in the wilderness, *were* at that time at the high place in Gibeon. ³⁰But David could not go before it to inquire of God, for he was afraid of the sword of the angel of the LORD.

David Prepares to Build the Temple

22 Then David said, "This *is* the house of the LORD God, and this *is* the altar of burnt offering for Israel." ²So David commanded to gather the aliens who *were* in the land of Israel; and he appointed masons to cut hewn stones to build the house of God. ³And David prepared iron in abundance for the nails of the doors of the gates and for the joints, and bronze in abundance beyond measure, ⁴and cedar trees in abundance; for the Sidonians and those from Tyre brought much cedar wood to David.

⁵Now David said, "Solomon my son *is* young and inexperienced, and the house to be built for the LORD *must be* exceedingly magnificent, famous and glorious throughout all countries. I will now make preparation for it." So David made abundant preparations before his death.

⁶Then he called for his son Solomon, and charged him to build a house for the LORD God of Israel. ⁷And David said to Solomon: "My son, as for me, it was in my mind to build a house to the name of the LORD my God; ⁸but the word of the LORD came to me, saying, 'You have shed much blood and have made great wars; you shall not build a house for My name, because you have shed much blood on the earth in My sight. ⁹Behold, a son shall be born to you, who shall be a man of rest; and I will give him rest from all his enemies all around. His name shall be Solomon,ᵃ for I will give peace and quietness to Israel in his days. ¹⁰He shall build a house for My name, and he shall be My son, and I *will be* his Father; and I will establish the throne of his kingdom over Israel forever.'
¹¹Now, my son, may the LORD be with you; and may you prosper, and build the house of the LORD your God, as He has said to you. ¹²Only may the LORD give you wisdom and understanding, and give you charge concerning Israel, that you may keep the law of the LORD your God. ¹³Then you will prosper, if you take care to fulfill the statutes and judgments with which the LORD charged Moses concerning Israel. Be strong and of good courage; do not fear nor be dismayed. ¹⁴Indeed I have taken much trouble to prepare for the house of the LORD one hundred thousand talents of gold and one million talents of silver, and bronze and iron beyond measure, for it is so abundant. I have prepared timber and stone also, and you may add to them. ¹⁵Moreover *there are* workmen with you in abundance: woodsmen and stonecutters, and all types of skillful men for every kind of work. ¹⁶Of gold and silver and bronze and iron *there is* no limit. Arise and begin working, and the LORD be with you."

¹⁷David also commanded all the leaders of Israel to help Solomon his son, *saying,* ¹⁸"*Is* not the LORD your God with you? And has He *not* given you rest on every side? For He has given the inhabitants of the land into my hand, and the land is subdued before the LORD and before His people. ¹⁹Now set your heart and your soul to seek the LORD your God. Therefore arise and build the sanctuary of the LORD God, to bring the ark of the covenant of the LORD and the holy articles of God into the house that is to be built for the name of the LORD."

The Divisions of the Levites

23 So when David was old and full of days, he made his son Solomon king over Israel.

²And he gathered together all the leaders of Israel, with the priests and the Levites. ³Now the Levites were numbered from the age of thirty

••••••••••••••••••
22:9 ᵃLiterally *Peaceful*

---

became the temple site (1 Chr. 21:1–26; 22:1). The center of worship was Gibeon (1 Chr. 21:29; 2 Chr. 1:3). The lifting of the plague played a significant role in identifying the future site of the temple, making this episode an important part of Chronicles. David is seen in his role as temple planner (1 Chr. 17:1–11).

22:2–5 Abundant preparations for the temple were made by David due to the inexperience of Solomon and the enormity of the building task (1 Chr. 29:1; see also 1 Kin. 7:51; 2 Chr. 5:1). Tyre and Sidon, Phoenician seaport cities, were well known for the greatness of their wealth and extensive trading (see 1 Kin. 5:1–10; 1 Chr. 14:1; Ezra 3:7).

22:11–16 Solomon is reminded that faithfulness yields prosperity and success (vv. 12, 13). Note the phrase "the LORD be with you" (vv. 11, 16) and the fourfold encouragement: "Be strong and of good courage" and "Do not fear nor be dis-

mayed" (v. 13; 1 Chr. 28:10, 20). This is followed by "Arise and begin working" (1 Chr. 22:16) and "arise and build" (v. 19). The framing phrase and the encouragements are common for God-given tasks (Deut. 31:6–8; Josh. 1:9; Hag. 1:13; 2:4, 5).

23:3–5 Duties were assigned to the majority of the Levites (24,000) for the house of the Lord. This work may have included the construction of the temple as well as conducting regular services of the temple. Twenty-four is a number common in the appointments made by David. He appointed 24 divisions of priests (1 Chr. 24:1–18), 24 groups of musicians (1 Chr. 25:7–31), 24 gatekeepers (1 Chr. 26:12–19), 24 military divisions (1 Chr. 27:1–15). Additional duties included 6,000 officers and judges (1 Chr. 26:29; see also Deut. 17:8–13; 2 Chr. 19:4–11; 34:13), 4,000 gatekeepers and 4,000 musicians. Under Moses, the Levites were numbered for service from the age of 30 years (1 Chr. 23:3; Num. 4:3, 23). Moses later low-

years and above; and the number of individual males was thirty-eight thousand. [4]Of these, twenty-four thousand *were* to look after the work of the house of the LORD, six thousand *were* officers and judges, [5]four thousand *were* gatekeepers, and four thousand praised the LORD with *musical* instruments, "which I made," *said David,* "for giving praise."

[6]Also David separated them into divisions among the sons of Levi: Gershon, Kohath, and Merari.

[7]Of the Gershonites: Laadan[a] and Shimei. [8]The sons of Laadan: the first Jehiel, then Zetham and Joel—three *in all.* [9]The sons of Shimei: Shelomith, Haziel, and Haran—three *in all.* These were the heads of the fathers' *houses* of Laadan. [10]And the sons of Shimei: Jahath, Zina,[a] Jeush, and Beriah. These *were* the four sons of Shimei. [11]Jahath was the first and Zizah the second. But Jeush and Beriah did not have many sons; therefore they were assigned as one father's house.

[12]The sons of Kohath: Amram, Izhar, Hebron, and Uzziel—four *in all.* [13]The sons of Amram: Aaron and Moses; and Aaron was set apart, he and his sons forever, that he should sanctify the most holy things, to burn incense before the LORD, to minister to Him, and to give the blessing in His name forever. [14]Now the sons of Moses the man of God were reckoned to the tribe of Levi. [15]The sons of Moses *were* Gershon[a] and Eliezer. [16]Of the sons of Gershon, Shebuel[a] *was* the first. [17]Of the descendants of Eliezer, Rehabiah was the first. And Eliezer had no other sons, but the sons of Rehabiah were very many. [18]Of the sons of Izhar, Shelomith *was* the first. [19]Of the sons of Hebron, Jeriah *was* the first, Amariah the second, Jahaziel the third, and Jekameam the fourth. [20]Of the sons of Uzziel, Michah *was* the first and Jesshiah the second.

[21]The sons of Merari *were* Mahli and Mushi. The sons of Mahli *were* Eleazar and Kish. [22]And Eleazar died, and had no sons, but only daughters; and their brethren, the sons of Kish, took them *as wives.* [23]The sons of Mushi *were* Mahli, Eder, and Jeremoth—three *in all.*

[24]These *were* the sons of Levi by their fathers' houses—the heads of the fathers' *houses* as they were counted individually by the number of their names, who did the work for the service of the house of the LORD, from the age of twenty years and above.

[25]For David said, "The LORD God of Israel has given rest to His people, that they may dwell in Jerusalem forever"; [26]and also to the Levites, "They shall no longer carry the tabernacle, or any of the articles for its service." [27]For by the last words of David the Levites *were* numbered from twenty years old and above; [28]because their duty *was* to help the sons of Aaron in the service of the house of the LORD, in the courts and in the chambers, in the purifying of all holy things and the work of the service of the house of God, [29]both with the showbread and the fine flour for the grain offering, with the unleavened cakes and *what is baked in* the pan, with what is mixed and with all kinds of measures and sizes; [30]to stand every morning to thank and praise the LORD, and likewise at evening; [31]and at every presentation of a burnt offering to the LORD on the Sabbaths and on the New Moons and on the set feasts, by number according to the ordinance governing them, regularly before the LORD; [32]and that they should attend to the needs of the tabernacle of meeting, the needs of the holy *place,* and the needs of the sons of Aaron their brethren in the work of the house of the LORD.

The Divisions of the Priests

24 Now *these are* the divisions of the sons of Aaron. The sons of Aaron *were* Nadab, Abihu, Eleazar, and Ithamar. [2]And Nadab and Abihu died before their father, and had no children; therefore Eleazar and Ithamar ministered as priests. [3]Then David with Zadok of the sons of Eleazar, and Ahimelech of the sons of Ithamar, divided them according to the schedule of their service.

23:7 [a]Spelled *Libni* in Exodus 6:17   **23:10** [a]Septuagint and Vulgate read *Zizah* (compare verse 11).   **23:15** [a]Hebrew *Gershom* (compare 6:16)   **23:16** [a]Spelled *Shubael* in 24:20

---

ered the age to 25 (Num. 8:24), then David to 20 years (1 Chr. 23:27). No reasons are given for the change, though during David's reign preparation for construction and upkeep on the projected temple would most certainly increase the work load.

23:6 This listing of the three Levitical families (Gershon, vv. 7–11; Kohath, vv. 12–20; Merari, vv. 21–23) differs from that of 1 Chronicles 6 due to a change in genealogical structure. Linear genealogy is used in 1 Chronicles 6 and segmented genealogy here (see 1 Chr. 1:1–4, note).

23:24 The Levites who carried the tabernacle were now assigned to serve under the priests of Aaron (Num. 1:50, 51). They were to assist with purification (Ex. 29; 30:22–33), with the showbread (Ex. 25:30; Lev. 24:5–9), with the grain offer-

ing (Lev. 2; 6:14–23), with morning and evening praises, and with burnt offerings (Lev. 1; 23:37, 38; Num. 10:10; 28:1—29:40). The notion of "rest" included dwelling in the Land and being in the presence of God (1 Chr. 23:25, 26).

24:1 Two legitimate priestly lines existed. Zadok represented the sons of Eleazar, and Ahimelech represented the sons of Ithamar (1 Chr. 24:3; see 1 Chr. 15:11, note). Zadok was the more prominent line. The 24 divisions were divided by lot in the presence of David and the leaders Zadok and Ahimelech (1 Chr. 24:5). An unknown scribe, Shemaiah, acted as recorder (v. 6). No details regarding the process of lots were given, but the method does indicate human objectivity and divine providence (v. 31; 1 Chr. 25:8; 26:13).

[4]There were more leaders found of the sons of Eleazar than of the sons of Ithamar, and *thus* they were divided. Among the sons of Eleazar *were* sixteen heads of *their* fathers' houses, and eight heads of their fathers' houses among the sons of Ithamar. [5]Thus they were divided by lot, one group as another, for there were officials of the sanctuary and officials *of the house* of God, from the sons of Eleazar and from the sons of Ithamar. [6]And the scribe, Shemaiah the son of Nethanel, *one of* the Levites, wrote them down before the king, the leaders, Zadok the priest, Ahimelech the son of Abiathar, and the heads of the fathers' *houses* of the priests and Levites, one father's house taken for Eleazar and *one* for Ithamar.

[7]Now the first lot fell to Jehoiarib, the second to Jedaiah, [8]the third to Harim, the fourth to Seorim, [9]the fifth to Malchijah, the sixth to Mijamin, [10]the seventh to Hakkoz, the eighth to Abijah, [11]the ninth to Jeshua, the tenth to Shecaniah, [12]the eleventh to Eliashib, the twelfth to Jakim, [13]the thirteenth to Huppah, the fourteenth to Jeshebeab, [14]the fifteenth to Bilgah, the sixteenth to Immer, [15]the seventeenth to Hezir, the eighteenth to Happizzez,[a] [16]the nineteenth to Pethahiah, the twentieth to Jehezekel,[a] [17]the twenty-first to Jachin, the twenty-second to Gamul, [18]the twenty-third to Delaiah, the twenty-fourth to Maaziah.

[19]This *was* the schedule of their service for coming into the house of the LORD according to their ordinance by the hand of Aaron their father, as the LORD God of Israel had commanded him.

Other Levites

[20]And the rest of the sons of Levi: of the sons of Amram, Shubael;[a] of the sons of Shubael, Jehdeiah. [21]Concerning Rehabiah, of the sons of Rehabiah, the first *was* Isshiah. [22]Of the Izharites, Shelomoth;[a] of the sons of Shelomoth, Jahath. [23]Of the sons *of Hebron,*[a] Jeriah *was the first,*[b] Amariah the second, Jahaziel the third, *and* Jekameam the fourth. [24]*Of* the sons of Uzziel, Michah; of the sons of Michah, Shamir. [25]The brother of Michah, Isshiah; of the sons of Isshiah, Zechariah. [26]The sons of Merari *were* Mahli and Mushi; the son of Jaaziah, Beno. [27]The sons of Merari by Jaaziah *were* Beno, Shoham, Zaccur, and Ibri. [28]Of Mahli: Eleazar, who had no sons. [29]Of Kish: the son of Kish, Jerahmeel.

[30]Also the sons of Mushi *were* Mahli, Eder, and Jerimoth. These *were* the sons of the Levites according to their fathers' houses.

[31]These also cast lots just as their brothers the sons of Aaron did, in the presence of King David, Zadok, Ahimelech, and the heads of the fathers' *houses* of the priests and Levites. The chief fathers *did* just as their younger brethren.

The Musicians

25 Moreover David and the captains of the army separated for the service *some* of the sons of Asaph, of Heman, and of Jeduthun, who *should* prophesy with harps, stringed instruments, and cymbals. And the number of the skilled men performing their service was: [2]Of the sons of Asaph: Zaccur, Joseph, Nethaniah, and Asharelah;[a] the sons of Asaph *were* under the direction of Asaph, who prophesied according to the order of the king. [3]Of Jeduthun, the sons of Jeduthun: Gedaliah, Zeri,[a] Jeshaiah, *Shimei,* Hashabiah, and Mattithiah, six,[b] under the direction of their father Jeduthun, who prophesied with a harp to give thanks and to praise the LORD. [4]Of Heman, the sons of Heman: Bukkiah, Mattaniah, Uzziel,[a] Shebuel,[b] Jerimoth,[c] Hananiah, Hanani, Eliathah, Giddalti, Romamti-Ezer, Joshbekashah, Mallothi, Hothir, *and* Mahazioth. [5]All these *were* the sons of Heman the king's seer in the words of God, to exalt his horn.[a] For God gave Heman fourteen sons and three daughters.

[6]All these *were* under the direction of their father for the music *in* the house of the LORD, with cymbals, stringed instruments, and harps, for the service of the house of God. Asaph, Jeduthun, and Heman *were* under the authority of the king. [7]So the number of them, with their brethren who were instructed in the songs of the LORD, all who were skillful, *was* two hundred and eighty-eight.

[8]And they cast lots for their duty, the small as well as the great, the teacher with the student.

[9]Now the first lot for Asaph came out for Joseph; the second for Gedaliah, him with his brethren and sons, twelve; [10]the third for Zaccur, his sons and his brethren, twelve; [11]the fourth for Jizri,[a] his sons and his brethren, twelve; [12]the fifth for Nethaniah, his sons and his brethren, twelve; [13]the sixth for Bukkiah, his sons and his brethren, twelve; [14]the seventh for Jesharelah,[a] his sons and

---

24:15 [a]Septuagint and Vulgate read *Aphses.* 24:16 [a]Masoretic Text reads *Jehezkel.* 24:20 [a]Spelled *Shebuel* in 23:16 24:22 [a]Spelled *Shelomith* in 23:18 24:23 [a]Supplied from 23:19 (following some Hebrew manuscripts and Septuagint manuscripts) [b]Supplied from 23:19 (following some Hebrew manuscripts and Septuagint manuscripts) 25:2 [a]Spelled *Jesharelah* in verse 14 25:3 [a]Spelled *Jizri* in verse 11 [b]*Shimei,* appearing in one Hebrew and several Septuagint manuscripts, completes the total of six sons (compare verse 17). 25:4 [a]Spelled *Azarel* in verse 18 [b]Spelled *Shubael* in verse 20 [c]Spelled *Jeremoth* in verse 22 25:5 [a]That is, to increase his power or influence 25:11 [a]Spelled *Zeri* in verse 3 25:14 [a]Spelled *Asharelah* in verse 2

25:1 **The musicians** served a principal role in the true worship of Israel. They were from the sons of Asaph, Heman, and Jeduthun (also called Ethan; see 1 Chr. 6:31, note). Lots were cast (see 1 Chr. 24:1, note), and they were divided into 24 divisions, each with 12 members (see 1 Chr. 23:3–5, note).

his brethren, twelve; [15]the eighth for Jeshaiah, his sons and his brethren, twelve; [16]the ninth for Mattaniah, his sons and his brethren, twelve; [17]the tenth for Shimei, his sons and his brethren, twelve; [18]the eleventh for Azarel,[a] his sons and his brethren, twelve; [19]the twelfth for Hashabiah, his sons and his brethren, twelve; [20]the thirteenth for Shubael,[a] his sons and his brethren, twelve; [21]the fourteenth for Mattithiah, his sons and his brethren, twelve; [22]the fifteenth for Jeremoth,[a] his sons and his brethren, twelve; [23]the sixteenth for Hananiah, his sons and his brethren, twelve; [24]the seventeenth for Joshbekashah, his sons and his brethren, twelve; [25]the eighteenth for Hanani, his sons and his brethren, twelve; [26]the nineteenth for Mallothi, his sons and his brethren, twelve; [27]the twentieth for Eliathah, his sons and his brethren, twelve; [28]the twenty-first for Hothir, his sons and his brethren, twelve; [29]the twenty-second for Giddalti, his sons and his brethren, twelve; [30]the twenty-third for Mahazioth, his sons and his brethren, twelve; [31]the twenty-fourth for Romamti-Ezer, his sons and his brethren, twelve.

The Gatekeepers

26 Concerning the divisions of the gatekeepers: of the Korahites, Meshelemiah the son of Kore, of the sons of Asaph. [2]And the sons of Meshelemiah were Zechariah the firstborn, Jediael the second, Zebadiah the third, Jathniel the fourth, [3]Elam the fifth, Jehohanan the sixth, Eliehoenai the seventh.

[4]Moreover the sons of Obed-Edom were Shemaiah the firstborn, Jehozabad the second, Joah the third, Sacar the fourth, Nethanel the fifth, [5]Ammiel the sixth, Issachar the seventh, Peulthai the eighth; for God blessed him.

[6]Also to Shemaiah his son were sons born who governed their fathers' houses, because they were men of great ability. [7]The sons of Shemaiah were Othni, Rephael, Obed, and Elzabad, whose brothers Elihu and Semachiah were able men. [8]All these were of the sons of Obed-Edom, they and their sons and their brethren, able men with strength for the work: sixty-two of Obed-Edom.

[9]And Meshelemiah had sons and brethren, eighteen able men.

[10]Also Hosah, of the children of Merari, had sons: Shimri the first (for though he was not the firstborn, his father made him the first), [11]Hilkiah the second, Tebaliah the third, Zechariah the fourth; all the sons and brethren of Hosah were thirteen.

[12]Among these were the divisions of the gatekeepers, among the chief men, having duties just like their brethren, to serve in the house of the LORD. [13]And they cast lots for each gate, the small as well as the great, according to their father's house. [14]The lot for the East Gate fell to Shelemiah. Then they cast lots for his son Zechariah, a wise counselor, and his lot came out for the North Gate; [15]to Obed-Edom the South Gate, and to his sons the storehouse.[a] [16]To Shuppim and Hosah the lot came out for the West Gate, with the Shallecheth Gate on the ascending highway—watchman opposite watchman. [17]On the east were six Levites, on the north four each day, on the south four each day, and for the storehouse[a] two by two. [18]As for the Parbar[a] on the west, there were four on the highway and two at the Parbar. [19]These were the divisions of the gatekeepers among the sons of Korah and among the sons of Merari.

The Treasuries and Other Duties

[20]Of the Levites, Ahijah was over the treasuries of the house of God and over the treasuries of the dedicated things. [21]The sons of Laadan, the descendants of the Gershonites of Laadan, heads of their fathers' houses, of Laadan the Gershonite: Jehieli. [22]The sons of Jehieli, Zetham and Joel his brother, were over the treasuries of the house of the LORD. [23]Of the Amramites, the Izharites, the Hebronites, and the Uzzielites: [24]Shebuel the son of Gershom, the son of Moses, was overseer of the treasuries. [25]And his brethren by Eliezer were Rehabiah his son, Jeshaiah his son, Joram his son, Zichri his son, and Shelomith his son.

[26]This Shelomith and his brethren were over all the treasuries of the dedicated things which King David and the heads of fathers' houses, the captains over thousands and hundreds, and the captains of the army, had dedicated. [27]Some of the spoils won in battles they dedicated to maintain the house of the LORD. [28]And all that Samuel the seer, Saul the son of Kish, Abner the son of Ner, and Joab the son of Zeruiah had dedicated, every dedicated thing, was under the hand of Shelomith and his brethren.

25:18 [a]Spelled *Uzziel* in verse 4   **25:20** [a]Spelled *Shebuel* in verse 4
25:22 [a]Spelled *Jerimoth* in verse 4   **26:15** [a]Hebrew *asuppim*   **26:17** [a]Hebrew *asuppim*   **26:18** [a]Probably a court or colonnade extending west of the temple

---

26:1 The gatekeepers were Levites assigned to protect the tabernacle (Num. 1:52, 53). Later they guarded the temple. The gatekeepers were from the Korahites (see Kohath, 1 Chr. 6:22) and Merarites. Obed-Edom was given prominence, although his Levitical connection is uncertain (1 Chr. 13:13, 14; 15:18; 16:38). The storehouse may refer to the treasuries of the king (1 Chr. 26:15, 20–28). The "Parbar" is unknown but may refer to a courtyard area west of the temple (v. 18).

26:20 The king's treasuries requiring administration were filled with the spoils of war (vv. 20, 26, 28; see 1 Chr. 9:26). Levites given charge over the treasuries were from the sons of Gershon and from four Kohathite families (see 1 Chr. 6:16, note). Among these is the family of Moses (Gershom, 1 Chr. 26:24; Eliezer, v. 25; Ex. 18:2–5). The family of Izhar had duties outside Jerusalem. The Hebronites looked after the king's affairs east and west of the Jordan (1 Chr. 26:30, 32).

²⁹Of the Izharites, Chenaniah and his sons *performed* duties as officials and judges over Israel outside Jerusalem.

³⁰Of the Hebronites, Hashabiah and his brethren, one thousand seven hundred able men, had the oversight of Israel on the west side of the Jordan for all the business of the Lord, and in the service of the king. ³¹Among the Hebronites, Jerijah *was* head of the Hebronites according to his genealogy of the fathers. In the fortieth year of the reign of David they were sought, and there were found among them capable men at Jazer of Gilead. ³²And his brethren *were* two thousand seven hundred able men, heads of fathers' *houses,* whom King David made officials over the Reubenites, the Gadites, and the half-tribe of Manasseh, for every matter pertaining to God and the affairs of the king.

The Military Divisions

27 And the children of Israel, according to their number, the heads of fathers' *houses,* the captains of thousands and hundreds and their officers, served the king in every matter of the *military* divisions. *These divisions* came in and went out month by month throughout all the months of the year, each division *having* twenty-four thousand.

²Over the first division for the first month *was* Jashobeam the son of Zabdiel, and in his division *were* twenty-four thousand; ³*he was* of the children of Perez, and the chief of all the captains of the army for the first month. ⁴Over the division of the second month *was* Dodai[a] an Ahohite, and of his division Mikloth also *was* the leader; in his division *were* twenty-four thousand. ⁵The third captain of the army for the third month *was* Benaiah, the son of Jehoiada the priest, who was chief; in his division *were* twenty-four thousand. ⁶This was the Benaiah *who was* mighty *among* the thirty, and was over the thirty; in his division *was* Ammizabad his son. ⁷The fourth *captain* for the fourth month *was* Asahel the brother of Joab, and Zebadiah his son after him; in his division *were* twenty-four thousand. ⁸The fifth captain for the fifth month *was* Shamhuth[a] the Izrahite; in his division *were* twenty-four thousand. ⁹The sixth *captain* for the sixth month *was* Ira the son of Ikkesh the Tekoite; in his division *were* twenty-four thousand. ¹⁰The seventh *captain* for the seventh month *was* Helez the Pelonite, of the children of Ephraim; in his division *were* twenty-four thousand. ¹¹The eighth *captain* for the eighth month *was* Sibbechai the Hushathite, of the Zarhites; in his division *were* twenty-four thousand. ¹²The ninth *captain* for the ninth month *was* Abiezer the Anathothite, of the Benjamites; in his division *were* twenty-four thousand. ¹³The tenth *captain* for the tenth month *was* Maharai the Netophathite, of the Zarhites; in his division *were* twenty-four thousand. ¹⁴The eleventh *captain* for the eleventh month *was* Benaiah the Pirathonite, of the children of Ephraim; in his division *were* twenty-four thousand. ¹⁵The twelfth *captain* for the twelfth month *was* Heldai[a] the Netophathite, of Othniel; in his division *were* twenty-four thousand.

Leaders of Tribes

¹⁶Furthermore, over the tribes of Israel: the officer over the Reubenites *was* Eliezer the son of Zichri; over the Simeonites, Shephatiah the son of Maachah; ¹⁷*over* the Levites, Hashabiah the son of Kemuel; over the Aaronites, Zadok; ¹⁸*over* Judah, Elihu, *one* of David's brothers; *over* Issachar, Omri the son of Michael; ¹⁹*over* Zebulun, Ishmaiah the son of Obadiah; *over* Naphtali, Jerimoth the son of Azriel; ²⁰*over* the children of Ephraim, Hoshea the son of Azaziah; *over* the half-tribe of Manasseh, Joel the son of Pedaiah; ²¹*over* the half-*tribe* of Manasseh in Gilead, Iddo the son of Zechariah; *over* Benjamin, Jaasiel the son of Abner; ²²*over* Dan, Azarel the son of Jeroham. These *were* the leaders of the tribes of Israel.

²³But David did not take the number of those twenty years old and under, because the Lord had said He would multiply Israel like the stars of the heavens. ²⁴Joab the son of Zeruiah began a census, but he did not finish, for wrath came upon Israel because of this census; nor was the number recorded in the account of the chronicles of King David.

Other State Officials

²⁵And Azmaveth the son of Adiel *was* over the king's treasuries; and Jehonathan the son of Uzziah *was* over the storehouses in the field, in the cities, in the villages, and in the fortresses. ²⁶Ezri the son of Chelub *was* over those who did the work of the field for tilling the ground. ²⁷And Shimei the Ramathite *was* over the vineyards, and

· · · · · · · · · · · · · · · · · ·

27:4 ᵃHebrew *Dodai,* usually spelled *Dodo* (compare 2 Samuel 23:9)
27:8 ᵃSpelled *Shammoth* in 11:27 and *Shammah* in 2 Samuel 23:11
27:15 ᵃSpelled *Heled* in 11:30 and *Heleb* in 2 Samuel 23:29

27:1 Protection of the kingdom was assigned to 12 military divisions, each with 24,000 men and each serving one month (see 1 Chr. 23:3–5, note). The captain of the armies of the first month, Jashobeam, descended from Perez, son of Judah (1 Chr. 27:2, 3). This shows the prominence of the tribe of Judah among all Israel. A head is appointed for each tribe (vv. 16–21). Note the absence of Gad and Asher—perhaps because the chronicler followed his usual form and structure of planning to limit his list to 12 tribes, which he already had; or he may not have had the names of their leaders available and omitted them for that reason (see 1 Chr. 2:3). The responsibilities are listed according to the treasury (1 Chr. 27:25), the produce of the land (vv. 26–28), and the livestock (vv. 29–31). David's uncle, Jehonathan, is otherwise unknown (v. 32).

Zabdi the Shiphmite was over the produce of the vineyards for the supply of wine. [28]Baal-Hanan the Gederite was over the olive trees and the sycamore trees that *were* in the lowlands, and Joash *was* over the store of oil. [29]And Shitrai the Sharonite *was* over the herds that fed in Sharon, and Shaphat the son of Adlai was over the herds *that were* in the valleys. [30]Obil the Ishmaelite *was* over the camels, Jehdeiah the Meronothite *was* over the donkeys, [31]and Jaziz the Hagrite *was* over the flocks. All these *were* the officials over King David's property.

[32]Also Jehonathan, David's uncle, *was* a counselor, a wise man, and a scribe; and Jehiel the son of Hachmoni *was* with the king's sons. [33]Ahithophel *was* the king's counselor, and Hushai the Archite *was* the king's companion. [34]After Ahithophel *was* Jehoiada the son of Benaiah, then Abiathar. And the general of the king's army *was* Joab.

Solomon Instructed to Build the Temple

28 Now David assembled at Jerusalem all the leaders of Israel: the officers of the tribes and the captains of the divisions who served the king, the captains over thousands and captains over hundreds, and the stewards over all the substance and possessions of the king and of his sons, with the officials, the valiant men, and all the mighty men of valor.

[2]Then King David rose to his feet and said, "Hear me, my brethren and my people: I *had* it in my heart to build a house of rest for the ark of the covenant of the LORD, and for the footstool of our God, and had made preparations to build it. [3]But God said to me, 'You shall not build a house for My name, because you *have been* a man of war and have shed blood.' [4]However the LORD God of Israel chose me above all the house of my father to be king over Israel forever, for He has chosen Judah *to be* the ruler. And of the house of Judah, the house of my father, and among the sons of my father, He was pleased with me to make *me* king over all Israel. [5]And of all my sons (for the LORD has given me many sons) He has chosen my son Solomon to sit on the throne of the kingdom of the LORD over Israel. [6]Now He said to me, 'It is your son Solomon *who* shall build My house and My courts; for I have chosen him *to be* My son, and I will be his Father. [7]Moreover I will establish his kingdom forever, if he is steadfast to observe My commandments and My judgments, as it is this

day.' [8]Now therefore, in the sight of all Israel, the assembly of the LORD, and in the hearing of our God, be careful to seek out all the commandments of the LORD your God, that you may possess this good land, and leave *it* as an inheritance for your children after you forever.

[9]"As for you, my son Solomon, know the God of your father, and serve Him with a loyal heart and with a willing mind; for the LORD searches all hearts and understands all the intent of the thoughts. If you seek Him, He will be found by you; but if you forsake Him, He will cast you off forever. [10]Consider now, for the LORD has chosen you to build a house for the sanctuary; be strong, and do it."

[11]Then David gave his son Solomon the plans for the vestibule, its houses, its treasuries, its upper chambers, its inner chambers, and the place of the mercy seat; [12]and the plans for all that he had by the Spirit, of the courts of the house of the LORD, of all the chambers all around, of the treasuries of the house of God, and of the treasuries for the dedicated things; [13]also for the division of the priests and the Levites, for all the work of the service of the house of the LORD, and for all the articles of service in the house of the LORD. [14]*He gave* gold by weight for *things* of gold, for all articles used in every kind of service; also *silver* for all articles of silver by weight, for all articles used in every kind of service; [15]the weight for the lampstands of gold, and their lamps of gold, by weight for each lampstand and its lamps; for the lampstands of silver by weight, for the lampstand and its lamps, according to the use of each lampstand. [16]And by weight *he gave* gold for the tables of the showbread, for each table, and silver for the tables of silver; [17]also pure gold for the forks, the basins, the pitchers of pure gold, and the golden bowls— *he gave gold* by weight for every bowl; and for the silver bowls, *silver* by weight for every bowl; [18]and refined gold by weight for the altar of incense, and for the construction of the chariot, that is, the gold cherubim that spread *their wings* and overshadowed the ark of the covenant of the LORD. [19]"All *this*," *said David*, "the LORD made me understand in writing, by *His* hand upon me, all the works of these plans."

[20]And David said to his son Solomon, "Be strong and of good courage, and do *it;* do not fear nor be dismayed, for the LORD God— my God— *will be* with you. He will not leave you nor forsake you, until you have finished all the work for the service

28:1 Solomon's building of the temple. This expanded and intensified record of 1 Chronicles 22 takes the form of a greater encouragement to Solomon. David legitimized Solomon's claim to the throne by tracing his heritage to Judah (1 Chr. 28:4, 5; see 1 Chr. 2:3). Solomon is chosen to sit on the throne (1 Chr. 28:5), to be God's son (v. 6), and to build the temple (v. 10). Solomon did fail in a key point, however. He did not obey steadfastly God's commandments as specified (v. 7). David's preparation for the temple is expanded to include the plans of God for the temple (vv. 11–21; Ex. 25:9, 40; 1 Chr. 22:14–16). All Israel joined in the building project with contributions (1 Chr. 29:6–9). The "daric" is a Persian coin probably named for King Darius of Persia (1 Chr. 29:7).

of the house of the LORD. [21]*Here are* the divisions of the priests and the Levites for all the service of the house of God; and every willing craftsman *will be* with you for all manner of workmanship, for every kind of service; also the leaders and all the people *will be* completely at your command."

Offerings for Building the Temple

29 Furthermore King David said to all the assembly: "My son Solomon, whom alone God has chosen, *is* young and inexperienced; and the work *is* great, because the temple[a] *is* not for man but for the LORD God. [2]Now for the house of my God I have prepared with all my might: gold for *things to be made of* gold, silver for *things of* silver, bronze for *things of* bronze, iron for *things of* iron, wood for *things of* wood, onyx stones, *stones* to be set, glistening stones of various colors, all kinds of precious stones, and marble slabs in abundance. [3]Moreover, because I have set my affection on the house of my God, I have given to the house of my God, over and above all that I have prepared for the holy house, my own special treasure of gold and silver: [4]three thousand talents of gold, of the gold of Ophir, and seven thousand talents of refined silver, to overlay the walls of the houses; [5]the gold for *things of* gold and the silver for *things of* silver, and for all kinds of work *to be done* by the hands of craftsmen. Who then is willing to consecrate himself this day to the LORD?"

[6]Then the leaders of the fathers' *houses*, leaders of the tribes of Israel, the captains of thousands and of hundreds, with the officers over the king's work, offered willingly. [7]They gave for the work of the house of God five thousand talents and ten thousand darics of gold, ten thousand talents of silver, eighteen thousand talents of bronze, and one hundred thousand talents of iron. [8]And whoever had *precious* stones gave *them* to the treasury of the house of the LORD, into the hand of Jehiel[a] the Gershonite. [9]Then the people rejoiced, for they had offered willingly, because with a loyal heart they had offered willingly to the LORD; and King David also rejoiced greatly.

David's Praise to God

[10]Therefore David blessed the LORD before all the assembly; and David said:

"Blessed are You, LORD God of Israel, our Father, forever and ever.
[11]Yours, O LORD, *is* the greatness,
The power and the glory,
The victory and the majesty;
For all *that is* in heaven and in earth *is Yours;*
Yours *is* the kingdom, O LORD,
And You are exalted as head over all.
[12]Both riches and honor *come* from You,
And You reign over all.
In Your hand *is* power and might;
In Your hand *it is* to make great
And to give strength to all.

[13]"Now therefore, our God,
We thank You
And praise Your glorious name.
[14]But who *am* I, and who *are* my people,
That we should be able to offer so willingly as this?
For all things *come* from You,
And of Your own we have given You.
[15]For we *are* aliens and pilgrims before You,
As *were* all our fathers;
Our days on earth *are* as a shadow,
And without hope.

[16]"O LORD our God, all this abundance that we have prepared to build You a house for Your holy name is from Your hand, and *is* all Your own. [17]I know also, my God, that You test the heart and have pleasure in uprightness. As for me, in the uprightness of my heart I have willingly offered all these *things;* and now with joy I have seen Your people, who are present here to offer willingly to You. [18]O LORD God of Abraham, Isaac, and Israel, our fathers, keep this forever in the intent of the

•••••••••••••••••••
29:1 [a]Literally *palace*   **29:8** [a]Possibly the same as *Jehieli* (compare 26:21, 22)

29:1 The tabernacle and temple are presented in the OT as one unit. The Lord has only one dwelling place on earth. Much of the language used here is reminiscent of the tabernacle passages (Ex. 25–31; 35–40; see chart, The Temples of the Bible).

29:5 Those who did the work (Heb. *charash,* lit. "worker," "skillful one") has particular reference to the "craftsmen" for the building of the tabernacle (Ex. 28:3; 31:1–11). The word "consecrate" (lit. "to fill the hand") is used to describe the setting apart to the priesthood (Ex. 28:41; 2 Chr. 13:9). Materials gathered are the same used in the tabernacle (1 Chr. 29:2–5, 7, 8; Ex. 25:3–7; 1 Chr. 28:14–18).

29:9 The generosity of the people to give for each building project is stressed. Forms of the Hebrew word *nadab* (lit. "offer voluntarily") occur in this passage (1 Chr. 28:21, "willing

craftsman"; 1 Chr. 29:5; Ex. 35:5, 21, 22, 29, "willing"; 1 Chr. 29:6, 9, "offered willingly"; Ex. 25:2, "willingly"). The heart is at the center of this voluntary giving (1 Chr. 29:9). Both Moses and David appealed to the people to make willing contributions to the building (vv. 1–5; Ex. 35:4–9). In both cases, the people respond from the heart (1 Chr. 29:6–9; Ex. 35:20–29). Everyone rejoiced over this "willing" response to the needs of the temple (see 2 Cor. 9, Giving).

29:17 The opportunity to give willingly to the building of the temple is cause for David's humility (see v. 9, note; vv. 14, 17). David requested that the people and Solomon remain faithful to the Lord and continue to be generous and joyful regarding the building of the temple. David's final words were about the temple, for which he had been preparing throughout his reign.

thoughts of the heart of Your people, and fix their heart toward You. [19]And give my son Solomon a loyal heart to keep Your commandments and Your testimonies and Your statutes, to do all *these things,* and to build the temple[a] for which I have made provision."

[20]Then David said to all the assembly, "Now bless the LORD your God." So all the assembly blessed the LORD God of their fathers, and bowed their heads and prostrated themselves before the LORD and the king.

Solomon Anointed King

[21]And they made sacrifices to the LORD and offered burnt offerings to the LORD on the next day: a thousand bulls, a thousand rams, a thousand lambs, with their drink offerings, and sacrifices in abundance for all Israel. [22]So they ate and drank before the LORD with great gladness on that day. And they made Solomon the son of David king the second time, and anointed *him* before the LORD *to be* the leader, and Zadok *to be* priest. [23]Then Solomon sat on the throne of the LORD as king instead of David his father, and pros-

pered; and all Israel obeyed him. [24]All the leaders and the mighty men, and also all the sons of King David, submitted themselves to King Solomon. [25]So the LORD exalted Solomon exceedingly in the sight of all Israel, and bestowed on him *such* royal majesty as had not been on any king before him in Israel.

The Close of David's Reign

[26]Thus David the son of Jesse reigned over all Israel. [27]And the period that he reigned over Israel *was* forty years; seven years he reigned in Hebron, and thirty-three *years* he reigned in Jerusalem. [28]So he died in a good old age, full of days and riches and honor; and Solomon his son reigned in his place. [29]Now the acts of King David, first and last, indeed they *are* written in the book of Samuel the seer, in the book of Nathan the prophet, and in the book of Gad the seer, [30]with all his reign and his might, and the events that happened to him, to Israel, and to all the kingdoms of the lands.

29:19 [a]Literally *palace*

29:21–25 The crowning of Solomon as king. The overwhelming generosity and joy of all Israel over building the temple is expressed in a religious celebration. In this context Solomon, the temple builder, was made king (vv. 21, 22). Contrast this account of the crowning of Solomon with that of 1 Kings 1 and 2. Here Solomon experienced no opposition, but even the "sons of King David" immediately were loyal to him (v. 24). All reference to the attempt of Adonijah to claim the throne was omitted (1 Kin. 1). Like David, Solomon enjoyed the unanimous support of "all Israel" (1 Chr. 11:1–3; 29:23, 25). David was an integral part of Solomon's accession to the throne. His name is mentioned three times (1 Chr. 29:22–24).

29:26–30 David, the temple planner, died as Solomon, the temple builder, was made king with the unanimous support of the people (vv. 23–25; see 1 Chr. 17:1, 11–15, notes). The naming of sources indicates the thorough and careful research of the chronicler (1 Chr. 29:29, 30). Nothing here suggests that the canon is incomplete or that any portion of these works is uninspired. These three titled works may well refer to portions of 1 and 2 Samuel and/or other works in the historical archives of Israel. Samuel (1 Sam. 3:19—4:1), Nathan (see 2 Sam. 12:1–15; 1 Chr. 17:1–15), and Gad (2 Sam. 24:10–19; 1 Chr. 21:9–19) are well known from David's life.

2 Chronicles

AUTHOR

Together, 1 and 2 Chronicles form one work of an author usually referred to as the "chronicler" (see 1 Chronicles, Introduction: Author).

DATE

Chronicles is a postexilic work with a date of completion about fifth century B.C.

BACKGROUND

See 1 Chronicles, Introduction: Background Information.

PURPOSE: In 2 Chronicles, the central focus is on Solomon's reign. Solomon's role in the history of the temple has been constructed around a specific Hebrew literary form in which passages parallel in content are repeated in the reverse order, bracketing a central passage. For example, passages concerning "house, tribute, building" (2 Chr. 1:1—4:22) are repeated in the reverse order, "building, tribute, house" (2 Chr. 8:1—9:28). The central section, "The temple and the covenant" (2 Chr. 5:1—7:22), then becomes the focal point of Solomon's reign. The covenant demanded that the people live in devotion to the Lord. An integral part of that devotion was loyalty to the temple and worship in the temple. This lifestyle was the way to blessing.

LITERARY CHARACTERISTICS: The history of the temple in Jerusalem as presented in 1 and 2 Chronicles is structured into four parts. After the important genealogies of 1 Chronicles 1—9, revealing God's sovereign election and preservation of Israel, the chronicler focused his history on David as the temple planner (1 Chr. 10—29), on Solomon as the temple builder (2 Chr. 1—9), and on Israel as the nation responsible for the temple (2 Chr. 10—36).

Throughout Chronicles, speeches are made by kings (1 Chr. 22:7–16; 2 Chr. 13:4–12; 14:11), by prophets (2 Chr. 15:1–7; 21:12–15), and by the Lord Himself (2 Chr. 7:12–22). Such speeches and prayers, many of which are unique to the chronicler, reinforce the chronicler's theology that devotion to the Lord, especially as exemplified in temple worship, is the means to blessing and prosperity. Anything less than complete devotion is sin. The chronicler repeatedly used specific vocabulary in speeches, prayers, and narrative sections to demonstrate Israel's faithfulness, or lack thereof, to the Lord. The reader will find frequent use of such words as "seek," "forsake," "turn," "humble," "trust," "worship" (bow down), "praise," "sanctify," and "pray."

The chronicler's use of numbers raises a perplexing question. Some numbers seem too large, and others seem to contradict those given in related passages. Solutions suggested often have their own difficulties and weaknesses. Yet exegetical, historical, and archaeological investigations have continued to clarify and explain. The numbers used may provide a literary device for the chronicler to accomplish his purpose.

King in his place. 'Now, O LORD God, let Your
promise to David my father be established, for
You have ...

THEMES

The themes of "all Israel," the centrality of the temple, the ideal reigns of David and
Solomon, and the theology of retribution are all present in 2 Chronicles (see also
1 Chronicles, Introduction: Themes).

OUTLINE

Solomon Requests Wisdom

1 Now Solomon the son of David was strengthened in his kingdom, and the LORD his God *was*
with him and exalted him exceedingly.

²And Solomon spoke to all Israel, to the captains of thousands and of hundreds, to the judges,
and to every leader in all Israel, the heads of the
fathers' *houses.* ³Then Solomon, and all the assembly with him, went to the high place that *was* at
Gibeon; for the tabernacle of meeting with God
was there, which Moses the servant of the LORD
had made in the wilderness. ⁴But David had
brought up the ark of God from Kirjath Jearim to
the place David had prepared for it, for he had

pitched a tent for it at Jerusalem. ⁵Now the bronze
altar that Bezalel the son of Uri, the son of Hur,
had made, he put ᵃ before the tabernacle of the
LORD; Solomon and the assembly sought Him
there. ⁶And Solomon went up there to the bronze
altar before the LORD, which *was* at the tabernacle
of meeting, and offered a thousand burnt offerings on it.

⁷On that night God appeared to Solomon, and
said to him, "Ask! What shall I give you?"

⁸And Solomon said to God: "You have shown
great mercy to David my father, and have made me

1:5 ᵃSome authorities read *it was there.*

1:1 Solomon fulfilled the promises God had made to David
that his son would build the house of the Lord and that the
Lord would build a house for David, that is, establish
David's heirs on the throne of Israel (1 Chr. 17:10–14; 22:10;
28:6, 7; 29:19, 23–25). The chronicler pictured an easy transition of power from David to Solomon (see 1 Chr. 23:1;
29:21–25, note). Solomon was a man of rest (1 Chr. 22:9).
Solomon's kingdom was established by God with wisdom
and prosperity (1 Chr. 22:10–13). The account of the chronicler gives little hint of Solomon's turning from the Lord and
of the resulting judgment for his sin (compare 1 Kin. 11:1–40
with 2 Chr. 8:11).

1:3 The 1 Kings account emphasizes Solomon's role in the sacrifice at Gibeon (1 Kin. 3:4). The chronicler emphasizes that it
was the king and all the assembly who went to Gibeon, showing all the people as actively supporting and participating in
Solomon's activities. During David's reign, Gibeon, a Levitical

city of Benjamin just north of Jerusalem, was the location of
the tabernacle that Moses had built (1 Chr. 21:29). A "high
place" was a worship site, usually an altar, built on an elevated
location such as a mountain or hill (Is. 65:7; Ezek. 6:13). The
high places of foreign gods were to be destroyed, but
nonetheless they were common throughout Israel (Deut.
12:1–14; 2 Chr. 14:3, 5).

1:5 Bezalel. The chronicler makes a direct association between
Bezalel, the builder of the tabernacle, and Solomon, the
builder of the temple (see Ex. 31:2–5; 35:30—36:7; 38:22;
1 Chr. 2:18–20). Bezalel built the bronze altar for the tabernacle according to the plans God had given Moses (Ex. 37:1; see
chart, The Furniture of the Tabernacle). Solomon built a
bronze altar for the temple of the Lord according to the plans
God had given David (2 Chr. 3:1; 4:1; see chart, The Plan of Solomon's Temple). Both men were from the tribe of Judah (Ex.
31:2; 1 Chr. 28:4, 5).

king in his place. ⁹Now, O LORD God, let Your promise to David my father be established, for You have made me king over a people like the dust of the earth in multitude. ¹⁰Now give me wisdom and knowledge, that I may go out and come in before this people; for who can judge this great people of Yours?"

¹¹Then God said to Solomon: "Because this was in your heart, and you have not asked riches or wealth or honor or the life of your enemies, nor have you asked long life—but have asked wisdom and knowledge for yourself, that you may judge My people over whom I have made you king— ¹²wisdom and knowledge *are* granted to you; and I will give you riches and wealth and honor, such as none of the kings have had who *were* before you, nor shall any after you have the like."

Solomon's Military and Economic Power

¹³So Solomon came to Jerusalem from the high place that *was* at Gibeon, from before the tabernacle of meeting, and reigned over Israel. ¹⁴And Solomon gathered chariots and horsemen; he had one thousand four hundred chariots and twelve thousand horsemen, whom he stationed in the chariot cities and with the king in Jerusalem. ¹⁵Also the king made silver and gold as common in Jerusalem as stones, and he made cedars as abundant as the sycamores which *are* in the lowland. ¹⁶And Solomon had horses imported from Egypt and Keveh; the king's merchants bought them in Keveh at the *current* price. ¹⁷They also acquired and imported from Egypt a chariot for six hundred *shekels* of silver, and a horse for one hundred and fifty; thus, through their agents,ᵃ they exported them to all the kings of the Hittites and the kings of Syria.

Solomon Prepares to Build the Temple

2 Then Solomon determined to build a temple for the name of the LORD, and a royal house for himself. ²Solomon selected seventy thousand men to bear burdens, eighty thousand to quarry *stone* in the mountains, and three thousand six hundred to oversee them.

³Then Solomon sent to Huramᵃ king of Tyre, saying:

As you have dealt with David my father, and sent him cedars to build himself a house to

dwell in, *so deal with me.* ⁴Behold, I am building a temple for the name of the LORD my God, to dedicate *it* to Him, to burn before Him sweet incense, for the continual showbread, for the burnt offerings morning and evening, on the Sabbaths, on the New Moons, and on the set feasts of the LORD our God. This *is an ordinance* forever to Israel.

⁵And the temple which I build *will be* great, for our God is greater than all gods. ⁶But who is able to build Him a temple, since heaven and the heaven of heavens cannot contain Him? Who *am* I then, that I should build Him a temple, except to burn sacrifice before Him?

⁷Therefore send me at once a man skillful to work in gold and silver, in bronze and iron, in purple and crimson and blue, who has skill to engrave with the skillful men who are with me in Judah and Jerusalem, whom David my father provided. ⁸Also send me cedar and cypress and algum logs from Lebanon, for I know that your servants have skill to cut timber in Lebanon; and indeed my servants *will be* with your servants, ⁹to prepare timber for me in abundance, for the temple which I am about to build *shall be* great and wonderful.

¹⁰And indeed I will give to your servants, the woodsmen who cut timber, twenty thousand kors of ground wheat, twenty thousand kors of barley, twenty thousand baths of wine, and twenty thousand baths of oil.

¹¹Then Hiram king of Tyre answered in writing, which he sent to Solomon:

Because the LORD loves His people, He has made you king over them.

¹²Hiramᵃ also said:

Blessed *be* the LORD God of Israel, who made heaven and earth, for He has given King David

•••••••••••••••••••••
1:17 ᵃLiterally *by their hands*   2:3 ᵃHebrew *Huram* (compare 1 Kings 5:1)   2:12 ᵃHebrew *Huram* (compare 1 Kings 5:1)

2:2 The labor force for the work of the temple is the subject of correspondence between Solomon and Hiram (see 1 Kin. 5:13, note). The chronicler's focus is on the aliens forced into labor and not on Israelite labor.

2:13, 14 Huram is presented as a "master craftsman" as was Aholiab, a tabernacle artisan. Huram seemingly is the only worker in bronze. The chronicler noted skills paralleling those of Aholiab and Bezalel (v. 7; Ex. 35:30–35). Aholiab worked on the tabernacle from the beginning (Ex. 31:1–11). Both Huram and Aholiab were from the tribe of Dan (2 Chr. 2:14; Ex. 31:6).

Huram's mother, though unnamed, is listed as being from the tribe of Dan. In another reference she is linked with the tribe of Naphtali (1 Kin. 7:13, 14). Though seemingly a contradiction, many reasonable explanations are proposed. One suggestion is that in Solomon's day the city of Dan and its territories were part of the general region of Naphtali, making it quite possible for Huram's mother, though living in Dan, to be from the tribe of Naphtali. Huram's father was Phoenician, which gave Huram a unique ability linguistically and culturally for dealing with the men of mixed nationalities working under him.

Speak little to creatures but speak much with God. He will make you truly wise.

St. Mary Mazzarello

a wise son, endowed with prudence and understanding, who will build a temple for the LORD and a royal house for himself!

13And now I have sent a skillful man, endowed with understanding, Hurama my masterb *craftsman* 14(the son of a woman of the daughters of Dan, and his father was a man of Tyre), skilled to work in gold and silver, bronze and iron, stone and wood, purple and blue, fine linen and crimson, and to make any engraving and to accomplish any plan which may be given to him, with your skillful men and with the skillful men of my lord David your father.

15Now therefore, the wheat, the barley, the oil, and the wine which my lord has spoken of, let him send to his servants. 16And we will cut wood from Lebanon, as much as you need; we will bring it to you in rafts by sea to Joppa, and you will carry it up to Jerusalem.

17Then Solomon numbered all the aliens who *were* in the land of Israel, after the census in which David his father had numbered them; and there were found to be one hundred and fifty-three thousand six hundred. 18And he made seventy thousand of them bearers of burdens, eighty thousand stonecutters in the mountain, and three thousand six hundred overseers to make the people work.

Solomon Builds the Temple

3 Now Solomon began to build the house of the LORD at Jerusalem on Mount Moriah, where *the LORD*a had appeared to his father David, at the place that David had prepared on the threshing floor of Ornanb the Jebusite. 2And he began to build on the second *day* of the second month in the fourth year of his reign.

3This is the foundation which Solomon laid for building the house of God: The length *was* sixty cubits (by cubits according to the former measure) and the width twenty cubits. 4And the

vestibule that *was* in front *of the sanctuary*a was twenty cubits long across the width of the house, and the height *was* one hundred andb twenty. He overlaid the inside with pure gold. 5The larger rooma he paneled with cypress which he overlaid with fine gold, and he carved palm trees and chainwork on it. 6And he decorated the house with precious stones for beauty, and the gold *was* gold from Parvaim. 7He also overlaid the house— the beams and doorposts, its walls and doors— with gold; and he carved cherubim on the walls.

8And he made the Most Holy Place. Its length was according to the width of the house, twenty cubits, and its width twenty cubits. He overlaid it with six hundred talents of fine gold. 9The weight of the nails *was* fifty shekels of gold; and he overlaid the upper area with gold. 10In the Most Holy Place he made two cherubim, fashioned by carving, and overlaid them with gold. 11The wings of the cherubim *were* twenty cubits in *overall* length: one wing *of the one cherub was* five cubits, touching the wall of the room, and the other wing *was* five cubits, touching the wing of the other cherub; 12*one* wing of the other cherub *was* five cubits, touching the wall of the room, and the other wing *also was* five cubits, touching the wing of the other cherub. 13The wings of these cherubim spanned twenty cubits overall. They stood on their feet, and they faced inward. 14And he made the veil of blue, purple, crimson, and fine linen, and wove cherubim into it.

15Also he made in front of the templea two pillars thirty-fiveb cubits high, and the capital that *was* on the top of each of *them* was five cubits. 16He made wreaths of chainwork, as in the inner sanctuary, and put *them* on top of the pillars; and

2:13 aSpelled *Hiram* in 1 Kings 7:13 bLiterally *father* (compare 1 Kings 7:13, 14) 3:1 aLiterally *He*, following Masoretic Text and Vulgate; Septuagint reads *the LORD*; Targum reads *the Angel of the LORD.* bSpelled *Araunah* in 2 Samuel 24:16ff 3:4 aThe main room of the temple; elsewhere called the holy place (compare 1 Kings 6:3) bFollowing Masoretic Text, Septuagint, and Vulgate; Arabic, some manuscripts of the Septuagint, and Syriac omit *one hundred and.* 3:5 aLiterally *house* 3:15 aLiterally *house* bOr *eighteen* (compare 1 Kings 7:15; 2 Kings 25:17; and Jeremiah 52:21)

3:1–17 The postexilic temple paled in comparison to the splendor and size of Solomon's temple (Hag. 2:3). Mount Moriah, the place of Abraham's offering of Isaac, only here in Scripture is associated with the temple site (2 Chr. 3:1; see Gen. 22:2). Among the many temple preparations made by David was the location of the temple site (see 1 Chr. 21:27–30, note). "Parvaim" is seemingly the name of a place, but its location is unknown (2 Chr. 3:6). The veil is a deliberate reference to the tabernacle (v. 14; Ex. 26:31–33). The significance of the names of the pillars is unclear (see chart, The Plan of Solomon's Temple). "Jachin" (a compound term using *Yahweh* and Heb. ku^-n, lit. "accomplish," "set up," "establish") may refer to the Lord as "He who established." "Boaz" may be a reference to the strength of the Lord (2 Chr. 3:17). Together they may form the exclamation, "He establishes in strength!"

he made one hundred pomegranates, and put *them* on the wreaths of chainwork. [17]Then he set up the pillars before the temple, one on the right hand and the other on the left; he called the name of the one on the right hand Jachin, and the name of the one on the left Boaz.

Furnishings of the Temple

4 Moreover he made a bronze altar: twenty cubits was its length, twenty cubits its width, and ten cubits its height.

[2]Then he made the Sea of cast *bronze*, ten cubits from one brim to the other; *it was* completely round. Its height *was* five cubits, and a line of thirty cubits measured its circumference. [3]And under it *was* the likeness of oxen encircling it all around, ten to a cubit, all the way around the Sea. The oxen *were* cast in two rows, when it was cast. [4]It stood on twelve oxen: three looking toward the north, three looking toward the west, three looking toward the south, and three looking toward the east; the Sea *was set* upon them, and all their back parts *pointed* inward. [5]It *was* a handbreadth thick; and its brim was shaped like the brim of a cup, *like* a lily blossom. It contained three thousand[a] baths.

[6]He also made ten lavers, and put five on the right side and five on the left, to wash in them; such things as they offered for the burnt offering they would wash in them, but the Sea *was* for the priests to wash in. [7]And he made ten lampstands of gold according to their design, and set *them* in the temple, five on the right side and five on the left. [8]He also made ten tables, and placed *them* in the temple, five on the right side and five on the left. And he made one hundred bowls of gold.

[9]Furthermore he made the court of the priests, and the great court and doors for the court; and he overlaid these doors with bronze. [10]He set the Sea on the right side, toward the southeast.

[11]Then Huram made the pots and the shovels and the bowls. So Huram finished doing the work that he was to do for King Solomon for the house of God: [12]the two pillars and the bowl-shaped capitals *that were* on top of the two pillars; the two networks covering the two bowl-shaped capitals which *were* on top of the pillars; [13]four hundred pomegranates for the two networks (two rows of pomegranates for each network, to cover the two bowl-shaped capitals that *were* on the pillars); [14]he also made carts and the lavers on the carts; [15]one Sea and twelve oxen under it; [16]also the pots, the shovels, the forks—and all their articles Huram his master[a] *craftsman* made of burnished bronze for King Solomon for the house of the LORD.

[17]In the plain of Jordan the king had them cast in clay molds, between Succoth and Zeredah.[a] [18]And Solomon had all these articles made in such great abundance that the weight of the bronze was not determined.

[19]Thus Solomon had all the furnishings made for the house of God: the altar of gold and the tables on which *was* the showbread; [20]the lampstands with their lamps of pure gold, to burn in the prescribed manner in front of the inner sanctuary, [21]with the flowers and the lamps and the wick-trimmers of gold, of purest gold; [22]the trimmers, the bowls, the ladles, and the censers of pure gold. As for the entry of the sanctuary, its inner doors to the Most Holy *Place*, and the doors of the main hall of the temple, *were* gold.

5 So all the work that Solomon had done for the house of the LORD was finished; and Solomon brought in the things which his father David had dedicated: the silver and the gold and all the furnishings. And he put *them* in the treasuries of the house of God.

The Ark Brought into the Temple

[2]Now Solomon assembled the elders of Israel and all the heads of the tribes, the chief fathers of the children of Israel, in Jerusalem, that they might bring the ark of the covenant of the LORD up from the City of David, which *is* Zion. [3]Therefore all the men of Israel assembled with the king at the feast, which *was* in the seventh month. [4]So all the elders of Israel came, and the Levites took up the ark. [5]Then they brought up the ark, the

4:5 [a]Or *two thousand* (compare 1 Kings 7:26)   **4:16** [a]Literally *father*
4:17 [a]Spelled *Zaretan* in 1 Kings 7:46

4:1–22 Temple furnishings. The "Sea" was for the ritual washing of the priests, and the "ten lavers" were for the washing of utensils used for sacrifices (vv. 2–6; Ex. 30:17–21). The "Sea" stood on "twelve oxen" (2 Chr. 4:4), probably symbolic of the 12 tribes of Israel. The "Sea" was of considerable size (v. 5; 3,000 baths equaling about 12,000 gallons). The "altar of gold" is the altar of incense (v. 19; Ex. 30:1–10; 37:25–28; 1 Chr. 28:18; see also chart, The Furniture of the Tabernacle).

5:1–14 The ark was brought from the city of David to the Most Holy Place of the temple with the same type of religious procession that accompanied David's bringing the ark to Jerusa-lem (see 1 Kin. 8:1–11; 1 Chr. 15:16, note; see also chart, The Furniture of the Tabernacle). In both processions all Israel gathered at Jerusalem (2 Chr. 5:2, 3); only the Levites carried the ark (vv. 4, 5; see 1 Chr. 15:2); joyful feasting and sacrificing accompanied the procession (2 Chr. 5:3; see 1 Chr. 16:2, 3); the ark was set in the place especially prepared for it (2 Chr. 5:7–10; see 1 Chr. 16:1); and the people were blessed (2 Chr. 6:3; see 1 Chr. 16:2). The feast in the seventh month is the Feast of Tabernacles (2 Chr. 5:3; 7:8–10; see Lev. 23:33–43; chart, The Feasts of Israel). Each procession was accompanied with music and singing (2 Chr. 5:11–13; see 1 Chr. 15:28).

tabernacle of meeting, and all the holy furnishings that *were* in the tabernacle. The priests and the Levites brought them up. 6Also King Solomon, and all the congregation of Israel who were assembled with him before the ark, were sacrificing sheep and oxen that could not be counted or numbered for multitude. 7Then the priests brought in the ark of the covenant of the LORD to its place, into the inner sanctuary of the temple,a to the Most Holy *Place,* under the wings of the cherubim. 8For the cherubim spread *their* wings over the place of the ark, and the cherubim overshadowed the ark and its poles. 9The poles extended so that the ends of the poles of the ark could be seen from *the holy place,* in front of the inner sanctuary; but they could not be seen from outside. And they are there to this day. 10Nothing was in the ark except the two tablets which Moses put *there* at Horeb, when the LORD made *a covenant* with the children of Israel, when they had come out of Egypt.

11And it came to pass when the priests came out of the *Most* Holy *Place* (for all the priests who *were* present had sanctified themselves, without keeping to their divisions), 12and the Levites *who were* the singers, all those of Asaph and Heman and Jeduthun, with their sons and their brethren, stood at the east end of the altar, clothed in white linen, having cymbals, stringed instruments and harps, and with them one hundred and twenty priests sounding with trumpets— 13indeed it came to pass, when the trumpeters and singers *were* as one, to make one sound to be heard in praising and thanking the LORD, and when they lifted up their voice with the trumpets and cymbals and instruments of music, and praised the LORD, *saying:*

"*For He is* good,
  For His mercy *endures* forever,"a

that the house, the house of the LORD, was filled with a cloud, 14so that the priests could not continue ministering because of the cloud; for the glory of the LORD filled the house of God.

6

Then Solomon spoke:

"The LORD said He would dwell in the dark cloud.
  2I have surely built You an exalted house,
  And a place for You to dwell in forever."

SOLOMON'S PRAYER

Prelude to Solomon's Prayer (2 Chr. 5:1–14)
  The completion of the temple (2 Chr. 5:1)
  A feast for the men of Israel (2 Chr. 5:2, 3)
  Sacrifices and music from the people (2 Chr. 5:4–12)
  Goodness and mercy from the Lord (2 Chr. 5:13)
  The glory of His presence in the temple (2 Chr. 5:14)

Solomon's Speech (2 Chr. 6:1–42)
  A blessing (2 Chr. 6:1–11)
  A prayer (2 Chr. 6:12–42)

Epilogue to Solomon's Prayer (2 Chr. 7:1–11)
  The "glory" of His presence (2 Chr. 7:1, 2)
  Goodness and mercy from the Lord (2 Chr. 7:3)
  Sacrifices and music from the people (2 Chr. 7:4–7)
  A seven-day feast (2 Chr. 7:8)
  A sacred assembly (2 Chr. 7:9, 10)
  A final note (2 Chr. 7:11)

The Lord's Answer (2 Chr. 7:12–22)
  Affirmation of the place of worship (2 Chr. 7:12)
  Promise to keep My covenant (2 Chr. 7:13–22)

Solomon's Speech upon Completion of the Work

3Then the king turned around and blessed the whole assembly of Israel, while all the assembly of Israel was standing. 4And he said: "Blessed *be* the LORD God of Israel, who has fulfilled with His hands *what* He spoke with His mouth to my father David, saying, 5'Since the day that I brought My people out of the land of Egypt, I have chosen no city from any tribe of Israel *in which* to build a house, that My name might be there, nor did I choose any man to be a ruler over My people Israel. 6Yet I have chosen Jerusalem, that My name may be there, and I have chosen David to be over My people Israel.' 7Now it was in the heart of my father David to build a templea for the name of the LORD God of Israel. 8But the LORD said to my father David, 'Whereas it was in your heart to build a temple for My name, you did well in that it was in your heart. 9Nevertheless you shall not build the temple, but your son who will come from your body, he shall build the temple for My name.' 10So the LORD has fulfilled His word which He spoke, and I have filled the position of my father David, and sit on the throne of Israel, as the LORD promised; and I have built the temple for the name of the LORD God of Israel. 11And there I have

5:7 aLiterally *house* 5:13 aCompare Psalm 106:1 6:7 aLiterally *house,* and so in verses 8–10

5:14 The glory of the Lord. As the ark was placed in the temple, the Most Holy Place was so filled with the presence of the Lord that the priests could not continue ministering. This "glory of the LORD" was represented by a cloud, signifying the dwelling place of the Lord (2 Chr. 6:1; 7:1, 2; see also Ex. 40:34–38).

6:1, 2 The presence of the Lord was pictured as a cloud at Sinai (Ex. 20:21; Deut. 5:22). In contrast to the transportable tabernacle, the temple at Jerusalem was the permanent dwelling place of the Lord (see chart, The Plan of Solomon's Temple).

put the ark, in which *is* the covenant of the LORD which He made with the children of Israel."

Solomon's Prayer of Dedication

[12]Then *Solomon*[a] stood before the altar of the LORD in the presence of all the assembly of Israel, and spread out his hands [13](for Solomon had made a bronze platform five cubits long, five cubits wide, and three cubits high, and had set it in the midst of the court; and he stood on it, knelt down on his knees before all the assembly of Israel, and spread out his hands toward heaven); [14]and he said: "LORD God of Israel, *there is* no God in heaven or on earth like You, who keep *Your* covenant and mercy with Your servants who walk before You with all their hearts. [15]You have kept what You promised Your servant David my father; You have both spoken with Your mouth and fulfilled *it* with Your hand, as *it is* this day. [16]Therefore, LORD God of Israel, now keep what You promised Your servant David my father, saying, 'You shall not fail to have a man sit before Me on the throne of Israel, only if your sons take heed to their way, that they walk in My law as you have walked before Me.' [17]And now, O LORD God of Israel, let Your word come true, which You have spoken to Your servant David.

[18]"But will God indeed dwell with men on the earth? Behold, heaven and the heaven of heavens cannot contain You. How much less this temple[a] which I have built! [19]Yet regard the prayer of Your servant and his supplication, O LORD my God, and listen to the cry and the prayer which Your servant is praying before You: [20]that Your eyes may be open toward this temple day and night, toward the place where *You* said *You would* put Your name, that You may hear the prayer which Your servant makes toward this place. [21]And may You hear the supplications of Your servant and of Your people Israel, when they pray toward this place. Hear from heaven Your dwelling place, and when You hear, forgive.

[22]"If anyone sins against his neighbor, and is forced to take an oath, and comes *and* takes an oath before Your altar in this temple, [23]then hear from heaven, and act, and judge Your servants, bringing retribution on the wicked by bringing his way on his own head, and justifying the righteous by giving him according to his righteousness.

[24]"Or if Your people Israel are defeated before an enemy because they have sinned against You,

and return and confess Your name, and pray and make supplication before You in this temple, [25]then hear from heaven and forgive the sin of Your people Israel, and bring them back to the land which You gave to them and their fathers.

[26]"When the heavens are shut up and there is no rain because they have sinned against You, when they pray toward this place and confess Your name, and turn from their sin because You afflict them, [27]then hear *in* heaven, and forgive the sin of Your servants, Your people Israel, that You may teach them the good way in which they should walk; and send rain on Your land which You have given to Your people as an inheritance.

[28]"When there is famine in the land, pestilence or blight or mildew, locusts or grasshoppers; when their enemies besiege them in the land of their cities; whatever plague or whatever sickness *there is;* [29]whatever prayer, whatever supplication is *made* by anyone, or by all Your people Israel, when each one knows his own burden and his own grief, and spreads out his hands to this temple: [30]then hear from heaven Your dwelling place, and forgive, and give to everyone according to all his ways, whose heart You know (for You alone know the hearts of the sons of men), [31]that they may fear You, to walk in Your ways as long as they live in the land which You gave to our fathers.

[32]"Moreover, concerning a foreigner, who is not of Your people Israel, but has come from a far country for the sake of Your great name and Your mighty hand and Your outstretched arm, when they come and pray in this temple; [33]then hear from heaven Your dwelling place, and do according to all for which the foreigner calls to You, that all peoples of the earth may know Your name and fear You, as *do* Your people Israel, and that they may know that this temple which I have built is called by Your name.

[34]"When Your people go out to battle against their enemies, wherever You send them, and when they pray to You toward this city which You have chosen and the temple which I have built for Your name, [35]then hear from heaven their prayer and their supplication, and maintain their cause.

[36]"When they sin against You (for *there is* no one who does not sin), and You become angry with them and deliver them to the enemy, and they take them captive to a land far or near; [37]*yet* when they come to themselves in the land where they

6:12 [a]Literally *he* (compare 1 Kings 8:22)   6:18 [a]Literally *house*

6:12–42 Solomon's prayer is that the Lord would remember His promises in the future just as His promises in the past had been fulfilled in the building of the temple (vv. 15–17). Note the necessity of the obedience of God's covenant people (v. 16; see chart, Models of Obedience and Disobedience). "The place where You said You would put Your name" (v. 20)

is where Solomon entreated the Lord to listen. The Lord listened at the temple, answered from heaven, and forgave (vv. 20, 21). Solomon's prayer was not grounded in the Exodus but rather in the temple, "Your resting place," and in the promises to David (v. 41; see 1 Kin. 8:50–53; chart, Solomon's Prayer).

were carried captive, and repent, and make supplication to You in the land of their captivity, saying, 'We have sinned, we have done wrong, and have committed wickedness'; [38]and *when* they return to You with all their heart and with all their soul in the land of their captivity, where they have been carried captive, and pray toward their land which You gave to their fathers, the city which You have chosen, and toward the temple which I have built for Your name: [39]then hear from heaven Your dwelling place their prayer and their supplications, and maintain their cause, and forgive Your people who have sinned against You. [40]Now, my God, I pray, let Your eyes be open and *let* Your ears *be* attentive to the prayer *made* in this place.

[41]"Now therefore,

Arise, O LORD God, to Your resting place,
You and the ark of Your strength.
Let Your priests, O LORD God, be clothed with
    salvation,
And let Your saints rejoice in goodness.

[42]"O LORD God, do not turn away the face of Your
    Anointed;
Remember the mercies of Your servant
    David."[a]

Solomon Dedicates the Temple

7 When Solomon had finished praying, fire came down from heaven and consumed the burnt offering and the sacrifices; and the glory of the LORD filled the temple.[a] [2]And the priests could not enter the house of the LORD, because the glory of the LORD had filled the LORD's house. [3]When all the children of Israel saw how the fire came down, and the glory of the LORD on the temple, they bowed their faces to the ground on the pavement, and worshiped and praised the LORD, *saying:*

"For *He is* good,
For His mercy *endures* forever."[a]

[4]Then the king and all the people offered sacrifices before the LORD. [5]King Solomon offered a sacrifice of twenty-two thousand bulls and one hundred and twenty thousand sheep. So the king and all the people dedicated the house of God. [6]And the priests attended to their services; the Levites also with instruments of the music of the LORD, which King David had made to praise the LORD, saying, "For His mercy *endures* forever,"[a] whenever David offered praise by their ministry. The priests sounded trumpets opposite them, while all Israel stood.

[7]Furthermore Solomon consecrated the middle of the court that *was* in front of the house of the LORD; for there he offered burnt offerings and the fat of the peace offerings, because the bronze al-

tar which Solomon had made was not able to receive the burnt offerings, the grain offerings, and the fat.

[8]At that time Solomon kept the feast seven days, and all Israel with him, a very great assembly from the entrance of Hamath to the Brook of Egypt.[a] [9]And on the eighth day they held a sacred assembly, for they observed the dedication of the altar seven days, and the feast seven days. [10]On the twenty-third day of the seventh month he sent the people away to their tents, joyful and glad of heart for the good that the LORD had done for David, for Solomon, and for His people Israel. [11]Thus Solomon finished the house of the LORD and the king's house; and Solomon successfully accomplished all that came into his heart to make in the house of the LORD and in his own house.

God's Second Appearance to Solomon

[12]Then the LORD appeared to Solomon by night, and said to him: "I have heard your prayer, and have chosen this place for Myself as a house of sacrifice. [13]When I shut up heaven and there is no rain, or command the locusts to devour the land, or send pestilence among My people, [14]if My people who are called by My name will humble themselves, and pray and seek My face, and turn from their wicked ways, then I will hear from heaven, and will forgive their sin and heal their land. [15]Now My eyes will be open and My ears attentive to prayer *made* in this place. [16]For now I have chosen and sanctified this house, that My name may be there forever; and My eyes and My heart will be there perpetually. [17]As for you, if you walk before Me as your father David walked, and do according to all that I have commanded you, and if you keep My statutes and My judgments, [18]then I will establish the throne of your kingdom, as I covenanted with David your father, saying, 'You shall not fail *to have* a man as ruler in Israel.'

[19]"But if you turn away and forsake My statutes and My commandments which I have set before you, and go and serve other gods, and worship them, [20]then I will uproot them from My land which I have given them; and this house which I have sanctified for My name I will cast out of My sight, and will make it a proverb and a byword among all peoples. [21]"And *as for* this house, which is exalted, everyone who passes by it will be astonished and say, 'Why has the LORD done thus to this land and this house?' [22]Then they will answer, 'Because they forsook the LORD God of their fathers, who brought them out of the land of Egypt, and embraced other gods, and worshiped them and served them;

6:42 [a]Compare Psalm 132:8–10   **7:1** [a]Literally *house*   **7:3** [a]Compare Psalm 106:1   **7:6** [a]Compare Psalm 106:1   **7:8** [a]That is, the Shihor (compare 1 Chronicles 13:5)

therefore He has brought all this calamity on them.'"

Solomon's Additional Achievements

8 It came to pass at the end of twenty years, when Solomon had built the house of the LORD and his own house, [2]that the cities which Hiram[a] had given to Solomon, Solomon built them; and he settled the children of Israel there. [3]And Solomon went to Hamath Zobah and seized it. [4]He also built Tadmor in the wilderness, and all the storage cities which he built in Hamath. [5]He built Upper Beth Horon and Lower Beth Horon, fortified cities *with* walls, gates, and bars, [6]also Baalath and all the storage cities that Solomon had, and all the chariot cities and the cities of the cavalry, and all that Solomon desired to build in Jerusalem, in Lebanon, and in all the land of his dominion.

[7]All the people *who were* left of the Hittites, Amorites, Perizzites, Hivites, and Jebusites, who *were* not of Israel— [8]that is, their descendants who were left in the land after them, whom the children of Israel did not destroy—from these Solomon raised forced labor, as it is to this day. [9]But Solomon did not make the children of Israel servants for his work. Some *were* men of war, captains of his officers, captains of his chariots, and his cavalry. [10]And others *were* chiefs of the officials of King Solomon: two hundred and fifty, who ruled over the people.

[11]Now Solomon brought the daughter of Pharaoh up from the City of David to the house he had built for her, for he said, "My wife shall not dwell in the house of David king of Israel, because *the places* to which the ark of the LORD has come are holy."

[12]Then Solomon offered burnt offerings to the LORD on the altar of the LORD which he had built before the vestibule, [13]according to the daily rate, offering according to the commandment of Moses, for the Sabbaths, the New Moons, and the three appointed yearly feasts—the Feast of Unleavened Bread, the Feast of Weeks, and the Feast of Tabernacles. [14]And, according to the order of David his father, he appointed the divisions of the priests for their service, the Levites for their duties (to praise and serve before the priests) as the duty of each day required, and the gatekeepers by their divisions at each gate; for so David the man of God had commanded. [15]They did not depart from the command of the king to the priests and Levites concerning any matter or concerning the treasuries.

[16]Now all the work of Solomon was well-ordered from[a] the day of the foundation of the house of the LORD until it was finished. So the house of the LORD was completed.

[17]Then Solomon went to Ezion Geber and Elath[a] on the seacoast, in the land of Edom. [18]And Hiram sent him ships by the hand of his servants, and servants who knew the sea. They went with the servants of Solomon to Ophir, and acquired four hundred and fifty talents of gold from there, and brought it to King Solomon.

The Queen of Sheba's Praise of Solomon

9 Now when the queen of Sheba heard of the fame of Solomon, she came to Jerusalem to test Solomon with hard questions, *having* a very great retinue, camels that bore spices, gold in abundance, and precious stones; and when she came to Solomon, she spoke with him about all that was in her heart. [2]So Solomon answered all her questions; there was nothing so difficult for Solomon that he could not explain it to her. [3]And when the queen of Sheba had seen the wisdom of

---

8:2 [a]Hebrew *Huram* (compare 2 Chronicles 2:3)   8:16 [a]Following Septuagint, Syriac, and Vulgate; Masoretic Text reads *as far as.* 8:17 [a]Hebrew *Eloth* (compare 2 Kings 14:22)

8:1, 2 The cities given by Hiram. The record noted that Solomon had surrendered 20 non-Israelite cities in Galilee to Hiram (1 Kin. 9:11–13)—perhaps as payment for building debts (see 2 Chr. 2:3–16). Apparently, Hiram did not want the cities, forcing Solomon to take them back (1 Kin. 9:12, 13).

8:3–6 Hamath was the northern border of Israel (2 Chr. 7:8). Tadmor (now Palmyra) is about 120 miles northeast of Damascus. Hamath and Tadmor together are indicative of Solomon's control over the land trade routes to the north. Upper and Lower Beth Horon overlooked a valley northwest of Jerusalem, providing access to another important trade and military route. The location of Baalath is uncertain, though in this context it seems to be near Gezer. It could be Baalah or Kirjath Jearim (see 1 Kin. 9:17; 1 Chr. 13:5, 6). Either way, Solomon fortified the military routes leading from Jerusalem.

8:11 Pharaoh's daughter was united with Solomon in a political marriage, and Solomon brought this wife from the City of David to a house prepared for her. The chronicler is unique in providing the reason for this action. Solomon was spiritually sensitive enough to avoid keeping his pagan wife's residence in a holy place (1 Kin. 11:1–4). The chronicler omitted any reference to Solomon's unfaithfulness to the holiness of the temple because of his foreign wives (see 1 Kin. 11, Solomon's Pagan Wives).

8:17—9:12 The queen of Sheba, a woman of great wisdom and enormous wealth, played a significant role in the economy and life of her world. Her visit to Solomon was not only for commercial reasons but also to test Solomon's God-given wisdom (1 Kin. 10:1). This passage is virtually a repetition of the account in 1 Kings and parallels Solomon's encounter with Hiram, king of Tyre. Both Gentile monarchs reacted to Solomon's wisdom and wealth with similar praise, "Blessed be the LORD your God" (2 Chr. 9:5–8; see 2 Chr. 2:12). Both saw Solomon's throne as evidence of God's great love for Israel (2 Chr. 9:8; see 2 Chr. 2:11), and both gave tribute to him (2 Chr. 9:9; see 2 Chr. 2:13–16). The queen of Sheba received honorable mention from Jesus (Matt. 12:38–42; Luke 11:29–32; see also 1 Kin. 10, The Queen of Sheba).

Solomon, the house that he had built, [4]the food on his table, the seating of his servants, the service of his waiters and their apparel, his cupbearers and their apparel, and his entryway by which he went up to the house of the LORD, there was no more spirit in her.

[5]Then she said to the king: "*It was* a true report which I heard in my own land about your words and your wisdom. [6]However I did not believe their words until I came and saw with my own eyes; and indeed the half of the greatness of your wisdom was not told me. You exceed the fame of which I heard. [7]Happy *are* your men and happy *are* these your servants, who stand continually before you and hear your wisdom! [8]Blessed be the LORD your God, who delighted in you, setting you on His throne *to be* king for the LORD your God! Because your God has loved Israel, to establish them forever, therefore He made you king over them, to do justice and righteousness."

[9]And she gave the king one hundred and twenty talents of gold, spices in great abundance, and precious stones; there never were any spices such as those the queen of Sheba gave to King Solomon.

[10]Also, the servants of Hiram and the servants of Solomon, who brought gold from Ophir, brought algum[a] wood and precious stones. [11]And the king made walkways *of* the algum[a] wood for the house of the LORD and for the king's house, also harps and stringed instruments for singers; and there were none such *as these* seen before in the land of Judah.

[12]Now King Solomon gave to the queen of Sheba all she desired, whatever she asked, *much more* than she had brought to the king. So she turned and went to her own country, she and her servants.

Solomon's Great Wealth

[13]The weight of gold that came to Solomon yearly was six hundred and sixty-six talents of gold, [14]besides *what* the traveling merchants and traders brought. And all the kings of Arabia and governors of the country brought gold and silver to Solomon. [15]And King Solomon made two hundred large shields of hammered gold; six hundred *shekels* of hammered gold went into each shield. [16]*He* also *made* three hundred shields of hammered gold; three hundred *shekels*[a] of gold went into each shield. The king put them in the House of the Forest of Lebanon.

[17]Moreover the king made a great throne of ivory, and overlaid it with pure gold. [18]The throne *had* six steps, with a footstool of gold, *which were* fastened to the throne; there were armrests on either side of the place of the seat, and two lions stood beside the armrests. [19]Twelve lions stood there, one on each side of the six steps; nothing like *this* had been made for any *other* kingdom.

[20]All King Solomon's drinking vessels *were* gold, and all the vessels of the House of the Forest of Lebanon *were* pure gold. Not *one was* silver, for this was accounted as nothing in the days of Solomon. [21]For the king's ships went to Tarshish with the servants of Hiram.[a] Once every three years the merchant ships[b] came, bringing gold, silver, ivory, apes, and monkeys.[c]

[22]So King Solomon surpassed all the kings of the earth in riches and wisdom. [23]And all the kings of the earth sought the presence of Solomon to hear his wisdom, which God had put in his heart. [24]Each man brought his present: articles of silver and gold, garments, armor, spices, horses, and mules, at a set rate year by year.

[25]Solomon had four thousand stalls for horses and chariots, and twelve thousand horsemen whom he stationed in the chariot cities and with the king at Jerusalem.

[26]So he reigned over all the kings from the River[a] to the land of the Philistines, as far as the border of Egypt. [27]The king made silver *as common* in Jerusalem as stones, and he made cedar trees as abundant as the sycamores which *are* in the lowland. [28]And they brought horses to Solomon from Egypt and from all lands.

Death of Solomon

[29]Now the rest of the acts of Solomon, first and last, *are* they not written in the book of Nathan the prophet, in the prophecy of Ahijah the Shilonite, and in the visions of Iddo the seer concerning Jeroboam the son of Nebat? [30]Solomon reigned in Jerusalem over all Israel forty years. [31]Then Solomon rested with his fathers, and was buried in the City of David his father. And Rehoboam his son reigned in his place.

....

9:10 [a]Or *almug* (compare 1 Kings 10:11, 12)   **9:11** [a]Or *almug* (compare 1 Kings 10:11, 12)   **9:16** [a]Or *three minas* (compare 1 Kings 10:17)   **9:21** [a]Hebrew *Huram* (compare 1 Kings 10:22)   [b]Literally *ships of Tarshish* (deep-sea vessels)   [c]Or *peacocks*   **9:26** [a]That is, the Euphrates

9:13–28 The wealth and extent of Solomon's kingdom and wisdom are extolled in these short summaries. This passage reveals the fulfillment of God's words to David regarding his son's kingdom (1 Chr. 17:10–14; 22:9–13; 28:6, 7). The extensive borders of Solomon's kingdom are noted (2 Chr. 9:26). The chronicler portrayed an ideal Solomon ruling an ideal kingdom with tremendous wealth, wisdom, and worldwide recognition within the context of the centrality of the temple for all Israel.

9:29 The death of Solomon. The writings to which the chronicler refers are unknown. (For the book of Nathan the prophet, see 1 Chr. 29:26–30. For Ahijah, see 1 Kin. 11:26–40; 12:12–15; 14:1–18; 15:29; 2 Chr. 10:15. For Iddo, see 2 Chr. 12:15; 13:22).

The Revolt Against Rehoboam

10 And Rehoboam went to Shechem, for all Israel had gone to Shechem to make him king. ²So it happened, when Jeroboam the son of Nebat heard *it* (he was in Egypt, where he had fled from the presence of King Solomon), that Jeroboam returned from Egypt. ³Then they sent for him and called him. And Jeroboam and all Israel came and spoke to Rehoboam, saying, ⁴"Your father made our yoke heavy; now therefore, lighten the burdensome service of your father and his heavy yoke which he put on us, and we will serve you."

⁵So he said to them, "Come back to me after three days." And the people departed.

⁶Then King Rehoboam consulted the elders who stood before his father Solomon while he still lived, saying, "How do you advise *me* to answer these people?"

⁷And they spoke to him, saying, "If you are kind to these people, and please them, and speak good words to them, they will be your servants forever."

⁸But he rejected the advice which the elders had given him, and consulted the young men who had grown up with him, who stood before him. ⁹And he said to them, "What advice do you give? How should we answer this people who have spoken to me, saying, 'Lighten the yoke which your father put on us'?"

¹⁰Then the young men who had grown up with him spoke to him, saying, "Thus you should speak to the people who have spoken to you, saying, 'Your father made our yoke heavy, but you make *it* lighter on us'—thus you shall say to them: 'My little *finger* shall be thicker than my father's waist! ¹¹And now, whereas my father put a heavy yoke on you, I will add to your yoke; my father chastised you with whips, but I *will chastise you* with scourges!' "ᵃ

¹²So Jeroboam and all the people came to Rehoboam on the third day, as the king had directed, saying, "Come back to me the third day." ¹³Then the king answered them roughly. King Rehoboam rejected the advice of the elders, ¹⁴and he spoke to them according to the advice of the young men, saying, "My fatherᵃ made your yoke heavy, but I will add to it; my father chastised you with whips, but I *will chastise you* with scourges!"ᵇ ¹⁵So the king did not listen to the people; for the turn *of events* was from God, that the LORD might fulfill His word, which He had spoken by the hand of Ahijah the Shilonite to Jeroboam the son of Nebat.

¹⁶Now when all Israel *saw* that the king did not listen to them, the people answered the king, saying:

"What share have we in David?
We have no inheritance in the son of Jesse.
Every man to your tents, O Israel!
Now see to your own house, O David!"

So all Israel departed to their tents. ¹⁷But Rehoboam reigned over the children of Israel who dwelt in the cities of Judah.

¹⁸Then King Rehoboam sent Hadoram, who *was* in charge of revenue; but the children of Israel stoned him with stones, and he died. Therefore King Rehoboam mounted *his* chariot in haste to flee to Jerusalem. ¹⁹So Israel has been in rebellion against the house of David to this day.

11 Now when Rehoboam came to Jerusalem, he assembled from the house of Judah and Benjamin one hundred and eighty thousand chosen *men* who were warriors, to fight against Israel, that he might restore the kingdom to Rehoboam. ²But the word of the LORD came to Shemaiah the man of God, saying, ³"Speak to Rehoboam the son of Solomon, king of Judah, and to all Israel in Judah and Benjamin, saying, ⁴'Thus says the LORD: "You shall not go up or fight against your brethren! Let every man return to his house, for this thing is from Me." ' " Therefore they obeyed the words of the LORD, and turned back from attacking Jeroboam.

Rehoboam Fortifies the Cities

⁵So Rehoboam dwelt in Jerusalem, and built cities for defense in Judah. ⁶And he built Bethlehem, Etam, Tekoa, ⁷Beth Zur, Sochoh, Adullam, ⁸Gath, Mareshah, Ziph, ⁹Adoraim, Lachish, Azekah, ¹⁰Zorah, Aijalon, and Hebron, which are in Judah and Benjamin, fortified cities. ¹¹And he fortified the strongholds, and put captains in them, and stores of food, oil, and wine. ¹²Also in every city *he put* shields and spears, and made them very strong, having Judah and Benjamin on his side.

Priests and Levites Move to Judah

¹³And from all their territories the priests and the Levites who *were* in all Israel took their stand with him. ¹⁴For the Levites left their commonlands and their possessions and came to Judah and

10:11 ᵃLiterally *scorpions* 10:14 ᵃFollowing many Hebrew manuscripts, Septuagint, Syriac, and Vulgate (compare verse 10 and 1 Kings 12:14); Masoretic Text reads *I.* ᵇLiterally *scorpions*

10:1 Rehoboam obeyed. The emphasis in 1 Kings is on Solomon's sin, which resulted in the split of his kingdom after his death (see 1 Kin. 11). However, the chronicler presents Solomon as the faithful temple builder. The reader is reminded of God's sovereign control of history (2 Chr. 10:15). The repetition of this story demonstrates Rehoboam's initial faithfulness to the Lord (1 Kin. 12:1-19, 21-24).

THE DIVIDED KINGDOM

GREAT SEA
(MEDITERRANEAN)

Litani River

Damascus

Tyre

Dan

Kedesh

ARAM
(SYRIA)

Jezebel died here.
(1 Kin. 21:23; 2 Kin. 9:30–37)

Jezebel had altars to Baal here.
(1 Kin. 16:29–33)

PHOENICIA

Acco

Hazor

Sea of
Chinnereth
(Galilee)

Ashtaroth

MT. CARMEL

MT. TABOR

Megiddo

Jezreel

Ramoth Gilead

Athaliah usurped the throne
here. (2 Kin. 8:26; 11:1–3)

Taanach

Jabesh Gilead

Tirzah

Samaria

Jordan River

Huldah prophesied. (2 Chr. 34:22)

MT. EBAL

MT.
GERIZIM

Shechem

Jabbok River

Mahanaim

AMMON

Shiloh

Jazer

Joppa

Bethel

Ashdod

Heshbon

Gezer

Jericho

MT. NEBO

Rabbah

Jerusalem

Gath

Bethlehem

Medeba

Ashkelon

Adullam

Tekoa

Hebron

Dibon

Gaza

Debir

Dead Sea

N

JUDAH

Kir Hareseth

PHILISTIA

Arad

MOAB

Beersheba

EDOM

0   30 Mi.

0

The united kingdom ended after the death of Solomon, whose son Rehoboam reigned over Judah in the south.
Jeroboam seized the throne of Israel in the north.

Jerusalem, for Jeroboam and his sons had rejected them from serving as priests to the LORD. [15]Then he appointed for himself priests for the high places, for the demons, and the calf idols which he had made. [16]And after *the Levites left,*[a] those from all the tribes of Israel, such as set their heart to seek the LORD God of Israel, came to Jerusalem to sacrifice to the LORD God of their fathers. [17]So they strengthened the kingdom of Judah, and made Rehoboam the son of Solomon strong for three years, because they walked in the way of David and Solomon for three years.

The Family of Rehoboam

[18]Then Rehoboam took for himself as wife Mahalath the daughter of Jerimoth the son of David, *and of* Abihail the daughter of Eliah the son of Jesse. [19]And she bore him children: Jeush, Shamariah, and Zaham. [20]After her he took Maachah the granddaughter[a] of Absalom; and she bore him Abijah, Attai, Ziza, and Shelomith. [21]Now Rehoboam loved Maachah the granddaughter of Absalom more than all his wives and his concubines; for he took eighteen wives and sixty concubines, and begot twenty-eight sons and sixty daughters. [22]And Rehoboam appointed Abijah the son of Maachah as chief, *to be* leader among his brothers; for he *intended* to make him king. [23]He dealt wisely, and dispersed some of his sons throughout all the territories of Judah and Benjamin, to every fortified city; and he gave them provisions in abundance. He also sought many wives *for them.*

Egypt Attacks Judah

12 Now it came to pass, when Rehoboam had established the kingdom and had strengthened himself, that he forsook the law of the LORD, and all Israel along with him. [2]And it happened in the fifth year of King Rehoboam *that* Shishak king of Egypt came up against Jerusalem, because they had transgressed against the LORD, [3]with twelve hundred chariots, sixty thousand horsemen, and people without number who came with him out of Egypt—the Lubim and the Sukkiim and the Ethiopians. [4]And he took the fortified cities of Judah and came to Jerusalem.

[5]Then Shemaiah the prophet came to Rehoboam and the leaders of Judah, who were gathered together in Jerusalem because of Shishak, and said to them, "Thus says the LORD: 'You have forsaken Me, and therefore I also have left you in the hand of Shishak.'"

[6]So the leaders of Israel and the king humbled themselves; and they said, "The LORD *is* righteous."

[7]Now when the LORD saw that they humbled themselves, the word of the LORD came to Shemaiah, saying, "They have humbled themselves; *therefore* I will not destroy them, but I will grant them some deliverance. My wrath shall not be poured out on Jerusalem by the hand of Shishak. [8]Nevertheless they will be his servants, that they may distinguish My service from the service of the kingdoms of the nations."

[9]So Shishak king of Egypt came up against Jerusalem, and took away the treasures of the house of the LORD and the treasures of the king's house; he took everything. He also carried away the gold shields which Solomon had made. [10]Then King Rehoboam made bronze shields in their place, and committed *them* to the hands of the captains of the guard, who guarded the doorway of the king's house. [11]And whenever the king entered the house of the LORD, the guard would go and bring them out; then they would take them back into the guardroom. [12]When he humbled himself, the wrath of the LORD turned from him, so as not to destroy *him* completely; and things also went well in Judah.

The End of Rehoboam's Reign

[13]Thus King Rehoboam strengthened himself in Jerusalem and reigned. Now Rehoboam *was* forty-one years old when he became king; and he reigned seventeen years in Jerusalem, the city which the LORD had chosen out of all the tribes of Israel, to put His name there. His mother's name *was* Naamah, an Ammonitess. [14]And he did evil, because he did not prepare his heart to seek the LORD.

[15]The acts of Rehoboam, first and last, *are* they not written in the book of Shemaiah the prophet,

---

11:16 [a]Literally *after them*   11:20 [a]Literally *daughter*, but in the broader sense of granddaughter (compare 2 Chronicles 13:2)

11:18–21 Maachah, Rehoboam's wife, was evidently a granddaughter of Absalom through his daughter Tamar and Uriel (2 Chr. 13:2, note; chart, The Queens of the Old Testament), making her a half-cousin to Rehoboam. Rehoboam willfully disobeyed the Lord by taking multiple wives (Deut. 17:17). His "eighteen wives" showed a complete disregard for God's Law and for the tragedies that came from his father Solomon's example (1 Kin. 11:1–4).

12:1 Because Rehoboam forsook the law (v. 1), he suffered defeat and lost the cities he had built (vv. 2–4; see also 2 Chr. 7:19–22). For emphasis, some derivation of "forsake" (Heb.,

'azab, translated "forsook," "forsaken," "left") is used three times (2 Chr. 12:1, 5). Shishak (Sheshonq I, 945–924 B.C.), a Libyan, overthrew the Egyptian king and established the 22nd dynasty in Egypt. He grew powerful after the disintegration of Solomon's great kingdom and attacked Judah at will (v. 2).

12:6 Repentance and forgiveness were always possible and resulted in blessing as the Lord faithfully restored His people (see vv. 5–8, 12).

12:15 These record books are unknown (see 2 Chr. 9:29, note).

and of Iddo the seer concerning genealogies? And *there were* wars between Rehoboam and Jeroboam all their days. [16]So Rehoboam rested with his fathers, and was buried in the City of David. Then Abijah[a] his son reigned in his place.

Abijah Reigns in Judah

13 In the eighteenth year of King Jeroboam, Abijah became king over Judah. [2]He reigned three years in Jerusalem. His mother's name *was* Michaiah[a] the daughter of Uriel of Gibeah.

And there was war between Abijah and Jeroboam. [3]Abijah set the battle in order with an army of valiant warriors, four hundred thousand choice men. Jeroboam also drew up in battle formation against him with eight hundred thousand choice men, mighty men of valor.

[4]Then Abijah stood on Mount Zemaraim, which *is* in the mountains of Ephraim, and said, "Hear me, Jeroboam and all Israel: [5]Should you not know that the LORD God of Israel gave the dominion over Israel to David forever, to him and his sons, by a covenant of salt? [6]Yet Jeroboam the son of Nebat, the servant of Solomon the son of David, rose up and rebelled against his lord. [7]Then worthless rogues gathered to him, and strengthened themselves against Rehoboam the son of Solomon, when Rehoboam was young and inexperienced and could not withstand them. [8]And now you think to withstand the kingdom of the LORD, which is in the hand of the sons of David; and you *are* a great multitude, and with you are the gold calves which Jeroboam made for you as gods. [9]Have you not cast out the priests of the LORD, the sons of Aaron, and the Levites, and made for yourselves priests, like the peoples of *other* lands, so that whoever comes to consecrate himself with a young bull and seven rams may be a priest of *things that are* not gods? [10]But as for us, the LORD *is* our God, and we have not forsaken Him; and the priests who minister to the LORD *are* the sons of Aaron, and the Levites *attend* to *their* duties. [11]And they burn to the LORD every morning and every evening burnt sacrifices and sweet incense; *they* also *set* the showbread *in order on* the pure *gold* table, and the lampstand of gold with its lamps to burn every evening; for we keep the command of the LORD our God, but you have forsaken Him. [12]Now look, God Himself is with us as *our* head, and His priests with sounding trumpets to sound the alarm against you. O children of Israel, do not fight against the LORD God of your fathers, for you shall not prosper!"

[13]But Jeroboam caused an ambush to go around behind them; so they were in front of Judah, and the ambush *was* behind them. [14]And when Judah looked around, to their surprise the battle line *was* at both front and rear; and they cried out to the LORD, and the priests sounded the trumpets. [15]Then the men of Judah gave a shout; and as the men of Judah shouted, it happened that God struck Jeroboam and all Israel before Abijah and Judah. [16]And the children of Israel fled before Judah, and God delivered them into their hand. [17]Then Abijah and his people struck them with a great slaughter; so five hundred thousand choice men of Israel fell slain. [18]Thus the children of Israel were subdued at that time; and the children of Judah prevailed, because they relied on the LORD God of their fathers.

[19]And Abijah pursued Jeroboam and took cities from him: Bethel with its villages, Jeshanah with its villages, and Ephrain[a] with its villages. [20]So Jeroboam did not recover strength again in the days of Abijah; and the LORD struck him, and he died.

[21]But Abijah grew mighty, married fourteen wives, and begot twenty-two sons and sixteen daughters. [22]Now the rest of the acts of Abijah, his ways, and his sayings *are* written in the annals of the prophet Iddo.

14 So Abijah rested with his fathers, and they buried him in the City of David. Then Asa his son reigned in his place. In his days the land was quiet for ten years.

Asa Reigns in Judah

[2]Asa did *what was* good and right in the eyes of the LORD his God, [3]for he removed the altars of

---

12:16 [a]Spelled *Abijam* in 1 Kings 14:31   **13:2** [a]Spelled *Maachah* in 11:20, 21 and 1 Kings 15:2   **13:19** [a]Or *Ephron*

13:2 The mother of Abijah, Michaiah (an alternate spelling of Maachah), was the beloved wife of Rehoboam (2 Chr. 11:18–21, note; 15:16). She was the daughter of Tamar and Uriel of Gibeah (2 Chr. 13:2), the granddaughter of Absalom (Abishalom, an alternate spelling for Absalom, 1 Kin. 15:10), and the grandmother of Asa. Maachah worshiped idols (see 2 Chr. 15:16, in which the term "mother" is used in a figurative sense). The chronicler often identified a king by his mother (see 2 Chr. 12:13; 13:2; 20:31; 22:10; 25:1; 26:3; 27:1; 29:1).

13:5 A covenant of salt describes the effective and permanent character of God's covenant with David (Num. 18:19; 2 Sam. 7; 1 Chr. 17). Some have suggested that the reference to "salt" is representative of a meal by which a covenant would be rati-

fied (Ex. 24:11), symbolic of a substance associated with the covenant (Lev. 2:13), or suggestive of permanence because of the fact that salt is used as a preservative and enhancer of flavor (Matt. 5:13).

14:3 Asa, the first temple reformer, removed illegitimate worship and brought the people back to the true worship of God by teaching them to observe the Law and to seek the Lord (vv. 3–5, 11; 2 Chr. 15:8, 11–13, 16). For the chronicler, the true Israel is all those living in Judah who are faithful to the temple and loyal to David's throne. For obedience, Asa was blessed with building projects (2 Chr. 14:6, 7), a strong army (v. 8), victory (vv. 9–15), honor (2 Chr. 15:9, 10), and rest (2 Chr. 15:15, 19).

the foreign *gods* and the high places, and broke down the *sacred* pillars and cut down the wooden images. [4]He commanded Judah to seek the LORD God of their fathers, and to observe the law and the commandment. [5]He also removed the high places and the incense altars from all the cities of Judah, and the kingdom was quiet under him. [6]And he built fortified cities in Judah, for the land had rest; he had no war in those years, because the LORD had given him rest. [7]Therefore he said to Judah, "Let us build these cities and make walls around *them*, and towers, gates, and bars, *while* the land *is* yet before us, because we have sought the LORD our God; we have sought *Him*, and He has given us rest on every side." So they built and prospered. [8]And Asa had an army of three hundred thousand from Judah who carried shields and spears, and from Benjamin two hundred and eighty thousand men who carried shields and drew bows; all these *were* mighty men of valor.

[9]Then Zerah the Ethiopian came out against them with an army of a million men and three hundred chariots, and he came to Mareshah. [10]So Asa went out against him, and they set the troops in battle array in the Valley of Zephathah at Mareshah. [11]And Asa cried out to the LORD his God, and said, "LORD, *it is* nothing for You to help, whether with many or with those who have no power; help us, O LORD our God, for we rest on You, and in Your name we go against this multitude. O LORD, You *are* our God; do not let man prevail against You!"

[12]So the LORD struck the Ethiopians before Asa and Judah, and the Ethiopians fled. [13]And Asa and the people who *were* with him pursued them to Gerar. So the Ethiopians were overthrown, and they could not recover, for they were broken before the LORD and His army. And they carried away very much spoil. [14]Then they defeated all the cities around Gerar, for the fear of the LORD came upon them; and they plundered all the cities, for there was exceedingly much spoil in them. [15]They also attacked the livestock enclosures, and carried off sheep and camels in abundance, and returned to Jerusalem.

The Reforms of Asa

15 Now the Spirit of God came upon Azariah the son of Oded. [2]And he went out to meet Asa, and said to him: "Hear me, Asa, and all Judah and Benjamin. The LORD *is* with you while you are with Him. If you seek Him, He will be found by you; but if you forsake Him, He will forsake you. [3]For a long time Israel *has been* without the true God, without a teaching priest, and without law; [4]but when in their trouble they turned to the LORD God of Israel, and sought Him, He was found by them. [5]And in those times *there was* no peace to the one who went out, nor to the one who came in, but great turmoil *was* on all the inhabitants of the lands. [6]So nation was destroyed by nation, and city by city, for God troubled them with every adversity. [7]But you, be strong and do not let your hands be weak, for your work shall be rewarded!"

[8]And when Asa heard these words and the prophecy of Oded[a] the prophet, he took courage, and removed the abominable idols from all the land of Judah and Benjamin and from the cities which he had taken in the mountains of Ephraim; and he restored the altar of the LORD that *was* before the vestibule of the LORD. [9]Then he gathered all Judah and Benjamin, and those who dwelt with them from Ephraim, Manasseh, and Simeon, for they came over to him in great numbers from Israel when they saw that the LORD his God *was* with him.

[10]So they gathered together at Jerusalem in the third month, in the fifteenth year of the reign of Asa. [11]And they offered to the LORD at that time seven hundred bulls and seven thousand sheep from the spoil they had brought. [12]Then they entered into a covenant to seek the LORD God of their fathers with all their heart and with all their soul; [13]and whoever would not seek the LORD God of Israel was to be put to death, whether small or great, whether man or woman. [14]Then they took an oath before the LORD with a loud voice, with shouting and trumpets and rams' horns. [15]And all Judah rejoiced at the oath, for they had sworn with all their heart and sought Him with all their soul; and He was found by them, and the LORD gave them rest all around.

[16]Also he removed Maachah, the mother of Asa the king, from *being* queen mother, because she had made an obscene image of Asherah;[a] and Asa

---

15:8 [a]Following Masoretic Text and Septuagint; Syriac and Vulgate read *Azariah the son of Oded* (compare verse 1).   **15:16** [a]A Canaanite deity

---

15:1–7 Azariah, the prophet restated the Lord's answer to Solomon's prayer to encourage Asa to continue to obey (see 2 Chr. 7:12–22; contrast 2 Chr. 16:7–10). What it means to forsake the Lord is illustrated (2 Chr. 15:3–6). Under Jeroboam I, Israel turned from God and knew only great turmoil (2 Chr. 11:13–16; 13:4–9). In contrast, Asa obeyed the word of the Lord (2 Chr. 15:8–19). The returned Jewish community would relate their time in Exile as a long time without the true God and be encouraged in their restored fellowship with God in which they were to seek Him and be rewarded.

15:16 The obscene image that Asa removed was most likely a sexually explicit image used in the worship of the fertility goddess Asherah (see Deut. 7:5, 6). The chronicler makes clear that early in his reign, Asa cleared the high places from Judah (2 Chr. 1:3, note; 14:3, 5) but that later on he failed to remove the high places from the land of Israel under his control. This fact sets the stage for Asa's sin (2 Chr. 16:1–14).

cut down her obscene image, then crushed and burned *it* by the Brook Kidron. [17]But the high places were not removed from Israel. Nevertheless the heart of Asa was loyal all his days.

[18]He also brought into the house of God the things that his father had dedicated and that he himself had dedicated: silver and gold and utensils. [19]And there was no war until the thirty-fifth year of the reign of Asa.

Asa's Treaty with Syria

16 In the thirty-sixth year of the reign of Asa, Baasha king of Israel came up against Judah and built Ramah, that he might let none go out or come in to Asa king of Judah. [2]Then Asa brought silver and gold from the treasuries of the house of the LORD and of the king's house, and sent to Ben-Hadad king of Syria, who dwelt in Damascus, saying, [3]"*Let there be* a treaty between you and me, as there was between my father and your father. See, I have sent you silver and gold; come, break your treaty with Baasha king of Israel, so that he will withdraw from me."

[4]So Ben-Hadad heeded King Asa, and sent the captains of his armies against the cities of Israel. They attacked Ijon, Dan, Abel Maim, and all the storage cities of Naphtali. [5]Now it happened, when Baasha heard *it*, that he stopped building Ramah and ceased his work. [6]Then King Asa took all Judah, and they carried away the stones and timber of Ramah, which Baasha had used for building; and with them he built Geba and Mizpah.

Hanani's Message to Asa

[7]And at that time Hanani the seer came to Asa king of Judah, and said to him: "Because you have relied on the king of Syria, and have not relied on the LORD your God, therefore the army of the king of Syria has escaped from your hand. [8]Were the Ethiopians and the Lubim not a huge army with very many chariots and horsemen? Yet, because you relied on the LORD, He delivered them into your hand. [9]For the eyes of the LORD run to and fro throughout the whole earth, to show Himself strong on behalf of *those* whose heart *is* loyal to Him. In this you have done foolishly; therefore from now on you shall have wars." [10]Then Asa was angry with the seer, and put him in prison, for *he was* enraged at him because of this. And Asa oppressed *some* of the people at that time.

Illness and Death of Asa

[11]Note that the acts of Asa, first and last, are indeed written in the book of the kings of Judah and Israel. [12]And in the thirty-ninth year of his reign, Asa became diseased in his feet, and his malady was severe; yet in his disease he did not seek the LORD, but the physicians. [13]So Asa rested with his fathers; he died in the forty-first year of his reign. [14]They buried him in his own tomb, which he had made for himself in the City of David; and they laid him in the bed which was filled with spices and various ingredients prepared in a mixture of ointments. They made a very great burning for him.

Jehoshaphat Reigns in Judah

17 Then Jehoshaphat his son reigned in his place, and strengthened himself against Israel. [2]And he placed troops in all the fortified cities of Judah, and set garrisons in the land of Judah and in the cities of Ephraim which Asa his father had taken. [3]Now the LORD was with Jehoshaphat, because he walked in the former ways of his father David; he did not seek the Baals, [4]but

---

16:1 Asa's sin. Judah was being oppressed by Baasha who built a blockade about five miles north of Jerusalem. Instead of seeking the Lord, Asa sought protection through a treaty with Ben-Hadad of Syria, emptying all the royal and religious treasuries in payment (vv. 2–6). Such foreign alliances were judged as failure to trust in the Lord (v. 7) in contrast to the times when Asa cried to the Lord for help (2 Chr. 14:11). Through the prophet Hanani, Asa was rebuked and punished with wars (2 Chr. 16:7–10; see 2 Chr. 19:2). Asa's failure to seek the Lord is heightened by the chronicler's report of his death. Asa, who had reformed temple worship and taught the people to follow the Lord (2 Chr. 14:2–5; 15:8–19), forsook the Lord and then died forsaken by Him (2 Chr. 15:2; 16:12–14).

16:14 A very great burning refers to the burning of precious spices as part of a funeral worthy of a great king (Jer. 34:5).

17:1 Jehoshaphat, a temple reformer. Two large sections are unique to the chronicler in the story of Jehoshaphat, both concerning Jehoshaphat's obedience to the Lord and subsequent blessing (2 Chr. 17:1—18:1; 19:1—20:30). Jehoshaphat's alliance with Ahab is also described in the Book of 1 Kings (1 Kin. 22:2–35; see 2 Chr. 18:2–34). First Kings focuses on Ahab's

punishment for unfaithfulness, while the chronicler shows that Jehoshaphat was saved when he cried to the Lord (2 Chr. 18:31). The chronicler stated that Jehoshaphat followed Asa, his father, in doing "right in the sight of the LORD" (2 Chr. 20:32). Both purged the land, brought about reforms, and were blessed (2 Chr. 14:2–15; 17:1—19:1). Both received an encouraging message of prophecy (2 Chr. 15:1–7; 19:2, 3), cried to the Lord in battle (2 Chr. 14:11; 18:31), made additional reforms (2 Chr. 15:8–19; 19:4–11), yet neglected to remove completely the high places (2 Chr. 1:3, note; 14:3; 15:17; 17:6; 20:33). Both kings sinned in making a foreign alliance (2 Chr. 18:1–6; 20:35, 36), were rebuked by a prophet (2 Chr. 18:7–10; 20:37), then were punished (2 Chr. 20:37). The way of Asa and Jehoshaphat is set in contrast to the way of Jehoram (2 Chr. 21:12–15).

17:1–19 The Lord was with Jehoshaphat, the reformer who rid Judah of illegitimate practices of worship and taught the people the Law of the Lord (vv. 6–9; Deut. 17:18–20). His kingdom was established by the Lord with great honor and riches (2 Chr. 17:5). He was blessed with peace (v. 10), foreign tribute (v. 11), building projects (v. 12), wealth (v. 13), and a great

sought the God[a] of his father, and walked in His commandments and not according to the acts of Israel. [5]Therefore the LORD established the kingdom in his hand; and all Judah gave presents to Jehoshaphat, and he had riches and honor in abundance. [6]And his heart took delight in the ways of the LORD; moreover he removed the high places and wooden images from Judah.

[7]Also in the third year of his reign he sent his leaders, Ben-Hail, Obadiah, Zechariah, Nethanel, and Michaiah, to teach in the cities of Judah. [8]And with them *he sent* Levites: Shemaiah, Nethaniah, Zebadiah, Asahel, Shemiramoth, Jehonathan, Adonijah, Tobijah, and Tobadonijah—the Levites; and with them Elishama and Jehoram, the priests. [9]So they taught in Judah, and *had* the Book of the Law of the LORD with them; they went throughout all the cities of Judah and taught the people.

[10]And the fear of the LORD fell on all the kingdoms of the lands that *were* around Judah, so that they did not make war against Jehoshaphat. [11]Also *some* of the Philistines brought Jehoshaphat presents and silver as tribute; and the Arabians brought him flocks, seven thousand seven hundred rams and seven thousand seven hundred male goats.

[12]So Jehoshaphat became increasingly powerful, and he built fortresses and storage cities in Judah. [13]He had much property in the cities of Judah; and the men of war, mighty men of valor, *were* in Jerusalem.

[14]These *are* their numbers, according to their fathers' houses. Of Judah, the captains of thousands: Adnah the captain, and with him three hundred thousand mighty men of valor; [15]and next to him *was* Jehohanan the captain, and with him two hundred and eighty thousand; [16]and next to him *was* Amasiah the son of Zichri, who willingly offered himself to the LORD, and with him two hundred thousand mighty men of valor. [17]Of Benjamin: Eliada a mighty man of valor, and with him two hundred thousand men armed with bow and shield; [18]and next to him *was* Jehozabad, and with him one hundred and eighty thousand prepared for war. [19]These served the king, besides those the king put in the fortified cities throughout all Judah.

Micaiah Warns Ahab

18 Jehoshaphat had riches and honor in abundance; and by marriage he allied himself with Ahab. [2]After some years he went down to *visit* Ahab in Samaria; and Ahab killed sheep and oxen in abundance for him and the people who were with him, and persuaded him to go up *with him* to Ramoth Gilead. [3]So Ahab king of Israel said to Jehoshaphat king of Judah, "Will you go with me *against* Ramoth Gilead?"

And he answered him, "I *am* as you *are,* and my people as your people; *we will be* with you in the war."

[4]Also Jehoshaphat said to the king of Israel, "Please inquire for the word of the LORD today."

[5]Then the king of Israel gathered the prophets together, four hundred men, and said to them, "Shall we go to war against Ramoth Gilead, or shall I refrain?"

So they said, "Go up, for God will deliver it into the king's hand."

[6]But Jehoshaphat said, "*Is there* not still a prophet of the LORD here, that we may inquire of Him?"[a]

[7]So the king of Israel said to Jehoshaphat, "*There is* still one man by whom we may inquire of the LORD; but I hate him, because he never prophesies good concerning me, but always evil. He *is* Micaiah the son of Imla."

And Jehoshaphat said, "Let not the king say such things!"

[8]Then the king of Israel called one *of his* officers and said, "Bring Micaiah the son of Imla quickly!"

[9]The king of Israel and Jehoshaphat king of Judah, clothed in *their* robes, sat each on his throne; and they sat at a threshing floor at the entrance of the gate of Samaria; and all the prophets prophesied before them. [10]Now Zedekiah the son of Chenaanah had made horns of iron for himself; and he said, "Thus says the LORD: 'With these you shall gore the Syrians until they are destroyed.'"

[11]And all the prophets prophesied so, saying, "Go up to Ramoth Gilead and prosper, for the LORD will deliver *it* into the king's hand."

[12]Then the messenger who had gone to call Micaiah spoke to him, saying, "Now listen, the words of the prophets with one accord encourage the king. Therefore please let your word be like *the word of* one of them, and speak encouragement."

[13]And Micaiah said, "*As* the LORD lives, whatever my God says, that I will speak."

[14]Then he came to the king; and the king said

17:4 [a]Septuagint reads LORD God.   18:6 [a]Or him

---

army (vv. 13–19). At this time, the worship of the Baals in the north was increasing with the influence of Ahab and Jezebel (1 Kin. 16:29—22:40). Although Jehoshaphat would ally himself with Ahab, he would not be caught up in the apostasy of Ahab (2 Chr. 19:2, 3; 20:32).

18:3 The alliance with Ahab. In this battle the chronicler's focus is on Jehoshaphat (see also 1 Kin. 22). The marriage alliance was forged between Jehoshaphat's son, Jehoram, and Athaliah, the daughter of Ahab and Jezebel (2 Chr. 21:6; 22:2). Ahab and Jezebel were characterized by their great wickedness and Baal worship, and the results were devastating (2 Chr. 21; 22).

to him, "Micaiah, shall we go to war against Ramoth Gilead, or shall I refrain?"

And he said, "Go and prosper, and they shall be delivered into your hand!"

15So the king said to him, "How many times shall I make you swear that you tell me nothing but the truth in the name of the LORD?"

16Then he said, "I saw all Israel scattered on the mountains, as sheep that have no shepherd. And the LORD said, 'These have no master. Let each return to his house in peace.' "

17And the king of Israel said to Jehoshaphat, "Did I not tell you he would not prophesy good concerning me, but evil?"

18Then *Micaiah* said, "Therefore hear the word of the LORD: I saw the LORD sitting on His throne, and all the host of heaven standing on His right hand and His left. 19And the LORD said, 'Who will persuade Ahab king of Israel to go up, that he may fall at Ramoth Gilead?' So one spoke in this manner, and another spoke in that manner. 20Then a spirit came forward and stood before the LORD, and said, 'I will persuade him.' The LORD said to him, 'In what way?' 21So he said, 'I will go out and be a lying spirit in the mouth of all his prophets.' And *the LORD* said, 'You shall persuade *him* and also prevail; go out and do so.' 22Therefore look! The LORD has put a lying spirit in the mouth of these prophets of yours, and the LORD has declared disaster against you."

23Then Zedekiah the son of Chenaanah went near and struck Micaiah on the cheek, and said, "Which way did the spirit from the LORD go from me to speak to you?"

24And Micaiah said, "Indeed you shall see on that day when you go into an inner chamber to hide!"

25Then the king of Israel said, "Take Micaiah, and return him to Amon the governor of the city and to Joash the king's son; 26and say, 'Thus says the king: "Put this *fellow* in prison, and feed him with bread of affliction and water of affliction, until I return in peace." ' "

27But Micaiah said, "If you ever return in peace, the LORD has not spoken by me." And he said, "Take heed, all you people!"

Ahab Dies in Battle

28So the king of Israel and Jehoshaphat the king of Judah went up to Ramoth Gilead. 29And the king of Israel said to Jehoshaphat, "I will disguise myself and go into battle; but you put on your robes." So the king of Israel disguised himself, and they went into battle.

30Now the king of Syria had commanded the captains of the chariots who *were* with him, saying, "Fight with no one small or great, but only with the king of Israel."

31So it was, when the captains of the chariots saw Jehoshaphat, that they said, "It *is* the king of Israel!" Therefore they surrounded him to attack; but Jehoshaphat cried out, and the LORD helped him, and God diverted them from him. 32For so it was, when the captains of the chariots saw that it was not the king of Israel, that they turned back from pursuing him. 33Now a certain man drew a bow at random, and struck the king of Israel between the joints of his armor. So he said to the driver of his chariot, "Turn around and take me out of the battle, for I am wounded." 34The battle increased that day, and the king of Israel propped *himself* up in *his* chariot facing the Syrians until evening; and about the time of sunset he died.

19 Then Jehoshaphat the king of Judah returned safely to his house in Jerusalem. 2And Jehu the son of Hanani the seer went out to meet him, and said to King Jehoshaphat, "Should you help the wicked and love those who hate the LORD? Therefore the wrath of the LORD *is* upon you. 3Nevertheless good things are found in you, in that you have removed the wooden images from the land, and have prepared your heart to seek God."

The Reforms of Jehoshaphat

4So Jehoshaphat dwelt at Jerusalem; and he went out again among the people from Beersheba to the mountains of Ephraim, and brought them back to the LORD God of their fathers. 5Then he set judges in the land throughout all the fortified cities of Judah, city by city, 6and said to the judges, "Take heed to what you are doing, for you do not judge for man but for the LORD, who *is* with you in the judgment. 7Now therefore, let the fear of the LORD be upon you; take care and do *it,* for *there is* no iniquity with the LORD our God, no partiality, nor taking of bribes."

8Moreover in Jerusalem, for the judgment of the LORD and for controversies, Jehoshaphat appointed some of the Levites and priests, and some of the chief fathers of Israel, when they returned to Jerusalem.a 9And he commanded them, saying, "Thus you shall act in the fear of the LORD, faithfully and with a loyal heart: 10Whatever case comes to you from your brethren who dwell in their cities, whether of bloodshed or offenses against law or commandment, against statutes or

---

19:8 aSeptuagint and Vulgate read *for the inhabitants of Jerusalem.*

19:4–11 Just as Asa had two reform efforts (2 Chr. 14:1–15; 15:8–19), Jehoshaphat entered into a second stage of reform (2 Chr. 17:1, note; 19:6–9), which centered on a system for judging the people (Deut. 16:18—17:13). The boundaries of Judah (2 Chr. 19:4, Beersheba to the south and the mountains to the north) show that all Israel was involved in this reform.

ATTRIBUTES OF GOD   *HE IS JUDGE*

A god who does not judge is a god of the imagination. God judges. Attempts are made to water down God's judgment, explain it away, or apologize for it, but God's judgment is a manifestation of the reaction of His holiness to evil (Is. 42:8). Judgment is an integral part of redemptive history as seen in the Fall (Gen. 3:14–19), the Flood (6:5–7), the plagues (Ex. 3:19, 20; 7:5; 11:4, 5), the conquest (Josh. 3:10), the destruction of Israel (2 Kin. 17:5–23), the destitution of Judah (25:1–21), the Great Tribulation (Matt. 24:21, 22), and the Great White Throne Judgment (Rev. 20:11–15). There are many references in Scripture to both His judgment and His love.

Judgment is necessary. Society recognizes that a judge who will not judge is a mockery. The Bible salutes God's judgments as "righteous" and "true" (Ps. 19:9), impartial (Rom. 2:11), perfect (Ps. 19:7), and complete (Rev. 15:1).

All sin starts when we determine that we want to be like God (Gen. 3:5, 6). This attitude of the will is judged (Is. 14:14, 15). The Cross did not do away with judgment; it served as the lightning rod (Col. 2:14). At the Cross judgment and mercy met, and both were victorious. Judgment is a necessity; the Cross has no meaning without it (Rom. 3:24–26). In judgment, our innermost attitudes will be revealed, and justice will be administered. We would do well to prepare our hearts (2 Cor. 5:9–11).

See also Ex. 34:6, 7; Deut. 32:4; Is. 16:5; Lam. 3:22, note; Dan. 4:37; Mark 9:43–48, note; Rom. 1:18; 3:23, note; 9:22; 12:19; chart on Judgments in the New Testament; notes on Attributes of God (Ex. 33; Deut. 4; 32; Job 23; 42; Ps. 25; 90; 102; 119; Is. 6; 65; Jer. 23; Rom. 2; Eph. 1; 1 John 5); The Fear of the Lord (Prov. 2); Rebellion (Num. 16)

---

ordinances, you shall warn them, lest they trespass against the LORD and wrath come upon you and your brethren. Do this, and you will not be guilty. [11]And take notice: Amariah the chief priest *is* over you in all matters of the LORD; and Zebadiah the son of Ishmael, the ruler of the house of Judah, for all the king's matters; also the Levites *will be* officials before you. Behave courageously, and the LORD will be with the good."

Ammon, Moab, and Mount Seir Defeated

20It happened after this *that* the people of Moab with the people of Ammon, and *others* with them besides the Ammonites,[a] came to battle against Jehoshaphat. [2]Then some came and told Jehoshaphat, saying, "A great multitude is coming against you from beyond the sea, from Syria;[a] and they are in Hazazon Tamar" (which *is* En Gedi). [3]And Jehoshaphat feared, and set himself to seek the LORD, and proclaimed a fast throughout all Judah. [4]So Judah gathered together to ask *help* from the LORD; and from all the cities of Judah they came to seek the LORD.

[5]Then Jehoshaphat stood in the assembly of Judah and Jerusalem, in the house of the LORD, before the new court, [6]and said: "O LORD God of our fathers, *are* You not God in heaven, and do You *not* rule over all the kingdoms of the nations, and in Your hand *is there not* power and might, so that no one is able to withstand You? [7]*Are* You not our

God, *who* drove out the inhabitants of this land before Your people Israel, and gave it to the descendants of Abraham Your friend forever? [8]And they dwell in it, and have built You a sanctuary in it for Your name, saying, [9]'If disaster comes upon us—sword, judgment, pestilence, or famine—we will stand before this temple and in Your presence (for Your name *is* in this temple), and cry out to You in our affliction, and You will hear and save.' [10]And now, here are the people of Ammon, Moab, and Mount Seir—whom You would not let Israel invade when they came out of the land of Egypt, but they turned from them and did not destroy them— [11]here they are, rewarding us by coming to throw us out of Your possession which You have given us to inherit. [12]O our God, will You not judge them? For we have no power against this great multitude that is coming against us; nor do we know what to do, but our eyes *are* upon You."

[13]Now all Judah, with their little ones, their wives, and their children, stood before the LORD.

[14]Then the Spirit of the LORD came upon Jahaziel the son of Zechariah, the son of Benaiah, the son of Jeiel, the son of Mattaniah, a Levite of the sons of Asaph, in the midst of the assembly. [15]And he said, "Listen, all you of Judah and you in-

20:1 [a]Following Masoretic Text and Vulgate; Septuagint reads *Meunites* (compare 26:7).   **20:2** [a]Following Masoretic Text, Septuagint, and Vulgate; some Hebrew manuscripts and Old Latin read *Edom.*

20:15 The report of this battle is unique to the chronicler, who has chosen not to include Jehoshaphat's battle against Moab (2 Kin. 3). The joint Transjordan forces of Moab, Ammon, and Mt. Seir had set themselves in battle against Judah (2 Chr. 20:10, 22). En Gedi is an oasis on the west side of the Dead Sea (v. 2). The temple singers, not military captains, led the army (v. 21). As a result of Jehoshaphat's reliance on the Lord, Judah was blessed with an abundance of spoil and with peace (vv. 25–27, 30).

habitants of Jerusalem, and you, King Jehoshaphat! Thus says the LORD to you: 'Do not be afraid nor dismayed because of this great multitude, for the battle *is* not yours, but God's. [16]Tomorrow go down against them. They will surely come up by the Ascent of Ziz, and you will find them at the end of the brook before the Wilderness of Jeruel. [17]You will not *need* to fight in this *battle.* Position yourselves, stand still and see the salvation of the LORD, who is with you, O Judah and Jerusalem!' Do not fear or be dismayed; tomorrow go out against them, for the LORD *is* with you."

[18]And Jehoshaphat bowed his head with *his* face to the ground, and all Judah and the inhabitants of Jerusalem bowed before the LORD, worshiping the LORD. [19]Then the Levites of the children of the Kohathites and of the children of the Korahites stood up to praise the LORD God of Israel with voices loud and high.

[20]So they rose early in the morning and went out into the Wilderness of Tekoa; and as they went out, Jehoshaphat stood and said, "Hear me, O Judah and you inhabitants of Jerusalem: Believe in the LORD your God, and you shall be established; believe His prophets, and you shall prosper." [21]And when he had consulted with the people, he appointed those who should sing to the LORD, and who should praise the beauty of holiness, as they went out before the army and were saying:

"Praise the LORD,
  For His mercy *endures* forever."[a]

[22]Now when they began to sing and to praise, the LORD set ambushes against the people of Ammon, Moab, and Mount Seir, who had come against Judah; and they were defeated. [23]For the people of Ammon and Moab stood up against the inhabitants of Mount Seir to utterly kill and destroy *them.* And when they had made an end of the inhabitants of Seir, they helped to destroy one another.

[24]So when Judah came to a place overlooking the wilderness, they looked toward the multitude; and there *were* their dead bodies, fallen on the earth. No one had escaped.

[25]When Jehoshaphat and his people came to take away their spoil, they found among them an abundance of valuables on the dead bodies,[a] and precious jewelry, which they stripped off for themselves, more than they could carry away; and they were three days gathering the spoil because there was so much. [26]And on the fourth day they assembled in the Valley of Berachah, for there they blessed the LORD; therefore the name of that place was called The Valley of Berachah[a] until this day. [27]Then they returned, every man of Judah and Jerusalem, with Jehoshaphat in front of them, to go back to Jerusalem with joy, for the LORD had made them rejoice over their enemies. [28]So they came to Jerusalem, with stringed instruments and harps and trumpets, to the house of the LORD. [29]And the fear of God was on all the kingdoms of *those* countries when they heard that the LORD had fought against the enemies of Israel. [30]Then the realm of Jehoshaphat was quiet, for his God gave him rest all around.

The End of Jehoshaphat's Reign

[31]So Jehoshaphat was king over Judah. *He was* thirty-five years old when he became king, and he reigned twenty-five years in Jerusalem. His mother's name *was* Azubah the daughter of Shilhi. [32]And he walked in the way of his father Asa, and did not turn aside from it, doing *what was* right in the sight of the LORD. [33]Nevertheless the high places were not taken away, for as yet the people had not directed their hearts to the God of their fathers.

[34]Now the rest of the acts of Jehoshaphat, first and last, indeed they *are* written in the book of Jehu the son of Hanani, which *is* mentioned in the book of the kings of Israel.

[35]After this Jehoshaphat king of Judah allied himself with Ahaziah king of Israel, who acted very wickedly. [36]And he allied himself with him to make ships to go to Tarshish, and they made the ships in Ezion Geber. [37]But Eliezer the son of Dodavah of Mareshah prophesied against Jehoshaphat, saying, "Because you have allied yourself with Ahaziah, the LORD has destroyed your works." Then the ships were wrecked, so that they were not able to go to Tarshish.

Jehoram Reigns in Judah

21 And Jehoshaphat rested with his fathers, and was buried with his fathers in the City

---

20:21 [a]Compare Psalm 106:1   20:25 [a]A few Hebrew manuscripts, Old Latin, and Vulgate read *garments;* Septuagint reads *armor.*   20:26 [a]Literally *Blessing*

20:35–37 Jehoshaphat allied himself with the wicked Ahaziah, and his ships were wrecked (v. 37; 1 Kin. 22:51–53). Such alliances were viewed as indicating a lack of trust in the Lord. Ahaziah's attempt at a second alliance was then rejected by Jehoshaphat (1 Kin. 22:49).

21:1 Jehoram and Ahaziah, two wicked kings, followed immediately after the parallel reigns of the temple reformers, Asa and Jehoshaphat (v. 6; 2 Chr. 22:3). The sin of and curses on Jehoram

and Ahaziah were the direct result of Jehoshaphat's alliance with Ahab, from which the house of David just barely survived (2 Chr. 18:1; 19:2; 21:6, 7; 22:2–5, 10–13). Jehoram's sin was against the throne of David and ultimately against the Lord (2 Chr. 21:4–7, 11). The curse of constant warfare was "because he had forsaken the LORD God of his fathers" (2 Chr. 21:10). The people, Jehoram's family, and Jehoram himself would all suffer (vv. 14, 15, 18–20). No one mourned his death (v. 20).

of David. Then Jehoram his son reigned in his place. ²He had brothers, the sons of Jehoshaphat: Azariah, Jehiel, Zechariah, Azaryahu, Michael, and Shephatiah; all these *were* the sons of Jehoshaphat king of Israel. ³Their father gave them great gifts of silver and gold and precious things, with fortified cities in Judah; but he gave the kingdom to Jehoram, because he *was* the firstborn.

⁴Now when Jehoram was established over the kingdom of his father, he strengthened himself and killed all his brothers with the sword, and also *others* of the princes of Israel.

⁵Jehoram *was* thirty-two years old when he became king, and he reigned eight years in Jerusalem. ⁶And he walked in the way of the kings of Israel, just as the house of Ahab had done, for he had the daughter of Ahab as a wife; and he did evil in the sight of the LORD. ⁷Yet the LORD would not destroy the house of David, because of the covenant that He had made with David, and since He had promised to give a lamp to him and to his sons forever.

⁸In his days Edom revolted against Judah's authority, and made a king over themselves. ⁹So Jehoram went out with his officers, and all his chariots with him. And he rose by night and attacked the Edomites who had surrounded him and the captains of the chariots. ¹⁰Thus Edom has been in revolt against Judah's authority to this day. At that time Libnah revolted against his rule, because he had forsaken the LORD God of his fathers. ¹¹Moreover he made high places in the mountains of Judah, and caused the inhabitants of Jerusalem to commit harlotry, and led Judah astray.

¹²And a letter came to him from Elijah the prophet, saying,

Thus says the LORD God of your father David: Because you have not walked in the ways of Jehoshaphat your father, or in the ways of Asa king of Judah, ¹³but have walked in the way of the kings of Israel, and have made Judah and the inhabitants of Jerusalem to play the harlot like the harlotry of the house of Ahab, and also have killed your brothers, those of your father's household, *who were* better than yourself, ¹⁴behold, the LORD will strike your people with a serious affliction—your children, your wives, and all your possessions; ¹⁵and you *will become* very sick with a disease of your

intestines, until your intestines come out by reason of the sickness, day by day.

¹⁶Moreover the LORD stirred up against Jehoram the spirit of the Philistines and the Arabians who *were* near the Ethiopians. ¹⁷And they came up into Judah and invaded it, and carried away all the possessions that were found in the king's house, and also his sons and his wives, so that there was not a son left to him except Jehoahaz,ª the youngest of his sons.

¹⁸After all this the LORD struck him in his intestines with an incurable disease. ¹⁹Then it happened in the course of time, after the end of two years, that his intestines came out because of his sickness; so he died in severe pain. And his people made no burning for him, like the burning for his fathers.

²⁰He was thirty-two years old when he became king. He reigned in Jerusalem eight years and, to no one's sorrow, departed. However they buried him in the City of David, but not in the tombs of the kings.

Ahaziah Reigns in Judah

22 Then the inhabitants of Jerusalem made Ahaziah his youngest son king in his place, for the raiders who came with the Arabians into the camp had killed all the older *sons*. So Ahaziah the son of Jehoram, king of Judah, reigned. ²Ahaziah *was* forty-twoª years old when he became king, and he reigned one year in Jerusalem. His mother's name *was* Athaliah the granddaughter of Omri. ³He also walked in the ways of the house of Ahab, for his mother advised him to do wickedly. ⁴Therefore he did evil in the sight of the LORD, like the house of Ahab; for they were his counselors after the death of his father, to his destruction. ⁵He also followed their advice, and went with Jehoramª the son of Ahab king of Israel to war against Hazael king of Syria at Ramoth Gilead; and the Syrians wounded Joram. ⁶Then he returned to Jezreel to recover from the wounds which he had received at Ramah, when he fought against Hazael king of Syria. And Azariahª the son

• • • • • • • • • • • • • • • • • •

21:17 ªElsewhere called *Ahaziah* (compare 2 Chronicles 22:1) **22:2** ªOr *twenty-two* (compare 2 Kings 8:26) **22:5** ªAlso spelled *Joram* (compare verses 5 and 7; 2 Kings 8:28; and elsewhere) **22:6** ªSome Hebrew manuscripts, Septuagint, Syriac, Vulgate, and 2 Kings 8:29 read *Ahaziah*.

22:1–9 The wickedness of Ahaziah (Jehoahaz; see chart, The Kings with Two Names) was the result of the direct influence of his mother and her family (v. 3; see 2 Chr. 18:3, note). Omri founded the first enduring dynasty of the northern kingdom (2 Chr. 22:2, 1 Kin. 16:21–28; chart, The Dynasties of Israel—Part 1). The influence of this wicked dynasty over the southern kingdom is evident (see 2 Chr. 20:35; 21:6; 22:3, 4).

Ahaziah was so influenced by his mother's family that he also experienced the judgment of Jehu on the house of Ahab (2 Chr. 22:7–9). Hazael, king of Syria, was a constant enemy of Judah (vv. 5, 6; see 2 Kin. 12:17, 18; 13:22–24). Jehoram and Joram are alternate spellings for the king of Israel (2 Chr. 22:5, not to be confused with Jehoram, king of Judah, 2 Chr. 21:1–20; see also chart, The Kings with Two Names).

of Jehoram, king of Judah, went down to see Jehoram the son of Ahab in Jezreel, because he was sick.

7His going to Joram was God's occasion for Ahaziah's downfall; for when he arrived, he went out with Jehoram against Jehu the son of Nimshi, whom the Lord had anointed to cut off the house of Ahab. 8And it happened, when Jehu was executing judgment on the house of Ahab, and found the princes of Judah and the sons of Ahaziah's brothers who served Ahaziah, that he killed them. 9Then he searched for Ahaziah; and they caught him (he was hiding in Samaria), and brought him to Jehu. When they had killed him, they buried him, "because," they said, "he is the son of Jehoshaphat, who sought the Lord with all his heart."

So the house of Ahaziah had no one to assume power over the kingdom.

Athaliah Reigns in Judah

10Now when Athaliah the mother of Ahaziah saw that her son was dead, she arose and destroyed all the royal heirs of the house of Judah. 11But Jehoshabeath,a the daughter of the king, took Joash the son of Ahaziah, and stole him away from among the king's sons who were being murdered, and put him and his nurse in a bedroom. So Jehoshabeath, the daughter of King Jehoram, the wife of Jehoiada the priest (for she was the sister of Ahaziah), hid him from Athaliah so that she did not kill him. 12And he was hidden with them in the house of God for six years, while Athaliah reigned over the land.

Joash Crowned King of Judah

23In the seventh year Jehoiada strengthened himself, and made a covenant with the captains of hundreds: Azariah the son of Jeroham, Ishmael the son of Jehohanan, Azariah the son of Obed, Maaseiah the son of Adaiah, and Elishaphat the son of Zichri. 2And they went throughout Judah and gathered the Levites from all the cities of Judah, and the chief fathers of Israel, and they came to Jerusalem.

3Then all the assembly made a covenant with the king in the house of God. And he said to them, "Behold, the king's son shall reign, as the Lord has said of the sons of David. 4This is what you shall do: One-third of you entering on the Sabbath, of the priests and the Levites, shall be keep-

ing watch over the doors; 5one-third shall be at the king's house; and one-third at the Gate of the Foundation. All the people shall be in the courts of the house of the Lord. 6But let no one come into the house of the Lord except the priests and those of the Levites who serve. They may go in, for they are holy; but all the people shall keep the watch of the Lord. 7And the Levites shall surround the king on all sides, every man with his weapons in his hand; and whoever comes into the house, let him be put to death. You are to be with the king when he comes in and when he goes out."

8So the Levites and all Judah did according to all that Jehoiada the priest commanded. And each man took his men who were to be on duty on the Sabbath, with those who were going off duty on the Sabbath; for Jehoiada the priest had not dismissed the divisions. 9And Jehoiada the priest gave to the captains of hundreds the spears and the large and small shields which had belonged to King David, that were in the temple of God. 10Then he set all the people, every man with his weapon in his hand, from the right side of the temple to the left side of the temple, along by the altar and by the temple, all around the king. 11And they brought out the king's son, put the crown on him, gave him the Testimony,a and made him king. Then Jehoiada and his sons anointed him, and said, "Long live the king!"

Death of Athaliah

12Now when Athaliah heard the noise of the people running and praising the king, she came to the people in the temple of the Lord. 13When she looked, there was the king standing by his pillar at the entrance; and the leaders and the trumpeters were by the king. All the people of the land were rejoicing and blowing trumpets, also the singers with musical instruments, and those who led in praise. So Athaliah tore her clothes and said, "Treason! Treason!"

14And Jehoiada the priest brought out the captains of hundreds who were set over the army, and said to them, "Take her outside under guard, and slay with the sword whoever follows her." For the priest had said, "Do not kill her in the house of the Lord."

22:11 aSpelled Jehosheba in 2 Kings 11:2   23:11 aThat is, the Law (compare Exodus 25:16, 21; 31:18)

22:10 The queen mother probably had some authoritative standing regarding the promotion of worship (see 2 Chr. 15:16). Athaliah, Judah's only queen and a Baal worshiper (2 Chr. 24:7), kept her son Ahaziah from following the Lord, which ultimately led to his destruction (2 Chr. 22:5–9). Jehoshaphat's marriage alliance with the house of Ahab started this chain of wickedness. Athaliah attempted to destroy the throne of David and paganize the nation of Judah by placing herself over Judah for six years (vv. 10–12).

22:10—24:1 All Israel made Joash king. The chronicler makes clear that the priests and Levites, as well as all Israel, participated in making Joash king (2 Chr. 23:1–6). Jehoshabeath (also called Jehosheba, 2 Kin. 11:2) is described as the wife of a priest (2 Chr. 22:11). The priests and the Levites gathered to prevent unauthorized, non-Levitical personnel from entering the sanctuary (2 Chr. 23:1, 2, 6). The legitimate king and his priest replaced the illegitimate queen and her priest (2 Chr. 23:12–17).

JEHOSHABEATH (JEHOSHEBA) *The Wife of a Priest*

Jehoshabeath (also called Jehosheba in 2 Kin. 11:2) was Ahaziah's sister. She may have been the daughter of Athaliah, but she was more likely Jehoram's daughter by an unrecorded wife. She was the wife of Jehoiada, a true priest of God, suggesting that she herself remained faithful to God.

The priesthood of Jehoshabeath's husband undoubtedly made her keenly aware of the need to rescue Joash from the sword of his murderous grandmother, Athaliah. The temple afforded her a place to keep the young child safe and an environment in which the boy could be prepared for future service as king. By rescuing Joash, Jehoshabeath became God's instrument in His sovereign plan to keep His promise that a son of David would always be king and part of the lineage of the Messiah.

Presumably, this courageous woman risked her own life to save the life of an innocent child marked for murder.

See also 2 Kin. 11:2; notes on Attributes of God (Job 23); Heroines (Heb. 11)

---

[15]So they seized her; and she went by way of the entrance of the Horse Gate *into* the king's house, and they killed her there.

[16]Then Jehoiada made a covenant between himself, the people, and the king, that they should be the LORD's people. [17]And all the people went to the temple[a] of Baal, and tore it down. They broke in pieces its altars and images, and killed Mattan the priest of Baal before the altars. [18]Also Jehoiada appointed the oversight of the house of the LORD to the hand of the priests, the Levites, whom David had assigned in the house of the LORD, to offer the burnt offerings of the LORD, as *it is* written in the Law of Moses, with rejoicing and with singing, *as it was established* by David. [19]And he set the gatekeepers at the gates of the house of the LORD, so that no one *who was* in any way unclean should enter.

[20]Then he took the captains of hundreds, the nobles, the governors of the people, and all the people of the land, and brought the king down from the house of the LORD; and they went through the Upper Gate to the king's house, and set the king on the throne of the kingdom. [21]So all the people of the land rejoiced; and the city was quiet, for they had slain Athaliah with the sword.

Joash Repairs the Temple

24 Joash *was* seven years old when he became king, and he reigned forty years in Jerusalem. His mother's name *was* Zibiah of Beersheba. [2]Joash did *what was* right in the sight of the LORD all the days of Jehoiada the priest. [3]And Jehoiada took two wives for him, and he had sons and daughters.

[4]Now it happened after this *that* Joash set his heart on repairing the house of the LORD. [5]Then he gathered the priests and the Levites, and said to them, "Go out to the cities of Judah, and gather from all Israel money to repair the house of your God from year to year, and see that you do it quickly."

However the Levites did not do it quickly. [6]So the king called Jehoiada the chief *priest,* and said to him, "Why have you not required the Levites to bring in from Judah and from Jerusalem the collection, *according to the commandment* of Moses the servant of the LORD and of the assembly of Israel, for the tabernacle of witness?" [7]For the sons of Athaliah, that wicked woman, had broken into the house of God, and had also presented all the dedicated things of the house of the LORD to the Baals.

[8]Then at the king's command they made a chest, and set it outside at the gate of the house of the LORD. [9]And they made a proclamation throughout Judah and Jerusalem to bring to the LORD the collection *that* Moses the servant of God *had imposed* on Israel in the wilderness. [10]Then all the leaders and all the people rejoiced, brought their contributions, and put *them* into the chest until all had given. [11]So it was, at that time, when the chest was brought to the king's official by the hand of the Levites, and when they saw that *there was* much money, that the king's scribe and the high priest's officer came and emptied the chest, and took it and returned it to its place. Thus they did day by day, and gathered money in abundance.

[12]The king and Jehoiada gave it to those who did the work of the service of the house of the LORD; and they hired masons and carpenters to repair the house of the LORD, and also those who worked in iron and bronze to restore the house of the LORD. [13]So the workmen labored, and the work was completed by them; they restored the house of God to its original condition and reinforced it. [14]When they had finished, they brought the rest of the money before the king and Jehoiada; they made from it articles for the house of the LORD, articles for serving and offering, spoons and vessels of gold and silver. And they offered burnt offerings in the house of the LORD continually all the days of Jehoiada.

23:17 [a]Literally *house*

Apostasy of Joash

[15]But Jehoiada grew old and was full of days, and he died; *he was* one hundred and thirty years old when he died. [16]And they buried him in the City of David among the kings, because he had done good in Israel, both toward God and His house.

[17]Now after the death of Jehoiada the leaders of Judah came and bowed down to the king. And the king listened to them. [18]Therefore they left the house of the LORD God of their fathers, and served wooden images and idols; and wrath came upon Judah and Jerusalem because of their trespass. [19]Yet He sent prophets to them, to bring them back to the LORD; and they testified against them, but they would not listen.

[20]Then the Spirit of God came upon Zechariah the son of Jehoiada the priest, who stood above the people, and said to them, "Thus says God: 'Why do you transgress the commandments of the LORD, so that you cannot prosper? Because you have forsaken the LORD, He also has forsaken you.' " [21]So they conspired against him, and at the command of the king they stoned him with stones in the court of the house of the LORD. [22]Thus Joash the king did not remember the kindness which Jehoiada his father had done to him, but killed his son; and as he died, he said, "The LORD look on *it,* and repay!"

Death of Joash

[23]So it happened in the spring of the year *that* the army of Syria came up against him; and they came to Judah and Jerusalem, and destroyed all the leaders of the people from among the people, and sent all their spoil to the king of Damascus. [24]For the army of the Syrians came with a small company of men; but the LORD delivered a very great army into their hand, because they had forsaken the LORD God of their fathers. So they executed judgment against Joash. [25]And when they had withdrawn from him (for they left him severely wounded), his own servants conspired against him because of the blood of the sons[a] of Jehoiada the priest, and killed him on his bed. So he died. And they buried him in the City of David, but they did not bury him in the tombs of the kings.

[26]These are the ones who conspired against him: Zabad[a] the son of Shimeath the Ammonitess, and Jehozabad the son of Shimrith[b] the Moabitess. [27]Now *concerning* his sons, and the many oracles about him, and the repairing of the house of God, indeed they *are* written in the annals of the book of the kings. Then Amaziah his son reigned in his place.

Amaziah Reigns in Judah

25 Amaziah *was* twenty-five years old *when* he became king, and he reigned twenty-nine years in Jerusalem. His mother's name *was* Jehoaddan of Jerusalem. [2]And he did *what was* right in the sight of the LORD, but not with a loyal heart.

[3]Now it happened, as soon as the kingdom was established for him, that he executed his servants who had murdered his father the king. [4]However he did not execute their children, but *did* as *it is* written in the Law in the Book of Moses, where the LORD commanded, saying, "The fathers shall not be put to death for their children, nor shall the children be put to death for their fathers; but a person shall die for his own sin."[a]

The War Against Edom

[5]Moreover Amaziah gathered Judah together and set over them captains of thousands and captains of hundreds, according to *their* fathers' houses, throughout all Judah and Benjamin; and he numbered them from twenty years old and above, and found them to be three hundred thou-

---

24:25 [a]Septuagint and Vulgate read *son* (compare verses 20–22).
24:26 [a]Or *Jozachar* (compare 2 Kings 12:21) [b]Or *Shomer* (compare 2 Kings 12:21) 25:4 [a]Deuteronomy 24:16

24:15 The death of Jehoiada. Joash rebuilt the temple while Jehoiada was alive but failed to teach the people the Law of the Lord as Asa and Jehoshaphat had done (vv. 15–18; 2 Chr. 14:2–4; 17:3–6). Jehoiada the priest, not the king, led the temple worship (2 Chr. 24:14). Joash was not fully dedicated to proper worship at the temple (v. 18). The report of Jehoiada's death is much more honorable and regal than that of King Joash (v. 25) and highlights the gravity of Joash's sin (vv. 18, 19). Jehoiada was "full of days" (v. 15) and was buried "among the kings" because he was devoted to the Lord (v. 16). No mention is made of Joash's age, and he was buried apart from the kings as his grandfather Jehoram had been (v. 25; 2 Chr. 21:20). Upon the death of Jehoiada, Joash forsook the temple (see 2 Chr. 24:17–27, note).

24:17–27 The details of the sin of Joash are unique to the chronicler. The Lord gave Joash an opportunity to repent (v. 19). Zechariah's father, Jehoiada, who had helped save Joash (v. 20; 2 Chr. 22:10–12), gathered all Israel to make Joash king (2 Chr. 23:1–21) and taught Joash the Law of the Lord (2 Kin. 12:2), but this did not stop Joash from ordering Zechariah's murder. Joash owed not only his power and throne but also his life to the loyalty and unselfishness of Jehoiada's protection. Because of his sin, Joash knew defeat (2 Chr. 24:24), disloyalty (v. 25), and death in shame (v. 25).

25:1–13 Amaziah followed Joash's half-hearted obedience to the Lord (v. 2; 2 Kin. 14:1–20). Amaziah acted in accord with the Law of the Lord (2 Chr. 25:3, 4; Deut. 24:16) and the "man of God" (an unknown prophet, 2 Chr. 25:5–10). The Valley of Salt is south of the Dead Sea (2 Chr. 25:11; 1 Chr. 18:12). The people of Seir were Edomites (2 Chr. 25:11, 14; see 1 Chr. 1:38–42). "Samaria to Beth Horon" designated the northern border of Amaziah's kingdom (2 Chr. 25:13). The attack by the soldiers discharged by Amaziah accounts for Amaziah's request for war (vv. 10, 13, 17).

sand choice *men, able* to go to war, who could handle spear and shield. [6]He also hired one hundred thousand mighty men of valor from Israel for one hundred talents of silver. [7]But a man of God came to him, saying, "O king, do not let the army of Israel go with you, for the LORD *is* not with Israel— *not with* any of the children of Ephraim. [8]But if you go, be gone! Be strong in battle! *Even so,* God shall make you fall before the enemy; for God has power to help and to overthrow."

[9]Then Amaziah said to the man of God, "But what *shall we* do about the hundred talents which I have given to the troops of Israel?"

And the man of God answered, "The LORD is able to give you much more than this." [10]So Amaziah discharged the troops that had come to him from Ephraim, to go back home. Therefore their anger was greatly aroused against Judah, and they returned home in great anger.

[11]Then Amaziah strengthened himself, and leading his people, he went to the Valley of Salt and killed ten thousand of the people of Seir. [12]Also the children of Judah took captive ten thousand alive, brought them to the top of the rock, and cast them down from the top of the rock, so that they all were dashed in pieces.

[13]But as for the soldiers of the army which Amaziah had discharged, so that they would not go with him to battle, they raided the cities of Judah from Samaria to Beth Horon, killed three thousand in them, and took much spoil.

[14]Now it was so, after Amaziah came from the slaughter of the Edomites, that he brought the gods of the people of Seir, set them up *to be* his gods, and bowed down before them and burned incense to them. [15]Therefore the anger of the LORD was aroused against Amaziah, and He sent him a prophet who said to him, "Why have you sought the gods of the people, which could not rescue their own people from your hand?"

[16]So it was, as he talked with him, that *the king* said to him, "Have we made you the king's counselor? Cease! Why should you be killed?"

Then the prophet ceased, and said, "I know that God has determined to destroy you, because you have done this and have not heeded my advice."

Israel Defeats Judah

[17]Now Amaziah king of Judah asked advice and sent to Joash[a] the son of Jehoahaz, the son of Jehu, king of Israel, saying, "Come, let us face one another *in battle.*"

[18]And Joash king of Israel sent to Amaziah king of Judah, saying, "The thistle that *was* in Lebanon sent to the cedar that was in Lebanon, saying, 'Give your daughter to my son as wife'; and a wild beast that *was* in Lebanon passed by and trampled the thistle. [19]Indeed you say that you have defeated the Edomites, and your heart is lifted up to boast. Stay at home now; why should you meddle with trouble, that you should fall—you and Judah with you?"

[20]But Amaziah would not heed, for it *came* from God, that He might give them into the hand *of their enemies,* because they sought the gods of Edom. [21]So Joash king of Israel went out; and he and Amaziah king of Judah faced one another at Beth Shemesh, which *belongs* to Judah. [22]And Judah was defeated by Israel, and every man fled to his tent. [23]Then Joash the king of Israel captured Amaziah king of Judah, the son of Joash, the son of Jehoahaz, at Beth Shemesh; and he brought him to Jerusalem, and broke down the wall of Jerusalem from the Gate of Ephraim to the Corner Gate—four hundred cubits. [24]And *he took* all the gold and silver, all the articles that were found in the house of God with Obed-Edom, the treasures of the king's house, and hostages, and returned to Samaria.

Death of Amaziah

[25]Amaziah the son of Joash, king of Judah, lived fifteen years after the death of Joash the son of Jehoahaz, king of Israel. [26]Now the rest of the acts of Amaziah, from first to last, indeed *are* they not written in the book of the kings of Judah and Israel? [27]After the time that Amaziah turned away from following the LORD, they made a conspiracy against him in Jerusalem, and he fled to Lachish; but they sent after him to Lachish and killed him there. [28]Then they brought him on horses and buried him with his fathers in the City of Judah.

Uzziah Reigns in Judah

26 Now all the people of Judah took Uzziah,[a] who *was* sixteen years old, and made him king instead of his father Amaziah. [2]He built Elath[a] and restored it to Judah, after the king rested with his fathers.

[3]Uzziah *was* sixteen years old when he became

25:17 [a]Spelled *Jehoash* in 2 Kings 14:8ff   **26:1** [a]Called *Azariah* in 2 Kings 14:21ff   **26:2** [a]Hebrew *Eloth*

26:1 Uzziah (Azariah) repeated his father Joash's pattern of obedience and blessing during the life of Zechariah the prophet (2 Chr. 26:4–15), followed by sin and punishment (vv. 16–21; see 1 Chr. 3:12; see Is. 1:1; 6:1; Hos. 1:1; Amos 1:1; chart, The Kings with Two Names). Uzziah's obedience was blessed with prosperity (2 Chr. 26:5), victory (vv. 6, 7), foreign tribute (v. 8), fame (vv. 8, 15), building projects (vv. 9, 10), abundance (v. 10), and a large army (vv. 11–14). Uzziah strengthened Judah's control of the south by building at the important gulf port of Elath (v. 2). Gath, Jabneh, and Ashdod were important Philistine cities (v. 6).

king, and he reigned fifty-two years in Jerusalem. His mother's name was Jecholiah of Jerusalem. ⁴And he did *what was* right in the sight of the LORD, according to all that his father Amaziah had done. ⁵He sought God in the days of Zechariah, who had understanding in the visionsª of God; and as long as he sought the LORD, God made him prosper.

⁶Now he went out and made war against the Philistines, and broke down the wall of Gath, the wall of Jabneh, and the wall of Ashdod; and he built cities *around* Ashdod and among the Philistines. ⁷God helped him against the Philistines, against the Arabians who lived in Gur Baal, and against the Meunites. ⁸Also the Ammonites brought tribute to Uzziah. His fame spread as far as the entrance of Egypt, for he became exceedingly strong.

⁹And Uzziah built towers in Jerusalem at the Corner Gate, at the Valley Gate, and at the corner buttress of the wall; then he fortified them. ¹⁰Also he built towers in the desert. He dug many wells, for he had much livestock, both in the lowlands and in the plains; *he also had* farmers and vinedressers in the mountains and in Carmel, for he loved the soil.

¹¹Moreover Uzziah had an army of fighting men who went out to war by companies, according to the number on their roll as prepared by Jeiel the scribe and Maaseiah the officer, under the hand of Hananiah, *one* of the king's captains. ¹²The total number of chief officersª of the mighty men of valor *was* two thousand six hundred. ¹³And under their authority *was* an army of three hundred and seven thousand five hundred, that made war with mighty power, to help the king against the enemy. ¹⁴Then Uzziah prepared for them, for the entire army, shields, spears, helmets, body armor, bows, and slings *to cast* stones. ¹⁵And he made devices in Jerusalem, invented by skillful men, to be on the towers and the corners, to shoot arrows and large stones. So his fame spread far and wide, for he was marvelously helped till he became strong.

The Penalty for Uzziah's Pride

¹⁶But when he was strong his heart was lifted up, to *his* destruction, for he transgressed against the LORD his God by entering the temple of the LORD to burn incense on the altar of incense. ¹⁷So Azariah the priest went in after him, and with him were eighty priests of the LORD—valiant men. ¹⁸And they withstood King Uzziah, and said to him, "*It is* not for you, Uzziah, to burn incense to the LORD, but for the priests, the sons of Aaron, who are consecrated to burn incense. Get out of the sanctuary, for you have trespassed! You *shall have* no honor from the LORD God."

¹⁹Then Uzziah became furious; and he *had* a censer in his hand to burn incense. And while he was angry with the priests, leprosy broke out on his forehead, before the priests in the house of the LORD, beside the incense altar. ²⁰And Azariah the chief priest and all the priests looked at him, and there, on his forehead, he *was* leprous; so they thrust him out of that place. Indeed he also hurried to get out, because the LORD had struck him.

²¹King Uzziah was a leper until the day of his death. He dwelt in an isolated house, because he was a leper; for he was cut off from the house of the LORD. Then Jotham his son *was* over the king's house, judging the people of the land.

²²Now the rest of the acts of Uzziah, from first to last, the prophet Isaiah the son of Amoz wrote. ²³So Uzziah rested with his fathers, and they buried him with his fathers in the field of burial which *belonged* to the kings, for they said, "He is a leper." Then Jotham his son reigned in his place.

Jotham Reigns in Judah

27 Jotham *was* twenty-five years old when he became king, and he reigned sixteen years in Jerusalem. His mother's name *was* Jerushahª the daughter of Zadok. ²And he did *what was* right in the sight of the LORD, according to all that his father Uzziah had done (although he did not enter the temple of the LORD). But still the people acted corruptly.

³He built the Upper Gate of the house of the LORD, and he built extensively on the wall of Ophel. ⁴Moreover he built cities in the mountains of Judah, and in the forests he built fortresses and towers. ⁵He also fought with the king of the Ammonites and defeated them. And the people of Ammon gave him in that year one hundred talents of silver, ten thousand kors of wheat, and ten thousand of barley. The people of Ammon paid this to him in the second and third years also. ⁶So Jotham became mighty, because he prepared his ways before the LORD his God.

⁷Now the rest of the acts of Jotham, and all his wars and his ways, indeed they *are* written in the book of the kings of Israel and Judah. ⁸He was twenty-five years old when he became king, and he reigned sixteen years in Jerusalem. ⁹So Jotham

---

26:5 ªSeveral Hebrew manuscripts, Septuagint, Syriac, Targum, and Arabic read *fear.* **26:12** ªLiterally *chief fathers* **27:1** ªSpelled *Jerusha* in 2 Kings 15:33

26:16–23 Uzziah's sin. In spite of great blessing for his obedience (vv. 1–15), Uzziah took it upon himself to perform the duties of the priest (v. 16). He refused to heed the word of the prophet (vv. 17, 18) and was smitten with leprosy and exiled from the temple (vv. 19–21; see Lev. 13:46). Uzziah's son, Jotham, then assumed all the royal duties (2 Chr. 26:21).

rested with his fathers, and they buried him in the City of David. Then Ahaz his son reigned in his place.

Ahaz Reigns in Judah

28 Ahaz *was* twenty years old when he became king, and he reigned sixteen years in Jerusalem; and he did not do *what was* right in the sight of the LORD, as his father David *had done.* ²For he walked in the ways of the kings of Israel, and made molded images for the Baals. ³He burned incense in the Valley of the Son of Hinnom, and burned his children in the fire, according to the abominations of the nations whom the LORD had cast out before the children of Israel. ⁴And he sacrificed and burned incense on the high places, on the hills, and under every green tree.

Syria and Israel Defeat Judah

⁵Therefore the LORD his God delivered him into the hand of the king of Syria. They defeated him, and carried away a great multitude of them as captives, and brought *them* to Damascus. Then he was also delivered into the hand of the king of Israel, who defeated him with a great slaughter. ⁶For Pekah the son of Remaliah killed one hundred and twenty thousand in Judah in one day, all valiant men, because they had forsaken the LORD God of their fathers. ⁷Zichri, a mighty man of Ephraim, killed Maaseiah the king's son, Azrikam the officer over the house, and Elkanah *who was* second to the king. ⁸And the children of Israel carried away captive of their brethren two hundred thousand women, sons, and daughters; and they also took away much spoil from them, and brought the spoil to Samaria.

Israel Returns the Captives

⁹But a prophet of the LORD was there, whose name *was* Oded; and he went out before the army that came to Samaria, and said to them: "Look, because the LORD God of your fathers was angry with Judah, He has delivered them into your hand; but you have killed them in a rage *that* reaches up to heaven. ¹⁰And now you propose to force the children of Judah and Jerusalem to be your male

and female slaves; *but are* you not also guilty before the LORD your God? ¹¹Now hear me, therefore, and return the captives, whom you have taken captive from your brethren, for the fierce wrath of the LORD *is* upon you."

¹²Then some of the heads of the children of Ephraim, Azariah the son of Johanan, Berechiah the son of Meshillemoth, Jehizkiah the son of Shallum, and Amasa the son of Hadlai, stood up against those who came from the war, ¹³and said to them, "You shall not bring the captives here, for we *already* have offended the LORD. You intend to add to our sins and to our guilt; for our guilt is great, and *there is* fierce wrath against Israel." ¹⁴So the armed men left the captives and the spoil before the leaders and all the assembly. ¹⁵Then the men who were designated by name rose up and took the captives, and from the spoil they clothed all who were naked among them, dressed them and gave them sandals, gave them food and drink, and anointed them; and they let all the feeble ones ride on donkeys. So they brought them to their brethren at Jericho, the city of palm trees. Then they returned to Samaria.

Assyria Refuses to Help Judah

¹⁶At the same time King Ahaz sent to the kings[a] of Assyria to help him. ¹⁷For again the Edomites had come, attacked Judah, and carried away captives. ¹⁸The Philistines also had invaded the cities of the lowland and of the South of Judah, and had taken Beth Shemesh, Aijalon, Gederoth, Sochoh with its villages, Timnah with its villages, and Gimzo with its villages; and they dwelt there. ¹⁹For the LORD brought Judah low because of Ahaz king of Israel, for he had encouraged moral decline in Judah and had been continually unfaithful to the LORD. ²⁰Also Tiglath-Pileser[a] king of Assyria came to him and distressed him, and did not assist him. ²¹For Ahaz took part *of the treasures* from the house of the LORD, from the house of the king, and from the leaders, and he gave *it* to the king of Assyria; but he did not help him.

28:16 [a]Septuagint, Syriac, and Vulgate read *king* (compare verse 20).
28:20 [a]Hebrew *Tilgath-Pilneser*

28:1 Ahaz, in his evil reign, countered the righteous reign of his father Jotham (2 Chr. 27:1–9) and forsook the Lord, abandoned the temple (2 Chr. 28:4, 22–25), worshiped idols (v. 2), and practiced human sacrifice (v. 3; Deut. 18:9–14). "The valley of the Son of Hinnom" was a place of idolatry located to the east below the southern edge of Jerusalem (2 Chr. 28:3; Jer. 7:28–31). Associated with Judah's most disgusting pagan practices (2 Chr. 33:6), the valley later became a place of refuse, and as such its perpetual fires were used to describe the place of eternal punishment in the NT (Mark 9:43). Ahaz was defeated by Israel and Syria (2 Chr. 28:5–15) but did not learn from his mistakes and sought help through another foreign

alliance (v. 16). Ahaz brought Judah to its lowest point. Under his leadership, the nation was united in wickedness and spiritual decline (vv. 2, 19). He was so wicked that he was not buried in the "tombs of the kings" (v. 27). From the ideal kings (David and Solomon), who remained faithful to temple worship and reigned over a united Israel, the chronicler has led the reader to the ultimate wicked king, who had completely forsaken the temple (2 Chr. 28:22–25) and who reigned over an Israel united in spiritual decline. This fact opens the way for the great temple reforms of Hezekiah (2 Chr. 29—32).

Apostasy and Death of Ahaz

²²Now in the time of his distress King Ahaz became increasingly unfaithful to the LORD. This *is that* King Ahaz. ²³For he sacrificed to the gods of Damascus which had defeated him, saying, "Because the gods of the kings of Syria help them, I will sacrifice to them that they may help me." But they were the ruin of him and of all Israel. ²⁴So Ahaz gathered the articles of the house of God, cut in pieces the articles of the house of God, shut up the doors of the house of the LORD, and made for himself altars in every corner of Jerusalem. ²⁵And in every single city of Judah he made high places to burn incense to other gods, and provoked to anger the LORD God of his fathers.

²⁶Now the rest of his acts and all his ways, from first to last, indeed they *are* written in the book of the kings of Judah and Israel. ²⁷So Ahaz rested with his fathers, and they buried him in the city, in Jerusalem; but they did not bring him into the tombs of the kings of Israel. Then Hezekiah his son reigned in his place.

Hezekiah Reigns in Judah

29 Hezekiah became king *when he was* twenty-five years old, and he reigned twenty-nine years in Jerusalem. His mother's name *was* Abijah[a] the daughter of Zechariah. ²And he did *what was* right in the sight of the LORD, according to all that his father David had done.

Hezekiah Cleanses the Temple

³In the first year of his reign, in the first month, he opened the doors of the house of the LORD and repaired them. ⁴Then he brought in the priests and the Levites, and gathered them in the East Square, ⁵and said to them: "Hear me, Levites! Now sanctify yourselves, sanctify the house of the LORD God of your fathers, and carry out the rubbish from the holy *place.* ⁶For our fathers have trespassed and done evil in the eyes of the LORD our God; they have forsaken Him, have turned their faces away from the dwelling place of the LORD, and turned *their* backs *on Him.* ⁷They have also shut up the doors of the vestibule, put out the lamps, and have not burned incense or offered burnt offerings in the holy *place* to the God of Israel. ⁸Therefore the wrath of the LORD fell upon Judah and Jerusalem, and He has given them up to trouble, to desolation, and to jeering, as you see with your eyes. ⁹For indeed, because of this our fathers have fallen by the sword; and our sons, our daughters, and our wives *are* in captivity.

¹⁰"Now *it is* in my heart to make a covenant with the LORD God of Israel, that His fierce wrath may turn away from us. ¹¹My sons, do not be negligent now, for the LORD has chosen you to stand before Him, to serve Him, and that you should minister to Him and burn incense."

¹²Then these Levites arose: Mahath the son of Amasai and Joel the son of Azariah, of the sons of the Kohathites; of the sons of Merari, Kish the son of Abdi and Azariah the son of Jehallelel; of the Gershonites, Joah the son of Zimmah and Eden the son of Joah; ¹³of the sons of Elizaphan, Shimri and Jeiel; of the sons of Asaph, Zechariah and Mattaniah; ¹⁴of the sons of Heman, Jehiel and Shimei; and of the sons of Jeduthun, Shemaiah and Uzziel.

¹⁵And they gathered their brethren, sanctified themselves, and went according to the commandment of the king, at the words of the LORD, to cleanse the house of the LORD. ¹⁶Then the priests went into the inner part of the house of the LORD to cleanse *it,* and brought out all the debris that they found in the temple of the LORD to the court of the house of the LORD. And the Levites took *it* out and carried *it* to the Brook Kidron.

¹⁷Now they began to sanctify on the first *day* of the first month, and on the eighth day of the month they came to the vestibule of the LORD. So they sanctified the house of the LORD in eight days, and on the sixteenth day of the first month they finished.

¹⁸Then they went in to King Hezekiah and said, "We have cleansed all the house of the LORD, the altar of burnt offerings with all its articles, and the table of the showbread with all its articles. ¹⁹Moreover all the articles which King Ahaz in his

29:1 ᵃSpelled *Abi* in 2 Kings 18:2

29:1 The great apostasy of Ahaz paved the way for the comprehensive reforms of Hezekiah (vv. 1–27). Hezekiah did what was right before the Lord "according to all that his father David had done" (v. 2). A king of Judah had not been compared to David since the days of Jehoshaphat, almost 150 years before (2 Chr. 17:3). Hezekiah's reign is described in language reminiscent of the faithful reigns of David and Solomon (2 Chr. 30:26). Hezekiah was a king who acted in complete faithfulness toward the temple, as had David and Solomon. He ordered the Levites to sanctify themselves (2 Chr. 29:5–17), restored the sacrifices (vv. 20–24), stationed musicians at the temple (vv. 25–30), and encouraged the full participation of all Israel in joyful temple worship (vv. 31–36; 2 Chr. 31:10). Hezekiah even kept a joyful feast for 14 days (2 Chr. 30:21–23). Passover (2 Chr. 29:5, 15) and Unleavened Bread (vv. 13, 21) are two separate feasts. However, because the Feast of Unleavened Bread follows immediately after Passover, both feasts are sometimes referred to as Passover. For celebrating the feasts, Hezekiah was blessed with prosperity, a strong army, victory, and tribute (2 Chr. 32:1–5, 6, 23). Through Hezekiah's example, the people learned of repentance, forgiveness, and restored blessing (2 Chr. 32:24–29). Hezekiah was highly honored at his death (2 Chr. 32:32, 33).

29:3 In whole-hearted reform, Hezekiah repaired the temple and called the people to obedience as well (vv. 5–11, 31; Deut. 17:18–20). "Captivity" refers to the scattering of the northern kingdom by Assyria (2 Chr. 29:9; 30:7).

reign had cast aside in his transgression we have prepared and sanctified; and there they *are,* before the altar of the LORD."

Hezekiah Restores Temple Worship

20Then King Hezekiah rose early, gathered the rulers of the city, and went up to the house of the LORD. 21And they brought seven bulls, seven rams, seven lambs, and seven male goats for a sin offering for the kingdom, for the sanctuary, and for Judah. Then he commanded the priests, the sons of Aaron, to offer *them* on the altar of the LORD. 22So they killed the bulls, and the priests received the blood and sprinkled *it* on the altar. Likewise they killed the rams and sprinkled the blood on the altar. They also killed the lambs and sprinkled the blood on the altar. 23Then they brought out the male goats *for* the sin offering before the king and the assembly, and they laid their hands on them. 24And the priests killed them; and they presented their blood on the altar as a sin offering to make an atonement for all Israel, for the king commanded *that* the burnt offering and the sin offering *be made* for all Israel.

25And he stationed the Levites in the house of the LORD with cymbals, with stringed instruments, and with harps, according to the commandment of David, of Gad the king's seer, and of Nathan the prophet; for thus *was* the commandment of the LORD by His prophets. 26The Levites stood with the instruments of David, and the priests with the trumpets. 27Then Hezekiah commanded *them* to offer the burnt offering on the altar. And when the burnt offering began, the song of the LORD *also* began, with the trumpets and with the instruments of David king of Israel. 28So all the assembly worshiped, the singers sang, and the trumpeters sounded; all *this continued* until the burnt offering was finished. 29And when they had finished offering, the king and all who were present with him bowed and worshiped. 30Moreover King Hezekiah and the leaders commanded the Levites to sing praise to the LORD with the words of David and of Asaph the seer. So they sang praises with gladness, and they bowed their heads and worshiped.

31Then Hezekiah answered and said, "Now *that* you have consecrated yourselves to the LORD, come near, and bring sacrifices and thank offerings into the house of the LORD." So the assembly brought in sacrifices and thank offerings, and as many as were of a willing heart *brought* burnt offerings. 32And the number of the burnt offerings which the assembly brought was seventy bulls, one hundred rams, *and* two hundred lambs; all these *were* for a burnt offering to the LORD. 33The consecrated things *were* six hundred bulls and three thousand sheep. 34But the priests were too few, so that they could not skin all the burnt offerings; therefore their brethren the Levites helped them until the work was ended and until the *other* priests had sanctified themselves, for the Levites were more diligent in sanctifying themselves than the priests. 35Also the burnt offerings *were* in abundance, with the fat of the peace offerings and *with* the drink offerings for *every* burnt offering.

So the service of the house of the LORD was set in order. 36Then Hezekiah and all the people rejoiced that God had prepared the people, since the events took place so suddenly.

Hezekiah Keeps the Passover

30And Hezekiah sent to all Israel and Judah, and also wrote letters to Ephraim and Manasseh, that they should come to the house of the LORD at Jerusalem, to keep the Passover to the LORD God of Israel. 2For the king and his leaders and all the assembly in Jerusalem had agreed to keep the Passover in the second month. 3For they could not keep it at the regular time,[a] because a sufficient number of priests had not consecrated themselves, nor had the people gathered together at Jerusalem. 4And the matter pleased the king and all the assembly. 5So they resolved to make a proclamation throughout all Israel, from Beersheba to Dan, that they should come to keep the Passover to the LORD God of Israel at Jerusalem, since they had not done *it* for a long *time* in the *prescribed* manner.

6Then the runners went throughout all Israel and Judah with the letters from the king and his leaders, and spoke according to the command of the king: "Children of Israel, return to the LORD God of Abraham, Isaac, and Israel; then He will return to the remnant of you who have escaped from the hand of the kings of Assyria. 7And do not be like your fathers and your brethren, who trespassed against the LORD God of their fathers, so that He gave them up to desolation, as you see. 8Now do not be stiff-necked, as your fathers *were,* but yield yourselves to the LORD; and enter His sanctuary, which He has sanctified forever, and

---

30:3 aThat is, the first month (compare Leviticus 23:5); literally *at that time*

30:1–27 Hezekiah celebrated Passover, a feast to which all Israel was invited "from Beersheba to Dan" (vv. 5, 10, 11). Ephraim and Manasseh are typical terms denoting the northern kingdom (v. 1). According to the Law, the celebration of the feast could be delayed until the second month (Num. 9:9–11). The celebration of Passover, recalling escape from Egypt, was appropriate since Judah had "escaped from the hand of the kings of Assyria" (2 Chr. 30:6; see also Ex. 12:1—13:10). Where there is sin, repentance and restoration may also be found (2 Chr. 30:6–9).

serve the LORD your God, that the fierceness of His wrath may turn away from you. [9]For if you return to the LORD, your brethren and your children *will be treated* with compassion by those who lead them captive, so that they may come back to this land; for the LORD your God *is* gracious and merciful, and will not turn *His* face from you if you return to Him."

[10]So the runners passed from city to city through the country of Ephraim and Manasseh, as far as Zebulun; but they laughed at them and mocked them. [11]Nevertheless some from Asher, Manasseh, and Zebulun humbled themselves and came to Jerusalem. [12]Also the hand of God was on Judah to give them singleness of heart to obey the command of the king and the leaders, at the word of the LORD.

[13]Now many people, a very great assembly, gathered at Jerusalem to keep the Feast of Unleavened Bread in the second month. [14]They arose and took away the altars that *were* in Jerusalem, and they took away all the incense altars and cast *them* into the Brook Kidron. [15]Then they slaughtered the Passover *lambs* on the fourteenth *day* of the second month. The priests and the Levites were ashamed, and sanctified themselves, and brought the burnt offerings to the house of the LORD. [16]They stood in their place according to their custom, according to the Law of Moses the man of God; the priests sprinkled the blood *received* from the hand of the Levites. [17]For *there were* many in the assembly who had not sanctified themselves; therefore the Levites had charge of the slaughter of the Passover *lambs* for everyone *who was* not clean, to sanctify *them* to the LORD. [18]For a multitude of the people, many from Ephraim, Manasseh, Issachar, and Zebulun, had not cleansed themselves, yet they ate the Passover contrary to what was written. But Hezekiah prayed for them, saying, "May the good LORD provide atonement for everyone [19]*who* prepares his heart to seek God, the LORD God of his fathers, though *he is* not *cleansed* according to the purification of the sanctuary." [20]And the LORD listened to Hezekiah and healed the people.

[21]So the children of Israel who were present at Jerusalem kept the Feast of Unleavened Bread seven days with great gladness; and the Levites and the priests praised the LORD day by day, *singing* to the LORD, accompanied by loud instruments. [22]And Hezekiah gave encouragement to all the Levites who taught the good knowledge of the LORD; and they ate throughout the feast seven days, offering peace offerings and making confession to the LORD God of their fathers.

[23]Then the whole assembly agreed to keep *the*

feast another seven days, and they kept it *another* seven days with gladness. [24]For Hezekiah king of Judah gave to the assembly a thousand bulls and seven thousand sheep, and the leaders gave to the assembly a thousand bulls and ten thousand sheep; and a great number of priests sanctified themselves. [25]The whole assembly of Judah rejoiced, also the priests and Levites, all the assembly that came from Israel, the sojourners who came from the land of Israel, and those who dwelt in Judah. [26]So there was great joy in Jerusalem, for since the time of Solomon the son of David, king of Israel, *there had* been nothing like this in Jerusalem. [27]Then the priests, the Levites, arose and blessed the people, and their voice was heard; and their prayer came *up* to His holy dwelling place, to heaven.

The Reforms of Hezekiah

31 Now when all this was finished, all Israel who were present went out to the cities of Judah and broke the *sacred* pillars in pieces, cut down the wooden images, and threw down the high places and the altars—from all Judah, Benjamin, Ephraim, and Manasseh—until they had utterly destroyed them all. Then all the children of Israel returned to their own cities, every man to his possession.

[2]And Hezekiah appointed the divisions of the priests and the Levites according to their divisions, each man according to his service, the priests and Levites for burnt offerings and peace offerings, to serve, to give thanks, and to praise in the gates of the camp[a] of the LORD. [3]The king also *appointed* a portion of his possessions for the burnt offerings: for the morning and evening burnt offerings, the burnt offerings for the Sabbaths and the New Moons and the set feasts, as *it is* written in the Law of the LORD.

[4]Moreover he commanded the people who dwelt in Jerusalem to contribute support for the priests and the Levites, that they might devote themselves to the Law of the LORD.

[5]As soon as the commandment was circulated, the children of Israel brought in abundance the firstfruits of grain and wine, oil and honey, and of all the produce of the field; and they brought in abundantly the tithe of everything. [6]And the children of Israel and Judah, who dwelt in the cities of Judah, brought the tithe of oxen and sheep; also the tithe of holy things which were consecrated to the LORD their God they laid in heaps.

[7]In the third month they began laying them in heaps, and they finished in the seventh month.

31:2 [a]That is, the temple

31:1 **Illegitimate worship** was removed from all Israel, and the system for proper worship was reinstated. Hezekiah's re-

forms paralleled the work of David and Solomon (v. 21; see 1 Chr. 23—26).

⁸And when Hezekiah and the leaders came and saw the heaps, they blessed the LORD and His people Israel. ⁹Then Hezekiah questioned the priests and the Levites concerning the heaps. ¹⁰And Azariah the chief priest, from the house of Zadok, answered him and said, "Since *the people* began to bring the offerings into the house of the LORD, we have had enough to eat and have plenty left, for the LORD has blessed His people; and what is left *is* this great abundance."

¹¹Now Hezekiah commanded *them* to prepare rooms in the house of the LORD, and they prepared them. ¹²Then they faithfully brought in the offerings, the tithes, and the dedicated things; Cononiah the Levite had charge of them, and Shimei his brother *was* the next. ¹³Jehiel, Azaziah, Nahath, Asahel, Jerimoth, Jozabad, Eliel, Ismachiah, Mahath, and Benaiah *were* overseers under the hand of Cononiah and Shimei his brother, at the commandment of Hezekiah the king and Azariah the ruler of the house of God. ¹⁴Kore the son of Imnah the Levite, the keeper of the East Gate, *was* over the freewill offerings to God, to distribute the offerings of the LORD and the most holy things. ¹⁵And under him *were* Eden, Miniamin, Jeshua, Shemaiah, Amariah, and Shecaniah, *his* faithful assistants in the cities of the priests, to distribute allotments to their brethren by divisions, to the great as well as the small.

¹⁶Besides those males from three years old and up who were written in the genealogy, they distributed to everyone who entered the house of the LORD his daily portion for the work of his service, by his division, ¹⁷and to the priests who were written in the genealogy according to their father's house, and to the Levites from twenty years old and up according to their work, by their divisions, ¹⁸and to all who were written in the genealogy—their little ones and their wives, their sons and daughters, the whole company of them—for in their faithfulness they sanctified themselves in holiness.

¹⁹Also for the sons of Aaron the priests, *who were* in the fields of the common-lands of their cities, in every single city, *there were* men who were designated by name to distribute portions to all the males among the priests and to all who were listed by genealogies among the Levites.

²⁰Thus Hezekiah did throughout all Judah, and he did what *was* good and right and true before the LORD his God. ²¹And in every work that he began in the service of the house of God, in the law

and in the commandment, to seek his God, he did *it* with all his heart. So he prospered.

Sennacherib Boasts Against the LORD

32 After these deeds of faithfulness, Sennacherib king of Assyria came and entered Judah; he encamped against the fortified cities, thinking to win them over to himself. ²And when Hezekiah saw that Sennacherib had come, and that his purpose was to make war against Jerusalem, ³he consulted with his leaders and commandersᵃ to stop the water from the springs which *were* outside the city; and they helped him. ⁴Thus many people gathered together who stopped all the springs and the brook that ran through the land, saying, "Why should the kingsᵃ of Assyria come and find much water?" ⁵And he strengthened himself, built up all the wall that was broken, raised *it* up to the towers, and *built* another wall outside; also he repaired the Milloᵃ *in* the City of David, and made weapons and shields in abundance. ⁶Then he set military captains over the people, gathered them together to him in the open square of the city gate, and gave them encouragement, saying, ⁷"Be strong and courageous; do not be afraid nor dismayed before the king of Assyria, nor before all the multitude that *is* with him; for *there are* more with us than with him. ⁸With him *is* an arm of flesh; but with us *is* the LORD our God, to help us and to fight our battles." And the people were strengthened by the words of Hezekiah king of Judah.

⁹After this Sennacherib king of Assyria sent his servants to Jerusalem (but he and all the forces with him *laid siege* against Lachish), to Hezekiah king of Judah, and to all Judah who *were* in Jerusalem, saying, ¹⁰"Thus says Sennacherib king of Assyria: 'In what do you trust, that you remain under siege in Jerusalem? ¹¹Does not Hezekiah persuade you to give yourselves over to die by famine and by thirst, saying, "The LORD our God will deliver us from the hand of the king of Assyria"? ¹²Has not the same Hezekiah taken away His high places and His altars, and commanded Judah and Jerusalem, saying, "You shall worship before one altar and burn incense on it"? ¹³Do you not know what I and my fathers have done to all the peoples of *other* lands? Were the gods of the nations of those

---

32:3 ᵃLiterally *mighty men*   **32:4** ᵃFollowing Masoretic Text and Vulgate; Arabic, Septuagint, and Syriac read *king*.   **32:5** ᵃLiterally *The Landfill*

32:1 Hezekiah found success in everything he did. Just as David encouraged Solomon, so Hezekiah encouraged his captains to "be strong and courageous" (v. 7; 1 Chr. 22:11–16; 28:1—29:9). The taunt of Sennacherib, king of Assyria, was meant to put fear and doubt into the hearts of the people (2 Chr. 32:9–19). The honor of both the Lord and the king are

called into question, but Hezekiah did not falter. In obedience, he called on the Lord and was saved (vv. 20, 21). Hezekiah humbled himself and repented (vv. 24–26) and was blessed with abundant wealth like Solomon (vv. 27–31) and with great honor at death (vv. 32, 33).

lands in any way able to deliver their lands out of my hand? [14]Who *was there* among all the gods of those nations that my fathers utterly destroyed that could deliver his people from my hand, that your God should be able to deliver you from my hand? [15]Now therefore, do not let Hezekiah deceive you or persuade you like this, and do not believe him; for no god of any nation or kingdom was able to deliver his people from my hand or the hand of my fathers. How much less will your God deliver you from my hand?' "

[16]Furthermore, his servants spoke against the LORD God and against His servant Hezekiah.

[17]He also wrote letters to revile the LORD God of Israel, and to speak against Him, saying, "As the gods of the nations of *other* lands have not delivered their people from my hand, so the God of Hezekiah will not deliver His people from my hand." [18]Then they called out with a loud voice in Hebrew[a] to the people of Jerusalem who *were* on the wall, to frighten them and trouble them, that they might take the city. [19]And they spoke against the God of Jerusalem, as against the gods of the people of the earth—the work of men's hands.

Sennacherib's Defeat and Death

[20]Now because of this King Hezekiah and the prophet Isaiah, the son of Amoz, prayed and cried out to heaven. [21]Then the LORD sent an angel who cut down every mighty man of valor, leader, and captain in the camp of the king of Assyria. So he returned shamefaced to his own land. And when he had gone into the temple of his god, some of his own offspring struck him down with the sword there.

[22]Thus the LORD saved Hezekiah and the inhabitants of Jerusalem from the hand of Sennacherib the king of Assyria, and from the hand of all *others*, and guided them[a] on every side. [23]And many brought gifts to the LORD at Jerusalem, and presents to Hezekiah king of Judah, so that he was exalted in the sight of all nations thereafter.

Hezekiah Humbles Himself

[24]In those days Hezekiah was sick and near death, and he prayed to the LORD; and He spoke to him and gave him a sign. [25]But Hezekiah did not repay according to the favor *shown* him, for his heart was lifted up; therefore wrath was looming over him and over Judah and Jerusalem. [26]Then Hezekiah humbled himself for the pride of his heart, he and the inhabitants of Jerusalem, so that the wrath of the LORD did not come upon them in the days of Hezekiah.

Hezekiah's Wealth and Honor

[27]Hezekiah had very great riches and honor. And he made himself treasuries for silver, for gold, for precious stones, for spices, for shields, and for all kinds of desirable items; [28]storehouses for the harvest of grain, wine, and oil; and stalls for all kinds of livestock, and folds for flocks.[a] [29]Moreover he provided cities for himself, and possessions of flocks and herds in abundance; for God had given him very much property. [30]This same Hezekiah also stopped the water outlet of Upper Gihon, and brought the water by tunnel[a] to the west side of the City of David. Hezekiah prospered in all his works.

[31]However, *regarding* the ambassadors of the princes of Babylon, whom they sent to him to inquire about the wonder that was *done* in the land, God withdrew from him, in order to test him, that He might know all *that was* in his heart.

Death of Hezekiah

[32]Now the rest of the acts of Hezekiah, and his goodness, indeed they *are* written in the vision of Isaiah the prophet, the son of Amoz, *and* in the book of the kings of Judah and Israel. [33]So Hezekiah rested with his fathers, and they buried him in the upper tombs of the sons of David; and all Judah and the inhabitants of Jerusalem honored him at his death. Then Manasseh his son reigned in his place.

Manasseh Reigns in Judah

33 Manasseh *was* twelve years old when he became king, and he reigned fifty-five years in Jerusalem. [2]But he did evil in the sight of the LORD, according to the abominations of the nations whom the LORD had cast out before the children of Israel. [3]For he rebuilt the high places which Hezekiah his father had broken down; he raised up altars for the Baals, and made wooden images; and he worshiped all the host of heaven[a] and served them. [4]He also built altars in the house of the LORD, of which the LORD had said, "In Jerusalem shall My name be forever." [5]And he built altars for all the host of heaven in the two courts of the house of the LORD. [6]Also he caused his sons to pass through the fire in the Valley of the Son of Hinnom; he practiced soothsaying, used witchcraft and sorcery, and consulted mediums and spiritists. He did much evil in the sight of the LORD, to provoke Him to anger. [7]He even set a carved image, the idol which he had made, in the house of God, of which God had said to David and to Solomon his son, "In this house and in Jerusalem, which I have chosen out of all the tribes of Israel, I will put My name forever; [8]and I will not again remove the foot of Israel from the land which I have appointed for your fathers—only if

---

32:18 [a]Literally *Judean* 32:22 [a]Septuagint reads *gave them rest;* Vulgate reads *gave them treasures.* 32:28 [a]Following Septuagint and Vulgate; Arabic and Syriac omit *folds for flocks;* Masoretic Text reads *flocks for sheepfolds.* 32:30 [a]Literally *brought it straight* (compare 2 Kings 20:20) 33:3 [a]The gods of the Assyrians

they are careful to do all that I have commanded them, according to the whole law and the statutes and the ordinances by the hand of Moses." ⁹So Manasseh seduced Judah and the inhabitants of Jerusalem to do more evil than the nations whom the LORD had destroyed before the children of Israel.

Manasseh Restored After Repentance

¹⁰And the LORD spoke to Manasseh and his people, but they would not listen. ¹¹Therefore the LORD brought upon them the captains of the army of the king of Assyria, who took Manasseh with hooks,ᵃ bound him with bronze *fetters,* and carried him off to Babylon. ¹²Now when he was in affliction, he implored the LORD his God, and humbled himself greatly before the God of his fathers, ¹³and prayed to Him; and He received his entreaty, heard his supplication, and brought him back to Jerusalem into his kingdom. Then Manasseh knew that the LORD *was* God.

¹⁴After this he built a wall outside the City of David on the west side of Gihon, in the valley, as far as the entrance of the Fish Gate; and *it* enclosed Ophel, and he raised it to a very great height. Then he put military captains in all the fortified cities of Judah. ¹⁵He took away the foreign gods and the idol from the house of the LORD, and all the altars that he had built in the mount of the house of the LORD and in Jerusalem; and he cast *them* out of the city. ¹⁶He also repaired the altar of the LORD, sacrificed peace offerings and thank offerings on it, and commanded Judah to serve the LORD God of Israel. ¹⁷Nevertheless the people still sacrificed on the high places, *but* only to the LORD their God.

Death of Manasseh

¹⁸Now the rest of the acts of Manasseh, his prayer to his God, and the words of the seers who spoke to him in the name of the LORD God of Israel, indeed they *are written* in the bookᵃ of the kings of Israel. ¹⁹Also his prayer and *how God* received his entreaty, and all his sin and trespass, and the sites where he built high places and set up wooden images and carved images, before he was humbled, indeed they *are* written among the sayings of Hozai.ᵃ ²⁰So Manasseh rested with his fathers, and they buried him in his own house. Then his son Amon reigned in his place.

Amon's Reign and Death

²¹Amon *was* twenty-two years old when he became king, and he reigned two years in Jerusalem. ²²But he did evil in the sight of the LORD, as his father Manasseh had done; for Amon sacrificed to all the carved images which his father Manasseh had made, and served them. ²³And he did not humble himself before the LORD, as his father Manasseh had humbled himself; but Amon trespassed more and more.

²⁴Then his servants conspired against him, and killed him in his own house. ²⁵But the people of the land executed all those who had conspired against King Amon. Then the people of the land made his son Josiah king in his place.

Josiah Reigns in Judah

34 Josiah *was* eight years old when he became king, and he reigned thirty-one years in Jerusalem. ²And he did *what was* right in the sight of the LORD, and walked in the ways of his father David; *he* did *not* turn aside to the right hand or to the left.

³For in the eighth year of his reign, while he was still young, he began to seek the God of his father David; and in the twelfth year he began to purge Judah and Jerusalem of the high places, the wooden images, the carved images, and the molded images. ⁴They broke down the altars of the Baals in his presence, and the incense altars which *were* above them he cut down; and the wooden images, the carved images, and the molded images he broke in pieces, and made dust of them and scattered *it* on the graves of those who had sacrificed to them. ⁵He also burned the bones of the priests on their altars, and cleansed Judah and Jerusalem. ⁶And *so he did* in the cities of Manasseh, Ephraim, and Simeon, as far as Naphtali and all around, with axes.ᵃ ⁷When he had broken down the altars and the wooden images, had beaten the carved images into powder, and cut down all the incense altars throughout all the land of Israel, he returned to Jerusalem.

Hilkiah Finds the Book of the Law

⁸In the eighteenth year of his reign, when he had purged the land and the temple,ᵃ he sent

---

33:11 ᵃThat is, nose hooks (compare 2 Kings 19:28)   **33:18** ᵃLiterally *words*   **33:19** ᵃSeptuagint reads *the seers.*   **34:6** ᵃLiterally *swords*   **34:8** ᵃLiterally *house*

34:1 Josiah, like other temple reformers, was characterized by walking "in the ways of his father David" (v. 2; 2 Chr. 17:3; 29:2). Josiah cleansed Judah, Jerusalem, and all Israel from illegitimate worship (2 Kin. 23:4–20; 2 Chr. 34:3–7) and reestablished the temple and temple worship (vv. 8–28). His twelfth year was a time of the weakening of the Assyrian Empire, which made reforms easier (v. 3). As a faithful king, Josiah taught the people the Law and led them in covenant renewal (vv. 29–33; see Deut. 17:18–22). He led them in the Passover, a celebration not seen in Israel since Samuel's time. He even exceeded Hezekiah's celebration of the Passover (2 Chr. 35:1–19). He made sure all Israel gave to the repairing of the temple and joined together in temple worship (2 Chr. 34:9, 29–33). The "Book of the Law" found has been associated with the Book of Deuteronomy (v. 14).

Shaphan the son of Azaliah, Maaseiah the governor of the city, and Joah the son of Joahaz the recorder, to repair the house of the LORD his God. 9When they came to Hilkiah the high priest, they delivered the money that was brought into the house of God, which the Levites who kept the doors had gathered from the hand of Manasseh and Ephraim, from all the remnant of Israel, from all Judah and Benjamin, and *which* they had brought back to Jerusalem. 10Then they put *it* in the hand of the foremen who had the oversight of the house of the LORD; and they gave it to the workmen who worked in the house of the LORD, to repair and restore the house. 11They gave *it* to the craftsmen and builders to buy hewn stone and timber for beams, and to floor the houses which the kings of Judah had destroyed. 12And the men did the work faithfully. Their overseers *were* Jahath and Obadiah the Levites, of the sons of Merari, and Zechariah and Meshullam, of the sons of the Kohathites, to supervise. *Others of* the Levites, all of whom were skillful with instruments of music, 13*were* over the burden bearers and *were* overseers of all who did work in any kind of service. And *some* of the Levites *were* scribes, officers, and gatekeepers.

14Now when they brought out the money that was brought into the house of the LORD, Hilkiah the priest found the Book of the Law of the LORD *given* by Moses. 15Then Hilkiah answered and said to Shaphan the scribe, "I have found the Book of the Law in the house of the LORD." And Hilkiah gave the book to Shaphan. 16So Shaphan carried the book to the king, bringing the king word, saying, "All that was committed to your servants they are doing. 17And they have gathered the money that was found in the house of the LORD, and have delivered it into the hand of the overseers and the workmen." 18Then Shaphan the scribe told the king, saying, "Hilkiah the priest has given me a book." And Shaphan read it before the king.

19Thus it happened, when the king heard the words of the Law, that he tore his clothes. 20Then the king commanded Hilkiah, Ahikam the son of Shaphan, Abdon[a] the son of Micah, Shaphan the scribe, and Asaiah a servant of the king, saying, 21"Go, inquire of the LORD for me, and for those who are left in Israel and Judah, concerning the words of the book that is found; for great *is* the wrath of the LORD that is poured out on us, because our fathers have not kept the word of the LORD, to do according to all that is written in this book."

22So Hilkiah and those the king *had appointed* went to Huldah the prophetess, the wife of Shallum the son of Tokhath,[a] the son of Hasrah,[b] keeper of the wardrobe. (She dwelt in Jerusalem in the Second Quarter.) And they spoke to her to that *effect.*

23Then she answered them, "Thus says the LORD God of Israel, 'Tell the man who sent you to Me, 24"Thus says the LORD: 'Behold, I will bring calamity on this place and on its inhabitants, all the curses that are written in the book which they have read before the king of Judah, 25because they have forsaken Me and burned incense to other gods, that they might provoke Me to anger with all the works of their hands. Therefore My wrath will be poured out on this place, and not be quenched.' " ' 26But as for the king of Judah, who sent you to inquire of the LORD, in this manner you shall speak to him, 'Thus says the LORD God of Israel: "*Concerning* the words which you have heard— 27because your heart was tender, and you humbled yourself before God when you heard His words against this place and against its inhabitants, and you humbled yourself before Me, and you tore your clothes and wept before Me, I also have heard *you*," says the LORD. 28"Surely I will gather you to your fathers, and you shall be gathered to your grave in peace; and your eyes shall not see all the calamity which I will bring on this place and its inhabitants." ' " So they brought back word to the king.

Josiah Restores True Worship

29Then the king sent and gathered all the elders of Judah and Jerusalem. 30The king went up to the house of the LORD, with all the men of Judah and the inhabitants of Jerusalem—the priests and the Levites, and all the people, great and small. And he read in their hearing all the words of the Book of the Covenant which had been found in the house of the LORD. 31Then the king stood in his place and made a covenant before the LORD, to follow the LORD, and to keep His commandments and His testimonies and His statutes with all his heart and all his soul, to perform the words of the covenant that were written in this book. 32And he made all who were present in Jerusalem and Benjamin take a stand. So the inhabitants of Jerusalem did according to the covenant of God, the God of their fathers. 33Thus Josiah removed all the abominations from all the country that *belonged* to the children of Israel, and made all who were present in Israel diligently serve the LORD their God. All his days they did not depart from following the LORD God of their fathers.

Josiah Keeps the Passover

35 Now Josiah kept a Passover to the LORD in Jerusalem, and they slaughtered the Passover *lambs* on the fourteenth *day* of the first month. 2And he set the priests in their duties and

34:20 [a]*Achbor the son of Michaiah* in 2 Kings 22:12　　**34:22** [a]Spelled *Tikvah* in 2 Kings 22:14　[b]Spelled *Harhas* in 2 Kings 22:14

encouraged them for the service of the house of the LORD. ³Then he said to the Levites who taught all Israel, who were holy to the LORD: "Put the holy ark in the house which Solomon the son of David, king of Israel, built. *It shall* no longer *be* a burden on *your* shoulders. Now serve the LORD your God and His people Israel. ⁴Prepare *yourselves* according to your fathers' houses, according to your divisions, following the written instruction of David king of Israel and the written instruction of Solomon his son. ⁵And stand in the holy *place* according to the divisions of the fathers' houses of your brethren the *lay* people, and *according to* the division of the father's house of the Levites. ⁶So slaughter the Passover *offerings*, consecrate yourselves, and prepare *them* for your brethren, that *they* may do according to the word of the LORD by the hand of Moses."

⁷Then Josiah gave the *lay* people lambs and young goats from the flock, all for Passover *offerings* for all who were present, to the number of thirty thousand, as well as three thousand cattle; these *were* from the king's possessions. ⁸And his leaders gave willingly to the people, to the priests, and to the Levites. Hilkiah, Zechariah, and Jehiel, rulers of the house of God, gave to the priests for the Passover *offerings* two thousand six hundred *from the flock,* and three hundred cattle. ⁹Also Conaniah, his brothers Shemaiah and Nethanel, and Hashabiah and Jeiel and Jozabad, chief of the Levites, gave to the Levites for Passover *offerings* five thousand *from the flock* and five hundred cattle.

¹⁰So the service was prepared, and the priests stood in their places, and the Levites in their divisions, according to the king's command. ¹¹And they slaughtered the Passover *offerings;* and the priests sprinkled *the blood* with their hands, while the Levites skinned *the animals.* ¹²Then they removed the burnt offerings that *they* might give them to the divisions of the fathers' houses of the *lay* people, to offer to the LORD, as *it is* written in the Book of Moses. And so *they did* with the cattle. ¹³Also they roasted the Passover *offerings* with fire according to the ordinance; but the *other* holy *offerings* they boiled in pots, in caldrons, and in pans, and divided *them* quickly among all the *lay* people. ¹⁴Then afterward they prepared portions for themselves and for the priests, because the priests, the sons of Aaron, *were busy* in offering burnt offerings and fat until night; therefore the Levites prepared portions for themselves and for the priests, the sons of Aaron. ¹⁵And the singers, the sons of Asaph, *were* in their places, according to the command of David, Asaph, Heman, and Jeduthun the king's seer. Also the gatekeepers were at each gate; they did not have to leave their position, because their brethren the Levites prepared portions for them.

¹⁶So all the service of the LORD was prepared the same day, to keep the Passover and to offer burnt offerings on the altar of the LORD, according to the command of King Josiah. ¹⁷And the children of Israel who were present kept the Passover at that time, and the Feast of Unleavened Bread for seven days. ¹⁸There had been no Passover kept in Israel like that since the days of Samuel the prophet; and none of the kings of Israel had kept such a Passover as Josiah kept, with the priests and the Levites, all Judah and Israel who were present, and the inhabitants of Jerusalem. ¹⁹In the eighteenth year of the reign of Josiah this Passover was kept.

Josiah Dies in Battle

²⁰After all this, when Josiah had prepared the temple, Necho king of Egypt came up to fight against Carchemish by the Euphrates; and Josiah went out against him. ²¹But he sent messengers to him, saying, "What have I to do with you, king of Judah? *I have* not *come* against you this day, but against the house with which I have war; for God commanded me to make haste. Refrain *from meddling with* God, who *is* with me, lest He destroy you." ²²Nevertheless Josiah would not turn his face from him, but disguised himself so that he might fight with him, and did not heed the words of Necho from the mouth of God. So he came to fight in the Valley of Megiddo.

²³And the archers shot King Josiah; and the king said to his servants, "Take me away, for I am severely wounded." ²⁴His servants therefore took him out of that chariot and put him in the second chariot that he had, and they brought him to Jerusalem. So he died, and was buried in *one of* the tombs of his fathers. And all Judah and Jerusalem mourned for Josiah.

²⁵Jeremiah also lamented for Josiah. And to this day all the singing men and the singing women speak of Josiah in their lamentations. They made it a custom in Israel; and indeed they *are* written in the Laments.

²⁶Now the rest of the acts of Josiah and his goodness, according to *what was* written in the Law of the LORD, ²⁷and his deeds from first to last, indeed they *are* written in the book of the kings of Israel and Judah.

35:20–27 King Josiah began well but ended his life in disobedience. Some suggest that his untimely death was immediate retribution for sin. The circumstances of his death are given but without clear explanation. Necho, king of Egypt, was responsible for the sudden death of this faithful king. Even Josiah was not exempt from punishment for disobedience.

The Reign and Captivity of Jehoahaz

36 Then the people of the land took Jehoahaz the son of Josiah, and made him king in his father's place in Jerusalem. ²Jehoahazᵃ *was* twenty-three years old when he became king, and he reigned three months in Jerusalem. ³Now the king of Egypt deposed him at Jerusalem; and he imposed on the land a tribute of one hundred talents of silver and a talent of gold. ⁴Then the king of Egypt made *Jehoahaz's*ᵃ brother Eliakim king over Judah and Jerusalem, and changed his name to Jehoiakim. And Necho took Jehoahazᵇ his brother and carried him off to Egypt.

The Reign and Captivity of Jehoiakim

⁵Jehoiakim *was* twenty-five years old when he became king, and he reigned eleven years in Jerusalem. And he did evil in the sight of the LORD his God. ⁶Nebuchadnezzar king of Babylon came up against him, and bound him in bronze *fetters* to carry him off to Babylon. ⁷Nebuchadnezzar also carried off *some* of the articles from the house of the LORD to Babylon, and put them in his temple at Babylon. ⁸Now the rest of the acts of Jehoiakim, the abominations which he did, and what was found against him, indeed they *are* written in the book of the kings of Israel and Judah. Then Jehoiachin his son reigned in his place.

The Reign and Captivity of Jehoiachin

⁹Jehoiachin *was* eightᵃ years old when he became king, and he reigned in Jerusalem three months and ten days. And he did evil in the sight of the LORD. ¹⁰At the turn of the year King Nebuchadnezzar summoned *him* and took him to Babylon, with the costly articles from the house of the LORD, and made Zedekiah, *Jehoiakim's*ᵃ brother, king over Judah and Jerusalem.

Zedekiah Reigns in Judah

¹¹Zedekiah *was* twenty-one years old when he became king, and he reigned eleven years in Jerusalem. ¹²He did evil in the sight of the LORD his God, *and* did not humble himself before Jeremiah the prophet, *who spoke* from the mouth of the LORD.

¹³And he also rebelled against King Nebuchadnezzar, who had made him swear *an oath* by God; but he stiffened his neck and hardened his heart against turning to the LORD God of Israel. ¹⁴Moreover all the leaders of the priests and the people transgressed more and more, *according* to all the abominations of the nations, and defiled the house of the LORD which He had consecrated in Jerusalem.

The Fall of Jerusalem

¹⁵And the LORD God of their fathers sent *warnings* to them by His messengers, rising up early and sending *them,* because He had compassion on His people and on His dwelling place. ¹⁶But they mocked the messengers of God, despised His words, and scoffed at His prophets, until the wrath of the LORD arose against His people, till *there was* no remedy.

¹⁷Therefore He brought against them the king of the Chaldeans, who killed their young men with the sword in the house of their sanctuary, and had no compassion on young man or virgin, on the aged or the weak; He gave *them* all into his hand. ¹⁸And all the articles from the house of God, great and small, the treasures of the house of the LORD, and the treasures of the king and of his leaders, all *these* he took to Babylon. ¹⁹Then they burned the house of God, broke down the wall of Jerusalem, burned all its palaces with fire, and destroyed all its precious possessions. ²⁰And those who escaped from the sword he carried away to Babylon, where they became servants to him and his sons until the rule of the kingdom of Persia, ²¹to fulfill the word of the LORD by the mouth of Jeremiah, until the land had enjoyed her Sabbaths. As long as she lay desolate she kept Sabbath, to fulfill seventy years.

The Proclamation of Cyrus

²²Now in the first year of Cyrus king of Persia, that the word of the LORD by the mouth of Jeremiah might be fulfilled, the LORD stirred up the spirit of Cyrus king of Persia, so that he made a

---

36:2 ᵃMasoretic Text reads *Joahaz.* 36:4 ᵃLiterally *his* ᵇMasoretic Text reads *Joahaz.* 36:9 ᵃSome Hebrew manuscripts, Septuagint, Syriac, and 2 Kings 24:8 read *eighteen.* 36:10 ᵃLiterally *his* (compare 2 Kings 24:17)

36:1 The Lord had promised Josiah that he would not have to endure the pain of the Exile (2 Chr. 34:26–28). Upon the death of Josiah, the chronicler, in swift and sweeping accounts, brings Judah to exile in Babylon. Note that all these kings experienced exile: Jehoahaz to Egypt (2 Chr. 36:2–4); Jehoiakim, Jehoiachin, and Zedekiah to Babylon (vv. 5, 6, 9–11, 17–20). That the Exile was justified is made clear by the Lord's repeated yet unheeded call for repentance through his prophets (vv. 15–21). The Exile was the fulfillment of what had been foretold by Jeremiah (Jer. 25:2–14; 29:10). The returned Jewish community was thus reminded that the Exile

came by the hand of the Lord as judgment for their unfaithfulness and continued until His purposes were accomplished. The returned community was not to follow the sins of the past.

36:22, 23 The decree of Cyrus. Just as the Exile was by the hand of the Lord, so the return from Exile was by the word of the Lord (Is. 44:24–28; Jer. 29:10). The Lord stirred the spirit of Cyrus, and the return to Judah is centered around the temple. The rebuilt temple in Jerusalem would be proof that the Exile was ended and that the covenant had been restored. The returned Jewish community would be encouraged with

proclamation throughout all his kingdom, and also *put it* in writing, saying,

²³Thus says Cyrus king of Persia:
All the kingdoms of the earth the LORD God of

heaven has given me. And He has commanded me to build Him a house at Jerusalem which is in Judah. Who *is* among you of all His people? May the LORD his God *be* with him, and let him go up!

---

this knowledge. As they looked forward to a renewed covenant relation with the Lord, they would understand that He required them to be faithful just as He had required faithfulness from their fathers before the Exile. Devotion to the

Lord would be the way to blessing. Chronicles ends on a positive note of hope and assurance for the future. God had not changed His way of dealing with His people. He remained faithful to His covenant.

Ezra

AUTHOR

Jewish tradition ascribes this book to Ezra, a scribe and a priest during the Exile of the Jews in Babylon. However, scholars continue to debate the authorship. In earlier manuscripts Ezra and Nehemiah were one book with similar characteristics in style and content. Possibly Chronicles, Ezra, and Nehemiah may have been edited by the same person, someone known as the chronicler. The section written in first person can be considered Ezra's (Ezra 7:28—9:15), but whether an editor compiled the book and inserted Ezra's writing or whether Ezra prepared the whole text is not documented. The available information allows no more than conjecture.

DATE

Set during the reign of Artaxerxes I (465–424 B.C.) and Ezra's presence in Judah, the book was most likely compiled sometime after 458 B.C. (Ezra 7:1; see chart, The Timeline for Ezra, Nehemiah, and Esther).

BACKGROUND

SETTING: The story begins in 538 B.C., during the first year of the rule of King Cyrus of Persia over Babylon. There were three major deportations in the Exile of the Jews from Jerusalem (605 B.C., 598 B.C., and 586 B.C.). Jerusalem and the temple had been destroyed by the invasion of Nebuchadnezzar and his Babylonian army. Many Jews were killed, others scattered to distant lands, and some were taken as prisoners to Babylon. Those taken into exile included the political, religious, and intellectual leaders of the Jewish community. Later, Cyrus overthrew the Babylonians, and the empire changed hands. Believing the worship of foreign gods to be a political advantage, Cyrus tolerated and even encouraged this practice, which resulted in an edict to the Jews to return to Jerusalem to rebuild the house of their God. This edict permitting the Jews to return to their homeland was inscribed on the Cyrus Cylinder (538 B.C.). Discovered in the nineteenth century, the cylinder parallels and affirms the biblical account of the benevolent treatment received by the Jews in captivity under Cyrus.

Earlier prophets such as Jeremiah and Isaiah had prophesied the events of both the Exile and the eventual return of the remnant to Jerusalem. However, the Jews believed the Davidic promise of a dynasty that would not end. When they no longer had a king on the throne, and worse yet, no country, they began to doubt the prophets. Some believed the Jews had committed an unforgivable sin, resulting in God's cancellation of their destiny. There was little hope in the hearts of the people of Israel prior to the reign of Cyrus, king of Persia.

PURPOSE: Ezra 1—6 was written to document the return of a small remnant of Jews to Jerusalem from Exile in Babylon in response to the decree of King Cyrus of Persia to rebuild the temple of God (see map, The Return from Exile). No less important is the purpose to preserve the details of the accomplishment of the task set before them and

to document God's providence in caring for His people and fulfilling His promises to them. Ezra 7—10 focused on the description of the ministry of Ezra as an expounder of God's Word (Ezra 7:6, 12), a man of faith (Ezra 8:20-22), an inspired leader (Ezra 7:27, 28), a man of prayer and piety (Ezra 8:21; 10:6).

LITERARY CHARACTERISTICS:

1) A definite chronological sequence cannot be determined in Ezra. Rather, the narrative provides a summary of events that transpired in order to emphasize certain themes.
2) The use of lists, inventories, written decrees, and memoirs emphasizes the historicity of the text. Of special interest is the repetition of the list of returning exiles (Ezra 2; Neh. 7).
3) The "memoirs" of Ezra are included (Ezra 7—10).
4) The earliest manuscripts were written in Hebrew with small portions in Aramaic, the official language of Persian diplomacy (Ezra 4:8—6:18; 7:12–26).

THEMES

Among the themes in Ezra are these:

1) *Yahweh* is sovereign and faithful to His covenant. His redemptive promises prevail.
2) Israel, as God's instrument, must remain separate from the pagan world. The transition of Israel from a nation to a community is presented as complete.
3) The written Law of Moses becomes the foundation of the faith and the mark of the Jew. Hope is restored to the people of God.

OUTLINE

I. The Return of the Exiles to Jerusalem to Build the Temple (1:1—3:7)
  A. The edict of Cyrus (1:1–4)
  B. The provision for those returning (1:5—2:70)
  C. The restoration of temple worship (3:1–7)
II. The Rebuilding of the Temple (3:8—6:22)
  A. The laying of the foundation (3:8–13)
  B. The interference from adversaries (4:1–24)
  C. Encouragement from Haggai and Zechariah (5:1—6:14)
  D. The completion and dedication of the temple (6:15–18)
  E. The celebration of Passover (6:19–22)
III. The Return of the Law of Moses to Jerusalem (7:1—10:44)
  A. Ezra's return to Jerusalem (7:1–10)
  B. The king's authorization of Ezra (7:11–28)

  C. Ezra's company of returning exiles (8:1–14)
  D. Equipping the temple (8:15–30)
    1. The Levites who will serve in the temple (8:15–20)
    2. Fasting and praying by the people (8:21–23)
    3. A freewill offering for the temple (8:24–30)
  E. The journey to Jerusalem (8:31–36)
  F. The reforms of Ezra (9:1—10:44)
    1. The problem of intermarriage with pagans (9:1–4)
    2. Ezra's intercession for the sins of the people (9:5–15)
    3. The response of the people (10:1–4)
    4. Ezra's call for repentance (10:5–16)
    5. The repentance of the people (10:17–44)

End of the Babylonian Captivity

1 Now in the first year of Cyrus king of Persia, that the word of the LORD by the mouth of Jeremiah might be fulfilled, the LORD stirred up the spirit of Cyrus king of Persia, so that he made a proclamation throughout all his kingdom, and also *put it* in writing, saying,

²Thus says Cyrus king of Persia:

All the kingdoms of the earth the LORD God of heaven has given me. And He has commanded me to build Him a house at Jerusalem which *is* in Judah. ³Who *is* among you of all His people? May his God be with him, and let him go up to Jerusalem which *is* in Judah, and build the house of the LORD God of Israel (He *is* God), which *is* in Jerusalem. ⁴And whoever is left in any place where he dwells, let the men of his place help him with silver and gold, with goods and livestock, besides the freewill offerings for the house of God which *is* in Jerusalem.

⁵Then the heads of the fathers' *houses* of Judah and Benjamin, and the priests and the Levites, with all whose spirits God had moved, arose to go up and build the house of the LORD which *is* in Jerusalem. ⁶And all those who *were* around them encouraged them with articles of silver and gold, with goods and livestock, and with precious things, besides all *that* was willingly offered.

⁷King Cyrus also brought out the articles of the house of the LORD, which Nebuchadnezzar had taken from Jerusalem and put in the temple of his gods; ⁸and Cyrus king of Persia brought them out by the hand of Mithredath the treasurer, and counted them out to Sheshbazzar the prince of Judah. ⁹This *is* the number of them:

thirty gold platters, one thousand silver platters, twenty-nine knives, ¹⁰thirty gold basins, four hundred and ten silver basins of a similar *kind, and* one thousand other articles. ¹¹All the articles of gold and silver *were* five thousand four hundred. All *these* Sheshbazzar took with the captives who were brought from Babylon to Jerusalem.

The Captives Who Returned to Jerusalem

2 Now[a] these *are* the people of the province who came back from the captivity, of those who had been carried away, whom Nebuchadnezzar the king of Babylon had carried away to Babylon, and who returned to Jerusalem and Judah, everyone to his *own* city.

²*Those* who came with Zerubbabel *were* Jeshua, Nehemiah, Seraiah, Reelaiah, Mordecai, Bilshan, Mispar,[a] Bigvai, Rehum,[b] *and* Baanah. The number of the men of the people of Israel: ³the people of Parosh, two thousand one hundred and seventy-two; ⁴the people of Shephatiah, three hundred and seventy-two; ⁵the people of Arah, seven hundred and seventy-five; ⁶the people of Pahath-Moab, of the people of Jeshua *and* Joab, two thousand eight hundred and twelve; ⁷the people of Elam, one thousand two hundred and fifty-four; ⁸the people of Zattu, nine hundred and forty-five; ⁹the people of Zaccai, seven hundred and sixty; ¹⁰the people of Bani,[a] six hundred and forty-two; ¹¹the people of Bebai, six hundred and twenty-three; ¹²the people of Azgad, one thousand two hundred and twenty-two; ¹³the people of Adonikam, six hundred and sixty-six; ¹⁴the people of Bigvai, two thousand and fifty-six; ¹⁵the people of Adin, four hundred and fifty-four; ¹⁶the people of Ater of Hezekiah,

2:1 [a]Compare this chapter with Nehemiah 7:6–73.   2:2 [a]Spelled *Mispereth* in Nehemiah 7:7 [b]Spelled *Nehum* in Nehemiah 7:7   2:10 [a]Spelled *Binnui* in Nehemiah 7:15

1:1 The first year of Cyrus is dated 538 B.C. The Word of the Lord as prophesied by Jeremiah was now being fulfilled (Jer. 29:10). A characteristic of the Book of Ezra is that much of its content is in the form of written documentation: decrees (Ezra 1:2–4; 6:3–12); genealogies (Ezra 7:1–5; 8:1–14; 10:18–43); lists (Ezra 1:9–11; 2:2–61, 65–70; 6:17); letters (Ezra 4:9–22; 5:6–17; 7:12–26); and Ezra's "memoirs" (Ezra 7—10).

1:1, 2 God wanted the temple rebuilt in Jerusalem so He could dwell in the midst of His people, His family—Israel. God accomplished His plans through people as He "stirred up the spirit" of Cyrus (v. 1). As a sovereign God, He does what He chooses, and even pagan kings are subject to Him (Prov. 21:1).

1:2–4 The edict of restoration is the first of two reports in Ezra of the decree issued by Cyrus for the return of the Jews to Jerusalem to rebuild the temple of God (see also 2 Chr. 36:22, 23; Ezra 6:3–12; map, The Return from Exile). As a pagan king, the intentions of Cyrus were self-serving. The Persians considered it politically advantageous to support the gods worshiped by the different cultures throughout the lands they had conquered (see reference to Cyrus Cylinder in Introduction: Setting).

1:5, 6 Only a few of the Jews who had been exiled to Babylon chose to return at this time. Many knew no other home. They were settled in careers and lifestyles, and many had become established as the elite of their communities. Those who remained encouraged those moved by God to make the journey by providing them with "silver and gold" and "precious things" (v. 6).

1:8 Cyrus appointed Sheshbazzar governor (Ezra 5:14). Whether he was governor of a separate section of Judah inhabited by those whom he had led from Exile or ruler of the entire district of Judah is unclear.

2:1 The people who came back were the exiles (Heb. *gola*). They were considered to be the "true Israel," the descendants of the families of ancient Israel. They were known also as the "remnant" (see chart, The Faithful Remnant).

2:2 Israel is the name used to define the group of people listed as returning from the Exile. Therefore, these returning exiles are given the stamp of authenticity by being called "Israel." They are the true descendants from the line of Jacob, the true nation of Israel.

ninety-eight; [17]the people of Bezai, three hundred and twenty-three; [18]the people of Jorah,[a] one hundred and twelve; [19]the people of Hashum, two hundred and twenty-three; [20]the people of Gibbar,[a] ninety-five; [21]the people of Bethlehem, one hundred and twenty-three; [22]the men of Netophah, fifty-six; [23]the men of Anathoth, one hundred and twenty-eight; [24]the people of Azmaveth,[a] forty-two; [25]the people of Kirjath Arim,[a] Chephirah, and Beeroth, seven hundred and forty-three; [26]the people of Ramah and Geba, six hundred and twenty-one; [27]the men of Michmas, one hundred and twenty-two; [28]the men of Bethel and Ai, two hundred and twenty-three; [29]the people of Nebo, fifty-two; [30]the people of Magbish, one hundred and fifty-six; [31]the people of the other Elam, one thousand two hundred and fifty-four; [32]the people of Harim, three hundred and twenty; [33]the people of Lod, Hadid, and Ono, seven hundred and twenty-five; [34]the people of Jericho, three hundred and forty-five; [35]the people of Senaah, three thousand six hundred and thirty.

[36]The priests: the sons of Jedaiah, of the house of Jeshua, nine hundred and seventy-three; [37]the sons of Immer, one thousand and fifty-two; [38]the sons of Pashhur, one thousand two hundred and forty-seven; [39]the sons of Harim, one thousand and seventeen.

[40]The Levites: the sons of Jeshua and Kadmiel, of the sons of Hodaviah,[a] seventy-four.

[41]The singers: the sons of Asaph, one hundred and twenty-eight.

[42]The sons of the gatekeepers: the sons of Shallum, the sons of Ater, the sons of Talmon, the sons of Akkub, the sons of Hatita, and the sons of Shobai, one hundred and thirty-nine *in* all.

[43]The Nethinim: the sons of Ziha, the sons of Hasupha, the sons of Tabbaoth, [44]the sons of Keros, the sons of Siaha,[a] the sons of Padon, [45]the sons of Lebanah, the sons of Hagabah, the sons of Akkub, [46]the sons of Hagab, the sons of Shalmai, the sons of Hanan, [47]the sons of Giddel, the sons of Gahar, the sons of Reaiah, [48]the sons of Rezin, the sons of Nekoda, the sons of Gazzam, [49]the sons of Uzza, the sons of Paseah, the sons of Besai, [50]the sons of Asnah, the sons of Meunim, the sons of Nephusim,[a] [51]the sons of Bakbuk, the sons of Hakupha, the sons of Harhur, [52]the sons of Bazluth,[a] the sons of Mehida, the sons of Harsha, [53]the sons of Barkos, the sons of Sisera, the sons of Tamah, [54]the sons of Neziah, and the sons of Hatipha.

[55]The sons of Solomon's servants: the sons of Sotai, the sons of Sophereth, the sons of Peruda,[a] [56]the sons of Jaala, the sons of Darkon, the sons of Giddel, [57]the sons of Shephatiah, the sons of Hattil, the sons of Pochereth of Zebaim, and the sons of Ami.[a] [58]All the Nethinim and the children of Solomon's servants were three hundred and ninety-two.

[59]And these *were* the ones who came up from Tel Melah, Tel Harsha, Cherub, Addan,[a] and Immer; but they could not identify their father's house or their genealogy,[b] whether they *were* of Israel: [60]the sons of Delaiah, the sons of Tobiah, and the sons of Nekoda, six hundred and fifty-two; [61]and of the sons of the priests: the sons of Habaiah, the sons of Koz,[a] and the sons of Barzillai, who took a wife of the daughters of Barzillai the Gileadite, and was called by their name. [62]These sought their listing *among* those who were registered by genealogy, but they were not found; therefore they *were excluded* from the priesthood as defiled. [63]And the governor[a] said to them that they should not eat of the most holy things till a priest could consult with the Urim and Thummim.

[64]The whole assembly together *was* forty-two thousand three hundred *and* sixty, [65]besides their male and female servants, of whom *there were* seven thousand three hundred and thirty-seven; and they had two hundred men and women singers. [66]Their horses *were* seven hundred and thirty-six, their mules two hundred and forty-five, [67]their camels four hundred and thirty-five, and *their* donkeys six thousand seven hundred and twenty.

[68]*Some* of the heads of the fathers' *houses*, when they came to the house of the LORD which *is* in Jerusalem, offered freely for the house of God, to erect it in its place: [69]According to their ability, they gave to the treasury for the work

---

2:18 [a]Called *Hariph* in Nehemiah 7:24   2:20 [a]Called *Gibeon* in Nehemiah 7:25   2:24 [a]Called *Beth Azmaveth* in Nehemiah 7:28   2:25 [a]Called *Kirjath Jearim* in Nehemiah 7:29   2:40 [a]Spelled *Hodevah* in Nehemiah 7:43   2:44 [a]Spelled *Sia* in Nehemiah 7:47   2:50 [a]Spelled *Nephishesim* in Nehemiah 7:52   2:52 [a]Spelled *Bazlith* in Nehemiah 7:54   2:55 [a]Spelled *Perida* in Nehemiah 7:57   2:57 [a]Spelled *Amon* in Nehemiah 7:59   2:59 [a]Spelled *Addon* in Nehemiah 7:61   [b]Literally *seed*   2:61[a]Or *Hakkoz*   2:63 [a]Hebrew *Tirshatha*

2:36–39 The priests were descendants of Aaron, who was from the tribe of Levi. Together with their sons, they were ordained to be responsible for temple sacrifice (Ex. 28; 29).

2:40 The Levites were descended from the tribe of Levi but not from the family of Aaron. They assisted the priests (Num. 3:5–13).

2:41, 42 The singers and gatekeepers had been chosen by King David from the Levite families and had been assigned special tasks (1 Chr. 25; 26).

2:43–55 The Nethinim were most likely "temple servants." Though considered the most menial of temple personnel, they served the Lord with utmost devotion.

2:63 The Urim and Thummim were consulted. These were used to help determine God's will in a matter (see Ex. 28:15, note).

As one person we can make only a small impact, but together we can become a mighty river, reaching a lost and needy world with the remarkable love of God.

Amy Roth

---

sixty-one thousand gold drachmas, five thousand minas of silver, and one hundred priestly garments.

70So the priests and the Levites, *some* of the people, the singers, the gatekeepers, and the Nethinim, dwelt in their cities, and all Israel in their cities.

Worship Restored at Jerusalem

3And when the seventh month had come, and the children of Israel *were* in the cities, the people gathered together as one man to Jerusalem. 2Then Jeshua the son of Jozadaka and his brethren the priests, and Zerubbabel the son of Shealtiel and his brethren, arose and built the altar of the God of Israel, to offer burnt offerings on it, as *it is* written in the Law of Moses the man of God. 3Though fear *had come* upon them because of the people of those countries, they set the altar on its bases; and they offered burnt offerings on it to the LORD, *both* the morning and evening burnt offerings. 4They also kept the Feast of Tabernacles, as *it is* written, and *offered* the daily burnt offerings in the number required by ordinance for each day. 5Afterwards *they offered* the regular burnt offering, and *those* for New Moons and for all the appointed feasts of the LORD that were consecrated, and *those* of everyone who willingly offered a freewill offering to the LORD. 6From the first day of the seventh month they began to offer burnt offerings to the LORD, although the foundation of the temple of the LORD had not been laid. 7They also gave money to the masons and the carpenters, and food, drink, and oil to the people of Sidon and Tyre to bring cedar logs from Lebanon to the sea, to Joppa, according to the permission which they had from Cyrus king of Persia.

Restoration of the Temple Begins

8Now in the second month of the second year of their coming to the house of God at Jerusalem, Zerubbabel the son of Shealtiel, Jeshua the son of Jozadak,a and the rest of their brethren the priests and the Levites, and all those who had come out of the captivity to Jerusalem, began *work* and appointed the Levites from twenty years old and above to oversee the work of the house of the LORD. 9Then Jeshua *with* his sons and brothers, Kadmiel *with* his sons, and the sons of Judah,a arose as one to oversee those working on the house of God: the sons of Henadad *with* their sons and their brethren the Levites.

10When the builders laid the foundation of the temple of the LORD, the priests stooda in their apparel with trumpets, and the Levites, the sons of Asaph, with cymbals, to praise the LORD, according to the ordinance of David king of Israel. 11And they sang responsively, praising and giving thanks to the LORD:

"For *He is* good,
    For His mercy *endures* forever toward Israel."a

Then all the people shouted with a great shout, when they praised the LORD, because the foundation of the house of the LORD was laid.

12But many of the priests and Levites and heads of the fathers' *houses,* old men who had seen the first temple, wept with a loud voice when the foundation of this temple was laid before their

---

3:2 aSpelled *Jehozadak* in 1 Chronicles 6:14   3:8 aSpelled *Jehozadak* in 1 Chronicles 6:14   3:9 aOr *Hodaviah* (compare 2:40)   3:10 aFollowing Septuagint, Syriac, and Vulgate; Masoretic Text reads *they stationed the priests.*   3:11 aCompare Psalm 136:1

3:1 They gathered in the seventh month of the first year. Tishri, equivalent to September/October, was the seventh month (see chart, The Jewish Sacred Calendar). One of the most important months in the Jewish year, Tishri marked *Rosh Hashanah* on its first day (the Jewish New Year's Day, Lev. 23:24), followed ten days later by *Yom Kippur* (the Day of Atonement, Lev. 23:27), then from the 15th to the 22nd day *Succoth* (the Feast of Tabernacles, Lev. 23:34–36; see also chart, The Feasts of Israel).

The people of Israel are depicted as complete only in community with one another. The temple and its worship activities were clearly the focal point of the people of God. Though they initially had gone to their own cities (Ezra 2:70), they soon returned to accomplish the task for which they came to Jerusalem—the building of the temple. When the foundation

was laid, their shouts of joy and the weeping of men, women, and children were mingled as one loud noise to those "afar off" (Ezra 3:13), indicating the deep emotions of the occasion. The memories of those who remembered the splendor of the temple of Solomon were mingled with the excitement of the preparing for a new temple.

3:2–6 The Law of Moses provided instructions for worship (Deut. 12:5, 6). Although these forms of worship had been practiced for approximately 400 years in the temple built during Solomon's reign (1 Kin. 6:37, 38), the Jews in exile did not practice the traditional forms of worship. Now, along with the rebuilding of the temple, worship and sacrifice are being restored to Israel. However, the sacrificial system never reached the same significance it had prior to the exile.

eyes. Yet many shouted aloud for joy, [13]so that the people could not discern the noise of the shout of joy from the noise of the weeping of the people, for the people shouted with a loud shout, and the sound was heard afar off.

Resistance to Rebuilding the Temple

4 Now when the adversaries of Judah and Benjamin heard that the descendants of the captivity were building the temple of the LORD God of Israel, [2]they came to Zerubbabel and the heads of the fathers' *houses,* and said to them, "Let us build with you, for we seek your God as you *do;* and we have sacrificed to Him since the days of Esarhaddon king of Assyria, who brought us here." [3]But Zerubbabel and Jeshua and the rest of the heads of the fathers' *houses* of Israel said to them, "You may do nothing with us to build a house for our God; but we alone will build to the LORD God of Israel, as King Cyrus the king of Persia has commanded us." [4]Then the people of the land tried to discourage the people of Judah. They troubled them in building, [5]and hired counselors against them to frustrate their purpose all the days of Cyrus king of Persia, even until the reign of Darius king of Persia.

Rebuilding of Jerusalem Opposed

[6]In the reign of Ahasuerus, in the beginning of his reign, they wrote an accusation against the inhabitants of Judah and Jerusalem.

[7]In the days of Artaxerxes also, Bishlam, Mithredath, Tabel, and the rest of their companions wrote to Artaxerxes king of Persia; and the letter *was* written in Aramaic script, and translated into the Aramaic language. [8]Rehum[a] the commander and Shimshai the scribe wrote a letter against Jerusalem to King Artaxerxes in this fashion:

[9]From[a] Rehum the commander, Shimshai the scribe, and the rest of their companions— *representatives* of the Dinaites, the Apharsathchites, the Tarpelites, the people of Persia and Erech and Babylon and Shushan,[b] the Dehavites, the Elamites, [10]and the rest of the nations whom the great and noble Osnapper took captive and settled in the cities of Samaria and the remainder beyond the River[a]— and so forth.[b]

[11](This *is* a copy of the letter that they sent him)

To King Artaxerxes from your servants, the men *of the region* beyond the River, and so forth:[a]

[12]Let it be known to the king that the Jews who came up from you have come to us at Jerusalem, and are building the rebellious and evil city, and are finishing *its* walls and repairing the foundations. [13]Let it now be known to the king that, if this city is built and the walls completed, they will not pay tax, tribute, or custom, and the king's treasury will be diminished. [14]Now because we receive support from the palace, it was not proper for us to see the king's dishonor; therefore we have sent and informed the king, [15]that search may be made in the book of the records of your fathers. And you will find in the book of the records and know that this city *is* a rebellious city, harmful to kings and provinces, and that they have incited sedition within the city in former times, for which cause this city was destroyed.

[16]We inform the king that if this city is rebuilt and its walls are completed, the result will be that you will have no dominion beyond the River.

[17]The king sent an answer:

To Rehum the commander, *to* Shimshai the scribe, *to* the rest of their companions who dwell in Samaria, and *to* the remainder beyond the River:

4:8 [a]The original language of Ezra 4:8 through 6:18 is Aramaic.   **4:9** [a]Literally *Then* [b]Or *Susa*   **4:10** [a]That is, the Euphrates [b]Literally *and now*   **4:11** [a]Literally *and now*

4:1 See Ezra 2:1, note.

4:2, 3 The people of God refused help. The heathen of the land had incorporated the worship of the God of the Jews along with a variety of other gods. Israel's refusal of the help offered by these pagan people in the Land underscored the importance of a pure faith in *Yahweh* (Ex. 20:3; Deut. 5:7). "The adversaries" were descendants of those imported to Samaria by King Esarhaddon of Assyria (681–669 B.C.; see 2 Kin. 17:24, note; chart, The Kings of Assyria).

4:6–23 A parenthetical section interrupts the chronological sequence of the events surrounding the temple building. In these verses, later kings are mentioned along with the difficulties that would ensue. Their work was made more difficult by the "people of the land," who continually harassed the workers, especially through "hired counselors," who must have been trained in techniques akin to psychological warfare (vv. 4, 5). The possible reasons for this insertion cannot be adequately addressed here, but perhaps the intent was to dispel any notion that the Jews were exaggerating the interference and aggressiveness of the enemies in the Land who were blatantly opposing the building of the house of God. Ahasuerus, also known as Xerxes, is the king depicted in the Book of Esther (486 B.C.; v. 6).

4:8—6:18 Aramaic language. This text and Ezra 7:12–26 both appear in the Aramaic language (the official diplomatic language of the Persians). The rest of Ezra is in Hebrew.

Peace, and so forth.[a]

[18]The letter which you sent to us has been clearly read before me. [19]And I gave the command, and a search has been made, and it was found that this city in former times has revolted against kings, and rebellion and sedition have been fostered in it. [20]There have also been mighty kings over Jerusalem, who have ruled over all *the region* beyond the River; and tax, tribute, and custom were paid to them. [21]Now give the command to make these men cease, that this city may not be built until the command is given by me.

[22]Take heed now that you do not fail to do this. Why should damage increase to the hurt of the kings?

[23]Now when the copy of King Artaxerxes' letter *was* read before Rehum, Shimshai the scribe, and their companions, they went up in haste to Jerusalem against the Jews, and by force of arms made them cease. [24]Thus the work of the house of God which *is* at Jerusalem ceased, and it was discontinued until the second year of the reign of Darius king of Persia.

Restoration of the Temple Resumed

5 Then the prophet Haggai and Zechariah the son of Iddo, prophets, prophesied to the Jews who *were* in Judah and Jerusalem, in the name of the God of Israel, *who was* over them. [2]So Zerubbabel the son of Shealtiel and Jeshua the son of Jozadak[a] rose up and began to build the house of God which *is* in Jerusalem; and the prophets of God *were* with them, helping them.

[3]At the same time Tattenai the governor of *the region* beyond the River[a] and Shethar-Boznai and their companions came to them and spoke thus to them: "Who has commanded you to build this temple and finish this wall?" [4]Then, accordingly, we told them the names of the men who were constructing this building. [5]But the eye of their God was upon the elders of the Jews, so that they could not make them cease till a report could go to Darius. Then a written answer was returned concern-

ing this *matter.* [6]This is a copy of the letter that Tattenai sent:

The governor of *the region* beyond the River, and Shethar-Boznai, and his companions, the Persians who *were in the region* beyond the River, to Darius the king.

[7](They sent a letter to him, in which was written thus)

To Darius the king:

All peace.

[8]Let it be known to the king that we went into the province of Judea, to the temple of the great God, which is being built with heavy stones, and timber is being laid in the walls; and this work goes on diligently and prospers in their hands.

[9]Then we asked those elders, *and* spoke thus to them: "Who commanded you to build this temple and to finish these walls?" [10]We also asked them their names to inform you, that we might write the names of the men who *were* chief among them.

[11]And thus they returned us an answer, saying: "We are the servants of the God of heaven and earth, and we are rebuilding the temple that was built many years ago, which a great king of Israel built and completed. [12]But because our fathers provoked the God of heaven to wrath, He gave them into the hand of Nebuchadnezzar king of Babylon, the Chaldean, *who* destroyed this temple and carried the people away to Babylon. [13]However, in the first year of Cyrus king of Babylon, King Cyrus issued a decree to build this house of God. [14]Also, the gold and silver articles of the house of God, which Nebuchadnezzar had taken from the temple that *was* in Jerusalem and carried into the temple of Babylon— those

---

4:17 [a]Literally *and now*   5:2 [a]Spelled *Jehozadak* in 1 Chronicles 6:14
5:3 [a]That is, the Euphrates

4:24 The aristocracy of Samaria believed the land of Judah belonged to them. Therefore, they resented the faithful Jews and their separatism, which even included refusing to associate with the unfaithful brethren among them. The harassment that began toward those building the temple finally caused them to cease working in 520 B.C. or approximately 16 years after the project began (v. 1).

5:1–5 God restored the building project. The Jews had lost interest in God's house while caring for their own houses, and God was not pleased (Hag. 1:7–11; 2:15–19). Therefore, He sent the prophets Haggai and Zechariah to encourage the Jews to

resume building the temple, which they did. Governor Tattenai questioned the building project. This time the attempt of enemies to interfere with the rebuilding was unsuccessful (Ezra 5:5).

5:3–6 The region beyond the River originally was merely a geographical term for the land west of the Euphrates River to the Mediterranean Sea, including Judah and Samaria. From Assyrian rule through the Persian rule, this phrase was an administrative designation for the same region. Finally, during the reign of Darius I, it became a province of its own with a governor named Tattenai.

King Cyrus took from the temple of Babylon, and they were given to one named Sheshbazzar, whom he had made governor. [15]And he said to him, 'Take these articles; go, carry them to the temple *site* that *is* in Jerusalem, and let the house of God be rebuilt on its former site.' [16]Then the same Sheshbazzar came *and* laid the foundation of the house of God which *is* in Jerusalem; but from that time even until now it has been under construction, and it is not finished."

[17]Now therefore, if *it seems* good to the king, let a search be made in the king's treasure house, which *is* there in Babylon, whether it is *so* that a decree was issued by King Cyrus to build this house of God at Jerusalem, and let the king send us his pleasure concerning this *matter.*

The Decree of Darius

6 Then King Darius issued a decree, and a search was made in the archives,[a] where the treasures were stored in Babylon. [2]And at Achmetha,[a] in the palace that *is* in the province of Media, a scroll was found, and in it a record *was* written thus:

[3]In the first year of King Cyrus, King Cyrus issued a decree *concerning* the house of God at Jerusalem: "Let the house be rebuilt, the place where they offered sacrifices; and let the foundations of it be firmly laid, its height sixty cubits *and* its width sixty cubits, [4]*with* three rows of heavy stones and one row of new timber. Let the expenses be paid from the king's treasury. [5]Also let the gold and silver articles of the house of God, which Nebuchadnezzar took from the temple which *is* in Jerusalem and brought to Babylon, be restored and taken back to the temple which *is* in Jerusalem, *each* to its place; and deposit *them* in the house of God"—

[6]Now *therefore,* Tattenai, governor of *the region* beyond the River, and Shethar-Boznai, and your companions the Persians who *are* beyond the River, keep yourselves far from there. [7]Let the work of this house of God alone; let the governor of the Jews and the elders of the Jews build this house of God on its site.

[8]Moreover I issue a decree *as to* what you shall do for the elders of these Jews, for the building of this house of God: Let the cost be paid at the king's expense from taxes *on the region* beyond the River; this is to be given immediately to these men, so that they are not hindered. [9]And whatever they need—young bulls, rams, and lambs for the burnt offerings of the God of heaven, wheat, salt, wine, and oil, according to the request of the priests who *are* in Jerusalem—let it be given them day by day without fail, [10]that they may offer sacrifices of sweet aroma to the God of heaven, and pray for the life of the king and his sons.

[11]Also I issue a decree that whoever alters this edict, let a timber be pulled from his house and erected, and let him be hanged on it; and let his house be made a refuse heap because of this. [12]And may the God who causes His name to dwell there destroy any king or people who put their hand to alter it, or to destroy this house of God which is in Jerusalem. I Darius issue a decree; let it be done diligently.

The Temple Completed and Dedicated

[13]Then Tattenai, governor of *the region* beyond the River, Shethar-Boznai, and their companions diligently did according to what King Darius had sent. [14]So the elders of the Jews built, and they prospered through the prophesying of Haggai the prophet and Zechariah the son of Iddo. And they built and finished *it,* according to the commandment of the God of Israel, and according to the command of Cyrus, Darius, and Artaxerxes king of Persia. [15]Now the temple was finished on the third day of the month of Adar, which was in the sixth year of the reign of King Darius. [16]Then the children of Israel, the priests and the Levites and the rest of the descendants of the captivity, celebrated the dedication of this house of God with joy. [17]And they offered sacrifices at the dedication of this house of God, one hundred bulls, two hundred rams, four hundred lambs, and as a sin offering for all Israel twelve male goats, according to the number of the tribes of Israel. [18]They assigned the priests to their divisions and the Levites to their

····················

6:1 [a]Literally *house of the scrolls*   6:2 [a]Probably *Ecbatana*, the ancient capital of Media

6:13–15 The temple was completed. In the month of Adar, 515 B.C., the temple was completed about 70 years after its destruction (see chart, The Jewish Sacred Calendar). Although no longer a nation, the remnant of Israel successfully established an identity in the region as the community of the Jerusalem temple.

6:16–22 They separated from the pagans of the Land. The prerequisite for seeking God was to separate from ungodly people. As worshipers of a holy God, the Jews were to be holy, too, which would be impossible if they participated in the practices of the surrounding heathen nations. Such practices included child sacrifice, fortune telling, consulting of mediums, and witchcraft (Deut. 18:9–14). The Jews who did not choose to separate themselves were given no place in this exclusive community. Unfortunately, the faithful spirit exhibited here failed to endure.

divisions, over the service of God in Jerusalem, as it is written in the Book of Moses.

The Passover Celebrated

[19]And the descendants of the captivity kept the Passover on the fourteenth *day* of the first month. [20]For the priests and the Levites had purified themselves; all of them *were ritually* clean. And they slaughtered the Passover *lambs* for all the descendants of the captivity, for their brethren the priests, and for themselves. [21]Then the children of Israel who had returned from the captivity ate together with all who had separated themselves from the filth of the nations of the land in order to seek the LORD God of Israel. [22]And they kept the Feast of Unleavened Bread seven days with joy; for the LORD made them joyful, and turned the heart of the king of Assyria toward them, to strengthen their hands in the work of the house of God, the God of Israel.

The Arrival of Ezra

7Now after these things, in the reign of Artaxerxes king of Persia, Ezra the son of Seraiah, the son of Azariah, the son of Hilkiah, [2]the son of Shallum, the son of Zadok, the son of Ahitub, [3]the son of Amariah, the son of Azariah, the son of Meraioth, [4]the son of Zerahiah, the son of Uzzi, the son of Bukki, [5]the son of Abishua, the son of Phinehas, the son of Eleazar, the son of Aaron the chief priest— [6]this Ezra came up from Babylon; and he *was* a skilled scribe in the Law of Moses, which the LORD God of Israel had given. The king granted him all his request, according to the hand of the LORD his God upon him. [7]*Some* of the children of Israel, the priests, the Levites, the singers, the gatekeepers, and the Nethinim came up to Jerusalem in the seventh year of King Artaxerxes. [8]And Ezra came to Jerusalem in the

fifth month, which *was* in the seventh year of the king. [9]On the first *day* of the first month he began *his* journey from Babylon, and on the first *day* of the fifth month he came to Jerusalem, according to the good hand of his God upon him. [10]For Ezra had prepared his heart to seek the Law of the LORD, and to do *it,* and to teach statutes and ordinances in Israel.

The Letter of Artaxerxes to Ezra

[11]This *is* a copy of the letter that King Artaxerxes gave Ezra the priest, the scribe, expert in the words of the commandments of the LORD, and of His statutes to Israel:

[12]Artaxerxes,[a] king of kings,

To Ezra the priest, a scribe of the Law of the God of heaven:

Perfect *peace,* and so forth.[b]

[13]I issue a decree that all those of the people of Israel and the priests and Levites in my realm, who volunteer to go up to Jerusalem, may go with you. [14]And whereas you are being sent by the king and his seven counselors to inquire concerning Judah and Jerusalem, with regard to the Law of your God which *is* in your hand; [15]and *whereas you are* to carry the silver and gold which the king and his counselors have freely offered to the God of Israel, whose dwelling *is* in Jerusalem; [16]and *whereas* all the silver and gold that you may find in all the province of Babylon, along with the freewill offering of the people and the priests, *are to be*

7:12 [a]The original language of Ezra 7:12–26 is Aramaic. [b]Literally *and now*

7:1–6 Preparation for Ezra's mission. Ezra was born a priest from the line of Aaron and was gifted as a scribe (v. 6). He studied the Law of the Lord, not just for academic purposes but in order to obey it and teach it. Originally, the main duty of a scribe was to recount information by writing it down. During the Exile in Babylon, the professions of scribe and priest merged; Ezra was both a priest and a scribe. He may have worked in the Babylonian courts on the affairs of the Jews. He was copyist, preserver, and interpreter of the Law. In NT times the profession of scribe belonged primarily to the group known as the Pharisees. However, they were a separate class and were often associated with the priests and elders. During the approximately 50 years following the completion of the temple in Jerusalem, morale in Judah reached a low point. The priests were poor leaders, and the Sabbath was not kept or the tithes paid. There was widespread divorce and intermarriage with the pagan population (Mal. 2:13–16). Still searching for an identity while being unduly influenced by the surrounding pagan world, the small Jewish community needed desperately to establish a direction. Israel needed help. Both Ezra and Nehemiah were sent to the rescue: one

for religious reform and the other for administrative direction (Neh. 2:5).

7:8 Artaxerxes sent Ezra. This marks the second of three major expeditions of returning exiles from Babylon. If this is Artaxerxes I, then the year is 458 B.C., which is the traditionally accepted date (see map, The Return from Exile).

7:11–26 The royal decree of Artaxerxes. Ezra sought to unite those who returned with him as one nation. The decree shows the support of this foreign king toward Ezra and those who chose to go with him. It also reveals a clear picture of God's grace toward the exiles when He used a pagan king to require three things Ezra needed to accomplish: An evaluation of lifestyle according to God's Law (v. 14), an understanding of the godly use of possessions (vv. 15–20), and the achievement of godly wisdom in leadership (vv. 25, 26). Ezra praised God and acknowledged His involvement and then obeyed, confident that "the hand of the LORD [*Yahweh*] my God was upon me" (vv. 27, 28).

7:12–26 See Ezra 4:8—6:18, note.

freely offered for the house of their God in Jerusalem— [17]now therefore, be careful to buy with this money bulls, rams, and lambs, with their grain offerings and their drink offerings, and offer them on the altar of the house of your God in Jerusalem.

[18]And whatever seems good to you and your brethren to do with the rest of the silver and the gold, do it according to the will of your God. [19]Also the articles that are given to you for the service of the house of your God, deliver in full before the God of Jerusalem. [20]And whatever more may be needed for the house of your God, which you may have occasion to provide, pay *for it* from the king's treasury.

[21]And I, *even* I, Artaxerxes the king, issue a decree to all the treasurers who *are in the region* beyond the River, that whatever Ezra the priest, the scribe of the Law of the God of heaven, may require of you, let it be done diligently, [22]up to one hundred talents of silver, one hundred kors of wheat, one hundred baths of wine, one hundred baths of oil, and salt without prescribed limit. [23]Whatever is commanded by the God of heaven, let it diligently be done for the house of the God of heaven. For why should there be wrath against the realm of the king and his sons?

[24]Also we inform you that it shall not be lawful to impose tax, tribute, or custom *on* any of the priests, Levites, singers, gatekeepers, Nethinim, or servants of this house of God. [25]And you, Ezra, according to your God-given wisdom, set magistrates and judges who may judge all the people who *are in the region* beyond the River, all such as know the laws of your God; and teach those who do not know *them.* [26]Whoever will not observe the law of your God and the law of the king, let judgment be executed speedily on him, whether *it be* death, or banishment, or confiscation of goods, or imprisonment.

[27]Blessed *be* the LORD God of our fathers, who has put *such a thing* as this in the king's heart, to beautify the house of the LORD which *is* in Jerusalem, [28]and has extended mercy to me before the king and his counselors, and before all the king's mighty princes.

So I was encouraged, as the hand of the LORD my God *was* upon me; and I gathered leading men of Israel to go up with me.

Heads of Families Who Returned with Ezra

8These *are* the heads of their fathers' *houses,* and *this is* the genealogy of those who went up with me from Babylon, in the reign of King Artaxerxes: [2]of the sons of Phinehas, Gershom; of the sons of Ithamar, Daniel; of the sons of David, Hattush; [3]of the sons of Shecaniah, of the sons of Parosh, Zechariah; and registered with him *were* one hundred and fifty males; [4]of the sons of Pahath-Moab, Eliehoenai the son of Zerahiah, and with him two hundred males; [5]of the sons of Shechaniah,[a] Ben-Jahaziel, and with him three hundred males; [6]of the sons of Adin, Ebed the son of Jonathan, and with him fifty males; [7]of the sons of Elam, Jeshaiah the son of Athaliah, and with him seventy males; [8]of the sons of Shephatiah, Zebadiah the son of Michael, and with him eighty males; [9]of the sons of Joab, Obadiah the son of Jehiel, and with him two hundred and eighteen males; [10]of the sons of Shelomith,[a] Ben-Josiphiah, and with him one hundred and sixty males; [11]of the sons of Bebai, Zechariah the son of Bebai, and with him twenty-eight males; [12]of the sons of Azgad, Johanan the son of Hakkatan, and with him one hundred and ten males; [13]of the last sons of Adonikam, whose names *are* these— Eliphelet, Jeiel, and Shemaiah— and with them sixty males; [14]also of the sons of Bigvai, Uthai and Zabbud, and with them seventy males.

Servants for the Temple

[15]Now I gathered them by the river that flows to Ahava, and we camped there three days. And I looked among the people and the priests, and found none of the sons of Levi there. [16]Then I sent for Eliezer, Ariel, Shemaiah, Elnathan, Jarib, Elnathan, Nathan, Zechariah, and Meshullam, leaders; also for Joiarib and Elnathan, men of understanding. [17]And I gave them a command for Iddo the chief man at the place Casiphia, and I told them what they should say to Iddo *and* his brethren[a] the Nethinim at the place Casiphia— that they should bring us servants for the house of our God. [18]Then, by the good hand of our God upon us, they brought us a man of understanding, of the sons of Mahli the son of Levi, the son of Is-

---

8:5 [a]Following Masoretic Text and Vulgate; Septuagint reads *the sons of Zatho, Shechaniah.* **8:10** [a]Following Masoretic Text and Vulgate; Septuagint reads *the sons of Banni, Shelomith.* **8:17** [a]Following Vulgate; Masoretic Text reads *to Iddo his brother;* Septuagint reads *to their brethren.*

8:2–14 Those who went with Ezra. The names on this list can be compared with those of the first group of returning exiles (Ezra 2:3–15). These repeated names may be descendants of those who returned some 80 years earlier. It was a dangerous, 1,000-mile trip across a bandit-filled desert. Even in the face of such danger, about 5,000 men, women, and children joined Ezra on his journey. Their safe arrival in Jerusalem was another indication of the hand of God upon them.

THE TIMELINE FOR EZRA, NEHEMIAH, AND ESTHER

Events Recorded in EZRA
(537–458 B.C.)

Events Recorded
in NEHEMIAH
(444-about 425 B.C.)

550 B.C.	525 B.C.	500 B.C.	475 B.C.	450 B.C.	425 B.C.

Events Recorded
in ESTHER
(483–471 B.C.)

537 B.C. – Zerubbabel
leads first return of
exiles (Ezra 1—6)

458 B.C. – Ezra leads
second return of
exiles (Ezra 7—10)

rael, namely Sherebiah, with his sons and brothers, eighteen men; [19]and Hashabiah, and with him Jeshaiah of the sons of Merari, his brothers and their sons, twenty men; [20]also of the Nethinim, whom David and the leaders had appointed for the service of the Levites, two hundred and twenty Nethinim. All of them were designated by name.

Fasting and Prayer for Protection

[21]Then I proclaimed a fast there at the river of Ahava, that we might humble ourselves before our God, to seek from Him the right way for us and our little ones and all our possessions. [22]For I was ashamed to request of the king an escort of soldiers and horsemen to help us against the enemy on the road, because we had spoken to the king, saying, "The hand of our God is upon all those for good who seek Him, but His power and His wrath are against all those who forsake Him." [23]So we fasted and entreated our God for this, and He answered our prayer.

Gifts for the Temple

[24]And I separated twelve of the leaders of the priests— Sherebiah, Hashabiah, and ten of their brethren with them— [25]and weighed out to them the silver, the gold, and the articles, the offering for the house of our God which the king and his counselors and his princes, and all Israel who were

present, had offered. [26]I weighed into their hand six hundred and fifty talents of silver, silver articles weighing one hundred talents, one hundred talents of gold, [27]twenty gold basins worth a thousand drachmas, and two vessels of fine polished bronze, precious as gold. [28]And I said to them, "You are holy to the LORD; the articles are holy also; and the silver and the gold are a freewill offering to the LORD God of your fathers. [29]Watch and keep them until you weigh them before the leaders of the priests and the Levites and heads of the fathers' houses of Israel in Jerusalem, in the chambers of the house of the LORD." [30]So the priests and the Levites received the silver and the gold and the articles by weight, to bring them to Jerusalem to the house of our God.

The Return to Jerusalem

[31]Then we departed from the river of Ahava on the twelfth day of the first month, to go to Jerusalem. And the hand of our God was upon us, and He delivered us from the hand of the enemy and from ambush along the road. [32]So we came to Jerusalem, and stayed there three days.

[33]Now on the fourth day the silver and the gold and the articles were weighed in the house of our God by the hand of Meremoth the son of Uriah the priest, and with him was Eleazar the son of Phinehas; with them were the Levites, Jozabad the son of Jeshua and Noadiah the son of Binnui,

---

8:21–31 Ezra, determined to trust God for the journey and not to seek help from the king, exercised godly leadership (see chart, Preparation for Leadership). Ezra knew that ultimately protection must come from God. Before the people began the journey, Ezra declared a time of fasting and prayer. The people humbled themselves before God to solicit His protection for themselves, their children, and their belongings. God proved faithful.

34with the number *and* weight of everything. All the weight was written down at that time.

35The children of those who had been carried away captive, who had come from the captivity, offered burnt offerings to the God of Israel: twelve bulls for all Israel, ninety-six rams, seventy-seven lambs, and twelve male goats *as* a sin offering. All *this was* a burnt offering to the Lord.

36And they delivered the king's orders to the king's satraps and the governors *in the region* beyond the River. So they gave support to the people and the house of God.

Intermarriage with Pagans

9 When these things were done, the leaders came to me, saying, "The people of Israel and the priests and the Levites have not separated themselves from the peoples of the lands, with respect to the abominations of the Canaanites, the Hittites, the Perizzites, the Jebusites, the Ammonites, the Moabites, the Egyptians, and the Amorites. 2For they have taken some of their daughters *as wives* for themselves and their sons, so that the holy seed is mixed with the peoples of *those* lands. Indeed, the hand of the leaders and rulers has been foremost in this trespass." 3So when I heard this thing, I tore my garment and my robe, and plucked out some of the hair of my head and beard, and sat down astonished. 4Then everyone who trembled at the words of the God of Israel assembled to me, because of the transgression of those who had been carried away captive, and I sat astonished until the evening sacrifice.

5At the evening sacrifice I arose from my fasting; and having torn my garment and my robe, I fell on my knees and spread out my hands to the Lord my God. 6And I said: "O my God, I am too ashamed and humiliated to lift up my face to You, my God; for our iniquities have risen higher than *our* heads, and our guilt has grown up to the heavens. 7Since the days of our fathers to this day we *have been* very guilty, and for our iniquities we, our kings, *and* our priests have been delivered into the hand of the kings of the lands, to the sword, to captivity, to plunder, and to humiliation, as *it is* this day. 8And now for a little while grace has been *shown* from the Lord our God, to leave us a remnant to escape, and to give us a peg in His holy place, that our God may enlighten our eyes and give us a measure of revival in our bondage. 9For we *were* slaves. Yet our God did not forsake us in our bondage; but He extended mercy to us in the sight of the kings of Persia, to revive us, to repair the house of our God, to rebuild its ruins, and to give us a wall in Judah and Jerusalem. 10And now, O our God, what shall we say after this? For we have forsaken Your commandments, 11which You commanded by Your servants the prophets, saying, 'The land which you are entering to possess is an unclean land, with the uncleanness of the peoples of the lands, with their abominations which have filled it from one end to another with their impurity. 12Now therefore, do not give your daughters as wives for their sons, nor take their daughters to your sons; and never seek their peace or prosperity, that you may be strong and eat the good of the land, and leave *it* as an inheritance to your children forever.' 13And after all that has come upon us for our evil deeds and for our great guilt, since You our God have punished us less than our iniquities *deserve,* and have given us *such* deliverance as this, 14should we again break Your commandments, and join in marriage with the people *committing* these abominations? Would You not be angry with us until You had consumed *us,* so that *there would be* no remnant or survivor? 15O Lord God of Israel, You

---

8:35 The children returned. "Children" is actually a reference to the descendants of those who had been taken to Babylon after the fall of Jerusalem in 586 b.c., nearly 150 years earlier. The words of the prophets were being fulfilled by their return (Is. 10:20–23).

9:1–2 Ezra discovered unfaithfulness (Heb. *ma*̓*al*, lit. "an act of unfaithfulness"). This word is understood as sin against God either by trespassing on holy things or violating a sworn oath. This same word for unfaithfulness is used to explain why "Judah was carried away captive to Babylon" (1 Chr. 9:1). Israel under covenant with God knew that they should not intermarry with pagan nations (Deut. 7:3, 4; Neh. 10, Interfaith Marriage). In Deuteronomy, the writer was referring to the surrounding nations, which are representative of those called "the peoples of the land" (Ezra 9:1). The concern over intermarriage spanned the history of the Israelites. First was the importance of remaining a faithful people. This nation had been promised that it would be a blessing to the whole world (Gen. 12:1–3, 7). The promise of "holy seed" is fulfilled in Jesus Christ (Is. 6:13; Matt. 1:1). Second, the pagan nations—their foreign gods and strange, as well as frequently immoral, religious practices—remained a constant threat to the faith and steadfastness of the Israelites toward their God, *Yahweh.*

9:3–5 Tearing the clothes, pulling the hair, and even sitting in stunned silence were traditional rituals for mourning. These outward displays of mourning implied that what the Jews had done was worthy of death and that God would be fully justified if He were to condemn them. The fact that Ezra tore his inner garment as well as his outer tunic emphasizes the seriousness of the trespass.

9:7—10:2 God had made a covenant promise that He would bless and never leave or forsake His people if they would trust Him and worship Him only (Ex. 19:5; Jer. 11:4). Through the years, the Israelites repeatedly failed to uphold their end of the agreement, but *Yahweh* remained faithful (Lam. 3:22, note). Ezra declared Israel to be a shameful people before God, but he also remembered that *Yahweh* is a righteous, just, and gracious God.

9:15 Those Jews who returned from the Exile in Babylon were very few. They were called the remnant, and their existence— no longer as a nation but as a small community of men, women, and children—was an act of restoration on God's part.

THE JEWISH SACRED CALENDAR

MONTH OF THE SACRED YEAR	NAME OF MONTH	CANAANITE EQUIVALENT	MODERN EQUIVALENT	NUMBER OF DAYS	REFERENCES
1	Nisan	Abib (Ex. 13:4; 23:15; 34:18; Deut. 16:1)	March–April	30	Neh. 2:1; Esth. 3:7
2	Iyar	Ziv (1 Kin. 6:1, 37)	April–May	29	
3	Sivan		May–June	30	Esth. 8:9
4	Tammuz		June–July	29	
5	Ab		July–August	30	
6	Elul		August–September	29	Neh. 6:15
7	Tishri	Ethanim (1 Kin. 8:2)	September–October	30	
8	Heshvan	Bul (1 Kin. 6:38)	October–November	29 or 30	
9	Chislev		November–December	29 or 30	Neh. 1:1; Zech. 7:1
10	Tebeth		December–January	29	Esth. 2:16
11	Shebat		January–February	30	Zech. 1:7
12	Adar		February–March	29 or 30	Ezra 6:15; Esth.3:7, 13; 8:12; 9:1,15, 17, 19, 21

Hebrew months were alternately 30 and 29 days long. The Hebrew year, shorter than ours, had 354 days. Therefore, about every 3 years (7 times in 19 years) an extra 29-day month, Veadar, was added between Adar and Nisan.

The Civil Calendar—official calendar for kings, childbirth, and contracts—differed somewhat from this Sacred Calendar.

---

are righteous, for we are left as a remnant, as *it is* this day. Here we *are* before You, in our guilt, though no one can stand before You because of this!"

Confession of Improper Marriages

10 Now while Ezra was praying, and while he was confessing, weeping, and bowing down before the house of God, a very large assembly of men, women, and children gathered to him from Israel; for the people wept very bitterly. ²And Shechaniah the son of Jehiel, *one* of the sons of Elam, spoke up and said to Ezra, "We have trespassed against our God, and have taken pagan wives from the peoples of the land; yet now there is hope in Israel in spite of this. ³Now therefore,

---

10:1 Ezra taught the Law (v. 3), fasted and prayed for the people (vv. 1, 6), shared in their shame (v. 6), responded to their request for help (v. 4), supported their plans (v. 7), declared the fact of their sinfulness (v. 10), called them to confession and obedience (vv. 11, 12), and delegated responsibilities while he worked side by side with others to accomplish the work (v. 16). Ezra was sent to teach the Law and bring reforms to the Jews. This chapter reveals that his mission was accomplished. In Jerusalem, the Davidic, kingly era was over, not to return until the Messiah would come. The people now were central figures of God's unfolding story. There remained no

hero types—simply God's people persevering day to day in the faith. Their hope remained in their holy God, *Yahweh,* whose deeds, prophetic promises, and commandments were found in the Law. The Law would mark them as a people separate from the other nations.

10:2 The Jews divorced their pagan wives. Perhaps Shechaniah had married an idolatrous wife. Or the "we" may be Shechaniah's way of identifying with the community, as Ezra sometimes used "we" rather than his own personal expression. If the person named Jehiel in this verse (v. 2) is the same

let us make a covenant with our God to put away all these wives and those who have been born to them, according to the advice of my master and of those who tremble at the commandment of our God; and let it be done according to the law. [4]Arise, for *this* matter *is* your *responsibility*. We also *are* with you. Be of good courage, and do *it*."

[5]Then Ezra arose, and made the leaders of the priests, the Levites, and all Israel swear an oath that they would do according to this word. So they swore an oath. [6]Then Ezra rose up from before the house of God, and went into the chamber of Jehohanan the son of Eliashib; and *when* he came there, he ate no bread and drank no water, for he mourned because of the guilt of those from the captivity.

[7]And they issued a proclamation throughout Judah and Jerusalem to all the descendants of the captivity, that they must gather at Jerusalem, [8]and that whoever would not come within three days, according to the instructions of the leaders and elders, all his property would be confiscated, and he himself would be separated from the assembly of those from the captivity.

[9]So all the men of Judah and Benjamin gathered at Jerusalem within three days. It *was* the ninth month, on the twentieth of the month; and all the people sat in the open square of the house of God, trembling because of *this* matter and because of heavy rain. [10]Then Ezra the priest stood up and said to them, "You have transgressed and have taken pagan wives, adding to the guilt of Israel. [11]Now therefore, make confession to the LORD God of your fathers, and do His will; separate yourselves from the peoples of the land, and from the pagan wives."

[12]Then all the assembly answered and said with a loud voice, "Yes! As you have said, so we must do. [13]But *there are* many people; *it is* the season for heavy rain, and we are not able to stand outside. Nor *is this* the work of one or two days, for *there are* many of us who have transgressed in this matter. [14]Please, let the leaders of our entire assembly stand; and let all those in our cities who have taken pagan wives come at appointed times, together with the elders and judges of their cities, until the fierce wrath of our God is turned away from us in this matter." [15]Only Jonathan the son of Asahel and Jahaziah the son of Tikvah opposed this, and Meshullam and Shabbethai the Levite gave them support.

[16]Then the descendants of the captivity did so. And Ezra the priest, *with* certain heads of the fathers' *households,* were set apart by the fathers' households, each of them by name; and they sat down on the first day of the tenth month to examine the matter. [17]By the first day of the first month they finished *questioning* all the men who had taken pagan wives.

Pagan Wives Put Away

[18]And among the sons of the priests who had taken pagan wives *the following* were found of the sons of Jeshua the son of Jozadak,[a] and his brothers: Maaseiah, Eliezer, Jarib, and Gedaliah. [19]And they gave their promise that they would put away their wives; and *being* guilty, *they presented* a ram of the flock as their trespass offering.

[20]Also of the sons of Immer: Hanani and Zebadiah; [21]of the sons of Harim: Maaseiah, Elijah, Shemaiah, Jehiel, and Uzziah; [22]of the sons of Pashhur: Elioenai, Maaseiah, Ishmael, Nethanel, Jozabad, and Elasah.

[23]Also of the Levites: Jozabad, Shimei, Kelaiah (the same *is* Kelita), Pethahiah, Judah, and Eliezer.

[24]Also of the singers: Eliashib; and of the gatekeepers: Shallum, Telem, and Uri.

[25]And others of Israel: of the sons of Parosh: Ramiah, Jeziah, Malchiah, Mijamin, Eleazar, Malchijah, and Benaiah; [26]of the sons of Elam: Mattaniah, Zechariah, Jehiel, Abdi, Jeremoth, and Eliah; [27]of the sons of Zattu: Elioenai, Eliashib, Mattaniah, Jeremoth, Zabad, and Aziza; [28]of the sons of Bebai: Jehohanan, Hananiah, Zabbai, *and* Athlai; [29]of the sons of Bani: Meshullam, Malluch, Adaiah, Jashub, Sheal, *and* Ramoth;[a] [30]of the sons of Pahath-Moab: Adna, Chelal, Benaiah, Maaseiah, Mattaniah, Bezalel,

---

10:18 [a]Spelled *Jehozadak* in 1 Chronicles 6:14   **10:29** [a]Or *Jeremoth*

Jehiel in verse 26 (see also v. 44), Shechaniah may have been consumed with guilt and concern about the actions of his own relative. Feeling guilt from disobedience or perhaps feeling that such marriages were invalid, he suggested his own plan to right the wrong done. He asked the people to dissolve their mixed marriages and send away their pagan wives as well as the children born to these mixed unions. Evidently Shechaniah believed this radical action was essential to reestablish a holy people.

This requirement for the Jews to divorce their pagan wives is not easy to understand. Divorce did occur in OT times (see Deut. 24:1–3). Many of these listed may have divorced their Jewish wives prior to marrying the pagan women (Mal. 2:10–16). However, we must be careful not to apply this means of describing how unfaithfulness in the OT was handled as prescribing a rule binding Christians in later generations (see Matt. 19, Divorce). Rather we must look to the clear and explicit instructions given in Scripture concerning God's plan for marriage (Gen. 2:24, note).

The Christian is not to leave an unbelieving spouse but rather to live in a manner that may win that spouse to the faith (1 Cor. 7:12–16; 1 Pet. 3:1–7). At the same time, the Bible warns the believer not to enter marriage with an unbeliever for one of the reasons that the Jews were not to do so—because it can weaken the faith of the believer. What is valuable and essential to a believer cannot be shared with an unbelieving spouse (see Neh. 10, Interfaith Marriage; 2 Cor. 6, Husbands).

Binnui, and Manasseh; ³¹*of* the sons of Harim: Eliezer, Ishijah, Malchijah, Shemaiah, Shimeon, ³²Benjamin, Malluch, *and* Shemariah; ³³of the sons of Hashum: Mattenai, Mattattah, Zabad, Eliphelet, Jeremai, Manasseh, *and* Shimei; ³⁴of the sons of Bani: Maadai, Amram, Uel, ³⁵Benaiah, Bedeiah, Cheluh,^a ³⁶Vaniah, Meremoth, Eliashib, ³⁷Mattaniah, Mattenai, Jaasai,^a ³⁸Bani, Binnui, Shimei, ³⁹Shelemiah, Nathan, Adaiah, ⁴⁰Mach-

nadebai, Shashai, Sharai, ⁴¹Azarel, Shelemiah, Shemariah, ⁴²Shallum, Amariah, *and* Joseph; ⁴³of the sons of Nebo: Jeiel, Mattithiah, Zabad, Zebina, Jaddai,^a Joel, *and* Benaiah.

⁴⁴All these had taken pagan wives, and *some* of them had wives *by whom* they had children.

• • • • • • • • • • • • • • • • •

10:35 ^aOr *Cheluhi*, or *Cheluhu*   **10:37** ^aOr *Jaasu*   **10:43** ^aOr *Jaddu*

Nehemiah

AUTHOR

Early Hebrew texts of the Old Testament (up to the fifteenth century A.D.) combined the books of Ezra and Nehemiah (also identified as Esdras B in the Greek Septuagint) and cited Ezra as the author, implying that Ezra also authored the work under the name of Nehemiah. However, many believe Nehemiah penned most of this book that bears his name.

The composite nature of the book suggests that it may have been put together from diverse lists and from Nehemiah's own memoirs of the great project of rebuilding the wall and the city of Jerusalem. His prayers are so markedly personal that they may have come from his own prayer journals. Detailed lists (ten are recorded in this book) show careful attention to people as individuals and to their jobs as being important efforts, preserved as mementos of the work of God.

Nehemiah was deeply moved when he heard of the dismal state of Jerusalem. Although he had achieved an influential position in the palace of the Persian King Artaxerxes I, he, like Moses, did not consider the luxuries of the palace as anything compared to the promises of God (Heb. 11:24–26). Nehemiah, as Queen Esther, must have believed that he had "come to the kingdom for such as time as this" (Esth. 4:14). As cupbearer to the king, he prayerfully but boldly asked for and received permission from the king to return to Jerusalem to rebuild the walls.

Throughout the book, Nehemiah displayed extraordinary leadership skills and abilities. He was a man of prayer who deeply depended on the Lord and knew how to draw strength and assurance from Him. He was a visionary who inspired others; yet he humbly worked alongside everyone else. He was steadfast under the pressures of an enormous task. He kept his priorities straight when confronting opposition, as well as when achieving success. In his humility, he was not afraid to admit and rectify his own mistakes. He was magnanimous and generous, sacrificially sharing from his table at his own expense. He refused to take advantage of his position to tax and burden the people. Nehemiah, whose name means the "the comfort of *Yahweh*," was a great leader who both blessed and comforted his people.

DATE

The events in this book span a period of approximately thirteen years from 446 B.C., when Nehemiah first heard about the condition of Jerusalem, until sometime after his second term as governor, when he returned to Jerusalem from Persia in 433 B.C. However, the book was probably written before the death of King Artaxerxes I in 424 B.C., since this important event was not mentioned. Thus the book was probably written sometime between 430 and 420 B.C.

SETTING: From the beginning, God had promised to bless the people of Israel if they obeyed Him and to curse them if they disobeyed Him. The periods of the captivities by the Assyrians (the northern kingdom fell in 722 B.C.), the Babylonians (the southern kingdom fell in 586 B.C.), and the Medo-Persians (they conquered the Babylonians in 539 B.C.) were times when God disciplined His people for their disobedience. The destruction and burning of Jerusalem and Solomon's temple by Nebuchadnezzar in 586 B.C. was a catastrophe that further threatened the worship of *Yahweh*. But the temple's destruction and its restoration seventy years later was predicted by Jeremiah the prophet (Jer. 25:11; 29:10) as assurance that God would preserve a faithful remnant of His people.

Although the Assyrians and Babylonians deported their captives to their empires, the Medo-Persians repatriated them. Thus, in 538 B.C. Cyrus issued orders to begin rebuilding the temple, and the first of three groups of postexilic Jews returned to Jerusalem under the leadership of Sheshbazzar and Zerubbabel. The temple was completed in 516 B.C. The second group returned in 458 B.C. with Ezra. In 445 B.C., King Artaxerxes I issued the decree for Nehemiah to lead the third group to begin the work of rebuilding the wall of Jerusalem.

This last decree of Artaxerxes I was of unique prophetic importance because it marked the beginning of the "seventy weeks" forecast by Daniel (Dan. 9:24–27). Understanding that the term "week" means "one week of years" or a period of seven years, this remarkable prophecy of Daniel marked the time from the decree to rebuild Jerusalem until the coming of the Messiah to be sixty-nine weeks (or 483 years). If these years are understood as Jewish lunar years of 360 days each, the sixty-nine week period would terminate in the precise year of the passion of Jesus (see chart, The Prophecy of Seventy Weeks).

PURPOSE: The Book of Nehemiah records not only the physical rebuilding of the wall but also the spiritual restoration of the people of Jerusalem. Nehemiah's reforms helped to preserve Jewish identity, protecting it from compromise with the pagan community until the arrival of the promised seed of Abraham, Jesus the Messiah. This book was the last recorded history of Israel in the Old Testament before the silent years of the intertestamental period.

Nehemiah was a man of prayer. Ten recorded prayers range from the quick "arrow prayer" (Neh. 2:4) to the Bible's longest recorded prayer (Neh. 9; see also chart, Solomon's Prayer). There are prayers of confession and repentance, delivered in mourning with sackcloth and ashes, and prayers of praise and adoration, delivered with jubilant singing and musical instruments. There are prayers of supplication in weakness (Neh. 6:9) and prayers for God's judgment on Nehemiah's enemies (Neh. 4:4, 5). Above all, Nehemiah desired the approval of God more than the approval of people.

The walk of faith is a balanced blend of prayer and action. Nehemiah prayed and then put his request before the king (Neh. 2:4, 5); he prayed and then "set a watch" (Neh. 4:9). He exhorted the people to "remember the Lord . . . and fight" (Neh. 4:14).

The opposition of enemies and spiritual warfare are inevitable when people are doing the work of God. Satan's purpose is to destroy God's people and God's work. Satan's tactics as seen in Nehemiah include: ridicule, slander, opposition from within and without, oppression and unrighteousness, discouragement, demoralization, distraction, and physical threat. Nehemiah combated these tactics with continual prayer, single-mindedness, wisdom, and righteous living. God's people in every age must employ these same weapons.

Becoming entrapped by sin through compromise (such as intermarriage with unbelievers) is easy, but escaping from that sin and its consequences can be difficult (see, for example, Tobiah's room in the temple, Neh. 13:4, 5).

Nehemiah Prays for His People

1 The words of Nehemiah the son of Hachaliah.
It came to pass in the month of Chislev, *in the* twentieth year, as I was in Shushan[a] the citadel, ²that Hanani one of my brethren came with men from Judah; and I asked them concerning the Jews who had escaped, who had survived the captivity, and concerning Jerusalem. ³And they said to me, "The survivors who are left from the captivity in the province *are* there in great distress and reproach. The wall of Jerusalem *is* also broken down, and its gates are burned with fire."

⁴So it was, when I heard these words, that I sat down and wept, and mourned *for many* days; I was fasting and praying before the God of heaven.

⁵And I said: "I pray, LORD God of heaven, O great and awesome God, *You* who keep *Your* covenant and mercy with those who love You[a] and observe Your[b] commandments, ⁶please let Your ear be attentive and Your eyes open, that You may hear the prayer of Your servant which I pray before You now, day and night, for the children of Israel Your servants, and confess the sins of the children of Israel which we have sinned against You. Both my father's house and I have sinned. ⁷We have acted very corruptly against You, and have not kept the commandments, the statutes, nor the ordinances which You commanded Your servant Moses. ⁸Remember, I pray, the word that You commanded Your servant Moses, saying, '*If* you are unfaithful, I will scatter you among the nations;[a] ⁹but *if* you return to Me, and keep My commandments and do them, though some of you were cast out to the farthest part of the heavens, *yet* I will gather them from there, and bring them to the place which I have chosen as a dwelling for My name.'[a] ¹⁰Now these *are* Your servants and Your people, whom You have redeemed by Your great power, and by Your

1:1 [a]Or *Susa* 1:5 [a]Literally *Him* [b]Literally *His* 1:8 [a]Leviticus 26:33
1:9 [a]Deuteronomy 30:2–5

1:1 The month of Chislev was November–December (see chart, The Jewish Sacred Calendar). King Artaxerxes I reigned from 465–424 B.C.; thus his "twentieth year" would be 445 B.C. His father was King Ahasuerus or Xerxes I, the husband of Queen Esther. The city of "Shushan" was the winter resort of the Persian kings and the place where Daniel had his vision more than 100 years earlier (Dan. 8:2).

1:3 A city without a wall was one with no security. Where the condition of the city walls was seen an indication of the strength of the people's gods, the state of the wall was a source of "reproach" from their neighbors for Yahweh, the God of the Hebrews.

1:4 Nehemiah equated the state of the wall with the state of his people's obedience to the Lord. He was grieved for God's reputation.

1:5 Nehemiah prayed a God-centered prayer, referring to God 34 times by name or pronoun. This classic prayer included adoration, confession, remembrance of God's commitment to His people, and petition (see also chart, Solomon's Prayer).

I can learn, with God's power and motivation, to daily make the choices that will lead me toward my goal of being a godly wife.

Linda Dillow

strong hand. [11]O Lord, I pray, please let Your ear be attentive to the prayer of Your servant, and to the prayer of Your servants who desire to fear Your name; and let Your servant prosper this day, I pray, and grant him mercy in the sight of this man."

For I was the king's cupbearer.

Nehemiah Sent to Judah

2 And it came to pass in the month of Nisan, in the twentieth year of King Artaxerxes, *when* wine *was* before him, that I took the wine and gave it to the king. Now I had never been sad in his presence before. [2]Therefore the king said to me, "Why *is* your face sad, since you *are* not sick? This *is* nothing but sorrow of heart."

So I became dreadfully afraid, [3]and said to the king, "May the king live forever! Why should my face not be sad, when the city, the place of my fathers' tombs, *lies* waste, and its gates are burned with fire?"

[4]Then the king said to me, "What do you request?"

So I prayed to the God of heaven. [5]And I said to the king, "If it pleases the king, and if your servant has found favor in your sight, I ask that you send me to Judah, to the city of my fathers' tombs, that I may rebuild it."

[6]Then the king said to me (the queen also sitting beside him), "How long will your journey be? And when will you return?" So it pleased the king to send me; and I set him a time.

[7]Furthermore I said to the king, "If it pleases the king, let letters be given to me for the governors *of the region* beyond the River,[a] that they must permit me to pass through till I come to Judah, [8]and a letter to Asaph the keeper of the king's forest, that he must give me timber to make beams for the gates of the citadel which *pertains* to the temple,[a] for the city wall, and for the house that I will occupy." And the king granted *them* to me according to the good hand of my God upon me.

[9]Then I went to the governors *in the region* beyond the River, and gave them the king's letters. Now the king had sent captains of the army and horsemen with me. [10]When Sanballat the Horonite and Tobiah the Ammonite official[a] heard *of it,* they were deeply disturbed that a man had

---

2:7 [a]That is, the Euphrates, and so elsewhere in this book   2:8 [a]Literally *house*   2:10 [a]Literally *servant,* and so elsewhere in this book

---

1:11 Nehemiah saw this whole endeavor from the spiritual perspective that God would initiate and accomplish His tasks to bring about His purposes through whomever He wished. Thus he revered the heavenly King far above the earthly one. Nehemiah had the trusted position of serving wine and of making sure it was not poisoned by tasting it first himself. This job allowed him to be present at top-level conferences and privy to state secrets as well as to the personal affairs of the king.

2:1 The month of Nisan was in March–April (see chart, The Jewish Sacred Calendar).

2:4 The quick prayer that Nehemiah prayed between the king's question and his own answer is often referred to as the "arrow prayer" because it was direct and to the point.

2:5 Treachery from governors of captive lands was common. The king's father Ahasuerus was killed in his private apartment by one of his own staff. Thus the king showed great trust and respect for Nehemiah in appointing this cupbearer to be the governor and rebuilder of Jerusalem.

2:6 Damaspia was the "queen," according to Greek historical sources. Mention of her presence may have meant that this was a private moment, as the queen did not usually attend public banquets (see Esth. 1:3, 9). Her presence may indicate her influence on the decision since women did have a strong influence in the court, or she could have been asked to witness the transaction (see Esth. 8).

2:7 While Ezra's return to Jerusalem was a religious mission, Nehemiah's return officially was a political one. Ezra went without any political protection (see Ezra 8). As the appointed governor of Jerusalem, Nehemiah had the king's letters assuring him safe passage. Otherwise, he probably would not have made it past Sanballat, the governor of Samaria, who opposed the work of Nehemiah (Neh. 2:10; 4:1).

2:10 Sanballat (Akkadian, *Sin-uballit,* lit. "Sin," the moon god, "has given life") was the governor of Samaria to the north of Jerusalem (Neh. 4:1, 2). He was a Horonite and may have been a syncretistic follower of the god of Horon and a native of Upper or Lower Beth Horon. His ancestry was from the mixed group that settled in Samaria after the Assyrian conquest. According to earlier Babylonian rule, Jerusalem and parts of Judah had been given to Samaria as territory; so Sanballat was loath to see it slip from his grasp. Tobiah (Heb., lit. *"Yahweh* is good"), who was referred to contemptuously as the Ammonite, may have been the governor of Ammon to the east of Jerusalem. He probably was at least half-Jewish. His syncretism and relationships through marriage gave him insidious access to privileged places (see Neh. 6:18; 13:4–7).

The response of Nehemiah when he heard of the neglected condition of the wall (Neh. 1:4) and the response of Sanballat and Tobiah when they heard that someone had come to rebuild the wall were the same: They were "deeply disturbed," though for entirely different reasons.

VOLUNTEERS WILLING SERVICE

The words "Here am I! Send me" (Is. 6:8) are the volunteer's motto. The Book of Nehemiah may be considered the volunteer's handbook. In rebuilding the walls of Jerusalem, Nehemiah demonstrates these principles of divinely inspired and highly effective volunteerism:

1. Recognize a project and make it your own (Neh. 1:3, 4).
2. Pray about the project (Neh. 1:4–11).
3. Determine how you are uniquely positioned to participate in the project (Neh. 1:11).
4. Bring the project to the attention of those in authority and gain their permission to pursue it (Neh. 2:1–10).
5. Gather information about the project (vv. 11–16).
6. Report your findings to maintain accountability and arouse interest (vv. 17–20).
7. Inspire others to join your cause (vv. 17, 18).
8. Organize others to help you do the work (Neh. 3:1–32).
9. Confront opposition directly and turn to God when discouraged (Neh. 4:1–23).
10. Celebrate what is accomplished and give God the glory (Neh. 12:27–47).

To offer ourselves freely to the kingdom's work provides great joy and needful service (Matt. 10:8; Gal. 5:13). See also Judg. 7:2–7; notes on Sacrificial Living (Mic. 7); Servanthood (Mark 10); Spiritual Gifts (Rom. 12); Time Management (Ps. 31); Women's Ministries (John 4; Acts 2; 1 Cor. 11; Eph. 2; 1 Tim. 3; Titus 2)

come to seek the well-being of the children of Israel.

Nehemiah Views the Wall of Jerusalem

¹¹So I came to Jerusalem and was there three days. ¹²Then I arose in the night, I and a few men with me; I told no one what my God had put in my heart to do at Jerusalem; nor was there any animal with me, except the one on which I rode. ¹³And I went out by night through the Valley Gate to the Serpent Well and the Refuse Gate, and viewed the walls of Jerusalem which were broken down and its gates which were burned with fire. ¹⁴Then I went on to the Fountain Gate and to the King's Pool, but *there was* no room for the animal under me to pass. ¹⁵So I went up in the night by the valley, and viewed the wall; then I turned back and entered by the Valley Gate, and so returned. ¹⁶And the officials did not know where I had gone or what I had done; I had not yet told the Jews, the priests, the nobles, the officials, or the others who did the work.

¹⁷Then I said to them, "You see the distress that we *are* in, how Jerusalem *lies* waste, and its gates are burned with fire. Come and let us build the wall of Jerusalem, that we may no longer be a reproach." ¹⁸And I told them of the hand of my God which had been good upon me, and also of the king's words that he had spoken to me.

So they said, "Let us rise up and build." Then they set their hands to *this* good *work*.

¹⁹But when Sanballat the Horonite, Tobiah the Ammonite official, and Geshem the Arab heard *of it,* they laughed at us and despised us, and said, "What *is* this thing that you are doing? Will you rebel against the king?"

²⁰So I answered them, and said to them, "The God of heaven Himself will prosper us; therefore we His servants will arise and build, but you have no heritage or right or memorial in Jerusalem."

Rebuilding the Wall

3 Then Eliashib the high priest rose up with his brethren the priests and built the Sheep Gate;

2:12 Nehemiah made a private nocturnal inspection of the wall (see also v. 16). As a discerning governor, he may have wanted to keep his enemies from knowing his plans. As a capable leader, he may have wanted to assess personally and privately the work that needed to be done. As a man of prayer, he may have wanted a time of solitude in which to dedicate himself and the site to God.

2:19 Geshem was probably the most powerful of the three enemies of Nehemiah. He is probably the man who, with his son, Kain, king of Kedor, united the northern Arabian tribes, extending their rule to Moab on the east and to Edom on the south of Jerusalem, along with territories near Egypt. Nehemiah and his countrymen were thus surrounded by hostile

neighbors to the north (Sanballat), to the east (Tobiah), and to the south (Geshem). The first attack on Nehemiah's work was ridicule and slander. Nehemiah repudiated his enemies as having "no heritage" or inheritance in Israel, no "right" or legal position over Jerusalem regardless of past treaties, and no "memorial" (or control over worship in the temple). This eliminated past, present, and future ties with Jerusalem.

3:1 Some forty sections of the wall are mentioned, showing Nehemiah's careful detailed planning of the project. Archaeologists have found that some parts of the rebuilt wall were as thick as eight feet. Since breaking down a gate was easier than destroying a piece of the wall, areas around the gates needed special repair and reinforcement.

they consecrated it and hung its doors. They built as far as the Tower of the Hundred,[a] *and* consecrated it, then as far as the Tower of Hananel. [2]Next to *Eliashib*[a] the men of Jericho built. And next to them Zaccur the son of Imri built.

[3]Also the sons of Hassenaah built the Fish Gate; they laid its beams and hung its doors with its bolts and bars. [4]And next to them Meremoth the son of Urijah, the son of Koz,[a] made repairs. Next to them Meshullam the son of Berechiah, the son of Meshezabel, made repairs. Next to them Zadok the son of Baana made repairs. [5]Next to them the Tekoites made repairs; but their nobles did not put their shoulders[a] to the work of their Lord.

[6]Moreover Jehoiada the son of Paseah and Meshullam the son of Besodeiah repaired the Old Gate; they laid its beams and hung its doors, with its bolts and bars. [7]And next to them Melatiah the Gibeonite, Jadon the Meronothite, the men of Gibeon and Mizpah, repaired the residence[a] of the governor *of the region* beyond the River. [8]Next to him Uzziel the son of Harhaiah, one of the goldsmiths, made repairs. Also next to him Hananiah, one[a] of the perfumers, made repairs; and they fortified Jerusalem as far as the Broad Wall. [9]And next to them Rephaiah the son of Hur, leader of half the district of Jerusalem, made repairs. [10]Next to them Jedaiah the son of Harumaph made repairs in front of his house. And next to him Hattush the son of Hashabniah made repairs.

[11]Malchijah the son of Harim and Hashub the son of Pahath-Moab repaired another section, as well as the Tower of the Ovens. [12]And next to him was Shallum the son of Hallohesh, leader of half the district of Jerusalem; he and his daughters made repairs.

[13]Hanun and the inhabitants of Zanoah repaired the Valley Gate. They built it, hung its doors with its bolts and bars, and *repaired* a thousand cubits of the wall as far as the Refuse Gate.

[14]Malchijah the son of Rechab, leader of the district of Beth Haccerem, repaired the Refuse Gate; he built it and hung its doors with its bolts and bars.

[15]Shallun the son of Col-Hozeh, leader of the district of Mizpah, repaired the Fountain Gate; he built it, covered it, hung its doors with its bolts

and bars, and repaired the wall of the Pool of Shelah by the King's Garden, as far as the stairs that go down from the City of David. [16]After him Nehemiah the son of Azbuk, leader of half the district of Beth Zur, made repairs as far as *the place* in front of the tombs[a] of David, to the man-made pool, and as far as the House of the Mighty.

[17]After him the Levites, *under* Rehum the son of Bani, made repairs. Next to him Hashabiah, leader of half the district of Keilah, made repairs for his district. [18]After him their brethren, *under* Bavai[a] the son of Henadad, leader of the *other* half of the district of Keilah, made repairs. [19]And next to him Ezer the son of Jeshua, the leader of Mizpah, repaired another section in front of the Ascent to the Armory at the buttress. [20]After him Baruch the son of Zabbai[a] carefully repaired the other section, from the buttress to the door of the house of Eliashib the high priest. [21]After him Meremoth the son of Urijah, the son of Koz,[a] repaired another section, from the door of the house of Eliashib to the end of the house of Eliashib.

[22]And after him the priests, the men of the plain, made repairs. [23]After him Benjamin and Hasshub made repairs opposite their house. After them Azariah the son of Maaseiah, the son of Ananiah, made repairs by his house. [24]After him Binnui the son of Henadad repaired another section, from the house of Azariah to the buttress, even as far as the corner. [25]Palal the son of Uzai *made repairs* opposite the buttress, and on the tower which projects from the king's upper house that *was* by the court of the prison. After him Pedaiah the son of Parosh *made repairs*.

[26]Moreover the Nethinim who dwelt in Ophel *made repairs* as far as *the place* in front of the Water Gate toward the east, and on the projecting tower. [27]After them the Tekoites repaired another section, next to the great projecting tower, and as far as the wall of Ophel.

3:1 [a]Hebrew *Hammeah*, also at 12:39   **3:2** [a]Literally *On his hand*   **3:4** [a]Or *Hakkoz*   **3:5** [a]Literally *necks*   **3:7** [a]Literally *throne*   **3:8** [a]Literally *the son*   **3:16** [a]Septuagint, Syriac, and Vulgate read *tomb*. **3:18** [a]Following Masoretic Text and Vulgate; some Hebrew manuscripts, Septuagint, and Syriac read *Binnui* (compare verse 24). **3:20** [a]A few Hebrew manuscripts, Syriac, and Vulgate read *Zaccai*. **3:21** [a]Or *Hakkoz*

The description of the rebuilding of the wall began with the high priest, Eliashib, showing the centrality of his position within the community. He rebuilt the "Sheep Gate," which was nearest the temple, the place through which the sacrifical sheep were brought. Eliashib was the son of Joiakim, the son of Jeshua who first went to Jerusalem with Zerubbabel. His grandson married Sanballat's daughter (see Neh. 13:28).

3:5 Unenthusiastic workers. Perhaps the "Tekoite" nobles did not work enthusiastically because they feared repercussions from Sanballat.

3:10 The wall was repaired. "Made repairs" (lit. "to make firm or strong") did not necessarily mean that they rebuilt the wall from scratch or restored it to the way it was.

Nehemiah assigned each person to work "in front of his house," which inspired each to do a good job as he saw the benefit to himself and his family. In this way, work progressed at various points along the wall simultaneously, instead of leaving huge unattended gaps that would pose a security risk.

3:12 Women worked on the wall of Jerusalem, carrying out a difficult and dangerous task. The contribution of the daughters of Shallum was valuable.

[28]Beyond the Horse Gate the priests made repairs, each in front of his *own* house. [29]After them Zadok the son of Immer made repairs in front of his *own* house. After him Shemaiah the son of Shechaniah, the keeper of the East Gate, made repairs. [30]After him Hananiah the son of Shelemiah, and Hanun, the sixth son of Zalaph, repaired another section. After him Meshullam the son of Berechiah made repairs in front of his dwelling. [31]After him Malchijah, one of the goldsmiths, made repairs as far as the house of the Nethinim and of the merchants, in front of the Miphkad[a] Gate, and as far as the upper room at the corner. [32]And between the upper room at the corner, as far as the Sheep Gate, the goldsmiths and the merchants made repairs.

The Wall Defended Against Enemies

4 But it so happened, when Sanballat heard that we were rebuilding the wall, that he was furious and very indignant, and mocked the Jews. [2]And he spoke before his brethren and the army of Samaria, and said, "What are these feeble Jews doing? Will they fortify themselves? Will they offer sacrifices? Will they complete it in a day? Will they revive the stones from the heaps of rubbish— stones that are burned?"

[3]Now Tobiah the Ammonite *was* beside him, and he said, "Whatever they build, if even a fox goes up *on it,* he will break down their stone wall."

[4]Hear, O our God, for we are despised; turn their reproach on their own heads, and give them as plunder to a land of captivity! [5]Do not cover their iniquity, and do not let their sin be blotted out from before You; for they have provoked *You* to anger before the builders.

[6]So we built the wall, and the entire wall was joined together up to half its *height,* for the people had a mind to work.

[7]Now it happened, when Sanballat, Tobiah, the Arabs, the Ammonites, and the Ashdodites heard that the walls of Jerusalem were being restored and the gaps were beginning to be closed, that they became very angry, [8]and all of them conspired together to come *and* attack Jerusalem and create confusion. [9]Nevertheless we made our prayer to our God, and because of them we set a watch against them day and night.

[10]Then Judah said, "The strength of the laborers is failing, and *there is* so much rubbish that we are not able to build the wall."

[11]And our adversaries said, "They will neither know nor see anything, till we come into their midst and kill them and cause the work to cease."

[12]So it was, when the Jews who dwelt near them came, that they told us ten times, "From whatever place you turn, *they will be* upon us."

[13]Therefore I positioned *men* behind the lower parts of the wall, at the openings; and I set the people according to their families, with their swords, their spears, and their bows. [14]And I looked, and arose and said to the nobles, to the leaders, and to the rest of the people, "Do not be afraid of them. Remember the Lord, great and awesome, and fight for your brethren, your sons, your daughters, your wives, and your houses."

[15]And it happened, when our enemies heard that it was known to us, and *that* God had brought their plot to nothing, that all of us returned to the wall, everyone to his work. [16]So it was, from that time on, *that* half of my servants worked at construction, while the other half held the spears, the shields, the bows, and *wore* armor; and the leaders *were* behind all the house of Judah. [17]Those who built on the wall, and those who carried burdens, loaded themselves so that with one hand they worked at construction, and with the other held a weapon. [18]Every one of the builders had his sword girded at his side as he built. And the one who sounded the trumpet *was* beside me. [19]Then I said to the nobles, the rulers, and the rest of the people, "The work *is* great and extensive, and we are separated far from one another on the wall. [20]Wherever you hear the sound of the trumpet, rally to us there. Our God will fight for us."

3:31 [a]Literally *Inspection* or *Recruiting*

4:1–5 Nehemiah's enemies tried to discourage the people by pointing out the immensity of the task and the weakness of the Jews. They were called "feeble" (lit. "withering or fading" or "hopeless"), but Nehemiah instead placed his hope in his God who hears and judges. When Nehemiah asked God to judge his enemies unmercifully, he was motivated more from spiritual than patriotic reasons. The enemies of God's people were the enemies of God.

4:7 Jerusalem was surrounded by enemies. The "Ashdodites" were the Philistines west of Jerusalem who became part of the Assyrian empire in 711 B.C. Thus Jerusalem was completely surrounded by her enemies: the Samaritans to the north, the Ammonites to the east, the Arabs to the south, and the Ashdodites to the west.

4:8–23 When Nehemiah's enemies realized that ridicule, slander, and discouragement did not dissuade the Jews from their work, they took a more direct approach. They planned to harm them physically. Nehemiah prayed and wisely took precautions to "set a watch." He armed and posted people in family groups at strategic areas on the wall, encouraging them to "remember the Lord . . . and fight" for their families. Half of the workers were full-time guards while the other half worked bearing arms. They worked with one hand on their weapons and slept in their clothes as a sign of the seriousness of the threat. The balance of faith with work, prayer with precaution, and trust with action is seen most graphically here.

4:20 Just as a person would rally the troops to fight a battle, he would alert people to pray, especially in times of danger or great need. This person is an invaluable link—whether in battle or prayer.

SPIRITUAL WARFARE: STRATEGIES

THE STRATEGIES OF NEHEMIAH	THE PLOYS OF HIS ENEMIES
He took up the work of God (Neh. 2:6–9).	They ridiculed him (Neh. 2:19).
He prayed, acknowledging God's sovereignty and noting the illegitimacy of his enemies (Neh. 2:20).	They mocked him (Neh. 4:1, 2).
He prayed, asking God to take note of his reproach and to refuse to forgive his enemies (Neh. 4:4, 5).	They conspired to attack and create confusion (Neh. 4:7, 8).
He prayed and set a watch (Neh. 4:9), taking necessary precautions (Neh. 4:13), reminding people to fight for their families (Neh. 4:14).	They used oppression from within, the fruit of their own unrighteousness (Neh. 5:1–5).
He led the people to confess, repent, and make restitution (Neh. 5:1–19).	They plotted to harm the leader (Neh. 6:1, 2).
He showed singlemindedness (Neh. 6:3).	They created a distraction (Neh. 6:4) and circulated slander to create fear (Neh. 6:5–7).
He refuted their slander (Neh. 6:8) and prayed for strength (Neh. 6:9).	They developed an insider plot to discredit the leader (Neh. 6:10).
He modeled righteousness (Neh. 6:11), received God's discernment (Neh. 6:12), and prayed, asking God to remember them (Neh. 6:14).	They used covert connections as Tobiah sent letters to frighten Nehemiah and desensitize the people (Neh. 6:19).
He suggested precautions for protecting the gates (Neh. 7:3).	They established insider alliances; Eliashib gave room to Tobiah (Neh. 13:4, 5).
He expelled the household goods of the enemy (Neh. 13:8).	They continued acts of unrighteousness (Neh. 13:10, 15, 16).
He contended with unrighteousness (Neh. 13:11, 17, 25, 28).	They used compromise, especially in intermarriage (Neh. 13:23–25).

Spiritual warfare begins when the enemy (Satan) perceives that someone is trying to seek God's purposes or to protect the well-being of God's people. Nehemiah drew the attention of his enemies, Sanballat and Tobiah, who were "deeply disturbed" when he began the work of rebuilding the walls of Jerusalem. They employed a variety of strategies to divert Nehemiah from his task. These strategies of the enemy have been used through the generations, even until now. Nehemiah's counterstrategies helped him to persevere and to finish his task. See also Eph. 6:10–19; notes on Adversity (Acts 5); Perseverance (Rev. 14); Spiritual Warfare (Eph. 6); Temptation (Heb. 2).

²¹So we labored in the work, and half of *the men*[a] held the spears from daybreak until the stars appeared. ²²At the same time I also said to the people, "Let each man and his servant stay at night in Jerusalem, that they may be our guard by night and a working party by day." ²³So neither I, my brethren, my servants, nor the men of the

4:21 [a]Literally *them*

4:22 **If people were allowed to return to the neighboring villages** for the night, they could easily be captured by the enemy. Also, movement in and out of the city might well provide opportunity for enemy infiltration.

guard who followed me took off our clothes, *except* that everyone took them off for washing.

Nehemiah Deals with Oppression

5 And there was a great outcry of the people and their wives against their Jewish brethren. ²For there were those who said, "We, our sons, and our daughters *are* many; therefore let us get grain, that we may eat and live."

³There were also *some* who said, "We have mortgaged our lands and vineyards and houses, that we might buy grain because of the famine."

⁴There were also those who said, "We have borrowed money for the king's tax *on* our lands and vineyards. ⁵Yet now our flesh *is* as the flesh of our brethren, our children as their children; and indeed we are forcing our sons and our daughters to be slaves, and *some* of our daughters have been brought into slavery. *It is* not in our power *to redeem them*, for other men have our lands and vineyards."

⁶And I became very angry when I heard their outcry and these words. ⁷After serious thought, I rebuked the nobles and rulers, and said to them, "Each of you is exacting usury from his brother." So I called a great assembly against them. ⁸And I said to them, "According to our ability we have redeemed our Jewish brethren who were sold to the nations. Now indeed, will you even sell your brethren? Or should they be sold to us?"

Then they were silenced and found nothing *to say.* ⁹Then I said, "What you are doing *is* not good. Should you not walk in the fear of our God because of the reproach of the nations, our enemies? ¹⁰I also, *with* my brethren and my servants, am lending them money and grain. Please, let us stop this usury! ¹¹Restore now to them, even this day, their lands, their vineyards, their olive groves, and their houses, also a hundredth of the money and the grain, the new wine and the oil, that you have charged them."

¹²So they said, "We will restore *it*, and will require nothing from them; we will do as you say."

Then I called the priests, and required an oath from them that they would do according to this promise. ¹³Then I shook out the fold of my garmentª and said, "So may God shake out each man from his house, and from his property, who does not perform this promise. Even thus may he be shaken out and emptied."

And all the assembly said, "Amen!" and praised the LORD. Then the people did according to this promise.

The Generosity of Nehemiah

¹⁴Moreover, from the time that I was appointed to be their governor in the land of Judah, from the twentieth year until the thirty-second year of King Artaxerxes, twelve years, neither I nor my brothers ate the governor's provisions. ¹⁵But the former governors who *were* before me laid burdens on the people, and took from them bread and wine, besides forty shekels of silver. Yes, even their servants bore rule over the people, but I did not do so, because of the fear of God. ¹⁶Indeed, I also continued the work on this wall, and weª did not buy any land. All my servants *were* gathered there for the work.

¹⁷And at my table *were* one hundred and fifty Jews and rulers, besides those who came to us from the nations around us. ¹⁸Now *that* which was prepared daily *was* one ox *and* six choice sheep. Also fowl were prepared for me, and once every ten days an abundance of all kinds of wine. Yet in spite of this I did not demand the governor's provisions, because the bondage was heavy on this people.

¹⁹Remember me, my God, for good, *according to* all that I have done for this people.

·················

5:13 ªLiterally *my lap*   5:16 ªFollowing Masoretic Text; Septuagint, Syriac, and Vulgate read *I*.

5:1 Although women usually stayed in the background, they are specifically mentioned in this protest. The economic problems of scarcity of food and heavy taxation were overwhelming (vv. 2–4). Perhaps this was due to the great stress upon them as they maintained homes and farms while their husbands worked and slept in Jerusalem (vv. 2, 3). Perhaps it was because the situation was so desperate that their own "children," and especially some daughters were sold into slavery (v. 5). Such unrighteous times demanded justice and awakened a cry from the women.

5:3–5 The people paid taxes to the king, the satrap of the province, the local governor, and a tithe to the temple. The heavy taxation burden forced many to borrow or mortgage their land and themselves to fellow Jews, who were harsh and exacting. The careful guidelines of Levitical law were clearly violated during these times (Ex. 21:7–11; 22:25–27; Lev. 25:39, 40; Deut. 24:10–13).

5:10 When faced with his own participation in the wrongdo-ing, Nehemiah did not try to cover up or make excuses. While he confessed to lending money, there is no indication that he participated in debt slavery. He insisted on the immediate reversal of the situation instead of waiting until the year of release (Deut. 15:1–6). He did not allow oppression from within to become a foothold for the opposition from without. Again he demonstrated his leadership in his willingness to admit a mistake and change.

5:11 A hundredth of the money charged was an interest rate of 1 percent monthly or 12 percent annually.

5:14 Nehemiah was governor of Jerusalem for 12 years; then he returned to the Persian court. He later came back to Jerusalem for a second term of unknown length.

5:17 Nehemiah's choice to refrain from taxing the people for his governor's food allotment was unprecedented throughout the Persian Empire and proved that he was truly seeking "the well-being of the children of Israel" (see Neh. 2:10).

Conspiracy Against Nehemiah

6 Now it happened when Sanballat, Tobiah, Geshem the Arab, and the rest of our enemies heard that I had rebuilt the wall, and *that* there were no breaks left in it (though at that time I had not hung the doors in the gates), ²that Sanballat and Geshem sent to me, saying, "Come, let us meet together among the villages in the plain of Ono." But they thought to do me harm.

³So I sent messengers to them, saying, "I *am* doing a great work, so that I cannot come down. Why should the work cease while I leave it and go down to you?"

⁴But they sent me this message four times, and I answered them in the same manner.

⁵Then Sanballat sent his servant to me as before, the fifth time, with an open letter in his hand. ⁶In it *was* written:

It is reported among the nations, and Geshem[a] says, *that* you and the Jews plan to rebel; therefore, according to these rumors, you are rebuilding the wall, that you may be their king. ⁷And you have also appointed prophets to proclaim concerning you at Jerusalem, saying, "*There is* a king in Judah!" Now these matters will be reported to the king. So come, therefore, and let us consult together.

⁸Then I sent to him, saying, "No such things as you say are being done, but you invent them in your own heart."

⁹For they all *were trying to* make us afraid, saying, "Their hands will be weakened in the work, and it will not be done."

Now therefore, *O God,* strengthen my hands.

¹⁰Afterward I came to the house of Shemaiah the son of Delaiah, the son of Mehetabel, who *was* a secret informer; and he said, "Let us meet to-gether in the house of God, within the temple, and let us close the doors of the temple, for they are coming to kill you; indeed, at night they will come to kill you."

¹¹And I said, "Should such a man as I flee? And who *is there* such as I who would go into the temple to save his life? I will not go in!" ¹²Then I perceived that God had not sent him at all, but that he pronounced *this* prophecy against me because Tobiah and Sanballat had hired him. ¹³For this reason he *was* hired, that I should be afraid and act that way and sin, so *that* they might have *cause* for an evil report, that they might reproach me.

¹⁴My God, remember Tobiah and Sanballat, according to these their works, and the prophetess Noadiah and the rest of the prophets who would have made me afraid.

The Wall Completed

¹⁵So the wall was finished on the twenty-fifth *day* of Elul, in fifty-two days. ¹⁶And it happened, when all our enemies heard *of it,* and all the nations around us saw *these things,* that they were very disheartened in their own eyes; for they perceived that this work was done by our God.

¹⁷Also in those days the nobles of Judah sent many letters to Tobiah, and *the letters of* Tobiah came to them. ¹⁸For many in Judah were pledged to him, because he was the son-in-law of Shechaniah the son of Arah, and his son Jehohanan had married the daughter of Meshullam the son of Berechiah. ¹⁹Also they reported his good deeds before me, and reported my words to him. Tobiah sent letters to frighten me.

7 Then it was, when the wall was built and I had hung the doors, when the gatekeepers, the

6:6 [a]Hebrew *Gashmu*

6:2 The plain of Ono was about 25 miles northwest of Jerusalem and was probably a neutral territory used to entice Nehemiah.

6:5–9 Sanballat's accusation included slandering Nehemiah by accusing him of high treason, saying that he was rebuilding Jerusalem so that he could be declared the king. This kind of rumor once put an end to the work of rebuilding the temple (Ezra 4). The fact that Sanballat sent a letter showed his intent to demoralize the people of Jerusalem. The messianic reference to the prophets' presence showed Sanballat's understanding of the Jewish religion and put Nehemiah personally at risk.

6:10–13 Nehemiah's enemies tried to trick him into a compromising position by using a "secret informer." Nehemiah escaped this plot by refusing to do wrong in order to save his life since it was against the Levitical law for anyone but the priests to go into the Holy Place (see Num. 18:7). Besides, taking refuge in the temple would not protect him from foreign enemies. God gave Nehemiah special discernment to see through the plot.

6:14 The prophetess Noadiah is not mentioned elsewhere. Presumably she was among the group of false prophets who were eager to displace Nehemiah's godly influence.

6:15, 16 The wall was completed, about 2,600 meters long. Although most of the work was restorative, the whole eastern wall was built from its foundation. The 52–day completion was recognized by all of Jerusalem's neighbors as a supernatural feat and "disheartened" those who had earlier tried so hard to discourage Nehemiah.

6:18 Although Nehemiah's enemies were thwarted when the wall was rebuilt, they still had a toehold in Jerusalem because of intermarriages. Tobiah and his son took Jewish wives from influential families, which eventually enabled Tobiah to have a room inside the temple itself (see Neh. 13:4–7). Sanballat's daughter married a son of the high priest Eliashib (see Neh. 13:28). These, along with many other intermarriages, provided conduits to the enemy that would continue to plague the people.

singers, and the Levites had been appointed, [2]that I gave the charge of Jerusalem to my brother Hanani, and Hananiah the leader of the citadel, for he *was* a faithful man and feared God more than many.

[3]And I said to them, "Do not let the gates of Jerusalem be opened until the sun is hot; and while they stand *guard,* let them shut and bar the doors; and appoint guards from among the inhabitants of Jerusalem, one at his watch station and another in front of his own house."

The Captives Who Returned to Jerusalem

[4]Now the city *was* large and spacious, but the people in it *were* few, and the houses *were* not rebuilt. [5]Then my God put it into my heart to gather the nobles, the rulers, and the people, that they might be registered by genealogy. And I found a register of the genealogy of those who had come up in the first *return,* and found written in it:

[6]These[a] *are* the people of the province who came back from the captivity, of those who had been carried away, whom Nebuchadnezzar the king of Babylon had carried away, and who returned to Jerusalem and Judah, everyone to his city.

[7]Those who came with Zerubbabel *were* Jeshua, Nehemiah, Azariah, Raamiah, Nahamani, Mordecai, Bilshan, Mispereth,[a] Bigvai, Nehum, and Baanah.

The number of the men of the people of Israel: [8]the sons of Parosh, two thousand one hundred and seventy-two;

[9]the sons of Shephatiah, three hundred and seventy-two;

[10]the sons of Arah, six hundred and fifty-two;

[11]the sons of Pahath-Moab, of the sons of Jeshua and Joab, two thousand eight hundred and eighteen;

[12]the sons of Elam, one thousand two hundred and fifty-four;

[13]the sons of Zattu, eight hundred and forty-five;

[14]the sons of Zaccai, seven hundred and sixty;

[15]the sons of Binnui,[a] six hundred and forty-eight;

[16]the sons of Bebai, six hundred and twenty-eight;

[17]the sons of Azgad, two thousand three hundred and twenty-two;

[18]the sons of Adonikam, six hundred and sixty-seven;

[19]the sons of Bigvai, two thousand and sixty-seven;

[20]the sons of Adin, six hundred and fifty-five;

[21]the sons of Ater of Hezekiah, ninety-eight;

[22]the sons of Hashum, three hundred and twenty-eight;

[23]the sons of Bezai, three hundred and twenty-four;

[24]the sons of Hariph,[a] one hundred and twelve;

[25]the sons of Gibeon,[a] ninety-five;

[26]the men of Bethlehem and Netophah, one hundred and eighty-eight;

[27]the men of Anathoth, one hundred and twenty-eight;

[28]the men of Beth Azmaveth,[a] forty-two;

[29]the men of Kirjath Jearim, Chephirah, and Beeroth, seven hundred and forty-three;

[30]the men of Ramah and Geba, six hundred and twenty-one;

[31]the men of Michmas, one hundred and twenty-two;

[32]the men of Bethel and Ai, one hundred and twenty-three;

[33]the men of the other Nebo, fifty-two;

[34]the sons of the other Elam, one thousand two hundred and fifty-four;

[35]the sons of Harim, three hundred and twenty;

[36]the sons of Jericho, three hundred and forty-five;

[37]the sons of Lod, Hadid, and Ono, seven hundred and twenty-one;

[38]the sons of Senaah, three thousand nine hundred and thirty.

[39]The priests: the sons of Jedaiah, of the house of Jeshua, nine hundred and seventy-three;

[40]the sons of Immer, one thousand and fifty-two;

[41]the sons of Pashhur, one thousand two hundred and forty-seven;

[42]the sons of Harim, one thousand and seventeen.

[43]The Levites: the sons of Jeshua, of Kadmiel, *and* of the sons of Hodevah,[a] seventy-four.

[44]The singers: the sons of Asaph, one hundred and forty-eight.

[45]The gatekeepers: the sons of Shallum, the sons of Ater, the sons of Talmon, the sons of Akkub,

---

7:6 [a]Compare verses 6–72 with Ezra 2:1–70   7:7 [a]Spelled *Mispar* in Ezra 2:2   7:15 [a]Spelled *Bani* in Ezra 2:10   7:24 [a]Called *Jorah* in Ezra 2:18   7:25 [a]Called *Gibbar* in Ezra 2:20   7:28 [a]Called *Azmaveth* in Ezra 2:24   7:43 [a]Spelled *Hodaviah* in Ezra 2:40

7:3 The city gates were usually opened at dawn, but these special precautions were taken so that the people would not be victims of a surprise attack while they were sleeping or changing guard.

the sons of Hatita,
the sons of Shobai, one hundred and thirty-eight.

[46]The Nethinim: the sons of Ziha,
the sons of Hasupha,
the sons of Tabbaoth,
[47]the sons of Keros,
the sons of Sia,[a]
the sons of Padon,
[48]the sons of Lebana,[a]
the sons of Hagaba,[b]
the sons of Salmai,[c]
[49]the sons of Hanan,
the sons of Giddel,
the sons of Gahar,
[50]the sons of Reaiah,
the sons of Rezin,
the sons of Nekoda,
[51]the sons of Gazzam,
the sons of Uzza,
the sons of Paseah,
[52]the sons of Besai,
the sons of Meunim,
the sons of Nephishesim,[a]
[53]the sons of Bakbuk,
the sons of Hakupha,
the sons of Harhur,
[54]the sons of Bazlith,[a]
the sons of Mehida,
the sons of Harsha,
[55]the sons of Barkos,
the sons of Sisera,
the sons of Tamah,
[56]the sons of Neziah,
and the sons of Hatipha.

[57]The sons of Solomon's servants: the sons of Sotai,
the sons of Sophereth,
the sons of Perida,[a]
[58]the sons of Jaala,
the sons of Darkon,
the sons of Giddel,
[59]the sons of Shephatiah,
the sons of Hattil,
the sons of Pochereth of Zebaim,
and the sons of Amon.[a]
[60]All the Nethinim, and the sons of Solomon's servants, *were* three hundred and ninety-two.

[61]And these *were* the ones who came up from Tel Melah, Tel Harsha, Cherub, Addon,[a] and Immer, but they could not identify their father's house nor their lineage, whether they *were* of Israel: [62]the sons of Delaiah,
the sons of Tobiah,
the sons of Nekoda, six hundred and forty-two;
[63]and of the priests: the sons of Habaiah,
the sons of Koz,[a]
the sons of Barzillai, who took a wife of the daughters of Barzillai the Gileadite, and was called by their name.
[64]These sought their listing *among* those who were registered by genealogy, but it was not found; therefore they were excluded from the priesthood as defiled. [65]And the governor[a] said to them that they should not eat of the most holy things till a priest could consult with the Urim and Thummim.

[66]Altogether the whole assembly *was* forty-two thousand three hundred and sixty, [67]besides their male and female servants, of whom *there were* seven thousand three hundred and thirty-seven; and they had two hundred and forty-five men and women singers. [68]Their horses were seven hundred and thirty-six, their mules two hundred and forty-five, [69]*their* camels four hundred and thirty-five, *and* donkeys six thousand seven hundred and twenty.

[70]And some of the heads of the fathers' houses gave to the work. The governor[a] gave to the treasury one thousand gold drachmas, fifty basins, and five hundred and thirty priestly garments. [71]Some of the heads of the fathers' *houses* gave to the treasury of the work twenty thousand gold drachmas, and two thousand two hundred silver minas. [72]And that which the rest of the people gave *was* twenty thousand gold drachmas, two thousand silver minas, and sixty-seven priestly garments.

[73]So the priests, the Levites, the gatekeepers, the singers, *some* of the people, the Nethinim, and all Israel dwelt in their cities.

Ezra Reads the Law

When the seventh month came, the children of Israel *were* in their cities.

8Now all the people gathered together as one man in the open square that *was* in front of the

· · · · · · · · · · · · · · · · · ·

7:47 [a]Spelled *Siaha* in Ezra 2:44   7:48 [a]Masoretic Text reads *Lebanah.* [b]Masoretic Text reads *Hogabah.* [c]Or *Shalmai,* or *Shamlai*
7:52 [a]Spelled *Nephusim* in Ezra 2:50   7:54 [a]Spelled *Bazluth* in Ezra 2:52   7:57 [a]Spelled *Peruda* in Ezra 2:55   7:59 [a]Spelled *Ami* in Ezra 2:57   7:61 [a]Spelled *Addan* in Ezra 2:59   7:63 [a]Or *Hakkoz*   7:65, 70 [a]Hebrew *Tirshatha*

8:1–3 All heard the Law. Women and children, though they did not participate in regular temple functions, came together on such solemn occasions (see Deut. 31:12; Josh. 8:35). Presumably "all who could hear with understanding" referred to chil-dren old enough to understand. This rediscovery of the Word of God was evidently meant for everyone in the family. Many may never have heard it before this time.

Water Gate; and they told Ezra the scribe to bring the Book of the Law of Moses, which the LORD had commanded Israel. [2]So Ezra the priest brought the Law before the assembly of men and women and all who *could* hear with understanding on the first day of the seventh month. [3]Then he read from it in the open square that *was* in front of the Water Gate from morning until midday, before the men and women and those who could understand; and the ears of all the people *were attentive* to the Book of the Law.

[4]So Ezra the scribe stood on a platform of wood which they had made for the purpose; and beside him, at his right hand, stood Mattithiah, Shema, Anaiah, Urijah, Hilkiah, and Maaseiah; and at his left hand Pedaiah, Mishael, Malchijah, Hashum, Hashbadana, Zechariah, *and* Meshullam. [5]And Ezra opened the book in the sight of all the people, for he was *standing* above all the people; and when he opened it, all the people stood up. [6]And Ezra blessed the LORD, the great God.

Then all the people answered, "Amen, Amen!" while lifting up their hands. And they bowed their heads and worshiped the LORD with *their* faces to the ground.

[7]Also Jeshua, Bani, Sherebiah, Jamin, Akkub, Shabbethai, Hodijah, Maaseiah, Kelita, Azariah, Jozabad, Hanan, Pelaiah, and the Levites, helped the people to understand the Law; and the people *stood* in their place. [8]So they read distinctly from the book, in the Law of God; and they gave the sense, and helped *them* to understand the reading.

[9]And Nehemiah, who *was* the governor,[a] Ezra the priest *and* scribe, and the Levites who taught the people said to all the people, "This day *is* holy to the LORD your God; do not mourn nor weep." For all the people wept, when they heard the words of the Law.

[10]Then he said to them, "Go your way, eat the fat, drink the sweet, and send portions to those for whom nothing is prepared; for *this* day *is* holy to our Lord. Do not sorrow, for the joy of the LORD is your strength."

[11]So the Levites quieted all the people, saying, "Be still, for the day *is* holy; do not be grieved." [12]And all the people went their way to eat and drink, to send portions and rejoice greatly, because they understood the words that were declared to them.

The Feast of Tabernacles

[13]Now on the second day the heads of the fathers' *houses* of all the people, with the priests and Levites, were gathered to Ezra the scribe, in order to understand the words of the Law. [14]And they found written in the Law, which the LORD had commanded by Moses, that the children of Israel should dwell in booths during the feast of the seventh month, [15]and that they should announce and proclaim in all their cities and in Jerusalem, saying, "Go out to the mountain, and bring olive branches, branches of oil trees, myrtle branches, palm branches, and branches of leafy trees, to make booths, as *it is* written."

[16]Then the people went out and brought *them* and made themselves booths, each one on the roof of his house, or in their courtyards or the courts of the house of God, and in the open square of the Water Gate and in the open square of the Gate of Ephraim. [17]So the whole assembly of those who had returned from the captivity made booths and sat under the booths; for since the days of Joshua the son of Nun until that day the children of Israel had not done so. And there was very great gladness. [18]Also day by day, from the first day until the last day, he read from the Book of the Law of God. And they kept the feast seven days; and on the eighth day *there was* a sacred assembly, according to the *prescribed* manner.

The People Confess Their Sins

9 Now on the twenty-fourth day of this month the children of Israel were assembled with fasting, in sackcloth, and with dust on their heads.[a] [2]Then those of Israelite lineage separated themselves from all foreigners; and they stood and con-

8:9 [a]Hebrew *Tirshatha*   9:1 [a]Literally *earth on them*

8:5–8 Understanding the Scripture. While Ezra read the Scripture from the Hebrew text, the Levites translated and explained the meaning in Aramaic, the language understood by the people. The people "stood" as a sign of reverence for the Word. This reading, interpretation, and even standing later became part of the synagogue worship services and can be seen in some Christian churches today.

8:9 Conviction of the Law. The people wept and mourned when they heard the Word because they realized how disobedient they had been. They were told not to weep but to enjoy celebrating the Feast of Trumpets (see Lev. 23:23–25; chart, The Feasts of the Lord). The reading and receiving of the Law was to be a joyous time.

8:14–17 The Feast of Tabernacles (also called the Feast of Booths or Ingathering) was one of the three main festivals for which all Jewish men were required to assemble at the temple in Jerusalem. It was celebrated as everyone lived in booths made from the limbs of trees, to commemorate the temporary dwellings of their forefathers in the wilderness (see also Deut. 31:10–13; chart, The Feasts of the Lord).

8:18 The public reading of Scripture achieved a new preeminence at this time as the guiding principle in Jewish life. Nehemiah and Ezra brought back the public reading of Scripture and gave it a prominent place in worship. The Word of God has power to convict, convert, and revive (see Heb. 4:12).

9:1 The signs of mourning. "Sackcloth" was worn during times of mourning, and "dust" thrown "on their heads" was symbolic of death or burial. Both these gestures were symbolic of deep mourning and human frailty.

fessed their sins and the iniquities of their fathers. ³And they stood up in their place and read from the Book of the Law of the LORD their God *for one-fourth* of the day; and *for another* fourth they confessed and worshiped the LORD their God.

⁴Then Jeshua, Bani, Kadmiel, Shebaniah, Bunni, Sherebiah, Bani, *and* Chenani stood on the stairs of the Levites and cried out with a loud voice to the LORD their God. ⁵And the Levites, Jeshua, Kadmiel, Bani, Hashabniah, Sherebiah, Hodijah, Shebaniah, *and* Pethahiah, said:

"Stand up and bless the LORD your God
    Forever and ever!

"Blessed be Your glorious name,
    Which is exalted above all blessing and praise!
⁶You alone *are* the LORD;
    You have made heaven,
    The heaven of heavens, with all their host,
    The earth and everything on it,
    The seas and all that is in them,
    And You preserve them all.
    The host of heaven worships You.

⁷"You *are* the LORD God,
    Who chose Abram,
    And brought him out of Ur of the Chaldeans,
    And gave him the name Abraham;
⁸You found his heart faithful before You,
    And made a covenant with him
    To give the land of the Canaanites,
    The Hittites, the Amorites,
    The Perizzites, the Jebusites,
    And the Girgashites—
    To give *it* to his descendants.
    You have performed Your words,
    For You *are* righteous.

⁹"You saw the affliction of our fathers in Egypt,
    And heard their cry by the Red Sea.
¹⁰You showed signs and wonders against
        Pharaoh,
    Against all his servants,
    And against all the people of his land.
    For You knew that they acted proudly against
        them.
    So You made a name for Yourself, as *it is* this day.

¹¹And You divided the sea before them,
    So that they went through the midst of the sea
        on the dry land;
    And their persecutors You threw into the deep,
    As a stone into the mighty waters.
¹²Moreover You led them by day with a cloudy
        pillar,
    And by night with a pillar of fire,
    To give them light on the road
    Which they should travel.

¹³"You came down also on Mount Sinai,
    And spoke with them from heaven,
    And gave them just ordinances and true laws,
    Good statutes and commandments.
¹⁴You made known to them Your holy Sabbath,
    And commanded them precepts, statutes and
        laws,
    By the hand of Moses Your servant.
¹⁵You gave them bread from heaven for their
        hunger,
    And brought them water out of the rock for
        their thirst,
    And told them to go in to possess the land
    Which You had sworn to give them.

¹⁶"But they and our fathers acted proudly,
    Hardened their necks,
    And did not heed Your commandments.
¹⁷They refused to obey,
    And they were not mindful of Your wonders
    That You did among them.
    But they hardened their necks,
    And in their rebellionª
    They appointed a leader
    To return to their bondage.
    But You *are* God,
    Ready to pardon,
    Gracious and merciful,
    Slow to anger,
    Abundant in kindness,
    And did not forsake them.

¹⁸"Even when they made a molded calf for
        themselves,

9:17 ªFollowing Masoretic Text and Vulgate; Septuagint reads *in Egypt.*

9:5 The Levites' prayer, which begins with this verse, is a chronicle of God's faithfulness to His people and their faithlessness to Him, beginning in Genesis with the creation and continuing through the period of the Judges, the Kings, and Chronicles until Nehemiah's day (v. 32; see also chart, Solomon's Prayer). Perhaps this showed how fresh the reading of the Scripture was in the minds of the Levites who led this prayer.

9:6–15 A righteous God. In this portion of the prayer, God is the subject of every sentence. Prayers that talk to God about Himself build a woman's faith as she sees herself in relation to the Lord. This section cites incidents from Genesis, Exodus, Numbers, and Deuteronomy where God is described as "righteous" (v. 8).

9:16–25 The subject alternates between "they" and "you," showing that although the people were disobedient and proud, God continued to bless them. This section cites incidents from Exodus, Numbers, Joshua, Judges, and 1 Chronicles where God is described as "ready to pardon, gracious and merciful, slow to anger" and "abundant in kindness" (Neh. 9:17).

And said, 'This *is* your god
That brought you up out of Egypt,'
And worked great provocations,
¹⁹Yet in Your manifold mercies
You did not forsake them in the wilderness.
The pillar of the cloud did not depart from
    them by day,
To lead them on the road;
Nor the pillar of fire by night,
To show them light,
And the way they should go.
²⁰You also gave Your good Spirit to instruct them,
And did not withhold Your manna from their
    mouth,
And gave them water for their thirst.
²¹Forty years You sustained them in the
    wilderness;
They lacked nothing;
Their clothes did not wear out^a
And their feet did not swell.

²²"Moreover You gave them kingdoms and
    nations,
And divided them into districts.^a
So they took possession of the land of Sihon,
The land of^b the king of Heshbon,
And the land of Og king of Bashan.
²³You also multiplied their children as the stars
    of heaven,
And brought them into the land
Which You had told their fathers
To go in and possess.
²⁴So the people went in
And possessed the land;
You subdued before them the inhabitants of
    the land,
The Canaanites,
And gave them into their hands,
With their kings
And the people of the land,
That they might do with them as they wished.
²⁵And they took strong cities and a rich land,
And possessed houses full of all goods,
Cisterns *already* dug, vineyards, olive groves,
And fruit trees in abundance.
So they ate and were filled and grew fat,
And delighted themselves in Your great
    goodness.

²⁶"Nevertheless they were disobedient
And rebelled against You,

Cast Your law behind their backs
And killed Your prophets, who testified against
    them
To turn them to Yourself;
And they worked great provocations.
²⁷Therefore You delivered them into the hand of
    their enemies,
Who oppressed them;
And in the time of their trouble,
When they cried to You,
You heard from heaven;
And according to Your abundant mercies
You gave them deliverers who saved them
From the hand of their enemies.

²⁸"But after they had rest,
They again did evil before You.
Therefore You left them in the hand of their
    enemies,
So that they had dominion over them;
Yet when they returned and cried out to
    You,
You heard from heaven;
And many times You delivered them according
    to Your mercies,
²⁹And testified against them,
That You might bring them back to Your law.
Yet they acted proudly,
And did not heed Your commandments,
But sinned against Your judgments,
'Which if a man does, he shall live by them.'^a
And they shrugged their shoulders,
Stiffened their necks,
And would not hear.
³⁰Yet for many years You had patience with
    them,
And testified against them by Your Spirit in
    Your prophets.
Yet they would not listen;
Therefore You gave them into the hand of the
    peoples of the lands.
³¹Nevertheless in Your great mercy
You did not utterly consume them nor forsake
    them;
For You *are* God, gracious and merciful.

³²"Now therefore, our God,
The great, the mighty, and awesome God,

·············
9:21 ^aCompare Deuteronomy 29:5 9:22 ^aLiterally *corners*
^bFollowing Masoretic Text and Vulgate; Septuagint omits *The land of.*
9:29 ^aLeviticus 18:5

9:26–31 A merciful God. This section covers the period of the Judges when the people rebelled time and time again despite the fact that God continually provided deliverers and prophets. God is described as "gracious and merciful" (v. 31).

9:32 The kings of Assyria were the first to conquer Israel and Judah after the bondage in Egypt in the mid-8th century B.C. These kings included Tiglath-Pileser III (known also as Pul,

1 Chr. 5:26), Shalmaneser V (2 Kin. 18:9), Sargon II (Is. 20:1), Sennacherib (2 Kin. 18:13), Esarhaddon (Ezra 4:2), and Ashurbanipal (known also as Osnapper, Ezra 4:10; see also chart, The Kings of Assyria). After the Assyrians, the Babylonians and later the Persians conquered Israel. After Nehemiah's time, the Greeks and then the Romans ruled over Israel.

Who keeps covenant and mercy:
Do not let all the trouble seem small before
       You
That has come upon us,
Our kings and our princes,
Our priests and our prophets,
Our fathers and on all Your people,
From the days of the kings of Assyria until this
       day.
³³However You *are* just in all that has befallen us;
For You have dealt faithfully,
But we have done wickedly.
³⁴Neither our kings nor our princes,
Our priests nor our fathers,
Have kept Your law,
Nor heeded Your commandments and Your
       testimonies,
With which You testified against them.
³⁵For they have not served You in their kingdom,
Or in the many good *things* that You gave them,
Or in the large and rich land which You set
       before them;
Nor did they turn from their wicked works.

³⁶"Here we *are*, servants today!
And the land that You gave to our fathers,
To eat its fruit and its bounty,
Here we *are*, servants in it!
³⁷And it yields much increase to the kings
You have set over us,
Because of our sins;
Also they have dominion over our bodies and
       our cattle
At their pleasure;
And we *are* in great distress.

³⁸"And because of all this,
We make a sure *covenant* and write *it;*
Our leaders, our Levites, *and* our priests seal
       it."

The People Who Sealed the Covenant

10Now those who placed *their* seal on *the document were:*
Nehemiah the governor, the son of Hacaliah,
and Zedekiah, ²Seraiah, Azariah, Jeremiah,
³Pashhur, Amariah, Malchijah, ⁴Hattush,

Shebaniah, Malluch, ⁵Harim, Meremoth,
Obadiah, ⁶Daniel, Ginnethon, Baruch,
⁷Meshullam, Abijah, Mijamin, ⁸Maaziah, Bilgai,
and Shemaiah. These *were* the priests.

⁹The Levites: Jeshua the son of Azaniah, Binnui
of the sons of Henadad, *and* Kadmiel.

¹⁰Their brethren: Shebaniah, Hodijah, Kelita,
Pelaiah, Hanan, ¹¹Micha, Rehob, Hashabiah,
¹²Zaccur, Sherebiah, Shebaniah, ¹³Hodijah,
Bani, *and* Beninu.

¹⁴The leaders of the people: Parosh, Pahath-
Moab, Elam, Zattu, Bani, ¹⁵Bunni, Azgad, Bebai,
¹⁶Adonijah, Bigvai, Adin, ¹⁷Ater, Hezekiah,
Azzur, ¹⁸Hodijah, Hashum, Bezai, ¹⁹Hariph,
Anathoth, Nebai, ²⁰Magpiash, Meshullam,
Hezir, ²¹Meshezabel, Zadok, Jaddua, ²²Pelatiah,
Hanan, Anaiah, ²³Hoshea, Hananiah, Hasshub,
²⁴Hallohesh, Pilha, Shobek, ²⁵Rehum,
Hashabnah, Maaseiah, ²⁶Ahijah, Hanan, Anan,
²⁷Malluch, Harim, *and* Baanah.

The Covenant That Was Sealed

²⁸Now the rest of the people—the priests, the
Levites, the gatekeepers, the singers, the Nethinim,
and all those who had separated themselves from
the peoples of the lands to the Law of God, their
wives, their sons, and their daughters, everyone
who had knowledge and understanding— ²⁹these
joined with their brethren, their nobles, and entered into a curse and an oath to walk in God's Law,
which was given by Moses the servant of God, and
to observe and do all the commandments of the
LORD our Lord, and His ordinances and His
statutes: ³⁰We would not give our daughters as
wives to the peoples of the land, nor take their
daughters for our sons; ³¹*if* the peoples of the land
brought wares or any grain to sell on the Sabbath
day, we would not buy it from them on the Sabbath,
or on a holy day; and we would forego the seventh
year's *produce* and the exacting of every debt.
³²Also we made ordinances for ourselves, to exact from ourselves yearly one-third of a shekel for
the service of the house of our God: ³³for the
showbread, for the regular grain offering, for the

10:32 The sanctuary tax in Exodus was one-half a shekel (Ex. 30:13), while one-third is required here in Nehemiah. The shekel in Exodus was the sanctuary shekel which was mea-sured as ten silver shekels to one gold shekel, while the Per-sian shekel of Nehemiah's day was measured as 15 to one.

10:33 The showbread was an offering to God placed on a table in the holy place (see Lev. 24:5–9; see chart, The Furniture of the Tabernacle). It consisted of 12 cakes, representing the 12 tribes. They were made by the Levites of fine unleavened wheat flour and were to be eaten only by the priests. The showbread was to be replaced each Sabbath.

The "grain offering" consisted of cakes made with unleav-ened fine flour, oil, and salt (see Lev. 2), and it was to signify a

person's thanksgiving to the Lord (see chart, The Offerings of the Lord). A memorial portion was to be burned on the altar, and the rest was for the priests. The offering was made in the morning and the evening with the "regular burnt offering," which could be either a bull, a lamb, or turtledoves. These were entirely burned except for the skin and were for pay-ment of sins in general. "Sin offerings" were burnt offerings of animals for sins that were committed unconsciously (Lev. 4).

Enumeration of these offerings shows the importance of the identity that helped to insure the continuance of the Jew-ish nation and worship.

INTERFAITH MARRIAGE
MARRYING OUTSIDE YOUR FAITH

God views marriage as a union of two people becoming one. The choice of partners becomes very important since each will identify with the other in their union. The Lord strictly warned the Jews against intermarriage because of its propensity to result in dangerous compromise and even tragic abandonment of their commitment to Him. Malachi, a contemporary of Nehemiah, spoke specifically against such marriages (Mal. 2:11).

In the history of Israel, interfaith marriages frequently led to the worship of other gods. The wise King Solomon ruled everything but his own heart wisely. His seven hundred wives and three hundred concubines not only continued to worship their false gods but also led him to worship their pagan deities. In the Book of Nehemiah, the demise of Jerusalem is directly linked to intermarriage, especially Tobiah and Sanballat, the opponents to the rebuilding of the city's walls (Neh. 6:17, 18; 13:28). Since marriages were arranged by parents, Nehemiah—and other leaders before and after him—warned parents specifically not to give their children to pagan unions.

What led the Hebrews to intermarry? Generally the pagan occupants of the lands they came to inhabit were the longstanding landowners and merchants. Much of the tendency to intermarry was not based upon love, romance, or any other intention other than to improve a family's economic and social position in life. The prophet Malachi spoke strongly against Hebrew men divorcing their Hebrew wives to marry "daughters of a foreign god" (Mal. 2:11–16).

The danger of interfaith marriage extended beyond a dilution of faith, a deviation from strict obedience, and a straying from pure worship of the One True and Living God. It generally included loss of language, thought, understanding, and expression at the most basic cultural level, including access to Scripture. Interfaith marriages blurred and eventually obliterated the "national identity," destroying the adherence to God's laws which were the moral code of the Hebrew people. Thus, in marrying "outside the faith," God's people destroyed their own identity and tainted the favored status they enjoyed as "the people of God."

In the New Testament, believers are cautioned against marrying outside the faith (1 Cor. 7:39; 2 Cor. 6:14). Such marriages are especially problematic and are prone to fail when both spouses are strong in their respective faiths. Guiding principles regarding those already married to unbelievers can also be found (1 Cor. 7:12–16; 1 Pet. 3:1, 2). Certainly the faith of your spouse and his expression of that faith must be respected as you simultaneously try to hold on to your own faith. If children are born to such a union, parents must discuss and agree upon how to nurture their children spiritually.

See also Neh. 13:23–27; notes on Divorce (Matt. 19); Husbands (Job 31; 2 Cor. 6); Marriage (Gen. 2; 2 Sam. 6; Prov. 5; Hos. 2; Amos 3; 2 Cor. 13; Heb. 12); Prejudice (Acts 15); Racial Relations (Acts 10); Wives (Prov. 31); portraits of Jezebel (1 Kin. 18); Samson's Pagan Bride (Judg. 14); Solomon's Pagan Wives (1 Kin. 11)

---

regular burnt offering of the Sabbaths, the New Moons, and the set feasts; for the holy things, for the sin offerings to make atonement for Israel, and all the work of the house of our God. ³⁴We cast lots among the priests, the Levites, and the people, for *bringing* the wood offering into the house of our God, according to our fathers' houses, at the appointed times year by year, to burn on the altar of the LORD our God as *it is* written in the Law.

³⁵And *we made ordinances* to bring the firstfruits of our ground and the firstfruits of all fruit of all trees, year by year, to the house of the LORD; ³⁶to bring the firstborn of our sons and our cattle, as *it is* written in the Law, and the firstborn of our herds and our flocks, to the house of our God, to the priests who minister in the house of our God;

³⁷to bring the firstfruits of our dough, our offerings, the fruit from all kinds of trees, *the* new wine and oil, to the priests, to the storerooms of the house of our God; and to bring the tithes of our land to the Levites, for the Levites should receive the tithes in all our farming communities. ³⁸And the priest, the descendant of Aaron, shall be with the Levites when the Levites receive tithes; and the Levites shall bring up a tenth of the tithes to the house of our God, to the rooms of the storehouse.

³⁹For the children of Israel and the children of Levi shall bring the offering of the grain, of the new wine and the oil, to the storerooms where the articles of the sanctuary *are, where* the priests who minister and the gatekeepers and the singers *are;* and we will not neglect the house of our God.

10:34 The wood offering was to be a continuous fire on the altar to aid in the offering of the other sacrifices (Lev. 6:12).

10:35 Because the people had neglected their tithes and of- **ferings** of firstfruits in which the first of the harvest was to be given to God, the maintenance of the Levites and the temple was lacking.

The People Dwelling in Jerusalem

11 Now the leaders of the people dwelt at Jerusalem; the rest of the people cast lots to bring one out of ten to dwell in Jerusalem, the holy city, and nine-tenths *were to dwell* in *other* cities. ²And the people blessed all the men who willingly offered themselves to dwell at Jerusalem.

³These *are* the heads of the province who dwelt in Jerusalem. (But in the cities of Judah everyone dwelt in his own possession in their cities—Israelites, priests, Levites, Nethinim, and descendants of Solomon's servants.) ⁴Also in Jerusalem dwelt *some* of the children of Judah and of the children of Benjamin.

The children of Judah: Athaiah the son of Uzziah, the son of Zechariah, the son of Amariah, the son of Shephatiah, the son of Mahalalel, of the children of Perez; ⁵and Maaseiah the son of Baruch, the son of Col-Hozeh, the son of Hazaiah, the son of Adaiah, the son of Joiarib, the son of Zechariah, the son of Shiloni. ⁶All the sons of Perez who dwelt at Jerusalem *were* four hundred and sixty-eight valiant men.

⁷And these are the sons of Benjamin: Sallu the son of Meshullam, the son of Joed, the son of Pedaiah, the son of Kolaiah, the son of Maaseiah, the son of Ithiel, the son of Jeshaiah; ⁸and after him Gabbai *and* Sallai, nine hundred and twenty-eight. ⁹Joel the son of Zichri *was* their overseer, and Judah the son of Senuah[a] *was* second over the city.

¹⁰Of the priests: Jedaiah the son of Joiarib, and Jachin; ¹¹Seraiah the son of Hilkiah, the son of Meshullam, the son of Zadok, the son of Meraioth, the son of Ahitub, *was* the leader of the house of God. ¹²Their brethren who did the work of the house *were* eight hundred and twenty-two; and Adaiah the son of Jeroham, the son of Pelaliah, the son of Amzi, the son of Zechariah, the son of Pashhur, the son of Malchijah, ¹³and his brethren, heads of the fathers' *houses, were* two hundred and forty-two; and Amashai the son of Azarel, the son of Ahzai, the son of Meshillemoth, the son of Immer, ¹⁴and their brethren, mighty men of valor, *were* one hundred and twenty-eight. Their overseer *was* Zabdiel the son of *one of* the great men.[a]

¹⁵Also of the Levites: Shemaiah the son of Hasshub, the son of Azrikam, the son of Hashabiah, the son of Bunni; ¹⁶Shabbethai and Jozabad, of the heads of the Levites, *had* the oversight of the business outside of the house of God; ¹⁷Mattaniah the son of Micha,[a] the son of Zabdi, the son of Asaph, the leader *who* began the thanksgiving with prayer; Bakbukiah, the second among his brethren; and Abda the son of Shammua, the son of Galal, the son of Jeduthun. ¹⁸All the Levites in the holy city *were* two hundred and eighty-four.

¹⁹Moreover the gatekeepers, Akkub, Talmon, and their brethren who kept the gates, *were* one hundred and seventy-two.

²⁰And the rest of Israel, of the priests *and* Levites, *were* in all the cities of Judah, everyone in his inheritance. ²¹But the Nethinim dwelt in Ophel. And Ziha and Gishpa *were* over the Nethinim.

²²Also the overseer of the Levites at Jerusalem *was* Uzzi the son of Bani, the son of Hashabiah, the son of Mattaniah, the son of Micha, of the sons of Asaph, the singers in charge of the service of the house of God. ²³For *it was* the king's command concerning them that a certain portion should be for the singers, a quota day by day. ²⁴Pethahiah the son of Meshezabel, of the children of Zerah the son of Judah, *was* the king's deputy[a] in all matters concerning the people.

The People Dwelling Outside Jerusalem

²⁵And as for the villages with their fields, *some* of the children of Judah dwelt in Kirjath Arba and its villages, Dibon and its villages, Jekabzeel and its villages; ²⁶in Jeshua, Moladah, Beth Pelet, ²⁷Hazar Shual, and Beersheba and its villages; ²⁸in Ziklag and Meconah and its villages; ²⁹in En Rimmon, Zorah, Jarmuth, ³⁰Zanoah, Adullam, and their villages; in Lachish and its fields; in Azekah and its villages. They dwelt from Beersheba to the Valley of Hinnom.

³¹Also the children of Benjamin from Geba *dwelt* in Michmash, Aija, and Bethel, and their villages; ³²in Anathoth, Nob, Ananiah; ³³in Hazor, Ramah, Gittaim; ³⁴in Hadid, Zeboim, Neballat; ³⁵in Lod, Ono, *and* the Valley of Craftsmen. ³⁶Some of the Judean divisions of Levites *were* in Benjamin.

The Priests and Levites

12 Now these *are* the priests and the Levites who came up with Zerubbabel the son of Shealtiel, and Jeshua: Seraiah, Jeremiah, Ezra, ²Amariah, Malluch, Hattush, ³Shechaniah, Rehum, Meremoth, ⁴Iddo, Ginnethoi,[a] Abijah, ⁵Mijamin, Maadiah, Bilgah, ⁶Shemaiah, Joiarib, Jedaiah, ⁷Sallu, Amok, Hilkiah, *and* Jedaiah.

11:9 [a]Or *Hassenuah* 11:14 [a]Or *the son of Haggedolim* 11:17 [a]Or *Michah* 11:24 [a]Literally *at the king's hand* 12:4 [a]Or *Ginnethon* (compare verse 16)

11:1 When people cast lots to see who should move to Jerusalem, they believed that God would choose those individuals through the sacred lots (see Prov. 16:33). Thus Nehemiah did not force them to relocate; God willed it. The list of those who returned showed that it was not a free-for-all land rush but an ordered and purposeful resettlement (Neh. 11:4–19).

11:3 Nethinim (Heb., lit. "dedicated" or "given" ones) were temple assistants who did the more menial tasks (see 1 Chr. 9:2, note).

SHOPPING *BARTERING AND BUYING*

Scripture refers to vendors in streets, squares, marketplaces, and near gates where farmers, artisans, merchants, and peddlers displayed their wares (see Neh. 13:17–22). Apparently bartering was prohibited on the Sabbath. The Bible gives little information about the quality of goods or regulation of trade (see Amos 8:5, 6). The method of transaction was often a barter system of exchange, although there is also evidence that items were purchased by weights of gold and silver.

Among the items traded in the Bible were oil, wine, grapes, figs, fish, animals, pottery, and clothing (1 Kin. 4:7; Neh. 13:15, 16). The people of Palestine exported grains and flour, oil and wine, cosmetics and medicinal products (Gen. 43:11; Ezek. 27:17).

The Law has very few references to buying and selling, the primary rules being to have honest weights and measures and to refrain from charging interest of fellow Israelites (Lev. 19:36; Deut. 25:13).

Solomon was the first king of Israel who promoted international trade. He entered into a profitable joint trading venture with Hiram, king of Tyre. During Solomon's reign, ancient trade routes were strictly controlled, and merchants were taxed heavily. The Queen of Sheba may very well have been the head of a trade delegation to establish closer relations with Israel (1 Kin. 10; 2 Chr. 9:1–12). In any case, just as those who shop today, she combined curiosity (2 Chr. 9:1) and commercial interest with buying power to meet her needs (2 Chr. 9:9–12).

Women obviously bought and sold goods, whether in the process of providing food and clothing for their households (Prov. 31:18, 24) or as a professional pursuit (Acts 16:14). Shopping required time (Prov. 31:14), planning (v. 21), good taste (v. 22), and stewardship (v. 13).

See also article on What They Left Behind; notes on Clothing (Ezek. 16); Cooking (Gen. 25); Financial Planning (Luke 19); Jewelry (Ex. 28)

These *were* the heads of the priests and their brethren in the days of Jeshua.

8Moreover the Levites *were* Jeshua, Binnui, Kadmiel, Sherebiah, Judah, *and* Mattaniah *who led* the thanksgiving *psalms,* he and his brethren. 9Also Bakbukiah and Unni, their brethren, *stood* across from them in *their* duties.

10Jeshua begot Joiakim, Joiakim begot Eliashib, Eliashib begot Joiada, 11Joiada begot Jonathan, and Jonathan begot Jaddua.

12Now in the days of Joiakim, the priests, the heads of the fathers' *houses were:* of Seraiah, Meraiah; of Jeremiah, Hananiah; 13of Ezra, Meshullam; of Amariah, Jehohanan; 14of Melichu,[a] Jonathan; of Shebaniah,[b] Joseph; 15of Harim,[a] Adna; of Meraioth,[b] Helkai; 16of Iddo, Zechariah; of Ginnethon, Meshullam; 17of Abijah, Zichri; *the son of* Minjamin;[a] of Moadiah,[b] Piltai; 18of Bilgah, Shammua; of Shemaiah, Jehonathan; 19of Joiarib, Mattenai; of Jedaiah, Uzzi; 20of Sallai,[a] Kallai; of Amok, Eber; 21of Hilkiah, Hashabiah; *and* of Jedaiah, Nethanel.

22During the reign of Darius the Persian, a record *was also kept* of the Levites and priests *who had been* heads of their fathers' *houses* in the days of Eliashib, Joiada, Johanan, and Jaddua. 23The sons of Levi, the heads of the fathers' *houses* until

the days of Johanan the son of Eliashib, *were* written in the book of the chronicles.

24And the heads of the Levites *were* Hashabiah, Sherebiah, and Jeshua the son of Kadmiel, with their brothers across from them, to praise *and* give thanks, group alternating with group, according to the command of David the man of God. 25Mattaniah, Bakbukiah, Obadiah, Meshullam, Talmon, and Akkub *were* gatekeepers keeping the watch at the storerooms of the gates. 26These *lived* in the days of Joiakim the son of Jeshua, the son of Jozadak,[a] and in the days of Nehemiah the governor, and of Ezra the priest, the scribe.

Nehemiah Dedicates the Wall

27Now at the dedication of the wall of Jerusalem they sought out the Levites in all their places, to bring them to Jerusalem to celebrate the dedication with gladness, both with thanksgivings and singing, *with* cymbals and stringed instruments and harps. 28And the sons of the singers gathered together from the countryside around Jerusalem,

12:14 [a]Or *Malluch* (compare verse 2) [b]Or *Shechaniah* (compare verse 3) **12:15** [a]Or *Rehum* (compare verse 3) [b]Or *Meremoth* (compare verse 3) **12:17** [a]Or *Mijamin* (compare verse 5) [b]Or *Maadiah* (compare verse 5) **12:20** [a]Or *Sallu* (compare verse 7) **12:26** [a]Spelled *Jehozadak* in 1 Chronicles 6:14

12:10, 22 Joiada's son married Sanballat's daughter, which made Eliashib's grandson Sanballat's son-in-law (see Neh. 13:28, note).

12:25 Meshullam's daughter married Jehohanan, Tobiah's son, which made Meshullam and Tobiah in-laws (Neh. 3:4, 30; see

6:18, note). As Meshullam was one of the "gatekeepers" who watched "the storerooms of the gates," he might have been useful to Tobiah in gaining access to the temple storeroom (see Neh. 13:4, 5).

from the villages of the Netophathites, [29]from the house of Gilgal, and from the fields of Geba and Azmaveth; for the singers had built themselves villages all around Jerusalem. [30]Then the priests and Levites purified themselves, and purified the people, the gates, and the wall.

[31]So I brought the leaders of Judah up on the wall, and appointed two large thanksgiving choirs. *One* went to the right hand on the wall toward the Refuse Gate. [32]After them went Hoshaiah and half of the leaders of Judah, [33]and Azariah, Ezra, Meshullam, [34]Judah, Benjamin, Shemaiah, Jeremiah, [35]and some of the priests' sons with trumpets— Zechariah the son of Jonathan, the son of Shemaiah, the son of Mattaniah, the son of Michaiah, the son of Zaccur, the son of Asaph, [36]and his brethren, Shemaiah, Azarel, Milalai, Gilalai, Maai, Nethanel, Judah, *and* Hanani, with the musical instruments of David the man of God. And Ezra the scribe *went* before them. [37]By the Fountain Gate, in front of them, they went up the stairs of the City of David, on the stairway of the wall, beyond the house of David, as far as the Water Gate eastward.

[38]The other thanksgiving choir went the opposite *way,* and I *was* behind them with half of the people on the wall, going past the Tower of the Ovens as far as the Broad Wall, [39]and above the Gate of Ephraim, above the Old Gate, above the Fish Gate, the Tower of Hananel, the Tower of the Hundred, as far as the Sheep Gate; and they stopped by the Gate of the Prison.

[40]So the two thanksgiving choirs stood in the house of God, likewise I and the half of the rulers with me; [41]and the priests, Eliakim, Maaseiah, Minjamin,[a] Michaiah, Elioenai, Zechariah, *and* Hananiah, with trumpets; [42]also Maaseiah, Shemaiah, Eleazar, Uzzi, Jehohanan, Malchijah, Elam, and Ezer. The singers sang loudly with Jezrahiah the director.

[43]Also that day they offered great sacrifices, and rejoiced, for God had made them rejoice with great joy; the women and the children also rejoiced, so that the joy of Jerusalem was heard afar off.

Temple Responsibilities

[44]And at the same time some were appointed over the rooms of the storehouse for the offerings, the firstfruits, and the tithes, to gather into them from the fields of the cities the portions specified by the Law for the priests and Levites; for Judah rejoiced over the priests and Levites

who ministered. [45]Both the singers and the gatekeepers kept the charge of their God and the charge of the purification, according to the command of David *and* Solomon his son. [46]For in the days of David and Asaph of old *there were* chiefs of the singers, and songs of praise and thanksgiving to God. [47]In the days of Zerubbabel and in the days of Nehemiah all Israel gave the portions for the singers and the gatekeepers, a portion for each day. They also consecrated *holy things* for the Levites, and the Levites consecrated *them* for the children of Aaron.

Principles of Separation

13 On that day they read from the Book of Moses in the hearing of the people, and in it was found written that no Ammonite or Moabite should ever come into the assembly of God, [2]because they had not met the children of Israel with bread and water, but hired Balaam against them to curse them. However, our God turned the curse into a blessing. [3]So it was, when they had heard the Law, that they separated all the mixed multitude from Israel.

The Reforms of Nehemiah

[4]Now before this, Eliashib the priest, having authority over the storerooms of the house of our God, *was* allied with Tobiah. [5]And he had prepared for him a large room, where previously they had stored the grain offerings, the frankincense, the articles, the tithes of grain, the new wine and oil, which were commanded *to be given* to the Levites and singers and gatekeepers, and the offerings for the priests. [6]But during all this I was not in Jerusalem, for in the thirty-second year of Artaxerxes king of Babylon I had returned to the king. Then after certain days I obtained leave from the king, [7]and I came to Jerusalem and discovered the evil that Eliashib had done for Tobiah, in preparing a room for him in the courts of the house of God. [8]And it grieved me bitterly; therefore I threw all the household goods of Tobiah out of the room. [9]Then I commanded them to cleanse the rooms; and I brought back into them the articles of the house of God, with the grain offering and the frankincense.

[10]I also realized that the portions for the Levites had not been given *them;* for each of the Levites and the singers who did the work had gone back to his field. [11]So I contended with the

12:41 [a]Or *Mijamin* (compare verse 5)

12:31 The choir was divided in half; one half was sent in one direction around the wall while the other half went in the opposite direction, both meeting at the temple (v. 38). Thus they encircled the city with their thanksgiving.

13:4–9 Cleansing the temple. Evil is never so content as when

it is firmly lodged in the very heart of the work of God. Nehemiah's cleansing of the temple calls to mind the zeal and righteous anger of Jesus when He cleansed the temple (see John 2:13–17; Mal. 3:5, note).

rulers, and said, "Why is the house of God forsaken?" And I gathered them together and set them in their place. ¹²Then all Judah brought the tithe of the grain and the new wine and the oil to the storehouse. ¹³And I appointed as treasurers over the storehouse Shelemiah the priest and Zadok the scribe, and of the Levites, Pedaiah; and next to them *was* Hanan the son of Zaccur, the son of Mattaniah; for they were considered faithful, and their task *was* to distribute to their brethren.

¹⁴Remember me, O my God, concerning this, and do not wipe out my good deeds that I have done for the house of my God, and for its services!

¹⁵In those days I saw *people* in Judah treading wine presses on the Sabbath, and bringing in sheaves, and loading donkeys with wine, grapes, figs, and all *kinds of* burdens, which they brought into Jerusalem on the Sabbath day. And I warned *them* about the day on which they were selling provisions. ¹⁶Men of Tyre dwelt there also, who brought in fish and all kinds of goods, and sold *them* on the Sabbath to the children of Judah, and in Jerusalem.

¹⁷Then I contended with the nobles of Judah, and said to them, "What evil thing *is* this that you do, by which you profane the Sabbath day? ¹⁸Did not your fathers do thus, and did not our God bring all this disaster on us and on this city? Yet you bring added wrath on Israel by profaning the Sabbath."

¹⁹So it was, at the gates of Jerusalem, as it began to be dark before the Sabbath, that I commanded the gates to be shut, and charged that they must not be opened till after the Sabbath. Then I posted *some* of my servants at the gates, *so that* no burdens would be brought in on the Sabbath day. ²⁰Now the merchants and sellers of all kinds of wares lodged outside Jerusalem once or twice.

²¹Then I warned them, and said to them, "Why do you spend the night around the wall? If you do *so* again, I will lay hands on you!" From that time on they came no *more* on the Sabbath. ²²And I commanded the Levites that they should cleanse themselves, and that they should go and guard the gates, to sanctify the Sabbath day.

Remember me, O my God, *concerning* this also, and spare me according to the greatness of Your mercy!

²³In those days I also saw Jews *who* had married women of Ashdod, Ammon, *and* Moab. ²⁴And half of their children spoke the language of Ashdod, and could not speak the language of Judah, but spoke according to the language of one or the other people.

²⁵So I contended with them and cursed them, struck some of them and pulled out their hair, and made them swear by God, *saying,* "You shall not give your daughters as wives to their sons, nor take their daughters for your sons or yourselves. ²⁶Did not Solomon king of Israel sin by these things? Yet among many nations there was no king like him, who was beloved of his God; and God made him king over all Israel. Nevertheless pagan women caused even him to sin. ²⁷Should we then hear of your doing all this great evil, transgressing against our God by marrying pagan women?"

²⁸And *one* of the sons of Joiada, the son of Eliashib the high priest, *was* a son-in-law of Sanballat the Horonite; therefore I drove him from me.

²⁹Remember them, O my God, because they have defiled the priesthood and the covenant of the priesthood and the Levites.

³⁰Thus I cleansed them of everything pagan. I also assigned duties to the priests and the Levites, each to his service, ³¹and *to bringing* the wood offering and the firstfruits at appointed times.

Remember me, O my God, for good!

13:23–27 A warning about intermarriage (see Ex. 34:14, 16; Deut. 7:3, 4; Ezra 9:12; Neh. 10, Interfaith Marriage; Mal. 3:5, note).

13:28 The marriage of a priest's son to a pagan woman was particularly grievous, and therefore every priest was told strictly to "take a virgin of his own people as wife" (Lev. 21:14; see Neh. 10, Interfaith Marriage). Since the sons of a priest would follow in their father's footsteps and become priests themselves, this command was for them as well. Thus when Eliashib's grandson married the daughter of Sanballat the Horonite, he was in effect making a treasonous alliance.

13:29–31 Celebration of the festivals placed special emphasis on remembrance. Nehemiah himself showed the importance of remembrance in his keen detailed lists of names. Remembrance could be negative, as in Nehemiah's request that God remember the priests who had defiled the priesthood and their special priestly covenant; the implication is that they deserved God's judgment. On the other hand, Nehemiah asked that he be remembered for good, implying God's blessing on him for his obedience. "Remember" (Heb. *zakar*, lit. "to meditate upon and pay attention to") implied that appropriate action would follow. Nehemiah used this word eight times, four of which were to ask God to remember him for good (vv. 14, 22, 31; Neh. 5:19), which was the only request he had for himself throughout the book. This singleminded desire to be remembered by the Lord revealed the purity of heart of a servant who wanted first and foremost to please his Master.

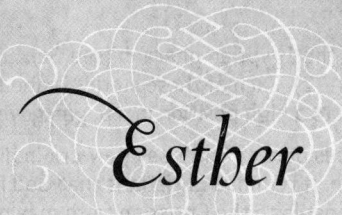

Esther

Although no one knows who wrote the Book of Esther, it was apparently written by a Jew who was familiar with Susa, the royal palace, and Persian customs. The Jewish Talmud attributes Esther to the "men of the Great Synagogue," anonymous teachers who lived in the period between the last prophets and the earliest rabbinic scholars.

Early church fathers, such as Clement of Alexandria, as well as Jewish authorities like Josephus, ascribed the book to Mordecai.

DATE

The date of the book's composition is also unknown. The events described in the story occurred during the reign of the Persian king Ahasuerus, whose name was rendered in Greek histories as Xerxes and who reigned 486–465 B.C. Although some scholars date its composition as late as the first century B.C., there is evidence to indicate the book was written shortly after the events it narrates and before the Persian empire fell to Alexander the Great in 331 B.C. The Hebrew of Esther is similar to that of the books of Chronicles and Daniel, which suggests that these three books were composed during the same period (see chart, Timeline for Ezra, Nehemiah, and Esther). The author's knowledge of Persian court life and customs and the book's linguistic evidence point to the late fifth century B.C.

BACKGROUND

SETTING: The story of Esther occurs during the Achaemenid period of biblical history (559–330 B.C.) in the court of the Persian king Ahasuerus, also known as Xerxes, who ruled Persia from 486–465 B.C. This places the events of the story at least fifty years after the decree of Cyrus (538 B.C.), which announced that the exiled Jews could return to Jerusalem, and about twenty-five years before Ezra's return to Jerusalem.

Esther and Mordecai were living in the royal city of Susa (Heb. *Shushan*). Susa had been an important political, cultural, and religious center for centuries. At the time of Esther, the city was one of the capital cities of a vast empire stretching from what is now India in the east to Turkey and Ethiopia in the west. The ruins of Susa are in Iran near its border with Iraq.

PURPOSE: As traditionally understood, the purpose of the book is to explain the origin of the Jewish holiday of Purim as a celebration of deliverance. From the Second Temple Period until now, the *Megillat Ester* (Heb., lit. "scroll of Esther") in its entirety is read in the assemblies of the Jews as the central rite of the observance of Purim. Although women are normally exempt from mandatory attendance at worship, they are required to be present for the reading of Esther.

The story has provided encouragement and hope for the Jews, who from that day until this, like Esther and Mordecai, have lived far from Jerusalem. The story of Esther is similar

to that of Joseph in the court of the Egyptian pharaoh (see Gen. 37—50) and of Daniel in the court at Babylon (see Dan. 1—2). Each of these stories is about a Jew who was delivered from a death plot and rose to a high position in a pagan government.

The book as Christian Scripture is part of God's saving work in history that culminated in the coming of Jesus the Messiah. It reminds Christians that God is never absent, even though those living in a world hostile to the Christian faith may not always be aware of His presence.

AUDIENCE: The events recorded concern the well-being of the Jews in Persia. Certainly Jews were the original audience, but whether the book was written for the Jews living in Persia or for Jews facing a similar situation elsewhere at another time is uncertain.

The book has long been included in the canon of Scripture for both Jews and Christians. Its message is relevant to readers in every generation.

LITERARY CHARACTERISTICS: The Book of Esther is a prose account of an event in the life of the Jewish people who lived under Persian rule. The opening words of the book (Heb. *wyhy,* lit. "now it came to pass") are also used to open the historical books of Joshua, Judges, and Samuel. The reference to "the chronicles of the kings of Media and Persia" implies that additional historical information about Mordecai was once available (Esth. 10:2).

Such features suggest that the author intended the story to be taken as history. Irony and humor are literary features appropriately used to dramatize historical events.

THEMES

A most conspicuous feature of the Book of Esther is the complete absence of any mention of God, the temple, Jerusalem, or the Law. In this sense, it appears to be a completely secular book, which relates its story on the purely human plane of history. Nevertheless, this book is about God's chosen people, and it appears in both the Jewish and Christian canon of Scripture. Therefore, the book must be understood in the canonical context of redemptive history.

The major theme of the book is God's sovereign power to work, even through pagans, in order to preserve and deliver His people. The enemies of God's people, portrayed possibly as Amalekites in the Book of Esther, cannot prevail over His purposes, even when God Himself seems strangely absent (see Esth. 3:1).

The name of the holiday, Purim (or the Feast of Lots), which celebrates this great deliverance, commemorates the theme that the destiny of God's people will not be determined by anything other than the purposes of God Himself.

OUTLINE

I. The Ascension of Esther to the Throne of Persia (1:1—2:18)
  A. A banquet given by the king (1:1–22)
    1. Queen Vashti's scandal (1:1–12)
    2. Queen Vashti's dethronement (1:13–22)
  B. The selection of a new queen (2:1–18)
    1. The search for candidates (2:1–8)
    2. The choosing of Esther (2:9–18)
II. The Conflict Between Mordecai and Haman (2:19—3:6)

  A. An assassination attempt foiled by Mordecai (2:19–23)
  B. Mordecai's refusal to bow to Haman (3:1–6)
III. Haman's Evil Plan to Annihilate the Jews (3:7—7:6)
  A. Haman's plot to destroy the Jews (3:7–15)
  B. Mordecai's appeal to Esther for help (4:1—5:8)

The King Dethrones Queen Vashti

1 Now it came to pass in the days of Ahasuerus[a] (this *was* the Ahasuerus who reigned over one hundred and twenty-seven provinces, from India to Ethiopia), ²in those days when King Ahasuerus sat on the throne of his kingdom, which *was* in Shushan[a] the citadel, ³*that* in the third year of his reign he made a feast for all his officials and servants—the powers of Persia and Media, the nobles, and the princes of the provinces *being* before him— ⁴when he showed the riches of his glorious kingdom and the splendor of his excellent majesty for many days, one hundred and eighty days *in all.*

⁵And when these days were completed, the king made a feast lasting seven days for all the people who were present in Shushan the citadel, from great to small, in the court of the garden of the king's palace. ⁶*There were* white and blue linen curtains fastened with cords of fine linen and purple on silver rods and marble pillars; *and the* couches *were* of gold and silver on a *mosaic* pavement of alabaster, turquoise, and white and black marble. ⁷And they served drinks in golden vessels, each vessel being different from the other, with royal wine in abundance, according to the generosity of the king. ⁸In accordance with the law, the drinking was not compulsory; for so the king had ordered all the officers of his household, that they should do according to each man's pleasure.

⁹Queen Vashti also made a feast for the women *in* the royal palace which *belonged* to King Ahasuerus.

¹⁰On the seventh day, when the heart of the king was merry with wine, he commanded Mehuman,

1:1 [a]Generally identified with Xerxes I (485–464 B.C.) 1:2 [a]Or *Susa,* and so throughout this book

---

1:1 **Ahasuerus** is the Hebrew equivalent of *Khshayarsha,* the king's Old Persian name. In Greek histories, he was known as Xerxes I (reigning 486–465 B.C.).

1:2 **Shushan** (also called Susa) had long been an important center of culture, religion, and politics. Darius (522–486 B.C.) chose Susa as his political and administrative capital. For Susa, see Nehemiah 1:1, note.

1:3 **Cyrus,** whose mother was a Mede and father a Persian, united the Median and Persian empires into one. Median customs were adopted by the Persian court, and Medes held prominent positions in the empire. At the time of Ahasuerus, Persia was dominant and therefore named first (compare to Esth. 10:2). The joint Persian-Median Empire lasted until 330 B.C. when Alexander the Great marched eastward. Ancient Persia was centered in the area known today as Iraq and Iran. The area known as ancient Media covers what is now the northwest part of Iran, Azerbaijan, Ardelan, and parts of Kurdistan.

1:5 **Lavish banquets** were given on many occasions (see Esth. 2:18). The date of this banquet (483/482 B.C.) and its length suggest the occasion may have been a war council to plan the ill-fated campaigns against Greece (482–479 B.C.).

1:6 **The palace at Shushan (Susa)** was built by Darius I, Ahasuerus' father. Archaeologists have found in its dedication inscription (housed at the Louvre in Paris), a confirmation of its lavish appointments and ornamentation. Excavation has determined that the king received visitors in a large hall separated from the king's private living quarters by a courtyard. The hall contained 36 columns and was flanked on three sides by porticoes, each having two rows of six columns. The remains of colorfully glazed decorative brick, which formed large mosaics of human figures, winged lions and bulls, sphinxes, and winged sun disks, have also been unearthed at Susa. The foundation charter describes the materials used to build the royal compound (cedar, gold, ivory, lapis lazuli, turquoise, and marble) as tribute coming from all parts of the Persian Empire.

1:9 **Greek historians** record that Amestris was the name of Xerxes' wife. Some have attempted to identify this name as the Greek spelling of Vashti (or even of Esther). Others believe Amestris was neither Vashti nor Esther and that Xerxes had more than one woman who was referred to as his "wife."

1:10 **Eunuchs** were castrated men employed to guard the harem. Because the legitimacy of the king's offspring was of

VASHTI *A Deposed Queen*

The pride and splendor of the Medo-Persian Empire were on display for 180 days before all of King Ahasuerus' officials and allies. Building support for his coming Greek campaign (482–479 B.C.), the king climaxed his lavish celebration with a seven-day banquet for citizens of Shushan, the site of his royal palace.

Persian monarchs insisted upon deference. Not even the queen was allowed into the throne room unless summoned. To be called by the king was a rigid order, not an invitation. On the final day of the feast such a bid was issued for Queen Vashti, who refused to come. She was hosting her own feast for the women of the palace when she was called to appear before the men. Her action could have been a response to the Near Eastern custom which dictated that the women, including the queen, be excluded from such revelry. Some historians believe she feared the gawking of a crowd of drunken officials and commoners; others suggest that she was pregnant at the time.

Vashti's decision to disobey the order of Ahasuerus, probably assuming he would forgive her later, was a serious miscalculation. The sovereign had announced her arrival in front of his guests, making her refusal equally public, and the king was humiliated in the presence of his subjects.

The king and his counselors realized immediately that disastrous repercussions could occur in every household, as other wives might follow the queen's precedent. The king acted upon the advice of his officials, whereas Vashti herself had apparently unwisely made the decision to defy her husband and king. A decree was sent out, and Vashti was eventually replaced by Queen Esther.

The two queens, one a Gentile and the other a Jewess, demonstrate diverse and antithetical responses. Unlike Esther, who courageously yet humbly disobeyed the king by appearing unsummoned, Vashti defiantly disregarded his command with no recorded apology or explanation. Esther acted in the best interests of her people whose lives were in her hands and at the request of her foster parent. Vashti apparently acted in her own interest and without counsel or petition of anyone. Yet each is used sovereignly to accomplish God's purposes. Vashti lives in history as the queen who was deposed for daring to challenge her husband as well as the irrevocable royal law of the Medes and Persians.

See also notes on Influence (Esth. 4); Submission (1 Pet. 3)

Biztha, Harbona, Bigtha, Abagtha, Zethar, and Carcas, seven eunuchs who served in the presence of King Ahasuerus, [11]to bring Queen Vashti before the king, *wearing* her royal crown, in order to show her beauty to the people and the officials, for she *was* beautiful to behold. [12]But Queen Vashti refused to come at the king's command *brought* by *his* eunuchs; therefore the king was furious, and his anger burned within him.

[13]Then the king said to the wise men who understood the times (for this *was* the king's manner toward all who knew law and justice, [14]those closest to him *being* Carshena, Shethar, Admatha, Tarshish, Meres, Marsena, and Memucan, the seven princes of Persia and Media, who had access to the king's presence, *and* who ranked highest in the kingdom): [15]"What *shall we* do to Queen Vashti, according to law, because she did not obey the command of King Ahasuerus *brought to her* by the eunuchs?"

[16]And Memucan answered before the king and the princes: "Queen Vashti has not only wronged the king, but also all the princes, and all the people who *are* in all the provinces of King Ahasuerus. [17]For the queen's behavior will become known to all women, so that they will despise their husbands in their eyes, when they report, 'King Ahasuerus commanded Queen Vashti to be brought in before him, but she did not come.' [18]This very day the *noble* ladies of Persia and Media will say to all the king's officials that they have heard of the behavior of the queen. Thus *there will be* excessive contempt and wrath. [19]If it pleases the king, let a royal decree go out from him, and let it be

---

paramount importance, no men except eunuchs were permitted contact with the harem.

1:12 Herodotus, a Greek historian of the Persian period, writes in less than flattering terms about Xerxes as a very impatient, easily angered ruler who had a widespread reputation as a voracious womanizer. The characterization of Ahasuerus in the Book of Esther is consistent with that (see v. 12; Esth. 2:1; 2:4; 7:7).

1:13, 14 The wise men were official advisors found in all the courts of the ancient Near East. "Understood the times" is a phrase used to suggest that the wise men could determine by divination and astrology the most opportune time for action (see Is. 47:13; Dan. 2:27; 5:15). Both Herodotus and Ezra 7:14 record that seven men formed the council of the king's closest advisors. Lesser officials, such as Haman, also had wise men to advise them (see Esth. 6:13).

1:19 Since Vashti had refused to come before the king, she would never again be permitted to enter his presence. Her act is interpreted by some as more than a queen's rebellion against her king (v. 16). The king's advisors surmised that

God understands our questioning, but if our questions keep us from trusting His goodness and wisdom, then we have forfeited His promised blessedness and peace.

Verna Birkey

recorded in the laws of the Persians and the Medes, so that it will not be altered, that Vashti shall come no more before King Ahasuerus; and let the king give her royal position to another who is better than she. ²⁰When the king's decree which he will make is proclaimed throughout all his empire (for it is great), all wives will honor their husbands, both great and small."

²¹And the reply pleased the king and the princes, and the king did according to the word of Memucan. ²²Then he sent letters to all the king's provinces, to each province in its own script, and to every people in their own language, that each man should be master in his own house, and speak in the language of his own people.

Esther Becomes Queen

2 After these things, when the wrath of King Ahasuerus subsided, he remembered Vashti, what she had done, and what had been decreed against her. ²Then the king's servants who attended him said: "Let beautiful young virgins be sought for the king; ³and let the king appoint officers in all the provinces of his kingdom, that they may gather all the beautiful young virgins to Shushan the citadel, into the women's quarters, under the custody of Hegai[a] the king's eunuch, custodian of the women. And let beauty preparations be given *them*. ⁴Then let the young woman

who pleases the king be queen instead of Vashti." This thing pleased the king, and he did so.

⁵In Shushan the citadel there was a certain Jew whose name *was* Mordecai the son of Jair, the son of Shimei, the son of Kish, a Benjamite. ⁶*Kish*[a] had been carried away from Jerusalem with the captives who had been captured with Jeconiah[b] king of Judah, whom Nebuchadnezzar the king of Babylon had carried away. ⁷And *Mordecai* had brought up Hadassah, that *is,* Esther, his uncle's daughter, for she had neither father nor mother. The young woman *was* lovely and beautiful. When her father and mother died, Mordecai took her as his own daughter.

⁸So it was, when the king's command and decree were heard, and when many young women were gathered at Shushan the citadel, *under* the custody of Hegai, that Esther also was taken to the king's palace, into the care of Hegai the custodian of the women. ⁹Now the young woman pleased him, and she obtained his favor; so he readily gave beauty preparations to her, besides her allowance. Then seven choice maidservants were provided for her from the king's palace, and he moved her and her maidservants to the best *place* in the house of the women.

2:3 [a]Hebrew *Hege* 2:6 [a]Literally *Who* [b]Same as *Jehoiachin,* 2 Kings 24:6 and elsewhere

---

Vashti's disrespectful attitude toward her monarch (who was also her husband) could well influence the way other women in the kingdom responded to their husbands, bringing widespread upheaval and discord in homes throughout the land (vv. 17, 18).

1:22 Many languages were spoken such as Old Persian, Elamite, and Babylonian dialects, as well as Assyrian, Arabic, and Indo-European dialects. Aramaic was the *lingua franca* used for trade and diplomacy across the empire. Inscriptions from the reign of Xerxes are mostly trilingual, in Old Persian, Babylonian (Akkadian), and Elamite. Throughout the empire there was an excellent postal system using horses and riders in relays (see Esth. 8:10).

2:3 Fathers may not have brought their daughters voluntarily to the palace (v. 2). Historical sources attest that the harems of two other Persian kings, Darius II and Artaxerxes II, were replenished by a mass gathering of virgins from throughout the empire.

2:5 Mordecai (lit."man of Marduk") is the Hebrew form of his Babylonian name, which contained the name of Marduk, the state god of Babylon. A common practice during the Diaspora was to give an individual both a Babylonian and Hebrew name (see Dan. 1:6, 7). In an undated document, possibly from the

reign of Ahasuerus, an official from Susa named Marduka, who may be this same Mordecai, is mentioned.

This first mention of the "Jews" in the book links this story to the history of Israel. The term "Jew" was used of the Israelites from the time of the Exile (see Josh., Terminology for the Land and People of God). The identification of Mordecai as a descendant of Kish, a Benjamite, reminds those familiar with the Bible of Israel's first king, Saul, who was also introduced as a Benjamite and the son of Kish (1 Sam. 9:1; 14:51). If Kish in both books refers to the same person, then it is being used as an ancestral family name. Otherwise, there may have been two men named Kish, one the father of Saul, the other a more recent ancestor of Mordecai. This genealogy sets the stage for the conflict that is to arise between Mordecai and Haman (see Esth. 3:1, note).

2:6 For Jeconiah, see 2 Kings 24:6–17; chart, The Kings with Two Names.

2:7 Hadassah, meaning "myrtle," is Esther's Hebrew name. The myrtle plant was used metaphorically in the OT to symbolize the Lord's forgiveness and acceptance of His people (see Is. 55:13). Her Babylonian name Esther (lit. "star") may be a form of the name Ishtar, the Babylonian goddess of love and war.

ADOPTION *CHOSEN CHILDREN*

In the process of adoption, an individual—whether relative or not—assumes parental responsibility for the child of another, as Mordecai adopted his young relative Esther after the death of her parents.

Joseph adopted Jesus to be recognized as his own son in the eyes of God and man. This gave all legal inheritance rights traceable through Joseph to Jesus (Matt. 1:1–25), assigning to Him legal claim to the Davidic throne. Spiritually, we are the children of God by adoption just as Jesus was the child of Joseph by adoption. This process of adoption gives to the one adopted full family standing and rights (Rom. 8:15–17). This transaction is a divinely authorized, God-blessed, and legally binding means for adding to the family unit and passing on the family inheritance (Gal. 4:5; Eph. 1:5).

Though the Bible does not present explicit legal process or rights and responsibilities demanded for adoption, Old Testament examples are found (Esther's adoption by Mordecai, Esth. 2:15; Moses by Pharaoh's daughter, Ex. 2:10) in addition to the use of the adoption motif in explaining God's relationship to His people Israel (Deut. 14:2). In the New Testament, adoption describes the believer's relationship with the Lord (Gal. 4:3–7; Eph. 1:1–6).

When a woman accepts Jesus as Savior, the Holy Spirit completes a transaction of adoption on her behalf. She becomes God's daughter and He, her *Abba* (Aramaic word) or "Daddy." As God's adopted daughters, we will inherit a perfect home with Him, and in the meantime we have immediate access to Him for comfort, direction, and provision. He adopted us with pleasure and will never revoke our adoption.

See also Matt. 18:3, note; Rom. 9:4; notes on Children (2 Sam. 21; Ps. 128; Prov. 22; Luke 15); Family (Gen. 32; 1 Sam. 3; Ps. 78; 127); Parenthood (Prov. 10); Salvation (Eph. 2)

---

¹⁰Esther had not revealed her people or family, for Mordecai had charged her not to reveal *it.* ¹¹And every day Mordecai paced in front of the court of the women's quarters, to learn of Esther's welfare and what was happening to her.

¹²Each young woman's turn came to go in to King Ahasuerus after she had completed twelve months' preparation, according to the regulations for the women, for thus were the days of their preparation apportioned: six months with oil of myrrh, and six months with perfumes and preparations for beautifying women. ¹³Thus *prepared, each* young woman went to the king, and she was given whatever she desired to take with her from the women's quarters to the king's palace. ¹⁴In the evening she went, and in the morning she returned to the second house of the women, to the custody of Shaashgaz, the king's eunuch who kept the concubines. She would not go in to the king again unless the king delighted in her and called for her by name.

¹⁵Now when the turn came for Esther the daughter of Abihail the uncle of Mordecai, who had taken her as his daughter, to go in to the king, she requested nothing but what Hegai the king's eunuch, the custodian of the women, advised. And Esther obtained favor in the sight of all who saw her. ¹⁶So Esther was taken to King Ahasuerus, into his royal palace, in the tenth month, which *is* the month of Tebeth, in the seventh year of his reign. ¹⁷The king loved Esther more than all the *other* women, and she obtained grace and favor in his

---

2:12 "Whatever she desired" may have been clothing and jewelry, which the young women in this process may have been allowed to keep as a "wedding" gift from the king.

2:13 The ancient beauty process referred to as "six months with perfumes" has been illuminated by the archaeological find of a cosmetic burner from this period. During the Persian period and even among some Arabian tribes in this century, women would build a small charcoal fire in a pit in the floor. A fragrant oil, such as that from sandalwood, cloves, myrrh, or rose, would be placed in the cosmetic burner and heated in the fire. The woman would crouch naked over the burner with her robe draped over her head and body to form a tent. As she perspired, her open pores absorbed the fragrance of the oil. By the time the fire burned out, her skin and clothing would be thoroughly perfumed. Aromatic oils and spices were Persia's major export.

2:14 The two different parts of the harem mentioned are the "house of the women" (v. 9) and the "second house of the women." The virgins were kept in the first area of the harem.

After a woman had sexual relations with the king, she was moved to the second area of the harem where the king's offspring were reared. From this area she would never depart—even to other areas of the palace—unless the king summoned her to his presence by name (see 2 Sam. 20:3). Both parts were securely guarded by eunuchs. The king's living quarters in the royal palace were separate from the harem but were within the same heavily guarded royal compound.

2:15 Abihail (Heb., lit. "my father is might"), Esther's father, is mentioned twice (v. 15; Esth. 9:29).

2:16 The month of Tebeth corresponds to December–January in the modern calendar (see chart, The Jewish Sacred Calendar). The "seventh year of his reign" would be December, 480 B.C., or January, 479 B.C. or some four years after Vashti was deposed (see Esth. 1:3). The king was occupied during these years by his disastrous war with Greece (482–479 B.C.).

2:17 The grace and favor Esther received from the king hinted at the influential role she would play. According to the Jewish

sight more than all the virgins; so he set the royal crown upon her head and made her queen instead of Vashti. ¹⁸Then the king made a great feast, the Feast of Esther, for all his officials and servants; and he proclaimed a holiday in the provinces and gave gifts according to the generosity of a king.

Mordecai Discovers a Plot

¹⁹When virgins were gathered together a second time, Mordecai sat within the king's gate. ²⁰Now Esther had not revealed her family and her people, just as Mordecai had charged her, for Esther obeyed the command of Mordecai as when she was brought up by him.

²¹In those days, while Mordecai sat within the king's gate, two of the king's eunuchs, Bigthan and Teresh, doorkeepers, became furious and sought to lay hands on King Ahasuerus. ²²So the matter became known to Mordecai, who told Queen Esther, and Esther informed the king in Mordecai's name. ²³And when an inquiry was made into the matter, it was confirmed, and both were hanged on a gallows; and it was written in the book of the chronicles in the presence of the king.

Haman's Conspiracy Against the Jews

3 After these things King Ahasuerus promoted Haman, the son of Hammedatha the Agagite, and advanced him and set his seat above all the princes who *were* with him. ²And all the king's servants who *were* within the king's gate bowed and paid homage to Haman, for so the king had commanded concerning him. But Mordecai would not bow or pay homage. ³Then the king's servants who *were* within the king's gate said to Mordecai, "Why do you transgress the king's command?" ⁴Now it happened, when they spoke to him daily and he would not listen to them, that they told *it* to Haman, to see whether Mordecai's words would stand; for *Mordecai* had told them that he *was* a Jew. ⁵When Haman saw that Mordecai did not bow or pay him homage, Haman was filled with wrath. ⁶But he disdained to lay hands on Mordecai alone, for they had told him of the people of Mordecai. Instead, Haman sought to destroy all the Jews who *were* throughout the whole kingdom of Ahasuerus— the people of Mordecai.

⁷In the first month, which is the month of Nisan, in the twelfth year of King Ahasuerus, they cast Pur (that *is*, the lot), before Haman to determine the day and the month,ᵃ until *it fell on the twelfth month*,ᵇ which *is* the month of Adar.

3:7 ᵃSeptuagint adds *to destroy the people of Mordecai in one day;* Vulgate adds *the nation of the Jews should be destroyed.* ᵇFollowing Masoretic Text and Vulgate; Septuagint reads *and the lot fell on the fourteenth of the month.*

Talmud, Esther was one of the four most beautiful women who ever lived, along with Rahab, Sarah, and Abigail. Evidently, the king had no desire to look further for a queen after he had seen Esther.

2:18 A holiday implies more than release from work. It may include the freeing of slaves, the forgiving of debt, and the remission of tribute or military service (see also Esth. 1:5, note).

2:20 Esther continued to listen to and be obedient to Mordecai even as the queen. For Esther to obey Mordecai's instruction to conceal her identity as a Jew, she would have had to eat, dress, and live in ways that probably would have violated Jewish ceremonial law. Interestingly, the Septuagint (LXX) adds a statement that Mordecai told Esther "to fear God and to perform His commandments." The Bible does not evaluate or commend her behavior in the Persian court in a direct way.

2:21 Mordecai sat within the king's gate. This phrase does not refer to a leisurely pastime but means Mordecai had gained an official position within the court of the king. Much administrative and judicial business was conducted in the gate, which was a large building forming the entrance to the royal compound (see Esth. 4:6, note). Mordecai's position gave him access to much of the royal compound but not to the harem or the palace.

3:1 Haman was associated with Agag, king of the Amalekites, whom Saul (a son of Kish, like Mordecai) had failed to kill when he defied God's command more than 500 years before (v. 1; Esth. 8:3, 5; 9:24; see 1 Sam. 15:1–9). The Amalekites were a nomadic people of the southern desert region who frequently raided the Israelites. They had a long history of animosity with Israel, which began when they were the first nation to war with Israel after the Exodus. (Ex. 17:8–16; see also Deut. 25:17–19). The name "Amalekite" came to refer to any indistinct group of Israel's enemies. The conflict between Mordecai and Haman is portrayed as a continuation of the conflict between Israel and the Amalekites.

3:2 The custom of bowing and paying homage to those ranking members of the court was common and widespread (see 1 Sam. 24:8; 2 Sam. 14:4; 1 Kin. 1:16). Mordecai's refusal may have been on the grounds that such an act would be considered idolatry (v. 4), or he, as a Jew, may have refused to bow to Haman, the Agagite (Amalekite), because the Amalekites were long-standing enemies of the Israelites.

3:7 The months of the Jewish calendar were renamed sometime during the Exile (see chart, The Jewish Sacred Calendar). Nisan, formerly Abib, was the month in which the Lord brought Israel out of Egypt and in which all subsequent generations of Jews have celebrated Passover (Deut. 16:1). While the Jews celebrated their deliverance from Egypt, Haman was casting the "lot" to determine when they would be destroyed. The appointed date would be March or April 474 B.C. a month before the next celebration of Passover. Esther had been queen about five years (see Esth. 2:16).

"Pur" is the singular form of an Akkadian word that was adopted into the Hebrew language referring to a little cube made of clay or glass with an inscription or dots on each side of the cube. The "purim" (Heb. plural) were used throughout the ancient Near East to solicit decisions from the gods. This practice was also used by the Israelites (see Josh. 18:6; Prov. 16:33). The celebration of that deliverance was named "Purim" (lit. "lots") to commemorate God's sovereignty over the "gods" of the oppressors (see chart, The Feast of Purim). A roll of the dice had no power to determine the destiny of God's people.

ESTHER *A Courageous Queen*

How could a modern-day woman imagine the fear and insecurity that would plague Queen Esther, who was chosen solely on the basis of her beauty and appeal to the king? She was no princess with the clout of her father's kingdom to enhance her position in the court. When she was not summoned for thirty days, she did not know if the king had found someone more pleasing or if she was merely losing her influence.

As a displaced, orphaned Jewess, Esther had been reared by Mordecai, an older relative. Whether at his bidding, by force of evil officials, or by her own choice, she had entered the beauty contest and won. Now Mordecai's sources informed Esther that the Jewish people were scheduled for extinction by the wicked Haman, a self-promoter who had elevated himself to vice-regent, second only to the monarch, King Ahasuerus.

Faced with a desperate challenge to survival, Esther pondered Mordecai's question: "Who knows whether you have come to the kingdom for such a time as this?" (Esth. 4:14). Three principles are embodied in his advice:

(1) No place of privilege can ever exempt a person from responsibility to respond to God's call.
(2) Although a situation may look hopeless, God is never helpless.
(3) A God-given opportunity is an individual's received privilege.

Courageously Esther formulated her plan, even if it meant dying in the effort. In the court she had been taught to prepare herself physically, but she had also learned to prepare herself spiritually, as was evidenced by her fasting (Esth. 4:16; 9:31). According to Near Eastern tradition, with patience the queen invited Ahasuerus and Haman to a pair of banquets. Then, seizing the right moment, she presented her case, not questioning the king's justice or righteousness but humbly asking for mercy for herself and her people.

Divine guidance seemingly directed Esther's thoughts, words, and actions. She had won the respect and the ear of her royal husband. In response, he assigned to her the task of re-writing the law (see Esth. 9:29), and she became quite properly the heroine of her people. To every woman she is a reminder of God's sovereignty. God used her beauty, her intelligence, and perhaps even her respectful attitude toward her husband, as well as her remarkable, fearless faith to accomplish His will. Through her obedience, Esther became a true "star" (the meaning of her Persian name) in the Kingdom.

See also notes on Heroines (Heb. 11); Influence (Esth. 4); Submission (1 Pet. 3); chart on Esther: A Leader of the Jews

---

⁸Then Haman said to King Ahasuerus, "There is a certain people scattered and dispersed among the people in all the provinces of your kingdom; their laws *are* different from all *other* people's, and they do not keep the king's laws. Therefore it *is* not fitting for the king to let them remain. ⁹If it pleases the king, let *a decree* be written that they be destroyed, and I will pay ten thousand talents of silver into the hands of those who do the work, to bring *it* into the king's treasuries."

¹⁰So the king took his signet ring from his hand and gave it to Haman, the son of Hammedatha the Agagite, the enemy of the Jews. ¹¹And the king said to Haman, "The money and the people *are* given to you, to do with them as seems good to you."

¹²Then the king's scribes were called on the thirteenth day of the first month, and *a decree* was written according to all that Haman commanded— to the king's satraps, to the governors who *were* over each province, to the officials of all people, to every province according to its script, and to every people in their language. In the name of King Ahasuerus it was written, and sealed with the king's signet ring. ¹³And the letters were sent by couriers into all the king's provinces, to destroy, to kill, and to annihilate all the Jews, both young and old, little children and women, in one day, on the thirteenth *day* of the twelfth month, which *is* the month of Adar, and to plunder their possessions.ᵃ ¹⁴A copy of

3:13 ᵃSeptuagint adds the text of the letter here.

3:9 Ten thousand talents of silver is an enormous amount—over two tons! The total income of the Persian Empire under Ahasuerus' father Darius was 14,560 talents. Haman offered to increase the king's treasury by about two-thirds the national income, presumably by plundering the wealth of the Jews (see Esth. 4:7, note).

3:10 The king's signet ring was the symbol of full executive power. Its imprint was the equivalent of a legally binding signature. By giving Haman his signet ring, the king was giving him the authority to issue a decree in the king's name (see Esth. 8:8).

3:12 The governing hierarchy of the Persian Empire was well organized. "Satraps," a Hebrew spelling of a Persian title, were rulers of large regions. "Governors" ruled over provinces within satrapies. Under Persian rule, Nehemiah was the governor of Judah (Neh. 5:14). "Officials" were local authorities. The decree with the king's seal was sent to all levels of the Persian government.

THE RETURN FROM EXILE

The residence of Esther (Esth. 2:5–7) and Nehemiah

Exiles led by Ezra depart from Babylon.

————————— Probable route of Ezra and Nehemiah (458 B.C.)
————————— Probable route of Sheshbazzar and Zerubbabel (537 B.C.)
See also chart, The Timeline for Ezra, Nehemiah, and Esther.

the document was to be issued as law in every province, being published for all people, that they should be ready for that day. [15] The couriers went out, hastened by the king's command; and the decree was proclaimed in Shushan the citadel. So the king and Haman sat down to drink, but the city of Shushan was perplexed.

Esther Agrees to Help the Jews

4 When Mordecai learned all that had happened, he tore his clothes and put on sackcloth and ashes, and went out into the midst of the city. He cried out with a loud and bitter cry. [2] He went as far as the front of the king's gate, for no one *might* enter the king's gate clothed with sackcloth. [3] And in every province where the king's command and decree arrived, *there was* great mourning among the Jews, with fasting, weeping, and wailing; and many lay in sackcloth and ashes.

[4] So Esther's maids and eunuchs came and told her, and the queen was deeply distressed. Then she sent garments to clothe Mordecai and take his sackcloth away from him, but he would not accept *them*. [5] Then Esther called Hathach, *one of* the king's eunuchs whom he had appointed to attend her, and she gave him a command concerning Mordecai, to learn what and why this *was*. [6] So Hathach went out to Mordecai in the city square that *was* in front of the king's gate. [7] And Mordecai told him all that had happened to him, and the sum of money that Haman had promised to pay into the king's treasuries to destroy the Jews. [8] He also gave him a copy of the written decree for their destruction, which was given at Shushan, that he might show it to Esther and explain it to her, and that he might command her to go in to the king to make supplication to him and plead before him for her people. [9] So Hathach returned and told Esther the words of Mordecai.

3:15 Herodotus, a Greek historian of the Persian period, explained that Persian kings customarily deliberated weighty matters of state while inebriated. When the "king and Haman sat down to drink," they were not necessarily celebrating but more probably were confirming deliberations on the matter.

4:1–3 Sackcloth and ashes were an almost universal sign of grief in the ancient Near East throughout the OT period (see 1 Kin. 21:27; Dan. 9:3; Jon. 3:6; Matt. 11:21). Although Mordecai had access to the royal compound, he could not enter while so attired.

4:6 Archaeologists have uncovered the king's gate—a large building, 131 by 92 feet, with a central room 69 feet square. The discovery that the gate opened onto a city square corroborates the accuracy of details such as that given in this verse.

4:7 Mordecai had heard of Haman's offer to increase the royal treasury enormously at the expense of the Jews; he apparently had not heard that the king refused the money (Esth. 3:11). Before marrying Esther, Xerxes had fought and lost a costly war with Greece (482–479 B.C.). Perhaps Mordecai reasoned that the fate of the Jews was sealed because Haman had made an offer the king could not afford to refuse (see Esth. 3:9, note).

INFLUENCE *MAKING YOUR MARK*

Women in Bible times are often thought of as being weak pawns in the world of mighty men. A careful study of the Bible, however, reveals women of enormous influence over their families, communities, and nations.

- Queen Esther was used of God to accomplish His purpose. She offered a moving petition for the lives of her people, swayed a king's opinion, and was given the authority and resources to devise a strategy for saving her people (Esth. 8:7–12).
- Deborah judged all of Israel and led a general into a victorious battle (Judg. 4:4–24).
- Jochebed cleverly defied the evil ruling of the pharaoh and put together a creative plan to save the life of her son, who eventually led his people out of slavery (Ex. 2:1–10).
- Rahab offered shelter to two spies, saving her family from the invaders who destroyed all others in her city. Ultimately, she committed herself to *Yahweh*, the God of Israel (Josh. 2:12–14; 6:22–25).
- Abigail worked creatively to circumvent her husband's foolishness and in so doing saved her family and servants from certain death, putting herself into a position of great influence (1 Sam. 25:3–42).
- Huldah, wife of the keeper of the king's wardrobe, boldly spoke as a prophetess of the Lord to her people (2 Kin. 22:14–20).

The same kind of influence is evident today among women all over the world who use their gifts and talents to lead movements, rear families, and nurture the body of Christ. Women have a real ability to impact society in their homes and in their professional lives by practicing the same sacrificial attitude of these women whose testimonies are found in Scripture. The issue is not whether women have influence but whether they will choose to use their influence for evil or good, to extend God's kingdom on the earth or attempt to destroy it.

See also Ruth 3:10, 11; Prov. 11:16; 31:10–31; Matt. 15:21–28; 26:6–13; 1 Pet. 3:15–17; notes on Feminine Leadership (1 Sam. 25); Intuition (Heb. 5); Motherhood (1 Sam. 1; Is. 49; Ezek. 16); Women's Ministries (John 4; Acts 2; 1 Cor. 11; Eph. 2; 1 Tim. 3; Titus 2); portraits of Abigail (1 Sam. 25); Deborah (Judg. 4); Esther (Esth. 2); Huldah (2 Kin. 22); Jochebed (Ex. 6); Rahab (Josh. 2)

---

[10]Then Esther spoke to Hathach, and gave him a command for Mordecai: [11]"All the king's servants and the people of the king's provinces know that any man or woman who goes into the inner court to the king, who has not been called, *he has* but one law: put *all* to death, except the one to whom the king holds out the golden scepter, that he may live. Yet I myself have not been called to go in to the king these thirty days." [12]So they told Mordecai Esther's words.

[13]And Mordecai told *them* to answer Esther: "Do not think in your heart that you will escape in the king's palace any more than all the other Jews. [14]For if you remain completely silent at this time, relief and deliverance will arise for the Jews from another place, but you and your father's house will perish. Yet who knows whether you have come to the kingdom for *such* a time as this?"

[15]Then Esther told *them* to reply to Mordecai: [16]"Go, gather all the Jews who are present in Shushan, and fast for me; neither eat nor drink for three days, night or day. My maids and I will fast likewise. And so I will go to the king, which *is* against the law; and if I perish, I perish!"

[17]So Mordecai went his way and did according to all that Esther commanded him.[a]

···················
4:17 [a]Septuagint adds a prayer of Mordecai here.

4:11 The law that no one, not even his family, could approach the king unsummoned was a defense against assassination. Anyone wishing to see the king was expected to send a message requesting an audience. A carved relief excavated from the royal city of Persepolis shows Darius I seated on his throne with the royal scepter in his right hand and Crown Prince Xerxes standing behind him. The royal bodyguards, complete with ax, sword, and bow, flank the throne. Because she had not been summoned by the king for 30 days, Esther was not expecting an opportunity to speak with him in the near future. Esther believed that she had to violate court protocol at the risk of her life because of the urgency of her mission (v. 16).

4:12–16 These verses most clearly express the book's theme: God works through human decisions (see Matt. 26:24; Acts 2:23 for NT expressions of the concurrence of God's sovereignty and human responsibility).

4:14 Mordecai's belief that the Jews would be delivered is rooted in the promises of God to preserve Israel while in Exile (see Jer. 29:1–14). Mordecai's remark, implying the improbability of an unknown Jewess becoming the wife of the Persian king, designates Esther herself as the means of their deliverance. Mordecai's remark is a veiled reference to God's providential work in orchestrating life's circumstances.

4:16 Fasting was closely associated with prayer (Ezra 8:23; Neh. 1:4; Dan. 9:3; see Matt. 6:16–18, note). The omission of any mention of prayer at this point is so conspicuous in its absence that the author, for whatever reason, may well have deliberately chosen to avoid all explicitly religious language.

Esther's Banquet

5 Now it happened on the third day that Esther put on *her* royal *robes* and stood in the inner court of the king's palace, across from the king's house, while the king sat on his royal throne in the royal house, facing the entrance of the house.[a] 2So it was, when the king saw Queen Esther standing in the court, *that* she found favor in his sight, and the king held out to Esther the golden scepter that *was* in his hand. Then Esther went near and touched the top of the scepter.

3And the king said to her, "What do you wish, Queen Esther? What *is* your request? It shall be given to you— up to half the kingdom!"

4So Esther answered, "If it pleases the king, let the king and Haman come today to the banquet that I have prepared for him."

5Then the king said, "Bring Haman quickly, that he may do as Esther has said." So the king and Haman went to the banquet that Esther had prepared.

6At the banquet of wine the king said to Esther, "What *is* your petition? It shall be granted you. What *is* your request, up to half the kingdom? It shall be done!"

7Then Esther answered and said, "My petition and request *is this:* 8If I have found favor in the sight of the king, and if it pleases the king to grant my petition and fulfill my request, then let the king and Haman come to the banquet which I will prepare for them, and tomorrow I will do as the king has said."

Haman's Plot Against Mordecai

9So Haman went out that day joyful and with a glad heart; but when Haman saw Mordecai in the king's gate, and that he did not stand or tremble before him, he was filled with indignation against Mordecai. 10Nevertheless Haman restrained himself and went home, and he sent and called for his friends and his wife Zeresh. 11Then Haman told them of his great riches, the multitude of his children, everything in which the king had promoted him, and how he had advanced him above the officials and servants of the king.

12Moreover Haman said, "Besides, Queen Esther invited no one but me to come in with the king to the banquet that she prepared; and tomorrow I am again invited by her, along with the king. 13Yet all this avails me nothing, so long as I see Mordecai the Jew sitting at the king's gate."

14Then his wife Zeresh and all his friends said to him, "Let a gallows be made, fifty cubits high, and in the morning suggest to the king that Mordecai be hanged on it; then go merrily with the king to the banquet."

And the thing pleased Haman; so he had the gallows made.

The King Honors Mordecai

6 That night the king could not sleep. So one was commanded to bring the book of the records of the chronicles; and they were read before the king. 2And it was found written that Mordecai had told of Bigthana and Teresh, two of the king's eunuchs, the doorkeepers who had sought to lay hands on King Ahasuerus. 3Then the king said, "What honor or dignity has been bestowed on Mordecai for this?"

And the king's servants who attended him said, "Nothing has been done for him."

4So the king said, "Who *is* in the court?" Now Haman had *just* entered the outer court of the king's palace to suggest that the king hang Mordecai on the gallows that he had prepared for him.

5:1 [a]Septuagint adds many extra details in verses 1 and 2.

5:1 Greek historians described the royal robes of the Persian king. The outer robe was dyed with Phoenician purple and embroidered with gold in patterns of fighting hawks or serpents. White or crimson trousers edged with purple were worn under the robe. Gold jeweled earrings, bracelets, and a filigree collar adorned the king. The king's sword, with a sheath reportedly made of a single precious stone, was supported by a belt made of gold. Bright color, precious gems, and abundant gold made the royal dress a glittering splendor. The queen's royal robes were no doubt commensurate with the riches of her position.

5:3 The phrase up to half the kingdom was a court idiom used by kings in the ancient Near East to indicate their generous disposition toward the person in view. It was probably not to be understood as a literal offer of half the riches or the power of the kingdom (v. 6; Esth. 7:2; see Mark 6:23).

5:14 In the Persian culture "gallows" would have been used to impale Mordecai for public display. The great height (about 75 feet), which is often taken as an exaggeration, may have been intended to assure that all in Susa would have a good view of Haman's revenge on Mordecai (see Esth. 9:13, 14, note).

Haman's wife Zeresh gave him advice similar to that given when Jezebel suggested to Ahab that he kill Naboth and seize his vineyard (1 Kin. 21). To readers familiar with that story, Zeresh's advice hints at a disastrous outcome.

6:1 The Greek historians reported that by law Persian officials kept archives of royal records which contained a detailed account of the business of the Persian kings. These "records of the chronicles" (see Esth. 2:23) were written on scrolls of leather or papyrus and were carefully filed in the royal archives (see Ezra 6:1–4; Esth. 10:2). It was a point of honor to Persian kings, as well as good politics, to reward amply anyone whose loyal action benefited the king. As much as five years had passed between the time when Mordecai had thwarted the assassination plot and when the king realized no reward had been given (Esth. 2:19–23). Fortunately, the king was disposed to reward Mordecai on the same day that Haman was preparing to kill him. This verse is the narrative center of the book, after which the plot turns to the Jews' favor.

⁵The king's servants said to him, "Haman is there, standing in the court."

And the king said, "Let him come in."

⁶So Haman came in, and the king asked him, "What shall be done for the man whom the king delights to honor?"

Now Haman thought in his heart, "Whom would the king delight to honor more than me?" ⁷And Haman answered the king, "For the man whom the king delights to honor, ⁸let a royal robe be brought which the king has worn, and a horse on which the king has ridden, which has a royal crest placed on its head. ⁹Then let this robe and horse be delivered to the hand of one of the king's most noble princes, that he may array the man whom the king delights to honor. Then parade him on horseback through the city square, and proclaim before him: 'Thus shall it be done to the man whom the king delights to honor!' "

¹⁰Then the king said to Haman, "Hurry, take the robe and the horse, as you have suggested, and do so for Mordecai the Jew who sits within the king's gate! Leave nothing undone of all that you have spoken."

¹¹So Haman took the robe and the horse, arrayed Mordecai and led him on horseback through the city square, and proclaimed before him, "Thus shall it be done to the man whom the king delights to honor!"

¹²Afterward Mordecai went back to the king's gate. But Haman hurried to his house, mourning and with his head covered. ¹³When Haman told his wife Zeresh and all his friends everything that had happened to him, his wise men and his wife Zeresh said to him, "If Mordecai, before whom you have begun to fall, is of Jewish descent, you will not prevail against him but will surely fall before him."

¹⁴While they were still talking with him, the king's eunuchs came, and hastened to bring Haman to the banquet which Esther had prepared.

Haman Hanged Instead of Mordecai

7 So the king and Haman went to dine with Queen Esther. ²And on the second day, at the banquet of wine, the king again said to Esther, "What is your petition, Queen Esther? It shall be granted you. And what is your request, up to half the kingdom? It shall be done!"

³Then Queen Esther answered and said, "If I have found favor in your sight, O king, and if it pleases the king, let my life be given me at my petition, and my people at my request. ⁴For we have been sold, my people and I, to be destroyed, to be killed, and to be annihilated. Had we been sold as male and female slaves, I would have held my tongue, although the enemy could never compensate for the king's loss."

⁵So King Ahasuerus answered and said to Queen Esther, "Who is he, and where is he, who would dare presume in his heart to do such a thing?"

⁶And Esther said, "The adversary and enemy is this wicked Haman!"

So Haman was terrified before the king and queen.

⁷Then the king arose in his wrath from the banquet of wine and went into the palace garden; but Haman stood before Queen Esther, pleading for his life, for he saw that evil was determined against him by the king. ⁸When the king returned from the palace garden to the place of the banquet of wine, Haman had fallen across the couch where Esther was. Then the king said, "Will he also assault the queen while I am in the house?"

As the word left the king's mouth, they covered Haman's face. ⁹Now Harbonah, one of the eunuchs, said to the king, "Look! The gallows, fifty cubits high, which Haman made for Mordecai, who spoke good on the king's behalf, is standing at the house of Haman."

Then the king said, "Hang him on it!"

¹⁰So they hanged Haman on the gallows that

6:8 A royal robe. It was a great honor to wear the king's robe in ancient times, for it symbolized special favor (see 1 Sam. 18:4). What is here called the "royal crest" on the king's horse is seen in the reliefs excavated from the palace in Persepolis. The horse's mane was arranged in a top-knot between his ears.

6:13 Invincibility of the Jews. The remark made by Haman's wife, Zeresh, and his wise men about the invincibility of the Jews and Haman's certain defeat hints at the reversal of fortune that is about to occur. Haman, the Agagite, was an Amalekite against whom stood a long tradition of biblical curses. At the beginning of the conflict between Israel and the Amalekites, the Lord swore that He would be at war with every generation of Amalekites (Ex. 17:16). Because Haman, an Amalekite, was warring against the Jews, as had his ancestors, he could expect nothing but defeat.

7:2 See Esth. 5:3, note.

7:8 A violation of harem protocol. It was a Persian custom to recline during a meal. Had Haman followed harem protocol, he would have left Esther's presence with the king. Although it was a common Near Eastern gesture of contrition to seize the feet or even kiss them, such behavior was completely inappropriate with a woman of the harem, much less the queen herself! So strict was harem protocol that the king's interpretation of Haman's behavior would have probably been the same even if Haman had merely knelt before Esther with no physical contact.

7:9, 10 Not only had Haman plotted against the queen's people and assaulted the queen, but he had also planned to murder Mordecai, who had previously foiled an assassination plot against the king. The king therefore saw Haman as a traitor. Haman's execution on the very gallows he had prepared for Mordecai is another of the book's ironic reversals of fortune.

ESTHER: A LEADER OF THE JEWS

EARLY YEARS	Her Hebrew name was Hadassah (lit. "myrtle"), but she was known by her Persian name Esther (lit. "star"). Her family was carried into captivity and chose to remain in Shushan. She was reared by her close relative (possibly cousin) Mordecai in Persia as part of a minority race (Esth. 2:5–7).
FAMILY STATUS	She was the orphaned daughter of Abihail of the tribe of Benjamin. Her close relative Mordecai was her guardian (Esth. 2:7, 15).
LEADERSHIP TRAINING	She possessed inner and outer beauty (Esth. 2:7, 9, 15, 17; 5:2). She was reared in the home of Mordecai, who sat within the king's gate, having at least an understanding of court life and probably some official responsibilities (Esth. 2:21–23). She disciplined herself to be obedient to authorities in her life (Esth. 2:8, 9, 20).
GOD'S CALL	The words of Mordecai, "…who knows whether you have come to the kingdom for such a time as this," presented her call (Esth. 4:13, 14).
GOD'S PROMISES	God's timing was perfect (Esth. 4:14). God's providence, which uses His people to accomplish His purposes, was certain (Esth. 4:14, 15). God's provision, including service, was not without cost (Esth. 4:16).
GOD'S INSTRUCTION	Mordecai delivered God's instruction (Esth. 2:22; 4:8–14).
THE PEOPLE'S AFFIRMATION	Esther's leadership was followed by palace staff (Esth. 4:5–9). Mordecai respected and responded to Esther (Esth. 4:17).
ESTHER'S LEADERSHIP	She accepted God's will (Esth. 4:16). She was confident of God's providence (Esth. 4:17). She was active in mobilizing her staff and others for "fasting"; prayer and fasting were usually done in concert in times of grief or anguish (Esth. 4:15, 16; see also 2 Sam. 12:16, 17; Ezra 8:23). She set an example of fasting herself (Esth. 4:16). She presented herself in humility and obedience (Esth. 5:1—6:14). She used creativity of effort and talent in her task (Esth. 5:3—6:14). She considered timing in her plan (Esth. 6:1–14). Her influence reflected extraordinary power and authority for a woman in Esther's historical setting; it traveled far and wide; it continued unto the generations after her death (Esth. 9:32). She wrote a decree that was entered in official records with full authority (Esth. 9:29, 32).
OBSERVATIONS	She was courageous and self-sacrificing (Esth. 4:14, 16). She was clever (Esth. 5:3, 4; 8:3). She was used of God to save her people.

he had prepared for Mordecai. Then the king's wrath subsided.

Esther Saves the Jews

8 On that day King Ahasuerus gave Queen Esther the house of Haman, the enemy of the Jews. And Mordecai came before the king, for Esther had told how he *was related* to her. ²So the king took off his signet ring, which he had taken from Haman, and gave it to Mordecai; and Esther appointed Mordecai over the house of Haman.

³Now Esther spoke again to the king, fell down at his feet, and implored him with tears to counteract the evil of Haman the Agagite, and the scheme which he had devised against the Jews. ⁴And the king held out the golden scepter toward Esther. So Esther arose and stood before the king, ⁵and said, "If it pleases the king, and if I have

8:1 The house of Haman. Herodotus and Josephus both recorded that the property of a traitor became the property of the king. Ahasuerus gave the confiscated property to Esther as restitution for the offense against her.

8:2 Mordecai's promotion. Not only is Mordecai's life spared from Haman's murderous attempts, but Mordecai is also pro-

moted as Haman's successor in the court. Haman's attempt to kill Mordecai leads only to Mordecai's exaltation and Haman's own destruction. Clearly this reversal is meant as a warning to the enemies of God's people and as an encouragement to those on whom God's promised protection rests.

8:4 See Esth. 4:11, note.

found favor in his sight and the thing *seems* right to the king and I am pleasing in his eyes, let it be written to revoke the letters devised by Haman, the son of Hammedatha the Agagite, which he wrote to annihilate the Jews who *are* in all the king's provinces. [6]For how can I endure to see the evil that will come to my people? Or how can I endure to see the destruction of my countrymen?"

[7]Then King Ahasuerus said to Queen Esther and Mordecai the Jew, "Indeed, I have given Esther the house of Haman, and they have hanged him on the gallows because he *tried to* lay his hand on the Jews. [8]You yourselves write *a decree* concerning the Jews, as you please, in the king's name, and seal *it* with the king's signet ring; for whatever is written in the king's name and sealed with the king's signet ring no one can revoke."

[9]So the king's scribes were called at that time, in the third month, which *is* the month of Sivan, on the twenty-third *day;* and it was written, according to all that Mordecai commanded, to the Jews, the satraps, the governors, and the princes of the provinces from India to Ethiopia, one hundred and twenty-seven provinces *in all,* to every province in its own script, to every people in their own language, and to the Jews in their own script and language. [10]And he wrote in the name of King Ahasuerus, sealed *it* with the king's signet ring, and sent letters by couriers on horseback, riding on royal horses bred from swift steeds.[a]

[11]By these letters the king permitted the Jews who *were* in every city to gather together and protect their lives—to destroy, kill, and annihilate all the forces of any people or province that would assault them, *both* little children and women, and to plunder their possessions, [12]on one day in all the provinces of King Ahasuerus, on the thirteenth *day* of the twelfth month, which *is* the month of Adar.[a] [13]A copy of the document was to be issued as a decree in every province and published for all people, so that the Jews would be ready on that day to avenge themselves on their enemies. [14]The couriers who rode on royal horses went out, hastened and pressed on by the king's command. And the decree was issued in Shushan the citadel.

[15]So Mordecai went out from the presence of the king in royal apparel of blue and white, with a great crown of gold and a garment of fine linen and purple; and the city of Shushan rejoiced and was glad. [16]The Jews had light and gladness, joy and honor. [17]And in every province and city, wherever the king's command and decree came, the Jews had joy and gladness, a feast and a holiday. Then many of the people of the land became Jews, because fear of the Jews fell upon them.

The Jews Destroy Their Tormentors

9 Now in the twelfth month, that *is,* the month of Adar, on the thirteenth day, *the time* came for the king's command and his decree to be executed. On the day that the enemies of the Jews had hoped to overpower them, the opposite occurred, in that the Jews themselves overpowered those who hated them. [2]The Jews gathered together in their cities throughout all the provinces of King Ahasuerus to lay hands on those who sought their harm. And no one could withstand them, because fear of them fell upon all people. [3]And all the officials of the provinces, the satraps, the governors, and all those doing the king's work, helped the Jews, because the fear of Mordecai fell upon them. [4]For Mordecai *was* great in the king's palace, and his fame spread throughout all the provinces; for this man Mordecai became increasingly prominent. [5]Thus the Jews defeated all their enemies with the stroke of the sword, with slaughter and destruction, and did what they pleased with those who hated them.

[6]And in Shushan the citadel the Jews killed and destroyed five hundred men. [7]Also Parshandatha, Dalphon, Aspatha, [8]Poratha, Adalia, Aridatha, [9]Parmashta, Arisai, Aridai, and Vajezatha— [10]the ten sons of Haman the son of Hammedatha, the enemy of the Jews—they killed; but they did not lay a hand on the plunder.

[11]On that day the number of those who were killed in Shushan the citadel was brought to the king. [12]And the king said to Queen Esther, "The Jews have killed and destroyed five hundred men in Shushan the citadel, and the ten sons of

---

8:10 [a]Literally *sons of the swift horses*   **8:12** [a]Septuagint adds the text of the letter here.

8:9 The third month . . . the twenty-third day. The month of Sivan corresponds with mid-May to mid-June on the modern calendar (see chart, The Jewish Sacred Calendar). The Jewish Feast of Pentecost (or Weeks), which, according to later Jewish tradition, celebrated the giving of the Law at Sinai, was celebrated in Sivan. This feast was primarily a harvest celebration. Two months and ten days after issuing his decree, Haman was dead and his decree was counteracted. But the appointed day of confrontation was still nine months away.

8:10 See Esth. 1:22, note.

8:11 Mordecai counteracts Haman's decree. Mordecai's decree protecting the Jews only gave them legal permission to defend themselves in the event that anyone should still wish to act upon Haman's edict of extermination. The fact that hostilities did occur and that so many people were killed indicates that many among the population wished to harm the Jews.

8:12 Thirteenth day of the twelfth month. The month of Adar corresponds to February–March (see chart, The Jewish Sacred Calendar).

9:5–10 The Jews defeated their enemies. This incident is the antithesis of Saul's disobedience to God. Saul failed to kill the Amalekites and took forbidden plunder (1 Sam. 15:1–23). He consequently lost the throne. The Jews took no plunder (Esth. 9:10). After this incident, Mordecai ascends to a position of leadership second only to the king himself (Esth. 10:3).

THE FEAST OF PURIM

NAME	Purim (Heb. *pur*, lit. "the lot")
REFERENCE	Esth. 9:16–32
TIME	The fourteenth day of Adar (Feb.–Mar.) by those in villages and unwalled towns and on the fifteenth day by those in fortified cities.
PURPOSE	(1) To commemorate the deliverance of the Jews from genocide through the efforts of Esther. (2) To rejoice together and distribute food and presents.

Haman. What have they done in the rest of the king's provinces? Now what *is* your petition? It shall be granted to you. Or what *is* your further request? It shall be done."

¹³Then Esther said, "If it pleases the king, let it be granted to the Jews who *are* in Shushan to do again tomorrow according to today's decree, and let Haman's ten sons be hanged on the gallows."

¹⁴So the king commanded this to be done; the decree was issued in Shushan, and they hanged Haman's ten sons.

¹⁵And the Jews who *were* in Shushan gathered together again on the fourteenth day of the month of Adar and killed three hundred men at Shushan; but they did not lay a hand on the plunder.

¹⁶The remainder of the Jews in the king's provinces gathered together and protected their lives, had rest from their enemies, and killed seventy-five thousand of their enemies; but they did not lay a hand on the plunder. ¹⁷*This was* on the thirteenth day of the month of Adar. And on the fourteenth of *the month*ᵃ they rested and made it a day of feasting and gladness.

The Feast of Purim

¹⁸But the Jews who *were* at Shushan assembled together on the thirteenth *day*, as well as on the fourteenth; and on the fifteenth of *the month*ᵃ they rested, and made it a day of feasting and gladness. ¹⁹Therefore the Jews of the villages who dwelt in the unwalled towns celebrated the fourteenth day of the month of Adar *with* gladness and feasting, as a holiday, and for sending presents to one another.

²⁰And Mordecai wrote these things and sent letters to all the Jews, near and far, who *were* in all the provinces of King Ahasuerus, ²¹to establish among them that they should celebrate yearly the fourteenth and fifteenth days of the month of Adar, ²²as the days on which the Jews had rest from their enemies, as the month which was turned from sorrow to joy for them, and from mourning to a holiday; that they should make them days of feasting and joy, of sending presents to one another and gifts to the poor. ²³So the Jews accepted the custom which they had begun, as Mordecai had written to them, ²⁴because Haman, the son of Hammedatha the Agagite, the enemy of all the Jews, had plotted against the Jews to annihilate them, and had cast Pur (that *is*, the lot), to consume them and destroy them; ²⁵but when *Esther*ᵃ came before the king, he commanded by letter that thisᵇ wicked plot which

9:17, 18 ᵃLiterally *it* 9:25 ᵃLiterally *she* or *it* ᵇLiterally *his*

9:13, 14 Haman's ten sons had been killed (v. 10). The request that they "be hanged on the gallows" would be understood as a request that their dead bodies be impaled for public viewing. The public humiliation of a dead enemy was a common practice in the ancient Near East (see 1 Sam. 31:8–13).

9:18, 19 Two days of celebration. Both the "Jews of the villages" and the Jews in Susa celebrated after the hostilities ceased. The "Jews of the villages" celebrated after one day of hostilities; the Jews in Susa after two days. Therefore, the village Jews celebrated on the fourteenth day of Adar and the Jews in Susa on the fifteenth day. In subsequent celebrations of Purim, both days were days of celebration (vv. 21, 22). Purim is now observed on the fifteenth of Adar in Jerusalem and on the fourteenth by Jews living elsewhere (see charts, The Jewish Sacred Calendar; The Feast of Purim).

9:21 The celebration of Purim (or the Feast of Lots) falls in late February or early March. It continues to be celebrated by the Jews with the reading of Esther in the synagogue accompanied by noisemakers and booing whenever Haman's name is read. It is the first Jewish festival to be observed without mention in the Torah (see charts, The Feasts of Israel; The Feast of Purim). The holiday is observed with masquerading, feasting, and games, similar to the carnival celebration preceding the Lenten season. The Jewish Talmud prescribes festive drinking on Purim until one cannot distinguish between "Haman be cursed!" and "Mordecai be blessed!"

9:23, 24 Haman, "the Agagite, the enemy of all the Jews," believed he could secure success for his plot by casting the lots. Purim celebrates the power of God working in history to preserve His people and to deliver them from destruction (Prov. 21:30, 31).

Haman had devised against the Jews should return on his own head, and that he and his sons should be hanged on the gallows.

26So they called these days Purim, after the name Pur. Therefore, because of all the words of this letter, what they had seen concerning this matter, and what had happened to them, 27the Jews established and imposed it upon themselves and their descendants and all who would join them, that without fail they should celebrate these two days every year, according to the written *instructions* and according to the *prescribed* time, 28*that* these days *should be* remembered and kept throughout every generation, every family, every province, and every city, that these days of Purim should not fail *to be observed* among the Jews, and *that* the memory of them should not perish among their descendants.

29Then Queen Esther, the daughter of Abihail, with Mordecai the Jew, wrote with full authority to confirm this second letter about Purim. 30And *Mordecai* sent letters to all the Jews, to the one hundred and twenty-seven provinces of the kingdom of Ahasuerus, *with* words of peace and truth, 31to confirm these days of Purim at their *appointed* time, as Mordecai the Jew and Queen Esther had prescribed for them, and as they had decreed for themselves and their descendants concerning matters of their fasting and lamenting. 32So the decree of Esther confirmed these matters of Purim, and it was written in the book.

Mordecai's Advancement

10And King Ahasuerus imposed tribute on the land and *on* the islands of the sea. 2Now all the acts of his power and his might, and the account of the greatness of Mordecai, to which the king advanced him, *are* they not written in the book of the chronicles of the kings of Media and Persia? 3For Mordecai the Jew *was* second to King Ahasuerus, and was great among the Jews and well received by the multitude of his brethren, seeking the good of his people and speaking peace to all his countrymen.[a]

·······················

10:3 [a]Literally *seed*. Septuagint and Vulgate add a dream of Mordecai here; Vulgate adds six more chapters.

9:31 The fast of Esther is observed by Jews today on the thirteenth of Adar in preparation for the Feast of Purim (see chart, The Feast of Purim).

9:32 The holiday is permanently established. Queen Esther institutionalized the celebration of Purim under Persian law. The phrase "it was written in the book" indicates that Esther's decree establishing a permanent observance of Purim throughout the empire was filed in the royal archives (see Esth. 6:1, note).

10:1 Replenishing the royal coffers. Xerxes fought and lost a costly war with Greece in 479 B.C. The imposition of "tribute" was a system of taxation, and perhaps forced labor, which would restore the depleted royal treasury.

10:3 The rise of Mordecai, a Jew, to the second highest position in a pagan court is a reminder of Daniel in Babylon and of Joseph in Pharaoh's Egyptian court much earlier in Israel's history. Mordecai joined these heroes of Israel's history as another example of how God's people lived victoriously even when scattered among the nations.

Job

The Book of Job is named after its principal character, around whom the events of the narrative revolve. The same is true of other Old Testament books like Joshua, Ruth, Samuel, Ezra, Nehemiah, Esther, Daniel, and Jonah.

AUTHOR

The author of the Book of Job is unknown, but he was obviously a wise and well-educated man with literary skills. He referred to such diverse subjects as mining, astronomy, animals, embryonic development, and hunting. Possibly the author was Job himself, in which case he wrote it after his restoration. Other suggested authors include Moses (according to Jewish tradition), Solomon, Hezekiah, Isaiah, Ezra, and Elihu.

DATE

The date of the events in Job is unknown. Evidence for a patriarchal setting includes Job's old age (more than 100 years, Job 42:16), the assessment of his wealth according to livestock and servants (Job 1:3), the unique vocabulary, and the lack of any reference to Israelite history or Mosaic Law. Proposed dates for the writing of Job vary from patriarchal to postexilic times, depending on the author assumed.

BACKGROUND

SETTING: The period of the patriarchs seems to be the most likely setting for the Book of Job. In the description of wealth and prosperity, great similarity exists between Job and Isaac (Job 1:3; see Gen. 26:13, 14). However, Job is not a descendant of Abraham, and he is not living in the land of Canaan. The text identifies his land as Uz (Job 1:1). Uz has been located either northeast of Palestine (in the region of Hauran or Trachonitis) or to the south (between Edom and northern Arabia). The latter seems more probable (see Lam. 4:21 and reference to "daughter of Edom," which points to Idumea).

PURPOSE: The book presents a "blameless and upright" man "who feared God" (Job 1:1). He was a patriarch secure in the midst of family and prosperity. The faith and perseverance of this extraordinary man were tested by Satan, but in the end Job was victorious, and his faith was rewarded. The author affirmed that God never abandons the one in the midst of suffering and that all suffering is not necessarily due to the personal sin of the one suffering. Also, suffering does not necessarily detach the one suffering from God. The book describes the kind of faith required of God and how that faith works itself out in the midst of the fires of suffering. Perhaps this was the author's way of vindicating God against the popular notions that have persisted from then until now. Suffering teaches us about our own insufficiency and leads us to greater faith in God. God requires of His saints a faith that perseveres patiently under adversity.

LITERARY CHARACTERISTICS: The Book of Job is usually classified as Wisdom Literature, but it differs from other books of Jewish wisdom in that it combines prose (as in the narrative of the Prologue, Job 1:1—2:13, and the Epilogue, Job 42:7–17), poetry (the speeches), and dialogue. The book is masterful in its structure, parallelism, vocabulary, imagery, and use of literary devices.

THEMES

Although the Book of Job seems to be about a righteous man who endures incredible suffering, it focuses more on God's wisdom and sovereignty. The grand themes of God's wisdom and justice overshadow the suffering and faith of Job. Deep questions that gnaw at the heart are raised: Why do the righteous suffer? Why would God allow such suffering? Why should a man believe in God? Why believe in God without visible benefit? The answers emphasize the limitations of human wisdom as contrasted with the vast wisdom of God.

The comfortable but not comforting answers of Job's friends are shown not only to be inadequate, but wrong (Job 42:7, 8). They speak from their experience and from a tradition limited to the doctrine of retribution or the belief that suffering is always punishment for sin. But there is a greater answer to Job's suffering founded on the wisdom of God.

In Job is a rare glimpse behind-the-scenes where God's control and limiting of Satan are evident. Job is singled out by God to be a tested man of faith. As Satan accuses God of bribing His servant to believe in Him (Job 1:9, 10), Job emerges without sin even in the face of crushing disaster and undeserved suffering (Job 1:22; 2:10). In the first thirteen chapters of Job, the question "Why?" is asked repeatedly but with no reply. The question demands an explanation and a justification. But even if Job could have comprehended God's answers, he would have known only "the mere edges of His ways" (Job 26:14). Thus, when faced with suffering, the question "Why?" is inappropriate.

The better question is "Who?" "Who is in charge?" In his reply to Job, God asks "Who?" at least twenty times (Job 38—41). When the "Who?" is God, then the gnawing "Why?" is moderated. The believer can be like "a weaned child with his mother," a child who has learned to wait for and trust in his mother to give him what he needs at the right time (Ps. 131:2).

Job rightly and steadfastly identified God as the One ultimately responsible for all his suffering. He never once blamed Satan, from whose direct hand he had received his blows (Job 2:10).

God Himself had said to Satan, "You incited Me against him, to destroy him without cause" (Job 2:3). God is not in charge of only the good things that happen, impotently observing as bad things happen, but He is sovereignly in control of all things, good *and* bad. He permits His children to endure testing. One who only accepts the good from God's hand risks rejecting Him completely when things do not work out as desired. Such a limited acceptance of God's wisdom is foolish.

Job recognized God in his trials, and though he was grief-stricken and bewildered, he tenaciously clung to God (Job 13:15). In his impoverished and depleted state, Job uttered a profound statement of faith (Job 19:25–27). In the face of hopelessness, Job did not lose his greatest hope.

Only the Lord knows all the whys and wherefores of human suffering. Until "I shall know just as I also am known," knowing Him is more than sufficient (see 1 Cor. 13:12; 2 Tim. 1:12; James 5:11).

Job and His Family in Uz

1 There was a man in the land of Uz, whose name *was* Job; and that man was blameless and upright, and one who feared God and shunned evil. ²And seven sons and three daughters were born to him. ³Also, his possessions were seven thousand sheep, three thousand camels, five hundred yoke of oxen, five hundred female donkeys, and a very large household, so that this man was the greatest of all the people of the East.

⁴And his sons would go and feast *in their* houses, each on his *appointed* day, and would send and invite their three sisters to eat and drink with them. ⁵So it was, when the days of feasting had run their course, that Job would send and sanctify them, and he would rise early in the morning and offer burnt offerings *according to* the number of them all. For Job said, "It may be that my sons have sinned and cursedᵃ God in their hearts." Thus Job did regularly.

1:5 ᵃLiterally *blessed*, but used here in the evil sense, and so in verse 11 and 2:5, 9

1:1 The location of Uz is uncertain (see Introduction: Setting). Though near a desert, Uz was in an area fertile enough for Job's considerable prosperity through agriculture and stock.

The meaning of the name "Job" is unknown. Unlike other patriarchs who are introduced with a genealogy, Job has none. Thus, the story of Job has universal appeal. He represents all the righteous who suffer. Other biblical references to Job are found in Ezek. 14:14, 20; James 5:11.

Job is "blameless" (lit. "without moral blemish," "having integrity") and "upright" (lit. "just," "straightforward") in regard to his way of life. He does not claim sinless perfection, admitting his own sins (Job 13:26; 14:16). Rather, he is marked by pure motivation and integrity. Although Job's friends argued otherwise, God used these same words to describe Job (Job 1:8; 2:3), which is the foundation of Job's testing by Satan (see Job 1:8; 2:9, notes).

1:2, 3 Prosperity and peace were viewed as signs of God's favor, while poverty and calamity signified God's punishment (see Introduction: Themes). This tradition had its roots in God's promise to bless obedience and curse disobedience. While God may and often does give prosperity, obedience does not necessarily produce prosperity. Conversely, calamity does not always indicate wickedness. The Book of Job with its emphasis on God's sovereignty and wisdom refutes the limited, traditional view of retribution.

1:5 To curse God was such a serious matter that people were reluctant even to utter such a phrase. In the Hebrew text, the word "curse" is actually "bless," though the phrase was an obvious euphemism for "cursing" (see Job 1:11; 2:5, 9). To "curse God" was the pivotal sin in the Book of Job. Satan predicted it (Job 1:11; 2:5); Job's wife suggested it (Job 2:9), but Job never did it (Job 1:22; 2:10).

S A T A N *THE ADVERSARY*

"Satan" (Heb., lit. "the adversary") is referenced as "the Satan," indicating a title more than a personal name. He is identified by this name only rarely in the Old Testament (v. 6; 1 Chr. 21:1; Zech. 3:1, 2).

In the Old Testament, Satan sought to bring out the worst in mankind. His character as the aggressive tempter of man and hated opponent of God is developed further in the New Testament. Satan revealed his brazenness in his speech with God and his perverseness in the way he imputed evil motives to Job. As a created being, Satan is not omnipotent, omniscient, or omnipresent. Although his powers are impressive and extensive, he acts only with the permission of God, who puts definite limits on him. Satan is always subordinate to God and ultimately will be defeated. He roams the earth like a king's spy, seeking disloyal subjects (Job 1:7). However, a believer need not fear Satan (see 2 Chr. 16:9).

The action against Job was attributed to the hand of God who permitted the action, even though Satan was the one working against Job (Job 1:11). The Lord was then ultimately responsible for what happened to Job. This confirmed that God's dominion extended over Satan and his fallen angels. There is nothing Satan can do that falls outside God's dominion. The God of the Bible is clearly the incomparable, peerless, matchless Creator who is superior over all His creation. Satan acknowledged God's sovereignty by his own words (v. 10).

God gave Satan power (lit. "in your hand"; compare Job 2:6) over Job for a purpose, but Satan's power and action were limited by God (Job 1:12). God's intention in allowing testing is to prove strength of character; whereas Satan's intention is to prove lack of character. Thus, every temptation has the potential for positive as well as negative effects, depending on the response to it. Nevertheless, the Lord promises that believers will not be tempted beyond what they can endure (1 Cor. 10:13; compare Rom. 8:28).

See also charts on The Names of Satan; A Portrait of the Adversary

Satan Attacks Job's Character

[6]Now there was a day when the sons of God came to present themselves before the LORD, and Satan[a] also came among them. [7]And the LORD said to Satan, "From where do you come?"

So Satan answered the LORD and said, "From going to and fro on the earth, and from walking back and forth on it."

[8]Then the LORD said to Satan, "Have you considered My servant Job, that *there is* none like him on the earth, a blameless and upright man, one who fears God and shuns evil?"

[9]So Satan answered the LORD and said, "Does Job fear God for nothing? [10]Have You not made a hedge around him, around his household, and around all that he has on every side? You have blessed the work of his hands, and his possessions have increased in the land. [11]But now, stretch out Your hand and touch all that he has, and he will surely curse You to Your face!"

[12]And the LORD said to Satan, "Behold, all that he has *is* in your power; only do not lay a hand on his *person.*"

So Satan went out from the presence of the LORD.

Job Loses His Property and Children

[13]Now there was a day when his sons and daughters *were* eating and drinking wine in their oldest brother's house; [14]and a messenger came to Job and said, "The oxen were plowing and the donkeys feeding beside them, [15]when the Sabeans[a] raided *them* and took them away— indeed they have killed the servants with the edge of the sword; and I alone have escaped to tell you!"

[16]While he *was* still speaking, another also came and said, "The fire of God fell from heaven and burned up the sheep and the servants, and consumed them; and I alone have escaped to tell you!"

[17]While he *was* still speaking, another also came and said, "The Chaldeans formed three bands, raided the camels and took them away, yes, and killed the servants with the edge of the sword; and I alone have escaped to tell you!"

[18]While he *was* still speaking, another also came and said, "Your sons and daughters *were* eating and drinking wine in their oldest brother's

· · · · · · · · · · · · · · · · · ·

1:6 [a]Literally *the Adversary,* and so throughout this book **1:15** [a]Literally *Sheba* (compare 6:19)

1:6 God's opinion of Job is presented in this section of the prologue as the backdrop against which all other opinions are measured (Job 1:6—2:8). The phrase "sons of God" refers to angelic beings who do God's bidding. These beings were created and thus limited and in no way equal to God. Here they are seen as gathered around the throne of God to report activities and to receive further orders.

1:8 My servant is a title of honor reserved for those uniquely committed to the Lord (Abraham, Ps. 105:6, 42; Jacob or Israel, Is. 41:8; Moses, Ex. 14:31; Joshua, Josh. 24:29; David, 2 Sam. 7:5, 8; Isaiah, Is. 20:3; and the prophets, 2 Kin. 9:7). In the NT, the Lord used this title to praise those who have done well (Matt. 25:21). The Lord Himself described Job to Satan (see v. 1, note; Job 2:3).

house, [19]and suddenly a great wind came from across[a] the wilderness and struck the four corners of the house, and it fell on the young people, and they are dead; and I alone have escaped to tell you!"

[20]Then Job arose, tore his robe, and shaved his head; and he fell to the ground and worshiped. [21]And he said:

"Naked I came from my mother's womb,
And naked shall I return there.
The LORD gave, and the LORD has taken away;
Blessed be the name of the LORD."

[22]In all this Job did not sin nor charge God with wrong.

Satan Attacks Job's Health

2 Again there was a day when the sons of God came to present themselves before the LORD, and Satan came also among them to present himself before the LORD. [2]And the LORD said to Satan, "From where do you come?"

Satan answered the LORD and said, "From going to and fro on the earth, and from walking back and forth on it."

[3]Then the LORD said to Satan, "Have you considered My servant Job, that *there is* none like him on the earth, a blameless and upright man, one who fears God and shuns evil? And still he holds fast to his integrity, although you incited Me against him, to destroy him without cause."

[4]So Satan answered the LORD and said, "Skin for skin! Yes, all that a man has he will give for his life. [5]But stretch out Your hand now, and touch his bone and his flesh, and he will surely curse You to Your face!"

[6]And the LORD said to Satan, "Behold, he *is* in your hand, but spare his life."

[7]So Satan went out from the presence of the LORD, and struck Job with painful boils from the sole of his foot to the crown of his head. [8]And he took for himself a potsherd with which to scrape himself while he sat in the midst of the ashes.

[9]Then his wife said to him, "Do you still hold fast to your integrity? Curse God and die!"

[10]But he said to her, "You speak as one of the foolish women speaks. Shall we indeed accept good from God, and shall we not accept adversity?" In all this Job did not sin with his lips.

Job's Three Friends

[11]Now when Job's three friends heard of all this adversity that had come upon him, each one came from his own place—Eliphaz the Temanite, Bildad the Shuhite, and Zophar the Naamathite. For they had made an appointment together to come and mourn with him, and to comfort him. [12]And when they raised their eyes from afar, and did not recognize him, they lifted their voices and wept; and each one tore his robe and sprinkled dust on his head toward heaven. [13]So they sat down with him on the ground seven days and seven nights, and no one spoke a word to him, for they saw that *his* grief was very great.

1:19 [a]Septuagint omits *across*.

1:20 Job shaved his head. The ancient Near Eastern custom of cutting the hair was a symbol of destitution, destruction, and disgrace inappropriate for the people of God. Job shaved his head as a deliberate action to show his devastation (see Introduction: Date). Job expressed his deepest grief without a hint of resentment or rebellion. He worshiped God with the only thing he had left—an humble, dependent, and devoted heart (see Deut. 12, Worship; Rom. 10, Access to God).

1:21 Job did not see his possessions as something he deserved but as God's gift to him. How could he begrudge the hand that removes these blessings when that same hand had bestowed them? Job never cursed or blamed the Sabeans, the fire, the Chaldeans, the wind, or his servants. He never wavered about who had given and taken in his life. Job's use of God's personal name (Heb. *Yahweh*, LORD) is repeated three times in this verse as a confession of Job's dependence on God.

1:22 Job did not sin. Suffering affords a person great opportunities to sin as he tries either to alleviate the suffering or to assign blame for it (see article, Reconciling Faith and Dogma). Job's acceptance of his suffering goes beyond that of Eli (1 Sam. 3:11–18) or David (2 Sam. 16:11). They suffered justly, while Job suffered unjustly. His faith, the very cause of his suffering, was his only comfort (Job 1:20–22).

2:7 The symptoms of Job's physical afflictions are noted: Boils and sores, the shedding of bleached skin, fever and chills (Job 30:30), intolerable itching, swollen limbs, ulcers that breed maggots (Job 7:5), halitosis (Job 19:17), choking, corroding bones, diarrhea, feelings of panic (Job 21:6), depression, and terrifying nightmares that led to insomnia.

2:9 Job's wife has been called "the helpmeet of the devil." Others have suggested that one of his trials was the sparing of his wife's life. Rabbinic literature treats her more compassionately. On the other hand, when grief and love are intertwined, the reasoning of any woman or man can be impaired. Job treated his wife with sensitivity and responded courteously to her bitter advice. He maintained the responsibility of spiritual leadership in responding to the immature faith of his wife, who was willing to accept good but not evil at the hand of God.

2:11 Eliphaz (lit. "God is gold" or "God is the victor") was from Teman, an Edomite city known for wisdom (Jer. 49:7). Bildad (lit. "son of Hadad" or "Baal is lord") was from Shuah, possibly farther south near the Euphrates River (see also Gen. 25:2, 6). Zophar (lit. "bird") was from Naamath in northwest Arabia. However, there is no consensus on these name meanings or site locations.

2:13 No one spoke. According to the Talmud, comforters were required to remain silent until the mourner addressed them. The friends did their most effective work of comforting when they kept silent.

JOB'S FOOLISH WIFE

Job's wife must have been under a great deal of stress as the catastrophic events unfolded upon her and her husband. She had led a life of privilege and ease and was respected as the wife of a righteous and wealthy man. Prosperity may cover a multitude of sins, but adversity uncovers them. While the flames of hardship distilled Job's true motives, they surfaced his wife's impure ones.

Satan's prediction to God was that if calamity befell Job, he would "surely curse You to Your face" (Job 1:11, 2:5). Is it mere coincidence when his own wife makes the suggestion, "Do you still hold fast to your integrity? Curse God and die!" (Job 2:9) Often those who are closest to a person can be used by Satan to discourage and divert them from the path of faith.

Job asked his wife, "Shall we indeed accept good from God, and shall we not accept adversity?" (Job 2:10) Can we trust God for the good but not the bad that comes into our lives? Is God still in control even when adversity hits? How do we accept adversity from God, even if Satan is directly behind it? Can we be shaken by the adverse circumstances yet be confident that God is still in control and has our best interest at heart? What is the difference between true faith and mere superstition? A person who trusts God only in the good times but not the bad is fooling herself about her trust in God. Job called his wife a "foolish woman" (Job 2:10).

Job's wife failed her husband at a time when he needed her support the most, making his suffering even greater as he faced it alone. Although he tried to correct her thinking, whether or not she repented is not recorded. She was not named with the three friends who in the end needed to repent, make an offering to God, and ask Job to pray for them. Perhaps she listened to Job's correction, or perhaps as Job's wife she was under her husband's righteous cover. We assume that she was the mother of the subsequent children born after Job's restoration, since by all indications Job was monogamous.

What Job really needed was comfort and compassion. Unfortunately, when a wife feels threatened by insecurity and instability, she often becomes consumed with her own fears and is unable to find the strength and courage to be affirming and compassionate. On the one hand, Job's wife was an ordinary, normal woman who failed to meet her husband's needs in an hour of adversity. On the other hand, she remained at her husband's side and endured affliction with him, losing children and possessions, and yet surviving.

See also Job 19:17; 31:10; notes on Change Points in Life (Eccl. 3); Wives (Prov. 31)

Job Deplores His Birth

3 After this Job opened his mouth and cursed the day of his *birth.* [2]And Job spoke, and said:

[3]"May the day perish on which I was born,
  And the night *in which* it was said,
  'A male child is conceived.'
[4]May that day be darkness;
  May God above not seek it,
  Nor the light shine upon it.
[5]May darkness and the shadow of death claim it;
  May a cloud settle on it;
  May the blackness of the day terrify it.
[6]*As for* that night, may darkness seize it;
  May it not rejoice[a] among the days of the year,
  May it not come into the number of the
    months.
[7]Oh, may that night be barren!
  May no joyful shout come into it!

[8]May those curse it who curse the day,
  Those who are ready to arouse Leviathan.
[9]May the stars of its morning be dark;
  May it look for light, but *have* none,
  And not see the dawning of the day;
[10]Because it did not shut up the doors of my
    mother's womb,
  Nor hide sorrow from my eyes.

[11]"Why did I not die at birth?
  Why did I *not* perish when I came from the
    womb?
[12]Why did the knees receive me?
  Or why the breasts, that I should nurse?
[13]For now I would have lain still and been quiet,
  I would have been asleep;
  Then I would have been at rest

• • • • • • • • • • • • • • • • •

3:6 [a]Septuagint, Syriac, Targum, and Vulgate read *be joined.*

3:1–26 Job's first speech to his friends is a lament, expressing Job's passionate grief over his present life. A lament expressed honest frustrations and grief to God—not so much to give information to God as to share feelings with Him.

3:12 The knees received me could be an allusion to the fact that women often knelt or bowed down to give birth (see 1 Sam. 4:19) or to the customary placing of a newborn child on

the knees of the father as assurance of the child's acceptance and legitimacy.

3:13 Job's longing for rest from his suffering motivated this speech. Job used four different terms: "lain still" (Heb. *shakah*), "quiet" (Heb. *shaqat*), "asleep" (Heb. *yashen*), and "rest" (Heb. *nuah*) to express this longing for rest.

[14]With kings and counselors of the earth,
Who built ruins for themselves,
[15]Or with princes who had gold,
Who filled their houses *with* silver;
[16]Or *why* was I not hidden like a stillborn child,
Like infants who never saw light?
[17]There the wicked cease *from* troubling,
And there the weary are at rest.
[18]*There* the prisoners rest together;
They do not hear the voice of the oppressor.
[19]The small and great are there,
And the servant *is* free from his master.

[20]"Why is light given to him who is in misery,
And life to the bitter of soul,
[21]Who long for death, but it does not *come,*
And search for it more than hidden treasures;
[22]Who rejoice exceedingly,
And are glad when they can find the grave?
[23]*Why is light given* to a man whose way is hidden,
And whom God has hedged in?
[24]For my sighing comes before I eat,[a]
And my groanings pour out like water.
[25]For the thing I greatly feared has come
upon me,
And what I dreaded has happened to me.
[26]I am not at ease, nor am I quiet;
I have no rest, for trouble comes."

Eliphaz: Job Has Sinned

4 Then Eliphaz the Temanite answered and said:

[2]"If one attempts a word with you, will you
become weary?
But who can withhold himself from speaking?
[3]Surely you have instructed many,
And you have strengthened weak hands.
[4]Your words have upheld him who was
stumbling,
And you have strengthened the feeble knees;
[5]But now it comes upon you, and you are weary;
It touches you, and you are troubled.
[6]*Is* not your reverence your confidence?
And the integrity of your ways your hope?

[7]"Remember now, who *ever* perished being
innocent?
Or where were the upright *ever* cut off?
[8]Even as I have seen,
Those who plow iniquity
And sow trouble reap the same.
[9]By the blast of God they perish,
And by the breath of His anger they are
consumed.
[10]The roaring of the lion,
The voice of the fierce lion,
And the teeth of the young lions are broken.
[11]The old lion perishes for lack of prey,
And the cubs of the lioness are scattered.

[12]"Now a word was secretly brought to me,
And my ear received a whisper of it.
[13]In disquieting thoughts from the visions of the
night,
When deep sleep falls on men,
[14]Fear came upon me, and trembling,
Which made all my bones shake.
[15]Then a spirit passed before my face;
The hair on my body stood up.
[16]It stood still,
But I could not discern its appearance.
A form *was* before my eyes;
There was silence;
Then I heard a voice *saying:*
[17]'Can a mortal be more righteous than God?
Can a man be more pure than his Maker?
[18]If He puts no trust in His servants,
If He charges His angels with error,
[19]How much more those who dwell in houses of
clay,
Whose foundation is in the dust,
Who are crushed before a moth?
[20]They are broken in pieces from morning till
evening;
They perish forever, with no one regarding.
[21]Does not their own excellence go away?
They die, even without wisdom.'

3:24 [a]Literally *my bread*

3:23 The heart of Satan's complaint was his perception that God had surrounded Job with a hedge of safety (Job 1:9, 10). Ironically, Job complained that God had hedged him into a turmoil from which there was no escape or help.

4:1—5:27 The argument of the first speech of Eliphaz, probably the oldest of the friends who spoke, described Job's outburst as impious and embarrassing. Many believers mistakenly think that disavowing or suppressing feelings of anguish and grief is essential in order to be pious. However, God never chastised Job for his lament (Job 3:1–26).

Eliphaz argued from his own personal experience that God punishes the wicked and rewards the righteous. He questioned whether any man could be righteous before God (Job 4:12–21). Therefore, he surmised sin must be at the root of Job's suffering and suggested that Job repent and learn from

God, who would then relent and restore him (Job 5:8–27). Although Eliphaz had general truth in some of his words, he was wrong about the reason for Job's suffering.

4:10, 11 The five different references to lion in these verses (lion, fierce lion, young lion, old lion, lioness) illustrate the comprehensiveness of God's wrath (v. 9).

4:12–16 Eliphaz's vision is similar to those of other OT prophets in that the vision is not self-initiated, and what is heard prevails over what is seen. However, no OT prophet is ever recorded as receiving a message from "a spirit" (v. 15). The atmosphere surrounding the "disquieting thoughts" is more frightening than awesome (v. 13). God's later condemnation of Eliphaz is affirmation that this secret whisper was not from God (Job 42:7).

Eliphaz: Job Is Chastened by God

5 "Call out now;
 Is there anyone who will answer you?
 And to which of the holy ones will you turn?
2For wrath kills a foolish man,
 And envy slays a simple one.
3I have seen the foolish taking root,
 But suddenly I cursed his dwelling place.
4His sons are far from safety,
 They are crushed in the gate,
 And *there is* no deliverer.
5Because the hungry eat up his harvest,
 Taking it even from the thorns,ª
 And a snare snatches their substance.ᵇ
6For affliction does not come from the dust,
 Nor does trouble spring from the ground;
7Yet man is born to trouble,
 As the sparks fly upward.

8"But as for me, I would seek God,
 And to God I would commit my cause—
9Who does great things, and unsearchable,
 Marvelous things without number.
10He gives rain on the earth,
 And sends waters on the fields.
11He sets on high those who are lowly,
 And those who mourn are lifted to safety.
12He frustrates the devices of the crafty,
 So that their hands cannot carry out their
  plans.
13He catches the wise in their own craftiness,
 And the counsel of the cunning comes quickly
  upon them.
14They meet with darkness in the daytime,
 And grope at noontime as in the night.
15But He saves the needy from the sword,
 From the mouth of the mighty,
 And from their hand.
16So the poor have hope,
 And injustice shuts her mouth.

17"Behold, happy *is* the man whom God corrects;
 Therefore do not despise the chastening of the
  Almighty.
18For He bruises, but He binds up;
 He wounds, but His hands make whole.
19He shall deliver you in six troubles,
 Yes, in seven no evil shall touch you.

20In famine He shall redeem you from death,
 And in war from the power of the sword.
21You shall be hidden from the scourge of the
  tongue,
 And you shall not be afraid of destruction
  when it comes.
22You shall laugh at destruction and famine,
 And you shall not be afraid of the beasts of the
  earth.
23For you shall have a covenant with the stones
  of the field,
 And the beasts of the field shall be at peace
  with you.
24You shall know that your tent *is* in peace;
 You shall visit your dwelling and find nothing
  amiss.
25You shall also know that your descendants *shall
  be* many,
 And your offspring like the grass of the earth.
26You shall come to the grave at a full age,
 As a sheaf of grain ripens in its season.
27Behold, this we have searched out;
 It *is* true.
 Hear it, and know for yourself."

Job: My Complaint Is Just

6 Then Job answered and said:

2"Oh, that my grief were fully weighed,
 And my calamity laid with it on the scales!
3For then it would be heavier than the sand of
  the sea—
 Therefore my words have been rash.
4For the arrows of the Almighty *are* within me;
 My spirit drinks in their poison;
 The terrors of God are arrayed against me.
5Does the wild donkey bray when it has grass,
 Or does the ox low over its fodder?
6Can flavorless food be eaten without salt?
 Or is there *any* taste in the white of an egg?
7My soul refuses to touch them;
 They *are* as loathsome food to me.

8"Oh, that I might have my request,

• • • • • • • • • • • • • • • • •

5:5 ªSeptuagint reads *They shall not be taken from evil men;* Vulgate
reads *And the armed man shall take him by violence.* ᵇSeptuagint
reads *The might shall draw them off;* Vulgate reads *And the thirsty
shall drink up their riches.*

5:1 The desire and need for a mediator recurs (Job 9:33; 16:19,
21). No one can stand before God without a mediator (1 Tim.
2:5).

6:1—7:21 Job's first reply expresses his longing for an end to
his suffering or even life itself. He complained that his friends
had not been helpful and had undermined his character as
well (Job 4:1—5:27). Job continued to maintain his righteousness. He did not entertain the idea that God had forsaken him
but instead wondered why God had chosen him as a target for
trouble.

6:4 The arrows of the Almighty (Heb. *Shaddai,* lit. "Almighty"
or "All-sufficient One"). Out of the many times this name is
used in the OT, most of those usages are in the Book of Job,
showing Job's deep dependence on God to meet all his needs.
Some might look at these events as the "fiery darts of the
wicked one" (Eph. 6:16), but Job chose to call them "arrows of
the Almighty."

6:8-10 Suicide was never an option, though Job longed for
death. Such self-inflicted tragedy would have aborted God's
plan to restore everything doubly in Job's life. Inherent is the

Affliction can be having what you do not want or wanting what you do not have.
— Dorothy Patterson

That God would grant *me* the thing that I long for!
⁹That it would please God to crush me,
That He would loose His hand and cut me off!
¹⁰Then I would still have comfort;
Though in anguish I would exult,
He will not spare;
For I have not concealed the words of the Holy One.

¹¹"What strength do I have, that I should hope?
And what *is* my end, that I should prolong my life?
¹²*Is* my strength the strength of stones?
Or is my flesh bronze?
¹³*Is* my help not within me?
And is success driven from me?

¹⁴"To him who is afflicted, kindness *should be shown* by his friend,
Even though he forsakes the fear of the Almighty.
¹⁵My brothers have dealt deceitfully like a brook,
Like the streams of the brooks that pass away,
¹⁶Which are dark because of the ice,
And into which the snow vanishes.
¹⁷When it is warm, they cease to flow;
When it is hot, they vanish from their place.
¹⁸The paths of their way turn aside,
They go nowhere and perish.
¹⁹The caravans of Tema look,
The travelers of Sheba hope for them.
²⁰They are disappointed because they were confident;
They come there and are confused.
²¹For now you are nothing,
You see terror and are afraid.
²²Did I ever say, 'Bring *something* to me'?
Or, 'Offer a bribe for me from your wealth'?
²³Or, 'Deliver me from the enemy's hand'?
Or, 'Redeem me from the hand of oppressors'?

²⁴"Teach me, and I will hold my tongue;
Cause me to understand wherein I have erred.
²⁵How forceful are right words!
But what does your arguing prove?
²⁶Do you intend to rebuke *my* words,
And the speeches of a desperate one, *which are* as wind?
²⁷Yes, you overwhelm the fatherless,
And you undermine your friend.
²⁸Now therefore, be pleased to look at me;
For I would never lie to your face.
²⁹Yield now, let there be no injustice!
Yes, concede, my righteousness still stands!
³⁰Is there injustice on my tongue?
Cannot my taste discern the unsavory?

Job: My Suffering Is Comfortless

7 "*Is there* not a time of hard service for man on earth?
Are not his days also like the days of a hired man?
²Like a servant who earnestly desires the shade,
And like a hired man who eagerly looks for his wages,
³So I have been allotted months of futility,
And wearisome nights have been appointed to me.
⁴When I lie down, I say, 'When shall I arise,
And the night be ended?'
For I have had my fill of tossing till dawn.
⁵My flesh is caked with worms and dust,
My skin is cracked and breaks out afresh.

⁶"My days are swifter than a weaver's shuttle,
And are spent without hope.
⁷Oh, remember that my life *is* a breath!
My eye will never again see good.
⁸The eye of him who sees me will see me no *more*;
While your eyes *are* upon me, I shall no longer be.

---

idea that both life and death are in God's hands (see Gen. 4, Euthanasia; Gen. 9, Sanctity of Life).

6:14 Kindness (Heb. *chesed*, lit. "pity" or "mercy") suggests loyal love and is usually used to describe God's steadfast love for His people. Thus Job wondered why his friends' fear of God would not compel them to be kind to him.

6:15–20 Job compared his friends to the desert streams (Heb. *wadi*) that ran through a rocky valley full of rain or melting snow in the spring but became dry in the summer (see Jer.

15:18). Even caravans have perished because they relied on the dependability of such streams and were caught "high and dry." This figure illustrates how hopes can be crushed. When Job needed his friends the most, they not only had nothing to give, but they were also abusive and condemning of him.

7:6 The fleeting character of life. An interesting play on words is found here as the Hebrew word for "hope" carries two levels of meaning. Its secondary meaning is "thread." Thus, both the weaver's shuttle and Job's days would come to an end without thread or hope.

EMOTIONAL PAIN *IN THE DEPTHS OF DESPAIR*

Lack of fulfillment in general and unfulfilled dreams in particular (Prov. 13:12) create emotional pain. Even in the presence of devoted love, sensitive areas in a person's life bring pain when "provoked." Hannah provides an illustration (1 Sam. 1:5, 6).

Emotional pain may exhibit itself in weeping, in altered appetite (1 Sam. 1:7), and in changed countenance (1 Sam. 1:18). This inward pain is described by the phrase "heart grieved" (1 Sam. 1:8), "bitterness of soul" (1 Sam. 1:10), and "grief" (1 Sam. 1:16).

Emotional pain is often misunderstood by others (1 Sam. 1:13, 14). Job's grief was harder to bear because his friends misunderstood him. This pain must be "poured out" to the Lord (1 Sam. 1:15), for Christ has "borne our griefs/And carried our sorrows" (Is. 53:4), and He does understand. This pain can be shared with someone He provides who is willing to listen and give support (1 Sam. 1:16, 17). That person needs to be a trusted person who has a "faithful spirit" (Prov. 11:13). God's children are to "bear one another's burdens" (Gal. 6:2). This support provides hope and lifts sadness (1 Sam. 1:18).

A helpful prayer for the person experiencing emotional pain is found in Romans 15:13.

See also Mark 5:2, note; notes on Abuse (Ps. 31); Conflict (Song 5; Matt. 18); Death (1 Cor. 15); Emotions (Ps. 42); Fear (Ps. 27); Grief (Is. 53); Healing (Ps. 13; 133; Eccl. 1; 2 Cor. 5; Gal. 6; James 5); Sorrow (Rev. 21); portrait of Hannah (1 Sam. 1)

⁹*As* the cloud disappears and vanishes away,
So he who goes down to the grave does not
come up.
¹⁰He shall never return to his house,
Nor shall his place know him anymore.

¹¹"Therefore I will not restrain my mouth;
I will speak in the anguish of my spirit;
I will complain in the bitterness of my soul.
¹²*Am* I a sea, or a sea serpent,
That You set a guard over me?
¹³When I say, 'My bed will comfort me,
My couch will ease my complaint,'
¹⁴Then You scare me with dreams
And terrify me with visions,
¹⁵So that my soul chooses strangling
And death rather than my body.ᵃ
¹⁶I loathe *my life;*
I would not live forever.
Let me alone,
For my days *are but* a breath.

¹⁷"What *is* man, that You should exalt him,
That You should set Your heart on him,
¹⁸That You should visit him every morning,
And test him every moment?
¹⁹How long?
Will You not look away from me,
And let me alone till I swallow my saliva?
²⁰Have I sinned?
What have I done to You, O watcher of men?
Why have You set me as Your target,
So that I am a burden to myself?ᵃ
²¹Why then do You not pardon my transgression,

And take away my iniquity?
For now I will lie down in the dust,
And You will seek me diligently,
But I *will* no longer *be.*"

Bildad: Job Should Repent

8 Then Bildad the Shuhite answered and said:

²"How long will you speak these *things,*
And the words of your mouth *be like* a strong
wind?
³Does God subvert judgment?
Or does the Almighty pervert justice?
⁴If your sons have sinned against Him,
He has cast them away for their transgression.
⁵If you would earnestly seek God
And make your supplication to the Almighty,
⁶If you *were* pure and upright,
Surely now He would awake for you,
And prosper your rightful dwelling place.
⁷Though your beginning was small,
Yet your latter end would increase
abundantly.

⁸"For inquire, please, of the former age,
And consider the things discovered by their
fathers;
⁹For we *were born* yesterday, and know nothing,
Because our days on earth *are* a shadow.
¹⁰Will they not teach you and tell you,
And utter words from their heart?

7:15 ᵃLiterally *my bones* **7:20** ᵃFollowing Masoretic Text, Targum,
and Vulgate; Septuagint and Jewish tradition read *to You.*

8:4 Bildad's argument that Job's children were punished for their sin was unjust. Not only was this contrary to the picture already given of Job's family (Job 1:1–5), but also Job's godliness, expressed in connection with his calamity, highlighted his undeserved suffering.

[11]"Can the papyrus grow up without a marsh?
 Can the reeds flourish without water?
[12]While it *is* yet green *and* not cut down,
 It withers before any *other* plant.
[13]So *are* the paths of all who forget God;
 And the hope of the hypocrite shall perish,
[14]Whose confidence shall be cut off,
 And whose trust *is* a spider's web.
[15]He leans on his house, but it does not stand.
 He holds it fast, but it does not endure.
[16]He grows green in the sun,
 And his branches spread out in his garden.
[17]His roots wrap around the rock heap,
 And look for a place in the stones.
[18]If he is destroyed from his place,
 Then *it* will deny him, *saying,* 'I have not seen
  you.'

[19]"Behold, this is the joy of His way,
 And out of the earth others will grow.
[20]Behold, God will not cast away the blameless,
 Nor will He uphold the evildoers.
[21]He will yet fill your mouth with laughing,
 And your lips with rejoicing.
[22]Those who hate you will be clothed with shame,
 And the dwelling place of the wicked will come
  to nothing."[a]

Job: There Is No Mediator

9 Then Job answered and said:

[2]"Truly I know *it is* so,
 But how can a man be righteous before God?
[3]If one wished to contend with Him,
 He could not answer Him one time out of a
  thousand.
[4]God is wise in heart and mighty in strength.
 Who has hardened *himself* against Him and
  prospered?
[5]He removes the mountains, and they do not
  know
 When He overturns them in His anger;
[6]He shakes the earth out of its place,
 And its pillars tremble;
[7]He commands the sun, and it does not rise;
 He seals off the stars;

[8]He alone spreads out the heavens,
 And treads on the waves of the sea;
[9]He made the Bear, Orion, and the Pleiades,
 And the chambers of the south;
[10]He does great things past finding out,
 Yes, wonders without number.
[11]If He goes by me, I do not see *Him;*
 If He moves past, I do not perceive Him;
[12]If He takes away, who can hinder Him?
 Who can say to Him, 'What are You doing?'
[13]God will not withdraw His anger,
 The allies of the proud[a] lie prostrate beneath
  Him.

[14]"How then can I answer Him,
 And choose my words *to reason* with Him?
[15]For though I were righteous, I could not
  answer Him;
 I would beg mercy of my Judge.
[16]If I called and He answered me,
 I would not believe that He was listening to my
  voice.
[17]For He crushes me with a tempest,
 And multiplies my wounds without cause.
[18]He will not allow me to catch my breath,
 But fills me with bitterness.
[19]If *it is a matter* of strength, indeed *He is* strong;
 And if of justice, who will appoint my day *in*
  court?
[20]Though I were righteous, my own mouth
  would condemn me;
 Though I *were* blameless, it would prove me
  perverse.

[21]"I am blameless, yet I do not know myself;
 I despise my life.
[22]It *is* all one *thing;*
 Therefore I say, 'He destroys the blameless and
  the wicked.'
[23]If the scourge slays suddenly,
 He laughs at the plight of the innocent.
[24]The earth is given into the hand of the wicked.
 He covers the faces of its judges.
 If it is not *He,* who else could it be?

8:22 [a]Literally *will not be*   **9:13** [a]Hebrew *rahab*

9:1 Job's second reply employed the imagery of a courtroom (vv. 19, 32), referring to God as the Judge (v. 15), to witnesses (Job 10:17), and even to a mediator (Job. 9:33). God's sovereignty over all creation is uncontestable. His ways are unknown and unquestionable. Job complained freely to the Lord, asking why he had been so incessantly and intensely scrutinized. Job recognized that God is the Creator, Preserver, and Destroyer of life. Job's questions were righteous inquiries directed to the One who knows the answers.

9:9 The stars and heavenly bodies. The "Bear" is the constellation of the Big Dipper in the north. "Orion" is a constellation recognized as the "Hunter's Belt" in the southern sky. "The Pleiades" is a grouping of stars in the constellation of Taurus

(see Amos 5:8), and the phrase "chambers of the south" refers to the hosts of stars in the southern sky. Although pagan cultures worshiped the stars and heavenly bodies, worshipers of *Yahweh* did not confuse the creation with the Creator (see Is. 45:9–13; 55:8, 9).

9:24 The existence of evil and suffering seems to question the character and power of God. On the surface God appears either powerless or indifferent in the face of wickedness. Job, however, knew God to be both all-good and all-powerful, allowing evil and suffering only for a time (Rev. 21:4). God uses even suffering and evil to bring about His greater purposes. This fact countered Bildad's argument that only the evildoer suffers (Job 8:1–22, especially v. 20).

²⁵"Now my days are swifter than a runner;
　They flee away, they see no good.
²⁶They pass by like swift ships,
　Like an eagle swooping on its prey.
²⁷If I say, 'I will forget my complaint,
　I will put off my sad face and wear a smile,'
²⁸I am afraid of all my sufferings;
　I know that You will not hold me innocent.
²⁹*If* I am condemned,
　Why then do I labor in vain?
³⁰If I wash myself with snow water,
　And cleanse my hands with soap,
³¹Yet You will plunge me into the pit,
　And my own clothes will abhor me.

³²"For *He* is not a man, as I *am*,
　That I may answer Him,
　And that we should go to court together.
³³Nor is there any mediator between us,
　Who may lay his hand on us both.
³⁴Let Him take His rod away from me,
　And do not let dread of Him terrify me.
³⁵*Then* I would speak and not fear Him,
　But it is not so with me.

Job: I Would Plead with God

10 "My soul loathes my life;
　I will give free course to my complaint,
　I will speak in the bitterness of my soul.
²I will say to God, 'Do not condemn me;
　Show me why You contend with me.
³*Does it* seem good to You that You should
　　oppress,
　That You should despise the work of Your
　　hands,
　And smile on the counsel of the wicked?
⁴Do You have eyes of flesh?
　Or do You see as man sees?
⁵*Are* Your days like the days of a mortal man?
　Are Your years like the days of a mighty man,
⁶That You should seek for my iniquity
　And search out my sin,
⁷Although You know that I am not wicked,
　And *there is* no one who can deliver from Your
　　hand?

⁸'Your hands have made me and fashioned
　　me,
　An intricate unity;
　Yet You would destroy me.
⁹Remember, I pray, that You have made me like
　　clay.
　And will You turn me into dust again?
¹⁰Did You not pour me out like milk,
　And curdle me like cheese,
¹¹Clothe me with skin and flesh,
　And knit me together with bones and
　　sinews?
¹²You have granted me life and favor,
　And Your care has preserved my spirit.

¹³'And these *things* You have hidden in Your
　　heart;
　I know that this *was* with You:
¹⁴If I sin, then You mark me,
　And will not acquit me of my iniquity.
¹⁵If I am wicked, woe to me;
　Even *if* I am righteous, I cannot lift up my
　　head.
　I am full of disgrace;
　See my misery!
¹⁶If *my head* is exalted,
　You hunt me like a fierce lion,
　And again You show Yourself awesome against
　　me.
¹⁷You renew Your witnesses against me,
　And increase Your indignation toward me;
　Changes and war are *ever* with me.

¹⁸'Why then have You brought me out of the
　　womb?
　Oh, that I had perished and no eye had seen
　　me!
¹⁹I would have been as though I had not been.
　I would have been carried from the womb to
　　the grave.
²⁰Are not my days few?
　Cease! Leave me alone, that I may take a little
　　comfort,
²¹Before I go *to the place from which* I shall not
　　return,

9:33 A mediator (Heb. *yakach*, lit. "judge or arbiter") suggests the role of an umpire or one who can arbitrate, negotiate, and help to reconcile two parties rather than one who is in a higher position judging between two parties. Job sensed the huge gap between God and man (v. 32) and intensely longed to restore his relationship with God. This Mediator is later fulfilled in Jesus Christ, who as God and man not only mediates but also forgives (see 1 Tim. 2:5).

10:8–12 Job is the handiwork of God (v. 3; Job 14:15). These verses affirm God's omniscience, omnipotence, and omnipresence in His creation and preservation of man (Ps. 139). Job expressed his ideas concerning the formation of life, describing the embryo with an analogy as did the ancients. The analogy between the conception of a person and the making

of "cheese" (v. 10, in the Hebrew text a *hapax legomenon* or one-time usage of the word) suggests the pouring of "milk" (semen) into the womb to curdle into a soft "cheese" (an embryo). The "skin and flesh" are outwardly visible clothes forming the exterior, while "bones and sinews" are the framework (v. 11). Job, the creature, reminded the Lord of how tenderly the Creator had created him and how He had not only given him "life" but also sustained that life because of His "favor" (Heb. *chesed*). The reasons God would now allow Job's destruction are known only to the heart of God (vv. 8, 13).

10:20 Job's distress was so great that he envisioned relief as God's ceasing to notice him.

The purpose of pruning is to improve the quality of the roses, not to hurt the bush.

Florence Littauer

To the land of darkness and the shadow of
death,
²²A land as dark as darkness *itself,*
As the shadow of death, without any order,
Where even the light *is* like darkness.' "

Zophar Urges Job to Repent

11 Then Zophar the Naamathite answered and
said:

²"Should not the multitude of words be
answered?
And should a man full of talk be vindicated?
³Should your empty talk make men hold their
peace?
And when you mock, should no one rebuke
you?
⁴For you have said,
"My doctrine *is* pure,
And I am clean in your eyes.'
⁵But oh, that God would speak,
And open His lips against you,
⁶That He would show you the secrets of
wisdom!
For *they would* double *your* prudence.
Know therefore that God exacts from you
Less than your iniquity *deserves.*

⁷"Can you search out the deep things of God?
Can you find out the limits of the Almighty?
⁸*They are* higher than heaven— what can you do?
Deeper than Sheol— what can you know?
⁹Their measure *is* longer than the earth
And broader than the sea.

¹⁰"If He passes by, imprisons, and gathers *to*
judgment,
Then who can hinder Him?
¹¹For He knows deceitful men;
He sees wickedness also.
Will He not then consider *it?*
¹²For an empty-headed man will be wise,
When a wild donkey's colt is born a man.

¹³"If you would prepare your heart,
And stretch out your hands toward Him;
¹⁴If iniquity *were* in your hand, *and you* put it far
away,
And would not let wickedness dwell in your
tents;
¹⁵Then surely you could lift up your face without
spot;
Yes, you could be steadfast, and not fear;
¹⁶Because you would forget *your* misery,
And remember *it* as waters *that have* passed
away,
¹⁷And *your* life would be brighter than noonday.
Though you were dark, you would be like the
morning.
¹⁸And you would be secure, because there is
hope;
Yes, you would dig *around you, and* take your
rest in safety.
¹⁹You would also lie down, and no one would
make *you* afraid;
Yes, many would court your favor.
²⁰But the eyes of the wicked will fail,
And they shall not escape,
And their hope— loss of life!"

Job Answers His Critics

12 Then Job answered and said:

²"No doubt you *are* the people,
And wisdom will die with you!
³But I have understanding as well as you;
I *am* not inferior to you.
Indeed, who does not *know* such things as
these?

⁴"I am one mocked by his friends,
Who called on God, and He answered him,
The just and blameless *who is* ridiculed.
⁵A lampᵃ is despised in the thought of one who
is at ease;

·················

12:5 ᵃOr *disaster*

11:1–20 The argument of Zophar's first speech implied that
Job was lying about his righteousness and that God had given
Job less punishment than he deserved (vv. 1–6). He suggested
that if Job would repent from his sins, God would surely restore him (vv. 13–20). Unlike Eliphaz, who argued from personal revelation (Job 4:1—5:27), and Bildad, who argued from
tradition (Job 8:1–22), Zophar spoke from his own simplistic
understanding of the world and God. Like the other two

friends, he maintained that the wicked, and not the righteous,
will always suffer.

12:1—14:22 Job's third reply voiced his impatience with his
friends and accused them of thoughtless speculation. Their
platitudes could not account for his misery. The sovereign
God was responsible, and Job longed to put his case before
Him. Job maintained his innocence and was certain of his
eventual vindication.

It is made ready for those whose feet slip.
⁶The tents of robbers prosper,
And those who provoke God are secure—
In what God provides by His hand.

⁷"But now ask the beasts, and they will teach
you;
And the birds of the air, and they will tell you;
⁸Or speak to the earth, and it will teach you;
And the fish of the sea will explain to you.
⁹Who among all these does not know
That the hand of the LORD has done this,
¹⁰In whose hand *is* the life of every living thing,
And the breath of all mankind?
¹¹Does not the ear test words
And the mouth taste its food?
¹²Wisdom *is* with aged men,
And with length of days, understanding.

¹³"With Him *are* wisdom and strength,
He has counsel and understanding.
¹⁴If He breaks *a thing* down, it cannot be rebuilt;
If He imprisons a man, there can be no release.
¹⁵If He withholds the waters, they dry up;
If He sends them out, they overwhelm the
earth.
¹⁶With Him *are* strength and prudence.
The deceived and the deceiver *are* His.
¹⁷He leads counselors away plundered,
And makes fools of the judges.
¹⁸He loosens the bonds of kings,
And binds their waist with a belt.
¹⁹He leads princesᵃ away plundered,
And overthrows the mighty.
²⁰He deprives the trusted ones of speech,
And takes away the discernment of the elders.
²¹He pours contempt on princes,
And disarms the mighty.
²²He uncovers deep things out of darkness,
And brings the shadow of death to light.
²³He makes nations great, and destroys them;
He enlarges nations, and guides them.
²⁴He takes away the understandingᵃ of the chiefs
of the people of the earth,
And makes them wander in a pathless
wilderness.
²⁵They grope in the dark without light,
And He makes them stagger like a drunken
man.

13 "Behold, my eye has seen all *this,*
My ear has heard and understood it.
²What you know, I also know;
I *am* not inferior to you.

³But I would speak to the Almighty,
And I desire to reason with God.
⁴But you forgers of lies,
You *are* all worthless physicians.
⁵Oh, that you would be silent,
And it would be your wisdom!
⁶Now hear my reasoning,
And heed the pleadings of my lips.
⁷Will you speak wickedly for God,
And talk deceitfully for Him?
⁸Will you show partiality for Him?
Will you contend for God?
⁹Will it be well when He searches you out?
Or can you mock Him as one mocks a man?
¹⁰He will surely rebuke you
If you secretly show partiality.
¹¹Will not His excellence make you afraid,
And the dread of Him fall upon you?
¹²Your platitudes *are* proverbs of ashes,
Your defenses are defenses of clay.

¹³"Hold your peace with me, and let me speak,
Then let come on me what *may!*
¹⁴Why do I take my flesh in my teeth,
And put my life in my hands?
¹⁵Though He slay me, yet will I trust Him.
Even so, I will defend my own ways before
Him.
¹⁶He also *shall* be my salvation,
For a hypocrite could not come before Him.
¹⁷Listen carefully to my speech,
And to my declaration with your ears.
¹⁸See now, I have prepared *my* case,
I know that I shall be vindicated.
¹⁹Who *is* he *who* will contend with me?
If now I hold my tongue, I perish.

Job's Despondent Prayer

²⁰"Only two *things* do not do to me,
Then I will not hide myself from You:
²¹Withdraw Your hand far from me,
And let not the dread of You make me afraid.
²²Then call, and I will answer;
Or let me speak, then You respond to me.
²³How many *are* my iniquities and sins?
Make me know my transgression and my sin.
²⁴Why do You hide Your face,
And regard me as Your enemy?
²⁵Will You frighten a leaf driven to and fro?
And will You pursue dry stubble?
²⁶For You write bitter things against me,

••••••••••••••••••••
12:19 ᵃLiterally *priests,* but not in a technical sense   12:24 ᵃLiterally
heart

12:9 The hand of the Lord has done this (see Job 1:14–19). The
motive or purpose, however, was the cause of speculation by
his friends and the source of anguish to Job.

13:24 The silence of God regarding the possible reasons for

his alienated state caused Job's suffering as well as his obvious afflictions. This perceived alienation was more heart-
breaking than the loss of his possessions and comforts. Job
cherished above all else his relationship with God.

I will never see the hand of God in all that happens to me, attributing nothing to individual people, who are but instruments used by Him in the work of our sanctification.

Blessed Raphaela Maria

And make me inherit the iniquities of my
  youth.
27You put my feet in the stocks,
  And watch closely all my paths.
  You set a limit[a] for the soles of my feet.

28"Man[a] decays like a rotten thing,
  Like a garment that is moth-eaten.

14 "Man *who is* born of woman
  Is of few days and full of trouble.
2He comes forth like a flower and fades away;
  He flees like a shadow and does not continue.
3And do You open Your eyes on such a one,
  And bring me[a] to judgment with Yourself?
4Who can bring a clean *thing* out of an unclean?
  No one!
5Since his days *are* determined,
  The number of his months *is* with You;
  You have appointed his limits, so that he
    cannot pass.
6Look away from him that he may rest,
  Till like a hired man he finishes his day.

7"For there is hope for a tree,
  If it is cut down, that it will sprout again,
  And that its tender shoots will not cease.
8Though its root may grow old in the earth,
  And its stump may die in the ground,
9Yet at the scent of water it will bud
  And bring forth branches like a plant.
10But man dies and is laid away;
  Indeed he breathes his last
  And where *is* he?
11As water disappears from the sea,
  And a river becomes parched and dries up,
12So man lies down and does not rise.
  Till the heavens *are* no more,
  They will not awake
  Nor be roused from their sleep.

13"Oh, that You would hide me in the grave,
  That You would conceal me until Your wrath is
    past,
  That You would appoint me a set time, and
    remember me!
14If a man dies, shall he live *again?*

All the days of my hard service I will wait,
  Till my change comes.
15You shall call, and I will answer You;
  You shall desire the work of Your hands.
16For now You number my steps,
  But do not watch over my sin.
17My transgression *is* sealed up in a bag,
  And You cover[a] my iniquity.

18"But *as* a mountain falls *and* crumbles away,
  And *as* a rock is moved from its place;
19As water wears away stones,
  And as torrents wash away the soil of the
    earth;
  So You destroy the hope of man.
20You prevail forever against him, and he passes
    on;
  You change his countenance and send him
    away.
21His sons come to honor, and he does not know
    it;
  They are brought low, and he does not perceive
    it.
22But his flesh will be in pain over it,
  And his soul will mourn over it."

Eliphaz Accuses Job of Folly

15 Then Eliphaz the Temanite answered and
  said:

2"Should a wise man answer with empty
    knowledge,
  And fill himself with the east wind?
3Should he reason with unprofitable talk,
  Or by speeches with which he can do no good?
4Yes, you cast off fear,
  And restrain prayer before God.
5For your iniquity teaches your mouth,
  And you choose the tongue of the crafty.
6Your own mouth condemns you, and not I;
  Yes, your own lips testify against you.

7"Are you the first man *who* was born?
  Or were you made before the hills?

·······················

13:27 [a]Literally *inscribe a print*   13:28 [a]Literally *He*   14:3 [a]Septuagint,
Syriac, and Vulgate read *him.*   14:17 [a]Literally *plaster over*

14:13, 14 Job was certainly weary of life, but suicide or euthanasia were not options. God's perfect timing and control of life includes the timing of death as well (see Gen. 4, Euthanasia; Gen. 9, Sanctity of Life).

⁸Have you heard the counsel of God?
  Do you limit wisdom to yourself?
⁹What do you know that we do not know?
  What do you understand that *is* not in us?
¹⁰Both the gray-haired and the aged *are* among
    us,
  Much older than your father.
¹¹*Are* the consolations of God too small for you,
  And the word *spoken* gentlyᵃ with you?
¹²Why does your heart carry you away,
  And what do your eyes wink at,
¹³That you turn your spirit against God,
  And let *such* words go out of your mouth?

¹⁴"What *is* man, that he could be pure?
  And *he who is* born of a woman, that he could
    be righteous?
¹⁵If *God* puts no trust in His saints,
  And the heavens are not pure in His sight,
¹⁶How much less man, *who is* abominable and
    filthy,
  Who drinks iniquity like water!

¹⁷"I will tell you, hear me;
  What I have seen I will declare,
¹⁸What wise men have told,
  Not hiding *anything received* from their fathers,
¹⁹To whom alone the land was given,
  And no alien passed among them:
²⁰The wicked man writhes with pain all *his* days,
  And the number of years is hidden from the
    oppressor.
²¹Dreadful sounds *are* in his ears;
  In prosperity the destroyer comes upon him.
²²He does not believe that he will return from
    darkness,
  For a sword is waiting for him.
²³He wanders about for bread, *saying,* 'Where *is*
    it?'
  He knows that a day of darkness is ready at his
    hand.
²⁴Trouble and anguish make him afraid;
  They overpower him, like a king ready for
    battle.
²⁵For he stretches out his hand against God,
  And acts defiantly against the Almighty,
²⁶Running stubbornly against Him
  With his strong, embossed shield.

²⁷"Though he has covered his face with his
    fatness,
  And made *his* waist heavy with fat,
²⁸He dwells in desolate cities,
  In houses which no one inhabits,
  Which are destined to become ruins.
²⁹He will not be rich,
  Nor will his wealth continue,
  Nor will his possessions overspread the earth.
³⁰He will not depart from darkness;

The flame will dry out his branches,
  And by the breath of His mouth he will go
    away.
³¹Let him not trust in futile *things,* deceiving
    himself,
  For futility will be his reward.
³²It will be accomplished before his time,
  And his branch will not be green.
³³He will shake off his unripe grape like a vine,
  And cast off his blossom like an olive tree.
³⁴For the company of hypocrites *will be* barren,
  And fire will consume the tents of bribery.
³⁵They conceive trouble and bring forth futility;
  Their womb prepares deceit."

Job Reproaches His Pitiless Friends

16 Then Job answered and said:

²"I have heard many such things;
  Miserable comforters *are* you all!
³Shall words of wind have an end?
  Or what provokes you that you answer?
⁴I also could speak as you *do,*
  If your soul were in my soul's place.
  I could heap up words against you,
  And shake my head at you;
⁵*But* I would strengthen you with my mouth,
  And the comfort of my lips would relieve *your*
    grief.

⁶"Though I speak, my grief is not relieved;
  And *if* I remain silent, how am I eased?
⁷But now He has worn me out;
  You have made desolate all my company.
⁸You have shriveled me up,
  And it is a witness *against me;*
  My leanness rises up against me
  And bears witness to my face.
⁹He tears *me* in His wrath, and hates me;
  He gnashes at me with His teeth;
  My adversary sharpens His gaze on me.
¹⁰They gape at me with their mouth,
  They strike me reproachfully on the cheek,
  They gather together against me.
¹¹God has delivered me to the ungodly,
  And turned me over to the hands of the
    wicked.
¹²I was at ease, but He has shattered me;
  He also has taken *me* by my neck, and shaken
    me to pieces;
  He has set me up for His target,
¹³His archers surround me.
  He pierces my heartᵃ and does not pity;
  He pours out my gall on the ground.
¹⁴He breaks me with wound upon wound;
  He runs at me like a warrior.ᵃ

15:11 ᵃSeptuagint reads *a secret thing.* 16:13 ᵃLiterally *kidneys*
16:14 ᵃVulgate reads *giant.*

HOW TO ENDURE SUFFERING

WRONG WAYS	RIGHT WAYS
Demand to know WHY.	Be content to know WHO is in charge (Rom. 8:28–30).
Withdraw from God.	Acknowledge that He is with you (Heb. 13:5). Pray all the more (1 Pet. 5:6, 7).
Withdraw from others.	Keep fellowship with believers (Heb. 10:24, 25).
Decide the limits to your own endurance.	Know that God sets and knows your limits (1 Cor. 10:13).
Be impatient with God.	Wait for His perfect timing (Ps. 31:14, 15).
Seek your own remedies (Prov. 14:12).	Trust in the Lord to guide (Prov. 3:5, 6).
Give up to despair.	Wait upon the Lord (Ps. 27).
Delude yourself.	Seek the truth (John 8:32).
Indulge yourself.	Keep pure (1 Pet. 2:11, 12).
Become angry.	Master the anger (James 1:19, 20).
Become depressed (Ps. 73).	Hope in the Lord (Job 13:15).

15"I have sewn sackcloth over my skin,
 And laid my head[a] in the dust.
16My face is flushed from weeping,
 And on my eyelids *is* the shadow of
   death;
17Although no violence *is* in my hands,
 And my prayer *is* pure.

18"O earth, do not cover my blood,
 And let my cry have no *resting* place!
19Surely even now my witness *is* in heaven,
 And my evidence *is* on high.
20My friends scorn me;
 My eyes pour out *tears* to God.
21Oh, that one might plead for a man with
   God,
 As a man *pleads* for his neighbor!
22For when a few years are finished,
 I shall go the way of no return.

Job Prays for Relief

17 "My spirit is broken,
 My days are extinguished,
 The grave *is ready* for me.
2*Are* not mockers with me?
 And does not my eye dwell on their provocation?

3"Now put down a pledge for me with Yourself.
 Who *is* he *who* will shake hands with me?
4For You have hidden their heart from
   understanding;
 Therefore You will not exalt *them*.
5He who speaks flattery to *his* friends,
 Even the eyes of his children will fail.

6"But He has made me a byword of the people,
 And I have become one in whose face men spit.

16:15 [a]Literally *horn*

16:15 The misery of mourning. Job donned sackcloth or coarse-haired cloth to symbolize the abasement, sorrow, and misery he felt in his humiliation (see Job 1:20). "Head" (lit. "horn") is used figuratively to denote strength and dignity. Thus, to lay your "head in the dust" indicated the loss of all honor and power and was also a sign of great humiliation, similar to the modern expression of "rubbing your face in the dirt."

16:19 The heavenly witness or advocate is a reference to God Himself, who testified from heaven of Job's innocence. Job appealed to God for vindication. He had been misjudged by his friends on earth. His prayer was for someone to plead his case. Not until Christ's coming would the heavenly Advocate be revealed (see 1 John 2:1, 2).

⁷My eye has also grown dim because of sorrow,
  And all my members *are* like shadows.
⁸Upright *men* are astonished at this,
  And the innocent stirs himself up against the
    hypocrite.
⁹Yet the righteous will hold to his way,
  And he who has clean hands will be stronger
    and stronger.

¹⁰"But please, come back again, all of you,ᵃ
  For I shall not find *one* wise *man* among you.
¹¹My days are past,
  My purposes are broken off,
  Even the thoughts of my heart.
¹²They change the night into day;
  'The light *is* near,' *they say,* in the face of
    darkness.
¹³If I wait *for* the grave *as* my house,
  If I make my bed in the darkness,
¹⁴If I say to corruption, 'You *are* my father,'
  And to the worm, 'You *are* my mother and my
    sister,'
¹⁵Where then *is* my hope?
  As for my hope, who can see it?
¹⁶*Will* they go down to the gates of Sheol?
  Shall *we have* rest together in the dust?"

Bildad: The Wicked Are Punished

18 Then Bildad the Shuhite answered and said:

²"How long *till* you put an end to words?
  Gain understanding, and afterward we will
    speak.
³Why are we counted as beasts,
  And regarded as stupid in your sight?
⁴You who tear yourself in anger,
  Shall the earth be forsaken for you?
  Or shall the rock be removed from its place?

⁵"The light of the wicked indeed goes out,
  And the flame of his fire does not shine.
⁶The light is dark in his tent,
  And his lamp beside him is put out.
⁷The steps of his strength are shortened,
  And his own counsel casts him down.
⁸For he is cast into a net by his own feet,
  And he walks into a snare.
⁹The net takes *him* by the heel,
  And a snare lays hold of him.
¹⁰A noose *is* hidden for him on the ground,

And a trap for him in the road.
¹¹Terrors frighten him on every side,
  And drive him to his feet.
¹²His strength is starved,
  And destruction *is* ready at his side.
¹³It devours patches of his skin;
  The firstborn of death devours his limbs.
¹⁴He is uprooted from the shelter of his tent,
  And they parade him before the king of
    terrors.
¹⁵They dwell in his tent *who are* none of his;
  Brimstone is scattered on his dwelling.
¹⁶His roots are dried out below,
  And his branch withers above.
¹⁷The memory of him perishes from the earth,
  And he has no name among the renowned.ᵃ
¹⁸He is driven from light into darkness,
  And chased out of the world.
¹⁹He has neither son nor posterity among his
    people,
  Nor any remaining in his dwellings.
²⁰Those in the west are astonished at his day,
  As those in the east are frightened.
²¹Surely such *are* the dwellings of the wicked,
  And this *is* the place *of him who* does not know
    God."

Job Trusts in His Redeemer

19 Then Job answered and said:

²"How long will you torment my soul,
  And break me in pieces with words?
³These ten times you have reproached me;
  You are not ashamed *that* you have wronged
    me.ᵃ
⁴And if indeed I have erred,
  My error remains with me.
⁵If indeed you exalt *yourselves* against me,
  And plead my disgrace against me,
⁶Know then that God has wronged me,
  And has surrounded me with His net.

⁷"If I cry out concerning wrong, I am not heard.
  If I cry aloud, *there is* no justice.
⁸He has fenced up my way, so that I cannot pass;
  And He has set darkness in my paths.

17:10 ᵃFollowing some Hebrew manuscripts, Septuagint, Syriac, and Vulgate; Masoretic Text and Targum read *all of them.* 18:17 ᵃLiterally *before the outside,* meaning distinguished, famous 19:3 ᵃA Jewish tradition reads *make yourselves strange to me.*

18:8–10 From the world of hunting, six words are used here to describe traps laid to ensnare the wicked man: A net that is primarily an instrument of capture to entangle the feet (v. 8); a snare or netting that forms a false floor over a hidden pit (v. 8); a net that grabs the victim's feet (v. 9); a snare that constricts (v. 9); a noose that catches and raises its victim off the ground (v. 10); and a trap, the term that is inclusive of all these devices (v. 10). Once again the writer revealed not only his literary ability but also his extensive knowledge of hunting.

19:1–29 Job's fifth reply recounted that God had set up his disasters (vv. 7–12) and that everyone had forsaken him (vv. 13–20). Pleading for pity, he yearned for his words to be recorded (vv. 23, 24). Maintaining his righteousness and believing that judgment belongs to God, Job longed for vindication by his Redeemer (vv. 23–29). He warned his friends about their own vulnerability to God's judgment (v. 29).

⁹He has stripped me of my glory,
  And taken the crown *from* my head.
¹⁰He breaks me down on every side,
  And I am gone;
  My hope He has uprooted like a tree.
¹¹He has also kindled His wrath against me,
  And He counts me as *one of* His enemies.
¹²His troops come together
  And build up their road against me;
  They encamp all around my tent.

¹³"He has removed my brothers far from me,
  And my acquaintances are completely
    estranged from me.
¹⁴My relatives have failed,
  And my close friends have forgotten me.
¹⁵Those who dwell in my house, and my
    maidservants,
  Count me as a stranger;
  I am an alien in their sight.
¹⁶I call my servant, but he gives no answer;
  I beg him with my mouth.
¹⁷My breath is offensive to my wife,
  And I am repulsive to the children of my own
    body.
¹⁸Even young children despise me;
  I arise, and they speak against me.
¹⁹All my close friends abhor me,
  And those whom I love have turned against me.
²⁰My bone clings to my skin and to my flesh,
  And I have escaped by the skin of my teeth.

²¹"Have pity on me, have pity on me, O you my
    friends,
  For the hand of God has struck me!
²²Why do you persecute me as God *does*,
  And are not satisfied with my flesh?

²³"Oh, that my words were written!
  Oh, that they were inscribed in a book!
²⁴That they were engraved on a rock
  With an iron pen and lead, forever!

²⁵For I know *that* my Redeemer lives,
  And He shall stand at last on the earth;
²⁶And after my skin is destroyed, this *I know,*
  That in my flesh I shall see God,
²⁷Whom I shall see for myself,
  And my eyes shall behold, and not another.
  How my heart yearns within me!
²⁸If you should say, 'How shall we persecute
    him?'—
  Since the root of the matter is found in me,
²⁹Be afraid of the sword for yourselves;
  For wrath *brings* the punishment of the sword,
  That you may know *there is* a judgment."

Zophar's Sermon on the Wicked Man

20 Then Zophar the Naamathite answered and
    said:

²"Therefore my anxious thoughts make me
    answer,
  Because of the turmoil within me.
³I have heard the rebuke that reproaches me,
  And the spirit of my understanding causes me
    to answer.

⁴"Do you *not* know this of old,
  Since man was placed on earth,
⁵That the triumphing of the wicked is short,
  And the joy of the hypocrite is *but* for a
    moment?
⁶Though his haughtiness mounts up to the
    heavens,
  And his head reaches to the clouds,
⁷*Yet* he will perish forever like his own refuse;
  Those who have seen him will say, 'Where is he?'
⁸He will fly away like a dream, and not be
    found;
  Yes, he will be chased away like a vision of the
    night.
⁹The eye *that* saw him will *see him* no more,
  Nor will his place behold him anymore.

19:17 The loss of those most dear. In light of the fact that all Job's children were dead (Job 1:18, 19), this reference could be to his own siblings or could be part of the general stereotypical language. The loathsome nature of the diseases afflicting Job had driven away those nearest and dearest to him. The emphasis is on the isolation felt by Job. Rejection from a wife would be the ultimate human tragedy.

19:23, 24 Job wanted his words to be recorded forever, as solid evidence would be in a court of law. Job's personal testimony was recorded here more indelibly than on a "rock" with an "iron pen" and "lives and abides forever" in Holy Scripture (1 Pet. 1:23).

19:25 The kinsman-redeemer (Heb. *go'el*) was the closest blood-relative. According to Levitical law, someone who was in debt or taken captive needed the "kinsman-redeemer" to pay his ransom or gain his release. In the OT, this relationship is most poignantly depicted by Boaz, who acted in behalf of Ruth's deceased husband. In the NT, Jesus Christ was the ulti-

mate "Kinsman-Redeemer." This term was also an OT title for God, who delivered His people from Egyptian bondage. This Redeemer would "stand" as Job's only faithful witness, to argue for his vindication. Job's sons were dead, and he had been deserted by the rest of his family and friends so that no earthly redeemer was present to defend Job. Job's testimony was sure: He would see God, and God would no longer be hidden from him (Job 9:11; 13:24). The hope of the afterlife was vivid and vital to Job (Job 19:26). Job fully expected to see God with his own eyes, that is, while clothed in his physical body as opposed to a disembodied spiritual state (v. 27).

20:1–29 The argument of Zophar's second speech. He felt compelled to answer Job's words (Job 19:1–29) and continued to insist that God unfailingly would punish the wicked (Job 20:4–29). Like the other friends, he declared Job's guilt without considering any other plea or evidence brought before him by Job (vv. 27–29).

¹⁰His children will seek the favor of the poor,
And his hands will restore his wealth.
¹¹His bones are full of his youthful vigor,
But it will lie down with him in the dust.

¹²"Though evil is sweet in his mouth,
And he hides it under his tongue,
¹³*Though* he spares it and does not forsake it,
But still keeps it in his mouth,
¹⁴*Yet* his food in his stomach turns sour;
It becomes cobra venom within him.
¹⁵He swallows down riches
And vomits them up again;
God casts them out of his belly.
¹⁶He will suck the poison of cobras;
The viper's tongue will slay him.
¹⁷He will not see the streams,
The rivers flowing with honey and cream.
¹⁸He will restore that for which he labored,
And will not swallow *it* down;
From the proceeds of business
He will get no enjoyment.
¹⁹For he has oppressed *and* forsaken the poor,
He has violently seized a house which he did
not build.

²⁰"Because he knows no quietness in his heart,ᵃ
He will not save anything he desires.
²¹Nothing is left for him to eat;
Therefore his well-being will not last.
²²In his self-sufficiency he will be in distress;
Every hand of misery will come against him.
²³*When* he is about to fill his stomach,
God will cast on him the fury of His wrath,
And will rain *it* on him while he is eating.
²⁴He will flee from the iron weapon;
A bronze bow will pierce him through.
²⁵It is drawn, and comes out of the body;
Yes, the glittering *point comes* out of his gall.
Terrors *come* upon him;
²⁶Total darkness *is* reserved for his treasures.
An unfanned fire will consume him;
It shall go ill with him who is left in his tent.
²⁷The heavens will reveal his iniquity,
And the earth will rise up against him.
²⁸The increase of his house will depart,
And his goods will flow away in the day of His
wrath.
²⁹This *is* the portion from God for a wicked man,
The heritage appointed to him by God."

Job's Discourse on the Wicked

21 Then Job answered and said:

²"Listen carefully to my speech,
And let this be your consolation.

³Bear with me that I may speak,
And after I have spoken, keep mocking.

⁴"As for me, *is* my complaint against man?
And if *it were,* why should I not be impatient?
⁵Look at me and be astonished;
Put *your* hand over *your* mouth.
⁶Even when I remember I am terrified,
And trembling takes hold of my flesh.
⁷Why do the wicked live *and* become old,
Yes, become mighty in power?
⁸Their descendants are established with them
in their sight,
And their offspring before their eyes.
⁹Their houses *are* safe from fear,
Neither *is* the rod of God upon them.
¹⁰Their bull breeds without failure;
Their cow calves without miscarriage.
¹¹They send forth their little ones like a flock,
And their children dance.
¹²They sing to the tambourine and harp,
And rejoice to the sound of the flute.
¹³They spend their days in wealth,
And in a moment go down to the grave.ᵃ
¹⁴Yet they say to God, 'Depart from us,
For we do not desire the knowledge of Your
ways.
¹⁵Who *is* the Almighty, that we should serve
Him?
And what profit do we have if we pray to
Him?'
¹⁶Indeed their prosperity *is* not in their hand;
The counsel of the wicked is far from me.

¹⁷"How often is the lamp of the wicked put out?
How often does their destruction come upon
them,
The sorrows God distributes in His anger?
¹⁸They are like straw before the wind,
And like chaff that a storm carries away.
¹⁹*They say,* 'God lays up one's,ᵃ iniquity for his
children';
Let Him recompense him, that he may know *it.*
²⁰Let his eyes see his destruction,
And let him drink of the wrath of the
Almighty.
²¹For what does he care about his household
after him,
When the number of his months is cut in
half?

²²"Can *anyone* teach God knowledge,
Since He judges those on high?

· · · · · · · · · · · · · · · · · · · ·
20:20 ᵃLiterally *belly*   **21:13** ᵃOr *Sheol*   **21:19** ᵃLiterally *his*

21:15 Satan's intent was to get Job to question the wisdom of
trusting God (Job 1:9–11). Here Job mocked the ungodly who
question the Almighty.

HOW TO COMFORT THE SUFFERING

WRONG WAYS	RIGHT WAYS
Pre-judge a situation.	Empathize with the sufferer (Rom. 12:15).
Have a know-it-all attitude.	Pray for yourself (James 1:5).
Try to solve the problem of the one suffering.	Pray for others (Phil. 4:6, 7).
Assume the cause of suffering is sin.	Listen to the sufferer (James 1:19).
	Consider causes other than the sin of the sufferer (Job 42:7; John 9:2, 3; Heb. 12:5–11).

²³One dies in his full strength,
  Being wholly at ease and secure;
²⁴His pails[a] are full of milk,
  And the marrow of his bones is moist.
²⁵Another man dies in the bitterness of his
    soul,
  Never having eaten with pleasure.
²⁶They lie down alike in the dust,
  And worms cover them.

²⁷"Look, I know your thoughts,
  And the schemes *with which* you would wrong
    me.
²⁸For you say,
  'Where *is* the house of the prince?
  And where *is* the tent,[a]
  The dwelling place of the wicked?'
²⁹Have you not asked those who travel the road?
  And do you not know their signs?
³⁰For the wicked are reserved for the day of
    doom;
  They shall be brought out on the day of wrath.
³¹Who condemns his way to his face?
  And who repays him *for what* he has done?
³²Yet he shall be brought to the grave,
  And a vigil kept over the tomb.
³³The clods of the valley shall be sweet to him;
  Everyone shall follow him,
  As countless *have gone* before him.
³⁴How then can you comfort me with empty
    words,
  Since falsehood remains in your answers?"

Eliphaz Accuses Job of Wickedness

22 Then Eliphaz the Temanite answered and said:

²"Can a man be profitable to God,
  Though he who is wise may be profitable to
    himself?
³*Is it* any pleasure to the Almighty that you are
    righteous?
  Or *is it* gain *to Him* that you make your ways
    blameless?

⁴"Is it because of your fear of Him that He
    corrects you,
  And enters into judgment with you?
⁵*Is* not your wickedness great,
  And your iniquity without end?
⁶For you have taken pledges from your brother
    for no reason,
  And stripped the naked of their clothing.
⁷You have not given the weary water to drink,
  And you have withheld bread from the hungry.
⁸But the mighty man possessed the land,
  And the honorable man dwelt in it.
⁹You have sent widows away empty,
  And the strength of the fatherless was crushed.
¹⁰Therefore snares *are* all around you,
  And sudden fear troubles you,
¹¹Or darkness *so that* you cannot see;
  And an abundance of water covers you.

21:24 [a]Septuagint and Vulgate read *bowels*; Syriac reads *sides*; Targum reads *breasts*.　**21:28** [a]Vulgate omits *the tent*.

22:1–30 The argument of Eliphaz's third speech brutally and bluntly accused Job of outright wrongdoing contrary to anything Job had ever done or stood for (vv. 4–11; contrast Job 29:12–17). Thus judgment was passed, and Job was declared guilty. The only recourse for such a situation was repentance (vv. 21–30). Eliphaz knew some truth but categorically misapplied it. He traced Job's suffering to Job's sin.

22:2 Eliphaz questioned how God could benefit from the righteousness of mankind as Job continually asked God why He allowed the righteous to suffer. To think that God needs man for anything would be to ascribe too much significance to man and too little to God. According to Eliphaz, God was interested only in punishing sin (vv. 4, 5; see Job 35:1–16, note).

12"Is not God in the height of heaven?
    And see the highest stars, how lofty they
        are!
13And you say, 'What does God know?
    Can He judge through the deep darkness?
14Thick clouds cover Him, so that He cannot
        see,
    And He walks above the circle of heaven.'
15Will you keep to the old way
    Which wicked men have trod,
16Who were cut down before their time,
    Whose foundations were swept away by a
        flood?
17They said to God, 'Depart from us!
    What can the Almighty do to them?'ᵃ
18Yet He filled their houses with good
        things;
    But the counsel of the wicked is far from
        me.

19"The righteous see it and are glad,
    And the innocent laugh at them:
20"Surely our adversariesᵃ are cut down,
    And the fire consumes their remnant.'

21"Now acquaint yourself with Him, and be at
        peace;
    Thereby good will come to you.
22Receive, please, instruction from His mouth,
    And lay up His words in your heart.
23If you return to the Almighty, you will be built
        up;
    You will remove iniquity far from your tents.
24Then you will lay your gold in the dust,
    And the gold of Ophir among the stones of the
        brooks.
25Yes, the Almighty will be your goldᵃ
    And your precious silver;
26For then you will have your delight in the
        Almighty,
    And lift up your face to God.
27You will make your prayer to Him,
    He will hear you,
    And you will pay your vows.
28You will also declare a thing,
    And it will be established for you;
    So light will shine on your ways.
29When they cast you down, and you say,
        'Exaltation will come!'
    Then He will save the humble person.
30He will even deliver one who is not innocent;
    Yes, he will be delivered by the purity of your
        hands."

Job Proclaims God's Righteous Judgments

23 Then Job answered and said:

2"Even today my complaint is bitter;
    Myᵃ hand is listless because of my groaning.
3Oh, that I knew where I might find Him,
    That I might come to His seat!
4I would present my case before Him,
    And fill my mouth with arguments.
5I would know the words which He would
        answer me,
    And understand what He would say to me.
6Would He contend with me in His great
        power?
    No! But He would take note of me.
7There the upright could reason with Him,
    And I would be delivered forever from my
        Judge.

8"Look, I go forward, but He is not there,
    And backward, but I cannot perceive Him;
9When He works on the left hand, I cannot
        behold Him;
    When He turns to the right hand, I cannot see
        Him.
10But He knows the way that I take;
    When He has tested me, I shall come forth as
        gold.
11My foot has held fast to His steps;
    I have kept His way and not turned aside.
12I have not departed from the commandment of
        His lips;
    I have treasured the words of His mouth
    More than my necessary food.

13"But He is unique, and who can make Him
        change?
    And whatever His soul desires, that He does.
14For He performs what is appointed for me,
    And many such things are with Him.
15Therefore I am terrified at His presence;
    When I consider this, I am afraid of Him.
16For God made my heart weak,
    And the Almighty terrifies me;
17Because I was not cut off from the presence of
        darkness,
    And He did not hide deep darkness from my
        face.

22:17 ᵃSeptuagint and Syriac read us.   22:20 ᵃSeptuagint reads substance.   22:25 ᵃThe ancient versions suggest defense; Hebrew
reads gold as in verse 24.   23:2 ᵃFollowing Masoretic Text, Targum,
and Vulgate; Septuagint and Syriac read His.

23:10 He knows the way that I take. Even in the face of so
much physical evidence against him, Job was still tenaciously
clinging to the belief that God knows and cares. God knew
that Job was blameless and that he would arise from this
calamity as gold (see 1 Pet. 1:6, 7).

23:17 This deep darkness must have been the deafening divine silence Job sensed to his questions and situation. What
Job feared and dreaded most was not so much his own actual
suffering as the disruption of his personal relationship with
God and evasive silence from the Creator.

Job Complains of Violence on the Earth

24 "*Since* times are not hidden from the Almighty,
Why do those who know Him see not His days?

²"*Some* remove landmarks;
They seize flocks violently and feed *on them;*
³They drive away the donkey of the fatherless;
They take the widow's ox as a pledge.
⁴They push the needy off the road;
All the poor of the land are forced to hide.
⁵Indeed, *like* wild donkeys in the desert,
They go out to their work, searching for food.
The wilderness *yields* food for them *and* for *their* children.
⁶They gather their fodder in the field
And glean in the vineyard of the wicked.
⁷They spend the night naked, without clothing,
And have no covering in the cold.
⁸They are wet with the showers of the mountains,
And huddle around the rock for want of shelter.

⁹"*Some* snatch the fatherless from the breast,
And take a pledge from the poor.
¹⁰They cause *the poor* to go naked, without clothing;
And they take away the sheaves from the hungry.
¹¹They press out oil within their walls,
And tread winepresses, yet suffer thirst.
¹²The dying groan in the city,
And the souls of the wounded cry out;
Yet God does not charge *them* with wrong.

¹³"There are those who rebel against the light;
They do not know its ways
Nor abide in its paths.
¹⁴The murderer rises with the light;
He kills the poor and needy;
And in the night he is like a thief.
¹⁵The eye of the adulterer waits for the twilight,
Saying, 'No eye will see me';
And he disguises *his* face.
¹⁶In the dark they break into houses
Which they marked for themselves in the daytime;

They do not know the light.
¹⁷For the morning is the same to them as the shadow of death;
If *someone* recognizes *them,*
They are in the terrors of the shadow of death.

¹⁸"*They should be* swift on the face of the waters,
Their portion *should be* cursed in the earth,
So that no *one would* turn into the way of their vineyards.
¹⁹As drought and heat consume the snow waters,
So the grave[a] *consumes those who* have sinned.
²⁰The womb *should* forget him,
The worm *should* feed sweetly on him;
He *should* be remembered no more,
And wickedness *should* be broken like a tree.
²¹For he preys on the barren *who* do not bear,
And does no good for the widow.

²²"But *God* draws the mighty away with His power;
He rises up, but no *man* is sure of life.
²³He gives them security, and they rely *on it;*
Yet His eyes *are* on their ways.
²⁴They are exalted for a little while,
Then they are gone.
They are brought low;
They are taken out of the way like all *others;*
They dry out like the heads of grain.

²⁵"Now if *it is* not *so,* who will prove me a liar,
And make my speech worth nothing?"

Bildad: How Can Man Be Righteous?

25 Then Bildad the Shuhite answered and said:

²"Dominion and fear *belong* to Him;
He makes peace in His high places.
³Is there any number to His armies?
Upon whom does His light not rise?
⁴How then can man be righteous before God?
Or how can he be pure *who is* born of a woman?
⁵If even the moon does not shine,
And the stars are not pure in His sight,
⁶How much less man, *who is* a maggot,
And a son of man, *who is* a worm?"

24:19 [a]Or *Sheol*

24:1 Specific periods of judgment are suggested by the word "times." Job did not complain that God does not judge; rather his concern was that God's judgment does not come at set times. The lesson for Job was that retribution does not operate on an earthly, human timetable but according to divine will.

24:18–25 The righteous and the wicked. The Hebrew text has been translated in different ways. Some suggest that Job capitulated to his friends' views. On the other hand, just because these words do not sound like Job's views about the

wicked does not necessarily mean that they are not his words. Job never claimed that the wicked *always* prosper and *never* receive punishment. He simply questioned why God treated the righteous and the wicked alike.

25:1–6 The argument of Bildad's third speech took a different tactic and asked how any man who is a "maggot" and a "worm" could claim to be righteous before a holy God (v. 6). If what Bildad maintained before was true, namely, that all the wicked suffer, then everyone would be suffering, and no one

ATTRIBUTES OF GOD *HE IS SOVEREIGN*

God alone is accountable to no one and is supreme in power, rank, authority, virtues, decrees, and work (Ps. 115:3). Strictly speaking, the title "Sovereign" belongs only to Him (Deut. 4:39).

Everything depends on God (Col. 1:16, 17), but He depends on nothing. Everything came from Him, but He came from nowhere because He has no beginning and no end (Ps. 90:2). He is the "I AM" (Ex. 3:14), the one of a kind (Is. 43:10, 11).

Since all life comes from Him, He rightfully retains ultimate authority (1 Tim. 6:15) and will do what He pleases (Ps. 135:6). He needs counsel from no one, and no one qualifies to give Him counsel (Rom. 9:20). The title "King of Kings" means just that. Even among kings, He is *The* King (Ps. 47:6, 7). This Sovereign One does not make occasional raids into our lives and world events; rather, He is intimately involved in the life of each person (Matt. 10:30) and rules the universe completely and perfectly (Is. 40:21–28).

See also 1 Chr. 29:11–13; Lam. 3:22, note; Rom. 11:33, 34; Eph. 1:11; 1 Tim. 6:15; notes on Attributes of God (Ex. 33; Deut. 4; 32; 2 Chr. 19; Job 42; Ps. 25; 90; 102; 119; Is. 6; 65; Jer. 23; Rom. 2; Eph. 1; 1 John 5); Authority (John 19); Fear of the Lord (Prov. 2); Goddess Religion (Ex. 20); Holiness (Lev. 20); Providence (Eccl. 7)

Job: Man's Frailty and God's Majesty

26 But Job answered and said:

²"How have you helped *him who is* without power?
How have you saved the arm *that has* no strength?
³How have you counseled *one who has* no wisdom?
And *how* have you declared sound advice to many?
⁴To whom have you uttered words?
And whose spirit came from you?

⁵"The dead tremble,
Those under the waters and those inhabiting them.
⁶Sheol *is* naked before Him,
And Destruction has no covering.
⁷He stretches out the north over empty space;
He hangs the earth on nothing.
⁸He binds up the water in His thick clouds,
Yet the clouds are not broken under it.
⁹He covers the face of *His* throne,
And spreads His cloud over it.
¹⁰He drew a circular horizon on the face of the waters,
At the boundary of light and darkness.
¹¹The pillars of heaven tremble,
And are astonished at His rebuke.
¹²He stirs up the sea with His power,
And by His understanding He breaks up the storm.

¹³By His Spirit He adorned the heavens;
His hand pierced the fleeing serpent.
¹⁴Indeed these *are* the mere edges of His ways,
And how small a whisper we hear of Him!
But the thunder of His power who can understand?"

Job Maintains His Integrity

27 Moreover Job continued his discourse, and said:

²"*As* God lives, *who* has taken away my justice,
And the Almighty, *who* has made my soul bitter,
³As long as my breath *is* in me,
And the breath of God in my nostrils,
⁴My lips will not speak wickedness,
Nor my tongue utter deceit.
⁵Far be it from me
That I should say you are right;
Till I die I will not put away my integrity from me.
⁶My righteousness I hold fast, and will not let it go;
My heart shall not reproach *me* as long as I live.

⁷"May my enemy be like the wicked,
And he who rises up against me like the unrighteous.
⁸For what is the hope of the hypocrite,
Though he may gain *much,*
If God takes away his life?
⁹Will God hear his cry
When trouble comes upon him?

---

would experience the prosperous life Bildad claimed belonged to the righteous.

26:7 An understanding of space that goes beyond the notions of his day is exhibited. The thinking of the day was that the earth was a flat disc surrounded by water (v. 10).

26:14 Job understood that his knowledge of God was limited and dependent on God's revelation of Himself. This view was in contrast to the all-encompassing and certain knowledge of his friends (Deut. 29:29).

[10]Will he delight himself in the Almighty?
Will he always call on God?

[11]"I will teach you about the hand of God;
What *is* with the Almighty I will not conceal.
[12]Surely all of you have seen *it;*
Why then do you behave with complete
nonsense?

[13]"This is the portion of a wicked man with God,
And the heritage of oppressors, received from
the Almighty:
[14]If his children are multiplied, *it is* for the
sword;
And his offspring shall not be satisfied with
bread.
[15]Those who survive him shall be buried in
death,
And their[a] widows shall not weep,
[16]Though he heaps up silver like dust,
And piles up clothing like clay—
[17]He may pile *it* up, but the just will wear *it,*
And the innocent will divide the silver.
[18]He builds his house like a moth,[a]
Like a booth *which* a watchman makes.
[19]The rich man will lie down,
But not be gathered *up;*[a]
He opens his eyes,
And he *is* no more.
[20]Terrors overtake him like a flood;
A tempest steals him away in the night.
[21]The east wind carries him away, and he is gone;
It sweeps him out of his place.
[22]It hurls against him and does not spare;
He flees desperately from its power.
[23]*Men* shall clap their hands at him,
And shall hiss him out of his place.

Job's Discourse on Wisdom

28 "Surely there is a mine for silver,
And a place *where* gold is refined.
[2]Iron is taken from the earth,
And copper *is* smelted *from* ore.
[3]*Man* puts an end to darkness,
And searches every recess
For ore in the darkness and the shadow of death.
[4]He breaks open a shaft away from people;
In places forgotten by feet
They hang far away from men;
They swing to and fro.
[5]*As for* the earth, from it comes bread,

But underneath it is turned up as by fire;
[6]Its stones *are* the source of sapphires,
And it contains gold dust.
[7]*That* path no bird knows,
Nor has the falcon's eye seen it.
[8]The proud lions[a] have not trodden it,
Nor has the fierce lion passed over it.
[9]He puts his hand on the flint;
He overturns the mountains at the roots.
[10]He cuts out channels in the rocks,
And his eye sees every precious thing.
[11]He dams up the streams from trickling;
What is hidden he brings forth to light.

[12]"But where can wisdom be found?
And where *is* the place of understanding?
[13]Man does not know its value,
Nor is it found in the land of the living.
[14]The deep says, *'It is* not in me';
And the sea says, *'It is* not with me.'
[15]It cannot be purchased for gold,
Nor can silver be weighed *for* its price.
[16]It cannot be valued in the gold of Ophir,
In precious onyx or sapphire.
[17]Neither gold nor crystal can equal it,
Nor can it be exchanged for jewelry of fine
gold.
[18]No mention shall be made of coral or quartz,
For the price of wisdom *is* above rubies.
[19]The topaz of Ethiopia cannot equal it,
Nor can it be valued in pure gold.

[20]"From where then does wisdom come?
And where *is* the place of understanding?
[21]It is hidden from the eyes of all living,
And concealed from the birds of the air.
[22]Destruction and Death say,
'We have heard a report about it with our ears.'
[23]God understands its way,
And He knows its place.
[24]For He looks to the ends of the earth,
And sees under the whole heavens,
[25]To establish a weight for the wind,
And apportion the waters by measure.
[26]When He made a law for the rain,
And a path for the thunderbolt,

27:15 [a]Literally *his*   **27:18** [a]Following Masoretic Text and Vulgate;
Septuagint and Syriac read *spider* (compare 8:14); Targum reads
decay.   **27:19** [a]Following Masoretic Text and Targum; Septuagint
and Syriac read *But shall not add* (that is, do it again); Vulgate reads
But take away nothing.   **28:8** [a]Literally *sons of pride*, figurative of
the great lions

28:1 Job's monologues began with a discourse on wisdom
(vv. 1–28). Wisdom is not found in the creation but in the Creator (vv. 20–28). As if for a court case, Job then presented:

1) His past blessed days when he was in obvious favor with
God and highly esteemed by men (Job 29:1–25);

2) His present time of loss and calamity when even worthless men taunted him (Job 30:1–31); and

3) His plaintiff cry for a future audience with the Almighty to
present his case (Job 31:1–40).

In recounting his blameless life, Job opened himself to
curses if he had misstepped or if he had hidden iniquity in his
heart.

²⁷Then He saw *wisdom*ᵃ and declared it;
He prepared it, indeed, He searched it out.
²⁸And to man He said,
'Behold, the fear of the Lord, that *is* wisdom,
And to depart from evil *is* understanding.' "

Job's Summary Defense

29 Job further continued his discourse, and said:

²"Oh, that I were as *in* months past,
As *in* the days *when* God watched over me;
³When His lamp shone upon my head,
And when by His light I walked *through* darkness;
⁴Just as I was in the days of my prime,
When the friendly counsel of God *was* over my tent;
⁵When the Almighty *was* yet with me,
When my children *were* around me;
⁶When my steps were bathed with cream,ᵃ
And the rock poured out rivers of oil for me!

⁷"When I went out to the gate by the city,
When I took my seat in the open square,
⁸The young men saw me and hid,
And the aged arose *and* stood;
⁹The princes refrained from talking,
And put *their* hand on their mouth;
¹⁰The voice of nobles was hushed,
And their tongue stuck to the roof of their mouth.
¹¹When the ear heard, then it blessed me,
And when the eye saw, then it approved me;
¹²Because I delivered the poor who cried out,
The fatherless and *the one who* had no helper.
¹³The blessing of a perishing *man* came upon me,
And I caused the widow's heart to sing for joy.
¹⁴I put on righteousness, and it clothed me;
My justice *was* like a robe and a turban.
¹⁵I *was* eyes to the blind,
And I *was* feet to the lame.
¹⁶I *was* a father to the poor,
And I searched out the case *that* I did not know.
¹⁷I broke the fangs of the wicked,
And plucked the victim from his teeth.

¹⁸"Then I said, 'I shall die in my nest,
And multiply *my* days as the sand.
¹⁹My root *is* spread out to the waters,
And the dew lies all night on my branch.
²⁰My glory *is* fresh within me,
And my bow is renewed in my hand.'

²¹"*Men* listened to me and waited,
And kept silence for my counsel.
²²After my words they did not speak again,
And my speech settled on them *as dew.*
²³They waited for me *as* for the rain,
And they opened their mouth wide *as* for the spring rain.
²⁴*If* I mocked at them, they did not believe *it,*
And the light of my countenance they did not cast down.
²⁵I chose the way for them, and sat as chief;
So I dwelt as a king in the army,
As one *who* comforts mourners.

30 "But now they mock at me, *men* younger than I,
Whose fathers I disdained to put with the dogs of my flock.
²Indeed, what *profit is* the strength of their hands to me?
Their vigor has perished.
³*They are* gaunt from want and famine,
Fleeing late to the wilderness, desolate and waste,
⁴Who pluck mallow by the bushes,
And broom tree roots *for* their food.
⁵They were driven out from among *men,*
They shouted at them as *at* a thief.
⁶*They had* to live in the clefts of the valleys,
In caves of the earth and the rocks.
⁷Among the bushes they brayed,
Under the nettles they nestled.
⁸*They were* sons of fools,
Yes, sons of vile men;
They were scourged from the land.

⁹"And now I am their taunting song;
Yes, I am their byword.
¹⁰They abhor me, they keep far from me;
They do not hesitate to spit in my face.
¹¹Because He has loosed myᵃ bowstring and afflicted me,
They have cast off restraint before me.
¹²At *my* right *hand* the rabble arises;
They push away my feet,
And they raise against me their ways of destruction.

························

28:27 ᵃLiterally *it*   29:6 ᵃMasoretic Text reads *wrath;* ancient versions and some Hebrew manuscripts read *cream* (compare 20:17). 30:11 ᵃFollowing Masoretic Text, Syriac, and Targum; Septuagint and Vulgate read *His.*

28:28 The fear of the Lord. Both Job and his friends claimed wisdom of themselves. Although personified, wisdom is clearly a manifestation of God Himself and not merely something to be obtained. Although believers can know and understand many things, they cannot attain to this level of Creator-wisdom. Job knew that true wisdom is not found in human understanding but is from God alone (Prov. 1:7; 9:10).

29:12–17 Job's righteous deeds are in marked contrast to Eliphaz's accusations (Job 22:5–9).

30:11 What God has done to Job is pictured as a loosed bowstring. Without a tight bowstring, the bow is useless and the archer powerless. Job felt useless, defenseless, and aggravated.

BIBLICAL MANHOOD AND WOMANHOOD

A MAN OF INTEGRITY (JOB 31:4–40)	A WOMAN OF STRENGTH (PROV. 31:10–31)
Stands in God's presence (Job 31:4)	Manages her household well (Prov. 31:10–12)
Exemplifies integrity (Job 31:5, 6)	Works willingly with her hands (Prov. 31:13)
Commits to personal purity (Job 31:7–12)	Serves her household (Prov. 31:14, 15)
Reflects justice in all dealings (Job 31:13–15)	Invests wisely (Prov. 31:16)
Gives generously to others (Job 31:16–20)	Strengthens herself through proper care of her body and spirit (Prov. 31:17)
Shows compassion to all (Job 31:21, 22)	Uses her gifts consistently and creatively (Prov. 31:18, 19)
Sets godly priorities in life (Job 31:23–25)	Gives generously to the poor (Prov. 31:20)
Lives out faith in God (Job 31:26–28)	Protects her children (Prov. 31:21)
Forgives others (Job 31:29, 30)	Dresses herself attractively (Prov. 31:22)
Opens home to the needy (Job 31:31, 32)	Represents her husband well (Prov. 31:23)
Walks with the Lord (Job 31:33–37)	Uses her time and energies efficiently (Prov. 31:24)
Seeks to do right (Job 31:38–40)	Exhibits a spirit of optimism (Prov. 31:25)
	Speaks with wisdom and kindness (Prov. 31:26)
	Exemplifies faithfulness and excellence (Prov. 31:27–29)
	Receives praise for her work (Prov. 31:30, 31)

These parallel passages present challenging patterns and examples for godly character and lifestyle.

¹³They break up my path,
They promote my calamity;
They have no helper.
¹⁴They come as broad breakers;
Under the ruinous storm they roll along.
¹⁵Terrors are turned upon me;
They pursue my honor as the wind,
And my prosperity has passed like a cloud.

¹⁶"And now my soul is poured out because of my
plight;

The days of affliction take hold of me.
¹⁷My bones are pierced in me at night,
And my gnawing pains take no rest.
¹⁸By great force my garment is disfigured;
It binds me about as the collar of my coat.
¹⁹He has cast me into the mire,
And I have become like dust and ashes.

²⁰"I cry out to You, but You do not answer me;
I stand up, and You regard me.
²¹*But* You have become cruel to me;

30:20–23 Job's afflictions were unbearable and yet bearable because they had been permitted by God, who, in Job's understanding, had suddenly turned against him without reason or disclosure. Job was baffled by the silence of God. The word translated "oppose" (Heb. *satam*, lit. "to act hatefully," v. 21) is probably a play on words with the name for Satan (Heb. *sa-*

tan, lit. "to accuse"; see Job 1:6–12; 2:1–7). Job felt that God was opposing him and acting hatefully toward him even as Satan would. Ironically, Job was accurate in that God had *permitted* Job's adversities, which were conceived and delivered by Satan.

HUSBANDS TREATED AS A GIFT

To a woman, a man is the most complex of all of God's creatures. He has high expectations for himself; when he fails to attain his dreams, he experiences emotions that are difficult to handle. At times he may be afraid of rejection, comparison to another man, the inability to satisfy his wife. He may feel inadequate, insecure, frustrated, and helpless as he faces the challenges of life. During these times of vulnerability, a man desperately needs an understanding helper (Gen. 2:18). He needs acceptance, appreciation, and affirmation.

A godly husband is going to show respect for his wife in the way he treats her. This begins with his thought life (Prov. 23:7) and moves to his lifestyle (1 Pet. 3:7) and communication (Eph. 4:29). Because women are responders, they generally will respond to efforts or lack of efforts from their husbands. This reciprocity is part of the mystery in sexuality.

God extended acceptance to all people in that He did not wait until we were worthy of His love. He simply loved us first (Rom. 5:8). A wife should treat her husband as if he is already the person God desires him to be.

- A husband needs to have the respect of his wife (Eph. 5:33). He needs her sincere *admiration.*
- A husband needs *appreciation.* To appreciate means to recognize worth, to hold in high regard or to respect (Eph. 5:33). A wife needs to express gratitude for her husband's life, faithfulness, work, provision, and care.
- A husband also needs *affirmation.* A wife should speak kind words (Prov. 31:26) and assure her husband of her love and fidelity (Prov. 31:11, 12).
- A husband needs *sexual fulfillment* and sensitivity on the part of his wife to this need (1 Cor. 7:3–5).
- A husband needs a home to which he can go for *comfort and peace* (Gen. 24:67).
- A husband needs to find his wife attractive and be proud of her (Prov. 31:28, 29). He needs to share *mutual fellowship* and fun with her.

A husband should be considered as a precious gift from God, to be treated with sensitivity, tenderness, and love. To meet his needs requires time—listening, touching, doing kind deeds, and creativity in doing the acts of love (see Eccl. 4:9–12).

See also chart on Biblical Manhood and Womanhood (Job 31); notes on Family (Gen. 32; 1 Sam. 3; Ps. 78; 127); Fatherhood (Eph. 5); Marriage (Gen. 2; 2 Sam. 6; Prov. 5; Hos. 2; Amos 3; 2 Cor. 13; Heb. 12); Masculinity (Gen. 2); Wives (Prov. 31)

With the strength of Your hand You oppose
  me.
22You lift me up to the wind and cause me to ride
  on it;
You spoil my success.
23For I know *that* You will bring me *to* death,
And *to* the house appointed for all living.

24"Surely He would not stretch out *His* hand
  against a heap of ruins,
If they cry out when He destroys *it.*
25Have I not wept for him who was in trouble?
Has *not* my soul grieved for the poor?
26But when I looked for good, evil came *to me;*
And when I waited for light, then came
  darkness.
27My heart is in turmoil and cannot rest;
Days of affliction confront me.
28I go about mourning, but not in the sun;

I stand up in the assembly *and* cry out for
  help.
29I am a brother of jackals,
And a companion of ostriches.
30My skin grows black and falls from me;
My bones burn with fever.
31My harp is *turned* to mourning,
And my flute to the voice of those who weep.

31 "I have made a covenant with my eyes;
Why then should I look upon a young
  woman?
2For what *is* the allotment of God from above,
And the inheritance of the Almighty from on
  high?
3*Is* it not destruction for the wicked,
And disaster for the workers of iniquity?
4Does He not see my ways,
And count all my steps?

30:31 Job's voice, like the harp and the flute, once sang tunes of joy and happiness, but now rendered dirges and mourning.

31:1–40 Job was desperate to proclaim his own righteousness. He invoked four curses to come upon himself if he was not found innocent (vv. 8, 10, 22, 40). In so doing, his blameless stand before God was all the more bold (vv. 35–37).

31:1 Job was careful not to let lust have a chance by covenanting with his eyes to remain blameless (James 1:14, 15). People fall into sin when they allow their desire to sin to be conceived and grow.

⁵"If I have walked with falsehood,
  Or if my foot has hastened to deceit,
⁶Let me be weighed on honest scales,
  That God may know my integrity.
⁷If my step has turned from the way,
  Or my heart walked after my eyes,
  Or if any spot adheres to my hands,
⁸Then let me sow, and another eat;
  Yes, let my harvest be rooted out.

⁹"If my heart has been enticed by a woman,
  Or if I have lurked at my neighbor's door,
¹⁰Then let my wife grind for another,
  And let others bow down over her.
¹¹For that would be wickedness;
  Yes, it would be iniquity deserving of judgment.
¹²For that would be a fire that consumes to
    destruction,
  And would root out all my increase.

¹³"If I have despised the cause of my male or
    female servant
  When they complained against me,
¹⁴What then shall I do when God rises up?
  When He punishes, how shall I answer Him?
¹⁵Did not He who made me in the womb make
    them?
  Did not the same One fashion us in the womb?

¹⁶"If I have kept the poor from their desire,
  Or caused the eyes of the widow to fail,
¹⁷Or eaten my morsel by myself,
  So that the fatherless could not eat of it
¹⁸(But from my youth I reared him as a father,
  And from my mother's womb I guided the
    widowᵃ);
¹⁹If I have seen anyone perish for lack of
    clothing,
  Or any poor man without covering;
²⁰If his heartᵃ has not blessed me,
  And if he was not warmed with the fleece of my
    sheep;
²¹If I have raised my hand against the fatherless,
  When I saw I had help in the gate;
²²Then let my arm fall from my shoulder,
  Let my arm be torn from the socket.
²³For destruction from God is a terror to me,
  And because of His magnificence I cannot
    endure.

²⁴"If I have made gold my hope,
  Or said to fine gold, 'You are my confidence';

²⁵If I have rejoiced because my wealth was
    great,
  And because my hand had gained much;
²⁶If I have observed the sunᵃ when it shines,
  Or the moon moving in brightness,
²⁷So that my heart has been secretly
    enticed,
  And my mouth has kissed my hand;
²⁸This also would be an iniquity deserving of
    judgment,
  For I would have denied God who is above.

²⁹"If I have rejoiced at the destruction of him who
    hated me,
  Or lifted myself up when evil found him
³⁰(Indeed I have not allowed my mouth to sin
  By asking for a curse on his soul);
³¹If the men of my tent have not said,
  "Who is there that has not been satisfied with
    his meat?'
³²(But no sojourner had to lodge in the street,
  For I have opened my doors to the travelerᵃ);
³³If I have covered my transgressions as
    Adam,
  By hiding my iniquity in my bosom,
³⁴Because I feared the great multitude,
  And dreaded the contempt of families,
  So that I kept silence
  And did not go out of the door—
³⁵Oh, that I had one to hear me!
  Here is my mark.
  Oh, that the Almighty would answer me,
  That my Prosecutor had written a book!
³⁶Surely I would carry it on my shoulder,
  And bind it on me like a crown;
³⁷I would declare to Him the number of my
    steps;
  Like a prince I would approach Him.

³⁸"If my land cries out against me,
  And its furrows weep together;
³⁹If I have eaten its fruitᵃ without money,
  Or caused its owners to lose their lives;
⁴⁰Then let thistles grow instead of wheat,
  And weeds instead of barley."

The words of Job are ended.

·····················

31:18 ᵃLiterally *her* (compare verse 16)   **31:20** ᵃLiterally *loins*   **31:26** ᵃLiterally *light*   **31:32** ᵃFollowing Septuagint, Syriac, Targum, and Vulgate; Masoretic Text reads *road*.   **31:39** ᵃLiterally *its strength*

31:9, 10 The sin of adultery, which involved a relationship with another man's wife, was serious because of its damage to the family. This section details sins to which strong men are exposed. Although the words for "grind" (Heb. *tachan*) and "bow down over" (Heb. *kara'*) may suggest the servitude of one to another, the sexual connotations of the context cannot be denied. This curse is particularly humiliating and heinous.

Adultery is described as a fire because of the destructiveness of illicit sexual passion (v. 12). For the wife to suffer because of her husband's adultery—a sin committed against her—is entirely comprehensible because of the nature of the family. Certainly this would explain partially Job's determination to avoid adultery.

Elihu Contradicts Job's Friends

32 So these three men ceased answering Job, because he *was* righteous in his own eyes. [2]Then the wrath of Elihu, the son of Barachel the Buzite, of the family of Ram, was aroused against Job; his wrath was aroused because he justified himself rather than God. [3]Also against his three friends his wrath was aroused, because they had found no answer, and *yet* had condemned Job.

[4]Now because they *were* years older than he, Elihu had waited to speak to Job.[a] [5]When Elihu saw that *there was* no answer in the mouth of these three men, his wrath was aroused.

[6]So Elihu, the son of Barachel the Buzite, answered and said:

"I *am* young in years, and you *are* very old;
Therefore I was afraid,
And dared not declare my opinion to you.
[7]I said, 'Age[a] should speak,
And multitude of years should teach wisdom.'
[8]But *there is* a spirit in man,
And the breath of the Almighty gives him
understanding.
[9]Great men[a] are not *always* wise,
Nor do the aged *always* understand justice.

[10]"Therefore I say, 'Listen to me,
I also will declare my opinion.'
[11]Indeed I waited for your words,
I listened to your reasonings, while you
searched out what to say.
[12]I paid close attention to you;
And surely not one of you convinced Job,
Or answered his words—
[13]Lest you say,
'We have found wisdom';
God will vanquish him, not man.
[14]Now he has not directed *his* words against me;
So I will not answer him with your words.

[15]"They are dismayed and answer no more;
Words escape them.
[16]And I have waited, because they did not speak,
Because they stood still *and* answered no
more.
[17]I also will answer my part,
I too will declare my opinion.

[18]For I am full of words;
The spirit within me compels me.
[19]Indeed my belly *is* like wine *that* has no vent;
It is ready to burst like new wineskins.
[20]I will speak, that I may find relief;
I must open my lips and answer.
[21]Let me not, I pray, show partiality to anyone;
Nor let me flatter any man.
[22]For I do not know how to flatter,
Else my Maker would soon take me away.

Elihu Contradicts Job

33 "But please, Job, hear my speech,
And listen to all my words.
[2]Now, I open my mouth;
My tongue speaks in my mouth.
[3]My words *come* from my upright heart;
My lips utter pure knowledge.
[4]The Spirit of God has made me,
And the breath of the Almighty gives me life.
[5]If you can answer me,
Set *your words* in order before me;
Take your stand.
[6]Truly I *am* as your spokesman[a] before God;
I also have been formed out of clay.
[7]Surely no fear of me will terrify you,
Nor will my hand be heavy on you.

[8]"Surely you have spoken in my hearing,
And I have heard the sound of *your* words,
saying,
[9]'I *am* pure, without transgression;
I *am* innocent, and *there is* no iniquity in me.
[10]Yet He finds occasions against me,
He counts me as His enemy;
[11]He puts my feet in the stocks,
He watches all my paths.'

[12]"Look, *in* this you are not righteous.
I will answer you,
For God is greater than man.
[13]Why do you contend with Him?
For He does not give an accounting of any of
His words.
[14]For God may speak in one way, or in another,

32:4 [a]Vulgate reads *till Job had spoken.* **32:7** [a]Literally *Days,* that is, years **32:9** [a]Or *Men of many years* **33:6** [a]Literally *as your mouth*

32:1 The significance of Elihu's speeches is greatly debated among scholars. Elihu was not implicated with the other three friends as having spoken wrongly and as having needed Job's prayers of intercession in the end. Therefore, some say that Elihu added another much needed dimension to the discussion on suffering, balancing out the dogmatic theology of the other three. Yet because of his arrogant tone, moralistic verbosity, and his lapse into accusations similar to the other friends against Job, other scholars do not deem his words as comprehensive or substantive.

Some suggest that Elihu's speech could be a later interpolation into the text because of its relatively inferior poetry when compared with the rest of the book and because there is no mention of him or his words before or after he speaks. Some consider his speech to be an untimely interruption that detracts from Job's impassioned challenge to God. Others think of the speech as preparation for Job to hear God. God's lack of comment on Elihu's words could be interpreted as either agreement with or indifference toward his words. At any rate, Elihu's speech is considered more positively than the speeches of the other three.

Yet man does not perceive it.
¹⁵In a dream, in a vision of the night,
When deep sleep falls upon men,
While slumbering on their beds,
¹⁶Then He opens the ears of men,
And seals their instruction.
¹⁷In order to turn man *from his* deed,
And conceal pride from man,
¹⁸He keeps back his soul from the Pit,
And his life from perishing by the sword.

¹⁹"*Man* is also chastened with pain on his bed,
And with strong *pain* in many of his bones,
²⁰So that his life abhors bread,
And his soul succulent food.
²¹His flesh wastes away from sight,
And his bones stick out *which once* were not seen.
²²Yes, his soul draws near the Pit,
And his life to the executioners.

²³"If there is a messenger for him,
A mediator, one among a thousand,
To show man His uprightness,
²⁴Then He is gracious to him, and says,
'Deliver him from going down to the Pit;
I have found a ransom';
²⁵His flesh shall be young like a child's,
He shall return to the days of his youth.
²⁶He shall pray to God, and He will delight in him,
He shall see His face with joy,
For He restores to man His righteousness.
²⁷Then he looks at men and says,
'I have sinned, and perverted *what was* right,
And it did not profit me.'
²⁸He will redeem his^a soul from going down to the Pit,
And his^b life shall see the light.

²⁹"Behold, God works all these *things*,
Twice, *in fact,* three *times* with a man,
³⁰To bring back his soul from the Pit,
That he may be enlightened with the light of life.

³¹"Give ear, Job, listen to me;
Hold your peace, and I will speak.
³²If you have anything to say, answer me;
Speak, for I desire to justify you.

³³If not, listen to me;
Hold your peace, and I will teach you wisdom."

Elihu Proclaims God's Justice

34 Elihu further answered and said:

²"Hear my words, you wise *men;*
Give ear to me, you who have knowledge.
³For the ear tests words
As the palate tastes food.
⁴Let us choose justice for ourselves;
Let us know among ourselves what *is* good.

⁵"For Job has said, 'I am righteous,
But God has taken away my justice;
⁶Should I lie concerning my right?
My wound *is* incurable, *though I am* without transgression.'
⁷What man *is* like Job,
Who drinks scorn like water,
⁸Who goes in company with the workers of iniquity,
And walks with wicked men?
⁹For he has said, 'It profits a man nothing
That he should delight in God.'

¹⁰"Therefore listen to me, you men of understanding:
Far be it from God *to do* wickedness,
And *from* the Almighty to *commit* iniquity.
¹¹For He repays man *according to* his work,
And makes man to find a reward according to *his* way.
¹²Surely God will never do wickedly,
Nor will the Almighty pervert justice.
¹³Who gave Him charge over the earth?
Or who appointed *Him over* the whole world?
¹⁴If He should set His heart on it,
If He should gather to Himself His Spirit and His breath,
¹⁵All flesh would perish together,
And man would return to dust.

¹⁶"If *you have* understanding, hear this;
Listen to the sound of my words:
¹⁷Should one who hates justice govern?
Will you condemn *Him who is* most just?

33:28 ^aOr *my* (Kethib) ^bOr *my* (Kethib)

33:23, 24 The way of God is to bring us back to Himself through repentance. In His grace He may send a "mediator" to help the sinner learn the lesson God wants him to learn and thus to "ransom" him from death. The passage may be pointing the way to the future Messiah-Mediator who truly ransoms, delivers, and redeems (see 1 Tim. 2:5, 6).

34:1 The argument of Elihu's second speech fiercely defended God's right to act sovereignly, a point never debated by Job. He accused Job of speaking in ignorance and rebellion, though God never chastised Job for such attitudes. He accused Job of complaining that there would be no profit to refraining from sin (a statement Satan had hoped to get Job to say, though Job refused). Yet, even if Job were being punished for maintaining his innocence, the question remains as to the nature of the sins for which he was being punished in the first place.

¹⁸*Is it fitting* to say to a king, '*You are* worthless,'
And to nobles, '*You are* wicked'?
¹⁹Yet He is not partial to princes,
Nor does He regard the rich more than the
poor;
For they *are* all the work of His hands.
²⁰In a moment they die, in the middle of the
night;
The people are shaken and pass away;
The mighty are taken away without a hand.

²¹"For His eyes *are* on the ways of man,
And He sees all his steps.
²²There is no darkness nor shadow of death
Where the workers of iniquity may hide
themselves.
²³For He need not further consider a man,
That he should go before God in judgment.
²⁴He breaks in pieces mighty men without
inquiry,
And sets others in their place.
²⁵Therefore He knows their works;
He overthrows *them* in the night,
And they are crushed.
²⁶He strikes them as wicked *men*
In the open sight of others,
²⁷Because they turned back from Him,
And would not consider any of His ways,
²⁸So that they caused the cry of the poor to
come to Him;
For He hears the cry of the afflicted.
²⁹When He gives quietness, who then can make
trouble?
And when He hides *His* face, who then can see
Him,
Whether *it is* against a nation or a man
alone?—
³⁰That the hypocrite should not reign,
Lest the people be ensnared.

³¹"For has *anyone* said to God,
'I have borne *chastening*;
I will offend no more;
³²Teach me *what* I do not see;
If I have done iniquity, I will do no more'?
³³Should He repay *it* according to your *terms,*
Just because you disavow it?
You must choose, and not I;
Therefore speak what you know.

³⁴"Men of understanding say to me,
Wise men who listen to me:
³⁵'Job speaks without knowledge,

His words *are* without wisdom.'
³⁶Oh, that Job were tried to the utmost,
Because *his* answers *are like* those of wicked
men!
³⁷For he adds rebellion to his sin;
He claps *his hands* among us,
And multiplies his words against God."

Elihu Condemns Self-Righteousness

35 Moreover Elihu answered and said:

²"Do you think this is right?
Do you say,
'My righteousness is more than God's'?
³For you say,
'What advantage will it be to You?
What profit shall I have, more than *if* I had
sinned?'

⁴"I will answer you,
And your companions with you.
⁵Look to the heavens and see;
And behold the clouds—
They are higher than you.
⁶If you sin, what do you accomplish against
Him?
Or, *if* your transgressions are multiplied, what
do you do to Him?
⁷If you are righteous, what do you give
Him?
Or what does He receive from your hand?
⁸Your wickedness affects a man such as you,
And your righteousness a son of man.

⁹"Because of the multitude of oppressions they
cry out;
They cry out for help because of the arm of the
mighty.
¹⁰But no one says, 'Where *is* God my Maker,
Who gives songs in the night,
¹¹Who teaches us more than the beasts of the
earth,
And makes us wiser than the birds of heaven?'
¹²There they cry out, but He does not answer,
Because of the pride of evil men.
¹³Surely God will not listen to empty *talk,*
Nor will the Almighty regard it.
¹⁴Although you say you do not see Him,
Yet justice *is* before Him, and you must wait for
Him.
¹⁵And now, because He has not punished in His
anger,

35:1–16 The argument of Elihu's third speech was that Job thought too much of himself when he protested his unjust punishment to God. Elihu claimed that a person's righteousness or unrighteousness affected mainly him and not God (vv. 7, 8). God receives nothing from man's righteousness (see Job 22:2, note). Thus Job's many words are meaningless. But Scripture teaches that while God is dependent on mankind for nothing, He is pleased with obedience (see Job 1:8; 2:3; Matt. 25:21, 23) and grieved by disobedience (see Ps. 78:40; Matt. 25:26, 30). Elihu's theology lacked this basic knowledge of the personal God.

Nor taken much notice of folly,
[16]Therefore Job opens his mouth in vain;
He multiplies words without knowledge."

Elihu Proclaims God's Goodness

36 Elihu also proceeded and said:

[2]"Bear with me a little, and I will show you
That *there are* yet words to speak on God's
behalf.
[3]I will fetch my knowledge from afar;
I will ascribe righteousness to my Maker.
[4]For truly my words *are* not false;
One who is perfect in knowledge *is* with you.

[5]"Behold, God *is* mighty, but despises *no one;*
He is mighty in strength of understanding.
[6]He does not preserve the life of the wicked,
But gives justice to the oppressed.
[7]He does not withdraw His eyes from the
righteous;
But *they are* on the throne with kings,
For He has seated them forever,
And they are exalted.
[8]And if *they are* bound in fetters,
Held in the cords of affliction,
[9]Then He tells them their work and their
transgressions—
That they have acted defiantly.
[10]He also opens their ear to instruction,
And commands that they turn from iniquity.
[11]If they obey and serve *Him,*
They shall spend their days in prosperity,
And their years in pleasures.
[12]But if they do not obey,
They shall perish by the sword,
And they shall die without knowledge.[a]

[13]"But the hypocrites in heart store up wrath;
They do not cry for help when He binds them.
[14]They die in youth,
And their life *ends* among the perverted
persons.[a]
[15]He delivers the poor in their affliction,
And opens their ears in oppression.

[16]"Indeed He would have brought you out of dire
distress,
Into a broad place where *there is* no restraint;
And what is set on your table *would be* full of
richness.
[17]But you are filled with the judgment due the
wicked;
Judgment and justice take hold *of you.*

[18]Because *there is* wrath, *beware* lest He take you
away with *one* blow;
For a large ransom would not help you avoid *it.*
[19]Will your riches,
Or all the mighty forces,
Keep you from distress?
[20]Do not desire the night,
When people are cut off in their place.
[21]Take heed, do not turn to iniquity,
For you have chosen this rather than affliction.

[22]"Behold, God is exalted by His power;
Who teaches like Him?
[23]Who has assigned Him His way,
Or who has said, 'You have done wrong'?

Elihu Proclaims God's Majesty

[24]"Remember to magnify His work,
Of which men have sung.
[25]Everyone has seen it;
Man looks on *it* from afar.

[26]"Behold, God *is* great, and we do not know *Him;*
Nor can the number of His years *be* discovered.
[27]For He draws up drops of water,
Which distill as rain from the mist,
[28]Which the clouds drop down
And pour abundantly on man.
[29]Indeed, can *anyone* understand the spreading
of clouds,
The thunder from His canopy?
[30]Look, He scatters His light upon it,
And covers the depths of the sea.
[31]For by these He judges the peoples;
He gives food in abundance.
[32]He covers *His* hands with lightning,
And commands it to strike.
[33]His thunder declares it,
The cattle also, concerning the rising *storm.*

37 "At this also my heart trembles,
And leaps from its place.
[2]Hear attentively the thunder of His voice,
And the rumbling *that* comes from His mouth.
[3]He sends it forth under the whole heaven,
His lightning to the ends of the earth.
[4]After it a voice roars;
He thunders with His majestic voice,
And He does not restrain them when His voice
is heard.

36:12 [a]Masoretic Text reads *as one* without knowledge.   **36:14**
[a]Hebrew *qedeshim*, that is, those practicing sodomy and prostitution
in religious rituals

36:1 The argument of Elihu's fourth speech continued to expound the theology of retribution both positively (God blesses the righteous, vv. 5–12) and negatively (God judges the wicked, vv. 13–21). He encouraged Job to listen and learn from God and repent. He ended by expounding about how God speaks in and through His magnificent creation, making Him worthy of our fear and awe. Although essentially Elihu did not say anything new, he did prepare Job for God's speeches.

⁵God thunders marvelously with His voice;
He does great things which we cannot
comprehend.
⁶For He says to the snow, 'Fall *on* the earth';
Likewise to the gentle rain and the heavy rain
of His strength.
⁷He seals the hand of every man,
That all men may know His work.
⁸The beasts go into dens,
And remain in their lairs.
⁹From the chamber *of the south* comes the
whirlwind,
And cold from the scattering winds *of the north.*
¹⁰By the breath of God ice is given,
And the broad waters are frozen.
¹¹Also with moisture He saturates the thick
clouds;
He scatters His bright clouds.
¹²And they swirl about, being turned by His
guidance,
That they may do whatever He commands
them
On the face of the whole earth.ᵃ
¹³He causes it to come,
Whether for correction,
Or for His land,
Or for mercy.

¹⁴"Listen to this, O Job;
Stand still and consider the wondrous works of
God.
¹⁵Do you know when God dispatches them,
And causes the light of His cloud to shine?
¹⁶Do you know how the clouds are balanced,
Those wondrous works of Him who is perfect
in knowledge?
¹⁷Why *are* your garments hot,
When He quiets the earth by the south *wind?*
¹⁸With Him, have you spread out the skies,
Strong as a cast metal mirror?

¹⁹"Teach us what we should say to Him,
For we can prepare nothing because of the
darkness.
²⁰Should He be told that I *wish to* speak?

If a man were to speak, surely he would be
swallowed up.
²¹Even now *men* cannot look at the light *when it is*
bright in the skies,
When the wind has passed and cleared them.
²²He comes from the north *as* golden *splendor;*
With God *is* awesome majesty.
²³*As for* the Almighty, we cannot find Him;
He is excellent in power,
In judgment and abundant justice;
He does not oppress.
²⁴Therefore men fear Him;
He shows no partiality to any *who are* wise of
heart."

The LORD Reveals His Omnipotence to Job

38 Then the LORD answered Job out of the
whirlwind, and said:
²"Who *is* this who darkens counsel
By words without knowledge?
³Now prepare yourself like a man;
I will question you, and you shall answer Me.

⁴"Where were you when I laid the foundations of
the earth?
Tell *Me,* if you have understanding.
⁵Who determined its measurements?
Surely you know!
Or who stretched the line upon it?
⁶To what were its foundations fastened?
Or who laid its cornerstone,
⁷When the morning stars sang together,
And all the sons of God shouted for joy?

⁸"Or *who* shut in the sea with doors,
When it burst forth *and* issued from the womb;
⁹When I made the clouds its garment,
And thick darkness its swaddling band;
¹⁰When I fixed My limit for it,
And set bars and doors;
¹¹When I said,
'This far you may come, but no farther,
And here your proud waves must stop!'

37:12 ᵃLiterally *the world of the earth*

38:1 God appeared to Job out of the whirlwind. This both hides and displays his power (compare Ezek. 1:1–4, 26–28). It is an awesome thing to be in the presence of the Lord (Ex. 19:10–25; 33:17–23). God began to ask Job rhetorical questions related to Creator-wisdom that Job could not answer (Job 38:1–3). His questions showed His dominion over the creation of the earth, the sea, time, death, light and darkness, the weather, the heavens, and the animals—both wild and domestic (Job 38:4—39:30). The one who cannot answer these questions about the universe dare not correct the One who planned and maintains it (Job 38:4–7).

That God speaks so much about nature rather than about moral issues is surprising, especially to western readers who have been taught a subtle bias against natural theology,

which claims that God is revealed through nature. The Book of Job shows no such aversion. Instead of trying to crush Job with His infinite knowledge and wisdom, God gave him dignity by speaking to him about these things. God's speeches emphasize that if Job can trust God to run the universe, he can trust God to run his life.

38:2, 3 Job showed a lack of understanding when he questioned God. His very words demonstrated a lack of wisdom. God asked the questions of Job.

38:7 The morning stars, perhaps Venus or Mercury, and the "sons of God" or angels together sang in joyful praise at the creation scene. How awesome it would be to hear the whole universe praising the Creator.

¹²"Have you commanded the morning since your
  days *began,*
  And caused the dawn to know its place,
¹³That it might take hold of the ends of the
  earth,
  And the wicked be shaken out of it?
¹⁴It takes on form like clay *under* a seal,
  And stands out like a garment.
¹⁵From the wicked their light is withheld,
  And the upraised arm is broken.

¹⁶"Have you entered the springs of the sea?
  Or have you walked in search of the depths?
¹⁷Have the gates of death been revealed to
  you?
  Or have you seen the doors of the shadow of
  death?
¹⁸Have you comprehended the breadth of the
  earth?
  Tell *Me,* if you know all this.

¹⁹"Where *is* the way *to* the dwelling of light?
  And darkness, where *is* its place,
²⁰That you may take it to its territory,
  That you may know the paths *to* its home?
²¹Do you know *it,* because you were born then,
  Or *because* the number of your days *is* great?

²²"Have you entered the treasury of snow,
  Or have you seen the treasury of hail,
²³Which I have reserved for the time of trouble,
  For the day of battle and war?
²⁴By what way is light diffused,
  Or the east wind scattered over the earth?

²⁵"Who has divided a channel for the overflowing
  water,
  Or a path for the thunderbolt,
²⁶To cause it to rain on a land *where there is* no
  one,
  A wilderness in which *there is* no man;
²⁷To satisfy the desolate waste,
  And cause to spring forth the growth of tender
  grass?
²⁸Has the rain a father?
  Or who has begotten the drops of dew?
²⁹From whose womb comes the ice?
  And the frost of heaven, who gives it birth?
³⁰The waters harden like stone,
  And the surface of the deep is frozen.

³¹"Can you bind the cluster of the Pleiades,
  Or loose the belt of Orion?
³²Can you bring out Mazzarothᵃ in its season?
  Or can you guide the Great Bear with its cubs?

³³Do you know the ordinances of the heavens?
  Can you set their dominion over the earth?

³⁴"Can you lift up your voice to the clouds,
  That an abundance of water may cover you?
³⁵Can you send out lightnings, that they may go,
  And say to you, 'Here we *are!*'?
³⁶Who has put wisdom in the mind?ᵃ
  Or who has given understanding to the
  heart?
³⁷Who can number the clouds by wisdom?
  Or who can pour out the bottles of heaven,
³⁸When the dust hardens in clumps,
  And the clods cling together?

³⁹"Can you hunt the prey for the lion,
  Or satisfy the appetite of the young lions,
⁴⁰When they crouch in *their* dens,
  Or lurk in their lairs to lie in wait?
⁴¹Who provides food for the raven,
  When its young ones cry to God,
  And wander about for lack of food?

39

"Do you know the time when the wild
  mountain goats bear young?
  Or can you mark when the deer gives birth?
²Can you number the months *that* they fulfill?
  Or do you know the time when they bear
  young?
³They bow down,
  They bring forth their young,
  They deliver their offspring.ᵃ
⁴Their young ones are healthy,
  They grow strong with grain;
  They depart and do not return to them.

⁵"Who set the wild donkey free?
  Who loosed the bonds of the onager,
⁶Whose home I have made the wilderness,
  And the barren land his dwelling?
⁷He scorns the tumult of the city;
  He does not heed the shouts of the driver.
⁸The range of the mountains *is* his pasture,
  And he searches after every green thing.

⁹"Will the wild ox be willing to serve you?
  Will he bed by your manger?
¹⁰Can you bind the wild ox in the furrow with
  ropes?
  Or will he plow the valleys behind you?
¹¹Will you trust him because his strength *is*
  great?

38:32 ᵃLiterally *Constellations*   **38:36** ᵃLiterally *inward parts*   **39:3**
ᵃLiterally *pangs,* figurative of offspring

38:31–33 Mazzaroth may refer to a particular constellation or
star but cannot be identified with certainty. The picture is one
of God leading the stars as if on a chain, binding or harnessing
them to cross the skies, then loosening them at the journey's
end. This figurative language displays God's sovereign power
over the heavenlies (see Job 9:9; Amos 5:8).

God can do anything, and He gets things done. However, He cannot lie (Titus 1:2); He can neither be tempted Himself nor tempt anyone with evil (James 1:13); He cannot be in fellowship with sin (Hab. 1:13). These are not weaknesses or inadequacies but rather are perfections of His power.

God is the source of His own power. Who else can create anything by mere words (Ps. 33:9)! From wonders viewed only by means of high-powered microscopes to those viewed through high-powered telescopes, God's power is on display for all to see (Ps. 19:1–4).

God uses His power for His children to conquer death, to provide salvation; to complete their transformation; to equip them for service; to protect, provide, and preserve them; and to secure their inheritance (Rom. 8:31).

If God were not all-powerful, His mercy would be helpless pity; His justice, an empty threat; His knowledge, useless information; and His love, pure frustration. Ultimate power has been coveted by both angels and mankind, but the throne is occupied (Rev. 4:2, 3), and there is no danger of a dethronement (Ps. 93:2–4). God reigns without rival (Ps. 86:8–10).

See also Gen. 17:1; 18:14; 1 Chr. 29:11–13; Ps. 115:3; 147:4–6; Jer. 32:17; Lam. 3:22, note; Matt. 19:26; Luke 1:37; Rev. 19:6; notes on Attributes of God (Ex. 33; Deut. 4; 32; 2 Chr. 19; Job 23; Ps. 25; 90; 102; 119; Is. 6; 65; Jer. 23; Rom. 2; Eph. 1; 1 John 5); Authority (John 19); Government and Citizenship (Rom. 13); Spiritual Warfare (Neh. 4; Eph. 6)

Or will you leave your labor to him?
12Will you trust him to bring home your grain,
And gather it to your threshing floor?

13"The wings of the ostrich wave proudly,
But are her wings and pinions *like the* kindly stork's?
14For she leaves her eggs on the ground,
And warms them in the dust;
15She forgets that a foot may crush them,
Or that a wild beast may break them.
16She treats her young harshly, as though *they were* not hers;
Her labor is in vain, without concern,
17Because God deprived her of wisdom,
And did not endow her with understanding.
18When she lifts herself on high,
She scorns the horse and its rider.

19"Have you given the horse strength?
Have you clothed his neck with thunder?a
20Can you frighten him like a locust?
His majestic snorting strikes terror.
21He paws in the valley, and rejoices in *his* strength;
He gallops into the clash of arms.
22He mocks at fear, and is not frightened;
Nor does he turn back from the sword.
23The quiver rattles against him,
The glittering spear and javelin.
24He devours the distance with fierceness and rage;

Nor does he come to a halt because the trumpet *has* sounded.
25At *the blast of* the trumpet he says, 'Aha!'
He smells the battle from afar,
The thunder of captains and shouting.

26"Does the hawk fly by your wisdom,
And spread its wings toward the south?
27Does the eagle mount up at your command,
And make its nest on high?
28On the rock it dwells and resides,
On the crag of the rock and the stronghold.
29From there it spies out the prey;
Its eyes observe from afar.
30Its young ones suck up blood;
And where the slain *are*, there it *is*."

40 Moreover the LORD answered Job, and said:

2"Shall the one who contends with the Almighty correct *Him*?
He who rebukes God, let him answer it."

Job's Response to God

3Then Job answered the LORD and said:

4"Behold, I am vile;
What shall I answer You?
I lay my hand over my mouth.
5Once I have spoken, but I will not answer;
Yes, twice, but I will proceed no further."

39:19 aOr *a mane*

39:13–18 The ostrich, which was thought to be stupid because of its awkward appearance, displayed God's sovereignty in creation. The ostrich also has a seemingly hazardous way of raising its young. Yet this heaviest of all birds, though unable to fly, can outrun a fast horse.

God's Challenge to Job

⁶Then the LORD answered Job out of the whirlwind, and said:

⁷"Now prepare yourself like a man;
I will question you, and you shall answer Me:

⁸"Would you indeed annul My judgment?
Would you condemn Me that you may be
justified?
⁹Have you an arm like God?
Or can you thunder with a voice like His?
¹⁰Then adorn yourself *with* majesty and splendor,
And array yourself with glory and beauty.
¹¹Disperse the rage of your wrath;
Look on everyone *who is* proud, and humble
him.
¹²Look on everyone *who is* proud, *and* bring him
low;
Tread down the wicked in their place.
¹³Hide them in the dust together,
Bind their faces in hidden *darkness.*
¹⁴Then I will also confess to you
That your own right hand can save you.

¹⁵"Look now at the behemoth,ᵃ which I made
along with you;
He eats grass like an ox.
¹⁶See now, his strength *is* in his hips,
And his power *is* in his stomach muscles.
¹⁷He moves his tail like a cedar;
The sinews of his thighs are tightly knit.
¹⁸His bones *are like* beams of bronze,
His ribs like bars of iron.
¹⁹He *is* the first of the ways of God;
Only He who made him can bring near His
sword.
²⁰Surely the mountains yield food for him,
And all the beasts of the field play there.
²¹He lies under the lotus trees,
In a covert of reeds and marsh.
²²The lotus trees cover him *with* their shade;
The willows by the brook surround him.
²³Indeed the river may rage,
Yet he is not disturbed;

He is confident, though the Jordan gushes into
his mouth,
²⁴*Though* he takes it in his eyes,
Or one pierces *his* nose with a snare.

41 "Can you draw out Leviathanᵃ with a hook,
Or *snare* his tongue with a line *which* you
lower?
²Can you put a reed through his nose,
Or pierce his jaw with a hook?
³Will he make many supplications to you?
Will he speak softly to you?
⁴Will he make a covenant with you?
Will you take him as a servant forever?
⁵Will you play with him as *with* a bird,
Or will you leash him for your maidens?
⁶Will *your* companions make a banquetᵃ of him?
Will they apportion him among the merchants?
⁷Can you fill his skin with harpoons,
Or his head with fishing spears?
⁸Lay your hand on him;
Remember the battle—
Never do it again!
⁹Indeed, *any* hope of *overcoming* him is false;
Shall *one not* be overwhelmed at the sight of
him?
¹⁰No one *is so* fierce that he would dare stir him
up.
Who then is able to stand against Me?
¹¹Who has preceded Me, that I should pay *him?*
Everything under heaven is Mine.

¹²"I will not concealᵃ his limbs,
His mighty power, or his graceful proportions.
¹³Who can remove his outer coat?
Who can approach *him* with a double bridle?
¹⁴Who can open the doors of his face,
With his terrible teeth all around?
¹⁵*His* rows of scales are *his* pride,
Shut up tightly *as with* a seal;
¹⁶One is so near another

40:15 ᵃA large animal, exact identity unknown   41:1 ᵃA large sea
creature, exact identity unknown   41:6 ᵃOr *bargain over him*
41:12 ᵃLiterally *keep silent about*

40:3–5 Job's first response to God. Suddenly aware of his own
base position, Job was stunned into silence. However, he did
not confess wrongdoing in what he had said.

40:6—41:34 The themes of God's second speech. Job did not
dare criticize the judgment of God. Job was not powerful
enough to judge the world; he was not even able to contend
with two of the most fierce and untamed of God's creatures—behemoth on the land and Leviathan in the sea. Job
could not harness God's handiwork (see Job 38:1, note). God's
speeches notably did not address any of the issues that Job
had been wanting to discuss, nor did they explain why all
these adversities had happened to Job. While we might expect
God to address Satan's propositions concerning Job, no such

words were offered. Job's greatest need was not to know why
things happened but to know Who was in control.

40:15 Behemoth, though unknown, is sometimes identified
with the hippopotamus. The language used is both poetic and
hyperbolic but nonetheless describes an animal of great
strength, which, though feared by man, is used of God for His
own purposes.

41:1 Leviathan, a great sea creature, is unknown, but the description seems to fit that of the crocodile. This is not necessarily a mythical creature. "Leviathan" is used symbolically as
the object of God's wrath (see Is. 27:1; compare Rev. 12:9). In
any case, the point made is that Job, and mankind, cannot
control such fearsome creatures. Yet God will use such a beast
for His own purposes.

JOB'S BEAUTIFUL DAUGHTERS

Job's first daughters must have lived a life of privilege and honor among their brothers. They were regularly invited to join their brothers in family feasts, and their father regularly interceded for their sins, known or unknown. However, when Satan began to try Job, all the children were killed as the roof literally crushed them during a banquet.

When Job had come through the trials, God restored to him everything he had lost twofold, except for the number of his children. Job was given the same number of children he originally had, seven sons and three daughters.

Of the new children Job was given, only the three daughters were mentioned by name. Jemimah means "turtle-dove," a name that was often used of a bride, describing her fine form and lovely voice. Keziah was the name of a fragrant plant, cassia, which was a prized variety of cinnamon. Keren-Happuch was a horn of eye paint, usually black, that was used to draw attention to a woman's eyes. This was probably the equivalent of modern day eyeliner. These daughters were known for their unparalleled beauty.

The naming of the daughters rather than the sons was unusual as was the fact that Job's daughters were given an inheritance along with their brothers. According to Israelite law, daughters were allowed to inherit if there were no sons (Num. 27:1–11; 36:1–13). Thus Job's gift of an inheritance to his daughters is a special act of grace. This inheritance would allow the daughters to remain in the midst of the family with their brothers and to continue the close affectionate relationships that existed among them. Some commentators speculate that such an inheritance was a sign of Job's new great wealth, while others thought it was a sign of a new generosity that came out of his sufferings. Still another has suggested that it was a sign of gratitude for his new family. Certainly throughout his ordeal, Job had learned to go beyond the letter of the Law to the Author of the Law, who in the end did not pay Job wages deserved but rewarded Job according to His grace.

See also Job 1:18; notes on Attributes of God (Ps. 25; Is. 65); Inheritance (Prov. 13)

That no air can come between them;
17They are joined one to another,
They stick together and cannot be parted.
18His sneezings flash forth light,
And his eyes *are* like the eyelids of the morning.
19Out of his mouth go burning lights;
Sparks of fire shoot out.
20Smoke goes out of his nostrils,
As *from* a boiling pot and burning rushes.
21His breath kindles coals,
And a flame goes out of his mouth.
22Strength dwells in his neck,
And sorrow dances before him.
23The folds of his flesh are joined together;
They are firm on him and cannot be moved.
24His heart is as hard as stone,
Even as hard as the lower *millstone.*
25When he raises himself up, the mighty are afraid;
Because of his crashings they are beside[a] themselves.
26*Though* the sword reaches him, it cannot avail;
Nor does spear, dart, or javelin.
27He regards iron as straw,
And bronze as rotten wood.
28The arrow cannot make him flee;
Slingstones become like stubble to him.

29Darts are regarded as straw;
He laughs at the threat of javelins.
30His undersides *are* like sharp potsherds;
He spreads pointed *marks* in the mire.
31He makes the deep boil like a pot;
He makes the sea like a pot of ointment.
32He leaves a shining wake behind him;
One would think the deep had white hair.
33On earth there is nothing like him,
Which is made without fear.
34He beholds every high *thing;*
He *is* king over all the children of pride."

Job's Repentance and Restoration

42 Then Job answered the LORD and said:

2"I know that You can do everything,
And that no purpose *of Yours* can be withheld from You.
3*You asked,* 'Who *is* this who hides counsel without knowledge?'
Therefore I have uttered what I did not understand,
Things too wonderful for me, which I did not know.
4Listen, please, and let me speak;

41:25 [a]Or *purify themselves*

42:1–6 Upon seeing God through the whirlwind, Job was completely humbled, and he repented (Job 38:1). Job finally realized that God, and God alone, runs the universe.

You said, 'I will question you, and you shall
    answer Me.'

⁵"I have heard of You by the hearing of the ear,
    But now my eye sees You.
⁶Therefore I abhor *myself,*
    And repent in dust and ashes."

⁷And so it was, after the Lord had spoken these
words to Job, that the Lord said to Eliphaz the Temanite, "My wrath is aroused against you and your
two friends, for you have not spoken of Me *what is*
right, as My servant Job *has.* ⁸Now therefore, take
for yourselves seven bulls and seven rams, go to
My servant Job, and offer up for yourselves a burnt
offering; and My servant Job shall pray for you.
For I will accept him, lest I deal with you *according
to your* folly; because you have not spoken of Me
what is right, as My servant Job *has.*"

⁹So Eliphaz the Temanite and Bildad the
Shuhite *and* Zophar the Naamathite went and did
as the Lord commanded them; for the Lord had
accepted Job. ¹⁰And the Lord restored Job's losses[a]
when he prayed for his friends. Indeed the Lord
gave Job twice as much as he had before. ¹¹Then
all his brothers, all his sisters, and all those who
had been his acquaintances before, came to him
and ate food with him in his house; and they con-
soled him and comforted him for all the adversity
that the Lord had brought upon him. Each one
gave him a piece of silver and each a ring of gold.
¹²Now the Lord blessed the latter *days* of Job
more than his beginning; for he had fourteen
thousand sheep, six thousand camels, one thousand yoke of oxen, and one thousand female donkeys. ¹³He also had seven sons and three daughters. ¹⁴And he called the name of the first
Jemimah, the name of the second Keziah, and the
name of the third Keren-Happuch. ¹⁵In all the land
were found no women *so* beautiful as the daughters of Job; and their father gave them an inheritance among their brothers.
¹⁶After this Job lived one hundred and forty
years, and saw his children and grandchildren *for*
four generations. ¹⁷So Job died, old and full of days.

42:10 [a]Literally *Job's captivity,* that is, what was captured from Job

---

42:6 Job did not claim to be sinless, but he was in right standing with God. He did not confess alleged overt sins as bringing
about his suffering. Yet he did confess his lack of faith in God
and his bitterness of attitude during the time of his suffering
(vv. 4–6).

42:7 God accused Job's three friends of speaking in a wrong
way about Him, His ways, and His reasons for allowing affliction. Although what they said about God was typical theological jargon, it was distorted and incomplete.

42:8 Seven bulls and seven rams was considered an excep-
tionally large sacrifice for three men, thus indicating how serious their sins were to God (see Ezek. 45:21–25). Although
Job's friends did not pray for him, Job was instructed to be
their intercessor. This privilege assigned to Job showed God's
high regard for him and vindicated Job from the guilt assigned to him by his friends. The words of Job's wife and of
the three friends were contrary to the wisdom of God (see Job
28:28; Prov. 9).

42:10 The restoration of a double portion of his losses was a
gracious gift from God, not a reward for Job's goodness or
restitution owed him.

42:11 The gifts are typical of the patriarchal period and are
customarily given after a calamity. However, Job was proper-
ous because of God, not because of the generosity of his family and friends.

42:7–17 The Lord vindicated Job, who took an active role in
restoring his three friends. God did not punish the three
friends but offered forgiveness. No complaints were heard
from Job.

Without the epilogue, one might get the idea that the
greatest result of faith was suffering, which could suggest a
sadistic faith in a sadistic God. Suffering itself has no intrinsic
value, but it does serve as a testing ground for true identity
and beliefs. It is also a "hothouse" for character growth and
development. While no one can deny that worship is wonderful when everything is going well, only the broken heart
knows a closeness with the Lord that is even more blessed.
Yet God will not leave His people broken or bewildered forever. The question is not whether God will reward the righteous and punish the wicked, but *when* He will do it. Whether
it happens sooner or later, on earth or in heaven, rewards will
indeed be given in God's perfect timing.

Psalms

AUTHOR

The Book of Psalms is a collection of worship songs written by a variety of authors over an extended period in Israel's history. The superscriptions, titles, or headings of some of the psalms identify them with certain individuals or groups. Other psalms contain no reference to authorship. The individual most frequently mentioned is David, and the entire Book of Psalms generally is associated with him. He was recognized as "the sweet psalmist of Israel" (2 Sam. 23:1). The phrase "of David" appearing in the titles of many psalms may also be translated "to David" or "for David," conveying the sense of belonging to the Davidic collection of psalms. Other individuals and groups associated with certain psalms include Asaph, Solomon, Ethan, Moses, and the sons of Korah.

DATE

The nature of the Book of Psalms as a collection of songs for use in Israel's worship makes it difficult to assign a date to the entire book. The psalms were written at various times throughout Israel's history. The superscriptions of some of the psalms identify the precise historical setting (see chart, The Types of Psalms). For example, Psalm 51, David's prayer for forgiveness after he committed adultery with Bathsheba, was probably composed during the tenth century B.C. In contrast, Psalm 137 is a song of God's people, who went into Babylonian captivity (586 B.C.) and remained in captivity until the 538 B.C. edict of King Cyrus of Persia permitted the exiles to return to their homeland. Certain psalms composed by individuals were probably modified later for use in the worship assembly. The Book of Psalms is a part of the section of the Hebrew canon known as the Writings.

BACKGROUND

SETTING: The psalms are derived from a variety of individual and corporate settings in Israel's history, and the superscriptions or headings of certain psalms identify their historical settings. For example, Psalm 3 is set during David's flight from his son Absalom. Ultimately, the psalms became a part of Israel's worship in the temple. Some of the psalms undoubtedly were composed specifically for temple worship.

PURPOSE: The Book of Psalms uniquely reflects individual responses to God's revelation of Himself (see chart, Images of God in Psalms). Women can identify with many of these poets who poured out their hearts to God in prayers, longings, confessions, laments, and thanksgivings. The Book of Psalms functioned as Israel's hymnbook of worship songs, sometimes identified as the Psalter (see charts, Musical Instruments of the Old Testament; Hymns and Songs Associated with Women).

AUDIENCE: The psalms, primarily addressed to the Lord God of Israel, played a significant role in the corporate life of Israel. They encompass a variety of positive and nega-

tive human experiences, thus revealing that we can approach God with all the experiences of our lives. God hears the cries of suffering and sin as well as the shouts of joy and gladness from His people (see chart, Psalms for Daily Living).

LITERARY CHARACTERISTICS: The Book of Psalms contains Hebrew poetry, which is recognized by rhythm rather than rhyme. Primary characteristics of Hebrew poetry include parallelism, meter, and strophic arrangement. Among the many types of parallelism are *synonymous*, in which the second line repeats the thought of the first line in slightly different words (Ps. 51:2); *antithetic*, in which the second line stands in contrast to the first (Ps. 1:6); or *synthetic*, in which the second line advances or completes the thought of the first line (Ps. 107:1).

Meter is determined by the number of accented syllables in a line of poetry. Strophic arrangement refers to the grouping of a psalm or psalms into stanzas by a recurring refrain (Ps. 42:5, 11; 43:5).

THEMES

The Book of Psalms contains responses to God by individuals and the community in worship. Various types of psalms have been identified, including hymns of praise, royal psalms, laments, thanksgivings, enthronement psalms, and wisdom psalms (see chart, The Types of Psalms). Above all, Psalms is a book of praise. A reading of the 150 psalms will shift the focus to the majesty of the God who is to be worshiped, for He is worthy of eternal praise.

OUTLINE

The Book of Psalms generally is outlined according to the various collections or books comprising the whole:

Book I   (Ps. 1—41)

Book II   (Ps. 42—72)

Book III (Ps. 73—89)

Book IV   (Ps. 90—106)

Book V   (Ps. 107—150)

Each of these five books ends with a doxology of praise to the Lord (see Ps. 41:13; 72:18, 19; 89:52; 106:48). The entirety of Psalm 150 functions as a doxology to Book V and also as a fitting conclusion to the Book of Psalms.

Book One: Psalms 1—41

PSALM 1

The Way of the Righteous and the End of the Ungodly

¹Blessed *is* the man
  Who walks not in the counsel of the ungodly,
    Nor stands in the path of sinners,
    Nor sits in the seat of the scornful;
²But his delight *is* in the law of the LORD,
    And in His law he meditates day and night.
³He shall be like a tree
    Planted by the rivers of water,
    That brings forth its fruit in its season,
    Whose leaf also shall not wither;
And whatever he does shall prosper.

⁴The ungodly *are* not so,
  But *are* like the chaff which the wind drives
    away.
⁵Therefore the ungodly shall not stand in the
    judgment,
  Nor sinners in the congregation of the
    righteous.

⁶For the LORD knows the way of the righteous,
  But the way of the ungodly shall perish.

PSALM 2

The Messiah's Triumph and Kingdom

¹Why do the nations rage,
  And the people plot a vain thing?
²The kings of the earth set themselves,
  And the rulers take counsel together,
  Against the LORD and against His Anointed,
    saying,
³"Let us break Their bonds in pieces
  And cast away Their cords from us."

⁴He who sits in the heavens shall laugh;
  The Lord shall hold them in derision.
⁵Then He shall speak to them in His wrath,
  And distress them in His deep displeasure:
⁶"Yet I have set My King
  On My holy hill of Zion."

⁷"I will declare the decree:
  The LORD has said to Me,
  'You *are* My Son,
  Today I have begotten You.
⁸Ask of Me, and I will give *You*
  The nations *for* Your inheritance,
  And the ends of the earth *for* Your possession.
⁹You shall break[a] them with a rod of iron;
  You shall dash them to pieces like a potter's
    vessel.'"

¹⁰Now therefore, be wise, O kings;
  Be instructed, you judges of the earth.
¹¹Serve the LORD with fear,
  And rejoice with trembling.
¹²Kiss the Son,[a] lest He[b] be angry,
  And you perish *in* the way,
  When His wrath is kindled but a little.
Blessed *are* all those who put their trust in
    Him.

PSALM 3

The LORD Helps His Troubled People

A Psalm of David when he fled from Absalom his son.

¹LORD, how they have increased who trouble me!
  Many *are* they who rise up against me.
²Many *are* they who say of me,
  "*There is* no help for him in God."   *Selah*

³But You, O LORD, *are* a shield for me,
  My glory and the One who lifts up my head.
⁴I cried to the LORD with my voice,
  And He heard me from His holy hill.   *Selah*

⁵I lay down and slept;
  I awoke, for the LORD sustained me.
⁶I will not be afraid of ten thousands of people
  Who have set *themselves* against me all
    around.
· · · · · · · · · · · · · · · · · · · ·

2:9 [a]Following Masoretic Text and Targum; Septuagint, Syriac, and Vulgate read *rule* (compare Revelation 2:27). **2:12** [a]Septuagint and Vulgate read *Embrace discipline;* Targum reads *Receive instruction.* [b]Septuagint reads *the LORD.*

1:1–3 The blessed individual is described in both negative and positive phrases in this wisdom psalm (see chart, The Choice Between Life and Death). The word "blessed" is plural in the Hebrew text, perhaps denoting the fullness of blessing that comes to the person who obeys the Lord (v. 1). To know and do the will of God is the essence of wisdom. Happiness and blessing belong to the individual who delights in and continually meditates on God's Word (v. 2). Such meditation is not primarily mental knowledge but a constant yielding to the will of God. Stability and fruitfulness belong to the individual who focuses continually on obedience to God (v. 3).

2:1–3 This royal psalm, most likely connected with the enthronement ceremony of a new king, contrasts the rebellion of earthly kings with the greatness and power of God (see chart, The Types of Psalms). The coronation of a new king in Israel apparently was accompanied by an outburst of unrest and rebellion on the part of nations subject to Israel. Therefore, the king of Israel asserted his authority as the anointed of God (v. 2, "Anointed," lit. "messiah"). Revolt against God's people is portrayed as rebellion against God.

3:3–6 David's flight from his son Absalom prompted this psalm (2 Sam. 15:13–17). In his turmoil, David expressed confidence in the Lord as a shield about him (see chart, Images of God in the Psalms). The small shield of leather or metal was carried by a warrior for protection against an enemy's sword or spear (see also Ps. 5:12). Like this shield, God protects His people. Paul described the shield of faith as providing our protection against the power of evil (Eph. 6:16).

THE CHOICE BETWEEN LIFE AND DEATH

THE WAY OF LIFE	THE WAY OF DEATH
1. Avoid destructive relationships (Ps. 1:1).	1. Experience instability (Ps. 1:4).
2. Delight continually in God's Word (Ps. 1:2).	2. Experience defeat and isolation (Ps. 1:5).
3. Achieve stability and productivity (Ps. 1:3).	3. Experience separation from God (Ps. 1:6).

⁷Arise, O Lord;
　Save me, O my God!
　For You have struck all my enemies on the
　　cheekbone;
　You have broken the teeth of the ungodly.
⁸Salvation *belongs* to the Lord.
　Your blessing *is* upon Your people.　　　*Selah*

PSALM 4

The Safety of the Faithful

To the Chief Musician. With stringed instruments. A Psalm of
David.

¹Hear me when I call, O God of my
　　righteousness!
　You have relieved me in *my* distress;
　Have mercy on me, and hear my
　　prayer.

²How long, O you sons of men,
　Will you turn my glory to shame?
　How long will you love worthlessness
　And seek falsehood?　　　　　　　*Selah*
³But know that the Lord has set apartª for
　　Himself him who is godly;
　The Lord will hear when I call to Him.

⁴Be angry, and do not sin.
　Meditate within your heart on your bed, and
　　be still.　　　　　　　　　　　　*Selah*
⁵Offer the sacrifices of righteousness,
　And put your trust in the Lord.

⁶*There are* many who say,
　"Who will show us *any* good?"

Lord, lift up the light of Your countenance
　upon us.
⁷You have put gladness in my heart,
　More than in the season that their grain and
　　wine increased.
⁸I will both lie down in peace, and sleep;
　For You alone, O Lord, make me dwell in
　　safety.

PSALM 5

A Prayer for Guidance

To the Chief Musician. With flutes.ª A Psalm of David.

¹Give ear to my words, O Lord,
　Consider my meditation.
²Give heed to the voice of my cry,
　My King and my God,
　For to You I will pray.
³My voice You shall hear in the morning,
　　O Lord;
　In the morning I will direct *it* to You,
　And I will look up.

⁴For You *are* not a God who takes pleasure in
　　wickedness,
　Nor shall evil dwell with You.
⁵The boastful shall not stand in Your sight;
　You hate all workers of iniquity.
⁶You shall destroy those who speak
　　falsehood;
　The Lord abhors the bloodthirsty and
　　deceitful man.

4:3 ªMany Hebrew manuscripts, Septuagint, Targum, and Vulgate
read *made wonderful.*　**5:title** ªHebrew *nehiloth*

4:4, 5 The poet's faith and trust in God is expressed in this
psalm (see also Ps. 3). "The sacrifices of righteousness" are
those offered with the right attitude (Ps. 4:5). The assurance
of God's protection comes to those who put their trust in Him,
and He is the true source of security in an insecure world
(v. 8).

5:7–12 Mercy describes God's steadfast love and His covenant
loyalty (v. 7). Experiencing God's "mercy" (Heb. *chesed,* lit.
"unfailing love") is a primary benefit of faith in Him. This reference to God's covenant love is often translated "loving-

kindness." God's love must be set in the context of His
covenant to emphasize the constancy and fidelity of His love
for His people. Through this "loving-kindness," God promises
forgiveness, compassion, and blessings. His benefits are
guaranteed to be unceasing. Such faith leads the believer to
"fear" the Lord in reverent obedience (v. 7). Joy, protection,
and blessing surround those who put their faith in the Lord
(vv. 11, 12). The large "shield" was designed to protect the entire body (v. 12; see also Ps. 3:3–6, note).

PROSPERITY *MORE THAN POSSESSIONS*

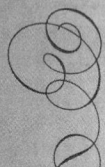

God desires His children to prosper in all things (Gen. 39:3), and He promises prosperity to the godly (Job 22:23–27). Biblical prosperity, however, means more than financial wealth or material possessions. True prosperity is total well-being and is dependent on a lifestyle of righteousness.

The righteous who meditate faithfully on God's Word are those who prosper abundantly (Ps. 1:1–3). Prosperity from God is reserved for those who do the will of God (Josh. 1:8)—keeping His statutes, His commandments, His judgments, and His testimonies (1 Kin. 2:3). Strength and courage as well as prosperity are offered to all who fulfill the statutes and judgments of the Lord (1 Chr. 22:13). Those who live God's way are in position to receive God's help and blessing.

While the Lord rejoices in the prosperity of His children (Ps. 35:27; Eccl. 7:14), He also warns believers about its dangers. As God's children enjoy the blessings of a prosperous life, they naturally tend to forget the source of their blessings (Deut. 8:10–18) and begin to rely on their possessions (including intangible possessions such as family, intelligence, or innate talents) for their identity, ability, and security. Christians are reminded to recognize always that it is God who gives the power to acquire material prosperity (James 1:17).

Jesus taught that material possessions are not a measure of a person's value or spiritual worthiness (Luke 12:15). Paul warned against a pursuit of prosperity as a person's primary motive or "love" (1 Tim. 6:9, 10). Christians should depend entirely on the Lord to provide all their needs (Matt. 6:25, 26) and should give Him thanks as He does.

See also 2 Chr. 26:5; Job 36:11; Prov. 28:25; Matt. 16:26, 27; 3 John 2; notes on Blessings (Gen. 12); Gratitude (Ps. 95); Wealth (1 Tim. 6); portraits of Claudia (2 Tim. 4); Lydia (Acts 16)

7But as for me, I will come into Your house in
   the multitude of Your mercy;
In fear of You I will worship toward Your holy
   temple.
8Lead me, O Lᴏʀᴅ, in Your righteousness
   because of my enemies;
Make Your way straight before my face.

9For *there is* no faithfulness in their mouth;
   Their inward part *is* destruction;
   Their throat *is* an open tomb;
   They flatter with their tongue.
10Pronounce them guilty, O God!
   Let them fall by their own counsels;
   Cast them out in the multitude of their
      transgressions,
   For they have rebelled against You.

11But let all those rejoice who put their trust in
   You;
   Let them ever shout for joy, because You
      defend them;
   Let those also who love Your name
   Be joyful in You.
12For You, O Lᴏʀᴅ, will bless the righteous;
   With favor You will surround him as *with a*
      shield.

PSALM 6

A Prayer of Faith in Time of Distress

To the Chief Musician. With stringed instruments.
On an eight-stringed harp.ᵃ A Psalm of David.

1O Lᴏʀᴅ, do not rebuke me in Your anger,
   Nor chasten me in Your hot displeasure.
2Have mercy on me, O Lᴏʀᴅ, for I *am*
   weak;
   O Lᴏʀᴅ, heal me, for my bones are
      troubled.
3My soul also is greatly troubled;
   But You, O Lᴏʀᴅ— how long?

4Return, O Lᴏʀᴅ, deliver me!
   Oh, save me for Your mercies' sake!
5For in death *there is* no remembrance of
      You;
   In the grave who will give You thanks?

6I am weary with my groaning;
   All night I make my bed swim;
   I drench my couch with my tears.
7My eye wastes away because of grief;
   It grows old because of all my enemies.

················

6:title ᵃHebrew *sheminith*

6:2–10 The seven penitential psalms recognized by the ancient church deal particularly with the nature of sin and forgiveness (Ps. 6; 32; 38; 51; 102; 130; 143; see chart, The Types of Psalms). The psalmist appealed to God's gracious mercy because his "bones" (lit. entire being) were troubled. In Hebrew thought, such suffering was generally connected directly with sin. Therefore, the psalmist's petition for healing constituted a plea for forgiveness. For God to hear the psalmist's prayer confirmed forgiveness (Ps. 6:9) and victory (v. 10), shifting the mood of the poem (vv. 1–7 in contrast to vv. 8–10). The psalmist did not assert his innocence; rather he appealed to the gracious nature of God for forgiveness (see charts, Journey to Forgiveness; Forgiveness: Your Path to Freedom).

THE NAMES OF GOD

NAME	DESCRIPTION	REFERENCE
Abba (Aram. *Abba*)	Daddy—a diminutive of father	Mark 14:36
Almighty (Heb. *Shaddai*)	The All Powerful God	*Ruth 1:20
Ancient of Days (Aram. *Attiq Yomin*)	God is active in history	Dan. 7:9
The Everlasting God (Heb. *'El Olam*)	The Eternal God	Gen. 21:33
Father (Heb. *'Ab*)	The first person of the Trinity	2 Sam. 7:14
God (Heb. *'Elohim*)	The Creator	*Gen. 3:3
God Most High (Heb. *'El 'Elyon*)	The Exalted One	Gen. 14:18–20
The-God-Who-Sees (Heb. *'El Roi*)	The Responder to needs	*Gen. 16:13
The Holy One of Israel (Heb. *Qedosh Yisra'el*)	The set-apart God of Israel	Is. 1:4
Judge (Heb. *Shapat*)	The Leader who pronounces judgments	Gen. 18:25
Lord (Heb. *'Adonai*)	The Master	Ps. 2:4
Lord (*Yahweh*) (Heb. *YHWH*)	The personal, most intimate name God assigned to Himself	*1 Sam. 1:20
The Lord is my Banner (Heb. *YHWH-Nissi*)	*Yahweh* protects	Ex. 17:15
The Lord of Hosts (Heb. *YHWH-Sabaoth*)	*Yahweh* of the armies	1 Sam. 1:3
The-Lord-is-Peace (Heb. *YHWH-Shalom*)	*Yahweh* is peace	Judg. 6:24
The-Lord-will-Provide (Heb. *YHWH-Yireh*)	*Yahweh* provides	Gen. 22:14
The Lord our Righteousness (Heb. *YHWH-Tsidekenu*)	The Righteous One	Jer. 23:6
The Lord is my Shepherd (Heb. *YHWH-Rohi*)	The God who provides loving care	Ps. 23:1
Most High (Aram. *Illaya*)	The Exalted One	Dan. 7:25

See also Lam. 3:22, note; notes on Attributes of God (Ex. 33; Deut. 4; 32; 2 Chr. 19; Job 23; 42; Ps. 25; 89; 90; 102; 119; Is. 6; 65; Jer. 23; Rom. 2; Eph. 1; 1 John 5); charts, Images of God in the Psalms; Names of Jesus.

*References in which a woman used this name.

---

⁸Depart from me, all you workers of iniquity;
For the Lord has heard the voice of my
weeping.
⁹The Lord has heard my supplication;

The Lord will receive my prayer.
¹⁰Let all my enemies be ashamed and greatly
troubled;
Let them turn back *and* be ashamed suddenly.

PSALM 7

Prayer and Praise for Deliverance from Enemies

A Meditation[a] of David, which he sang to the LORD concerning the words of Cush, a Benjamite.

¹O LORD my God, in You I put my trust;
Save me from all those who persecute me;
And deliver me,
²Lest they tear me like a lion,
Rending *me* in pieces, while *there is* none to deliver.

³O LORD my God, if I have done this:
If there is iniquity in my hands,
⁴If I have repaid evil to him who was at peace with me,
Or have plundered my enemy without cause,
⁵Let the enemy pursue me and overtake *me;*
Yes, let him trample my life to the earth,
And lay my honor in the dust.   Selah

⁶Arise, O LORD, in Your anger;
Lift Yourself up because of the rage of my enemies;
Rise up for me[a] *to* the judgment You have commanded!
⁷So the congregation of the peoples shall surround You;
For their sakes, therefore, return on high.
⁸The LORD shall judge the peoples;
Judge me, O LORD, according to my righteousness,
And according to my integrity within me.

⁹Oh, let the wickedness of the wicked come to an end,
But establish the just;
For the righteous God tests the hearts and minds.
¹⁰My defense *is* of God,
Who saves the upright in heart.

¹¹God *is* a just judge,
And God is angry *with the wicked* every day.
¹²If he does not turn back,
He will sharpen His sword;
He bends His bow and makes it ready.
¹³He also prepares for Himself instruments of death;
He makes His arrows into fiery shafts.

¹⁴Behold, *the wicked* brings forth iniquity;
Yes, he conceives trouble and brings forth falsehood.
¹⁵He made a pit and dug it out,
And has fallen into the ditch *which* he made.
¹⁶His trouble shall return upon his own head,
And his violent dealing shall come down on his own crown.

¹⁷I will praise the LORD according to His righteousness,
And will sing praise to the name of the LORD Most High.

PSALM 8

The Glory of the LORD in Creation

To the Chief Musician. On the instrument of Gath.[a] A Psalm of David.

¹O LORD, our Lord,
How excellent *is* Your name in all the earth,
Who have set Your glory above the heavens!

²Out of the mouth of babes and nursing infants
You have ordained strength,
Because of Your enemies,
That You may silence the enemy and the avenger.

³When I consider Your heavens, the work of Your fingers,
The moon and the stars, which You have ordained,
⁴What is man that You are mindful of him,
And the son of man that You visit him?
⁵For You have made him a little lower than the angels,[a]
And You have crowned him with glory and honor.

⁶You have made him to have dominion over the works of Your hands;
You have put all *things* under his feet,
⁷All sheep and oxen—
Even the beasts of the field,

• • • • • • • • • • • • • • • • •

7:title [a]Hebrew *Shiggaion*   7:6 [a]Following Masoretic Text, Targum, and Vulgate; Septuagint reads *O LORD my God.*   8:title [a]Hebrew *Al Gittith*   8:5 [a]Hebrew *Elohim, God;* Septuagint, Syriac, Targum, and Jewish tradition translate as *angels.*

7:1–17 An innocent plea for protection from the false accusations of enemies is reflected, but the psalmist also asked that his enemies overcome him if he was in the wrong (vv. 4, 5). The psalmist's enemies were viewed as the enemies of the Lord (v. 16). "The LORD Most High" (lit. "the Exalted One, LORD over all") is a title found only twice in the Psalms (v. 17; see also Ps. 47:2; chart, Images of God in the Psalms).

8:1 An exaltation of the majestic name of the Lord is the refrain that both begins and ends this poem (vv. 1, 9). While the primary emphasis is on the excellence of God, a secondary emphasis falls on the worth and dignity of those created in God's image. God created us in His image. He also re-created believers (2 Cor. 5:17).

[8]The birds of the air,
And the fish of the sea
That pass through the paths of the seas.

[9]O LORD, our Lord,
How excellent *is* Your name in all the earth!

PSALM 9

Prayer and Thanksgiving for the LORD's Righteous Judgments
To the Chief Musician. To *the tune of* "Death of the Son."[a]
A Psalm of David.

[1]I will praise *You,* O LORD, with my whole heart;
I will tell of all Your marvelous works.
[2]I will be glad and rejoice in You;
I will sing praise to Your name, O Most High.

[3]When my enemies turn back,
They shall fall and perish at Your presence.
[4]For You have maintained my right and my
cause;
You sat on the throne judging in
righteousness.
[5]You have rebuked the nations,
You have destroyed the wicked;
You have blotted out their name forever and
ever.

[6]O enemy, destructions are finished forever!
And you have destroyed cities;
Even their memory has perished.
[7]But the LORD shall endure forever;
He has prepared His throne for judgment.
[8]He shall judge the world in righteousness,
And He shall administer judgment for the
peoples in uprightness.

[9]The LORD also will be a refuge for the
oppressed,
A refuge in times of trouble.
[10]And those who know Your name will put their
trust in You;
For You, LORD, have not forsaken those who
seek You.

[11]Sing praises to the LORD, who dwells in Zion!
Declare His deeds among the people.
[12]When He avenges blood, He remembers them;
He does not forget the cry of the
humble.

[13]Have mercy on me, O LORD!
Consider my trouble from those who hate me,

IMAGES OF GOD IN THE PSALMS	
IMAGES OF GOD AS	REFERENCE IN PSALMS
Shield	3:3; 28:7; 119:114
Rock	18:2; 42:9; 95:1
King	5:2; 44:4; 74:12
Shepherd	23:1; 80:1
Judge	7:11
Refuge	46:1; 62:7
Fortress	31:3; 71:3
Avenger	26:1
Creator	8:1, 6
Deliverer	37:39, 40
Healer	30:2
Protector	5:11
Provider	78:23–29
Redeemer	107:2

You who lift me up from the gates of death,
[14]That I may tell of all Your praise
In the gates of the daughter of Zion.
I will rejoice in Your salvation.

[15]The nations have sunk down in the pit *which*
they made;
In the net which they hid, their own foot is
caught.
[16]The LORD is known *by* the judgment He
executes;
The wicked is snared in the work of his own
hands.
Meditation.[a]   *Selah*

9:title [a]Hebrew *Muth Labben*   **9:16** [a]Hebrew *Higgaion*

9:9–11 This psalm of thankful praise celebrates the Lord's righteous judgments. Psalms 9 and 10, closely related in form and language, appear as a single psalm in the Septuagint (a Greek translation of the Hebrew OT). Both psalms express confidence in God's victory over evil. "To know" refers to personal, intimate knowledge. Therefore, those who possess such knowledge and put their trust in the Lord experience His protection during troubled times, prompting the psalmist to encourage his listeners to "sing praises to the LORD!" (Ps. 9:11).

IMAGE OF GOD *HIS REFLECTION IN US*

What a magnificent concept—God's creation of mankind in His image—patterned after Him, mirroring a family resemblance of Him (2 Cor. 3:18). This does not pertain to the physical nature but rather to the spiritual and moral nature.

How are we like God?

- We are capable of communicating, and in so doing, we can bless or curse (James 3:9).
- We are creative, and creativity gives us joy and satisfaction (Prov. 31:13–22).
- We experience emotions and feelings; we long for relationship and fellowship (Ps. 16:11).
- We discern between right and wrong (Is. 6:5).
- We act and are responsible for our actions (John 3:18).
- We long to pursue Him. Mary sat at Jesus' feet, listening to Him. Jesus let her know that sitting at His feet was important (Luke 10:42).

Even though the original intimate relationship between God and humanity was severed by the Fall (Gen. 3:5–7), God has pursued His children down through the ages, sending His Son that we might be reconciled to Him and become His daughters and sons, His heirs (Rom. 8:14–17). His image can be reflected in us. Through Christ the image is brought back into focus so that His glory shines from the reflection.

See also Gen. 1:26; 9:6; Ps. 100:3; Eph. 4:24; chart on Biblical Manhood and Womanhood (Job 31); notes on Biblical Equality (Eph. 5); Fall of Creation (Gen. 3); Femininity (Ps. 144); Masculinity (Gen. 2)

17The wicked shall be turned into hell,
And all the nations that forget God.
18For the needy shall not always be forgotten;
The expectation of the poor shall *not* perish
forever.

19Arise, O LORD,
Do not let man prevail;
Let the nations be judged in Your sight.
20Put them in fear, O LORD,
That the nations may know themselves *to be but*
men.   *Selah*

PSALM 10

A Song of Confidence in God's Triumph over Evil
1Why do You stand afar off, O LORD?
Why do You hide in times of trouble?
2The wicked in *his* pride persecutes the poor;
Let them be caught in the plots which they
have devised.

3For the wicked boasts of his heart's desire;
He blesses the greedy *and* renounces the LORD.
4The wicked in his proud countenance does not
seek *God;*
God *is* in none of his thoughts.

5His ways are always prospering;
Your judgments *are* far above, out of his sight;
As for all his enemies, he sneers at them.
6He has said in his heart, "I shall not be moved;
I shall never be in adversity."
7His mouth is full of cursing and deceit and
oppression;
Under his tongue *is* trouble and iniquity.

8He sits in the lurking places of the villages;
In the secret places he murders the innocent;
His eyes are secretly fixed on the helpless.
9He lies in wait secretly, as a lion in his den;
He lies in wait to catch the poor;
He catches the poor when he draws him into
his net.
10So he crouches, he lies low,
That the helpless may fall by his strength.
11He has said in his heart,
"God has forgotten;
He hides His face;
He will never see."

12Arise, O LORD!
O God, lift up Your hand!
Do not forget the humble.
13Why do the wicked renounce God?
He has said in his heart,
"You will not require *an account.*"

14But You have seen, for You observe trouble and
grief,
To repay *it* by Your hand.
The helpless commits himself to You;
You are the helper of the fatherless.
15Break the arm of the wicked and the evil *man;*
Seek out his wickedness *until* You find none.

16The LORD *is* King forever and ever;
The nations have perished out of His land.
17LORD, You have heard the desire of the
humble;
You will prepare their heart;
You will cause Your ear to hear,

To sin is human, but to persist in sin is devilish.

St. Catherine of Siena

---

[18]To do justice to the fatherless and the
oppressed,
That the man of the earth may oppress no
more.

PSALM 11

Faith in the LORD's Righteousness

To the Chief Musician. *A Psalm* of David.

[1]In the LORD I put my trust;
How can you say to my soul,
"Flee *as* a bird to your mountain"?
[2]For look! The wicked bend *their* bow,
They make ready their arrow on the string,
That they may shoot secretly at the upright in
heart.
[3]If the foundations are destroyed,
What can the righteous do?

[4]The LORD *is* in His holy temple,
The LORD's throne *is* in heaven;
His eyes behold,
His eyelids test the sons of men.
[5]The LORD tests the righteous,
But the wicked and the one who loves violence
His soul hates.
[6]Upon the wicked He will rain coals;
Fire and brimstone and a burning wind
Shall be the portion of their cup.

[7]For the LORD *is* righteous,
He loves righteousness;
His countenance beholds the upright.[a]

PSALM 12

Man's Treachery and God's Constancy

To the Chief Musician. On an eight-stringed harp.[a]
A Psalm of David.

[1]Help, LORD, for the godly man ceases!
For the faithful disappear from among the
sons of men.
[2]They speak idly everyone with his neighbor;
With flattering lips *and* a double heart they
speak.

[3]May the LORD cut off all flattering lips,
And the tongue that speaks proud things,
[4]Who have said,
"With our tongue we will prevail;
Our lips *are* our own;
Who *is* lord over us?"

[5]"For the oppression of the poor, for the sighing
of the needy,
Now I will arise," says the LORD;
"I will set *him* in the safety for which he yearns."

[6]The words of the LORD *are* pure words,
Like silver tried in a furnace of earth,
Purified seven times.
[7]You shall keep them, O LORD,
You shall preserve them from this generation
forever.

[8]The wicked prowl on every side,
When vileness is exalted among the sons of
men.

PSALM 13

Trust in the Salvation of the LORD

To the Chief Musician. A Psalm of David.

[1]How long, O LORD? Will You forget me forever?
How long will You hide Your face from me?
[2]How long shall I take counsel in my soul,
Having sorrow in my heart daily?
How long will my enemy be exalted over me?

[3]Consider *and* hear me, O LORD my God;
Enlighten my eyes,
Lest I sleep the *sleep of* death;
[4]Lest my enemy say,
"I have prevailed against him";
Lest those who trouble me rejoice when I am
moved.

[5]But I have trusted in Your mercy;
My heart shall rejoice in Your salvation.

11:7 [a]Or *The upright beholds His countenance*   12:title [a]Hebrew
sheminith

12:1 All alone in his combat against evil, the poet felt that no
good and faithful individual existed in his world (see Jer. 5:1–5;
Mic. 7:2). The poet's cry for help is a cry for salvation or deliverance. God responds to the cries of His people, reassuring
them of His presence (Ps. 12:5).

13:5, 6 The longing for the Lord's deliverance from sickness
and from enemies is echoed throughout the Book of Psalms
(see Ps. 6:3; 79:5; 89:46). An abrupt change of tone occurs in
this psalm when the psalmist confidently asserted that he
was trusting in the Lord's mercy (Heb.,*chesed*: Ps. 13:5; see
5:7–12, note).

TESTING   THE STRENGTHENING OF YOUR FAITH

In a sense, every day of life is a test of our relationship with God. But to each person come seasons of special joy or adversity. Both good times and bad times present opportunities for testing our trust in the Lord.

For the Christian this is not like a classroom exam. God is not watching us with grade book in hand, waiting to "pass" or "fail" us based on our performance. Since all have sinned, no human being on earth could pass such a test (Rom. 6:23). Testing comes through the circumstances of our lives so that we can know our own hearts more insightfully and appreciate God's grace more deeply. In such times of testing, we become aware of our thoughts, attitudes, and emotions. Through this self-awareness, God shows us where we must yet yield to Him in trusting obedience.

As the psalmist has written, when God exposes our hearts through testing, He is leading us away from the ways of the world and into the way that is everlasting (Ps. 139:23, 24).

The same kinds of joy and adversity come to believers as to unbelievers. The unbeliever can make little sense of life and her response to it. The Christian can walk through the testing of life's joys and sorrows with full assurance that in Jesus Christ she is becoming the woman God created her to be.

See also Ps. 7:9; Prov. 17:3; 1 Thess. 2:4; James 1:3; notes on Adversity (Acts 5); Conscience (2 Cor. 1); Decision Making (1 Cor. 8); Temptation (Heb. 2)

---

⁶I will sing to the LORD,
Because He has dealt bountifully with me.

PSALM 14

Folly of the Godless, and God's Final Triumph
To the Chief Musician. *A Psalm* of David.

¹The fool has said in his heart,
"*There is* no God."
They are corrupt,
They have done abominable works,
There is none who does good.

²The LORD looks down from heaven upon the
children of men,
To see if there are any who understand, who
seek God.
³They have all turned aside,
They have together become corrupt;
There is none who does good,
No, not one.

⁴Have all the workers of iniquity no knowledge,
Who eat up my people *as* they eat bread,
And do not call on the LORD?
⁵There they are in great fear,
For God *is* with the generation of the
righteous.

⁶You shame the counsel of the poor,
But the LORD *is* his refuge.

⁷Oh, that the salvation of Israel *would come* out
of Zion!
When the LORD brings back the captivity of His
people,
Let Jacob rejoice *and* Israel be glad.

PSALM 15

The Character of Those Who May Dwell with the LORD
A Psalm of David.

¹LORD, who may abide in Your tabernacle?
Who may dwell in Your holy hill?

²He who walks uprightly,
And works righteousness,
And speaks the truth in his heart;
³He *who* does not backbite with his tongue,
Nor does evil to his neighbor,
Nor does he take up a reproach against his
friend;
⁴In whose eyes a vile person is despised,
But he honors those who fear the LORD;
He *who* swears to his own hurt and does not
change;
⁵He *who* does not put out his money at usury,

14:1 The foolish individual (Heb.*nabal*) lacks spiritual discernment, not intelligence, denying the existence of God and living as if God did not exist. The opposite of folly or foolishness in the OT is not intelligence but rather steadfast devotion to the Lord. Paul's use of Psalm 14 emphasizes that we are all foolish as long as we choose to separate ourselves from the wisdom of God found in the gospel of Christ (1 Cor. 1:18–25; compare Ps. 14 with Ps. 53).

15:1–5 Requirements for worshiping God include experiencing fellowship with God. The tabernacle or holy hill refers to the designated place of worship (v. 1). Acceptable worship comes in living blamelessly, doing righteousness, and speaking truth from the heart (v. 2). An individual who "walks uprightly" makes God the focal point of life in both action and words and practices right living daily in her relationships with others (vv. 3–5). This psalm demands self-examination in preparation for worship.

THE TYPES OF PSALMS

CATEGORY OF PSALMS	REFERENCES	DESCRIPTION
Lament	Prayers for God's deliverance; comfort in times of desperation and despair.	Ps. 3—5; 7; 12; 13; 22; 25—28; 35; 37—40; 42—44; 54—57; 59—61; 63; 64; 69—71; 74; 79; 80; 83; 85; 86; 88; 90; 109; 120; 123; 140—142
Penitential	Prayers centering upon the nature of sin and forgiveness.	Ps. 6; 32; 38; 51; 102; 130; 143
Thanksgiving	Praise to God for His gracious acts; gratitude for God's many blessings.	Ps. 8; 18; 19; 29; 30; 32—34; 36; 40; 41; 66; 103—106; 111
Hallel	Psalms of praise to be sung in relation to Holy Days.	Ps. 113—118
Enthronement	Description of God's sovereign rule; acknowledgment of God as powerful Creator and sovereign Lord.	Ps. 47; 93; 96—99
Pilgrimage (or ascent or degrees)	Songs of worship by travelers to Jewish festivals; expression of reverence and celebration.	Ps. 43; 46; 48; 76; 84; 87; 120—134
Royal	Proclamation of the reign of the earthly king and the heavenly King; reflection of need to make the Lord the sovereign ruler in daily life.	Ps. 2; 18; 20; 21; 45; 72; 89; 101; 110; 132; 144
Wisdom	Instruction in the way of righteousness; determination to seek God's will and direction in time of decision.	Ps. 1; 37; 119
Imprecatory	Request for God's wrath and judgment against enemies; expression of honest feelings about others and resolution of conflict.	Ps. 7; 35; 40; 55; 58; 59; 69; 79; 109; 137; 139; 144

Note: The Book of Psalms is a collection of prayers, poems, and hymns focusing thoughts on God in praise and adoration. Some of the Psalms were used as hymns in the worship services of ancient Israel. This chart represents one system of categorization.

Nor does he take a bribe against the
innocent.

He who does these *things* shall never be
moved.

PSALM 16

The Hope of the Faithful, and the Messiah's Victory

A Michtam of David.

¹Preserve me, O God, for in You I put my trust.

²O my soul, you have said to the LORD,
"You *are* my Lord,
  My goodness is nothing apart from You."
³As for the saints who *are* on the earth,
"They are the excellent ones, in whom is all my
  delight."

⁴Their sorrows shall be multiplied who hasten
  after another *god;*
Their drink offerings of blood I will not offer,
Nor take up their names on my lips.

EMOTIONAL HEALING   RESTORING THE POSITIVE

Emotions are God-given, spontaneous responses to events. A person perceives an event in a particular way, and an emotion is aroused that leads to one of at least three responses: The emotion is allowed to escalate so that it becomes destructive to yourself or others; its validity is denied; or it is directed in a manner appropriate and healthy for the situation. Emotions themselves are neither good nor bad. The problem lies in the thoughts that produce emotions and in behaviors resulting from emotions.

Because they are spontaneous, emotions do not last for an extended period unless they are nurtured by the mind and will. Emotions are a caution light reminding us to re-examine what we are thinking. Thus, Paul does not condemn anger (an emotion indicating a boundary has been crossed) but counsels the Ephesians to deal with it quickly. Anger, when wedded with hurt and shame, can develop into bitterness and provide fertile ground for further temptation (Eph. 4:26, 27, 31; Heb. 12:15).

When a person is shamed for having an emotional response such as fear or anger, her tendency is to protect herself by blocking these emotions from conscious awareness. She, being bound by shame, is unable to express the emotion in appropriate, healthy ways. Since emotions are interconnected, denying painful emotions also necessitates burying pleasant ones, and the result is often emotional numbness.

Scripture challenges you to identify your emotions (Ps. 13:1–3; 77:1–6) and to learn how to channel them into positive behaviors. As painful memories surface, you can bring them to God for healing and restoration, allowing Him to remove the shame that has been linked to those memories.

See also Mark 5:2, note; notes on Emotions (Ps. 42); Forgiveness (Ps. 51; Luke 17); Healing (Ps. 133; Eccl. 1; 2 Cor. 5; Gal. 6; James 5)

---

⁵O Lord, *You are* the portion of my inheritance
  and my cup;
 You maintain my lot.
⁶The lines have fallen to me in pleasant
  places;
 Yes, I have a good inheritance.

⁷I will bless the Lord who has given me
  counsel;
 My heart also instructs me in the night
  seasons.
⁸I have set the Lord always before me;
 Because *He is* at my right hand I shall not be
  moved.

⁹Therefore my heart is glad, and my glory
  rejoices;
 My flesh also will rest in hope.
¹⁰For You will not leave my soul in Sheol,
 Nor will You allow Your Holy One to see
  corruption.
¹¹You will show me the path of life;
 In Your presence *is* fullness of joy;
 At Your right hand *are* pleasures forevermore.

PSALM 17

Prayer with Confidence in Final Salvation

A Prayer of David.

¹Hear a just cause, O Lord,
 Attend to my cry;
 Give ear to my prayer *which is* not from
  deceitful lips.
²Let my vindication come from Your presence;
 Let Your eyes look on the things that are
  upright.

³You have tested my heart;
 You have visited *me* in the night;
 You have tried me and have found
  nothing;
 I have purposed that my mouth shall not
  transgress.
⁴Concerning the works of men,
 By the word of Your lips,
 I have kept away from the paths of the
  destroyer.
⁵Uphold my steps in Your paths,
 That my footsteps may not slip.

16:8–11 The psalmist's faith, reflected in this prayer for preservation, cannot be shaken (v. 10). God is present in all the experiences of life with help, counsel, and guidance. Lifelong fellowship with God brings joy (vv. 9, 11). These verses are also a foretelling of the bodily Resurrection of Christ (vv. 9–11; see Acts 2:25–28, 31; 13:35–37).

17:5–7 David was confident that the Lord would protect him as an innocent person facing difficult circumstances (v. 6; see

Ps. 1; chart, the Choice Between Life and Death). This psalm is the first to be identified as a prayer in its heading or superscription. Having walked in the paths of God and chosen the way of life, the psalmist expressed confidence that God would hear his cry for help uttered under extreme pressure (Ps. 17:5). For "lovingkindness" (Heb. *chesed,* v. 7), see Psalm 5:7–12, note. The language reflects Israel's song of deliverance at the time of the Exodus when the Lord defeated the Egyptian army (Ps. 17:7; see Ex. 15:11–13).

⁶I have called upon You, for You will hear me,
O God;
Incline Your ear to me, *and* hear my speech.
⁷Show Your marvelous lovingkindness by Your
right hand,
O You who save those who trust *in You*
From those who rise up *against them.*
⁸Keep me as the apple of Your eye;
Hide me under the shadow of Your wings,
⁹From the wicked who oppress me,
From my deadly enemies who surround me.

¹⁰They have closed up their fat *hearts;*
With their mouths they speak proudly.
¹¹They have now surrounded us in our steps;
They have set their eyes, crouching down to
the earth,
¹²As a lion is eager to tear his prey,
And like a young lion lurking in secret places.

¹³Arise, O LORD,
Confront him, cast him down;
Deliver my life from the wicked with Your
sword,
¹⁴With Your hand from men, O LORD,
From men of the world *who have* their portion
in *this* life,
And whose belly You fill with Your hidden
treasure.
They are satisfied with children,
And leave the rest of their *possession* for their
babes.

¹⁵As for me, I will see Your face in righteousness;
I shall be satisfied when I awake in Your likeness.

PSALM 18

God the Sovereign Savior

To the Chief Musician. *A Psalm* of David the servant of the LORD,
who spoke to the LORD the words of this song on the day that the
LORD delivered him from the hand of all his enemies and from the
hand of Saul. And he said:

¹I will love You, O LORD, my strength.
²The LORD is my rock and my fortress and my
deliverer;

My God, my strength, in whom I will trust;
My shield and the horn of my salvation, my
stronghold.
³I will call upon the LORD, *who is worthy* to be
praised;
So shall I be saved from my enemies.

⁴The pangs of death surrounded me,
And the floods of ungodliness made me afraid.
⁵The sorrows of Sheol surrounded me;
The snares of death confronted me.
⁶In my distress I called upon the LORD,
And cried out to my God;
He heard my voice from His temple,
And my cry came before Him, *even* to His ears.

⁷Then the earth shook and trembled;
The foundations of the hills also quaked and
were shaken,
Because He was angry.
⁸Smoke went up from His nostrils,
And devouring fire from His mouth;
Coals were kindled by it.
⁹He bowed the heavens also, and came down
With darkness under His feet.
¹⁰And He rode upon a cherub, and flew;
He flew upon the wings of the wind.
¹¹He made darkness His secret place;
His canopy around Him *was* dark waters
And thick clouds of the skies.
¹²From the brightness before Him,
His thick clouds passed with hailstones and
coals of fire.

¹³The LORD thundered from heaven,
And the Most High uttered His voice,
Hailstones and coals of fire.ᵃ
¹⁴He sent out His arrows and scattered the foe,
Lightnings in abundance, and He vanquished
them.
¹⁵Then the channels of the sea were seen,
The foundations of the world were uncovered
At Your rebuke, O LORD,

18:13 ᵃFollowing Masoretic Text, Targum, and Vulgate; a few Hebrew
manuscripts and Septuagint omit *Hailstones and coals of fire.*

17:8 God's keeping power is illustrated in tender imagery. "Apple of Your eye" (lit. "pupil") denotes something most dear and precious. "Under the shadow of Your wings" may refer to the ark of the covenant as a symbol of God's presence or to the protection by which God brought Israel to Himself (Ex. 19:4–6).

18:1–3 David offered this hymn of gratitude for his deliverance from the hand of Saul and all his other enemies (see 2 Sam. 22). David began by declaring his love for the Lord and exalting the Lord as his "strength," "rock," "fortress," "deliverer," "shield," "horn of my salvation," and "stronghold" (Ps. 18:1, 2; see chart, Images of God in the Psalms). God is worthy

of devotion and praise because of who He is. "Love" (lit. "to have mercy" and translated "tender mercies" in Ps. 51:1) indicates intimate relationship (Ps. 18:1) and is closely associated with a mother's care for her children (see chart, Female Metaphors for God). This eloquent expression describes the quality by which God expresses His Fatherhood and empathizes with our human frailties (Ps. 103:13). It is the ultimate expression of God's presence and His closeness to His children. "Love" (Heb. *rachamim*, lit. "to have compassion on," always plural in Hebrew text) is the moving force for restoration and salvation and expresses the restraint of God's anger by His love. God's "mercy" is based on His gracious character (see Ps. 89, Attributes of God).

DISTRESS A TIME TO CALL UPON THE LORD

Many were the distresses of the psalmist. Without exception, however, the psalmist turned to the Lord God to be the source of his deliverance in those difficult times (Ps. 18:3, 6). Many of the psalms reflect the pattern found in Psalm 18:

- The psalmist declared his love for the Lord, whom he knows has proven to be sufficient (vv. 1, 2).
- He called out to the Lord to save him from his enemies, confident that God heard him (vv. 3, 6).
- He expressed a heartfelt longing for God's deliverance (v. 19).
- He acknowledged that God is in control despite all the catastrophes he experienced (vv. 16, 17).
- He remained confident even in the midst of delays that kept him from immediate deliverance (vv. 28, 29, 33, 35, 36).
- He glorified God when deliverance came or his enemies were defeated (vv. 43, 47–50).

In the midst of the trials and difficulties that inevitably come, believers can be confident that they are loved, that they will be ultimately delivered, that every delay will be used to edify and make them better, and that deliverance is assured (Rom. 8:31–39).

See also notes on Depression (1 Sam. 16); Emotions (Ps. 42); Stress Management (Phil. 4); Suffering (Ps. 33; 113; Is. 43; 1 Pet. 5); Worry (Rom. 8).

At the blast of the breath of Your
    nostrils.

16He sent from above, He took me;
    He drew me out of many waters.
17He delivered me from my strong enemy,
    From those who hated me,
    For they were too strong for me.
18They confronted me in the day of my calamity,
    But the LORD was my support.
19He also brought me out into a broad place;
    He delivered me because He delighted in me.

20The LORD rewarded me according to my
    righteousness;
    According to the cleanness of my hands
    He has recompensed me.
21For I have kept the ways of the LORD,
    And have not wickedly departed from my God.
22For all His judgments *were* before me,
    And I did not put away His statutes from me.
23I was also blameless before Him,
    And I kept myself from my iniquity.
24Therefore the LORD has recompensed me
    according to my righteousness,
    According to the cleanness of my hands in His
    sight.

25With the merciful You will show Yourself
    merciful;
    With a blameless man You will show Yourself
    blameless;
26With the pure You will show Yourself pure;
    And with the devious You will show Yourself
    shrewd.

27For You will save the humble people,
    But will bring down haughty looks.

28For You will light my lamp;
    The LORD my God will enlighten my
    darkness.
29For by You I can run against a troop,
    By my God I can leap over a wall.
30*As for* God, His way *is* perfect;
    The word of the LORD is proven;
    He *is* a shield to all who trust in Him.

31For who *is* God, except the LORD?
    And who *is* a rock, except our God?
32*It is* God who arms me with strength,
    And makes my way perfect.
33He makes my feet like the *feet of* deer,
    And sets me on my high places.
34He teaches my hands to make war,
    So that my arms can bend a bow of bronze.

35You have also given me the shield of Your
    salvation;
    Your right hand has held me up,
    Your gentleness has made me great.
36You enlarged my path under me,
    So my feet did not slip.

37I have pursued my enemies and overtaken
    them;
    Neither did I turn back again till they were
    destroyed.
38I have wounded them,
    So that they could not rise;
    They have fallen under my feet.

18:30 God's way means integrity, soundness and wholeness, utter reliability, and trustworthiness. God functions as a shield of protection for those who take refuge in Him (see Ps. 3:3–6, note; Prov. 30:5).

³⁹For You have armed me with strength for the battle;
You have subdued under me those who rose up against me.
⁴⁰You have also given me the necks of my enemies,
So that I destroyed those who hated me.
⁴¹They cried out, but *there was* none to save;
Even to the LORD, but He did not answer them.
⁴²Then I beat them as fine as the dust before the wind;
I cast them out like dirt in the streets.

⁴³You have delivered me from the strivings of the people;
You have made me the head of the nations;
A people I have not known shall serve me.
⁴⁴As soon as they hear of me they obey me;
The foreigners submit to me.
⁴⁵The foreigners fade away,
And come frightened from their hideouts.

⁴⁶The LORD lives!
Blessed *be* my Rock!
Let the God of my salvation be exalted.
⁴⁷*It is* God who avenges me,
And subdues the peoples under me;
⁴⁸He delivers me from my enemies.
You also lift me up above those who rise against me;
You have delivered me from the violent man.
⁴⁹Therefore I will give thanks to You, O LORD, among the Gentiles,
And sing praises to Your name.

⁵⁰Great deliverance He gives to His king,
And shows mercy to His anointed,
To David and his descendants forevermore.

PSALM 19

The Perfect Revelation of the LORD
To the Chief Musician. A Psalm of David.

¹The heavens declare the glory of God;
And the firmament shows His handiwork.
²Day unto day utters speech,
And night unto night reveals knowledge.

³*There is* no speech nor language
Where their voice is not heard.
⁴Their line^a has gone out through all the earth,
And their words to the end of the world.

In them He has set a tabernacle for the sun,
⁵Which *is* like a bridegroom coming out of his chamber,
And rejoices like a strong man to run its race.
⁶Its rising *is* from one end of heaven,
And its circuit to the other end;
And there is nothing hidden from its heat.

⁷The law of the LORD *is* perfect, converting the soul;
The testimony of the LORD *is* sure, making wise the simple;
⁸The statutes of the LORD *are* right, rejoicing the heart;
The commandment of the LORD *is* pure, enlightening the eyes;
⁹The fear of the LORD *is* clean, enduring forever;
The judgments of the LORD *are* true *and* righteous altogether.
¹⁰More to be desired *are they* than gold,
Yea, than much fine gold;
Sweeter also than honey and the honeycomb.
¹¹Moreover by them Your servant is warned,
And in keeping them *there is* great reward.

¹²Who can understand *his* errors?
Cleanse me from secret *faults.*
¹³Keep back Your servant also from presumptuous *sins;*
Let them not have dominion over me.
Then I shall be blameless,
And I shall be innocent of great transgression.

¹⁴Let the words of my mouth and the meditation of my heart
Be acceptable in Your sight,
O LORD, my strength and my Redeemer.

19:4 ^aSeptuagint, Syriac, and Vulgate read *sound;* Targum reads *business.*

19:1 God reveals Himself through the beauty of His creation just as a master artist is known by his work. The heavens reveal God's glory (Heb. *kabod,* lit. "heavy," having the connotation of weightiness). God's glory is His imprimatur or signature in His world, His revelation of Himself to His creation, the physical manifestation of His divine presence, and the external form of His majesty, preeminence, and dignity. Everyone can observe this channel of God's revelation and in so doing cannot miss the awesome Creator, who by His very presence makes a difference and wields the incomparable influence of one who ultimately determines events and makes decisions. The beauty of creation should lead all to worship the Creator and not the creation itself (Rom. 1:20). "Glory" is that essential possession and characteristic of God which all recognize and to which all may respond in confession, worship, and praise.

19:7–9 God's Law provides true wisdom, in revealing how to live a life pleasing to God (Deut. 29:14–29). The "simple" person is one whose mind is open to God's truth (Ps. 19:7). "Fear" is the attitude of reverent obedience (v. 9). Compare Psalm 19:7–14 with Psalm 119, which praises the majesty of God's Word.

PSALM 20

The Assurance of God's Saving Work
To the Chief Musician. A Psalm of David.

[1]May the LORD answer you in the day of trouble;
May the name of the God of Jacob defend you;
[2]May He send you help from the sanctuary,
And strengthen you out of Zion;
[3]May He remember all your offerings,
And accept your burnt sacrifice.   Selah

[4]May He grant you according to your heart's
desire,
And fulfill all your purpose.
[5]We will rejoice in your salvation,
And in the name of our God we will set up our
banners!
May the LORD fulfill all your petitions.

[6]Now I know that the LORD saves His anointed;
He will answer him from His holy heaven
With the saving strength of His right hand.

[7]Some trust in chariots, and some in horses;
But we will remember the name of the LORD
our God.
[8]They have bowed down and fallen;
But we have risen and stand upright.

[9]Save, LORD!
May the King answer us when we call.

PSALM 21

Joy in the Salvation of the LORD
To the Chief Musician. A Psalm of David.

[1]The king shall have joy in Your strength,
O LORD;
And in Your salvation how greatly shall he
rejoice!
[2]You have given him his heart's desire,
And have not withheld the request of his
lips.   Selah

[3]For You meet him with the blessings of
goodness;
You set a crown of pure gold upon his head.
[4]He asked life from You, and You gave it to
him—
Length of days forever and ever.
[5]His glory is great in Your salvation;

Honor and majesty You have placed upon him.
[6]For You have made him most blessed forever;
You have made him exceedingly glad with Your
presence.
[7]For the king trusts in the LORD,
And through the mercy of the Most High he
shall not be moved.

[8]Your hand will find all Your enemies;
Your right hand will find those who hate You.
[9]You shall make them as a fiery oven in the time
of Your anger;
The LORD shall swallow them up in His wrath,
And the fire shall devour them.
[10]Their offspring You shall destroy from the
earth,
And their descendants from among the sons of
men.
[11]For they intended evil against You;
They devised a plot which they are not able to
perform.
[12]Therefore You will make them turn their back;
You will make ready Your arrows on Your string
toward their faces.

[13]Be exalted, O LORD, in Your own strength!
We will sing and praise Your power.

PSALM 22

The Suffering, Praise, and Posterity of the Messiah
To the Chief Musician. Set to "The Deer of the Dawn."[a]
A Psalm of David.

[1]My God, My God, why have You forsaken Me?
Why are You so far from helping Me,
And from the words of My groaning?
[2]O My God, I cry in the daytime, but You do not
hear;
And in the night season, and am not silent.

[3]But You are holy,
Enthroned in the praises of Israel.
[4]Our fathers trusted in You;
They trusted, and You delivered them.
[5]They cried to You, and were delivered;
They trusted in You, and were not ashamed.

[6]But I am a worm, and no man;
A reproach of men, and despised by the people.

22:title [a]Hebrew Aijeleth Hashahar

20:1–4 The king's need for the assurance of God's presence, perhaps when preparing for battle, is the theme of this psalm. The prayer includes a plea for safety, power, and victory. "The name of the God of Jacob" is a reminder of God's deliverance of Jacob in his time of distress (v. 1; Gen. 35:3). Names are important in identification and relationships (Ps. 20:7; Is. 45, Naming of Children; chart, The Names of God). God does not grant every desire of our hearts, but neither does He withhold the desires of our hearts when they are in tune with His purposes (Ps. 20:4).

22:1–31 This great messianic psalm is fulfilled in Christ on the Cross. The suffering of the victim is depicted (vv. 1–21) as the triumph of faith is portrayed (vv. 22–31). Jesus quoted this psalm of victory from the Cross (v. 1; see Matt. 27:46; Mark 15:34).

After the verb "to love," "to help" is the most beautiful verb in the world.

Bertha Von Suttner

---

⁷All those who see Me ridicule Me;
They shoot out the lip, they shake the head,
   saying,
⁸"He trusted^a in the LORD, let Him rescue Him;
Let Him deliver Him, since He delights in Him!"

⁹But You *are* He who took Me out of the womb;
You made Me trust *while* on My mother's
   breasts.
¹⁰I was cast upon You from birth.
From My mother's womb
You *have been* My God.
¹¹Be not far from Me,
For trouble *is* near;
For *there is* none to help.

¹²Many bulls have surrounded Me;
Strong *bulls* of Bashan have encircled Me.
¹³They gape at Me *with* their mouths,
Like a raging and roaring lion.

¹⁴I am poured out like water,
And all My bones are out of joint;
My heart is like wax;
It has melted within Me.
¹⁵My strength is dried up like a potsherd,
And My tongue clings to My jaws;
You have brought Me to the dust of death.

¹⁶For dogs have surrounded Me;
The congregation of the wicked has enclosed
   Me.
They pierced^a My hands and My feet;
¹⁷I can count all My bones.
They look *and* stare at Me.
¹⁸They divide My garments among them,
And for My clothing they cast lots.

¹⁹But You, O LORD, do not be far from Me;
O My Strength, hasten to help Me!
²⁰Deliver Me from the sword,
My precious *life* from the power of the dog.
²¹Save Me from the lion's mouth
And from the horns of the wild oxen!

You have answered Me.

²²I will declare Your name to My brethren;
In the midst of the assembly I will praise You.
²³You who fear the LORD, praise Him!
All you descendants of Jacob, glorify Him,
And fear Him, all you offspring of Israel!
²⁴For He has not despised nor abhorred the
   affliction of the afflicted;
Nor has He hidden His face from Him;
But when He cried to Him, He heard.

²⁵My praise *shall be* of You in the great assembly;
I will pay My vows before those who fear Him.
²⁶The poor shall eat and be satisfied;
Those who seek Him will praise the LORD.
Let your heart live forever!

²⁷All the ends of the world
Shall remember and turn to the LORD,
And all the families of the nations
Shall worship before You.^a
²⁸For the kingdom *is* the LORD's,
And He rules over the nations.

²⁹All the prosperous of the earth
Shall eat and worship;
All those who go down to the dust
Shall bow before Him,
Even he who cannot keep himself alive.

³⁰A posterity shall serve Him.
It will be recounted of the Lord to the *next*
   generation,
³¹They will come and declare His righteousness
   to a people who will be born,
That He has done *this.*

PSALM 23

The LORD the Shepherd of His People
A Psalm of David.

¹The LORD *is* my shepherd;
I shall not want.

· · · · · · · · · · · · · · · ·

22:8 ^aSeptuagint, Syriac, and Vulgate read *hoped;* Targum reads *praised.* **22:16** ^aFollowing some Hebrew manuscripts, Septuagint, Syriac, Vulgate; Masoretic Text reads *Like a lion.* **22:27** ^aFollowing Masoretic Text, Septuagint, and Targum; Arabic, Syriac, and Vulgate read *Him.*

23:1–6 The imagery of the shepherd and sheep in this poem reflects our total dependence on God. A shepherd's chief concern is to do everything to insure the well-being of his flock. The emphasis of this psalm is trust in God to meet our needs (see Phil. 4:19). As the Good Shepherd, God provides for our physical, mental, and spiritual well-being (see John 10:7–18). He provides refreshment in the difficult experiences of life. His "rod" and "staff" lovingly guide, protect, and discipline His sheep. God's "mercy" (Heb. *chesed,* Ps. 23:6) describes His steadfast love (see Ps. 5:7–12, note).

ATTRIBUTES OF GOD · HE IS GOOD

God not only does good; He is the originator of goodness (Gen. 1:31). We have no innate goodness in ourselves; there is no source of goodness outside God (Ps. 16:2; 119:68). To say God is good is to say that He is absolutely pure. There is not a hint of evil or even neutrality. The moment we call Him less than good, we see Him as less than God. Jesus defines "goodness" in one word—God (Matt. 19:16, 17).

Goodness is not one of God's part-time activities (Ps. 136:1). He abounds in it (Ex. 34:6). It is the drive behind His blessings and the reason for His compassion, kindness, and generosity (Ps. 84:11). God does not give out of obligation, for He is never in anyone's debt. He gives out of His goodness. God's goodness is for this life (Ps. 27:13) as well as eternity (Ps. 31:19). It gives hope (Ps. 27:13), leads to repentance (Rom. 2:4), and produces thankfulness (Ps. 136:1). God has started a good work in each believer and has committed Himself to completing His work (Phil. 1:6).

See also Ps. 34:8; 100:5; Lam. 3:22, note; John 10:11; notes on Attributes of God (Ex. 33; Deut. 4; 32; 2 Chr. 19; Job 23; 42; Ps. 90; 102; 119; Is. 6; 65; Jer. 23; Rom. 2; Eph. 1; 1 John 5); Blessings (Gen. 12); Fruit of the Spirit (Ps. 86; Rom. 5; 15; 1 Cor. 10; 13; Gal. 5; Eph. 4; Col. 3; 2 Thess. 1; Rev. 2); Promises of God (2 Pet. 1); Prosperity (Ps. 2)

²He makes me to lie down in green pastures;
He leads me beside the still waters.
³He restores my soul;
He leads me in the paths of righteousness
For His name's sake.

⁴Yea, though I walk through the valley of the
shadow of death,
I will fear no evil;
For You *are* with me;
Your rod and Your staff, they comfort me.

⁵You prepare a table before me in the presence
of my enemies;
You anoint my head with oil;
My cup runs over.
⁶Surely goodness and mercy shall follow me
All the days of my life;
And I will dwell[a] in the house of the LORD
Forever.

PSALM 24

The King of Glory and His Kingdom
A Psalm of David.

¹The earth *is* the LORD's, and all its fullness,
The world and those who dwell therein.
²For He has founded it upon the seas,
And established it upon the waters.

³Who may ascend into the hill of the
LORD?
Or who may stand in His holy place?
⁴He who has clean hands and a pure heart,
Who has not lifted up his soul to an idol,
Nor sworn deceitfully.
⁵He shall receive blessing from the LORD,
And righteousness from the God of his
salvation.

⁶This *is* Jacob, the generation of those who seek
Him,
Who seek Your face.   *Selah*

⁷Lift up your heads, O you gates!
And be lifted up, you everlasting doors!
And the King of glory shall come in.
⁸Who *is* this King of glory?
The LORD strong and mighty,
The LORD mighty in battle.
⁹Lift up your heads, O you gates!
Lift up, you everlasting doors!
And the King of glory shall come in.
¹⁰Who is this King of glory?
The LORD of hosts,
He *is* the King of glory.   *Selah*

PSALM 25

A Plea for Deliverance and Forgiveness
A Psalm of David.

¹To You, O LORD, I lift up my soul.
²O my God, I trust in You;
Let me not be ashamed;
Let not my enemies triumph over me.
³Indeed, let no one who waits on You be
ashamed;
Let those be ashamed who deal treacherously
without cause.

⁴Show me Your ways, O LORD;
Teach me Your paths.
⁵Lead me in Your truth and teach me,
For You *are* the God of my salvation;
On You I wait all the day.

23:6 ᵃFollowing Septuagint, Syriac, Targum, and Vulgate; Masoretic
Text reads *return*.

⁶Remember, O Lᴏʀᴅ, Your tender mercies and
Your lovingkindnesses,
For they *are* from of old.
⁷Do not remember the sins of my youth, nor my
transgressions;
According to Your mercy remember me,
For Your goodness' sake, O Lᴏʀᴅ.

⁸Good and upright *is* the Lᴏʀᴅ;
Therefore He teaches sinners in the way.
⁹The humble He guides in justice,
And the humble He teaches His way.
¹⁰All the paths of the Lᴏʀᴅ *are* mercy and
truth,
To such as keep His covenant and His
testimonies.
¹¹For Your name's sake, O Lᴏʀᴅ,
Pardon my iniquity, for it *is* great.

¹²Who *is* the man that fears the Lᴏʀᴅ?
Him shall Heᵃ teach in the way Heᵇ chooses.
¹³He himself shall dwell in prosperity,
And his descendants shall inherit the earth.
¹⁴The secret of the Lᴏʀᴅ *is* with those who fear
Him,
And He will show them His covenant.
¹⁵My eyes *are* ever toward the Lᴏʀᴅ,
For He shall pluck my feet out of the net.

¹⁶Turn Yourself to me, and have mercy on me,
For I *am* desolate and afflicted.
¹⁷The troubles of my heart have enlarged;
Bring me out of my distresses!
¹⁸Look on my affliction and my pain,
And forgive all my sins.
¹⁹Consider my enemies, for they are many;
And they hate me with cruel hatred.
²⁰Keep my soul, and deliver me;
Let me not be ashamed, for I put my trust in
You.
²¹Let integrity and uprightness preserve me,
For I wait for You.

²²Redeem Israel, O God,
Out of all their troubles!

PSALM 26

A Prayer for Divine Scrutiny and Redemption
A Psalm of David.

¹Vindicate me, O Lᴏʀᴅ,
For I have walked in my integrity.
I have also trusted in the Lᴏʀᴅ;
I shall not slip.

²Examine me, O Lᴏʀᴅ, and prove me;
Try my mind and my heart.
³For Your lovingkindness *is* before my eyes,
And I have walked in Your truth.
⁴I have not sat with idolatrous mortals,
Nor will I go in with hypocrites.
⁵I have hated the assembly of evildoers,
And will not sit with the wicked.

⁶I will wash my hands in innocence;
So I will go about Your altar, O Lᴏʀᴅ,
⁷That I may proclaim with the voice of
thanksgiving,
And tell of all Your wondrous works.
⁸Lᴏʀᴅ, I have loved the habitation of Your house,
And the place where Your glory dwells.

⁹Do not gather my soul with sinners,
Nor my life with bloodthirsty men,
¹⁰In whose hands *is* a sinister scheme,
And whose right hand is full of bribes.

¹¹But as for me, I will walk in my integrity;
Redeem me and be merciful to me.
¹²My foot stands in an even place;
In the congregations I will bless the Lᴏʀᴅ.

PSALM 27

An Exuberant Declaration of Faith
A Psalm of David.

¹The Lᴏʀᴅ *is* my light and my salvation;
Whom shall I fear?
The Lᴏʀᴅ *is* the strength of my life;
Of whom shall I be afraid?
²When the wicked came against me
To eat up my flesh,
My enemies and foes,
They stumbled and fell.
³Though an army may encamp against me,
My heart shall not fear;
Though war may rise against me,
In this I *will be* confident.

⁴One *thing* I have desired of the Lᴏʀᴅ,
That will I seek:
That I may dwell in the house of the Lᴏʀᴅ
All the days of my life,
To behold the beauty of the Lᴏʀᴅ,
And to inquire in His temple.
⁵For in the time of trouble

. . . .

25:12 ᵃOr *he* ᵇOr *he*

27:1–3 The poet declared his confident faith, affirming the
Lord as his "light," "salvation," and "strength." God's presence provides the inner resources to overcome fear in difficult
experiences (Ps. 23:4). God's love even transcends the love

parents have for their children (Ps. 27:10). This psalm does
not suggest abandonment by God but rather the committing
of oneself to God in utter dependence upon Him.

INTEGRITY *SINGLENESS OF HEART*

Some mistakenly associate the word "integrity" only with reputation—an external appearance. True integrity is a quality of character—an inward reality that refers to singleness of heart or mind, the development of a blameless character by adhering to an exemplary moral code. The biblical model of integrity is marked by several distinct features:

- innocent actions (Gen. 20:5);
- a clear conscience (Acts 24:16; Heb. 13:18);
- fear of God, truthfulness, and opposition to covetousness (Ex. 18:21);
- blamelessness and uprightness (Job 2:3; Ps. 25:21);
- righteousness (Ps. 7:8);
- freedom from that which is shameful, crafty, or deceitful (2 Cor. 4:2);
- refusal to serve idols (Ps. 24:3–5);
- disassociation with evil doers (Ps. 26:4);
- honorable behavior (2 Cor. 8:21; 1 Pet. 2:12).

The Hebrews understood that:

- integrity of heart guides a person into right and rewarding situations (Prov. 11:3);
- integrity is more acceptable to the Lord than sacrifice (Prov. 21:3); and
- a person's integrity silences critics (1 Pet. 2:13–17).

Integrity provides a "mind set" toward righteousness and an abiding intent to do the will of God and to walk in His ways.

See also Gen. 6:9; 17:1; 1 Kin. 9:4; Job 31:1–40; Matt. 5:8; James 1:6–8; 4:8; notes on Conscience (2 Cor. 1); Fear of the Lord (Prov. 2); Purity (1 John 3)

He shall hide me in His pavilion;
In the secret place of His tabernacle
He shall hide me;
He shall set me high upon a rock.

⁶And now my head shall be lifted up above my
  enemies all around me;
Therefore I will offer sacrifices of joy in His
  tabernacle;
I will sing, yes, I will sing praises to the LORD.

⁷Hear, O LORD, *when* I cry with my voice!
Have mercy also upon me, and answer me.
⁸*When You said,* "Seek My face,"
My heart said to You, "Your face, LORD, I will
  seek."
⁹Do not hide Your face from me;
Do not turn Your servant away in anger;
You have been my help;
Do not leave me nor forsake me,
O God of my salvation.
¹⁰When my father and my mother forsake me,
Then the LORD will take care of me.

¹¹Teach me Your way, O LORD,
And lead me in a smooth path, because of my
  enemies.

¹²Do not deliver me to the will of my adversaries;
For false witnesses have risen against me,
And such as breathe out violence.
¹³*I would have lost heart,* unless I had believed
That I would see the goodness of the LORD
In the land of the living.

¹⁴Wait on the LORD;
Be of good courage,
And He shall strengthen your heart;
Wait, I say, on the LORD!

PSALM 28

Rejoicing in Answered Prayer
A Psalm of David.

¹To You I will cry, O LORD my Rock:
Do not be silent to me,
Lest, if You *are* silent to me,
I become like those who go down to the pit.
²Hear the voice of my supplications
When I cry to You,
When I lift up my hands toward Your holy
  sanctuary.

³Do not take me away with the wicked
And with the workers of iniquity,

28:1 The psalmist cried out to God in a time of need. His reference to "the pit" (or death) shows that he felt totally alone and abandoned by God in his experience (v. 1). The poem's tone dramatically changed as the psalmist blessed the Lord for hearing his cry (v. 6) and glorified the Lord as his strength and shield (v. 7).

Who speak peace to their neighbors,
But evil *is* in their hearts.
[4]Give them according to their deeds,
And according to the wickedness of their
endeavors;
Give them according to the work of their
hands;
Render to them what they deserve.
[5]Because they do not regard the works of the
LORD,
Nor the operation of His hands,
He shall destroy them
And not build them up.

[6]Blessed *be* the LORD,
Because He has heard the voice of my
supplications!
[7]The LORD *is* my strength and my shield;
My heart trusted in Him, and I am helped;
Therefore my heart greatly rejoices,
And with my song I will praise Him.

[8]The LORD *is* their strength,[a]
And He *is* the saving refuge of His anointed.
[9]Save Your people,
And bless Your inheritance;
Shepherd them also,
And bear them up forever.

PSALM 29

Praise to God in His Holiness and Majesty
A Psalm of David.

[1]Give unto the LORD, O you mighty ones,
Give unto the LORD glory and strength.
[2]Give unto the LORD the glory due to His name;
Worship the LORD in the beauty of holiness.

[3]The voice of the LORD *is* over the waters;
The God of glory thunders;
The LORD *is* over many waters.
[4]The voice of the LORD *is* powerful;
The voice of the LORD *is* full of majesty.

[5]The voice of the LORD breaks the cedars,
Yes, the LORD splinters the cedars of Lebanon.
[6]He makes them also skip like a calf,
Lebanon and Sirion like a young wild ox.
[7]The voice of the LORD divides the flames of
fire.

[8]The voice of the LORD shakes the wilderness;
The LORD shakes the Wilderness of Kadesh.

[9]The voice of the LORD makes the deer give
birth,
And strips the forests bare;
And in His temple everyone says, "Glory!"

[10]The LORD sat *enthroned* at the Flood,
And the LORD sits as King forever.
[11]The LORD will give strength to His people;
The LORD will bless His people with peace.

PSALM 30

The Blessedness of Answered Prayer
A Psalm. A Song at the dedication of the house of David.

[1]I will extol You, O LORD, for You have lifted me
up,
And have not let my foes rejoice over me.
[2]O LORD my God, I cried out to You,
And You healed me.
[3]O LORD, You brought my soul up from the
grave;
You have kept me alive, that I should not go
down to the pit.[a]

[4]Sing praise to the LORD, you saints of His,
And give thanks at the remembrance of His
holy name.[a]
[5]For His anger *is but for* a moment,
His favor *is for* life;
Weeping may endure for a night,
But joy *comes* in the morning.

[6]Now in my prosperity I said,
"I shall never be moved."
[7]LORD, by Your favor You have made my
mountain stand strong;
You hid Your face, *and* I was troubled.

[8]I cried out to You, O LORD;
And to the LORD I made supplication:
[9]"What profit *is there* in my blood,
When I go down to the pit?
Will the dust praise You?
Will it declare Your truth?
[10]Hear, O LORD, and have mercy on me;
LORD, be my helper!"

[11]You have turned for me my mourning into
dancing;

28:8 [a]Following Masoretic Text and Targum; Septuagint, Syriac, and Vulgate read *the strength of His people.* 30:3 [a]Following Qere and Targum; Kethib, Septuagint, Syriac, and Vulgate read *from those who descend to the pit.* 30:4 [a]Or *His holiness*

29:1, 2 A revelation of the Lord's majesty is experienced by the palmist in a powerful thunderstorm. David called to the "mighty ones" or heavenly beings to give to the Lord the glory (lit. "heaviness"; see Ps. 19:1, note) and worship (lit. "bowing down") due Him. We worship the Lord when we submit ourselves to His will and purpose for our lives (see Ps. 96:7–9; 1 Chr. 16:28–30).

30:11, 12 The psalmist was critically ill, and the Lord heard his prayer and healed him (vv. 2, 3). Because of the close associa-

FEAR *SHUTTING GOD OUT*

The admonition to "fear not" is frequently repeated in Scripture. Fear is described as bondage (Rom. 8:15), torment (1 John 4:18), and a snare (Prov. 29:25). Often the phrase "nor be dismayed" (lit. "torn apart," "panicked") accompanies the command to "fear not."

Scripture offers a long list of things about which believers are not to worry: provision (Matt. 6:25), enemies (Deut. 1:21), other gods (2 Kin. 17:35), death (Ps. 23:4), armies and wars (Ps. 27:3), reputation (Ps. 71:24), evil days (Ps. 49:5), children (Ps. 127:3), the future (Ps. 139:1–6), sudden terror (Prov. 3:25, 26), safety (Matt. 10:28), events beyond your control (Matt. 8:26), health (2 Cor. 12:7–10), fearful thoughts (Phil. 4:6, 7), words of others (1 Pet. 3:14), and suffering (Rev. 2:10).

Reasons are also given for not fearing: You are His creation (Is. 44:2); He fights for you (Ex. 14:13); you are loved (1 John 4:9); He is your helper (Heb. 13:6); you are more valuable than the sparrows (Luke 12:7). The reason given most often is God's presence (Gen. 26:24; Deut. 31:8; Rom. 8:15). You do not need to ask for God's presence—He is with you; you have His word on it. But you often need to ask for an awareness of His presence (Is. 41:10, 13). This awareness is most often prompted by remembering His faithfulness in the past (Deut. 7:18, 19).

See also Josh. 1:9; Matt. 14:27; notes on Death (1 Cor. 15); Emotions (Ps. 42); Persecution (2 Cor. 4); Providence (Eccl. 7); Testing (Ps. 12); Worry (Rom. 8); Fear of the Lord (Prov. 2)

You have put off my sackcloth and clothed me
    with gladness,
[12]To the end that *my* glory may sing praise to You
    and not be silent.
O Lord my God, I will give thanks to You
    forever.

PSALM 31

The Lord a Fortress in Adversity

To the Chief Musician. A Psalm of David.

[1]In You, O Lord, I put my trust;
    Let me never be ashamed;
    Deliver me in Your righteousness.
[2]Bow down Your ear to me,
    Deliver me speedily;
    Be my rock of refuge,
    A fortress of defense to save me.

[3]For You *are* my rock and my fortress;
    Therefore, for Your name's sake,
    Lead me and guide me.
[4]Pull me out of the net which they have secretly
    laid for me,
    For You *are* my strength.
[5]Into Your hand I commit my spirit;
    You have redeemed me, O Lord God of truth.

[6]I have hated those who regard useless idols;
    But I trust in the Lord.
[7]I will be glad and rejoice in Your mercy,
    For You have considered my trouble;
    You have known my soul in adversities,

[8]And have not shut me up into the hand of the
    enemy;
    You have set my feet in a wide place.

[9]Have mercy on me, O Lord, for I am in trouble;
    My eye wastes away with grief,
    Yes, my soul and my body!
[10]For my life is spent with grief,
    And my years with sighing;
    My strength fails because of my iniquity,
    And my bones waste away.
[11]I am a reproach among all my enemies,
    But especially among my neighbors,
    And *am* repulsive to my acquaintances;
    Those who see me outside flee from me.
[12]I am forgotten like a dead man, out of mind;
    I am like a broken vessel.
[13]For I hear the slander of many;
    Fear *is* on every side;
    While they take counsel together against me,
    They scheme to take away my life.

[14]But as for me, I trust in You, O Lord;
    I say, "You *are* my God."
[15]My times *are* in Your hand;
    Deliver me from the hand of my enemies,
    And from those who persecute me.
[16]Make Your face shine upon Your servant;
    Save me for Your mercies' sake.
[17]Do not let me be ashamed, O Lord, for I have
    called upon You;
    Let the wicked be ashamed;

tion of sin and illness in Hebrew thought, God's healing, to the psalmist, undoubtedly meant God's forgiveness. The psalmist had felt secure when he enjoyed prosperity and everything was going well (v. 7). He failed to depend on God because of his own self-sufficiency. But in the midst of calamity, he turned to God for help, and God was faithful to hear his prayer (v. 10). Difficult experiences do come to an end (v. 5), and a joyful morning follows a period of sorrow (vv. 5, 11, 12; see also chart, The Bible and Abuse).

31:5 The psalmist's cry for deliverance is based on God's faithfulness (vv. 1–4). A keynote of the psalm is the poet's faith and commitment to the Lord, as he makes the Lord the overseer of his life. Jesus' last words from the Cross included this prayer of faith (Luke 23:46).

THE BIBLE AND ABUSE

PEOPLE UNDER AUTHORITY	COMMAND FROM GOD	PEOPLE IN AUTHORITY	COMMAND TO COUNTERACT POTENTIAL ABUSE
1. Children	Obey (Eph. 6:1; Col. 3:20).	1. Parents	Do not exasperate or embitter a child (Eph. 6:4; Col. 3:21).
2. Slaves	Obey, submit, serve whole-heartedly (Eph. 6:6, 7; Col. 3:22; 1 Tim. 6:1; 1 Pet. 2:18).	2. Masters	Treat slaves well; do not show partiality; provide what is right and fair; do not threaten them (Eph. 6:9; Col. 4:1).
3. Citizens	Submit, obey (Rom. 13:1; Titus 3:1; 1 Pet. 3:13–19).	3. Governing Authorities	God will regulate behavior of government (Prov. 21:1; Rom. 13:1–14).
4. Wives	Submit, obey, respect (Eph. 5:22–24; Col. 3:18; Titus 2:5; 1 Pet. 3:1).	4. Husbands	Be considerate; treat with respect; do not be harsh; love as Christ loved (Eph. 5:25–29; Col. 3:19; 1 Pet. 3:7).
5. Believers	Submit, respect (1 Thess. 5:12; Heb. 13:17; 1 Pet. 5:5).	5. Pastors	Do not "lord over" the flock; be examples; lead by serving (1 Pet. 5:3–5).

Hierarchical structure cannot be dismissed as evil simply because of potential or real abuse.

The New Testament does not present a society without authority or submission but rather an orderly structure ordained of God and functioning in a manner that fulfills the teaching of the New Testament. Christ is the PERFECT MODEL both of willing submission and loving authority.

The Bible nowhere commends slavery. If it gives instruction for the regulation of even slavery, how much more important are its directives concerning relationships Scripture does commend?

Let them be silent in the grave.
[18]Let the lying lips be put to silence,
 Which speak insolent things proudly and
  contemptuously against the righteous.

[19]Oh, how great *is* Your goodness,
 Which You have laid up for those who fear You,
 Which You have prepared for those who trust
  in You
 In the presence of the sons of men!
[20]You shall hide them in the secret place of Your
  presence
 From the plots of man;
 You shall keep them secretly in a pavilion
 From the strife of tongues.

[21]Blessed *be* the LORD,
 For He has shown me His marvelous kindness
  in a strong city!
[22]For I said in my haste,

"I am cut off from before Your eyes";
 Nevertheless You heard the voice of my
  supplications
 When I cried out to You.

[23]Oh, love the LORD, all you His saints!
 For the LORD preserves the faithful,
 And fully repays the proud person.
[24]Be of good courage,
 And He shall strengthen your heart,
 All you who hope in the LORD.

PSALM 32

The Joy of Forgiveness

A Psalm of David. A Contemplation.[a]

[1]Blessed *is he whose* transgression *is* forgiven,
 Whose sin *is* covered.

32:title [a]Hebrew *Maschil*

32:1, 2 The blessedness of forgiveness is celebrated in this penitential psalm of thanksgiving (see Ps. 6:2–10, note; chart, The Types of Psalms). Such forgiveness comes by confessing sin, not denying it. Three words describe sin: "transgression"

ABUSE RITUALISTIC HARM

Abuse—the ritualistic harm or self-gratifying use of a living being—is inflicted by wicked individuals, never by the Lord God or by those who truly follow in His ways. God's loving concern for His people and the value He places on every life is in sharp contrast to abuse. Three of the foremost manifestations of abuse in the Scriptures are:

1. *Disdain and rejection.* Sterility was considered a curse (see 1 Sam. 1:6), and thus a barren woman became the focus of society's contempt. Children born out of marriage were called names, shunned, treated with severe hostility, and forbidden entrance into the assembly (Deut. 23:2).
2. *Slavery.* The Mosaic Code contained various regulations to protect slaves from abuse (see Ex. 20:10; Deut. 16:10, 11; 23:15, 16), but slaves under Roman rule had no such protection.
3. *Torture.* Christians were often the bloody, lacerated victims of Roman gladiatorial shows. Forced to fight wild beasts in amphitheaters for the amusement of Roman spectators, the games ended only upon the Christian's gruesome death. Paul refers to this practice (1 Cor. 15:32).

See also Gen. 16:6; 34:1, 2; Deut. 23:15, 16; 2 Sam. 13:1–22; chart on The Bible and Abuse; notes on Battered Wives (Deut. 22); Conflict (Song 5; Matt. 18); Date Rape (2 Sam. 13); Pain (Job 7; 2 Cor. 12); Rape (Gen. 34); Sanctity of Life (Gen. 9); Suffering (Ps. 33; 113; Is. 43; 1 Pet. 5); portraits of The Levite's Defenseless Concubine (Judg. 19); Tamar (2 Sam. 13)

²Blessed *is* the man to whom the LORD does not
impute iniquity,
And in whose spirit *there is* no deceit.

³When I kept silent, my bones grew old
Through my groaning all the day long.
⁴For day and night Your hand was heavy upon
me;
My vitality was turned into the drought of
summer. *Selah*
⁵I acknowledged my sin to You,
And my iniquity I have not hidden.
I said, "I will confess my transgressions to the
LORD,"
And You forgave the iniquity of my sin. *Selah*

⁶For this cause everyone who is godly shall pray
to You
In a time when You may be found;
Surely in a flood of great waters
They shall not come near him.
⁷You *are* my hiding place;
You shall preserve me from trouble;

You shall surround me with songs of
deliverance. *Selah*

⁸I will instruct you and teach you in the way you
should go;
I will guide you with My eye.
⁹Do not be like the horse *or* like the mule,
Which have no understanding,
Which must be harnessed with bit and bridle,
Else they will not come near you.

¹⁰Many sorrows *shall be* to the wicked;
But he who trusts in the LORD, mercy shall
surround him.
¹¹Be glad in the LORD and rejoice, you
righteous;
And shout for joy, all *you* upright in heart!

PSALM 33

The Sovereignty of the LORD in Creation and History
¹Rejoice in the LORD, O you righteous!
For praise from the upright is beautiful.
²Praise the LORD with the harp;

(lit. "rebellion"); "sin" (lit. "miss the mark" or "go wrong"); "iniquity" (lit. "moral crookedness" or "perversion"). The threefold expression of forgiveness also indicates the completeness of God's forgiveness: "forgiven" (lit. "lift" or "take away"); "covered" (lit. "hide" or "conceal"); "does not impute" (lit. "count" or "reckon"). Such forgiveness comes to the individual who, though at one time refusing to have his sin covered, then honestly confessed it to God. (See charts, Journey to Forgiveness; Forgiveness: Your Path to Freedom).

32:10, 11 This proverb of wisdom presents two ways: the way of sorrow for those who persist in their sin and the way of blessedness for those who confess their sin and trust in the Lord (compare Ps. 1; see chart, The Choice Between Life and Death).

33:1–9 This hymn of praise celebrates the greatness of the Lord as Creator. Psalms 32 and 33 were once linked (v. 1; Ps. 32:11). The expression "new song" may designate the freshness that should always characterize our worship (Ps. 33:3; see Rev. 5:9). God spoke and His word came to pass (Ps. 33:6, 7, 9). A good example of synonymous parallelism occurs in verse 8 (see Introduction: Literary Characteristics). The second line of this verse repeats the thought of the first line in slightly different words. Thus "fear" in the first line corresponds to "stand in awe" in the second line. Fear of the Lord is reverence for Him that leads to obedience.

JOURNEY TO FORGIVENESS

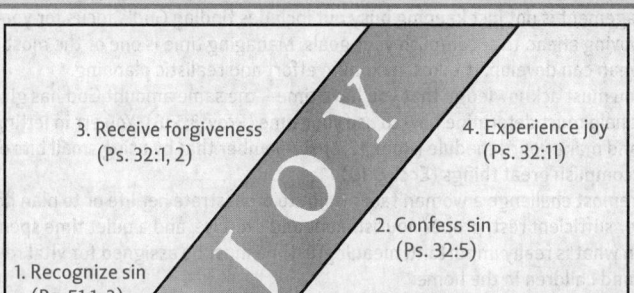

3. Receive forgiveness
(Ps. 32:1, 2)

4. Experience joy
(Ps. 32:11)

JOY

2. Confess sin
(Ps. 32:5)

1. Recognize sin
(Ps. 51:1, 2)

Make melody to Him with an instrument of ten
strings.
³Sing to Him a new song;
Play skillfully with a shout of joy.

⁴For the word of the LORD *is* right,
And all His work *is done* in truth.
⁵He loves righteousness and justice;
The earth is full of the goodness of the LORD.

⁶By the word of the LORD the heavens were
made,
And all the host of them by the breath of His
mouth.
⁷He gathers the waters of the sea together as a
heap;ᵃ
He lays up the deep in storehouses.

⁸Let all the earth fear the LORD;
Let all the inhabitants of the world stand in
awe of Him.
⁹For He spoke, and it was *done;*
He commanded, and it stood fast.

¹⁰The LORD brings the counsel of the nations to
nothing;
He makes the plans of the peoples of no
effect.
¹¹The counsel of the LORD stands forever,
The plans of His heart to all generations.
¹²Blessed *is* the nation whose God *is* the LORD,
The people He has chosen as His own
inheritance.

¹³The LORD looks from heaven;
He sees all the sons of men.

¹⁴From the place of His dwelling He looks
On all the inhabitants of the earth;
¹⁵He fashions their hearts individually;
He considers all their works.

¹⁶No king *is* saved by the multitude of an army;
A mighty man is not delivered by great
strength.
¹⁷A horse *is* a vain hope for safety;
Neither shall it deliver *any* by its great
strength.

¹⁸Behold, the eye of the LORD *is* on those who
fear Him,
On those who hope in His mercy,
¹⁹To deliver their soul from death,
And to keep them alive in famine.

²⁰Our soul waits for the LORD;
He *is* our help and our shield.
²¹For our heart shall rejoice in Him,
Because we have trusted in His holy name.
²²Let Your mercy, O LORD, be upon us,
Just as we hope in You.

PSALM 34

The Happiness of Those Who Trust in God
A Psalm of David when he pretended madness before Abimelech,
who drove him away, and he departed.

¹I will bless the LORD at all times;
His praise *shall* continually *be* in my mouth.
²My soul shall make its boast in the LORD;
The humble shall hear *of it* and be glad.

33:7 ᵃSeptuagint, Targum, and Vulgate read *in a vessel.*

34:1–3 The historical setting of this psalm is identified in its
superscription as the time when David feigned insanity before Abimelech, who was identified as Achish (1 Sam.

21:10–15). "Abimelech" may be a general title for Philistine
kings, just as "pharaoh" was applied to Egyptian kings.

TIME MANAGEMENT   USING GOD'S GIFT OF TIME

Time management is not just keeping busy but includes finding God's focus for you—choosing a direction and moving ahead to accomplish your goals. Managing time is one of the most difficult yet helpful skills a woman can develop. It takes maximum effort and realistic planning.

First, you must acknowledge that you have time—the same amount God has given to everyone. You, with God's help must determine how to use your time (Prov. 3:5, 6). You err in letting others decide your priorities and make your schedule (Rom. 12:2). Remember that by using small bits of time faithfully, you can accomplish great things (Eccl. 9:10).

The foremost challenge a woman faces is not to orchestrate her life or to plan her year but to order each day, allowing for sufficient rest, proper nourishment and exercise, and a quiet time spent exclusively with the Lord. To focus on what is really important, meaningful time must be assigned for vital relationships, especially with a spouse and children in the home.

The "woman of strength" arose early to plan for the day's activities (Prov. 31:15). Just as she had "maidservants," women today have appliances, vehicles, as well as utility and telephone services. These blessings of God are ready to help and serve women in daily, mundane tasks, giving them a maximum amount of time to spend with the Lord and to serve others!

To the Hebrews, a day began in the evening—with rest, family fellowship, as well as study and meditation in God's Word (Ps. 55:17). Jesus said, "Seek first the kingdom of God and His righteousness" (Matt. 6:33). One way to do that is to devote the evening hours to quiet rest, reflection, and "inner preparing"—in other words, to prepare yourself in the evening for the coming day as well as to plan your day's schedule upon rising in the morning.

See also Eccl. 3:1–8; 9:11; 11:6; Eph. 5:16; 1 Thess. 4:10–12; notes on Decision Making (1 Cor. 8); Organization (John 9); Priorities (Matt. 6)

---

³Oh, magnify the LORD with me,
And let us exalt His name together.

⁴I sought the LORD, and He heard me,
And delivered me from all my fears.
⁵They looked to Him and were radiant,
And their faces were not ashamed.
⁶This poor man cried out, and the LORD heard
him,
And saved him out of all his troubles.
⁷The angel[a] of the LORD encamps all around
those who fear Him,
And delivers them.

⁸Oh, taste and see that the LORD is good;
Blessed is the man who trusts in Him!
⁹Oh, fear the LORD, you His saints!
There is no want to those who fear Him.
¹⁰The young lions lack and suffer hunger;
But those who seek the LORD shall not lack any
good thing.

¹¹Come, you children, listen to me;
I will teach you the fear of the LORD.
¹²Who is the man who desires life,
And loves many days, that he may see good?
¹³Keep your tongue from evil,
And your lips from speaking deceit.
¹⁴Depart from evil and do good;
Seek peace and pursue it.

¹⁵The eyes of the LORD are on the righteous,
And His ears are open to their cry.
¹⁶The face of the LORD is against those who do
evil,
To cut off the remembrance of them from the
earth.

¹⁷The righteous cry out, and the LORD hears,
And delivers them out of all their troubles.
¹⁸The LORD is near to those who have a broken
heart,

34:7 ᵃOr Angel

34:4–10 David gave thanks because the Lord responded to his cry for help and delivered him from his fears in the sense of snatching away, as one might snatch the prey at the last minute from the mouth of an animal. Jacob utilized this same verb when he prayed that God would "deliver" him from the power of Esau (Gen. 32:11). Thus the poet's face is radiant with victory rather than shameful with defeat (Ps. 34:5). "The angel of the LORD" is the Lord's special messenger appearing at various times in the OT (see chart, The Angel of the Lord). Sometimes He is identified with God Himself (Gen. 22:11, 15,

16; 48:16; Ex. 23:20, 21; Judg. 6:11–23). The poet reminded those who sought the Lord that they would never lack the experience of God's goodness, even in difficult times (Ps. 34:8).

34:11–14 The fear of the Lord is regarded as the essence of wisdom (Prov. 1:7; 3:7; 9:10). The psalmist offered words for wise living, including keeping your tongue from evil, doing good, and pursuing peace. Similar counsel is offered to Christians in the practical Book of James in the NT (see James 3:2, 13; 4:1, 2).

And saves such as have a contrite
   spirit.

¹⁹Many *are* the afflictions of the righteous,
   But the LORD delivers him out of them all.
²⁰He guards all his bones;
   Not one of them is broken.
²¹Evil shall slay the wicked,
   And those who hate the righteous shall be
   condemned.
²²The LORD redeems the soul of His servants,
   And none of those who trust in Him shall be
   condemned.

PSALM 35

The LORD the Avenger of His People
A Psalm of David.

¹Plead *my cause,* O LORD, with those who strive
   with me;
   Fight against those who fight against me.
²Take hold of shield and buckler,
   And stand up for my help.
³Also draw out the spear,
   And stop those who pursue me.
   Say to my soul,
   "I *am* your salvation."

⁴Let those be put to shame and brought to
   dishonor
   Who seek after my life;
   Let those be turned back and brought to
   confusion
   Who plot my hurt.
⁵Let them be like chaff before the wind,
   And let the angelᵃ of the LORD chase *them.*
⁶Let their way be dark and slippery,
   And let the angel of the LORD pursue them.
⁷For without cause they have hidden their net
   for me *in* a pit,
   Which they have dug without cause for my life.
⁸Let destruction come upon him unexpectedly,
   And let his net that he has hidden catch
   himself;
   Into that very destruction let him fall.

⁹And my soul shall be joyful in the LORD;
   It shall rejoice in His salvation.
¹⁰All my bones shall say,
   "LORD, who *is* like You,

Delivering the poor from him who is too
   strong for him,
   Yes, the poor and the needy from him who
   plunders him?"

¹¹Fierce witnesses rise up;
   They ask me *things* that I do not know.
¹²They reward me evil for good,
   To the sorrow of my soul.
¹³But as for me, when they were sick,
   My clothing *was* sackcloth;
   I humbled myself with fasting;
   And my prayer would return to my own heart.
¹⁴I paced about as though *he were* my friend *or*
   brother;
   I bowed down heavily, as one who mourns *for*
   his mother.

¹⁵But in my adversity they rejoiced
   And gathered together;
   Attackers gathered against me,
   And I did not know *it;*
   They tore *at me* and did not cease;
¹⁶With ungodly mockers at feasts
   They gnashed at me with their teeth.

¹⁷Lord, how long will You look on?
   Rescue me from their destructions,
   My precious *life* from the lions.
¹⁸I will give You thanks in the great assembly;
   I will praise You among many people.

¹⁹Let them not rejoice over me who are
   wrongfully my enemies;
   Nor let them wink with the eye who hate me
   without a cause.
²⁰For they do not speak peace,
   But they devise deceitful matters
   Against *the* quiet ones in the land.
²¹They also opened their mouth wide against
   me,
   And said, "Aha, aha!
   Our eyes have seen *it.*"

²²*This* You have seen, O LORD;
   Do not keep silence.
   O Lord, do not be far from me.
²³Stir up Yourself, and awake to my vindication,

35:5 ᵃOr *Angel*

34:19–22 The righteous, those rightly related to the Lord, often suffer much affliction (v. 19). We are to rejoice in suffering for the sake of Christ (2 Tim. 3:12; 1 Pet. 4:12–16; see Ps. 33, Suffering; charts, How to Comfort the Suffering; How to Endure Suffering; Suffering in Divine Perspective). The psalmist realized that faith in the Lord does not offer immunity from adversity (see Acts 5, Adversity). Ultimately victory belongs to those who follow the Lord (see Ps. 1; chart, The Choice Between Life and Death).

35:5, 6 The psalmist experienced suffering from his enemies, who are also God's enemies. He prayed vengeance on his enemies (vv. 5, 6; see Ps. 1:4). Jesus warned His disciples that the world hated Him without reason (John 15:25; see Ps. 35:19). However, this psalm's purpose of calling for vengeance on enemies was transformed in the life of Christ, who taught His followers to love their enemies and to pray for their well-being (Matt. 5:43–48). Jesus displayed an attitude of loving concern toward His enemies (see Luke 22:49–51).

SUFFERING *THE DILEMMA OF HELPLESSNESS*

Perhaps the most brutal and degrading form of suffering is violent ill-treatment. The subject of rape appears in the story of King David's daughter, Tamar (2 Sam. 13:1–22). The subject of death is met in the account of Jephthah's daughter (Judg. 11:29–40). Jephthah, quite apart from God's will, makes a vow that if he were to win in battle he would offer as a burnt offering the first person to greet him on his return home. His only daughter became this person, and to save face, he carried out his vow. The tragic irony for Jephthah was the fact that God wished to give him the victory without any such deal. In the end, his daughter gained the true victory because in her obedience to her father her name was perpetuated among the women of Israel in a way in which neither her father nor any subsequent offspring could ever have insured.

The Bible does not present an easy solution to the problem of suffering. Rather, the suffering of Christ is our model. By participating in our suffering through His own suffering and by rising from its absolute destruction, Jesus Christ has shown us that beyond the awfulness of human suffering is a way to victory that serves somehow to transform our fallen world to its former glory (see 2 Tim. 3:12; Heb. 5:8).

See also notes on Abuse (Ps. 31); Adversity (Acts 5); Rape (Gen. 34); Suffering (Ps. 113; Is. 43; 1 Pet. 5); portrait of Jephthah's Obedient Daughter (Judg. 11); Tamar (2 Sam. 13)

To my cause, my God and my Lord.
24Vindicate me, O LORD my God, according to
Your righteousness;
And let them not rejoice over me.
25Let them not say in their hearts, "Ah, so we
would have it!"
Let them not say, "We have swallowed him up."

26Let them be ashamed and brought to mutual
confusion
Who rejoice at my hurt;
Let them be clothed with shame and dishonor
Who exalt themselves against me.

27Let them shout for joy and be glad,
Who favor my righteous cause;
And let them say continually,
"Let the LORD be magnified,
Who has pleasure in the prosperity of His
servant."
28And my tongue shall speak of Your
righteousness
And of Your praise all the day long.

PSALM 36

Man's Wickedness and God's Perfections

To the Chief Musician. *A Psalm* of David the servant of the LORD.

1An oracle within my heart concerning the
transgression of the wicked:
There is no fear of God before his eyes.

2For he flatters himself in his own eyes,
When he finds out his iniquity *and* when he
hates.
3The words of his mouth *are* wickedness and
deceit;
He has ceased to be wise *and* to do good.
4He devises wickedness on his bed;
He sets himself in a way *that is* not good;
He does not abhor evil.

5Your mercy, O LORD, *is* in the heavens;
Your faithfulness *reaches* to the clouds.
6Your righteousness *is* like the great mountains;
Your judgments *are* a great deep;
O LORD, You preserve man and beast.

7How precious *is* Your lovingkindness, O God!
Therefore the children of men put their trust
under the shadow of Your wings.
8They are abundantly satisfied with the fullness
of Your house,
And You give them drink from the river of
Your pleasures.
9For with You *is* the fountain of life;
In Your light we see light.

10Oh, continue Your lovingkindness to those who
know You,
And Your righteousness to the upright in
heart.
11Let not the foot of pride come against me,

36:5–10 The poet extolled God's great love against the background of human evil. The psalm begins and ends with references to the wicked (vv. 1–4, 11, 12). In between these references is a poignant description of the Lord's love and mercy (vv. 5–10). For "mercy" or "lovingkindness" (Heb. *chesed,* lit. "steadfast love," vv. 5, 7, 10), see Psalm 5:7–12, note. For "the shadow of Your wings" (Ps. 36:7), see Psalm 17:8, note. God's unchanging love is seen in His constancy or faithfulness (Ps. 36:5), His justice (v. 6), His deliverance or preservation (v. 6), and His abundant provision (v. 8). God is the source of life and light (v. 9). The abundance of His love is poured out on all those who "know" Him, referring to a personal, intimate relationship (v. 10).

And let not the hand of the wicked drive me
away.
¹²There the workers of iniquity have fallen;
They have been cast down and are not able to
rise.

PSALM 37

The Heritage of the Righteous and the Calamity of the Wicked
A Psalm of David.

¹Do not fret because of evildoers,
Nor be envious of the workers of iniquity.
²For they shall soon be cut down like the grass,
And wither as the green herb.

³Trust in the LORD, and do good;
Dwell in the land, and feed on His faithfulness.
⁴Delight yourself also in the LORD,
And He shall give you the desires of your
heart.

⁵Commit your way to the LORD,
Trust also in Him,
And He shall bring *it* to pass.
⁶He shall bring forth your righteousness as the
light,
And your justice as the noonday.

⁷Rest in the LORD, and wait patiently for Him;
Do not fret because of him who prospers in his
way,
Because of the man who brings wicked
schemes to pass.
⁸Cease from anger, and forsake wrath;
Do not fret—*it* only *causes* harm.

⁹For evildoers shall be cut off;
But those who wait on the LORD,
They shall inherit the earth.
¹⁰For yet a little while and the wicked *shall be* no
more;
Indeed, you will look carefully for his place,
But it *shall be* no *more.*
¹¹But the meek shall inherit the earth,
And shall delight themselves in the abundance
of peace.

¹²The wicked plots against the just,
And gnashes at him with his teeth.

¹³The Lord laughs at him,
For He sees that his day is coming.
¹⁴The wicked have drawn the sword
And have bent their bow,
To cast down the poor and needy,
To slay those who are of upright conduct.
¹⁵Their sword shall enter their own heart,
And their bows shall be broken.

¹⁶A little that a righteous man has
Is better than the riches of many wicked.
¹⁷For the arms of the wicked shall be broken,
But the LORD upholds the righteous.

¹⁸The LORD knows the days of the upright,
And their inheritance shall be forever.
¹⁹They shall not be ashamed in the evil time,
And in the days of famine they shall be
satisfied.
²⁰But the wicked shall perish;
And the enemies of the LORD,
Like the splendor of the meadows, shall
vanish.
Into smoke they shall vanish away.

²¹The wicked borrows and does not repay,
But the righteous shows mercy and gives.
²²For *those* blessed by Him shall inherit the
earth,
But *those* cursed by Him shall be cut off.

²³The steps of a *good* man are ordered by the
LORD,
And He delights in his way.
²⁴Though he fall, he shall not be utterly cast
down;
For the LORD upholds *him with* His hand.

²⁵I have been young, and *now* am old;
Yet I have not seen the righteous forsaken,
Nor his descendants begging bread.
²⁶*He is* ever merciful, and lends;
And his descendants *are* blessed.

²⁷Depart from evil, and do good;
And dwell forevermore.
²⁸For the LORD loves justice,
And does not forsake His saints;
They are preserved forever,

37:1–11 This collection of wisdom teachings promotes the traditional OT viewpoint: The righteous will prosper, and the wicked will suffer (see Deut. 28). This wisdom teacher instructed his hearers to trust in the Lord (Ps. 37:3), to delight in Him (v. 4), to commit their way to Him (v. 5), to rest in Him (v. 7), and to wait patiently for the Lord (v. 7). The other side of his admonition is the command not to be agitated by evildoers, since their success is temporary (v. 10). Eventually, the "meek" (or humble) will inherit the earth (v. 11; see Matt. 5:5).

This inheritance comes as the gift of God, to whom the meek have committed themselves and before whom they humbly submit themselves (Ps. 24:1). The righteous fail and fall down; yet they never experience total defeat (Ps. 37:23, 24). From personal observation the poet drew the conclusion that God never abandons His children (v. 25). Though they may experience the heartaches of a fallen world, God's children are never completely forsaken. In fact, His blessings will extend to the next generation (v. 26).

BROKENHEARTEDNESS · A SHATTERED LIFE

The psalmist speaks of a "broken heart" and a "contrite spirit" (Ps. 34:18). A broken heart is experienced when someone else causes a breach in a relationship with us, while a contrite spirit results when we feel sorrow for having caused such a breach, against either God or another human being.

The woman who experiences a broken heart, in many ways, is a "victim" in the wake of another person's actions, whether intentional or unintentional. The broken heart she experiences may be the result of abandonment, rejection, oppression, abuse, or even death. Regardless of the cause, the typical feeling is one of being devastated or feeling as if life has been shattered. Three other emotions are usually quick to arise: fear, loneliness, and despair. In many ways, a broken heart is a "broken spirit," in which you may lose the will to live, to love, or to trust.

One of the foremost roles of the Messiah, and one which Jesus embraced wholeheartedly (Luke 4:18), was to "heal the brokenhearted" (Is. 61:1–3). Jesus very specifically addressed the underlying nature of a broken heart on several occasions. He dealt with fear (Mark 5:36), rejection and feelings of isolation (John 14:16), despair and a loss of will (John 14:1).

The brokenhearted woman finds healing when she chooses to believe again—to believe that she will live, to believe that she will experience love again, to believe that God has a future purpose and plan for her life, or to believe that God will be with her always, even in the darkest hours of her hurt and sorrow (Jer. 29:11–14). In embracing fully the promise of Christ Jesus to heal her broken heart, she finds strength for reaching out to others, trusting that God still has "something new" for her (Lam. 3:22–24).

See also Ps. 147:3; Prov. 15:13; Mark 5:2, note; notes on Abuse (Ps. 31); Distress (Ps. 18); Fear (Ps. 27); Grief (Is. 53); Healing (Ps. 13; 133; Eccl. 1; 2 Cor. 5; Gal. 6; James 5); Loneliness (Eccl. 4); Sorrow (Rev. 21); Tears (Ps. 56)

But the descendants of the wicked shall be cut off.
29 The righteous shall inherit the land,
And dwell in it forever.

30 The mouth of the righteous speaks wisdom,
And his tongue talks of justice.
31 The law of his God *is* in his heart;
None of his steps shall slide.

32 The wicked watches the righteous,
And seeks to slay him.
33 The LORD will not leave him in his hand,
Nor condemn him when he is judged.

34 Wait on the LORD,
And keep His way,
And He shall exalt you to inherit the land;
When the wicked are cut off, you shall see *it.*
35 I have seen the wicked in great power,
And spreading himself like a native green tree.
36 Yet he passed away,[a] and behold, he *was* no more;
Indeed I sought him, but he could not be found.

37 Mark the blameless *man,* and observe the upright;
For the future of *that* man *is* peace.
38 But the transgressors shall be destroyed together;
The future of the wicked shall be cut off.

39 But the salvation of the righteous *is* from the LORD;
He is their strength in the time of trouble.
40 And the LORD shall help them and deliver them;
He shall deliver them from the wicked,
And save them,
Because they trust in Him.

PSALM 38

Prayer in Time of Chastening
A Psalm of David. To bring to remembrance.

1 O LORD, do not rebuke me in Your wrath,
Nor chasten me in Your hot displeasure!
2 For Your arrows pierce me deeply,
And Your hand presses me down.

••••••••••••••••••

37:36 [a]Following Masoretic Text, Septuagint, and Targum; Syriac and Vulgate read *I passed by.*

38:1–22 This psalmist felt isolated from God, as well as from family and friends, in his suffering (v. 11). He attributed his illness to divine displeasure and viewed his sufferings as God's chastening (see chart, Suffering in Divine Perspective). Although sickness in general is a result of sin in the world, all illness or infirmity is not due to the sin of the afflicted individual (see John 9:1–3). On the other hand, some suffering directly results from specific sins in our lives. We cannot judge others when they are suffering; we can only seek to discern the reasons for our own sufferings (see charts, How to Comfort the Suffering; How to Endure Suffering). The psalmist saw a direct connection between his suffering and his sin, which had overwhelmed him completely. His sense of alienation was compounded by the presence of strong enemies (Ps. 38:19,

³*There is* no soundness in my flesh
  Because of Your anger,
  Nor *any* health in my bones
  Because of my sin.
⁴For my iniquities have gone over my head;
  Like a heavy burden they are too heavy for
    me.
⁵My wounds are foul *and* festering
  Because of my foolishness.

⁶I am troubled, I am bowed down greatly;
  I go mourning all the day long.
⁷For my loins are full of inflammation,
  And *there is* no soundness in my flesh.
⁸I am feeble and severely broken;
  I groan because of the turmoil of my heart.

⁹Lord, all my desire *is* before You;
  And my sighing is not hidden from You.
¹⁰My heart pants, my strength fails me;
  As for the light of my eyes, it also has gone
    from me.

¹¹My loved ones and my friends stand aloof from
    my plague,
  And my relatives stand afar off.
¹²Those also who seek my life lay snares *for me;*
  Those who seek my hurt speak of destruction,
  And plan deception all the day long.

¹³But I, like a deaf *man,* do not hear;
  And *I am* like a mute *who* does not open his
    mouth.
¹⁴Thus I am like a man who does not hear,
  And in whose mouth *is* no response.

¹⁵For in You, O LORD, I hope;
  You will hear, O Lord my God.
¹⁶For I said, *"Hear me,* lest they rejoice over me,
  Lest, when my foot slips, they exalt *themselves*
    against me."

¹⁷For I *am* ready to fall,
  And my sorrow *is* continually before me.
¹⁸For I will declare my iniquity;
  I will be in anguish over my sin.
¹⁹But my enemies *are* vigorous, *and* they are
    strong;
  And those who hate me wrongfully have
    multiplied.
²⁰Those also who render evil for good,

They are my adversaries, because I follow *what
    is* good.

²¹Do not forsake me, O LORD;
  O my God, be not far from me!
²²Make haste to help me,
  O Lord, my salvation!

PSALM 39

Prayer for Wisdom and Forgiveness
To the Chief Musician. To Jeduthun. A Psalm of David.

¹I said, "I will guard my ways,
  Lest I sin with my tongue;
  I will restrain my mouth with a muzzle,
  While the wicked are before me."
²I was mute with silence,
  I held my peace *even* from good;
  And my sorrow was stirred up.
³My heart was hot within me;
  While I was musing, the fire burned.
  Then I spoke with my tongue:

⁴"LORD, make me to know my end,
  And what *is* the measure of my days,
  That I may know how frail I *am.*
⁵Indeed, You have made my days *as*
    handbreadths,
  And my age *is* as nothing before You;
  Certainly every man at his best state *is* but
    vapor.   *Selah*
⁶Surely every man walks about like a shadow;
  Surely they busy themselves in vain;
  He heaps up *riches,*
  And does not know who will gather them.

⁷"And now, Lord, what do I wait for?
  My hope *is* in You.
⁸Deliver me from all my transgressions;
  Do not make me the reproach of the foolish.
⁹I was mute, I did not open my mouth,
  Because it was You who did *it.*
¹⁰Remove Your plague from me;
  I am consumed by the blow of Your hand.
¹¹When with rebukes You correct man for
    iniquity,
  You make his beauty melt away like a moth;
  Surely every man *is* vapor.   *Selah*

¹²"Hear my prayer, O LORD,
  And give ear to my cry;

20). The poet believed that God's nearness would bring him healing and forgiveness. Despite his despair, he continued to pray, as we must continue to call on God in times of suffering and loneliness (see Ps. 6:2–10, note; chart, The Types of Psalms).

39:4–6 The transitory nature of life is described as a "vapor" (v. 5) and a "shadow" (v. 6). The suffering psalmist searched to find the meaning of this brief time on earth. The days of life are as "handbreadths," a reference to the width of four fingers (v. 5; see chart, Money and Measurements in the Bible). The tone is similar to that of Ecclesiastes (Eccl. 1:12—12:8), but here the psalmist affirmed that his only hope rested in the Lord and His forgiveness (Ps. 39:7, 8).

DEBT   A FORM OF BONDAGE

From a biblical perspective, debt puts a person into a form of bondage—the indebted person is a "servant" to the lender (Prov. 22:7). One of the most significant problems with debt is that it always presumes upon the future (see Job 8:9). When a person chooses to borrow, she presumes that she will have means available to repay her debt in an uncertain and unknown future. James 4:13–16 warns against the assumption that you will be able to control future events. The point is that the future is in God's hands (Acts 1:7).

To borrow without repaying is not an option for a Christian (Ps. 37:21). Two of Jesus' parables deal with the matter of repaying money that has been loaned (Luke 16:1–8; 19:12–27). Believers were instructed that borrowed items were always to be returned (Ex. 22:7–15; 2 Kin. 6:5). Lenders are admonished to be generous in loaning to the poor (Ps. 37:26). The Law provided for the poor who were unable to repay a debt to have that debt canceled every seventh year (Deut. 15:7–11)—a reminder that God is bigger than all problems, including financial ones. Going into debt may deny God the opportunity to work (Is. 55:8, 9). He can work in exciting ways if we trust Him to do so.

See also Ex. 22:25–27; Rom. 13:8; notes on Financial Planning (Luke 19); Prosperity (Ps. 2); Wealth (1 Tim. 6)

Do not be silent at my tears;
For I *am* a stranger with You,
A sojourner, as all my fathers *were*.
[13]Remove Your gaze from me, that I may regain
      strength,
Before I go away and am no more."

PSALM 40

Faith Persevering in Trial
To the Chief Musician. A Psalm of David.

[1]I waited patiently for the LORD;
  And He inclined to me,
  And heard my cry.
[2]He also brought me up out of a horrible pit,
  Out of the miry clay,
  And set my feet upon a rock,
  And established my steps.
[3]He has put a new song in my mouth—
  Praise to our God;
  Many will see *it* and fear,
  And will trust in the LORD.

[4]Blessed *is* that man who makes the LORD his
      trust,
  And does not respect the proud, nor such as
      turn aside to lies.
[5]Many, O LORD my God, *are* Your wonderful
      works
  Which You have done;
  And Your thoughts toward us

Cannot be recounted to You in order;
If I would declare and speak *of them,*
  They are more than can be numbered.

[6]Sacrifice and offering You did not desire;
  My ears You have opened.
  Burnt offering and sin offering You did not
      require.
[7]Then I said, "Behold, I come;
  In the scroll of the book *it is* written of me.
[8]I delight to do Your will, O my God,
  And Your law *is* within my heart."

[9]I have proclaimed the good news of
      righteousness
  In the great assembly;
  Indeed, I do not restrain my lips,
  O LORD, You Yourself know.
[10]I have not hidden Your righteousness within
      my heart;
  I have declared Your faithfulness and Your
      salvation;
  I have not concealed Your lovingkindness and
      Your truth
  From the great assembly.

[11]Do not withhold Your tender mercies from me,
      O LORD;
  Let Your lovingkindness and Your truth
      continually preserve me.
[12]For innumerable evils have surrounded me;

40:1–3 All those who wait on the Lord in patient expectation will discover security and refreshing newness in fellowship with Him. This poet began by praising the Lord for answered prayer. He had waited on the Lord in patient expectation and was not disappointed. The Lord responded to his cry for help and gave him stability and a "new song," which became his testimony to others (v. 3). The Lord gave the poet firm footing, a new stability resulting from his relationship with the Lord.

40:6 The OT sacrificial system is not rejected, but sacrifice and offering are worthless if not presented to God with the right attitude. Acts of worship are meaningless ritual if not accompanied by obedience (see 1 Sam. 15:22). The sacrifice of self-will and self-importance is the primary sacrifice that God desires (see Ps. 51:16, 17).

Disorder in society is the result of disorder in the family.

St. Angela Merici

My iniquities have overtaken me, so that I am
not able to look up;
They are more than the hairs of my head;
Therefore my heart fails me.

¹³Be pleased, O LORD, to deliver me;
O LORD, make haste to help me!
¹⁴Let them be ashamed and brought to mutual
confusion
Who seek to destroy my life;
Let them be driven backward and brought to
dishonor
Who wish me evil.
¹⁵Let them be confounded because of their shame,
Who say to me, "Aha, aha!"

¹⁶Let all those who seek You rejoice and be glad
in You;
Let such as love Your salvation say continually,
"The LORD be magnified!"
¹⁷But I *am* poor and needy;
Yet the LORD thinks upon me.
You *are* my help and my deliverer;
Do not delay, O my God.

PSALM 41

The Blessing and Suffering of the Godly

To the Chief Musician. A Psalm of David.

¹Blessed *is* he who considers the poor;
The LORD will deliver him in time of trouble.
²The LORD will preserve him and keep him alive,
And he will be blessed on the earth;
You will not deliver him to the will of his
enemies.
³The LORD will strengthen him on his bed of
illness;
You will sustain him on his sickbed.

⁴I said, "LORD, be merciful to me;
Heal my soul, for I have sinned against You."
⁵My enemies speak evil of me:

"When will he die, and his name perish?"
⁶And if he comes to see *me,* he speaks lies;
His heart gathers iniquity to itself;
When he goes out, he tells *it.*

⁷All who hate me whisper together against me;
Against me they devise my hurt.
⁸"An evil disease," *they say,* "clings to him.
And *now* that he lies down, he will rise up no
more."
⁹Even my own familiar friend in whom I
trusted,
Who ate my bread,
Has lifted up *his* heel against me.

¹⁰But You, O LORD, be merciful to me, and raise
me up,
That I may repay them.
¹¹By this I know that You are well pleased with
me,
Because my enemy does not triumph over me.
¹²As for me, You uphold me in my integrity,
And set me before Your face forever.

¹³Blessed *be* the LORD God of Israel
From everlasting to everlasting!
Amen and Amen.

Book Two: Psalms 42—72

PSALM 42

Yearning for God in the Midst of Distresses

To the Chief Musician. A Contemplation[a] of the sons of Korah.

¹As the deer pants for the water brooks,
So pants my soul for You, O God.
²My soul thirsts for God, for the living God.
When shall I come and appear before God?[a]
³My tears have been my food day and night,

· · · · · · · · · · · · · · · · ·

42:title [a]Hebrew *Maschil*   42:2 [a]Following Masoretic Text and
Vulgate; some Hebrew manuscripts, Septuagint, Syriac, and Targum
read *I see the face of God.*

41:1–3 A beatitude noting the blessing on the individual who
gives attention to the poor opens this psalm (see Matt. 5:7;
chart, Beatitudes for Women). James reminded his hearers
that true religion involves the outward dimension of visiting
orphans and widows and meeting the needs of the helpless
members of society (James 1:27). The psalm reminds us that
the Lord rewards those who show compassion toward others
(Ps. 41:1–3). Jesus taught His followers that ministering to the

needs of the poor with compassion was serving Him (see
Matt. 25:31–46).

41:13 This benediction or doxology may be regarded as a con-
clusion to Book I of the Psalms (see Introduction: Outline).
Note the benedictions at the end of Book II (Ps. 72:18, 19),
Book III (Ps. 89:52), and Book IV (Ps. 106:48).

42:1, 2 This poet felt that God was remote and distant. He expressed his deep longing for God as being comparable to the

EMOTIONS *EXPRESSING WHAT IS WITHIN*

Emotions are at the core of our being and reflect one profound aspect of the wonder of being made in the image of God (Num. 32:10; Is. 53:3; John 11:33). More than anything else they reflect our attitudes and behavior. Emotions often express outwardly our innermost beliefs. For instance, if we believe in God's sovereignty and ultimate control, we exchange fear and worry for peace and contentment.

God makes Himself known to us not only in truth and by decree but in the way He reveals His heart. God is passionate in His pursuit of us, and that passion is expressed in a variety of emotions: grief at the rebellion of His children (Hos. 11:8, 9), anger at their idolatry (Jer. 2:11–13), and delight upon their return to Him (Luke 15:11–32). God's longing for an unhindered relationship with His children is found all through Scripture (Jer. 17:9, 10).

Women, too, who are made in His image not only think and choose—they feel. Their personalities are interwoven with an intricate mix of mind, will, and emotions. To be able to experience pain or joy, sadness or anger is to feel alive. You not only do yourself damage and limit your potential in Christ when you deny or suppress your emotions, you reduce your understanding of who God is. Emotion—that is passionate, heartfelt desire—is part of the energy that bonds believers to God and to each other in a rich, meaningful way.

Emotions are a gift from God intended to compel us to take action. For example, our anger at a "wrong" committed against us or someone else can compel us to seek justice. As important as our emotions are, we must never be ruled by them—rather, we must subject our emotions to a will that is yielded to God. All emotions are intended to be expressed in a godly manner so as not to cause hurt to other people or result in manipulation of other people.

See also Ex. 15:1–18; Ps. 66:1–20; Nahum 1:6, 7; Eph. 5:25–32; notes on Anger (Eccl. 7); Depression (1 Sam. 16); Grief (Is. 53); Healing (Ps. 13); Mental Health (John 10)

While they continually say to me,
"Where *is* your God?"

⁴When I remember these *things,*
I pour out my soul within me.
For I used to go with the multitude;
I went with them to the house of God,
With the voice of joy and praise,
With a multitude that kept a pilgrim feast.

⁵Why are you cast down, O my soul?
And *why* are you disquieted within me?
Hope in God, for I shall yet praise Him
For the help of His countenance.ᵃ

⁶O my God,ᵃ my soul is cast down within me;
Therefore I will remember You from the land
    of the Jordan,
And from the heights of Hermon,
From the Hill Mizar.
⁷Deep calls unto deep at the noise of Your
    waterfalls;
All Your waves and billows have gone over me.
⁸The LORD will command His lovingkindness in
    the daytime,
And in the night His song *shall be* with me—
A prayer to the God of my life.

⁹I will say to God my Rock,

"Why have You forgotten me?
Why do I go mourning because of the
    oppression of the enemy?"
¹⁰*As* with a breaking of my bones,
My enemies reproach me,
While they say to me all day long,
"Where *is* your God?"

¹¹Why are you cast down, O my soul?
And why are you disquieted within me?
Hope in God;
For I shall yet praise Him,
The help of my countenance and my
    God.

PSALM 43

Prayer to God in Time of Trouble

¹Vindicate me, O God,
And plead my cause against an ungodly
    nation;
Oh, deliver me from the deceitful and unjust
    man!
²For You *are* the God of my strength;

. . . .

42:5 ᵃFollowing Masoretic Text and Targum; a few Hebrew manuscripts, Septuagint, Syriac, and Vulgate read *The help of my countenance, my God.*   42:6 ᵃFollowing Masoretic Text and Targum; a few Hebrew manuscripts, Septuagint, Syriac, and Vulgate put *my God* at the end of verse 5.

---

intense thirst of a deer for water during a time of severe drought. The poet longed to enjoy once more the assurance of God's presence with him. All who belong to God experience times when God seems absent, and they long for the reassurance of His presence. Psalms 42 and 43 provide guidance in such times.

Why do You cast me off?
Why do I go mourning because of the
   oppression of the enemy?

³Oh, send out Your light and Your truth!
Let them lead me;
Let them bring me to Your holy hill
And to Your tabernacle.
⁴Then I will go to the altar of God,
To God my exceeding joy;
And on the harp I will praise You,
O God, my God.

⁵Why are you cast down, O my soul?
And why are you disquieted within me?
Hope in God;
For I shall yet praise Him,
The help of my countenance and my God.

PSALM 44

Redemption Remembered in Present Dishonor

To the Chief Musician. A Contemplation³ of the sons of Korah.

¹We have heard with our ears, O God,
Our fathers have told us,
The deeds You did in their days,
In days of old:
²You drove out the nations with Your hand,
But them You planted;
You afflicted the peoples, and cast them out.
³For they did not gain possession of the land by
   their own sword,
Nor did their own arm save them;
But it was Your right hand, Your arm, and the
   light of Your countenance,
Because You favored them.

⁴You are my King, O God;ᵃ
Commandᵇ victories for Jacob.
⁵Through You we will push down our enemies;
Through Your name we will trample those who
   rise up against us.
⁶For I will not trust in my bow,
Nor shall my sword save me.
⁷But You have saved us from our enemies,
And have put to shame those who hated us.
⁸In God we boast all day long,
And praise Your name forever.   *Selah*

⁹But You have cast *us* off and put us to shame,
And You do not go out with our armies.

¹⁰You make us turn back from the enemy,
And those who hate us have taken spoil for
   themselves.
¹¹You have given us up like sheep *intended* for
   food,
And have scattered us among the nations.
¹²You sell Your people for *next to* nothing,
And are not enriched by selling them.

¹³You make us a reproach to our neighbors,
A scorn and a derision to those all around
   us.
¹⁴You make us a byword among the nations,
A shaking of the head among the peoples.
¹⁵My dishonor *is* continually before me,
And the shame of my face has covered me,
¹⁶Because of the voice of him who reproaches
   and reviles,
Because of the enemy and the avenger.

¹⁷All this has come upon us;
But we have not forgotten You,
Nor have we dealt falsely with Your
   covenant.
¹⁸Our heart has not turned back,
Nor have our steps departed from Your way;
¹⁹But You have severely broken us in the place of
   jackals,
And covered us with the shadow of death.

²⁰If we had forgotten the name of our God,
Or stretched out our hands to a foreign
   god,
²¹Would not God search this out?
For He knows the secrets of the heart.
²²Yet for Your sake we are killed all day long;
We are accounted as sheep for the slaughter.

²³Awake! Why do You sleep, O Lord?
Arise! Do not cast *us* off forever.
²⁴Why do You hide Your face,
And forget our affliction and our oppression?
²⁵For our soul is bowed down to the dust;
Our body clings to the ground.
²⁶Arise for our help,
And redeem us for Your mercies' sake.

• • • • • • • • • • • • • • • • • •

44:title ᵃHebrew *Maschil*   44:4 ᵃFollowing Masoretic Text and
Targum; Septuagint and Vulgate read *and my God.* ᵇFollowing
Masoretic Text and Targum; Septuagint, Syriac, and Vulgate read
Who commands.

44:21–26 National calamity for Israel, probably a time of military defeat, may have prompted this psalm. The psalmist reflected on the military victories God had accomplished for His people in the past (vv. 2, 3), calling to mind God's acts on behalf of His people when they entered the Promised Land under Joshua's leadership. The psalmist expected God to bring military victory for His people in the present just as He had in the past (vv. 1–8). Instead, God's people experienced calamity (vv. 9–16), despite their faithfulness to the Lord (vv. 17–22). The apostle Paul stressed that God is always with His children even in the midst of suffering, making them more than conquerors (Rom. 8:36–39). The poet concluded by calling on the Lord to arise and deliver His people (Ps. 44:20–26).

It is such a joy when I awaken to salute God by singing.

Blessed Teresa of the Andes

PSALM 45

The Glories of the Messiah and His Bride

To the Chief Musician. Set to "The Lilies."[a]
A Contemplation[b] of the sons of Korah. A Song of Love.

[1]My heart is overflowing with a good theme;
I recite my composition concerning the
King;
My tongue *is* the pen of a ready writer.

[2]You are fairer than the sons of men;
Grace is poured upon Your lips;
Therefore God has blessed You forever.
[3]Gird Your sword upon *Your* thigh, O Mighty
One,
With Your glory and Your majesty.
[4]And in Your majesty ride prosperously because
of truth, humility, *and* righteousness;
And Your right hand shall teach You awesome
things.
[5]Your arrows *are* sharp in the heart of the King's
enemies;
The peoples fall under You.

[6]Your throne, O God, *is* forever and ever;
A scepter of righteousness *is* the scepter of
Your kingdom.
[7]You love righteousness and hate wickedness;
Therefore God, Your God, has anointed You
With the oil of gladness more than Your
companions.
[8]All Your garments *are scented* with myrrh and
aloes *and* cassia,
Out of the ivory palaces, by which they have
made You glad.
[9]Kings' daughters *are* among Your honorable
women;
At Your right hand stands the queen in gold
from Ophir.

[10]Listen, O daughter,
Consider and incline your ear;

Forget your own people also, and your father's
house;
[11]So the King will greatly desire your beauty;
Because He *is* your Lord, worship Him.
[12]And the daughter of Tyre *will come* with a gift;
The rich among the people will seek your
favor.

[13]The royal daughter *is* all glorious within *the
palace;*
Her clothing *is* woven with gold.
[14]She shall be brought to the King in robes of
many colors;
The virgins, her companions who follow her,
shall be brought to You.
[15]With gladness and rejoicing they shall be
brought;
They shall enter the King's palace.

[16]Instead of Your fathers shall be Your sons,
Whom You shall make princes in all the earth.
[17]I will make Your name to be remembered in all
generations;
Therefore the people shall praise You forever
and ever.

PSALM 46

God the Refuge of His People and Conqueror of the Nations

To the Chief Musician. *A Psalm* of the sons of Korah. A Song for
Alamoth.

[1]God *is* our refuge and strength,
A very present help in trouble.
[2]Therefore we will not fear,
Even though the earth be removed,
And though the mountains be carried into the
midst of the sea;
[3]*Though* its waters roar *and* be troubled,
Though the mountains shake with its swelling.
Selah

....

45:title [a]Hebrew *Shoshannim* [b]Hebrew *Maschil*

45:6, 7 The royal wedding of a great king, an ethical leader loving right and hating evil, is celebrated in this psalm. The robes, spices, fragrance (v. 8), royal daughters, and the royal bride all enhance this special anointing of the son of David. The queen (bride) of foreign descent was encouraged to submit to her husband as a token of her ultimate association with the people of God (v. 11; see Ruth 1:16). The "daughter of Tyre" is a personification for the people of Tyre. The bride was comforted by the honor of being counted among the people of God (Ps. 45:12–17). This reference is also used for the Messiah

(Heb. 1:8, 9). As God's son, His throne is forever, and His kingdom is righteousness (Ps. 45:6).

46:1–3 The psalmist exhibited a confident faith in God as his refuge in troublesome times. The psalm's background may be the crisis of 701 B.C., when God miraculously delivered the city of Jerusalem from the armies of Sennacherib, king of Assyria (see 2 Kin. 18; 19). The words inspired Martin Luther's hymn, "A Mighty Fortress Is Our God."

⁴*There is* a river whose streams shall make glad
   the city of God,
The holy *place* of the tabernacle of the Most
   High.
⁵God *is* in the midst of her, she shall not be
   moved;
God shall help her, just at the break of dawn.
⁶The nations raged, the kingdoms were
   moved;
He uttered His voice, the earth melted.

⁷The Lord of hosts *is* with us;
   The God of Jacob *is* our refuge.   *Selah*

⁸Come, behold the works of the Lord,
   Who has made desolations in the earth.
⁹He makes wars cease to the end of the earth;
   He breaks the bow and cuts the spear in two;
   He burns the chariot in the fire.

¹⁰Be still, and know that I *am* God;
   I will be exalted among the nations,
   I will be exalted in the earth!

¹¹The Lord of hosts *is* with us;
   The God of Jacob *is* our refuge.   *Selah*

PSALM 47

Praise to God, the Ruler of the Earth

To the Chief Musician. A Psalm of the sons of Korah.

¹Oh, clap your hands, all you peoples!
   Shout to God with the voice of triumph!
²For the Lord Most High *is* awesome;
   He is a great King over all the earth.
³He will subdue the peoples under us,
   And the nations under our feet.
⁴He will choose our inheritance for us,
   The excellence of Jacob whom He loves. *Selah*

⁵God has gone up with a shout,
   The Lord with the sound of a trumpet.
⁶Sing praises to God, sing praises!
   Sing praises to our King, sing praises!
⁷For God *is* the King of all the earth;
   Sing praises with understanding.

⁸God reigns over the nations;
   God sits on His holy throne.
⁹The princes of the people have gathered
   together,
   The people of the God of Abraham.

PSALMS FOR DAILY LIVING

LIFE SITUATION	REFERENCE
1. In a time of fear	Ps. 27
2. In a time of doubt	Ps. 73
3. In a time of illness	Ps. 6
4. In a time of trouble	Ps. 46
5. In a time of sin	Ps. 51
6. In a time of thanksgiving for forgiveness	Ps. 32
7. In a time of loneliness	Ps. 12

For the shields of the earth *belong* to God;
   He is greatly exalted.

PSALM 48

The Glory of God in Zion

A Song. A Psalm of the sons of Korah.

¹Great *is* the Lord, and greatly to be praised
   In the city of our God,
   In His holy mountain.
²Beautiful in elevation,
   The joy of the whole earth,
   Is Mount Zion *on* the sides of the north,
   The city of the great King.
³God *is* in her palaces;
   He is known as her refuge.

⁴For behold, the kings assembled,
   They passed by together.
⁵They saw *it, and* so they marveled;
   They were troubled, they hastened away.
⁶Fear took hold of them there,
   And pain, as of a woman in birth pangs,
⁷*As when* You break the ships of Tarshish
   With an east wind.

⁸As we have heard,
   So we have seen
   In the city of the Lord of hosts,
   In the city of our God:
   God will establish it forever.   *Selah*

46:10 Be still (lit. "to sink" or "to relax") encourages the hearer to stop all struggle and find the peace of faith. Such peace comes only as we acknowledge God's Lordship in our lives and surrender to His will.

48:1–3 The security that belongs to those who place their faith in the Lord is celebrated in this psalm (see also Ps. 46).

God's people believed that Jerusalem, "the city of our God," could never be conquered because God's presence would always protect it (Ps. 48:1). The city of Jerusalem, however, fell to the Babylonians in 586 B.C., at which time God's people learned through bitter experience the importance of a faith in Him that reflects itself in moral and ethical living.

⁹We have thought, O God, on Your
  lovingkindness,
 In the midst of Your temple.
¹⁰According to Your name, O God,
 So *is* Your praise to the ends of the earth;
 Your right hand is full of righteousness.
¹¹Let Mount Zion rejoice,
 Let the daughters of Judah be glad,
 Because of Your judgments.

¹²Walk about Zion,
 And go all around her.
 Count her towers;
¹³Mark well her bulwarks;
 Consider her palaces;
 That you may tell *it* to the generation
  following.
¹⁴For this *is* God,
 Our God forever and ever;
 He will be our guide
 Even to death.^a

PSALM 49

The Confidence of the Foolish

To the Chief Musician. A Psalm of the sons of Korah.

¹Hear this, all peoples;
 Give ear, all inhabitants of the world,
²Both low and high,
 Rich and poor together.
³My mouth shall speak wisdom,
 And the meditation of my heart *shall give*
  understanding.
⁴I will incline my ear to a proverb;
 I will disclose my dark saying on the harp.

⁵Why should I fear in the days of evil,
 When the iniquity at my heels surrounds
  me?
⁶Those who trust in their wealth
 And boast in the multitude of their riches,
⁷None *of them* can by any means redeem *his*
  brother,
 Nor give to God a ransom for him—
⁸For the redemption of their souls *is* costly,
 And it shall cease forever—
⁹That he should continue to live eternally,
 And not see the Pit.

¹⁰For he sees wise men die;
 Likewise the fool and the senseless person
  perish,
 And leave their wealth to others.
¹¹Their inner thought *is that* their houses *will*
  last forever,^a

Their dwelling places to all generations;
 They call *their* lands after their own names.
¹²Nevertheless man, *though* in honor, does not
  remain;^a
 He is like the beasts *that* perish.

¹³This is the way of those who *are* foolish,
 And of their posterity who approve their
  sayings.   *Selah*
¹⁴Like sheep they are laid in the grave;
 Death shall feed on them;
 The upright shall have dominion over them in
  the morning;
 And their beauty shall be consumed in the
  grave, far from their dwelling.
¹⁵But God will redeem my soul from the power
  of the grave,
 For He shall receive me.   *Selah*

¹⁶Do not be afraid when one becomes rich,
 When the glory of his house is increased;
¹⁷For when he dies he shall carry nothing away;
 His glory shall not descend after him.
¹⁸Though while he lives he blesses himself
 (For *men* will praise you when you do well for
  yourself),
¹⁹He shall go to the generation of his fathers;
 They shall never see light.
²⁰A man *who is* in honor, yet does not
  understand,
 Is like the beasts *that* perish.

PSALM 50

God the Righteous Judge

A Psalm of Asaph.

¹The Mighty One, God the Lord,
 Has spoken and called the earth
 From the rising of the sun to its going down.
²Out of Zion, the perfection of beauty,
 God will shine forth.
³Our God shall come, and shall not keep silent;
 A fire shall devour before Him,
 And it shall be very tempestuous all around
  Him.

⁴He shall call to the heavens from above,
 And to the earth, that He may judge His
  people:
⁵"Gather My saints together to Me,

••••••••••••••••••••••••••••••••••••••

48:14 ^aFollowing Masoretic Text and Syriac; Septuagint and Vulgate read *Forever.* **49:11** ^aSeptuagint, Syriac, Targum, and Vulgate read *Their graves shall be their houses forever.* **49:12** ^aFollowing Masoretic Text and Targum; Septuagint, Syriac, and Vulgate read *understand* (compare verse 20).

49:5–12 The certainty of death and the inadequacy of wealth are the subject of this wisdom psalm, emphasizing the folly of depending on material riches (v. 10). Wealth cannot buy the precious gift of life, which comes from God alone (Luke 12:15; see Ps. 2, Prosperity).

Those who have made a covenant with Me by
sacrifice."
[6]Let the heavens declare His righteousness,
For God Himself *is* Judge.   Selah

[7]"Hear, O My people, and I will speak,
O Israel, and I will testify against you;
I *am* God, your God!
[8]I will not rebuke you for your sacrifices
Or your burnt offerings,
Which are continually before Me.
[9]I will not take a bull from your house,
Nor goats out of your folds.
[10]For every beast of the forest *is* Mine,
And the cattle on a thousand hills.
[11]I know all the birds of the mountains,
And the wild beasts of the field *are* Mine.

[12]"If I were hungry, I would not tell you;
For the world *is* Mine, and all its fullness.
[13]Will I eat the flesh of bulls,
Or drink the blood of goats?
[14]Offer to God thanksgiving,
And pay your vows to the Most High.
[15]Call upon Me in the day of trouble;
I will deliver you, and you shall glorify
Me."

[16]But to the wicked God says:
"What *right* have you to declare My statutes,
Or take My covenant in your mouth,
[17]Seeing you hate instruction
And cast My words behind you?
[18]When you saw a thief, you consented[a] with
him,
And have been a partaker with adulterers.
[19]You give your mouth to evil,
And your tongue frames deceit.
[20]You sit *and* speak against your brother;
You slander your own mother's son.
[21]These *things* you have done, and I kept silent;
You thought that I was altogether like you;

But I will rebuke you,
And set *them* in order before your eyes.

[22]"Now consider this, you who forget God,
Lest I tear *you* in pieces,
And *there be* none to deliver:
[23]Whoever offers praise glorifies Me;
And to him who orders *his* conduct *aright*
I will show the salvation of God."

PSALM 51

A Prayer of Repentance

To the Chief Musician. A Psalm of David when Nathan the prophet
went to him, after he had gone in to Bathsheba.

[1]Have mercy upon me, O God,
According to Your lovingkindness;
According to the multitude of Your tender
mercies,
Blot out my transgressions.
[2]Wash me thoroughly from my iniquity,
And cleanse me from my sin.

[3]For I acknowledge my transgressions,
And my sin *is* always before me.
[4]Against You, You only, have I sinned,
And done *this* evil in Your sight—
That You may be found just when You speak,[a]
And blameless when You judge.

[5]Behold, I was brought forth in iniquity,
And in sin my mother conceived me.
[6]Behold, You desire truth in the inward parts,
And in the hidden *part* You will make me to
know wisdom.

[7]Purge me with hyssop, and I shall be clean;
Wash me, and I shall be whiter than snow.
[8]Make me hear joy and gladness,

50:18 [a]Septuagint, Syriac, Targum, and Vulgate read *ran.*   **51:4**
[a]Septuagint, Targum, and Vulgate read *in Your words.*

50:7–15 All the earth belongs to the Lord (see Ps. 24). The
people mistakenly assumed that God needed their sacrifices
and offerings, but God reminded them that every beast, cow,
and bird already belong to Him. There is no lack in God; He
needs nothing. We worship to meet our need, not God's. We
need to experience the joy of sharing and giving. God desires
our sincere worship and thanksgiving (Ps. 50:14). He wants us
to depend on Him (v. 15).

51:1 The superscription of this penitential psalm identifies it
as David's prayer for forgiveness after Nathan had confronted
him regarding his adultery with Bathsheba (see 2 Sam. 11; 12;
Ps. 6:2–10, note; chart, The Types of Psalms). The use of imperatives reveals the heaviness with which David viewed his
sin and his broken fellowship with God (Ps. 51:1, 2). "Have
mercy" (lit. "to show unmerited favor") is a plea based on the
character of God. For "lovingkindness," see Psalm 5:7–12,
note. For "tender mercies" see Psalm 18:1–3, note. For "trans-

gression," "iniquity," and "sin," see Psalm 32:1, 2, note.
"Against You, You only, have I sinned" (Ps. 51:4) does not mean
that David had not sinned against Bathsheba and Uriah,
rather that sin always is directed primarily against God
(2 Sam. 12:13; see also Ex. 20:13, 14).

51:5, 6 David's experience paralleled that of Isaiah, who recognized his human frailty and sinfulness when he saw God's
holiness (Is. 6:5). Whatever sins we cover, God will uncover;
what we uncover, God will cover (Prov. 28:13). Psalm 51:5 does
not teach that sin is passed along through the genes nor that
sexual intimacy within marriage is sinful. It is not intended to
support celibacy or to imply that David himself was born out
of wedlock. Rather, the verse emphasizes human frailty in the
constant battle against sin. "Hyssop," a small plant that grew
on the walls, was used to sprinkle blood on the doorposts of
Hebrew homes at the first Passover and later in purification
ceremonies (Ex. 12:22; 1 Kin. 4:33).

FORGIVENESS   GOD'S EXTENDED MERCY

All human beings are sinners and thus the victims of sin's deadly consequences (Ps. 51:5; Rom. 3:23; 1 John 1:8–10). Ultimately, sin breaks the fellowship between God and mankind. God's forgiveness is the divine means of removing sin and restoring fellowship. His forgiveness is complete (Ps. 103:12; Is. 1:18; Mic. 7:19); it is everlasting (Is. 44:22; Jer. 31:34; Heb. 10:17); it is always available (Ps. 86:5; 1 John 1:9). Various terms are used to describe this process, including cleansing, purifying, purging, and washing (Ps. 51:4–9; Is. 1:16; 43:25; Jer. 33:8). Those who fail to seek God's forgiveness are subject to being "blotted out" of God's Book of Life (Ps. 69:28; Rev. 3:5).

Although priestly functions related to forgiveness are prescribed in the Bible (Lev. 4:26), forgiveness is ultimately granted solely by God. Sacrifices are a means of obtaining forgiveness for inadvertent errors (Num. 15:22–29) but do not cover blatant contempt of God (Num. 15:30, 31; Mark 3:29). All rituals related to forgiveness in the Bible are expected to be accompanied by contrition and compassion, as well as penitence and confession (Lev. 5:5, 6; 16:21; Num. 5:6, 7). Rituals and sacrifices alone, however, do not bring forgiveness. We must humble ourselves, acknowledge our wrongs, and resolve to depart from sin (1 Kin. 21:27–29; Is. 1:16, 17; Joel 2:12, 13). When we do this, God gives each one of us a new heart and spirit—a desire and an ability to keep His statutes (Ezek. 36:24–27).

An emphasis is always placed on the translation of true remorse into a positive course of action. Those forgiven cease to do evil (Ps. 15; 24:3–5), begin to do good (Is. 1:17; Jer. 7:3), incline their hearts to the Lord (Josh. 24:23), and, in sum, turn from sin and embrace righteousness. This is "repentance." When we repent, God forgives (Num. 14:18–20; 2 Chr. 7:14; Is. 55:7; 1 John 1:9). He pardons sin (Mic. 7:18), removes it completely (Ps. 103:12), and remembers it no more (Ps. 25:7). Jesus' death on the cross provides redemption to all who will accept what He has done on their behalf (Eph. 1:7, 8; Col. 1:14).

See also Ps. 32; 103:11–17; Jer. 31:34; Lam. 3:22, note; Luke 24:47, note; notes on Attributes of God (Ex. 33; Deut. 4; 32; 2 Chr. 19; Job 23; 42; Ps. 25; 90; 102; 119; Is. 6; 65; Jer. 23; Luke 18; Rom. 2; Eph. 1; 1 John 5); Forgiveness (Luke 17)

That the bones You have broken may rejoice.
⁹Hide Your face from my sins,
And blot out all my iniquities.

¹⁰Create in me a clean heart, O God,
And renew a steadfast spirit within me.
¹¹Do not cast me away from Your presence,
And do not take Your Holy Spirit from me.

¹²Restore to me the joy of Your salvation,
And uphold me *by Your* generous Spirit.
¹³*Then* I will teach transgressors Your ways,
And sinners shall be converted to You.

¹⁴Deliver me from the guilt of bloodshed, O God,
The God of my salvation,
And my tongue shall sing aloud of Your righteousness.
¹⁵O Lord, open my lips,
And my mouth shall show forth Your praise.
¹⁶For You do not desire sacrifice, or else I would give *it*;

You do not delight in burnt offering.
¹⁷The sacrifices of God *are* a broken spirit,
A broken and a contrite heart—
These, O God, You will not despise.

¹⁸Do good in Your good pleasure to Zion;
Build the walls of Jerusalem.
¹⁹Then You shall be pleased with the sacrifices of righteousness,
With burnt offering and whole burnt offering;
Then they shall offer bulls on Your altar.

PSALM 52

The End of the Wicked and the Peace of the Godly

To the Chief Musician. A Contemplation[a] of David when Doeg the Edomite went and told Saul, and said to him, "David has gone to the house of Ahimelech."

¹Why do you boast in evil, O mighty man?
The goodness of God *endures* continually.

••••••••••••••••••••

52:title [a]Hebrew *Maschil*

51:10–13 Create is the same word used in Genesis 1:1, emphasizing that the radical cleansing requested can come only from God (see 2 Cor. 5:17). Because of the joy that he had experienced, David wanted to share the good news of forgiveness with others (Ps. 51:13; Ps. 32, Forgiveness; see charts, Journey to Forgiveness; Forgiveness: Your Path to Freedom).

51:16, 17 The OT sacrificial system was not rejected. Rather, the Law did not prescribe sacrifices for murder or adultery, sins which David had committed. For these presumptuous sins, the sinner could only cast himself on the mercy of God (see 2 Sam. 12:13, 14). The Lord accepts and forgives those who are honest with Him, who are humble before Him, and who recognize their dependence on His grace.

²Your tongue devises destruction,
  Like a sharp razor, working deceitfully.
³You love evil more than good,
  Lying rather than speaking righteousness.
  Selah

⁴You love all devouring words,
  You deceitful tongue.

⁵God shall likewise destroy you forever;
  He shall take you away, and pluck you out of
    your dwelling place,
  And uproot you from the land of the living.
  Selah

⁶The righteous also shall see and fear,
  And shall laugh at him, *saying,*
⁷"Here is the man *who* did not make God his
    strength,
  But trusted in the abundance of his riches,
  And strengthened himself in his wickedness."

⁸But I *am* like a green olive tree in the house of
    God;
  I trust in the mercy of God forever and ever.
⁹I will praise You forever,
  Because You have done *it;*
  And in the presence of Your saints
  I will wait on Your name, for *it is* good.

PSALM 53

Folly of the Godless, and the Restoration of Israel

To the Chief Musician. Set to "Mahalath." A Contemplation[a]
of David.

¹The fool has said in his heart,
"*There is* no God."
  They are corrupt, and have done abominable
    iniquity;
  There is none who does good.

²God looks down from heaven upon the
    children of men,
  To see if there are *any* who understand, who
    seek God.
³Every one of them has turned aside;
  They have together become corrupt;
  There is none who does good,
  No, not one.

⁴Have the workers of iniquity no knowledge,
  Who eat up my people *as* they eat bread,
  And do not call upon God?
⁵There they are in great fear
  Where no fear was,

For God has scattered the bones of him who
    encamps against you;
  You have put *them* to shame,
  Because God has despised them.

⁶Oh, that the salvation of Israel would come out
    of Zion!
  When God brings back the captivity of His
    people,
  Let Jacob rejoice *and* Israel be glad.

PSALM 54

Answered Prayer for Deliverance from Adversaries

To the Chief Musician. With stringed instruments.[a] A
Contemplation[b] of David when the Ziphites went and said to Saul,
"Is David not hiding with us?"

¹Save me, O God, by Your name,
  And vindicate me by Your strength.
²Hear my prayer, O God;
  Give ear to the words of my mouth.
³For strangers have risen up against me,
  And oppressors have sought after my life;
  They have not set God before them.   *Selah*

⁴Behold, God *is* my helper;
  The Lord *is* with those who uphold my life.
⁵He will repay my enemies for their evil.
  Cut them off in Your truth.

⁶I will freely sacrifice to You;
  I will praise Your name, O LORD, for *it is*
    good.
⁷For He has delivered me out of all trouble;
  And my eye has seen *its desire* upon my
    enemies.

PSALM 55

Trust in God Concerning the Treachery of Friends

To the Chief Musician. With stringed instruments.[a] A
Contemplation[b] of David.

¹Give ear to my prayer, O God,
  And do not hide Yourself from my supplication.
²Attend to me, and hear me;
  I am restless in my complaint, and moan
    noisily,
³Because of the voice of the enemy,
  Because of the oppression of the wicked;

53:title [a]Hebrew *Maschil* 54:title; 55:title [a]Hebrew *neginoth*
[b]Hebrew *Maschil*

53:1–6 The foolish person lacks spiritual discernment not intelligence (see Ps. 14:1, note). The opposite of folly is steadfast devotion to the Lord.

54:1–7 David affirmed his faith in God as his Helper. The superscription connects this psalm with a time when the Ziphites betrayed David's hideout to Saul (see 1 Sam. 23:15–23). David prayed for deliverance from his enemies, calling on God's name (for the sake of God's reputation or character).

For they bring down trouble upon me,
And in wrath they hate me.

[4]My heart is severely pained within me,
And the terrors of death have fallen upon me.
[5]Fearfulness and trembling have come upon me,
And horror has overwhelmed me.
[6]So I said, "Oh, that I had wings like a dove!
I would fly away and be at rest.
[7]Indeed, I would wander far off,
And remain in the wilderness.   *Selah*
[8]I would hasten my escape
From the windy storm *and* tempest."

[9]Destroy, O Lord, *and* divide their tongues,
For I have seen violence and strife in the
city.
[10]Day and night they go around it on its walls;
Iniquity and trouble *are* also in the midst of it.
[11]Destruction *is* in its midst;
Oppression and deceit do not depart from its
streets.

[12]For *it is* not an enemy *who* reproaches me;
Then I could bear *it*.
Nor *is it* one *who* hates me who has exalted
himself against me;
Then I could hide from him.
[13]But *it was* you, a man my equal,
My companion and my acquaintance.
[14]We took sweet counsel together,
And walked to the house of God in the
throng.

[15]Let death seize them;
Let them go down alive into hell,
For wickedness *is* in their dwellings *and* among
them.

[16]As for me, I will call upon God,
And the LORD shall save me.
[17]Evening and morning and at noon
I will pray, and cry aloud,
And He shall hear my voice.
[18]He has redeemed my soul in peace from the
battle *that was* against me,
For there were many against me.
[19]God will hear, and afflict them,
Even He who abides from of old.   *Selah*
Because they do not change,
Therefore they do not fear God.

[20]He has put forth his hands against those who
were at peace with him;
He has broken his covenant.
[21]*The words* of his mouth were smoother than
butter,
But war *was* in his heart;
His words were softer than oil,
Yet they *were* drawn swords.

[22]Cast your burden on the LORD,
And He shall sustain you;
He shall never permit the righteous to be
moved.

[23]But You, O God, shall bring them down to the
pit of destruction;
Bloodthirsty and deceitful men shall not live
out half their days;
But I will trust in You.

PSALM 56

Prayer for Relief from Tormentors

To the Chief Musician. Set to "The Silent Dove in Distant
Lands."[a] A Michtam of David when the Philistines captured
him in Gath.

[1]Be merciful to me, O God, for man would
swallow me up;
Fighting all day he oppresses me.
[2]My enemies would hound *me* all day,
For *there are* many who fight against me,
O Most High.

[3]Whenever I am afraid,
I will trust in You.
[4]In God (I will praise His word),
In God I have put my trust;
I will not fear.
What can flesh do to me?

[5]All day they twist my words;
All their thoughts *are* against me for evil.
[6]They gather together,
They hide, they mark my steps,
When they lie in wait for my life.
[7]Shall they escape by iniquity?
In anger cast down the peoples, O God!

···
56:title [a]Hebrew *Jonath Elem Rechokim*

55:9–15 The poet lashed out at his enemies, but the betrayal of his friend hurt the most (vv. 13, 14). Jesus faced this same heartbreak when Judas, one of His 12 disciples, betrayed Him (John 18:1–12).

55:22 The psalmist did the right thing in pouring out his grief to God who always remains faithful (see 1 Pet. 5:5-7). Those who trust in Him will remain firmly established in life's difficult times. They will not be shaken.

56:3, 4 No one can overcome the individual who trusts in God (see Rom. 8:31-39). The superscription identifies this psalm with David's capture by the Philistines in Gath (see 1 Sam. 21:10—22:1). Although not actually seized, David was frightened by the pursuit.

[8]You number my wanderings;
  Put my tears into Your bottle;
  Are they not in Your book?
[9]When I cry out *to You,*
  Then my enemies will turn back;
  This I know, because God *is* for me.
[10]In God (I will praise *His* word),
  In the LORD (I will praise *His* word),
[11]In God I have put my trust;
  I will not be afraid.
  What can man do to me?

[12]Vows *made* to You *are binding* upon me, O God;
  I will render praises to You,
[13]For You have delivered my soul from death.
  Have You not *kept* my feet from falling,
  That I may walk before God
  In the light of the living?

PSALM 57

Prayer for Safety from Enemies

To the Chief Musician. Set to "Do Not Destroy."[a] A Michtam of
David when he fled from Saul into the cave.

[1]Be merciful to me, O God, be merciful to me!
  For my soul trusts in You;
  And in the shadow of Your wings I will make
    my refuge,
  Until *these* calamities have passed by.

[2]I will cry out to God Most High,
  To God who performs *all things* for me.
[3]He shall send from heaven and save me;
  He reproaches the one who would swallow me
    up.   *Selah*
  God shall send forth His mercy and His truth.

[4]My soul *is* among lions;
  I lie *among* the sons of men
  Who are set on fire,
  Whose teeth *are* spears and arrows,
  And their tongue a sharp sword.
[5]Be exalted, O God, above the heavens;
  Let Your glory *be* above all the earth.

[6]They have prepared a net for my steps;
  My soul is bowed down;

They have dug a pit before me;
  Into the midst of it they *themselves* have fallen.
                                           Selah

[7]My heart is steadfast, O God, my heart is
    steadfast;
  I will sing and give praise.
[8]Awake, my glory!
  Awake, lute and harp!
  I will awaken the dawn.

[9]I will praise You, O Lord, among the peoples;
  I will sing to You among the nations.
[10]For Your mercy reaches unto the heavens,
  And Your truth unto the clouds.

[11]Be exalted, O God, above the heavens;
  Let Your glory *be* above all the earth.

PSALM 58

The Just Judgment of the Wicked

To the Chief Musician. Set to "Do Not Destroy."[a]
A Michtam of David.

[1]Do you indeed speak righteousness, you silent
    ones?
  Do you judge uprightly, you sons of men?
[2]No, in heart you work wickedness;
  You weigh out the violence of your hands in
    the earth.

[3]The wicked are estranged from the womb;
  They go astray as soon as they are born,
    speaking lies.
[4]Their poison *is* like the poison of a serpent;
  They are like the deaf cobra *that* stops its ear,
[5]Which will not heed the voice of charmers,
  Charming ever so skillfully.

[6]Break their teeth in their mouth, O God!
  Break out the fangs of the young lions, O LORD!
[7]Let them flow away as waters *which* run
    continually;
  When he bends *his bow,*
  Let his arrows be as if cut in pieces.

57:title; 58:title [a]Hebrew *Al Tashcheth*

57:1–11 The poet began with a cry for mercy from God in whom he trusted, using lovely imagery to describe taking refuge in the shadow of God's wings until the storms have passed (Ps. 17:8; 63:7). The heading associates this poem with a time when David escaped from King Saul into a cave in the wilderness of En Gedi: either his escape to the cave of Adullam (1 Sam. 22:1, 2) or the encounter at the Rocks of the Wild Goats where he could have killed Saul (1 Sam. 24:1–7). The psalmist had experienced the actions of God in his behalf in the past and was thus confident of His deliverance from present difficulties. God is to be exalted for His glory (see Ps. 19:1, note; 108:1–6).

58:11 The psalmist expressed anger over the apparent lack of judgment on the wicked, yet asserted that there is a God who judges the earth (see 2 Chr. 19, Attributes of God). The wicked devise evil from birth, and there is never evidence of good in their hearts (Ps. 58:3). The problem confronted by the psalmist appears similar to the question raised in the Book of Job: Why do the righteous suffer and the wicked continue in prosperity? The poet ended the psalm with certainty that the score would be evened out in the end. God is the righteous Judge who will reward the faithful and bring vengeance on the wicked (see chart, Suffering in Divine Perspective).

TEARS A CRY FROM THE HEART

People are brought to tears for a multitude of reasons. Tears have always been closely intertwined with the human heart and may express such diverse emotions as grief and joy.

In the Old Testament, tears were often an expression of remorse (Lam. 2:18, 19). Esther wept with a troubled soul over the plight of her people (Esth. 8:3). Hannah shed tears from a heart that grieved and a soul that was bitter (1 Sam. 1:8, 10). Mary and Martha wept over the loss of their brother Lazarus (John 11:31). The sinful woman at the feet of Christ shed tears, not from remorse, anxiety, or grief, but rather in humility as a grateful response to God's mercy and love toward her (Luke 7:38–50).

All of us will experience circumstances in our lives that will move us to tears. In those times, let us hold fast to the promise that a day is coming when God will "wipe away every tear . . . there shall be no more . . . crying" (Rev. 7:17; 21:4; see Is. 25:8). Until that time, may our desire be for tears of repentance, adoration, thankfulness, and joy (see Ps. 6:4–8; 126:5; 2 Tim. 1:3–5).

See also Ps. 56:8, 9; 2 Tim. 1:3–5; notes on Death (1 Cor. 15); Emotions (Ps. 42); Fruit of the Spirit (Rom. 15); Grief (Is. 53); Sorrow (Rev. 21)

---

[8]Let them be like a snail which melts away as it goes,
Like a stillborn child of a woman, that they may not see the sun.

[9]Before your pots can feel the burning thorns,
He shall take them away as with a whirlwind,
As in His living and burning wrath.
[10]The righteous shall rejoice when he sees the vengeance;
He shall wash his feet in the blood of the wicked,
[11]So that men will say,
"Surely there is a reward for the righteous;
Surely He is God who judges in the earth."

PSALM 59

The Assured Judgment of the Wicked

To the Chief Musician. Set to "Do Not Destroy."[a] A Michtam of David when Saul sent men, and they watched the house in order to kill him.

[1]Deliver me from my enemies, O my God;
Defend me from those who rise up against me.
[2]Deliver me from the workers of iniquity,
And save me from bloodthirsty men.

[3]For look, they lie in wait for my life;
The mighty gather against me,
Not for my transgression nor for my sin,
O LORD.
[4]They run and prepare themselves through no fault of mine.

Awake to help me, and behold!

[5]You therefore, O LORD God of hosts, the God of Israel,
Awake to punish all the nations;
Do not be merciful to any wicked transgressors.   Selah

[6]At evening they return,
They growl like a dog,
And go all around the city.
[7]Indeed, they belch with their mouth;
Swords are in their lips;
For they say, "Who hears?"

[8]But You, O LORD, shall laugh at them;
You shall have all the nations in derision.
[9]I will wait for You, O You his Strength;[a]
For God is my defense.
[10]My God of mercy[a] shall come to meet me;
God shall let me see my desire on my enemies.

[11]Do not slay them, lest my people forget;
Scatter them by Your power,
And bring them down,
O Lord our shield.
[12]For the sin of their mouth and the words of their lips,
Let them even be taken in their pride,
And for the cursing and lying which they speak.

••••••••••••••••••

59:title [a]Hebrew Al Tashcheth   **59:9** [a]Following Masoretic Text and Syriac; some Hebrew manuscripts, Septuagint, Targum, and Vulgate read my Strength.   **59:10** [a]Following Qere; some Hebrew manuscripts, Septuagint, and Vulgate read My God, His mercy; Kethib, some Hebrew manuscripts and Targum read O God, my mercy; Syriac reads O God, Your mercy.

59:11–17 God is the only source of power and strength for David. The superscription associates this song with a time when King Saul sent men to kill David (1 Sam. 19:11–17). David desired deliverance from these destructive enemies ("dogs," Ps. 59:6, 14) who sought his life. The poet also asserted his in-nocence and declared that he had not rebelled against the Lord ("transgression," v. 3) or missed God's mark for his life ("sin," v. 3; see Ps. 32:1, 2; 51:1, notes). The song ends on a confident note, as the psalmist praises God as his defense and refuge.

¹³Consume *them* in wrath, consume *them,*
 That they *may* not *be;*
 And let them know that God rules in Jacob
 To the ends of the earth. *Selah*

¹⁴And at evening they return,
 They growl like a dog,
 And go all around the city.
¹⁵They wander up and down for food,
 And howl^a if they are not satisfied.

¹⁶But I will sing of Your power;
 Yes, I will sing aloud of Your mercy in the
 morning;
 For You have been my defense
 And refuge in the day of my trouble.
¹⁷To You, O my Strength, I will sing praises;
 For God *is* my defense,
 My God of mercy.

PSALM 60

Urgent Prayer for the Restored Favor of God

To the Chief Musician. Set to "Lily of the Testimony."^a A Michtam of
David. For teaching. When he fought against Mesopotamia and
Syria of Zobah, and Joab returned and killed twelve thousand
Edomites in the Valley of Salt.

¹O God, You have cast us off;
 You have broken us down;
 You have been displeased;
 Oh, restore us again!
²You have made the earth tremble;
 You have broken it;
 Heal its breaches, for it is shaking.
³You have shown Your people hard things;
 You have made us drink the wine of confusion.

⁴You have given a banner to those who fear
 You,
 That it may be displayed because of the truth.
 Selah
⁵That Your beloved may be delivered,
 Save *with* Your right hand, and hear me.

⁶God has spoken in His holiness:
 "I will rejoice;
 I will divide Shechem
 And measure out the Valley of Succoth.
⁷Gilead *is* Mine, and Manasseh *is* Mine;
 Ephraim also *is* the helmet for My head;
 Judah *is* My lawgiver.
⁸Moab *is* My washpot;

Over Edom I will cast My shoe;
 Philistia, shout in triumph because of Me."

⁹Who will bring me *to* the strong city?
 Who will lead me to Edom?
¹⁰*Is it* not You, O God, *who* cast us off?
 And You, O God, *who* did not go out with our
 armies?
¹¹Give us help from trouble,
 For the help of man *is* useless.
¹²Through God we will do valiantly,
 For *it is* He *who* shall tread down our enemies.^a

PSALM 61

Assurance of God's Eternal Protection

To the Chief Musician. On a stringed instrument.^a A Psalm of David.

¹Hear my cry, O God;
 Attend to my prayer.
²From the end of the earth I will cry to You,
 When my heart is overwhelmed;
 Lead me to the rock that is higher than I.

³For You have been a shelter for me,
 A strong tower from the enemy.
⁴I will abide in Your tabernacle forever;
 I will trust in the shelter of Your wings. *Selah*

⁵For You, O God, have heard my vows;
 You have given *me* the heritage of those who
 fear Your name.
⁶You will prolong the king's life,
 His years as many generations.
⁷He shall abide before God forever.
 Oh, prepare mercy and truth, *which* may
 preserve him!

⁸So I will sing praise to Your name forever,
 That I may daily perform my vows.

PSALM 62

A Calm Resolve to Wait for the Salvation of God

To the Chief Musician. To Jeduthun. A Psalm of David.

¹Truly my soul silently *waits* for God;
 From Him *comes* my salvation.
²He only *is* my rock and my salvation;
 He is my defense;
 I shall not be greatly moved.

· ·
59:15 ^aFollowing Septuagint and Vulgate; Masoretic Text, Syriac, and
Targum read *spend the night.* **60:title** ^aHebrew *Shushan Eduth*
60:12 ^aCompare verses 5–12 with 108:6–13 **61:title** ^aHebrew *neginah*

61:1–8 The poet sought safety in God's presence during difficult times. "From the end of the earth" suggests that the
psalmist had reached the end of his rope. In any case, he experienced despair over the apparent absence of God in his life
(v. 2). He longed to be guided to "the rock that is higher than
I," probably a reference to God Himself (Ps. 18:2). Note the
change in tone (Ps. 61:3). The psalmist recognized that the

safety and security of God's presence he had enjoyed in the
past would remain, and thus the psalm ends on a note of gratitude to God (vv. 5–8).

62:1–7 Quiet waiting enables us to reflect on the greatness of
God (see Ps. 46:10) and ensures steadfastness (Ps. 62:2, 6; see
1:3). The psalmist's soul, his total being, waits expectantly on

SINGLENESS ALONE BUT NOT LONELY

Loneliness, which usually refers to a lack of companionship and fellowship, is part of every human life, not just that of the single person. Loneliness may well accompany special missions, moments of decision, bereavement, betrayal, separation from the community of faith, and misfortune (see Gen. 32:24; Jer. 15:17; Job 12:4; Luke 7:12; 22:45, 46, 48; 24:17).

The faith-filled single woman responds to loneliness by focusing her devotion on Jesus and by drawing near to the community of faith for support and wisdom. The single woman who immerses herself in God's Word and prayer can experience great comfort and joy. Although single, a person need never stand without God, who is the constant companion and ever-present guide for every believer (John 16:7, 8).

In many ways, singleness may be a call to holiness—either for a period in one's life or for the whole of one's life. Holiness is a call to be like God. It includes acknowledging your place in Him and His role in your life. It means knowing Jesus and believing in Him (John 17:3). Spiritual strength that comes from knowing Jesus enables a single person to do the work of God in the world and to be happy regardless of whether she is married or single (Gal. 5:22).

Holiness is not self-direction rooted in pride and ambition, but divine guidance by the Holy Spirit. Nor is holiness limited to listening attentively to the Lord, but includes rousing yourself to do whatever He tells you (John 2:5). Holiness, thus, is directly related to knowing and applying the whole of God's Word to the whole of your life.

The promise of God's Word is that we will experience the fullness of His presence in our lives as we seek to know the Lord, love the Lord, and obey His Word. We may be single, but we are never alone. We may be holy—separated for God's indwelling and use—but we never have to be isolated from others or live without a sense of purpose and fulfillment.

See also Ps. 37:4; 69:20; notes on Holiness (Lev. 20); Prayer (Jer. 33, Heb. 4; 1 John 5; 3 John); Friendship (Luke 1); Loneliness (Eccl. 4); Singleness (John 2; 1 Cor. 7); Suffering (Ps. 33; 113; Is. 43; 1 Pet. 5); Sacrificial Living (Mic. 7)

---

³How long will you attack a man?
 You shall be slain, all of you,
 Like a leaning wall and a tottering fence.
⁴They only consult to cast *him* down from his
   high position;
 They delight in lies;
 They bless with their mouth,
 But they curse inwardly.   *Selah*

⁵My soul, wait silently for God alone,
 For my expectation *is* from Him.
⁶He only *is* my rock and my salvation;
 He is my defense;
 I shall not be moved.
⁷In God *is* my salvation and my glory;
 The rock of my strength,
 And my refuge, *is* in God.

⁸Trust in Him at all times, you people;
 Pour out your heart before Him;
 God *is* a refuge for us.   *Selah*

⁹Surely men of low degree *are* a vapor,
 Men of high degree *are* a lie;

If they are weighed on the scales,
 They *are* altogether *lighter* than vapor.
¹⁰Do not trust in oppression,
 Nor vainly hope in robbery;
 If riches increase,
 Do not set *your* heart *on them*.

¹¹God has spoken once,
 Twice I have heard this:
 That power *belongs* to God.
¹²Also to You, O Lord, *belongs* mercy;
 For You render to each one according to his
   work.

PSALM 63

Joy in the Fellowship of God

A Psalm of David when he was in the wilderness of Judah.

¹O God, You *are* my God;
 Early will I seek You;
 My soul thirsts for You;
 My flesh longs for You
 In a dry and thirsty land
 Where there is no water.

God as he extolled the nature of the God on whom he waited. He is "my rock," "my salvation," "my defense," "my glory," "my strength," and "my refuge" (see chart, Images of God in the Psalms). In a whirl of activity, we find it difficult to wait on God or anyone else, much less to wait alone in silence. The

psalmist would remain firmly established because of his faith in God (see Ps. 1:3).

63:1–11 The psalm begins with the confession of faith that God is "my God." The psalm's superscription identifies it with an occasion when David was in the wilderness of Judah

²So I have looked for You in the sanctuary,
To see Your power and Your glory.

³Because Your lovingkindness *is* better than
life,
My lips shall praise You.
⁴Thus I will bless You while I live;
I will lift up my hands in Your name.
⁵My soul shall be satisfied as with marrow and
fatness,
And my mouth shall praise *You* with joyful lips.

⁶When I remember You on my bed,
I meditate on You in the *night* watches.
⁷Because You have been my help,
Therefore in the shadow of Your wings I will
rejoice.
⁸My soul follows close behind You;
Your right hand upholds me.

⁹But those *who* seek my life, to destroy *it,*
Shall go into the lower parts of the earth.
¹⁰They shall fall by the sword;
They shall be a portion for jackals.

¹¹But the king shall rejoice in God;
Everyone who swears by Him shall glory;
But the mouth of those who speak lies shall be
stopped.

PSALM 64

Oppressed by the Wicked but Rejoicing in the Lord

To the Chief Musician. A Psalm of David.

¹Hear my voice, O God, in my meditation;
Preserve my life from fear of the enemy.
²Hide me from the secret plots of the wicked,
From the rebellion of the workers of iniquity,
³Who sharpen their tongue like a sword,
And bend *their bows to shoot* their arrows—
bitter words,
⁴That they may shoot in secret at the blameless;
Suddenly they shoot at him and do not
fear.

⁵They encourage themselves *in* an evil
matter;
They talk of laying snares secretly;
They say, "Who will see them?"
⁶They devise iniquities:
"We have perfected a shrewd scheme."
Both the inward thought and the heart of man
are deep.

⁷But God shall shoot at them *with* an arrow;
Suddenly they shall be wounded.
⁸So He will make them stumble over their own
tongue;
All who see them shall flee away.
⁹All men shall fear,
And shall declare the work of God;
For they shall wisely consider His doing.

¹⁰The righteous shall be glad in the Lord, and
trust in Him.
And all the upright in heart shall glory.

PSALM 65

Praise to God for His Salvation and Providence

To the Chief Musician. A Psalm of David. A Song.

¹Praise is awaiting You, O God, in Zion;
And to You the vow shall be performed.
²O You who hear prayer,
To You all flesh will come.
³Iniquities prevail against me;
As for our transgressions,
You will provide atonement for them.

⁴Blessed *is the man* You choose,
And cause to approach *You,*
That he may dwell in Your courts.
We shall be satisfied with the goodness of Your
house,
Of Your holy temple.

⁵*By* awesome deeds in righteousness You will
answer us,
O God of our salvation,

(perhaps 1 Sam. 23 or 2 Sam. 15–18). David acknowledged a personal, intimate relationship with God in which his longing for God is as intense as the longing of dry, parched lips for water (Ps. 63:1). Through his disciplined practice of worship in the sanctuary, David experienced God's strength and glory as wonderfully real to him. He had experienced God's "lov- ingkindness" (Heb. *chesed,* "steadfast love" or "covenant loyalty," v. 3; see Ps. 5:7–12, note). The poet praised God for His faithful love, which was more dear to him than life itself (Ps. 63:3–5).

64:1–10 The poet felt overwhelmed by the secrets of the en- emy against him. Evidently, the psalmist is experiencing slan- der from his enemies (vv. 3, 4). Their words were like arrows aimed to destroy him. The Hebrews viewed words as living forces carrying the power to fulfill their purposes. The spoken

word was like an arrow shot from a bow. It could not be re- called. These verses remind us of the importance of guarding our speech (see James 3:1–12).

65:1–13 This hymn of joyful thanksgiving may have been sung at a spring festival celebrating God's salvation and His boun- tiful provision in the earth. The tone of the hymn is one of joy. All persons can come to God and experience His forgiveness (vv. 1–4; Ps. 51, Forgiveness; chart, Journey to Forgiveness). God hears our prayers and responds to them. God is to be praised because He forgives our sins. God also merits praise because He is the great Creator who establishes the moun- tains, controls the seas, and sends rain to water the crops. The poet described the wonder of God's provision in picturesque language (Ps. 65:9–13). Even nature itself participates in praise of God's abundant provision (vv. 11–13).

You who are the confidence of all the ends of
    the earth,
And of the far-off seas;
6Who established the mountains by His
    strength,
Being clothed with power;
7You who still the noise of the seas,
The noise of their waves,
And the tumult of the peoples.
8They also who dwell in the farthest parts are
    afraid of Your signs;
You make the outgoings of the morning and
    evening rejoice.

9You visit the earth and water it,
You greatly enrich it;
The river of God is full of water;
You provide their grain,
For so You have prepared it.
10You water its ridges abundantly,
You settle its furrows;
You make it soft with showers,
You bless its growth.

11You crown the year with Your goodness,
And Your paths drip *with* abundance.
12They drop *on* the pastures of the wilderness,
And the little hills rejoice on every side.
13The pastures are clothed with flocks;
The valleys also are covered with grain;
They shout for joy, they also sing.

PSALM 66

Praise to God for His Awesome Works
To the Chief Musician. A Song. A Psalm.

1Make a joyful shout to God, all the earth!
2Sing out the honor of His name;
    Make His praise glorious.
3Say to God,
"How awesome are Your works!
Through the greatness of Your power
Your enemies shall submit themselves to You.
4All the earth shall worship You
And sing praises to You;
They shall sing praises *to* Your name."   *Selah*

5Come and see the works of God;
He is awesome *in His* doing toward the sons of
    men.

6He turned the sea into dry *land;*
They went through the river on foot.
There we will rejoice in Him.
7He rules by His power forever;
His eyes observe the nations;
Do not let the rebellious exalt themselves.
    Selah

8Oh, bless our God, you peoples!
And make the voice of His praise to be heard,
9Who keeps our soul among the living,
And does not allow our feet to be moved.
10For You, O God, have tested us;
You have refined us as silver is refined.
11You brought us into the net;
You laid affliction on our backs.
12You have caused men to ride over our heads;
We went through fire and through water;
But You brought us out to rich *fulfillment.*

13I will go into Your house with burnt offerings;
I will pay You my vows,
14Which my lips have uttered
And my mouth has spoken when I was in trouble.
15I will offer You burnt sacrifices of fat animals,
With the sweet aroma of rams;
I will offer bulls with goats.   *Selah*

16Come *and* hear, all you who fear God,
And I will declare what He has done for my
    soul.
17I cried to Him with my mouth,
And He was extolled with my tongue.
18If I regard iniquity in my heart,
The Lord will not hear.
19*But* certainly God has heard *me;*
He has attended to the voice of my prayer.

20Blessed *be* God,
Who has not turned away my prayer,
Nor His mercy from me!

PSALM 67

An Invocation and a Doxology
To the Chief Musician. On stringed instruments.a A Psalm. A Song.

1God be merciful to us and bless us,
And cause His face to shine upon us,   *Selah*

67:title aHebrew *neginoth*

66:1–9 All peoples of the earth are invited to praise God (see Ps. 100:1). One of God's great deeds was the deliverance of His people from Egypt (Ps. 66:6; see Ex. 14). The God who has brought His people through confidence great crises is worthy of glorious praise (Ps. 66:8–12). Such appropriate praise is defined by the offering of sacrifices and the payment of promised vows (Ps. 66:13–15).

67:1–7 This psalm has a missionary focus. It begins with a ref-

erence to the blessing or benediction of Aaron (see Num. 6:24–26). The poet repeatedly calls all people and all nations to praise God, the righteous Ruler and Judge of the earth (Ps. 67:4). God is presented here as the God of all nations, not just the God of Israel. Gratitude for all God has done for us is an appropriate motivation for sharing the gospel with others. The ideal result of God's blessing on His people is that "all the ends of the earth" should fear or reverence Him (v. 7).

²That Your way may be known on earth,
Your salvation among all nations.

³Let the peoples praise You, O God;
Let all the peoples praise You.
⁴Oh, let the nations be glad and sing for joy!
For You shall judge the people righteously,
And govern the nations on earth.   *Selah*

⁵Let the peoples praise You, O God;
Let all the peoples praise You.
⁶*Then* the earth shall yield her increase;
God, our own God, shall bless us.
⁷God shall bless us,
And all the ends of the earth shall fear Him.

PSALM 68

The Glory of God in His Goodness to Israel

To the Chief Musician. A Psalm of David. A Song.

¹Let God arise,
Let His enemies be scattered;
Let those also who hate Him flee before Him.
²As smoke is driven away,
So drive *them* away;
As wax melts before the fire,
So let the wicked perish at the presence of
God.
³But let the righteous be glad;
Let them rejoice before God;
Yes, let them rejoice exceedingly.

⁴Sing to God, sing praises to His name;
Extol Him who rides on the clouds,ª
By His name YAH,
And rejoice before Him.

⁵A father of the fatherless, a defender of
widows,
Is God in His holy habitation.
⁶God sets the solitary in families;
He brings out those who are bound into
prosperity;
But the rebellious dwell in a dry *land.*

⁷O God, when You went out before Your
people,
When You marched through the wilderness,
                                          Selah
⁸The earth shook;

The heavens also dropped *rain* at the presence
of God;
Sinai itself *was moved* at the presence of God,
the God of Israel.
⁹You, O God, sent a plentiful rain,
Whereby You confirmed Your inheritance,
When it was weary.
¹⁰Your congregation dwelt in it;
You, O God, provided from Your goodness for
the poor.

¹¹The Lord gave the word;
Great *was* the company of those who
proclaimed *it:*
¹²"Kings of armies flee, they flee,
And she who remains at home divides the
spoil.
¹³Though you lie down among the sheepfolds,
You will be like the wings of a dove covered with
silver,
And her feathers with yellow gold."
¹⁴When the Almighty scattered kings in it,
It was *white* as snow in Zalmon.

¹⁵A mountain of God *is* the mountain of Bashan;
A mountain *of many* peaks *is* the mountain of
Bashan.
¹⁶Why do you fume with envy, you mountains of
many peaks?
This is the mountain *which* God desires to dwell
in;
Yes, the LORD will dwell *in it* forever.

¹⁷The chariots of God *are* twenty thousand,
Even thousands of thousands;
The Lord is among them *as in* Sinai, in the
Holy *Place.*
¹⁸You have ascended on high,
You have led captivity captive;
You have received gifts among men,
Even *from* the rebellious,
That the LORD God might dwell *there.*

¹⁹Blessed *be* the Lord,
Who daily loads us *with benefits,*
The God of our salvation!   *Selah*

···························
68:4 ªMasoretic Text reads *deserts;* Targum reads *heavens* (compare
verse 34 and Isaiah 19:1).

68:4–6 God cares for the poor and helpless. He is the father
of the orphan and the defender of the widow. He provides
homes for the homeless and delivers those in bondage into
blessing ("prosperity," v. 6). Those who rebel against God fail
to realize His bountiful care and dwell in a "dry land." Verse 4
refers to the Lord as *Yah,* a shortened form of *Yahweh,* the
covenant name of Israel's God. This familiar expression is
found in *hallelujah* (Heb., lit. "praise the Lord").

68:7–10 God revealed His presence with His people by per-

forming great and mighty acts in their behalf. Following the
Exodus from Egypt, He revealed Himself during the journey
in the wilderness and through the giving of the Law at Mt.
Sinai (Ex. 13:21; 19:16–18).

68:18 As victor, the ascended Christ gave spiritual gifts to His
disciples (Eph. 4:7–16). In this imagery, a king comes home
from battle, leading a triumphant procession as he returns
with the defeated captives.

²⁰Our God *is* the God of salvation;
And to GOD the Lord *belong* escapes from death.

²¹But God will wound the head of His enemies,
The hairy scalp of the one who still goes on in
his trespasses.
²²The Lord said, "I will bring back from Bashan,
I will bring *them* back from the depths of the
sea,
²³That your foot may crush *them*^a in blood,
And the tongues of your dogs *may have* their
portion from *your* enemies."

²⁴They have seen Your procession, O God,
The procession of my God, my King, into the
sanctuary.
²⁵The singers went before, the players on
instruments *followed* after;
Among *them were* the maidens playing timbrels.
²⁶Bless God in the congregations,
The Lord, from the fountain of Israel.
²⁷There *is* little Benjamin, their leader,
The princes of Judah *and* their company,
The princes of Zebulun *and* the princes of
Naphtali.

²⁸Your God has commanded^a your strength;
Strengthen, O God, what You have done for
us.
²⁹Because of Your temple at Jerusalem,
Kings will bring presents to You.
³⁰Rebuke the beasts of the reeds,
The herd of bulls with the calves of the
peoples,
Till everyone submits himself with pieces of
silver.
Scatter the peoples *who* delight in war.
³¹Envoys will come out of Egypt;
Ethiopia will quickly stretch out her hands to
God.

³²Sing to God, you kingdoms of the earth;
Oh, sing praises to the Lord,   *Selah*
³³To Him who rides on the heaven of heavens,
which were of old!
Indeed, He sends out His voice, a mighty voice.
³⁴Ascribe strength to God;
His excellence *is* over Israel,
And His strength *is* in the clouds.

³⁵O God, *You are* more awesome than Your holy
places.
The God of Israel *is* He who gives strength and
power to *His* people.

Blessed *be* God!

PSALM 69

An Urgent Plea for Help in Trouble

To the Chief Musician. Set to "The Lilies."^a
A Psalm of David.

¹Save me, O God!
For the waters have come up to *my* neck.
²I sink in deep mire,
Where *there is* no standing;
I have come into deep waters,
Where the floods overflow me.
³I am weary with my crying;
My throat is dry;
My eyes fail while I wait for my God.

⁴Those who hate me without a cause
Are more than the hairs of my head;
They are mighty who would destroy me,
Being my enemies wrongfully;
Though I have stolen nothing,
I *still* must restore *it.*

⁵O God, You know my foolishness;
And my sins are not hidden from You.
⁶Let not those who wait for You, O Lord GOD of
hosts, be ashamed because of me;
Let not those who seek You be confounded
because of me, O God of Israel.
⁷Because for Your sake I have borne reproach;
Shame has covered my face.
⁸I have become a stranger to my brothers,
And an alien to my mother's children;
⁹Because zeal for Your house has eaten me up,
And the reproaches of those who reproach You
have fallen on me.
¹⁰When I wept *and chastened* my soul with
fasting,
That became my reproach.

••••••••••••••••••

68:23 ^aSeptuagint, Syriac, Targum, and Vulgate read *you may dip
your foot.* **68:28** ^aSeptuagint, Syriac, Targum, and Vulgate read
Command, O God. **69:title** ^aHebrew *Shoshannim*

68:33–35 The presence of this awesome God with His people,
now as in the past, is a marvel to ponder until its reality
changes our lives. The psalmist called on others to worship
the great and good God who gives power and strength to His
people (v. 34).

69:7–9 The poet suffered because of his commitment to the
Lord. John used this psalm when referring to Jesus cleansing
the temple (John 2:17; see also Mark 3:21; John 7:3–5). Jesus
even experienced alienation from His own family.

69:29–36 After denouncing his enemies (vv. 22–28), the poet
returned to his plea for God's deliverance (see vv. 1–3). He is
assured of deliverance as he vowed to praise and magnify the
Lord (v. 32). Despite the dark perspective the psalmist had
expressed in his words in the earlier part of the psalm, he
ended on a positive note of praise. We can pour out our hearts
to God in confidence that He will hear us.

As I live in awareness of, growth in, and gratitude for God's grace and mercy, my life will bring glory to Him.

Sandy Smith

¹¹I also made sackcloth my garment;
I became a byword to them.
¹²Those who sit in the gate speak against me,
And I *am* the song of the drunkards.

¹³But as for me, my prayer *is* to You,
O Lord, *in* the acceptable time;
O God, in the multitude of Your mercy,
Hear me in the truth of Your salvation.
¹⁴Deliver me out of the mire,
And let me not sink;
Let me be delivered from those who hate me,
And out of the deep waters.
¹⁵Let not the floodwater overflow me,
Nor let the deep swallow me up;
And let not the pit shut its mouth on me.

¹⁶Hear me, O Lord, for Your lovingkindness *is* good;
Turn to me according to the multitude of Your tender mercies.
¹⁷And do not hide Your face from Your servant,
For I am in trouble;
Hear me speedily.
¹⁸Draw near to my soul, *and* redeem it;
Deliver me because of my enemies.

¹⁹You know my reproach, my shame, and my dishonor;
My adversaries *are* all before You.
²⁰Reproach has broken my heart,
And I am full of heaviness;
I looked *for someone* to take pity, but *there was* none;
And for comforters, but I found none.
²¹They also gave me gall for my food,
And for my thirst they gave me vinegar to drink.

²²Let their table become a snare before them,
And their well-being a trap.
²³Let their eyes be darkened, so that they do not see;
And make their loins shake continually.
²⁴Pour out Your indignation upon them,
And let Your wrathful anger take hold of them.
²⁵Let their dwelling place be desolate;
Let no one live in their tents.

²⁶For they persecute the *ones* You have struck,
And talk of the grief of those You have wounded.
²⁷Add iniquity to their iniquity,
And let them not come into Your righteousness.
²⁸Let them be blotted out of the book of the living,
And not be written with the righteous.

²⁹But I *am* poor and sorrowful;
Let Your salvation, O God, set me up on high.
³⁰I will praise the name of God with a song,
And will magnify Him with thanksgiving.
³¹*This* also shall please the Lord better than an ox *or* bull,
Which has horns and hooves.
³²The humble shall see *this and* be glad;
And you who seek God, your hearts shall live.
³³For the Lord hears the poor,
And does not despise His prisoners.

³⁴Let heaven and earth praise Him,
The seas and everything that moves in them.
³⁵For God will save Zion
And build the cities of Judah,
That they may dwell there and possess it.
³⁶Also, the descendants of His servants shall inherit it,
And those who love His name shall dwell in it.

PSALM 70

Prayer for Relief from Adversaries
To the Chief Musician. *A Psalm* of David.
To bring to remembrance.

¹*Make haste*, O God, to deliver me!
Make haste to help me, O Lord!

²Let them be ashamed and confounded
Who seek my life;
Let them be turned back[a] and confused
Who desire my hurt.

70:2 [a]Following Masoretic Text, Septuagint, Targum, and Vulgate; some Hebrew manuscripts and Syriac read *be appalled* (compare 40:15).

70:1–5 The sense of urgency in the psalmist's plea is reflected in both the first words and the last words of this brief poem (vv. 1, 5). The poet recognized both his own helplessness and the greatness of God (see Ps. 40:13–17).

WIDOWHOOD *DEPENDENCE ON GOD*

A woman does not choose to become a widow. The loss of a beloved husband is a devastating experience that leaves a woman brokenhearted and emotionally drained. Her planned future suddenly seems dim and fading, and fears can become life-consuming (2 Kin. 4:1). With major support systems and financial resources often no longer available, widows must become sole providers for their children and homes no matter what their abilities, training, or resources. Perhaps at no other time in her life does a woman face as many major decisions with fewer emotional resources.

Through Elisha, God asked a seemingly hopeless widow what she would like Him to do for her. Although omnipotent and knowing her need, the Lord wanted this woman specifically to assess her situation and define reachable goals for her future. How purposeful God is and how practical He teaches us to be (Ps. 32:8).

This widow's simple response to Elisha indicated the deep level of trust and faith in her heart. She did not chide Elisha for asking foolish questions or infringing on her personal rights. Rather, from a deep and abiding faith in God, this new widow, by her willing response, indicated to a friend whom she knew was sent by her heavenly Father, her own expectancy of divine intervention on her behalf (2 Kin. 4:5, 6; see also Deut. 10:18).

Widows today need that same total dependence on a sovereign Lord (Deut. 10:18). Through Christlike friends, the Lord sends loving concern and practical sympathy (James 1:17). As part of His healing process, He encourages us to speak of our grief—to pour out our heartache, fear, anxiety, and pain—so that He in turn can pour into us His strength and peace (Is. 40:29–31; 2 Cor. 1: 3, 4). He does heal broken hearts (Ps. 147:3).

See also Matt. 18:3, note; notes on Brokenheartedness (Ps. 34); Children (2 Sam. 21; 2 Kin. 4; Ps. 128; Prov. 22; Luke 15); Death (1 Cor. 15); Family (Gen. 32; 1 Sam. 3; Ps. 78; 127); Grief (Is. 53); Tears (Ps. 56); Widowhood (Jer. 29; 1 Cor. 2); portraits of The Prophet's Widow (2 Kin. 4); Widow of Zarephath (1 Kin. 17)

³Let them be turned back because of their
    shame,
Who say, "Aha, aha!"

⁴Let all those who seek You rejoice and be glad
    in You;
And let those who love Your salvation say
    continually,
"Let God be magnified!"

⁵But I *am* poor and needy;
Make haste to me, O God!
You *are* my help and my deliverer;
O Lord, do not delay.

PSALM 71

God the Rock of Salvation

¹In You, O Lord, I put my trust;
Let me never be put to shame.
²Deliver me in Your righteousness, and cause
    me to escape;
Incline Your ear to me, and save me.
³Be my strong refuge,
To which I may resort continually;

You have given the commandment to save
    me,
For You *are* my rock and my fortress.

⁴Deliver me, O my God, out of the hand of the
    wicked,
Out of the hand of the unrighteous and cruel
    man.
⁵For You are my hope, O Lord God;
You are my trust from my youth.
⁶By You I have been upheld from birth;
You are He who took me out of my mother's
    womb.
My praise *shall be* continually of You.

⁷I have become as a wonder to many,
But You *are* my strong refuge.
⁸Let my mouth be filled *with* Your praise
And with Your glory all the day.

⁹Do not cast me off in the time of old age;
Do not forsake me when my strength fails.
¹⁰For my enemies speak against me;
And those who lie in wait for my life take
    counsel together,

71:1–24 A senior citizen's prayer. Although experiencing distress and longing for deliverance, this older person trusted God as his rock, fortress, refuge, and hope (see Is. 46, Aging). He affirmed his trust in God from his youth, even from his birth (Ps. 71:5, 6; Is. 46:3, 4). The God who sustained and carried him through life is worshiped. Our faith should not be a burden to us; it should provide us with a lift. The poet praised God either because He had already responded to his prayer or because God's answer was certain to come. What wonderful words on the lips of a person whose total commitment to God echoes throughout the verses of this psalm! How wonderful to come to the end of life with a positive outlook of joy in the Lord! As we look back at the Lord's faithfulness in the past, we can continue to trust Him for whatever the future may bring.

¹¹Saying, "God has forsaken him;
Pursue and take him, for *there is* none to deliver
    him."

¹²O God, do not be far from me;
O my God, make haste to help me!
¹³Let them be confounded *and* consumed
Who are adversaries of my life;
Let them be covered *with* reproach and
    dishonor
Who seek my hurt.

¹⁴But I will hope continually,
And will praise You yet more and more.
¹⁵My mouth shall tell of Your righteousness
And Your salvation all the day,
For I do not know *their* limits.
¹⁶I will go in the strength of the Lord God;
I will make mention of Your righteousness, of
    Yours only.

¹⁷O God, You have taught me from my
    youth;
And to this *day* I declare Your wondrous
    works.
¹⁸Now also when *I am* old and grayheaded,
O God, do not forsake me,
Until I declare Your strength to *this*
    generation,
Your power to everyone *who* is to come.

¹⁹Also Your righteousness, O God, *is* very
    high,
You who have done great things;
O God, who *is* like You?
²⁰*You,* who have shown me great and severe
    troubles,
Shall revive me again,
And bring me up again from the depths of the
    earth.
²¹You shall increase my greatness,
And comfort me on every side.

²²Also with the lute I will praise You—
And Your faithfulness, O my God!
To You I will sing with the harp,
O Holy One of Israel.
²³My lips shall greatly rejoice when I sing to
    You,
And my soul, which You have redeemed.
²⁴My tongue also shall talk of Your righteousness
    all the day long;
For they are confounded,
For they are brought to shame
Who seek my hurt.

PSALM 72

Glory and Universality of the Messiah's Reign
A Psalm of Solomon.

¹Give the king Your judgments, O God,
And Your righteousness to the king's Son.
²He will judge Your people with righteousness,
And Your poor with justice.
³The mountains will bring peace to the people,
And the little hills, by righteousness.
⁴He will bring justice to the poor of the people;
He will save the children of the needy,
And will break in pieces the oppressor.

⁵They shall fear You[a]
As long as the sun and moon endure,
Throughout all generations.
⁶He shall come down like rain upon the grass
    before mowing,
Like showers *that* water the earth.
⁷In His days the righteous shall flourish,
And abundance of peace,
Until the moon is no more.

⁸He shall have dominion also from sea to sea,
And from the River to the ends of the earth.
⁹Those who dwell in the wilderness will bow
    before Him,
And His enemies will lick the dust.
¹⁰The kings of Tarshish and of the isles
Will bring presents;
The kings of Sheba and Seba
Will offer gifts.
¹¹Yes, all kings shall fall down before Him;
All nations shall serve Him.

¹²For He will deliver the needy when he cries,
The poor also, and *him* who has no helper.
¹³He will spare the poor and needy,
And will save the souls of the needy.
¹⁴He will redeem their life from oppression and
    violence;
And precious shall be their blood in His sight.

¹⁵And He shall live;
And the gold of Sheba will be given to Him;
Prayer also will be made for Him continually,
And daily He shall be praised.

¹⁶There will be an abundance of grain in the earth,
On the top of the mountains;
Its fruit shall wave like Lebanon;

72:5 [a]Following Masoretic Text and Targum; Septuagint and Vulgate read *They shall continue.*

72:1–4 The superscription links this psalm with Solomon, who requested understanding or wisdom with which to judge God's people (1 Kin. 3:5–10). Nature itself, the mountains and hills, will participate in the delight of a righteous ruler (Ps. 72:3).

GRANDPARENTHOOD MINISTRY OF LOVE

Grandparents have an opportunity for ministry to their grandchildren that parents may not have time to do. Grandparents can be a prime channel of spiritual education, especially in homes of single parents or homes in which both parents are employed. Here are some suggestions for investing in the next generation:

- Share how God spoke to you (or other family members) through the years, and how you obeyed His commands. This vital testimony gives grandchildren "know-how" and spiritual roots as well as keeping family history alive (Ps. 45:17; 79:13). Provide wise counsel, time-tested insights, and your knowledge at appropriate times (Prov. 1:5).
- Explain your own salvation experience and lead your grandchildren to Christ (Deut. 6:7–9).
- Pray for your grandchildren, using Paul's prayers as examples (Eph. 3:14–21; Phil. 1:9–11; Col. 1:9–11). Pray for their protection (Ps. 121:1–8), both physically and spiritually.
- Pray with your grandchildren.
- Give your grandchildren Christian books, tapes, and videos (Prov. 3:27).
- Read the Bible together, sitting shoulder to shoulder (Ps. 119:9–11).
- Find ways to reinforce godly lessons taught by parents with examples from your own life, building bridges from one generation to another (Ps. 78:1, 2).
- Teach them that they are important to God not because of what they do but because of who lives inside them.
- Teach them that God is in control; nothing is too difficult or too big for the Lord (Jer. 32:17).
- Teach them that God is loving, compassionate, and understanding (Lam. 3:22, 23).
- Demonstrate the joys of tithing (Prov. 3:9; Mal. 3:10).
- If living apart, find ways to communicate to each grandchild that she is special (Prov. 15:23; 16:24). Leave a solid spiritual legacy (a worn Bible with special notes, a handmade article, happy memories), not just money, as an inheritance (Prov. 13:22).

In many ways, grandparents are strong role models for their grandchildren (2 Tim. 1:5). As such, grandparents have a powerful influence in exemplifying these messages:

- Forgiveness is the highest form of giving (Eph. 4:32).
- Right and wrong are defined by God's Word (Prov. 14:12).
- Great joy can be experienced in living each day, rather than dwelling on the past or future (Neh. 8:10, Ps. 118:24).

As a grandparent, don't complain about your aches and pains. Instead, praise God for your long life. You will be happier, and so will people around you (1 Thess. 5:18). Stay active and maintain interests outside the family (Col. 2:6,7). Be careful not to undermine parental authority. Be there, but do not meddle.

And what about the great rewards of being a grandparent? They are many! The crowns of grandparenting include:

- Hearing again the spontaneous joy and laughter of a little child,
- Collecting humorous stories and anecdotes about your grandchild as well as having an eager audience with whom to share firsthand experiences from your own childhood,
- Receiving the tender love and sweet comfort from a child who is untouched by the busyness of the rest of the world,
- Sensing pride in making your mark and extending your influence to the next generation (Prov. 17:6; Is. 51:1),
- Allowing God to channel His love through you into the lives of your grandchildren (Ps. 78:6),
- Having your life renewed and faith revitalized (Ruth 4:15).

See also chart on Praying for Your Children (Phil. 1); notes on Aging (Is. 46); Blessings (Gen. 12); Family (Gen. 32; 1 Sam. 3; Ps. 78; 127); Prayer (Jer. 33; Heb. 4; 1 John 5; 3 John); Traditions (1 Sam. 7); Inheritance (Prov. 13); Influence (Esth. 4); portraits of Naomi (Ruth 1); Lois and Eunice (2 Tim. 1)

And *those* of the city shall flourish like grass of
the earth.

17His name shall endure forever;
His name shall continue as long as the sun.

And *men* shall be blessed in Him;
All nations shall call Him blessed.

18Blessed *be* the LORD God, the God of Israel,
Who only does wondrous things!

¹⁹And blessed *be* His glorious name forever!
And let the whole earth be filled *with* His glory.
Amen and Amen.

²⁰The prayers of David the son of Jesse are
ended.

Book Three: Psalms 73—89

PSALM 73

The Tragedy of the Wicked, and the Blessedness of Trust in God

A Psalm of Asaph.

¹Truly God *is* good to Israel,
To such as are pure in heart.
²But as for me, my feet had almost stumbled;
My steps had nearly slipped.
³For I *was* envious of the boastful,
When I saw the prosperity of the wicked.

⁴For *there are* no pangs in their death,
But their strength *is* firm.
⁵They *are* not in trouble *as other* men,
Nor are they plagued like *other* men.
⁶Therefore pride serves as their necklace;
Violence covers them *like* a garment.
⁷Their eyes bulge[a] with abundance;
They have more than heart could wish.
⁸They scoff and speak wickedly *concerning*
oppression;
They speak loftily.
⁹They set their mouth against the heavens,
And their tongue walks through the earth.

¹⁰Therefore his people return here,
And waters of a full *cup* are drained by them.
¹¹And they say, "How does God know?
And is there knowledge in the Most High?"
¹²Behold, these *are* the ungodly,
Who are always at ease;
They increase *in* riches.
¹³Surely I have cleansed my heart *in* vain,
And washed my hands in innocence.
¹⁴For all day long I have been plagued,
And chastened every morning.

¹⁵If I had said, "I will speak thus,"
Behold, I would have been untrue to the
generation of Your children.

¹⁶When I thought *how* to understand this,
It *was* too painful for me—
¹⁷Until I went into the sanctuary of God;
Then I understood their end.

¹⁸Surely You set them in slippery places;
You cast them down to destruction.
¹⁹Oh, how they are *brought* to desolation, as in a
moment!
They are utterly consumed with terrors.
²⁰As a dream when *one* awakes,
So, Lord, when You awake,
You shall despise their image.

²¹Thus my heart was grieved,
And I was vexed in my mind.
²²I *was* so foolish and ignorant;
I was *like* a beast before You.
²³Nevertheless I *am* continually with You;
You hold *me* by my right hand.
²⁴You will guide me with Your counsel,
And afterward receive me *to* glory.

²⁵Whom have I in heaven *but You*?
And *there is* none upon earth *that* I desire
besides You.
²⁶My flesh and my heart fail;
But God *is* the strength of my heart and my
portion forever.

²⁷For indeed, those who are far from You shall
perish;
You have destroyed all those who desert You
for harlotry.
²⁸But *it is* good for me to draw near to God;
I have put my trust in the Lord GOD,
That I may declare all Your works.

PSALM 74

A Plea for Relief from Oppressors

A Contemplation[a] of Asaph.

¹O God, why have You cast *us* off forever?
Why does Your anger smoke against the sheep
of Your pasture?
²Remember Your congregation, *which* You have
purchased of old,

73:7 [a]Targum reads *face bulges;* Septuagint, Syriac, and Vulgate read *iniquity bulges.*   **74:title** [a]Hebrew *Maschil*

72:18, 19 A doxology marks the end of Book II of the Psalms (see Introduction: Outline). The words emphasize that God is to be blessed forever and throughout the whole earth. "Glory" refers to God's character, presence, and influence (see Ps. 19:1, note).

73:25–28 The psalmist expressed his human weakness (vv. 2, 3). His feet had nearly slipped. He saw the prosperity of the ungodly and was envious of the wicked who never seemed to suffer for their wrongdoing (vv. 4–14). Life did not seem fair.

The psalmist began to reflect the viewpoint of faith as he entered the sanctuary and worshiped God (vv. 15–17). He began to put life in perspective. He realized the devastating end of the wicked (vv. 18–20), which led him to pour out his heart in praise to God (vv. 25–28). The poet did not receive a comprehensive answer to the unanswerable question of evil. He did receive great assurance of the presence of God.

74:1–11 God's people felt rejected and punished because God's sanctuary had been destroyed. This psalm is probably

The tribe of Your inheritance, *which* You have
  redeemed—
This Mount Zion where You have dwelt.
³Lift up Your feet to the perpetual desolations.
  The enemy has damaged everything in the
    sanctuary.
⁴Your enemies roar in the midst of Your
  meeting place;
  They set up their banners *for* signs.
⁵They seem like men who lift up
  Axes among the thick trees.
⁶And now they break down its carved work, all
  at once,
  With axes and hammers.
⁷They have set fire to Your sanctuary;
  They have defiled the dwelling place of Your
    name to the ground.
⁸They said in their hearts,
  "Let us destroy them altogether."
  They have burned up all the meeting places of
    God in the land.

⁹We do not see our signs;
  There is no longer any prophet;
  Nor *is there* any among us who knows how long.
¹⁰O God, how long will the adversary reproach?
  Will the enemy blaspheme Your name forever?
¹¹Why do You withdraw Your hand, even Your
  right hand?
  Take it out of Your bosom and destroy *them.*
¹²For God *is* my King from of old,
  Working salvation in the midst of the earth.
¹³You divided the sea by Your strength;
  You broke the heads of the sea serpents in the
    waters.
¹⁴You broke the heads of Leviathan in pieces,
  And gave him *as* food to the people inhabiting
    the wilderness.
¹⁵You broke open the fountain and the flood;
  You dried up mighty rivers.
¹⁶The day *is* Yours, the night also *is* Yours;
  You have prepared the light and the sun.
¹⁷You have set all the borders of the earth;
  You have made summer and winter.

¹⁸Remember this, *that* the enemy has
  reproached, O LORD,
  And *that* a foolish people has blasphemed Your
    name.
¹⁹Oh, do not deliver the life of Your turtledove to
  the wild beast!

Do not forget the life of Your poor forever.
²⁰Have respect to the covenant;
  For the dark places of the earth are full of the
    haunts of cruelty.
²¹Oh, do not let the oppressed return
  ashamed!
  Let the poor and needy praise Your name.

²²Arise, O God, plead Your own cause;
  Remember how the foolish man reproaches
    You daily.
²³Do not forget the voice of Your enemies;
  The tumult of those who rise up against You
    increases continually.

PSALM 75

Thanksgiving for God's Righteous Judgment
To the Chief Musician. Set to "Do Not Destroy."[a]
A Psalm of Asaph. A Song.

¹We give thanks to You, O God, we give thanks!
  For Your wondrous works declare *that* Your
    name is near.

²"When I choose the proper time,
  I will judge uprightly.
³The earth and all its inhabitants are dissolved;
  I set up its pillars firmly.   *Selah*

⁴"I said to the boastful, 'Do not deal boastfully,'
  And to the wicked, 'Do not lift up the horn.
⁵Do not lift up your horn on high;
  Do *not* speak with a stiff neck.' "

⁶For exaltation *comes* neither from the east
  Nor from the west nor from the south.
⁷But God *is* the Judge:
  He puts down one,
  And exalts another.
⁸For in the hand of the LORD *there is* a cup,
  And the wine is red;
  It is fully mixed, and He pours it out;
  Surely its dregs shall all the wicked of the
    earth
  Drain *and* drink down.

⁹But I will declare forever,
  I will sing praises to the God of Jacob.

75:title ªHebrew *Al Tashcheth*

framed immediately following the destruction of Jerusalem
by the Babylonians in 586 B.C. Israel did not believe that God
would ever allow Jerusalem or the temple to be destroyed.
They claimed that the presence of the temple in itself en-
sured them of protection from their enemies. However, the
prophet Jeremiah, among others, had warned the people of
Jerusalem's pending destruction if the people did not repent

of their evil ways and turn to God (see Jer. 7). Because God's
people failed to repent, destruction came upon them.

75:1–10 God's righteous judgment. That God alone can judge
rightly and fairly is the theme of this psalm. He alone knows
our hearts and all the circumstances, and thus He alone can
judge correctly. This psalm warns us against judging others.

¹⁰"All the horns of the wicked I will also cut off,
But the horns of the righteous shall be
exalted."

PSALM 76

The Majesty of God in Judgment

To the Chief Musician. On stringed instruments.^a
A Psalm of Asaph. A Song.

¹In Judah God *is* known;
His name *is* great in Israel.
²In Salem^a also is His tabernacle,
And His dwelling place in Zion.
³There He broke the arrows of the bow,
The shield and sword of battle.   *Selah*

⁴You *are* more glorious and excellent
Than the mountains of prey.
⁵The stouthearted were plundered;
They have sunk into their sleep;
And none of the mighty men have found the
use of their hands.
⁶At Your rebuke, O God of Jacob,
Both the chariot and horse were cast into a
dead sleep.

⁷You, Yourself, *are* to be feared;
And who may stand in Your presence
When once You are angry?
⁸You caused judgment to be heard from heaven;
The earth feared and was still,
⁹When God arose to judgment,
To deliver all the oppressed of the earth.   *Selah*

¹⁰Surely the wrath of man shall praise You;
With the remainder of wrath You shall gird
Yourself.

¹¹Make vows to the LORD your God, and pay *them;*
Let all who are around Him bring presents to
Him who ought to be feared.
¹²He shall cut off the spirit of princes;
He is awesome to the kings of the earth.

PSALM 77

The Consoling Memory of God's Redemptive Works

To the Chief Musician. To Jeduthun. A Psalm of Asaph.

¹I cried out to God with my voice—
To God with my voice;
And He gave ear to me.
²In the day of my trouble I sought the Lord;

My hand was stretched out in the night
without ceasing;
My soul refused to be comforted.
³I remembered God, and was troubled;
I complained, and my spirit was overwhelmed.
Selah

⁴You hold my eyelids *open;*
I am so troubled that I cannot speak.
⁵I have considered the days of old,
The years of ancient times.
⁶I call to remembrance my song in the night;
I meditate within my heart,
And my spirit makes diligent search.

⁷Will the Lord cast off forever?
And will He be favorable no more?
⁸Has His mercy ceased forever?
Has *His* promise failed forevermore?
⁹Has God forgotten to be gracious?
Has He in anger shut up His tender mercies?
Selah

¹⁰And I said, "This *is* my anguish;
But I will remember the years of the right hand
of the Most High."
¹¹I will remember the works of the LORD;
Surely I will remember Your wonders of old.
¹²I will also meditate on all Your work,
And talk of Your deeds.
¹³Your way, O God, *is* in the sanctuary;
Who *is* so great a God as *our* God?
¹⁴You *are* the God who does wonders;
You have declared Your strength among the
peoples.
¹⁵You have with *Your* arm redeemed Your people,
The sons of Jacob and Joseph.   *Selah*

¹⁶The waters saw You, O God;
The waters saw You, they were afraid;
The depths also trembled.
¹⁷The clouds poured out water;
The skies sent out a sound;
Your arrows also flashed about.
¹⁸The voice of Your thunder *was* in the
whirlwind;
The lightnings lit up the world;
The earth trembled and shook.
¹⁹Your way *was* in the sea,
Your path in the great waters,

76:title ^aHebrew *neginoth*   **76:2** ^aThat is, Jerusalem

76:1–6 God's victory over Israel's enemies and the deliverance of His people is celebrated (see Ps. 46; 48). God's people knew Him by personal experience as the God who repeatedly brought victory into their lives. "Salem" and "Zion" refer to Jerusalem (Ps. 76:2).

77:10–15 The poet wondered about the presence of God in his difficulties (vv. 1–9). But when he remembered the past goodness of God, then he hoped for the future. He both meditated on and talked about God's works (v. 12). This focus on God's greatness led the poet to realize that God was the only true God (v. 13). Faith in the only true God enables His people to see things in proper perspective.

And Your footsteps were not known.
²⁰You led Your people like a flock
  By the hand of Moses and Aaron.

PSALM 78

God's Kindness to Rebellious Israel

A Contemplationᵃ of Asaph.

¹Give ear, O my people, *to* my law;
  Incline your ears to the words of my mouth.
²I will open my mouth in a parable;
  I will utter dark sayings of old,
³Which we have heard and known,
  And our fathers have told us.
⁴We will not hide *them* from their children,
  Telling to the generation to come the praises
    of the LORD,
  And His strength and His wonderful works
    that He has done.

⁵For He established a testimony in Jacob,
  And appointed a law in Israel,
  Which He commanded our fathers,
  That they should make them known to their
    children;
⁶That the generation to come might know *them,*
  The children *who* would be born,
  That they may arise and declare *them* to their
    children,
⁷That they may set their hope in God,
  And not forget the works of God,
  But keep His commandments;
⁸And may not be like their fathers,
  A stubborn and rebellious generation,
  A generation *that* did not set its heart aright,
  And whose spirit was not faithful to God.

⁹The children of Ephraim, *being* armed *and*
    carrying bows,
  Turned back in the day of battle.
¹⁰They did not keep the covenant of God;
  They refused to walk in His law,
¹¹And forgot His works
  And His wonders that He had shown them.

¹²Marvelous things He did in the sight of their
    fathers,
  In the land of Egypt, *in* the field of Zoan.
¹³He divided the sea and caused them to pass
    through;
  And He made the waters stand up like a heap.
¹⁴In the daytime also He led them with the
    cloud,

And all the night with a light of fire.
¹⁵He split the rocks in the wilderness,
  And gave *them* drink in abundance like the
    depths.
¹⁶He also brought streams out of the rock,
  And caused waters to run down like rivers.

¹⁷But they sinned even more against Him
  By rebelling against the Most High in the
    wilderness.
¹⁸And they tested God in their heart
  By asking for the food of their fancy.
¹⁹Yes, they spoke against God:
  They said, "Can God prepare a table in the
    wilderness?
²⁰Behold, He struck the rock,
  So that the waters gushed out,
  And the streams overflowed.
  Can He give bread also?
  Can He provide meat for His people?"

²¹Therefore the LORD heard *this* and was
    furious;
  So a fire was kindled against Jacob,
  And anger also came up against Israel,
²²Because they did not believe in God,
  And did not trust in His salvation.
²³Yet He had commanded the clouds above,
  And opened the doors of heaven,
²⁴Had rained down manna on them to eat,
  And given them of the bread of heaven.
²⁵Men ate angels' food;
  He sent them food to the full.

²⁶He caused an east wind to blow in the heavens;
  And by His power He brought in the south
    wind.
²⁷He also rained meat on them like the dust,
  Feathered fowl like the sand of the seas;
²⁸And He let *them* fall in the midst of their camp,
  All around their dwellings.
²⁹So they ate and were well filled,
  For He gave them their own desire.
³⁰They were not deprived of their craving;
  But while their food *was* still in their mouths,
³¹The wrath of God came against them,
  And slew the stoutest of them,
  And struck down the choice *men* of Israel.

³²In spite of this they still sinned,
  And did not believe in His wondrous works.

78:title ᵃHebrew *Maschil*

78:1–4 The poet called on his generation to learn a lesson from the mistakes of Israel's forefathers. God's people had disobeyed Him even in the face of all the mighty acts He performed on their behalf (the Exodus from Egypt, vv. 12–14, 42–53; the wilderness experience, vv. 15–33; the conquest of the Land, vv. 54, 55). They responded not with faith, but with ingratitude (Ps. 106:6–46). The rebellion of people against God, despite His abundant mercy, remains as great a mystery now as it was in the time of the psalmist.

³³Therefore their days He consumed in futility,
And their years in fear.

³⁴When He slew them, then they sought Him;
And they returned and sought earnestly for
God.
³⁵Then they remembered that God *was* their
rock,
And the Most High God their Redeemer.
³⁶Nevertheless they flattered Him with their
mouth,
And they lied to Him with their tongue;
³⁷For their heart was not steadfast with Him,
Nor were they faithful in His covenant.
³⁸But He, *being* full of compassion, forgave *their*
iniquity,
And did not destroy *them*.
Yes, many a time He turned His anger away,
And did not stir up all His wrath;
³⁹For He remembered that they *were but* flesh,
A breath that passes away and does not come
again.

⁴⁰How often they provoked Him in the
wilderness,
And grieved Him in the desert!
⁴¹Yes, again and again they tempted God,
And limited the Holy One of Israel.
⁴²They did not remember His power:
The day when He redeemed them from the
enemy,
⁴³When He worked His signs in Egypt,
And His wonders in the field of Zoan;
⁴⁴Turned their rivers into blood,
And their streams, that they could not
drink.
⁴⁵He sent swarms of flies among them, which
devoured them,
And frogs, which destroyed them.
⁴⁶He also gave their crops to the caterpillar,
And their labor to the locust.
⁴⁷He destroyed their vines with hail,
And their sycamore trees with frost.
⁴⁸He also gave up their cattle to the hail,
And their flocks to fiery lightning.
⁴⁹He cast on them the fierceness of His anger,
Wrath, indignation, and trouble,
By sending angels of destruction *among them*.
⁵⁰He made a path for His anger;
He did not spare their soul from death,
But gave their life over to the plague,
⁵¹And destroyed all the firstborn in Egypt,
The first of *their* strength in the tents of Ham.

⁵²But He made His own people go forth like
sheep,
And guided them in the wilderness like a flock;
⁵³And He led them on safely, so that they did not
fear;
But the sea overwhelmed their enemies.
⁵⁴And He brought them to His holy border,
This mountain *which* His right hand had
acquired.
⁵⁵He also drove out the nations before them,
Allotted them an inheritance by survey,
And made the tribes of Israel dwell in their
tents.

⁵⁶Yet they tested and provoked the Most High
God,
And did not keep His testimonies,
⁵⁷But turned back and acted unfaithfully like
their fathers;
They were turned aside like a deceitful bow.
⁵⁸For they provoked Him to anger with their
high places,
And moved Him to jealousy with their carved
images.
⁵⁹When God heard *this,* He was furious,
And greatly abhorred Israel,
⁶⁰So that He forsook the tabernacle of Shiloh,
The tent He had placed among men,
⁶¹And delivered His strength into captivity,
And His glory into the enemy's hand.
⁶²He also gave His people over to the sword,
And was furious with His inheritance.
⁶³The fire consumed their young men,
And their maidens were not given in marriage.
⁶⁴Their priests fell by the sword,
And their widows made no lamentation.

⁶⁵Then the Lord awoke as *from* sleep,
Like a mighty man who shouts because of wine.
⁶⁶And He beat back His enemies;
He put them to a perpetual reproach.

⁶⁷Moreover He rejected the tent of Joseph,
And did not choose the tribe of Ephraim,
⁶⁸But chose the tribe of Judah,
Mount Zion which He loved.
⁶⁹And He built His sanctuary like the heights,
Like the earth which He has established
forever.
⁷⁰He also chose David His servant,
And took him from the sheepfolds;
⁷¹From following the ewes that had young He
brought him,

79:1–13 The destruction of Jerusalem is vivid in the psalmist's mind. The historical background behind this psalm is the Babylonian conquest of Jerusalem in 586 B.C. (see Ps. 74). Because the people believed Jerusalem would never be destroyed, the poet must have experienced difficulty comprehending the present reality (Jer. 7:33, 34). He wondered how long God would continue to reject His people (Ps. 79:5) and called on God to turn His anger toward the enemies of His people (v. 6) in order to vindicate His name (vv. 9, 10).

FAMILY WORSHIP

SHARING A SPIRITUAL HERITAGE

The home must provide a vital, living example of true Christianity. Children must be taught to talk to God about everything from major decisions in their lives to simply finding a parking space uptown (Matt. 18:19, 20). Faith must become a part of everyday life. Effective ways to do this are to have times of family prayer and Bible reading on a regular basis and to infuse faith into the routines of family life—gathering to sing hymns, playing Bible games, and engaging in discussions about the Lord, the Bible, and ways to apply Christian principles to life's everyday circumstances.

A spiritual heritage builds a wall of security and protection around the home. What a beautiful responsibility and privilege for women, as mothers and wives, to provide an atmosphere such as this for their loved ones (Prov. 31:18). The privilege of passing on that kind of spiritual heritage goes beyond the walls of the immediate family circle. The repercussions of a truly Christian home can be widespread and persist long after the initial influence. We remain faithful to God because He remains faithful to us (Ps. 89:1).

Family devotions do not have to be long and drawn out—just a simple Bible reading or a brief prayer. Reading Scripture and praying are important enough for Mommy and Daddy to keep on trying to instill them as a family habit, even if interruptions, failures, and minor disasters occasionally disrupt (Deut. 6:7).

Few Christian families spend time together in prayer and Bible reading. Yet what a priceless experience to have your parents share spiritual truths from the Word of God and to hear your mother or father asking God's blessing and protection on each person in the family. Finding the time, discovering the best formula, and being patient and persistent are all common challenges associated with family devotions. Strive to be consistent. Your children will develop a love for Scripture and a habitual reliance on the power of prayer. Every family heritage of faithfulness must begin with someone. Perhaps the beginning will be with you.

See also Ps. 16:3, 6; Dan. 2:23, note; notes on Family (Gen. 32; 1 Sam. 3; Ps. 78; 127); Inheritance (Prov. 13); Spiritual Discipline (2 Pet. 3); Traditions (1 Sam. 7)

To shepherd Jacob His people,
And Israel His inheritance.
⁷²So he shepherded them according to the
integrity of his heart,
And guided them by the skillfulness of his
hands.

PSALM 79

A Dirge and a Prayer for Israel, Destroyed by Enemies

A Psalm of Asaph.

¹O God, the nations have come into Your
inheritance;
Your holy temple they have defiled;
They have laid Jerusalem in heaps.
²The dead bodies of Your servants
They have given as food for the birds of the
heavens,
The flesh of Your saints to the beasts of the
earth.
³Their blood they have shed like water all
around Jerusalem,
And there was no one to bury them.
⁴We have become a reproach to our neighbors,
A scorn and derision to those who are
around us.

⁵How long, LORD?
Will You be angry forever?
Will Your jealousy burn like fire?
⁶Pour out Your wrath on the nations that do not
know You,

And on the kingdoms that do not call on Your
name.
⁷For they have devoured Jacob,
And laid waste his dwelling place.

⁸Oh, do not remember former iniquities against
us!
Let Your tender mercies come speedily to meet
us,
For we have been brought very low.
⁹Help us, O God of our salvation,
For the glory of Your name;
And deliver us, and provide atonement for our
sins,
For Your name's sake!
¹⁰Why should the nations say,
"Where is their God?"
Let there be known among the nations in our
sight
The avenging of the blood of Your servants
which has been shed.

¹¹Let the groaning of the prisoner come before
You;
According to the greatness of Your
power
Preserve those who are appointed to die;
¹²And return to our neighbors sevenfold into
their bosom
Their reproach with which they have
reproached You, O Lord.

¹³So we, Your people and sheep of Your pasture,
  Will give You thanks forever;
  We will show forth Your praise to all
    generations.

PSALM 80

Prayer for Israel's Restoration

To the Chief Musician. Set to "The Lilies."ᵃ A Testimonyᵇ of Asaph.
A Psalm.

¹Give ear, O Shepherd of Israel,
  You who lead Joseph like a flock;
  You who dwell *between* the cherubim, shine
    forth!
²Before Ephraim, Benjamin, and Manasseh,
  Stir up Your strength,
  And come *and* save us!

³Restore us, O God;
  Cause Your face to shine,
  And we shall be saved!

⁴O LORD God of hosts,
  How long will You be angry
  Against the prayer of Your people?
⁵You have fed them with the bread of tears,
  And given them tears to drink in great measure.
⁶You have made us a strife to our neighbors,
  And our enemies laugh among themselves.

⁷Restore us, O God of hosts;
  Cause Your face to shine,
  And we shall be saved!

⁸You have brought a vine out of Egypt;
  You have cast out the nations, and planted it.
⁹You prepared *room* for it,
  And caused it to take deep root,
  And it filled the land.
¹⁰The hills were covered with its shadow,
  And the mighty cedars with its boughs.
¹¹She sent out her boughs to the Sea,ᵃ
  And her branches to the River.ᵇ

¹²Why have You broken down her hedges,
  So that all who pass by the way pluck her *fruit?*
¹³The boar out of the woods uproots it,
  And the wild beast of the field devours it.

¹⁴Return, we beseech You, O God of hosts;
  Look down from heaven and see,
  And visit this vine
¹⁵And the vineyard which Your right hand has
    planted,
  And the branch *that* You made strong for
    Yourself.
¹⁶*It is* burned with fire, *it is* cut down;
  They perish at the rebuke of Your
    countenance.
¹⁷Let Your hand be upon the man of Your right
    hand,
  Upon the son of man *whom* You made strong
    for Yourself.
¹⁸Then we will not turn back from You;
  Revive us, and we will call upon Your name.

¹⁹Restore us, O LORD God of hosts;
  Cause Your face to shine,
  And we shall be saved!

PSALM 81

An Appeal for Israel's Repentance

To the Chief Musician. On an instrument of Gath.ᵃ
A Psalm of Asaph.

¹Sing aloud to God our strength;
  Make a joyful shout to the God of Jacob.
²Raise a song and strike the timbrel,
  The pleasant harp with the lute.

³Blow the trumpet at the time of the New
    Moon,
  At the full moon, on our solemn feast day.
⁴For this *is* a statute for Israel,
  A law of the God of Jacob.
⁵This He established in Joseph *as* a testimony,
  When He went throughout the land of Egypt,
  Where I heard a language I did not understand.

⁶"I removed his shoulder from the burden;
  His hands were freed from the baskets.
⁷You called in trouble, and I delivered you;
  I answered you in the secret place of thunder;
  I tested you at the waters of Meribah.   *Selah*

80:title ᵃHebrew *Shoshannim* ᵇHebrew *Eduth* **80:11** ᵃThat is, the
Mediterranean ᵇThat is, the Euphrates **81:title** ᵃHebrew *Al Gittith*

80:1–19 Presenting God as the Shepherd of His people reminds the reader of Psalm 23, in which the poet identified the Lord as his personal Shepherd. "Joseph" is a reference to the northern kingdom of Israel (Ps. 80:1). This psalm originated in a time of crisis when God's people were suffering at the hands of their enemies. God as Shepherd was called to care for and restore His people because they were dependent on Him. God's dwelling place was "between the cherubim" (see v. 1). God invisibly dwelt above the ark of the covenant (or ark of the Testimony; Ex. 25:10–22; see Ps. 99:1). The repeated plea

is reminiscent of the blessing of Aaron (Ps. 80:3, 7, 19; see also Num. 6:24–26). Israel's hope lay in the delivering presence of the Lord, who tenderly shepherds His flock.

81:1–7 The trumpet or ram's horn reminded the people of God's presence (Num. 10:10). This psalm was probably used in worship during the Feast of Booths or Tabernacles, the harvest festival in the fall of the year (Ex. 23:14–19; Deut. 16:13–17). The poem begins with a call to praise God by singing, shouting, and playing musical instruments (see chart, Musical Instruments of the Old Testament).

8"Hear, O My people, and I will admonish
you!
O Israel, if you will listen to Me!
9There shall be no foreign god among you;
Nor shall you worship any foreign god.
10I *am* the LORD your God,
Who brought you out of the land of Egypt;
Open your mouth wide, and I will fill it.

11"But My people would not heed My voice,
And Israel would *have* none of Me.
12So I gave them over to their own stubborn
heart,
To walk in their own counsels.

13"Oh, that My people would listen to Me,
That Israel would walk in My ways!
14I would soon subdue their enemies,
And turn My hand against their adversaries.
15The haters of the LORD would pretend
submission to Him,
But their fate would endure forever.
16He would have fed them also with the finest of
wheat;
And with honey from the rock I would have
satisfied you."

PSALM 82

A Plea for Justice

A Psalm of Asaph.

1God stands in the congregation of the
mighty;
He judges among the gods.ᵃ
2How long will you judge unjustly,
And show partiality to the wicked?   *Selah*
3Defend the poor and fatherless;
Do justice to the afflicted and needy.
4Deliver the poor and needy;
Free *them* from the hand of the wicked.

5They do not know, nor do they understand;
They walk about in darkness;
All the foundations of the earth are unstable.

6I said, "You *are* gods,ᵃ
And all of you *are* children of the Most High.
7But you shall die like men,
And fall like one of the princes."

8Arise, O God, judge the earth;
For You shall inherit all nations.

PSALM 83

Prayer to Frustrate Conspiracy Against Israel

A Song. A Psalm of Asaph.

1Do not keep silent, O God!
Do not hold Your peace,
And do not be still, O God!
2For behold, Your enemies make a tumult;
And those who hate You have lifted up their
head.
3They have taken crafty counsel against Your
people,
And consulted together against Your sheltered
ones.
4They have said, "Come, and let us cut them off
from *being* a nation,
That the name of Israel may be remembered
no more."

5For they have consulted together with one
consent;
They form a confederacy against You:
6The tents of Edom and the Ishmaelites;
Moab and the Hagrites;
7Gebal, Ammon, and Amalek;
Philistia with the inhabitants of Tyre;
8Assyria also has joined with them;
They have helped the children of Lot.   *Selah*

9Deal with them as *with* Midian,
As *with* Sisera,
As *with* Jabin at the Brook Kishon,
10Who perished at En Dor,
Who became *as* refuse on the earth.
11Make their nobles like Oreb and like Zeeb,
Yes, all their princes like Zebah and Zalmunna,
12Who said, "Let us take for ourselves
The pastures of God for a possession."

13O my God, make them like the whirling dust,
Like the chaff before the wind!
14As the fire burns the woods,
And as the flame sets the mountains on fire,
15So pursue them with Your tempest,
And frighten them with Your storm.
16Fill their faces with shame,
That they may seek Your name, O LORD.
17Let them be confounded and dismayed
forever;
Yes, let them be put to shame and perish,

82:1, 6 ᵃHebrew *elohim, mighty ones;* that is, the judges

81:8–16 The psalmist reminded the people of the importance of hearing and obeying God (v. 8). In the OT, hearing God's voice is usually associated with heeding His word. As a result of their disobedience, God's people missed His greatest blessings (v. 16).

82:1–8 The psalmist called on God to judge the earth (v. 8). The "gods" have been identified variously as angels, idols, and corrupt human judges (vv. 1, 6). These unjust judges received God's condemnation for showing partiality to the wicked and failing to see that justice was extended to the helpless in society.

18That they may know that You, whose name
　　alone *is* the LORD,
Are the Most High over all the earth.

PSALM 84

The Blessedness of Dwelling in the House of God
To the Chief Musician. On an instrument of Gath.ᵃ
A Psalm of the sons of Korah.

1How lovely *is* Your tabernacle,
　O LORD of hosts!
2My soul longs, yes, even faints
　For the courts of the LORD;
　My heart and my flesh cry out for the living
　　God.

3Even the sparrow has found a home,
　And the swallow a nest for herself,
　Where she may lay her young—
　Even Your altars, O LORD of hosts,
　My King and my God.
4Blessed *are* those who dwell in Your house;
　They will still be praising You.　　　*Selah*

5Blessed *is* the man whose strength *is* in You,
　Whose heart *is* set on pilgrimage.
6*As they* pass through the Valley of Baca,
　They make it a spring;
　The rain also covers it with pools.
7They go from strength to strength;
　Each one appears before God in Zion.ᵃ

8O LORD God of hosts, hear my prayer;
　Give ear, O God of Jacob!　　　*Selah*
9O God, behold our shield,
　And look upon the face of Your anointed.

10For a day in Your courts *is* better than a
　　thousand.
　I would rather be a doorkeeper in the house of
　　my God
　Than dwell in the tents of wickedness.
11For the LORD God *is* a sun and shield;
　The LORD will give grace and glory;
　No good *thing* will He withhold
　From those who walk uprightly.

12O LORD of hosts,
　Blessed *is* the man who trusts in You!

PSALM 85

Prayer that the LORD Will Restore Favor to the Land
To the Chief Musician. A Psalm of the sons of Korah.

1LORD, You have been favorable to Your land;
　You have brought back the captivity of Jacob.
2You have forgiven the iniquity of Your people;
　You have covered all their sin.　　　*Selah*
3You have taken away all Your wrath;
　You have turned from the fierceness of Your
　　anger.

4Restore us, O God of our salvation,
　And cause Your anger toward us to cease.
5Will You be angry with us forever?
　Will You prolong Your anger to all generations?
6Will You not revive us again,
　That Your people may rejoice in You?
7Show us Your mercy, LORD,
　And grant us Your salvation.

8I will hear what God the LORD will speak,
　For He will speak peace
　To His people and to His saints;
　But let them not turn back to folly.
9Surely His salvation *is* near to those who fear
　　Him,
　That glory may dwell in our land.

10Mercy and truth have met together;
　Righteousness and peace have kissed.
11Truth shall spring out of the earth,
　And righteousness shall look down from
　　heaven.
12Yes, the LORD will give *what is* good;
　And our land will yield its increase.
13Righteousness will go before Him,
　And shall make His footsteps *our* pathway.

PSALM 86

Prayer for Mercy, with Meditation on the Excellencies of the LORD
A Prayer of David.

1Bow down Your ear, O LORD, hear me;
　For I *am* poor and needy.

84:title ᵃHebrew *Al Gittith*　**84:7** ᵃSeptuagint, Syriac, and Vulgate read *The God of gods shall be seen.*

84:1–4 This psalm celebrates the beauty of God's dwelling place. The poet's "soul," that is, his whole being, longed to bask in the blessing of God's presence (v. 2). The feeling of belonging that derives from being in God's presence brings great joy and satisfaction.
84:5–9 Those who make the pilgrimage to the temple for worship find joy. The woman who depends on God for strength has resources on which to rely in life's difficult pilgrimage. She continually experiences renewal and refreshment because God is with her. Zion is Jerusalem (v. 7).

85:4–7 God's people requested that He graciously restore them, just as He had done in the past. Calamities were viewed as a sign of God's anger because of sin; mercy and salvation were needed. God's people still need the revival that comes from a fresh encounter with the living Lord.
86:1–7 A personal prayer for deliverance. The poet began with a plea for the Lord to "bow down" (lit. "bend") His ear toward him. He identified himself as both godly and in need of help. The Lord is "my God," and the psalmist is "Your servant who trusts in You." Because the Lord is good, forgiving,

FRUIT OF THE SPIRIT   LONGSUFFERING

Longsuffering encompasses patience, endurance, steadfastness, and forbearance. It is an active response to opposition, not a passive resignation to the inevitable. An important word in both Hebrew and Greek, "longsuffering" is an attribute of God (Ps. 86:15), a fruit of the Holy Spirit (Gal. 5:22), and an attitude all women should reflect (1 Cor. 13:4).

The apostle Paul prayed that his Colossian friends might possess patience and longsuffering as well as joy (Col. 1:9–12). Patience (Gk. *hupomone*, lit. "bearing up under") is getting under a burden or affliction and turning it into glory. This word for patience is most often applied to people. God's people are to be patient with others, especially when facing adversity (Rom. 5:3–5). Patience is a characteristic of true love (1 Cor. 13:4, 7).

"Longsuffering" (Gk. *makrothumia*) is a quality most often applied to God. Its root means to "put fury far off while suffering wrong or injustice." Only God can be completely longsuffering. He alone is "slow to anger" (Ps. 86:15; Joel 2:13). However, Christians can become longsuffering through the power of the Holy Spirit. Believers who walk in the Spirit develop a longsuffering attitude that no circumstance can destroy and patience that no person can defeat (Eph. 4:1–3).

See also Ps. 130:5, 6; Is. 40:31; Lam. 3:25, 26; Col. 3:12; 2 Pet. 3:15; notes on Anger (Eccl. 7); Attributes of God (Rom. 2); Fruit of the Spirit (Rom. 5; 15; 1 Cor. 10; 13; Gal. 5; Eph. 4; Col. 3; 2 Thess. 1; Rev. 2); Suffering (Ps. 33; 113; Is. 43; 1 Pet. 5); Testing (Ps. 12)

²Preserve my life, for I *am* holy;
You are my God;
Save Your servant who trusts in You!
³Be merciful to me, O Lord,
For I cry to You all day long.
⁴Rejoice the soul of Your servant,
For to You, O Lord, I lift up my soul.
⁵For You, Lord, *are* good, and ready to forgive,
And abundant in mercy to all those who call
upon You.

⁶Give ear, O LORD, to my prayer;
And attend to the voice of my supplications.
⁷In the day of my trouble I will call upon You,
For You will answer me.

⁸Among the gods *there is* none like You, O Lord;
Nor *are there any works* like Your works.
⁹All nations whom You have made
Shall come and worship before You, O Lord,
And shall glorify Your name.
¹⁰For You *are* great, and do wondrous things;
You alone *are* God.

¹¹Teach me Your way, O LORD;
I will walk in Your truth;
Unite my heart to fear Your name.
¹²I will praise You, O Lord my God, with all my
heart,
And I will glorify Your name forevermore.
¹³For great *is* Your mercy toward me,

And You have delivered my soul from the
depths of Sheol.

¹⁴O God, the proud have risen against me,
And a mob of violent *men* have sought my
life,
And have not set You before them.
¹⁵But You, O Lord, *are* a God full of compassion,
and gracious,
Longsuffering and abundant in mercy and
truth.

¹⁶Oh, turn to me, and have mercy on me!
Give Your strength to Your servant,
And save the son of Your maidservant.
¹⁷Show me a sign for good,
That those who hate me may see *it* and be
ashamed,
Because You, LORD, have helped me and
comforted me.

PSALM 87

The Glories of the City of God
A Psalm of the sons of Korah. A Song.

¹His foundation *is* in the holy mountains.
²The LORD loves the gates of Zion
More than all the dwellings of Jacob.
³Glorious things are spoken of you,
O city of God!   *Selah*

and merciful (Heb. *chesed*: see Ps. 5:7–12, note), the psalmist was assured that God would answer his cry in the day of trouble.

86:11–13 God's law is His instruction to us regarding how to live. "Teach" (lit. "to throw" or "to shoot") is related to the Hebrew

Torah (lit. "law," "direction," or "instruction"). To "walk" in truth refers to a lifestyle of commitment to the Lord, and to "fear" God's name indicates reverent obedience to Him (v. 11).

87:1–4 This psalm praises Jerusalem, the city of God, the spiritual center of the world (see Ps. 137:3–5). "Jacob" is an alter-

⁴"I will make mention of Rahab and Babylon to
those who know Me;
Behold, O Philistia and Tyre, with Ethiopia:
'This *one* was born there.'"

⁵And of Zion it will be said,
"This *one* and that *one* were born in her;
And the Most High Himself shall establish
her."
⁶The LORD will record,
When He registers the peoples:
"This *one* was born there."   *Selah*

⁷Both the singers and the players on
instruments *say,*
"All my springs *are* in you."

PSALM 88

A Prayer for Help in Despondency

A Song. A Psalm of the sons of Korah. To the Chief Musician. Set to
"Mahalath Leannoth." A Contemplation^a of Heman the Ezrahite.

¹O LORD, God of my salvation,
I have cried out day and night before You.
²Let my prayer come before You;
Incline Your ear to my cry.

³For my soul is full of troubles,
And my life draws near to the grave.
⁴I am counted with those who go down to the pit;
I am like a man *who has* no strength,
⁵Adrift among the dead,
Like the slain who lie in the grave,
Whom You remember no more,
And who are cut off from Your hand.

⁶You have laid me in the lowest pit,
In darkness, in the depths.
⁷Your wrath lies heavy upon me,
And You have afflicted *me* with all Your waves.
                                              Selah
⁸You have put away my acquaintances far from
me;
You have made me an abomination to them;
I am shut up, and I cannot get out;
⁹My eye wastes away because of affliction.

LORD, I have called daily upon You;
I have stretched out my hands to You.

¹⁰Will You work wonders for the dead?
Shall the dead arise *and* praise You?   *Selah*
¹¹Shall Your lovingkindness be declared in the
grave?
Or Your faithfulness in the place of
destruction?
¹²Shall Your wonders be known in the dark?
And Your righteousness in the land of
forgetfulness?

¹³But to You I have cried out, O LORD,
And in the morning my prayer comes before
You.
¹⁴LORD, why do You cast off my soul?
Why do You hide Your face from me?
¹⁵I *have been* afflicted and ready to die from *my*
youth;
I suffer Your terrors;
I am distraught.
¹⁶Your fierce wrath has gone over me;
Your terrors have cut me off.
¹⁷They came around me all day long like
water;
They engulfed me altogether.
¹⁸Loved one and friend You have put far from
me,
And my acquaintances into darkness.

PSALM 89

*Remembering the Covenant with David, and Sorrow
for Lost Blessings*

A Contemplation^a of Ethan the Ezrahite.

¹I will sing of the mercies of the LORD
forever;
With my mouth will I make known Your
faithfulness to all generations.
²For I have said, "Mercy shall be built up
forever;
Your faithfulness You shall establish in the
very heavens."

³"I have made a covenant with My chosen,
I have sworn to My servant David:
⁴'Your seed I will establish forever,
And build up your throne to all generations.'"
                                              Selah

88:title; 89:title ^aHebrew *Maschil*

---

nate name for Israel (Ps. 87:2). God is the God of all nations,
not just Israel (v. 4). "Rahab" refers to Egypt (v. 4; see Is.
30:7).

88:1–18 This psalm reflects the intense sadness and gloom of
a despondent poet with no echoes of deliverance or hope.
This poet had prayed constantly but had experienced no deliverance (v. 1). He felt that death was near (v. 3). Yet faith is
evident in the fact that the poet continued to cry out to the
Lord.

89:1–52 This royal psalm relates to a time of national crisis
(see chart, The Types of Psalms). A major theme of the psalm
is the Lord's covenant with David in the past as hope for present deliverance (2 Sam. 7:1–17). Note the repeated appeals to
God's "mercy" (Heb. *chesed,* Ps. 89:1, 2, 14, 24, 28; "lovingkindness" vv. 33, 49; see Ps. 5:7–12, note) and "faithfulness" (Ps. 89:1, 2, 5, 8, 24, 33, 37; lit "steadfastness," "fidelity") in this time of calamity (vv. 38–45). The doxology of
verse 52 marks the end of Book III of the Psalms (see Introduction: Outline).

5And the heavens will praise Your wonders,
O Lord;
Your faithfulness also in the assembly of the
saints.
6For who in the heavens can be compared to the
Lord?
Who among the sons of the mighty can be
likened to the Lord?
7God is greatly to be feared in the assembly of
the saints,
And to be held in reverence by all *those* around
Him.
8O Lord God of hosts,
Who *is* mighty like You, O Lord?
Your faithfulness also surrounds You.
9You rule the raging of the sea;
When its waves rise, You still them.
10You have broken Rahab in pieces, as one who is
slain;
You have scattered Your enemies with Your
mighty arm.

11The heavens *are* Yours, the earth also *is* Yours;
The world and all its fullness, You have
founded them.
12The north and the south, You have created
them;
Tabor and Hermon rejoice in Your name.
13You have a mighty arm;
Strong is Your hand, *and* high is Your right
hand.
14Righteousness and justice *are* the foundation
of Your throne;
Mercy and truth go before Your face.
15Blessed *are* the people who know the joyful
sound!
They walk, O Lord, in the light of Your
countenance.
16In Your name they rejoice all day long,
And in Your righteousness they are exalted.
17For You *are* the glory of their strength,
And in Your favor our horn is exalted.
18For our shield *belongs* to the Lord,
And our king to the Holy One of Israel.

19Then You spoke in a vision to Your holy
one,[a]
And said: "I have given help to *one who is*
mighty;
I have exalted one chosen from the people.
20I have found My servant David;
With My holy oil I have anointed him,
21With whom My hand shall be established;
Also My arm shall strengthen him.
22The enemy shall not outwit him,
Nor the son of wickedness afflict him.
23I will beat down his foes before his face,
And plague those who hate him.

24"But My faithfulness and My mercy *shall be* with
him,
And in My name his horn shall be exalted.
25Also I will set his hand over the sea,
And his right hand over the rivers.
26He shall cry to Me, 'You *are* my Father,
My God, and the rock of my salvation.'
27Also I will make him *My* firstborn,
The highest of the kings of the earth.
28My mercy I will keep for him forever,
And My covenant shall stand firm with him.
29His seed also I will make *to endure* forever,
And his throne as the days of heaven.

30"If his sons forsake My law
And do not walk in My judgments,
31If they break My statutes
And do not keep My commandments,
32Then I will punish their transgression with the
rod,
And their iniquity with stripes.
33Nevertheless My lovingkindness I will not
utterly take from him,
Nor allow My faithfulness to fail.
34My covenant I will not break,
Nor alter the word that has gone out of My
lips.
35Once I have sworn by My holiness;
I will not lie to David:
36His seed shall endure forever,
And his throne as the sun before Me;
37It shall be established forever like the moon,
Even *like* the faithful witness in the sky." *Selah*

38But You have cast off and abhorred,
You have been furious with Your anointed.
39You have renounced the covenant of Your
servant;
You have profaned his crown *by casting it* to the
ground.
40You have broken down all his hedges;
You have brought his strongholds to ruin.
41All who pass by the way plunder him;
He is a reproach to his neighbors.
42You have exalted the right hand of his
adversaries;
You have made all his enemies rejoice.
43You have also turned back the edge of his
sword,
And have not sustained him in the battle.
44You have made his glory cease,
And cast his throne down to the ground.
45The days of his youth You have shortened;
You have covered him with shame. *Selah*

·····················
89:19 [a]Following many Hebrew manuscripts; Masoretic Text,
Septuagint, Targum, and Vulgate read *holy ones.*

MUSICAL INSTRUMENTS OF THE OLD TESTAMENT

CATEGORY	BIBLICAL INSTRUMENT	MODERN EQUIVALENT	SCRIPTURE REFERENCES
PERCUSSION an instrument sounded by striking, shaking, or scraping	Cymbals	Cymbals	2 Sam. 6:5; 2 Chr. 5:12, 13; Ps. 150:5
	Sistrum	Rattlers	2 Sam. 6:5
	Tambourines	Tambourines	2 Sam. 6:5; Job 21:12; Is. 5:12; 24:8
	Timbrels	Timbrels	Gen. 31:27; Ex. 15:20; Judg. 11:34; Ps. 81:2; 150:4
STRING an instrument played by strumming or stroking with a bow	Harp	Harp	Gen. 4:21; 1 Sam. 16:16; Ps. 33:2; 98:5; Is. 5:12
	Lute	Lute	Ps. 71:22; 92:3
	Lyre	Lyre	Dan. 3:5, 7, 10, 15
	Psaltery	Zither	Dan. 3:5, 10, 15
	Stringed instruments	Violin or any of the above	Ps. 150:5; Is. 14:11; Amos 5:23
WIND an instrument sounded by blowing air	Flute	Flute	Gen. 4:21; Job 21:12; Ps. 150:4; Dan. 3:5
	Horn	Cornet	1 Kin. 1:34; Dan. 3:5, 7, 10, 15
	Trumpet	Trumpet	Num. 10:2–10; Judg. 3:27; 6:34; 2 Chr. 5:12, 13; Neh. 4:18, 20

⁴⁶How long, LORD?
 Will You hide Yourself forever?
 Will Your wrath burn like fire?
⁴⁷Remember how short my time is;
 For what futility have You created all the
  children of men?
⁴⁸What man can live and not see death?
 Can he deliver his life from the power of the
  grave? *Selah*

⁴⁹Lord, where *are* Your former lovingkindnesses,
 Which You swore to David in Your truth?
⁵⁰Remember, Lord, the reproach of Your
  servants—
 How I bear in my bosom *the reproach of* all the
  many peoples,
⁵¹With which Your enemies have reproached,
  O LORD,
 With which they have reproached the footsteps
  of Your anointed.

⁵²Blessed *be* the LORD forevermore!
 Amen and Amen.

Book Four: Psalms 90—106

PSALM 90

The Eternity of God, and Man's Frailty
A Prayer of Moses the man of God.

¹Lord, You have been our dwelling place[a] in all
  generations.
²Before the mountains were brought forth,
 Or ever You had formed the earth and the
  world,
 Even from everlasting to everlasting, You *are*
  God.

³You turn man to destruction,
 And say, "Return, O children of men."
⁴For a thousand years in Your sight
 Are like yesterday when it is past,
 And *like* a watch in the night.
⁵You carry them away *like* a flood;
 They are like a sleep.

90:1 ᵃSeptuagint, Targum, and Vulgate read *refuge.*

90:1–17 God is eternal. This poem marks the beginning of Book IV and is the only psalm associated with Moses (see Introduction: Outline). The poet contrasted the nature of God with the nature of humanity. God is from everlasting to ever-lasting (v. 2), while the brevity of human life is compared to a flood, a dream, and grass (vv. 5, 6). Only faith in the eternal God can make life meaningful (vv. 13–17).

ATTRIBUTES OF GOD   *HE IS ETERNAL*

God has no beginning and no ending. He is the only self-existent Being. He existed before time and creation began (Ps. 90:2). Everything about God is "always" (Ps. 102:12). He had no youth, has no age, and will never be a senior citizen (Heb. 1:10–12). "Everlasting" is not the same as "long-lasting," which suggests a beginning and demands dealing with time and eternity. Time dwells within God. He causes, affects, and controls it, but time has no hold on Him (Ps. 90:4–6).

God's attributes bask in His eternality. Since eternity neither wears out nor runs out, neither do His attributes (Is. 40:25–28). God describes His love as "everlasting" (Jer. 31:3).

Eternity is God's signature—it is who He is (Is. 63:16). His name, "I Am," expresses clearly His unconditional and independent existence and encompasses the idea of His continuous presence (Ex. 3:14) because He simply "is." Unlike His creatures who are bound by time with life that is brief and fleeting, the Creator is eternal. Everything in existence is dependent on Him (Col. 1:15–17).

See also Gen. 21:33; Is. 9:6; 43:10, 11; 57:15; Jer. 10:10; Lam. 3:22, note; notes on Attributes of God (Ex. 33; Deut. 4; 32; 2 Chr. 19; Job 23; 42; Ps. 25; 102; 119; Is. 6; 65; Jer. 23; Rom. 2; Eph. 1; 1 John 5); Heaven (2 Tim. 4)

In the morning they are like grass *which* grows
  up:
6In the morning it flourishes and grows up;
In the evening it is cut down and withers.

7For we have been consumed by Your anger,
  And by Your wrath we are terrified.
8You have set our iniquities before You,
  Our secret *sins* in the light of Your
    countenance.
9For all our days have passed away in Your
    wrath;
  We finish our years like a sigh.
10The days of our lives *are* seventy years;
  And if by reason of strength *they are* eighty
    years,
  Yet their boast *is* only labor and sorrow;
  For it is soon cut off, and we fly away.
11Who knows the power of Your anger?
  For as the fear of You, *so is* Your wrath.
12So teach *us* to number our days,
  That we may gain a heart of wisdom.

13Return, O LORD!
  How long?
  And have compassion on Your servants.
14Oh, satisfy us early with Your mercy,
  That we may rejoice and be glad all our days!
15Make us glad according to the days *in which*
    You have afflicted us,
  The years *in which* we have seen evil.
16Let Your work appear to Your servants,
  And Your glory to their children.
17And let the beauty of the LORD our God be
  upon us,

And establish the work of our hands for us;
Yes, establish the work of our hands.

PSALM 91

Safety of Abiding in the Presence of God
1He who dwells in the secret place of the Most
  High
Shall abide under the shadow of the Almighty.
2I will say of the LORD, "*He is* my refuge and my
    fortress;
  My God, in Him I will trust."

3Surely He shall deliver you from the snare of
    the fowler[a]
  And from the perilous pestilence.
4He shall cover you with His feathers,
  And under His wings you shall take refuge;
  His truth *shall be your* shield and buckler.
5You shall not be afraid of the terror by night,
  Nor of the arrow *that* flies by day,
6*Nor* of the pestilence *that* walks in darkness,
  Nor of the destruction *that* lays waste at
    noonday.

7A thousand may fall at your side,
  And ten thousand at your right hand;
  But it shall not come near you.
8Only with your eyes shall you look,
  And see the reward of the wicked.

9Because you have made the LORD, *who is* my
    refuge,
  Even the Most High, your dwelling place,

91:3 [a] That is, one who catches birds in a trap or snare

91:1–16 Those who trust in the Lord experience His protection. The poet builds image upon image to express the security found in a relationship with the Lord. The Lord is the "Most High" and "Almighty," a "refuge" and a "fortress" (vv. 1, 2). He delivers His people from the trap and protects His own from pestilence (v. 3). The imagery is that of a mother bird protecting her young under her wings (v. 4; see Matt. 23:37). Nothing can match the security of knowing we are safe in the arms of God! Psalm 91:11 and 12 were misused by Satan when Jesus was tempted in the wilderness (see Matt. 4:6; Luke 4:10, 11).

Without the burden of afflictions it is impossible to reach the height of grace.
The gifts of grace increase as the struggles increase.

St. Rose of Lima

---

¹⁰No evil shall befall you,
  Nor shall any plague come near your dwelling;
¹¹For He shall give His angels charge over you,
  To keep you in all your ways.
¹²In *their* hands they shall bear you up,
  Lest you dash your foot against a stone.
¹³You shall tread upon the lion and the cobra,
  The young lion and the serpent you shall
    trample underfoot.

¹⁴"Because he has set his love upon Me, therefore
    I will deliver him;
  I will set him on high, because he has known
    My name.
¹⁵He shall call upon Me, and I will answer him;
  I *will be* with him in trouble;
  I will deliver him and honor him.
¹⁶With long life I will satisfy him,
  And show him My salvation."

PSALM 92

Praise to the LORD for His Love and Faithfulness
A Psalm. A Song for the Sabbath day.

¹*It is* good to give thanks to the LORD,
  And to sing praises to Your name, O Most
    High;
²To declare Your lovingkindness in the
    morning,
  And Your faithfulness every night,
³On an instrument of ten strings,
  On the lute,
  And on the harp,
  With harmonious sound.
⁴For You, LORD, have made me glad through
    Your work;
  I will triumph in the works of Your hands.

⁵O LORD, how great are Your works!
  Your thoughts are very deep.
⁶A senseless man does not know,
  Nor does a fool understand this.
⁷When the wicked spring up like grass,
  And when all the workers of iniquity flourish,
  It is that they may be destroyed forever.

⁸But You, LORD, *are* on high forevermore.
⁹For behold, Your enemies, O LORD,

For behold, Your enemies shall perish;
  All the workers of iniquity shall be scattered.

¹⁰But my horn You have exalted like a wild ox;
  I have been anointed with fresh oil.
¹¹My eye also has seen *my desire* on my enemies;
  My ears hear *my desire* on the wicked
  Who rise up against me.

¹²The righteous shall flourish like a palm
    tree,
  He shall grow like a cedar in Lebanon.
¹³Those who are planted in the house of the
    LORD
  Shall flourish in the courts of our God.
¹⁴They shall still bear fruit in old age;
  They shall be fresh and flourishing,
¹⁵To declare that the LORD is upright;
  He is my rock, and *there is* no unrighteousness
    in Him.

PSALM 93

The Eternal Reign of the LORD
¹The LORD reigns, He is clothed with majesty;
  The LORD is clothed,
  He has girded Himself with strength.
  Surely the world is established, so that it
    cannot be moved.
²Your throne *is* established from of old;
  You *are* from everlasting.

³The floods have lifted up, O LORD,
  The floods have lifted up their voice;
  The floods lift up their waves.
⁴The LORD on high *is* mightier
  Than the noise of many waters,
  Than the mighty waves of the sea.

⁵Your testimonies are very sure;
  Holiness adorns Your house,
  O LORD, forever.

PSALM 94

God the Refuge of the Righteous
¹O LORD God, to whom vengeance belongs—
  O God, to whom vengeance belongs, shine
    forth!
²Rise up, O Judge of the earth;

93:1, 2 The Lord reigns. This enthronement psalm celebrates the eternal reign of the Lord and was used in Israel's worship (see Ps. 97; 99; chart, The Types of Psalms). The majestic Lord is affirmed as sovereign over all His creation and King forever. These enthronement psalms played a significant role in Israel's worship in affirming the truth that God is in control.

ATTRIBUTES OF GOD   *HE IS MERCIFUL*

Mercy differs from grace in that grace gives what is not deserved, while mercy does not give what is deserved. Mercy is compassion in action toward sinners who have no claim or right to receive such treatment. "Deserving mercy" is a contradictory term (Eph. 2:4–9).

Mercy is only for sinners. Angels do not experience it; they do not need it. Mercy is God's idea (2 Cor. 1:3). It is available to everyone, but only through Christ's sacrifice on the Cross.

God's mercy is great (1 Kin. 3:6), tender (Luke 1:78), abundant (1 Pet. 1:3), and everlasting (Ps. 103:17). Mercy is interwoven with all other attributes of God. His lovingkindness initiates mercy (Eph. 2:4–7); His holiness insures its integrity (Ex. 34:6, 7); His truth guarantees its reliability (Is. 16:5); His power assures its duration (Ps. 89:2); and His faithfulness demands its constancy (Ps. 36:5).

The results of mercy are forgiveness (Is. 55:7), restoration (Ps 51:2, 10, 11), and praise on the part of those who experience mercy (Ps. 89:1).

See also Deut. 4:31; Ps. 86:15; 103:8, 11; Lam. 3:22, note; Titus 3:5; notes on Attributes of God (Ex. 33; Deut. 4; 32; 2 Chr. 19; Job 23; 42; Ps. 25; 90; 102; 119; Is. 6; 65; Jer. 23; Rom. 2; Eph. 1; 1 John 5); Access to God (Rom. 10); Forgiveness (Ps. 51; Luke 17); Guilt (2 Cor. 7); Heaven (2 Tim. 4); Promises of God (2 Pet. 1)

Render punishment to the proud.
³LORD, how long will the wicked,
How long will the wicked triumph?

⁴They utter speech, *and* speak insolent things;
All the workers of iniquity boast in themselves.
⁵They break in pieces Your people, O LORD,
And afflict Your heritage.
⁶They slay the widow and the stranger,
And murder the fatherless.
⁷Yet they say, "The LORD does not see,
Nor does the God of Jacob understand."

⁸Understand, you senseless among the people;
And *you* fools, when will you be wise?
⁹He who planted the ear, shall He not hear?
He who formed the eye, shall He not see?
¹⁰He who instructs the nations, shall He not correct,
He who teaches man knowledge?
¹¹The LORD knows the thoughts of man,
That they *are* futile.

¹²Blessed *is* the man whom You instruct, O LORD,
And teach out of Your law,
¹³That You may give him rest from the days of adversity,
Until the pit is dug for the wicked.
¹⁴For the LORD will not cast off His people,
Nor will He forsake His inheritance.
¹⁵But judgment will return to righteousness,
And all the upright in heart will follow it.

¹⁶Who will rise up for me against the evildoers?
Who will stand up for me against the workers of iniquity?
¹⁷Unless the LORD *had been* my help,
My soul would soon have settled in silence.
¹⁸If I say, "My foot slips,"
Your mercy, O LORD, will hold me up.
¹⁹In the multitude of my anxieties within me,
Your comforts delight my soul.

²⁰Shall the throne of iniquity, which devises evil by law,
Have fellowship with You?
²¹They gather together against the life of the righteous,
And condemn innocent blood.
²²But the LORD has been my defense,
And my God the rock of my refuge.
²³He has brought on them their own iniquity,
And shall cut them off in their own wickedness;
The LORD our God shall cut them off.

PSALM 95

A Call to Worship and Obedience

¹Oh come, let us sing to the LORD!
Let us shout joyfully to the Rock of our salvation.
²Let us come before His presence with thanksgiving;
Let us shout joyfully to Him with psalms.
³For the LORD *is* the great God,
And the great King above all gods.
⁴In His hand *are* the deep places of the earth;

95:6–11 God is worthy of worship because He is the Creator of all people (vv. 6, 7; 100:3). We worship Him who made us in His image. The proof of genuine worship is faithful obedience. The poet urged the current generation not to live in rebellion as their fathers had (Ps. 95:8–11). Just as Israel failed to enter the Promised Land due to lack of faith (v. 11), God's people have often failed to enter into the "restful" joy of fellowship with Him because of their lack of trust (Heb. 3:7–19; 4:3, 5, 7).

The heights of the hills *are* His also.
5The sea *is* His, for He made it;
And His hands formed the dry *land.*

6Oh come, let us worship and bow down;
Let us kneel before the LORD our Maker.
7For He *is* our God,
And we *are* the people of His pasture,
And the sheep of His hand.

Today, if you will hear His voice:
8"Do not harden your hearts, as in the rebellion,[a]
As *in* the day of trial[b] in the wilderness,
9When your fathers tested Me;
They tried Me, though they saw My work.
10For forty years I was grieved with *that* generation,
And said, 'It *is* a people who go astray in their hearts,
And they do not know My ways.'
11So I swore in My wrath,
'They shall not enter My rest.' "

PSALM 96

A Song of Praise to God Coming in Judgment
1Oh, sing to the LORD a new song!
Sing to the LORD, all the earth.
2Sing to the LORD, bless His name;
Proclaim the good news of His salvation from day to day.
3Declare His glory among the nations,
His wonders among all peoples.

4For the LORD *is* great and greatly to be praised;
He *is* to be feared above all gods.
5For all the gods of the peoples *are* idols,
But the LORD made the heavens.
6Honor and majesty *are* before Him;
Strength and beauty *are* in His sanctuary.

7Give to the LORD, O families of the peoples,
Give to the LORD glory and strength.
8Give to the LORD the glory *due* His name;
Bring an offering, and come into His courts.
9Oh, worship the LORD in the beauty of holiness!
Tremble before Him, all the earth.

10Say among the nations, "The LORD reigns;
The world also is firmly established,
It shall not be moved;
He shall judge the peoples righteously."

11Let the heavens rejoice, and let the earth be glad;
Let the sea roar, and all its fullness;
12Let the field be joyful, and all that *is* in it.
Then all the trees of the woods will rejoice before the LORD.
13For He is coming, for He is coming to judge the earth.
He shall judge the world with righteousness,
And the peoples with His truth.

PSALM 97

A Song of Praise to the Sovereign LORD
1The LORD reigns;
Let the earth rejoice;
Let the multitude of isles be glad!

2Clouds and darkness surround Him;
Righteousness and justice *are* the foundation of His throne.
3A fire goes before Him,
And burns up His enemies round about.
4His lightnings light the world;
The earth sees and trembles.
5The mountains melt like wax at the presence of the LORD,
At the presence of the Lord of the whole earth.
6The heavens declare His righteousness,
And all the peoples see His glory.

7Let all be put to shame who serve carved images,
Who boast of idols.
Worship Him, all *you* gods.
8Zion hears and is glad,
And the daughters of Judah rejoice
Because of Your judgments, O LORD.
9For You, LORD, *are* most high above all the earth;
You are exalted far above all gods.

10You who love the LORD, hate evil!
He preserves the souls of His saints;
He delivers them out of the hand of the wicked.
11Light is sown for the righteous,
And gladness for the upright in heart.
12Rejoice in the LORD, you righteous,

95:8 [a]Or *Meribah* [b]Or *Massah*

96:1–13 Worshipers are called to sing a new song to the Lord who is exalted above all gods (vv. 4, 5; 1 Chr. 16:23–33). Other gods are mere idols, but the Lord is the Creator. Therefore, all people are to worship the Lord, give to Him the honor due His name, and bring to Him their offerings (Ps. 96:7–9). They are to proclaim the universal rule of the righteous Judge among the nations (v. 10).

97:1–6 This enthronement psalm celebrates God's universal rule as King (see Ps. 93; 99). God has revealed Himself in majesty with clouds, darkness, fire, lightnings, and earth tremors (Ps. 97:2–4; see Ex. 19:16–18). All creation reveals the awesome mystery of His presence (Ps. 97:6; Ps. 19:1).

GRATITUDE *A THANKFUL SPIRIT*

Gratitude begins by acknowledging who God is and what He has done. This heartfelt emotion is not dependent on the response of another person or on the nature of what is received as a gift. Ingratitude, on the other hand, begins with a heart that refuses to be satisfied, that rejects the Giver as well as His gift (Rom. 1:21).

Life itself is a gracious gift from God. There is no gratitude except what is built on this foundation. A spirit of gratitude must be cultivated, then passed on to others, especially to those in your own household, by example. These are some ways to accomplish this:

- Remember that a grateful person is humble and focused on God, while the ungrateful heart is full of pride and focused on self. Ruth beautifully emulated such a spirit of gratitude and humility (Ruth 2:10). She responded graciously even to the smallest kindness.
- Do not take for granted the small and ordinary daily blessings (Matt. 6:11).
- Look for blessings from God, being careful not to overlook the hidden, subtle, indirect gifts from God (Col. 4:2). Recognize that not every gift you desire may be beneficial to you. God is the all-wise Giver. Consider His plan and priorities for your life, being careful not to lose sight of the big picture because of a tragic but small interruption.
- Remember to thank God even in the midst of adversity and trials (Hab. 3:17–19; 1 Cor. 10:31; Phil. 1:3; 2:14; 1 Thess. 5:18).
- Gratitude to God and others should be expressed not only regularly but also publicly (Ps. 35:18; John 11:41, 42). Family members and close friends should not be taken for granted.
- Record your blessings and keep a record of God's faithfulness to you.
- Complete the cycle of gratitude by reaching out to give to others in the Spirit of Christ (2 Cor. 9:12).

A grateful spirit and thankful heart are an integral part of the holy life. The woman who is thankful and has a heart full of praise brings joy to the Father and glory to His name. An attitude of gratitude will bring to your heart a host of blessings and make you a channel of blessing to others.

See also 2 Cor. 2:14; 9:15; Phil. 4:6; Col. 3:15; notes on Blessings (Gen. 12); Fruit of the Spirit (Ps. 86; Rom. 5; 15; 1 Cor. 10; 13; Gal. 5; Eph. 4; Col. 3; 2 Thess. 1; Rev. 2); Giving (2 Cor. 9); Graciousness (Prov. 11); Prosperity (Ps. 2); Stewardship (Luke 16)

And give thanks at the remembrance of His
    holy name.[a]

PSALM 98

A Song of Praise to the LORD for His Salvation and Judgment

A Psalm.

1 Oh, sing to the LORD a new song!
    For He has done marvelous things;
    His right hand and His holy arm have gained
        Him the victory.
2 The LORD has made known His salvation;
    His righteousness He has revealed in the sight
        of the nations.
3 He has remembered His mercy and His
        faithfulness to the house of Israel;
    All the ends of the earth have seen the
        salvation of our God.

4 Shout joyfully to the LORD, all the earth;
    Break forth in song, rejoice, and sing praises.

5 Sing to the LORD with the harp,
    With the harp and the sound of a psalm,
6 With trumpets and the sound of a horn;
    Shout joyfully before the LORD, the King.

7 Let the sea roar, and all its fullness,
    The world and those who dwell in it;
8 Let the rivers clap *their* hands;
    Let the hills be joyful together before the
        LORD,
9 For He is coming to judge the earth.
    With righteousness He shall judge the world,
    And the peoples with equity.

PSALM 99

Praise to the LORD for His Holiness

1 The LORD reigns;
    Let the peoples tremble!

97:12 [a]Or *His holiness*

98:1–9 The basis for this new song is God's reign as the righteous King and Judge (vv. 6, 9). He is worthy of praise for His mighty acts (see Ps. 96). The Lord's "right hand" is a reference to His power (Ps. 98:1; see Ps. 89:13; Ex. 15:6, 12). He alone had brought victory to His people. All the earth, even nature, participates in the joy of worshiping the Lord as King (Ps. 98:4–8; compare verses 7–9 with Psalm 96:11–13).

99:1–9 This enthronement psalm celebrates God's eternal

He dwells *between* the cherubim;
Let the earth be moved!
[2]The LORD *is* great in Zion,
And He *is* high above all the peoples.
[3]Let them praise Your great and awesome
name—
He *is* holy.

[4]The King's strength also loves justice;
You have established equity;
You have executed justice and righteousness in
Jacob.
[5]Exalt the LORD our God,
And worship at His footstool—
He *is* holy.

[6]Moses and Aaron were among His priests,
And Samuel was among those who called upon
His name;
They called upon the LORD, and He answered
them.
[7]He spoke to them in the cloudy pillar;
They kept His testimonies and the ordinance
He gave them.

[8]You answered them, O LORD our God;
You were to them God-Who-Forgives,
Though You took vengeance on their
deeds.
[9]Exalt the LORD our God,
And worship at His holy hill;
For the LORD our God *is* holy.

PSALM 100

A Song of Praise for the Faithfulness to His People
A Psalm of Thanksgiving.

[1]Make a joyful shout to the LORD, all you lands!
[2]Serve the LORD with gladness;
Come before His presence with singing.
[3]Know that the LORD, He *is* God;
It is He *who* has made us, and not we ourselves;[a]
We are His people and the sheep of His pasture.

[4]Enter into His gates with thanksgiving,
And into His courts with praise.

Be thankful to Him, *and* bless His
name.
[5]For the LORD *is* good;
His mercy *is* everlasting,
And His truth *endures* to all generations.

PSALM 101

Promised Faithfulness to the LORD
A Psalm of David.

[1]I will sing of mercy and justice;
To You, O LORD, I will sing praises.

[2]I will behave wisely in a perfect way.
Oh, when will You come to me?
I will walk within my house with a perfect
heart.

[3]I will set nothing wicked before my eyes;
I hate the work of those who fall away;
It shall not cling to me.
[4]A perverse heart shall depart from me;
I will not know wickedness.

[5]Whoever secretly slanders his neighbor,
Him I will destroy;
The one who has a haughty look and a proud
heart,
Him I will not endure.

[6]My eyes *shall be* on the faithful of the land,
That they may dwell with me;
He who walks in a perfect way,
He shall serve me.
[7]He who works deceit shall not dwell within my
house;
He who tells lies shall not continue in my
presence.
[8]Early I will destroy all the wicked of the
land,
That I may cut off all the evildoers from the
city of the LORD.

100:3 [a]Following Kethib, Septuagint, and Vulgate; Qere, many
Hebrew manuscripts, and Targum read *we are His*.

reign of holiness (vv. 3, 5, 9; see Ps. 93; 97). The people are to
submit to His holy rule and are to worship and exalt Him because "He is holy." The holy place of the Lord's dwelling, "between the cherubim" (Ps. 99:1), refers to the ark of the
covenant where the Lord was enthroned (see Ex. 25:22;
1 Sam. 4:4; Ps. 80:1). God's holiness refers to His otherness—
His separateness from His creation—and involves both the
judgment of sin and forgiveness (Ps. 99:8).

100:1–5 The Book of Psalms is a hymnbook, a book of praise
to the Lord. Repeatedly, these poets emphasized praising God
and serving Him. This psalm of thanksgiving stresses the joy
experienced in praising the Lord. All are invited to praise the
Lord because He alone is God (v. 1), the Creator (v. 3; Ps. 95:7).

We are dependent on Him. He is also the good Shepherd who
cares for His people. His "mercy" (Heb. *chesed*: see Ps. 5:7–12,
note) and His "truth" (faithfulness; see Ps. 89) are extended
to all generations.

101:1–8 The Davidic king's promise of faithfulness to the Lord
is the focus of this psalm. The king pledged to "behave wisely
in a perfect way" (v. 2). "Perfect" (lit. "unimpaired," "blameless") is used to describe an individual of integrity (see also
v. 6). The king appointed by God promised to rule wisely and
with integrity and to reject wickedness in himself, in others
(vv. 3–5), and in his administration (vv. 6–8). Modern politicians make promises to the voters. This king made promises
to God.

PSALM 102

The LORD's Eternal Love

A Prayer of the afflicted, when he is overwhelmed and pours out his
complaint before the LORD.

¹Hear my prayer, O LORD,
And let my cry come to You.
²Do not hide Your face from me in the day of
my trouble;
Incline Your ear to me;
In the day that I call, answer me speedily.

³For my days are consumed like smoke,
And my bones are burned like a hearth.
⁴My heart is stricken and withered like grass,
So that I forget to eat my bread.
⁵Because of the sound of my groaning
My bones cling to my skin.
⁶I am like a pelican of the wilderness;
I am like an owl of the desert.
⁷I lie awake,
And am like a sparrow alone on the housetop.

⁸My enemies reproach me all day long;
Those who deride me swear an oath against
me.
⁹For I have eaten ashes like bread,
And mingled my drink with weeping,
¹⁰Because of Your indignation and Your wrath;
For You have lifted me up and cast me away.
¹¹My days are like a shadow that lengthens,
And I wither away like grass.

¹²But You, O LORD, shall endure forever,
And the remembrance of Your name to all
generations.
¹³You will arise and have mercy on Zion;
For the time to favor her,
Yes, the set time, has come.
¹⁴For Your servants take pleasure in her stones,
And show favor to her dust.
¹⁵So the nations shall fear the name of the LORD,
And all the kings of the earth Your glory.

¹⁶For the LORD shall build up Zion;
He shall appear in His glory.
¹⁷He shall regard the prayer of the destitute,
And shall not despise their prayer.

¹⁸This will be written for the generation to
come,
That a people yet to be created may praise the
LORD.
¹⁹For He looked down from the height of His
sanctuary;
From heaven the LORD viewed the earth,
²⁰To hear the groaning of the prisoner,
To release those appointed to death,
²¹To declare the name of the LORD in Zion,
And His praise in Jerusalem,
²²When the peoples are gathered together,
And the kingdoms, to serve the LORD.

²³He weakened my strength in the way;
He shortened my days.
²⁴I said, "O my God,
Do not take me away in the midst of my days;
Your years are throughout all generations.
²⁵Of old You laid the foundation of the earth,
And the heavens are the work of Your hands.
²⁶They will perish, but You will endure;
Yes, they will all grow old like a garment;
Like a cloak You will change them,
And they will be changed.
²⁷But You are the same,
And Your years will have no end.
²⁸The children of Your servants will continue,
And their descendants will be established
before You."

PSALM 103

Praise for the LORD's Mercies

A Psalm of David.

¹Bless the LORD, O my soul;
And all that is within me, bless His holy name!
²Bless the LORD, O my soul,

102:1–7 This psalm is the prayer of one who is afflicted and crying out to God (see the superscription; vv. 3–7). It is one of seven penitential psalms on the nature of sin and forgiveness (see Ps. 6, 32, 38, 51, 130, 143; chart, The Types of Psalms). The malady that afflicted this psalmist cannot be identified. He may simply be describing extreme mental anguish in physical terms, as he feels isolated from God and tormented constantly by his enemies (Ps. 102:6–11). Because of the close connection with sin, suffering generally was viewed as an expression of God's wrath against sins the tormented individual had committed. When an individual suffered, the assumption was that he had sinned. The Book of Job refutes the universal or careless application of this assumption.

102:18–28 The psalmist expressed faith in the midst of his lament. Even though the poet's days (of his life) are few (v. 11; see vv. 1–7, note), the Lord will endure forever. God's great-

ness stands in contrast to human weakness. His plan transcends a lifetime. Other generations will come to stand in awe of the Lord and will serve Him (vv. 18–22). This testimony of faith in a difficult situation reflects confidence in God's sovereignty. Recognizing God's eternal presence puts a new perspective on life.

103:1–5 The psalmist instructed his whole being to offer joyful praise to the Lord (note the repeated phrase, v. 22; see also Ps. 104:1, 35). The Lord forgives all iniquities and brings healing to life (see Ps. 32:1, 2; 51:1, notes). He redeems from destruction. "Redeems" is the word used for Boaz's role as the kinsman-redeemer of Ruth (Ps. 103:4; see Ruth 4). God does for us what we cannot do for ourselves. For "lovingkindness" (Heb. chesed, lit. "steadfast love"), see Psalm 5:7–12, note; for "tender mercies," see Psalm 18:1–3, note. Nothing else can satisfy like a relationship with the Lord (Ps. 103:5).

FORGIVENESS: YOUR PATH TO FREEDOM

GOD'S ACTION	OUR REACTIONS	HIS WORD
His Forgiveness	Because God forgives you, you can forgive others.	Ps. 103:10–12; Eph. 1:7; Heb. 10:17, 18; 1 John 1:9
His Call	Forgiveness is an act of obedience to God.	Matt. 6:14; Luke 17:3, 4; Eph. 4:32; Col. 3:13
His Character	When you forgive, you allow God to work in your life.	Gen. 50:20; Deut. 32:4; Rom. 8:28, 29, 38, 39
His Perspective	If you are willing to obey, you will forgive in God's way.	Matt. 5:44; Acts 20:35; Rom. 12:17–21; 1 Cor. 13:5
His Provision	What God calls you to do, He will equip you to do.	Matt. 19:26; Phil. 1:6; 4:13; 1 Thess. 5:24

And forget not all His benefits:
³Who forgives all your iniquities,
  Who heals all your diseases,
⁴Who redeems your life from destruction,
  Who crowns you with lovingkindness and
    tender mercies,
⁵Who satisfies your mouth with good *things*,
  So that your youth is renewed like the eagle's.

⁶The LORD executes righteousness
  And justice for all who are oppressed.
⁷He made known His ways to Moses,
  His acts to the children of Israel.
⁸The LORD *is* merciful and gracious,
  Slow to anger, and abounding in mercy.
⁹He will not always strive *with us*,
  Nor will He keep *His anger* forever.
¹⁰He has not dealt with us according to our sins,
  Nor punished us according to our iniquities.

¹¹For as the heavens are high above the earth,
  So great is His mercy toward those who fear
    Him;

¹²As far as the east is from the west,
  So far has He removed our transgressions from
    us.
¹³As a father pities *his* children,
  So the LORD pities those who fear Him.
¹⁴For He knows our frame;
  He remembers that we *are* dust.

¹⁵*As for* man, his days *are* like grass;
  As a flower of the field, so he flourishes.
¹⁶For the wind passes over it, and it is gone,
  And its place remembers it no more.ª
¹⁷But the mercy of the LORD *is* from everlasting
    to everlasting
  On those who fear Him,
  And His righteousness to children's
    children,
¹⁸To such as keep His covenant,
  And to those who remember His
    commandments to do them.

103:16 ªCompare Job 7:10

103:6–12 The Lord is righteous and just to all who are oppressed, as is evident in His revelation of Himself to Moses and in His deeds on Israel's behalf. He is "merciful and gracious, slow to anger, and abounding in mercy" (Heb. *chesed,* lit. "lovingkindness," v. 8; see Ex. 34:6, 7; see Ps. 5:7–12, note). God does not hold a grudge against His people (Ps. 103:9). God does not treat us the way we deserve to be treated. He does not mete out the punishment according to our sins; instead He forgives. God's mercy is pictured in geographical dimensions as great as the distance separating the heavens from the earth and as far as the east is from the west, the distance which separates sunrise and sunset (vv. 11, 12). He removes our "transgressions" (lit. "rebellion against God"; see Ps. 32:1, 2; 51:1; notes).

103:13–18 God is a compassionate and tender Father toward His children (v. 13). He created us from the dust of the earth (Gen. 2:7), and He knows our make-up. The Lord has compassion on our human frailty (Ps. 103:15, 16). In contrast to our weaknesses and the brevity of our lives, God's "mercy" (Heb. *chesed,* lit. "lovingkindness"; see Ps. 5:7–12, note) is everlasting and unchanging. All those who take His covenant seriously and live by His commands experience the wonderful reality of His unchanging love.

MEALTIME TOTAL NOURISHMENT

Descriptions of food are found throughout the Bible from the fruit of the Garden of Eden (Gen. 2:16; 3:3) to the elements of the Lord's Supper in the New Testament (1 Cor. 11:23–26). Careful dietary laws are given (see Lev.11:1–47). Mealtimes were often celebrations (see Luke 15:11–32).

As in Solomon's day, so it is in today's high-stress society; peaceful mealtimes aid both the digestion and the disposition. Perhaps the most meaningful and effective way to bring an air of peace and grace to mealtime is to make a habit of inviting God to be present. To offer a prayer of thanksgiving together before you begin to eat creates an attitude of gratitude and peace (see Ps. 100:4, 5; 1 Thess. 5:18). Turning off distracting noises creates an air of calm and allows conversation to focus on building relationships, generating peace, expressing love, and providing encouragement (Prov. 15:17; James 3:18). Even when dining alone, mealtime can be a time to rest, to reflect on God's blessings, or to enjoy scenic beauty.

Women have long been associated with mealtime in a special way. For example, the "virtuous wife" or "woman of strength" described in Proverbs 31:10–31 is willing to expend great effort to provide physical nurture for her family (Ps. 104:14, 15). Scripture also emphasizes that food must be shared in a regular and timely way (see Ps. 104:27; Matt. 24:45). There is no more beautiful time to nourish the family and others than in those regularly appointed gatherings that provide physical sustenance and spiritual nurture.

Brother Lawrence, a member of the humble barefooted Carmelite monks in the 1600s expressed the special opportunity in service at mealtime in his prayer: "Lord of all pots and pans and things . . . make me a saint by getting meals and washing up the plates! The time of business does not with me differ from the time of prayer, and in the noise and clatter of my kitchen . . . I possess God in as great tranquility as if I were upon my knees at the blessed sacrament."

See also Ps. 136:25, 26; Prov. 17:1; Matt. 6:11; notes on Cooking (Gen. 25); Family (Gen. 32; 1 Sam. 3; Ps. 78; 127); Hospitality (1 Pet. 4); Nutrition (Lev. 11)

19The LORD has established His throne in
 heaven,
 And His kingdom rules over all.

20Bless the LORD, you His angels,
 Who excel in strength, who do His word,
 Heeding the voice of His word.
21Bless the LORD, all *you* His hosts,
 You ministers of His, who do His pleasure.
22Bless the LORD, all His works,
 In all places of His dominion.

Bless the LORD, O my soul!

PSALM 104

*Praise to the Sovereign LORD for His Creation
and Providence*

1Bless the LORD, O my soul!

O LORD my God, You are very great:
You are clothed with honor and majesty,
2Who cover *Yourself* with light as *with* a
 garment,
Who stretch out the heavens like a curtain.

3He lays the beams of His upper chambers in
 the waters,
Who makes the clouds His chariot,
Who walks on the wings of the wind,
4Who makes His angels spirits,
His ministers a flame of fire.

5*You who* laid the foundations of the earth,
So *that* it should not be moved forever,
6You covered it with the deep as *with* a garment;
The waters stood above the mountains.
7At Your rebuke they fled;
At the voice of Your thunder they hastened
 away.
8They went up over the mountains;
They went down into the valleys,
To the place which You founded for them.
9You have set a boundary that they may not pass
 over,
That they may not return to cover the earth.

10He sends the springs into the valleys;
They flow among the hills.
11They give drink to every beast of the field;

104:1–23 The greatness of God is the theme of the poem. This psalm has the same marvelous phrase for both introduction and conclusion (vv. 1, 35; see Ps. 103:1, 22). The lengthy poem is a description of the greatness of God as Creator. The poet begins with the heavens as the dwelling place of the Lord (Ps. 104:2). The poet next extolled the Lord as He who established the foundations of the earth (v. 5), putting creation under His control. He harnessed the waters for the benefit of His creation (vv. 9–13). God provided food and home, time and seasons for all His creatures (vv. 14–23). God provided meaning and purpose for the lives of His people (v. 23).

The wild donkeys quench their thirst.
¹²By them the birds of the heavens have their home;
They sing among the branches.
¹³He waters the hills from His upper chambers;
The earth is satisfied with the fruit of Your works.

¹⁴He causes the grass to grow for the cattle,
And vegetation for the service of man,
That he may bring forth food from the earth,
¹⁵And wine *that* makes glad the heart of man,
Oil to make *his* face shine,
And bread *which* strengthens man's heart.
¹⁶The trees of the LORD are full *of sap,*
The cedars of Lebanon which He planted,
¹⁷Where the birds make their nests;
The stork has her home in the fir trees.
¹⁸The high hills *are* for the wild goats;
The cliffs are a refuge for the rock badgers.ᵃ

¹⁹He appointed the moon for seasons;
The sun knows its going down.
²⁰You make darkness, and it is night,
In which all the beasts of the forest creep about.
²¹The young lions roar after their prey,
And seek their food from God.
²²*When* the sun rises, they gather together
And lie down in their dens.
²³Man goes out to his work
And to his labor until the evening.

²⁴O LORD, how manifold are Your works!
In wisdom You have made them all.
The earth is full of Your possessions—
²⁵This great and wide sea,
In which *are* innumerable teeming things,
Living things both small and great.
²⁶There the ships sail about;
There is that Leviathan
Which You have made to play there.

²⁷These all wait for You,
That You may give *them* their food in due season.
²⁸*What* You give them they gather in;
You open Your hand, they are filled with good.
²⁹You hide Your face, they are troubled;

You take away their breath, they die and return to their dust.
³⁰You send forth Your Spirit, they are created;
And You renew the face of the earth.

³¹May the glory of the LORD endure forever;
May the LORD rejoice in His works.
³²He looks on the earth, and it trembles;
He touches the hills, and they smoke.

³³I will sing to the LORD as long as I live;
I will sing praise to my God while I have my being.
³⁴May my meditation be sweet to Him;
I will be glad in the LORD.
³⁵May sinners be consumed from the earth,
And the wicked be no more.

Bless the LORD, O my soul!
Praise the LORD!

PSALM 105

The Eternal Faithfulness of the LORD

¹Oh, give thanks to the LORD!
Call upon His name;
Make known His deeds among the peoples!
²Sing to Him, sing psalms to Him;
Talk of all His wondrous works!
³Glory in His holy name;
Let the hearts of those rejoice who seek the LORD!
⁴Seek the LORD and His strength;
Seek His face evermore!
⁵Remember His marvelous works which He has done,
His wonders, and the judgments of His mouth,
⁶O seed of Abraham His servant,
You children of Jacob, His chosen ones!

⁷He *is* the LORD our God;
His judgments *are* in all the earth.
⁸He remembers His covenant forever,
The word *which* He commanded, for a thousand generations,
⁹*The covenant* which He made with Abraham,
And His oath to Isaac,

104:18 ᵃOr *rock hyrax* (compare Leviticus 11:5)

104:24–30 God is the source of life. He made the seas and all forms of sea life. "Leviathan" refers to a great sea creature (v. 26). All creatures depend on God for their existence and sustenance. God renews the entire earth, both plant and animal life, for life is the gift of the Lord. Every mother understands vividly the importance of the regular provision of food (v. 27). Nature is dependent on God, who gives and sustains life (v. 30). The poem ends as it began with a call to praise (vv. 33–35). The psalmist vowed to sing praise to God as long as he lived (v. 33), expressing his joy in the Lord

(v. 34). He prayed that the wicked who spoil the beauty and purpose of God's creation may exist no more.

105:1–6 The Lord is to be praised for His wonderful works on behalf of His chosen people throughout history. The first 15 verses of this psalm were used as a psalm of thanksgiving to the Lord when David brought the ark to Jerusalem (1 Chr. 16).

105:7–25 God made His covenant of promise with Abraham, Isaac, and Jacob to give the Land of Canaan to His people as their inheritance (vv. 8–12; see Gen. 12:1–3). God protected

¹⁰And confirmed it to Jacob for a statute,
To Israel as an everlasting covenant,
¹¹Saying, "To you I will give the land of Canaan
As the allotment of your inheritance,"
¹²When they were few in number,
Indeed very few, and strangers in it.

¹³When they went from one nation to another,
From one kingdom to another people,
¹⁴He permitted no one to do them wrong;
Yes, He rebuked kings for their sakes,
¹⁵Saying, "Do not touch My anointed ones,
And do My prophets no harm."

¹⁶Moreover He called for a famine in the land;
He destroyed all the provision of bread.
¹⁷He sent a man before them—
Joseph—who was sold as a slave.
¹⁸They hurt his feet with fetters,
He was laid in irons.
¹⁹Until the time that his word came to pass,
The word of the LORD tested him.
²⁰The king sent and released him,
The ruler of the people let him go free.
²¹He made him lord of his house,
And ruler of all his possessions,
²²To bind his princes at his pleasure,
And teach his elders wisdom.

²³Israel also came into Egypt,
And Jacob dwelt in the land of Ham.
²⁴He increased His people greatly,
And made them stronger than their enemies.
²⁵He turned their heart to hate His people,
To deal craftily with His servants.

²⁶He sent Moses His servant,
And Aaron whom He had chosen.
²⁷They performed His signs among them,
And wonders in the land of Ham.
²⁸He sent darkness, and made it dark;
And they did not rebel against His word.
²⁹He turned their waters into blood,
And killed their fish.
³⁰Their land abounded with frogs,
Even in the chambers of their kings.

³¹He spoke, and there came swarms of flies,
And lice in all their territory.
³²He gave them hail for rain,
And flaming fire in their land.
³³He struck their vines also, and their fig trees,
And splintered the trees of their territory.
³⁴He spoke, and locusts came,
Young locusts without number,
³⁵And ate up all the vegetation in their land,
And devoured the fruit of their ground.
³⁶He also destroyed all the firstborn in their
land,
The first of all their strength.

³⁷He also brought them out with silver and gold,
And there was none feeble among His tribes.
³⁸Egypt was glad when they departed,
For the fear of them had fallen upon them.
³⁹He spread a cloud for a covering,
And fire to give light in the night.
⁴⁰The people asked, and He brought quail,
And satisfied them with the bread of heaven.
⁴¹He opened the rock, and water gushed out;
It ran in the dry places like a river.

⁴²For He remembered His holy promise,
And Abraham His servant.
⁴³He brought out His people with joy,
His chosen ones with gladness.
⁴⁴He gave them the lands of the Gentiles,
And they inherited the labor of the nations,
⁴⁵That they might observe His statutes
And keep His laws.

Praise the LORD!

PSALM 106

Joy in Forgiveness of Israel's Sins
¹Praise the LORD!

Oh, give thanks to the LORD, for He is good!
For His mercy endures forever.

²Who can utter the mighty acts of the LORD?
Who can declare all His praise?

Abraham, Isaac, and Jacob, while they were wandering nomads, from the kings of other nations (Ps. 105:12, 13; see Gen. 12:10–20; 20:1-18). God's covenant with the patriarchs, who were also identified as prophets, was an unconditional covenant (Ps. 105:15; see Gen. 20:7). Joseph, sold by his brothers, became a powerful ruler in Egypt. The Lord used Joseph to save His people from terrible famine by bringing Jacob and his family to Egypt, where they multiplied but eventually were enslaved (Ps. 105:16–25; see Gen. 46—50).

105:26–41 This recital of Israel's history under the leadership of Moses refreshed the people's memories with all the reasons they had to give thanks to the Lord. The plagues that fell on Egypt before Pharaoh let the Hebrew people go are re-

counted (see chart, The Ten Plagues on Egypt in Exodus). God provided guidance for His people in the wilderness, giving them meat (quail), manna (bread from heaven), and water from the rock (vv. 40, 41).

105:42–45 God's people should respond in obedience to His numerous acts on their behalf (v. 45). Privilege always brings with it responsibility. God's goodness to His people should lead believers in every generation to obedience as the proper response of a grateful heart.

106:1–6 The focus is on Israel's unfaithfulness as incidents from Israel's history are related (see Psalm 78). The Lord is praised for His goodness and mercy (Heb. *chesed*, Ps. 106:1;

Worship is not an experience. Worship is an act, and this takes discipline.

Elisabeth Elliot

---

[3]Blessed *are* those who keep justice,
And he who does[a] righteousness at all times!

[4]Remember me, O LORD, with the favor *You have toward* Your people.
Oh, visit me with Your salvation,
°[5]That I may see the benefit of Your chosen ones,
That I may rejoice in the gladness of Your nation,
That I may glory with Your inheritance.

[6]We have sinned with our fathers,
We have committed iniquity,
We have done wickedly.
[7]Our fathers in Egypt did not understand Your wonders;
They did not remember the multitude of Your mercies,
But rebelled by the sea— the Red Sea.

[8]Nevertheless He saved them for His name's sake,
That He might make His mighty power known.
[9]He rebuked the Red Sea also, and it dried up;
So He led them through the depths,
As through the wilderness.
[10]He saved them from the hand of him who hated *them*,
And redeemed them from the hand of the enemy.
[11]The waters covered their enemies;
There was not one of them left.
[12]Then they believed His words;
They sang His praise.

[13]They soon forgot His works;
They did not wait for His counsel,
[14]But lusted exceedingly in the wilderness,
And tested God in the desert.
[15]And He gave them their request,
But sent leanness into their soul.

[16]When they envied Moses in the camp,
And Aaron the saint of the LORD,
[17]The earth opened up and swallowed Dathan,

And covered the faction of Abiram.
[18]A fire was kindled in their company;
The flame burned up the wicked.

[19]They made a calf in Horeb,
And worshiped the molded image.
[20]Thus they changed their glory
Into the image of an ox that eats grass.
[21]They forgot God their Savior,
Who had done great things in Egypt,
[22]Wondrous works in the land of Ham,
Awesome things by the Red Sea.
[23]Therefore He said that He would destroy them,
Had not Moses His chosen one stood before Him in the breach,
To turn away His wrath, lest He destroy *them*.

[24]Then they despised the pleasant land;
They did not believe His word,
[25]But complained in their tents,
And did not heed the voice of the LORD.
[26]Therefore He raised His hand *in an oath* against them,
To overthrow them in the wilderness,
[27]To overthrow their descendants among the nations,
And to scatter them in the lands.

[28]They joined themselves also to Baal of Peor,
And ate sacrifices made to the dead.
[29]Thus they provoked *Him* to anger with their deeds,
And the plague broke out among them.
[30]Then Phinehas stood up and intervened,
And the plague was stopped.
[31]And that was accounted to him for righteousness
To all generations forevermore.

[32]They angered *Him* also at the waters of strife,[a]
So that it went ill with Moses on account of them;

106:3 [a]Septuagint, Syriac, Targum, and Vulgate read *those who do.*
106:32 [a]Or *Meribah*

---

see Ps. 5:7-12, note). The poet longed to experience God's salvation or deliverance (Ps. 106:4, 5). The poet recalled numerous times when Israel disobeyed the Lord after He delivered them from Egypt (vv. 7-46). Yet the Lord remained faithful to His people (vv. 40-46), forgiving and delivering them again and again. He faithfully kept the covenant that His people broke. No wonder the poet issued a call to praise (v. 47). The doxology of verse 48 marks the conclusion to Book IV of the Psalms (see Introduction: Outline).

ATTRIBUTES OF GOD   HE IS IMMUTABLE

Believers can be sure of God. His character, truth, ways, purposes, love, and promises never vary (Is. 46:9–11). He has never been less than what He is, nor will He be more (Mal. 3:6).

People change because of inadequate ability, lack of knowledge, change of circumstances, or loss of interest. God lacks no ability (Gen. 18:14), He knows everything, controls everything, and is involved in everything (Is. 40:11–14).

God does nothing partially (Is. 41:4), never changes moods (Heb. 13:8), nor does He cool off in His affections (Jer. 31:3) or enthusiasm (Phil. 1:6). His attitude toward sin is the same as it was in the garden of Eden, and His love is the same as it was when He displayed it on the Cross (Rom. 5:17).

God never alters His plans because they are made with complete knowledge and control (Ps. 33:11). What He does in time He planned in eternity, and what He planned in eternity He carries out in time (Is. 46:9–11). God does not change because He is bigger than all causes.

See also Is. 14:24; Lam. 3:22, note; Heb. 1:11, 12; James 1:17; notes on Attributes of God (Ex. 33; Deut. 4; 32; 2 Chr. 19; Job 23; 42; Ps. 25; 90; 119; Is. 6; 65; Jer. 23; Luke 18; Rom. 2; Eph. 1; 1 John 5); Commitment (Matt. 16); Holiness (Lev. 20); God's Will (Eph. 5); Promises of God (2 Pet. 1); Vows (Num. 30)

33Because they rebelled against His Spirit,
So that he spoke rashly with his lips.

34They did not destroy the peoples,
Concerning whom the LORD had commanded them,
35But they mingled with the Gentiles
And learned their works;
36They served their idols,
Which became a snare to them.
37They even sacrificed their sons
And their daughters to demons,
38And shed innocent blood,
The blood of their sons and daughters,
Whom they sacrificed to the idols of Canaan;
And the land was polluted with blood.
39Thus they were defiled by their own works,
And played the harlot by their own deeds.

40Therefore the wrath of the LORD was kindled against His people,
So that He abhorred His own inheritance.
41And He gave them into the hand of the Gentiles,
And those who hated them ruled over them.
42Their enemies also oppressed them,
And they were brought into subjection under their hand.
43Many times He delivered them;
But they rebelled in their counsel,
And were brought low for their iniquity.

44Nevertheless He regarded their affliction,

When He heard their cry;
45And for their sake He remembered His covenant,
And relented according to the multitude of His mercies.
46He also made them to be pitied
By all those who carried them away captive.

47Save us, O LORD our God,
And gather us from among the Gentiles,
To give thanks to Your holy name,
To triumph in Your praise.

48Blessed be the LORD God of Israel
From everlasting to everlasting!
And let all the people say, "Amen!"

Praise the LORD!

Book Five: Psalms 107—150

PSALM 107

Thanksgiving to the LORD for His Great Works of Deliverance
1Oh, give thanks to the LORD, for *He is* good!
For His mercy *endures* forever.
2Let the redeemed of the LORD say *so,*
Whom He has redeemed from the hand of the enemy,
3And gathered out of the lands,
From the east and from the west,
From the north and from the south.

4They wandered in the wilderness in a desolate way;

107:1–3 The call to give thanks (v. 1) is based on the Lord's enduring "mercy" (Heb. *chesed*: see Ps. 5:7–12, note), demonstrated as He has "redeemed" His people (Ps. 107:2; see Ps. 103:1–5, note). This same term was used to describe Boaz as the kinsman-redeemer in the Book of Ruth (see Ps. 103:1–5, note). God does for His people what they cannot do for themselves by redeeming them from the power of their enemies (Ps. 107:2). Those who have experienced God's deliverance should speak up, letting others know of their praise to God for His wonderful works of deliverance (vv. 4–42). Psalm 107 marks the beginning of Book V (see Introduction: Outline).

They found no city to dwell in.
⁵Hungry and thirsty,
  Their soul fainted in them.
⁶Then they cried out to the LORD in their
    trouble,
  And He delivered them out of their
    distresses.
⁷And He led them forth by the right way,
  That they might go to a city for a dwelling
    place.
⁸Oh, that *men* would give thanks to the LORD *for*
    His goodness,
  And *for* His wonderful works to the children of
    men!
⁹For He satisfies the longing soul,
  And fills the hungry soul with goodness.

¹⁰Those who sat in darkness and in the shadow
    of death,
  Bound in affliction and irons—
¹¹Because they rebelled against the words of
    God,
  And despised the counsel of the Most
    High,
¹²Therefore He brought down their heart with
    labor;
  They fell down, and *there was* none to help.
¹³Then they cried out to the LORD in their
    trouble,
  And He saved them out of their distresses.
¹⁴He brought them out of darkness and the
    shadow of death,
  And broke their chains in pieces.
¹⁵Oh, that *men* would give thanks to the LORD *for*
    His goodness,
  And *for* His wonderful works to the children of
    men!
¹⁶For He has broken the gates of bronze,
  And cut the bars of iron in two.

¹⁷Fools, because of their transgression,
  And because of their iniquities, were
    afflicted.
¹⁸Their soul abhorred all manner of food,
  And they drew near to the gates of death.
¹⁹Then they cried out to the LORD in their
    trouble,
  And He saved them out of their distresses.
²⁰He sent His word and healed them,
  And delivered *them* from their destructions.
²¹Oh, that *men* would give thanks to the LORD *for*
    His goodness,
  And *for* His wonderful works to the children of
    men!
²²Let them sacrifice the sacrifices of
    thanksgiving,
  And declare His works with rejoicing.

²³Those who go down to the sea in ships,
  Who do business on great waters,
²⁴They see the works of the LORD,
  And His wonders in the deep.
²⁵For He commands and raises the stormy wind,
  Which lifts up the waves of the sea.
²⁶They mount up to the heavens,
  They go down again to the depths;
  Their soul melts because of trouble.
²⁷They reel to and fro, and stagger like a
    drunken man,
  And are at their wits' end.
²⁸Then they cry out to the LORD in their trouble,
  And He brings them out of their distresses.
²⁹He calms the storm,
  So that its waves are still.
³⁰Then they are glad because they are quiet;
  So He guides them to their desired haven.
³¹Oh, that *men* would give thanks to the LORD *for*
    His goodness,
  And *for* His wonderful works to the children of
    men!
³²Let them exalt Him also in the assembly of the
    people,
  And praise Him in the company of the
    elders.

³³He turns rivers into a wilderness,
  And the watersprings into dry ground;
³⁴A fruitful land into barrenness,
  For the wickedness of those who dwell in it.
³⁵He turns a wilderness into pools of water,
  And dry land into watersprings.
³⁶There He makes the hungry dwell,
  That they may establish a city for a dwelling
    place,
³⁷And sow fields and plant vineyards,
  That they may yield a fruitful harvest.
³⁸He also blesses them, and they multiply
    greatly;
  And He does not let their cattle decrease.

³⁹When they are diminished and brought
    low
  Through oppression, affliction and sorrow,
⁴⁰He pours contempt on princes,
  And causes them to wander in the wilderness
    where there is no way;
⁴¹Yet He sets the poor on high, far from
    affliction,
  And makes *their* families like a flock.
⁴²The righteous see *it* and rejoice,
  And all iniquity stops its mouth.

⁴³Whoever *is* wise will observe these *things*,
  And they will understand the lovingkindness
    of the LORD.

PSALM 108

Assurance of God's Victory over Enemies
A Song. A Psalm of David.

¹O God, my heart is steadfast;
I will sing and give praise, even with my glory.
²Awake, lute and harp!
I will awaken the dawn.
³I will praise You, O Lord, among the peoples,
And I will sing praises to You among the
nations.
⁴For Your mercy is great above the heavens,
And Your truth reaches to the clouds.

⁵Be exalted, O God, above the heavens,
And Your glory above all the earth;
⁶That Your beloved may be delivered,
Save with Your right hand, and hear me.

⁷God has spoken in His holiness:
"I will rejoice;
I will divide Shechem
And measure out the Valley of Succoth.
⁸Gilead is Mine; Manasseh is Mine;
Ephraim also is the helmet for My head;
Judah is My lawgiver.
⁹Moab is My washpot;
Over Edom I will cast My shoe;
Over Philistia I will triumph."

¹⁰Who will bring me into the strong city?
Who will lead me to Edom?
¹¹Is it not You, O God, who cast us off?
And You, O God, who did not go out with our
armies?
¹²Give us help from trouble,
For the help of man is useless.
¹³Through God we will do valiantly,
For it is He who shall tread down our enemies.[a]

PSALM 109

Plea for Judgment of False Accusers
To the Chief Musician. A Psalm of David.

¹Do not keep silent,
O God of my praise!
²For the mouth of the wicked and the mouth of
the deceitful
Have opened against me;
They have spoken against me with a lying
tongue.

³They have also surrounded me with words of
hatred,
And fought against me without a cause.
⁴In return for my love they are my accusers,
But I give myself to prayer.
⁵Thus they have rewarded me evil for good,
And hatred for my love.

⁶Set a wicked man over him,
And let an accuser[a] stand at his right hand.
⁷When he is judged, let him be found guilty,
And let his prayer become sin.
⁸Let his days be few,
And let another take his office.
⁹Let his children be fatherless,
And his wife a widow.
¹⁰Let his children continually be vagabonds, and
beg;
Let them seek their bread[a] also from their
desolate places.
¹¹Let the creditor seize all that he has,
And let strangers plunder his labor.
¹²Let there be none to extend mercy to him,
Nor let there be any to favor his fatherless
children.
¹³Let his posterity be cut off,
And in the generation following let their name
be blotted out.

¹⁴Let the iniquity of his fathers be remembered
before the Lord,
And let not the sin of his mother be blotted
out.
¹⁵Let them be continually before the Lord,
That He may cut off the memory of them from
the earth;
¹⁶Because he did not remember to show
mercy,
But persecuted the poor and needy man,
That he might even slay the broken in heart.
¹⁷As he loved cursing, so let it come to him;
As he did not delight in blessing, so let it be
far from him.
¹⁸As he clothed himself with cursing as with his
garment,
So let it enter his body like water,
And like oil into his bones.

·················

108:13 [a]Compare verses 6–13 with 60:5–12   109:6 [a]Hebrew *satan*
109:10 [a]Following Masoretic Text and Targum; Septuagint and
Vulgate read *be cast out*.

108:1–6 The poet praised God with a steadfast heart and prayed for deliverance, knowing that ultimately only God could bring the deliverance for which he longed. The first five verses of this psalm are found in Psalm 57:7–11, and Psalm 108:6–13 also appear in Psalm 60:5–12.

109:21–31 This psalm reveals the humanity of the psalmist and reflects the common belief that the poet's enemies were God's enemies. The poet was concerned for God's name or reputation. The longest section of this angry poet's harsh prayer for God to curse his enemies (vv. 6–20, in which v. 8 was applied to Judas; see Acts 1:20). In contrast to the attitudes reflected in this psalm, Jesus taught His followers to love their enemies (Matt. 5:44).

¹⁹Let it be to him like the garment which covers
  him,
  And for a belt with which he girds himself
    continually.
²⁰*Let* this *be* the LORD's reward to my accusers,
  And to those who speak evil against my person.

²¹But You, O GOD the Lord,
  Deal with me for Your name's sake;
  Because Your mercy *is* good, deliver me.
²²For I *am* poor and needy,
  And my heart is wounded within me.
²³I am gone like a shadow when it lengthens;
  I am shaken off like a locust.
²⁴My knees are weak through fasting,
  And my flesh is feeble from lack of fatness.
²⁵I also have become a reproach to them;
  When they look at me, they shake their heads.

²⁶Help me, O LORD my God!
  Oh, save me according to Your mercy,
²⁷That they may know that this *is* Your hand—
  That You, LORD, have done it!
²⁸Let them curse, but You bless;
  When they arise, let them be ashamed,
  But let Your servant rejoice.
²⁹Let my accusers be clothed with shame,
  And let them cover themselves with their own
    disgrace as with a mantle.

³⁰I will greatly praise the LORD with my
  mouth;
  Yes, I will praise Him among the multitude.
³¹For He shall stand at the right hand of the
  poor,
  To save *him* from those who condemn him.

PSALM 110

Announcement of the Messiah's Reign
A Psalm of David.

¹The LORD said to my Lord,
  "Sit at My right hand,
  Till I make Your enemies Your footstool."
²The LORD shall send the rod of Your strength
  out of Zion.
  Rule in the midst of Your enemies!

³Your people *shall be* volunteers
  In the day of Your power;

In the beauties of holiness, from the womb of
  the morning,
  You have the dew of Your youth.
⁴The LORD has sworn
  And will not relent,
  "You *are* a priest forever
  According to the order of Melchizedek."

⁵The Lord *is* at Your right hand;
  He shall execute kings in the day of His
    wrath.
⁶He shall judge among the nations,
  He shall fill *the places* with dead bodies,
  He shall execute the heads of many countries.
⁷He shall drink of the brook by the wayside;
  Therefore He shall lift up the head.

PSALM 111

Praise to God for His Faithfulness and Justice
¹Praise the LORD!

I will praise the LORD with *my* whole heart,
  In the assembly of the upright and *in the*
    congregation.

²The works of the LORD *are* great,
  Studied by all who have pleasure in them.
³His work *is* honorable and glorious,
  And His righteousness endures forever.
⁴He has made His wonderful works to be
  remembered;
  The LORD *is* gracious and full of compassion.
⁵He has given food to those who fear Him;
  He will ever be mindful of His covenant.
⁶He has declared to His people the power of His
  works,
  In giving them the heritage of the nations.

⁷The works of His hands *are* verity and
  justice;
  All His precepts *are* sure.
⁸They stand fast forever and ever,
  And are done in truth and uprightness.
⁹He has sent redemption to His people;
  He has commanded His covenant forever:
  Holy and awesome *is* His name.

¹⁰The fear of the LORD *is* the beginning of
  wisdom;

110:1–7 This psalm was used during the coronation ceremony of kings from David's line, emphasizing that the king's authority derived from the Lord Himself (vv. 1, 2). As God's special representative to the people, the king served in a priestly role (v. 4). Melchizedek, king of Salem and priest of God Most High, blessed Abraham after the rescue of Lot (see Gen. 14:18–20). Psalm 110 is frequently quoted in the NT in relation to Christ (see Matt. 22:44; Acts 2:34, 35; Heb. 1:13; 5:6; 7:17). Jesus is both our great High Priest and King.

111:1 The psalmist testified that he would praise the Lord with his whole being for many reasons (vv. 2–9). "Fear," which marks the beginning of wisdom, is an awesome reverence of God, not a cringing fear. This is the praise of a wise and understanding person living in a right relationship with the Lord (see Prov. 1:7; 9:10). Psalm 111, as is Psalm 112, is an example of a Hebrew acrostic poem. Each of the 22 lines begins with a successive letter of the Hebrew alphabet.

INFERTILITY   *CHILDLESS IS NOT LESS*

Most couples anticipate children after marriage. Indeed, children are a part of God's plan for a man and woman united in marriage since God instructed Adam and Eve to "be fruitful and multiply" (Gen. 1:28). Scripture teaches that children are a heritage from the Lord, a reward from God (Ps. 127:3–5). Therefore, it can become very confusing and disconcerting to a married couple when children are not conceived as planned or desired. This was especially true in Bible times.

Barrenness is not merely a personal pain in the Bible. Children were a sign of *material* blessing (Psalm 127:3–5). They provided caregivers for older family members. Offspring were a sign of *spiritual* blessing: the "family-line" continued because there were family representatives in the land of the living. A person lived on through her descendants. Barrenness, then, carried with it a sense of termination.

Infertility is defined by the medical community as the inability to achieve pregnancy after a year or more of regular sexual relations without contraception or the inability to carry repeated pregnancies to live birth. About 15 percent of all married couples today are infertile. Although there are numerous causes of infertility in women and men, medical advances have made it possible to diagnose and treat many of them. Still, some couples remain childless despite years of treatment. A couple's decision to manage the timing of conception, pursue fertility measures, or adopt a child is a responsibility they share before God, the Author of life. "Childless" is not "less" if that is God's perfect will for a couple. Infertile couples have not been abandoned by God.

Couples who face infertility can experience a wide range of emotions. Like Sarai (Gen. 11:30), Rachel (Gen. 30:1), Hannah (1 Sam. 1:2), and Elizabeth (Luke 1:36), a childless woman often feels a wide range of emotions: disappointment, helplessness, anger, self-pity, grief, low self-esteem, or guilt. Regardless of how infertility impacts the couple, the personal pain is often great. Fellow Christians can help heal this pain by offering encouragement and understanding, by respecting the couple's efforts to explore their options, and by talking freely about infertility when the subject is introduced. Most importantly, the church needs to accept childless couples and encourage them to discover and pursue outlets for ministry.

God does not give children to every couple. God may have other blessings in store for the childless. Though we can only speculate as to their family lives, none of these notable women in the Bible are associated with the bearing of children: Miriam, Esther, Priscilla, Mary and Martha, Mary Magdalene. Once a woman realizes that the rearing of children is not the only responsibility God assigns to Christian couples, she often finds true joy in embracing her personal assignment from God.

See also Gen. 16:1, 2; Ps. 113:9; Matt. 18:3, Luke 2:36–38; notes on Bitterness (Heb. 12); Marriage (Gen. 2; 2 Sam. 6; Prov. 5; Hos. 2; Amos 3; 2 Cor. 13; Heb. 12); Miscarriage (Ex. 21); Motherhood (1 Sam. 1; Is. 49; Ezek. 16); Pregnancy (Judg. 13); Self-Esteem (2 Cor. 10); Pain (Job 7); portraits of Hannah (1 Sam. 1); Rachel (Gen. 29); Sarai (Gen. 11); Elizabeth (Luke 1:5–25).

A good understanding have all those who do
    His commandments.
His praise endures forever.

PSALM 112

The Blessed State of the Righteous

¹Praise the LORD!

Blessed *is* the man *who* fears the LORD,
Who delights greatly in His commandments.

²His descendants will be mighty on earth;
    The generation of the upright will be
      blessed.
³Wealth and riches *will be* in his house,
    And his righteousness endures forever.

⁴Unto the upright there arises light in the
    darkness;
He is gracious, and full of compassion, and
    righteous.
⁵A good man deals graciously and lends;
    He will guide his affairs with discretion.
⁶Surely he will never be shaken;
    The righteous will be in everlasting
      remembrance.
⁷He will not be afraid of evil tidings;
    His heart is steadfast, trusting in the LORD.
⁸His heart *is* established;
    He will not be afraid,
Until he sees *his desire* upon his enemies.

⁹He has dispersed abroad,
    He has given to the poor;

112:1, 2 This acrostic poem is a wisdom psalm contrasting the blessings of the righteous with the fate of the wicked (see Ps. 1; 111:1, note). The person who holds the Lord in awesome reverence and obeys His commands would receive His blessing (Ps. 112:1–9). The righteous person would enjoy descendants to carry on his name, prosperity, and security. In contrast, the punishment of the wicked person is described: He would experience frustration, grief, and instability (v. 10).

His righteousness endures forever;
His horn will be exalted with honor.
¹⁰The wicked will see *it* and be grieved;
He will gnash his teeth and melt away;
The desire of the wicked shall perish.

PSALM 113

The Majesty and Condescension of God
¹Praise the LORD!

Praise, O servants of the LORD,
Praise the name of the LORD!
²Blessed be the name of the LORD
From this time forth and forevermore!
³From the rising of the sun to its going down
The LORD's name *is* to be praised.

⁴The LORD *is* high above all nations,
His glory above the heavens.
⁵Who *is* like the LORD our God,
Who dwells on high,
⁶Who humbles Himself to behold
The things that are in the heavens and in the
earth?

⁷He raises the poor out of the dust,
And lifts the needy out of the ash heap,
⁸That He may seat *him* with princes—
With the princes of His people.
⁹He grants the barren woman a home,
Like a joyful mother of children.

Praise the LORD!

PSALM 114

The Power of God in His Deliverance of Israel
¹When Israel went out of Egypt,
The house of Jacob from a people of strange
language,
²Judah became His sanctuary,
And Israel His dominion.

³The sea saw *it* and fled;
Jordan turned back.
⁴The mountains skipped like rams,

The little hills like lambs.
⁵What ails you, O sea, that you fled?
O Jordan, *that* you turned back?
⁶O mountains, *that* you skipped like rams?
O little hills, like lambs?

⁷Tremble, O earth, at the presence of the Lord,
At the presence of the God of Jacob,
⁸Who turned the rock *into* a pool of water,
The flint into a fountain of waters.

PSALM 115

The Futility of Idols and the Trustworthiness of God
¹Not unto us, O LORD, not unto us,
But to Your name give glory,
Because of Your mercy,
Because of Your truth.
²Why should the Gentiles say,
"So where *is* their God?"

³But our God *is* in heaven;
He does whatever He pleases.
⁴Their idols *are* silver and gold,
The work of men's hands.
⁵They have mouths, but they do not
speak;
Eyes they have, but they do not see;
⁶They have ears, but they do not hear;
Noses they have, but they do not smell;
⁷They have hands, but they do not handle;
Feet they have, but they do not walk;
Nor do they mutter through their throat.
⁸Those who make them are like them;
So is everyone who trusts in them.

⁹O Israel, trust in the LORD;
He *is* their help and their shield.
¹⁰O house of Aaron, trust in the LORD;
He *is* their help and their shield.
¹¹You who fear the LORD, trust in the LORD;
He *is* their help and their shield.

¹²The LORD has been mindful of *us;*
He will bless us;
He will bless the house of Israel;
He will bless the house of Aaron.

113:1–9 **This poem exalts** both God's majesty and His compassion. "Hallel" (Heb., lit. "praise") psalms were sung in connection with major Jewish feasts and holy days (Ps. 113–118; see chart, The Types of Psalms). Psalms 113 and 114 were sung before the Passover meal, while Psalms 115–118 were part of the worship experience following the meal (see Matt. 26:30). Repeatedly, the psalmist noted that the Lord's "name," a reference to His character, is to be praised (Ps. 113:1, 2, 3), for no god compares to the Lord in His majestic splendor and in His concern for the poor, the needy, and the outcast. Compare verse 7 with Hannah's prayer (1 Sam. 2:8) and Mary's song (Luke 1:48). In ancient times, childlessness was considered a disgrace (Ps. 113:9; see Gen. 11, Infertility). A barren woman

was often rejected by her husband, ridiculed by other women, and critical of herself (Gen. 16:2; 20:18; 1 Sam. 1:6; Luke 1:25). God's goodness also would overcome this tragedy.

114:1–8 **This hallel psalm** celebrates God's mighty acts of deliverance on behalf of His people (see Psalm 113:1–9, note; chart, The Types of Psalms). The Lord delivered them from bondage in Egypt, He parted the sea as they came out of Egypt, and He parted the Jordan River when they entered the Promised Land. Nature joyfully responds to the presence of the Lord (Ps. 114:4–6). God's majestic presence should still prompt His people to tremble in awe before Him (v. 7).

¹³He will bless those who fear the LORD,
Both small and great.

¹⁴May the LORD give you increase more and
more,
You and your children.
¹⁵May you be blessed by the LORD,
Who made heaven and earth.

¹⁶The heaven, even the heavens, are the LORD's;
But the earth He has given to the children of
men.
¹⁷The dead do not praise the LORD,
Nor any who go down into silence.
¹⁸But we will bless the LORD
From this time forth and forevermore.

Praise the LORD!

PSALM 116

Thanksgiving for Deliverance from Death

¹I love the LORD, because He has heard
My voice and my supplications.
²Because He has inclined His ear to me,
Therefore I will call upon Him as long as I
live.

³The pains of death surrounded me,
And the pangs of Sheol laid hold of me;
I found trouble and sorrow.
⁴Then I called upon the name of the LORD:
"O LORD, I implore You, deliver my soul!"

⁵Gracious is the LORD, and righteous;
Yes, our God is merciful.
⁶The LORD preserves the simple;
I was brought low, and He saved me.
⁷Return to your rest, O my soul,
For the LORD has dealt bountifully with you.

⁸For You have delivered my soul from death,
My eyes from tears,
And my feet from falling.
⁹I will walk before the LORD

In the land of the living.
¹⁰I believed, therefore I spoke,
"I am greatly afflicted."
¹¹I said in my haste,
"All men are liars."

¹²What shall I render to the LORD
For all His benefits toward me?
¹³I will take up the cup of salvation,
And call upon the name of the LORD.
¹⁴I will pay my vows to the LORD
Now in the presence of all His people.

¹⁵Precious in the sight of the LORD
Is the death of His saints.

¹⁶O LORD, truly I am Your servant;
I am Your servant, the son of Your maid
servant;
You have loosed my bonds.
¹⁷I will offer to You the sacrifice of thanksgiving,
And will call upon the name of the LORD.

¹⁸I will pay my vows to the LORD
Now in the presence of all His people,
¹⁹In the courts of the LORD's house,
In the midst of you, O Jerusalem.

Praise the LORD!

PSALM 117

Let All Peoples Praise the LORD

¹Praise the LORD, all you Gentiles!
Laud Him, all you peoples!
²For His merciful kindness is great toward us,
And the truth of the LORD endures forever.

Praise the LORD!

PSALM 118

Praise to God for His Everlasting Mercy

¹Oh, give thanks to the LORD, for He is good!
For His mercy endures forever.

115:1–11 The poet emphasized the praise due God's name in this hallel psalm (vv. 1–3). The psalm was most likely sung by Jesus and His disciples following the Passover meal (Mark 14:26; see Ps. 113:1–9, note; chart, The Types of Psalms). By contrast, the idols of Israel's neighbors were powerless and worthy of ridicule (Ps. 115:4–7), and those who worshiped them were also helpless (v. 8; see Ps. 135:15–18; Is. 40:18–20; 44:9–17).

116:1–19 The poet cried out to the Lord for deliverance from sheol (Heb., lit. "death," v. 3). God heard and answered his prayer. Death remains an area in which believers have many questions (see 1 Cor. 15, Death). This verse is a loving assurance that, for the believer, physical death is an ushering into the presence of Jesus and an entrance into a more abundant life. The poet vowed his love and service to the Lord as an ex-

pression of gratitude for what He had done for him (see Ps. 113:1–9, note; chart, The Types of Psalms).

117:1, 2 This shortest poem in the Book of Psalms is a powerful universal call to worship (see Ps. 113:1–9, note; chart, The Types of Psalms). All nations and peoples are called on to praise the Lord for His love and faithfulness (Rom. 15:11).

118:1–4 This psalm praises God for His mercy (Heb. chesed: see Ps. 5:7–12, note), which endures forever (see Ps. 113:1–9, note). What a wonderful reason to give thanks to Him! Verses 22, 23 are applied to Christ, the chief cornerstone (see Matt. 21:42; Mark 12:10, 11; Luke 20:17; Acts 4:11; 1 Pet. 2:7). Psalm 118:25, 26 were chanted by those who welcomed Christ at His triumphal entry into Jerusalem ("save now I pray" from Heb. hoshiana or Gk. hosanna: see Matt. 21:9; Mark 11:9; John 12:13).

²Let Israel now say,
"His mercy *endures* forever."
³Let the house of Aaron now say,
"His mercy *endures* forever."
⁴Let those who fear the LORD now say,
"His mercy *endures* forever."

⁵I called on the LORD in distress;
The LORD answered me *and set me* in a broad
place.
⁶The LORD *is* on my side;
I will not fear.
What can man do to me?
⁷The LORD is for me among those who help
me;
Therefore I shall see *my desire* on those who
hate me.
⁸*It is* better to trust in the LORD
Than to put confidence in man.
⁹*It is* better to trust in the LORD
Than to put confidence in princes.

¹⁰All nations surrounded me,
But in the name of the LORD I will destroy
them.
¹¹They surrounded me,
Yes, they surrounded me;
But in the name of the LORD I will destroy
them.
¹²They surrounded me like bees;
They were quenched like a fire of thorns;
For in the name of the LORD I will destroy
them.
¹³You pushed me violently, that I might fall,
But the LORD helped me.
¹⁴The LORD *is* my strength and song,
And He has become my salvation.ᵃ

¹⁵The voice of rejoicing and salvation
Is in the tents of the righteous;
The right hand of the LORD does valiantly.
¹⁶The right hand of the LORD is exalted;
The right hand of the LORD does valiantly.
¹⁷I shall not die, but live,
And declare the works of the LORD.
¹⁸The LORD has chastened me severely,
But He has not given me over to death.

¹⁹Open to me the gates of righteousness;
I will go through them,
And I will praise the LORD.
²⁰This is the gate of the LORD,
Through which the righteous shall enter.

²¹I will praise You,
For You have answered me,
And have become my salvation.

²²The stone *which* the builders rejected
Has become the chief cornerstone.
²³This was the LORD's doing;
It *is* marvelous in our eyes.
²⁴This *is* the day the LORD has made;
We will rejoice and be glad in it.

²⁵Save now, I pray, O LORD;
O LORD, I pray, send now prosperity.
²⁶Blessed *is* he who comes in the name of the
LORD!
We have blessed you from the house of the
LORD.
²⁷God *is* the LORD,
And He has given us light;
Bind the sacrifice with cords to the horns of
the altar.
²⁸You *are* my God, and I will praise You;
You are my God, I will exalt You.

²⁹Oh, give thanks to the LORD, for *He is* good!
For His mercy *endures* forever.

PSALM 119

Meditations on the Excellencies of the Word of God

א ALEPH
¹Blessed *are* the undefiled in the way,
Who walk in the law of the LORD!
²Blessed *are* those who keep His testimonies,
Who seek Him with the whole heart!
³They also do no iniquity;
They walk in His ways.
⁴You have commanded *us*
To keep Your precepts diligently.
⁵Oh, that my ways were directed
To keep Your statutes!
⁶Then I would not be ashamed,
When I look into all Your commandments.
⁷I will praise You with uprightness of heart,
When I learn Your righteous judgments.
⁸I will keep Your statutes;
Oh, do not forsake me utterly!

ב BETH
⁹How can a young man cleanse his way?
By taking heed according to Your word.

118:14 ᵃCompare Exodus 15:2

119:1–8 The theme of this acrostic poem is a celebration of God's Law. Each paragraph of the psalm begins with a successive letter of the Hebrew alphabet. This poem is the longest psalm in the Book of Psalms, as well as the longest chapter in the Bible. This hymn of praise magnifies and extols the Word of God. Various terms used for the Law of the Lord include "word" (v. 9), "testimonies" (v. 46), "precepts" (v. 28), "statutes" (v. 33), "commandments" (v. 60), and "judgments" (v. 102). Those who obey God's Law experience His blessing and are protected from sin (v. 11; see Matt. 4:1–11). God's Word stands forever (Ps. 119:89; see Is. 40:8; 1 Pet. 1:24, 25), providing light and guidance through life (see John 8:12).

ATTRIBUTES OF GOD *HE IS TRUTH*

Every word God speaks is true (John 17:17). He is unable to speak an untruth (Heb. 6:17, 18), and He is never mistaken (Deut. 32:4). He knows all things as they really are and sees what has happened, is happening, and will happen (Is. 46:9, 10). Since He is responsible for everything, all accurate knowledge comes from Him. He is the standard for all truth; He is that by which all else is measured.

Truth not only describes what He knows; it also describes all He does and says, including judgment (Is. 16:5), creation (Ps. 146:6), redemption (Ps. 31:5), and each detail of every promise He makes (Josh. 23:14).

Truth is so identified with God that Jesus simply states, "I am . . . the truth" (John 14:6), identifying Himself as the only way to the understanding of genuine truth (1 John 5:20).

The fact that God is Truth is the basis of faith because the opposite of having faith in God is calling God a liar (Rom. 3:4). He is not only dependably accurate, but He is also accurately dependable.

See also Num. 23:19; Josh. 21:45; Ps. 86:15; 119:142; Lam. 3:22, note; John 8:32; 16:13; 17:3; Titus 1:2; Rev. 19:11; notes on Attributes of God (Ex. 33; Deut. 4; 32; 2 Chr. 19; Job 23; 42; Ps. 25; 90; 102; Is. 6; 65; Jer. 23; Rom. 2; Eph. 1; 1 John 5); Holiness (Lev. 20); Fear of the Lord (Prov. 2); Cults (2 Cor. 11); the Occult (Deut. 18); Promises of God (2 Pet. 1)

---

¹⁰With my whole heart I have sought You;
Oh, let me not wander from Your
commandments!
¹¹Your word I have hidden in my heart,
That I might not sin against You.
¹²Blessed *are* You, O LORD!
Teach me Your statutes.
¹³With my lips I have declared
All the judgments of Your mouth.
¹⁴I have rejoiced in the way of Your testimonies,
As *much as* in all riches.
¹⁵I will meditate on Your precepts,
And contemplate Your ways.
¹⁶I will delight myself in Your statutes;
I will not forget Your word.

ℷ GIMEL
¹⁷Deal bountifully with Your servant,
That I may live and keep Your word.
¹⁸Open my eyes, that I may see
Wondrous things from Your law.
¹⁹I *am* a stranger in the earth;
Do not hide Your commandments from me.
²⁰My soul breaks with longing
For Your judgments at all times.
²¹You rebuke the proud—the cursed,
Who stray from Your commandments.
²²Remove from me reproach and contempt,
For I have kept Your testimonies.
²³Princes also sit *and* speak against me,
But Your servant meditates on Your statutes.
²⁴Your testimonies also *are* my delight
And my counselors.

ℸ DALETH
²⁵My soul clings to the dust;
Revive me according to Your word.
²⁶I have declared my ways, and You answered me;

Teach me Your statutes.
²⁷Make me understand the way of Your
precepts;
So shall I meditate on Your wonderful works.
²⁸My soul melts from heaviness;
Strengthen me according to Your word.
²⁹Remove from me the way of lying,
And grant me Your law graciously.
³⁰I have chosen the way of truth;
Your judgments I have laid *before me.*
³¹I cling to Your testimonies;
O LORD, do not put me to shame!
³²I will run the course of Your commandments,
For You shall enlarge my heart.

ה HE
³³Teach me, O LORD, the way of Your statutes,
And I shall keep it *to* the end.
³⁴Give me understanding, and I shall keep Your
law;
Indeed, I shall observe it with *my* whole heart.
³⁵Make me walk in the path of Your
commandments,
For I delight in it.
³⁶Incline my heart to Your testimonies,
And not to covetousness.
³⁷Turn away my eyes from looking at worthless
things,
And revive me in Your way.ᵃ
³⁸Establish Your word to Your servant,
Who *is devoted* to fearing You.
³⁹Turn away my reproach which I dread,
For Your judgments *are* good.
⁴⁰Behold, I long for Your precepts;
Revive me in Your righteousness.

• • • • • • • • • • • • • • • • • •

119:37 ᵃFollowing Masoretic Text, Septuagint, and Vulgate; Targum
reads *Your words.*

ו WAW

⁴¹Let Your mercies come also to me, O LORD—
  Your salvation according to Your word.
⁴²So shall I have an answer for him who
      reproaches me,
  For I trust in Your word.
⁴³And take not the word of truth utterly out of
      my mouth,
  For I have hoped in Your ordinances.
⁴⁴So shall I keep Your law continually,
  Forever and ever.
⁴⁵And I will walk at liberty,
  For I seek Your precepts.
⁴⁶I will speak of Your testimonies also before
      kings,
  And will not be ashamed.
⁴⁷And I will delight myself in Your
      commandments,
  Which I love.
⁴⁸My hands also I will lift up to Your
      commandments,
  Which I love,
  And I will meditate on Your statutes.

ז ZAYIN

⁴⁹Remember the word to Your servant,
  Upon which You have caused me to hope.
⁵⁰This *is* my comfort in my affliction,
  For Your word has given me life.
⁵¹The proud have me in great derision,
  Yet I do not turn aside from Your law.
⁵²I remembered Your judgments of old, O LORD,
  And have comforted myself.
⁵³Indignation has taken hold of me
  Because of the wicked, who forsake Your law.
⁵⁴Your statutes have been my songs
  In the house of my pilgrimage.
⁵⁵I remember Your name in the night, O LORD,
  And I keep Your law.
⁵⁶This has become mine,
  Because I kept Your precepts.

ח HETH

⁵⁷*You are* my portion, O LORD;
  I have said that I would keep Your words.
⁵⁸I entreated Your favor with *my* whole heart;
  Be merciful to me according to Your word.
⁵⁹I thought about my ways,
  And turned my feet to Your testimonies.
⁶⁰I made haste, and did not delay
  To keep Your commandments.
⁶¹The cords of the wicked have bound me,
  But I have not forgotten Your law.
⁶²At midnight I will rise to give thanks to
      You,
  Because of Your righteous judgments.
⁶³I *am* a companion of all who fear You,
  And of those who keep Your precepts.

⁶⁴The earth, O LORD, is full of Your mercy;
  Teach me Your statutes.

ט TETH

⁶⁵You have dealt well with Your servant,
  O LORD, according to Your word.
⁶⁶Teach me good judgment and knowledge,
  For I believe Your commandments.
⁶⁷Before I was afflicted I went astray,
  But now I keep Your word.
⁶⁸You *are* good, and do good;
  Teach me Your statutes.
⁶⁹The proud have forged a lie against me,
  But I will keep Your precepts with *my* whole
      heart.
⁷⁰Their heart is as fat as grease,
  But I delight in Your law.
⁷¹*It is* good for me that I have been afflicted,
  That I may learn Your statutes.
⁷²The law of Your mouth *is* better to me
  Than thousands of *coins of* gold and silver.

י YOD

⁷³Your hands have made me and fashioned me;
  Give me understanding, that I may learn Your
      commandments.
⁷⁴Those who fear You will be glad when they see
      me,
  Because I have hoped in Your word.
⁷⁵I know, O LORD, that Your judgments *are* right,
  And *that* in faithfulness You have afflicted me.
⁷⁶Let, I pray, Your merciful kindness be for my
      comfort,
  According to Your word to Your servant.
⁷⁷Let Your tender mercies come to me, that I
      may live;
  For Your law *is* my delight.
⁷⁸Let the proud be ashamed,
  For they treated me wrongfully with
      falsehood;
  But I will meditate on Your precepts.
⁷⁹Let those who fear You turn to me,
  Those who know Your testimonies.
⁸⁰Let my heart be blameless regarding Your
      statutes,
  That I may not be ashamed.

כ KAPH

⁸¹My soul faints for Your salvation,
  But I hope in Your word.
⁸²My eyes fail *from searching* Your word,
  Saying, "When will You comfort me?"
⁸³For I have become like a wineskin in smoke,
  Yet I do not forget Your statutes.
⁸⁴How many *are* the days of Your servant?
  When will You execute judgment on those who
      persecute me?
⁸⁵The proud have dug pits for me,

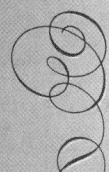

SHAME FEELING UNWORTHY

Shame is a deep inner response to the potential for, or the actual experience of, being exposed as deficient or unworthy in another's eyes. The word "shame" is closely related to "mortified," which is derived from the French word meaning "death." Shame is the experience of profound embarrassment, a feeling of wanting "to curl up and die" on the inside.

Shame is one of the first human emotions recorded in Scripture (Gen. 3:10). Adam and Eve felt shame when God exposed their deception. Their response is common to us all: they hid behind a facade of their own making (Gen. 3:7); and, when confronted, they tried to shift the blame to someone other than themselves (Gen. 3:12, 13).

Understanding your shame leads to a richer appreciation for the work of Christ. Scripture declares that He bore your sin and your shame on the Cross (Heb. 12:2) so that you might live in free, unhindered relationship with Him and each other.

See also Ps. 119:116; Mark 5:2, note; Rom. 3:23, note; Phil. 3:19; notes on Forgiveness (Ps. 51; Luke 17); Guilt (2 Cor. 7); Healing (Ps. 13; 133; Eccl. 1; 2 Cor 5; Gal. 6; James 5); Humility (Phil. 2)

Which *is* not according to Your law.
⁸⁶All Your commandments *are* faithful;
They persecute me wrongfully;
Help me!
⁸⁷They almost made an end of me on earth,
But I did not forsake Your precepts.
⁸⁸Revive me according to Your lovingkindness,
So that I may keep the testimony of Your
mouth.

ל LAMED
⁸⁹Forever, O LORD,
Your word is settled in heaven.
⁹⁰Your faithfulness *endures* to all generations;
You established the earth, and it abides.
⁹¹They continue this day according to Your
ordinances,
For all *are* Your servants.
⁹²Unless Your law *had been* my delight,
I would then have perished in my affliction.
⁹³I will never forget Your precepts,
For by them You have given me life.
⁹⁴I *am* Yours, save me;
For I have sought Your precepts.
⁹⁵The wicked wait for me to destroy me,
But I will consider Your testimonies.
⁹⁶I have seen the consummation of all perfection,
But Your commandment *is* exceedingly broad.

מ MEM
⁹⁷Oh, how I love Your law!
It *is* my meditation all the day.
⁹⁸You, through Your commandments, make me
wiser than my enemies;
For they *are* ever with me.
⁹⁹I have more understanding than all my
teachers,
For Your testimonies *are* my meditation.
¹⁰⁰I understand more than the ancients,
Because I keep Your precepts.

¹⁰¹I have restrained my feet from every evil way,
That I may keep Your word.
¹⁰²I have not departed from Your judgments,
For You Yourself have taught me.
¹⁰³How sweet are Your words to my taste,
Sweeter than honey to my mouth!
¹⁰⁴Through Your precepts I get understanding;
Therefore I hate every false way.

נ NUN
¹⁰⁵Your word *is* a lamp to my feet
And a light to my path.
¹⁰⁶I have sworn and confirmed
That I will keep Your righteous judgments.
¹⁰⁷I am afflicted very much;
Revive me, O LORD, according to Your word.
¹⁰⁸Accept, I pray, the freewill offerings of my
mouth, O LORD,
And teach me Your judgments.
¹⁰⁹My life *is* continually in my hand,
Yet I do not forget Your law.
¹¹⁰The wicked have laid a snare for me,
Yet I have not strayed from Your precepts.
¹¹¹Your testimonies I have taken as a heritage
forever,
For they *are* the rejoicing of my heart.
¹¹²I have inclined my heart to perform Your
statutes
Forever, to the very end.

ס SAMEK
¹¹³I hate the double-minded,
But I love Your law.
¹¹⁴You *are* my hiding place and my shield;
I hope in Your word.
¹¹⁵Depart from me, you evildoers,
For I will keep the commandments of my God!
¹¹⁶Uphold me according to Your word, that I may
live;
And do not let me be ashamed of my hope.

117Hold me up, and I shall be safe,
And I shall observe Your statutes continually.
118You reject all those who stray from Your
statutes,
For their deceit *is* falsehood.
119You put away all the wicked of the earth *like*
dross;
Therefore I love Your testimonies.
120My flesh trembles for fear of You,
And I am afraid of Your judgments.

ע AYIN

121I have done justice and righteousness;
Do not leave me to my oppressors.
122Be surety for Your servant for good;
Do not let the proud oppress me.
123My eyes fail *from seeking* Your salvation
And Your righteous word.
124Deal with Your servant according to Your
mercy,
And teach me Your statutes.
125I *am* Your servant;
Give me understanding,
That I may know Your testimonies.
126*It is* time for *You* to act, O LORD,
For they have regarded Your law as void.
127Therefore I love Your commandments
More than gold, yes, than fine gold!
128Therefore all *Your* precepts *concerning* all *things*
I consider *to be* right;
I hate every false way.

פ PE

129Your testimonies are wonderful;
Therefore my soul keeps them.
130The entrance of Your words gives light;
It gives understanding to the simple.
131I opened my mouth and panted,
For I longed for Your commandments.
132Look upon me and be merciful to me,
As Your custom *is* toward those who love Your
name.
133Direct my steps by Your word,
And let no iniquity have dominion over me.
134Redeem me from the oppression of man,
That I may keep Your precepts.
135Make Your face shine upon Your servant,
And teach me Your statutes.
136Rivers of water run down from my eyes,
Because *men* do not keep Your law.

צ TSADDE

137Righteous *are* You, O LORD,
And upright *are* Your judgments.
138Your testimonies, *which* You have commanded,
Are righteous and very faithful.
139My zeal has consumed me,
Because my enemies have forgotten Your
words.

140Your word *is* very pure;
Therefore Your servant loves it.
141I *am* small and despised,
Yet I do not forget Your precepts.
142Your righteousness *is* an everlasting
righteousness,
And Your law *is* truth.
143Trouble and anguish have overtaken me,
Yet Your commandments *are* my delights.
144The righteousness of Your testimonies *is*
everlasting;
Give me understanding, and I shall live.

ק QOPH

145I cry out with *my* whole heart;
Hear me, O LORD!
I will keep Your statutes.
146I cry out to You;
Save me, and I will keep Your testimonies.
147I rise before the dawning of the morning,
And cry for help;
I hope in Your word.
148My eyes are awake through the *night* watches,
That I may meditate on Your word.
149Hear my voice according to Your
lovingkindness;
O LORD, revive me according to Your justice.
150They draw near who follow after wickedness;
They are far from Your law.
151You *are* near, O LORD,
And all Your commandments *are* truth.
152Concerning Your testimonies,
I have known of old that You have founded
them forever.

ר RESH

153Consider my affliction and deliver me,
For I do not forget Your law.
154Plead my cause and redeem me;
Revive me according to Your word.
155Salvation *is* far from the wicked,
For they do not seek Your statutes.
156Great *are* Your tender mercies, O LORD;
Revive me according to Your judgments.
157Many *are* my persecutors and my enemies,
Yet I do not turn from Your testimonies.
158I see the treacherous, and am disgusted,
Because they do not keep Your word.
159Consider how I love Your precepts;
Revive me, O LORD, according to Your
lovingkindness.
160The entirety of Your word *is* truth,
And every one of Your righteous judgments
endures forever.

ש SHIN

161Princes persecute me without a cause,
But my heart stands in awe of Your word.

Perspective by Nancy Leigh DeMoss

THE WORD OF GOD: A PRECIOUS TREASURE (From *A Place of Quiet Rest*, 146–149)

Even more important than what we think of the Word of God is what God says about His own Word. According to the Bible, the Word of the Lord is true (Ps. 33:4, 119:160); it is pure (Ps. 12:6; 19:9; 119:140 KJV; Prov. 30:5 KJV); it is righteous and fully trustworthy (Ps. 119:138); it is eternal and stands firm in the heavens (Ps. 119:89); it is divinely inspired (2 Tim. 3:16); it is perfect (Ps. 19:7); it is of greater value than any amount of gold or silver (Ps. 119:72); it is sweet to the taste (Ps. 19:10; 119:103; Ezek. 3:3).

The power and authority of God's Word infinitely surpass that of any other book that has ever been written. As a troubled young seminary professor being pursued by the "Hound of Heaven," Martin Luther experienced the supernatural, transforming power of the Word that later led him to write, "The Bible is alive, it speaks to me; it has feet, it runs after me; it has hands, it lays hold on me."

When we pick up a copy of the Bible, do we realize what it is that we are holding in our hands? Do we ever stop to think that this is actually the *Word of God?* As Augustine reminds us, "When the Bible speaks, *God* speaks!" In the West we have been blessed with such easy access to the Word that it is hard not to take it for granted. Proverbs tells us that "A satisfied soul loathes the honeycomb, but to a hungry soul every bitter thing is sweet" (27:7). To hungry souls in parts of the world that have never been allowed to own a Bible, the Word of God is exceedingly precious. But to those of us who can turn on the radio and hear the Word preached every hour of the day, who can walk into any bookstore and find the Bible of our choice, who have Bibles located every several inches on the backs of our pews, and whose shelves are bursting with Bibles, some of them unused—we may find ourselves in danger of adopting a casual attitude toward the Word of God.

The Scripture says that God has exalted His Word above even His own name (Ps. 138:2 KJV). If God esteems His Word that highly, what should be our attitude toward the Word? In Psalm 119, David speaks of loving the Word, reverencing it, delighting in it, longing for it, trusting it, and fearing it. God says through the prophet Isaiah, "But on this one will I look: on him who is poor and of a contrite spirit, and who *trembles* at My word" (Is.66:2, emphasis added; cf. Ps. 119:161). What does is mean to tremble at the Word of the Lord? It means to have an attitude of reverential awe and fear. It is the opposite of a cavalier attitude toward the Word.

In Psalm 119, David can scarcely contain his joy as he rehearses the blessings and benefits he has received from the Word of God. We learn that the Word of God has the power to keep us from sin (Ps. 119:9, 11), to strengthen us when we are grieving (v. 28), to comfort us when we are suffering (vv. 50, 52), to grant us freedom (v. 45), to give us understanding and light for our path (v. 104), and to give us peace and keep us from stumbling (v. 165).

The Word of God will light your way; it will help you make right choices; it will heal your wounds and settle your heart; it will warn you of danger; it will protect and cleanse you from sin; it will lead you; it will make you wise. It is bread; it is water; it is a counselor; it is life. It is satisfying; it is sufficient; it is supreme; it is supernatural. The hymn writer put it this way:

> Holy Bible, book divine;
>> Precious treasure, thou art mine;
> Mine to tell me whence I came;
>> Mine to teach me what I am.
>
> Mine to chide me when I rove;
>> Mine to show a Savior's love;
> Mine thou art to guide and guard;
>> Mine to punish or reward.
>
> Mine to comfort in distress,
>> Suff'ring in this wilderness;
> Mine to show, by living faith,
>> Man can triumph over death.
>
> Mine to tell of joys to come,
>> And the rebel sinner's doom;
> O thou Holy Book divine,
>> Precious treasure, thou art mine.

—John Burton (1773–1822)

¹⁶²I rejoice at Your word
  As one who finds great treasure.
¹⁶³I hate and abhor lying,
  But I love Your law.
¹⁶⁴Seven times a day I praise You,
  Because of Your righteous judgments.
¹⁶⁵Great peace have those who love Your law,
  And nothing causes them to stumble.
¹⁶⁶LORD, I hope for Your salvation,
  And I do Your commandments.
¹⁶⁷My soul keeps Your testimonies,
  And I love them exceedingly.
¹⁶⁸I keep Your precepts and Your
    testimonies,
  For all my ways *are* before You.

ת TAU
¹⁶⁹Let my cry come before You, O LORD;
  Give me understanding according to Your
    word.
¹⁷⁰Let my supplication come before You;
  Deliver me according to Your word.
¹⁷¹My lips shall utter praise,
  For You teach me Your statutes.
¹⁷²My tongue shall speak of Your word,
  For all Your commandments *are* righteousness.
¹⁷³Let Your hand become my help,
  For I have chosen Your precepts.
¹⁷⁴I long for Your salvation, O LORD,
  And Your law *is* my delight.
¹⁷⁵Let my soul live, and it shall praise You;
  And let Your judgments help me.
¹⁷⁶I have gone astray like a lost sheep;
  Seek Your servant,
  For I do not forget Your commandments.

PSALM 120

Plea for Relief from Bitter Foes
A Song of Ascents.

¹In my distress I cried to the LORD,
  And He heard me.
²Deliver my soul, O LORD, from lying lips
  And from a deceitful tongue.

³What shall be given to you,
  Or what shall be done to you,
  You false tongue?

⁴Sharp arrows of the warrior,
  With coals of the broom tree!

⁵Woe is me, that I dwell in Meshech,
  That I dwell among the tents of Kedar!
⁶My soul has dwelt too long
  With one who hates peace.
⁷I *am for* peace;
  But when I speak, they *are* for war.

PSALM 121

God the Help of Those Who Seek Him
A Song of Ascents.

¹I will lift up my eyes to the hills—
  From whence comes my help?
²My help *comes* from the LORD,
  Who made heaven and earth.

³He will not allow your foot to be moved;
  He who keeps you will not slumber.
⁴Behold, He who keeps Israel
  Shall neither slumber nor sleep.

⁵The LORD *is* your keeper;
  The LORD *is* your shade at your right hand.
⁶The sun shall not strike you by day,
  Nor the moon by night.

⁷The LORD shall preserve you from all evil;
  He shall preserve your soul.
⁸The LORD shall preserve your going out and
    your coming in
  From this time forth, and even forevermore.

PSALM 122

The Joy of Going to the House of the LORD
A Song of Ascents. Of David.

¹I was glad when they said to me,
  "Let us go into the house of the LORD."
²Our feet have been standing
  Within your gates, O Jerusalem!

³Jerusalem is built
  As a city that is compact together,
⁴Where the tribes go up,

120:1, 2 Psalms 120—134 are called "the songs of ascents," "the songs of degrees," or "the songs of pilgrimage" (see chart, The Types of Psalms). They probably were sung by worshipers as they went up to Jerusalem to celebrate the great festivals each year. The poet found himself in a hostile environment. He cried out for deliverance from the deceitful tongue of his enemies (v. 2). The psalmist longed for peace (Heb. *shalom*, lit. "well-being" or "wholeness"), but his enemies wanted conflict.

121:1–8 The poet lifted up his eyes to look for the only source of help (vv. 1, 2; see Ps. 120:1, 2, note). The "hills" may refer to the terrain around Jerusalem (Ps. 121:1). The Lord, the Creator, is the guardian and protector of His people (vv. 3–7). He never sleeps but watches over His own continuously (vv. 3–6; Phil. 4:7).

122:1, 2 A prayer for Jerusalem's peace (Heb. *shalom*, lit. "well-being"). Jerusalem, the place for worship of God, plays a significant role in the religious and political lives of God's people (vv. 1, 4, 5; see Ps. 120:1, 2, note). Some link this psalm with Jesus' entry into Jerusalem (Luke 19:41, 42).

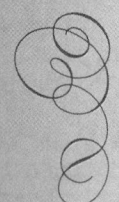

CHILDREN THE VALUE OF CHILDREN

One of the characteristics that distinguishes the Jews from other people of the Bible is the value they placed on children. They had learned well *Yahweh*'s absolute prohibition of child sacrifice (Deut. 12:31, 32) and the importance He placed on teaching children to love and serve Him (Deut. 6:7–9). Jesus responded in anger to the disciples' denial of the worth of children in the kingdom (Mark 10:13–16). Jesus went so far as to say that people are better off dead than to cause children to fall (Mark 9:42). He taught that to receive children is to receive Him (Mark 9:37); to give to children is to give to Him (Matt. 10:42); and to become like a child is the secret to conversion (Mark 10:15). Jesus invited children to come to Himself (Mark 10:14).

Children are a blessing from God (Ps. 128:3). Psalm 128 has been called "the Builder's Psalm" because to the Israelite the home was an opportunity to pursue the holy task of "building" sons and daughters. This picture is shown in the Hebrew language itself (*banah*, lit. "to build"; *ben*, "son"; *bat*, "daughter"). This concept clearly portrays what the Creator had in mind as parents are to work at "building" their children—laying the foundation of faith in living before them as Christians, honoring Jesus, nurturing and undergirding them with prayer, polishing them with the teaching of God's Word. Then, if well "built" in the Lord, these children will themselves become builders of sons and daughters, continuing godly seed unto the generations.

Children then are the most valuable fruit of the kingdom. They are generally sensitive and pliable—open to the gospel. They are fresh and energetic with years of service to offer in the kingdom. Children are part of the heritage God gives (Ps. 127:3–5). When we devalue them, we have crossed swords with the Almighty.

See also Matt. 18:3, note; 19:13–15; Luke 17:1, 2; 18:15–17; notes on Adoption (Esth. 2); Birth Control (Ps. 139); Child Care (John 14); Children (2 Sam. 21; Prov. 22; Luke 15); Family (Gen. 32; 1 Sam. 3; Ps. 78; 127); Naming of Children (Is. 45); Parenthood (Prov. 10); Sanctity of Life (Gen. 9)

The tribes of the LORD,
To the Testimony of Israel,
To give thanks to the name of the LORD.
⁵For thrones are set there for judgment,
The thrones of the house of David.

⁶Pray for the peace of Jerusalem:
"May they prosper who love you.
⁷Peace be within your walls,
Prosperity within your palaces."
⁸For the sake of my brethren and
companions,
I will now say, "Peace *be* within you."
⁹Because of the house of the LORD our God
I will seek your good.

PSALM 123

Prayer for Relief from Contempt
A Song of Ascents.

¹Unto You I lift up my eyes,
O You who dwell in the heavens.
²Behold, as the eyes of servants *look* to the hand
of their masters,
As the eyes of a maid to the hand of her
mistress,
So our eyes *look* to the LORD our God,
Until He has mercy on us.

³Have mercy on us, O LORD, have mercy on
us!
For we are exceedingly filled with contempt.
⁴Our soul is exceedingly filled
With the scorn of those who are at ease,
With the contempt of the proud.

PSALM 124

The LORD the Defense of His People
A Song of Ascents. Of David.

¹"If it had not been the LORD who was on our
side,"
Let Israel now say—
²"If it had not been the LORD who was on our
side,
When men rose up against us,
³Then they would have swallowed us alive,
When their wrath was kindled against us;
⁴Then the waters would have overwhelmed
us,
The stream would have gone over our
soul;
⁵Then the swollen waters
Would have gone over our soul."

⁶Blessed *be* the LORD,
Who has not given us *as* prey to their teeth.

124:1–8 God received credit for bringing victory to His people in this psalm of ascents (see Ps. 120:1, 2, note; chart, The Types of Psalms). Had the Lord not been on Israel's side, the nation would have been swallowed up by its enemies (Ps.

124:3). Instead, they were preserved from a flood (vv. 4, 5) and escaped the fowler's snare (vv. 6, 7; compare also v. 8 with Ps. 121:2). God often seeks to bring us to His side so that He may reveal Himself as One who is totally for us.

[7]Our soul has escaped as a bird from the snare
of the fowlers;[a]
The snare is broken, and we have escaped.
[8]Our help *is* in the name of the LORD,
Who made heaven and earth.

PSALM 125

The LORD the Strength of His People
A Song of Ascents.

[1]Those who trust in the LORD
Are like Mount Zion,
Which cannot be moved, *but* abides forever.
[2]As the mountains surround Jerusalem,
So the LORD surrounds His people
From this time forth and forever.

[3]For the scepter of wickedness shall not rest
On the land allotted to the righteous,
Lest the righteous reach out their hands to
iniquity.

[4]Do good, O LORD, to *those who are* good,
And to *those who are* upright in their hearts.

[5]As for such as turn aside to their crooked ways,
The LORD shall lead them away
With the workers of iniquity.

Peace *be* upon Israel!

PSALM 126

A Joyful Return to Zion
A Song of Ascents.

[1]When the LORD brought back the captivity of
Zion,
We were like those who dream.
[2]Then our mouth was filled with laughter,
And our tongue with singing.
Then they said among the nations,
"The LORD has done great things for them."
[3]The LORD has done great things for us,
And we are glad.

[4]Bring back our captivity, O LORD,
As the streams in the South.

[5]Those who sow in tears
Shall reap in joy.
[6]He who continually goes forth weeping,
Bearing seed for sowing,
Shall doubtless come again with rejoicing,
Bringing his sheaves *with him.*

PSALM 127

Laboring and Prospering with the LORD
A Song of Ascents. Of Solomon.

[1]Unless the LORD builds the house,
They labor in vain who build it;
Unless the LORD guards the city,
The watchman stays awake in vain.
[2]*It is* vain for you to rise up early,
To sit up late,
To eat the bread of sorrows;
For so He gives His beloved sleep.

[3]Behold, children *are* a heritage from the LORD,
The fruit of the womb *is* a reward.
[4]Like arrows in the hand of a warrior,
So *are* the children of one's youth.
[5]Happy *is* the man who has his quiver full of
them;
They shall not be ashamed,
But shall speak with their enemies in the gate.

PSALM 128

Blessings of Those Who Fear the LORD
A Song of Ascents.

[1]Blessed *is* every one who fears the LORD,
Who walks in His ways.

[2]When you eat the labor of your hands,
You *shall be* happy, and *it shall be* well with you.

· · · · · · · · · · · · · · ·
124:7 [a]That is, persons who catch birds in a trap or snare

125:1–5 The Lord provides strength and assurance for His people in difficult times (see Ps. 120:1, 2, note). Those who trust in the Lord are as secure and immovable as Mount Zion, on which the temple was built. They are surrounded by His protection. The power of the wicked will not last forever.

126:1–6 The people are encouraged to persevere in the knowledge that God will again restore His people (vv. 5, 6; see Ps. 120:1, 2, note). The historical setting of this psalm focuses around the return of the exiles from captivity in Babylon as permitted by the decree of King Cyrus of Persia in 538 B.C. (see Ezra 1:1–4). Joy accompanied this release from captivity.

127:1, 2 God gives genuine rest to those who depend on Him (v. 2; see Ps. 120:1, 2, note). The word pictures of building a house and guarding a city are employed to stress the neces-

sity of depending on the Lord (Ps. 127:1). All human effort is worthless ("vain") without the blessing of the Lord.

127:3–5 Children are a gift from the Lord (see Ps. 128, Children). The Hebrews regarded children as a blessing from the Lord (see Gen. 13:16; Ruth 4:13–16; 1 Sam. 1:11). They are a reward and heritage, bringing joy to their parents. Rearing a child is a sacred responsibility, and parents must depend on the Lord to help them guide their children.

128:1–6 Those who fear the Lord reap the rewards of labor, a good marriage, and a happy family (see Ps. 127, Family). These blessings, not material possessions, constitute life's greatest values (see Ps. 120:1, 2, note). To fear the Lord involves reverence, obedience, and walking "in His ways" (Ps. 128:1).

FAMILY   GOD'S OBJECT LESSON

A Christ-centered home offers unlimited potential to study the Bible, to learn theology through object lessons built into the structure of the home, and to give a "word about God" to the world through the testimony of their lives and interactions of family members. Incarnational living, in which parents make it possible for their children to see the sanctification process in their own lives, is crucial (Deut. 6:7–9).

God's plan for marriage is presented in Genesis (Gen. 2:24). In Exodus each commandment of the Decalogue touches on behavior within the family circle. In Leviticus, the Law contains the death penalty for those who prostitute the home. In Numbers, the numbering of the people is done by family units (Num. 4:1, 2). Deuteronomy emphasizes parental instruction (Deut. 6:1–12). Joshua describes the godly patriarch who led his family to follow *Yahweh* God (Josh. 24:15); whereas Judges records the account of Samson's selfish, unbridled lust. Ruth records a beautiful story of romantic love and godly marriage (Ruth 1:16, 17).

In the books of Samuel, Kings, and Chronicles, the history of Israel notes the influence of the home on the kings. The wickedness of Ahab was extended and magnified by his wife Jezebel (1 Kin. 21:5–16); whereas the greatness of Samuel and his unusual sensitivity to God certainly was partly due to the influence of the devout Hannah (1 Sam. 1:27, 28). In Ezra, Nehemiah, and Esther a godly seed was preserved through the family unit (Esth. 2:20; 4:14).

Job reveals Satan's attack on the home through death, disease, poverty, and internal strife (Job 1:13–21; 2:7–10). Psalms contains promises for the home (Ps. 127); Proverbs and Ecclesiastes abound in maxims about family and interpersonal relationships (Prov. 14:1; 22:6; Eccl. 4:9–12). The Song is an explicit account of a holy and exclusive love between a man and a woman (Song 4:1–7).

The prophetic books allude to the open violation of godly principles in families (Is. 3:12–26; Jer. 31:29–30; Lam. 4:10; Ezek. 16:44–45; Hos. 4:1–5; Joel 2:28, 29; Mic. 7:5–6; Mal. 2:14–16).

In the New Testament, the synoptic Gospels present Jesus' teachings concerning the family (Matt. 19:3–9), and John records His first miracle at a wedding in Cana (John 2:1–11). Acts makes mention of the home, together with the synagogue, as a center for worship (Acts 2:46; 12:12). The Epistles, too, are full of teachings concerning the family (1 Cor. 11:1–16; Eph. 5:21—6:4; Col. 3:18–21; 1 Thess. 4:1–7; 1 Tim. 3:1–12; Titus 2:1–5; Heb. 12:5–11; 1 Pet. 3:1–7). Even the Apocalypse has its message for the home (Rev. 3:20).

God commands husbands to love their wives as Christ loved the church by assuming leadership and responsibility. Wives were created to be helpers to their own respective husbands (Gen. 2:18), supplementing and not supplanting, complementing and not commanding.

Husbands and wives who enter parenthood are admonished to take seriously their responsibilities to teach God's Word to their children at every opportunity (Deut. 6:4–9, 20–25; Josh. 4:6, 7). Grandparents, aunts, uncles, and cousins, were included in the extended family. The same loving commitment enjoined for husbands and wives is projected unto the generations (see Ruth 1:16, 17).

See also Num. 36:8; Ps. 128:1–6; Matt. 18:3, note; notes on Children (2 Sam. 21; Ps. 128; Prov. 22; Luke 15); Fatherhood (Eph. 5); Grandparenthood (Ps. 71); Homemaking (Prov. 24); Husbands (Job 31; 2 Cor. 6); Marriage (Gen. 2; 2 Sam. 6; Prov. 5; Hos. 2; Amos 3; 2 Cor. 13; Heb. 12); Motherhood (1 Sam. 1; Is. 49; Ezek. 16); Wives (Prov. 31)

---

³Your wife *shall be* like a fruitful vine
In the very heart of your house,
Your children like olive plants
All around your table.
⁴Behold, thus shall the man be blessed
Who fears the LORD.

⁵The LORD bless you out of Zion,
And may you see the good of Jerusalem
All the days of your life.
⁶Yes, may you see your children's children.

Peace *be* upon Israel!

PSALM 129

Song of Victory over Zion's Enemies

A Song of Ascents.

¹"Many a time they have afflicted me from my
    youth,"
    Let Israel now say—
²"Many a time they have afflicted me from my
    youth;
    Yet they have not prevailed against me.
³The plowers plowed on my back;
    They made their furrows long."
⁴The LORD *is* righteous;

129:1–8 Israel had repeatedly suffered at the hands of their enemies, and God repeatedly had delivered them. Israel recalled those who had afflicted the people of God in the past

(see Ps. 120:1, 2, note). The poem concludes with a threefold curse on Israel's enemies, who are viewed also as the enemies of the Lord.

He has cut in pieces the cords of the
  wicked.

⁵Let all those who hate Zion
  Be put to shame and turned back.
⁶Let them be as the grass *on* the housetops,
  Which withers before it grows up,
⁷With which the reaper does not fill his hand,
  Nor he who binds sheaves, his arms.
⁸Neither let those who pass by them say,
  "The blessing of the Lord *be* upon you;
  We bless you in the name of the Lord!"

PSALM 130

Waiting for the Redemption of the Lord
A Song of Ascents.

¹Out of the depths I have cried to You, O Lord;
²Lord, hear my voice!
  Let Your ears be attentive
  To the voice of my supplications.

³If You, Lord, should mark iniquities,
  O Lord, who could stand?
⁴But *there is* forgiveness with You,
  That You may be feared.

⁵I wait for the Lord, my soul waits,
  And in His word I do hope.
⁶My soul *waits* for the Lord
  More than those who watch for the morning—
  Yes, more than those who watch for the
  morning.

⁷O Israel, hope in the Lord;
  For with the Lord *there is* mercy,
  And with Him *is* abundant redemption.
⁸And He shall redeem Israel
  From all his iniquities.

PSALM 131

Simple Trust in the Lord
A Song of Ascents. Of David.

¹Lord, my heart is not haughty,
  Nor my eyes lofty.

Neither do I concern myself with great
  matters,
  Nor with things too profound for me.

²Surely I have calmed and quieted my soul,
  Like a weaned child with his mother;
  Like a weaned child *is* my soul within me.

³O Israel, hope in the Lord
  From this time forth and forever.

PSALM 132

The Eternal Dwelling of God in Zion
A Song of Ascents.

¹Lord, remember David
  And all his afflictions;
²How he swore to the Lord,
  And vowed to the Mighty One of Jacob:
³"Surely I will not go into the chamber of my
  house,
  Or go up to the comfort of my bed;
⁴I will not give sleep to my eyes
  Or slumber to my eyelids,
⁵Until I find a place for the Lord,
  A dwelling place for the Mighty One of Jacob."

⁶Behold, we heard of it in Ephrathah;
  We found it in the fields of the woods.ᵃ
⁷Let us go into His tabernacle;
  Let us worship at His footstool.
⁸Arise, O Lord, to Your resting place,
  You and the ark of Your strength.
⁹Let Your priests be clothed with righteousness,
  And let Your saints shout for joy.

¹⁰For Your servant David's sake,
  Do not turn away the face of Your Anointed.

¹¹The Lord has sworn *in* truth to David;
  He will not turn from it:
  "I will set upon your throne the fruit of your
  body.
¹²If your sons will keep My covenant

132:6 ᵃHebrew *Jaar*

130:1–8 The poet urgently cried out in his despair for the Lord to hear his prayer for forgiveness. His sins overwhelmed him as though he were drowning. But rather than recording sins and meting out justice accordingly, God forgives. In this penitential psalm, gratitude for His forgiveness leads the worshiper to reverent fear and obedience (v. 4; see Ps. 6:2–10, note; chart, The Types of Psalms). Thus, the poet waited expectantly, as watchmen wait for the dawn, for the Lord's forgiveness and deliverance. He encouraged others to wait confidently and expectantly for the God who abundantly forgives.

131:1–3 The poet no longer felt torn apart by inner nagging and turmoil. He had come to terms with himself and thus ex-

perienced inner peace (v. 2; see Ps. 120:1, 2, note). The psalmist used a metaphor easily understood by mothers to describe his new found serenity. A child that is weaned (Heb. *gamul*) no longer struggles for milk when held on its mother's breast, but this would also be true of a baby that has been satisfied with the mother's milk. However, the picture is one of contentment, regardless of age. The psalmist advised Israel to trust in the Lord and not to depend on themselves. Only then would God's people know true serenity, security, and contentment.

132:1–18 The worshipers are reminded of David's desire to build a house for the Lord (vv. 1–5; 2 Sam. 7:1, 2; see chart, The Types of Psalms). God's promise to establish the Davidic

HEALING RELATIONSHIPS · *LIVING TOGETHER IN UNITY*

The psalmist speaks warmly of believers living together in unity (Ps. 133:1–3), and Jesus said that Christians should be identified by their love for one another (John 13:35). Nevertheless, the Bible records numerous instances of broken relationships. These began when sin entered at the Fall, as demonstrated by Adam and Eve's blame-shifting (Gen. 3:11–13) and Cain's anger with and murder of his brother Abel (Gen. 4:5–8).

The key to healing broken relationships is forgiveness (Eph. 4:31, 32; Col. 3:12–15). Forgiveness needs to be based on a truthful view of the offenses, neither exaggerating nor minimizing them. It accurately recognizes three things: the true nature of the offense; the emotional wounding that occurred (feeling shamed, worthless, abandoned); and the consequences of the offense that has played out over time (physical or emotional injury from abuse or loss).

In forgiving, a woman needs

1) to acknowledge that she has been hurt or wronged, including emotional wounds and losses she may have suffered;
2) to forgive freely the offenses and to release the offender from any obligation to make up for them (Luke 6:37);
3) to confess as sin any bitterness and resentment she may have harbored as a result of the offense.

This threefold process puts the woman in a frame of heart, mind, and will to approach her offender with godly love and compassion, seeking ways in which the relationship might be restored.

See also Mark 5:2, note; notes on Conflict (Song 5; Matt. 18); Forgiveness (Ps. 51; Luke 17); Healing (Ps. 13; Eccl. 1; 2 Cor. 5; Gal. 6; James 5)

And My testimony which I shall teach them,
Their sons also shall sit upon your throne
forevermore."

13For the Lord has chosen Zion;
He has desired *it* for His dwelling place:
14"This *is* My resting place forever;
Here I will dwell, for I have desired it.
15I will abundantly bless her provision;
I will satisfy her poor with bread.
16I will also clothe her priests with salvation,
And her saints shall shout aloud for joy.
17There I will make the horn of David grow;
I will prepare a lamp for My Anointed.
18His enemies I will clothe with shame,
But upon Himself His crown shall flourish."

PSALM 133

Blessed Unity of the People of God
A Song of Ascents. Of David.

1Behold, how good and how pleasant *it is*
For brethren to dwell together in unity!

2*It is* like the precious oil upon the
head,
Running down on the beard,
The beard of Aaron,

Running down on the edge of his garments.
3*It is* like the dew of Hermon,
Descending upon the mountains of Zion;
For there the Lord commanded the blessing—
Life forevermore.

PSALM 134

Praising the Lord in His House at Night
A Song of Ascents.

1Behold, bless the Lord,
All *you* servants of the Lord,
Who by night stand in the house of the
Lord!
2Lift up your hands *in* the sanctuary,
And bless the Lord.
3The Lord who made heaven and earth
Bless you from Zion!

---

dynasty is recalled (Ps. 132:11–18; see 2 Sam. 7:8–17). Although David was not permitted to build a house for the Lord, the Lord promised to build a house (dynasty) for David. This messianic promise is fulfilled in Christ (Luke 1:32, 33).

133:1–3 God's blessing involves unity among the members in His family (see Ps. 120:1, 2, note). In this poem, the psalmist illustrated the sweet spirit of unity with the fragrant oil used to anoint the priests and the life-giving dew of Mount Hermon. Such harmony within the family of God renews our energies as we share life with Him and with one another.

134:1–3 Worship involves willingness to serve (v. 1). This final song of ascents, degrees, or pilgrimage is a fitting conclusion to the group of 15 psalms (see Ps. 120:1, 2, note; chart, The Types of Psalms). The first two verses of this psalm call the worshipers to bless the Lord and to praise Him. The third verse is a benediction requesting the Lord's blessing on His servants. God's blessings include wonderful gifts that money cannot purchase, gifts such as peace of mind, unity, fellowship, and joy (see Gal. 5:22, 23).

PSALM 135

Praise to God in Creation and Redemption

¹Praise the LORD!

Praise the name of the LORD;
Praise *Him*, O you servants of the LORD!
²You who stand in the house of the LORD,
In the courts of the house of our God,
³Praise the LORD, for the LORD *is* good;
Sing praises to His name, for *it is* pleasant.
⁴For the LORD has chosen Jacob for Himself,
Israel for His special treasure.

⁵For I know that the LORD *is* great,
And our Lord *is* above all gods.
⁶Whatever the LORD pleases He does,
In heaven and in earth,
In the seas and in all deep places.
⁷He causes the vapors to ascend from the ends
    of the earth;
He makes lightning for the rain;
He brings the wind out of His treasuries.

⁸He destroyed the firstborn of Egypt,
Both of man and beast.
⁹He sent signs and wonders into the midst of
    you, O Egypt,
Upon Pharaoh and all his servants.
¹⁰He defeated many nations
And slew mighty kings—
¹¹Sihon king of the Amorites,
Og king of Bashan,
And all the kingdoms of Canaan—
¹²And gave their land *as* a heritage,
A heritage to Israel His people.

¹³Your name, O LORD, *endures* forever,
Your fame, O LORD, throughout all generations.
¹⁴For the LORD will judge His people,
And He will have compassion on His servants.

¹⁵The idols of the nations *are* silver and gold,
The work of men's hands.
¹⁶They have mouths, but they do not speak;
Eyes they have, but they do not see;
¹⁷They have ears, but they do not hear;
Nor is there *any* breath in their mouths.
¹⁸Those who make them are like them;
So is everyone who trusts in them.

¹⁹Bless the LORD, O house of Israel!
Bless the LORD, O house of Aaron!

²⁰Bless the LORD, O house of Levi!
You who fear the LORD, bless the LORD!
²¹Blessed be the LORD out of Zion,
Who dwells in Jerusalem!

Praise the LORD!

PSALM 136

Thanksgiving to God for His Enduring Mercy

¹Oh, give thanks to the LORD, for *He is* good!
For His mercy *endures* forever.
²Oh, give thanks to the God of gods!
For His mercy *endures* forever.
³Oh, give thanks to the Lord of lords!
For His mercy *endures* forever:

⁴To Him who alone does great wonders,
For His mercy *endures* forever;
⁵To Him who by wisdom made the heavens,
For His mercy *endures* forever;
⁶To Him who laid out the earth above the
    waters,
For His mercy *endures* forever;
⁷To Him who made great lights,
For His mercy *endures* forever—
⁸The sun to rule by day,
For His mercy *endures* forever;
⁹The moon and stars to rule by night,
For His mercy *endures* forever.

¹⁰To Him who struck Egypt in their firstborn,
For His mercy *endures* forever;
¹¹And brought out Israel from among them,
For His mercy *endures* forever;
¹²With a strong hand, and with an outstretched
    arm,
For His mercy *endures* forever;
¹³To Him who divided the Red Sea in two,
For His mercy *endures* forever;
¹⁴And made Israel pass through the midst of it,
For His mercy *endures* forever;
¹⁵But overthrew Pharaoh and his army in the
    Red Sea,
For His mercy *endures* forever;
¹⁶To Him who led His people through the
    wilderness,
For His mercy *endures* forever;
¹⁷To Him who struck down great kings,
For His mercy *endures* forever;
¹⁸And slew famous kings,
For His mercy *endures* forever—
¹⁹Sihon king of the Amorites,

135:1–4 God's people bring special joy to Him. This psalm is a call to worship the Lord who is good (v. 3). "Jacob" and "Israel" refer to God's people, who are His "special treasure" (lit. "valued property" or "precious possession," v. 4).

137:1–6 This poet poured out his feelings of homesickness and his longings for Jerusalem. He must have been among those who experienced exile and captivity in Babylon following the fall of Jerusalem to the Babylonians in 586 B.C. Unable to sing, the poet vowed never to forget his homeland. He would not be a traitor to Jerusalem, his spiritual home! As Christians, we can learn to sing a song of praise to the Lord regardless of the difficult circumstances we encounter.

BIRTH CONTROL *THE STEWARDSHIP OF PROCREATION*

Certain biblical premises must be recognized before making any decision regarding birth control. First, children are regarded by God as a blessing to be welcomed into the home of a married couple (Ps. 127:3). God is intricately involved in the formation of life in the womb (Ps. 139:13–16), and He plans that life before the child is born (Jer. 1:5).

Birth control, when viewed as a stewardship of procreation is neither categorically affirmed nor expressly forbidden by Scripture. A decision to limit or plan the bearing of children should be a directive from God and not merely a decision based on self-centered convenience. For example, birth control is not acceptable to prevent the consequences of sins like fornication and adultery, which are condemned by God (Ex. 20:14; 1 Cor. 6:15–20).

Sexual relations within the context of marriage are designed by God for the expression of intimacy and love as well as for procreation. A Christian must seek God's leadership before using any natural or artificial means of birth control. No method of birth control that brings death to an innocent human life is moral. In addition, irreversible forms of birth control should be weighed seriously. While the Bible does not condemn childlessness, a married couple should recognize that fruitful marriage is a biblical norm, and they would do well to consider the heritage God may have planned for them in ushering in and rearing the generation to come.

See also Gen. 38:8, 9; Matt. 18:3, note; notes on Abortion (Jer. 1); Childbirth (John 16); Children (2 Sam. 21; Ps. 128; Prov. 22; Luke 15); Pregnancy (Judg. 13); Sanctity of Life (Gen. 9)

For His mercy *endures* forever;
20And Og king of Bashan,
  For His mercy *endures* forever—
21And gave their land as a heritage,
  For His mercy *endures* forever;
22A heritage to Israel His servant,
  For His mercy *endures* forever.

23Who remembered us in our lowly state,
  For His mercy *endures* forever;
24And rescued us from our enemies,
  For His mercy *endures* forever;
25Who gives food to all flesh,
  For His mercy *endures* forever.

26Oh, give thanks to the God of heaven!
  For His mercy *endures* forever.

PSALM 137

Longing for Zion in a Foreign Land

1By the rivers of Babylon,
  There we sat down, yea, we wept
  When we remembered Zion.
2We hung our harps
  Upon the willows in the midst of it.
3For there those who carried us away captive
    asked of us a song,
  And those who plundered us *requested* mirth,
  Saying, "Sing us *one* of the songs of Zion!"

4How shall we sing the LORD's song
  In a foreign land?

5If I forget you, O Jerusalem,
  Let my right hand forget *its skill!*
6If I do not remember you,
  Let my tongue cling to the roof of my mouth—
  If I do not exalt Jerusalem
  Above my chief joy.

7Remember, O LORD, against the sons of Edom
  The day of Jerusalem,
  Who said, "Raze *it,* raze *it,*
  To its very foundation!"

8O daughter of Babylon, who are to be
    destroyed,
  Happy the one who repays you as you have
    served us!
9Happy the one who takes and dashes
  Your little ones against the rock!

PSALM 138

The LORD's Goodness to the Faithful

A Psalm of David.

1I will praise You with my whole heart;
  Before the gods I will sing praises to You.
2I will worship toward Your holy temple,
  And praise Your name
  For Your lovingkindness and Your truth;
  For You have magnified Your word above all
    Your name.
3In the day when I cried out, You answered me,
  And made me bold *with* strength in my soul.

138:1–8 This poet's hymn arose out of a grateful heart. The "gods" may refer to pagan idols (v. 1). The Lord is praised for His "lovingkindness" (Heb. *chesed*; see Ps. 5:7–12, note) and "truth" (Ps. 138:2). God had answered the poet's prayer and strengthened him (v. 3). The psalmist had complete confidence that the Lord would complete His work in him (Phil. 1:6).

⁴All the kings of the earth shall praise You, O
LORD,
When they hear the words of Your mouth.
⁵Yes, they shall sing of the ways of the LORD,
For great *is* the glory of the LORD.
⁶Though the LORD *is* on high,
Yet He regards the lowly;
But the proud He knows from afar.

⁷Though I walk in the midst of trouble, You will
revive me;
You will stretch out Your hand
Against the wrath of my enemies,
And Your right hand will save me.
⁸The LORD will perfect *that which* concerns me;
Your mercy, O LORD, *endures* forever;
Do not forsake the works of Your hands.

PSALM 139

God's Perfect Knowledge of Man
For the Chief Musician. A Psalm of David.

¹O LORD, You have searched me and known *me.*
²You know my sitting down and my rising up;
You understand my thought afar off.
³You comprehend my path and my lying down,
And are acquainted with all my ways.
⁴For *there is* not a word on my tongue,
But behold, O LORD, You know it altogether.
⁵You have hedged me behind and before,
And laid Your hand upon me.
⁶*Such* knowledge *is* too wonderful for me;
It is high, I cannot *attain* it.

⁷Where can I go from Your Spirit?
Or where can I flee from Your presence?
⁸If I ascend into heaven, You *are* there;
If I make my bed in hell, behold, You *are there.*
⁹*If* I take the wings of the morning,
And dwell in the uttermost parts of the sea,
¹⁰Even there Your hand shall lead me,
And Your right hand shall hold me.
¹¹If I say, "Surely the darkness shall fallᵃ on me,"
Even the night shall be light about me;
¹²Indeed, the darkness shall not hide from You,

But the night shines as the day;
The darkness and the light *are* both alike *to You.*

¹³For You formed my inward parts;
You covered me in my mother's womb.
¹⁴I will praise You, for I am fearfully *and*
wonderfully made;ᵃ
Marvelous are Your works,
And *that* my soul knows very well.
¹⁵My frame was not hidden from You,
When I was made in secret,
And skillfully wrought in the lowest parts of
the earth.
¹⁶Your eyes saw my substance, being yet
unformed.
And in Your book they all were written,
The days fashioned for me,
When *as yet there were* none of them.

¹⁷How precious also are Your thoughts to me, O
God!
How great is the sum of them!
¹⁸*If* I should count them, they would be more in
number than the sand;
When I awake, I am still with You.

¹⁹Oh, that You would slay the wicked, O God!
Depart from me, therefore, you bloodthirsty
men.
²⁰For they speak against You wickedly;
Your enemies take *Your name* in vain.ᵃ
²¹Do I not hate them, O LORD, who hate You?
And do I not loathe those who rise up against
You?
²²I hate them with perfect hatred;
I count them my enemies.

²³Search me, O God, and know my heart;
Try me, and know my anxieties;
²⁴And see if *there is any* wicked way in me,
And lead me in the way everlasting.

139:11 ᵃVulgate and Symmachus read *cover.* **139:14** ᵃFollowing
Masoretic Text and Targum; Septuagint, Syriac, and Vulgate read
You are fearfully wonderful. **139:20** ᵃSeptuagint and Vulgate read
They take your cities in vain.

139:7–12 We cannot escape God's presence (vv. 8–10) or be separated from Him (vv. 11, 12). We can have the assurance of God's presence wherever we go. "Hell" (Heb. *sheol*) is here a reference to "the place of the dead" (v. 8). We have great assurance and security in the knowledge that God is always present (vv. 7–12; see Ps. 23:4; Rom. 8:35).

139:13–18 God has His eye on us before we are born. These verses avow that personhood does exist from the moment of conception. The psalmist affirms God's knowledge of his life from the pre-embryonic stage through death. The Lord weaves and knits together our beings in the wombs of our mothers (v. 13; see Gen. 9, Sanctity of Life; Jer. 1, Abortion). We are in a real sense "prescription babies" in that God has a custom design for every individual, equipping each for specific

achievement and purpose (see Is. 43:7, 21; Rom. 9:20; 1 Thess. 1:4). Even the greatest tragedies can be overruled or transformed to good within the providence of God (Rom. 8:28). We praise God for the wonderful way in which He fashioned our bodies, our minds, and our spirits. We marvel at the magnitude of His thoughts (vv. 17, 18). We are grateful that He never finishes His edification process (Eph. 2:10; 1 Pet. 5:10). Even our worst negative traits can be transformed into positive qualities (Rom. 12:2).

139:23, 24 Praise for God's unlimited knowledge, power, and presence leads the psalmist to invite God to search his heart (vv. 1–22). God is the only Judge who judges our hearts correctly. He alone knows us as we are and understands our true thoughts and motives. He knows us better than we know

FEMININITY *THE NATURE OF A WOMAN*

Femininity is a reality of God's design and making—His precious gift to every woman—and, in a very different way, His gracious gift to men as well. The difference between men and women is not a mere matter of biology. Throughout the millennia of human history, up until the past several decades, people took for granted that the differences were so obvious as to need no comment. Yet never as now have we more needed Paul's reminder to the Roman Christians not to let the world squeeze us into its own mold but to let God remold our minds from within (Rom. 12:2).

Surrender is a key ingredient in femininity. As a bride, a woman in marriage surrenders her independence, her name, her destiny, her will, and ultimately, in the marriage chamber, her body, to the bridegroom. As a mother, she surrenders in a very real sense her life for the life of the child. As a single woman, she surrenders herself in a unique way for service to her Lord and for service to family and community.

Femininity receives. It takes what God gives. In other words, women are to receive the given as Mary did (Luke 1:38), not to insist on the not-given, as Eve did (Gen. 3:1–6). This does not imply that a woman should surrender to evils such as coercion or violent conquest.

The gentle and quiet spirit of which Peter speaks is the ornament of femininity (1 Pet. 3:4), which found its epitome in Mary, the mother of Jesus. She was willing to be a vessel, hidden, unknown, except as Somebody's mother. This maternity is available to every woman who humbles herself before the Lord, not simply as a biological role but as an attitude of selflessness in her own heart and submission to the Lord.

The challenge of biblical femininity for you is to be a woman, holy through and through, asking for nothing but what God wants to give you, receiving with both hands and with all your heart whatever that is. Femininity is a precious treasure to be guarded and nourished each and every day.

See also Prov. 31:10–31; 1 Pet. 3:1–7; notes on Biblical Equality (Eph. 5); Masculinity (Gen. 2); Surrender (James 4)

PSALM 140

Prayer for Deliverance from Evil Men

To the Chief Musician. A Psalm of David.

¹Deliver me, O LORD, from evil men;
Preserve me from violent men,
²Who plan evil things in *their* hearts;
They continually gather together *for* war.
³They sharpen their tongues like a serpent;
The poison of asps *is* under their lips.   *Selah*

⁴Keep me, O LORD, from the hands of the
  wicked;
Preserve me from violent men,
Who have purposed to make my steps stumble.
⁵The proud have hidden a snare for me, and
  cords;
They have spread a net by the wayside;
They have set traps for me.   *Selah*

⁶I said to the LORD: "You *are* my God;
Hear the voice of my supplications, O LORD.
⁷O GOD the Lord, the strength of my salvation,
You have covered my head in the day of battle.
⁸Do not grant, O LORD, the desires of the
  wicked;

Do not further his *wicked* scheme,
  Lest they be exalted.   *Selah*

⁹"*As for* the head of those who surround me,
Let the evil of their lips cover them;
¹⁰Let burning coals fall upon them;
Let them be cast into the fire,
Into deep pits, that they rise not up again.
¹¹Let not a slanderer be established in the earth;
Let evil hunt the violent man to overthrow
  him."

¹²I know that the LORD will maintain
The cause of the afflicted,
And justice for the poor.
¹³Surely the righteous shall give thanks to Your
  name;
The upright shall dwell in Your presence.

PSALM 141

Prayer for Safekeeping from Wickedness

A Psalm of David.

¹LORD, I cry out to You;
Make haste to me!
Give ear to my voice when I cry out to You.

---

ourselves. If we truly want to walk in the Lord's way and enjoy His presence, we must be dependent on God to lead us in the right way.

141:1–10 Looking to God and depending on Him enables us to resist temptation (v. 8). Apparently, this poet feared the influ-

ence of evil persons in his life and cried out to the Lord for immediate assistance in dealing with the temptation. He requested that his prayer be accepted as incense offered to the Lord (see Ex. 30:7, 8). He asked that God guard his lips that he might not speak or even think about evil (Ps. 141:3, 4)—an

²Let my prayer be set before You *as* incense,
  The lifting up of my hands *as* the evening
    sacrifice.

³Set a guard, O LORD, over my mouth;
  Keep watch over the door of my lips.
⁴Do not incline my heart to any evil thing,
  To practice wicked works
  With men who work iniquity;
  And do not let me eat of their delicacies.

⁵Let the righteous strike me;
  It shall be a kindness.
  And let him rebuke me;
  It shall be as excellent oil;
  Let my head not refuse it.

  For still my prayer *is* against the deeds of the
    wicked.
⁶Their judges are overthrown by the sides of
    the cliff,
  And they hear my words, for they are sweet.
⁷Our bones are scattered at the mouth of the
    grave,
  As when one plows and breaks up the earth.

⁸But my eyes *are* upon You, O GOD the Lord;
  In You I take refuge;
  Do not leave my soul destitute.
⁹Keep me from the snares they have laid for me,
  And from the traps of the workers of iniquity.
¹⁰Let the wicked fall into their own nets,
  While I escape safely.

PSALM 142

A Plea for Relief from Persecutors

A Contemplation[a] of David. A Prayer when he was in the cave.

¹I cry out to the LORD with my voice;
  With my voice to the LORD I make my
    supplication.
²I pour out my complaint before Him;
  I declare before Him my trouble.

³When my spirit was overwhelmed within me,
  Then You knew my path.
  In the way in which I walk
  They have secretly set a snare for me.
⁴Look on *my* right hand and see,
  For *there is* no one who acknowledges me;
  Refuge has failed me;
  No one cares for my soul.

⁵I cried out to You, O LORD:
  I said, "You *are* my refuge,
  My portion in the land of the living.

⁶Attend to my cry,
  For I am brought very low;
  Deliver me from my persecutors,
  For they are stronger than I.
⁷Bring my soul out of prison,
  That I may praise Your name;
  The righteous shall surround me,
  For You shall deal bountifully with me."

PSALM 143

An Earnest Appeal for Guidance and Deliverance

A Psalm of David.

¹Hear my prayer, O LORD,
  Give ear to my supplications!
  In Your faithfulness answer me,
  And in Your righteousness.
²Do not enter into judgment with Your servant,
  For in Your sight no one living is righteous.

³For the enemy has persecuted my soul;
  He has crushed my life to the ground;
  He has made me dwell in darkness,
  Like those who have long been dead.
⁴Therefore my spirit is overwhelmed within me;
  My heart within me is distressed.

⁵I remember the days of old;
  I meditate on all Your works;
  I muse on the work of Your hands.
⁶I spread out my hands to You;
  My soul *longs* for You like a thirsty land.   *Selah*

⁷Answer me speedily, O LORD;
  My spirit fails!
  Do not hide Your face from me,
  Lest I be like those who go down into the pit.
⁸Cause me to hear Your lovingkindness in the
    morning,
  For in You do I trust;
  Cause me to know the way in which I should
    walk,
  For I lift up my soul to You.

⁹Deliver me, O LORD, from my enemies;
  In You I take shelter.[a]
¹⁰Teach me to do Your will,
  For You *are* my God;
  Your Spirit *is* good.
  Lead me in the land of uprightness.

¹¹Revive me, O LORD, for Your name's sake!
  For Your righteousness' sake bring my soul out
    of trouble.

142:title [a]Hebrew *Maschil*   **143:9** [a]Septuagint and Vulgate read *To
You I flee.*

---

appropriate prayer for most of us. How easy it is to speak
words that we later regret! We need God to help us learn to
discipline the tongue, and we must rely on His Spirit to help us
control the words we speak (James 3:8–12).

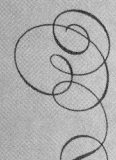

MUSIC *MAKING MELODY IN YOUR HEART*

Music played a prominent part of the battle plan between Jehoshaphat and the enemies of Judah (2 Chr. 20:20–23). Not only did that music strengthen the morale of the Hebrew soldiers, it also signaled defeat to God's enemies. Believers, as they lift their voices in singing are engaging in spiritual warfare! Music was used to drive away the evil spirit that terrorized King Saul (1 Sam. 16:16, 17, 23). As David played skillfully, Saul was soothed.

Music was also used to create a holy environment for the ark—the symbol of God's presence—in the tabernacle of David (2 Chr. 5:11–13). Psalms 98 and 100 tell us to praise God with music of all kinds.

Musical praise is not limited to singing; cymbals, trumpets, horns, and harps are all pleasing to God when used as instruments of praise.

Music is for all believers—that they might have a melody in their hearts to give them courage to defeat evil and make space for the Lord (Eph. 5:19). Musical praise is not restricted to those who are gifted or formally trained. The battle cry of victory begins in the heart as worship and can be expressed by anyone with a melody of praise.

See also 2 Sam. 6:21; 1 Chr. 16:5, 9; 2 Chr. 7:6; 30:21; Ps. 98:1; 100:2; notes on Family Worship (Ps. 78); Praise (Ps. 150); Spiritual Gifts (Rom. 12); Worship (Deut. 12).

---

[12]In Your mercy cut off my enemies,
  And destroy all those who afflict my soul;
  For I *am* Your servant.

PSALM 144

A Song to the LORD Who Preserves and Prospers His People

A Psalm of David.

[1]Blessed *be* the LORD my Rock,
  Who trains my hands for war,
  And my fingers for battle—
[2]My lovingkindness and my fortress,
  My high tower and my deliverer,
  My shield and *the One* in whom I take refuge,
  Who subdues my people[a] under me.

[3]LORD, what *is* man, that You take knowledge of
    him?
  Or the son of man, that You are mindful of
    him?
[4]Man is like a breath;
  His days *are* like a passing shadow.

[5]Bow down Your heavens, O LORD, and come
    down;
  Touch the mountains, and they shall smoke.
[6]Flash forth lightning and scatter them;
  Shoot out Your arrows and destroy them.
[7]Stretch out Your hand from above;

Rescue me and deliver me out of great waters,
  From the hand of foreigners,
[8]Whose mouth speaks lying words,
  And whose right hand *is* a right hand of
    falsehood.

[9]I will sing a new song to You, O God;
  On a harp of ten strings I will sing praises to
    You,
[10]*The One* who gives salvation to kings,
  Who delivers David His servant
  From the deadly sword.

[11]Rescue me and deliver me from the hand of
    foreigners,
  Whose mouth speaks lying words,
  And whose right hand *is* a right hand of
    falsehood—
[12]That our sons *may be* as plants grown up in
    their youth;
  That our daughters *may be* as pillars,
  Sculptured in palace style;
[13]*That* our barns *may be* full,
  Supplying all kinds of produce;
  That our sheep may bring forth thousands
  And ten thousands in our fields;

•••••••••••••••••••
144:2 [a]Following Masoretic Text, Septuagint, and Vulgate; Syriac and Targum read *the peoples* (compare 18:47).

144:1–10 The Lord is praised for the preparation of His king for battle. The poet described the Lord variously as his "Rock," trainer, "lovingkindness" (Heb. *chesed,* see Ps. 5:7–12, note), "fortress," "high tower," "deliverer," "shield," and "refuge." All indicate God's protective strength. In contrast to the great power and stability of God is the frailty of mankind (Ps. 144:3, 4; see Ps. 8:4). Human life is like a fleeting breath or passing shadow. God alone brings deliverance to His people (Ps. 144:9, 10).

144:11–15 God prospers His people. In ancient Hebrew thought, material prosperity indicated God's blessing; so the poet prayed for vigorous sons and stately daughters, for bountiful crops and multiplied flocks, and for peace in the land. "Happy" (or blessed) "are the people whose God is the LORD!" The poet began this psalm by blessing the Lord; he ended by observing the blessing that the Lord sends on His people.

¹⁴*That* our oxen *may be* well laden;
  That there be no breaking in or going out;
  That there be no outcry in our streets.
¹⁵Happy *are* the people who are in such a state;
  Happy *are* the people whose God *is* the LORD!

PSALM 145

A Song of God's Majesty and Love
A Praise of David.

¹I will extol You, my God, O King;
  And I will bless Your name forever and ever.
²Every day I will bless You,
  And I will praise Your name forever and
  ever.
³Great *is* the LORD, and greatly to be praised;
  And His greatness *is* unsearchable.

⁴One generation shall praise Your works to
  another,
  And shall declare Your mighty acts.
⁵Iª will meditate on the glorious splendor of
  Your majesty,
  And on Your wondrous works.ᵇ
⁶*Men* shall speak of the might of Your awesome
  acts,
  And I will declare Your greatness.
⁷They shall utter the memory of Your great
  goodness,
  And shall sing of Your righteousness.

⁸The LORD *is* gracious and full of compassion,
  Slow to anger and great in mercy.
⁹The LORD *is* good to all,
  And His tender mercies *are* over all His works.

¹⁰All Your works shall praise You, O LORD,
  And Your saints shall bless You.
¹¹They shall speak of the glory of Your kingdom,
  And talk of Your power,
¹²To make known to the sons of men His mighty
  acts,
  And the glorious majesty of His kingdom.
¹³Your kingdom *is* an everlasting kingdom,
  And Your dominion *endures* throughout all
  generations.ª

¹⁴The LORD upholds all who fall,
  And raises up all *who are* bowed down.
¹⁵The eyes of all look expectantly to You,
  And You give them their food in due season.

LISTEN FOR GOD'S REPLIES
When you want to live successfully (Rom. 12:1–21)
When having a good time seems too important (Gal. 5:1–26)
When you want inward peace (Rom. 8:1–39)
When you are discouraged (Ps. 23; 42)
When friends are unfaithful (1 Cor. 13:1–13)
When tempted to do wrong (Ps. 19:1–14)
When you seem too busy (Eccl. 3:1–15)
When a crisis comes (Job 28:12–28)
When you are jealous (James 3:1–12)
When you are impatient (Ps. 40:1–17)
When you are bored (Ps. 103)
When you have a grudge (2 Cor. 4:1–18)
When you are disobedient (Luke 5:1–11)
When your faith is weak (Ps. 146)
When God seems far away (Ps. 25)

¹⁶You open Your hand
  And satisfy the desire of every living thing.

¹⁷The LORD *is* righteous in all His ways,
  Gracious in all His works.
¹⁸The LORD *is* near to all who call upon Him,
  To all who call upon Him in truth.
¹⁹He will fulfill the desire of those who fear
  Him;

· · · · · · · · · · · · · · · · · ·

145:5 ªFollowing Masoretic Text and Targum; Dead Sea Scrolls, Septuagint, Syriac, and Vulgate read *They.* ᵇLiterally *on the words of Your wondrous works* 145:13 ªFollowing Masoretic Text and Targum; Dead Sea Scrolls, Septuagint, Syriac, and Vulgate add *The LORD is faithful in all His words, And holy in all His works.*

145:1–21 Praising God for His greatness and love. This is an acrostic poem with each verse beginning with a succeeding letter of the Hebrew alphabet. Daily and forever, the psalmist's heart is filled with praise for the goodness and majesty of the Lord (v. 1, 2). The instruction one generation gives to the next is crucial in God's plan (vv. 4–7; Ps. 22:30, 31; 78:4–6). The very essence of transmitting redemptive history is the sharing of the story of redemption from one generation to the next (Prov. 13, Inheritance). "Tender mercies" (Ps. 145:9) comes from the same root as the word translated "womb." It may indicate a mother's compassion toward the child of her womb (see Ps. 18:1–3; 51:1, notes). God is accessible to those who seek Him (Ps. 145:18). He fulfills our desires, delivers us, and preserves us (vv. 18–20). Therefore, He is worthy of praise (v. 21).

PRAISE *ADORATION FROM THE HEART*

Praising God is not something that comes naturally to anyone. Praise runs an aggravating interference pattern against your nature. Occasionally, praise feels more like a duty, an obligatory lip service performed at the opening of prayer. With persistence every believer can learn to praise God in all things.

Who is to praise God? All of God's people, all of creation (Ps. 145:4, 5; Is. 55:12). *Where* do you praise God? Praise is fitting wherever you are (Ps. 96:3). *How* do you praise God? Praise is expressed through words and music (Ps. 33:1–3). *When* do you praise God? God should be praised at all times (Ps. 34:1). *What* do you praise God for? God is praised for His greatness (Ps. 150:2). *Why* do you praise God? God is worthy of your praise (Rev. 5:12).

Praise is your best weapon against Satan. When you praise God, you are showing the heavenly hosts, powers, principalities, demons of darkness, and angels of light that your great God is worthy of praise—no matter what your circumstances. Praise produces victory, and victory evokes praise. The process is cyclical.

Genuine praise must flow from your heart even during times of sorrow, discouragement, trial, and temptation (Ps. 42:5). The praise of His people brings glory to God. What a privilege it is to bring God joy!

See also Ex. 15:2; Ps. 63:5, 6; 1 Pet. 2:9; notes on Blessings (Gen. 12); Gratitude (Ps. 95); Music (Ps. 147); Prayer (Jer. 33; Heb. 4; 1 John 5; 3 John 2); Worship (Deut. 12)

He also will hear their cry and save them.
20The LORD preserves all who love Him,
But all the wicked He will destroy.
21My mouth shall speak the praise of the LORD,
And all flesh shall bless His holy name
Forever and ever.

PSALM 146

The Happiness of Those Whose Help Is the LORD
1Praise the LORD!

Praise the LORD, O my soul!
2While I live I will praise the LORD;
I will sing praises to my God while I have my
being.

3Do not put your trust in princes,
Nor in a son of man, in whom *there is* no help.
4His spirit departs, he returns to his earth;
In that very day his plans perish.

5Happy *is he* who *has* the God of Jacob for his
help,
Whose hope *is* in the LORD his God,
6Who made heaven and earth,
The sea, and all that *is* in them;
Who keeps truth forever,
7Who executes justice for the oppressed,
Who gives food to the hungry.
The LORD gives freedom to the prisoners.

8The LORD opens *the eyes of* the blind;
The LORD raises those who are bowed down;

The LORD loves the righteous.
9The LORD watches over the strangers;
He relieves the fatherless and widow;
But the way of the wicked He turns upside
down.

10The LORD shall reign forever—
Your God, O Zion, to all generations.

Praise the LORD!

PSALM 147

Praise to God for His Word and Providence
1Praise the LORD!
For *it is* good to sing praises to our God;
For *it is* pleasant, *and* praise is beautiful.

2The LORD builds up Jerusalem;
He gathers together the outcasts of Israel.
3He heals the brokenhearted
And binds up their wounds.
4He counts the number of the stars;
He calls them all by name.
5Great *is* our Lord, and mighty in power;
His understanding *is* infinite.
6The LORD lifts up the humble;
He casts the wicked down to the ground.

7Sing to the LORD with thanksgiving;
Sing praises on the harp to our God,
8Who covers the heavens with clouds,
Who prepares rain for the earth,

146:1–4 Praise the Lord! Psalms 146—150 each begin and end with *hallelujah* (Heb., lit. "praise the Lord"). How fitting that praise is the focus of the last five psalms of this book. The poet of Psalm 146 exhorted his listeners to trust in God, not people. God is the great Creator, who cares for the needy and helpless.

147:1–6 God is praised for building up and protecting Jerusalem and for creating and sustaining the universe in this second hallelujah psalm. Knowledge of God's wonderful works should lead us to praise Him. For "statutes" and "judgments," see Deuteronomy 6:1, note.

Who makes grass to grow on the mountains.
⁹He gives to the beast its food,
And to the young ravens that cry.

¹⁰He does not delight in the strength of the
  horse;
He takes no pleasure in the legs of a man.
¹¹The LORD takes pleasure in those who fear
  Him,
In those who hope in His mercy.

¹²Praise the LORD, O Jerusalem!
Praise your God, O Zion!
¹³For He has strengthened the bars of your
  gates;
He has blessed your children within you.
¹⁴He makes peace *in* your borders,
And fills you with the finest wheat.

¹⁵He sends out His command *to the* earth;
His word runs very swiftly.
¹⁶He gives snow like wool;
He scatters the frost like ashes;
¹⁷He casts out His hail like morsels;
Who can stand before His cold?
¹⁸He sends out His word and melts them;
He causes His wind to blow, *and* the waters
  flow.

¹⁹He declares His word to Jacob,
His statutes and His judgments to Israel.
²⁰He has not dealt thus with any nation;
And *as for His* judgments, they have not known
  them.

Praise the LORD!

PSALM 148

Praise to the LORD from Creation
¹Praise the LORD!

Praise the LORD from the heavens;
Praise Him in the heights!
²Praise Him, all His angels;
Praise Him, all His hosts!
³Praise Him, sun and moon;
Praise Him, all you stars of light!
⁴Praise Him, you heavens of heavens,
And you waters above the heavens!

⁵Let them praise the name of the LORD,
For He commanded and they were
  created.

⁶He also established them forever and ever;
He made a decree which shall not pass away.

⁷Praise the LORD from the earth,
You great sea creatures and all the depths;
⁸Fire and hail, snow and clouds;
Stormy wind, fulfilling His word;
⁹Mountains and all hills;
Fruitful trees and all cedars;
¹⁰Beasts and all cattle;
Creeping things and flying fowl;
¹¹Kings of the earth and all peoples;
Princes and all judges of the earth;
¹²Both young men and maidens;
Old men and children.

¹³Let them praise the name of the LORD,
For His name alone is exalted;
His glory *is* above the earth and heaven.
¹⁴And He has exalted the horn of His people,
The praise of all His saints—
Of the children of Israel,
A people near to Him.

Praise the LORD!

PSALM 149

Praise to God for His Salvation and Judgment
¹Praise the LORD!

Sing to the LORD a new song,
And His praise in the assembly of saints.

²Let Israel rejoice in their Maker;
Let the children of Zion be joyful in their King.
³Let them praise His name with the dance;
Let them sing praises to Him with the timbrel
  and harp.
⁴For the LORD takes pleasure in His people;
He will beautify the humble with salvation.

⁵Let the saints be joyful in glory;
Let them sing aloud on their beds.
⁶*Let* the high praises of God *be* in their mouth,
And a two-edged sword in their hand,
⁷To execute vengeance on the nations,
And punishments on the peoples;
⁸To bind their kings with chains,
And their nobles with fetters of iron;
⁹To execute on them the written judgment—
This honor have all His saints.

Praise the LORD!

148:1–14 Creation sings (see Ps. 146:1–4, note). This psalm is a series of calls to all creation from the height of the heavens to the depths of the sea to praise the Lord. Such praise of the Creator is the obligation, great joy, and privilege of creation.

149:1–9 Saints sing (see Ps. 146:1–4, note). God receives praise both for His salvation and judgment through the music of His people (Ps. 149:2). The Lord takes pleasure in His people and saves them (vv. 3, 4). The people praised God for military victory over their enemies (vv. 6–9).

PSALM 150

Let All Things Praise the LORD

¹Praise the LORD!

Praise God in His sanctuary;
Praise Him in His mighty firmament!

²Praise Him for His mighty acts;
Praise Him according to His excellent
greatness!

³Praise Him with the sound of the trumpet;
Praise Him with the lute and harp!
⁴Praise Him with the timbrel and dance;
Praise Him with stringed instruments and
flutes!
⁵Praise Him with loud cymbals;
Praise Him with clashing cymbals!

⁶Let everything that has breath praise the LORD.

Praise the LORD!

150:1–6 This psalm constitutes a pinnacle of praise and functions as a doxology to Book V and as a fitting conclusion of the Book of Psalms (see Ps. 146:1–4, note; Introduction: Outline). "Praise" appears 13 times in these six brief verses. The psalmist instructed us where the Lord is to be praised (Ps. 150:1), why (v. 2), how (vv. 3–5), and who is to sing His praise (v. 6).

Proverbs

Solomon, king of Israel, was the son of David and Bathsheba. He was about twenty when he took the throne, and he reigned for forty years from 971–931 B.C. About 3,000 proverbs and 1,005 songs are attributed to Solomon. That he authored most of the Book of Proverbs is appropriate since he was acclaimed the wisest person in his time (1 Kin. 4:29–32). Nothing is known of Agur, to whom Proverbs 30 is ascribed, or of Lemuel, whose words are found in Proverbs 31. Solomon's strengths were not on the battlefield but in the realm of the mind: meditation, organization, planning, and negotiation. Except for Moses, Solomon wrote more of the Old Testament than any other man. The writing of the Song of Solomon is assigned to his youth, Proverbs to his mature years when he was at the height of his power, and Ecclesiastes to his later years as he reflected on his life and experience.

DATE

Most of this collection of proverbs was gathered during the tenth century B.C. and took its final form from 729 to 686 B.C.

The purpose of the Book of Proverbs is to develop in men and women (and especially the young) a wise, skillful way of living (Prov. 1:7; 9:10). To be wise in the biblical sense means beginning with a right relationship to God. Such wisdom applies practical knowledge about God in order to live skillfully. Proverbs are precepts for practical prudence.

BACKGROUND

LITERARY CHARACTERISTICS: The name of this book expresses its writing style. A "proverb" (Heb. *mashal,* lit. "to be like" or "to be compared with") is a statement that makes a comparison, usually in the form of a brief saying instead of many words. These are brief but vivid statements taken from everyday life; they are practical guidelines for successful living. A proverb does not argue; it assumes. Its primary purpose is not to explain a matter but to give pointed expression to the idea. Many of the proverbial maxims should be recognized as guidelines, not necessarily absolutes. What is stated is generally true, although there may be exceptions.

THEMES

Proverbs refers often to the "path" and the "way," indicating conduct and lifestyle and providing both a goal and a means to reach that goal. The goal is successful living, and the route to that goal is the way of wisdom. Along the route, almost every facet of important human relationships is mentioned. The Book of Proverbs is as relevant now as when it was written. Wisdom concerning relationships is timeless, just as the nature of sin and foolishness never changes. Running throughout the practical philosophy of these proverbs is an awareness of the perpetual struggle between good and evil in our lives. Powerful contrasts are used to show why wisdom is the answer. Set in vivid contrast are

the ideas of wisdom vs. folly, good vs. evil, life vs. death, fidelity vs. adultery, truth vs. falsehood, prudence vs. rashness, prosperity vs. poverty, industry vs. indolence. Truths of eternal importance are set forth:

- Wisdom (godly living) is more valuable than jewels or wealth.
- Wisdom originates with God.
- Wisdom is available to all, but each woman and man must *choose* the path of wisdom.
- The wise are rewarded for their righteousness.
- The foolish reap the consequences of their evil deeds.

OUTLINE

The Beginning of Knowledge

1 The proverbs of Solomon the son of David, king of Israel:

²To know wisdom and instruction,
  To perceive the words of understanding,
³To receive the instruction of wisdom,
  Justice, judgment, and equity;
⁴To give prudence to the simple,
  To the young man knowledge and discretion—

⁵A wise *man* will hear and increase learning,
And a man of understanding will attain wise counsel,
⁶To understand a proverb and an enigma,
The words of the wise and their riddles.

⁷The fear of the LORD *is* the beginning of knowledge,
  But fools despise wisdom and instruction.

1:2 Wisdom (Heb. *hokmah*) is found repeatedly in the Book of Proverbs. In the OT, this word was used to describe the skill of craftsmen, artists, and counselors (see Ex. 28:3; 31:3, 6; 35:26; 36:1). In the spiritual realm, a wise person lived life according to God's commandments, applying knowledge about God in a practical and successful way. "Instruction" suggests that wisdom is gained through time and discipline.

1:4 Prudence or "shrewdness" is a safeguard against being

misled. "Simple" (lit. "to be wide open"), a common designation in Proverbs, suggests someone who is naive, gullible, and susceptible to good and bad influences.

1:7 Fear in Proverbs is best understood as reverent obedience expressed in a submissive spirit rather than as terrifying dread. "Fear of the Lord" is the beginning point of becoming a woman of wisdom (v. 29; Prov. 2:5; 9:10; 14:26, 27; 15:33; 22:4). A "fool" is morally rather than intellectually defective.

GIRLHOOD   *THE BUD OF WOMANHOOD*

A surface reading of the Bible may leave a young girl with the impression that this Book is of little relevance to her today. Only a few times are young girls specifically mentioned in the history of God's dealings with His people.

Rebekah in her youth was beautiful and charming as well as gracious and resourceful. She became the wife of the patriarch Isaac (Gen. 24:15–67). Naaman's young maidservant was not only obedient and helpful but also spiritually perceptive as she was responsible for introducing her pagan master to the God of Israel (2 Kin. 5:1–14). The daughter of Jairus was a member of a prominent and wealthy household, but she was also valuable to the Savior who restored her to life (Mark 5:21–43). The girl Rhoda was alert and sensitive to the working of the Lord in delivering Peter from prison, and she refused to doubt even when others questioned her faith (Acts 12:13–15).

In addition to these examples is the vibrant testimony of Mary, the mother of our Lord. In her youth—probably in her teens—she showed remarkable faith and commitment as she responded with obedience to God's call to her (Luke 1:26–38).

Scripture clearly affirms the relevance and sufficiency of the Bible for all Christians of all times (1 Tim. 3:16; 2 Pet. 1:3) because the most fundamental issues of human life resurface in every generation. Proverbs, the only book addressed specifically to young people, is essentially a book about pure living and wise decision making. Its advice for boys is equally appropriate for girls. The Book of Numbers is primarily the story of the Israelites in the wilderness in their "time between" leaving Mt. Sinai and entering the Promised Land, but a close study of it can offer girls insights into the trials that they are likely to face as they mature from girlhood to womanhood.

Girlhood is a time of identity formation, self-discovery, friendship, and growth, and God's Word is sufficient to guide girls in all these areas.

See also Matt. 18:3, note; notes on Adolescence (Luke 2); Children (2 Sam. 21; Ps. 128; Prov. 22; Luke 15); Femininity (Ps. 144); Motherhood (Ezek. 16); portraits of Dinah (Gen. 34); Miriam (Ex. 15); Naaman's Maidservant (2 Kin. 5); Rhoda (Acts 12)

Shun Evil Counsel

8My son, hear the instruction of your father,
  And do not forsake the law of your mother;
9For they *will be* a graceful ornament on your
    head,
  And chains about your neck.

10My son, if sinners entice you,
  Do not consent.
11If they say, "Come with us,
  Let us lie in wait to *shed* blood;
  Let us lurk secretly for the innocent without
    cause;
12Let us swallow them alive like Sheol,a
  And whole, like those who go down to the Pit;
13We shall find all *kinds* of precious possessions,
  We shall fill our houses with spoil;
14Cast in your lot among us,

Let us all have one purse"—
15My son, do not walk in the way with them,
  Keep your foot from their path;
16For their feet run to evil,
  And they make haste to shed blood.
17Surely, in vain the net is spread
  In the sight of any bird;
18But they lie in wait for their *own* blood,
  They lurk secretly for their *own* lives.
19So *are* the ways of everyone who is greedy for
    gain;
  It takes away the life of its owners.

The Call of Wisdom

20Wisdom calls aloud outside;
  She raises her voice in the open squares.

1:12 aOr *the grave*

1:8—9:18 The contrast of good and evil is found in the first major section of the book (see chart, The Choice Between Life and Death). The father-teacher pleaded with his son (and ultimately with all who would listen) to understand the difference between the path of good (wisdom) and the path of evil (sin). This section provides the theological foundation for understanding chapters 10—31.

1:8 The mother, along with the father, is a teacher of the children in the biblical model (see also Prov. 6:20). She is to instruct her children in her home according to established principles (Deut. 6:6, 7; see Deut. 6, Education). The fact that

both parents are mentioned is a tribute to the prominent role of Israel's mothers. Such reference to the mother as teacher would be rare, if present at all, in Egyptian or other wisdom literature.

1:12 Sheol (Heb., lit. "the place of the dead" or "the grave") is used several times in Proverbs as the place to which the path of the foolish leads.

1:20–23 Wisdom is explained through a figure of speech. Such language can be God's chosen means for revealing Himself and His plans more effectively. If such figures are altered or

WISDOM ITS FOUNDATION AND EXPRESSION

"Fear of the Lord" is the foundation for wisdom, the prerequisite for obedience, and the accompaniment of love (Deut. 10:12). Fearing the Lord and loving Him are not antithetical but inseparable responses. The Book of Proverbs is permeated with these admonitions (Prov. 1:7; 31:30). Other wisdom literature supports the plea (Eccl. 12:13), the prophets echo the same (Mic. 6:8), and the New Testament picks up this emphasis in its description of "a gentle and quiet spirit" (1 Pet. 3:4).

"Fear" in this sense indicates submissive reverence and not stark terror. To reject this awe, which inspires respectful obedience, is to determine to go your own way (Prov. 1:31) and turn away from God's way (Is. 55:8).

The promised results of fearing Him are goodness, riches, honor and satisfaction (Ps. 31:19), a right relationship with others (Lev. 25:17), long life (Deut. 6:2), mercy (Ps. 103:17), strong confidence (Prov. 14:26), and God's constant attention (Ps. 34:7).

See also Gen. 22:12; Deut. 5:29; Josh. 4:24; Ps. 19:9; 25:14; 33:8, 18; 103:11; 115:13; Prov. 3:7; 9:10; 10:27; Dan. 2:23, note; Luke 1:50; Rev. 15:4; notes on God's Will (Eph. 5); Obedience (Philem.); Spiritual Discipline (2 Pet. 3); Wisdom (James 1); portrait of Mary of Nazareth (Luke 1)

²¹She cries out in the chief concourses,ᵃ
  At the openings of the gates in the city
  She speaks her words:
²²"How long, you simple ones, will you love
    simplicity?
  For scorners delight in their scorning,
  And fools hate knowledge.
²³Turn at my rebuke;
  Surely I will pour out my spirit on you;
  I will make my words known to you.
²⁴Because I have called and you refused,
  I have stretched out my hand and no one
    regarded,
²⁵Because you disdained all my counsel,
  And would have none of my rebuke,
²⁶I also will laugh at your calamity;
  I will mock when your terror comes,
²⁷When your terror comes like a storm,
  And your destruction comes like a whirlwind,
  When distress and anguish come upon you.

²⁸"Then they will call on me, but I will not answer;
  They will seek me diligently, but they will not
    find me.
²⁹Because they hated knowledge
  And did not choose the fear of the LORD,
³⁰They would have none of my counsel
  And despised my every rebuke.
³¹Therefore they shall eat the fruit of their own
    way,
  And be filled to the full with their own fancies.

³²For the turning away of the simple will slay
    them,
  And the complacency of fools will destroy
    them;
³³But whoever listens to me will dwell safely,
  And will be secure, without fear of evil."

The Value of Wisdom

2 My son, if you receive my words,
  And treasure my commands within you,
²So that you incline your ear to wisdom,
  And apply your heart to understanding;
³Yes, if you cry out for discernment,
  And lift up your voice for understanding,
⁴If you seek her as silver,
  And search for her as for hidden treasures;
⁵Then you will understand the fear of the LORD,
  And find the knowledge of God.
⁶For the LORD gives wisdom;
  From His mouth come knowledge and
    understanding;
⁷He stores up sound wisdom for the upright;
  He is a shield to those who walk uprightly;
⁸He guards the paths of justice,
  And preserves the way of His saints.
⁹Then you will understand righteousness and
    justice,
  Equity and every good path.

··················

1:21 ᵃSeptuagint, Syriac, and Targum read *top of the walls*; Vulgate reads *the head of multitudes.*

---

changed, the understanding of God's purpose is thwarted (see Prov. 8:1–36, note; 9).

2:1–4 Single-hearted devotion to discovering and doing what is right is implied in the verbs "receive," "treasure," "incline," "apply," "cry out," "lift up," "seek," and "search." The three "ifs" in these verses show the importance of our choices. We are instructed to do our part in seeking wisdom in order to reap the wonderful, promised results. God grants wisdom as a

gift to those who truly seek it, and He bestows understanding and knowledge (v. 5).

2:2 The heart was the seat of the intellect and of life itself in Hebrew thought. Not only must the ear be inclined to wisdom, but the heart (inclusive of the mind in Hebrew thought; see Prov. 4:20–27, note) must diligently seek to understand wisdom. Obedience is a life-long endeavor.

¹⁰When wisdom enters your heart,
  And knowledge is pleasant to your soul,
¹¹Discretion will preserve you;
  Understanding will keep you,
¹²To deliver you from the way of evil,
  From the man who speaks perverse things,
¹³From those who leave the paths of uprightness
  To walk in the ways of darkness;
¹⁴Who rejoice in doing evil,
  And delight in the perversity of the wicked;
¹⁵Whose ways *are* crooked,
  And *who are* devious in their paths;
¹⁶To deliver you from the immoral woman,
  From the seductress *who* flatters with her
    words,
¹⁷Who forsakes the companion of her youth,
  And forgets the covenant of her God.
¹⁸For her house leads down to death,
  And her paths to the dead;
¹⁹None who go to her return,
  Nor do they regain the paths of life—
²⁰So you may walk in the way of goodness,
  And keep *to* the paths of righteousness.
²¹For the upright will dwell in the land,
  And the blameless will remain in it;
²²But the wicked will be cut off from the
    earth,
  And the unfaithful will be uprooted from it.

Guidance for the Young

3 My son, do not forget my law,
  But let your heart keep my commands;
²For length of days and long life
  And peace they will add to you.

³Let not mercy and truth forsake you;
  Bind them around your neck,
  Write them on the tablet of your heart,
⁴*And* so find favor and high esteem
  In the sight of God and man.

⁵Trust in the Lord with all your heart,
  And lean not on your own understanding;
⁶In all your ways acknowledge Him,
  And He shall direct^a your paths.

⁷Do not be wise in your own eyes;
  Fear the Lord and depart from evil.
⁸It will be health to your flesh,^a
  And strength^b to your bones.

⁹Honor the Lord with your possessions,
  And with the firstfruits of all your increase;
¹⁰So your barns will be filled with plenty,
  And your vats will overflow with new wine.

¹¹My son, do not despise the chastening of the
    Lord,
  Nor detest His correction;
¹²For whom the Lord loves He corrects,
  Just as a father the son *in whom* he delights.

¹³Happy *is* the man *who* finds wisdom,
  And the man *who* gains understanding;
¹⁴For her proceeds *are* better than the profits of
    silver,
  And her gain than fine gold.
¹⁵She *is* more precious than rubies,
  And all the things you may desire cannot
    compare with her.
¹⁶Length of days *is* in her right hand,
  In her left hand riches and honor.
¹⁷Her ways *are* ways of pleasantness,
  And all her paths *are* peace.
¹⁸She *is* a tree of life to those who take hold of her,
  And happy *are all* who retain her.

¹⁹The Lord by wisdom founded the earth;
  By understanding He established the heavens;
²⁰By His knowledge the depths were broken up,
  And clouds drop down the dew.

²¹My son, let them not depart from your eyes—
  Keep sound wisdom and discretion;
²²So they will be life to your soul
  And grace to your neck.
²³Then you will walk safely in your way,
  And your foot will not stumble.
²⁴When you lie down, you will not be afraid;
  Yes, you will lie down and your sleep will be
    sweet.
²⁵Do not be afraid of sudden terror,
  Nor of trouble from the wicked when it comes;
²⁶For the Lord will be your confidence,
  And will keep your foot from being caught.

²⁷Do not withhold good from those to whom it is
    due,

·······················

3:6 ^aOr *make smooth* or *straight* **3:8** ^aLiterally *navel*, figurative of the body ^bLiterally *drink* or *refreshment*

3:2 The practical benefits of wisdom include a lack of anxiety, which brings peace to the soul as well as vigorous physical health.

3:6 Direct (Heb. *yashar*, lit. "to make smooth, straight, right"), includes the idea of removing obstacles that are in the way. God will straighten the stressful paths. He does not say when or how; He just promises that He will.

3:1–12 This passage lists commands in the odd-numbered

verses and the blessings that come from obedience in the even-numbered verses. Wisdom and obedience bring longevity and exemplary reputation (vv. 2, 4), God's guidance (v. 6), physical well-being (v. 8), prosperity (v. 10), and discipline (v. 12; compare vv. 13–18). Three actions are required on our part: "trust" God, "lean not" to our own understanding, and "acknowledge" His leadership (vv. 5, 6). God responds with His action, which is to "direct" (v. 6, note).

BEAUTY — MORE THAN AN APPEALING FACE

The Bible has a great deal to say about both inner and outer beauty. Many women in the Bible are noted for their lovely appearance, such as Sarah, Rebekah, Rachel, Abigail, Bathsheba, and Esther (Gen. 12:11; 24:16; 29:17; 1 Sam 25:3; 2 Sam. 11:2; Esth. 2:7). Queen Esther had a beauty regimen (Esth. 2:3, 12). In fact, the account of a beauty pageant is found in the Book of Esther (Esth. 2).

A Christian woman's appearance should be a complement to her inner spirit and never a hindrance to the kingdom of God. Beauty is more than an appealing face or the latest fashion. For a godly woman, good hygiene, healthy skin care, appropriate attire, and gracious manners are all expected to be a means of presenting an outward appearance that attracts others toward her life and ultimately gives opportunity for sharing a testimony of the Christ who dwells within her (2 Cor. 3:2, 3).

A woman's countenance is often a mirror of her heart. When she abides in God's love, her facial features tend to soften and lines become tempered. An inner peace and joy are reflected on her face. A woman's actions and attitudes are often an indication of where her roots are planted. When a woman's heart is rooted in peace and joy (Gal. 5:22, 23), her outward countenance radiates vitality, enthusiasm, love, and a deep sense of well-being—something no amount of make-up, perfume, professional styling, high fashion, or personal fitness program can create. Having the Holy Spirit within empowers a woman with vitality and enthusiasm, making her a magnet to other people.

True beauty comes from within and is manifested by pure motives and a generous, unselfish spirit toward others. Jesus alone can establish such a wellspring of love (see 1 Chr. 16:29) when a woman yields her life to Him. No beautification regimen or stylish clothes can mask an unattractive heart, unkind words, or hurtful actions.

See also 2 Cor. 2:14–15; 1 Pet. 3:3, 4; notes on Appearance (2 Cor. 3); Femininity (Ps. 144); Graciousness (Prov. 11); Modesty (Is. 3)

When it is in the power of your hand to do *so.*
28 Do not say to your neighbor,
"Go, and come back,
And tomorrow I will give *it,*"
When *you have* it with you.
29 Do not devise evil against your neighbor,
For he dwells by you for safety's sake.
30 Do not strive with a man without cause,
If he has done you no harm.

31 Do not envy the oppressor,
And choose none of his ways;
32 For the perverse *person is* an abomination to the LORD,
But His secret counsel *is* with the upright.
33 The curse of the LORD *is* on the house of the wicked,
But He blesses the home of the just.
34 Surely He scorns the scornful,
But gives grace to the humble.
35 The wise shall inherit glory,
But shame shall be the legacy of fools.

Security in Wisdom

4 Hear, *my* children, the instruction of a father,
And give attention to know understanding;
2 For I give you good doctrine:
Do not forsake my law.
3 When I was my father's son,

Tender and the only one in the sight of my mother,
4 He also taught me, and said to me:
"Let your heart retain my words;
Keep my commands, and live.
5 Get wisdom! Get understanding!
Do not forget, nor turn away from the words of my mouth.
6 Do not forsake her, and she will preserve you;
Love her, and she will keep you.
7 Wisdom *is* the principal thing;
Therefore get wisdom.
And in all your getting, get understanding.
8 Exalt her, and she will promote you;
She will bring you honor, when you embrace her.
9 She will place on your head an ornament of grace;
A crown of glory she will deliver to you."

10 Hear, my son, and receive my sayings,
And the years of your life will be many.
11 I have taught you in the way of wisdom;
I have led you in right paths.
12 When you walk, your steps will not be hindered,
And when you run, you will not stumble.
13 Take firm hold of instruction, do not let go;
Keep her, for she *is* your life.

3:27–35 Five principles concerning relationships with others, each beginning with the words "do not," appear in this passage. These principles are specific examples of what it means to acknowledge God in everything (v. 6). The Lord's "secret counsel" (lit. "confidential, intimate speech") is strong motivation for maintaining a distance from the wicked (vv. 31–35).

¹⁴Do not enter the path of the wicked,
  And do not walk in the way of evil.
¹⁵Avoid it, do not travel on it;
  Turn away from it and pass on.
¹⁶For they do not sleep unless they have done
    evil;
  And their sleep is taken away unless they make
    someone fall.
¹⁷For they eat the bread of wickedness,
  And drink the wine of violence.

¹⁸But the path of the just *is* like the shining sun,^a
  That shines ever brighter unto the perfect day.
¹⁹The way of the wicked *is* like darkness;
  They do not know what makes them stumble.

²⁰My son, give attention to my words;
  Incline your ear to my sayings.
²¹Do not let them depart from your eyes;
  Keep them in the midst of your heart;
²²For they *are* life to those who find them,
  And health to all their flesh.
²³Keep your heart with all diligence,
  For out of it *spring* the issues of life.
²⁴Put away from you a deceitful mouth,
  And put perverse lips far from you.
²⁵Let your eyes look straight ahead,
  And your eyelids look right before you.
²⁶Ponder the path of your feet,
  And let all your ways be established.
²⁷Do not turn to the right or the left;
  Remove your foot from evil.

The Peril of Adultery

5 My son, pay attention to my wisdom;
  Lend your ear to my understanding,
²That you may preserve discretion,
  And your lips may keep knowledge.
³For the lips of an immoral woman drip honey,

  And her mouth *is* smoother than oil;
⁴But in the end she is bitter as wormwood,
  Sharp as a two-edged sword.
⁵Her feet go down to death,
  Her steps lay hold of hell.^a
⁶Lest you ponder *her* path of life—
  Her ways are unstable;
  You do not know *them.*

⁷Therefore hear me now, *my* children,
  And do not depart from the words of my
    mouth.
⁸Remove your way far from her,
  And do not go near the door of her house,
⁹Lest you give your honor to others,
  And your years to the cruel *one;*
¹⁰Lest aliens be filled with your wealth,
  And your labors *go* to the house of a foreigner;
¹¹And you mourn at last,
  When your flesh and your body are consumed,
¹²And say:
  "How I have hated instruction,
  And my heart despised correction!
¹³I have not obeyed the voice of my teachers,
  Nor inclined my ear to those who
    instructed me!
¹⁴I was on the verge of total ruin,
  In the midst of the assembly and
    congregation."

¹⁵Drink water from your own cistern,
  And running water from your own well.
¹⁶Should your fountains be dispersed abroad,
  Streams of water in the streets?
¹⁷Let them be only your own,
  And not for strangers with you.
¹⁸Let your fountain be blessed,

4:18 ^aLiterally *light*   5:5 ^aOr *Sheol*

4:18, 19 A contrast between light and darkness illustrates the paths of the wise and the wicked (see chart, The Choice Between Life and Death). The path of the wise is like the dawn's first rays of light that gradually increase to greater brightness. The path of the wicked is characterized by complete and utter darkness that causes instability and stumbling.

4:20–27 Heart is a term that includes mind, emotions, and will. The decision is made in the inner being (v. 21) but quickly shows forth in outer actions (see Luke 6:43–45). Therefore, the heart must be guarded carefully (Prov. 4:23). Keeping the heart involves what is said (v. 24), what is seen (v. 25), and what is done (vv. 26, 27).

5:4 Wormwood is a plant used as a biblical symbol for that which is harmful and bitter (see chart, The Herbs of the Bible). Its root meaning, though not used in Scripture, is understood to be "curse." The words of the adulteress may sound sweet but in reality she is a "bitter curse."

5:7–14 The father-teacher pleaded with his son not to turn away from his words but to turn away from the adulteress. The temptations of the adulteress are to be resisted through

the strength of wisdom, which dictates that a man not even go near the house of an adulteress. Failure to turn from such a woman results in the loss of strength (v. 9) and health (v. 11) and in misery and ruin (vv. 12–14). Contrast with the blessings of Proverbs 3 and 4; compare with the blessings of obedience and the curses of disobedience (Deut. 28). Two ways are given to resist the adulteress: Avoid her and do not go near her house (Prov. 5:8), and enjoy a vital and exciting sexual relationship with your wife (vv. 15, 18).

5:15–20 God's view of sex in marriage. A beautiful parallel is drawn between the quenching of thirst by drinks of cool, fresh water and the satisfaction of a couple's sexual thirst with regular, exciting sexual intimacy in marriage. "Rejoice with the wife of your youth" indicates that the sexual relationship is to provide the marriage partners great pleasure (v. 18). The wife is described as tender, charming, loving, and satisfying. God's view of the sexual relationship in marriage is of an exciting, erotic, intoxicating, and loving partnership. Such a relationship is the most effective means of preventing infidelity.

MARRIAGE *THE FACETS OF LOVE*

Love has several aspects, and each is designed to be an integral part of a marriage relationship. There is first the magnetic drawing of two people together, which is usually termed desire (Gen. 29:18) and which should remain a very important facet of every marriage (Prov. 5:17–19). Love also has a facet of romance—strong, sweet, and absorbing (Gen. 26:8, 9). Genuine love is marked by contentment with each other, and a sense of assurance and belonging that enables partners to care for one another and to give the promise of total loyalty (Ruth 3:9–11). The fourth facet of love is friendship, with an emphasis on communicating and being close, sharing thoughts and feelings, and dreaming together (Song 2:14).

These four aspects of love are held together with God's love, which is absolutely essential if the marriage is going to endure. God's love is unconditional; it is given with no thought of response. Self-sacrificing love (Gk. *Agapē*) is an act of the will and not the emotions (1 Cor. 13:4–8). *Agapē* love is unselfish and undemanding, realizes the value of the loved one, recognizes responsibility for the beloved, continues to grow, never fades, and is pure (1 Cor. 13:12, 13).

God demands permanence in marriage (Mal. 2:16), but He intended for it to be a growing, loving relationship from beginning to end (Eccl. 9:9). This is a truth bound up in God's will, and thus it is possible for Christians to accomplish it.

As all five aspects of love come to find expression in a marriage relationship, permanence is assured. The house will be built, established, and filled with precious and pleasant riches (Prov. 14:1; 24:3, 4).

See also notes on Fruit of the Spirit (1 Cor. 13); Love (1 John 4); Marriage (Gen. 2; 2 Sam. 6; Hos. 2; Amos 3; 2 Cor. 13; 1 Tim. 3; Heb. 12); Romance (Song 2)

And rejoice with the wife of your youth.
¹⁹ *As a* loving deer and a graceful doe,
Let her breasts satisfy you at all times;
And always be enraptured with her love.
²⁰For why should you, my son, be enraptured by
an immoral woman,
And be embraced in the arms of a seductress?

²¹For the ways of man *are* before the eyes of the
LORD,
And He ponders all his paths.
²²His own iniquities entrap the wicked *man*,
And he is caught in the cords of his sin.
²³He shall die for lack of instruction,
And in the greatness of his folly he shall go
astray.

Dangerous Promises

6 My son, if you become surety for your friend,
If you have shaken hands in pledge for a
stranger,
²You are snared by the words of your mouth;

You are taken by the words of your mouth.
³So do this, my son, and deliver yourself;
For you have come into the hand of your
friend:
Go and humble yourself;
Plead with your friend.
⁴Give no sleep to your eyes,
Nor slumber to your eyelids.
⁵Deliver yourself like a gazelle from the hand *of
the hunter,*
And like a bird from the hand of the fowler.^a

The Folly of Indolence

⁶Go to the ant, you sluggard!
Consider her ways and be wise,
⁷Which, having no captain,
Overseer or ruler,
⁸Provides her supplies in the summer,
And gathers her food in the harvest.
⁹How long will you slumber, O sluggard?

....
6:5 ^aThat is, one who catches birds in a trap or snare

5:21–23 God ponders all the paths (lit. "habits") of the wicked. The course of life chosen by the wicked entraps in ignorance and sin and leads to death. Judgment is of the Lord. People may talk about being "free" to do whatever they feel like doing, but in reality sin takes away all freedom.

6:1–5 The warning is against being held accountable for another person's loan. Putting up security is often mentioned in Proverbs (Prov. 11:15; 17:18; 20:16; 22:26, 27; 27:13). Two strong expressions are used to encourage the release of a person who has become surety for a friend (Prov. 6:3). "Humble yourself" (lit. "trample upon yourself") suggests it is better, if

necessary, to be humiliated in order to secure release from a pledge. "Plead" (lit. "urge with troublesome persistence") advises strong and continuous argument until your neighbor is willing to release you.

6:6–11 The sluggard is mentioned a number of times in Proverbs. His procrastination and lack of initiative are strongly condemned (Prov. 26:13). His foolishness is evident in his lack of preparation for the future. Rather he prefers to stay in bed (Prov. 6:9, 10). As he waits and does nothing, opportunities slip away, and without notice his poverty and need overwhelm him.

When will you rise from your sleep?
[10]A little sleep, a little slumber,
A little folding of the hands to sleep—
[11]So shall your poverty come on you like a
prowler,
And your need like an armed man.

The Wicked Man

[12]A worthless person, a wicked man,
Walks with a perverse mouth;
[13]He winks with his eyes,
He shuffles his feet,
He points with his fingers;
[14]Perversity *is* in his heart,
He devises evil continually,
He sows discord.
[15]Therefore his calamity shall come suddenly;
Suddenly he shall be broken without remedy.

[16]These six *things* the LORD hates,
Yes, seven *are* an abomination to Him:
[17]A proud look,
A lying tongue,
Hands that shed innocent blood,
[18]A heart that devises wicked plans,
Feet that are swift in running to evil,
[19]A false witness *who* speaks lies,
And one who sows discord among brethren.

Beware of Adultery

[20]My son, keep your father's command,
And do not forsake the law of your mother.
[21]Bind them continually upon your heart;
Tie them around your neck.
[22]When you roam, they[a] will lead you;
When you sleep, they will keep you;
And *when* you awake, they will speak with you.
[23]For the commandment *is* a lamp,
And the law a light;

Reproofs of instruction *are* the way of life,
[24]To keep you from the evil woman,
From the flattering tongue of a seductress.
[25]Do not lust after her beauty in your heart,
Nor let her allure you with her eyelids.
[26]For by means of a harlot
A man is reduced to a crust of bread;
And an adulteress[a] will prey upon his precious
life.
[27]Can a man take fire to his bosom,
And his clothes not be burned?
[28]Can one walk on hot coals,
And his feet not be seared?
[29]So *is* he who goes in to his neighbor's wife;
Whoever touches her shall not be innocent.

[30]*People* do not despise a thief
If he steals to satisfy himself when he is
starving.
[31]Yet *when* he is found, he must restore
sevenfold;
He may have to give up all the substance of his
house.
[32]Whoever commits adultery with a woman lacks
understanding;
He *who* does so destroys his own soul.
[33]Wounds and dishonor he will get,
And his reproach will not be wiped away.
[34]For jealousy *is* a husband's fury;
Therefore he will not spare in the day of
vengeance.
[35]He will accept no recompense,
Nor will he be appeased though you give many
gifts.

7 My son, keep my words,
And treasure my commands within you.

6:22 [a]Literally *it*   6:26 [a]Literally *a man's wife*, that is, of another

---

6:12–19 God hates not just the murderer or adulterer but also the one who "sows discord" (vv. 14, 19). Interestingly, among the two lists of things that are an abomination to the Lord, several are sins of attitude ("winks with his eyes," v. 13; "a proud look," v. 17) and sins of the tongue ("a perverse mouth," v. 12; "a lying tongue," v. 17; "a false witness," v. 19).

6:20–23 The mother is described as a teacher of her children (see Prov. 1:8). God's Word is a lamp to your feet and a light to your path (Ps. 119:105). Parental commands, like the Word of God, are a lamp and a light, giving wise guidance to the child's life. This analogy shows parents the importance of teaching according to God's Word. That parents can only teach their children what they themselves know and are applying in their own lives is a sobering fact!

6:24–27 Following the godly wisdom of parents offers protection from an evil woman (vv. 20–23; see also Prov. 9 regarding the foolish woman). The Talmud identifies the heart and eye as agents of sin. To permit your mind to become obsessed with lustful thoughts is to put yourself willingly in the way of temptation. Adultery could be called a type of suicide. The

person who enters into an adulterous relationship, embracing foolishness rather than godly wisdom, will surely pay the consequences. His own soul will be destroyed (see Prov. 6:32; 7).

7:1–27 The portrait of adultery in this chapter sounds like a repeat of previous chapters because Solomon three times previously has addressed the problem of sexual immorality as a metaphor for turning from wisdom and following after folly (Prov. 2:16–19; 5:1–23; 6:20–35). Here, the ways of the seductress and the consequences of involvement with her are graphically illustrated. She is disloyal in heart (Prov. 7:5), provocatively dressed (v. 10), boisterous and rebellious (v. 11), and restless and unfulfilled (vv. 11, 12). She uses flattering speech (v. 21; see Prov. 5:3) and destroys her captive (Prov. 7:21–23, 26, 27). The way of folly at its root gives no thought to the path of life (see Prov. 5:6). The consequences of a lack of wisdom in life are dreadfully real. In these verses, the plea is to treat the parent's commandments as a treasure, to burn them into the heart that they might be remembered. Wisdom, when chosen to be an intimate friend, protects from the folly of immorality (Prov. 7:4, 5).

THE ADULTERESS OF PROVERBS

Proverbs 5—7 is a trio of chapters warning against the immoral woman whose character is not only shallow but also evil. Her conscience is seared, her dress seductive, and her heart crafty. The deceptive words from her lips are enticing, as sweet as honey (the sweetest food in ancient Israel) and smoother than olive oil (the smoothest consistency). She is an adulteress, an unfaithful wife whose restless, unstable feet do not stay at home.

Belligerently flaunting her marriage vows and defiant against God's Law, she uses tactics of surprise and flattery. With vivid descriptions of a perfumed bed waiting for a night of exhilarating lovemaking, she uses her energies to lure the naive, foolish man to her bedchamber.

Her evil character and lifestyle result from not pondering the path of life (Prov. 5:6). Instead, she leads her victims on the path to destruction, leading to the utter ruin of a man's strength and vigor and the depletion of his material possessions. Ultimately, his folly will cost him his life (Prov. 7:23).

Three ways are given by the father-teacher to avoid this woman "whose house is the way to hell, descending to the chambers of death" (Prov. 7:27):

1. Observe the commandment of your father and do not forsake the teaching of your mother (Prov. 6:20).
2. Resist temptation by removing yourself from the seductress; keep your way far from her, and do not go near the door of her house (Prov. 5:8).
3. Be exhilarated with the sexual love of your wife (vv. 15–20).

The adulteress seeks and offers quick but unsatisfying pleasures. She is unstable; she has no anchor of godly character to direct her paths. She not only follows a road to destruction herself but also leads others down that avenue. She not only destroys her own family and loses their fellowship, but also she often brings to ruin other homes as well. Yet, however great has been the folly of such a woman, she has but to turn to Christ in order to experience forgiveness and to reach for the "fear of the Lord" in order to achieve the blessings of wisdom.

See also Prov. 6:20–35; 7:4–27; notes on Adultery (Hos. 3); Sexual Purity (1 Cor. 7); Temptation (Heb. 2)

---

²Keep my commands and live,
  And my law as the apple of your eye.
³Bind them on your fingers;
  Write them on the tablet of your heart.
⁴Say to wisdom, "You *are* my sister,"
  And call understanding *your* nearest kin,
⁵That they may keep you from the immoral
      woman,
  From the seductress *who* flatters with her
      words.

The Crafty Harlot

⁶For at the window of my house
  I looked through my lattice,
⁷And saw among the simple,
  I perceived among the youths,
  A young man devoid of understanding,
⁸Passing along the street near her corner;
  And he took the path to her house
⁹In the twilight, in the evening,
  In the black and dark night.

¹⁰And there a woman met him,
  With the attire of a harlot, and a crafty heart.
¹¹She *was* loud and rebellious,
  Her feet would not stay at home.
¹²At times *she was* outside, at times in the open
      square,
  Lurking at every corner.

¹³So she caught him and kissed him;
  With an impudent face she said to him:
¹⁴"*I have* peace offerings with me;
  Today I have paid my vows.
¹⁵So I came out to meet you,
  Diligently to seek your face,
  And I have found you.
¹⁶I have spread my bed with tapestry,
  Colored coverings of Egyptian linen.
¹⁷I have perfumed my bed
  With myrrh, aloes, and cinnamon.
¹⁸Come, let us take our fill of love until
      morning;
  Let us delight ourselves with love.
¹⁹For my husband *is* not at home;
  He has gone on a long journey;
²⁰He has taken a bag of money with him,
  And will come home on the appointed day."

²¹With her enticing speech she caused him to
      yield,
  With her flattering lips she seduced him.
²²Immediately he went after her, as an ox goes to
      the slaughter,
  Or as a fool to the correction of the stocks,ᵃ
²³Till an arrow struck his liver.

•••••••••••••••••••••••••••

7:22 ᵃSeptuagint, Syriac, and Targum read *as a dog to bonds;* Vulgate reads *as a lamb . . . to bonds.*

SEXUAL IMMORALITY *A PATHWAY TO TRAGEDY*

In the New Testament, sexual immorality (Gk. *porneia*) refers to the voluntary sexual intercourse of an unmarried person with anyone of the opposite sex (Col. 3:5; 1 Thess. 4:3). The term is also used to describe prostitution (Rev. 2:14) and all forms of inappropriate sexual behavior (John 8:41; 1 Cor. 5:1; 6:13, 18). Adultery (Gk. *moicheia*) identified extra-marital infidelity. The two terms later were used interchangeably (Matt. 15:19; Mark 7:21; John 8:3; Gal. 5:19).

Sexual immorality covers a number of sins and came to be used as a general term to cover all sexual sins. Though all these actions forbidden by Scripture were despicable in God's eyes, none is unforgivable. Sexual intimacy is a special gift from God to express the deepest physical and spiritual unity between husband and wife as well as being God's seal on the marriage. Thus, God expects us to take very seriously the safeguards He has established for that exclusive and intimate union.

Sexual immorality has tragic consequences:

- God's gift of sexuality (Gen. 2:24; Song 3:4, 5; Matt. 19:5), which is a good and unifying communication of love, is abused;
- The bodies that God created to be His temple, the dwelling place for the Holy Spirit, are degraded (1 Cor. 3:16, 17);
- As does any sin, those who participate separate themselves from God, break their fellowship with other believers, and bring hurt to the kingdom of God (Amos 3:3; Rom. 3:23);
- Those with whom the perpetrator commits such acts are exploited and violated (2 Sam. 13:14–19);
- The natural and holy intimacy God has designed in a permanent, monogamous relationship is denied (Gen. 24:67; Mark 10:6–9).

Still all must remember God's mercy and forgiveness. Any woman who has engaged in sexual immorality can find forgiveness and healing at the foot of the Cross (John 8:3–11).

See also Prov. 5—7; Rom. 3:23, note; 1 Cor. 5:1–13; notes on Adultery (Hos. 3); Forgiveness (Ps. 51; Luke 17); Incest (Lev. 18); Sexuality (Song 4); Sexual Purity (1 Cor. 7)

As a bird hastens to the snare,
He did not know it *would cost* his life.

²⁴Now therefore, listen to me, *my* children;
Pay attention to the words of my mouth:
²⁵Do not let your heart turn aside to her ways,
Do not stray into her paths;
²⁶For she has cast down many wounded,
And all who were slain by her were strong *men.*
²⁷Her house *is* the way to hell,ᵃ
Descending to the chambers of death.

The Excellence of Wisdom

8 Does not wisdom cry out,
And understanding lift up her voice?
²She takes her stand on the top of the high hill,
Beside the way, where the paths meet.

³She cries out by the gates, at the entry of the city,
At the entrance of the doors:
⁴"To you, O men, I call,
And my voice *is* to the sons of men.
⁵O you simple ones, understand prudence,
And you fools, be of an understanding heart.
⁶Listen, for I will speak of excellent things,
And from the opening of my lips *will come* right things;
⁷For my mouth will speak truth;
Wickedness *is* an abomination to my lips.
⁸All the words of my mouth *are* with righteousness;
Nothing crooked or perverse *is* in them.
⁹They *are* all plain to him who understands,

7:27 ᵃOr *Sheol*

8:1–36 Wisdom has credentials! Chapter 8 is a beautiful contrast to chapter 7, showing that folly ends in death and destruction, while wisdom's call is brilliant, emotional, poetic, and convincing. However, some confusion has arisen over the personification of "wisdom" as a woman in this chapter. The literary device of personification (the representing as a person a quality that is recognized by all as not actually being a person) is often seen in Wisdom Literature. Though personified, wisdom is clearly an attribute, *not* a person. The "wisdom" in Proverbs 8 refers to wisdom that is an attribute of God Himself, going beyond understanding and right decisions. Unfortunately, some have elevated this personification into a goddess, whom they say was associated with *Yahweh* at creation. They even go so far as to subordinate the Son to the Father by claiming that Jesus is the incarnation of divine wisdom and *not* God Himself in flesh. Wisdom is *not* God, although when portrayed as a person, she acts and speaks as God does. Wisdom invites all men and women to choose her path of life. She calls the foolish and the simple because they need her most (vv. 4, 5; see Matt. 9:12, 13). Wisdom is available to all but acquired only by those who love her (Prov. 8:21) and seek her (v. 17).

COUNSELING *HELPING OTHERS HELP THEMSELVES*

Human beings were created by God with a variety of needs: physical, emotional, intellectual, psychological, and spiritual. These needs God is ready and able to supply (Phil. 4:19). We find His help in prayer, study of Scripture, guidance of the Holy Spirit (Gk. *paraklētos*, "comforter," lit. one "called alongside"), and from the counsel of godly and wise individuals—whether family, friends, or professionals.

God may choose to meet a need through an individual or "people helper" within an organization or institution or through particular circumstances. When making important or life-changing decisions, we do well to seek counsel from wise, mature Christians (Prov. 11:14).

When life needs are not met in appropriate and effective ways, mental anguish occurs. When this anguish results in serious disruptions of daily activities or damage to relationships, counseling is necessary. To seek biblical counseling is often helpful and should not bring shame or embarrassment. Christian counseling provides the individual with healing, integration, balance, and wholeness through a variety of methods but is always marked by reliance on the Lord as the Great Physician. Jesus assured His followers of the indwelling presence of the Holy Spirit, the Comforter, the Helper, the resident Counselor for every believer (John 16:13).

See also Job 12:13; Ps. 16:7, 8; 73:24; 106:13–15; Mark 5:2, note; John 14:26; notes on God's Will (Eph. 5); Healing (Ps. 13; 133; Eccl. 1; 2 Cor. 5; Gal. 6; James 5); Holy Spirit (John 14); Problem Solving (John 5)

And right to those who find knowledge.
¹⁰Receive my instruction, and not silver,
And knowledge rather than choice gold;
¹¹For wisdom *is* better than rubies,
And all the things one may desire cannot be
compared with her.

¹²"I, wisdom, dwell with prudence,
And find out knowledge *and* discretion.
¹³The fear of the LORD *is* to hate evil;
Pride and arrogance and the evil way
And the perverse mouth I hate.
¹⁴Counsel *is* mine, and sound wisdom;
I *am* understanding, I have strength.
¹⁵By me kings reign,
And rulers decree justice.
¹⁶By me princes rule, and nobles,
All the judges of the earth.ᵃ
¹⁷I love those who love me,
And those who seek me diligently will find
me.
¹⁸Riches and honor *are* with me,
Enduring riches and righteousness.
¹⁹My fruit *is* better than gold, yes, than fine
gold,
And my revenue than choice silver.
²⁰I traverse the way of righteousness,
In the midst of the paths of justice,
²¹That I may cause those who love me to inherit
wealth,
That I may fill their treasuries.

²²"The LORD possessed me at the beginning of
His way,
Before His works of old.
²³I have been established from everlasting,
From the beginning, before there was ever an
earth.
²⁴When *there were* no depths I was brought forth,
When *there were* no fountains abounding with
water.
²⁵Before the mountains were settled,
Before the hills, I was brought forth;
²⁶While as yet He had not made the earth or the
fields,
Or the primal dust of the world.
²⁷When He prepared the heavens, I *was* there,
When He drew a circle on the face of the deep,
²⁸When He established the clouds above,
When He strengthened the fountains of the
deep,
²⁹When He assigned to the sea its limit,
So that the waters would not transgress His
command,
When He marked out the foundations of the
earth,
³⁰Then I was beside Him *as* a master craftsman;ᵃ
And I was daily *His* delight,
Rejoicing always before Him,

· · · · · · · · · · · · · · · · ·

8:16 ᵃMasoretic Text, Syriac, Targum, and Vulgate read *righteousness;* Septuagint, Bomberg, and some manuscripts and editions read *earth.*   **8:30** ᵃA Jewish tradition reads *one brought up.*

8:22–31 Wisdom is seen here figuratively as a personification of God's attribute of wisdom. Some scholars suggest that wisdom in chapter 8 refers to Christ. Although Christ was with God before creation and all wisdom resides in Christ (Col. 2:3), these verses give no indication that Jesus Christ Himself is the one referred to as wisdom. Some have suggested that if wisdom is replaced by Christ in chapter 8, then wisdom should be replaced with Christ throughout the Book of Proverbs. Wisdom was present before creation (Prov. 8:24–26) and at creation (vv. 27–29), and wisdom rejoiced at creation as the "master craftsman" (vv. 30, 31).

THE PERSONIFICATION OF WISDOM

ORIGIN OF WISDOM	VIRTUES OF WISDOM	VALUE OF WISDOM
In God (Prov. 8:22)	Prudence (Prov. 8:5, 12)	The wise receive riches and honor (Prov. 8:18)
From everlasting (Prov. 8:23)	Understanding (Prov. 8:5)	The wise have fruit better than gold and silver (Prov. 8:19)
Before all things (Prov. 8:22–31)	Excellence (Prov. 8:6)	The wise are blessed (Prov. 8:32, 34)
	Truth (Prov. 8:7)	The wise find life (Prov. 8:35)
	Righteousness (Prov. 8:8)	
	Knowledge (Prov. 8:12)	
	Discretion (Prov. 8:12)	
	Fear of the Lord (Prov. 8:13)	

Note: Wisdom is personified in the Proverbs and acts as God's dynamic Word. In the New Testament Jesus is the Wisdom and Word of God.

³¹Rejoicing in His inhabited world,
And my delight *was* with the sons of men.

³²"Now therefore, listen to me, *my* children,
For blessed *are those who* keep my ways.
³³Hear instruction and be wise,
And do not disdain *it.*
³⁴Blessed is the man who listens to me,
Watching daily at my gates,
Waiting at the posts of my doors.
³⁵For whoever finds me finds life,
And obtains favor from the LORD;
³⁶But he who sins against me wrongs his own soul;
All those who hate me love death."

The Way of Wisdom

9 Wisdom has built her house,
She has hewn out her seven pillars;
²She has slaughtered her meat,
She has mixed her wine,
She has also furnished her table.
³She has sent out her maidens,
She cries out from the highest places of the city,
⁴"Whoever *is* simple, let him turn in here!"
As for him who lacks understanding, she says to him,
⁵"Come, eat of my bread
And drink of the wine I have mixed.
⁶Forsake foolishness and live,
And go in the way of understanding.

⁷"He who corrects a scoffer gets shame for himself,
And he who rebukes a wicked *man only* harms himself.
⁸Do not correct a scoffer, lest he hate you;
Rebuke a wise *man,* and he will love you.
⁹Give *instruction* to a wise *man,* and he will be still wiser;

8:32–36 Wisdom's call is to discipleship. Following wisdom is an act of faithful and obedient service. This is reminiscent of Joshua's call to the people of Israel to serve the Lord and forsake other gods (Josh. 24:14, 15). Wisdom offers long-term satisfaction and leads to life, while folly, which brings immediate gratification, ultimately leads to death.

9:1–6 Wisdom prepares her home, as would a resourceful woman. The "house" is considered by some to be a reference to the world (Job 38:6; Ps. 104:5). The "seven pillars" are imagery describing the house (Prov. 9:1). Perhaps the number "seven" suggests that wisdom is essential for a perfect world (see chart, The Significance of Numbers in Scripture).

9:7–9 The wise accept rebuke, learn from it, and become even wiser. A scoffer will never accept correction and therefore cannot grow or change.

WISDOM PERSONIFIED

Wisdom, together with the virtuous wife (Prov. 31) and the adulteress of folly (Prov. 5—7), is one of the three dominant personifications in the Book of Proverbs. This literary device does not present a literal woman or goddess but is a means of picturing the contrast between good and evil and between wisdom and folly.

This divine attribute and activity is personified as a dignified and noble woman who is warm, caring, and competent. She offers life with long-term satisfaction (Prov. 1:33; 8:34, 35). In contrast, her rival or "counter-wisdom," called "folly" (Prov. 15:21), provides immediate gratification but ultimate ruin.

Wisdom pleads with her hearers, begging them to follow her and learn how to take their knowledge about God and apply it to their lives in a practical and successful way (Prov. 8:1–11). She sets forth her virtues and her rewards. She is incomparable, better than rubies (Prov. 8:11); her instructions more precious than silver and her knowledge exceeding the worth of choice gold (Prov. 8:10). Excellent things from her lips lead to life, and her followers are blessed materially and spiritually (Prov. 8:17–21).

After detailing why wisdom and not folly is the appropriate choice, Wisdom invites all who wish to sit at her banquet, to eat of the fruits of wisdom, to forsake foolishness, and to go in the way of life and understanding (Prov. 9:1–6). The shining and winsome godliness of Wisdom set against the dark and evil seductiveness of the adulteress shows the path of wisdom in all its beauty. Wisdom, in fact, foreshadows the divine wisdom found in Jesus Christ (see Col. 1:9, 16–18).

When women move away from Scripture as their sole authority and rather claim a collection of extra-biblical texts as authority in order to establish a biblical deity, they are reconstructing the basic foundation of theology itself. For example, to introduce goddess worship through creating a feminine deity named Wisdom or "Sophia" (a transliteration of the Greek word for "wisdom") is using language loosely in order to blur the distinction between the Word of God and pagan ritual. We must reject any union of Christianity and paganism. A careful look at Wisdom points directly to the God who names Himself by revealing to us who He is (Ex. 3:14).

See also Prov. 1; 8; notes on Decision Making (1 Cor. 8); Wisdom (James 1)

Teach a just *man,* and he will increase in
 learning.
[10]"The fear of the LORD *is* the beginning of
 wisdom,
And the knowledge of the Holy One *is*
 understanding.
[11]For by me your days will be multiplied,
And years of life will be added to you.
[12]If you are wise, you are wise for yourself,
And *if* you scoff, you will bear *it* alone."

The Way of Folly

[13]A foolish woman is clamorous;
She is simple, and knows nothing.
[14]For she sits at the door of her house,
On a seat *by* the highest places of the city,
[15]To call to those who pass by,
Who go straight on their way:

[16]"Whoever *is* simple, let him turn in here";
And *as for* him who lacks understanding, she
 says to him,
[17]"Stolen water is sweet,
And bread *eaten* in secret is pleasant."
[18]But he does not know that the dead *are*
 there,
That her guests *are* in the depths of hell.[a]

Wise Sayings of Solomon

10 The proverbs of Solomon:

A wise son makes a glad father,
But a foolish son *is* the grief of his mother.

[2]Treasures of wickedness profit nothing,
But righteousness delivers from death.

9:18 [a]Or *Sheol*

9:13–18 The foolish woman tries in secretive and deceptive ways to imitate wisdom in order to deceive all but those who are most discerning (v. 3). She is loud (v. 13); she is without discipline and void of knowledge (v. 13). Ignorance in Proverbs is a reference to the lack of moral understanding. She tries to convince the simple that only "stolen water," synonymous with an adulterous relationship, is exciting (v. 17). Many today have accepted this erroneous viewpoint that something gained unjustly and secretly is better. Such a life of folly runs contrary to God's plan of wisdom and inevitably will end in death (v. 18).

10:1—31:31 The theological groundwork of Proverbs 1—9 is ended, and what remains is the purely practical. The emphasis in chapters 10—31 is on the application of wisdom, on how to fear the Lord in daily life. Continuing with the theme of the righteous (wisdom) and the wicked (folly), these chapters contain short contrasting proverbs emphasizing the radical difference between the wise living of the righteous and the evil living of the wicked. In many cases, the second line of the verse begins with the word "but."

10:1 In this example of a contrasting proverb (see Prov. 10:1—31:31, note), the use of father in one line and mother in the

[3]The LORD will not allow the righteous soul to famish,
But He casts away the desire of the wicked.

[4]He who has a slack hand becomes poor,
But the hand of the diligent makes rich.
[5]He who gathers in summer *is* a wise son;
He who sleeps in harvest *is* a son who causes shame.

[6]Blessings *are* on the head of the righteous,
But violence covers the mouth of the wicked.
[7]The memory of the righteous *is* blessed,
But the name of the wicked will rot.

[8]The wise in heart will receive commands,
But a prating fool will fall.

[9]He who walks with integrity walks securely,
But he who perverts his ways will become known.

[10]He who winks with the eye causes trouble,
But a prating fool will fall.

[11]The mouth of the righteous *is* a well of life,
But violence covers the mouth of the wicked.

[12]Hatred stirs up strife,
But love covers all sins.

[13]Wisdom is found on the lips of him who has understanding,
But a rod *is* for the back of him who is devoid of understanding.

[14]Wise *people* store up knowledge,
But the mouth of the foolish *is* near destruction.

[15]The rich man's wealth *is* his strong city;
The destruction of the poor *is* their poverty.

[16]The labor of the righteous *leads* to life,
The wages of the wicked to sin.

[17]He who keeps instruction *is in* the way of life,
But he who refuses correction goes astray.

[18]Whoever hides hatred *has* lying lips,
And whoever spreads slander *is* a fool.

[19]In the multitude of words sin is not lacking,
But he who restrains his lips *is* wise.
[20]The tongue of the righteous *is* choice silver;
The heart of the wicked *is worth* little.
[21]The lips of the righteous feed many,
But fools die for lack of wisdom.[a]

[22]The blessing of the LORD makes *one* rich,
And He adds no sorrow with it.

[23]To do evil *is* like sport to a fool,
But a man of understanding has wisdom.
[24]The fear of the wicked will come upon him,
And the desire of the righteous will be granted.
[25]When the whirlwind passes by, the wicked *is* no *more*,
But the righteous *has* an everlasting foundation.

[26]As vinegar to the teeth and smoke to the eyes,
So *is* the lazy *man* to those who send him.

[27]The fear of the LORD prolongs days,
But the years of the wicked will be shortened.
[28]The hope of the righteous *will be* gladness,
But the expectation of the wicked will perish.
[29]The way of the LORD *is* strength for the upright,
But destruction *will come* to the workers of iniquity.

[30]The righteous will never be removed,
But the wicked will not inhabit the earth.
[31]The mouth of the righteous brings forth wisdom,
But the perverse tongue will be cut out.
[32]The lips of the righteous know what is acceptable,
But the mouth of the wicked *what is* perverse.

10:21 [a]Literally *heart*

10:11 **The tongue** is one of Solomon's favorite subjects (vv. 11, 13, 14, 18–21, 31, 32). What is said and how it is said are good indicators and measures of wisdom.

10:19 **Silence brings healing.** "Restrains his lips" (lit. "keeps a check on his tongue") confirms the adage that "the less said the better." Rabbinic sayings also address silence: "Silence is a healing for all ailments"; "Silence is good for the wise; how much more so for the foolish."

other indicates that just as both parents are involved in teaching their children, both share in the joy and grief associated with parenting (see Prov. 1:8; 4:3, 4; 6:20).

10:27 **Proverbs are not necessarily promises** or absolutes but guidelines (compare Ps. 73:12). Usually the righteous will live longer than the wicked because the lifestyle of the wise brings peace, security, and a lack of anxiety. These blessings of wisdom contribute to the wise person's health and longevity.

10:31 **What a wonderful epitaph** to have on a gravestone, "The mouth of this woman brought forth wisdom." The phrase "brings forth" (lit. "bears fruit") illustrates clearly that wisdom is a reflection of righteousness. Just as a tree naturally brings forth fruit of its own kind, so words of wisdom are a natural result of righteousness.

PARENTHOOD A GOD-GIVEN RESPONSIBILITY

Something must be incredibly basic, important, and possible in parenthood if being parents is part of the primary command God gave to the mother and father of the human race (Gen. 1:28). True, reproduction was necessary to continue the generations, but to see children as simply the by-product of a biological function is to miss completely the divine significance attached to parenthood (Ps. 127; 128).

God made us in His image (Gen. 1:27), and nothing reveals the true nature of His deity any more than God's loving creation of human life. How could man and woman more unambiguously reflect that characteristic of God than in their own loving procreation of a child?

The Bible contains clear principles for rearing children in the nurture and admonition of the Lord.

- Parents are to demonstrate God's pattern for Christian marriage (1 Tim. 3:4, 12; Titus 2:1–5). A loving relationship between mother and father is a living object lesson for the child in how a husband and wife are to relate in marriage.
- Parents are responsible for teaching their children spiritual truths (Deut. 6:4–9; Ps. 78:1–8; 2 Tim. 1:3–5; Eph. 6:4). Such an important task cannot be left to the church and Christian school.
- Parents must lead their children to go God's way through loving and consistent discipline (Prov. 13:24; 19:18; 20:30; 22:15; Heb. 12:5–8, 11). This is not merely administering punishment but careful nurture to make "disciples" out of their children, teaching them how to live the Christian life by word and example.

See also Matt. 18:3, note; charts on In-Law or In-Love; The Rod of Discipline; notes on Child Care (John 14); Children (2 Sam. 21; Ps. 128; Prov. 22; Luke 15); Family (Gen. 32; 1 Sam. 3; Ps. 78; 127); Fatherhood (Eph. 5); Motherhood (1 Sam. 1; Is. 49; Ezek. 16)

11 Dishonest scales *are* an abomination to the LORD,
But a just weight *is* His delight.

[2] When pride comes, then comes shame;
But with the humble *is* wisdom.

[3] The integrity of the upright will guide them,
But the perversity of the unfaithful will destroy them.
[4] Riches do not profit in the day of wrath,
But righteousness delivers from death.
[5] The righteousness of the blameless will direct[a] his way aright,
But the wicked will fall by his own wickedness.
[6] The righteousness of the upright will deliver them,
But the unfaithful will be caught by *their* lust.

[7] When a wicked man dies, *his* expectation will perish,
And the hope of the unjust perishes.
[8] The righteous is delivered from trouble,
And it comes to the wicked instead.
[9] The hypocrite with *his* mouth destroys his neighbor,
But through knowledge the righteous will be delivered.
[10] When it goes well with the righteous, the city rejoices;
And when the wicked perish, *there is* jubilation.
[11] By the blessing of the upright the city is exalted,
But it is overthrown by the mouth of the wicked.

[12] He who is devoid of wisdom despises his neighbor,
But a man of understanding holds his peace.

[13] A talebearer reveals secrets,
But he who is of a faithful spirit conceals a matter.

[14] Where *there is* no counsel, the people fall;
But in the multitude of counselors *there is* safety.

[15] He who is surety for a stranger will suffer,
But one who hates being surety is secure.

················

11:5 [a] Or *make smooth* or *straight*

11:2 **Self-centered pride brings disgrace to the person and dishonor to God.** This theme is common in Proverbs. In contrast, the wise display humility. To be humble is to be submissive to God and to the authorities He places in your life (see Mic. 6:8).

11:13 **The mouth is a destroyer of people and places** (vv. 9, 11).

One of the most terrible forms of destruction by the mouth is gossip (v. 13). The divulging of a secret by a "talebearer" (lit. "one who goes about in slander") is a betrayal of trust (Prov. 16:28; 17:9; 26:20–22).

11:14 **Counsel** (lit. "steering" or "guidance") carries the idea of giving wise direction on the course of life.

¹⁶A gracious woman retains honor,
But ruthless *men* retain riches.
¹⁷The merciful man does good for his own soul,
But *he who is* cruel troubles his own flesh.
¹⁸The wicked *man* does deceptive work,
But he who sows righteousness *will have* a sure reward.
¹⁹As righteousness *leads* to life,
So he who pursues evil *pursues it* to his own death.
²⁰Those who are of a perverse heart *are* an abomination to the LORD,
But *the* blameless in their ways *are* His delight.
²¹*Though they join* forces,ᵃ the wicked will not go unpunished;
But the posterity of the righteous will be delivered.

²²*As* a ring of gold in a swine's snout,
So is a lovely woman who lacks discretion.

²³The desire of the righteous *is* only good,
But the expectation of the wicked *is* wrath.

²⁴There is *one* who scatters, yet increases more;
And there is *one* who withholds more than is right,
But it *leads* to poverty.
²⁵The generous soul will be made rich,
And he who waters will also be watered himself.
²⁶The people will curse him who withholds grain,
But blessing *will be* on the head of him who sells *it.*

²⁷He who earnestly seeks good finds favor,
But trouble will come to him who seeks *evil.*

²⁸He who trusts in his riches will fall,
But the righteous will flourish like foliage.

²⁹He who troubles his own house will inherit the wind,
And the fool *will be* servant to the wise of heart.

³⁰The fruit of the righteous *is a* tree of life,
And he who wins souls *is* wise.

³¹If the righteous will be recompensed on the earth,
How much more the ungodly and the sinner.

12 Whoever loves instruction loves knowledge,
But he who hates correction *is* stupid.

²A good *man* obtains favor from the LORD,
But a man of wicked intentions He will condemn.

³A man is not established by wickedness,
But the root of the righteous cannot be moved.

⁴An excellentᵃ wife *is* the crown of her husband,
But she who causes shame *is* like rottenness in his bones.

⁵The thoughts of the righteous *are* right,
But the counsels of the wicked *are* deceitful.
⁶The words of the wicked *are,* "Lie in wait for blood,"
But the mouth of the upright will deliver them.

⁷The wicked are overthrown and *are* no more,
But the house of the righteous will stand.

⁸A man will be commended according to his wisdom,

11:21 ᵃLiterally *hand to hand*   12:4 ᵃLiterally *A wife of valor*

11:16 **A gracious woman** is described by contrasting the quiet victories of a beautiful character, which are honor and approval, with the ruthless victories won by force, which consist in making and holding riches. Women of commendable character are mentioned elsewhere (Prov. 12:4; 14:1; 19:14; 31:10–31; see also chart, Biblical Manhood and Womanhood).

11:22 **The women of Israel wore nose rings as ornaments** in the same way that women wear earrings and finger rings (see Ex. 28, Jewelry). The swine were considered unclean animals, thus making the example of a ring of gold in a pig's nose ludicrous. A gold ring could not beautify a dirty pig. Similarly, to suppose that a woman's physical beauty can cover her lack of discretion (or moral perception) is ridiculous. Outward beauty with indiscreet conduct has no value and actually turns beauty into ugliness (see Prov. 4, Beauty).

12:4 **A wife affects her husband.** She either becomes a crown to him or brings him to ruin like a horrible disease that weakens the body. "Excellent" (Heb. *chayil,* lit. "strength") can also

be understood as a reference to moral character. This wife possesses a strong and virtuous character. She is a woman of ability and worth. "Crown" suggests that this wife of quality enables her husband to realize his potential. Because of her character and resourcefulness, her husband is greatly admired by others (see Prov. 31:10; Ruth 3:11). In contrast is the woman who puts her husband to shame before the world. While the wife of quality helps her husband reach the fullness of his abilities, the shameful wife will drag her husband down all his days, and he will never command respect nor win influence in the community. To have such a wife is like enduring an infestation of maggots in the bones. It is a horrible irritant and a fatal disease.

12:5 **Thoughts may break into words at any time!** We eventually become that on which we allow our minds to dwell (Prov. 23:7). The apostle Paul encouraged us to dwell on the positive, good, lovely, excellent, and praiseworthy (Phil. 4:8, 9).

EDUCATION · STUDYING WITH HIM

The Lord is our ultimate Teacher (Ex. 4:15; Ps. 25:8, 9, 12); we are His students (Job 6:24). The first and foremost textbook is to be His Word—His commandments, the inspired account of the life of Jesus, and the divine revelation of the Holy Spirit (Prov. 6:23; Luke 12:12; John 14:26). The curriculum includes:

- Fear of the Lord (Ps. 34:11–14)—His laws and the outworking of those laws;
- His truth (Ps. 86:11)—the nature of the Lord and His promises to us;
- Right judgment (Is. 28:26)—the ability to distinguish between good and evil, right and wrong;
- The way to profit from His blessings (Is. 48:17–19) and to be in a position to receive all His benefits, including peace, righteousness, and righteous children;
- The difference between what is holy and unholy (Ezek. 44:23, 24)—how to discern what is of God;
- Wisdom (James 1:5)—the way in which to live in good relationship with both God and man.

We as students are to be humble (Ps. 25:9), eager to learn (Prov. 12:1), and obedient (2 Tim. 3:14). We are to share generously our worldly goods with those who teach us God's Word (Gal. 6:6). We are to remember His lessons and diligently do what He has taught us to do (Deut. 4:9). Above all, we are to learn with our wills as well as with our minds. We are to live out, not simply know, His laws.

See also Eccl. 12:11, 12; Matt. 18:3, note; notes on Children (2 Sam. 21; Ps. 128; Prov. 22; Luke 15); Education (Deut. 6; 2 Tim. 3); Fear of the Lord (Prov. 2); Spiritual Discipline (2 Pet. 3); Wisdom (James 1)

But he who is of a perverse heart will be despised.

9Better *is the one* who is slighted but has a servant,
Than he who honors himself but lacks bread.

10A righteous *man* regards the life of his animal,
But the tender mercies of the wicked *are* cruel.

11He who tills his land will be satisfied with bread,
But he who follows frivolity *is* devoid of understanding.ᵃ

12The wicked covet the catch of evil *men*,
But the root of the righteous yields *fruit*.

13The wicked is ensnared by the transgression of *his* lips,
But the righteous will come through trouble.

14A man will be satisfied with good by the fruit of *his* mouth,
And the recompense of a man's hands will be rendered to him.

15The way of a fool *is* right in his own eyes,
But he who heeds counsel *is* wise.

16A fool's wrath is known at once,
But a prudent *man* covers shame.

17He *who* speaks truth declares righteousness,
But a false witness, deceit.

18There is one who speaks like the piercings of a sword,
But the tongue of the wise *promotes* health.

19The truthful lip shall be established forever,
But a lying tongue *is* but for a moment.

20Deceit is in the heart of those who devise evil,
But counselors of peace have joy.

21No grave trouble will overtake the righteous,
But the wicked shall be filled with evil.

22Lying lips *are* an abomination to the LORD,
But those who deal truthfully *are* His delight.

23A prudent man conceals knowledge,
But the heart of fools proclaims foolishness.

24The hand of the diligent will rule,
But the lazy *man* will be put to forced labor.

25Anxiety in the heart of man causes depression,
But a good word makes it glad.

••••••••••••••••••••

12:11 ᵃLiterally *heart*

12:12–15 Words, as deeds, bear fruit. Words can bring satisfaction when they are wise or disaster when they are unwise. Wicked words will trap a woman or man.

12:17–22 Words heal or hurt. "Piercings," containing the notion of the quick thrustings of a sword (v. 18), is a fitting picture for the verb "speak" (Heb. *batah*, lit. "speak rashly or unadvisedly," v. 18; see Ps. 106:33). Once spoken, words cannot be taken back. Jesus said that each man and woman will be accountable for every carelessly spoken word (Matt. 12:36, 37). If Jesus was so concerned about careless words, what would He think of rash words that thrust like a sword? The contrast in this verse is shown in the wonderful healing power of the words of the wise.

12:25 Good words help someone want to be a better person, even when life is tough. God tells us to cast all our cares on Him (1 Pet. 5:7) and not to be anxious (Phil. 4:6). Yet how uplifting it is in the midst of a trial to hear a word of encouragement! Encouragement stirs up, provokes, incites people in a given direction.

THE ROD OF DISCIPLINE

PURPOSE	GUIDELINES
• To express loving parental concern (Prov. 13:24)	• Administer "promptly" before behavior patterns become set (Prov. 13:24)
• To offer hope for the most effective development of the child (Prov. 19:18)	• Temper firmness with tenderness (Prov. 4:3; 15:32)
• To cleanse the child of willfulness and disobedience (Prov. 20:30)	• Explain clearly the offense for which the child is being punished (Prov. 4:4, 11)
• To drive out foolishness, which in Proverbs is the opposite of wisdom and centers in the spiritual realm (Prov. 20:30; 22:15)	• Reflect grief with the child for his act of disobedience (Prov. 17:25; Jer. 4:18, 22; Matt. 23:37; Heb. 3:10, 17)
• To break the rebellious heart and deliver the child from eternal punishment (Prov. 23:13, 14)	• Remain with the child until the fellowship and the relationship have been restored (Ps. 51:7–12)
• To teach (Prov. 10:13; 29:15)	• Avoid unnecessary severity (Eph. 6:4)
• To give a parent rest and satisfaction (Prov. 29:17)	
• To underscore the responsibility of the individual for personal attitudes, actions, and reactions (Ps. 53:3; Jer. 17:10; Ezek. 18:4, 20; Rom. 3:10, 23; 14:12; Col. 3:25)	

²⁶The righteous should choose his friends
    carefully,
For the way of the wicked leads them astray.

²⁷The lazy *man* does not roast what he took in
    hunting,
But diligence *is* man's precious possession.

²⁸In the way of righteousness *is* life,
And in *its* pathway *there is* no death.

13 A wise son *heeds* his father's instruction,
But a scoffer does not listen to rebuke.

²A man shall eat well by the fruit of *his* mouth,
But the soul of the unfaithful feeds on violence.
³He who guards his mouth preserves his life,
But he who opens wide his lips shall have
    destruction.

⁴The soul of a lazy *man* desires, and *has* nothing;
But the soul of the diligent shall be made rich.

⁵A righteous *man* hates lying,
But a wicked *man* is loathsome and comes to
    shame.
⁶Righteousness guards *him whose* way is
    blameless,
But wickedness overthrows the sinner.

⁷There is one who makes himself rich, yet *has*
    nothing;
And one who makes himself poor, yet *has* great
    riches.

⁸The ransom of a man's life *is* his riches,
But the poor does not hear rebuke.

⁹The light of the righteous rejoices,
But the lamp of the wicked will be put out.

¹⁰By pride comes nothing but strife,
But with the well-advised *is* wisdom.

¹¹Wealth *gained by* dishonesty will be diminished,
But he who gathers by labor will increase.

¹²Hope deferred makes the heart sick,
But *when* the desire comes, *it is* a tree of life.

13:7 Money is only a small ingredient of both wealth and poverty. A person may be rich in material goods but have nothing of wisdom. In Proverbs, "great riches" are not measured by money (see Prov. 8:1–36, note).

13:12 Hope deferred (lit. "long drawn out" or "delayed in fulfillment") can cause disappointment and depression in body and spirit. The realization of hope gives encouragement just

INHERITANCE PASSING IT ON

Every home should provide a storehouse of happy memories. God knows us even before we are formed. Aunts, uncles, grandparents, and parents should be challenged to link hand and heart to provide a vital, living example of what true Christianity is all about (Ps. 78:4–6).

God's plan is for godly heritage to begin before birth. The privileges and blessings of the extended family provide untold blessings. The influence of grandparents in forming values and character cannot be underestimated. The valuable advice of parents, the care and concern of brothers and sisters, the influence of all the family members on the children is vitally important to the development of godly character in a child.

The unique privileges and tremendous responsibility of providing influence and atmosphere are not confined to the walls of the parental home. The potential influence of a faithful grandparent and God-fearing parent is unending. Principles and precepts are shared in the family's faith journey from generation to generation by parents, grandparents, and great-grandparents—the godly men and women who make up our spiritual heritage (Deut. 5:29) and who consider the "passing on" of the instructions given to Moses a priority (Deut. 6:6, 7). Such a spiritual inheritance will outlive its own generation, bringing strength and joy to our children's children as they experience ups and downs, difficulties, problems, and, of course, the faithfulness of God.

Deuteronomy 6 directs parents to pass along their spiritual heritage throughout the course of any given day—when working in the kitchen, carpooling to school, sitting around the breakfast table, or watching TV in the evenings. There are no set times or specific locations to pass on our values and spiritual legacy. This passage implies a lifestyle modeling and discussion of those things that are deeply important to us. If these values are not woven through the everyday cloth of normal life, then the fabric of life is weak indeed.

Our task is not to showcase perfect families within our communities but rather to allow an unbelieving world to see ordinary families struggling with real issues, yet finding strength and wisdom in a loving, sufficient Savior.

See also Ps. 102:12–28; notes on Family (Gen. 32; 1 Sam. 3; Ps. 127); Family Worship (Ps. 78); Fatherhood (Eph. 5); Grandparenthood (Ps. 71); Motherhood (1 Sam. 1; Is. 49; Ezek. 16); Parenthood (Prov. 10); Traditions (1 Sam. 7)

13He who despises the word will be destroyed,
But he who fears the commandment will be rewarded.
14The law of the wise *is* a fountain of life,
To turn *one* away from the snares of death.

15Good understanding gains favor,
But the way of the unfaithful *is* hard.
16Every prudent *man* acts with knowledge,
But a fool lays open *his* folly.

17A wicked messenger falls into trouble,
But a faithful ambassador *brings* health.

18Poverty and shame *will come* to him who disdains correction,
But he who regards a rebuke will be honored.

19A desire accomplished is sweet to the soul,
But *it is* an abomination to fools to depart from evil.

20He who walks with wise *men* will be wise,
But the companion of fools will be destroyed.

21Evil pursues sinners,
But to the righteous, good shall be repaid.

22A good *man* leaves an inheritance to his children's children,
But the wealth of the sinner is stored up for the righteous.

23Much food *is in* the fallow *ground* of the poor,
And for lack of justice there is waste.[a]

24He who spares his rod hates his son,
But he who loves him disciplines him promptly.

25The righteous eats to the satisfying of his soul,
But the stomach of the wicked shall be in want.

················

13:23 [a]Literally *what is swept away*

---

like a tree that gives life. It brings new vitality to the body and the spirit.

13:24 God disciplines His children, and earthly parents are instructed to do the same (Prov. 3:11, 12; 22:6, note; Heb. 12:5, 6). Loving parents inflict temporary discomfort on their children to keep them from the long-range tragedy that inevitably accompanies lives without discipline. God disciplines us for our

good that we might share His holiness and learn to live wisely and righteously (Heb. 12:10, 11). Parents discipline their children for these same reasons (see Prov. 22, Children). The method of discipline mentioned in this verse and throughout Proverbs is spanking with a "rod" (Heb. *shevet;* see chart, The Rod of Discipline). "Hates" is used figuratively in the sense that refusal to discipline a child is to act as his enemy. Over-

14
The wise woman builds her house,
But the foolish pulls it down with her hands.

[2]He who walks in his uprightness fears the
LORD,
But *he who is* perverse in his ways despises
Him.

[3]In the mouth of a fool *is* a rod of pride,
But the lips of the wise will preserve
them.

[4]Where no oxen *are,* the trough *is* clean;
But much increase *comes* by the strength of an
ox.

[5]A faithful witness does not lie,
But a false witness will utter lies.

[6]A scoffer seeks wisdom and does not *find it,*
But knowledge *is* easy to him who understands.
[7]Go from the presence of a foolish man,
When you do not perceive *in him* the lips of
knowledge.
[8]The wisdom of the prudent *is* to understand
his way,
But the folly of fools *is* deceit.

[9]Fools mock at sin,
But among the upright *there is* favor.

[10]The heart knows its own bitterness,
And a stranger does not share its joy.

[11]The house of the wicked will be overthrown,
But the tent of the upright will flourish.

[12]There is a way *that seems* right to a man,
But its end *is* the way of death.

[13]Even in laughter the heart may sorrow,
And the end of mirth *may be* grief.

[14]The backslider in heart will be filled with his
own ways,
But a good man *will be satisfied* from above.[a]

[15]The simple believes every word,
But the prudent considers well his steps.
[16]A wise *man* fears and departs from evil,
But a fool rages and is self-confident.
[17]A quick-tempered *man* acts foolishly,
And a man of wicked intentions is hated.
[18]The simple inherit folly,
But the prudent are crowned with knowledge.
[19]The evil will bow before the good,
And the wicked at the gates of the righteous.

[20]The poor *man* is hated even by his own
neighbor,
But the rich *has* many friends.
[21]He who despises his neighbor sins;
But he who has mercy on the poor, happy *is*
he.
[22]Do they not go astray who devise evil?
But mercy and truth *belong* to those who devise
good.

[23]In all labor there is profit,
But idle chatter[a] *leads* only to poverty.

[24]The crown of the wise is their riches,
But the foolishness of fools *is* folly.

[25]A true witness delivers souls,
But a deceitful *witness* speaks lies.

14:14 [a]Literally *from above himself*   14:23 [a]Literally *talk of the lips*

looking faults, ignoring disobedience, and refusing to administer discipline does not influence a child to go the right way but rather allows the child's self-will to gain control over life and actions (Prov. 1:31; 3:5, 6; 12:15; 16:9, 25; 19:18, note; 21:2; 30:12). Love is the balance and tempering force in discipline. Love is always to be the greatest motivation for discipline (see Prov. 29:17).

14:1 A wise woman builds. The fact that this woman is called "wise" indicates that she fears and reverences the Lord. She conscientiously builds her house, making her entire household thrive, because she has learned that wisdom brings the happiness and prosperity she desires for her family. The wise woman cares for her home, causing it to flourish and become a haven to those who live there. She builds her home by making wise choices in her relationships with her husband and children. She works on her marriage, knowing that intimacy does not happen naturally but must be developed. All building takes time, picturing brick set on brick until a sturdy safe home is constructed. In contrast, the foolish woman does not build. She tears down both her possessions and her relation-

ships. She destroys by her own efforts—with her hands, her tongue, her idleness, and her lack of interest.

14:4 Where there is no progress, there are no problems. Some disturbance is necessary for growth and accomplishment to occur.

14:12 The right way. The figure is that of a journey, in which the traveler imagines that he is pursuing a straight path that will lead him to his desired goal of success and happiness. Sin is often able to hide its own character and disguise its bitter end. He finds, too late, that the easy path leads to an early death. Human wisdom (folly) is the "way of death" (see Eccl. 1:12—12:8), the path that a person determines to be right, without regard for God. The path of life is submissive obedience to the will of the Lord. That is true wisdom (see Prov. 1:7; 9:10).

14:14 The backslider (lit. "proven to be unfaithful") is a person who has turned away from God in his heart and instead is seeking his own way. Sadly, he will reap what he sows (Gal. 6:7). He will never find true satisfaction.

GRACIOUSNESS A COMPLEMENT TO BEAUTY

A gracious spirit enhances a woman's demeanor, while a selfish heart tarnishes her appearance and limits her effectiveness. The word "gracious" is used to describe God Himself (Ex. 34:6; Neh. 9:17; Ps. 111:4).

Abigail was a gracious woman. She realized and accepted her husband's weak habits (1 Sam. 25:23–31). She poised herself before David with respect, kindness, and courtesy. Yet in so doing she showed deference to her husband and others by taking upon herself responsibility for the lack of hospitality.

The Moabitess Ruth was a quiet woman whose perseverance complemented her beauty. She was gracious to her mother-in-law even when Naomi was absorbed in bitterness and self-pity (Ruth 2:2). Her strong character and gracious manner were eventually rewarded with a devoted husband and important offspring (4:13).

Having experienced God's forgiveness and love should increase a woman's sensitivity to another's needs. A condescending or resentful attitude does not exemplify graciousness. Believers are challenged to be gracious, kind, merciful, and forgiving (Neh. 9:17).

A Christian reflects God's kingdom by words spoken. Wise words are gracious, but foolish words are damaging (Eccl. 10:12). Believers are also admonished to speak with kindness and truth (Col. 3:12, 13). Words can scar the heart and forever damage a reputation and relationship. To possess graciousness is to showcase His love and channel His care to a needy world.

As an end in itself, graciousness or charm is merely a pleasing manner which has been developed through painstaking determination to do certain things in order to win the favor of family and friends. In other words, it is an outward polish or refinement. However, if this graciousness is the fruit of godly character, springing from a heart committed to the Lord, then such charm becomes a tool for drawing others to the Savior and for service to Christ in the kingdom. Such a "gracious" woman retains a great honor.

See also Prov. 11:25; notes on Beauty (Prov. 4); Femininity (Ps. 144); Fruit of the Spirit (Eph. 4); portraits of Abigail (1 Sam. 25); Ruth (Ruth 2)

---

²⁶In the fear of the LORD *there is* strong confidence,
And His children will have a place of refuge.
²⁷The fear of the LORD *is* a fountain of life,
To turn *one* away from the snares of death.

²⁸In a multitude of people *is* a king's honor,
But in the lack of people *is* the downfall of a prince.

²⁹He who is slow to wrath has great understanding,
But *he who is* impulsive^a exalts folly.

³⁰A sound heart *is* life to the body,
But envy *is* rottenness to the bones.

³¹He who oppresses the poor reproaches his Maker,

But he who honors Him has mercy on the needy.

³²The wicked is banished in his wickedness,
But the righteous has a refuge in his death.

³³Wisdom rests in the heart of him who has understanding,
But *what is* in the heart of fools is made known.
³⁴Righteousness exalts a nation,
But sin *is* a reproach to *any* people.

³⁵The king's favor *is* toward a wise servant,
But his wrath *is against* him who causes shame.

15 A soft answer turns away wrath,
But a harsh word stirs up anger.
²The tongue of the wise uses knowledge rightly,

14:29 ^aLiterally *short of spirit*

14:26, 27 The fear of the Lord brings blessing (Prov. 1:7; 9:10), including a "strong confidence" (security) and a "fountain of life" (source of spiritual vitality). With wisdom, there is refuge in the Lord and escape from death. The children, too, will learn from their mother and father the benefits of a wise life lived in reverence before God.

14:29 Patience is evidence of wisdom, but the "impulsive" (lit. "short of spirit" or "impatient"), quick-tempered person

shows folly. Patience produces increased wisdom, that is, the "righteousness of God" (James 1:19, 20).

14:30 A sound heart could be translated as a "healthy, tranquil mind" (see Prov. 4:20–27; note). A healthy mind produces a healthy body. But envy destroys physical health (see Phil. 4:11–13).

15:1–33 A woman's words, the tongue that speaks them, and the heart that chooses them reveal much about her (vv. 2, 4,

But the mouth of fools pours forth
   foolishness.

3The eyes of the Lord *are* in every place,
   Keeping watch on the evil and the good.

4A wholesome tongue *is* a tree of life,
   But perverseness in it breaks the spirit.

5A fool despises his father's instruction,
   But he who receives correction is prudent.

6*In* the house of the righteous *there is* much
   treasure,
   But in the revenue of the wicked is trouble.

7The lips of the wise disperse knowledge,
   But the heart of the fool *does* not *do* so.

8The sacrifice of the wicked *is* an abomination
   to the Lord,
   But the prayer of the upright *is* His delight.
9The way of the wicked *is* an abomination to the
   Lord,
   But He loves him who follows righteousness.

10Harsh discipline *is* for him who forsakes the
   way,
   And he who hates correction will die.

11Hell[a] and Destruction[b] *are* before the Lord;
   So how much more the hearts of the sons of
   men.

12A scoffer does not love one who corrects him,
   Nor will he go to the wise.

13A merry heart makes a cheerful countenance,
   But by sorrow of the heart the spirit is
   broken.

14The heart of him who has understanding seeks
   knowledge,
   But the mouth of fools feeds on foolishness.

15All the days of the afflicted *are* evil,
   But he who is of a merry heart *has* a continual
   feast.

16Better *is* a little with the fear of the Lord,
   Than great treasure with trouble.
17Better *is* a dinner of herbs[a] where love is,
   Than a fatted calf with hatred.

18A wrathful man stirs up strife,
   But *he who is* slow to anger allays contention.

19The way of the lazy *man is* like a hedge of
   thorns,
   But the way of the upright *is* a highway.

20A wise son makes a father glad,
   But a foolish man despises his mother.

21Folly *is* joy *to him who is* destitute of
   discernment,
   But a man of understanding walks uprightly.

22Without counsel, plans go awry,
   But in the multitude of counselors they are
   established.

23A man has joy by the answer of his mouth,
   And a word *spoken* in due season, how good *it
   is!*

24The way of life *winds* upward for the wise,
   That he may turn away from hell[a] below.

25The Lord will destroy the house of the proud,
   But He will establish the boundary of the
   widow.

26The thoughts of the wicked *are* an abomination
   to the Lord,
   But *the words* of the pure *are* pleasant.

15:11 [a]Or *Sheol* [b]Hebrew *Abaddon*   **15:17** [a]Or *vegetables*   **15:24** [a]Or
Sheol

7, 14, 23, 26, 28). An ideal of conduct is urged in the comments on how we should say what we say (v. 1). A soft answer is a conciliatory answer, often relieving a tense situation by dissolving a person's anger. Such responses require kindness, self-control, patience, love, peace—all the fruit of the Spirit (see Gal. 5, Fruit of the Spirit).

15:13–15 Attitude is an inward feeling expressed by outward behavior. Attitude can be seen without the speaking of a word. Attitude can produce a "merry" (lit. "joyful" or "cheerful") face (v. 13). Attitudes also color a person's whole experience (v. 15)! Happiness and depression are issues of the heart. What a person is on the inside has more impact on his emotional state than the circumstances.

15:17 Lavish hospitality is not necessarily an indication of goodwill. Behind the stimulating conversation of a good host-

ess may lie ulterior motives. A simple meal with love, honesty, and true fellowship is far better than a sumptuous feast amid wealth with hatred (see 1 Pet. 4, Hospitality; chart, Hospitality or Entertainment).

15:25 God cares for the woman who is alone. He is the champion of the defenseless and will secure the land belonging to the widow (see Ps. 68, Widowhood). Land was kept in a family, and its boundaries were important. A widow was easy prey to thieves who might steal her land; so the Lord promised that He would protect her boundaries. God did this for Naomi when He provided Ruth as a dutiful daughter-in-law and established her borders in Israel (Ruth 1:7–18; 4:14–17). The contrast is between the proud and humble. The proud woman would depend on her own resources, but the widow (usually in humble circumstances) would depend on the Lord.

ENVY · DISCONTENT WITH WHAT YOU HAVE

Envy begins when contentment is interrupted by an awareness of the advantages enjoyed by another followed by the determination to seize such advantage—whether in social standing, material possessions, or personal praise (Gen. 26:14; 30:1; Ps. 73:3). To want what others have has become a part of our culture of abundant things accompanied by the expectation that life should continually escalate to something better, easier, and more affluent.

Scripture says that envy co-exists with "every evil thing." Envy is commonly included in the New Testament vice list, and the list is ugly: striving, self-seeking, malice, deceit, hypocrisy, and evil speaking (Phil. 1:15; James 3:14–16; 1 Pet. 2:1–3). Envy is a disastrous emotion because it displaces our trust that God knows best and will supply our needs.

Even a Christian woman is capable of envying the good that others have received from God—whether a leadership position, spiritual power, family relationships (especially children), or spiritual gifts. In so doing, she generally fails to reach her own potential in Christ Jesus. In seeking more that does not rightfully belong to her, she actually is diminished, a state described in Scripture as "leanness [of] soul" and "rottenness to the bones" (Ps. 106:13–15; Prov. 14:30).

You escape envy only by giving your desires to God so that He might satisfy them in His timing and by His methods. When you do so, you find that the love of God transforms your emotions. Contentment with what you have and in whatever state you find yourself replaces envy (Phil. 4:11). You will receive a new long-range perspective of what is really important.

See also Matt. 27:18; 1 Cor. 13:4; 1 Tim. 6:3–5; notes on Bitterness (Heb. 12); Covetousness (Prov. 30); Fruit of the Spirit (Ps. 86; Rom. 5; 15; 1 Cor. 10; 13; Gal. 5; Eph. 4; Col. 3; 2 Thess. 1; Rev. 2); Jealousy (Song 8)

---

²⁷He who is greedy for gain troubles his own
  house,
  But he who hates bribes will live.

²⁸The heart of the righteous studies how to
  answer,
  But the mouth of the wicked pours forth evil.

²⁹The Lord *is* far from the wicked,
  But He hears the prayer of the righteous.

³⁰The light of the eyes rejoices the heart,
  And a good report makes the bones healthy.ᵃ

³¹The ear that hears the rebukes of life
  Will abide among the wise.
³²He who disdains instruction despises his own
  soul,
  But he who heeds rebuke gets understanding.

³³The fear of the Lord *is* the instruction of
  wisdom,
  And before honor *is* humility.

16 The preparations of the heart *belong* to
  man,
  But the answer of the tongue *is* from the
  Lord.

²All the ways of a man *are* pure in his own eyes,
  But the Lord weighs the spirits.

³Commit your works to the Lord,
  And your thoughts will be established.

⁴The Lord has made all for Himself,
  Yes, even the wicked for the day of doom.
  •••••••••••••••••

15:30 ᵃLiterally *fat*

15:28 To open our mouths with wisdom requires study. The wise person ponders and thinks carefully by studying other people, the situation, and the impact of the potential words before answering. In contrast, a foolish person gushes out evil words like the water that bubbles forth out of a spring.

16:1—22:16 Wise living was emphasized by contrast using the key word "but" (Prov. 10—15; see Prov. 10:1—31:31, note). Beginning in Proverbs 16, wise living is encouraged by the use of the word "and." For example, "pride goes before destruction, and a haughty spirit before a fall" (Prov. 16:18).

16:1–9 Dependence on God is the crucial ingredient for the outworking of the wisdom of Proverbs in life (Prov. 1:7; 3:5, 6; 9:10). God is the blessed controller of all things (1 Tim. 6:15). He is sovereign with absolute authority and power

(Prov. 16:33). These verses emphasize God's role as sovereign King of the universe. We may make plans, but the answers are from God (v. 1). We think our ways are pure, but God weighs the motives of each one of us (v. 2). We may commit our works to the Lord, but God establishes the plans (v. 3). God has made everything for His own purpose (v. 4). We may plan the way but God directs each step (v. 9). What appears to be chance in reality is part of God's sovereign plan (v. 33).

16:3 Commit (lit. "roll" or "roll away") carries the idea that each woman should roll her efforts or roll away her burdens on the Lord. The Lord already clearly has charge of them (1 Pet. 5:7).

16:4 God's sovereignty is shown in the way He has shaped the world. The mysteries of God's sovereign plan are obviously

[5]Everyone proud in heart *is* an abomination to
the L ORD;
Though they join forces,[a] none will go
unpunished.

[6]In mercy and truth
Atonement is provided for iniquity;
And by the fear of the L ORD *one* departs from
evil.

[7]When a man's ways please the L ORD,
He makes even his enemies to be at peace with
him.

[8]Better *is* a little with righteousness,
Than vast revenues without justice.

[9]A man's heart plans his way,
But the L ORD directs his steps.

[10]Divination *is* on the lips of the king;
His mouth must not transgress in judgment.
[11]Honest weights and scales *are* the L ORD's;
All the weights in the bag *are* His work.
[12]*It is* an abomination for kings to commit
wickedness,
For a throne is established by righteousness.
[13]Righteous lips *are* the delight of kings,
And they love him who speaks *what is* right.
[14]As messengers of death *is* the king's wrath,
But a wise man will appease it.
[15]In the light of the king's face *is* life,
And his favor *is* like a cloud of the latter
rain.

[16]How much better to get wisdom than gold!
And to get understanding is to be chosen
rather than silver.

[17]The highway of the upright *is* to depart from
evil;
He who keeps his way preserves his soul.

[18]Pride *goes* before destruction,
And a haughty spirit before a fall.

[19]Better *to be* of a humble spirit with the lowly,
Than to divide the spoil with the proud.

[20]He who heeds the word wisely will find good,
And whoever trusts in the L ORD, happy *is* he.

[21]The wise in heart will be called prudent,
And sweetness of the lips increases learning.

[22]Understanding *is* a wellspring of life to him
who has it.
But the correction of fools *is* folly.

[23]The heart of the wise teaches his mouth,
And adds learning to his lips.

[24]Pleasant words *are like* a honeycomb,
Sweetness to the soul and health to the bones.

[25]There is a way *that seems* right to a man,
But its end *is* the way of death.

[26]The person who labors, labors for himself,
For his *hungry* mouth drives him *on.*

[27]An ungodly man digs up evil,
And *it is* on his lips like a burning fire.
[28]A perverse man sows strife,
And a whisperer separates the best of friends.
[29]A violent man entices his neighbor,
And leads him in a way *that is* not good.
[30]He winks his eye to devise perverse things;
He purses his lips *and* brings about evil.

[31]The silver-haired head *is* a crown of glory,
If it is found in the way of righteousness.

[32]*He who is* slow to anger *is* better than the
mighty,
And he who rules his spirit than he who takes
a city.

[33]The lot is cast into the lap,
But its every decision *is* from the L ORD.

16:5 [a]Literally *hand to hand*

---

beyond our comprehension and, sometimes, our inclinations.
Theologians often categorize the will of God into two broad
aspects, His effective or directive will, which encompasses His
plan to produce certain events by means of His own power,
and His permissive will, which is defined as His willingness to
allow certain events. Both aspects of His will are equally certain, and He is always sovereign over all. The success of evil
and existence of suffering are part of a fallen world. We must
be cautious not to expect our earthly perspectives to overshadow or dictate heavenly purposes. The Lord "made" the
wicked in the sense that in His plan He allowed evil. However,
all will ultimately conform to His good and loving purpose
(see Acts 2:23; Rom. 8:28–39). God's judgment of sin reveals
His justice as well as His sovereignty.

16:18 The sin of pride is strongly condemned because it violates the first principle of wisdom, which is to fear the Lord.
Our abilities, appearance, success, and wealth are not of our
own efforts and energy but come from God. The sin of pride is
attributing to ourselves that which comes by the mercy and
will of God.

16:32 Having strength over tempers is honored above physical
strength. The "mighty" man (lit. "strong and valiant") subdues his might and exercises self-control. This was an unbe-
lievable statement in a place and time when military might
was greatly admired and when safety and security depended
on might in warfare. Being able to conquer temperament is
more highly prized than conquering a city!

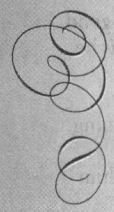

HUMOR   A TIME TO LAUGH

The psalmist declares that God Himself sits in the heavens and laughs (Ps. 2:4), and the writer of Proverbs describes the "woman of strength" as one who rejoices (lit. "laughs at") times to come (Prov. 31:25). Life can become taxing at times, and moments come when we desperately need a change. Laughter is one way the Creator gave us to switch gears and punctuate monotony with joy. Humor is an exit from the mundane "road of life." Laughter is a simple yet reasonable prescription for some of life's ills and most of its tedium (Prov. 17:22). Physicians have assigned healing properties to humor, especially in cases of mental illness, such as depression. Certainly humor defuses tensions and helps put at ease.

With so much tragedy in life, choosing humor instead of despair is good scriptural advice. Humor generally involves an acceptance of the ups and downs of life and the determination not to take ourselves too seriously. To combat stress, to relieve tension, and even to provide delightful diversion in the midst of trials and sufferings, laughter and a keen sense of humor may prove to be precious possessions.

Jesus Himself was unpredictable and witty and full of life in His responses. He used irony, word play, and hyperbole to get across His messages (see Matt. 22:15–22, in which Jesus cleverly eludes the trap of the Pharisees and unmasks their hypocrisy). Jesus asks a Pharisee for a coin with an image of Caesar and an inscription proclaiming Caesar to be god, knowing that to carry such a coin was breaking two commandments (Ex. 20:3, 4).

At the end of life's road we may all end up in the same place someday, but because of laughter along the way, some will have enjoyed the journey and arrived more refreshed.

See also notes on Celebrations and Holidays (Ex. 12); Fruit of the Spirit (Rom. 15); Praise (Ps. 150)

17 Better *is* a dry morsel with quietness,
Than a house full of feasting[a] *with* strife.

[2] A wise servant will rule over a son who causes shame,
And will share an inheritance among the brothers.

[3] The refining pot *is* for silver and the furnace for gold,
But the LORD tests the hearts.

[4] An evildoer gives heed to false lips;
A liar listens eagerly to a spiteful tongue.

[5] He who mocks the poor reproaches his Maker;
He who is glad at calamity will not go unpunished.

[6] Children's children *are* the crown of old men,
And the glory of children *is* their father.

[7] Excellent speech is not becoming to a fool,
Much less lying lips to a prince.

[8] A present *is* a precious stone in the eyes of its possessor;
Wherever he turns, he prospers.

[9] He who covers a transgression seeks love,
But he who repeats a matter separates friends.

[10] Rebuke is more effective for a wise *man*
Than a hundred blows on a fool.

[11] An evil *man* seeks only rebellion;
Therefore a cruel messenger will be sent against him.

[12] Let a man meet a bear robbed of her cubs,
Rather than a fool in his folly.

[13] Whoever rewards evil for good,
Evil will not depart from his house.

[14] The beginning of strife *is like* releasing water;
Therefore stop contention before a quarrel starts.

······························

17:1 [a] Or *sacrificial meals*

17:1 Peace and contentment within are more important than material possessions. A home full of anger, however elegant, is a place of misery.

17:9 Gossip destroys friendship. Silence is never more golden than when one refuses to discuss the weaknesses of a friend (see Prov. 11:13; 18:8, notes; 25, Gossip).

17:14 A quarrel begins like a tiny hole in a reservoir that releases only a trickle of water. If not stopped, however, the trickle becomes a flood. An issue of conflict should be dropped before a dispute can even begin; nothing should be allowed to fester. This excellent advice will keep peace in all relationships.

GOD ANSWERS DIFFICULT QUESTIONS

YOUR QUESTION	HIS ANSWER
Where was God when this happened to me?	He was there—He sees everything (Prov. 15:3).
Didn't He care?	Yes, He did and still does (Nah. 1:7; 1 Pet. 5:6, 7).
How could a loving God allow this to happen?	God gave His creations freedom of choice. He did not make people like puppets (Deut. 30:15–20).
Does the Lord understand how I feel?	Yes, more than anyone (Is. 53:3; Heb. 4:15).
Is recovery possible?	With God all things are possible (Matt. 19:26). Yes, He wants to bring healing to you (Jer. 17:14).
How can I be healed?	Trust God to be faithful to His Word (Ps. 18:25).
Where do I begin?	God hears you—confess your hurt (Ps. 34:17, 18). Give your hurt to Him (1 Pet. 5:7). Forgive the one who has grieved you (Col. 3:13).
Isn't forgiveness difficult?	Yes, but what God commands you to do, He will equip you to do (1 Thess. 5:24). Realize that God has forgiven you (Eph. 4:32).
Then what do I do?	Don't take revenge—God will deal with the violator (Rom. 12:19). Let go—move on with life (Is. 43:18, 19). Look for the good that will come out of the bad (Rom. 8:28).
When will I heal?	Healing of deep hurt takes time (Eccl. 3:3). It is a process of: • facing the harm (Ps. 51:6). • acknowledging your feelings (Eccl. 3:4–8). • applying God's truth from His Word (Ps. 107:20).

¹⁵He who justifies the wicked, and he who
    condemns the just,
  Both of them alike *are* an abomination to the
    LORD.

¹⁶Why *is there* in the hand of a fool the purchase
    price of wisdom,
  Since *he has* no heart *for it?*

¹⁷A friend loves at all times,
  And a brother is born for
    adversity.

¹⁸A man devoid of understanding shakes hands
    in a pledge,
  And becomes surety for his friend.

¹⁹He who loves transgression loves strife,
  And he who exalts his gate seeks destruction.

²⁰He who has a deceitful heart finds no good,
  And he who has a perverse tongue falls into evil.

²¹He who begets a scoffer *does so* to his sorrow,
  And the father of a fool has no joy.

17:17 A true friend, like a brother, loves "at all times," in joy and sorrow, sickness and health, when communication is easy and when communication requires hard work. "At all times" means there are no times when one does not love a friend. A genuine friend multiplies the joys and divides the sorrows (Eccl. 4:9–12, note; see Luke 1, Friendship).

17:21 Foolish sons and daughters bring bitterness, grief, sorrow, and a lack of joy to parents. "Scoffer" refers to one who is dull and thickheaded, while "fool" refers to one who lacks spiritual perception and sensitivity. The child with such characteristics brings sorrow and brokenness to the parents (see also v. 25).

COMMUNICATION EXCHANGING IDEAS

Communication is the exchange of ideas and information by talk, gestures, or writing. It is an active process present in all meaningful relationships. Communication is not only talking but also listening, looking, and feeling. Though individuals have different communication styles, spiritually mature believers are to seek continually to improve their communication with other people and with God.

Speech is powerful. The spoken word can either encourage or discourage. Scripture teaches believers to control the tongue (James 3:1–12) and speak only words of kindness (Eph. 4:29, 32). The Book of Proverbs discusses the importance of listening with understanding to others who speak (Prov. 11:12; 18:2, 13; 29:20).

Words alone cannot fully express meaning. Body language, facial expression, tone of voice, and other means of nonverbal communication are essentials for effectiveness. Those who study communication patterns have concluded that two-thirds of the intent of a message is communicated non-verbally, while only one-third of the message is communicated through words.

Obviously, communication is more than conveying information. Women especially use communication to express feelings more than facts, to establish rapport more than to give a report.

Paul underscores the significance of communication and gives advice about verbal behavior (Eph. 4:25–32). Christians are to

- speak the truth in love (vv. 15, 25),
- control angry words (v. 26),
- speak words of encouragement and healing (v. 29),
- avoid unkind or bitter speech (v. 29),
- speak words of forgiveness (v. 32).

Mature believers realize that clear, loving communication is important in conveying the message of salvation effectively.

See also Prov. 15:1, 23; 16:23, 24; 17:7; 18:4; 29:11; James 3:1–12; notes on Conflict (Matt. 18); Marriage (Gen. 2; 2 Sam. 6; Prov. 5; Hos. 2; Amos 3; 2 Cor. 13; Heb. 13); Prayer (Jer. 33; Heb. 4; 1 John 5; 3 John)

---

²²A merry heart does good, *like* medicine,ᵃ
But a broken spirit dries the bones.

²³A wicked *man* accepts a bribe behind the backᵃ
To pervert the ways of justice.

²⁴Wisdom *is* in the sight of him who has understanding,
But the eyes of a fool *are* on the ends of the earth.

²⁵A foolish son *is* a grief to his father,
And bitterness to her who bore him.

²⁶Also, to punish the righteous *is* not good,
Nor to strike princes for *their* uprightness.

²⁷He who has knowledge spares his words,

And a man of understanding is of a calm spirit.
²⁸Even a fool is counted wise when he holds his peace;
When he shuts his lips, *he is considered* perceptive.

18 A man who isolates himself seeks his own desire;
He rages against all wise judgment.

²A fool has no delight in understanding,
But in expressing his own heart.

³When the wicked comes, contempt comes also;
And with dishonor *comes* reproach.

·······················
17:22 ᵃOr *makes medicine even better*   **17:23** ᵃLiterally *from the bosom*

17:22 Inner-life affects physical well-being; attitude affects countenance (Prov. 15:13, 15, 30; 18:14). A broken, depressed spirit may be attributed to many things: family strife (v. 1), gossip (v. 9), quarrels (v. 14), or a foolish child (vv. 21, 25). How can you have a "merry heart" in the midst of grief and brokenness? The apostle Paul admonished us to trust God even within the tragedy and choose to dwell on what is good in the person or situation (Phil. 4:6–9).

18:1—19:29 Pleasing the Lord in our interactions with others is

the subject of these two chapters. These principles are applicable in our relationships with spouses, children, parents, colleagues, and friends.

18:2 The wise speak because they have something to say, fools because they have to say something. A fool's nature is revealed in his speech. He *must* air his personal opinions, based on nothing but his own folly. He takes no pleasure in receiving wisdom.

⁴The words of a man's mouth *are* deep waters;
The wellspring of wisdom *is* a flowing brook.

⁵*It is* not good to show partiality to the wicked,
Or to overthrow the righteous in judgment.

⁶A fool's lips enter into contention,
And his mouth calls for blows.
⁷A fool's mouth *is* his destruction,
And his lips *are* the snare of his soul.
⁸The words of a talebearer *are* like tasty
trifles,ᵃ
And they go down into the inmost body.

⁹He who is slothful in his work
Is a brother to him who is a great destroyer.

¹⁰The name of the LORD *is* a strong tower;
The righteous run to it and are safe.
¹¹The rich man's wealth *is* his strong city,
And like a high wall in his own esteem.

¹²Before destruction the heart of a man is
haughty,
And before honor *is* humility.

¹³He who answers a matter before he hears *it,*
It *is* folly and shame to him.

¹⁴The spirit of a man will sustain him in
sickness,
But who can bear a broken spirit?

¹⁵The heart of the prudent acquires
knowledge,
And the ear of the wise seeks knowledge.

¹⁶A man's gift makes room for him,
And brings him before great men.

¹⁷The first *one* to plead his cause *seems* right,
Until his neighbor comes and examines him.

¹⁸Casting lots causes contentions to cease,
And keeps the mighty apart.

¹⁹A brother offended *is harder to win* than a
strong city,
And contentions *are* like the bars of a castle.

²⁰A man's stomach shall be satisfied from the
fruit of his mouth;
From the produce of his lips he shall be filled.

²¹Death and life *are* in the power of the tongue,
And those who love it will eat its fruit.

²²*He who* finds a wife finds a good *thing,*
And obtains favor from the LORD.

²³The poor *man* uses entreaties,
But the rich answers roughly.

²⁴A man *who has* friends must himself be
friendly,ᵃ
But there is a friend *who* sticks closer than a
brother.

19 Better *is* the poor who walks in his
integrity
Than *one who is* perverse in his lips, and is a
fool.

²Also it is not good *for* a soul *to be* without
knowledge,
And he sins who hastens with *his* feet.

³The foolishness of a man twists his way,
And his heart frets against the LORD.

⁴Wealth makes many friends,
But the poor is separated from his friend.

⁵A false witness will not go unpunished,
And *he who* speaks lies will not escape.

⁶Many entreat the favor of the nobility,

18:8 ᵃA Jewish tradition reads *wounds.*   18:24 ᵃFollowing Greek
manuscripts, Syriac, Targum, and Vulgate; Masoretic Text reads *may
come to ruin.*

18:8 A gossip's words are like "tasty trifles" (lit. "things
greedily devoured"). Slanderous words do not make a superficial impression but penetrate into the innermost recesses of
the listener's mind where they are thoroughly digested (see
Prov. 11:13; 17:9, notes; 25, Gossip).

18:10, 11 The name of the LORD is often used in the OT for God
Himself (Ps. 20:7). The righteous or wise person makes the
Lord his refuge (Prov. 18:10). The rich falsely put their security
in their wealth (v. 11). The message is that God alone is a sure
refuge.

18:13 Warnings against forming hasty opinions are given
(vv. 2, 13, 17). Listening to the other person's "heart" as well as
his words is an important aspect of interpersonal relationships (v. 13).

18:21 The strong words "death" and "life" refer to the impact
of speech on others. The *Midrash* notes that the evil tongue
destroys three individuals, "the slanderer, the slandered, and
the listener." Obviously, the "death" caused by malicious,
backbiting, gossiping, or harsh words is not a physical death
but is more deadly because it cannot always be seen.

18:22 A good wife is understood to be one pleasing to God and
thus helpful to her husband and a joy to all. The parallel structure adds emphasis as the second line of the verse explains
the first. In other words, the finding of a wife is a sign of
God's favor. That every wife is not a good wife is implicit here
and this is the "good" wife (Heb. *tov,* lit. "fortune" or "favor")
whose price is far above rubies (Prov. 31:10).

HAPPINESS *A POSITIVE CHOICE*

Happiness can be defined as a feeling of spiritual contentment that will carry you through the triumphs, pitfalls, or even heartaches of life with calm stability, serenity, peace of mind, and tranquility (Matt. 5:3–12). Happiness may or may not be related to the happenings in your life. In many instances, the outward happenings in a life affect our attitudes. However, happiness is also an act of the will (Ps. 144:15). We all have things "happen" in our lives that give us reason to be unhappy, but we have the power through Christ to make our own response to those happenings. Happiness is a potential positive choice.

Jesus gives some characteristics that promote a response of happiness (meekness, righteousness, merciful, peacemakers; Matt. 5:8–11). A believer must concentrate not on doing, but on BEING and LIVING! Total commitment to the Lord will result in a believer's instinctive Christlike response to various happenings as they occur. You must appropriate the tools God has given (His Word and His indwelling Spirit) in order to pursue happiness (Prov. 3:13; 29:18). When a believer's faith and conduct are balanced, happiness will always result. Happiness is enjoying everything the Lord has given you and not fretting about the things that have been taken away or withheld (Matt. 6:33, 34). Happiness is trusting in God's sovereignty and omniscience. You must believe that in every "happening" God will work for your good (Rom. 8:28). Happiness comes from daily obedience and faith in the Lord.

See also Ps. 144:15; Prov. 3:13; 14:21; 29:18; Matt. 5:3–10; Rom. 14:22; notes on Blessings (Gen. 12); Contentment (1 Tim. 6); Fruit of the Spirit (Ps. 86; Rom. 5; 15; 1 Cor. 10; 13; Gal. 5; Eph. 4; Col. 3; 2 Thess. 1; Rev. 2); Hospitality (1 Pet. 4); Humor (Prov. 17); Promises of God (2 Pet. 1); Self-esteem (2 Cor. 10); Worry (Rom. 8)

And every man *is* a friend to one who gives gifts.
⁷All the brothers of the poor hate him;
How much more do his friends go far from him!
He may pursue *them with* words, *yet* they abandon *him*.

⁸He who gets wisdom loves his own soul;
He who keeps understanding will find good.

⁹A false witness will not go unpunished,
And *he who* speaks lies shall perish.

¹⁰Luxury is not fitting for a fool,
Much less for a servant to rule over princes.

¹¹The discretion of a man makes him slow to anger,
And his glory *is* to overlook a transgression.

¹²The king's wrath *is* like the roaring of a lion,
But his favor *is* like dew on the grass.

¹³A foolish son *is* the ruin of his father,
And the contentions of a wife *are* a continual dripping.

¹⁴Houses and riches *are* an inheritance from fathers,
But a prudent wife *is* from the LORD.

¹⁵Laziness casts *one* into a deep sleep,
And an idle person will suffer hunger.

¹⁶He who keeps the commandment keeps his soul,
But he who is careless[a] of his ways will die.

¹⁷He who has pity on the poor lends to the LORD,
And He will pay back what he has given.

¹⁸Chasten your son while there is hope,
And do not set your heart on his destruction.[a]

•••••••••••••••••••••••••••

19:16 [a]Literally *despises,* figurative of recklessness or carelessness
19:18 [a]Literally *to put him to death;* a Jewish tradition reads *on his crying.*

19:13 The ingredients of a tragic and miserable home are presented here: a foolish son and a nagging wife. This is the first of five references in Proverbs to a quarrelsome wife (Prov. 21:9, 19; 25:24; 27:15). "Contentious" is also translated "quarrelsome." The continual dripping that drives one to distraction is like an irritating mosquito buzzing in the night. Sleep is almost found when the buzzing begins again. More than one person has been forced from his bed by a bug! A man can be driven to distraction (or away) by raindrops, a tiny bug, or a nagging, contentious wife. An Arab proverb uses three words that rhyme to convey this point. "Three things

make a house uninhabitable: *tak* (leakage of rain), *nak* (a woman's nagging), and *bak* (bugs)."

19:14 The prudent wife is in contrast to the contentious wife (v. 13; see Prov. 18:22, note). A prudent wife is cautious and possesses good judgment and discretion. She is a good manager of her home (Prov. 31:10–31; see Prov. 24, Homemaking; chart, Homemaking in the Bible). She is a woman of practical wisdom. Here the contrast is between wealth inherited and a gift from God. Unhappy marriages are not addressed. The writer confirmed that God should be credited when the marriage is good.

¹⁹*A man of* great wrath will suffer punishment;
For if you rescue *him,* you will have to do it
again.

²⁰Listen to counsel and receive instruction,
That you may be wise in your latter days.

²¹There are many plans in a man's heart,
Nevertheless the LORD's counsel— that will
stand.

²²What is desired in a man is kindness,
And a poor man is better than a liar.

²³The fear of the LORD *leads* to life,
And *he who has it* will abide in satisfaction;
He will not be visited with evil.

²⁴A lazy *man* buries his hand in the bowl,^a
And will not so much as bring it to his mouth
again.

²⁵Strike a scoffer, and the simple will become
wary;
Rebuke one who has understanding, *and* he
will discern knowledge.

²⁶He who mistreats *his* father *and* chases away *his*
mother
Is a son who causes shame and brings reproach.

²⁷Cease listening to instruction, my son,
And you will stray from the words of
knowledge.

²⁸A disreputable witness scorns justice,
And the mouth of the wicked devours
iniquity.

²⁹Judgments are prepared for scoffers,
And beatings for the backs of fools.

20 Wine *is* a mocker,
Strong drink *is* a brawler,
And whoever is led astray by it is not wise.

²The wrath^a of a king *is* like the roaring of a
lion;
Whoever provokes him to anger sins *against* his
own life.

³*It is* honorable for a man to stop striving,
Since any fool can start a quarrel.

⁴The lazy *man* will not plow because of winter;
He will beg during harvest and *have* nothing.

⁵Counsel in the heart of man *is like* deep
water,
But a man of understanding will draw it out.

⁶Most men will proclaim each his own
goodness,
But who can find a faithful man?

⁷The righteous *man* walks in his integrity;
His children *are* blessed after him.

⁸A king who sits on the throne of judgment
Scatters all evil with his eyes.

⁹Who can say, "I have made my heart clean,
I am pure from my sin"?

- - - - - - - - - - - - - - - - -

19:24 ^aSeptuagint and Syriac read *bosom;* Targum and Vulgate read
armpit.　20:2 ^aLiterally *fear* or *terror* which is produced by the
king's wrath

19:21 God's plans stand. The Book of Proverbs enables us to
gain wisdom and take that knowledge and apply it in a practical way in our own lives. We can acquire wisdom by our own
means, but our wisdom will always be finite compared to the
limitless wisdom and power of God. Because God is absolutely
right and because He has the necessary power to bring His
plans or "counsel" about, He always succeeds. Our "plans"
are many and uncertain, and the success of our plans depends on the will of God. Only plans that God approves will
succeed (see Ps. 33:10, 11; Prov. 16:9; Is. 14:26, 27).

19:22 Kindness (Heb. *chesed,* lit. "lovingkindness") is an attribute that people desire in others and God desires in us (see
Ps. 5:7–12, note). Certainly every wife should know that kindness in her husband. Such kindness is an evidence of wisdom
and should be demonstrated in godly lives (Ps. 36:7; Mic. 6:8,
translated "mercy"). Anyone practicing unfailing loving-kindness will draw others to himself. Loyal love is of much greater
value than wealth; even poverty would be preferable over the
absence of this unfailing love. A man's kindness is one of the
things that enables his wife to trust him.

20:1 Wine mocks the one who drinks it, and the strong drink

makes him loud, aggressive, and without self-control. Intoxicating drinks have often led to great misery and suffering.
They can lead people astray and cause them to do foolish and
abusive things. Though Scripture mentions the medicinal
value of a small amount of wine (1 Tim. 5:23), unquestionably
its excessive use and any form of intoxication were expressly
forbidden for God's people (Prov. 23:20; 31:4–7). Also clear is
how quickly its use moves to become a snare and destroyer
(see Gen. 9:20, 21; 19:30–36; Prov. 23:29–35).

20:7 The children of the righteous are blessed. These children
see in righteous and blameless parents the model of integrity
in their home. They are encouraged by this godly example of
parents who live out their faith, and they are challenged to
become wise themselves.

20:9 Scripture has many affirmations of our sinfulness (Gen.
6:5; 1 Kin. 8:46; Ps. 143:2). No man or woman can say, "I am
perfect and without sin." Two levels are addressed: faultless-
ness in motive and thoughts (having a "pure" heart) and perfection in moral actions (being "clean"). Because of sin, we all
need Jesus Christ as Savior (Rom. 3:23).

ALCOHOLISM   *THE BONDAGE OF STRONG DRINK*

The Bible clearly warns about the consequences of using strong drink (Prov. 20:1). Society today encourages the use of alcohol at almost every occasion. Drinking is not limited to specific amounts, to certain rituals or times of the year. The use of alcohol is increasingly romanticized and idealized by younger age groups. The impact of the consumption of alcohol on individuals, families, employers, and churches is devastating.

Those who choose to follow Christ are exhorted to "not be drunk with wine, in which is dissipation" (Eph. 5:18). The world encourages the use of strong drink by promising good times, many friends, and great glamour. What happens to those who continue to drink over a period of time is the exact opposite: bad times, fewer and fewer friends, and physical deterioration—and generally a host of other woes such as depression, broken family relationships, and financial as well as legal difficulties. Abstinence is not only possible but desirable for two reasons:

1) The person who drinks may not be able to determine if she can stop drinking until after she is addicted to alcohol. Genetic and other physical and emotional factors can play a large part in a person's inability to quit after one or two drinks.
2) The unbeliever needs to see the believer as a model of Christ who chooses to be filled only with the Holy Spirit because believers have discovered the Spirit to be sufficient in meeting all their emotional needs.

See also Prov. 23:21, 29–35; 31:4, 5; Mark 5:2, note; Gal. 5:19–21; 1 Pet. 4:3; notes on Addictions (2 Pet. 2); Codependency (Gen. 27); Decision Making (1 Cor. 8); Healing (Ps. 13; 133; Eccl. 1; 2 Cor. 5; Gal. 6; James 5); Health (Prov. 3); Substance Abuse (Prov. 23); Temptation (Heb. 2)

---

¹⁰Diverse weights *and* diverse measures,
They *are* both alike, an abomination to the
LORD.

¹¹Even a child is known by his deeds,
Whether what he does *is* pure and right.

¹²The hearing ear and the seeing eye,
The LORD has made them both.

¹³Do not love sleep, lest you come to poverty;
Open your eyes, *and* you will be satisfied with
bread.

¹⁴"*It is* good for nothing,"ᵃ cries the buyer;
But when he has gone his way, then he boasts.

¹⁵There is gold and a multitude of rubies,
But the lips of knowledge *are* a precious jewel.

¹⁶Take the garment of one who is surety *for* a
stranger,
And hold it as a pledge *when it* is for a
seductress.

¹⁷Bread gained by deceit *is* sweet to a man,
But afterward his mouth will be filled with
gravel.

¹⁸Plans are established by counsel;
By wise counsel wage war.

¹⁹He who goes about *as* a talebearer reveals
secrets;
Therefore do not associate with one who
flatters with his lips.

²⁰Whoever curses his father or his mother,
His lamp will be put out in deep darkness.

²¹An inheritance gained hastily at the
beginning
Will not be blessed at the end.

²²Do not say, "I will recompense evil";
Wait for the LORD, and He will save you.

²³Diverse weights *are* an abomination to the
LORD,
And dishonest scales *are* not good.

²⁴A man's steps *are* of the LORD;
How then can a man understand his own
way?

20:14 ᵃLiterally *evil, evil*

20:11 Character is recognized, even in childhood. A child's actions and conduct reveal what he is like. Parents must be alert to evaluate the actions of their children and thus mold them through discipline, teaching, and example.

20:19 See Proverbs 11:13, note; 25, Gossip.

20:22 Vengeance should be left to God. Only God is able to

deliver just vengeance (Rom. 12:19). Deliverance of the righteous does involve judgment of the wicked. Nevertheless, punishment for injustice must be left in God's hands.

20:24 Although we can try to understand God's sovereignty, we will never fully comprehend the incomprehensible God (see Is. 55:8, 9).

²⁵*It is* a snare for a man to devote rashly *something*
as holy,
And afterward to reconsider *his* vows.

²⁶A wise king sifts out the wicked,
And brings the threshing wheel over them.

²⁷The spirit of a man *is* the lamp of the Lᴏʀᴅ,
Searching all the inner depths of his heart.ᵃ

²⁸Mercy and truth preserve the king,
And by lovingkindness he upholds his throne.

²⁹The glory of young men *is* their strength,
And the splendor of old men *is* their gray
head.

³⁰Blows that hurt cleanse away evil,
As *do* stripes the inner depths of the heart.ᵃ

21 The king's heart *is* in the hand of the
Lᴏʀᴅ,
Like the rivers of water; He turns it wherever
He wishes.

²Every way of a man *is* right in his own eyes,
But the Lᴏʀᴅ weighs the hearts.

³To do righteousness and justice
Is more acceptable to the Lᴏʀᴅ than sacrifice.

⁴A haughty look, a proud heart,
And the plowingᵃ of the wicked *are* sin.

⁵The plans of the diligent *lead* surely to plenty,
But *those of* everyone *who is* hasty, surely to
poverty.

⁶Getting treasures by a lying tongue
Is the fleeting fantasy of those who seek
death.ᵃ

⁷The violence of the wicked will destroy them,ᵃ
Because they refuse to do justice.

⁸The way of a guilty man *is* perverse;ᵃ
But *as for* the pure, his work *is* right.

⁹Better to dwell in a corner of a housetop,
Than in a house shared with a contentious
woman.

¹⁰The soul of the wicked desires evil;
His neighbor finds no favor in his eyes.

¹¹When the scoffer is punished, the simple is
made wise;
But when the wise is instructed, he receives
knowledge.

¹²The righteous *God* wisely considers the house
of the wicked,
Overthrowing the wicked for *their* wickedness.

¹³Whoever shuts his ears to the cry of the poor
Will also cry himself and not be heard.

¹⁴A gift in secret pacifies anger,
And a bribe behind the back,ᵃ strong wrath.

¹⁵*It is* a joy for the just to do justice,
But destruction *will come* to the workers of
iniquity.

¹⁶A man who wanders from the way of
understanding
Will rest in the assembly of the dead.

20:27, 30 ᵃLiterally *the rooms of the belly* 21:4 ᵃOr *lamp* 21:6
ᵃSeptuagint reads *Pursue vanity on the snares of death;* Vulgate
reads *Is vain and foolish, and shall stumble on the snares of death;*
Targum reads *They shall be destroyed, and they shall fall who seek
death.* 21:7 ᵃLiterally *drag them away* 21:8 ᵃOr *The way of a man
is perverse and strange* 21:14 ᵃLiterally *in the bosom*

20:27 God reveals what is in the depths of a person's heart (thoughts, attitudes, desires, will) in the same way a lamp reveals what is in the darkness. He discerns our motives and evaluates our actions. God's Spirit enables us to know and please God, functioning far beyond the human conscience.

20:30 The purpose of discipline is not to wound or cause pain but to heal a person of evil and lead him to maturity (see Prov. 13:24, note). Sometimes when the conscience is slow to work, physical discipline is needed to break the most stubborn self-will. There is absolutely no hint of abuse, since cruel correction is forbidden and since the worth of the child is consistently affirmed (Ps. 127:3–5, note; 128, Children; chart, The Rod of Discipline).

21:1 Rivers (lit. "streams" or "divisions") refers to watercourses or irrigation ditches dug to direct the water. In the same way, God, in His sovereignty, directs the hearts of kings (see Prov. 16:1, 9). Cyrus (Is. 44:28; 45:1–7), Artaxerxes (Ezra

7:21), and Pharaoh (Ex. 10:1, 2) are examples of kings whose hearts were directed by the King of Kings.

21:9 The portrait of marriage God paints in Scripture is a most intimate relationship in which husband and wife grow to become lovers and best friends (see Gen. 2, Marriage). The husband is commanded to love his wife as Christ loved the church and to love her as his own body (see Job 31, Husbands). The wife is commanded to respond to her husband and to respect him (Eph. 5:22, 23; see Prov. 31, Wives). A contentious spirit in a wife says, "I will not respond to you and I do not respect you" (see Prov. 19:13, note). Instead of being like the excellent, prudent wife who is a blessing to her husband by her words and her works, the contentious wife makes life in the home miserable (see Prov. 12:4; 31:10–31, notes). The man living with a contentious woman would rather live on the rooftop, exposed to the elements, or in a small dusty attic that is hot in the summer and cold in the winter. The joys of intimate companionship are nonexistent with such a wife.

PMS (PREMENSTRUAL SYNDROME) COPING WITH YOUR BODY CYCLE

PMS (premenstrual syndrome) includes a wide variety of physical and psychological symptoms that may recur during the menstrual cycle. Traits such as being argumentative, combative, angry, and vexing (Prov. 21:19) are commonplace among women suffering from PMS. Medical studies reveal that only 10 percent of the menstruating-aged female population are completely free of PMS symptoms; the other 90 percent struggle to some degree.

Would it really be better to live alone, hungry, and thirsty in a desert rather than to live with a woman who exhibits these characteristics? Some husbands think so (Prov. 12:4; 19:13; 21:9, 19; 25:24; 27:15). If you suffer from the extreme symptoms of PMS, realize that it is a physical illness and should be given serious medical attention. Severe PMS can even lead to alarming problems such as child abuse, marital conflict, divorce, depression, and suicide. Seek out a physician who can help you take care of your body, which is the temple of the Lord (2 Cor. 6:16).

See also Lev. 15:19–30; notes on Anger (Eccl. 7); Depression (1 Sam. 16); Distress (Ps. 18); Health (Prov. 3); Menstrual Cycle (Lev. 15); Mental Health (John 10); Stress Management (Phil. 4)

17He who loves pleasure *will be* a poor man;
He who loves wine and oil will not be rich.

18The wicked *shall be* a ransom for the righteous,
And the unfaithful for the upright.

19Better to dwell in the wilderness,
Than with a contentious and angry woman.

20*There is* desirable treasure,
And oil in the dwelling of the wise,
But a foolish man squanders it.

21He who follows righteousness and mercy
Finds life, righteousness, and honor.

22A wise *man* scales the city of the mighty,
And brings down the trusted stronghold.

23Whoever guards his mouth and tongue
Keeps his soul from troubles.

24A proud *and* haughty *man*—"Scoffer" *is* his name;
He acts with arrogant pride.

25The desire of the lazy *man* kills him,
For his hands refuse to labor.

26He covets greedily all day long,
But the righteous gives and does not spare.

27The sacrifice of the wicked *is* an abomination;
How much more *when* he brings it with wicked intent!

28A false witness shall perish,
But the man who hears *him* will speak endlessly.

29A wicked man hardens his face,
But *as for* the upright, he establishesª his way.

30*There is* no wisdom or understanding
Or counsel against the Lord.

31The horse *is* prepared for the day of battle,
But deliverance *is* of the Lord.

22

A *good* name is to be chosen rather than great riches,
Loving favor rather than silver and gold.

2The rich and the poor have this in common,
The Lord *is* the maker of them all.

3A prudent *man* foresees evil and hides himself,
But the simple pass on and are punished.

4By humility *and* the fear of the Lord
Are riches and honor and life.

5Thorns *and* snares *are* in the way of the perverse;
He who guards his soul will be far from them.

....

21:29 ªQere and Septuagint read *understands.*

22:1 A good name is the reward of good behavior, a token of the esteem of family and community, and one of wisdom's most valuable prizes. Living wisely and traveling the path of wisdom results in a good name. Solomon chose wisdom, walked this path, and received a "good name." After years of walking the wise path, Solomon tragically compromised his convictions about God and wisdom. In the end, all his wealth and power could not salvage his "good name" (1 Kin. 11:1–13). This admonition urges us to keep our eyes on the Lord, trusting Him to give us the power and strength to keep walking in the path of wisdom.

⁶Train up a child in the way he should go,
  And when he is old he will not depart from it.

⁷The rich rules over the poor,
  And the borrower *is* servant to the lender.

⁸He who sows iniquity will reap sorrow,
  And the rod of his anger will fail.

⁹He who has a generous eye will be blessed,
  For he gives of his bread to the poor.

¹⁰Cast out the scoffer, and contention will leave;
  Yes, strife and reproach will cease.

¹¹He who loves purity of heart
  And has grace on his lips,
  The king *will be* his friend.

¹²The eyes of the Lord preserve knowledge,
  But He overthrows the words of the faithless.

¹³The lazy *man* says, "*There is* a lion outside!
  I shall be slain in the streets!"

¹⁴The mouth of an immoral woman *is* a deep pit;
  He who is abhorred by the Lord will fall there.

¹⁵Foolishness *is* bound up in the heart of a child;
  The rod of correction will drive it far from him.

¹⁶He who oppresses the poor to increase his *riches,*
  And he who gives to the rich, *will* surely *come* to poverty.

Sayings of the Wise

¹⁷Incline your ear and hear the words of the wise,
  And apply your heart to my knowledge;

¹⁸For *it is* a pleasant thing if you keep them within you;
  Let them all be fixed upon your lips,

¹⁹So that your trust may be in the Lord;
  I have instructed you today, even you.

²⁰Have I not written to you excellent things
  Of counsels and knowledge,

²¹That I may make you know the certainty of the words of truth,
  That you may answer words of truth
  To those who send to you?

²²Do not rob the poor because he *is* poor,
  Nor oppress the afflicted at the gate;

²³For the Lord will plead their cause,
  And plunder the soul of those who plunder them.

²⁴Make no friendship with an angry man,
  And with a furious man do not go,

²⁵Lest you learn his ways
  And set a snare for your soul.

²⁶Do not be one of those who shakes hands in a pledge,
  One of those who is surety for debts;

²⁷If you have nothing *with which* to pay,
  Why should he take away your bed from under you?

²⁸Do not remove the ancient landmark
  Which your fathers have set.

²⁹Do you see a man *who* excels in his work?
  He will stand before kings;
  He will not stand before unknown *men.*

23 When you sit down to eat with a ruler,
  Consider carefully what *is* before you;
²And put a knife to your throat
  If you *are* a man given to appetite.
³Do not desire his delicacies,
  For they *are* deceptive food.

22:6 The interpretation of this verse as a promise to "good parents" that training their children in God's way would result in "good children" has caused heartache and feelings of failure for many parents who have trusted God, yet watched their children stray. Though generally wise parents produce wise children, there are exceptions. God has given every individual the freedom to choose his own way. "Train up" (Heb. *chanak,* lit. "to put something into the mouth") also describes the breaking and bringing into submission of a wild horse by a rope in the mouth. In Solomon's time, the term was used to describe the way a midwife, after delivering a child, would dip her fingers into crushed dates and massage the gums of the newborn with her sweet-tasting fingers to stimulate sucking. Then when placed at the mother's breast, the infant would begin to feed. Some suggest "in the way" alludes to "God's way" or "the path of wisdom"; others believe the phrase is a call for parents to discover the child's "natural bent." Yet children of godly parents sometimes are determined to choose the path of foolishness, and their choices bring heartache and deep grief to their parents. This verse is not necessarily a promise but more likely a warning to parents to break the willfulness of their children and direct them to God's way.

22:17—24:34 Sayings of the wise are to be heard and heeded. The appeal in this section is to act on the knowledge learned from the statements describing wise and foolish living (Prov. 10:1—22:16). Many of the proverbs in these chapters are warnings. These proverbs are similar to those with the personal father-son appeals (Prov. 1—9).

22:17-21 Applying the words of the wise is important. Memorized, they will be on our lips. Our trust in the Lord will increase, and we will be convinced of the certainty of the words and know how to give a good answer to those who ask.

GLUTTONY *AN UNDISCIPLINED APPETITE*

Scripture speaks especially harshly about gluttony—linking it with poverty. Gluttony can indicate excessive eating and drinking, and it does refer to a ravenous, nearly unstoppable, appetite. It is to food what greed is to material wealth, a craving that cannot be satisfied.

More specifically, in Scripture gluttony is associated with eating foods forbidden to the Israelites, the meat and delicacies that are called "deceptive food" (Prov. 23:1–3, 20, 21). It was also associated with a loose and undisciplined lifestyle—disobedience, stubbornness, and rebellion (Deut. 21:20). The fruits of gluttony were laziness and poverty to the glutton (Prov. 23:21) and shame to others (Prov. 28:7).

Gluttony has been smiled upon in modern times. Though never listed on the death certificate, you would probably be amazed at how many diseases have gluttony as a root cause. Solomon prescribed drastic measures if a person is "given to appetite." He said, "Put a knife to your throat" (Prov. 23:2), a stern and severe way of dealing with an undesirable habit or a health problem.

Daniel recognized that food and drink affected nutrition and health (Dan. 1:8, 12–16), and Solomon speaks of deceitful "delicacies" and warns us not to desire them (Prov. 23:3). Many modern foods have been robbed of their vital nutrients and contain ingredients that may fill our bodies with elements that take the place of nutritious foods. The gluttonous use of foods high in sugar and fat takes away from the nutritional balance of milk, fruit, vegetables, meat, and bread, which contain fiber and other nutrients for good digestion and health.

First and foremost, we are not to satisfy our selfish and harmful appetites but rather use our bodies to bring glory to God (1 Cor. 6:19, 20).

See also notes on Addictions (2 Pet. 2); Eating Disorders (Lev. 26); Fruit of the Spirit (1 Cor. 10); Health (Prov. 3); Nutrition (Lev. 11)

⁴Do not overwork to be rich;
  Because of your own understanding, cease!
⁵Will you set your eyes on that which is not?
  For *riches* certainly make themselves wings;
  They fly away like an eagle *toward* heaven.

⁶Do not eat the bread of a miser,ᵃ
  Nor desire his delicacies;
⁷For as he thinks in his heart, so *is* he.
  "Eat and drink!" he says to you,
  But his heart is not with you.
⁸The morsel you have eaten, you will vomit up,
  And waste your pleasant words.

⁹Do not speak in the hearing of a fool,
  For he will despise the wisdom of your words.

¹⁰Do not remove the ancient landmark,
  Nor enter the fields of the fatherless;
¹¹For their Redeemer *is* mighty;
  He will plead their cause against you.

¹²Apply your heart to instruction,
  And your ears to words of knowledge.

¹³Do not withhold correction from a child,
  For *if* you beat him with a rod, he will not die.
¹⁴You shall beat him with a rod,
  And deliver his soul from hell.ᵃ

¹⁵My son, if your heart is wise,
  My heart will rejoice— indeed, I myself;
¹⁶Yes, my inmost being will rejoice
  When your lips speak right things.

¹⁷Do not let your heart envy sinners,
  But *be zealous* for the fear of the LORD all the day;
¹⁸For surely there is a hereafter,
  And your hope will not be cut off.

¹⁹Hear, my son, and be wise;
  And guide your heart in the way.

23:6 ᵃLiterally *one who has an evil eye* 23:14 ᵃOr *Sheol*

23:4, 5 In the quest for wealth, we are encouraged to remember that the first priority in life is not work (see Is. 26, Balancing Home and Career). This is not speaking against industriousness and hard work but rather warning against overwork for the sake of accumulating riches. A wise person realizes that wealth is temporary and unstable; it can fly away like an eagle soars to the heavens (see 1 Tim. 6, Wealth).

23:13, 14 One of the strongest admonitions to parents in Proverbs is to discipline their children that they might be delivered from physical death (see Prov. 13:24; 20:30, notes). Discipline enables a child to live the fullest and happiest life.

23:15, 16 Great rejoicing occurs in the hearts of mothers and fathers when their adult children choose the path of wisdom (vv. 24, 25). This child should be honored with praise for wise choices. How easy for parents to speak loudly and often when a child is being foolish but fail to speak words of praise when she walks wisely.

SUBSTANCE ABUSE *THE DEVASTATION OF DRUGS*

Drugs are used by many as a way to avoid emotional pain—the pain of past or present hurts, or future fears. The impact of drugs on the individual, her family, and others is devastating. Family and friends, however, often find themselves unwittingly aiding the abuser in her denial process by making excuses or refusing to accept that she is harming herself and them. As long as she is able to deny her behavior, she will not see the need for change.

Although alcohol is the drug to which most frequent reference is made in the Bible and also the one more often used by people today, Scripture refers to two other situations where drugs may well have been involved: witchcraft or sorcery, and idolatry. Grim warning is given to those who practice those activities (Gal. 5:19–21).

God encourages us as believers to bring our cares to Him (Ps. 55:22; 1 Pet. 5:6, 7) instead of trying to handle them alone or escape from them by using chemicals or any other artificial means. He stands willing to forgive those who have been involved with drugs or any other harmful substance if we ask for His forgiveness (1 John 1:9).

Believers are exhorted to be filled with and to walk by the Spirit instead of being dependent on wine (Gal. 5:16, 25; Eph. 5:18). What is said about wine applies to the use of any chemical that alters behavior and has the potential to become addictive.

Facing the problem of substance abuse and giving it over to God, confident that He is able to deliver you and bring you through the pain and out of the bondage, puts a person on the road to recovery and victory (Rom. 4:20, 21).

See also Gen. 9:20, 21; Prov. 20:1; 23:19–21; Mark 5:2, note; Rom. 12:1, 2; 1 Cor. 6:12, 19, 20; 8:13; 10:23; Gal. 5:19–21; notes on Alcoholism (Prov. 20); Abuse (Ps. 30); Addictions (2 Pet. 2); Decision Making (1 Cor. 8); Healing (Ps. 13; 133; Eccl. 1; 2 Cor. 5; Gal. 6; James 5); Temptation (Heb. 2)

---

²⁰Do not mix with winebibbers,
   Or with gluttonous eaters of meat;
²¹For the drunkard and the glutton will come to
   poverty,
   And drowsiness will clothe *a man* with rags.

²²Listen to your father who begot you,
   And do not despise your mother when she is
   old.

²³Buy the truth, and do not sell *it,*
   Also wisdom and instruction and
   understanding.

²⁴The father of the righteous will greatly
   rejoice,
   And he who begets a wise *child* will delight in
   him.
²⁵Let your father and your mother be glad,
   And let her who bore you rejoice.

²⁶My son, give me your heart,
   And let your eyes observe my ways.
²⁷For a harlot *is* a deep pit,
   And a seductress *is* a narrow well.

²⁸She also lies in wait as *for* a victim,
   And increases the unfaithful among
   men.

²⁹Who has woe?
   Who has sorrow?
   Who has contentions?
   Who has complaints?
   Who has wounds without cause?
   Who has redness of eyes?
³⁰Those who linger long at the wine,
   Those who go in search of mixed wine.
³¹Do not look on the wine when it is red,
   When it sparkles in the cup,
   When it swirls around smoothly;
³²At the last it bites like a serpent,
   And stings like a viper.
³³Your eyes will see strange things,
   And your heart will utter perverse things.
³⁴Yes, you will be like one who lies down in the
   midst of the sea,
   Or like one who lies at the top of the mast,
   saying:
³⁵"They have struck me, *but* I was not hurt;
   They have beaten me, but I did not feel *it.*

23:29–35 This vivid portrait describes a drunkard. Often drunkenness is characterized by laughter, partying, and great fun. The devastating picture here is exactly the opposite. This person is beset by problems, quarrels, anxiety, hallucinations, and poor health. How many marriages, homes, and businesses have been wrecked because a man or woman became enslaved to drink. Even though the drunkard described is miserable, he cannot wait to wake up so he can have another drink (v. 35). The admonition is to refuse to allow your eyes to look at the wine (v. 31). Outwardly it sparkles, but it is as deadly as a poisonous snake (see Prov. 20, Alcoholism).

CHILDREN   DISCIPLINE FROM PARENTS

Parenthood involves a process of "making disciples" of your own children. Parents teach obedience not just to bring children under parental authority but in order to bring them to salvation and spiritual discipleship (Heb. 12:11). While punishment may sometimes be a part of discipline, much more is involved in moving a child from parent-controlled behavior to self-controlled, independent decision making and ultimately to a God-controlled lifestyle in which the child learns to make wise, God-honoring decisions on his own (Heb. 12:10–11). Godly discipline provides an umbrella of protection under which a child learns to obey God during the days of vulnerability.

Willful defiance is a deliberate act of disobedience in which a child knows what his parents expect, then chooses to do the opposite (Prov. 29:1). This is to be distinguished from childish irresponsibility, resulting from forgetting, making mistakes, having a short attention span or low frustration tolerance, or immaturity.

To nurture and control children demands enough firmness to correct unacceptable behavior (Prov. 22:15) but not so much as to injure or damage a child (Eph. 6:4). Loving parents, who exhibit a tenderness, kindness, and gentleness no matter what the child's behavior, err when they intervene to protect the child from reaping the consequences of that behavior (Prov. 13:24).

Guidelines are given for administering the "rod" of discipline, which, as a symbol of the parent's loving care and concern, should be administered only in love. The rod underscores the responsibility of the individual for his own attitudes, actions, and reactions (Ezek. 18:20; Rom. 3:23; 14:12). Correction shows the child the error of his way and pulls him to the right way.

Discipline should be delivered "promptly" at the time of the offense (Prov. 13:24), catching wrong behavior patterns before they become set. The child must understand clearly that the behavior was wrong (Col. 3:25) and that the authority violated is not merely that of the earthly parent, but of God. The child must be led to evaluate his action as sin, and he must be led to see the need of seeking forgiveness and changing direction. The child should see grief reflected in the parent (Prov. 17:25), who should remain with the child until their fellowship has been restored (Ps. 51:7–12).

In this light, Proverbs 22:6 is not just a promise to good parents that consistent spiritual nurture ultimately assures their children of godly lives, but it is also a warning that leaving a child to the willfulness of going his own way is the path to destruction (Prov. 3:5, 6), laying a foundation for self-willed living from which the child will not depart (Judg. 21:25; Prov. 3:5; 12:15; 14:12; 21:2; 29:15; Is. 53:6).

See also Ex. 20:12; Prov. 3:11, 12; 10:13; 19:18; 20:30; 23:13, 14; 29:17; Matt. 18:3, note; Heb. 12:5–8; notes on Authority (John 19); Children (2 Sam. 21; Ps. 128; Luke 15); Obedience (Philem.); Parenthood (Prov. 10); Spiritual Discipline (2 Pet. 3)

When shall I awake, that I may seek another
　　drink?"

24 Do not be envious of evil men,
　　Nor desire to be with them;
²For their heart devises violence,
　　And their lips talk of troublemaking.

³Through wisdom a house is built,
　　And by understanding it is established;
⁴By knowledge the rooms are filled
　　With all precious and pleasant riches.

⁵A wise man *is* strong,
　　Yes, a man of knowledge increases strength;

⁶For by wise counsel you will wage your own
　　war,
　　And in a multitude of counselors *there is*
　　safety.

⁷Wisdom *is* too lofty for a fool;
　　He does not open his mouth in the gate.

⁸He who plots to do evil
　　Will be called a schemer.
⁹The devising of foolishness *is* sin,
　　And the scoffer *is* an abomination to men.

¹⁰*If* you faint in the day of adversity,
　　Your strength *is* small.

24:3, 4 A house is built, not with wallpaper, drapes, and throw pillows but with wisdom, understanding, and knowledge. "Wisdom" is the ability to take the knowledge about God concerning life and apply it in a practical and successful way in our homes. It takes godly skill (wisdom) to build a godly home. "Understanding" is discernment. Of utmost importance in the relationships of life is the ability to be discerning. "Knowledge" for knowledge's sake alone is meaningless. But knowledge about God enables a woman to fill her home and her relationships with "precious and pleasant riches." The word "built" (Heb. *banah*) is also used to describe the creation of the woman (Gen. 2:22), in which God took Adam's rib and "rebuilt" the bone and made Eve. It is never too late to begin applying this verse and using wisdom, understanding, and knowledge as mortar to join the bricks in building the home!

[11]Deliver *those who* are drawn toward death,
And hold back *those* stumbling to the
slaughter.
[12]If you say, "Surely we did not know this,"
Does not He who weighs the hearts consider
it?
He who keeps your soul, does He *not* know *it?*
And will He *not* render to *each* man according
to his deeds?

[13]My son, eat honey because *it is* good,
And the honeycomb *which is* sweet to your
taste;
[14]So *shall* the knowledge of wisdom *be* to your
soul;
If you have found *it,* there is a prospect,
And your hope will not be cut off.

[15]Do not lie in wait, O wicked *man,* against the
dwelling of the righteous;
Do not plunder his resting place;
[16]For a righteous *man* may fall seven times
And rise again,
But the wicked shall fall by calamity.

[17]Do not rejoice when your enemy falls,
And do not let your heart be glad when he
stumbles;
[18]Lest the LORD see *it,* and it displease Him,
And He turn away His wrath from him.

[19]Do not fret because of evildoers,
Nor be envious of the wicked;
[20]For there will be no prospect for the evil *man;*
The lamp of the wicked will be put out.

[21]My son, fear the LORD and the king;
Do not associate with those given to change;
[22]For their calamity will rise suddenly,
And who knows the ruin those two can bring?

Further Sayings of the Wise

[23]These *things* also *belong* to the wise:

It is not good to show partiality in judgment.

[24]He who says to the wicked, "You *are* righteous,"
Him the people will curse;
Nations will abhor him.
[25]But those who rebuke *the wicked* will have
delight,
And a good blessing will come upon them.

[26]He who gives a right answer kisses the lips.

[27]Prepare your outside work,
Make it fit for yourself in the field;
And afterward build your house.

[28]Do not be a witness against your neighbor
without cause,
For would you deceive[a] with your lips?
[29]Do not say, "I will do to him just as he has done
to me;
I will render to the man according to his work."

[30]I went by the field of the lazy *man,*
And by the vineyard of the man devoid of
understanding;
[31]And there it was, all overgrown with thorns;
Its surface was covered with nettles;
Its stone wall was broken down.
[32]When I saw *it,* I considered *it* well;
I looked on *it and* received instruction:
[33]A little sleep, a little slumber,
A little folding of the hands to rest;
[34]So shall your poverty come *like* a prowler,
And your need like an armed man.

Further Wise Sayings of Solomon

25 These also *are* proverbs of Solomon which
the men of Hezekiah king of Judah copied:

[2]*It is* the glory of God to conceal a matter,
But the glory of kings *is* to search out a matter.

[3]*As* the heavens for height and the earth for
depth,
So the heart of kings *is* unsearchable.

24:28 [a]Septuagint and Vulgate read *Do not deceive.*

24:10 Trusting God is easy when life is going smoothly but difficult when adversity attacks. Some say that a woman never shows her colors as truly as in crisis. A crisis will either tear a marriage apart or cause a couple to pull together. Proverbs offers good advice on how to be strong in adversity (see Acts 5, Adversity).

24:13, 14 As honey is to the lips, so wisdom is to the soul. Sweet satisfaction comes from the freedom wisdom gives. To know what to do and to do it brings joy. Parents should strive to impart wisdom so that it appears sweet to the child! The woman who finds wisdom will hope with a hope that endures to the end.

25:1 Hezekiah, king of Judah, reigned about 250 years after Solomon. Hezekiah walked the way of wisdom and thus be-came one of the greatest kings since Solomon. King Hezekiah led a revival in the Land and restored temple service (2 Chr. 29:20–35). He wisely commissioned a group of his counselors and scholars to compile the proverbs of Solomon (Prov. 25—27). Many of these proverbs use the literary device of comparison to teach truth. A stated likeness between objects of different classes using "like" or "as" is often found.

25:2 God has chosen not to reveal everything about Himself. God conceals some things, but what is needed in order to obey Him is revealed clearly (Deut. 29:29). The king must investigate God's revelation to lead his people rightly (Deut. 17:18–20). These verses praise not academic research but administrative ability. A king needs godly wisdom so that he can make wise decisions.

HOMEMAKING *AN EXPRESSION OF CREATIVITY AND LOVE*

King Solomon identified three great foundation stones of a home:

1) wisdom—knowledge of God's ways and the ability to make right choices in both practical and ethical matters,
2) understanding—an ability to apply God's principles, especially to relationships, and
3) knowledge—very practical skills in specific areas (Prov. 24:3, 4).

The home is the primary place where children and parents learn God's wisdom and how to apply it to their lives, where loving relationships are built on mutual communication and understanding, and where children and adults both learn and grow in the basic practical skills needed for life to function smoothly.

A woman's role involved helping family members get along with one another in the context of the home and creating an environment in which each family member might feel fully at ease, nurtured, and safe. Home is expected to be a place of refuge from life's storms.

A woman's homemaking ability should be infused with creativity and love so that her home reflects her own personal style. Homemaking skills were highly prized in Bible times, and the training of young women focused primarily on the care of husbands, children, and home (Titus 2:3–5).

Homemaking from a biblical perspective, however, is not limited to the care of physical property or the meeting of physical needs but extends to the creation of a nurturing and satisfying environment in which a family might flourish emotionally and spiritually. In the context of such a home our identities are forged in a healthy and positive way, and we truly become equipped to minister to others. A home built on the Lord Jesus and nurtured by a woman who spends time seeking wisdom, understanding, and knowledge with the Lord each day will stand strong in the storms of life.

See also Prov. 31:10–31; Titus 2:3–5; notes on Creativity (Col. 1); Hospitality (1 Pet. 4); Mealtime (Ps. 104); Family (Gen. 32; 1 Sam. 3; Ps. 78; 127); Wives (Prov. 31); portrait of the Virtuous Wife (Prov. 31)

⁴Take away the dross from silver,
And it will go to the silversmith *for* jewelry.
⁵Take away the wicked from before the king,
And his throne will be established in righteousness.

⁶Do not exalt yourself in the presence of the king,
And do not stand in the place of the great;
⁷For *it is* better that he say to you,
"Come up here,"
Than that you should be put lower in the presence of the prince,
Whom your eyes have seen.

⁸Do not go hastily to court;
For what will you do in the end,
When your neighbor has put you to shame?
⁹Debate your case with your neighbor,
And do not disclose the secret to another;
¹⁰Lest he who hears *it* expose your shame,
And your reputation be ruined.

¹¹A word fitly spoken *is like* apples of gold
In settings of silver.

¹²*Like* an earring of gold and an ornament of fine gold
Is a wise rebuker to an obedient ear.

¹³Like the cold of snow in time of harvest
Is a faithful messenger to those who send him,
For he refreshes the soul of his masters.

¹⁴Whoever falsely boasts of giving
Is like clouds and wind without rain.

¹⁵By long forbearance a ruler is persuaded,
And a gentle tongue breaks a bone.

¹⁶Have you found honey?
Eat only as much as you need,
Lest you be filled with it and vomit.

¹⁷Seldom set foot in your neighbor's house,
Lest he become weary of you and hate you.

¹⁸A man who bears false witness against his neighbor
Is like a club, a sword, and a sharp arrow.

25:12 A rebuke given in love and received with intent to obey at the right time, in the right place, and in the right way is more valuable than gold.

25:16, 17 Overdoing anything can be a problem. A disastrous difference exists between healthy appetite and greed or gluttony (v. 16). False thinking suggests "ecstasy," not "nausea," is ahead. "Seldom" (lit. "make precious") carries the idea that a visit becomes more valuable when rare. Good manners take into consideration the feelings of others. Do not visit so often that you become a nuisance, but visit often enough that the visit is made special. As the saying goes, familiarity breeds contempt.

[19]Confidence in an unfaithful *man* in time of
   trouble
   Is like a bad tooth and a foot out of joint.

[20]*Like* one who takes away a garment in cold
   weather,
   And like vinegar on soda,
   Is one who sings songs to a heavy heart.

[21]If your enemy is hungry, give him bread to eat;
   And if he is thirsty, give him water to drink;
[22]For *so* you will heap coals of fire on his head,
   And the LORD will reward you.

[23]The north wind brings forth rain,
   And a backbiting tongue an angry
   countenance.

[24]*It is* better to dwell in a corner of a housetop,
   Than in a house shared with a contentious
   woman.

[25]*As* cold water to a weary soul,
   So *is* good news from a far country.

[26]A righteous *man* who falters before the wicked
   Is like a murky spring and a polluted well.

[27]*It is* not good to eat much honey;
   So to seek one's own glory *is not* glory.

[28]Whoever *has* no rule over his own spirit
   Is like a city broken down, without walls.

26 As snow in summer and rain in harvest,
   So honor is not fitting for a fool.

[2]Like a flitting sparrow, like a flying swallow,
   So a curse without cause shall not alight.

[3]A whip for the horse,
   A bridle for the donkey,
   And a rod for the fool's back.

[4]Do not answer a fool according to his folly,
   Lest you also be like him.
[5]Answer a fool according to his folly,
   Lest he be wise in his own eyes.
[6]He who sends a message by the hand of a fool
   Cuts off *his own* feet *and* drinks violence.
[7]*Like* the legs of the lame that hang limp
   Is a proverb in the mouth of fools.
[8]Like one who binds a stone in a sling
   Is he who gives honor to a fool.
[9]*Like* a thorn *that* goes into the hand of a
   drunkard
   Is a proverb in the mouth of fools.
[10]The great *God* who formed everything
   Gives the fool *his* hire and the transgressor *his*
   wages.[a]
[11]As a dog returns to his own vomit,
   So a fool repeats his folly.
[12]Do you see a man wise in his own eyes?
   There is more hope for a fool than for him.

[13]The lazy *man* says, "*There is* a lion in the road!
   A fierce lion *is* in the streets!"
[14]*As* a door turns on its hinges,
   So *does* the lazy *man* on his bed.
[15]The lazy *man* buries his hand in the bowl;[a]
   It wearies him to bring it back to his mouth.
[16]The lazy *man is* wiser in his own eyes
   Than seven men who can answer sensibly.

[17]He who passes by *and* meddles in a quarrel not
   his own
   Is like one who takes a dog by the ears.

[18]Like a madman who throws firebrands, arrows,
   and death,
[19]*Is* the man *who* deceives his neighbor,
   And says, "I was only joking!"

[20]Where *there is* no wood, the fire goes out;
   And where *there is* no talebearer, strife ceases.

26:10 [a]The Hebrew is difficult; ancient and modern translators differ
greatly.   26:15 [a]Compare 19:24

25:21, 22 Caring and compassion, not revenge, should characterize Christians. Kindness makes an enemy ashamed and invokes a blessing from God (see Rom. 12:20). "Coals of fire" are the feelings of guilt, which are far better felt now as shame than later as punishment. When a person shows compassion to his enemy, the Lord rewards him.

25:23 What is happening inwardly affects the outward appearance both positively and negatively (see Prov. 18:6, 7, note). Of all the things a woman wears, her expression is the most important. A woman who possesses a calm and gentle spirit has a peaceful countenance (1 Pet. 3:4).

26:1–12 The fool is graphically painted as a ludicrous individual. A fool must be controlled by a "rod" or physical force because he cannot be reached through his intellect, and he does not respond to reason (v. 3). A fool cannot be trusted with a message (v. 6), and wisdom is as useless to a fool as the para-

lyzed limbs of a lame man (v. 7). A fool cannot learn from experience. Even though his habits are disgusting, he returns to repeat them (v. 11). The fool has the possibility of learning; a conceited individual is more hopeless (v. 12).

26:13–16 The lazy person is a tragic figure glued to his bed (v. 14). He gives ridiculous excuses to get out of work (v. 13) and is totally helpless (vv. 15, 16; see Prov. 6:6–11, note). He is called a sluggard and described as a person who neither begins nor completes things (Prov. 6:9, 10; 12:27). His slothfulness causes him to be restless (Prov. 13:4; 21:25, 26). He is truly pathetic.

26:17–28 Speech is a popular topic in Proverbs. The negative impact of words said without thinking or with evil intent cannot be underestimated: quarrels (vv. 17, 20, 21), deceit (vv. 18, 19, 26), gossip (vv. 20–22; see Prov. 25, Gossip), and lying (Prov. 26:23–28; see also Prov. 15, Communication).

GOSSIP CONTROLLING YOUR TONGUE

Most of us are not strangers to gossip—we have listened to it, spread it, and been the victim of it. Rumors have a dangerous edge in that people do not feel responsible for that which they simply pass on as hearsay, making accountability and damage control much more difficult. Gossip can run the gamut from talk of a personal, sensational, or intimate nature to statements that defame or injure the reputation or well-being of a person. Often our conversations are full of judgments. The Lord lists gossips together with the untrustworthy, unloving, unrighteous, murderers, and haters of God (Rom. 1:28–32). The Bible is clear about the damage (Prov. 11:13; 16:28; 18:6–8; 26:20) and consequences of gossip and slander (Ps. 101:5; Prov. 8:13; 17:9; Matt. 12:36, 37; 1 Tim. 5:13).

Not only the spreading of lies but also the telling of partially or entirely true facts may yet fall under the wrath of God. Sharing anything about a person that does not help or edify may be considered gossip. God has His own plan for dealing with someone in sin (Matt. 18:15). We are to go to an offending individual and no one else to begin a longsuffering effort for their restoration to God if we are concerned about their eternal welfare (Gal. 6:1). Listening to gossip is just as bad as spreading the words of hurt (1 Sam. 24:9; Prov. 17:4). A mark of spiritual maturity is to have control over your tongue (James 1:26). Gossip and slander are tools of Satan.

In Paul's discussion of the holy lifestyle in which spiritually mature women are to teach younger women, he includes a warning about slander and admonishes the women not to accuse others (Gk. *diabolous,* "the accuser," a title assigned to Satan 34 times in Scripture), thus refraining from being "devils" in their relationships. Nothing is a sharper sword with which to wound another than hurtful words. Gossip is never an act of kindness: it diminishes the person about whom you are talking; it degrades any Christian who would do such a thing; it serves as a temptation and snare to any listener who would join in such unkindness.

See also Ex. 20:16; 23:1; Deut. 5:20; Ps. 50:20; Prov. 6:19; 14:5; 19:5; 20:19; Matt. 15:19; 19:18; 1 Tim. 3:11; 2 Tim. 3:3; Titus 2:3; James 4:11; notes on Communication (Prov. 15); Conflict (Song 5; Matt. 18); Friendship (Luke 1); Influence (Esth. 4); Jealousy (Song 8)

21*As* charcoal *is* to burning coals, and wood to
    fire,
So *is* a contentious man to kindle strife.
22The words of a talebearer *are* like tasty
    trifles,
And they go down into the inmost body.

23Fervent lips with a wicked heart
Are like earthenware covered with silver dross.

24He who hates, disguises *it* with his lips,
And lays up deceit within himself;
25When he speaks kindly, do not believe him,
For *there are* seven abominations in his heart;
26*Though his* hatred is covered by deceit,
His wickedness will be revealed before the
    assembly.

27Whoever digs a pit will fall into it,
And he who rolls a stone will have it roll back
    on him.

28A lying tongue hates *those who are* crushed by
    it,
And a flattering mouth works ruin.

27 Do not boast about tomorrow,
For you do not know what a day may bring
    forth.

2Let another man praise you, and not your own
    mouth;
A stranger, and not your own lips.

3A stone *is* heavy and sand *is* weighty,
But a fool's wrath *is* heavier than both of
    them.

4Wrath *is* cruel and anger a torrent,
But who *is* able to stand before jealousy?

5Open rebuke *is* better
Than love carefully concealed.

26:20–22 Destructive words create strife and wound deeply. Inestimable damage is done by those who deliberately use their speech to harm the reputations of other people (see Prov. 25, Gossip). Just as a fire goes out when there is no fuel, a quarrel dies down when there is no gossip. Gossip spreads like a fire; it is untamable (see Prov. 11:13, note).

27:1, 2 The uncertainty of the future makes it presumptuous to predict what tomorrow will bring. This does not discourage wise planning for the future and, in fact, encourages wise use of today. Therefore, it is prideful to assert that anyone has knowledge of tomorrow (James 4:13–16). Another form of pride is self-praise. It is far wiser to let another issue your praise.

27:5, 6 Open rebuke suggests constructive criticism or loving correction and is the evidence of the love of a true friend. Concealed love is too cowardly to admit that rebuke and correction are necessary ingredients in the edification that is a part of genuine friendship.

⁶Faithful *are* the wounds of a friend,
But the kisses of an enemy *are* deceitful.

⁷A satisfied soul loathes the honeycomb,
But to a hungry soul every bitter thing *is*
sweet.

⁸Like a bird that wanders from its nest
Is a man who wanders from his place.

⁹Ointment and perfume delight the heart,
And the sweetness of a man's friend *gives
delight* by hearty counsel.

¹⁰Do not forsake your own friend or your
father's friend,
Nor go to your brother's house in the day of
your calamity;
Better *is* a neighbor nearby than a brother far
away.

¹¹My son, be wise, and make my heart glad,
That I may answer him who reproaches me.

¹²A prudent *man* foresees evil *and* hides himself;
The simple pass on *and* are punished.

¹³Take the garment of him who is surety for a
stranger,
And hold it in pledge *when* he is surety for a
seductress.

¹⁴He who blesses his friend with a loud voice,
rising early in the morning,
It will be counted a curse to him.

¹⁵A continual dripping on a very rainy day
And a contentious woman are alike;
¹⁶Whoever restrains her restrains the wind,
And grasps oil with his right hand.

¹⁷*As* iron sharpens iron,
So a man sharpens the countenance of his
friend.

¹⁸Whoever keeps the fig tree will eat its fruit;
So he who waits on his master will be honored.

¹⁹As in water face *reflects* face,
So a man's heart *reveals* the man.

²⁰Hell^a and Destruction^b are never full;
So the eyes of man are never satisfied.

²¹The refining pot *is* for silver and the furnace
for gold,
And a man *is valued* by what others say of him.

²²Though you grind a fool in a mortar with a
pestle along with crushed grain,
Yet his foolishness will not depart from him.

²³Be diligent to know the state of your flocks,
And attend to your herds;
²⁴For riches *are* not forever,
Nor does a crown *endure* to all generations.
²⁵*When* the hay is removed, and the tender grass
shows itself,
And the herbs of the mountains are gathered
in,
²⁶The lambs *will provide* your clothing,
And the goats the price of a field;
²⁷*You shall have* enough goats' milk for your food,
For the food of your household,
And the nourishment of your maidservants.

28¹The wicked flee when no one pursues,
But the righteous are bold as a lion.

²Because of the transgression of a land, many
are its princes;
But by a man of understanding *and* knowledge
Right will be prolonged.

³A poor man who oppresses the poor
Is like a driving rain which leaves no food.

27:20 ^aOr *Sheol* ^bHebrew *Abaddon*

27:9 Hearty counsel (lit. "advice of the soul") is saturated with compassion. It gives delight, edifies, and encourages.

27:10 Long-term friendship is precious indeed. It is not intended to demean the help of a brother but to emphasize that of a trusted friend (see Luke 1, Friendship). We cannot choose brothers or sisters, but a friend, freely chosen, can sometimes be closer than a blood relative. Often a relative lives far away, and a friend who is nearby is an immediate help in time of trial.

27:15, 16 A contentious woman is as untameable as the wind and as slippery as oil (see Prov. 19:13, note). Her character is unsteady, and she cannot be restrained. "Restrains" (lit. "hide") suggests that this woman's contentious character cannot be hidden from neighbors and friends. Concealing her contentious spirit is like attempting to enclose the wind.

27:17 Constructive criticism can be a precious link between two friends. Iron rubbed against iron shapes and sharpens it. In the same way, discussion and soul-searching interaction between friends bring obvious changes. A woman's thinking and even her face are shaped and sharpened as a result of her "rubbing together" with another.

27:23–27 Care and diligent concern over what God has provided to meet the needs of life is the practical message of these verses. Such care takes hard work and effort and is evidence of great wisdom. The pastoral scene beautifully calls to remembrance that money does not last (v. 24). Deep satisfaction arises naturally for a job well done (v. 23).

28:9 Those who do not listen to God cannot expect God to listen to them. "Turns away his ear" indicates a decision to turn from the path of wisdom. The activities of such a person, even his prayers, are an "abomination" to the Lord.

FAVORITISM *THE NEED FOR EQUAL LOVE*

Though a parent may feel a special rapport with a child—same interests, similar physical characteristics, compatible goals—a parent errs in consistently offering special consideration, responsibility, or privilege to one child to the exclusion of another (Gen. 25:28). Some parents favor beauty or intellect; others elevate the child who is difficult or a troublemaker. Some seek to undercut the brighter child or more spiritually sensitive child in order to compensate for her sibling who is not gifted in the same way.

One child may be showered with attention and the others ignored (Gen. 37:3). Anger, resentment, and insecurity will arise in the child denied (v. 4); guilt and defensiveness or even tyranny may characterize the one singled out for attention (vv. 5–11). A child may also be singled out for criticism and unrealistic expectations with the burden of never being able to measure up (Prov. 11:29).

Each child should be given praise and recognition in inclusive, not exclusive, ways (Prov. 25:11). A parent should build on a child's strengths, allowing for differences (Prov. 24:3). A child should be enjoyed and accepted for who she is, not what she may do for you. Comparison must be avoided (2 Cor. 10:12). A parent does well to love equally but appreciate individually (Ps. 32:8). Fair and equal are not synonymous, but both are necessary in relating to children.

See also Matt. 18:3, note; notes on Children (2 Sam. 21; Ps. 128; Prov. 22; Luke 15); Family (Gen. 32); Parenthood (Prov. 10); Siblings (Gen. 37)

4Those who forsake the law praise the
  wicked,
But such as keep the law contend with
  them.

5Evil men do not understand justice,
But those who seek the LORD understand all.

6Better *is* the poor who walks in his integrity
Than one perverse *in his* ways, though he *be*
  rich.

7Whoever keeps the law *is* a discerning son,
But a companion of gluttons shames his father.

8One who increases his possessions by usury
  and extortion
Gathers it for him who will pity the poor.

9One who turns away his ear from hearing the
  law,
Even his prayer *is* an abomination.

10Whoever causes the upright to go astray in an
  evil way,
He himself will fall into his own pit;
But the blameless will inherit good.

11The rich man *is* wise in his own eyes,
But the poor who has understanding searches
  him out.

12When the righteous rejoice, *there is* great glory;
But when the wicked arise, men hide
  themselves.

13He who covers his sins will not prosper,
But whoever confesses and forsakes *them* will
  have mercy.

14Happy *is* the man who is always reverent,
But he who hardens his heart will fall into
  calamity.

15*Like* a roaring lion and a charging bear
Is a wicked ruler over poor people.

16A ruler who lacks understanding *is* a great
  oppressor,
But he who hates covetousness will prolong *his*
  days.

17A man burdened with bloodshed will flee into
  a pit;
Let no one help him.

28:11 The rich person's success does not mean he has obtained wisdom. The poor person who is wise and has understanding can see through the pretentious facade of one who seems "to have it all."

28:13 Covers his sin carries with it the notion of refusing to admit guilt. King David found that hiding sin only led to negative physical, emotional, and spiritual consequences. His body wasted away, he groaned all day long, and his vitality was drained (Ps. 32:3, 4). The same consequences will fall on any man or woman who refuses to admit guilt. But confession brings peace and joy as sin is first uncovered and then covered by God with His forgiveness (Ps. 32:1, 5; 51:5, 6, note). "Confess" and "forsake" imply a changing of mind about sin. The name of the Lord is confessed as the sin is forgiven (1 John 1:9).

28:14 Reverence here is the awesome fear and dread of sin and its consequences (contrast Prov. 1:7, referring to the "fear of the Lord"). The one who "hardens his heart" disregards such fear and does what he pleases. He gives no thought to God's punishment of sin.

¹⁸Whoever walks blamelessly will be saved,
But *he who is* perverse *in his* ways will suddenly fall.

¹⁹He who tills his land will have plenty of bread,
But he who follows frivolity will have poverty enough!

²⁰A faithful man will abound with blessings,
But he who hastens to be rich will not go unpunished.

²¹To show partiality *is* not good,
Because for a piece of bread a man will transgress.

²²A man with an evil eye hastens after riches,
And does not consider that poverty will come upon him.

²³He who rebukes a man will find more favor afterward
Than he who flatters with the tongue.

²⁴Whoever robs his father or his mother,
And says, "*It is* no transgression,"
The same *is* companion to a destroyer.

²⁵He who is of a proud heart stirs up strife,
But he who trusts in the Lord will be prospered.

²⁶He who trusts in his own heart is a fool,
But whoever walks wisely will be delivered.

²⁷He who gives to the poor will not lack,
But he who hides his eyes will have many curses.

²⁸When the wicked arise, men hide themselves;
But when they perish, the righteous increase.

29

He who is often rebuked, *and* hardens *his* neck,
Will suddenly be destroyed, and that without remedy.

²When the righteous are in authority, the people rejoice;
But when a wicked *man* rules, the people groan.

³Whoever loves wisdom makes his father rejoice,
But a companion of harlots wastes *his* wealth.

⁴The king establishes the land by justice,
But he who receives bribes overthrows it.

⁵A man who flatters his neighbor
Spreads a net for his feet.

⁶By transgression an evil man is snared,
But the righteous sings and rejoices.

⁷The righteous considers the cause of the poor,
But the wicked does not understand *such* knowledge.

⁸Scoffers set a city aflame,
But wise *men* turn away wrath.

⁹*If* a wise man contends with a foolish man,
Whether *the fool* rages or laughs, *there is* no peace.

¹⁰The bloodthirsty hate the blameless,
But the upright seek his well-being.[a]

¹¹A fool vents all his feelings,[a]
But a wise *man* holds them back.

¹²If a ruler pays attention to lies,
All his servants *become* wicked.

¹³The poor *man* and the oppressor have this in common:
The Lord gives light to the eyes of both.

¹⁴The king who judges the poor with truth,
His throne will be established forever.

29:10 [a]Literally *soul*   29:11 [a]Literally *spirit*

29:7 A compassionate attitude toward those in need demonstrates a godly character. The "woman of strength" extends her hands to the poor (Prov. 31:20).

29:11 The slave to impulse has no power to keep back the expression of what he feels. Every feeling is voiced; every emotion or gripe is vented. Such a person has no control over his words and actions. In contrast, the wise person keeps himself under control. Although he feels irritation, he is characterized by self-control; his irritation does not explode in anger. "Hold them back" (lit. "soothe" or "still") is the calming of the storm of emotions.

29:15 The rebuke (verbal discipline) and the rod (physical discipline) are tools used to make children wise (Prov. 17:10). The "child left to himself" lives without restriction, allowed to run wild and go unchecked (see Prov. 22, Children). This child brings shame to his mother. How difficult to find the balance. Often, parents are inconsistent—not faithful in discipline or too severe in punishment. Much prayer, patience, and perseverance is needed to be a parent with the right mixture of love and discipline. But it is worth the effort (Prov. 29:17).

BOLDNESS *A MEMORABLE PRESENCE*

Biblical boldness (Gk. *parrēsia*, lit. "all speech") describes clear communication unhindered by fear (Phil. 1:14). A woman can be frank in her speech because of confidence in her spirit (Phil. 1:20). Such determination to make your opinions known gives memorable presence and makes your influence felt.

Boldness should not be equated with obnoxious or aggressive personalities. It is a gift to be sought by every believer. We ask and receive boldness from God (Acts 4:29–31). New Testament boldness is not found in safe and secure places but rather where God's Word needs to be on the cutting edge to penetrate the hearts and minds of the individuals to whom we relate.

God uses boldness for His own purpose. Our weakness is used of God to prove His strength (Acts 4:13). Rahab, the prostitute, acted to aid God's people and save herself and her family. Her boldness brought forgiveness for her sins and a place in the genealogy of the Messiah (Josh. 6:17, 22–25; Matt. 1:5). Abigail, the wife of an abusive husband, acted redemptively in making a bold personal appeal to David for the lives of her husband and their servants (1 Sam. 25:23–35). Ruth, the Gentile widow, accepted her mother-in-law's plan and boldly asked Boaz to be her kinsman-redeemer and become her husband (Ruth 3:1–11).

Queen Esther knew that God was in control of the king (Prov. 21:1), and she made her intercession for her people first to the Lord (Esth. 4:15, 16). She continued to be sensitive to God's timing and patiently waited for the ideal opportunity to make her bold request to Ahasuerus (Esth. 5—8). Esther did not attempt to usurp the authority of her husband the king, nor did she seek to deceive him or the court, nor did she devise a plan of manipulation (Esth. 5:2–8).

Submission and boldness are not antithetical. When boldness is founded on unwavering confidence in the Lord and kept within the boundaries God has set, a woman can stand for right even in the face of overwhelming opposition and receive the blessing and favor of God.

See also Eph. 3:12; 1 Thess. 2:2; Heb. 4:16; 10:19; 13:6; 1 John 2:28; 4:17; notes on Authority (John 19); Confidence (Is. 30); Evangelism (Matt. 28; John 6; Col. 4; 1 Pet. 3); Submission (1 Pet. 3); portraits of Abigail (1 Sam. 25); Deborah (Judg. 4); Esther (Esth. 2); Priscilla (Acts 18); Rahab (Josh. 2); Ruth (Ruth 2)

---

[15]The rod and rebuke give wisdom,
But a child left *to himself* brings shame to his mother.

[16]When the wicked are multiplied, transgression increases;
But the righteous will see their fall.

[17]Correct your son, and he will give you rest;
Yes, he will give delight to your soul.

[18]Where *there is* no revelation,[a] the people cast off restraint;
But happy *is* he who keeps the law.

[19]A servant will not be corrected by mere words;
For though he understands, he will not respond.

[20]Do you see a man hasty in his words?
There is more hope for a fool than for him.

[21]He who pampers his servant from childhood
Will have him as a son in the end.

[22]An angry man stirs up strife,
And a furious man abounds in transgression.

[23]A man's pride will bring him low,
But the humble in spirit will retain honor.

[24]Whoever is a partner with a thief hates his own life;
He swears to tell the truth,[a] but reveals nothing.

[25]The fear of man brings a snare,
But whoever trusts in the Lord shall be safe.

[26]Many seek the ruler's favor,
But justice for man *comes* from the Lord.

[27]An unjust man *is* an abomination to the righteous,
And *he who is* upright in the way *is* an abomination to the wicked.

The Wisdom of Agur

30The words of Agur the son of Jakeh, *his* utterance. This man declared to Ithiel—to Ithiel and Ucal:

....

29:18 [a]Or *prophetic vision*   **29:24** [a]Literally *hears the adjuration*

30:1–33 The words of Agur form a separate collection of Proverbs and are somewhat different in tone from the rest of

the book. A variety of literary forms have been used, including prayer, argument, instruction, and enchanting numerical say-

²Surely I *am* more stupid than *any* man,
  And do not have the understanding of a man.
³I neither learned wisdom
  Nor have knowledge of the Holy One.

⁴Who has ascended into heaven, or descended?
  Who has gathered the wind in His fists?
  Who has bound the waters in a garment?
  Who has established all the ends of the earth?
  What *is* His name, and what *is* His Son's name,
  If you know?

⁵Every word of God *is* pure;
  He *is* a shield to those who put their trust in
    Him.
⁶Do not add to His words,
  Lest He rebuke you, and you be found a liar.

⁷Two *things* I request of You
  (Deprive me not before I die):
⁸Remove falsehood and lies far from me;
  Give me neither poverty nor riches—
  Feed me with the food allotted to me;
⁹Lest I be full and deny *You,*
  And say, "Who *is* the LORD?"
  Or lest I be poor and steal,
  And profane the name of my God.

¹⁰Do not malign a servant to his master,
  Lest he curse you, and you be found guilty.

¹¹*There is* a generation *that* curses its father,
  And does not bless its mother.
¹²*There is* a generation *that is* pure in its own eyes,
  Yet is not washed from its filthiness.
¹³*There is* a generation— oh, how lofty are their
    eyes!
  And their eyelids are lifted up.
¹⁴*There is* a generation whose teeth *are like*
    swords,
  And whose fangs *are like* knives,
  To devour the poor from off the earth,
  And the needy from *among* men.

¹⁵The leech has two daughters—
  Give *and* Give!

THE ANSWER TO INAPPROPRIATE ANGER

MEMORIZE AND MEDITATE ON THESE SCRIPTURES.

Don't give full vent to your anger (Prov. 29:11).

Don't take revenge on a violator (Rom. 12:19).

Don't get caught up in name-calling (Matt. 5:22).

Don't expect perfection from people (Rom. 3:10, 23).

Seek out the source of your anger (Ps. 139:23, 24).

Ask your wise God for His wisdom (James 1:5).

Be slow to speak if angry (James 1:19, 20).

Release your right to stay angry (Col. 3:8).

Give your anger to God (1 Pet. 5:7).

Pray for those who persecute you (Matt. 5:44).

Forgive as the Lord forgave you (Col. 3:13).

Trust God to bring good from your trials (Rom. 8:28).

Stay ready to forgive anyone for anything (Eph. 4:31, 32).

Lord, I see that "anger" is one little letter away from "danger."

There are three *things that* are never satisfied,
  Four never say, "Enough!":
¹⁶The grave,ᵃ
  The barren womb,

30:16 ᵃOr *Sheol*

---

ings that are more like puzzles than proverbs. The questions of verse 4 remind us of Job 38—41. Nothing is known of Agur, but he was apparently a well-known sage. Ithiel and Ucal were evidently his students or possibly his sons. Agur shows a spirit of humility (Prov. 30:1–9). Genuine humility is seen in Scripture as a sign of wisdom and greatness (see Prov. 22:4).

30:2–4 Words of doubt and skepticism seem to belong to the Book of Job or Ecclesiastes more than to the Book of Proverbs. These words show that part of the ministry of the teachers, along with their instruction in the path of wisdom, was dealing with uncertainties of faith. Agur says that he is incapable of comprehending the mind of finite man. How could he presume to try to understand the workings of God's infinite mind! There is no evidence that Agur has not applied himself

to the study of wisdom but rather that after all his study, he still has not mastered the subject (v. 3).

30:7–9 The numerical sayings are introduced here by the words "two things." Agur's humility (vv. 2, 3) is reaffirmed as he was more concerned with character than with wealth and an easy life. He acknowledged his own frailty and asked for circumstances that would enable him to keep his eyes on God.

30:11–14 A generation is used here to depict a certain group who possess the common characteristics of the disrespectful (v. 11), the hypocrite (v. 12), the proud (v. 13), and the greedy (v. 14).

30:15, 16 Greed, symbolized by the "leech," is the theme of these verses. The "two daughters" refer to the two suckers of

COVETOUSNESS *A HEART OF GREED*

A materialistic society demands that we constantly be in a state of acquisition for more and more. We often are mentally assaulted by messages that say, "You don't have enough, nor will you ever."

"Feed me with the food allotted to me" (Prov. 30:8) is a refreshing cry of the heart. To realize that we can trust God to give us our portion, and that it will be sufficient, is a relief (Matt. 6:8).

When David became involved with Bathsheba, their adultery and ultimately the murder of Uriah were not his only sins. His root sin was covetousness (2 Sam. 12:1–8). God reminded David of all the people, power, and prosperity he had received. He continued, "And if that had been too little, I also would have given you much more!" An ungrateful heart and eyes that continue to seek more can lead to deadly consequences.

To free your heart of covetousness:

- Repent of a discontented heart (Phil. 4:11, 12).
- Set your heart on things eternal (1 John 2:15–17).
- Trust that God will keep His promises (Phil. 4:19; Heb. 13:5).
- Yield to God's plan for your life (2 Cor. 9:8–10).

See also notes on Contentment (1 Tim. 6); Envy (Prov. 14); Gratitude (Ps. 95); Jealousy (Song 8); Prosperity (Ps. 2)

The earth *that* is not satisfied with water—
And the fire never says, "Enough!"

17The eye *that* mocks *his* father,
And scorns obedience to *his* mother,
The ravens of the valley will pick it out,
And the young eagles will eat it.

18There are three *things which* are too wonderful
for me,
Yes, four *which* I do not understand:
19The way of an eagle in the air,
The way of a serpent on a rock,
The way of a ship in the midst of the sea,
And the way of a man with a virgin.

20This *is* the way of an adulterous woman:
She eats and wipes her mouth,
And says, "I have done no wickedness."

21For three *things* the earth is perturbed,
Yes, for four it cannot bear up:
22For a servant when he reigns,
A fool when he is filled with food,
23A hateful *woman* when she is married,
And a maidservant who succeeds her mistress.

24There are four *things which* are little on the
earth,
But they *are* exceedingly wise:
25The ants *are* a people not strong,

Yet they prepare their food in the summer;
26The rock badgers[a] are a feeble folk,
Yet they make their homes in the crags;
27The locusts have no king,
Yet they all advance in ranks;
28The spider[a] skillfully grasps with its hands,
And it is in kings' palaces.

29There are three *things which* are majestic in
pace,
Yes, four *which* are stately in walk:
30A lion, *which is* mighty among beasts
And does not turn away from any;
31A greyhound,[a]
A male goat also,
And a king *whose* troops *are* with him.[b]

32If you have been foolish in exalting yourself,
Or if you have devised evil, *put your* hand on
your mouth.
33For *as* the churning of milk produces butter,
And wringing the nose produces blood,
So the forcing of wrath produces strife.

The Words of King Lemuel's Mother

31 The words of King Lemuel, the utterance
which his mother taught him:

••••••••••••••••••••

30:26 [a]Or *hyraxes*   30:28 [a]Or *lizard*   30:31 [a]Exact identity unknown   [b]A Jewish tradition reads *a king against whom there is no uprising.*

---

the leech, who cry "Give, Give" and whose voracious appetites are never satisfied.

30:23 When a "hateful" woman like the ill-tempered, contentious woman described marries, she brings her unpleasant-

ness to the marriage relationship, and her husband and children suffer the consequences (see Prov. 19:13, note).

31:1–31 The fear of the Lord brings purpose and meaning to this earthly existence. Throughout Proverbs, wisdom is por-

WIVES   CALLED TO BE STRONG AND AFFIRMING

Being a godly wife begins with the right priorities—nourishing your personal relationship to God (Matt. 6:33), ministering to your husband (Prov. 18:22; 19:14), nurturing your children (2 Tim. 1:5), keeping your home (Titus 2:5), then adding whatever other activities time and energy permit (Prov. 31:10–31).

This passage praises a "virtuous wife" (lit. "woman of strength") in the form of an acrostic, with each successive verse beginning with one of the twenty-two letters in the Hebrew alphabet. This divinely inspired portrait of an ideal wife includes: pleasant appearance (v. 22, giving her husband a sense of pride), godly character (vv. 10–12, 17, 25, 30, 31, without a materialistic mindset), efficiency in homemaking (vv. 13–15, 21, 27, seeing value in the mundane household tasks), helpfulness to her husband (vv. 11, 23, 28, especially when he is emotionally and spiritually drained), attentiveness to her children (v. 28, understanding the awesome task of producing the next generation), interest in her community (vv. 20, 26), willingness to use energies and creativity (vv. 16, 18, 19, 24), and determination to be worthy of honor and commendation (vv. 28–31).

These very positive qualities are contrasted with the "contentious" wife (Prov. 19:13; 21:9, 19) and "immoral" (in some translations "strange") woman elsewhere (Prov. 5:3–14, 20; 6:24–32; 7:6–27).

A wife also has unique needs that are best met by her own husband:

- Spiritual leadership, including family worship of prayer and Bible study (1 Pet. 3:7)
- Personal affirmation (Eph. 5:25)
- Tender loving care, including touching, courtesies, and loving words (Prov. 5:19)
- Intimate, sensitive, and understanding communication (Song 2:16)
- Integrity worthy of respect and transparency so that nothing is hidden (Gen. 2:25)
- Provision and sustenance as well as protection (Gen. 2:15)
- Commitment of loyal devotion (Eccl. 9:9)

Scripture describes the creation of woman with the word "made" (Heb. *banah*, lit. "build"). God planned and supervised this "building" of the woman with the intent that she would be a "helper comparable to the man" (Heb '*ezer kenegdo*). Unlike the animals, the woman was of the same nature as the man (Gen. 2:23). The word "helper" is also used to describe God (Ps. 33:20). It is a term of function rather than worth. A woman does not lose value as a person by humbly assuming the role of a helper.

The wife then has the assignment of being her husband's helper: (1) as a spiritual partner, assisting him in obeying the Word of God and in doing spiritual ministries, (2) as a counterpart in linking hands with the Creator to continue the generations, (3) as a confidant to offer comfort and fellowship (Gen. 2:23, 24), and (4) as a companion to provide encouragement and inspiration.

See also Gen. 2:18–25; 3:1–16; 1 Kin. 11:4; Esth. 1:20; Jer. 29:6; Eph. 5:22–33; Col. 3:18, 19; 1 Tim. 3:11; notes on Biblical Equality (Eph. 5); Family (Gen. 32; 1 Sam. 3; Ps. 78; 127); Husbands (Job 31; 2 Cor. 6); Marriage (Gen. 2; 2 Sam. 6; Prov. 5; Hos. 2; Amos 3; 2 Cor. 13; Heb. 12); Submission (1 Pet. 3); portrait of the Virtuous Wife of Proverbs (Prov. 31)

²What, my son?
And what, son of my womb?
And what, son of my vows?
³Do not give your strength to women,
Nor your ways to that which destroys kings.

⁴*It is* not for kings, O Lemuel,
It is not for kings to drink wine,
Nor for princes intoxicating drink;
⁵Lest they drink and forget the law,
And pervert the justice of all the afflicted.
⁶Give strong drink to him who is perishing,

And wine to those who are bitter of
    heart.
⁷Let him drink and forget his poverty,
And remember his misery no more.

⁸Open your mouth for the speechless,
In the cause of all *who are* appointed to
    die.ᵃ
⁹Open your mouth, judge righteously,
And plead the cause of the poor and needy.

31:8 ᵃLiterally *sons of passing away*

trayed through contrasts between the wise and the foolish (the good and the evil), giving practical, everyday advice for living and relating to people. The excellent wife lives and embodies wisdom in her home, in her community, and in her relationships (Prov. 31:10–31). The key to all she has become is clear: She has feared and reverenced the Lord (vv. 30, 31; Prov. 1:7; 9:10).

THE VIRTUOUS WIFE OF PROVERBS

Many outstanding godly women appear throughout the Bible, but the virtuous wife described here merits special praise (Prov. 31:29). This woman was a wife and mother. For centuries women have been amazed and challenged by her life (v. 31).

The passage describes what kind of wife a woman should be and what kind of woman a man should choose to marry. An acrostic poem, each of the twenty-two verses begins with a successive letter of the Hebrew alphabet, encouraging the memorization of this literary masterpiece. We are told not who she was but what she was. This woman of strength comes alive.

This rare woman was a paragon of virtue: trustworthy, industrious, organized, and loving. Yet amazingly she was able to order the priorities of her world. Her husband totally trusted her; her grown children voluntarily praised her, and her home was a model of efficiency. Still she found time to reach out to her community, to help the poor, and even to increase her family's resources through wise investments and productive management of all placed in her care. Moreover, she was as outwardly beautiful as she was inwardly wise.

The portrait of the virtuous wife closes with the key to her success (v. 30). Illustrating the theme of wisdom found throughout Proverbs, this woman first feared and reverenced God. Therefore, relationships and responsibilities were wisely balanced. She exemplifies the truth spoken by Jesus Christ, "Seek first the kingdom of God and His righteousness, and all these things shall be added to you" (Matt. 6:33). A close look at this woman can prove invaluable in helping every woman set her own priorities in managing the time, resources, and giftedness God has given.

See also notes on Femininity (Ps. 144); Heroines (Heb. 11); Influence (Esth. 4)

The Virtuous Wife

[10]Who[a] can find a virtuous[b] wife?
For her worth *is* far above rubies.
[11]The heart of her husband safely trusts her;
So he will have no lack of gain.
[12]She does him good and not evil
All the days of her life.
[13]She seeks wool and flax,
And willingly works with her hands.
[14]She is like the merchant ships,
She brings her food from afar.
[15]She also rises while it is yet night,
And provides food for her household,
And a portion for her maidservants.
[16]She considers a field and buys it;
From her profits she plants a vineyard.
[17]She girds herself with strength,
And strengthens her arms.
[18]She perceives that her merchandise *is* good,
And her lamp does not go out by night.
[19]She stretches out her hands to the distaff,
And her hand holds the spindle.
[20]She extends her hand to the poor,
Yes, she reaches out her hands to the needy.
[21]She is not afraid of snow for her household,
For all her household *is* clothed with scarlet.

[22]She makes tapestry for herself;
Her clothing *is* fine linen and purple.
[23]Her husband is known in the gates,
When he sits among the elders of the land.
[24]She makes linen garments and sells *them*,
And supplies sashes for the merchants.
[25]Strength and honor *are* her clothing;
She shall rejoice in time to come.
[26]She opens her mouth with wisdom,
And on her tongue *is* the law of kindness.
[27]She watches over the ways of her
household,
And does not eat the bread of idleness.
[28]Her children rise up and call her blessed;
Her husband *also,* and he praises her:
[29]"Many daughters have done well,
But you excel them all."
[30]Charm *is* deceitful and beauty *is* passing,
But a woman *who* fears the Lord, she shall be
praised.
[31]Give her of the fruit of her hands,
And let her own works praise her in the
gates.

• • • • • • • • • • • • • • • • • • •

31:10 [a]Verses 10 through 31 are an alphabetic acrostic in Hebrew (compare Psalm 119). [b]Literally *a wife of valor,* in the sense of all forms of excellence

---

31:10–12 A virtuous woman (lit. "a woman of strength") is trustworthy and would never do anything to bring dishonor to her husband's name. "All the days of her life" indicates her "forever" commitment to her husband.

31:28, 29 This description of the wise woman of strength ends with the testimony of those who knew her best: her husband and her children. Her children blessed her for their early training. Her husband praised her for her excellence among women. The praise from family was the most meaningful because they were the ones who had observed her in every situation and truly knew her character. Such praise should encourage every woman to follow in the steps and acquire wisdom as did this extraordinary woman.

Ecclesiastes

The Hebrew title (*qoheleth,* "the Preacher," lit. "one who calls together an assembly") is from the root *qahal,* meaning "assembly" or "congregation" (Eccl. 12:8). *Qoheleth* appears nowhere else in Scripture. The English title of the book is a transliteration of the Greek *ekklesiastes* (lit. "one who calls an assembly"), which is the book's title in the Septuagint (a Greek translation of the Old Testament).

Tradition is strong in ascribing the authorship of Ecclesiastes to King Solomon. The book itself supports this view by asserting that the words are those of "the son of David, king in Jerusalem" (Eccl. 1:1). The author identified himself as "the Preacher," as king reigning over Israel in Jerusalem (Eccl. 1:1, 12), as a wealthy individual (Eccl. 2:7, 8), and as a lover of proverbs (Eccl. 12:9). These characteristics lend further weight to Solomonic author-ship.

However, because the name Solomon never appears in Ecclesiastes, Solomonic author-ship has been questioned. Martin Luther, in the sixteenth century, was the first to assert non-Solomonic authorship. One basis for the rejection of Solomonic authorship is the interpretation of the author's words as indicating that he was writing at a time when he was no longer king over Israel. However, the phrase translated "was king" could also be translated "have been king," suggesting that the penning of Ecclesiastes came late in Solomon's life (Eccl. 1:12). Solomon "reigned in Jerusalem over all Israel" until his death (1 Kin. 11:42, 43). Furthermore, the author expressed helplessness before the nation's injustices (Eccl. 4:1–3). As king, Solomon had authority to correct such problems. On the other hand, to express helplessness is not the same as being helpless. From what is known of Solomon's life, the Book of Ecclesiastes certainly reflects much of what King Solomon could have taught from his vast experience.

Those who reject Solomonic authorship date the book as late as the fourth or third cen-tury B.C. According to the traditional view of Solomonic authorship, however, the Book of Ecclesiastes was written during the tenth century B.C. when Solomon reigned. This tradi-tion was unquestioned until the sixteenth century and has the stronger support.

SETTING: As Wisdom Literature, Ecclesiastes may have been used in an educational setting.

PURPOSE: Ecclesiastes records *Qoheleth's* observations as he searched for meaning in life. *Qoheleth* concluded that human wisdom, apart from God is vanity or emptiness. Yet

the Preacher ended on a positive note as he observed that the ultimate meaning of life is found only in a right relationship with God.

AUDIENCE: The audience of *Qoheleth* may have been his pupils. "My son" was the typical way a teacher addressed his students (see Eccl. 12:12).

LITERARY CHARACTERISTICS: The Book of Ecclesiastes is classified as Wisdom Literature. Wisdom teachers drew conclusions about life from their observations. The wisdom teacher *Qoheleth* was pessimistic or skeptical in his outlook as he drew conclusions about the meaning of life from human wisdom. *Qoheleth* employed the literary forms of the proverb, the parable, and repeated refrains ("all is vanity," "under the sun").

THEMES

The theme of Ecclesiastes is the search for life's meaning. Is life worth living, or is it just a meaningless existence that ends in futility? *Qoheleth* set out to investigate thoroughly what makes life worth living. He discovered that the meaning of life does not lie in labor, luxury, lust, leisure, learning, or liquor. Ultimately, the author realized that a life worth living can be found only in a relationship with the Lord (Eccl. 12:13, 14) and that a life not focused on the Lord is futile and empty. Ecclesiastes reflects the skeptical, pessimistic assessment of human life projected by *Qoheleth,* yet ends with a declaration of the ultimate purpose of life, which is to obey and glorify God.

OUTLINE

The Vanity of Life

1 The words of the Preacher, the son of David, king in Jerusalem.

2 "Vanity[a] of vanities," says the Preacher;
"Vanity of vanities, all *is* vanity."

3 What profit has a man from all his labor
In which he toils under the sun?
4 *One* generation passes away, and *another* generation comes;
But the earth abides forever.
5 The sun also rises, and the sun goes down,
And hastens to the place where it arose.
6 The wind goes toward the south,
And turns around to the north;
The wind whirls about continually,
And comes again on its circuit.
7 All the rivers run into the sea,
Yet the sea *is* not full;
To the place from which the rivers come,
There they return again.
8 All things *are* full of labor;
Man cannot express *it.*
The eye is not satisfied with seeing,
Nor the ear filled with hearing.

9 That which has been *is* what will be,
That which *is* done is what will be done,
And *there is* nothing new under the sun.
10 Is there anything of which it may be said,
"See, this *is* new"?
It has already been in ancient times before us.
11 *There is* no remembrance of former *things,*
Nor will there be any remembrance of *things*
that are to come
By *those* who will come after.

The Grief of Wisdom

12 I, the Preacher, was king over Israel in Jerusalem. 13 And I set my heart to seek and search out by wisdom concerning all that is done under heaven;

this burdensome task God has given to the sons of man, by which they may be exercised. 14 I have seen all the works that are done under the sun; and indeed, all *is* vanity and grasping for the wind.

15 *What is* crooked cannot be made straight,
And what is lacking cannot be numbered.

16 I communed with my heart, saying, "Look, I have attained greatness, and have gained more wisdom than all who were before me in Jerusalem. My heart has understood great wisdom and knowledge." 17 And I set my heart to know wisdom and to know madness and folly. I perceived that this also is grasping for the wind.

18 For in much wisdom *is* much grief,
And he who increases knowledge increases sorrow.

The Vanity of Pleasure

2 I said in my heart, "Come now, I will test you with mirth; therefore enjoy pleasure"; but surely, this also *was* vanity. 2 I said of laughter—"Madness!"; and of mirth, "What does it accomplish?" 3 I searched in my heart *how* to gratify my flesh with wine, while guiding my heart with wisdom, and how to lay hold on folly, till I might see what *was* good for the sons of men to do under heaven all the days of their lives.

4 I made my works great, I built myself houses, and planted myself vineyards. 5 I made myself gardens and orchards, and I planted all *kinds* of fruit trees in them. 6 I made myself water pools from which to water the growing trees of the grove. 7 I acquired male and female servants, and had servants born in my house. Yes, I had greater possessions of herds and flocks than all who were in Jerusalem before me. 8 I also gathered for myself

---

1:2 [a]Or *Absurdity, Frustration, Futility, Nonsense;* and so throughout this book

---

1:2 Vanity (Heb. *hebel,* lit. "vapor" or "breath") is used figuratively to describe that which is without substance or transitory. It carries the concept of ultimate meaninglessness, emptiness, or worthlessness. The Preacher began on a less than positive note by declaring that earthly life was hollow and meaningless.

1:3–11 Life is meaningless because it is as a treadmill going nowhere. The word translated "profit" (v. 3) refers to the gain accrued from a business transaction. *Qoheleth* cited evidence to support his evaluation of the vanity of all human effort. Generation follows generation in a monotonous fashion (v. 4); the sun rises, sets, and comes up again. The wind whirls about on its own circular route. Even the movement of waters on the earth's surface follows a routine, monotonous pattern (vv. 5–7). The author viewed life as constantly in motion but never achieving a meaningful goal (vv. 4–7).

1:9 Under the sun is a frequent and significant phrase of *Qoheleth* (v. 14; Eccl. 2:11, 18, 19, 20, 22; 3:16; 4:3, 7, 15; 5:13, 18; 6:1, 12; 8:9, 15, 17; 9:3, 6, 9, 11, 13; 10:5). The phrase indicates the limited focus of his vision. As an earthly observer, he could not seem to get his eyes above the limited perspective of life on earth.

1:13–18 Searching for human wisdom alone is a futile quest. *Qoheleth* determined to make a thorough investigation (v. 13). He ventured to test the competence of human wisdom to discover the principles on which the world is ordered. Solomonic authorship receives strong support since King Solomon was uniquely noted for his great wisdom (v. 16; see 1 Kin. 3; 4:30, 31). *Qoheleth* concluded that mere human wisdom or knowledge brought only disillusionment and grief (Eccl. 1:18). He evaluated human wisdom as resulting only in increased sorrow and heartache rather than in the achievement of real success.

HEALING OF MEMORIES A PERSONAL STOREHOUSE

Memories may be either conscious or unconscious; they are stored in our brains and may include thoughts, feelings, and sensory perceptions. Paul realized that he could have hidden thoughts and motives (1 Cor. 4:1–5), and David asked God to search his heart for known anxieties and any hidden wicked way (lit. "way of pain"; Ps. 139:23, 24).

Memories filled with pain are frequently healed when a woman asks the Holy Spirit to touch a known memory or bring to light a hidden memory. In response to this request, God sometimes allows a person to re-experience in varying degrees the hurt stored in the memory. He then enables her to choose to forgive those who victimized her and to repent of any sin of her own. As she brings her deep wound to Him for healing, He touches her and, over a period of time, takes away the pain. In its place the Lord gives her the love, acceptance, tenderness, or encouragement that she lacked from others in that situation. He does not alter the facts of the past; rather, He alters her perception of these facts. Then she is able to move forward with courage and victory in greater wholeness.

See also Ps. 42:4; Mark 5:2, note; notes on Forgiveness (Ps. 51; Luke 17); Healing (Ps. 13; 133; 2 Cor. 5; Gal. 6; James 5); Incest (Lev. 18); Pain (Job 7); Rape (Gen. 34)

silver and gold and the special treasures of kings and of the provinces. I acquired male and female singers, the delights of the sons of men, *and* musical instruments[a] of all kinds.

⁹So I became great and excelled more than all who were before me in Jerusalem. Also my wisdom remained with me.

¹⁰Whatever my eyes desired I did not keep from them.
  I did not withhold my heart from any pleasure,
  For my heart rejoiced in all my labor;
  And this was my reward from all my labor.
¹¹Then I looked on all the works that my hands had done
  And on the labor in which I had toiled;
  And indeed all *was* vanity and grasping for the wind.
  There was no profit under the sun.

The End of the Wise and the Fool

¹²Then I turned myself to consider wisdom and madness and folly;
  For what *can* the man *do* who succeeds the king?—
  Only what he has already done.
¹³Then I saw that wisdom excels folly
  As light excels darkness.
¹⁴The wise man's eyes *are* in his head,
  But the fool walks in darkness.

Yet I myself perceived
  That the same event happens to them all.

¹⁵So I said in my heart,
  "As it happens to the fool,
  It also happens to me,
  And why was I then more wise?"
  Then I said in my heart,
  "This also *is* vanity."
¹⁶For *there is* no more remembrance of the wise than of the fool forever,
  Since all that now *is* will be forgotten in the days to come.
  And how does a wise *man* die?
  As the fool!

¹⁷Therefore I hated life because the work that was done under the sun *was* distressing to me, for all *is* vanity and grasping for the wind.
¹⁸Then I hated all my labor in which I had toiled under the sun, because I must leave it to the man who will come after me. ¹⁹And who knows whether he will be wise or a fool? Yet he will rule over all my labor in which I toiled and in which I have shown myself wise under the sun. This also *is* vanity. ²⁰Therefore I turned my heart and despaired of all the labor in which I had toiled under the sun. ²¹For there is a man whose labor *is* with

2:8 ᵃExact meaning unknown

2:14–16 Qoheleth made a clear distinction between the wise and the foolish. The fool walks in darkness, while the wise focuses on the eternal dimensions of life. The biblical definition of a fool is one who leaves God out of his life in all his actions and thoughts (see Ps. 14:1, note; 53:1). Those who are genuinely wise make God the focus of life. A wise woman orders her daily life in tune with the purposes of God. Yet from *Qoheleth's* earthly perspective, the wise and the fool would come to a very similar ending. Both would die and soon be forgotten! Thus for *Qoheleth*, vanity or meaninglessness prevailed.

2:17–23 Dwelling on the negative reflected a lack of faith and finally left *Qoheleth* in despair. As long as he was still searching for meaning in temporary, worldly things, he met only profitlessness and disappointment (v. 11). He viewed the emptiness or futility of human toil, which upon death must be left as an inheritance to others (vv. 18–23). His heirs might turn out to be shiftless, lazy men who would soon squander what he had worked so long to gain. Thus, *Qoheleth* faced the ultimate realization that material possessions could not be carried away with the decedent on his death (see Ps. 49).

wisdom, knowledge, and skill; yet he must leave his heritage to a man who has not labored for it. This also *is* vanity and a great evil. [22]For what has man for all his labor, and for the striving of his heart with which he has toiled under the sun? [23]For all his days *are* sorrowful, and his work burdensome; even in the night his heart takes no rest. This also *is* vanity.

[24]Nothing *is* better for a man *than* that he should eat and drink, and *that* his soul should enjoy good in his labor. This also, I saw, was from the hand of God. [25]For who can eat, or who can have enjoyment, more than I?[a] [26]For *God* gives wisdom and knowledge and joy to a man who *is* good in His sight; but to the sinner He gives the work of gathering and collecting, that he may give to *him who is* good before God. This also *is* vanity and grasping for the wind.

Everything Has Its Time

3 To everything *there is* a season,
A time for every purpose under heaven:

[2]A time to be born,
  And a time to die;
 A time to plant,
   And a time to pluck *what is* planted;
[3]A time to kill,
   And a time to heal;
 A time to break down,
   And a time to build up;
[4]A time to weep,
   And a time to laugh;
 A time to mourn,
   And a time to dance;
[5]A time to cast away stones,
   And a time to gather stones;
 A time to embrace,
   And a time to refrain from embracing;
[6]A time to gain,

And a time to lose;
 A time to keep,
   And a time to throw away;
[7]A time to tear,
   And a time to sew;
 A time to keep silence,
   And a time to speak;
[8]A time to love,
   And a time to hate;
 A time of war,
   And a time of peace.

The God-Given Task

[9]What profit has the worker from that in which he labors? [10]I have seen the God-given task with which the sons of men are to be occupied. [11]He has made everything beautiful in its time. Also He has put eternity in their hearts, except that no one can find out the work that God does from beginning to end.

[12]I know that nothing *is* better for them than to rejoice, and to do good in their lives, [13]and also that every man should eat and drink and enjoy the good of all his labor—it *is* the gift of God.

[14]I know that whatever God does,
 It shall be forever.
 Nothing can be added to it,
 And nothing taken from it.
 God does *it,* that men should fear before Him.
[15]That which is has already been,
 And what is to be has already been;
 And God requires an account of what is past.

Injustice Seems to Prevail

[16]Moreover I saw under the sun:

• • • • • • • • • • • • • • • •

2:25 [a]Following Masoretic Text, Targum, and Vulgate; some Hebrew manuscripts, Septuagint, and Syriac read *without Him.*

2:24–26 Qoheleth drew a tentative conclusion about the futility of life in these verses. One should enjoy food, drink, and work, capitalizing on whatever joy he can find. The sovereignty of God is the most important factor in the distribution of gifts (v. 26). A great mystery emerges from the fact that some have wealth and power, while others do not.

3:1–8 Every activity has its proper time as ordained by God. These rhythmic verses affirm that God definitely has a plan. Notice that each verse of this poem cites a characteristic activity of life matched with its opposite (vv. 2–8). Every activity has an appointed time (see Ps. 31, Time Management). We can accept God's timetable or be crushed by it. The God who ordains the routine events of our lives is a compassionate, gracious, faithful God. We must trust His will and rest in Him. Birth and death, sowing and harvesting, weeping and laughing, mourning and dancing, speaking and keeping silent, and war and peace are common occurrences in life. We must fit ourselves appropriately into God's plan for our lives (see Change Points in Life).

3:5 To cast away stones may be a euphemism for marital sex, while "to gather stones" may be a reference to refraining from that activity. Others suggest that these phrases literally refer to throwing stones into a field to prevent its cultivation and collecting the stones so the field can be utilized for planting. A third possibility is that of scattering stones from an old building that has been destroyed, while all the time collecting good stones to build a new structure. The meaning of these verses remains obscure.

3:11 God has imposed limitations on life. As finite beings, we can catch only a small glimpse of God's majestic works. Thus, in recognition of our limitations, we should at least enjoy food, drink, and the results of our labor as God's gifts (vv. 12, 13). Enjoyment itself is a gift from God.

3:14, 15 God's actions cannot be changed by mankind. Therefore, we should live in fear or reverence of Him (v. 14). The cyclical nature of life is now described by Qoheleth (v. 15). Thus, life appears to be just a wearisome treadmill (compare Eccl. 1:3–11, note).

CHANGE POINTS OF LIFE *TIMES OF TRANSITION*

Change is an inevitable part of life! While knowledge, experience, and routine foster security, the uncertainty of change is uncomfortable for many people. When circumstances are changing, Christian women can depend on God for strength, guidance, and constancy. He never changes (see Heb. 1:10–12). In times of transition, we can trust a sovereign and loving God to order all the events in our lives according to His purposes (Rom. 8:28).

Every life includes nearly constant contact with change—marriage, career, children, illness, relocations, divorce, retirement. Some changes are voluntary; others are forced by circumstances. Some changes bring joy; others, sorrow and confusion. All changes can become positive, strengthening experiences for those under God's authority.

Women respond to life's changes in different ways. Sometimes there is fear about the unknown. Often women lack self-confidence in times of transition. Others experience frustration, loneliness, and pain. The antidote for these feelings is faith and active obedience. Christian women are challenged to accept the reality of change and provide words of encouragement to those experiencing change.

The study of Scripture is especially important when facing change. Inner strength from God during times of distress results in God's richest blessings forever (2 Cor. 4:7–18). Change can be a gift from God to heighten, deepen, and widen your personal relationship with the Lord. Changes in life are cause to remember that God is faithful yesterday, today, and forever (Heb. 13:8).

See also Dan. 2:20–23; Acts 1:7, 8; 1 Thess. 5:1; notes on Adversity (Acts 5); Aging (Is. 46); Flexibility (Deut. 10); Premenstrual Syndrome (Prov. 21)

In the place of judgment,
Wickedness *was* there;
And *in* the place of righteousness,
Iniquity *was* there.

[17]I said in my heart,

"God shall judge the righteous and the wicked,
For *there is* a time there for every purpose and
    for every work."

[18]I said in my heart, "Concerning the condition of the sons of men, God tests them, that they may see that they themselves are *like* animals." [19]For what happens to the sons of men also happens to animals; one thing befalls them: as one dies, so dies the other. Surely, they all have one breath; man has no advantage over animals, for all *is* vanity. [20]All go to one place: all are from the dust, and all return to dust. [21]Who knows the spirit of the sons of men, which goes upward, and the spirit of the animal, which goes down to the earth?[a] [22]So I perceived that nothing *is* better than that a man should rejoice in his own works, for that *is* his heritage. For who can bring him to see what will happen after him?

4 Then I returned and considered all the oppression that is done under the sun:

And look! The tears of the oppressed,
But they have no comforter—
On the side of their oppressors *there is* power,
But they have no comforter.
[2]Therefore I praised the dead who were already
    dead,
More than the living who are still alive.
[3]Yet, better than both *is he* who has never
    existed,
Who has not seen the evil work that is done
    under the sun.

The Vanity of Selfish Toil

[4]Again, I saw that for all toil and every skillful work a man is envied by his neighbor. This also *is* vanity and grasping for the wind.

[5]The fool folds his hands
And consumes his own flesh.

••••••••••••••••••

3:21 [a]Septuagint, Syriac, Targum, and Vulgate read *Who knows whether the spirit . . . goes upward, and whether . . . goes downward to the earth?*

3:16—4:6 The oppressed seem to be powerless in confronting their oppressors. The author of Ecclesiastes pondered the prevalence of injustice and oppression in the world. This important fact supported *Qoheleth's* conclusions regarding the vanity or emptiness of human existence. Life does not seem to deal fairly with people. Equity is hardly upheld in the courts of law (Eccl. 3:16). Thus, *Qoheleth* could only conclude that God would bring about justice in His own time and way (Eccl.

3:17). Whether or not *Qoheleth* understood about life after death is not altogether clear (Eccl. 3:21). The prevalent view within Hebrew opinion was that meaningful life really ends at death. From this consideration, *Qoheleth* drew another temporary conclusion: Enjoy your work, for no one knows what lies ahead (Eccl. 3:22).

4:4–6 Emptiness and vanity result from selfish toil (v. 4). *Qoheleth* might be saying that working to get ahead of a neigh-

⁶Better a handful *with* quietness
Than both hands full, *together with* toil and
grasping for the wind.

⁷Then I returned, and I saw vanity under the
sun:

⁸There is one alone, without companion:
He has neither son nor brother.
Yet *there is* no end to all his labors,
Nor is his eye satisfied with riches.
But he never asks,
"For whom do I toil and deprive myself of
good?"
This also *is* vanity and a grave misfortune.

The Value of a Friend

⁹Two *are* better than one,
Because they have a good reward for their
labor.
¹⁰For if they fall, one will lift up his companion.
But woe to him *who is* alone when he falls,
For *he has* no one to help him up.
¹¹Again, if two lie down together, they will keep
warm;
But how can one be warm *alone?*
¹²Though one may be overpowered by another,
two can withstand him.
And a threefold cord is not quickly broken.

Popularity Passes Away

¹³Better a poor and wise youth
Than an old and foolish king who will be
admonished no more.
¹⁴For he comes out of prison to be king,
Although he was born poor in his kingdom.
¹⁵I saw all the living who walk under the sun;
They were with the second youth who stands
in his place.
¹⁶*There was* no end of all the people over whom
he was made king;

Yet those who come afterward will not rejoice
in him.
Surely this also *is* vanity and grasping for the
wind.

Fear God, Keep Your Vows

5 Walk prudently when you go to the house of
God; and draw near to hear rather than to give
the sacrifice of fools, for they do not know that
they do evil.

²Do not be rash with your mouth,
And let not your heart utter anything hastily
before God.
For God *is* in heaven, and you on earth;
Therefore let your words be few.
³For a dream comes through much activity,
And a fool's voice *is known* by *his* many words.

⁴When you make a vow to God, do not delay to
pay it;
For *He has* no pleasure in fools.
Pay what you have vowed—
⁵Better not to vow than to vow and not pay.

⁶Do not let your mouth cause your flesh to sin, nor
say before the messenger *of God* that it *was* an error. Why should God be angry at your excuseᵃ and
destroy the work of your hands? ⁷For in the multitude of dreams and many words *there is* also vanity.
But fear God.

The Vanity of Gain and Honor

⁸If you see the oppression of the poor, and the
violent perversion of justice and righteousness in
a province, do not marvel at the matter; for high
official watches over high official, and higher officials are over them.

5:6 ᵃLiterally *voice*

---

bor is poor motivation or that the envy of a neighbor under-
mines the satisfaction the laborer should receive from his toil.
Two proverbs are suggested (vv. 5, 6). The first is a warning
against laziness (v. 5). The folding of the hands is a gesture of
the lazy (see Prov. 6:9–11). Consuming one's own flesh may refer to bringing about personal ruin by constantly consuming
instead of producing. The second proverb suggests that while
laziness must be avoided, so also must be the drive to work
just to get ahead of other people. Satisfaction with a handful
is better than to have an abundance motivated by envy (v. 6).
The man who works endlessly out of a sense of greed never
ends up satisfied with what he has acquired. Work for the
sake of work alone is mere vanity (1 Tim. 6:10).

4:9–12 The value of companionship and friendship is the focus of these verses. The selfish individual works in competition with others (v. 8). He misses the reward of cooperation
(vv. 9–12). God Himself realized that it was not good for us to
be alone (Gen. 2:18; see Loneliness). He made provisions from
the beginning for our need of companionship and fellowship
with others (see Luke 1, Friendship).

4:13–16 Earthly fame and popularity quickly fade and are not
remembered. To make them our chief goals is vanity or
emptiness. *Qoheleth* viewed fame or popularity as an unworthy end in itself. Even a prestigious position never provides
lasting happiness and contentment.

**5:1–7 Qoheleth warned against a casual approach to
worship.** He focused on the meaninglessness of insincerity
and irreverence in worship. How easy it is to go to church on
Sunday and sit through the entire service with our minds far
from God. *Qoheleth* instructed us to listen when we worship
(v. 1). Listening in Hebrew thought carried the meaning of
obedience. When we read the Scripture and sing the hymns of
faith in worship, our words must be sincere (v. 2). Excessive
words sometimes indicate a lack of sincerity (v. 3; see Matt.
6:7, 8). We also sin with our speech when we make a pledge
we do not keep (Eccl. 5:4–7). *Qoheleth* ended this section
with the admonition to "fear God" (v. 7). Such fear does not
refer to cringing servitude but to reverent obedience.

LONELINESS — NEVER ALONE

Before God created Eve, He told Adam, "It is not good that man should be alone" (Gen. 2:18). Though not actually alone (for the animals were there), Adam was incomplete without human companionship. Central to God's purpose for His people are relationships with Him and with others (1 John 1:3, 7). Outside this fellowship is loneliness, a sense of isolation, as Adam and Eve were to discover when they disobeyed God (Gen. 3:22–24).

Loneliness, the result of broken relationships, is not the same as aloneness. In order to have a deeply intimate relationship with Christ, we must withdraw periodically from human companionship in order to meet with Him. Such aloneness with Christ is desirable and quite different from the pain of loneliness. We are never truly alone because of our friend Jesus (Prov. 18:24; John 15:15).

Jesus experienced aloneness when He was tempted in the wilderness (Mark 1:12, 13); when He traveled (Matt. 8:19, 20); and when His disciples forsook Him (Mark 14:50). However, He was only lonely once—when on the Cross He was made sin for us (Matt. 27:46).

See also Matt. 25:31–46; notes on Communication (Prov. 15); Friendship (Luke 1); Self-esteem (2 Cor. 10); Singleness (Ps. 62)

9Moreover the profit of the land is for all; *even* the king is served from the field.

10He who loves silver will not be satisfied with silver;
Nor he who loves abundance, with increase.
This also *is* vanity.

11When goods increase,
They increase who eat them;
So what profit have the owners
Except to see *them* with their eyes?

12The sleep of a laboring man *is* sweet,
Whether he eats little or much;
But the abundance of the rich will not permit him to sleep.

13There is a severe evil *which* I have seen under the sun:
Riches kept for their owner to his hurt.
14But those riches perish through misfortune;
When he begets a son, *there is* nothing in his hand.
15As he came from his mother's womb, naked shall he return,
To go as he came;

And he shall take nothing from his labor
Which he may carry away in his hand.

16And this also *is* a severe evil—
Just exactly as he came, so shall he go.
And what profit has he who has labored for the wind?
17All his days he also eats in darkness,
And *he has* much sorrow and sickness and anger.

18Here is what I have seen: *It is* good and fitting *for one* to eat and drink, and to enjoy the good of all his labor in which he toils under the sun all the days of his life which God gives him; for it *is* his heritage. 19As for every man to whom God has given riches and wealth, and given him power to eat of it, to receive his heritage and rejoice in his labor—this *is* the gift of God. 20For he will not dwell unduly on the days of his life, because God keeps *him* busy with the joy of his heart.

6There is an evil which I have seen under the sun, and it *is* common among men: 2A man to whom God has given riches and wealth and honor, so that he lacks nothing for himself of all he desires; yet God does not give him power to eat of it, but a foreigner consumes it. This *is* vanity, and it *is* an evil affliction.

5:8–20 Qoheleth warned that the pursuit of wealth or power would lead to the exploitation of the helpless members of society (vv. 8, 9). Wealth never brings inner satisfaction (vv. 10–12). Thus, the accumulation of riches is vanity or emptiness. Riches may disappear at any time (vv. 13–17) so that those who are wealthy today may end up in poverty tomorrow. Ultimately, death comes to us all, and we all face the grave empty-handed. Qoheleth instructed us that wise living consists of enjoying what God has provided (vv. 18–20). Qoheleth's philosophy is that we should learn to accept and enjoy our lot or position in life, whatever it may be. The transi-

tory nature of life should not prevent us from enjoying God's gifts.

6:1–6 The possession of riches, wealth, and honor does not guarantee joy or pleasure in life (v. 2). For the phrase "under the sun," see Ecclesiastes 1:9, note. The phrase "to eat" means "to enjoy" or "to utilize" (Eccl. 6:2). Many children and a long life were signs of God's blessing (Ps. 127:3–5, note; Prov. 3:16). The stillborn child who never had opportunity to enjoy life's benefits is better off than the individual who never knew how to enjoy what he already possessed.

PHILOSOPHIES OF LIFE

BOOK	PHILOSOPHY	THE WORLD'S VIEW	GOD'S VIEW
Ecclesiastes	Life of emptiness Search for God Reach for faith (Eccl. 12:1)	Wisdom (Eccl. 1:12–18) Pleasure (Eccl. 2:1–3) Ambition (Eccl. 2:4–17) Work (Eccl. 2:18–23) Religion (Eccl. 5:1–7) Wealth (Eccl. 5:8–20)	Wisdom (Eccl. 9:16–18) Purity of life (Eccl. 5:1–6; 9:9) Self-control (Eccl. 11:10; 12:13) Work (Eccl. 3:13; 9:10) Spiritual values (Eccl. 6:13–15) Wise stewardship (Eccl. 3:1–8) Friendships (Eccl. 4:9–12)
Job	Life of suffering Struggle with God Pursuit of hope (Job 19:25–27)	Wisdom—knowing all the answers (Job 11:1—12:2) Suffering for the righteous— unjust (Job 9:14–24) Decision making with feelings more than will (Job 6:2–4) Self-reliance (Job 32:10) Answers demanded from God (Job 10:18)	Wisdom—listening and respond- ing to God (Job 42:1–6) Suffering accepted as a channel for edification and spiritual growth (Job 13:13–19) Determination that faith in God will govern human feelings (Job 13:15, 16)
Song of Solomon	Life of love Presence of God Realization of joy (Song 2:3)	Love is a feeling Love can die Love is what you do for me Love is passive Love never allows suffering	Love is action (Song 1:15, 16; 2:2, 3) Love lives and grows (Song 4:12, 16; 7:12; 8:11, 12) Love acts in behalf of another (Song 8:6) Love requires work (Song 3:1, 2) Love comforts the one suffering (Song 1:5, 6)

³If a man begets a hundred *children* and lives many years, so that the days of his years are many, but his soul is not satisfied with goodness, or indeed he has no burial, I say *that* a stillborn child *is* better than he— ⁴for it comes in vanity and departs in darkness, and its name is covered with darkness. ⁵Though it has not seen the sun or known *anything,* this has more rest than that man, ⁶even if he lives a thousand years twice—but has not seen goodness. Do not all go to one place?

⁷All the labor of man *is* for his mouth,
And yet the soul is not satisfied.
⁸For what more has the wise *man* than the fool?
What does the poor man have,
Who knows *how* to walk before the living?
⁹Better *is* the sight of the eyes than the
wandering of desire.
This also *is* vanity and grasping for the wind.

¹⁰Whatever one is, he has been named already,
For it is known that he *is* man;
And he cannot contend with Him who is
mightier than he.
¹¹Since there are many things that increase
vanity,
How *is* man the better?

¹²For who knows what *is* good for man in life, all the days of his vain life which he passes like a shadow? Who can tell a man what will happen after him under the sun?

The Value of Practical Wisdom

7 A good name is better than precious
ointment,
And the day of death than the day of one's
birth;
²Better to go to the house of mourning

6:7–12 A person should enjoy the present rather than continually longing for more possessions and greater achievements in the future. *Qoheleth* questioned the value of a man's labor. He worked to feed himself but would be hungry again. He never would be satisfied permanently. Thus, *Qoheleth* stated his philosophy: "Enjoy life now" (v. 9). "The sight of the eyes" refers to the tangible present (v. 9). *Qo-*

heleth expressed a deterministic viewpoint. He believed that life was part of a prearranged system that could not be changed (vv. 10–12). All we could do in such a system would be to enjoy the present because no one would know what the future might bring.

7:1–29 Vanity of human wisdom. In these reflections on practical wisdom *Qoheleth* stressed the value of moderation. In a

ANGER ACT OR REACT

Anger can most often be defined as an emotional response to a perceived wrong or injustice. Hence, anger is normally expressed when a woman misinterprets circumstances, makes a mistake in judgment, or reacts quickly because she feels threatened or hurt. This anger is unjustified and sinful. This anger, in effect, denies the power of God to care for your needs and hurts and can even completely take over your life. There are many warnings about the danger of anger in Scripture (Eccl. 7:9; Matt. 5:22; Eph. 4:26, 31). Most often, you should leave your anger or wrath at the feet of Jesus and allow Him to act in your behalf.

God's anger is always perfectly controlled and expressed (Ps. 30:5; 78:38). There are examples of righteous anger given in Scripture, such as Moses' anger toward the children of Israel for not trusting God and following Him (Ex. 32:19). Righteous anger can be described as one that results when God's laws and His will are knowingly disobeyed. The concern must be for righteousness and reconciliation, never for personal vengeance coming out of our own hurts. We must be careful to take our anger to the Lord for Him to analyze and manage.

Do you act or *react*? The answer to this simple question will most likely reveal any weaknesses you have in expressing the emotion of anger. A person who *acts* knows who she is, what she believes, and how she should behave (Col. 3:23, 24). She not only knows this information, but she chooses to act on it. Another person's actions do not dictate her reactions, but rather the wisdom of the Lord is her mainstay (Col. 3:16, 17).

See also Ps. 85:4–7; 103:8, 9; Prov. 15:1; 22:24; 29:22; Matt. 5:22; Eph. 4:26, 31; chart on The Emotions of Jesus (Mark 1); notes on Attributes of God (Deut. 32); Bitterness (Heb. 12); Competition (1 Cor. 4); Conflict (Song 5; Matt. 18); Emotions (Ps. 42); Forgiveness (Ps. 51; Luke 17); Fruit of the Spirit (Ps. 86; Rom. 5; 15; 1 Cor. 10; 13; Gal. 5; Eph. 4; Col. 3; 2 Thess. 1; Rev. 2); Jealousy (Song 8)

Than to go to the house of feasting,
For that *is* the end of all men;
And the living will take *it* to heart.
³Sorrow *is* better than laughter,
For by a sad countenance the heart is made
better.
⁴The heart of the wise *is* in the house of
mourning,
But the heart of fools *is* in the house of mirth.

⁵*It is* better to hear the rebuke of the wise
Than for a man to hear the song of fools.
⁶For like the crackling of thorns under a pot,
So *is* the laughter of the fool.
This also is vanity.
⁷Surely oppression destroys a wise *man's* reason,
And a bribe debases the heart.

⁸The end of a thing *is* better than its beginning;

The patient in spirit *is* better than the proud
in spirit.
⁹Do not hasten in your spirit to be angry,
For anger rests in the bosom of fools.
¹⁰Do not say,
"Why were the former days better than these?"
For you do not inquire wisely concerning this.

¹¹Wisdom *is* good with an inheritance,
And profitable to those who see the sun.
¹²For wisdom *is* a defense *as* money *is* a defense,
But the excellence of knowledge *is that* wisdom
gives life to those who have it.

¹³Consider the work of God;
For who can make straight what He has made
crooked?
¹⁴In the day of prosperity be joyful,
But in the day of adversity consider:

---

series of proverbs *Qoheleth* mentioned certain values that are to be sought. These godly values were not just rules but a way of life that would bring happiness and fulfillment.

7:1 A good name was equated with one's character or reputation in Hebrew thought (see Prov. 22:1). Death is preferred over birth because the newborn has had no chance to develop a good reputation, but the man on his deathbed may rejoice in having earned a good name.

7:3 Sorrow or grief is better than laughter, for sorrow leads to reflection about the serious nature of life and its ultimate meaning. We also learn lessons from sorrow that we can learn in no other way. Sorrow accepted in the right way draws us closer to the Lord and closer to other people. Grief can help us get priorities in order (Is. 53, Grief).

7:8 The success of a particular venture can only be evaluated properly at its end. How an endeavor ends is much more important than how it began (see 1 Kin. 20:11). Thus, a wise man or woman is content to wait patiently and not demand immediate results. Patience is necessary to accomplish any successful achievement. The spirit of patience is preferable to the spirit of false pride.

7:9 Anger can cause us to act foolishly. The wise woman controls her temper rather than being controlled by it. Undisciplined anger can destroy our lives. *Qoheleth* warns us not to get angry too quickly (see Prov. 14:7; James 1:19; chart, The Answer to Inappropriate Anger).

Surely God has appointed the one as well as
the other,
So that man can find out nothing *that will come*
after him.

¹⁵I have seen everything in my days of vanity:

There is a just *man* who perishes in his
righteousness,
And there is a wicked *man* who prolongs *life* in
his wickedness.

¹⁶Do not be overly righteous,
Nor be overly wise:
Why should you destroy yourself?
¹⁷Do not be overly wicked,
Nor be foolish:
Why should you die before your time?
¹⁸*It is* good that you grasp this,
And also not remove your hand from the
other;
For he who fears God will escape them all.

¹⁹Wisdom strengthens the wise
More than ten rulers of the city.

²⁰For *there is* not a just man on earth who does
good
And does not sin.

²¹Also do not take to heart everything people
say,
Lest you hear your servant cursing you.
²²For many times, also, your own heart has
known
That even you have cursed others.

²³All this I have proved by wisdom.
I said, "I will be wise";
But it *was* far from me.

²⁴As for that which is far off and exceedingly
deep,
Who can find it out?
²⁵I applied my heart to know,
To search and seek out wisdom and the reason
of things,
To know the wickedness of folly,
Even of foolishness *and* madness.
²⁶And I find more bitter than death
The woman whose heart *is* snares and nets,
Whose hands *are* fetters.
He who pleases God shall escape from her,
But the sinner shall be trapped by her.

²⁷"Here is what I have found," says the Preacher,
"*Adding* one thing to the other to find out the
reason,
²⁸Which my soul still seeks but I cannot find:
One man among a thousand I have found,
But a woman among all these I have not
found.
²⁹Truly, this only I have found:
That God made man upright,
But they have sought out many schemes."

8Who *is* like a wise *man?*
And who knows the interpretation of a thing?
A man's wisdom makes his face shine,
And the sternness of his face is changed.

Obey Authorities for God's Sake

²I *say,* "Keep the king's commandment for the
sake of your oath to God. ³Do not be hasty to go
from his presence. Do not take your stand for an
evil thing, for he does whatever pleases him."

⁴Where the word of a king *is, there is* power;
And who may say to him, "What are you
doing?"

7:16–18 Life is filled with mysteries we cannot comprehend
(see Providence). The righteous die young, and the wicked
live a long life (v. 15). Therefore, *Qoheleth* recommended
moderation. If you live in moderation and fear God, according
to *Qoheleth*, you will come out all right in the end. No one
does good all the time (v. 20).

7:21, 22 Qoheleth's advice is not to take what others say about
you too seriously. An individual may praise you to your face
and condemn you behind your back. *Qoheleth* reminded us
that we have been guilty of speaking evil things of others. We
should not be too surprised to hear bad things being spoken
about us because we are all a mixture of good and evil.

**7:23–29 Qoheleth does not deny the existence of an upright
woman.** However, he does note that a good woman is hard to
find (v. 28). *Qoheleth* confessed that he himself had not
found wisdom. What he denied to women, he did not claim for
himself. Few women or men measure up to *Qoheleth's* definition of what constitutes a wise individual. The wise woman or
man avoids wickedness. A wise woman is to be a motivator,
not a manipulator. Her lifestyle is not "snares and nets" that

entrap but Christlike character that attracts. "The woman
whose heart is snares and nets" used her beauty to seduce
and manipulate to get her own way. *Qoheleth* found this kind
of woman to be "more bitter than death." It was difficult to
escape her grasp. A man who does not flee from such a
woman is a fool (Prov. 7:5, 21). Solomon had learned through
experience the tragedy of ignoring God's plan for marriage by
building up an extensive royal harem instead of settling for
one good wife (Eccl. 7:26; see also Eccl. 9:9; Prov. 31:10–31).
God created people good, but they have made themselves evil
by their own schemes (Eccl. 7:29).

8:2–9 Wisdom involves submission to authorities. People employed in the service of the government wisely obey even
when a task is personally unpleasant (v. 3). Yet the wise man
will choose the best manner and the proper time for carrying
out a command (vv. 5, 6) and accept the fact that he will not
like everything he will have to do. *Qoheleth* also reminded us
of another inevitability to which we must all submit—the reality of death (v. 8). Note the phrase "under the sun" (Eccl.
1:9, note).

PROVIDENCE PATIENT WAITING

The theme of God's providential care for His created order is woven throughout Scripture. In the Sermon on the Mount, Jesus assured His hearers of His presence in the midst of their trials (Matt. 6:25–34).

God's eternal and unfailing purpose is to sustain and direct His created beings (Matt. 6:10) from the beginning of creation into eternity (John 5:17). He has shown His providential care again and again (2 Tim. 1:12), extending it from the least to the greatest, covering the sinner and the saved.

Esther was simultaneously the humble Jewess, honoring her husband, and the queen of Persia, delivering her people. The God who controlled the cruel and despotic Ahasuerus of Persia has ultimate power over every situation. God's control is all-inclusive and absolutely certain, but at the same time every individual is responsible for her own decisions and actions. Still, no one can defeat the plans of God since all actions are included in His active or permissive will.

We are not under the tyranny of blind fate or an inviolable law of cause and effect, which by definition would seem to imply that there is a realm into which God cannot enter (Prov. 16:33). The events of our universe are ordered by a compassionate, gracious, longsuffering, faithful God (Ps. 16:9–11).

God has not promised that everything happening to us will be what we consider good. However, if tragedy strikes, we have only to wait patiently for His hour of redemption. God is able to cause even unfortunate happenings to work for good to those who love the Lord (Rom. 8:28). Nothing can happen to us apart from God's knowledge, presence, and love so that even in the most desperate circumstances we can be assured that God is working on our behalf for our eternal good. God is for us; He is not against us (Rom. 8:31, 32). In the tension between blessing and adversity, we recognize our complete dependence on Him, as well as His sovereignty over our own decisions and actions.

See also Gen. 45:5–8; Ruth 2:12; Esth. 4:14; 6:1–3; Ps. 24:1; Eccl. 3:1–8; Lam. 3:22, note; Acts 24:2; Eph. 1:11; notes on Blessings (Gen. 12); Fruit of the Spirit (Ps. 86); Promises of God (2 Pet. 1); God's Will (Eph. 5); Suffering (Ps. 33; 113; Is. 43; 1 Pet. 5); portrait of Esther (Esth. 2)

---

[5]He who keeps his command will experience
nothing harmful;
And a wise man's heart discerns both time and
judgment,
[6]Because for every matter there is a time and
judgment,
Though the misery of man increases greatly.
[7]For he does not know what will happen;
So who can tell him when it will occur?
[8]No one has power over the spirit to retain the
spirit,
And no one has power in the day of death.
There is no release from that war,
And wickedness will not deliver those who are
given to it.

[9]All this I have seen, and applied my heart to every work that is done under the sun: *There is* a time in which one man rules over another to his own hurt.

Death Comes to All

[10]Then I saw the wicked buried, who had come and gone from the place of holiness, and they were forgotten[a] in the city where they had so done. This also *is* vanity. [11]Because the sentence against an evil work is not executed speedily, therefore the heart of the sons of men is fully set in them to do evil. [12]Though a sinner does evil a hundred *times,* and his *days* are prolonged, yet I surely know that it will be well with those who fear God, who fear before Him. [13]But it will not be well with the wicked; nor will he prolong *his* days,

8:10 [a]Some Hebrew manuscripts, Septuagint, and Vulgate read *praised.*

8:10–17 The success of the wicked is soon forgotten. *Qoheleth* wondered why the world was so full of inequities. Why do the wicked prosper and the righteous suffer? The general principle is that those who reverence God will experience well-being, while those who reject God will not prosper; yet observations do not confirm this general principle. Good men have experienced disaster, while the wicked have gone on practicing evil undisturbed (v. 14; see Ps. 1, Prosperity). This philosophy of life sometimes is termed the "deuteronomic formula" (Deut. 4:40; 5:29, 32, 33; 28:1, 2). According to this philosophy, living right and practicing good will result in blessings of prosperity in this life. On the other hand, doing evil will reap only suffering and negative repercussions in this life (Deut. 28:15, 58–63). While the "deuteronomic formula" expresses a basic principle of life (we reap what we sow), we know many exceptions exist. Bad things do happen to good people, and the wicked do not immediately get the punishment they deserve (see chart, Suffering in Divine Perspective). The Book of Job deals with the mystery of the suffering of the righteous. According to Job, this mystery of life's inequities can be surmounted only by faith, not by reason.

which are as a shadow, because he does not fear before God.

[14]There is a vanity which occurs on earth, that there are just *men* to whom it happens according to the work of the wicked; again, there are wicked *men* to whom it happens according to the work of the righteous. I said that this also *is* vanity.

[15]So I commended enjoyment, because a man has nothing better under the sun than to eat, drink, and be merry; for this will remain with him in his labor *all* the days of his life which God gives him under the sun.

[16]When I applied my heart to know wisdom and to see the business that is done on earth, even though one sees no sleep day or night, [17]then I saw all the work of God, that a man cannot find out the work that is done under the sun. For though a man labors to discover *it,* yet he will not find *it;* moreover, though a wise *man* attempts to know *it,* he will not be able to find *it.*

9 For I considered all this in my heart, so that I could declare it all: that the righteous and the wise and their works *are* in the hand of God. People know neither love nor hatred *by* anything *they see* before them. [2]All things *come* alike to all:

One event *happens* to the righteous and the
　　wicked;
To the good,[a] the clean, and the unclean;
To him who sacrifices and him who does not
　　sacrifice.
As is the good, so *is* the sinner;
He who takes an oath as *he* who fears an oath.

[3]This *is* an evil in all that is done under the sun: that one thing *happens* to all. Truly the hearts of the sons of men are full of evil; madness *is* in their hearts while they live, and after that *they* go to the dead. [4]But for him who is joined to all the living there is hope, for a living dog is better than a dead lion.

[5]For the living know that they will die;
　　But the dead know nothing,

And they have no more reward,
　　For the memory of them is forgotten.
[6]Also their love, their hatred, and their envy
　　　　have now perished;
Nevermore will they have a share
　　In anything done under the sun.

[7]Go, eat your bread with joy,
　　And drink your wine with a merry heart;
　　For God has already accepted your works.
[8]Let your garments always be white,
　　And let your head lack no oil.

[9]Live joyfully with the wife whom you love all the days of your vain life which He has given you under the sun, all your days of vanity; for that *is* your portion in life, and in the labor which you perform under the sun. [10]Whatever your hand finds to do, do *it* with your might; for *there is* no work or device or knowledge or wisdom in the grave where you are going.
[11]I returned and saw under the sun that—

The race *is* not to the swift,
　　Nor the battle to the strong,
　　Nor bread to the wise,
　　Nor riches to men of understanding,
　　Nor favor to men of skill;
　　But time and chance happen to them all.
[12]For man also does not know his time:
　　Like fish taken in a cruel net,
　　Like birds caught in a snare,
So the sons of men *are* snared in an evil time,
　　When it falls suddenly upon them.

Wisdom Superior to Folly

[13]This wisdom I have also seen under the sun, and it *seemed* great to me: [14]*There was* a little city with few men in it; and a great king came against it, besieged it, and built great snares[a] around it. [15]Now there was found in it a poor wise man, and

---

9:2 [a]Septuagint, Syriac, and Vulgate read *good and bad.*　**9:14** [a]Septuagint, Syriac, and Vulgate read *bulwarks.*

8:15 *Qoheleth's* **advice** is to enjoy the simple daily pleasures of life. "Eat, drink, and be merry" (v. 15; 2:24; 5:18). For "under the sun," see Ecclesiastes 1:9, note.

9:2–12 Death comes to all (vv. 2, 3). Death functions as the great leveler. Thus, *Qoheleth* concluded that it is better to be alive than dead (v. 4). Contrast this thought with *Qoheleth's* viewpoint in Ecclesiastes 4:2, 3. The Preacher's depression and despair caused him to sway back and forth in his opinions. The people of Palestine viewed the lion as a noble beast, while they utterly despised the dog as an unclean scavenger (Eccl. 9:4; 1 Sam. 17:43; Prov. 26:11). The most miserable life is better than the grandest death because only in life is there hope (Eccl. 9:5, 6). Note the repetition of "under the sun"

(vv. 3, 6, 9, 11; see Eccl. 1:9, note). As long as one is alive, hope exists that life can get better.

9:7–10 Enjoy earthly pleasures while life lasts because death brings the end of pleasure (v. 7). Enjoy relationships with others and enjoy your work (vv. 9, 10). *Qoheleth* did not have the concept of an afterlife that we as Christians have. *Sheol* (Heb., lit. "grave" or "place of the dead") was viewed as a shadowy existence (v. 10). Everybody, both good and bad, went to *Sheol.*

9:13–18 The superiority of wisdom. Note the phrase "under the sun" (v. 13; see Eccl. 1:9, note). *Qoheleth* related a parable about a poor wise man who was able to deliver his city from a powerful enemy but was forgotten (Eccl. 9:14, 15). Yet,

EMPLOYMENT THE CHALLENGE OF A CAREER

The woman who manages a profitable career while watching over the affairs of her household has a tremendous challenge. Frequently, her career activities take her into male-dominated arenas in which she seeks to achieve success with strength and dignity. Often her determination to seek employment is an economic necessity.

Career success does not often come easily. A woman frequently works long, hard hours and sacrifices a great deal of personal time in order to do all her jobs well. This demands unique creativity in order to maintain priorities and fulfill legitimate expectations with home and family (Eccl. 10:10). Wisdom from the Lord enables a woman to prepare herself to accomplish her tasks in a way so that time and energy are used most efficiently and effectively.

By focusing on God's unconditional love a woman can keep from demanding perfection of herself. Jesus Himself finished His life on earth without healing every person who was sick or preaching to everyone who was lost (John 4:34). The challenge for women with careers is to make sure that first they are women who fear the Lord and then that their work is ordered according to the priorities and plan the Lord has given.

Where does a career woman place her focus? Paul admonished women and men to seek in all pursuits to "[please] . . . God" (1 Thess. 2:4–6). Focus on pleasing God, and He will enable you not only to please others and meet their needs but also to bring honor to Him through your pursuits. In other words, He is the source of wisdom and strength to do all in a Christ-honoring way. The Lord will go with and in you to your job, and He is totally capable of helping you with any problems. He can make an enormous difference in your focus, attitude, and motivations (Col. 3:23, 24).

See also notes on Employment (2 Cor. 2; Col. 3; 1 Pet. 2); Organization (John 9); Priorities (Matt. 6); Time Management (Ps. 31)

---

he by his wisdom delivered the city. Yet no one remembered that same poor man.

¹⁶Then I said:

"Wisdom *is* better than strength.
Nevertheless the poor man's wisdom *is* despised,
And his words are not heard.
¹⁷Words of the wise, *spoken* quietly, *should be* heard
Rather than the shout of a ruler of fools.
¹⁸Wisdom *is* better than weapons of war;
But one sinner destroys much good."

10 Dead flies putrefy[a] the perfumer's ointment,
And cause it to give off a foul odor;
So does a little folly to one respected for wisdom *and* honor.
²A wise man's heart *is* at his right hand,
But a fool's heart at his left.
³Even when a fool walks along the way,
He lacks wisdom,

And he shows everyone *that* he *is* a fool.
⁴If the spirit of the ruler rises against you,
Do not leave your post;
For conciliation pacifies great offenses.

⁵There is an evil I have seen under the sun,
As an error proceeding from the ruler:
⁶Folly is set in great dignity,
While the rich sit in a lowly place.
⁷I have seen servants on horses,
While princes walk on the ground like servants.

⁸He who digs a pit will fall into it,
And whoever breaks through a wall will be bitten by a serpent.
⁹He who quarries stones may be hurt by them,
And he who splits wood may be endangered by it.
¹⁰If the ax is dull,
And one does not sharpen the edge,

······················

10:1 [a]Targum and Vulgate omit *putrefy.*

Qoheleth praised the value of wisdom. Wisdom is better than strength (Eccl. 7:19), better than the powerful weapons of war. However, much of the good done by the wise can be undermined by the wicked (Eccl. 9:18). Every individual has a tremendous influence for good or evil in this world.

10:1—11:8 A collection of wisdom sayings was recorded. Note the identification of the right hand with good and the left hand with evil (Eccl. 10:2; see Matt. 25:33). A fool is easy to

recognize (Eccl. 10:3). The values of the world are often mixed up and are the reverse of what they should be (Eccl. 10:6, 7). Any worthwhile endeavor involves a risk (Eccl. 10:8, 9). The possibility of failure is always present. Wisdom involves using brains and not just brawn (Eccl. 10:10). The fool shows no restraint in speech (Eccl. 10:14). Our words reveal our character (see Matt. 12:34). A familiar warning against laziness is given (Eccl. 10:18). Money does have power (Eccl. 10:19)! Be careful what you say (Eccl. 10:20). Word does get around!

Then he must use more strength;
But wisdom brings success.

[11] A serpent may bite when *it is* not charmed;
The babbler is no different.
[12] The words of a wise man's mouth *are* gracious,
But the lips of a fool shall swallow him up;
[13] The words of his mouth begin with
foolishness,
And the end of his talk *is* raving madness.
[14] A fool also multiplies words.
No man knows what is to be;
Who can tell him what will be after him?
[15] The labor of fools wearies them,
For they do not even know how to go to the
city!

[16] Woe to you, O land, when your king *is* a child,
And your princes feast in the morning!
[17] Blessed *are* you, O land, when your king *is* the
son of nobles,
And your princes feast at the proper time—
For strength and not for drunkenness!
[18] Because of laziness the building decays,
And through idleness of hands the house
leaks.
[19] A feast is made for laughter,
And wine makes merry;
But money answers everything.

[20] Do not curse the king, even in your thought;
Do not curse the rich, even in your bedroom;
For a bird of the air may carry your voice,
And a bird in flight may tell the matter.

The Value of Diligence

11 Cast your bread upon the waters,
For you will find it after many days.
[2] Give a serving to seven, and also to eight,
For you do not know what evil will be on the
earth.

[3] If the clouds are full of rain,
They empty *themselves* upon the earth;
And if a tree falls to the south or the north,

In the place where the tree falls, there it shall
lie.
[4] He who observes the wind will not sow,
And he who regards the clouds will not reap.

[5] As you do not know what *is* the way of the
wind,[a]
Or how the bones *grow* in the womb of her who
is with child,
So you do not know the works of God who
makes everything.
[6] In the morning sow your seed,
And in the evening do not withhold your hand;
For you do not know which will prosper,
Either this or that,
Or whether both alike *will be* good.

[7] Truly the light is sweet,
And *it is* pleasant for the eyes to behold the
sun;
[8] But if a man lives many years
And rejoices in them all,
Yet let him remember the days of darkness,
For they will be many.
All that is coming *is* vanity.

Seek God in Early Life

[9] Rejoice, O young man, in your youth,
And let your heart cheer you in the days of
your youth;
Walk in the ways of your heart,
And in the sight of your eyes;
But know that for all these
God will bring you into judgment.
[10] Therefore remove sorrow from your heart,
And put away evil from your flesh,
For childhood and youth *are* vanity.

12 Remember now your Creator in the days
of your youth,
Before the difficult days come,
And the years draw near when you say,
"I have no pleasure in them":

11:5 [a] Or *spirit*

11:1–8 We do not know what the future holds. Yet we still must act on our limited knowledge (v. 6). We must take risks and have faith. Life is a precious gift (see vv. 7, 8). *Qoheleth* ended here on a note of emptiness, for he still had not grasped the ultimate meaning of life (v. 8).

12:1–8 Remember your Creator so that you can live a fruitful life of obedience to Him. The difficult (lit. "evil") days in verse 1 may refer to times of trouble or to the infirmities of old age. A series of metaphors is used to describe the characteristics of old age (vv. 2–6). Old age as the winter season of life is a time of darkness (v. 2). The "keepers of the house" represent arms, the "strong men" suggest the legs, the "grinders" are the teeth, and the "windows" represent the eyes (v. 3). The "doors" may represent the lips or the ears (v. 4). "Daughters

of music" must be a reference to singing women (v. 4; see 2 Sam. 19:35). The singing women may no longer move him, or perhaps he could no longer hear them clearly. The verse could also suggest that the aged man described was unable to sing, uttering only a dreary moaning noise. Fear often accompanies old age (Eccl. 12:5). The "almond tree blossoms" refer to the elderly individual's white hair (v. 5). The "eternal home" is the grave, indicating the finality of death (v. 5). The reference to mourners indicates a funeral. There are four references to death, all symbolizing life poured out and ended in death (v. 6). At death the body returns to the dust from which it came, and the spirit or breath returns to God who gave it (see Gen. 2:7; Job 34:14, 15). To *Qoheleth*, who saw only human wisdom, this is vanity, meaningless and empty (Eccl. 12:8).

[2]While the sun and the light,
The moon and the stars,
Are not darkened,
And the clouds do not return after the rain;
[3]In the day when the keepers of the house
tremble,
And the strong men bow down;
When the grinders cease because they are
few,
And those that look through the windows
grow dim;
[4]When the doors are shut in the streets,
And the sound of grinding is low;
When one rises up at the sound of a bird,
And all the daughters of music are brought
low.
[5]Also they are afraid of height,
And of terrors in the way;
When the almond tree blossoms,
The grasshopper is a burden,
And desire fails.
For man goes to his eternal home,
And the mourners go about the streets.

[6]*Remember your Creator* before the silver cord is
loosed,[a]
Or the golden bowl is broken,
Or the pitcher shattered at the fountain,
Or the wheel broken at the well.

[7]Then the dust will return to the earth as it was,
And the spirit will return to God who gave it.

[8]"Vanity of vanities," says the Preacher,
"All *is* vanity."

The Whole Duty of Man

[9]And moreover, because the Preacher was wise, he still taught the people knowledge; yes, he pondered and sought out *and* set in order many proverbs. [10]The Preacher sought to find acceptable words; and *what was* written *was* upright—words of truth. [11]The words of the wise are like goads, and the words of scholars[a] are like well-driven nails, given by one Shepherd. [12]And further, my son, be admonished by these. Of making many books *there is* no end, and much study *is* wearisome to the flesh.

[13]Let us hear the conclusion of the whole matter:

Fear God and keep His commandments,
For this is man's all.
[14]For God will bring every work into judgment,
Including every secret thing,
Whether good or evil.

12:6 [a]Following Qere and Targum; Kethib reads *removed;* Septuagint and Vulgate read *broken.*   12:11 [a]Literally *masters of the assemblies*

12:11-14 Teachers of the wise function as goads and nails. They prod or motivate us to search out the meaning of life, and they present foundational truths for living. The Shepherd is God (v. 11). Students can identify with verse 12. "My son" is the typical way a wise man addressed his disciples

(see Prov. 1:8, 10). *Qoheleth* came to his ultimate conclusion regarding a proper approach to life (Eccl. 12:13, 14). The essence of wisdom is to show fear or reverence to God by obedience (Job 28:28; Prov. 31:30). We are accountable to Him!

Song of Solomon

TITLE

The Hebrew title (*Shir Hashirim,* lit "song of songs") is an expression of the superlative, meaning "the best song." The Latin name is Canticles (lit. "songs"). The Hebrew Bible places the Song in the *megilloth* (Heb., lit. "scrolls"), a collection of books read on feast days of the Jews. Ruth, Esther, Ecclesiastes, and Lamentations are also included in this group.

AUTHOR

King Solomon (Heb., lit. "peace"), the son of David and Bathsheba, claims authorship of the book (Song 1:1). The wisest man of his day, he authored 1,005 songs (see 1 Kin. 4:32). The Song is consonant with his great wisdom and skill. Solomon's name appears repeatedly in the book (Song 1:1, 5; 3:7, 9, 11; 8:11, 12), and the events occur in a royal setting. Also the book's geographic references seem to assume a united kingdom (see map, Locations in the Song).

DATE

The Song was written during Solomon's forty-year reign (971–931 B.C.), probably during the early years of his reign.

BACKGROUND

SETTING: Solomon presided over the royal court in Jerusalem. However, many geographical locations throughout the kingdom are mentioned (see map, Locations in the Song). Solomon's authorship has been questioned, though not until the nineteenth century, and arguments suggested against Solomonic authorship have been inconclusive. Most evangelical scholars remain in support of Solomonic authorship.

PURPOSE: The Song is an *epithalamium* or nuptial song, an expression of love between a bride and her bridegroom. Biblical scholars have debated whether the Song should be read figuratively or literally. Many Jewish and Christian scholars have interpreted this poetic expression of human physical love as a historical relationship that could also be interpreted as a divine parable.

Ancient Jewish scholars often regarded the story as a picture of *Yahweh* and His love for Israel. According to early church fathers such as Augustine, Origen, Jerome, and Bernard of Clairvaux, the Song revealed the love between Christ and His church.

As dissatisfaction with allegorical interpretations grew, evangelical scholars adopted the more literal reading as primary. Thus, the Song of Solomon was viewed as extoling human sexuality within the bounds of marriage, with a secondary application to Christ and His bride, the church.

LITERARY CHARACTERISTICS: Ancient Near Eastern lyrical poetry served as both entertainment and a catalyst for philosophical discussion. The metaphorical language

delights and enhances the senses, while it illuminates the understanding. The poet's intent was to underscore the most profound emotions in the human experience. The intensity of longing and loving, the rehearsal of searching and finding, vows of constancy and lavish praise for the one loved are literary conventions that evoke universal response.

No other Old Testament book is so full of technical terms for spices, plants, and shrubs (see charts, Animal Life, Flowers and Plants, Gems and Minerals). The Song of Solomon, part of the Old Testament wisdom literature (including Job, Psalms, Proverbs, and Ecclesiastes), is not mentioned in the New Testament, and the book contains no definite reference to God. The Song contains no explicit doctrinal theology, but it does reflect monotheism in its celebration of God's creation. In its praise of the joys of human love, the Song echoes Psalm 45 with its pastoral touch.

THEMES

The Song stresses the themes of love and devotion between a man and a woman committed to one another, while also echoing the loving relationship between *Yahweh* and His people Israel and between Christ and His church. With aesthetic imagery, Solomon skillfully highlighted the splendor and majesty of God. No traces of the polytheism that appears in other poetry of this time period is found in the Song.

For women, the Song pictures a bride who is healthy, balanced, and truly loved. In contrast to many contemporary writers who depict female weakness or victimization as inevitable and absolute, God presents a portrait of wholeness and hope. A reflection of the intimate relationship between the man and woman in the Garden of Eden can be traced as mutual devotion and respect between a husband and wife develop and as they are related harmoniously with the natural world around them.

The dialogue forms five poetic units, each a renewal of feeling and growing intimacy. Refrains are interspersed with interjections by friends and supporters who celebrate with the couple. This maturation of married love may be outlined as follows.

OUTLINE

Introduction: Title (1:1)

I. A Song of Longing and Invitation (1:2—3:5)
   A. The yearning of the Shulamite (1:2–6)
   B. A teasing interchange between the lovers (1:7–11)
   C. An expression of admiration (1:12—2:7)
   D. The invitation of the Shulamite (2:8—3:5)

II. A Song of Fulfillment in the Marriage Procession (3:6—5:1)
   A. A description of the bride (3:6–11)
   B. The groom's adoration of the bride (4:1–15)
   C. The couple's toast to one another (4:16—5:1)

III. Songs of Frustration and Delight (5:2—6:3)
   A. A dream sequence (5:2–8)
   B. The bride's description of her husband's assets (5:9—6:3)

IV. An Antiphonal Song of Celebration (6:4—8:4)
   A. The beloved's praise of his bride and her response (6:4—7:9)
   B. The bride's invitation to her beloved (7:10—8:4)

V. A Song of Commitment (8:5–14)
   A. The bride's reflections (8:5–11)
   B. An exchange of admiration (8:12–14)

Song of Solomon

1
The song of songs, which *is* Solomon's.

The Banquet

The Shulamite[a]
²Let him kiss me with the kisses of his mouth—
For your[b] love *is* better than wine.
³Because of the fragrance of your good
  ointments,
Your name *is* ointment poured forth;
Therefore the virgins love you.
⁴Draw me away!

The Daughters of Jerusalem
We will run after you.[a]

The Shulamite
The king has brought me into his chambers.

The Daughters of Jerusalem
We will be glad and rejoice in you.[b]

We will remember your[c] love more than wine.

The Shulamite
Rightly do they love you.[d]

⁵I *am* dark, but lovely,
O daughters of Jerusalem,
Like the tents of Kedar,
Like the curtains of Solomon.
⁶Do not look upon me, because I *am* dark,
Because the sun has tanned me.
My mother's sons were angry with me;
They made me the keeper of the vineyards,
But my own vineyard I have not kept.

(To Her Beloved)
⁷Tell me, O you whom I love,
Where you feed *your flock,*
Where you make *it* rest at noon.
For why should I be as one who veils herself[a]
By the flocks of your companions?

The Beloved
⁸If you do not know, O fairest among women,
  Follow in the footsteps of the flock,
  And feed your little goats
  Beside the shepherds' tents.
⁹I have compared you, my love,
  To my filly among Pharaoh's chariots.
¹⁰Your cheeks are lovely with ornaments,
  Your neck with chains *of gold.*

The Daughters of Jerusalem
¹¹We will make you[a] ornaments of gold
  With studs of silver.

The Shulamite
¹²While the king *is* at his table,
  My spikenard sends forth its fragrance.
¹³A bundle of myrrh *is* my beloved to me,
  That lies all night between my breasts.
¹⁴My beloved *is* to me a cluster of henna *blooms*
  In the vineyards of En Gedi.

·················

1:2 [a]A young woman from the town of Shulam or Shunem (compare 6:13). The speaker and audience are identified according to the number, gender, and person of the Hebrew words. Occasionally the identity is not certain. [b]Masculine singular, that is, the Beloved **1:4** [a]Masculine singular, that is, the Beloved [b]Feminine singular, that is, the Shulamite [c]Masculine singular, that is, the Beloved [d]Masculine singular, that is, the Beloved **1:7** [a]Septuagint, Syriac, and Vulgate read *wanders.* **1:11** [a]Feminine singular, that is, the Shulamite

---

1:2 The Hebrew idiom "love is better than wine" compares every joy and pleasure to wine. Banquets for pleasure were often described as simply "wine" (see Esth. 7:2) because wine was a metaphor for pleasure, intoxication, sweetness, and exhilaration (Song 4:10). Thus, this expression suggests that the Shulamite's love (Heb. *dodim*) of her beloved brought her indescribable and incomparable joy and delight. The plural form could suggest the expression of love in multiple caresses and kisses.

1:3 Your name is ointment (lit. "your very self is oil wafted about") is a reference to the purification oil used by women. Such an interpretation would identify the Hebrew verb as feminine, and the reference would be to the Shulamite. However, most scholars seem to view the verb as masculine and thus a reference to the lover's name as a fragrant ointment (see Eccl. 7:1). Names were far more important in the ancient Near Eastern culture than they are today (see Is. 45, Naming of Children). The mere mention of the lover's name was a symbol of worth and wealth and awakened pleasurable thoughts and great affection.

1:5 The Shulamite's dark but lovely complexion was the result of her exposure to the sun and was in contrast to the fair-skinned, privileged ladies of the court. She compared herself

to the "tents of Kedar," a reference to the tents of black or dark brown goat's hair used by the nomadic Ishmaelite tribe from a territory southeast of Damascus (see Ps. 120:5). The Shulamite acknowledged her darkness but was not unaware of her beauty. She compared herself to the "curtains of Solomon." The palace curtains would be richly ornamented and noted for their great beauty.

1:6 My own vineyard is a picture of the Shulamite's body as she toiled in the fields, often neglecting her grooming. Since vineyards were sometimes a metaphor for sexual intimacy, this expression could have referred to the delaying of her marriage.

1:7 During the heat of the day ("at noon"), the Shulamite's lover, as a herdsman, would be in a shady spot. There the Shulamite wished to be as well. The Shulamite distanced herself from a harlot or a leper, both of whom would be heavily veiled.

1:9 For "filly," see chart, Animal Life.

1:14 En Gedi, a fresh water spring, lay on the western shore of the Dead Sea in the territory of Judah (see map, Locations in the Song). Archaeologists have uncovered evidence that a perfume industry was located there.

THE SHULAMITE BRIDE

From the lyrical pen of King Solomon, a beautiful and sensuous young woman emerged. Much of her person was revealed, but she was not named, simply called the "Shulamite." Southeast of the Sea of Galilee in the fertile uplands of rich alluvial soil, the town of Shunem was probably the home of the king's beloved. Her knowledge of and fondness for the plant and animal world colored every statement; her heart throbbed with the natural world where she spent her youth.

Recounting her childhood, the Shulamite spoke of her brothers, who assigned to her manual field labor. The fact that she mentioned her mother's home and made no reference to her father probably indicates that her father had died, which, according to traditional Israelite practice, would have placed the young woman under the authority of her brothers. Her darker skin probably set her apart from the other women of the royal court. She was, obviously, beautiful of face and form.

Ancient Near Eastern families, as an index of the family's morality, guarded the chastity of their unmarried women with vigor. Moreover, the Torah spoke specifically on the subject (see Deut. 22:13–30). In poetic language, the Shulamite is called a "wall" and a "door." The figures described her virginity, a "wall" which her brothers protected, a "door" behind which they enclosed her (Song 8:8, 9).

Since the king apparently had a summer palace in Lebanon (see Song 8:11), he first may have seen the Shulamite as he traveled to or from this property. He memorialized his deep love for her in a series of songs, typical of the delicate handling of personal and erotic human feelings, which has been honored by its inclusion in the canon of Holy Writ.

The Shulamite loved and was loved passionately. Every fiber of her being echoed with responsive, adoring affection. She rejoiced in her husband's commitment to her (Song 2:4); she was enraptured by his desire for her (Song 7:10); she was secure in her husband's pledge of enduring commitment (Song 8:6, 7). The Shulamite is God's portrait of bridal bliss to be found within a permanent monogamous relationship.

See also notes on Commitment (Matt. 16); Conflict (Song 5); Sexual Purity (1 Cor. 7)

The Beloved
15Behold, you *are* fair, my love!
　Behold, you *are* fair!
　You *have* dove's eyes.

The Shulamite
16Behold, you *are* handsome, my beloved!
　Yes, pleasant!
　Also our bed *is* green.
17The beams of our houses *are* cedar,
　And our rafters of fir.

2 I *am* the rose of Sharon,
　And the lily of the valleys.

The Beloved
2Like a lily among thorns,
　So is my love among the daughters.

The Shulamite
3Like an apple tree among the trees of the
　woods,
　So *is* my beloved among the sons.

I sat down in his shade with great delight,
And his fruit *was* sweet to my taste.

The Shulamite to the Daughters of Jerusalem
4He brought me to the banqueting house,
　And his banner over me *was* love.
5Sustain me with cakes of raisins,
　Refresh me with apples,
　For I *am* lovesick.

6His left hand *is* under my head,
　And his right hand embraces me.
7I charge you, O daughters of Jerusalem,
　By the gazelles or by the does of the field,
　Do not stir up nor awaken love
　Until it pleases.

The Beloved's Request

The Shulamite
8The voice of my beloved!
　Behold, he comes
　Leaping upon the mountains,
　Skipping upon the hills.

2:4 A standard or flag ("his banner") identified and led a military encampment or a large procession of people. The banner was a public display showing the army or people where they belonged or where they were to go. The Shulamite was brought to Solomon's banquet table by virtue of his love (Song 6:4, 10). She was made at ease by her lover's protective banner of love.

2:7 A recurring refrain throughout the Song is "Do not stir up nor awaken love until it pleases." The phrase often closes one section and opens another. Several interpretations concerning its significance have been suggested: a warning against forcing the development of love; an admonition to the women of the court not to interrupt the lovers; or a caution against premature arousal of sexual passions. The latter interpretation is

⁹My beloved is like a gazelle or a young stag.
  Behold, he stands behind our wall;
  He is looking through the windows,
  Gazing through the lattice.

¹⁰My beloved spoke, and said to me:
  "Rise up, my love, my fair one,
  And come away.
¹¹For lo, the winter is past,
  The rain is over *and* gone.
¹²The flowers appear on the earth;
  The time of singing has come,
  And the voice of the turtledove
  Is heard in our land.
¹³The fig tree puts forth her green figs,
  And the vines *with* the tender grapes
  Give a *good* smell.
  Rise up, my love, my fair one,
  And come away!

¹⁴"O my dove, in the clefts of the rock,
  In the secret *places* of the cliff,
  Let me see your face,
  Let me hear your voice;
  For your voice *is* sweet,
  And your face *is* lovely."

Her Brothers
¹⁵Catch us the foxes,
  The little foxes that spoil the vines,
  For our vines *have* tender grapes.

The Shulamite
¹⁶My beloved *is* mine, and I *am* his.
  He feeds *his flock* among the lilies.

(To Her Beloved)
¹⁷Until the day breaks
  And the shadows flee away,
  Turn, my beloved,
  And be like a gazelle

Or a young stag
Upon the mountains of Bether.ª

A Troubled Night

The Shulamite
3 By night on my bed I sought the one I love;
  I sought him, but I did not find him.
²"I will rise now," *I said,*
  "And go about the city;
  In the streets and in the squares
  I will seek the one I love."
  I sought him, but I did not find him.
³The watchmen who go about the city found
    me;
I said,
  "Have you seen the one I love?"

⁴Scarcely had I passed by them,
  When I found the one I love.
  I held him and would not let him go,
  Until I had brought him to the house of my
    mother,
  And into the chamber of her who conceived
    me.

⁵I charge you, O daughters of Jerusalem,
  By the gazelles or by the does of the field,
  Do not stir up nor awaken love
  Until it pleases.

The Coming of Solomon

The Shulamite
⁶Who *is* this coming out of the wilderness
  Like pillars of smoke,
  Perfumed with myrrh and frankincense,
  With all the merchant's fragrant powders?
⁷Behold, it *is* Solomon's couch,
  With sixty valiant men around it,
  Of the valiant of Israel.

2:17 ªLiterally *Separation*

---

more natural and affirms the premarital chastity that is encouraged throughout the Song and all of Scripture (Song 4:12; 8:8–12; see 1 Cor. 7, Sexual Purity).

2:15 Foxes that spoil the vines is a reference to small marauders that were a common pestilence for vineyard keepers (see chart, Animal Life). These "foxes" would represent the problems and differences found in any intimate relationship. In marriage, a commitment to work through such difficulties and to protect the relationship must be in place (see Romance; Song 5, Conflict).

2:17 Bether, an obscure word, has been translated variously. The idea is probably one of "cutting" or "dividing." No place is known by this name. The phrase may simply read "mountains of separation," a metaphor describing the separation of the lovers. In this love poem, some see the "mountains" as a reference to the Shulamite's breasts and to her deep longing for her lover.

3:4 House of my mother presents evidence of legitimate es-

pousal in that the Shulamite's lover was approved by her family.

3:5 Daughters of Jerusalem has been variously understood to identify friends of the bride or women of the royal court of Israel. The epithets used by the Shulamite (vv. 10, 11) are apparently parallel phrases used to address Hebrew women who showed allegiance to the king. Perhaps Jesus had this reference in mind when He addressed the weeping women on His way to Golgotha (Luke 23:28).

3:7 Solomon's couch (Heb. *mittah*) was a sedan or litter that allowed the occupant to recline. The king was attended by bodyguards to protect him from raiders. The *hapax legomenon* (a word used only once in the text) "palanquin" (Heb. *'appiryon*) seems to be a reference to the same piece of furniture (v. 9). The description is clear that this was an enclosed, portable chair/sofa constructed of wood from Lebanon and probably carried by members of the king's elite guard.

ROMANCE *THE ACTS OF LOVE*

Scripture approves of romance unreservedly. Marriages, even when arranged, were often recorded as love matches (Gen. 24:67), and Proverbs 30:19 speaks wonderingly of the mystery of romance. Three books in Scripture—Ruth, Esther, and the Song of Solomon—have romance at their center. These books are three of the five traditionally read at Jewish celebrations of the covenant between God and His people, suggesting that they have an extra dimension—they do, indeed, picture the wooing of the soul by God. Ezekiel 16:4–14 recounts God's wooing of Israel; the New Testament reveals that God's love for the church is a romance that ends in marriage (2 Cor. 11:2; Rev. 21:2). Romance provides a balanced picture of God's calling of the soul: The beloved is not forced to respond but desires to respond willingly to the love offered.

Romance offers the lover an opportunity to focus on responsibilities rather than privileges. Rather than dwelling on selfish needs and what others should do, the romantic lover is ever conscious of what he or she can do to show love for the other person (see Matt. 16:24–26). Everyone needs the acts of love for life and growth.

What are some basic elements of romance? Sincere admiration must be felt and shared on a regular basis (Song 1:8–10; 2:3). Differences between men and women must be acknowledged. Romance moves beyond the needs of the lover to minister to the beloved.

See also notes on Dating (1 Tim. 4); Love (1 John 4); Marriage (Gen. 2; 2 Sam. 6; Prov. 5; Hos. 2; Amos 3; 2 Cor. 13; Heb. 12)

8They all hold swords,
Being expert in war.
Every man *has* his sword on his thigh
Because of fear in the night.

9Of the wood of Lebanon
Solomon the King
Made himself a palanquin:a
10He made its pillars *of* silver,
Its support *of* gold,
Its seat *of* purple,
Its interior paved *with* love
By the daughters of Jerusalem.
11Go forth, O daughters of Zion,
And see King Solomon with the crown
With which his mother crowned him
On the day of his wedding,
The day of the gladness of his heart.

The Bridegroom Praises the Bride

The Beloved

4 Behold, you *are* fair, my love!
Behold, you *are* fair!

You *have* dove's eyes behind your veil.
Your hair *is* like a flock of goats,
Going down from Mount Gilead.
2Your teeth *are* like a flock of shorn *sheep*
Which have come up from the washing,
Every one of which bears twins,
And none *is* barren among them.
3Your lips *are* like a strand of scarlet,
And your mouth is lovely.
Your temples behind your veil
Are like a piece of pomegranate.
4Your neck *is* like the tower of David,
Built for an armory,
On which hang a thousand bucklers,
All shields of mighty men.
5Your two breasts *are* like two fawns,
Twins of a gazelle,
Which feed among the lilies.

6Until the day breaks
And the shadows flee away,

···················
3:9 ªA portable enclosed chair

3:10 The palanquin or wedding carriage was luxurious. No expense was spared in preparing for the king's wedding. Even the interior was beautifully prepared with expressions of love.

3:11 Solomon could have worn a crown of jewels, but this was probably the customary garland made by the ancients for festive occasions, especially weddings, and appropriately placed on the king's head by the queen mother.

4:1 Women sometimes wore a small veil over the lower face, but this word also denotes a hairnet (see chart, Head Coverings for Women). Mount Gilead, a chain of mountains east of the Jordan River, intersected with numerous valleys where shiny black goats were habitually seen descending in the sun-

light (Song 6:5; see chart, Animal Life; map, Locations in the Song).

4:4 The Shulamite's erect posture and shapely neck adorned with jewelry evoked a military vision, which would be natural for Solomon, possibly conveying the idea of strength and the suggestion of a model for others to follow (see chart, Gems and Minerals).

4:5 The reference to her two breasts is clearly an expression of erotic desire on the part of the lover who envisioned stroking or touching, as he would be drawn to pet a soft, young deer (see chart, Animal Life).

I will go my way to the mountain of myrrh
And to the hill of frankincense.

⁷You *are* all fair, my love,
  And *there is* no spot in you.
⁸Come with me from Lebanon, *my* spouse,
  With me from Lebanon.
  Look from the top of Amana,
  From the top of Senir and Hermon,
  From the lions' dens,
  From the mountains of the leopards.

⁹You have ravished my heart,
  My sister, *my* spouse;
You have ravished my heart
  With one *look* of your eyes,
  With one link of your necklace.
¹⁰How fair is your love,
  My sister, *my* spouse!
  How much better than wine is your love,
  And the scent of your perfumes
  Than all spices!
¹¹Your lips, O *my* spouse,
  Drip as the honeycomb;
  Honey and milk *are* under your tongue;
  And the fragrance of your garments
  Is like the fragrance of Lebanon.

¹²A garden enclosed
  Is my sister, *my* spouse,
  A spring shut up,
  A fountain sealed.
¹³Your plants *are* an orchard of pomegranates
  With pleasant fruits,
  Fragrant henna with spikenard,
¹⁴Spikenard and saffron,
  Calamus and cinnamon,
  With all trees of frankincense,
  Myrrh and aloes,
  With all the chief spices—
¹⁵A fountain of gardens,
  A well of living waters,
  And streams from Lebanon.

The Shulamite
¹⁶Awake, O north *wind,*
  And come, O south!
  Blow upon my garden,
  That its spices may flow out.
  Let my beloved come to his garden
  And eat its pleasant fruits.

The Beloved
5 I have come to my garden, my sister, *my*
    spouse;
  I have gathered my myrrh with my spice;
  I have eaten my honeycomb with my
    honey;
  I have drunk my wine with my milk.

(To His Friends)
  Eat, O friends!
  Drink, yes, drink deeply,
  O beloved ones!

The Shulamite's Troubled Evening

The Shulamite
²I sleep, but my heart is awake;
  It is the voice of my beloved!
  He knocks, *saying,*
  "Open for me, my sister, my love,
  My dove, my perfect one;
  For my head is covered with dew,
  My locks with the drops of the
    night."

³I have taken off my robe;
  How can I put it on *again?*
  I have washed my feet;
  How can I defile them?
⁴My beloved put his hand
  By the latch *of the door,*
  And my heart yearned for him.
⁵I arose to open for my beloved,
  And my hands dripped *with* myrrh,
  My fingers with liquid myrrh,
  On the handles of the lock.

4:8 Amana is a hill in the Anti-Lebanon Mountains facing the plain of Damascus (see map, Locations in the Song). All the places mentioned are in northern Israel. Senir and Hermon were the two highest peaks in this range of mountains.

4:12 The Shulamite's garden (Heb. *gan,* lit. "a covered place") was probably an enclosed and protected place of beauty and shade. Since water was scarce, private land owners sealed their fountains with clay, which would harden in the sun and serve as a protection for the water supply. Both metaphors suggest limited access, and the image is that the bride is a virgin. The Shulamite had indeed kept herself for her beloved, testifying to her own commitment to the faithfulness of marriage partners and to their exclusive monogamous physical intimacy. Though Solomon later violated this commitment, the purposes of God for marriage have not changed (see chart, God's Plan for Marriage).

4:16 The bridegroom would not enter the bridal chamber until invited. Here the Shulamite modestly invited him.

5:1, 2 The Shulamite was no longer a sealed garden because her beloved gained his rightful entrance. The relationship between the Shulamite and her lover was obviously personal and private. An interval occurred, during which the marriage was consummated (v. 1). Then the Shulamite spoke, perhaps as in a fitful dream, revealing her feelings. Every relationship experiences periods of apathy or indifference. However, the Shulamite did not remain in that state but repented (vv. 6–8), had a reawakening of her affections for her lover (vv. 10–16), and changed her heart, leading to reconciliation (Song 6:1–13).

5:4 The latch was a small hole in the door, enabling a woman to look out while remaining inside unexposed to view.

THE DAUGHTERS OF JERUSALEM

The phrase, "daughters of Jerusalem," especially as used in the Song of Solomon, has been variously understood to identify friends of the bride, women of the royal court of Israel, or merely a personification of the audience for the Shulamite and her lover (that is, a literary device rather than a group of real people). The epithets used by the Shulamite (Song 3:5, 11) are apparently parallel phrases used to address Hebrew women who show allegiance to the king. Perhaps Jesus Himself had this reference in the Song in mind when He addressed the weeping women on His way to Golgotha (Luke 23:28). He showed compassion as He addressed them with this tender and intimate phrase, "daughters of Jerusalem." These women were probably not His exclusive inner circle of disciples but inhabitants of Jerusalem. They showed sensitivity to His suffering, but Jesus gently pointed them beyond their emotional sympathy for Him to contemplation of their own innermost spiritual needs.

Certainly, there is a lesson to be learned. Only as women move out from themselves and look to Christ can they see the Savior's incomparable beauty and glory and experience His redeeming love and grace. The women mentioned in the Song were characterized by a willing spirit as they worked to make the palanquin (a portable canopy chair or bed) very beautiful for the king, and the women Jesus addressed showed sensitive hearts as they responded to His suffering with their tears. Women ought to emulate the "daughters of Jerusalem" with willing spirits to work for the Savior and with sensitive hearts in response to all He has done for them.

See also Song 1:5; 2:7; 5:8, 16; 8:4; Luke 23:28; note on Weddings (John 2)

---

⁶I opened for my beloved,
But my beloved had turned away *and* was gone.
My heart leaped up when he spoke.
I sought him, but I could not find him;
I called him, but he gave me no answer.
⁷The watchmen who went about the city found me.
They struck me, they wounded me;
The keepers of the walls
Took my veil away from me.
⁸I charge you, O daughters of Jerusalem,
If you find my beloved,
That you tell him I *am* lovesick!

The Daughters of Jerusalem
⁹What *is* your beloved
More than *another* beloved,
O fairest among women?
What *is* your beloved
More than *another* beloved,
That you so charge us?

The Shulamite
¹⁰My beloved *is* white and ruddy,
Chief among ten thousand.
¹¹His head *is like* the finest gold;
His locks *are* wavy,
And black as a raven.
¹²His eyes *are* like doves
By the rivers of waters,
Washed with milk,
And fitly set.

¹³His cheeks *are* like a bed of spices,
Banks of scented herbs.
His lips *are* lilies,
Dripping liquid myrrh.
¹⁴His hands *are* rods of gold
Set with beryl.
His body *is* carved ivory
Inlaid *with* sapphires.
¹⁵His legs *are* pillars of marble
Set on bases of fine gold.
His countenance *is* like Lebanon,
Excellent as the cedars.
¹⁶His mouth *is* most sweet,
Yes, he *is* altogether lovely.
This *is* my beloved,
And this *is* my friend,
O daughters of Jerusalem!

The Daughters of Jerusalem
6 Where has your beloved gone,
O fairest among women?
Where has your beloved turned aside,
That we may seek him with you?

The Shulamite
²My beloved has gone to his garden,
To the beds of spices,
To feed *his flock* in the gardens,
And to gather lilies.
³I *am* my beloved's,

5:7 Night patrols were charged with clearing the streets of wanton women. A large silk mantle or "veil" was often thrown over other garments for warmth (see chart, Head Coverings of Women).

5:15 This hyperbole pictures Solomon as rising far above common men, like the tall cedars on the awe-inspiring Mount Lebanon.

6:3 Mutual commitment is firmly stated, despite fluctuating

LOCATIONS IN THE SONG

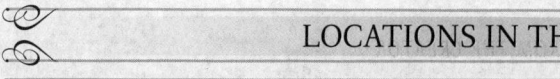

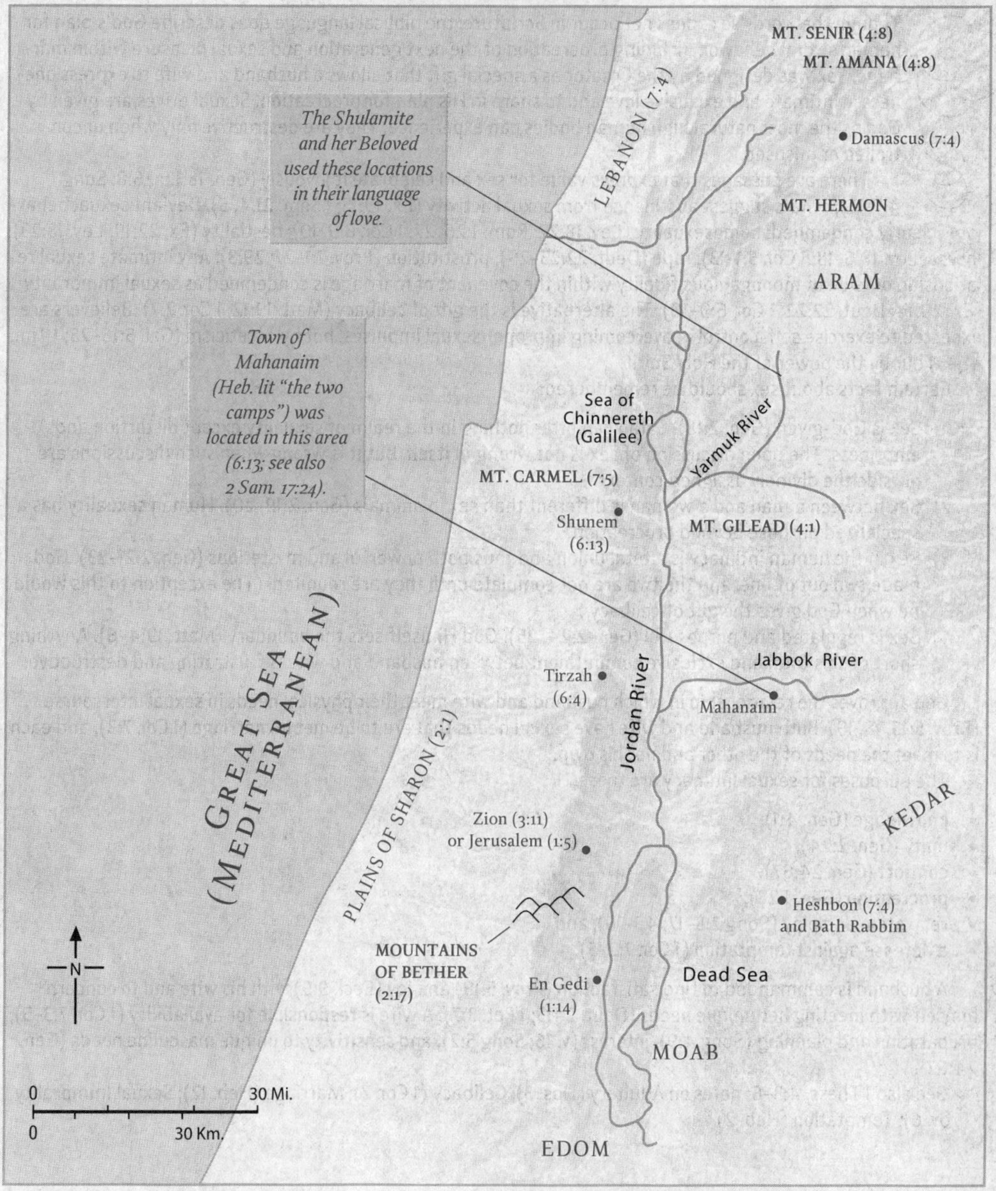

MT. SENIR (4:8)

MT. AMANA (4:8)

• Damascus (7:4)

The Shulamite and her Beloved used these locations in their language of love.

LEBANON (7:4)

MT. HERMON

ARAM

Town of Mahanaim (Heb. lit "the two camps") was located in this area (6:13; see also 2 Sam. 17:24).

Sea of Chinnereth (Galilee)

Yarmuk River

MT. CARMEL (7:5)

Shunem (6:13)

MT. GILEAD (4:1)

Jabbok River

GREAT SEA (MEDITERRANEAN)

Tirzah (6:4)

Jordan River

Mahanaim

KEDAR

PLAINS OF SHARON (2:1)

Zion (3:11) or Jerusalem (1:5)

Heshbon (7:4) and Bath Rabbim

—N—

MOUNTAINS OF BETHER (2:17)

En Gedi (1:14)

Dead Sea

MOAB

0   30 Mi.

0   30 Km.

EDOM

And my beloved *is* mine.
He feeds *his flock* among the lilies.

Praise of the Shulamite's Beauty

The Beloved

⁴O my love, you *are as* beautiful as Tirzah,
Lovely as Jerusalem,

Awesome as *an army* with banners!
⁵Turn your eyes away from me,
For they have overcome me.
Your hair *is* like a flock of goats
Going down from Gilead.
⁶Your teeth *are* like a flock of sheep
Which have come up from the washing;

---

feelings and misunderstandings (see Gen. 2, God's Plan for Marriage).

6:4 Tirzah, an old Canaanite city, was famed for its beauty and royal residences.

SEXUALITY *A GIFT FROM THE CREATOR*

Though the word "sex" does not occur in Scripture, the biblical language does describe God's plan for human sexual behavior, including procreation of the next generation and sexual pleasure within marriage. Sex was designed by the Creator as a special gift that allows a husband and wife to express oneness in intimate and exclusive love and to share in His plan for procreation. Sexual drives are given by God as the most natural high human bodies can experience. They are destructive only when uncontrolled or misused.

There are passages that express value for sex and celebrate it joyously (Gen. 18:12; 26:8; Song 4:1–16); others suggest abstinence from sexual activity (Ex. 19:15; 1 Sam. 21:4, 5). Deviant sexual behavior is clearly condemned: homosexuality (Lev. 18:22; Rom. 1:26, 27; 1 Cor. 6:9, 10); bestiality (Ex. 22:19; Lev. 18:23); incest (Lev. 18:6–18; 1 Cor. 5:1–13); rape (Deut. 22:23–29); prostitution (Prov. 7:1–27; 29:3). Any intimate sexual relationship outside of monogamous fidelity within the covenant of marriage is condemned as sexual immorality (Ex. 20:14; Deut. 22:22; 1 Cor. 6:9–10). The alternative is the gift of celibacy (Matt. 19:12; 1 Cor. 7:7). Believers are expected to exercise self-control in overcoming improper sexual impulses, not by asceticism (Gal. 5:16–25; 1 Tim. 4:1–5) but by the power of the Holy Spirit.

Certain facts about sex should be remembered:

1) Sex is God-given (Gen. 2:18). Satan can offer nothing in the realm of sexuality except distortion and emptiness. The open discussion of sex is not wrong in itself, but it is wrong when such discussions are outside the divinely assigned context.
2) Sex between a man and a woman is different than sex in animals (Gen. 2:19, 20). Human sexuality has a specialized purpose beyond procreation.
3) Sex in the human intimacy is a total union and thus both powerful and mysterious (Gen. 2:21–23). God made two out of one, and the two are not complete until they are reunited. (The exception to this would be when God gives the gift of celibacy.)
4) Sex is regulated and purposeful (Gen. 2:24, 25). God Himself sets the boundary (Matt. 19:4–6). Anything short of this total and exclusive commitment between husband and wife is frustrating and destructive.

God approves the relationship in which husband and wife meet their physical needs in sexual intercourse (Prov. 5:15, 18, 19). Both husband and wife have sexual needs that are to be met in marriage (1 Cor. 7:3), and each is to meet the needs of the other and not his own.

The purposes for sexual intimacy are these:

- knowledge (Gen. 4:1),
- unity (Gen. 2:24),
- comfort (Gen. 24:67),
- procreation (Gen. 1:28),
- relaxation and play (Song 2:8–17; 4:1–16), and
- a defense against temptation (1 Cor. 7:2–5).

A husband is commanded to find satisfaction (Prov. 5:19) and joy (Eccl. 9:9) with his wife and to concern himself with meeting her unique needs (Deut. 24:5; 1 Pet. 3:7). A wife is responsible for availability (1 Cor. 7:3–5), preparation and planning (Song 4:9), interest (v. 16; Song 5:2), and sensitivity to unique masculine needs (Gen. 24:67).

See also 1 Thess. 4:3–6; notes on Adultery (Hos. 3); Celibacy (1 Cor. 7); Marriage (Heb. 12); Sexual Immorality (Prov. 6); Temptation (Heb. 2)

Every one bears twins,
And none *is* barren among them.
⁷Like a piece of pomegranate
Are your temples behind your veil.

⁸There are sixty queens
And eighty concubines,
And virgins without number.

⁹My dove, my perfect one,
Is the only one,
The only one of her mother,
The favorite of the one who bore her.
The daughters saw her
And called her blessed,
The queens and the concubines,
And they praised her.

6:8 Solomon's royal position gave him access to as many   women as he wanted, but he had chosen the Shulamite.

ANIMAL LIFE

In ancient Near Eastern culture, animals were vital in maintaining subsistence. The Song uses them in poetic imagery to highlight characteristics of each lover.

ANIMAL	DESCRIPTION
Flock	This term is used repeatedly since the nation's economy was agricultural, involving flocks and herds. Shepherding patterns intertwine the expressions of love. The Shulamite looked for her beloved "at noon" because he would be resting with his flock in the heat of the day (Song 1:7). He responded with advice to follow the footsteps of the flock (Song 1:8).
Goats	Probably the Nubian ibex, with glossy black hair, still found in this area (Song 1:8; 4:1; 6:5).
Sheep	The whiteness of newly washed wool serves as a description of her teeth (Song 4:2; 6:6), perfectly matching ("twins") and evenly set.
Dove	This bird personified innocence and purity and described the young maiden as a term of endearment (Song 1:15). The Shulamite quoted him as thus addressing her (Song 5:2). She imagined the king urging her to come and alluded to the shy nature of doves as they rested high in the clefts of large rocks (Song 2:14).
Turtledove	This bird is the wild pigeon that passes through Palestine announcing springtime (Song 2:12).
Raven	The shiny feathers of this sleek, black bird are used to describe the royal hair (Song 5:11).
Fawns Gazelles Stags	These designations of deer were found commonly in poetry of this period. Gazelles were graceful and thus a symbol of feminine beauty. Three times a stanza closes with an oath to emphasize the serious nature of marriage (Song 2:7; 3:5; 8:4). Each lover used this analogy for the other. She saw him as a nimble stag (Song 2:9, 17). Her breasts evoked his memory of young fawns feeding (Song 4:5; 7:3).
Filly	The comparison of the Shulamite with the king's filly was intended as a high compliment, since Solomon introduced to the kingdom the finest thoroughbred Egyptian horses, strong and carefully groomed (Song 1:9).
Foxes	These are probably the abundant jackals, canines which were crafty and swift. They are used to denote apprehension that someone would thwart the expressions of the couple's love (Song 2:15).
Lion Leopard	Symbolically, the lion is seen as a threat, stalking its prey; the leopard (panther) is highly intelligent and treacherous. Both lived in mountainous areas (Song 4:8).

[10]Who is she who looks forth as the morning,
Fair as the moon,
Clear as the sun,
Awesome as *an army* with banners?

The Shulamite
[11]I went down to the garden of nuts
To see the verdure of the valley,
To see whether the vine had budded
And the pomegranates had bloomed.

[12]Before I was even aware,
My soul had made me
As the chariots of my noble people.[a]

The Beloved and His Friends
[13]Return, return, O Shulamite;
Return, return, that we may look upon you!

6:12 [a]Hebrew *Ammi Nadib*

6:12 **The king's love** had transformed the Shulamite, in her mind, from a simple maiden into a queen.

MARITAL CONFLICT *CONFRONTING IN LOVE*

Conflicts are usually the symptom of a wedge that has already been driven somehow in the past. Disagreements between spouses appear a number of times in Scripture. Solomon's poetic description of his misunderstanding with his new bride demonstrates a difference of feeling, awkward communication, and poor timing in learning to live together in love. Abraham and Sarah quarreled over her childlessness (Gen. 16:5), as did Jacob and Rachel (Gen. 30:1, 2). Job's wife disagreed with his response to his illness (Job 2:9, 10). The prophet Malachi denounced the priests who had broken, and not mended, their wedding vows (Mal. 2:14–16).

Disagreements are common, but Scripture also provides guidance. Both Paul and Peter give clues to the prevention and settlement of domestic clashes. To discordant couples in Corinth Paul wrote "God has called us to peace" (1 Cor. 7:15). That is the ultimate objective. Peter advised wives experiencing strained relations with unbelieving husbands to win them through consistently gentle and quiet spirits (1 Pet. 3:1–4).

Human nature has not changed. Competition and contention lead only to harsh consequences. Love, on the other hand, "bears . . . believes . . . hopes . . . endures all things" (1 Cor. 13:7). Jesus taught us to remove the plank in our own eyes before we try to get rid of the specks of dust in the eyes of others (Matt. 7:3–5).

Mercy is a vital part of relaxing tensions. A patient, forgiving, tolerant spirit eases confrontations (Mic. 6:8). Sensitivity in timing also recaptures warm affection. We should not let problems fester into bitterness. The New Testament cautions us to address anger before the sun goes down (Eph. 4:26). Even if all cannot be resolved, the peace process is begun.

Finally, we must choose to forgive. Calm settles over us when we allow Christ to control hurts. He modeled forgiveness (1 Pet. 2:23), and He alone can give us strength to bury revenge and to restore harmony in relationships. Believers are to be peacemakers (Matt. 5:9).

See also Amos 3:3; notes on Communication (Prov. 15); Conflict (Matt. 18); Forgiveness (Ps. 51; Luke 17); Interfaith Marriage (Neh. 10); Marriage (Gen. 2; 2 Sam. 6; Prov. 5; Hos. 2; Amos 3; 2 Cor. 13; Heb. 12)

The Shulamite
What would you see in the Shulamite—
As it were, the dance of the two camps?[a]

Expressions of Praise

The Beloved

7 How beautiful are your feet in sandals,
O prince's daughter!
The curves of your thighs *are* like jewels,
The work of the hands of a skillful
workman.
²Your navel *is* a rounded goblet;
It lacks no blended beverage.
Your waist *is* a heap of wheat
Set about with lilies.
³Your two breasts *are* like two fawns,
Twins of a gazelle.
⁴Your neck *is* like an ivory tower,
Your eyes *like* the pools in Heshbon
By the gate of Bath Rabbim.
Your nose *is* like the tower of Lebanon
Which looks toward Damascus.
⁵Your head *crowns* you like *Mount* Carmel,

And the hair of your head *is* like purple;
A king *is* held captive by *your* tresses.

⁶How fair and how pleasant you are,
O love, with your delights!
⁷This stature of yours is like a palm tree,
And your breasts *like* its clusters.
⁸I said, "I will go up to the palm tree,
I will take hold of its branches."
Let now your breasts be like clusters of the
vine,
The fragrance of your breath like apples,
⁹And the roof of your mouth like the best wine.

The Shulamite
The wine goes *down* smoothly for my beloved,
Moving gently the lips of sleepers.[a]
¹⁰I *am* my beloved's,
And his desire *is* toward me.

••••••••••••••••••

6:13 [a]Hebrew *Mahanaim*   7:9 [a]Septuagint, Syriac, and Vulgate read
lips and teeth.

7:1 The king extolled the Shulamite's beauty from her feet upward to her head. His passions were awakened. The Shulamite might be dancing before her husband.

7:4 The Amorite king Sihon established his ancient capital at Heshbon about 50 miles east of Jerusalem near modern Madaba (Num. 21:25–30; see map, Locations in the Song of Solomon). Beautiful reservoirs and fertile land made the city fa-

mous. Bath Rabbim was one of the gates of the ancient city. The king found rest in the Shulamite's eyes as a busy traveler who entered the city by the gate would find rest in the refreshing pools.

7:8 I will go up is a poetic expression of Solomon's intention to fulfill his sexual longing for the Shulamite. She was confident of his love as well (v. 10).

[11]Come, my beloved,
Let us go forth to the field;
Let us lodge in the villages.
[12]Let us get up early to the vineyards;
Let us see if the vine has budded,
Whether the grape blossoms are open,
And the pomegranates are in bloom.
There I will give you my love.
[13]The mandrakes give off a fragrance,
And at our gates *are* pleasant *fruits*,
All manner, new and old,
Which I have laid up for you, my beloved.

8 Oh, that you were like my brother,
Who nursed at my mother's breasts!
If I should find you outside,
I would kiss you;
I would not be despised.
[2]I would lead you *and* bring you
Into the house of my mother,
She *who* used to instruct me.
I would cause you to drink of spiced wine,
Of the juice of my pomegranate.

(To the Daughters of Jerusalem)
[3]His left hand *is* under my head,
And his right hand embraces me.
[4]I charge you, O daughters of Jerusalem,
Do not stir up nor awaken love
Until it pleases.

Love Renewed in Lebanon

A Relative
[5]Who *is* this coming up from the wilderness,
Leaning upon her beloved?

I awakened you under the apple tree.
There your mother brought you forth;
There she *who* bore you brought *you* forth.

The Shulamite to Her Beloved
[6]Set me as a seal upon your heart,

As a seal upon your arm;
For love *is as* strong as death,
Jealousy *as* cruel as the grave;[a]
Its flames *are* flames of fire,
A most vehement[b] flame.

[7]Many waters cannot quench love,
Nor can the floods drown it.
If a man would give for love
All the wealth of his house,
It would be utterly despised.

The Shulamite's Brothers
[8]We have a little sister,
And she has no breasts.
What shall we do for our sister
In the day when she is spoken for?
[9]If she *is* a wall,
We will build upon her
A battlement of silver;
And if she *is* a door,
We will enclose her
With boards of cedar.

The Shulamite
[10]I *am* a wall,
And my breasts like towers;
Then I became in his eyes
As one who found peace.
[11]Solomon had a vineyard at Baal Hamon;
He leased the vineyard to keepers;
Everyone was to bring for its fruit
A thousand silver *coins*.

(To Solomon)
[12]My own vineyard *is* before me.
You, O Solomon, *may have* a thousand,
And those who tend its fruit two hundred.

8:6 [a]Or *Sheol* [b]Literally *A flame of* YAH (a poetic form of *YHWH, the* LORD)

7:13 The Shulamite had planned sensual pleasures carefully for her beloved. She would give her love to him in ways new and old.

8:1 The ancient Near Eastern culture made improper all public expressions of love except to family members. The Shulamite wished her beloved was like her brother so that she could kiss him in public without shame and disgrace.

8:6 The Shulamite desired permanence and security from her lover. The seal was a mark of ownership and official commitment. The Shulamite wanted to be a "seal" on her lover's heart because the nearness to the seat of his affection gave her security. She wanted to be a "seal" on his arm to remind her of his protection and strength. The phrase "as strong as death" suggested that finality and immutability of his love. The reference to "jealousy" was a reminder of the exclusive intensity of his love, which could be described as a "waterproof torch" (v. 7).

8:8 These words of the concerned brothers of the Shulamite indicate that the future of every Israelite girl depended on her virginity.

8:9 The wall is a picture of a barrier, indicating virtue. The "door" represents promiscuity or the indiscriminate yielding of the body. The brothers are held responsible since a sister's lifestyle would reflect on her family. If the Shulamite were a "door," the brothers would step in and protect her; if she were a "wall," they would trust and praise her.

8:10 The Shulamite testified that she was a virgin. Thus, she had found favor with Solomon.

8:11 The location of Baal Hamon (lit. "owner of a multitude") is undetermined (see chart, Locations in the Song). The reference is to Solomon's wealth and royal status.

8:12 Metaphorical language suggests the abundant profit the Shulamite would be to Solomon. Though her first loyalty was

JEALOUSY — ADVERSARY OR ADVOCATE?

Jealousy, unlike envy (Prov. 14:30) and covetousness, can have a positive connotation. In Scripture, the term is used to describe God's intolerance of unfaithfulness on the part of His people, especially as concerns their tendency to be drawn away by other gods (Ex. 20:5; 34:14). God's protection of His people from their enemies is the fruit of this holy jealousy (Ezek. 39:25–28).

Jealousy that is the result of pride or self-centeredness is not a positive quality. It may describe the suspicions of a husband or wife in a marriage where there is unfaithfulness (see Num. 5:11–31). Such human jealousy, often translated in Scripture as "envy," easily becomes hostility toward one considered to be a rival and as such found a listing among the vices or "works of the flesh" (see Rom. 13:13; 2 Cor. 12:20; Gal. 5:20, 21).

Such jealousy among women is not a feeling restricted to modern times. God-fearing women of old also had to deal with those feelings. Hannah longed for a child. Though she was barren, she had the devoted love of her husband Elkanah; yet the jealous and more fruitful Peninnah tormented Hannah constantly (1 Sam. 1:2–8). Peninnah's jealousy led her to treat Hannah in hurtful ways. Likewise, Rachel and Leah bickered out of jealousy (Gen. 30:15). Sarah was cruel to Hagar (Gen. 16:5, 6), jealous of her fruitfulness in bearing a son to Abraham. Instead of being advocates for one another, these women were adversaries because of their jealousies.

Luke 1:41–45 is perhaps the best example of how women might respond appropriately to one another. Elizabeth did not argue over whose child was more important. She was not envious of Mary's child; neither was Mary jealous of Elizabeth's position or marital status. Rather than snipe at each other, they encouraged and became advocates for each other.

Women who are in Christ are joint-heirs to all that belongs to Christ, which is beyond what they deserve or can even imagine (1 Cor. 2:9). They are to focus on honoring and praising God (Col. 3:1–4) and not dwell on what they do not have or what others have, which inevitably leads to jealousy, envy, and covetousness (Ex. 20:17; 2 Cor. 10:12).

See also James 3:14–16; notes on Attributes of God (Deut. 4); Bitterness (Heb. 12); Covetousness (Prov. 30); Envy (Prov. 14); portraits of Elizabeth (Luke 1); Mary of Nazareth (Luke 1)

The Beloved

13You who dwell in the gardens,
The companions listen for your
voice—
Let me hear it!

The Shulamite

14Make haste, my beloved,
And be like a gazelle
Or a young stag
On the mountains of spices.

---

to Solomon, she did not forget the family who reared and nurtured her. The Shulamite's brothers had leased Solomon's vineyard. However, the Shulamite asked Solomon to reward her brothers for protecting her through the years by paying her brothers 20 percent or 200 of 1,000 silver coins, which

would represent the traditional percentage of profit due a vineyard's caretakers. This would be Solomon's payment to her brothers for preserving and caring for the Shulamite and for keeping her pure for him (v. 12). Marriage eluded her no longer (see Song 1:6, note).

FLOWERS AND PLANTS

The pastoral setting for this ancient song is authenticated by prolific references to the flora of northern Israel.

PLANT	REFERENCE	DESCRIPTION
Spikenard	Song 1:12; 4:13, 14	Plant with scented roots from which fragrant oil was extracted.
Myrrh	Song 1:13; 3:6; 4:6, 14; 5:1, 13	Short, stubby tree that dripped gum, highly prized for its aromatic qualities used for holy anointing oil, female purification, and cosmetics, as well as in burial shrouds.
Henna	Song 1:14; 4:13	Shrub with fragrant white blossoms, growing to height of 12 feet. Leaves were made into paste and used to color hair and nails as well as the manes and tails of horses, especially by pagan populations.
Cedar	Song 1:17; 5:15	Coniferous tree esteemed for its durability and resistance to larvae as well as its aroma. Grows to 140 feet with 40-foot girth. Used in constructing Solomon's palace and sedan carriage.
Fir	Song 1:17	Evergreen tree used for ships, buildings, and musical instruments. A symbol of the desert's fertility.
Rose of Sharon	Song 2:1	Humble meadow flower resembling a tulip with sweet fragrance. Found in abundance on plain of Sharon.
Lily of the Valley	Song 2:1, 2; 4:5; 5:13; 6:2, 3	Probably a type of hyacinth. Described as "glowing red," a variety akin to red anemone. The common "madonna lily" plentiful in Palestine.
Apple Tree	Song 2:3, 5; 7:8	Symbol of strength, sweetness, and fragrance.
Flowers	Song 2:12	Reference to wildflowers, which appear after the rains of March and April.
Fig Tree/ Green Figs	Song 2:13	Denoting figs that ripen at various times from August onward, some remaining until the following spring.
Grapevines	Song 2:13, 15	Early stage of grape growth when blossoms are fragrant.
Frankincense	Song 3:6; 4:6, 14	Tree that exudes clear resin from incisions in the bark, hardening into small yellow beads with strong odor. A symbol of religious fervor.
Wood of Lebanon	Song 1:17; 3:9	Cedar here symbolizing holiness, truth, and perseverance.
Pomegranate	Song 4:3, 13; 6:7, 11; 7:12; 8:2	Apple-shaped fruit with thin, hard skin, containing pulp of rosy color. Often used symbolically in Oriental poetry.
Saffron	Song 4:14	Dried stigma of the autumn crocus, producing aroma and orange dye. Used in foods as well as therapeutically.
Calamus	Song 4:14	Tawny-colored, reed-like stem grown in wet places in India. Use here obscure, but from context apparently the stem had a flower with a sweet smell.
Cinnamon	Song 4:14	Similar to modern spice used in foods. Also used with other spices as deodorant and disinfectant.

FLOWERS AND PLANTS (cont.)

PLANT	REFERENCE	DESCRIPTION
Aloes	Song 4:14	From a large, aromatic tree that produces resin and oil for making perfume.
Wheat	Song 7:2	Pale, newly threshed, and winnowed wheat, often used to describe ideal skin color.
Palm	Song 7:8	Stately trees found in oases along with graceful cypress and tall cedar, often used as poetic images.
Mandrakes	Song 7:13	Dark green, low-growing plant, like lettuce, with purple flower and forked root. Bright red fruit ripens in May and is the size of a small apple.

See also charts on Flowers of the Bible; Vegetables of the Bible; Bitter Herbs of the Bible; Herbs of the Bible.

GEMS AND MINERALS

The rustic lifestyle of the Israelites brought them close to the elements of the earth, to which frequent references are made in the Song.

GEM OR MINERAL	DESCRIPTION
Silver Gold	These precious metals are mentioned together (Song 1:11; 3:10), first spoken by the "daughters of Jerusalem" as the Shulamite anticipated the king's gifts of jewelry to her. Later, in the wedding procession, the description of the royal carriage contained costly supporting framework. Gold was also part of her description of the king's hands and feet (a figure of speech for excellence). Silver was mentioned by her brothers in describing their protection of the Shulamite's purity.
Ivory	This mark of wealth and luxury was procured from the tusks of Syrian elephants, which roamed the upper Euphrates or were imported from India. The bride likened her husband's body to ivory (Song 5:14), and he described her neck similarly (Song 7:4).
Marble	Close-grained crystalline limestone described in the Song was probably white or cream-colored, possibly veined in red or green, and imported from locations near the Gulf of Suez and in southern Greece. It was used for fine statuary, which, no doubt, prompted the Shulamite to describe the legs of her beloved as "pillars of marble" (Song 5:15).
Sapphires Jewels	In their mutual descriptions of each other, the lovers employed extravagant imagery. Sapphires, which are identified by some as lapis lazuli, might have been encrusted on the royal girdle (Song 5:14). His reference to jewels in the description of her thigh (Song 7:1) is linked by scholars to movement, literally, "twisting and winding of the upper part of the body by means of the thigh-joint." Beryl, a chrysolite found in ancient Spain, adorned the royal hands (Songs 5:14).

See also note on Jewelry (Ex. 28)

Isaiah

AUTHOR

Critical scholars in the eighteenth century began questioning the unity of Isaiah with arguments that are impressive to some. Traditionally, however, authorship of the Book of Isaiah has been ascribed to the eighth century B.C. prophet bearing that name. Reasons for maintaining this position include:

- An understanding of the superscription as applicable to the entire book (Is. 1:1);
- The marks of Isaiah's style throughout the book (such as his use of "the Holy One of Israel");
- The New Testament references affirming Isaianic authorship (Matt. 3:3; Luke 3:4; John 1:23; Acts 8:28; Rom. 10:16–20);
- The testimony of Jesus (Matt. 8:17; 12:17; Luke 4:17; John 12:38).

Isaiah (lit. *"Yahweh* saves" or *"Yahweh* is salvation") preached God's message to the southern kingdom of Judah during the latter half of the eighth century B.C. Isaiah was the son of Amoz (Is. 1:1), not to be confused with the eighth century B.C. prophet Amos. Isaiah married a woman called "the prophetess," who bore him two sons (Is. 8:3).

Isaiah's two sons received names that bore a direct connection to his ministry and functioned as walking sermons to the people of Judah. Maher-Shalal-Hash-Baz (Heb., lit. "the spoil speeds, the prey hastens" or "speeding to the spoil, hastening to the prey") bore in his name the message of judgment (Is. 8:3, 4). God would judge His people Judah because of their sin (Is. 1:2–4). The name Shear-Jashub (Heb., lit. "a remnant will return") carried a message of judgment in Isaiah's early ministry but later became a message of hope with the assurance that a remnant of the people would survive God's judgment (Is. 7:3). Tradition indicates that Isaiah was martyred by being sawn in two during the reign of the wicked king Manasseh (see Heb. 11:37).

DATE

Isaiah delivered God's message to the people of Judah during the reigns of Uzziah, Jotham, Ahaz, and Hezekiah (Is. 1:1). He served as adviser to these kings of Judah. Isaiah's ministry generally has been dated between approximately 740 and 700 B.C. His prophetic activity focused around three major crises in Judah's history.

- *The Syro-Ephraimitic Crisis* (734 B.C.). Rezin, king of Syria, and Pekah, king of Ephraim or Israel, joined forces against Assyria. They wanted King Ahaz of Judah to join with them. Isaiah counseled Judah not to join the coalition but rather to have faith in the Lord (see Is. 7). Although Judah did not join, Ahaz appealed to Assyria for help and protection. The Assyrians conquered Damascus, the capital of Syria, in 732 B.C. Ephraim, alternately known as Israel, Samaria, or the northern kingdom, fell to the Assyrians in 722 B.C. (see chart, The Terminology for the Divided Kingdom).

- *The Ashdod Rebellion* (714–711 B.C.). The ruler of the Philistine city of Ashdod led the Philistines to revolt against Assyria. He was assisted by the Egyptians. The five major Philistine cities, located near the coast in the southwestern part of Canaan, were Ashdod, Ashkelon, Gaza, Ekron, and Gath. The Philistines provided a major threat to Israel from the time of Israel's initial settlement in the Land. Isaiah bitterly opposed any participation on the part of Judah in this rebellion (see Is. 20:1–6).
- *The Sennacherib Crisis* (701 B.C.). King Hezekiah of Judah revolted against Sennacherib (705–681 B.C.), king of Assyria, who came to Judah and besieged Jerusalem. As in every crisis, Isaiah counseled faith in the Lord. He prophesied that God would deliver the city from the hands of the Assyrians. The Lord fulfilled His promise. The "angel of the LORD" killed 185,000 Assyrians, and Sennacherib returned home to Nineveh (see 2 Kin. 18—19 and Is. 36—37). Because of this experience, God's people came to believe that Jerusalem could never be destroyed.

BACKGROUND

SETTING: The setting of chapters 1—39 is in and around Jerusalem. The content of chapters 40—66 reflects the Exile in Babylon and beyond.

PURPOSE: The Book of Isaiah has several key messages the Lord's people needed to hear. Much of Isaiah's teaching comes out of his initial calling (see Is. 6).

- *The Lord is the sovereign God* (Is. 6:1). He is the only God. No other gods exist. The technical term for this teaching is monotheism, the belief that only one God exists (see Is. 45:14–25).
- *God is holy.* He is separate from man. He is perfect moral purity (Is. 6:3). "The Holy One of Israel," one of Isaiah's favorite designations for God, appears repeatedly throughout the Book of Isaiah (see Is. 5:19, 24; 10:20; 12:6; 30:12; 41:14, 20; 43:3; 45:11; 47:4; 49:7; 55:5).
- *The nature of sin is uncleanness* (Is. 6:5), rebellion against God (Is. 1:2); it is universal in scope (Is. 6:5); it is forgiven only by God since sacrifices do not remove sin (Is. 6:6, 7).
- *Faith in the Lord* is the essential need of everyone (Is. 7:9).
- *God preserves a remnant* of His people (Is. 6:13).
- *The Messiah is identified* as a kingly figure who reigns in righteousness (see Is. 1—39, especially Is. 7; 9; 11; 32). The Messiah is also identified as the Suffering Servant who suffers not for any wrong He has done but on behalf of others (Is. 40—66; see 42:1–4; 49:1–6; 50:4–9; 52:13—53:12).

AUDIENCE: Isaiah addressed God's people in Judah in the eighth century B.C. He pronounced judgment on the inhabitants of Judah, not because they lacked religious activity but because they failed in moral and ethical living (see Is. 1:16, 17). Isaiah also had a message of future comfort and hope for the exiles in Babylon.

LITERARY CHARACTERISTICS: The Book of Isaiah consists of historical narratives (see Is. 36—39) and prophetic pronouncements or oracles against Judah and Jerusalem (Is. 1—12), as well as oracles against foreign nations (Is. 13—23). Much of Isaiah appears in poetic rather than narrative form. Hebrew poetry is characterized by rhythm rather than by rhyme.

THEMES

The primary theme of Isaiah 1—39 is a message of judgment on the Lord's people. The main theme of Isaiah 40—66 is a message of comfort and hope (see also Purpose).

1 The vision of Isaiah the son of Amoz, which he saw concerning Judah and Jerusalem in the days of Uzziah, Jotham, Ahaz, *and* Hezekiah, kings of Judah.

The Wickedness of Judah

²Hear, O heavens, and give ear, O earth!
For the LORD has spoken:
"I have nourished and brought up children,
And they have rebelled against Me;
³The ox knows its owner
And the donkey its master's crib;
But Israel does not know,
My people do not consider."

⁴Alas, sinful nation,
A people laden with iniquity,
A brood of evildoers,
Children who are corrupters!
They have forsaken the LORD,
They have provoked to anger
The Holy One of Israel,
They have turned away backward.

⁵Why should you be stricken again?
You will revolt more and more.

The whole head is sick,
And the whole heart faints.
⁶From the sole of the foot even to the head,
There is no soundness in it,
But wounds and bruises and putrefying sores;
They have not been closed or bound up,
Or soothed with ointment.

⁷Your country *is* desolate,
Your cities *are* burned with fire;
Strangers devour your land in your presence;
And *it is* desolate, as overthrown by strangers.
⁸So the daughter of Zion is left as a booth in a vineyard,
As a hut in a garden of cucumbers,
As a besieged city.
⁹Unless the LORD of hosts
Had left to us a very small remnant,
We would have become like Sodom,
We would have been made like Gomorrah.

¹⁰Hear the word of the LORD,
You rulers of Sodom;
Give ear to the law of our God,
You people of Gomorrah:

1:1 For the identity of the prophet, see Introduction: Author; chart, Women in the Minor Prophets.

1:2, 3 God's people lacked the sense that even domestic animals possess. The ox and donkey know their masters, but God's people did not recognize Him as their Creator. "Know" indicates intimate, personal relationship. God's children had rebelled against the One who created and sustained them. "Israel" probably designated Judah, the southern kingdom (v. 3; see chart, The Terminology for the Divided Kingdom). At the conclusion of Solomon's reign in 931 B.C., the kingdom split between the northern ten tribes designated "Israel" and two southern tribes called "Judah." "Rebelled" suggests deliberate revolt (v. 2).

1:4–9 Isaiah pictured God's people as weighted down with their sin or "iniquity" (lit. "moral crookedness" or "perversion," v. 4). Again deliberate action is indicated. God's children had forsaken Him instead of turning toward Him in repentance. "The Holy One of Israel" was one of Isaiah's favorite designations for God (v. 4; see chart, The Names of

God). This title appears repeatedly throughout the Book of Isaiah (Is. 5:19, 24; 10:20; 12:6; 30:12; 41:14, 20; 43:3; 45:11; 47:4; 49:7; 55:5). As the Great Physician, the Lord diagnosed the nation's illness (Is. 1:5–8). Yet the people refused to turn to Him for healing. The few remaining survivors demonstrated God's grace (v. 9). For Sodom and Gomorrah, see verses 10–17, note.

1:10–17 True religion has both an inward and an outward dimension. "Rulers of Sodom" and "people of Gomorrah" are figurative designations for the leaders and inhabitants of Judah, indicating that the nation's sin was as great as that of Sodom and Gomorrah, two cities on which the Lord rained brimstone and fire in Abraham's time (v. 10; see Gen. 19:24). The Lord had rejected the sacrifices and the religious observances of His people (Is. 1:11–15). The sacrifices are described as "futile" or "worthless" because the people were not living by the moral and ethical demands of their covenant relationship with the Lord (v. 13). The essence of real religion would be to live in moral and ethical purity and to meet the needs of the helpless in society (vv. 16, 17).

11"To what purpose *is* the multitude of your
　　sacrifices to Me?"
Says the LORD.
"I have had enough of burnt offerings of
　　rams
And the fat of fed cattle.
I do not delight in the blood of bulls,
Or of lambs or goats.

12"When you come to appear before Me,
　　Who has required this from your hand,
　　To trample My courts?
13Bring no more futile sacrifices;
Incense is an abomination to Me.
The New Moons, the Sabbaths, and the calling
　　of assemblies—
I cannot endure iniquity and the sacred
　　meeting.
14Your New Moons and your appointed feasts
My soul hates;
They are a trouble to Me,
I am weary of bearing *them.*
15When you spread out your hands,
I will hide My eyes from you;
Even though you make many prayers,
I will not hear.
Your hands are full of blood.

16"Wash yourselves, make yourselves clean;
Put away the evil of your doings from before
　　My eyes.
Cease to do evil,
17Learn to do good;
Seek justice,
Rebuke the oppressor;[a]
Defend the fatherless,
Plead for the widow.

18"Come now, and let us reason together,"
Says the LORD,
"Though your sins are like scarlet,
They shall be as white as snow;
Though they are red like crimson,
They shall be as wool.
19If you are willing and obedient,
You shall eat the good of the land;
20But if you refuse and rebel,
You shall be devoured by the sword";
For the mouth of the LORD has spoken.

The Degenerate City

21How the faithful city has become a harlot!
It was full of justice;
Righteousness lodged in it,
But now murderers.
22Your silver has become dross,
Your wine mixed with water.
23Your princes *are* rebellious,
And companions of thieves;
Everyone loves bribes,
And follows after rewards.
They do not defend the fatherless,
Nor does the cause of the widow come before
　　them.

24Therefore the Lord says,
The LORD of hosts, the Mighty One of
　　Israel,
"Ah, I will rid Myself of My adversaries,
And take vengeance on My enemies.
25I will turn My hand against you,
And thoroughly purge away your dross,
And take away all your alloy.
26I will restore your judges as at the first,
And your counselors as at the beginning.
Afterward you shall be called the city of
　　righteousness, the faithful city."

27Zion shall be redeemed with justice,
And her penitents with righteousness.
28The destruction of transgressors and of
　　sinners *shall be* together,
And those who forsake the LORD shall be
　　consumed.
29For they[a] shall be ashamed of the terebinth
　　trees
Which you have desired;
And you shall be embarrassed because of the
　　gardens
Which you have chosen.
30For you shall be as a terebinth whose leaf
　　fades,
And as a garden that has no water.
31The strong shall be as tinder,
And the work of it as a spark;

····························

1:17 [a]Some ancient versions read *the oppressed.* 1:29 [a]Following
Masoretic Text, Septuagint, and Vulgate; some Hebrew manuscripts
and Targum read *you.*

1:18–20 Let us reason together is a legal term. A play on the
verb "to eat" is clearly evident in the Hebrew text (vv. 19, 20).
If the people obeyed, they would "eat the good of the land"
(v. 19). But if they rebelled, they would be eaten or "devoured" by the sword (v. 20).

1:21–26 This lament over Jerusalem appears in the *Qinah* meter, a Hebrew poetic device used to express lamentation
(v. 21). The prophet pictured the funeral of Jerusalem

(vv. 21–23). The faithful city of God had become an unfaithful
harlot. Righteousness and justice had been replaced with
murder, impurity, and bribery. The inhabitants had failed in
moral, ethical, and social dimensions. The defenseless members of society, the fatherless and the widows, suffered because of the city's wickedness (see also James 1:27). Because
of Jerusalem's wickedness, God would bring a purifying judgment on her inhabitants (Is. 1:24–26). Then Jerusalem would
again be a faithful city (v. 26).

Both will burn together,
And no one shall quench *them*.

The Future House of God

2 The word that Isaiah the son of Amoz saw concerning Judah and Jerusalem.

[2] Now it shall come to pass in the latter days
That the mountain of the LORD's house
Shall be established on the top of the
    mountains,
And shall be exalted above the hills;
And all nations shall flow to it.
[3] Many people shall come and say,
"Come, and let us go up to the mountain of the
    LORD,
To the house of the God of Jacob;
He will teach us His ways,
And we shall walk in His paths."
For out of Zion shall go forth the law,
And the word of the LORD from Jerusalem.
[4] He shall judge between the nations,
And rebuke many people;
They shall beat their swords into plowshares,
And their spears into pruning hooks;
Nation shall not lift up sword against nation,
Neither shall they learn war anymore.

The Day of the LORD

[5] O house of Jacob, come and let us walk
In the light of the LORD.

[6] For You have forsaken Your people, the house
    of Jacob,
Because they are filled with eastern ways;
They *are* soothsayers like the Philistines,
And they are pleased with the children of
    foreigners.
[7] Their land is also full of silver and gold,
And there is no end to their treasures;
Their land is also full of horses,
And there is no end to their chariots.
[8] Their land is also full of idols;
They worship the work of their own
    hands,
That which their own fingers have made.
[9] People bow down,
And each man humbles himself;
Therefore do not forgive them.

[10] Enter into the rock, and hide in the dust,
From the terror of the LORD
And the glory of His majesty.
[11] The lofty looks of man shall be humbled,
The haughtiness of men shall be bowed
    down,
And the LORD alone shall be exalted in that
    day.

[12] For the day of the LORD of hosts
Shall come upon everything proud and lofty,
Upon everything lifted up—
And it shall be brought low—
[13] Upon all the cedars of Lebanon *that are* high
    and lifted up,
And upon all the oaks of Bashan;
[14] Upon all the high mountains,
And upon all the hills *that are* lifted up;
[15] Upon every high tower,
And upon every fortified wall;
[16] Upon all the ships of Tarshish,
And upon all the beautiful sloops.
[17] The loftiness of man shall be bowed down,
And the haughtiness of men shall be brought
    low;
The LORD alone will be exalted in that
    day,
[18] But the idols He shall utterly abolish.

[19] They shall go into the holes of the rocks,
And into the caves of the earth,
From the terror of the LORD
And the glory of His majesty,
When He arises to shake the earth mightily.

[20] In that day a man will cast away his idols of
    silver
And his idols of gold,
Which they made, *each* for himself to worship,
To the moles and bats,
[21] To go into the clefts of the rocks,
And into the crags of the rugged rocks,
From the terror of the LORD
And the glory of His majesty,
When He arises to shake the earth mightily.

[22] Sever yourselves from such a man,
Whose breath *is* in his nostrils;
For of what account is he?

2:1–4 Future peace was envisioned "in the latter days" (v. 2). In the messianic age all nations are pictured as supernaturally streaming uphill to Zion, and the Law or teaching of the Lord will be the focus in this time of peace (v. 4). Instruments of war (swords, spears) will become instruments of peace (plowshares, pruning hooks). Compare Micah 4:1–3 for a similar prophecy, and note Joel 3:10 for a reversal of part of this prophecy.

2:5–22 The day of the Lord would hold terror for the disobedient. As a general rule, God's people viewed the day of the Lord as a day of victory for themselves and a day of defeat and judgment for their enemies. The 8th century B.C. prophet Amos, who probably delivered his message prior to Isaiah's ministry, reversed that concept, teaching that the day of the Lord would also be a day of judgment for God's people since they had rebelled against Him (see Amos 5:18–20). Isaiah called the house of Jacob (Israel) to walk in the light of the Lord because the day of the Lord would hold terror for those who rebelled against Him (Is. 2:5).

MODESTY · A MEASURE OF PROPRIETY

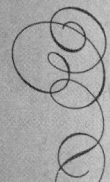

Before their disobedience in the Garden, Adam and Eve "were both naked . . . and were not ashamed," but afterward they were afraid. Their sense of shame and fear is at the core of modesty—the need to cover our bodies. In His grace God provided clothing for the first couple, and ever since, believers who fear God have covered themselves (Gen. 3:21).

The word modesty (Lat. *modus*, lit. "measure") is quantitative in its original meaning. It has come to mean a measure of propriety or humility, characterized by reserve and freedom from excess. In the New Testament, modesty carries the idea of arrangement, not only adornment of dress but also harmony of the inner life. Its biblical meaning is a sensitive withdrawal from anything that is indelicate or impure.

Throughout the Bible, lack of modesty is most often connected with an intent to commit sexual sin. Noah cursed his grandson Canaan because of the immodest actions of his father Ham (Gen. 9:21-25). Isaiah chided the women of Israel for exhibitionism (Is. 3:16). Hosea's allegory of unfaithful marriage contained reference to shameless behavior with a sexual connotation (Hos. 2:5).

Paul's writing in the New Testament refers more specifically to proper dress for believers. He teaches that the Christian should know when the boundaries of decency are being overstepped. Paul assumed in teaching on spiritual gifts and proper decorum in church that certain parts of the body are to be covered (1 Cor. 12:23; 1 Tim. 2:9).

The culture into which she is born and the Christian society in which she lives are factors in judging decency, but ultimately a woman's sense of modesty is to be regulated by her personal relationship with Jesus Christ and His purity.

See also Gen. 3:10, 21; notes on Appearance (2 Cor. 3); Femininity (Ps. 144); Graciousness (Prov. 11); Purity (1 John 3)

Judgment on Judah and Jerusalem

3 For behold, the Lord, the Lord of hosts,
Takes away from Jerusalem and from Judah
The stock and the store,
The whole supply of bread and the whole
supply of water;
[2] The mighty man and the man of war,
The judge and the prophet,
And the diviner and the elder;
[3] The captain of fifty and the honorable man,
The counselor and the skillful artisan,
And the expert enchanter.

[4] "I will give children *to be* their princes,
And babes shall rule over them.
[5] The people will be oppressed,
Every one by another and every one by his
neighbor;
The child will be insolent toward the elder,
And the base toward the honorable."

[6] When a man takes hold of his brother
In the house of his father, *saying,*
"You have clothing;
You be our ruler,

And *let* these ruins *be* under your power,"[a]
[7] In that day he will protest, saying,
"I cannot cure *your* ills,
For in my house *is* neither food nor clothing;
Do not make me a ruler of the people."

[8] For Jerusalem stumbled,
And Judah is fallen,
Because their tongue and their doings
Are against the Lord,
To provoke the eyes of His glory.
[9] The look on their countenance witnesses
against them,
And they declare their sin as Sodom;
They do not hide *it.*
Woe to their soul!
For they have brought evil upon themselves.

[10] "Say to the righteous that *it shall be* well *with
them,*
For they shall eat the fruit of their doings.
[11] Woe to the wicked! *It shall be* ill *with him,*
For the reward of his hands shall be given him.

• • • • • • • • • • • • • • • • •

3:6 [a] Literally *hand*

3:1-15 The Lord is identified as "the Lord of hosts," perhaps signifying His role as Captain of the armies of Judah. He is the One bringing judgment on Jerusalem and Judah (v. 1). Judah cannot escape judgment. The supply of food and water would be exhausted (v. 1); leaders would be lost (vv. 2-12). Judah's leaders had been condemned for living in luxury while oppressing the people (vv. 13-15; compare Is. 1:23). Isaiah, together with the other 8th century B.C. prophets, was especially concerned about social justice. God's judgment came on Judah partly in the form of permitting internal decay.

[12]*As for* My people, children *are* their oppressors,
And women rule over them.
O My people! Those who lead you cause *you* to err,
And destroy the way of your paths."

Oppression and Luxury Condemned

[13]The LORD stands up to plead,
And stands to judge the people.
[14]The LORD will enter into judgment
With the elders of His people
And His princes:
"For you have eaten up the vineyard;
The plunder of the poor *is* in your houses.
[15]What do you mean by crushing My people
And grinding the faces of the poor?"
Says the Lord GOD of hosts.

[16]Moreover the LORD says:

"Because the daughters of Zion are haughty,
And walk with outstretched necks
And wanton eyes,
Walking and mincing *as* they go,
Making a jingling with their feet,
[17]Therefore the Lord will strike with a scab
The crown of the head of the daughters of Zion,
And the LORD will uncover their secret parts."

[18]In that day the Lord will take away the finery:
The jingling anklets, the scarves, and the crescents;
[19]The pendants, the bracelets, and the veils;
[20]The headdresses, the leg ornaments, and the headbands;
The perfume boxes, the charms,
[21]and the rings;
The nose jewels,
[22]the festal apparel, and the mantles;
The outer garments, the purses,

[23]and the mirrors;
The fine linen, the turbans, and the robes.

[24]And so it shall be:

Instead of a sweet smell there will be a stench;
Instead of a sash, a rope;
Instead of well-set hair, baldness;
Instead of a rich robe, a girding of sackcloth;
And branding instead of beauty.
[25]Your men shall fall by the sword,
And your mighty in the war.

[26]Her gates shall lament and mourn,
And she *being* desolate shall sit on the ground.

4 And in that day seven women shall take hold of one man, saying,
"We will eat our own food and wear our own apparel;
Only let us be called by your name,
To take away our reproach."

The Renewal of Zion

[2]In that day the Branch of the LORD shall be beautiful and glorious;
And the fruit of the earth *shall be* excellent and appealing
For those of Israel who have escaped.

[3]And it shall come to pass that *he who is* left in Zion and remains in Jerusalem will be called holy—everyone who is recorded among the living in Jerusalem. [4]When the Lord has washed away the filth of the daughters of Zion, and purged the blood of Jerusalem from her midst, by the spirit of judgment and by the spirit of burning, [5]then the LORD will create above every dwelling place of Mount Zion, and above her assemblies, a cloud and smoke by day and the shining of a flaming fire by night. For over all the glory there *will be* a

---

3:16—4:1 The arrogant women of Jerusalem were judged by Isaiah. Amos had condemned the women of Samaria in the northern kingdom for their greed and oppression of the poor ("cows of Bashan," Amos 4:1–3, note). These prophets realized the importance of the character of women for the well-being of society. The aristocratic women of Jerusalem played a role in the ethical and moral collapse of Judah. They were condemned as vain, immodest, self-indulgent, and full of false pride. They engaged in vulgar and shameful behavior. The judgment on these women matched their sin. They were stripped of their fine garments, beauty, and jewels (Is. 3:18–24). Instead of holding their heads high in pride, they bowed them in shame. Part of their judgment included the fact that much of the male population of Jerusalem would die in battle (Is. 3:25, 26). The number "seven" is not literal but represents a large number of women (Is. 4:1; see chart, The Significance of Numbers in Scripture). Childlessness was viewed as a disgrace or "reproach" (Is. 54:4). The women are so desperate for husbands that they are willing to support

themselves rather than looking to their husbands for support. Moral decay that reaches the women of society can gain a strong foothold in the home, where the most formative influence on the younger generation is found. When moral corruption reaches the home, the nation is headed for disaster.

4:2–6 Isaiah painted a picture of hope on the backdrop of a situation of gloom and despair. "In that day" points toward a time beyond the coming judgment (v. 2). "Branch" may refer to the Messiah or to the righteous remnant who survive the judgment (v. 2). It may also indicate new growth or the fertility of the Land and thus parallel the phrase "the fruit of the earth." This holy (lit. "set apart") remnant would experience not only God's forgiveness but also His care and protection (vv. 5, 6). The cloud by day and the fire by night are reminders of how the Lord guided and protected His people as they journeyed through the wilderness (v. 5; see Ex. 13:21, 22; Num. 9:15–23). Genuine security does not depend on national leaders but is God's gift of His presence to His people (Is. 4:6).

FEMINISM A SOCIAL IDEOLOGY

Feminism is somewhat difficult to define, for the term means different things to different people. Some who call themselves feminists are merely interested in promoting the dignity and worth of women. Others seek to promote a specific socio-political ideology that goes far beyond this. Feminists raise many valid concerns: the verbal and physical abuse of women, the degradation of women through pornography, and the attitude that women are of less worth or value than men.

Feminist philosophers propose that the solution to these problems lies in women's claiming the right to "name" or decree meaning for themselves. They encourage women to decide who they are, what the world should be like, or who or what God is. Scripture stands against this solution. The Bible teaches that God—and God alone—has the right to define these things. God made the earth and created man and woman, and He has determined who they are and how they should live (Is. 45:10–13; Rom. 9:20, 21).

Women are made in the image of God (Gen. 1:27); therefore, they ought to be treated with the same dignity and respect as men. The Bible does describe, however, basic differences between men and women that are to be honored as part of God's design (1 Cor. 11:3–16). The Bible does not support the degradation or abuse of women. At the same time, it does not support the right of women (or men) to put themselves above God's plan and do as they please. Christians need to respond to the real problems that feminists identify, but they must do so without compromising the plan for male and female that God has revealed in His Word.

See also notes on Biblical Equality (Eph. 5); Femininity (Ps. 144)

covering. ⁶And there will be a tabernacle for shade in the daytime from the heat, for a place of refuge, and for a shelter from storm and rain.

God's Disappointing Vineyard

5 Now let me sing to my Well-beloved
A song of my Beloved regarding His vineyard:

My Well-beloved has a vineyard
On a very fruitful hill.
²He dug it up and cleared out its stones,
And planted it with the choicest vine.
He built a tower in its midst,
And also made a winepress in it;
So He expected *it* to bring forth *good* grapes,
But it brought forth wild grapes.

³"And now, O inhabitants of Jerusalem and men of Judah,
Judge, please, between Me and My vineyard.
⁴What more could have been done to My vineyard
That I have not done in it?
Why then, when I expected *it* to bring forth *good* grapes,

Did it bring forth wild grapes?
⁵And now, please let Me tell you what I will do to My vineyard:
I will take away its hedge, and it shall be burned;
And break down its wall, and it shall be trampled down.
⁶I will lay it waste;
It shall not be pruned or dug,
But there shall come up briers and thorns.
I will also command the clouds
That they rain no rain on it."

⁷For the vineyard of the LORD of hosts *is* the house of Israel,
And the men of Judah are His pleasant plant.
He looked for justice, but behold, oppression;
For righteousness, but behold, a cry *for help*.

Impending Judgment on Excesses

⁸Woe to those who join house to house;
They add field to field,
Till *there is* no place
Where they may dwell alone in the midst of the land!

5:1, 2 Isaiah's parable of the vineyard, utilizing the form of a love song, may have been sung by the prophet during one of the harvest festivals. A message that might be rejected if delivered in a sermon might be received in a song. "Beloved" is a reference to the owner of the vineyard (v. 1).

5:3–7 The Lord is the vineyard owner. The vineyard represents God's people. God had lavished loving care on His people and expected positive results. He was sorely disappointed. A play on words is evident (v. 7). The words for "justice" (Heb. *mishpat*) and "oppression" (Heb. *mispak*) are similar. The words for "righteousness" (Heb. *tsedaqah*) and "a cry" (Heb.

tse'aqah) are also similar. The technical term for such a word-play is paranomasia. God still looks for justice and righteousness that are exhibited in moral and ethical living from His people.

5:8–25 Woe can carry the idea of a curse, a reproach, or a funeral lament (vv. 8, 11, 18, 20–22). Here the word is used to announce judgment.

5:8–10 This first woe is a condemnation of those greedy for land and wealth. Despite their increased land holdings, production would decrease significantly (vv. 9, 10). God's judgment would strike the object of their greed.

⁹In my hearing the Lord of hosts *said,*
"Truly, many houses shall be desolate,
  Great and beautiful ones, without inhabitant.
¹⁰For ten acres of vineyard shall yield one bath,
  And a homer of seed shall yield one ephah."

¹¹Woe to those who rise early in the morning,
  That they may follow intoxicating drink;
  Who continue until night, *till* wine inflames
    them!
¹²The harp and the strings,
  The tambourine and flute,
  And wine are in their feasts;
  But they do not regard the work of the Lord,
  Nor consider the operation of His hands.

¹³Therefore my people have gone into captivity,
  Because *they have* no knowledge;
  Their honorable men *are* famished,
  And their multitude dried up with thirst.
¹⁴Therefore Sheol has enlarged itself
  And opened its mouth beyond measure;
  Their glory and their multitude and their
    pomp,
  And he who is jubilant, shall descend into it.
¹⁵People shall be brought down,
  Each man shall be humbled,
  And the eyes of the lofty shall be humbled.
¹⁶But the Lord of hosts shall be exalted in
    judgment,
  And God who is holy shall be hallowed in
    righteousness.
¹⁷Then the lambs shall feed in their pasture,
  And in the waste places of the fat ones
    strangers shall eat.

¹⁸Woe to those who draw iniquity with cords of
    vanity,
  And sin as if with a cart rope;
¹⁹That say, "Let Him make speed *and* hasten His
    work,
  That we may see *it;*

And let the counsel of the Holy One of Israel
    draw near and come,
  That we may know *it.*"

²⁰Woe to those who call evil good, and good evil;
  Who put darkness for light, and light for
    darkness;
  Who put bitter for sweet, and sweet for bitter!

²¹Woe to *those who are* wise in their own eyes,
  And prudent in their own sight!

²²Woe to men mighty at drinking wine,
  Woe to men valiant for mixing intoxicating
    drink,
²³Who justify the wicked for a bribe,
  And take away justice from the righteous man!

²⁴Therefore, as the fire devours the stubble,
  And the flame consumes the chaff,
  So their root will be as rottenness,
  And their blossom will ascend like dust;
  Because they have rejected the law of the Lord
    of hosts,
  And despised the word of the Holy One of
    Israel.
²⁵Therefore the anger of the Lord is aroused
    against His people;
  He has stretched out His hand against them
  And stricken them,
  And the hills trembled.
  Their carcasses *were* as refuse in the midst of
    the streets.

For all this His anger is not turned away,
  But His hand *is* stretched out still.

²⁶He will lift up a banner to the nations from
    afar,
  And will whistle to them from the end of the
    earth;
  Surely they shall come with speed, swiftly.

5:11–17 The second woe is upon Judah's drunken inhabitants, who pursue intoxicating drink from dawn to dark. This intoxication even occurred at religious festivals (v. 12). In their drunken stupor, the inhabitants of Judah were not aware that God was at work in their midst, probably a reference to God's work of judgment (v. 12). The wise men of Israel condemned excessive drinking (see Prov. 20, Alcoholism; 21:17; 23:29–35; 31:4, 5). The coming exile of God's people is predicted. *She'ol* (Heb.) refers to the place of the dead (Is. 5:14).

5:18, 19 The third woe is directed toward those who mocked God by continuing in their sin while challenging God to prove Himself to them. They implied that the Lord no longer had power to act. For "The Holy One of Israel," see Isaiah 1:4–9, note.

5:20 The fourth woe encompassed those living in such confusion that they had lost the power of moral discernment. They were no longer able to distinguish between good and evil.

5:21 The fifth woe is aimed at the proud and arrogant who have cut themselves off from God, the source of true wisdom (see James 1:5; 3:17). Claiming to be wise and totally self-sufficient, they were, in reality, fools (see Rom. 1:22).

5:22–25 The sixth woe, iike the second, condemned those who became intoxicated through drink and those who perverted justice by accepting bribes (see vv. 11–17). The guilty went free, while the innocent were condemned.

5:24, 25 Because Judah had rejected the Lord, He had rejected them. These verses may belong only with the sixth woe or may apply to all six woes. Judgment was inevitable. The "law of the Lord" refers to His revelation of His will (v. 24).

5:26–30 The sovereign Lord would command a foreign power to come against Judah. Assyria, though not identified by name in this passage, was that power (see Is. 10:5, 6). The Lord is in control of history and will accomplish His purposes.

ATTRIBUTES OF GOD *HE IS HOLY*

God is not one among many; He is the One and Only (Is. 40:25). The word holy (Heb. *qadosh*) means "unique, set apart, unlike all others."

God's holiness is a powerful study of contrasts. The threefold "holy, holy, holy" of the seraphim expresses the superlative degree. This not only emphatically separates God from sin but also emphasizes His righteousness in contrast to our sinfulness.

Holiness is not what God does but who He is. The Lord swears by His holiness (Amos 4:2), and He swears by Himself (Amos 6:8)—they are the same. All God's attributes flow out of His holiness. That is why He is incapable of the slightest hint of impurity, unrighteousness, untruth, injustice, or questionable use of power (Gen. 18:25).

Two consistent responses spring from those who have seen God's holiness: they thirst for more (see Ex. 33:17–23; Ps. 42:1, 2; Phil. 3:10), and they know with certainty that He is God and they are not (Ps. 100:3).

See also Ps. 99:9; 111:9; Is. 57:15; Lam. 3:22, note; Luke 1:49; Rev. 15:4; notes on Attributes of God (Ex. 33; Deut. 4; 32; 2 Chr. 19; Job 23; 42; Ps. 25; 90; 102; 119; Is. 65; Jer. 23; Rom. 2; Eph. 1; 1 John 5); Holiness (Lev. 20); Praise (Ps. 149); Worship (Deut. 12).

²⁷No one will be weary or stumble among
    them,
No one will slumber or sleep;
Nor will the belt on their loins be loosed,
Nor the strap of their sandals be broken;
²⁸Whose arrows *are* sharp,
And all their bows bent;
Their horses' hooves will seem like flint,
And their wheels like a whirlwind.
²⁹Their roaring *will be* like a lion,
They will roar like young lions;
Yes, they will roar
And lay hold of the prey;
They will carry *it* away safely,
And no one will deliver.
³⁰In that day they will roar against them
Like the roaring of the sea.
And if *one* looks to the land,
Behold, darkness *and* sorrow;
And the light is darkened by the clouds.

Isaiah Called to Be a Prophet

6 In the year that King Uzziah died, I saw the Lord sitting on a throne, high and lifted up, and the train of His *robe* filled the temple. ²Above it stood seraphim; each one had six wings: with two he covered his face, with two he covered his feet, and with two he flew. ³And one cried to another and said:

"Holy, holy, holy *is* the Lord of hosts;
    The whole earth *is* full of His glory!"

⁴And the posts of the door were shaken by the voice of him who cried out, and the house was filled with smoke.

⁵So I said:

"Woe *is* me, for I am undone!
Because I *am* a man of unclean lips,
And I dwell in the midst of a people of unclean
    lips;
For my eyes have seen the King,
The Lord of hosts."

⁶Then one of the seraphim flew to me, having in his hand a live coal *which* he had taken with the tongs from the altar. ⁷And he touched my mouth *with it,* and said:

"Behold, this has touched your lips;
Your iniquity is taken away,
And your sin purged."

⁸Also I heard the voice of the Lord, saying:

"Whom shall I send,
And who will go for Us?"

6:1–4 The seraphim, who guarded God's holiness, were fiery creatures with six wings (v. 2). With two wings the seraphim covered their faces, indicating reverence, and with two wings they covered their feet, depicting modesty or humility. With the other two wings the creatures flew, demonstrating their readiness for service. The seraphim focused on the holiness of God (v. 3).

6:5 Humility, not pride, should result from any genuine experience with the Lord. Isaiah viewed sin as uncleanness (v. 5), one of his key teachings about sin. Sin is also rebellion (Is. 1:2).

A focus on the tools for speech occurred in this encounter with God, pointing to the nature of Isaiah's ministry as a spokesman for God.

6:6, 7 The fiery seraph (singular form of seraphim) touched the live coal directly to Isaiah's mouth in a symbolic act of forgiveness. This action suggests that no painless cure exists for sin. Nevertheless, forgiveness came from God, not from the burning coal. Only God can forgive sin.

6:8 Isaiah responded out of gratitude for what the Lord had done for him. Moses made several excuses when God called

Then I said, "Here *am* I! Send me."
[9]And He said, "Go, and tell this people:

'Keep on hearing, but do not understand;
Keep on seeing, but do not perceive.'

[10]"Make the heart of this people dull,
And their ears heavy,
And shut their eyes;
Lest they see with their eyes,
And hear with their ears,
And understand with their heart,
And return and be healed."

[11]Then I said, "Lord, how long?"
And He answered:

"Until the cities are laid waste and without
  inhabitant,
The houses are without a man,
The land is utterly desolate,
[12]The LORD has removed men far away,
And the forsaken places *are* many in the midst
  of the land.
[13]But yet a tenth *will be* in it,
And will return and be for consuming,
As a terebinth tree or as an oak,
Whose stump *remains* when it is cut down.
So the holy seed *shall be* its stump."

Isaiah Sent to King Ahaz

7 Now it came to pass in the days of Ahaz the son of Jotham, the son of Uzziah, king of Judah, *that* Rezin king of Syria and Pekah the son of Remaliah, king of Israel, went up to Jerusalem to *make* war against it, but could not prevail against it. [2]And it was told to the house of David, saying, "Syria's forces are deployed in Ephraim." So his heart and the heart of his people were moved as the trees of the woods are moved with the wind.

[3]Then the LORD said to Isaiah, "Go out now to meet Ahaz, you and Shear-Jashub[a] your son, at the end of the aqueduct from the upper pool, on the highway to the Fuller's Field, [4]and say to him: 'Take heed, and be quiet; do not fear or be faint-hearted for these two stubs of smoking firebrands, for the fierce anger of Rezin and Syria, and the son of Remaliah. [5]Because Syria, Ephraim, and the son of Remaliah have plotted evil against you, saying, [6]"Let us go up against Judah and trouble it, and let us make a gap in its wall for ourselves, and set a king over them, the son of Tabel"— [7]thus says the Lord GOD:

"It shall not stand,
  Nor shall it come to pass.
[8]For the head of Syria *is* Damascus,
  And the head of Damascus *is* Rezin.
Within sixty-five years Ephraim will be broken,
  So that it will not *be* a people.
[9]The head of Ephraim *is* Samaria,
  And the head of Samaria *is* Remaliah's son.
If you will not believe,
  Surely you shall not be established." ' "

The Immanuel Prophecy

[10]Moreover the LORD spoke again to Ahaz, saying, [11]"Ask a sign for yourself from the LORD your God; ask it either in the depth or in the height above."

[12]But Ahaz said, "I will not ask, nor will I test the LORD!"

7:3 [a]Literally *A Remnant Shall Return*

---

him because he did not really want to do the task God was calling him to do (see Ex. 3; 4). Jeremiah claimed that he was only a youth and could not speak well when he heard God call (Jer. 1:6). In contrast, Isaiah willingly volunteered to meet the need that the Lord had revealed to him.

6:11–13 Isaiah questioned how long he would be required to continue this difficult ministry. The Lord's answer indicated that Isaiah was to preach until the destruction came and the northern kingdom of Israel fell under Assyrian domination in 722 B.C. (vv. 11, 12). Although the destruction would be extensive, a remnant would survive (v. 13). Early in Isaiah's ministry, the teaching about the remnant singularly emphasized judgment. After the judgment, Isaiah's teaching about the remnant became a message of hope. The Lord's people would not be destroyed totally. A remnant would be spared.

7:1–9 The Syro-Ephraimitic Crisis occurred around 735 or 734 B.C. Syro refers to Syria, while Ephraimitic refers to the northern kingdom or Israel, sometimes designated Ephraim (see chart, The Terminology for the Divided Kingdom). Ahaz was king of Judah at this time. Rezin, king of Syria, and Pekah, king of Israel, formed a coalition against Assyria. They wanted Judah to join with them and she refused. Rezin and Pekah planned to force Judah to join with them by waging war against Judah. Through His prophet Isaiah, the Lord told Ahaz not to be afraid of Rezin or Pekah (vv. 3–8). In this instance (as was true in every crisis the nation faced), Isaiah counseled the people and leaders to have faith in the Lord. God was in control. A play on words appears in the latter part of verse 9. The Hebrew words translated "believe" and "be established" come from the same root word transliterated "amen." God's people must place their faith in Him, not in political alliances. Although Judah did not join the alliance, Ahaz appealed to Assyria for help, looking to men instead of to the Lord for assistance. Judah suffered as a result of Ahaz's foolish decision. Damascus, the capital of Syria, fell in 732 B.C. Samaria, the capital of the northern kingdom or Israel, fell in 722 B.C. (see 2 Kin. 16).

7:10–17 The Lord told Ahaz to request a sign, but he piously refused, implying that asking for a sign would be putting God to a test wrongly. The offer of a sign was linked with a word from God, and Ahaz did not want to hear God's message. His refusal to ask for a sign indicated his lack of faith in the Lord. The Lord gave Ahaz a sign anyway (vv. 14–16). This sign had a double significance—a special meaning for Isaiah's time but also a looking toward the future birth of the Messiah.

THE VIRGIN BIRTH *A MIRACLE OF THE SPIRIT*

A virgin is one who has not engaged in sexual intercourse. The "virgin birth" describes the birth of the Savior, who was conceived in the womb of the young virgin Mary through the miraculous work of the Holy Spirit and without the presence of an earthly father. God chose this mystery, which is beyond human understanding, to bring His Son into the world (Matt. 1:18; Luke 1:34, 35).

Belief in the virgin birth is foundational to the Christian faith because this affirms and guarantees the perfect union of the human and divine in Jesus, the God-Man (Is. 9:6, 7); this identifies Jesus as the "New Adam" (Rom. 5:14, 15); this enables Jesus in His sinless nature as the Son of God and His perfect obedience as the Son of Man to meet the requirements for redemption (Heb. 2:17; 1 John 2:1, 2; 4:9, 10).

Being misunderstood is always painful, particularly when all the circumstantial evidence stacks up against you. Young, unmarried, and pregnant in a society that highly valued sexual purity and virginity, Mary surely was among the most misunderstood of women.

Mary's response to the angel's announcement to her must be seen in light of this tremendously high personal cost (Luke 1:38). She made a monumental declaration of faith. God asked Mary to bear the shame of pregnancy out of wedlock with only the knowledge of the truth as her strength—the truth that she was in fact a virgin despite all appearances. Mary accepted God's Word that by His power alone the Holy Child would be planted inside her body, receiving Him in faith and giving witness to His presence.

See also notes on Childbirth (John 16); Christology (Gal. 4); Obedience (Philem.); Submission (1 Pet. 3); Testing (Ps. 12)

---

[13]Then he said, "Hear now, O house of David! *Is it* a small thing for you to weary men, but will you weary my God also? [14]Therefore the Lord Himself will give you a sign: Behold, the virgin shall conceive and bear a Son, and shall call His name Immanuel.[a] [15]Curds and honey He shall eat, that He may know to refuse the evil and choose the good. [16]For before the Child shall know to refuse the evil and choose the good, the land that you dread will be forsaken by both her kings. [17]The LORD will bring the king of Assyria upon you and your people and your father's house—days that have not come since the day that Ephraim departed from Judah."

[18]And it shall come to pass in that day
That the LORD will whistle for the fly
That *is* in the farthest part of the rivers of
Egypt,
And for the bee that *is* in the land of Assyria.
[19]They will come, and all of them will rest
In the desolate valleys and in the clefts of the
rocks,
And on all thorns and in all pastures.

[20]In the same day the Lord will shave with a
hired razor,
With those from beyond the River,[a] with the
king of Assyria,
The head and the hair of the legs,
And will also remove the beard.

[21]It shall be in that day
That a man will keep alive a young cow and two
sheep;
[22]So it shall be, from the abundance of milk they
give,
That he will eat curds;
For curds and honey everyone will eat who is
left in the land.

[23]It shall happen in that day,
That wherever there could be a thousand
vines
Worth a thousand *shekels* of silver,
It will be for briers and thorns.
[24]With arrows and bows men will come there,

7:14 [a]Literally *God-With-Us*   **7:20** [a]That is, the Euphrates

---

7:14 Two Hebrew words can be translated virgin. *'Almah* (Heb.) is the more general term, designating a young woman of marriageable age. *Bethulah* (Heb.) is a very specific word for "virgin," though not used exclusively in this way. However, in all its OT usages, the word can be, though does not have to be, translated in this way. Isaiah's use of *'almah* indicates a double fulfillment of this prophecy. Isaiah's son Shear-Jashub was a sign to Ahaz (vv. 3, 4) and the child Immanuel (Heb., lit. "God with us") was a sign to the whole world (vv. 14–16). The emphasis fell on the promise of God's presence in times of crisis. This promise ultimately was fulfilled in Christ (Matt. 1:22, 23).

7:18–25 Because of their lack of faith, judgment was coming on Judah. Isaiah described the devastation of the Land that would result from Ahaz's unwise policy. Four times in this brief passage reference is made to "that day" as the day of judgment (vv. 18, 20, 21, 23). The enemies of Judah are pictured metaphorically as swarming flies, stinging bees, and a hired razor. Disgrace, devastation, and despair would accompany Judah's defeat. The sovereign Lord would be in control of this judgment on His people (vv. 18, 20).

Because all the land will become briers and
　　thorns.

²⁵And to any hill which could be dug with the
　　hoe,
You will not go there for fear of briers and
　　thorns;
But it will become a range for oxen
And a place for sheep to roam.

Assyria Will Invade the Land

8 Moreover the LORD said to me, "Take a large
scroll, and write on it with a man's pen concerning Maher-Shalal-Hash-Baz.ª ²And I will take for
Myself faithful witnesses to record, Uriah the
priest and Zechariah the son of Jeberechiah."
　³Then I went to the prophetess, and she conceived and bore a son. Then the LORD said to me,
"Call his name Maher-Shalal-Hash-Baz; ⁴for before
the child shall have knowledge to cry 'My father'
and 'My mother,' the riches of Damascus and the
spoil of Samaria will be taken away before the
king of Assyria."
　⁵The LORD also spoke to me again, saying:

⁶"Inasmuch as these people refused
　　The waters of Shiloah that flow softly,
　　And rejoice in Rezin and in Remaliah's son;
⁷Now therefore, behold, the Lord brings up
　　over them
　　The waters of the River,ª strong and mighty—
　　The king of Assyria and all his glory;
　　He will go up over all his channels
　　And go over all his banks.
⁸He will pass through Judah,
　　He will overflow and pass over,
　　He will reach up to the neck;
　　And the stretching out of his wings
　　Will fill the breadth of Your land,
　　　O Immanuel.ª

⁹"Be shattered, O you peoples, and be broken in
　　pieces!
　　Give ear, all you from far countries.
　　Gird yourselves, but be broken in pieces;
　　Gird yourselves, but be broken in pieces.
¹⁰Take counsel together, but it will come to
　　nothing;

Speak the word, but it will not stand,
For God is with us."ª

Fear God, Heed His Word

¹¹For the LORD spoke thus to me with a strong
hand, and instructed me that I should not walk in
the way of this people, saying:

¹²"Do not say, 'A conspiracy,'
　　Concerning all that this people call a
　　　conspiracy,
　　Nor be afraid of their threats, nor be troubled.
¹³The LORD of hosts, Him you shall hallow;
　　Let Him be your fear,
　　And let Him be your dread.
¹⁴He will be as a sanctuary,
　　But a stone of stumbling and a rock of offense
　　To both the houses of Israel,
　　As a trap and a snare to the inhabitants of Jerusalem.
¹⁵And many among them shall stumble;
　　They shall fall and be broken,
　　Be snared and taken."

¹⁶Bind up the testimony,
　　Seal the law among my disciples.
¹⁷And I will wait on the LORD,
　　Who hides His face from the house of Jacob;
　　And I will hope in Him.
¹⁸Here am I and the children whom the LORD has
　　given me!
　　We are for signs and wonders in Israel
　　From the LORD of hosts,
　　Who dwells in Mount Zion.

¹⁹And when they say to you, "Seek those who
are mediums and wizards, who whisper and mutter," should not a people seek their God? Should
they seek the dead on behalf of the living? ²⁰To the
law and to the testimony! If they do not speak according to this word, it is because there is no light
in them.
　²¹They will pass through it hard-pressed and
hungry; and it shall happen, when they are hungry, that they will be enraged and curse their king

8:1 ªLiterally Speed the Spoil, Hasten the Booty　8:7 ªThat is, the
Euphrates　8:8 ªLiterally God-With-Us　8:10 ªHebrew Immanuel

8:1–4 Isaiah's wife is identified as the prophetess (v. 3),
though no reason for this designation is specifically given in
the text. She may have been thus identified because she was
the wife of a prophet or because she, as the mother of children bearing prophetic names, was involved in delivering
God's message. The latter seems less likely since there is no
additional textual evidence to affirm that. Isaiah's son Maher-
Shalal-Hash-Baz (lit. "speeding to the spoil" or "hastening to
the prey") functioned as a walking sermon to indicate that
judgment was coming. The name sounds a note of judgment.
Prophecy was fulfilled in 732 B.C. when Damascus, the capital

of Syria, fell to the Assyrians and in 722 B.C. when Samaria,
the capital of Israel, was conquered by Assyria (v. 4).

**8:11–15 God is described as either a sanctuary or a stumbling
stone** (v. 14). To those who reverently feared Him, He would
be a sanctuary. To those who feared men and rejected the
Lord, He would be a stumbling stone, a trap, and a snare.
Every woman has a choice regarding how she will respond to
God's revelation, but each is responsible for the consequences
of her choice. Without faith, no victory is possible.

and their God, and look upward. ²²Then they will look to the earth, and see trouble and darkness, gloom of anguish; and *they will be* driven into darkness.

The Government of the Promised Son

9 Nevertheless the gloom *will* not *be* upon her who *is* distressed,
As when at first He lightly esteemed
The land of Zebulun and the land of Naphtali,
And afterward more heavily oppressed *her,*
By the way of the sea, beyond the Jordan,
In Galilee of the Gentiles.
²The people who walked in darkness
Have seen a great light;
Those who dwelt in the land of the shadow of death,
Upon them a light has shined.

³You have multiplied the nation
And increased its joy;ᵃ
They rejoice before You
According to the joy of harvest,
As *men* rejoice when they divide the spoil.
⁴For You have broken the yoke of his burden
And the staff of his shoulder,
The rod of his oppressor,
As in the day of Midian.
⁵For every warrior's sandal from the noisy battle,
And garments rolled in blood,
Will be used for burning *and* fuel of fire.

⁶For unto us a Child is born,
Unto us a Son is given;
And the government will be upon His shoulder.
And His name will be called
Wonderful, Counselor, Mighty God,
Everlasting Father, Prince of Peace.
⁷Of the increase of *His* government and peace
There will be no end,
Upon the throne of David and over His kingdom,

To order it and establish it with judgment and justice
From that time forward, even forever.
The zeal of the Lord of hosts will perform this.

The Punishment of Samaria

⁸The Lord sent a word against Jacob,
And it has fallen on Israel.
⁹All the people will know—
Ephraim and the inhabitant of Samaria—
Who say in pride and arrogance of heart:
¹⁰"The bricks have fallen down,
But we will rebuild with hewn stones;
The sycamores are cut down,
But we will replace *them* with cedars."
¹¹Therefore the LORD shall set up
The adversaries of Rezin against him,
And spur his enemies on,
¹²The Syrians before and the Philistines behind;
And they shall devour Israel with an open mouth.

For all this His anger is not turned away,
But His hand *is* stretched out still.

¹³For the people do not turn to Him who strikes them,
Nor do they seek the LORD of hosts.
¹⁴Therefore the LORD will cut off head and tail from Israel,
Palm branch and bulrush in one day.
¹⁵The elder and honorable, he *is* the head;
The prophet who teaches lies, he *is* the tail.
¹⁶For the leaders of this people cause *them* to err,
And *those who are* led by them are destroyed.
¹⁷Therefore the Lord will have no joy in their young men,
Nor have mercy on their fatherless and widows;

•••••••••••••••••••••••••

9:3 ᵃFollowing Qere and Targum; Kethib and Vulgate read *not increased joy;* Septuagint reads *Most of the people You brought down in Your joy.*

9:1–5 The lands of Zebulun and Naphtali in northern Galilee had suffered greatly at the hands of the Assyrians who had annexed these two areas around 732 B.C. The joy of deliverance is portrayed in imagery of harvest and of military victory in this song of thanksgiving to celebrate God's action on behalf of His people (vv. 3–5). The "day of Midian" recalled the story of Gideon's defeat of the Midianites through only a small army of men (v. 4; see Judg. 6—8). In the same way, God would bring a mighty victory to His people despite their weakness and helplessness. Clearly no king of Judah ever fulfilled these hopes.

9:6, 7 The messianic King would usher in the ideal age of peace (v. 5). Four titles describe the Messiah (v. 6): "Wonderful, Counselor" (one with great wisdom and leadership) is actually a single designation; "Mighty God" indicates His deity; "Everlasting Father" describes His unceasingly tender, loving relationship

with His people; and "Prince of Peace" refers to a rich, harmonious life. Most glorious of all, His reign will never end (v. 7).

9:8—10:4 The stretching out of the Lord's hand, a refrain repeated throughout this passage, signifies judgment, not compassion (Is. 9:12, 17, 21; 10:4). Alternate designations for the northern kingdom are suggested: Jacob, Israel, Ephraim, and Samaria (Is. 9:8, 9; see chart, The Terminology of the Divided Kingdom). Even though calamity had come upon the northern kingdom, the inhabitants still maintained their stubborn pride and self-sufficiency (Is. 9:9, 10). As a result, God would impose even harsher discipline upon His people Israel (Is. 9:12; see Ex. 6:6; Jer. 21:5). Isaiah sang a funeral hymn over the dying nation (Is. 10:1–4). God's judgment on Israel had failed to produce a reform movement in Judah.

For everyone *is* a hypocrite and an evildoer,
And every mouth speaks folly.

For all this His anger is not turned away,
But His hand *is* stretched out still.

[18]For wickedness burns as the fire;
It shall devour the briers and thorns,
And kindle in the thickets of the forest;
They shall mount up *like* rising smoke.
[19]Through the wrath of the LORD of hosts
The land is burned up,
And the people shall be as fuel for the fire;
No man shall spare his brother.
[20]And he shall snatch on the right hand
And be hungry;
He shall devour on the left hand
And not be satisfied;
Every man shall eat the flesh of his own arm.
[21]Manasseh *shall devour* Ephraim, and Ephraim
Manasseh;
Together they *shall be* against Judah.

For all this His anger is not turned away,
But His hand *is* stretched out still.

10 "Woe to those who decree unrighteous
decrees,
Who write misfortune,
Which they have prescribed
[2]To rob the needy of justice,
And to take what is right from the poor of My
people,
That widows may be their prey,
And *that* they may rob the fatherless.
[3]What will you do in the day of punishment,
And in the desolation *which* will come from
afar?
To whom will you flee for help?
And where will you leave your glory?
[4]Without Me they shall bow down among the
prisoners,
And they shall fall among the slain."

For all this His anger is not turned away,
But His hand *is* stretched out still.

Arrogant Assyria Also Judged

[5]"Woe to Assyria, the rod of My anger
And the staff in whose hand is My indignation.
[6]I will send him against an ungodly nation,
And against the people of My wrath
I will give him charge,
To seize the spoil, to take the prey,
And to tread them down like the mire of the
streets.

[7]Yet he does not mean so,
Nor does his heart think so;
But *it is* in his heart to destroy,
And cut off not a few nations.
[8]For he says,
'*Are* not my princes altogether kings?
[9]*Is* not Calno like Carchemish?
Is not Hamath like Arpad?
Is not Samaria like Damascus?
[10]As my hand has found the kingdoms of the
idols,
Whose carved images excelled those of Jerusa-
lem and Samaria,
[11]As I have done to Samaria and her idols,
Shall I not do also to Jerusalem and her idols?' "

[12]Therefore it shall come to pass, when the
Lord has performed all His work on Mount Zion
and on Jerusalem, *that He will say*, "I will punish the
fruit of the arrogant heart of the king of Assyria,
and the glory of his haughty looks."
[13]For he says:

"By the strength of my hand I have done *it*,
And by my wisdom, for I am prudent;
Also I have removed the boundaries of the
people,
And have robbed their treasuries;
So I have put down the inhabitants like a
valiant *man*.
[14]My hand has found like a nest the riches of the
people,
And as one gathers eggs *that are* left,
I have gathered all the earth;
And there was no one who moved *his* wing,
Nor opened *his* mouth with even a peep."

[15]Shall the ax boast itself against him who chops
with it?
Or shall the saw exalt itself against him who
saws with it?
As if a rod could wield *itself* against those who
lift it up,
Or as if a staff could lift up, *as if it were* not
wood!
[16]Therefore the Lord, the Lord[a] of hosts,
Will send leanness among his fat ones;
And under his glory
He will kindle a burning
Like the burning of a fire.
[17]So the Light of Israel will be for a fire,
And his Holy One for a flame;
It will burn and devour

• • • • • • • • • • • • • • • •
10:16 [a]Following Bomberg; Masoretic Text and Dead Sea Scrolls read
YHWH (*the* LORD).

10:5–19 **God used Assyria** to judge His people (v. 5). But the
prophet clearly revealed that God would judge Assyria also
(vv. 12–19). Nineveh, the capital of Assyria, fell in 612 B.C. Discipline is an expression of the Lord's love for His people.

His thorns and his briers in one day.

[18]And it will consume the glory of his forest and
of his fruitful field,
Both soul and body;
And they will be as when a sick man wastes
away.
[19]Then the rest of the trees of his forest
Will be so few in number
That a child may write them.

The Returning Remnant of Israel

[20]And it shall come to pass in that day
That the remnant of Israel,
And such as have escaped of the house of Jacob,
Will never again depend on him who defeated
them,
But will depend on the LORD, the Holy One of
Israel, in truth.
[21]The remnant will return, the remnant of Jacob,
To the Mighty God.
[22]For though your people, O Israel, be as the
sand of the sea,
A remnant of them will return;
The destruction decreed shall overflow with
righteousness.
[23]For the Lord GOD of hosts
Will make a determined end
In the midst of all the land.

[24]Therefore thus says the Lord GOD of hosts:
"O My people, who dwell in Zion, do not be afraid
of the Assyrian. He shall strike you with a rod and
lift up his staff against you, in the manner of
Egypt. [25]For yet a very little while and the indignation will cease, as will My anger in their destruction." [26]And the LORD of hosts will stir up a
scourge for him like the slaughter of Midian at
the rock of Oreb; *as* His rod was on the sea, so will
He lift it up in the manner of Egypt.

[27]It shall come to pass in that day
That his burden will be taken away from your
shoulder,
And his yoke from your neck,
And the yoke will be destroyed because of the
anointing oil.

[28]He has come to Aiath,
He has passed Migron;
At Michmash he has attended to his
equipment.
[29]They have gone along the ridge,
They have taken up lodging at Geba.

Ramah is afraid,
Gibeah of Saul has fled.
[30]Lift up your voice,
O daughter of Gallim!
Cause it to be heard as far as Laish—
O poor Anathoth![a]
[31]Madmenah has fled,
The inhabitants of Gebim seek refuge.
[32]As yet he will remain at Nob that day;
He will shake his fist at the mount of the
daughter of Zion,
The hill of Jerusalem.

[33]Behold, the Lord,
The LORD of hosts,
Will lop off the bough with terror;
Those of high stature *will be* hewn down,
And the haughty will be humbled.
[34]He will cut down the thickets of the forest
with iron,
And Lebanon will fall by the Mighty One.

The Reign of Jesse's Offspring

11 There shall come forth a Rod from the
stem of Jesse,
And a Branch shall grow out of his roots.
[2]The Spirit of the LORD shall rest upon Him,
The Spirit of wisdom and understanding,
The Spirit of counsel and might,
The Spirit of knowledge and of the fear of the
LORD.

[3]His delight *is* in the fear of the LORD,
And He shall not judge by the sight of His
eyes,
Nor decide by the hearing of His ears;
[4]But with righteousness He shall judge the
poor,
And decide with equity for the meek of the
earth;
He shall strike the earth with the rod of His
mouth,
And with the breath of His lips He shall slay
the wicked.
[5]Righteousness shall be the belt of His loins,
And faithfulness the belt of His waist.

[6]"The wolf also shall dwell with the lamb,
The leopard shall lie down with the young
goat,

· ·

10:30 [a]Following Masoretic Text, Targum, and Vulgate; Septuagint
and Syriac read *Listen to her, O Anathoth.*

11:1–9 The messianic King is described as a "Rod" or shoot
from the "stem" or stump of Jesse, the father of David from
whom the Messiah would come. The coming Messiah is pictured as a messianic King with the Spirit of the Lord resting
upon Him, possessing wisdom and leadership, and having intimacy with God. "Knowledge" signifies an intimate, personal

relationship (v. 2). "Fear of the Lord" describes reverent obedience, not cringing fear (v. 2). The messianic King would delight in doing the Lord's will (v. 3). He would rule with equity.
The social and ethical aspects of His reign were emphasized.
The Messiah would bring a time of peace with harmony, even
among natural enemies (vv. 6, 7).

The calf and the young lion and the fatling
together;
And a little child shall lead them.
⁷The cow and the bear shall graze;
Their young ones shall lie down together;
And the lion shall eat straw like the ox.
⁸The nursing child shall play by the cobra's
hole,
And the weaned child shall put his hand in the
viper's den.
⁹They shall not hurt nor destroy in all My holy
mountain,
For the earth shall be full of the knowledge of
the LORD
As the waters cover the sea.

¹⁰"And in that day there shall be a Root of Jesse,
Who shall stand as a banner to the people;
For the Gentiles shall seek Him,
And His resting place shall be glorious."

¹¹It shall come to pass in that day
That the Lord shall set His hand again the
second time
To recover the remnant of His people who are
left,
From Assyria and Egypt,
From Pathros and Cush,
From Elam and Shinar,
From Hamath and the islands of the sea.

¹²He will set up a banner for the nations,
And will assemble the outcasts of Israel,
And gather together the dispersed of Judah
From the four corners of the earth.
¹³Also the envy of Ephraim shall depart,
And the adversaries of Judah shall be cut off;
Ephraim shall not envy Judah,
And Judah shall not harass Ephraim.
¹⁴But they shall fly down upon the shoulder of
the Philistines toward the west;
Together they shall plunder the people of the
East;
They shall lay their hand on Edom and Moab;
And the people of Ammon shall obey them.
¹⁵The LORD will utterly destroy[a] the tongue of
the Sea of Egypt;

With His mighty wind He will shake His fist
over the River,[b]
And strike it in the seven streams,
And make *men* cross over dryshod.
¹⁶There will be a highway for the remnant of His
people
Who will be left from Assyria,
As it was for Israel
In the day that he came up from the land of
Egypt.

A Hymn of Praise

12 And in that day you will say:

"O LORD, I will praise You;
Though You were angry with me,
Your anger is turned away, and You comfort
me.
²Behold, God *is* my salvation,
I will trust and not be afraid;
'For YAH, the LORD, *is* my strength and song;
He also has become my salvation.' "[a]

³Therefore with joy you will draw water
From the wells of salvation.

⁴And in that day you will say:

"Praise the LORD, call upon His name;
Declare His deeds among the peoples,
Make mention that His name is exalted.
⁵Sing to the LORD,
For He has done excellent things;
This *is* known in all the earth.
⁶Cry out and shout, O inhabitant of Zion,
For great *is* the Holy One of Israel in your
midst!"

Proclamation Against Babylon

13 The burden against Babylon which Isaiah
the son of Amoz saw.

²"Lift up a banner on the high mountain,
Raise your voice to them;

11:15 [a]Following Masoretic Text and Vulgate; Septuagint, Syriac, and
Targum read *dry up.* [b]That is, the Euphrates　**12:2** [a]Exodus 15:2

11:10–16 In that day, a phrase used by the prophets to describe
future times, is eschatological language. The "Root of Jesse"
is another designation for the Messiah (v. 10). The imagery of
the Exodus from Egypt is employed to describe the Lord's future deliverance of His people (vv. 15, 16).

12:1–6 The joyful response of the Lord's people is anticipated
in that future day when God would deliver them. After the
disciplining judgment of the Lord was past, His people would
look to Him in praise and trust Him as their salvation (v. 2).
Yah is the abbreviated form of *Yahweh,* the Lord's personal
name (v. 2; compare Is. 12:2 with Ex. 15:2). The Lord's praise
would be proclaimed joyously among the nations. The Lord's

name represents His character (Is. 12:4). The Lord was
praised for His great acts and also for His presence with His
people. For "the Holy One of Israel," see Isaiah 1:4–9, note.
Compare the words of this song of praise with Psalm 66:2;
67:2; and 148:13.

13:1–22 God proclaimed judgment on Babylon, a significant
foe of God's people in ancient times (Is. 13; 14). The southern
kingdom of Judah fell to the Babylonians in 586 B.C. In the NT,
the term Babylon symbolizes the oppression of Rome (see
1 Pet. 5:13; Rev. 14:8). While Isaiah 1—12 is concerned primarily
with judgment on Judah and Jerusalem, chapters 13—23 concern prophecies against various nations. "The day of the

Wave your hand, that they may enter the gates
of the nobles.
³I have commanded My sanctified ones;
I have also called My mighty ones for My
anger—
Those who rejoice in My exaltation."

⁴The noise of a multitude in the mountains,
Like that of many people!
A tumultuous noise of the kingdoms of nations
gathered together!
The LORD of hosts musters
The army for battle.
⁵They come from a far country,
From the end of heaven—
The LORD and His weapons of indignation,
To destroy the whole land.

⁶Wail, for the day of the LORD *is* at hand!
It will come as destruction from the Almighty.
⁷Therefore all hands will be limp,
Every man's heart will melt,
⁸And they will be afraid.
Pangs and sorrows will take hold of *them;*
They will be in pain as a woman in childbirth;
They will be amazed at one another;
Their faces *will be like* flames.

⁹Behold, the day of the LORD comes,
Cruel, with both wrath and fierce anger,
To lay the land desolate;
And He will destroy its sinners from it.
¹⁰For the stars of heaven and their constellations
Will not give their light;
The sun will be darkened in its going forth,
And the moon will not cause its light to shine.

¹¹"I will punish the world for *its* evil,
And the wicked for their iniquity;
I will halt the arrogance of the proud,
And will lay low the haughtiness of the
terrible.
¹²I will make a mortal more rare than fine gold,
A man more than the golden wedge of Ophir.
¹³Therefore I will shake the heavens,
And the earth will move out of her place,
In the wrath of the LORD of hosts
And in the day of His fierce anger.
¹⁴It shall be as the hunted gazelle,
And as a sheep that no man takes up;
Every man will turn to his own people,
And everyone will flee to his own land.

¹⁵Everyone who is found will be thrust through,
And everyone who is captured will fall by the
sword.
¹⁶Their children also will be dashed to pieces
before their eyes;
Their houses will be plundered
And their wives ravished.

¹⁷"Behold, I will stir up the Medes against them,
Who will not regard silver;
And *as for* gold, they will not delight in it.
¹⁸Also *their* bows will dash the young men to
pieces,
And they will have no pity on the fruit of the
womb;
Their eye will not spare children.
¹⁹And Babylon, the glory of kingdoms,
The beauty of the Chaldeans' pride,
Will be as when God overthrew Sodom and
Gomorrah.
²⁰It will never be inhabited,
Nor will it be settled from generation to
generation;
Nor will the Arabian pitch tents there,
Nor will the shepherds make their sheepfolds
there.
²¹But wild beasts of the desert will lie there,
And their houses will be full of owls;
Ostriches will dwell there,
And wild goats will caper there.
²²The hyenas will howl in their citadels,
And jackals in their pleasant palaces.
Her time *is* near to come,
And her days will not be prolonged."

Mercy on Jacob

14 For the LORD will have mercy on Jacob, and
will still choose Israel, and settle them in
their own land. The strangers will be joined with
them, and they will cling to the house of Jacob.
²Then people will take them and bring them to
their place, and the house of Israel will possess
them for servants and maids in the land of the
LORD; they will take them captive whose captives
they were, and rule over their oppressors.

Fall of the King of Babylon

³It shall come to pass in the day the LORD gives
you rest from your sorrow, and from your fear and
the hard bondage in which you were made to
serve, ⁴that you will take up this proverb against
the king of Babylon, and say:

Lord" would be a day of destruction (Is. 13:6, 9). According to
this prophecy, Babylon would become like Sodom and Gomorrah (v. 19), cities on which the Lord rained fire and brimstone
in the time of Abraham (Gen. 19:24, 25). Babylon's defeat by
the Medes was prophesied (Is. 13:17), and it occurred in 539
B.C.

14:3–23 Babylon, the capital of the ancient nation of Babylonia, was located between the Tigris and Euphrates rivers.
The fall, or death, of the king of Babylon was celebrated in
the form of a mocking song. The reference to "hell" is literally
a reference to *She'ol* (Heb.), the shadowy place of the dead
(v. 9). The Lord Himself would bring about the fall of Babylon

A PORTRAIT OF THE ADVERSARY

DESCRIPTION OF HIS CHARACTER AND WORK	SCRIPTURE REFERENCES
His Character	
• Cunning	Gen. 3:1
• Proud	Is. 14:13, 16; Ezek. 28:2, 4, 5, 17
• Created with superior wisdom	Is. 14:13, 16; Ezek. 28:2, 3, 12
• Appears to be beautiful	Is 14:12, 13; Ezek. 28:12
• Resident of Eden	Gen. 3:1 (as serpent); Ezek. 28:13
• Essentially evil	Ezek. 28:15
• Liar and violent	Gen. 3:4; John 8:44
• Originally created as one of the heavenly beings	Ezek. 28:15
• Ambitious to be as God	Is. 14:13, 14; Ezek. 28:2, 3, 6; Luke 4:6–8; 2 Thess. 2:3, 4
• Deceptive in appearance	Gen. 3:1; Ezek. 28:14; 2 Cor. 11:14; Acts 5:3
• Repulsive to those who know him	Is. 14:16, 17; Ezek. 28:19
• He is not omniscient, omnipresent, or omnipotent.	Eph. 6:11; 1 Cor. 10:13; James 4:7; 1 Pet. 5:9
His Work	
• Urges people to renounce God	Gen. 3:4, 5
• Perverts and distorts Scripture	Gen. 3:1, 4, 5; Matt. 4:6
• Opposes the work of God	John 8:44; 13:2, 27; 2 Cor. 2:11; 1 Thess. 2:18; 1 Tim. 3:7; 2 Tim. 2:26; 1 Pet. 5:8
• Hinders the Gospel	Matt. 13:19; 16:23
• Performs miracles to deceive people	Rev. 16:14
• He lost his position and is under judgment because of his rebellion against God.	Is. 14:12, 15; Ezek. 28:7, 8, 10, 16–18; Matt. 25:41; Rev. 19:20, 21; 20:13–15

See Gen. 3:1, 3, 5; Ezek. 28:13, notes; chart, The Names of Satan.

"How the oppressor has ceased,
The golden[a] city ceased!
⁵The LORD has broken the staff of the wicked,
The scepter of the rulers;
⁶He who struck the people in wrath with a
continual stroke,
He who ruled the nations in anger,
Is persecuted *and* no one hinders.
⁷The whole earth is at rest *and* quiet;
They break forth into singing.
⁸Indeed the cypress trees rejoice over you,
And the cedars of Lebanon,

Saying, 'Since you were cut down,
No woodsman has come up against us.'

⁹"Hell from beneath is excited about you,
To meet *you* at your coming;
It stirs up the dead for you,
All the chief ones of the earth;
It has raised up from their thrones
All the kings of the nations.
¹⁰They all shall speak and say to you:

· · · · · · · · · · · · · · · ·

14:4 ᵃOr *insolent*

---

because of the pride of the king of Babylon, who tried to ascend into heaven and be like the Most High (vv. 13, 15; see chart, A Portrait of the Adversary). Both in Genesis 11 at the Tower of Babel and in Isaiah 14, pride resulted in the downfall of a people. Isaiah 14:12–21 has been interpreted typologically as a description of the fall of Satan, but the fall of Babylon because of its pride is the primary event in view in the context of this passage. The Lord of Hosts, the God of the armies, guaranteed the defeat of Babylon (vv. 22, 23), and the Babylonian Empire fell to the Medes and Persians in 539 B.C.

'Have you also become as weak as we?
Have you become like us?
[11]Your pomp is brought down to Sheol,
And the sound of your stringed instruments;
The maggot is spread under you,
And worms cover you.'

The Fall of Lucifer

[12]"How you are fallen from heaven,
O Lucifer,[a] son of the morning!
How you are cut down to the ground,
You who weakened the nations!
[13]For you have said in your heart:
'I will ascend into heaven,
I will exalt my throne above the stars of God;
I will also sit on the mount of the congregation
On the farthest sides of the north;
[14]I will ascend above the heights of the clouds,
I will be like the Most High.'
[15]Yet you shall be brought down to Sheol,
To the lowest depths of the Pit.

[16]"Those who see you will gaze at you,
And consider you, *saying:*
'*Is* this the man who made the earth tremble,
Who shook kingdoms,
[17]Who made the world as a wilderness
And destroyed its cities,
Who did not open the house of his prisoners?'

[18]"All the kings of the nations,
All of them, sleep in glory,
Everyone in his own house;
[19]But you are cast out of your grave
Like an abominable branch,
Like the garment of those who are slain,
Thrust through with a sword,
Who go down to the stones of the pit,
Like a corpse trodden underfoot.
[20]You will not be joined with them in burial,
Because you have destroyed your land
And slain your people.
The brood of evildoers shall never be named.
[21]Prepare slaughter for his children
Because of the iniquity of their fathers,
Lest they rise up and possess the land,
And fill the face of the world with cities."

Babylon Destroyed

[22]"For I will rise up against them," says the LORD
of hosts,

"And cut off from Babylon the name and
remnant,
And offspring and posterity," says the LORD.
[23]"I will also make it a possession for the
porcupine,
And marshes of muddy water;
I will sweep it with the broom of destruction,"
says the LORD of hosts.

Assyria Destroyed

[24]The LORD of hosts has sworn, saying,
"Surely, as I have thought, so it shall come to
pass,
And as I have purposed, *so* it shall stand:
[25]That I will break the Assyrian in My land,
And on My mountains tread him underfoot.
Then his yoke shall be removed from them,
And his burden removed from their shoulders.
[26]This *is* the purpose that is purposed against
the whole earth,
And this *is* the hand that is stretched out over
all the nations.
[27]For the LORD of hosts has purposed,
And who will annul *it?*
His hand *is* stretched out,
And who will turn it back?"

Philistia Destroyed

[28]This is the burden which came in the year
that King Ahaz died.

[29]"Do not rejoice, all you of Philistia,
Because the rod that struck you is broken;
For out of the serpent's roots will come forth a
viper,
And its offspring *will be* a fiery flying serpent.
[30]The firstborn of the poor will feed,
And the needy will lie down in safety;
I will kill your roots with famine,
And it will slay your remnant.
[31]Wail, O gate! Cry, O city!
All you of Philistia *are* dissolved;
For smoke will come from the north,
And no one *will be* alone in his appointed
times."

[32]What will they answer the messengers of the
nation?
That the LORD has founded Zion,

14:12 [a]Literally *Day Star*

14:24–27 The Lord of Hosts would bring about the fall of Assyria. The northern kingdom completely fell to Assyrian domination in 722 B.C. The Assyrians dominated Palestine during the years 745-650 B.C. The Lord would also bring His judgment finally on the Assyrians (see Is. 10:5-19, note).

14:28–32 The Philistines, a major threat to Israel from soon after the time of Israel's initial settlement in the Land, inhab-

ited the southwestern coast of Canaan. The five major Philistine cities were Ashdod, Ashkelon, Gaza, Ekron, and Gath. Isaiah announced the certain doom of the Philistine revolt against Assyria and bitterly opposed Judah's participation in this rebellion (see Is. 20:1-6). In each crisis that Judah encountered, Isaiah counseled faith in the Lord rather than dependence on military alliances (see Introduction: Date).

And the poor of His people shall take refuge in
it.

Proclamation Against Moab

15 The burden against Moab.

Because in the night Ar of Moab is laid waste
And destroyed,
Because in the night Kir of Moab is laid waste
And destroyed,
[2]He has gone up to the temple[a] and Dibon,
To the high places to weep.
Moab will wail over Nebo and over Medeba;
On all their heads *will be* baldness,
And every beard cut off.
[3]In their streets they will clothe themselves
with sackcloth;
On the tops of their houses
And in their streets
Everyone will wail, weeping bitterly.
[4]Heshbon and Elealeh will cry out,
Their voice shall be heard as far as Jahaz;
Therefore the armed soldiers[a] of Moab will cry
out;
His life will be burdensome to him.

[5]"My heart will cry out for Moab;
His fugitives *shall flee* to Zoar,
Like a three-year-old heifer.[a]
For by the Ascent of Luhith
They will go up with weeping;
For in the way of Horonaim
They will raise up a cry of destruction,
[6]For the waters of Nimrim will be desolate,
For the green grass has withered away;
The grass fails, there is nothing green.
[7]Therefore the abundance they have gained,
And what they have laid up,
They will carry away to the Brook of the
Willows.
[8]For the cry has gone all around the borders of
Moab,
Its wailing to Eglaim
And its wailing to Beer Elim.
[9]For the waters of Dimon[a] will be full of
blood;
Because I will bring more upon Dimon,[b]
Lions upon him who escapes from Moab,
And on the remnant of the land."

Moab Destroyed

16 Send the lamb to the ruler of the land,
From Sela to the wilderness,
To the mount of the daughter of Zion.

[2]For it shall be as a wandering bird thrown out
of the nest;
So shall be the daughters of Moab at the fords
of the Arnon.

[3]"Take counsel, execute judgment;
Make your shadow like the night in the middle
of the day;
Hide the outcasts,
Do not betray him who escapes.
[4]Let My outcasts dwell with you, O Moab;
Be a shelter to them from the face of the
spoiler.
For the extortioner is at an end,
Devastation ceases,
The oppressors are consumed out of the
land.
[5]In mercy the throne will be established;
And One will sit on it in truth, in the
tabernacle of David,
Judging and seeking justice and hastening
righteousness."

[6]We have heard of the pride of Moab—
He is very proud—
Of his haughtiness and his pride and his wrath;
But his lies *shall* not *be* so.
[7]Therefore Moab shall wail for Moab;
Everyone shall wail.
For the foundations of Kir Hareseth you shall
mourn;
Surely *they are* stricken.

[8]For the fields of Heshbon languish,
And the vine of Sibmah;
The lords of the nations have broken down its
choice plants,
Which have reached to Jazer
And wandered through the wilderness.
Her branches are stretched out,
They are gone over the sea.
[9]Therefore I will bewail the vine of Sibmah,
With the weeping of Jazer;
I will drench you with my tears,
O Heshbon and Elealeh;
For battle cries have fallen
Over your summer fruits and your harvest.

15:2 [a]Hebrew *bayith,* literally *house*   **15:4** [a]Following Masoretic
Text, Targum, and Vulgate; Septuagint and Syriac read *loins.*   **15:5**
[a]Or *The Third Eglath,* an unknown city (compare Jeremiah 48:34)
15:9 [a]Following Masoretic Text and Targum; Dead Sea Scrolls and
Vulgate read *Dibon;* Septuagint reads *Rimon.* [b]Following Masoretic
Text and Targum; Dead Sea Scrolls and Vulgate read *Dibon;*
Septuagint reads *Rimon.*

15:1—16:14 This lengthy proclamation against Moab announced the doom of that nation. Moab, whose inhabitants
descended from Lot (Gen. 19:30-38), was located east of the
Salt Sea. Moab opposed the Israelites when they prepared to
enter Canaan (Num. 22—24) and was later overrun by Sargon, king of Assyria. Pride and arrogance are associated with
Moab's fall (Is. 16:6, 7).

¹⁰Gladness is taken away,
And joy from the plentiful field;
In the vineyards there will be no singing,
Nor will there be shouting;
No treaders will tread out wine in the
presses;
I have made their shouting cease.
¹¹Therefore my heart shall resound like a harp
for Moab,
And my inner being for Kir Heres.

¹²And it shall come to pass,
When it is seen that Moab is weary on the high
place,
That he will come to his sanctuary to pray;
But he will not prevail.

¹³This *is* the word which the LORD has spoken
concerning Moab since that time. ¹⁴But now the
LORD has spoken, saying, "Within three years, as
the years of a hired man, the glory of Moab will be
despised with all that great multitude, and the
remnant *will be* very small *and* feeble."

Proclamation Against Syria and Israel

17 The burden against Damascus.

"Behold, Damascus will cease from *being* a city,
And it will be a ruinous heap.
²The cities of Aroer *are* forsaken;ᵃ
They will be for flocks
Which lie down, and no one will make *them*
afraid.
³The fortress also will cease from Ephraim,
The kingdom from Damascus,
And the remnant of Syria;
They will be as the glory of the children of
Israel,"
Says the LORD of hosts.
⁴"In that day it shall come to pass
That the glory of Jacob will wane,
And the fatness of his flesh grow lean.
⁵It shall be as when the harvester gathers the
grain,
And reaps the heads with his arm;
It shall be as he who gathers heads of grain
In the Valley of Rephaim.
⁶Yet gleaning grapes will be left in it,
Like the shaking of an olive tree,
Two *or* three olives at the top of the uppermost
bough,
Four *or* five in its most fruitful branches,"
Says the LORD God of Israel.

⁷In that day a man will look to his Maker,
And his eyes will have respect for the Holy One
of Israel.
⁸He will not look to the altars,
The work of his hands;
He will not respect what his fingers have
made,
Nor the wooden imagesᵃ nor the incense
altars.

⁹In that day his strong cities will be as a
forsaken boughᵃ
And an uppermost branch,ᵇ
Which they left because of the children of
Israel;
And there will be desolation.

¹⁰Because you have forgotten the God of your
salvation,
And have not been mindful of the Rock of your
stronghold,
Therefore you will plant pleasant plants
And set out foreign seedlings;
¹¹In the day you will make your plant to
grow,
And in the morning you will make your seed to
flourish;
But the harvest *will be* a heap of ruins
In the day of grief and desperate sorrow.

¹²Woe to the multitude of many people
Who make a noise like the roar of the seas,
And to the rushing of nations
That make a rushing like the rushing of
mighty waters!
¹³The nations will rush like the rushing of many
waters;
But *God* will rebuke them and they will flee far
away,
And be chased like the chaff of the mountains
before the wind,
Like a rolling thing before the whirlwind.
¹⁴Then behold, at eventide, trouble!
And before the morning, he *is* no more.
This *is* the portion of those who plunder us,
And the lot of those who rob us.

•••••••••••••••••

17:2 ᵃFollowing Masoretic Text and Vulgate; Septuagint reads *It shall
be forsaken forever;* Targum reads *Its cities shall be forsaken and
desolate.* **17:8** ᵃHebrew *Asherim,* Canaanite deities **17:9**
ᵃSeptuagint reads *Hivites;* Targum reads *laid waste;* Vulgate reads *as
the plows.* ᵇSeptuagint reads *Amorites;* Targum reads *in ruins;*
Vulgate reads *corn.*

17:1–6 Damascus, the capital of Syria, was located northeast
of Israel. Ephraim and Jacob in this passage are alternate designations for Israel, the northern kingdom (see chart, The
Terminology for the Divided Kingdom). The message of this
passage is associated with the Syro-Ephraimitic Crisis in 734

B.C. (see Introduction: Date). Just as Syria and Ephraim united
themselves and tried to force Judah into coalition with them
against Assyria, they were united in receiving condemnation.
Syria fell in 732 B.C. Ephraim or Israel ultimately fell to the Assyrians in 722 B.C.

Proclamation Against Ethiopia

18 Woe to the land shadowed with buzzing wings,
Which *is* beyond the rivers of Ethiopia,
[2] Which sends ambassadors by sea,
Even in vessels of reed on the waters, *saying,*
"Go, swift messengers, to a nation tall and smooth *of skin,*
To a people terrible from their beginning onward,
A nation powerful and treading down,
Whose land the rivers divide."

[3] All inhabitants of the world and dwellers on the earth:
When he lifts up a banner on the mountains, you see *it;*
And when he blows a trumpet, you hear *it.*
[4] For so the LORD said to me,
"I will take My rest,
And I will look from My dwelling place
Like clear heat in sunshine,
Like a cloud of dew in the heat of harvest."
[5] For before the harvest, when the bud is perfect
And the sour grape is ripening in the flower,
He will both cut off the sprigs with pruning hooks
And take away *and* cut down the branches.
[6] They will be left together for the mountain birds of prey
And for the beasts of the earth;
The birds of prey will summer on them,
And all the beasts of the earth will winter on them.

[7] In that time a present will be brought to the LORD of hosts
From[a] a people tall and smooth *of skin,*
And from a people terrible from their beginning onward,
A nation powerful and treading down,
Whose land the rivers divide—
To the place of the name of the LORD of hosts,
To Mount Zion.

Proclamation Against Egypt

19 The burden against Egypt.

Behold, the LORD rides on a swift cloud,
And will come into Egypt;

The idols of Egypt will totter at His presence,
And the heart of Egypt will melt in its midst.

[2] "I will set Egyptians against Egyptians;
Everyone will fight against his brother,
And everyone against his neighbor,
City against city, kingdom against kingdom.
[3] The spirit of Egypt will fail in its midst;
I will destroy their counsel,
And they will consult the idols and the charmers,
The mediums and the sorcerers.
[4] And the Egyptians I will give
Into the hand of a cruel master,
And a fierce king will rule over them,"
Says the Lord, the LORD of hosts.

[5] The waters will fail from the sea,
And the river will be wasted and dried up.
[6] The rivers will turn foul;
The brooks of defense will be emptied and dried up;
The reeds and rushes will wither.
[7] The papyrus reeds by the River,[a] by the mouth of the River,
And everything sown by the River,
Will wither, be driven away, and be no more.
[8] The fishermen also will mourn;
All those will lament who cast hooks into the River,
And they will languish who spread nets on the waters.
[9] Moreover those who work in fine flax
And those who weave fine fabric will be ashamed;
[10] And its foundations will be broken.
All who make wages *will be* troubled of soul.

[11] Surely the princes of Zoan *are* fools;
Pharaoh's wise counselors give foolish counsel.
How do you say to Pharaoh, "I *am* the son of the wise,
The son of ancient kings?"
[12] Where *are* they?
Where are your wise men?
Let them tell you now,
And let them know what the LORD of hosts has purposed against Egypt.

18:7 [a]Following Dead Sea Scrolls, Septuagint, and Vulgate; Masoretic Text omits *From;* Targum reads *To.*   19:7 [a]That is, the Nile

---

18:1–7 The designations Egypt and Ethiopia are used almost synonymously in the Book of Isaiah. Egypt was ruled by an Ethiopian dynasty during the latter part of the 8th century and the first half of the 7th century B.C. Egyptians experienced new hope for the supremacy of their nation under Ethiopian leadership, but that hope ended when the Assyrians conquered Thebes, the capital city of Egypt, in the 7th century B.C.

19:1–17 Egypt, the ancient enemy of God's people, would once again face God's judgment, just as the armies of Pharaoh met devastation by the power of the Lord at the sea (Ex. 14; 15). The drying up of the Nile River, the source of Egypt's life, would seal the destruction of the nation (Is. 19:5–10). The city of Zoan is also known as Tanis or Raamses. Noph is an alternate name for the city of Memphis. Both cities had served as Egypt's capital.

¹³The princes of Zoan have become fools;
The princes of Noph[a] are deceived;
They have also deluded Egypt,
Those who are the mainstay of its tribes.
¹⁴The LORD has mingled a perverse spirit in her
midst;
And they have caused Egypt to err in all her
work,
As a drunken man staggers in his vomit.
¹⁵Neither will there be *any* work for Egypt,
Which the head or tail,
Palm branch or bulrush, may do.[a]

¹⁶In that day Egypt will be like women, and will
be afraid and fear because of the waving of the
hand of the LORD of hosts, which He waves over it.
¹⁷And the land of Judah will be a terror to Egypt;
everyone who makes mention of it will be afraid
in himself, because of the counsel of the LORD of
hosts which He has determined against it.

Egypt, Assyria, and Israel Blessed

¹⁸In that day five cities in the land of Egypt
will speak the language of Canaan and swear by
the LORD of hosts; one will be called the City of
Destruction.[a]
¹⁹In that day there will be an altar to the LORD
in the midst of the land of Egypt, and a pillar to
the LORD at its border. ²⁰And it will be for a sign
and for a witness to the LORD of hosts in the land
of Egypt; for they will cry to the LORD because of
the oppressors, and He will send them a Savior
and a Mighty One, and He will deliver them.
²¹Then the LORD will be known to Egypt, and the
Egyptians will know the LORD in that day, and will
make sacrifice and offering; yes, they will make a
vow to the LORD and perform *it.* ²²And the LORD
will strike Egypt, He will strike and heal *it;* they
will return to the LORD, and He will be entreated
by them and heal them.
²³In that day there will be a highway from
Egypt to Assyria, and the Assyrian will come into
Egypt and the Egyptian into Assyria, and the
Egyptians will serve with the Assyrians.
²⁴In that day Israel will be one of three with
Egypt and Assyria—a blessing in the midst of the
land, ²⁵whom the LORD of hosts shall bless, saying,

"Blessed *is* Egypt My people, and Assyria the work
of My hands, and Israel My inheritance."

The Sign Against Egypt and Ethiopia

20In the year that Tartan[a] came to Ashdod,
when Sargon the king of Assyria sent him,
and he fought against Ashdod and took it, ²at the
same time the LORD spoke by Isaiah the son of
Amoz, saying, "Go, and remove the sackcloth from
your body, and take your sandals off your feet."
And he did so, walking naked and barefoot.
³Then the LORD said, "Just as My servant Isaiah
has walked naked and barefoot three years *for* a
sign and a wonder against Egypt and Ethiopia, ⁴so
shall the king of Assyria lead away the Egyptians
as prisoners and the Ethiopians as captives, young
and old, naked and barefoot, with their buttocks
uncovered, to the shame of Egypt. ⁵Then they
shall be afraid and ashamed of Ethiopia their expectation and Egypt their glory. ⁶And the inhabitant of this territory will say in that day, 'Surely
such *is* our expectation, wherever we flee for help
to be delivered from the king of Assyria; and how
shall we escape?'"

The Fall of Babylon Proclaimed

21The burden against the Wilderness of the Sea.

As whirlwinds in the South pass through,
So it comes from the desert, from a terrible
land.
²A distressing vision is declared to me;
The treacherous dealer deals treacherously,
And the plunderer plunders.
Go up, O Elam!
Besiege, O Media!
All its sighing I have made to cease.

³Therefore my loins are filled with pain;
Pangs have taken hold of me, like the pangs of
a woman in labor.
I was distressed when *I* heard *it;*
I was dismayed when *I* saw *it.*

· · · · · · · · · · · · · · · · · ·

19:13 [a]That is, ancient Memphis   19:15 [a]Compare Isaiah 9:14–16
19:18 [a]Some Hebrew manuscripts, Arabic, Dead Sea Scrolls, Targum,
and Vulgate read *Sun;* Septuagint reads *Asedek* (literally
Righteousness).   20:1 [a]Or *the Commander in Chief*

19:18–25 The day would come when the Lord would bless
Egypt, Assyria, and Israel. The inhabitants of Egypt and Assyria would become worshipers of the Lord, the God of Israel,
who would be recognized as the God of the whole earth. A
tremendous missionary emphasis appears in this passage.
The future would bring the fulfillment of the promise made to
Abram (Gen. 12:1–3). Egypt and Assyria, two of the worst enemies of God's people, would be partners with Israel in serving
as a blessing to the world.

20:1–6 Isaiah employed a symbolic act to emphasize vividly
God's judgment on Egypt and Ethiopia. Isaiah's action of
walking naked and barefoot symbolized a captive being taken

into exile. The setting of this passage is the Ashdod Rebellion
(714–711 B.C.). The ruler of Ashdod led the Philistines to revolt
against Assyria. Isaiah bitterly opposed any participation on
the part of Judah in this rebellion, for in every crisis he counseled Judah to have faith in the Lord instead of trusting in political alliances. Evidently Judah did not become involved in
this rebellion (see Is. 14:28–32, note).

21:1–10 Babylon, who led forces against Assyrian power, fell to
Cyrus of Persia in 539 B.C. (see Is. 14:3–23, note). The message
to Judah was clear: God's people should trust in the Lord, not
in political or military alliances.

[4]My heart wavered, fearfulness frightened me;
The night for which I longed He turned into
fear for me.
[5]Prepare the table,
Set a watchman in the tower,
Eat and drink.
Arise, you princes,
Anoint the shield!

[6]For thus has the Lord said to me:
"Go, set a watchman,
Let him declare what he sees."
[7]And he saw a chariot *with* a pair of horsemen,
A chariot of donkeys, *and* a chariot of camels,
And he listened earnestly with great care.
[8]Then he cried, "A lion,[a] my Lord!
I stand continually on the watchtower in the
daytime;
I have sat at my post every night.
[9]And look, here comes a chariot of men *with* a
pair of horsemen!"
Then he answered and said,
"Babylon is fallen, is fallen!
And all the carved images of her gods
He has broken to the ground."

[10]Oh, my threshing and the grain of my
floor!
That which I have heard from the LORD of
hosts,
The God of Israel,
I have declared to you.

Proclamation Against Edom

[11]The burden against Dumah.

He calls to me out of Seir,
"Watchman, what of the night?
Watchman, what of the night?"
[12]The watchman said,
"The morning comes, and also the night.
If you will inquire, inquire;
Return! Come back!"

Proclamation Against Arabia

[13]The burden against Arabia.

In the forest in Arabia you will lodge,
O you traveling companies of Dedanites.

[14]O inhabitants of the land of Tema,
Bring water to him who is thirsty;
With their bread they met him who fled.
[15]For they fled from the swords, from the drawn
sword,
From the bent bow, and from the distress of
war.

[16]For thus the LORD has said to me: "Within a
year, according to the year of a hired man, all the
glory of Kedar will fail; [17]and the remainder of the
number of archers, the mighty men of the people
of Kedar, will be diminished; for the LORD God of
Israel has spoken *it*."

Proclamation Against Jerusalem

22 The burden against the Valley of Vision.

What ails you now, that you have all gone up to
the housetops,
[2]You who are full of noise,
A tumultuous city, a joyous city?
Your slain *men are* not slain with the sword,
Nor dead in battle.
[3]All your rulers have fled together;
They are captured by the archers.
All who are found in you are bound together;
They have fled from afar.
[4]Therefore I said, "Look away from me,
I will weep bitterly;
Do not labor to comfort me
Because of the plundering of the daughter of
my people."

[5]For *it is* a day of trouble and treading down and
perplexity
By the Lord GOD of hosts
In the Valley of Vision—
Breaking down the walls
And of crying to the mountain.
[6]Elam bore the quiver
With chariots of men *and* horsemen,
And Kir uncovered the shield.
[7]It shall come to pass *that* your choicest valleys
Shall be full of chariots,
And the horsemen shall set themselves in array
at the gate.

· ·

21:8 [a]Dead Sea Scrolls read *Then the observer cried.*

21:11–17 Dumah is probably a reference to Edom as indicated
by the further reference to Seir, an alternate designation for
Edom (v. 11). The Edomites were descendants of Esau. The oracle or prophecy of an uncertain future is indicated for Edom
(vv. 11, 12). The Dedanites, the inhabitants of Tema, and the
people of Kedar are all apparently associated with the area of
Arabia (vv. 13–17).

22:1–25 In the Sennacherib Crisis of 701 B.C., the third major
crisis in Judah's history, King Sennacherib of Assyria laid siege

to Jerusalem (2 Kin. 18; 19). God's message through His
prophet Isaiah was that the king of Assyria would not enter
the city of Jerusalem (2 Kin. 19:32–34). God did deliver the
city (2 Kin. 19:35). The inhabitants of Jerusalem engaged in
boisterous celebration (Is. 22:1, 2), to which Isaiah responded
with disappointment because God's people had not learned
the lesson God intended for them to learn. They did not repent and change their lifestyles but came to view Jerusalem
as indestructible. In this oracle God assured them that they
would not escape judgment because of their sin (v. 14).

8He removed the protection of Judah.
You looked in that day to the armor of the
House of the Forest;
9You also saw the damage to the city of
David,
That it was great;
And you gathered together the waters of the
lower pool.
10You numbered the houses of Jerusalem,
And the houses you broke down
To fortify the wall.
11You also made a reservoir between the two
walls
For the water of the old pool.
But you did not look to its Maker,
Nor did you have respect for Him who
fashioned it long ago.

12And in that day the Lord GOD of hosts
Called for weeping and for mourning,
For baldness and for girding with sackcloth.
13But instead, joy and gladness,
Slaying oxen and killing sheep,
Eating meat and drinking wine:
"Let us eat and drink, for tomorrow we die!"

14Then it was revealed in my hearing by the
LORD of hosts,
"Surely for this iniquity there will be no
atonement for you,
Even to your death," says the Lord GOD of
hosts.

The Judgment on Shebna

15Thus says the Lord GOD of hosts:

"Go, proceed to this steward,
To Shebna, who is over the house, and say:
16'What have you here, and whom have you here,
That you have hewn a sepulcher here,
As he who hews himself a sepulcher on high,
Who carves a tomb for himself in a rock?
17Indeed, the LORD will throw you away
violently,
O mighty man,
And will surely seize you.
18He will surely turn violently and toss you like a
ball
Into a large country;
There you shall die, and there your glorious
chariots
Shall be the shame of your master's house.
19So I will drive you out of your office,
And from your position he will pull you down.a

20'Then it shall be in that day,
That I will call My servant Eliakim the son of
Hilkiah;
21I will clothe him with your robe
And strengthen him with your belt;
I will commit your responsibility into his hand.
He shall be a father to the inhabitants of
Jerusalem
And to the house of Judah.
22The key of the house of David
I will lay on his shoulder;
So he shall open, and no one shall shut;
And he shall shut, and no one shall open.
23I will fasten him as a peg in a secure place,
And he will become a glorious throne to his
father's house.

24'They will hang on him all the glory of his father's house, the offspring and the posterity, all
vessels of small quantity, from the cups to all the
pitchers. 25In that day,' says the LORD of hosts, 'the
peg that is fastened in the secure place will be removed and be cut down and fall, and the burden
that was on it will be cut off; for the LORD has spoken.'"

Proclamation Against Tyre

23 The burden against Tyre.

Wail, you ships of Tarshish!
For it is laid waste,
So that there is no house, no harbor;
From the land of Cyprusa it is revealed to
them.

2Be still, you inhabitants of the coastland,
You merchants of Sidon,
Whom those who cross the sea have filled.a
3And on great waters the grain of Shihor,
The harvest of the River,a is her revenue;
And she is a marketplace for the nations.

4Be ashamed, O Sidon;
For the sea has spoken,
The strength of the sea, saying,
"I do not labor, nor bring forth children;
Neither do I rear young men,
Nor bring up virgins."

22:19 aSeptuagint omits he will pull you down; Syriac, Targum, and Vulgate read I will pull you down. 23:1 aHebrew Kittim, western lands, especially Cyprus 23:2 aFollowing Masoretic Text and Vulgate; Septuagint and Targum read Passing over the water; Dead Sea Scrolls read Your messengers passing over the sea. 23:3 aThat is, the Nile

23:1–18 This prophetic oracle pronounced God's judgment on Tyre and Sidon, Phoenician seacoast cities located north of Israel. In contrast with the oracles on the nations pro-nounced by Amos (see Amos 1; 2), the message of judgment in Isaiah continued even after God announced judgment on His own people (Is. 22). Israel had depended on the Phoeni-cians, sailors engaging in overseas trade, for international trade.

⁵When the report *reaches* Egypt,
They also will be in agony at the report of
Tyre.

⁶Cross over to Tarshish;
Wail, you inhabitants of the coastland!
⁷*Is* this your joyous *city,*
Whose antiquity *is* from ancient days,
Whose feet carried her far off to dwell?
⁸Who has taken this counsel against Tyre, the
crowning *city,*
Whose merchants *are* princes,
Whose traders *are* the honorable of the
earth?
⁹The LORD of hosts has purposed it,
To bring to dishonor the pride of all glory,
To bring into contempt all the honorable of
the earth.

¹⁰Overflow through your land like the River,ᵃ
O daughter of Tarshish;
There is no more strength.
¹¹He stretched out His hand over the sea,
He shook the kingdoms;
The LORD has given a commandment against
Canaan
To destroy its strongholds.
¹²And He said, "You will rejoice no more,
O you oppressed virgin daughter of Sidon.
Arise, cross over to Cyprus;
There also you will have no rest."

¹³Behold, the land of the Chaldeans,
This people *which* was not;
Assyria founded it for wild beasts of the
desert.
They set up its towers,
They raised up its palaces,
And brought it to ruin.

¹⁴Wail, you ships of Tarshish!
For your strength is laid waste.

¹⁵Now it shall come to pass in that day that
Tyre will be forgotten seventy years, according to
the days of one king. At the end of seventy years it
will happen to Tyre as *in* the song of the harlot:

¹⁶"Take a harp, go about the city,
You forgotten harlot;
Make sweet melody, sing many songs,
That you may be remembered."

¹⁷And it shall be, at the end of seventy years,
that the LORD will deal with Tyre. She will return
to her hire, and commit fornication with all the
kingdoms of the world on the face of the earth.
¹⁸Her gain and her pay will be set apart for the
LORD; it will not be treasured nor laid up, for her
gain will be for those who dwell before the LORD,
to eat sufficiently, and for fine clothing.

Impending Judgment on the Earth

24 Behold, the LORD makes the earth empty
and makes it waste,
Distorts its surface
And scatters abroad its inhabitants.
²And it shall be:
As with the people, so with the priest;
As with the servant, so with his master;
As with the maid, so with her mistress;
As with the buyer, so with the seller;
As with the lender, so with the borrower;
As with the creditor, so with the debtor.
³The land shall be entirely emptied and utterly
plundered,
For the LORD has spoken this word.

⁴The earth mourns *and* fades away,
The world languishes *and* fades away;
The haughty people of the earth languish.
⁵The earth is also defiled under its inhabitants,
Because they have transgressed the laws,
Changed the ordinance,
Broken the everlasting covenant.
⁶Therefore the curse has devoured the earth,
And those who dwell in it are desolate.
Therefore the inhabitants of the earth are
burned,
And few men *are* left.

⁷The new wine fails, the vine languishes,
All the merry-hearted sigh.
⁸The mirth of the tambourine ceases,
The noise of the jubilant ends,
The joy of the harp ceases.
⁹They shall not drink wine with a song;
Strong drink is bitter to those who drink it.
¹⁰The city of confusion is broken down;
Every house is shut up, so that none may go in.
¹¹*There is* a cry for wine in the streets,
All joy is darkened,
The mirth of the land is gone.

23:10 ᵃThat is, the Nile

24:1—27:13 The little apocalypse holds prophecies of both
judgment and redemption (Is. 24—27). Disaster would come
upon the entire earth, for the everlasting covenant with the
Lord had been broken (Is. 24:5; see Gen. 9:16). The 8th century B.C. prophet Hosea also observed that the Land mourned
because of the broken covenant with the Lord (Compare Is.

24:4, 5 with Hos. 4:1–3). The Lord would be praised because
of His victory over all His enemies and because of His care for
His people (Is. 25; 26). The Lord's people looked forward to
restoration after the judgment was past, though such restoration would not be automatic but dependent upon their response in obedience to Him (Is. 27).

ECOLOGICAL CONCERNS *OUR HABITAT FOR LIFE*

The Lord God created the earth to be a habitat for life (Is. 45:18). He blessed the earth and put it under our care (Gen. 1:26). But something went terribly wrong with this scenario when Adam and Eve rebelled against their Creator. To this day the earth is still groaning under the curse of our sinfulness (Rom. 8:19–25).

Jesus Christ came to redeem His creation from sin. The earth will share in that redemption when, at the end of history, He comes, freeing both the earth and its inhabitants from sin. The Bible speaks of an environmental restoration of global magnitude: a recreated earth (Rev. 21:1).

Until that time, we have a responsibility to God to be good stewards of the earth He entrusted to us. We cannot exploit the earth's resources in greed and technological ambition. Nor must we care for the environment more than we care for people. In our attempt to protect the environment, we cannot forget that God created the earth in order to sustain the traffic of life upon it (Ps. 24:1).

While we must take our stewardship responsibilities seriously, we must also keep in mind that in the ultimate sense only Jesus Christ can restore the perfect balance between a new earth and a new humanity. Until that time, believers are challenged to be wise stewards of God's good creation—to be fruitful, multiply, and fill the earth even as we subdue it and take dominion over it (Gen. 1:28).

See also charts on Flowers of the Bible; Vegetables of the Bible; Bitter Herbs of the Bible; Herbs of the Bible; Flowers and Plants (Song 8); Fall of Creation (Gen. 3)

¹²In the city desolation is left,
And the gate is stricken with destruction.
¹³When it shall be thus in the midst of the land
among the people,
It shall be like the shaking of an olive tree,
Like the gleaning of grapes when the vintage
is done.

¹⁴They shall lift up their voice, they shall
sing;
For the majesty of the LORD
They shall cry aloud from the sea.
¹⁵Therefore glorify the LORD in the dawning
light,
The name of the LORD God of Israel in the
coastlands of the sea.
¹⁶From the ends of the earth we have heard
songs:
"Glory to the righteous!"
But I said, "I am ruined, ruined!
Woe to me!
The treacherous dealers have dealt
treacherously,
Indeed, the treacherous dealers have dealt very
treacherously."

¹⁷Fear and the pit and the snare
Are upon you, O inhabitant of the earth.
¹⁸And it shall be
That he who flees from the noise of the fear
Shall fall into the pit,
And he who comes up from the midst of the
pit
Shall be caught in the snare;
For the windows from on high are open,
And the foundations of the earth are shaken.

¹⁹The earth is violently broken,
The earth is split open,
The earth is shaken exceedingly.
²⁰The earth shall reel to and fro like a drunkard,
And shall totter like a hut;
Its transgression shall be heavy upon it,
And it will fall, and not rise again.

²¹It shall come to pass in that day
That the LORD will punish on high the host of
exalted ones,
And on the earth the kings of the earth.
²²They will be gathered together,
As prisoners are gathered in the pit,
And will be shut up in the prison;
After many days they will be punished.
²³Then the moon will be disgraced
And the sun ashamed;
For the LORD of hosts will reign
On Mount Zion and in Jerusalem
And before His elders, gloriously.

Praise to God

25 O LORD, You *are* my God.
I will exalt You,
I will praise Your name,
For You have done wonderful *things;*
Your counsels of old *are* faithfulness *and* truth.
²For You have made a city a ruin,
A fortified city a ruin,
A palace of foreigners to be a city no more;
It will never be rebuilt.
³Therefore the strong people will glorify You;
The city of the terrible nations will fear You.
⁴For You have been a strength to the poor,
A strength to the needy in his distress,

A refuge from the storm,
A shade from the heat;
For the blast of the terrible ones *is* as a storm
   against the wall.
⁵You will reduce the noise of aliens,
As heat in a dry place;
As heat in the shadow of a cloud,
The song of the terrible ones will be
   diminished.

⁶And in this mountain
The Lord of hosts will make for all people
A feast of choice pieces,
A feast of wines on the lees,
Of fat things full of marrow,
Of well-refined wines on the lees.
⁷And He will destroy on this mountain
The surface of the covering cast over all
   people,
And the veil that is spread over all nations.
⁸He will swallow up death forever,
And the Lord God will wipe away tears from all
   faces;
The rebuke of His people
He will take away from all the earth;
For the Lord has spoken.

⁹And it will be said in that day:
"Behold, this *is* our God;
We have waited for Him, and He will save us.
This *is* the Lord;
We have waited for Him;
We will be glad and rejoice in His salvation."

¹⁰For on this mountain the hand of the Lord will
   rest,
And Moab shall be trampled down under Him,
As straw is trampled down for the refuse heap.
¹¹And He will spread out His hands in their midst
As a swimmer reaches out to swim,
And He will bring down their pride
Together with the trickery of their hands.
¹²The fortress of the high fort of your walls
He will bring down, lay low,
And bring to the ground, down to the dust.

A Song of Salvation

26 In that day this song will be sung in the land of Judah:

"We have a strong city;
God will appoint salvation *for* walls and
   bulwarks.
²Open the gates,
That the righteous nation which keeps the
   truth may enter in.
³You will keep *him* in perfect peace,
Whose mind *is* stayed *on You,*

Because he trusts in You.
⁴Trust in the Lord forever,
For in Yah, the Lord, *is* everlasting strength.^a
⁵For He brings down those who dwell on high,
The lofty city;
He lays it low,
He lays it low to the ground,
He brings it down to the dust.
⁶The foot shall tread it down—
The feet of the poor
And the steps of the needy."

⁷The way of the just *is* uprightness;
O Most Upright,
You weigh the path of the just.
⁸Yes, in the way of Your judgments,
O Lord, we have waited for You;
The desire of *our* soul *is* for Your name
And for the remembrance of You.
⁹With my soul I have desired You in the night,
Yes, by my spirit within me I will seek You
   early;
For when Your judgments *are* in the earth,
The inhabitants of the world will learn
   righteousness.

¹⁰Let grace be shown to the wicked,
Yet he will not learn righteousness;
In the land of uprightness he will deal unjustly,
And will not behold the majesty of the Lord.
¹¹Lord, *when* Your hand is lifted up, they will not
   see.
But they will see and be ashamed
For *their* envy of people;
Yes, the fire of Your enemies shall devour
   them.

¹²Lord, You will establish peace for us,
For You have also done all our works in us.
¹³O Lord our God, masters besides You
Have had dominion over us;
But by You only we make mention of Your
   name.
¹⁴*They are* dead, they will not live;
They are deceased, they will not rise.
Therefore You have punished and destroyed
   them,
And made all their memory to perish.
¹⁵You have increased the nation, O Lord,
You have increased the nation;
You are glorified;
You have expanded all the borders of the land.

¹⁶Lord, in trouble they have visited You,
They poured out a prayer *when* Your
   chastening *was* upon them.

26:4 ^aOr *Rock of Ages*

¹⁷As a woman with child
Is in pain and cries out in her pangs,
When she draws near the time of her delivery,
So have we been in Your sight, O LORD.
¹⁸We have been with child, we have been in pain;
We have, as it were, brought forth wind;
We have not accomplished any deliverance in
    the earth,
Nor have the inhabitants of the world fallen.

¹⁹Your dead shall live;
Together with my dead body[a] they shall arise.
Awake and sing, you who dwell in dust;
For your dew *is like* the dew of herbs,
And the earth shall cast out the dead.

Take Refuge from the Coming Judgment

²⁰Come, my people, enter your chambers,
And shut your doors behind you;
Hide yourself, as it were, for a little moment,
Until the indignation is past.
²¹For behold, the LORD comes out of His place
To punish the inhabitants of the earth for
    their iniquity;
The earth will also disclose her blood,
And will no more cover her slain.

27 In that day the LORD with His severe sword,
    great and strong,
Will punish Leviathan the fleeing serpent,
Leviathan that twisted serpent;
And He will slay the reptile that *is* in the sea.

The Restoration of Israel

²In that day sing to her,
"A vineyard of red wine![a]
³I, the LORD, keep it,
I water it every moment;
Lest any hurt it,
I keep it night and day.
⁴Fury *is* not in Me.
Who would set briers *and* thorns
Against Me in battle?
I would go through them,
I would burn them together.
⁵Or let him take hold of My strength,
That he may make peace with Me;
And he shall make peace with Me."

⁶Those who come He shall cause to take root in
    Jacob;
Israel shall blossom and bud,
And fill the face of the world with fruit.

⁷Has He struck Israel as He struck those who
    struck him?

Or has He been slain according to the
    slaughter of those who were slain by Him?
⁸In measure, by sending it away,
You contended with it.
He removes *it* by His rough wind
In the day of the east wind.
⁹Therefore by this the iniquity of Jacob will be
    covered;
And this *is* all the fruit of taking away his sin:
When he makes all the stones of the altar
Like chalkstones that are beaten to dust,
Wooden images[a] and incense altars shall not
    stand.

¹⁰Yet the fortified city *will be* desolate,
The habitation forsaken and left like a
    wilderness;
There the calf will feed, and there it will lie
    down
And consume its branches.
¹¹When its boughs are withered, they will be
    broken off;
The women come *and* set them on fire.
For it *is* a people of no understanding;
Therefore He who made them will not have
    mercy on them,
And He who formed them will show them no
    favor.

¹²And it shall come to pass in that day
That the LORD will thresh,
From the channel of the River[a] to the Brook of
    Egypt;
And you will be gathered one by one,
O you children of Israel.

¹³So it shall be in that day:
The great trumpet will be blown;
They will come, who are about to perish in the
    land of Assyria,
And they who are outcasts in the land of
    Egypt,
And shall worship the LORD in the holy mount
    at Jerusalem.

Woe to Ephraim and Jerusalem

28 Woe to the crown of pride, to the drunkards
    of Ephraim,
Whose glorious beauty *is* a fading flower

•••••••••••••••••••••

26:19 [a]Following Masoretic Text and Vulgate; Syriac and Targum read *their dead bodies;* Septuagint reads *those in the tombs.* **27:2** [a]Following Masoretic Text (Kittel's *Biblia Hebraica*), Bomberg, and Vulgate; Masoretic Text (*Biblia Hebraica Stuttgartensia*), some Hebrew manuscripts, and Septuagint read *delight;* Targum reads *choice vineyard.* **27:9** [a]Hebrew *Asherim,* Canaanite deities **27:12** [a]That is, the Euphrates

---

28:1–13 The drunken leaders of the Lord's people were condemned. Ephraim is an alternate designation for Israel or the northern kingdom (v. 1). "The crown of pride" usually is interpreted as the city of Samaria, located on a hill (v. 1). The city

Which *is* at the head of the verdant valleys,
To those who are overcome with wine!
[2]Behold, the Lord has a mighty and strong one,
Like a tempest of hail and a destroying storm,
Like a flood of mighty waters overflowing,
Who will bring *them* down to the earth with
His hand.
[3]The crown of pride, the drunkards of Ephraim,
Will be trampled underfoot;
[4]And the glorious beauty is a fading flower
Which *is* at the head of the verdant valley,
Like the first fruit before the summer,
Which an observer sees;
He eats it up while it is still in his hand.

[5]In that day the LORD of hosts will be
For a crown of glory and a diadem of beauty
To the remnant of His people,
[6]For a spirit of justice to him who sits in
judgment,
And for strength to those who turn back the
battle at the gate.

[7]But they also have erred through wine,
And through intoxicating drink are out of the
way;
The priest and the prophet have erred through
intoxicating drink,
They are swallowed up by wine,
They are out of the way through intoxicating
drink;
They err in vision, they stumble *in* judgment.
[8]For all tables are full of vomit *and* filth;
No place *is clean.*

[9]"Whom will he teach knowledge?
And whom will he make to understand the
message?
Those *just* weaned from milk?
Those *just* drawn from the breasts?
[10]For precept *must be* upon precept, precept
upon precept,
Line upon line, line upon line,
Here a little, there a little."

[11]For with stammering lips and another tongue
He will speak to this people,
[12]To whom He said, "This *is* the rest *with which*
You may cause the weary to rest,"
And, "This *is* the refreshing";

Yet they would not hear.
[13]But the word of the LORD was to them,
"Precept upon precept, precept upon precept,
Line upon line, line upon line,
Here a little, there a little,"
That they might go and fall backward, and be
broken
And snared and caught.

[14]Therefore hear the word of the LORD, you
scornful men,
Who rule this people who *are* in Jerusalem,
[15]Because you have said, "We have made a
covenant with death,
And with Sheol we are in agreement.
When the overflowing scourge passes through,
It will not come to us,
For we have made lies our refuge,
And under falsehood we have hidden
ourselves."

A Cornerstone in Zion

[16]Therefore thus says the Lord GOD:

"Behold, I lay in Zion a stone for a foundation,
A tried stone, a precious cornerstone, a sure
foundation;
Whoever believes will not act hastily.
[17]Also I will make justice the measuring line,
And righteousness the plummet;
The hail will sweep away the refuge of lies,
And the waters will overflow the hiding place.
[18]Your covenant with death will be annulled,
And your agreement with Sheol will not stand;
When the overflowing scourge passes through,
Then you will be trampled down by it.
[19]As often as it goes out it will take you;
For morning by morning it will pass over,
And by day and by night;
It will be a terror just to understand the
report."

[20]For the bed is too short to stretch out *on,*
And the covering so narrow that one cannot
wrap himself *in it.*
[21]For the LORD will rise up as *at* Mount Perazim,
He will be angry as in the Valley of Gibeon—
That He may do His work, His awesome work,
And bring to pass His act, His unusual act.
[22]Now therefore, do not be mockers,

---

of Samaria did fall to the Assyrians in 722 B.C. The genuine
crown of God's people is the Lord Himself (v. 5). "In that day"
is eschatological language looking toward a glorious future
time when the Lord of Hosts would be an everlasting crown of
glory to the remnant of His people (v. 5). The sinful priests
and prophets were no longer capable of guiding the Lord's
people (vv. 7–13). Because the leaders of God's people had refused to hear the Lord's message in their own language, the
Lord would speak to them in Assyrian (v. 11).

28:14–22 Isaiah addressed the political leaders of Jerusalem,
who sought security in foreign alliances, believing their alliances would afford them protection from calamity (v. 15).
But judgment did come on the nation. Faith is a key element
in Isaiah's preaching. God's judgment on His people was predicted (v. 20).

EMPLOYMENT RELATIONSHIPS IN THE WORKPLACE AND AT HOME

A woman who is employed outside her home faces numerous decisions on a daily basis about how to juggle various obligations and priorities. As a woman evaluates her priorities and decisions, these guidelines may be helpful:

- Careers are usually based on contracts that are temporary; family relationships are covenants with spiritual commitment and are thus eternal. Employees and employers come and go, but a mother's children are hers for the rest of her life.
- Careers provide only part of a woman's identity. Ultimately, a woman is not what she does but who she is, which is largely determined by her relationships to God and to others.

When the inevitable feelings of guilt come, as the result of less than perfect choices, these principles of Scripture offer comfort: God created you and gave you the gifts and talents you choose to use in your career (Matt. 25:14–29). God's criterion for success is faithfulness with what you have been given to the task He has assigned (1 Cor. 4:2). You, as well as others, may expect perfection. Perfection is never possible, of course, but faithfulness is. God honors your efforts and intentions. He knows your weaknesses as well as your strengths. Neither your family members nor your colleagues in the workplace see the big picture of your life. Only God does. Conversely, He alone knows the way to meet all of the needs of those with whom you live or work.

A woman who is employed must acknowledge that she is obligated in certain ways to her employer, regardless of their spiritual state. For example, she owes her employer hard work (Prov. 10:4, 26; 15:19). A Christian should always give a full day's work and never take advantage of employers by cheating them out of time and work that is owed to them (Eccl. 9:10; 2 Tim. 2:15). She must be careful not to steal from our employers, doing everything she can to conserve their resources—both time and material assets (Prov. 1:19). She owes her employer loyalty. A Christian should not be found slandering or gossiping about her employer (see Titus 2:3).

Just as a woman must be willing to give an employer what is rightfully belonging to the employer, she must also give to God what is God's. For example, we do not owe our employer dishonesty of any sort, even if that employer should demand such (Prov. 2:12–15; 20:17). God requires a life of integrity and honesty, and an employer has no right to ask an employee to lie or deceive in any way.

A woman does not owe her employer participation in any activity that is dishonorable (1 Cor. 10:31). That includes social occasions marked by lewd conversation or sinful behavior. No employer has a right to require an employee to take part in sexually or morally compromising situations in order to keep a job.

Also, while a woman owes her employer an honest day's work, she does not owe all of her energy and time. She not only owes time and resources to God, but also God expects a balanced lifestyle with family and home priorities firmly established according to His divine order.

See also Eccl. 3:17; notes on Child Care (John 15); Decision Making (1 Cor. 8); Employment (Eccl. 9; Acts 18; 2 Cor. 2; Col. 3; 1 Pet. 2); Motherhood (1 Sam. 1; Is. 49; Ezek. 16); Priorities (Matt. 6); Wives (Prov. 31)

Lest your bonds be made strong;
For I have heard from the Lord God of hosts,
A destruction determined even upon the whole
    earth.

Listen to the Teaching of God

23Give ear and hear my voice,
    Listen and hear my speech.
24Does the plowman keep plowing all day to sow?
    Does he keep turning his soil and breaking the
        clods?
25When he has leveled its surface,
    Does he not sow the black cummin
    And scatter the cummin,

Plant the wheat in rows,
    The barley in the appointed place,
    And the spelt in its place?
26For He instructs him in right judgment,
    His God teaches him.

27For the black cummin is not threshed with a
        threshing sledge,
    Nor is a cartwheel rolled over the cummin;
    But the black cummin is beaten out with a
        stick,
    And the cummin with a rod.
28Bread *flour* must be ground;
    Therefore he does not thresh it forever,

28:23–29 Isaiah employed a parable regarding the farmer who practiced wisdom as he went about his work. The farmer knew when to till the soil and when and where to plant the seed. His cultivating, planting, and harvesting were in tune with the seasons or cycle of nature. Surely then God knew the needs of His people at each particular time in their existence. He knew when they needed chastening and when that discipline had accomplished His ultimate purpose—the salvation of His people.

Break *it with* his cartwheel,
Or crush it *with* his horsemen.
²⁹This also comes from the LORD of hosts,
Who is wonderful in counsel *and* excellent in
guidance.

Woe to Jerusalem

29 "Woe to Ariel,ᵃ to Ariel, the city *where* David
dwelt!
Add year to year;
Let feasts come around.
²Yet I will distress Ariel;
There shall be heaviness and sorrow,
And it shall be to Me as Ariel.
³I will encamp against you all around,
I will lay siege against you with a mound,
And I will raise siegeworks against you.
⁴You shall be brought down,
You shall speak out of the ground;
Your speech shall be low, out of the dust;
Your voice shall be like a medium's, out of the
ground;
And your speech shall whisper out of the dust.

⁵"Moreover the multitude of your foes
Shall be like fine dust,
And the multitude of the terrible ones
Like chaff that passes away;
Yes, it shall be in an instant, suddenly.
⁶You will be punished by the LORD of hosts
With thunder and earthquake and great noise,
With storm and tempest
And the flame of devouring fire.
⁷The multitude of all the nations who fight
against Ariel,
Even all who fight against her and her fortress,
And distress her,
Shall be as a dream of a night vision.
⁸It shall even be as when a hungry man dreams,
And look—he eats;
But he awakes, and his soul is still empty;
Or as when a thirsty man dreams,
And look—he drinks;
But he awakes, and indeed *he is* faint,
And his soul still craves:
So the multitude of all the nations shall be,
Who fight against Mount Zion."

The Blindness of Disobedience

⁹Pause and wonder!
Blind yourselves and be blind!
They are drunk, but not with wine;
They stagger, but not with intoxicating drink.
¹⁰For the LORD has poured out on you
The spirit of deep sleep,
And has closed your eyes, namely, the prophets;
And He has covered your heads, *namely,* the
seers.

¹¹The whole vision has become to you like the
words of a book that is sealed, which *men* deliver
to one who is literate, saying, "Read this, please."
And he says, "I cannot, for it *is* sealed."
¹²Then the book is delivered to one who is illiterate, saying, "Read this, please."
And he says, "I am not literate."
¹³Therefore the Lord said:

"Inasmuch as these people draw near with their
mouths
And honor Me with their lips,
But have removed their hearts far from Me,
And their fear toward Me is taught by the
commandment of men,
¹⁴Therefore, behold, I will again do a marvelous
work
Among this people,
A marvelous work and a wonder;
For the wisdom of their wise *men* shall perish,
And the understanding of their prudent *men*
shall be hidden."

¹⁵Woe to those who seek deep to hide their
counsel far from the LORD,
And their works are in the dark;
They say, "Who sees us?" and, "Who knows us?"
¹⁶Surely you have things turned around!
Shall the potter be esteemed as the clay;
For shall the thing made say of him who made it,
"He did not make me"?
Or shall the thing formed say of him who
formed it,
"He has no understanding"?

29:1 ᵃThat is, Jerusalem

29:1–8 Ariel probably refers to Jerusalem as the "altar of
God." Isaiah described a day of judgment on Jerusalem, the
city David captured from the Jebusites and established as his
capital (vv. 1–4; see 2 Sam. 5:6–9). The Lord brought both
judgment and deliverance to His people. Zion originally referred to the fortified hill of the city. The temple was built on
Mount Zion. Eventually Zion came to be a designation for the
city of Jerusalem itself (see chart, The Terminology for the Divided Kingdom).

29:9–16 This prophecy probably was delivered shortly before
the Sennacherib Crisis in 701 B.C. (see Introduction: Date). The

people went through all the motions of religion (v. 13); yet
their hearts were far from the Lord. Blindness was not the result intended by God but the inevitable result of continuing in
the way of disobedience to the Lord. Personal experience
with God was missing from the lives of God's people, a condition compared to a deep sleep (v. 10). Disobedience had made
God's people incapable of understanding His message. God
would awaken His people by performing a marvelous work in
their midst (v. 14). Judah's leaders were condemned for their
spiritual lethargy and disobedience to the Lord (vv. 10, 15, 16).

GOAL SETTING *PLOTTING A COURSE*

Goals are dreams with a deadline. In life's pursuits, you either move ahead or find yourself falling back; there is no middle ground! Some goals express good desires but cannot be measured and have no deadlines and thus are not achievable.

Meaningful vision and realistic goals must include: an explanation of the goal (what will it take to reach the goal?), and a date for completion (what is the deadline?).

The ardent and relentless pursuit of a goal was important to Paul! He spoke of pressing "toward the goal for the prize" (Phil. 3:14) and of running toward a prize and disciplining himself to "obtain" that prize (1 Cor. 9:24, 25). In both cases, however, Paul was speaking of achieving that which is imperishable: the crown that belongs to those who answer the upward call of God in Christ Jesus. The Lord is not at all opposed to your achievement—He simply calls upon you to direct your achievement toward right and eternal things!

Biblical guidelines determine goals (1 Cor. 10:31). All goals must be consistent with the written Word of God (2 Tim. 3:14–17) and like-minded with Jesus Christ (Phil. 2:5). Goal setting is appropriate for any age from youth through adulthood (1 Tim. 4:12–16), for all God-ordained relationships, and in all areas of life.

Certain commitments are involved in setting goals: Priorities must be specific or measurable (Heb. 6:10); goals should be realistic (Phil. 3:13, 14); a plan must be developed to get the work done (1 Cor. 9:24–27); time must be set aside to complete the task (Acts 20:24); and evaluation of the goal reached ought to be included (2 Tim. 4:7).

To accomplish an ultimate purpose or goal, steps are important. You first ask for direction from God (Prov. 3:5, 6). This establishes objectives for what is to be done (Ps. 37:23, 24) and determines a program for how you are going to accomplish your goal (Prov. 16:9). You must schedule when you are going to do what God has put in your heart to do (see 1 Chr. 12:32) and budget how much time and money is required.

A Christian's ultimate goal is always to please God. Discover His priorities (Matt. 22:36–40); study His principles (Ps. 119:105); determine His plans (Ps. 16:7–11); note His way of evaluating progress (Gal. 6:3, 4); remember His promise for help (Phil. 1:6); commit to His way of problem-solving (Ps. 37:4–9).

See also Phil. 3:12–14; Heb. 12:1, 2; notes on Organization (John 9); Priorities (Matt. 6); Time Management (Ps. 31)

Future Recovery of Wisdom

17Is it not yet a very little while
　Till Lebanon shall be turned into a fruitful
　　field,
　And the fruitful field be esteemed as a forest?
18In that day the deaf shall hear the words of the
　　book,
　And the eyes of the blind shall see out of
　　obscurity and out of darkness.
19The humble also shall increase *their* joy in the
　　LORD,
　And the poor among men shall rejoice
　　In the Holy One of Israel.
20For the terrible one is brought to nothing,
　The scornful one is consumed,
　And all who watch for iniquity are cut off—
21Who make a man an offender by a word,
　And lay a snare for him who reproves in the
　　gate,
　And turn aside the just by empty words.

22Therefore thus says the LORD, who redeemed
Abraham, concerning the house of Jacob:

"Jacob shall not now be ashamed,
　Nor shall his face now grow pale;
23But when he sees his children,
　The work of My hands, in his midst,
　They will hallow My name,
　And hallow the Holy One of Jacob,
　And fear the God of Israel.
24These also who erred in spirit will come to
　　understanding,
　And those who complained will learn
　　doctrine."

Futile Confidence in Egypt

30 "Woe to the rebellious children," says the
　　LORD,
"Who take counsel, but not of Me,
　And who devise plans, but not of My Spirit,
　That they may add sin to sin;
2Who walk to go down to Egypt,
　And have not asked My advice,
　To strengthen themselves in the strength of
　　Pharaoh,
　And to trust in the shadow of Egypt!

30:1–7 God's people would experience humiliation and shame because they trusted in Egypt instead of the Lord. Isaiah referred to Egypt as "Rahab-Hem-Shebeth," or as "Rahab who sits still" or "remains idle" (v. 7). Rahab refers to a primeval monster or dragon. Egypt's help was worthless.

³Therefore the strength of Pharaoh
Shall be your shame,
And trust in the shadow of Egypt
Shall be *your* humiliation.
⁴For his princes were at Zoan,
And his ambassadors came to Hanes.
⁵They were all ashamed of a people *who* could
not benefit them,
Or be help or benefit,
But a shame and also a reproach."

⁶The burden against the beasts of the South.

Through a land of trouble and anguish,
From which *came* the lioness and lion,
The viper and fiery flying serpent,
They will carry their riches on the backs of
young donkeys,
And their treasures on the humps of camels,
To a people *who* shall not profit;
⁷For the Egyptians shall help in vain and to no
purpose.
Therefore I have called her
Rahab-Hem-Shebeth.^a

A Rebellious People

⁸Now go, write it before them on a tablet,
And note it on a scroll,
That it may be for time to come,
Forever and ever:
⁹That this *is* a rebellious people,
Lying children,
Children *who* will not hear the law of the
LORD;
¹⁰Who say to the seers, "Do not see,"
And to the prophets, "Do not prophesy to us
right things;
Speak to us smooth things, prophesy
deceits.
¹¹Get out of the way,
Turn aside from the path,
Cause the Holy One of Israel
To cease from before us."

¹²Therefore thus says the Holy One of
Israel:

"Because you despise this word,
And trust in oppression and perversity,
And rely on them,
¹³Therefore this iniquity shall be to you
Like a breach ready to fall,
A bulge in a high wall,
Whose breaking comes suddenly, in an
instant.
¹⁴And He shall break it like the breaking of the
potter's vessel,
Which is broken in pieces;
He shall not spare.
So there shall not be found among its
fragments
A shard to take fire from the hearth,
Or to take water from the cistern."

¹⁵For thus says the Lord GOD, the Holy One of
Israel:

"In returning and rest you shall be saved;
In quietness and confidence shall be your
strength."
But you would not,
¹⁶And you said, "No, for we will flee on horses"—
Therefore you shall flee!
And, "We will ride on swift *horses*"—
Therefore those who pursue you shall be
swift!

¹⁷One thousand *shall flee* at the threat of one,
At the threat of five you shall flee,
Till you are left as a pole on top of a mountain
And as a banner on a hill.

God Will Be Gracious

¹⁸Therefore the LORD will wait, that He may be
gracious to you;

- - - - - - - - - - - - - - - -

30:7 ^aLiterally *Rahab Sits Idle*

30:8–17 The rebellious and unfaithful nature of God's people was to be written down as a testimony for future generations. Isaiah announced the coming judgment using two familiar images. Disaster would come like a crack in a wall, causing a sudden collapse, or like a worthless vessel that a potter smashes into tiny pieces. Bits of broken pottery or shards were used in Isaiah's time for such purposes as dipping water or writing messages. Isaiah described a vessel so shattered that no fragments could be salvaged, emphasizing that judgment would be both sudden and complete. Trust in God, not dependence on foreign alliances, was the desperate need of God's people (vv. 15, 16). "Horses" may refer to dependence on military cavalry (v. 16). Egypt and Assyria had horses (Is. 31:3). The folly of dependence on foreign alliances and military might was again indicated (Is. 30:15–17).

30:18–26 God's people were assured of His love for them in the midst of His discipline. Nevertheless, as the all-wise Parent, the Lord knows that His discipline is essential for His children's spiritual health. The verb "to be gracious" carries the idea of unmerited favor and denotes the attitude of a superior toward those under him (v. 18). "Mercy" is related closely to the Hebrew word for "womb," denoting the tender compassion that a mother shows to the child of her womb or the brotherly feeling of those born from the same womb (v. 18; see chart, Female Metaphors for God). "In that day" when the disciplining judgment would be past, the Lord would bountifully provide for His people (v. 23, see Is. 11:10–16, note). Agricultural imagery is used to picture the restoration of Zion (Is. 30:19) as a time of abundant provision (vv. 23, 24) and as a time of healing (v. 26). The Lord's judgment or discipline was intended to draw His people closer to Himself.

And therefore He will be exalted, that He may
    have mercy on you.
For the LORD *is* a God of justice;
Blessed *are* all those who wait for Him.

¹⁹For the people shall dwell in Zion at
    Jerusalem;
You shall weep no more.
He will be very gracious to you at the sound of
    your cry;
When He hears it, He will answer you.
²⁰And *though* the Lord gives you
The bread of adversity and the water of
    affliction,
Yet your teachers will not be moved into a
    corner anymore,
But your eyes shall see your teachers.
²¹Your ears shall hear a word behind you, saying,
"This *is* the way, walk in it,"
Whenever you turn to the right hand
Or whenever you turn to the left.
²²You will also defile the covering of your images
    of silver,
And the ornament of your molded images of
    gold.
You will throw them away as an unclean thing;
You will say to them, "Get away!"

²³Then He will give the rain for your seed
With which you sow the ground,
And bread of the increase of the earth;
It will be fat and plentiful.
In that day your cattle will feed
In large pastures.
²⁴Likewise the oxen and the young donkeys that
    work the ground
Will eat cured fodder,
Which has been winnowed with the shovel and
    fan.
²⁵There will be on every high mountain
And on every high hill
Rivers *and* streams of waters,
In the day of the great slaughter,
When the towers fall.
²⁶Moreover the light of the moon will be as the
    light of the sun,
And the light of the sun will be sevenfold,

As the light of seven days,
In the day that the LORD binds up the bruise of
    His people
And heals the stroke of their wound.

Judgment on Assyria

²⁷Behold, the name of the LORD comes from
    afar,
Burning *with* His anger,
And *His* burden *is* heavy;
His lips are full of indignation,
And His tongue like a devouring fire.
²⁸His breath is like an overflowing stream,
Which reaches up to the neck,
To sift the nations with the sieve of futility;
And *there shall be* a bridle in the jaws of the
    people,
Causing *them* to err.

²⁹You shall have a song
As in the night *when* a holy festival is kept,
And gladness of heart as when one goes with a
    flute,
To come into the mountain of the LORD,
To the Mighty One of Israel.
³⁰The LORD will cause His glorious voice to be
    heard,
And show the descent of His arm,
With the indignation of *His* anger
And the flame of a devouring fire,
With scattering, tempest, and hailstones.
³¹For through the voice of the LORD
Assyria will be beaten down,
As He strikes with the rod.
³²And *in* every place where the staff of
    punishment passes,
Which the LORD lays on him,
It will be with tambourines and harps;
And in battles of brandishing He will fight
    with it.
³³For Tophet *was* established of old,
Yes, for the king it is prepared.
He has made *it* deep and large;
Its pyre *is* fire with much wood;
The breath of the LORD, like a stream of
    brimstone,
Kindles it.

30:27–33 The Lord's judgment on Assyria takes the form of a theophany (an appearance of God in bodily form). "The name of the LORD" is another way of expressing the concept of God's presence and power (v. 27). God's name represents His character. God's tender compassion toward His people was emphasized (vv. 18–20), and God's wrath toward Assyria was revealed (vv. 27–33). The response of the Lord's people to Him, obedience or disobedience, determined which aspect of the Lord's character—mercy or wrath—would apply in any given situation. The description of the coming of the Lord in these verses is reminiscent of the description of His theo-

phany on Mount Sinai when Israel received the Law (see Ex. 19:16–18). The reference to the tambourines and harps may indicate the rejoicing of God's people as the Lord brings judgment on their enemies (Is. 30:32; see chart, Musical Instruments of the Old Testament). Assyria previously had served as the instrument of God's discipline on His people, and the time had come for Assyria to experience God's judgment (see Is. 10:5–19, note). "Tophet," literally a "hearth" or "burning place," refers to the place where human sacrifices were made to the pagan god Molech (Is. 30:33). In this case, the king of Assyria would be the sacrificial victim.

The Folly of Not Trusting God

31 Woe to those who go down to Egypt for help,
And rely on horses,
Who trust in chariots because *they are* many,
And in horsemen because they are very strong,
But who do not look to the Holy One of Israel,
Nor seek the LORD!
[2]Yet He also *is* wise and will bring disaster,
And will not call back His words,
But will arise against the house of evildoers,
And against the help of those who work
iniquity.
[3]Now the Egyptians *are* men, and not God;
And their horses are flesh, and not spirit.
When the LORD stretches out His hand,
Both he who helps will fall,
And he who is helped will fall down;
They all will perish together.

God Will Deliver Jerusalem

[4]For thus the LORD has spoken to me:

"As a lion roars,
And a young lion over his prey
(When a multitude of shepherds is summoned
against him,
He will not be afraid of their voice
Nor be disturbed by their noise),
So the LORD of hosts will come down
To fight for Mount Zion and for its hill.
[5]Like birds flying about,
So will the LORD of hosts defend Jerusalem.
Defending, He will also deliver *it;*
Passing over, He will preserve *it.*"

[6]Return *to Him* against whom the children of
Israel have deeply revolted. [7]For in that day every
man shall throw away his idols of silver and his
idols of gold—sin, which your own hands have
made for yourselves.

[8]"Then Assyria shall fall by a sword not of man,
And a sword not of mankind shall devour him.
But he shall flee from the sword,
And his young men shall become forced
labor.
[9]He shall cross over to his stronghold for fear,
And his princes shall be afraid of the banner,"
Says the LORD,
Whose fire *is* in Zion
And whose furnace *is* in Jerusalem.

A Reign of Righteousness

32 Behold, a king will reign in righteousness,
And princes will rule with justice.
[2]A man will be as a hiding place from the
wind,
And a cover from the tempest,
As rivers of water in a dry place,
As the shadow of a great rock in a weary
land.
[3]The eyes of those who see will not be dim,
And the ears of those who hear will listen.
[4]Also the heart of the rash will understand
knowledge,
And the tongue of the stammerers will be
ready to speak plainly.

[5]The foolish person will no longer be called
generous,
Nor the miser said *to be* bountiful;
[6]For the foolish person will speak foolishness,
And his heart will work iniquity:
To practice ungodliness,
To utter error against the LORD,
To keep the hungry unsatisfied,
And he will cause the drink of the thirsty to
fail.
[7]Also the schemes of the schemer *are* evil;
He devises wicked plans
To destroy the poor with lying words,
Even when the needy speaks justice.
[8]But a generous man devises generous
things,
And by generosity he shall stand.

31:4–9 The imagery of the lion may express the Lord's commitment to hold Jerusalem in His control regardless of how hard the shepherds (perhaps a reference to foreign kings) tried to snatch Jerusalem away. The Lord's commitment to the defense of His city may be pictured in the imagery of a mother bird protecting her young (v. 5; see chart, Female Metaphors for God). The Hebrew word translated "passing over" comes from the same root as the noun "Passover" (v. 5; see Ex. 12:1–30). Repentance was encouraged on the basis of God's love and grace, not on the basis of fear and punishment. Returning to the Lord involved casting away false gods (Is. 31:7, see 2:20). Isaiah 31:8, 9 acknowledges that God, not men, would defeat the Assyrians. This promise of deliverance found fulfillment when the Lord delivered Jerusalem from the armies of Sennacherib in 701 B.C. (see Introduction: Date).

32:1–8 The ideal of kingship is set forth. This prophecy was fulfilled in Christ but may also be interpreted as a description of good government, indicating what the nation would be like if its leaders were righteous men. Good leaders practice justice and righteousness and render right judgments. "Righteousness" carries the idea of meeting the demands of a relationship. Righteous leaders wisely fulfill the duties and obligations of their offices. Good leaders protect their people (vv. 1–5). Under the guidance of such leaders, truth can be distinguished from falsehood. The foolish person can be distinguished from the wise and noble individual. The "generous" person is one who operates with no ulterior motive (v. 8), making decisions objectively on the basis of what is best for the whole nation rather than on the basis of personal interests. This quality of nobility or generosity is associated closely with the qualities of justice and righteousness.

CONFIDENCE INWARD ASSURANCE

In the Old Testament, the words "confidence" and "assurance" are different forms of the same Hebrew word. Isaiah adds the concept of "quietness": "In quietness and confidence" (Is. 30:15) we find our strength. Isaiah also tells us that "quietness and assurance" are the effect of righteousness (Is. 32:17). In the New Testament, the Greek words translated "assurance" (Col. 2:2), "persuaded" (Rom. 8:38), and "convinced" (Rom. 14:5) convey the same idea as similar words in the Old Testament.

Assurance is not based on optimism about your own abilities. Rather it is an inward peace based on God's righteous work in you. Such confidence is not *self*-confidence, for that would be false security and reliance on something unreliable (Prov. 14:16; Jer. 9:23, 24). Scripture states that those who have confidence in their own strength (Is. 30:12), beauty (Ezek. 16:15), or righteousness (Ezek. 33:12) are to be considered fools (Prov. 28:26).

True confidence—rooted in the Lord's capabilities and His relationship with His children—is a quiet strength that brings "great reward" (Heb. 10:35, 36), a lasting security that is fully satisfying.

See also Ps. 115:8–11; 118:8; Jer. 17:5, 7; Col. 4:12; 1 Thess. 1:5; Heb. 6:11; 10:22; notes on Access to God (Rom. 10); Boldness (Prov. 28); Fruit of the Spirit (Rom. 5)

Consequences of Complacency

[9]Rise up, you women who are at ease,
Hear my voice;
You complacent daughters,
Give ear to my speech.
[10]In a year and *some* days
You will be troubled, you complacent women;
For the vintage will fail,
The gathering will not come.
[11]Tremble, you *women* who are at ease;
Be troubled, you complacent ones;
Strip yourselves, make yourselves bare,
And gird *sackcloth* on *your* waists.

[12]People shall mourn upon their breasts
For the pleasant fields, for the fruitful vine.
[13]On the land of my people will come up thorns
and briers,
Yes, on all the happy homes *in* the joyous city;
[14]Because the palaces will be forsaken,
The bustling city will be deserted.
The forts and towers will become lairs forever,
A joy of wild donkeys, a pasture of flocks—
[15]Until the Spirit is poured upon us from on
high,

And the wilderness becomes a fruitful field,
And the fruitful field is counted as a forest.

The Peace of God's Reign

[16]Then justice will dwell in the wilderness,
And righteousness remain in the fruitful field.
[17]The work of righteousness will be peace,
And the effect of righteousness, quietness and
assurance forever.
[18]My people will dwell in a peaceful habitation,
In secure dwellings, and in quiet resting
places,
[19]Though hail comes down on the forest,
And the city is brought low in humiliation.

[20]Blessed *are* you who sow beside all waters,
Who send out freely the feet of the ox and the
donkey.

A Prayer in Deep Distress

33 Woe to you who plunder, though you *have*
not *been* plundered;
And you who deal treacherously, though they
have not dealt treacherously with you!
When you cease plundering,
You will be plundered;

32:9–14 A challenge is issued to complacent women. The prophet challenged the women of his day to take heed of the current political situation. God's women must not be complacent and at ease in familiar surroundings. They must not look to externals as sources of security and trust. The Lord is the only true source of security for His people. Isaiah predicted trouble ahead for God's people! He foresaw a time of lamentation and mourning. Distress would come upon the happy homes of Jerusalem. This prophecy ultimately reached fulfillment in the destruction of Jerusalem by the Babylonians in 586 B.C. The women of Jerusalem had an important role to play in helping their nation find true security in the Lord.

32:15–20 The scene shifts from that of judgment to that of salvation (vv. 9–14). Justice, righteousness, and peace are the

effects of God's reign in the lives of His people. No longer would God's people feel a frantic need to seek a false security in military alliances. Genuine security results from a right relationship with the Lord (v. 18). Normal activities of daily living would be resumed in this time of peace (v. 20). God's gracious blessing of salvation reversed the destruction resulting from judgment.

33:1–9 The unnamed enemy on whom woe had been pronounced was identified as the Assyrians. The destroyer would now experience destruction. "Be gracious" carries the idea of unmerited favor and denotes the attitude of a superior toward those under him (v. 2). A note in the text indicates that the Septuagint (a Greek translation of the Hebrew OT) omits the word "their" preceding "arm" (v. 2). Other translations of

When you make an end of dealing
  treacherously,
They will deal treacherously with you.

2O Lord, be gracious to us;
  We have waited for You.
  Be their[a] arm every morning,
  Our salvation also in the time of trouble.
3At the noise of the tumult the people shall
  flee;
  When You lift Yourself up, the nations shall be
  scattered;
4And Your plunder shall be gathered
  Like the gathering of the caterpillar;
  As the running to and fro of locusts,
  He shall run upon them.

5The Lord is exalted, for He dwells on high;
  He has filled Zion with justice and
  righteousness.
6Wisdom and knowledge will be the stability of
  your times,
  And the strength of salvation;
  The fear of the Lord is His treasure.

7Surely their valiant ones shall cry outside,
  The ambassadors of peace shall weep bitterly.
8The highways lie waste,
  The traveling man ceases.
  He has broken the covenant,
  He has despised the cities,[a]
  He regards no man.
9The earth mourns and languishes,
  Lebanon is shamed and shriveled;
  Sharon is like a wilderness,
  And Bashan and Carmel shake off their
  fruits.

Impending Judgment on Zion

10"Now I will rise," says the Lord;
  "Now I will be exalted,
  Now I will lift Myself up.
11You shall conceive chaff,
  You shall bring forth stubble;
  Your breath, as fire, shall devour you.
12And the people shall be like the burnings of
  lime;
  Like thorns cut up they shall be burned in the
  fire.

13Hear, you who are afar off, what I have done;
  And you who are near, acknowledge My might."

14The sinners in Zion are afraid;
  Fearfulness has seized the hypocrites:
  "Who among us shall dwell with the devouring
  fire?
  Who among us shall dwell with everlasting
  burnings?"
15He who walks righteously and speaks
  uprightly,
  He who despises the gain of oppressions,
  Who gestures with his hands, refusing bribes,
  Who stops his ears from hearing of bloodshed,
  And shuts his eyes from seeing evil:
16He will dwell on high;
  His place of defense will be the fortress of
  rocks;
  Bread will be given him,
  His water will be sure.

The Land of the Majestic King

17Your eyes will see the King in His beauty;
  They will see the land that is very far off.
18Your heart will meditate on terror:
  "Where is the scribe?
  Where is he who weighs?
  Where is he who counts the towers?"
19You will not see a fierce people,
  A people of obscure speech, beyond
  perception,
  Of a stammering tongue that you cannot
  understand.

20Look upon Zion, the city of our appointed
  feasts;
  Your eyes will see Jerusalem, a quiet home,
  A tabernacle that will not be taken down;
  Not one of its stakes will ever be removed,
  Nor will any of its cords be broken.
21But there the majestic Lord will be for us
  A place of broad rivers and streams,
  In which no galley with oars will sail,
  Nor majestic ships pass by
22(For the Lord is our Judge,

33:2 aSeptuagint omits their; Syriac, Targum, and Vulgate read our.
33:8 aFollowing Masoretic Text and Vulgate; Dead Sea Scrolls read witnesses; Septuagint omits cities; Targum reads They have been removed from their cities.

the OT, such as the Syriac and the Latin Vulgate, read "our arm" instead of "their arm." The reading "our arm" fits the context of the verse with its predominant use of first person plural pronouns. If "our arm" is the correct reading, then the cry is for God to be the arm or strength of His people, their salvation in the time of trouble. The exalted Lord established Zion (Jerusalem) as the city of justice and righteousness (see Is. 32:1–8, note). "The fear of the Lord" refers not to cringing fear, but to reverent obedience (Is. 33:6).

33:17–24 This eschatological passage looks toward a future time when God's people will celebrate His majestic reign and enjoy the glories of the New Jerusalem. The terror of foreign domination would be past (vv. 18, 19). Jerusalem would become the immovable and secure dwelling place of the righteous (v. 20). The Lord would be recognized as the great Judge, Lawgiver, and King (v. 22). In that future day, happiness would abound as sickness is healed and sin is forgiven, reflecting the close association between sin and sickness in Hebrew thought (v. 24).

The LORD *is* our Lawgiver,
The LORD *is* our King;
He will save us);
23 Your tackle is loosed,
They could not strengthen their mast,
They could not spread the sail.

Then the prey of great plunder is divided;
The lame take the prey.
24 And the inhabitant will not say, "I am sick";
The people who dwell in it *will be* forgiven *their*
iniquity.

Judgment on the Nations

34 Come near, you nations, to hear;
And heed, you people!
Let the earth hear, and all that is in it,
The world and all things that come forth from
it.
2 For the indignation of the LORD *is* against all
nations,
And *His* fury against all their armies;
He has utterly destroyed them,
He has given them over to the slaughter.
3 Also their slain shall be thrown out;
Their stench shall rise from their corpses,
And the mountains shall be melted with their
blood.
4 All the host of heaven shall be dissolved,
And the heavens shall be rolled up like a scroll;
All their host shall fall down
As the leaf falls from the vine,
And as *fruit* falling from a fig tree.

5 "For My sword shall be bathed in heaven;
Indeed it shall come down on Edom,
And on the people of My curse, for judgment.
6 The sword of the LORD is filled with blood,
It is made overflowing with fatness,
With the blood of lambs and goats,
With the fat of the kidneys of rams.
For the LORD has a sacrifice in Bozrah,
And a great slaughter in the land of Edom.
7 The wild oxen shall come down with them,
And the young bulls with the mighty bulls;
Their land shall be soaked with blood,
And their dust saturated with fatness."

8 For *it is* the day of the LORD's vengeance,
The year of recompense for the cause of Zion.

9 Its streams shall be turned into pitch,
And its dust into brimstone;
Its land shall become burning pitch.
10 It shall not be quenched night or day;
Its smoke shall ascend forever.
From generation to generation it shall lie waste;
No one shall pass through it forever and ever.
11 But the pelican and the porcupine shall possess
it,
Also the owl and the raven shall dwell in it.
And He shall stretch out over it
The line of confusion and the stones of
emptiness.
12 They shall call its nobles to the kingdom,
But none *shall be* there, and all its princes shall
be nothing.

13 And thorns shall come up in its palaces,
Nettles and brambles in its fortresses;
It shall be a habitation of jackals,
A courtyard for ostriches.
14 The wild beasts of the desert shall also meet
with the jackals,
And the wild goat shall bleat to its companion;
Also the night creature shall rest there,
And find for herself a place of rest.
15 There the arrow snake shall make her nest and
lay *eggs*
And hatch, and gather *them* under her shadow;
There also shall the hawks be gathered,
Every one with her mate.

16 "Search from the book of the LORD, and read:
Not one of these shall fail;
Not one shall lack her mate.
For My mouth has commanded it, and His
Spirit has gathered them.
17 He has cast the lot for them,
And His hand has divided it among them with
a measuring line.
They shall possess it forever;
From generation to generation they shall dwell
in it."

The Future Glory of Zion

35 The wilderness and the wasteland shall be
glad for them,
And the desert shall rejoice and blossom as the
rose;

**34:1–4 The entire earth was called to witness the fury of the
Lord.** The slain bodies of God's enemies would not receive
burial, a sign of great tragedy or disrespect from the Hebrew
perspective. This judgment is described as apocalyptic in nature because it is connected with the end of world history
(v. 4; see Zech., Introduction: Literary Characteristics). The
sovereignty of the Lord is emphasized.

34:5–17 Edom is singled out for judgment because of that nation's intense hatred of God's people. Edom, located south-

east of Judah, is associated with Esau (see Gen. 36:1). Constant hostility existed between God's people and Edom during
the time of the kings. The Edomites assisted the Babylonians
in their destruction of Jerusalem in 586 B.C. Amos condemned
the Edomites for their hostility toward God's people (Amos
1:11, 12), and the theme of Obadiah is the destruction of Edom.

35:1–10 This proclamation of new life from the Lord provides
the background for the commission given to the prophet
(vv. 3, 4). This new message of hope would strengthen the

²It shall blossom abundantly and rejoice,
Even with joy and singing.
The glory of Lebanon shall be given to it,
The excellence of Carmel and Sharon.
They shall see the glory of the LORD,
The excellency of our God.

³Strengthen the weak hands,
And make firm the feeble knees.
⁴Say to those *who are* fearful-hearted,
"Be strong, do not fear!
Behold, your God will come *with* vengeance,
With the recompense of God;
He will come and save you."

⁵Then the eyes of the blind shall be opened,
And the ears of the deaf shall be unstopped.
⁶Then the lame shall leap like a deer,
And the tongue of the dumb sing.
For waters shall burst forth in the wilderness,
And streams in the desert.
⁷The parched ground shall become a pool,
And the thirsty land springs of water;
In the habitation of jackals, where each lay,
There shall be grass with reeds and rushes.

⁸A highway shall be there, and a road,
And it shall be called the Highway of Holiness.
The unclean shall not pass over it,
But it *shall be* for others.
Whoever walks the road, although a fool,
Shall not go astray.
⁹No lion shall be there,
Nor shall *any* ravenous beast go up on it;
It shall not be found there.
But the redeemed shall walk *there,*
¹⁰And the ransomed of the LORD shall return,
And come to Zion with singing,
With everlasting joy on their heads.
They shall obtain joy and gladness,
And sorrow and sighing shall flee away.

Sennacherib Boasts Against the LORD

36 Now it came to pass in the fourteenth year of King Hezekiah *that* Sennacherib king of Assyria came up against all the fortified cities of Judah and took them. ²Then the king of Assyria sent *the* Rabshakeh[a] with a great army from Lachish to King Hezekiah at Jerusalem. And he stood by the aqueduct from the upper pool, on the highway to the Fuller's Field. ³And Eliakim the son of Hilkiah, who was over the household, Shebna the scribe, and Joah the son of Asaph, the recorder, came out to him.

⁴Then *the* Rabshakeh said to them, "Say now to Hezekiah, 'Thus says the great king, the king of Assyria: "What confidence is this in which you trust? ⁵I say you speak of having plans and power for war; but *they are* mere words. Now in whom do you trust, that you rebel against me? ⁶Look! You are trusting in the staff of this broken reed, Egypt, on which if a man leans, it will go into his hand and pierce it. So *is* Pharaoh king of Egypt to all who trust in him.
⁷"But if you say to me, 'We trust in the LORD our God,' *is it* not He whose high places and whose altars Hezekiah has taken away, and said to Judah and Jerusalem, 'You shall worship before this altar'?" ' ⁸Now therefore, I urge you, give a pledge to my master the king of Assyria, and I will give you two thousand horses—if you are able on your part to put riders on them! ⁹How then will you repel one captain of the least of my master's servants, and put your trust in Egypt for chariots and horsemen? ¹⁰Have I now come up without the LORD against this land to destroy it? The LORD said to me, 'Go up against this land, and destroy it.' "

¹¹Then Eliakim, Shebna, and Joah said to *the* Rabshakeh, "Please speak to your servants in Aramaic, for we understand *it;* and do not speak to us in Hebrew[a] in the hearing of the people who *are* on the wall."

¹²But *the* Rabshakeh said, "Has my master sent me to your master and to you to speak these words, and not to the men who sit on the wall, who will eat and drink their own waste with you?"

¹³Then *the* Rabshakeh stood and called out with a loud voice in Hebrew, and said, "Hear the words of the great king, the king of Assyria!

36:2 [a]A title, probably *Chief of Staff* or *Governor*   **36:11** [a]Literally *Judean*

---

weak and fearful. God would defeat His people's enemies and bring His people salvation (v. 4). The desert symbolizes life without God. God's highway would provide a safe and joyful way for His people to journey to Zion (vv. 8–10), signifying the everlasting joy and security He would bring to the lives of His people. This chapter shares themes common to Isaiah 40–66 such as the joy of God's redeemed people, the transformation of the desert, the preparation of the highway, and the message of comfort and hope.

36:1—37:38 Sennacherib ascended the throne in 705 B.C. after the death of his father Sargon II, king of Assyria. A rebellion involving the entire Assyrian Empire occurred early in Sennacherib's reign. Hezekiah, king of Judah, joined the revolt.

Sennacherib and his army marched westward to put down the rebellion. Rabshakeh is a title designating the chief officer of the Assyrian army (Is. 36:2). Isaiah prophesied that the Assyrian king would return to his own land and die by the sword, and he did (Is. 37:37, 38). Jerusalem was spared for the sake of the Lord's name or reputation and also for the sake of the Lord's servant David.

36:1—39:8 A historical interlude functions as a bridge between Isaiah 35 and 40 (see 2 Kin. 18:13—20:19; 2 Chr. 32). Chapters 36—39 of Isaiah deal with events surrounding the illness of Hezekiah and the Sennacherib Crisis in 701 B.C. (see Introduction: Date).

14Thus says the king: 'Do not let Hezekiah deceive you, for he will not be able to deliver you; 15nor let Hezekiah make you trust in the LORD, saying, "The LORD will surely deliver us; this city will not be given into the hand of the king of Assyria." ' 16Do not listen to Hezekiah; for thus says the king of Assyria: 'Make *peace* with me *by a* present and come out to me; and every one of you eat from his own vine and every one from his own fig tree, and every one of you drink the waters of his own cistern; 17until I come and take you away to a land like your own land, a land of grain and new wine, a land of bread and vineyards. 18*Beware* lest Hezekiah persuade you, saying, "The LORD will deliver us." Has any one of the gods of the nations delivered its land from the hand of the king of Assyria? 19Where *are* the gods of Hamath and Arpad? Where *are* the gods of Sepharvaim? Indeed, have they delivered Samaria from my hand? 20Who among all the gods of these lands have delivered their countries from my hand, that the LORD should deliver Jerusalem from my hand?' "

21But they held their peace and answered him not a word; for the king's commandment was, "Do not answer him." 22Then Eliakim the son of Hilkiah, who *was* over the household, Shebna the scribe, and Joah the son of Asaph, the recorder, came to Hezekiah with *their* clothes torn, and told him the words of *the* Rabshakeh.

Isaiah Assures Deliverance

37 And so it was, when King Hezekiah heard *it*, that he tore his clothes, covered himself with sackcloth, and went into the house of the LORD. 2Then he sent Eliakim, who *was* over the household, Shebna the scribe, and the elders of the priests, covered with sackcloth, to Isaiah the prophet, the son of Amoz. 3And they said to him, "Thus says Hezekiah: 'This day *is* a day of trouble and rebuke and blasphemy; for the children have come to birth, but *there is* no strength to bring them forth. 4It may be that the LORD your God will hear the words of *the* Rabshakeh, whom his master the king of Assyria has sent to reproach the living God, and will rebuke the words which the LORD your God has heard. Therefore lift up *your* prayer for the remnant that is left.' "

5So the servants of King Hezekiah came to Isaiah. 6And Isaiah said to them, "Thus you shall say to your master, 'Thus says the LORD: "Do not be afraid of the words which you have heard, with which the servants of the king of Assyria have blasphemed Me. 7Surely I will send a spirit upon him, and he shall hear a rumor and return to his own land; and I will cause him to fall by the sword in his own land." ' "

Sennacherib's Threat and Hezekiah's Prayer

8Then *the* Rabshakeh returned, and found the king of Assyria warring against Libnah, for he heard that he had departed from Lachish. 9And the king heard concerning Tirhakah king of Ethiopia, "He has come out to make war with you." So when he heard *it*, he sent messengers to Hezekiah, saying, 10"Thus you shall speak to Hezekiah king of Judah, saying: 'Do not let your God in whom you trust deceive you, saying, "Jerusalem shall not be given into the hand of the king of Assyria." 11Look! You have heard what the kings of Assyria have done to all lands by utterly destroying them; and shall you be delivered? 12Have the gods of the nations delivered those whom my fathers have destroyed, Gozan and Haran and Rezeph, and the people of Eden who *were* in Telassar? 13Where *is* the king of Hamath, the king of Arpad, and the king of the city of Sepharvaim, Hena, and Ivah?' "

14And Hezekiah received the letter from the hand of the messengers, and read it; and Hezekiah went up to the house of the LORD, and spread it before the LORD. 15Then Hezekiah prayed to the LORD, saying: 16"O LORD of hosts, God of Israel, *the* One who dwells *between* the cherubim, You *are* God, You alone, of all the kingdoms of the earth. You have made heaven and earth. 17Incline Your ear, O LORD, and hear; open Your eyes, O LORD, and see; and hear all the words of Sennacherib, which he has sent to reproach the living God. 18Truly, LORD, the kings of Assyria have laid waste all the nations and their lands, 19and have cast their gods into the fire; for they *were* not gods, but the work of men's hands— wood and stone. Therefore they destroyed them. 20Now therefore, O LORD our God, save us from his hand, that all the kingdoms of the earth may know that You *are* the LORD, You alone."

The Word of the LORD Concerning Sennacherib

21Then Isaiah the son of Amoz sent to Hezekiah, saying, "Thus says the LORD God of Israel, 'Because you have prayed to Me against Sennacherib king of Assyria, 22this *is* the word which the LORD has spoken concerning him:

"The virgin, the daughter of Zion,
Has despised you, laughed you to scorn;
The daughter of Jerusalem
Has shaken *her* head behind your back!

23"Whom have you reproached and blasphemed?
Against whom have you raised *your* voice,
And lifted up your eyes on high?
Against the Holy One of Israel.
24By your servants you have reproached the
Lord,

And said, 'By the multitude of my chariots
I have come up to the height of the mountains,
To the limits of Lebanon;
I will cut down its tall cedars
And its choice cypress trees;
I will enter its farthest height,
To its fruitful forest.
25I have dug and drunk water,
And with the soles of my feet I have dried up
All the brooks of defense.'

26"Did you not hear long ago
How I made it,
From ancient times that I formed it?
Now I have brought it to pass,
That you should be
For crushing fortified cities *into* heaps of
ruins.
27Therefore their inhabitants *had* little power;
They were dismayed and confounded;
They were *as* the grass of the field
And the green herb,
As the grass on the housetops
And grain blighted before it is grown.

28"But I know your dwelling place,
Your going out and your coming in,
And your rage against Me.
29Because your rage against Me and your tumult
Have come up to My ears,
Therefore I will put My hook in your nose
And My bridle in your lips,
And I will turn you back
By the way which you came." '

30"This *shall be* a sign to you:

You shall eat this year such as grows of itself,
And the second year what springs from the
same;
Also in the third year sow and reap,
Plant vineyards and eat the fruit of them.
31And the remnant who have escaped of the
house of Judah
Shall again take root downward,
And bear fruit upward.
32For out of Jerusalem shall go a remnant,
And those who escape from Mount Zion.
The zeal of the LORD of hosts will do this.

33"Therefore thus says the LORD concerning
the king of Assyria:

'He shall not come into this city,
Nor shoot an arrow there,
Nor come before it with shield,
Nor build a siege mound against it.
34By the way that he came,
By the same shall he return;
And he shall not come into this city,'
Says the LORD.
35'For I will defend this city, to save it
For My own sake and for My servant David's
sake.' "

Sennacherib's Defeat and Death

36Then the angel[a] of the LORD went out, and killed in the camp of the Assyrians one hundred and eighty-five thousand; and when *people* arose early in the morning, there were the corpses—all dead. 37So Sennacherib king of Assyria departed and went away, returned *home,* and remained at Nineveh. 38Now it came to pass, as he was worshiping in the house of Nisroch his god, that his sons Adrammelech and Sharezer struck him down with the sword; and they escaped into the land of Ararat. Then Esarhaddon his son reigned in his place.

Hezekiah's Life Extended

38 In those days Hezekiah was sick and near death. And Isaiah the prophet, the son of Amoz, went to him and said to him, "Thus says the LORD: 'Set your house in order, for you shall die and not live.' "

2Then Hezekiah turned his face toward the wall, and prayed to the LORD, 3and said, "Remember now, O LORD, I pray, how I have walked before You in truth and with a loyal heart, and have done *what is* good in Your sight." And Hezekiah wept bitterly.

4And the word of the LORD came to Isaiah, saying, 5"Go and tell Hezekiah, 'Thus says the LORD, the God of David your father: "I have heard your prayer, I have seen your tears; surely I will add to your days fifteen years. 6I will deliver you and this city from the hand of the king of Assyria, and I will defend this city." ' 7And this *is* the sign to you from the LORD, that the LORD will do this thing which He has spoken: 8Behold, I will bring the shadow on the sundial, which has gone down with the sun on the sundial of Ahaz, ten degrees backward." So the sun

37:36 [a]Or Angel

38:1–22 King Hezekiah went to the Lord in prayer after Isaiah delivered the news of his impending death. As a wise king, Hezekiah took both personal and national crises to the Lord (see Is. 37:14–20). The Lord, who alone has power over life and death, added 15 years to Hezekiah's life. Hezekiah offered a prayer of thanksgiving for healing (Is. 38:10–20).

Hezekiah not only prayed in the difficult times of life, but he also offered praise for the Lord's deliverance and salvation. Insight into the Hebrew concept of death is provided (v. 18). Those in "Sheol" lived a shadowy kind of existence, lacking hope and no longer praising God.

returned ten degrees on the dial by which it had gone down.

⁹This is the writing of Hezekiah king of Judah, when he had been sick and had recovered from his sickness:

¹⁰I said,
"In the prime of my life
  I shall go to the gates of Sheol;
  I am deprived of the remainder of my years."
¹¹I said,
"I shall not see YAH,
  The LORDᵃ in the land of the living;
  I shall observe man no more among the
    inhabitants of the world.ᵇ
¹²My life span is gone,
  Taken from me like a shepherd's tent;
  I have cut off my life like a weaver.
  He cuts me off from the loom;
  From day until night You make an end of me.
¹³I have considered until morning—
  Like a lion,
  So He breaks all my bones;
  From day until night You make an end of me.
¹⁴Like a crane *or* a swallow, so I chattered;
  I mourned like a dove;
  My eyes fail *from looking* upward.
  O LORD,ᵃ I am oppressed;
  Undertake for me!

¹⁵"What shall I say?
  He has both spoken to me,ᵃ
  And He Himself has done *it*.
  I shall walk carefully all my years
  In the bitterness of my soul.
¹⁶O Lord, by these *things men* live;
  And in all these *things is* the life of my spirit;
  So You will restore me and make me live.
¹⁷Indeed *it was* for *my own* peace
  That I had great bitterness;
  But You have lovingly *delivered* my soul from
    the pit of corruption,
  For You have cast all my sins behind Your back.
¹⁸For Sheol cannot thank You,
  Death cannot praise You;
  Those who go down to the pit cannot hope for
    Your truth.
¹⁹The living, the living man, he shall praise You,
  As I *do* this day;
  The father shall make known Your truth to the
    children.

²⁰"The LORD *was ready* to save me;
  Therefore we will sing my songs with stringed
    instruments

All the days of our life, in the house of the
  LORD."

²¹Now Isaiah had said, "Let them take a lump of figs, and apply *it* as a poultice on the boil, and he shall recover."

²²And Hezekiah had said, "What *is* the sign that I shall go up to the house of the LORD?"

The Babylonian Envoys

39 At that time Merodach-Baladanᵃ the son of Baladan, king of Babylon, sent letters and a present to Hezekiah, for he heard that he had been sick and had recovered. ²And Hezekiah was pleased with them, and showed them the house of his treasures—the silver and gold, the spices and precious ointment, and all his armory—all that was found among his treasures. There was nothing in his house or in all his dominion that Hezekiah did not show them.

³Then Isaiah the prophet went to King Hezekiah, and said to him, "What did these men say, and from where did they come to you?"

So Hezekiah said, "They came to me from a far country, from Babylon."

⁴And he said, "What have they seen in your house?"

So Hezekiah answered, "They have seen all that *is* in my house; there is nothing among my treasures that I have not shown them."

⁵Then Isaiah said to Hezekiah, "Hear the word of the LORD of hosts: ⁶'Behold, the days are coming when all that *is* in your house, and what your fathers have accumulated until this day, shall be carried to Babylon; nothing shall be left,' says the LORD. ⁷'And they shall take away *some* of your sons who will descend from you, whom you will beget; and they shall be eunuchs in the palace of the king of Babylon.' "

⁸So Hezekiah said to Isaiah, "The word of the LORD which you have spoken *is* good!" For he said, "At least there will be peace and truth in my days."

God's People Are Comforted

40 "Comfort, yes, comfort My people!"
  Says your God.
²"Speak comfort to Jerusalem, and cry out to her,
  That her warfare is ended,

- - - - - - - - - - - - - - - - - -

38:11 ᵃHebrew *YAH, YAH* ᵇFollowing some Hebrew manuscripts; Masoretic Text and Vulgate read *rest*; Septuagint omits *among the inhabitants of the world*; Targum reads *land*. **38:14** ᵃFollowing Bomberg; Masoretic Text and Dead Sea Scrolls read *Lord*. **38:15** ᵃFollowing Masoretic Text and Vulgate; Dead Sea Scrolls and Targum read *And shall I say to Him*; Septuagint omits first half of this verse. **39:1** ᵃSpelled *Berodach-Baladan* in 2 Kings 20:12

39:1–8 After Hezekiah's recovery, he trusted in human resources instead of putting his faith in the Lord. Isaiah prophesied the coming Exile in Babylon. Hezekiah's response reflects his selfish attitude. He did not seem too concerned about the coming judgment as long as it did not affect him

personally (v. 8). The reference to Babylon in this chapter provides a link with the remainder of the Book of Isaiah.

40:1–11 The Lord had heard the cries of His people in Exile (cf. Ex. 2:23–25). Through His prophet, He delivered a message of

That her iniquity is pardoned;
For she has received from the LORD's hand
Double for all her sins."

³The voice of one crying in the wilderness:
"Prepare the way of the LORD;
Make straight in the desert[a]
A highway for our God.
⁴Every valley shall be exalted
And every mountain and hill brought low;
The crooked places shall be made straight
And the rough places smooth;
⁵The glory of the LORD shall be revealed,
And all flesh shall see *it* together;
For the mouth of the LORD has spoken."

⁶The voice said, "Cry out!"
And he[a] said, "What shall I cry?"

"All flesh *is* grass,
And all its loveliness *is* like the flower of the
field.
⁷The grass withers, the flower fades,
Because the breath of the LORD blows upon it;
Surely the people *are* grass.
⁸The grass withers, the flower fades,
But the word of our God stands forever."

⁹O Zion,
You who bring good tidings,
Get up into the high mountain;
O Jerusalem,
You who bring good tidings,
Lift up your voice with strength,
Lift *it* up, be not afraid;
Say to the cities of Judah, "Behold your God!"

¹⁰Behold, the Lord GOD shall come with a strong
hand,
And His arm shall rule for Him;
Behold, His reward *is* with Him,
And His work before Him.
¹¹He will feed His flock like a shepherd;
He will gather the lambs with His arm,
And carry *them* in His bosom,
And gently lead those who are with
young.

THE HEART OF THE BOOK OF ISAIAH		
CONTRAST	ISAIAH 1–39	ISAIAH 40–66
Locale	Around Jerusalem	Babylonian Exile
Message	Judgment	Comfort and hope
View of Messiah	Messianic King	Suffering Servant

¹²Who has measured the waters[a] in the hollow of
His hand,
Measured heaven with a span
And calculated the dust of the earth in a
measure?
Weighed the mountains in scales
And the hills in a balance?
¹³Who has directed the Spirit of the LORD,
Or *as* His counselor has taught Him?
¹⁴With whom did He take counsel, and *who*
instructed Him,
And taught Him in the path of justice?
Who taught Him knowledge,
And showed Him the way of understanding?

¹⁵Behold, the nations *are* as a drop in a bucket,
And are counted as the small dust on the
scales;
Look, He lifts up the isles as a very little thing.
¹⁶And Lebanon *is* not sufficient to burn,
Nor its beasts sufficient for a burnt offering.
¹⁷All nations before Him *are* as nothing,
And they are counted by Him less than
nothing and worthless.

¹⁸To whom then will you liken God?
Or what likeness will you compare to Him?
¹⁹The workman molds an image,
The goldsmith overspreads it with gold,
And the silversmith casts silver chains.

40:3 ᵃFollowing Masoretic Text, Targum, and Vulgate; Septuagint
omits *in the desert.*   40:6 ᵃFollowing Masoretic Text and Targum;
Dead Sea Scrolls, Septuagint, and Vulgate read *I.*   40:12 ᵃFollowing
Masoretic Text, Septuagint, and Vulgate; Dead Sea Scrolls read
waters of the sea; Targum reads *waters of the world.*

comfort to them regarding their return from captivity. Captivity and Exile had resulted from the sins of God's people (Is. 40:2). "Speak comfort to Jerusalem" (lit. "speak upon the heart of Jerusalem") carries the picture of bringing encouragement, reassurance, and tender compassion to the people of Jerusalem (v. 2). "All flesh" indicates that through His act of deliverance, God would reveal Himself to all peoples, not just to His own (v. 5). For "glory" (lit. "to be heavy" or "to be weighty"; see Psalm 19:1, note). Isaiah 40:8 underlines the necessity of focusing on the dependability of God's Word, not on the unreliability of mankind. The Lord is revealed as One who is both strong and tender (vv. 10, 11). The essence of comfort

for the Lord's people would be God's presence in their midst (v. 9).

40:12–26 The prophet proclaimed the majesty of the Lord over the idols worshiped by other nations. The great Creator God, the Lord, intimately knows the universe He has created (v. 12). No one instructs the Lord; He is the all-knowing God (vv. 13, 14). Satire is evident in the suggestion that one could even think of comparing the great Creator God to an image made out of a tree, itself part of God's creative handiwork (vv. 18–20). The great Creator is separate from His creation (v. 22). "Created" (Heb. *bara'*), appearing a number of times

FATIGUE REFUELING FOR RENEWED SERVICE

Fatigue can make a "nag" of anyone! Nothing goes further to make a woman less able to cope with unruly children, household or job crises, and thousands of other mundane irritations. Scripture offers ways for women to reduce fatigue and avoid weariness.

- Support from an understanding husband or close friend helps you handle pressure and stress more effectively. Knowing that someone not only knows about the burden but comes alongside to help you bear up under the load (Is. 50:4; Gal. 6:2) makes every crisis more tolerable.
- Women are refreshed and invigorated by being able to walk away from burdens even for a few hours. Such time for yourself can provide renewal of energies and revival of spirit and can produce creativity and re-create productivity (Eccl. 5:18).
- Women need to guard against overcommitment. Even good and godly pursuits must be weighed against the purposes of God (Heb. 12:1). You must learn to say "no," determine to slow your frantic pace, resist the temptation to add more and more to your schedule. Busyness is not necessarily godliness. Perhaps your "R and R" should become Reprioritizing responsibilities (Matt. 6:33) and Rethinking free time (Eccl. 3:1–8).

Being tired is a physical affliction. Being weary, on the other hand, is a spiritual attitude that results in part from blaming God for your own sinfulness. Life will never free you from fatigue, but fatigue can bring you to the point of setting aside the mundane cares of the world in order to open your heart and soul to the Lord (Eccl. 12:12).

God can use fatigue:

1) to cause you to look to Him for satisfaction (Is. 28:12, 13),
2) to administer correction (Heb. 12:5) as He pulls back His hand of strength to force your body to slow down for refueling, and
3) to prepare you for a greater challenge (Jer. 12:5).

God has promised to satisfy fully the weary soul and replenish faithfully the sorrowful heart (Jer. 31:25). Sometimes that means, "He makes me to lie down" (Ps. 23:2). Physical frailties may cause you to miss earthly fun and fellowship, but spiritual resources will enable you to grow stronger on the bed of affliction.

See also 2 Sam. 16:14; 17:2; Job 3:17; Ps. 6:6; 69:3; notes on Fitness (Phil. 1); Health (Prov. 3); Leisure (Mark 6); The Lord's Day (Ex. 23); Renewal (Hab. 3)

²⁰Whoever *is* too impoverished for *such a* contribution
Chooses a tree *that* will not rot;
He seeks for himself a skillful workman
To prepare a carved image *that* will not totter.

²¹Have you not known?
Have you not heard?
Has it not been told you from the beginning?
Have you not understood from the foundations of the earth?
²²*It is* He who sits above the circle of the earth,
And its inhabitants *are* like grasshoppers,

Who stretches out the heavens like a curtain,
And spreads them out like a tent to dwell in.
²³He brings the princes to nothing;
He makes the judges of the earth useless.

²⁴Scarcely shall they be planted,
Scarcely shall they be sown,
Scarcely shall their stock take root in the earth,
When He will also blow on them,
And they will wither,
And the whirlwind will take them away like stubble.

---

in Isaiah 40–66, suggests the idea of creation out of nothing because it is always used with God as subject. *Bara'* refers to something only God can do.

40:27–31 The Lord's people, referred to as Jacob and as Israel, felt that He had forgotten them. They were discouraged and afraid because their concept of God was too small. The prophet reminded them of the greatness of the Lord. The greatest human strength is insufficient to meet the challenges of life. The powerful Creator God *gives* power (v. 29). "Renew" actually means "to exchange." Those who wait or

depend on the Lord will exchange their weakness for God's strength. Neither soaring with wings as eagles nor running is pictured as the climax; rather the sought-after prize of walking is presented as the mainstay of Christian experience. Serving God in the mountain-top experiences of life when His people can soar with Him is not so difficult. The most difficult times of service can be in the monotonous, everyday grind of life when God's people feel like they are spinning their wheels and going nowhere. The Lord's children can exchange their weaknesses for God's strength in the daily walk of life.

²⁵"To whom then will you liken Me,
Or *to whom* shall I be equal?" says the Holy One.
²⁶Lift up your eyes on high,
And see who has created these *things*,
Who brings out their host by number;
He calls them all by name,
By the greatness of His might
And the strength of *His* power;
Not one is missing.

²⁷Why do you say, O Jacob,
And speak, O Israel:
"My way is hidden from the LORD,
And my just claim is passed over by my God"?
²⁸Have you not known?
Have you not heard?
The everlasting God, the LORD,
The Creator of the ends of the earth,
Neither faints nor is weary.
His understanding is unsearchable.
²⁹He gives power to the weak,
And to *those who have* no might He increases
    strength.
³⁰Even the youths shall faint and be weary,
And the young men shall utterly fall,
³¹But those who wait on the LORD
Shall renew *their* strength;
They shall mount up with wings like eagles,
They shall run and not be weary,
They shall walk and not faint.

Israel Assured of God's Help

41 "Keep silence before Me, O coastlands,
And let the people renew *their* strength!
Let them come near, then let them speak;
Let us come near together for judgment.

²"Who raised up one from the east?
Who in righteousness called him to His feet?
Who gave the nations before him,
And made *him* rule over kings?
Who gave *them* as the dust *to* his sword,
As driven stubble to his bow?
³Who pursued them, *and* passed safely
By the way *that* he had not gone with his feet?
⁴Who has performed and done *it*,
Calling the generations from the beginning?

'I, the LORD, am the first;
And with the last I *am* He.' "

⁵The coastlands saw *it* and feared,
The ends of the earth were afraid;
They drew near and came.
⁶Everyone helped his neighbor,
And said to his brother,
"Be of good courage!"
⁷So the craftsman encouraged the goldsmith;
He who smooths *with* the hammer *inspired* him
    who strikes the anvil,
Saying, "It *is* ready for the soldering";
Then he fastened it with pegs,
That it might not totter.

⁸"But you, Israel, *are* My servant,
Jacob whom I have chosen,
The descendants of Abraham My friend.
⁹*You* whom I have taken from the ends of the
    earth,
And called from its farthest regions,
And said to you,
'You *are* My servant,
I have chosen you and have not cast you away:
¹⁰Fear not, for I *am* with you;
Be not dismayed, for I *am* your God.
I will strengthen you,
Yes, I will help you,
I will uphold you with My righteous right
    hand.'

¹¹"Behold, all those who were incensed against
    you
Shall be ashamed and disgraced;
They shall be as nothing,
And those who strive with you shall perish.
¹²You shall seek them and not find them—
Those who contended with you.
Those who war against you
Shall be as nothing,
As a nonexistent thing.
¹³For I, the LORD your God, will hold your right
    hand,
Saying to you, 'Fear not, I will help you.'

¹⁴"Fear not, you worm Jacob,
You men of Israel!

41:1–7 A court scene is envisioned, and legal arguments are employed to demonstrate the incomparable nature of the Lord over the gods of the other nations. The "one from the east" is Cyrus, king of Persia, who began to rule over Babylon in 539 B.C. (v. 2). The edict or decree of Cyrus allowed captives to return to their homelands (see Ezra 1:1–4). The Lord in His sovereignty permitted Cyrus to rule. The Lord has always been in control of history. Fear fell on the nations when they heard of the success of Cyrus (Is. 41:5–7). A satire on the folly of idol worship appears in these verses as, in panic, the nations try to make more powerful gods.

41:8–20 Israel is identified as the Lord's servant (v. 8), providing reassurance to the Lord's people that He has not given up on them or abandoned them. The Lord's election of His people still stands (Ex. 19:1–6). To be God's servant means to belong to the Lord and to give allegiance only to Him. The Lord's servant has no reason to fear, for the Lord provides security and protection for His own (Is. 41:10, 13, 14). Jacob is an alternate designation for the nation Israel (see chart, Terminology for the People of God). The patriarch Jacob received the name Israel after he wrestled with the Man of God at Peniel (see Gen. 32:22–32). For "the Holy One of Israel," see Isaiah 1:4–9, note.

IDOLATRY *WORSHIPING PSEUDO-GODS*

An idol—that is, an image or a phantom—in ancient times was often cast as the actual physical image of a god. Idolatry is a direct attack against the basic nature of God. In the New Testament, idolatry is associated with sexual sin (Gal. 5:19–20), evil desires, covetousness (1 Cor. 5:11; Eph. 5:5; Col. 3:5), and anything else that causes people to deviate from the gospel of Jesus Christ (1 John 5:18–21).

An idol is whatever claims the loyalty and glory that belong to God alone (Ps. 95:3; Is. 42:8). For that reason, idols are detestable in God's sight (Jer. 4:1). They arouse His jealousy (Ps. 78:58), anger (Deut. 32:16), and even hatred (Jer. 44:4).

Idols are nonentities that are crafted and fashioned out of human imagination (Ps. 31:6; 1 Cor. 8:4). Nevertheless, they are associated with witchcraft and contain demonic potencies that constitute a very real spiritual menace (2 Chr. 33:5–7; Mic. 5:12–13; Gal. 5:20). Idolatry and Christianity are totally and utterly incompatible (2 Cor. 6:16), and believers are thus admonished to keep themselves free from idols (1 John 5:21).

See also Is. 44:9–20; John 1:4, note; notes on Goddess Religion (Ex. 20); Heresies (1 Cor. 1); the Occult (Deut. 18); Paganism (Jer. 7); Witchcraft (1 Sam. 15)

I will help you," says the LORD
And your Redeemer, the Holy One of Israel.
¹⁵"Behold, I will make you into a new threshing
    sledge with sharp teeth;
You shall thresh the mountains and beat *them*
    small,
And make the hills like chaff.
¹⁶You shall winnow them, the wind shall carry
    them away,
And the whirlwind shall scatter them;
You shall rejoice in the LORD,
And glory in the Holy One of Israel.

¹⁷"The poor and needy seek water, but *there is*
    none,
Their tongues fail for thirst.
I, the LORD, will hear them;
I, the God of Israel, will not forsake them.
¹⁸I will open rivers in desolate heights,
And fountains in the midst of the valleys;
I will make the wilderness a pool of water,
And the dry land springs of water.
¹⁹I will plant in the wilderness the cedar and the
    acacia tree,
The myrtle and the oil tree;
I will set in the desert the cypress tree *and* the
    pine
And the box tree together,
²⁰That they may see and know,
And consider and understand together,
That the hand of the LORD has done this,
And the Holy One of Israel has created it.

The Futility of Idols

²¹"Present your case," says the LORD.
"Bring forth your strong *reasons*," says the King
    of Jacob.

²²"Let them bring forth and show us what will
    happen;
Let them show the former things, what they
    were,
That we may consider them,
And know the latter end of them;
Or declare to us things to come.
²³Show the things that are to come hereafter,
That we may know that you *are* gods;
Yes, do good or do evil,
That we may be dismayed and see *it*
    together.
²⁴Indeed you *are* nothing,
And your work *is* nothing;
He who chooses you *is* an abomination.

²⁵"I have raised up one from the north,
And he shall come;
From the rising of the sun he shall call on My
    name;
And he shall come against princes as *though*
    mortar,
As the potter treads clay.
²⁶Who has declared from the beginning, that we
    may know?
And former times, that we may say, '*He is*
    righteous'?
Surely *there is* no one who shows,
Surely *there is* no one who declares,
Surely *there is* no one who hears your words.
²⁷The first time *I said* to Zion,
'Look, there they are!'
And I will give to Jerusalem one who brings
    good tidings.
²⁸For I looked, and *there was* no man;
I looked among them, but *there was* no
    counselor,

41:21–29 Again in a courtroom scene the Lord challenged the false gods of the nations to prove whether they could control history. The silence of the idols indicated their worthlessness and lack of power. In contrast, the Lord had raised up Cyrus as ruler and had directed world history.

Who, when I asked of them, could answer a
word.
[29]Indeed they *are* all worthless;[a]
Their works *are* nothing;
Their molded images *are* wind and confusion.

The Servant of the LORD

42 "Behold! My Servant whom I uphold,
My Elect One *in whom* My soul delights!
I have put My Spirit upon Him;
He will bring forth justice to the Gentiles.
[2]He will not cry out, nor raise *His voice,*
Nor cause His voice to be heard in the
street.
[3]A bruised reed He will not break,
And smoking flax He will not quench;
He will bring forth justice for truth.
[4]He will not fail nor be discouraged,
Till He has established justice in the earth;
And the coastlands shall wait for His law."

[5]Thus says God the LORD,
Who created the heavens and stretched them
out,
Who spread forth the earth and that which
comes from it,
Who gives breath to the people on it,
And spirit to those who walk on it:
[6]"I, the LORD, have called You in righteousness,
And will hold Your hand;
I will keep You and give You as a covenant to
the people,
As a light to the Gentiles,
[7]To open blind eyes,
To bring out prisoners from the prison,
Those who sit in darkness from the prison
house.
[8]I *am* the LORD, that *is* My name;
And My glory I will not give to another,
Nor My praise to carved images.
[9]Behold, the former things have come to
pass,
And new things I declare;
Before they spring forth I tell you of them."

Praise to the LORD

[10]Sing to the LORD a new song,
And His praise from the ends of the earth,
You who go down to the sea, and all that is in
it,
You coastlands and you inhabitants of
them!
[11]Let the wilderness and its cities lift up *their
voice,*
The villages *that* Kedar inhabits.
Let the inhabitants of Sela sing,
Let them shout from the top of the mountains.
[12]Let them give glory to the LORD,
And declare His praise in the coastlands.
[13]The LORD shall go forth like a mighty man;
He shall stir up *His* zeal like a man of war.
He shall cry out, yes, shout aloud;
He shall prevail against His enemies.

Promise of the LORD's Help

[14]"I have held My peace a long time,
I have been still and restrained Myself.
Now I will cry like a woman in labor,
I will pant and gasp at once.
[15]I will lay waste the mountains and hills,
And dry up all their vegetation;
I will make the rivers coastlands,
And I will dry up the pools.
[16]I will bring the blind by a way they did not
know;
I will lead them in paths they have not
known.
I will make darkness light before them,
And crooked places straight.
These things I will do for them,
And not forsake them.
[17]They shall be turned back,
They shall be greatly ashamed,
Who trust in carved images,
Who say to the molded images,
'You *are* our gods.'

41:29 [a]Following Masoretic Text and Vulgate; Dead Sea Scrolls,
Syriac, and Targum read *nothing;* Septuagint omits the first line.

42:1–4 A series of servant songs or poems have been identified in Isaiah 40—66 (Is. 42:1-4 or 42:1-9; 49:1-6; 50:4-9; 52:13—53:12). Who is the servant of these passages? The Lord put His Spirit upon His servant to equip him for ministry (Is. 42:1-4). His servant had the mission of bringing justice to the Gentiles, to all the earth. The servant was to accomplish the Lord's purpose in a gentle and patient manner (vv. 2, 3). In context, some identify the servant described in this passage as the Lord's people Israel (see Is. 41:8), who were intended to be a light to the nations (Is. 42:6). The Lord called Abram or Abraham in order that He might bless all the families of the earth through him (Gen. 12:1-3). The Lord's purpose from the beginning was for His people to function as instruments of His salvation (see Ex. 19:1-6). Others see the servant as an individual who would bring salvation to Israel. The NT seems to apply the messianic "servant" passages to Jesus (see Matt. 12:17-20). In any case, the servant mission given to Israel was perfectly fulfilled in Jesus. The identification of the servant with Israel would certainly point to ultimate fulfillment in Jesus Christ.

42:14–17 God's intervention on behalf of His people will have a negative effect on idol worshipers (vv. 14-17). God presented Himself using the metaphor of a pregnant woman in labor. The Hebrew text suggest a breathless and convulsive condition (v. 14; see chart, Female Metaphors for God). The "blind" are the Lord's people (v. 16). They are designated as blind because they felt that their future was hopeless. Though they were blind, the Lord would lead them along the right paths.

SUFFERING — EXPERIENCING GOD'S GOODNESS IN THE MIDST

God's goodness is nowhere more apparent than in the midst of suffering. His history of providential care and deliverance for His people remains a constant reminder in every generation that He is to carry us *through* every adversity and trial. His presence is sufficient to banish fear. His power is enough to deliver from despair. His ultimate purpose is always for our good (Rom. 8:28).

Much of our suffering as human beings is rooted either in circumstances beyond our control, or in relationships.

Everyone is affected by circumstances that bring suffering. Mary Magdalene, for example, had been possessed of demons. She testified to the suffering of body and mind she endured before meeting Jesus. The outpouring of devotion that she showed in following Jesus to the cross (Mark 15:40, 47), as well as the unutterable joy she displayed to Jesus at the Garden after His resurrection (John 20:1, 11–18), left little doubt that she had known at a very deep level a response of love from our Lord that had liberated her from the demon possession she had previously suffered. In the light of His love, she experienced status, acceptance, and peace.

The Scriptures have a number of stories of suffering that are rooted in a woman's relationships: mother, wife, sister, daughter, friend. One example is Mary, the mother of Jesus. As a result of her openness and obedience to God, she exposed herself to the suffering that was to manifest itself in various ways: She endangered her engagement to Joseph (Matt. 1:18–25); she fled into exile once Jesus was born in order to safeguard His life (Matt. 2:14–15); she suffered the rejection of Jesus as He moved out of the exclusiveness of His family to the inclusiveness of the kingdom of God (Mark 3:31–35); and finally, she suffered the agonies of watching her Son's cruel death on Calvary. As with other biblical motifs, suffering, however, does not have the final word; for with the Resurrection of the Lord, the arrows that pierced Mary's soul were turned to the joy that every believer will experience at the Lord's return.

In the story of the Shunammite mother and her son is an insight into the profound suffering that comes peculiarly to mothers who experience the death of a dearly loved child (2 Kin. 4:8–37). Pathos and tragedy combine in the growing relationship between a family from Shunem and Elisha the prophet. Elisha received hospitality from a wealthy woman from Shunem. Her barrenness obviously had not made her bitter because she was profoundly hospitable. As a result of her hospitality to Elisha, she was blessed with a son. What greater joy could a woman know than the blessing of a child, and yet what greater pain could she endure than to lose this son through death. As with many biblical presentations of suffering, the pain is not belittled, but the promise of life broke through in her faith and obedience, which led to her son being raised to life.

See also notes on Adversity (Acts 5); Family (Gen. 32; 1 Sam. 3; Ps. 78; 127); Prejudice (Acts 15); Friendship (Luke 1); Husbands (Job 31; 2 Cor. 6); Suffering (Ps. 33; 113; 1 Pet. 5); Wives (Prov. 31), Prisoners (Is. 61)

18"Hear, you deaf;
 And look, you blind, that you may see.
19Who *is* blind but My servant,
 Or deaf as My messenger *whom* I send?
 Who *is* blind as *he who is* perfect,
 And blind as the LORD's servant?
20Seeing many things, but you do not observe;
 Opening the ears, but he does not hear."

Israel's Obstinate Disobedience

21The LORD is well pleased for His righteousness' sake;
 He will exalt the law and make *it* honorable.
22But this *is* a people robbed and plundered;
 All of them are snared in holes,
 And they are hidden in prison houses;

They are for prey, and no one delivers;
 For plunder, and no one says, "Restore!"

23Who among you will give ear to this?
 Who will listen and hear for the time to come?
24Who gave Jacob for plunder, and Israel to the robbers?
 Was it not the LORD,
 He against whom we have sinned?
 For they would not walk in His ways,
 Nor were they obedient to His law.
25Therefore He has poured on him the fury of His anger
 And the strength of battle;
 It has set him on fire all around,
 Yet he did not know;

42:18–25 The Lord's people had not been sensitive to His mission for them. They had forsaken His law. They believed the Lord had chosen them for privilege and were blind to the responsibility that accompanied the Lord's choice of the nation. The people blamed the Lord for their defeat and captivity, though the prophet clearly indicated that defeat occurred because of the people's sin. The Lord was neither blind nor deaf to His servant; rather the Lord's servant was blind and deaf to Him.

And it burned him,
Yet he did not take *it* to heart.

The Redeemer of Israel

43 But now, thus says the LORD, who created
you, O Jacob,
And He who formed you, O Israel:
"Fear not, for I have redeemed you;
I have called *you* by your name;
You *are* Mine.
2When you pass through the waters, I *will be*
with you;
And through the rivers, they shall not overflow
you.
When you walk through the fire, you shall not
be burned,
Nor shall the flame scorch you.
3For I *am* the LORD your God,
The Holy One of Israel, your Savior;
I gave Egypt for your ransom,
Ethiopia and Seba in your place.
4Since you were precious in My sight,
You have been honored,
And I have loved you;
Therefore I will give men for you,
And people for your life.
5Fear not, for I *am* with you;
I will bring your descendants from the east,
And gather you from the west;
6I will say to the north, 'Give them up!'
And to the south, 'Do not keep them back!'
Bring My sons from afar,
And My daughters from the ends of the
earth—
7Everyone who is called by My name,
Whom I have created for My glory;
I have formed him, yes, I have made him."

8Bring out the blind people who have eyes,
And the deaf who have ears.
9Let all the nations be gathered together,
And let the people be assembled.
Who among them can declare this,
And show us former things?
Let them bring out their witnesses, that they
may be justified;
Or let them hear and say, "*It is* truth."
10"You *are* My witnesses," says the LORD,
"And My servant whom I have chosen,
That you may know and believe Me,

And understand that I *am* He.
Before Me there was no God formed,
Nor shall there be after Me.
11I, *even* I, *am* the LORD,
And besides Me *there is* no savior.
12I have declared and saved,
I have proclaimed,
And *there was* no foreign *god* among you;
Therefore you *are* My witnesses,"
Says the LORD, "that I *am* God.
13Indeed before the day *was*, I *am* He;
And *there is* no one who can deliver out of My
hand;
I work, and who will reverse it?"

14Thus says the LORD, your Redeemer,
The Holy One of Israel:
"For your sake I will send to Babylon,
And bring them all down as fugitives—
The Chaldeans, who rejoice in their ships.
15I *am* the LORD, your Holy One,
The Creator of Israel, your King."

16Thus says the LORD, who makes a way in the
sea
And a path through the mighty waters,
17Who brings forth the chariot and horse,
The army and the power
(They shall lie down together, they shall not
rise;
They are extinguished, they are quenched like
a wick):
18"Do not remember the former things,
Nor consider the things of old.
19Behold, I will do a new thing,
Now it shall spring forth;
Shall you not know it?
I will even make a road in the wilderness
And rivers in the desert.
20The beast of the field will honor Me,
The jackals and the ostriches,
Because I give waters in the wilderness
And rivers in the desert,
To give drink to My people, My chosen.
21This people I have formed for Myself;
They shall declare My praise.

Pleading with Unfaithful Israel

22"But you have not called upon Me, O Jacob;
And you have been weary of Me, O Israel.

43:1–7 Jacob is an alternate designation for Israel (v. 1; see
chart, The Terminology for the People of God). Comforting and
encouraging words are provided for the Lord's people. Israel
belonged to God by right of creation, redemption, and naming
(v. 1). Just as the Lord brought the Hebrew slaves safely through
the waters of the sea (Ex. 14:1–31), so He would continue to
bring His people "through" when they encountered troubled
times (Is. 43:2). The Lord named His people and they are His
(v. 1). The Hebrew concept of naming implies having power or

control over that which is named (See Is. 45, Naming of Children). For "the Holy One of Israel," see Isaiah 1:4–9, note.

43:8–13 The prophet turned to the courtroom scene again to
demonstrate the greatness of the Lord. The Lord's people are
called as witnesses to the fact that there is no other like the
Lord.

43:22–28 The Lord condemned His people for their unfaithfulness. The designation "Jacob" may be a reminder that they

²³You have not brought Me the sheep for your
    burnt offerings,
Nor have you honored Me with your sacrifices.
I have not caused you to serve with grain
    offerings,
Nor wearied you with incense.
²⁴You have bought Me no sweet cane with
    money,
Nor have you satisfied Me with the fat of your
    sacrifices;
But you have burdened Me with your sins,
You have wearied Me with your iniquities.

²⁵"I, *even* I, *am* He who blots out your
    transgressions for My own sake;
And I will not remember your sins.
²⁶Put Me in remembrance;
Let us contend together;
State your *case,* that you may be acquitted.
²⁷Your first father sinned,
And your mediators have transgressed against
    Me.
²⁸Therefore I will profane the princes of the
    sanctuary;
I will give Jacob to the curse,
And Israel to reproaches.

God's Blessing on Israel

44 "Yet hear me now, O Jacob My servant,
And Israel whom I have chosen.
²Thus says the LORD who made you
And formed you from the womb, *who* will help
    you:
'Fear not, O Jacob My servant;
And you, Jeshurun, whom I have chosen.
³For I will pour water on him who is thirsty,
And floods on the dry ground;
I will pour My Spirit on your descendants,
And My blessing on your offspring;
⁴They will spring up among the grass
Like willows by the watercourses.'
⁵One will say, 'I *am* the LORD's';

Another will call *himself* by the name of Jacob;
Another will write *with* his hand, 'The LORD's,'
And name *himself* by the name of Israel.

There Is No Other God

⁶"Thus says the LORD, the King of Israel,
And his Redeemer, the LORD of hosts:
'I *am* the First and I *am* the Last;
Besides Me *there is* no God.
⁷And who can proclaim as I do?
Then let him declare it and set it in order for
    Me,
Since I appointed the ancient people.
And the things that are coming and shall
    come,
Let them show these to them.
⁸Do not fear, nor be afraid;
Have I not told you from that time, and
    declared *it?*
You *are* My witnesses.
Is there a God besides Me?
Indeed *there is* no other Rock;
I know not *one.*' "

Idolatry Is Foolishness

⁹Those who make an image, all of them *are*
    useless,
And their precious things shall not profit;
They *are* their own witnesses;
They neither see nor know, that they may be
    ashamed.
¹⁰Who would form a god or mold an image
That profits him nothing?
¹¹Surely all his companions would be ashamed;
And the workmen, they *are* mere men.
Let them all be gathered together,
Let them stand up;
Yet they shall fear,
They shall be ashamed together.

¹²The blacksmith with the tongs works one in
    the coals,

---

were imitating the character of their deceitful ancestor Jacob, whose name was later changed to Israel (v. 22). The Lord's requirements for His people were not overly demanding; yet the people failed to meet those basic requirements. Instead they burdened the Lord with their sins (v. 24). The people had come to view the Lord as their servant rather than as their Lord. The Lord had not failed in the covenant relationship with Israel; His people had failed Him. The Lord repeatedly had forgiven their sins (v. 25). "Transgressions" also can be translated "rebellion" (v. 25). The Lord's people had deliberately rebelled against Him.

44:1–5 God's people had sinned from the beginning of their existence (see Is. 43:27); yet the people of Israel had also remained the Lord's chosen instrument from the beginning of their existence (Is. 44:2). "Jeshurun" (Heb. lit. "upright") is a positive title the Lord gave His people, indicating His ideal for His own (v. 2). Note the contrast in verse 2 between the desig-

nations "Jacob" (lit. "trickster") and "Jeshurun" (lit. "upright one"). As water brings life to dry ground, so the Lord's Spirit will bring new life to His people. Verse 5 may be a reference to the increase of the Lord's people through proselytizing among the nations.

44:9–20 The folly of worshiping idols is described with sarcasm. The Hebrew word "useless" is the same word used to describe the emptiness or formlessness of the world in the beginning (v. 9; see Gen. 1:2). The prophet indicated that those who practice idol worship are empty-headed. The satire reaches its height when the craftsman cuts down a tree and uses part of it to build a fire to cook his meal and warm himself (Is. 44:15–17). With the rest of the wood the craftsman makes an idol before which he bows and cries for deliverance! Such a person is deluded and deceived, and he "feeds on ashes" (v. 20).

Fashions it with hammers,
And works it with the strength of his arms.
Even so, he is hungry, and his strength
 fails;
He drinks no water and is faint.

¹³The craftsman stretches out *his* rule,
He marks one out with chalk;
He fashions it with a plane,
He marks it out with the compass,
And makes it like the figure of a man,
According to the beauty of a man, that it may
 remain in the house.
¹⁴He cuts down cedars for himself,
And takes the cypress and the oak;
He secures *it* for himself among the trees of
 the forest.
He plants a pine, and the rain nourishes *it.*

¹⁵Then it shall be for a man to burn,
For he will take some of it and warm himself;
Yes, he kindles *it* and bakes bread;
Indeed he makes a god and worships *it;*
He makes it a carved image, and falls down to
 it.
¹⁶He burns half of it in the fire;
With this half he eats meat;
He roasts a roast, and is satisfied.
He even warms *himself* and says,
"Ah! I am warm,
I have seen the fire."
¹⁷And the rest of it he makes into a god,
His carved image.
He falls down before it and worships *it,*
Prays to it and says,
"Deliver me, for you *are* my god!"

¹⁸They do not know nor understand;
For He has shut their eyes, so that they cannot
 see,
And their hearts, so that they cannot
 understand.
¹⁹And no one considers in his heart,
Nor *is there* knowledge nor understanding to
 say,
"I have burned half of it in the fire,
Yes, I have also baked bread on its coals;
I have roasted meat and eaten *it;*
And shall I make the rest of it an abomination?
Shall I fall down before a block of wood?"
²⁰He feeds on ashes;
A deceived heart has turned him aside;
And he cannot deliver his soul,
Nor say, "*Is there* not a lie in my right
 hand?"

Israel Is Not Forgotten

²¹"Remember these, O Jacob,
And Israel, for you *are* My servant;
I have formed you, you *are* My servant;
O Israel, you will not be forgotten by Me!
²²I have blotted out, like a thick cloud, your
 transgressions,
And like a cloud, your sins.
Return to Me, for I have redeemed you."

²³Sing, O heavens, for the Lord has done *it!*
Shout, you lower parts of the earth;
Break forth into singing, you mountains,
O forest, and every tree in it!
For the Lord has redeemed Jacob,
And glorified Himself in Israel.

Judah Will Be Restored

²⁴Thus says the Lord, your Redeemer,
And He who formed you from the womb:
"I *am* the Lord, who makes all *things,*
Who stretches out the heavens all alone,
Who spreads abroad the earth by Myself;
²⁵Who frustrates the signs of the babblers,
And drives diviners mad;
Who turns wise men backward,
And makes their knowledge foolishness;
²⁶Who confirms the word of His servant,
And performs the counsel of His messengers;
Who says to Jerusalem, 'You shall be inhabited,'
To the cities of Judah, 'You shall be built,'
And I will raise up her waste places;
²⁷Who says to the deep, 'Be dry!
And I will dry up your rivers';
²⁸Who says of Cyrus, '*He is* My shepherd,
And he shall perform all My pleasure,
Saying to Jerusalem, "You shall be built,"
And to the temple, "Your foundation shall be
 laid." '

Cyrus, God's Instrument

45 "Thus says the Lord to His anointed,
To Cyrus, whose right hand I have held—
To subdue nations before him
And loose the armor of kings,
To open before him the double doors,
So that the gates will not be shut:
²I will go before you
And make the crooked places[a] straight;
I will break in pieces the gates of bronze
And cut the bars of iron.

45:2 [a]Dead Sea Scrolls and Septuagint read *mountains;* Targum
reads *I will trample down the walls;* Vulgate reads *I will humble the
great ones of the earth.*

45:1–13 The Lord chose Cyrus, king of Persia, to be His instrument in accomplishing His purposes, even though Cyrus did not acknowledge the Lord (vv. 4, 5). The Hebrew practice was to anoint with oil those who assumed positions of leadership (v. 1). The right hand is the hand of strength or power (v. 1).

NAMING OF CHILDREN WHAT'S IN A NAME?

The Hebrews believed that naming something was to encompass and control it. Names of children, thus, spoke of the "essence" of children—their attributes, identities, or distinguishing characteristics.

In the Old Testament, there are more than fifty examples in which children are given names that have a meaning. Some of these relate to events associated with the child's birth or conception (Gen. 17:19; 25:26; 1 Sam. 4:21). The Lord commanded Hosea to name his children as part of a prophetic message to Israel (Hos. 1:4, 6, 9)—Jezreel meaning "my punishment," Lo-Ruhamah meaning "not loved," and Lo-Ammi meaning "not my people."

Names also frequently referred to a child's lineage. The Aramaic word "bar" means "the son of"—so that Bartimaeus means "son of Timaeus" (Mark 10:46). The Hebrew word "ben" also means "son" and is frequently linked to a circumstance or situation. For example, Ben-ammi means the "son of my people," Benoni is "the son of my trouble," and Benjamin is "the son of my right hand" (see Gen. 19:38, 35:18).

In some cases, parents in the Bible are told specifically what to name their children, perhaps most notably in the case of John the Baptist (Luke 1:57–66) and Jesus (Luke 2:21). A change in a person's name nearly always refers to a change in that person's character or identity, such as when Jesus changed the name of Simon to Peter (John 1:42).

See also Matt. 18:3, note; notes on Children (2 Sam. 21; Ps. 128; Prov. 22; Luke 15); Family (Gen. 32; 1 Sam. 3; Ps. 78; 127); Inheritance (Prov. 13); Traditions (1 Sam. 7)

³I will give you the treasures of darkness
And hidden riches of secret places,
That you may know that I, the LORD,
Who call *you* by your name,
Am the God of Israel.
⁴For Jacob My servant's sake,
And Israel My elect,
I have even called you by your name;
I have named you, though you have not known Me.
⁵I *am* the LORD, and *there is* no other;
There is no God besides Me.
I will gird you, though you have not known Me,
⁶That they may know from the rising of the sun to its setting
That *there is* none besides Me.
I *am* the LORD, and *there is* no other;
⁷I form the light and create darkness,
I make peace and create calamity;
I, the LORD, do all these *things.*'

⁸"Rain down, you heavens, from above,
And let the skies pour down righteousness;
Let the earth open, let them bring forth salvation,
And let righteousness spring up together.
I, the LORD, have created it.

⁹"Woe to him who strives with his Maker!
Let the potsherd *strive* with the potsherds of the earth!
Shall the clay say to him who forms it, 'What are you making?'
Or shall your handiwork *say,* 'He has no hands'?
¹⁰Woe to him who says to *his* father, 'What are you begetting?'
Or to the woman, 'What have you brought forth?'"

¹¹Thus says the LORD,
The Holy One of Israel, and his Maker:
"Ask Me of things to come concerning My sons;
And concerning the work of My hands, you command Me.
¹²I have made the earth,
And created man on it.
I—My hands—stretched out the heavens,
And all their host I have commanded.
¹³I have raised him up in righteousness,
And I will direct all his ways;
He shall build My city
And let My exiles go free,
Not for price nor reward,"
Says the LORD of hosts.

The LORD, the Only Savior

¹⁴Thus says the LORD:

"The labor of Egypt and merchandise of Cush
And of the Sabeans, men of stature,
Shall come over to you, and they shall be yours;
They shall walk behind you,
They shall come over in chains;
And they shall bow down to you.
They will make supplication to you, *saying,*
'Surely God *is* in you,
And *there is* no other;
There is no other God.'"

¹⁵Truly You *are* God, who hide Yourself,
O God of Israel, the Savior!
¹⁶They shall be ashamed

And also disgraced, all of them;
They shall go in confusion together,
Who are makers of idols.
¹⁷*But* Israel shall be saved by the Lord
With an everlasting salvation;
You shall not be ashamed or disgraced
Forever and ever.

¹⁸For thus says the Lord,
Who created the heavens,
Who is God,
Who formed the earth and made it,
Who has established it,
Who did not create it in vain,
Who formed it to be inhabited:
"I *am* the Lord, and *there is* no other.
¹⁹I have not spoken in secret,
In a dark place of the earth;
I did not say to the seed of Jacob,
'Seek Me in vain';
I, the Lord, speak righteousness,
I declare things that are right.

²⁰"Assemble yourselves and come;
Draw near together,
You *who have* escaped from the nations.
They have no knowledge,
Who carry the wood of their carved image,
And pray to a god *that* cannot save.
²¹Tell and bring forth *your case;*
Yes, let them take counsel together.
Who has declared this from ancient time?
Who has told it from that time?
Have not I, the Lord?
And *there is* no other God besides Me,
A just God and a Savior;
There is none besides Me.

²²"Look to Me, and be saved,
All you ends of the earth!
For I *am* God, and *there is* no other.
²³I have sworn by Myself;
The word has gone out of My mouth *in*
    righteousness,
And shall not return,
That to Me every knee shall bow,
Every tongue shall take an oath.
²⁴He shall say,
'Surely in the Lord I have righteousness and
    strength.
To Him *men* shall come,
And all shall be ashamed
Who are incensed against Him.

²⁵In the Lord all the descendants of Israel
Shall be justified, and shall glory.' "

Dead Idols and the Living God

46 Bel bows down, Nebo stoops;
Their idols were on the beasts and on the
    cattle.
Your carriages *were* heavily loaded,
A burden to the weary *beast.*
²They stoop, they bow down together;
They could not deliver the burden,
But have themselves gone into captivity.

³"Listen to Me, O house of Jacob,
And all the remnant of the house of Israel,
Who have been upheld *by Me* from birth,
Who have been carried from the womb:
⁴Even to *your* old age, I *am* He,
And *even* to gray hairs I will carry *you!*
I have made, and I will bear;
Even I will carry, and will deliver *you.*

⁵"To whom will you liken Me, and make *Me*
    equal
And compare Me, that we should be alike?
⁶They lavish gold out of the bag,
And weigh silver on the scales;
They hire a goldsmith, and he makes it a god;
They prostrate themselves, yes, they worship.
⁷They bear it on the shoulder, they carry it
And set it in its place, and it stands;
From its place it shall not move.
Though *one* cries out to it, yet it cannot
    answer
Nor save him out of his trouble.

⁸"Remember this, and show yourselves men;
Recall to mind, O you transgressors.
⁹Remember the former things of old,
For I *am* God, and *there is* no other;
I am God, and *there is* none like Me,
¹⁰Declaring the end from the beginning,
And from ancient times *things* that are not *yet*
    done,
Saying, 'My counsel shall stand,
And I will do all My pleasure,'
¹¹Calling a bird of prey from the east,
The man who executes My counsel, from a far
    country.
Indeed I have spoken *it;*
I will also bring it to pass.
I have purposed *it;*
I will also do it.

46:1–13 The prophet drew a startling contrast between the Lord and idols. Bel and Nebo were Babylonian gods (v. 1). When the Persians conquered Babylon, the fleeing people loaded their idols on their already overburdened beasts. The idols could not deliver their worshipers; instead they provided an additional burden for those trying to escape their captors. What a mighty contrast to the Lord of Israel! His people do not carry Him; rather, He carries them (vv. 3, 4). He had carried the people of Israel since their birth as a nation (see Ex. 19:4). He would continue to carry them to old age.

ATTRIBUTES OF GOD HE IS OMNISCIENT

God knows everything from eternity past to eternity future simultaneously. He learns from no one, is never surprised, and never forgets (Is. 46:9, 10).

God knows His creation completely. He names the stars (Ps. 147:4, 5), places the clouds (Job 37:16), tracks activity in the oceans (Job 38:16), clothes the fields (Matt. 6:28), and is aware of every creature and its activities at all times (Matt. 10:29).

God knows each woman fully (Ps. 33:15)—her past (Rev. 2:2, 3), where she goes, what she does, thinks, says, (Ps. 33:13–15), and even her motivations (1 Sam. 16:7).

The comforting news is that God knows and loves you anyway (Ps. 103:14). He knows the number of hairs on your head (Matt. 10:30), your needs (Matt. 6:8), your feelings (Is. 40:28, 29), and your future (John 14:2, 3). You can take comfort in these words in Scripture, "O Lord God, You know" (Ezek. 37:3).

See also Job 28:24; 36:5; Ps. 139:1–16; Prov. 15:3; Is. 29:15, 16; Lam. 3:22, note; Heb. 4:13; notes on Attributes of God (Ex. 33; Deut. 4; 32; 2 Chr. 19; Job 23; 42; Ps. 25; 90; 102; 119; Is. 6; Jer. 23; Rom. 2; Eph. 1; 1 John 5); Decision Making (1 Cor. 8); Fear of the Lord (Prov. 2); God's Will (Eph. 5); Wisdom (James 1)

12"Listen to Me, you stubborn-hearted,
  Who *are* far from righteousness:
13I bring My righteousness near, it shall not be
    far off;
  My salvation shall not linger.
  And I will place salvation in Zion,
  For Israel My glory.

The Humiliation of Babylon

47 "Come down and sit in the dust,
  O virgin daughter of Babylon;
  Sit on the ground without a throne,
  O daughter of the Chaldeans!
  For you shall no more be called
  Tender and delicate.
2Take the millstones and grind meal.
  Remove your veil,
  Take off the skirt,
  Uncover the thigh,
  Pass through the rivers.
3Your nakedness shall be uncovered,
  Yes, your shame will be seen;
  I will take vengeance,
  And I will not arbitrate with a man."

4*As for* our Redeemer, the LORD of hosts *is* His
    name,
  The Holy One of Israel.

5"Sit in silence, and go into darkness,
  O daughter of the Chaldeans;
  For you shall no longer be called
  The Lady of Kingdoms.
6I was angry with My people;
  I have profaned My inheritance,
  And given them into your hand.

You showed them no mercy;
  On the elderly you laid your yoke very heavily.
7And you said, 'I shall be a lady forever,'
  So that you did not take these *things* to heart,
  Nor remember the latter end of them.

8"Therefore hear this now, *you who are* given to
    pleasures,
  Who dwell securely,
  Who say in your heart, 'I *am,* and *there is* no one
    else besides me;
  I shall not sit *as* a widow,
  Nor shall I know the loss of children';
9But these two *things* shall come to you
  In a moment, in one day:
  The loss of children, and widowhood.
  They shall come upon you in their fullness
  Because of the multitude of your sorceries,
  For the great abundance of your
    enchantments.

10"For you have trusted in your wickedness;
  You have said, 'No one sees me';
  Your wisdom and your knowledge have warped
    you;
  And you have said in your heart,
  "I *am,* and *there is* no one else besides me.'
11Therefore evil shall come upon you;
  You shall not know from where it arises.
  And trouble shall fall upon you;
  You will not be able to put it off.
  And desolation shall come upon you suddenly,
  Which you shall not know.

12"Stand now with your enchantments
  And the multitude of your sorceries,

47:1–15 The prophet predicted the downfall of Babylon. God used Babylon to discipline His people. But Persia would conquer wicked Babylon, and the Lord would rescue His people. Babylon, in its arrogance, made a claim for itself that belonged only to the Lord (see vv. 8, 10; see Is. 45:14, 18). Babylon became the symbol of evil in Scripture (see Rev. 17; 18). For "the Holy One of Israel," see Isaiah 1:4–9, note.

In which you have labored from your youth—
Perhaps you will be able to profit,
Perhaps you will prevail.
¹³You are wearied in the multitude of your
    counsels;
Let now the astrologers, the stargazers,
And the monthly prognosticators
Stand up and save you
From what shall come upon you.
¹⁴Behold, they shall be as stubble,
The fire shall burn them;
They shall not deliver themselves
From the power of the flame;
It shall not *be* a coal to be warmed by,
Nor a fire to sit before!
¹⁵Thus shall they be to you
With whom you have labored,
Your merchants from your youth;
They shall wander each one to his quarter.
No one shall save you.

Israel Refined for God's Glory

48 ¹"Hear this, O house of Jacob,
Who are called by the name of Israel,
And have come forth from the wellsprings of
    Judah;
Who swear by the name of the LORD,
And make mention of the God of Israel,
But not in truth or in righteousness;
²For they call themselves after the holy city,
And lean on the God of Israel;
The LORD of hosts *is* His name:

³"I have declared the former things from the
    beginning;
They went forth from My mouth, and I caused
    them to hear it.
Suddenly I did *them,* and they came to pass.
⁴Because I knew that you *were* obstinate,
And your neck *was* an iron sinew,
And your brow bronze,
⁵Even from the beginning I have declared *it* to
    you;
Before it came to pass I proclaimed *it* to you,
Lest you should say, 'My idol has done them,
And my carved image and my molded image
Have commanded them.'

⁶"You have heard;
See all this.
And will you not declare *it?*
I have made you hear new things from this
    time,

Even hidden things, and you did not know
    them.
⁷They are created now and not from the
    beginning;
And before this day you have not heard them,
Lest you should say, 'Of course I knew them.'
⁸Surely you did not hear,
Surely you did not know;
Surely from long ago your ear was not opened.
For I knew that you would deal very
    treacherously,
And were called a transgressor from the womb.

⁹"For My name's sake I will defer My anger,
And *for* My praise I will restrain it from you,
So that I do not cut you off.
¹⁰Behold, I have refined you, but not as silver;
I have tested you in the furnace of affliction.
¹¹For My own sake, for My own sake, I will do *it;*
For how should *My name* be profaned?
And I will not give My glory to another.

God's Ancient Plan to Redeem Israel

¹²"Listen to Me, O Jacob,
And Israel, My called:
I *am* He, I *am* the First,
I *am* also the Last.
¹³Indeed My hand has laid the foundation of the
    earth,
And My right hand has stretched out the
    heavens;
When I call to them,
They stand up together.

¹⁴"All of you, assemble yourselves, and hear!
Who among them has declared these *things?*
The LORD loves him;
He shall do His pleasure on Babylon,
And His arm *shall be against* the Chaldeans.
¹⁵I, *even* I, have spoken;
Yes, I have called him,
I have brought him, and his way will prosper.

¹⁶"Come near to Me, hear this:
I have not spoken in secret from the
    beginning;
From the time that it was, I *was* there.
And now the Lord GOD and His Spirit
Have[a] sent Me."

¹⁷Thus says the LORD, your Redeemer,
· ·

48:16 [a]The Hebrew verb is singular.

48:1–8 The Lord's people, alternately referred to as Jacob, Israel, and Judah, are described as obstinate, stiff-necked or stubborn, idol worshipers, deaf, treacherous, and rebellious (vv. 1, 4, 5, 8). "Transgressor" refers to one who rebels against the Lord (v. 8). The Lord's people gave the appearance of being religious (vv. 1, 2), but they did not obey the Lord's commands. They closed their ears to the words of the Lord (v. 8). Genuine faith in the Lord, as the 8th century B.C. prophets repeatedly emphasized, makes a difference in the way a person lives every day.

AGING THE PASSING OF YEARS

The Bible offers repeated assurances that the process we call aging is completely secure in God's hand. Looks, health, and circumstances change with time and often in ways we would not desire. Many cope with the stress of aging by trying to cling to outward beauty, youthful strength, or vocational achievement. Yet, only when we realize that God has made each of us and, in accordance with His plan, carries us through the changing seasons of life, do we come to peace with the inevitability of getting older.

Just as each season of nature has its beauty and purpose by God's design, so there is no season of life in which the Christian should despair of living. Though opportunities and abilities may decline with age, each day of life that God gives is purposefully ordained according to His perfect wisdom. God's plan includes people of every age. Miriam was a young girl when she stood by a river and watched her baby brother, Moses. Many years later, she helped her brother lead God's people across another body of water to freedom. Mary was a teenager when Gabriel announced her motherhood and middle-aged when she witnessed His Crucifixion and Resurrection, and the sending of the Holy Spirit to the early church. Sarah was well past menopause when she gave birth to her son, Isaac. Those who live each day for Christ will bear fruit not only in youth but in old age as well (Ps. 92:12–15).

See also notes on Change Points in Life (Eccl. 3); Children (2 Kin. 4); Death (1 Cor. 15); Grandparenthood (Ps. 71); Widowhood (Ps. 68; Jer. 29; 1 Cor. 2)

The Holy One of Israel:
"I *am* the LORD your God,
Who teaches you to profit,
Who leads you by the way you should go.
18 Oh, that you had heeded My commandments!
Then your peace would have been like a river,
And your righteousness like the waves of the sea.
19 Your descendants also would have been like the sand,
And the offspring of your body like the grains of sand;
His name would not have been cut off
Nor destroyed from before Me."

20 Go forth from Babylon!
Flee from the Chaldeans!
With a voice of singing,
Declare, proclaim this,
Utter it to the end of the earth;
Say, "The LORD has redeemed
His servant Jacob!"
21 And they did not thirst
When He led them through the deserts;
He caused the waters to flow from the rock for them;

He also split the rock, and the waters gushed out.

22 "*There is* no peace," says the LORD, "for the wicked."

The Servant, the Light to the Gentiles

49 "Listen, O coastlands, to Me,
And take heed, you peoples from afar!
The LORD has called Me from the womb;
From the matrix of My mother He has made mention of My name.
2 And He has made My mouth like a sharp sword;
In the shadow of His hand He has hidden Me,
And made Me a polished shaft;
In His quiver He has hidden Me."

3 "And He said to me,
'You *are* My servant, O Israel,
In whom I will be glorified.'
4 Then I said, 'I have labored in vain,
I have spent my strength for nothing and in vain;
Yet surely my just reward *is* with the LORD,
And my work with my God.' "

49:1–6 In the second servant passage, a tension exists regarding the identity of the servant (see Is. 42:1–4, note). The servant himself speaks, testifying how the Lord had called him and prepared him for his task (Is. 49:1, 2). The Lord hid His servant (v. 2), indicating the Lord's care and protection. In verse 3 the servant is called "Israel." The Lord did indeed choose Israel to be His instrument in making Himself known to the entire world. Verse 4 may reflect the complaint of the servant (or the people of Israel) that their mission was too great and they were too weak. Ultimately, this Servant is the Lord Himself, and certainly His earthly ministry in many ways was disappointing to Him since the fruit borne was small in light of the sacrifice made. Yet He willingly left the results in the Father's hand. Verses 5 and 6 increase the tension in this passage regarding the identity of the servant. If the servant is identified as Israel (v. 3), the servant here is said to have a mission to bring Jacob or Israel back to the Lord (vv. 5, 6). The servant could be a remnant or a part of Israel. Verse 6 further extends the mission of this servant as overwhelming and far beyond any human agent. The servant is to bring Israel back to the Lord and bring the Lord's salvation to the Gentiles, not only as the bearer of that salvation but as the Savior (v. 6). For this reason, it seems more prudent to identify the Servant as none other than Jesus Christ (see John 8:12).

[5]"And now the LORD says,
Who formed Me from the womb *to be* His
Servant,
To bring Jacob back to Him,
So that Israel is gathered to Him[a]
(For I shall be glorious in the eyes of the LORD,
And My God shall be My strength),

[6]Indeed He says,
'It is too small a thing that You should be My
Servant
To raise up the tribes of Jacob,
And to restore the preserved ones of Israel;
I will also give You as a light to the Gentiles,
That You should be My salvation to the ends of
the earth.' "

[7]Thus says the LORD,
The Redeemer of Israel, their Holy One,
To Him whom man despises,
To Him whom the nation abhors,
To the Servant of rulers:
"Kings shall see and arise,
Princes also shall worship,
Because of the LORD who is faithful,
The Holy One of Israel;
And He has chosen You."

[8]Thus says the LORD:

"In an acceptable time I have heard You,
And in the day of salvation I have helped You;
I will preserve You and give You
As a covenant to the people,
To restore the earth,
To cause them to inherit the desolate
heritages;
[9]That You may say to the prisoners, 'Go forth,'
To those who *are* in darkness, 'Show
yourselves.'

"They shall feed along the roads,
And their pastures *shall be* on all desolate
heights.
[10]They shall neither hunger nor thirst,
Neither heat nor sun shall strike them;
For He who has mercy on them will lead them,
Even by the springs of water He will guide
them.
[11]I will make each of My mountains a road,
And My highways shall be elevated.
[12]Surely these shall come from afar;
Look! Those from the north and the
west,
And these from the land of Sinim."

[13]Sing, O heavens!
Be joyful, O earth!
And break out in singing, O mountains!
For the LORD has comforted His people,
And will have mercy on His afflicted.

God Will Remember Zion

[14]But Zion said, "The LORD has forsaken me,
And my Lord has forgotten me."

[15]"Can a woman forget her nursing child,
And not have compassion on the son of her
womb?
Surely they may forget,
Yet I will not forget you.
[16]See, I have inscribed you on the palms *of My
hands;*
Your walls *are* continually before Me.
[17]Your sons[a] shall make haste;
Your destroyers and those who laid you waste
Shall go away from you.
[18]Lift up your eyes, look around and see;
All these gather together *and* come to you.
As I live," says the LORD,
"You shall surely clothe yourselves with them all
as an ornament,
And bind them *on you* as a bride *does.*

[19]"For your waste and desolate places,
And the land of your destruction,
Will even now be too small for the inhabitants;
And those who swallowed you up will be far
away.
[20]The children you will have,
After you have lost the others,
Will say again in your ears,
'The place *is* too small for me;
Give me a place where I may dwell.'
[21]Then you will say in your heart,
'Who has begotten these for me,
Since I have lost my children and am desolate,
A captive, and wandering to and fro?
And who has brought these up?
There I was, left alone;
But these, where *were* they?' "

[22]Thus says the Lord GOD:

"Behold, I will lift My hand in an oath to the
nations,
And set up My standard for the peoples;

49:5 [a]Qere, Dead Sea Scrolls, and Septuagint read *is gathered to Him*; Kethib reads *is not gathered.*   **49:17** [a]Dead Sea Scrolls, Septuagint, Targum, and Vulgate read *builders.*

49:7–26 The prophet encouraged the Lord's people. For "the Holy One of Israel," see Isaiah 1:4–9, note. In the allusion to a mother and the child of her womb, the Lord's loving concern for His people goes even beyond that of the most devoted mother (Is. 49:15; see chart, Female Metaphors for God).

CULTURE *THE JUDEO-CHRISTIAN HERITAGE*

The culture of a people includes its language, customs, laws, mores, traditions, music and art, symbols, artifacts—everything that points toward the best of a group of people and those things which the group desires to pass on to future generations. The Bible may very well be considered the handbook for Judeo-Christian culture since it clearly defines the essence of what it means to be "God's people" (Is. 51:16).

The Bible clearly states that the culture of God's people is to have these hallmarks:

- *To live in obedience to the Law by faith.* To follow God's commands is to be in a position to receive God's blessings; to disobey God's laws is to experience God's wrath (Ex. 15:26; Deut. 28:1–14).
- *To have a heart for the one true and living God plus a heart for your neighbor.* The Law's purpose is to reveal a heart for God and for others (Matt. 22:37–40).
- *To maintain family alliances.* God's people dwell in a community that has a family orientation. Inheritances are to be kept within a tribe (Deut. 32:6–9).

God's people are strongly warned against diluting their culture through intermarriage with nonbelievers (2 Cor. 6:14–16) and endangering their culture through situations making them vulnerable to captivity and slavery (Deut. 7:2–5). Conversely, God's people are admonished to *spread* their culture to others (Acts 10:34–43) and to be a moral light to the nations (Acts 13:47). Women in the history of God's people held a unique responsibility for the transmission of culture within the family context. Religious descent among the Hebrews is matrilineal. If the mother is Jewish, then so is the child. Women are also responsible for preparing the most important "cultural" celebration: the *Shabbat* or Sabbath feast.

See also Deut. 11:1–12; Is. 29:13–16; chart on Terminology for the People of God; notes on Celebrations and Holidays (Ex. 12); Family (Gen. 32; 1 Sam. 3; Ps. 78; 127); Inheritance (Prov. 13); Patriarchy (Gen. 28); Traditions (1 Sam. 7)

They shall bring your sons in *their* arms,
And your daughters shall be carried on *their*
  shoulders;
23Kings shall be your foster fathers,
And their queens your nursing mothers;
They shall bow down to you with *their* faces to
  the earth,
And lick up the dust of your feet.
Then you will know that I *am* the LORD,
For they shall not be ashamed who wait for
  Me."

24Shall the prey be taken from the mighty,
Or the captives of the righteousª be delivered?

25But thus says the LORD:

"Even the captives of the mighty shall be taken
  away,
And the prey of the terrible be delivered;
For I will contend with him who contends with
  you,
And I will save your children.
26I will feed those who oppress you with their
  own flesh,
And they shall be drunk with their own blood
  as with sweet wine.
All flesh shall know

That I, the LORD, *am* your Savior,
And your Redeemer, the Mighty One of Jacob."

The Servant, Israel's Hope

50Thus says the LORD:

"Where *is* the certificate of your mother's
  divorce,
Whom I have put away?
Or which of My creditors *is it* to whom I have
  sold you?
For your iniquities you have sold yourselves,
And for your transgressions your mother has
  been put away.
2Why, when I came, *was there* no man?
Why, when I called, *was there* none to answer?
Is My hand shortened at all that it cannot
  redeem?
Or have I no power to deliver?
Indeed with My rebuke I dry up the sea,
I make the rivers a wilderness;
Their fish stink because *there is* no water,
And die of thirst.
3I clothe the heavens with blackness,
And I make sackcloth their covering."

••••••••••••••••••

49:24 ªFollowing Masoretic Text and Targum; Dead Sea Scrolls, Syriac, and Vulgate read *the mighty;* Septuagint reads *unjustly.*

50:1–3 That the Lord's people suffered defeat was not a sign that He had forgotten them. The people had brought calamity

upon themselves by their sins. He had not divorced them; He had not sold them into slavery.

⁴"The Lord God has given Me
The tongue of the learned,
That I should know how to speak
A word in season to *him who is* weary.
He awakens Me morning by morning,
He awakens My ear
To hear as the learned.
⁵The Lord God has opened My ear;
And I was not rebellious,
Nor did I turn away.
⁶I gave My back to those who struck *Me*,
And My cheeks to those who plucked out the
beard;
I did not hide My face from shame and
spitting.

⁷"For the Lord God will help Me;
Therefore I will not be disgraced;
Therefore I have set My face like a flint,
And I know that I will not be ashamed.
⁸*He is* near who justifies Me;
Who will contend with Me?
Let us stand together.
Who *is* My adversary?
Let him come near Me.
⁹Surely the Lord God will help Me;
Who *is* he *who* will condemn Me?
Indeed they will all grow old like a
garment;
The moth will eat them up.

¹⁰"Who among you fears the Lord?
Who obeys the voice of His Servant?
Who walks in darkness
And has no light?
Let him trust in the name of the Lord
And rely upon his God.
¹¹Look, all you who kindle a fire,
Who encircle *yourselves* with sparks:
Walk in the light of your fire and in the sparks
you have kindled—
This you shall have from My hand:
You shall lie down in torment.

The Lord Comforts Zion

51 "Listen to Me, you who follow after
righteousness,
You who seek the Lord:
Look to the rock *from which* you were hewn,
And to the hole of the pit *from which* you were
dug.
²Look to Abraham your father,
And to Sarah *who* bore you;

For I called him alone,
And blessed him and increased him."

³For the Lord will comfort Zion,
He will comfort all her waste places;
He will make her wilderness like Eden,
And her desert like the garden of the Lord;
Joy and gladness will be found in it,
Thanksgiving and the voice of melody.

⁴"Listen to Me, My people;
And give ear to Me, O My nation:
For law will proceed from Me,
And I will make My justice rest
As a light of the peoples.
⁵My righteousness *is* near,
My salvation has gone forth,
And My arms will judge the peoples;
The coastlands will wait upon Me,
And on My arm they will trust.
⁶Lift up your eyes to the heavens,
And look on the earth beneath.
For the heavens will vanish away like smoke,
The earth will grow old like a garment,
And those who dwell in it will die in like
manner;
But My salvation will be forever,
And My righteousness will not be abolished.

⁷"Listen to Me, you who know righteousness,
You people in whose heart *is* My law:
Do not fear the reproach of men,
Nor be afraid of their insults.
⁸For the moth will eat them up like a garment,
And the worm will eat them like wool;
But My righteousness will be forever,
And My salvation from generation to
generation."

⁹Awake, awake, put on strength,
O arm of the Lord!
Awake as in the ancient days,
In the generations of old.
Are You not *the arm* that cut Rahab apart,
And wounded the serpent?

¹⁰*Are* You not *the One* who dried up the sea,
The waters of the great deep;
That made the depths of the sea a road
For the redeemed to cross over?
¹¹So the ransomed of the Lord shall return,
And come to Zion with singing,
With everlasting joy on their heads.

50:4–9 In the third servant passage, the servant had an encouraging word from the Lord for those around him (v. 4; see Is. 42:1–4; 49:1–6, notes). The servant suffered persecution willingly and without complaint (Is. 50:6). The servant expressed faith that the Lord would help him and vindicate him (vv. 7–9).

The servant's fellowship with the Lord brought him confidence in the most difficult situations. Again Jesus in His perfect obedience to the Father fit the description of this servant.

GRIEF   SORROW OF SOUL

Sorrow of soul, such as the disciples experienced at the imminent death of Jesus, is a very real thing (Luke 22:45). God expects us to grieve when we are brokenhearted (John 11:19, 31–35).

Unexpressed grief often brings complex emotional and physical illness. Release from grief and inner happiness comes only when you offer your unique circumstances to God so that He can cause them to bear fruit on your behalf (John 7:37, 38). As Jesus used the words of the prophet Isaiah to describe Himself and His messianic role, He included the replacement of the signs of sorrow—ashes, mourning, or the spirit of heaviness—with the marks of victory—beauty, joy, and the garment of praise (Is. 61:1–3; Luke 4:18–21).

Jesus identifies with your broken heart because He is "a Man of sorrows and acquainted with grief" (Is. 53:3). He understands when you hurt (Is. 53:4).

Jesus wept (John 11:35) and taught His children by example at the Cross to express openly feelings of protest, sadness, anxieties, and fears (Matt. 26:39; 27:46).

For women, grief is not confined to the death of a loved one. It also includes sorrow at the tearing apart of anything that they have thought to be secure, such as a marriage, possessions, job, health, relationships, or finances.

Believers must remember that grief is not forever. It is healed through a deliberate, personal, lived-out experience of the unfailing grace of God (2 Cor. 12:9).

See also notes on Brokenheartedness (Ps. 34); Death (1 Cor. 15); Emotions (Ps. 42); Sorrow (Rev. 21); Widowhood (Ps. 68; Jer. 29; 1 Cor. 2); portraits of Rizpah (2 Sam. 3); the Widow of Nain (Luke 7); the Widow of Zarephath (1 Kin. 17)

They shall obtain joy and gladness;
Sorrow and sighing shall flee away.

12"I, *even* I, *am* He who comforts you.
Who *are* you that you should be afraid
Of a man *who* will die,
And of the son of a man *who* will be made like
grass?
13And you forget the LORD your Maker,
Who stretched out the heavens
And laid the foundations of the earth;
You have feared continually every day
Because of the fury of the oppressor,
When *he has* prepared to destroy.
And where *is* the fury of the oppressor?
14The captive exile hastens, that he may be
loosed,
That he should not die in the pit,
And that his bread should not fail.
15But I *am* the LORD your God,
Who divided the sea whose waves roared—
The LORD of hosts *is* His name.
16And I have put My words in your mouth;
I have covered you with the shadow of My
hand,
That I may plant the heavens,
Lay the foundations of the earth,
And say to Zion, 'You *are* My people.' "

God's Fury Removed

17Awake, awake!
Stand up, O Jerusalem,
You who have drunk at the hand of the LORD

The cup of His fury;
You have drunk the dregs of the cup of
trembling,
And drained *it* out.
18*There is* no one to guide her
Among all the sons she has brought forth;
Nor *is there any* who takes her by the hand
Among all the sons she has brought up.
19These two *things* have come to you;
Who will be sorry for you?—
Desolation and destruction, famine and
sword—
By whom will I comfort you?
20Your sons have fainted,
They lie at the head of all the streets,
Like an antelope in a net;
They are full of the fury of the LORD,
The rebuke of your God.

21Therefore please hear this, you afflicted,
And drunk but not with wine.
22Thus says your Lord,
The LORD and your God,
Who pleads the cause of His people:
"See, I have taken out of your hand
The cup of trembling,
The dregs of the cup of My fury;
You shall no longer drink it.
23But I will put it into the hand of those who
afflict you,
Who have said to you,[a]

51:23 [a]Literally *your soul*

'Lie down, that we may walk over you.'
And you have laid your body like the ground,
And as the street, for those who walk over."

God Redeems Jerusalem

52 Awake, awake!
Put on your strength, O Zion;
Put on your beautiful garments,
O Jerusalem, the holy city!
For the uncircumcised and the unclean
Shall no longer come to you.
²Shake yourself from the dust, arise;
Sit down, O Jerusalem!
Loose yourself from the bonds of your neck,
O captive daughter of Zion!

³For thus says the LORD:

"You have sold yourselves for nothing,
And you shall be redeemed without money."

⁴For thus says the Lord GOD:

"My people went down at first
Into Egypt to dwell there;
Then the Assyrian oppressed them without
cause.
⁵Now therefore, what have I here," says the
LORD,
"That My people are taken away for nothing?
Those who rule over them
Make them wail,"ᵃ says the LORD,
"And My name *is* blasphemed continually every
day.
⁶Therefore My people shall know My name;
Therefore *they shall know* in that day
That I *am* He who speaks:
'Behold, *it is* I.' "

⁷How beautiful upon the mountains
Are the feet of him who brings good news,
Who proclaims peace,
Who brings glad tidings of good *things,*
Who proclaims salvation,
Who says to Zion,

"Your God reigns!"
⁸Your watchmen shall lift up *their* voices,
With their voices they shall sing together;
For they shall see eye to eye
When the LORD brings back Zion.
⁹Break forth into joy, sing together,
You waste places of Jerusalem!
For the LORD has comforted His people,
He has redeemed Jerusalem.
¹⁰The LORD has made bare His holy arm
In the eyes of all the nations;
And all the ends of the earth shall see
The salvation of our God.

¹¹Depart! Depart! Go out from there,
Touch no unclean *thing;*
Go out from the midst of her,
Be clean,
You who bear the vessels of the LORD.
¹²For you shall not go out with haste,
Nor go by flight;
For the LORD will go before you,
And the God of Israel *will be* your rear guard.

The Sin-Bearing Servant

¹³Behold, My Servant shall deal prudently;
He shall be exalted and extolled and be very
high.
¹⁴Just as many were astonished at you,
So His visage was marred more than any
man,
And His form more than the sons of men;
¹⁵So shall He sprinkleᵃ many nations.
Kings shall shut their mouths at Him;
For what had not been told them they shall
see,
And what they had not heard they shall
consider.

53 Who has believed our report?
And to whom has the arm of the LORD been
revealed?

52:5 ᵃDead Sea Scrolls read *Mock;* Septuagint reads *Marvel and wail;*
Targum reads *Boast themselves;* Vulgate reads *Treat them unjustly.*
52:15 ᵃOr *startle*

**52:1–12 A recollection of the oppression the Lord's people had
experienced** in Egypt and at the hands of the Assyrians is presented (v. 4). The northern kingdom fell completely to Assyrian domination in 722 B.C. and ceased to exist as a nation. The
Lord would act on behalf of His people out of concern for His
name (character or reputation, vv. 5, 6). A watchman's song
describes the joy of Jerusalem in the Lord's redemption and
deliverance of His people (vv. 7–10). Paul quoted verse 7 in describing those who preach the gospel of Christ (Rom. 10:15).
As He led His people out of captivity, the Lord would go before them and also be their rear guard.

52:13—53:12 The final servant song or poem consists of five
stanzas (Is. 52:13–15; 53:1–3, 4–6, 7–9, 10–12; see also Is.
42:1–4, note). A vivid picture of the nature and work of the

servant is presented. Clearly the picture portrayed reached
fulfillment in the life and work of Jesus, the Messiah.

52:13–15 The servant's changed status from humiliation to exaltation is noted in the first stanza (see chart, Jesus' Pilgrimage). The people were astonished at the servant because his
suffering had left him disfigured. "Sprinkle" is associated
with the priestly function of cleansing from sin. An alternate
reading for "sprinkle" is "startle." In this case, the meaning
may be that the servant would startle the nations by his sudden rise from humiliation to exaltation.

53:1–3 The servant's humble beginning made His exaltation
difficult to believe. He had no outward splendor to attract
others to himself.

²For He shall grow up before Him as a tender
plant,
And as a root out of dry ground.
He has no form or comeliness;
And when we see Him,
There is no beauty that we should desire Him.
³He is despised and rejected by men,
A Man of sorrows and acquainted with grief.
And we hid, as it were, *our* faces from Him;
He was despised, and we did not esteem Him.

⁴Surely He has borne our griefs
And carried our sorrows;
Yet we esteemed Him stricken,
Smitten by God, and afflicted.
⁵But He *was* wounded for our transgressions,
He was bruised for our iniquities;
The chastisement for our peace *was* upon Him,
And by His stripes we are healed.
⁶All we like sheep have gone astray;
We have turned, every one, to his own way;
And the LORD has laid on Him the iniquity of
us all.

⁷He was oppressed and He was afflicted,
Yet He opened not His mouth;
He was led as a lamb to the slaughter,
And as a sheep before its shearers is silent,
So He opened not His mouth.
⁸He was taken from prison and from judgment,
And who will declare His generation?
For He was cut off from the land of the living;
For the transgressions of My people He was
stricken.
⁹And they³ made His grave with the wicked—
But with the rich at His death,
Because He had done no violence,
Nor *was any* deceit in His mouth.

¹⁰Yet it pleased the LORD to bruise Him;
He has put *Him* to grief.
When You make His soul an offering for sin,

He shall see *His* seed, He shall prolong *His*
days,
And the pleasure of the LORD shall prosper in
His hand.
¹¹He shall see the labor of His soul,³ *and* be
satisfied.
By His knowledge My righteous Servant shall
justify many,
For He shall bear their iniquities.
¹²Therefore I will divide Him a portion with the
great,
And He shall divide the spoil with the strong,
Because He poured out His soul unto death,
And He was numbered with the transgressors,
And He bore the sin of many,
And made intercession for the transgressors.

A Perpetual Covenant of Peace

54 "Sing, O barren,
You *who* have not borne!
Break forth into singing, and cry aloud,
You *who* have not labored with child!
For more *are* the children of the desolate
Than the children of the married woman," says
the LORD.
²"Enlarge the place of your tent,
And let them stretch out the curtains of your
dwellings;
Do not spare;
Lengthen your cords,
And strengthen your stakes.
³For you shall expand to the right and to the
left,
And your descendants will inherit the nations,
And make the desolate cities inhabited.

⁴"Do not fear, for you will not be ashamed;
Neither be disgraced, for you will not be put to
shame;

53:9 ³Literally *he* or *He*   **53:11** ³Following Masoretic Text, Targum, and Vulgate; Dead Sea Scrolls and Septuagint read *From the labor of His soul He shall see light.*

53:4–6 The servant was described as carrying the griefs and sorrows of those who looked on him as rejected by God in this third stanza of the poem. The Hebrew or Jewish people observed a close, sometimes extreme, relationship between sin and suffering. Any suffering individual was viewed as having committed a specific sin that resulted in his sickness or suffering (see John 9:1–3; Job, Introduction: Purpose). This servant of Isaiah 53 suffered not for any wrong that he had done, but vicariously for the sake of others. "Iniquity" (lit. "twistedness" or "moral crookedness") is a reference to sin as the universal condition of the human race.

53:10–12 The servant's death did not result in defeat, but victory. The one who died would live again. The servant successfully completed His mission (v. 11). He would possess the spoils of victory after the battle had been won (v. 12). Truly none other than Jesus of Nazareth perfectly fulfilled these stanzas of this servant song.

54:1–17 The Lord's redemption of His people was celebrated. Verses 1–3 focus on how the multiplication of the Lord's people had been like a widow without children, but the Lord would again multiply His people as He promised Abraham (vv. 1–3; Gen. 15:5). Redeemed Israel is compared to an unfaithful wife who will be restored to her husband, the Lord. The imagery in this passage is similar to that found in the Book of Hosea. The Lord will show everlasting kindness and mercy on His people (Is. 54:8). "Kindness" refers to covenant love or loyalty (see Ps. 5:7–12, note). "I will have mercy" is related closely to the Hebrew word for "womb" (see chart, Female Metaphors for God). The Lord's mercy is like the tender compassion a mother shows toward the child of her womb. God is making a new beginning with His people so startling that it can only be compared to the new beginning and the new covenant He made with Noah (Is. 54:9, 10).

FULFILLED PROPHECIES FROM ISAIAH

THE PROPHECY	THE FULFILLMENT
The Messiah . . .	Jesus Christ . . .
will be born of a virgin (Is. 7:14).	was born of a virgin named Mary (Luke 1:26–31).
will have a Galilean ministry (Is. 9:1, 2).	ministered in Galilee to the Gentiles (Matt. 4:13–16).
will be an heir to the throne of David (Is. 9:7).	was given the throne of His father David (Luke 1:32, 33).
will have His way prepared (Is. 40:3–5).	was announced by John the Baptist (John 1:19–28).
will be spat on and struck (Is. 50:6).	was spat on and beaten (Matt. 26:67).
will be exalted (Is. 52:13).	was highly exalted by God and the people (Phil. 2:9, 10).
will be disfigured by suffering (Is. 52:14; 53:2).	was scourged by the soldiers, who gave Him a crown of thorns (Mark 15:15–19).
will make a blood atonement (Is. 53:5).	shed His blood to atone for our sins (1 Pet. 1:2).
will be widely rejected (Is. 53:1, 3).	was not accepted by many (John 12:37, 38).
will bear our sins and sorrows (Is. 53:4, 5).	died because of our sins (Rom. 4:25; 1 Pet. 2:24, 25).
will be our substitute (Is. 53:6, 8).	died in our place (Rom. 5:6, 8; 2 Cor. 5:21).
will voluntarily accept our guilt and punishment (Is. 53:7, 8).	was silent about our sin (Mark 15:4, 5; John 10:11; 19:30).
will be buried in a rich man's tomb (Is. 53:9).	was buried in the tomb of Joseph, a rich man from Arimathea (Matt. 27:57–60; John 19:38–42).
will save us who believe in Him (Is. 53:10, 11).	provided salvation for all who believe (John 3:16; Acts 16:31).
will die with transgressors (Is. 53:12).	was numbered with the transgressors (Mark 15:27, 28; Luke 22:37).
will heal the brokenhearted (Is. 61:1, 2).	healed the brokenhearted (Luke 4:18, 19).

For you will forget the shame of your youth,
And will not remember the reproach of your
    widowhood anymore.
⁵For your Maker *is* your husband,
The LORD of hosts *is* His name;
And your Redeemer *is* the Holy One of
    Israel;
He is called the God of the whole earth.
⁶For the LORD has called you
Like a woman forsaken and grieved in spirit,
Like a youthful wife when you were refused,"

Says your God.
⁷"For a mere moment I have forsaken you,
But with great mercies I will gather you.
⁸With a little wrath I hid My face from you for a
    moment;
But with everlasting kindness I will have mercy
    on you,"
Says the LORD, your Redeemer.

⁹"For this *is* like the waters of Noah to Me;
For as I have sworn

That the waters of Noah would no longer cover
    the earth,
So have I sworn
That I would not be angry with you, nor rebuke
    you.
10For the mountains shall depart
    And the hills be removed,
But My kindness shall not depart from you,
    Nor shall My covenant of peace be removed,"
Says the LORD, who has mercy on you.

11"O you afflicted one,
    Tossed with tempest, *and* not comforted,
Behold, I will lay your stones with colorful
    gems,
    And lay your foundations with sapphires.
12I will make your pinnacles of rubies,
    Your gates of crystal,
    And all your walls of precious stones.
13All your children *shall be* taught by the LORD,
    And great *shall be* the peace of your children.
14In righteousness you shall be established;
    You shall be far from oppression, for you shall
        not fear;
    And from terror, for it shall not come near you.
15Indeed they shall surely assemble, *but* not
        because of Me.
Whoever assembles against you shall fall for
    your sake.

16"Behold, I have created the blacksmith
    Who blows the coals in the fire,
    Who brings forth an instrument for his work;
And I have created the spoiler to destroy.
17No weapon formed against you shall prosper,
    And every tongue *which* rises against you in
        judgment
    You shall condemn.
This *is* the heritage of the servants of the
    LORD,
    And their righteousness *is* from Me,"
Says the LORD.

An Invitation to Abundant Life

55 "Ho! Everyone who thirsts,
    Come to the waters;
And you who have no money,
    Come, buy and eat.

Yes, come, buy wine and milk
    Without money and without price.
2Why do you spend money for *what is* not bread,
    And your wages for *what* does not satisfy?
Listen carefully to Me, and eat *what is* good,
    And let your soul delight itself in abundance.
3Incline your ear, and come to Me.
    Hear, and your soul shall live;
    And I will make an everlasting covenant with
        you—
    The sure mercies of David.
4Indeed I have given him *as* a witness to the
        people,
    A leader and commander for the people.
5Surely you shall call a nation you do not
        know,
And nations *who* do not know you shall run to
    you,
    Because of the LORD your God,
    And the Holy One of Israel;
    For He has glorified you."

6Seek the LORD while He may be found,
    Call upon Him while He is near.
7Let the wicked forsake his way,
    And the unrighteous man his thoughts;
Let him return to the LORD,
    And He will have mercy on him;
And to our God,
    For He will abundantly pardon.

8"For My thoughts *are* not your thoughts,
    Nor *are* your ways My ways," says the LORD.
9"For *as* the heavens are higher than the earth,
    So are My ways higher than your ways,
    And My thoughts than your thoughts.

10"For as the rain comes down, and the snow from
        heaven,
    And do not return there,
But water the earth,
    And make it bring forth and bud,
That it may give seed to the sower
    And bread to the eater,
11So shall My word be that goes forth from My
        mouth;
It shall not return to Me void,
    But it shall accomplish what I please,

55:1–5 The invitation in this passage is extended to everyone. "Come," "buy," and "eat" are imperatives which express the specific invitation. The language employed is that of the marketplace or street vendor. Due to the scarcity of water, its vendors were common in the Near East. In these verses, the call is issued by the Lord Himself. Not only does He offer water, the basic necessity of life, but He also offers all that brings overwhelming satisfaction or abundance to life. Best of all, the invitation is extended to those who have no money. The Lord freely offers everything necessary to give His people an abundant life (cf. John 10:10). The vendors required money, but

their products did not satisfy. "Listen" carries the idea of obedience. If the people would respond to Him in obedience, they would enjoy the good life.

55:10–13 God's word never fails to accomplish His purpose. The Hebrews viewed the spoken word as having a power of its own once it left the mouth of the speaker. Like the arrow shot from the bow, the spoken word could not be recalled. God remains faithful to His word. His word restores life to His people as surely as the rain coming down from the heavens brings new life to the earth.

And it shall prosper *in the thing* for which I sent
it.

¹²"For you shall go out with joy,
And be led out with peace;
The mountains and the hills
Shall break forth into singing before you,
And all the trees of the field shall clap *their*
hands.
¹³Instead of the thorn shall come up the cypress
tree,
And instead of the brier shall come up the
myrtle tree;
And it shall be to the LORD for a name,
For an everlasting sign *that* shall not be cut
off."

Salvation for the Gentiles

56 Thus says the LORD:

"Keep justice, and do righteousness,
For My salvation *is* about to come,
And My righteousness to be revealed.
²Blessed *is* the man *who* does this,
And the son of man *who* lays hold on it;
Who keeps from defiling the Sabbath,
And keeps his hand from doing any evil."

³Do not let the son of the foreigner
Who has joined himself to the LORD
Speak, saying,
"The LORD has utterly separated me from His
people";
Nor let the eunuch say,
"Here I am, a dry tree."
⁴For thus says the LORD:
"To the eunuchs who keep My Sabbaths,
And choose what pleases Me,
And hold fast My covenant,
⁵Even to them I will give in My house
And within My walls a place and a name
Better than that of sons and daughters;
I will give them^a an everlasting name
That shall not be cut off.

⁶"Also the sons of the foreigner
Who join themselves to the LORD, to serve Him,
And to love the name of the LORD, to be His
servants—
Everyone who keeps from defiling the Sabbath,

And holds fast My covenant—
⁷Even them I will bring to My holy mountain,
And make them joyful in My house of prayer.
Their burnt offerings and their sacrifices
Will be accepted on My altar;
For My house shall be called a house of prayer
for all nations."
⁸The Lord GOD, who gathers the outcasts of
Israel, says,
"Yet I will gather to him
Others besides those who are gathered to him."

Israel's Irresponsible Leaders

⁹All you beasts of the field, come to devour,
All you beasts in the forest.
¹⁰His watchmen *are* blind,
They are all ignorant;
They *are* all dumb dogs,
They cannot bark;
Sleeping, lying down, loving to slumber.
¹¹Yes, *they are* greedy dogs
Which never have enough.
And they *are* shepherds
Who cannot understand;
They all look to their own way,
Every one for his own gain,
From his *own* territory.
¹²"Come," *one says,* "I will bring wine,
And we will fill ourselves with intoxicating
drink;
Tomorrow will be as today,
And much more abundant."

Israel's Futile Idolatry

57 The righteous perishes,
And no man takes *it* to heart;
Merciful men *are* taken away,
While no one considers
That the righteous is taken away from evil.
²He shall enter into peace;
They shall rest in their beds,
Each one walking *in* his uprightness.

³"But come here,
You sons of the sorceress,
You offspring of the adulterer and the harlot!
⁴Whom do you ridicule?
Against whom do you make a wide mouth

56:5 ^aLiterally *him*

56:1–8 The Lord's salvation is available to all, including those
with physical disabilities (as a eunuch) and those from various
racial or ethnic backgrounds (as the son of the foreigner). The
Lord gathers to Himself all who respond to Him in faith and
obedience. His people likewise are to demonstrate attitudes
of inclusiveness rather than exclusiveness. The Lord's house is
to be a house of prayer for all peoples (v. 7). Jesus quoted this
verse when He cleansed the temple (see Matt. 21:13; Luke
19:46).

56:9–12 The prophet harshly condemned the leaders of God's
people. These irresponsible leaders are portrayed as beasts
preying on the people, as blind watchmen, and as lazy, greedy,
and drunken. The Lord's people needed protection from their
own leaders! Irresponsible leaders are accountable to the
Lord for their failure to render service.

And stick out the tongue?
Are you not children of transgression,
Offspring of falsehood,
⁵Inflaming yourselves with gods under every
    green tree,
Slaying the children in the valleys,
Under the clefts of the rocks?
⁶Among the smooth *stones* of the stream
Is your portion;
They, they, *are* your lot!
Even to them you have poured a drink
    offering,
You have offered a grain offering.
Should I receive comfort in these?

⁷"On a lofty and high mountain
You have set your bed;
Even there you went up
To offer sacrifice.
⁸Also behind the doors and their posts
You have set up your remembrance;
For you have uncovered yourself *to those other*
    than Me,
And have gone up to them;
You have enlarged your bed
And made *a covenant* with them;
You have loved their bed,
Where you saw *their* nudity.ᵃ
⁹You went to the king with ointment,
And increased your perfumes;
You sent your messengers far off,
And *even* descended to Sheol.
¹⁰You are wearied in the length of your way;
Yet you did not say, 'There is no hope.'
You have found the life of your hand;
Therefore you were not grieved.

¹¹"And of whom have you been afraid, or feared,
That you have lied
And not remembered Me,
Nor taken *it* to your heart?
Is it not because I have held My peace from of
    old
That you do not fear Me?
¹²I will declare your righteousness

And your works,
For they will not profit you.
¹³When you cry out,
Let your collection *of idols* deliver you.
But the wind will carry them all away,
A breath will take *them*.
But he who puts his trust in Me shall possess
    the land,
And shall inherit My holy mountain."

Healing for the Backslider

¹⁴And one shall say,
"Heap it up! Heap it up!
Prepare the way,
Take the stumbling block out of the way of My
    people."

¹⁵For thus says the High and Lofty One
Who inhabits eternity, whose name *is* Holy:
"I dwell in the high and holy *place,*
With him *who* has a contrite and humble spirit,
To revive the spirit of the humble,
And to revive the heart of the contrite ones.
¹⁶For I will not contend forever,
Nor will I always be angry;
For the spirit would fail before Me,
And the souls *which* I have made.
¹⁷For the iniquity of his covetousness
I was angry and struck him;
I hid and was angry,
And he went on backsliding in the way of his
    heart.
¹⁸I have seen his ways, and will heal him;
I will also lead him,
And restore comforts to him
And to his mourners.
¹⁹"I create the fruit of the lips:
Peace, peace to *him who is* far off and to *him*
    who is near,"
Says the LORD,
"And I will heal him."
²⁰But the wicked *are* like the troubled sea,

•••••••••••••••••••••••

57:8 ᵃLiterally *hand*, a euphemism

57:14–21 The Lord tempered His judgment with mercy. Those who respond to the Lord with a contrite heart and humble spirit would experience the blessing of His presence (v. 15; see Matt. 5:3–5). Paul quoted Isaiah 57:19 in his reference to the work of Christ (Eph. 2:17). The repetition of the word "peace," the Lord's gift to those who respond to Him in faith, indicated complete peace or perfect peace (Is. 57:19). The wicked, in contrast, cannot experience peace (vv. 20, 21).

58:1–12 Fasting in biblical times was a spontaneous expression of grief at the time of death or great trouble (see Matt. 6:16–18, note). Evidence indicates that fasting also accompanied repentance (see Jon. 3:6–9). In the time of the NT, the Pharisees observed fasting as a ritual. The Lord told the prophet to declare to His people their transgressions or rebel-

lion against the Lord (Is. 58:1). The people practiced religious observances faithfully (v. 2). They had fasted, but the Lord did not seem to notice. The prophet announced several reasons why the Lord had not responded to their fasting:

1) They sought their own pleasure in fasting (v. 3).
2) They oppressed their slaves in fasting (v. 3).
3) They quarreled and fought in their fasting (v. 4).

Their fasting did not draw them closer to the Lord. The Lord wanted the kind of fast that seeks to do good to others (vv. 6, 7). He wanted His people to relieve the oppressed, to share their food with the hungry, and to provide housing for the poor and clothing for the naked. Genuine faith is focused outward in ministry and service.

When it cannot rest,
Whose waters cast up mire and dirt.

²¹"*There is* no peace,"
Says my God, "for the wicked."

Fasting that Pleases God

58 "Cry aloud, spare not;
Lift up your voice like a trumpet;
Tell My people their transgression,
And the house of Jacob their sins.
²Yet they seek Me daily,
And delight to know My ways,
As a nation that did righteousness,
And did not forsake the ordinance of their
God.
They ask of Me the ordinances of justice;
They take delight in approaching God.
³'Why have we fasted,' *they say,* 'and You have not
seen?
Why have we afflicted our souls, and You take
no notice?'

"In fact, in the day of your fast you find
pleasure,
And exploit all your laborers.
⁴Indeed you fast for strife and debate,
And to strike with the fist of wickedness.
You will not fast as *you do* this day,
To make your voice heard on high.
⁵Is it a fast that I have chosen,
A day for a man to afflict his soul?
Is it to bow down his head like a bulrush,
And to spread out sackcloth and ashes?
Would you call this a fast,
And an acceptable day to the LORD?

⁶"*Is* this not the fast that I have chosen:
To loose the bonds of wickedness,
To undo the heavy burdens,
To let the oppressed go free,
And that you break every yoke?
⁷*Is it* not to share your bread with the hungry,
And that you bring to your house the poor who
are cast out;
When you see the naked, that you cover him,
And not hide yourself from your own flesh?
⁸Then your light shall break forth like the
morning,
Your healing shall spring forth speedily,
And your righteousness shall go before you;
The glory of the LORD shall be your rear guard.

⁹Then you shall call, and the LORD will answer;
You shall cry, and He will say, 'Here I *am.*'

"If you take away the yoke from your midst,
The pointing of the finger, and speaking
wickedness,
¹⁰*If* you extend your soul to the hungry
And satisfy the afflicted soul,
Then your light shall dawn in the darkness,
And your darkness shall *be* as the noonday.
¹¹The LORD will guide you continually,
And satisfy your soul in drought,
And strengthen your bones;
You shall be like a watered garden,
And like a spring of water, whose waters do not
fail.
¹²Those from among you
Shall build the old waste places;
You shall raise up the foundations of many
generations;
And you shall be called the Repairer of the
Breach,
The Restorer of Streets to Dwell In.

¹³"If you turn away your foot from the Sabbath,
From doing your pleasure on My holy day,
And call the Sabbath a delight,
The holy *day* of the LORD honorable,
And shall honor Him, not doing your own
ways,
Nor finding your own pleasure,
Nor speaking *your own* words,
¹⁴Then you shall delight yourself in the LORD;
And I will cause you to ride on the high hills of
the earth,
And feed you with the heritage of Jacob your
father.
The mouth of the LORD has spoken."

Separated from God

59 Behold, the LORD's hand is not shortened,
That it cannot save;
Nor His ear heavy,
That it cannot hear.
²But your iniquities have separated you from
your God;
And your sins have hidden *His* face from you,
So that He will not hear.
³For your hands are defiled with blood,
And your fingers with iniquity;
Your lips have spoken lies,
Your tongue has muttered perversity.

58:13, 14 Obedience brought blessing. After the destruction of the temple, Sabbath observance became an identifying mark of the Lord's people (see chart, The Principle of the Sabbath).

59:1–8 God's people were doubting His goodness and power in their experience of distress. The prophet put the situation in its proper perspective. The Lord had not changed. He re-

mained the all-powerful God. Instead the iniquities and sins of the people had separated them from God. "Iniquities" indicated moral crookedness or perversion (v. 2). "Sins" referred to missing the mark (v. 2). The people were walking in crooked ways and were missing the Lord's target or mark for their lives.

4No one calls for justice,
   Nor does *any* plead for truth.
   They trust in empty words and speak lies;
   They conceive evil and bring forth iniquity.
5They hatch vipers' eggs and weave the spider's
      web;
   He who eats of their eggs dies,
   And *from* that which is crushed a viper breaks
      out.

6Their webs will not become garments,
   Nor will they cover themselves with their
      works;
   Their works *are* works of iniquity,
   And the act of violence *is* in their hands.
7Their feet run to evil,
   And they make haste to shed innocent blood;
   Their thoughts *are* thoughts of iniquity;
   Wasting and destruction *are* in their paths.
8The way of peace they have not known,
   And *there is* no justice in their ways;
   They have made themselves crooked paths;
   Whoever takes that way shall not know peace.

Sin Confessed

9Therefore justice is far from us,
   Nor does righteousness overtake us;
   We look for light, but there is darkness!
   For brightness, *but* we walk in blackness!
10We grope for the wall like the blind,
   And we grope as if *we had* no eyes;
   We stumble at noonday as at twilight;
   We are as dead *men* in desolate places.
11We all growl like bears,
   And moan sadly like doves;
   We look for justice, but *there is* none;
   For salvation, *but* it is far from us.
12For our transgressions are multiplied before
      You,
   And our sins testify against us;
   For our transgressions *are* with us,
   And *as for* our iniquities, we know them:
13In transgressing and lying against the LORD,
   And departing from our God,
   Speaking oppression and revolt,
   Conceiving and uttering from the heart words
      of falsehood.
14Justice is turned back,
   And righteousness stands afar off;

For truth is fallen in the street,
   And equity cannot enter.
15So truth fails,
   And he *who* departs from evil makes himself a
      prey.

The Redeemer of Zion

Then the LORD saw *it*, and it displeased Him
   That *there was* no justice.
16He saw that *there was* no man,
   And wondered that *there was* no intercessor;
   Therefore His own arm brought salvation for
      Him;
   And His own righteousness, it sustained Him.
17For He put on righteousness as a breastplate,
   And a helmet of salvation on His head;
   He put on the garments of vengeance for
      clothing,
   And was clad with zeal as a cloak.
18According to *their* deeds, accordingly He will
      repay,
   Fury to His adversaries,
   Recompense to His enemies;
   The coastlands He will fully repay.
19So shall they fear
   The name of the LORD from the west,
   And His glory from the rising of the sun;
   When the enemy comes in like a flood,
   The Spirit of the LORD will lift up a standard
      against him.

20"The Redeemer will come to Zion,
   And to those who turn from transgression in
      Jacob,"
   Says the LORD.

21"As for Me," says the LORD, "this *is* My
covenant with them: My Spirit who *is* upon you,
and My words which I have put in your mouth,
shall not depart from your mouth, nor from the
mouth of your descendants, nor from the mouth
of your descendants' descendants," says the LORD,
"from this time and forevermore."

The Gentiles Bless Zion

60 Arise, shine;
   For your light has come!
   And the glory of the LORD is risen upon you.
2For behold, the darkness shall cover the earth,

59:9–15 The people's disobedience brought misery and disillusionment. "Transgressions" indicates rebellion (v. 12). For "sins" and "iniquities," see verses 1–8, note. The threefold reference to sin signifies completeness. Complete confession is essential in order to experience forgiveness.

59:16–21 The Lord responded to the prayer of confession. He forgives sin, bringing His salvation. Human failure cannot defeat the purposes of God. God faithfully maintained His covenant with His people (v. 21).

60:1–22 The Lord's people are commanded to reflect the light that the Lord has shone upon them. They are to be His witnesses to all nations. The initial command is not to go, but rather first to reflect clearly the light of God's glory. The Lord is the everlasting light of His people (v. 19). Compare this chapter with Revelation 21. For "the Holy One of Israel," see Isaiah 1:4–9, note.

61:1–3 Some have identified these verses as a fifth servant song or poem (see Is. 42:1–4, note). Jesus read part of this

And deep darkness the people;
But the LORD will arise over you,
And His glory will be seen upon you.
³The Gentiles shall come to your light,
And kings to the brightness of your rising.

⁴"Lift up your eyes all around, and see:
They all gather together, they come to you;
Your sons shall come from afar,
And your daughters shall be nursed at *your*
side.
⁵Then you shall see and become radiant,
And your heart shall swell with joy;
Because the abundance of the sea shall be
turned to you,
The wealth of the Gentiles shall come to you.
⁶The multitude of camels shall cover your *land,*
The dromedaries of Midian and Ephah;
All those from Sheba shall come;
They shall bring gold and incense,
And they shall proclaim the praises of the LORD.
⁷All the flocks of Kedar shall be gathered
together to you,
The rams of Nebaioth shall minister to you;
They shall ascend with acceptance on My altar,
And I will glorify the house of My glory.

⁸"Who *are* these *who* fly like a cloud,
And like doves to their roosts?
⁹Surely the coastlands shall wait for Me;
And the ships of Tarshish *will come* first,
To bring your sons from afar,
Their silver and their gold with them,
To the name of the LORD your God,
And to the Holy One of Israel,
Because He has glorified you.

¹⁰"The sons of foreigners shall build up your
walls,
And their kings shall minister to you;
For in My wrath I struck you,
But in My favor I have had mercy on you.
¹¹Therefore your gates shall be open continually;
They shall not be shut day or night,
That *men* may bring to you the wealth of the
Gentiles,
And their kings in procession.
¹²For the nation and kingdom which will not
serve you shall perish,
And *those* nations shall be utterly ruined.

¹³"The glory of Lebanon shall come to you,
The cypress, the pine, and the box tree
together,

To beautify the place of My sanctuary;
And I will make the place of My feet glorious.
¹⁴Also the sons of those who afflicted you
Shall come bowing to you,
And all those who despised you shall fall
prostrate at the soles of your feet;
And they shall call you The City of the LORD,
Zion of the Holy One of Israel.

¹⁵"Whereas you have been forsaken and hated,
So that no one went through *you,*
I will make you an eternal excellence,
A joy of many generations.
¹⁶You shall drink the milk of the Gentiles,
And milk the breast of kings;
You shall know that I, the LORD, *am* your Savior
And your Redeemer, the Mighty One of Jacob.

¹⁷"Instead of bronze I will bring gold,
Instead of iron I will bring silver,
Instead of wood, bronze,
And instead of stones, iron.
I will also make your officers peace,
And your magistrates righteousness.
¹⁸Violence shall no longer be heard in your land,
Neither wasting nor destruction within your
borders;
But you shall call your walls Salvation,
And your gates Praise.

God the Glory of His People

¹⁹"The sun shall no longer be your light by day,
Nor for brightness shall the moon give light to
you;
But the LORD will be to you an everlasting
light,
And your God your glory.
²⁰Your sun shall no longer go down,
Nor shall your moon withdraw itself;
For the LORD will be your everlasting light,
And the days of your mourning shall be ended.
²¹Also your people *shall* all *be* righteous;
They shall inherit the land forever,
The branch of My planting,
The work of My hands,
That I may be glorified.
²²A little one shall become a thousand,
And a small one a strong nation.
I, the LORD, will hasten it in its time."

The Good News of Salvation

61 "The Spirit of the Lord GOD *is* upon Me,
Because the LORD has anointed Me
To preach good tidings to the poor;

---

passage in the synagogue at Nazareth and interpreted it as a reference to Himself (Luke 4:16–21). The Lord's salvation will bring a reversal in the fortunes of His people. Joy will replace mourning. Liberty will take the place of bondage. This pas-

sage also reveals the positive nature of the ministry the Lord wants His people to perform.

61:4–11 The ruined cities will be rebuilt in the time of salvation (v. 4). The Lord's people will serve as priests to all nations

PRISONERS — REACHING BEYOND BARS

Prisoners are those accused and convicted, whether justly or unjustly, of criminal activity. Joseph was imprisoned in Egypt (Gen. 39:20). The prophet Jeremiah had perhaps the worst experience as he was confined to a muddy cistern or underground dungeon (Jer. 37:16). John the Baptist was murdered while in prison (Matt. 14:3–12).

Paul, who was thrown in jail for his faith, often called himself a prisoner of Jesus Christ (Acts 16:23, 24). The apostle was delivered from spiritual imprisonment on accepting Christ as his Savior; he then submitted himself to physical imprisonment that the Word of God might move forward.

Causes for imprisonment ranged from offending the king (Gen. 40:1–3) or differing with his policies (2 Chr. 16:10) to an accusation of treason (Jer. 37:11–15). Treatment of prisoners was harsh (Judg. 16:21; Jer. 29:26).

Prison is Satan's domain over which he has ruled through the ages. Yet the Light dispels darkness. Those who suffer for the gospel's sake will be delivered (Ps. 146:7). Believers are reminded to give love and support to those under persecution because of their work for Christ and to share the gospel with all prisoners (Acts 16:25).

Individuals who reach out to prisoners in loving compassion demonstrate the spirit of Christ, for His own description of His messianic task taken from the prophet Isaiah (61:1–3) included "the opening of the prison" (Matt. 25:34–44; Luke 4:18–21). Salvation opened the spiritual prison, but our Lord also showed His compassion for those languishing in an earthly prison. They, too, need the gospel and loving concern.

See also Rom. 3:23, note; Eph. 3:1; 2 Tim 1:8; Phil 1:1; notes on Evangelism (John 6; Col. 4; 1 Pet. 3); Prejudice (Acts 15)

He has sent Me to heal the brokenhearted,
To proclaim liberty to the captives,
And the opening of the prison to *those who are*
    bound;
²To proclaim the acceptable year of the LORD,
And the day of vengeance of our God;
To comfort all who mourn,
³To console those who mourn in Zion,
To give them beauty for ashes,
The oil of joy for mourning,
The garment of praise for the spirit of
    heaviness;
That they may be called trees of righteousness,
The planting of the LORD, that He may be
    glorified."

⁴And they shall rebuild the old ruins,
They shall raise up the former desolations,
And they shall repair the ruined cities,
The desolations of many generations.
⁵Strangers shall stand and feed your flocks,
And the sons of the foreigner
Shall be your plowmen and your vinedressers.
⁶But you shall be named the priests of the
    LORD,
They shall call you the servants of our God.
You shall eat the riches of the Gentiles,
And in their glory you shall boast.
⁷Instead of your shame *you shall have* double
    honor,

And *instead of* confusion they shall rejoice in
    their portion.
Therefore in their land they shall possess
    double;
Everlasting joy shall be theirs.

⁸"For I, the LORD, love justice;
I hate robbery for burnt offering;
I will direct their work in truth,
And will make with them an everlasting
    covenant.
⁹Their descendants shall be known among the
    Gentiles,
And their offspring among the people.
All who see them shall acknowledge them,
That they *are* the posterity *whom* the LORD has
    blessed."

¹⁰I will greatly rejoice in the LORD,
My soul shall be joyful in my God;
For He has clothed me with the garments of
    salvation,
He has covered me with the robe of
    righteousness,
As a bridegroom decks *himself* with
    ornaments,
And as a bride adorns *herself* with her jewels.
¹¹For as the earth brings forth its bud,
As the garden causes the things that are sown
    in it to spring forth,

(v. 6). The reference to a double portion in verse 7 is reminiscent of Isaiah 40:2 where comfort is announced to the Lord's people because they have received double for all their sins. The concept of the double portion also suggests Israel's role as the firstborn among the nations. The firstborn son received

a double portion of the inheritance (see Deut. 21:17). The Lord will make an everlasting covenant with His people. Their descendants will be recognized among the nations as the people whom the Lord has blessed. A hymn of rejoicing describes their joy as being like the joy at a wedding feast (Is. 61:10, 11).

So the Lord God will cause righteousness and
praise to spring forth before all the
nations.

Assurance of Zion's Salvation

62 For Zion's sake I will not hold My peace,
And for Jerusalem's sake I will not rest,
Until her righteousness goes forth as
brightness,
And her salvation as a lamp *that* burns.
2The Gentiles shall see your righteousness,
And all kings your glory.
You shall be called by a new name,
Which the mouth of the Lord will name.
3You shall also be a crown of glory
In the hand of the Lord,
And a royal diadem
In the hand of your God.
4You shall no longer be termed Forsaken,
Nor shall your land any more be termed
Desolate;
But you shall be called Hephzibah,ᵃ and your
land Beulah;ᵇ
For the Lord delights in you,
And your land shall be married.
5For *as* a young man marries a virgin,
So shall your sons marry you;
And *as* the bridegroom rejoices over the bride,
So shall your God rejoice over you.

6I have set watchmen on your walls,
O Jerusalem;
They shall never hold their peace day or night.
You who make mention of the Lord, do not
keep silent,
7And give Him no rest till He establishes
And till He makes Jerusalem a praise in the
earth.

8The Lord has sworn by His right hand
And by the arm of His strength:
"Surely I will no longer give your grain

As food for your enemies;
And the sons of the foreigner shall not drink
your new wine,
For which you have labored.
9But those who have gathered it shall eat it,
And praise the Lord;
Those who have brought it together shall
drink it in My holy courts."

10Go through,
Go through the gates!
Prepare the way for the people;
Build up,
Build up the highway!
Take out the stones,
Lift up a banner for the peoples!

11Indeed the Lord has proclaimed
To the end of the world:
"Say to the daughter of Zion,
'Surely your salvation is coming;
Behold, His reward *is* with Him,
And His work before Him.' "
12And they shall call them The Holy People,
The Redeemed of the Lord;
And you shall be called Sought Out,
A City Not Forsaken.

The Lord in Judgment and Salvation

63 Who *is* this who comes from Edom,
With dyed garments from Bozrah,
This *One who is* glorious in His apparel,
Traveling in the greatness of His strength?—

"I who speak in righteousness, mighty to save."

2Why *is* Your apparel red,
And Your garments like one who treads in the
winepress?

62:4 ᵃLiterally *My Delight Is in Her* ᵇLiterally *Married*

62:1–12 The Lord would rejoice over His people as a bride-groom rejoices over his bride. The Lord would change their name, signifying that His people belong to Him. A play on words in the Hebrew illustrates a change of character through the change of a name (v. 4). They would no longer be called "Forsaken" (Heb., *Azubah*, the name of Jehoshaphat's mother, 1 Kin. 22:42) or their land "Desolate" (Heb. *she-mamah*), but they would be called *Heph-zibah* (Heb., lit. "My Delight Is in Her," the name of Manasseh's mother, 2 Kin. 21:1) and their land *Beulah* (Heb., lit. "Married"). The negative is rejected for the positive. Though it is not possible to be married to a land, marriage is a strong figure to portray loyalty between the people and land. Imagery of the husband-wife relationship between the Lord and His people also appears in the Book of Hosea (Hos. 1:2; 2:2). See also Revelation 21:2, 9 where the Lord's people are pictured as His bride. The Lord had established watchmen to protect His people (Is. 62:6, 7). Foreigners would no longer confiscate His people's harvest

(vv. 8, 9). The people were encouraged to prepare a highway for the Lord who would bring salvation to His people (vv. 10–12; see Is. 40:3).

62:5 The analogy of love between a young man and a virgin illustrates the relationship between the Lord and Israel. *Ba'al* (Heb.) can be translated "marry" or "take possession of." Sons do not marry mothers. However, the secondary meaning "possess" does fit the context with the understanding that the young man would marry in the sense of possessing the virgin. Israel would then no longer be desolate or abandoned but possessed and filled by her spiritual sons. The Lord would rejoice in Zion just as a bridegroom would rejoice in his bride.

63:1–6 The prophet observed a lone figure with red-stained garments coming from Edom, which represented the enemies of God's people. That figure was the Lord, who alone and in His own strength defeated the enemy of His people. He is able to fulfill all His promises.

3"I have trodden the winepress alone,
And from the peoples no one *was* with Me.
For I have trodden them in My anger,
And trampled them in My fury;
Their blood is sprinkled upon My garments,
And I have stained all My robes.
4For the day of vengeance *is* in My heart,
And the year of My redeemed has come.
5I looked, but *there was* no one to help,
And I wondered
That *there was* no one to uphold;
Therefore My own arm brought salvation for
Me;
And My own fury, it sustained Me.
6I have trodden down the peoples in My anger,
Made them drunk in My fury,
And brought down their strength to the
earth."

God's Mercy Remembered

7I will mention the lovingkindnesses of the LORD
And the praises of the LORD,
According to all that the LORD has bestowed on
us,
And the great goodness toward the house of
Israel,
Which He has bestowed on them according to
His mercies,
According to the multitude of His
lovingkindnesses.
8For He said, "Surely they *are* My people,
Children *who* will not lie."
So He became their Savior.
9In all their affliction He was afflicted,
And the Angel of His Presence saved them;
In His love and in His pity He redeemed them;
And He bore them and carried them
All the days of old.
10But they rebelled and grieved His Holy Spirit;
So He turned Himself against them as an
enemy,
And He fought against them.

11Then he remembered the days of old,
Moses *and* his people, *saying*:

"Where *is* He who brought them up out of the
sea
With the shepherd of His flock?
Where *is* He who put His Holy Spirit within
them,
12Who led *them* by the right hand of Moses,
With His glorious arm,
Dividing the water before them
To make for Himself an everlasting name,
13Who led them through the deep,
As a horse in the wilderness,
That they might not stumble?"

14As a beast goes down into the valley,
And the Spirit of the LORD causes him to rest,
So You lead Your people,
To make Yourself a glorious name.

A Prayer of Penitence

15Look down from heaven,
And see from Your habitation, holy and
glorious.
Where *are* Your zeal and Your strength,
The yearning of Your heart and Your mercies
toward me?
Are they restrained?
16Doubtless You *are* our Father,
Though Abraham was ignorant of us,
And Israel does not acknowledge us.
You, O LORD, *are* our Father;
Our Redeemer from Everlasting *is* Your
name.
17O LORD, why have You made us stray from Your
ways,
And hardened our heart from Your fear?
Return for Your servants' sake,
The tribes of Your inheritance.
18Your holy people have possessed *it* but a little
while;
Our adversaries have trodden down Your
sanctuary.
19We have become *like* those of old, over whom
You never ruled,
Those who were never called by Your
name.

63:7–14 This prayer reviewed the Lord's goodness to His people in history, although they rebelled against Him, and provided the basis for the prophet's intercession for the people. The prophet focused upon the great goodness, mercies, and loving-kindnesses of the Lord (v. 7). The term "lovingkindnesses" (Heb. *chesed*) refers to the Lord's covenant loyalty or steadfast love to His people. "Mercies" comes from the same Hebrew root as the word "womb" (v. 7; see chart, Female Metaphors of God). Thus "mercies" may indicate the compassion a mother shows to the child of her womb or the brotherly feeling of those born from the same womb. The plural form may add emphasis to the fullness of God's mercy. The Lord shared the suffering of His people in Egypt and sent His angel to rescue them (vv. 8, 9; see Ex. 3:7–10; 14:19). Like a parent

the Lord cared for His people and carried them in their helplessness. Yet His people responded in rebellion, and the Lord became His people's enemy (Is. 63:10).

63:15—64:12 The people cried out to Him for help. They longed for Him to reveal Himself to them. They acknowledged Him as their compassionate Father and their everlasting Redeemer. According to the Hebrew concept of the Lord's sovereignty, no secondary causes existed, and thus everything that happened was due to God's will. The Lord had let His people suffer the consequences of their sin, which had separated them from the presence of the Lord (Is. 64:7). The Lord is identified as both Father and potter, indicating His role as both Father and Creator (Is. 63:8; see Jer. 18:6).

64 Oh, that You would rend the heavens!
That You would come down!
That the mountains might shake at Your
presence—
[2] As fire burns brushwood,
As fire causes water to boil—
To make Your name known to Your adversaries,
That the nations may tremble at Your presence!
[3] When You did awesome things *for which* we did
not look,
You came down,
The mountains shook at Your presence.
[4] For since the beginning of the world
Men have not heard nor perceived by the ear,
Nor has the eye seen any God besides You,
Who acts for the one who waits for Him.
[5] You meet him who rejoices and does
righteousness,
Who remembers You in Your ways.
You are indeed angry, for we have sinned—
In these ways we continue;
And we need to be saved.

[6] But we are all like an unclean *thing,*
And all our righteousnesses *are* like filthy
rags;
We all fade as a leaf,
And our iniquities, like the wind,
Have taken us away.
[7] And *there is* no one who calls on Your
name,
Who stirs himself up to take hold of You;
For You have hidden Your face from us,
And have consumed us because of our
iniquities.

[8] But now, O Lord,
You *are* our Father;
We *are* the clay, and You our potter;
And all we *are* the work of Your hand.
[9] Do not be furious, O Lord,
Nor remember iniquity forever;
Indeed, please look— we all *are* Your people!
[10] Your holy cities are a wilderness,
Zion is a wilderness,
Jerusalem a desolation.
[11] Our holy and beautiful temple,
Where our fathers praised You,
Is burned up with fire;
And all our pleasant things are laid waste.
[12] Will You restrain Yourself because of these
things, O Lord?
Will You hold Your peace, and afflict us very
severely?

The Righteousness of God's Judgment

65 "I was sought by *those who* did not ask *for*
Me;
I was found by *those who* did not seek Me.
I said, 'Here I am, here I am,'
To a nation *that* was not called by My name.
[2] I have stretched out My hands all day long to a
rebellious people,
Who walk in a way *that is* not good,
According to their own thoughts;
[3] A people who provoke Me to anger continually
to My face;
Who sacrifice in gardens,
And burn incense on altars of brick;
[4] Who sit among the graves,
And spend the night in the tombs;
Who eat swine's flesh,
And the broth of abominable things is *in* their
vessels;
[5] Who say, 'Keep to yourself,
Do not come near me,
For I am holier than you!'
These *are* smoke in My nostrils,
A fire that burns all the day.

[6] "Behold, *it is* written before Me:
I will not keep silence, but will repay—
Even repay into their bosom—
[7] Your iniquities and the iniquities of your
fathers together,"
Says the Lord,
"Who have burned incense on the mountains
And blasphemed Me on the hills;
Therefore I will measure their former work
into their bosom."

[8] Thus says the Lord:

"As the new wine is found in the cluster,
And *one* says, 'Do not destroy it,
For a blessing *is* in it,'
So will I do for My servants' sake,
That I may not destroy them all.
[9] I will bring forth descendants from Jacob,
And from Judah an heir of My mountains;
My elect shall inherit it,
And My servants shall dwell there.
[10] Sharon shall be a fold of flocks,
And the Valley of Achor a place for herds to lie
down,
For My people who have sought Me.

[11] "But you *are* those who forsake the Lord,
Who forget My holy mountain,

65:1–16 The Lord is the righteous Judge. He responded to the prayer of His people. He would not destroy all His people (vv. 8–16). The faithful servants would receive the Lord's blessing, while the unfaithful would experience His judgment. The blessings on the righteous are contrasted with the curses on the wicked (vv. 13–15; see Luke 6:20–26). The promises the Lord made to the patriarch Abraham would be fulfilled in the lives of the faithful remnant (Is. 65:16; see Gen. 12:1–3).

MOTHERHOOD A NOBLE MINISTRY

A mother is one who bears and/or rears children. References to motherhood are found throughout Scripture: conception (Gen. 4:1), pregnancy (Luke 1:24), childbirth (Is. 66:7–9), breastfeeding (1 Sam. 1:23). Mothers were to be respected and obeyed (Ex. 20:12).

More than a job or responsibility, mothering is ministry. Most assuredly it takes work! It means sacrifice. Children do not come off an assembly line, nor are they the by-product of an impersonal biological process; they are to be lovingly nurtured by their mothers (2 Tim. 1:3–5). Mothers divide time among their children but multiply their love for all their children. To this they add the care of the home, often subtracting many extras in order to do so.

When Isaiah the prophet searched for an illustration of God's constant love for His people, the best example he could find was a new baby's mother (Is. 49:15). Mothers have enduring love that even the most trying circumstances or rebellious child cannot dim. As a mother lets go of her own life for the sake of her child, she is reminded of the depth and height and breadth of God's love for her, and in a unique way she experiences the true joy of motherhood. This is a truth that will transform any suffering or sacrifice into reward and joy (1 John 3:16).

There are caring mothers in the Bible: Hagar, wandering in the wilderness, wept for her child, and God responded to the cry of her heart by revealing a well of water nearby to quench the thirst of her and her child (Gen. 21:16, 19). Jochebed defied Pharaoh in order to save the life of her son (Ex. 2:1–8). The mother who appealed to Solomon was willing to let another woman enjoy her child rather than see the child murdered (1 Kin. 3:26). The mother from Shunem loved her child so devotedly that she made the difficult journey to find the prophet and inspired him to come and seek life for her child (2 Kin. 4:22–35). Hannah was devoted to her son, yet willingly offered him to the Lord (1 Sam. 1:27, 28). On the other hand, there are wicked mothers such as Athaliah, the idolatrous mother of King Ahaziah, who guided her son into devotion to evil (2 Kin. 8:26, 27).

God has a plan for mothers (Ex. 2:1–10). The high calling is an all-consuming task (Deut. 6:6, 7): in the morning, you can read God's Word to your child; at mealtime you are to give attention to meeting physical needs; as you are outside, you can teach your child about the beauty of creation; at bedtime you can pray for your child and give assurance. The reward is worth the effort (Prov. 31:28).

Godly mothers are the nation's greatest treasure, the Lord's best helpers, and the most blessed among women.

See also Gen. 27:5–46; Ezek. 16:44; Matt. 18:3, note; 2 Cor. 4:7–12; 11:27–30; Gal. 4:19; notes on Childbirth (John 16); Child Care (John 15); Children (2 Sam. 21; Ps. 128; Prov. 22; Luke 15); Family (Gen. 32; 1 Sam. 3; Ps. 78; 127); Fatherhood (Eph. 5); Motherhood (1 Sam. 1; Ezek. 16); portraits of Athaliah (2 Kin. 11); Hannah (1 Sam. 1); Herodias and Salome (Matt. 14); Jochebed (Ex. 6); Samson's Confident Mother (Judg. 13); the Shunammite Woman (2 Kin. 4)

Who prepare a table for Gad,[a]
And who furnish a drink offering for Meni.[b]
¹²Therefore I will number you for the sword,
And you shall all bow down to the slaughter;
Because, when I called, you did not answer;
When I spoke, you did not hear,
But did evil before My eyes,
And chose *that* in which I do not delight."

¹³Therefore thus says the Lord GOD:

"Behold, My servants shall eat,
But you shall be hungry;
Behold, My servants shall drink,
But you shall be thirsty;
Behold, My servants shall rejoice,
But you shall be ashamed;
¹⁴Behold, My servants shall sing for joy of heart,
But you shall cry for sorrow of heart,

And wail for grief of spirit.
¹⁵You shall leave your name as a curse to My
   chosen;
For the Lord GOD will slay you,
And call His servants by another name;
¹⁶So that he who blesses himself in the
   earth
Shall bless himself in the God of truth;
And he who swears in the earth
Shall swear by the God of truth;
Because the former troubles are forgotten,
And because they are hidden from My eyes.

The Glorious New Creation

¹⁷"For behold, I create new heavens and a new
   earth;

·······················

65:11 [a]Literally *Troop* or *Fortune*, a pagan deity [b]Literally *Number* or *Destiny*, a pagan deity

---

65:17–25 The faithful remnant will enjoy the Lord's new creation. "Create" (Heb. *bara'*) refers to activity only God can perform. Joy, not sorrow, will characterize the lives of the Lord's people (vv. 18, 19). The righteous will live to a full old

And the former shall not be remembered or
   come to mind.
[18]But be glad and rejoice forever in what I
   create;
For behold, I create Jerusalem *as* a rejoicing,
   And her people a joy.
[19]I will rejoice in Jerusalem,
   And joy in My people;
The voice of weeping shall no longer be heard
   in her,
Nor the voice of crying.

[20]"No more shall an infant from there *live but a few*
   days,
Nor an old man who has not fulfilled his days;
For the child shall die one hundred years old,
But the sinner *being* one hundred years old
   shall be accursed.
[21]They shall build houses and inhabit *them;*
   They shall plant vineyards and eat their fruit.
[22]They shall not build and another inhabit;
   They shall not plant and another eat;
For as the days of a tree, *so shall be* the days of
   My people,
And My elect shall long enjoy the work of their
   hands.
[23]They shall not labor in vain,
   Nor bring forth children for trouble;
For they *shall be* the descendants of the blessed
   of the LORD,
And their offspring with them.

[24]"It shall come to pass
   That before they call, I will answer;
And while they are still speaking, I will hear.
[25]The wolf and the lamb shall feed together,
   The lion shall eat straw like the ox,
And dust *shall be* the serpent's food.
They shall not hurt nor destroy in all My holy
   mountain,"
   Says the LORD.

True Worship and False

66 Thus says the LORD:

"Heaven *is* My throne,
   And earth *is* My footstool.
Where *is* the house that you will build Me?
   And where *is* the place of My rest?

[2]For all those *things* My hand has made,
   And all those *things* exist,"
   Says the LORD.
"But on this *one* will I look:
   On *him who is* poor and of a contrite spirit,
   And who trembles at My word.

[3]"He who kills a bull *is as if* he slays a man;
   He who sacrifices a lamb, *as if* he breaks a dog's
     neck;
He who offers a grain offering, *as if he offers*
     swine's blood;
He who burns incense, *as if* he blesses an
     idol.
Just as they have chosen their own ways,
   And their soul delights in their abominations,
[4]So will I choose their delusions,
   And bring their fears on them;
Because, when I called, no one answered,
   When I spoke they did not hear;
But they did evil before My eyes,
   And chose *that* in which I do not delight."

The LORD Vindicates Zion

[5]Hear the word of the LORD,
   You who tremble at His word:
"Your brethren who hated you,
   Who cast you out for My name's sake, said,
"Let the LORD be glorified,
   That we may see your joy.'
But they shall be ashamed."

[6]The sound of noise from the city!
   A voice from the temple!
The voice of the LORD,
   Who fully repays His enemies!

[7]"Before she was in labor, she gave birth;
   Before her pain came,
   She delivered a male child.
[8]Who has heard such a thing?
   Who has seen such things?
Shall the earth be made to give birth in one
   day?
Or shall a nation be born at once?
For as soon as Zion was in labor,
   She gave birth to her children.
[9]Shall I bring to the time of birth, and not cause
   delivery?" says the LORD.

---

age (v. 20). Their work will not be in vain (contrast vv. 21–23 with Zeph. 1:13). The Lord will answer the prayers of His people (Is. 65:24). Finally, peace among enemies in the natural order will occur in the glorious future of the Lord's people (v. 25; see Is. 11:6–9).

66:1–4 The internal dimension of faith is what matters. The Lord hears those who cry to Him with an humble and contrite heart. Without the proper inner attitude, sacrifices and other ritual observances are worthless (see Ps. 51:16, 17). Those

whom the Lord blesses are those who respond in obedience to Him. Those who choose against the Lord reap the evil consequences of their choices (Is. 66:3, 4).

66:5, 6 The Lord will bring judgment on His enemies. These verses assume a split among the Lord's people. The faithful believers were being cast out. The terminology "cast out" later came to mean excommunication from the synagogue (see John 9:34, 35). The Lord will judge the unfaithful among His people.

"Shall I who cause delivery shut up *the womb?*"
 says your God.
[10]"Rejoice with Jerusalem,
 And be glad with her, all you who love her;
 Rejoice for joy with her, all you who mourn for
  her;
[11]That you may feed and be satisfied
 With the consolation of her bosom,
 That you may drink deeply and be delighted
 With the abundance of her glory."

[12]For thus says the LORD:

"Behold, I will extend peace to her like a river,
 And the glory of the Gentiles like a flowing
  stream.
 Then you shall feed;
 On *her* sides shall you be carried,
 And be dandled on *her* knees.
[13]As one whom his mother comforts,
 So I will comfort you;
 And you shall be comforted in Jerusalem."

The Reign and Indignation of God

[14]When you see *this,* your heart shall rejoice,
 And your bones shall flourish like grass;
 The hand of the LORD shall be known to His
  servants,
 And *His* indignation to His enemies.
[15]For behold, the LORD will come with fire
 And with His chariots, like a whirlwind,
 To render His anger with fury,
 And His rebuke with flames of fire.
[16]For by fire and by His sword
 The LORD will judge all flesh;
 And the slain of the LORD shall be many.

[17]"Those who sanctify themselves and purify
  themselves,
 To go to the gardens
 After an *idol* in the midst,

Eating swine's flesh and the abomination and
 the mouse,
Shall be consumed together," says the LORD.

[18]"For I *know* their works and their thoughts. It
shall be that I will gather all nations and tongues;
and they shall come and see My glory. [19]I will set a
sign among them; and those among them who escape I will send to the nations: *to* Tarshish and Pul[a]
and Lud, who draw the bow, and Tubal and Javan,
to the coastlands afar off who have not heard My
fame nor seen My glory. And they shall declare My
glory among the Gentiles. [20]Then they shall bring
all your brethren for an offering to the LORD out
of all nations, on horses and in chariots and in lit-
ters, on mules and on camels, to My holy mountain
Jerusalem," says the LORD, "as the children of Israel bring an offering in a clean vessel into the
house of the LORD. [21]And I will also take some of
them for priests *and* Levites," says the LORD.

[22]"For as the new heavens and the new earth
 Which I will make shall remain before Me,"
  says the LORD,
"So shall your descendants and your name
  remain.
[23]And it shall come to pass
 That from one New Moon to another,
 And from one Sabbath to another,
 All flesh shall come to worship before Me,"
  says the LORD.

[24]"And they shall go forth and look
 Upon the corpses of the men
 Who have transgressed against Me.
 For their worm does not die,
 And their fire is not quenched.
 They shall be an abhorrence to all flesh."

•••••••••••••••••••••••••••••••••••

66:19 [a]Following Masoretic Text and Targum; Septuagint reads *Put*
(compare Jeremiah 46:9).

66:17–24 All nations would see and experience the glory of
the Lord. All nations would worship Him. Even foreigners
would serve the Lord (v. 21). This passage begins and ends
with a pronouncement of judgment (vv. 17, 24). In between

these verses lies a glorious picture of salvation. The new creation of God is revealed (vv. 22, 23). These verses challenge
the Lord's children in every age to reach out into all the world
with the Good News of the gospel (Matt. 28:18–20).

Jeremiah

The Book of Jeremiah is titled after its author. Its pages record the ministry and personal life of the prophet in greater depth and detail than any other Old Testament prophet except perhaps Moses. Jeremiah devotedly served the God who called him, but he experienced deep emotional conflict as God set before him one difficult task after another. He suffered not only resistance to his ministry and persecution by God's own people, but he also witnessed the downfall of Jerusalem and the temple.

Jeremiah's name may mean *"Yahweh* exalts" or *"Yahweh* loosens [the womb]," depending on the Hebrew root with which the name is associated. Jeremiah's hometown was Anathoth. He was born into the priestly family of Hilkiah, although no evidence exists to suggest that he himself was a priest (1 Kin. 2:26, 27). Jeremiah was unique among the writing prophets in that he was commanded not to marry and produce offspring because of the impending judgment on the nation (Jer. 16:1–4). The faithful scribe Baruch recorded the words of the prophet (Jer. 36:4) and accompanied him into Egypt (Jer. 43:6, 7). Baruch may have been responsible for the final compilation of the book and the addendum of the historical material in Jeremiah 52.

Jeremiah provided a portrait of a great man of God. Yet he was not a superman or the stoic ideal who allowed the currents of life to wash around him with no effect. Rather, Jeremiah was a real person with a complex personality, who nonetheless remained true to his calling and to God. He experienced fear and despair, joy and praise. Called the "weeping prophet," Jeremiah agonized over Judah's sin and coming judgment. In a series of prayers labeled "confessions," Jeremiah honestly confronted the meaning of his messages and complained to God in a spirit of humility (Jer. 11:18–23; 12:1–4; 15:10–21; 17:14–18; 18:18–23; 20:7–18). However, God did rebuke Jeremiah for worthless talk (Jer. 15:19). His prayers against his enemies recall the imprecatory psalms (see Jer. 12:1–3; 18:19–23; Ps. 35), so zealous was Jeremiah for the glory and reputation of God. As Jeremiah dealt with his conflicting emotions, he turned to God to receive encouragement. Jeremiah's words reflect a man in rich, honest dialogue with God.

The approximate dates of Jeremiah's ministry are 626 to 586 B.C. Jeremiah received God's call in the thirteenth year of King Josiah's reign (Jer. 1:2). He was a contemporary of Zephaniah, Ezekiel, Habakkuk, and perhaps Obadiah. It is difficult to determine the amount of interaction that such prophets would have had (compare Obad. 1–4 with Jer. 49:14–16). The northern kingdom of Israel had disappeared into exile approximately one hundred years before Jeremiah's call. After that event, the southern kingdom of Judah sometimes is designated Israel (see chart, Terminology for the Divided Kingdom).

Jeremiah's writing ministry is dated from the fourth year of Jehoiakim in 605 B.C. (Jer. 36:1, 2), though portions of the Book of Jeremiah may have been written earlier. The

book was completed sometime after the fall of Jerusalem. The events recorded in the Book of Jeremiah are not in chronological order.

BACKGROUND

SETTING: The dates of Jeremiah's ministry encompass a world experiencing great change. The three great powers of that time were Assyria, Babylon, and Egypt. The strength of Assyria and Egypt was on the wane, and the power of Babylon was rising. Much of what happened to God's people and the surrounding states happened in the context of the struggle among these powers, a struggle in which Babylon and the dynasty of Nabopolassar would dominate (see chart, The Kings of Babylon). Judah, located on a major route used by invading armies, was particularly vulnerable since whoever controlled Syria-Palestine could attack Egypt. At such times, the smaller city states were under great pressure to declare for one power or the other and usually chose either the one represented by the nearest army or the one most likely to win. A wrong choice would have serious consequences. Judah's rebellion against Babylon, despite Jeremiah's counsel to surrender, contributed, in human terms, to the destruction of Jerusalem.

LITERARY CHARACTERISTICS: The Book of Jeremiah contains lengthy prose sections, both narrative and discourse (Jer. 7; 11; 16; 19; 21; 24—29; 32—45), but much of the work is poetic in form. The poetry of Jeremiah reflects skillful use of the Hebrew language. Jeremiah was particularly adept at using poetic repetition, as well as "living metaphors." These living metaphors were actions taken by the prophet to reflect or embody symbolically his message. Other prophets, especially Jeremiah's contemporary, Ezekiel, used this technique. Examples include the ruined sash (Jer. 13:1–11), God's command not to marry and raise a family (Jer. 16:1–4), the prohibition against participating in a funeral meal or feast (Jer. 16:5–9), the smashed flask (Jer. 19:1–15), the bonds and yokes (Jer. 27:1–22), the purchase of his relative's field in Anathoth (Jer. 32:6–15), and the hidden stones (Jer. 43:8–13). All these directives involved actual objects and actions in Jeremiah's life. God also revealed Himself to Jeremiah in ordinary experiences of life such as a visit to the potter's house (Jer.18:1–11) and two baskets of figs (Jer. 24).

The composition of the book is not chronological, but rather loosely thematic. The Book of Jeremiah should be viewed as a collection of the writings and sermons of the prophet, which, when read together, form a powerful, unitary whole.

THEMES

The skillfully combined writings effectively communicate the controlling theme of Jeremiah, clearly summarized in Jeremiah 1:10. God used Jeremiah to proclaim His word of both judgment and hope to the nations. Verbs of destruction predominate in this verse, indicating that Jeremiah's message would be primarily one of judgment. Constructive verbs, "to build" and "to plant," indicate that Jeremiah's message also contained an element of hope, such as that found in the New Covenant passage (Jer. 31:31–34).

OUTLINE

I. The Making of a Prophet (1:1–19)
   A. The historical setting (1:1–3)
   B. Jeremiah's prophetic role (1:4–19)
II. The Prophet's Warnings and Exhortations (2:1—35:19)
   A. Israel's guilt and punishment (2:1—6:30)

B. False religion and its judgment (7:1—10:25)
C. Warnings and judgment (11:1—15:9)
D. Confessions, symbolic actions, and sermons (15:10—25:38)
E. Foretelling of the Babylonian Exile (26:1—29:32)

1 The words of Jeremiah the son of Hilkiah, of the priests who *were* in Anathoth in the land of Benjamin, ²to whom the word of the LORD came in the days of Josiah the son of Amon, king of Judah, in the thirteenth year of his reign. ³It came also in the days of Jehoiakim the son of Josiah, king of Judah, until the end of the eleventh year of Zedekiah the son of Josiah, king of Judah, until the carrying away of Jerusalem captive in the fifth month.

The Prophet Is Called

⁴Then the word of the LORD came to me, saying:

⁵"Before I formed you in the womb I knew you;
Before you were born I sanctified you;
I ordained you a prophet to the nations."

⁶Then said I:

"Ah, Lord GOD!
Behold, I cannot speak, for I *am* a youth."

⁷But the LORD said to me:

"Do not say, 'I *am* a youth,'
For you shall go to all to whom I send you,
And whatever I command you, you shall speak.
⁸Do not be afraid of their faces,
For I *am* with you to deliver you," says the LORD.

⁹Then the LORD put forth His hand and touched my mouth, and the LORD said to me:

"Behold, I have put My words in your mouth.
¹⁰See, I have this day set you over the nations and over the kingdoms,

1:2 The word of the Lord is a common way of introducing a divine oracle at the beginning of a prophetic book (see Ezek. 1:3; Hos. 1:1; Joel 1:1; Jon. 1:1; Mic. 1:1; Zeph. 1:1; Hag. 1:1; Zech. 1:1). Fulfillment of Jeremiah's prophecy provided evidence of the authenticity of his call. Jeremiah heard the Lord's call in the 13th year of Josiah's reign (640 to 609 B.C.). Thus, Jeremiah's ministry began about 626 B.C. and extended beyond the fall of Jerusalem (586 B.C.).

1:5 God's call of Jeremiah preceded the prophet's birth. "Formed," "knew," "sanctified," and "ordained" are verbs that illustrate the extent to which God was active in Jeremiah's life, preparing him for a ministry that would involve every aspect of his being. "Formed" (Heb. *yatsar*) revealed that God, the ultimate life-giving source, is involved intimately with the birth process. Even before Jeremiah's forma-

tion in the womb, God "knew" (Heb. *yada'*) him, implying an active foreknowledge grounded in God's sovereign purposes (see Ps. 139:13–18, note). "Sanctified" (Heb. *qadash*) means to set apart for God's special use.

1:6 Jeremiah's reluctance to assume the prophetic ministry stemmed from his perception of his youth and his inability to speak. Moses experienced a similar sense of inadequacy (Ex. 3:11; 4:10–13).

1:9, 10 Jeremiah's ministry would have both a negative (judgment) and positive (grace) aspect, expressed here with verbs drawn from agriculture and construction (v. 10). The predominance of destructive verbs indicated Jeremiah's message would be mainly one of judgment. But an element of hope is present also in the verbs "to build" and "to plant." This verse summarizes the major themes of the book.

ABORTION — DEFENDING THE INNOCENT

Although the Bible does not specifically address the subject of abortion, Scripture clearly regards the unborn child as fully human life. This life is to be protected in the same way that God calls us to defend the lives of all innocent human beings.

Jesus affirmed the value of unborn life in the womb through His Incarnation—coming as a baby rather than arriving on earth as an adult (Matt. 1:20, 21, 25). Other passages of Scripture also affirm the extension of the sanctity of life to the unborn. The psalmist speaks of God's care for the baby while still in the womb (Ps. 139:13–16), and the Mosaic Law punished violence done to the unborn the same as violence done to a full-grown adult (Ex. 21:22–25).

The existence of a person is established at conception. God had plans for you before you were born (Jer. 1:4, 5), and He tells you He has been your God since before your birth (Ps. 22:10). John the Baptist "leaped" while in the womb of his mother Elizabeth as she acknowledged the coming of the Messiah (Luke 1:41–45). These verses all speak of the unborn child as an *actual* human being, not a mere *potential* that will become a human being at birth.

The unborn child is to be protected because the child is a life (Ex. 21:22–25); God does get angry over the killing of unborn children (Amos 1:13). An unintended pregnancy can be difficult for a woman and her family, but God wants both the woman and her unborn child to be protected and cherished.

However, a woman who has had an abortion, for whatever reason, needs to know that Jesus still loves her and stands ready to forgive her just as He freely forgave women who erred against His law in other ways (John 8:1–11).

See also Matt. 18:3, note; notes on Childbirth (John 16); Children (2 Sam. 21; Ps. 128; Prov. 22; Luke 15); Image of God (Ps. 8); Miscarriage (Ex. 21); Sanctity of Life (Gen. 9)

To root out and to pull down,
To destroy and to throw down,
To build and to plant."

11Moreover the word of the LORD came to me, saying, "Jeremiah, what do you see?"

And I said, "I see a branch of an almond tree."

12Then the LORD said to me, "You have seen well, for I am ready to perform My word."

13And the word of the LORD came to me the second time, saying, "What do you see?"

And I said, "I see a boiling pot, and it is facing away from the north."

14Then the LORD said to me:

"Out of the north calamity shall break forth
On all the inhabitants of the land.
15For behold, I am calling
All the families of the kingdoms of the north,"
    says the LORD;
"They shall come and each one set his throne
At the entrance of the gates of Jerusalem,
Against all its walls all around,
And against all the cities of Judah.
16I will utter My judgments

Against them concerning all their wickedness,
Because they have forsaken Me,
Burned incense to other gods,
And worshiped the works of their own hands.

17"Therefore prepare yourself and arise,
And speak to them all that I command you.
Do not be dismayed before their faces,
Lest I dismay you before them.
18For behold, I have made you this day
A fortified city and an iron pillar,
And bronze walls against the whole land—
Against the kings of Judah,
Against its princes,
Against its priests,
And against the people of the land.
19They will fight against you,
But they shall not prevail against you.
For I *am* with you," says the LORD, "to deliver you."

God's Case Against Israel

2 Moreover the word of the LORD came to me, saying, 2"Go and cry in the hearing of Jerusalem, saying, 'Thus says the LORD:

1:11, 12 In a Hebraic play on words, "almond" (Heb. *shaqed*) and "I am ready" (Heb. *shoqed*, lit., "watching") are remarkably similar. The almond was the first tree to awaken to life in the spring, signifying that God is awake, watching over His word to bring it to pass.

1:13 God spoke to Jeremiah through the ordinary experiences of life. The boiling pot suggests God's judgment waiting to be

poured out on Judah. The pot is tilted southward, indicating that an enemy would come on God's people from the north.

1:14–16 God revealed to Jeremiah His intent to use a foreign power to judge the people of Judah for idolatry. Later Jeremiah identified the Babylonians as the enemy from the north.

2:2 The kindness (Heb. *chesed*) of Israel's youth indicated the

"I remember you,
The kindness of your youth,
The love of your betrothal,
When you went after Me in the wilderness,
In a land not sown.
[3]Israel *was* holiness to the LORD,
The firstfruits of His increase.
All that devour him will offend;
Disaster will come upon them," says the LORD.' "

[4]Hear the word of the LORD, O house of Jacob and all the families of the house of Israel. [5]Thus says the LORD:

"What injustice have your fathers found in Me,
That they have gone far from Me,
Have followed idols,
And have become idolaters?
[6]Neither did they say, 'Where *is* the LORD,
Who brought us up out of the land of Egypt,
Who led us through the wilderness,
Through a land of deserts and pits,
Through a land of drought and the shadow of
death,
Through a land that no one crossed
And where no one dwelt?'
[7]I brought you into a bountiful country,
To eat its fruit and its goodness.
But when you entered, you defiled My land
And made My heritage an abomination.
[8]The priests did not say, 'Where *is* the LORD?'
And those who handle the law did not know
Me;
The rulers also transgressed against Me;
The prophets prophesied by Baal,
And walked after *things that* do not profit.

[9]"Therefore I will yet bring charges against you,"
says the LORD,
"And against your children's children I will
bring charges.
[10]For pass beyond the coasts of Cyprus[a] and see,
Send to Kedar[b] and consider diligently,
And see if there has been such *a thing.*
[11]Has a nation changed *its* gods,
Which *are* not gods?
But My people have changed their Glory
For *what* does not profit.
[12]Be astonished, O heavens, at this,
And be horribly afraid;
Be very desolate," says the LORD.
[13]"For My people have committed two evils:
They have forsaken Me, the fountain of living
waters,
And hewn themselves cisterns—broken cisterns
that can hold no water.

[14]*Is* Israel a servant?
Is he a homeborn *slave?*
Why is he plundered?
[15]The young lions roared at him, *and* growled;
They made his land waste;
His cities are burned, without inhabitant.
[16]Also the people of Noph[a] and Tahpanhes
Have broken the crown of your head.
[17]Have you not brought this on yourself,
In that you have forsaken the LORD your
God
When He led you in the way?

2:10 [a]Hebrew *Kittim,* western lands, especially Cyprus [b]In the northern Arabian desert, representative of the eastern cultures 2:16 [a]That is, Memphis in ancient Egypt

intimacy of the covenantal relationship between God and Israel, denoting a high degree of loyalty, love, and unfailing devotion. Israel is pictured as a young bride, accepting the Lord as her husband with full confidence and entering into a new life with Him. Israel's trust in God led her to follow Him into the wilderness. Jeremiah idealized the desert period of Israel's history much the same way as did Hosea (Hos. 2:14, 15; 9:10).

2:3 Israel was God's firstfruits of His harvest of the nations. Thus, anyone who touched God's special possession would suffer the consequences. According to OT law, the first yield of the harvest belonged to God as a way of acknowledging the abundance of God's providence.

2:4–13 Jeremiah unfolded a three-point progression repeated throughout his book: Israel's devotion to God; Israel's apostasy; the results of Israel's apostasy. Israel sometimes is used to refer to the southern kingdom of Judah after the northern kingdom fell in 722 B.C.

2:5 Idols (Heb. *hevel*) implied a worthless vanity or emptiness. By following idols, the people had pursued emptiness and become empty themselves. Sin results in emptiness. People become like whatever they worship (see also v. 13).

2:9 The Hebrew legal term translated "bring charges" intro-

duced the lawsuit God brought against Israel. God's judgment ultimately came in 586 B.C. when Jerusalem fell completely to Nebuchadnezzar, king of Babylon (2 Kin. 24—25).

2:10, 11 Jeremiah detailed the enormity of Israel's crime by drawing evidence from surrounding nations. The rhetorical question in verse 11 anticipated a negative answer and emphasized the enormity of Israel's sin. From Cyprus in the west to Kedar in the east, no nation had ever turned against its pagan gods; yet Israel had forsaken the living God.

2:13 The people of Israel had the full resources of God, the living water; yet they turned aside to worthless substitutes and entrusted themselves to powerless deities that could not meet their spiritual needs.

2:15 While lions may be understood literally (2 Kin. 17:25, 26), they are most likely a reference to Assyria. Devastation of land and destruction of cities may refer to the numerous Assyrian campaigns.

2:16 Noph traditionally is identified with Memphis, the ancient capital of lower Egypt. Tahpanhes may refer to the city of Daphne, also located in Egypt. To break (or graze) the crown of the head may be a figurative reference to the disgrace and death of King Josiah of Judah in 609 B.C. (see 2 Kin. 23:29). He was killed by the Egyptian Pharaoh Necho.

[18]And now why take the road to Egypt,
To drink the waters of Sihor?
Or why take the road to Assyria,
To drink the waters of the River?[a]
[19]Your own wickedness will correct you,
And your backslidings will rebuke you.
Know therefore and see that *it is* an evil and
bitter *thing*
That you have forsaken the LORD your God,
And the fear of Me *is* not in you,"
Says the Lord GOD of hosts.

[20]"For of old I have broken your yoke *and* burst
your bonds;
And you said, 'I will not transgress,'
When on every high hill and under every green
tree
You lay down, playing the harlot.
[21]Yet I had planted you a noble vine, a seed of
highest quality.
How then have you turned before Me
Into the degenerate plant of an alien vine?
[22]For though you wash yourself with lye, and use
much soap,
Yet your iniquity is marked before Me," says the
Lord GOD.

[23]"How can you say, 'I am not polluted,
I have not gone after the Baals'?
See your way in the valley;
Know what you have done:
You are a swift dromedary breaking loose in her
ways,
[24]A wild donkey used to the wilderness,
That sniffs at the wind in her desire;
In her time of mating, who can turn her
away?
All those who seek her will not weary
themselves;
In her month they will find her.

[25]Withhold your foot from being unshod, and
your throat from thirst.
But you said, 'There is no hope.
No! For I have loved aliens, and after them I
will go.'

[26]"As the thief is ashamed when he is found out,
So is the house of Israel ashamed;
They and their kings and their princes, and
their priests and their prophets,
[27]Saying to a tree, 'You *are* my father,'
And to a stone, 'You gave birth to me.'
For they have turned *their* back to Me, and not
their face.
But in the time of their trouble
They will say, 'Arise and save us.'
[28]But where *are* your gods that you have made
for yourselves?
Let them arise,
If they can save you in the time of your trouble;
For *according to* the number of your cities
Are your gods, O Judah.

[29]"Why will you plead with Me?
You all have transgressed against Me," says the
LORD.
[30]"In vain I have chastened your children;
They received no correction.
Your sword has devoured your prophets
Like a destroying lion.

[31]"O generation, see the word of the LORD!
Have I been a wilderness to Israel,
Or a land of darkness?
Why do My people say, 'We are lords;
We will come no more to You'?
[32]Can a virgin forget her ornaments,
Or a bride her attire?

2:18 [a]That is, the Euphrates

2:18 Sihor (Heb., lit. "black") may refer to the Nile River. In a play on words, Jeremiah could be slighting the Nile River god. Jeremiah rebuked the people who had taken roads to a broken cistern or a black river when they had living water.

2:19 Assyria and Egypt were not responsible for Israel's disaster. The nation's own sin, the repeated breach of the covenant with God, resulted in calamity. Israel had shown more respect to earthly rulers than to God.

2:20–29 Seven illustrations show the collapse of Israel's loyalty:
1) an ox that breaks its yoke (v. 20);
2) an unfaithful wife who has played the harlot (v. 20);
3) God's planting of a noble vine that has become a degenerate plant (v. 21);
4) someone unable to cleanse his iniquity even with lye or soap (v. 22);
5) a wild camel wandering with no direction (v. 23);
6) a female donkey in heat wildly pursuing a mate (v. 24); and
7) a thief caught and ashamed (v. 26).

The phrase "plead with Me" (v. 29) is a legal term used here to show how ironic it was for Israel to bring charges against God.

2:23, 24 Israel is graphically compared to a dromedary and a female donkey in heat. Young female camels are altogether unreliable and easily disturbed. When confused, they dash about in a disorganized fashion. A female donkey in heat is very wild. She tracks the male donkeys, pursuing them relentlessly. This is an extremely vivid picture of Israel recklessly, shamelessly chasing after the Baals, in stark contrast to Deuteronomy 28:14, where God commanded her to turn neither to the right or left but to obey God and follow Him. However, there was no hope Israel would continue after her first love, and she would ultimately be led thirsty and shameless (as pictured here) into Babylonian captivity.

2:32 Jeremiah asked a rhetorical question, while giving an indictment against Israel. That a bride would forget the wedding sash or girdle that signified her status is highly unlikely.

THE TIMELINE FOR JEREMIAH

YEAR	EVENT	REFERENCE
640–609 B.C.	Josiah was king of Judah.	2 Kin. 22:1—23:30
628/627 B.C.	Josiah's reform began with the removal of high places and all vestiges of foreign cults.	2 Chr. 34:1-7
627 B.C.	Ashurbanipal, last of the great Assyrian rulers, died.	Jer. 1:1, 2
627/626 B.C.	Jeremiah was called by God to prophetic office.	
626 B.C.	Nabopolassar, gaining independence from Assyria, founded the Neo-Babylonian Empire.	
622 B.C.	Josiah repaired the temple; the Book of the Law was found.	2 Kin. 23:1-25; 2 Chr. 34:8—35:19
612 B.C.	Nineveh, the capital of Assyria, fell to the Media-Babylonian coalition.	
614 B.C.	Medes, led by Cyaxares, captured Asshur, the old Assyrian capital.	
609–605 B.C.	Egypt ruled Palestine and Syria.	
609 B.C.	Josiah was killed by the Egyptian army at the Battle of Megiddo.	2 Kin. 23:29; 2 Chr. 35:20-25
609 B.C.	Jehoahaz (Shallum) ruled Judah for three months. His reign marked a turn in the court's attitude toward Jeremiah.	2 Kin. 23:31-34; 2 Chr. 36:1-4; Jer. 22:11, 12
609–598 B.C.	Jehoiakim (Eliakim) was king of Judah.	2 Kin. 23:34—24:7
609–598 B.C.	Jeremiah's scroll was read in the temple and palace and burned during reign of Jehoiakim.	Jer. 7:1-15; 26:1-24; 36:1-26
608 B.C.	The temple in Jerusalem was destroyed.	Jer. 26:1-24
605 B.C.	Babylon gained supremacy in the Near East by defeating Egypt at the Battle of Carchemish.	Jer. 25:1; 46:2
605 B.C.	Deportation in which Daniel was taken.	
605 B.C.	Jeremiah summarized his work to Baruch.	Jer. 45:1-5
602 B.C.	Jehoiakim rebelled against Nebuchadnezzar.	2 Kin. 24:1
598/597 B.C.	Nebuchadnezzar retaliated; deportation of Jews to Babylon in which Ezekiel was taken.	2 Kin. 24:8-16
598–597 B.C.	Jehoiachin (Jeconiah) ruled Judah for three months before being deported to Babylon.	2 Kin. 24:8-16; 2 Chr. 36:9, 10; Jer. 22:24-30
597–586 B.C.	Zedekiah (Mattaniah) ruled Judah.	2 Kin. 24:17—25:7; 2 Chr. 36:11-14; Jer. 52:1-11
594 B.C.	Seraiah visited Babylon in the midst of revolt and unrest.	Jer. 51:59
588 B.C.	Jeremiah was in a cistern while Jerusalem was under siege.	2 Kin. 25:1; Jer. 32:1, 2; 37:1—38:28; 39:1; 52:4; Ezek. 24:1, 2
587 B.C.	Jeremiah purchased a field at Anathoth.	Jer. 32:6-15
586 B.C.	Jerusalem was destroyed; the Jews were deported to Babylon; Jeremiah was released.	2 Kin. 25:2-10; Jer. 39:1—40:7; 52:5-27
587–582 B.C.	The governor Gedaliah was murdered. Some Jews fled to Egypt, taking Jeremiah with them.	2 Kin. 25:22-26
582 B.C.	Deportation of Jews to Babylon.	Jer. 52:30
561 B.C.	Jehoiachin was released from prison.	2 Kin. 25:27; Jer. 52:31

Yet My people have forgotten Me days without
    number.

³³"Why do you beautify your way to seek love?
    Therefore you have also taught
    The wicked women your ways.
³⁴Also on your skirts is found
    The blood of the lives of the poor innocents.
    I have not found it by secret search,
    But plainly on all these things.
³⁵Yet you say, 'Because I am innocent,
    Surely His anger shall turn from me.'
    Behold, I will plead My case against you,
    Because you say, 'I have not sinned.'
³⁶Why do you gad about so much to change your
    way?
    Also you shall be ashamed of Egypt as you were
    ashamed of Assyria.
³⁷Indeed you will go forth from him
    With your hands on your head;
    For the LORD has rejected your trusted allies,
    And you will not prosper by them.

Israel Is Shameless

3 "They say, 'If a man divorces his wife,
    And she goes from him
    And becomes another man's,
    May he return to her again?'
    Would not that land be greatly polluted?
    But you have played the harlot with many
      lovers;
    Yet return to Me," says the LORD.

²"Lift up your eyes to the desolate heights and
    see:
    Where have you not lain *with men?*
    By the road you have sat for them
    Like an Arabian in the wilderness;
    And you have polluted the land

    With your harlotries and your wickedness.
³Therefore the showers have been withheld,
    And there has been no latter rain.
    You have had a harlot's forehead;
    You refuse to be ashamed.
⁴Will you not from this time cry to Me,
    'My Father, You *are* the guide of my youth?
⁵Will He remain angry forever?
    Will He keep it to the end?'
    Behold, you have spoken and done evil things,
    As you were able."

A Call to Repentance

⁶The LORD said also to me in the days of Josiah
the king: "Have you seen what backsliding Israel
has done? She has gone up on every high mountain and under every green tree, and there played
the harlot. ⁷And I said, after she had done all these
things, 'Return to Me.' But she did not return. And
her treacherous sister Judah saw it. ⁸Then I saw
that for all the causes for which backsliding Israel
had committed adultery, I had put her away and
given her a certificate of divorce; yet her treacherous sister Judah did not fear, but went and played
the harlot also. ⁹So it came to pass, through her
casual harlotry, that she defiled the land and committed adultery with stones and trees. ¹⁰And yet
for all this her treacherous sister Judah has not
turned to Me with her whole heart, but in pretense," says the LORD.

¹¹Then the LORD said to me, "Backsliding Israel
has shown herself more righteous than treacherous Judah. ¹²Go and proclaim these words toward
the north, and say:

'Return, backsliding Israel,' says the LORD;
'I will not cause My anger to fall on you.
For I *am* merciful,' says the LORD;
'I will not remain angry forever.

Yet for countless days Israel, God's bride, had forgotten her wedding adornment—God Himself.

2:36, 37 Both Egypt and Assyria were fickle and unreliable. Already Assyria had taken the northern kingdom captive. Judah was under heavy tribute. God had rejected Israel's allies. Prosperity and deliverance would only come from God. The phrase "your hands on your head" probably indicates subjection to a foreign power. Archaeological evidence depicts captives being led into slavery with their hands over their heads.

3:1 After forsaking God and taking many lovers, Israel found reconciliation with God impossible. Yet as in Hosea 2:2—3:5, God pleaded with His people for their true repentance and return. God's grace makes reconciliation possible. Jeremiah applied Deuteronomy 24:1–4 to Israel, God's betrothed wife.

3:2, 3 A close link existed between sin and the Land's productivity in OT thought (Lev. 18:24–28; Deut. 24:4; Hos. 4:2, 3; Amos 4:6–10). Drought was a consequence of Israel's sin. Showers that fell normally in October or November as well as the late rain in March and April were withheld. Yet Judah refused to be ashamed or humiliated because of idolatry. An-

other reference to droughts during the time of Jeremiah's ministry is found in Jeremiah 14:1–6.

3:6, 7 The northern kingdom of Israel became the paradigm of backsliding or apostasy, as Judah watched (see Ezek. 23). The hilltops and leafy trees were the chosen site for those practicing fertility rites.

3:8 Samaria or Israel fell to Assyria in 722 B.C. (2 Kin. 17:1–18). Judah understood this fall of the northern kingdom as judgment for sin; yet Judah continued to play the harlot.

3:9 A warning is issued against treating sin lightly. Stones and trees were significant instruments in the fertility cult (Jer. 2:27). Judah exchanged the God of living water for the gods of trees and stones.

3:12–14 God's judgment is restrained by His mercy to provide ample time for Israel's repentance and return to Him. Husband-wife imagery is used to describe the Lord's relationship with His people (vv. 14, 20). Israel is portrayed as an unfaithful wife. Similar imagery appears in the Book of Hosea (Hos. 2).

¹³Only acknowledge your iniquity,
That you have transgressed against the LORD
    your God,
And have scattered your charms
To alien deities under every green tree,
And you have not obeyed My voice,' says the
    LORD.

¹⁴"Return, O backsliding children," says the
LORD; "for I am married to you. I will take you, one
from a city and two from a family, and I will bring
you to Zion. ¹⁵And I will give you shepherds according to My heart, who will feed you with
knowledge and understanding.

¹⁶"Then it shall come to pass, when you are
multiplied and increased in the land in those
days," says the LORD, "that they will say no more,
'The ark of the covenant of the LORD.' It shall not
come to mind, nor shall they remember it, nor
shall they visit it, nor shall it be made anymore.

¹⁷"At that time Jerusalem shall be called The
Throne of the LORD, and all the nations shall be
gathered to it, to the name of the LORD, to Jerusalem. No more shall they follow the dictates of
their evil hearts.

¹⁸"In those days the house of Judah shall walk
with the house of Israel, and they shall come together out of the land of the north to the land
that I have given as an inheritance to your fathers.

¹⁹"But I said:

'How can I put you among the children
And give you a pleasant land,
A beautiful heritage of the hosts of nations?'

"And I said:

'You shall call Me, "My Father,"
And not turn away from Me.'
²⁰Surely, as a wife treacherously departs from
    her husband,
So have you dealt treacherously with Me,
O house of Israel," says the LORD.

²¹A voice was heard on the desolate heights,
Weeping and supplications of the children of
    Israel.
For they have perverted their way;
They have forgotten the LORD their God.

²²"Return, you backsliding children,
And I will heal your backslidings."

"Indeed we do come to You,
For You are the LORD our God.
²³Truly, in vain is salvation hoped for from the
    hills,
And from the multitude of mountains;
Truly, in the LORD our God
Is the salvation of Israel.
²⁴For shame has devoured
The labor of our fathers from our youth—
Their flocks and their herds,
Their sons and their daughters.
²⁵We lie down in our shame,
And our reproach covers us.
For we have sinned against the LORD our God,
We and our fathers,
From our youth even to this day,
And have not obeyed the voice of the LORD our
    God."

4 "If you will return, O Israel," says the LORD,
"Return to Me;
And if you will put away your abominations out
    of My sight,
Then you shall not be moved.
²And you shall swear, 'The LORD lives,'
In truth, in judgment, and in righteousness;
The nations shall bless themselves in Him,
And in Him they shall glory."

³For thus says the LORD to the men of Judah
and Jerusalem:

"Break up your fallow ground,
And do not sow among thorns.
⁴Circumcise yourselves to the LORD,
And take away the foreskins of your hearts,
You men of Judah and inhabitants of
    Jerusalem,
Lest My fury come forth like fire,
And burn so that no one can quench it,
Because of the evil of your doings."

An Imminent Invasion

⁵Declare in Judah and proclaim in Jerusalem,
and say:

3:16 In those days refers to the messianic age (v. 18; Jer. 31:29).
The ark of the covenant, which designated God's royal presence, will be irrelevant when the Messiah is seated upon His
throne in Jerusalem (see 1 Sam. 4:3). Since the ark was the
center of OT worship, for an OT prophet to suggest its absence would be shocking.

3:21 Baal worship took place on bare hilltops. Josiah's reform
destroyed these Baal sanctuaries. Yet the bare hills or high
places still attracted God's people to perversion, casting
doubt on the sincerity of their repentance.

4:2 Israel's true repentance would have far-reaching consequences for mankind in general (Is. 1:16, 17; 42:6; 49:6). Jeremiah clearly had God's promise to Abraham in mind here
(Gen. 12:2, 3).

4:3, 4 The necessity of deep and radical repentance is portrayed in both agricultural and ceremonial imagery. "Fallow
ground" refers to unplowed ground. Breaking up hardened or
weed-covered earth was no easy task on the rocky slopes of
Judah. The radical change necessary in Judah's inhabitants is
illustrated further by the call to circumcision of the heart, a
radical change in the total inner being.

"Blow the trumpet in the land;
Cry, 'Gather together,'
And say, 'Assemble yourselves,
And let us go into the fortified cities.'
6Set up the standard toward Zion.
Take refuge! Do not delay!
For I will bring disaster from the north,
And great destruction."

7The lion has come up from his thicket,
And the destroyer of nations is on his way.
He has gone forth from his place
To make your land desolate.
Your cities will be laid waste,
Without inhabitant.
8For this, clothe yourself with sackcloth,
Lament and wail.
For the fierce anger of the LORD
Has not turned back from us.

9"And it shall come to pass in that day," says the
LORD,
"That the heart of the king shall perish,
And the heart of the princes;
The priests shall be astonished,
And the prophets shall wonder."

10Then I said, "Ah, Lord GOD!
Surely You have greatly deceived this people
and Jerusalem,
Saying, 'You shall have peace,'
Whereas the sword reaches to the heart."

11At that time it will be said
To this people and to Jerusalem,
"A dry wind of the desolate heights blows in the
wilderness
Toward the daughter of My people—
Not to fan or to cleanse—
12A wind too strong for these will come for Me;
Now I will also speak judgment against them."

13"Behold, he shall come up like clouds,
And his chariots like a whirlwind.
His horses are swifter than eagles.
Woe to us, for we are plundered!"

14O Jerusalem, wash your heart from wickedness,
That you may be saved.

How long shall your evil thoughts lodge within
you?
15For a voice declares from Dan
And proclaims affliction from Mount Ephraim:
16"Make mention to the nations,
Yes, proclaim against Jerusalem,
That watchers come from a far country
And raise their voice against the cities of
Judah.
17Like keepers of a field they are against her all
around,
Because she has been rebellious against Me,"
says the LORD.
18"Your ways and your doings
Have procured these things for you.
This is your wickedness,
Because it is bitter,
Because it reaches to your heart."

Sorrow for the Doomed Nation

19O my soul, my soul!
I am pained in my very heart!
My heart makes a noise in me;
I cannot hold my peace,
Because you have heard, O my soul,
The sound of the trumpet,
The alarm of war.
20Destruction upon destruction is cried,
For the whole land is plundered.
Suddenly my tents are plundered,
And my curtains in a moment.
21How long will I see the standard,
And hear the sound of the trumpet?

22"For My people are foolish,
They have not known Me.
They are silly children,
And they have no understanding.
They are wise to do evil,
But to do good they have no knowledge."

23I beheld the earth, and indeed it was without
form, and void;
And the heavens, they had no light.
24I beheld the mountains, and indeed they
trembled,
And all the hills moved back and forth.
25I beheld, and indeed there was no man,
And all the birds of the heavens had fled.

4:7 The invading lion is not named but has been identified variously as the Scythian, Assyrian, or Babylonian armies. The enemy is described as the "destroyer." Jeremiah painted a vivid picture of the utter devastation the invasion would bring. Observe that the Lord is behind this judgment on His people (v. 6).

4:10 You have greatly deceived is a reference to the sovereignty of God that permitted the people to be deceived. The phrase "you shall have peace" was quoted often by false

prophets who propagated the view that all was well in Judah (Jer. 6:14; 14:13; 23:16, 17).

4:23–26 The repetition of "I beheld" at the beginning of each of these verses gives them a unity which emphasizes the visionary nature of the poetry. As Jeremiah viewed the utter destruction of his nation, he used the imagery of creation in reverse. "Without form, and void" is found only in Genesis 1:2. A return to the darkness and chaos of the pre-creation state is pictured in these verses.

²⁶I beheld, and indeed the fruitful land *was* a wilderness,
And all its cities were broken down
At the presence of the LORD,
By His fierce anger.

²⁷For thus says the LORD:

"The whole land shall be desolate;
Yet I will not make a full end.
²⁸For this shall the earth mourn,
And the heavens above be black,
Because I have spoken.
I have purposed and will not relent,
Nor will I turn back from it.
²⁹The whole city shall flee from the noise of the horsemen and bowmen.
They shall go into thickets and climb up on the rocks.
Every city *shall be* forsaken,
And not a man shall dwell in it.

³⁰"And *when* you *are* plundered,
What will you do?
Though you clothe yourself with crimson,
Though you adorn *yourself* with ornaments of gold,
Though you enlarge your eyes with paint,
In vain you will make yourself fair;
Your lovers will despise you;
They will seek your life.

³¹"For I have heard a voice as of a woman in labor,
The anguish as of her who brings forth her first child,
The voice of the daughter of Zion bewailing herself;
She spreads her hands, *saying,*
'Woe *is* me now, for my soul is weary
Because of murderers!'

The Justice of God's Judgment

5 "Run to and fro through the streets of Jerusalem;
See now and know;
And seek in her open places
If you can find a man,
If there is *anyone* who executes judgment,
Who seeks the truth,
And I will pardon her.
²Though they say, '*As* the LORD lives,'
Surely they swear falsely."

³O LORD, *are* not Your eyes on the truth?
You have stricken them,
But they have not grieved;
You have consumed them,
But they have refused to receive correction.
They have made their faces harder than rock;
They have refused to return.

⁴Therefore I said, "Surely these *are* poor.
They are foolish;
For they do not know the way of the LORD,
The judgment of their God.
⁵I will go to the great men and speak to them,
For they have known the way of the LORD,
The judgment of their God."

But these have altogether broken the yoke
And burst the bonds.
⁶Therefore a lion from the forest shall slay them,
A wolf of the deserts shall destroy them;
A leopard will watch over their cities.
Everyone who goes out from there shall be torn in pieces,
Because their transgressions are many;
Their backslidings have increased.

⁷"How shall I pardon you for this?
Your children have forsaken Me
And sworn by *those that are* not gods.
When I had fed them to the full,
Then they committed adultery
And assembled themselves by troops in the harlots' houses.
⁸They were *like* well-fed lusty stallions;
Every one neighed after his neighbor's wife.

4:30, 31 Jerusalem is portrayed as a woman who, though adorning herself for suitors, welcomes her foe. The description of such ornamentation is that of a harlot seeking to lure lovers. To "paint" (lit. "to tear") the eyes with black antimony to make them appear larger is a practice still common in the Middle East (see Ex. 30, Cosmetics). "Lovers" designates those with whom Judah has entered into political alliances, particularly the Babylonians.

5:1 Two terms in prophetic literature denote qualities that should characterize those in covenantal relationship with God—"judgment" (Heb. *mishpat,* lit. "justice") and "truth" (Heb. *'emunah,* lit. "faithfulness"). God promised to spare Sodom for the sake of ten such men (Gen. 18:23–32). Here he offered much more lenient terms for Jerusalem, despite her greater sin.

5:2, 3 To swear by God is to invoke His name as a guarantee of the obligation to be undertaken. If the agreement is broken, God is expected to afflict the covenant breaker with judgment, with the intent of bringing His people to repentance. In stubbornness the people of Jerusalem rejected "correction" or discipline and made their faces harder than rock, a vivid illustration of rebellion.

5:7, 8 During Manasseh's reign, cult-prostitution was practiced widely. The sexual activities destroyed by Josiah's reform in the sanctuaries moved to the brothels. The people turned from God who "fed" or satisfied them to immorality and adulterous lust (Jer. 2:20–37). Adultery, punishable then by death, is a particularly grievous sin against the covenant foundation of the family and society (see Hos. 3, Adultery).

⁹Shall I not punish *them* for these *things?*" says
the LORD.
"And shall I not avenge Myself on such a nation
as this?

¹⁰"Go up on her walls and destroy,
But do not make a complete end.
Take away her branches,
For they *are* not the LORD's.
¹¹For the house of Israel and the house of Judah
Have dealt very treacherously with Me," says
the LORD.

¹²They have lied about the LORD,
And said, "*It is* not He.
Neither will evil come upon us,
Nor shall we see sword or famine.
¹³And the prophets become wind,
For the word *is* not in them.
Thus shall it be done to them."

¹⁴Therefore thus says the LORD God of hosts:

"Because you speak this word,
Behold, I will make My words in your mouth
fire,
And this people wood,
And it shall devour them.
¹⁵Behold, I will bring a nation against you from
afar,
O house of Israel," says the LORD.
"It *is* a mighty nation,
It *is* an ancient nation,
A nation whose language you do not know,
Nor can you understand what they say.
¹⁶Their quiver *is* like an open tomb;
They *are* all mighty men.
¹⁷And they shall eat up your harvest and your
bread,
Which your sons and daughters should eat.
They shall eat up your flocks and your herds;
They shall eat up your vines and your fig trees;
They shall destroy your fortified cities,
In which you trust, with the sword.

¹⁸"Nevertheless in those days," says the LORD, "I
will not make a complete end of you. ¹⁹And it will
be when you say, 'Why does the LORD our God do
all these *things* to us?' then you shall answer them,
'Just as you have forsaken Me and served foreign
gods in your land, so you shall serve aliens in a
land *that is* not yours.'

²⁰"Declare this in the house of Jacob
And proclaim it in Judah, saying,
²¹'Hear this now, O foolish people,
Without understanding,
Who have eyes and see not,
And who have ears and hear not:
²²Do you not fear Me?' says the LORD.
'Will you not tremble at My presence,
Who have placed the sand as the bound of the
sea,
By a perpetual decree, that it cannot pass
beyond it?
And though its waves toss to and fro,
Yet they cannot prevail;
Though they roar, yet they cannot pass over it.
²³But this people has a defiant and rebellious
heart;
They have revolted and departed.
²⁴They do not say in their heart,
"Let us now fear the LORD our God,
Who gives rain, both the former and the latter,
in its season.
He reserves for us the appointed weeks of the
harvest."
²⁵Your iniquities have turned these *things* away,
And your sins have withheld good from you.

²⁶'For among My people are found wicked
men;
They lie in wait as one who sets snares;
They set a trap;
They catch men.
²⁷As a cage is full of birds,
So their houses *are* full of deceit.
Therefore they have become great and grown
rich.
²⁸They have grown fat, they are sleek;
Yes, they surpass the deeds of the wicked;
They do not plead the cause,
The cause of the fatherless;
Yet they prosper,
And the right of the needy they do not
defend.
²⁹Shall I not punish *them* for these *things?*' says
the LORD.
'Shall I not avenge Myself on such a nation as
this?'

³⁰"An astonishing and horrible thing
Has been committed in the land:
³¹The prophets prophesy falsely,
And the priests rule by their *own* power;

5:17 The outcome of Nebuchadnezzar's invasion is depicted in
graphic language by the prophet. Destruction of the cities of
Judah is affirmed by archaeological evidence. Many cities
never were occupied again.

5:18, 19 A remnant would be preserved (v. 10; Jer. 4:27). Jeremiah poetically reiterated the fact that, while the destruction
would be severe, God's righteous judgment would be tempered with grace.

5:30, 31 Even the religious leaders entrusted with the moral
and spiritual guidance of God's people were corrupt. "Astonishing" (Heb. *shammah*) denotes a horrified amazement that
the prophets and priests in their unholy alliance would falsify
God's truth and that the people would love this corruption despite Jeremiah's pleas. "What will you do in the end" refers to
the coming judgment.

And My people love *to have it* so.
But what will you do in the end?

Impending Destruction from the North

6 "O you children of Benjamin,
Gather yourselves to flee from the midst of
Jerusalem!
Blow the trumpet in Tekoa,
And set up a signal-fire in Beth Haccerem;
For disaster appears out of the north,
And great destruction.
²I have likened the daughter of Zion
To a lovely and delicate woman.
³The shepherds with their flocks shall come to
her.
They shall pitch *their* tents against her all
around.
Each one shall pasture in his own place."

⁴"Prepare war against her;
Arise, and let us go up at noon.
Woe to us, for the day goes away,
For the shadows of the evening are
lengthening.
⁵Arise, and let us go by night,
And let us destroy her palaces."

⁶For thus has the LORD of hosts said:

"Cut down trees,
And build a mound against Jerusalem.
This *is* the city to be punished.
She *is* full of oppression in her midst.
⁷As a fountain wells up with water,
So she wells up with her wickedness.
Violence and plundering are heard in her.
Before Me continually *are* grief and wounds.
⁸Be instructed, O Jerusalem,
Lest My soul depart from you;
Lest I make you desolate,
A land not inhabited."

⁹Thus says the LORD of hosts:

"They shall thoroughly glean as a vine the
remnant of Israel;
As a grape-gatherer, put your hand back into
the branches."

¹⁰To whom shall I speak and give warning,
That they may hear?
Indeed their ear *is* uncircumcised,
And they cannot give heed.
Behold, the word of the LORD is a reproach to
them;
They have no delight in it.
¹¹Therefore I am full of the fury of the
LORD.
I am weary of holding *it* in.
"I will pour it out on the children outside,
And on the assembly of young men
together;
For even the husband shall be taken with the
wife,
The aged with *him who is* full of days.
¹²And their houses shall be turned over to
others,
Fields and wives together;
For I will stretch out My hand
Against the inhabitants of the land," says the
LORD.
¹³"Because from the least of them even to the
greatest of them,
Everyone *is* given to covetousness;
And from the prophet even to the priest,
Everyone deals falsely.
¹⁴They have also healed the hurt of My people
slightly,
Saying, 'Peace, peace!'
When *there is* no peace.
¹⁵Were they ashamed when they had committed
abomination?
No! They were not at all ashamed;
Nor did they know how to blush.
Therefore they shall fall among those who
fall;
At the time I punish them,
They shall be cast down," says the LORD.

¹⁶Thus says the LORD:

"Stand in the ways and see,
And ask for the old paths, where the good way
is,
And walk in it;
Then you will find rest for your souls.
But they said, 'We will not walk *in it*.'

6:1 The warning came to Jeremiah's own tribe of Benjamin. Tekoa, located approximately 12 miles south of Jerusalem, was the home village of the prophet Amos (Amos 1:1). Disaster in Jerusalem appeared imminent despite the ancient cultic beliefs that Jerusalem's walls were impregnable. The belief that Jerusalem would never be destroyed developed because of the Lord's deliverance of the city during the Sennacherib Crisis in 701 B.C. (see 2 Kin. 18:17—19:37).

6:10 The ears of God's people were closed (lit. "uncircumcised"), denoting willful rebellion and refusal to hear. They no longer delighted in the Lord's Word.

6:14 The message of the false prophets was "peace," a false hope because no peace existed. Judah's religious leaders treated the people's sin superficially, thereby implicitly encouraging their waywardness.

6:16 Old paths refer to the ways of faith and obedience, the ways followed by Moses and the patriarchs. "Walk" indicates lifestyle (Ps. 1:1). Jeremiah encouraged the people not only to remember the old traditions of faith but also to live them.

PAGANISM *FOLLOWING FALSE GODS*

Solomon was a man of great God-given wisdom; yet his heart was turned away from the Lord by his foreign wives (1 Kin. 11:1–8). Even though God had appeared to Solomon twice, warning him of the danger of following false gods, ultimately Solomon did not listen and chose to follow his own sinful heart instead of God (vv. 9, 10).

Likewise, Israel's King Ahab was influenced by his Sidonian wife, Jezebel, to worship Baal (1 Kin. 16:31). Jezebel opposed the worship of the Lord God of Israel, and on one occasion she demanded the slaying of all the prophets of the Lord she could find (1 Kin. 18:4). Her threats upon the life of Elijah, because he had executed the prophets of Baal, sent the prophet into hiding and deep depression (1 Kin. 19:1–4).

Not only foreign women, but the women of Israel themselves, influenced God's people to embrace pagan gods (Jer. 7:16–18; Ezek. 8:14). With the full permission of their husbands, the women of Israel and Judah baked cakes to offer to the queen of heaven; they also burned incense and poured out drink offerings to her. These men and women were totally unrepentant when confronted with their sin. Therefore, God pronounced judgment upon them through Jeremiah (Jer. 44:15–29).

In recent times, a renewed interest in paganism has arisen among many women. Focus has been placed upon such ancient goddesses as Gaia, the earth goddess, and Sophia, the goddess of wisdom. Some women's organizations, even within the church, are introducing women to goddesses and pagan elements of worship and theology.

Christian women must guard their hearts and minds against these influences. The power of their persuasion must be used to turn the hearts of men, women, and children not away from but toward the one true God as revealed in Jesus Christ.

See also 1 Kin. 11:1–10; Jer. 10:3–6, note; 44:15–25; Ezek. 8:12–16; chart, Graeco-Roman Goddesses; notes on Feminine Leadership (1 Sam. 25); Goddess Religion (Ex. 20); Idolatry (Is. 42); Influence (Esth. 4); the Occult (Deut. 18); Witchcraft (1 Sam. 15); portrait of Jezebel (1 Kin. 18)

---

¹⁷Also, I set watchmen over you, *saying,*
 'Listen to the sound of the trumpet!'
But they said, 'We will not listen.'
¹⁸Therefore hear, you nations,
 And know, O congregation, what *is* among
  them.
¹⁹Hear, O earth!
 Behold, I will certainly bring calamity on this
  people—
 The fruit of their thoughts,
 Because they have not heeded My words
 Nor My law, but rejected it.
²⁰For what purpose to Me
 Comes frankincense from Sheba,
 And sweet cane from a far country?
 Your burnt offerings *are* not acceptable,
 Nor your sacrifices sweet to Me."

²¹Therefore thus says the LORD:

"Behold, I will lay stumbling blocks before this
  people,
 And the fathers and the sons together shall
  fall on them.

 The neighbor and his friend shall
  perish."

²²Thus says the LORD:

"Behold, a people comes from the north
  country,
 And a great nation will be raised from the
  farthest parts of the earth.
²³They will lay hold on bow and spear;
 They *are* cruel and have no mercy;
 Their voice roars like the sea;
 And they ride on horses,
 As men of war set in array against you,
  O daughter of Zion."

²⁴We have heard the report of it;
 Our hands grow feeble.
 Anguish has taken hold of us,
 Pain as of a woman in labor.
²⁵Do not go out into the field,
 Nor walk by the way.
 Because of the sword of the enemy,

6:17 Watchmen are true prophets who give warning to a city about to be destroyed (Ezek. 33). The true prophets were in direct opposition to the prophets who presented the false hope of peace (see Jer. 6:14).

6:20 No offering could substitute for obedience. "Frankincense" was imported from Sheba, located in Arabia, and

"sweet cane" may have been brought from India. "Burnt offerings" indicated those in which the entire animal was consumed. "Sacrifices" were those in which only choice portions of the animal were offered, while the rest was consumed by the worshipers (see Amos 5:21–24).

Fear *is* on every side.

²⁶O daughter of my people,
Dress in sackcloth
And roll about in ashes!
Make mourning *as for* an only son, most bitter
　　lamentation;
For the plunderer will suddenly come upon us.

²⁷"I have set you *as* an assayer *and* a fortress
　　among My people,
That you may know and test their way.
²⁸They *are* all stubborn rebels, walking as
　　slanderers.
They are bronze and iron,
They *are* all corrupters;
²⁹The bellows blow fiercely,
The lead is consumed by the fire;
The smelter refines in vain,
For the wicked are not drawn off.
³⁰*People* will call them rejected silver,
Because the LORD has rejected them."

Trusting in Lying Words

7 The word that came to Jeremiah from the LORD, saying, ²"Stand in the gate of the LORD's house, and proclaim there this word, and say, 'Hear the word of the LORD, all *you of* Judah who enter in at these gates to worship the LORD!' " ³Thus says the LORD of hosts, the God of Israel: "Amend your ways and your doings, and I will cause you to dwell in this place. ⁴Do not trust in these lying words, saying, 'The temple of the LORD, the temple of the LORD, the temple of the LORD *are* these.'

⁵"For if you thoroughly amend your ways and your doings, if you thoroughly execute judgment between a man and his neighbor, ⁶*if* you do not oppress the stranger, the fatherless, and the widow, and do not shed innocent blood in this place, or walk after other gods to your hurt, ⁷then I will cause you to dwell in this place, in the land that I gave to your fathers forever and ever.

⁸"Behold, you trust in lying words that cannot profit. ⁹Will you steal, murder, commit adultery, swear falsely, burn incense to Baal, and walk after other gods whom you do not know, ¹⁰and *then* come and stand before Me in this house which is called by My name, and say, 'We are delivered to do all these abominations'? ¹¹Has this house, which is called by My name, become a den of thieves in your eyes? Behold, I, even I, have seen *it*," says the LORD.

¹²"But go now to My place which *was* in Shiloh, where I set My name at the first, and see what I did to it because of the wickedness of My people Israel. ¹³And now, because you have done all these works," says the LORD, "and I spoke to you, rising up early and speaking, but you did not hear, and I called you, but you did not answer, ¹⁴therefore I will do to the house which is called by My name, in which you trust, and to this place which I gave to you and your fathers, as I have done to Shiloh. ¹⁵And I will cast you out of My sight, as I have cast out all your brethren—the whole posterity of Ephraim.

¹⁶"Therefore do not pray for this people, nor lift up a cry or prayer for them, nor make intercession to Me; for I will not hear you. ¹⁷Do you not see what they do in the cities of Judah and in the streets of Jerusalem? ¹⁸The children gather wood, the fathers kindle the fire, and the women knead dough, to make cakes for the queen of heaven; and *they* pour out drink offerings to other gods, that they may provoke Me to anger. ¹⁹Do they provoke Me to anger?" says the LORD. "*Do they* not *provoke* themselves, to the shame of their own faces?"

²⁰Therefore thus says the Lord GOD: "Behold, My anger and My fury will be poured out on this place—on man and on beast, on the trees of the field and on the fruit of the ground. And it will burn and not be quenched."

²¹Thus says the LORD of hosts, the God of Israel: "Add your burnt offerings to your sacrifices and eat meat. ²²For I did not speak to your fathers, or command them in the day that I brought them out of the land of Egypt, concerning burnt offerings or sacrifices. ²³But this is what I commanded them, saying, 'Obey My voice, and I will be your God, and you shall be My people. And walk in all

---

6:29, 30 The ancient metallurgical process of refining raw ore to pure silver is applied metaphorically to the people of Judah, who were hopelessly impure and beyond refining.

7:4 False prophets deceived the people with the promise that God would not allow the temple, His earthly dwelling place, to be destroyed. This delusion was strengthened by the miraculous deliverance of Jerusalem during the reign of Hezekiah (2 Kin. 19:20–36) and by the promise that David and his descendants would have a kingdom forever (2 Sam. 7:10–13).

7:12 Under Joshua the tabernacle was erected in Shiloh, located in the territory of Ephraim in the northern kingdom. Archaeological evidence indicates that it was destroyed by the Philistines around 1050 B.C. (1 Sam. 4).

7:15 The Assyrian exile of the northern kingdom occurred in 722 B.C. (2 Kin. 17:22, 23). For Ephraim, see chart, Terminology for the Divided Kingdom.

7:18 Queen of heaven is a reference to the Assyro-Babylonian Astarte or Ishtar, an ancient cult practiced throughout the Orient (see Jer. 44:15–19, note). The queen of heaven was the goddess of love and fertility (see chart, Graeco-Roman Goddesses). Such worship involved a pinch of incense, a cake in the shape of a woman, a crescent moon or a star, or a libation. Apparently this goddess was worshiped primarily by women (Jer. 44:15–19), but this idolatry evidently spread throughout the land and was practiced not only by women but by entire families, including children.

7:22 All sacrifices are not rejected, but they are meaningless without true repentance and obedience (see 1 Sam. 15:22).

the ways that I have commanded you, that it may be well with you.' ²⁴Yet they did not obey or incline their ear, but followed the counsels *and* the dictates of their evil hearts, and went backward and not forward. ²⁵Since the day that your fathers came out of the land of Egypt until this day, I have even sent to you all My servants the prophets, daily rising up early and sending *them.* ²⁶Yet they did not obey Me or incline their ear, but stiffened their neck. They did worse than their fathers.

²⁷"Therefore you shall speak all these words to them, but they will not obey you. You shall also call to them, but they will not answer you.

Judgment on Obscene Religion

²⁸"So you shall say to them, 'This *is* a nation that does not obey the voice of the LORD their God nor receive correction. Truth has perished and has been cut off from their mouth. ²⁹Cut off your hair and cast *it* away, and take up a lamentation on the desolate heights; for the LORD has rejected and forsaken the generation of His wrath.' ³⁰For the children of Judah have done evil in My sight," says the LORD. "They have set their abominations in the house which is called by My name, to pollute it. ³¹And they have built the high places of Tophet, which *is* in the Valley of the Son of Hinnom, to burn their sons and their daughters in the fire, which I did not command, nor did it come into My heart.

³²"Therefore behold, the days are coming," says the LORD, "when it will no more be called Tophet, or the Valley of the Son of Hinnom, but the Valley of Slaughter; for they will bury in Tophet until there is no room. ³³The corpses of this people will be food for the birds of the heaven and for the beasts of the earth. And no one will frighten *them away.* ³⁴Then I will cause to cease from the cities of Judah and from the streets of Jerusalem the

voice of mirth and the voice of gladness, the voice of the bridegroom and the voice of the bride. For the land shall be desolate.

8 "At that time," says the LORD, "they shall bring out the bones of the kings of Judah, and the bones of its princes, and the bones of the priests, and the bones of the prophets, and the bones of the inhabitants of Jerusalem, out of their graves. ²They shall spread them before the sun and the moon and all the host of heaven, which they have loved and which they have served and after which they have walked, which they have sought and which they have worshiped. They shall not be gathered nor buried; they shall be like refuse on the face of the earth. ³Then death shall be chosen rather than life by all the residue of those who remain of this evil family, who remain in all the places where I have driven them," says the LORD of hosts.

The Peril of False Teaching

⁴"Moreover you shall say to them, 'Thus says the LORD:

"Will they fall and not rise?
 Will one turn away and not return?
⁵Why has this people slidden back,
 Jerusalem, in a perpetual backsliding?
 They hold fast to deceit,
 They refuse to return.
⁶I listened and heard,
 But they do not speak aright.
 No man repented of his wickedness,
 Saying, 'What have I done?'
 Everyone turned to his own course,
 As the horse rushes into the battle.

⁷"Even the stork in the heavens
 Knows her appointed times;
 And the turtledove, the swift, and the swallow

7:29 Cutting the hair was a sign of mourning (Job 1:20; Mic. 1:16; see 2 Sam. 14, Hair). The long hair of the Nazirite was a sign of his consecration to God (Num. 6:1, 2, 3–8, notes). Judah had abandoned her consecration to God and was now seen lamenting on the barren hills where so many of her evils had been committed.

7:31 The Valley of the Son of Hinnom (NT *Gehenna*), south of Jerusalem, was the site of the worship of Molech, to which children were sacrificed. Tophet, located near the eastern end of the southern part of the Valley of Hinnom, was commonly used to designate a place of child sacrifice. Hebrew scribes often translated the word as "shameful thing" because of the hideous practices that took place there. High places were the scenes of such pagan rites during the reigns of Ahaz (2 Kin. 16:2, 3) and Manasseh (2 Kin. 21:6). Human sacrifice was strictly forbidden under Mosaic Law (Lev. 18:21; 20:2–5).

7:32 The valley where Israel sacrificed her children to Molech would become her own graveyard, called the "Valley of Slaughter." The Babylonian army would destroy Judah in judgment for her wickedness.

7:33 This judgment was one of the curses for breaking the covenant (Deut. 28:26). For a body to be unburied was an abomination. Even the bodies of criminals were buried (Deut. 21:22, 23).

8:2 The sun, moon, and host of heaven were astral deities worshiped by Judah before, during, and following the reign of Manasseh (2 Kin. 21:3, 5; 23:11). Ironically, the bones of those who worshiped these pagan gods would be spread before the astral deities and denied the decency of burial.

8:4 Turn away . . . return is a word play in which the Hebrew verb forms are identical. Jeremiah emphasized the irrationality of the people's behavior.

8:6 To repent (Heb. *nacham*) is to be sorry, to mourn for one's sin. Instead of turning from their sin, the people rushed to embrace it.

8:7 Drawing from nature, Jeremiah noted that even the birds obey their God-given instincts. Similarly obedience to the covenant should be natural for God's people (see Is. 1:2, 3).

Observe the time of their coming.
But My people do not know the judgment of
the LORD.

⁸"How can you say, 'We *are* wise,
And the law of the LORD *is* with us'?
Look, the false pen of the scribe certainly
works falsehood.
⁹The wise men are ashamed,
They are dismayed and taken.
Behold, they have rejected the word of the
LORD;
So what wisdom do they have?
¹⁰Therefore I will give their wives to others,
And their fields to those who will inherit *them;*
Because from the least even to the greatest
Everyone is given to covetousness;
From the prophet even to the priest
Everyone deals falsely.
¹¹For they have healed the hurt of the daughter
of My people slightly,
Saying, 'Peace, peace!'
When *there is* no peace.
¹²Were they ashamed when they had committed
abomination?
No! They were not at all ashamed,
Nor did they know how to blush.
Therefore they shall fall among those who fall;
In the time of their punishment
They shall be cast down," says the LORD.

¹³"I will surely consume them," says the LORD.
"No grapes *shall be* on the vine,
Nor figs on the fig tree,
And the leaf shall fade;
And *the things* I have given them shall pass away
from them." ' "

¹⁴"Why do we sit still?
Assemble yourselves,
And let us enter the fortified cities,
And let us be silent there.
For the LORD our God has put us to silence
And given us water of gall to drink,
Because we have sinned against the LORD.

¹⁵"*We* looked for peace, but no good *came;*
And for a time of health, and there was
trouble!
¹⁶The snorting of His horses was heard from
Dan.
The whole land trembled at the sound of the
neighing of His strong ones;
For they have come and devoured the land and
all that is in it,
The city and those who dwell in it."

¹⁷"For behold, I will send serpents among you,
Vipers which cannot be charmed,
And they shall bite you," says the LORD.

The Prophet Mourns for the People

¹⁸I would comfort myself in sorrow;
My heart *is* faint in me.
¹⁹Listen! The voice,
The cry of the daughter of my people
From a far country:
"*Is* not the LORD in Zion?
Is not her King in her?"

"Why have they provoked Me to anger
With their carved images—
With foreign idols?"

²⁰"The harvest is past,
The summer is ended,
And we are not saved!"

²¹For the hurt of the daughter of my people I am
hurt.
I am mourning;
Astonishment has taken hold of me.
²²*Is there* no balm in Gilead,
Is there no physician there?
Why then is there no recovery
For the health of the daughter of my people?

9 Oh, that my head were waters,
And my eyes a fountain of tears,
That I might weep day and night
For the slain of the daughter of my people!

8:8, 9 The scribes manipulated God's Law in order to twist its meaning to suit their own purposes (see chart, Jewish Sects). They wanted the people to believe that they could sin without consequence. This reference to "scribes" as an organized group may be the earliest (see 1 Chr. 2:55). The scribes copied, studied, and interpreted the law.

8:11 Jeremiah criticized the false prophets for fostering a false hope of security in the people. Hypnotized by the comfortable and profitable doctrine of prosperity and peace (Heb. *shalom*, lit. "completeness, well-being, and contentment"), they neglected the repentance and obedience that would bring healing.

8:16 Dan lies at the northern border of Israel, near the headwaters of the Jordan (1 Kin. 4:25). The army of the invading foe was so numerous that the snorting and neighing of their stallions made the ground shake. The Lord had warned that destruction would come from the north (Jer. 1:14, 15).

8:17 Vipers were sent by God in judgment, reminiscent of Numbers 21:6–9. Although deliverance came in Moses' day, none would come in Jeremiah's time.

8:20 This popular proverb was used in everyday life to depict the loss of all hope of deliverance.

8:22 Gilead, on the eastern side of the Jordan River, was well known for its healing balms (Gen. 37:25). The "balm" came from the turpentine and pistachio trees.

9:1 Jeremiah is known as the weeping prophet. Although his message was one of doom and destruction, he mourned over

²Oh, that I had in the wilderness
A lodging place for travelers;
That I might leave my people,
And go from them!
For they *are* all adulterers,
An assembly of treacherous men.

³"And *like* their bow they have bent their tongues
for lies.
They are not valiant for the truth on the earth.
For they proceed from evil to evil,
And they do not know Me," says the LORD.
⁴"Everyone take heed to his neighbor,
And do not trust any brother;
For every brother will utterly supplant,
And every neighbor will walk with slanderers.
⁵Everyone will deceive his neighbor,
And will not speak the truth;
They have taught their tongue to speak lies;
They weary themselves to commit iniquity.
⁶Your dwelling place *is* in the midst of deceit;
Through deceit they refuse to know Me," says
the LORD.

⁷Therefore thus says the LORD of hosts:

"Behold, I will refine them and try them;
For how shall I deal with the daughter of My
people?
⁸Their tongue *is* an arrow shot out;
It speaks deceit;
One speaks peaceably to his neighbor with his
mouth,
But in his heart he lies in wait.
⁹Shall I not punish them for these *things?*" says
the LORD.
"Shall I not avenge Myself on such a nation as
this?"

¹⁰I will take up a weeping and wailing for the
mountains,
And for the dwelling places of the wilderness a
lamentation,
Because they are burned up,
So that no one can pass through;
Nor can *men* hear the voice of the cattle.
Both the birds of the heavens and the beasts
have fled;
They are gone.

¹¹"I will make Jerusalem a heap of ruins, a den of
jackals.

I will make the cities of Judah desolate,
without an inhabitant."

¹²Who *is* the wise man who may understand this? And *who is he* to whom the mouth of the LORD has spoken, that he may declare it? Why does the land perish *and* burn up like a wilderness, so that no one can pass through?
¹³And the LORD said, "Because they have forsaken My law which I set before them, and have not obeyed My voice, nor walked according to it, ¹⁴but they have walked according to the dictates of their own hearts and after the Baals, which their fathers taught them," ¹⁵therefore thus says the LORD of hosts, the God of Israel: "Behold, I will feed them, this people, with wormwood, and give them water of gall to drink. ¹⁶I will scatter them also among the Gentiles, whom neither they nor their fathers have known. And I will send a sword after them until I have consumed them."

The People Mourn in Judgment

¹⁷Thus says the LORD of hosts:

"Consider and call for the mourning women,
That they may come;
And send for skillful *wailing* women,
That they may come.
¹⁸Let them make haste
And take up a wailing for us,
That our eyes may run with tears,
And our eyelids gush with water.
¹⁹For a voice of wailing is heard from Zion:
'How we are plundered!
We are greatly ashamed,
Because we have forsaken the land,
Because we have been cast out of our
dwellings.' "

²⁰Yet hear the word of the LORD, O women,
And let your ear receive the word of His
mouth;
Teach your daughters wailing,
And everyone her neighbor a lamentation.
²¹For death has come through our windows,
Has entered our palaces,
To kill off the children—*no longer to be* outside!
And the young men—*no longer* on the streets!

²²Speak, "Thus says the LORD:

---

the sufferings of his people out of his deep compassion for them.

9:2 Jeremiah sought a lodging place, probably little more than a simple shelter in the wilderness, as an escape from the sight of the people's degradation that sickened his heart.

9:12–14 Judah had forsaken God's Law and soon would be destroyed. The reference to the covenant is clear. These verses offer an explanation of the judgment on Judah.

9:15 Wormwood denotes bitterness, while "water of gall" is poisoned water (see Prov. 5:4, note; chart, The Herbs of the Bible). Moses had warned the Israelites centuries before about similar consequences of idolatry (Deut. 29:18).

9:17–20 Mourning women (Heb. *qonen*) are professional mourners. So great will be the need for mourners that mothers are encouraged to teach their daughters to lament.

9:22 Jeremiah lamented that the dead were too numerous to

Those who call to mind the sufferings of Christ and who offer up their own to God through His passion find their pains sweet and pleasant.

St. Mary Magdalene dei Pazzi

'Even the carcasses of men shall fall as refuse
     on the open field,
Like cuttings after the harvester,
And no one shall gather *them.*'"

23Thus says the LORD:

"Let not the wise *man* glory in his wisdom,
Let not the mighty *man* glory in his might,
Nor let the rich *man* glory in his riches;
24But let him who glories glory in this,
That he understands and knows Me,
That I *am* the LORD, exercising lovingkindness,
     judgment, and righteousness in the earth.
For in these I delight," says the LORD.

25"Behold, the days are coming," says the LORD, "that I will punish all *who are* circumcised with the uncircumcised— 26Egypt, Judah, Edom, the people of Ammon, Moab, and all *who are* in the farthest corners, who dwell in the wilderness. For all *these* nations *are* uncircumcised, and all the house of Israel *are* uncircumcised in the heart."

Idols and the True God

10 Hear the word which the LORD speaks to you, O house of Israel.
2Thus says the LORD:

"Do not learn the way of the Gentiles;
Do not be dismayed at the signs of heaven,
For the Gentiles are dismayed at them.
3For the customs of the peoples *are* futile;
For *one* cuts a tree from the forest,
The work of the hands of the workman, with
     the ax.
4They decorate it with silver and gold;
They fasten it with nails and hammers
So that it will not topple.
5They *are* upright, like a palm tree,
And they cannot speak;
They must be carried,

Because they cannot go *by themselves.*
Do not be afraid of them,
For they cannot do evil,
Nor can they do any good."

6Inasmuch as *there is* none like You, O LORD
(You *are* great, and Your name *is* great in
     might),
7Who would not fear You, O King of the
     nations?
For this is Your rightful due.
For among all the wise *men* of the nations,
And in all their kingdoms,
There is none like You.
8But they are altogether dull-hearted and
     foolish;
A wooden idol *is* a worthless doctrine.
9Silver is beaten into plates;
It is brought from Tarshish,
And gold from Uphaz,
The work of the craftsman
And of the hands of the metalsmith;
Blue and purple *are* their clothing;
They *are* all the work of skillful *men.*
10But the LORD *is* the true God;
He *is* the living God and the everlasting King.
At His wrath the earth will tremble,
And the nations will not be able to endure His
     indignation.

11Thus you shall say to them: "The gods that have not made the heavens and the earth shall perish from the earth and from under these heavens."

12He has made the earth by His power,
He has established the world by His wisdom,
And has stretched out the heavens at His
     discretion.
13When He utters His voice,
There is a multitude of waters in the heavens:

---

be buried. Unburied corpses were viewed as a particularly loathsome degradation (see Jer. 8:2; 16:4–6; 25:33).

9:23, 24 This beautiful poem on wisdom is in the best tradition of wisdom literature. The absolute superiority of the true knowledge of God over the best of human thinking is a recurring theme of Jeremiah (Jer. 2:8; 4:22; 9:2–5; 22:16; 24:7). "To know" in Hebrew thought indicates intimate, personal relationship. True religion consists of acknowledging the complete sovereignty of God in every facet of life. The lives of those who know God will reflect His attributes: lovingkindness, justice, and righteousness.

10:2 To learn (lit. "to adopt") has overtones of discipleship. The "way" refers to religious customs. "Signs of heaven" are the heavenly bodies created by God for His purposes (Gen. 1:14–18). Unusual natural phenomena associated with the heavens were considered portents of good and evil and often were part of idolatrous worship.

10:8 Dull-hearted (Heb. *ba'ar*) can mean "stupid" or "unreceptive." Teaching received from idolaters is as worthless as the idols themselves.

"And He causes the vapors to ascend from the
   ends of the earth.
He makes lightning for the rain,
He brings the wind out of His treasuries."[a]

[14]Everyone is dull-hearted, without knowledge;
Every metalsmith is put to shame by an image;
For his molded image *is* falsehood,
And *there is* no breath in them.
[15]They *are* futile, a work of errors;
In the time of their punishment they shall
   perish.
[16]The Portion of Jacob *is* not like them,
For He *is* the Maker of all *things,*
And Israel *is* the tribe of His inheritance;
The Lord of hosts *is* His name.

The Coming Captivity of Judah

[17]Gather up your wares from the land,
O inhabitant of the fortress!

[18]For thus says the Lord:

"Behold, I will throw out at this time
The inhabitants of the land,
And will distress them,
That they may find *it so.*"

[19]Woe is me for my hurt!
My wound is severe.
But I say, "Truly this *is* an infirmity,
And I must bear it."
[20]My tent is plundered,
And all my cords are broken;
My children have gone from me,
And they *are* no more.
There is no one to pitch my tent anymore,
Or set up my curtains.

[21]For the shepherds have become dull-hearted,
And have not sought the Lord;
Therefore they shall not prosper,
And all their flocks shall be scattered.
[22]Behold, the noise of the report has come,
And a great commotion out of the north
   country,
To make the cities of Judah desolate, a den of
   jackals.

[23]O Lord, I know the way of man *is* not in
   himself;

It is not in man who walks to direct his own
   steps.
[24]O Lord, correct me, but with justice;
Not in Your anger, lest You bring me to
   nothing.
[25]Pour out Your fury on the Gentiles, who do not
   know You,
And on the families who do not call on Your
   name;
For they have eaten up Jacob,
Devoured him and consumed him,
And made his dwelling place desolate.

The Broken Covenant

11 The word that came to Jeremiah from the
Lord, saying, [2]"Hear the words of this
covenant, and speak to the men of Judah and to
the inhabitants of Jerusalem; [3]and say to them,
'Thus says the Lord God of Israel: "Cursed *is* the
man who does not obey the words of this covenant
[4]which I commanded your fathers in the day I
brought them out of the land of Egypt, from the
iron furnace, saying, 'Obey My voice, and do according to all that I command you; so shall you be
My people, and I will be your God,' [5]that I may establish the oath which I have sworn to your fathers, to give them 'a land flowing with milk and
honey,'[a] as *it is* this day." ' "

And I answered and said, "So be it, Lord."

[6]Then the Lord said to me, "Proclaim all these
words in the cities of Judah and in the streets of
Jerusalem, saying: 'Hear the words of this
covenant and do them. [7]For I earnestly exhorted
your fathers in the day I brought them up out of
the land of Egypt, until this day, rising early and
exhorting, saying, "Obey My voice." [8]Yet they did
not obey or incline their ear, but everyone followed the dictates of his evil heart; therefore I
will bring upon them all the words of this
covenant, which I commanded *them* to do, but
which they have not done.' "

[9]And the Lord said to me, "A conspiracy has
been found among the men of Judah and among
the inhabitants of Jerusalem. [10]They have turned
back to the iniquities of their forefathers who refused to hear My words, and they have gone after
other gods to serve them; the house of Israel and
the house of Judah have broken My covenant
which I made with their fathers."

•••••••••••••••••••••••

10:13 [a]Psalm 135:7   11:5 [a]Exodus 3:8

10:16 The "portion" refers to anything that rightfully belongs
to an individual. In this context, God chose Israel to be His inheritance, and He was Israel's "portion." The essence of the
covenant relationship between Israel and the Lord is that God
calls them "My people," and they call Him "our God" (Ex. 6:6,
7).

10:22 The great commotion out of the north refers to the

Babylonian army. Indeed, Nebuchadnezzar's invasion around
586 b.c. carried widespread destruction. Many cities destroyed in the 6th century never were inhabited again.

11:1, 2 The covenant, a typical Middle Eastern treaty, was comprised of stipulations, curses, blessings, and witnesses. Under
oath, the subject promised obedience, which brought blessing, while disobedience brought a curse.

¹¹Therefore thus says the LORD: "Behold, I will surely bring calamity on them which they will not be able to escape; and though they cry out to Me, I will not listen to them. ¹²Then the cities of Judah and the inhabitants of Jerusalem will go and cry out to the gods to whom they offer incense, but they will not save them at all in the time of their trouble. ¹³For *according to* the number of your cities were your gods, O Judah; and *according to* the number of the streets of Jerusalem you have set up altars to *that* shameful thing, altars to burn incense to Baal.

¹⁴"So do not pray for this people, or lift up a cry or prayer for them; for I will not hear *them* in the time that they cry out to Me because of their trouble.

¹⁵"What has My beloved to do in My house,
Having done lewd deeds with many?
And the holy flesh has passed from you.
When you do evil, then you rejoice.
¹⁶The LORD called your name,
Green Olive Tree, Lovely *and* of Good Fruit.
With the noise of a great tumult
He has kindled fire on it,
And its branches are broken.

¹⁷"For the LORD of hosts, who planted you, has pronounced doom against you for the evil of the house of Israel and of the house of Judah, which they have done against themselves to provoke Me to anger in offering incense to Baal."

Jeremiah's Life Threatened

¹⁸Now the LORD gave me knowledge *of it,* and I know *it;* for You showed me their doings. ¹⁹But I *was* like a docile lamb brought to the slaughter; and I did not know that they had devised schemes against me, *saying,* "Let us destroy the tree with its fruit, and let us cut him off from the land of the living, that his name may be remembered no more."

²⁰But, O LORD of hosts,
You who judge righteously,
Testing the mind and the heart,

Let me see Your vengeance on them,
For to You I have revealed my cause.

²¹"Therefore thus says the LORD concerning the men of Anathoth who seek your life, saying, 'Do not prophesy in the name of the LORD, lest you die by our hand'— ²²therefore thus says the LORD of hosts: 'Behold, I will punish them. The young men shall die by the sword, their sons and their daughters shall die by famine; ²³and there shall be no remnant of them, for I will bring catastrophe on the men of Anathoth, *even* the year of their punishment.'"

Jeremiah's Question

12 Righteous *are* You, O LORD, when I plead with You;
Yet let me talk with You about *Your* judgments.
Why does the way of the wicked prosper?
Why are those happy who deal so treacherously?
²You have planted them, yes, they have taken root;
They grow, yes, they bear fruit.
You *are* near in their mouth
But far from their mind.

³But You, O LORD, know me;
You have seen me,
And You have tested my heart toward You.
Pull them out like sheep for the slaughter,
And prepare them for the day of slaughter.
⁴How long will the land mourn,
And the herbs of every field wither?
The beasts and birds are consumed,
For the wickedness of those who dwell there,
Because they said, "He will not see our final end."

The LORD Answers Jeremiah

⁵"If you have run with the footmen, and they have wearied you,
Then how can you contend with horses?
And *if* in the land of peace,
In which you trusted, *they wearied you,*

11:11, 12 Judah would be judged as surely as Israel had been judged earlier. Doom came upon Israel in 722 B.C. by the hands of the Assyrian army. Jerusalem was destroyed and the inhabitants of Judah taken into captivity in 586 B.C. by Babylon.

11:18–23 Jeremiah learned of a plot against his life. Some from his own family and community threatened his life. Jeremiah's lament is similar to some psalms of complaint (Ps. 44; 55). This passage reads like excerpts from his spiritual journal. The man behind the message is revealed.

11:19 Like a docile lamb brought to the slaughter are words reminiscent of Jeremiah 51:40 and Isaiah 53:7. Isaiah's portrait of the Suffering Servant was fulfilled in Christ (Is. 53:7; Acts 8:32).

12:1 Why do the wicked prosper? This age-old question greatly perplexed the faithful of Israel—Job (Job 21; 24), David (Ps. 37), and Asaph (Ps. 73). That the wicked could not prosper was a widely held belief in ancient Israel (see Ps. 1). Only the righteous would take root and become a sturdy tree. However, Jeremiah's experience, as well as that of others, challenged that assumption.

12:5, 6 God answered Jeremiah's question about the prosperity of the wicked by telling him that the worst was yet to come. Jeremiah needed endurance if he was to withstand the struggle. "Footmen" may refer to other prophets or enemies or conspirators he faced. "Wearied" (Heb. *la'ah*) implies exhaustion. "Horses" may allude to the military power of Babylon (Jer. 4:13;

Then how will you do in the floodplain[a] of the Jordan?

[6]For even your brothers, the house of your father,
Even they have dealt treacherously with you;
Yes, they have called a multitude after you.
Do not believe them,
Even though they speak smooth words to you.

[7]"I have forsaken My house, I have left My heritage;
I have given the dearly beloved of My soul into the hand of her enemies.
[8]My heritage is to Me like a lion in the forest;
It cries out against Me;
Therefore I have hated it.
[9]My heritage is to Me like a speckled vulture;
The vultures all around are against her.
Come, assemble all the beasts of the field,
Bring them to devour!

[10]"Many rulers[a] have destroyed My vineyard,
They have trodden My portion underfoot;
They have made My pleasant portion a desolate wilderness.
[11]They have made it desolate;
Desolate, it mourns to Me;
The whole land is made desolate,
Because no one takes it to heart.
[12]The plunderers have come
On all the desolate heights in the wilderness,
For the sword of the LORD shall devour
From one end of the land to the other end of the land;
No flesh shall have peace.
[13]They have sown wheat but reaped thorns;
They have put themselves to pain but do not profit.
But be ashamed of your harvest
Because of the fierce anger of the LORD."

[14]Thus says the LORD: "Against all My evil neighbors who touch the inheritance which I have caused My people Israel to inherit— behold, I will pluck them out of their land and pluck out the house of Judah from among them. [15]Then it shall be, after I have plucked them out, that I will return and have compassion on them and bring them back, everyone to his heritage and everyone to his land. [16]And it shall be, if they will learn carefully the ways of My people, to swear by My name, 'As the LORD lives,' as they taught My people to swear by Baal, then they shall be established in the midst of My people. [17]But if they do not obey, I will utterly pluck up and destroy that nation," says the LORD.

Symbol of the Linen Sash

13 Thus the LORD said to me: "Go and get yourself a linen sash, and put it around your waist, but do not put it in water." [2]So I got a sash according to the word of the LORD, and put it around my waist.

[3]And the word of the LORD came to me the second time, saying, [4]"Take the sash that you acquired, which is around your waist, and arise, go to the Euphrates,[a] and hide it there in a hole in the rock." [5]So I went and hid it by the Euphrates, as the LORD commanded me.

[6]Now it came to pass after many days that the LORD said to me, "Arise, go to the Euphrates, and take from there the sash which I commanded you to hide there." [7]Then I went to the Euphrates and dug, and I took the sash from the place where I had hidden it; and there was the sash, ruined. It was profitable for nothing.

[8]Then the word of the LORD came to me, saying, [9]"Thus says the LORD: 'In this manner I will ruin the pride of Judah and the great pride of Jerusalem. [10]This evil people, who refuse to hear My words, who follow the dictates of their hearts, and walk after other gods to serve them and worship them, shall be just like this sash which is profitable for nothing. [11]For as the sash clings to the waist of a man, so I have caused the whole house of Israel and the whole house of Judah to cling to Me,' says the LORD, 'that they may become My people, for renown, for praise, and for glory; but they would not hear.'

Symbol of the Wine Bottles

[12]"Therefore you shall speak to them this word: 'Thus says the LORD God of Israel: "Every bottle shall be filled with wine." '

"And they will say to you, 'Do we not certainly know that every bottle will be filled with wine?'

12:5 [a]Or thicket 12:10 [a]Literally shepherds or pastors 13:4 [a]Hebrew Perath

---

8:16). The "floodplain" or thicket of Jordan was a place of jungle growth and a lair of lions (Jer. 49:19; 50:44).

12:10 Rulers were leaders from foreign countries. They had ravaged the vineyard of the Lord—the people and land of Judah (Jer. 2:21; 5:10).

12:14–17 Israel's faith moved within the confines of a narrow nationalism, Yet God's sovereignty included His desire for the salvation of even Israel's worst enemies if they would repent (Ps. 67).

13:1 The sash of linen, an expensive material used in priestly attire, was worn around the prophet's waist as a symbol of the intimacy of Judah's covenantal relationship with God (see chart, The High Priest's Clothing).

13:12 Jeremiah used the imagery of a popular proverb "Every bottle shall be filled with wine" to announce that since the people no longer were filled with the glory of God, God would fill them with the wine of His wrath.

[13]"Then you shall say to them, 'Thus says the LORD: "Behold, I will fill all the inhabitants of this land—even the kings who sit on David's throne, the priests, the prophets, and all the inhabitants of Jerusalem—with drunkenness! [14]And I will dash them one against another, even the fathers and the sons together," says the LORD. "I will not pity nor spare nor have mercy, but will destroy them." ' "

Pride Precedes Captivity

[15]Hear and give ear:
　Do not be proud,
　For the LORD has spoken.
[16]Give glory to the LORD your God
　Before He causes darkness,
　And before your feet stumble
　On the dark mountains,
　And while you are looking for light,
　He turns it into the shadow of death
　And makes *it* dense darkness.
[17]But if you will not hear it,
　My soul will weep in secret for *your* pride;
　My eyes will weep bitterly
　And run down with tears,
　Because the LORD's flock has been taken
　　captive.

[18]Say to the king and to the queen mother,
　"Humble yourselves;
　Sit down,
　For your rule shall collapse, the crown of your
　　glory."
[19]The cities of the South shall be shut up,
　And no one shall open *them;*
　Judah shall be carried away captive, all of it;
　It shall be wholly carried away captive.

[20]Lift up your eyes and see
　Those who come from the north.
　Where *is* the flock *that* was given to you,
　Your beautiful sheep?
[21]What will you say when He punishes you?
　For you have taught them
　To be chieftains, to be head over you.
　Will not pangs seize you,
　Like a woman in labor?

[22]And if you say in your heart,
　"Why have these things come upon me?"
　For the greatness of your iniquity
　Your skirts have been uncovered,
　Your heels made bare.
[23]Can the Ethiopian change his skin or the
　　leopard its spots?
　Then may you also do good who are
　　accustomed to do evil.

[24]"Therefore I will scatter them like stubble
　That passes away by the wind of the
　　wilderness.
[25]This is your lot,
　The portion of your measures from Me," says
　　the LORD,
　"Because you have forgotten Me
　And trusted in falsehood.
[26]Therefore I will uncover your skirts over your
　　face,
　That your shame may appear.
[27]I have seen your adulteries
　And your *lustful* neighings,
　The lewdness of your harlotry,
　Your abominations on the hills in the fields.
　Woe to you, O Jerusalem!
　Will you still not be made clean?"

Sword, Famine, and Pestilence

14 The word of the LORD that came to Jeremiah concerning the droughts.

[2]"Judah mourns,
　And her gates languish;
　They mourn for the land,
　And the cry of Jerusalem has gone up.
[3]Their nobles have sent their lads for water;
　They went to the cisterns *and* found no water.
　They returned with their vessels empty;
　They were ashamed and confounded
　And covered their heads.
[4]Because the ground is parched,
　For there was no rain in the land,
　The plowmen were ashamed;
　They covered their heads.
[5]Yes, the deer also gave birth in the field,
　But left because there was no grass.

13:15–17 This brief elegy or poem of lament expresses in a few sensitive words both the prophet's message and his feelings. To "give glory" to the Lord is to acknowledge God in the fullness of His revelation, an important element in repentance. The phrase is often used as an idiom for "confess your sins" (Josh. 7:19; John 9:24).

13:18 The king may be Jehoiachin, who reigned for three months (598–597 B.C.) He was taken captive to Babylon with his mother, Nehushta, and 10,000 other prominent citizens of Judah (see chart, The Queens of the Old Testament).

13:22 To uncover a woman's skirts (lit. "to tear off the skirts")

was a common way to bring shame to a prostitute in Israel (Hos. 2:3–10). Israel's prostitution to other gods is a dominant theme in Jeremiah's message.

13:23 This rhetorical question required a negative answer in the literature of Jeremiah's day. It showed the utter hopelessness of Israel's ability to repent.

14:1–6 Droughts were one of the curses threatened for disobedience to the covenant (Lev. 26:19, 20; Deut. 28:22–24). Jeremiah graphically portrayed the most pathetic aspects of nature in a time of drought: empty wells, parched farmlands, and starving wild animals.

⁶And the wild donkeys stood in the desolate heights;
They sniffed at the wind like jackals;
Their eyes failed because *there was* no grass."

⁷O Lᴏʀᴅ, though our iniquities testify against us,
Do it for Your name's sake;
For our backslidings are many,
We have sinned against You.
⁸O the Hope of Israel, his Savior in time of trouble,
Why should You be like a stranger in the land,
And like a traveler *who* turns aside to tarry for a night?
⁹Why should You be like a man astonished,
Like a mighty one *who* cannot save?
Yet You, O Lᴏʀᴅ, *are* in our midst,
And we are called by Your name;
Do not leave us!

¹⁰Thus says the Lᴏʀᴅ to this people:

"Thus they have loved to wander;
They have not restrained their feet.
Therefore the Lᴏʀᴅ does not accept them;
He will remember their iniquity now,
And punish their sins."

¹¹Then the Lᴏʀᴅ said to me, "Do not pray for this people, for *their* good. ¹²When they fast, I will not hear their cry; and when they offer burnt offering and grain offering, I will not accept them. But I will consume them by the sword, by the famine, and by the pestilence."

¹³Then I said, "Ah, Lord Gᴏᴅ! Behold, the prophets say to them, 'You shall not see the sword, nor shall you have famine, but I will give you assured peace in this place.'"

¹⁴And the Lᴏʀᴅ said to me, "The prophets prophesy lies in My name. I have not sent them, commanded them, nor spoken to them; they prophesy to you a false vision, divination, a worthless thing, and the deceit of their heart. ¹⁵Therefore thus says the Lᴏʀᴅ concerning the prophets who prophesy in My name, whom I did not send, and who say, 'Sword and famine shall not be in this land'— 'By sword and famine those prophets shall be consumed! ¹⁶And the people to whom they prophesy shall be cast out in the streets of Jerusalem because of the famine and the sword; they will have no one to bury them— them nor their wives, their sons nor their daughters— for I will pour their wickedness on them.'

¹⁷"Therefore you shall say this word to them:

'Let my eyes flow with tears night and day,
And let them not cease;
For the virgin daughter of my people
Has been broken with a mighty stroke, with a very severe blow.
¹⁸If I go out to the field,
Then behold, those slain with the sword!
And if I enter the city,
Then behold, those sick from famine!
Yes, both prophet and priest go about in a land they do not know.'"

The People Plead for Mercy

¹⁹Have You utterly rejected Judah?
Has Your soul loathed Zion?
Why have You stricken us so that *there is* no healing for us?
We looked for peace, but *there was* no good;
And for the time of healing, and there was trouble.
²⁰We acknowledge, O Lᴏʀᴅ, our wickedness
And the iniquity of our fathers,
For we have sinned against You.
²¹Do not abhor *us,* for Your name's sake;
Do not disgrace the throne of Your glory.
Remember, do not break Your covenant with us.
²²Are there any among the idols of the nations that can cause rain?
Or can the heavens give showers?
Are You not He, O Lᴏʀᴅ our God?
Therefore we will wait for You,
Since You have made all these.

The Lᴏʀᴅ Will Not Relent

15 Then the Lᴏʀᴅ said to me, "*Even* if Moses and Samuel stood before Me, My mind *would* not *be* favorable toward this people. Cast *them* out of My sight, and let them go forth. ²And

---

14:7–9 Jeremiah's appeal for God's help and deliverance was powerful. He questioned the balance of judgment and mercy in the character of God. The Lord was as equally God of the covenant when He fulfilled the curses of the covenant as when He fulfilled the blessings.

14:9 The assertion that the people were "called" by God's "name" was an attempt to invoke God's covenantal protection and presence. In ancient Near Eastern treaties, the inferior party pledged obedience, and the superior pledged to protect the weaker (see Ex. 19:5, note). Judah had rejected God and so invalidated any hope of divine protection.

14:15, 16 The people of Judah had not obeyed the Lord's com-

mand to put false prophets to death (Deut. 13:1–5; 18:20). Rather, they had welcomed them. Therefore, God would destroy both prophets and people by reversing the false prophecy of deliverance and turning it into a death sentence.

14:21 God is petitioned, for the sake of His name or His glory, not to reject His people. God's name represents His character or reputation. This confession is a typical lament and a concise summary of many of the themes of Jeremiah's prophecy: the people's sin; the covenant; God's superiority to the idols; and God's glory (lit. "weightiness"; see Ps. 19:1–15, note).

15:1 Two of Israel's great intercessors are used to illustrate the depth of the people's sin and the irrevocability of God's

it shall be, if they say to you, 'Where should we go?' then you shall tell them, 'Thus says the LORD:

"Such as *are* for death, to death;
And such as *are* for the sword, to the sword;
And such as *are* for the famine, to the famine;
And such as *are* for the captivity, to the captivity." '

³"And I will appoint over them four forms *of destruction*," says the LORD: "the sword to slay, the dogs to drag, the birds of the heavens and the beasts of the earth to devour and destroy. ⁴I will hand them over to trouble, to all kingdoms of the earth, because of Manasseh the son of Hezekiah, king of Judah, for what he did in Jerusalem.

⁵"For who will have pity on you, O Jerusalem?
Or who will bemoan you?
Or who will turn aside to ask how you are doing?
⁶You have forsaken Me," says the LORD,
"You have gone backward.
Therefore I will stretch out My hand against you and destroy you;
I am weary of relenting!
⁷And I will winnow them with a winnowing fan in the gates of the land;
I will bereave *them* of children;
I will destroy My people,
Since they do not return from their ways.
⁸Their widows will be increased to Me more than the sand of the seas;
I will bring against them,
Against the mother of the young men,
A plunderer at noonday;
I will cause anguish and terror to fall on them suddenly.
⁹"She languishes who has borne seven;

She has breathed her last;
Her sun has gone down
While *it was* yet day;
She has been ashamed and confounded.
And the remnant of them I will deliver to the sword
Before their enemies," says the LORD.

Jeremiah's Dejection

¹⁰Woe is me, my mother,
That you have borne me,
A man of strife and a man of contention to the whole earth!
I have neither lent for interest,
Nor have men lent to me for interest.
Every one of them curses me.

¹¹The LORD said:

"Surely it will be well with your remnant;
Surely I will cause the enemy to intercede with you
In the time of adversity and in the time of affliction.
¹²Can anyone break iron,
The northern iron and the bronze?
¹³Your wealth and your treasures
I will give as plunder without price,
Because of all your sins,
Throughout your territories.
¹⁴And I will make *you* cross over with[a] your enemies
Into a land *which* you do not know;
For a fire is kindled in My anger,
Which shall burn upon you."
¹⁵O LORD, You know;
Remember me and visit me,

15:14 [a]Following Masoretic Text and Vulgate; Septuagint, Syriac, and Targum read *cause you to serve* (compare 17:4).

---

judgment. Moses pleaded with God for rebellious Israel (Ex. 32:11–14, 30–32), and his intercession was heard. Samuel, too, pleaded for Israel (1 Sam. 7:8, 9; 12:19–25), and God answered.

15:3 Four forms of destruction project a poetic description of the complete judgment of Judah. The imagery of beasts and birds devouring human flesh vividly portrays an unclean death.

15:4 Manasseh, son of the good king Hezekiah, is considered Judah's most wicked king (2 Kin. 21:1–18). He led the people into grotesque forms of sin and idolatry, and so is credited as being a primary cause of Judah's eventual destruction.

15:6 God enforced the moral law of the covenant with grief. "Relenting" (Heb. *naham*) may include the ideas of pity and compassion. Judgment had come. The Lord's hand indicated His power.

15:8, 9 Grief is one of the results of war women must bear. The image of widows more numerous than the sands of the sea is a tragic reversal of the Abrahamic covenant, which promised

innumerable offspring (Gen. 22:17). The "mother of the young men" was honored and considered to be blessed greatly (Ruth 4:15). The mother with "seven" sons would have her happiness complete (see chart, The Significance of Numbers in Scripture), but this mother would lose all (Jer. 15:9).

15:10–21 Both Jeremiah's weakness and God's reassurance were revealed. The prophet's addressing his mother illustrates the tenderness of his own character. The text implies that she was still living. Jeremiah's grief was intensified as he was reminded of his mother's sorrow and suffering on his behalf (see 1 Sam. 1, Motherhood; see also Luke 2:35). The Lord dealt with Jeremiah differently than He did with the people. They have been judged as beyond repentance. Jeremiah was given hope and encouragement. Jeremiah 15:12–14 was fulfilled when the temple and the city of Jerusalem were plundered (see Jer. 52). Jeremiah 15:20 and 21 contain the same vocabulary found in Jeremiah's original call (see Jer. 1:8, 18, 19).

And take vengeance for me on my persecutors.
In Your enduring patience, do not take me away.
Know that for Your sake I have suffered rebuke.
¹⁶Your words were found, and I ate them,
And Your word was to me the joy and rejoicing of my heart;
For I am called by Your name,
O Lord God of hosts.
¹⁷I did not sit in the assembly of the mockers,
Nor did I rejoice;
I sat alone because of Your hand,
For You have filled me with indignation.
¹⁸Why is my pain perpetual
And my wound incurable,
Which refuses to be healed?
Will You surely be to me like an unreliable stream,
As waters *that* fail?

The Lord Reassures Jeremiah

¹⁹Therefore thus says the Lord:

"If you return,
Then I will bring you back;
You shall stand before Me;
If you take out the precious from the vile,
You shall be as My mouth.
Let them return to you,
But you must not return to them.
²⁰And I will make you to this people a fortified bronze wall;
And they will fight against you,
But they shall not prevail against you;
For I *am* with you to save you
And deliver you," says the Lord.
²¹"I will deliver you from the hand of the wicked,
And I will redeem you from the grip of the terrible."

Jeremiah's Life-Style and Message

16 The word of the Lord also came to me, saying, ²"You shall not take a wife, nor shall you have sons or daughters in this place." ³For thus says the Lord concerning the sons and daughters who are born in this place, and concerning their mothers who bore them and their fathers who begot them in this land: ⁴"They shall die gruesome deaths; they shall not be lamented nor shall they be buried, *but* they shall be like refuse on the face of the earth. They shall be consumed by the sword and by famine, and their corpses shall be meat for the birds of heaven and for the beasts of the earth."

⁵For thus says the Lord: "Do not enter the house of mourning, nor go to lament or bemoan them; for I have taken away My peace from this people," says the Lord, "lovingkindness and mercies. ⁶Both the great and the small shall die in this land. They shall not be buried; neither shall men lament for them, cut themselves, nor make themselves bald for them. ⁷Nor shall *men* break *bread* in mourning for them, to comfort them for the dead; nor shall *men* give them the cup of consolation to drink for their father or their mother. ⁸Also you shall not go into the house of feasting to sit with them, to eat and drink."

⁹For thus says the Lord of hosts, the God of Israel: "Behold, I will cause to cease from this place, before your eyes and in your days, the voice of mirth and the voice of gladness, the voice of the bridegroom and the voice of the bride.

¹⁰"And it shall be, when you show this people all these words, and they say to you, 'Why has the Lord pronounced all this great disaster against us? Or what *is* our iniquity? Or what *is* our sin that we have committed against the Lord our God?' ¹¹then you shall say to them, 'Because your fathers have forsaken Me,' says the Lord; 'they have walked after other gods and have served them and worshiped them, and have forsaken Me and not kept My law. ¹²And you have done worse than your fathers, for behold, each one follows the dictates of his own evil heart, so that no one listens to Me. ¹³Therefore I will cast you out of this land into a land that you do not know, neither you nor your fathers; and there you shall serve other gods day and night, where I will not show you favor.'

God Will Restore Israel

¹⁴"Therefore behold, the days are coming," says the Lord, "that it shall no more be said, 'The Lord lives who brought up the children of Israel from the land of Egypt,' ¹⁵but, 'The Lord lives who brought up the children of Israel from the land of

---

16:2 The prophetic word often is proclaimed through the life of a prophet. Jeremiah's call to celibacy is unique in the OT. In the ancient Near East, marriage was considered the natural state, and children were viewed as a blessing (Gen. 22:17; Ps. 127:3–5). Sterility and barrenness were regarded as a curse (1 Sam. 1:6–8). Jeremiah's celibacy was a dramatic witness that Judah's end was near. He faced life with God as his sole comfort and support.

16:5 Jeremiah, as well as Ezekiel, was commanded by God not to mourn (Ezek. 24:16, 17, 22, 23). To "cut themselves" and to "make themselves bald" were acts of self-mutilation closely associated with pagan cults (Jer. 16:6). Though they were expressly forbidden in Israel, the people practiced these acts (Lev. 19:27, 28; 21:5).

16:12 The sin of Judah was individual as well as corporate. Judgment would not be blamed on the sins of previous generations. Individual responsibility was a major teaching of Jeremiah (Jer. 31:30) and Ezekiel (Ezek. 18:1–4).

16:14, 15 The future restoration of Israel would surpass the ancient deliverance from Egypt. The "land of the north" refers to the Babylonian Empire.

An iron is fashioned by fire and on an anvil, so in fire of suffering and under the weight of trials, our souls receive the form which our Lord desires them to have.

St. Madeleine Sophie Barat

the north and from all the lands where He had driven them.' For I will bring them back into their land which I gave to their fathers.

¹⁶"Behold, I will send for many fishermen," says the LORD, "and they shall fish them; and afterward I will send for many hunters, and they shall hunt them from every mountain and every hill, and out of the holes of the rocks. ¹⁷For My eyes *are* on all their ways; they are not hidden from My face, nor is their iniquity hidden from My eyes. ¹⁸And first I will repay double for their iniquity and their sin, because they have defiled My land; they have filled My inheritance with the carcasses of their detestable and abominable idols."

¹⁹O LORD, my strength and my fortress,
   My refuge in the day of affliction,
   The Gentiles shall come to You
   From the ends of the earth and say,
   "Surely our fathers have inherited lies,
   Worthlessness and unprofitable *things*."
²⁰Will a man make gods for himself,
   Which *are* not gods?

²¹"Therefore behold, I will this once cause them
      to know,
   I will cause them to know
   My hand and My might;
   And they shall know that My name *is* the
   LORD.

Judah's Sin and Punishment

17 "The sin of Judah *is* written with a pen of
      iron;
   With the point of a diamond *it is* engraved
   On the tablet of their heart,
   And on the horns of your altars,
²While their children remember
   Their altars and their wooden images[a]
   By the green trees on the high hills.

³O My mountain in the field,
   I will give as plunder your wealth, all your
      treasures,
And your high places of sin within all your
      borders.
⁴And you, even yourself,
   Shall let go of your heritage which I gave you;
   And I will cause you to serve your enemies
   In the land which you do not know;
   For you have kindled a fire in My anger *which*
      shall burn forever."

⁵Thus says the LORD:

"Cursed *is* the man who trusts in man
   And makes flesh his strength,
   Whose heart departs from the LORD.
⁶For he shall be like a shrub in the desert,
   And shall not see when good comes,
   But shall inhabit the parched places in the
      wilderness,
In a salt land *which is* not inhabited.

⁷"Blessed *is* the man who trusts in the LORD,
   And whose hope is the LORD.
⁸For he shall be like a tree planted by the
      waters,
   Which spreads out its roots by the river,
   And will not fear[a] when heat comes;
   But its leaf will be green,
   And will not be anxious in the year of drought,
   Nor will cease from yielding fruit.

⁹"The heart *is* deceitful above all *things*,
   And desperately wicked;
   Who can know it?
¹⁰I, the LORD, search the heart,

. . . .

17:2 [a]Hebrew *Asherim*, Canaanite deities   **17:8** [a]Qere and Targum read *see*.

16:19–21 Israel's future restoration not only would bring God's people back to their Promised Land, but it also would bring the offer of salvation to the nations.

17:1 Judah's sin is entrenched deeply. It is compared to an inscription carved into a rock face that cannot be erased. Only when God writes His law on the people's hearts can obedience replace rebellion (Jer. 31:31–34).

17:3 My mountain refers to Mt. Zion, the location of the temple in Jerusalem. "High places" were the locations of idol worship.

17:5–8 The curse of trusting in human strength is contrasted

with the blessings of trusting in God (vv. 5–13). The truth that the person who trusts in the Lord of the covenant and surrenders to Him will be blessed is here affirmed with illustrations. These words bear a marked similarity to Psalm 1.

17:9, 10 The heart (Heb. *leb*) refers to the mind, the source of thinking, feeling, and action. The Hebrews viewed the heart as the center of life. It is desperately deceitful and incurably sick. Yet God not only knows the heart, He searches it. The "heart" and the "mind" encompass human emotions and together cover the hidden elements in a person's character and personality.

I test the mind,
Even to give every man according to his ways,
According to the fruit of his doings.

[11]"*As* a partridge that broods but does not hatch,
So is he who gets riches, but not by right;
It will leave him in the midst of his days,
And at his end he will be a fool."

[12]A glorious high throne from the beginning
Is the place of our sanctuary.
[13]O LORD, the hope of Israel,
All who forsake You shall be ashamed.

"Those who depart from Me
Shall be written in the earth,
Because they have forsaken the LORD,
The fountain of living waters."

Jeremiah Prays for Deliverance

[14]Heal me, O LORD, and I shall be healed;
Save me, and I shall be saved,
For You *are* my praise.
[15]Indeed they say to me,
"Where *is* the word of the LORD?
Let it come now!"
[16]As for me, I have not hurried away from *being* a
shepherd *who* follows You,
Nor have I desired the woeful day;
You know what came out of my lips;
It was right there before You.
[17]Do not be a terror to me;
You *are* my hope in the day of doom.
[18]Let them be ashamed who persecute me,
But do not let me be put to shame;
Let them be dismayed,
But do not let me be dismayed.
Bring on them the day of doom,
And destroy them with double destruction!

Hallow the Sabbath Day

[19]Thus the LORD said to me: "Go and stand in
the gate of the children of the people, by which
the kings of Judah come in and by which they go
out, and in all the gates of Jerusalem; [20]and say to
them, 'Hear the word of the LORD, you kings of Judah, and all Judah, and all the inhabitants of Jerusalem, who enter by these gates. [21]Thus says the
LORD: "Take heed to yourselves, and bear no burden on the Sabbath day, nor bring *it* in by the
gates of Jerusalem; [22]nor carry a burden out of
your houses on the Sabbath day, nor do any work,
but hallow the Sabbath day, as I commanded your
fathers. [23]But they did not obey nor incline their
ear, but made their neck stiff, that they might not
hear nor receive instruction.

[24]"And it shall be, if you heed Me carefully,"
says the LORD, "to bring no burden through the
gates of this city on the Sabbath day, but hallow
the Sabbath day, to do no work in it, [25]then shall
enter the gates of this city kings and princes sitting on the throne of David, riding in chariots and
on horses, they and their princes, accompanied by
the men of Judah and the inhabitants of Jerusalem; and this city shall remain forever. [26]And they
shall come from the cities of Judah and from the
places around Jerusalem, from the land of Benjamin and from the lowland, from the mountains
and from the South, bringing burnt offerings and
sacrifices, grain offerings and incense, bringing
sacrifices of praise to the house of the LORD.

[27]"But if you will not heed Me to hallow the
Sabbath day, such as not carrying a burden when
entering the gates of Jerusalem on the Sabbath
day, then I will kindle a fire in its gates, and it
shall devour the palaces of Jerusalem, and it shall
not be quenched." ' "

The Potter and the Clay

18 The word which came to Jeremiah from the
LORD, saying: [2]"Arise and go down to the
potter's house, and there I will cause you to hear
My words." [3]Then I went down to the potter's
house, and there he was, making something at the
wheel. [4]And the vessel that he made of clay was
marred in the hand of the potter; so he made it
again into another vessel, as it seemed good to the
potter to make.

[5]Then the word of the LORD came to me, saying: [6]"O house of Israel, can I not do with you as
this potter?" says the LORD. "Look, as the clay *is* in
the potter's hand, so *are* you in My hand, O house

17:11 This simile of nature portrays the prosperity of the
wicked as a foolish delusion. Popular belief held that a "partridge" would hatch eggs that were not her own. When the
young recognized the difference, they would abandon the
mother.

17:13 Written in the earth perhaps means "written in the sand"
and thus soon forgotten, referring to the death of those who
had forsaken God (Ex. 32:32). In contrast, note those who are
"written in the Book of Life" (Dan. 12:1, 2; Rev. 20:11–15).

17:19–27 Keeping the Sabbath was vitally important for the
future of Judah (see Ex. 20:8–11; Deut. 5:12–15). If the people
guarded this day, as God had instructed, then the Land would
be blessed. If they violated its sanctity, then Jerusalem would

be destroyed. The keeping of the Sabbath had become to the
people of Judah a symbol of their entire relationship with God.

18:1–3 The prophets heard God speak in the simple events of
daily life. Jeremiah had heard the word of the Lord while observing an almond tree (Jer. 1:11, 12) and a boiling pot (Jer. 1:13,
14), and now while watching a potter shape clay.

18:4–6 God is in control (see 1 Tim. 6:15). "Marred" (Heb.
nishchath) suggests two variations in meaning: "morally corrupt" (Gen. 6:11) or "physically ruined" (Jer. 13:7). The marred
clay would be used for another purpose. As a potter has absolute authority over the clay to fashion it into whatever he
wishes, so the Lord God of Israel has the power to do what He
chooses with His people.

of Israel! ⁷The instant I speak concerning a nation and concerning a kingdom, to pluck up, to pull down, and to destroy *it*, ⁸if that nation against whom I have spoken turns from its evil, I will relent of the disaster that I thought to bring upon it. ⁹And the instant I speak concerning a nation and concerning a kingdom, to build and to plant *it*, ¹⁰if it does evil in My sight so that it does not obey My voice, then I will relent concerning the good with which I said I would benefit it.

¹¹"Now therefore, speak to the men of Judah and to the inhabitants of Jerusalem, saying, 'Thus says the LORD: "Behold, I am fashioning a disaster and devising a plan against you. Return now every one from his evil way, and make your ways and your doings good." ' "

God's Warning Rejected

¹²And they said, "That is hopeless! So we will walk according to our own plans, and we will every one obey the dictates of his evil heart."

¹³Therefore thus says the LORD:

"Ask now among the Gentiles,
   Who has heard such things?
The virgin of Israel has done a very horrible
   thing.
¹⁴Will *a man* leave the snow water of
   Lebanon,
Which comes from the rock of the field?
Will the cold flowing waters be forsaken for
   strange waters?

¹⁵"Because My people have forgotten Me,
   They have burned incense to worthless idols.
And they have caused themselves to stumble in
   their ways,
From the ancient paths,
To walk in pathways and not on a highway,
¹⁶To make their land desolate *and* a perpetual
   hissing;
Everyone who passes by it will be astonished
And shake his head.
¹⁷I will scatter them as with an east wind before
   the enemy;
I will show themᵃ the back and not the face
In the day of their calamity."

Jeremiah Persecuted

¹⁸Then they said, "Come and let us devise plans against Jeremiah; for the law shall not perish from the priest, nor counsel from the wise, nor the word from the prophet. Come and let us attack him with the tongue, and let us not give heed to any of his words."

¹⁹Give heed to me, O LORD,
   And listen to the voice of those who contend
      with me!
²⁰Shall evil be repaid for good?
   For they have dug a pit for my life.
Remember that I stood before You
   To speak good for them,
To turn away Your wrath from them.
²¹Therefore deliver up their children to the
      famine,
And pour out their *blood*
   By the force of the sword;
Let their wives *become* widows
   And bereaved of their children.
Let their men be put to death,
   Their young men *be* slain
By the sword in battle.
²²Let a cry be heard from their houses,
   When You bring a troop suddenly upon them;
For they have dug a pit to take me,
   And hidden snares for my feet.
²³Yet, LORD, You know all their counsel
   Which is against me, to slay *me.*
Provide no atonement for their iniquity,
   Nor blot out their sin from Your sight;
But let them be overthrown before You.
   Deal *thus* with them
In the time of Your anger.

The Sign of the Broken Flask

19 Thus says the LORD: "Go and get a potter's earthen flask, and *take* some of the elders of the people and some of the elders of the priests. ²And go out to the Valley of the Son of Hinnom, which *is* by the entry of the Potsherd Gate; and proclaim there the words that I will tell you, ³and

---

18:17 ᵃFollowing Septuagint, Syriac, Targum, and Vulgate; Masoretic Text reads *look them in.*

18:13 Israel did not remain chaste as a "virgin" awaiting her husband. Instead, she corrupted herself with the practices of pagan religions, usually through participating in some of the sexually oriented, Canaanite rituals. Jeremiah noted Israel's behavior with astonishment. The peoples of the ancient Near East considered their gods to be one with their culture and national identity. To abandon a "god" would be to deny themselves of their personal identity. Yet Israel had abandoned the living God.

18:16, 17 God withheld His face or His grace from His people. Ancient Near Eastern cultures were more shame-based than

modern western peoples. To face scorn and degradation would have been to endure physical pain and loss.

18:18–23 Jeremiah's prayer was an honest and heartfelt response to the wickedness plotted against him. He called upon God to allow the curses of the broken covenant to take effect. Jeremiah found comfort in the Lord's knowledge of his situation.

19:2 The Potsherd Gate is identified with the Dung or Refuse Gate (Neh. 2:13), which indicated that the city dump was nearby. Potsherds are broken pieces of pottery.

say, 'Hear the word of the LORD, O kings of Judah and inhabitants of Jerusalem. Thus says the LORD of hosts, the God of Israel: "Behold, I will bring such a catastrophe on this place, that whoever hears of it, his ears will tingle.

4"Because they have forsaken Me and made this an alien place, because they have burned incense in it to other gods whom neither they, their fathers, nor the kings of Judah have known, and have filled this place with the blood of the innocents 5(they have also built the high places of Baal, to burn their sons with fire *for* burnt offerings to Baal, which I did not command or speak, nor did it come into My mind), 6therefore behold, the days are coming," says the LORD, "that this place shall no more be called Tophet or the Valley of the Son of Hinnom, but the Valley of Slaughter. 7And I will make void the counsel of Judah and Jerusalem in this place, and I will cause them to fall by the sword before their enemies and by the hands of those who seek their lives; their corpses I will give as meat for the birds of the heaven and for the beasts of the earth. 8I will make this city desolate and a hissing; everyone who passes by it will be astonished and hiss because of all its plagues. 9And I will cause them to eat the flesh of their sons and the flesh of their daughters, and everyone shall eat the flesh of his friend in the siege and in the desperation with which their enemies and those who seek their lives shall drive them to despair." '

10"Then you shall break the flask in the sight of the men who go with you, 11and say to them, 'Thus says the LORD of hosts: "Even so I will break this people and this city, as *one* breaks a potter's vessel, which cannot be made whole again; and they shall bury *them* in Tophet till *there is* no place to bury. 12Thus I will do to this place," says the LORD, "and to its inhabitants, and make this city like Tophet. 13And the houses of Jerusalem and the houses of the kings of Judah shall be defiled like the place of Tophet, because of all the houses on whose roofs they have burned incense to all the host of heaven, and poured out drink offerings to other gods." ' "

14Then Jeremiah came from Tophet, where the LORD had sent him to prophesy; and he stood in the court of the Lord's house and said to all the people, 15"Thus says the LORD of hosts, the God of Israel: 'Behold, I will bring on this city and on all her towns all the doom that I have pronounced against it, because they have stiffened their necks that they might not hear My words.' "

The Word of God to Pashhur

20 Now Pashhur the son of Immer, the priest who *was* also chief governor in the house of the LORD, heard that Jeremiah prophesied these things. 2Then Pashhur struck Jeremiah the prophet, and put him in the stocks that *were* in the high gate of Benjamin, which *was* by the house of the LORD.

3And it happened on the next day that Pashhur brought Jeremiah out of the stocks. Then Jeremiah said to him, "The LORD has not called your name Pashhur, but Magor-Missabib.a 4For thus says the LORD: 'Behold, I will make you a terror to yourself and to all your friends; and they shall fall by the sword of their enemies, and your eyes shall see *it*. I will give all Judah into the hand of the king of Babylon, and he shall carry them captive to Babylon and slay them with the sword. 5Moreover I will deliver all the wealth of this city, all its produce, and all its precious things; all the treasures of the kings of Judah I will give into the hand of their enemies, who will plunder them, seize them, and carry them to Babylon. 6And you, Pashhur, and all who dwell in your house, shall go

20:3 aLiterally *Fear on Every Side*

19:4–6 Abandoning the true God and following idols was not only a violation of the first commandment but also involved a host of corollary sins included in pagan worship with the worst being human sacrifice.

19:8 Hissing was then, as it still is in the Middle East, a sign of derision. "Desolate" (Heb. *shamah*) may be translated "waste" or "horror."

19:9 The people had destroyed one another by participation in ritual human sacrifice. God's judgment would confirm them in mutual self-destruction. Eating flesh was one of the curses for disobedience (Deut. 28:53–57). This prophecy was literally fulfilled first in 586 B.C. and again in A.D. 70, as recorded by the historian Josephus. Under pressure of siege, the people of Jerusalem ate the flesh of their children and devoured one another (Lam. 2:20; 4:10).

19:10, 11 Jeremiah completed the parable. God commanded Jeremiah to break the flask and in the name of the Lord to predict the destruction of the city. The first analogy emphasizes

God's sovereignty over His people (Jer. 18:1–6); the image here underscores God's power to accomplish His purposes.

20:1–6 Jeremiah faced opposition because he faithfully proclaimed the word of the Lord. The religious leaders, who should have been the first to respond to Jeremiah's message, ironically were the ones who most vehemently opposed it. This passage is the first record of physical violence against Jeremiah (v. 2) and the first time the title "prophet" was applied to him.

20:3 To name something, in Hebrew thought, is to control it, to own it, or to bring out its true essence (Gen. 2:19–23; Dan. 1:6, 7). Here, God's renaming of Pashhur, a high official in the temple, shows God's power over him in judgment (see Is. 45, Naming of Children). The name Magor-Missabib means "Fear on Every Side."

20:4 The king of Babylon was Nebuchadnezzar, who assumed the throne of Babylon in 605 B.C. (see chart, The Kings of Babylon). As the time of destruction drew near, Jeremiah became more specific concerning the details of Judah's demise.

into captivity. You shall go to Babylon, and there you shall die, and be buried there, you and all your friends, to whom you have prophesied lies.' "

Jeremiah's Unpopular Ministry

[7]O LORD, You induced me, and I was persuaded;
You are stronger than I, and have prevailed.
I am in derision daily;
Everyone mocks me.
[8]For when I spoke, I cried out;
I shouted, "Violence and plunder!"
Because the word of the LORD was made to me
A reproach and a derision daily.
[9]Then I said, "I will not make mention of Him,
Nor speak anymore in His name."
But *His word* was in my heart like a burning fire
Shut up in my bones;
I was weary of holding *it* back,
And I could not.
[10]For I heard many mocking:
"Fear on every side!"
"Report," *they say,* "and we will report it!"
All my acquaintances watched for my stumbling, *saying,*
"Perhaps he can be induced;
Then we will prevail against him,
And we will take our revenge on him."

[11]But the LORD *is* with me as a mighty, awesome One.
Therefore my persecutors will stumble, and will not prevail.
They will be greatly ashamed, for they will not prosper.
Their everlasting confusion will never be forgotten.
[12]But, O LORD of hosts,
You who test the righteous,
And see the mind and heart,

Let me see Your vengeance on them;
For I have pleaded my cause before You.

[13]Sing to the LORD! Praise the LORD!
For He has delivered the life of the poor
From the hand of evildoers.

[14]Cursed *be* the day in which I was born!
Let the day not be blessed in which my mother bore me!
[15]Let the man *be* cursed
Who brought news to my father, saying,
"A male child has been born to you!"
Making him very glad.
[16]And let that man be like the cities
Which the LORD overthrew, and did not relent;
Let him hear the cry in the morning
And the shouting at noon,
[17]Because he did not kill me from the womb,
That my mother might have been my grave,
And her womb always enlarged *with me.*
[18]Why did I come forth from the womb to see labor and sorrow,
That my days should be consumed with shame?

Jerusalem's Doom Is Sealed

21 The word which came to Jeremiah from the LORD when King Zedekiah sent to him Pashhur the son of Melchiah, and Zephaniah the son of Maaseiah, the priest, saying, [2]"Please inquire of the LORD for us, for Nebuchadnezzar[a] king of Babylon makes war against us. Perhaps the LORD will deal with us according to all His wonderful works, that *the king* may go away from us."

[3]Then Jeremiah said to them, "Thus you shall say to Zedekiah, [4]Thus says the LORD God of Israel: "Behold, I will turn back the weapons of war that *are* in

21:2 [a]Hebrew *Nebuchadrezzar,* and so elsewhere

20:7–18 This last and longest of Jeremiah's confessions is similar to the psalms of lament. The progression is the same: Jeremiah first complained about the consequences of his call to ministry, then found hope in the Lord his God (see Ps. 22).

20:9 The imagery here is a powerful way of portraying the inner psychological necessity that Jeremiah felt. As a hungry fire must consume everything it touches, so the word of God in Jeremiah had to find an outlet. The verb "weary" in Hebrew thought implies a struggle to the point of exhaustion.

20:13 Contemplation of the promise of protection led Jeremiah to an outburst of praise. God is the God who protects the "poor," those who are in need and cannot help themselves.

20:14, 15 Jeremiah's crisis reached its peak. He avoided cursing either God or his parents, capital offenses in Israel (Lev. 20:9; 24:10–16), by cursing the day he was born (see Job 3:3).

20:14–18 Jeremiah again lapsed into despair, even after re-

membering the promise of God and praising Him for it. Note the balanced order of this lament: complaint (vv. 7–10); promise and praise (vv. 11–13); complaint (vv. 14–18). The placing of the promise and praise in the central position of this triad suggests that this was the most important element of the section. Jeremiah lamented, while acknowledging God's sovereignty and grace, which took priority over his difficult circumstances.

21:1 Pashhur, son of Melchiah, is not the same Pashhur of Jeremiah 20:1-6 (see Jer. 38:1). The priest Zephaniah is not the same person as the prophet Zephaniah (see Jer. 29:25, 29; 37:3; 52:24; Zeph. 1:1). King Zedekiah finally acknowledged Jeremiah as a true prophet and sought his intercession, but it was too little too late.

21:2 To inquire of the Lord is to request knowledge, not necessarily help. Nebuchadnezzar, the most famous ruler of the Babylonian Empire (605-562 B.C.), attacked Jerusalem because Zedekiah rebelled against Babylon.

your hands, with which you fight against the king of Babylon and the Chaldeans[a] who besiege you outside the walls; and I will assemble them in the midst of this city. [5]I Myself will fight against you with an outstretched hand and with a strong arm, even in anger and fury and great wrath. [6]I will strike the inhabitants of this city, both man and beast; they shall die of a great pestilence. [7]And afterward," says the LORD, "I will deliver Zedekiah king of Judah, his servants and the people, and such as are left in this city from the pestilence and the sword and the famine, into the hand of Nebuchadnezzar king of Babylon, into the hand of their enemies, and into the hand of those who seek their life; and he shall strike them with the edge of the sword. He shall not spare them, or have pity or mercy." '

[8]"Now you shall say to this people, 'Thus says the LORD: "Behold, I set before you the way of life and the way of death. [9]He who remains in this city shall die by the sword, by famine, and by pestilence; but he who goes out and defects to the Chaldeans who besiege you, he shall live, and his life shall be as a prize to him. [10]For I have set My face against this city for adversity and not for good," says the LORD. "It shall be given into the hand of the king of Babylon, and he shall burn it with fire." '

Message to the House of David

[11]"And concerning the house of the king of Judah, *say,* 'Hear the word of the LORD, [12]O house of David! Thus says the LORD:

"Execute judgment in the morning;
And deliver *him who is* plundered
Out of the hand of the oppressor,
Lest My fury go forth like fire
And burn so that no one can quench *it,*
Because of the evil of your doings.

[13]"Behold, I *am* against you, O inhabitant of the
valley,
And rock of the plain," says the LORD,
"Who say, 'Who shall come down against us?

Or who shall enter our dwellings?'
[14]But I will punish you according to the fruit of
your doings," says the LORD;
"I will kindle a fire in its forest,
And it shall devour all things around it." ' "

22Thus says the LORD: "Go down to the house of the king of Judah, and there speak this word, [2]and say, 'Hear the word of the LORD, O king of Judah, you who sit on the throne of David, you and your servants and your people who enter these gates! [3]Thus says the LORD: "Execute judgment and righteousness, and deliver the plundered out of the hand of the oppressor. Do no wrong and do no violence to the stranger, the fatherless, or the widow, nor shed innocent blood in this place. [4]For if you indeed do this thing, then shall enter the gates of this house, riding on horses and in chariots, accompanied by servants and people, kings who sit on the throne of David. [5]But if you will not hear these words, I swear by Myself," says the LORD, "that this house shall become a desolation." ' "

[6]For thus says the LORD to the house of the king of Judah:

"You *are* Gilead to Me,
The head of Lebanon;
Yet I surely will make you a wilderness,
Cities *which* are not inhabited.
[7]I will prepare destroyers against you,
Everyone with his weapons;
They shall cut down your choice cedars
And cast *them* into the fire.

[8]And many nations will pass by this city; and everyone will say to his neighbor, 'Why has the LORD done so to this great city?' [9]Then they will answer, 'Because they have forsaken the covenant of the LORD their God, and worshiped other gods and served them.' "

•••••••••••••••••••••
21:4 [a]Or *Babylonians*

21:5 The divine Warrior image, which portrays God as fighting on behalf of His people, is reversed (Josh. 10:9–15). Not only would God not perform marvelous works on behalf of Judah, He would actively oppose His people.

21:7 This prophecy of doom was fulfilled (Jer. 52:8–11, 24–27; see Ezek. 12:10–14).

21:9, 10 The way of life was the way of submission to the Lord's will. Paradoxically, obedience to the Lord no longer meant fighting, but submitting to Judah's enemies. Jeremiah 21:9 was fulfilled (Jer. 39:9; 52:15).

22:1 The king of Judah is probably Zedekiah (Jer. 21:3, 7).

22:3, 4 Kings of Israel and Judah are evaluated according to whether they did good or evil in the sight of the Lord. The Books of Kings and Chronicles record the various fortunes of these kings. Under a wicked king, idolatry and various forms

of sin raged unchecked, especially oppression of the needy and injustice to the most vulnerable in society, and most of the people gave themselves wholeheartedly to such activities (see Mal. 3:5; Luke 4, Poverty; 9, the Homeless). Under a righteous king, these activities were severely limited, although not totally eliminated. God had delayed judgment on Judah because of the reforms of righteous kings (Hezekiah, 2 Kin. 19:14—20:21; Josiah, 2 Kin. 22:1—23:25).

22:5 This prophecy was fulfilled (Jer. 52:13).

22:9 The pagan nations would know why Jerusalem had been destroyed and its inhabitants deported. God preserved His witness to the world as much in His judgment of Judah as in His kindness toward His people. Worshiping and serving other gods violated the first two commandments of the Sinai covenant (Ex. 20:3–5).

¹⁰Weep not for the dead, nor bemoan him;
Weep bitterly for him who goes away,
For he shall return no more,
Nor see his native country.

Message to the Sons of Josiah

¹¹For thus says the LORD concerning Shallumᵃ the son of Josiah, king of Judah, who reigned instead of Josiah his father, who went from this place: "He shall not return here anymore, ¹²but he shall die in the place where they have led him captive, and shall see this land no more.

¹³"Woe to him who builds his house by
   unrighteousness
And his chambers by injustice,
Who uses his neighbor's service without wages
And gives him nothing for his work,
¹⁴Who says, 'I will build myself a wide house with
   spacious chambers,
And cut out windows for it,
Paneling *it* with cedar
And painting *it* with vermilion.'

¹⁵"Shall you reign because you enclose *yourself* in
   cedar?
Did not your father eat and drink,
And do justice and righteousness?
Then *it was* well with him.
¹⁶He judged the cause of the poor and needy;
Then *it was* well.
Was not this knowing Me?" says the LORD.
¹⁷"Yet your eyes and your heart *are* for nothing
   but your covetousness,
For shedding innocent blood,
And practicing oppression and violence."

¹⁸Therefore thus says the LORD concerning Jehoiakim the son of Josiah, king of Judah:

"They shall not lament for him,
Saying, 'Alas, my brother!' or 'Alas, my sister!'
They shall not lament for him,
Saying, 'Alas, master!' or 'Alas, his glory!'
¹⁹He shall be buried with the burial of a
   donkey,
Dragged and cast out beyond the gates of
   Jerusalem.

²⁰"Go up to Lebanon, and cry out,
And lift up your voice in Bashan;
Cry from Abarim,
For all your lovers are destroyed.
²¹I spoke to you in your prosperity,
But you said, 'I will not hear.'
This *has been* your manner from your youth,
That you did not obey My voice.
²²The wind shall eat up all your rulers,
And your lovers shall go into captivity;
Surely then you will be ashamed and
   humiliated
For all your wickedness.
²³O inhabitant of Lebanon,
Making your nest in the cedars,
How gracious will you be when pangs come
   upon you,
Like the pain of a woman in labor?

Message to Coniah

²⁴"*As* I live," says the LORD, "though Coniahᵃ the son of Jehoiakim, king of Judah, were the signet on My right hand, yet I would pluck you off; ²⁵and I will give you into the hand of those who seek your life, and into the hand *of those* whose face you fear—the hand of Nebuchadnezzar king of Babylon and the hand of the Chaldeans. ²⁶So I will cast you out, and your mother who bore you, into another country where you were not born; and there you shall die. ²⁷But to the land to which they desire to return, there they shall not return.

²⁸"Is this man Coniah a despised, broken idol—
A vessel in which *is* no pleasure?
Why are they cast out, he and his descendants,
And cast into a land which they do not know?
²⁹O earth, earth, earth,
Hear the word of the LORD!
³⁰Thus says the LORD:
'Write this man down as childless,

22:11 ᵃAlso called *Jehoahaz* 22:24 ᵃAlso called *Jeconiah* and *Jehoiachin*

22:10–19 The dead refers to Josiah who was mourned long after he was killed at the Battle of Megiddo in 609 B.C. (2 Chr. 35:20–25). Shallum is the one who went away. He was carried to Egypt in 609 B.C. and died in exile. Shallum is an alternate name of Jehoahaz (see chart, The Kings With Two Names). Two poems draw a contrast between Josiah and his successors, Shallum and Jehoiakim. The first contrast invites pity (Jer. 22:10–12); the second invites scorn (Jer. 22:13–19). Both Shallum (Jehoahaz) and Jehoiakim were sons of Josiah.

22:20–23 Bashan is in the Transjordan toward the northeast of Israel. Abarim is a mountainous region in Moab to the southeast. It includes Mt. Nebo where Moses first saw the Promised Land (Deut. 32:49). Judah's "lovers" are the political allies to whom she turned for help. Jerusalem is personified as a woman in this lament. When calamity came, she would experience the pain of a woman in childbirth.

22:24 Coniah also is known as Jehoiachin or Jeconiah (Jer. 24:1; see chart, The Kings With Two Names). The removal of the signet ring, which was used to authenticate all official documents, edicts, and correspondence, signified a rejection of Jehoiachin's kingship, but the Davidic monarchy would be reestablished through the Messiah (see Hag. 2:25).

22:30 Jehoiachin had heirs, but none of his offspring sat on the Davidic throne (1 Chr. 3:16, 17).

ATTRIBUTES OF GOD *HE IS OMNIPRESENT*

The active presence of God, both in places and in relationships, is one of the chief presuppositions running through Scripture. There is no place without God, no place beyond Him (2 Chr. 6:18), and He is everywhere simultaneously (Eph. 4:6). Yet God is not bound by, nor dependent upon, any place or anyone (Jer. 23:23, 24).

God's universal presence encompasses all space—extending to every geographical location (Ps. 33:18; 34:15; 121:1–8), creation (Ps. 104), and all human affairs (Is. 40:21–23). This in no way suggests that He is immersed *in* His creation, as pantheism suggests. God is always distinct from His creation because He, as the Creator, brought all into existence (Gen. 1:31). His relational presence is experienced only by believers. He indwells His children (1 Cor. 6:19, 20). In "taking up residence," He establishes ownership, provision, love, workmanship, guidance, teaching, and personal friendship (Ps. 139).

Jesus reveals what God's presence is like. In a created universe filled with energy and wonder, God's passion was and is to have a relationship with every man and woman (John 1:1–18). God does not come and go in our lives—rather, we live and move and have our being in Him (Acts 17:27, 28; Phil. 1:6).

See also Josh. 1:5, 9; Ps. 16:11; 23:1–6; Prov. 15:3; Lam. 3:22, note; Matt. 28:20; Heb. 13:5; notes on Attributes of God (Ex. 33; Deut. 4; 32; 2 Chr. 19; Job 23; 42; Ps. 25; 89; 90; 102; 119; Is. 6; 65; Rom. 2; Eph. 1; 1 John 5); Access to God (Rom. 10); Promises of God (2 Pet. 1); Providence (Eccl. 7); Spiritual Warfare (Eph. 6)

A man *who* shall not prosper in his days;
For none of his descendants shall prosper,
Sitting on the throne of David,
And ruling anymore in Judah.'"

The Branch of Righteousness

23 "Woe to the shepherds who destroy and scatter the sheep of My pasture!" says the LORD. ²Therefore thus says the LORD God of Israel against the shepherds who feed My people: "You have scattered My flock, driven them away, and not attended to them. Behold, I will attend to you for the evil of your doings," says the LORD. ³"But I will gather the remnant of My flock out of all countries where I have driven them, and bring them back to their folds; and they shall be fruitful and increase. ⁴I will set up shepherds over them who will feed them; and they shall fear no more, nor be dismayed, nor shall they be lacking," says the LORD.

⁵"Behold, *the* days are coming," says the LORD,
"That I will raise to David a Branch of
    righteousness;
A King shall reign and prosper,

And execute judgment and righteousness in
    the earth.
⁶In His days Judah will be saved,
And Israel will dwell safely;
Now this *is* His name by which He will be
    called:

THE LORD OUR RIGHTEOUSNESS.ᵃ

⁷"Therefore, behold, *the* days are coming," says the LORD, "that they shall no longer say, 'As the LORD lives who brought up the children of Israel from the land of Egypt,' ⁸but, 'As the LORD lives who brought up and led the descendants of the house of Israel from the north country and from all the countries where I had driven them.' And they shall dwell in their own land."

False Prophets and Empty Oracles

⁹My heart within me is broken
Because of the prophets;
All my bones shake.
I am like a drunken man,
And like a man whom wine has overcome,

••
23:6 ᵃHebrew *YHWH Tsidkenu*

23:1, 2 Jeremiah continued the theme of the wicked rulers, employing the familiar ancient Near Eastern metaphor of the shepherd with his sheep. Unlike the good shepherd who cared for his flock and protected his investment, the rulers of Israel had scattered the people through their unrighteous acts.

23:3, 4 God's people had been scattered, but they would be restored to the Land, and the righteous would have an abundant life. Part of this blessing would include leaders who would treat the people of God according to God's standards. This theme of a second Exodus was frequent among the prophets of the Exile (Is. 49:8-26; Ezek. 36:24—37:14).

23:5, 6 The Davidic line would be restored, and a king after the heart of David would reign (see Ezek. 37:24, 25). The Jews interpreted such passages as a reference to the Messiah and the golden age over which He would reign. The writers of the NT saw Jesus Christ as the fulfillment of these verses (Luke 3:31; Rom. 1:1-4; Rev. 22:16). "THE LORD OUR RIGHTEOUSNESS" is a fit designation for the ruler of Israel.

23:7, 8 The second Exodus would be greater than the first, becoming the paradigm to the nations of God's grace and lovingkindness to His people. The first Exodus was a witness to Egypt and surrounding nations; the second a witness to the nations of the earth.

Because of the LORD,
And because of His holy words.
[10]For the land is full of adulterers;
For because of a curse the land mourns.
The pleasant places of the wilderness are dried
    up.
Their course of life is evil,
And their might *is* not right.

[11]"For both prophet and priest are profane;
Yes, in My house I have found their
    wickedness," says the LORD.
[12]"Therefore their way shall be to them
Like slippery *ways;*
In the darkness they shall be driven on
And fall in them;
For I will bring disaster on them,
The year of their punishment," says the LORD.
[13]"And I have seen folly in the prophets of
    Samaria:
They prophesied by Baal
And caused My people Israel to err.
[14]Also I have seen a horrible thing in the
    prophets of Jerusalem:
They commit adultery and walk in lies;
They also strengthen the hands of evildoers,
So that no one turns back from his wickedness.
All of them are like Sodom to Me,
And her inhabitants like Gomorrah.

[15]"Therefore thus says the LORD of hosts concerning the prophets:

'Behold, I will feed them with wormwood,
And make them drink the water of gall;
For from the prophets of Jerusalem
Profaneness has gone out into all the land.' "

[16]Thus says the LORD of hosts:

"Do not listen to the words of the prophets who
    prophesy to you.
They make you worthless;
They speak a vision of their own heart,
Not from the mouth of the LORD.
[17]They continually say to those who despise Me,
'The LORD has said, "You shall have peace" ';
And *to* everyone who walks according to the
    dictates of his own heart, they say,
'No evil shall come upon you.' "

[18]For who has stood in the counsel of the LORD,
And has perceived and heard His word?
Who has marked His word and heard *it?*
[19]Behold, a whirlwind of the LORD has gone forth
    in fury—
A violent whirlwind!
It will fall violently on the head of the wicked.
[20]The anger of the LORD will not turn back
Until He has executed and performed the
    thoughts of His heart.
In the latter days you will understand it
    perfectly.

[21]"I have not sent these prophets, yet they ran.
I have not spoken to them, yet they prophesied.
[22]But if they had stood in My counsel,
And had caused My people to hear My words,
Then they would have turned them from their
    evil way
And from the evil of their doings.

[23]"*Am* I a God near at hand," says the LORD,
"And not a God afar off?
[24]Can anyone hide himself in secret places,
So I shall not see him?" says the LORD;
"Do I not fill heaven and earth?" says the LORD.

[25]"I have heard what the prophets have said who prophesy lies in My name, saying, 'I have dreamed, I have dreamed!' [26]How long will *this* be in the heart of the prophets who prophesy lies? Indeed *they are* prophets of the deceit of their own heart, [27]who try to make My people forget My name by their dreams which everyone tells his neighbor, as their fathers forgot My name for Baal.

[28]"The prophet who has a dream, let him tell a
    dream;
And he who has My word, let him speak My
    word faithfully.
What *is* the chaff to the wheat?" says the LORD.
[29]"*Is* not My word like a fire?" says the LORD,
"And like a hammer *that* breaks the rock in
    pieces?

[30]"Therefore behold, I *am* against the prophets," says the LORD, "who steal My words every one from his neighbor. [31]Behold, I *am*

23:14 Sodom and Gomorrah were primary examples of wickedness in the OT. Sodom was judged not only for immoral sexual practices (Gen. 19) but also for pride and failure to care for the poor (Ezek. 16:49, 50).

23:16–22 The false prophets sinned by declaring their own thoughts to be the message of the Lord. Their message of peace ran directly counter to the truth, leading the people into a false security.

23:23, 24 Common conceptions of deity focused on localized deities who, largely restricted to their own temples, had no knowledge beyond the range of sight (see 1 Kin. 18:27). In contrast, the true God sees and knows all.

23:25–29 God used dreams and visions, oral preaching, and the written word as modes of revelation (Num. 12:6). However, the false prophets were preaching daydreams. The genuine Word of God has a powerful effect (Jer. 23:29; see Is. 55:10, 11).

23:30–40 The people were responsible for listening to a prophet's message and discerning whether it was of the Lord.

against the prophets," says the LORD, "who use their tongues and say, 'He says.' ³²Behold, I *am* against those who prophesy false dreams," says the LORD, "and tell them, and cause My people to err by their lies and by their recklessness. Yet I did not send them or command them; therefore they shall not profit this people at all," says the LORD.

³³"So when these people or the prophet or the priest ask you, saying, 'What is the oracle of the LORD?' you shall then say to them, 'What oracle?'ª I will even forsake you," says the LORD. ³⁴"And *as for* the prophet and the priest and the people who say, 'The oracle of the LORD!' I will even punish that man and his house. ³⁵Thus every one of you shall say to his neighbor, and every one to his brother, 'What has the LORD answered?' and, 'What has the LORD spoken?' ³⁶And the oracle of the LORD you shall mention no more. For every man's word will be his oracle, for you have perverted the words of the living God, the LORD of hosts, our God. ³⁷Thus you shall say to the prophet, 'What has the LORD answered you?' and, 'What has the LORD spoken?' ³⁸But since you say, 'The oracle of the LORD!' therefore thus says the LORD: 'Because you say this word, "The oracle of the LORD!" and I have sent to you, saying, "Do not say, 'The oracle of the LORD!' " ³⁹therefore behold, I, even I, will utterly forget you and forsake you, and the city that I gave you and your fathers, and *will cast you* out of My presence. ⁴⁰And I will bring an everlasting reproach upon you, and a perpetual shame, which shall not be forgotten.' "

The Sign of Two Baskets of Figs

24 The LORD showed me, and there were two baskets of figs set before the temple of the LORD, after Nebuchadnezzar king of Babylon had carried away captive Jeconiah the son of Jehoiakim, king of Judah, and the princes of Judah with the craftsmen and smiths, from Jerusalem, and had brought them to Babylon. ²One basket *had* very good figs, like the figs *that are* first ripe; and the other basket *had* very bad figs which could not be eaten, they were so bad. ³Then the LORD said to me, "What do you see, Jeremiah?"

And I said, "Figs, the good figs, very good; and the bad, very bad, which cannot be eaten, they are so bad."

⁴Again the word of the LORD came to me, saying, ⁵"Thus says the LORD, the God of Israel: 'Like these good figs, so will I acknowledge those who are carried away captive from Judah, whom I have sent out of this place for *their own* good, into the land of the Chaldeans. ⁶For I will set My eyes on them for good, and I will bring them back to this land; I will build them and not pull *them* down, and I will plant them and not pluck *them* up. ⁷Then I will give them a heart to know Me, that I *am* the LORD; and they shall be My people, and I will be their God, for they shall return to Me with their whole heart.

⁸'And as the bad figs which cannot be eaten, they are so bad'—surely thus says the LORD—'so will I give up Zedekiah the king of Judah, his princes, the residue of Jerusalem who remain in this land, and those who dwell in the land of Egypt. ⁹I will deliver them to trouble into all the kingdoms of the earth, for *their* harm, *to be* a reproach and a byword, a taunt and a curse, in all places where I shall drive them. ¹⁰And I will send the sword, the famine, and the pestilence among them, till they are consumed from the land that I gave to them and their fathers.' "

Seventy Years of Desolation

25 The word that came to Jeremiah concerning all the people of Judah, in the fourth year of

23:33 ªSeptuagint, Targum, and Vulgate read 'You are the burden.'

False prophets were to be punished by death (Deut. 13:1–5). Not only would the false prophets be judged, but those who listened to them as well.

23:30 Steal My words indicates that the false prophets would twist the true Word of God in order to deceive the people. Heresy may sound like the truth, but it is not the truth.

24:1 Nebuchadnezzar took captive the leaders of the people and the skilled craftsmen. Highly selective, the Babylonians were interested in those who would benefit the empire (see Dan. 1:3–5). The poorest and least educated people would have been left behind to till the land (Jer. 39:10).

24:2–10 Through the vision of the good and bad figs, God revealed His plans for His people in Exile. The Exile actually became a means of protecting the true remnant and rejecting the faithless, such as Zedekiah and his followers. Through the ministry of men such as Daniel and Nehemiah, God's word came even to the pagan kings of the Babylonian and Persian empires. God's purposes are accomplished despite the failure of His people. He is faithful, though people fail.

24:6 The heart of Jeremiah's preaching included verbs like "build up," "plant," "pull down," and "pluck up" (see Jer. 1:10; see also 31:27, 28). Both elements of judgment and hope were included in his message.

24:7 A heart to know Me suggests not just outward conformity but complete inward renewal. Language similar to that of the initial establishment of the covenant is used but with an added spiritual dimension (Ex. 6:6–8).

24:8 Archaeological discoveries on the island of Elephantine have shown that a community of Jews existed in Egypt at Syene (modern Aswan), surviving until postexilic times and possibly dating from this period. They even built a temple to the Lord and sought approval and advice from Jerusalem. What eventually happened to them is unknown. Centuries later Jewish communities developed in Alexandria and elsewhere in Egypt from the policy of Alexander the Great and his generals, who encouraged the resettlement of the Jews as an economic stimulus.

25:1 The fourth year of Jehoiakim and the first of Nebuchadnezzar was 605 B.C.

Jehoiakim the son of Josiah, king of Judah (which *was* the first year of Nebuchadnezzar king of Babylon), ²which Jeremiah the prophet spoke to all the people of Judah and to all the inhabitants of Jerusalem, saying: ³"From the thirteenth year of Josiah the son of Amon, king of Judah, even to this day, this *is* the twenty-third year in which the word of the Lord has come to me; and I have spoken to you, rising early and speaking, but you have not listened. ⁴And the Lord has sent to you all His servants the prophets, rising early and sending *them,* but you have not listened nor inclined your ear to hear. ⁵They said, 'Repent now everyone of his evil way and his evil doings, and dwell in the land that the Lord has given to you and your fathers forever and ever. ⁶Do not go after other gods to serve them and worship them, and do not provoke Me to anger with the works of your hands; and I will not harm you.' ⁷Yet you have not listened to Me," says the Lord, "that you might provoke Me to anger with the works of your hands to your own hurt.

⁸"Therefore thus says the Lord of hosts: 'Because you have not heard My words, ⁹behold, I will send and take all the families of the north,' says the Lord, 'and Nebuchadnezzar the king of Babylon, My servant, and will bring them against this land, against its inhabitants, and against these nations all around, and will utterly destroy them, and make them an astonishment, a hissing, and perpetual desolations. ¹⁰Moreover I will take from them the voice of mirth and the voice of gladness, the voice of the bridegroom and the voice of the bride, the sound of the millstones and the light of the lamp. ¹¹And this whole land shall be a desolation *and* an astonishment, and these nations shall serve the king of Babylon seventy years.

¹²"Then it will come to pass, when seventy years are completed, *that* I will punish the king of Babylon and that nation, the land of the Chaldeans, for their iniquity,' says the Lord; 'and I will make it a perpetual desolation. ¹³So I will bring on that land all My words which I have pronounced against it, all that is written in this book, which Jeremiah has prophesied concerning all the nations. ¹⁴(For many nations and great kings shall be served by them also; and I will repay them according to their deeds and according to the works of their own hands.)' "

Judgment on the Nations

¹⁵For thus says the Lord God of Israel to me: "Take this wine cup of fury from My hand, and cause all the nations, to whom I send you, to drink it. ¹⁶And they will drink and stagger and go mad because of the sword that I will send among them."

¹⁷Then I took the cup from the Lord's hand, and made all the nations drink, to whom the Lord had sent me: ¹⁸Jerusalem and the cities of Judah, its kings and its princes, to make them a desolation, an astonishment, a hissing, and a curse, as *it is* this day; ¹⁹Pharaoh king of Egypt, his servants, his princes, and all his people; ²⁰all the mixed multitude, all the kings of the land of Uz, all the kings of the land of the Philistines (namely, Ashkelon, Gaza, Ekron, and the remnant of Ashdod); ²¹Edom, Moab, and the people of Ammon; ²²all the kings of Tyre, all the kings of Sidon, and the kings of the coastlands which *are* across the sea; ²³Dedan, Tema, Buz, and all *who are* in the farthest corners; ²⁴all the kings of Arabia and all the kings of the mixed multitude who dwell in the desert; ²⁵all the kings of Zimri, all the kings of Elam, and all the kings of the Medes; ²⁶all the kings of the north, far and near, one with another; and all the kingdoms of the world which *are* on the face of the earth. Also the king of Sheshach[a] shall drink after them.

²⁷"Therefore you shall say to them, 'Thus says the Lord of hosts, the God of Israel: "Drink, be drunk, and vomit! Fall and rise no more, because of the sword which I will send among you." ' ²⁸And it shall be, if they refuse to take the cup from your hand to drink, then you shall say to them, 'Thus says the Lord of hosts: "You shall certainly drink! ²⁹For behold, I begin to bring calamity on the city which is called by My name, and should you be utterly unpunished? You shall not be unpunished, for I will call for a sword on all the inhabitants of the earth," says the Lord of hosts.'

25:26 ᵃA code word for Babylon (compare 51:41)

25:3–7 The people of Judah were not in trouble for lack of revelation and knowledge of the truth. In fact, God had been faithful to send them prophets to declare the truth. The problem was not lack of knowledge, but willful rebellion. The 13th year of Josiah (v. 3) dated the beginning of Jeremiah's prophetic ministry around 626 B.C. (Jer. 1:2).

25:11, 12 The seventy years of Babylonian Exile lasted from approximately 605 to 538 B.C. Babylon, though the instrument of the Lord to accomplish His judgment against Judah, was a pagan nation full of idolatry and sin and under divine condemnation. Babylon was conquered by Cyrus of Persia in 539 B.C. This message would have been a comfort to the remnant.

25:15 The cup of fury symbolizes divine judgment. Isaiah, Ezekiel, and Habakkuk used similar terminology (Is. 51:17, 21, 22; Ezek. 23:32–34; Hab. 2:16).

25:15–38 God would judge not only Judah, but pagan nations as well. This passage anticipates the oracles against the nations (Jer. 46:1—51:64). God's judgment was focused on His people, who were His chief representatives to these nations.

25:26 Sheshach is possibly a cipher or code name for Babylon written as an *Atbash,* a literary device which exchanges the letters of a name counted from the beginning of the alphabet for letters counted from the end.

³⁰"Therefore prophesy against them all these words, and say to them:

'The LORD will roar from on high,
And utter His voice from His holy habitation;
He will roar mightily against His fold.
He will give a shout, as those who tread *the grapes,*
Against all the inhabitants of the earth.
³¹A noise will come to the ends of the earth—
For the LORD has a controversy with the nations;
He will plead His case with all flesh.
He will give those *who are* wicked to the sword,'
says the LORD."

³²Thus says the LORD of hosts:

"Behold, disaster shall go forth
From nation to nation,
And a great whirlwind shall be raised up
From the farthest parts of the earth.

³³"And at that day the slain of the LORD shall be from *one* end of the earth even to the *other* end of the earth. They shall not be lamented, or gathered, or buried; they shall become refuse on the ground.

³⁴"Wail, shepherds, and cry!
Roll about *in the ashes,*
You leaders of the flock!
For the days of your slaughter and your dispersions are fulfilled;
You shall fall like a precious vessel.
³⁵And the shepherds will have no way to flee,
Nor the leaders of the flock to escape.
³⁶A voice of the cry of the shepherds,
And a wailing of the leaders to the flock *will be heard.*
For the LORD has plundered their pasture,
³⁷And the peaceful dwellings are cut down
Because of the fierce anger of the LORD.
³⁸He has left His lair like the lion;
For their land is desolate
Because of the fierceness of the Oppressor,
And because of His fierce anger."

Jeremiah Saved from Death

26 In the beginning of the reign of Jehoiakim the son of Josiah, king of Judah, this word came from the LORD, saying, ²"Thus says the LORD: 'Stand in the court of the LORD's house, and speak to all the cities of Judah, which come to worship *in* the LORD's house, all the words that I command you to speak to them. Do not diminish a word. ³Perhaps everyone will listen and turn from his evil way, that I may relent concerning the calamity which I purpose to bring on them because of the evil of their doings.' ⁴And you shall say to them, 'Thus says the LORD: "If you will not listen to Me, to walk in My law which I have set before you, ⁵to heed the words of My servants the prophets whom I sent to you, both rising up early and sending *them* (but you have not heeded), ⁶then I will make this house like Shiloh, and will make this city a curse to all the nations of the earth." ' "

⁷So the priests and the prophets and all the people heard Jeremiah speaking these words in the house of the LORD. ⁸Now it happened, when Jeremiah had made an end of speaking all that the LORD had commanded *him* to speak to all the people, that the priests and the prophets and all the people seized him, saying, "You will surely die! ⁹Why have you prophesied in the name of the LORD, saying, 'This house shall be like Shiloh, and this city shall be desolate, without an inhabitant'?" And all the people were gathered against Jeremiah in the house of the LORD.

¹⁰When the princes of Judah heard these things, they came up from the king's house to the house of the LORD and sat down in the entry of the New Gate of the LORD's *house.* ¹¹And the priests and the prophets spoke to the princes and all the people, saying, "This man deserves to die! For he has prophesied against this city, as you have heard with your ears."

¹²Then Jeremiah spoke to all the princes and all the people, saying: "The LORD sent me to prophesy against this house and against this city with all the words that you have heard. ¹³Now therefore, amend your ways and your doings, and obey the voice of the LORD your God; then the LORD will relent concerning the doom that He has

---

26:2 Jeremiah was called to proclaim God's word in the temple of the Lord, the focal point of Judah's religion. Paradoxically, the temple had become a hotbed of idolatry and falsehood hostile to God's purposes rather than a place of true worship and righteous teaching. Facing such opposition required great courage from Jeremiah (see Jer. 7).

26:3 God knew what the people's response would be and earlier had described their inability to change (Jer. 13:23) and the inevitability of judgment (Jer. 17:1–4). The language here, however, reflects the covenantal language (see Deut. 30:10–20). In His mercy, God gave His people every opportunity to repent.

26:7–9 The false prophets, the priests, and the people ironically accused Jeremiah of prophesying falsely and were willing to put him to death (see Deut. 13:5). In their depravity the people called evil "good" and good "evil." To speak of the destruction of the temple, which was considered inviolate, was equal to blasphemy. The sanctuary at Shiloh had been destroyed by the Philistines in the time of Samuel (see 1 Sam. 4).

26:12–19 Jeremiah successfully conducted his defense by forcefully claiming God as his authority. Micah the prophet, who predicted the destruction of Jerusalem in the time of Hezekiah (715–686 B.C.), was cited as a precedent (Mic. 3:12). Micah's life had been spared.

pronounced against you. [14]As for me, here I am, in your hand; do with me as seems good and proper to you. [15]But know for certain that if you put me to death, you will surely bring innocent blood on yourselves, on this city, and on its inhabitants; for truly the LORD has sent me to you to speak all these words in your hearing."

[16]So the princes and all the people said to the priests and the prophets, "This man does not deserve to die. For he has spoken to us in the name of the LORD our God."

[17]Then certain of the elders of the land rose up and spoke to all the assembly of the people, saying: [18]"Micah of Moresheth prophesied in the days of Hezekiah king of Judah, and spoke to all the people of Judah, saying, 'Thus says the LORD of hosts:

"Zion shall be plowed *like* a field,
Jerusalem shall become heaps of ruins,
And the mountain of the temple[a]
Like the bare hills of the forest." '[b]

[19]Did Hezekiah king of Judah and all Judah ever put him to death? Did he not fear the LORD and seek the LORD's favor? And the LORD relented concerning the doom which He had pronounced against them. But we are doing great evil against ourselves."

[20]Now there was also a man who prophesied in the name of the LORD, Urijah the son of Shemaiah of Kirjath Jearim, who prophesied against this city and against this land according to all the words of Jeremiah. [21]And when Jehoiakim the king, with all his mighty men and all the princes, heard his words, the king sought to put him to death; but when Urijah heard *it*, he was afraid and fled, and went to Egypt. [22]Then Jehoiakim the king sent men to Egypt: Elnathan the son of Achbor, and *other* men *who went* with him to Egypt. [23]And they brought Urijah from Egypt and brought him to Jehoiakim the king, who killed him with the sword and cast his dead body into the graves of the common people.

[24]Nevertheless the hand of Ahikam the son of Shaphan was with Jeremiah, so that they should not give him into the hand of the people to put him to death.

Symbol of the Bonds and Yokes

27In the beginning of the reign of Jehoiakim[a] the son of Josiah, king of Judah, this word came to Jeremiah from the LORD, saying,[b] [2]"Thus says the LORD to me: 'Make for yourselves bonds and yokes, and put them on your neck, [3]and send them to the king of Edom, the king of Moab, the king of the Ammonites, the king of Tyre, and the king of Sidon, by the hand of the messengers who come to Jerusalem to Zedekiah king of Judah. [4]And command them to say to their masters, "Thus says the LORD of hosts, the God of Israel—thus you shall say to your masters: [5]I have made the earth, the man and the beast that *are* on the ground, by My great power and by My outstretched arm, and have given it to whom it seemed proper to Me. [6]And now I have given all these lands into the hand of Nebuchadnezzar the king of Babylon, My servant; and the beasts of the field I have also given him to serve him. [7]So all nations shall serve him and his son and his son's son, until the time of his land comes; and then many nations and great kings shall make him serve them. [8]And it shall be, *that* the nation and kingdom which will not serve Nebuchadnezzar the king of Babylon, and which will not put its neck under the yoke of the king of Babylon, that nation I will punish,' says the LORD, 'with the sword, the famine, and the pestilence, until I have consumed them by his hand. [9]Therefore do not listen to your prophets, your diviners, your dreamers, your soothsayers, or your sorcerers, who speak to you, saying, "You shall not serve the king of Babylon." [10]For they prophesy a lie to you, to remove you far from your land; and I will drive you out, and you will perish. [11]But the nations that bring their necks under the yoke of the king of Babylon and serve him, I will let them remain in their own land,' says the LORD, 'and they shall till it and dwell in it.' " ' "

26:18 [a]Literally *house* [b]Compare Micah 3:12 **27:1** [a]Following Masoretic Text, Targum, and Vulgate; some Hebrew manuscripts, Arabic, and Syriac read *Zedekiah* (compare 27:3, 12; 28:1). [b]Septuagint omits verse 1.

26:20–24 The threat of death was real. Nothing is known of Urijah, except what is recorded here. This passage clearly reveals that at least one other prophet was declaring God's word in Judah during Jeremiah's time. Jeremiah is the best known because his sermons and observations have been preserved in writing.

27:2–6 Bonds and yokes were symbols of political submission. The sovereign Lord is in control of all nations.

27:5 God's authority over the nations is based on His role as Creator of all. God's decisions are rooted in His eternal plan. He always acts according to His wisdom ("proper") and power ("My great power").

27:6 Nebuchadnezzar was identified as the Lord's servant. He was the instrument through whom God would judge His people. That even the "beasts" would serve the king of Babylon shows the extent of power God would grant Nebuchadnezzar.

27:9, 14 The court or royal prophets, who served the kings of the nations, were most likely prophetic puppets. They served the social function of making the gods favorable to the current regime. Thus, in the face of invaders, they might proclaim victory or peace, whichever seemed most likely to please the king. Sadly, the descendants of David had yielded to the temptation to employ such a pagan practice in Judah.

W I D O W H O O D   *TRUSTING GOD TO PROVIDE*

God sometimes asks questions that reveal truths otherwise unseen. To the penniless widow with two sons for whom to care, God asked what she had in the house. Though the widow's response was that she had "nothing in the house but a jar of oil" (2 Kin. 4:2), she was touched by the living God at this turning point in her life. Like the widow, when all else is gone, God's children always have the oil of His Spirit within (1 Cor. 3:16, 17). It is to be used only as He personally directs (1 Cor. 6:19, 20).

When Elisha requested the widow to act in order to meet her needs, he undoubtedly rekindled hope in her heart (2 Kin. 4:3). God never leaves His children without resources for all circumstances. The answer may not be what was expected, but by listening to His heart the believing woman will come to understand that He is providing for her good and His glory (Jer. 29:11; Phil. 4:19).

Widows without means of support became the responsibility for the people as a whole, just as the Levites, strangers, and orphans (Deut. 14:29). This concept of care for widows was readily embraced by the early church. Paul gave very specific advice to Timothy about the definition and care of widows (1 Tim. 5:3–16).

Widows face unending challenges. By relying on God's character and determining to become more like Him, their lives are forever changed. The widow to whom God sent Elisha never hesitated or questioned the prophet's unusual request. She listened intently (2 Kin. 4:5). She remembered his instructions. And she immediately "went from him" into active work she knew to be God's plan for her. She had all the resources she would ever need—God's presence within (see Phil. 4:13). Widows—and all women—have that same power available as they face the complexities of an ever-changing world.

Everyone in the church is called to care for widows—both materially and spiritually (Acts 6:1). The church should undergird and provide support for those who have no means of support and should give freely of time and life to widows. As part of giving to widows, an active effort should be made to include them in all activities of the church and to invite them to be a part of celebrations within the church family.

See also Matt. 18:3, note; notes on Brokenheartedness (Ps. 34); Children (2 Sam. 21; Ps. 128; Prov. 22; Luke 15); Death (1 Cor. 15); Family (Gen. 32; 1 Sam. 3; Ps. 78; 127); Grief (Is. 53); Providence (Eccl. 7); Sorrow (Rev. 21); Widowhood (Ps. 68; 1 Cor. 2); portraits of the Prophet's Widow (2 Kin. 4); the Widow of Zarephath (1 Kin. 17)

---

[12]I also spoke to Zedekiah king of Judah according to all these words, saying, "Bring your necks under the yoke of the king of Babylon, and serve him and his people, and live! [13]Why will you die, you and your people, by the sword, by the famine, and by the pestilence, as the LORD has spoken against the nation that will not serve the king of Babylon? [14]Therefore do not listen to the words of the prophets who speak to you, saying, 'You shall not serve the king of Babylon,' for they prophesy a lie to you; [15]for I have not sent them," says the LORD, "yet they prophesy a lie in My name, that I may drive you out, and that you may perish, you and the prophets who prophesy to you."

[16]Also I spoke to the priests and to all this people, saying, "Thus says the LORD: 'Do not listen to the words of your prophets who prophesy to you, saying, "Behold, the vessels of the LORD's house will now shortly be brought back from Babylon"; for they prophesy a lie to you. [17]Do not listen to them; serve the king of Babylon, and live! Why should this city be laid waste? [18]But if they *are* prophets, and if the word of the LORD is with

them, let them now make intercession to the LORD of hosts, that the vessels which are left in the house of the LORD, *in* the house of the king of Judah, and at Jerusalem, do not go to Babylon.'

[19]"For thus says the LORD of hosts concerning the pillars, concerning the Sea, concerning the carts, and concerning the remainder of the vessels that remain in this city, [20]which Nebuchadnezzar king of Babylon did not take, when he carried away captive Jeconiah the son of Jehoiakim, king of Judah, from Jerusalem to Babylon, and all the nobles of Judah and Jerusalem— [21]yes, thus says the LORD of hosts, the God of Israel, concerning the vessels that remain in the house of the LORD, and in the house of the king of Judah and of Jerusalem: [22]'They shall be carried to Babylon, and there they shall be until the day that I visit them,' says the LORD. 'Then I will bring them up and restore them to this place.' "

Hananiah's Falsehood and Doom

28 And it happened in the same year, at the beginning of the reign of Zedekiah king of Ju-

---

27:16–22 The vessels of the Lord's house were the various furnishings and utensils used in the worship and service of the temple. Taking such items was viewed as the victory of the gods of the conqueror over the gods of the defeated.

28:1–4 A fascinating interaction occurred between two

prophets in Judah—Jeremiah the true prophet and Hananiah the false. False prophets often act and speak much like true representatives of the Lord. Hananiah invoked the name of the Lord and preached a message that pleased his hearers.

dah, in the fourth year *and* in the fifth month, *that* Hananiah the son of Azur the prophet, who *was* from Gibeon, spoke to me in the house of the LORD in the presence of the priests and of all the people, saying, ²"Thus speaks the LORD of hosts, the God of Israel, saying: 'I have broken the yoke of the king of Babylon. ³Within two full years I will bring back to this place all the vessels of the LORD's house, that Nebuchadnezzar king of Babylon took away from this place and carried to Babylon. ⁴And I will bring back to this place Jeconiah the son of Jehoiakim, king of Judah, with all the captives of Judah who went to Babylon,' says the LORD, 'for I will break the yoke of the king of Babylon.'"

⁵Then the prophet Jeremiah spoke to the prophet Hananiah in the presence of the priests and in the presence of all the people who stood in the house of the LORD, ⁶and the prophet Jeremiah said, "Amen! The LORD do so; the LORD perform your words which you have prophesied, to bring back the vessels of the LORD's house and all who were carried away captive, from Babylon to this place. ⁷Nevertheless hear now this word that I speak in your hearing and in the hearing of all the people: ⁸The prophets who have been before me and before you of old prophesied against many countries and great kingdoms—of war and disaster and pestilence. ⁹As for the prophet who prophesies of peace, when the word of the prophet comes to pass, the prophet will be known *as* one whom the LORD has truly sent."

¹⁰Then Hananiah the prophet took the yoke off the prophet Jeremiah's neck and broke it. ¹¹And Hananiah spoke in the presence of all the people, saying, "Thus says the LORD: 'Even so I will break the yoke of Nebuchadnezzar king of Babylon from the neck of all nations within the space of two full years.'" And the prophet Jeremiah went his way.

¹²Now the word of the LORD came to Jeremiah, after Hananiah the prophet had broken the yoke from the neck of the prophet Jeremiah, saying,

¹³"Go and tell Hananiah, saying, 'Thus says the LORD: "You have broken the yokes of wood, but you have made in their place yokes of iron." ¹⁴For thus says the LORD of hosts, the God of Israel: "I have put a yoke of iron on the neck of all these nations, that they may serve Nebuchadnezzar king of Babylon; and they shall serve him. I have given him the beasts of the field also." ' "

¹⁵Then the prophet Jeremiah said to Hananiah the prophet, "Hear now, Hananiah, the LORD has not sent you, but you make this people trust in a lie. ¹⁶Therefore thus says the LORD: 'Behold, I will cast you from the face of the earth. This year you shall die, because you have taught rebellion against the LORD.' "

¹⁷So Hananiah the prophet died the same year in the seventh month.

Jeremiah's Letter to the Captives

29 Now these *are* the words of the letter that Jeremiah the prophet sent from Jerusalem to the remainder of the elders who were carried away captive—to the priests, the prophets, and all the people whom Nebuchadnezzar had carried away captive from Jerusalem to Babylon. ²(This happened after Jeconiah the king, the queen mother, the eunuchs, the princes of Judah and Jerusalem, the craftsmen, and the smiths had departed from Jerusalem.) ³*The letter was sent* by the hand of Elasah the son of Shaphan, and Gemariah the son of Hilkiah, whom Zedekiah king of Judah sent to Babylon, to Nebuchadnezzar king of Babylon, saying,

⁴Thus says the LORD of hosts, the God of Israel, to all who were carried away captive, whom I have caused to be carried away from Jerusalem to Babylon:

⁵Build houses and dwell *in them;* plant gardens and eat their fruit. ⁶Take wives and beget

---

28:6–9 Jeremiah spoke "Amen" with measured sarcasm. He would like to believe Hananiah's message; clearly he could not. Jeremiah noted that such optimistic prophecy was opposed diametrically to his own and typical of other prophets of the day. A test of the true prophet is that his prophecy of peace is verified by history (v. 9). Jeremiah knew that his nation was headed for catastrophe because of the people's sins. Nothing short of radical repentance could possibly alter that course. Genuine prophecy is ethically conditioned.

28:10 Jeremiah had placed this yoke around his neck according to God's command as a witness of the approaching victory of the Babylonians (Jer. 27:2). False prophets also employed symbolic actions.

28:15–17 By Hananiah's preaching and his actions, he set himself up as a personal enemy of Jeremiah and therefore of God. He was rebellious, and he taught others to rebel. God therefore singled him out for special judgment and sentenced him to imminent death (for Korah's rebellion, see Num. 16).

29:3 The Assyrian and Babylonian empires had reasonably well developed systems for delivering official messages and military instructions. Private messages, however, normally were sent by a personal envoy. In this case, Jeremiah sent his letter by royal messengers, high ranking members of the priestly class, possibly carrying tribute for the king of Babylon.

29:4–9 Babylon was going to be the home of the exiles for approximately 70 years (v. 10). Therefore the exiles were instructed not only to seek personal prosperity but also the well-being of the city. God would improve the welfare of the city due to the presence and prayers of His people. God's "common grace" (or His creation-based blessings to unbelievers) often is connected with His special grace to His people, so that the presence of His people in a community improves the community as a whole.

sons and daughters; and take wives for your sons and give your daughters to husbands, so that they may bear sons and daughters—that you may be increased there, and not diminished. [7]And seek the peace of the city where I have caused you to be carried away captive, and pray to the LORD for it; for in its peace you will have peace. [8]For thus says the LORD of hosts, the God of Israel: Do not let your prophets and your diviners who are in your midst deceive you, nor listen to your dreams which you cause to be dreamed. [9]For they prophesy falsely to you in My name; I have not sent them, says the LORD.

[10]For thus says the LORD: After seventy years are completed at Babylon, I will visit you and perform My good word toward you, and cause you to return to this place. [11]For I know the thoughts that I think toward you, says the LORD, thoughts of peace and not of evil, to give you a future and a hope. [12]Then you will call upon Me and go and pray to Me, and I will listen to you. [13]And you will seek Me and find *Me*, when you search for Me with all your heart. [14]I will be found by you, says the LORD, and I will bring you back from your captivity; I will gather you from all the nations and from all the places where I have driven you, says the LORD, and I will bring you to the place from which I cause you to be carried away captive.

[15]Because you have said, "The LORD has raised up prophets for us in Babylon"— [16]therefore thus says the LORD concerning the king who sits on the throne of David, concerning all the people who dwell in this city, and concerning your brethren who have not gone out with you into captivity— [17]thus says the LORD of hosts: Behold, I will send on them the sword, the famine, and the pestilence, and will make them like rotten figs that cannot be eaten, they are so bad. [18]And I will pursue them with the sword, with famine, and with pestilence; and I will deliver them to trouble among all the kingdoms of the earth—to be a curse, an astonishment, a hissing, and a reproach among all the nations where I have driven them, [19]because they have not heeded My words, says the LORD, which I sent to them by My servants the prophets, rising up early and sending *them;* neither would you heed, says the LORD. [20]Therefore hear the word of the LORD, all

you of the captivity, whom I have sent from Jerusalem to Babylon.

[21]Thus says the LORD of hosts, the God of Israel, concerning Ahab the son of Kolaiah, and Zedekiah the son of Maaseiah, who prophesy a lie to you in My name: Behold, I will deliver them into the hand of Nebuchadnezzar king of Babylon, and he shall slay them before your eyes. [22]And because of them a curse shall be taken up by all the captivity of Judah who *are* in Babylon, saying, "The LORD make you like Zedekiah and Ahab, whom the king of Babylon roasted in the fire"; [23]because they have done disgraceful things in Israel, have committed adultery with their neighbors' wives, and have spoken lying words in My name, which I have not commanded them. Indeed I know, and *am* a witness, says the LORD.

[24]You shall also speak to Shemaiah the Nehelamite, saying, [25]Thus speaks the LORD of hosts, the God of Israel, saying: You have sent letters in your name to all the people who *are* at Jerusalem, to Zephaniah the son of Maaseiah the priest, and to all the priests, saying, [26]"The LORD has made you priest instead of Jehoiada the priest, so that there should be officers *in* the house of the LORD over every man *who* is demented and considers himself a prophet, that you should put him in prison and in the stocks. [27]Now therefore, why have you not rebuked Jeremiah of Anathoth who makes himself a prophet to you? [28]For he has sent to us *in* Babylon, saying, 'This *captivity is* long; build houses and dwell *in them,* and plant gardens and eat their fruit.' "

[29]Now Zephaniah the priest read this letter in the hearing of Jeremiah the prophet. [30]Then the word of the LORD came to Jeremiah, saying: [31]Send to all those in captivity, saying, Thus says the LORD concerning Shemaiah the Nehelamite: Because Shemaiah has prophesied to you, and I have not sent him, and he has caused you to trust in a lie— [32]therefore thus says the LORD: Behold, I will punish Shemaiah the Nehelamite and his family: he shall not have anyone to dwell among this people, nor shall he see the good that I will do for My people, says the LORD, because he has taught rebellion against the LORD.

29:16–19 The judgment on those who had not gone to Babylon stands in contrast to the blessing on the faithful remnant. The remnant in Babylon would receive peace, prosperity, and re-turn to the Land. The others would experience war, famine and disease, and permanent exile.

Restoration of Israel and Judah

30 The word that came to Jeremiah from the LORD, saying, ²"Thus speaks the LORD God of Israel, saying: 'Write in a book for yourself all the words that I have spoken to you. ³For behold, the days are coming,' says the LORD, 'that I will bring back from captivity My people Israel and Judah,' says the LORD. 'And I will cause them to return to the land that I gave to their fathers, and they shall possess it.'"

⁴Now these *are* the words that the LORD spoke concerning Israel and Judah.

⁵"For thus says the LORD:

'We have heard a voice of trembling,
Of fear, and not of peace.
⁶Ask now, and see,
Whether a man is ever in labor with child?
So why do I see every man *with* his hands on his loins
Like a woman in labor,
And all faces turned pale?
⁷Alas! For that day *is* great,
So that none *is* like it;
And it *is* the time of Jacob's trouble,
But he shall be saved out of it.

'For it shall come to pass in that day,'
Says the LORD of hosts,
'*That* I will break his yoke from your neck,
And will burst your bonds;
Foreigners shall no more enslave them.
⁹But they shall serve the LORD their God,
And David their king,
Whom I will raise up for them.

¹⁰"Therefore do not fear, O My servant Jacob,' says the LORD,
'Nor be dismayed, O Israel;
For behold, I will save you from afar,
And your seed from the land of their captivity.
Jacob shall return, have rest and be quiet,
And no one shall make *him* afraid.
¹¹For I *am* with you,' says the LORD, 'to save you;
Though I make a full end of all nations where I have scattered you,
Yet I will not make a complete end of you.

But I will correct you in justice,
And will not let you go altogether unpunished.'

¹²"For thus says the LORD:

'Your affliction *is* incurable,
Your wound *is* severe.
¹³*There is* no one to plead your cause,
That you may be bound up;
You have no healing medicines.
¹⁴All your lovers have forgotten you;
They do not seek you;
For I have wounded you with the wound of an enemy,
With the chastisement of a cruel one,
For the multitude of your iniquities,
Because your sins have increased.
¹⁵Why do you cry about your affliction?
Your sorrow *is* incurable.
Because of the multitude of your iniquities,
Because your sins have increased,
I have done these things to you.

¹⁶'Therefore all those who devour you shall be devoured;
And all your adversaries, every one of them, shall go into captivity;
Those who plunder you shall become plunder,
And all who prey upon you I will make a prey.
¹⁷For I will restore health to you
And heal you of your wounds,' says the LORD,
'Because they called you an outcast *saying:*
"This *is* Zion;
No one seeks her."'

¹⁸"Thus says the LORD:

'Behold, I will bring back the captivity of Jacob's tents,
And have mercy on his dwelling places;
The city shall be built upon its own mound,
And the palace shall remain according to its own plan.
¹⁹Then out of them shall proceed thanksgiving
And the voice of those who make merry;

30:2 Jeremiah was commissioned as a writing prophet (see Jer. 26:2; 45:1). Jeremiah recorded various portions of his message at different times. Baruch may have been responsible for the final compilation of the book (see Introduction: Author). "Book" (Heb. *sepher,* lit. "writing" or "document") is probably understood here as an ancient scroll-book.

30:8, 9 The people of God are encouraged that God would fulfill His covenant promises to them and to the house of David (2 Sam. 7:12–16).

30:11 God's discipline of His covenant people is not like His judgment on those outside His covenantal protection. Rather this discipline is designed for correction. It is a mark of sonship and an act of love (Prov. 3:11, 12).

30:12–17 The desolate state of the remnant is described in vivid detail. "Incurable" affliction and "severe" wounds indicate the depth of their sin and depravity. Human aid would not help in this affliction (vv. 13, 14). "Lovers" may refer to political allies or to the idols in Judah. These "lovers" had left and could offer no hope. Although Judah had lost all hope, God declared that He would do what was impossible for any one else: deliver, heal, and restore them to Himself.

I will multiply them, and they shall not
    diminish;
I will also glorify them, and they shall not be
    small.
²⁰Their children also shall be as before,
    And their congregation shall be established
      before Me;
    And I will punish all who oppress them.
²¹Their nobles shall be from among them,
    And their governor shall come from their
      midst;
    Then I will cause him to draw near,
    And he shall approach Me;
    For who *is* this who pledged his heart to
      approach Me?' says the LORD.
²²'You shall be My people,
    And I will be your God.' "

²³Behold, the whirlwind of the LORD
Goes forth with fury,
A continuing whirlwind;
It will fall violently on the head of the wicked.
²⁴The fierce anger of the LORD will not return
    until He has done it,
And until He has performed the intents of His
    heart.

In the latter days you will consider it.

The Remnant of Israel Saved

31 "At the same time," says the LORD, "I will be
the God of all the families of Israel, and
they shall be My people."
²Thus says the LORD:

"The people who survived the sword
    Found grace in the wilderness—
Israel, when I went to give him rest."

³The LORD has appeared of old to me, *saying*:
"Yes, I have loved you with an everlasting love;
    Therefore with lovingkindness I have drawn you.
⁴Again I will build you, and you shall be rebuilt,
    O virgin of Israel!

You shall again be adorned with your
    tambourines,
And shall go forth in the dances of those who
    rejoice.
⁵You shall yet plant vines on the mountains of
    Samaria;
The planters shall plant and eat *them* as
    ordinary food.
⁶For there shall be a day
When the watchmen will cry on Mount
    Ephraim,
'Arise, and let us go up *to* Zion,
To the LORD our God.' "

⁷For thus says the LORD:

"Sing with gladness for Jacob,
    And shout among the chief of the nations;
Proclaim, give praise, and say,
    'O LORD, save Your people,
    The remnant of Israel!'
⁸Behold, I will bring them from the north
    country,
And gather them from the ends of the earth,
Among them the blind and the lame,
The woman with child
And the one who labors with child, together;
A great throng shall return there.
⁹They shall come with weeping,
    And with supplications I will lead them.
I will cause them to walk by the rivers of
    waters,
In a straight way in which they shall not
    stumble;
For I am a Father to Israel,
    And Ephraim *is* My firstborn.

¹⁰"Hear the word of the LORD, O nations,
    And declare *it* in the isles afar off, and say,
'He who scattered Israel will gather him,
    And keep him as a shepherd *does* his flock.'
¹¹For the LORD has redeemed Jacob,
    And ransomed him from the hand of one
    stronger than he.

30:23, 24 A storm of judgment awaits the wicked or those who oppose God. Those who reject the Lord's salvation experience His storm.

31:3 God has never ceased to love His people, and all that He has done for them has been rooted in that love. The Hebrew word translated "love" sometimes indicates the love that initiates relationships. "Lovingkindness" (Heb. *chesed*) refers to God's steadfast love or covenant loyalty (see Ps. 5:7–12, note).

31:4–6 The metaphor of the building was applied to God's people. God's people are seen as His dwelling place. The remaining imagery here suggests a rich, abundant life filled with rejoicing. In the OT, the blessing of God's people often is described in material terms and is tied particularly to the Land.

31:7–9 A crowd greater than that which was taken from the Land is portrayed returning to the Land. In this second Exodus, even the "blind," the "lame," and the "woman with child" would not stumble. Unlike the first Exodus with its 40 years of wandering, the people would return "in a straight way" to the Promised Land. This instance is among the few in which "Father" is a title given to the Lord God. The image could refer to His fatherly protection of the returning remnant or to rebirth imagery in which God granted a radically new beginning for His people.

31:11 Redeemed and ransomed are Exodus terms, metaphorically applied to God's work in rescuing His people from their enemies. The Israelites were slaves in Egypt whom God bought back with His mighty power. The sacrificial system God instituted was meant in part to remind the people of

¹²Therefore they shall come and sing in the
    height of Zion,
Streaming to the goodness of the LORD—
For wheat and new wine and oil,
For the young of the flock and the herd;
Their souls shall be like a well-watered garden,
And they shall sorrow no more at all.

¹³"Then shall the virgin rejoice in the dance,
And the young men and the old, together;
For I will turn their mourning to joy,
Will comfort them,
And make them rejoice rather than sorrow.
¹⁴I will satiate the soul of the priests with
    abundance,
And My people shall be satisfied with My
    goodness, says the LORD."

Mercy on Ephraim

¹⁵Thus says the LORD:

"A voice was heard in Ramah,
Lamentation *and* bitter weeping,
Rachel weeping for her children,
Refusing to be comforted for her children,
Because they *are* no more."

¹⁶Thus says the LORD:

"Refrain your voice from weeping,
And your eyes from tears;
For your work shall be rewarded, says the
    LORD,
And they shall come back from the land of the
    enemy.
¹⁷There is hope in your future, says the LORD,
That *your* children shall come back to their
    own border.

¹⁸"I have surely heard Ephraim bemoaning
    himself:
'You have chastised me, and I was chastised,
Like an untrained bull;
Restore me, and I will return,
For You *are* the LORD my God.
¹⁹Surely, after my turning, I repented;

And after I was instructed, I struck myself on
    the thigh;
I was ashamed, yes, even humiliated,
Because I bore the reproach of my youth.'
²⁰*Is* Ephraim My dear son?
Is he a pleasant child?
For though I spoke against him,
I earnestly remember him still;
Therefore My heart yearns for him;
I will surely have mercy on him, says the LORD.

²¹"Set up signposts,
Make landmarks;
Set your heart toward the highway,
The way in *which* you went.
Turn back, O virgin of Israel,
Turn back to these your cities.
²²How long will you gad about,
O you backsliding daughter?
For the LORD has created a new thing in the
    earth—
A woman shall encompass a man."

Future Prosperity of Judah

²³Thus says the LORD of hosts, the God of Israel: "They shall again use this speech in the land
of Judah and in its cities, when I bring back their
captivity: 'The LORD bless you, O home of justice,
and mountain of holiness!' ²⁴And there shall dwell
in Judah itself, and in all its cities together, farmers and those going out with flocks. ²⁵For I have
satiated the weary soul, and I have replenished
every sorrowful soul."

²⁶After this I awoke and looked around, and my
sleep was sweet to me.

²⁷"Behold, the days are coming, says the LORD,
that I will sow the house of Israel and the house of
Judah with the seed of man and the seed of beast.
²⁸And it shall come to pass, *that* as I have watched
over them to pluck up, to break down, to throw
down, to destroy, and to afflict, so I will watch
over them to build and to plant, says the LORD. ²⁹In
those days they shall say no more:

'The fathers have eaten sour grapes,
And the children's teeth are set on edge.'

---

their deliverance. In the NT, Jesus Christ became the literal
sacrifice for His people, to purchase them from the kingdom
of darkness (Titus 2:13, 14).

31:15 This verse was quoted by Matthew when he commented
on Herod's murder of the innocent children of Bethlehem and
the surrounding area as he sought to destroy the Messiah
(Matt. 2:17, 18). Rachel was the favored wife of Jacob, the
mother of Joseph and Benjamin.

31:22 The new thing probably refers to the fact that virgin Israel would encompass or cling to her divine Bridegroom. For
God's people to express faithful devotion to Him certainly
would be something new.

31:23–28 The prosperity of the messianic period is described
again, primarily in agricultural terms. The depleted population of Israel would be replenished, and the people's lives
would be characterized by justice and holiness, precisely
those elements that the people of Judah in Jeremiah's time
lacked. The verbs of verse 28 refer to both the negative and
positive aspects of Jeremiah's ministry—judgment and hope
(Jer. 1:10).

31:29, 30 The new concept of individual responsibility is a key
teaching of Jeremiah. Each person must bear responsibility
for his sins.

³⁰But every one shall die for his own iniquity; every man who eats the sour grapes, his teeth shall be set on edge.

A New Covenant

³¹"Behold, the days are coming, says the LORD, when I will make a new covenant with the house of Israel and with the house of Judah— ³²not according to the covenant that I made with their fathers in the day *that* I took them by the hand to lead them out of the land of Egypt, My covenant which they broke, though I was a husband to them,^a says the LORD. ³³But this *is* the covenant that I will make with the house of Israel after those days, says the LORD: I will put My law in their minds, and write it on their hearts; and I will be their God, and they shall be My people. ³⁴No more shall every man teach his neighbor, and every man his brother, saying, 'Know the LORD,' for they all shall know Me, from the least of them to the greatest of them, says the LORD. For I will forgive their iniquity, and their sin I will remember no more."

³⁵Thus says the LORD,
Who gives the sun for a light by day,
The ordinances of the moon and the stars for a
    light by night,
Who disturbs the sea,
And its waves roar
(The LORD of hosts *is* His name):

³⁶"If those ordinances depart
From before Me, says the LORD,
Then the seed of Israel shall also cease
From being a nation before Me forever."

³⁷Thus says the LORD:

"If heaven above can be measured,
And the foundations of the earth searched out
    beneath,
I will also cast off all the seed of Israel
For all that they have done, says the LORD.

³⁸"Behold, the days are coming, says the LORD, that the city shall be built for the LORD from the Tower of Hananel to the Corner Gate. ³⁹The sur-

veyor's line shall again extend straight forward over the hill Gareb; then it shall turn toward Goath. ⁴⁰And the whole valley of the dead bodies and of the ashes, and all the fields as far as the Brook Kidron, to the corner of the Horse Gate toward the east, *shall be* holy to the LORD. It shall not be plucked up or thrown down anymore forever."

Jeremiah Buys a Field

32The word that came to Jeremiah from the LORD in the tenth year of Zedekiah king of Judah, which was the eighteenth year of Nebuchadnezzar. ²For then the king of Babylon's army besieged Jerusalem, and Jeremiah the prophet was shut up in the court of the prison, which *was in* the king of Judah's house. ³For Zedekiah king of Judah had shut him up, saying, "Why do you prophesy and say, 'Thus says the LORD: "Behold, I will give this city into the hand of the king of Babylon, and he shall take it; ⁴and Zedekiah king of Judah shall not escape from the hand of the Chaldeans, but shall surely be delivered into the hand of the king of Babylon, and shall speak with him face to face,^a and see him eye to eye; ⁵then he shall lead Zedekiah to Babylon, and there he shall be until I visit him," says the LORD; "though you fight with the Chaldeans, you shall not succeed" ?' "

⁶And Jeremiah said, "The word of the LORD came to me, saying, ⁷"Behold, Hanamel the son of Shallum your uncle will come to you, saying, 'Buy my field which *is* in Anathoth, for the right of redemption *is* yours to buy *it*.' ' ⁸Then Hanamel my uncle's son came to me in the court of the prison according to the word of the LORD, and said to me, 'Please buy my field that *is* in Anathoth, which *is* in the country of Benjamin; for the right of inheritance *is* yours, and the redemption yours; buy *it* for yourself.' Then I knew that this was the word of the LORD. ⁹So I bought the field from Hanamel, the son of my uncle who *was* in Anathoth, and weighed *out to* him the money—seventeen shekels of silver. ¹⁰And I signed the deed and sealed *it,* took witnesses, and weighed the money on the

· · · · · · · · · · · · · · · ·

31:32 ^aFollowing Masoretic Text, Targum, and Vulgate; Septuagint and Syriac read *and I turned away from them.* **32:4** ^aLiterally *mouth to mouth*

31:31–34 God would establish a new covenant with His people. Unlike the covenant at Sinai which demanded outward obedience to external laws, this covenant would consist of inward spiritual renewal, which would enable the people to live in a right covenantal relationship with God. The new covenant is internal, universal, and unconditional. All people have the opportunity for an intimate personal relationship with the Lord. A primary element of this new covenant is forgiveness (Heb. *salach*). God would remember their sins no more. NT writers find the fulfillment of this prophecy in Jesus Christ (Heb. 8:7–13).

31:35–37 The foundation of the new covenant is as sure as the

God who providentially maintains creation. These rhetorical statements underscore the certainty of the prophecy.

32:2–5 Jeremiah had violated the cultural ethic of court prophets, committing the equivalent of treason by preaching the truth. Zedekiah threw him in prison.

32:7–15 Jeremiah was instructed to buy a field, a foolish decision in human terms. But this was God's sign that the Land eventually would be restored. Similarly, Abraham purchased ground in Canaan to bury Sarah, land which the Israelites eventually returned to reclaim (Gen. 23:1–20).

scales. [11]So I took the purchase deed, *both* that which was sealed *according* to the law and custom, and that which was open; [12]and I gave the purchase deed to Baruch the son of Neriah, son of Mahseiah, in the presence of Hanamel my uncle's *son,* and in the presence of the witnesses who signed the purchase deed, before all the Jews who sat in the court of the prison.

[13]"Then I charged Baruch before them, saying, [14]'Thus says the LORD of hosts, the God of Israel: "Take these deeds, both this purchase deed which is sealed and this deed which is open, and put them in an earthen vessel, that they may last many days." [15]For thus says the LORD of hosts, the God of Israel: "Houses and fields and vineyards shall be possessed again in this land." '

Jeremiah Prays for Understanding

[16]"Now when I had delivered the purchase deed to Baruch the son of Neriah, I prayed to the LORD, saying: [17]'Ah, Lord GOD! Behold, You have made the heavens and the earth by Your great power and outstretched arm. There is nothing too hard for You. [18]*You* show lovingkindness to thousands, and repay the iniquity of the fathers into the bosom of their children after them—the Great, the Mighty God, whose name *is* the LORD of hosts. [19]*You are* great in counsel and mighty in work, for Your eyes *are* open to all the ways of the sons of men, to give everyone according to his ways and according to the fruit of his doings. [20]You have set signs and wonders in the land of Egypt, to this day, and in Israel and among *other* men; and You have made Yourself a name, as it is this day. [21]You have brought Your people Israel out of the land of Egypt with signs and wonders, with a strong hand and an outstretched arm, and with great terror; [22]You have given them this land, of which You swore to their fathers to give them—"a land flowing with milk and honey."[a] [23]And they came in and took possession of it, but they have not obeyed Your voice or walked in Your law. They have done nothing of all that You commanded them to do; therefore You have caused all this calamity to come upon them.

[24]'Look, the siege mounds! They have come to the city to take it; and the city has been given into the hand of the Chaldeans who fight against it, because of the sword and famine and pestilence. What You have spoken has happened; there You see *it!* [25]And You have said to me, O Lord GOD, "Buy the field for money, and take witnesses"!—

yet the city has been given into the hand of the Chaldeans.' "

God's Assurance of the People's Return

[26]Then the word of the LORD came to Jeremiah, saying, [27]"Behold, I *am* the LORD, the God of all flesh. Is there anything too hard for Me? [28]Therefore thus says the LORD: 'Behold, I will give this city into the hand of the Chaldeans, into the hand of Nebuchadnezzar king of Babylon, and he shall take it. [29]And the Chaldeans who fight against this city shall come and set fire to this city and burn it, with the houses on whose roofs they have offered incense to Baal and poured out drink offerings to other gods, to provoke Me to anger; [30]because the children of Israel and the children of Judah have done only evil before Me from their youth. For the children of Israel have provoked Me only to anger with the work of their hands,' says the LORD. [31]'For this city has been to Me *a provocation of* My anger and My fury from the day that they built it, even to this day; so I will remove it from before My face [32]because of all the evil of the children of Israel and the children of Judah, which they have done to provoke Me to anger—they, their kings, their princes, their priests, their prophets, the men of Judah, and the inhabitants of Jerusalem. [33]And they have turned to Me the back, and not the face; though I taught them, rising up early and teaching *them,* yet they have not listened to receive instruction. [34]But they set their abominations in the house which is called by My name, to defile it. [35]And they built the high places of Baal which *are* in the Valley of the Son of Hinnom, to cause their sons and their daughters to pass through *the fire* to Molech, which I did not command them, nor did it come into My mind that they should do this abomination, to cause Judah to sin.'

[36]"Now therefore, thus says the LORD, the God of Israel, concerning this city of which you say, 'It shall be delivered into the hand of the king of Babylon by the sword, by the famine, and by the pestilence: [37]Behold, I will gather them out of all countries where I have driven them in My anger, in My fury, and in great wrath; I will bring them back to this place, and I will cause them to dwell safely. [38]They shall be My people, and I will be their God; [39]then I will give them one heart and one way, that they may fear Me forever, for the

---

32:22 [a]Exodus 3:8

32:16–25 Jeremiah seemed to doubt what God had instructed him to do, even though he had preached the answer (see v. 15). But he responded by asking for God's help, providing insight into his prayer life. The prayer consisted almost entirely of praise, acknowledging God for His sovereign lovingkindness and His marvelous deeds in redeeming Israel. Jeremiah took his doubts to the Lord.

32:26–44 The answer God gave is a summary of everything He had proclaimed through Jeremiah to this point—His judgment on the sin of Judah and His promise to restore them in the future. What Jeremiah needed was a reminder. This principle of remembrance and repetition of truth is a biblical one (Deut. 6:4–9, 20–25).

PRAYER   ROOTED IN GOD'S PROMISES

Prayer is one way in which the believer claims the promises of God. Through prayer God reveals His character and His blessings. His precious promises are apparent to believers as they pray (2 Pet. 1:2–4).

God makes several promises to His children who are committed to prayer. First and foremost, He promises a *response*. God promises to hear and to answer the prayer of every sinner who seek forgiveness and to act on the request of every believer who asks in faith. Jesus told His disciples that the Father would do anything asked in His name (John 14:13, 14).

To the believer, God's answer at first may be unclear or different from the answer expected or desired, or the answer may be delayed. God's answers include "yes," "no," and "wait." You must recognize in praying that sometimes you ask the Lord to do things that are not for your good, the good of others, or the ultimate fulfillment of God's plan. You see life from a limited, finite viewpoint; He alone can see the beginning and ending of all things. The Lord alone knows how your prayer requests fit into His purpose—which is both for your good and the good of all other believers.

Second, God promises His *presence* through prayer. When you are called by name, you should respond with attention. When you call God by name, He gives you His ear. From the time of salvation, a believer is promised the presence of the Holy Spirit as Helper, Tutor, and Guide (Acts 2:33). The Holy Spirit through His presence fulfills the promises of God to and in believers.

Third, God promises His *wisdom* as believers pray. Often during a time of crisis, a believer does not know how to pray. At other times a believer may not know what to pray. You can take heart at those times in knowing that the Holy Spirit helps the believer to pray (Jude 20). God promises to answer the sincere intent of the heart, even if you cannot find the "right words." When a believer prays in faith, God does even more than He is asked (Jer. 33:3). He answers us liberally, abundantly, and generously.

See also Dan. 2:33, note; John 14:13, 14; notes on Prayer (Heb. 4; 1 John 5; 3 John); Promises of God (2 Pet. 1)

good of them and their children after them. ⁴⁰And I will make an everlasting covenant with them, that I will not turn away from doing them good; but I will put My fear in their hearts so that they will not depart from Me. ⁴¹Yes, I will rejoice over them to do them good, and I will assuredly plant them in this land, with all My heart and with all My soul.'

⁴²"For thus says the LORD: 'Just as I have brought all this great calamity on this people, so I will bring on them all the good that I have promised them. ⁴³And fields will be bought in this land of which you say, "*It is* desolate, without man or beast; it has been given into the hand of the Chaldeans." ⁴⁴Men will buy fields for money, sign deeds and seal *them,* and take witnesses, in the land of Benjamin, in the places around Jerusalem, in the cities of Judah, in the cities of the mountains, in the cities of the lowland, and in the cities of the South; for I will cause their captives to return,' says the LORD."

Excellence of the Restored Nation

33 Moreover the word of the LORD came to Jeremiah a second time, while he was still shut up in the court of the prison, saying, ²"Thus says the LORD who made it, the LORD who formed it to establish it (the LORD *is* His name): ³'Call to Me, and I will answer you, and show you great and mighty things, which you do not know.'

⁴"For thus says the LORD, the God of Israel, concerning the houses of this city and the houses of the kings of Judah, which have been pulled down *to fortify*ᵃ against the siege mounds and the sword: ⁵'They come to fight with the Chaldeans, but *only* to fill their placesᵃ with the dead bodies of men whom I will slay in My anger and My fury, all for whose wickedness I have hidden My face from this city. ⁶Behold, I will bring it health and healing; I will heal them and reveal to them the abundance of peace and truth. ⁷And I will cause the captives of Judah and the captives of Israel to return, and will rebuild those places as at the first. ⁸I will cleanse them from all their iniquity by which they have sinned against Me, and I will pardon all their iniquities by which they have sinned and by which they have transgressed against Me. ⁹Then it shall be to Me a name of joy, a praise, and

· · · · · · · · · · · · · · · · ·
33:4 ᵃCompare Isaiah 22:10   **33:5** ᵃCompare 2 Kings 23:14

33:3 Call to Me is a sign of the great love of God for His prophet. He invited Jeremiah to pray and then promised an answer to that prayer beyond Jeremiah's present understanding. God's people are invited to do the same (John 15:16).

33:6–18 The time of restoration would bring joy such as that

of the bride and bridegroom at a wedding feast. As is common in prophetic literature, the passage begins with the current situation and then merges seamlessly with the messianic age. The elements of forgiveness of sin, healing, restoration, and prosperity appear.

an honor before all nations of the earth, who shall hear all the good that I do to them; they shall fear and tremble for all the goodness and all the prosperity that I provide for it.'

10"Thus says the LORD: 'Again there shall be heard in this place— of which you say, "It *is* desolate, without man and without beast"— in the cities of Judah, in the streets of Jerusalem that are desolate, without man and without inhabitant and without beast, 11the voice of joy and the voice of gladness, the voice of the bridegroom and the voice of the bride, the voice of those who will say:

"Praise the LORD of hosts,
For the LORD *is* good,
For His mercy *endures* forever"—

and of those *who will* bring the sacrifice of praise into the house of the LORD. For I will cause the captives of the land to return as at the first,' says the LORD.

12"Thus says the LORD of hosts: 'In this place which is desolate, without man and without beast, and in all its cities, there shall again be a dwelling place of shepherds causing *their* flocks to lie down. 13In the cities of the mountains, in the cities of the lowland, in the cities of the South, in the land of Benjamin, in the places around Jerusalem, and in the cities of Judah, the flocks shall again pass under the hands of him who counts *them*,' says the LORD.

14'Behold, the days are coming,' says the LORD, 'that I will perform that good thing which I have promised to the house of Israel and to the house of Judah:

15'In those days and at that time
I will cause to grow up to David
A Branch of righteousness;
He shall execute judgment and righteousness
    in the earth.
16In those days Judah will be saved,
And Jerusalem will dwell safely.
And this *is the name* by which she will be
    called:

THE LORD OUR RIGHTEOUSNESS.'a

17"For thus says the LORD: 'David shall never lack a man to sit on the throne of the house of Israel; 18nor shall the priests, the Levites, lack a man to offer burnt offerings before Me, to kindle grain offerings, and to sacrifice continually.' "

The Permanence of God's Covenant

19And the word of the LORD came to Jeremiah, saying, 20"Thus says the LORD: 'If you can break My covenant with the day and My covenant with the night, so that there will not be day and night in their season, 21then My covenant may also be broken with David My servant, so that he shall not have a son to reign on his throne, and with the Levites, the priests, My ministers. 22As the host of heaven cannot be numbered, nor the sand of the sea measured, so will I multiply the descendants of David My servant and the Levites who minister to Me.' "

23Moreover the word of the LORD came to Jeremiah, saying, 24"Have you not considered what these people have spoken, saying, 'The two families which the LORD has chosen, He has also cast them off'? Thus they have despised My people, as if they should no more be a nation before them.

25"Thus says the LORD: 'If My covenant *is* not with day and night, *and if* I have not appointed the ordinances of heaven and earth, 26then I will cast away the descendants of Jacob and David My servant, *so* that I will not take *any* of his descendants *to be* rulers over the descendants of Abraham, Isaac, and Jacob. For I will cause their captives to return, and will have mercy on them.' "

Zedekiah Warned by God

34 The word which came to Jeremiah from the LORD, when Nebuchadnezzar king of Babylon and all his army, all the kingdoms of the earth under his dominion, and all the people, fought against Jerusalem and all its cities, saying, 2"Thus says the LORD, the God of Israel: 'Go and speak to Zedekiah king of Judah and tell him, "Thus says the LORD: 'Behold, I will give this city into the hand of the king of Babylon, and he shall burn it with fire. 3And you shall not escape from his hand, but shall surely be taken and delivered into his hand; your eyes shall see the eyes of the king of Babylon, he shall speak with you face to face,a and you shall go to Babylon.' " ' 4Yet hear the word of the LORD, O Zedekiah king of Judah! Thus says the LORD concerning you: 'You shall not die by the sword. 5You shall die in peace; as in the ceremonies of your fathers, the former kings who were before you, so they shall burn *incense* for you and lament for you, *saying,* "Alas, lord!" For I have pronounced the word, says the LORD.' "

33:16 aCompare 23:5, 6   **34:3** aLiterally *mouth to mouth*

33:17, 18 Jesus, as Priest and King, fulfills both offices in the NT.

33:22 The Davidic covenant is a renewal of the covenant given to Abraham (Gen. 22:17). In the NT, Jesus is the further fulfillment of this covenant (Matt. 1:1).

34:1–7 God in His grace and justice often seems to respond to individuals in the measure they turn to Him. God showed a certain measure of grace to Zedekiah. This was in keeping with a partial repentance (see vv. 18–22) after the pattern of Ahab's shallow, albeit sincere, repentance (1 Kin. 21:27–29).

⁶Then Jeremiah the prophet spoke all these words to Zedekiah king of Judah in Jerusalem, ⁷when the king of Babylon's army fought against Jerusalem and all the cities of Judah that were left, against Lachish and Azekah; for *only* these fortified cities remained of the cities of Judah.

Treacherous Treatment of Slaves

⁸*This is* the word that came to Jeremiah from the LORD, after King Zedekiah had made a covenant with all the people who *were* at Jerusalem to proclaim liberty to them: ⁹that every man should set free his male and female slave—a Hebrew man or woman—that no one should keep a Jewish brother in bondage. ¹⁰Now when all the princes and all the people, who had entered into the covenant, heard that everyone should set free his male and female slaves, that no one should keep them in bondage anymore, they obeyed and let *them* go. ¹¹But afterward they changed their minds and made the male and female slaves return, whom they had set free, and brought them into subjection as male and female slaves.

¹²Therefore the word of the LORD came to Jeremiah from the LORD, saying, ¹³"Thus says the LORD, the God of Israel: 'I made a covenant with your fathers in the day that I brought them out of the land of Egypt, out of the house of bondage, saying, ¹⁴"At the end of seven years let every man set free his Hebrew brother, who has been sold to him; and when he has served you six years, you shall let him go free from you." But your fathers did not obey Me nor incline their ear. ¹⁵Then you recently turned and did what was right in My sight—every man proclaiming liberty to his neighbor; and you made a covenant before Me in the house which is called by My name. ¹⁶Then you turned around and profaned My name, and every one of you brought back his male and female slaves, whom you had set at liberty, at their pleasure, and brought them back into subjection, to be your male and female slaves.'

¹⁷"Therefore thus says the LORD: 'You have not obeyed Me in proclaiming liberty, every one to his brother and every one to his neighbor. Behold, I proclaim liberty to you,' says the LORD—'to the sword, to pestilence, and to famine! And I will deliver you to trouble among all the kingdoms of the earth. ¹⁸And I will give the men who have transgressed My covenant, who have not performed the words of the covenant which they made before Me, when they cut the calf in two and passed between the parts of it— ¹⁹the princes of Judah, the princes of Jerusalem, the eunuchs, the priests, and all the people of the land who passed between the parts of the calf— ²⁰I will give them into the hand of their enemies and into the hand of those who seek their life. Their dead bodies shall be for meat for the birds of the heaven and the beasts of the earth. ²¹And I will give Zedekiah king of Judah and his princes into the hand of their enemies, into the hand of those who seek their life, and into the hand of the king of Babylon's army which has gone back from you. ²²Behold, I will command,' says the LORD, 'and cause them to return to this city. They will fight against it and take it and burn it with fire; and I will make the cities of Judah a desolation without inhabitant.'"

The Obedient Rechabites

35 The word which came to Jeremiah from the LORD in the days of Jehoiakim the son of Josiah, king of Judah, saying, ²"Go to the house of the Rechabites, speak to them, and bring them into the house of the LORD, into one of the chambers, and give them wine to drink."

³Then I took Jaazaniah the son of Jeremiah, the son of Habazziniah, his brothers and all his sons, and the whole house of the Rechabites, ⁴and I brought them into the house of the LORD, into the chamber of the sons of Hanan the son of Igdaliah, a man of God, which *was* by the chamber of the princes, above the chamber of Maaseiah the son of Shallum, the keeper of the door. ⁵Then I set be-

---

34:8–22 The attempt to release all the slaves and fulfill Leviticus 25:54 was halfhearted at best. To reenslave them was worse than not releasing them at all and so earned a harsher judgment. The institution of slavery in Israel was quite different from slavery in the western world. Rather than racially based, slavery was an economic provision intended to prevent absolute destitution of those who had no other recourse. Strict laws protected the rights of slaves. Though a foreigner theoretically could be kept a slave in perpetuity (since he was not a member of God's people), a fellow Israelite had to be freed in the Year of Jubilee, unless he decided to remain a slave out of love for his master (Lev. 25:39–55; see chart, The Principle of the Sabbath).

34:18 To cut a covenant is a literal Hebrew expression that refers to the making of a covenant. The two parties butchered an animal, divided it into several parts, and walked between the pieces, reciting the terms of the covenant (Gen.

15:9–18). The idea here is "may God so do to me as we have done to this animal if I do not fulfill the terms of the covenant." God would punish His people for their failure to obey Him by freeing the slaves (Jer. 34:18–20).

35:1 Jehoiakim began to rule in 609 B.C. and Zedekiah in 597 B.C. The placement of this passage (recording events some 10 years earlier than the previous chapters) illustrates the nonchronological nature of the Book of Jeremiah (see Introduction: Date).

35:2 The Rechabites were descendants of Jonadab, the son of Rechab, who taught his relatives to abstain from wine, building houses, and agriculture. Jonadab was a strong opponent of Baal worship. The Baals were fertility gods. Jonadab's instructions were meant to guard against his descendants becoming involved in Baal worship (2 Kin. 10:15–28). All Jonadab's descendants faithfully had carried out his instructions.

fore the sons of the house of the Rechabites bowls full of wine, and cups; and I said to them, "Drink wine."

⁶But they said, "We will drink no wine, for Jonadab the son of Rechab, our father, commanded us, saying, 'You shall drink no wine, you nor your sons, forever. ⁷You shall not build a house, sow seed, plant a vineyard, nor have *any of these;* but all your days you shall dwell in tents, that you may live many days in the land where you are sojourners.' ⁸Thus we have obeyed the voice of Jonadab the son of Rechab, our father, in all that he charged us, to drink no wine all our days, we, our wives, our sons, or our daughters, ⁹nor to build ourselves houses to dwell in; nor do we have vineyard, field, or seed. ¹⁰But we have dwelt in tents, and have obeyed and done according to all that Jonadab our father commanded us. ¹¹But it came to pass, when Nebuchadnezzar king of Babylon came up into the land, that we said, 'Come, let us go to Jerusalem for fear of the army of the Chaldeans and for fear of the army of the Syrians.' So we dwell at Jerusalem."

¹²Then came the word of the LORD to Jeremiah, saying, ¹³"Thus says the LORD of hosts, the God of Israel: 'Go and tell the men of Judah and the inhabitants of Jerusalem, "Will you not receive instruction to obey My words?" says the LORD. ¹⁴"The words of Jonadab the son of Rechab, which he commanded his sons, not to drink wine, are performed; for to this day they drink none, and obey their father's commandment. But although I have spoken to you, rising early and speaking, you did not obey Me. ¹⁵I have also sent to you all My servants the prophets, rising up early and sending *them,* saying, 'Turn now everyone from his evil way, amend your doings, and do not go after other gods to serve them; then you will dwell in the land which I have given you and your fathers.' But you have not inclined your ear, nor obeyed Me. ¹⁶Surely the sons of Jonadab the son of Rechab have performed the commandment of their father, which he commanded them, but this people has not obeyed Me." '

¹⁷"Therefore thus says the LORD God of hosts, the God of Israel: 'Behold, I will bring on Judah and on all the inhabitants of Jerusalem all the doom that I have pronounced against them; because I have spoken to them but they have not heard, and I have called to them but they have not answered.' "

¹⁸And Jeremiah said to the house of the Rechabites, "Thus says the LORD of hosts, the God of Israel: 'Because you have obeyed the commandment of Jonadab your father, and kept all his precepts and done according to all that he commanded you, ¹⁹therefore thus says the LORD of hosts, the God of Israel: "Jonadab the son of Rechab shall not lack a man to stand before Me forever." ' "

The Scroll Read in the Temple

36 Now it came to pass in the fourth year of Jehoiakim the son of Josiah, king of Judah, *that* this word came to Jeremiah from the LORD, saying: ²"Take a scroll of a book and write on it all the words that I have spoken to you against Israel, against Judah, and against all the nations, from the day I spoke to you, from the days of Josiah even to this day. ³It may be that the house of Judah will hear all the adversities which I purpose to bring upon them, that everyone may turn from his evil way, that I may forgive their iniquity and their sin."

⁴Then Jeremiah called Baruch the son of Neriah; and Baruch wrote on a scroll of a book, at the instruction of Jeremiah,ᵃ all the words of the LORD which He had spoken to him. ⁵And Jeremiah commanded Baruch, saying, "I *am* confined, I cannot go into the house of the LORD. ⁶You go, therefore, and read from the scroll which you have written at my instruction,ᵃ the words of the LORD, in the hearing of the people in the LORD's house on the day of fasting. And you shall also read them in the hearing of all Judah who come from their cities. ⁷It may be that they will present their supplication before the LORD, and everyone will turn from his evil way. For great *is* the anger and the fury that the LORD has pronounced against this people." ⁸And Baruch the son of Neriah did according to all that Jeremiah the prophet commanded him, reading from the book the words of the LORD in the LORD's house.

⁹Now it came to pass in the fifth year of Jehoiakim the son of Josiah, king of Judah, in the ninth month, *that* they proclaimed a fast before the LORD to all the people in Jerusalem, and to all the people who came from the cities of Judah to Jerusalem. ¹⁰Then Baruch read from the book the words of Jeremiah in the house of the LORD, in the

36:4 ᵃLiterally *from Jeremiah's mouth*   36:6 ᵃLiterally *from my mouth*

35:14 Father often is used of a remote ancestor. The faithfulness of the Rechabites became an example and a rebuke to the people of Judah. If the Rechabites were willing to obey their earthly ancestor, how much more the Israelites should obey God, who created and redeemed them.

36:4 Baruch acted as Jeremiah's amanuensis—a secretary or assistant.

36:6 The ability to read in ancient times often was restricted to the upper classes and those with special training, such as scribes. Only at such public gatherings would the common people hear the Word of God (or any written work) read.

36:9 Fasting was common, particularly in times of distress. Isaiah rebuked the merely outward ritual of fasting that lacked heartfelt repentance (Is. 58; see Matt. 6:16–18, note).

chamber of Gemariah the son of Shaphan the scribe, in the upper court at the entry of the New Gate of the LORD's house, in the hearing of all the people.

The Scroll Read in the Palace

[11]When Michaiah the son of Gemariah, the son of Shaphan, heard all the words of the LORD from the book, [12]he then went down to the king's house, into the scribe's chamber; and there all the princes were sitting—Elishama the scribe, Delaiah the son of Shemaiah, Elnathan the son of Achbor, Gemariah the son of Shaphan, Zedekiah the son of Hananiah, and all the princes. [13]Then Michaiah declared to them all the words that he had heard when Baruch read the book in the hearing of the people. [14]Therefore all the princes sent Jehudi the son of Nethaniah, the son of Shelemiah, the son of Cushi, to Baruch, saying, "Take in your hand the scroll from which you have read in the hearing of the people, and come." So Baruch the son of Neriah took the scroll in his hand and came to them. [15]And they said to him, "Sit down now, and read it in our hearing." So Baruch read it in their hearing.

[16]Now it happened, when they had heard all the words, that they looked in fear from one to another, and said to Baruch, "We will surely tell the king of all these words." [17]And they asked Baruch, saying, "Tell us now, how did you write all these words—at his instruction?"[a]

[18]So Baruch answered them, "He proclaimed with his mouth all these words to me, and I wrote them with ink in the book."

[19]Then the princes said to Baruch, "Go and hide, you and Jeremiah; and let no one know where you are."

The King Destroys Jeremiah's Scroll

[20]And they went to the king, into the court; but they stored the scroll in the chamber of Elishama the scribe, and told all the words in the hearing of the king. [21]So the king sent Jehudi to bring the scroll, and he took it from Elishama the scribe's chamber. And Jehudi read it in the hearing of the king and in the hearing of all the princes who stood beside the king. [22]Now the king was sitting in the winter house in the ninth month, with a fire burning on the hearth before him. [23]And it happened, when Jehudi had read three or four columns, that the king cut it with the scribe's knife and cast it into the fire that was on the hearth, until all the scroll was consumed in the fire that was on the hearth. [24]Yet they were not afraid, nor did they tear their garments, the king nor any of his servants who heard all these words. [25]Nevertheless Elnathan, Delaiah, and Gemariah implored the king not to burn the scroll; but he would not listen to them. [26]And the king commanded Jerahmeel the king's[a] son, Seraiah the son of Azriel, and Shelemiah the son of Abdeel, to seize Baruch the scribe and Jeremiah the prophet, but the LORD hid them.

Jeremiah Rewrites the Scroll

[27]Now after the king had burned the scroll with the words which Baruch had written at the instruction of Jeremiah,[a] the word of the LORD came to Jeremiah, saying: [28]"Take yet another scroll, and write on it all the former words that were in the first scroll which Jehoiakim the king of Judah has burned. [29]And you shall say to Jehoiakim king of Judah, 'Thus says the LORD: "You have burned this scroll, saying, 'Why have you written in it that the king of Babylon will certainly come and destroy this land, and cause man and beast to cease from here?' " [30]Therefore thus says the LORD concerning Jehoiakim king of Judah: "He shall have no one to sit on the throne of David, and his dead body shall be cast out to the heat of the day and the frost of the night. [31]I will punish him, his family, and his servants for their iniquity; and I will bring on them, on the inhabitants of Jerusalem, and on the men of Judah all the doom that I have pronounced against them; but they did not heed." ' "

[32]Then Jeremiah took another scroll and gave it to Baruch the scribe, the son of Neriah, who wrote on it at the instruction of Jeremiah[a] all the words of the book which Jehoiakim king of Judah had burned in the fire. And besides, there were added to them many similar words.

Zedekiah's Vain Hope

37 Now King Zedekiah the son of Josiah reigned instead of Coniah the son of Jehoiakim, whom Nebuchadnezzar king of Babylon made king in the land of Judah. [2]But neither he

....

36:17 [a]Literally with his mouth   36:26 [a]Hebrew Hammelech   36:27 [a]Literally from Jeremiah's mouth   36:32 [a]Literally from Jeremiah's mouth

---

36:11–19 The princes, whether sympathetic to Jeremiah or not, realized the political import of Jeremiah's message and the potential danger to him. They, therefore, warned him to hide in order to escape the king's wrath. Their suspicions were well-founded.

36:27–32 God's Word cannot be destroyed. God instructed Jeremiah to rewrite the scroll, adding to it. The attempt to sup-

press God's Word resulted in its increase (v. 32). For his act of rebellion, the king received a punishment reserved for the worst of the kings of Israel and Judah—the complete overthrow of his dynasty (1 Kin. 21:20–23).

37:1 The Babylonians, as later did the Romans, left much of the local power structure and religion of a conquered people intact, as long as they submitted by paying tribute and by

nor his servants nor the people of the land gave heed to the words of the LORD which He spoke by the prophet Jeremiah.

³And Zedekiah the king sent Jehucal the son of Shelemiah, and Zephaniah the son of Maaseiah, the priest, to the prophet Jeremiah, saying, "Pray now to the LORD our God for us." ⁴Now Jeremiah was coming and going among the people, for they had not *yet* put him in prison. ⁵Then Pharaoh's army came up from Egypt; and when the Chaldeans who were besieging Jerusalem heard news of them, they departed from Jerusalem.

⁶Then the word of the LORD came to the prophet Jeremiah, saying, ⁷"Thus says the LORD, the God of Israel, 'Thus you shall say to the king of Judah, who sent you to Me to inquire of Me: "Behold, Pharaoh's army which has come up to help you will return to Egypt, to their own land. ⁸And the Chaldeans shall come back and fight against this city, and take it and burn it with fire." ' ⁹Thus says the LORD: 'Do not deceive yourselves, saying, "The Chaldeans will surely depart from us," for they will not depart. ¹⁰For though you had defeated the whole army of the Chaldeans who fight against you, and there remained *only* wounded men among them, they would rise up, every man in his tent, and burn the city with fire.' "

Jeremiah Imprisoned

¹¹And it happened, when the army of the Chaldeans left *the siege* of Jerusalem for fear of Pharaoh's army, ¹²that Jeremiah went out of Jerusalem to go into the land of Benjamin to claim his property there among the people. ¹³And when he was in the Gate of Benjamin, a captain of the guard *was* there whose name *was* Irijah the son of Shelemiah, the son of Hananiah; and he seized Jeremiah the prophet, saying, "You are defecting to the Chaldeans!"

¹⁴Then Jeremiah said, "False! I am not defecting to the Chaldeans." But he did not listen to him.

So Irijah seized Jeremiah and brought him to the princes. ¹⁵Therefore the princes were angry with Jeremiah, and they struck him and put him in prison in the house of Jonathan the scribe. For they had made that the prison.

¹⁶When Jeremiah entered the dungeon and the cells, and Jeremiah had remained there many days, ¹⁷then Zedekiah the king sent and took him *out.*

The king asked him secretly in his house, and said, "Is there *any* word from the LORD?"

And Jeremiah said, "There is." Then he said, "You shall be delivered into the hand of the king of Babylon!"

¹⁸Moreover Jeremiah said to King Zedekiah, "What offense have I committed against you, against your servants, or against this people, that you have put me in prison? ¹⁹Where now *are* your prophets who prophesied to you, saying, 'The king of Babylon will not come against you or against this land'? ²⁰Therefore please hear now, O my lord the king. Please, let my petition be accepted before you, and do not make me return to the house of Jonathan the scribe, lest I die there."

²¹Then Zedekiah the king commanded that they should commit Jeremiah to the court of the prison, and that they should give him daily a piece of bread from the bakers' street, until all the bread in the city was gone. Thus Jeremiah remained in the court of the prison.

Jeremiah in the Dungeon

38 Now Shephatiah the son of Mattan, Gedaliah the son of Pashhur, Jucalᵃ the son of Shelemiah, and Pashhur the son of Malchiah heard the words that Jeremiah had spoken to all the people, saying, ²"Thus says the LORD: 'He who remains in this city shall die by the sword, by famine, and by pestilence; but he who goes over to the Chaldeans shall live; his life shall be as a prize to him, and he shall live.'ᵃ ³Thus says the LORD: 'This city shall surely be given into the hand of the king of Babylon's army, which shall take it.' "

⁴Therefore the princes said to the king, "Please, let this man be put to death, for thus he weakens the hands of the men of war who remain in this city, and the hands of all the people, by speaking such words to them. For this man does not seek the welfare of this people, but their harm."

⁵Then Zedekiah the king said, "Look, he *is* in your hand. For the king can *do* nothing against you." ⁶So they took Jeremiah and cast him into the dungeon of Malchiah the king'sᵃ son, which *was* in the court of the prison, and they let Jeremiah down with ropes. And in the dungeon *there was* no water, but mire. So Jeremiah sank in the mire.

38:1 ᵃSame as *Jehucal* (compare 37:3)   **38:2** ᵃCompare 21:9   **38:6** ᵃHebrew *Hammelech*

37:3 Zedekiah sought Jeremiah's intervention under the pressure of the impending attack. Though there was temporary reprieve, the prophecy of destruction remained in effect.

38:4 Jeremiah was charged with treason because he counseled surrender to the Babylonians. The princes' response to Jeremiah's preaching reveals their lack of faith and their rebellion against God.

supporting the greater interests of the empire. Zedekiah must have agreed to similar stipulations with Nebuchadnezzar, but he later broke the agreement and came under the emperor's wrath. The breaking of the human covenant and its consequences parallels the breaking of the divine covenant and the resulting judgment.

⁷Now Ebed-Melech the Ethiopian, one of the eunuchs, who was in the king's house, heard that they had put Jeremiah in the dungeon. When the king was sitting at the Gate of Benjamin, ⁸Ebed-Melech went out of the king's house and spoke to the king, saying: ⁹"My lord the king, these men have done evil in all that they have done to Jeremiah the prophet, whom they have cast into the dungeon, and he is likely to die from hunger in the place where he is. For *there is* no more bread in the city." ¹⁰Then the king commanded Ebed-Melech the Ethiopian, saying, "Take from here thirty men with you, and lift Jeremiah the prophet out of the dungeon before he dies." ¹¹So Ebed-Melech took the men with him and went into the house of the king under the treasury, and took from there old clothes and old rags, and let them down by ropes into the dungeon to Jeremiah. ¹²Then Ebed-Melech the Ethiopian said to Jeremiah, "Please put these old clothes and rags under your armpits, under the ropes." And Jeremiah did so. ¹³So they pulled Jeremiah up with ropes and lifted him out of the dungeon. And Jeremiah remained in the court of the prison.

Zedekiah's Fears and Jeremiah's Advice

¹⁴Then Zedekiah the king sent and had Jeremiah the prophet brought to him at the third entrance of the house of the LORD. And the king said to Jeremiah, "I will ask you something. Hide nothing from me."

¹⁵Jeremiah said to Zedekiah, "If I declare *it* to you, will you not surely put me to death? And if I give you advice, you will not listen to me."

¹⁶So Zedekiah the king swore secretly to Jeremiah, saying, "*As* the LORD lives, who made our very souls, I will not put you to death, nor will I give you into the hand of these men who seek your life."

¹⁷Then Jeremiah said to Zedekiah, "Thus says the LORD, the God of hosts, the God of Israel: 'If you surely surrender to the king of Babylon's princes, then your soul shall live; this city shall not be burned with fire, and you and your house shall live. ¹⁸But if you do not surrender to the king of Babylon's princes, then this city shall be given into the hand of the Chaldeans; they shall burn it with fire, and you shall not escape from their hand.' "

¹⁹And Zedekiah the king said to Jeremiah, "I am afraid of the Jews who have defected to the Chaldeans, lest they deliver me into their hand, and they abuse me."

²⁰But Jeremiah said, "They shall not deliver *you.* Please, obey the voice of the LORD which I speak to you. So it shall be well with you, and your soul shall live. ²¹But if you refuse to surrender, this *is* the word that the LORD has shown me: ²²'Now behold, all the women who are left in the king of Judah's house *shall be* surrendered to the king of Babylon's princes, and those *women* shall say:

"Your close friends have set upon you
  And prevailed against you;
Your feet have sunk in the mire,
  And they have turned away again."

²³'So they shall surrender all your wives and children to the Chaldeans. You shall not escape from their hand, but shall be taken by the hand of the king of Babylon. And you shall cause this city to be burned with fire.' "

²⁴Then Zedekiah said to Jeremiah, "Let no one know of these words, and you shall not die. ²⁵But if the princes hear that I have talked with you, and they come to you and say to you, 'Declare to us now what you have said to the king, and also what the king said to you; do not hide *it* from us, and we will not put you to death,' ²⁶then you shall say to them, 'I presented my request before the king, that he would not make me return to Jonathan's house to die there.' "

²⁷Then all the princes came to Jeremiah and asked him. And he told them according to all these words that the king had commanded. So they stopped speaking with him, for the conversation had not been heard. ²⁸Now Jeremiah remained in the court of the prison until the day that Jerusalem was taken. And he was *there* when Jerusalem was taken.

The Fall of Jerusalem

39In the ninth year of Zedekiah king of Judah, in the tenth month, Nebuchadnezzar king of Babylon and all his army came against Jerusalem, and besieged it. ²In the eleventh year of Zedekiah, in the fourth month, on the ninth *day* of the month, the city was penetrated.

³Then all the princes of the king of Babylon came in and sat in the Middle Gate: Nergal-Sharezer, Samgar-Nebo, Sarsechim, Rabsaris,ª Nergal-Sarezer, Rabmag,ᵇ with the rest of the princes of the king of Babylon.

• • • • • • • • • • • • • • • • • •

39:3 ªA title, probably *Chief Officer;* also verse 13 ᵇA title, probably *Troop Commander;* also verse 13

38:7 Ebed-Melech (Heb., lit. "servant of the king") is likely a title rather than a personal name. Ironically, a foreigner, rather than one of God's own people, led the attempt to rescue Jeremiah.

38:14 Zedekiah, to his credit, listened sincerely to Jeremiah's message, though he did not obey. This attitude also may have contributed to God's mercy shown to him (see Jer. 34:4, 5).

39:1 Jeremiah and his message were vindicated by the historical reality of the fall of Jerusalem in 586 B.C. The treatment accorded Jerusalem is typical imperial punishment for a city in rebellion.

39:3 The elders would sit in the gate and conduct the government of a small town. This action of the princes of the Babylonian king indicated their control of the city.

⁴So it was, when Zedekiah the king of Judah and all the men of war saw them, that they fled and went out of the city by night, by way of the king's garden, by the gate between the two walls. And he went out by way of the plain.ᵃ ⁵But the Chaldean army pursued them and overtook Zedekiah in the plains of Jericho. And when they had captured him, they brought him up to Nebuchadnezzar king of Babylon, to Riblah in the land of Hamath, where he pronounced judgment on him. ⁶Then the king of Babylon killed the sons of Zedekiah before his eyes in Riblah; the king of Babylon also killed all the nobles of Judah. ⁷Moreover he put out Zedekiah's eyes, and bound him with bronze fetters to carry him off to Babylon. ⁸And the Chaldeans burned the king's house and the houses of the people with fire, and broke down the walls of Jerusalem. ⁹Then Nebuzaradan the captain of the guard carried away captive to Babylon the remnant of the people who remained in the city and those who defected to him, with the rest of the people who remained. ¹⁰But Nebuzaradan the captain of the guard left in the land of Judah the poor people, who had nothing, and gave them vineyards and fields at the same time.

Jeremiah Goes Free

¹¹Now Nebuchadnezzar king of Babylon gave charge concerning Jeremiah to Nebuzaradan the captain of the guard, saying, ¹²"Take him and look after him, and do him no harm; but do to him just as he says to you." ¹³So Nebuzaradan the captain of the guard sent Nebushasban, Rabsaris, Nergal-Sharezer, Rabmag, and all the king of Babylon's chief officers; ¹⁴then they sent *someone* to take Jeremiah from the court of the prison, and committed him to Gedaliah the son of Ahikam, the son of Shaphan, that he should take him home. So he dwelt among the people.

¹⁵Meanwhile the word of the LORD had come to Jeremiah while he was shut up in the court of the prison, saying, ¹⁶"Go and speak to Ebed-Melech the Ethiopian, saying, 'Thus says the LORD of hosts, the God of Israel: "Behold, I will bring My words upon this city for adversity and not for good, and they shall be *performed* in that day before you. ¹⁷But I will deliver you in that day," says the LORD, "and you shall not be given into the hand of the men of whom you *are* afraid. ¹⁸For I will surely deliver you, and you shall not fall by the sword; but your life shall be as a prize to you, because you have put your trust in Me," says the LORD.'"

Jeremiah with Gedaliah the Governor

40 The word that came to Jeremiah from the LORD after Nebuzaradan the captain of the guard had let him go from Ramah, when he had taken him bound in chains among all who were carried away captive from Jerusalem and Judah, who were carried away captive to Babylon.

²And the captain of the guard took Jeremiah and said to him: "The LORD your God has pronounced this doom on this place. ³Now the LORD has brought *it,* and has done just as He said. Because you *people* have sinned against the LORD, and not obeyed His voice, therefore this thing has come upon you. ⁴And now look, I free you this day from the chains that *were* on your hand. If it seems good to you to come with me to Babylon, come, and I will look after you. But if it seems wrong for you to come with me to Babylon, remain here. See, all the land *is* before you; wherever it seems good and convenient for you to go, go there."

⁵Now while Jeremiah had not yet gone back, *Nebuzaradan said,* "Go back to Gedaliah the son of Ahikam, the son of Shaphan, whom the king of Babylon has made governor over the cities of Judah, and dwell with him among the people. Or go wherever it seems convenient for you to go." So the captain of the guard gave him rations and a gift and let him go. ⁶Then Jeremiah went to Gedaliah the son of Ahikam, to Mizpah, and dwelt with him among the people who were left in the land.

⁷And when all the captains of the armies who *were* in the fields, they and their men, heard that the king of Babylon had made Gedaliah the son of Ahikam governor in the land, and had committed to him men, women, children, and the poorest of the land who had not been carried away captive to Babylon, ⁸then they came to Gedaliah at Mizpah—Ishmael the son of Nethaniah, Johanan and Jonathan the sons of Kareah, Seraiah the son of Tanhumeth,

39:4 ᵃOr *the Arabah,* that is, the Jordan Valley

39:5, 6 Zedekiah's suffering was indeed great. Jeremiah had not prophesied that Zedekiah would escape suffering, since his sins were grievous, but that Zedekiah would die in peace and receive a burial fit for a king (Jer. 34:5).

39:12 Jeremiah's preaching and actions undoubtedly had been reported to the king of Babylon. As one of the few who openly advocated submission to Nebuchadnezzar, Jeremiah was seen as faithful to the covenant between Judah and Babylon, and so was rewarded (as in Jer. 40). In this case, Jeremiah's faithfulness to the covenant of God paralleled his faithfulness to surrender to Nebuchadnezzar.

40:2, 3 For pagans to acknowledge the God of Israel and recognize His power, even in a qualified measure, was a rebuke to the disbelief of the people. Here in Jeremiah and several times in other exilic writings (particularly Daniel), the king of the pagan empire or one of his high ranking officials is seen speaking in respectful or even positive terms of the God of Israel. These pronouncements do not mean that they were true believers; they simply had found room for another god in their pantheon.

the sons of Ephai the Netophathite, and Jezaniah[a] the son of a Maachathite, they and their men. [9]And Gedaliah the son of Ahikam, the son of Shaphan, took an oath before them and their men, saying, "Do not be afraid to serve the Chaldeans. Dwell in the land and serve the king of Babylon, and it shall be well with you. [10]As for me, I will indeed dwell at Mizpah and serve the Chaldeans who come to us. But you, gather wine and summer fruit and oil, put *them* in your vessels, and dwell in your cities that you have taken." [11]Likewise, when all the Jews who *were* in Moab, among the Ammonites, in Edom, and who *were* in all the countries, heard that the king of Babylon had left a remnant of Judah, and that he had set over them Gedaliah the son of Ahikam, the son of Shaphan, [12]then all the Jews returned out of all places where they had been driven, and came to the land of Judah, to Gedaliah at Mizpah, and gathered wine and summer fruit in abundance.

[13]Moreover Johanan the son of Kareah and all the captains of the forces that *were* in the fields came to Gedaliah at Mizpah, [14]and said to him, "Do you certainly know that Baalis the king of the Ammonites has sent Ishmael the son of Nethaniah to murder you?" But Gedaliah the son of Ahikam did not believe them.

[15]Then Johanan the son of Kareah spoke secretly to Gedaliah in Mizpah, saying, "Let me go, please, and I will kill Ishmael the son of Nethaniah, and no one will know *it*. Why should he murder you, so that all the Jews who are gathered to you would be scattered, and the remnant in Judah perish?"

[16]But Gedaliah the son of Ahikam said to Johanan the son of Kareah, "You shall not do this thing, for you speak falsely concerning Ishmael."

Insurrection Against Gedaliah

41 Now it came to pass in the seventh month *that* Ishmael the son of Nethaniah, the son of Elishama, of the royal family and of the officers of the king, came with ten men to Gedaliah the son of Ahikam, at Mizpah. And there they ate bread together in Mizpah. [2]Then Ishmael the son of Nethaniah, and the ten men who were with him, arose and struck Gedaliah the son of Ahikam,

the son of Shaphan, with the sword, and killed him whom the king of Babylon had made governor over the land. [3]Ishmael also struck down all the Jews who were with him, *that is,* with Gedaliah at Mizpah, and the Chaldeans who were found there, the men of war.

[4]And it happened, on the second day after he had killed Gedaliah, when as yet no one knew *it,* [5]that certain men came from Shechem, from Shiloh, and from Samaria, eighty men with their beards shaved and their clothes torn, having cut themselves, with offerings and incense in their hand, to bring *them* to the house of the LORD. [6]Now Ishmael the son of Nethaniah went out from Mizpah to meet them, weeping as he went along; and it happened as he met them that he said to them, "Come to Gedaliah the son of Ahikam!" [7]So it was, when they came into the midst of the city, that Ishmael the son of Nethaniah killed them *and cast them* into the midst of a pit, he and the men who were with him. [8]But ten men were found among them who said to Ishmael, "Do not kill us, for we have treasures of wheat, barley, oil, and honey, in the field." So he desisted and did not kill them among their brethren. [9]Now the pit into which Ishmael had cast all the dead bodies of the men whom he had slain, because of Gedaliah, *was* the same one Asa the king had made for fear of Baasha king of Israel. Ishmael the son of Nethaniah filled it with *the* slain. [10]Then Ishmael carried away captive all the rest of the people who *were* in Mizpah, the king's daughters and all the people who remained in Mizpah, whom Nebuzaradan the captain of the guard had committed to Gedaliah the son of Ahikam. And Ishmael the son of Nethaniah carried them away captive and departed to go over to the Ammonites.

[11]But when Johanan the son of Kareah and all the captains of the forces that *were* with him heard of all the evil that Ishmael the son of Nethaniah had done, [12]they took all the men and went to fight with Ishmael the son of Nethaniah; and they found him by the great pool that *is* in Gibeon. [13]So it was, when all the people who *were* with Ishmael saw Johanan the son of Kareah, and all the cap-

40:8 [a]Spelled *Jaazaniah* in 2 Kings 25:23

40:9–12 Gedaliah, too, swore the oath of covenantal allegiance to Babylon, and unlike Zedekiah, was faithful for his short tenure. Gedaliah's faithfulness resulted in a sort of precursor to the restoration, as Jews scattered throughout nearby countries returned. Submission to Babylon paralleled submission to God, and so God began to reward Gedaliah.

40:13—41:2 Ishmael murdered Gedaliah. Gedaliah apparently was too trusting of his enemies (Jer. 40:16). This trust cost him his life.

41:2 The insurrection was ultimately against the king of Babylon, who had appointed Gedaliah as governor over the Land.

Ishmael and his followers probably prided themselves on being patriots, but in fact they were rebelling against the Lord's command to submit to the Babylonians. Paradoxically, true patriotism meant submitting to Nebuchadnezzar.

41:4–10 Ishmael pretended to welcome the 80 pilgrims, but he deceived them. He murdered 70 of them. Ten escaped death by claiming to have treasures of grain, oil, and honey, products which Ishmael needed. Ishmael carried away a number of captives.

tains of the forces who *were* with him, that they were glad. [14]Then all the people whom Ishmael had carried away captive from Mizpah turned around and came back, and went to Johanan the son of Kareah. [15]But Ishmael the son of Nethaniah escaped from Johanan with eight men and went to the Ammonites.

[16]Then Johanan the son of Kareah, and all the captains of the forces that were with him, took from Mizpah all the rest of the people whom he had recovered from Ishmael the son of Nethaniah after he had murdered Gedaliah the son of Ahikam—the mighty men of war and the women and the children and the eunuchs, whom he had brought back from Gibeon. [17]And they departed and dwelt in the habitation of Chimham, which is near Bethlehem, as they went on their way to Egypt, [18]because of the Chaldeans; for they were afraid of them, because Ishmael the son of Nethaniah had murdered Gedaliah the son of Ahikam, whom the king of Babylon had made governor in the land.

The Flight to Egypt Forbidden

42 Now all the captains of the forces, Johanan the son of Kareah, Jezaniah the son of Hoshaiah, and all the people, from the least to the greatest, came near [2]and said to Jeremiah the prophet, "Please, let our petition be acceptable to you, and pray for us to the LORD your God, for all this remnant (since we are left *but* a few of many, as you can see), [3]that the LORD your God may show us the way in which we should walk and the thing we should do."

[4]Then Jeremiah the prophet said to them, "I have heard. Indeed, I will pray to the LORD your God according to your words, and it shall be, *that* whatever the LORD answers you, I will declare *it* to you. I will keep nothing back from you."

[5]So they said to Jeremiah, "Let the LORD be a true and faithful witness between us, if we do not do according to everything which the LORD your God sends us by you. [6]Whether *it is* pleasing or displeasing, we will obey the voice of the LORD our God to whom we send you, that it may be well with us when we obey the voice of the LORD our God."

[7]And it happened after ten days that the word of the LORD came to Jeremiah. [8]Then he called Johanan the son of Kareah, all the captains of the

forces which *were* with him, and all the people from the least even to the greatest, [9]and said to them, "Thus says the LORD, the God of Israel, to whom you sent me to present your petition before Him: [10]'If you will still remain in this land, then I will build you and not pull *you* down, and I will plant you and not pluck *you* up. For I relent concerning the disaster that I have brought upon you. [11]Do not be afraid of the king of Babylon, of whom you are afraid; do not be afraid of him,' says the LORD, 'for I *am* with you, to save you and deliver you from his hand. [12]And I will show you mercy, that he may have mercy on you and cause you to return to your own land.'

[13]"But if you say, 'We will not dwell in this land,' disobeying the voice of the LORD your God, [14]saying, 'No, but we will go to the land of Egypt where we shall see no war, nor hear the sound of the trumpet, nor be hungry for bread, and there we will dwell'— [15]Then hear now the word of the LORD, O remnant of Judah! Thus says the LORD of hosts, the God of Israel: 'If you wholly set your faces to enter Egypt, and go to dwell there, [16]then it shall be *that* the sword which you feared shall overtake you there in the land of Egypt; the famine of which you were afraid shall follow close after you there *in* Egypt; and there you shall die. [17]So shall it be with all the men who set their faces to go to Egypt to dwell there. They shall die by the sword, by famine, and by pestilence. And none of them shall remain or escape from the disaster that I will bring upon them.'

[18]"For thus says the LORD of hosts, the God of Israel: 'As My anger and My fury have been poured out on the inhabitants of Jerusalem, so will My fury be poured out on you when you enter Egypt. And you shall be an oath, an astonishment, a curse, and a reproach; and you shall see this place no more.'

[19]"The LORD has said concerning you, O remnant of Judah, 'Do not go to Egypt!' Know certainly that I have admonished you this day. [20]For you were hypocrites in your hearts when you sent me to the LORD your God, saying, 'Pray for us to the LORD our God, and according to all that the LORD your God says, so declare to us and we will do *it*.' [21]And I have this day declared *it* to you, but you have not obeyed the voice of the LORD your God, or anything which He has sent you by me. [22]Now therefore, know certainly that you shall die

---

41:16–18 Johanan rescued the people whom Ishmael had kidnapped, but his fear of retaliation from the Babylonians motivated him and his followers to flee toward Egypt, an enemy of Babylon.

42:10–22 The temptation to flee to Egypt was an attractive option to Johanan and his followers. Fleeing appeared to be the safe and logical thing to do because Ishmael's rebellion once again had made Nebuchadnezzar the enemy. Such ac-

tion, however, ran directly counter to God's will. The peace and safety they desired could not be found in Egypt. Obedience to their higher sovereign, the Lord Himself, demanded that they stay in the Land and offer Nebuchadnezzar their allegiance. Returning to Egypt, whether in Moses' time or later, always was seen as a reversal of God's purposes for His people. Only by remaining in the Land could they experience the Lord's building and planting them as a people (see Jer. 1:10).

by the sword, by famine, and by pestilence in the place where you desire to go to dwell."

Jeremiah Taken to Egypt

43 Now it happened, when Jeremiah had stopped speaking to all the people all the words of the Lᴏʀᴅ their God, for which the Lᴏʀᴅ their God had sent him to them, all these words, ²that Azariah the son of Hoshaiah, Johanan the son of Kareah, and all the proud men spoke, saying to Jeremiah, "You speak falsely! The Lᴏʀᴅ our God has not sent you to say, 'Do not go to Egypt to dwell there.' ³But Baruch the son of Neriah has set you against us, to deliver us into the hand of the Chaldeans, that they may put us to death or carry us away captive to Babylon." ⁴So Johanan the son of Kareah, all the captains of the forces, and all the people would not obey the voice of the Lᴏʀᴅ, to remain in the land of Judah. ⁵But Johanan the son of Kareah and all the captains of the forces took all the remnant of Judah who had returned to dwell in the land of Judah, from all nations where they had been driven— ⁶men, women, children, the king's daughters, and every person whom Nebuzaradan the captain of the guard had left with Gedaliah the son of Ahikam, the son of Shaphan, and Jeremiah the prophet and Baruch the son of Neriah. ⁷So they went to the land of Egypt, for they did not obey the voice of the Lᴏʀᴅ. And they went as far as Tahpanhes.

⁸Then the word of the Lᴏʀᴅ came to Jeremiah in Tahpanhes, saying, ⁹"Take large stones in your hand, and hide them in the sight of the men of Judah, in the clay in the brick courtyard which *is* at the entrance to Pharaoh's house in Tahpanhes; ¹⁰and say to them, 'Thus says the Lᴏʀᴅ of hosts, the God of Israel: "Behold, I will send and bring Nebuchadnezzar the king of Babylon, My servant, and will set his throne above these stones that I have hidden. And he will spread his royal pavilion over them. ¹¹When he comes, he shall strike the land of Egypt *and deliver* to death *those appointed* for death, and to captivity *those appointed* for cap-

tivity, and to the sword *those appointed* for the sword. ¹²Iᵃ will kindle a fire in the houses of the gods of Egypt, and he shall burn them and carry them away captive. And he shall array himself with the land of Egypt, as a shepherd puts on his garment, and he shall go out from there in peace. ¹³He shall also break the *sacred* pillars of Beth Shemeshᵃ that *are* in the land of Egypt; and the houses of the gods of the Egyptians he shall burn with fire." ' "

Israelites Will Be Punished in Egypt

44 The word that came to Jeremiah concerning all the Jews who dwell in the land of Egypt, who dwell at Migdol, at Tahpanhes, at Noph,ᵃ and in the country of Pathros, saying, ²"Thus says the Lᴏʀᴅ of hosts, the God of Israel: 'You have seen all the calamity that I have brought on Jerusalem and on all the cities of Judah; and behold, this day they *are* a desolation, and no one dwells in them, ³because of their wickedness which they have committed to provoke Me to anger, in that they went to burn incense *and* to serve other gods whom they did not know, they nor you nor your fathers. ⁴However I have sent to you all My servants the prophets, rising early and sending *them,* saying, "Oh, do not do this abominable thing that I hate!" ⁵But they did not listen or incline their ear to turn from their wickedness, to burn no incense to other gods. ⁶So My fury and My anger were poured out and kindled in the cities of Judah and in the streets of Jerusalem; and they are wasted *and* desolate, as it is this day.'

⁷"Now therefore, thus says the Lᴏʀᴅ, the God of hosts, the God of Israel: 'Why do you commit *this* great evil against yourselves, to cut off from you man and woman, child and infant, out of Judah, leaving none to remain, ⁸in that you provoke Me to wrath with the works of your hands, burn-

---

43:12 ᵃFollowing Masoretic Text and Targum; Septuagint, Syriac, and Vulgate read *He.* 43:13 ᵃLiterally *House of the Sun,* ancient On; later called Heliopolis 44:1 ᵃThat is, ancient Memphis

---

43:1–3 This vehement response revealed the rebellious hearts of the people. They already had made up their minds to disobey and simply were hoping for a message from God that would confirm what they desired.

43:9 Tahpanhes was a garrison city and not the capital of Egypt, though Pharaoh maintained a statehouse or royal residence there.

43:10, 11 Nebuchadnezzar invaded Egypt about 568 B.C. The Egyptians maintained a peaceful relationship with the Babylonians following the invasion.

44:1 The Jews would include Johanan's group as well as others deported earlier (2 Kin. 23:34). Groups of refugees probably had been migrating since the Babylonian invasion became imminent.

44:2–6 In the fashion of covenant indictment, Jeremiah re-

cited the recent history of God's dealings with Judah. The title "Lᴏʀᴅ of hosts" portrays the Lord as the commander of armies (v. 2).

44:7 A remnant ideally would have been left not only in Babylon, but in the Land as well. Instead, those who returned after the years of Babylonian captivity found a group of mixed Jewish and pagan descent who were quite hostile to rebuilding Jerusalem (see Ezra 9—10; Neh. 4:1–3). This situation had resulted in part from the resettlement policies of the Assyrians, who always transplanted conquered peoples to other lands to reduce the risk of rebellion.

44:8 Their stubborn sin of idolatry explains the Jews' unwillingness to submit to the Word of God. The essence of idolatry is to place something in place of God in the center of one's affections. The people who fled to Egypt were as corrupt as those who had been judged and deported.

ing incense to other gods in the land of Egypt where you have gone to dwell, that you may cut yourselves off and be a curse and a reproach among all the nations of the earth? ⁹Have you forgotten the wickedness of your fathers, the wickedness of the kings of Judah, the wickedness of their wives, your own wickedness, and the wickedness of your wives, which they committed in the land of Judah and in the streets of Jerusalem? ¹⁰They have not been humbled, to this day, nor have they feared; they have not walked in My law or in My statutes that I set before you and your fathers.'

¹¹"Therefore thus says the LORD of hosts, the God of Israel: 'Behold, I will set My face against you for catastrophe and for cutting off all Judah. ¹²And I will take the remnant of Judah who have set their faces to go into the land of Egypt to dwell there, and they shall all be consumed *and* fall in the land of Egypt. They shall be consumed by the sword *and* by famine. They shall die, from the least to the greatest, by the sword and by famine; and they shall be an oath, an astonishment, a curse and a reproach! ¹³For I will punish those who dwell in the land of Egypt, as I have punished Jerusalem, by the sword, by famine, and by pestilence, ¹⁴so that none of the remnant of Judah who have gone into the land of Egypt to dwell there shall escape or survive, lest they return to the land of Judah, to which they desire to return and dwell. For none shall return except those who escape.' "

¹⁵Then all the men who knew that their wives had burned incense to other gods, with all the women who stood by, a great multitude, and all the people who dwelt in the land of Egypt, in Pathros, answered Jeremiah, saying: ¹⁶"*As for* the word that you have spoken to us in the name of the LORD, we will not listen to you! ¹⁷But we will certainly do whatever has gone out of our own mouth, to burn incense to the queen of heaven and pour out drink offerings to her, as we have done, we and our fathers, our kings and our princes, in the cities of Judah and in the streets of Jerusalem. For *then* we had plenty of food, were well-off, and saw no trouble. ¹⁸But since we stopped burning incense to the queen of heaven and pouring out drink offerings to her, we have lacked everything and have been consumed by the sword and by famine."

¹⁹*The women also said,* "And when we burned incense to the queen of heaven and poured out drink offerings to her, did we make cakes for her, to worship her, and pour out drink offerings to her without our husbands' *permission?*"

²⁰Then Jeremiah spoke to all the people—the men, the women, and all the people who had given him *that* answer—saying: ²¹"The incense that you burned in the cities of Judah and in the streets of Jerusalem, you and your fathers, your kings and your princes, and the people of the land, did not the LORD remember them, and did it *not* come into His mind? ²²So the LORD could no longer bear *it,* because of the evil of your doings *and* because of the abominations which you committed. Therefore your land is a desolation, an astonishment, a curse, and without an inhabitant, as *it is* this day. ²³Because you have burned incense and because you have sinned against the LORD, and have not obeyed the voice of the LORD or walked in His law, in His statutes or in His testimonies, therefore this calamity has happened to you, as *at* this day."

²⁴Moreover Jeremiah said to all the people and to all the women, "Hear the word of the LORD, all Judah who *are* in the land of Egypt! ²⁵Thus says the LORD of hosts, the God of Israel, saying: 'You and your wives have spoken with your mouths and fulfilled with your hands, saying, "We will surely keep our vows that we have made, to burn incense to the queen of heaven and pour out drink offerings to her." You will surely keep your vows and perform your vows!' ²⁶Therefore hear the word of the LORD, all Judah who dwell in the land of Egypt: 'Behold, I have sworn by My great name,' says the LORD, 'that My name shall no more be named in the mouth of any man of Judah in all the land of Egypt, saying, "The Lord GOD lives." ²⁷Behold, I will watch over them for adversity and not for good. And all the men of Judah who *are* in the land of Egypt shall be consumed by the sword and by famine, until there is an end to them. ²⁸Yet a small number who escape the sword shall return from the land of Egypt to the land of Judah; and all the remnant of Judah, who have gone to the land of Egypt to dwell there, shall know whose words will stand, Mine or theirs. ²⁹And this *shall be* a sign to you,' says the LORD, 'that I will punish you in this place, that you may know that My words will surely stand against you for adversity.'

³⁰"Thus says the LORD: 'Behold, I will give Pharaoh Hophra king of Egypt into the hand of his enemies and into the hand of those who seek his life, as I gave Zedekiah king of Judah into the hand of Nebuchadnezzar king of Babylon, his enemy who sought his life.' "

44:15–19 Both women and men defied Jeremiah. They were practicing idolatry openly and even seeking to justify it. The prominence of women in this worship may have been because of Astarte, the queen of heaven, who was the goddess of fertility (see Jer. 7:18, note; chart, the Graeco-Roman Goddesses). The women sarcastically responded to Jeremiah by justifying their worship of the queen of heaven on the grounds that they did so with the knowledge and approval of their husbands (Jer. 44:19; see Num. 30, Vows). However, nowhere in Scripture is there a higher authority in personal spiritual matters than *Yahweh* God Himself. He acts consistently with His Word, but He expects complete obedience.

Assurance to Baruch

45 The word that Jeremiah the prophet spoke to Baruch the son of Neriah, when he had written these words in a book at the instruction of Jeremiah,[a] in the fourth year of Jehoiakim the son of Josiah, king of Judah, saying, [2]"Thus says the LORD, the God of Israel, to you, O Baruch: [3]'You said, "Woe is me now! For the LORD has added grief to my sorrow. I fainted in my sighing, and I find no rest." '

[4]"Thus you shall say to him, 'Thus says the LORD: "Behold, what I have built I will break down, and what I have planted I will pluck up, that is, this whole land. [5]And do you seek great things for yourself? Do not seek *them;* for behold, I will bring adversity on all flesh," says the LORD. "But I will give your life to you as a prize in all places, wherever you go." ' "

Judgment on Egypt

46 The word of the LORD which came to Jeremiah the prophet against the nations. [2]Against Egypt.

Concerning the army of Pharaoh Necho, king of Egypt, which was by the River Euphrates in Carchemish, and which Nebuchadnezzar king of Babylon defeated in the fourth year of Jehoiakim the son of Josiah, king of Judah:

[3]"Order the buckler and shield,
And draw near to battle!
[4]Harness the horses,
And mount up, you horsemen!
Stand forth with *your* helmets,
Polish the spears,
Put on the armor!
[5]Why have I seen them dismayed *and* turned
    back?
Their mighty ones are beaten down;
They have speedily fled,
And did not look back,
For fear *was* all around," says the LORD.
[6]"Do not let the swift flee away,
Nor the mighty man escape;
They will stumble and fall
Toward the north, by the River Euphrates.

[7]"Who *is* this coming up like a flood,
Whose waters move like the rivers?
[8]Egypt rises up like a flood,

And *its* waters move like the rivers;
And he says, 'I will go up *and* cover the earth,
I will destroy the city and its inhabitants.'
[9]Come up, O horses, and rage, O chariots!
And let the mighty men come forth:
The Ethiopians and the Libyans who handle
    the shield,
And the Lydians who handle *and* bend the bow.
[10]For this *is* the day of the Lord GOD of hosts,
A day of vengeance,
That He may avenge Himself on His
    adversaries.
The sword shall devour;
It shall be satiated and made drunk with their
    blood;
For the Lord GOD of hosts has a sacrifice
In the north country by the River Euphrates.

[11]"Go up to Gilead and take balm,
O virgin, the daughter of Egypt;
In vain you will use many medicines;
You shall not be cured.
[12]The nations have heard of your shame,
And your cry has filled the land;
For the mighty man has stumbled against the
    mighty;
They both have fallen together."

Babylonia Will Strike Egypt

[13]The word that the LORD spoke to Jeremiah the prophet, how Nebuchadnezzar king of Babylon would come *and* strike the land of Egypt.

[14]"Declare in Egypt, and proclaim in Migdol;
Proclaim in Noph[a] and in Tahpanhes;
Say, 'Stand fast and prepare yourselves,
For the sword devours all around you.'
[15]Why are your valiant *men* swept away?
They did not stand
Because the LORD drove them away.
[16]He made many fall;
Yes, one fell upon another.
And they said, 'Arise!
Let us go back to our own people
And to the land of our nativity
From the oppressing sword.'
[17]They cried there,

45:1 [a]Literally *from Jeremiah's mouth* 46:14 [a]That is, ancient Memphis

---

45:5 The Lord's assurance to Baruch is recorded. What did Baruch expect for himself? Perhaps he thought he would be to Jeremiah as Elisha was to Elijah. His great expectations, however, were not to be met. Jeremiah told Baruch that his proper expectation should be the preservation of his own life.

46:1—51:64 Oracles or prophecies addressed to various nations near Israel are included. These neighbors received God's judgment for cruelty toward Israel or for idolatry. A major

theme of this section is God's sovereignty over all nations, regardless of their power and standing in the world (see Ps. 2; Amos 1:3—2:16).

46:2 Nebuchadnezzar's forces met the forces of Pharaoh Necho at Carchemish on the Euphrates in 605 B.C. Necho was soundly defeated, and the power of Egypt never returned to its former heights. The result of this battle revealed the folly of the exiles who fled to Egypt (see Jer. 42:10–22, note).

'Pharaoh, king of Egypt, *is but* a noise.
He has passed by the appointed time!'

18"*As* I live," says the King,
Whose name *is* the LORD of hosts,
"Surely as Tabor *is* among the mountains
And as Carmel by the sea, *so* he shall come.
19O you daughter dwelling in Egypt,
Prepare yourself to go into captivity!
For Noph[a] shall be waste and desolate, without
inhabitant.

20"Egypt *is* a very pretty heifer,
But destruction comes, it comes from the
north.
21Also her mercenaries are in her midst like fat
bulls,
For they also are turned back,
They have fled away together.
They did not stand,
For the day of their calamity had come upon
them,
The time of their punishment.
22Her noise shall go like a serpent,
For they shall march with an army
And come against her with axes,
Like those who chop wood.

23"They shall cut down her forest," says the LORD,
"Though it cannot be searched,
Because they *are* innumerable,
And more numerous than grasshoppers.
24The daughter of Egypt shall be ashamed;
She shall be delivered into the hand
Of the people of the north."

25The LORD of hosts, the God of Israel, says:
"Behold, I will bring punishment on Amon[a] of No,[b]
and Pharaoh and Egypt, with their gods and their
kings—Pharaoh and those who trust in him. 26And
I will deliver them into the hand of those who
seek their lives, into the hand of Nebuchadnezzar
king of Babylon and the hand of his servants. Afterward it shall be inhabited as in the days of old,"
says the LORD.

God Will Preserve Israel

27"But do not fear, O My servant Jacob,
And do not be dismayed, O Israel!

For behold, I will save you from afar,
And your offspring from the land of their
captivity;
Jacob shall return, have rest and be at ease;
No one shall make *him* afraid.
28Do not fear, O Jacob My servant," says the
LORD,
"For I *am* with you;
For I will make a complete end of all the
nations
To which I have driven you,
But I will not make a complete end of you.
I will rightly correct you,
For I will not leave you wholly unpunished."

Judgment on Philistia

47 The word of the LORD that came to Jeremiah the prophet against the Philistines,
before Pharaoh attacked Gaza.
2Thus says the LORD:

"Behold, waters rise out of the north,
And shall be an overflowing flood;
They shall overflow the land and all that is in
it,
The city and those who dwell within;
Then the men shall cry,
And all the inhabitants of the land shall
wail.
3At the noise of the stamping hooves of his
strong horses,
At the rushing of his chariots,
At the rumbling of his wheels,
The fathers will not look back for *their*
children,
Lacking courage,
4Because of the day that comes to plunder all
the Philistines,
To cut off from Tyre and Sidon every helper
who remains;
For the LORD shall plunder the Philistines,
The remnant of the country of Caphtor.
5Baldness has come upon Gaza,
Ashkelon is cut off
With the remnant of their valley.
How long will you cut yourself?

46:19 aThat is, ancient Memphis 46:25 aA sun god bThat is, ancient
Thebes

46:27, 28 The destruction of Egypt did not mean the destruction of God's people. All the nations of the ancient Near East
would be destroyed, but God faithfully would preserve His
remnant (see Jer. 30:10, 11).

47:1 Disaster would come on Philistia, Judah's immediate
neighbor, from the north (v. 2; see Jer. 1:13-16). Five major
Philistine cities mentioned elsewhere in the OT were Ashdod,
Ashkelon, Gaza, Ekron, and Gath (see 1 Sam. 6:17; Amos

1:6-8). The cities of Tyre and Sidon were located in Phoenicia,
an ally of Philistia (Jer. 47:4). Amos condemned Gath, Philistia, and Phoenicia for their involvement in slave trade (Amos
1:6-10).

47:5 Baldness (referring either to hair or beard) signified
shame or great distress in ancient Near Eastern culture
(2 Sam. 10:4, 5; 2 Kin. 2:23; Is. 15:2).

6"O you sword of the LORD,
    How long until you are quiet?
    Put yourself up into your scabbard,
    Rest and be still!
7How can it be quiet,
    Seeing the LORD has given it a charge
    Against Ashkelon and against the seashore?
    There He has appointed it."

Judgment on Moab

48Against Moab.
    Thus says the LORD of hosts, the God of Israel:

"Woe to Nebo!
    For it is plundered,
    Kirjathaim is shamed *and* taken;
    The high stronghold[a] is shamed and
        dismayed—
2No more praise of Moab.
    In Heshbon they have devised evil against
        her:
    'Come, and let us cut her off as a nation.'
    You also shall be cut down, O Madmen![a]
    The sword shall pursue you;
3A voice of crying *shall be* from Horonaim:
    'Plundering and great destruction!'

4"Moab is destroyed;
    Her little ones have caused a cry to be heard;[a]
5For in the Ascent of Luhith they ascend with
        continual weeping;
    For in the descent of Horonaim the enemies
        have heard a cry of destruction.

6"Flee, save your lives!
    And be like the juniper[a] in the wilderness.
7For because you have trusted in your works
        and your treasures,
    You also shall be taken.
    And Chemosh shall go forth into captivity,
    His priests and his princes together.
8And the plunderer shall come against every
        city;
    No one shall escape.
    The valley also shall perish,
    And the plain shall be destroyed,
    As the LORD has spoken.

9"Give wings to Moab,
    That she may flee and get away;
    For her cities shall be desolate,
    Without any to dwell in them.

10Cursed *is* he who does the work of the LORD
        deceitfully,
    And cursed *is* he who keeps back his sword
        from blood.

11"Moab has been at ease from his[a] youth;
    He has settled on his dregs,
    And has not been emptied from vessel to
        vessel,
    Nor has he gone into captivity.
    Therefore his taste remained in him,
    And his scent has not changed.

12"Therefore behold, the days are coming," says
        the LORD,
    "That I shall send him wine-workers
    Who will tip him over
    And empty his vessels
    And break the bottles.
13Moab shall be ashamed of Chemosh,
    As the house of Israel was ashamed of Bethel,
        their confidence.

14"How can you say, 'We *are* mighty
    And strong men for the war'?
15Moab is plundered and gone up *from* her cities;
    Her chosen young men have gone down to the
        slaughter," says the King,
    Whose name *is* the LORD of hosts.

16"The calamity of Moab *is* near at hand,
    And his affliction comes quickly.
17Bemoan him, all you who are around him;
    And all you who know his name,
    Say, 'How the strong staff is broken,
    The beautiful rod!'

18"O daughter inhabiting Dibon,
    Come down from *your* glory,
    And sit in thirst;
    For the plunderer of Moab has come against
        you,
    He has destroyed your strongholds.
19O inhabitant of Aroer,
    Stand by the way and watch;
    Ask him who flees
    And her who escapes;
    Say, 'What has happened?'

•••••••••••••••••

48:1 [a]Hebrew *Misgab*   **48:2** [a]A city of Moab   **48:4** [a]Following Masoretic Text, Targum, and Vulgate; Septuagint reads *Proclaim it in Zoar.*   **48:6** [a]Or *Aroer,* a city of Moab   **48:11** [a]The Hebrew uses masculine and feminine pronouns interchangeably in this chapter.

47:6 The Philistine hope of being spared apparently is voiced here. It does not indicate repentance—merely the Philistine perception that the God of Israel was superior to their own idols and must be appeased (1 Sam. 5; 6). The Lord's sword represents His righteous judgments.

48:13 Moab was proud of its culture and deity, as was any nation of the ancient world (see v. 11). Chemosh was the national god of both Moab and Ammon. The comparison here may indicate that Moab gloated over the destruction of its enemy Israel, but Moab would be subject to the same fate.

20Moab is shamed, for he is broken down.
　Wail and cry!
　Tell it in Arnon, that Moab is plundered.

21"And judgment has come on the plain country:
　On Holon and Jahzah and Mephaath,
22On Dibon and Nebo and Beth Diblathaim,
23On Kirjathaim and Beth Gamul and Beth
　　Meon,
24On Kerioth and Bozrah,
　On all the cities of the land of Moab,
　Far or near.
25The horn of Moab is cut off,
　And his arm is broken," says the LORD.

26"Make him drunk,
　Because he exalted *himself* against the LORD.
　Moab shall wallow in his vomit,
　And he shall also be in derision.
27For was not Israel a derision to you?
　Was he found among thieves?
　For whenever you speak of him,
　You shake *your head in scorn.*
28You who dwell in Moab,
　Leave the cities and dwell in the rock,
　And be like the dove *which* makes her nest
　In the sides of the cave's mouth.

29"We have heard the pride of Moab
　(He *is* exceedingly proud),
　Of his loftiness and arrogance and pride,
　And of the haughtiness of his heart."

30"I know his wrath," says the LORD,
　"But it *is* not right;
　His lies have made nothing right.
31Therefore I will wail for Moab,
　And I will cry out for all Moab;
　I[a] will mourn for the men of Kir Heres.
32O vine of Sibmah! I will weep for you with the
　　weeping of Jazer.
　Your plants have gone over the sea,
　They reach to the sea of Jazer.
　The plunderer has fallen on your summer fruit
　　and your vintage.
33Joy and gladness are taken
　From the plentiful field
　And from the land of Moab;
　I have caused wine to fail from the
　　winepresses;
　No one will tread with joyous shouting—
　Not joyous shouting!

34"From the cry of Heshbon to Elealeh and to
　Jahaz

They have uttered their voice,
From Zoar to Horonaim,
Like a three-year-old heifer;[a]
For the waters of Nimrim also shall be
　desolate.

35"Moreover," says the LORD,
　"I will cause to cease in Moab
　The one who offers *sacrifices* in the high
　　places
　And burns incense to his gods.
36Therefore My heart shall wail like flutes for
　　Moab,
　And like flutes My heart shall wail
　For the men of Kir Heres.
　Therefore the riches they have acquired have
　　perished.

37"For every head *shall be* bald, and every beard
　　clipped;
　On all the hands *shall be* cuts, and on the loins
　　sackcloth—
38A general lamentation
　On all the housetops of Moab,
　And in its streets;
　For I have broken Moab like a vessel in which *is*
　　no pleasure," says the LORD.
39"They shall wail:
　"How she is broken down!
　How Moab has turned her back with shame!'
　So Moab shall be a derision
　And a dismay to all those about her."

40For thus says the LORD:

"Behold, one shall fly like an eagle,
　And spread his wings over Moab.
41Kerioth is taken,
　And the strongholds are surprised;
　The mighty men's hearts in Moab on that day
　　shall be
　Like the heart of a woman in birth pangs.
42And Moab shall be destroyed as a people,
　Because he exalted *himself* against the LORD.
43Fear and the pit and the snare *shall be* upon
　　you,
　O inhabitant of Moab," says the LORD.
44"He who flees from the fear shall fall into the
　　pit,
　And he who gets out of the pit shall be caught
　　in the snare.

48:31 [a]Following Dead Sea Scrolls, Septuagint, and Vulgate;
Masoretic Text reads *He*.　48:34 [a]Or *The Third Eglath*, an unknown
city (compare Isaiah 15:5)

48:29 The essence of Moab's sin was pride, haughtiness toward God and the people of Israel. Not every nation or ruler in
ancient times expressed such haughtiness. The queen of

Sheba and King Hiram of Tyre showed sincere respect for the
God of Israel (2 Chr. 2:11, 12; 9:1–12).

For upon Moab, upon it I will bring
The year of their punishment," says the
LORD.

45"Those who fled stood under the shadow of
Heshbon
Because of exhaustion.
But a fire shall come out of Heshbon,
A flame from the midst of Sihon,
And shall devour the brow of Moab,
The crown of the head of the sons of tumult.
46Woe to you, O Moab!
The people of Chemosh perish;
For your sons have been taken captive,
And your daughters captive.

47"Yet I will bring back the captives of Moab
In the latter days," says the LORD.

Thus far *is* the judgment of Moab.

Judgment on Ammon

49 Against the Ammonites.
Thus says the LORD:

"Has Israel no sons?
Has he no heir?
Why *then* does Milcom^a inherit Gad,
And his people dwell in its cities?
2Therefore behold, the days are coming," says
the LORD,
"That I will cause to be heard an alarm of war
In Rabbah of the Ammonites;
It shall be a desolate mound,
And her villages shall be burned with fire.
Then Israel shall take possession of his
inheritance," says the LORD.

3"Wail, O Heshbon, for Ai is plundered!
Cry, you daughters of Rabbah,
Gird yourselves with sackcloth!
Lament and run to and fro by the walls;
For Milcom shall go into captivity
With his priests and his princes together.
4Why do you boast in the valleys,
Your flowing valley, O backsliding daughter?
Who trusted in her treasures, *saying,*
'Who will come against me?'
5Behold, I will bring fear upon you,"
Says the Lord GOD of hosts,
"From all those who are around you;
You shall be driven out, everyone headlong,
And no one will gather those who wander off.
6But afterward I will bring back

The captives of the people of Ammon," says the
LORD.

Judgment on Edom

7Against Edom.
Thus says the LORD of hosts:

"*Is* wisdom no more in Teman?
Has counsel perished from the prudent?
Has their wisdom vanished?
8Flee, turn back, dwell in the depths,
O inhabitants of Dedan!
For I will bring the calamity of Esau upon him,
The time *that* I will punish him.
9If grape-gatherers came to you,
Would they not leave *some* gleaning grapes?
If thieves by night,
Would they not destroy until they have
enough?
10But I have made Esau bare;
I have uncovered his secret places,^a
And he shall not be able to hide himself.
His descendants are plundered,
His brethren and his neighbors,
And he *is* no more.
11Leave your fatherless children,
I will preserve *them* alive;
And let your widows trust in Me."

12For thus says the LORD: "Behold, those whose
judgment *was* not to drink of the cup have assuredly drunk. And *are* you the one who will altogether go unpunished? You shall not go unpunished, but you shall surely drink *of it.* 13For I have
sworn by Myself," says the LORD, "that Bozrah
shall become a desolation, a reproach, a waste, and
a curse. And all its cities shall be perpetual
wastes."

14I have heard a message from the LORD,
And an ambassador has been sent to the
nations:
"Gather together, come against her,
And rise up to battle!

15"For indeed, I will make you small among
nations,
Despised among men.
16Your fierceness has deceived you,
The pride of your heart,
O you who dwell in the clefts of the rock,

••••••••••••••••••••••••

49:1 ^aHebrew *Malcam,* literally *their king,* a god of the Ammonites;
also called *Molech* (compare verse 3)   49:10 ^aCompare Obadiah 5, 6

48:47 Though the destruction of Moab is regarded in almost
absolute terms, the judgment is not permanent. In some distant future, Moab would be restored. The Moabites descended from Lot, Abraham's nephew (Gen. 19:30–38).

49:6 The Ammonites were given the same future hope as the
Egyptians and the Moabites (Jer. 46:25, 26; 48:47).

Who hold the height of the hill!
Though you make your nest as high as the
   eagle,
I will bring you down from there," says the
   LORD.[a]

17"Edom also shall be an astonishment;
Everyone who goes by it will be astonished
And will hiss at all its plagues.
18As in the overthrow of Sodom and Gomorrah
And their neighbors," says the LORD,
"No one shall remain there,
Nor shall a son of man dwell in it.

19"Behold, he shall come up like a lion from the
   floodplain[a] of the Jordan
Against the dwelling place of the strong;
But I will suddenly make him run away from
   her.
And who is a chosen man that I may appoint
   over her?
For who is like Me?
Who will arraign Me?
And who is that shepherd
Who will withstand Me?"

20Therefore hear the counsel of the LORD that
   He has taken against Edom,
And His purposes that He has proposed
   against the inhabitants of Teman:
Surely the least of the flock shall draw them
   out;
Surely He shall make their dwelling places
   desolate with them.
21The earth shakes at the noise of their fall;
At the cry its noise is heard at the Red Sea.
22Behold, He shall come up and fly like the eagle,
And spread His wings over Bozrah;
The heart of the mighty men of Edom in that
   day shall be
Like the heart of a woman in birth pangs.

Judgment on Damascus

23Against Damascus.

"Hamath and Arpad are shamed,
For they have heard bad news.
They are fainthearted;
There is trouble on the sea;
It cannot be quiet.
24Damascus has grown feeble;
She turns to flee,
And fear has seized her.

Anguish and sorrows have taken her like a
   woman in labor.
25Why is the city of praise not deserted, the city
   of My joy?
26Therefore her young men shall fall in her
   streets,
And all the men of war shall be cut off in that
   day," says the LORD of hosts.
27"I will kindle a fire in the wall of Damascus,
And it shall consume the palaces of Ben-Hadad."[a]

Judgment on Kedar and Hazor

28Against Kedar and against the kingdoms of
Hazor, which Nebuchadnezzar king of Babylon
shall strike.
   Thus says the LORD:

"Arise, go up to Kedar,
And devastate the men of the East!
29Their tents and their flocks they shall take
   away.
They shall take for themselves their curtains,
All their vessels and their camels;
And they shall cry out to them,
'Fear is on every side!'

30"Flee, get far away! Dwell in the depths,
O inhabitants of Hazor!" says the LORD.
"For Nebuchadnezzar king of Babylon has taken
   counsel against you,
And has conceived a plan against you.

31"Arise, go up to the wealthy nation that dwells
   securely," says the LORD,
"Which has neither gates nor bars,
Dwelling alone.
32Their camels shall be for booty,
And the multitude of their cattle for plunder.
I will scatter to all winds those in the farthest
   corners,
And I will bring their calamity from all its
   sides," says the LORD.
33"Hazor shall be a dwelling for jackals, a
   desolation forever;
No one shall reside there,
Nor son of man dwell in it."

Judgment on Elam

34The word of the LORD that came to Jeremiah
the prophet against Elam, in the beginning of the

49:16 [a]Compare Obadiah 3, 4   49:19 [a]Or thicket   49:27 [a]Compare
Amos 1:4

49:17, 18 No future hope was given to the Edomites. Edom's
destruction is pictured as being as total as that of Sodom and
Gomorrah. The prophet Obadiah revealed that this judgment
was due to their overwhelming pride and mistreatment of the
Israelites (see Obad. 3, 4, 10, 12, 18, 19).

49:23-39 Damascus was the capital of Aram or Syria, an ancient enemy of Israel. Kedar and Hazor apparently were nomadic peoples, since they possessed "tents" and "flocks" and
lacked city "gates" or "bars." Elam, located east of Babylon,
would experience restoration after disaster (v. 39; see Jer.
48:47; 49:6).

reign of Zedekiah king of Judah, saying, ³⁵"Thus says the LORD of hosts:

'Behold, I will break the bow of Elam,
The foremost of their might.
³⁶Against Elam I will bring the four winds
From the four quarters of heaven,
And scatter them toward all those winds;
There shall be no nations where the outcasts
of Elam will not go.
³⁷For I will cause Elam to be dismayed before
their enemies
And before those who seek their life.
I will bring disaster upon them,
My fierce anger,' says the LORD;
'And I will send the sword after them
Until I have consumed them.
³⁸I will set My throne in Elam,
And will destroy from there the king and the
princes,' says the LORD.

³⁹'But it shall come to pass in the latter days:
I will bring back the captives of Elam,' says the
LORD."

Judgment on Babylon and Babylonia

50 The word that the LORD spoke against Babylon *and* against the land of the Chaldeans by Jeremiah the prophet.

²"Declare among the nations,
Proclaim, and set up a standard;
Proclaim— do not conceal *it*—
Say, 'Babylon is taken, Bel is shamed.
Merodach[a] is broken in pieces;
Her idols are humiliated,
Her images are broken in pieces.'
³For out of the north a nation comes up against
her,
Which shall make her land desolate,
And no one shall dwell therein.
They shall move, they shall depart,
Both man and beast.

⁴"In those days and in that time," says the
LORD,
"The children of Israel shall come,
They and the children of Judah together;
With continual weeping they shall come,
And seek the LORD their God.
⁵They shall ask the way to Zion,
With their faces toward it, *saying,*
'Come and let us join ourselves to the LORD
In a perpetual covenant
That will not be forgotten.'

⁶"My people have been lost sheep.
Their shepherds have led them astray;
They have turned them away *on* the mountains.
They have gone from mountain to hill;
They have forgotten their resting place.
⁷All who found them have devoured them;
And their adversaries said, 'We have not
offended,
Because they have sinned against the LORD, the
habitation of justice,
The LORD, the hope of their fathers.'

⁸"Move from the midst of Babylon,
Go out of the land of the Chaldeans;
And be like the rams before the flocks.
⁹For behold, I will raise and cause to come up
against Babylon
An assembly of great nations from the north
country,
And they shall array themselves against her;
From there she shall be captured.
Their arrows *shall be* like *those* of an expert
warrior;[a]
None shall return in vain.
¹⁰And Chaldea shall become plunder;
All who plunder her shall be satisfied," says the
LORD.

¹¹"Because you were glad, because you rejoiced,
You destroyers of My heritage,
Because you have grown fat like a heifer
threshing grain,
And you bellow like bulls,
¹²Your mother shall be deeply ashamed;
She who bore you shall be ashamed.
Behold, the least of the nations *shall be* a
wilderness,
A dry land and a desert.
¹³Because of the wrath of the LORD
She shall not be inhabited,
But she shall be wholly desolate.
Everyone who goes by Babylon shall be
horrified
And hiss at all her plagues.

¹⁴"Put yourselves in array against Babylon all
around,
All you who bend the bow;
Shoot at her, spare no arrows,
For she has sinned against the LORD.
¹⁵Shout against her all around;

50:2 ªA Babylonian god; sometimes spelled *Marduk* 50:9
ªFollowing some Hebrew manuscripts, Septuagint, and Syriac;
Masoretic Text, Targum, and Vulgate read *a warrior who makes childless.*

50:1 Babylon was God's tool to punish Judah and the surrounding nations. Babylon, too, would experience God's judgment. Bel and Merodach (Mardut) were Babylonian idols.

She has given her hand,
Her foundations have fallen,
Her walls are thrown down;
For it *is* the vengeance of the LORD.
Take vengeance on her.
As she has done, so do to her.
¹⁶Cut off the sower from Babylon,
And him who handles the sickle at harvest
time.
For fear of the oppressing sword
Everyone shall turn to his own people,
And everyone shall flee to his own land.

¹⁷"Israel *is* like scattered sheep;
The lions have driven *him* away.
First the king of Assyria devoured him;
Now at last this Nebuchadnezzar king of
Babylon has broken his bones."

¹⁸Therefore thus says the LORD of hosts, the
God of Israel:

"Behold, I will punish the king of Babylon and
his land,
As I have punished the king of Assyria.
¹⁹But I will bring back Israel to his home,
And he shall feed on Carmel and Bashan;
His soul shall be satisfied on Mount Ephraim
and Gilead.
²⁰In those days and in that time," says the LORD,
"The iniquity of Israel shall be sought, but *there
shall be* none;
And the sins of Judah, but they shall not be
found;
For I will pardon those whom I preserve.

²¹"Go up against the land of Merathaim, against
it,
And against the inhabitants of Pekod.
Waste and utterly destroy them," says the
LORD,
"And do according to all that I have commanded
you.
²²A sound of battle *is* in the land,
And of great destruction.
²³How the hammer of the whole earth has been
cut apart and broken!
How Babylon has become a desolation among
the nations!
²⁴I have laid a snare for you;
You have indeed been trapped, O Babylon,
And you were not aware;
You have been found and also caught,
Because you have contended against the LORD.
²⁵The LORD has opened His armory,

And has brought out the weapons of His
indignation;
For this *is* the work of the Lord GOD of hosts
In the land of the Chaldeans.
²⁶Come against her from the farthest border;
Open her storehouses;
Cast her up as heaps of ruins,
And destroy her utterly;
Let nothing of her be left.
²⁷Slay all her bulls,
Let them go down to the slaughter.
Woe to them!
For their day has come, the time of their
punishment.
²⁸The voice of those who flee and escape from
the land of Babylon
Declares in Zion the vengeance of the LORD our
God,
The vengeance of His temple.

²⁹"Call together the archers against Babylon.
All you who bend the bow, encamp against it
all around;
Let none of them escape.ᵃ
Repay her according to her work;
According to all she has done, do to her;
For she has been proud against the LORD,
Against the Holy One of Israel.
³⁰Therefore her young men shall fall in the
streets,
And all her men of war shall be cut off in that
day," says the LORD.
³¹"Behold, I *am* against you,
O most haughty one!" says the Lord GOD of
hosts;
"For your day has come,
The time *that* I will punish you.ᵃ
³²The most proud shall stumble and fall,
And no one will raise him up;
I will kindle a fire in his cities,
And it will devour all around him."

³³Thus says the LORD of hosts:

"The children of Israel *were* oppressed,
Along with the children of Judah;
All who took them captive have held them fast;
They have refused to let them go.
³⁴Their Redeemer *is* strong;
The LORD of hosts *is* His name.
He will thoroughly plead their case,

50:29 ᵃQere, some Hebrew manuscripts, Septuagint, and Targum
add *to her.* 50:31 ᵃFollowing Masoretic Text and Targum;
Septuagint and Vulgate read *The time of your punishment.*

50:31, 32 The pride of the Babylonians was their most notable
sin—a theme also found in the Book of Daniel (Dan. 4:28–30;
5:22–23).

50:34 God is the Redeemer (Heb. *go'el*) of His people. The
term was used in the OT to describe the nearest of kin who
had the duties of blood revenge, redeeming property in danger

That He may give rest to the land,
And disquiet the inhabitants of Babylon.

35"A sword *is* against the Chaldeans," says the
LORD,
"Against the inhabitants of Babylon,
And against her princes and her wise men.
36A sword *is* against the soothsayers, and they
will be fools.
A sword *is* against her mighty men, and they
will be dismayed.
37A sword *is* against their horses,
Against their chariots,
And against all the mixed peoples who *are* in
her midst;
And they will become like women.
A sword *is* against her treasures, and they will
be robbed.
38A drought[a] *is* against her waters, and they will
be dried up.
For it *is* the land of carved images,
And they are insane with *their* idols.

39"Therefore the wild desert beasts shall dwell
there with the jackals,
And the ostriches shall dwell in it.
It shall be inhabited no more forever,
Nor shall it be dwelt in from generation to
generation.
40As God overthrew Sodom and Gomorrah
And their neighbors," says the LORD,
"*So* no one shall reside there,
Nor son of man dwell in it.

41"Behold, a people shall come from the north,
And a great nation and many kings
Shall be raised up from the ends of the earth.
42They shall hold the bow and the lance;
They *are* cruel and shall not show mercy.
Their voice shall roar like the sea;
They shall ride on horses,
Set in array, like a man for the battle,
Against you, O daughter of Babylon.

43"The king of Babylon has heard the report
about them,
And his hands grow feeble;
Anguish has taken hold of him,
Pangs as of a woman in childbirth.

44"Behold, he shall come up like a lion from the
floodplain[a] of the Jordan
Against the dwelling place of the strong;

But I will make them suddenly run away from
her.
And who *is* a chosen *man that* I may appoint
over her?
For who *is* like Me?
Who will arraign Me?
And who *is* that shepherd
Who will withstand Me?"

45Therefore hear the counsel of the LORD that
He has taken against Babylon,
And His purposes that He has proposed
against the land of the Chaldeans:
Surely the least of the flock shall draw them out;
Surely He will make their dwelling place
desolate with them.
46At the noise of the taking of Babylon
The earth trembles,
And the cry is heard among the nations.

The Utter Destruction of Babylon

51 Thus says the LORD:

"Behold, I will raise up against Babylon,
Against those who dwell in Leb Kamai,[a]
A destroying wind.
2And I will send winnowers to Babylon,
Who shall winnow her and empty her land.
For in the day of doom
They shall be against her all around.
3Against *her* let the archer bend his bow,
And lift himself up against *her* in his armor.
Do not spare her young men;
Utterly destroy all her army.
4Thus the slain shall fall in the land of the
Chaldeans,
And *those* thrust through in her streets.
5For Israel is not forsaken, nor Judah,
By his God, the LORD of hosts,
Though their land was filled with sin against
the Holy One of Israel."

6Flee from the midst of Babylon,
And every one save his life!
Do not be cut off in her iniquity,
For this *is* the time of the LORD's vengeance;
He shall recompense her.
7Babylon *was* a golden cup in the LORD's hand,
That made all the earth drunk.

50:38 [a]Following Masoretic Text, Targum, and Vulgate; Syriac reads
sword; Septuagint omits *A drought is.*   50:44 [a]Or *thicket*   51:1 [a]A
code word for Chaldea (Babylonia); may be translated *The Midst of
Those Who Rise Up Against Me*

---

of being lost to the family, and providing the deceased with an
heir. The full revelation of God as Redeemer is in Christ. The
fate of Babylon is compared with that of Sodom and Gomorrah (see Gen. 19:24, 25).

51:5 Despite outward appearances, God has neither forgotten

nor forsaken His people. God's purpose in raising up Babylon
was to chastise and purify His people. "The Holy One of Israel," a favorite designation for God used by Isaiah, emphasizes God as perfect moral purity (see Is. 17:7; 29:19; 30:12;
41:14; 43:3, 14).

The nations drank her wine;
Therefore the nations are deranged.
[8]Babylon has suddenly fallen and been
destroyed.
Wail for her!
Take balm for her pain;
Perhaps she may be healed.

[9]We would have healed Babylon,
But she is not healed.
Forsake her, and let us go everyone to his own
country;
For her judgment reaches to heaven and is
lifted up to the skies.
[10]The LORD has revealed our righteousness.
Come and let us declare in Zion the work of
the LORD our God.

[11]Make the arrows bright!
Gather the shields!
The LORD has raised up the spirit of the kings
of the Medes.
For His plan is against Babylon to destroy it,
Because it is the vengeance of the LORD,
The vengeance for His temple.
[12]Set up the standard on the walls of Babylon;
Make the guard strong,
Set up the watchmen,
Prepare the ambushes.
For the LORD has both devised and done
What He spoke against the inhabitants of
Babylon.
[13]O you who dwell by many waters,
Abundant in treasures,
Your end has come,
The measure of your covetousness.
[14]The LORD of hosts has sworn by Himself:
"Surely I will fill you with men, as with locusts,
And they shall lift up a shout against you."

[15]He has made the earth by His power;
He has established the world by His wisdom,
And stretched out the heaven by His
understanding.
[16]When He utters His voice—
There is a multitude of waters in the heavens:
"He causes the vapors to ascend from the ends
of the earth;
He makes lightnings for the rain;
He brings the wind out of His treasuries."[a]

[17]Everyone is dull-hearted, without knowledge;
Every metalsmith is put to shame by the
carved image;
For his molded image is falsehood,
And there is no breath in them.

[18]They are futile, a work of errors;
In the time of their punishment they shall
perish.
[19]The Portion of Jacob is not like them,
For He is the Maker of all things;
And Israel is the tribe of His inheritance.
The LORD of hosts is His name.

[20]"You are My battle-ax and weapons of war:
For with you I will break the nation in pieces;
With you I will destroy kingdoms;
[21]With you I will break in pieces the horse and
its rider;
With you I will break in pieces the chariot and
its rider;
[22]With you also I will break in pieces man and
woman;
With you I will break in pieces old and young;
With you I will break in pieces the young man
and the maiden;
[23]With you also I will break in pieces the
shepherd and his flock;
With you I will break in pieces the farmer and
his yoke of oxen;
And with you I will break in pieces governors
and rulers.

[24]"And I will repay Babylon
And all the inhabitants of Chaldea
For all the evil they have done
In Zion in your sight," says the LORD.

[25]"Behold, I am against you, O destroying
mountain,
Who destroys all the earth," says the LORD.
"And I will stretch out My hand against you,
Roll you down from the rocks,
And make you a burnt mountain.
[26]They shall not take from you a stone for a
corner
Nor a stone for a foundation,
But you shall be desolate forever," says the
LORD.

[27]Set up a banner in the land,
Blow the trumpet among the nations!
Prepare the nations against her,
Call the kingdoms together against her:
Ararat, Minni, and Ashkenaz.
Appoint a general against her;
Cause the horses to come up like the bristling
locusts.
[28]Prepare against her the nations,
With the kings of the Medes,

51:16 [a]Psalm 135:7

51:17–19 Almighty God the Creator is contrasted with the worthless idols of Babylon (see Is. 40:18–20). The difference is simple: He is real and they are not. Absolute dependence on any other than the true God is a vain hope.

Its governors and all its rulers,
All the land of his dominion.
29And the land will tremble and sorrow;
For every purpose of the LORD shall be
performed against Babylon,
To make the land of Babylon a desolation
without inhabitant.
30The mighty men of Babylon have ceased
fighting,
They have remained in their strongholds;
Their might has failed,
They became *like* women;
They have burned her dwelling places,
The bars of her *gate* are broken.
31One runner will run to meet another,
And one messenger to meet another,
To show the king of Babylon that his city is
taken on *all* sides;
32The passages are blocked,
The reeds they have burned with fire,
And the men of war are terrified.

33For thus says the LORD of hosts, the God of Israel:

"The daughter of Babylon *is* like a threshing
floor
When it is time to thresh her;
Yet a little while
And the time of her harvest will come."

34"Nebuchadnezzar the king of Babylon
Has devoured me, he has crushed me;
He has made me an empty vessel,
He has swallowed me up like a monster;
He has filled his stomach with my delicacies,
He has spit me out.
35Let the violence *done* to me and my flesh *be*
upon Babylon,"
The inhabitant of Zion will say;
"And my blood be upon the inhabitants of
Chaldea!"
Jerusalem will say.

36Therefore thus says the LORD:

"Behold, I will plead your case and take
vengeance for you.
I will dry up her sea and make her springs dry.
37Babylon shall become a heap,
A dwelling place for jackals,
An astonishment and a hissing,
Without an inhabitant.
38They shall roar together like lions,
They shall growl like lions' whelps.
39In their excitement I will prepare their feasts;
I will make them drunk,

That they may rejoice,
And sleep a perpetual sleep
And not awake," says the LORD.
40"I will bring them down
Like lambs to the slaughter,
Like rams with male goats.

41"Oh, how Sheshach[a] is taken!
Oh, how the praise of the whole earth is
seized!
How Babylon has become desolate among the
nations!
42The sea has come up over Babylon;
She is covered with the multitude of its waves.
43Her cities are a desolation,
A dry land and a wilderness,
A land where no one dwells,
Through which no son of man passes.
44I will punish Bel in Babylon,
And I will bring out of his mouth what he has
swallowed;
And the nations shall not stream to him
anymore.
Yes, the wall of Babylon shall fall.

45"My people, go out of the midst of her!
And let everyone deliver himself from the
fierce anger of the LORD.
46And lest your heart faint,
And you fear for the rumor that *will be* heard in
the land
(A rumor will come *one* year,
And after that, in *another* year
A rumor *will come*,
And violence in the land,
Ruler against ruler),
47Therefore behold, the days are coming
That I will bring judgment on the carved
images of Babylon;
Her whole land shall be ashamed,
And all her slain shall fall in her midst.
48Then the heavens and the earth and all that *is*
in them
Shall sing joyously over Babylon;
For the plunderers shall come to her from the
north," says the LORD.

49As Babylon *has caused* the slain of Israel to fall,
So at Babylon the slain of all the earth shall
fall.
50You who have escaped the sword,
Get away! Do not stand still!
Remember the LORD afar off,
And let Jerusalem come to your mind.

51:41 [a]A code word for Babylon (compare Jeremiah 25:26)

51:36 God is pictured as the divine advocate who would plead on Israel's behalf. Disaster would fall on Babylon.

⁵¹We are ashamed because we have heard
reproach.
    Shame has covered our faces,
    For strangers have come into the sanctuaries
        of the LORD's house.

⁵²"Therefore behold, the days are coming," says
        the LORD,
    "That I will bring judgment on her carved
        images,
    And throughout all her land the wounded shall
        groan.
⁵³Though Babylon were to mount up to heaven,
    And though she were to fortify the height of
        her strength,
    Yet from Me plunderers would come to her,"
        says the LORD.

⁵⁴The sound of a cry comes from Babylon,
    And great destruction from the land of the
        Chaldeans,
⁵⁵Because the LORD is plundering Babylon
    And silencing her loud voice,
    Though her waves roar like great waters,
    And the noise of their voice is uttered,
⁵⁶Because the plunderer comes against her,
        against Babylon,
    And her mighty men are taken.
    Every one of their bows is broken;
    For the LORD is the God of recompense,
    He will surely repay.

⁵⁷"And I will make drunk
    Her princes and wise men,
    Her governors, her deputies, and her mighty
        men.
    And they shall sleep a perpetual sleep
    And not awake," says the King,
    Whose name is the LORD of hosts.

⁵⁸Thus says the LORD of hosts:

"The broad walls of Babylon shall be utterly
        broken,
    And her high gates shall be burned with fire;
    The people will labor in vain,
    And the nations, because of the fire;
    And they shall be weary."

Jeremiah's Command to Seraiah

⁵⁹The word which Jeremiah the prophet commanded Seraiah the son of Neriah, the son of
Mahseiah, when he went with Zedekiah the king

of Judah to Babylon in the fourth year of his reign.
And Seraiah was the quartermaster. ⁶⁰So Jeremiah
wrote in a book all the evil that would come upon
Babylon, all these words that are written against
Babylon. ⁶¹And Jeremiah said to Seraiah, "When
you arrive in Babylon and see it, and read all these
words, ⁶²then you shall say, 'O LORD, You have spoken against this place to cut it off, so that none
shall remain in it, neither man nor beast, but it
shall be desolate forever.' ⁶³Now it shall be, when
you have finished reading this book, that you shall
tie a stone to it and throw it into the Euphrates. ⁶⁴Then you shall say, 'Thus Babylon shall
sink and not rise from the catastrophe that I will
bring upon her. And they shall be weary.' "

Thus far are the words of Jeremiah.

The Fall of Jerusalem Reviewed

52 Zedekiah was twenty-one years old when he
became king, and he reigned eleven years in
Jerusalem. His mother's name was Hamutal the
daughter of Jeremiah of Libnah. ²He also did evil
in the sight of the LORD, according to all that Jehoiakim had done. ³For because of the anger of
the LORD this happened in Jerusalem and Judah,
till He finally cast them out from His presence.
Then Zedekiah rebelled against the king of Babylon.

⁴Now it came to pass in the ninth year of his
reign, in the tenth month, on the tenth day of the
month, that Nebuchadnezzar king of Babylon and
all his army came against Jerusalem and encamped
against it; and they built a siege wall against it all
around. ⁵So the city was besieged until the
eleventh year of King Zedekiah. ⁶By the fourth
month, on the ninth day of the month, the famine
had become so severe in the city that there was no
food for the people of the land. ⁷Then the city wall
was broken through, and all the men of war fled
and went out of the city at night by way of the
gate between the two walls, which was by the
king's garden, even though the Chaldeans were
near the city all around. And they went by way of
the plain.ᵃ

⁸But the army of the Chaldeans pursued the
king, and they overtook Zedekiah in the plains of
Jericho. All his army was scattered from him. ⁹So
they took the king and brought him up to the
king of Babylon at Riblah in the land of Hamath,
and he pronounced judgment on him. ¹⁰Then the
king of Babylon killed the sons of Zedekiah before

52:7 ᵃOr the Arabah, that is, the Jordan Valley

51:56 People reap what they sow (see Gal. 6:7). At the root of
all God's activities of judgment recorded in Jeremiah is the reality of His justice.

52:1–34 The material in this chapter is strikingly similar to
that recorded in 2 Kings 24:18—25:30. The chapter provides a

fitting capstone for the ministry of Jeremiah. This appendix
may have been included to demonstrate the fulfillment of
God's word proclaimed through His prophet Jeremiah.

his eyes. And he killed all the princes of Judah in Riblah. [11]He also put out the eyes of Zedekiah; and the king of Babylon bound him in bronze fetters, took him to Babylon, and put him in prison till the day of his death.

The Temple and City Plundered and Burned

[12]Now in the fifth month, on the tenth *day* of the month (which *was* the nineteenth year of King Nebuchadnezzar king of Babylon), Nebuzaradan, the captain of the guard, *who* served the king of Babylon, came to Jerusalem. [13]He burned the house of the LORD and the king's house; all the houses of Jerusalem, that is, all the houses of the great, he burned with fire. [14]And all the army of the Chaldeans who *were* with the captain of the guard broke down all the walls of Jerusalem all around. [15]Then Nebuzaradan the captain of the guard carried away captive *some* of the poor people, the rest of the people who remained in the city, the defectors who had deserted to the king of Babylon, and the rest of the craftsmen. [16]But Nebuzaradan the captain of the guard left *some* of the poor of the land as vinedressers and farmers.

[17]The bronze pillars that *were* in the house of the LORD, and the carts and the bronze Sea that *were* in the house of the LORD, the Chaldeans broke in pieces, and carried all their bronze to Babylon. [18]They also took away the pots, the shovels, the trimmers, the bowls, the spoons, and all the bronze utensils with which the *priests* ministered. [19]The basins, the firepans, the bowls, the pots, the lampstands, the spoons, and the cups, whatever *was* solid gold and whatever *was* solid silver, the captain of the guard took away. [20]The two pillars, one Sea, the twelve bronze bulls which *were* under *it, and* the carts, which King Solomon had made for the house of the LORD—the bronze of all these articles was beyond measure. [21]Now *concerning* the pillars: the height of one pillar *was* eighteen cubits, a measuring line of twelve cubits could measure its circumference, and its thickness *was* four fingers; *it was* hollow. [22]A capital of bronze *was* on it; and the height of one capital *was* five cubits, with a network and pomegranates all around the capital, all of bronze. The second pillar, with pomegranates was the same. [23]There

were ninety-six pomegranates on the sides; all the pomegranates, all around on the network, *were* one hundred.

The People Taken Captive to Babylonia

[24]The captain of the guard took Seraiah the chief priest, Zephaniah the second priest, and the three doorkeepers. [25]He also took out of the city an officer who had charge of the men of war, seven men of the king's close associates who were found in the city, the principal scribe of the army who mustered the people of the land, and sixty men of the people of the land who were found in the midst of the city. [26]And Nebuzaradan the captain of the guard took these and brought them to the king of Babylon at Riblah. [27]Then the king of Babylon struck them and put them to death at Riblah in the land of Hamath. Thus Judah was carried away captive from its own land.

[28]These *are* the people whom Nebuchadnezzar carried away captive: in the seventh year, three thousand and twenty-three Jews; [29]in the eighteenth year of Nebuchadnezzar he carried away captive from Jerusalem eight hundred and thirty-two persons; [30]in the twenty-third year of Nebuchadnezzar, Nebuzaradan the captain of the guard carried away captive of the Jews seven hundred and forty-five persons. All the persons *were* four thousand six hundred.

Jehoiachin Released from Prison

[31]Now it came to pass in the thirty-seventh year of the captivity of Jehoiachin king of Judah, in the twelfth month, on the twenty-fifth *day* of the month, *that* Evil-Merodach[a] king of Babylon, in the *first* year of his reign, lifted up the head of Jehoiachin king of Judah and brought him out of prison. [32]And he spoke kindly to him and gave him a more prominent seat than those of the kings who *were* with him in Babylon. [33]So Jehoiachin changed from his prison garments, and he ate bread regularly before the king all the days of his life. [34]And as for his provisions, there was a regular ration given him by the king of Babylon, a portion for each day until the day of his death, all the days of his life.

52:31[a]Or *Awil-Marduk*

52:27 **The word of the Lord** through His faithful prophet has come to pass (see Jer. 13—16). The kingdom of Judah has fallen because of its sin.

52:31 **A king in the ancient Near East** customarily eliminated

his enemies and showed mercy on those who no longer would pose a threat to him. Jehoiachin, after being released from prison, lived the rest of his life dependent on the king of Babylon and received the Babylonian king's favor (v. 34).

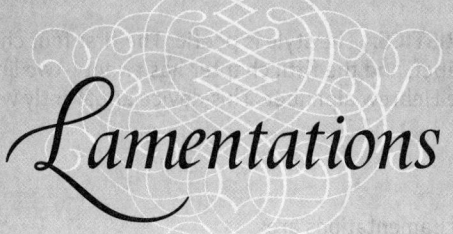

Lamentations

AUTHOR

Though not directly stated in the text, traditionally Jeremiah is viewed as the author. In the Latin Vulgate this book is entitled "The Lamentations of Jeremiah." The close similarity between Lamentations and Jeremiah and the nature of the subject matter suggest Jeremiah could be the author. Second Chronicles 35:24, 25 also has been cited in support of Jeremiah's authorship of Lamentations.

DATE

Jeremiah (Heb., lit. "the Lord exalts" or "the Lord loosens [the womb]") ministered forty years, from 626 B.C. to 586 B.C. He prophesied during the reigns of Josiah, Jehoahaz, Jehoiakim, Jehoiachin, and Zedekiah, kings of Judah. The Book of Lamentations was written at the end of Jeremiah's ministry in 586 B.C.

BACKGROUND

SETTING: Assyria had ceased to be a dominant world power. Babylon and Egypt were in a power struggle for control. Nebuchadnezzar, king of Babylon, had utterly destroyed Judah, including the city of Jerusalem and the temple in 586 B.C.

Jeremiah noted three deportations of the Jews to Babylon, occurring respectively in 597, 586, and 582 B.C. (see Jer. 52:28–30). Those exiled were a relatively small portion of the population, but they were the best of their country's political, ecclesiastical, and intellectual leadership. The poorest peasants of Judah were allowed to remain in the Land. Those left behind experienced lack of leadership and the loss of all their identity as a people. They faced battle, execution, starvation, and disease.

PURPOSE: The author's purpose was to examine honestly the causes, responsibilities, and future possibilities connected with the fall of Jerusalem. "How does one maintain faith in God in the midst of great calamity?" is a major concern of Jeremiah. Jeremiah's grief was both personal and universal as he recounted the events surrounding the capture and fall of Jerusalem. Lamentations is a lament for what had been lost. Both the temple and the throne were gone; their destruction seemed to mark the end of the Davidic kingdom, which God had promised would have no end (see 2 Sam. 7:16). Jeremiah mourned this demise and the fate of those left behind. He acknowledged the sin of the people and the justice of God in bringing judgment.

AUDIENCE: The book reminded those left after the fall of Jerusalem, as well as believers throughout history, that God is faithful to His promise to judge—and to restore. Lamentations is read annually by the Jewish people on the "Ninth of Ab," a day of fasting (see chart, The Jewish Sacred Calendar).

LITERARY CHARACTERISTICS: The style is poetic. The first four chapters are an acrostic of the Hebrew alphabet, and the fifth chapter has twenty-two lines, which is the number of letters in the Hebrew alphabet. This device apparently was used to aid the memory.

THEMES

Two primary themes of Lamentations are:

- the sovereignty of God and the justice of His judgments
- the hope of restoration after judgment.

OUTLINE

I. The Image of Destruction (1:1–22)
II. Judgment from God (2:1–22)

III. The Hope of Restoration (3:1–66)
IV. The Reality of Destruction (4:1—5:22)

Jerusalem in Affliction

1 How lonely sits the city
That was full of people!
How like a widow is she,
Who *was* great among the nations!
The princess among the provinces
Has become a slave!

²She weeps bitterly in the night,
Her tears *are* on her cheeks;
Among all her lovers
She has none to comfort *her*.
All her friends have dealt treacherously with
her;
They have become her enemies.

³Judah has gone into captivity,
Under affliction and hard servitude;
She dwells among the nations,
She finds no rest;
All her persecutors overtake her in dire straits.

⁴The roads to Zion mourn
Because no one comes to the set feasts.
All her gates are desolate;
Her priests sigh,
Her virgins are afflicted,
And she *is* in bitterness.

⁵Her adversaries have become the master,
Her enemies prosper;

For the LORD has afflicted her
Because of the multitude of her
transgressions.
Her children have gone into captivity before
the enemy.

⁶And from the daughter of Zion
All her splendor has departed.
Her princes have become like deer
That find no pasture,
That flee without strength
Before the pursuer.

⁷In the days of her affliction and roaming,
Jerusalem remembers all her pleasant things
That she had in the days of old.
When her people fell into the hand of the
enemy,
With no one to help her,
The adversaries saw her
And mocked at her downfall.ᵃ

⁸Jerusalem has sinned gravely,
Therefore she has become vile.ᵃ
All who honored her despise her
Because they have seen her
nakedness;
Yes, she sighs and turns away.

· · · · · · · · · · · · · · · · · ·

1:7 ᵃVulgate reads *her Sabbaths.*   **1:8** ᵃSeptuagint and Vulgate read *moved* or *removed.*

1:1 Jerusalem is personified as a woman. An alternate translation of the Hebrew phrase "full of people" is "mistress of the nations." The same Hebrew word may be translated as the noun "mistress" or as an adjective meaning "much, many, great"—hence "full." The former fits the female imagery of the verse. In either case, note the contrasts. She who had "many" or was "full" was filled with loneliness. She who had been a princess was now a slave. The term "widow" is appropriate. The widow, as a helpless member of society, often was rejected and treated poorly (see Ps. 68, Widowhood).

⁹Her uncleanness *is* in her skirts;
  She did not consider her destiny;
Therefore her collapse was awesome;
  She had no comforter.
"O Lᴏʀᴅ, behold my affliction,
  For *the* enemy is exalted!"

¹⁰The adversary has spread his hand
  Over all her pleasant things;
For she has seen the nations enter her
    sanctuary,
Those whom You commanded
  Not to enter Your assembly.

¹¹All her people sigh,
  They seek bread;
They have given their valuables for food to
    restore life.
"See, O Lᴏʀᴅ, and consider,
  For I am scorned."

¹²"*Is it* nothing to you, all you who pass by?
  Behold and see
If there is any sorrow like my sorrow,
  Which has been brought on me,
Which the Lᴏʀᴅ has inflicted
  In the day of His fierce anger.

¹³"From above He has sent fire into my bones,
  And it overpowered them;
He has spread a net for my feet
  And turned me back;
He has made me desolate
  And faint all the day.

¹⁴"The yoke of my transgressions was bound;[a]
  They were woven together by His hands,
And thrust upon my neck.
  He made my strength fail;
The Lord delivered me into the hands of *those*
    whom I am not able to withstand.

¹⁵"The Lord has trampled underfoot all my
    mighty *men* in my midst;
He has called an assembly against me
  To crush my young men;
The Lord trampled *as* in a winepress
  The virgin daughter of Judah.

¹⁶"For these *things* I weep;
  My eye, my eye overflows with water;
Because the comforter, who should restore my
    life,

Is far from me.
  My children are desolate
Because the enemy prevailed."

¹⁷Zion spreads out her hands,
  But no one comforts her;
The Lᴏʀᴅ has commanded concerning Jacob
  That those around him *become* his adversaries;
Jerusalem has become an unclean thing among
    them.

¹⁸"The Lᴏʀᴅ is righteous,
  For I rebelled against His commandment.
Hear now, all peoples,
  And behold my sorrow;
My virgins and my young men
  Have gone into captivity.

¹⁹"I called for my lovers,
  But they deceived me;
My priests and my elders
  Breathed their last in the city,
While they sought food
  To restore their life.

²⁰"See, O Lᴏʀᴅ, that I *am* in distress;
  My soul is troubled;
My heart is overturned within me,
  For I have been very rebellious.
Outside the sword bereaves,
  At home *it is* like death.

²¹"They have heard that I sigh,
  But no one comforts me.
All my enemies have heard of my trouble;
  They are glad that You have done *it.*
Bring on the day You have announced,
  That they may become like me.

²²"Let all their wickedness come before You,
  And do to them as You have done to me
For all my transgressions;
  For my sighs *are* many,
And my heart *is* faint."

God's Anger with Jerusalem

2 How the Lord has covered the daughter of
  Zion
With a cloud in His anger!
  He cast down from heaven to the earth

1:14 ᵃFollowing Masoretic Text and Targum; Septuagint, Syriac, and Vulgate read *watched over.*

1:18 A turning point in the chapter is marked by this verse. The focus moves from circumstances to God and then outward to "all peoples." Jeremiah did not soften the message in the verses that follow (vv. 19–22). The situation had not changed, but the city that had appeared a victim now assumed responsibility for her rebellion.

2:1–9 God is central. More than 40 references to God, either His title "Lord" or the pronouns "He" and "His," appear in these verses. The message concerns His righteous anger against "the daughter of Zion" (v. 8).

The beauty of Israel,
And did not remember His footstool
In the day of His anger.

²The Lord has swallowed up and has not pitied
All the dwelling places of Jacob.
He has thrown down in His wrath
The strongholds of the daughter of Judah;
He has brought *them* down to the ground;
He has profaned the kingdom and its princes.

³He has cut off in fierce anger
Every horn of Israel;
He has drawn back His right hand
From before the enemy.
He has blazed against Jacob like a flaming fire
Devouring all around.

⁴Standing like an enemy, He has bent His bow;
With His right hand, like an adversary,
He has slain all *who were* pleasing to His eye;
On the tent of the daughter of Zion,
He has poured out His fury like fire.

⁵The Lord was like an enemy.
He has swallowed up Israel,
He has swallowed up all her palaces;
He has destroyed her strongholds,
And has increased mourning and lamentation
In the daughter of Judah.

⁶He has done violence to His tabernacle,
As if it were a garden;
He has destroyed His place of assembly;
The Lord has caused
The appointed feasts and Sabbaths to be
    forgotten in Zion.
In His burning indignation He has spurned the
    king and the priest.

⁷The Lord has spurned His altar,
He has abandoned His sanctuary;
He has given up the walls of her palaces
Into the hand of the enemy.
They have made a noise in the house of the
    Lord
As on the day of a set feast.

⁸The Lord has purposed to destroy
The wall of the daughter of Zion.
He has stretched out a line;
He has not withdrawn His hand from
    destroying;
Therefore He has caused the rampart and wall
    to lament;
They languished together.

⁹Her gates have sunk into the ground;
He has destroyed and broken her bars.
Her king and her princes *are* among the
    nations;
The Law *is* no *more*,
And her prophets find no vision from the
    Lord.

¹⁰The elders of the daughter of Zion
Sit on the ground *and* keep silence;
They throw dust on their heads
And gird themselves with sackcloth.
The virgins of Jerusalem
Bow their heads to the ground.

¹¹My eyes fail with tears,
My heart is troubled;
My bile is poured on the ground
Because of the destruction of the daughter of
    my people,
Because the children and the infants
Faint in the streets of the city.

¹²They say to their mothers,
"Where *is* grain and wine?"
As they swoon like the wounded
In the streets of the city,
As their life is poured out
In their mothers' bosom.

¹³How shall I console you?
To what shall I liken you,
O daughter of Jerusalem?
What shall I compare with you, that I may
    comfort you,
O virgin daughter of Zion?
For your ruin *is* spread wide as the sea;
Who can heal you?

¹⁴Your prophets have seen for you
False and deceptive visions;
They have not uncovered your iniquity,
To bring back your captives,
But have envisioned for you false prophecies
    and delusions.

¹⁵All who pass by clap *their* hands at you;
They hiss and shake their heads
At the daughter of Jerusalem:
"*Is* this the city that is called
'The perfection of beauty,
The joy of the whole earth'?"

¹⁶All your enemies have opened their mouth
    against you;

2:10 Sackcloth, a rough fabric, originally made of goat's hair, was worn as an expression of grief or penitence. Mourning behavior included assuming a position of prostration as well as wearing ashes or dust on the head. "Elders" are city officials.

*Pain is God's beautiful gift to make us lean harder
on Him, when He knows we need it.*

Anne Ortlund

They hiss and gnash *their* teeth.
They say, "We have swallowed *her* up!
Surely this *is* the day we have waited for;
We have found *it,* we have seen *it!*"

17The LORD has done what He purposed;
He has fulfilled His word
Which He commanded in days of old.
He has thrown down and has not pitied,
And He has caused an enemy to rejoice over
    you;
He has exalted the horn of your adversaries.

18Their heart cried out to the Lord,
"O wall of the daughter of Zion,
Let tears run down like a river day and night;
Give yourself no relief;
Give your eyes no rest.

19"Arise, cry out in the night,
At the beginning of the watches;
Pour out your heart like water before the face
    of the Lord.
Lift your hands toward Him
For the life of your young children,
Who faint from hunger at the head of every
    street."

20"See, O LORD, and consider!
To whom have You done this?
Should the women eat their offspring,
The children they have cuddled?a
Should the priest and prophet be slain
In the sanctuary of the Lord?

21"Young and old lie
On the ground in the streets;
My virgins and my young men
Have fallen by the sword;
You have slain *them* in the day of Your anger,
You have slaughtered *and* not pitied.

22"You have invited as to a feast day
The terrors that surround me.
In the day of the LORD's anger
There was no refugee or survivor.
Those whom I have borne and brought up
My enemies have destroyed."

The Prophet's Anguish and Hope

3 I *am* the man *who* has seen affliction by the
    rod of His wrath.
2He has led me and made *me* walk
In darkness and not *in* light.
3Surely He has turned His hand against me
Time and time again throughout the day.

4He has aged my flesh and my skin,
And broken my bones.
5He has besieged me
And surrounded *me* with bitterness and
    woe.
6He has set me in dark places
Like the dead of long ago.

7He has hedged me in so that I cannot get out;
He has made my chain heavy.
8Even when I cry and shout,
He shuts out my prayer.
9He has blocked my ways with hewn stone;
He has made my paths crooked.

10He *has been* to me a bear lying in wait,
Like a lion in ambush.
11He has turned aside my ways and torn me in
    pieces;
He has made me desolate.
12He has bent His bow
And set me up as a target for the arrow.

13He has caused the arrows of His quiver
To pierce my loins.a
14I have become the ridicule of all my
    people—
Their taunting song all the day.
15He has filled me with bitterness,
He has made me drink wormwood.

16He has also broken my teeth with gravel,
And covered me with ashes.
17You have moved my soul far from peace;
I have forgotten prosperity.
18And I said, "My strength and my hope
Have perished from the LORD."

2:20 aVulgate reads *a span long.*   **3:13** aLiterally *kidneys*

2:17 God promised or covenanted with Moses to judge sin (see Deut. 28:15, 16). The destruction witnessed is a fulfillment of that promise.

3:1–18 Jeremiah gave a personal testimony which paralleled the experience of the city as a whole (see Lam. 1; 2). The people felt forsaken by the Lord.

¹⁹Remember my affliction and roaming,
The wormwood and the gall.
²⁰My soul still remembers
And sinks within me.
²¹This I recall to my mind,
Therefore I have hope.

²²*Through* the LORD's mercies we are not
consumed,
Because His compassions fail not.
²³*They are* new every morning;
Great *is* Your faithfulness.
²⁴"The LORD *is* my portion," says my soul,
"Therefore I hope in Him!"

²⁵The LORD *is* good to those who wait for Him,
To the soul *who* seeks Him.
²⁶*It is* good that *one* should hope and wait quietly
For the salvation of the LORD.
²⁷*It is* good for a man to bear
The yoke in his youth.

²⁸Let him sit alone and keep silent,
Because *God* has laid *it* on him;
²⁹Let him put his mouth in the dust—
There may yet be hope.
³⁰Let him give *his* cheek to the one who strikes
him,
And be full of reproach.

³¹For the Lord will not cast off forever.
³²Though He causes grief,
Yet He will show compassion
According to the multitude of His mercies.
³³For He does not afflict willingly,
Nor grieve the children of men.

³⁴To crush under one's feet
All the prisoners of the earth,
³⁵To turn aside the justice *due* a man

Before the face of the Most High,
³⁶Or subvert a man in his cause—
The Lord does not approve.

³⁷Who *is* he *who* speaks and it comes to pass,
When the Lord has not commanded *it?*
³⁸*Is it* not from the mouth of the Most High
That woe and well-being proceed?
³⁹Why should a living man complain,
A man for the punishment of his sins?

⁴⁰Let us search out and examine our ways,
And turn back to the LORD;
⁴¹Let us lift our hearts and hands
To God in heaven.
⁴²We have transgressed and rebelled;
You have not pardoned.

⁴³You have covered *Yourself* with anger
And pursued us;
You have slain *and* not pitied.
⁴⁴You have covered Yourself with a cloud,
That prayer should not pass through.
⁴⁵You have made us an offscouring and refuse
In the midst of the peoples.

⁴⁶All our enemies
Have opened their mouths against us.
⁴⁷Fear and a snare have come upon us,
Desolation and destruction.
⁴⁸My eyes overflow with rivers of water
For the destruction of the daughter of my
people.

⁴⁹My eyes flow and do not cease,
Without interruption,
⁵⁰Till the LORD from heaven
Looks down and sees.
⁵¹My eyes bring suffering to my soul
Because of all the daughters of my city.

3:19, 20 Wormwood is a bitter plant (see Prov. 5:4, note; chart, The Herbs of the Bible). Gall, also bitter, is a secretion of the liver. Both suggest the extent of Jeremiah's sorrowful and painful experience.

3:21–24 Jeremiah had reached the point of despair. Verse 21 is a pivotal statement. Here Jeremiah turned toward God. His remembrance of God's faithfulness marked the turning point. The Hebrew word translated "mercies" (v. 22) refers to the steadfast love or covenant loyalty of the Lord (see Ps. 5:7–12, note). Every woman will have times of discouragement and even depression during which she must remember and even cling to God's faithfulness (see 1 Sam. 16, Depression)

3:22 God's faithfulness is a commitment on His part and is as dependable as the scheduled appearances of the sun and moon (Ps. 89:2, 5, 36, 37). When you wake up in the morning, God will always be there. Family and friends may disappoint; heroes and heroines may fail to live up to expectations. Nevertheless, God is ever faithful.

The root meaning of faithfulness (Heb. *'emunah*) is "cer-

tainty" and "dependability." Faithfulness describes who God is (1 Cor. 1:9). No matter what you do, God cannot be unfaithful because He cannot deny Himself (2 Tim. 2:13). He is steadfast and trustworthy. He keeps His promises (Heb. 10:23).

God's presence is assured, even if you are unaware of it (Matt. 28:20). His faithfulness is experienced in His protection (2 Thess. 3:3), mercy (Ps. 89:2), preservation (1 Thess. 5:23, 24), love (Rom. 8:35–39), and discipline (Ps. 89:32, 33); it is revealed in all His promises (Josh. 23:14). What a comfort and encouragement to experience His faithfulness (see Ex. 33; Deut. 4; 32; 2 Chr. 19; Job 23; 42; Ps. 25; 90; 102; 119; Is. 6; 65; Jer. 23; Rom. 2; Eph. 1; 1 John 4, Attributes of God).

3:25–41 The prophet's job was to speak on behalf of God. Having reconciled his own sorrow in the previous verses (see vv. 21–24), Jeremiah turned his attention outward and preached to the people of Judah. His message urged them to accept what was from the hand of God without complaint and hope in His mercy.

⁵²My enemies without cause
  Hunted me down like a bird.
⁵³They silenced[a] my life in the pit
  And threw stones at me.
⁵⁴The waters flowed over my head;
  I said, "I am cut off!"

⁵⁵I called on Your name, O Lord,
  From the lowest pit.
⁵⁶You have heard my voice:
  "Do not hide Your ear
  From my sighing, from my cry for help."
⁵⁷You drew near on the day I called on You,
  And said, "Do not fear!"

⁵⁸O Lord, You have pleaded the case for my
    soul;
  You have redeemed my life.
⁵⁹O Lord, You have seen how I am wronged;
  Judge my case.
⁶⁰You have seen all their vengeance,
  All their schemes against me.

⁶¹You have heard their reproach, O Lord,
  All their schemes against me,
⁶²The lips of my enemies
  And their whispering against me all the day.
⁶³Look at their sitting down and their rising up;
  I am their taunting song.

⁶⁴Repay them, O Lord,
  According to the work of their hands.
⁶⁵Give them a veiled[a] heart;
  Your curse be upon them!
⁶⁶In Your anger,
  Pursue and destroy them
  From under the heavens of the Lord.

The Degradation of Zion

4 How the gold has become dim!
  How changed the fine gold!
  The stones of the sanctuary are scattered
  At the head of every street.

²The precious sons of Zion,
  Valuable as fine gold,
  How they are regarded as clay pots,
  The work of the hands of the potter!

³Even the jackals present their breasts
  To nurse their young;
  But the daughter of my people is cruel,
  Like ostriches in the wilderness.

⁴The tongue of the infant clings
  To the roof of its mouth for thirst;
  The young children ask for bread,
  But no one breaks it for them.

⁵Those who ate delicacies
  Are desolate in the streets;
  Those who were brought up in scarlet
  Embrace ash heaps.

⁶The punishment of the iniquity of the
    daughter of my people
  Is greater than the punishment of the sin of
    Sodom,
  Which was overthrown in a moment,
  With no hand to help her!

⁷Her Nazirites[a] were brighter than snow
  And whiter than milk;
  They were more ruddy in body than rubies,
  Like sapphire in their appearance.

⁸Now their appearance is blacker than soot;
  They go unrecognized in the streets;
  Their skin clings to their bones,
  It has become as dry as wood.

⁹Those slain by the sword are better off
  Than those who die of hunger;
  For these pine away,
  Stricken for lack of the fruits of the field.

¹⁰The hands of the compassionate women
  Have cooked their own children;
  They became food for them
  In the destruction of the daughter of my
    people.

¹¹The Lord has fulfilled His fury,
  He has poured out His fierce anger.

3:53 [a]Septuagint reads put to death.   3:65 [a]A Jewish tradition reads sorrow of.   4:7 [a]Or nobles

---

4:1 The temple was destroyed with the fall of Jerusalem in 586 b.c. The reference is to the people of Israel as God's sanctuary. God's people were the real treasure of the city. God's true dwelling place is among His people, not in fine buildings.

4:6 God destroyed Sodom quickly and without human intervention (see Gen. 19:24, 25). Jerusalem was left in the hands of her captors, making her destruction neither quick nor merciful.

4:7 The Nazirites in ancient Israel had strict religious convictions. They took vows to abstain from wine and strong drink, contact with unclean objects such as dead bodies, and use of the razor. They were not to cut their hair (see Num. 6:1–8). This verse may refer to any class of nobility. Its significance lies in the fact that no group of society was spared destruction.

4:10 During the severe siege, the plight of the children was especially tragic (vv. 2–4). The ultimate degradation came when mothers boiled and ate their children because food was so scarce (Lam. 2:20). The practice of cannibalism emphasizes the horror of the siege.

He kindled a fire in Zion,
And it has devoured its foundations.

¹²The kings of the earth,
And all inhabitants of the world,
Would not have believed
That the adversary and the enemy
Could enter the gates of Jerusalem—

¹³Because of the sins of her prophets
And the iniquities of her priests,
Who shed in her midst
The blood of the just.

¹⁴They wandered blind in the streets;
They have defiled themselves with blood,
So that no one would touch their garments.

¹⁵They cried out to them,
"Go away, unclean!
Go away, go away,
Do not touch us!"
When they fled and wandered,
Those among the nations said,
"They shall no longer dwell *here.*"

¹⁶The face[a] of the LORD scattered them;
He no longer regards them.
The people do not respect the priests
Nor show favor to the elders.

¹⁷Still our eyes failed us,
Watching vainly for our help;
In our watching we watched
For a nation *that* could not save *us.*

¹⁸They tracked our steps
So that we could not walk in our
streets.
Our end was near;
Our days were over,
For our end had come.

¹⁹Our pursuers were swifter
Than the eagles of the heavens.
They pursued us on the mountains
And lay in wait for us in the wilderness.

²⁰The breath of our nostrils, the anointed of the
LORD,
Was caught in their pits,
Of whom we said, "Under his shadow
We shall live among the nations."

²¹Rejoice and be glad, O daughter of Edom,
You who dwell in the land of Uz!
The cup shall also pass over to you
And you shall become drunk and make yourself
naked.

²²*The punishment of* your iniquity is accomplished,
O daughter of Zion;
He will no longer send you into captivity.
He will punish your iniquity,
O daughter of Edom;
He will uncover your sins!

A Prayer for Restoration

5 Remember, O LORD, what has come upon us;
Look, and behold our reproach!
²Our inheritance has been turned over to aliens,
And our houses to foreigners.
³We have become orphans and waifs,
Our mothers *are* like widows.

⁴We pay for the water we drink,
And our wood comes at a price.
⁵*They* pursue at our heels;[a]
We labor *and* have no rest.
⁶We have given our hand *to* the Egyptians
And the Assyrians, to be satisfied with bread.

⁷Our fathers sinned *and are* no more,
But we bear their iniquities.
⁸Servants rule over us;
There is none to deliver *us* from their hand.
⁹We get our bread *at the risk* of our lives,
Because of the sword in the wilderness.

¹⁰Our skin is hot as an oven,
Because of the fever of famine.
¹¹They ravished the women in Zion,
The maidens in the cities of Judah.
¹²Princes were hung up by their hands,
And elders were not respected.
¹³Young men ground at the millstones;
Boys staggered under *loads of* wood.
¹⁴The elders have ceased *gathering at* the
gate,
And the young men from their music.

¹⁵The joy of our heart has ceased;
Our dance has turned into mourning.
¹⁶The crown has fallen *from* our head.
Woe to us, for we have sinned!

················· **4:16** [a]Targum reads *anger.*   **5:5** [a]Literally *necks*

4:21, 22 The Edomites were descendants of Esau and long-time enemies of Israel. Edom was located south of the Dead Sea. These verses emphasize that God would judge Israel's enemies in His time (see also Obadiah).

5:1–18 The reality of bondage for those who survived deporta-tion to Babylon included extreme hardship, sexual abuse, hu-miliation, and servitude. This passage is viewed by others as a description of the terrible conditions in Jerusalem after its capture.

17Because of this our heart is faint;
Because of these *things* our eyes grow dim;
18Because of Mount Zion which is desolate,
With foxes walking about on it.

19You, O Lord, remain forever;
Your throne from generation to generation.

20Why do You forget us forever,
And forsake us for so long a time?
21Turn us back to You, O Lord, and we will be restored;
Renew our days as of old,
22Unless You have utterly rejected us,
And are very angry with us!

5:19–22 Lamentations ends with a plea to God to restore and renew. The conclusion affirms the unchangeable nature of the Lord (see Lam. 3:22, note). He remains sovereign on His throne.

Ezekiel

The prophet Ezekiel (Heb., lit. "God strengthens") was born into a priestly family who probably lived in Jerusalem (Ezek. 1:3). Ezekiel descended from the accepted priestly line of Zadok (see 1 Kin. 2:35) in contrast to Jeremiah, who descended from the rejected priestly line of Abiathar. In 597 B.C., Ezekiel was carried into exile by the Babylonians with King Jehoiachin of Judah and ten thousand other prominent citizens, including military leaders, artisans, and craftsmen (2 Kin. 24:8–16).

Ezekiel lived with other Jewish exiles in a settlement called Tel Abib, located near the Chebar River and the ancient site of Nippur, southeast of Babylon (Ezek. 1:1–3). He prophesied among the exiles for at least twenty-two years from 593 to 571 B.C. Little more is known of Ezekiel's circumstances. He was married, although his wife died shortly before the fall of Jerusalem in 586 B.C. (Ezek. 24:15–18). He had his own house, where he was visited on occasion by elders of his community seeking a word from God (Ezek. 8:1).

Ezekiel was an unusual figure among the Lord's prophets. More than any other prophet, Ezekiel's preaching was accompanied by numerous, striking symbolic acts (see Ezek. 3:1, 2; 4:1–17; 5:1–4; 12:3–7). Sensitive to ritual defilement as a result of his priestly upbringing (Ezek. 4:14, 15), Ezekiel nonetheless could use shockingly graphic language to depict the sins of the people (Ezek. 23:20, 21). The vocabulary, phraseology, and theology of his book bear the imprint of a singular and powerful mind and argue for a single author. For a book of its size, containing prophecies spanning more than two decades, the Book of Ezekiel displays an amazing consistency of language, perspective, and purpose.

DATE

This prophetic book, as the Book of Haggai, contains an orderly sequence of dates. Various visions and prophecies are dated, including the year, month, and day. With one exception, the dates follow a scheme based on the year in which King Jehoiachin of Judah was taken into captivity by the Babylonians (Ezek. 1:1). Based on archaeological records and astronomical data, scholars can give precise equivalents in the modern calendar for these dates with reasonable confidence. The beginning of Ezekiel's prophetic ministry is dated 593 B.C. Ezekiel's last dated prophecy was delivered April 26, 571 B.C. (Ezek. 29:17). The book was probably compiled by Ezekiel into its final form shortly thereafter.

BACKGROUND

SETTING: Ezekiel prophesied during a period of great turmoil. The people of Judah had reverted to idolatry and lawlessness after the death of King Josiah in 609 B.C. The Exile of King Jehoiachin caused a great stir among God's people, who had believed that the Lord would always deliver Jerusalem from the armies of the nations. False prophets were

preaching that the Lord soon would overthrow the Babylonians and return Jehoiachin to his throne. In Judah, the prophet Jeremiah proclaimed that Nebuchadnezzar, the Babylonian king, was God's instrument of judgment on the nation for its sins (Jer. 34:1–3).

Under King Zedekiah, the leaders of Judah revolted against Babylon around 589 B.C. In response, the Babylonians ravaged Judah. After a siege of eighteen months, they destroyed even Jerusalem and the temple in 586 B.C. and carried all but the poorest survivors into Exile (Jer. 39:1, 2). This catastrophe weakened the faith of many exiles in Ezekiel's community. Some grumbled about the justice of God (Ezek. 18:2). Others despaired, thinking that God had rejected His people forever (Ezek. 37:11; see Ps. 137).

PURPOSE: Like most of the Lord's prophets, Ezekiel's message consisted of two elements: judgment and hope. Prior to the fall of Jerusalem (586 B.C.), Ezekiel primarily proclaimed coming judgment because of the people's sins. After the fall of Jerusalem, Ezekiel focused on the message of hope, which included restoration for God's people and judgment on their enemies. Ezekiel also proclaimed the concept of individual responsibility (Ezek. 18:1–32). Each person is responsible for his own sins.

AUDIENCE: Ezekiel was called to preach to "the house of Israel" (Ezek. 3:4). This designation applied to the inhabitants of Judah, also known as the southern kingdom. Though the designation "Israel" usually applied to the northern kingdom, after the nation was destroyed by the Assyrians, its inhabitants disappeared into Exile (722 B.C.). After that time, Israel was sometimes used to designate the southern kingdom (see chart, Terminology for the Divided Kingdom). Ezekiel ministered to God's people in Babylon, though in some of his visions he was transported to Jerusalem. Although the leaders came to hear him (Ezek. 14:1; 20:1; 33:30–32), the majority of the exiles failed to accept his preaching (Ezek. 33:32).

LITERARY CHARACTERISTICS: The Book of Ezekiel consists almost entirely of visions and prophetic oracles. The book can be divided roughly into three sections: judgment on God's people (Ezek. 1—24), judgment on the nations (Ezek. 25—32), and salvation for God's people (Ezek. 33—48).

The Book of Ezekiel consists of both prose and poetry. The prophet used such literary devices as parables, allegories, and rhetorical questions. Several unusual stylistic features appear in the Book of Ezekiel. The prophet utilized popular religious sayings to introduce his teachings. Symbolic actions and pantomines were employed as a means of conveying the Lord's word. Ezekiel repeatedly is referred to as "son of man" (over 80 times), a phrase emphasizing the humanness of the prophet. Ezekiel's choice of language and his preaching appear to have been influenced by the Mosaic Law.

THEMES

A major theme of the Book of Ezekiel is the Lord's revelation of His holiness and majesty by the fulfillment of His Word in the history of God's people and the nations. Throughout the book the Lord proclaimed that after He fulfilled His Word, people would "know that I am the LORD" (see Ezek. 6:10, 13; 7:4, 9, 27; 11:12).

Another major theme is the Lord's judgment on Judah and Jerusalem because of the people's sins. Although God delighted in His people, gave Himself to them, and proved Himself worthy of their exclusive devotion, they turned to other gods and other nations for security and blessing (Ezek. 16; 23). Their unfaithfulness and impurity obscured His holiness in the eyes of the nations. Therefore, the Lord would restore His honor or glory by bringing judgment. Ezekiel also taught the concept of individual responsibility: "The soul who sins shall die" (Ezek. 18:4; see also 7:27; 18:30; 24:14; 33:20; 36:19).

Ezekiel emphasized future hope and forgiveness for the Lord's people. Chapters 33—39 consist of restoration messages, while chapters 40—48 provide a picture of the restored community. For Ezekiel, the revelation of God's glory was connected closely to the temple. The coming of God to dwell in the temple (Ezek. 43) foreshadowed the coming of the Holy Spirit to the church as the spiritual temple of God (Eph. 2:19–22). The Book of Ezekiel also contains a new covenant passage (Ezek. 36:22–32) similar to that found in the Book of Jeremiah (Jer. 31:31–34).

OUTLINE

I. Judgment on Judah and Jerusalem (1:1—24:27)
  A. Ezekiel's call to prophesy (1:1—3:27)
    1. His vision of God's glory (1:1–28)
    2. His commissioning (2:1—3:15)
    3. His appointment as a watchman (3:16–27)
  B. Symbolic acts of judgment on God's people (4:1—5:17)
  C. Oracles of judgment on God's people (6:1—7:27)
  D. A vision of judgment at the temple (8:1—11:25)
    1. Idolatrous practices (8:1–18)
    2. The release of executioners in Jerusalem (9:1–11)
    3. The departure of God's glory from the temple (10:1–22)
    4. The inheritance of the Land by the exiles (11:1–25)
  E. Symbolic acts regarding the Exile (12:1–28)
  F. More oracles of judgment on God's People (13:1—24:27)
    1. A word against false prophets (13:1–23)
    2. The judgment against ineffective intercessors (14:1–23)
    3. The figure of the burned vine (15:1–8)
    4. The parable of the harlot (16:1–63)
    5. The parable of the eagles and branches (17:1–24)
    6. An explanation of God's justice (18:1–32)
    7. A lament for the princes of Israel (19:1–14)
    8. A history of God's rebellious people (20:1–49)

    9. The sword of the Lord's judgment (21:1–32)
    10. God's judgment on Jerusalem (22:1–31)
    11. The parable of two sisters (23:1–49)
    12. The figure of the cooking pot (24:1–14)
    13. The death of the beloved (24:15–27)
II. God's Judgment on the Nations (25:1—32:32)
  A. Oracles of retribution on Ammon, Moab, Edom, and Philistia (25:1–17)
  B. Oracles against Tyre (26:1—28:19)
  C. Oracle against Sidon (28:20–26)
  D. Oracles against Egypt (29:1—32:32)
III. Salvation for God's People (33:1—48:35)
  A. A defense of God's justice (33:1–20)
  B. The unworthiness of God's people (33:21–33)
  C. The evil shepherds vs. the Good Shepherd (34:1–31)
  D. Mount Seir vs. the mountains of Israel (35:1—36:38)
  E. The vision of the valley of dry bones (37:1–28)
  F. The judgment on Gog (38:1—39:29)
  G. A vision of the restored kingdom (40:1—48:35)
    1. The new temple (40:1—43:27)
    2. The regulations for worship (44:1—46:24)
    3. New conditions in the Land (47:1–23)
    4. New allotments for the tribes of Israel (48:1–35)

Ezekiel's Vision of God

1 Now it came to pass in the thirtieth year, in the fourth *month,* on the fifth *day* of the month, as I *was* among the captives by the River Chebar, *that* the heavens were opened and I saw visions[a] of God. [2]On the fifth *day* of the month, which *was* in the fifth year of King Jehoiachin's captivity, [3]the word of the LORD came expressly to Ezekiel the priest, the son of Buzi, in the land of the Chaldeans[a] by the River Chebar; and the hand of the LORD was upon him there.

[4]Then I looked, and behold, a whirlwind was coming out of the north, a great cloud with raging fire engulfing itself; and brightness *was* all around it and radiating out of its midst like the color of amber, out of the midst of the fire. [5]Also from within it *came* the likeness of four living creatures. And this *was* their appearance: they had the likeness of a man. [6]Each one had four faces, and each one had four wings. [7]Their legs *were* straight, and the soles of their feet *were* like the soles of calves' feet. They sparkled like the color of burnished bronze. [8]The hands of a man *were* under their wings on their four sides; and each of the four had faces and wings. [9]Their wings touched one another. *The creatures* did not turn when they went, but each one went straight forward.

[10]As for the likeness of their faces, *each* had the face of a man; each of the four had the face of a lion on the right side, each of the four had the face of an ox on the left side, and each of the four had the face of an eagle. [11]Thus *were* their faces. Their wings stretched upward; two *wings* of each one touched one another, and two covered their bodies. [12]And each one went straight forward; they went wherever the spirit wanted to go, and they did not turn when they went.

[13]As for the likeness of the living creatures, their appearance *was* like burning coals of fire, like the appearance of torches going back and forth among the living creatures. The fire was bright, and out of the fire went lightning. [14]And the living creatures ran back and forth, in appearance like a flash of lightning.

[15]Now as I looked at the living creatures, behold, a wheel *was* on the earth beside each living creature with its four faces. [16]The appearance of the wheels and their workings *was* like the color of beryl, and all four had the same likeness. The appearance of their workings *was,* as it were, a wheel in the middle of a wheel. [17]When they moved, they went toward any one of four directions; they did not turn aside when they went. [18]As for their rims, they were so high they were awesome; and their rims *were* full of eyes, all around the four of them. [19]When the living creatures went, the wheels went beside them; and when the living creatures were lifted up from the earth, the wheels were lifted up. [20]Wherever the spirit wanted to go, they went, *because* there the spirit went; and the wheels were lifted together with them, for the spirit of the living creatures[a] *was* in the wheels. [21]When those went, *these* went; when those stood, *these* stood; and when those were lifted up from the earth, the wheels were lifted up together with them, for the spirit of the living creatures[a] *was* in the wheels.

[22]The likeness of the firmament above the heads of the living creatures[a] *was* like the color of an awesome crystal, stretched out over their heads. [23]And under the firmament their wings *spread out* straight, one toward another. Each one had two which covered one side, and each one had two which covered the other side of the body. [24]When they went, I heard the noise of their wings, like the noise of many waters, like the voice of the Almighty, a tumult like the noise of an

1:1 [a]Following Masoretic Text, Septuagint, and Vulgate; Syriac and Targum read *a vision.* 1:3 [a]Or *Babylonians,* and so elsewhere in this book 1:20 [a]Literally *living creature;* Septuagint and Vulgate read *spirit of life;* Targum reads *creatures.* 1:21 [a]Literally *living creature;* Septuagint and Vulgate read *spirit of life;* Targum reads *creatures.* 1:22 [a]Following Septuagint, Targum, and Vulgate; Masoretic Text reads *living creature.*

1:1 **The thirtieth year** may refer to the 30th year of Josiah's reform, which began in 622 B.C., or to the age of Ezekiel himself. The latter interpretation is more likely. Ezekiel may have had in mind the special significance of the 30th year for himself as a member of a priestly family. The 30th year was the usual age for a man to assume the full responsibilities of the priesthood (Num. 4:3). If this be the case, then at the precise time Ezekiel would have assumed his priestly responsibilities, the Lord called him to be a prophet to His people in Exile.

1:2, 3 **King Jehoiachin's captivity** is used as a reference point for dating. That captivity began in 597 B.C. Thus, Ezekiel's call to be a prophet came around 593 B.C. The River Chebar was an irrigation canal off the Euphrates River. It left the Euphrates north of Babylon and flowed to the southeast of Babylon, passing through the city of Nippur before it re-entered the Euphrates.

1:4–28 **Ezekiel's account of his vision** of God began with a physical description of a storm cloud "coming out of the north." As it drew closer, an outline emerged in which four "living creatures," along with intersecting wheels, supported a brilliant expanse above which stood a sapphire throne. According to Jewish tradition the four faces of the living creatures (man, lion, ox, eagle) were chosen for their places of honor in their respective domains. Despite their dignified status, all served under God's chariot. The description of intersecting wheels with rims full of eyes may indicate both the omnipresence and omniscience of God.

As the theophany or vision of God drew nearer, Ezekiel's description became more vague as he attempted to portray the glory of God. Precision gave way to approximations (note the multiple uses of "appearance" and "likeness" in vv. 26–28) until Ezekiel fell on his face in recognition of "the appearance of the likeness of the glory of the LORD" (v. 28).

army; and when they stood still, they let down their wings. ²⁵A voice came from above the firmament that *was* over their heads; whenever they stood, they let down their wings.

²⁶And above the firmament over their heads *was* the likeness of a throne, in appearance like a sapphire stone; on the likeness of the throne *was* a likeness with the appearance of a man high above it. ²⁷Also from the appearance of His waist and upward I saw, as it were, the color of amber with the appearance of fire all around within it; and from the appearance of His waist and downward I saw, as it were, the appearance of fire with brightness all around. ²⁸Like the appearance of a rainbow in a cloud on a rainy day, so *was* the appearance of the brightness all around it. This *was* the appearance of the likeness of the glory of the LORD.

Ezekiel Sent to Rebellious Israel

So when I saw *it*, I fell on my face, and I heard a voice of One speaking.

2 And He said to me, "Son of man, stand on your feet, and I will speak to you." ²Then the Spirit entered me when He spoke to me, and set me on my feet; and I heard Him who spoke to me. ³And He said to me: "Son of man, I am sending you to the children of Israel, to a rebellious nation that has rebelled against Me; they and their fathers have transgressed against Me to this very day. ⁴For *they are* impudent and stubborn children. I am sending you to them, and you shall say to them, 'Thus says the Lord GOD.' ⁵As for them, whether they hear or whether they refuse—for they *are* a rebellious house—yet they will know that a prophet has been among them.

⁶"And you, son of man, do not be afraid of them nor be afraid of their words, though briers and thorns *are* with you and you dwell among scorpions; do not be afraid of their words or dismayed by their looks, though they *are* a rebellious house. ⁷You shall speak My words to them, whether they hear or whether they refuse, for they *are* rebellious. ⁸But you, son of man, hear what I say to you.

Do not be rebellious like that rebellious house; open your mouth and eat what I give you."

⁹Now when I looked, there was a hand stretched out to me; and behold, a scroll of a book *was* in it. ¹⁰Then He spread it before me; and *there was* writing on the inside and on the outside, and written on it *were* lamentations and mourning and woe.

3 Moreover He said to me, "Son of man, eat what you find; eat this scroll, and go, speak to the house of Israel." ²So I opened my mouth, and He caused me to eat that scroll.

³And He said to me, "Son of man, feed your belly, and fill your stomach with this scroll that I give you." So I ate, and it was in my mouth like honey in sweetness.

⁴Then He said to me: "Son of man, go to the house of Israel and speak with My words to them. ⁵For you *are* not sent to a people of unfamiliar speech and of hard language, *but* to the house of Israel, ⁶not to many people of unfamiliar speech and of hard language, whose words you cannot understand. Surely, had I sent you to them, they would have listened to you. ⁷But the house of Israel will not listen to you, because they will not listen to Me; for all the house of Israel *are* impudent and hard-hearted. ⁸Behold, I have made your face strong against their faces, and your forehead strong against their foreheads. ⁹Like adamant stone, harder than flint, I have made your forehead; do not be afraid of them, nor be dismayed at their looks, though they *are* a rebellious house."

¹⁰Moreover He said to me: "Son of man, receive into your heart all My words that I speak to you, and hear with your ears. ¹¹And go, get to the captives, to the children of your people, and speak to them and tell them, 'Thus says the Lord GOD,' whether they hear, or whether they refuse."

¹²Then the Spirit lifted me up, and I heard behind me a great thunderous voice: "Blessed *is* the glory of the LORD from His place!" ¹³*I* also *heard* the noise of the wings of the living creatures that

---

1:28 Ezekiel's vision contained several important messages for both the prophet and his fellow exiles. God's people associated God's glory and enthronement with the temple in Jerusalem (1 Kin. 8:10–13); but here, God's glory appeared to the priest Ezekiel while he was in Exile. God was made manifest in His mobile chariot throne in splendor and majesty. God revealed to Ezekiel that He was far superior to any earthly king or kingdom. Certainly, His glory exceeded that of Nebuchadnezzar. The God of Israel had come in victory to His exiled people. The natural question in the minds of those in Exile was, "What does the appearance of God's glory mean for Jerusalem and the temple?" Obviously, God could not be limited to the temple. He is omnipresent and omnipotent. The message of impending judgment for Jerusalem was also delivered. God was removing His glory (the manifestation of His presence) in order to allow Nebuchadnezzar to destroy His city and to remove from His people the false sense of security

they had developed. Nevertheless, there was also hope that ultimately His glory would return, bringing restoration to His people and His city.

2:1 Ezekiel's title "son of man" was God's way of addressing Ezekiel in order to emphasize his status as a mortal in contrast to the divine glory he had just witnessed. This title appears approximately 90 times in the book.

3:1–6 The eating of the scroll graphically portrayed the divine origin of Ezekiel's message as well as his own acceptance of that message. The message must become part of the prophet's life. The words that Ezekiel would preach to his fellow exiles were God's words. As such, a rejection of them by the exilic community was not so much a rejection of the prophet as it was a rejection of God Himself. Note that "house of Israel" referred to God's covenant people who lived in Judah.

touched one another, and the noise of the wheels beside them, and a great thunderous noise. [14]So the Spirit lifted me up and took me away, and I went in bitterness, in the heat of my spirit; but the hand of the LORD was strong upon me. [15]Then I came to the captives at Tel Abib, who dwelt by the River Chebar; and I sat where they sat, and remained there astonished among them seven days.

Ezekiel Is a Watchman

[16]Now it came to pass at the end of seven days that the word of the LORD came to me, saying, [17]"Son of man, I have made you a watchman for the house of Israel; therefore hear a word from My mouth, and give them warning from Me: [18]When I say to the wicked, 'You shall surely die,' and you give him no warning, nor speak to warn the wicked from his wicked way, to save his life, that same wicked *man* shall die in his iniquity; but his blood I will require at your hand. [19]Yet, if you warn the wicked, and he does not turn from his wickedness, nor from his wicked way, he shall die in his iniquity; but you have delivered your soul.

[20]"Again, when a righteous *man* turns from his righteousness and commits iniquity, and I lay a stumbling block before him, he shall die; because you did not give him warning, he shall die in his sin, and his righteousness which he has done shall not be remembered; but his blood I will require at your hand. [21]Nevertheless if you warn the righteous *man* that the righteous should not sin, and he does not sin, he shall surely live because he took warning; also you will have delivered your soul."

[22]Then the hand of the LORD was upon me there, and He said to me, "Arise, go out into the plain, and there I shall talk with you."

[23]So I arose and went out into the plain, and behold, the glory of the LORD stood there, like the glory which I saw by the River Chebar; and I fell on my face. [24]Then the Spirit entered me and set me on my feet, and spoke with me and said to me: "Go, shut yourself inside your house. [25]And you, O son of man, surely they will put ropes on you and bind you with them, so that you cannot go out among them. [26]I will make your tongue cling to the roof of your mouth, so that you shall be mute and not be one to rebuke them, for they *are* a rebellious house. [27]But when I speak with you, I will open your mouth, and you shall say to them, 'Thus says the Lord GOD.' He who hears, let him hear; and he who refuses, let him refuse; for they *are* a rebellious house.

The Siege of Jerusalem Portrayed

4 "You also, son of man, take a clay tablet and lay it before you, and portray on it a city, Jerusalem. [2]Lay siege against it, build a siege wall against it, and heap up a mound against it; set camps against it also, and place battering rams against it all around. [3]Moreover take for yourself an iron plate, and set it *as* an iron wall between you and the city. Set your face against it, and it shall be besieged, and you shall lay siege against it. This *will be* a sign to the house of Israel.

[4]"Lie also on your left side, and lay the iniquity of the house of Israel upon it. *According* to the number of the days that you lie on it, you shall bear their iniquity. [5]For I have laid on you the years of their iniquity, according to the number of the days, three hundred and ninety days; so you shall bear the iniquity of the house of Israel. [6]And when you have completed them, lie again on your right side; then you shall bear the iniquity of the house of Judah forty days. I have laid on you a day for each year.

[7]"Therefore you shall set your face toward the siege of Jerusalem; your arm *shall be* uncovered, and you shall prophesy against it. [8]And surely I will restrain you so that you cannot turn from one

---

3:14, 15 The expression in the heat of my spirit may refer to the prophet's knowledge that his ministry would be largely one of rejection and pain. He experienced the same type of anger that the Lord had toward His rebellious people. Tel Abib means "mound left by the flood" in Akkadian, probably referring to mounds covering buried cities. It was not uncommon for exiles to occupy such ruins (see Ezra 2:59; Neh. 7:61). Ezekiel's "seven days" may refer symbolically to the traditional time of mourning for the dead (see Gen. 50:10; Num. 19:11; Job 2:13), as well as to the period of consecration for a priest (see Lev. 8:33).

3:16–21 Ezekiel was commissioned as a watchman with the responsibility to warn the exilic community of impending danger. These verses emphasize Ezekiel's need to be faithful regardless of the response of the people.

3:24–27 The Lord afflicted Ezekiel with muteness (v. 26), which lasted until the fall of Jerusalem (Ezek. 33:21, 22), except for brief periods when God commanded him to speak.

4:1 Ezekiel's ministry began with a series of symbolic acts, providing a message for the exilic community (Ezek. 4:1–6:7). Ezekiel repeatedly emphasized God's impending judgment on Jerusalem, the site of Judah's hope, in an attempt to break the people's ironclad belief that God would never allow Jerusalem to be harmed.

4:3 Ezekiel used a common household cooking tool to symbolize the impassable barrier between God and Jerusalem. The people would cry out to God when the invading army besieged Jerusalem, but their prayers would go unheeded.

4:4–6 God's judgment on His chosen city Jerusalem occurred because of the people's unfaithfulness. The command for Ezekiel to lie on his side for a total of 430 days probably is understood best as something Ezekiel was to do for part of each day. Obviously from the text, Ezekiel was to do other things, such as to prepare bread and drink. These unusual actions symbolized God's punishment on both the northern kingdom ("House of Israel") and the southern kingdom ("House of Judah").

side to another till you have ended the days of your siege.

⁹"Also take for yourself wheat, barley, beans, lentils, millet, and spelt; put them into one vessel, and make bread of them for yourself. *During* the number of days that you lie on your side, three hundred and ninety days, you shall eat it. ¹⁰And your food which you eat *shall be* by weight, twenty shekels a day; from time to time you shall eat it. ¹¹You shall also drink water by measure, one-sixth of a hin; from time to time you shall drink. ¹²And you shall eat it *as* barley cakes; and bake it using fuel of human waste in their sight."

¹³Then the LORD said, "So shall the children of Israel eat their defiled bread among the Gentiles, where I will drive them."

¹⁴So I said, "Ah, Lord GOD! Indeed I have never defiled myself from my youth till now; I have never eaten what died of itself or was torn by beasts, nor has abominable flesh ever come into my mouth."

¹⁵Then He said to me, "See, I am giving you cow dung instead of human waste, and you shall prepare your bread over it."

¹⁶Moreover He said to me, "Son of man, surely I will cut off the supply of bread in Jerusalem; they shall eat bread by weight and with anxiety, and shall drink water by measure and with dread, ¹⁷that they may lack bread and water, and be dismayed with one another, and waste away because of their iniquity.

A Sword Against Jerusalem

5 "And you, son of man, take a sharp sword, take it as a barber's razor, and pass *it* over your head and your beard; then take scales to weigh and divide the *hair.* ²You shall burn with fire one-third in the midst of the city, when the days of the siege are finished; then you shall take one-third and strike around *it* with the sword, and one-third you shall scatter in the wind: I will draw out a sword after them. ³You shall also take a small number of them and bind them in the edge of your *garment.* ⁴Then take some of them again and throw them into the midst of the fire, and burn them in the fire. From there a fire will go out into all the house of Israel.

⁵"Thus says the Lord GOD: 'This *is* Jerusalem; I

have set her in the midst of the nations and the countries all around her. ⁶She has rebelled against My judgments by doing wickedness more than the nations, and against My statutes more than the countries that *are* all around her; for they have refused My judgments, and they have not walked in My statutes.' ⁷Therefore thus says the Lord GOD: 'Because you have multiplied *disobedience* more than the nations that *are* all around you, have not walked in My statutes nor kept My judgments, nor even doneᵃ according to the judgments of the nations that *are* all around you'— ⁸therefore thus says the Lord GOD: 'Indeed I, even I, *am* against you and will execute judgments in your midst in the sight of the nations. ⁹And I will do among you what I have never done, and the like of which I will never do again, because of all your abominations. ¹⁰Therefore fathers shall eat *their* sons in your midst, and sons shall eat their fathers; and I will execute judgments among you, and all of you who remain I will scatter to all the winds.

¹¹"Therefore, *as* I live,' says the Lord GOD, 'surely, because you have defiled My sanctuary with all your detestable things and with all your abominations, therefore I will also diminish *you;* My eye will not spare, nor will I have any pity. ¹²One-third of you shall die of the pestilence, and be consumed with famine in your midst; and one-third shall fall by the sword all around you; and I will scatter another third to all the winds, and I will draw out a sword after them.

¹³"Thus shall My anger be spent, and I will cause My fury to rest upon them, and I will be avenged; and they shall know that I, the LORD, have spoken *it* in My zeal, when I have spent My fury upon them. ¹⁴Moreover I will make you a waste and a reproach among the nations that *are* all around you, in the sight of all who pass by.

¹⁵"So itᵃ shall be a reproach', a taunt, a lesson, and an astonishment to the nations that *are* all around you, when I execute judgments among you in anger and in fury and in furious rebukes. I, the LORD, have spoken. ¹⁶When I send against them the terrible arrows of famine which shall be for

---

5:7 ᵃFollowing Masoretic Text, Septuagint, Targum, and Vulgate; many Hebrew manuscripts and Syriac read *but have done* (compare 11:12).   **5:15** ᵃSeptuagint, Syriac, Targum, and Vulgate read *you.*

4:9–11 Ezekiel's sparse rations highlight the meager food supply during a long siege. "Twenty shekels" of food would be eight or nine ounces, and "one-sixth of a hin" is a little more than a pint (see chart, Money and Measurements in the Bible). Whether this amount was all Ezekiel was permitted to consume is uncertain.

4:12–15 The Lord's command for Ezekiel to use human waste was unthinkable for his priestly sensibilities regarding ritual purity, even though cow dung was and still is used commonly for fuel in the Near East. God allowed him to use cow dung,

which still underscored the message of future adversity for Jerusalem.

5:1–4 Ezekiel's final symbolic enactment regarding Jerusalem's impending danger is recorded. For the Israelites, shaving the head was an indication of both shame (see 2 Sam. 10:4, 5) and grief (see Is. 15:2; Jer. 41:5, 6; 48:37).

5:10 Cannibalism is cited in the Pentateuch as one of the curses associated with God's punishment for covenant breaking (see Lev. 26:27–29; Deut. 28:53). Such practices actually occurred when Jerusalem fell (Lam. 4:10).

destruction, which I will send to destroy you, I will increase the famine upon you and cut off your supply of bread. [17]So I will send against you famine and wild beasts, and they will bereave you. Pestilence and blood shall pass through you, and I will bring the sword against you. I, the LORD, have spoken.' "

Judgment on Idolatrous Israel

6Now the word of the LORD came to me, saying: [2]"Son of man, set your face toward the mountains of Israel, and prophesy against them, [3]and say, 'O mountains of Israel, hear the word of the Lord GOD! Thus says the Lord GOD to the mountains, to the hills, to the ravines, and to the valleys: "Indeed I, *even* I, will bring a sword against you, and I will destroy your high places. [4]Then your altars shall be desolate, your incense altars shall be broken, and I will cast down your slain *men* before your idols. [5]And I will lay the corpses of the children of Israel before their idols, and I will scatter your bones all around your altars. [6]In all your dwelling places the cities shall be laid waste, and the high places shall be desolate, so that your altars may be laid waste and made desolate, your idols may be broken and made to cease, your incense altars may be cut down, and your works may be abolished. [7]The slain shall fall in your midst, and you shall know that I *am* the LORD.

[8]"Yet I will leave a remnant, so that you may have *some* who escape the sword among the nations, when you are scattered through the countries. [9]Then those of you who escape will remember Me among the nations where they are carried captive, because I was crushed by their adulterous heart which has departed from Me, and by their eyes which play the harlot after their idols; they will loathe themselves for the evils which they committed in all their abominations. [10]And they shall know that I *am* the LORD; I have not said in vain that I would bring this calamity upon them."

[11]"Thus says the Lord GOD: "Pound your fists and stamp your feet, and say, 'Alas, for all the evil abominations of the house of Israel! For they shall fall by the sword, by famine, and by pestilence. [12]He who is far off shall die by the pestilence, he who is near shall fall by the sword, and he who remains and is besieged shall die by the famine. Thus will I spend My fury upon them. [13]Then you shall know that I *am* the LORD, when their slain are among their idols all around their altars, on every high hill, on all the mountaintops, under every green tree, and under every thick oak, wherever they offered sweet incense to all their idols. [14]So I will stretch out My hand against them and make the land desolate, yes, more desolate than the wilderness toward Diblah, in all their dwelling places. Then they shall know that I *am* the LORD.' " ' "

Judgment on Israel Is Near

7Moreover the word of the LORD came to me, saying, [2]"And you, son of man, thus says the Lord GOD to the land of Israel:

'An end! The end has come upon the four
   corners of the land.
[3]Now the end *has come* upon you,
  And I will send My anger against you;
  I will judge you according to your ways,
  And I will repay you for all your abominations.
[4]My eye will not spare you,
  Nor will I have pity;
  But I will repay your ways,
  And your abominations will be in your midst;
  Then you shall know that I *am* the LORD!'

[5]"Thus says the Lord GOD:

'A disaster, a singular disaster;
  Behold, it has come!
[6]An end has come,
  The end has come;
  It has dawned for you;
  Behold, it has come!
[7]Doom has come to you, you who dwell in the
   land;
  The time has come,
  A day of trouble *is* near,
  And not of rejoicing in the mountains.
[8]Now upon you I will soon pour out My fury,
  And spend My anger upon you;

6:3, 4 The high places repeatedly were condemned throughout the OT as representing a compromising combination of Canaanite idol worship and the true worship of the Lord (see 1 Kin. 14:23; 2 Kin. 17:9, 10). The "altars" were used for burning animal sacrifices to various idols; "incense altars" were small stands holding bowls of aromatic spices, herbs, and other materials.

6:8–10 The survival of a remnant also is proclaimed in the midst of Ezekiel's pronouncement of looming judgment. The adversity of the Exile, hunger, and sword would eventually result in strengthening the people.

6:14 The identification of Diblah is uncertain. Some suggest it refers either to Almon Diblathaim (Num. 33:46) or Beth Diblathaim (Jer. 48:22). Several Hebrew manuscripts read "Riblah," which was a city north of Damascus. The Hebrew letters for "R" and "D" are so similar that a scribal change could have easily occurred. Either way, the point of utter destruction remains the same.

7:7 The day (see vv. 10, 12), a common expression in prophetic writings, refers to the "day of the Lord," a time of decisive judgment (see Amos 5:18–20; Obad. 15).

7:8 Pour out My fury is a common expression used by the prophets to describe God's judgments. The imagery is that of a cup filled to overflowing and then poured out (see Hos. 5:10; Ezek. 23:31–34).

I will judge you according to your ways,
And I will repay you for all your abominations.

[9]"My eye will not spare,
Nor will I have pity;
I will repay you according to your ways,
And your abominations will be in your
midst.
Then you shall know that I *am* the LORD who
strikes.

[10]"Behold, the day!
Behold, it has come!
Doom has gone out;
The rod has blossomed,
Pride has budded.
[11]Violence has risen up into a rod of wickedness;
None of them *shall remain*,
None of their multitude,
None of them;
Nor *shall there be* wailing for them.
[12]The time has come,
The day draws near.

'Let not the buyer rejoice,
Nor the seller mourn,
For wrath *is* on their whole multitude.
[13]For the seller shall not return to what has been
sold,
Though he may still be alive;
For the vision concerns the whole multitude,
And it shall not turn back;
No one will strengthen himself
Who lives in iniquity.

[14]"They have blown the trumpet and made
everyone ready,
But no one goes to battle;
For My wrath *is* on all their multitude.
[15]The sword *is* outside,
And the pestilence and famine within.
Whoever *is* in the field
Will die by the sword;
And whoever *is* in the city,
Famine and pestilence will devour him.

[16]"Those who survive will escape and be on the
mountains
Like doves of the valleys,
All of them mourning,
Each for his iniquity.
[17]Every hand will be feeble,
And every knee will be *as* weak *as* water.
[18]They will also be girded with sackcloth;
Horror will cover them;

Shame *will be* on every face,
Baldness on all their heads.

[19]"They will throw their silver into the streets,
And their gold will be like refuse;
Their silver and their gold will not be able to
deliver them
In the day of the wrath of the LORD;
They will not satisfy their souls,
Nor fill their stomachs,
Because it became their stumbling block of
iniquity.

[20]'As for the beauty of his ornaments,
He set it in majesty;
But they made from it
The images of their abominations—
Their detestable things;
Therefore I have made it
Like refuse to them.
[21]I will give it as plunder
Into the hands of strangers,
And to the wicked of the earth as spoil;
And they shall defile it.
[22]I will turn My face from them,
And they will defile My secret place;
For robbers shall enter it and defile it.

[23]Make a chain,
For the land is filled with crimes of blood,
And the city is full of violence.
[24]Therefore I will bring the worst of the
Gentiles,
And they will possess their houses;
I will cause the pomp of the strong to cease,
And their holy places shall be defiled.
[25]Destruction comes;
They will seek peace, but *there shall be* none.
[26]Disaster will come upon disaster,
And rumor will be upon rumor.
Then they will seek a vision from a prophet;
But the law will perish from the priest,
And counsel from the elders.

[27]"The king will mourn,
The prince will be clothed with desolation,
And the hands of the common people will
tremble.
I will do to them according to their way,
And according to what they deserve I will
judge them;
Then they shall know that I *am* the LORD!'"

Abominations in the Temple

8 And it came to pass in the sixth year, in the
sixth *month*, on the fifth *day* of the month, as I

7:10–12 The rod has blossomed and "violence has arisen" imply that God's judgment included the unbridled fruition of sinful human behavior. Normal commercial activity would cease when God came in judgment (v. 12). The daily routine of life as God's people had known it would end.

7:22 My secret place refers to the temple in Jerusalem.

8:1 In the sixth year, in the sixth month, on the fifth day introduces Ezekiel's vision dated September 17, 592 B. C. (see Ezek. 1:2; 40:1). This date is approximately 14 months after Ezekiel's initial vision.

sat in my house with the elders of Judah sitting before me, that the hand of the Lord GOD fell upon me there. ²Then I looked, and there was a likeness, like the appearance of fire—from the appearance of His waist and downward, fire; and from His waist and upward, like the appearance of brightness, like the color of amber. ³He stretched out the form of a hand, and took me by a lock of my hair; and the Spirit lifted me up between earth and heaven, and brought me in visions of God to Jerusalem, to the door of the north gate of the inner *court,* where the seat of the image of jealousy *was,* which provokes to jealousy. ⁴And behold, the glory of the God of Israel *was* there, like the vision that I saw in the plain.

⁵Then He said to me, "Son of man, lift your eyes now toward the north." So I lifted my eyes toward the north, and there, north of the altar gate, was this image of jealousy in the entrance.

⁶Furthermore He said to me, "Son of man, do you see what they are doing, the great abominations that the house of Israel commits here, to make Me go far away from My sanctuary? Now turn again, you will see greater abominations." ⁷So He brought me to the door of the court; and when I looked, there was a hole in the wall. ⁸Then He said to me, "Son of man, dig into the wall"; and when I dug into the wall, there was a door.

⁹And He said to me, "Go in, and see the wicked abominations which they are doing there." ¹⁰So I went in and saw, and there—every sort of creeping thing, abominable beasts, and all the idols of the house of Israel, portrayed all around on the walls. ¹¹And there stood before them seventy men of the elders of the house of Israel, and in their midst stood Jaazaniah the son of Shaphan. Each man had a censer in his hand, and a thick cloud of incense went up. ¹²Then He said to me, "Son of man, have you seen what the elders of the house of Israel do in the dark, every man in the room of his idols? For they say, 'The LORD does not see us, the LORD has forsaken the land.'"

¹³And He said to me, "Turn again, *and* you will see greater abominations that they are doing." ¹⁴So He brought me to the door of the north gate of the LORD's house; and to my dismay, women were sitting there weeping for Tammuz.

¹⁵Then He said to me, "Have you seen *this,* O son of man? Turn again, you will see greater abominations than these." ¹⁶So He brought me into the inner court of the LORD's house; and there, at the door of the temple of the LORD, between the porch and the altar, *were* about twenty-five men with their backs toward the temple of the LORD and their faces toward the east, and they were worshiping the sun toward the east.

¹⁷And He said to me, "Have you seen *this,* O son of man? Is it a trivial thing to the house of Judah to commit the abominations which they commit here? For they have filled the land with violence; then they have returned to provoke Me to anger. Indeed they put the branch to their nose. ¹⁸Therefore I also will act in fury. My eye will not spare nor will I have pity; and though they cry in My ears with a loud voice, I will not hear them."

The Wicked Are Slain

9 Then He called out in my hearing with a loud voice, saying, "Let those who have charge over the city draw near, each *with* a deadly weapon in his hand." ²And suddenly six men came from the direction of the upper gate, which faces north, each with his battle-ax in his hand. One man among them *was* clothed with linen and had a writer's inkhorn at his side. They went in and stood beside the bronze altar.

³Now the glory of the God of Israel had gone up from the cherub, where it had been, to the threshold of the temple.ᵃ And He called to the man clothed with linen, who *had* the writer's inkhorn at his side; ⁴and the LORD said to him, "Go through the midst of the city, through the midst

9:3 ᵃLiterally *house*

8:3 **The image of jealousy** has been identified with an image of the Canaanite fertility goddess, Asherah, which Manasseh had set up in the temple area (2 Kin. 21:1–7; 2 Chr. 33:7). Though it had been removed during Josiah's reform (2 Kin. 23:6), the idolatry apparently had been reinstated after Josiah's death.

8:4 **Amidst the details of Ezekiel's vision of the temple** in Jerusalem was the progressive movement of God's glory (symbolizing His presence) from within the temple to a mountain on the east side of the city (see Ezek. 9:3; 10:14–19; 11:23). This mountain has been identified as the Mount of Olives.

8:7–13 **Ezekiel depicted the failure of the elders of Judah** to worship the Lord properly. Instead, they secretly and defiantly practiced idolatry. The mention of Jaazaniah, the son of Shaphan, emphasized the extent of the apostasy, for Shaphan had been a leader in Josiah's reforms (see 2 Kin. 22:3–20).

8:14 **Tammuz was the Babylonian god** of nature or of vegetation (the husband and brother of Ishtar) who supposedly died in summer and came back to life in the spring (see chart, Graeco-Roman Goddesses). Ezekiel's vision occurred in September when Palestine was so parched that the women were crying for relief and fertility in the Land. The involvement of Israelite women in the ritual of weeping for Tammuz at the entrance to God's sanctuary was further indication of blatant idolatry. Later the Jewish calendar named a month Tammuz.

8:16, 17 **These men were probably priests.** By standing with their backs toward the sanctuary, they deliberately were rejecting God in favor of some sort of sun worship (see Joel 2:17). "They put the branch to their nose" is an obscure Hebrew idiom, probably referring to some offensive or insulting gesture.

9:4 **Marking a person in the ancient Near East** indicated that the individual was the object of another's protection or mercy (see Gen. 4:15). Those grieved over Judah's sin received the mark.

of Jerusalem, and put a mark on the foreheads of the men who sigh and cry over all the abominations that are done within it."

⁵To the others He said in my hearing, "Go after him through the city and kill; do not let your eye spare, nor have any pity. ⁶Utterly slay old *and* young men, maidens and little children and women; but do not come near anyone on whom *is* the mark; and begin at My sanctuary." So they began with the elders who *were* before the temple. ⁷Then He said to them, "Defile the temple, and fill the courts with the slain. Go out!" And they went out and killed in the city.

⁸So it was, that while they were killing them, I was left *alone;* and I fell on my face and cried out, and said, "Ah, Lord God! Will You destroy all the remnant of Israel in pouring out Your fury on Jerusalem?"

⁹Then He said to me, "The iniquity of the house of Israel and Judah *is* exceedingly great, and the land is full of bloodshed, and the city full of perversity; for they say, 'The Lord has forsaken the land, and the Lord does not see!' ¹⁰And as for Me also, My eye will neither spare, nor will I have pity, *but* I will recompense their deeds on their own head."

¹¹Just then, the man clothed with linen, who *had* the inkhorn at his side, reported back and said, "I have done as You commanded me."

The Glory Departs from the Temple

10 And I looked, and there in the firmament that was above the head of the cherubim, there appeared something like a sapphire stone, having the appearance of the likeness of a throne. ²Then He spoke to the man clothed with linen, and said, "Go in among the wheels, under the cherub, fill your hands with coals of fire from among the cherubim, and scatter *them* over the city." And he went in as I watched.

³Now the cherubim were standing on the south side of the temple[a] when the man went in, and the cloud filled the inner court. ⁴Then the glory of the Lord went up from the cherub, *and paused* over the threshold of the temple; and the house was filled with the cloud, and the court was full of the brightness of the Lord's glory. ⁵And the sound of the wings of the cherubim was heard *even* in the outer court, like the voice of Almighty God when He speaks.

⁶Then it happened, when He commanded the man clothed in linen, saying, "Take fire from among the wheels, from among the cherubim," that he went in and stood beside the wheels. ⁷And the cherub stretched out his hand from among the cherubim to the fire that *was* among the cherubim, and took *some of it* and put *it* into the hands of the *man* clothed with linen, who took *it* and went out. ⁸The cherubim appeared to have the form of a man's hand under their wings.

⁹And when I looked, there were four wheels by the cherubim, one wheel by one cherub and another wheel by each other cherub; the wheels appeared *to have* the color of a beryl stone. ¹⁰*As for* their appearance, all four looked alike—as it were, a wheel in the middle of a wheel. ¹¹When they went, they went toward *any of* their four directions; they did not turn aside when they went, but followed in the direction the head was facing. They did not turn aside when they went. ¹²And their whole body, with their back, their hands, their wings, and the wheels that the four had, *were* full of eyes all around. ¹³As for the wheels, they were called in my hearing, "Wheel."

¹⁴Each one had four faces: the first face *was* the face of a cherub, the second face the face of a man, the third the face of a lion, and the fourth the face of an eagle. ¹⁵And the cherubim were lifted up. This *was* the living creature I saw by the River Chebar. ¹⁶When the cherubim went, the wheels went beside them; and when the cherubim lifted their wings to mount up from the earth, the same wheels also did not turn from beside them. ¹⁷When *the cherubim*[a] stood still, *the wheels* stood still, and when one[b] was lifted up, *the other*[c] lifted itself up, for the spirit of the living creature *was* in them.

¹⁸Then the glory of the Lord departed from the threshold of the temple and stood over the cherubim. ¹⁹And the cherubim lifted their wings and mounted up from the earth in my sight. When they went out, the wheels *were* beside them; and they stood at the door of the east gate of the Lord's house, and the glory of the God of Israel *was* above them.

²⁰This *is* the living creature I saw under the God of Israel by the River Chebar, and I knew they *were* cherubim. ²¹Each one had four faces and each one four wings, and the likeness of the hands of a man *was* under their wings. ²²And the likeness of their faces *was* the same *as* the faces which I had seen by the River Chebar, their appearance and their persons. They each went straight forward.

Judgment on Wicked Counselors

11 Then the Spirit lifted me up and brought me to the East Gate of the Lord's house,

10:3 ᵃLiterally *house,* also in verses 4 and 18   10:17 ᵃLiterally *they* ᵇLiterally *they* ᶜLiterally *they*

9:6 **This scene of judgment** paralleled the Exodus Passover. In both instances those without the mark of safety were slain (see Ex. 12:13).

10:2 **The command to scatter the coals of fire** over the city symbolized God's purifying judgment (see Gen. 19:24; Is. 6:6, 7).

which faces eastward; and there at the door of the gate were twenty-five men, among whom I saw Jaazaniah the son of Azzur, and Pelatiah the son of Benaiah, princes of the people. ²And He said to me: "Son of man, these *are* the men who devise iniquity and give wicked counsel in this city, ³who say, '*The time is* not near to build houses; this *city is* the caldron, and we *are* the meat.' ⁴Therefore prophesy against them, prophesy, O son of man!"

⁵Then the Spirit of the LORD fell upon me, and said to me, "Speak! 'Thus says the LORD: "Thus you have said, O house of Israel; for I know the things that come into your mind. ⁶You have multiplied your slain in this city, and you have filled its streets with the slain." ⁷Therefore thus says the Lord GOD: "Your slain whom you have laid in its midst, they *are* the meat, and this *city is* the caldron; but I shall bring you out of the midst of it. ⁸You have feared the sword; and I will bring a sword upon you," says the Lord GOD. ⁹"And I will bring you out of its midst, and deliver you into the hands of strangers, and execute judgments on you. ¹⁰You shall fall by the sword. I will judge you at the border of Israel. Then you shall know that I *am* the LORD. ¹¹This *city* shall not be your caldron, nor shall you be the meat in its midst. I will judge you at the border of Israel. ¹²And you shall know that I *am* the LORD; for you have not walked in My statutes nor executed My judgments, but have done according to the customs of the Gentiles which *are* all around you." ' "

¹³Now it happened, while I was prophesying, that Pelatiah the son of Benaiah died. Then I fell on my face and cried with a loud voice, and said, "Ah, Lord GOD! Will You make a complete end of the remnant of Israel?"

God Will Restore Israel

¹⁴Again the word of the LORD came to me, saying, ¹⁵"Son of man, your brethren, your relatives, your countrymen, and all the house of Israel in its entirety, *are* those about whom the inhabitants of Jerusalem have said, 'Get far away from the LORD; this land has been given to us as a possession.' ¹⁶Therefore say, 'Thus says the Lord GOD: "Although I have cast them far off among the Gentiles, and although I have scattered them among the countries, yet I shall be a little sanctuary for them in the countries where they have gone." ' ¹⁷Therefore say, 'Thus says the Lord GOD: "I will

gather you from the peoples, assemble you from the countries where you have been scattered, and I will give you the land of Israel." ' ¹⁸And they will go there, and they will take away all its detestable things and all its abominations from there. ¹⁹Then I will give them one heart, and I will put a new spirit within them,ᵃ and take the stony heart out of their flesh, and give them a heart of flesh, ²⁰that they may walk in My statutes and keep My judgments and do them; and they shall be My people, and I will be their God. ²¹But *as for those* whose hearts follow the desire for their detestable things and their abominations, I will recompense their deeds on their own heads," says the Lord GOD.

²²So the cherubim lifted up their wings, with the wheels beside them, and the glory of the God of Israel *was* high above them. ²³And the glory of the LORD went up from the midst of the city and stood on the mountain, which *is* on the east side of the city.

²⁴Then the Spirit took me up and brought me in a vision by the Spirit of God into Chaldea,ᵃ to those in captivity. And the vision that I had seen went up from me. ²⁵So I spoke to those in captivity of all the things the LORD had shown me.

Judah's Captivity Portrayed

12 Now the word of the LORD came to me, saying: ²"Son of man, you dwell in the midst of a rebellious house, which has eyes to see but does not see, and ears to hear but does not hear; for they *are* a rebellious house.

³"Therefore, son of man, prepare your belongings for captivity, and go into captivity by day in their sight. You shall go from your place into captivity to another place in their sight. It may be that they will consider, though they *are* a rebellious house. ⁴By day you shall bring out your belongings in their sight, as though going into captivity; and at evening you shall go in their sight, like those who go into captivity. ⁵Dig through the wall in their sight, and carry *your belongings* out through it. ⁶In their sight you shall bear *them* on *your* shoulders *and* carry *them* out at twilight; you shall cover your face, so that you cannot see the ground, for I have made you a sign to the house of Israel."

11:19 ᵃLiterally *you*   11:24 ᵃOr *Babylon*, and so elsewhere in this book

---

11:6–9 For these reckless leaders God had prepared a special punishment that would take place outside the confines of the city (see Amos 7:17).

11:13 The death of Pelatiah (Heb., lit. "the Lord's remnant" or "the Lord delivers") confirmed Ezekiel's prophecy. At the same time, Ezekiel feared again that no remnant would survive.

11:16 The proud survivors in Jerusalem were left an empty shell

of a sanctuary once God's glory departed (see Ezek. 11:23). God promised to be a sanctuary to the scattered remnant in Babylon by helping them in their distress.

11:23 God's glory departed. In the final stage before its departure from Jerusalem, the glory of God rested on the Mount of Olives east of the city (2 Sam. 15:30). On this same mountain Jesus wept over Jerusalem (Luke 19:41); here He ascended and will return (Acts 1:9–12).

⁷So I did as I was commanded. I brought out my belongings by day, as though going into captivity, and at evening I dug through the wall with my hand. I brought *them* out at twilight, *and* I bore *them* on *my* shoulder in their sight.

⁸And in the morning the word of the LORD came to me, saying, ⁹"Son of man, has not the house of Israel, the rebellious house, said to you, 'What are you doing?' ¹⁰Say to them, 'Thus says the Lord GOD: "This burden *concerns* the prince in Jerusalem and all the house of Israel who are among them." ' ¹¹Say, 'I *am* a sign to you. As I have done, so shall it be done to them; they shall be carried away into captivity.' ¹²And the prince who *is* among them shall bear *his belongings* on *his* shoulder at twilight and go out. They shall dig through the wall to carry *them* out through it. He shall cover his face, so that he cannot see the ground with *his* eyes. ¹³I will also spread My net over him, and he shall be caught in My snare. I will bring him to Babylon, *to* the land of the Chaldeans; yet he shall not see it, though he shall die there. ¹⁴I will scatter to every wind all who *are* around him to help him, and all his troops; and I will draw out the sword after them.

¹⁵"Then they shall know that I *am* the LORD, when I scatter them among the nations and disperse them throughout the countries. ¹⁶But I will spare a few of their men from the sword, from famine, and from pestilence, that they may declare all their abominations among the Gentiles wherever they go. Then they shall know that I *am* the LORD."

Judgment Not Postponed

¹⁷Moreover the word of the LORD came to me, saying, ¹⁸"Son of man, eat your bread with quaking, and drink your water with trembling and anxiety. ¹⁹And say to the people of the land, 'Thus says the Lord GOD to the inhabitants of Jerusalem *and* to the land of Israel: "They shall eat their bread with anxiety, and drink their water with dread, so that her land may be emptied of all who are in it, because of the violence of all those who dwell in it. ²⁰Then the cities that are inhabited shall be laid waste, and the land shall become desolate; and you shall know that I *am* the LORD." ' "

²¹And the word of the LORD came to me, saying, ²²"Son of man, what *is* this proverb *that* you

people have about the land of Israel, which says, 'The days are prolonged, and every vision fails'? ²³Tell them therefore, 'Thus says the Lord GOD: "I will lay this proverb to rest, and they shall no more use it as a proverb in Israel." ' But say to them, ' "The days are at hand, and the fulfillment of every vision. ²⁴For no more shall there be any false vision or flattering divination within the house of Israel. ²⁵For I *am* the LORD. I speak, and the word which I speak will come to pass; it will no more be postponed; for in your days, O rebellious house, I will say the word and perform it," says the Lord GOD.' "

²⁶Again the word of the LORD came to me, saying, ²⁷"Son of man, look, the house of Israel is saying, 'The vision that he sees *is* for many days *from now,* and he prophesies of times far off.' ²⁸Therefore say to them, 'Thus says the Lord GOD: "None of My words will be postponed any more, but the word which I speak will be done," says the Lord GOD.' "

Woe to Foolish Prophets

13 And the word of the LORD came to me, saying, ²"Son of man, prophesy against the prophets of Israel who prophesy, and say to those who prophesy out of their own heart, 'Hear the word of the LORD!' "

³Thus says the Lord GOD: "Woe to the foolish prophets, who follow their own spirit and have seen nothing! ⁴O Israel, your prophets are like foxes in the deserts. ⁵You have not gone up into the gaps to build a wall for the house of Israel to stand in battle on the day of the LORD. ⁶They have envisioned futility and false divination, saying, 'Thus says the LORD!' But the LORD has not sent them; yet they hope that the word may be confirmed. ⁷Have you not seen a futile vision, and have you not spoken false divination? You say, 'The LORD says,' but I have not spoken."

⁸Therefore thus says the Lord GOD: "Because you have spoken nonsense and envisioned lies, therefore I *am* indeed against you," says the Lord GOD. ⁹"My hand will be against the prophets who envision futility and who divine lies; they shall not be in the assembly of My people, nor be written in the record of the house of Israel, nor shall they enter into the land of Israel. Then you shall know that I *am* the Lord GOD.

12:10 The prince of Jerusalem probably refers to Zedekiah, the puppet king whose rebellion against Babylon led to the destruction of Jerusalem (see 2 Kin. 24:17—25:2).

12:12, 13 When Zedekiah attempted to flee Jerusalem after its capture by the Babylonians, he was caught, blinded, and taken to Babylon (see 2 Kin. 25:4–7).

12:18 Ezekiel's eating and drinking, as if in mortal terror, symbolized the coming fear that those in Jerusalem would experience during the siege of the city.

13:5 The true prophet of the Lord was one who went "into the gaps to build a wall." Such a prophet would strengthen the moral and spiritual defenses of God's people. This military metaphor assumed a knowledge of the defense of a walled city. If a city wall was breached by a siege engine, a repair team would be sent under guard to repair the hole. The guards would hold off any intruders while repairs were being completed. A true prophet would undergird and fortify God's people by calling them back to the Lord. Most of all a true prophet spoke the truth as God gave it.

10"Because, indeed, because they have seduced My people, saying, 'Peace!' when *there is* no peace—and one builds a wall, and they plaster it with untempered *mortar*— 11say to those who plaster *it* with untempered *mortar,* that it will fall. There will be flooding rain, and you, O great hailstones, shall fall; and a stormy wind shall tear *it* down. 12Surely, when the wall has fallen, will it not be said to you, 'Where *is* the mortar with which you plastered *it?*' "

13Therefore thus says the Lord GOD: "I will cause a stormy wind to break forth in My fury; and there shall be a flooding rain in My anger, and great hailstones in fury to consume *it.* 14So I will break down the wall you have plastered with untempered *mortar,* and bring it down to the ground, so that its foundation will be uncovered; it will fall, and you shall be consumed in the midst of it. Then you shall know that I *am* the LORD.

15"Thus will I accomplish My wrath on the wall and on those who have plastered it with untempered *mortar;* and I will say to you, 'The wall *is* no *more,* nor those who plastered it, 16*that is,* the prophets of Israel who prophesy concerning Jerusalem, and who see visions of peace for her when *there is* no peace,' " says the Lord GOD.

17"Likewise, son of man, set your face against the daughters of your people, who prophesy out of their own heart; prophesy against them, 18and say, 'Thus says the Lord GOD: "Woe to the *women* who sew *magic* charms on their sleevesa and make veils for the heads of people of every height to hunt souls! Will you hunt the souls of My people, and keep yourselves alive? 19And will you profane Me among My people for handfuls of barley and for pieces of bread, killing people who should not die, and keeping people alive who should not live, by your lying to My people who listen to lies?"

20'Therefore thus says the Lord GOD: "Behold, I *am* against your *magic* charms by which you hunt souls there like birds. I will tear them from your arms, and let the souls go, the souls you hunt like birds. 21I will also tear off your veils and deliver My people out of your hand, and they shall no longer be as prey in your hand. Then you shall know that I *am* the LORD.

22"Because with lies you have made the heart of the righteous sad, whom I have not made sad; and you have strengthened the hands of the wicked, so that he does not turn from his wicked way to save his life. 23Therefore you shall no longer envision futility nor practice divination; for I will deliver My people out of your hand, and you shall know that I *am* the LORD." ' "

Idolatry Will Be Punished

14 Now some of the elders of Israel came to me and sat before me. 2And the word of the LORD came to me, saying, 3"Son of man, these men have set up their idols in their hearts, and put before them that which causes them to stumble into iniquity. Should I let Myself be inquired of at all by them?

4"Therefore speak to them, and say to them, 'Thus says the Lord GOD: "Everyone of the house of Israel who sets up his idols in his heart, and puts before him what causes him to stumble into iniquity, and then comes to the prophet, I the LORD will answer him who comes, according to the multitude of his idols, 5that I may seize the house of Israel by their heart, because they are all estranged from Me by their idols." '

6"Therefore say to the house of Israel, 'Thus says the Lord GOD: "Repent, turn away from your idols, and turn your faces away from all your abominations. 7For anyone of the house of Israel, or of the strangers who dwell in Israel, who separates himself from Me and sets up his idols in his heart and puts before him what causes him to stumble into iniquity, then comes to a prophet to inquire of him concerning Me, I the LORD will answer him by Myself. 8I will set My face against that man and make him a sign and a proverb, and I will cut him off from the midst of My people. Then you shall know that I *am* the LORD.

9"And if the prophet is induced to speak

13:18 aLiterally *over all the joints of My hands;* Vulgate reads *under every elbow;* Septuagint and Targum read *on all elbows of the hands.*

13:10 Plaster also means whitewash. The imagery of this verse assumes a wall of stone or brick built without a bonding agent. The wall was then plastered in such a way that it appeared strong. The false prophets who misled the people by proclaiming peace were like those who whitewashed or plastered a weak wall, making it appear strong. When the storm of God's judgment struck Judah, the nation would fall (vv. 13, 14).

13:17 Daughters of your people were evidently women who practiced crude magic as prophecy in the name of the Lord for personal gain (vv. 18, 19). Though female prophets were rare in Israel, Miriam, Deborah, and Huldah are identified as filling such a role in the Lord's service (see Ex. 15:20; Judg. 4:4; 2 Kin. 22:14).

13:19 Barley and bread were used as payment for magical services rendered. Many with superstitious fears were being exploited by the false prophetesses.

13:23 The Canaanites practiced many types of "divination" (see Ezek. 21:21, note) in stark contrast to the prophets of the Lord, who were forbidden to use such methods (see Deut. 18:9–14).

14:3, 4 The elders of Ezekiel's community, despite being in Exile because of idolatry, still practiced some sort of idolatry *secretly.* They came to Ezekiel anticipating an oracular decision but instead were given a word of judgment.

CLOTHING GARMENTS IN BIBLE TIMES

The Bible teaches that believers are not to fret over what they are going to wear (Matt. 6:25–30), they are not to judge others by what they wear, nor are they to show favor based on how well someone is dressed (James 2:2–4). They are to be generous in clothing the poor (Matt. 25:36, 44). Embroidered cloth, leather sandals, and fine linen were typical clothing (Is. 3:18–23; Ezek. 16:9–13). Gold and silver jewelry included bracelets, necklaces, earrings, crowns, and even nose rings—often encrusted with jewels.

Both men and women in Bible times wore tunics as their primary garments. These were loose-fitting, dresslike garments with sleeves to the mid-forearm. They were tucked at the waist, sometimes by a money pocket, a belt, or, more commonly, a sash. Women's tunics were usually decorated with embroidery. A man was forbidden by the Law to wear a woman's garment, and vice versa (Deut. 22:5).

Fabrics mentioned in Scripture include goat and camel hair (Matt. 3:4), leather (Matt. 3:4), linen (Lev. 16:4; Ezek. 16:10; Rev. 18:12; 19:14), and wool (Job 31:20). In Bible times, the texture of a garment was a sign of wealth. Rough-textured garments were worn by the poor. Since dyes were expensive, garments generally were in the natural colors. The Israelites, however, did weave colored threads—including gold thread—into the fabrics of special garments (Ex. 39:3).

Head Coverings included veils that were used to hide a woman's beauty from strangers until she was united with her husband in marriage. Once married, an Israelite woman was not bound to wear a veil, but she generally continued to cover her face in the presence of strangers (Gen. 24:65). High priests covered their heads in the temple, and women also were admonished to cover their heads in worship services of the first-century church (1 Cor. 11:5, 6).

Footwear, especially sandals, provided protection from scorching sands and rocky paths but were not worn inside homes. Hosts showed kindness to their guests by removing their shoes at the home's entrance and washing their feet (Luke 7:44; John 13:5). Shoes were also removed in the temple and on "holy ground" and were not worn during times of mourning. Footwear also has symbolic meaning in the Scriptures. Boaz sealed his marriage contract with Ruth using a shoe (Ruth 4:7–10). To lift up your shoe to show its sole or heel to another person was considered an insult (Ps. 41:9).

See also charts on The High Priest's Clothing; Head Coverings in the Bible; notes on Appearance (2 Cor. 3); Beauty (Prov. 4); Cosmetics (Ex. 30); Femininity (Ps. 144)

anything, I the LORD have induced that prophet, and I will stretch out My hand against him and destroy him from among My people Israel. [10]And they shall bear their iniquity; the punishment of the prophet shall be the same as the punishment of the one who inquired, [11]that the house of Israel may no longer stray from Me, nor be profaned anymore with all their transgressions, but that they may be My people and I may be their God," says the Lord GOD.' "

Judgment on Persistent Unfaithfulness

[12]The word of the LORD came again to me, saying: [13]"Son of man, when a land sins against Me by persistent unfaithfulness, I will stretch out My hand against it; I will cut off its supply of bread, send famine on it, and cut off man and beast from it. [14]Even if these three men, Noah, Daniel, and Job, were in it, they would deliver only themselves by their righteousness," says the Lord GOD.

[15]"If I cause wild beasts to pass through the land, and they empty it, and make it so desolate that no man may pass through because of the beasts, [16]even though these three men were in it, as I live," says the Lord GOD, "they would deliver neither sons nor daughters; only they would be delivered, and the land would be desolate.

[17]"Or if I bring a sword on that land, and say, 'Sword, go through the land,' and I cut off man and beast from it, [18]even though these three men were in it, as I live," says the Lord GOD, "they would deliver neither sons nor daughters, but only they themselves would be delivered.

[19]"Or if I send a pestilence into that land and pour out My fury on it in blood, and cut off from it man and beast, [20]even though Noah, Daniel, and Job were in it, as I live," says the Lord GOD, "they would deliver neither son nor daughter; they would deliver only themselves by their righteousness."

[21]For thus says the Lord GOD: "How much more it shall be when I send My four severe judg-

---

14:14 Noah, Daniel, and Job were well-known examples of true righteousness. Noah is described as just and blameless (Gen. 6:9) and Job as blameless and upright (Job 1:1). Daniel was a contemporary of Ezekiel (Dan. 1:1–6).

14:16 A prevalent misconception was that Jerusalem would be spared because of a righteous remnant. Ezekiel dispelled this falsehood by announcing that the presence of three proverbially righteous men could not save the city.

ments on Jerusalem—the sword and famine and wild beasts and pestilence—to cut off man and beast from it? [22]Yet behold, there shall be left in it a remnant who will be brought out, *both* sons and daughters; surely they will come out to you, and you will see their ways and their doings. Then you will be comforted concerning the disaster that I have brought upon Jerusalem, all that I have brought upon it. [23]And they will comfort you, when you see their ways and their doings; and you shall know that I have done nothing without cause that I have done in it," says the Lord God.

The Outcast Vine

15Then the word of the Lord came to me, saying: [2]"Son of man, how is the wood of the vine *better* than any other wood, the vine branch which is among the trees of the forest? [3]Is wood taken from it to make any object? Or can *men* make a peg from it to hang any vessel on? [4]Instead, it is thrown into the fire for fuel; the fire devours both ends of it, and its middle is burned. Is it useful for *any* work? [5]Indeed, when it was whole, no object could be made from it. How much less will it be useful for *any* work when the fire has devoured it, and it is burned?

[6]"Therefore thus says the Lord God: 'Like the wood of the vine among the trees of the forest, which I have given to the fire for fuel, so I will give up the inhabitants of Jerusalem; [7]and I will set My face against them. They will go out from *one* fire, but *another* fire shall devour them. Then you shall know that I *am* the Lord, when I set My face against them. [8]Thus I will make the land desolate, because they have persisted in unfaithfulness,' says the Lord God."

God's Love for Jerusalem

16Again the word of the Lord came to me, saying, [2]"Son of man, cause Jerusalem to know her abominations, [3]and say, 'Thus says the Lord God to Jerusalem: "Your birth and your nativity *are* from the land of Canaan; your father *was* an Amorite and your mother a Hittite. [4]*As for* your nativity, on the day you were born your navel cord was not cut, nor were you washed in water to cleanse *you;* you were not rubbed with salt nor wrapped in swaddling cloths. [5]No eye pitied you, to do any of these things for you, to have compassion on you; but you were thrown out into the open field, when you yourself were loathed on the day you were born.

[6]"And when I passed by you and saw you struggling in your own blood, I said to you in your blood, 'Live!' Yes, I said to you in your blood, 'Live!' [7]I made you thrive like a plant in the field; and you grew, matured, and became very beautiful. *Your* breasts were formed, your hair grew, but you *were* naked and bare.

[8]"When I passed by you again and looked upon you, indeed your time *was* the time of love; so I spread My wing over you and covered your nakedness. Yes, I swore an oath to you and entered into a covenant with you, and you became Mine," says the Lord God.

[9]"Then I washed you in water; yes, I thoroughly washed off your blood, and I anointed you with oil. [10]I clothed you in embroidered cloth and gave you sandals of badger skin; I clothed you with fine linen and covered you with silk. [11]I adorned you with ornaments, put bracelets on your wrists, and a chain on your neck. [12]And I put a jewel in your nose, earrings in your ears, and a beautiful crown on your head. [13]Thus you were adorned with gold and silver, and your clothing *was of* fine linen, silk, and embroidered cloth. You ate *pastry of* fine flour, honey, and oil. You were exceedingly beautiful, and succeeded to royalty. [14]Your fame went out among the nations because of your beauty, for it *was* perfect through My splendor which I had bestowed on you," says the Lord God.

15:2 The image of a vine is used in Scripture to depict Israel's standing before God. Normally, the picture is that of a vine tended and protected by the Lord (see Is. 5:1-10; Jer. 2:21; Hos. 10:1). Ezekiel focused on the uselessness of the wood of the vine (Ezek. 15:3, 4). Such wood served only to fuel a fire. Likewise, Jerusalem would experience the fire of God's judgment because of the people's unfaithfulness to the Lord.

15:7 They will go out from one fire may refer to the siege under Jehoiachin. "Another fire" points to the coming destruction of the city (see 2 Kin. 24:10-16; 25:1-10).

16:3 Ezekiel began this section of historical narrative with a reminder that Jerusalem's past was rooted in Canaanite history. Ezekiel drew a condemning comparison between the Jews and the idolatrous Canaanite inhabitants of Jerusalem in the days before Israel captured the city. The Amorites were Semitic inhabitants of Canaan before the conquest. The Hittites were non-Semitic peoples who settled in Canaan before the conquest (see Gen. 9:25; Josh. 15:63; Judg. 1:21).

16:4–6 Rubbing the infant with salt, water, and oil and wrapping the baby in cloth strips for seven days and repeating the process for 40 days after the umbilical cord had been cut was done for hygienic purposes (v. 4). This process promoted the good health of the baby. Unwanted newborns, especially girls, often were abandoned to die in the ancient world. The female child depicted in these verses was deprived of the normal postnatal cleansing and health care procedures.

16:8 Wing also referred to the corner or extremity of a garment. In the ancient Near East, clothing often served a symbolic function. The spreading of one's garment over another symbolized entry into a marriage relationship (see Deut. 22:30; Ruth 3:9).

16:10–12 God used the imagery of the bridal costume to describe His care for His people. According to what the family could afford, brides wore lavish clothing, expensive jewelry, and a crown (see Ps. 45:13, 14; Song 3:11).

MOTHERHOOD MOTHERS AND DAUGHTERS

Mothers often fail to savor the precious, fleeting moments with their daughters. In rushing through life, they sometimes take time only for the high spots, while the small, daily experiences that give life its character and the most delicious and meaningful moments are all but lost in the shuffle. The lasting and eternal are engulfed in triviality.

There is no better opportunity to enjoy life's small, mundane responsibilities than to invest time and energy in lifestyle teaching of your daughter—giving her instruction on how to care for younger children, to fix family meals, to study the art and method of homemaking, even teaching her to set a table with care and creativity (see Titus 2:3–5). Sensing pleasure and significance in caring for the simple needs of the family is caught as well as taught (2 Cor. 3:2, 3) so that irksome, bothersome, and irritating chores become meaningful, delightful, and rewarding opportunities for service.

There are many practical ways of spending time together without making elaborate plans. In the biblical story of Mary and Martha, Martha was not rebuked by the Lord for setting the table, cooking, sweeping the floor, or decorating the house. She was not doing anything wrong, but her priorities were not right at that time. Busy with good things, she missed her opportunity for the best thing (Luke 10:38–42). Many mothers today are busy with good things, but miss the opportunity for the best thing—investing time in a daughter (Ps. 127:3–5).

Childhood cannot be used over again for another set of memories (Deut 6:10–25). Therefore, the spending of time is an irrevocable act that cannot be used again (Eph. 5:15–17). No day or even hour can be recaptured. What greater delight than to work side by side with your daughters, mentoring and modeling and sharing.

See also Ezek. 16:20, 21, 44–63; Matt. 14:6–11; 15:21–28; Titus 2:3–5; 1 Pet. 3:5, 6; notes on Adolescence (Luke 2); Family (Gen. 32; 1 Sam. 3; Ps. 78; 127); Femininity (Ps. 144); Girlhood (Prov. 1); Motherhood (1 Sam. 1; Is. 49); Parenthood (Prov. 10); Siblings (Gen. 37); portraits of Herodias and Salome (Matt. 14); Lois and Eunice (2 Tim.1)

Jerusalem's Harlotry

15"But you trusted in your own beauty, played the harlot because of your fame, and poured out your harlotry on everyone passing by who *would have* it. 16You took some of your garments and adorned multicolored high places for yourself, and played the harlot on them. *Such things should not happen, nor be.* 17You have also taken your beautiful jewelry from My gold and My silver, which I had given you, and made for yourself male images and played the harlot with them. 18You took your embroidered garments and covered them, and you set My oil and My incense before them. 19Also My food which I gave you—the pastry of fine flour, oil, and honey *which* I fed you—you set it before them as sweet incense; and *so* it was," says the Lord GOD.

20"Moreover you took your sons and your daughters, whom you bore to Me, and these you sacrificed to them to be devoured. *Were* your *acts* of harlotry a small matter, 21that you have slain My children and offered them up to them by causing them to pass through *the fire?* 22And in all your abominations and acts of harlotry you did not remember the days of your youth, when you were naked and bare, struggling in your blood.

23"Then it was so, after all your wickedness—'Woe, woe to you!' says the Lord GOD— 24*that* you also built for yourself a shrine, and made a high place for yourself in every street. 25You built your high places at the head of every road, and made your beauty to be abhorred. You offered yourself to everyone who passed by, and multiplied your acts of harlotry. 26You also committed harlotry with the Egyptians, your very fleshly neighbors,

16:15 The accusation that Israel "played the harlot" is significant in two ways. First, in the OT this language often describes turning away from the Lord to worship other gods. Second, worship in Canaanite fertility cults involved prostitution (see Hos. 2:2–13; 4:11, 12). Jerusalem had been crowned with beauty and fame but began to trust in her own devices instead of the God who had given her all she had. Thus, her gifts merely led to her downfall.

16:17 The beloved wife is charged with taking the gifts of precious jewelry and exquisite garments lavished on her by her husband and turning them into male images and worshiping these images with incense and offerings to satisfy her lusts.

16:20–22 Child sacrifice, part of Canaanite cultic rituals, was practiced to some extent by Israel, even though this practice

was expressly prohibited in the Law (Lev. 18:21; Deut. 12:31). This crime appears in its starkest horror by contrasting God's rescue of Israel when she was abandoned to infanticide with the nation's subsequent sacrifice of its own children (see Judg. 11:39; 2 Kin. 16:3). Anyone who would slaughter a helpless child has forgotten that children are a blessing from God (see Ps. 128, Children). Every generation has had to deal with this issue (see Gen. 9, Sanctity of Life; Jer. 1, Abortion). Children are indeed a precious gift from the Creator and an awesome responsibility in the kingdom (Is. 49, Motherhood).

16:23–29 Israel repeatedly had been warned to avoid political alliances because such alliances often resulted in idol worship (see Josh. 24:14, 15; 2 Chr. 7:19–22).

and increased your acts of harlotry to provoke Me to anger.

27"Behold, therefore, I stretched out My hand against you, diminished your allotment, and gave you up to the will of those who hate you, the daughters of the Philistines, who were ashamed of your lewd behavior. 28You also played the harlot with the Assyrians, because you were insatiable; indeed you played the harlot with them and still were not satisfied. 29Moreover you multiplied your acts of harlotry as far as the land of the trader, Chaldea; and even then you were not satisfied.

30"How degenerate is your heart!" says the Lord GOD, "seeing you do all these *things*, the deeds of a brazen harlot.

Jerusalem's Adultery

31"You erected your shrine at the head of every road, and built your high place in every street. Yet you were not like a harlot, because you scorned payment. 32*You are* an adulterous wife, *who* takes strangers instead of her husband. 33Men make payment to all harlots, but you made your payments to all your lovers, and hired them to come to you from all around for your harlotry. 34You are the opposite of *other* women in your harlotry, because no one solicited you to be a harlot. In that you gave payment but no payment was given you, therefore you are the opposite."

Jerusalem's Lovers Will Abuse Her

35'Now then, O harlot, hear the word of the LORD! 36Thus says the Lord GOD: "Because your filthiness was poured out and your nakedness uncovered in your harlotry with your lovers, and with all your abominable idols, and because of the blood of your children which you gave to them, 37surely, therefore, I will gather all your lovers with whom you took pleasure, all those you loved, *and* all those you hated; I will gather them from all around against you and will uncover your nakedness to them, that they may see all your nakedness. 38And I will judge you as women who break wedlock or shed blood are judged; I will bring blood upon you in fury and jealousy. 39I will also give you into their hand, and they shall throw

down your shrines and break down your high places. They shall also strip you of your clothes, take your beautiful jewelry, and leave you naked and bare.

40"They shall also bring up an assembly against you, and they shall stone you with stones and thrust you through with their swords. 41They shall burn your houses with fire, and execute judgments on you in the sight of many women; and I will make you cease playing the harlot, and you shall no longer hire lovers. 42So I will lay to rest My fury toward you, and My jealousy shall depart from you. I will be quiet, and be angry no more. 43Because you did not remember the days of your youth, but agitated Me[a] with all these *things*, surely I will also recompense your deeds on *your own* head," says the Lord GOD. "And you shall not commit lewdness in addition to all your abominations.

More Wicked than Samaria and Sodom

44"Indeed everyone who quotes proverbs will use *this* proverb against you: 'Like mother, like daughter!' 45You *are* your mother's daughter, loathing husband and children; and you *are* the sister of your sisters, who loathed their husbands and children; your mother *was* a Hittite and your father an Amorite.

46"Your elder sister *is* Samaria, who dwells with her daughters to the north of you; and your younger sister, who dwells to the south of you, *is* Sodom and her daughters. 47You did not walk in their ways nor act according to their abominations; but, as *if that were* too little, you became more corrupt than they in all your ways.

48"*As* I live," says the Lord GOD, "neither your sister Sodom nor her daughters have done as you and your daughters have done. 49Look, this was the iniquity of your sister Sodom: She and her daughter had pride, fullness of food, and abundance of idleness; neither did she strengthen the hand of the poor and needy. 50And they were haughty and committed abomination before Me; therefore I took them away as I saw *fit*.[a]

16:43 [a]Following Septuagint, Syriac, Targum, and Vulgate; Masoretic Text reads *were agitated with Me*. 16:50 [a]Vulgate reads *you saw*; Septuagint reads *he saw*; Targum reads *as was revealed to Me*.

16:33, 34 The senselessness of Israel's apostasy is highlighted. Unlike those who practiced prostitution in exchange for compensation, Israel practiced "prostitution" for pleasure and was willing to compensate others rather than to receive payment herself.

16:37 The woman, representing Israel or Jerusalem, was stripped of her clothing. Her nakedness served as a reminder of the exposed and unattended situation in which God found her (v. 7).

16:38 The death penalty was proscribed by God Himself, acting as the husband, as judgment for adultery (see Lev. 20:10; Deut. 22:21–24).

16:44 The proverbial saying, "Like mother, like daughter!" was meant to cause sober reflection, as it drove home Jerusalem's Canaanite origins (see v. 3). The phrase refers to the fact that God's people were pagan and immoral like the original residents of Canaan. Mothers in every generation do well to consider their unique influence on their daughters.

16:46, 47 Sodom served as a type for the sinful city in the OT because of its rampant sexual perversion, violence, and injustice (Gen. 18:20; 19:24, 25). Ezekiel could not have used stronger language to depict the depths of Jerusalem's depravity than to say that the city was worse than Sodom (see Deut. 29:23; 32:32; Is. 1:9, 10; Jer. 23:14).

51"Samaria did not commit half of your sins; but you have multiplied your abominations more than they, and have justified your sisters by all the abominations which you have done. 52You who judged your sisters, bear your own shame also, because the sins which you committed were more abominable than theirs; they are more righteous than you. Yes, be disgraced also, and bear your own shame, because you justified your sisters.

53"When I bring back their captives, the captives of Sodom and her daughters, and the captives of Samaria and her daughters, then *I will also bring back* the captives of your captivity among them, 54that you may bear your own shame and be disgraced by all that you did when you comforted them. 55When your sisters, Sodom and her daughters, return to their former state, and Samaria and her daughters return to their former state, then you and your daughters will return to your former state. 56For your sister Sodom was not a byword in your mouth in the days of your pride, 57before your wickedness was uncovered. It was like the time of the reproach of the daughters of Syriaa and all *those* around her, and of the daughters of the Philistines, who despise you everywhere. 58You have paid for your lewdness and your abominations," says the LORD. 59For thus says the Lord GOD: "I will deal with you as you have done, who despised the oath by breaking the covenant.

An Everlasting Covenant

60"Nevertheless I will remember My covenant with you in the days of your youth, and I will establish an everlasting covenant with you. 61Then you will remember your ways and be ashamed, when you receive your older and your younger sisters; for I will give them to you for daughters, but not because of My covenant with you. 62And I will establish My covenant with you. Then you shall know that I *am* the LORD, 63that you may remember and be ashamed, and never open your mouth anymore because of your shame, when I provide you an atonement for all you have done," says the Lord GOD.' "

The Eagles and the Vine

17 And the word of the LORD came to me, saying, 2"Son of man, pose a riddle, and speak a parable to the house of Israel, 3and say, 'Thus says the Lord GOD:

"A great eagle with large wings and long pinions,
Full of feathers of various colors,
Came to Lebanon
And took from the cedar the highest branch.
4He cropped off its topmost young twig
And carried it to a land of trade;
He set it in a city of merchants.
5Then he took some of the seed of the land
And planted it in a fertile field;
He placed *it* by abundant waters
And set it like a willow tree.
6And it grew and became a spreading vine of low stature;
Its branches turned toward him,
But its roots were under it.
So it became a vine,
Brought forth branches,
And put forth shoots.

7"But there was anothera great eagle with large wings and many feathers;
And behold, this vine bent its roots toward him,
And stretched its branches toward him,
From the garden terrace where it had been planted,
That he might water it.
8It was planted in good soil by many waters,
To bring forth branches, bear fruit,
And become a majestic vine." '

9"Say, 'Thus says the Lord GOD:

"Will it thrive?
Will he not pull up its roots,
Cut off its fruit,
And leave it to wither?
All of its spring leaves will wither,
And no great power or many people
Will be needed to pluck it up by its roots.
10Behold, *it is* planted,
Will it thrive?
Will it not utterly wither when the east wind touches it?
It will wither in the garden terrace where it grew." ' "

··
16:57 aFollowing Masoretic Text, Septuagint, Targum, and Vulgate; many Hebrew manuscripts and Syriac read *Edom.* 17:7 aFollowing Septuagint, Syriac, and Vulgate; Masoretic Text and Targum read *one.*

17:2–4 **The riddle** or parable which Ezekiel was commanded to speak is presented (vv. 3–10), and the divine interpretation is given (vv. 11–21). The first "great eagle" is identified as Nebuchadnezzar, king of Babylon. The land of trade is Babylonia (v. 4). The "topmost young twig" (v. 4) represented King Jehoiachin taken from Jerusalem into Exile in 597 B.C. (2 Kin. 24:10–12).

17:5–10 **The seed of the Land** symbolized Zedekiah, Jehoiachin's uncle, whom Nebuchadnezzar installed as puppet king over Judah (see 2 Kin. 24:17). The second "great eagle" (Ezek. 17:7) referred to an Egyptian pharaoh, either Pharaoh Hophra (see Jer. 44:30) or Pharaoh Psammetichus II. The point was that Zedekiah broke his vassal oath to Nebuchadnezzar by looking to Egypt for help (see 2 Kin. 24:20). Political alliance

[11]Moreover the word of the LORD came to me, saying, [12]"Say now to the rebellious house: 'Do you not know what these *things mean?*' Tell *them*, 'Indeed the king of Babylon went to Jerusalem and took its king and princes, and led them with him to Babylon. [13]And he took the king's offspring, made a covenant with him, and put him under oath. He also took away the mighty of the land, [14]that the kingdom might be brought low and not lift itself up, *but* that by keeping his covenant it might stand. [15]But he rebelled against him by sending his ambassadors to Egypt, that they might give him horses and many people. Will he prosper? Will he who does such *things* escape? Can he break a covenant and still be delivered?

[16]'*As* I live,' says the Lord GOD, 'surely in the place *where* the king *dwells* who made him king, whose oath he despised and whose covenant he broke—with him in the midst of Babylon he shall die. [17]Nor will Pharaoh with *his* mighty army and great company do anything in the war, when they heap up a siege mound and build a wall to cut off many persons. [18]Since he despised the oath by breaking the covenant, and in fact gave his hand and still did all these *things*, he shall not escape.' "

[19]Therefore thus says the Lord GOD: "*As* I live, surely My oath which he despised, and My covenant which he broke, I will recompense on his own head. [20]I will spread My net over him, and he shall be taken in My snare. I will bring him to Babylon and try him there for the treason which he committed against Me. [21]All his fugitives[a] with all his troops shall fall by the sword, and those who remain shall be scattered to every wind; and you shall know that I, the LORD, have spoken."

Israel Exalted at Last

[22]Thus says the Lord GOD: "I will take also *one* of the highest branches of the high cedar and set *it* out. I will crop off from the topmost of its young twigs a tender one, and will plant *it* on a high and prominent mountain. [23]On the mountain height of Israel I will plant it; and it will bring forth boughs, and bear fruit, and be a majestic cedar. Under it will dwell birds of every sort; in the shadow of its branches they will dwell. [24]And all the trees of the field shall know that I, the LORD, have brought down the high tree and exalted the low tree, dried up the green tree and made the dry tree flourish; I, the LORD, have spoken and have done *it*."

A False Proverb Refuted

18 The word of the LORD came to me again, saying, [2]"What do you mean when you use this proverb concerning the land of Israel, saying:

'The fathers have eaten sour grapes,
  And the children's teeth are set on edge'?

[3]"*As* I live," says the Lord GOD, "you shall no longer use this proverb in Israel.

[4]"Behold, all souls are Mine;
  The soul of the father
  As well as the soul of the son is Mine;
  The soul who sins shall die.
[5]But if a man is just
  And does what is lawful and right;
[6]If he has not eaten on the mountains,
  Nor lifted up his eyes to the idols of the house
      of Israel,
  Nor defiled his neighbor's wife,
  Nor approached a woman during her impurity;
[7]If he has not oppressed anyone,
  But has restored to the debtor his pledge;
  Has robbed no one by violence,
  But has given his bread to the hungry
  And covered the naked with clothing;
[8]If he has not exacted usury
  Nor taken any increase,
  But has withdrawn his hand from iniquity
  And executed true judgment between man and
      man;
[9]*If* he has walked in My statutes
  And kept My judgments faithfully—
  He *is* just;

17:21 [a]Following Masoretic Text and Vulgate; many Hebrew manuscripts and Syriac read *choice men;* Targum reads *mighty men;* Septuagint omits *All his fugitives.*

---

with Egypt would result in the destruction of the vine, that is, Judah's kings (Ezek. 17:10).

17:15–20 Zedekiah's disloyalty to Nebuchadnezzar involved oath-breaking and therefore required punishment (see v. 18). In the ancient Near East, oaths between countries were sworn in the names of their respective gods. Therefore, Zedekiah was breaking an oath he had sworn in the name of the Lord (see v. 19). He also violated God's covenant with Israel by looking to Egypt for help. Zedekiah had committed treason against the Lord by refusing to submit to Babylon (2 Chr. 36:11–13). As a result, God employed the angry Babylonians as His instruments of retribution.

17:22 The reference to a twig, shoot, or branch is a common OT metaphor for the messianic king (see Is. 11:1–5; 53:2; Jer. 23:5–8; Zech. 3:8–10).

18:2 This popular proverb probably arose out of a bitter twisting of the concept of corporate responsibility (see Ex. 20:5; 34:7). It had come into popular use among the exiles as a confession of innocence (that is, we are suffering for the sins of earlier generations) or as a protest against God's perceived injustice (see Jer. 31:29).

18:6 The principle of individual responsibility is here presented. The righteous person was expected to guard moral purity and honor marital commitments (Ex. 20:14; Lev. 15:19–30).

He shall surely live!"
Says the Lord GOD.

10"If he begets a son *who is* a robber
Or a shedder of blood,
Who does any of these *things*
11And does none of those *duties,*
But has eaten on the mountains
Or defiled his neighbor's wife;
12If he has oppressed the poor and needy,
Robbed by violence,
Not restored the pledge,
Lifted his eyes to the idols,
Or committed abomination;
13If he has exacted usury
Or taken increase—
Shall he then live?
He shall not live!
If he has done any of these abominations,
He shall surely die;
His blood shall be upon him.

14"*If,* however, he begets a son
Who sees all the sins which his father has
done,
And considers but does not do likewise;
15*Who* has not eaten on the mountains,
Nor lifted his eyes to the idols of the house of
Israel,
Nor defiled his neighbor's wife;
16Has not oppressed anyone,
Nor withheld a pledge,
Nor robbed by violence,
But has given his bread to the hungry
And covered the naked with clothing;
17*Who* has withdrawn his hand from the poor[a]
And not received usury or increase,
But has executed My judgments
And walked in My statutes—
He shall not die for the iniquity of his father;
He shall surely live!

18"*As for* his father,
Because he cruelly oppressed,
Robbed his brother by violence,
And did what *is* not good among his people,
Behold, he shall die for his iniquity.

Turn and Live

19"Yet you say, 'Why should the son not bear the guilt of the father?' Because the son has done what is lawful and right, and has kept all My statutes and observed them, he shall surely live. 20The soul who sins shall die. The son shall not bear the guilt of the father, nor the father bear the guilt of the son. The righteousness of the righteous shall be upon himself, and the wickedness of the wicked shall be upon himself.

21"But if a wicked man turns from all his sins which he has committed, keeps all My statutes, and does what is lawful and right, he shall surely live; he shall not die. 22None of the transgressions which he has committed shall be remembered against him; because of the righteousness which he has done, he shall live. 23Do I have any pleasure at all that the wicked should die?" says the Lord GOD, "*and* not that he should turn from his ways and live?

24"But when a righteous man turns away from his righteousness and commits iniquity, and does according to all the abominations that the wicked *man* does, shall he live? All the righteousness which he has done shall not be remembered; because of the unfaithfulness of which he is guilty and the sin which he has committed, because of them he shall die.

25"Yet you say, 'The way of the Lord is not fair.' Hear now, O house of Israel, is it not My way which is fair, and your ways which are not fair? 26When a righteous *man* turns away from his righteousness, commits iniquity, and dies in it, it is because of the iniquity which he has done that he dies. 27Again, when a wicked *man* turns away from the wickedness which he committed, and does what is lawful and right, he preserves himself alive. 28Because he considers and turns away from all the transgressions which he committed, he shall surely live; he shall not die. 29Yet the house of Israel says, 'The way of the Lord is not fair.' O house of Israel, is it not My ways which are fair, and your ways which are not fair?

30"Therefore I will judge you, O house of Israel, every one according to his ways," says the Lord GOD. "Repent, and turn from all your transgressions, so that iniquity will not be your ruin. 31Cast away from you all the transgressions which you have committed, and get yourselves a new heart and a new spirit. For why should you die, O house of Israel? 32For I have no pleasure in the death of one who dies," says the Lord GOD. "Therefore turn and live!"

•••••••••••••••••••••••

18:17 aFollowing Masoretic Text, Targum, and Vulgate; Septuagint reads *iniquity* (compare verse 8).

18:21–24 Ezekiel shifted his focus to the present state of affairs with an individual. Past guilt could not nullify current repentance, and past righteousness could not excuse present rebellion. By stressing their present response to God, Ezekiel sought to bring the exiles to a better understanding of their current opportunities and responsibilities.

18:31, 32 God manifested His patience and love as He sent the prophets repeatedly to preach repentance in light of Israel's sin and coming judgment. Note the emphasis on the need for a new heart and spirit (v. 31; see Jer. 31:31–34).

*Parents will not rear righteous children in the midst
of their own unrighteous standards.*

Dorothy Kelley Patterson

Israel Degraded

19"Moreover take up a lamentation for the princes of Israel, [2]and say:

'What *is* your mother? A lioness:
  She lay down among the lions;
  Among the young lions she nourished her
    cubs.
[3]She brought up one of her cubs,
  And he became a young lion;
  He learned to catch prey,
  And he devoured men.
[4]The nations also heard of him;
  He was trapped in their pit,
  And they brought him with chains to the land
    of Egypt.

[5]When she saw that she waited, *that* her hope
    was lost,
  She took another of her cubs *and* made him a
    young lion.
[6]He roved among the lions,
  And became a young lion;
  He learned to catch prey;
  He devoured men.
[7]He knew their desolate places,[a]
  And laid waste their cities;
  The land with its fullness was desolated
  By the noise of his roaring.
[8]Then the nations set against him from the
      provinces on every side,
  And spread their net over him;
  He was trapped in their pit.
[9]They put him in a cage with chains,
  And brought him to the king of Babylon;
  They brought him in nets,
  That his voice should no longer be heard on
    the mountains of Israel.

[10]Your mother *was* like a vine in your bloodline,[a]
  Planted by the waters,

Fruitful and full of branches
  Because of many waters.
[11]She had strong branches for scepters of
    rulers.
  She towered in stature above the thick
    branches,
  And was seen in her height amid the dense
    foliage.
[12]But she was plucked up in fury,
  She was cast down to the ground,
  And the east wind dried her fruit.
  Her strong branches were broken and
    withered;
  The fire consumed them.
[13]And now she *is* planted in the wilderness,
  In a dry and thirsty land.
[14]Fire has come out from a rod of her branches
  And devoured her fruit,
  So that she has no strong branch—a scepter
    for ruling.' "

This *is* a lamentation, and has become a lamentation.

The Rebellions of Israel

20It came to pass in the seventh year, in the fifth *month,* on the tenth *day* of the month, *that* certain of the elders of Israel came to inquire of the LORD, and sat before me. [2]Then the word of the LORD came to me, saying, [3]"Son of man, speak to the elders of Israel, and say to them, 'Thus says the Lord GOD: "Have you come to inquire of Me? *As* I live," says the Lord GOD, "I will not be inquired of by you." ' [4]Will you judge them, son of man, will you judge *them?* Then make known to them the abominations of their fathers.

19:7 [a]Septuagint reads *He stood in insolence;* Targum reads *He destroyed its palaces;* Vulgate reads *He learned to make widows.* **19:10** [a]Literally *blood,* following Masoretic Text, Syriac, and Vulgate; Septuagint reads *like a flower on a pomegranate tree;* Targum reads *in your likeness.*

19:1 Take up a lamentation indicated to the people that Ezekiel was singing a funeral dirge. The prophets commonly employed this type of song in their proclamations of judgment (see Jer. 7:29; Amos 5:1–3).

19:3, 4 These verses refer to Jehoahaz, Josiah's son, who reigned only three months before he was deported to Egypt by Pharaoh Necho (see 2 Kin. 23:31–34).

19:5–9 The identity of this second cub is uncertain. It may refer to Jehoiakim, Jehoiachin, or Zedekiah, Judah's last three kings. Or instead of representing specific rulers, the lions may represent a composite picture of Judah's kings. Such kings forfeited their power by acting irresponsibly.

19:10–14 This lament emphasized the death of the vine representing Judah or Judah's rulers. The reason for the fall of Judah and the Davidic line resulted from internal, not external, factors. Judah's own foolishness and the poor leadership of its kings brought disaster on the nation (v. 14).

20:1 This prophecy dated August 9, 591 B.C. was given approximately one year after the vision of the temple in Jerusalem (Ezek. 8:1).

⁵"Say to them, 'Thus says the Lord GOD: "On the day when I chose Israel and raised My hand in an oath to the descendants of the house of Jacob, and made Myself known to them in the land of Egypt, I raised My hand in an oath to them, saying, 'I *am* the LORD your God.' ⁶On that day I raised My hand in an oath to them, to bring them out of the land of Egypt into a land that I had searched out for them, 'flowing with milk and honey,'ᵃ the glory of all lands. ⁷Then I said to them, 'Each of you, throw away the abominations which are before his eyes, and do not defile yourselves with the idols of Egypt. I *am* the LORD your God.' ⁸But they rebelled against Me and would not obey Me. They did not all cast away the abominations which were before their eyes, nor did they forsake the idols of Egypt. Then I said, 'I will pour out My fury on them and fulfill My anger against them in the midst of the land of Egypt.' ⁹But I acted for My name's sake, that it should not be profaned before the Gentiles among whom they *were,* in whose sight I had made Myself known to them, to bring them out of the land of Egypt.

¹⁰"Therefore I made them go out of the land of Egypt and brought them into the wilderness. ¹¹And I gave them My statutes and showed them My judgments, 'which, *if* a man does, he shall live by them.'ᵃ ¹²Moreover I also gave them My Sabbaths, to be a sign between them and Me, that they might know that I *am* the LORD who sanctifies them. ¹³Yet the house of Israel rebelled against Me in the wilderness; they did not walk in My statutes; they despised My judgments, 'which, *if* a man does, he shall live by them';ᵃ and they greatly defiled My Sabbaths. Then I said I would pour out My fury on them in the wilderness, to consume them. ¹⁴But I acted for My name's sake, that it should not be profaned before the Gentiles, in whose sight I had brought them out. ¹⁵So I also raised My hand in an oath to them in the wilderness, that I would not bring them into the land which I had given *them,* 'flowing with milk and honey,'ᵃ the glory of all lands, ¹⁶because they despised My judgments and did not walk in My statutes, but profaned My Sabbaths; for their heart went after their idols. ¹⁷Nevertheless My eye spared them from destruction. I did not make an end of them in the wilderness.

¹⁸"But I said to their children in the wilderness, 'Do not walk in the statutes of your fathers, nor observe their judgments, nor defile yourselves with their idols. ¹⁹I *am* the LORD your God: Walk in My statutes, keep My judgments, and do them; ²⁰hallow My Sabbaths, and they will be a sign between Me and you, that you may know that I *am* the LORD your God.'

²¹"Notwithstanding, the children rebelled against Me; they did not walk in My statutes, and were not careful to observe My judgments, 'which, *if* a man does, he shall live by them';ᵃ but they profaned My Sabbaths. Then I said I would pour out My fury on them and fulfill My anger against them in the wilderness. ²²Nevertheless I withdrew My hand and acted for My name's sake, that it should not be profaned in the sight of the Gentiles, in whose sight I had brought them out. ²³Also I raised My hand in an oath to those in the wilderness, that I would scatter them among the Gentiles and disperse them throughout the countries, ²⁴because they had not executed My judgments, but had despised My statutes, profaned My Sabbaths, and their eyes were fixed on their fathers' idols.

²⁵"Therefore I also gave them up to statutes *that were* not good, and judgments by which they could not live; ²⁶and I pronounced them unclean because of their ritual gifts, in that they caused all their firstborn to pass through *the fire,* that I might make them desolate and that they might know that I am the LORD." '

²⁷"Therefore, son of man, speak to the house of Israel, and say to them, 'Thus says the Lord GOD: "In this too your fathers have blasphemed Me, by being unfaithful to Me. ²⁸When I brought them into the land *concerning* which I had raised My hand in an oath to give them, and they saw all the high hills and all the thick trees, there they offered their sacrifices and provoked Me with their offerings. There they also sent up their sweet aroma and poured out their drink offerings. ²⁹Then I said to them, 'What *is* this high place to which you go?' So its name is called Bamahᵃ to this day." ' ³⁰Therefore say to the house of Israel, 'Thus

· · · · · · · · · · · · · · · · · · ·
20:6, 15 ᵃExodus 3:8   20:11, 13, 21 ᵃLeviticus 18:5   20:29 ᵃLiterally *High Place*

20:5–9 God recounted the history of Israel's election, beginning with bondage in Egypt. Despite God's sworn oath to His people, they continued to worship the gods of Egypt (see chart, The Goddesses of Egypt).

20:9 A name signified character or reputation in Hebrew thought. The Lord chose Israel to reveal His character; thus the nation's demise would lead to the profaning of His name. God acted to preserve His reputation (see vv. 14, 22, 44; Ex. 32:12).

20:12 The Sabbath marked the Israelites as a people conse-

crated to God among all the nations (see Ex. 19:4–6; Deut. 14:2; chart, The Principle of the Sabbath).

20:25 God's laws, though given to lead to life, brought death (see v. 11). Such radical judgment occurs when God gives people up to their own sinful desires and their hearts become hardened (see Rom. 1:18–32).

20:33, 34 Using language clearly reminiscent of the first Exodus, God's answer to the blatant disobedience of His people was to begin again by gathering Israel out of Exile and reaffirming His love and plan for Israel (Ex. 3:19; 6:6).

says the Lord GOD: "Are you defiling yourselves in the manner of your fathers, and committing harlotry according to their abominations? [31]For when you offer your gifts and make your sons pass through the fire, you defile yourselves with all your idols, even to this day. So shall I be inquired of by you, O house of Israel? *As* I live," says the Lord GOD, "I will not be inquired of by you. [32]What you have in your mind shall never be, when you say, 'We will be like the Gentiles, like the families in other countries, serving wood and stone.'

God Will Restore Israel

[33]"*As* I live," says the Lord GOD, "surely with a mighty hand, with an outstretched arm, and with fury poured out, I will rule over you. [34]I will bring you out from the peoples and gather you out of the countries where you are scattered, with a mighty hand, with an outstretched arm, and with fury poured out. [35]And I will bring you into the wilderness of the peoples, and there I will plead My case with you face to face. [36]Just as I pleaded My case with your fathers in the wilderness of the land of Egypt, so I will plead My case with you," says the Lord GOD.

[37]"I will make you pass under the rod, and I will bring you into the bond of the covenant; [38]I will purge the rebels from among you, and those who transgress against Me; I will bring them out of the country where they dwell, but they shall not enter the land of Israel. Then you will know that I *am* the LORD.

[39]"As for you, O house of Israel," thus says the Lord GOD: "Go, serve every one of you his idols— and hereafter— if you will not obey Me; but profane My holy name no more with your gifts and your idols. [40]For on My holy mountain, on the mountain height of Israel," says the Lord GOD, "there all the house of Israel, all of them in the land, shall serve Me; there I will accept them, and there I will require your offerings and the firstfruits of your sacrifices, together with all your holy things. [41]I will accept you as a sweet aroma when I bring you out from the peoples and gather you out of the countries where you have been scattered; and I will be hallowed in you before the Gentiles. [42]Then you shall know that I *am* the LORD, when I bring you into the land of Israel, into the country *for* which I raised My hand in an oath

to give to your fathers. [43]And there you shall remember your ways and all your doings with which you were defiled; and you shall loathe yourselves in your own sight because of all the evils that you have committed. [44]Then you shall know that I *am* the LORD, when I have dealt with you for My name's sake, not according to your wicked ways nor according to your corrupt doings, O house of Israel," says the Lord GOD.' "

Fire in the Forest

[45]Furthermore the word of the LORD came to me, saying, [46]"Son of man, set your face toward the south; preach against the south and prophesy against the forest land, the South,[a] [47]and say to the forest of the South, 'Hear the word of the LORD! Thus says the Lord GOD: "Behold, I will kindle a fire in you, and it shall devour every green tree and every dry tree in you; the blazing flame shall not be quenched, and all faces from the south to the north shall be scorched by it. [48]All flesh shall see that I, the LORD, have kindled it; it shall not be quenched." ' "

[49]Then I said, "Ah, Lord GOD! They say of me, 'Does he not speak parables?' "

Babylon, the Sword of God

21 And the word of the LORD came to me, saying, [2]"Son of man, set your face toward Jerusalem, preach against the holy places, and prophesy against the land of Israel; [3]and say to the land of Israel, 'Thus says the LORD: "Behold, I *am* against you, and I will draw My sword out of its sheath and cut off both righteous and wicked from you. [4]Because I will cut off both righteous and wicked from you, therefore My sword shall go out of its sheath against all flesh from south *to* north, [5]that all flesh may know that I, the LORD, have drawn My sword out of its sheath; it shall not return anymore." '
[6]Sigh therefore, son of man, with a breaking heart, and sigh with bitterness before their eyes. [7]And it shall be when they say to you, 'Why are you sighing?' that you shall answer, 'Because of the news; when it comes, every heart will melt, all hands will be feeble, every spirit will faint, and all knees will be weak *as* water. Behold, it is coming and shall be brought to pass,' says the Lord GOD."

20:46 [a]Hebrew *Negev*

20:37 Pass under the rod refers to the way a shepherd counted or separated his flock (see Matt. 25:31–46).

20:46 The south refers to Jerusalem, which is located almost directly west of Babylon (see Ezek. 21:2). However, the Syrian desert, which lies between the two nations, forced travelers to take a northward arc along the Fertile Crescent. As a result, a traveler from Babylon would be heading south in approaching Jerusalem.

21:1–5 A parable is explained (see Ezek. 20:45–49). "Holy

places" included, along with the temple, numerous high places on which idolatrous worship was practiced (Ezek. 21:2). The reference to "righteous and wicked" does not contradict Ezekiel's earlier statements about individual responsibility before God (v. 3; see Ezek. 14:12–23; 18:1–32). The earlier statements do not mean that the righteous person has an ironclad exemption from suffering. Some members of the righteous remnant, including Ezekiel, had not escaped the judgment of deportation.

⁸Again the word of the LORD came to me, saying, ⁹"Son of man, prophesy and say, 'Thus says the LORD!' Say:

'A sword, a sword is sharpened
And also polished!
¹⁰Sharpened to make a dreadful slaughter,
Polished to flash like lightning!
Should we then make mirth?
It despises the scepter of My son,
As it does all wood.
¹¹And He has given it to be polished,
That it may be handled;
This sword is sharpened, and it is polished
To be given into the hand of the slayer.'

¹²"Cry and wail, son of man;
For it will be against My people,
Against all the princes of Israel.
Terrors including the sword will be against My
people;
Therefore strike *your* thigh.

¹³"Because *it is* a testing,
And what if *the sword* despises even the
scepter?
The scepter shall be no *more*,"

says the Lord GOD.

¹⁴"You therefore, son of man, prophesy,
And strike *your* hands together.
The third time let the sword do double
damage.
It *is* the sword *that* slays,
The sword that slays the great *men*,
That enters their private chambers.
¹⁵I have set the point of the sword against all
their gates,
That the heart may melt and many may
stumble.
Ah! *It is* made bright;
It is grasped for slaughter:

¹⁶"Swords at the ready!
Thrust right!
Set your blade!
Thrust left—
Wherever your edge is ordered!

¹⁷"I also will beat My fists together,
And I will cause My fury to rest;
I, the LORD, have spoken."

¹⁸The word of the LORD came to me again, saying: ¹⁹"And son of man, appoint for yourself two ways for the sword of the king of Babylon to go; both of them shall go from the same land. Make a sign; put *it* at the head of the road to the city. ²⁰Appoint a road for the sword to go to Rabbah of the Ammonites, and to Judah, into fortified Jerusalem. ²¹For the king of Babylon stands at the parting of the road, at the fork of the two roads, to use divination: he shakes the arrows, he consults the images, he looks at the liver. ²²In his right hand is the divination for Jerusalem: to set up battering rams, to call for a slaughter, to lift the voice with shouting, to set battering rams against the gates, to heap up a *siege* mound, and to build a wall. ²³And it will be to them like a false divination in the eyes of those who have sworn oaths with them; but he will bring their iniquity to remembrance, that they may be taken.

²⁴"Therefore thus says the Lord GOD: 'Because you have made your iniquity to be remembered, in that your transgressions are uncovered, so that in all your doings your sins appear— because you have come to remembrance, you shall be taken in hand.

²⁵'Now to you, O profane, wicked prince of Israel, whose day has come, whose iniquity *shall* end, ²⁶thus says the Lord GOD:

"Remove the turban, and take off the crown;
Nothing *shall remain* the same.
Exalt the humble, and humble the exalted.
²⁷Overthrown, overthrown,
I will make it overthrown!
It shall be no *longer*,
Until He comes whose right it is,
And I will give it *to Him*." '

A Sword Against the Ammonites

²⁸"And you, son of man, prophesy and say, 'Thus says the Lord GOD concerning the Ammonites and concerning their reproach,' and say:

'A sword, a sword *is* drawn,
Polished for slaughter,

21:12 Strike your thigh was an action expressing mourning, hopelessness, and despair (see Jer. 31:19).

21:14 Clapping or striking the hands indicated a summons, exultation over an enemy, or sorrow (see Nah. 3:19).

21:20 Rabbah was the capital of the Ammonite nation, which had joined with Judah in revolt against Babylon.

21:21 Magical methods to determine the will of the gods were used extensively in Babylon. Examinations of the livers of animals had been an established practice for centuries. Ancient

soothsayers would cut up an animal, observe the shape and condition of the liver, and use elaborate tables to determine what the omen revealed about the will of the gods. Other methods included shaking arrows marked affirmatively and negatively and consulting images or household gods (see Deut. 18, The Occult).

21:27 The threefold repetition of "overthrown" denotes complete ruin. The phrase "until He comes whose right it is" has been understood to refer to the Messiah, the rightful Ruler.

These . . . events are permitted and guided by thy wisdom,
which solely is light. We are in darkness and must be thankful that
our knowledge is not {needed} to perfect thy work.

St. Elizabeth Seton

For consuming, for flashing—
²⁹While they see false visions for you,
While they divine a lie to you,
To bring you on the necks of the wicked, the
    slain
Whose day has come,
Whose iniquity *shall* end.

³⁰'Return *it* to its sheath.
I will judge you
In the place where you were created,
In the land of your nativity.
³¹I will pour out My indignation on you;
I will blow against you with the fire of My
    wrath,
And deliver you into the hands of brutal men
    who are skillful to destroy.
³²You shall be fuel for the fire;
Your blood shall be in the midst of the land.
You shall not be remembered,
For I the LORD have spoken.' "

Sins of Jerusalem

22 Moreover the word of the LORD came to me,
saying, ²"Now, son of man, will you judge,
will you judge the bloody city? Yes, show her all
her abominations! ³Then say, 'Thus says the Lord
GOD: "The city sheds blood in her own midst, that
her time may come; and she makes idols within
herself to defile herself. ⁴You have become guilty
by the blood which you have shed, and have defiled yourself with the idols which you have made.
You have caused your days to draw near, and have
come to *the end of* your years; therefore I have
made you a reproach to the nations, and a mockery
to all countries. ⁵*Those* near and *those* far from you
will mock you as infamous *and* full of tumult.

⁶"Look, the princes of Israel: each one has used
his power to shed blood in you. ⁷In you they have
made light of father and mother; in your midst
they have oppressed the stranger; in you they
have mistreated the fatherless and the widow.
⁸You have despised My holy things and profaned

My Sabbaths. ⁹In you are men who slander to
cause bloodshed; in you are those who eat on the
mountains; in your midst they commit lewdness.
¹⁰In you men uncover their fathers' nakedness; in
you they violate women who are set apart during
their impurity. ¹¹One commits abomination with
his neighbor's wife; another lewdly defiles his
daughter-in-law; and another in you violates his
sister, his father's daughter. ¹²In you they take
bribes to shed blood; you take usury and increase;
you have made profit from your neighbors by extortion, and have forgotten Me," says the Lord
GOD.

¹³"Behold, therefore, I beat My fists at the dishonest profit which you have made, and at the
bloodshed which has been in your midst. ¹⁴Can
your heart endure, or can your hands remain
strong, in the days when I shall deal with you? I,
the LORD, have spoken, and will do *it*. ¹⁵I will scatter you among the nations, disperse you throughout the countries, and remove your filthiness completely from you. ¹⁶You shall defile yourself in the
sight of the nations; then you shall know that I *am*
the LORD." ' "

Israel in the Furnace

¹⁷The word of the LORD came to me, saying,
¹⁸"Son of man, the house of Israel has become
dross to Me; they *are* all bronze, tin, iron, and lead,
in the midst of a furnace; they have become dross
from silver. ¹⁹Therefore thus says the Lord GOD:
'Because you have all become dross, therefore behold, I will gather you into the midst of Jerusalem.
²⁰*As men* gather silver, bronze, iron, lead, and tin
into the midst of a furnace, to blow fire on it, to
melt *it;* so I will gather *you* in My anger and in My
fury, and I will leave *you there* and melt you. ²¹Yes, I
will gather you and blow on you with the fire of
My wrath, and you shall be melted in its midst.
²²As silver is melted in the midst of a furnace, so
shall you be melted in its midst; then you shall
know that I, the LORD, have poured out My fury on
you.' "

22:7 In Israel's patriarchal, agricultural society, those without
the economic and legal protection of a male head of household were objects of God's special care. Specific laws were instituted by God to ensure that the fatherless and widow received justice. The stranger also was to be treated right (see
Deut. 14:29; 16:11; 24:19–21; 26:12–15).

22:29 The people of the Land, oppressed by their leaders, became oppressors of those weaker than themselves.

22:30 For standing in the gap, see Ezekiel 13:5, note.

Israel's Wicked Leaders

23And the word of the LORD came to me, saying, 24"Son of man, say to her: 'You *are* a land that is not cleansed[a] or rained on in the day of indignation.' 25The conspiracy of her prophets[a] in her midst is like a roaring lion tearing the prey; they have devoured people; they have taken treasure and precious things; they have made many widows in her midst. 26Her priests have violated My law and profaned My holy things; they have not distinguished between the holy and unholy, nor have they made known *the difference* between the unclean and the clean; and they have hidden their eyes from My Sabbaths, so that I am profaned among them. 27Her princes in her midst *are* like wolves tearing the prey, to shed blood, to destroy people, and to get dishonest gain. 28Her prophets plastered them with untempered *mortar,* seeing false visions, and divining lies for them, saying, 'Thus says the Lord GOD,' when the LORD had not spoken. 29The people of the land have used oppressions, committed robbery, and mistreated the poor and needy; and they wrongfully oppress the stranger. 30So I sought for a man among them who would make a wall, and stand in the gap before Me on behalf of the land, that I should not destroy it; but I found no one. 31Therefore I have poured out My indignation on them; I have consumed them with the fire of My wrath; and I have recompensed their deeds on their own heads," says the Lord GOD.

Two Harlot Sisters

23 The word of the LORD came again to me, saying:

2"Son of man, there were two women,
   The daughters of one mother.
3They committed harlotry in Egypt,
   They committed harlotry in their youth;
   Their breasts were there embraced,
   Their virgin bosom was there pressed.
4Their names: Oholah[a] the elder and Oholibah[b]
   her sister;
   They were Mine,
   And they bore sons and daughters.
   As for their names,
   Samaria *is* Oholah, and Jerusalem *is* Oholibah.

The Older Sister, Samaria

5"Oholah played the harlot even though she was Mine;

And she lusted for her lovers, the neighboring
   Assyrians,
6*Who were* clothed in purple,
   Captains and rulers,
   All of them desirable young men,
   Horsemen riding on horses.
7Thus she committed her harlotry with them,
   All of them choice men of Assyria;
   And with all for whom she lusted,
   With all their idols, she defiled herself.
8She has never given up her harlotry *brought*
   from Egypt,
   For in her youth they had lain with her,
   Pressed her virgin bosom,
   And poured out their immorality upon her.

9"Therefore I have delivered her
   Into the hand of her lovers,
   Into the hand of the Assyrians,
   For whom she lusted.
10They uncovered her nakedness,
   Took away her sons and daughters,
   And slew her with the sword;
   She became a byword among women,
   For they had executed judgment on her.

The Younger Sister, Jerusalem

11"Now although her sister Oholibah saw *this,* she became more corrupt in her lust than she, and in her harlotry more corrupt than her sister's harlotry.

12"She lusted for the neighboring Assyrians,
   Captains and rulers,
   Clothed most gorgeously,
   Horsemen riding on horses,
   All of them desirable young men.
13Then I saw that she was defiled;
   Both *took* the same way.
14But she increased her harlotry;
   She looked at men portrayed on the wall,
   Images of Chaldeans portrayed in vermilion,
15Girded with belts around their waists,
   Flowing turbans on their heads,
   All of them looking like captains,
   In the manner of the Babylonians of Chaldea,
   The land of their nativity.
16As soon as her eyes saw them,

·················

22:24 [a]Following Masoretic Text, Syriac, and Vulgate; Septuagint reads *showered upon.*   22:25 [a]Following Masoretic Text and Vulgate; Septuagint reads *princes;* Targum reads *scribes.*   23:4 [a]Literally *Her Own Tabernacle* [b]Literally *My Tabernacle Is in Her*

23:1–49 In this allegory of two sisters, Oholah and Oholibah, respectively, represent Samaria and Jerusalem, the capital cities of the northern and southern kingdoms. Ezekiel employed shocking sexual metaphors to describe how the two nations violated the covenant with the Lord. Through this parable Ezekiel emphasized the horror of idolatry.

23:4 Ohola and Oholibah are variant forms meaning "tent-dweller," perhaps referring to Israel's origin as a nation without a land (see vv. 1–49, note). Marital imagery is employed to describe the relationship between God and Israel.

She lusted for them
And sent messengers to them in
    Chaldea.

17"Then the Babylonians came to her, into the bed
    of love,
And they defiled her with their immorality;
So she was defiled by them, and alienated
    herself from them.
18She revealed her harlotry and uncovered her
    nakedness.
Then I alienated Myself from her,
As I had alienated Myself from her sister.

19"Yet she multiplied her harlotry
In calling to remembrance the days of her
    youth,
When she had played the harlot in the land of
    Egypt.
20For she lusted for her paramours,
Whose flesh *is like* the flesh of donkeys,
And whose issue *is like* the issue of horses.
21Thus you called to remembrance the lewdness
    of your youth,
When the Egyptians pressed your bosom
Because of your youthful breasts.

Judgment on Jerusalem

22"Therefore, Oholibah, thus says the Lord GOD:

'Behold, I will stir up your lovers against you,
From whom you have alienated yourself,
And I will bring them against you from every
    side:
23The Babylonians,
All the Chaldeans,
Pekod, Shoa, Koa,
All the Assyrians with them,
All of them desirable young men,
Governors and rulers,
Captains and men of renown,
All of them riding on horses.
24And they shall come against you
With chariots, wagons, and war-horses,
With a horde of people.
They shall array against you
Buckler, shield, and helmet all around.

'I will delegate judgment to them,
And they shall judge you according to their
    judgments.
25I will set My jealousy against you,
And they shall deal furiously with you;

They shall remove your nose and your ears,
And your remnant shall fall by the sword;
They shall take your sons and your
    daughters,
And your remnant shall be devoured by fire.
26They shall also strip you of your clothes
And take away your beautiful jewelry.

27"Thus I will make you cease your lewdness and
    your harlotry
Brought from the land of Egypt,
So that you will not lift your eyes to them,
Nor remember Egypt anymore.'

28"For thus says the Lord GOD: 'Surely I will deliver you into the hand of those you hate, into the
hand *of those* from whom you alienated yourself.
29They will deal hatefully with you, take away all
you have worked for, and leave you naked and
bare. The nakedness of your harlotry shall be uncovered, both your lewdness and your harlotry. 30I
will do these *things* to you because you have gone
as a harlot after the Gentiles, because you have become defiled by their idols. 31You have walked in
the way of your sister; therefore I will put her cup
in your hand.'
32"Thus says the Lord GOD:

'You shall drink of your sister's cup,
The deep and wide one;
You shall be laughed to scorn
And held in derision;
It contains much.
33You will be filled with drunkenness and
    sorrow,
The cup of horror and desolation,
The cup of your sister Samaria.
34You shall drink and drain it,
You shall break its shards,
And tear at your own breasts;
For I have spoken,'
Says the Lord GOD.

35"Therefore thus says the Lord GOD:

'Because you have forgotten Me and cast Me
    behind your back,
Therefore you shall bear the *penalty*
Of your lewdness and your harlotry.' "

Both Sisters Judged

36The LORD also said to me: "Son of man, will
you judge Oholah and Oholibah? Then declare to

23:23 Chaldeans were the inhabitants of a region in southern
Babylonia. The term also referred to the final dynasty of Babylon in the 7th and 6th centuries B.C. Pekod, Shoa, and Koa
were tribes located on the eastern border of the Babylonian
Empire. Some have identified their tribesmen as mercenaries.

23:25 The removal of nose and ears was a horrifying
penalty. Although not widely practiced in Israel, mutilation
was a frequent punishment for prisoners of war in the ancient Near East. Both Babylonians and Egyptians practiced
mutilation.

THE WIFE OF EZEKIEL

Ezekiel's wife is unnamed, but we may assume that she was a godly woman who helped the priest Ezekiel serve the Lord in a colony of Jewish exiles at Tel Abib on a canal of the Euphrates called Chebar. The details of her life are undisclosed; yet her death was the symbol of Ezekiel's most poignant message depicting the destruction in Israel.

Ezekiel's wife was taken quite suddenly in what may have been a stroke. Ezekiel was forewarned of his wife's death, but he was forbidden to display any public sign of mourning (Ezek. 24:15–17). He was expected to bear his grief silently. Indeed, on the morning of the day his wife died, the prophet spoke to his people about the coming destruction of Jerusalem (vv. 18–21). Just as he was losing his wife, "the desire of his eyes," so they would lose God's sanctuary and their loved ones remaining in Jerusalem—the desire of their eyes (vv. 16, 21). The people were instructed to restrain their grief as well. In this sense, Ezekiel and his wife became a heart-breaking sign to God's people of the grief and loss they would endure.

See also note on Adversity (Acts 5)

them their abominations. ³⁷For they have committed adultery, and blood *is* on their hands. They have committed adultery with their idols, and even sacrificed their sons whom they bore to Me, passing them through *the fire*, to devour *them.* ³⁸Moreover they have done this to Me: They have defiled My sanctuary on the same day and profaned My Sabbaths. ³⁹For after they had slain their children for their idols, on the same day they came into My sanctuary to profane it; and indeed thus they have done in the midst of My house.

⁴⁰"Furthermore you sent for men to come from afar, to whom a messenger *was* sent; and there they came. And you washed yourself for them, painted your eyes, and adorned yourself with ornaments. ⁴¹You sat on a stately couch, with a table prepared before it, on which you had set My incense and My oil. ⁴²The sound of a carefree multitude *was* with her, and Sabeans *were* brought from the wilderness with men of the common sort, who put bracelets on their wrists and beautiful crowns on their heads. ⁴³Then I said concerning *her who had grown old in adulteries,* 'Will they commit harlotry with her now, and she *with them?*' ⁴⁴Yet they went in to her, as men go in to a woman who plays the harlot; thus they went in to Oholah and Oholibah, the lewd women. ⁴⁵But righteous men will judge them after the manner of adulteresses, and after the manner of women who shed blood, because they *are* adulteresses, and blood *is* on their hands.

⁴⁶"For thus says the Lord God: 'Bring up an assembly against them, give them up to trouble and plunder. ⁴⁷The assembly shall stone them with stones and execute them with their swords; they shall slay their sons and their daughters, and burn their houses with fire. ⁴⁸Thus I will cause lewdness to cease from the land, that all women may be taught not to practice your lewdness. ⁴⁹They shall repay you for your lewdness, and you shall pay for your idolatrous sins. Then you shall know that I *am* the Lord God.' "

Symbol of the Cooking Pot

24 Again, in the ninth year, in the tenth month, on the tenth *day* of the month, the word of the Lord came to me, saying, ²"Son of man, write down the name of the day, this very day—the king of Babylon started his siege against Jerusalem this very day. ³And utter a parable to the rebellious house, and say to them, 'Thus says the Lord God:

"Put on a pot, set it on,
And also pour water into it.
⁴Gather pieces *of meat* in it,
Every good piece,
The thigh and the shoulder.
Fill *it* with choice cuts;
⁵Take the choice of the flock.
Also pile *fuel* bones under it,
Make it boil well,
And let the cuts simmer in it."

⁶'Therefore thus says the Lord God:

23:37 Child sacrifice in the pagan cultures around Israel was done partially to provide food for the gods. Israel's children belonged to the Lord (see Ps. 127:3).

23:45 The terminology righteous men, as applying to Assyria and Babylon, is puzzling. These pagan nations were certainly not righteous in the sense of meeting God's requirements for salvation. However, they were "righteous" in their execution of God's proscribed judgment against Samaria and Jerusalem, respectively.

24:1 This prophecy is dated January 15, 588 B.C., which became a day of fasting to commemorate Jerusalem's fall (Zech. 8:19).

24:3–14 This parable is an ironic reversal of the figure of the pot and the flesh used by the leaders of Judah. In Ezekiel 11:3 the emphasis was on military activity and preparation for war. The emphasis here falls on the destruction of Jerusalem.

"Woe to the bloody city,
To the pot whose scum *is* in it,
And whose scum is not gone from it!
Bring it out piece by piece,
On which no lot has fallen.
[7]For her blood is in her midst;
She set it on top of a rock;
She did not pour it on the ground,
To cover it with dust.
[8]That it may raise up fury and take
     vengeance,
I have set her blood on top of a rock,
That it may not be covered."

[9]"Therefore thus says the Lord GOD:

"Woe to the bloody city!
I too will make the pyre great.
[10]Heap on the wood,
Kindle the fire;
Cook the meat well,
Mix in the spices,
And let the cuts be burned up.

[11]"Then set the pot empty on the coals,
That it may become hot and its bronze may
     burn,
That its filthiness may be melted in it,
That its scum may be consumed.
[12]She has grown weary with lies,
And her great scum has not gone from her.
Let her scum *be* in the fire!
[13]In your filthiness *is* lewdness.
Because I have cleansed you, and you were not
     cleansed,
You will not be cleansed of your filthiness
     anymore,
Till I have caused My fury to rest upon
     you.
[14]I, the LORD, have spoken *it;*
It shall come to pass, and I will do *it;*
I will not hold back,
Nor will I spare,
Nor will I relent;
According to your ways
And according to your deeds
They[a] will judge you,"
Says the Lord GOD.' "

The Prophet's Wife Dies

[15]Also the word of the LORD came to me, saying,
[16]"Son of man, behold, I take away from you the
desire of your eyes with one stroke; yet you shall
neither mourn nor weep, nor shall your tears run
down. [17]Sigh in silence, make no mourning for the
dead; bind your turban on your head, and put your
sandals on your feet; do not cover *your* lips, and do
not eat man's bread *of sorrow.*"

[18]So I spoke to the people in the morning, and
at evening my wife died; and the next morning I
did as I was commanded.

[19]And the people said to me, "Will you not tell
us what these *things signify* to us, that you behave
so?"

[20]Then I answered them, "The word of the
LORD came to me, saying, [21]'Speak to the house of
Israel, "Thus says the Lord GOD: 'Behold, I will profane My sanctuary, your arrogant boast, the desire
of your eyes, the delight of your soul; and your
sons and daughters whom you left behind shall
fall by the sword. [22]And you shall do as I have
done; you shall not cover *your* lips nor eat man's
bread *of sorrow.* [23]Your turbans shall be on your
heads and your sandals on your feet; you shall neither mourn nor weep, but you shall pine away in
your iniquities and mourn with one another.
[24]Thus Ezekiel is a sign to you; according to all
that he has done you shall do; and when this
comes, you shall know that I *am* the Lord GOD.' "

[25]'And you, son of man—*will it* not *be* in the day
when I take from them their stronghold, their joy
and their glory, the desire of their eyes, and that
on which they set their minds, their sons and
their daughters: [26]*that* on that day one who escapes will come to you to let *you* hear *it* with *your*
ears? [27]On that day your mouth will be opened to
him who has escaped; you shall speak and no
longer be mute. Thus you will be a sign to them,
and they shall know that I *am* the LORD.' "

Proclamation Against Ammon

25 The word of the LORD came to me, saying,
[2]"Son of man, set your face against the Ammonites, and prophesy against them. [3]Say to the

---

24:14 [a]Septuagint, Syriac, Targum, and Vulgate read *I.*

24:7 The spilled blood of an innocent person was evidence of
injustice visible to God. The moral insensitivity of the inhabitants of Jerusalem was so great that they practiced corruption openly and shamelessly (see Gen. 4:10).

24:15–18 The death of Ezekiel's wife must have been unbe-
lievably difficult for the prophet, but he faithfully responded
to this tragedy as God directed (vv. 16, 18; see The Wife of
Ezekiel). The cause of her death was described as "one
stroke," usually a reference to a plague or disease (v. 16; see
also Ex. 9:14, 15). Ezekiel was forbidden the usual procedures
of public mourning. His suffering had to be in silence (Ezek.

24:17). This unnatural response must have been a powerful
testimony to the people (v. 19).

25:2 The Ammonites, longstanding enemies of Israel, lived
east of the Jordan River north of Moab and south of Gad's
tribal allotment.

25:3 Ammon joined a coalition of nations, including Judah,
who planned to revolt against Babylon. The term "Aha" indicates that the Ammonites gloated over the misfortune of
God's people. They would reap the consequences of their evil
attitudes (vv. 4, 5).

Ammonites, 'Hear the word of the Lord GOD! Thus says the Lord GOD: "Because you said, 'Aha!' against My sanctuary when it was profaned, and against the land of Israel when it was desolate, and against the house of Judah when they went into captivity, [4]indeed, therefore, I will deliver you as a possession to the men of the East, and they shall set their encampments among you and make their dwellings among you; they shall eat your fruit, and they shall drink your milk. [5]And I will make Rabbah a stable for camels and Ammon a resting place for flocks. Then you shall know that I *am* the LORD."

[6]'For thus says the Lord GOD: "Because you clapped *your* hands, stamped your feet, and rejoiced in heart with all your disdain for the land of Israel, [7]indeed, therefore, I will stretch out My hand against you, and give you as plunder to the nations; I will cut you off from the peoples, and I will cause you to perish from the countries; I will destroy you, and you shall know that I *am* the LORD."

Proclamation Against Moab

[8]'Thus says the Lord GOD: "Because Moab and Seir say, 'Look! The house of Judah *is* like all the nations,' [9]therefore, behold, I will clear the territory of Moab of cities, of the cities on its frontier, the glory of the country, Beth Jeshimoth, Baal Meon, and Kirjathaim. [10]To the men of the East I will give it as a possession, together with the Ammonites, that the Ammonites may not be remembered among the nations. [11]And I will execute judgments upon Moab, and they shall know that I *am* the LORD."

Proclamation Against Edom

[12]'Thus says the Lord GOD: "Because of what Edom did against the house of Judah by taking

vengeance, and has greatly offended by avenging itself on them," [13]therefore thus says the Lord GOD: "I will also stretch out My hand against Edom, cut off man and beast from it, and make it desolate from Teman; Dedan shall fall by the sword. [14]I will lay My vengeance on Edom by the hand of My people Israel, that they may do in Edom according to My anger and according to My fury; and they shall know My vengeance," says the Lord GOD.

Proclamation Against Philistia

[15]'Thus says the Lord GOD: "Because the Philistines dealt vengefully and took vengeance with a spiteful heart, to destroy because of the old hatred," [16]therefore thus says the Lord GOD: "I will stretch out My hand against the Philistines, and I will cut off the Cherethites and destroy the remnant of the seacoast. [17]I will execute great vengeance on them with furious rebukes; and they shall know that I *am* the LORD, when I lay My vengeance upon them." ' "

Proclamation Against Tyre

26 And it came to pass in the eleventh year, on the first *day* of the month, *that* the word of the LORD came to me, saying, [2]"Son of man, because Tyre has said against Jerusalem, 'Aha! She is broken who *was* the gateway of the peoples; now she is turned over to me; I shall be filled; she is laid waste.'

[3]"Therefore thus says the Lord GOD: 'Behold, I *am* against you, O Tyre, and will cause many nations to come up against you, as the sea causes its waves to come up. [4]And they shall destroy the walls of Tyre and break down her towers; I will

---

25:8 Moab, on the east coast of the Dead Sea, sent representatives to a council of nations planning to revolt against Babylon (see Jer. 27:3). Seir is identified with Edom (v. 12).

25:9 Beth Jeshimoth, Baal Meon, and Kirjathaim were in territory that was formerly part of Reuben's tribal allotment (see Josh. 13:15–20). Moab and Israel fought for control of this territory. During the time of Ezekiel, these cities were Moabite defensive fortresses.

25:12, 13 Edom, descended from Esau and occupying the territory southeast of the Dead Sea, sent representatives to the council on revolt (see Jer. 27:3). Edom joined with the Babylonians against Judah (see Jer. 49:7–22). Teman was a district in northern Edom. Dedan was an area on the southern end of Edom. The entire nation would experience destruction.

25:15 The animosity between Israel and Philistia was perpetual. The Philistine nation consisted of a confederacy of five city-states (Gaza, Ashkelon, Ashdod, Ekron, and Gath) on the Mediterranean coast west of Judah. "Old hatred" may refer to the wars between Israel and Philistia in the days of Samuel, Saul, and David (see 1 Sam. 1—7; 14; 17; 31; 2 Sam. 5:17–25; 8:1).

25:16 The Cherethites may be synonymous with the Philistines, a part of the "sea peoples" that migrated from the

Agean area. This group may originally have come from Caphtor, identified with Crete by most or with Cappadocia in Asia Minor by others (Jer. 47:4).

26:1—32:32 Oracles against two of Israel's neighbors, Phoenicia and Egypt, are contained in these chapters. Tyre was a significant seaport of the Phoenicians. Much space is devoted to prophecies about these two great powers. They were both resisting Nebuchadnezzar, whom Ezekiel recognized as God's instrument of judgment (see Ezek. 29:19, 20).

26:1 This prophecy against Tyre is dated 587/586 B.C., the year Jerusalem fell.

26:2 Tyre was a wealthy port on the Mediterranean coast north of Israel. It was the home base of the sprawling Phoenician commercial empire. By virtue of their enterprising spirit, advanced sailing technology, and powerful navy, the Phoenicians had dominated sea-going trade in the Mediterranean for centuries and as a result had amassed vast wealth. The city itself was built partly on the mainland and partly on a heavily fortified island.

26:4 Alexander the Great destroyed Tyre in 332 B.C., fulfilling the prophecy of this verse. The punishment of being reduced to bare "rock" is an ironic play on the name Tyre. This port city sat on rocky terrain (lit. "rock").

also scrape her dust from her, and make her like the top of a rock. [5]It shall be *a place for* spreading nets in the midst of the sea, for I have spoken,' says the Lord GOD; 'it shall become plunder for the nations. [6]Also her daughter *villages* which *are* in the fields shall be slain by the sword. Then they shall know that I am the LORD.'

[7]"For thus says the Lord GOD: 'Behold, I will bring against Tyre from the north Nebuchadnezzar[a] king of Babylon, king of kings, with horses, with chariots, and with horsemen, and an army with many people. [8]He will slay with the sword your daughter *villages* in the fields; he will heap up a siege mound against you, build a wall against you, and raise a defense against you. [9]He will direct his battering rams against your walls, and with his axes he will break down your towers. [10]Because of the abundance of his horses, their dust will cover you; your walls will shake at the noise of the horsemen, the wagons, and the chariots, when he enters your gates, as men enter a city that has been breached. [11]With the hooves of his horses he will trample all your streets; he will slay your people by the sword, and your strong pillars will fall to the ground. [12]They will plunder your riches and pillage your merchandise; they will break down your walls and destroy your pleasant houses; they will lay your stones, your timber, and your soil in the midst of the water. [13]I will put an end to the sound of your songs, and the sound of your harps shall be heard no more. [14]I will make you like the top of a rock; you shall be *a place for* spreading nets, and you shall never be rebuilt, for I the LORD have spoken,' says the Lord GOD.

[15]"Thus says the Lord GOD to Tyre: 'Will the coastlands not shake at the sound of your fall, when the wounded cry, when slaughter is made in the midst of you? [16]Then all the princes of the sea will come down from their thrones, lay aside their robes, and take off their embroidered garments; they will clothe themselves with trembling; they will sit on the ground, tremble *every* moment, and be astonished at you. [17]And they will take up a lamentation for you, and say to you:

"How you have perished,
O one inhabited by seafaring men,

O renowned city,
Who was strong at sea,
She and her inhabitants,
Who caused their terror *to be* on all her inhabitants!
[18]Now the coastlands tremble on the day of your fall;
Yes, the coastlands by the sea are troubled at your departure."

[19]"For thus says the Lord GOD: 'When I make you a desolate city, like cities that are not inhabited, when I bring the deep upon you, and great waters cover you, [20]then I will bring you down with those who descend into the Pit, to the people of old, and I will make you dwell in the lowest part of the earth, in places desolate from antiquity, with those who go down to the Pit, so that you may never be inhabited; and I shall establish glory in the land of the living. [21]I will make you a terror, and you *shall be* no *more;* though you are sought for, you will never be found again,' says the Lord GOD."

Lamentation for Tyre

27 The word of the LORD came again to me, saying, [2]"Now, son of man, take up a lamentation for Tyre, [3]and say to Tyre, 'You who are situated at the entrance of the sea, merchant of the peoples on many coastlands, thus says the Lord GOD:

"O Tyre, you have said,
'I *am* perfect in beauty.'
[4]Your borders *are* in the midst of the seas.
Your builders have perfected your beauty.
[5]They made all *your* planks of fir trees from Senir;
They took a cedar from Lebanon to make you a mast.
[6]*Of* oaks from Bashan they made your oars;
The company of Ashurites have inlaid your planks
With ivory from the coasts of Cyprus.[a]

26:7 [a]Hebrew *Nebuchadrezzar,* and so elsewhere in this book   27:6 [a]Hebrew *Kittim,* western lands, especially Cyprus

26:6 Daughter villages referred to settlements on the mainland dependent on Tyre.

26:7 The Babylonian king attacked Tyre sometime around 585 B.C. The Jewish historian Josephus reported that Nebuchadnezzar besieged Tyre for 13 years.

26:20 Ezekiel employed an analogy with the "Pit" between the destruction of Tyre and the burial of the dead to convey the finality of the city's doom.

27:2 The lament or funeral song for Tyre exhibits the following characteristics: a remembrance of the former circumstances of the deceased, a description of her death, a descrip-

tion of the reaction to her death, and a contrast between her former glory and her current tragic condition. A prose description of Tyre's trading relationships also appears (vv. 12–24).

27:4 The Phoenicians made contact with much of the known ancient world by way of the sea. Ezekiel described Tyre using the figure of one of her trading vessels.

27:5 Senir is another name for Mount Hermon in southern Lebanon. The mountain range is famous for its cedars (Deut. 3:9).

⁷Fine embroidered linen from Egypt was what
you spread for your sail;
Blue and purple from the coasts of Elishah was
what covered you.

⁸"Inhabitants of Sidon and Arvad were your
oarsmen;
Your wise men, O Tyre, were in you;
They became your pilots.
⁹Elders of Gebal and its wise men
Were in you to caulk your seams;
All the ships of the sea
And their oarsmen were in you
To market your merchandise.

¹⁰"Those from Persia, Lydia,ᵃ and Libyaᵇ
Were in your army as men of war;
They hung shield and helmet in you;
They gave splendor to you.
¹¹Men of Arvad with your army were on your
walls all around,
And the men of Gammad were in your
towers;
They hung their shields on your walls all
around;
They made your beauty perfect.

¹²"Tarshish was your merchant because of your
many luxury goods. They gave you silver, iron, tin,
and lead for your goods. ¹³Javan, Tubal, and
Meshech were your traders. They bartered human
lives and vessels of bronze for your merchandise.
¹⁴Those from the house of Togarmah traded for
your wares with horses, steeds, and mules. ¹⁵The
men of Dedan were your traders; many isles were
the market of your hand. They brought you ivory
tusks and ebony as payment. ¹⁶Syria was your merchant because of the abundance of goods you
made. They gave you for your wares emeralds,
purple, embroidery, fine linen, corals, and rubies.
¹⁷Judah and the land of Israel were your traders.

They traded for your merchandise wheat of Minnith, millet, honey, oil, and balm. ¹⁸Damascus was
your merchant because of the abundance of goods
you made, because of your many luxury items,
with the wine of Helbon and with white wool.
¹⁹Dan and Javan paid for your wares, traversing
back and forth. Wrought iron, cassia, and cane
were among your merchandise. ²⁰Dedan was your
merchant in saddlecloths for riding. ²¹Arabia and
all the princes of Kedar were your regular merchants. They traded with you in lambs, rams, and
goats. ²²The merchants of Sheba and Raamah were
your merchants. They traded for your wares the
choicest spices, all kinds of precious stones, and
gold. ²³Haran, Canneh, Eden, the merchants of
Sheba, Assyria, and Chilmad were your merchants.
²⁴These were your merchants in choice items—in
purple clothes, in embroidered garments, in
chests of multicolored apparel, in sturdy woven
cords, which were in your marketplace.

²⁵"The ships of Tarshish were carriers of your
merchandise.
You were filled and very glorious in the midst
of the seas.
²⁶Your oarsmen brought you into many
waters,
But the east wind broke you in the midst of the
seas.

²⁷"Your riches, wares, and merchandise,
Your mariners and pilots,
Your caulkers and merchandisers,
All your men of war who are in you,
And the entire company which is in your midst,
Will fall into the midst of the seas on the day
of your ruin.
²⁸The common-land will shake at the sound of
the cry of your pilots.

••••••••••••••••••••••

27:10 ᵃHebrew Lud ᵇHebrew Put

27:7 **Elishah** was a region or city of the island of Cyprus.

27:8, 9 **Sidon, Arvad, and Gebal** were Phoenician cities and rivals of Tyre. Gebal is modern Byblos. As part of the metaphor
comparing the trade of Tyre to the sailing of a vessel, the best
trained seamen of Sidon, Arvad, and Gebal were given menial
tasks to perform. However, the "wise men" or intelligentsia of
Tyre performed the skilled task of piloting the ship. This distinction highlighted the dominance of Tyre over her sister
cities.

27:10 **The Phoenicians** hired mercenary soldiers to help defend themselves. This list suggests their broad influence. Persia is modern Iran, Lydia was a kingdom in Asia Minor, and
Libya lay west of Egypt in North Africa.

27:12 **The location of Tarshish** is still disputed. Many scholars
identify it with the Phoenician port of Tartessus, Spain. However, recent archaeological excavations suggest that the location could be in the Far East or South America because of the
exotic nature of the cargo and the possibility of the roundtrip

length of the voyage extending to three years (see Jon. 1:3,
note).

27:13 **Javan** refers to Greece. Tubal was located in the eastern
region of Asia Minor, and Meshech was located in the central
region of Asia Minor.

27:14 **Togarmah** was a region in eastern Asia Minor, the location of modern Armenia.

27:15 **Dedan** may refer to an Arab tribe in Edom.

27:17 **Minnith** was a city of the Ammonites.

27:18 **Helbon** was a famous wine-producing center near Damascus.

27:21 **Kedar** referred to a group of nomads in the Arabian
desert.

27:22 **Sheba and Raamah** were located in southwestern Arabia.

27:23 **Canneh and Eden** were located south of Haran in
Mesopotamia. Chilmad is an unknown reference.

²⁹"All who handle the oar,
　The mariners,
　All the pilots of the sea
　Will come down from their ships *and* stand on
　　the shore.
³⁰They will make their voice heard because of
　　you;
　They will cry bitterly and cast dust on their
　　heads;
　They will roll about in ashes;
³¹They will shave themselves completely bald
　　because of you,
　Gird themselves with sackcloth,
　And weep for you
　With bitterness of heart *and* bitter wailing.
³²In their wailing for you
　They will take up a lamentation,
　And lament for you:
　'What *city is* like Tyre,
　Destroyed in the midst of the sea?

³³'When your wares went out by sea,
　You satisfied many people;
　You enriched the kings of the earth
　With your many luxury goods and your
　　merchandise.
³⁴But you are broken by the seas in the depths of
　　the waters;
　Your merchandise and the entire company will
　　fall in your midst.
³⁵All the inhabitants of the isles will be
　　astonished at you;
　Their kings will be greatly afraid,
　And *their* countenance will be troubled.
³⁶The merchants among the peoples will hiss at
　　you;
　You will become a horror, and *be* no more
　　forever.' " ' "

Proclamation Against the King of Tyre

28 The word of the LORD came to me again,
saying, ²"Son of man, say to the prince of
Tyre, 'Thus says the Lord GOD:

"Because your heart *is* lifted up,
　And you say, 'I *am* a god,

I sit *in* the seat of gods,
In the midst of the seas,'
Yet you *are* a man, and not a god,
Though you set your heart as the heart of a god
³(Behold, you *are* wiser than Daniel!
There is no secret that can be hidden from
　you!
⁴With your wisdom and your understanding
You have gained riches for yourself,
And gathered gold and silver into your
　treasuries;
⁵By your great wisdom in trade you have
　increased your riches,
And your heart is lifted up because of your
　riches),"

⁶'Therefore thus says the Lord GOD:

"Because you have set your heart as the heart of
　a god,
⁷Behold, therefore, I will bring strangers
　against you,
The most terrible of the nations;
And they shall draw their swords against the
　beauty of your wisdom,
And defile your splendor.
⁸They shall throw you down into the Pit,
And you shall die the death of the slain
In the midst of the seas.

⁹"Will you still say before him who slays you,
　'I *am* a god'?
But you *shall be* a man, and not a god,
In the hand of him who slays you.
¹⁰You shall die the death of the uncircumcised
By the hand of aliens;
For I have spoken," says the Lord GOD.' "

Lamentation for the King of Tyre

¹¹Moreover the word of the LORD came to me,
saying, ¹²"Son of man, take up a lamentation for
the king of Tyre, and say to him, 'Thus says the
Lord GOD:

"You *were* the seal of perfection,
　Full of wisdom and perfect in beauty.

27:30, 31 These acts were traditional ways of expressing grief
in the ancient Near East.

27:36 Hissing indicated astonishment or derision.

28:10 To die the death of the uncircumcised indicated a
shameful and dishonorable death. Circumcision was a sign of
the covenant. To be uncircumcised was to stand outside God's
covenant (see Gen. 17, Circumcision).

28:12–19 This lament over the king of Tyre employs imagery
drawn from the creation story (Gen. 2) and ancient Near
Eastern mythology. The most logical understanding is that
these verses were a funeral lament for the king of Tyre. Many
interpreters have also seen a description of Satan in the hy-

perbolic language used by Ezekiel (see charts, The Names
for Satan; A Portrait of the Adversary). Parts of the description do point to more than a human creature: "anointed
cherub" (v. 14), previous resident "on the holy mountain of
God" rather than on the earth (v. 14), and one who "walked
. . . in the midst of fiery stones" (Ezek. 28:14). It is also possible that Ezekiel moved his focus from the historical king of
Tyre to the figurative character. No doubt Ezekiel meant to
associate the king of Tyre with an exalted cherub in order to
emphasize the gravity of the king's sin. Ezekiel's purpose
was to describe the judgment of Tyre. Tyre's sin was that of
pride and self-exaltation (v. 17). The lament warns against
false pride.

[13]You were in Eden, the garden of God;
Every precious stone *was* your covering:
The sardius, topaz, and diamond,
Beryl, onyx, and jasper,
Sapphire, turquoise, and emerald with gold.
The workmanship of your timbrels and pipes
Was prepared for you on the day you were
created.

[14]"You *were* the anointed cherub who covers;
I established you;
You were on the holy mountain of God;
You walked back and forth in the midst of fiery
stones.
[15]You *were* perfect in your ways from the day you
were created,
Till iniquity was found in you.

[16]"By the abundance of your trading
You became filled with violence within,
And you sinned;
Therefore I cast you as a profane thing
Out of the mountain of God;
And I destroyed you, O covering cherub,
From the midst of the fiery stones.

[17]"Your heart was lifted up because of your
beauty;
You corrupted your wisdom for the sake of
your splendor;
I cast you to the ground,
I laid you before kings,
That they might gaze at you.

[18]"You defiled your sanctuaries
By the multitude of your iniquities,
By the iniquity of your trading;
Therefore I brought fire from your midst;
It devoured you,
And I turned you to ashes upon the earth
In the sight of all who saw you.
[19]All who knew you among the peoples are
astonished at you;
You have become a horror,
And *shall be* no more forever." ' "

Proclamation Against Sidon

[20]Then the word of the LORD came to me, saying, [21]"Son of man, set your face toward Sidon, and prophesy against her, [22]and say, 'Thus says the Lord GOD:

"Behold, I *am* against you, O Sidon;
I will be glorified in your midst;
And they shall know that I *am* the LORD,
When I execute judgments in her and am
hallowed in her.
[23]For I will send pestilence upon her,
And blood in her streets;
The wounded shall be judged in her midst
By the sword against her on every side;
Then they shall know that I *am* the LORD.

[24]"And there shall no longer be a pricking brier or a painful thorn for the house of Israel from among all *who are* around them, who despise them. Then they shall know that I *am* the Lord GOD."

Israel's Future Blessing

[25]"Thus says the Lord GOD: "When I have gathered the house of Israel from the peoples among whom they are scattered, and am hallowed in them in the sight of the Gentiles, then they will dwell in their own land which I gave to My servant Jacob. [26]And they will dwell safely there, build houses, and plant vineyards; yes, they will dwell securely, when I execute judgments on all those around them who despise them. Then they shall know that I *am* the LORD their God." ' "

Proclamation Against Egypt

29 In the tenth year, in the tenth *month,* on the twelfth *day* of the month, the word of the LORD came to me, saying, [2]"Son of man, set your face against Pharaoh king of Egypt, and prophesy against him, and against all Egypt. [3]Speak, and say, 'Thus says the Lord GOD:

"Behold, I *am* against you,
O Pharaoh king of Egypt,
O great monster who lies in the midst of his
rivers,
Who has said, 'My River[a] *is* my own;
I have made *it* for myself.'
[4]But I will put hooks in your jaws,
And cause the fish of your rivers to stick to
your scales;
I will bring you up out of the midst of your
rivers,
And all the fish in your rivers will stick to your
scales.

••••••••••••••••••••••••
29:3 [a]That is, the Nile

28:13 The glory of the king of Tyre is denoted by the reference to precious stones. The high priest's breastplate contained various precious stones (Ex. 28:15–21; see chart, The Breastplate of the High Priest).

28:14 The king of Tyre held an exalted status and enjoyed God's presence, according to the imagery of this verse.

28:18 Fire represents judgment (see Amos 1:4, 7, 10).

28:21 For Sidon, see Ezekiel 27:8, 9, note.

29:1 This prophecy, the first of several against Egypt, is dated 587 B.C.

29:3 The monster, with whom Pharaoh is compared, is most likely a Nile crocodile. The "River" is the Nile.

⁵I will leave you in the wilderness,
  You and all the fish of your rivers;
  You shall fall on the open field;
  You shall not be picked up or gathered.ᵃ
  I have given you as food
  To the beasts of the field
  And to the birds of the heavens.

⁶"Then all the inhabitants of Egypt
  Shall know that I *am* the LORD,
  Because they have been a staff of reed to the
    house of Israel.
⁷When they took hold of you with the hand,
  You broke and tore all their shoulders;ᵃ
  When they leaned on you,
  You broke and made all their backs quiver."

⁸'Therefore thus says the Lord GOD: "Surely I will bring a sword upon you and cut off from you man and beast. ⁹And the land of Egypt shall become desolate and waste; then they will know that I *am* the LORD, because she said, 'The River *is* mine, and I have made *it*.' ¹⁰Indeed, therefore, I *am* against you and against your rivers, and I will make the land of Egypt utterly waste and desolate, from Migdolᵃ *to* Syene, as far as the border of Ethiopia. ¹¹Neither foot of man shall pass through it nor foot of beast pass through it, and it shall be uninhabited forty years. ¹²I will make the land of Egypt desolate in the midst of the countries *that are* desolate; and among the cities *that are* laid waste, her cities shall be desolate forty years; and I will scatter the Egyptians among the nations and disperse them throughout the countries."

¹³'Yet, thus says the Lord GOD: "At the end of forty years I will gather the Egyptians from the peoples among whom they were scattered. ¹⁴I will bring back the captives of Egypt and cause them to return to the land of Pathros, to the land of their origin, and there they shall be a lowly king-dom. ¹⁵It shall be the lowliest of kingdoms; it shall never again exalt itself above the nations, for I will diminish them so that they will not rule over the nations anymore. ¹⁶No longer shall it be the confidence of the house of Israel, but will remind them of *their* iniquity when they turned to follow them. Then they shall know that I *am* the Lord GOD." ' "

Babylonia Will Plunder Egypt

¹⁷And it came to pass in the twenty-seventh year, in the first *month,* on the first *day* of the month, *that* the word of the LORD came to me, saying, ¹⁸"Son of man, Nebuchadnezzar king of Babylon caused his army to labor strenuously against Tyre; every head *was* made bald, and every shoulder rubbed raw; yet neither he nor his army received wages from Tyre, for the labor which they expended on it. ¹⁹Therefore thus says the Lord GOD: 'Surely I will give the land of Egypt to Nebuchadnezzar king of Babylon; he shall take away her wealth, carry off her spoil, and remove her pillage; and that will be the wages for his army. ²⁰I have given him the land of Egypt *for* his labor, because they worked for Me,' says the Lord GOD.

²¹'In that day I will cause the horn of the house of Israel to spring forth, and I will open your mouth to speak in their midst. Then they shall know that I *am* the LORD.' "

Egypt and Her Allies Will Fall

30 The word of the LORD came to me again, saying, ²"Son of man, prophesy and say, 'Thus says the Lord GOD:

  "Wail, 'Woe to the day!'
³For the day *is* near,

29:5 ᵃFollowing Masoretic Text, Septuagint, and Vulgate; some Hebrew manuscripts and Targum read *buried.*   29:7 ᵃFollowing Masoretic Text and Vulgate; Septuagint and Syriac read *hand.* 29:10 ᵃOr *tower*

29:5–7 To be left unburied after death was a sign of great disgrace. This fate was an especially fitting judgment for the pharaohs, whose bodies were preserved by mummification. Such an end was viewed as jeopardizing possible entrance into their afterlife.

29:10 Migdol to Syene was a common designation for the whole of Egypt. Since Egypt is mostly desert, only a thin strip of land on either side of the Nile would support human settlement. Migdol was located in the extreme north, near the Nile Delta. Syene is Aswan in the south. In similar fashion "Dan to Beersheba" signified the land of Israel (Judg. 20:1).

29:12–16 The judgment on Egypt is cast in terms parallel to the judgment on Judah: desolate land (Ezek. 6:14), people exiled (Ezek. 12:15), 40 years of punishment (Ezek. 4:6), and finally a return to the Land (Ezek. 28:25). The crucial difference is that Egypt would be restored in weakness as a reminder of God's judgment.

29:17 This prophecy is the prophecy with the latest date in the Book of Ezekiel. The month is March/April (see chart, The Jewish Sacred Calendar), and the year would have been 573–571 B.C., depending on the technical chronology used.

29:18 Nebuchadnezzar's attack on Tyre apparently did not result in the wholesale pillage and destruction that chapter 26 seems to predict. Historical evidence indicates that the siege of Tyre failed. At least it appeared unsuccessful from an economic perspective. Perhaps the prophecy (Ezek. 26) was conditioned on Tyre's continued rebellion against Nebuchadnezzar, just as the prophecies against Judah were conditioned on her refusal to repent. Perhaps Tyre submitted to Nebuchadnezzar and was spared the full extent of God's wrath.

29:19 A civil war broke out in Egypt a few years after this prophecy. Nebuchadnezzar seized this opportunity to invade Egypt. Egypt would be given as wages to the Babylonians. Nebuchadnezzar, as an employee of the Lord, would receive the wealth of Egypt to compensate for his losses in Tyre. The sovereignty of God over all nations is evident.

30:3 The day of the Lord refers to that time in history when the Lord would vindicate Himself. God's people typically had

Even the day of the LORD *is* near;
It will be a day of clouds, the time of the
Gentiles.
[4]The sword shall come upon Egypt,
And great anguish shall be in Ethiopia,
When the slain fall in Egypt,
And they take away her wealth,
And her foundations are broken down.

[5]"Ethiopia, Libya,[a] Lydia,[b] all the mingled people, Chub, and the men of the lands who are allied,
shall fall with them by the sword."

[6]Thus says the LORD:

"Those who uphold Egypt shall fall,
And the pride of her power shall come down.
From Migdol *to* Syene
Those within her shall fall by the sword,"
Says the Lord GOD.

[7]"They shall be desolate in the midst of the
desolate countries,
And her cities shall be in the midst of the
cities *that are* laid waste.
[8]Then they will know that I *am* the LORD,
When I have set a fire in Egypt
And all her helpers are destroyed.
[9]On that day messengers shall go forth from Me
in ships
To make the careless Ethiopians afraid,
And great anguish shall come upon them,
As on the day of Egypt;
For indeed it is coming!"

[10]Thus says the Lord GOD:

"I will also make a multitude of Egypt to cease
By the hand of Nebuchadnezzar king of
Babylon.
[11]He and his people with him, the most terrible
of the nations,
Shall be brought to destroy the land;
They shall draw their swords against Egypt,
And fill the land with the slain.
[12]I will make the rivers dry,
And sell the land into the hand of the wicked;
I will make the land waste, and all that is in it,
By the hand of aliens.
I, the LORD, have spoken."

[13]Thus says the Lord GOD:

"I will also destroy the idols,
And cause the images to cease from Noph;[a]
There shall no longer be princes from the land
of Egypt;
I will put fear in the land of Egypt.
[14]I will make Pathros desolate,
Set fire to Zoan,
And execute judgments in No.[a]
[15]I will pour My fury on Sin,[a] the strength of
Egypt;
I will cut off the multitude of No,
[16]And set a fire in Egypt;
Sin shall have great pain,
No shall be split open,
And Noph *shall be in* distress daily.
[17]The young men of Aven[a] and Pi Beseth shall
fall by the sword,
And these *cities* shall go into captivity.
[18]At Tehaphnehes[a] the day shall also be
darkened,[b]
When I break the yokes of Egypt there.
And her arrogant strength shall cease in her;
As for her, a cloud shall cover her,
And her daughters shall go into captivity.
[19]Thus I will execute judgments on Egypt,
Then they shall know that I *am* the LORD." ' "

Proclamation Against Pharaoh

[20]And it came to pass in the eleventh year, in
the first *month,* on the seventh *day* of the month,
that the word of the LORD came to me, saying,
[21]"Son of man, I have broken the arm of Pharaoh
king of Egypt; and see, it has not been bandaged
for healing, nor a splint put on to bind it, to make
it strong enough to hold a sword. [22]Therefore
thus says the Lord GOD: 'Surely I *am* against
Pharaoh king of Egypt, and will break his arms,
both the strong one and the one that was broken;
and I will make the sword fall out of his hand. [23]I
will scatter the Egyptians among the nations, and
disperse them throughout the countries. [24]I will
strengthen the arms of the king of Babylon and
put My sword in his hand; but I will break
Pharaoh's arms, and he will groan before him with
the groanings of a mortally wounded *man.* [25]Thus

30:5 [a]Hebrew *Put* [b]Hebrew *Lud*   **30:13** [a]That is, ancient Memphis
30:14 [a]That is, ancient Thebes   **30:15** [a]That is, ancient Pelusium
30:17 [a]That is, ancient On (Heliopolis)   **30:18** [a]Spelled *Tahpanhes* in
Jeremiah 43:7 and elsewhere   [b]Following many Hebrew manuscripts,
Bomberg, Septuagint, Syriac, Targum, and Vulgate; Masoretic Text
reads *refrained.*

---

viewed that Day as a time of victory for themselves and of defeat for their enemies. Amos (in the 8th century B.C.) presented the day of the Lord as also a day of judgment for God's
people (see Amos 5:16–20).

30:5 Egypt's allies supplied mercenary troops for their protection.

30:9 The ships were actually papyrus boats sent up the Nile.

30:20 This prophecy against Pharaoh is dated April 587 B.C.

30:21 I have broken the arm is a reference to Egypt's recent
military defeats. The background of this verse is Jerusalem's
siege that began in approximately 588 B.C. Pharaoh Hophra
sent an army to assist Jerusalem's inhabitants against the
Babylonians. Egypt's army was weak and ineffective. Nebuchadnezzar routed the Egyptians (Jer. 37:5–8).

I will strengthen the arms of the king of Babylon, but the arms of Pharaoh shall fall down; they shall know that I *am* the LORD, when I put My sword into the hand of the king of Babylon and he stretches it out against the land of Egypt. [26]I will scatter the Egyptians among the nations and disperse them throughout the countries. Then they shall know that I *am* the LORD.' "

Egypt Cut Down Like a Great Tree

31 Now it came to pass in the eleventh year, in the third *month,* on the first *day* of the month, *that* the word of the LORD came to me, saying, [2]"Son of man, say to Pharaoh king of Egypt and to his multitude:

'Whom are you like in your greatness?
[3]Indeed Assyria *was* a cedar in Lebanon,
  With fine branches that shaded the
    forest,
  And of high stature;
  And its top was among the thick boughs.
[4]The waters made it grow;
  Underground waters gave it height,
  With their rivers running around the place
    where it was planted,
  And sent out rivulets to all the trees of the
    field.

[5]'Therefore its height was exalted above all the
    trees of the field;
  Its boughs were multiplied,
  And its branches became long because of the
    abundance of water,
  As it sent them out.
[6]All the birds of the heavens made their nests
    in its boughs;
  Under its branches all the beasts of the field
    brought forth their young;
  And in its shadow all great nations made their
    home.
[7]'Thus it was beautiful in greatness and in the
    length of its branches,
  Because its roots reached to abundant
    waters.
[8]The cedars in the garden of God could not
    hide it;
  The fir trees were not like its boughs,
  And the chestnut[a] trees were not like its
    branches;
  No tree in the garden of God was like it in
    beauty.
[9]I made it beautiful with a multitude of
    branches,

So that all the trees of Eden envied it,
  That *were* in the garden of God.'

[10]"Therefore thus says the Lord GOD: 'Because you have increased in height, and it set its top among the thick boughs, and its heart was lifted up in its height, [11]therefore I will deliver it into the hand of the mighty one of the nations, and he shall surely deal with it; I have driven it out for its wickedness. [12]And aliens, the most terrible of the nations, have cut it down and left it; its branches have fallen on the mountains and in all the valleys; its boughs lie broken by all the rivers of the land; and all the peoples of the earth have gone from under its shadow and left it.

[13]'On its ruin will remain all the birds of the
    heavens,
  And all the beasts of the field will come to its
    branches—

[14]'So that no trees by the waters may ever again exalt themselves for their height, nor set their tops among the thick boughs, that no tree which drinks water may ever be high enough to reach up to them.

'For they have all been delivered to death,
  To the depths of the earth,
  Among the children of men who go down to
    the Pit.'

[15]"Thus says the Lord GOD: 'In the day when it went down to hell, I caused mourning. I covered the deep because of it. I restrained its rivers, and the great waters were held back. I caused Lebanon to mourn for it, and all the trees of the field wilted because of it. [16]I made the nations shake at the sound of its fall, when I cast it down to hell together with those who descend into the Pit; and all the trees of Eden, the choice and best of Lebanon, all that drink water, were comforted in the depths of the earth. [17]They also went down to hell with it, with those slain by the sword; and *those who were* its *strong* arm dwelt in its shadows among the nations.

[18]'To which of the trees in Eden will you then be likened in glory and greatness? Yet you shall be brought down with the trees of Eden to the depths of the earth; you shall lie in the midst of the uncircumcised, with *those* slain by the sword.

• • • • • • • • • • • • • • • • •

31:8 [a]Hebrew *armon*

31:1 This prophecy against Egypt is dated in the third month 587 B.C. (see chart, The Jewish Sacred Calendar).

31:3 Parables using a plant to symbolize a nation or leader appear in many parts of Scripture. Assyria dominated and terri-

fied the ancient Near East for over a century, until the Babylonians and the Medes overran the nation in 612–610 B.C. The same fate that Assyria experienced awaited Egypt (see Judg. 9:7–15; Ps. 80:8–11; Is. 5:1–7; Matt. 13:31–32).

This *is* Pharaoh and all his multitude,' says the Lord GOD."

Lamentation for Pharaoh and Egypt

32And it came to pass in the twelfth year, in the twelfth *month,* on the first *day* of the month, *that* the word of the LORD came to me, saying, [2]"Son of man, take up a lamentation for Pharaoh king of Egypt, and say to him:

'You are like a young lion among the nations,
And you *are* like a monster in the seas,
Bursting forth in your rivers,
Troubling the waters with your feet,
And fouling their rivers.

[3]'Thus says the Lord GOD:

"I will therefore spread My net over you with a
    company of many people,
And they will draw you up in My net.
[4]Then I will leave you on the land;
I will cast you out on the open fields,
And cause to settle on you all the birds of the
    heavens.
And with you I will fill the beasts of the whole
    earth.
[5]I will lay your flesh on the mountains,
And fill the valleys with your carcass.

[6]"I will also water the land with the flow of your
    blood,
Even to the mountains;
And the riverbeds will be full of you.
[7]When *I* put out your light,
I will cover the heavens, and make its stars
    dark;
I will cover the sun with a cloud,
And the moon shall not give her light.
[8]All the bright lights of the heavens I will make
    dark over you,
And bring darkness upon your land,"
Says the Lord GOD.

[9]'I will also trouble the hearts of many peoples, when I bring your destruction among the nations, into the countries which you have not known. [10]Yes, I will make many peoples astonished at you, and their kings shall be horribly afraid of you when I brandish My sword before them; and they shall tremble *every* moment, every man for his own life, in the day of your fall.

[11]'For thus says the Lord GOD: "The sword of the king of Babylon shall come upon you. [12]By the swords of the mighty warriors, all of them the most terrible of the nations, I will cause your multitude to fall.

"They shall plunder the pomp of Egypt,
And all its multitude shall be destroyed.
[13]Also I will destroy all its animals
From beside its great waters;
The foot of man shall muddy them no more,
Nor shall the hooves of animals muddy them.
[14]Then I will make their waters clear,
And make their rivers run like oil,"
Says the Lord GOD.

[15]"When I make the land of Egypt desolate,
And the country is destitute of all that once
    filled it,
When I strike all who dwell in it,
Then they shall know that I *am* the LORD.

[16]"This *is* the lamentation
With which they shall lament her;
The daughters of the nations shall lament her;
They shall lament for her, for Egypt,
And for all her multitude,"
Says the Lord GOD.'"

Egypt and Others Consigned to the Pit

[17]It came to pass also in the twelfth year, on the fifteenth *day* of the month, *that* the word of the LORD came to me, saying:

[18]"Son of man, wail over the multitude of Egypt,
And cast them down to the depths of the
    earth,
Her and the daughters of the famous nations,
With those who go down to the Pit:
[19]'Whom do you surpass in beauty?
Go down, be placed with the uncircumcised.'

[20]"They shall fall in the midst of *those* slain by the
    sword;
She is delivered to the sword,
Drawing her and all her multitudes.
[21]The strong among the mighty
Shall speak to him out of the midst of hell

32:1 This lamentation for Pharaoh is dated March 585 B.C., more than a year and a half after Jerusalem fell.

32:17–32 The Pit is repeatedly mentioned (vv. 18, 23, 24, 25, 29, 30). The imagery Ezekiel used to describe this place of the dead is part of a larger constellation of ideas about the afterlife found in the OT. In the popular conception of the time, all the dead dwelt in the depths of the earth. Sometimes the words "grave" and "hell" (Heb. *She'ol*) refer to this place.

Other OT writers gave descriptions of the place of the dead (Job 26:5, 6; Ps. 88:10–12; Is. 14:9–20). Ezekiel employed the concept of "the Pit" to show the human frailty of Pharaoh and his armies. The NT provides a clearer revelation of the afterlife.

32:17 A funeral lament against Egypt was given sometime in 586–585 B.C.

With those who help him:
'They have gone down,
They lie with the uncircumcised, slain by the
sword.'
²²"Assyria *is* there, and all her company,
With their graves all around her,
All of them slain, fallen by the sword.
²³Her graves are set in the recesses of the Pit,
And her company is all around her grave,
All of them slain, fallen by the sword,
Who caused terror in the land of the living.

²⁴"There *is* Elam and all her multitude,
All around her grave,
All of them slain, fallen by the sword,
Who have gone down uncircumcised to the
lower parts of the earth,
Who caused their terror in the land of the
living;
Now they bear their shame with those who go
down to the Pit.
²⁵They have set her bed in the midst of the slain,
With all her multitude,
With her graves all around it,
All of them uncircumcised, slain by the sword;
Though their terror was caused
In the land of the living,
Yet they bear their shame
With those who go down to the Pit;
It was put in the midst of the slain.

²⁶"There *are* Meshech and Tubal and all their
multitudes,
With all their graves around it,
All of them uncircumcised, slain by the sword,
Though they caused their terror in the land of
the living.
²⁷They do not lie with the mighty
Who are fallen of the uncircumcised,
Who have gone down to hell with their
weapons of war;
They have laid their swords under their heads,
But their iniquities will be on their bones,
Because of the terror of the mighty in the land
of the living.

²⁸Yes, you shall be broken in the midst of the
uncircumcised,
And lie with *those* slain by the sword.

²⁹"There *is* Edom,
Her kings and all her princes,
Who despite their might
Are laid beside *those* slain by the sword;
They shall lie with the uncircumcised,
And with those who go down to the Pit.
³⁰There *are* the princes of the north,
All of them, and all the Sidonians,
Who have gone down with the slain
In shame at the terror which they caused by
their might;
They lie uncircumcised with *those* slain by the
sword,
And bear their shame with those who go down
to the Pit.

³¹"Pharaoh will see them
And be comforted over all his multitude,
Pharaoh and all his army,
Slain by the sword,"
Says the Lord GOD.

³²"For I have caused My terror in the land of the
living;
And he shall be placed in the midst of the
uncircumcised
With *those* slain by the sword,
Pharaoh and all his multitude,"
Says the Lord GOD.

The Watchman and His Message

33 Again the word of the LORD came to me,
saying, ²"Son of man, speak to the children
of your people, and say to them: 'When I bring the
sword upon a land, and the people of the land take
a man from their territory and make him their
watchman, ³when he sees the sword coming upon
the land, if he blows the trumpet and warns the
people, ⁴then whoever hears the sound of the
trumpet and does not take warning, if the sword
comes and takes him away, his blood shall be on
his *own* head. ⁵He heard the sound of the trumpet,

32:24 Elam was situated east of Babylon.

32:26 For Meshech and Tubal, see Ezekiel 27:13, note.

33:2 The focus of Ezekiel's message shifted from judgment to salvation and restoration in chapter 33. The commissioning of Ezekiel as a watchman marked the beginning of a new emphasis in his prophetic ministry. Ezekiel's first commissioning was primarily a call to warn the people of impending judgment (Ezek. 3:17–21). This commissioning, coming before the announcement of Jerusalem's destruction was given prior to the wonderful message of hope for their future restoration, which would come after several more messages of warning (see Ezek. 33:21).

33:3 The watchman's duty was to monitor the surrounding countryside and warn the city's inhabitants of approaching enemies. Sometimes the watchman would shout out information, but in case of coming danger he would often blow a ram's horn to alert the people (see 2 Sam. 13:34–36; 18:24–27; 2 Kin. 9:17–20; Jer. 4:5, 19, 21; 6:1, 17; Joel 2:1; Amos 3:6).

33:4 His blood shall be on his own head refers to the responsibility placed on an individual for his own sin. Some interpreters suggest that the expression arises from the Oriental custom of transporting loads atop the head.

but did not take warning; his blood shall be upon himself. But he who takes warning will save his life. ⁶But if the watchman sees the sword coming and does not blow the trumpet, and the people are not warned, and the sword comes and takes *any* person from among them, he is taken away in his iniquity; but his blood I will require at the watchman's hand.'

⁷"So you, son of man: I have made you a watchman for the house of Israel; therefore you shall hear a word from My mouth and warn them for Me. ⁸When I say to the wicked, 'O wicked *man,* you shall surely die!' and you do not speak to warn the wicked from his way, that wicked *man* shall die in his iniquity; but his blood I will require at your hand. ⁹Nevertheless if you warn the wicked to turn from his way, and he does not turn from his way, he shall die in his iniquity; but you have delivered your soul.

¹⁰"Therefore you, O son of man, say to the house of Israel: 'Thus you say, "If our transgressions and our sins *lie* upon us, and we pine away in them, how can we then live?" ' ¹¹Say to them: '*As* I live,' says the Lord GOD, 'I have no pleasure in the death of the wicked, but that the wicked turn from his way and live. Turn, turn from your evil ways! For why should you die, O house of Israel?'

The Fairness of God's Judgment

¹²"Therefore you, O son of man, say to the children of your people: 'The righteousness of the righteous man shall not deliver him in the day of his transgression; as for the wickedness of the wicked, he shall not fall because of it in the day that he turns from his wickedness; nor shall the righteous be able to live because of *his righteousness* in the day that he sins.' ¹³When I say to the righteous *that* he shall surely live, but he trusts in his own righteousness and commits iniquity, none of his righteous works shall be remembered; but because of the iniquity that he has committed, he shall die. ¹⁴Again, when I say to the wicked, 'You shall surely die,' if he turns from his sin and does what is lawful and right, ¹⁵if the wicked restores

the pledge, gives back what he has stolen, and walks in the statutes of life without committing iniquity, he shall surely live; he shall not die. ¹⁶None of his sins which he has committed shall be remembered against him; he has done what is lawful and right; he shall surely live.

¹⁷"Yet the children of your people say, 'The way of the LORD is not fair.' But it is their way which is not fair! ¹⁸When the righteous turns from his righteousness and commits iniquity, he shall die because of it. ¹⁹But when the wicked turns from his wickedness and does what is lawful and right, he shall live because of it. ²⁰Yet you say, 'The way of the LORD is not fair.' O house of Israel, I will judge every one of you according to his own ways."

The Fall of Jerusalem

²¹And it came to pass in the twelfth year of our captivity, in the tenth *month,* on the fifth *day* of the month, *that* one who had escaped from Jerusalem came to me and said, "The city has been captured!"

²²Now the hand of the LORD had been upon me the evening before the man came who had escaped. And He had opened my mouth; so when he came to me in the morning, my mouth was opened, and I was no longer mute.

The Cause of Judah's Ruin

²³Then the word of the LORD came to me, saying: ²⁴"Son of man, they who inhabit those ruins in the land of Israel are saying, 'Abraham was only one, and he inherited the land. But we *are* many; the land has been given to us as a possession.'

²⁵"Therefore say to them, 'Thus says the Lord GOD: "You eat *meat* with blood, you lift up your eyes toward your idols, and shed blood. Should you then possess the land? ²⁶You rely on your sword, you commit abominations, and you defile one another's wives. Should you then possess the land?" '

²⁷"Say thus to them, 'Thus says the Lord GOD: "*As* I live, surely those who *are* in the ruins shall fall by the sword, and the one who *is* in the open

---

33:11 The rhetorical question of Ezekiel 18:23 is answered emphatically in this verse. God desires that the wicked turn from their evil and live (see Ezek. 14:6; 18:30; 18:32).

33:12–20 These same concerns are expressed in Ezekiel 18:21–29. The present state of affairs is what matters with God. The person weighed down with an evil past is not beyond hope, nor is the one with a righteous history beyond peril.

33:15 A garment (outer cloak) taken in pledge from the poor by a lender was to be returned by nightfall (Ex. 22:26). For a poor Israelite, the cloak served both as a garment and a blanket (Deut. 24:12, 13; Amos 2:7, 8, note).

33:21 Jerusalem fell to the Babylonians about 586 B.C. An eyewitness bearing the news came to Ezekiel some months later.

33:22 Ezekiel's divinely-imposed muteness was lifted (see Ezek. 3:26, 27). The period of silence had lasted seven and a half years. The prophet did speak during this silent period when God gave him specific messages to deliver. Now he would function as a regular prophet—a spokesman for God.

33:24 Those who remained in Jerusalem after its destruction about 586 B.C. still assumed that they were God's elect, with whom the future of Israel lay. Their appeal to God's promises to Abraham revealed their misplaced confidence in their physical lineage and their misunderstanding of covenant obedience (see Ezek. 11:15).

33:27 Sword, beasts, and pestilence are mentioned specifically as curses to be inflicted on the Israelites for not keeping God's laws (Lev. 26:21–33; Deut. 28:15–26).

field I will give to the beasts to be devoured, and those who *are* in the strongholds and caves shall die of the pestilence. [28]For I will make the land most desolate, her arrogant strength shall cease, and the mountains of Israel shall be so desolate that no one will pass through. [29]Then they shall know that I *am* the LORD, when I have made the land most desolate because of all their abominations which they have committed." '

Hearing and Not Doing

[30]"As for you, son of man, the children of your people are talking about you beside the walls and in the doors of the houses; and they speak to one another, everyone saying to his brother, 'Please come and hear what the word is that comes from the LORD.' [31]So they come to you as people do, they sit before you *as* My people, and they hear your words, but they do not do them; for with their mouth they show much love, *but* their hearts pursue their *own* gain. [32]Indeed you *are* to them as a very lovely song of one who has a pleasant voice and can play well on an instrument; for they hear your words, but they do not do them. [33]And when this comes to pass—surely it will come—then they will know that a prophet has been among them."

Irresponsible Shepherds

34 And the word of the LORD came to me, saying, [2]"Son of man, prophesy against the shepherds of Israel, prophesy and say to them, 'Thus says the Lord GOD to the shepherds: "Woe to the shepherds of Israel who feed themselves! Should not the shepherds feed the flocks? [3]You eat the fat and clothe yourselves with the wool; you slaughter the fatlings, *but* you do not feed the flock. [4]The weak you have not strengthened, nor have you healed those who were sick, nor bound up the broken, nor brought back what was driven away, nor sought what was lost; but with force and cruelty you have ruled them. [5]So they were scattered because *there was* no shepherd; and they became food for all the beasts of the field when they were scattered. [6]My sheep wandered through all

the mountains, and on every high hill; yes, My flock was scattered over the whole face of the earth, and no one was seeking or searching *for* them."

[7]'Therefore, you shepherds, hear the word of the LORD: [8]"*As* I live," says the Lord GOD, "surely because My flock became a prey, and My flock became food for every beast of the field, because *there was* no shepherd, nor did My shepherds search for My flock, but the shepherds fed themselves and did not feed My flock"— [9]therefore, O shepherds, hear the word of the LORD! [10]Thus says the Lord GOD: "Behold, I *am* against the shepherds, and I will require My flock at their hand; I will cause them to cease feeding the sheep, and the shepherds shall feed themselves no more; for I will deliver My flock from their mouths, that they may no longer be food for them."

God, the True Shepherd

[11]'For thus says the Lord GOD: "Indeed I Myself will search for My sheep and seek them out. [12]As a shepherd seeks out his flock on the day he is among his scattered sheep, so will I seek out My sheep and deliver them from all the places where they were scattered on a cloudy and dark day. [13]And I will bring them out from the peoples and gather them from the countries, and will bring them to their own land; I will feed them on the mountains of Israel, in the valleys and in all the inhabited places of the country. [14]I will feed them in good pasture, and their fold shall be on the high mountains of Israel. There they shall lie down in a good fold and feed in rich pasture on the mountains of Israel. [15]I will feed My flock, and I will make them lie down," says the Lord GOD. [16]"I will seek what was lost and bring back what was driven away, bind up the broken and strengthen what was sick; but I will destroy the fat and the strong, and feed them in judgment."

[17]'And *as for* you, O My flock, thus says the Lord GOD: "Behold, I shall judge between sheep and sheep, between rams and goats. [18]*Is it* too little for you to have eaten up the good pasture, that you must tread down with your feet the residue of

---

34:2, 3 Shepherds referred to the rulers of Israel. This designation commonly was used in the ancient Near East for royalty, prophets, and priests (2 Sam. 7:7; Is. 56:11; Jer. 22:22; 23:9–11; 25:34–36; 50:6). Instead of caring for the flock, Israel's rulers enriched themselves by the use of their power.

34:5, 6 The scattering of the sheep referred to the dispersal of the people by the Exile (see Ezek. 11:16, 17; 22:15).

34:10 God judged the irresponsible shepherds or leaders of Israel for misusing their power for personal gain. In the midst of God's judgment against the shepherds, a promise of deliverance for the sheep is offered.

34:12 The Lord shepherds His people (Ps. 23:1; 77:20; 80:1; Is. 40:10, 11). Jesus described Himself as the Good Shepherd

(John 10:7–18). "Cloudy and dark day" is typical language describing the day of the Lord (see Amos 5:16–27, note).

34:17 God's proclamation of judgment turned to the flock itself. Although the leaders were judged for their misuse of power, the flock was not without guilt. The judgment was not between sheep and goats but between sheep and sheep. Israelites who brutally had exploited their fellow Israelites were not going to escape punishment. The fact that Israel had poor leaders did not excuse God's people from their individual responsibilities (see Ezek. 18; 33).

34:18, 19 Judgment occurred on the basis of how others were treated (vv. 20–22). Not being satisfied with securing the best pastures and water for themselves, the evil sheep spitefully rendered the water and pasture useless for others.

your pasture—and to have drunk of the clear waters, that you must foul the residue with your feet? ¹⁹And *as for* My flock, they eat what you have trampled with your feet, and they drink what you have fouled with your feet."

²⁰"Therefore thus says the Lord GOD to them: "Behold, I Myself will judge between the fat and the lean sheep. ²¹Because you have pushed with side and shoulder, butted all the weak ones with your horns, and scattered them abroad, ²²therefore I will save My flock, and they shall no longer be a prey; and I will judge between sheep and sheep. ²³I will establish one shepherd over them, and he shall feed them— My servant David. He shall feed them and be their shepherd. ²⁴And I, the LORD, will be their God, and My servant David a prince among them; I, the LORD, have spoken.

²⁵"I will make a covenant of peace with them, and cause wild beasts to cease from the land; and they will dwell safely in the wilderness and sleep in the woods. ²⁶I will make them and the places all around My hill a blessing; and I will cause showers to come down in their season; there shall be showers of blessing. ²⁷Then the trees of the field shall yield their fruit, and the earth shall yield her increase. They shall be safe in their land; and they shall know that I *am* the LORD, when I have broken the bands of their yoke and delivered them from the hand of those who enslaved them. ²⁸And they shall no longer be a prey for the nations, nor shall beasts of the land devour them; but they shall dwell safely, and no one shall make *them* afraid. ²⁹I will raise up for them a garden of renown, and they shall no longer be consumed with hunger in the land, nor bear the shame of the Gentiles anymore. ³⁰Thus they shall know that I, the LORD their God, *am* with them, and they, the house of Israel, *are* My people," says the Lord GOD.'

³¹"You are My flock, the flock of My pasture; you *are* men, *and* I *am* your God," says the Lord GOD.

Judgment on Mount Seir

35 Moreover the word of the LORD came to me, saying, ²"Son of man, set your face against Mount Seir and prophesy against it, ³and say to it, 'Thus says the Lord GOD:

"Behold, O Mount Seir, I *am* against you;
I will stretch out My hand against you,
And make you most desolate;
⁴I shall lay your cities waste,
And you shall be desolate.
Then you shall know that I *am* the LORD.

⁵"Because you have had an ancient hatred, and have shed *the blood of* the children of Israel by the power of the sword at the time of their calamity, when their iniquity *came to an* end, ⁶therefore, *as* I live," says the Lord GOD, "I will prepare you for blood, and blood shall pursue you; since you have not hated blood, therefore blood shall pursue you. ⁷Thus I will make Mount Seir most desolate, and cut off from it the one who leaves and the one who returns. ⁸And I will fill its mountains with the slain; on your hills and in your valleys and in all your ravines those who are slain by the sword shall fall. ⁹I will make you perpetually desolate, and your cities shall be uninhabited; then you shall know that I *am* the LORD.

¹⁰"Because you have said, 'These two nations and these two countries shall be mine, and we will possess them,' although the LORD was there, ¹¹therefore, *as* I live," says the Lord GOD, "I will do according to your anger and according to the envy which you showed in your hatred against them; and I will make Myself known among them when I judge you. ¹²Then you shall know that I *am* the LORD. I have heard all your blasphemies which you have spoken against the mountains of Israel, saying, 'They are desolate; they are given to us to consume.' ¹³Thus with your mouth you have boasted against Me and multiplied your words against Me; I have heard *them.*"

¹⁴"Thus says the Lord GOD: "The whole earth will rejoice when I make you desolate. ¹⁵As you rejoiced because the inheritance of the house of Israel was desolate, so I will do to you; you shall be desolate, O Mount Seir, as well as all of Edom— all of it! Then they shall know that I *am* the LORD."'

Blessing on Israel

36 "And you, son of man, prophesy to the mountains of Israel, and say, 'O mountains of Israel, hear the word of the LORD! ²Thus says the Lord GOD: "Because the enemy has said of you,

---

34:23 My servant David refers to a messianic King from the Davidic line (2 Sam. 7:1-16).

34:25–31 The covenant of peace anticipated a time when people would live in harmony with God, with one another, and with themselves. The New Covenant (see Ezek. 36:26–36; Jer. 31:31–34) is a "covenant of peace." This coming age is described in terms of agricultural productivity and harmony in the natural world (see Is. 11:1–11). Physical and political blessings accompany this time of peace. This passage ultimately will be fulfilled in Christ. Through Christ, God offers a covenant relationship that brings peace with God, with self,

and with others (see John 14:27). Upon His return, Christ will establish everlasting peace.

35:2 This oracle against Edom is paired with the oracle to the mountains of Israel in chapter 36 (see Ezek. 25:8, note). The oracles addressed the issue of Israel's return from the Exile to reoccupy its land. In the aftermath of the fall of Jerusalem, Edomites began moving into southern Judah (Ezek. 35:10). They also killed Jewish refugees (v. 5; see Obad. 14).

36:1 This oracle, given after the fall of Jerusalem, is to be contrasted with the oracle in Ezekiel 6. Whereas chapter 6 is a

'Aha! The ancient heights have become our possession,' " ' ³therefore prophesy, and say, 'Thus says
the Lord GOD: "Because they made *you* desolate
and swallowed you up on every side, so that you
became the possession of the rest of the nations,
and you are taken up by the lips of talkers and
slandered by the people"— ⁴therefore, O mountains of Israel, hear the word of the Lord GOD!
Thus says the Lord GOD to the mountains, the
hills, the rivers, the valleys, the desolate wastes,
and the cities that have been forsaken, which became plunder and mockery to the rest of the nations all around— ⁵therefore thus says the Lord
GOD: "Surely I have spoken in My burning jealousy
against the rest of the nations and against all
Edom, who gave My land to themselves as a possession, with wholehearted joy *and* spiteful minds,
in order to plunder its open country." '

⁶"Therefore prophesy concerning the land of
Israel, and say to the mountains, the hills, the
rivers, and the valleys, 'Thus says the Lord GOD:
"Behold, I have spoken in My jealousy and My fury,
because you have borne the shame of the nations."
⁷Therefore thus says the Lord GOD: "I have raised
My hand in an oath that surely the nations that *are*
around you shall bear their own shame. ⁸But you,
O mountains of Israel, you shall shoot forth your
branches and yield your fruit to My people Israel,
for they are about to come. ⁹For indeed I *am* for
you, and I will turn to you, and you shall be tilled
and sown. ¹⁰I will multiply men upon you, all the
house of Israel, all of it; and the cities shall be inhabited and the ruins rebuilt. ¹¹I will multiply
upon you man and beast; and they shall increase
and bear young; I will make you inhabited as in
former times, and do better *for you* than at your
beginnings. Then you shall know that I *am* the
LORD. ¹²Yes, I will cause men to walk on you, My
people Israel; they shall take possession of you,
and you shall be their inheritance; no more shall
you bereave them *of children.*"

¹³Thus says the Lord GOD: "Because they say to
you, 'You devour men and bereave your nation *of
children,*' ¹⁴therefore you shall devour men no
more, nor bereave your nation anymore," says the
Lord GOD. ¹⁵Nor will I let you hear the taunts of
the nations anymore, nor bear the reproach of the
peoples anymore, nor shall you cause your nation
to stumble anymore," says the Lord GOD.' "

The Renewal of Israel

¹⁶Moreover the word of the LORD came to me,
saying: ¹⁷"Son of man, when the house of Israel
dwelt in their own land, they defiled it by their
own ways and deeds; to Me their way was like the
uncleanness of a woman in her customary impurity. ¹⁸Therefore I poured out My fury on them for
the blood they had shed on the land, and for their
idols *with which* they had defiled it. ¹⁹So I scattered them among the nations, and they were dispersed throughout the countries; I judged them
according to their ways and their deeds. ²⁰When
they came to the nations, wherever they went,
they profaned My holy name—when they said of
them, 'These *are* the people of the LORD, *and* yet
they have gone out of His land.' ²¹But I had concern for My holy name, which the house of Israel
had profaned among the nations wherever they
went.

²²"Therefore say to the house of Israel, 'Thus
says the Lord GOD: "I do not do *this* for your sake,
O house of Israel, but for My holy name's sake,
which you have profaned among the nations wherever you went. ²³And I will sanctify My great
name, which has been profaned among the nations, which you have profaned in their midst; and
the nations shall know that I *am* the LORD," says
the Lord GOD, "when I am hallowed in you before
their eyes. ²⁴For I will take you from among the
nations, gather you out of all countries, and bring
you into your own land. ²⁵Then I will sprinkle
clean water on you, and you shall be clean; I will
cleanse you from all your filthiness and from all
your idols. ²⁶I will give you a new heart and put a
new spirit within you; I will take the heart of
stone out of your flesh and give you a heart of
flesh. ²⁷I will put My Spirit within you and cause
you to walk in My statutes, and you will keep My
judgments and do *them.* ²⁸Then you shall dwell in
the land that I gave to your fathers; you shall be
My people, and I will be your God. ²⁹I will deliver
you from all your uncleannesses. I will call for the
grain and multiply it, and bring no famine upon
you. ³⁰And I will multiply the fruit of your trees
and the increase of your fields, so that you need
never again bear the reproach of famine among
the nations. ³¹Then you will remember your evil
ways and your deeds that *were* not good; and you
will loathe yourselves in your own sight, for your

---

message of judgment, chapter 36 is a message of restoration.
In both passages Ezekiel addressed "the mountains of Israel."

36:17 Bodily discharges such as a woman's menstruation or a
man's semen were declared to cause ritual impurity in the
Mosaic Law (see Lev. 15, Menstrual Cycle). A person with a
discharge was unable to come into the presence of the Lord
until ritually purified, even though no moral blame was attached to the individual. Israel had made herself impure willfully, and therefore deserved to be cast from God's presence.

36:24–38 The return from the Exile in Babylon was a partial
fulfillment of this messianic passage. It looks forward to the
coming of Christ to inaugurate the New Covenant. The New
Covenant is internal and unconditional. All who respond to
God in faith can have a personal, intimate relationship with
Him (see Jer. 31:31–34).

iniquities and your abominations. [32]Not for your sake do I do *this*," says the Lord GOD, "let it be known to you. Be ashamed and confounded for your own ways, O house of Israel!"

[33]"Thus says the Lord GOD: "On the day that I cleanse you from all your iniquities, I will also enable *you* to dwell in the cities, and the ruins shall be rebuilt. [34]The desolate land shall be tilled instead of lying desolate in the sight of all who pass by. [35]So they will say, 'This land that was desolate has become like the garden of Eden; and the wasted, desolate, and ruined cities *are now* fortified *and* inhabited.' [36]Then the nations which are left all around you shall know that I, the LORD, have rebuilt the ruined places *and* planted what was desolate. I, the LORD, have spoken *it,* and I will do *it.*"

[37]"Thus says the Lord GOD: "I will also let the house of Israel inquire of Me to do this for them: I will increase their men like a flock. [38]Like a flock *offered as* holy *sacrifices,* like the flock at Jerusalem on its feast days, so shall the ruined cities be filled with flocks of men. Then they shall know that I *am* the LORD." ' "

The Dry Bones Live

37 The hand of the LORD came upon me and brought me out in the Spirit of the LORD, and set me down in the midst of the valley; and it *was* full of bones. [2]Then He caused me to pass by them all around, and behold, *there were* very many in the open valley; and indeed *they were* very dry. [3]And He said to me, "Son of man, can these bones live?"

So I answered, "O Lord GOD, You know."

[4]Again He said to me, "Prophesy to these bones, and say to them, 'O dry bones, hear the word of the LORD! [5]Thus says the Lord GOD to these bones: "Surely I will cause breath to enter into you, and you shall live. [6]I will put sinews on you and bring flesh upon you, cover you with skin and put breath in you; and you shall live. Then you shall know that I *am* the LORD." ' "

[7]So I prophesied as I was commanded; and as I prophesied, there was a noise, and suddenly a rattling; and the bones came together, bone to bone. [8]Indeed, as I looked, the sinews and the flesh came upon them, and the skin covered them over; but *there was* no breath in them.

[9]Also He said to me, "Prophesy to the breath, prophesy, son of man, and say to the breath, 'Thus says the Lord GOD: "Come from the four winds, O breath, and breathe on these slain, that they may live." ' " [10]So I prophesied as He commanded me, and breath came into them, and they lived, and stood upon their feet, an exceedingly great army.

[11]Then He said to me, "Son of man, these bones are the whole house of Israel. They indeed say, 'Our bones are dry, our hope is lost, and we ourselves are cut off!' [12]Therefore prophesy and say to them, 'Thus says the Lord GOD: "Behold, O My people, I will open your graves and cause you to come up from your graves, and bring you into the land of Israel. [13]Then you shall know that I *am* the LORD, when I have opened your graves, O My people, and brought you up from your graves. [14]I will put My Spirit in you, and you shall live, and I will place you in your own land. Then you shall know that I, the LORD, have spoken *it* and performed *it,*" says the LORD.' "

One Kingdom, One King

[15]Again the word of the LORD came to me, saying, [16]"As for you, son of man, take a stick for yourself and write on it: 'For Judah and for the children of Israel, his companions.' Then take another stick and write on it, 'For Joseph, the stick of Ephraim, and *for* all the house of Israel, his companions.' [17]Then join them one to another for yourself into one stick, and they will become one in your hand.

[18]"And when the children of your people speak to you, saying, 'Will you not show us what you *mean* by these?'— [19]say to them, 'Thus says the Lord GOD: "Surely I will take the stick of Joseph, which *is* in the hand of Ephraim, and the tribes of

---

37:1 In the valley of dry bones, Ezekiel was confronted with a scene of death. The corpses had been there for some time, picked clean by the birds and baked in the hot sun. According to verse 11, these bones symbolized the whole nation of Israel. The restoration was more than a return to the Land. It also had a spiritual dimension in a renewed covenant. Though the concept of the resurrection is not fully developed in the OT, obviously there is some concept of the resurrection in this chapter.

37:9 Breath (Heb. *ruah,* lit. "wind" or "spirit") is part of a word play. It is used 10 times in verses 1–14. The Spirit of the Lord is like "breath" or "wind" because He cannot be seen or contained but moves throughout the world (see John 3:4–8).

37:11 Although this vision is not dated, the note of utter despair displayed by the words of the exiles indicated that the vision was given sometime after Jerusalem's destruction

about 586 B.C. God's Spirit allowed Ezekiel to see Israel in its dead state and in its future resurrection and restoration.

37:12–14 The divine interpretation of Ezekiel's vision is a message of hope regarding Israel's restoration. Ezekiel spoke of that glorious future in terms of re-establishment in the Land. The passage anticipates also a spiritual restoration based on a New Covenant with the Lord (v. 14).

37:16 Again Ezekiel was commanded to act out his message for the people. The designations Joseph and Judah represent the northern and southern kingdoms. Ephraim, the leading tribe in the northern kingdom, often was used as a designation for that kingdom. The northern kingdom also was identified as Israel, a term Ezekiel used for the nation as a whole (see chart, Terminology for the Divided Kingdom). Once again, this prophecy awaits complete fulfillment.

Israel, his companions; and I will join them with it, with the stick of Judah, and make them one stick, and they will be one in My hand." ' [20]And the sticks on which you write will be in your hand before their eyes.

[21]"Then say to them, 'Thus says the Lord GOD: "Surely I will take the children of Israel from among the nations, wherever they have gone, and will gather them from every side and bring them into their own land; [22]and I will make them one nation in the land, on the mountains of Israel; and one king shall be king over them all; they shall no longer be two nations, nor shall they ever be divided into two kingdoms again. [23]They shall not defile themselves anymore with their idols, nor with their detestable things, nor with any of their transgressions; but I will deliver them from all their dwelling places in which they have sinned, and will cleanse them. Then they shall be My people, and I will be their God.

[24]"David My servant *shall be* king over them, and they shall all have one shepherd; they shall also walk in My judgments and observe My statutes, and do them. [25]Then they shall dwell in the land that I have given to Jacob My servant, where your fathers dwelt; and they shall dwell there, they, their children, and their children's children, forever; and My servant David *shall be* their prince forever. [26]Moreover I will make a covenant of peace with them, and it shall be an everlasting covenant with them; I will establish them and multiply them, and I will set My sanctuary in their midst forevermore. [27]My tabernacle also shall be with them; indeed I will be their God, and they shall be My people. [28]The nations also will know that I, the LORD, sanctify Israel, when My sanctuary is in their midst forevermore." ' "

Gog and Allies Attack Israel

38 Now the word of the LORD came to me, saying, [2]"Son of man, set your face against Gog, of the land of Magog, the prince of Rosh,[a] Meshech, and Tubal, and prophesy against him,

[3]and say, 'Thus says the Lord GOD: "Behold, I *am* against you, O Gog, the prince of Rosh, Meshech, and Tubal. [4]I will turn you around, put hooks into your jaws, and lead you out, with all your army, horses, and horsemen, all splendidly clothed, a great company *with* bucklers and shields, all of them handling swords. [5]Persia, Ethiopia,[a] and Libya[b] are with them, all of them *with* shield and helmet; [6]Gomer and all its troops; the house of Togarmah *from* the far north and all its troops— many people *are* with you.

[7]"Prepare yourself and be ready, you and all your companies that are gathered about you; and be a guard for them. [8]After many days you will be visited. In the latter years you will come into the land of those brought back from the sword *and* gathered from many people on the mountains of Israel, which had long been desolate; they were brought out of the nations, and now all of them dwell safely. [9]You will ascend, coming like a storm, covering the land like a cloud, you and all your troops and many peoples with you."

[10]Thus says the Lord GOD: "On that day it shall come to pass *that* thoughts will arise in your mind, and you will make an evil plan: [11]You will say, 'I will go up against a land of unwalled villages; I will go to a peaceful people, who dwell safely, all of them dwelling without walls, and having neither bars nor gates'— [12]to take plunder and to take booty, to stretch out your hand against the waste places *that are again* inhabited, and against a people gathered from the nations, who have acquired livestock and goods, who dwell in the midst of the land. [13]Sheba, Dedan, the merchants of Tarshish, and all their young lions will say to you, 'Have you come to take plunder? Have you gathered your army to take booty, to carry away silver and gold, to take away livestock and goods, to take great plunder?' " '

[14]"Therefore, son of man, prophesy and say to

38:2 [a]Targum, Vulgate, and Aquila read *chief prince of* (also verse 3).
38:5 [a]Hebrew *Cush* [b]Hebrew *Put*

37:22 The nation of Israel had divided into two kingdoms shortly after the death of Solomon in 931 B.C. (1 Kin. 12). Around 722 B.C. the 10 tribes of the northern kingdom were destroyed and carried into exile by the Assyrians. The promise given here is one of a reunified nation re-established in the Land.

37:24 For My servant David, see Ezekiel 34:23, note.

37:26–28 Despite Israel's sinful past, God had not rejected His people but instead promised to establish His sanctuary in their midst. This theme is developed in Ezekiel 40—48. The repetition of the word "forevermore" in Ezekiel 37:26–28 emphasized the irreversible nature of the promise ("covenant of peace"; see Ezek. 34:25–31, note).

38:2 The identity of Gog is uncertain (see Ezek. 38; 39; Rev. 20:8). Some identify him with Gyges, prince of Lydia, a

kingdom in southwestern Asia Minor in the 7th century B.C. Some suggest that the land of Magog is a veiled reference to Babylon, the only major enemy of the Israelites about which no oracle of judgment is given in the Book of Ezekiel (see Ezek. 25—32; see also Gen. 10:2). As a captive in Babylon, Ezekiel may have felt the need to write cryptically. Ezekiel 38:16, 17 seem to suggest that for years the prophets had prophesied concerning Gog.

38:2 The identity of prince of Rosh (Heb., lit. "chief") is not clear. No land or people called "Rosh" have been identified in Ezekiel's time. Many scholars translate this phrase "the chief prince."

38:6 Gomer refers to a region north of the Black Sea.

38:13 For Sheba, Dedan, and Tarshish, see Ezekiel 27:12, 15, 22, notes.

Gog, 'Thus says the Lord GOD: "On that day when My people Israel dwell safely, will you not know *it?* ¹⁵Then you will come from your place out of the far north, you and many peoples with you, all of them riding on horses, a great company and a mighty army. ¹⁶You will come up against My people Israel like a cloud, to cover the land. It will be in the latter days that I will bring you against My land, so that the nations may know Me, when I am hallowed in you, O Gog, before their eyes." ¹⁷Thus says the Lord GOD: "Are *you* he of whom I have spoken in former days by My servants the prophets of Israel, who prophesied for years in those days that I would bring you against them?

Judgment on Gog

¹⁸"And it will come to pass at the same time, when Gog comes against the land of Israel," says the Lord GOD, "*that* My fury will show in My face. ¹⁹For in My jealousy *and* in the fire of My wrath I have spoken: 'Surely in that day there shall be a great earthquake in the land of Israel, ²⁰so that the fish of the sea, the birds of the heavens, the beasts of the field, all creeping things that creep on the earth, and all men who *are* on the face of the earth shall shake at My presence. The mountains shall be thrown down, the steep places shall fall, and every wall shall fall to the ground.' ²¹I will call for a sword against Gog throughout all My mountains," says the Lord GOD. "Every man's sword will be against his brother. ²²And I will bring him to judgment with pestilence and bloodshed; I will rain down on him, on his troops, and on the many peoples who *are* with him, flooding rain, great hailstones, fire, and brimstone. ²³Thus I will magnify Myself and sanctify Myself, and I will be known in the eyes of many nations. Then they shall know that I *am* the LORD." '

Gog's Armies Destroyed

39 "And you, son of man, prophesy against Gog, and say, 'Thus says the Lord GOD: "Behold, I *am* against you, O Gog, the prince of Rosh,ᵃ Meshech, and Tubal; ²and I will turn you around and lead you on, bringing you up from the far north, and bring you against the mountains of Israel. ³Then I will knock the bow out of your left hand, and cause the arrows to fall out of your right hand. ⁴You shall fall upon the mountains of Israel, you and all your troops and the peoples who *are* with you; I will give you to birds of prey of every

sort and *to* the beasts of the field to be devoured. ⁵You shall fall on the open field; for I have spoken," says the Lord GOD. ⁶"And I will send fire on Magog and on those who live in security in the coastlands. Then they shall know that I *am* the LORD. ⁷So I will make My holy name known in the midst of My people Israel, and I will not *let them* profane My holy name anymore. Then the nations shall know that *I am* the LORD, the Holy One in Israel. ⁸Surely it is coming, and it shall be done," says the Lord GOD. "This *is* the day of which I have spoken.

⁹"Then those who dwell in the cities of Israel will go out and set on fire and burn the weapons, both the shields and bucklers, the bows and arrows, the javelins and spears; and they will make fires with them for seven years. ¹⁰They will not take wood from the field nor cut down *any* from the forests, because they will make fires with the weapons; and they will plunder those who plundered them, and pillage those who pillaged them," says the Lord GOD.

The Burial of Gog

¹¹"It will come to pass in that day *that* I will give Gog a burial place there in Israel, the valley of those who pass by east of the sea; and it will obstruct travelers, because there they will bury Gog and all his multitude. Therefore they will call *it* the Valley of Hamon Gog.ᵃ ¹²For seven months the house of Israel will be burying them, in order to cleanse the land. ¹³Indeed all the people of the land will be burying, and they will gain renown for it on the day that I am glorified," says the Lord GOD. ¹⁴"They will set apart men regularly employed, with the help of a search party,ᵃ to pass through the land and bury those bodies remaining on the ground, in order to cleanse it. At the end of seven months they will make a search. ¹⁵The search party will pass through the land; and *when anyone* sees a man's bone, he shall set up a marker by it, till the buriers have buried it in the Valley of Hamon Gog. ¹⁶*The* name of *the* city *will* also *be* Hamonah. Thus they shall cleanse the land." '

A Triumphant Festival

¹⁷"And as for you, son of man, thus says the Lord GOD, 'Speak to every sort of bird and to every beast of the field:

· · · · · · · · · · · · · · · · ·
39:1 ᵃTargum, Vulgate and Aquila read *chief prince of.* **39:11** ᵃLiterally *The Multitude of Gog* **39:14** ᵃLiterally *those who pass through*

38:17 The invasion by Gog evidently had been predicted earlier by the Lord's prophets, though which prophets were intended remains unclear (see Num. 24:17-24; Deut. 32:43; Jer. 4:5-31; Dan. 2:44, 45; Joel 3:1-16; Zeph. 1:14-18).

38:22, 23 This list of curses against Gog is similar to the covenant curses pronounced on Israel (Deut. 32:23, 24, 42).

39:1 For the prince of Rosh, see Ezekiel 38:2, note.

39:9 Seven is a number often used in apocalyptic passages to symbolize completeness and finality. Here it refers to the completeness of God's judgment (see chart, The Significance of Numbers in Scripture).

39:12 According to the law, dead bodies were ritually impure; therefore, the Land needed cleansing (see Lev. 5:2; 22:4). For "seven," see Ezekiel 39:9, note.

"Assemble yourselves and come;
Gather together from all sides to My sacrificial
meal
Which I am sacrificing for you,
A great sacrificial meal on the mountains of
Israel,
That you may eat flesh and drink blood.
[18]You shall eat the flesh of the mighty,
Drink the blood of the princes of the earth,
Of rams and lambs,
Of goats and bulls,
All of them fatlings of Bashan.
[19]You shall eat fat till you are full,
And drink blood till you are drunk,
At My sacrificial meal
Which I am sacrificing for you.
[20]You shall be filled at My table
With horses and riders,
With mighty men
And with all the men of war," says the Lord
GOD.

Israel Restored to the Land

[21]"I will set My glory among the nations; all the
nations shall see My judgment which I have executed, and My hand which I have laid on them.
[22]So the house of Israel shall know that I *am* the
LORD their God from that day forward. [23]The Gentiles shall know that the house of Israel went into
captivity for their iniquity; because they were unfaithful to Me, therefore I hid My face from them.
I gave them into the hand of their enemies, and
they all fell by the sword. [24]According to their uncleanness and according to their transgressions I
have dealt with them, and hidden My face from
them.' '

[25]"Therefore thus says the Lord GOD: 'Now I
will bring back the captives of Jacob, and have
mercy on the whole house of Israel; and I will be
jealous for My holy name— [26]after they have
borne their shame, and all their unfaithfulness in
which they were unfaithful to Me, when they
dwelt safely in their *own* land and no one made
them afraid. [27]When I have brought them back
from the peoples and gathered them out of their
enemies' lands, and I am hallowed in them in the
sight of many nations, [28]then they shall know that

I *am* the LORD their God, who sent them into captivity among the nations, but also brought them
back to their land, and left none of them captive
any longer. [29]And I will not hide My face from
them anymore; for I shall have poured out My
Spirit on the house of Israel,' says the Lord GOD."

A New City, a New Temple

40 In the twenty-fifth year of our captivity, at
the beginning of the year, on the tenth *day*
of the month, in the fourteenth year after the city
was captured, on the very same day the hand of
the LORD was upon me; and He took me there. [2]In
the visions of God He took me into the land of Israel and set me on a very high mountain; on it toward the south *was* something like the structure
of a city. [3]He took me there, and behold, *there was*
a man whose appearance *was* like the appearance
of bronze. He had a line of flax and a measuring
rod in his hand, and he stood in the gateway.

[4]And the man said to me, "Son of man, look
with your eyes and hear with your ears, and fix
your mind on everything I show you; for you *were*
brought here so that I might show *them* to you.
Declare to the house of Israel everything you see."
[5]Now there was a wall all around the outside of
the temple.[a] In the man's hand was a measuring
rod six cubits *long, each being a* cubit and a handbreadth; and he measured the width of the wall
structure, one rod; and the height, one rod.

The Eastern Gateway of the Temple

[6]Then he went to the gateway which faced
east; and he went up its stairs and measured the
threshold of the gateway, *which was* one rod wide,
and the other threshold *was* one rod wide. [7]Each
gate chamber *was* one rod long and one rod wide;
between the gate chambers *was a space of* five cubits; and the threshold of the gateway by the
vestibule of the inside gate *was* one rod. [8]He also
measured the vestibule of the inside gate, one
rod. [9]Then he measured the vestibule of the gateway, eight cubits; and the gateposts, two cubits.
The vestibule of the gate *was* on the inside. [10]In
the eastern gateway *were* three gate chambers on

40:5 [a]Literally *house*, and so elsewhere in this book

40:1–4 This vision occurred in April 573 B.C. Just as the Book of
Ezekiel opens with a vision (Ezek. 1—3), so it closes with one
(Ezek. 40—48). This vision included a diagram of the temple
(see charts, The Plan for Ezekiel's Temple; The Temples of the
Bible). Ezekiel 40—48 present a picture of the restored com-
munity of God.

40:3 Bronze suggests the person was an angel (Dan. 10:6;
Rev. 1:15). The "line of flax" was used for measuring long distances, the "measuring rod" for short measurements.

40:5 The cubit, an ancient measurement, was normally about
18 inches (see chart, Money and Measurements in the Bible).

For a long time, however, ancient Near Eastern builders also
used a longer cubit, about 21 inches. Apparently, the longer
cubit was used for Solomon's temple (2 Chr. 3:3; see chart,
The Plan of Solomon's Temple). The longer cubit equaled the
shorter cubit (18 in.) plus a handbreadth (about 3 in.).

40:6 The temple of Ezekiel's vision had eastern (v. 6), northern (v. 20), and southern (v. 24) gateways. There was no gateway on the western side at the back of the temple (see chart,
The Plan for Ezekiel's Temple). The gates were designed to
withstand assault and to provide protection.

40:10 These gate chambers were for temple guards, who

THE PLAN FOR EZEKIEL'S TEMPLE

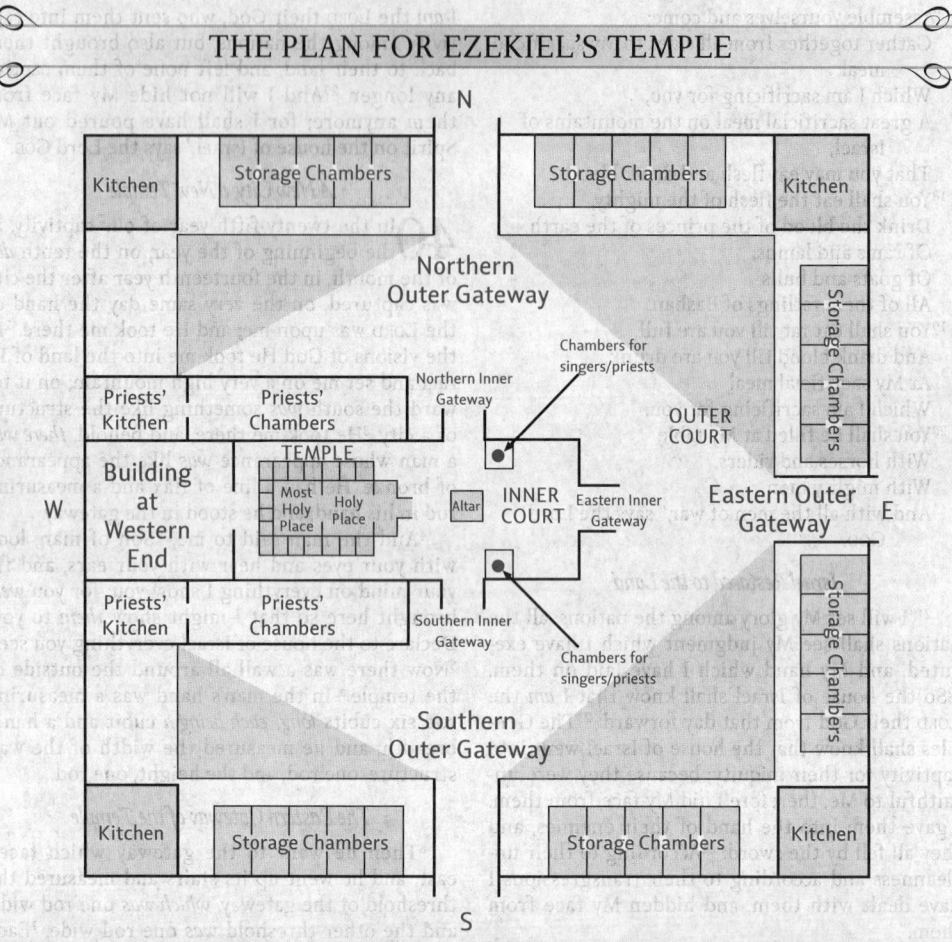

N

Kitchen | Storage Chambers | Storage Chambers | Kitchen

Northern Outer Gateway

Storage Chambers

Priests' Kitchen | Priests' Chambers

Northern Inner Gateway

Chambers for singers/priests

OUTER COURT

W

Building at Western End

TEMPLE

Most Holy Place | Holy Place

Altar | INNER COURT | Eastern Inner Gateway

Eastern Outer Gateway

E

Priests' Kitchen | Priests' Chambers

Southern Inner Gateway

Chambers for singers/priests

Storage Chambers

Southern Outer Gateway

Kitchen | Storage Chambers | Storage Chambers | Kitchen

S

one side and three on the other; the three *were* all the same size; also the gateposts were of the same size on this side and that side.

¹¹He measured the width of the entrance to the gateway, ten cubits; *and* the length of the gate, thirteen cubits. ¹²*There was* a space in front of the gate chambers, one cubit *on this side* and one cubit on that side; the gate chambers *were* six cubits on this side and six cubits on that side. ¹³Then he measured the gateway from the roof of *one* gate chamber to the roof of the other; the width *was* twenty-five cubits, as door faces door. ¹⁴He measured the gateposts, sixty cubits high, and the court all around the gateway *extended* to the gatepost. ¹⁵*From* the front of the entrance gate to the front of the vestibule of the inner gate *was*

fifty cubits. ¹⁶*There were* beveled window *frames* in the gate chambers and in their intervening archways on the inside of the gateway all around, and likewise in the vestibules. *There were* windows all around on the inside. And on each gatepost *were* palm trees.

The Outer Court

¹⁷Then he brought me into the outer court; and *there were* chambers and a pavement made all around the court; thirty chambers faced the pavement. ¹⁸The pavement was by the side of the gateways, corresponding to the length of the gateways; *this was* the lower pavement. ¹⁹Then he measured the width from the front of the lower gateway to the front of the inner court exterior,

were needed to control crowds and preserve order during the festivals. The alcoves were built into the walls of the gates.

40:16 Solomon's temple had similar decorations (see Ezek. 41:18; 1 Kin. 6:29; chart, The Plan of Solomon's Temple).

40:17 These rooms or storage chambers probably were used by worshipers not permitted to enter the inner court (see chart, The Plan for Ezekiel's Temple).

one hundred cubits toward the east and the north.

The Northern Gateway

20On the outer court was also a gateway facing north, and he measured its length and its width. 21Its gate chambers, three on this side and three on that side, its gateposts and its archways, had the same measurements as the first gate; its length was fifty cubits and its width twenty-five cubits. 22Its windows and those of its archways, and also its palm trees, had the same measurements as the gateway facing east; it was ascended by seven steps, and its archway was in front of it. 23A gate of the inner court was opposite the northern gateway, just as the eastern gateway; and he measured from gateway to gateway, one hundred cubits.

The Southern Gateway

24After that he brought me toward the south, and there a gateway was facing south; and he measured its gateposts and archways according to these same measurements. 25There were windows in it and in its archways all around like those windows; its length was fifty cubits and its width twenty-five cubits. 26Seven steps led up to it, and its archway was in front of them; and it had palm trees on its gateposts, one on this side and one on that side. 27There was also a gateway on the inner court, facing south; and he measured from gateway to gateway toward the south, one hundred cubits.

Gateways of the Inner Court

28Then he brought me to the inner court through the southern gateway; he measured the southern gateway according to these same measurements. 29Also its gate chambers, its gateposts, and its archways were according to these same measurements; there were windows in it and in its archways all around; it was fifty cubits long and twenty-five cubits wide. 30There were archways all around, twenty-five cubits long and five cubits wide. 31Its archways faced the outer court, palm trees were on its gateposts, and going up to it were eight steps.

32And he brought me into the inner court facing east; he measured the gateway according to these same measurements. 33Also its gate chambers, its gateposts, and its archways were accord-

ing to these same measurements; and there were windows in it and in its archways all around; it was fifty cubits long and twenty-five cubits wide. 34Its archways faced the outer court, and palm trees were on its gateposts on this side and on that side; and going up to it were eight steps.

35Then he brought me to the north gateway and measured it according to these same measurements— 36also its gate chambers, its gateposts, and its archways. It had windows all around; its length was fifty cubits and its width twenty-five cubits. 37Its gateposts faced the outer court, palm trees were on its gateposts on this side and on that side, and going up to it were eight steps.

Where Sacrifices Were Prepared

38There was a chamber and its entrance by the gateposts of the gateway, where they washed the burnt offering. 39In the vestibule of the gateway were two tables on this side and two tables on that side, on which to slay the burnt offering, the sin offering, and the trespass offering. 40At the outer side of the vestibule, as one goes up to the entrance of the northern gateway, were two tables; and on the other side of the vestibule of the gateway were two tables. 41Four tables were on this side and four tables on that side, by the side of the gateway, eight tables on which they slaughtered the sacrifices. 42There were also four tables of hewn stone for the burnt offering, one cubit and a half long, one cubit and a half wide, and one cubit high; on these they laid the instruments with which they slaughtered the burnt offering and the sacrifice. 43Inside were hooks, a handbreadth wide, fastened all around; and the flesh of the sacrifices was on the tables.

Chambers for Singers and Priests

44Outside the inner gate were the chambers for the singers in the inner court, one facing south at the side of the northern gateway, and the other facing north at the side of the southerna gateway. 45Then he said to me, "This chamber which faces south is for the priests who have charge of the temple. 46The chamber which faces north is for the priests who have charge of the altar; these are the sons of Zadok, from the sons of Levi, who come near the LORD to minister to Him."

40:44 aFollowing Septuagint; Masoretic Text and Vulgate read eastern.

40:28 The temple consisted of an outer court (vv. 5–27) and an inner court (vv. 28–37). The entire temple structure revealed a careful symmetry of design (see chart, The Plan for Ezekiel's Temple). Since there were gates, there must have been a wall around the inner court, even though it is not mentioned. Only priests were permitted to enter the inner court. The measurement of the inner court was 100 cubits square.

40:45, 46 The priests who had charge of the temple were the Levites. The priests who had charge of the altar were descendants of Zadok. Zadok, along with Abiathar, served as priest during David's reign (2 Sam. 8:17; 15:24; 1 Kin. 1:1–39). He became the sole high priest after Abiathar was dismissed for sedition and exiled by Solomon (1 Kin. 2:26, 27, 35). According to 1 Chronicles, Zadok descended from Eleazer, Aaron's son (1 Chr. 6:1–8; see also Ezek. 44:15, note).

Dimensions of the Inner Court and Vestibule

47And he measured the court, one hundred cubits long and one hundred cubits wide, foursquare. The altar *was* in front of the temple. 48Then he brought me to the vestibule of the temple and measured the doorposts of the vestibule, five cubits on this side and five cubits on that side; and the width of the gateway was three cubits on this side and three cubits on that side. 49The length of the vestibule *was* twenty cubits, and the width eleven cubits; and by the steps which led up to it *there were* pillars by the doorposts, one on this side and another on that side.

Dimensions of the Sanctuary

41 Then he brought me into the sanctuarya and measured the doorposts, six cubits wide on one side and six cubits wide on the other side—the width of the tabernacle. 2The width of the entryway *was* ten cubits, and the side walls of the entrance *were* five cubits on this side and five cubits on the other side; and he measured its length, forty cubits, and its width, twenty cubits. 3Also he went inside and measured the doorposts, two cubits; and the entrance, six cubits *high;* and the width of the entrance, seven cubits. 4He measured the length, twenty cubits; and the width, twenty cubits, beyond the sanctuary; and he said to me, "This *is* the Most Holy *Place.*"

The Side Chambers on the Wall

5Next, he measured the wall of the temple, six cubits. The width of each side chamber all around the temple *was* four cubits on every side. 6The side chambers *were* in three stories, one above the other, thirty chambers in each story; they rested on ledges which *were* for the side chambers all around, that they might be supported, but not fastened to the wall of the temple. 7As one went up from story to story, the side chambers became wider all around, because their supporting ledges in the wall of the temple ascended like steps; therefore the width of the structure increased as one went up *from* the lowest *story* to the highest by way of the middle one. 8I also saw an elevation all around the temple; it was the foundation of the side chambers, a full rod, *that is,* six cubits *high.* 9The thickness of the outer wall of the side chambers *was* five cubits, and so also the remaining terrace by the place of the side chambers of the temple. 10And between *it and* the *wall* chambers was a width of twenty cubits all around the temple on every side. 11The doors of the side chambers opened on the terrace, one door toward the north and another toward the south; and the width of the terrace *was* five cubits all around.

The Building at the Western End

12The building that faced the separating courtyard at its western end *was* seventy cubits wide; the wall of the building *was* five cubits thick all around, and its length ninety cubits.

Dimensions and Design of the Temple Area

13So he measured the temple, one hundred cubits long; and the separating courtyard with the building and its walls *was* one hundred cubits long; 14also the width of the eastern face of the temple, including the separating courtyard, *was* one hundred cubits. 15He measured the length of the building behind it, facing the separating courtyard, with its galleries on the one side and on the other side, one hundred cubits, as well as the inner temple and the porches of the court, 16their doorposts and the beveled window frames. And the galleries all around their three stories opposite the threshold were paneled with wood from the ground to the windows—the windows were covered— 17from the space above the door, even to the inner room,a as well as outside, and on every wall all around, inside and outside, by measure.

18And *it was* made with cherubim and palm trees, a palm tree between cherub and cherub. *Each* cherub had two faces, 19so that the face of a man *was* toward a palm tree on one side, and the face of a young lion toward a palm tree on the other side; thus *it was* made throughout the temple all around. 20From the floor to the space above the door, and on the wall of the sanctuary, cherubim and palm trees *were* carved.

21The doorposts of the temple *were* square, *as was* the front of the sanctuary; their appearance was similar. 22The altar *was* of wood, three cubits

· · · · · · · · · · · · · · · · · · · ·

41:1 aHebrew *heykal,* here the main room of the temple, sometimes called the *holy place* (compare Exodus 26:33)   41:17 aLiterally *house,* here *the Most Holy Place*

40:48—41:4 Ezekiel was led through the temple proper, moving through three rooms: the vestibule, the sanctuary or holy place, and the Most Holy Place. Each had a doorway. As he approached the Most Holy Place, the doorways became smaller, perhaps focusing the worshiper's eyes to the center of worship—the presence of God in the Most Holy Place. No one was permitted to enter the Most Holy Place except the high priest once a year on the Day of Atonement (Lev. 16).

41:6 The 90 rooms built into the side of the temple were used to store tithes and offerings, as well as temple equipment and furnishings.

41:18 The cherubim function as guardians of God's holiness. Here, the cherubim have two faces, unlike Ezekiel's earlier vision (see Ezek. 10:14). The cherubim and palm tree motifs were used in Solomon's temple (see 1 Kin. 6:29–35).

41:22 The altar could hardly have been used to burn sacrifices, since it was made of wood. The description suggests that this table was for the bread of the Presence.

high, and its length two cubits. Its corners, its length, and its sides *were* of wood; and he said to me, "This *is* the table that *is* before the LORD."

[23]The temple and the sanctuary had two doors. [24]The doors had two panels *apiece,* two folding panels: two *panels* for one door and two panels for the other *door.* [25]Cherubim and palm trees *were* carved on the doors of the temple just as they *were* carved on the walls. A wooden canopy *was* on the front of the vestibule outside. [26]*There were* beveled window *frames* and palm trees on one side and on the other, on the sides of the vestibule— also on the side chambers of the temple and on the canopies.

The Chambers for the Priests

42 Then he brought me out into the outer court, by the way toward the north; and he brought me into the chamber which *was* opposite the separating courtyard, and which *was* opposite the building toward the north. [2]Facing the length, which *was* one hundred cubits (the width was fifty cubits), was the north door. [3]Opposite the inner court of twenty *cubits,* and opposite the pavement of the outer court, *was* gallery against gallery in three *stories.* [4]In front of the chambers, toward the inside, *was* a walk ten cubits wide, at a distance of one cubit; and their doors faced north. [5]Now the upper chambers *were* shorter, because the galleries took away *space* from them more than from the lower and middle stories of the building. [6]For they *were* in three *stories* and did not have pillars like the pillars of the courts; therefore *the upper level* was shortened more than the lower and middle levels from the ground up. [7]And a wall which *was* outside ran parallel to the chambers, at the front of the chambers, toward the outer court; its length *was* fifty cubits. [8]The length of the chambers toward the outer court *was* fifty cubits, whereas that facing the temple *was* one hundred cubits. [9]At the lower chambers *was* the entrance on the east side, as one goes into them from the outer court.

[10]Also *there were* chambers in the thickness of the wall of the court toward the east, opposite the separating courtyard and opposite the building. [11]*There was* a walk in front of them also, and their appearance *was* like the chambers which *were* to-

ward the north; they *were* as long and as wide as the others, and all their exits and entrances *were* according to plan. [12]And corresponding to the doors of the chambers that *were* facing south, as one enters them, *there was* a door in front of the walk, the way directly in front of the wall toward the east.

[13]Then he said to me, "The north chambers *and* the south chambers, which *are* opposite the separating courtyard, *are* the holy chambers where the priests who approach the LORD shall eat the most holy offerings. There they shall lay the most holy offerings— the grain offering, the sin offering, and the trespass offering— for the place *is* holy. [14]When the priests enter them, they shall not go out of the holy *chamber* into the outer court; but there they shall leave their garments in which they minister, for they *are* holy. They shall put on other garments; then they may approach *that* which *is* for the people."

Outer Dimensions of the Temple

[15]Now when he had finished measuring the inner temple, he brought me out through the gateway that faces toward the east, and measured it all around. [16]He measured the east side with the measuring rod,[a] five hundred rods by the measuring rod all around. [17]He measured the north side, five hundred rods by the measuring rod all around. [18]He measured the south side, five hundred rods by the measuring rod. [19]He came around to the west side *and* measured five hundred rods by the measuring rod. [20]He measured it on the four sides; it had a wall all around, five hundred *cubits* long and five hundred wide, to separate the holy areas from the common.

The Temple, the LORD's Dwelling Place

43 Afterward he brought me to the gate, the gate that faces toward the east. [2]And behold, the glory of the God of Israel came from the way of the east. His voice *was* like the sound of many waters; and the earth shone with His glory. [3]*It was* like the appearance of the vision which I saw— like the vision which I saw when I[a] came to

42:16 [a]Compare 40:5   43:3 [a]Some Hebrew manuscripts and Vulgate read *He.*

42:1 There were two chambers for the priests (see chart, The Plan for Ezekiel's Temple). These chambers were located opposite one another on the north and south sides of the temple, possibly between the inner and the outer courts. Each chamber was a complex structure. The chambers functioned as protective barriers to prevent defilement of the most sacred areas.

42:13 The priests who approached the Lord were the descendants of Zakok (see Ezek. 40:45, 46; 44:15, notes).

42:14 The priestly clothing used in divine service was to be

kept separate from the people due to the holiness of God (see chart, The High Priest's Clothing).

42:15–20 The boundary of the entire temple complex formed a perfect square (see chart, The Plan for Ezekiel's Temple).

43:2 The return of God's glory formed a climax to the temple vision, witnessed by Ezekiel 19 years after he saw God's departure. The Lord returned by the way He left, from the east (see Ezek. 11:23). The Hebrew word translated "glory" comes from a root meaning "to be heavy" or "weighty"(see Ps. 19:1, note).

destroy the city. The visions *were* like the vision which I saw by the River Chebar; and I fell on my face. ⁴And the glory of the LORD came into the temple by way of the gate which faces toward the east. ⁵The Spirit lifted me up and brought me into the inner court; and behold, the glory of the LORD filled the temple.

⁶Then I heard *Him* speaking to me from the temple, while a man stood beside me. ⁷And He said to me, "Son of man, *this is* the place of My throne and the place of the soles of My feet, where I will dwell in the midst of the children of Israel forever. No more shall the house of Israel defile My holy name, they nor their kings, by their harlotry or with the carcasses of their kings on their high places. ⁸When they set their threshold by My threshold, and their doorpost by My doorpost, with a wall between them and Me, they defiled My holy name by the abominations which they committed; therefore I have consumed them in My anger. ⁹Now let them put their harlotry and the carcasses of their kings far away from Me, and I will dwell in their midst forever.

¹⁰"Son of man, describe the temple to the house of Israel, that they may be ashamed of their iniquities; and let them measure the pattern. ¹¹And if they are ashamed of all that they have done, make known to them the design of the temple and its arrangement, its exits and its entrances, its entire design and all its ordinances, all its forms and all its laws. Write *it* down in their sight, so that they may keep its whole design and all its ordinances, and perform them. ¹²This *is* the law of the temple: The whole area surrounding the mountaintop *is* most holy. Behold, this *is* the law of the temple.

Dimensions of the Altar

¹³"These are the measurements of the altar in cubits (the *cubit is* one cubit and a handbreadth): the base one cubit high and one cubit wide, with a rim all around its edge of one span. This *is* the height of the altar: ¹⁴from the base on the ground to the lower ledge, two cubits; the width of the ledge, one cubit; from the smaller ledge to the larger ledge, four cubits; and the width of the ledge, *one* cubit. ¹⁵The altar hearth *is* four cubits high, with four horns extending upward from the hearth. ¹⁶The altar hearth *is* twelve cubits long, twelve wide, square at its four corners; ¹⁷the ledge, fourteen *cubits* long and fourteen wide on its four sides, with a rim of half a cubit around it; its base, one cubit all around; and its steps face toward the east."

Consecrating the Altar

¹⁸And He said to me, "Son of man, thus says the Lord GOD: 'These *are* the ordinances for the altar on the day when it is made, for sacrificing burnt offerings on it, and for sprinkling blood on it. ¹⁹You shall give a young bull for a sin offering to the priests, the Levites, who are of the seed of Zadok, who approach Me to minister to Me,' says the Lord GOD. ²⁰You shall take some of its blood and put *it* on the four horns of the altar, on the four corners of the ledge, and on the rim around it; thus you shall cleanse it and make atonement for it. ²¹Then you shall also take the bull of the sin offering, and burn it in the appointed place of the temple, outside the sanctuary. ²²On the second day you shall offer a kid of the goats without blemish for a sin offering; and they shall cleanse the altar, as they cleansed *it* with the bull. ²³When you have finished cleansing *it,* you shall offer a young bull without blemish, and a ram from the flock without blemish. ²⁴When you offer them before the LORD, the priests shall throw salt on them, and they will offer them up *as* a burnt offering to the LORD. ²⁵Every day for seven days you shall prepare a goat *for* a sin offering; they shall also prepare a young bull and a ram from the flock, both without blemish. ²⁶Seven days they shall make atonement for the altar and purify it, and so consecrate *it.* ²⁷When these days are over it shall be, on the eighth day and thereafter, that the priests shall offer your burnt offerings and your peace offerings on the altar; and I will accept you,' says the Lord GOD."

The East Gate and the Prince

44 Then He brought me back to the outer gate of the sanctuary which faces toward the

---

43:5 The Lord's glory filled the temple. As in Solomon's temple, God's presence entered the temple (1 Kin. 8:10, 11).

43:7 Carcasses of kings on high places may refer to the graves of Manasseh and Amon, who were buried close to the temple precincts (2 Kin. 21:18, 26). Actually some 14 kings had been buried in the area of the palace and temple. These tombs were viewed as an impingement on the Lord's holy place. In the temple area, the phrase also may refer to memorials set up in honor of kings. In any case, the temple complex had been defiled.

43:13 The altar was built of several layers with each successive level smaller than the preceding one (Ezek. 40:47; 43:13–27; see chart, The Plan for Ezekiel's Temple). The description of the altar follows the return of God's presence to indicate the way of access to Him.

43:17 These steps of the altar illustrated one of the differences between the millennial altar and the Mosaic altar of sacrifice in which ascending by steps was forbidden (Ex. 20:26). The millennial altar was so large that steps were needed (approximately 3½ feet at the base and 19¼ feet high; see Ezek. 43:13–17; charts, Money and Measurements in the Bible; The Plan for Ezekiel's Temple).

43:25 This period of consecration is similar to that for the altar of sacrifice in the tabernacle (Ex. 29:37).

east, but it *was* shut. [2]And the LORD said to me, "This gate shall be shut; it shall not be opened, and no man shall enter by it, because the LORD God of Israel has entered by it; therefore it shall be shut. [3]*As for* the prince, *because* he *is* the prince, he may sit in it to eat bread before the LORD; he shall enter by way of the vestibule of the gateway, and go out the same way."

Those Admitted to the Temple

[4]Also He brought me by way of the north gate to the front of the temple; so I looked, and behold, the glory of the LORD filled the house of the LORD; and I fell on my face. [5]And the LORD said to me, "Son of man, mark well, see with your eyes and hear with your ears, all that I say to you concerning all the ordinances of the house of the LORD and all its laws. Mark well who may enter the house and all who go out from the sanctuary.

[6]"Now say to the rebellious, to the house of Israel, 'Thus says the Lord GOD: "O house of Israel, let Us have no more of all your abominations. [7]When you brought in foreigners, uncircumcised in heart and uncircumcised in flesh, to be in My sanctuary to defile it—My house—and when you offered My food, the fat and the blood, then they broke My covenant because of all your abominations. [8]And you have not kept charge of My holy things, but you have set *others* to keep charge of My sanctuary for you." [9]Thus says the Lord GOD: "No foreigner, uncircumcised in heart or uncircumcised in flesh, shall enter My sanctuary, including any foreigner who *is* among the children of Israel.

Laws Governing Priests

[10]"And the Levites who went far from Me, when Israel went astray, who strayed away from Me after their idols, they shall bear their iniquity. [11]Yet they shall be ministers in My sanctuary, *as* gatekeepers of the house and ministers of the house; they shall slay the burnt offering and the sacrifice

for the people, and they shall stand before them to minister to them. [12]Because they ministered to them before their idols and caused the house of Israel to fall into iniquity, therefore I have raised My hand in an oath against them," says the Lord GOD, "that they shall bear their iniquity. [13]And they shall not come near Me to minister to Me as priest, nor come near any of My holy things, nor into the Most Holy *Place;* but they shall bear their shame and their abominations which they have committed. [14]Nevertheless I will make them keep charge of the temple, for all its work, and for all that has to be done in it.

[15]"But the priests, the Levites, the sons of Zadok, who kept charge of My sanctuary when the children of Israel went astray from Me, they shall come near Me to minister to Me; and they shall stand before Me to offer to Me the fat and the blood," says the Lord GOD. [16]"They shall enter My sanctuary, and they shall come near My table to minister to Me, and they shall keep My charge. [17]And it shall be, whenever they enter the gates of the inner court, that they shall put on linen garments; no wool shall come upon them while they minister within the gates of the inner court or within the house. [18]They shall have linen turbans on their heads and linen trousers on their bodies; they shall not clothe themselves with *anything that causes* sweat. [19]When they go out to the outer court, to the outer court to the people, they shall take off their garments in which they have ministered, leave them in the holy chambers, and put on other garments; and in their holy garments they shall not sanctify the people.

[20]"They shall neither shave their heads, nor let their hair grow long, but they shall keep their hair well trimmed. [21]No priest shall drink wine when he enters the inner court. [22]They shall not take as wife a widow or a divorced woman, but take virgins of the descendants of the house of Israel, or widows of priests.

[23]"And they shall teach My people *the difference* between the holy and the unholy, and cause them

---

44:2 The east gate of the outer court was to remain closed out of reverence for the Lord's future return through that gate. The shut gate also may indicate that God promised not to leave the temple again.

44:3 The prince was Ezekiel's designation for a king (Ezek. 28:2; 38:2). The king was granted this one privilege of eating bread before the Lord in recognition of his special role. The regulation addressed the tendency of the kings to usurp temple worship for their own purposes (2 Chr. 26:16–23). The temple belonged to the Lord. This prince also has been identified as King David or as the Messiah (Ezek. 34:24; 37:25).

44:7–9 The Israelites had defiled the temple by bringing in foreigners. Some foreigners had been charged with care of the sanctuary (v. 8). God's people failed to appreciate that the temple epitomized their special covenant relationship with God (Deut. 23:3). Foreigners who accepted the Lord as

their God were received in Israel. Ruth the Moabitess is an example. She even became a part of the ancestry of the Messiah. In most cases, however, foreigners corrupted Israel with their idols.

44:10–14 The Levites would be punished for their idolatrous practices by being restricted to menial tasks such as guarding the gates and killing the sacrificial animals. The Levites had contributed to the corruption and fall of Jerusalem.

44:15 The sons of Zadok were not included in Ezekiel's indictments of the priests (Ezek. 8:16; 22:26; see also 40:45, 46, note).

44:17 The priestly regulations are similar to those in Leviticus and Numbers. These restrictions highlighted the holiness of the priestly office.

44:19 For priestly garments, see Ezekiel 42:14, note.

to discern between the unclean and the clean. [24]In controversy they shall stand as judges, *and* judge it according to My judgments. They shall keep My laws and My statutes in all My appointed meetings, and they shall hallow My Sabbaths.

[25]"They shall not defile *themselves* by coming near a dead person. Only for father or mother, for son or daughter, for brother or unmarried sister may they defile themselves. [26]After he is cleansed, they shall count seven days for him. [27]And on the day that he goes to the sanctuary to minister in the sanctuary, he must offer his sin offering in the inner court," says the Lord GOD.

[28]"It shall be, in regard to their inheritance, *that* I *am* their inheritance. You shall give them no possession in Israel, for I *am* their possession. [29]They shall eat the grain offering, the sin offering, and the trespass offering; every dedicated thing in Israel shall be theirs. [30]The best of all firstfruits of any kind, and every sacrifice of any kind from all your sacrifices, shall be the priest's; also you shall give to the priest the first of your ground meal, to cause a blessing to rest on your house. [31]The priests shall not eat anything, bird or beast, that died naturally or was torn *by wild beasts*.

The Holy District

45 "Moreover, when you divide the land by lot into inheritance, you shall set apart a district for the LORD, a holy section of the land; its length *shall be* twenty-five thousand *cubits,* and the width ten thousand. It *shall be* holy throughout its territory all around. [2]Of this there shall be a square plot for the sanctuary, five hundred by five hundred *rods,* with fifty cubits around it for an open space. [3]So this is the district you shall measure: twenty-five thousand *cubits* long and ten thousand wide; in it shall be the sanctuary, the Most Holy *Place.* [4]It shall be a holy *section* of the land, belonging to the priests, the ministers of the sanctuary, who come near to minister to the LORD; it shall be a place for their houses and a holy place for the sanctuary. [5]*An area* twenty-five thousand *cubits* long and ten thousand wide shall belong to the Levites, the ministers of the temple; they shall have twenty chambers as a possession.[a]

Properties of the City and the Prince

[6]"You shall appoint as the property of the city *an area* five thousand *cubits* wide and twenty-five

thousand long, adjacent to the district of the holy *section;* it shall belong to the whole house of Israel.

[7]"The prince shall have *a section* on one side and the other of the holy district and the city's property; and bordering on the holy district and the city's property, extending westward on the west side and eastward on the east side, the length *shall be* side by side with one of the *tribal* portions, from the west border to the east border. [8]The land shall be his possession in Israel; and My princes shall no more oppress My people, but they shall give *the rest of* the land to the house of Israel, according to their tribes."

Laws Governing the Prince

[9]"Thus says the Lord GOD: "Enough, O princes of Israel! Remove violence and plundering, execute justice and righteousness, and stop dispossessing My people," says the Lord GOD. [10]"You shall have honest scales, an honest ephah, and an honest bath. [11]The ephah and the bath shall be of the same measure, so that the bath contains one-tenth of a homer, and the ephah one-tenth of a homer; their measure shall be according to the homer. [12]The shekel *shall be* twenty gerahs; twenty shekels, twenty-five shekels, *and* fifteen shekels shall be your mina.

[13]"This *is* the offering which you shall offer: you shall give one-sixth of an ephah from a homer of wheat, and one-sixth of an ephah from a homer of barley. [14]The ordinance concerning oil, the bath of oil, *is* one-tenth of a bath from a kor. *A kor is* a homer or ten baths, for ten baths *are* a homer. [15]And one lamb shall be given from a flock of two hundred, from the rich pastures of Israel. These shall be for grain offerings, burnt offerings, and peace offerings, to make atonement for them," says the Lord GOD. [16]"All the people of the land shall give this offering for the prince in Israel. [17]Then it shall be the prince's part *to give* burnt offerings, grain offerings, and drink offerings, at the feasts, the New Moons, the Sabbaths, and at all the appointed seasons of the house of Israel. He shall prepare the sin offering, the grain offering, the burnt offering, and the peace offerings to make atonement for the house of Israel."

•••••••••••••••••••

45:5 [a]Following Masoretic Text, Targum, and Vulgate; Septuagint reads *a possession, cities of dwelling.*

45:1–6 Three sections of land in Jerusalem—one for the temple and priesthood (vv. 1–4), one for the Levites (v. 5), and one for all the house of Israel (v. 6)—are described.

45:8 The prince or king was warned not to expropriate land for royal use (see 1 Kin. 21). This warning was necessary because the expropriation of lands deprived families in Israel of their lawful inheritance. No one was to lose his property (see Ezek. 46:18).

45:10 The ephah was a dry measure. The "bath" was a liquid measure (see chart, Money and Measurements in the Bible).

45:11, 12 The homer was a dry measure. The "shekel" was a dry measure equaling about two-fifths ounce. The "mina" was a dry measure, here equal to 60 shekels. It was commonly 50 shekels in the Canaanite system (see chart, Money and Measurements in the Bible). Ezekiel was following the Babylonian system.

Keeping the Feasts

¹⁸"Thus says the Lord GOD: "In the first *month*, on the first *day* of the month, you shall take a young bull without blemish and cleanse the sanctuary. ¹⁹The priest shall take some of the blood of the sin offering and put *it* on the doorposts of the temple, on the four corners of the ledge of the altar, and on the gateposts of the gate of the inner court. ²⁰And so you shall do on the seventh *day* of the month for everyone who has sinned unintentionally or in ignorance. Thus you shall make atonement for the temple.

²¹"In the first *month*, on the fourteenth day of the month, you shall observe the Passover, a feast of seven days; unleavened bread shall be eaten. ²²And on that day the prince shall prepare for himself and for all the people of the land a bull *for* a sin offering. ²³On the seven days of the feast he shall prepare a burnt offering to the LORD, seven bulls and seven rams without blemish, daily for seven days, and a kid of the goats daily *for* a sin offering. ²⁴And he shall prepare a grain offering of one ephah for each bull and one ephah for each ram, together with a hin of oil for each ephah.

²⁵"In the seventh *month*, on the fifteenth day of the month, at the feast, he shall do likewise for seven days, according to the sin offering, the burnt offering, the grain offering, and the oil."

The Manner of Worship

46 ¹"Thus says the Lord GOD: "The gateway of the inner court that faces toward the east shall be shut the six working days; but on the Sabbath it shall be opened, and on the day of the New Moon it shall be opened. ²The prince shall enter by way of the vestibule of the gateway from the outside, and stand by the gatepost. The priests shall prepare his burnt offering and his peace offerings. He shall worship at the threshold of the gate. Then he shall go out, but the gate shall not be shut until evening. ³Likewise the people of the land shall worship at the entrance to this gateway before the LORD on the Sabbaths and the New Moons. ⁴The burnt offering that the prince offers to the LORD on the Sabbath day *shall be* six lambs without blemish, and a ram without blemish; ⁵and the grain offering *shall be one* ephah for a ram, and the grain offering for the lambs, as much as he

wants to give, as well as a hin of oil with every ephah. ⁶On the day of the New Moon *it shall be* a young bull without blemish, six lambs, and a ram; they shall be without blemish. ⁷He shall prepare a grain offering of an ephah for a bull, an ephah for a ram, as much as he wants to give for the lambs, and a hin of oil with every ephah. ⁸When the prince enters, he shall go in by way of the vestibule of the gateway, and go out the same way.

⁹"But when the people of the land come before the LORD on the appointed feast days, whoever enters by way of the north gate to worship shall go out by way of the south gate; and whoever enters by way of the south gate shall go out by way of the north gate. He shall not return by way of the gate through which he came, but shall go out through the opposite gate. ¹⁰The prince shall then be in their midst. When they go in, he shall go in; and when they go out, he shall go out. ¹¹At the festivals and the appointed feast days the grain offering shall be an ephah for a bull, an ephah for a ram, as much as he wants to give for the lambs, and a hin of oil with every ephah.

¹²"Now when the prince makes a voluntary burnt offering or voluntary peace offering to the LORD, the gate that faces toward the east shall then be opened for him; and he shall prepare his burnt offering and his peace offerings as he did on the Sabbath day. Then he shall go out, and after he goes out the gate shall be shut.

¹³"You shall daily make a burnt offering to the LORD *of* a lamb of the first year without blemish; you shall prepare it every morning. ¹⁴And you shall prepare a grain offering with it every morning, a sixth of an ephah, and a third of a hin of oil to moisten the fine flour. This grain offering is a perpetual ordinance, to be made regularly to the LORD. ¹⁵Thus they shall prepare the lamb, the grain offering, and the oil, *as* a regular burnt offering every morning."

The Prince and Inheritance Laws

¹⁶"Thus says the Lord GOD: "If the prince gives a gift *of some* of his inheritance to any of his sons, it shall belong to his sons; it is their possession by inheritance. ¹⁷But if he gives a gift of some of his inheritance to one of his servants, it shall be his until the year of liberty, after which it shall return to the prince. But his inheritance shall belong to

---

45:18—46:24 Regulations for feast days, worship, and inheritance are discussed in this section. Many of these regulations differ from those found in the Mosaic Law. For example, the Feast of Harvest (Ex. 23:16) is not mentioned as part of the annual cycle of feasts (see chart, The Feasts of Israel). The return of the sacrificial system and feast day celebrations in the millennial earthly kingdom would point to the saving work of Christ on the Cross as the Mosaic sacrificial system had pointed to His atonement on the Cross. Sacrifices have always

been symbols that point to Christ. They in themselves have never been efficacious (Heb. 9:12). The Mosaic covenant would be fulfilled in the messianic kingdom in which Israel would be God's holy people and He would be their God (Ezek. 37:15–28).

46:17 Year of liberty is probably a reference to the Year of Jubilee (see Lev. 25:8–17; see chart, The Principle of the Sabbath).

his sons; it shall become theirs. ¹⁸Moreover the prince shall not take any of the people's inheritance by evicting them from their property; he shall provide an inheritance for his sons from his own property, so that none of My people may be scattered from his property." ' "

How the Offerings Were Prepared

¹⁹Now he brought me through the entrance, which *was* at the side of the gate, into the holy chambers of the priests which face toward the north; and there a place *was* situated at their extreme western end. ²⁰And he said to me, "This *is* the place where the priests shall boil the trespass offering and the sin offering, *and* where they shall bake the grain offering, so that they do not bring *them* out into the outer court to sanctify the people."

²¹Then he brought me out into the outer court and caused me to pass by the four corners of the court; and in fact, in every corner of the court *there was another* court. ²²In the four corners of the court *were* enclosed courts, forty *cubits* long and thirty wide; all four corners *were* the same size. ²³*There was* a row *of building stones* all around in them, all around the four of them; and cooking hearths were made under the rows of stones all around. ²⁴And he said to me, "These *are* the kitchens where the ministers of the temple shall boil the sacrifices of the people."

The Healing Waters and Trees

47Then he brought me back to the door of the temple; and there was water, flowing from under the threshold of the temple toward the east, for the front of the temple faced east; the water was flowing from under the right side of the temple, south of the altar. ²He brought me out by way of the north gate, and led me around on the outside to the outer gateway that faces

east; and there was water, running out on the right side.

³And when the man went out to the east with the line in his hand, he measured one thousand cubits, and he brought me through the waters; the water *came up to my* ankles. ⁴Again he measured one thousand and brought me through the waters; the water *came up to my* knees. Again he measured one thousand and brought me through; the water *came up to my* waist. ⁵Again he measured one thousand, *and it was* a river that I could not cross; for the water was too deep, water in which one must swim, a river that could not be crossed. ⁶He said to me, "Son of man, have you seen *this?*" Then he brought me and returned me to the bank of the river.

⁷When I returned, there, along the bank of the river, *were* very many trees on one side and the other. ⁸Then he said to me: "This water flows toward the eastern region, goes down into the valley, and enters the sea. *When it* reaches the sea, *its* waters are healed. ⁹And it shall be *that* every living thing that moves, wherever the rivers go, will live. There will be a very great multitude of fish, because these waters go there; for they will be healed, and everything will live wherever the river goes. ¹⁰It shall be *that* fishermen will stand by it from En Gedi to En Eglaim; they will be *places* for spreading their nets. Their fish will be of the same kinds as the fish of the Great Sea, exceedingly many. ¹¹But its swamps and marshes will not be healed; they will be given over to salt. ¹²Along the bank of the river, on this side and that, will grow all *kinds of* trees used for food; their leaves will not wither, and their fruit will not fail. They will bear fruit every month, because their water flows from the sanctuary. Their fruit will be for food, and their leaves for medicine."

Borders of the Land

¹³Thus says the Lord GOD: "These *are* the borders by which you shall divide the land as an in-

---

46:18 For limitations on the prince or king, see Ezekiel 45:8, note.

46:19–24 Kitchens used by the priests to cook sacrifices were described by Ezekiel (see chart, The Plan for Ezekiel's Temple). Another set of kitchens in the corners of the outer court was dedicated to cooking sacrifices that the people were allowed to eat.

47:1 The stream under the temple is a reminder of the river that flowed out of the Garden of Eden (Gen. 2:10). It represents life flowing out from God to His creation. The woman of Samaria took of this life-giving water (see John 4:14). The image of the temple and Jerusalem as the source of life-giving waters appears in several prophetic books (see Is. 33:20, 21; Rev. 22). The only natural spring known to have existed in Jerusalem in biblical times was the Gihon spring in the Kidron Valley (2 Chr. 32:2–4).

47:3–5 One thousand cubits equals approximately one-third

of a mile (see chart, Money and Measurements in the Bible). The volume of water increased miraculously (no tributaries are mentioned) as the stream proceeded out of the city.

47:8 The mighty river from the temple changed the salty Dead Sea into a sea of life. The power of God transforms death into life.

47:10 En Gedi is an oasis west of the Dead Sea. The location of En Eglaim is uncertain. The Great Sea is another name for the Mediterranean Sea (see vv. 15, 19, 20).

47:12 John used this verse to describe the "tree of life" in Revelation 22, showing that God's goal for His eternal kingdom is to realize the glory creation would have achieved under Adam and Eve, if not corrupted by sin.

47:13 The Levites received no separate portion of the Land (Ezek. 44:28; see Josh. 13:14). Joseph's two sons, Ephraim and Manasseh, each received a portion, making a total of 12 portions (see Gen. 48:17–20).

heritance among the twelve tribes of Israel. Joseph *shall have two* portions. [14]You shall inherit it equally with one another; for I raised My hand in an oath to give it to your fathers, and this land shall fall to you as your inheritance.

[15]"This *shall be* the border of the land on the north: from the Great Sea, *by* the road to Hethlon, as one goes to Zedad, [16]Hamath, Berothah, Sibraim (which *is* between the border of Damascus and the border of Hamath), to Hazar Hatticon (which *is* on the border of Hauran). [17]Thus the boundary shall be from the Sea to Hazar Enan, the border of Damascus; and as for the north, northward, it is the border of Hamath. *This is* the north side.

[18]"On the east side you shall mark out the border from between Hauran and Damascus, and between Gilead and the land of Israel, along the Jordan, and along the eastern side of the sea. *This is* the east side.

[19]"The south side, toward the South,[a] *shall be* from Tamar to the waters of Meribah by Kadesh, along the brook to the Great Sea. *This is* the south side, toward the South.

[20]"The west side *shall be* the Great Sea, from the *southern* boundary until one comes to a point opposite Hamath. This *is* the west side.

[21]"Thus you shall divide this land among yourselves according to the tribes of Israel. [22]It shall be that you will divide it by lot as an inheritance for yourselves, and for the strangers who dwell among you and who bear children among you. They shall be to you as native-born among the children of Israel; they shall have an inheritance with you among the tribes of Israel. [23]And it shall be *that* in whatever tribe the stranger dwells, there you shall give *him* his inheritance," says the Lord GOD.

Division of the Land

48 "Now these *are* the names of the tribes: From the northern border along the road to Hethlon at the entrance of Hamath, to Hazar Enan, the border of Damascus northward, in the direction of Hamath, *there shall be* one *section for* Dan from its east to its west side; [2]by the border of Dan, from the east side to the west, one *section for* Asher; [3]by the border of Asher, from the east side to the west, one *section for* Naphtali; [4]by the border of Naphtali, from the east side to the west, one *section for* Manasseh; [5]by the border of Manasseh, from the east side to the west, one *section for* Ephraim; [6]by the border of Ephraim, from the east side to the west, one *section for* Reuben; [7]by the border of Reuben, from the east side to the west, one *section for* Judah; [8]by the border of Judah, from the east side to the west, shall be the district which you shall set apart, twenty-five thousand *cubits* in width, and *in* length the same as one of the *other* portions, from the east side to the west, with the sanctuary in the center.

[9]"The district that you shall set apart for the LORD *shall be* twenty-five thousand *cubits* in length and ten thousand in width. [10]To these—to the priests—the holy district shall belong: on the north twenty-five thousand *cubits in length,* on the west ten thousand in width, on the east ten thousand in width, and on the south twenty-five thousand in length. The sanctuary of the LORD shall be in the center. [11]*It shall be* for the priests of the sons of Zadok, who are sanctified, who have kept My charge, who did not go astray when the children of Israel went astray, as the Levites went astray. [12]And *this* district of land that is set apart shall be to them a thing most holy by the border of the Levites.

[13]"Opposite the border of the priests, the Levites *shall have an area* twenty-five thousand *cubits* in length and ten thousand in width; its entire length *shall be* twenty-five thousand and its width ten thousand. [14]And they shall not sell or exchange

47:19 [a]Hebrew *Negev*

47:15–20 The boundaries of the Land of Promise are approximately those described in Numbers 34. Ezekiel did not mention any land east of the Jordan River. See Joshua 13 for an account of the division of the land east of the Jordan River (see map, The Division of the Land of Israel).

47:19 Meribah was the site in the wilderness where Moses brought forth water for the people. The brook to the Great Sea, the modern *Wadi el 'Arish* is elsewhere "the brook of Egypt" (see Num. 34:5; Josh. 15:4; 1 Kin. 8:65).

47:22 The mention of strangers (foreigners) sharing in the inheritance of the Land is striking. It reflects the reality of the conquest under Joshua, in which some foreigners such as Caleb inherited land in Israel (Josh. 14:6–15). It also points forward to the inclusion of the Gentiles in the New Covenant.

48:1–12 Tribal territories in the new arrangement are grouped according to the status of their ancestral mother. The sons of Leah and Rachel are closest to the temple and city. Dan and Naphtali were sons of Rachel's maidservant, Bilhah (vv. 1, 3;

Gen. 35:25). Gad and Asher were sons of Leah's maidservant, Zilpah (Ezek. 48:2, 27; Gen. 35:26). Reuben, Judah, Simeon, Issachar, and Zebulun were sons of Leah (Ezek. 48:6, 7, 24–26; Gen. 35:23). Benjamin and Joseph (Manasseh and Ephraim) were sons of Rachel (Ezek. 48:4, 5, 23; Gen. 35:24).

48:7 Judah borders on the north of the consecrated district and the lands of the prince (vv. 8–22). In Judah's case, the messianic promise made it proper for Judah's tribal territory to be located near the prince's lands (Gen. 49:8–12).

48:8–22 The temple, the Lord's dwelling place, would be in the center of a special district. This district would be in the form of a perfect square set apart for the Lord in the midst of the land of Israel (see Ezek. 45:1–8; chart, The Plan for Ezekiel's Temple). Ezekiel's millennial temple and its sacrifices are a step forward in God's preparation of His people for worshiping Him in heaven (see chart, The Temples of the Bible).

48:11 See Ezekiel 44:15, note.

THE TEMPLES OF THE BIBLE

THE TEMPLE	DATE	DESCRIPTION	REFERENCE
The Tabernacle (Mobile Temple)	about 1444 B.C.	Detailed plan received by Moses from the Lord Constructed by divinely appointed artisans Desecrated by Nadab and Abihu	Ex. 25—30; Ex. 35:30—40:38; Lev. 10:1-7
Solomon's Temple	966–586 B.C.	Planned by David Constructed by Solomon Destroyed by Nebuchadnezzar	2 Sam. 7:1-29; 1 Kin. 8:1-66; Jer. 32:28-44
Zerubbabel's Temple	516–169 B.C.	Envisioned by Zerubbabel Constructed by Zerubbabel and the elders of the Jews Desecrated by Antiochus Epiphanes	Ezra 6:1-22; Ezra 3:1-8; 4:1-14; Matt. 24:15
Herod's Temple	19 B.C.–A.D. 70	Zerubbabel's temple restored by Herod the Great Destroyed by the Romans	Mark 13:2, 14-23; Luke 1:11-20; 2:22-38; 2:42-51; 4:21-24; Acts 21:27-33
The Present Temple	Present Age	Found in the heart of the believer The body of the believer is the Lord's only temple until the Messiah returns	1 Cor. 6:19, 20; 2 Cor. 6:16-18
The Temple of Revelation 11	Tribulation Period	To be constructed during the Tribulation by the Antichrist To be desecrated and destroyed	Dan. 9:2; Matt. 24:15; 2 Thess. 2:4; Rev. 17:18
Ezekiel's (Millennial) Temple	Millennium	Envisioned by the prophet Ezekiel To be built by the Messiah during His millennial reign	Ezek. 40:1—42:20; Zech. 6:12, 13
The Eternal Temple of His Presence	The Eternal Kingdom	The greatest temple of all ("The Lord God Almighty and the Lamb are its temple") A spiritual temple	Rev. 21:22; Rev. 22:1-21

The temple (Gk. *hieron*) is a place of worship, a sacred or holy space built primarily for the national worship of God.

See also charts on The Plan of the Tabernacle; The Plan of Solomon's Temple; The Plan for Ezekiel's Temple; The Plan of Herod's Temple.

any of it; they may not alienate this best *part* of the land, for *it is* holy to the LORD.

15"The five thousand *cubits* in width that remain, along the edge of the twenty-five thousand, shall be for general use by the city, for dwellings and common-land; and the city shall be in the center. 16These *shall be* its measurements: the north side four thousand five hundred *cubits,* the south side four thousand five hundred, the east side four thousand five hundred, and the west side four thousand five hundred. 17The common-land of the city shall be: to the north two hundred and fifty *cubits,* to the south two hundred and fifty, to the east two hundred and fifty, and to the west two hundred and fifty. 18The rest of the length, alongside the district of the holy *section, shall be*

ten thousand *cubits* to the east and ten thousand to the west. It shall be adjacent to the district of the holy *section,* and its produce shall be food for the workers of the city. [19]The workers of the city, from all the tribes of Israel, shall cultivate it. [20]The entire district *shall be* twenty-five thousand *cubits* by twenty-five thousand *cubits,* foursquare. You shall set apart the holy district with the property of the city.

[21]"The rest *shall belong* to the prince, on one side and on the other of the holy district and of the city's property, next to the twenty-five thousand *cubits* of the *holy* district as far as the eastern border, and westward next to the twenty-five thousand as far as the western border, adjacent to the *tribal* portions; *it shall belong* to the prince. It shall be the holy district, and the sanctuary of the temple *shall be* in the center. [22]Moreover, apart from the possession of the Levites and the possession of the city *which are* in the midst of what *belongs* to the prince, *the area* between the border of Judah and the border of Benjamin shall belong to the prince.

[23]"As for the rest of the tribes, from the east side to the west, Benjamin *shall have* one *section;* [24]by the border of Benjamin, from the east side to the west, Simeon *shall have* one *section;* [25]by the border of Simeon, from the east side to the west, Issachar *shall have* one *section;* [26]by the border of Issachar, from the east side to the west, Zebulun *shall have* one *section;* [27]by the border of Zebulun, from the east side to the west, Gad *shall have* one *section;* [28]by the border of Gad, on the south side, toward the South,[a] the border shall be from Tamar *to* the waters of Meribah *by* Kadesh, along the brook to the Great Sea. [29]This *is* the land which you shall divide by lot as an inheritance among the tribes of Israel, and these *are* their portions," says the Lord GOD.

The Gates of the City and Its Name

[30]"These *are* the exits of the city. On the north side, measuring four thousand five hundred *cubits* [31](the gates of the city *shall be* named after the tribes of Israel), the three gates northward: one gate for Reuben, one gate for Judah, and one gate for Levi; [32]on the east side, four thousand five hundred *cubits,* three gates: one gate for Joseph, one gate for Benjamin, and one gate for Dan; [33]on the south side, measuring four thousand five hundred *cubits,* three gates: one gate for Simeon, one gate for Issachar, and one gate for Zebulun; [34]on the west side, four thousand five hundred *cubits* with their three gates: one gate for Gad, one gate for Asher, and one gate for Naphtali. [35]All the way around *shall be* eighteen thousand *cubits;* and the name of the city from *that* day *shall be:* THE LORD *IS* THERE."[a]

···················
48:28 [a]Hebrew *Negev*   **48:35** [a]Hebrew *YHWH Shammah*

48:28 See Ezekiel 47:19, note.

48:31–35 John's description of the gates leading into the heavenly Jerusalem in Revelation 21 compares to Ezekiel's vision.

48:35 This title of the city provides assurance that God has fulfilled His covenant promise to dwell with His people (see Ex. 6:7; 29:45, 46).

Daniel

AUTHOR

The author is Daniel (Heb., lit. "God is my judge"), a contemporary of Jeremiah and Ezekiel, who was taken into Exile in Babylon along with other young men of high birth. The internal evidence of the book supports the authorship of Daniel (see Dan. 8:1; 9:2, 20; 10:2). Additionally, Jesus assumed the authenticity of Daniel's authorship and his prophecies (Matt. 24:15). Daniel's authorship was essentially unquestioned, except for Porphyry in the third century, until higher criticism appeared in the seventeenth century.

Daniel was probably in his late teens when he and his friends were taken to Babylon to serve in Nebuchadnezzar's court, possibly in 605 B.C. during the first of several deportations. Additional deportations followed in 597 B.C. and 586 B.C.

DATE

For most of Christian history, biblical scholars proposed that Daniel wrote the book during his own lifetime. Events recorded in the book span the period between 605 and 536 B.C., the third year of Cyrus' reign. His book was most likely completed by the year 530 B.C.

Although some contend that the Book of Daniel was written during the second century B.C. (Maccabean Period), recent archaeological discoveries strongly support a sixth century date for the writing of Daniel (see also Dan. 5:31, note).

BACKGROUND

SETTING: Because of its geographical location, the land occupied by God's chosen people was constantly the target of conquest. For many years Judah was threatened by the Assyrians. Then finally it was conquered by the Babylonians under Nebuchadnezzar. Promising youth, of royal lineage or prominent families, were trained for service in the government of the Babylonian Empire to serve as advisers to the king regarding the customs and beliefs of the different people in his empire. The book was written in Babylon, where Daniel spent all of his adult life in the service of three different rulers. The events recorded by Daniel span the time from 605 B.C. into the third year of the reign of King Cyrus the Great of Persia (536 B.C.).

PURPOSE: The events recorded and prophesied in the Book of Daniel encouraged and comforted the Jews of Daniel's day. Though they were defeated and scattered in Exile, their God was still in control of history. To those who served other gods, the message of the sovereignty of the God of Israel over all other gods was clearly delivered.

RELATIONSHIP TO SECULAR HISTORY: During the period of the events recorded in Daniel, the Babylonian Empire reached its height, began its decline, then fell to the Medo-Persian army under Cyrus. Many of the events recorded in Daniel are corroborated in secular records of the same period.

LITERARY CHARACTERISTICS: Interestingly, the Book of Daniel is written in two languages: Aramaic (Dan. 2:4—7:28) and Hebrew (Dan. 1:1—2:4; 8:1—12:13). Aramaic was the official and legal language of the empire. Even now official Jewish documents are written in Aramaic.

THEMES

The book is generally divided into two major sections. The first section records stories of Daniel and his friends and is primarily historical narrative. The second half features the dreams and visions of the future and is primarily predictive prophecy. The Book of Daniel belongs to apocalyptic (Gk. *apokalupsis,* lit. "revelation" or "disclosure") literature, the contents of which concern "revelations," especially those communicated through dreams and visions or symbols.

One cannot read the Book of Daniel without recognizing the clear message that Daniel's God is sovereign and His kingdom everlasting. He rules over the events of individual lives, and He is sovereign over all history. That message not only comforted and strengthened the Jews in Daniel's day, it has also provided comfort and strength through the generations for the uncertainties of every age.

OUTLINE

I. Daniel's Life and Work in Babylon (1:1—6:28)
  A. Nebuchadnezzar's capture of Jerusalem and deportation of promising youth to Babylon (1:1–21)
  B. Daniel's interpretation of Nebuchadnezzar's dream (2:1–49)
  C. The preservation of Daniel's three friends in the fiery furnace (3:1–30)
  D. Daniel's interpretation of Nebuchadnezzar's second dream (4:1–37)
  E. Daniel's interpretation of the handwriting on the wall (5:1–31)
  F. Daniel's survival of the plot against his life and deliverance from the lion's den (6:1–28)

II. Daniel's Prophecies Concerning Israel and the End of Time (7:1—12:13)
  A. Daniel's vision of the four beasts (7:1–28)
  B. The vision of the ram and goat (8:1–27)
  C. Daniel's prayer for his people (9:1–27)
  D. The vision by the Tigris River (10:1–21)
  E. Israel's suffering between opposing armies of warring kingdoms (11:1–45)
  F. Daniel's prophecy of the end of time (12:1–13)

Daniel and His Friends Obey God

1 In the third year of the reign of Jehoiakim king of Judah, Nebuchadnezzar king of Babylon came to Jerusalem and besieged it. ²And the Lord gave Jehoiakim king of Judah into his hand, with some of the articles of the house of God, which he carried into the land of Shinar to the house of his god; and he brought the articles into the treasure house of his god.

³Then the king instructed Ashpenaz, the master of his eunuchs, to bring some of the children of Israel and some of the king's descendants and some of the nobles, ⁴young men in whom *there was* no blemish, but good-looking, gifted in all wisdom, possessing knowledge and quick to understand, who *had* ability to serve in the king's palace, and whom they might teach the language and literature of the Chaldeans. ⁵And the king appointed for them a daily provision of the king's delicacies and of the wine which he drank, and three years of training for them, so that at the end of *that time* they might serve before the king. ⁶Now from among those of the sons of Judah were Daniel, Hananiah, Mishael, and Azariah. ⁷To them the chief of the eunuchs gave names: he gave Daniel *the name* Belteshazzar; to Hananiah, Shadrach; to Mishael, Meshach; and to Azariah, Abed-Nego.

⁸But Daniel purposed in his heart that he would not defile himself with the portion of the king's delicacies, nor with the wine which he drank; therefore he requested of the chief of the eunuchs that he might not defile himself. ⁹Now God had brought Daniel into the favor and goodwill of the chief of the eunuchs. ¹⁰And the chief of the eunuchs said to Daniel, "I fear my lord the king, who has appointed your food and drink. For why should he see your faces looking worse than the young men who *are* your age? Then you would endanger my head before the king."

¹¹So Daniel said to the steward[a] whom the chief of the eunuchs had set over Daniel, Hananiah, Mishael, and Azariah, ¹²"Please test your servants for ten days, and let them give us vegetables to eat and water to drink. ¹³Then let our appearance be examined before you, and the appearance of the young men who eat the portion of the king's delicacies; and as you see fit, *so* deal with your servants." ¹⁴So he consented with them in this matter, and tested them ten days.

¹⁵And at the end of ten days their features appeared better and fatter in flesh than all the young men who ate the portion of the king's delicacies. ¹⁶Thus the steward took away their portion of delicacies and the wine that they were to drink, and gave them vegetables.

¹⁷As for these four young men, God gave them knowledge and skill in all literature and wisdom; and Daniel had understanding in all visions and dreams.

¹⁸Now at the end of the days, when the king had said that they should be brought in, the chief of the eunuchs brought them in before Nebuchadnezzar. ¹⁹Then the king interviewed[a] them, and among them all none was found like Daniel, Hananiah, Mishael, and Azariah; therefore they served before the king. ²⁰And in all matters of wisdom *and* understanding about which the king examined them, he found them ten times better than all the magicians *and* astrologers who *were* in all his realm. ²¹Thus Daniel continued until the first year of King Cyrus.

Nebuchadnezzar's Dream

2 Now in the second year of Nebuchadnezzar's reign, Nebuchadnezzar had dreams; and his spirit was *so* troubled that his sleep left him. ²Then the

•••••••••••••••••••

1:11 ªHebrew *Melzar*, also in verse 16   1:19 ªLiterally *talked with them*

1:1 Daniel dates Nebuchadnezzar's siege of Jerusalem as the third year of Jehoiakim's reign over Judah. Jeremiah, the fourth year of Jehoiakim's reign (Jer. 25:1). This difference is explained by the variation in the Babylonian and Judean systems of dating a king's reign. In Judah, the year of accession to the throne was counted as the first year; in Babylon it was not.

1:2 Removing some of the articles of the house of God and taking them to "the treasure house of his god" was symbolic of the supposedly superior strength of Nebuchadnezzar's god over the God of Israel. The act introduces the primary theme of the Book of Daniel—the sovereignty of God.

1:4 Training promising youth, as Daniel and his friends, from conquered nations was common in Nebuchadnezzar's reign. No mention is made of Daniel's parents who may not have been taken to Babylon. To suggest that these parents had prepared their children well for such times of testing, is not unreasonable speculation since their sons remained faithful to God. "Chaldeans" is another reference for the Babylonians as a whole. In this book it is also used to refer to pagan priests

who practiced the old traditions of astrology and classical Babylonian philosophy.

1:6, 7 All four names of the Jewish youth contained some form or variation of the Hebrew names for God—Daniel, "God is my judge"; Mishael, "Who is like God?"; Hananiah, *"Yahweh is gracious"*; Azariah, *"Yahweh is my helper."* Their new Babylonian names contained some reference to pagan gods. In spite of pagan surroundings and new names, these youth had clear understandings of who they were and where their loyalties belonged (see Is. 45, Naming of Children).

1:8 Daniel did not want to defile himself by eating the type of food that was unclean or what had been offered to pagan idols before being put on the king's table (see Lev. 10, Clean vs. Unclean). Eating the food offered to a pagan god was an indication of loyalty to that god. We must marvel at the deep commitment to the faith of these young men that enabled them to take the stands they took. Perhaps these young men bore testimony to the faithfulness of mothers and fathers who ingrained in them a deep understanding of the central issues of obedience and faithfulness.

king gave the command to call the magicians, the astrologers, the sorcerers, and the Chaldeans to tell the king his dreams. So they came and stood before the king. ³And the king said to them, "I have had a dream, and my spirit is anxious to know the dream."

⁴Then the Chaldeans spoke to the king in Aramaic,ᵃ "O king, live forever! Tell your servants the dream, and we will give the interpretation."

⁵The king answered and said to the Chaldeans, "My decision is firm: if you do not make known the dream to me, and its interpretation, you shall be cut in pieces, and your houses shall be made an ash heap. ⁶However, if you tell the dream and its interpretation, you shall receive from me gifts, rewards, and great honor. Therefore tell me the dream and its interpretation."

⁷They answered again and said, "Let the king tell his servants the dream, and we will give its interpretation."

⁸The king answered and said, "I know for certain that you would gain time, because you see that my decision is firm: ⁹if you do not make known the dream to me, *there is only* one decree for you! For you have agreed to speak lying and corrupt words before me till the time has changed. Therefore tell me the dream, and I shall know that you can give me its interpretation."

¹⁰The Chaldeans answered the king, and said, "There is not a man on earth who can tell the king's matter; therefore no king, lord, or ruler has *ever* asked such things of any magician, astrologer, or Chaldean. ¹¹*It is* a difficult thing that the king requests, and there is no other who can tell it to the king except the gods, whose dwelling is not with flesh."

¹²For this reason the king was angry and very furious, and gave the command to destroy all the wise *men* of Babylon. ¹³So the decree went out, and they began killing the wise *men;* and they sought Daniel and his companions, to kill *them.*

God Reveals Nebuchadnezzar's Dream

¹⁴Then with counsel and wisdom Daniel answered Arioch, the captain of the king's guard, who had gone out to kill the wise *men* of Babylon; ¹⁵he answered and said to Arioch the king's captain, "Why is the decree from the king so urgent?" Then Arioch made the decision known to Daniel.

¹⁶So Daniel went in and asked the king to give him time, that he might tell the king the interpretation. ¹⁷Then Daniel went to his house, and made the decision known to Hananiah, Mishael, and Azariah, his companions, ¹⁸that they might seek mercies from the God of heaven concerning this secret, so that Daniel and his companions might not perish with the rest of the wise *men* of Babylon. ¹⁹Then the secret was revealed to Daniel in a night vision. So Daniel blessed the God of heaven.

²⁰Daniel answered and said:

"Blessed be the name of God forever and ever,
    For wisdom and might are His.
²¹And He changes the times and the seasons;
    He removes kings and raises up kings;
    He gives wisdom to the wise
    And knowledge to those who have
        understanding.
²²He reveals deep and secret things;
    He knows what *is* in the darkness,
    And light dwells with Him.

²³"I thank You and praise You,
    O God of my fathers;
    You have given me wisdom and might,
    And have now made known to me what we
        asked of You,
    For You have made known to us the king's
        demand."

2:4 ᵃThe original language of Daniel 2:4b through **7:28** is Aramaic.

2:2 Dreams were considered important for foretelling the future and communicating the will of the gods in ancient cultures. Great effort was therefore expended in the proper interpretation of dreams, and many books and formulas were used specifically in the interpretation of dreams. The chief responsibilities of the magicians, sorcerers, and astrologers in the king's court included interpreting the meaning of the king's dreams. Although not every dream was thought to be from God, dreams often revealed the future to God's people. Symbolic meanings had to be interpreted carefully. There is no indication that Nebuchadnezzar's behavior was altered by this dream, though it is obvious he considered the understanding of the dream's meaning important.

2:23 A personal devotional life was modeled by Daniel so that he "purposed in his heart that he would not defile himself" with the riches and delicacies offered to him by the king (Dan. 1:8–17). He openly refrained from these luxuries offered to him, exhibiting the strength of his convictions. As a result God gave Daniel and his friends—Shadrach, Meshach, and Abed-

nego—"knowledge and skill in all literature and wisdom." To Daniel he also gave understanding in visions and dreams.

One of Daniel's foremost lifestyle choices was a decision to pray and give thanks to God—which he had done three times a day since his "early days" (Dan. 6:10). Daniel kept this personal devotional commitment even in the face of a royal decree that sought to prohibit the worship of *Yahweh* (Dan. 6:3–5). Daniel was also quick to ask for God's wisdom, to seek the counsel of godly advisers, and to praise God for the revelations of His wisdom. Daniel's life exhibited a commitment to hearing and knowing God's Word, then living it out in practical ways. Jesus taught this same pattern: hearing and doing (Matt. 7:24).

Devotion to knowing and doing the work of God—refraining from being pulled into the sinfulness of the world—enables one to inherit the grace, love, and wisdom that God offers those who give themselves totally to Him (Matt. 22:37; see Matt. 6:16–18, note; 6, Priorities; Rom. 10, Access to God).

Daniel Explains the Dream

²⁴Therefore Daniel went to Arioch, whom the king had appointed to destroy the wise *men* of Babylon. He went and said thus to him: "Do not destroy the wise *men* of Babylon; take me before the king, and I will tell the king the interpretation."

²⁵Then Arioch quickly brought Daniel before the king, and said thus to him, "I have found a man of the captives[a] of Judah, who will make known to the king the interpretation."

²⁶The king answered and said to Daniel, whose name *was* Belteshazzar, "Are you able to make known to me the dream which I have seen, and its interpretation?"

²⁷Daniel answered in the presence of the king, and said, "The secret which the king has demanded, the wise *men*, the astrologers, the magicians, and the soothsayers cannot declare to the king. ²⁸But there is a God in heaven who reveals secrets, and He has made known to King Nebuchadnezzar what will be in the latter days. Your dream, and the visions of your head upon your bed, were these: ²⁹As for you, O king, thoughts came *to* your *mind while* on your bed, *about* what would come to pass after this; and He who reveals secrets has made known to you what will be. ³⁰But as for me, this secret has not been revealed to me because I have more wisdom than anyone living, but for *our* sakes who make known the interpretation to the king, and that you may know the thoughts of your heart.

³¹"You, O king, were watching; and behold, a great image! This great image, whose splendor *was* excellent, stood before you; and its form *was* awesome. ³²This image's head *was* of fine gold, its chest and arms of silver, its belly and thighs[a] of bronze, ³³its legs of iron, its feet partly of iron and partly of clay.[a] ³⁴You watched while a stone was cut out without hands, which struck the image on its feet of iron and clay, and broke them in pieces. ³⁵Then the iron, the clay, the bronze, the silver, and the gold were crushed together, and became like chaff from the summer threshing floors; the wind carried them away so that no trace of them was found. And the stone that struck the image

became a great mountain and filled the whole earth.

³⁶"This *is* the dream. Now we will tell the interpretation of it before the king. ³⁷You, O king, *are* a king of kings. For the God of heaven has given you a kingdom, power, strength, and glory; ³⁸and wherever the children of men dwell, or the beasts of the field and the birds of the heaven, He has given *them* into your hand, and has made you ruler over them all—you *are* this head of gold. ³⁹But after you shall arise another kingdom inferior to yours; then another, a third kingdom of bronze, which shall rule over all the earth. ⁴⁰And the fourth kingdom shall be as strong as iron, inasmuch as iron breaks in pieces and shatters everything; and like iron that crushes, *that kingdom* will break in pieces and crush all the others. ⁴¹Whereas you saw the feet and toes, partly of potter's clay and partly of iron, the kingdom shall be divided; yet the strength of the iron shall be in it, just as you saw the iron mixed with ceramic clay. ⁴²And *as* the toes of the feet *were* partly of iron and partly of clay, *so* the kingdom shall be partly strong and partly fragile. ⁴³As you saw iron mixed with ceramic clay, they will mingle with the seed of men; but they will not adhere to one another, just as iron does not mix with clay. ⁴⁴And in the days of these kings the God of heaven will set up a kingdom which shall never be destroyed; and the kingdom shall not be left to other people; it shall break in pieces and consume all these kingdoms, and it shall stand forever. ⁴⁵Inasmuch as you saw that the stone was cut out of the mountain without hands, and that it broke in pieces the iron, the bronze, the clay, the silver, and the gold—the great God has made known to the king what will come to pass after this. The dream is certain, and its interpretation is sure."

Daniel and His Friends Promoted

⁴⁶Then King Nebuchadnezzar fell on his face, prostrate before Daniel, and commanded that they should present an offering and incense to him. ⁴⁷The king answered Daniel, and said, "Truly

---

2:25 [a]Literally *of the sons of the captivity*   2:32 [a]Or *sides*   2:33 [a]Or *baked clay*, and so in verses 34, 35, and 42

2:31–45 In interpreting the dream, Daniel identified Nebuchadnezzar as the head of gold. The succeeding kingdoms were not specifically identified in this dream or its interpretation, but subsequent dreams and visions added additional and more specific identifying details. Scholars who accept a 6th century B.C. date of authorship take this dream as predictive and generally identify the four kingdoms as Babylon, the Medo-Persian Empire, Greece, and Rome (see chart, Dreams and Visions).

2:43 Will mingle with the seed of men is a probable reference to marriages, for political purposes, between stronger politi-

cal families and weaker ones. These alliances would prove to be unstable, just as the iron and clay mixture was unstable.

2:44, 45 For all the value and strength represented by the metals in the image, they were neither enduring nor strong when compared with the stone representing the kingdom of God, which overrules all earthly powers and endures forever.

2:47 Though Nebuchadnezzar made this statement about Daniel's God, remember that as a polytheist (worshiper of many gods), the king could easily add one more deity to the pantheon of gods he worshiped.

When we pray, we talk to God; but when we read His Word, He talks to us. As our "listening" skills improve, so do our "conversation" skills.

Joy P. Gage

your God *is* the God of gods, the Lord of kings, and a revealer of secrets, since you could reveal this secret." [48]Then the king promoted Daniel and gave him many great gifts; and he made him ruler over the whole province of Babylon, and chief administrator over all the wise *men* of Babylon. [49]Also Daniel petitioned the king, and he set Shadrach, Meshach, and Abed-Nego over the affairs of the province of Babylon; but Daniel *sat* in the gate[a] of the king.

The Image of Gold

3 Nebuchadnezzar the king made an image of gold, whose height *was* sixty cubits *and* its width six cubits. He set it up in the plain of Dura, in the province of Babylon. [2]And King Nebuchadnezzar sent *word* to gather together the satraps, the administrators, the governors, the counselors, the treasurers, the judges, the magistrates, and all the officials of the provinces, to come to the dedication of the image which King Nebuchadnezzar had set up. [3]So the satraps, the administrators, the governors, the counselors, the treasurers, the judges, the magistrates, and all the officials of the provinces gathered together for the dedication of the image that King Nebuchadnezzar had set up; and they stood before the image that Nebuchadnezzar had set up. [4]Then a herald cried aloud: "To you it is commanded, O peoples, nations, and languages, [5]*that* at the time you hear the sound of the horn, flute, harp, lyre, *and* psaltery, in symphony with all kinds of music, you shall fall down and worship the gold image that King Nebuchadnezzar has set up; [6]and whoever does not fall down and worship shall be cast immediately into the midst of a burning fiery furnace."

[7]So at that time, when all the people heard the

sound of the horn, flute, harp, *and* lyre, in symphony with all kinds of music, all the people, nations, and languages fell down *and* worshiped the gold image which King Nebuchadnezzar had set up.

Daniel's Friends Disobey the King

[8]Therefore at that time certain Chaldeans came forward and accused the Jews. [9]They spoke and said to King Nebuchadnezzar, "O king, live forever! [10]You, O king, have made a decree that everyone who hears the sound of the horn, flute, harp, lyre, *and* psaltery, in symphony with all kinds of music, shall fall down and worship the gold image; [11]and whoever does not fall down and worship shall be cast into the midst of a burning fiery furnace. [12]There are certain Jews whom you have set over the affairs of the province of Babylon: Shadrach, Meshach, and Abed-Nego; these men, O king, have not paid due regard to you. They do not serve your gods or worship the gold image which you have set up."

[13]Then Nebuchadnezzar, in rage and fury, gave the command to bring Shadrach, Meshach, and Abed-Nego. So they brought these men before the king. [14]Nebuchadnezzar spoke, saying to them, "*Is it* true, Shadrach, Meshach, and Abed-Nego, *that* you do not serve my gods or worship the gold image which I have set up? [15]Now if you are ready at the time you hear the sound of the horn, flute, harp, lyre, *and* psaltery, in symphony with all kinds of music, and you fall down and worship the image which I have made, *good!* But if you do not worship, you shall be cast immediately into the midst of a burning fiery furnace. And who *is* the god who will deliver you from my hands?"

[16]Shadrach, Meshach, and Abed-Nego answered

2:49 [a]That is, the king's court

3:1–7 Nebuchadnezzar's action in making an image of gold, 90 feet high and 9 feet wide, is indicative of both his own arrogance and his lack of understanding of Daniel's God. He may have intended the image to be symbolic of himself. On the other hand, since verse 3 indicates that all the government officials from across the empire were summoned, he might have been trying to unify all the various nations under his rule by imposing a common religion. As is generally the case with idolatry, the idol served the goals and purposes of the one who made it.

3:5, 7 The use of three Greek words in the listing of musical instruments does not indicate that the book was written some time after the conquests of Alexander the Great. Commercial

trading activities by the Greeks were prevalent throughout the Middle East from the 8th century B.C. onward. That various Greek musical instruments would have been known by their Greek names in Babylon in the 6th century is entirely reasonable.

3:9 O, king, live forever was not a prayer that the king would indeed live forever, but rather a typical greeting.

3:12 The three Jewish youth obeyed God's command, even at the risk of their lives (Ex. 20:3–5). Their reply in Daniel 3:17, 18 is a powerful testimony to their faith in God and their willingness to trust His will, regardless of the cost.

and said to the king, "O Nebuchadnezzar, we have no need to answer you in this matter. [17]If that *is* the case, our God whom we serve is able to deliver us from the burning fiery furnace, and He will deliver *us* from your hand, O king. [18]But if not, let it be known to you, O king, that we do not serve your gods, nor will we worship the gold image which you have set up."

Saved in Fiery Trial

[19]Then Nebuchadnezzar was full of fury, and the expression on his face changed toward Shadrach, Meshach, and Abed-Nego. He spoke and commanded that they heat the furnace seven times more than it was usually heated. [20]And he commanded certain mighty men of valor who *were* in his army to bind Shadrach, Meshach, and Abed-Nego, *and* cast *them* into the burning fiery furnace. [21]Then these men were bound in their coats, their trousers, their turbans, and their *other* garments, and were cast into the midst of the burning fiery furnace. [22]Therefore, because the king's command was urgent, and the furnace exceedingly hot, the flame of the fire killed those men who took up Shadrach, Meshach, and Abed-Nego. [23]And these three men, Shadrach, Meshach, and Abed-Nego, fell down bound into the midst of the burning fiery furnace.

[24]Then King Nebuchadnezzar was astonished; and he rose in haste *and* spoke, saying to his counselors, "Did we not cast three men bound into the midst of the fire?"

They answered and said to the king, "True, O king."

[25]"Look!" he answered, "I see four men loose, walking in the midst of the fire; and they are not hurt, and the form of the fourth is like the Son of God."[a]

Nebuchadnezzar Praises God

[26]Then Nebuchadnezzar went near the mouth of the burning fiery furnace *and* spoke, saying, "Shadrach, Meshach, and Abed-Nego, servants of the Most High God, come out, and come *here*." Then Shadrach, Meshach, and Abed-Nego came from the midst of the fire. [27]And the satraps, administrators, governors, and the king's counselors gathered together, and they saw these men on whose bodies the fire had no power; the hair of their head was not singed nor were their garments affected, and the smell of fire was not on them.

[28]Nebuchadnezzar spoke, saying, "Blessed be the God of Shadrach, Meshach, and Abed-Nego, who sent His Angel[a] and delivered His servants who trusted in Him, and they have frustrated the king's word, and yielded their bodies, that they should not serve nor worship any god except their own God! [29]Therefore I make a decree that any people, nation, or language which speaks anything amiss against the God of Shadrach, Meshach, and Abed-Nego shall be cut in pieces, and their houses shall be made an ash heap; because there is no other God who can deliver like this."

[30]Then the king promoted Shadrach, Meshach, and Abed-Nego in the province of Babylon.

Nebuchadnezzar's Second Dream

4 Nebuchadnezzar the king,

To all peoples, nations, and languages that dwell in all the earth:

Peace be multiplied to you.

[2]I thought it good to declare the signs and wonders that the Most High God has worked for me.

[3]How great *are* His signs,
And how mighty His wonders!
His kingdom *is* an everlasting kingdom,
And His dominion *is* from generation to generation.

[4]I, Nebuchadnezzar, was at rest in my house, and flourishing in my palace. [5]I saw a dream which made me afraid, and the thoughts on my bed and the visions of my head troubled me. [6]Therefore I issued a decree to bring in all the wise *men* of Babylon before me, that they might make known to me the interpretation of the dream. [7]Then the magicians, the astrologers, the Chaldeans, and the soothsayers came in, and I told them the dream; but they did not make known to me its interpretation. [8]But at last Daniel came before me (his name *is* Belteshazzar, according to the

•••••••••••••••••••
3:25 [a]Or *a son of the gods* **3:28** [a]Or *angel*

3:25–30 Nebuchadnezzar is astonished and forced to admit that there is a "Most High God" who is even more powerful than he is.

4:1–37 Another disquieting dream caused Nebuchadnezzar to call for his astrologers and magicians, who once again proved inadequate to tell him what the dream meant. Then Daniel was called to explain the vision. Despite having seen with his own eyes the power of God in the deliverance of the three Jewish youth from the fiery furnace, Nebuchadnezzar still did not personally recognize the limits of his own power and intelligence. After being warned that "the Most High rules in the kingdom of men" and "gives it to whomever He will," the king endured the painful humiliation of insanity before he finally acknowledged the sovereignty of the God of Israel over the affairs of humanity.

name of my god; in him *is* the Spirit of the Holy God), and I told the dream before him, *saying:* ⁹"Belteshazzar, chief of the magicians, because I know that the Spirit of the Holy God *is* in you, and no secret troubles you, explain to me the visions of my dream that I have seen, and its interpretation.

¹⁰"These *were* the visions of my head *while* on my bed:

I was looking, and behold,
A tree in the midst of the earth,
And its height was great.
¹¹The tree grew and became strong;
Its height reached to the heavens,
And it could be seen to the ends of all the earth.
¹²Its leaves *were* lovely,
Its fruit abundant,
And in it *was* food for all.
The beasts of the field found shade under it,
The birds of the heavens dwelt in its branches,
And all flesh was fed from it.

¹³"I saw in the visions of my head *while* on my bed, and there was a watcher, a holy one, coming down from heaven. ¹⁴He cried aloud and said thus:

'Chop down the tree and cut off its branches,
Strip off its leaves and scatter its fruit.
Let the beasts get out from under it,
And the birds from its branches.
¹⁵Nevertheless leave the stump and roots in the earth,
Bound with a band of iron and bronze,
In the tender grass of the field.
Let it be wet with the dew of heaven,
And *let* him graze with the beasts
On the grass of the earth.
¹⁶Let his heart be changed from *that of* a man,
Let him be given the heart of a beast,
And let seven timesᵃ pass over him.

¹⁷'This decision *is* by the decree of the watchers,
And the sentence by the word of the holy ones,
In order that the living may know
That the Most High rules in the kingdom of men,
Gives it to whomever He will,
And sets over it the lowest of men.'

¹⁸"This dream I, King Nebuchadnezzar, have seen. Now you, Belteshazzar, declare its interpretation, since all the wise *men* of my kingdom are not able to make known to me the interpretation; but you *are* able, for the Spirit of the Holy God *is* in you."

Daniel Explains the Second Dream

¹⁹Then Daniel, whose name *was* Belteshazzar, was astonished for a time, and his thoughts troubled him. *So* the king spoke, and said, "Belteshazzar, do not let the dream or its interpretation trouble you." Belteshazzar answered and said, "My lord, *may* the dream concern those who hate you, and its interpretation concern your enemies!

²⁰"The tree that you saw, which grew and became strong, whose height reached to the heavens and which *could be* seen by all the earth, ²¹whose leaves *were* lovely and its fruit abundant, in which *was* food for all, under which the beasts of the field dwelt, and in whose branches the birds of the heaven had their home— ²²it *is* you, O king, who have grown and become strong; for your greatness has grown and reaches to the heavens, and your dominion to the end of the earth.

²³"And inasmuch as the king saw a watcher, a holy one, coming down from heaven and saying, 'Chop down the tree and destroy it, but leave its stump and roots in the earth, *bound* with a band of iron and bronze in the tender grass of the field; let it be wet with the dew of heaven, and let him graze with the beasts of the field, till seven times pass over him'; ²⁴this is the interpretation, O king, and this is the decree of the Most High, which has come upon my lord the king: ²⁵They shall drive you from men, your dwelling shall be with the beasts of the field, and they shall make you eat grass like oxen. They shall wet you with the dew of heaven, and seven times shall pass over you, till you know that the Most High rules in the kingdom of men, and gives it to whomever He chooses.

²⁶"And inasmuch as they gave the command to leave the stump *and* roots of the tree, your kingdom shall be assured to you, after you come to know that Heaven rules. ²⁷Therefore, O king, let my advice be acceptable to you; break off your sins by *being* righteous, and your iniquities by showing mercy to *the* poor.

4:16 ᵃPossibly *seven years*, and so in verses 23, 25, and 32

4:27 God's grace extends to all, as evidenced in His intervention in the life of this pagan king. Daniel pleaded with the king to change his ways, hoping that the consequences portrayed in the vision might be allayed. Apparently Nebuchadnezzar ignored Daniel's plea.

Perhaps there may be a lengthening of your prosperity."

Nebuchadnezzar's Humiliation

²⁸All *this* came upon King Nebuchadnezzar. ²⁹At the end of the twelve months he was walking about the royal palace of Babylon. ³⁰The king spoke, saying, "Is not this great Babylon, that I have built for a royal dwelling by my mighty power and for the honor of my majesty?"

³¹While the word *was still* in the king's mouth, a voice fell from heaven: "King Nebuchadnezzar, to you it is spoken: the kingdom has departed from you! ³²And they shall drive you from men, and your dwelling *shall be* with the beasts of the field. They shall make you eat grass like oxen; and seven times shall pass over you, until you know that the Most High rules in the kingdom of men, and gives it to whomever He chooses."

³³That very hour the word was fulfilled concerning Nebuchadnezzar; he was driven from men and ate grass like oxen; his body was wet with the dew of heaven till his hair had grown like eagles' *feathers* and his nails like birds' *claws.*

Nebuchadnezzar Praises God

³⁴And at the end of the time[a] I, Nebuchadnezzar, lifted my eyes to heaven, and my understanding returned to me; and I blessed the Most High and praised and honored Him who lives forever:

For His dominion *is* an everlasting dominion,
And His kingdom *is* from generation to
      generation.
³⁵All the inhabitants of the earth *are* reputed as
      nothing;
He does according to His will in the army of
      heaven
And *among* the inhabitants of the earth.
No one can restrain His hand
Or say to Him, "What have You done?"

³⁶At the same time my reason returned to me, and for the glory of my kingdom, my honor and splendor returned to me. My counselors and nobles resorted to me, I was restored to my kingdom, and excellent majesty was added to me. ³⁷Now I, Nebuchadnezzar, praise and extol and honor the King of heaven, all of whose works *are* truth, and His ways justice. And those who walk in pride He is able to put down.

Belshazzar's Feast

5 Belshazzar the king made a great feast for a thousand of his lords, and drank wine in the presence of the thousand. ²While he tasted the wine, Belshazzar gave the command to bring the gold and silver vessels which his father Nebuchadnezzar had taken from the temple which *had been* in Jerusalem, that the king and his lords, his wives, and his concubines might drink from them. ³Then they brought the gold vessels that had been taken from the temple of the house of God which *had been* in Jerusalem; and the king and his lords, his wives, and his concubines drank from them. ⁴They drank wine, and praised the gods of gold and silver, bronze and iron, wood and stone.

⁵In the same hour the fingers of a man's hand appeared and wrote opposite the lampstand on the plaster of the wall of the king's palace; and the king saw the part of the hand that wrote. ⁶Then the king's countenance changed, and his thoughts troubled him, so that the joints of his hips were loosened and his knees knocked against each other. ⁷The king cried aloud to bring in the astrologers, the Chaldeans, and the soothsayers. The king spoke, saying to the wise *men* of Babylon, "Whoever reads this writing, and tells me its interpretation, shall be clothed with purple and *have* a chain of gold around his neck; and he shall be the third ruler in the kingdom." ⁸Now all the king's wise *men* came, but they could not read the writing, or make known to the king its interpretation. ⁹Then King Belshazzar was greatly troubled,

···················

4:34 [a]Literally *days*

4:30, 31 Instead of humbling himself before the Most High, Nebuchadnezzar displayed remarkable personal arrogance. While surveying the palace and its environs, he boasted of and revelled in his own power and majesty. At that moment the judgment of God took effect by the loss of sanity, and for "seven times" the king lived like an animal, and was an outcast from humanity (v. 32). The number seven frequently signifies completeness in that the time of insanity was completed. It could also indicate seven years.

5:2 Even pagans were superstitious enough not to use articles plundered from temples. In a drunken orgy, however, Belshazzar committed a great blasphemy. During the feast, he and his guests drank from the sacred articles that Nebuchad-

nezzar had taken from the temple in Jerusalem while they praised their pagan idols (see Dan. 1:2).

5:2 The Aramaic word for "father" was also frequently used for "grandfather," "ancestor," or "predecessor." Belshazzar was the oldest son of Nabonidus, the last king of Babylon, and therefore the grandson of Nebuchadnezzar. Because Nabonidus was away on campaigns for more than half of his reign, his son Belshazzar served as co-regent in his father's absence.

5:7 Third ruler in the kingdom indicates that Belshazzar understood himself to be the second ruler, as co-regent with his father.

his countenance was changed, and his lords were astonished.

[10]The queen, because of the words of the king and his lords, came to the banquet hall. The queen spoke, saying, "O king, live forever! Do not let your thoughts trouble you, nor let your countenance change. [11]There is a man in your kingdom in whom *is* the Spirit of the Holy God. And in the days of your father, light and understanding and wisdom, like the wisdom of the gods, were found in him; and King Nebuchadnezzar your father—your father the king—made him chief of the magicians, astrologers, Chaldeans, *and* soothsayers. [12]Inasmuch as an excellent spirit, knowledge, understanding, interpreting dreams, solving riddles, and explaining enigmas[a] were found in this Daniel, whom the king named Belteshazzar, now let Daniel be called, and he will give the interpretation."

The Writing on the Wall Explained

[13]Then Daniel was brought in before the king. The king spoke, and said to Daniel, "*Are* you that Daniel who is one of the captives[a] from Judah, whom my father the king brought from Judah? [14]I have heard of you, that the Spirit of God *is* in you, and *that* light and understanding and excellent wisdom are found in you. [15]Now the wise *men*, the astrologers, have been brought in before me, that they should read this writing and make known to me its interpretation, but they could not give the interpretation of the thing. [16]And I have heard of you, that you can give interpretations and explain enigmas. Now if you can read the writing and make known to me its interpretation, you shall be clothed with purple and *have* a chain of gold around your neck, and shall be the third ruler in the kingdom."

[17]Then Daniel answered, and said before the king, "Let your gifts be for yourself, and give your rewards to another; yet I will read the writing to the king, and make known to him the interpretation. [18]O king, the Most High God gave Nebuchadnezzar your father a kingdom and majesty, glory and honor. [19]And because of the majesty that He gave him, all peoples, nations, and languages trembled and feared before him. Whomever he wished, he executed; whomever he wished, he kept alive; whomever he wished, he set up; and whomever he wished, he put down. [20]But when his heart was lifted up, and his spirit was hardened in pride, he was deposed from his kingly throne, and they took his glory from him. [21]Then he was driven from the sons of men, his heart was made like the beasts, and his dwelling *was* with the wild donkeys. They fed him with grass like oxen, and his body was wet with the dew of heaven, till he knew that the Most High God rules in the kingdom of men, and appoints over it whomever He chooses.

[22]"But you his son, Belshazzar, have not humbled your heart, although you knew all this. [23]And you have lifted yourself up against the Lord of heaven. They have brought the vessels of His house before you, and you and your lords, your wives and your concubines, have drunk wine from them. And you have praised the gods of silver and gold, bronze and iron, wood and stone, which do not see or hear or know; and the God who *holds* your breath in His hand and owns all your ways, you have not glorified. [24]Then the fingers[a] of the hand were sent from Him, and this writing was written.

[25]"And this is the inscription that was written:

MENE,[a] MENE, TEKEL,[b] UPHARSIN.[c]

[26]This *is* the interpretation of *each* word. MENE: God has numbered your kingdom, and finished it; [27]TEKEL: You have been weighed in the balances, and found wanting; [28]PERES: Your kingdom has been divided, and given to the Medes and Persians."[a] [29]Then Belshazzar gave the command, and they clothed Daniel with purple and *put* a chain of gold around his neck, and made a proclamation concerning him that he should be the third ruler in the kingdom.

Belshazzar's Fall

[30]That very night Belshazzar, king of the Chaldeans, was slain. [31]And Darius the Mede received the kingdom, *being* about sixty-two years old.

5:12 [a]Literally *untying knots,* and so in verse 16   5:13 [a]Literally *of the sons of the captivity*   5:24 [a]Literally *palm*   5:25 [a]Literally *a mina* (50 shekels) from the verb "to number"   [b]Literally *a shekel* from the verb "to weigh"   [c]Literally *and half-shekels* from the verb "to divide"   5:28 [a]Aramaic *Paras,* consonant with *Peres*

5:10 Since Belshazzar's wives and concubines were already present at the feasting (v. 2), the woman who came to the banquet hall may have been the widow of Nebuchadnezzar, or his daughter, and Belshazzar's own mother, the wife of Nabonidus.

5:22 The word for son was often used for "grandson" or "successor" in the OT. This family history made Belshazzar's own sins of pride and disobedience even more reprehensible.

5:25 Daniel interpreted these three words as roots of Aramaic

verbs. *Mene* comes from the verb "to number." *Tekel* comes from the verb "to weigh." *Upharsin* comes from the verb "to divide." While the common meaning of the verbs was well known, special insights were necessary for Daniel to apply them to the current situation.

5:30 Belshazzar was killed that very night. While the king and his officials were feasting and drinking, the city of Babylon, thought by many to be impregnable, fell to the Persians. In October 539 B.C., according to the historian Herodotus, Cyrus

The Plot Against Daniel

6 It pleased Darius to set over the kingdom one hundred and twenty satraps, to be over the whole kingdom; [2]and over these, three governors, of whom Daniel *was* one, that the satraps might give account to them, so that the king would suffer no loss. [3]Then this Daniel distinguished himself above the governors and satraps, because an excellent spirit *was* in him; and the king gave thought to setting him over the whole realm. [4]So the governors and satraps sought to find *some* charge against Daniel concerning the kingdom; but they could find no charge or fault, because he *was* faithful; nor was there any error or fault found in him. [5]Then these men said, "We shall not find any charge against this Daniel unless we find *it* against him concerning the law of his God."

[6]So these governors and satraps thronged before the king, and said thus to him: "King Darius, live forever! [7]All the governors of the kingdom, the administrators and satraps, the counselors and advisors, have consulted together to establish a royal statute and to make a firm decree, that whoever petitions any god or man for thirty days, except you, O king, shall be cast into the den of lions. [8]Now, O king, establish the decree and sign the writing, so that it cannot be changed, according to the law of the Medes and Persians, which does not alter." [9]Therefore King Darius signed the written decree.

Daniel in the Lions' Den

[10]Now when Daniel knew that the writing was signed, he went home. And in his upper room, with his windows open toward Jerusalem, he knelt down on his knees three times that day, and prayed and gave thanks before his God, as was his custom since early days. [11]Then these men assembled and found Daniel praying and making supplication before his God. [12]And they went before the king, and spoke concerning the king's decree: "Have you not signed a decree that every man who petitions any god or man within thirty days, except you, O king, shall be cast into the den of lions?"

The king answered and said, "The thing *is* true, according to the law of the Medes and Persians, which does not alter."

[13]So they answered and said before the king, "That Daniel, who is one of the captives[a] from Judah, does not show due regard for you, O king, or for the decree that you have signed, but makes his petition three times a day."

[14]And the king, when he heard *these* words, was greatly displeased with himself, and set *his* heart on Daniel to deliver him; and he labored till the going down of the sun to deliver him. [15]Then these men approached the king, and said to the king, "Know, O king, that *it is* the law of the Medes and Persians that no decree or statute which the king establishes may be changed."

[16]So the king gave the command, and they brought Daniel and cast *him* into the den of lions. *But* the king spoke, saying to Daniel, "Your God, whom you serve continually, He will deliver you." [17]Then a stone was brought and laid on the mouth of the den, and the king sealed it with his own signet ring and with the signets of his lords, that the purpose concerning Daniel might not be changed.

Daniel Saved from the Lions

[18]Now the king went to his palace and spent the night fasting; and no musicians[a] were brought before him. Also his sleep went from him. [19]Then the king arose very early in the morning and went in haste to the den of lions. [20]And when he came to the den, he cried out with a lamenting voice to Daniel. The king spoke, saying to Daniel, "Daniel, servant of the living God, has your God, whom you serve continually, been able to deliver you from the lions?"

[21]Then Daniel said to the king, "O king, live forever! [22]My God sent His angel and shut the lions' mouths, so that they have not hurt me, because I was found innocent before Him; and also, O king, I have done no wrong before you."

[23]Now the king was exceedingly glad for him,

•••••••••••••••••••

6:13 [a]Literally *of the sons of the captivity* **6:18** [a]Exact meaning unknown

---

and his forces diverted the waters from the Euphrates River and entered the city by way of the nearly dry river bed. The Cyrus Cylinder and Babylonian Chronicle agree on the invasion but attribute it to treason within, which resulted in the opening of the gates to the invaders.

5:31 Darius the Mede remains one of the unsolved mysteries in the Book of Daniel. Historical evidence is clear that the Babylonian Empire was conquered by the Persians under Cyrus. Some scholars have used Darius as evidence for a late date of writing, saying that a 6th century B.C. writer would have been aware of these historical facts (see Introduction: Date). According to this argument, whoever wrote the book in the 2nd

century B.C. simply was not an accurate historian. However, archaeological discoveries have continued to substantiate Daniel's accuracy and to support an early writing date. Use of the words "received the kingdom" leaves room for the possibility that Darius was made ruler over the conquered Babylonian territories by someone else, that is, Cyrus. Daniel was clearly aware of Cyrus (Dan. 6:28). Some scholars believe that Darius was a different name for Gubaru, who is named in some ancient texts (such as the Nabonidus Chronicle) as governor of Babylon and could well have been appointed to serve over Babylon during Cyrus' absence (see Dan. 6:1, 2); or it may be that the word "Darius" was a title meaning "the Royal One." At this point there is not enough evidence to be certain.

and commanded that they should take Daniel up out of the den. So Daniel was taken up out of the den, and no injury whatever was found on him, because he believed in his God.

Darius Honors God

24And the king gave the command, and they brought those men who had accused Daniel, and they cast *them* into the den of lions— them, their children, and their wives; and the lions overpowered them, and broke all their bones in pieces before they ever came to the bottom of the den.

25Then King Darius wrote:

To all peoples, nations, and languages that dwell in all the earth:

Peace be multiplied to you.

26I make a decree that in every dominion of my kingdom *men must* tremble and fear before the God of Daniel.

For He *is* the living God,
And steadfast forever;
His kingdom *is the one* which shall not be destroyed,
And His dominion *shall endure* to the end.
27He delivers and rescues,
And He works signs and wonders
In heaven and on earth,
Who has delivered Daniel from the power of the lions.

28So this Daniel prospered in the reign of Darius and in the reign of Cyrus the Persian.

Vision of the Four Beasts

7 In the first year of Belshazzar king of Babylon, Daniel had a dream and visions of his head *while* on his bed. Then he wrote down the dream, telling the main facts.a

2Daniel spoke, saying, "I saw in my vision by night, and behold, the four winds of heaven were stirring up the Great Sea. 3And four great beasts came up from the sea, each different from the other. 4The first *was* like a lion, and had eagle's wings. I watched till its wings were plucked off; and it was lifted up from the earth and made to stand on two feet like a man, and a man's heart was given to it.

5"And suddenly another beast, a second, like a bear. It was raised up on one side, and *had* three ribs in its mouth between its teeth. And they said thus to it: 'Arise, devour much flesh!'

6"After this I looked, and there was another, like a leopard, which had on its back four wings of a bird. The beast also had four heads, and dominion was given to it.

7"After this I saw in the night visions, and behold, a fourth beast, dreadful and terrible, exceedingly strong. It had huge iron teeth; it was devouring, breaking in pieces, and trampling the residue with its feet. It *was* different from all the beasts that *were* before it, and it had ten horns. 8I was

7:1 aLiterally *the head* (or *chief*) *of the words*

7:1 The second major section of the Book of Daniel, which features visions and dreams and their related prophecies, begins with this chapter. The first year of Belshazzar was about 553 B.C., over 50 years from Daniel's deportation from Jerusalem. The dreams and visions of these last six chapters took place during the time period covered by the first six chapters. Much of the imagery has parallels or similarities in either the Book of Ezekiel (see Ezek. 17:3) or in the Book of Revelation (see Rev. 13:12). The identification of the empires or kingdoms portrayed by the various animals has generally been less difficult than the interpretation of the events and specific times predicted for the end times. While Christians have an interest in ascertaining the meanings of these prophecies, the believer's faith is not dependent on knowing the precise events that will take place as human history moves toward conclusion. Rather, faith is based on a personal relationship with the Lord of history, and that relationship requires faithfulness and obedience now, just as in Daniel's day.

7:2–28 The sea is frequently used in biblical visions as a symbol for the nations of the world in tumult (Is. 17:12, 13); "four winds" are used to indicate the four cardinal directions— north, south, east, and west—and symbolize the whole earth. Each of the "great beasts" represents a kingdom, corresponding with the kingdoms related to Nebuchadnezzar's image. Daniel then saw a great throne room, where the God of history would deliver His judgment against the beasts, and their

kingdoms are given to "One like the Son of Man" (see chart, Dreams and Visions).

7:4 The winged lion represented the Babylonian Empire and Nebuchadnezzar. Jeremiah also used the imagery of the lion and the eagle (Jer. 49:19–22).

7:5 The bear "raised up on one side" with "three ribs in its mouth" represents the Medo-Persian Empire, with Persia as the stronger and the ribs possibly representing the primary nations it conquered: Lydia, Babylon, and Egypt.

7:6 The leopard, with wings and four heads, symbolizes a kingdom which was realized by Greek dominion under Alexander the Great, who swept through the then known world with astonishing speed and power (as with "wings"). Historians record that Alexander wept that there were no more worlds to conquer. After his death, Alexander's great empire was eventually divided among four of his generals (four heads): Seleucus, Ptolemy, Lysimachus, and Cassander.

7:7 The fourth animal, while not described by name, was "dreadful and terrible, exceedingly strong," with teeth of iron, the same metal which represented the Roman Empire in the image in Nebuchadnezzar's dream (Dan. 2:40). As that image had ten toes, this one had ten horns, representing great and unusual power (see Rev. 13:1, 2).

7:8 The message of Daniel's dreams is clear: God's kingdom will prevail over the kingdoms of earth, and it will never pass

considering the horns, and there was another horn, a little one, coming up among them, before whom three of the first horns were plucked out by the roots. And there, in this horn, *were* eyes like the eyes of a man, and a mouth speaking pompous words.

Vision of the Ancient of Days

[9]"I watched till thrones were put in place,
And the Ancient of Days was seated;
His garment *was* white as snow,
And the hair of His head *was* like pure wool.
His throne *was* a fiery flame,
Its wheels a burning fire;
[10]A fiery stream issued
And came forth from before Him.
A thousand thousands ministered to Him;
Ten thousand times ten thousand stood before Him.
The court[a] was seated,
And the books were opened.

[11]"I watched then because of the sound of the pompous words which the horn was speaking; I watched till the beast was slain, and its body destroyed and given to the burning flame. [12]As for the rest of the beasts, they had their dominion taken away, yet their lives were prolonged for a season and a time.

[13]"I was watching in the night visions,
And behold, *One* like the Son of Man,
Coming with the clouds of heaven!
He came to the Ancient of Days,
And they brought Him near before Him.
[14]Then to Him was given dominion and glory and a kingdom,
That all peoples, nations, and languages should serve Him.
His dominion *is* an everlasting dominion,
Which shall not pass away,
And His kingdom the one
Which shall not be destroyed.

Daniel's Visions Interpreted

[15]"I, Daniel, was grieved in my spirit within *my* body, and the visions of my head troubled me. [16]I came near to one of those who stood by, and asked him the truth of all this. So he told me and made

known to me the interpretation of these things: [17]'Those great beasts, which are four, *are* four kings[a] *which* arise out of the earth. [18]But the saints of the Most High shall receive the kingdom, and possess the kingdom forever, even forever and ever.'

[19]"Then I wished to know the truth about the fourth beast, which was different from all the others, exceedingly dreadful, *with* its teeth of iron and its nails of bronze, *which* devoured, broke in pieces, and trampled the residue with its feet; [20]and the ten horns that *were* on its head, and the other *horn* which came up, before which three fell, namely, that horn which had eyes and a mouth which spoke pompous words, whose appearance *was* greater than his fellows.

[21]"I was watching; and the same horn was making war against the saints, and prevailing against them, [22]until the Ancient of Days came, and a judgment was made *in favor* of the saints of the Most High, and the time came for the saints to possess the kingdom.

[23]"Thus he said:

'The fourth beast shall be
A fourth kingdom on earth,
Which shall be different from all *other* kingdoms,
And shall devour the whole earth,
Trample it and break it in pieces.
[24]The ten horns *are* ten kings
Who shall arise from this kingdom.
And another shall rise after them;
He shall be different from the first *ones,*
And shall subdue three kings.
[25]He shall speak *pompous* words against the Most High,
Shall persecute[a] the saints of the Most High,
And shall intend to change times and law.
Then *the saints* shall be given into his hand
For a time and times and half a time.

[26]'But the court shall be seated,
And they shall take away his dominion,
To consume and destroy *it* forever.
[27]Then the kingdom and dominion,

7:10 [a]Or *judgment* 7:17 [a]Representing their kingdoms (compare verse 23) 7:25 [a]Literally *wear out*

---

away. Scholars agree that some elements of this part of Daniel's vision refer to the rise and rule of the first Roman Empire, while other elements refer to a future political power. For example, it seems clear that this little horn refers to a world ruler, at some future time, who will be so powerful that he will cause great suffering to God's people and even challenge God Himself (see Dan. 11:36, 37; 2 Thess. 2:3–12; Rev. 13:5, 6).

7:9 The Ancient of Days refers to God the Father (see also

v. 13). This title expresses God's eternal existence. The kingdoms of this world will be judged by God.

7:13 The Son of Man is a designation Jesus later used of Himself (Matt. 8:20; 9:6; Mark 14:62). Rather than being like one of the beasts mentioned—lion (Dan. 7:4), bear (v. 5), leopard (v. 6)—or incomparably horrible, the divine King of Kings will come in human form; yet He will be the perfect representative of humanity. This One is the Son of Man and the Son of God—our Lord Jesus Christ. All kingdoms serve Him (Phil. 2:10).

And the greatness of the kingdoms under the
  whole heaven,
Shall be given to the people, the saints of the
  Most High.
His kingdom *is* an everlasting kingdom,
And all dominions shall serve and obey Him.'

[28]"This *is* the end of the account.[a] As for me,
Daniel, my thoughts greatly troubled me, and my
countenance changed; but I kept the matter in my
heart."

Vision of a Ram and a Goat

8 In the third year of the reign of King
Belshazzar a vision appeared *to* me—to me,
Daniel—after the one that appeared to me the first
time. [2]I saw in the vision, and it so happened while I
was looking, that I *was* in Shushan, the citadel,
which *is* in the province of Elam; and I saw in the
vision that I was by the River Ulai. [3]Then I lifted my
eyes and saw, and there, standing beside the river,
was a ram which had two horns, and the two horns
were high; but one *was* higher than the other, and
the higher *one* came up last. [4]I saw the ram pushing
westward, northward, and southward, so that no
animal could withstand him; nor *was there any* that
could deliver from his hand, but he did according to
his will and became great.

[5]And as I was considering, suddenly a male
goat came from the west, across the surface of the
whole earth, without touching the ground; and
the goat *had* a notable horn between his eyes.
[6]Then he came to the ram that had two horns,
which I had seen standing beside the river, and
ran at him with furious power. [7]And I saw him
confronting the ram; he was moved with rage
against him, attacked the ram, and broke his two
horns. There was no power in the ram to withstand him, but he cast him down to the ground

and trampled him; and there was no one that
could deliver the ram from his hand.
[8]Therefore the male goat grew very great; but
when he became strong, the large horn was broken, and in place of it four notable ones came up
toward the four winds of heaven. [9]And out of one
of them came a little horn which grew exceedingly great toward the south, toward the east, and
toward the Glorious *Land.* [10]And it grew up to the
host of heaven; and it cast down *some* of the host
and *some* of the stars to the ground, and trampled
them. [11]He even exalted *himself* as high as the
Prince of the host; and by him the daily *sacrifices*
were taken away, and the place of His sanctuary
was cast down. [12]Because of transgression, an
army was given over *to the horn* to oppose the daily
sacrifices; and he cast truth down to the ground.
He did *all this* and prospered.
[13]Then I heard a holy one speaking; and *another*
holy one said to that certain *one* who was speaking, "How long *will* the vision *be, concerning* the
daily *sacrifices* and the transgression of desolation,
the giving of both the sanctuary and the host to
be trampled underfoot?"
[14]And he said to me, "For two thousand three
hundred days;[a] then the sanctuary shall be
cleansed."

Gabriel Interprets the Vision

[15]Then it happened, when I, Daniel, had seen
the vision and was seeking the meaning, that suddenly there stood before me one having the appearance of a man. [16]And I heard a man's voice between *the banks of* the Ulai, who called, and said,
"Gabriel, make this *man* understand the vision."
[17]So he came near where I stood, and when he
came I was afraid and fell on my face; but he said

• • • • • • • • • • • • • • • • •

7:28 [a]Literally *the word*   **8:14** [a]Literally *evening-mornings*

8:1–27 The third year was about 550 B.C. The date is significant because it is the year Cyrus established the joint state of
the Medes and Persians. Beginning with this chapter, the language reverts to Hebrew, and its message relates primarily to
the Jews. The writer records the interpretation of his vision
given to him by the angel Gabriel (one of only two good angels named in the Bible). It deals with only two of the four
empires which Daniel saw in his vision (Dan. 7). The primary
focus is "the time of the end" (Dan. 8:17).

8:3, 4 The ram represents the Medo-Persian Empire (v. 20),
with the larger horn referring to the predominance of Persia.
Within a period of ten years after this vision, Cyrus had indeed
pushed "westward, northward and southward" (see Dan. 7:5,
note).

8:5–8 The male goat image represents pagan political powers.
In this vision, the male goat represents the Greek Empire
(v. 21) with Alexander the Great as its principal ruler. This empire was subsequently divided into four kingdoms after an extended power struggle by four of Alexander's generals (v. 22),
none of whom was as powerful as he.

8:9–12 The little horn mentioned here arises from the 3rd
kingdom and is therefore not identical to the one in Daniel 7,
which rose from the 4th kingdom. This one is generally accepted to symbolize Antiochus IV Epiphanes, of the Seleucid
line who took over Asia Minor, Syria, and the western part of
Alexander's empire after his death (Dan. 8:23, 24). This occurred in the 2nd century B.C., a period of much conflict in
Palestine (the "Glorious Land," v. 9) as the Jews resisted the
process of Hellenization of their land and society. History
records that, in his efforts at various times to subdue the
Jews, Antiochus was brutal and ruthless. Calling himself
"Epiphanes" (which means "God manifest"), Antiochus
stopped the daily sacrifices in the temple in Jerusalem, built
an altar there to the Greek god Jupiter, and offered swine on
the altar. Reading of the Scripture, observance of the Sabbath, and circumcision were forbidden. In his ruthlessness
against the people of God, Antiochus foreshadowed the Antichrist of the end times.

8:27 Daniel resumed his service. Though he was physically affected by the implications of the vision, it was characteristic

to me, "Understand, son of man, that the vision *refers* to the time of the end."

[18]Now, as he was speaking with me, I was in a deep sleep with my face to the ground; but he touched me, and stood me upright. [19]And he said, "Look, I am making known to you what shall happen in the latter time of the indignation; for at the appointed time the end *shall be.* [20]The ram which you saw, having the two horns—*they are* the kings of Media and Persia. [21]And the male goat *is* the kingdom[a] of Greece. The large horn that *is* between its eyes *is* the first king. [22]As for the broken *horn* and the four that stood up in its place, four kingdoms shall arise out of that nation, but not with its power.

[23]"And in the latter time of their kingdom,
　When the transgressors have reached their
　　fullness,
　A king shall arise,
　Having fierce features,
　Who understands sinister schemes.
[24]His power shall be mighty, but not by his own
　　power;
　He shall destroy fearfully,
　And shall prosper and thrive;
　He shall destroy the mighty, and *also* the holy
　　people.

[25]"Through his cunning
　He shall cause deceit to prosper under his
　　rule;[a]
　And he shall exalt *himself* in his heart.
　He shall destroy many in *their* prosperity.
　He shall even rise against the Prince of
　　princes;
　But he shall be broken without *human* means.[b]

[26]"And the vision of the evenings and mornings
　Which was told is true;
　Therefore seal up the vision,
　For *it refers* to many days *in the future.*"

[27]And I, Daniel, fainted and was sick for days; afterward I arose and went about the king's business. I was astonished by the vision, but no one understood it.

Daniel's Prayer for the People

9 In the first year of Darius the son of Ahasuerus, of the lineage of the Medes, who was made king over the realm of the Chaldeans— [2]in the first year

of his reign I, Daniel, understood by the books the number of the years *specified* by the word of the LORD through Jeremiah the prophet, that He would accomplish seventy years in the desolations of Jerusalem.

[3]Then I set my face toward the Lord God to make request by prayer and supplications, with fasting, sackcloth, and ashes. [4]And I prayed to the LORD my God, and made confession, and said, "O Lord, great and awesome God, who keeps His covenant and mercy with those who love Him, and with those who keep His commandments, [5]we have sinned and committed iniquity, we have done wickedly and rebelled, even by departing from Your precepts and Your judgments. [6]Neither have we heeded Your servants the prophets, who spoke in Your name to our kings and our princes, to our fathers and all the people of the land. [7]O Lord, righteousness *belongs* to You, but to us shame of face, as *it is* this day—to the men of Judah, to the inhabitants of Jerusalem and all Israel, those near and those far off in all the countries to which You have driven them, because of the unfaithfulness which they have committed against You.

[8]"O Lord, to us *belongs* shame of face, to our kings, our princes, and our fathers, because we have sinned against You. [9]To the Lord our God *belong* mercy and forgiveness, though we have rebelled against Him. [10]We have not obeyed the voice of the LORD our God, to walk in His laws, which He set before us by His servants the prophets. [11]Yes, all Israel has transgressed Your law, and has departed so as not to obey Your voice; therefore the curse and the oath written in the Law of Moses the servant of God have been poured out on us, because we have sinned against Him. [12]And He has confirmed His words, which He spoke against us and against our judges who judged us, by bringing upon us a great disaster; for under the whole heaven such has never been done as what has been done to Jerusalem.

[13]"As *it is* written in the Law of Moses, all this disaster has come upon us; yet we have not made our prayer before the LORD our God, that we might turn from our iniquities and understand Your truth. [14]Therefore the LORD has kept the disaster in mind, and brought it upon us; for the LORD our God *is* righteous in all the works which He does, though we have not obeyed His voice.

••

8:21 [a]Literally *king,* representing his kingdom (compare 7:17, 23)
8:25 [a]Literally *hand* [b]Literally *hand*

of Daniel's life that he "arose and went about the king's business," maintaining his habits of faithful service. Daniel, just as those in succeeding generations, was obviously bewildered over his lack of understanding of what was to come, since some of the events prophesied obviously would remain in the future. However, Daniel believed that God knew the future and controlled it. Believers have that same assurance.

9:1–19 Daniel knew Jeremiah's promise to the Jews that their captivity would last 70 years (v. 2), and he realized that the time was nearly completed. This event is dated approximately 539 B.C., during the first year of the reign of Darius (or Gubaru; v. 1; see also Dan. 5:31, note), the son of Ahasuerus (not the Persian husband of Queen Esther). He immediately began a season of prayer and fasting (see Matt. 6:16–18, note;

THE PROPHECY OF SEVENTY WEEKS

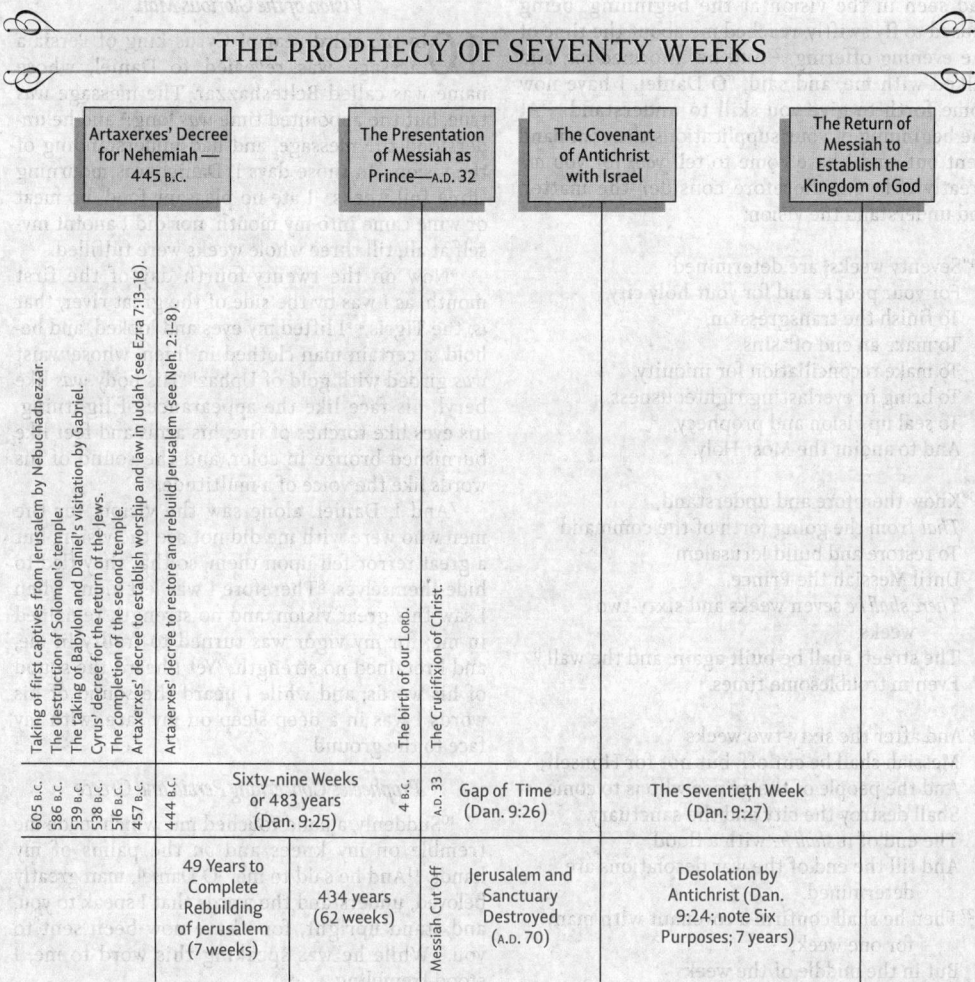

						The Presentation of Messiah as Prince—A.D. 32	The Covenant of Antichrist with Israel	The Return of Messiah to Establish the Kingdom of God

Artaxerxes' Decree for Nehemiah— 445 B.C.

Taking of first captives from Jerusalem by Nebuchadnezzar.
The destruction of Solomon's temple.
The taking of Babylon and Daniel's visitation by Gabriel.
Cyrus' decree for the return of the Jews.
The completion of the second temple.
Artaxerxes' decree to establish worship and law in Judah (see Ezra 7:13–16).
Artaxerxes' decree to restore and rebuild Jerusalem (see Neh. 2:1–8).
The birth of our LORD.
The Crucifixion of Christ.

605 B.C. 586 B.C. 539 B.C. 538 B.C. 516 B.C. 457 B.C.	444 B.C.	Sixty-nine Weeks or 483 years (Dan. 9:25)	4 B.C.	A.D. 33	Gap of Time (Dan. 9:26)	The Seventieth Week (Dan. 9:27)
		49 Years to Complete Rebuilding of Jerusalem (7 weeks)	434 years (62 weeks)	Messiah Cut Off	Jerusalem and Sanctuary Destroyed (A.D. 70)	Desolation by Antichrist (Dan. 9:24; note Six Purposes; 7 years)

15And now, O Lord our God, who brought Your people out of the land of Egypt with a mighty hand, and made Yourself a name, as *it is* this day—we have sinned, we have done wickedly!

16"O Lord, according to all Your righteousness, I pray, let Your anger and Your fury be turned away from Your city Jerusalem, Your holy mountain; because for our sins, and for the iniquities of our fathers, Jerusalem and Your people *are* a reproach to all *those* around us. 17Now therefore, our God, hear the prayer of Your servant, and his supplications, and for the Lord's sake cause Your face to shine on Your sanctuary, which is desolate. 18O my God, incline Your ear and hear; open Your eyes and see our desolations, and the city which is called by Your name; for we do not present our supplications before You because of our righteous deeds, but because of Your great mercies. 19O Lord, hear! O Lord, forgive! O Lord, listen and act! Do not delay for Your own sake, my God, for Your city and Your people are called by Your name."

The Seventy-Weeks Prophecy

20Now while I *was* speaking, praying, and confessing my sin and the sin of my people Israel, and presenting my supplication before the LORD my God for the holy mountain of my God, 21yes, while I *was* speaking in prayer, the man Gabriel, whom I

chart, Lessons from the Model Prayer). Daniel pleaded with God to remember His promise. He openly acknowledged the sinfulness of his own people. He knew that they deserved the judgment of captivity, but he also reminded God that His own

righteousness and mercy were at stake in the fulfilling of the promise.

9:21–27 God sent the angel Gabriel in response to Daniel's prayers to give Daniel "skill to understand" and to assure him

had seen in the vision at the beginning, being caused to fly swiftly, reached me about the time of the evening offering. [22]And he informed *me,* and talked with me, and said, "O Daniel, I have now come forth to give you skill to understand. [23]At the beginning of your supplications the command went out, and I have come to tell *you,* for you *are* greatly beloved; therefore consider the matter, and understand the vision:

[24]"Seventy weeks[a] are determined
For your people and for your holy city,
To finish the transgression,
To make an end of[b] sins,
To make reconciliation for iniquity,
To bring in everlasting righteousness,
To seal up vision and prophecy,
And to anoint the Most Holy.

[25]"Know therefore and understand,
That from the going forth of the command
To restore and build Jerusalem
Until Messiah the Prince,
There shall be seven weeks and sixty-two
    weeks;
The street[a] shall be built again, and the wall,[b]
Even in troublesome times.

[26]"And after the sixty-two weeks
Messiah shall be cut off, but not for Himself;
And the people of the prince who is to come
Shall destroy the city and the sanctuary.
The end of it *shall be* with a flood,
And till the end of the war desolations are
    determined.
[27]Then he shall confirm a covenant with many
    for one week;
But in the middle of the week
He shall bring an end to sacrifice and offering.
And on the wing of abominations shall be one
    who makes desolate,
Even until the consummation, which is
    determined,
Is poured out on the desolate."

Vision of the Glorious Man

10 In the third year of Cyrus king of Persia a message was revealed to Daniel, whose name was called Belteshazzar. The message *was* true, but the appointed time *was* long;[a] and he understood the message, and had understanding of the vision. [2]In those days I, Daniel, was mourning three full weeks. [3]I ate no pleasant food, no meat or wine came into my mouth, nor did I anoint myself at all, till three whole weeks were fulfilled.

[4]Now on the twenty-fourth day of the first month, as I was by the side of the great river, that is, the Tigris,[a] [5]I lifted my eyes and looked, and behold, a certain man clothed in linen, whose waist *was* girded with gold of Uphaz! [6]His body *was* like beryl, his face like the appearance of lightning, his eyes like torches of fire, his arms and feet like burnished bronze in color, and the sound of his words like the voice of a multitude.

[7]And I, Daniel, alone saw the vision, for the men who were with me did not see the vision; but a great terror fell upon them, so that they fled to hide themselves. [8]Therefore I was left alone when I saw this great vision, and no strength remained in me; for my vigor was turned to frailty in me, and I retained no strength. [9]Yet I heard the sound of his words; and while I heard the sound of his words I was in a deep sleep on my face, with my face to the ground.

Prophecies Concerning Persia and Greece

[10]Suddenly, a hand touched me, which made me tremble on my knees and *on* the palms of my hands. [11]And he said to me, "O Daniel, man greatly beloved, understand the words that I speak to you, and stand upright, for I have now been sent to you." While he was speaking this word to me, I stood trembling.

[12]Then he said to me, "Do not fear, Daniel, for

···············

9:24 [a]Literally *sevens,* and so throughout the chapter [b]Following Qere, Septuagint, Syriac, and Vulgate; Kethib and Theodotion read *To seal up.*   **9:25** [a]Or *open square* [b]Or *moat*   **10:1** [a]Or *and of great conflict*   **10:4** [a]Hebrew *Hiddekel*

that he was "greatly beloved" by God. The revelation that Gabriel gave involved "seventy weeks," with a "week" representing seven years, making a total of 490 years. Some scholars feel that the number should be taken symbolically; others have developed fairly detailed schedules of events, culminating in the Crucifixion of Jesus or His yet future return (see chart, The Prophecy of Seventy Weeks). Regardless of the various interpretations, however, clearly God is in control of the timetable of human history.

10:1–21 The third year of Cyrus king of Persia was about 536 B.C. The first group of exiles had returned to Jerusalem, but Daniel remained in Babylon. The purpose of this vision was to give Daniel another word about his people and their future (v. 14). Before he could receive the vision, however, Daniel needed strength and encouragement. Several references are

made in this chapter (and in previous chapters) to the fact that the visions left Daniel in a state of weakness caused by the awe, wholesome fear, and sometimes sorrow, attendant to a heavenly vision or being in the presence of a heavenly being. That he was specifically told "do not fear" (v. 12) and that he was reminded on two different occasions (vv. 11, 19) that he was greatly loved must be an indication of the degree of his fear and anxiety in the experience of this vision.

10:5, 6 The glorious man of this vision may simply be an angel sent to deliver a message to Daniel. Some would identify the angel as Gabriel (Dan. 8:16; 9:21). Yet others point to Daniel's unusual response (Dan. 10:7–10, 15) and suggest that the man dressed in linen was God Himself appearing in a Christophany (an appearance of the preincarnate Christ). There are similarities between these verses and Revelation 1:12–16.

from the first day that you set your heart to understand, and to humble yourself before your God, your words were heard; and I have come because of your words. ¹³But the prince of the kingdom of Persia withstood me twenty-one days; and behold, Michael, one of the chief princes, came to help me, for I had been left alone there with the kings of Persia. ¹⁴Now I have come to make you understand what will happen to your people in the latter days, for the vision *refers* to *many* days yet *to come.*"

¹⁵When he had spoken such words to me, I turned my face toward the ground and became speechless. ¹⁶And suddenly, *one* having the likeness of the sons^a of men touched my lips; then I opened my mouth and spoke, saying to him who stood before me, "My lord, because of the vision my sorrows have overwhelmed me, and I have retained no strength. ¹⁷For how can this servant of my lord talk with you, my lord? As for me, no strength remains in me now, nor is any breath left in me."

¹⁸Then again, *the one* having the likeness of a man touched me and strengthened me. ¹⁹And he said, "O man greatly beloved, fear not! Peace *be* to you; be strong, yes, be strong!"

So when he spoke to me I was strengthened, and said, "Let my lord speak, for you have strengthened me."

²⁰Then he said, "Do you know why I have come to you? And now I must return to fight with the prince of Persia; and when I have gone forth, indeed the prince of Greece will come. ²¹But I will tell you what is noted in the Scripture of Truth. (No one upholds me against these, except Michael your prince.

11 "Also in the first year of Darius the Mede, I, *even* I, stood up to confirm and strengthen him.) ²And now I will tell you the truth: Behold, three more kings will arise in Persia, and the fourth shall be far richer than *them* all; by his strength, through his riches, he shall stir up all against the realm of Greece. ³Then a mighty king shall arise, who shall rule with great dominion, and do according to his will. ⁴And when he has arisen, his kingdom shall be broken up and divided toward the four winds of heaven, but not among his posterity nor according to his dominion with which he ruled; for his kingdom shall be uprooted, even for others besides these.

Warring Kings of North and South

⁵"Also the king of the South shall become strong, as well as *one* of his princes; and he shall gain power over him and have dominion. His dominion *shall be* a great dominion. ⁶And at the end of *some* years they shall join forces, for the daughter of the king of the South shall go to the king of the North to make an agreement; but she shall not retain the power of her authority,^a and neither he nor his authority^b shall stand; but she shall be given up, with those who brought her, and with him who begot her, and with him who strengthened her in *those* times. ⁷But from a branch of her roots *one* shall arise in his place, who shall come with an army, enter the fortress of the king of the North, and deal with them and prevail. ⁸And he shall also carry their gods captive to Egypt, with their princes^a *and* their precious

10:16 ^aTheodotion and Vulgate read *the son;* Septuagint reads *a hand.*
11:6 ^aLiterally *arm* ^bLiterally *arm*   11:8 ^aOr *molded images*

10:13 The prince of the kingdom of Persia was not a human king. The clear implication is that, just as God is concerned with the affairs of humanity and works for the well-being of His people, so also Satan is actively at work to subvert and thwart the will of God in the lives of individuals and nations, and particularly to hinder the welfare of God's people (see Eph. 6:11, 12; chart, A Portrait of the Adversary). Just as Satan sends emissaries to work his evil will, so also God sends His heavenly messengers to assist His people. In this case, Michael was sent to help. There are only two angels named in the Bible, Michael and Gabriel; both appear in the Book of Daniel.

11:2–35 The events that the messenger prophesied in this chapter were fulfilled and recorded in secular histories with amazing accuracy. As in the previous vision, this one also dealt with only two of the four kingdoms, Persia and Greece, though the primary concern was the time of oppression of God's people.

11:2 The accuracy of detail is amazing concerning the history of nations after the Persian and Alexandrian states had passed. The kings of Persia to come were to be Cambyses (529–522 B.C.), Smerdis or Pseudo-Smerdis (522–512 B.C.), Darius Hystaspis (521–486 B.C.; see Ezra 5; 6), and Xerxes I or Ahasuerus (486–465 B.C.; see Ezra 4:6). The omission of the

names of kings after Xerxes could well have been due to their unimportance to the author's purpose.

11:3 The mighty king of Greece was Alexander the Great, whose kingdom was divided among four of his generals (see Dan. 7:6, note).

11:5–9 South of Palestine was Egypt, which came under the rule of the Ptolemies, the "king of the South." North and east of Palestine was Syria, under the rule of the Seleucids, the "king of the North." The Jewish homeland was caught in the middle and often suffered at the hands of competing political forces, though at least while under the control of the Ptolemies the Jews were free to practice their faith.

11:6 The daughter of the king of the South was an unfortunate pawn in the game of political alliance. The prophecy was fulfilled by the daughter of Ptolemy II, Egyptian princess Berenice, who was married to Antiochus II of Syria, thus sealing a treaty between Egypt and Syria. As she was subsequently murdered by her husband's former wife, she in fact did not "retain the power of her authority." The "agreement" between Egypt and Syria did not last, and the power struggle resumed.

11:7 Berenice's brother Ptolemy Euergetes, "a branch of her roots," attacked Syria and prevailed, avenging his sister's death and conquering part of Syria.

articles of silver and gold; and he shall continue *more* years than the king of the North.

⁹"Also *the king of the North* shall come to the kingdom of the king of the South, but shall return to his own land. ¹⁰However his sons shall stir up strife, and assemble a multitude of great forces; and *one* shall certainly come and overwhelm and pass through; then he shall return to his fortress and stir up strife.

¹¹"And the king of the South shall be moved with rage, and go out and fight with him, with the king of the North, who shall muster a great multitude; but the multitude shall be given into the hand of his *enemy*. ¹²When he has taken away the multitude, his heart will be lifted up; and he will cast down tens of thousands, but he will not prevail. ¹³For the king of the North will return and muster a multitude greater than the former, and shall certainly come at the end of some years with a great army and much equipment.

¹⁴"Now in those times many shall rise up against the king of the South. Also, violent menᵃ of your people shall exalt themselves in fulfillment of the vision, but they shall fall. ¹⁵So the king of the North shall come and build a siege mound, and take a fortified city; and the forcesᵃ of the South shall not withstand *him*. Even his choice troops *shall have* no strength to resist. ¹⁶But he who comes against him shall do according to his own will, and no one shall stand against him. He shall stand in the Glorious Land with destruction in his power.ᵃ

¹⁷"He shall also set his face to enter with the strength of his whole kingdom, and upright onesᵃ with him; thus shall he do. And he shall give him the daughter of women to destroy it; but she shall not stand *with him,* or be for him. ¹⁸After this he shall turn his face to the coastlands, and shall take many. But a ruler shall bring the reproach against them to an end; and with the reproach removed, he shall turn back on him. ¹⁹Then he shall turn his face toward the fortress of his own land; but he shall stumble and fall, and not be found.

²⁰"There shall arise in his place one who imposes taxes *on* the glorious kingdom; but within a few days he shall be destroyed, but not in anger or in battle. ²¹And in his place shall arise a vile person, to whom they will not give the honor of royalty; but he shall come in peaceably, and seize the kingdom by intrigue. ²²With the forceᵃ of a flood they shall be swept away from before him and be broken, and also the prince of the covenant. ²³And after the league *is made* with him he shall act deceitfully, for he shall come up and become strong with a small *number of* people. ²⁴He shall enter peaceably, even into the richest places of the province; and he shall do *what* his fathers have not done, nor his forefathers: he shall disperse among them the plunder, spoil, and riches; and he shall devise his plans against the strongholds, but *only* for a time.

²⁵"He shall stir up his power and his courage against the king of the South with a great army. And the king of the South shall be stirred up to battle with a very great and mighty army; but he shall not stand, for they shall devise plans against him. ²⁶Yes, those who eat of the portion of his delicacies shall destroy him; his army shall be swept away, and many shall fall down slain. ²⁷Both these kings' hearts *shall be* bent on evil, and they shall speak lies at the same table; but it shall not prosper, for the end *will* still *be* at the appointed time. ²⁸While returning to his land with great riches, his heart shall be *moved* against the holy covenant; so he shall do *damage* and return to his own land.

The Northern King's Blasphemies

²⁹"At the appointed time he shall return and go toward the south; but it shall not be like the for-

---

11:14 ᵃOr *robbers,* literally *sons of breakage*   11:15, 22 ᵃLiterally *arms*   11:16 ᵃLiterally *hand*   11:17 ᵃOr *bring equitable terms*

11:9–15 The picture in these verses is one of constant incursions by the armies of Egypt and Syria against each other. The reality for the Jews was a continual flow of opposing troops back and forth through their homeland.

11:16–20 The Seleucid king Antiochus III was successful, after many attempts, in overcoming Ptolemy V of Egypt. The control of the "Glorious Land" (Palestine) passed from Egypt to Syria. These political changes also meant changes of a drastic nature for the Jews, as the new high priest was determined to change Jerusalem into a Greek city. Great turmoil and resistance followed as the Jews refused what they saw as pagan ways.

11:17 The daughter of women was Antiochus's daughter Cleopatra, whom he gave in marriage to Ptolemy V. This is the second mention in the Book of Daniel of a marriage for political purposes (see v. 6).

11:21–35 The coming of Antiochus IV Epiphanes is generally thought to be predicted in this section. It also has implications

for future times. Antiochus was a real historical figure, whose harsh treatment of the Jews and desecrations of the temple are well documented; he was also an example of political power against God's people that will recur until Christ returns. When the Jews rebelled against the high priest whom he had installed in Jerusalem, Antiochus IV sent an army to put down the rebellion (v. 30) and forbade the Jews to carry out the practices of their faith. He ended the daily sacrifices in the temple (v. 31), rededicated the temple to Jupiter, and offered swine on the altar. This forcible worship of another god was the "abomination of desolation" to which Jesus referred (Matt. 24:15; Luke 21:20). Having stood all that they could stand, the "people who know their God" (faithful Jews) revolted (Dan. 11:32). With able leadership given by Mattathias Maccabeus and his son Judas, they were able to "carry out great exploits" in defense of their homeland and their faith.

DREAMS AND VISIONS

	NEBUCHADNEZZAR'S DREAM (DAN. 2:1–13)	DANIEL'S DREAM (DAN. 7:1–14)	DANIEL'S VISION (DAN. 8:1–27)	KINGDOM REPRESENTED
Dreams and Visions	Head of fine gold (Dan. 2:32).	Like a lion with eagle's wings (Dan. 7:4).		Babylon
	Chest and arms of silver (Dan. 2:32).	Like a bear (Dan. 7:5).	A ram with two horns, one higher than the other (Dan. 8:3).	Media-Persia
	Belly and thighs of bronze (Dan. 2:2).	Like a leopard with four wings and four heads (Dan. 7:6).	A male goat with one great horn, four horns, and a little horn (Dan. 8:5, 8, 9).	Greece (Macedonia)
	Legs of iron, feet of iron and clay (Dan. 2:33).	Incomparable beast with ten horns and a little horn (Dan. 7:7, 9).		Rome
Interpretation	The statue represented successive world empires, which would be defeated (Dan. 2:39, 40). Ultimately, however, God's kingdom would conquer this kingdom (Dan. 2:35).	Rome would defeat the Greeks, but eventually the Messiah would come and receive the kingdom with His saints (Dan. 7:19–22).	Greece would defeat the Medes and Persians (Dan. 8:20, 21).	Kingdom of God

Nebuchadnezzar's second dream (Dan. 4:1–18) is not included because it does not concern the prophecies about the nations.

mer or the latter. ³⁰For ships from Cyprusᵃ shall come against him; therefore he shall be grieved, and return in rage against the holy covenant, and do *damage.*

"So he shall return and show regard for those who forsake the holy covenant. ³¹And forcesᵃ shall be mustered by him, and they shall defile the sanctuary fortress; then they shall take away the daily *sacrifices,* and place *there* the abomination of desolation. ³²Those who do wickedly against the covenant he shall corrupt with flattery; but the people who know their God shall be strong, and carry out *great exploits.* ³³And those of the people who understand shall instruct many; yet *for many* days they shall fall by sword and flame, by captiv-

ity and plundering. ³⁴Now when they fall, they shall be aided with a little help; but many shall join with them by intrigue. ³⁵And *some* of those of understanding shall fall, to refine them, purify *them,* and make *them* white, *until* the time of the end; because *it is* still for the appointed time.

³⁶"Then the king shall do according to his own will: he shall exalt and magnify himself above every god, shall speak blasphemies against the God of gods, and shall prosper till the wrath has been accomplished; for what has been determined shall be done. ³⁷He shall regard neither the Godᵃ

11:30 ᵃHebrew *Kittim,* western lands, especially Cyprus   **11:31** ᵃLiterally *arms*   **11:37** ᵃOr *gods*

11:36–45 The similarity to Antiochus IV and his oppression of the Jews decreases, and the emphasis moves, in this transitional section, to the end times and a focus on the final evil ruler who dares to "exalt and magnify himself above every god," including the God of the universe (v. 36). He will use force, deception, and idolatry in his campaign to rule and to cause suffering to the people of God. When seemingly evil has

triumphed, the God of history will intervene. The evil one and those who allied themselves with him "shall come to his end, and no one will help him" (v. 45). God's judgment against evil will be sure and everlasting, and His kingdom of righteousness will last forever. That sure knowledge gives hope to the people of God.

of his fathers nor the desire of women, nor regard any god; for he shall exalt himself above *them* all. [38]But in their place he shall honor a god of fortresses; and a god which his fathers did not know he shall honor with gold and silver, with precious stones and pleasant things. [39]Thus he shall act against the strongest fortresses with a foreign god, which he shall acknowledge, *and* advance *its* glory; and he shall cause them to rule over many, and divide the land for gain.

The Northern King's Conquests

[40]"At the time of the end the king of the South shall attack him; and the king of the North shall come against him like a whirlwind, with chariots, horsemen, and with many ships; and he shall enter the countries, overwhelm *them*, and pass through. [41]He shall also enter the Glorious Land, and many *countries* shall be overthrown; but these shall escape from his hand: Edom, Moab, and the prominent people of Ammon. [42]He shall stretch out his hand against the countries, and the land of Egypt shall not escape. [43]He shall have power over the treasures of gold and silver, and over all the precious things of Egypt; also the Libyans and Ethiopians *shall follow* at his heels. [44]But news from the east and the north shall trouble him; therefore he shall go out with great fury to destroy and annihilate many. [45]And he shall plant the tents of his palace between the seas and the glorious holy mountain; yet he shall come to his end, and no one will help him.

Prophecy of the End Time

12 "At that time Michael shall stand up,
The great prince who stands *watch* over the
sons of your people;
And there shall be a time of trouble,
Such as never was since there was a nation,
Even to that time.
And at that time your people shall be
delivered,

Every one who is found written in the book.
[2]And many of those who sleep in the dust of the
earth shall awake,
Some to everlasting life,
Some to shame *and* everlasting contempt.
[3]Those who are wise shall shine
Like the brightness of the firmament,
And those who turn many to righteousness
Like the stars forever and ever.

[4]"But you, Daniel, shut up the words, and seal the book until the time of the end; many shall run to and fro, and knowledge shall increase."

[5]Then I, Daniel, looked; and there stood two others, one on this riverbank and the other on that riverbank. [6]And *one* said to the man clothed in linen, who *was* above the waters of the river, "How long shall the fulfillment of these wonders *be?*"

[7]Then I heard the man clothed in linen, who *was* above the waters of the river, when he held up his right hand and his left hand to heaven, and swore by Him who lives forever, that *it shall be* for a time, times, and half *a time;* and when the power of the holy people has been completely shattered, all these *things* shall be finished.

[8]Although I heard, I did not understand. Then I said, "My lord, what *shall be* the end of these *things?*"

[9]And he said, "Go *your way,* Daniel, for the words *are* closed up and sealed till the time of the end. [10]Many shall be purified, made white, and refined, but the wicked shall do wickedly; and none of the wicked shall understand, but the wise shall understand.

[11]"And from the time *that* the daily *sacrifice* is taken away, and the abomination of desolation is set up, *there shall be* one thousand two hundred and ninety days. [12]Blessed *is* he who waits, and comes to the one thousand three hundred and thirty-five days.

[13]"But you, go *your way* till the end; for you shall rest, and will arise to your inheritance at the end of the days."

12:1–4 God's final triumph over evil will come after a period of intense suffering, particularly for God's people, who will be delivered in the midst of their suffering by Michael.

12:2–4 Everlasting life is mentioned here for the first time in the Bible and the only time in the OT, though there are other OT references to the concept of resurrection (see Ps. 16:10; Is. 25:8; 26:19). Mention of "shame and everlasting contempt" indicates that not all will spend eternity in the presence of God. The sealing is in anticipation of the One who is able to unseal Daniel's vision. Jesus Christ ultimately will make the vision clear.

12:5–13 Some see the 70th week in the prophecy as being fulfilled without any intervening time period and culminating in the Crucifixion of Christ and the ultimate destruction of Jerusalem in A.D. 70. Other interpreters attribute this 70th week to the future (see Dan. 9:27; chart, The Prophecy of Seventy Weeks). According to this view, a future for the Jew-

ish people includes building a temple and establishing a protective covenant with the "prince who is to come" (Dan. 9:26). This reference is to the Antichrist of the Tribulation period, who breaks his covenant with Israel at the mid-point of the 70th week, desecrates the temple, and makes war with God's children until "the consummation which is determined" (Dan. 9:27). God's people (Israel) would undergo dreadful suffering for a "time, times, and half a time" (three and a half years or half of the seven years represented by the 70th week; see Dan. 9:21–27, note).

The "words are closed up and sealed," perhaps to keep believers in every generation from dwelling on the end times to the exclusion of living responsibly each day (Dan. 12:9). Daniel's life was characterized by faithfulness and obedience (Dan. 12:13). The book ends, despite the message of great turmoil, suffering, and unrest, on a note of peace and hope for Daniel and for all who find refuge in the Lord.

WOMEN IN THE MINOR PROPHETS

PROPHET	DATE OF MINISTRY	KINGS OF ISRAEL	KINGS OF JUDAH	KINGS OF ASSYRIA	KINGS OF BABYLON	KEY FEMALE FIGURE
Hosea	755–725 B.C.	Jeroboam II Zechariah Shallum Menahem Pekahiah Pekah Hoshea	Uzziah Jotham Ahaz Hezekiah	Tiglath-Pileser III Shalmaneser V		Gomer (Hos. 1—3)
Joel	about 835 B.C.	Jehu	Joash (Jehoash)	Shalmaneser III		God's maidservants received His Spirit (Joel 2:29).
Amos	about 760 B.C.	Jeroboam II	Uzziah	Ashur-dan III		"Cows of Bashan," the greedy women of Samaria (Amos 4:1).
Obadiah	about 586 B.C.		Zedekiah		Nebuchadnezzar II	
Jonah	800–750 B.C.	Jeroboam II	Uzziah	Adad-nirari III Shalmaneser IV Ashur-dan III		
Micah	750–686 B.C.	Jeroboam II Zechariah Shallum Menahem Pekahiah Pekah Hoshea	Jotham Ahaz Hezekiah	Tiglath-Pileser III Shalmaneser V		Future triumph of the Lord's people identified as the daughter of Zion (Mic. 4:6–13).
Nahum	Sometime between 663–612 B.C.		Manasseh Amon Josiah	Ashurbanipal	Nabopolassar	Nineveh as a great harlot had enticed other nations (Nah. 3:4).
Habakkuk	609–605 B.C.		Jehoiakim		Nabopolassar	
Zephaniah	about 625 B.C.		Josiah	Ashurbanipal	Nabopolassar	Faithful remnant as the "daughter of Zion" will rejoice in the Lord's faithfulness (Zeph. 3:14, 15).
				Kings of Persia		
Haggai	520 B.C.		Zerubbabel (governor of Judah)	Darius I		
Zechariah	about 520 B.C.		Zerubbabel (governor of Judah)	Darius I		Vision of woman in basket who stands for evil (Zech. 5:5–11).
Malachi	about 435 B.C.		Nehemiah (governor of Judah)	Artaxerxes I		"The wife of your youth" (Mal. 2:14–16).

See also charts, The Kings of Assyria; The Kings of Babylon; The Kings of Israel and Judah; The Kings of Syria.

Hosea

AUTHOR

Hosea marked a new stage in Hebrew prophecy because he was one of the first prophets to put his prophecies into writing. His book is placed at the beginning of the scroll of the twelve prophets, which the Jews have designated "The Twelve." They are sometimes called the Minor Prophets, "minor" referring to their brevity rather than their importance.

Hosea appeared to have been a native of the northern kingdom of Israel, since he was well acquainted with the geography and details of the political, religious, and social life there. Except for the text of the Book of Hosea itself, the Old Testament is silent about the man Hosea. He simply identified himself as "the son of Beeri" (Hos. 1:1). Because of his knowledge of the work of a baker, some have conjectured that baking was his profession (Hos. 7:4). The most outstanding feature about Hosea is his marriage and family life. His marriage to Gomer, at God's command to take a "wife of harlotry," provided the setting for God to present the nature of His covenant with His people and how they had defiled that covenant (Hos. 1:2, note). It also allowed Hosea to register the vivid and painful emotions of love betrayed and to record the steps he took to redeem the woman who had so wronged him. That action, of course, is representative of the redemptive love of God, which is so passionately revealed in the prophecies God entrusted to Hosea.

DATE

Hosea recorded the reigning kings in both Israel and Judah when the word of the Lord came to him. Thus, there is a way to determine when his prophetic activity occurred. He mentioned the reigns of four kings in Judah (Hos. 1:1): Uzziah (792–740 B.C.), Jotham (750–731 B.C.), Ahaz (735–715 B.C.), and Hezekiah (715–686 B.C. as well as the coregency with Ahaz, 729–715 B.C.). In the northern kingdom, Jeroboam II reigned (793–753 B.C.). After him came the last six kings of Israel, whose rules Hosea witnessed, although he did not name these kings in his prophecy. They were Zechariah (753–752 B.C.), Shallum (752 B.C.), Menahem (752–742 B.C.), Pekahiah (742–740 B.C.), Pekah (740–732 B.C.), and Hoshea (732–722 B.C.), and they represent a time of political instability and moral collapse in the nation of Israel. For Hosea to have been a witness to this part of history, his prophetic activity had to occur not earlier than 760 B.C. His ministry occurred in the same period as that of Amos in the northern kingdom and Isaiah and Micah in the southern kingdom.

BACKGROUND

SETTING: Hosea's preaching took place against a background of extreme political and spiritual decline in Israel. After Jeroboam II (793–753 B.C.) institutionalized idolatry, the life of the people was characterized in every way by unfaithfulness to the covenant God had made with them. As external political pressures exerted themselves, the kings of Israel sought help and protection not from God but from alliances with Egypt and

Assyria. In addition, the people were lured into the worship of idols, forsaking their allegiance to God and manifesting in their lives every type of immorality and impurity. Hosea lived and preached among a nation that had lost its heart for God.

PURPOSE: Hosea warned Israel of the tragedy of her betrayal of God and the sure judgment that would follow if she did not return to Him. He included a note of joy even in the midst of judgment. Israel's time of sorrow and judgment would be followed by happiness and restoration (Hos. 1:10; 2:14, 15).

AUDIENCE: God's people living in Israel, the northern kingdom, were the ones to whom Hosea addressed his prophecies, although occasionally he included the southern kingdom of Judah in his warnings.

LITERARY CHARACTERISTICS: Hosea used a variety of literary devices to deliver his prophetic message. There are numerous judgment and salvation speeches, which provide a rhythmic structure to the book. In addition, Hosea used proverbs, metaphors, and similes to give life to his message. A feeling of spontaneity, freedom, and passion marks the movement of his words.

THEMES

As one who personally had known the agony of a broken covenant, Hosea wrote movingly of God's redeeming love for Israel. The marriage he embraced with Gomer is a living demonstration of how far true love will go in order to keep its covenant. The book simmers with the wild vacillations in the heart of the one betrayed: an acknowledgment of the sin and the anger it arouses, the appropriateness of punishment, yet a steadfast, unwavering desire for reconciliation and a promise of loving restoration. No one before Hosea had spoken so repeatedly of God's love for His people; neither had anyone couched divine grace in the terms of marital intimacy.

OUTLINE

I. Hosea's Marriage: The Making of a Prophet, the Breaking of a Covenant (1:1—3:5)
  A. The faithful husband, the harlot wife (1:1—2:1)
  B. The punishment for unfaithfulness accompanied by a quest for restoration (2:2–23)
  C. Gomer's redemption, Israel's hope (3:1–5)
II. Hosea's Preaching: A Revelation of God's Love (4:1—14:9)
  A. God's condemnation of an unrepentant Israel (4:1—7:16)
    1. The charges against Israel (4:1–19)
    2. The judgment on Israel and Judah (5:1–15)

    3. An invitation to repentance (6:1–3)
    4. The consequences of Israel's sin (6:4—7:16)
  B. Israel's judgment following condemnation (8:1—10:15)
    1. The certainty of judgment (8:1–14)
    2. The nature of the judgment (9:1–17)
    3. The Exile of Israel into captivity (10:1–15)
  C. Israel's restoration because of God's love (11:1—14:9)
    1. God as Israel's true Father (11:1–11)
    2. The guilt of Judah (11:12—12:14)
    3. The spurning of God's love by Ephraim (13:1–16)
    4. The triumph of God's grace (14:1–9)

GOMER   *A Selfish Harlot*

During a time when the nation of Israel defiantly turned her back on God and gave herself to idolatry, God called Hosea to pursue an unusual prophetic role among His people. Hosea's job was to prophesy by both words and actions—he was commanded to marry Gomer (Hos. 1:2). Gomer was apparently pure when she married Hosea, but she had harlotry in her heart. The life Hosea and Gomer had together was symbolic of the relationship between God and His people.

Gomer conducted her harlotry in a shamefully flagrant manner, judging from Hosea's descriptions. What drove her to this sin? Whatever her reasons, the consequences of her actions, especially the agony she caused her husband and children (see Hos. 2), were the unavoidable realities of her selfish behavior. Gomer sought her own enjoyment so irresponsibly that she ultimately wound up in some sort of bondage from which she had to be redeemed (see Hos. 3:1–3). As Hosea paid the price for her and took her back to himself, he restored her as his wife after a preliminary period of discipline to help her direct her life afresh to the vows she had made to Hosea in marriage.

The meaning for all who love God is profound: God Himself likewise paid the price to redeem His people, demonstrating that the aim of His love is reconciliation, restoration, and forgiveness (see Titus 2:14).

See also notes on Adultery (Hos. 3); Forgiveness (Ps. 51; 103; Luke 17)

1 The word of the LORD that came to Hosea the son of Beeri, in the days of Uzziah, Jotham, Ahaz, *and* Hezekiah, kings of Judah, and in the days of Jeroboam the son of Joash, king of Israel.

The Family of Hosea

²When the LORD began to speak by Hosea, the LORD said to Hosea:

"Go, take yourself a wife of harlotry
And children of harlotry,
For the land has committed great harlotry
By departing from the LORD."

³So he went and took Gomer the daughter of Dib-

laim, and she conceived and bore him a son. ⁴Then the LORD said to him:

"Call his name Jezreel,
For in a little *while*
I will avenge the bloodshed of Jezreel on the
house of Jehu,
And bring an end to the kingdom of the house
of Israel.
⁵It shall come to pass in that day
That I will break the bow of Israel in the Valley
of Jezreel."

⁶And she conceived again and bore a daughter. Then *God* said to him:

1:1 God's people were divided into two kingdoms at the time of Hosea's prophecies. Sometimes the northern kingdom is referred to as "Ephraim," its most influential tribe, or as "Samaria," its capital city (see chart, Terminology for the Divided Kingdom). Hosea was probably a resident of the northern kingdom.

1:2 Hosea's marriage is interwoven with his prophetic work. Hosea was to understand Israel's unfaithfulness to the Lord in all its tragedy through the betrayal of his own wife Gomer, described here as "a wife of harlotry." To consider the marriage allegorical, is highly unlikely because of the details presented in the narrative, which are not symbolic and are presented as historical facts (vv. 3, 8; Hos. 3:2). Others suggest that the marriage actually occurred and that Gomer was unchaste, perhaps even a temple prostitute, at the time. However, again this does not seem an appropriate conclusion since genuine affection on the part of Hosea for Gomer would seem difficult if not impossible under such circumstances. Hosea as a prophet would have been sensitive to the law forbidding such a union (Lev. 21:7, 14). Thus, it seems more likely that Hosea married Gomer, who was presumably chaste at the time, and she bore Hosea a son. In this case, the description is taken proleptically (with the future act presented as already

existing). After Gomer married Hosea, she allowed harlotry to rule in her heart. The children she bore were given names symbolic of the severe break in the covenant relationship between God and His unfaithful people. This latter view also more closely paralleled God's experience with His people Israel (Hos. 1:2, 6, 7, 9; 2:2–13). Israel was presented to *Yahweh* as chaste (Jer. 2:2, 3), but He knew that she would play the harlot and become unfaithful.

1:4 At Jezreel (lit. "God will scatter") Jehu was swept to power through bloodthirsty acts (see 2 Kin. 9:21, 37; 10:1–11). Jehu's extermination of the house of Ahab and his efforts to remove Baalism were commanded and commended by God (2 Kin. 9:1–10; 10:30). Jehu, nevertheless, was wrong in the way he carried out God's commands (2 Kin. 10:31–36). The blood of Naboth was shed by Ahab and Jezebel at Jezreel (1 Kin. 21:1–16), resulting in God's curse and the complete extermination of the house of Ahab (1 Kin. 21:19–24). Jehu's continuation in idolatry would keep him in the line of judgment (2 Kin. 10:31). God avenged that terrible act by bringing an end to that dynasty of kings through the murder of Zechariah (2 Kin. 15:8–10; see chart, The Dynasties of Israel—Part 2) and the fall of Samaria, which scattered Israel into exile (see 2 Kin. 17:5, 6).

"Call her name Lo-Ruhamah,[a]
    For I will no longer have mercy on the house of
        Israel,
    But I will utterly take them away.[b]
[7]Yet I will have mercy on the house of Judah,
    Will save them by the LORD their God,
    And will not save them by bow,
    Nor by sword or battle,
    By horses or horsemen."

[8]Now when she had weaned Lo-Ruhamah, she conceived and bore a son. [9]Then *God* said:

"Call his name Lo-Ammi,[a]
    For you *are* not My people,
    And I will not be your *God*.

The Restoration of Israel

[10]"Yet the number of the children of Israel
    Shall be as the sand of the sea,
    Which cannot be measured or numbered.
    And it shall come to pass
    In the place where it was said to them,
    'You *are* not My people,'[a]
    There it shall be said to them,
    '*You are* sons of the living God.'
[11]Then the children of Judah and the children of
        Israel
    Shall be gathered together,
    And appoint for themselves one head;
    And they shall come up out of the land,
    For great *will be* the day of Jezreel!

2 Say to your brethren, 'My people,'[a]
    And to your sisters, 'Mercy[b] *is shown.*'

God's Unfaithful People

[2]"Bring charges against your mother, bring
        charges;
    For she *is* not My wife, nor *am* I her Husband!
    Let her put away her harlotries from her sight,
    And her adulteries from between her breasts;
[3]Lest I strip her naked
    And expose her, as in the day she was born,

And make her like a wilderness,
    And set her like a dry land,
    And slay her with thirst.
[4]"I will not have mercy on her children,
    For they *are* the children of harlotry.
[5]For their mother has played the harlot;
    She who conceived them has behaved
        shamefully.
    For she said, 'I will go after my lovers,
    Who give *me* my bread and my water,
    My wool and my linen,
    My oil and my drink.'

[6]"Therefore, behold,
    I will hedge up your way with thorns,
    And wall her in,
    So that she cannot find her paths.
[7]She will chase her lovers,
    But not overtake them;
    Yes, she will seek them, but not find *them*.
    Then she will say,
    'I will go and return to my first husband,
    For then *it was* better for me than now.'
[8]For she did not know
    That I gave her grain, new wine, and oil,
    And multiplied her silver and gold—
    Which they prepared for Baal.

[9]"Therefore I will return and take away
    My grain in its time
    And My new wine in its season,
    And will take back My wool and My linen,
    Given to cover her nakedness.
[10]Now I will uncover her lewdness in the sight of
        her lovers,
    And no one shall deliver her from My hand.
[11]I will also cause all her mirth to cease,
    Her feast days,

1:6 Lo-Ruhamah (lit. "she has not shown compassion") indicates that the harlot Israel would suffer her punishment to the full.

1:9 The waywardness of the people, as well as God's response of separating Himself from them are indicated in the name of the third child, "Lo-Ammi" (lit. "not my people").

1:10 The name changes portray a move from judgment to blessing. "Lo" (Heb., lit. "no" or "not") removed from "Lo-Ruhamah" and "Lo-Ammi" is then "my people" (*Ammi*) and "mercy is shown" (*Ruhamah*), pointing to Israel's future restoration (Rom. 9:25, 26).

2:2 God brought an indictment against Israel: The charge was adultery, a flagrant violation of the covenant of love. Gomer also betrayed Hosea and offered herself to those to whom she

did not belong. Hosea's personal experience of having an unfaithful wife enabled him to understand in part God's heartbreak over His unfaithful people.

2:8 Baal (lit. "lord," "husband," or "owner") was a reference to the Canaanite gods of the autumn and winter rains that were so vital to good crops. Using the analogy of Baal as a husband fertilizing the land, temple prostitution was practiced with the hope that such acts would induce Baal to fertilize the earth. The people refused to recognize God as the source of their blessings of grain, wine, and oil (basic household needs) as well as silver and gold (metals used in trade). They failed to express gratitude to God for these; then they actually used God's blessings (silver and gold) to fashion idols.

MARRIAGE A METAPHOR OF UNION WITH GOD

Throughout Scripture the marriage union is a metaphor or picture of the relationship between God and His people. In the Old Testament, Israel is pictured as the wife of *Yahweh*. When Israel became unfaithful and worshiped other gods, she was described as a harlot (Jer. 3:1; Ezek. 23). Her spiritual adultery became so despicable in God's sight that He issued a writing of divorcement (Jer. 3:8). Actually, this was a separation, as God in His great love for His chosen people could not bear to cut off Israel without a promise of renewal (Hos. 2:14–20; 5:15).

In the Epistles and in Revelation, the church is described as the Bride of Christ. The experience of obtaining a bride is similar for both Adam and Christ—Adam was put to sleep; Christ was laid in a tomb. When Christ came to earth in human form, He left His Father. When He began His earthly ministry and ultimately died on the Cross, He left His mother. This was for the purpose of cleaving to the object of His love—His people. As He is received into the heart of each sinner, they become one flesh (Gen. 2:24; 1 Cor. 6:15).

The whole focus and course of a life is changed both by marriage and a personal experience with Jesus Christ. Marriage (1 Cor. 7:3) and becoming a child of God (Mark 8:34; 1 Cor. 6:20; 7:23) both demand death to self and accountability to God and to others. A wife or husband cannot be faithful to more than one partner, as a Christian cannot serve any other God (Matt. 6:24). Believers should have no hesitation in giving themselves in totality to God because of the high price He paid for them (1 Pet. 1:18, 19). God has given all He has to give; He now expects our all in response (Rom. 12:1, 2).

In marriage two hearts are grafted together, making them dependent on one another for life. This is depicted in John 15, with Jesus as the vine and believers the branches. Through the infilling of the Holy Spirit and His control in the life of both partners, this picture of marriage and the parallel relationship of Christ and His Bride come into focus. The Holy Spirit fills and fulfills both.

See also notes on Adultery (Hos. 3); Divorce (Matt. 19); Family (Gen. 32; 1 Sam. 3; Ps. 78; 127); Marriage (Gen. 2; 2 Sam. 6; Prov. 5; Amos 3; 2 Cor. 13; Heb. 12)

Her New Moons,
Her Sabbaths—
All her appointed feasts.

12"And I will destroy her vines and her fig trees,
Of which she has said,
'These *are* my wages that my lovers have given me.'
So I will make them a forest,
And the beasts of the field shall eat them.
13I will punish her
For the days of the Baals to which she burned incense.
She decked herself with her earrings and jewelry,
And went after her lovers;
But Me she forgot," says the LORD.

God's Mercy on His People

14"Therefore, behold, I will allure her,
Will bring her into the wilderness,
And speak comfort to her.
15I will give her her vineyards from there,
And the Valley of Achor as a door of hope;
She shall sing there,
As in the days of her youth,

As in the day when she came up from the land of Egypt.

16"And it shall be, in that day,"
Says the LORD,
"*That* you will call Me 'My Husband,'[a]
And no longer call Me 'My Master,'[b]
17For I will take from her mouth the names of the Baals,
And they shall be remembered by their name no more.
18In that day I will make a covenant for them
With the beasts of the field,
With the birds of the air,
And *with* the creeping things of the ground.
Bow and sword of battle I will shatter from the earth,
To make them lie down safely.

19"I will betroth you to Me forever;
Yes, I will betroth you to Me
In righteousness and justice,
In lovingkindness and mercy;

2:16 [a]Hebrew *Ishi* [b]Hebrew *Baali*

2:19, 20 The ingredients of the betrothal relationship included "righteousness and justice" as the legal requirement, "lovingkindness and mercy" as the personal ties of affection, and "faithfulness" as the seal of exclusive and permanent commitment. These qualities should mark every marital union (see John 2, Weddings; chart, God's Plan for Marriage).

[20]I will betroth you to Me in faithfulness,
And you shall know the LORD.

[21]"It shall come to pass in that day
That I will answer," says the LORD;
"I will answer the heavens,
And they shall answer the earth.
[22]The earth shall answer
With grain,
With new wine,
And with oil;
They shall answer Jezreel.[a]
[23]Then I will sow her for Myself in the
earth,
And I will have mercy on *her who had* not
obtained mercy;[a]
Then I will say to *those who were* not My
people,[b]
'You *are* My people!'
And they shall say, '*You are* my God!' "

Israel Will Return to God

3 Then the LORD said to me, "Go again, love a
woman *who is* loved by a lover[a] and is committing adultery, just like the love of the LORD for the
children of Israel, who look to other gods and love
the raisin cakes *of the pagans.*"

[2]So I bought her for myself for fifteen *shekels* of
silver, and one and one-half homers of barley. [3]And
I said to her, "You shall stay with me many days;
you shall not play the harlot, nor shall you have a
man—so, too, *will* I *be* toward you."

[4]For the children of Israel shall abide many days
without king or prince, without sacrifice or *sacred*
pillar, without ephod or teraphim. [5]Afterward the
children of Israel shall return and seek the LORD

their God and David their king. They shall fear
the LORD and His goodness in the latter days.

God's Charge Against Israel

4 Hear the word of the LORD,
You children of Israel,
For the LORD *brings* a charge against the
inhabitants of the land:

"There is no truth or mercy
Or knowledge of God in the land.
[2]*By* swearing and lying,
Killing and stealing and committing
adultery,
They break all restraint,
With bloodshed upon bloodshed.
[3]Therefore the land will mourn;
And everyone who dwells there will waste away
With the beasts of the field
And the birds of the air;
Even the fish of the sea will be taken away.

[4]"Now let no man contend, or rebuke another;
For your people *are* like those who contend
with the priest.
[5]Therefore you shall stumble in the day;
The prophet also shall stumble with you in the
night;
And I will destroy your mother.
[6]My people are destroyed for lack of knowledge.
Because you have rejected knowledge,
I also will reject you from being priest for
Me;

2:22 [a]Literally *God Will Sow* 2:23 [a]Hebrew *lo-ruhamah* [b]Hebrew *lo-ammi* 3:1 [a]Literally *friend* or *husband*

3:1 God commanded Hosea to demonstrate in his marriage to Gomer the same kind of steadfast, redeeming love that He had for His idolatrous people Israel. "The raisin cakes of the pagans" were sweetmeats made of pressed grapes, an integral part of worship in many Canaanite cultic festivals.

3:2 The measure of shekels here refers to a weight of silver, about 0.4 ounces, not coins. A "homer" was a measure of cereal, roughly equal to about five bushels (see chart, Money and Measurements in the Bible).

3:3 The reciprocity in commitment is essential. Hosea directed Gomer to return home and resume her responsibilities as wife and mother, and he committed himself to remain faithful to her as his wife and only love. Forgiveness and restoration are possible only for one who is absolutely committed to going God's way.

3:4 The waiting period imposed on Gomer after Hosea bought her back is analogous to Israel's coming exile. The "ephod" was part of the garment worn by the high priest when he inquired of the Lord (see chart, The High Priest's Clothing); whereas the "teraphim" were household idols used as a means of divination (see Gen. 31:19, note).

3:5 The northern kingdom, under their own king (1 Kin. 12:20)

and with their own centers for worship (1 Kin. 12:28, 29), was in rebellion against the Davidic covenant (2 Sam. 7:1–16; see 1 Chr. 17:7–12). Christian and Jewish scholars interpret this as a reference to the Messiah since David had long been dead at the time of this prophecy. The "latter days" refers to the messianic era.

4:1 Hosea announced that the Lord would take His people to court to focus the attention of all Israel on the magnitude of its crime. God charged Israel with a breach in the covenant. "Truth" is nowhere to be found because the people of Israel had not sustained or supported their covenant with God. "Mercy" (Heb. *chesed*; see Ps. 5:7–12, note) is the term for God's covenant love that Israel experienced when God redeemed His people from Egypt. They would know that love again when God would call the contrite nation back to Himself. The "knowledge of God" that expressed covenantal intimacy had been completely abandoned.

4:5 The designation your mother identifies the nation Israel, which gave birth to the people (Hos. 1:2; 3:2–5). The northern kingdom had been destroyed and had disappeared completely as an entity. Since the priests had ignored or "forgotten" God's Law, God would "forget" their descendants (Hos. 4:6).

ADULTERY UNFAITHFULNESS IN MARRIAGE

A theme running throughout Scripture is God's intent for husbands and wives to be faithful to each other. Fidelity in marriage is God's plan for His kingdom and God's purpose for His children. Adultery—when a husband or wife willfully engages in sexual intercourse with someone other than the marriage partner—is prohibited (Ex. 20:14; Deut. 5:18). Many Old Testament regulations prescribed severe punishment for adultery (Lev. 20:10; Deut. 22:22). In the New Testament, Jesus condemned adultery (Mark 10:11, 12; Luke 16:18), and Paul denounced it as one of the "works of the flesh" (Gal. 5:19).

Adulterers can receive God's forgiveness (John 8:3–11) from extra-marital sexual infidelity, which is an act of unfaithfulness. Believers are to practice faithfulness to God and in their personal relationships. A spouse who is able to forgive adulterous behavior on the part of a mate is encouraged to remain within a marriage. At the same time, in Scripture, adultery is regarded as such a severe breach of trust and fidelity that it is noted as *permissible* grounds for divorce (Matt. 5:32).

Jesus taught that adultery begins in the heart (Matt. 5:27, 28; 19:18, 19) and is rooted in lust. Many a marriage has suffered greatly because of "emotional adultery," which Jesus taught was just as serious as sexual immorality.

In part, adultery was dealt with so harshly in Scripture because it distorts one of God's illustrations about Himself and His intentions toward His creation. God wants to use the faithfulness between husband and wife to illustrate His faithfulness to His people. For this reason, adultery is likened to idolatry in the Old Testament. To commit adultery is to distort the very relationship God wants with those whom He loves.

See also Job 24:15; Prov. 5—7; James 4:4; notes on Divorce (Matt. 19); Marriage (Gen. 2; 2 Sam. 6; Prov. 5; Hos. 2; Amos 3; 2 Cor. 13; Heb. 12); Seduction (Judg. 16); Sexual Immorality (Prov. 6); Sexual Purity (Eph. 5); portraits of the Adulteress of Proverbs (Prov. 5); Gomer (Hos. 2)

Because you have forgotten the law of your
  God,
I also will forget your children.

⁷"The more they increased,
The more they sinned against Me;
I will change[a] their glory[b] into shame.
⁸They eat up the sin of My people;
They set their heart on their iniquity.
⁹And it shall be: like people, like priest.
So I will punish them for their ways,
And reward them for their deeds.
¹⁰For they shall eat, but not have enough;
They shall commit harlotry, but not
  increase;
Because they have ceased obeying the LORD.

The Idolatry of Israel

¹¹"Harlotry, wine, and new wine enslave the heart.
¹²My people ask counsel from their wooden *idols*,
And their staff informs them.
For the spirit of harlotry has caused *them* to
  stray,

And they have played the harlot against their
  God.
¹³They offer sacrifices on the mountaintops,
And burn incense on the hills,
Under oaks, poplars, and terebinths,
Because their shade *is* good.
Therefore your daughters commit harlotry,
And your brides commit adultery.

¹⁴"I will not punish your daughters when they
  commit harlotry,
Nor your brides when they commit adultery;
For *the* men themselves go apart with harlots,
And offer sacrifices with a ritual harlot.[a]
Therefore people *who* do not understand will
  be trampled.

¹⁵"Though you, Israel, play the harlot,
Let not Judah offend.

• •

4:7 [a]Following Masoretic Text, Septuagint, and Vulgate; scribal tradition, Syriac, and Targum read *They will change.* [b]Following Masoretic Text, Septuagint, Syriac, Targum, and Vulgate; scribal tradition reads *My glory.* 4:14 [a]Compare Deuteronomy 23:18

4:13, 14 Israel's practice of pagan ritual was described. The people were slaying and offering sacrifices as well as burning incense. These practices were performed on elevated sites instead of in Jerusalem where God had commanded sacrifices were to be offered. Hosea mockingly referred to the only true benefit of choosing these sites for their abominations: good shade. As if these abominations were not enough, the leaders of Israel allowed their daughters and daughters-in-law (Heb. *kallah*, lit. "bride") to participate in cultic prostitution. God in

His justice would not punish these young women, while the men were pursuing cultic prostitutes without penalty. With immorality on such a grand scale, among both the leaders of Israel and the general population, it is no surprise that Hosea predicted the ruin of Israel: they were without understanding and were consequently headed for certain disaster.

4:15 Hosea presented Israel as an example to the people of Judah and warned them not to make pilgrimages to the north, a practice common at the time. Gilgal and Beth Aven (or

God promises to make the vale of trouble a door of hope.

Jill Briscoe

Do not come up to Gilgal,
Nor go up to Beth Aven,
Nor swear an oath, *saying,* 'As the LORD lives'—

16"For Israel is stubborn
Like a stubborn calf;
Now the LORD will let them forage
Like a lamb in open country.

17"Ephraim *is* joined to idols,
Let him alone.
18Their drink is rebellion,
They commit harlotry continually.
Her rulers dearly[a] love dishonor.
19The wind has wrapped her up in its wings,
And they shall be ashamed because of their
sacrifices.

Impending Judgment on Israel and Judah

5 "Hear this, O priests!
Take heed, O house of Israel!
Give ear, O house of the king!
For yours *is* the judgment,
Because you have been a snare to Mizpah
And a net spread on Tabor.
2The revolters are deeply involved in slaughter,
Though I rebuke them all.
3I know Ephraim,
And Israel is not hidden from Me;
For now, O Ephraim, you commit harlotry;
Israel is defiled.

4"They do not direct their deeds
Toward turning to their God,
For the spirit of harlotry is in their midst,
And they do not know the LORD.
5The pride of Israel testifies to his face;

Therefore Israel and Ephraim stumble in their
iniquity;
Judah also stumbles with them.

6"With their flocks and herds
They shall go to seek the LORD,
But they will not find *Him;*
He has withdrawn Himself from them.
7They have dealt treacherously with the LORD,
For they have begotten pagan children.
Now a New Moon shall devour them and their
heritage.

8"Blow the ram's horn in Gibeah,
The trumpet in Ramah!
Cry aloud *at* Beth Aven,
'*Look* behind you, O Benjamin!'
9Ephraim shall be desolate in the day of rebuke;
Among the tribes of Israel I make known what
is sure.

10"The princes of Judah are like those who
remove a landmark;
I will pour out My wrath on them like water.
11Ephraim is oppressed *and* broken in judgment,
Because he willingly walked by *human* precept.
12Therefore I *will be* to Ephraim like a moth,
And to the house of Judah like rottenness.

13"When Ephraim saw his sickness,
And Judah *saw* his wound,
Then Ephraim went to Assyria
And sent to King Jareb;
Yet he cannot cure you,

4:18 [a]Hebrew is difficult; a Jewish tradition reads *Her rulers shamefully love, 'Give!'*

Bethel) were cities considered to be heavily infected with idolatry (see Amos 4:4; 5:5). Beth Aven (Heb., lit "house of nothingness") is actually Hosea's contemptuous renaming of Bethel (Heb., lit. "house of God").

5:1 Israel's impending judgment would start with the priests and the king, the two primary entities of covenant leadership. The failure of Israel's leaders negatively affected the people. Hosea referred to Mizpah (a site on Samuel's circuit of judging; see 1 Sam. 7:5–11) and Tabor (a famous mountain in north central Palestine, south of the Lebanese border) as two places where evil was perpetrated.

5:6 The Lord withdrew from His people. The judgment here was complete. In vain Israel would seek the Lord; He would withdraw from them. The futility of their idolatrous devotion with all its sacrifices was profound. The people sought God's

favor through sacrifices, here symbolized in the two words "flocks" (small cattle like sheep and goats) and "herds" (larger cattle such as cows and oxen). However, true faith involved the heart's devotion and not just outward ritual.

5:8 The soundings of the ram's horn and trumpet were standard warning systems that alerted the people working in the fields to take protection behind the city walls and get ready for battle. Hosea furnished his audience with a glimpse of the doom about to overtake them in the form of an attack from Assyria.

5:13 In the day of judgment, Ephraim's immediate response was to seek aid not from God but from the king of Assyria. King Jareb (lit. "great king") is a reference to the king of Assyria, possibly Tiglath-pileser III (see chart, The Kings of Assyria).

Nor heal you of your wound.
14For I *will be* like a lion to Ephraim,
And like a young lion to the house of Judah.
I, *even* I, will tear *them* and go away;
I will take *them* away, and no one shall rescue.
15I will return again to My place
Till they acknowledge their offense.
Then they will seek My face;
In their affliction they will earnestly seek Me."

A Call to Repentance

6 Come, and let us return to the LORD;
For He has torn, but He will heal us;
He has stricken, but He will bind us up.
2After two days He will revive us;
On the third day He will raise us up,
That we may live in His sight.
3Let us know,
Let us pursue the knowledge of the LORD.
His going forth is established as the morning;
He will come to us like the rain,
Like the latter *and* former rain to the earth.

Impenitence of Israel and Judah

4"O Ephraim, what shall I do to you?
O Judah, what shall I do to you?
For your faithfulness is like a morning cloud,
And like the early dew it goes away.
5Therefore I have hewn *them* by the prophets,
I have slain them by the words of My mouth;
And your judgments *are like* light *that* goes
forth.
6For I desire mercy and not sacrifice,
And the knowledge of God more than burnt
offerings.

7"But like mena they transgressed the covenant;
There they dealt treacherously with Me.
8Gilead *is* a city of evildoers
And defiled with blood.
9As bands of robbers lie in wait for a man,
So the company of priests murder on the way
to Shechem;
Surely they commit lewdness.

10I have seen a horrible thing in the house of
Israel:
There *is* the harlotry of Ephraim;
Israel is defiled.
11Also, O Judah, a harvest is appointed for you,
When I return the captives of My people.

7"When I would have healed Israel,
Then the iniquity of Ephraim was uncovered,
And the wickedness of Samaria.
For they have committed fraud;
A thief comes in;
A band of robbers takes spoil outside.
2They do not consider in their hearts
That I remember all their wickedness;
Now their own deeds have surrounded them;
They are before My face.
3They make a king glad with their wickedness,
And princes with their lies.

4"They *are* all adulterers.
Like an oven heated by a baker—
He ceases stirring *the fire* after kneading the
dough,
Until it is leavened.
5In the day of our king
Princes have made *him* sick, inflamed with
wine;
He stretched out his hand with scoffers.
6They prepare their heart like an oven,
While they lie in wait;
Their bakera sleeps all night;
In the morning it burns like a flaming fire.
7They are all hot, like an oven,
And have devoured their judges;
All their kings have fallen.
None among them calls upon Me.

8"Ephraim has mixed himself among the
peoples;
Ephraim is a cake unturned.

••••••••••••••••••••••••••••

6:7 aOr *like Adam* 7:6 aFollowing Masoretic Text and Vulgate; Syriac
and Targum read *Their anger;* Septuagint reads *Ephraim.*

6:2 Israel hoped for mercy. Although the call to repentance
that begins in verse 1, on Israel's part, appears to be an acknowledgment of God's just judgment on them, it is not
enough (see vv. 4, 5 and God's rejection). The crucial requirement of admitting guilt is lacking. This contrasts sharply with
Hosea's closing song of penitence (see Hos. 14:1–3). The verbs
"revive" and "raise" up anticipate God's restoration of His
people.

**6:6 God has always wanted religious activity to reflect what is
in the heart** (see Matt. 9:13; 12:7). The importance of the sacrificial system, which God Himself had given, is not denied; but
God's plan for sacrifice, which was to be an outward manifestation of inner faith, is defined. The outward rituals are
meaningless to Him unless "mercy" and the "knowledge of
God" form the inward reality.

7:1 God's gracious intention to heal and restore Israel was
blocked by the realities of Ephraim's rebellion. The charge
here reiterated murder and looting by priests (Hos. 6:7–9).
God wanted to renew the nation. However, the wickedness of
one segment, Ephraim, and its corrupt capital Samaria made
that renewal impossible (see Hos. 1:1, note).

7:4 Adultery was mentioned specifically. Though primarily a
reference to spiritual adultery, unfaithfulness to marital vows
must have also been in view because of the cultic prostitution
associated with Baalism. Hosea compared the lustful release
of all moral restraints that characterized the religious and
moral life of Israel to the heating of leavened bread in the
oven. The heat of the oven was so intense that it needed no
tending during the night and still could be revived for baking
on the morrow.

*Your marriage is the guidepost by which your children
will establish their standards for their own marriage.*

Catherine Hickem

---

⁹Aliens have devoured his strength,
But he does not know *it;*
Yes, gray hairs are here and there on him,
Yet he does not know *it.*
¹⁰And the pride of Israel testifies to his face,
But they do not return to the LORD their God,
Nor seek Him for all this.

Futile Reliance on the Nations

¹¹"Ephraim also is like a silly dove, without
sense—
They call to Egypt,
They go to Assyria.
¹²Wherever they go, I will spread My net on
them;
I will bring them down like birds of the air;
I will chastise them
According to what their congregation has
heard.
¹³"Woe to them, for they have fled from Me!
Destruction to them,
Because they have transgressed against Me!
Though I redeemed them,
Yet they have spoken lies against Me.
¹⁴They did not cry out to Me with their heart
When they wailed upon their beds.

"They assemble together for[a] grain and new
wine,
They rebel against Me;[b]
¹⁵Though I disciplined *and* strengthened their
arms,
Yet they devise evil against Me;
¹⁶They return, *but* not to the Most High;[a]
They are like a treacherous bow.
Their princes shall fall by the sword
For the cursings of their tongue.
This *shall be* their derision in the land of Egypt.

The Apostasy of Israel

8 "Set the trumpet[a] to your mouth!
He shall come like an eagle against the house of
the LORD,

Because they have transgressed My covenant
And rebelled against My law.
²Israel will cry to Me,
'My God, we know You!'
³Israel has rejected the good;
The enemy will pursue him.

⁴"They set up kings, but not by Me;
They made princes, but I did not acknowledge
them.
From their silver and gold
They made idols for themselves—
That they might be cut off.
⁵Your calf is rejected, O Samaria!
My anger is aroused against them—
How long until they attain to innocence?
⁶For from Israel *is* even this:
A workman made it, and it *is* not God;
But the calf of Samaria shall be broken to
pieces.

⁷"They sow the wind,
And reap the whirlwind.
The stalk has no bud;
It shall never produce meal.
If it should produce,
Aliens would swallow it up.
⁸Israel is swallowed up;
Now they are among the Gentiles
Like a vessel in which *is* no pleasure.
⁹For they have gone up to Assyria,
Like a wild donkey alone by itself;
Ephraim has hired lovers.
¹⁰Yes, though they have hired among the nations,
Now I will gather them;
And they shall sorrow a little,[a]
Because of the burden[b] of the king of princes.

7:14 [a]Following Masoretic Text and Targum; Vulgate reads *thought
upon;* Septuagint reads *slashed themselves for* (compare 1 Kings
18:28). [b]Following Masoretic Text, Syriac, and Targum; Septuagint
omits *They rebel against Me;* Vulgate reads *They departed from Me.*
7:16 [a]Or *upward*   **8:1** [a]Hebrew *shophar,* ram's horn   **8:10** [a]Or *begin
to diminish* [b]Or *oracle*

7:11 The complete failure of Ephraim to worship her true God,
in time of trouble, led to a senseless foreign policy in which she
sought help from her natural enemies Egypt and Assyria. Subsequently, Israel's ruler Pekah went to Egypt for assistance
while under the vassalship of Assyria, a fatal move that led to
the loss of both his country and his life (see 2 Kin. 15:29, 30).

8:5, 6 God's anger burned against His people. The "calf of
Samaria," in all likelihood, was situated and housed in the

royal shrine at Bethel. As a symbol of Israel's embracing forbidden cults, these calves had been fashioned by men to take
the place of *Yahweh* and were an abomination before the
Lord (1 Kin. 12:28). Though the people had rationalized that
they were still honoring God, their worship at this shrine was
rejected by Him.

11"Because Ephraim has made many altars for sin,
They have become for him altars for sinning.
12I have written for him the great things of My law,
But they were considered a strange thing.
13*For* the sacrifices of My offerings they sacrifice flesh and eat *it*,
But the LORD does not accept them.
Now He will remember their iniquity and punish their sins.
They shall return to Egypt.

14"For Israel has forgotten his Maker,
And has built temples;ᵃ
Judah also has multiplied fortified cities;
But I will send fire upon his cities,
And it shall devour his palaces."

Judgment of Israel's Sin

9 Do not rejoice, O Israel, with joy like *other* peoples,
For you have played the harlot against your God.
You have made love *for* hire on every threshing floor.
2The threshing floor and the winepress
Shall not feed them,
And the new wine shall fail in her.

3They shall not dwell in the LORD's land,
But Ephraim shall return to Egypt,
And shall eat unclean *things* in Assyria.
4They shall not offer wine *offerings* to the LORD,
Nor shall their sacrifices be pleasing to Him.
It shall be like bread of mourners to them;
All who eat it shall be defiled.
For their bread *shall be* for their *own* life;
It shall not come into the house of the LORD.

5What will you do in the appointed day,
And in the day of the feast of the LORD?
6For indeed they are gone because of destruction.
Egypt shall gather them up;
Memphis shall bury them.

Nettles shall possess their valuables of silver;
Thorns *shall be* in their tents.

7The days of punishment have come;
The days of recompense have come.
Israel knows!
The prophet *is* a fool,
The spiritual man *is* insane,
Because of the greatness of your iniquity and great enmity.
8The watchman of Ephraim *is* with my God;
But the prophet *is* a fowler'sᵃ snare in all his ways—
Enmity in the house of his God.
9They are deeply corrupted,
As in the days of Gibeah.
He will remember their iniquity;
He will punish their sins.

10"I found Israel
Like grapes in the wilderness;
I saw your fathers
As the firstfruits on the fig tree in its first season.
But they went to Baal Peor,
And separated themselves *to that* shame;
They became an abomination like the thing they loved.
11*As for* Ephraim, their glory shall fly away like a bird—
No birth, no pregnancy, and no conception!
12Though they bring up their children,
Yet I will bereave them to the last man.
Yes, woe to them when I depart from them!
13Just as I saw Ephraim like Tyre, planted in a pleasant place,
So Ephraim will bring out his children to the murderer."

14Give them, O LORD—
What will You give?

·····················

8:14 ᵃOr *palaces* **9:8** ᵃThat is, one who catches birds in a trap or snare

---

9:1 Israel's rejection of God was complete. The Israelites, through their devotion to cultic practices, had put their hopes in Baal to provide material blessing. That blessing was thought to be guaranteed in exchange for ritual prostitution practiced at the shrines, which here were connected to "threshing floors" (see Hos. 2:8, note).

9:6 Any who attempted to find refuge in Egypt from the destruction brought on Israel by Assyria would not find it. Instead, they would be collected and buried in Memphis (a city in northern Egypt), where extensive burial grounds and ancient pyramids were located. All their cultic paraphernalia would have been abandoned when they fled; "nettles" and "thorns" were all that would remain.

9:10 God's joy over Israel when they first formed their covenant with Him in the wilderness is likened to the joy of both a hungry traveler who finds grapes growing in the desert and a gardener who finds the first ripe fig of the season. But He also recalled the time when Israel corrupted herself by committing adultery with the Moabites and devoting herself to their idols (see Num. 25:1–9). The punishment for adultery was death.

9:11 God's judgment of Israel would be so severe that it would strip them of their "glory," which in this context refers to their offspring. The future generation would have assured their continuity in the Land, but they would be cut off from that. To emphasize the barrenness that would affect the Land, God mentioned all three stages of human development. God's people would be painfully denied the children for whom they most longed.

God's love is so delightful–any other pleasure seems dismal in comparison with it.

St. Catherine of Genoa

Give them a miscarrying womb
And dry breasts!

[15]"All their wickedness *is* in Gilgal,
For there I hated them.
Because of the evil of their deeds
I will drive them from My house;
I will love them no more.
All their princes *are* rebellious.
[16]Ephraim is stricken,
Their root is dried up;
They shall bear no fruit.
Yes, were they to bear children,
I would kill the darlings of their womb."

[17]My God will cast them away,
Because they did not obey Him;
And they shall be wanderers among the
nations.

Israel's Sin and Captivity

10Israel empties *his* vine;
He brings forth fruit for himself.
According to the multitude of his fruit
He has increased the altars;
According to the bounty of his land
They have embellished *his* sacred pillars.
[2]Their heart is divided;
Now they are held guilty.
He will break down their altars;
He will ruin their sacred pillars.

[3]For now they say,
"We have no king,
Because we did not fear the LORD.
And as for a king, what would he do for us?"
[4]They have spoken words,
Swearing falsely in making a covenant.
Thus judgment springs up like hemlock in the
furrows of the field.

[5]The inhabitants of Samaria fear
Because of the calf[a] of Beth Aven.
For its people mourn for it,
And its priests shriek for it—

Because its glory has departed from it.
[6]*The idol* also shall be carried to Assyria
As a present for King Jareb.
Ephraim shall receive shame,
And Israel shall be ashamed of his own counsel.

[7]*As for* Samaria, her king is cut off
Like a twig on the water.
[8]Also the high places of Aven, the sin of Israel,
Shall be destroyed.
The thorn and thistle shall grow on their
altars;
They shall say to the mountains, "Cover us!"
And to the hills, "Fall on us!"

[9]"O Israel, you have sinned from the days of
Gibeah;
There they stood.
The battle in Gibeah against the children of
iniquity[a]
Did not overtake them.
[10]When *it is* My desire, I will chasten them.
Peoples shall be gathered against them
When I bind them for their two
transgressions.[a]
[11]Ephraim *is* a trained heifer
That loves to thresh *grain;*
But I harnessed her fair neck,
I will make Ephraim pull *a plow.*
Judah shall plow;
Jacob shall break his clods."

[12]Sow for yourselves righteousness;
Reap in mercy;
Break up your fallow ground,
For *it is* time to seek the LORD,
Till He comes and rains righteousness on you.

[13]You have plowed wickedness;
You have reaped iniquity.
You have eaten the fruit of lies,

10:5 [a]Literally *calves* **10:9** [a]So read many Hebrew manuscripts, Septuagint, and Vulgate; Masoretic Text reads *unruliness.* **10:10** [a]Or *in their two habitations*

10:4 Samaria's kings had attempted to find security, not in faithfulness to God but in alliances and treaties with foreign powers. Thus, Samaria had sowed the seeds of her own judgment, which were now sprouting like poisonous weeds throughout the Land.

10:8 The execution of God's judgment would produce such a terror in Israel that the people would cry out for the mountains to cover them and the hills to fall on them. About 700 years later, Jesus used this imagery to describe how the Jews would react to their destruction by Rome (Luke 23:30); also, those in the Great Tribulation, at the end of time, will likewise utilize this cry (see Rev. 6:16).

Because you trusted in your own way,
In the multitude of your mighty men.
[14]Therefore tumult shall arise among your
people,
And all your fortresses shall be plundered
As Shalman plundered Beth Arbel in the day of
battle—
A mother dashed in pieces upon *her* children.
[15]Thus it shall be done to you, O Bethel,
Because of your great wickedness.
At dawn the king of Israel
Shall be cut off utterly.

God's Continuing Love for Israel

11 "When Israel *was* a child, I loved him,
And out of Egypt I called My son.
[2]*As* they called them,[a]
So they went from them;[b]
They sacrificed to the Baals,
And burned incense to carved images.

[3]"I taught Ephraim to walk,
Taking them by their arms;[a]
But they did not know that I healed them.
[4]I drew them with gentle cords,[a]
With bands of love,
And I was to them as those who take the yoke
from their neck.[b]
I stooped *and* fed them.

[5]"He shall not return to the land of Egypt;
But the Assyrian shall be his king,
Because they refused to repent.
[6]And the sword shall slash in his cities,
Devour his districts,
And consume *them,*
Because of their own counsels.
[7]My people are bent on backsliding from Me.
Though they call to the Most High,[a]
None at all exalt *Him.*

[8]"How can I give you up, Ephraim?
How can I hand you over, Israel?
How can I make you like Admah?
How can I set you like Zeboiim?

My heart churns within Me;
My sympathy is stirred.
[9]I will not execute the fierceness of My anger;
I will not again destroy Ephraim.
For I *am* God, and not man,
The Holy One in your midst;
And I will not come with terror.[a]

[10]"They shall walk after the LORD.
He will roar like a lion.
When He roars,
Then *His* sons shall come trembling from the
west;
[11]They shall come trembling like a bird from
Egypt,
Like a dove from the land of Assyria.
And I will let them dwell in their houses,"
Says the LORD.

God's Charge Against Ephraim

[12]"Ephraim has encircled Me with lies,
And the house of Israel with deceit;
But Judah still walks with God,
Even with the Holy One[a] *who is* faithful.

12 "Ephraim feeds on the wind,
And pursues the east wind;
He daily increases lies and desolation.
Also they make a covenant with the Assyrians,
And oil is carried to Egypt.

[2]"The LORD also *brings* a charge against Judah,
And will punish Jacob according to his ways;
According to his deeds He will recompense
him.
[3]He took his brother by the heel in the womb,
And in his strength he struggled with God.[a]
[4]Yes, he struggled with the Angel and prevailed;

·················

11:2 [a]Following Masoretic Text and Vulgate; Septuagint reads *Just as I called them;* Targum interprets as *I sent prophets to a thousand of them.* [b]Following Masoretic Text, Targum, and Vulgate; Septuagint reads *from My face.* 11:3 [a]Some Hebrew manuscripts, Septuagint, Syriac, and Vulgate read *My arms.* 11:4 [a]Literally *cords of a man* [b]Literally *jaws* 11:7 [a]Or *upward* 11:9 [a]Or *I will not enter a city* 11:12 [a]Or *holy ones* 12:3 [a]Compare Genesis 32:28

11:1–4 God revealed another dimension of His love for Israel in these verses. In addition to loving her as a husband loves a wife, He loved her as a devoted and nurturing parent. Israel's rejection of God's love seemed even more outrageous in light of the tender care and interest He has always had for His cherished children.

11:8 God had sympathy for His people. God did not want to see His people utterly destroyed, as were Admah and Zeboiim, the cities of the plain, destroyed with Sodom and Gomorrah (see Gen. 10:19; 19:24; Deut. 29:23).

11:11 God's repentant people will be returned to their Land. The "lion" simile is used for God. The "roar" of the "lion" suggests a clear and loud call from God to His people.

Christ is the Lion of Judah (Rev. 5:5). The "bird" and "dove" images represent Israel. "Bird" and "dove" suggest the swiftness of the future return of God's people. These images strengthen the pictures of divine authority ("lion," Hos. 11:10), violated by Israel's rebellion (v. 12). This return of God's chastened and obedient people took place after they had served their time of punishment in Exile.

12:1 The foolishness of Ephraim's desertion of God culminated in a senseless and ultimately dangerous foreign policy. Here Ephraim is shown courting two foreign powers that were each other's enemy. She made a "covenant" with Assyria, while at the same time paying a tribute of olive "oil" to Egypt. This madness would eventually lead to Ephraim's destruction by these two volatile forces.

The ultimate expectation in Marriage is not in our consensus that we are one, but in our commitment to something bigger than any of us.

Gloria Gaither

He wept, and sought favor from Him.
He found Him *in* Bethel,
And there He spoke to us—
[5]That is, the LORD God of hosts.
The LORD *is* His memorable name.
[6]So you, by *the help of* your God, return;
Observe mercy and justice,
And wait on your God continually.

[7]"A cunning Canaanite!
Deceitful scales *are* in his hand;
He loves to oppress.
[8]And Ephraim said,
'Surely I have become rich,
I have found wealth for myself;
In all my labors
They shall find in me no iniquity that *is* sin.'

[9]"But I *am* the LORD your God,
Ever since the land of Egypt;
I will again make you dwell in tents,
As in the days of the appointed feast.
[10]I have also spoken by the prophets,
And have multiplied visions;
I have given symbols through the witness of
the prophets."

[11]Though Gilead *has* idols—
Surely they are vanity—
Though they sacrifice bulls in Gilgal,
Indeed their altars *shall be* heaps in the furrows
of the field.

[12]Jacob fled to the country of Syria;
Israel served for a spouse,
And for a wife he tended *sheep.*
[13]By a prophet the LORD brought Israel out of
Egypt,
And by a prophet he was preserved.
[14]Ephraim provoked *Him* to anger most bitterly;
Therefore his Lord will leave the guilt of his
bloodshed upon him,
And return his reproach upon him.

Relentless Judgment on Israel

13 When Ephraim spoke, trembling,
He exalted *himself* in Israel;

But when he offended through Baal *worship,* he
died.
[2]Now they sin more and more,
And have made for themselves molded images,
Idols of their silver, according to their skill;
All of it *is* the work of craftsmen.
They say of them,
"Let the men who sacrifice[a] kiss the calves!"
[3]Therefore they shall be like the morning cloud
And like the early dew that passes away,
Like chaff blown off from a threshing floor
And like smoke from a chimney.

[4]"Yet I *am* the LORD your God
Ever since the land of Egypt,
And you shall know no God but Me;
For *there is* no savior besides Me.
[5]I knew you in the wilderness,
In the land of great drought.
[6]When they had pasture, they were filled;
They were filled and their heart was exalted;
Therefore they forgot Me.

[7]"So I will be to them like a lion;
Like a leopard by the road I will lurk;
[8]I will meet them like a bear deprived *of her cubs;*
I will tear open their rib cage,
And there I will devour them like a lion.
The wild beast shall tear them.

[9]"O Israel, you are destroyed,[a]
But your help[b] *is* from Me.
[10]I will be your King;[a]
Where *is any other,*
That he may save you in all your cities?
And your judges to whom you said,
'Give me a king and princes'?
[11]I gave you a king in My anger,
And took *him* away in My wrath.

[12]"The iniquity of Ephraim *is* bound up;
His sin *is* stored up.
[13]The sorrows of a woman in childbirth shall
come upon him.

13:2 [a]Or *those who offer human sacrifice* **13:9** [a]Literally *it* or *he destroyed you* [b]Literally *in your help* **13:10** [a]Septuagint, Syriac, Targum, and Vulgate read *Where is your king?*

12:10 God had not left His people without guidance, warning, and instruction. He had given words and visions to the prophets, as well as using their lives as living parables of His teachings. Hosea's marriage to Gomer is an obvious example.

13:13 God used the familiar figure of a woman giving birth to alert Israel to the fact that the sufferings and calamities she was experiencing ("sorrows of a woman in childbirth") are meant as refining judgments, which could lead Israel to a new

He *is* an unwise son,
For he should not stay long where children are
born.

[14]"I will ransom them from the power of the
grave;[a]
I will redeem them from death.
O Death, I will be your plagues![b]
O Grave,[c] I will be your destruction![d]
Pity is hidden from My eyes."

[15]Though he is fruitful among *his* brethren,
An east wind shall come;
The wind of the LORD shall come up from the
wilderness.
Then his spring shall become dry,
And his fountain shall be dried up.
He shall plunder the treasury of every
desirable prize.
[16]Samaria is held guilty,[a]
For she has rebelled against her God.
They shall fall by the sword,
Their infants shall be dashed in pieces,
And their women with child ripped open.

Israel Restored at Last

14 O Israel, return to the LORD your God,
For you have stumbled because of your
iniquity;
[2]Take words with you,
And return to the LORD.
Say to Him,
"Take away all iniquity;
Receive *us* graciously,
For we will offer the sacrifices[a] of our
lips.
[3]Assyria shall not save us,
We will not ride on horses,

Nor will we say anymore to the work of our
hands, '*You are* our gods.'
For in You the fatherless finds mercy."

[4]"I will heal their backsliding,
I will love them freely,
For My anger has turned away from him.
[5]I will be like the dew to Israel;
He shall grow like the lily,
And lengthen his roots like Lebanon.
[6]His branches shall spread;
His beauty shall be like an olive
tree,
And his fragrance like Lebanon.
[7]Those who dwell under his shadow shall
return;
They shall be revived *like* grain,
And grow like a vine.
Their scent[a] *shall be* like the wine of
Lebanon.

[8]"Ephraim *shall say*, 'What have I to do anymore
with idols?'
I have heard and observed him.
I *am* like a green cypress tree;
Your fruit is found in Me."
[9]Who *is* wise?
Let him understand these things.
Who is prudent?
Let him know them.
For the ways of the LORD *are* right;
The righteous walk in them,
But transgressors stumble in them.

•••••••••••••••••

13:14 [a]Or *Sheol* [b]Septuagint reads *where is your punishment?* [c]Or *Sheol* [d]Septuagint reads *where is your sting?* **13:16** [a]Septuagint reads *shall be disfigured* **14:2** [a]Literally *bull calves;* Septuagint reads *fruit.* **14:7** [a]Literally *remembrance*

---

birth. Unwisely, the child refused to heed the signals of birth, and so the womb became a grave.

13:14 God promised to redeem His people even from all-powerful "death." God has authority over death and the "grave." The apostle Paul quoted this verse in his teaching on the Resurrection, where Christ's power over death and *hades* (Gk., lit. "the place of the dead," the equivalent of Heb. *she'ol*) is final (see 1 Cor. 15:55, 56).

13:16 Because Samaria rebelled against her covenant with God, she would no longer enjoy His protection when the wrath of her enemies (the "east wind" of Assyria, v. 15) fell upon her. The viciousness of this attack was revealed in the horrific picture of Israel's infants, born and unborn, falling victim to the onslaught.

14:1–3 Hosea issued one final call for true repentance, characterized by both the correct words and the correct actions. Israel must know that only in acknowledging guilt and putting her faith in God alone would she be able to find her Father's mercy.

14:4–7 Hosea portrayed Israel's beautiful restoration. Although Hosea's prophecies have boiled with warnings and threats of God's judgment, which subsequently were fulfilled, he ended his book on a note of hope. The ultimate reunion Hosea and Gomer experienced in their marriage was a picture of Israel's future restoration with the Lord. God's healing and restoring love would endure forever.

HOSEA'S MARRIAGE AND ISRAEL'S APOSTASY

HOSEA'S MARRIAGE	ADVICE FROM ISRAEL'S PROPHETS
The betrothal	Remember "the love of your betrothed" (Jer. 2:2).
Marriage (Hos. 1:2)	Protect and provide for your bride (Ezek. 16:8–14).
Children (Hos. 1:3)	Beware of neglecting your sons and daughters (Ezek. 16:20, 21).
Adultery (Hos. 3:1)	Remain faithful to the covenant of marriage (Jer. 5:7; Ezek. 16:15–34).
Estrangement (Hos. 3:3, 4)	Resolve conflict and rebuild intimacy (Jer. 3:8–10; Ezek. 16:35–52).
Restoration (Hos. 3:5)	Renew marriage vows and rebuild relationship (Ezek. 16:53–63).

Note: The stages in Hosea's relationship with Gomer are illustrative of the stages in Israel's relationship with Yahweh as depicted by the prophets.

Joel

AUTHOR

Joel (Heb. *"Yahweh* is God"), the son of Pethuel, states that this prophecy is "the word of the LORD" (Joel 1:1). Most scholars agree that Joel was highly educated, perhaps a member of the priesthood, and that he lived in or around Jerusalem. He is mentioned nowhere else in Scripture.

DATE

Several dates have been proposed, ranging from the preexilic time of King Joash (835–796 B.C.) to the postexilic period after or during the restoration of the wall of Jerusalem (400 B.C.), but no date is given in the text. The earlier traditional date has been favored for these reasons:

- the absence of the influence of a king or government in the book (King Joash ascended the throne as a child, and the priest Jehoiada actually ruled);
- the strong influence of the priesthood;
- the names of foreign nations found in the book.

The books of Joel and Amos have similar material (compare Joel 2:2 with Amos 5:18; Joel 3:16 with Amos 2:2; Joel 3:18 with Amos 9:13). These similarities could suggest an eighth century B.C. date for Joel, that Amos preached from the writings of Joel, or that both were inspired with the same prophecies. Fortunately, an understanding of Joel's message does not depend on a precise dating of its composition.

BACKGROUND

SETTING: Joel apparently was a prophet in Judah, the southern kingdom. The capital of Judah was Jerusalem. Joel's frequent references to the temple and its rituals suggest that he was a resident of Jerusalem, and perhaps a priest.

PURPOSE: Joel's prophecy stressed that calamities were judgments from God and warnings of the final judgment to come. He strongly proclaimed that judgment was coming on Judah because of sin, and he exhorted the covenant people to observe the events around them, to repent, and to return wholeheartedly to God. Finally, he wanted to impress on all people that the coming culmination of history would put the scales of God's justice in perfect balance.

AUDIENCE: Joel's message was first to the people in Jerusalem and Judah—they would be judged first and restored first. He boldly identified their sins and called for repentance. Then he expanded his prophecy to include all people—Jew and Gentile, present and future.

LITERARY CHARACTERISTICS: Joel wove together the three concepts of ruin, repentance, and restoration. His literary style is exceptional and unique in this respect. The focus and clarity of his images are almost lifelike. He builds toward the denouement (the

revelation or outcome), and the book is tied together with the powerful and beautiful concluding image of believers living in the presence of a loving and eternal God.

THEMES

Three themes are evident:

- God judges sin;
- God demands repentance; and
- God restores and blesses those who repent and commit themselves to Him.

Overriding these is the dominant idea that God is merciful and patient as seen in His repeated warnings; but there will be an end to His favor. He will judge the unrepentant (those who choose to stand against Him), while blessing the faithful.

OUTLINE

1 The word of the LORD that came to Joel the son of Pethuel.

The Land Laid Waste

²Hear this, you elders,
And give ear, all you inhabitants of the land!
Has *anything like* this happened in your days,
Or even in the days of your fathers?
³Tell your children about it,
Let your children *tell* their children,
And their children another generation.

⁴What the chewing locust[a] left, the swarming locust has eaten;
What the swarming locust left, the crawling locust has eaten;
And what the crawling locust left, the consuming locust has eaten.

••••••••••••••••••••

1:4 [a]Exact identity of these locusts is unknown.

1:1 **Prophets** were responsible for both "forthtelling" the Word of God and "foretelling" the future events ordained by God. Joel (Heb. "Yahweh is God") was the son of Pethuel.

1:2, 3 **Joel warned the people** not to be lulled into a false sense of security by the good life they had enjoyed. The prophet drew a direct correlation between the devotion and obedience of the people to God and the social and agricultural conditions in the Land (see Lev. 26). The disaster that had occurred must be taught from generation to generation as a reminder that God's final judgment would come surely and swiftly.

1:4 **Four kinds of locusts** are mentioned: "gnawer," "licker" or "hopper," "devourer" or "stripper," and "masses," describing the activities of the locusts. What the first onslaught of locusts missed, the second would devour, and so on until nothing was left. Locusts multiply at an alarming rate and swarm together in clouds that block the sun. Joel used the locust imagery to describe the final judgment. Strong emphasis is placed on the totality of the destruction that occurred. Joel recognized that as horrific as this calamity was, even more disasters would come unless the people made a complete and immediate return to their exclusive covenant with *Yahweh*.

⁵Awake, you drunkards, and weep;
  And wail, all you drinkers of wine,
  Because of the new wine,
  For it has been cut off from your mouth.
⁶For a nation has come up against My land,
  Strong, and without number;
  His teeth *are* the teeth of a lion,
  And he has the fangs of a fierce lion.
⁷He has laid waste My vine,
  And ruined My fig tree;
  He has stripped it bare and thrown *it* away;
  Its branches are made white.

⁸Lament like a virgin girded with sackcloth
  For the husband of her youth.
⁹The grain offering and the drink offering
  Have been cut off from the house of the
    LORD;
  The priests mourn, who minister to the LORD.
¹⁰The field is wasted,
  The land mourns;
  For the grain is ruined,
  The new wine is dried up,
  The oil fails.

¹¹Be ashamed, you farmers,
  Wail, you vinedressers,
  For the wheat and the barley;
  Because the harvest of the field has perished.
¹²The vine has dried up,
  And the fig tree has withered;
  The pomegranate tree,
  The palm tree also,
  And the apple tree—
  All the trees of the field are withered;
  Surely joy has withered away from the sons of
    men.

Mourning for the Land

¹³Gird yourselves and lament, you priests;
  Wail, you who minister before the altar;
  Come, lie all night in sackcloth,
  You who minister to my God;
  For the grain offering and the drink offering
  Are withheld from the house of your God.
¹⁴Consecrate a fast,
  Call a sacred assembly;
  Gather the elders
  And all the inhabitants of the land
  Into the house of the LORD your God,
  And cry out to the LORD.

¹⁵Alas for the day!
  For the day of the LORD *is* at hand;
  It shall come as destruction from the Almighty.
¹⁶Is not the food cut off before our eyes,
  Joy and gladness from the house of our God?
¹⁷The seed shrivels under the clods,
  Storehouses are in shambles;
  Barns are broken down,
  For the grain has withered.
¹⁸How the animals groan!
  The herds of cattle are restless,
  Because they have no pasture;
  Even the flocks of sheep suffer punishment.[a]

¹⁹O LORD, to You I cry out;
  For fire has devoured the open pastures,
  And a flame has burned all the trees of the field.
²⁰The beasts of the field also cry out to You,
  For the water brooks are dried up,
  And fire has devoured the open pastures.

•••••••••••••••••••

1:18 [a]Septuagint and Vulgate read *are made desolate.*

1:5 The prophet wanted the people to understand why God sent the locust plague to impact the drunkards, farmers, and priests (vv. 5–13) and how this plague would affect God's purpose for His people (vv. 14–20). Because the vineyards, which were not inherently evil, had been consumed by the locusts, there was no wine, a sign that God's blessing had departed from the Land.

1:6 Far worse than the scourge of locusts were the Assyrian (8th century B.C.) and Babylonian (6th century B.C.) invasions that came upon Israel and Judah. The plague was judgment in the present and warning for the future. Prosperity had lulled the people into complacency and moral decadence.

1:7 The fig tree and vine are references to ancient Israel (see Is. 5:1–7; Matt. 21:18, 19).

1:8 The Jewish nation is described as a virgin throughout Scripture (see Jer. 14:17). Sackcloth (usually woven of black goat's hair) was worn during times of mourning. Joel described the inconsolable grief of a virgin at the death of her betrothed prior to consummation of the marriage. Her opportunities for marriage would be almost non-existent. Israel's grief would be likewise inconsolable.

1:9, 10 The priests and the farmers were to mourn, not only for their livelihood, which had been destroyed, but also because the sacrifices and feasts of the Lord had been reduced or canceled by the devastation. Grain, wine, and oil were essential elements of sacrifice, and the locust plague destroyed them. The sacrifices were prerequisite for God to meet with His people. For Israel, suspension of the daily sacrifices implied a break in their fellowship with God.

1:11, 12 The nation faced starvation, for the grains (wheat and barley) and fruits (dates, apples, grapes, figs, and pomegranates) had been destroyed. Since abundant crops and food were signs of God's blessing, the destruction of the harvest was a severe indictment.

1:14 This key verse instructs all to repent, to fast, and to cry out to the Lord. God never leaves His people without recourse.

1:15 In Egypt the plague of locusts came before the plagues of darkness and death (Ex. 10:21–29; 11; 12:29, 30). Joel viewed this locust plague as a harbinger of worse things to come. God protected and delivered His people when He brought plagues on the Egyptians. Now His own people would experience a taste of what it was like to be an enemy of God.

The Day of the LORD

2 Blow the trumpet in Zion,
And sound an alarm in My holy mountain!
Let all the inhabitants of the land tremble;
For the day of the LORD is coming,
For it is at hand:
[2]A day of darkness and gloominess,
A day of clouds and thick darkness,
Like the morning *clouds* spread over the
    mountains.
A people *come,* great and strong,
The like of whom has never been;
Nor will there ever be any *such* after them,
Even for many successive generations.

[3]A fire devours before them,
And behind them a flame burns;
The land *is* like the Garden of Eden before
    them,
And behind them a desolate wilderness;
Surely nothing shall escape them.
[4]Their appearance is like the appearance of
    horses;
And like swift steeds, so they run.
[5]With a noise like chariots
Over mountaintops they leap,
Like the noise of a flaming fire that devours
    the stubble,
Like a strong people set in battle array.

[6]Before them the people writhe in pain;
All faces are drained of color.[a]
[7]They run like mighty men,
They climb the wall like men of war;
Every one marches in formation,
And they do not break ranks.
[8]They do not push one another;
Every one marches in his own column.[a]

Though they lunge between the weapons,
They are not cut down.[b]
[9]They run to and fro in the city,
They run on the wall;
They climb into the houses,
They enter at the windows like a thief.

[10]The earth quakes before them,
The heavens tremble;
The sun and moon grow dark,
And the stars diminish their brightness.
[11]The LORD gives voice before His army,
For His camp is very great;
For strong *is the One* who executes His word.
For the day of the LORD *is* great and very
    terrible;
Who can endure it?

A Call to Repentance

[12]"Now, therefore," says the LORD,
"Turn to Me with all your heart,
With fasting, with weeping, and with
    mourning."
[13]So rend your heart, and not your garments;
Return to the LORD your God,
For He *is* gracious and merciful,
Slow to anger, and of great kindness;
And He relents from doing harm.
[14]Who knows *if* He will turn and relent,
And leave a blessing behind Him—
A grain offering and a drink offering
For the LORD your God?

[15]Blow the trumpet in Zion,
Consecrate a fast,
Call a sacred assembly;

••••••••••••••••••••
2:6 [a]Septuagint, Targum, and Vulgate read *gather blackness.* **2:8**
[a]Literally *his own highway* [b]That is, they are not halted by losses

2:1 The trumpet (Heb. *shophar*) was a ram's horn, blown to alert people of impending danger, the start of the Sabbath, the beginning of the month, and the celebration of various feasts. The holy mount is the Temple Mount in Jerusalem. At this point, Joel shifted images from that of an army of locusts to an actual invading army. Locust invasions were normally from the south or southeast, but this army came out of the north and was the instrument of the Lord for destruction to turn the people back to Him (v. 20).

2:1 The day of the Lord may refer to any time God intervenes actively to judge or to bless but always points to that final day of judgment at the end of history. The phrase is particularly associated with the latter days and that "great and awesome day of the LORD" (Joel 2:31; see also Ezek. 30:3; Acts 2:20; 2 Pet. 3:10).

2:3–11 Another description of the day of the Lord is revealed, more terrible than the previous one when the locusts covered the land. This description vividly pictures the invasion of a foreign army, the captivity of Israel, and the punishment of Judah. However, even this calamity pales in comparison to the final divine judgment of those who refuse Christ.

2:10, 11 This description of cosmic disturbance depicted the divine commander as the leader, initiator, and conductor of judgment (Is. 13:13).

2:12–17 This appeal for a change of heart was initiated by the Lord. In the face of calamity, the only effective response was to call on the Lord Almighty.

2:13 When tragedy occurred, the proper expression of mourning was to smear the head with ashes, tear garments, and put on sackcloth. God instructed the people that He was not interested in outward expressions but in a broken and contrite heart (1 Sam. 16:7).

2:13, 14 Sin breaks the heart of God more than the rules of God. God seeks your repentance and the restoration of your relationship to Him. In His sovereignty, He can bring blessings from the most tragic and traumatic situations (Rom. 8:28–30). By mentioning the grain and drink offering, the prophet indicated that it is a privilege and a blessing to worship God.

¹⁶Gather the people,
Sanctify the congregation,
Assemble the elders,
Gather the children and nursing babes;
Let the bridegroom go out from his chamber,
And the bride from her dressing room.
¹⁷Let the priests, who minister to the Lord,
Weep between the porch and the altar;
Let them say, "Spare Your people, O Lord,
And do not give Your heritage to reproach,
That the nations should rule over them.
Why should they say among the peoples,
'Where is their God?' "

The Land Refreshed

¹⁸Then the Lord will be zealous for His land,
And pity His people.
¹⁹The Lord will answer and say to His people,
"Behold, I will send you grain and new wine and
oil,
And you will be satisfied by them;
I will no longer make you a reproach among
the nations.

²⁰"But I will remove far from you the northern
army,
And will drive him away into a barren and
desolate land,
With his face toward the eastern sea
And his back toward the western sea;
His stench will come up,
And his foul odor will rise,
Because he has done monstrous things."

²¹Fear not, O land;
Be glad and rejoice,
For the Lord has done marvelous things!
²²Do not be afraid, you beasts of the field;
For the open pastures are springing up,
And the tree bears its fruit;
The fig tree and the vine yield their
strength.
²³Be glad then, you children of Zion,
And rejoice in the Lord your God;

For He has given you the former rain
faithfully,^a
And He will cause the rain to come down for
you—
The former rain,
And the latter rain in the first *month*.
²⁴The threshing floors shall be full of wheat,
And the vats shall overflow with new wine and
oil.

²⁵"So I will restore to you the years that the
swarming locust has eaten,
The crawling locust,
The consuming locust,
And the chewing locust,^a
My great army which I sent among you.
²⁶You shall eat in plenty and be satisfied,
And praise the name of the Lord your God,
Who has dealt wondrously with you;
And My people shall never be put to shame.
²⁷Then you shall know that I *am* in the midst of
Israel:
I *am* the Lord your God
And there is no other.
My people shall never be put to shame.

God's Spirit Poured Out

²⁸"And it shall come to pass afterward
That I will pour out My Spirit on all flesh;
Your sons and your daughters shall
prophesy,
Your old men shall dream dreams,
Your young men shall see visions.
²⁹And also on *My* menservants and on *My*
maidservants
I will pour out My Spirit in those days.

³⁰"And I will show wonders in the heavens and in
the earth:
Blood and fire and pillars of smoke.
³¹The sun shall be turned into darkness,
And the moon into blood,

••••••••••••••••••••••••••••••••••••

2:23 ^aOr *the teacher of righteousness*   2:25 ^aCompare 1:4

2:16 All were to gather at the sacred assembly to weep and pray (v. 17). None was exempt, not even those normally excused, such as nursing mothers and children and those about to be married (see Deut. 24:5). Extreme urgency was expressed in the tone of the words.

2:18–25 When God's people repented, the Land would be restored. This theme of sin and restoration permeates Scripture (Gen. 3:13–24; Lev. 26:3, 4). Sin never occurs in isolation; it is always social in nature and influence.

2:25–27 God's grace would return the time spent in judgment. The statement implied that when repentance occurred, joy would be of such magnitude that former times of sorrow and pain would be erased.

2:28, 29 After judgment, God's Spirit would be poured out on

all His people, regardless of age, sex, or social class. Twice Joel stated that the outpouring of the Spirit would include women. Paul reinforced this principle of equality in Christ (Gal. 3:28). This outpouring differed from the OT pattern, in which God poured out His Spirit on an individual for a particular task. This prophecy declared that God's Spirit would be given to all believers. Peter quoted this passage at Pentecost (Acts 2:17–21) to explain the manifestation of the Holy Spirit upon believers. Jesus anticipated this same outpouring of the Spirit upon His followers (John 14:15–17; 16:7–15).

2:30, 31 Cosmic cataclysm announced the "day of the Lord." The progression is from the locusts (whether in Egypt or in Joel's time) to the invading army, to any time of judgment, to the final judgment. Every calamity is a reminder of the great and final judgment.

You cannot be half a saint. You must be a whole saint or no saint at all.

St. Therese of Lisieux

Before the coming of the great and awesome
day of the LORD.
32And it shall come to pass
That whoever calls on the name of the LORD
Shall be saved.
For in Mount Zion and in Jerusalem there shall
be deliverance,
As the LORD has said,
Among the remnant whom the LORD calls.

God Judges the Nations

3 "For behold, in those days and at that time,
When I bring back the captives of Judah and
Jerusalem,
2I will also gather all nations,
And bring them down to the Valley of
Jehoshaphat;
And I will enter into judgment with them
there
On account of My people, My heritage Israel,
Whom they have scattered among the nations;
They have also divided up My land.
3They have cast lots for My people,
Have given a boy *as payment* for a harlot,
And sold a girl for wine, that they may drink.

4"Indeed, what have you to do with Me,
O Tyre and Sidon, and all the coasts of
Philistia?
Will you retaliate against Me?
But if you retaliate against Me,
Swiftly and speedily I will return your
retaliation upon your own head;
5Because you have taken My silver and My gold,
And have carried into your temples My prized
possessions.
6Also the people of Judah and the people of
Jerusalem

You have sold to the Greeks,
That you may remove them far from their
borders.

7"Behold, I will raise them
Out of the place to which you have sold them,
And will return your retaliation upon your own
head.
8I will sell your sons and your daughters
Into the hand of the people of Judah,
And they will sell them to the Sabeans,a
To a people far off;
For the LORD has spoken."

9Proclaim this among the nations:
"Prepare for war!
Wake up the mighty men,
Let all the men of war draw near,
Let them come up.
10Beat your plowshares into swords
And your pruning hooks into spears;
Let the weak say, 'I *am* strong.' "
11Assemble and come, all you nations,
And gather together all around.
Cause Your mighty ones to go down there,
O LORD.

12"Let the nations be wakened, and come up to
the Valley of Jehoshaphat;
For there I will sit to judge all the surrounding
nations.
13Put in the sickle, for the harvest is ripe.
Come, go down;
For the winepress is full,
The vats overflow—
For their wickedness *is* great."

3:8 aLiterally *Shebaites* (compare Isaiah 60:6 and Ezekiel 27:22)

2:32 The salvation of God is available to all who call on the name of the Lord. There is salvation in no other name (John 3:36; Acts 4:12; Rom. 10:13). God is Creator, Jesus is Lord and Redeemer, and the Holy Spirit is Sustainer.

3:1 God will restore the Jews to their Land, their fortunes, and the covenant He made with them (Jer. 30:18; 31:23). God will judge the nations concerning their treatment of His people (Rom. 11:25, 26). God will initiate the final day of judgment, and He will bring all the nations to the Valley of Jehoshaphat (lit., *"Yahweh* judges"). This valley's importance is more theological than topographical. The character of the judgment, not the location, is emphasized (Joel 3:12).

3:4 The neighbors who perennially harassed Judah included Tyre, Sidon, Philistia, Egypt, and Edom (v. 19). Many of these

nations engaged in slave trade. Punishment would be delivered especially for two crimes—the looting of treasures (probably from the temple in Jerusalem) and the selling of God's people into slavery.

3:9–12 Joel deliberately reversed the commands in which the peace and blessings of the messianic kingdom were anticipated (Is. 2:4; Mic. 4:3). The time for peace had not yet arrived. The present time, declared Joel, would be a time for war. The nations would gather their forces, but the Sovereign Lord would not be anxious or moved. He would be the final judge. Joel 3:12 offers great hope for the believer.

3:13 Joel used an agricultural theme throughout the book. Now the harvest imagery changed from grains and wine to the destruction and judgment of the enemies of God.

¹⁴Multitudes, multitudes in the valley of
    decision!
For the day of the LORD *is* near in the valley of
    decision.
¹⁵The sun and moon will grow dark,
    And the stars will diminish their brightness.
¹⁶The LORD also will roar from Zion,
    And utter His voice from Jerusalem;
    The heavens and earth will shake;
    But the LORD will be a shelter for His
       people,
    And the strength of the children of Israel.

¹⁷"So you shall know that I *am* the LORD your
    God,
    Dwelling in Zion My holy mountain.
    Then Jerusalem shall be holy,
    And no aliens shall ever pass through her
      again."

God Blesses His People

¹⁸And it will come to pass in that day
    That the mountains shall drip with new wine,
    The hills shall flow with milk,
    And all the brooks of Judah shall be flooded
      with water;
    A fountain shall flow from the house of the LORD
    And water the Valley of Acacias.

¹⁹"Egypt shall be a desolation,
    And Edom a desolate wilderness,
    Because of violence *against* the people of Judah,
    For they have shed innocent blood in their
      land.
²⁰But Judah shall abide forever,
    And Jerusalem from generation to generation.
²¹For I will acquit them of the guilt of
      bloodshed, whom I had not acquitted;
    For the LORD dwells in Zion."

3:14–16 The valley of decision (which may be the same as the Valley of Jehoshaphat) refers to the verdict of the Lord as He carried out His divine judgment on the nations. The time for decisions by individuals is past—now God would judge and decree punishment. One of the saddest features in these verses is the reference to "multitudes," suggesting innumerable people. The certainty of final judgment must prompt believers to commit themselves to God and to call unbelievers to repentance.

3:16 The climax of the battle is described in poetic terms, enabling the reader to picture the judgment of God more vividly. While the heavens and earth are shaking, the Lord will be a shelter for His people.

3:17–21 The prophet described the hope and goal of all prophecy—a time when God would dwell with His people and the joy of His presence would exist forever (Rev. 21:3, 4). Joel emphasized that the people of God would dwell in the holy place of God (Jerusalem) in the beautiful Promised Land.

3:18 Joel spoke of the same river the prophet John mentioned (Rev. 22:1, 2).

3:20, 21 The judgment for sin will finally be over. Atonement for the enormous bloodguilt of God's people was finally and completely made by Jesus Christ in His death on the Cross (Heb. 9:28; 10:10). Joel reiterated the promise that the people of God would return to their Land and to Jerusalem, and God would reign and live in Zion with His people forever.

Amos

Traditionally, authorship of the Book of Amos has been ascribed to the eighth century B.C. prophet bearing that name (Amos 1:1). Amos laid claim to God's call to prophesy (Amos 7:14, 15), but he denied association with the group of professional prophets, many of whom made their living by prophesying only what the people and leaders of Israel wanted to hear. Amos earned his living as a sheepbreeder, and he had a seasonal job as a tender of sycamore fruit, slitting the "poor man's figs" to make them sweeter and softer for market (Amos 7:14). He was a native of Tekoa, a city located in Judah, approximately ten miles south of Jerusalem. Amos was not necessarily a poor man. Yet he left all when the Lord called him to go as a foreign missionary from the southern kingdom to the northern kingdom of Israel. Amos (lit. "burdened" or "burden bearer") delivered a weighty message from the Lord to His wayward people.

DATE

Amos' prophecy is placed during the reigns of Uzziah in Judah (792–740 B.C.) and Jeroboam II in Israel (793–753 B.C.; see Amos 1:1). A definite date for his initial prophecy is noted as "two years before the earthquake" (Amos 1:1), but an exact date for the quake is not known. It is placed in the reign of Uzziah (Zech. 14:5). Archaeological evidence from the excavation at Hazor suggests a date of 765–760 B.C. for the earthquake. A specific prophecy regarding the imminent doom of "the house of Jeroboam" (Amos 7:9) would also support a date for Amos' ministry near the end of Jeroboam's reign around 760 B.C.

BACKGROUND

SETTING: Israel was enjoying a golden age of peace and prosperity in its history. Jeroboam II had extended Israel's borders (2 Kin. 14:23–25). The nation was free from external pressures. In this pleasant environment, God's people had forgotten Him. They had divided themselves into a two-class society—the wealthy and the poor. They were religious but not righteous, tracing their wayward religious practices back to Jeroboam I, who set up pagan worship centers in Dan and Bethel.

PURPOSE: Amos indicted Israel for four major sins: inhumane treatment of others, mistreatment of the poor, false pride in their wealth and race, and insincere worship. Although God's people regularly participated in religious activities, their lives did not demonstrate what they professed. Thus, Amos announced Israel's day of judgment, which he designated "the day of the Lord" (Amos 5:18–20).

AUDIENCE: Amos' audience consisted of the inhabitants of the northern kingdom of Israel.

LITERARY CHARACTERISTICS: Much of the Book of Amos is written in Hebrew poetry, characterized by rhythm instead of rhyme. Amos utilized a numerical pattern in the oracles or prophecies against the nations (Amos 1—2).

The primary theme of the Book of Amos is the Lord's judgment on His people. Israel would face God's judgment and go into exile because of sin (Amos 7:17). They acted with injustice toward the poor and needy. The message of Amos is relevant for affluent societies in all generations. Amos appropriately is designated "the prophet of God's justice" (see Amos 5:24).

1 The words of Amos, who was among the sheep-breeders[a] of Tekoa, which he saw concerning Israel in the days of Uzziah king of Judah, and in the days of Jeroboam the son of Joash, king of Israel, two years before the earthquake.

2And he said:

"The LORD roars from Zion,
And utters His voice from Jerusalem;
The pastures of the shepherds mourn,
And the top of Carmel withers."

Judgment on the Nations

3Thus says the LORD:

"For three transgressions of Damascus, and for four,
I will not turn away its *punishment*,
Because they have threshed Gilead with implements of iron.
4But I will send a fire into the house of Hazael,

. . . .

1:1 [a]Compare 2 Kings 3:4

1:3—2:3 Amos described the reasons for God's judgment on six neighbors of Israel and Judah. These nations were condemned primarily for their inhumane treatment of others. The basic structure for each announcement of judgment is as follows: the introductory formula, the charge, the specific punishment, and the concluding formula. God would not revoke or "turn away" His judgment on the nations (Amos 1:3, 6, 9, 11, 13; 2:1).

1:3 A specific pattern is generally repeated with each announcement of judgment on a nation. "For three transgressions . . . and for four" begins each oracle (vv. 3, 6, 9, 11, 13; Amos 2:1, 4, 6). The phrase "three transgressions" indicates

that the Lord has had enough of the people's sin. "Transgressions" often refers to rebellion or deliberate revolt (see Ps. 32:1, 2, note). "Four" represents the fact that their sin is overflowing and intolerable. Damascus had sinned again and again. They had reached the limit, and God's judgment upon them was now certain. Most mothers have felt frustration similar to this when a child disobeys again and again and correction is made with boundaries clearly defined. Finally, punishment comes swiftly and effectively.

1:3–5 Damascus, the capital of Syria, was indicted for cruelty in warfare toward Gilead, their less powerful neighbors to the south. "Implements of iron," normally used to thresh grain,

ORACLES AGAINST THE NATIONS

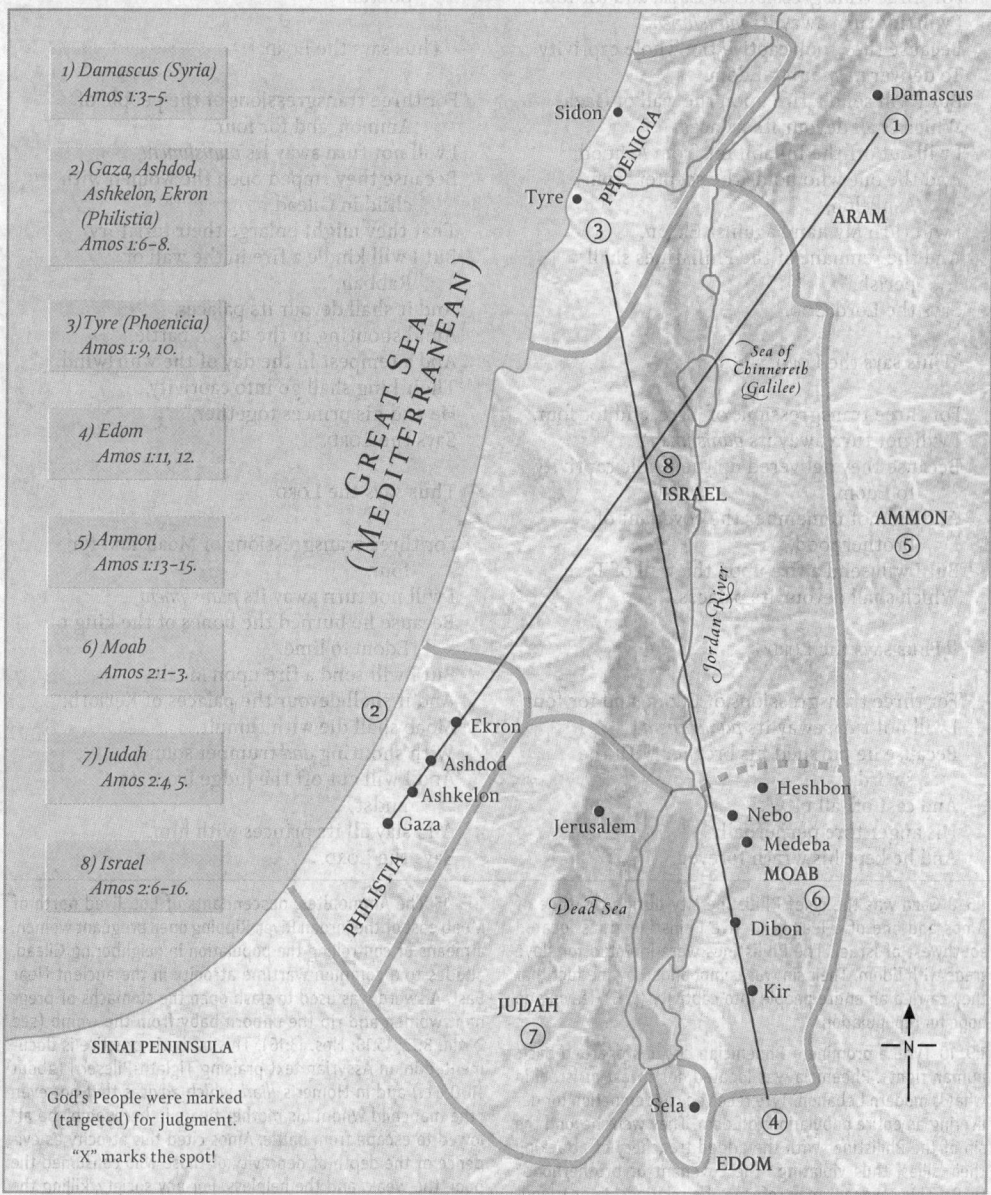

1) Damascus (Syria)
   Amos 1:3–5.

2) Gaza, Ashdod,
   Ashkelon, Ekron
   (Philistia)
   Amos 1:6–8.

3) Tyre (Phoenicia)
   Amos 1:9, 10.

4) Edom
   Amos 1:11, 12.

5) Ammon
   Amos 1:13–15.

6) Moab
   Amos 2:1–3.

7) Judah
   Amos 2:4, 5.

8) Israel
   Amos 2:6–16.

SINAI PENINSULA

God's People were marked
(targeted) for judgment.

"X" marks the spot!

GREAT SEA
(MEDITERRANEAN)

Sidon
PHOENICIA
Tyre

Damascus
①

ARAM

③

Sea of
Chinnereth
(Galilee)

⑧
ISRAEL

AMMON
⑤

Jordan River

②
Ekron
Ashdod
Ashkelon
Gaza

PHILISTIA

Jerusalem

Heshbon
Nebo
Medeba
MOAB
⑥

Dibon

Kir

Dead Sea

JUDAH
⑦

Sela
④

EDOM

—N—

Which shall devour the palaces of Ben-Hadad.
⁵I will also break the *gate* bar of Damascus,
And cut off the inhabitant from the Valley of
   Aven,

And the one who holds the scepter from Beth
   Eden.
The people of Syria shall go captive to Kir,"
Says the LORD.

---

may have been used by the Syrians to rake over their prisoners of war. Hazael murdered Ben-Hadad and succeeded him
as king of Syria. Both led border wars against Israel (v. 4; see

2 Kin. 6:24, 25; 8:7–15; 10:32, 33; 13:3; see chart, The Kings of
Syria). "Fire" symbolizes warfare.

⁶Thus says the LORD:

"For three transgressions of Gaza, and for four,
I will not turn away its *punishment*,
Because they took captive the whole captivity
To deliver *them* up to Edom.
⁷But I will send a fire upon the wall of Gaza,
Which shall devour its palaces.
⁸I will cut off the inhabitant from Ashdod,
And the one who holds the scepter from
Ashkelon;
I will turn My hand against Ekron,
And the remnant of the Philistines shall
perish,"
Says the Lord GOD.

⁹Thus says the LORD:

"For three transgressions of Tyre, and for four,
I will not turn away its *punishment*,
Because they delivered up the whole captivity
to Edom,
And did not remember the covenant of
brotherhood.
¹⁰But I will send a fire upon the wall of Tyre,
Which shall devour its palaces."

¹¹Thus says the LORD:

"For three transgressions of Edom, and for four,
I will not turn away its *punishment*,
Because he pursued his brother with the
sword,
And cast off all pity;
His anger tore perpetually,
And he kept his wrath forever.

¹²But I will send a fire upon Teman,
Which shall devour the palaces of
Bozrah."

¹³Thus says the LORD:

"For three transgressions of the people of
Ammon, and for four,
I will not turn away its *punishment*,
Because they ripped open the women with
child in Gilead,
That they might enlarge their territory.
¹⁴But I will kindle a fire in the wall of
Rabbah,
And it shall devour its palaces,
Amid shouting in the day of battle,
And a tempest in the day of the whirlwind.
¹⁵Their king shall go into captivity,
He and his princes together,"
Says the LORD.

2 Thus says the LORD:

"For three transgressions of Moab, and for
four,
I will not turn away its *punishment*,
Because he burned the bones of the king of
Edom to lime.
²But I will send a fire upon Moab,
And it shall devour the palaces of Kerioth;
Moab shall die with tumult,
With shouting *and* trumpet sound.
³And I will cut off the judge from its
midst,
And slay all its princes with him,"
Says the LORD.

1:6–8 Gaza was the chief Philistine city during the time of Amos and one of a league of five Philistine cities located southwest of Israel. The Philistines were indicted for slave trade with Edom. Their sin was compounded by the fact that they carried an entire people into captivity (v. 6), leaving no hope for repopulation.

1:9, 10 Tyre, a prominent Phoenician city, disregarded basic human rights. Phoenicia was located northwest of Israel in what is modern Lebanon. Tyre received condemnation for delivering an entire population to Edom. They went beyond the sin of the Philistines with the added treachery of attacking their allies, thus violating "the covenant of brotherhood" (v. 9). This covenant may refer to the relationship of friendship and mutual assistance established between kings David and Solomon of Israel and Hiram of Tyre (v. 9; see 2 Sam. 5:11; 1 Kin. 5:1–11).

1:11, 12 The inhabitants of Edom descended from Esau, the brother of Jacob. Hostility between the twins Jacob and Esau began in their mother's womb, persisted throughout their lives, and continued in their descendants. The Edomites refused passage through their land to the children of Israel bound for Canaan (Num. 20:14–21). They served as the intermediary for the slave trade between the Philistines and Phoenicians and distant nations (Amos 1:11).

1:13–15 The Ammonites, descendants of Lot, lived north of Moab east of the Jordan River. Ripping open pregnant women, a means of controlling the population in neighboring Gilead, alludes to a common wartime atrocity in the ancient Near East. A sword was used to slash open the stomachs of pregnant women and rip the unborn baby from the womb (see 2 Kin. 8:12; 15:16; Hos. 13:16). This barbaric practice is documented in an Assyrian text praising Tiglath-Pileser I (about 1100 B.C.) and in Homer's *Iliad*, which advises that not even "the manchild whom his mother bears in her womb" be allowed to escape from battle. Amos cited this atrocity as evidence of the depth of depravity of those who consumed the poor, the weak, and the helpless. For any society, killing the unborn child is the ultimate sin against the helpless (see Gen. 9, Sanctity of Life; Jer. 1, Abortion). The Ammonites engaged in this cruelty for the purpose of enlarging their own borders. Rabbah served as the capital of Ammon (Amos 1:14).

2:1–3 Moab was situated east of the Dead Sea between Ammon and Edom. The Moabites descended from Lot. The exact nature of Moab's crime is unclear. Probably the reference is to violating the sanctity of a tomb and treating the remains of a dead Edomite king with indignity. Punishment came in the form of "fire" or warfare (v. 2). Kerioth was a major city of Moab (Jer. 48:41).

Judgment on Judah

4Thus says the Lord:

"For three transgressions of Judah, and for four,
  I will not turn away its *punishment,*
Because they have despised the law of the
    Lord,
  And have not kept His commandments.
Their lies lead them astray,
Lies which their fathers followed.
5But I will send a fire upon Judah,
  And it shall devour the palaces of Jerusalem."

Judgment on Israel

6Thus says the Lord:

"For three transgressions of Israel, and for four,
  I will not turn away its *punishment,*
Because they sell the righteous for silver,
  And the poor for a pair of sandals.
7They pant aftera the dust of the earth *which is*
    on the head of the poor,
  And pervert the way of the humble.
A man and his father go in to the *same* girl,
  To defile My holy name.
8They lie down by every altar on clothes taken
    in pledge,
  And drink the wine of the condemned *in* the
    house of their god.

9"Yet *it was* I *who* destroyed the Amorite before
    them,
  Whose height *was* like the height of the
    cedars,

And he *was as* strong as the oaks;
  Yet I destroyed his fruit above
  And his roots beneath.
10Also *it was* I *who* brought you up from the land
    of Egypt,
  And led you forty years through the
    wilderness,
  To possess the land of the Amorite.
11I raised up some of your sons as prophets,
  And some of your young men as Nazirites.
  Is it not so, O you children of Israel?"
  Says the Lord.
12"But you gave the Nazirites wine to drink,
  And commanded the prophets saying,
  'Do not prophesy!'

13"Behold, I am weighed down by you,
  As a cart full of sheaves is weighed down.
14Therefore flight shall perish from the swift,
  The strong shall not strengthen his power,
  Nor shall the mighty deliver himself;
15He shall not stand who handles the bow,
  The swift of foot shall not escape,
  Nor shall he who rides a horse deliver
    himself.
16The most courageous men of might
  Shall flee naked in that day,"
  Says the Lord.

Authority of the Prophet's Message

3 Hear this word that the Lord has spoken
against you, O children of Israel, against the

2:7 aOr trample on

2:4, 5 Amos denounced Judah, having the rapt attention of his audience in Israel. The inhabitants of Judah, who had sunk to the level of the pagan nations, were condemned because they "despised the law of the Lord" (the revelation of God's will and way) and did not obey the *Torah.* "Lies" refers to idolatry (v. 4). The Lord's people were held accountable for the greater revelation they had received.

2:6–16 The indictment against Israel is the most lengthy of Amos' pronouncements against the nations. The prophet especially pointed out the crimes against their own countrymen. The poor of the land were being sold for money (silver) or property (represented by "a pair of sandals," the most insignificant item) because they could not pay debts owed to wealthy creditors (see also Ruth 4:7, note, for another reference to the sandal).

2:7, 8 Both son and father consorted sexually with the same maiden, a practice forbidden in Israel (Lev. 18:8, 15; 20:11; Deut. 22:30; 23:17, 18). They compounded their sin of sensual indulgence with idolaltry, perhaps the practice of cultic prostitution associated with the worship of Baal. Here the worshipers lay down by the altars for luxurious religious feasts on garments taken in pledge, in order to keep their own clothing clean. The borrowed clothes were to have been returned before sundown so that the owners would not be deprived of their coverings (Ex. 22:26, 27). The idol worshipers indulged

themselves at the expense of the poor. They went to the place of worship but defied God's Law and brought more misery to the least of His people.

2:9–12 The Lord rehearsed His mighty acts on behalf of His people accompanied by a note of His exasperation with their disobedience (vv. 13–16). God raised up prophets to instruct His people in righteousness and Nazirites to be an example of devotion to the Lord by separating themselves from wine or strong drink, the razor, and dead bodies (v. 12; Num. 6:1–8). The Israelites rejected the message of the prophets and ridiculed the Nazirite vow (Amos 2:12). Amos had experienced firsthand Israel's sin of commanding the prophets not to prophesy (v. 12, see Amos 7:12, 13, 16).

2:13–16 The Lord's judgment on Israel was inevitable and inescapable. A cart weighed down with sheaves would have been a common sight and illustrated graphically how God was burdened with the sins of His people (v. 13). The tragic irony lay in the fact that the Lord had used Israel to destroy the sinful Amorites who previously occupied the Land (v. 10). Now Israel had fallen into the same sins as the Amorites. They, too, would face God's judgment at the hands of an invading nation.

3:1, 2 The people of Israel had experienced a unique, covenant relationship with the Lord because He had elected them from

MARRIAGE *PRINCIPLES FROM GOD*

Marriage is the oldest relationship in the world, established by a sovereign Creator in the Garden of Eden. In that beautiful, perfect setting, God organized the home by assigning roles and defining responsibilities to Adam and Eve.

Adam was to be the provider ("to tend" the garden), the protector ("and keep" the garden), and the leader ("the Lord God commanded the man . . ."). His assigned occupation was to care for the garden and those in it (Gen. 2:15–17). This demanded the type of servant leadership emulated by Jesus (see Eph. 5:21–33). Certainly there is no room for abuse or tyranny directed to a wife on the part of her husband, nor is there the option of a wife's willful disregard for her husband's leadership.

The woman's responsibilities were several: She was to be a "helper" (Gen. 2:18), a comforter (Gen. 24:67), and an encourager (Prov. 31:12, 26). Eve was Adam's partner for carrying out God's purpose to multiply and replenish the earth (Gen. 1:28). She was to be his closest earthly companion, relieving his loneliness (Gen. 2:18).

When sin entered the world, chaos followed. God's plan did not change, but it was distorted by the sinful choices of Adam and Eve and their descendants. God let Adam and Eve choose to sin, but He did not let them choose sin's consequences. Fear emerged; they were afraid to face God because of their disobedience (Gen. 3:10). They were cast out of their idyllic home with this foretelling: Adam's work would become difficult because he would have to contend with thorns and thistles (Gen. 3:17, 18), and Eve would suffer pain in childbirth (Gen. 3:16). Adam and Eve and their posterity would have spiritual warfare until the end of time.

Despite the failure of Adam and Eve, God's principles for marriage have remained the same—according to their God-defined roles, husbands are to use their God-given authority to provide, to protect, and to love (Gen. 2:15–17; Eph. 5:25), and wives are to help their husbands and submit to their God-directed leadership (Gen. 2:18; Eph. 5:23, 24). Husbands and wives can ignore God's program for the home, but when a spiritual principle is violated, division is the result. They can seek to redefine God's plan according to their own desires and circumstances, but ultimately human wisdom cannot compete with the all-wise God. There can be no unity, no contentment, and no peace—only a house divided—in a marriage that defies God's principles. Husbands and wives are challenged to spend time, energy, and creativity looking for ways to conform to servant leadership and Christlike submission.

See also notes on Commitment (Matt. 16); Biblical Equality (Eph. 5); Husbands (Job 31; 2 Cor. 6); Marriage (Gen. 2; 2 Sam. 6; Prov. 5; Hos. 2; 2 Cor. 13; Heb. 12); Submission (1 Pet. 3); Wives (Prov. 31)

---

whole family which I brought up from the land of Egypt, saying:

²"You only have I known of all the families of the earth;
Therefore I will punish you for all your iniquities."

³Can two walk together, unless they are agreed?
⁴Will a lion roar in the forest, when he has no prey?
Will a young lion cry out of his den, if he has caught nothing?
⁵Will a bird fall into a snare on the earth, where there is no trap for it?

Will a snare spring up from the earth, if it has caught nothing at all?
⁶If a trumpet is blown in a city, will not the people be afraid?
If there is calamity in a city, will not the LORD have done *it?*

⁷Surely the Lord GOD does nothing,
Unless He reveals His secret to His servants the prophets.
⁸A lion has roared!
Who will not fear?
The Lord GOD has spoken!
Who can but prophesy?

---

among all the nations to be His people. They had forgotten that along with covenant promise comes covenant responsibility. Israel's special relationship with the Lord did not result in immunity from the Lord's judgment. Instead His suzerainty covenant (between unequal parties) formed the basis for God's judgment of His people (see Ex. 19:5, note). If God had not judged His people, He would have been in violation of His own covenant. "Iniquities" refers to moral crookedness and perversion (Amos. 3:2; see Ps. 32:1, 2, note).

3:3–8 The rhetorical questions raised reveal that events do not occur in nature or history without causes. The first six questions needed no response. However, the 7th did: Can God bring about calamity (Is. 45:7; see Ex. 14; Josh. 6, Justice)? God had pronounced certain disaster: The appointment had been made, the lion had roared, the trap had been set, and the trumpet had blown (Amos 3:7, 8). Amos explained the cause behind His preaching as the call of the Lord (v. 8). The Lord desired to disclose Himself and His ways to His servants the prophets so they could deliver His words before God carried out His judgment (v. 7). This principle provided a method of authenticating a prophet's ministry.

Punishment of Israel's Sins

⁹"Proclaim in the palaces at Ashdod,ᵃ
  And in the palaces in the land of Egypt, and
      say:
  'Assemble on the mountains of Samaria;
  See great tumults in her midst,
  And the oppressed within her.
¹⁰For they do not know to do right,'
  Says the LORD,
  'Who store up violence and robbery in their
      palaces.' "

¹¹Therefore thus says the Lord GOD:

"An adversary *shall be* all around the
      land;
  He shall sap your strength from you,
  And your palaces shall be plundered."

¹²Thus says the LORD:

"As a shepherd takes from the mouth of a lion
  Two legs or a piece of an ear,
  So shall the children of Israel be taken out
  Who dwell in Samaria—
  In the corner of a bed and on the edgeᵃ of a
      couch!
¹³Hear and testify against the house of
      Jacob,"
  Says the Lord GOD, the God of hosts,
¹⁴"That in the day I punish Israel for their
      transgressions,
  I will also visit *destruction* on the altars of
      Bethel;
  And the horns of the altar shall be cut off
  And fall to the ground.
¹⁵I will destroy the winter house along with the
      summer house;
  The houses of ivory shall perish,
  And the great houses shall have an end,"
  Says the LORD.

4 Hear this word, you cows of Bashan, who *are*
  on the mountain of Samaria,
  Who oppress the poor,
  Who crush the needy,
  Who say to your husbands,ᵃ "Bring *wine,* let us
      drink!"
²The Lord GOD has sworn by His holiness:
"Behold, the days shall come upon you
  When He will take you away with fishhooks,
  And your posterity with fishhooks.
³You will go out *through* broken *walls,*
  Each one straight ahead of her,
  And you will be cast into Harmon,"
  Says the LORD.

⁴"Come to Bethel and transgress,
  At Gilgal multiply transgression;
  Bring your sacrifices every morning,
  Your tithes every three days.ᵃ
⁵Offer a sacrifice of thanksgiving with leaven,
  Proclaim *and* announce the freewill offerings;
  For this you love,
  You children of Israel!"
  Says the Lord GOD.

Israel Did Not Accept Correction

⁶"Also I gave you cleanness of teeth in all your
      cities,
  And lack of bread in all your places;
  Yet you have not returned to Me,"
  Says the LORD.

⁷"I also withheld rain from you,
  When *there were* still three months to the
      harvest.
  I made it rain on one city,
  I withheld rain from another city.

- - - - - - - - - - - -

3:9 ᵃFollowing Masoretic Text; Septuagint reads *Assyria.*   **3:12** ᵃThe Hebrew is uncertain.   **4:1** ᵃLiterally *their lords* or *their masters* **4:4** ᵃOr *years* (compare Deuteronomy 14:28)

3:13–15 Houses of ivory have an interesting archaeological corroboration. Numerous fragments of ivory, some dating from the 8th century B.C., have been uncovered in Samaria. Some scholars believe these were inlays in the furniture and wall paneling of the homes of the wealthy Israelites against whom Amos prophesied. When God destroyed Samaria at the hands of the Assyrians, the ivory was smashed and the ruins of this wealthy society lay buried for many generations. God's pronouncement of impending disaster was fulfilled in history exactly as spoken by Amos.

4:1–3 In this stinging indictment of Israel's women, the designation "cows of Bashan" refers to the insensitive wives of wealthy officials living in luxury. Although they may not have oppressed the poor overtly, these women pressured their husbands to provide them with luxuries to satisfy their self-indulgence at the expense of the poor and needy. They had forfeited their right to be respected (Is. 3:16—4:1). The Lord's judgment on them takes the form of an oath (Amos 4:2).

Bashan was a fertile, well-watered region (now the Golan Heights; see Deut. 32:14; Ps. 22:12; Mic. 7:14) where sheep and cattle grazed in lush pastures. Animals for cultic sacrifice were raised here. Just as the fattening cattle were oblivious to their sure but pending slaughter, the Israelite women were living in luxury unaware of the catastrophe about to crush them. The Lord would lead them away like slaves with fishhooks, a humiliating captivity.

4:4, 5 Bethel, one of the sites where Jeroboam I had set up a golden calf, was Israel's primary worship center in Amos' time (Amos 7:13). It had become a center for idolatry. Gilgal was the second most important place for worship. Amos' invitation to "come" and "offer" thanks was a form of satire. The religious practices of the people did not draw them closer to God, but rather led them further from Him. Their worship resulted in multiplied transgression or rebellion against the Lord.

One part was rained upon,
And where it did not rain the part
   withered.
⁸So two *or* three cities wandered to another city
   to drink water,
But they were not satisfied;
Yet you have not returned to Me,"
Says the LORD.

⁹"I blasted you with blight and mildew.
When your gardens increased,
Your vineyards,
Your fig trees,
And your olive trees,
The locust devoured *them;*
Yet you have not returned to Me,"
Says the LORD.

¹⁰"I sent among you a plague after the manner of
   Egypt;
Your young men I killed with a sword,
Along with your captive horses;
I made the stench of your camps come up into
   your nostrils;
Yet you have not returned to Me,"
Says the LORD.

¹¹"I overthrew *some* of you,
As God overthrew Sodom and Gomorrah,
And you were like a firebrand plucked from
   the burning;
Yet you have not returned to Me,"
Says the LORD.

¹²"Therefore thus will I do to you, O Israel;
Because I will do this to you,
Prepare to meet your God, O Israel!"

¹³For behold,
He who forms mountains,
And creates the wind,
Who declares to man what his[a] thought *is,*
And makes the morning darkness,
Who treads the high places of the earth—
The LORD God of hosts *is* His name.

A Lament for Israel

5 Hear this word which I take up against you, a
lamentation, O house of Israel:

²The virgin of Israel has fallen;
She will rise no more.
She lies forsaken on her land;
There is no one to raise her up.

³For thus says the Lord GOD:

"The city that goes out by a thousand
Shall have a hundred left,
And that which goes out by a hundred
Shall have ten left to the house of Israel."

A Call to Repentance

⁴For thus says the LORD to the house of Israel:

"Seek Me and live;
⁵But do not seek Bethel,
Nor enter Gilgal,
Nor pass over to Beersheba;
For Gilgal shall surely go into captivity,
And Bethel shall come to nothing.
⁶Seek the LORD and live,
Lest He break out like fire *in* the house of
   Joseph,
And devour *it,*
With no one to quench *it* in Bethel—
⁷You who turn justice to wormwood,
And lay righteousness to rest in the earth!"

⁸He made the Pleiades and Orion;
He turns the shadow of death into morning
And makes the day dark as night;
He calls for the waters of the sea
And pours them out on the face of the earth;
The LORD *is* His name.
⁹He rains ruin upon the strong,
So that fury comes upon the fortress.

¹⁰They hate the one who rebukes in the gate,
And they abhor the one who speaks uprightly.

4:13 ᵃOr *His*

5:1–3 A funeral song over the "house of Israel," the northern kingdom is found here. The house of Israel is designated as "the virgin of Israel" (v. 2). This phrase represents the earliest reference to Israel as a woman and indicates youthfulness as well as virginity. Israel was doomed for untimely destruction. Failure to live according to God's holy Law would bring about the tithe of a remnant: "a hundred left" out of "a thousand"; "ten left" out of "a hundred" (v. 3).

5:4–7 The Lord's people could find life only by seeking Him, not by performing the prescribed ritual at traditional religious sites such as Bethel and Gilgal, for these cities had become centers for idolatry.

5:8, 9 The Pleiades and Orion are two primary constellations (see Job 9:9, note). The stars were worshiped by many ancient peoples, but they are created objects, not gods.

5:10–13 The elders and judges of the city officially met at the "gate" where legal transactions took place (see vv. 10, 12; see Ruth 4:1, 7). "Evil time" probably refers to a time of calamity (Amos 5:13). They would not benefit from any of their labors because they had denied justice to the poor, who could not pay the "bribes."

¹¹Therefore, because you tread down the poor
And take grain taxes from him,
Though you have built houses of hewn stone,
Yet you shall not dwell in them;
You have planted pleasant vineyards,
But you shall not drink wine from them.
¹²For I know your manifold transgressions
And your mighty sins:
Afflicting the just *and* taking bribes;
Diverting the poor *from justice* at the gate.
¹³Therefore the prudent keep silent at that time,
For it *is* an evil time.

¹⁴Seek good and not evil,
That you may live;
So the LORD God of hosts will be with you,
As you have spoken.
¹⁵Hate evil, love good;
Establish justice in the gate.
It may be that the LORD God of hosts
Will be gracious to the remnant of Joseph.

The Day of the LORD

¹⁶Therefore the LORD God of hosts, the Lord,
says this:

"*There shall be* wailing in all streets,
And they shall say in all the highways,
'Alas! Alas!'
They shall call the farmer to mourning,
And skillful lamenters to wailing.
¹⁷In all vineyards *there shall be* wailing,
For I will pass through you,"
Says the LORD.

¹⁸Woe to you who desire the day of the LORD!
For what good *is* the day of the LORD to you?
It *will be* darkness, and not light.
¹⁹It *will be* as though a man fled from a lion,
And a bear met him!
Or *as though* he went into the house,
Leaned his hand on the wall,

And a serpent bit him!
²⁰*Is* not the day of the LORD darkness, and not
light?
Is it not very dark, with no brightness in it?

²¹"I hate, I despise your feast days,
And I do not savor your sacred assemblies.
²²Though you offer Me burnt offerings and your
grain offerings,
I will not accept *them,*
Nor will I regard your fattened peace
offerings.
²³Take away from Me the noise of your songs,
For I will not hear the melody of your stringed
instruments.
²⁴But let justice run down like water,
And righteousness like a mighty stream.

²⁵"Did you offer Me sacrifices and offerings
In the wilderness forty years, O house of Israel?
²⁶You also carried Sikkuthᵃ your kingᵇ
And Chiun,ᶜ your idols,
The star of your gods,
Which you made for yourselves.
²⁷Therefore I will send you into captivity beyond
Damascus,"
Says the LORD, whose name *is* the God of hosts.

Warnings to Zion and Samaria

6 Woe to you *who are* at ease in Zion,
And trust in Mount Samaria,
Notable persons in the chief nation,
To whom the house of Israel comes!
²Go over to Calneh and see;
And from there go to Hamath the great;
Then go down to Gath of the Philistines.
Are you better than these kingdoms?
Or is their territory greater than your
territory?

· · · · · · · · · · · · · · · · · ·

5:26 ᵃA pagan deity ᵇSeptuagint and Vulgate read *tabernacle of Moloch.* ᶜA pagan deity

---

5:14, 15 The way of life lies in seeking God and doing right. The way of death is to persist in sinning. Each woman chooses the way she will take (see Ps. 1; chart, The Choice Between Life and Death).

5:16–27 The people of Israel perceived the day of the Lord as a day of victory for themselves and a day of judgment for their enemies. Amos corrected that popular misconception. He presented the day of the Lord as a day of judgment for the Lord's people. Their judgment would be greater because they had received greater revelation (see Amos 3:1, 2, note). The Israelites misunderstood and asked for the day of the Lord (Amos 5:18), but Amos warned that this "day" would not bring "brightness" or blessing but doom and "darkness" (v. 20). The Israelites kept "feast days," attended "sacred assemblies," and offered "burnt offerings" but neglected justice and righteousness (vv. 21, 22).

5:18—6:7 Oracles of Woe (Heb. *hoy,* lit. "pain" or "bereave-

ment") were delivered by Amos against the Israelites. Jesus used this same form of address in a series of woes against the scribes and Pharisees (Matt. 23:13–36; see chart, Jewish Sects). The self-righteous Jews saw themselves as fulfilling all the Law, but Jesus said that they "neglected the weightier matters of the law" (see Matt. 23:23). God wanted justice and righteousness from His people (Amos 5:24).

6:1–7 Amos condemned the rich, powerful leaders for living in luxury gained through violence and for ignoring the poor of the Land. Israel felt safe on the mountain of Samaria. Similarly, Judah felt at "ease in Zion." The ruling class felt secure in their religion because they went through the prescribed rituals. The people had blinded themselves to the serious nature of their sin, which had made them indistinguishable from the pagan nations. Israel was not exempt from God's judgment (see Luke 12:48).

³*Woe to* you who put far off the day of
doom,
Who cause the seat of violence to come
near;
⁴Who lie on beds of ivory,
Stretch out on your couches,
Eat lambs from the flock
And calves from the midst of the stall;
⁵Who sing idly to the sound of stringed
instruments,
And invent for yourselves musical instruments
like David;
⁶Who drink wine from bowls,
And anoint yourselves with the best ointments,
But are not grieved for the affliction of Joseph.
⁷Therefore they shall now go captive as the first
of the captives,
And those who recline at banquets shall be
removed.

⁸The Lord GOD has sworn by Himself,
The LORD God of hosts says:
"I abhor the pride of Jacob,
And hate his palaces;
Therefore I will deliver up *the* city
And all that is in it."

⁹Then it shall come to pass, that if ten men remain in one house, they shall die. ¹⁰And when a
relative *of the dead,* with one who will burn *the bodies,* picks up the bodiesᵃ to take them out of the
house, he will say to one inside the house, "*Are
there* any more with you?"
Then someone will say, "None."
And he will say, "Hold your tongue! For we dare
not mention the name of the LORD."

¹¹For behold, the LORD gives a command:
He will break the great house into bits,
And the little house into pieces.

¹²Do horses run on rocks?
Does *one* plow *there* with oxen?
Yet you have turned justice into gall,
And the fruit of righteousness into
wormwood,
¹³You who rejoice over Lo Debar,ᵃ
Who say, "Have we not taken Karnaimᵇ for
ourselves
By our own strength?"

¹⁴"But, behold, I will raise up a nation against you,
O house of Israel,"
Says the LORD God of hosts;
"And they will afflict you from the entrance of
Hamath
To the Valley of the Arabah."

Vision of the Locusts

7 Thus the Lord GOD showed me: Behold, He
formed locust swarms at the beginning of the
late crop; indeed *it was* the late crop after the
king's mowings. ²And so it was, when they had finished eating the grass of the land, that I said:

"O Lord GOD, forgive, I pray!
Oh, that Jacob may stand,
For he *is* small!"
³*So* the LORD relented concerning this.
"It shall not be," said the LORD.

Vision of the Fire

⁴Thus the Lord GOD showed me: Behold, the
Lord GOD called for conflict by fire, and it consumed the great deep and devoured the territory.
⁵Then I said:

"O Lord GOD, cease, I pray!
Oh, that Jacob may stand,
For he *is* small!"
⁶*So* the LORD relented concerning this.
"This also shall not be," said the Lord GOD.

Vision of the Plumb Line

⁷Thus He showed me: Behold, the Lord stood
on a wall *made* with a plumb line, with a plumb
line in His hand. ⁸And the LORD said to me, "Amos,
what do you see?"
And I said, "A plumb line."
Then the Lord said:

"Behold, I am setting a plumb line
In the midst of My people Israel;
I will not pass by them anymore.
⁹The high places of Isaac shall be desolate,
And the sanctuaries of Israel shall be laid
waste.
I will rise with the sword against the house of
Jeroboam."

6:10 ᵃLiterally *bones*   **6:13** ᵃLiterally *Nothing* ᵇLiterally *Horns*, symbol of strength

---

7:1–3 In Amos' first vision, he saw "locust swarms" in the
spring after the king's crop but before the people harvested
their crop. Amos interceded with one-word prayers: "forgive"
(v. 2) and "cease" (v. 5). The Lord "relented," altered His
course, and canceled the judgment (vv. 3, 6). Between "it shall
come to pass" and "it came to pass" stands God's mercy.

7:4–6 Fire referred to war or drought. Again Amos asked the
Lord to cease His judgment (see vv. 1–3, note) because Jacob

or Israel (see Gen. 32:28; chart, Terminology for the Divided
Kingdom) could not survive the devastation. Again the Lord
relented.

7:7–9 God as a building inspector set a plumb line in the midst
of Israel. To test the straightness of a wall, the builder used a
plumb line, a cord with a heavy weight at one end. Israel
failed God's test of straightness or righteousness. Therefore,
impending judgment was inevitable.

*All the wealth in the world cannot be compared
with the happiness of living together happily united.*
—St. Margaret of Youville

Amaziah's Complaint

¹⁰Then Amaziah the priest of Bethel sent to Jeroboam king of Israel, saying, "Amos has conspired against you in the midst of the house of Israel. The land is not able to bear all his words. ¹¹For thus Amos has said:

'Jeroboam shall die by the sword,
 And Israel shall surely be led away captive
 From their own land.' "

¹²Then Amaziah said to Amos:

"Go, you seer!
 Flee to the land of Judah.
 There eat bread,
 And there prophesy.
¹³But never again prophesy at Bethel,
 For it *is* the king's sanctuary,
 And it *is* the royal residence."

¹⁴Then Amos answered, and said to Amaziah:

"I *was* no prophet,
 Nor *was* I a son of a prophet,
 But I *was* a sheepbreeder[a]
 And a tender of sycamore fruit.
¹⁵Then the LORD took me as I followed the flock,
 And the LORD said to me,
 'Go, prophesy to My people Israel.'
¹⁶Now therefore, hear the word of the LORD:
 You say, 'Do not prophesy against Israel,
 And do not spout against the house of Isaac.'

¹⁷"Therefore thus says the LORD:

'Your wife shall be a harlot in the city;

Your sons and daughters shall fall by the
 sword;
Your land shall be divided by *survey* line;
You shall die in a defiled land;
And Israel shall surely be led away captive
From his own land.' "

Vision of the Summer Fruit

8 Thus the Lord GOD showed me: Behold, a basket of summer fruit. ²And He said, "Amos, what do you see?"

So I said, "A basket of summer fruit."
 Then the LORD said to me:

"The end has come upon My people Israel;
 I will not pass by them anymore.
³And the songs of the temple
 Shall be wailing in that day,"
 Says the Lord GOD—
"Many dead bodies everywhere,
 They shall be thrown out in silence."

⁴Hear this, you who swallow up[a] the needy,
 And make the poor of the land fail,

⁵Saying:

"When will the New Moon be past,
 That we may sell grain?
 And the Sabbath,
 That we may trade wheat?
 Making the ephah small and the shekel
 large,
 Falsifying the scales by deceit,
⁶That we may buy the poor for silver,

···············

7:14 ªCompare 2 Kings 3:4   8:4 ªOr *trample on* (compare 2:7)

7:10–17 This encounter between Amos and Amaziah occurred at Bethel, the king's sanctuary (v. 13). Amaziah the priest, who probably had been appointed by the king, accused Amos of being a traitor. The authorities at Bethel (Heb., lit. "house of God") could not tolerate the prophet of God. Amaziah strongly encouraged Amos to return to Judah and earn his living as a prophet there (see Introduction: Author). Amos refused to flee. His authority was from God, not men. The Lord's judgment would fall on Amaziah as well as on Israel (v. 17). Amaziah, as chief priest in the northern kingdom, was rejecting the authority of God, not of Amos. Thus, the consequences would be both personal and national (v. 17).

8:1–14 Judgment was an accomplished fact in this vision. Amos used a play on words to convey his message: "summer fruit" (Heb. *qayits*, v. 1) and "end" (Heb. *qets*, v. 2) sound similar in

Hebrew. Like the "summer fruit," the end had come for Israel. The vision was followed by the indictment of Israel (vv. 4–14). The charges included insincere worship, mistreatment of the poor, and unethical business practices. "That day" refers to the day of the Lord (v. 9; see Amos 5:16–27, note). Egypt had once known such desperate "mourning" when the Lord struck down the firstborn in every family (Ex. 12:30); now Israel would also know this "bitter day" of God's judgment (Amos 8:10). Because the people rejected the Word of God, God would make His Word scarce (v. 11). "Fair virgins and strong young men" indicates that the vigor and attraction of youth alone cannot provide strength to meet moral and spiritual crises (v. 13). Only God's Word can do this (v. 11).

And the needy for a pair of sandals—
Even sell the bad wheat?"

[7]The LORD has sworn by the pride of Jacob:
"Surely I will never forget any of their works.
[8]Shall the land not tremble for this,
And everyone mourn who dwells in it?
All of it shall swell like the River,[a]
Heave and subside
Like the River of Egypt.

[9]"And it shall come to pass in that day," says the
Lord GOD,
"That I will make the sun go down at noon,
And I will darken the earth in broad daylight;
[10]I will turn your feasts into mourning,
And all your songs into lamentation;
I will bring sackcloth on every waist,
And baldness on every head;
I will make it like mourning for an only *son*,
And its end like a bitter day.

[11]"Behold, the days are coming," says the Lord
GOD,
"That I will send a famine on the land,
Not a famine of bread,
Nor a thirst for water,
But of hearing the words of the LORD.
[12]They shall wander from sea to sea,
And from north to east;
They shall run to and fro, seeking the word of
the LORD,
But shall not find *it*.

[13]"In that day the fair virgins
And strong young men
Shall faint from thirst.
[14]Those who swear by the sin[a] of Samaria,
Who say,
'As your god lives, O Dan!'
And, 'As the way of Beersheba lives!'
They shall fall and never rise again."

The Destruction of Israel

9 I saw the Lord standing by the altar, and He
said:

"Strike the doorposts, that the thresholds may
shake,
And break them on the heads of them all.
I will slay the last of them with the sword.

He who flees from them shall not get away,
And he who escapes from them shall not be
delivered.

[2]"Though they dig into hell,[a]
From there My hand shall take them;
Though they climb up to heaven,
From there I will bring them down;
[3]And though they hide themselves on top of
Carmel,
From there I will search and take them;
Though they hide from My sight at the bottom
of the sea,
From there I will command the serpent, and it
shall bite them;
[4]Though they go into captivity before their
enemies,
From there I will command the sword,
And it shall slay them.
I will set My eyes on them for harm and not for
good."

[5]The Lord GOD of hosts,
He who touches the earth and it melts,
And all who dwell there mourn;
All of it shall swell like the River,[a]
And subside like the River of Egypt.
[6]He who builds His layers in the sky,
And has founded His strata in the earth;
Who calls for the waters of the sea,
And pours them out on the face of the earth—
The LORD *is* His name.

[7]"*Are* you not like the people of Ethiopia to Me,
O children of Israel?" says the LORD.
"Did I not bring up Israel from the land of
Egypt,
The Philistines from Caphtor,
And the Syrians from Kir?

[8]"Behold, the eyes of the Lord GOD *are* on the
sinful kingdom,
And I will destroy it from the face of the earth;
Yet I will not utterly destroy the house of
Jacob,"
Says the LORD.

··········

8:8 [a]That is, the Nile; some Hebrew manuscripts, Septuagint, Syriac,
Targum, and Vulgate read *River;* Masoretic Text reads *the light.*
8:14 [a]Or *Ashima,* a Syrian goddess   **9:2** [a]Or *Sheol*   **9:5** [a]That is, the
Nile

9:1–10 The Lord appeared at the altar to announce the total
devastation of Israel in this final vision of Amos. None would
be able to escape the Lord's judgment, which began with
those who claimed to believe Him as Israel had believed. The
sovereignty of the Lord permitted no hiding place. "Hell"
(Heb. *sheol*), is the place of the dead (v. 2). Compare the list
of hiding places in verses 2–4 with those of Psalm 139:7–12. In
Psalm 139 the Lord's omnipresence is related to His benevo-

lent care for His people. In Amos 9:1–10 the Lord's omnipresence is related to His judgment. Israel could not claim privileged status with the Lord (v. 7). The Lord's sovereignty was
behind the movement of Israel's enemies, the Philistines and
the Syrians, just as the Lord had initiated Israel's deliverance
from Egypt. God's eyes focused on His people for calamity
and not for good (vv. 4, 8). Judgment would fall on those who
least expected it (v. 10).

9"For surely I will command,
And will sift the house of Israel among all
    nations,
As *grain* is sifted in a sieve;
Yet not the smallest grain shall fall to the
    ground.
10All the sinners of My people shall die by the
    sword,
Who say, 'The calamity shall not overtake nor
    confront us.'

Israel Will Be Restored

11"On that day I will raise up
The tabernacle[a] of David, which has fallen
    down,
And repair its damages;
I will raise up its ruins,
And rebuild it as in the days of old;
12That they may possess the remnant of Edom,[a]
And all the Gentiles who are called by My name,"
Says the LORD who does this thing.

13"Behold, the days are coming," says the LORD,
"When the plowman shall overtake the reaper,
And the treader of grapes him who sows
    seed;
The mountains shall drip with sweet wine,
And all the hills shall flow *with it.*
14I will bring back the captives of My people
    Israel;
They shall build the waste cities and inhabit
    them;
They shall plant vineyards and drink wine
    from them;
They shall also make gardens and eat fruit
    from them.
15I will plant them in their land,
And no longer shall they be pulled up
From the land I have given them,"
Says the LORD your God.

9:11 [a]Literally *booth*, figure of a deposed dynasty   9:12 [a]Septuagint
reads *mankind.*

9:11–15 Hope existed for Israel beyond judgment. "The days are coming" (v. 13) is language used in the OT to describe the future blessings and hope of the messianic age (see Jer. 31:31–34). The judgment message of Amos 5:11 stands in contrast to the restoration message of Amos 9:14. Amos saw the restoration of Israel as complete and permanent (v. 15). The Lord's judgments have a redemptive purpose in the lives of His people.

Obadiah

AUTHOR

Several individuals named Obadiah (Heb., lit. "servant or worshiper of the Lord") are mentioned in the Old Testament (see 1 Kin. 18:3–16; 1 Chr. 7:3; 8:38; 9:16, 44; 2 Chr. 17:7; 34:12; Ezra 8:9; Neh. 10:5; 12:25). There is not enough evidence to identify positively any of these individuals with the author of the book.

DATE

Since the book offers no specific date, internal evidence, coupled with information given in other Old Testament references, are considerations in dating Obadiah. The prophet refers to an attack on Jerusalem (Obad. 11–14). Assaults on Jerusalem recorded in the Old Testament include those by Shishak, king of Egypt (925 B.C.; 1 Kin. 14:25, 26; 2 Chr. 12:2–9); by the Philistines and Arabs during the reign of Jehoram (around 850 B.C.; 2 Chr. 21:8–10, 16, 17); by Jehoash, king of Israel (around 790 B.C.; 2 Chr. 25); and by Nebuchadnezzar, king of Babylon (586 B.C.; 2 Kin. 25:1, 2).

Most scholars date the book after Nebuchadnezzar's destruction of Jerusalem in 586 B.C. Edom aided and abetted the attack on Jerusalem by Nebuchadnezzar, looted the city, and prevented its inhabitants from fleeing (see Ps. 137:7; Lam. 4:21, 22; Ezek. 35:1–15).

BACKGROUND

SETTING: Obadiah, a prophet ministering to the southern kingdom of Judah (or to its exiles if the book is dated after 586 B.C.), is also God's messenger to Edom, Judah's hostile neighbor across the Dead Sea to the southeast. The Old Testament recounts a history of conflict between these two nations (see Num. 20:14–21; 2 Chr. 28:17; Ps. 83:1–6; 137:7; Ezek. 35; Joel 3:19).

PURPOSE: Obadiah proclaimed God's judgment on Edom for injustices done to Judah and God's future blessings on His people. Sometime in the sixth or fifth century B.C. the kingdom of Edom fell, probably to Arab tribes. The surviving Edomites relocated to the Negev (southern Judah). During the intertestamental period they came under Jewish and then Roman domination.

AUDIENCE: The prophecy seems to be delivered to those who experienced or observed the overrunning of Jerusalem by a foreign army that conspired with the Edomites. The book contains a prophetic oracle against Edom and also a message of hope for God's people.

LITERARY CHARACTERISTICS: The structure is tripartite in form, revolving around a central passage (Obad. 10–14) that presents the evidence from which judgments in verses 1–9 and verses 15–21 are derived.

The primary theme of this shortest Old Testament book is that of reciprocity (see Obad. 15): God punished Edom by doing the same things to her that she had done to Judah. Because Edom stands as a representative figure for all who oppose the Lord, Obadiah's pronouncement of judgment against Edom warns of the destruction of all who oppose God and His people. Another closely related theme is God's promise of deliverance to His people. Both themes find ultimate fulfillment in Christ, who suffered God's judgment on behalf of His people (see Is. 53; Rom. 3:21–26; 2 Cor. 5:21). Christ will return as final Judge to try every individual and nation and to set up His eternal kingdom at the consummation of the age (see Matt. 19:28; 25:31–46; Rev. 11:15).

OUTLINE

The Coming Judgment on Edom

The vision of Obadiah.

Thus says the Lord GOD concerning Edom
(We have heard a report from the LORD,
And a messenger has been sent among the
    nations, *saying,*
"Arise, and let us rise up against her for battle"):

²"Behold, I will make you small among the
    nations;
You shall be greatly despised.
³The pride of your heart has deceived you,
You who dwell in the clefts of the rock,
Whose habitation *is* high;
You who say in your heart, 'Who will bring me
    down to the ground?'
⁴Though you ascend *as* high as the eagle,
And though you set your nest among the stars,
From there I will bring you down," says the
    LORD.

⁵"If thieves had come to you,
If robbers by night—

Oh, how you will be cut off!—
Would they not have stolen till they had
    enough?
If grape-gatherers had come to you,
Would they not have left *some* gleanings?

⁶"Oh, how Esau shall be searched out!
How his hidden treasures shall be sought after!
⁷All the men in your confederacy
Shall force you to the border;
The men at peace with you
Shall deceive you *and* prevail against you.
Those who eat your bread shall lay a trapᵃ for
    you.
No one is aware of it.

⁸"Will I not in that day," says the LORD,
"Even destroy the wise *men* from Edom,
And understanding from the mountains of
    Esau?
⁹Then your mighty men, O Teman, shall be
    dismayed,

7 ᵃOr *wound,* or *plot*

---

1 The nation Edom descended from Esau, Jacob's brother. Esau and Jacob were twins whose rivalry began in the womb as the younger Jacob held Esau's heel at birth (Gen. 25:22–26), thus depicting the struggle between the two brothers. The rivalry between the two was repeated in the history of the two nations that descended from them. Obadiah announced that Edom's day of reckoning had come as God summoned the nations as instruments of His wrath (see Num. 20:14–21; 1 Kin. 11:15–17; 2 Kin. 8:20–22; 2 Chr. 28:17).

3, 4 Rock (Heb. *sela*) may refer to Sela, Edom's capital city. The city was built on a hill surrounded by steep cliffs and was

well supplied with water in case of siege. But the Edomites' strongest defense would not secure them against God's judgment.

5 Obadiah used rhetorical questions to emphasize the completeness of God's judgment. Unlike "robbers" or "grape-gatherers" the nations brought against Edom will leave nothing behind.

6 Esau here refers to the nation of Edom (see v. 1, note).

9 Teman (lit. "south") is another name for the entire country of Edom.

To the end that everyone from the mountains
   of Esau
May be cut off by slaughter.

Edom Mistreated His Brother

10"For violence against your brother Jacob,
   Shame shall cover you,
And you shall be cut off forever.
11In the day that you stood on the other side—
   In the day that strangers carried captive his
     forces,
When foreigners entered his gates
And cast lots for Jerusalem—
Even you *were* as one of them.

12"But you should not have gazed on the day of
   your brother
In the day of his captivity;ᵃ
Nor should you have rejoiced over the children
   of Judah
In the day of their destruction;
Nor should you have spoken proudly
In the day of distress.
13You should not have entered the gate of My
   people
In the day of their calamity.
Indeed, you should not have gazed on their
   affliction
In the day of their calamity,
Nor laid *hands* on their substance
In the day of their calamity.
14You should not have stood at the crossroads
To cut off those among them who escaped;
Nor should you have delivered up those among
   them who remained
In the day of distress.

15"For the day of the LORD upon all the nations *is*
   near;
As you have done, it shall be done to you;
Your reprisal shall return upon your own
   head.
16For as you drank on My holy mountain,
So shall all the nations drink continually;
Yes, they shall drink, and swallow,
And they shall be as though they had never
   been.

Israel's Final Triumph

17"But on Mount Zion there shall be
   deliverance,
And there shall be holiness;
The house of Jacob shall possess their
   possessions.
18The house of Jacob shall be a fire,
And the house of Joseph a flame,
But the house of Esau *shall be* stubble;
They shall kindle them and devour them,
And no survivor shall *remain* of the house of
   Esau,"
For the LORD has spoken.

19The Southᵃ shall possess the mountains of
   Esau,
And the Lowland shall possess Philistia.
They shall possess the fields of Ephraim
And the fields of Samaria.
Benjamin *shall possess* Gilead.
20And the captives of this host of the children of
   Israel

12 ªLiterally *on the day he became a foreigner*   19 ªHebrew *Negev*

10 **Your brother Jacob** refers to the common ancestry between Edom and Israel. On the basis of this family tie, God commanded Israel to treat Edom with special consideration (Deut. 23:7). Edom's violation of this special relationship made her crimes more heinous.

11–14 **The Lord charged Edom,** through the words of Obadiah, with a series of crimes against Israel, each more reprehensible than the last, climaxing in murder and betrayal.

15 **The day of the Lord** is an expression frequently used by the prophets. It refers to any period of history in which God acts spectacularly to display His glory. It may also refer to God's final, climactic, universal action to judge the nations and save His people. This thematic verse affirms that what is sown will be reaped (Gal. 6:7).

16 **So all the nations will drink** is a metaphor often employed by the prophets for experiencing God's judgment. Jesus used the same metaphor to describe His sufferings on the Cross when He took God's judgment upon Himself (see Matt. 26:42). Everyone will "drink" a "cup" from God—either the cup of the New Covenant, which is offered freely to all, or the cup of God's wrath (see Luke 22:20; 1 Cor. 11:25, 26; Rev. 14:9, 10).

18 **House of Jacob and House of Joseph** refer to the united nation of Israel, including both Judah and the ten northern tribes which had been exiled by the Assyrians in 722 B.C. (see Ps. 77:15). The fire imagery indicates that God's people will be His instrument of judgment on Edom. Israel will be revived in the latter days to fulfill this prophecy (Amos. 9:11, 12). Some who do not anticipate a literal fulfillment of these prophecies would see this as only the promise of the ultimate victory of good over evil (see chart, Millennial Views).

19 **The place names** mentioned indicate that Obadiah envisioned an almost complete restoration of the ancient borders of Israel (see Num. 34:2–15). The "Lowland" refers to the region of Judah bordering Philistia. The Philistines were ancient enemies of the Israelites (see 1 Sam. 31:1–10). Ephraim and Samaria refer either to all the territory included in the old northern kingdom of Israel or to the southern section of that kingdom occupied by the tribe of Ephraim. After its conquest in 722 B.C., this section was made into an Assyrian province called Samaria (see Josh. 16:5–10). Gilead refers to territory east of the Jordan once occupied by the tribe of Gad and the half-tribe of Manasseh (see Josh. 13:24–32; chart, Terminology for the Divided Kingdom).

20 **Israel and Jerusalem** refer to the exiles of the northern and southern kingdoms who would reclaim possession of their in-

Shall possess the land of the Canaanites
As far as Zarephath.
The captives of Jerusalem who are in
 Sepharad
Shall possess the cities of the South.[a]

[21]Then saviors[a] shall come to Mount Zion
 To judge the mountains of Esau,
 And the kingdom shall be the LORD's.

20 [a]Hebrew *Negev*   21 [a]Or *deliverers*

heritance, territories that they had lost to their enemies because of their disobedience. Zarephath was a Phoenician town on the Mediterranean coast between Tyre and Sidon.

The location of Sepharad is disputed. The most common identification is with Sardis in Asia Minor (modern-day Turkey).

Jonah

AUTHOR

Though this book does not cite a specific author, tradition ascribes the authorship to its main character, the prophet Jonah, son of Amittai (Jon. 1:1). Jonah (Heb., lit. "dove") was a real person from Gath Hepher near Nazareth (2 Kin. 14:25). This Hebrew prophet was called by God to proclaim His message to the pagan nation of Assyria, while God used other prophets (Amos, Hosea, Isaiah, and Micah) to prophesy to Israel during the same time period.

DATE

The date of the prophet Jonah's ministry is generally accepted as between 800 and 750 B.C. Nothing about the book is incompatible with an eighth century B.C. composition. Some scholars support a later time after the Babylonian exile or the destruction of Nineveh, although these arguments are not conclusive. The Book of Jonah records historical events that occurred before the great city of Nineveh, the capital of Assyria, was destroyed (about 612 B.C.; see Jon. 3:3). Jeroboam II was king of Israel (782–753 B.C.; 2 Kin. 14:25) and Uzziah was king in Judah (792–740 B.C.). During this period, the Assyrian king was probably Ashur-dan III (772–755 B.C.; see chart, The Kings of Assyria).

BACKGROUND

SETTING: The Book of Jonah was initially set in Israel, where the prophet lived in the town of Gath Hepher near Nazareth. When Jonah fled from God's assignment in Nineveh, he went to Joppa, a port city along the Mediterranean Sea to catch a ship sailing in the opposite direction to Tarshish. After his brief encounter with the "great fish," Jonah returned to land. The last two chapters of the book were set in Assyria (present-day Iraq) after the prophet journeyed in obedience to Nineveh.

PURPOSE: The Book of Jonah teaches that only true repentance can bring salvation, and it also demonstrates God's compassion toward all (Jon. 4:2, 11; see Mic. 1:1, note). God wants all people truly to repent and receive salvation. Readers will discover Jonah to be a minor prophet with a major message.

AUDIENCE: While the original audience of the Book of Jonah is unidentified, clearly the Lord gave Jonah a message of hope for the wicked Assyrians and a message of restoration for believers who rebel. Taking that message to the enemies proved to be Jonah's greatest challenge. The impact of the Book of Jonah has continued through the generations, even among the Jews. The book is read in its entirety in the synagogues in the afternoon of *Yom Kippur* (the Day of Atonement; see chart, The Feasts of Israel). This liturgical use of the book is helpful in understanding its message of hope and assurance for God's chosen people.

LITERARY CHARACTERISTICS: The Book of Jonah is a historical account of a major event in Jonah's life. Most of Jonah is narrative with almost no proclamation, while other

prophets are almost all proclamation and little narrative. In the New Testament, Jesus Christ verified the historical significance of the prophet Jonah and this book (Matt. 12:39–41; Luke 11:29, 30).

Several significant, but sometimes overlooked, themes are found in the Book of Jonah. Though only forty-eight verses in length, the message of Jonah is important. The following are among its obvious themes:

Salvation comes only from the Lord. The Book of Jonah teaches that salvation is not by works, but by grace through faith (Jon. 2:8, 9; see also Eph. 2:8).

The God of the Hebrews has always expressed concern for the whole world. Jonah explained that Yahweh God lovingly offers salvation even to people we would prefer to hate (Jon. 4:9–11).

God is a God of beginning anew. The prophet experienced God's forgiveness when he was unfaithful and was offered another opportunity for obedience (Jon. 3:1). Nineveh likewise received the opportunity to repent.

Jesus used the experience of Jonah in the belly of the fish to explain His death, burial, and Resurrection (Jon. 1:17; Matt. 12:38–41).

I. God's Call to Jonah (1:1–17)
   A. The command from God (1:1–3)
   B. The storm at sea (1:4–17)
II. God's Forgiveness of Jonah (2:1–10)
   A. Jonah's prayer for mercy (2:1–9)
   B. Jonah's deliverance (2:10)

III. God's Use of Jonah (3:1–10)
   A. The response of Jonah (3:1–4)
   B. The response of the Ninevites (3:5–10)
IV. God's Chastening of Jonah (4:1–11)
   A. Jonah's anger (4:1–5)
   B. God's mercy (4:6–11)

Jonah's Disobedience

1 Now the word of the LORD came to Jonah the son of Amittai, saying, [2]"Arise, go to Nineveh, that great city, and cry out against it; for their wickedness has come up before Me." [3]But Jonah arose to flee to Tarshish from the presence of the LORD. He went down to Joppa, and found a ship going to Tarshish; so he paid the fare, and went down into it, to go with them to Tarshish from the presence of the LORD.

The Storm at Sea

[4]But the LORD sent out a great wind on the sea, and there was a mighty tempest on the sea, so that the ship was about to be broken up. [5]Then the mariners were afraid; and every man cried out to his god, and threw the cargo that was in the ship into the sea, to lighten the load.[a] But

....

1:5 [a]Literally from upon them

1:2 Built by Nimrod (Gen. 10:9–12), the great city of Nineveh was the Assyrian capital and the residence of many Assyrian kings. Located in northeastern Mesopotamia on the Tigris River, Nineveh flourished from 800 to 612 B.C., when it was destroyed by the Medes. The city limits spread widely along the river making it a great city both in size and influence.

1:3 While the exact location of Tarshish is uncertain, it is clear that Jonah's direction was opposite from the destination to which God had directed him (see Ezek. 27:12, note).

1:4 God did not accept Jonah's deliberate disobedience. While Jonah felt safe as he fled from God's call, God intervened supernaturally and caused a storm at sea.

Jonah had gone down into the lowest parts of the ship, had lain down, and was fast asleep.

⁶So the captain came to him, and said to him, "What do you mean, sleeper? Arise, call on your God; perhaps your God will consider us, so that we may not perish."

⁷And they said to one another, "Come, let us cast lots, that we may know for whose cause this trouble *has come* upon us." So they cast lots, and the lot fell on Jonah. ⁸Then they said to him, "Please tell us! For whose cause *is* this trouble upon us? What is your occupation? And where do you come from? What is your country? And of what people are you?"

⁹So he said to them, "I *am* a Hebrew; and I fear the LORD, the God of heaven, who made the sea and the dry *land.*"

Jonah Thrown into the Sea

¹⁰Then the men were exceedingly afraid, and said to him, "Why have you done this?" For the men knew that he fled from the presence of the LORD, because he had told them. ¹¹Then they said to him, "What shall we do to you that the sea may be calm for us?"—for the sea was growing more tempestuous.

¹²And he said to them, "Pick me up and throw me into the sea; then the sea will become calm for you. For I know that this great tempest *is* because of me."

¹³Nevertheless the men rowed hard to return to land, but they could not, for the sea continued to grow more tempestuous against them. ¹⁴Therefore they cried out to the LORD and said, "We pray, O LORD, please do not let us perish for this man's life, and do not charge us with innocent blood; for You, O LORD, have done as it pleased You." ¹⁵So they picked up Jonah and threw him into the sea,

and the sea ceased from its raging. ¹⁶Then the men feared the LORD exceedingly, and offered a sacrifice to the LORD and took vows.

Jonah's Prayer and Deliverance

¹⁷Now the LORD had prepared a great fish to swallow Jonah. And Jonah was in the belly of the fish three days and three nights.

2 Then Jonah prayed to the LORD his God from the fish's belly. ²And he said:

"I cried out to the LORD because of my
    affliction,
 And He answered me.

"Out of the belly of Sheol I cried,
 And You heard my voice.
³For You cast me into the deep,
 Into the heart of the seas,
 And the floods surrounded me;
 All Your billows and Your waves passed over
    me.
⁴Then I said, 'I have been cast out of Your
    sight;
 Yet I will look again toward Your holy temple.'
⁵The waters surrounded me, *even* to my soul;
 The deep closed around me;
 Weeds were wrapped around my head.
⁶I went down to the moorings of the mountains;
 The earth with its bars *closed* behind me
    forever;
 Yet You have brought up my life from the
    pit,
 O LORD, my God.

⁷"When my soul fainted within me,
 I remembered the LORD;

1:6–8 The storm and the sailors were used by God to confront a rebellious Jonah. While the prophet was trying to run from God, the captain forced him to call on God for help.

1:10 The sailors, though filled with fear, realized that there was no escape from God. While Jonah confessed his attempt to run from God's presence, the storm reminded him of God's constant presence.

1:12 Jonah realized that his rebellion from God had brought danger to all aboard the ship. God has many ways to get our attention. Jonah's admission of guilt was the first step in his return to God.

1:14 The sailors themselves called out to Jonah's God for help when their attempt to steer the ship back to shore failed. They did not want to die as a result of Jonah's sin or to receive blame for his death. The great fish was the means for God's gracious deliverance of Jonah from death.

1:15, 16 The sailors saw Jonah as being punished by his angry God. They did not see the "great fish" as God's means for deliverance. The text does not state that these Phoenician sailors committed themselves to *Yahweh,* but it does indicate that they received a powerful witness.

1:17 Many scholars have investigated the exact type of fish in which a man could be preserved for several days. While discussion continues and though several similar experiences have been reported in modern times, the issue is not finding a similar event but acknowledging the power of God to perform miracles. God intervened through nature to challenge Jonah's disobedience and to deliver Jonah from death. Jonah's encounter with the fish was later mentioned by Jesus (Matt. 12:40; Luke 11:30).

2:2–9 Jonah began his prayer from the belly of the fish with praise and thanksgiving for God's previous work in his life (see chart, Lessons from the Model Prayer). This prayer is structured as a psalm of thanksgiving, verifying that Jonah was not petitioning God for help but thanking Him for undeserved deliverance. This thanksgiving for his undeserved deliverance stands in stark contrast to his own anger when God later delivered undeserving Nineveh. Like the poetic style of the psalms, this prayer is a beautiful flow of Jonah's heartfelt thoughts (see Ps. 120:1). Jonah's use of *Sheol* (Heb., lit. "the place of the dead" or "the grave") indicates that he thought he was at death's door (Jon. 2:2). Again, the Lord rescued Jonah from physical death.

And my prayer went *up* to You,
Into Your holy temple.

8"Those who regard worthless idols
Forsake their own Mercy.
9But I will sacrifice to You
With the voice of thanksgiving;
I will pay what I have vowed.
Salvation *is* of the LORD."

10So the LORD spoke to the fish, and it vomited Jonah onto dry *land.*

Jonah Preaches at Nineveh

3 Now the word of the LORD came to Jonah the second time, saying, 2"Arise, go to Nineveh, that great city, and preach to it the message that I tell you." 3So Jonah arose and went to Nineveh, according to the word of the LORD. Now Nineveh was an exceedingly great city, a three-day journey[a] *in extent.* 4And Jonah began to enter the city on the first day's walk. Then he cried out and said, "Yet forty days, and Nineveh shall be overthrown!"

The People of Nineveh Believe

5So the people of Nineveh believed God, proclaimed a fast, and put on sackcloth, from the greatest to the least of them. 6Then word came to the king of Nineveh; and he arose from his throne and laid aside his robe, covered *himself* with sackcloth and sat in ashes. 7And he caused *it* to be proclaimed and published throughout Nineveh by the decree of the king and his nobles, saying,

Let neither man nor beast, herd nor flock, taste anything; do not let them eat, or drink water. 8But let man and beast be covered with sackcloth, and cry mightily to God; yes, let every one turn from his evil way and from the violence that is in his hands. 9Who can tell *if* God will turn and relent, and turn away from His fierce anger, so that we may not perish?

10Then God saw their works, that they turned from their evil way; and God relented from the disaster that He had said He would bring upon them, and He did not do it.

Jonah's Anger and God's Kindness

4 But it displeased Jonah exceedingly, and he became angry. 2So he prayed to the LORD, and said, "Ah, LORD, was not this what I said when I was still in my country? Therefore I fled previously to Tarshish; for I know that You *are* a gracious and merciful God, slow to anger and abundant in lovingkindness, One who relents from doing harm. 3Therefore now, O LORD, please take my life from me, for *it is* better for me to die than to live!"

4Then the LORD said, "*Is it* right for you to be angry?"

5So Jonah went out of the city and sat on the east side of the city. There he made himself a shelter and sat under it in the shade, till he might see what would become of the city. 6And the LORD God prepared a plant[a] and made it come up over Jonah, that it might be shade for his head to deliver him

---

3:3 [a]Exact meaning unknown　　4:6 [a]Hebrew *kikayon*, exact identity unknown

---

3:1 Though Jonah deliberately disobeyed God the first time (Jon. 1:3), he was given another opportunity to follow God's call to Nineveh, illustrating that God saves the undeserving and offers a second chance for service (Num. 12, Second Chances). Jonah's initial rejection of God's plan did not disqualify or excuse him from later service.

3:4 The reluctant prophet finally entered Nineveh and proclaimed God's warning loudly. Since the Assyrians were a hated, barbaric people, Jonah probably hoped they would ignore his warning and experience God's judgment. Though Jonah expected a destruction like that of Sodom and Gomorrah (Gen. 19:25; Lam. 4:6; Amos 4:11), God announced a turning around or repentance for Nineveh. Jonah's prophetic word was beautifully fulfilled but in a completely different sense than Jonah expected.

3:5 The pagan people of Nineveh believed (Heb. *'aman,* lit. "to stand firm, trust, believe") the message from God and were saved from destruction. The word "amen," is used most often to conclude a prayer by affirming, "so be it." All the Ninevites demonstrated their belief in God by humbling themselves before God and fasting (see Matt. 6:16–18, note). The inclusion of animals in the fast is documented in extrabiblical sources such as Herodotus (Jon. 3:7, 8). Perhaps it is the same idea as expressed in more recent funeral processions when horses drawing the funeral carriage are draped in black.

3:10 As a result of the genuine repentance of the people of Nineveh, God chose to spare them from divine punishment (see v. 4, note). When we change our wills, God wills a change. When we choose to repent, God may choose to relent.

4:2 The repentant prophet Jonah affirmed the nature of God in the same terms as Moses had centuries before (see Ex. 34:6). The Hebrews recognized that God is "gracious" (used only of God in the OT), favoring even the undeserving; He is "merciful," forgiving and compassionate toward His children; He is "slow to anger," patient with the disobedient; He is "abundant in lovingkindness," personal and consistent, demonstrating unconditional tenderness, love, and mercy (Heb. *chesed;* see Ps. 5:7–12, note); and He "relents from doing harm," responding to repentance. This prayer is Jonah's second confession of faith.

4:3, 4 Jonah thought God should destroy the Ninevites. Jonah preferred to die rather than live to see this pagan nation saved. For God to forgive the rebellious Assyrians did not seem fair even though God had forgiven him, a rebellious prophet! For Jonah to wish to die (vv. 3, 8) when he had just been so thankful for his own deliverance from death was ironic. Human logic questions fairness when evil is forgiven. But in so doing, it fails to see that if evil were not graciously forgiven, everyone would be destroyed.

from his misery. So Jonah was very grateful for the plant. [7]But as morning dawned the next day God prepared a worm, and it *so* damaged the plant that it withered. [8]And it happened, when the sun arose, that God prepared a vehement east wind; and the sun beat on Jonah's head, so that he grew faint. Then he wished death for himself, and said, "*It is* better for me to die than to live."

[9]Then God said to Jonah, "*Is it* right for you to be angry about the plant?"

And he said, "*It is* right for me to be angry, even to death!"

[10]But the LORD said, "You have had pity on the plant for which you have not labored, nor made it grow, which came up in a night and perished in a night. [11]And should I not pity Nineveh, that great city, in which are more than one hundred and twenty thousand persons who cannot discern between their right hand and their left—and much livestock?"

4:7 God appointed a worm to destroy the plant and teach another lesson to Jonah. God showed His compassion for Jonah as He did for Job and Jeremiah, who, in their own agonies, had accused God (see Jer. 15:15–18). The morning after the weary prophet found comfort under a plant provided by God, his shady covering withered. Jonah met a God-appointed worm, with a God-appointed task, at a God-appointed time, to yield God-appointed results. God chooses us, gives us a job at an appropriate time, and promises victory.

4:11 The Lord clearly confirms His right to destroy or deliver His children, who themselves often lack moral judgment. God's direct question abruptly ends the book. Only one other book of the Bible, Nahum, ends with a question. In both books the divine message is to the people of Nineveh.

Micah

Micah is a shortened form of Micaiah (lit. "Who is like *Yahweh?*"). The name is an expression of praise and awe for the God of Israel. Micah lived in Moresheth, a small village in Judah. The author of this book is not the prophet Micaiah, son of Imlah, who prophesied in the northern kingdom during the reign of Ahab (874–853 B.C.; see 1 Kin. 22:8–28; 2 Chr. 18:3–27).

Micah prophesied in Judah during the reigns of Jotham (750–735 B.C.), Ahaz (735–715 B.C.), and Hezekiah (715–686 B.C., plus coregency with Ahaz 729–715 B.C.), which places him on the scene during the disastrous invasion of Israel and Judah by the Assyrians. Micah was a contemporary of the prophet Isaiah in the southern kingdom and of Amos and Hosea in the northern kingdom.

SETTING: The leaders and people of Judah had mixed the worship of *Yahweh* with the idolatrous practices of their pagan neighbors. Some of Judah's kings, like Hezekiah, were God-fearing but had not been able to effect the needed spiritual reformation. Idolatry still flourished, even in Jerusalem. God announced, through Micah, that He would send Assyria to bring calamity upon His people. After the judgment, He promised restoration and blessing.

PURPOSE: Micah had been sent to declare God's judgment and call the people to repentance. He was to some extent successful. Hezekiah responded to the message, and Jerusalem was spared from assault by the Assyrians (Jer. 26:18).

AUDIENCE: Micah's message concerned both the northern and southern kingdoms, but the prophet delivered his message in Judah. Although Micah was not a court prophet like Isaiah, he probably spoke God's message to the leaders of Jerusalem as well as to the people themselves.

LITERARY CHARACTERISTICS: Considered one of the most remarkable prophetic books in form, the book was written in eloquent poetic verse, characterized by alliteration and word play. The prophet's anger and urgency are tempered by his tenderness, sympathy, and sorrow for his nation.

The major theme of Micah's prophecies is that the people of Judah had become as spiritually and ethically corrupt as the apostate northern kingdom of Israel. The heirs to David's throne were practicing the same abominations as the illegitimate kings of the northern kingdom (see Mic. 1:5; 2 Kin. 16:1–10). A time of prosperity had hardened the

rich, who were oppressing the poor to the extent of denying them justice in the courts (Mic. 2:1, 2; 6:9–12; 7:2, 3). The priests and prophets were performing the religious rituals as prescribed by *Yahweh,* but for a fee. Micah cried out against the ethical and social corruption of his society. He announced impending disaster from the Lord and called for more than external repentance. He called God's people to do justly, to love mercy, and to walk humbly with their God (Mic. 6:8).

OUTLINE

1 The word of the LORD that came to Micah of Moresheth in the days of Jotham, Ahaz, *and* Hezekiah, kings of Judah, which he saw concerning Samaria and Jerusalem.

The Coming Judgment on Israel

²Hear, all you peoples!
Listen, O earth, and all that is in it!
Let the Lord GOD be a witness against you,
The Lord from His holy temple.

³For behold, the LORD is coming out of His place;
He will come down
And tread on the high places of the earth.
⁴The mountains will melt under Him,
And the valleys will split
Like wax before the fire,
Like waters poured down a steep place.

⁵All this is for the transgression of Jacob
And for the sins of the house of Israel.
What *is* the transgression of Jacob?
Is it not Samaria?
And what *are* the high places of Judah?
Are they not Jerusalem?

⁶"Therefore I will make Samaria a heap of ruins
in the field,
Places for planting a vineyard;
I will pour down her stones into the valley,
And I will uncover her foundations.
⁷All her carved images shall be beaten to pieces,
And all her pay as a harlot shall be burned with
the fire;
All her idols I will lay desolate,
For she gathered *it* from the pay of a harlot,
And they shall return to the pay of a
harlot."

1:2–5 The announcement that God had a case against Judah as well as Israel must have come as a shock. The people of Judah proudly believed that they had God's perpetual favor because of the covenant He had made with David (2 Sam. 7:16).

But God pronounced Judah (Jerusalem) no better than Israel (Samaria). The entire people of God had become corrupt and idolatrous.

Mourning for Israel and Judah

[8]Therefore I will wail and howl,
  I will go stripped and naked;
  I will make a wailing like the jackals
  And a mourning like the ostriches,
[9]For her wounds *are* incurable.
  For it has come to Judah;
  It has come to the gate of My people—
  To Jerusalem.

[10]Tell *it* not in Gath,
  Weep not at all;
  In Beth Aphrah[a]
  Roll yourself in the dust.
[11]Pass by in naked shame, you inhabitant of
    Shaphir;
  The inhabitant of Zaanan[a] does not go out.
  Beth Ezel mourns;
  Its place to stand is taken away from you.

[12]For the inhabitant of Maroth pined[a] for good,
  But disaster came down from the LORD
  To the gate of Jerusalem.
[13]O inhabitant of Lachish,
  Harness the chariot to the swift steeds
  (She *was* the beginning of sin to the daughter
    of Zion),
  For the transgressions of Israel were found in
    you.

[14]Therefore you shall give presents to
    Moresheth Gath;[a]
  The houses of Achzib[b] *shall be* a lie to the kings
    of Israel.
[15]I will yet bring an heir to you, O inhabitant of
    Mareshah;[a]

The glory of Israel shall come to
    Adullam.
[16]Make yourself bald and cut off your hair,
  Because of your precious children;
  Enlarge your baldness like an eagle,
  For they shall go from you into captivity.

Woe to Evildoers

2 Woe to those who devise iniquity,
  And work out evil on their beds!
  At morning light they practice it,
  Because it is in the power of their hand.
[2]They covet fields and take *them* by violence,
  Also houses, and seize *them*.
  So they oppress a man and his house,
  A man and his inheritance.

[3]Therefore thus says the LORD:

"Behold, against this family I am devising
    disaster,
  From which you cannot remove your necks;
  Nor shall you walk haughtily,
  For this *is* an evil time.
[4]In that day *one* shall take up a proverb against
    you,
  And lament with a bitter lamentation,
    saying:
'We are utterly destroyed!
  He has changed the heritage of my people;
  How He has removed *it* from me!
  To a turncoat He has divided our fields.' "

·················

1:10 [a]Literally *House of Dust* 1:11 [a]Literally *Going Out* 1:12
[a]Literally *was sick* 1:14 [a]Literally *Possession of Gath* [b]Literally *Lie*
1:15 [a]Literally *Inheritance*

1:8, 9 The prophet demonstrated urgency and grief in his lament. Micah showed his grief at the coming disaster by wailing and adopting all the signs of mourning. Jesus wept over Jerusalem with similar grief, remembering how it had suffered for rejecting the prophets and how the city would suffer even more for rejecting Him (Matt. 23:37–39). The prophetic specificity of verse 9 is confirmed by history—the Assyrians came right up to the gate of Jerusalem, but God turned them back when Hezekiah and Isaiah interceded (2 Kin. 18:17—19:37).

1:10–16 The Israelites would suffer the anguish of ridicule by their gloating enemies in Gath. With poetic eloquence Micah named towns that would suffer the impending invasion. The comment on each town is a play on words in the Hebrew. Beth Aphrah ("house of dust") puns the command to its inhabitants to "roll yourself in the dust," as an expression of grief over humiliation and defeat (v. 10). "Tell it not in Gath" (that is, among the Philistines) expresses the fear that these perennial enemies of Judah will gloat over her suffering. All these towns Micah mentioned were destroyed by the Assyrians under Sennacherib in 701 B.C. (vv. 10–16).

2:1 The prophet identified those targeted for judgment because of their sin. Corrupt political leaders were indicted be-

cause of their misuse of power to satisfy their own greed. They dreamed of ways to satisfy their lustful appetites, then ran to carry out their plans. The unjust seizing of the Land was a particularly heinous crime because the Land had been given to the respective tribes by God as their perpetual inheritance (see 1 Kin. 21).

2:3 The Lord warned that He was devising disaster against those who devise evil (v. 1). God's disaster had a purpose to punish for sin and to correct ungodly behavior. The disaster God devised came in the form of Assyria's cruel military forces and the accompanying deportation of the people. God was giving His people over to the violent and arrogant Assyrians.

2:4, 5 The prophet warned that the Assyrians would seize the Land, which would be ironic because land-grabbers from among God's chosen people had taken the Land by force from the poor. What had been Israel's exclusive possession would be lost in a humiliating way to her enemies. The siege would be so devastating that the average observer would declare that God had removed His favor from His children. Not only would they lose everything, but God's people would be delivered into the hands of the most evil and corrupt enemies on the face of the earth.

[5]Therefore you will have no one to determine
boundaries[a] by lot
In the assembly of the LORD.

Lying Prophets

[6]"Do not prattle," *you say to those* who prophesy.
So they shall not prophesy to you;[a]
They shall not return insult for insult.[b]
[7]*You who are* named the house of Jacob:
"Is the Spirit of the LORD restricted?
Are these His doings?
Do not My words do good
To him who walks uprightly?

[8]"Lately My people have risen up as an enemy—
You pull off the robe with the garment
From those who trust *you,* as they pass by,
Like men returned from war.
[9]The women of My people you cast out
From their pleasant houses;
From their children
You have taken away My glory forever.

[10]"Arise and depart,
For this *is* not *your* rest;
Because it is defiled, it shall destroy,
Yes, with utter destruction.
[11]If a man should walk in a false spirit
And speak a lie, *saying,*
'I will prophesy to you of wine and drink,'
Even he would be the prattler of this people.

Israel Restored

[12]"I will surely assemble all of you, O Jacob,
I will surely gather the remnant of Israel;
I will put them together like sheep of the fold,[a]
Like a flock in the midst of their pasture;
They shall make a loud noise because of *so
many* people.
[13]The one who breaks open will come up before
them;
They will break out,
Pass through the gate,
And go out by it;
Their king will pass before them,
With the LORD at their head."

Wicked Rulers and Prophets

3 And I said:

"Hear now, O heads of Jacob,
And you rulers of the house of Israel:
Is it not for you to know justice?
[2]You who hate good and love evil;
Who strip the skin from My people,[a]
And the flesh from their bones;
[3]Who also eat the flesh of My people,
Flay their skin from them,
Break their bones,
And chop *them* in pieces
Like *meat* for the pot,
Like flesh in the caldron."

[4]Then they will cry to the LORD,
But He will not hear them;
He will even hide His face from them at that
time,
Because they have been evil in their deeds.

[5]Thus says the LORD concerning the prophets
Who make my people stray;
Who chant "Peace"
While they chew with their teeth,
But who prepare war against him
Who puts nothing into their mouths:
[6]"Therefore you shall have night without vision,
And you shall have darkness without
divination;
The sun shall go down on the prophets,
And the day shall be dark for them.
[7]So the seers shall be ashamed,
And the diviners abashed;
Indeed they shall all cover their lips;
For *there is* no answer from God."

[8]But truly I am full of power by the Spirit of the
LORD,
And of justice and might,
To declare to Jacob his transgression

2:5 [a]Literally *one casting a surveyor's line*   **2:6** [a]Literally *to these*
[b]Vulgate reads *He shall not take shame.*   **2:12** [a]Hebrew *Bozrah*   **3:2**
[a]Literally *them*

2:12 Micah concluded this first announcement of calamity with a promise that the Shepherd-King would protect and gather a remnant of the people. After God had dealt with the Israelites, both Judah and Israel, He would restore them to enjoy God's best fully (Ps. 23:2). Although they had sinned, His love for them and commitment to them would be permanent. Their fellowship with Him had been broken, but their relationship to Him would remain forever. They would never cease to be His children.

3:1–4 The rulers of Judah, princes and priests who were supposed to know right from wrong, were ruthless in their abuse of the people. Micah compared them to a large beast devouring the flesh of a smaller one. For that reason, the Lord would

not hear the cries of the princes and priests in their own time of great tribulation.

3:5–7 Because the prophets spoke lies for profit, God would take away their prophetic gift. They would be unable to offer God's word to the suffering people. This humiliation would place their prophetic calling in jeopardy, since prophets are authenticated by their ability to hear from God and to speak about that which is to come (Ezek. 14:6–11). The withdrawal of prophecy was a severe judgment against the nation.

3:8–12 Rulers took bribes, priests ministered for profit, and prophets spoke only for pay. In spite of their sin, they possessed a false sense of safety, assuming that because they were chosen of God, they had no reason to fear His retribution.

> *Quiet is a blessed gift. We must cherish every moment of it,*
> *and carve it out for ourselves every chance we get.*
>
> Anne Ortlund

And to Israel his sin.
⁹Now hear this,
You heads of the house of Jacob
And rulers of the house of Israel,
Who abhor justice
And pervert all equity,
¹⁰Who build up Zion with bloodshed
And Jerusalem with iniquity:
¹¹Her heads judge for a bribe,
Her priests teach for pay,
And her prophets divine for money.
Yet they lean on the LORD, and say,
"Is not the LORD among us?
No harm can come upon us."
¹²Therefore because of you
Zion shall be plowed *like* a field,
Jerusalem shall become heaps of ruins,
And the mountain of the templeᵃ
Like the bare hills of the forest.

The LORD's Reign in Zion

4 Now it shall come to pass in the latter days
That the mountain of the LORD's house
Shall be established on the top of the
mountains,
And shall be exalted above the hills;
And peoples shall flow to it.
²Many nations shall come and say,
"Come, and let us go up to the mountain of the
LORD,
To the house of the God of Jacob;
He will teach us His ways,
And we shall walk in His paths."
For out of Zion the law shall go forth,
And the word of the LORD from Jerusalem.
³He shall judge between many peoples,
And rebuke strong nations afar off;
They shall beat their swords into plowshares,
And their spears into pruning hooks;
Nation shall not lift up sword against nation,
Neither shall they learn war anymore.ᵃ

⁴But everyone shall sit under his vine and under
his fig tree,
And no one shall make *them* afraid;
For the mouth of the LORD of hosts has
spoken.
⁵For all people walk each in the name of his
god,
But we will walk in the name of the LORD our
God
Forever and ever.

Zion's Future Triumph

⁶"In that day," says the LORD,
"I will assemble the lame,
I will gather the outcast
And those whom I have afflicted;
⁷I will make the lame a remnant,
And the outcast a strong nation;
So the LORD will reign over them in Mount
Zion
From now on, even forever.
⁸And you, O tower of the flock,
The stronghold of the daughter of Zion,
To you shall it come,
Even the former dominion shall come,
The kingdom of the daughter of Jerusalem."

⁹Now why do you cry aloud?
Is there no king in your midst?
Has your counselor perished?
For pangs have seized you like a woman in
labor.
¹⁰Be in pain, and labor to bring forth,
O daughter of Zion,
Like a woman in birth pangs.
For now you shall go forth from the city,
You shall dwell in the field,
And to Babylon you shall go.
There you shall be delivered;

3:12 ᵃLiterally *house*   4:3 ᵃCompare Isaiah 2:2–4

4:1–8 Although Jerusalem was threatened with destruction, Micah reassured God's covenant people that the Lord would yet reign from Zion. When He assumed the throne, war between nations would cease (v. 3), and each person would enjoy the security of life free from fear (v. 4).

4:10 Micah here predicted that the people of Judah would go into captivity. Astonishingly, the Lord would deliver and redeem the remnant from their enemies in Babylon. Because of Hezekiah's repentance, Jerusalem did not fall to the Assyrians. Over a century later Jerusalem was destroyed by the Babylonians and the people were taken into Exile in

Babylon. Many interpret these words of Micah as a clear statement that the Exile must take place before the messianic age.

4:11–13 The Assyrians arrogantly assumed they could take Jerusalem, because no other city had withstood their advance (see 2 Kin. 18:33). God would use their siege of Jerusalem to slay them. King Hezekiah turned to the Lord in repentance, and God spared Jerusalem by slaughtering the besieging army (see 2 Kin. 19:1–7, 35). However, Hezekiah's repentance brought only a temporary reprieve; almost a century later Jerusalem finally fell to the Babylonians.

There the LORD will redeem you
From the hand of your enemies.

[11]Now also many nations have gathered against
you,
Who say, "Let her be defiled,
And let our eye look upon Zion."
[12]But they do not know the thoughts of the
LORD,
Nor do they understand His counsel;
For He will gather them like sheaves to the
threshing floor.

[13]"Arise and thresh, O daughter of Zion;
For I will make your horn iron,
And I will make your hooves bronze;
You shall beat in pieces many peoples;
I will consecrate their gain to the LORD,
And their substance to the Lord of the whole
earth."

5 Now gather yourself in troops,
O daughter of troops;
He has laid siege against us;
They will strike the judge of Israel with a rod
on the cheek.

The Coming Messiah

[2]"But you, Bethlehem Ephrathah,
Though you are little among the thousands of
Judah,
Yet out of you shall come forth to Me
The One to be Ruler in Israel,
Whose goings forth *are* from of old,
From everlasting."

[3]Therefore He shall give them up,
Until the time *that* she who is in labor has
given birth;
Then the remnant of His brethren

Shall return to the children of Israel.
[4]And He shall stand and feed *His flock*
In the strength of the LORD,
In the majesty of the name of the LORD His
God;
And they shall abide,
For now He shall be great
To the ends of the earth;
[5]And this *One* shall be peace.

Judgment on Israel's Enemies

When the Assyrian comes into our land,
And when he treads in our palaces,
Then we will raise against him
Seven shepherds and eight princely men.
[6]They shall waste with the sword the land of
Assyria,
And the land of Nimrod at its entrances;
Thus He shall deliver *us* from the Assyrian,
When he comes into our land
And when he treads within our borders.

[7]Then the remnant of Jacob
Shall be in the midst of many peoples,
Like dew from the LORD,
Like showers on the grass,
That tarry for no man
Nor wait for the sons of men.
[8]And the remnant of Jacob
Shall be among the Gentiles,
In the midst of many peoples,
Like a lion among the beasts of the
forest,
Like a young lion among flocks of sheep,
Who, if he passes through,
Both treads down and tears in pieces,
And none can deliver.
[9]Your hand shall be lifted against your
adversaries,
And all your enemies shall be cut off.

5:1 Daughter of troops describes Jerusalem as a warlike city, perhaps a reference to its renown for hostility to the less fortunate. The city would suffer siege because of its sinful actions.

5:2 The birthplace of the Shepherd-King would be the city of Bethlehem. King David, a man after God's own heart, had been born in Bethlehem centuries before. The intervening kings had failed to follow the Lord. By predicting a new King from Bethlehem, Micah was invoking the covenant God made with David (2 Sam. 7). Centuries later when Jesus was born, this prophecy was quoted in answer to the question of the wise men concerning where the Christ was to be born (Mic. 5:2; Matt 2:1–6).

5:3–6 A nation was only as secure as the strength of its king in the ancient Near East. Judah's kings were insufficient to assure lasting peace for God's chosen people. Micah spoke of a king who would come in such greatness and strength that his power would reach to the ends of the earth. Under such a king the people would abide in complete safety and peace. The enemy would be impotent against this king, who would

destroy them. The gospel writers identify Jesus as this great King of Israel, who is our peace.

5:7 God would not stop with only redeeming the remnant of Israel; He would use them to bless many. The presence of God's people would be to the nations what the morning dew and rain were to parched soil. The dew and rain were given by God as a sign of blessing. This metaphor must have been clearly understood by people who each morning saw the dew as the source that watered their crops. The prophet here said that the remnant of Jacob would be to the nations like life-giving water from heaven.

5:8 After depicting the remnant of Jacob as life-giving water (v. 7), the prophet now revealed that they would also be like a "lion" among the Gentiles. Assyrian kings likened themselves to the lion, and Assyrian art reflects this national symbol. In a dramatic reversal, Micah portrayed God's people as the "lion" who would prevail. This dual portrayal of God's people as both life and death to the nations is used by Paul as he described the church (2 Cor. 2:14–16).

[10]"And it shall be in that day," says the LORD,
"That I will cut off your horses from your midst
And destroy your chariots.
[11]I will cut off the cities of your land
And throw down all your strongholds.
[12]I will cut off sorceries from your hand,
And you shall have no soothsayers.
[13]Your carved images I will also cut off,
And your sacred pillars from your midst;
You shall no more worship the work of your
hands;
[14]I will pluck your wooden images[a] from your
midst;
Thus I will destroy your cities.
[15]And I will execute vengeance in anger and
fury
On the nations that have not heard."[a]

God Pleads with Israel

6 Hear now what the LORD says:

"Arise, plead your case before the mountains,
And let the hills hear your voice.
[2]Hear, O you mountains, the LORD's complaint,
And you strong foundations of the earth;
For the LORD has a complaint against His
people,
And He will contend with Israel.

[3]"O My people, what have I done to you?
And how have I wearied you?
Testify against Me.
[4]For I brought you up from the land of Egypt,
I redeemed you from the house of bondage;
And I sent before you Moses, Aaron, and
Miriam.
[5]O My people, remember now
What Balak king of Moab counseled,
And what Balaam the son of Beor answered
him,
From Acacia Grove[a] to Gilgal,
That you may know the righteousness of the
LORD."

[6]With what shall I come before the LORD,
And bow myself before the High God?

Shall I come before Him with burnt offerings,
With calves a year old?
[7]Will the LORD be pleased with thousands of
rams,
Ten thousand rivers of oil?
Shall I give my firstborn *for* my transgression,
The fruit of my body *for* the sin of my soul?

[8]He has shown you, O man, what *is* good;
And what does the LORD require of you
But to do justly,
To love mercy,
And to walk humbly with your God?

Punishment of Israel's Injustice

[9]The LORD's voice cries to the city—
Wisdom shall see Your name:

"Hear the rod!
Who has appointed it?
[10]Are there yet the treasures of wickedness
In the house of the wicked,
And the short measure *that is* an abomination?
[11]Shall I count pure *those* with the wicked scales,
And with the bag of deceitful weights?
[12]For her rich men are full of violence,
Her inhabitants have spoken lies,
And their tongue is deceitful in their mouth.

[13]"Therefore I will also make *you* sick by striking
you,
By making *you* desolate because of your sins.
[14]You shall eat, but not be satisfied;
Hunger[a] *shall be* in your midst.
You may carry *some* away,[b] but shall not save
them;
And what you do rescue I will give over to the
sword.

[15]"You shall sow, but not reap;
You shall tread the olives, but not anoint
yourselves with oil;
And *make* sweet wine, but not drink wine.

....

5:14 [a]Hebrew *Asherim,* Canaanite deities   5:15 [a]Or *obeyed*   6:5
[a]Hebrew *Shittim* (compare Numbers 25:1; Joshua 2:1; 3:1)   6:14 [a]Or
Emptiness or *Humiliation* [b]Targum and Vulgate read *You shall take
hold.*

6:1, 2 The Lord used a series of rhetorical questions to help
His people understand the reality of their sin. The Hebrew
word translated "complaint" is the word used for a legal court
case. Because of God's covenant with His people, God had a
legal case against them for violation of the covenant. He
called the hills and mountains, who had witnessed Israel's
transgressions, to hear the case.

6:3–5 God asked His people what He had done to deserve the
rejection of His covenant, as evidenced by their wickedness
and idolatry. He reminded the people of Judah that they
would not exist had He not supernaturally redeemed them
from slavery in Egypt. He reminded them of events during
their wilderness journey that revealed His righteousness and

power. God's people gave no explanation to His question as to
how He had failed them.

6:6–8 Although Judah had become corrupt, the people were
religiously practicing sacrifice to the Lord in the delusion that
this would satisfy His demands. God corrected His people
through Micah by demanding justice, not burnt offerings;
mercy, not calves and oil; humble obedience, not sacrifice.
Justice, mercy, and obedience were precisely those qualities
lacking in Judah. These verses actually summarize the messages of the 8th century B.C. prophets: Amos called for justice;
Hosea emphasized kindness; Isaiah exhorted the people to
obey or to walk humbly with God.

SACRIFICIAL LIVING *HERE IS MY LIFE*

A sacrifice is an offering rendered acceptable to God. To live sacrificially is to offer your entire life to God. Such a sacrifice is acceptable to God only because of Christ's work in you; He is the final and complete Sacrifice for the atonement of sin (Heb. 7:26, 27).

Micah knew lavish offerings were not acceptable to God (Mic. 6:6–8). David and Isaiah knew acceptability with God was "a contrite heart" (Ps. 51:17; Is. 66:2). Paul described this transaction as "a living sacrifice" (Rom. 12:1). Although you can never match Christ's sacrificial death—and indeed, are not asked to do so—your self-giving is to be complete and wholehearted. Being a living sacrifice means obeying the greatest commandments: giving God all your love, will, reason, and body (Mark 12:29–31), borne out in practical, daily service to others (Matt. 25:34–40). No expression of love, however costly, matches the price paid by Christ. The forgiven woman poured out expensive, fragrant oil to anoint Jesus' feet, but her gift also involved the recognition of her past and the risk of disclosure of her sin. Her example of sacrificial giving did not go unnoticed (Luke 7: 36–50).

See also Dan. 2:23, note; Luke 10:25–37; 21:1–4; 1 Pet. 2:5; notes on Commitment (Matt. 16); Servanthood (Mark 10); Suffering (Ps. 33; 113; Is. 43; 1 Pet. 5); Surrender (James 4)

16For the statutes of Omri are kept;
All the works of Ahab's house *are done;*
And you walk in their counsels,
That I may make you a desolation,
And your inhabitants a hissing.
Therefore you shall bear the reproach of My people."a

Sorrow for Israel's Sins

7 Woe is me!
For I am like those who gather summer fruits,
Like those who glean vintage grapes;
There is no cluster to eat
Of the first-ripe fruit *which* my soul desires.
2The faithful *man* has perished from the earth,
And *there is* no one upright among men.
They all lie in wait for blood;
Every man hunts his brother with a net.

3That they may successfully do evil with both hands—
The prince asks *for gifts,*
The judge *seeks* a bribe,
And the great *man* utters his evil desire;
So they scheme together.
4The best of them *is* like a brier;
The most upright *is sharper* than a thorn hedge;

The day of your watchman and your punishment comes;
Now shall be their perplexity.

5Do not trust in a friend;
Do not put your confidence in a companion;
Guard the doors of your mouth
From her who lies in your bosom.
6For son dishonors father,
Daughter rises against her mother,
Daughter-in-law against her mother-in-law;
A man's enemies *are* the men of his own household.
7Therefore I will look to the LORD;
I will wait for the God of my salvation;
My God will hear me.

Israel's Confession and Comfort

8Do not rejoice over me, my enemy;
When I fall, I will arise;
When I sit in darkness,
The LORD *will be* a light to me.
9I will bear the indignation of the LORD,
Because I have sinned against Him,
Until He pleads my case

6:16 aFollowing Masoretic Text, Targum, and Vulgate; Septuagint reads *of nations.*

6:16 Omri and his son Ahab ruled the northern kingdom of Israel more than a century before Micah. Their violence, injustice, and apostasy were legendary. Now the southern kingdom of Judah had followed that same wicked path. Just as the apostate northern kingdom would fall to Assyria, Judah's sentence of destruction was here made final. Ahab is credited with establishing idolatry as the national religion.

7:1–7 Micah lamented the sorry state of his society where evil was so pervasive that no one could be trusted. All preyed on their neighbors. Sin had so saturated the moral fiber of God's people that even those in the most intimate relationships would not be trusted. Micah stated boldly that only God could right such wrong (v. 7). Christ warned the disciples that similar conditions would exist during the last days (Matt. 24:10–12).

7:8–13 Micah portrayed Jerusalem as speaking to the enemy who would assault her, "Though you may win this battle, I will win the war because of the Lord." Micah encouraged the people that though their suffering in judgment was certain, it was also temporary. God's plan for His people would not ultimately be thwarted by their sin.

And executes justice for me.
He will bring me forth to the light;
I will see His righteousness.
¹⁰Then *she who is* my enemy will see,
And shame will cover her who said to me,
"Where is the LORD your God?"
My eyes will see her;
Now she will be trampled down
Like mud in the streets.

¹¹*In* the day when your walls are to be built,
In that day the decree shall go far and wide.ᵃ
¹²*In* that day theyᵃ shall come to you
From Assyria and the fortified cities,ᵇ
From the fortressᶜ to the River,ᵈ
From sea to sea,
And mountain *to* mountain.
¹³Yet the land shall be desolate
Because of those who dwell in it,
And for the fruit of their deeds.

God Will Forgive Israel

¹⁴Shepherd Your people with Your staff,
The flock of Your heritage,
Who dwell solitarily *in* a woodland,
In the midst of Carmel;
Let them feed *in* Bashan and Gilead,
As in days of old.

¹⁵"As in the days when you came out of the land of
Egypt,
I will show themᵃ wonders."

¹⁶The nations shall see and be ashamed of all
their might;
They shall put *their* hand over *their*
mouth;
Their ears shall be deaf.
¹⁷They shall lick the dust like a serpent;
They shall crawl from their holes like
snakes of the earth.
They shall be afraid of the LORD our
God,
And shall fear because of You.
¹⁸Who *is* a God like You,
Pardoning iniquity
And passing over the transgression of the
remnant of His heritage?

He does not retain His anger forever,
Because He delights *in* mercy.
¹⁹He will again have compassion on us,
And will subdue our iniquities.

You will cast all ourᵃ sins
Into the depths of the sea.
²⁰You will give truth to Jacob
And mercy to Abraham,
Which You have sworn to our fathers
From days of old.

7:11 ᵃOr *the boundary shall be extended*　**7:12** ᵃLiterally *he,* collective
of the captives　ᵇHebrew *arey mazor,* possibly *cities of Egypt*
ᶜHebrew *mazor,* possibly *Egypt*　ᵈThat is, the Euphrates　**7:15**
ᵃLiterally *him,* collective for the captives　**7:19** ᵃLiterally *their*

7:14 Micah prayed for the protection of God. He conceded that dark days lay ahead. He prayed that God would continue to shepherd them, comfort them, and hold to His covenant promise. He looked ahead to the day when God's people would dwell, as they did in the past, in the fertile land, represented by Carmel, Bashan, and Gilead. These regions were known for their fertile soils and rich pastures, the sign of divine blessing.

7:18–20 Micah was overcome with praise for a God who could work salvation beyond sin. The question "Who is a God like you?" is an expression of awe and wonder and is reminiscent of the prophet's name (v. 18). The compassion and persistence of the Lord caused the prophet to worship Him even in the midst of disaster. Micah remembered God's faithfulness in Judah's history since the days of His promise to Abraham. Asshur, the national god of Assyria, is now unknown, but the God of Israel still reigns. Nineveh, the capital of Assyria, lies beneath the soils of the ages, but Jerusalem abides. The Lord may judge His people, but He utterly destroys the enemies of His people.

Nahum

AUTHOR

Little is known about Nahum (Heb., lit. "comfort") except what he tells about himself. Nahum's message was intended to comfort Judah. He called himself the Elkoshite, which suggests he was a native of Elkosh, a small village of uncertain location. The lack of personal information does not obscure the message of the prophecy.

DATE

The exact time period of Nahum's prophecy is not known, but his references to certain events suggest a date between 663–612 B.C. Apparently the Assyrian Empire was still intact, which places the prophecy before 612 B.C., when Nineveh fell to the Medes and Babylonians.

BACKGROUND

SETTING: Nahum's entire prophecy was concerned with God's judgment and the destruction of Nineveh, the capital city of the great Assyrian Empire. More than a century earlier, the prophet Jonah had reluctantly gone to the city of Nineveh and preached a message that caused spiritual revival in the city. But the revival was short-lived, and the people soon returned to their former arrogant practice of evil. It is unlikely that Nahum delivered his prophecy in Nineveh. Rather, the prophecy was given to the people of Judah as reassurance of the ultimate destruction of their cruel Assyrian oppressors.

The Book of Nahum stands as a strong testament to the power and faithfulness of God, who judges evil wherever it is found. The Lord is able to bring down the greatest stronghold and will always protect His people. Unlike the message to God's people, which promised restoration and deliverance, no promise of hope existed for Assyria because of that nation's wickedness.

PURPOSE: The Book of Nahum conveys a single message: The great Assyrian Empire will be destroyed. Evildoers will have their day of reckoning with God, no matter how mighty their power may seem.

AUDIENCE: Nahum is addressing the people of Judah, with a message concerning the destruction of Nineveh.

LITERARY CHARACTERISTIC: Nahum's prophecy is presented in eloquent Hebrew poetry.

THEMES

Two themes run throughout the Book of Nahum:

1) Evildoers will be destroyed;
2) God is loyal to His people, even in their waywardness, and He will avenge their enemies.

1 The burden[a] against Nineveh. The book of the vision of Nahum the Elkoshite.

God's Wrath on His Enemies

2God *is* jealous, and the LORD avenges;
The LORD avenges and *is* furious.
The LORD will take vengeance on His
  adversaries,
And He reserves *wrath* for His enemies;
3The LORD *is* slow to anger and great in power,
And will not at all acquit *the wicked.*

The LORD has His way
In the whirlwind and in the storm,
And the clouds *are* the dust of His feet.
4He rebukes the sea and makes it dry,
And dries up all the rivers.
Bashan and Carmel wither,
And the flower of Lebanon wilts.
5The mountains quake before Him,
The hills melt,
And the earth heaves[a] at His presence,
Yes, the world and all who dwell in it.

6Who can stand before His indignation?
And who can endure the fierceness of His
  anger?
His fury is poured out like fire,
And the rocks are thrown down by Him.

7The LORD *is* good,
A stronghold in the day of trouble;
And He knows those who trust in Him.
8But with an overflowing flood
He will make an utter end of its place,
And darkness will pursue His enemies.

9What do you conspire against the LORD?
He will make an utter end *of it.*
Affliction will not rise up a second time.
10For while tangled *like* thorns,
And while drunken *like* drunkards,
They shall be devoured like stubble fully
  dried.
11From you comes forth *one*
Who plots evil against the LORD,
A wicked counselor.

12Thus says the LORD:

"Though *they are* safe, and likewise many,
Yet in this manner they will be cut down
When he passes through.
Though I have afflicted you,
I will afflict you no more;
13For now I will break off his yoke from you,
And burst your bonds apart."

•••••••••••••••••••

1:1 [a]Or *oracle*   1:5 [a]Targum reads *burns.*

1:1 **Nineveh,** the capital of Assyria, was known for its cruel deportation and torture of the Israelites. The Book of Nahum is often considered a companion book to Jonah as it is a sequel to the story of Jonah's journey to Nineveh to preach repentance. When Jonah declared the message of the Lord to the people of Nineveh some 100 years earlier, the Ninevites repented (see Jon. 3:5, 10, notes). However, they reverted to their wicked lifestyle, marked by violence and evil. The prophet Nahum now pronounced God's judgment against the city, a mission quite different from that of Jonah.

1:2 **God's jealousy** is not to be confused with human jealousy. People may jealously desire the possessions of another, but God is zealous to protect the interest and well-being of that which is His. The prophet, in declaring to the Ninevites that God is jealous, meant that God was displeased with the capture and abuse of His people and that Nineveh would be de-

stroyed as a result. Though God disciplined His chosen nation through Assyria's political ambitions, Assyria was nevertheless responsible to God for its arrogance, evil, and violence. The enemies of Judah were God's enemies.

1:3–5 **Bashan and Carmel** had both been known for their fertile soils, flowers, and fruit vines. The abundance of the Land was considered a sign of God's blessing. Lebanon was noted for its cedars. Nahum, recognizing that he was speaking to people filled with pride and arrogance, emphasized that God used the failure of natural elements and vegetation to judge the nations. At the time Nahum wrote, Assyria had already destroyed Lebanon, as well as Bashan and Carmel, which were part of the northern kingdom of Israel.

1:12–14 **Assyria had long threatened the existence of Judah.** God announced to Judah that He would subdue her enemy. God had

¹⁴The Lᴏʀᴅ has given a command concerning
you:
"Your name shall be perpetuated no longer.
Out of the house of your gods
I will cut off the carved image and the molded
image.
I will dig your grave,
For you are vile."

¹⁵Behold, on the mountains
The feet of him who brings good tidings,
Who proclaims peace!
O Judah, keep your appointed feasts,
Perform your vows.
For the wicked one shall no more pass through
you;
He is utterly cut off.

The Destruction of Nineveh

2 He who scatters[a] has come up before your
face.
Man the fort!
Watch the road!
Strengthen *your* flanks!
Fortify *your* power mightily.

²For the Lᴏʀᴅ will restore the excellence of
Jacob
Like the excellence of Israel,
For the emptiers have emptied them out
And ruined their vine branches.

³The shields of his mighty men *are* made red,
The valiant men *are* in scarlet.
The chariots *come* with flaming torches
In the day of his preparation,
And the spears are brandished.[a]
⁴The chariots rage in the streets,
They jostle one another in the broad roads;
They seem like torches,
They run like lightning.

⁵He remembers his nobles;
They stumble in their walk;
They make haste to her walls,

And the defense is prepared.
⁶The gates of the rivers are opened,
And the palace is dissolved.
⁷It is decreed:[a]
She shall be led away captive,
She shall be brought up;
And her maidservants shall lead *her* as with the
voice of doves,
Beating their breasts.

⁸Though Nineveh of old *was* like a pool of
water,
Now they flee away.
"Halt! Halt!" *they cry;*
But no one turns back.
⁹Take spoil of silver!
Take spoil of gold!
There is no end of treasure,
Or wealth of every desirable prize.
¹⁰She is empty, desolate, and waste!
The heart melts, and the knees shake;
Much pain *is* in every side,
And all their faces are drained of color.[a]

¹¹Where *is* the dwelling of the lions,
And the feeding place of the young lions,
Where the lion walked, the lioness *and* lion's
cub,
And no one made *them* afraid?
¹²The lion tore in pieces enough for his
cubs,
Killed for his lionesses,
Filled his caves with prey,
And his dens with flesh.

¹³"Behold, I *am* against you," says the Lᴏʀᴅ of
hosts, "I will burn your[a] chariots in smoke, and the
sword shall devour your young lions; I will cut off
your prey from the earth, and the voice of your
messengers shall be heard no more."

····················

2:1 [a]Vulgate reads *He who destroys.* **2:3** [a]Literally *the cypresses are shaken;* Septuagint and Syriac read *the horses rush about;* Vulgate reads *the drivers are stupefied.* **2:7** [a]Hebrew *Huzzab* **2:10** [a]Compare Joel 2:6 **2:13** [a]Literally *her*

---

allowed the Assyrians to attack His people because they had turned from Him. Now that the Lord had judged Judah, He would deliver His people from Assyrian domination. Nineveh would be destroyed. This event occurred in 612 B.C. The Assyrians were overrun by an alliance of the Medes and Babylonians, and Nineveh was sacked. Within a few years, the Assyrian Empire had vanished from the earth.

2:1 Nahum warned the Assyrians that they were about to face their toughest opposition. He suggested that the Assyrians, known for their military prowess and savage attacks, have their weapons in good supply, keep watch continually, and take special measures to strengthen themselves. They would need to be at their greatest strength if they had any thought of standing against *Yahweh*. Nahum used irony here, since he

knew that the Assyrians could do nothing to make themselves less vulnerable under the attack of almighty God.

2:2 This promised end to oppression was to motivate Judah's faithfulness to the covenant as expressed in keeping the appointed feasts (Nah. 1:15). To Judah, word of Assyria's imminent downfall meant their own liberation.

2:11–13 The lion was a symbol of Assyria. Lions were plentiful in the vicinity of Nineveh and became a public menace during Ashurbanipal's reign. To demonstrate their courage and strength, Assyrian kings hunted lions for sport. Several Assyrian kings referred to themselves as lions on the attack. God was mocking Assyria with a rhetorical question (v. 11). Though Assyria had been as strong and ferocious as a lion, the nation would not stand when the Lord of Hosts came against it.

The Woe of Nineveh

3 Woe to the bloody city!
It *is* all full of lies *and* robbery.
Its victim never departs.
²The noise of a whip
And the noise of rattling wheels,
Of galloping horses,
Of clattering chariots!
³Horsemen charge with bright sword and
glittering spear.
There is a multitude of slain,
A great number of bodies,
Countless corpses—
They stumble over the corpses—
⁴Because of the multitude of harlotries of the
seductive harlot,
The mistress of sorceries,
Who sells nations through her harlotries,
And families through her sorceries.

⁵"Behold, I *am* against you," says the LORD of
hosts;
"I will lift your skirts over your face,
I will show the nations your nakedness,
And the kingdoms your shame.
⁶I will cast abominable filth upon you,
Make you vile,
And make you a spectacle.
⁷It shall come to pass *that* all who look upon you
Will flee from you, and say,
'Nineveh is laid waste!
Who will bemoan her?'
Where shall I seek comforters for you?"

⁸Are you better than No Amonª
That was situated by the River,ᵇ
That had the waters around her,
Whose rampart *was* the sea,
Whose wall *was* the sea?
⁹Ethiopia and Egypt *were* her strength,
And *it was* boundless;
Put and Lubim were yourª helpers.
¹⁰Yet she *was* carried away,

She went into captivity;
Her young children also were dashed to
pieces
At the head of every street;
They cast lots for her honorable men,
And all her great men were bound in chains.
¹¹You also will be drunk;
You will be hidden;
You also will seek refuge from the enemy.

¹²All your strongholds *are* fig trees with ripened
figs:
If they are shaken,
They fall into the mouth of the eater.
¹³Surely, your people in your midst *are*
women!
The gates of your land are wide open for your
enemies;
Fire shall devour the bars of your *gates.*

¹⁴Draw your water for the siege!
Fortify your strongholds!
Go into the clay and tread the mortar!
Make strong the brick kiln!
¹⁵There the fire will devour you,
The sword will cut you off;
It will eat you up like a locust.

Make yourself many— like the locust!
Make yourself many— like the *swarming*
locusts!
¹⁶You have multiplied your merchants more than
the stars of heaven.
The locust plunders and flies away.
¹⁷Your commanders *are* like *swarming* locusts,
And your generals like great grasshoppers,
Which camp in the hedges on a cold day;
When the sun rises they flee away,
And the place where they *are* is not
known.

3:8 ªThat is, ancient Thebes; Targum and Vulgate read *populous Alexandria.* ᵇLiterally *rivers,* that is, the Nile and the surrounding canals 3:9 ªSeptuagint reads *her.*

3:4–7 Assyria, like a harlot selling her services, had hired out her vicious military forces against small, defenseless nations. Then she would devour her ally as well. Harlotry is often associated with sorcery in the OT. From thousands of clay tablet inscriptions, Assyria was apparently superstitious and steeped in the occult.

3:8–11 The Ninevites foolishly believed they were invincible. Nahum reminded them of the legendary fall of Egypt, whose capital is noted as No Amon (Thebes). The ancient Egyptian Empire had geographical defenses that Nineveh did not have. Situated on the Nile, its military forces were inferior to none, with innumerable soldiers. Though believed to be invincible, Thebes was sacked by the Assyrians in 663 B.C. Nahum's point was this: What happened to invincible Thebes would also happen to Nineveh. Ironically Nahum used one of Assyria's own victims to predict the nation's fate.

3:12 The Ninevites would prove powerless under the wrath of God, like the stem of a ripened fig, brittle and frail. To bring them down would require no tug, only a slight jolt. The Ninevites would fall into the clutches of their enemies, who would devour them.

3:14–17 Ancient cities were often secured by an outer wall erected to ensure safety. Attacking armies would surround the walls, hoping to starve the people or to break the walls. When the threat of war loomed, the people would strengthen the bricks of the wall by filling any cracks in the mortar, and they would store up water and food for the siege. The prophet, of course, understood that despite their preparations, nothing the Ninevites could do would save them. Although they had proved mighty against other earthly kingdoms, they were no match for God's judgment.

18Your shepherds slumber, O king of Assyria;
Your nobles rest *in the dust.*
Your people are scattered on the mountains,
And no one gathers them.
19Your injury *has* no healing,

Your wound is severe.
All who hear news of you
Will clap *their* hands over you,
For upon whom has not your wickedness
passed continually?

3:18, 19 The destruction was complete; the leaders ("shepherds") were dead; the Assyrian people had fled in terror to the mountains. Assyria would not recover from this attack; its demise was certain. These verses were addressed to the king of Assyria. Assyria had been so cruel to the surrounding nations that all who heard of its defeat would applaud. The defeat of the Assyrian Empire occurred in 612 B.C. when an alliance of the Medes and Babylonians destroyed Nineveh.

Habakkuk

AUTHOR

Little is known about the author of this book. The name "Habakkuk" is not a typical Hebrew name and occurs only twice in the Old Testament (Hab. 1:1; 3:1). Some rabbis have related the name to the word translated "embrace" (see 2 Kin. 4:16), in which case his name suggests a prophet who loved his people and sought to draw them to himself in comfort. Others have described the prophet as one who wrestled with God. Accordingly, St. Jerome nicknamed him "the wrestler." The name may also derive from an Akkadian word referring to a type of garden plant. The musical notations in Habakkuk 3 suggest that Habakkuk may have been a levitical priest who gave direction to music in the temple. In any case, nothing is recorded concerning the prophet and his personal life.

DATE

The content of the book indicates that it was written just prior to the destruction of Jerusalem by the Babylonians in 586 B.C. Most scholars date it between 625 and 587 B.C.

BACKGROUND

SETTING: After the reigns of the evil kings Manasseh and Ammon of Judah, God raised up Josiah. Coming to the throne at eight years of age, Josiah was the last good king to reign over Judah. The godly Josiah began to implement sweeping reforms. During the restoration of the temple, a copy of the Law was found and read to the king. Josiah, concerned that God's judgment would fall upon his nation, sent for the prophetess Huldah (see 2 Kin. 22, Huldah). The privilege of bringing a word from God to the king was given to a woman, even though Josiah could have turned to Jeremiah, Nahum, Habakkuk, or Zephaniah, all of whom were prophets at this time. The king ordered the book of the Law to be read in the hearing of all the people (2 Kin. 22; 23).

Josiah's reforms and godly influence died with him. Social injustice and moral corruption became rampant again. The people were cruel and corrupt. False gods were worshiped and very little honor was given to *Yahweh*.

On the international scene, the Babylonians (Chaldeans) had destroyed the Assyrian forces, which left the Chaldean nation the undisputed master of the east. The Chaldeans, who inhabited southern Babylon, were expanding their empire by the violent conquest of smaller nations. Judah's existence was threatened.

PURPOSE: Habakkuk called his nation to that same trust in God he had found in the midst of life's certain disasters (see Hab. 2:4; 3:16–19). The book continues to be a message of hope and comfort for God's people.

AUDIENCE: Habakkuk, unlike the other prophets, spoke to God about the people. He expected God to respond by bringing the people to repentance and obedience. Habakkuk asked God questions and received answers.

LITERARY CHARACTERISTICS: The book presents a dialogue between Habakkuk and God (Hab. 1:1—2:5). Habakkuk 3 is a psalm, including musical instructions (Hab. 3:1–19). The book also includes vivid metaphors and idiomatic phrases.

THEMES

Habakkuk, perplexed by the impending destruction of his nation by the Babylonians, found his faith faltering. Questioning God's goodness and wisdom, he called out to the Lord for hope and answers. He learned that he who puts his faith in the faithful God will endure to the end (Hab. 2:4). Habakkuk recorded his own experiences and told his own story. He was a man with honest doubts who had endured trials and learned to wait on God in the midst of all. He ended the book with a hymn of steadfast faith and joy born out of trial and trouble. God had called Habakkuk to embrace what he called him to endure, and the prophet did just that with joy.

OUTLINE

I. Is God There? (1:1–11)
  A. The Lord's reply (1:1–5)
    1. God is in control (1:1–4)
    2. God is active (1:5)
  B. God's instrument, the Chaldeans (1:6–11)
    1. A bitter and nasty nation (1:6)
    2. A self-sufficient people (1:7)
    3. A nation materially equipped for war (1:8)
    4. A violent, conquering nation (1:9)
    5. An arrogant and proud nation (1:10, 11)
II. Is God Fair? (1:12–17)
  A. The character of God explained (1:12, 13)
  B. The actions of God challenged (1:14)
  C. The analogy of the fish (1:15–17)
III. The Lord's Reply (2:1–20)
  A. An admonition to write the message clearly (2:1)

  B. A vision for the future (2:2–4)
  C. An exhortation (2:5)
  D. Five woes (2:6–20)
    1. Against the embezzlers (2:6–8)
    2. Against the extortionists (2:9–11)
    3. Against the tyrants (2:12–14)
    4. Against the drunkards (2:15–17)
    5. Against the idolaters (2:18–20)
IV. Habakkuk's Psalm (3:1–19)
  A. A vision of God (3:1–16)
    1. Coming in intercession (3:1, 2)
    2. Coming from Teman (3:3)
    3. Coming as a warrior (3:4)
    4. Coming with power over pestilence (3:5)
    5. Coming in sovereignty over the nations (3:6)
    6. Coming with salvation for His people (3:7–16)
  B. A hymn of joy (3:17–19)

1 The burden[a] which the prophet Habakkuk saw.

The Prophet's Question

[2]O LORD, how long shall I cry,
And You will not hear?
Even cry out to You, "Violence!"
And You will not save.
[3]Why do You show me iniquity,
And cause *me* to see trouble?
For plundering and violence *are* before me;
There is strife, and contention arises.
[4]Therefore the law is powerless,
And justice never goes forth.
For the wicked surround the righteous;
Therefore perverse judgment proceeds.

The LORD's Reply

[5]"Look among the nations and watch—
Be utterly astounded!
For *I will* work a work in your days
Which you would not believe, though it were
told *you.*
[6]For indeed I am raising up the Chaldeans,
A bitter and hasty nation
Which marches through the breadth of the
earth,
To possess dwelling places *that are* not theirs.
[7]They are terrible and dreadful;
Their judgment and their dignity proceed
from themselves.
[8]Their horses also are swifter than leopards,
And more fierce than evening wolves.
Their chargers charge ahead;
Their cavalry comes from afar;
They fly as the eagle *that* hastens to eat.

[9]"They all come for violence;
Their faces are set *like* the east wind.
They gather captives like sand.
[10]They scoff at kings,
And princes are scorned by them.

They deride every stronghold,
For they heap up earthen *mounds* and seize it.
[11]Then *his* mind[a] changes, and he transgresses;
He commits offense,
Ascribing this power to his god."

The Prophet's Second Question

[12]Are You not from everlasting,
O LORD my God, my Holy One?
We shall not die.
O LORD, You have appointed them for
judgment;
O Rock, You have marked them for correction.
[13]*You are* of purer eyes than to behold evil,
And cannot look on wickedness.
Why do You look on those who deal
treacherously,
And hold Your tongue when the wicked devours
A *person* more righteous than he?
[14]*Why* do You make men like fish of the sea,
Like creeping things *that have* no ruler over
them?

[15]They take up all of them with a hook,
They catch them in their net,
And gather them in their dragnet.
Therefore they rejoice and are glad.
[16]Therefore they sacrifice to their net,
And burn incense to their dragnet;
Because by them their share *is* sumptuous
And their food plentiful.
[17]Shall they therefore empty their net,
And continue to slay nations without
pity?

2 I will stand my watch
And set myself on the rampart,
And watch to see what He will say to me,
And what I will answer when I am corrected.

· ·

1:1 [a]Or *oracle*   1:11 [a]Literally *spirit* or *wind*

1:1–4 Habakkuk had doubts. Although the prophets formerly had declared the certainties of God's love for His people, Habakkuk began to doubt the unchanging character of God. In the divine government of the universe, Habakkuk's intellect and faith were faced with a moral problem for which he could find no solution. Like many in such turmoil, he asked, "Why is God inactive? Why doesn't He do something?" Habakkuk was deeply worried about the threatening international situation, Judah's spiritual decline, and his own faltering faith.

1:5–11 God's reply reminds us that His ways are not our ways. When we, like the prophet, ask, "Is God there, does He care, or is He fair?" we might have to struggle to trust His integrity, despite all evidence to the contrary.

1:8 The Babylonians were a terrifying threat to Habakkuk and his people. "Their horses also are swifter than leopards" suggests the rapidity with which the Babylonians struck. "More fierce than evening wolves" describes their voracious appetite for killing. "They fly as the eagle that hastens to eat" conjures

up a vivid picture of a bird of prey swooping down from the sky upon its helpless victim.

1:14–17 The fish in the nets is a comparison Habakkuk used to get his point across. The Babylonians treated lesser nations in the same way fish in the net were handled. Fish could not protect themselves, and neither can the hapless souls who fall prey to the assault of the invading Babylonians. The prophet described different nets: a small casting "net" that was thrown on the surface of the water and the "dragnet" that was lowered to the bottom of the sea with floats on top. Nothing escaped the nets. This imagery indicates the overwhelming force of the invading Babylonians.

2:1 Habakkuk settled down to wait for an answer from the Lord. Neither "watch" nor "rampart" need be taken literally but rather as an allusion to Habakkuk's prophetic place of responsibility. In a solitary position away from the mundane pressures of life, Habakkuk would patiently wait for God's revelation. He was confused and distressed, but in his doubt

The Just Live by Faith

²Then the Lord answered me and said:

"Write the vision
And make *it* plain on tablets,
That he may run who reads it.
³For the vision *is* yet for an appointed time;
But at the end it will speak, and it will not lie.
Though it tarries, wait for it;
Because it will surely come,
It will not tarry.

⁴"Behold the proud,
His soul is not upright in him;
But the just shall live by his faith.

Woe to the Wicked

⁵"Indeed, because he transgresses by wine,
He is a proud man,
And he does not stay at home.
Because he enlarges his desire as hell,ᵃ
And he *is* like death, and cannot be satisfied,
He gathers to himself all nations
And heaps up for himself all peoples.

⁶"Will not all these take up a proverb against
    him,
And a taunting riddle against him, and say,
'Woe to him who increases
What is not his— how long?
And to him who loads himself with many
    pledges'?ᵃ
⁷Will not your creditorsᵃ rise up suddenly?
Will they not awaken who oppress you?
And you will become their booty.
⁸Because you have plundered many nations,
All the remnant of the people shall plunder
    you,
Because of men's blood
And the violence of the land *and* the city,
And of all who dwell in it.

⁹"Woe to him who covets evil gain for his house,
That he may set his nest on high,
That he may be delivered from the power of
    disaster!
¹⁰You give shameful counsel to your house,
Cutting off many peoples,

And sin *against* your soul.
¹¹For the stone will cry out from the wall,
And the beam from the timbers will answer it.

¹²"Woe to him who builds a town with bloodshed,
Who establishes a city by iniquity!
¹³Behold, *is it* not of the Lord of hosts
That the peoples labor to feed the fire,ᵃ
And nations weary themselves in vain?
¹⁴For the earth will be filled
With the knowledge of the glory of the Lord,
As the waters cover the sea.

¹⁵"Woe to him who gives drink to his neighbor,
Pressingᵃ *him to* your bottle,
Even to make *him* drunk,
That you may look on his nakedness!
¹⁶You are filled with shame instead of glory.
You also— drink!
And be exposed as uncircumcised!ᵃ
The cup of the Lord's right hand *will be* turned
    against you,
And utter shame will be on your glory.
¹⁷For the violence *done to* Lebanon will cover
    you,
And the plunder of beasts *which* made them
    afraid,
Because of men's blood
And the violence of the land *and* the city,
And of all who dwell in it.

¹⁸"What profit is the image, that its maker should
    carve it,
The molded image, a teacher of lies,
That the maker of its mold should trust in it,
To make mute idols?
¹⁹Woe to him who says to wood, 'Awake!'
To silent stone, 'Arise! It shall teach!'
Behold, it is overlaid with gold and silver,
Yet in it there is no breath at all.

²⁰"But the Lord is in His holy temple.
Let all the earth keep silence before Him."

· ·

2:5 ᵃOr *Sheol* **2:6** ᵃSyriac and Vulgate read *thick clay.* **2:7** ᵃLiterally *those who bite you* **2:13** ᵃLiterally *for what satisfies fire,* that is, for what is of no lasting value **2:15** ᵃLiterally *Attaching* or *Joining* **2:16** ᵃDead Sea Scrolls and Septuagint read *And reel!;* Syriac and Vulgate read *And fall fast asleep!*

---

he did not abandon his prophetic calling. Instead, his doubt drove him to seek an answer from the Lord.

2:2 Some ancient texts were written on huge clay, stone, or metal tablets for display. Habakkuk was commanded to write the Lord's answer on such tablets for the benefit of others (Is. 8:1; 30:8). As a prophet, Habakkuk was obligated to preserve and deliver the Lord's message to the people as a source of hope for the future. The message was to be conspicuously displayed.

2:6-20 The five woes described were upon the Babylonians,

who, by vicious conquest of lands to which they had no moral right, continued to build their empire. The woes covered dishonesty and covetousness (vv. 6, 9), robbery and embezzlement (vv. 6-8), exploitation and extortion (vv. 9-11), tyranny (vv. 12-14), debauchery (vv. 15-17), and idolatry (vv. 18-20). This promise of the eventual destruction of Judah's enemy was the Lord's answer of hope to Habakkuk's question, "Is God fair to use an evil empire to judge His own people?" When God's people find themselves victims of oppression, injustice, or violence, Habakkuk's message recalls God's ultimate faithfulness to destroy all sin and evil.

*Feelings come and feelings leave you, but the disciplines of life
are what get you to where you want to go.*

Anne Ortlund

The Prophet's Prayer

3 A prayer of Habakkuk the prophet, on Shig-
ionoth.ᵃ

2 O LORD, I have heard Your speech *and* was
afraid;
O LORD, revive Your work in the midst of the
years!
In the midst of the years make *it* known;
In wrath remember mercy.

3 God came from Teman,
The Holy One from Mount Paran. *Selah*

His glory covered the heavens,
And the earth was full of His praise.
4 *His* brightness was like the light;
He had rays *flashing* from His hand,
And there His power *was* hidden.
5 Before Him went pestilence,
And fever followed at His feet.

6 He stood and measured the earth;
He looked and startled the nations.
And the everlasting mountains were scattered,
The perpetual hills bowed.
His ways *are* everlasting.
7 I saw the tents of Cushan in affliction;
The curtains of the land of Midian trembled.

8 O LORD, were *You* displeased with the rivers,
Was Your anger against the rivers,
Was Your wrath against the sea,
That You rode on Your horses,
Your chariots of salvation?
9 Your bow was made quite ready;
Oaths were sworn over *Your* arrows.ᵃ *Selah*

You divided the earth with rivers.
10 The mountains saw You *and* trembled;

The overflowing of the water passed by.
The deep uttered its voice,
And lifted its hands on high.
11 The sun and moon stood still in their
habitation;
At the light of Your arrows they went,
At the shining of Your glittering spear.

12 You marched through the land in indignation;
You trampled the nations in anger.
13 You went forth for the salvation of Your
people,
For salvation with Your Anointed.
You struck the head from the house of the
wicked,
By laying bare from foundation to neck. *Selah*

14 You thrust through with his own arrows
The head of his villages.
They came out like a whirlwind to scatter me;
Their rejoicing was like feasting on the poor in
secret.
15 You walked through the sea with Your horses,
Through the heap of great waters.

16 When I heard, my body trembled;
My lips quivered at *the* voice;
Rottenness entered my bones;
And I trembled in myself,
That I might rest in the day of trouble.
When he comes up to the people,
He will invade them with his troops.

A Hymn of Faith

17 Though the fig tree may not blossom,
Nor fruit be on the vines;
Though the labor of the olive may fail,
And the fields yield no food;

3:1 ᵃExact meaning unknown   **3:9** ᵃLiterally *rods* or *tribes* (compare
verse 14)

3:3–16 Habakkuk had a vision of the Holy One coming from
Teman and Mount Paran, a reference to Moses' final blessing
on Israel (see Deut. 32:1–4). God's glory filled the world and
all nature was convulsed before Him. The prophet was first
devastated by this vision but then resolved to be faithful, joyful, and watchful whatever his circumstances. Encouraged by
the vision of a God who would prevail, Habakkuk changed his
question from "Why does God allow it?" to "Who is this God
who will sustain me in the things He allows?" After taking a
good look at God, Habakkuk found Him sufficient.

3:16 Doubt was turned to faith. Habakkuk accepted the ap-

proaching disaster, believing God was in control and justice
would prevail in the end. His love for God was not based on
what God would give him. Even if God sent him suffering and
loss, he resolved to rejoice, not in the situation but in the Savior who is sovereign and would be his strength (vv. 18, 19). By
taking a good look at God, Habakkuk was able to put the Babylonian invasion in perspective. The prophet found a spirit of
faith and joy born out of this deeply traumatic spiritual experience (v. 19).

3:17–19 This hymn of faith is one of the most beautiful psalms
in the Bible. The poem was composed under great emotional

RENEWAL   RETURNING TO THE LORD

The corruption of the church seems to be increasing. The pattern found in Scripture and throughout church history, however, is this Again and again God's people have done what is right in their own eyes (Judg. 21:25), and God must call them back to obedience. The Law is given and the prophets are sent. The message of John the Baptist, then Jesus, is delivered to the lost sheep of Israel: "Repent, for the kingdom of heaven is at hand" (Matt. 3:2). Admonitions against apostasy, disunity, and immorality fill the New Testament epistles. The prophet Hosea's longsuffering love for Gomer is a parable of the price God will pay to woo His people back to Him (Hos. 3:1-5).

One of the key roles of Christ today is to sanctify and cleanse the church (Eph. 5:25-27). Scripture strongly condemns religious leaders who lead others astray (see Matt. 23:24, 27, 33). The biblical view of the church is not of a club that we can easily leave when problems arise (1 Cor. 12:21). Instead, we must labor as Paul did (1 Cor. 11:1).

See also Luke 24:47, note; 2 Cor. 3:2-4; Rev. 1:4—3:22; chart on Spiritual Warfare; notes on Attributes of God (Eph. 1); Commitment (Matt. 16); Forgiveness (Ps. 51; Luke 17); Spiritual Discipline (2 Pet. 3); Spiritual Warfare (Eph. 6)

Though the flock may be cut off from the fold,
And there be no herd in the stalls—
[18]Yet I will rejoice in the LORD,
I will joy in the God of my salvation.

[19]The LORD God[a] is my strength;
He will make my feet like deer's *feet*,

And He will make me walk on my high
hills.

To the Chief Musician. With my stringed instruments.

3:19 [a]Hebrew *YHWH Adonai*

---

pressure. The prophet glanced back to Israel's journey from Egypt to Sinai. Then he saw the Lord coming again to help and to save His people from complete destruction. Invasion, plagues, and pestilence are pictured as judgments of the Lord upon sin, wherever it is found.

3:17 Believers can know joy in the midst of desolation. This verse describes the desolation of the Land and the consequential famine caused by the Babylonian invasion. All of the plants and animals mentioned were staples of life, and their destruction indicated God's judgment on His people for their sin. Because God's judgment was just and temporary, Habakkuk could nevertheless rejoice in the God who saved him. This joyous confidence might be graphically pictured as

jumping for joy in the Lord, spinning around for delight in God.

3:18 Habakkuk's joy lay completely in his confidence in God. As with the prophet, our confidence in God grows as we come to know Him more intimately day by day.

3:19 True faith means loving and serving God regardless of the circumstances. Habakkuk learned that fear would turn to faith when he depended upon a dependable God. This faith, in turn, brought unspeakable joy. Habakkuk pictured himself with deer's feet, picking his way through the cracks of trouble, sure-footed because he was "sure-faithed"! This is an image of victory and triumph in precarious times.

Zephaniah

Zephaniah (lit. "the Lord has hidden") may refer to Zephaniah's protection by God from the oppressive and idolatrous reign of Manasseh (686–642 B.C.) or to the message of God's protection, in the midst of His punishment, for those who repent.

Zephaniah probably proclaimed his message between the first reform (about 628 B.C.) and the second more sweeping reform of King Josiah six years later. His prophecies can be dated roughly between 628 B.C. and 622 B.C., overlapping the ministry of Jeremiah.

SETTING: When Josiah became king of Judah, the international political relationships of the surrounding powers—Assyria, Babylon, and Egypt—gradually allowed a period of peace and expansion in the southern kingdom. Judah was suffering the effects of the idolatrous and wicked practices of her former kings—Ahaz, Manasseh, and Amon. After the prophecies of Isaiah and Micah, at least a half century of prophetic silence occurred during the reigns of Manasseh and Amon. This silence was broken by Zephaniah's message.

PURPOSE: Zephaniah preached the need to seek the Lord in view of the approaching judgment of Judah referred to as the day of the Lord. He also delivered God's promise to establish a purified remnant of His people.

AUDIENCE: The prophecies were delivered to the nation of Judah.

LITERARY CHARACTERISTICS: The book is a prophetic declaration, mostly in poetic form.

The theme is the coming "day of the LORD" (Zeph. 1:7). In the Old Testament, this theme involved God's intervention in history to bring both punishment for the wicked and peace to the righteous. In the New Testament, this theme will culminate in the return of Jesus Christ, who will destroy sin and death and establish a new heaven and a new earth.

Introduction (1:1)
  I. Messages of Judgment (1:2—2:15)
    A. The cosmic scope of the judgment (1:2, 3)
    B. The judgment on Judah (1:4—2:3)
      1. The pronouncement of the judgment (1:4–18)

      2. The protection from the judgment for the repentant (2:1–3)
    C. The judgment on neighboring nations (2:4–15)
  II. The Sins of Jerusalem (3:1–7)
    A. The sins of disobedience and rebellion (3:1, 2)

1 The word of the LORD which came to Zephaniah the son of Cushi, the son of Gedaliah, the son of Amariah, the son of Hezekiah, in the days of Josiah the son of Amon, king of Judah.

The Great Day of the LORD

2"I will utterly consume everything
From the face of the land,"
Says the LORD;
3"I will consume man and beast;
I will consume the birds of the heavens,
The fish of the sea,
And the stumbling blocks[a] along with the
   wicked.
I will cut off man from the face of the land,"
Says the LORD.

4"I will stretch out My hand against Judah,
And against all the inhabitants of Jerusalem.
I will cut off every trace of Baal from this
   place,
The names of the idolatrous priests[a] with the
   pagan priests—
5Those who worship the host of heaven on the
   housetops;

Those who worship and swear *oaths* by the
   LORD,
But who *also* swear by Milcom;[a]
6Those who have turned back from *following* the
   LORD,
And have not sought the LORD, nor inquired of
   Him."

7Be silent in the presence of the Lord GOD;
For the day of the LORD *is* at hand,
For the LORD has prepared a sacrifice;
He has invited[a] His guests.

8"And it shall be,
In the day of the LORD's sacrifice,
That I will punish the princes and the king's
   children,
And all such as are clothed with foreign
   apparel.
9In the same day I will punish
All those who leap over the threshold,[a]

• • • • • • • • • • • • • •

1:3 [a]Figurative of idols   1:4 [a]Hebrew *chemarim*   1:5 [a]Or *Malcam*, an Ammonite god, also called *Molech* (compare Leviticus 18:21)   1:7 [a]Literally *set apart, consecrated*   1:9 [a]Compare 1 Samuel 5:5

1:1 **Zephaniah** is the only one of the 16 writing prophets who traced his genealogy back through four generations to King Hezekiah. Possibly he wanted to document his royal lineage to substantiate his awareness of the sins committed by Jerusalem's leaders.

1:2, 3 **The language about destruction** is similar to that used in the description of Noah's flood (Gen. 6:7; 7:23). The context shows that the devastation of the "land" encompasses that of the whole world (Zeph. 1:2).

1:4—2:3 **The addressees** are the inhabitants of Judah (see chart, Terminology for the People of God).

1:4 **Baal** (lit. "master," "husband," "possessor") worship was a pagan cult with a variety of deities introduced by Israel's King Ahab and revived by Judah's King Manasseh after Hezekiah's eradication of the Baal idols (2 Kin. 21:1–3).

1:5 **Milcom is the Ammonite deity** (1 Kin. 11:5, 33; 2 Kin. 23:13).

1:7 **The metaphor of a sacrificial ritual** is used by Zephaniah to portray graphically the judgment coming in the day of the Lord. The sacrificial victim represented the people of Judah, while the guests were the Babylonian enemies, who were to slay the sacrifice and serve as instruments of God's judgment (Is. 13:3). The unrepentant sinner, as the victim of his own sins, would become a sacrifice.

1:8 **The princes** are the royal officials of Judah. The "king's children" are literally "the sons of the kings," perhaps a reference to the sons of Josiah—Jehoahaz, Jehoiakim, and Zedekiah (2 Kin. 23:31, 36; 24:18) or to the royal family in general (2 Kin. 10:1), including the children of Josiah. The latter is more likely. In 605 B.C., the Babylonians attacked Jerusalem and carried its noble young men to Babylon in the first of several deportations (2 Kin. 24:1; Dan. 1:1–6). In 597 B.C., Josiah's grandson King Jehoiachin, together with the royal family and the royal officers, was deported to Babylon (2 Kin. 24:8–12). In 586 B.C., King Nebuchadnezzar killed the sons of Zedekiah in front of him, took Zedekiah captive, and gouged out his eyes (2 Kin. 25:3–7). Wearing foreign apparel included the adoption of Gentile customs, lifestyle, moral behavior, and religious practices.

1:9 **Apparently, the leaders of Judah had adopted** this Philistine custom of jumping superstitiously over the doorstep of the entrance to Dagon's temple (1 Sam. 5:1–5). Not only were God's people adopting pagan practices, but their morality had also been corrupted. They had filled their homes with goods taken by means of violence and fraud.

Who fill their masters' houses with violence
and deceit.

10"And there shall be on that day," says the
LORD,
"The sound of a mournful cry from the Fish
Gate,
A wailing from the Second Quarter,
And a loud crashing from the hills.
11Wail, you inhabitants of Maktesh!a
For all the merchant people are cut down;
All those who handle money are cut off.

12"And it shall come to pass at that time
That I will search Jerusalem with lamps,
And punish the men
Who are settled in complacency,a
Who say in their heart,
'The LORD will not do good,
Nor will He do evil.'
13Therefore their goods shall become booty,
And their houses a desolation;
They shall build houses, but not inhabit them;
They shall plant vineyards, but not drink their
wine."

14The great day of the LORD is near;
It is near and hastens quickly.
The noise of the day of the LORD is bitter;
There the mighty men shall cry out.
15That day is a day of wrath,
A day of trouble and distress,
A day of devastation and desolation,
A day of darkness and gloominess,
A day of clouds and thick darkness,
16A day of trumpet and alarm
Against the fortified cities
And against the high towers.

17"I will bring distress upon men,
And they shall walk like blind men,
Because they have sinned against the
LORD;
Their blood shall be poured out like dust,
And their flesh like refuse."

18Neither their silver nor their gold
Shall be able to deliver them
In the day of the LORD's wrath;
But the whole land shall be devoured
By the fire of His jealousy,
For He will make speedy riddance
Of all those who dwell in the land.

A Call to Repentance

2 Gather yourselves together, yes, gather
together,
O undesirablea nation,
2Before the decree is issued,
Or the day passes like chaff,
Before the LORD's fierce anger comes upon you,
Before the day of the LORD's anger comes upon
you!
3Seek the LORD, all you meek of the earth,
Who have upheld His justice.
Seek righteousness, seek humility.
It may be that you will be hidden
In the day of the LORD's anger.

Judgment on Nations

4For Gaza shall be forsaken,
And Ashkelon desolate;
They shall drive out Ashdod at noonday,
And Ekron shall be uprooted.

1:11 aLiterally *Mortar*, a market district of Jerusalem   1:12 aLiterally
on their lees, that is, settled like the dregs of wine   2:1 aOr *shameless*

1:10, 11 The Fish Gate, the "Second Quarter," "the hills," and
the "Maktesh" cannot be located exactly. The sense portrayed in these verses is that Jerusalem faced widespread
devastation.

1:14–17 The day of the Lord suggests an ominous time of judgment reflected in words like "wrath," "trouble," "distress,"
"devastation," "darkness," and "gloominess" (v. 15). Its description is vividly portrayed as destructive military conflict.
Clearly there is no escape for those who have sinned against
the Lord (v. 17; see Amos 5:18–20; Rom. 1:18–25).

2:1–3 The nation (Heb. *goy*), usually a reference to Gentile nations (v. 1), here is Judah because of her pagan-like sinfulness.
Zephaniah admonishes those who have walked in the way of
righteousness to continue with a wholehearted pursuit of
God, not because the day of judgment would not come but so
that the penitent would be protected during the inevitable
time of destruction (v. 3).

2:4 The noonday downfall describes the shortness of the
siege and indicates the unpredictable timing of judgment.

2:4–7 Nebuchadnezzar of Babylon overran Ashkelon in 604
B.C. By 601 B.C., Babylon must have taken all of Philistia be-

cause its seacoast was used as a launching site to invade
Egypt. Verses 6 and 7 may have had the return from the Babylonian captivity in view, but like other predictive prophecies
having both near and future references, this passage refers
also to a later fulfillment.

2:4–15 The nations around Judah would also be the object of
punishment for threatening God's people (vv. 8, 10) and for
their pride (v. 15). The indicted nations are the Philistines to
the west (Gaza, Ashkelon, Ashdod, Ekron), Moab and Ammon
to the east, Ethiopia to the southwest, and Assyria (Nineveh)
to the northeast. Though the Moabites and Ammonites were
blood relatives of the Israelites, they had a long history of animosity with Israel (Gen. 19:30–38). Ethiopia, which roughly
corresponds to the present northern Sudan, is the southernmost edge of biblical geography and of the historical ancient
Near East. Assyria, centered in what is presently Iran and Iraq,
is often considered geographically to the north because the
Assyrians had to invade Palestine from that direction. The
designation of these border nations portrayed the widespread scope of God's judgment.

⁵Woe to the inhabitants of the seacoast,
  The nation of the Cherethites!
  The word of the LORD *is* against you,
  O Canaan, land of the Philistines:
  "I will destroy you;
  So there shall be no inhabitant."

⁶The seacoast shall be pastures,
  With shelters[a] for shepherds and folds for
    flocks.
⁷The coast shall be for the remnant of the
    house of Judah;
  They shall feed *their* flocks there;
  In the houses of Ashkelon they shall lie down
    at evening.
  For the LORD their God will intervene for
    them,
  And return their captives.

⁸"I have heard the reproach of Moab,
  And the insults of the people of Ammon,
  With which they have reproached My people,
  And made arrogant threats against their
    borders.
⁹Therefore, as I live,"
  Says the LORD of hosts, the God of Israel,
  "Surely Moab shall be like Sodom,
  And the people of Ammon like Gomorrah—
  Overrun with weeds and saltpits,
  And a perpetual desolation.
  The residue of My people shall plunder
    them,
  And the remnant of My people shall possess
    them."

¹⁰This they shall have for their pride,
  Because they have reproached and made
    arrogant threats
  Against the people of the LORD of hosts.
¹¹The LORD *will be* awesome to them,
  For He will reduce to nothing all the gods of
    the earth;
  People shall worship Him,
  Each one from his place,
  Indeed all the shores of the nations.

¹²"You Ethiopians also,
  You shall be slain by My sword."

¹³And He will stretch out His hand against the
    north,
  Destroy Assyria,
  And make Nineveh a desolation,
  As dry as the wilderness.
¹⁴The herds shall lie down in her midst,
  Every beast of the nation.
  Both the pelican and the bittern
  Shall lodge on the capitals *of* her *pillars;*
  Their voice shall sing in the windows;
  Desolation *shall be* at the threshold;
  For He will lay bare the cedar work.
¹⁵This is the rejoicing city
  That dwelt securely,
  That said in her heart,
  "I *am it,* and *there is* none besides me."
  How has she become a desolation,
  A place for beasts to lie down!
  Everyone who passes by her
  Shall hiss and shake his fist.

The Wickedness of Jerusalem

3 Woe to her who is rebellious and polluted,
  To the oppressing city!
²She has not obeyed *His* voice,
  She has not received correction;
  She has not trusted in the LORD,
  She has not drawn near to her God.

³Her princes in her midst *are* roaring lions;
  Her judges *are* evening wolves
  That leave not a bone till morning.
⁴Her prophets are insolent, treacherous people;
  Her priests have polluted the sanctuary,
  They have done violence to the law.
⁵The LORD *is* righteous in her midst,
  He will do no unrighteousness.
  Every morning He brings His justice to light;
  He never fails,
  But the unjust knows no shame.

···

2:6 ᵃLiterally *excavations,* either underground huts or cisterns

---

2:5 The Cherethites were immigrants from Crete who settled with the Philistines along the seacoast of Palestine (Ezek. 25:16).

2:9 Sodom and Gomorrah were completely destroyed by God due to their extreme unrighteousness (Gen. 19:24, 25). They are often used as an example of wickedness and as the recipients of God's wrath toward evil (Jer. 23:14; Matt. 10:15).

The saltpits allowed water from the Dead Sea to seep in and fill them. When the water evaporated, the deposits of salt left behind were sold. Saltpits have been associated with desolation, barrenness, and unfruitfulness.

2:11 A future time is proclaimed when every person in the world will bow before the Lord (see Phil. 2:9–11; Rev. 5:13).

2:13, 14 Nineveh was the capital of Assyria. Although not precisely identified, "pelican" and "bittern" present an image of wild animals frequenting a desolate place. The statements about broken "capitals" and "cedar work" of fine buildings support this picture. "Capitals" refers to the carved top parts of columns that had supported the roofs and had fallen to the ground, while the cedar beams of the walls or ceilings were exposed due to destruction. In 612 B.C., the secure, proud, and prosperous city of Nineveh fell. By 609 B.C., the whole Assyrian Empire had collapsed under the Medo-Babylonian alliance. In 401 B.C., Xenophon, a Greek adventurer, passed through the ruins of the once proud city of Nineveh and did not find any trace of its existence.

⁶"I have cut off nations,
　Their fortresses are devastated;
　I have made their streets desolate,
　With none passing by.
　Their cities are destroyed;
　There is no one, no inhabitant.
⁷I said, 'Surely you will fear Me,
　You will receive instruction'—
　So that her dwelling would not be cut off,
　Despite everything for which I punished her.
　But they rose early and corrupted all their
　　deeds.

A Faithful Remnant

⁸"Therefore wait for Me," says the LORD,
　"Until the day I rise up for plunder;ª
　My determination *is* to gather the nations
　To My assembly of kingdoms,
　To pour on them My indignation,
　All My fierce anger;
　All the earth shall be devoured
　With the fire of My jealousy.

⁹"For then I will restore to the peoples a pure
　　language,
　That they all may call on the name of the LORD,
　To serve Him with one accord.
¹⁰From beyond the rivers of Ethiopia
　My worshipers,
　The daughter of My dispersed ones,
　Shall bring My offering.
¹¹In that day you shall not be shamed for any of
　　your deeds
　In which you transgress against Me;
　For then I will take away from your midst
　Those who rejoice in your pride,
　And you shall no longer be haughty
　In My holy mountain.
¹²I will leave in your midst
　A meek and humble people,

And they shall trust in the name of the LORD.
¹³The remnant of Israel shall do no
　　unrighteousness
　And speak no lies,
　Nor shall a deceitful tongue be found in their
　　mouth;
　For they shall feed *their* flocks and lie down,
　And no one shall make *them* afraid."

Joy in God's Faithfulness

¹⁴Sing, O daughter of Zion!
　Shout, O Israel!
　Be glad and rejoice with all *your* heart,
　O daughter of Jerusalem!
¹⁵The LORD has taken away your judgments,
　He has cast out your enemy.
　The King of Israel, the LORD, *is* in your midst;
　You shall seeª disaster no more.

¹⁶In that day it shall be said to Jerusalem:
　"Do not fear;
　Zion, let not your hands be weak.
¹⁷The LORD your God in your midst,
　The Mighty One, will save;
　He will rejoice over you with gladness,
　He will quiet *you* with His love,
　He will rejoice over you with singing."

¹⁸"I will gather those who sorrow over the
　　appointed assembly,
　Who are among you,
　To whom its reproach *is* a burden.
¹⁹Behold, at that time
　I will deal with all who afflict you;
　I will save the lame,

3:8 ªSeptuagint and Syriac read *for witness;* Targum reads *for the day of My revelation for judgment;* Vulgate reads *for the day of My resurrection that is to come.* **3:15** ªSome Hebrew manuscripts, Septuagint, and Bomberg read *see;* Masoretic Text and Vulgate read *fear.*

3:6, 7 God's chastisement of other nations should have brought the people of Judah to their senses. But they "rose early," becoming more persistent and more eager in the pursuit of sin (v. 7).

3:9 God had already announced that all the nations would worship Him (Zeph. 2:11). Lips or "language" became unclean with the worship of pagan gods. Here a turn of the hearts of all the Gentiles is foreseen, expressed through a change to "pure language," that is, a change from calling on the name of false gods to calling on the name of the Lord (see Gen. 11:1–9). This passage anticipates the NT outpouring of the Holy Spirit after the ascension of Christ when the Gentiles from many nations would call upon the name of the Lord (see Acts 2:1–47).

3:10 Beyond the rivers of Ethiopia refers to the most remote place.

3:10–17 Zephaniah painted another picture of hope in the day of the Lord's coming even in the midst of the predicted devastation. The day of the Lord would mean destruction of evil,

but it would also mean that the people of God would worship Him and would be forgiven, humbled, and sanctified (vv. 10–13). God would be the victorious King and Warrior dwelling with His people and providing salvation, security, and peace. Thus, Zephaniah summoned the people of Jerusalem to rejoice. With similar emotions, the Mighty God would find joy in His formerly wayward people (vv. 14–17).

3:14 The word daughter combined with the name of a place or people is a figure of speech referring to the inhabitants of that place (see Is. 23:10, 12; Jer. 46:11). Thus, the "daughter of Zion" and "daughter of Jerusalem" both refer to the population of Jerusalem (see Song 3, The Daughters of Jerusalem). Zion is another name for Jerusalem because the original Jerusalem or City of David was built on Mount Zion. By the time of Josiah, Zion had expanded to include the western hill and the area north of the City of David on which the temple was built.

3:18–20 When the destruction of Jerusalem occurred, its population was deported to Babylon (2 Kin. 24, 25). These verses refer to a remnant of dispersed and afflicted people whom

And gather those who were driven out;
I will appoint them for praise and fame
In every land where they were put to shame.
20At that time I will bring you back,
Even at the time I gather you;

For I will give you fame and praise
Among all the peoples of the earth,
When I return your captives before your
eyes,"
Says the LORD.

God would bring back from Babylon to Jerusalem after 70 years of exile. This restoration began in 539 B.C. when Cyrus issued his decree that allowed the Jews to return to their homeland. The return of the Jews to Judah in fulfillment of Zephaniah's prophecy foreshadows the final redemption of the earth.

Haggai

TITLE

Nothing is known of Haggai's life or background. He appears on the biblical scene without introduction and disappears just as quickly. Haggai (Heb., "feast of *Yahweh*") may have been born on a special feast day and thus given this name to commemorate that event. According to ancient Jewish tradition, Haggai saw Solomon's temple before the Exile (Hag. 2:3) and so was quite old as he returned to the Land. Ancient Christian tradition holds that Haggai was born in exile and was young when he returned to Jerusalem. Others believe that Haggai never went into exile but instead stayed in the Land. In any case, Haggai was well acquainted with the situation of his day and spoke with such effectiveness that the people were moved to action. Haggai was a contemporary of Zechariah (Ezra 5:1; 6:14), although neither prophet mentioned the other.

DATE

All utterances in this prophecy are given specific dates in the year 520 B.C.; so Haggai's recorded ministry lasted only four months. The compilation of the prophet's oracles may have been done in that year or at a later time.

BACKGROUND

SETTING: In 539 B.C., Cyrus, king of Persia, decreed that all exiled Jews could return from Babylon to Jerusalem to rebuild that devastated city and the temple of the Lord. This decree by Cyrus is corroborated as authentic by extrabiblical sources such as the Cyrus Cylinder, now housed in the British Museum. Enough people returned for the rebuilding project to proceed. However, due to opposition by the Samaritans, work on the temple ceased after the foundation was laid (536 B.C.). The city and temple remained in ruins. By 520 B.C., a new king, Darius I, brought stability to the Persian Empire and to Judah as well. This new political situation allowed the work of rebuilding Jerusalem to resume. In 520 B.C., Haggai encouraged the people to resume the building.

PURPOSE: Haggai admonished the people to obey the Lord by rebuilding the temple. Haggai also announced renewed promises for the future.

AUDIENCE: Haggai's message was directed specifically to Zerubbabel, the governor of Judah; to Joshua, the high priest; and to the Jewish community that had returned from the Exile.

LITERARY CHARACTERISTICS: Haggai, the second shortest book of the Old Testament, is concise and simple in style. Rhetorical questions are used repeatedly (Hag. 1:4; 2:3, 12, 13, 19). Affirmation that Haggai's words are the words of the Lord is repeated about thirty times.

The Command to Build God's House

1 In the second year of King Darius, in the sixth month, on the first day of the month, the word of the LORD came by Haggai the prophet to Zerubbabel the son of Shealtiel, governor of Judah, and to Joshua the son of Jehozadak, the high priest, saying, ²"Thus speaks the LORD of hosts, saying: 'This people says, "The time has not come, the time that the LORD's house should be built." ' "

³Then the word of the LORD came by Haggai the prophet, saying, ⁴"Is it time for you yourselves to dwell in your paneled houses, and this temple^a to lie in ruins?" ⁵Now therefore, thus says the LORD of hosts: "Consider your ways!

⁶"You have sown much, and bring in little;
You eat, but do not have enough;
You drink, but you are not filled with drink;
You clothe yourselves, but no one is warm;

And he who earns wages,
Earns wages to put into a bag with holes."

⁷Thus says the LORD of hosts: "Consider your ways! ⁸Go up to the mountains and bring wood and build the temple, that I may take pleasure in it and be glorified," says the LORD. ⁹"You looked for much, but indeed it came to little; and when you brought it home, I blew it away. Why?" says the LORD of hosts. "Because of My house that is in ruins, while every one of you runs to his own house. ¹⁰Therefore the heavens above you withhold the dew, and the earth withholds its fruit. ¹¹For I called for a drought on the land and the mountains, on the grain and the new wine and the oil, on whatever the ground brings forth, on men and livestock, and on all the labor of your hands."

- - - - - - - - - - - - - - - - - - - -

1:4 ^aLiterally house, and so in verse 8

1:1 **Haggai is more precise** and chronological in his dating than any other prophet (see charts, The Jewish Sacred Calendar; Dating the Prophecies of Haggai and Zechariah). The first day of the sixth month of the second year of King Darius Hystaspes (522–486 B.C.) was about August 29, 520 B.C. The first day of each month was a holy day of special offering to the Lord when the people would have gathered around the altar (Num. 28:11–13). This time was appropriate for the prophet to address the people. A fast had occurred during the fifth month to mourn the destruction of the temple in 586 B.C. Thoughts of the temple would have been fresh in the minds of the people, and 24 days later the rebuilding of the temple began (about Sept. 21, 520 B.C.; Hag. 1:15). For Zerubbabel and Joshua, see Haggai 1:12, note.

1:2 **God's displeasure** is expressed in the phrase, "this people." Israel, living in obedience, was called "My people" (Ex. 5:1,

Ezek. 36:28; Zech. 8:8). Living in disobedience, Israel became "not My people" (Hos. 1:9). Haggai's reference to the temple as the Lord's "house" contrasts the "house" of the Lord with the "houses" of the people.

1:4 **Paneled houses** indicate that either the houses had paneled roofs or richly decorated walls. The people lived in completed houses or in luxury, while the house of the Lord lay in ruin.

1:6–11 Apparently unconcerned about their relationship to God, the people neglected the temple. They were experiencing the curses of that disobedience (Deut. 28:18, 22, 38–42). The economic plight of the people was an indictment against them but reassuring proof of the continuation of the covenant (Hag. 2:15–19).

DATING THE PROPHECIES OF HAGGAI AND ZECHARIAH

THE EVENT	THE BIBLICAL DATE*	REFERENCE	DATE**
The command to rebuild again	1st day of 6th month (Elul) in the 2nd year of King Darius (1-6-2)	Hag. 1:1	Aug. 29, 520 B.C.
The beginning of rebuilding	24th day of 6th month (Elul) in the 2nd year of King Darius (24-6-2)	Hag. 1:15	Sept. 21, 520 B.C.
The announcement of coming glory	21st day of 7th month (Tishri) in the 2nd year of King Darius (21-7-2)	Hag. 2:1	Oct. 17, 520 B.C.
A call to repentance	8th month (Heshvan) of the 2nd year of King Darius (8-2)	Zech. 1:1	Oct./Nov., 520 B.C.
The command to be clean	24th day of 9th month (Chislev) of the 2nd year of King Darius (24-9-2)	Hag. 2:10	Dec. 18, 520 B.C.
The announcement of Zerubbabel	24th day of 9th month (Chislev) of the 2nd year of King Darius (24-9-2)	Hag. 2:20	Dec. 18, 520 B.C.
The night visions	24th day of 11th month (Shebat) of the 2nd year of King Darius (24-11-2)	Zech. 1:7	Feb. 15, 519 B.C.
A question about fasting	4th day of the 9th month (Chislev) of the 4th year of King Darius (4-9-4)	Zech. 7:1	Dec. 7, 518 B.C.
The completion of the temple	3rd day of the 12th month (Adar) of the 6th year of King Darius (3-12-6)	Ezra 6:14, 15	Mar. 12, 516 B.C.

* *The dating is set according to the year within the reign of the Persian monarch, in this case Darius I. The months are according to The Jewish sacred calendar and not the Persian (see also chart, The Jewish Sacred Calendar).*
** *These modern dates are approximate; the Jewish dating encompasses parts of two months in our calendar.*

The People's Obedience

¹²Then Zerubbabel the son of Shealtiel, and Joshua the son of Jehozadak, the high priest, with all the remnant of the people, obeyed the voice of the LORD their God, and the words of Haggai the prophet, as the LORD their God had sent him; and the people feared the presence of the LORD. ¹³Then Haggai, the LORD's messenger, spoke the LORD's message to the people, saying, "I *am* with you, says the LORD." ¹⁴So the LORD stirred up the spirit of Zerubbabel the son of Shealtiel, governor of Judah, and the spirit of Joshua the son of Jehozadak, the high priest, and the spirit of all the remnant of the people; and they came and worked on the house of the LORD of hosts, their God, ¹⁵on the twenty-fourth day of the sixth month, in the second year of King Darius.

The Coming Glory of God's House

2 In the seventh *month*, on the twenty-first of the month, the word of the LORD came by Haggai

1:12 **Zerubbabel** was listed as the son of Shealtiel (see Matt. 1:12; Luke 3:27) but elsewhere as the son of Pedaiah (brother of Shealtiel; see 1 Chr. 3:17–19). The difference has been explained by Zerubbabel's status as legal son of the childless Shealtiel and biological son of Pedaiah, or that Zerubbabel was the son of a levirate marriage (see Deut. 25:5, 6). In any case, Zerubbabel is a descendant of King David through his grandfather, King Jehoiachin (or Jeconiah), justifying the reference to his leadership and later messianic lineage. Joshua, the high priest, is the son of Jehozadak, who was carried into exile (1 Chr. 6:15) and the grandson of Seraiah (1 Chr. 6:14). He was responsible for the religious affairs of the Jewish community of returning exiles. Zerubbabel and Joshua were important to Haggai as he addressed the concerns regarding David's throne and the temple.

The "remnant" identifies those who are committed to living in obedience to the covenant, not simply those who have survived the Exile.

2:1 **The people were to gather in Jerusalem** for the Feast of Tabernacles (Lev. 23:39–44; Deut. 16:13–17), an appropriate

the prophet, saying: [2]"Speak now to Zerubbabel the son of Shealtiel, governor of Judah, and to Joshua the son of Jehozadak, the high priest, and to the remnant of the people, saying: [3]'Who is left among you who saw this temple[a] in its former glory? And how do you see it now? In comparison with it, *is this* not in your eyes as nothing? [4]Yet now be strong, Zerubbabel,' says the LORD; 'and be strong, Joshua, son of Jehozadak, the high priest; and be strong, all you people of the land,' says the LORD, 'and work; for I *am* with you,' says the LORD of hosts. [5]*According to* the word that I covenanted with you when you came out of Egypt, so My Spirit remains among you; do not fear!'

[6]"For thus says the LORD of hosts: 'Once more (it *is* a little while) I will shake heaven and earth, the sea and dry land; [7]and I will shake all nations, and they shall come to the Desire of All Nations,[a] and I will fill this temple with glory,' says the LORD of hosts. [8]'The silver *is* Mine, and the gold *is* Mine,' says the LORD of hosts. [9]'The glory of this latter temple shall be greater than the former,' says the LORD of hosts. 'And in this place I will give peace,' says the LORD of hosts."

The People Are Defiled

[10]On the twenty-fourth *day* of the ninth *month*, in the second year of Darius, the word of the LORD came by Haggai the prophet, saying, [11]"Thus says the LORD of hosts: 'Now, ask the priests *concerning the* law, saying, [12]"If one carries holy meat in the fold of his garment, and with the edge he touches bread or stew, wine or oil, or any food, will it become holy?"' "

Then the priests answered and said, "No."

[13]And Haggai said, "If *one who is* unclean *because* of a dead body touches any of these, will it be unclean?"

So the priests answered and said, "It shall be unclean."

[14]Then Haggai answered and said, " 'So is this people, and so is this nation before Me,' says the LORD, 'and so is every work of their hands; and what they offer there is unclean.

Promised Blessing

[15]'And now, carefully consider from this day forward: from before stone was laid upon stone in the temple of the LORD— [16]since those *days*, when one came to a heap of twenty ephahs, there were *but* ten; when *one* came to the wine vat to draw out fifty baths from the press, there were *but* twenty. [17]I struck you with blight and mildew and hail in all the labors of your hands; yet you did not *turn* to Me,' says the LORD. [18]'Consider now from this day forward, from the twenty-fourth day of the ninth month, from the day that the foundation of the LORD's temple was laid— consider it: [19]Is the seed still in the barn? As yet the vine, the fig tree, the pomegranate, and the olive tree have not yielded *fruit. But* from this day I will bless *you.*' "

Zerubbabel Chosen as a Signet

[20]And again the word of the LORD came to Haggai on the twenty-fourth day of the month, saying, [21]"Speak to Zerubbabel, governor of Judah, saying:

'I will shake heaven and earth.
[22]I will overthrow the throne of kingdoms;
I will destroy the strength of the Gentile kingdoms.
I will overthrow the chariots
And those who ride in them;
The horses and their riders shall come down,
Every one by the sword of his brother.

[23]'In that day,' says the LORD of hosts, 'I will take you, Zerubbabel My servant, the son of Shealtiel,' says the LORD, 'and will make you like a signet *ring;* for I have chosen you,' says the LORD of hosts."

· · · · · · · · · · · · · · · ·
2:3 [a]Literally *house,* and so in verses 7 and 9   **2:7** [a]Or *the desire of all nations*

---

time for Haggai to speak regarding the future glory of the temple. The 21st day of the 7th month (about Oct. 17, 520 B.C.) is the 7th day of the Feast of Tabernacles.

2:6–9 The promise is for a greater glory in the temple to come (see chart, The Temples of the Bible). The temple of Zerubbabel was probably leveled during Herod's renovation. Both are identified as the "second temple." These "shakings" of the nations would prepare the way for the Messiah and His kingdom (Luke 24:47; Acts 1:8). The first "shaking" took place when God gave Moses the Law at Sinai (Ex. 19:16). Another of cosmic dimensions would be coming at the end (see Hag. 2:21; Heb. 12:26–28).

2:10–14 The twenty-fourth day of the ninth month (Dec. 18, 520 B.C.) seems to be an official day of proclamation that God would again accept their worship at the temple. The priests were asked rhetorical questions regarding the transmission of purity and impurity (see Lev. 6:27; 11:28). The holy meat

made the garment holy, but the garment was unable to transmit that holiness to anything it touched. The man who touched a dead body became unclean, and whatever he touched also became unclean. The priest's answers showed the people to be unclean (Hag. 2:12), affirming Haggai's word that holiness could not be caught from participation in temple worship.

2:23 The signet ring was a symbol of the authority of the king. Zerubbabel's grandfather, Jehoiachin (Jeconiah), was like the Lord's signet ring, which He pulled from His hand when Jehoiachin went into Exile (Jer. 22:24–30). Zerubbabel was like a signet ring placed on the hand of the Lord once again. He was an heir to David's throne. This promise did not stipulate that Zerubbabel would become king but rather that the Lord had not disregarded David's throne. "My servant" (Zerubbabel) confirmed the Davidic, messianic lineage (1 Kin. 11:34; Ps. 78:70; Is. 52:13).

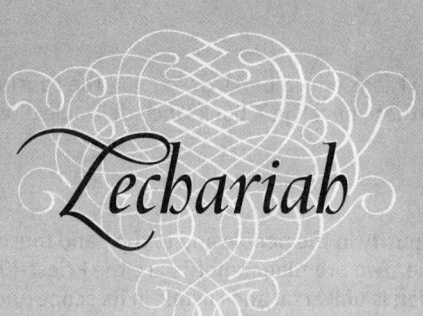

Zechariah

The name Zechariah (Heb., lit. *"Yahweh* remembers") is common in the Old Testament with more than twenty-eight men bearing that designation. The title of the book is appropriate, as the prophecies therein reassured those who had returned from the Exile that they were still God's covenant people. This Zechariah is the son of Berechiah and the grandson of Iddo (Zech. 1:1, 7; see Ezra 5:1). Nothing is known of Zechariah's father, but his grandfather was listed among the priests and Levites returning to the Land from the Exile (Neh. 12:1–47). Ezra's identification of Zechariah as the "son" of his grand-father probably indicates that Zechariah's father died before Iddo, making Zechariah his grandfather's successor as head of the family. Some suggest that Zechariah was born in Exile and returned to the Land as a boy. No compelling reason to doubt Zechariah's authorship of the entire book exists. Zechariah's prophetic ministry overlapped but extended beyond that of Haggai. Both prophets are mentioned in Ezra 5:1 and 6:14, but neither prophet mentioned the other.

The prophecies of the first eight chapters of Zechariah are explicitly dated between 520 B.C. and 518 B.C. Chapters 9—14 are undated but are most likely from the period about 516–500 B.C. when the Persian Empire was beginning to fall.

SETTING: Zechariah ministered to the residents of Jerusalem after their return from Exile in Babylon. Joshua was the newly appointed high priest, and Zerubbabel was the governor. Temple rebuilding had begun anew as a result of Haggai's prophetic ministry. The people were beginning to experience again the blessings of obedience. Zechariah encouraged the people to live in obedience as the necessary prerequisite to continued enjoyment of covenant blessings. Thus, the call to repent opened Zechariah's prophecy (Zech. 1—6). By 518 B.C., work on the temple was progressing, but once again the people needed to be called to obedience and purity (Zech. 7—8). Toward the end of Zechariah's ministry, the Greeks defeated Persia at Marathon (490 B.C.) and again at Salamis (481 B.C.), weakening the position of the Persian Empire. This period of political uncertainty and insecurity prompted new prophecies (Zech. 9—14).

PURPOSE: Zechariah's purpose was to comfort and encourage God's people to remain faithful in times of distress and perplexity. He encouraged them to rebuild the temple. Zechariah focused the attention of the people on the Lord's promises for the future.

AUDIENCE: Zechariah directly addressed the returned Jewish community in Judah, the Jews still in Exile, and the nations.

LITERARY CHARACTERISTICS: Zechariah is one of the two lengthier books of the Minor Prophets. It is often thought to be obscure and difficult to understand. Zechariah is an example of apocalyptic literature (the content of which concerns "revelations" often

communicated through visions or symbols), describing the consummation of history with graphic imagery. Other apocalyptic books include Daniel, Revelation, and portions of Ezekiel.

THEMES

Zechariah insisted that purity in the people and in the Land must accompany the restoration of the temple. Two prominent motifs are the Priest-King and the Shepherd. The message of Zechariah is universal and cosmic in its scope and pictures God's final victory as an accomplished fact. Because Zechariah is frequently referenced in the New Testament, the book is especially worthy of study and careful attention. The gospel writers quoted Zechariah more than any other minor prophet, which indicates Zechariah's strong messianic concerns as he looked to the future of God's people.

OUTLINE

A Call to Repentance

1 In the eighth month of the second year of Darius, the word of the LORD came to Zechariah the son of Berechiah, the son of Iddo the prophet, saying, ²"The LORD has been very angry with your fathers. ³Therefore say to them, 'Thus says the LORD of hosts: "Return to Me," says the LORD of hosts, "and I will return to you," says the LORD of hosts. ⁴"Do not be like your fathers, to whom the former prophets preached, saying, 'Thus says the LORD of hosts: "Turn now from your evil ways and your evil deeds." ' But they did not hear nor heed Me," says the LORD.

⁵"Your fathers, where are they?
  And the prophets, do they live forever?
⁶Yet surely My words and My statutes,
  Which I commanded My servants the prophets,
  Did they not overtake your fathers?

"So they returned and said:

1:1 The prophecies of Zechariah 1—8 are dated during the early years of the reign of Darius Hystaspes, king of the Persian Empire (522–486 B.C.; vv. 1, 7; Zech. 7:1). Darius reaffirmed Cyrus' decree (539 B.C.), permitting the rebuilding of the temple in Jerusalem.

1:2–6 The use of "your fathers" reminded the people that the Exile was judgment for sin and linked them with the past. The verb "return" is repeated several times in these verses, emphasizing the call to repentance. The same message given to their fathers by the former prophets went unheeded (v. 3; Is. 31:6; Jer. 18:11; Hos. 14:1, 2; Joel 2:12, 13). The returned community would experience similar judgment if they failed to heed this warning.

'Just as the LORD of hosts determined to do to
us,
According to our ways and according to our
deeds,
So He has dealt with us.' " ' "

Vision of the Horses

⁷On the twenty-fourth day of the eleventh
month, which is the month Shebat, in the second
year of Darius, the word of the LORD came to Zechariah the son of Berechiah, the son of Iddo the
prophet: ⁸I saw by night, and behold, a man riding
on a red horse, and it stood among the myrtle
trees in the hollow; and behind him *were* horses:
red, sorrel, and white. ⁹Then I said, "My lord, what
are these?" So the angel who talked with me said
to me, "I will show you what they *are.*"

¹⁰And the man who stood among the myrtle
trees answered and said, "These *are the ones* whom
the LORD has sent to walk to and fro throughout
the earth."

¹¹So they answered the Angel of the LORD, who
stood among the myrtle trees, and said, "We have
walked to and fro throughout the earth, and behold, all the earth is resting quietly."

The LORD Will Comfort Zion

¹²Then the Angel of the LORD answered and
said, "O LORD of hosts, how long will You not have
mercy on Jerusalem and on the cities of Judah,
against which You were angry these seventy
years?"

¹³And the LORD answered the angel who talked
to me, *with* good *and* comforting words. ¹⁴So the
angel who spoke with me said to me, "Proclaim,
saying, 'Thus says the LORD of hosts:

"I am zealous for Jerusalem

And for Zion with great zeal.
¹⁵I am exceedingly angry with the nations at
ease;
For I was a little angry,
And they helped— *but* with evil *intent.*"

¹⁶'Therefore thus says the LORD:

"I am returning to Jerusalem with mercy;
My house shall be built in it," says the LORD of
hosts,
"And a *surveyor's* line shall be stretched out over
Jerusalem." '

¹⁷"Again proclaim, saying, 'Thus says the LORD
of hosts:

"My cities shall again spread out through
prosperity;
The LORD will again comfort Zion,
And will again choose Jerusalem." ' "

Vision of the Horns

¹⁸Then I raised my eyes and looked, and there
were four horns. ¹⁹And I said to the angel who
talked with me, "What *are* these?"

So he answered me, "These *are* the horns that
have scattered Judah, Israel, and Jerusalem."

²⁰Then the LORD showed me four craftsmen.
²¹And I said, "What are these coming to do?"

So he said, "These *are* the horns that scattered
Judah, so that no one could lift up his head; but
the craftsmenᵃ are coming to terrify them, to cast
out the horns of the nations that lifted up *their*
horn against the land of Judah to scatter it."

· · · · · · · · · · · · · · · · · ·

1:21 ᵃLiterally *these*

1:7—6:8 Observing the visions with Zechariah was an interpreting angel (Zech. 1:9, 13, 14, 19; 2:3; 4:1, 4, 5; 5:5, 10; 6:4, 5).
All these visions except the fourth (Zech. 3:1–5) follow the
same literary pattern, in which the prophet described what he
saw, asked for an interpretation from the angel, then received
an explanation. Five of the visions were accompanied by a
prophetic oracle that amplified its message on purity and
leadership. Each built on the other, and all eight should be
viewed together as a whole.

1:8 The man on the red horse standing "among the myrtle
trees in the hollow" was probably to be identified as the "Angel of the LORD" (v. 11), a special manifestation of *Yahweh's*
presence in the OT and thought by some to be the pre-
incarnate Christ (Gen. 16:7–13; Ex. 3:1–6, Judg. 13:3–22; see
chart, The Angel of the Lord). With the man were horses of
different colors (see chart, Colors in the Bible).

1:12 Have mercy (Heb. *racham*) is a cognate of the noun
meaning "womb," a reference to the tenderness and compassion a mother shows toward the child of her womb (see Ps.
18:1–3, note; chart, Female Metaphors for God). Note the contrast regarding the Lord's zeal and His anger. He is "zealous

... with great zeal" toward Israel but "exceedingly angry" (lit.
"angry with great anger") toward the "nations at ease"
(Zech. 1:14, 15). Both Israel and the nations experienced the
Lord's anger, but their respective relationships with Him are
qualitatively different.

1:18, 19 A horned animal uses its horns for defense of itself
and as offense against an enemy. The horn therefore was a
symbol of strength and power. The "four horns" could be the
four world powers mentioned in Daniel 2 and 7 (Babylon,
Medo-Persia, Greece, and Rome) or the earlier powers (Assyria, Egypt, Babylon, and Medo-Persia). They are symbolic of
the totality of world power that had attempted, without success, to defeat the purposes of the Lord.

1:20–21 The symbolism of the craftsmen is unclear, though
they could represent Medo-Persia, Greece, Rome, and the
Messiah, since they were the destroyers of the earlier world
empires; or they could represent the nations used by God to
destory Israel's enemies (for example, Egypt, Babylonia, Persia, and Greece). Whatever the symbolism, clearly all Israel's
enemies would ultimately be defeated.

Vision of the Measuring Line

2 Then I raised my eyes and looked, and behold, a man with a measuring line in his hand. ²So I said, "Where are you going?"

And he said to me, "To measure Jerusalem, to see what *is* its width and what *is* its length."

³And there *was* the angel who talked with me, going out; and another angel was coming out to meet him, ⁴who said to him, "Run, speak to this young man, saying: 'Jerusalem shall be inhabited *as* towns without walls, because of the multitude of men and livestock in it. ⁵For I,' says the LORD, 'will be a wall of fire all around her, and I will be the glory in her midst.' "

Future Joy of Zion and Many Nations

⁶"Up, up! Flee from the land of the north," says the LORD; "for I have spread you abroad like the four winds of heaven," says the LORD. ⁷"Up, Zion! Escape, you who dwell with the daughter of Babylon."

⁸For thus says the LORD of hosts: "He sent Me after glory, to the nations which plunder you; for he who touches you touches the apple of His eye. ⁹For surely I will shake My hand against them, and they shall become spoil for their servants. Then you will know that the LORD of hosts has sent Me.

¹⁰"Sing and rejoice, O daughter of Zion! For behold, I am coming and I will dwell in your midst," says the LORD. ¹¹"Many nations shall be joined to the LORD in that day, and they shall become My people. And I will dwell in your midst. Then you will know that the LORD of hosts has sent Me to you. ¹²And the LORD will take possession of Judah as His inheritance in the Holy Land, and will again choose Jerusalem. ¹³Be silent, all flesh, before the LORD, for He is aroused from His holy habitation!"

Vision of the High Priest

3 Then he showed me Joshua the high priest standing before the Angel of the LORD, and Satan standing at his right hand to oppose him. ²And the LORD said to Satan, "The LORD rebuke you, Satan! The LORD who has chosen Jerusalem rebuke you! *Is* this not a brand plucked from the fire?"

³Now Joshua was clothed with filthy garments, and was standing before the Angel.

⁴Then He answered and spoke to those who stood before Him, saying, "Take away the filthy garments from him." And to him He said, "See, I have removed your iniquity from you, and I will clothe you with rich robes."

⁵And I said, "Let them put a clean turban on his head."

So they put a clean turban on his head, and they put the clothes on him. And the Angel of the LORD stood by.

The Coming Branch

⁶Then the Angel of the LORD admonished Joshua, saying, ⁷"Thus says the LORD of hosts:

'If you will walk in My ways,
    And if you will keep My command,
    Then you shall also judge My house,
    And likewise have charge of My courts;
    I will give you places to walk
    Among these who stand here.

⁸"Hear, O Joshua, the high priest,
    You and your companions who sit before
        you,
    For they are a wondrous sign;
    For behold, I am bringing forth My Servant the
        BRANCH.

2:1 Jerusalem could not be measured because it would be filled with such a great multitude that no walls could ever contain it.

2:5 Without walls, Jerusalem would be defenseless. The Lord Himself would be a "wall of fire" to protect Jerusalem, and He would be "glory in her midst." These expressions of the Lord's protective care and presence are reminiscent of the pillars of cloud and fire that accompanied God's people during the Exodus from Egypt (Ex. 13:22; 40:34–38).

2:6 Although Babylon was east of Judah, the route of travel from Judah to Babylon was to the north in order to avoid the desert. Thus, in the context of this prophecy "the land of the north" was Babylon. Jeremiah predicted the invasion of Judah would come from the north (Jer. 6:22; 10:22) and that the people would return from the north (Jer. 3:18; 23:8). This call was extended to the many Jews who had not yet returned to Jerusalem.

2:10 For Daughter of Zion, see Zephaniah 3:14; Zechariah 9:9, 10, notes.

3:1–5 Joshua, the religious leader of the returned community, stood before the Angel of the Lord as high priest, interceding

on behalf of the people (see Hag. 1:12, note). Accusing Joshua was Satan (Heb., *satan*, lit. "accuser" or "adversary"; see chart, The Names of Satan; see also Job 1:6–12; 2:1–6). This vision took place within the heavenly council, not in the earthly temple. The Lord was reinstating the office of high priest through this vision.

3:2 Twice the Lord rebuked Satan on the basis of the covenant because Joshua was a "brand plucked from the fire." This proverbial saying connotes the idea of being saved from complete destruction. A remnant had been saved from the fire of the Exile (see also Deut. 4:20; Jer. 11:4; Amos 4:11).

3:4, 5 Joshua's filthy clothes, soiled as if by human excrement, were replaced with "rich robes," symbolizing the removal of iniquity (v. 3). The high priest wore a special turban as part of his official dress (Ex. 28:36–38; Lev. 8:9; see chart, The High Priest's Clothing), but the word used here by Zechariah is a different word of uncertain meaning (see Job 29:14; Is. 62:3), perhaps to connote righteousness. Joshua was righteous before God in spite of Satan's accusations.

3:8 Joshua's companions, his fellow priests, served as a "wondrous sign" or symbol of what was to come. This future Priest, "My Servant, the BRANCH" (see Zech. 6:12, 13), would be the

⁹For behold, the stone
That I have laid before Joshua:
Upon the stone *are* seven eyes.
Behold, I will engrave its inscription,'
Says the LORD of hosts,
'And I will remove the iniquity of that land in
   one day.
¹⁰In that day,' says the LORD of hosts,
'Everyone will invite his neighbor
Under his vine and under his fig tree.' "

Vision of the Lampstand and Olive Trees

4 Now the angel who talked with me came back
and wakened me, as a man who is wakened out
of his sleep. ²And he said to me, "What do you see?"
So I said, "I am looking, and there *is* a lampstand of solid gold with a bowl on top of it, and on
the *stand* seven lamps with seven pipes to the
seven lamps. ³Two olive trees *are* by it, one at the
right of the bowl and the other at its left." ⁴So I
answered and spoke to the angel who talked with
me, saying, "What *are* these, my lord?"
⁵Then the angel who talked with me answered
and said to me, "Do you not know what these are?"
And I said, "No, my lord."
⁶So he answered and said to me:

"This *is* the word of the LORD to Zerubbabel:
'Not by might nor by power, but by My Spirit,'
Says the LORD of hosts.
⁷'Who *are* you, O great mountain?
Before Zerubbabel *you shall become* a plain!
And he shall bring forth the capstone
With shouts of "Grace, grace to it!" ' "

⁸Moreover the word of the LORD came to me,
saying:

⁹"The hands of Zerubbabel
Have laid the foundation of this temple;ª
His hands shall also finish *it*.
Then you will know
That the LORD of hosts has sent Me to you.
¹⁰For who has despised the day of small things?
For these seven rejoice to see
The plumb line in the hand of Zerubbabel.
They are the eyes of the LORD,
Which scan to and fro throughout the whole
   earth."

¹¹Then I answered and said to him, "What *are*
these two olive trees—at the right of the lampstand and at its left?" ¹²And I further answered
and said to him, "What *are these* two olive branches
that *drip* into the receptaclesª of the two gold
pipes from which the golden *oil* drains?"
¹³Then he answered me and said, "Do you not
know what these *are?*"
And I said, "No, my lord."
¹⁴So he said, "These *are* the two anointed ones,
who stand beside the Lord of the whole earth."

Vision of the Flying Scroll

5 Then I turned and raised my eyes, and saw
there a flying scroll.
²And he said to me, "What do you see?"
So I answered, "I see a flying scroll. Its length *is*
twenty cubits and its width ten cubits."
³Then he said to me, "This *is* the curse that
goes out over the face of the whole earth: 'Every
thief shall be expelled,' according *to* this side of
the scroll; and, 'Every perjurer shall be expelled,'
according *to* that side of it."

····················
4:9 ªLiterally *house*   **4:12** ªLiterally *into the hands of*

Priest-King who would judge and execute justice, embody righteousness, reign, bear the transgression of others, justify many, and intercede on their behalf (Jer. 23:5–8; 33:14–18). The NT refers to Jesus Christ as the long-awaited King-Priest.

3:9 The stone, variously interpreted, may be a reference to the Messiah (Ps. 118:22; Matt. 21:42; Eph. 2:20; 1 Pet. 2:6). The "seven eyes" may be symbolic of the fullness of the Godhead (Is. 11:2; Col. 2:3, 9).

3:10 Under his vine and under his fig tree is an OT image referring to a place of safety and peace where there is no fear (1 Kin. 4:25; 2 Kin. 18:31; Mic. 4:4).

4:2, 3 The tabernacle lampstand was to be tended by a priest from evening to morning, serving as a perpetual light in the otherwise dark tabernacle (Ex. 27:20, 21). Zechariah's lampstand, also a continual light, required no such priestly servicing. The tabernacle lampstand had seven lamps (Ex. 25:37). Zechariah's lampstand had seven lamps and seven spouts or a total of 49 wicks, giving forth a much more abundant light. Both lamps were fueled with olive oil (Ex. 27:20), which was used for consecration and anointing and, as such, a symbol for the Holy Spirit. In the OT, specially chosen people and things were anointed with oil (Ex. 40:9–15; 1 Sam. 9:27—10:1;

16:1, 11–13). In the NT, those chosen by God were anointed by the Holy Spirit (Acts 4:27; 10:38; 2 Cor. 1:21, 22).

4:7 The message of the prophecy is clear whether the mountain represents Jerusalem after its destruction or a picture of opposition to the rebuilding. All obstacles will be removed, and the temple will be completed.

4:10 Some felt disappointment with the new temple, which, though incomplete, lacked the splendor of Solomon's temple (see 2 Chr. 3; 4; see also Ezra 3:12, 13; Hag. 2:3; charts, The Plan of Solomon's Temple; The Plan for Ezekiel's Temple; The Temples of the Bible). Although lacking glory in appearance, this new temple would be the cause of the greatest rejoicing.

4:14 The two anointed ones (Heb., lit. "sons of oil"), were the civil and religious leaders, Zerubbabel and Joshua (see Zech. 3:1–5; Hag. 1:12, notes). Zerubbabel and Joshua are the "two olive trees" (Zech. 4:14), through whom the Holy Spirit (the oil; see v. 6) provided for the faithful people (the light) the encouragement they needed in order to rebuild the temple. To the world the people became witnesses or lights of the presence of God among them.

5:1–3 A scroll was a roll of writing material on which copies of biblical books were written in OT times. In Zechariah's vision

4"I will send out *the curse*," says the LORD of hosts;
"It shall enter the house of the thief
And the house of the one who swears falsely by
My name.
It shall remain in the midst of his house
And consume it, with its timber and stones."

Vision of the Woman in a Basket

5Then the angel who talked with me came out and said to me, "Lift your eyes now, and see what this *is* that goes forth."

6So I asked, "What *is* it?" And he said, "It *is* a basketª that is going forth."

He also said, "This *is* their resemblance throughout the earth: 7Here *is* a lead disc lifted up, and this *is* a woman sitting inside the basket"; 8then he said, "This *is* Wickedness!" And he thrust her down into the basket, and threw the lead coverª over its mouth. 9Then I raised my eyes and looked, and there *were* two women, coming with the wind in their wings; for they had wings like the wings of a stork, and they lifted up the basket between earth and heaven.

10So I said to the angel who talked with me, "Where are they carrying the basket?"

11And he said to me, "To build a house for it in the land of Shinar;ª when it is ready, *the basket* will be set there on its base."

Vision of the Four Chariots

6Then I turned and raised my eyes and looked, and behold, four chariots *were* coming from between two mountains, and the mountains *were* mountains of bronze. 2With the first chariot *were* red horses, with the second chariot black horses,

3with the third chariot white horses, and with the fourth chariot dappled horses—strong *steeds.* 4Then I answered and said to the angel who talked with me, "What *are* these, my lord?"

5And the angel answered and said to me, "These *are* four spirits of heaven, who go out from *their* station before the Lord of all the earth. 6The one with the black horses is going to the north country, the white are going after them, and the dappled are going toward the south country." 7Then the strong *steeds* went out, eager to go, that they might walk to and fro throughout the earth. And He said, "Go, walk to and fro throughout the earth." So they walked to and fro throughout the earth. 8And He called to me, and spoke to me, saying, "See, those who go toward the north country have given rest to My Spirit in the north country."

The Command to Crown Joshua

9Then the word of the LORD came to me, saying: 10"Receive *the gift* from the captives—from Heldai, Tobijah, and Jedaiah, who have come from Babylon—and go the same day and enter the house of Josiah the son of Zephaniah. 11Take the silver and gold, make an elaborate crown, and set *it* on the head of Joshua the son of Jehozadak, the high priest. 12Then speak to him, saying, 'Thus says the LORD of hosts, saying:

"Behold, the Man whose name *is* the BRANCH!
From His place He shall branch out,
And He shall build the temple of the LORD;

5:6 ªHebrew *ephah*, a measuring container, and so elsewhere **5:8** ªLiterally *stone* **5:11** ªThat is, Babylon

---

a scroll of considerable size (30' x 15') is already set in motion for judgment. Its designation as "the curse" indicates its relation to covenant Law (see Jer. 36:1–4, 27–32; Ezek. 2:8—3:7; Rev. 5:1–7). The two sins named represent breaking the entire Law, (see Matt. 22:36–40).

5:6 Some identify "their" with the sinners of the previous vision (v. 3). Others consider the pronoun a reference to any who participate in wickedness (v. 8). Still others change "resemblance" (Heb. lit. "eye") to "iniquity" (a slight alteration of one Hebrew letter), which better fits the context of the verse. The removal of sin is clearly the focus of this vision (see vv. 7, 8; 9–11, notes).

5:7, 8 Both positive and negative concepts are personified by a woman in the OT (see Prov. 1:20, 21). Such a metaphor in no way suggests degrading or oppressing women. In Revelation 21:9, the metaphor "bride" is used of the body of Christ, in which both women and men are included. Similarly, when the metaphor of a woman as "wickedness" (a word that happens to be a feminine noun in Hebrew) is used, both women and men are to be understood as sharing equally in the picture.

5:9–11 The stork is a large, migratory bird capable of traveling great distances. Thus, "wickedness" was being carried far away from the place God had chosen for Himself to the "land of Shinar," the ancient Mesopotamian name for the region of

Babylon where the Tower of Babel once stood (Gen. 11:2; Dan. 1:2). In Scripture, Babylon is the appropriate place for wickedness to dwell because it is outside the Promised Land (see Rev. 17:1–6, 15–18).

6:1–3 Horses and chariots indicate armies and war, power and judgment. God, the divine Warrior, is often pictured as coming in such style (Ps. 68:17; Is. 66:15, 16; Hab. 3:8). The chariots of this vision came from symbolic "mountains of bronze." Since God was pictured as dwelling in His mountain (Ps. 48:1–3) and since the entrance of the temple, God's earthly dwelling place, was made of bronze (1 Kin. 7:13–22), the image was of chariots coming to earth from the heavenly dwelling place.

6:9–11 The crown was placed on Joshua's head, indicating the joining of the royal and priestly offices.

6:12, 13 The crowning of the priest was not a re-establishment of the throne in Jerusalem but a promise for a future Priest-King. This crowned priest represents "the BRANCH" (Zech. 3:8–10), who would build the temple of the Lord. This merging of the offices of priest and king is distinctive (see Ps. 110). Previously the offices were maintained separately. As Priest, the Priest-King would build the temple; as King, He would rule on His throne (see chart, The Temples of the Bible).

Every little glimpse that can be gained of God exceeds every pain and every joy that man can conceive without it.

St. Catherine of Genoa

13Yes, He shall build the temple of the
  LORD.
He shall bear the glory,
And shall sit and rule on His throne;
So He shall be a priest on His throne,
And the counsel of peace shall be between
  them both." '

14"Now the elaborate crown shall be for a memorial in the temple of the LORD for Helem,[a] Tobijah, Jedaiah, and Hen the son of Zephaniah. 15Even those from afar shall come and build the temple of the LORD. Then you shall know that the LORD of hosts has sent Me to you. And *this* shall come to pass if you diligently obey the voice of the LORD your God."

Obedience Better than Fasting

7Now in the fourth year of King Darius it came to pass *that* the word of the LORD came to Zechariah, on the fourth *day* of the ninth month, Chislev, 2when *the people*[a] sent Sherezer,[b] with Regem-Melech and his men, *to* the house of God,[c] to pray before the LORD, 3*and* to ask the priests who *were* in the house of the LORD of hosts, and the prophets, saying, "Should I weep in the fifth month and fast as I have done for so many years?"

4Then the word of the LORD of hosts came to me, saying, 5"Say to all the people of the land, and to the priests: 'When you fasted and mourned in the fifth and seventh *months* during those seventy years, did you really fast for Me—for Me? 6When you eat and when you drink, do you not eat and drink *for yourselves?* 7*Should you* not *have obeyed* the words which the LORD proclaimed through the former prophets when Jerusalem and the cities around it were inhabited and prosperous, and the South[a] and the Lowland were inhabited?' "

Disobedience Resulted in Captivity

8Then the word of the LORD came to Zechariah, saying, 9"Thus says the LORD of hosts:

'Execute true justice,
  Show mercy and compassion
  Everyone to his brother.
10Do not oppress the widow or the fatherless,
  The alien or the poor.
  Let none of you plan evil in his heart
  Against his brother.'

11"But they refused to heed, shrugged their shoulders, and stopped their ears so that they could not hear. 12Yes, they made their hearts like flint, refusing to hear the law and the words which the LORD of hosts had sent by His Spirit through the former prophets. Thus great wrath came from the LORD of hosts. 13Therefore it happened, *that* just as He proclaimed and they would not hear, so they called out and I would not listen," says the LORD of hosts. 14"But I scattered them with a whirlwind among all the nations which they had not known. Thus the land became desolate after them, so that no one passed through or returned; for they made the pleasant land desolate."

Jerusalem, Holy City of the Future

8Again the word of the LORD of hosts came, saying, 2"Thus says the LORD of hosts:

'I am zealous for Zion with great zeal;
  With great fervor I am zealous for her.'

6:14 [a]Following Masoretic Text, Targum, and Vulgate; Syriac reads *for Heldai* (compare verse 10); Septuagint reads *for the patient ones.* 7:2 [a]Literally *they* (compare verse 5) [b]Or *Sar-Ezer* [c]Hebrew *Bethel* 7:7 [a]Hebrew *Negev*

6:14, 15 Joshua's crown would not remain on his head but was to be placed in the temple for a memorial to all who returned from the Exile. The crown would serve as a reminder of the promise of the Priest-King, who is called "the BRANCH" (see vv. 12, 13, note). The temple which Zerubbabel would build would act as surety for that promise. Just as the Lord's promise that the temple would be rebuilt was being fulfilled, so the people could be sure that the promise regarding "the BRANCH" would likewise come to pass.

7:1–3 The third and final date is given (see Zech. 1:1, note). It corresponds to December 7, 518 B.C. Two years have passed since temple reconstruction resumed and since the night visions occurred (Zech. 1:7—6:15). During the Exile, certain

fasts were celebrated throughout the year as a remembrance of the humiliation of being taken into Exile. The fast in the fifth month commemorated the destruction of the temple in 586 B.C. (Zech. 7:5).

7:4–14 While in exile, the people fasted, not because of sorrow for their sins, but for their own personal satisfaction. Even the activities of daily life were not lived to the honor of God. Righteous living was the theme of God's prophetic word both before and after the Exile (vv. 9, 10; Is. 1:10–17; Mic. 6:6–8). The Lord's message to His people remained the same.

8:1–23 Rather than concentrating on past judgment with fasting and mourning, the community of returned exiles was

³"Thus says the LORD:

'I will return to Zion,
  And dwell in the midst of Jerusalem.
Jerusalem shall be called the City of Truth,
  The Mountain of the LORD of hosts,
  The Holy Mountain.'

⁴"Thus says the LORD of hosts:

'Old men and old women shall again sit
  In the streets of Jerusalem,
Each one with his staff in his hand
  Because of great age.
⁵The streets of the city
  Shall be full of boys and girls
  Playing in its streets.'

⁶"Thus says the LORD of hosts:

'If it is marvelous in the eyes of the remnant of
    this people in these days,
Will it also be marvelous in My eyes?'
Says the LORD of hosts.

⁷"Thus says the LORD of hosts:

'Behold, I will save My people from the land of
    the east
  And from the land of the west;
⁸I will bring them *back*,
  And they shall dwell in the midst of
    Jerusalem.
They shall be My people
  And I will be their God,
  In truth and righteousness.'

⁹"Thus says the LORD of hosts:

'Let your hands be strong,
  You who have been hearing in these days
These words by the mouth of the prophets,
  Who *spoke* in the day the foundation was
    laid
  For the house of the LORD of hosts,
  That the temple might be built.
¹⁰For before these days
  There were no wages for man nor any hire for
    beast;
There was no peace from the enemy for
    whoever went out or came in;
  For I set all men, everyone, against his
    neighbor.

¹¹But now I *will* not *treat* the remnant of this
people as in the former days,' says the LORD of
hosts.

¹²"For the seed *shall be* prosperous,
  The vine shall give its fruit,
  The ground shall give her increase,
  And the heavens shall give their dew—
I will cause the remnant of this people
  To possess all these.
¹³And it shall come to pass
  That just as you were a curse among the
    nations,
O house of Judah and house of Israel,
  So I will save you, and you shall be a blessing.
Do not fear,
  Let your hands be strong.'

¹⁴"For thus says the LORD of hosts:

'Just as I determined to punish you
  When your fathers provoked Me to wrath,'
Says the LORD of hosts,
  'And I would not relent,
¹⁵So again in these days
  I am determined to do good
To Jerusalem and to the house of Judah.
  Do not fear.
¹⁶These *are* the things you shall do:
  Speak each man the truth to his neighbor;
  Give judgment in your gates for truth, justice,
    and peace;
¹⁷Let none of you think evil in your[a] heart
    against your neighbor;
  And do not love a false oath.
For all these *are things* that I hate,'
Says the LORD."

¹⁸Then the word of the LORD of hosts came to
me, saying, ¹⁹"Thus says the LORD of hosts:

'The fast of the fourth *month*,
  The fast of the fifth,
  The fast of the seventh,
  And the fast of the tenth,
Shall be joy and gladness and cheerful feasts
  For the house of Judah.
Therefore love truth and peace.'

²⁰"Thus says the LORD of hosts:

8:17 [a]Literally *his*

·····················

---

encouraged to live righteously in the present as future blessings were promised. A number of promises, each beginning
with the phrase "Thus says the LORD of Hosts," or a variation
of it, repeated a previous message of Zechariah.

8:18–23 Weeping and fasting were not to be continued because weeping had turned to "joy and gladness" and fasting
to "cheerful feasts" as Jerusalem was restored. When the nations would see this change, they would come to Jerusalem in
crowds to seek the Lord and to pray.

'Peoples shall yet come,
   Inhabitants of many cities;
²¹The inhabitants of one *city* shall go to another,
      saying,
   "Let us continue to go and pray before the
      LORD,
   And seek the LORD of hosts.
   I myself will go also."
²²Yes, many peoples and strong nations
   Shall come to seek the LORD of hosts in
      Jerusalem,
   And to pray before the LORD.'

²³"Thus says the LORD of hosts: 'In those days
ten men from every language of the nations shall
grasp the sleeve of a Jewish man, saying, "Let us
go with you, for we have heard *that* God *is* with
you." ' "

Israel Defended Against Enemies

9 The burden[a] of the word of the LORD
   Against the land of Hadrach,
   And Damascus its resting place
   (For the eyes of men
   And all the tribes of Israel
   Are on the LORD);
²Also *against* Hamath, *which* borders on it,
   And *against* Tyre and Sidon, though they are
      very wise.

³For Tyre built herself a tower,
   Heaped up silver like the dust,
   And gold like the mire of the streets.
⁴Behold, the Lord will cast her out;
   He will destroy her power in the sea,
   And she will be devoured by fire.

⁵Ashkelon shall see *it* and fear;
   Gaza also shall be very sorrowful;
   And Ekron, for He dried up her
      expectation.
   The king shall perish from Gaza,
   And Ashkelon shall not be inhabited.

⁶"A mixed race shall settle in Ashdod,
   And I will cut off the pride of the Philistines.
⁷I will take away the blood from his mouth,
   And the abominations from between his teeth.
   But he who remains, even he *shall be* for our
      God,
   And shall be like a leader in Judah,
   And Ekron like a Jebusite.
⁸I will camp around My house
   Because of the army,
   Because of him who passes by and him who
      returns.
   No more shall an oppressor pass through
      them,
   For now I have seen with My eyes.

The Coming King

⁹"Rejoice greatly, O daughter of Zion!
   Shout, O daughter of Jerusalem!
   Behold, your King is coming to you;
   He *is* just and having salvation,
   Lowly and riding on a donkey,
   A colt, the foal of a donkey.
¹⁰I will cut off the chariot from Ephraim
   And the horse from Jerusalem;
   The battle bow shall be cut off.
   He shall speak peace to the nations;
   His dominion *shall be* 'from sea to sea,
   And from the River to the ends of the earth.'[a]

God Will Save His People

¹¹"As for you also,
   Because of the blood of your covenant,
   I will set your prisoners free from the
      waterless pit.
¹²Return to the stronghold,
   You prisoners of hope.
   Even today I declare
   That I will restore double to you.
¹³For I have bent Judah, My *bow,*
   Fitted the bow with Ephraim,

9:1 [a]Or *oracle*   9:10 [a]Psalm 72:8

9:1 The burden introduces prophecies of judgment. Considerable time had lapsed since Zechariah's last recorded prophecy. The rebuilding of the temple had been completed. The once strong Persian Empire was beginning to crumble.

9:1–7 The cities mentioned here are the target of other prophecies of judgment (see Amos 1:3–10). They represent the most extensive borders of the Land, which, though promised, were never conquered by Israel (Josh. 13:1–6; Ezek. 47:13–20). The "land of Hadrach" was probably a region near the Syrian capital of Damascus. Tyre was noted for its wisdom, wealth, trade, and impregnable fortress (Zech. 9:2, 3). Ashkelon, Gaza, Ekron, and Ashdod were Philistine cities, which would tremble when they saw the terrible fate of Tyre. The goal of judgment is always repentance (v. 7).

9:9, 10 This royal procession of the victorious King is met with spontaneous shouts of exclamation from His people. It is the triumphant entry of the King, riding a donkey, coming to Jerusalem to dwell with His people (see Zech. 2:10). Chariots, war horses, and weapons are no longer needed. This King, whose kingdom is the whole earth "from sea to sea, from the river to the ends of the earth"), brings with Him everlasting peace. Verse 9 is used in the NT to speak of Jesus' entry into Jerusalem (Matt. 21:4, 5; John 12:12–19).

9:11–13 Blood is a vital part of God's covenants (Gen. 15:7–10, 17, 18; Ex. 24:6–8; Mark 14:24; 1 Cor. 11:25, 26; Heb. 9:22). In OT times, an animal sacrifice often ratified political treaties or covenants. The "prisoners" to be freed were the remaining exiles in Babylon. They cannot remain prisoners forever because of their covenant with *Yahweh.* Jesus spoke of Himself as the sacrifice whose blood would ratify a new covenant, setting free those who would come to Christ in faith (Mark 14:24).

And raised up your sons, O Zion,
Against your sons, O Greece,
And made you like the sword of a mighty man."

¹⁴Then the LORD will be seen over them,
And His arrow will go forth like lightning.
The Lord GOD will blow the trumpet,
And go with whirlwinds from the south.
¹⁵The LORD of hosts will defend them;
They shall devour and subdue with slingstones.
They shall drink *and* roar as if with wine;
They shall be filled *with blood* like basins,
Like the corners of the altar.
¹⁶The LORD their God will save them in that day,
As the flock of His people.
For they *shall be like* the jewels of a crown,
Lifted like a banner over His land—
¹⁷For how great is its° goodness
And how great itsᵇ beauty!
Grain shall make the young men thrive,
And new wine the young women.

Restoration of Judah and Israel

10Ask the LORD for rain
In the time of the latter rain.°
The LORD will make flashing clouds;
He will give them showers of rain,
Grass in the field for everyone.

²For the idols° speak delusion;
The diviners envision lies,
And tell false dreams;
They comfort in vain.
Therefore *the people* wend their way like sheep;
They are in trouble because *there is* no shepherd.

³"My anger is kindled against the shepherds,
And I will punish the goatherds.
For the LORD of hosts will visit His flock,
The house of Judah,
And will make them as His royal horse in the battle.
⁴From him comes the cornerstone,
From him the tent peg,
From him the battle bow,
From him every ruler° together.
⁵They shall be like mighty men,
Who tread down *their enemies*

In the mire of the streets in the battle.
They shall fight because the LORD is with them,
And the riders on horses shall be put to shame.

⁶"I will strengthen the house of Judah,
And I will save the house of Joseph.
I will bring them back,
Because I have mercy on them.
They shall be as though I had not cast them aside;
For I *am* the LORD their God,
And I will hear them.
⁷*Those of* Ephraim shall be like a mighty man,
And their heart shall rejoice as if with wine.
Yes, their children shall see *it* and be glad;
Their heart shall rejoice in the LORD.
⁸I will whistle for them and gather them,
For I will redeem them;
And they shall increase as they once increased.

⁹"I will sow them among the peoples,
And they shall remember Me in far countries;
They shall live, together with their children,
And they shall return.
¹⁰I will also bring them back from the land of Egypt,
And gather them from Assyria.
I will bring them into the land of Gilead and Lebanon,
Until no *more room* is found for them.
¹¹He shall pass through the sea with affliction,
And strike the waves of the sea:
All the depths of the River° shall dry up.
Then the pride of Assyria shall be brought down,
And the scepter of Egypt shall depart.

¹²"So I will strengthen them in the LORD,
And they shall walk up and down in His name,"
Says the LORD.

Desolation of Israel

11Open your doors, O Lebanon,
That fire may devour your cedars.
²Wail, O cypress, for the cedar has fallen,

· · · · · · · · · · · · · · · · ·
9:17 °Or *His* ᵇOr *His* **10:1** °That is, spring rain **10:2** °Hebrew *teraphim* **10:4** °Or *despot* **10:11** °That is, the Nile

---

10:1, 2 Instead of seeking the Lord through the prophets, the leaders of the people used illegitimate means to gain knowledge of the future (see Deut. 18:9–22). "Idols" were statuettes revered as household gods. The leaders failed to lead effectively, and the people strayed like sheep "because there is no shepherd."

10:3–5 The Lord would visit the leaders ("shepherds") in anger, but He would strengthen His people ("flock"). Note the many images of the people as strong and mighty in battle against their enemies (vv. 4–11). For example, "cornerstone"

and "tent peg" indicate that on which all else depends—steadfast strength (v. 4).

10:6, 7 After the kingdom divided (931 B.C.), distinctions between the southern kingdom Judah and the northern kingdom Israel were significant (see chart, Terminology for the Divided Kingdom). After the return from the Exile, God renewed His covenant with all His people; Judah, Joseph, and Ephraim emphasize this inclusiveness.

Because the mighty *trees* are ruined.
Wail, O oaks of Bashan,
For the thick forest has come down.
³*There is* the sound of wailing shepherds!
For their glory is in ruins.
There is the sound of roaring lions!
For the pride[a] of the Jordan is in ruins.

Prophecy of the Shepherds

⁴Thus says the LORD my God, "Feed the flock for slaughter, ⁵whose owners slaughter them and feel no guilt; those who sell them say, 'Blessed be the LORD, for I am rich'; and their shepherds do not pity them. ⁶For I will no longer pity the inhabitants of the land," says the LORD. "But indeed I will give everyone into his neighbor's hand and into the hand of his king. They shall attack the land, and I will not deliver *them* from their hand."

⁷So I fed the flock for slaughter, in particular the poor of the flock.[a] I took for myself two staffs: the one I called Beauty,[b] and the other I called Bonds;[c] and I fed the flock. ⁸I dismissed the three shepherds in one month. My soul loathed them, and their soul also abhorred me. ⁹Then I said, "I will not feed you. Let what is dying die, and what is perishing perish. Let those that are left eat each other's flesh." ¹⁰And I took my staff, Beauty, and cut it in two, that I might break the covenant which I had made with all the peoples. ¹¹So it was broken on that day. Thus the poor[a] of the flock, who were watching me, knew that it *was* the word of the LORD. ¹²Then I said to them, "If it is agreeable to you, give *me* my wages; and if not, refrain." So they weighed out for my wages thirty *pieces* of silver.

¹³And the LORD said to me, "Throw it to the potter"—that princely price they set on me. So I took the thirty *pieces* of silver and threw them into the house of the LORD for the potter. ¹⁴Then I cut in two my other staff, Bonds, that I might break the brotherhood between Judah and Israel.

¹⁵And the LORD said to me, "Next, take for yourself the implements of a foolish shepherd. ¹⁶For indeed I will raise up a shepherd in the land who will not care for those who are cut off, nor seek the young, nor heal those that are broken, nor feed those that still stand. But he will eat the flesh of the fat and tear their hooves in pieces.

¹⁷"Woe to the worthless shepherd,
Who leaves the flock!
A sword *shall be* against his arm
And against his right eye;
His arm shall completely wither,
And his right eye shall be totally blinded."

The Coming Deliverance of Judah

12 The burden[a] of the word of the LORD against Israel. Thus says the LORD, who stretches out the heavens, lays the foundation of the earth, and forms the spirit of man within him: ²"Behold, I will make Jerusalem a cup of drunkenness to all the surrounding peoples, when they lay siege against Judah and Jerusalem. ³And it shall happen in that day that I will make Jerusalem a very heavy stone for all peoples; all who would heave it away will surely be cut in pieces, though all nations of the earth are gathered against it. ⁴In that day," says the LORD, "I will strike every horse with confusion, and its rider with madness; I will open My eyes on the house of Judah, and will strike every horse of the peoples with blindness. ⁵And the governors of Judah shall say in their heart, 'The inhabitants of Jerusalem *are* my strength in the LORD of hosts, their God.' ⁶In that day I will make the governors of Judah like a firepan in the woodpile, and like a fiery torch in the sheaves; they shall devour all the surrounding peoples on the right hand and on the left, but Jerusalem shall be inhabited again in her own place—Jerusalem.

⁷"The LORD will save the tents of Judah first, so that the glory of the house of David and the glory of the inhabitants of Jerusalem shall not become greater than that of Judah. ⁸In that day the LORD will defend the inhabitants of Jerusalem; the one who is feeble among them in that day shall be like David, and the house of David *shall be* like God, like the Angel of the LORD before them. ⁹It shall be in that day *that* I will seek to destroy all the nations that come against Jerusalem.

11:3 ªOr *floodplain, thicket*　11:7 ªFollowing Masoretic Text, Targum, and Vulgate; Septuagint reads *for the Canaanites.* ᵇOr *Grace,* and so in verse 10　ᶜOr *Unity,* and so in verse 14　11:11 ªFollowing Masoretic Text, Targum, and Vulgate; Septuagint reads *the Canaanites.*　12:1 ªOr *oracle*

11:4–17 Zechariah was to play the part of a shepherd who leads the sheep rightly. The staffs, "Beauty" (or grace) and "Bonds" (or unity), were the tools of the good shepherd. The people who suffered from bad leadership nonetheless despised and rejected godly leadership (see chart, Preparation for Leadership). The breaking of the staffs of the good shepherd signaled that God would give the people to the "foolish shepherd." The people received the leader they wanted and deserved. The later rejection of Jesus Christ as the Shepherd-King was the culmination of Israel's long history of rejecting God's leadership through the prophets.

12:2–5 The attackers of Jerusalem would become like drunken men, powerless and unable to function properly. Though they expected Jerusalem to fall easily, they would be rendered impotent in their attack. Jerusalem would also be like a "heavy stone," which would injure its foes when they tried to lift it. The protective activity of the Lord on behalf of Jerusalem was a source of encouragement for the people.

12:8 The Lord would so strengthen Jerusalem and Judah that even the "feeble among them" would be "like David," a strong and mighty warrior and Israel's ideal king. For the "Angel of the LORD," see Zech. 1:8, note.

Mourning for the Pierced One

¹⁰"And I will pour on the house of David and on the inhabitants of Jerusalem the Spirit of grace and supplication; then they will look on Me whom they pierced. Yes, they will mourn for Him as one mourns for *his* only *son,* and grieve for Him as one grieves for a firstborn. ¹¹In that day there shall be a great mourning in Jerusalem, like the mourning at Hadad Rimmon in the plain of Megiddo.ᵃ ¹²And the land shall mourn, every family by itself: the family of the house of David by itself, and their wives by themselves; the family of the house of Nathan by itself, and their wives by themselves; ¹³the family of the house of Levi by itself, and their wives by themselves; the family of Shimei by itself, and their wives by themselves; ¹⁴all the families that remain, every family by itself, and their wives by themselves.

Idolatry Cut Off

13 "In that day a fountain shall be opened for the house of David and for the inhabitants of Jerusalem, for sin and for uncleanness.

²"It shall be in that day," says the LORD of hosts, "*that* I will cut off the names of the idols from the land, and they shall no longer be remembered. I will also cause the prophets and the unclean spirit to depart from the land. ³It shall come to pass *that* if anyone still prophesies, then his father and mother who begot him will say to him, 'You shall not live, because you have spoken lies in the name of the LORD.' And his father and mother who begot him shall thrust him through when he prophesies.

⁴"And it shall be in that day *that* every prophet will be ashamed of his vision when he prophesies; they will not wear a robe of coarse hair to deceive. ⁵But he will say, 'I *am* no prophet, I *am* a farmer; for a man taught me to keep cattle from my youth.' ⁶And *one* will say to him, 'What are these wounds between your arms?'ᵃ Then he will answer,

'*Those* with which I was wounded in the house of my friends.'

The Shepherd Savior

⁷"Awake, O sword, against My Shepherd,
  Against the Man who is My Companion,"
  Says the LORD of hosts.
"Strike the Shepherd,
  And the sheep will be scattered;
  Then I will turn My hand against the little
    ones.
⁸And it shall come to pass in all the land,"
  Says the LORD,
"*That* two-thirds in it shall be cut off *and* die,
  But *one*-third shall be left in it:
⁹I will bring the *one*-third through the fire,
  Will refine them as silver is refined,
  And test them as gold is tested.
  They will call on My name,
  And I will answer them.
  I will say, 'This *is* My people';
  And each one will say, 'The LORD *is* my God.'"

The Day of the LORD

14 Behold, the day of the LORD is coming,
  And your spoil will be divided in your
    midst.
²For I will gather all the nations to battle
    against Jerusalem;
  The city shall be taken,
  The houses rifled,
  And the women ravished.
  Half of the city shall go into captivity,
  But the remnant of the people shall not be cut
    off from the city.

³Then the LORD will go forth
  And fight against those nations,
  As He fights in the day of battle.

···················

12:11 ᵃHebrew *Megiddon*   **13:6** ᵃOr *hands*

12:10 Through the work of the Holy Spirit, the people will see clearly the one "whom they pierced." They would mourn in repentance for their actions (Luke 23:48) with the gravest of emotions ("as one mourns for his only son"). And "they will look on Me" (the Lord). The context demands that "Me" be identified as the Messiah (see Is. 53:5; John 19:34–37; Rev. 1:7).

12:11–14 An identification of Hadad Rimmon cannot be made with certainty. Apparently, it was associated with infamous mourning. Josiah, a righteous king of Judah, was mortally wounded at Megiddo (2 Chr. 35:20–25). If Hadad Rimmon is the name of a place, perhaps it was the site of this Megiddo battle where the people mourned the death of their righteous king. The name may also refer to a person or to a pagan deity. "Their wives by themselves" probably emphasizes the sincerity of their mourning. These were not professional mourners. Such sorrow revealed their genuine repentance for sin.

13:2–6 Just as God cuts off idols from the Land, He will cut off false prophets, who deserved death (Deut. 13:6–10; 18:20–22).

So serious was this matter, that even a mother and father would not allow a son to live if he persisted in delivering false prophecy. The distinctive clothing of the prophet was a "robe of coarse hair" (worn by Elijah, Elisha, John the Baptist), which the false prophet would discard to avoid judgment. However, self-inflicted "wounds," characteristic of idol worship, would identify him (1 Kin. 18:28).

13:7–9 The Shepherd was struck, and the sheep were scattered. The Lord directed that His Shepherd be put to death (Is. 53:10; Acts 2:23). Jesus quoted this verse on the night He was betrayed and arrested (Matt. 26:31; Mark 14:27).

14:1–21 Clearly Jerusalem is the dominant city of the world and most precious to the Lord, who reigns in Jerusalem as the King over all the earth. However, there are a wide range of opinions regarding the interpretation of this difficult chapter.

4And in that day His feet will stand on the
Mount of Olives,
Which faces Jerusalem on the east.
And the Mount of Olives shall be split in
two,
From east to west,
Making a very large valley;
Half of the mountain shall move toward the
north
And half of it toward the south.

5Then you shall flee *through* My mountain
valley,
For the mountain valley shall reach to
Azal.
Yes, you shall flee
As you fled from the earthquake
In the days of Uzziah king of Judah.

Thus the LORD my God will come,
And all the saints with You.[a]

6It shall come to pass in that day
That there will be no light;
The lights will diminish.
7It shall be one day
Which is known to the LORD—
Neither day nor night.
But at evening time it shall happen
That it will be light.

8And in that day it shall be
That living waters shall flow from Jerusalem,
Half of them toward the eastern sea
And half of them toward the western sea;
In both summer and winter it shall occur.
9And the LORD shall be King over all the earth.
In that day it shall be—
"The LORD *is* one,"[a]
And His name one.

10All the land shall be turned into a plain from
Geba to Rimmon south of Jerusalem. *Jerusalem*[a]
shall be raised up and inhabited in her place from
Benjamin's Gate to the place of the First Gate and
the Corner Gate, and *from* the Tower of Hananel to
the king's winepresses.

11*The people* shall dwell in it;
And no longer shall there be utter destruction,
But Jerusalem shall be safely inhabited.

12And this shall be the plague with which the
LORD will strike all the people who fought against
Jerusalem:

Their flesh shall dissolve while they stand on
their feet,
Their eyes shall dissolve in their sockets,
And their tongues shall dissolve in their
mouths.

13It shall come to pass in that day
That a great panic from the LORD will be
among them.
Everyone will seize the hand of his neighbor,
And raise his hand against his neighbor's
hand;
14Judah also will fight at Jerusalem.
And the wealth of all the surrounding nations
Shall be gathered together:
Gold, silver, and apparel in great abundance.

15Such also shall be the plague
On the horse *and* the mule,
On the camel and the donkey,
And on all the cattle that will be in those
camps.
So *shall* this plague *be.*

The Nations Worship the King

16And it shall come to pass *that* everyone who is
left of all the nations which came against Jerusalem shall go up from year to year to worship the
King, the LORD of hosts, and to keep the Feast of
Tabernacles. 17And it shall be *that* whichever of
the families of the earth do not come up to Jerusalem to worship the King, the LORD of hosts, on
them there will be no rain. 18If the family of Egypt
will not come up and enter in, they *shall have* no
rain; they shall receive the plague with which the
LORD strikes the nations who do not come up to

14:5 [a]Or *you;* Septuagint, Targum, and Vulgate read *Him.* **14:9**
[a]Compare Deuteronomy 6:4 **14:10** [a]Literally *She*

14:4 The Mount of Olives dominates a range of hills running
from north to southeast of Jerusalem. Departure from the city
toward the east is thus slow and difficult. Zechariah pictured
the Mount of Olives split in two, creating a valley of quick escape from the city.

14:5 The inhabitants of the city were to flee through the valley formed by the split mountain (v. 4). Azal's exact identification is unknown, but as the farthest point of the valley to
the east of the city, it is named the place of safety.

14:10 The Judean mountains surrounding Jerusalem would be
leveled from Geba in the north to Rimmon in the south. Jeru-

salem would become the high point of the entire region. The
entire city would be raised and fully inhabited, as indicated by
the gates named, which define the fullest area of the city in
every direction (Zech. 1:17; 2:4; 8:3–5).

14:16–19 The Feast of Tabernacles was one of the three feasts
that required male attendance in Jerusalem (Deut. 16:16; see
chart, The Feasts of Israel). Zechariah foresaw the celebration of this feast by peoples from "all the nations" and not
just by the Jews. A remnant of Gentiles from the nations
would join God's chosen covenant people.

keep the Feast of Tabernacles. [19]This shall be the punishment of Egypt and the punishment of all the nations that do not come up to keep the Feast of Tabernacles.

[20]In that day "HOLINESS TO THE LORD" shall be *engraved* on the bells of the horses. The pots in the LORD's house shall be like the bowls before the altar. [21]Yes, every pot in Jerusalem and Judah shall be holiness to the LORD of hosts.[a] Everyone who sacrifices shall come and take them and cook in them. In that day there shall no longer be a Canaanite in the house of the LORD of hosts.

·············

14:21 [a]Or *on every pot . . . shall be (engraved) "HOLINESS TO THE LORD OF HOSTS"*

14:20, 21 The priest had HOLINESS TO THE LORD engraved on a gold plate on the turban he wore as a reminder and expression of his consecration (Ex. 28:36–38; see chart, The High Priest's Clothing). "In that day" even the most common and ordinary things would be holy. All of life would be consecrated to the Lord. There would be no "Canaanite" because no person outside of the covenant would be in the house of the Lord.

Malachi

AUTHOR

The identity of the author of Malachi (Heb., lit. "my messenger" or "my angel") is uncertain. The author's identity revolves around whether Malachi is a proper name or a common noun used as a title. The book offers no biographical information about the prophet. Therefore, some scholars believe that Malachi is not the personal name of the prophet. If the name of the prophet is unknown, Malachi would be the only "anonymous" book in the prophetic section. Tradition suggests that Malachi refers to Ezra the scribe. However, Ezra was never called a "prophet" or "messenger." A fourth century A.D. Jewish writing conjectures that Malachi was the name of a prophet who might have been from a place called Sopha. After reviewing the evidence, the best conclusion is that the prophet named Malachi was the author of this book.

DATE

The Book of Malachi deals with the destruction of the Edomite Empire, impure sacrifices, a corrupt priesthood, and intermarriages with pagans. Malachi also used Persian terms such as *pehah* (governor). The language and concerns of the book are similar to those of Nehemiah (see Mal. 3:5, note). Therefore, the majority of scholars date Malachi from the first half of the fifth century B.C., after the Jews had returned to Jerusalem from the Exile and the temple had been rebuilt.

BACKGROUND

SETTING: Although a remnant had returned to Jerusalem from Babylon and had rebuilt the temple, God's people were in a state of spiritual apathy. With the exception of Sabbath-breaking, Malachi spoke against the same sins as did Nehemiah (Neh. 13:6–31). Foreigners had been received into the community without conversion, mixed marriages and divorces were prevalent, and the temple offerings were being neglected. These sins were precisely what the people had promised not to commit when they had rededicated the temple and renewed the covenant (Neh. 10:28–39). The people expected God to reward them for half-hearted religious performances and to disregard their unfaithfulness.

PURPOSE: God's people were directed to return to Him and to renew their faithfulness to the covenant.

AUDIENCE: Malachi prophesied to postexilic Israel. However, his message is relevant for any believer whose commitment is half-hearted.

LITERARY CHARACTERISTICS: The book was composed in prose, using prophetic dialogue. In this series of dialogues, each begins with "yet you say." Most of the fifty-five verses are in the first person, with the Lord Himself directly addressing His people. This offers a vividness of personal encounter with the Lord.

There are four major themes in Malachi:

- God's love for His people, despite their unfaithfulness and hypocrisy.
- The importance of serving God in the proper manner and with the right attitude.
- The importance of protecting and maintaining the sacred vows of marriage.
- The coming of the Messiah, His forerunner, and the day of the Lord.

I. God's Choice of Israel (1:1–5)
  A. A prophetic oracle (1:1)
  B. God's love for Jacob (1:2)
  C. Edom's destiny (1:3–5)
II. The Failures of the People (1:6—2:17)
  A. Unholy offerings (1:6—2:9)
    1. The dishonor to God (1:6)
    2. The unacceptable offerings (1:7–14)
    3. The corrupt priesthood (2:1–9)
  B. Unholy marriages (2:10–17)
    1. Marrying foreign wives (2:10–12)
    2. Divorcing Jewish wives (2:13–16)
    3. Living in moral confusion (2:17)

III. A Prophecy of the Last Day (3:1—4:6)
  A. The announcement of Messiah (3:1–7)
  B. The robbing of God (3:8—4:6)
    1. The blessings of tithing (3:8–12)
    2. The complaints of the wicked (3:13–18)
    3. The destiny of the wicked (4:1)
    4. The blessing of the righteous (4:2, 3)
    5. A reminder of the importance of the Mosaic Law (4:4)
    6. The prophecy of the messenger (4:5, 6)

1 The burden[a] of the word of the LORD to Israel by Malachi.

Israel Beloved of God

[2]"I have loved you," says the LORD.
"Yet you say, 'In what way have You loved us?'
Was not Esau Jacob's brother?"
Says the LORD.
"Yet Jacob I have loved;
[3]But Esau I have hated,
And laid waste his mountains and his heritage
For the jackals of the wilderness."

[4]Even though Edom has said,
"We have been impoverished,
But we will return and build the desolate
    places,"

Thus says the LORD of hosts:

"They may build, but I will throw down;
They shall be called the Territory of
    Wickedness,
And the people against whom the LORD will
    have indignation forever.
[5]Your eyes shall see,
And you shall say,

· · · · · · · · · · · · · · · · ·

1:1 [a]Or *oracle*

1:1 Burden (Heb. *massa'*, lit. "judgment" or "oracle") is used in prophetic books to introduce a message that originates from God (see Is. 13:1; 15:1; Nah. 1:1; Hab. 1:1; Zech. 9:1; 12:1).

1:2, 3 God's love is unconditional, personal, and undeserved, but His sovereign choice of Jacob over Esau was tantamount to "hating" Esau. God does not hate in the common usage of the term. Hate is a term used to describe comparative treatment. Jacob (Israel) and Esau (Edom) were brothers. God chose Jacob to inherit the covenant blessing and to procreate the nation upon whom He would set His love. Such choice implied selection for service. Israel was chosen to be the avenue of God's blessing to all the world. Esau remained outside of the Lord's covenant relationship with His people (Gen. 25:29–34; 27:1–40). The Lord was reminding His peo-

ple that by choosing them He had loved them with an everlasting love not bestowed on any other peoples. The fact that "Jacob" was "loved" implies by contrast that "Esau" was "hated."

1:4, 5 The nation Edom was located across the Jordan valley southeast of Jerusalem. The Edomites descended from Esau, Jacob's brother, and thus were kinsmen of God's people. Nevertheless, the relationship between Israel and Edom was characterized by enmity throughout their history. The Edomite destruction is foretold in other books (see Jer. 25:15–26; Amos 1:11, 12: Obad.). Regardless of efforts to rebuild, the Edomites would be unsuccessful because the Lord was against them. God is sovereign even over nations who are not in covenant with Him.

'The Lᴏʀᴅ is magnified beyond the border of
Israel.'

Polluted Offerings

6"A son honors *his* father,
And a servant *his* master.
If then I am the Father,
Where *is* My honor?
And if I *am* a Master,
Where *is* My reverence?
Says the Lᴏʀᴅ of hosts
To you priests who despise My name.
Yet you say, 'In what way have we despised Your
name?'

7"You offer defiled food on My altar,
But say,
'In what way have we defiled You?'
By saying,
'The table of the Lᴏʀᴅ is contemptible.'
8And when you offer the blind as a sacrifice,
Is it not evil?
And when you offer the lame and sick,
Is it not evil?
Offer it then to your governor!
Would he be pleased with you?
Would he accept you favorably?"
Says the Lᴏʀᴅ of hosts.

9"But now entreat God's favor,
That He may be gracious to us.
While this is being *done* by your hands,
Will He accept you favorably?"
Says the Lᴏʀᴅ of hosts.
10"Who *is there* even among you who would shut
the doors,
So that you would not kindle fire *on* My altar in
vain?
I have no pleasure in you,"
Says the Lᴏʀᴅ of hosts,
"Nor will I accept an offering from your hands.
11For from the rising of the sun, even to its
going down,
My name *shall be* great among the Gentiles;
In every place incense *shall be* offered to My
name,
And a pure offering;

For My name shall be great among the
nations,"
Says the Lᴏʀᴅ of hosts.

12"But you profane it,
In that you say,
'The table of the Lᴏʀᴅᵃ is defiled;
And its fruit, its food, *is* contemptible.'
13You also say,
'Oh, what a weariness!'
And you sneer at it,"
Says the Lᴏʀᴅ of hosts.
"And you bring the stolen, the lame, and the
sick;
Thus you bring an offering!
Should I accept this from your hand?"
Says the Lᴏʀᴅ.
14"But cursed *be* the deceiver
Who has in his flock a male,
And takes a vow,
But sacrifices to the Lord what is blemished—
For I *am* a great King,"
Says the Lᴏʀᴅ of hosts,
"And My name *is to be* feared among the nations.

Corrupt Priests

2 "And now, O priests, this commandment is for
you.
2If you will not hear,
And if you will not take *it* to heart,
To give glory to My name,"
Says the Lᴏʀᴅ of hosts,
"I will send a curse upon you,
And I will curse your blessings.
Yes, I have cursed them already,
Because you do not take *it* to heart.

3"Behold, I will rebuke your descendants
And spread refuse on your faces,
The refuse of your solemn feasts;
And *one* will take you away with it.
4Then you shall know that I have sent this
commandment to you,
That My covenant with Levi may continue,"
Says the Lᴏʀᴅ of hosts.

1:12 ᵃFollowing Bomberg; Masoretic Text reads *Lord.*

1:6–14 If a son honors his father and a servant his master, then
God, being the supreme Father and Master, deserves supreme
honor. But the priests were despising God by offering Him defective animals in sacrifice. Such shameful expressions of
"honor" would be rejected by the governor. How much more
God is justified in rejecting them! Yet even while offering contemptuous sacrifices, the priests were entreating God's favor
(see Mal. 3:5, note).

1:10 Because of their contempt for God and the Mosaic Law,
they would be wiser to close the temple doors than to offer
polluted sacrifices. God does not want sacrifices for sin from
people intent on sinning.

1:11 In contrast to Israel, people of other nations will honor the
name of God and worship Him purely. Incense was used in
temple worship to accompany prayers. The acceptable worship of *Yahweh* would extend beyond Israel even to the Gentiles.

2:1–9 Priests were expected to be obedient and lead the people in the way of godliness. They were messengers of God to
the people. The people would not be led to a right relationship with God unless the priests first turned back to the
Lord.

⁵"My covenant was with him, *one* of life and
        peace,
    And I gave them to him *that he might* fear *Me;*
    So he feared Me
    And was reverent before My name.
⁶The law of truthª was in his mouth,
    And injustice was not found on his lips.
    He walked with Me in peace and equity,
    And turned many away from iniquity.

⁷"For the lips of a priest should keep knowledge,
    And *people* should seek the law from his mouth;
    For he is the messenger of the LORD of hosts.
⁸But you have departed from the way;
    You have caused many to stumble at the law.
    You have corrupted the covenant of Levi,"
    Says the LORD of hosts.
⁹"Therefore I also have made you contemptible
        and base
    Before all the people,
    Because you have not kept My ways
    But have shown partiality in the law."

Treachery of Infidelity

¹⁰Have we not all one Father?
    Has not one God created us?
    Why do we deal treacherously with one
        another
    By profaning the covenant of the fathers?
¹¹Judah has dealt treacherously,
    And an abomination has been committed in
        Israel and in Jerusalem,
    For Judah has profaned
    The LORD's holy *institution* which He loves:
    He has married the daughter of a foreign god.
¹²May the LORD cut off from the tents of Jacob

The man who does this, being awake and
        aware,ª
    Yet who brings an offering to the LORD of
        hosts!

¹³And this is the second thing you do:
    You cover the altar of the LORD with tears,
    With weeping and crying;
    So He does not regard the offering anymore,
    Nor receive *it* with goodwill from your hands.
¹⁴Yet you say, "For what reason?"
    Because the LORD has been witness
    Between you and the wife of your youth,
    With whom you have dealt treacherously;
    Yet she is your companion
    And your wife by covenant.
¹⁵But did He not make *them* one,
    Having a remnant of the Spirit?
    And why one?
    He seeks godly offspring.
    Therefore take heed to your spirit,
    And let none deal treacherously with the wife
        of his youth.

¹⁶"For the LORD God of Israel says
    That He hates divorce,
    For it covers one's garment with violence,"
    Says the LORD of hosts.
    "Therefore take heed to your spirit,
    That you do not deal treacherously."

¹⁷You have wearied the LORD with your words;
    Yet you say,

·············

2:6 ªOr *true instruction*   **2:12** ªTalmud and Vulgate read *teacher and student.*

2:5–9 God established that the Levites, who assisted the priests in the temple, would have no inheritance of land because their livelihood would come from the animals and fruits offered by the people (Num. 18:21–24). Nowhere in the OT is there mention of God making a specific covenant with Levi. In the time of Malachi, the people's offerings at the temple were so scanty and of such poor quality that the Levites could not be supported. They were forced to farm the land for themselves; hence the temple service deteriorated further (Neh. 10:37; 13:10). God was commanding that proper offerings be restored so that the Levites might have sufficient livelihood to devote themselves to their work at the temple (Mal. 2:5). In return, the Levites were to be teachers of the knowledge of the Lord and were to lead sincere and proper worship of *Yahweh.*

2:10–12 Mixed marriages were against the Mosaic Law. A divorce broke the marriage covenant, which had been witnessed by God. That the people must marry within the chosen nation was one of the terms of the covenant relationship between God and Israel (Deut. 7:1–4). Foreigners could join themselves to the chosen nation by forsaking their gods and worshiping *Yahweh* alone, as did Ruth the Moabitess (Ruth 1:16, 17). The social problem addressed by Malachi was marriage to foreign women who continued to practice idolatry. In-

termarriage with unbelievers and divorces were matters of concern to Ezra and Nehemiah as well because these acts of disobedience represented dangerous spiritual compromise (Ezra 9:12, note; Neh. 13:23–27, 28; see Mal. 3:5, note). "The daughter of a foreign god" could be a reference to marriage to a foreigner or to the fact that God's people adopted pagan religious practices (Mal. 2:11). Malachi invoked a curse that such unions might produce no offspring, thus cutting off that mixed line in order to preserve the purity of the chosen people ("the tents of Jacob," v. 12).

2:13–16 Divorce was also a problem in Israel. Couples in which husband and wife were both members of the covenant community were ending their marriages in divorce. Throughout the ancient Near East, all marriages were legally binding contracts. Only Israel upheld marriage as a spiritual covenant worthy of life-long commitment. Though the people had permitted and regulated divorce by the Law (Deut. 24:1–4), God expressly rejected the breaking of marital vows in any way (see Matt. 19, Divorce).

2:17 Longsuffering is an attribute of God, but the people had "wearied" the Lord by claiming that evil was good and that God was unjust. The people had drifted so far from God's instructive Law that they were morally confused.

We cannot expect the Church to exhibit more godliness than its leaders.

Mary Lou Whitlock

"In what way have we wearied *Him?*"
In that you say,
"Everyone who does evil
Is good in the sight of the LORD,
And He delights in them,"
Or, "Where *is* the God of justice?"

The Coming Messenger

3 "Behold, I send My messenger,
And he will prepare the way before Me.
And the Lord, whom you seek,
Will suddenly come to His temple,
Even the Messenger of the covenant,
In whom you delight.
Behold, He is coming,"
Says the LORD of hosts.

2 "But who can endure the day of His coming?
And who can stand when He appears?
For He *is* like a refiner's fire
And like launderers' soap.
3 He will sit as a refiner and a purifier of silver;
He will purify the sons of Levi,
And purge them as gold and silver,
That they may offer to the LORD
An offering in righteousness.

4 "Then the offering of Judah and Jerusalem
Will be pleasant to the LORD,
As in the days of old,
As in former years.
5 And I will come near you for judgment;

I will be a swift witness
Against sorcerers,
Against adulterers,
Against perjurers,
Against those who exploit wage earners and
widows and orphans,
And against those who turn away an alien—
Because they do not fear Me,"
Says the LORD of hosts.

6 "For I *am* the LORD, I do not change;
Therefore you are not consumed, O sons of
Jacob.
7 Yet from the days of your fathers
You have gone away from My ordinances
And have not kept *them.*
Return to Me, and I will return to you,"
Says the LORD of hosts.
"But you said,
'In what way shall we return?'

Do Not Rob God

8 "Will a man rob God?
Yet you have robbed Me!
But you say,
'In what way have we robbed You?'
In tithes and offerings.
9 You are cursed with a curse,
For you have robbed Me,
Even this whole nation.
10 Bring all the tithes into the storehouse,
That there may be food in My house,

3:1–5 In their apathy, the people had lost sight of the value of their relationship with the Lord. Malachi reminded them that the Lord was not far off, and He was aware of the sins of His people. He would be coming to purge and purify them of their unrighteousness (see Mal. 3:5, note). God Himself, accused by the people of delighting in those who do evil (Mal. 2:17), would come to judge the people for grievous sins. His purpose was to restore holiness to His people and renew covenant faithfulness. God came and judged the sinner worthy of death when Jesus bore the penalty of that death Himself. The messenger who heralded the ministry of the Messiah was later revealed as John the Baptist (Matt. 11:10–15).

3:2 We can identify with purifying agents: fire for metals and soap for clothing. The refiner's fire is a metaphor used often for spiritual purification (Job 23:10; Ps. 66:10; Is. 1:25; 48:10; Dan. 12:10; Zech. 13:9). The Lord promised to purify Levites in the last days so they could carry out their ministries effectively (Mal. 3:3).

3:5 A comparison of Malachi and Nehemiah shows that both address these issues:
• Perversion of the priesthood (Mal. 1:6—2:9; Neh. 13:4–9);
• Mixed marriages (Mal. 2:11–16; Neh. 13:23–27);
• Problems in society (Mal. 3:5; Neh. 5:1–13);
• Disobedience of principles governing giving (Mal. 3:8–11; Neh. 13:10–14).

3:6, 7 Because of God's character, His people were not consumed, though their sins had made them worthy of death (see Rom. 6:23). Their existence rested upon the covenant promises of the unchangeable God.

3:8–12 Israel was robbing God. God had already provided specific directions for the offerings and tithes (Num. 18:21–24). The tithes were used to support the Levites and their families, who were ministers of the covenant. The tithes being presented, which consisted of animals and produce, were of poor quality and thus reflected a poor attitude. The entire nation was cursed. The people began by robbing God, but in the end they robbed themselves.

And try Me now in this,"
Says the LORD of hosts,
"If I will not open for you the windows of
heaven
And pour out for you *such* blessing
That *there will* not *be room* enough *to receive it.*

[11]"And I will rebuke the devourer for your sakes,
So that he will not destroy the fruit of your
ground,
Nor shall the vine fail to bear fruit for you in
the field,"
Says the LORD of hosts;
[12]And all nations will call you blessed,
For you will be a delightful land,"
Says the LORD of hosts.

The People Complain Harshly

[13]"Your words have been harsh against Me,"
Says the LORD,
"Yet you say,
'What have we spoken against You?'
[14]You have said,
'It is useless to serve God;
What profit *is it* that we have kept His
ordinance,
And that we have walked as mourners
Before the LORD of hosts?
[15]So now we call the proud blessed,
For those who do wickedness are raised up;
They even tempt God and go free.' "

A Book of Remembrance

[16]Then those who feared the LORD spoke to one
another,
And the LORD listened and heard *them;*
So a book of remembrance was written before
Him

For those who fear the LORD
And who meditate on His name.

[17]"They shall be Mine," says the LORD of hosts,
"On the day that I make them My jewels.[a]
And I will spare them
As a man spares his own son who serves
him."
[18]Then you shall again discern
Between the righteous and the wicked,
Between one who serves God
And one who does not serve Him.

The Great Day of God

4 "For behold, the day is coming,
Burning like an oven,
And all the proud, yes, all who do wickedly will
be stubble.
And the day which is coming shall burn them
up,"
Says the LORD of hosts,
"That will leave them neither root nor branch.
[2]But to you who fear My name
The Sun of Righteousness shall arise
With healing in His wings;
And you shall go out
And grow fat like stall-fed calves.
[3]You shall trample the wicked,
For they shall be ashes under the soles of your
feet
On the day that I do *this,*"
Says the LORD of hosts.

[4]"Remember the Law of Moses, My servant,
Which I commanded him in Horeb for all Israel,
With the statutes and judgments.

·····················
3:17 [a]Literally *special treasure*

3:10–12 God asked the people to prove His word because they questioned His holiness and righteousness. If they would bring the full tithe as required, divine blessing would be renewed. God would restore their agricultural abundance, remove pestilence, and increase the respect of the nations for His people. Israel would be a delight and winsome witness to other nations (see v. 5, note).

3:13–15 God's people had become cynical and spoke harsh words against Him. They maintained that the wicked prospered, the proud were blessed, and evildoers escaped judgment from God. They concluded that it was worthless to serve God.

3:16 A few among God's chosen nation still feared the Lord and heeded Malachi's warnings. The Lord was not far off but was so close to His people that He overheard their conversation. Ancient Near Eastern kings customarily recorded the names and deeds of people who were particularly loyal. This loyalty was usually lavishly recompensed (Esth. 6:1–11).

3:17 The Lord's jewels (Heb. *segullah*) is a reference found in ancient covenant contracts in regard to a valuable possession

acquired by a powerful king in covenant with a vassal nation. God was claiming these faithful people as His special possession under the terms of His covenant with Israel (see also Ex. 19:5; 1 Pet. 2:9).

3:18 The people had claimed there was no difference between those who worshiped the Lord and those who did not. The wicked still prospered, and the faithful suffered. But God's people must not be deceived by appearances. The day would come when it would be clear to everyone that there is an eternal difference between those who serve God and those who do not.

4:1–3 The coming day of the Lord would be like a burning furnace, consuming the wicked. For those who feared the Lord, this Day would be a day of joy when the "Sun of Righteousness," the Messiah, would rise with healing in His wings.

4:4–6 The righteous Law came through Moses. It was fitting that Israel's last prophet before the messianic age should call the people to remember the covenant commandments. The promise that Elijah would come to herald the day of the Lord offered hope that God would yet speak to Israel. Jesus identi-

[5]Behold, I will send you Elijah the prophet
  Before the coming of the great and dreadful
      day of the LORD.
[6]And he will turn

The hearts of the fathers to the children,
  And the hearts of the children to their
      fathers,
Lest I come and strike the earth with a curse."

---

fied John the Baptist as the Elijah who heralded the Messiah (Matt. 17:10–13). Moses and Elijah appeared with Jesus on the Mount of Transfiguration (Matt. 17:1–3).

4:6 Malachi's last word to God's people is "curse." Had God left His redemptive plan unfinished, the earth would have been destroyed by God's curse. The promise of an Elijah yet to come offered hope that a curse would not be God's last word. In Jesus, God's grace and not His curse is the final word (Rev. 22:21).

FLOWERS AND PLANTS OF THE BIBLE

God created plants on the third day (Gen. 1:11–13), and, when God created man, He placed him in a garden to tend and keep it (Gen. 2:15). One of the final moments of our Lord's life was spent in a garden—praying and seeking His Father's will (Matt. 26:36). The Bible says that Jesus often brought His disciples there. Every year the spring rains turn the parched and dry hillsides of Palestine into a vivid blaze of wildflowers and bulbous plants. Although ancient writers as well as biblical scholars debate some references to flora as to specifically which species is referenced, the following chart can help you visualize how the plants mentioned in the Bible may have looked.

See also Gen. 1:29, 31; 2:5, 8; Luke 22:39, 40; John 18:1, 2; chart on Flowers and Plants in the Song

FLOWERS OF THE BIBLE

FLOWERS	REFERENCE/ BIBLICAL TERM	DESCRIPTION/USE
Anemone	Matt. 6:28, 29 Luke 12:27, 28 "Lilies"	The single-flowered poppy anemone or windflower covers the hillsides of Palestine with dazzling color each spring.
Crocus	Song 4:14 "Saffron"	Four thousand stigmas and upper portions of the style of the saffron crocus are needed to make an ounce of saffron, a valuable dye in biblical times and even in the modern era.
Cyclamen	Matt. 6:28–30 Luke 12:27, 28 "Lilies"	Also called Solomon's crown and another possibility for "lily of the field." It is often given at Christmas time because of its glorious blooms (pinks and reds) and deep biblical roots.
Hyacinth	Song 2:1, 2, 16 Song 6:2, 3 "Lilies"	Native to eastern Mediterranean where it flowers in the wild with deep blue perfumed spikes.

FLOWERS OF THE BIBLE (cont.)

FLOWERS	REFERENCE/ BIBLICAL TERM	DESCRIPTION/USE
Iris Yellow Flag	Hos. 14:5 *"Lilies"*	In Palestine it grows in masses along streams and waterways.
Scarlet Turk's Cap Lily	Song 5:13 *"Lilies"*	Probably refers to the scarlet lily, since the passage refers to the lips. Grows wild in the woods in Palestine.
Madonna Lily	Song 6:2 *"Lilies"*	Grows wild in upper Galilee. Used in religious paintings to symbolize chastity, purity, and eternal beauty.
Narcissus	Is. 35:1 *"Rose"*	Sweet smelling, it grows commonly in Palestine. Some scholars believe it to be Isaiah's "rose."
Star of Bethlehem	2 Kin. 6:25 *"Dove Droppings"*	This bulbous and delicate plant dots fields and hillsides with prolific white blossoms that resemble dove droppings.
Tulip	Song 2:1 *"Rose"*	The "Rose of Sharon" is believed to be the mountain tulip. The deep red flowers grow wild in the sandy plains of Sharon.

The garden (Heb. *gan* or Gk. *kepos,* lit. "a covered or hidden place") has been an important part of Near Eastern culture as well as a delightful place of repose throughout the generations. In biblical literature, frequent references appear to the garden, picturing an enclosed or walled plot with vegetation and water, shade and quiet, beauty and utility. Enough drawings are extant of ancient gardens to confirm these general features: Planning for aesthetic effect and convenience of using water supplies (Gen. 13:10; Jer. 31:12); Beauty and fragrance of flowers and fruits (Gen. 2:9); Shelter and shade (Song 6:11; Luke 13:19); Pleasure, such as the meeting place for friends (John 18:1, 2) or site for social events (Esth. 1:5); Provision of food (Jer. 29:5, 28; Amos 9:14); Protection (Song 4:12); Retreat for quiet meditation (Esth. 7:7; Matt. 26:36–46).

The garden took time and effort to prepare; yet it offered rewards in return. In Genesis 2, the Lord chose to use the garden for a metaphor to describe the first home He established for Adam and Eve. That home was to be a place of shelter and delight (Gen. 2:8, note).

Biblical gardens include: The Garden of Eden or Garden of the Lord (Gen. 2; 3; Ezek. 28:13; 31:8, 9; 36:35); The Shulamite's figurative garden (Song 4:12–16); Solomon's gardens (Eccl. 2:5, 6); The King's Garden in Jerusalem (2 Kin. 25:4; Neh. 3:15; Jer. 39:4; 52:7); the garden in the palace of Ahasuerus (Esth. 1:5; 7:7, 8); Gethsemane (Matt. 26:36; Mark 14:32; John 18:2).

VEGETABLES OF THE BIBLE

VEGETABLES	REFERENCE/ BIBLICAL TERM	DESCRIPTION/USE
Cucumber	Num. 11:4–6 Is. 1:8 "Cucumbers"	Grown along the Nile, a major food of the poor centuries before Christ. A "cooling fruit" enjoyed in Egypt during the summer heat.
Melon Muskmelon Watermelon	Num. 11:5 "Melons"	Commentators believe the word "melons" refers to both the muskmelon and watermelon since both grew in Egypt prior to Israel's deliverance. Served as an alternative to water, largely consumed by the poor.
Leek	Num. 11:5 "Leeks"	The leek's delicate flavor replaced the stronger tasting onion in cooking. Regarded as a "sacred plant" for its multi-medicinal value.
Onion	Num. 11:5 "Onions"	The "Egyptian Onion" was sweet and mild. It was highly esteemed and worshiped by the Egyptians; it flourished more than any other plant in tomb paintings.

VEGETABLES OF THE BIBLE (cont.)

VEGETABLES	REFERENCE/ BIBLICAL TERM	DESCRIPTION/USE
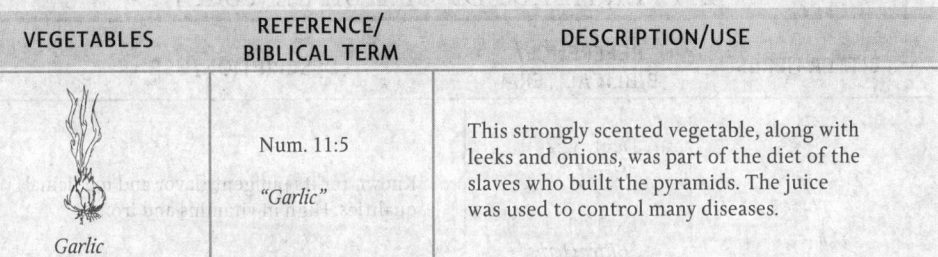 Garlic	Num. 11:5 "Garlic"	This strongly scented vegetable, along with leeks and onions, was part of the diet of the slaves who built the pyramids. The juice was used to control many diseases.

BITTER HERBS OF THE BIBLE

BITTER HERBS*	REFERENCE/ BIBLICAL TERM	DESCRIPTION/USE
Chicory	Num. 9:11 "Bitter Herbs"	Called "liver's friend" by the Egyptians and consumed in large amounts. It was thought to purify the blood and liver.
Dandelion	Ex. 12:8 Num. 9:11 "Bitter Herbs"	Leaves were used as a vegetable and the root for making medicine.
Endive	Ex. 12:8 Num. 9:11 "Bitter Herbs" Gen. 2:5 "Herb"	Bitter tasting, a tall leafy plant related to chicory. Used as salad greens.
Lettuce	Num. 9:11 Ex. 12:8 "Bitter Herbs"	A weedy, bitter-tasting plant with yellow flower heads.
Sorrel	Ex. 9:25 "Herb" Num. 9:11 "Bitter Herbs"	Known to Israelites as sheep's sorrel. Its sharp bitter taste combined well with other greens to improve their flavor.

BITTER HERBS OF THE BIBLE (cont.)

BITTER HERBS*	REFERENCE/ BIBLICAL TERM	DESCRIPTION/USE
Watercress	Deut. 32:2 "Herb" Ex. 12:8 "Bitter Herbs"	Known for its pungent flavor and medicinal qualities. High in vitamins and iron.

"Bitter herbs" are bitter-tasting plants that grew in ancient Egypt and were eaten by Moses and the Israelites during Passover. Many botanical scholars feel these six plants are among the bitter herbs referenced in Scripture. Sometimes the text uses general terms for classification instead of specific species. Today these herbs are more commonly known as vegetables.

HERBS OF THE BIBLE

Herbs were cultivated by the ancients for practical purposes ranging from the making of essential oils and culinary uses to the healing purposes of medicine (Gen. 1:29). The latter was the most important.

See also Gen. 1:11, 12, 31; 2:5, 8–15; 3:23; 1 Kin. 21:1–16; Song 4:12–16; 6:11

HERBS	REFERENCE/ BIBLICAL TERM	USAGE	DESCRIPTION/USE
Aloe	John 19:39 Ps. 45:8 "Aloes" Mark 14:4, 5 "Fragrant oil"	* TP MD	Sap from the leaves is added to other spices to make anointing oil (Matt. 26:7). Used in religious rites and for purifying bodies of the dead.
Coriander	Ex. 16:31 Num. 11:7 "Coriander seed"	A CUL MD	One of the most ancient herbs. Valued for both its seasoning and medicinal properties. The fruit is similar to the "Israelites' manna."
Cumin Tithing Herb	Is. 28:25–27 Matt. 23:23 "Cummin"	A CUL	Native to the Mediterranean region since the days of Isaiah. Used in unleavened bread and for digestive disorders.

HERBS	REFERENCE/ BIBLICAL TERM	USAGE	DESCRIPTION/USE
Dill *Tithing Herb*	Matt. 23:23 *"Anise"*	A MD CUL	Experts agree this "anise" is the dill of our day. Used by the ancients for flavoring and in medicine.
Fennel	Is. 28:25–27 *"Black Cummin"*	A CUL	The aromatic hot-tasting seeds were an Eastern substitute for black pepper. The spicy oil from the seeds increased the appetite and saliva flow.
Frankincense *Incense*	Ex. 30:34 Lev. 24:7 Song 3:6 Matt. 2:11 *"Frankincense"*		A ceremonial plant valued for the gum resin it produced. It symbolized holiness.
Hyssop	Ex. 12:21, 22 Num. 19:6, 18 1 Kin. 4:33 Ps. 51:7 *"Hyssop"*	TP CUL	Believed to be Syrian marjoram. This bushy herb was used by the Egyptians to cleanse the temples. Known as the holy herb because of its use in rituals as a symbol of purification.
Marjoram	*see Hyssop		
Mint *Tithing Herb*	Matt. 23:23 Luke 11:42 *"Mint"*	HP CUL MD	Probably horsemint. Used for cooking, medicine, and worship. Often strewn in synagogues to reduce bad odors.
Myrrh *Incense*	Ps. 45:8 Song 3:6; 4:14 Matt. 2:11 *"Myrrh"*		A gum resin highly valued as a perfume and as an incense. Used as a symbol of Christ's future suffering.

HERBS	REFERENCE/ BIBLICAL TERM	USAGE	DESCRIPTION/USE
Rue Tithing Herb	Luke 11:42 "Rue"	HP O MD	The "herb of grace" was scattered in public buildings for protection against diseases. Valued for its strong unusual taste and for its medicinal properties.
Saffron	*see Crocus on Flower chart.		
Sage	Ex. 37:17, 18 "Lampstand"	HP CUL MD	Cultivated in the Mediterranean for its fragrant oil. Also used in biblical times as a cure for many ailments. Blossoms of the sage plant served as inspiration for the gold lampstand.
Wormwood	Deut. 29:18 Prov. 5:4 Jer. 9:15; 23:15 Lam. 3:15, 19 "Wormwood"	HP O	This silvery white plant is a symbol of bitter experience, calamity, and sorrow.

*Key A—Annual   HP—Hardy Perennial   MD—Medicinal

   TP—Tender Perennial CUL—Culinary   O—Ornamental

The New Testament

Matthew

AUTHOR

Though the author of this gospel is unnamed, the early church consistently considered it to be the work of the apostle Matthew (also known as Levi). Though a Jew by birth, his duties as a Roman tax collector would have made fluency in Greek necessary as a complement to his Aramaic. Recent literary critics have argued that the writer of Matthew used Mark as his source. However, the early church, together with many evangelical scholars through the generations, has argued for the priority of Matthew.

DATE

The evidence for the date of Matthew is inconclusive. Because the book was written primarily to the Jews, many scholars feel it was written before the fall of Jerusalem in A.D. 70.

BACKGROUND

SETTING: A city along the coast of Phoenicia or Syria, such as Antioch, is generally accepted as the place where Matthew wrote his book (see Matt. 17:24, 27). Though a Greek-speaking city, Antioch had a large Jewish population. The book does not state specifically where it was written; yet it is probable that it originated somewhere in Rome's Syrian province.

PURPOSE: The author sought to show that the Messiah, whom the prophets predicted in the Old Testament, had come in the Person of Jesus.

AUDIENCE: The Gospel of Matthew, though one of four accounts covering the life and ministry of Jesus, was written especially for the Jews, who knew the Old Testament prophecies. The promised kingdom was first offered to them, and they were foremost among those responsible for spreading the Good News.

LITERARY CHARACTERISTICS: Matthew is the bridge between the Old Testament and New Testament. It contains more than 50 direct quotations from the Old Testament—more than the other three gospels combined—as well as many other affirming statements such as "you have heard," "it is written," and "that which was spoken."

The book is chronologically arranged, yet with a topical structure. Many of Jesus' teachings, as well as His healings, other miracles, and the parables concerning the kingdom, are grouped together.

THEMES

The major theme is that what the Old Testament foretold about the Messiah has been **fulfilled** in Jesus, and thus the book pays detailed attention to the lineage of Christ (Matt. 1). Because the lineage of royalty was important to the Jews, Matthew traced Jesus not only to Abraham, the father of the Jews, but also to the kingly lineage of David.

The book also delineates what a disciple's life should be. The Sermon on the Mount and related teachings give not only the code of conduct God requires but, more importantly, the quality of the relationship Jesus desired with His disciples.

Related to the discipleship theme is the key phrase, "the kingdom of heaven." This theme encompasses both the daily life of each disciple and the future coming of Christ.

OUTLINE

The Genealogy of Jesus Christ

1 The book of the genealogy of Jesus Christ, the Son of David, the Son of Abraham:

[2]Abraham begot Isaac, Isaac begot Jacob, and Jacob begot Judah and his brothers. [3]Judah begot Perez and Zerah by Tamar, Perez begot Hezron, and Hezron begot Ram. [4]Ram begot Amminadab, Amminadab begot Nahshon, and Nahshon begot Salmon. [5]Salmon begot Boaz by Rahab, Boaz begot Obed by Ruth, Obed begot Jesse, [6]and Jesse begot David the king.

David the king begot Solomon by her *who had* been the *wife*[a] of Uriah. [7]Solomon begot Rehoboam, Rehoboam begot Abijah, and Abijah begot Asa.[a] [8]Asa begot Jehoshaphat, Jehoshaphat begot Joram, and Joram begot Uzziah. [9]Uzziah begot Jotham, Jotham begot Ahaz, and Ahaz begot Hezekiah. [10]Hezekiah begot Manasseh, Manasseh begot Amon,[a] and Amon begot Josiah. [11]Josiah begot Jeconiah and his brothers about the time they were carried away to Babylon.

· · · · · · · · · · · · · · ·

1:6 [a]Words in italic type have been added for clarity. They are not found in the original Greek.   1:7 [a]NU-Text reads *Asaph.*   1:10 [a]NU-Text reads *Amos.*

1:1 In the lineage of the Messiah, Matthew highlighted the calling of one man (Abraham) to father the Jewish nation and the calling of one man from that nation (David) to father the line of the kings. If there had been any doubts about Jesus being a son of David, His claim to kingship would have been invalid. "Begot" can mean direct descent instead of direct parentage (v. 2).

1:2–6 Although the ancestral list does not include everyone, five women are mentioned: Tamar, Rahab, Ruth, Uriah's wife (Bathsheba), and Mary. Tamar, Rahab, and Bathsheba were connected with sexual sins; Rahab and Ruth were not Jewish, and Ruth belonged to the nation of Moab, which had its origin in incest (see Gen. 19:30–37; Deut. 23:3); Mary was an humble Jewish maiden. The fact that Gentile women were included showed in a dramatic way the inclusion of the Gentiles in the blessings of God's redemptive plan. These women were part of God's unique providence in preparing for and bringing the Messiah to His people.

¹²And after they were brought to Babylon, Jeconiah begot Shealtiel, and Shealtiel begot Zerubbabel. ¹³Zerubbabel begot Abiud, Abiud begot Eliakim, and Eliakim begot Azor. ¹⁴Azor begot Zadok, Zadok begot Achim, and Achim begot Eliud. ¹⁵Eliud begot Eleazar, Eleazar begot Matthan, and Matthan begot Jacob. ¹⁶And Jacob begot Joseph the husband of Mary, of whom was born Jesus who is called Christ.

¹⁷So all the generations from Abraham to David *are* fourteen generations, from David until the captivity in Babylon *are* fourteen generations, and from the captivity in Babylon until the Christ *are* fourteen generations.

Christ Born of Mary

¹⁸Now the birth of Jesus Christ was as follows: After His mother Mary was betrothed to Joseph, before they came together, she was found with child of the Holy Spirit. ¹⁹Then Joseph her husband, being a just *man,* and not wanting to make her a public example, was minded to put her away secretly. ²⁰But while he thought about these things, behold, an angel of the Lord appeared to him in a dream, saying, "Joseph, son of David, do not be afraid to take to you Mary your wife, for that which is conceived in her is of the Holy Spirit. ²¹And she will bring forth a Son, and you shall call His name JESUS, for He will save His people from their sins."

²²So all this was done that it might be fulfilled which was spoken by the Lord through the prophet, saying: ²³"*Behold, the virgin shall be with child, and bear a Son, and they shall call His name Immanuel,*"ᵃ which is translated, "God with us."

²⁴Then Joseph, being aroused from sleep, did as the angel of the Lord commanded him and took to him his wife, ²⁵and did not know her till she had brought forth her firstborn Son.ᵃ And he called His name JESUS.

Wise Men from the East

2 Now after Jesus was born in Bethlehem of Judea in the days of Herod the king, behold, wise men from the East came to Jerusalem, ²saying, "Where is He who has been born King of the Jews? For we have seen His star in the East and have come to worship Him."

³When Herod the king heard *this,* he was troubled, and all Jerusalem with him. ⁴And when he had gathered all the chief priests and scribes of the people together, he inquired of them where the Christ was to be born.

⁵So they said to him, "In Bethlehem of Judea, for thus it is written by the prophet:

⁶'*But you, Bethlehem, in the land of Judah,*
Are not the least among the rulers of Judah;
For out of you shall come a Ruler
Who will shepherd My people Israel.' "ᵃ

⁷Then Herod, when he had secretly called the wise men, determined from them what time the star appeared. ⁸And he sent them to Bethlehem and said, "Go and search carefully for the young Child, and when you have found *Him,* bring back word to me, that I may come and worship Him also."

1:23 ᵃIsaiah 7:14. Words in oblique type in the New Testament are quoted from the Old Testament. 1:25 ᵃNU-Text reads *a Son.* 2:6 ᵃMicah 5:2

1:19 The engagement period was legally binding, requiring a divorce to break it. The engagement period lasted as long as a year, perhaps to provide assurance that the woman was not pregnant by another man (see Engagement). Matthew, as Luke, affirms the virgin conception (vv. 18–25; Luke 1:26–38) and attributes that conception to the Holy Spirit (see Is. 7, The Virgin Birth). Only through the virgin conception could Jesus be both God and man and thus make atonement for sin.

1:21 Jesus is the Greek form of Joshua (Heb., lit. *Yahweh* saves); Christ (Gk. *christos*) or Messiah (Heb. *mashiach*) is His title, meaning "anointed one." The royal lineage of Jesus is through Mary, the mother who gave Him birth, and her husband Joseph, who was Jesus' legal father (v. 20). Most important, Jesus was God's eternal Son (see Matt. 2:15).

1:23 The process of naming in biblical times was important in expressing the character and work of the person named (see Is. 45, Naming of Children).

2:1 The account of the Magi is found only in Matthew, the book that presents Jesus as the Jewish King. The "wise men" (Gk. *magoi*) were magicians or astrologers. They probably came from Persia or Babylon (where wise men were part of the priestly order). Historians had predicted a world ruler from Judea at this time. The belief that a phenomenon of stars announced special births was widely held. The names of the wise men are not given, but three gifts are mentioned: gold, associated with royalty; frankincense, a costly incense; and myrrh, a prized perfume (v. 11). These men viewed the phenomenon of stars at the time of Jesus' birth in a distant land, and they could have taken up to two years to reach Judea. The wise men came to the house, not the stable (v. 11), and saw the Child, not the baby (vv. 9, 11).

2:3, 4 The chief priests and scribes were the ones who had supposedly been watching for this event for hundreds of years. Scribes practiced the highly prized skill of writing and specialized in copying official records, Scripture, and commentaries on Scripture. They had developed additional laws and traditions first to explain Scripture and ultimately to be obeyed as Scripture. For them, Jesus did not qualify as the Messiah because He did not fit these new laws and traditions. They were numbered among the chief opponents to the One about whom Scripture spoke (see Matt. 23:1–39; 26:57; 27:17–26, 39–43).

2:5, 6 Bethlehem is the place where Ruth (the great grandmother of David) met Boaz (Ruth 1:22—2:6) and where David was born and reared (1 Sam. 16:1, 12, 13; see also 2 Sam. 5:2; Mic. 5:2). This small hamlet is within walking distance of Jerusalem, less than ten miles away.

ENGAGEMENT *A STEP IN COMMITMENT*

Engagement or betrothal, in Jewish culture, was a formal bond between a man and a woman, almost as binding as marriage itself, yet without physical intimacy. According to the Law of Moses, the penalty for carelessly breaking this commitment through fornication, adultery, incest, or rape was death by stoning (Deut. 22:23–30). Under some circumstances, the engagement could be broken by a bill of divorcement.

The time period for an engagement was usually about a year. Mary and Joseph were betrothed or engaged but did not live together during that engagement period. Joseph is called Mary's "husband" (Matt. 1:19), although the relationship was still physically celibate.

In modern culture, engagement is considered a couple's promise of intent for uniting in marriage, although it is not binding. In fact, engagement is seen as the time of deepening intimacy in which a couple has the freedom to make sure that marriage is the step they ought to take. Becoming engaged is the first step toward the joining of two lives, the blending of two personalities and families, replete with the potential of many generations to come.

See also Gen. 24:1–67; 29:15—30:43; notes on Commitment (Matt. 16); Dating (1 Tim. 4); Dowry (1 Kin. 9); Marriage (Gen. 2; 2 Sam. 6; Prov. 5; Hos. 2; Amos 3; 2 Cor. 13; Heb. 12); Romance (Song 2); Weddings (John 2); portrait of Rebekah (Gen. 24)

⁹When they heard the king, they departed; and behold, the star which they had seen in the East went before them, till it came and stood over where the young Child was. ¹⁰When they saw the star, they rejoiced with exceedingly great joy. ¹¹And when they had come into the house, they saw the young Child with Mary His mother, and fell down and worshiped Him. And when they had opened their treasures, they presented gifts to Him: gold, frankincense, and myrrh.

¹²Then, being divinely warned in a dream that they should not return to Herod, they departed for their own country another way.

The Flight into Egypt

¹³Now when they had departed, behold, an angel of the Lord appeared to Joseph in a dream, saying, "Arise, take the young Child and His mother, flee to Egypt, and stay there until I bring you word; for Herod will seek the young Child to destroy Him."

¹⁴When he arose, he took the young Child and His mother by night and departed for Egypt, ¹⁵and was there until the death of Herod, that it might be fulfilled which was spoken by the Lord through the prophet, saying, *"Out of Egypt I called My Son."*ᵃ

Massacre of the Innocents

¹⁶Then Herod, when he saw that he was deceived by the wise men, was exceedingly angry; and he sent forth and put to death all the male children who were in Bethlehem and in all its districts, from two years old and under, according to the time which he had determined from the wise men. ¹⁷Then was fulfilled what was spoken by Jeremiah the prophet, saying:

¹⁸*"A voice was heard in Ramah,*
Lamentation, weeping, and great mourning,
Rachel weeping for her children,
Refusing to be comforted,
*Because they are no more."*ᵃ

The Home in Nazareth

¹⁹Now when Herod was dead, behold, an angel of the Lord appeared in a dream to Joseph in Egypt, ²⁰saying, "Arise, take the young Child and His mother, and go to the land of Israel, for those who sought the young Child's life are dead." ²¹Then he arose, took the young Child and His mother, and came into the land of Israel.

²²But when he heard that Archelaus was reigning over Judea instead of his father Herod, he was afraid to go there. And being warned by God in a dream, he turned aside into the region of Galilee. ²³And he came and dwelt in a city called Nazareth, that it might be fulfilled which was spoken by the prophets, "He shall be called a Nazarene."

2:15 ªHosea 11:1   2:18 ªJeremiah 31:15

2:16 Herod the Great built the temple in Jerusalem and also completed various palaces and numerous public works projects. His love for power and heavy taxation pleased Rome but alienated the Jews. A man of terrible paranoia, he did not hesitate to eliminate anyone who might threaten his position (see chart, The Family Tree of Herod the Great). Slaughtering a group of Jewish toddlers in a small town would have been typical of Herod.

2:23 Mary received the announcement of Jesus' birth in Nazareth, where she and Joseph had been reared (Luke 1:26, 27; 2:39; see also Matt. 13:53–58).

THE FAMILY TREE OF HEROD THE GREAT

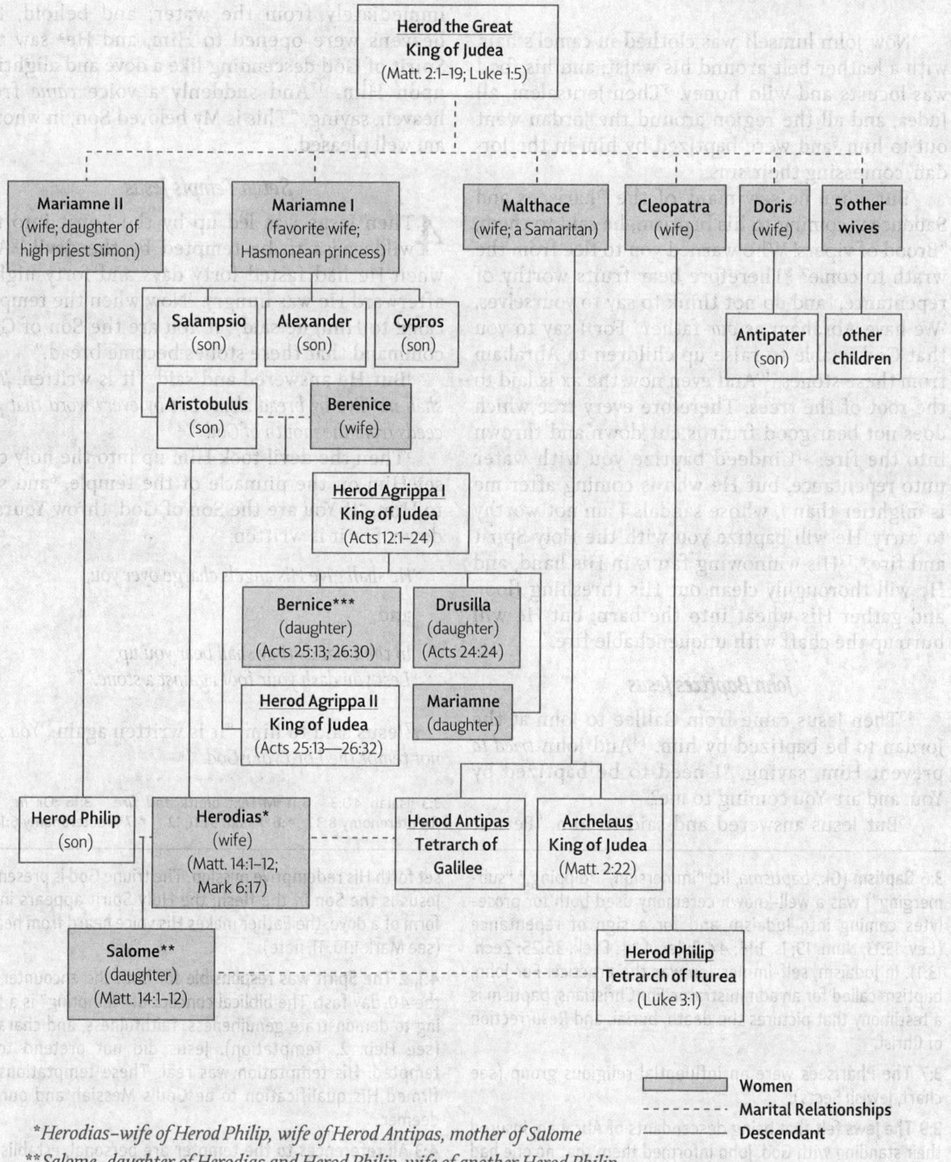

Herod the Great
King of Judea
(Matt. 2:1–19; Luke 1:5)

Mariamne II
(wife; daughter of high priest Simon)

Mariamne I
(favorite wife; Hasmonean princess)

Malthace
(wife; a Samaritan)

Cleopatra
(wife)

Doris
(wife)

5 other wives

Salampsio
(son)

Alexander
(son)

Cypros
(son)

Antipater
(son)

other children

Aristobulus
(son)

Berenice
(wife)

Herod Agrippa I
King of Judea
(Acts 12:1–24)

Bernice*
(daughter)
(Acts 25:13; 26:30)

Drusilla
(daughter)
(Acts 24:24)

Herod Agrippa II
King of Judea
(Acts 25:13—26:32)

Mariamne
(daughter)

Herod Philip
(son)

Herodias*
(wife)
(Matt. 14:1–12;
Mark 6:17)

Herod Antipas
Tetrarch of Galilee

Archelaus
King of Judea
(Matt. 2:22)

Salome**
(daughter)
(Matt. 14:1–12)

Herod Philip
Tetrarch of Iturea
(Luke 3:1)

	Women
- - - - -	Marital Relationships
———	Descendant

*Herodias–wife of Herod Philip, wife of Herod Antipas, mother of Salome
**Salome–daughter of Herodias and Herod Philip, wife of another Herod Philip
***Bernice–daughter of Herod Agrippa I, mistress of Titus, consort of Herod Agrippa II

John the Baptist Prepares the Way

 In those days John the Baptist came preaching in the wilderness of Judea, ²and saying, "Repent, for the kingdom of heaven is at hand!" ³For this is he who was spoken of by the prophet Isaiah, saying:

3:1 John was born to the priest Zacharias and his wife Elizabeth, a relative of Jesus' mother Mary, in their old age. John is similar to Elijah in that he was sent by God, he did not hesitate to point out evil, he offended many, his message called the people back to God's righteous ways, and he pointed beyond himself to the Messiah (see Mal. 4:3–6; Matt. 17:1–3).

"The voice of one crying in the wilderness:
'Prepare the way of the Lord;
Make His paths straight.' "[a]

[4]Now John himself was clothed in camel's hair, with a leather belt around his waist; and his food was locusts and wild honey. [5]Then Jerusalem, all Judea, and all the region around the Jordan went out to him [6]and were baptized by him in the Jordan, confessing their sins.

[7]But when he saw many of the Pharisees and Sadducees coming to his baptism, he said to them, "Brood of vipers! Who warned you to flee from the wrath to come? [8]Therefore bear fruits worthy of repentance, [9]and do not think to say to yourselves, 'We have Abraham as *our* father.' For I say to you that God is able to raise up children to Abraham from these stones. [10]And even now the ax is laid to the root of the trees. Therefore every tree which does not bear good fruit is cut down and thrown into the fire. [11]I indeed baptize you with water unto repentance, but He who is coming after me is mightier than I, whose sandals I am not worthy to carry. He will baptize you with the Holy Spirit and fire.[a] [12]His winnowing fan *is* in His hand, and He will thoroughly clean out His threshing floor, and gather His wheat into the barn; but He will burn up the chaff with unquenchable fire."

John Baptizes Jesus

[13]Then Jesus came from Galilee to John at the Jordan to be baptized by him. [14]And John *tried to* prevent Him, saying, "I need to be baptized by You, and are You coming to me?" [15]But Jesus answered and said to him, "Permit it to be so now, for thus it is fitting for us to fulfill all righteousness." Then he allowed Him.

[16]When He had been baptized, Jesus came up immediately from the water; and behold, the heavens were opened to Him, and He[a] saw the Spirit of God descending like a dove and alighting upon Him. [17]And suddenly a voice *came* from heaven, saying, "This is My beloved Son, in whom I am well pleased."

Satan Tempts Jesus

[4] Then Jesus was led up by the Spirit into the wilderness to be tempted by the devil. [2]And when He had fasted forty days and forty nights, afterward He was hungry. [3]Now when the tempter came to Him, he said, "If You are the Son of God, command that these stones become bread."

[4]But He answered and said, "It is written, 'Man *shall not live by bread alone, but by every word that proceeds from the mouth of God.' "*[a]

[5]Then the devil took Him up into the holy city, set Him on the pinnacle of the temple, [6]and said to Him, "If You are the Son of God, throw Yourself down. For it is written:

'He shall give His angels charge over you,'

and,

'In their hands they shall bear you up,
Lest you dash your foot against a stone.' "[a]

[7]Jesus said to him, "It is written again, *'You shall not tempt the Lord your God.' "*[a]

···················
3:3 [a]Isaiah 40:3   **3:11** [a]M-Text omits *and fire.*   **3:16** [a]Or *he*   **4:4** [a]Deuteronomy 8:3   **4:6** [a]Psalm 91:11, 12   **4:7** [a]Deuteronomy 6:16

3:6 Baptism (Gk. *baptisma,* lit. "immersion," "dipping," "submerging") was a well-known ceremony used both for proselytes coming into Judaism and for a sign of repentance (Lev. 15:13; Num. 19; Is. 1:16; 44:3; Jer. 4:14; Ezek. 36:25; Zech. 13:1). In Judaism, self-immersion was the practice. For John, baptism called for an administrator. For Christians, baptism is a testimony that pictures the death, burial, and Resurrection of Christ.

3:7 The Pharisees were an influential religious group (see chart, Jewish Sects).

3:9 The Jews felt that being descendants of Abraham insured their standing with God. John informed them that no one had special privileges with God, and no one was indispensable (Matt. 21:43).

3:10–12 The severity and immediacy of judgment is indicated by two metaphors: the ax at the root of the tree and the winnowing or separating the grain from the chaff. When tossed in the air, the grain would fall to the ground while the empty shells or chaff blew away. This separation process is also pictured as the division of the sons of the kingdom from the sons of the wicked one (Matt. 13:38), the wise from the foolish (Matt. 7:24–27), and the sheep from the goats (Matt. 25:31–46).

3:16 Through Jesus' baptism He proclaimed publicly His sonship, identified Himself with the people He came to save, and set forth His redemptive mission. The triune God is presented: Jesus is the Son in the flesh; the Holy Spirit appears in the form of a dove; the Father makes His voice heard from heaven (see Mark 1:10, 11, note).

4:1, 2 The Spirit was responsible for both the encounter and the 40-day fast. The biblical concept of "tempting" is a testing to demonstrate genuineness, faithfulness, and character (see Heb. 2, Temptation). Jesus did not pretend to be tempted; His temptation was real. These temptations affirmed His qualification to be God's Messiah and our Redeemer.

4:3 All references to the tempter are personal, establishing beyond doubt that Satan is not just an evil influence but a person (see chart, A Portrait of the Adversary).

4:3–10 Jesus' defense consisted of two things:

• Scripture—The first words of Jesus as He entered His public ministry were, "It is written" (v. 4).

• Immediate obedience.

These same weapons are available to believers. Satan did not attempt to argue with Scripture. Jesus eventually received from the Father all Satan had offered to Him: the provision of bread (Matt. 14:13–21), angels to minister to Him (Matt. 4:11), and rule over both earth and heaven (Matt. 28:18).

MARY'S TRAVEL

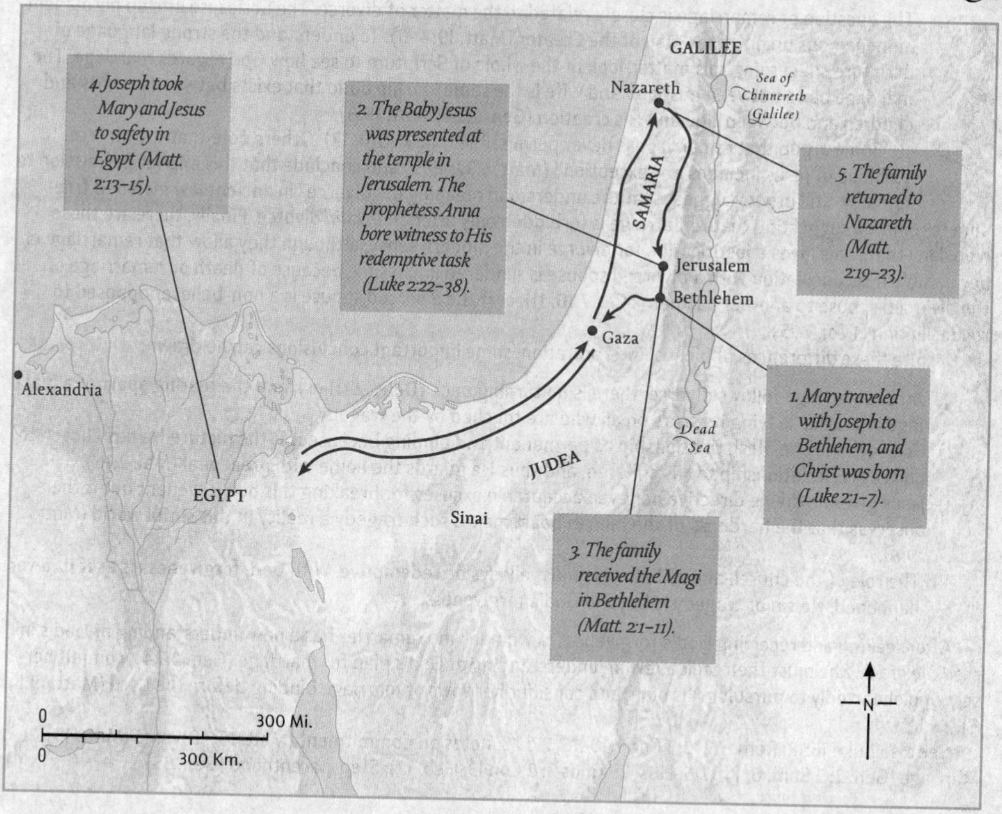

4. Joseph took Mary and Jesus to safety in Egypt (Matt. 2:13–15).

2. The Baby Jesus was presented at the temple in Jerusalem. The prophetess Anna bore witness to His redemptive task (Luke 2:22–38).

5. The family returned to Nazareth (Matt. 2:19–23).

1. Mary traveled with Joseph to Bethlehem, and Christ was born (Luke 2:1–7).

3. The family received the Magi in Bethlehem (Matt. 2:1–11).

GALILEE
Nazareth
Sea of Chinnereth (Galilee)
SAMARIA
Jerusalem
Bethlehem
Gaza
Alexandria
Dead Sea
JUDEA
EGYPT
Sinai

0   300 Mi.
0   300 Km.

—N→

⁸Again, the devil took Him up on an exceedingly high mountain, and showed Him all the kingdoms of the world and their glory. ⁹And he said to Him, "All these things I will give You if You will fall down and worship me."

¹⁰Then Jesus said to him, "Away with you,ᵃ Satan! For it is written, *'You shall worship the Lᴏʀᴅ your God, and Him only you shall serve.'* "ᵇ

¹¹Then the devil left Him, and behold, angels came and ministered to Him.

Jesus Begins His Galilean Ministry

¹²Now when Jesus heard that John had been put in prison, He departed to Galilee. ¹³And leaving Nazareth, He came and dwelt in Capernaum, which is by the sea, in the regions of Zebulun and Naphtali, ¹⁴that it might be fulfilled which was spoken by Isaiah the prophet, saying:

¹⁵"*The land of Zebulun and the land of Naphtali,*

By the way of the sea, beyond the Jordan,
Galilee of the Gentiles:
¹⁶ *The people who sat in darkness have seen a great*
    light,
And upon those who sat in the region and shadow of
    death
Light has dawned."ᵃ

¹⁷From that time Jesus began to preach and to say, "Repent, for the kingdom of heaven is at hand."

Four Fishermen Called as Disciples

¹⁸And Jesus, walking by the Sea of Galilee, saw two brothers, Simon called Peter, and Andrew his brother, casting a net into the sea; for they were fishermen. ¹⁹Then He said to them, "Follow Me,

4:10 ᵃM-Text reads *Get behind Me.* ᵇDeuteronomy 6:13   4:16 ᵃIsaiah 9:1, 2

4:11 Though Satan finally departed, this occasion was not the sum of Jesus' earthly temptations. Jesus was tempted many

other times (Matt. 26:38; Mark 8:33; Luke 22:28; John. 6:15; 7:1–9; Heb. 2:18; 4:15, 16).

REMARRIAGE AN AWESOME CHALLENGE

The question of remarriage is closely related to the matter of divorce. The Scripture lifts up permanent, monogamous union as the plan of the Creator (Matt. 19:4–6). To understand the strong language of Scripture concerning this matter, look at the whole of Scripture to see how God regards marriage. The marriage bond between husband and wife is the same kinship bond that exists between parents and children and between God and His creation (Gen. 2:24; Matt. 19:6).

Some argue that remarriage is never permissible (Mark 10:11, 12). Others note that the divorce teaching of Jesus includes an "exception" (Matt. 5:32; 19:9) and conclude that this implies permission to remarry. Still others suggest that the understood meaning of "divorce" in ancient law included freedom to remarry, suggesting that remarriage is forbidden only after an *invalid* divorce. Finally, there are those who deny that Jesus gives a justification for divorce in the modern sense, although they allow that remarriage is permissible if reconciliation with a divorced spouse is rendered impossible because of death or remarriage of the divorced spouse to another partner (1 Cor. 7:10, 11), or if the divorced spouse is a non-believer opposed to reconciliation (1 Cor. 7:15).

Despite these differences of biblical interpretation, some important conclusions can be drawn:

1) Once remarriage follows divorce, there is no turning back (Deut. 24:1–4), and the tearing apart of a marriage is painful, leaving its scars on all who are touched by the tragedy.
2) God sees the one-flesh relationship as permanent and binding because it is the picture He has chosen to portray His relationship to His children, and thus He guards the home with great zeal (Mal. 2:16).
3) Jesus gives no divine directive nor even acceptable excuses for breaking this holy covenant but rather observes that the hardness of the human heart makes such tragedy a reality in this sinful world (Matt. 19:8).
4) The role of the church and of believers must always be redemptive. With God, forgiveness is as if it never happened. No sin or tragedy is beyond God's forgiveness.

After seeking and receiving God's forgiveness, a woman who remarries has a new understanding of God's incredible grace. She must then seek anew an understanding of God's plan for marriage (Gen. 2:24), commit herself wholeheartedly to pursuing His plan, and consider her vows of marriage binding before the Lord (Matt. 19:5, 6).

See also Luke 16:18; Rom. 7:2, 3; 1 Cor. 7:10–16, 27, 28; notes on Commitment (Matt. 16); Divorce (Matt. 19); Marriage (Gen. 2; 2 Sam. 6; Prov. 5; Hos. 2; Amos 3; 2 Cor. 13; Heb. 12); Step-parenthood (Gen. 35)

---

and I will make you fishers of men." [20]They immediately left *their* nets and followed Him.

[21]Going on from there, He saw two other brothers, James *the son* of Zebedee, and John his brother, in the boat with Zebedee their father, mending their nets. He called them, [22]and immediately they left the boat and their father, and followed Him.

Jesus Heals a Great Multitude

[23]And Jesus went about all Galilee, teaching in their synagogues, preaching the gospel of the kingdom, and healing all kinds of sickness and all kinds of disease among the people. [24]Then His fame went throughout all Syria; and they brought to Him all sick people who were afflicted with various diseases and torments, and those who were demon-possessed, epileptics, and paralytics; and He healed them. [25]Great multitudes followed Him— from Galilee, and *from* Decapolis, Jerusalem, Judea, and beyond the Jordan.

The Beatitudes

5 And seeing the multitudes, He went up on a mountain, and when He was seated His disciples came to Him. [2]Then He opened His mouth and taught them, saying:

[3]"Blessed *are* the poor in spirit,
For theirs is the kingdom of heaven.
[4]Blessed *are* those who mourn,
For they shall be comforted.

5:1—7:29 The Sermon on the Mount is the first in a series of five discourses about the Christian life, both present and future. Its basic premise is that the Christian life has no neutral zones free from God. The Lord is sovereign, all-powerful, and omnipresent (see Job 23; 42; Jer. 23, Attributes of God). Believers do not *make* Him the Sovereign or Lord of their lives; He already *is*. Whether or not they are living as His subjects does not affect His sovereignty; their obedience or lack of it simply determines what kind of kingdom subjects they are.

5:3–12 Beatitudes are found elsewhere in Scripture, most often in the Psalms, though there are usually no more than two or three together (see chart, Beatitudes in the Book of Revelation). The distinctiveness of these Beatitudes is that they

BEATITUDES FOR WOMEN

BLESSED ARE . . .	CHARACTER QUALITY	DESCRIPTION	REFERENCES
those who are poor in spirit (Matt. 5:3)	Humility	Stripped of pride and sensitive to God's ministry in their behalf	Is. 61:1; Luke 4:16–21; 7:22
those who mourn (Matt. 5:4)	Sensitivity	Responsive to personal sinfulness and tender-hearted toward one another	Is. 61:2; Eccl. 3:1–8; Luke 19:41; John 11:33, 35
those who are meek (Matt. 5:5)	Meekness	Demonstration of self-control and submission	Matt. 6:33; 1 Pet. 3:1–7
those who hunger and thirst for righteousness (Matt. 5:6)	Obedience	Desire to hear and do the will of God	Luke 1:53
those who are merciful (Matt. 5:7)	Compassion	Outworking of faith to meet the needs of others	Luke 1:58
those who are pure in heart (Matt. 5:8)	Holiness	Lifestyle of set-apartness, including thoughts and actions	Ps. 24:4–6
those who are peace-makers (Matt. 5:9)	Reconciliation	Forbearance instead of retaliation; forgiveness of wrongs; restoration of fellowship	Rom. 3:25; 12:18; Eph. 4:32; Phil. 1:3–5; Titus 3:2; 1 John 1:7
those who are perse-cuted for righteousness' sake (Matt. 5:10)	Commitment	Steadfast loyalty that cannot be broken	Luke 13:35; 2 Thess. 2:15–17; 2 Tim. 2:3
those who are reviled and persecuted (Matt. 5:11)	Patience	Willingness to endure suffering	1 Pet. 2:19–21; 3:14; Rev. 12:11

⁵Blessed *are* the meek,
For they shall inherit the earth.
⁶Blessed *are* those who hunger and thirst for righteousness,
For they shall be filled.
⁷Blessed *are* the merciful,
For they shall obtain mercy.
⁸Blessed *are* the pure in heart,
For they shall see God.

⁹Blessed *are* the peacemakers,
For they shall be called sons of God.
¹⁰Blessed *are* those who are persecuted for righteousness' sake,
For theirs is the kingdom of heaven.

¹¹"Blessed are you when they revile and persecute you, and say all kinds of evil against you falsely for My sake. ¹²Rejoice and be exceedingly glad, for

are directly related to the kingdom of heaven, and the blessings promised are due to the presence and activity of Jesus (see chart, Beatitudes for Women).

great *is* your reward in heaven, for so they persecuted the prophets who were before you.

Believers Are Salt and Light

13"You are the salt of the earth; but if the salt loses its flavor, how shall it be seasoned? It is then good for nothing but to be thrown out and trampled underfoot by men.

14"You are the light of the world. A city that is set on a hill cannot be hidden. 15Nor do they light a lamp and put it under a basket, but on a lampstand, and it gives light to all *who are* in the house. 16Let your light so shine before men, that they may see your good works and glorify your Father in heaven.

Christ Fulfills the Law

17"Do not think that I came to destroy the Law or the Prophets. I did not come to destroy but to fulfill. 18For assuredly, I say to you, till heaven and earth pass away, one jot or one tittle will by no means pass from the law till all is fulfilled. 19Whoever therefore breaks one of the least of these commandments, and teaches men so, shall be called least in the kingdom of heaven; but whoever does and teaches *them,* he shall be called great in the kingdom of heaven. 20For I say to you, that unless your righteousness exceeds *the righteousness* of the scribes and Pharisees, you will by no means enter the kingdom of heaven.

Murder Begins in the Heart

21"You have heard that it was said to those of old, *'You shall not murder,*a and whoever murders will be in danger of the judgment.' 22But I say to you that whoever is angry with his brother without a causea shall be in danger of the judgment. And whoever says to his brother, 'Raca!' shall be in danger of the council. But whoever says, 'You fool!' shall be in danger of hell fire. 23Therefore if you bring your gift to the altar, and there remember that your brother has something against you, 24leave your gift there before the altar, and go your way. First be reconciled to your brother, and then come and offer your gift. 25Agree with your adversary quickly, while you are on the way with him, lest your adversary deliver you to the judge, the judge hand you over to the officer, and you be thrown into prison. 26Assuredly, I say to you, you will by no means get out of there till you have paid the last penny.

Adultery in the Heart

27"You have heard that it was said to those of old,a *'You shall not commit adultery.'*b 28But I say to you that whoever looks at a woman to lust for her has already committed adultery with her in his heart. 29If your right eye causes you to sin, pluck it out and cast *it* from you; for it is more profitable for you that one of your members perish, than for your whole body to be cast into hell. 30And if your right hand causes you to sin, cut it off and cast *it* from you; for it is more profitable for you that one of your members perish, than for your whole body to be cast into hell.

Marriage Is Sacred and Binding

31"Furthermore it has been said, 'Whoever divorces his wife, let him give her a certificate of divorce.' 32But I say to you that whoever divorces his wife for any reason except sexual immoralitya causes her to commit adultery; and whoever marries a woman who is divorced commits adultery.

Jesus Forbids Oaths

33"Again you have heard that it was said to those of old, 'You shall not swear falsely, but shall perform your oaths to the Lord.' 34But I say to you, do not swear at all: neither by heaven, for it is God's throne; 35nor by the earth, for it is His footstool; nor by Jerusalem, for it is the city of the great King. 36Nor shall you swear by your head, because you cannot make one hair white or black. 37But let your 'Yes' be 'Yes,' and your 'No,' 'No.' For whatever is more than these is from the evil one.

Go the Second Mile

38"You have heard that it was said, *'An eye for an eye and a tooth for a tooth.'*a 39But I tell you not to resist an evil person. But whoever slaps you on your right cheek, turn the other to him also. 40If any-

••••••••••••••••••

5:21 aExodus 20:13; Deuteronomy 5:17   5:22 aNU-Text omits *without a cause.*   5:27 aNU-Text and M-Text omit *to those of old.* bExodus 20:14; Deuteronomy 5:18   5:32 aOr *fornication*   5:38 aExodus 21:24; Leviticus 24:20; Deuteronomy 19:21

─────────────────────────

5:13–16 Both salt and light are forces that change an alien environment permanently. Salt enhances flavor and preserves or slows decay only if the salt itself stays pure. Sodium chloride, a stable compound, cannot lose its saltiness, but it can lose its effectiveness by being diluted. This point is the application for Christians. Light symbolizes purity and divine revelation. If Christians were only slowing the decay, their mission would seem rather bleak, but they are also to be beacons of light to those who will respond.

5:17 The Law and the Prophets refers to the OT. Jesus is the subject and the goal of the OT and the fulfillment of its prophecies (Matt. 1:22; 2:6, 15, 17, 18, 23; 3:3; 4:14–16).

5:21–43 Jesus repudiated wrong thoughts and attitudes with astounding severity. "Raca" (Aram., lit. "empty headed") was a term of dehumanization (v. 22). "Fool" (Gk. *moros*) may also be understood as "rebel." Jesus identified wrong attitudes as triggering other sins (vv. 21, 22). A woman's personal relationships directly affect her relationship (though not her position) with God (see Matt. 6:14, 15).

5:31, 32 The OT allowed a man to give his wife a "certificate of divorce" if she found no favor because of uncleanness (Deut. 24:1). This permission was abused, and men divorced their wives for many different reasons. Jesus rejected this practice because of the sanctity of marriage (see Matt. 19, Divorce).

one wants to sue you and take away your tunic, let him have *your* cloak also. [41]And whoever compels you to go one mile, go with him two. [42]Give to him who asks you, and from him who wants to borrow from you do not turn away.

Love Your Enemies

[43]"You have heard that it was said, *'You shall love your neighbor*[a] and hate your enemy.' [44]But I say to you, love your enemies, bless those who curse you, do good to those who hate you, and pray for those who spitefully use you and persecute you,[a] [45]that you may be sons of your Father in heaven; for He makes His sun rise on the evil and on the good, and sends rain on the just and on the unjust. [46]For if you love those who love you, what reward have you? Do not even the tax collectors do the same? [47]And if you greet your brethren[a] only, what do you do more *than others?* Do not even the tax collectors[b] do so? [48]Therefore you shall be perfect, just as your Father in heaven is perfect.

Do Good to Please God

6 "Take heed that you do not do your charitable deeds before men, to be seen by them. Otherwise you have no reward from your Father in heaven. [2]Therefore, when you do a charitable deed, do not sound a trumpet before you as the hypocrites do in the synagogues and in the streets, that they may have glory from men. Assuredly, I say to you, they have their reward. [3]But when you do a charitable deed, do not let your left hand know what your right hand is doing, [4]that your charitable deed may be in secret; and your Father who sees in secret will Himself reward you openly.[a]

The Model Prayer

[5]"And when you pray, you shall not be like the hypocrites. For they love to pray standing in the synagogues and on the corners of the streets, that they may be seen by men. Assuredly, I say to you, they have their reward. [6]But you, when you pray, go into your room, and when you have shut your door, pray to your Father who *is* in the secret *place;* and your Father who sees in secret will reward you openly.[a] [7]And when you pray, do not use vain repetitions as the heathen *do.* For they think that they will be heard for their many words.

[8]"Therefore do not be like them. For your Father knows the things you have need of before you ask Him. [9]In this manner, therefore, pray:

> Our Father in heaven,
> Hallowed be Your name.
> [10]Your kingdom come.
> Your will be done
> On earth as *it is* in heaven.
> [11]Give us this day our daily bread.
> [12]And forgive us our debts,
> As we forgive our debtors.
> [13]And do not lead us into temptation,
> But deliver us from the evil one.
> For Yours is the kingdom and the power and
> the glory forever. Amen.[a]

[14]"For if you forgive men their trespasses, your heavenly Father will also forgive you. [15]But if you do not forgive men their trespasses, neither will your Father forgive your trespasses.

Fasting to Be Seen Only by God

[16]"Moreover, when you fast, do not be like the hypocrites, with a sad countenance. For they

· · · · · · · · · · · · · · · · · ·

5:43 [a]Compare Leviticus 19:18   **5:44** [a]NU-Text omits three clauses from this verse, leaving, *"But I say to you, love your enemies and pray for those who persecute you."*   **5:47** [a]M-Text reads *friends.* [b]NU-Text reads *Gentiles.*   **6:4, 6** [a]NU-Text omits *openly.*   **6:13** [a]NU-Text omits *For Yours* through *Amen.*

6:9–13 The model prayer illustrates *how* to pray rather than prescribing necessary words to use (see chart, Lessons from the Model Prayer). The Jews did not address God directly as Father but used this personal title to describe God's relationship to Israel or to refer to Him as Creator. "Our Father" was a new title used by Jesus, who chose the term "Abba" (carrying the more intimate sense of "daddy") and invited all who belong to Him to do the same (see Gal. 4:6).

6:16–18 Fasting (v. 18), together with prayer (v. 6) and good deeds (v. 2), are outworkings of the Christian life that are exclusively between the believer and God. Fasting (Heb. *tsum,* lit. "to cover over"—as the mouth; Gk. *nesteia,* lit. "to abstain from food") could be observed completely for a short time or from certain foods for a longer period (Dan. 10:3). The ancient Israelites practiced fasting on the Day of Atonement (Lev. 16:29–31; 23:27–32, in which "afflict your souls" is a reference to fasting). At various other times fasting was practiced as a sign of mourning (1 Sam. 31:13; Esth. 4:1–3), as an act of personal or corporate repentance (1 Sam. 7:6; Dan. 9:3–19), as a means of gaining God's attention on behalf of

suffering or sickness (2 Sam. 12:16–23), in a critical time of decision making (2 Chr. 20:1–18; Esth. 4:16; 1 Cor. 7:5), or as the natural result of urgent prayer (2 Cor. 6:5; 11:27).

Jesus assumed that His disciples would fast. He Himself fasted for forty days to prepare for His ministry and to fortify His soul for His confrontation with Satan (Matt. 4:1, 2). He affirmed fasting as an accompaniment to times of intense prayer (Matt. 17:21). Early Christians fasted in preparation for major events (Acts 13:2, 3; 14:23).

The purpose of a spiritual fast is always the same: to draw the believer closer to God (Joel 2:12–15). From the most humble circumstances, one reaches out to God. The Lord is not moved by fasting itself but rather by the turning of the hearts of His people toward righteousness (Acts 10:30–33). The Bible repeatedly cautions that true fasting is not merely abstinence from food (Matt. 9:14, 15). Fasting must be accompanied by sincere repentance and good works (Is. 58:3–7) and must never be done to impress others, as mere ritualism or as a source of spiritual pride (Luke 18:10–14; see also Dan. 2:23, note; Luke 24:47, note; Jer. 33; Heb. 4; 1 John 5; 3 John, Prayer; Eph. 6, Spiritual Warfare; Esth. 2, Esther).

Often women are overwhelmed by too many things to do (see Luke 10:40) because there are many good choices concerning how to apportion their time (Eccl. 3:1–8). To set priorities is to determine what is important to you and how your time is to be apportioned—that is, who and what will take precedence over other parts of life.

Scripture contains guidelines for God's order (Ps. 119:105, 130):

- • Your personal relationship to Jesus Christ (Matt. 6:33; Phil 3:8);
- • Your commitment to home and family—especially spouse and children (Gen. 2:24; Ps. 127:3; Eph. 5:22, 25; 6:4; 1 Tim. 3:2–5; 5:8; 1 Pet. 3:7) and even to the extended family, as so beautifully portrayed in the relationship between Ruth and Naomi (Ruth 1:16, 17);
- • Your responsibility to employer and tasks assigned (see 1 Thess. 4:11, 12); and
- • Your service to God through ministries in the church and involvement in the community (see Col. 3:17).

Once you have these divinely appointed criteria in mind, you are ready to sort out the opportunities that come (Ps. 32:8) and move forward in the most effective and productive management of time and resources. A very practical way of accomplishing this is to list all the tasks before you, consider each prayerfully as to merit and timeliness (see Col 2:5), arrange them in order of importance, then proceed to do the most important things first (see 1 Cor. 14:40).

To be consistent in your priorities, consider these admonitions: assign God first place (Matt. 6:33); consult with the Father regularly in your quiet time (Ps. 55:17; Luke 5:15, 16); examine your own heart (Eccl. 3:1); and keep yourself spiritually fit (Is. 30:15). Jesus met with the Father in intensive prayer and meditation to determine His priorities and to prepare Himself for each day (see Luke 5:15, 16).

Note also these cautions: Put people before things (see 2 Cor. 8:5). Do not limit your investment in those you love, and others who cross your path, to money and gifts. Look for ways to invest yourself, your time, your energies. Family must be more important than occupation since Scripture clearly states that there is no success if the family is lost (1 Tim. 3:5; 5:8; Titus 2:4, 5). Sometimes you must say "no," as did even Jesus when some seemingly good requests for His time did not fit the overall plan for His ministry (Luke 4:42, 43). The underlying principle in determining priorities is always that spiritual values must overshadow worldly pursuits (2 Cor. 4:18).

See also Prov. 16:3; Luke 12:31; Eph 5:15, 16; notes on Goal Setting (Is. 58); Organization (John 9); Time Management (Ps. 31)

disfigure their faces that they may appear to men to be fasting. Assuredly, I say to you, they have their reward. [17]But you, when you fast, anoint your head and wash your face, [18]so that you do not appear to men to be fasting, but to your Father who *is* in the secret *place;* and your Father who sees in secret will reward you openly.[a]

Lay Up Treasures in Heaven

[19]"Do not lay up for yourselves treasures on earth, where moth and rust destroy and where thieves break in and steal; [20]but lay up for yourselves treasures in heaven, where neither moth nor rust destroys and where thieves do not break in and steal. [21]For where your treasure is, there your heart will be also.

The Lamp of the Body

[22]"The lamp of the body is the eye. If therefore your eye is good, your whole body will be full of light. [23]But if your eye is bad, your whole body will be full of darkness. If therefore the light that is in you is darkness, how great *is* that darkness!

You Cannot Serve God and Riches

[24]"No one can serve two masters; for either he will hate the one and love the other, or else he will be loyal to the one and despise the other. You cannot serve God and mammon.

Do Not Worry

[25]"Therefore I say to you, do not worry about your life, what you will eat or what you will drink; nor about your body, what you will put on. Is not life more than food and the body more than clothing? [26]Look at the birds of the air, for they neither sow nor reap nor gather into barns; yet your heavenly Father feeds them. Are you not of more value

••••••••••••••••••••

6:18 [a]NU-Text and M-Text omit *openly.*

6:24 Mammon (Aram.), a reference to wealth and riches, is offered as one of two options: a relationship with God or with possessions (see vv. 19–21).

6:25 Worry has the connotation of dividing, separating, and distracting. A woman cannot worry and trust God at the same time because worry destroys the single-hearted devotion Jesus described (v. 33).

LESSONS FROM THE MODEL PRAYER

Prepare
- Pure heart and motive (Matt. 6:5–8).
- Private conversation intent on invoking His presence (Matt. 6:6).
- Meaningful communication (Matt. 6:7, 8; Luke 18:1–8).
- Presentation of specific requests (Matt. 6:9–13; see 1 Sam. 12:23, 24).

Pray

PHRASE	MEANING	REFERENCES
"Our Father in heaven" (Matt. 6:9).	Recognize who He is—the PERSON.	Rom. 8:15; see Is. 64:8
"Hallowed be Your name" (Matt. 6:9).	Adore Him because of who He is—PRAISE.	Ps. 18:3; 96:8
"Your kingdom come/Your will be done" (Matt. 6:10).	Seek and do God's will. His Word is the path to finding His will—PURPOSE.	1 John 5:14
"Give us this day our daily bread" (Matt. 6:11).	Ask God to meet even your most mundane needs to accomplish your spiritual duties—PETITION.	Phil. 4:9
"And forgive us" (Matt. 6:12).	Ask God to forgive your debts or your failures to give obedience due Him—PARDON.	Ps. 66:18; Hos. 14:2
"And do not lead us into temptation" (Matt. 6:13).	Seek a way of escape from the evil of temptation—PROTECTION, not removal from any trials but from judgment that comes when you are overcome by trials.	1 Cor. 10:13; James 1:2, 3
"For Yours is the kingdom" (Matt. 6:13).	This benediction is also a doxology—PRAISE AND PERSON.	

This model teaches the manner and method of prayer and shares matters for which to pray.

---

than they? ²⁷Which of you by worrying can add one cubit to his stature?

²⁸"So why do you worry about clothing? Consider the lilies of the field, how they grow: they neither toil nor spin; ²⁹and yet I say to you that even Solomon in all his glory was not arrayed like one of these. ³⁰Now if God so clothes the grass of the field, which today is, and tomorrow is thrown into the oven, *will He* not much more *clothe* you, O you of little faith?

³¹"Therefore do not worry, saying, 'What shall we eat?' or 'What shall we drink?' or 'What shall we wear?' ³²For after all these things the Gentiles seek. For your heavenly Father knows that you need all these things. ³³But seek first the kingdom of God and His righteousness, and all these things shall be added to you. ³⁴Therefore do not worry about tomorrow, for tomorrow will worry about its own things. Sufficient for the day *is* its own trouble.

Do Not Judge

7 "Judge not, that you be not judged. ²For with what judgment you judge, you will be judged;

7:1–6 Judge (Gk. *krinō*) here has the sense of "condemn" or "avenge." The reference is not to a legal judgment but to a critical spirit. The foolishness of a judgmental attitude is illustrated in the hyperbole of the speck and the plank (vv. 3–5).

PETER'S MOTHER-IN-LAW

Each of the synoptic gospels includes the account of Jesus' healing the mother of Peter's wife. The significance of the story is twofold: first, the immediate restoration to health, and second, its symbolic nature. Matthew uses the incident to stress Christ's sovereignty; Mark, to illustrate His servanthood; Luke, to demonstrate His compassionate humanity.

In a home in Capernaum, described by Mark as that of Peter and Andrew, the woman lay ill. Luke, the physician, informs us that her fever was high, and the accounts together tell us that the family requested Jesus to heal her. She was important to them as well as to Jesus. He took her by the hand, her strength returned immediately, and she got up and began serving the guests.

The value of a mother to a family has always been substantial, and Jesus certainly understood this family's potential loss. But His miracle also reinforced His valuation of women in a society where many considered them to be inferior.

The healing also calls attention to Jesus' pity for His own race. He displayed His power to a Jewish mother, a symbol of His deep desire that His own nation return to their covenant-keeping God. It is one more touch of God's indescribable love. The woman responded by serving Him, a stellar example to every woman who feels His touch.

See also Mark 1:29–31; Luke 4:38, 39; charts on In-Law or In-Love; Women and Jesus

and with the measure you use, it will be measured back to you. ³And why do you look at the speck in your brother's eye, but do not consider the plank in your own eye? ⁴Or how can you say to your brother, 'Let me remove the speck from your eye'; and look, a plank *is* in your own eye? ⁵Hypocrite! First remove the plank from your own eye, and then you will see clearly to remove the speck from your brother's eye.

⁶"Do not give what is holy to the dogs; nor cast your pearls before swine, lest they trample them under their feet, and turn and tear you in pieces.

Keep Asking, Seeking, Knocking

⁷"Ask, and it will be given to you; seek, and you will find; knock, and it will be opened to you. ⁸For everyone who asks receives, and he who seeks finds, and to him who knocks it will be opened. ⁹Or what man is there among you who, if his son asks for bread, will give him a stone? ¹⁰Or if he asks for a fish, will he give him a serpent? ¹¹If you then, being evil, know how to give good gifts to your children, how much more will your Father who is in heaven give good things to those who ask Him! ¹²Therefore, whatever you want men to do to you, do also to them, for this is the Law and the Prophets.

The Narrow Way

¹³"Enter by the narrow gate; for wide *is* the gate and broad *is* the way that leads to destruction, and there are many who go in by it. ¹⁴Because[a] narrow *is* the gate and difficult *is* the way which leads to life, and there are few who find it.

You Will Know Them by Their Fruits

¹⁵"Beware of false prophets, who come to you in sheep's clothing, but inwardly they are ravenous wolves. ¹⁶You will know them by their fruits. Do men gather grapes from thornbushes or figs from thistles? ¹⁷Even so, every good tree bears

············

7:14 [a]NU-Text and M-Text read *How . . . !*

Jesus also used the term "hypocrite" (Gk., lit. "to judge under") to describe the insincerity of the Pharisees and scribes (see chart, Jewish Sects). Though a critical spirit is condemned, discernment enables the believer to confront and restore fellow believers who have erred. Dogs were wild animals, and swine were the ultimate example of sacrilege for the Jews. They picture all that is vicious, unclean, and abominable; they describe committed God-haters, of whom we are to be aware and from whom we are to separate ourselves (vv. 15–20).

7:7 Continual prayer is the secret to accomplishment: asking, seeking, and knocking. The goal is not a fixed time of prayer but rather a lifestyle in which prayer becomes like the air we breathe. The promise is absolute. Even if the instructions previously given seem impossible to follow, God will give believ-

ers the ability to follow them when they abide in Him (John 15:4–7). Answered prayer is guaranteed because these prayers are based upon the relationship of the disciples of Jesus with God, who responds to them as Father. Their prayers may not be answered as specifically requested because they do not have the Father's perspective on what is ultimately best.

7:12 Jesus framed this principle, known as "The Golden Rule," positively, rather than negatively. By doing so, He included omissions (what should not be done) as well as commissions (what should be done). This epigram expresses the heart of the Christian life.

7:15–20 The criteria for judging or the means for discerning what is truth and what is not is set forth here. These verses might seem in conflict with the admonition to avoid a judg-

> *Worry . . . compromises your joy, cramps your peace, and confines your freedom.*
>
> June Hunt

good fruit, but a bad tree bears bad fruit. [18]A good tree cannot bear bad fruit, nor *can* a bad tree bear good fruit. [19]Every tree that does not bear good fruit is cut down and thrown into the fire. [20]Therefore by their fruits you will know them.

I Never Knew You

[21]"Not everyone who says to Me, 'Lord, Lord,' shall enter the kingdom of heaven, but he who does the will of My Father in heaven. [22]Many will say to Me in that day, 'Lord, Lord, have we not prophesied in Your name, cast out demons in Your name, and done many wonders in Your name?' [23]And then I will declare to them, 'I never knew you; depart from Me, you who practice lawlessness!'

Build on the Rock

[24]"Therefore whoever hears these sayings of Mine, and does them, I will liken him to a wise man who built his house on the rock: [25]and the rain descended, the floods came, and the winds blew and beat on that house; and it did not fall, for it was founded on the rock.

[26]"But everyone who hears these sayings of Mine, and does not do them, will be like a foolish man who built his house on the sand: [27]and the rain descended, the floods came, and the winds blew and beat on that house; and it fell. And great was its fall."

[28]And so it was, when Jesus had ended these sayings, that the people were astonished at His teaching, [29]for He taught them as one having authority, and not as the scribes.

Jesus Cleanses a Leper

8 When He had come down from the mountain, great multitudes followed Him. [2]And behold, a leper came and worshiped Him, saying, "Lord, if You are willing, You can make me clean."

[3]Then Jesus put out *His* hand and touched him,

saying, "I am willing; be cleansed." Immediately his leprosy was cleansed.

[4]And Jesus said to him, "See that you tell no one; but go your way, show yourself to the priest, and offer the gift that Moses commanded, as a testimony to them."

Jesus Heals a Centurion's Servant

[5]Now when Jesus had entered Capernaum, a centurion came to Him, pleading with Him, [6]saying, "Lord, my servant is lying at home paralyzed, dreadfully tormented."

[7]And Jesus said to him, "I will come and heal him."

[8]The centurion answered and said, "Lord, I am not worthy that You should come under my roof. But only speak a word, and my servant will be healed. [9]For I also am a man under authority, having soldiers under me. And I say to this *one*, 'Go,' and he goes; and to another, 'Come,' and he comes; and to my servant, 'Do this,' and he does *it.*"

[10]When Jesus heard *it,* He marveled, and said to those who followed, "Assuredly, I say to you, I have not found such great faith, not even in Israel! [11]And I say to you that many will come from east and west, and sit down with Abraham, Isaac, and Jacob in the kingdom of heaven. [12]But the sons of the kingdom will be cast out into outer darkness. There will be weeping and gnashing of teeth." [13]Then Jesus said to the centurion, "Go your way; and as you have believed, *so* let it be done for you." And his servant was healed that same hour.

Peter's Mother-in-Law Healed

[14]Now when Jesus had come into Peter's house, He saw his wife's mother lying sick with a fever. [15]So He touched her hand, and the fever left her. And she arose and served them.[a]

• • • • • • • • • • • • • • • •

8:15 [a]NU-Text and M-Text read *Him.*

---

mental spirit (vv. 1–5), but the intervening passage concerning prayer serves as a bridge. Through prayer, believers determine their own faults. Once they deal with themselves, they have access to a clear view of problems in others. Only God is the ultimate Judge (vv. 21, 22).

8:2, 3 Whether the leprosy of that time is the same as the modern disease is uncertain. The disease was destructive, debilitating, and highly infectious. To the Jews, leprosy also was a sign of being cursed (Num. 12:10–12) and resulted in ceremonial defilement (Lev. 13:3; 22:4; see Lev. 10, Clean vs. Un-

clean). Jesus again demonstrated His uniqueness by making the unclean clean.

8:5 Centurions were Roman military officers, typically in charge of 100 soldiers, representing the emperor's authority (see Mark 15:39; Acts 10; 27:3). Usually they pursued military service as a career.

8:11, 12 Instead of limiting the kingdom to the physical descendants of Abraham (as the Jews did), Jesus taught that it was open to all. Faith alone would determine a position in God's family (see Matt. 3:9, note).

Many Healed in the Evening

[16]When evening had come, they brought to Him many who were demon-possessed. And He cast out the spirits with a word, and healed all who were sick, [17]that it might be fulfilled which was spoken by Isaiah the prophet, saying:

"He Himself took our infirmities
And bore our sicknesses."[a]

The Cost of Discipleship

[18]And when Jesus saw great multitudes about Him, He gave a command to depart to the other side. [19]Then a certain scribe came and said to Him, "Teacher, I will follow You wherever You go."

[20]And Jesus said to him, "Foxes have holes and birds of the air *have* nests, but the Son of Man has nowhere to lay *His* head."

[21]Then another of His disciples said to Him, "Lord, let me first go and bury my father."

[22]But Jesus said to him, "Follow Me, and let the dead bury their own dead."

Wind and Wave Obey Jesus

[23]Now when He got into a boat, His disciples followed Him. [24]And suddenly a great tempest arose on the sea, so that the boat was covered with the waves. But He was asleep. [25]Then His disciples came to *Him* and awoke Him, saying, "Lord, save us! We are perishing!"

[26]But He said to them, "Why are you fearful, O you of little faith?" Then He arose and rebuked the winds and the sea, and there was a great calm. [27]So the men marveled, saying, "Who can this be, that even the winds and the sea obey Him?"

Two Demon-Possessed Men Healed

[28]When He had come to the other side, to the country of the Gergesenes,[a] there met Him two demon-possessed *men*, coming out of the tombs, exceedingly fierce, so that no one could pass that way. [29]And suddenly they cried out, saying, "What have we to do with You, Jesus, You Son of God? Have You come here to torment us before the time?"

[30]Now a good way off from them there was a herd of many swine feeding. [31]So the demons begged Him, saying, "If You cast us out, permit us to go away[a] into the herd of swine."

[32]And He said to them, "Go." So when they had come out, they went into the herd of swine. And suddenly the whole herd of swine ran violently down the steep place into the sea, and perished in the water.

[33]Then those who kept *them* fled; and they went away into the city and told everything, including what *had happened* to the demon-possessed *men*. [34]And behold, the whole city came out to meet Jesus. And when they saw Him, they begged *Him* to depart from their region.

Jesus Forgives and Heals a Paralytic

9 So He got into a boat, crossed over, and came to His own city. [2]Then behold, they brought to Him a paralytic lying on a bed. When Jesus saw their faith, He said to the paralytic, "Son, be of good cheer; your sins are forgiven you."

[3]And at once some of the scribes said within themselves, "This Man blasphemes!"

[4]But Jesus, knowing their thoughts, said, "Why do you think evil in your hearts? [5]For which is easier, to say, '*Your* sins are forgiven you,' or to say, 'Arise and walk'? [6]But that you may know that the Son of Man has power on earth to forgive sins"— then He said to the paralytic, "Arise, take up your bed, and go to your house." [7]And he arose and departed to his house.

[8]Now when the multitudes saw *it,* they marveled[a] and glorified God, who had given such power to men.

Matthew the Tax Collector

[9]As Jesus passed on from there, He saw a man named Matthew sitting at the tax office. And He said to him, "Follow Me." So he arose and followed Him.

[10]Now it happened, as Jesus sat at the table in the house, *that* behold, many tax collectors and sinners came and sat down with Him and His disciples. [11]And when the Pharisees saw *it,* they said to His disciples, "Why does your Teacher eat with tax collectors and sinners?"

[12]When Jesus heard *that,* He said to them, "Those who are well have no need of a physician, but those who are sick. [13]But go and learn what *this* means: '*I desire mercy and not sacrifice.'*[a] For I did not come to call the righteous, but sinners, to repentance."[b]

• • • • • • • • • • • • • • • •

8:17 [a]Isaiah 53:4   **8:28** [a]NU-Text reads *Gadarenes.*   **8:31** [a]NU-Text reads *send us.*   **9:8** [a]NU-Text reads *were afraid.*   **9:13** [a]Hosea 6:6   [b]NU-Text omits *to repentance.*

8:28–34 The region of the Gergesenes lay in the Gentile territory of the Decapolis. This fact explains the presence of pigs, which would have been repulsive to the Jews. Jesus was seeking rest, not ministry. Two men are mentioned here, while only one is cited in the record of the same incident in Mark and Luke. Perhaps Matthew had personal knowledge of a second man, or one man may have been more prominent and thus the only one of two mentioned. Demon possession is to be distinguished from mental or emotional illness. It involves evil spirits who, though unseen, indwell and control individuals and their actions. The demons in these verses spoke and were spoken to, but they were no match for Jesus.

WOMEN HEALED BY JESUS

WOMAN	HER FAITH	JESUS' RESPONSE	HER RESPONSE
Peter's mother-in-law (Matt. 8:14, 15; Mark 1:30, 31; Luke 4:38, 39).	None stated, although her family's faith was demonstrated.	He saw, touched, and healed her fever.	She arose and served those present.
All who were sick (Matt. 8:16, 17; Mark 1:32–34).	The people came in faith.	He cast out the spirits and healed all who were sick.	None stated.
The hemorrhaging woman (Matt. 9:20–22; Mark 5:25–34; Luke 8:43–48).	Her faith caught the attention of Jesus.	He felt her touch, saw her, and healed her.	She must have rejoiced in the healing she sought.
The Canaanite woman's daughter (Matt. 15:21–28; Mark 7:24–30).	The mother expressed her faith by her persistence. She worshiped Jesus.	He heard and answered her request and healed her daughter.	None stated.
The infirm woman (Luke 13:11–13).	Her faith was not stated.	He saw, called, and healed her.	She responded to His healing, being made straight and glorifying God.

Jesus Is Questioned About Fasting

¹⁴Then the disciples of John came to Him, saying, "Why do we and the Pharisees fast often,ᵃ but Your disciples do not fast?"

¹⁵And Jesus said to them, "Can the friends of the bridegroom mourn as long as the bridegroom is with them? But the days will come when the bridegroom will be taken away from them, and then they will fast. ¹⁶No one puts a piece of unshrunk cloth on an old garment; for the patch pulls away from the garment, and the tear is made worse. ¹⁷Nor do they put new wine into old wineskins, or else the wineskins break, the wine is spilled, and the wineskins are ruined. But they put new wine into new wineskins, and both are preserved."

A Girl Restored to Life and a Woman Healed

¹⁸While He spoke these things to them, behold, a ruler came and worshiped Him, saying, "My daughter has just died, but come and lay Your hand on her and she will live." ¹⁹So Jesus arose and followed him, and so *did* His disciples.

²⁰And suddenly, a woman who had a flow of blood for twelve years came from behind and touched the hem of His garment. ²¹For she said to

---

9:14 ᵃNU-Text brackets *often* as disputed.

9:14 Eating in biblical times had ramifications beyond physical nourishment or social enjoyment. It could have religious significance when accompanying worship, festivals, and covenant-making. Fasting (or "afflicting" the soul) could also have religious significance such as repentance (Lev. 16:29–31), obedience, responding to a loss (2 Sam. 1:12), preparation for a great event (1 Sam. 7:6), and preparation for communication with God (Deut. 9:9; see Matt. 6:16–18, note).

9:20–22 The woman had several things against her:

1) She was a woman (see The Hemorrhaging Woman);

2) She approached Jesus at one of the busiest times of His ministry; and

3) Her bleeding was considered unclean, and rabbis were not to touch or to be touched by someone bleeding (Lev. 15:25–33).

The other gospels give more details (Mark 5:25–34; Luke 8:43–48). Though the woman was healed when she touched Jesus, she needed an encounter with Him. She is the only person Jesus addressed as daughter.

THE HEMORRHAGING WOMAN WHO WAS HEALED

For twelve years this woman had suffered with chronic hemorrhaging. Visiting physicians had only given her more pain, depleted her funds, and left her worse than when she began. She had tried everything. She could have become a legitimate cynic. Then she heard about Jesus.

Her approach to Jesus was different from most. She came from behind and touched the edge of His outer garment, hoping no one, including Jesus, would notice. We are not told whether she felt unworthy to talk to Him, fearful because of her uncleanness (see Lev. 15:25–33), or concerned that there would be no chance of an audience with Him in such a crowd. We are told that she had enough faith in the person of Christ to believe that just touching His clothes would prove life-changing, and she was right. Though the passage makes clear that her body was healed at the time she reached out to him, that was not enough for Jesus. He wanted to give her more.

Jesus came to an abrupt halt and demanded, "Who touched Me?" The disciples were incredulous. "What was He talking about?" They saw the many, but He saw the one. Power had gone out of Him, but His power had not been depleted. The healing had not been completed. She was more than a hemorrhaging body; she was a needy woman. When this woman contacted God—He knew and she knew, though no other was aware. Jesus would not move until she approached Him.

Her approach was three-faceted: She came forward trembling with fear, fell down at His feet, and told the whole truth. He gave her a fourfold response: He called her "daughter" (an intimate and endearing term), assured her that her body was healed (by her faith, not His clothes), sent her away free from all anxiety (go in peace), and healed (Gk. *sōzō*, "saved," Mark 5:34) her soul.

Between the healing of a demon-possessed man and the raising of a dead girl, this woman's situation could be considered a lesser concern by human measurements, but not by Christ. He stops for everyone.

See also Mark 5:25–34; Luke 8:43–48; notes on Healing (James 5)

---

herself, "If only I may touch His garment, I shall be made well." ²²But Jesus turned around, and when He saw her He said, "Be of good cheer, daughter; your faith has made you well." And the woman was made well from that hour.

²³When Jesus came into the ruler's house, and saw the flute players and the noisy crowd wailing, ²⁴He said to them, "Make room, for the girl is not dead, but sleeping." And they ridiculed Him. ²⁵But when the crowd was put outside, He went in and took her by the hand, and the girl arose. ²⁶And the report of this went out into all that land.

Two Blind Men Healed

²⁷When Jesus departed from there, two blind men followed Him, crying out and saying, "Son of David, have mercy on us!"

²⁸And when He had come into the house, the blind men came to Him. And Jesus said to them, "Do you believe that I am able to do this?"

They said to Him, "Yes, Lord."

²⁹Then He touched their eyes, saying, "According to your faith let it be to you." ³⁰And their eyes were opened. And Jesus sternly warned them, saying, "See *that* no one knows *it*." ³¹But when they had departed, they spread the news about Him in all that country.

A Mute Man Speaks

³²As they went out, behold, they brought to Him a man, mute and demon-possessed. ³³And when the demon was cast out, the mute spoke. And the multitudes marveled, saying, "It was never seen like this in Israel!"

³⁴But the Pharisees said, "He casts out demons by the ruler of the demons."

The Compassion of Jesus

³⁵Then Jesus went about all the cities and villages, teaching in their synagogues, preaching the gospel of the kingdom, and healing every sickness and every disease among the people.ᵃ ³⁶But when He saw the multitudes, He was moved with compassion for them, because they were wearyᵃ and scattered, like sheep having no shepherd. ³⁷Then He said to His disciples, "The harvest truly *is* plentiful, but the laborers *are* few. ³⁸Therefore pray

---

9:35 ᵃNU-Text omits *among the people.* 9:36 ᵃNU-Text and M-Text read *harassed.*

9:25 **Peter, James, and John** were the only ones invited to be at the Transfiguration and at the intimate prayer time in Gethsemane. Perhaps this occasion was considered as important because it was the first time Jesus raised someone from the dead. Jesus had shown His power over diseases, physical infirmities, supernatural beings, and nature. Here He showed

His power over death (see Mark 5, Jairus' Resurrected Daughter).

9:35 **Jesus healed** every kind of sickness, not necessarily every case of sickness.

*People before things, people before projects; family before friends;
husband before children; husband before parents; tithe before wants;
Bible before opinions; Jesus before all.*

Jo Ann Leavell

---

the Lord of the harvest to send out laborers into His harvest."

The Twelve Apostles

10 And when He had called His twelve disciples to *Him,* He gave them power *over* unclean spirits, to cast them out, and to heal all kinds of sickness and all kinds of disease. ²Now the names of the twelve apostles are these: first, Simon, who is called Peter, and Andrew his brother; James the *son* of Zebedee, and John his brother; ³Philip and Bartholomew; Thomas and Matthew the tax collector; James the *son* of Alphaeus, and Lebbaeus, whose surname was[a] Thaddaeus; ⁴Simon the Cananite,[a] and Judas Iscariot, who also betrayed Him.

Sending Out the Twelve

⁵These twelve Jesus sent out and commanded them, saying: "Do not go into the way of the Gentiles, and do not enter a city of the Samaritans. ⁶But go rather to the lost sheep of the house of Israel. ⁷And as you go, preach, saying, 'The kingdom of heaven is at hand.' ⁸Heal the sick, cleanse the lepers, raise the dead,[a] cast out demons. Freely you have received, freely give. ⁹Provide neither gold nor silver nor copper in your money belts, ¹⁰nor bag for *your* journey, nor two tunics, nor sandals, nor staffs; for a worker is worthy of his food.

¹¹"Now whatever city or town you enter, inquire who in it is worthy, and stay there till you go out. ¹²And when you go into a household, greet it. ¹³If the household is worthy, let your peace come upon it. But if it is not worthy, let your peace return to you. ¹⁴And whoever will not receive you nor hear your words, when you depart from that house or city, shake off the dust from your feet. ¹⁵Assuredly, I say to you, it will be more tolerable for the land of Sodom and Gomorrah in the day of judgment than for that city!

Persecutions Are Coming

¹⁶"Behold, I send you out as sheep in the midst of wolves. Therefore be wise as serpents and harmless as doves. ¹⁷But beware of men, for they will deliver you up to councils and scourge you in their synagogues. ¹⁸You will be brought before governors and kings for My sake, as a testimony to them and to the Gentiles. ¹⁹But when they deliver you up, do not worry about how or what you should speak. For it will be given to you in that hour what you should speak; ²⁰for it is not you who speak, but the Spirit of your Father who speaks in you.

²¹"Now brother will deliver up brother to death, and a father *his* child; and children will rise up against parents and cause them to be put to death. ²²And you will be hated by all for My name's sake. But he who endures to the end will be saved. ²³When they persecute you in this city, flee to another. For assuredly, I say to you, you will not have gone through the cities of Israel before the Son of Man comes.

²⁴"A disciple is not above *his* teacher, nor a servant above his master. ²⁵It is enough for a disciple that he be like his teacher, and a servant like his master. If they have called the master of the house Beelzebub,[a] how much more *will they call* those of his household! ²⁶Therefore do not fear them. For there is nothing covered that will not be revealed, and hidden that will not be known.

Jesus Teaches the Fear of God

²⁷"Whatever I tell you in the dark, speak in the light; and what you hear in the ear, preach on the housetops. ²⁸And do not fear those who kill the body but cannot kill the soul. But rather fear Him who is able to destroy both soul and body in hell.

10:3 [a]NU-Text omits *Lebbaeus, whose surname was.*   **10:4** [a]NU-Text reads *Cananaean.*   **10:8** [a]NU-Text reads *raise the dead, cleanse the lepers;* M-Text omits *raise the dead.*   **10:25** [a]NU-Text and M-Text read *Beelzebul.*

10:1 Jesus' disciples first learned about Him; then He sent them out. In each list of the Twelve, Peter is first and Judas Iscariot is last (see Mark 3:16–19; Luke 6:14–16). These men with such diverse personalities, backgrounds, education, and vocations were not the usual choices for a religious movement.

10:9–19 Their mission was to be shared by others who would offer them hospitality and support. The worthiness of a person was determined by his response to Jesus (see vv. 37, 38). To turn the disciples away meant they were turning away the Messiah, which meant the Messiah would turn away from them (see v. 33). Sodom and Gomorrah pictured the certainty and completeness of God's judgment.

²⁹Are not two sparrows sold for a copper coin? And not one of them falls to the ground apart from your Father's will. ³⁰But the very hairs of your head are all numbered. ³¹Do not fear therefore; you are of more value than many sparrows.

Confess Christ Before Men

³²"Therefore whoever confesses Me before men, him I will also confess before My Father who is in heaven. ³³But whoever denies Me before men, him I will also deny before My Father who is in heaven.

Christ Brings Division

³⁴"Do not think that I came to bring peace on earth. I did not come to bring peace but a sword. ³⁵For I have come to *'set a man against his father, a daughter against her mother, and a daughter-in-law against her mother-in-law';* ³⁶and *'a man's enemies will be those of his own household.'*ᵃ ³⁷He who loves father or mother more than Me is not worthy of Me. And he who loves son or daughter more than Me is not worthy of Me. ³⁸And he who does not take his cross and follow after Me is not worthy of Me. ³⁹He who finds his life will lose it, and he who loses his life for My sake will find it.

A Cup of Cold Water

⁴⁰"He who receives you receives Me, and he who receives Me receives Him who sent Me. ⁴¹He who receives a prophet in the name of a prophet shall receive a prophet's reward. And he who receives a righteous man in the name of a righteous man shall receive a righteous man's reward. ⁴²And whoever gives one of these little ones only a cup of cold *water* in the name of a disciple, assuredly, I say to you, he shall by no means lose his reward."

John the Baptist Sends Messengers to Jesus

11 Now it came to pass, when Jesus finished commanding His twelve disciples, that He departed from there to teach and to preach in their cities.

²And when John had heard in prison about the works of Christ, he sent two ofᵃ his disciples ³and said to Him, "Are You the Coming One, or do we look for another?"

⁴Jesus answered and said to them, "Go and tell John the things which you hear and see: ⁵*The* blind see and *the* lame walk; *the* lepers are cleansed and *the* deaf hear; *the* dead are raised up and *the* poor have the gospel preached to them. ⁶And blessed is he who is not offended because of Me."

⁷As they departed, Jesus began to say to the multitudes concerning John: "What did you go out into the wilderness to see? A reed shaken by the wind? ⁸But what did you go out to see? A man clothed in soft garments? Indeed, those who wear soft *clothing* are in kings' houses. ⁹But what did you go out to see? A prophet? Yes, I say to you, and more than a prophet. ¹⁰For this is *he* of whom it is written:

'Behold, I send My messenger before Your face,
*Who will prepare Your way before You.'*ᵃ

¹¹"Assuredly, I say to you, among those born of women there has not risen one greater than John the Baptist; but he who is least in the kingdom of heaven is greater than he. ¹²And from the days of John the Baptist until now the kingdom of heaven suffers violence, and the violent take it by force. ¹³For all the prophets and the law prophesied until John. ¹⁴And if you are willing to receive *it*, he is Elijah who is to come. ¹⁵He who has ears to hear, let him hear!

¹⁶"But to what shall I liken this generation? It is like children sitting in the marketplaces and calling to their companions, ¹⁷and saying:

'We played the flute for you,
And you did not dance;
We mourned to you,
And you did not lament.'

¹⁸For John came neither eating nor drinking, and they say, 'He has a demon.' ¹⁹The Son of Man came eating and drinking, and they say, 'Look, a glutton and a winebibber, a friend of tax collectors and sinners!' But wisdom is justified by her children."ᵃ

Woe to the Impenitent Cities

²⁰Then He began to rebuke the cities in which most of His mighty works had been done, because

---

10:36 ᵃMicah 7:6   **11:2** ᵃNU-Text reads *by* for *two of*.   **11:10** ᵃMalachi 3:1   **11:19** ᵃNU-Text reads *works*.

10:37 God is in a category separate from all else. He does not ask any woman to love her family less. However, even the closest human relationship must not stand between or supersede an individual's primary loyalty to the Lord (Matt. 16:24).

10:39 Sacrifice indicates a deliberate act of bringing a possession to the altar—abdicating all rights, stepping away, and leaving it there. Jesus asked His followers to sacrifice financial security (vv. 9, 10), personal defense (vv. 19–21), physical safety (vv. 22–31), earthly status (vv. 32, 33), family relationships (v. 37), personal agendas (v. 38), and even life itself (v. 39). The rewards promised are great: the meeting of personal needs (Matt. 6:30, 31); the ability to deliver God's words (Matt. 10:19, 20); The Lord's eternal protection (v. 28); value in the eyes of the Father (v. 31); membership in God's family (Matt. 12:49, 50); a role in His agenda (Matt. 10:24–26); and genuine life (v. 39).

11:10, 11 Although John's mission was to announce the coming of the Messiah, his understanding was veiled. The disciples who witnessed the Crucifixion, the Resurrection, the Ascension, and the glorification of Jesus had an even greater message to share.

WOMEN AND THE PARABLES OF JESUS

PARABLE	AUDIENCE	APPLICATION
The lamp under a basket (Matt. 5:14–16; Mark 4:21, 22; Luke 8:16, 17).	To the disciples.	Life and words should give personal testimony to God's redemptive and transforming grace.
The marriage (Matt. 9:15; Mark 2:19, 20; Luke 5:34, 35).	To the Pharisees and the disciples of John.	Joy will be found in Christ's companionship.
The patched garment (Matt. 9:16; Mark 2:21; Luke 5:36).	To the Pharisees and the disciples of John.	Jesus did not come to adapt to the old order of legalism but to make all things new.
The children in the marketplace (Matt. 11:16, 17; Luke 7:31, 32).	To the multitudes concerning John the Baptist.	Those who rejected Jesus and John could not be pleased. Beware of focusing on personal whims.
The leaven (Matt. 13:33; Luke 13:20, 21).	To the multitude on the seashore.	Beware of sin that makes its way into life to corrupt and draw away from the good and true.
The pearl of great price (Matt. 13:45, 46).	To the disciples.	The relative value of the gospel exceeded all else.
The wedding garment (Matt. 22:10–14).	To the chief priests and the Pharisees.	Keep your life pure and holy.
The wise and foolish virgins (Matt. 25:1–13).	To the disciples on the Mount of Olives.	Always be prepared and watchful.
The wedding feast (Matt. 22:2–9; Luke 14:16–23).	To the chief priests and the Pharisees.	Do not reject God's invitation to salvation.
The lost coin** (Luke 15:8–10).	To the Pharisees and scribes.	Remember Christ's love for sinners and His determination to draw them to Himself.
The persistent widow (Luke 18:1–8).	To the disciples.	Persevere in prayer.

**Biblical women often wore a frontlet (Heb. semedi) on their foreheads. This adornment was made of coins (perhaps part of the woman's dowry) and signified betrothal or marriage. The monetary value of the coins was not as important as the sentimental value and symbolism of commitment.*

A parable is a lesson from daily life that teaches a spiritual truth. Jesus often told parables to provide an understanding of life, especially life in God's kingdom. Thirty-five percent of all gospel teaching is written in parables.

they did not repent: [21]"Woe to you, Chorazin! Woe to you, Bethsaida! For if the mighty works which were done in you had been done in Tyre and Sidon, they would have repented long ago in sackcloth and ashes. [22]But I say to you, it will be more tolerable for Tyre and Sidon in the day of judgment than for you. [23]And you, Capernaum, who are exalted to heaven, will be[a] brought down to Hades; for if the mighty works which were done in you had been done in Sodom, it would have remained until this day. [24]But I say to you that it shall be more tolerable for the land of Sodom in the day of judgment than for you."

Jesus Gives True Rest

[25]At that time Jesus answered and said, "I thank You, Father, Lord of heaven and earth, that You have hidden these things from *the* wise and prudent and have revealed them to babes. [26]Even so, Father, for so it seemed good in Your sight. [27]All things have been delivered to Me by My Father, and no one knows the Son except the Father. Nor does anyone know the Father except the Son, and *the one* to whom the Son wills to reveal *Him.* [28]Come to Me, all *you* who labor and are heavy laden, and I will give you rest. [29]Take My yoke upon you and learn from Me, for I am gentle and lowly in heart, and you will find rest for your souls. [30]For My yoke *is* easy and My burden is light."

Jesus Is Lord of the Sabbath

12 At that time Jesus went through the grainfields on the Sabbath. And His disciples were hungry, and began to pluck heads of grain and to eat. [2]And when the Pharisees saw *it,* they said to Him, "Look, Your disciples are doing what is not lawful to do on the Sabbath!"

[3]But He said to them, "Have you not read what David did when he was hungry, he and those who were with him: [4]how he entered the house of God and ate the showbread which was not lawful for him to eat, nor for those who were with him, but only for the priests? [5]Or have you not read in the law that on the Sabbath the priests in the temple profane the Sabbath, and are blameless? [6]Yet I say to you that in this place there is *One* greater than the temple. [7]But if you had known what *this* means, '*I desire mercy and not sacrifice,*'[a] you would not have condemned the guiltless. [8]For the Son of Man is Lord even[a] of the Sabbath."

Healing on the Sabbath

[9]Now when He had departed from there, He went into their synagogue. [10]And behold, there was a man who had a withered hand. And they asked Him, saying, "Is it lawful to heal on the Sabbath?"—that they might accuse Him.

[11]Then He said to them, "What man is there among you who has one sheep, and if it falls into a pit on the Sabbath, will not lay hold of it and lift *it* out? [12]Of how much more value then is a man than a sheep? Therefore it is lawful to do good on the Sabbath." [13]Then He said to the man, "Stretch out your hand." And he stretched *it* out, and it was restored as whole as the other. [14]Then the Pharisees went out and plotted against Him, how they might destroy Him.

Behold, My Servant

[15]But when Jesus knew *it,* He withdrew from there. And great multitudes[a] followed Him, and He healed them all. [16]Yet He warned them not to make Him known, [17]that it might be fulfilled which was spoken by Isaiah the prophet, saying:

[18]"Behold! My Servant whom I have chosen,
    My Beloved in whom My soul is well pleased!
    I will put My Spirit upon Him,
    And He will declare justice to the Gentiles.
[19]He will not quarrel nor cry out,
    Nor will anyone hear His voice in the streets.
[20]A bruised reed He will not break,
    And smoking flax He will not quench,
    Till He sends forth justice to victory;
[21]And in His name Gentiles will trust."[a]

•••••••••••••••••••

11:23 [a]NU-Text reads *will you be exalted to heaven? No, you will be.*
12:7 [a]Hosea 6:6   12:8 [a]NU-Text and M-Text omit *even.*   12:15 [a]NU-Text brackets *multitudes* as disputed.   12:21 [a]Isaiah 42:1–4

11:25 The kingdom Jesus offered is available and understandable to anyone who is interested. The "wise and prudent" were those who were self-sufficient and prided themselves on their great understanding of spiritual things (see Matt. 9:12).

11:27 Jesus claimed to have an exclusive relationship with the Father and to be the exclusive Way to the Father (see John 10:15; 14:6).

11:28, 29 Jesus is the touchstone for everything. Individuals are to "come" and "take" His yoke, and He does the rest. A person who labors is struggling, and one with a heavy burden is overloaded. The yoke was a double harness in which two animals pulled together. Often, one harness was larger and meant for the stronger, more experienced animal, while the smaller was used for the animal being trained. The yoke of Jesus clearly implies that even though individuals are free from the Law, they are not to make their own rules. Rather, they are to be harnessed to Him, living life His way.

12:1–8 The yoke the religious leaders had put on the people is illustrated. The rules God gave concerning the Sabbath were few and to the point. By contrast, the Jewish additions were numerous and detailed. At the heart of this system was an effort to manipulate God. The idea was that if one could keep and enforce all the added rules, God would have no choice but to bless Israel. This religious system was given precedence over everything, including God's glory and the welfare of His people.

*A child's security is based not on how much his parents love him,
but on how much his parents love each other.*

Susan Alexander Yates

A House Divided Cannot Stand

22Then one was brought to Him who was demon-possessed, blind and mute; and He healed him, so that the blind and[a] mute man both spoke and saw. 23And all the multitudes were amazed and said, "Could this be the Son of David?"

24Now when the Pharisees heard *it* they said, "This *fellow* does not cast out demons except by Beelzebub,[a] the ruler of the demons."

25But Jesus knew their thoughts, and said to them: "Every kingdom divided against itself is brought to desolation, and every city or house divided against itself will not stand. 26If Satan casts out Satan, he is divided against himself. How then will his kingdom stand? 27And if I cast out demons by Beelzebub, by whom do your sons cast *them* out? Therefore they shall be your judges. 28But if I cast out demons by the Spirit of God, surely the kingdom of God has come upon you. 29Or how can one enter a strong man's house and plunder his goods, unless he first binds the strong man? And then he will plunder his house. 30He who is not with Me is against Me, and he who does not gather with Me scatters abroad.

The Unpardonable Sin

31"Therefore I say to you, every sin and blasphemy will be forgiven men, but the blasphemy *against* the Spirit will not be forgiven men. 32Anyone who speaks a word against the Son of Man, it will be forgiven him; but whoever speaks against the Holy Spirit, it will not be forgiven him, either in this age or in the *age* to come.

A Tree Known by Its Fruit

33"Either make the tree good and its fruit good, or else make the tree bad and its fruit bad; for a tree is known by *its* fruit. 34Brood of vipers! How can you, being evil, speak good things? For out of the abundance of the heart the mouth speaks. 35A good man out of the good treasure of his heart[a] brings forth good things, and an evil man out of the evil treasure brings forth evil things. 36But I say to you that for every idle word men may speak, they will give account of it in the day of judgment. 37For by your words you will be justified, and by your words you will be condemned."

The Scribes and Pharisees Ask for a Sign

38Then some of the scribes and Pharisees answered, saying, "Teacher, we want to see a sign from You."

39But He answered and said to them, "An evil and adulterous generation seeks after a sign, and no sign will be given to it except the sign of the prophet Jonah. 40For as Jonah was three days and three nights in the belly of the great fish, so will the Son of Man be three days and three nights in the heart of the earth. 41The men of Nineveh will rise up in the judgment with this generation and condemn it, because they repented at the preaching of Jonah; and indeed a greater than Jonah *is* here. 42The queen of the South will rise up in the judgment with this generation and condemn it, for she came from the ends of the earth to hear the wisdom of Solomon; and indeed a greater than Solomon *is* here.

An Unclean Spirit Returns

43"When an unclean spirit goes out of a man, he goes through dry places, seeking rest, and finds none. 44Then he says, 'I will return to my house from which I came.' And when he comes, he finds *it* empty, swept, and put in order. 45Then he goes and takes with him seven other spirits more wicked than himself, and they enter and dwell there; and the last *state* of that man is worse than

---

12:22 [a]NU-Text omits *blind and.*   **12:24** [a]NU-Text and M-Text read *Beelzebul.*   **12:35** [a]NU-Text and M-Text omit *of his heart.*

12:31 The unpardonable sin is defined as continually attributing the work of the Holy Spirit to Satan in full knowledge that the work is God's. All sin can and will be forgiven when there is genuine repentance. Even blasphemy, or profaning God's name in some way, can be forgiven when God's forgiveness is sought. However, blasphemy of the Holy Spirit ascribes to Satan what is done by God, and that cannot be forgiven. To be against Jesus in this way requires that the perpetrator know precisely what he is doing and knowingly and willingly credit Satan rather than the Holy Spirit with the work of God. Why would someone do this? Because to admit these miracles were from God would require acknowledging and following Jesus as Messiah, resulting in abandoning his own way (see Is. 53:6).

12:38–40 In the face of miracles, healings, and deliverances from demon possession, the Pharisees and scribes wanted yet another "sign." They were not seeking the truth but were seeking to entrap. As He often did, Jesus gave new meaning to a simple historical event with which His hearers were familiar (Jon. 1:17—2:10). The remarkable deliverance of Jonah from the fish after three days was presented as a precursor of Jesus' death, burial, and His Resurrection on the third day (Matt. 12:40).

the first. So shall it also be with this wicked generation."

Jesus' Mother and Brothers Send for Him

[46]While He was still talking to the multitudes, behold, His mother and brothers stood outside, seeking to speak with Him. [47]Then one said to Him, "Look, Your mother and Your brothers are standing outside, seeking to speak with You."

[48]But He answered and said to the one who told Him, "Who is My mother and who are My brothers?" [49]And He stretched out His hand toward His disciples and said, "Here are My mother and My brothers! [50]For whoever does the will of My Father in heaven is My brother and sister and mother."

The Parable of the Sower

13[On] the same day Jesus went out of the house and sat by the sea. [2]And great multitudes were gathered together to Him, so that He got into a boat and sat; and the whole multitude stood on the shore.

[3]Then He spoke many things to them in parables, saying: "Behold, a sower went out to sow. [4]And as he sowed, some *seed* fell by the wayside; and the birds came and devoured them. [5]Some fell on stony places, where they did not have much earth; and they immediately sprang up because they had no depth of earth. [6]But when the sun was up they were scorched, and because they had no root they withered away. [7]And some fell among thorns, and the thorns sprang up and choked them. [8]But others fell on good ground and yielded a crop: some a hundredfold, some sixty, some thirty. [9]He who has ears to hear, let him hear!"

The Purpose of Parables

[10]And the disciples came and said to Him, "Why do You speak to them in parables?"

[11]He answered and said to them, "Because it has been given to you to know the mysteries of the kingdom of heaven, but to them it has not been given. [12]For whoever has, to him more will be given, and he will have abundance; but whoever does not have, even what he has will be taken away from him. [13]Therefore I speak to them in parables, because seeing they do not see, and hearing they do not hear, nor do they understand. [14]And in them the prophecy of Isaiah is fulfilled, which says:

'Hearing you will hear and shall not understand,
  And seeing you will see and not perceive;
[15]For the hearts of this people have grown dull.
  Their ears are hard of hearing,
  And their eyes they have closed,
  Lest they should see with their eyes and hear with
    their ears,
  Lest they should understand with their hearts and
    turn,
  So that I should[a] heal them.'[b]

[16]But blessed *are* your eyes for they see, and your ears for they hear; [17]for assuredly, I say to you that many prophets and righteous *men* desired to see what you see, and did not see *it*, and to hear what you hear, and did not hear *it*.

The Parable of the Sower Explained

[18]"Therefore hear the parable of the sower: [19]When anyone hears the word of the kingdom, and does not understand *it*, then the wicked *one* comes and snatches away what was sown in his heart. This is he who received seed by the wayside. [20]But he who received the seed on stony places, this is he who hears the word and immediately receives it with joy; [21]yet he has no root in himself, but endures only for a while. For when tribulation or persecution arises because of the word, immediately he stumbles. [22]Now he who received seed among the thorns is he who hears the word, and the cares of this world and the deceitfulness of riches choke the word, and he becomes

·····················
13:15 [a]NU-Text and M-Text read *would*. [b]Isaiah 6:9, 10

12:46–50 Jesus was not diminishing the importance of family ties, nor was He anything other than caring and courteous in relating to His mother and other family members (see Matt. 10:37, note). Rather, He introduced an entirely new category of spiritual commitment. Jesus knew that He must give priority to doing the Father's will.

13:3 Parables (Gk. *parabolē*, lit. "a placing beside") are simple, short stories in the form of a "type," "figure," or "illustration" with two levels of meaning. They present a comparison or contrast in order to stimulate thought, decision, and action. Parables are the most difficult yet powerful form of literature to create (see chart, Women and the Parables of Jesus). Their power comes both in the simplicity and brevity of their teaching as well as in the memory tool they provide. Approximately one-third of Jesus' teaching was done in parables that revealed the nature of the kingdom of God. Here, the first four

were given to the general public, and the last four were given to the disciples.

13:3–9 The foundational parable is set apart from the others since it is the key to the rest. The kingdom of God that Jesus offered to the Jews involved their receiving this message. The parable of the soils is a parable of hearing. This parable warned that unless the mind and the heart would hear and accept the Word of God, the teaching of parables would be meaningless.

13:10–15 Jesus' parables were a teaching method designed to reveal spiritual truths in such a way that those who wanted to respond would understand and receive more (vv. 9, 12, 43). Those who chose not to respond would not completely understand, and what little understanding they did have would disappear.

Proper parenting God's way is to ponder and pray.

Joyce Rogers

unfruitful. ²³But he who received seed on the good ground is he who hears the word and understands *it*, who indeed bears fruit and produces: some a hundredfold, some sixty, some thirty."

The Parable of the Wheat and the Tares

²⁴Another parable He put forth to them, saying: "The kingdom of heaven is like a man who sowed good seed in his field; ²⁵but while men slept, his enemy came and sowed tares among the wheat and went his way. ²⁶But when the grain had sprouted and produced a crop, then the tares also appeared. ²⁷So the servants of the owner came and said to him, 'Sir, did you not sow good seed in your field? How then does it have tares?' ²⁸He said to them, 'An enemy has done this.' The servants said to him, 'Do you want us then to go and gather them up?' ²⁹But he said, 'No, lest while you gather up the tares you also uproot the wheat with them. ³⁰Let both grow together until the harvest, and at the time of harvest I will say to the reapers, "First gather together the tares and bind them in bundles to burn them, but gather the wheat into my barn." ' "

The Parable of the Mustard Seed

³¹Another parable He put forth to them, saying: "The kingdom of heaven is like a mustard seed, which a man took and sowed in his field, ³²which indeed is the least of all the seeds; but when it is grown it is greater than the herbs and becomes a tree, so that the birds of the air come and nest in its branches."

The Parable of the Leaven

³³Another parable He spoke to them: "The kingdom of heaven is like leaven, which a woman took and hid in three measures[a] of meal till it was all leavened."

Prophecy and the Parables

³⁴All these things Jesus spoke to the multitude in parables; and without a parable He did not speak to them, ³⁵that it might be fulfilled which was spoken by the prophet, saying:

*"I will open My mouth in parables;
I will utter things kept secret from the foundation of
the world."[a]*

The Parable of the Tares Explained

³⁶Then Jesus sent the multitude away and went into the house. And His disciples came to Him, saying, "Explain to us the parable of the tares of the field."

³⁷He answered and said to them: "He who sows the good seed is the Son of Man. ³⁸The field is the world, the good seeds are the sons of the kingdom, but the tares are the sons of the wicked *one.* ³⁹The enemy who sowed them is the devil, the harvest is the end of the age, and the reapers are the angels. ⁴⁰Therefore as the tares are gathered and burned in the fire, so it will be at the end of this age. ⁴¹The Son of Man will send out His angels, and they will gather out of His kingdom all things that offend, and those who practice lawlessness, ⁴²and will cast them into the furnace of fire. There will be wailing and gnashing of teeth. ⁴³Then the righteous will shine forth as the sun in the kingdom of their Father. He who has ears to hear, let him hear!

The Parable of the Hidden Treasure

⁴⁴"Again, the kingdom of heaven is like treasure hidden in a field, which a man found and hid; and for joy over it he goes and sells all that he has and buys that field.

The Parable of the Pearl of Great Price

⁴⁵"Again, the kingdom of heaven is like a merchant seeking beautiful pearls, ⁴⁶who, when he had found one pearl of great price, went and sold all that he had and bought it.

The Parable of the Dragnet

⁴⁷"Again, the kingdom of heaven is like a dragnet that was cast into the sea and gathered some of every kind, ⁴⁸which, when it was full, they drew to shore; and they sat down and gathered the good into vessels, but threw the bad away. ⁴⁹So it will be at the end of the age. The angels will come forth, separate the wicked from among the just, ⁵⁰and cast them into the furnace of fire. There will be wailing and gnashing of teeth."

⁵¹Jesus said to them,[a] "Have you understood all these things?"

They said to Him, "Yes, Lord."[b]

⁵²Then He said to them, "Therefore every scribe instructed concerning[a] the kingdom of heaven is like a householder who brings out of his treasure *things* new and old."

13:33 [a]Greek *sata*, approximately two pecks in all   **13:35** [a]Psalm 78:2
13:51 [a]NU-Text omits *Jesus said to them.* [b]NU-Text omits *Lord.*
13:52 [a]Or *for*

HERODIAS AND SALOME

A Manipulative Mother and Seductive Daughter

Herodias, who lived in Tiberias, the capital city built by her husband on the southwest shore of the Sea of Galilee, was a woman out of control. Crafty, ambitious, greedy, and politically astute, Herodias would stop at nothing to attain what she wanted.

Herodias and her first husband, her uncle Philip, had a daughter named Salome. When Herod Antipas, the brother of Philip and the stepbrother of Herodias' father Aristobulus, visited Philip, he and Herodias were immediately attracted to one another. Herod Antipas was a far more powerful man than Philip. Herodias saw her chance for more power, a better position, and an increase in wealth. She insisted Herod divorce his wife; she divorced her husband, and they married. This incestuous marriage was very offensive to the Jews.

Herodias definitely brought out the worst in Herod as is apparent in the account of the beheading of the fearless preacher John the Baptist, the only one who dared to stand up and reprove this unscrupulous couple. Herodias hated John the Baptist because he did not hesitate publicly to call her alliance with Herod "sin." She wanted to sentence John to death (Mark 6:19), but Herod was awed and fascinated by John. He liked to hear him speak, even though John confronted him with the truth, and he feared the reaction of the people if this popular preacher were harmed.

Herodias' resentment and anger festered like a sore. Her opportunity for revenge finally came on Herod's birthday. The military and political leaders came to help him celebrate at a great feast in his palace at Machaerus. Herodias' sensuous teenaged daughter, Salome, danced so alluringly that Herod loudly offered the girl anything she wanted up to half his kingdom. Her mother was ready with what she wanted, and it was not half a kingdom. Herodias knew that her husband was an unprincipled, cruel man. He was also boisterous and proud, and the embarrassment of backing down on his offer to Salome in front of all these people would be a humiliation he could not tolerate, even at the expense of an innocent man's life. Sometimes a woman's manipulation can outdo all the political maneuvers and power available to men.

Obviously, Herodias had entangled her daughter Salome in her obsession since the daughter added to her mother's request. Not only did Salome ask for John's head, but she also demanded it "immediately" and "on a platter." Obsessions of hate not only take over a person's life but usually infect others as well. By example, influence, and manipulation, Herodias led her young daughter into sin—as an accomplice in the murder of a godly preacher. Her husband and daughter were merely tools in the hand of Herodias, who had planned and orchestrated the tragic crime.

See also Mark 6:14–29; Luke 3:19, 20; notes on Dancing (Ex. 15); Family (1 Sam. 3); Motherhood (Ezek. 16)

Jesus Rejected at Nazareth

53Now it came to pass, when Jesus had finished these parables, that He departed from there. 54When He had come to His own country, He taught them in their synagogue, so that they were astonished and said, "Where did this *Man* get this wisdom and *these* mighty works? 55Is this not the carpenter's son? Is not His mother called Mary? And His brothers James, Joses,[a] Simon, and Judas? 56And His sisters, are they not all with us? Where then did this *Man* get all these things?" 57So they were offended at Him.

But Jesus said to them, "A prophet is not without honor except in his own country and in his own house." 58Now He did not do many mighty works there because of their unbelief.

John the Baptist Beheaded

14At that time Herod the tetrarch heard the report about Jesus 2and said to his servants, "This is John the Baptist; he is risen from the dead, and therefore these powers are at work in him." 3For Herod had laid hold of John and bound him, and put *him* in prison for the sake of Herodias, his brother Philip's wife. 4Because John had said to him, "It is not lawful for you to have her." 5And although he wanted to put him to death, he feared the multitude, because they counted him as a prophet.

6But when Herod's birthday was celebrated, the daughter of Herodias danced before them and

13:55 aNU-Text reads *Joseph.*

14:1 Herod the tetrarch or Antipas was the ruler responsible for the death of John the Baptist (see chart, The Family Tree of Herod the Great). "Herod" was a dynastic title used to describe many different rulers. This family was ruthless with each other as well as with outsiders. No one was safe. Herod the Great, the father of Antipas, had numerous members of his own family put to death, including his favorite wife Mariamne. To have ascended to power in such a family revealed the ruthlessness and ingenuity of Herod Antipas. He helped depose his brother Archelaus, stole his brother Philip's wife Herodias, and was devoted to whomever had the most power in Rome at the time (see Herodias and Salome).

If you can't feed a hundred, feed one.

Mother Teresa

pleased Herod. [7]Therefore he promised with an oath to give her whatever she might ask.

[8]So she, having been prompted by her mother, said, "Give me John the Baptist's head here on a platter."

[9]And the king was sorry; nevertheless, because of the oaths and because of those who sat with him, he commanded *it* to be given *to her.* [10]So he sent and had John beheaded in prison. [11]And his head was brought on a platter and given to the girl, and she brought *it* to her mother. [12]Then his disciples came and took away the body and buried it, and went and told Jesus.

Feeding the Five Thousand

[13]When Jesus heard *it,* He departed from there by boat to a deserted place by Himself. But when the multitudes heard it, they followed Him on foot from the cities. [14]And when Jesus went out He saw a great multitude; and He was moved with compassion for them, and healed their sick. [15]When it was evening, His disciples came to Him, saying, "This is a deserted place, and the hour is already late. Send the multitudes away, that they may go into the villages and buy themselves food." [16]But Jesus said to them, "They do not need to go away. You give them something to eat."

[17]And they said to Him, "We have here only five loaves and two fish."

[18]He said, "Bring them here to Me." [19]Then He commanded the multitudes to sit down on the grass. And He took the five loaves and the two fish, and looking up to heaven, He blessed and broke and gave the loaves to the disciples; and the disciples gave to the multitudes. [20]So they all ate and were filled, and they took up twelve baskets full of the fragments that remained. [21]Now those who had eaten were about five thousand men, besides women and children.

Jesus Walks on the Sea

[22]Immediately Jesus made His disciples get into the boat and go before Him to the other side, while He sent the multitudes away. [23]And when He had sent the multitudes away, He went up on the mountain by Himself to pray. Now when evening came, He was alone there. [24]But the boat was now in the middle of the sea,[a] tossed by the waves, for the wind was contrary.

[25]Now in the fourth watch of the night Jesus went to them, walking on the sea. [26]And when the disciples saw Him walking on the sea, they were troubled, saying, "It is a ghost!" And they cried out for fear.

[27]But immediately Jesus spoke to them, saying, "Be of good cheer! It is I; do not be afraid."

[28]And Peter answered Him and said, "Lord, if it is You, command me to come to You on the water."

[29]So He said, "Come." And when Peter had come down out of the boat, he walked on the water to go to Jesus. [30]But when he saw that the wind *was* boisterous,[a] he was afraid; and beginning to sink he cried out, saying, "Lord, save me!"

[31]And immediately Jesus stretched out *His* hand and caught him, and said to him, "O you of little faith, why did you doubt?" [32]And when they got into the boat, the wind ceased.

[33]Then those who were in the boat came and[a] worshiped Him, saying, "Truly You are the Son of God."

Many Touch Him and Are Made Well

[34]When they had crossed over, they came to the land of[a] Gennesaret. [35]And when the men of that place recognized Him, they sent out into all that surrounding region, brought to Him all who were sick, [36]and begged Him that they might only touch the hem of His garment. And as many as touched *it* were made perfectly well.

Defilement Comes from Within

15 Then the scribes and Pharisees who were from Jerusalem came to Jesus, saying, [2]"Why do Your disciples transgress the tradition of the elders? For they do not wash their hands when they eat bread."

14:24 [a]NU-Text reads *many furlongs away from the land.* **14:30** [a]NU-Text brackets *that* and *boisterous* as disputed. **14:33** [a]NU-Text omits *came and.* **14:34** [a]NU-Text reads *came to land at.*

14:13 Solitude was an important part of Jesus' life (see Matt. 4:1–11; 14:23; Mark 1:35; Luke 4:42; 5:16; John 17).

14:21 The size of a crowd was often numbered only by counting the men (in this case, 5,000). The number could possibly have been three times as great when women and children were included. The feeding of the 5,000, one of three mira-

cles through which food or drink was provided (Matt. 15:32–38; John 2:1–10), is the only miracle recorded in all four gospels (Mark 6:35–44; Luke 9:12–17; John 6:5–13).

15:1–7 The Pharisees' chief concern was to keep their own traditions, while Jesus' concern was to do God's will. The food regulations were a prominent part of the Pharisees' traditions

SYRO-PHOENICIAN WOMAN

A mother's heart is one of the most potent motivators known. A Syro-Phoenician (or Canaanite) woman exhibited this during one of Jesus' teaching tours. We do not know her name, but we do know this mother had insight, courage, persistence, and initiative.

Obviously, Jesus' reputation had reached beyond Palestine. Most likely His healing ministry had made the news in Tyre and Sidon, but few would cross cultural and religious lines to approach Him. This woman was one of the few. What motivated her to take such initiative on her own? Her mother's heart.

There were at least three barriers that could have discouraged her from accomplishing her task: She was a Gentile (Matt. 15:24); she was a Canaanite (see v. 22, note); and she was a woman (John 4:27). But the magnitude of a mother's love pulled her as irresistibly as the moon pulls the tides.

This mother used a threefold approach: She acknowledged Jesus as the rightful King by calling Him "Son of David" (see Matt. 15:22, note); she acknowledged Him as her King and Master by calling Him Lord; and she prayed the simple prayer, "Have mercy on me" (v. 22), "help me" (v. 25). These expressions are irresistible to God.

Her persistence during this brief encounter with Jesus revealed not only a mother's determination but also her growing faith. Notice: It was not her love for her daughter that impressed Him the most (though that surely pleased Him) but her great faith (v. 28).

There is an uncanny parallel between this woman and Rahab in the Old Testament (Josh. 2). Both women came from the hopelessly perverted Canaanites; both showed a strong love for family; both showed courage, persistence, and boldness by stepping away from their religious backgrounds on their own; both evaluated Israel's God and found Him superior to their gods (in fact, they gave Yahweh more credit than the Israelites did); both made a commitment to Israel's God; and both received what they were seeking.

God has a special understanding for the mother's heart (Is. 49:15; 66:12, 13; Luke 13:34). More than anything else we remember this woman's persistent, even obstinate, faith. She would not give up.

See also Mark 7:24–30; notes on Motherhood (Is. 49); Perseverance (Rev. 14); Prayer (Jer. 33)

³He answered and said to them, "Why do you also transgress the commandment of God because of your tradition? ⁴For God commanded, saying, *'Honor your father and your mother';*ᵃ and, *'He who curses father or mother, let him be put to death.'*ᵇ ⁵But you say, 'Whoever says to his father or mother, "Whatever profit you might have received from me *is* a gift *to God"*— ⁶then he need not honor his father or mother.'ᵃ Thus you have made the commandmentᵇ of God of no effect by your tradition. ⁷Hypocrites! Well did Isaiah prophesy about you, saying:

⁸*'These people draw near to Me with their mouth,*
  Andᵃ honor Me with their lips,
  But their heart is far from Me.
⁹*And in vain they worship Me,*
  Teaching as doctrines the commandments
    *of men.'*ᵃ

¹⁰When He had called the multitude to *Himself,* He said to them, "Hear and understand: ¹¹Not what goes into the mouth defiles a man; but what comes out of the mouth, this defiles a man."

¹²Then His disciples came and said to Him, "Do You know that the Pharisees were offended when they heard this saying?"

¹³But He answered and said, "Every plant which My heavenly Father has not planted will be uprooted. ¹⁴Let them alone. They are blind leaders of the blind. And if the blind leads the blind, both will fall into a ditch."

¹⁵Then Peter answered and said to Him, "Explain this parable to us."

¹⁶So Jesus said, "Are you also still without understanding? ¹⁷Do you not yet understand that whatever enters the mouth goes into the stomach and is eliminated? ¹⁸But those things which proceed out of the mouth come from the heart, and they defile a man. ¹⁹For out of the heart proceed

15:4 ᵃExodus 20:12; Deuteronomy 5:16 ᵇExodus 21:17 **15:6** ᵃNU-Text omits *or mother.* ᵇNU-Text reads *word.* **15:8** ᵃNU-Text omits *draw near to Me with their mouth, And.* **15:9** ᵃIsaiah 29:13

(see Lev. 10, Clean vs. Unclean). Jesus condemned the Pharisees for putting their traditions before God's commandments and the people's good. He referred to a practice called "Corban" in which a person dedicated selected possessions to God, while still having the use of them (see Mark 7:8–13). If someone (even parents) had a need, the individual would claim the injunction instructing him not to break vows (Num.

30:2). Such action elevated the law of "Corban" above God's Law to "Honor your father and your mother" (Ex. 20:12).

15:7 The Pharisees were described as "hypocrites" by Jesus. This theatrical term described an actor who played a part "underneath the mask." Jesus accused the Pharisees of putting on a mask of holiness.

*In raising children, all you can do is your best . . . we take care
of the possible and leave the impossible to God.*

Ruth Bell Graham

evil thoughts, murders, adulteries, fornications, thefts, false witness, blasphemies. 20These are *the things* which defile a man, but to eat with unwashed hands does not defile a man."

A Gentile Shows Her Faith

21Then Jesus went out from there and departed to the region of Tyre and Sidon. 22And behold, a woman of Canaan came from that region and cried out to Him, saying, "Have mercy on me, O Lord, Son of David! My daughter is severely demon-possessed."

23But He answered her not a word.

And His disciples came and urged Him, saying, "Send her away, for she cries out after us."

24But He answered and said, "I was not sent except to the lost sheep of the house of Israel."

25Then she came and worshiped Him, saying, "Lord, help me!"

26But He answered and said, "It is not good to take the children's bread and throw *it* to the little dogs."

27And she said, "Yes, Lord, yet even the little dogs eat the crumbs which fall from their masters' table."

28Then Jesus answered and said to her, "O woman, great *is* your faith! Let it be to you as you desire." And her daughter was healed from that very hour.

Jesus Heals Great Multitudes

29Jesus departed from there, skirted the Sea of Galilee, and went up on the mountain and sat down there. 30Then great multitudes came to Him, having with them *the* lame, blind, mute, maimed, and many others; and they laid them down at Jesus' feet, and He healed them. 31So the multitude marveled when they saw *the* mute speaking, *the* maimed made whole, *the* lame walking, and *the* blind seeing; and they glorified the God of Israel.

Feeding the Four Thousand

32Now Jesus called His disciples to *Himself* and said, "I have compassion on the multitude, because they have now continued with Me three days and have nothing to eat. And I do not want to send them away hungry, lest they faint on the way."

33Then His disciples said to Him, "Where could we get enough bread in the wilderness to fill such a great multitude?"

34Jesus said to them, "How many loaves do you have?"

And they said, "Seven, and a few little fish."

35So He commanded the multitude to sit down on the ground. 36And He took the seven loaves and the fish and gave thanks, broke *them* and gave *them* to His disciples; and the disciples *gave* to the multitude. 37So they all ate and were filled, and they took up seven large baskets full of the fragments that were left. 38Now those who ate were four thousand men, besides women and children. 39And He sent away the multitude, got into the boat, and came to the region of Magdala.[a]

The Pharisees and Sadducees Seek a Sign

16 Then the Pharisees and Sadducees came, and testing Him asked that He would show them a sign from heaven. 2He answered and said to them, "When it is evening you say, '*It will be* fair weather, for the sky is red'; 3and in the morning, '*It will be* foul weather today, for the sky is red and threatening.' Hypocrites![a] You know how to discern the face of the sky, but you cannot *discern* the signs of the times. 4A wicked and adulterous generation seeks after a sign, and no sign shall be given to it except the sign of the prophet[a] Jonah." And He left them and departed.

·················

15:39 [a]NU-Text reads *Magadan*. 16:3 [a]NU-Text omits *Hypocrites*. 16:4 [a]NU-Text omits *the prophet*.

15:21–28 See Syro-Phoenician Woman.

15:22 The Canaanites were Israel's ancient enemies. They were a perverse people who were in the land when Abraham arrived. Because of the atrocities they practiced in their religion, such as temple prostitution and child sacrifice, and because of their refusal to repent and turn to Him, God had ordered their destruction (see Num. 33:50–55; Deut. 7:1–11). The Jews reserved "Son of David" for the legitimate king of Israel. A Canaanite would not want to recognize such a title.

15:32–39 The feeding of the 4,000 had many similarities to the feeding described in Matthew 14:13–21. The people had been listening to His teaching; they were in a rural area; the food was the same; Jesus blessed and broke it; the disciples served it. But there are also marked differences: The number of people; the time they spent with Him; the different seashore; the initial amount of food; the amount left over.

COMMITMENT *FOLLOWING JESUS*

"Following Jesus" is the definition of "commitment." Commitment demands a choice. Jesus wasted no time getting to the heart of commitment: Either the disciples would be committed to Him and deny their own desires, or they would be determined to go their own ways and deny Him (Matt. 10:32–37). The choice to commit is the same for all believers—either we deny ourselves or deny Him; either we go His way, or we pursue our way.

Talk about Christ would be meaningless without the walk with Him. The disciples were to take up their crosses. Carrying the cross beam was a public declaration of Rome's authority. Jesus challenged them to put themselves voluntarily under God's authority, doing His will His way. Commitment demands action; it cannot be divorced from responsibility. It extends beyond our relationship to the heavenly Father to other areas of life. Ruth's words of commitment to Naomi did not speak as loudly as did her actions. She left her family and homeland to return with Naomi to Bethlehem (Ruth 1:16, 17).

Commitment definitely limits choices because it is exclusive. For example, in a commitment to marriage, God's plan is for one woman and one man to commit to each other exclusively and permanently (Matt. 19:5, 6).

Jesus demonstrated in the Garden of Gethsemane that the Father's will always takes precedence over His. The next day, He picked up His Cross, demonstrating that He would do the Father's will the Father's way.

Commitment builds up faith and develops character. It is a spiritual discipline (Prov. 16:3). It is a lifetime venture, requiring time, work, and determination (Matt. 16:24).

See also Eccl. 5:4, 5; Matt. 5:33, 37; Mark 8:34, Luke 9:62; 14:27; notes on Decision Making (1 Cor. 8); Integrity (Ps. 27); Marriage (Gen. 2; 2 Sam. 6; Prov. 5; Hos. 2; Amos 3; 2 Cor. 13; Heb. 12); Salvation (Eph. 2); Vows (Num. 30); portrait of Ruth (Ruth 2)

The Leaven of the Pharisees and Sadducees

5Now when His disciples had come to the other side, they had forgotten to take bread. 6Then Jesus said to them, "Take heed and beware of the leaven of the Pharisees and the Sadducees."

7And they reasoned among themselves, saying, "*It is* because we have taken no bread."

8But Jesus, being aware of *it,* said to them, "O you of little faith, why do you reason among yourselves because you have brought no bread?a 9Do you not yet understand, or remember the five loaves of the five thousand and how many baskets you took up? 10Nor the seven loaves of the four thousand and how many large baskets you took up? 11How is it you do not understand that I did not speak to you concerning bread?—*but* to beware of the leaven of the Pharisees and Sadducees." 12Then they understood that He did not tell *them* to beware of the leaven of bread, but of the doctrine of the Pharisees and Sadducees.

Peter Confesses Jesus as the Christ

13When Jesus came into the region of Caesarea Philippi, He asked His disciples, saying, "Who do men say that I, the Son of Man, am?"

14So they said, "Some *say* John the Baptist, some Elijah, and others Jeremiah or one of the prophets."

15He said to them, "But who do you say that I am?"

16Simon Peter answered and said, "You are the Christ, the Son of the living God."

17Jesus answered and said to him, "Blessed are you, Simon Bar-Jonah, for flesh and blood has not revealed *this* to you, but My Father who is in heaven. 18And I also say to you that you are Peter, and on this rock I will build My church, and the gates of Hades shall not prevail against it. 19And I will give you the keys of the kingdom of heaven,

16:8 aNU-Text reads *you have no bread.*

16:5–12 Leaven or yeast was a small substance that permeated the entire product (see Luke 12:1, note).

16:16 Peter declared that Jesus was not one among many—He was someone set apart from all others. "The Christ" is the Greek title for the promised Messiah for whom the Jews had been waiting. "Son of the living God" was a new title. In the OT, divine sonship referred to angels (as special messengers of God), to Israel (as a nation elected to perform the service of God), or to a king (one who had been given authority by God over Israel and other nations). Peter not only affirmed Jesus to be the Messiah; he identified the Messiah as the Son of God. Though the disciples had heard the Father call Jesus His beloved Son (Matt. 3:17) and had heard Jesus address God as

Father numerous times (Matt. 11:27), this confession went beyond that to express the understanding of their hearts.

16:18 Simon was Peter's given name; he was the son (Aram. *bar*) of Jonah (v. 17). The two words for "rock" differ: "You are Peter" (Gk. *petros*, lit. "a small stone"); and "on this rock" (Gk. *petra,* lit. "a massive rock"). There are three possible interpretations:

1) If Jesus were speaking in Aramaic and both references were *Cephas,* Peter is identified as the "rock";

2) Peter is the "small rock" (Gk. *petros*), and Jesus is the "massive boulder" (Gk. *petra*) upon whom the church is built (see 1 Cor. 3:11); or

and whatever you bind on earth will be bound in heaven, and whatever you loose on earth will be loosed[a] in heaven."

²⁰Then He commanded His disciples that they should tell no one that He was Jesus the Christ.

Jesus Predicts His Death and Resurrection

²¹From that time Jesus began to show to His disciples that He must go to Jerusalem, and suffer many things from the elders and chief priests and scribes, and be killed, and be raised the third day. ²²Then Peter took Him aside and began to rebuke Him, saying, "Far be it from You, Lord; this shall not happen to You!"

²³But He turned and said to Peter, "Get behind Me, Satan! You are an offense to Me, for you are not mindful of the things of God, but the things of men."

Take Up the Cross and Follow Him

²⁴Then Jesus said to His disciples, "If anyone desires to come after Me, let him deny himself, and take up his cross, and follow Me. ²⁵For whoever desires to save his life will lose it, but whoever loses his life for My sake will find it. ²⁶For what profit is it to a man if he gains the whole world, and loses his own soul? Or what will a man give in exchange for his soul? ²⁷For the Son of Man will come in the glory of His Father with His angels, and then He will reward each according to his works.

Jesus Transfigured on the Mount

²⁸Assuredly, I say to you, there are some standing here who shall not taste death till they see the Son of Man coming in His kingdom."

17 Now after six days Jesus took Peter, James, and John his brother, led them up on a high mountain by themselves; ²and He was transfigured before them. His face shone like the sun, and His clothes became as white as the light. ³And behold, Moses and Elijah appeared to them, talking with Him. ⁴Then Peter answered and said to Jesus, "Lord, it is good for us to be here; if You wish, let us[a] make here three tabernacles: one for You, one for Moses, and one for Elijah."

⁵While he was still speaking, behold, a bright cloud overshadowed them; and suddenly a voice came out of the cloud, saying, "This is My beloved Son, in whom I am well pleased. Hear Him!" ⁶And when the disciples heard it, they fell on their faces and were greatly afraid. ⁷But Jesus came and touched them and said, "Arise, and do not be afraid." ⁸When they had lifted up their eyes, they saw no one but Jesus only.

⁹Now as they came down from the mountain, Jesus commanded them, saying, "Tell the vision to no one until the Son of Man is risen from the dead."

¹⁰And His disciples asked Him, saying, "Why

16:19 [a]Or *will have been bound . . . will have been loosed*   **17:4** [a]NU-Text reads *I will.*

---

3) Peter is addressed, and his confession is the *petra* or "rock" on which the church would be built.

Hades (Gk., lit. "the place of the dead") was often used as an idiom for the powers of death. Jesus' point is that death itself cannot destroy the church or keep it from going forward.

16:19 The binding and loosing is a reference to the distribution of the gospel. Peter and all believers were given the gospel ("the keys of the kingdom") to introduce women and men to Christ and His salvation and thereby build the church (see Matt. 28:19, 20).

16:22, 23 Peter was unwittingly doing the same thing Satan tried to do in the wilderness temptation—urging Jesus to act on His own apart from the Father. Jesus' words did not fit Peter's agenda, just as His words and deeds did not fit the agenda of the Pharisees, scribes, and Sadducees. Jesus had only one purpose—to do the Father's will (Phil. 2:8; Heb. 10:7).

16:28 Three major interpretations are suggested:

1) The coming of Christ in judgment to destroy the temple in A.D. 70;

2) a reference to Jesus' Resurrection, Ascension, and the sending of the Holy Spirit to indwell believers;

3) a pointing to the Transfiguration in which three of these men would see Jesus in His glorified state.

The latter seems most likely because of the proximity of the Transfiguration account (Matt. 17:1–5).

17:1 The Transfiguration took place within a week of Christ's prediction that He would die. The three disciples included were the ones He allowed to witness the raising of Jairus' daughter (Mark 5:37); they later would accompany Him to the Garden of Gethsemane (Mark 14:33). Though tradition long held this "high mountain" to be Mt. Tabor, there is no record that Jesus was near Mt. Tabor at this time. In addition, archaeological excavations discovered here a fortified city dating to this time, which would have made it difficult for them to have been in seclusion. Mt. Hermon seems a more likely place. Three events took place: Jesus' body was transfigured (v. 2); Moses, the giver of the Law and deliverer from bondage in Egypt, and Elijah, the forerunner of John the Baptist and representative of the prophets in the OT, appeared (v. 3); and God spoke from a cloud (v. 5).

17:5 At Jesus' baptism the disciples heard God saying the same thing (Matt. 3:17). The message is repeated near the end of His ministry: God is still pleased with His Son. This time the admonition "Hear Him" was added, but they still were not listening.

17:9 The message must have been confusing. The Transfiguration was not for the masses but for His followers. The timing of this event was important. The disciples were at the crucial point of commitment to Jesus. Everything hinged on who He was to them. In fact, He had recently challenged them with this question (Matt. 16:15). They needed to be prepared for what would seem to be defeat—the Cross.

CONFLICT   RESOLVING DISAGREEMENTS

Conflict is inevitable in personal relationships. It is humanly impossible to live in total harmony with others at all times. Jesus told His disciples how to settle disputes between believers (Matt. 18:15–20). Paul resolved his conflict with John Mark, which had developed between the first and second missionary journeys (Acts 15:36–41). John warned Christians not to hate each other (1 John 4:20, 21).

The Bible offers several steps to resolving conflict and settling disagreements among people:

1) Scripture admonishes the believer to face the conflict—acknowledge its existence and accept its impact. Christ advised His disciples to go immediately and directly to the person and discuss the grievance (Matt. 18:15). Others should be enlisted to mediate the conflict only if the conflict cannot be resolved one-to-one (Matt. 18:16, 17).

2) Scripture instructs the believer to forgive the conflict—to put the disagreement behind and move ahead in harmony once it has been resolved. Euodia and Syntyche were encouraged to replace their bitterness with gentleness and to live in peaceful harmony, rejoicing in the Lord (Phil. 4:2–7).

3) Scripture encourages the believer to move beyond the conflict. Paul resolved his grudge against Mark and sought opportunities to minister with him (compare Acts 15:36–41 with 2 Tim. 4:9–11; see Eccl. 1, Healing).

Jesus reminded the Pharisees of the greatest commandments—to love the Lord and love your neighbor (Matt. 22:37–40). The desire of God is for His children to live in harmony. Christians are to resolve conflict with others by replacing discord with love. The emphasis is not punitive but redemptive (see 2 Cor. 2:5–11; 2 Thess. 3:14, 15).

See also 1 John 3:10–18; notes on Communication (Prov. 15); Conflict (Song 5); Forgiveness (Ps. 51; Luke 17); Marriage (Gen. 2; 2 Sam. 6; Prov. 5; Hos. 2; Amos 3; 2 Cor. 13; Heb. 12)

then do the scribes say that Elijah must come first?"

[11]Jesus answered and said to them, "Indeed, Elijah is coming first[a] and will restore all things. [12]But I say to you that Elijah has come already, and they did not know him but did to him whatever they wished. Likewise the Son of Man is also about to suffer at their hands." [13]Then the disciples understood that He spoke to them of John the Baptist.

A Boy Is Healed

[14]And when they had come to the multitude, a man came to Him, kneeling down to Him and saying, [15]"Lord, have mercy on my son, for he is an epileptic[a] and suffers severely; for he often falls into the fire and often into the water. [16]So I brought him to Your disciples, but they could not cure him."

[17]Then Jesus answered and said, "O faithless and perverse generation, how long shall I be with you? How long shall I bear with you? Bring him here to Me." [18]And Jesus rebuked the demon, and it came out of him; and the child was cured from that very hour.

[19]Then the disciples came to Jesus privately and said, "Why could we not cast it out?"

[20]So Jesus said to them, "Because of your unbelief;[a] for assuredly, I say to you, if you have faith as a mustard seed, you will say to this mountain, 'Move from here to there,' and it will move; and nothing will be impossible for you. [21]However, this kind does not go out except by prayer and fasting."[a]

Jesus Again Predicts His Death and Resurrection

[22]Now while they were staying[a] in Galilee, Jesus said to them, "The Son of Man is about to be betrayed into the hands of men, [23]and they will kill Him, and the third day He will be raised up." And they were exceedingly sorrowful.

Peter and His Master Pay Their Taxes

[24]When they had come to Capernaum,[a] those who received the *temple* tax came to Peter and said, "Does your Teacher not pay the *temple* tax?"

[25]He said, "Yes."

And when he had come into the house, Jesus anticipated him, saying, "What do you think, Simon? From whom do the kings of the earth take customs or taxes, from their sons or from strangers?"

17:11 [a]NU-Text omits *first*.   17:15 [a]Literally *moonstruck*   17:20 [a]NU-Text reads *little faith*.   17:21 [a]NU-Text omits this verse.   17:22 [a]NU-Text reads *gathering together*.   17:24 [a]NU-Text reads *Capharnaum* (here and elsewhere).

17:24–27 The tax in question was not a Roman tax but a Jewish temple tax that paid for the care of the temple (see Ex. 30:12–14; 38:26; 2 Chr. 24:6).

> *The pleasure of sex, the communication of love,
> and the desire for children are uniquely linked.*
> Charlene Kaemmerling

[26]Peter said to Him, "From strangers."

Jesus said to him, "Then the sons are free. [27]Nevertheless, lest we offend them, go to the sea, cast in a hook, and take the fish that comes up first. And when you have opened its mouth, you will find a piece of money;[a] take that and give it to them for Me and you."

Who Is the Greatest?

18 At that time the disciples came to Jesus, saying, "Who then is greatest in the kingdom of heaven?"

[2]Then Jesus called a little child to Him, set him in the midst of them, [3]and said, "Assuredly, I say to you, unless you are converted and become as little children, you will by no means enter the kingdom of heaven. [4]Therefore whoever humbles himself as this little child is the greatest in the kingdom of heaven. [5]Whoever receives one little child like this in My name receives Me.

Jesus Warns of Offenses

[6]"But whoever causes one of these little ones who believe in Me to sin, it would be better for him if a millstone were hung around his neck, and he were drowned in the depth of the sea. [7]Woe to the world because of offenses! For offenses must come, but woe to that man by whom the offense comes!

[8]"If your hand or foot causes you to sin, cut it off and cast *it* from you. It is better for you to enter into life lame or maimed, rather than having two hands or two feet, to be cast into the everlasting fire. [9]And if your eye causes you to sin, pluck it out and cast *it* from you. It is better for you to enter into life with one eye, rather than having two eyes, to be cast into hell fire.

The Parable of the Lost Sheep

[10]"Take heed that you do not despise one of these little ones, for I say to you that in heaven their angels always see the face of My Father who is in heaven. [11]For the Son of Man has come to save that which was lost.[a]

[12]"What do you think? If a man has a hundred sheep, and one of them goes astray, does he not leave the ninety-nine and go to the mountains to seek the one that is straying? [13]And if he should find it, assuredly, I say to you, he rejoices more over that *sheep* than over the ninety-nine that did not go astray. [14]Even so it is not the will of your Father who is in heaven that one of these little ones should perish.

Dealing with a Sinning Brother

[15]"Moreover if your brother sins against you, go and tell him his fault between you and him alone. If he hears you, you have gained your brother. [16]But if he will not hear, take with you one or two more, that 'by the mouth of two or three witnesses every word may be established.'[a] [17]And if he refuses to hear them, tell *it* to the church. But if he refuses even to hear the church, let him be to you like a heathen and a tax collector.

[18]"Assuredly, I say to you, whatever you bind on earth will be bound in heaven, and whatever you loose on earth will be loosed in heaven.

[19]"Again I say[a] to you that if two of you agree on earth concerning anything that they ask, it will be done for them by My Father in heaven. [20]For where two or three are gathered together in My name, I am there in the midst of them."

The Parable of the Unforgiving Servant

[21]Then Peter came to Him and said, "Lord, how often shall my brother sin against me, and I forgive him? Up to seven times?"

17:27 [a]Greek *stater*, the exact amount to pay the temple tax (didrachma) for two   18:11 [a]NU-Text omits this verse.   18:16 [a]Deuteronomy 19:15   18:19 [a]NU-Text and M-Text read *Again, assuredly, I say.*

18:3 The evangelism of children must be a priority for home and church. Jesus used children as illustrations of the faith (trust in and loyalty to) and humility (putting oneself under God's authority) required to become part of His kingdom. Though God has gifted some with special abilities to teach children, all believers have the assignment to live a godly life before them, tell them about the Lord, and love them (Deut. 6; Matt. 19:14; Eph. 6:4; Titus 2:4).

The gospel is to be given to all, and a response is required by all who are old enough to know the difference between right and wrong (Matt. 28:19, 20). Nowhere in Scripture is there the suggestion that children are incapable of responding to God or of engaging in praise, worship, prayer, and thanksgiving. In fact, Jesus emphasized that, in coming to the Father, children are not required to become like adults, but rather, adults are to become as children.

18:8, 9 Jesus was not advocating physical mutilation; the body is not responsible for sin. Lust begins in the heart as does pride (see Matt. 5:29, 30). Believers are to cut out of their lives anything that causes them or others to sin.

18:10 Guardian angels are not promised for each child, although Scripture does teach that angels are concerned about believers and minister to them (see Ps. 91:11; Heb. 1:14).

18:21 Rabbinical tradition taught a repeated sin should be forgiven three times, but on the fourth, there was to be no

DIVORCE BREAKING ASUNDER

In interpreting the decree of Moses on divorce (Deut. 24:1), the followers of the Rabbi Shammai believed that divorce should be granted only because of infidelity; while the followers of Rabbi Hillel argued that Mosaic Law permitted divorce for virtually any reason. Jesus shocked His disciples by rejecting both sides of the rabbinic debate (Matt. 19:10). Rather than going immediately to the contested text (Deut. 24:1), Jesus referred back to the beginning of marriage (Matt. 19:4–6). Ultimately the answer to this problematic issue does not lie in legal codes, traditional practices, or human solutions but in God's creative design (Gen. 2:24). God never accommodates or compromises His principles, but He does redeem and restore any who seek His forgiveness.

Jesus' view of divorce (Gk. *apostasion*, from *apoluÿ*, "to send away," meaning "to remove from the center of a relationship" or "to break fellowship") can be understood only against the background of His view of permanent monogamy, one man and one woman together for a lifetime. The plan for permanence is clear in the "one-flesh" metaphor used by the Lord. Moses allowed divorce as a human device to protect ill-treated Hebrew women from unscrupulous men who sought to manipulate the betrothal process. The Pharisees took the "permission" of the Law and turned it into a "command" that made human frailty a justification for circumventing God's divine plan and purpose.

Jesus did not teach that the innocent party must divorce the unfaithful one. The purpose of the "exception" clause in the Mosaic Law, which is repeated again in Jesus' explanation, is not to encourage divorce. The binding commitment of marriage does not depend upon human wills or upon what any individual does or does not do but rather upon God's original design and purpose for marriage (Hos. 3:1–3).

God rejects divorce for these reasons:

1) Marriage is a divine institution the Lord used to teach His children about their relationship to Him (Gen. 1:27; Matt. 19:4).
2) Marriage is by express command of the Creator and carries His imprimatur (Matt. 19:4, 5).
3) Marriage brings two people together as one flesh, testifying to the permanence God planned for this most intimate union (Matt. 19:6).
4) Jesus points to the example of the first couple (Matt. 19:8).
5) Evil consequences are inevitable when separation comes (Matt. 19:9).

Divorce is never God's choice. Indeed, God hates divorce (Mal. 2:16). However, whenever divorce occurs for whatever reason, God desires to work redemptively when the person who has experienced this tragedy is repentant and desires reconciliation to God.

See also Ex. 21:7–11; Esth. 1:10–22; Jer. 3:1; Mal. 2:14–16; Luke 16:18; 1 Cor. 7:10–17; notes on Adultery (Hos. 3); Commitment (Matt. 16); Husbands (Job 31; 2 Cor. 6); Marriage (Gen. 2; 2 Sam. 6; Prov. 5; Hos. 2; Amos 3; 2 Cor. 13; Heb. 12); Remarriage (Matt. 5); Vows (Num. 30); Wives (Prov. 31).

---

²²Jesus said to him, "I do not say to you, up to seven times, but up to seventy times seven. ²³Therefore the kingdom of heaven is like a certain king who wanted to settle accounts with his servants. ²⁴And when he had begun to settle accounts, one was brought to him who owed him ten thousand talents. ²⁵But as he was not able to pay, his master commanded that he be sold, with his wife and children and all that he had, and that payment be made. ²⁶The servant therefore fell down before him, saying, 'Master, have patience with me, and I will pay you all.' ²⁷Then the master of that servant was moved with compassion, released him, and forgave him the debt.

²⁸"But that servant went out and found one of his fellow servants who owed him a hundred denarii; and he laid hands on him and took *him* by the throat, saying, 'Pay me what you owe!' ²⁹So his fellow servant fell down at his feet[a] and begged him, saying, 'Have patience with me, and I will pay you all.'[b] ³⁰And he would not, but went and threw him into prison till he should pay the debt. ³¹So

•••••••••••••••••••

18:29 [a]NU-Text omits *at his feet.* [b]NU-Text and M-Text omit *all.*

---

forgiveness. Peter probably thought he was being generous to forgive "seven times." Jesus' answer suggested forgiving an unlimited number of times. He amplified that answer in a parable. The comparison of the debt owed the king and the debt owed the servant is almost ridiculous (see chart, Money and Measurements in the Bible). The picture is clear: God has forgiven believers an immense debt; they dare not refuse to forgive others for small offenses. The lack of forgiveness is another subtle form of playing god and puts believers in direct opposition to God. Those who are forgiven must forgive if they are to receive forgiveness (see Ps. 51; Luke 17, Forgiveness; chart, Your Path to Freedom).

when his fellow servants saw what had been done, they were very grieved, and came and told their master all that had been done. [32]Then his master, after he had called him, said to him, 'You wicked servant! I forgave you all that debt because you begged me. [33]Should you not also have had compassion on your fellow servant, just as I had pity on you?' [34]And his master was angry, and delivered him to the torturers until he should pay all that was due to him.

[35]"So My heavenly Father also will do to you if each of you, from his heart, does not forgive his brother his trespasses."[a]

Marriage and Divorce

19Now it came to pass, when Jesus had finished these sayings, *that* He departed from Galilee and came to the region of Judea beyond the Jordan. [2]And great multitudes followed Him, and He healed them there.

[3]The Pharisees also came to Him, testing Him, and saying to Him, "Is it lawful for a man to divorce his wife for *just* any reason?"

[4]And He answered and said to them, "Have you not read that He who made[a] *them* at the beginning *'made them male and female,'*[b] [5]and said, *'For this reason a man shall leave his father and mother and be joined to his wife, and the two shall become one flesh'?*[a] [6]So then, they are no longer two but one flesh. Therefore what God has joined together, let not man separate."

[7]They said to Him, "Why then did Moses command to give a certificate of divorce, and to put her away?"

[8]He said to them, "Moses, because of the hardness of your hearts, permitted you to divorce your wives, but from the beginning it was not so. [9]And I say to you, whoever divorces his wife, except for sexual immorality,[a] and marries another, commits adultery; and whoever marries her who is divorced commits adultery."

[10]His disciples said to Him, "If such is the case of the man with *his* wife, it is better not to marry."

Jesus Teaches on Celibacy

[11]But He said to them, "All cannot accept this saying, but only *those* to whom it has been given: [12]For there are eunuchs who were born thus from *their* mother's womb, and there are eunuchs who were made eunuchs by men, and there are eunuchs who have made themselves eunuchs for the kingdom of heaven's sake. He who is able to accept *it*, let him accept *it.*"

Jesus Blesses Little Children

[13]Then little children were brought to Him that He might put *His* hands on them and pray, but the disciples rebuked them. [14]But Jesus said, "Let the little children come to Me, and do not forbid them; for of such is the kingdom of heaven." [15]And He laid *His* hands on them and departed from there.

Jesus Counsels the Rich Young Ruler

[16]Now behold, one came and said to Him, "Good[a] Teacher, what good thing shall I do that I may have eternal life?"

[17]So He said to him, "Why do you call Me good?[a] No one *is* good but One, *that is,* God.[b] But if you want to enter into life, keep the commandments."

[18]He said to Him, "Which ones?"

Jesus said, " *'You shall not murder,' 'You shall not commit adultery,' 'You shall not steal,' 'You shall not bear false witness,'* [19]*'Honor your father and your mother,'*[a] and, *'You shall love your neighbor as yourself.'*"[b]

[20]The young man said to Him, "All these things I have kept from my youth.[a] What do I still lack?"

[21]Jesus said to him, "If you want to be perfect, go, sell what you have and give to the poor, and

---

18:35 [a]NU-Text omits *his trespasses.*   19:4 [a]NU-Text reads *created.* [b]Genesis 1:27; 5:2   19:5 [a]Genesis 2:24   19:9 [a]Or *fornication*   19:16 [a]NU-Text omits *Good.*   19:17 [a]NU-Text reads *Why do you ask Me about what is good?* [b]NU-Text reads *There is One who is good.* 19:19 [a]Exodus 20:12–16; Deuteronomy 5:16–20   [b]Leviticus 19:18 19:20 [a]NU-Text omits *from my youth.*

19:9 Sexual immorality (Gk. *porneia*) is a broad term, referring to a wide range of illicit sexual practices. The presupposition here is that immorality breaks the one-flesh union, which God declared to be part of the marriage relationship. For some, such a violation is a legitimate reason for divorce. However, Jesus was not requiring divorce, even in this case; He was simply noting that Moses gave this permission clause (Deut. 24:1–4) because of "the hardness of…hearts" (Matt. 19:8).

19:10, 11 Jesus was not condemning either marriage or single life but rather pointing out that both had advantages. Singleness may mean more time for kingdom work, but not everyone can handle single life (see Ps 62; John 2; 1 Cor. 7; 12, Singleness).

19:12 The reference is not to physical castration, but to God-directed, self-imposed celibacy (see 1 Cor. 7, Celibacy).

19:13 Customarily children were brought to rabbis and elders for blessing. The disciples appeared to be rude and thoughtless, especially in the light of Jesus' recent teaching (Matt. 18:2–6). They may have been annoyed that their private discussion with the Lord was interrupted by the seeming triviality of blessing children.

19:16–22 Luke identified this young man as a ruler (Luke 8:18). The ruler's question revealed his problem. He wanted to know what to *do* to earn eternal life. Jesus' emphasis was always on the attitude of the heart, not on deeds. Jesus showed the young man that he had failed, even in the areas in which he thought he had done well. His wealth was not his problem; his divided heart was (see Matt. 6:24). The vital message Jesus gave the man was not "Go, sell what you have," but "Come, follow Me" (see Matt. 5:29, 30; 16:15; 17:9; 18:8, 9).

ZEBEDEE'S AMBITIOUS WIFE

When Jesus taught His disciples, the mother of James and John listened with pride in her two sons. Naturally talented and dedicated to the Lord, they were included in Jesus' inner circle. James was a born leader (see Acts 12:17; 15:13). John was commonly called the disciple "whom Jesus loved" (see John 13:23).

This mother's pride also included human ambition, and she knelt before Jesus, requesting special favors (Matt. 20:21). Three times Jesus had foretold that He would be condemned to death, then rise the third day; yet at the Crucifixion, most of His disciples deserted Him, proving that they had heard Him selectively. They heard only the promise that His followers would sit on thrones (Matt. 19:28).

James and John may have urged their mother to speak, but neither they nor their mother understood the basic requirements for spiritual responsibility. Jesus listened to her request, but He posed His question to her sons (see also Mark 10:36). "You do not know what you ask. Are you able to drink the cup that I am about to drink, and be baptized with the baptism that I am baptized with?" (Matt. 20:22). They assured Him that they were, and Jesus proceeded to teach them and their mother elementary truths about servant leadership. Jesus did not reject this mother's request for her sons, but rather He corrected it in an unexpected way (vv. 23, 26).

This woman, who undoubtedly loved the Lord passionately, having joined the women who attended Him, is thought to be Salome (see Mark 15:40). She followed Jesus to the Cross and to the grave. Her highest fulfillment was to give her two sons to Christ, and the influence of a godly mother is certainly evident in these sons. But like many believers, she failed to grasp the essence of greatness—true humility. To follow Him is to take up one's own cross (see Luke 9:23, 24). Salome teaches us the importance of imitating Christ Who "did not come to be served, but to serve" (Mark 10:45).

See also Matt. 27:56; Mark 10:35–45; 15:40; 16:1; notes on Favoritism (Prov. 28); Motherhood (1 Sam. 1)

---

you will have treasure in heaven; and come, follow Me."

²²But when the young man heard that saying, he went away sorrowful, for he had great possessions.

With God All Things Are Possible

²³Then Jesus said to His disciples, "Assuredly, I say to you that it is hard for a rich man to enter the kingdom of heaven. ²⁴And again I say to you, it is easier for a camel to go through the eye of a needle than for a rich man to enter the kingdom of God."

²⁵When His disciples heard *it,* they were greatly astonished, saying, "Who then can be saved?"

²⁶But Jesus looked at *them* and said to them, "With men this is impossible, but with God all things are possible."

²⁷Then Peter answered and said to Him, "See,

we have left all and followed You. Therefore what shall we have?"

²⁸So Jesus said to them, "Assuredly I say to you, that in the regeneration, when the Son of Man sits on the throne of His glory, you who have followed Me will also sit on twelve thrones, judging the twelve tribes of Israel. ²⁹And everyone who has left houses or brothers or sisters or father or mother or wifeª or children or lands, for My name's sake, shall receive a hundredfold, and inherit eternal life. ³⁰But many *who are* first will be last, and the last first.

The Parable of the Workers in the Vineyard

20 "For the kingdom of heaven is like a landowner who went out early in the morning to hire laborers for his vineyard. ²Now when he had agreed with the laborers for a denarius a

··················

19:29 ªNU-Text omits *or wife.*

19:23–26 Jesus was not condemning wealthy people. For example, Abraham, Isaac, Jacob, David, Solomon, and Joseph of Arimathea were wealthy. But the Jews often interpreted wealth as a sign of God's blessing in the sense of a sure ticket to heaven. Instead, Jesus saw the dangers inherent in wealth and taught that only a few, with God's help (v. 26), could handle wealth properly. The camel was the largest animal commonly seen, and the eye of a needle was the smallest opening. Jesus used a figure of speech that demonstrated the dangers of wealth.

19:28, 29 Whether or not the twelve disciples would have a special assignment of judging Israel because of Israel's rejection of the Messiah is not clear. Jesus elsewhere said *all* His

followers would have a part in judging (Luke 22:30; 1 Cor. 6:2). Clearly, all who have responded to His call to follow Him will receive not only eternal life but also hundredfold rewards.

20:1 The parable of the laborers is found only in Matthew. Jesus illustrated why and how the last can become the first. Everything God has done for humanity is grace; individuals do not earn His favor, and He is never in their debt. God is sovereign—He is in charge. Rank, position, and reward are His to give to whomever He chooses. This parable illustrates two other points: God's concern with far more than the amount of work done; the people's anger with God because He is viewed as generous with others while only being fair with them.

day, he sent them into his vineyard. ³And he went out about the third hour and saw others standing idle in the marketplace, ⁴and said to them, 'You also go into the vineyard, and whatever is right I will give you.' So they went. ⁵Again he went out about the sixth and the ninth hour, and did likewise. ⁶And about the eleventh hour he went out and found others standing idle,ᵃ and said to them, 'Why have you been standing here idle all day?' ⁷They said to him, 'Because no one hired us.' He said to them, 'You also go into the vineyard, and whatever is right you will receive.'ᵃ

⁸"So when evening had come, the owner of the vineyard said to his steward, 'Call the laborers and give them *their* wages, beginning with the last to the first.' ⁹And when those came who *were hired* about the eleventh hour, they each received a denarius. ¹⁰But when the first came, they supposed that they would receive more; and they likewise received each a denarius. ¹¹And when they had received *it,* they complained against the landowner, ¹²saying, 'These last *men* have worked *only* one hour, and you made them equal to us who have borne the burden and the heat of the day.' ¹³But he answered one of them and said, 'Friend, I am doing you no wrong. Did you not agree with me for a denarius? ¹⁴Take *what is* yours and go your way. I wish to give to this last man *the same* as to you. ¹⁵Is it not lawful for me to do what I wish with my own things? Or is your eye evil because I am good?' ¹⁶So the last will be first, and the first last. For many are called, but few chosen."ᵃ

Jesus a Third Time Predicts His Death and Resurrection

¹⁷Now Jesus, going up to Jerusalem, took the twelve disciples aside on the road and said to them, ¹⁸"Behold, we are going up to Jerusalem, and the Son of Man will be betrayed to the chief priests and to the scribes; and they will condemn Him to death, ¹⁹and deliver Him to the Gentiles to mock and to scourge and to crucify. And the third day He will rise again."

Greatness Is Serving

²⁰Then the mother of Zebedee's sons came to Him with her sons, kneeling down and asking something from Him.

²¹And He said to her, "What do you wish?"

She said to Him, "Grant that these two sons of mine may sit, one on Your right hand and the other on the left, in Your kingdom."

²²But Jesus answered and said, "You do not know what you ask. Are you able to drink the cup that I am about to drink, and be baptized with the baptism that I am baptized with?"ᵃ

They said to Him, "We are able."

²³So He said to them, "You will indeed drink My cup, and be baptized with the baptism that I am baptized with;ᵃ but to sit on My right hand and on My left is not Mine to give, but *it is for those* for whom it is prepared by My Father."

²⁴And when the ten heard *it,* they were greatly displeased with the two brothers. ²⁵But Jesus called them to *Himself* and said, "You know that the rulers of the Gentiles lord it over them, and those who are great exercise authority over them. ²⁶Yet it shall not be so among you; but whoever desires to become great among you, let him be your servant. ²⁷And whoever desires to be first among you, let him be your slave— ²⁸just as the Son of Man did not come to be served, but to serve, and to give His life a ransom for many."

Two Blind Men Receive Their Sight

²⁹Now as they went out of Jericho, a great multitude followed Him. ³⁰And behold, two blind men sitting by the road, when they heard that Jesus was passing by, cried out, saying, "Have mercy on us, O Lord, Son of David!"

³¹Then the multitude warned them that they

20:6 ᵃNU-Text omits *idle.*   **20:7** ᵃNU-Text omits the last clause of this verse.   **20:16** ᵃNU-Text omits the last sentence of this verse.   **20:22** ᵃNU-Text omits *and be baptized with the baptism that I am baptized with.*   **20:23** ᵃNU-Text omits *and be baptized with the baptism that I am baptized with.*

20:20–24 A few days before Jesus' entry into Jerusalem, Zebedee's wife made a request for her sons James and John. Though her request suggested dangerous ambition on her part, the angry response of the other ten disciples was also unwise and reflected similar self-interest. "The cup" was a common expression for great suffering (vv. 22; Matt. 26:39; John 18:11; Ps. 75:8; Is. 51:17). Just as His suffering and death must come before His rule, so also their suffering would come before their ruling with Him. Even though they would suffer for Christ, the positions, ranks, and rewards of the kingdom were a matter of God's sovereign choice (see Matt. 20:1–16). Jesus wanted His disciples to approach Him freely with their requests, but He was disappointed in their inflated view of their own importance and with their lack of spiritual sensitivity in understanding His mission. They were reaching for glory

without a willingness to endure the prerequisite sufferings. The brothers were confident that they were willing to share Jesus' mission, and indeed Jesus prophesied that they would endure great suffering for the gospel (Acts 12:2; Rev. 1:9).

20:25 The Jews used the term "Gentiles" to refer to anyone who was not ethnically a Jew. In common usage this term also included the idea that they were pagans, since they usually did not worship the God of Israel.

20:26, 27 Greatness in His kingdom is servanthood—the opposite of the world's view of greatness. Servanthood begins in the heart. Again, Jesus is concerned more about the attitudes in the hearts of His followers than with their works (see John 13:1–17).

should be quiet; but they cried out all the more, saying, "Have mercy on us, O Lord, Son of David!"

³²So Jesus stood still and called them, and said, "What do you want Me to do for you?"

³³They said to Him, "Lord, that our eyes may be opened." ³⁴So Jesus had compassion and touched their eyes. And immediately their eyes received sight, and they followed Him.

The Triumphal Entry

21 Now when they drew near Jerusalem, and came to Bethphage,[a] at the Mount of Olives, then Jesus sent two disciples, ²saying to them, "Go into the village opposite you, and immediately you will find a donkey tied, and a colt with her. Loose *them* and bring *them* to Me. ³And if anyone says anything to you, you shall say, 'The Lord has need of them,' and immediately he will send them."

⁴All[a] this was done that it might be fulfilled which was spoken by the prophet, saying:

⁵"Tell the daughter of Zion,
  'Behold, your King is coming to you,
  Lowly, and sitting on a donkey,
  A colt, the foal of a donkey.'"[a]

⁶So the disciples went and did as Jesus commanded them. ⁷They brought the donkey and the colt, laid their clothes on them, and set *Him*[a] on them. ⁸And a very great multitude spread their clothes on the road; others cut down branches from the trees and spread *them* on the road. ⁹Then the multitudes who went before and those who followed cried out, saying:

"Hosanna to the Son of David!
  'Blessed is He who comes in the name of the LORD!'[a]
  Hosanna in the highest!"

¹⁰And when He had come into Jerusalem, all the city was moved, saying, "Who is this?"

¹¹So the multitudes said, "This is Jesus, the prophet from Nazareth of Galilee."

Jesus Cleanses the Temple

¹²Then Jesus went into the temple of God[a] and drove out all those who bought and sold in the temple, and overturned the tables of the money changers and the seats of those who sold doves. ¹³And He said to them, "It is written, '*My house shall be called a house of prayer,*'[a] but you have made it a '*den of thieves.*'"[b]

¹⁴Then *the* blind and *the* lame came to Him in the temple, and He healed them. ¹⁵But when the chief priests and scribes saw the wonderful things that He did, and the children crying out in the temple and saying, "Hosanna to the Son of David!" they were indignant ¹⁶and said to Him, "Do You hear what these are saying?"

And Jesus said to them, "Yes. Have you never read,

'*Out of the mouth of babes and nursing infants
  You have perfected praise'?* "[a]

¹⁷Then He left them and went out of the city to Bethany, and He lodged there.

The Fig Tree Withered

¹⁸Now in the morning, as He returned to the city, He was hungry. ¹⁹And seeing a fig tree by the road, He came to it and found nothing on it but leaves, and said to it, "Let no fruit grow on you ever again." Immediately the fig tree withered away.

The Lesson of the Withered Fig Tree

²⁰And when the disciples saw *it,* they marveled, saying, "How did the fig tree wither away so soon?"

²¹So Jesus answered and said to them, "Assuredly, I say to you, if you have faith and do not doubt, you will not only do what was done to the fig tree, but also if you say to this mountain, 'Be removed and be cast into the sea,' it will be done. ²²And whatever things you ask in prayer, believing, you will receive."

Jesus' Authority Questioned

²³Now when He came into the temple, the chief priests and the elders of the people confronted

---

21:1 [a]M-Text reads *Bethsphage.* 21:4 [a]NU-Text omits *All.* 21:5 [a]Zechariah 9:9 21:7 [a]NU-Text reads *and He sat.* 21:9 [a]Psalm 118:26 21:12 [a]NU-Text omits *of God.* 21:13 [a]Isaiah 56:7 [b]Jeremiah 7:11 21:16 [a]Psalm 8:2

21:5 The Triumphal Entry is the culmination of the offering of the kingdom by Jesus (see Mark 11:2–8, note).

21:9 See Mark 11:9, note.

21:12, 13 When people came to worship at the temple, they needed animal sacrifices, wood, oil, and other items. Stalls were set up at the temple to sell these necessities, but since these objects sold for temple currency, the people needed to exchange their money. The temple, designed as a house of prayer, had become a marketplace where money changing and bargaining took place.

21:18, 19 The tree looked like it was bearing figs, but no fruit was there. Just as in Jesus' cleansing of the temple, His striking of the tree indicated the imminence of judgment. This miracle of destruction could be understood as an illustrated parable or teaching device. In this case, the fig tree represented Israel (see Hos. 9:10; Nah. 3:12; Zech. 10:2). The tree with its leaves had the marks of fruitfulness, but it bore no fruit. Israel was likewise practicing hypocrisy (Mark 7:6), and for this reason the nation was in line for judgment. Jesus might also have been illustrating religious hypocrites like the ones He had just thrown out of the temple (Matt. 6:2, 5, 16; 7:5; 15:7, 8; 22:18).

To love your child unconditionally is to determine that no matter what, you will always seek his highest good, not your own.

Jan Silvious

Him as He was teaching, and said, "By what authority are You doing these things? And who gave You this authority?"

²⁴But Jesus answered and said to them, "I also will ask you one thing, which if you tell Me, I likewise will tell you by what authority I do these things: ²⁵The baptism of John—where was it from? From heaven or from men?"

And they reasoned among themselves, saying, "If we say, 'From heaven,' He will say to us, 'Why then did you not believe him?' ²⁶But if we say, 'From men,' we fear the multitude, for all count John as a prophet." ²⁷So they answered Jesus and said, "We do not know."

And He said to them, "Neither will I tell you by what authority I do these things.

The Parable of the Two Sons

²⁸"But what do you think? A man had two sons, and he came to the first and said, 'Son, go, work today in my vineyard.' ²⁹He answered and said, 'I will not,' but afterward he regretted it and went. ³⁰Then he came to the second and said likewise. And he answered and said, 'I *go*, sir,' but he did not go. ³¹Which of the two did the will of *his* father?"

They said to Him, "The first."

Jesus said to them, "Assuredly, I say to you that tax collectors and harlots enter the kingdom of God before you. ³²For John came to you in the way of righteousness, and you did not believe him; but tax collectors and harlots believed him; and when you saw *it*, you did not afterward relent and believe him.

The Parable of the Wicked Vinedressers

³³"Hear another parable: There was a certain landowner who planted a vineyard and set a hedge around it, dug a winepress in it and built a tower. And he leased it to vinedressers and went into a far country. ³⁴Now when vintage-time drew near, he sent his servants to the vinedressers, that they

might receive its fruit. ³⁵And the vinedressers took his servants, beat one, killed one, and stoned another. ³⁶Again he sent other servants, more than the first, and they did likewise to them. ³⁷Then last of all he sent his son to them, saying, 'They will respect my son.' ³⁸But when the vinedressers saw the son, they said among themselves, 'This is the heir. Come, let us kill him and seize his inheritance.' ³⁹So they took him and cast *him* out of the vineyard and killed *him*.

⁴⁰"Therefore, when the owner of the vineyard comes, what will he do to those vinedressers?"

⁴¹They said to Him, "He will destroy those wicked men miserably, and lease *his* vineyard to other vinedressers who will render to him the fruits in their seasons."

⁴²Jesus said to them, "Have you never read in the Scriptures:

'The stone which the builders rejected
Has become the chief cornerstone.
This was the LORD's doing,
And it is marvelous in our eyes'? ᵃ

⁴³"Therefore I say to you, the kingdom of God will be taken from you and given to a nation bearing the fruits of it. ⁴⁴And whoever falls on this stone will be broken; but on whomever it falls, it will grind him to powder."

⁴⁵Now when the chief priests and Pharisees heard His parables, they perceived that He was speaking of them. ⁴⁶But when they sought to lay hands on Him, they feared the multitudes, because they took Him for a prophet.

The Parable of the Wedding Feast

22 And Jesus answered and spoke to them again by parables and said: ²"The kingdom of heaven is like a certain king who arranged a marriage

* * *

21:42 ᵃPsalm 118:22, 23

* * *

21:28–32 Jesus clearly applied this parable to the religious leaders confronting Him. The tax collector's status was similar to that of a prostitute in society. Jesus taught that the outcasts of society could enter His kingdom if they would repent; while those who had lived a "religious" life but would not repent were the real outcasts.

21:33–41 The components of the parable are obvious: The landowner is God; the vineyard is Israel; the vinedressers are the religious leaders; the servants are the prophets (including John the Baptist); and the son is Jesus. The vinedressers have

attempted to usurp the authority of the owner and make the property their own—the essence of rebellion against God. To do so they must kill the son. Jesus had been telling His followers the leaders would kill Him; here He confronted the leaders with the same message.

21:42–46 The line was clearly drawn and supported by the OT (Ps. 118:22, 23; Is. 28:16). To reject Jesus was and is to reject God (Acts 4:11, 12).

for his son, ³and sent out his servants to call those who were invited to the wedding; and they were not willing to come. ⁴Again, he sent out other servants, saying, 'Tell those who are invited, "See, I have prepared my dinner; my oxen and fatted cattle *are* killed, and all things *are* ready. Come to the wedding." ' ⁵But they made light of it and went their ways, one to his own farm, another to his business. ⁶And the rest seized his servants, treated *them* spitefully, and killed *them.* ⁷But when the king heard *about it,* he was furious. And he sent out his armies, destroyed those murderers, and burned up their city. ⁸Then he said to his servants, 'The wedding is ready, but those who were invited were not worthy. ⁹Therefore go into the highways, and as many as you find, invite to the wedding.' ¹⁰So those servants went out into the highways and gathered together all whom they found, both bad and good. And the wedding *hall* was filled with guests.

¹¹"But when the king came in to see the guests, he saw a man there who did not have on a wedding garment. ¹²So he said to him, 'Friend, how did you come in here without a wedding garment?' And he was speechless. ¹³Then the king said to the servants, 'Bind him hand and foot, take him away, andª cast *him* into outer darkness; there will be weeping and gnashing of teeth.'

¹⁴"For many are called, but few *are* chosen."

The Pharisees: Is It Lawful to Pay Taxes to Caesar?

¹⁵Then the Pharisees went and plotted how they might entangle Him in *His* talk. ¹⁶And they sent to Him their disciples with the Herodians, saying, "Teacher, we know that You are true, and teach the way of God in truth; nor do You care about anyone, for You do not regard the person of men. ¹⁷Tell us, therefore, what do You think? Is it lawful to pay taxes to Caesar, or not?"

¹⁸But Jesus perceived their wickedness, and said, "Why do you test Me, *you* hypocrites? ¹⁹Show Me the tax money."

So they brought Him a denarius.

²⁰And He said to them, "Whose image and inscription *is* this?"

²¹They said to Him, "Caesar's."

And He said to them, "Render therefore to Caesar the things that are Caesar's, and to God the things that are God's." ²²When they had heard *these words,* they marveled, and left Him and went their way.

The Sadducees: What About the Resurrection?

²³The same day the Sadducees, who say there is no resurrection, came to Him and asked Him, ²⁴saying: "Teacher, Moses said that if a man dies, having no children, his brother shall marry his wife and raise up offspring for his brother. ²⁵Now there were with us seven brothers. The first died after he had married, and having no offspring, left his wife to his brother. ²⁶Likewise the second also, and the third, even to the seventh. ²⁷Last of all the woman died also. ²⁸Therefore, in the resurrection, whose wife of the seven will she be? For they all had her."

²⁹Jesus answered and said to them, "You are mistaken, not knowing the Scriptures nor the power of God. ³⁰For in the resurrection they neither marry nor are given in marriage, but are like angels of Godª in heaven. ³¹But concerning the resurrection of the dead, have you not read what was spoken to you by God, saying, ³²*I am the God of Abraham, the God of Isaac, and the God of Jacob'?*ª God is not the God of the dead, but of the living." ³³And when the multitudes heard *this,* they were astonished at His teaching.

The Scribes: Which Is the First Commandment of All?

³⁴But when the Pharisees heard that He had silenced the Sadducees, they gathered together. ³⁵Then one of them, a lawyer, asked *Him a question,* testing Him, and saying, ³⁶"Teacher, which *is* the great commandment in the law?"

³⁷Jesus said to him, " *You shall love the* LORD *your God with all your heart, with all your soul, and with all your mind.'*ª ³⁸This is *the* first and great commandment. ³⁹And *the* second *is* like it: *'You shall love your neighbor as yourself.'*ª ⁴⁰On these two commandments hang all the Law and the Prophets."

•••••••••••••••••••••••

22:13 ªNU-Text omits *take him away, and.* **22:30** ªNU-Text omits *of God.* **22:32** ªExodus 3:6, 15 **22:37** ªDeuteronomy 6:5 **22:39** ªLeviticus 19:18

22:17–19 The trap seemed masterful—His answer would have to support either a rebellion against Rome or a rebellion against God. He effectively diffused their trap, while addressing an issue with which the conquered Jews wrestled—paying taxes to Rome (see Mark 12:14, note).

22:23–33 The Sadducees accepted only the Torah and thus rejected the Resurrection, which is not mentioned in the Pentateuch (Acts 23:8; see chart, Jewish Sects). By appealing to levirate marriage (Matt. 22:25–27; see Deut. 25:5, 6, note) in which a brother marries the childless widow of his deceased brother in order to perpetuate the brother's lineage, the Sadducees created a hypothetical worst-case scenario to entrap Jesus. Jesus pointed to their misunderstanding of God's power

and ignorance of Scripture and its teaching on the Resurrection (Matt. 22:29; see Is. 26:19). Though marriage as we know it will not exist in heaven, the lack of sexual relationships will in no way hinder the heavenly happiness and fulfillment God has planned for that blessed place. In fact, all relationships will surely surpass even the most joyous pleasure of intimacy on earth.

22:37–40 The scribes were experts in both theology and legal matters and thus the crafters of a hotly debated test question for Jesus. Jesus answered by linking the two commandments because the first is not possible without the second (see 1 John 4:20), any more than the second could stand without the first. This wholehearted devotion to God is at the heart of

CHRIST'S LAST DAYS IN JERUSALEM

Women looked on, waiting to minister to him (Matt. 27:55, 56).

"Gordon's Calvary" and the Garden Tomb.

from Mizpeh

from Ramah

Triumphal entry on Palm Sunday, fulfilling Isaiah's prophecy to "the daughter of Zion" (Matt. 21:1–11).

Pilate pronounced judgment despite warning from his wife (Matt. 27:19–26).

Pools of Bethesda

from Emmaus

from Bethany

Church of the Holy Sepulcher (Catholic site for Calvary and tomb).

Praetorium

Mishneh

Temple

Mt. of Olives

Preached and cleansed temple (Matt. 21:12, 13).

Royal Portico

Palace of Herod Antipas

Herod's Palace

Wall during the time of Christ

Theater

Upper City

"pinnacle of the temple"

Caiaphas' house—servant girls taunted Peter, and he denied Christ (Matt. 26:69–75).

Spring of Gihon

Kidron Valley

Lower City

Jesus arrested in Garden of Gethsemane (Matt. 26:47–56).

Essene Gate

Pool of Siloam

Refuse Gate

Water Gate

—N—

from Bethlehem

Hinnom Valley

Jesus: How Can David Call His Descendant Lord?

⁴¹While the Pharisees were gathered together, Jesus asked them, ⁴²saying, "What do you think about the Christ? Whose Son is He?"

They said to Him, "*The Son* of David."

⁴³He said to them, "How then does David in the Spirit call Him '*Lord*,' saying:

⁴⁴'*The LORD said to my Lord,*
"*Sit at My right hand,*
Till I make Your enemies Your footstool" '?ᵃ

⁴⁵If David then calls Him '*Lord*,' how is He his Son?"

⁴⁶And no one was able to answer Him a word, nor from that day on did anyone dare question Him anymore.

Woe to the Scribes and Pharisees

23 Then Jesus spoke to the multitudes and to His disciples, ²saying: "The scribes and the Pharisees sit in Moses' seat. ³Therefore whatever they tell you to observe,ᵃ *that* observe and do, but do not do according to their works; for they say, and do not do. ⁴For they bind heavy burdens, hard to bear, and lay *them* on men's shoulders; but they *themselves* will not move them with one of their fingers. ⁵But all their works they do to be seen by men. They make their phylacteries broad and enlarge the borders of their garments. ⁶They love the best places at feasts, the best seats in the synagogues, ⁷greetings in the marketplaces, and to be

22:44 ᵃPsalm 110:1 23:3 ᵃNU-Text omits *to observe.*

the OT Law and the teachings of Jesus. A right relationship to God is the beginning of everything and produces a right relationship to others.

22:41–46 Prior to this time Jesus had primarily talked about the religious leaders to His disciples and others. In these last confrontations and parables He had dealt with them directly. They have seen Him and heard the truth and now must answer the most important question: "What do you think about the Christ? Whose son is He?" "The Son of David" was not a sufficient answer (v. 42). This title was used for the Messiah

in reference to descent from the line of David, but many had not understood (or believed) that the Messiah would also be God's Son.

23:5 Phylacteries were leather boxes containing Scripture. They were worn by Jewish men during prayer time on the arm or the forehead. Biblical commands were written on small scrolls and placed in the OT frontlets or NT phylacteries (Ex. 13:9, 16; Deut. 6:8; 11:18). The Pharisees and scribes made their phylacteries showpieces, drawing attention to their supposed adherence to Scripture.

called by men, 'Rabbi, Rabbi.' [8]But you, do not be called 'Rabbi'; for One is your Teacher, the Christ,[a] and you are all brethren. [9]Do not call anyone on earth your father; for One is your Father, He who is in heaven. [10]And do not be called teachers; for One is your Teacher, the Christ. [11]But he who is greatest among you shall be your servant. [12]And whoever exalts himself will be humbled, and he who humbles himself will be exalted.

[13]"But woe to you, scribes and Pharisees, hypocrites! For you shut up the kingdom of heaven against men; for you neither go in *yourselves,* nor do you allow those who are entering to go in. [14]Woe to you, scribes and Pharisees, hypocrites! For you devour widows' houses, and for a pretense make long prayers. Therefore you will receive greater condemnation.[a]

[15]"Woe to you, scribes and Pharisees, hypocrites! For you travel land and sea to win one proselyte, and when he is won, you make him twice as much a son of hell as yourselves.

[16]"Woe to you, blind guides, who say, 'Whoever swears by the temple, it is nothing; but whoever swears by the gold of the temple, he is obliged *to perform it.'* [17]Fools and blind! For which is greater, the gold or the temple that sanctifies[a] the gold? [18]And, 'Whoever swears by the altar, it is nothing; but whoever swears by the gift that is on it, he is obliged *to perform it.'* [19]Fools and blind! For which is greater, the gift or the altar that sanctifies the gift? [20]Therefore he who swears by the altar, swears by it and by all things on it. [21]He who swears by the temple, swears by it and by Him who dwells[a] in it. [22]And he who swears by heaven, swears by the throne of God and by Him who sits on it.

[23]"Woe to you, scribes and Pharisees, hypocrites! For you pay tithe of mint and anise and cummin, and have neglected the weightier *matters* of the law: justice and mercy and faith. These you ought to have done, without leaving the others undone. [24]Blind guides, who strain out a gnat and swallow a camel!

[25]"Woe to you, scribes and Pharisees, hypocrites! For you cleanse the outside of the cup and dish, but inside they are full of extortion and self-indulgence.[a] [26]Blind Pharisee, first cleanse the inside of the cup and dish, that the outside of them may be clean also.

[27]"Woe to you, scribes and Pharisees, hypocrites! For you are like whitewashed tombs which indeed appear beautiful outwardly, but inside are full of dead *men's* bones and all uncleanness. [28]Even so you also outwardly appear righteous to men, but inside you are full of hypocrisy and lawlessness.

[29]"Woe to you, scribes and Pharisees, hypocrites! Because you build the tombs of the prophets and adorn the monuments of the righteous, [30]and say, 'If we had lived in the days of our fathers, we would not have been partakers with them in the blood of the prophets.'

[31]"Therefore you are witnesses against yourselves that you are sons of those who murdered the prophets. [32]Fill up, then, the measure of your fathers' *guilt.* [33]Serpents, brood of vipers! How can you escape the condemnation of hell? [34]Therefore, indeed, I send you prophets, wise men, and scribes: *some* of them you will kill and crucify, and *some* of them you will scourge in your synagogues and persecute from city to city, [35]that on you may come all the righteous blood shed on the earth, from the blood of righteous Abel to the blood of Zechariah, son of Berechiah, whom you murdered between the temple and the altar. [36]Assuredly, I say to you, all these things will come upon this generation.

Jesus Laments over Jerusalem

[37]"O Jerusalem, Jerusalem, the one who kills the prophets and stones those who are sent to her! How often I wanted to gather your children together, as a hen gathers her chicks under *her* wings, but you were not willing! [38]See! Your house is left to you desolate; [39]for I say to you, you shall see Me no more till you say, '*Blessed is He who comes in the name of the LORD!*' "[a]

Jesus Predicts the Destruction of the Temple

24 Then Jesus went out and departed from the temple, and His disciples came up to show Him the buildings of the temple. [2]And Jesus said to them, "Do you not see all these things? Assuredly, I say to you, not *one* stone shall be left here upon another, that shall not be thrown down."

The Signs of the Times and the End of the Age

[3]Now as He sat on the Mount of Olives, the disciples came to Him privately, saying, "Tell us, when

---

23:8 [a]NU-Text omits *the Christ.* 23:14 [a]NU-Text omits this verse.
23:17 [a]NU-Text reads *sanctified.* 23:21 [a]M-Text reads *dwelt.*
23:25 [a]M-Text reads *unrighteousness.* 23:39 [a]Psalm 118:26

23:8–10 Only Jesus was qualified to sit in Moses' seat.

23:13–36 Jesus pronounced seven woes, condemning the rejection of the kingdom, false teaching of Scripture, attempts at purification, and attitudes toward the prophets God had sent. Jesus' language had been strong and pointed. Nevertheless, His heart ached over the situation, and He yearned to forgive and heal (v. 37).

24:1, 2 The destruction of the temple was literally fulfilled in A.D. 70 when the Romans destroyed Jerusalem.

24:3 The disciples knew that Jesus was the Messiah (Matt. 16:16–20), the temple would be destroyed, and the kingdom was coming (Matt. 20:20–28). Since they did not understand other events must also occur—Jesus' Crucifixion and death—they might have thought the events Jesus mentioned would all

ABOMINATION OF DESOLATION

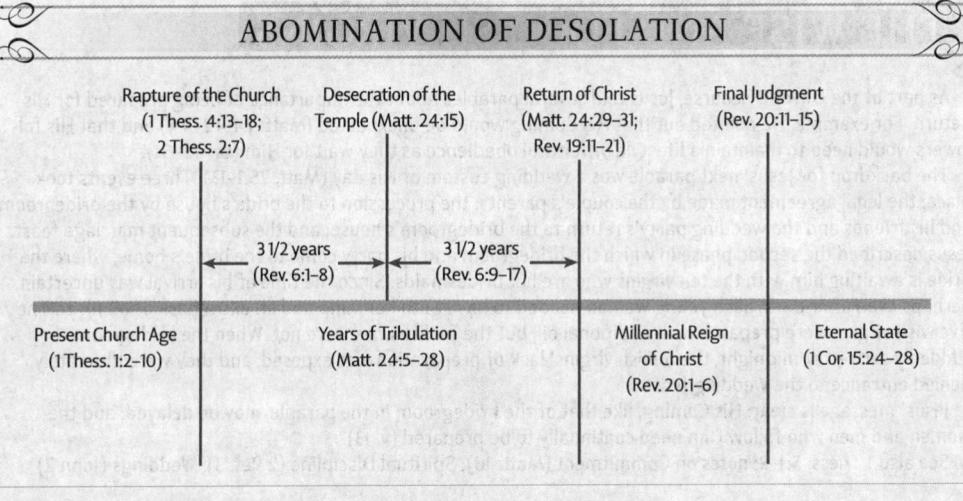

Rapture of the Church (1 Thess. 4:13–18; 2 Thess. 2:7)	Desecration of the Temple (Matt. 24:15)	Return of Christ (Matt. 24:29–31; Rev. 19:11–21)	Final Judgment (Rev. 20:11–15)
	3 1/2 years (Rev. 6:1–8) ← →	3 1/2 years (Rev. 6:9–17) →	
Present Church Age (1 Thess. 1:2–10)	Years of Tribulation (Matt. 24:5–28)	Millennial Reign of Christ (Rev. 20:1–6)	Eternal State (1 Cor. 15:24–28)

*See also Dan. 9:27; 2 Thess. 2:2–4.

will these things be? And what *will be* the sign of Your coming, and of the end of the age?"

⁴And Jesus answered and said to them: "Take heed that no one deceives you. ⁵For many will come in My name, saying, 'I am the Christ,' and will deceive many. ⁶And you will hear of wars and rumors of wars. See that you are not troubled; for allᵃ *these things* must come to pass, but the end is not yet. ⁷For nation will rise against nation, and kingdom against kingdom. And there will be famines, pestilences,ᵃ and earthquakes in various places. ⁸All these *are* the beginning of sorrows.

⁹"Then they will deliver you up to tribulation and kill you, and you will be hated by all nations for My name's sake. ¹⁰And then many will be offended, will betray one another, and will hate one another. ¹¹Then many false prophets will rise up and deceive many. ¹²And because lawlessness will abound, the love of many will grow cold. ¹³But he who endures to the end shall be saved. ¹⁴And this gospel of the kingdom will be preached in all the world as a witness to all the nations, and then the end will come.

The Great Tribulation

¹⁵"Therefore when you see the 'abomination of desolation,'ᵃ spoken of by Daniel the prophet, standing in the holy place" (whoever reads, let him understand), ¹⁶"then let those who are in Judea flee to the mountains. ¹⁷Let him who is on the housetop not go down to take anything out of his house. ¹⁸And let him who is in the field not go back to get his clothes. ¹⁹But woe to those who are pregnant and to those who are nursing babies in those days! ²⁰And pray that your flight may not be in winter or on the Sabbath. ²¹For then there will be great tribulation, such as has not been since the beginning of the world until this time, no, nor

24:6 ᵃNU-Text omits *all.* 24:7 ᵃNU-Text omits *pestilences.* 24:15 ᵃDaniel 11:31; 12:11

happen soon. Jesus told them they would see some of these things happen in a comparatively short time (persecution, abomination at the temple, destruction of Jerusalem and the temple), but He also made it clear that there would be a time lapse before it all came to pass. The events described obviously demanded a longer period to transpire: the coming of false prophets, wars and rumors of wars, kingdom rising against kingdom, famine, earthquakes, and the extension of the gospel to the entire world before the kingdom would come literally. The emphasis then would be upon the necessity of faith and obedience even in times of suffering and sorrow rather than on a timetable of events.

24:4–14 Jesus described the overall future of the world that would include natural disasters, persecution, false prophets, hatred of Christians, betrayal, defection, lawlessness, and lack of love. The gospel would be spread despite all this.

24:15 The abomination of desolation prophesied by the prophet Daniel (Dan. 9:27; 11:31; 12:11; see chart, Abomination of Desolation) is a good example of a prophecy with more than one fulfillment. The term refers to the defilement of the temple, especially the altar of sacrifice. The altar was a picture of the sacrifice of Christ as the only atonement for sin. The "abomination" would cast aside what represented Christ and offer sacrifices to other gods. In 168 B.C. Antiochus Epiphanes sacked the temple, erected a statue to Zeus above the altar, and sacrificed swine (unclean animals). Jesus predicted that similar events would happen again.

24:16–28 Jesus described events that would occur in Jerusalem in the future. There would be a Great Tribulation before He would come to set up His physical kingdom (see Rev. 6; chart, Millennial Views).

THE WISE AND FOOLISH VIRGINS

As part of the Olivet Discourse, Jesus told several parables about the importance of being prepared for His Return. For example, He pointed out that His Coming would be unexpected (Matt. 24:42–44) and that His followers would need to maintain a lifestyle of faithful obedience as they wait for Him (vv. 45–51).

The backdrop for Jesus' next parable was a wedding custom of His day (Matt. 25:1–13). Three events took place: the legal agreement made by the couple's parents; the procession to the bride's house by the bridegroom and his friends and the wedding party's return to the bridegroom's house; and the subsequent marriage feast. Jesus described the second phase in which the bridegroom and his party come to the bride's home, where the bride is awaiting him with the ten virgins who are her bridesmaids. Since the time of his arrival was uncertain, perhaps even after dark, each young woman needed to have both her lamp and an extra flask of oil for it. The five wise virgins were prepared with additional oil, but the foolish ones were not. When the bridegroom suddenly arrived at midnight, the foolish virgins' lack of preparation was exposed, and they were ultimately denied entrance to the wedding feast.

Jesus' message is clear: His Coming, like that of the bridegroom in the parable, may be delayed; and the women and men who follow Him need continually to be prepared (v. 13).

See also 1 Thess. 5:1–3; notes on Commitment (Matt. 16); Spiritual Discipline (2 Pet. 3); Weddings (John 2)

---

ever shall be. ²²And unless those days were shortened, no flesh would be saved; but for the elect's sake those days will be shortened.

²³"Then if anyone says to you, 'Look, here *is* the Christ!' or 'There!' do not believe *it.* ²⁴For false christs and false prophets will rise and show great signs and wonders to deceive, if possible, even the elect. ²⁵See, I have told you beforehand.

²⁶"Therefore if they say to you, 'Look, He is in the desert!' do not go out; *or* 'Look, *He is* in the inner rooms!' do not believe *it.* ²⁷For as the lightning comes from the east and flashes to the west, so also will the coming of the Son of Man be. ²⁸For wherever the carcass is, there the eagles will be gathered together.

The Coming of the Son of Man

²⁹"Immediately after the tribulation of those days the sun will be darkened, and the moon will not give its light; the stars will fall from heaven, and the powers of the heavens will be shaken. ³⁰Then the sign of the Son of Man will appear in heaven, and then all the tribes of the earth will mourn, and they will see the Son of Man coming on the clouds of heaven with power and great glory. ³¹And He will send His angels with a great sound of a trumpet, and they will gather together His elect from the four winds, from one end of heaven to the other.

The Parable of the Fig Tree

³²"Now learn this parable from the fig tree: When its branch has already become tender and puts forth leaves, you know that summer *is* near. ³³So you also, when you see all these things, know that it[a] is near—at the doors! ³⁴Assuredly, I say to you, this generation will by no means pass away till all these things take place. ³⁵Heaven and earth will pass away, but My words will by no means pass away.

No One Knows the Day or Hour

³⁶"But of that day and hour no one knows, not even the angels of heaven,[a] but My Father only. ³⁷But as the days of Noah *were,* so also will the coming of the Son of Man be. ³⁸For as in the days before the flood, they were eating and drinking, marrying and giving in marriage, until the day that Noah entered the ark, ³⁹and did not know until the flood came and took them all away, so also will the coming of the Son of Man be. ⁴⁰Then two *men* will be in the field: one will be taken and the

••••••••••••••••••••

24:33 [a]Or He   24:36 [a]NU-Text adds *nor the Son.*

24:30 Jesus' Incarnation was relatively quiet and uneventful. Only a few witnessed the unusual events: Mary and Joseph had angelic visits; a group of shepherds heard an angelic choir; wise men from another nation saw a phenomenal star. Jesus came as the Lamb of God to make peace between God and man. When He would come again to set up His kingdom, heaven and earth would dramatically announce Him, and all would see the display. He would come as King in power and glory and declare war against His enemies (see Rev. 6).

24:34 Generation (Gk. *genea*) may refer to the nation Israel,

suggesting her continued existence until the last days; it may mean "age" or "time period," referring to the dispensation of grace; or it may mean the time period of 30 years. If the latter is the case, then the text would indicate that these signs would *begin* to be fulfilled before that generation would end.

24:36–44 Jesus made it clear that while a general time may be determined for His return (when all these events occur), only the Father knows the day and hour. Christ's coming will surprise everyone. The believers' responsibility is not to attempt to guess the day but always to be ready.

I like to define forgiveness as giving up the right to punish the one who has hurt you." That's what Jesus did on the cross.

Jan Silvious

other left. ⁴¹Two *women will be* grinding at the mill: one will be taken and the other left. ⁴²Watch therefore, for you do not know what hourª your Lord is coming. ⁴³But know this, that if the master of the house had known what hour the thief would come, he would have watched and not allowed his house to be broken into. ⁴⁴Therefore you also be ready, for the Son of Man is coming at an hour you do not expect.

The Faithful Servant and the Evil Servant

⁴⁵"Who then is a faithful and wise servant, whom his master made ruler over his household, to give them food in due season? ⁴⁶Blessed *is* that servant whom his master, when he comes, will find so doing. ⁴⁷Assuredly, I say to you that he will make him ruler over all his goods. ⁴⁸But if that evil servant says in his heart, 'My master is delaying his coming,'ª ⁴⁹and begins to beat *his* fellow servants, and to eat and drink with the drunkards, ⁵⁰the master of that servant will come on a day when he is not looking for *him* and at an hour that he is not aware of, ⁵¹and will cut him in two and appoint *him* his portion with the hypocrites. There shall be weeping and gnashing of teeth.

The Parable of the Wise and Foolish Virgins

25 "Then the kingdom of heaven shall be likened to ten virgins who took their lamps and went out to meet the bridegroom. ²Now five of them were wise, and five *were* foolish. ³Those who *were* foolish took their lamps and took no oil with them, ⁴but the wise took oil in their vessels with their lamps. ⁵But while the bridegroom was delayed, they all slumbered and slept.

⁶"And at midnight a cry was *heard:* 'Behold, the bridegroom is coming;ª go out to meet him!' ⁷Then all those virgins arose and trimmed their lamps. ⁸And the foolish said to the wise, 'Give us *some* of your oil, for our lamps are going out.' ⁹But the wise answered, saying, '*No,* lest there should not be enough for us and you; but go rather to those who sell, and buy for yourselves.' ¹⁰And while they went to buy, the bridegroom came, and those who were ready went in with him to the wedding; and the door was shut.

¹¹"Afterward the other virgins came also, saying, 'Lord, Lord, open to us!' ¹²But he answered and said, 'Assuredly, I say to you, I do not know you.'

¹³"Watch therefore, for you know neither the day nor the hourª in which the Son of Man is coming.

The Parable of the Talents

¹⁴"For *the kingdom of heaven is* like a man traveling to a far country, *who* called his own servants and delivered his goods to them. ¹⁵And to one he gave five talents, to another two, and to another one, to each according to his own ability; and immediately he went on a journey. ¹⁶Then he who had received the five talents went and traded with them, and made another five talents. ¹⁷And likewise he who *had received* two gained two more also. ¹⁸But he who had received one went and dug in the ground, and hid his lord's money. ¹⁹After a long time the lord of those servants came and settled accounts with them.

²⁰"So he who had received five talents came and brought five other talents, saying, 'Lord, you delivered to me five talents; look, I have gained five more talents besides them.' ²¹His lord said to him, 'Well *done,* good and faithful servant; you

---

24:42 ªNU-Text reads *day.* 24:48 ªNU-Text omits *his coming.* 25:6 ªNU-Text omits *is coming.* 25:13 ªNU-Text omits the rest of this verse.

24:45–51 The servant's assignment was to be faithful in caring for the household and distributing food. Similarly, the priests and teachers had been given the assignment of caring for the people of Israel. When they failed in their assignment and abused the members of God's household, their punishment was severe.

25:1–13 The parable of the ten virgins is found only in Matthew (see The Wise and Foolish Virgins). Jesus taught this parable a few days before the Crucifixion. He had recently taught about the timing of the kingdom's appearance (see Matt. 24). Here He used three parables to teach the importance of personal preparation for it.

25:14–30 The parable of the talents is connected to the previ-

ous parable of the ten virgins, as it illustrates *how* to prepare for His coming. A talent could be of gold, silver, or copper. It was measured and valued according to the type of metal and its weight. A Roman-Attic talent is thought to have been worth 6,000 denarii—the amount a day laborer would need 20 years to earn (see chart, Money and Measurements in the Bible). Each person according to his own ability was expected to use what he had been given. The one given five talents and another given two talents both used their talents and received the same reward. The person given one talent did not even try to fulfill the responsibility the master gave him. His talent was taken away; he received no reward; the relationship between him and his master was destroyed.

were faithful over a few things, I will make you ruler over many things. Enter into the joy of your lord.' ²²He also who had received two talents came and said, 'Lord, you delivered to me two talents; look, I have gained two more talents besides them.' ²³His lord said to him, 'Well *done,* good and faithful servant; you have been faithful over a few things, I will make you ruler over many things. Enter into the joy of your lord.'

²⁴"Then he who had received the one talent came and said, 'Lord, I knew you to be a hard man, reaping where you have not sown, and gathering where you have not scattered seed. ²⁵And I was afraid, and went and hid your talent in the ground. Look, *there* you have *what is* yours.'

²⁶"But his lord answered and said to him, 'You wicked and lazy servant, you knew that I reap where I have not sown, and gather where I have not scattered seed. ²⁷So you ought to have deposited my money with the bankers, and at my coming I would have received back my own with interest. ²⁸Therefore take the talent from him, and give *it* to him who has ten talents.

²⁹"For to everyone who has, more will be given, and he will have abundance; but from him who does not have, even what he has will be taken away. ³⁰And cast the unprofitable servant into the outer darkness. There will be weeping and gnashing of teeth.'

The Son of Man Will Judge the Nations

³¹"When the Son of Man comes in His glory, and all the holyᵃ angels with Him, then He will sit on the throne of His glory. ³²All the nations will be gathered before Him, and He will separate them one from another, as a shepherd divides *his* sheep from the goats. ³³And He will set the sheep on His right hand, but the goats on the left. ³⁴Then the King will say to those on His right hand, 'Come, you blessed of My Father, inherit the kingdom prepared for you from the foundation of the world: ³⁵for I was hungry and you gave Me food; I was thirsty and you gave Me drink; I was a stranger and you took Me in; ³⁶I *was* naked and you clothed Me; I was sick and you visited Me; I was in prison and you came to Me.'

³⁷"Then the righteous will answer Him, saying, 'Lord, when did we see You hungry and feed *You,* or thirsty and give *You* drink? ³⁸When did we see You a stranger and take *You* in, or naked and clothe *You?* ³⁹Or when did we see You sick, or in prison, and come to You?' ⁴⁰And the King will answer and say to them, 'Assuredly, I say to you, inasmuch as you did *it* to one of the least of these My brethren, you did *it* to Me.'

⁴¹"Then He will also say to those on the left hand, 'Depart from Me, you cursed, into the everlasting fire prepared for the devil and his angels: ⁴²for I was hungry and you gave Me no food; I was thirsty and you gave Me no drink; ⁴³I was a stranger and you did not take Me in, naked and you did not clothe Me, sick and in prison and you did not visit Me.'

⁴⁴"Then they also will answer Him,ᵃ saying, 'Lord, when did we see You hungry or thirsty or a stranger or naked or sick or in prison, and did not minister to You?' ⁴⁵Then He will answer them, saying, 'Assuredly, I say to you, inasmuch as you did not do *it* to one of the least of these, you did not do *it* to Me.' ⁴⁶And these will go away into everlasting punishment, but the righteous into eternal life."

The Plot to Kill Jesus

26 Now it came to pass, when Jesus had finished all these sayings, *that* He said to His disciples, ²"You know that after two days is the Passover, and the Son of Man will be delivered up to be crucified."

³Then the chief priests, the scribes,ᵃ and the elders of the people assembled at the palace of the high priest, who was called Caiaphas, ⁴and plotted to take Jesus by trickery and kill *Him.* ⁵But they said, "Not during the feast, lest there be an uproar among the people."

The Anointing at Bethany

⁶And when Jesus was in Bethany at the house of Simon the leper, ⁷a woman came to Him having

---

25:31 ᵃNU-Text omits *holy.*   25:44 ᵃNU-Text and M-Text omit *Him.*
26:3 ᵃNU-Text omits *the scribes.*

25:31–46 The separation of the sheep and goats illustrates a truth. God knows who belongs to Him (see Matt. 13:24). God's children can be detected in how they treat "the least of these My brethren" (Matt. 25:40). Reaching out to Jesus' brethren does not enable a person to attain salvation; that comes only through confession of Jesus (Matt. 10:32). Reaching out is a result of salvation because it is a matter of responding to His love by obeying His commands.

26:1, 2 The Passover was an annual celebration of the ceremony Moses instituted the night before the people left Egypt (Ex. 12).

26:1–46 The Lord's Passion is described in this section. Jesus

prepared His disciples for the trial, sentencing, and Crucifixion; His enemies prepared their plans for taking Him; a woman prepared His body for burial; Judas prepared to betray Him; and Jesus prepared Himself in prayer. These events probably took place late Tuesday evening (actually Wednesday, as days ended at sunset) before His death (see chart, The Last Week in the Life of Jesus).

26:3 The chief priests, the scribes, and the elders of the people were the ones who tried to challenge Jesus. He had met their challenges and repeatedly defeated and unmasked them.

26:6–13 Two anointings took place—this one in Bethany and

SERVANT GIRL

Just as a master craftsman knows how to put a small amount of pressure in the right place at the right time in order to reveal weaknesses, God often uses small things to reveal the weaknesses of an individual.

Peter was sure that he, of all the disciples, would never desert Jesus (Matt. 26:35). He may not have had the sensitivity of John, the literary gifts of Matthew, or the servant's heart of Andrew, but the one thing he did have was courage. He proved his courage when he swung his sword at the priest's servant in the Garden of Gethsemane. However, only a few hours later he met the servant girl and denied he ever knew Jesus. What the powerful temple rulers could not make Peter do one moment, a seemingly insignificant servant girl accomplished the next.

The girl's name or from where she came is unknown. She belonged to the household of the high priest (Mark 14:66), and one of her duties was to meet people at the door (John 18:17). God used her in one brief encounter to put the right amount of pressure at the right time on one of His children in order to bring his weakness to the forefront. Just as with David's small stone (see 1 Sam. 17:49), God often combines little things with His strength to overpower the weaknesses in the lives of His children.

See also Mark 14:66–68; Luke 22:56, 57; John 18:17; notes on Girlhood (Prov. 1); Testing (Ps. 12); Vows (Num. 30)

an alabaster flask of very costly fragrant oil, and she poured *it* on His head as He sat *at the table.* [8]But when His disciples saw *it,* they were indignant, saying, "Why this waste? [9]For this fragrant oil might have been sold for much and given to *the* poor."

[10]But when Jesus was aware of *it,* He said to them, "Why do you trouble the woman? For she has done a good work for Me. [11]For you have the poor with you always, but Me you do not have always. [12]For in pouring this fragrant oil on My body, she did *it* for My burial. [13]Assuredly, I say to you, wherever this gospel is preached in the whole world, what this woman has done will also be told as a memorial to her."

Judas Agrees to Betray Jesus

[14]Then one of the twelve, called Judas Iscariot, went to the chief priests [15]and said, "What are you willing to give me if I deliver Him to you?" And they counted out to him thirty pieces of silver. [16]So from that time he sought opportunity to betray Him.

Jesus Celebrates Passover with His Disciples

[17]Now on the first *day of the Feast* of the Unleavened Bread the disciples came to Jesus, saying to Him, "Where do You want us to prepare for You to eat the Passover?"

[18]And He said, "Go into the city to a certain man, and say to him, 'The Teacher says, "My time is at hand; I will keep the Passover at your house with My disciples." ' "

[19]So the disciples did as Jesus had directed them; and they prepared the Passover.

[20]When evening had come, He sat down with the twelve. [21]Now as they were eating, He said, "Assuredly, I say to you, one of you will betray Me."

[22]And they were exceedingly sorrowful, and each of them began to say to Him, "Lord, is it I?"

[23]He answered and said, "He who dipped *his* hand with Me in the dish will betray Me. [24]The Son of Man indeed goes just as it is written of Him, but woe to that man by whom the Son of Man is betrayed! It would have been good for that man if he had not been born."

[25]Then Judas, who was betraying Him, answered and said, "Rabbi, is it I?"

He said to him, "You have said it."

---

an earlier one in Galilee (Luke 7:36). To honor a revered rabbi in this manner was not an uncommon event. The oil was costly (about 300 denarii), worth about a year's wages (see chart, Money and Measurements in the Bible). Mary of Bethany is identified as the woman (John 12:1–8). Though the text does not actually say Mary fully understood that Jesus was going to die, her actions may indicate she had a better grasp of what was taking place than did the disciples. Jesus understood her act as one of devout preparation and distinguished it as something set apart from mere good works.

26:14 Judas' motivation for betrayal is not indicated. Perhaps he was offended by Jesus' earlier rebuke or by the finality of Jesus' words, which indicated that He would not seek an earthly kingdom; even the money itself could have entered into consideration. In any case, Judas' decision to betray Jesus stands in sharp contrast to Mary's devotion.

26:15 Thirty pieces of silver was the value of a male or female slave gored to death accidentally by an ox (Ex. 21:32).

26:17 The first day of the Feast of Unleavened Bread was the beginning of the Passover celebration. Jews were to rid the house of all leaven and use only unleavened bread during the celebration (Lev. 23:6).

Jesus Institutes the Lord's Supper

²⁶And as they were eating, Jesus took bread, blessedᵃ and broke *it*, and gave *it* to the disciples and said, "Take, eat; this is My body."

²⁷Then He took the cup, and gave thanks, and gave *it* to them, saying, "Drink from it, all of you. ²⁸For this is My blood of the newᵃ covenant, which is shed for many for the remission of sins. ²⁹But I say to you, I will not drink of this fruit of the vine from now on until that day when I drink it new with you in My Father's kingdom."

³⁰And when they had sung a hymn, they went out to the Mount of Olives.

Jesus Predicts Peter's Denial

³¹Then Jesus said to them, "All of you will be made to stumble because of Me this night, for it is written:

'I will strike the Shepherd,
And the sheep of the flock will be scattered.'ᵃ

³²But after I have been raised, I will go before you to Galilee."

³³Peter answered and said to Him, "Even if all are made to stumble because of You, I will never be made to stumble."

³⁴Jesus said to him, "Assuredly, I say to you that this night, before the rooster crows, you will deny Me three times."

³⁵Peter said to Him, "Even if I have to die with You, I will not deny You!"

And so said all the disciples.

The Prayer in the Garden

³⁶Then Jesus came with them to a place called Gethsemane, and said to the disciples, "Sit here while I go and pray over there." ³⁷And He took with Him Peter and the two sons of Zebedee, and He began to be sorrowful and deeply distressed. ³⁸Then He said to them, "My soul is exceedingly sorrowful, even to death. Stay here and watch with Me."

³⁹He went a little farther and fell on His face, and prayed, saying, "O My Father, if it is possible, let this cup pass from Me; nevertheless, not as I will, but as You *will.*"

⁴⁰Then He came to the disciples and found them sleeping, and said to Peter, "What! Could you not watch with Me one hour? ⁴¹Watch and pray, lest you enter into temptation. The spirit indeed *is* willing, but the flesh *is* weak."

⁴²Again, a second time, He went away and prayed, saying, "O My Father, if this cup cannot pass away from Me unlessᵃ I drink it, Your will be done." ⁴³And He came and found them asleep again, for their eyes were heavy.

⁴⁴So He left them, went away again, and prayed the third time, saying the same words. ⁴⁵Then He came to His disciples and said to them, "Are *you* still sleeping and resting? Behold, the hour is at hand, and the Son of Man is being betrayed into the hands of sinners. ⁴⁶Rise, let us be going. See, My betrayer is at hand."

Betrayal and Arrest in Gethsemane

⁴⁷And while He was still speaking, behold, Judas, one of the twelve, with a great multitude with swords and clubs, came from the chief priests and elders of the people.

⁴⁸Now His betrayer had given them a sign, saying, "Whomever I kiss, He is the One; seize Him." ⁴⁹Immediately he went up to Jesus and said, "Greetings, Rabbi!" and kissed Him.

···············

26:26 ᵃM-Text reads *gave thanks for.*   26:28 ᵃNU-Text omits *new.* 26:31 ᵃZechariah 13:7   26:42 ᵃNU-Text reads *if this may not pass away unless.*

26:24 Though the betrayal by one of the disciples was foretold, Judas was still personally responsible for his actions.

26:26–29 Jesus instituted the Lord's Supper by using two symbols—bread and the fruit of the vine. The unleavened bread was a reminder of the hasty departure of God's people from Egypt (Ex. 12). Jesus gave the bread new meaning by associating it with His body, which would be broken (Matt. 26:26). This object lesson pointed to His death on the Cross. The original Passover ceremony used several "cups" (Ex. 6:6, 7). Jesus gave new meaning to the cup as well (Matt. 26:28, 29). It would stand for His blood, which would be shed on the Cross. After His Resurrection, this celebration would look back to Jesus' death on the Cross and forward to His return. The hymn would probably be from one of the Hallel psalms (see Ps. 114–118; see chart, The Types of Psalms). Jesus reminded them there would be a kingdom, and He would be with them again.

26:31 Jesus also referred to Himself as the Shepherd who would give His life for His sheep (John 10:1–15; see also Zech. 13:7).

26:36–44 Gethsemane (lit. "oil press"), the garden located across the Kidron on the Mount of Olives, was likely so named because of the abundance of olive trees. There, in prayer, Jesus fought His greatest battle. The intense sorrow was not primarily over the physical torture or dying, for He had been telling them for months He was willing to die (vv. 21–23). Rather, it was over needing to experience God's "cup of wrath." In the OT God's cup of wrath was poured out on sinners resulting in desolation, waste, and becoming a curse (Jer. 25:13–18; 49:12, 13). He, the pure, sinless Son of God, would become sin, which would result in separation between Himself and the Father. It was this separation that He dreaded (Matt. 27:46). Because He was obedient, He experienced something no Christian would ever experience—separation from God (Rom. 8:38, 39).

26:47–56 A series of predictions were fulfilled: Judas betrayed Him, the priests and elders seized Him, and the disciples fled. The central character, of course, was Jesus. His amazing calmness and willingness to endure what faced Him reflected the results of His prayer battle in the garden.

WOMEN AND JESUS IN HIS LAST DAYS

THE WOMAN	THE EVENT	HER MINISTRY TO JESUS	REFERENCE
Unnamed woman (See John 11, Mary of Bethany)	The anointing of Jesus at Bethany	She used expensive and fragrant oil to anoint Jesus' head.	Matt. 26:6–13
Unnamed servant girl	The testing of Peter	She asked Peter about his association with Jesus.	Matt. 26:69, 70
Another girl	The testing of Peter	She asked Peter about his association with Jesus.	Matt. 26:71, 72
Pilate's wife	The trial of Jesus	She pleaded with her husband to release Jesus.	Matt. 27:17–19
Unnamed women	The journey to the Crucifixion site	They mourned for Jesus.	Luke 23:26–29
Mary (Jesus' mother); Mary (the wife of Clopas and the aunt of Jesus); Mary Magdalene	The Crucifixion	They stood by the Cross, suffering with Jesus.	John 19:25–27
Women from Galilee: Mary Magdalene; Mary (the mother of James and Joses); Salome (the wife of Zebedee)	The Crucifixion and burial	They ministered to Jesus in His last days, including preparing His body for burial.	Matt. 27:55, 56
Mary Magdalene; Mary (the mother of James); Joanna	The Resurrection	They were the first to announce His Resurrection.	Matt. 28:1–10; Luke 24:1–12

⁵⁰But Jesus said to him, "Friend, why have you come?"

Then they came and laid hands on Jesus and took Him. ⁵¹And suddenly, one of those *who were* with Jesus stretched out *his* hand and drew his sword, struck the servant of the high priest, and cut off his ear.

⁵²But Jesus said to him, "Put your sword in its place, for all who take the sword will perishᵃ by the sword. ⁵³Or do you think that I cannot now pray to My Father, and He will provide Me with more than twelve legions of angels? ⁵⁴How then could the Scriptures be fulfilled, that it must happen thus?"

⁵⁵In that hour Jesus said to the multitudes, "Have you come out, as against a robber, with swords and clubs to take Me? I sat daily with you, teaching in the temple, and you did not seize Me. ⁵⁶But all this was done that the Scriptures of the prophets might be fulfilled."

Then all the disciples forsook Him and fled.

Jesus Faces the Sanhedrin

⁵⁷And those who had laid hold of Jesus led *Him* away to Caiaphas the high priest, where the scribes and the elders were assembled. ⁵⁸But Peter followed Him at a distance to the high priest's courtyard. And he went in and sat with the servants to see the end.

26:52 ᵃM-Text reads *die*.

26:59, 60 The chief priests, the elders, and all the council would constitute the Jews' highest court, known as the Sanhedrin. Scholars have discussed at length what parts of Jesus' trials were illegal. For example, the proceedings took place at the high priest's home rather than the courts; no one spoke for His defense; and the trial was at night. Whether or not these were illegal, the calling of false witnesses certainly was a travesty in legal proceedings.

PILATE'S INTUITIVE WIFE

Only one verse in the Bible refers to Pilate's wife (Matt. 27:19); yet it tells much. She appeared at Jesus' trials when all Jerusalem was divided over His fate, "What then shall I do with Jesus who is called Christ?" (v. 22). Some were hiding, most were condemning, and a few—almost all women—were following at a distance (vv. 55, 56).

Her husband was on precarious ground. He was not popular with the Jewish people he governed and had few, if any, diplomatic skills (brute force was his style). The danger of rebellion continually bubbled beneath the surface, and Pilate had learned to avoid offending the Jewish leaders unless personally threatened. Releasing Jesus would mean no political gain; in fact, the opposite was true. Yet he tried. Obviously, he was impressed by this man (v. 14) and considered Him innocent (v. 18). Then his wife had a dream.

Whether her dream was divinely inspired or a result of her own feelings is unknown. She was disturbed enough to send a note in the middle of the trial procedures. She described Jesus as a "just Man," giving a clue to her dream. Convinced of His innocence, she encouraged her husband to an action that was politically unsound.

Did she actually respond to Christ? No evidence is presented. But she had, at least one time in her life, faced the universal decision, "What then shall I do with Jesus?" and responded with conviction and courage.

See also notes on Decision Making (1 Cor. 8); Influence (Esth. 4)

---

[59]Now the chief priests, the elders,[a] and all the council sought false testimony against Jesus to put Him to death, [60]but found none. Even though many false witnesses came forward, they found none.[a] But at last two false witnesses[b] came forward [61]and said, "This *fellow* said, 'I am able to destroy the temple of God and to build it in three days.' "

[62]And the high priest arose and said to Him, "Do You answer nothing? What *is it* these men testify against You?" [63]But Jesus kept silent. And the high priest answered and said to Him, "I put You under oath by the living God: Tell us if You are the Christ, the Son of God!"

[64]Jesus said to him, "*It is as* you said. Nevertheless, I say to you, hereafter you will see the Son of Man sitting at the right hand of the Power, and coming on the clouds of heaven."

[65]Then the high priest tore his clothes, saying, "He has spoken blasphemy! What further need do we have of witnesses? Look, now you have heard His blasphemy! [66]What do you think?"

They answered and said, "He is deserving of death."

[67]Then they spat in His face and beat Him; and others struck *Him* with the palms of their hands, [68]saying, "Prophesy to us, Christ! Who is the one who struck You?"

Peter Denies Jesus, and Weeps Bitterly

[69]Now Peter sat outside in the courtyard. And a servant girl came to him, saying, "You also were with Jesus of Galilee."

[70]But he denied it before *them* all, saying, "I do not know what you are saying."

[71]And when he had gone out to the gateway, another *girl* saw him and said to those *who were* there, "This *fellow* also was with Jesus of Nazareth."

[72]But again he denied with an oath, "I do not know the Man!"

[73]And a little later those who stood by came up and said to Peter, "Surely you also are *one* of them, for your speech betrays you."

[74]Then he began to curse and swear, *saying*, "I do not know the Man!"

Immediately a rooster crowed. [75]And Peter remembered the word of Jesus who had said to him, "Before the rooster crows, you will deny Me three times." So he went out and wept bitterly.

Jesus Handed Over to Pontius Pilate

27 When morning came, all the chief priests and elders of the people plotted against Jesus to put Him to death. [2]And when they had bound Him, they led Him away and delivered Him to Pontius[a] Pilate the governor.

Judas Hangs Himself

[3]Then Judas, His betrayer, seeing that He had been condemned, was remorseful and brought back the thirty pieces of silver to the chief priests and elders, [4]saying, "I have sinned by betraying innocent blood."

And they said, "What *is that* to us? You see *to it!*"

26:59 [a]NU-Text omits *the elders.* **26:60** [a]NU-Text puts a comma after *but found none,* does not capitalize *Even,* and omits *they found none.* [b]NU-Text omits *false witnesses.* **27:2** [a]NU-Text omits *Pontius.*

27:1, 2 The Sanhedrin had found Jesus guilty of blasphemy, a capital offense for the Jews, though not for the Romans. The Jews, however, were restricted in carrying out a death penalty.

The Romans would have to do executions. The Roman trial eventually centered on Jesus' kingship—something Rome did take seriously.

⁵Then he threw down the pieces of silver in the temple and departed, and went and hanged himself.

⁶But the chief priests took the silver pieces and said, "It is not lawful to put them into the treasury, because they are the price of blood." ⁷And they consulted together and bought with them the potter's field, to bury strangers in. ⁸Therefore that field has been called the Field of Blood to this day. ⁹Then was fulfilled what was spoken by Jeremiah the prophet, saying, *"And they took the thirty pieces of silver, the value of Him who was priced,* whom they of the children of Israel priced, ¹⁰*and gave them for the potter's field, as the* Lord *directed me."*ᵃ

Jesus Faces Pilate

¹¹Now Jesus stood before the governor. And the governor asked Him, saying, "Are You the King of the Jews?"

Jesus said to him, *"It is as* you say." ¹²And while He was being accused by the chief priests and elders, He answered nothing.

¹³Then Pilate said to Him, "Do You not hear how many things they testify against You?" ¹⁴But He answered him not one word, so that the governor marveled greatly.

Taking the Place of Barabbas

¹⁵Now at the feast the governor was accustomed to releasing to the multitude one prisoner whom they wished. ¹⁶And at that time they had a notorious prisoner called Barabbas.ᵃ ¹⁷Therefore, when they had gathered together, Pilate said to them, "Whom do you want me to release to you? Barabbas, or Jesus who is called Christ?" ¹⁸For he knew that they had handed Him over because of envy.

¹⁹While he was sitting on the judgment seat, his wife sent to him, saying, "Have nothing to do with that just Man, for I have suffered many things today in a dream because of Him."

²⁰But the chief priests and elders persuaded the multitudes that they should ask for Barabbas and destroy Jesus. ²¹The governor answered and said to them, "Which of the two do you want me to release to you?"

They said, "Barabbas!"

²²Pilate said to them, "What then shall I do with Jesus who is called Christ?"

They all said to him, "Let Him be crucified!"

²³Then the governor said, "Why, what evil has He done?"

But they cried out all the more, saying, "Let Him be crucified!"

²⁴When Pilate saw that he could not prevail at all, but rather *that* a tumult was rising, he took water and washed *his* hands before the multitude, saying, "I am innocent of the blood of this just Person.ᵃ You see *to it."*

²⁵And all the people answered and said, "His blood *be* on us and on our children."

²⁶Then he released Barabbas to them; and when he had scourged Jesus, he delivered *Him* to be crucified.

The Soldiers Mock Jesus

²⁷Then the soldiers of the governor took Jesus into the Praetorium and gathered the whole garrison around Him. ²⁸And they stripped Him and put a scarlet robe on Him. ²⁹When they had twisted a crown of thorns, they put *it* on His head, and a reed in His right hand. And they bowed the knee before Him and mocked Him, saying, "Hail, King of the Jews!" ³⁰Then they spat on Him, and took the reed and struck Him on the head. ³¹And when they had mocked Him, they took the robe off Him, put His *own* clothes on Him, and led Him away to be crucified.

The King on a Cross

³²Now as they came out, they found a man of Cyrene, Simon by name. Him they compelled to bear His cross. ³³And when they had come to a place called Golgotha, that is to say, Place of a Skull, ³⁴they gave Him sourᵃ wine mingled with

27:10 ᵃJeremiah 32:6–9   27:16 ᵃNU-Text reads *Jesus Barabbas.* 27:24 ᵃNU-Text omits *just.*   27:34 ᵃNU-Text omits *sour.*

27:6, 7 Blood money could not be used in the treasury (Deut. 23:18); so they bought a field to be used for the burial of foreigners.

27:11 In the first step of a Roman trial, the magistrate listened to the charges and gave the accused opportunity for rebuttal. Pilate asked the first question, "Are You the King of the Jews?" Jesus' answer was the reason for the inscription later put on the Cross.

27:15–20 Pilate obviously thought Jesus was innocent, and he offered His accusers a way out, while not backing down himself. His offer for "Passover amnesty" was rejected. He underestimated their hatred.

27:32–38 The Crucifixion of Jesus by Pilate is well docu-mented not only in the gospels, but also by non-Christian writers (Tacitus, Josephus, Mara bar Serapion, and Thallus). Crucifixion was a cruel form of death since it did not damage any vital organs or cause excessive bleeding but caused a long, slow death, mostly from asphyxiation or shock. This cruel and humiliating execution was reserved for foreigners, not Roman citizens. It was always a public affair, becoming an especially useful deterrent to those who might be entertaining thoughts of insurrection. The Jews detested this inhumane act of execution, not only for its cruelty, but because the OT clearly stated that anyone who hangs on a tree is "accursed of God" (Deut. 21:22, 23). And Jesus, of course, was accursed of God for our sins (chart, Prophecies Fulfilled at the Cross).

MARY   *The Mother of James*

Jesus had many "behind the scene" followers. All four gospels describe a group of women who were devoted to special ministries to the Savior. These women served, supported, and even traveled in order to prepare the way for Jesus and the Twelve. Mary, the mother of James the Less and Joses, was one of these women. In fact, she was one of the few followers (mostly women) who did not desert Jesus at the Cross. She remained for the entire tragic ordeal. Imagine the wrenching of her heart as she helplessly watched the hideous torture, humiliation, and Crucifixion of the One she had found so understanding and gentle.

Staying behind when the crowds left the death scene, she and a few of this loyal group followed Joseph of Arimathea as he took Jesus' body to the tomb. Though they saw Him die, they could not let Him go—not yet. They needed to know where His body would rest.

After the Sabbath, these women spent hours gathering the spices used for burial—they still served Him. With heavy hearts they got up early in the morning, packed the spices, and trudged toward the tomb. When they arrived, there was an eerie silence, not the silence of death but rather of wonder—the tomb was open and empty.

God had honored these faithful women in a special way. At the lowest point of Christianity, Mary and her companions were the first to receive the news that revolutionized the world. Composers, writers, and artists through the centuries have celebrated the message they, alone, heard that morning—"He is risen."

Mary is a prime example of the reward of faithfulness. Every act of service done for the Master counts.

See also Mark 15:40, 47; 16:1; Luke 24:10; notes on Influence (Esth. 4); Motherhood (1 Sam. 1)

---

gall to drink. But when He had tasted *it*, He would not drink.

[35]Then they crucified Him, and divided His garments, casting lots,[a] that it might be fulfilled which was spoken by the prophet:

*"They divided My garments among them,
And for My clothing they cast lots."*[b]

[36]Sitting down, they kept watch over Him there. [37]And they put up over His head the accusation written against Him:

THIS IS JESUS
THE KING OF THE JEWS.

[38]Then two robbers were crucified with Him, one on the right and another on the left.

[39]And those who passed by blasphemed Him, wagging their heads [40]and saying, "You who destroy the temple and build *it* in three days, save Yourself! If You are the Son of God, come down from the cross."

[41]Likewise the chief priests also, mocking with the scribes and elders,[a] said, [42]"He saved others; Himself He cannot save. If He is the King of Israel,[a] let Him now come down from the cross, and we will believe Him.[b] [43]He trusted in God; let

Him deliver Him now if He will have Him; for He said, 'I am the Son of God.' "

[44]Even the robbers who were crucified with Him reviled Him with the same thing.

Jesus Dies on the Cross

[45]Now from the sixth hour until the ninth hour there was darkness over all the land. [46]And about the ninth hour Jesus cried out with a loud voice, saying, "Eli, Eli, lama sabachthani?" that is, *"My God, My God, why have You forsaken Me?"*[a]

[47]Some of those who stood there, when they heard *that*, said, "This Man is calling for Elijah!" [48]Immediately one of them ran and took a sponge, filled *it* with sour wine and put *it* on a reed, and offered it to Him to drink.

[49]The rest said, "Let Him alone; let us see if Elijah will come to save Him."

[50]And Jesus cried out again with a loud voice, and yielded up His spirit.

[51]Then, behold, the veil of the temple was torn in two from top to bottom; and the earth quaked,

27:35 [a]NU-Text and M-Text omit the rest of this verse. [b]Psalm 22:18
27:41 [a]M-Text reads *with the scribes, the Pharisees, and the elders.*
27:42 [a]NU-Text reads *He is the King of Israel!* [b]NU-Text and M-Text read *we will believe in Him.*   27:46 [a]Psalm 22:1

27:40–43 Jesus stayed on the Cross because He *was* the Son of God obeying His Father. Had Jesus saved Himself, He would not have been able to save others. The Resurrection demonstrated God's powerful work in His Son.

27:45 From the sixth hour to the ninth would be from noon until 3:00 in the afternoon. The darkness was a sign of judgment and a reminder that mankind does not know fully what

transpired on the Cross. Matthew only stated the reason for His suffering and death.

27:51 The veil of the temple was the heavily woven curtain that hung between the holy place and the Most Holy Place (see Luke 23:45, note; Heb. 9:3). Its presence was a continual reminder of the separation between mankind and God. The author of Hebrews stated that the veil represented Jesus'

and the rocks were split, [52]and the graves were opened; and many bodies of the saints who had fallen asleep were raised; [53]and coming out of the graves after His resurrection, they went into the holy city and appeared to many.

[54]So when the centurion and those with him, who were guarding Jesus, saw the earthquake and the things that had happened, they feared greatly, saying, "Truly this was the Son of God!"

[55]And many women who followed Jesus from Galilee, ministering to Him, were there looking on from afar, [56]among whom were Mary Magdalene, Mary the mother of James and Joses,[a] and the mother of Zebedee's sons.

Jesus Buried in Joseph's Tomb

[57]Now when evening had come, there came a rich man from Arimathea, named Joseph, who himself had also become a disciple of Jesus. [58]This man went to Pilate and asked for the body of Jesus. Then Pilate commanded the body to be given to him. [59]When Joseph had taken the body, he wrapped it in a clean linen cloth, [60]and laid it in his new tomb which he had hewn out of the rock; and he rolled a large stone against the door of the tomb, and departed. [61]And Mary Magdalene was there, and the other Mary, sitting opposite the tomb.

Pilate Sets a Guard

[62]On the next day, which followed the Day of Preparation, the chief priests and Pharisees gathered together to Pilate, [63]saying, "Sir, we remember, while He was still alive, how that deceiver said, 'After three days I will rise.' [64]Therefore command that the tomb be made secure until the third day, lest His disciples come by night[a] and steal Him *away,* and say to the people, 'He has risen from the dead.' So the last deception will be worse than the first."

[65]Pilate said to them, "You have a guard; go your way, make *it* as secure as you know how." [66]So they went and made the tomb secure, sealing the stone and setting the guard.

He Is Risen

28 Now after the Sabbath, as the first *day* of the week began to dawn, Mary Magdalene and the other Mary came to see the tomb. [2]And behold, there was a great earthquake; for an angel of the Lord descended from heaven, and came and rolled back the stone from the door,[a] and sat on it. [3]His countenance was like lightning, and his clothing as white as snow. [4]And the guards shook for fear of him, and became like dead *men.*

[5]But the angel answered and said to the women, "Do not be afraid, for I know that you seek Jesus who was crucified. [6]He is not here; for He is risen, as He said. Come, see the place where the Lord lay. [7]And go quickly and tell His disciples that He is risen from the dead, and indeed He is going before you into Galilee; there you will see Him. Behold, I have told you."

[8]So they went out quickly from the tomb with fear and great joy, and ran to bring His disciples word.

The Women Worship the Risen Lord

[9]And as they went to tell His disciples,[a] behold, Jesus met them, saying, "Rejoice!" So they came and held Him by the feet and worshiped Him. [10]Then Jesus said to them, "Do not be afraid. Go *and* tell My brethren to go to Galilee, and there they will see Me."

The Soldiers Are Bribed

[11]Now while they were going, behold, some of the guard came into the city and reported to the chief priests all the things that had happened. [12]When they had assembled with the elders and consulted together, they gave a large sum of money to the soldiers, [13]saying, "Tell them, 'His disciples came at night and stole Him *away* while we slept.' [14]And if this comes to the governor's ears, we will appease him and make you secure."

27:56 [a]NU-Text reads *Joseph.*   27:64 [a]NU-Text omits *by night.*
28:2 [a]NU-Text omits *from the door.*   28:9 [a]NU-Text omits the first clause of this verse.

---

body (Heb. 10:19, 20). The tearing signified the removal of the barrier between God and anyone who would accept Jesus' sacrifice (Heb. 4:16; 6:19).

27:55, 56 The women faithfully stayed through the Crucifixion and followed His body to the tomb (see chart, Women and Jesus in His Last Days).

27:57 Only a rich man could have owned ground so close to the city. Many think Joseph was a member of the Sanhedrin who had believed in Christ. He had to be a man of influence in order to approach Pilate.

27:61 Mourning for a victim of a Roman execution was not allowed. The women would have had to grieve silently.

28:5–10 The women, not the guards, were addressed by the angel. His first words were to quiet their fears. When Jesus

walked on the water and the disciples expressed fear, He told them not to fear (Matt. 14:27). Here the angel again used the Person of Jesus as the reason for dismissing fear. The second thing the angel wanted to make clear was that Resurrection had taken place. No other explanation was possible. The grave was opened not to let Jesus out but to let His followers see that the tomb was empty. The angel declared Jesus would actually be seen in Galilee, just as He promised (Matt. 26:32). The women who remained at the Cross and followed to see where He was buried were the ones privileged to first share this earth-shattering news and the first to see and worship Him. The Lord Himself gave the message of the Resurrection to the women to take to the disciples.

28:11–15 The guards who reported to the chief priests must have been temple police (v. 11).

EVANGELISM WOMEN AND THE GREAT COMMISSION

When Christ gave the Great Commission, He did not consider gender, just as gender is not a consideration when the Holy Spirit imparts spiritual gifts. God has chosen every believing woman to carry His message to her sphere of influence as she is filled and controlled by the Holy Spirit and anointed and equipped with His power (Acts 1:8). The mission of every believer in Jesus Christ is to communicate to the world who Jesus is and to extend to all His offer of salvation and spiritual refuge. Jesus has commissioned all believers to go to the most distant and remote points of the earth—as well as to their neighbors next door—to reach the lost with the gospel message of redemption and reconciliation. We are to make the Savior known

- through the spoken word (Rom. 10:14, 15),
- through good works (James 2:14–17),
- through the example of a new character (Matt. 5:16, 20).

The single woman, the wife, the mother, the grandmother, the widow are called to "go into all the world." "Going" does not necessarily mean leaving home and family, but it does mean making yourself totally available to serve wherever, whenever, and however He directs. The foremost manifestation of the Holy Spirit in a believer's life is that she will be a witness of the Lord's life and commandments (Acts 1:8). She is to be ready at all times to speak His name, tell of His marvelous works, give a defense of the reason for our hope, and tell others about His sacrifice and the abundant life He provides now and for all eternity (1 Pet. 3:15).

The New Testament gives certain requirements for soul-winning. The first, of course, is a genuine experience of grace through a personal relationship with Jesus Christ (1 John 1:1–3). A love for Christ and for people is also essential (Ps. 126:6), as is a willingness to be used by the Holy Spirit in sharing the gospel (Acts 8:29). An effective soul-winner will determine to live a separated life (2 Cor. 6:17) since lifestyle testimony is also a key ingredient. Creativity in using every opportunity for saying a word about Christ is also helpful (1 Pet. 3:15), as is a diligence in the study of God's Word, which enables the believer to explain more effectively the way of salvation (Ps. 51:13; 1 Pet. 2:2). All must be undergirded with specific and unceasing prayer (1 Thess. 5:17). Any woman willing to commit herself to this high and holy responsibility will indeed be rewarded (Dan. 12:3).

When unbelievers see those in the church generously giving their time, resources, and love to carry out the Great Commission, they are compelled to glorify the Father (Matt 5:16).

See also 1 Pet. 3:15; notes on Evangelism (John 6; Col. 4; 1 Pet. 3); Salvation (Eph. 2); Spiritual Gifts (Rom. 12); Women's Ministries (John 4; Acts 2; 1 Cor. 11; Eph. 2; 1 Tim. 3; Titus 2); portrait of The Samaritan Woman (John 4)

---

[15]So they took the money and did as they were instructed; and this saying is commonly reported among the Jews until this day.

The Great Commission

[16]Then the eleven disciples went away into Galilee, to the mountain which Jesus had appointed for them. [17]When they saw Him, they worshiped Him; but some doubted.

[18]And Jesus came and spoke to them, saying,

"All authority has been given to Me in heaven and on earth. [19]Go therefore[a] and make disciples of all the nations, baptizing them in the name of the Father and of the Son and of the Holy Spirit, [20]teaching them to observe all things that I have commanded you; and lo, I am with you always, *even* to the end of the age." Amen.[a]

··················

28:19 [a]M-Text omits *therefore.*   **28:20** [a]NU-Text omits *Amen.*

28:18 The first man, Adam, was given rule over the earth in the Garden of Eden but abdicated that responsibility through his sin. In the wilderness, Satan offered Jesus that rulership, but Jesus refused (Matt. 4:1–11). Jesus not only regained that rule by obedience to the Father but also was given the rule over all the heavens (see Phil. 2:8–11).

28:19 Jesus called His disciples to Himself first, where they would learn about Him, and He then would send them out. "Baptizing" and "teaching" are specified as part of the process of discipleship.

28:20 The Master closed His time on earth with the disciples with the one promise required to make all His teaching effective—His presence. He had made this promise before when He invited His followers to join in His yoke (Matt. 11:28–30). "Always" has the sense here of "the whole of every day." Jesus' commission did not end here at the end of the gospel; it was just beginning.

NEW TESTAMENT POLITICAL RULERS

NAME	POSITION	BIBLICAL EVENT	REFERENCE	KEY WOMEN
Augustus Caesar (31 B.C.–A.D. 14)	Roman Emperor	Census that took Mary and Joseph to Bethlehem; Birth of Jesus	Luke 2:1–7	Mary (Luke 2:5–7)
Claudius (A.D. 41–54)	Roman Emperor	Expelling of residents from Rome (including Priscilla and Aquila)	Acts 11:28; 17:7; 18:2	Priscilla (Acts 18:2)
Felix (A.D. 52–60)	Procurator of Judea	Trial of Paul	Acts 23:25— 24:27	Drusilla (Acts 24:24)
Festus (A.D. 60–62)	Procurator of Judea	Trial of Paul when he appealed to Caesar	Acts 24:27; 25:1–27	Bernice (Acts 25:13)
Herod Agrippa I (A.D. 37–44)	King of Judea	Persecution of the early church; Murder of James, the brother of John; Imprisonment of Peter	Acts 12:1–24	Mary, the mother of John Mark Rhoda (Acts 12:12, 13)
Herod Agrippa II (A.D. 48–70)	Tetrarch of Chalcis and northern territory	Ministry of Paul; Interrogation of Paul in Caesarea	Acts 25:13— 26:32	Bernice (Acts 25:13)
Herod Antipas (4 B.C.–A.D. 39)	Tetrarch of Galilee and Perea	Murder of John the Baptist; Trial and torture of Jesus	Matt. 14:1–11; Mark 6:14–29; Luke 3:1, 19; 13:31–35; 23:7–12	Herodias (Matt. 14:3) Salome (Matt. 14:6–11)
Herod Archelaus (4 B.C.–A.D. 6)	Ethnarch of Judea, Samaria, and Idumea	Flight into Egypt of Mary and Joseph with Jesus.	Matt. 2:13–15, 22	Mary (Matt. 2:14)
Herod the Great (37–4 B.C.)	King over all Palestine (Judea)	Birth of Jesus; Visit from the Magi; Massacre of innocents	Matt. 2:1–21; Luke 1:5	Mary (Matt. 2:11)
Herod Philip II (4 B.C.–A.D. 34)	Tetrarch of Iturea, Trachonitus, Gaulanitis, Auranitis, and Batahea	Ministry of John the Baptist	Luke 3:1–20	Herodias (Luke 3:19)
Nero (A.D. 54–68)	Roman Emperor	Persecution of Christians in Rome; Martyrdom of Peter and Paul	Acts 25:1–12; 28:19; Phil. 4:22	
Pontius Pilate (A.D. 26–36)	Roman Procurator	Public ministry of Jesus; Trial and Crucifixion of Jesus	Matt. 27:11–26; Luke 3:1; 23:1–25	Pilate's wife (Matt. 27:19)
Tiberius Caesar (A.D. 14–37)	Roman Emperor	Public ministry of Jesus; Crucifixion of Jesus	Luke 3:1	

Mark

AUTHOR

Early Christian testimony leaves little doubt that John (Hebrew name) Mark (Roman name), the son of Mary and kinsman of Barnabas, was the author of the gospel that bears his name (Acts 12:12; Col. 4:10). Though Mark was not one of the original twelve disciples, he witnessed much of what happened in the early church, especially in Jerusalem. Many scholars believe that Mark described himself in the book (Mark 14:51, 52). He traveled with Paul and Barnabas and spent much time with Peter, who called him "my son" (1 Pet. 5:13). This affectionate designation could refer to a spiritual relationship, if Peter had introduced Mark to Christ, or merely to a close working relationship. Some have identified Mark as an "interpreter" for Peter, and certainly Peter's preaching and testimony are sources for the information Mark recorded (Acts 15:36–40; Col. 4:10; 2 Tim. 4:11; Philem. 24; 1 Pet. 5:13).

DATE

The Gospel of Mark was probably written before the destruction of the temple and Jerusalem (A.D. 70), since a catastrophe of such magnitude would surely have been mentioned. Although the actual date is uncertain, a date between A.D. 65 and 68 seems reasonable.

BACKGROUND

SETTING: The Gospel of Mark is usually uniquely associated with Rome (see Introduction: Audience), where a sizable Christian community was located.

PURPOSE: Mark wanted to tell the Good News of Jesus (Mark 1:1). Unlike the gospels of Matthew and Luke, which begin with Jesus' birth, or John, which opens with the presentation of the pre-incarnate Christ, the Gospel of Mark begins with Jesus' ministry. Essentially evangelistic, the events and teachings of Mark present the Cross and the Resurrection as central.

AUDIENCE: Mark was written primarily for Gentiles, especially Roman believers. Note his careful explanation of Jewish customs (Mark 7:2–4) and his effort to translate Aramaic words or phrases (Mark 3:17; 5:41). Unlike the Gospel of Matthew, written especially for Jewish readers, few references to the Old Testament appear in Mark. The prominence given to persecution and martyrdom would also have appealed to the Roman Christians who had suffered greatly under Nero and other emperors (Mark 13:9–13).

LITERARY CHARACTERISTICS: Mark is a book of action. "Immediately" ("straightway" in some translations) introduces most of its section divisions and is used more in Mark than in any other New Testament book. Mark frequently uses verbs in the present tense to suggest a vivid, moving drama of the Lord's ministry on earth. The shortest of the four gospels, the Gospel of Mark often presents in a few verses what other gospels

would describe in a chapter (compare Jesus' wilderness temptation, Mark 1:12, 13 with Matthew 4:1–11). Although the events in Mark are in an overall chronological order, he arranged much of the book topically.

THEMES

The emphasis in the Gospel of Mark is more on the activities of Jesus than on His teachings. Mark presented the gospel as relevant even in the midst of uncertainties and crises. He presented Jesus as present and active among His people (Mark 10:45).

OUTLINE

I. Jesus' Preparation for Ministry (1:1–13)
  A. His introduction by John the Baptist (1:1–8)
  B. His baptism by John the Baptist (1:9–11)
  C. His temptation in the wilderness (1:12, 13)

II. The Galilean Ministry (1:14—8:30)
  A. A call to the first disciples (1:14–20)
  B. A series of healings (1:21—2:5)
    1. The casting out of an unclean spirit (1:21–28)
    2. The healing of Peter's mother-in-law (1:29–31)
    3. The healing of many (1:32–34)
    4. The healing of a leper (1:35–45)
    5. The healing of the paralytic (2:1–5)
  C. The conflict with religious leaders (2:6—3:6)
    1. Conflict over forgiving sin (2:6–12)
    2. Conflict over the people with whom He associated (2:13–17)
    3. Conflict over fasting (2:18–22)
    4. Conflict over the Sabbath (2:23—3:6)
  D. The choosing of twelve disciples (3:7–19)
  E. False accusations (3:20–35)
  F. Parables about the kingdom of God (4:1–34)
    1. The parable of the sower (4:1–9)
    2. The mystery of the kingdom (4:10–12)
    3. The interpretation of the parable of the sower (4:13–20)
    4. The parable of the lamp (4:21–25)
    5. The parable of the growing seed (4:26–29)
    6. The parable of the mustard seed (4:30–34)
  G. A series of miracles (4:35—5:43)
    1. The calming of the sea (4:35–41)
    2. The healing of the demon-possessed man (5:1–20)
    3. The healing of the hemorrhaging woman (5:21–34)
    4. The healing of Jairus' daughter (5:35–43)
  H. Jesus' rejection in His hometown (6:1–6)
  I. The sending out of the Twelve (6:7–13)
  J. The death of John the Baptist (6:14–29)
  K. More miracles and teachings (6:30—8:26)
    1. The feeding of the five thousand (6:30–44)
    2. Jesus' walking on the water (6:45–52)
    3. The healings near Gennesaret (6:53–56)
    4. A collision of the commands of God and traditions of mankind (7:1–13)
    5. The nature of sin (7:14–23)
    6. The healing of the Syro-Phoenician woman's daughter (7:24–30)
    7. The healing of a deaf and mute man (7:31–37)
    8. The feeding of the four thousand (8:1–10)
    9. A request from the Pharisees (8:11–21)
    10. The healing of a blind man (8:22–26)
  L. Peter's confession of faith (8:27–30)

III. The Jerusalem Ministry (8:31—13:37)
  A. The journey to Jerusalem (8:31—10:52)
    1. The first prediction of His death and Resurrection (8:31–33)
    2. The requirements of discipleship (8:34—9:1)
    3. The Transfiguration (9:2–13)

John the Baptist Prepares the Way

1 The beginning of the gospel of Jesus Christ, the Son of God. [2]As it is written in the Prophets:[a]

"Behold, I send My messenger before Your face,
Who will prepare Your way before You."[b]

[3]"The voice of one crying in the wilderness:

'Prepare the way of the LORD;
Make His paths straight.' "[a]

[4]John came baptizing in the wilderness and preaching a baptism of repentance for the remission of sins. [5]Then all the land of Judea, and those

1:2 [a]NU-Text reads *Isaiah the prophet.* [b]Malachi 3:1   1:3 [a]Isaiah 40:3

1:1 Mark begins his gospel account with Jesus' public ministry. "Jesus" is the transliteration of the Greek form of the Hebrew name "Joshua" (lit. "salvation of *Yahweh*" or "*Yahweh* saves"). "Christ" (Gk. *Christos*, lit. "anointed one") is equivalent to the Hebrew title "Messiah" (*mashiach*). "Son of God" is an important theme in the book, highlighting Christ's character as well as His essence. In all four gospels, Jesus addressed God as "Father," and the Father addressed Him as "My Son."

1:2, 3 Mark was laying the groundwork for understanding Jesus as the One about whom the OT spoke. The phrase "It is written" is in the perfect tense, which refers to something that happened in the past but with present results, emphasizing the authoritative nature of what is about to be said.

1:4 John the Baptist fulfilled these prophecies. All four gospels recognized his appearance as heralding the beginning of Jesus' ministry. John's father Zacharias was a priest,

and his mother Elizabeth was a relative of Mary, the mother of Jesus. Even before his conception, John had been appointed to announce the coming of the Messiah (Luke 1:5–25). "To baptize" (Gk. *baptizō*) can mean "to place into" and is used to describe something or someone placed into a new environment or union, thereby changing its relationship with the old environment. John clearly stated that his baptism was not the same as Jesus' baptism. The heart of John's message was to call people to repentance for sins. Repentance (Gk. *metanoia*, lit. "change of mind") called for a deliberate turning from the old ways of life. Genuine repentance resulted in the forgiveness of sin (see Luke 24:47, note). Though John may well have had contacts with the ascetic Qumran community, his differences with them were too distinct to make that passing contact important. There is certainly no evidence that John's baptismal method or emphasis on repentance and judgment came from this Essene community (see chart, Jewish Sects).

THE EMOTIONS OF JESUS

INCIDENT	EMOTION	CAUSE	JESUS' ACTION
He met a leper (Mark 1:41).	Compassion	The leper begged for healing.	He touched and healed him.
5,000 followed Him (Matt. 14:14; Mark 6:34).	Compassion	They had no shepherd.	He fed and taught them.
4,000 followed Him (Mark 8:2).	Compassion	They were hungry.	He supplied food.
He preached among the villages (Matt. 9:35, 36).	Compassion	They were weary and scattered without a shepherd.	He instructed the disciples to pray and go out to minister.
The multitudes followed Him (Matt. 20:34).	Compassion	Two blind men begged for healing.	He healed them.
A funeral passed (Luke 7:13–15).	Compassion	The widow lost her only son.	He raised her son to life.
The rich young ruler came to Him (Mark 10:21).	Love	He conversed with the young man.	He pointed out the one thing lacking.
The 70 returned from a preaching tour (Luke 10:21).	Joy	The Father revealed truth to the untutored.	He thanked the Father.
The people brought children to Jesus (Matt. 19:13; Mark 10:14; Luke 18:15).	Anger	The disciples rebuked the people and tried to keep the children away.	He rebuked the disciples, embraced the children, and blessed them.
The centurion approached Jesus for the healing of his servant (Matt. 8:10; Luke 7:9).	Wonder, awe	He understood who Jesus was.	He drew attention to faith and healed the servant.
He healed on the Sabbath (Mark 3:5).	Anger, grief	The Pharisees had hard hearts.	He challenged the Pharisees and healed the man.
The Pharisees demanded a sign (Mark 8:11).	Distress	They were trying to entrap Him.	He left them.
He met Mary and Martha after Lazarus' death (John 11:35).	Grief	He saw their tears and felt the loss of a friend.	He wept with them.
He approached Lazarus' tomb (John 11:38).	Grief	Jesus fielded questions concerning why He had not healed Lazarus and eliminated death itself.	He raised Lazarus.
He entered Jerusalem (Matt. 23:27; Luke 19:41).	Sorrow	Jerusalem rejected Him and faced coming destruction.	He wept over the city.
He hosted the Last Supper (John 13:1).	Love	He knew He was leaving.	He washed their feet.
He hosted the Last Supper (John 13:21).	Distress	Judas betrayed Him.	He singled out the betrayer and told him to act quickly.
He went to the Garden of Gethsemane (Mark 14:32).	Distress	He knew of His coming separation from the ones He loved.	He asked the disciples to wait and watch. He prayed.

DISABILITIES   *FRIENDS WITH SPECIAL NEEDS*

More than anything else disabled people need friends—acquaintances, casual, close, or especially intimate. No matter what form of impairment the disabled person has, she needs friends who give unconditional love.

The faith, creativity, and commitment of friends helped a paralyzed man experience the healing power of Jesus. Four concerned friends took their paralyzed friend to see Jesus (Mark 2:1–12). After overcoming a seemingly insurmountable hurdle, the friends laid the paralytic at the feet of Jesus. When Jesus healed the man, He took special note of the faith exhibited by the four friends.

The disabled person needs friends who give more comfort than advice. Friends should continue giving of self despite barriers—architectural or attitudinal—involving persons with disabilities in activities and in ministry. Integrate people with impairments with the able-bodied in worship. Evangelize disabled friends. Look past the gizmos, gadgets, and electrical wizardry to get to know the individual as a person. Have the attitude, "If I don't reach out to this individual with the gospel and God's love, who will?"

Tender mercies, kindness, humility, meekness, and longsuffering are essential to friendship with a disabled person. However, able-bodied Christians are also challenged to rise above all these obstacles and "put on love" (Col. 3:12–14). Unconditional love overlooks physical or mental handicaps and focuses on the true person, a special object of God's care and concern. An intimate relationship with a disabled friend or family member can be a special way to discover what real love is all about.

See also notes on Friendship (Luke 1); Love (1 John 4); Spiritual Gifts (Rom. 12)

---

from Jerusalem, went out to him and were all baptized by him in the Jordan River, confessing their sins.

6Now John was clothed with camel's hair and with a leather belt around his waist, and he ate locusts and wild honey. 7And he preached, saying, "There comes One after me who is mightier than I, whose sandal strap I am not worthy to stoop down and loose. 8I indeed baptized you with water, but He will baptize you with the Holy Spirit."

John Baptizes Jesus

9It came to pass in those days *that* Jesus came from Nazareth of Galilee, and was baptized by John in the Jordan. 10And immediately, coming up froma the water, He saw the heavens parting and the Spirit descending upon Him like a dove. 11Then a voice came from heaven, "You are My beloved Son, in whom I am well pleased."

Satan Tempts Jesus

12Immediately the Spirit drove Him into the wilderness. 13And He was there in the wilderness forty days, tempted by Satan, and was with the wild beasts; and the angels ministered to Him.

Jesus Begins His Galilean Ministry

14Now after John was put in prison, Jesus came to Galilee, preaching the gospel of the kingdoma of God, 15and saying, "The time is fulfilled, and the kingdom of God is at hand. Repent, and believe in the gospel."

Four Fishermen Called as Disciples

16And as He walked by the Sea of Galilee, He saw Simon and Andrew his brother casting a net into the sea; for they were fishermen. 17Then Jesus said to them, "Follow Me, and I will make you become fishers of men." 18They immediately left their nets and followed Him.

19When He had gone a little farther from there, He saw James the *son* of Zebedee, and John his brother, who also *were* in the boat mending their nets. 20And immediately He called them, and

··················

1:10 aNU-Text reads *out of.*   1:14 aNU-Text omits *of the kingdom.*

1:10, 11 The presence of the Trinity is emphasized: Jesus the Son in the flesh, the Holy Spirit in the form of a dove, and the Father whose voice was heard from heaven. The Father declared His pleasure with His Son *before* the wilderness temptation and *before* He taught, performed any miracles or healings, or died on the Cross. The Father publicly declared Jesus' authority to be as His own.

1:12, 13 Mark agreed with the other writers that the Spirit was responsible for both the encounter with Satan and the 40-day fast (see Matt. 4:1–11). Both Moses (Ex. 24:18) and Elijah

(1 Kin. 19:8) spent 40 days in the wilderness during their respective ministries.

1:16–20 Andrew had been one of John's followers (see John 1:35–42). Jesus called all four by encouraging each to "follow" (Gk. *akoloutheō,* lit. "to walk the same road" or "to accompany"; see Mark 8:34). This call had the connotation of attaching oneself to another and accepting that person's leadership. All four men responded "immediately." Obviously God had been working in them; when Jesus called, they were ready.

they left their father Zebedee in the boat with the hired servants, and went after Him.

Jesus Casts Out an Unclean Spirit

²¹Then they went into Capernaum, and immediately on the Sabbath He entered the synagogue and taught. ²²And they were astonished at His teaching, for He taught them as one having authority, and not as the scribes.

²³Now there was a man in their synagogue with an unclean spirit. And he cried out, ²⁴saying, "Let us alone! What have we to do with You, Jesus of Nazareth? Did You come to destroy us? I know who You are— the Holy One of God!"

²⁵But Jesus rebuked him, saying, "Be quiet, and come out of him!" ²⁶And when the unclean spirit had convulsed him and cried out with a loud voice, he came out of him. ²⁷Then they were all amazed, so that they questioned among themselves, saying, "What is this? What new doctrine is this? For with authorityᵃ He commands even the unclean spirits, and they obey Him." ²⁸And immediately His fame spread throughout all the region around Galilee.

Peter's Mother-in-Law Healed

²⁹Now as soon as they had come out of the synagogue, they entered the house of Simon and Andrew, with James and John. ³⁰But Simon's wife's mother lay sick with a fever, and they told Him about her at once. ³¹So He came and took her by the hand and lifted her up, and immediately the fever left her. And she served them.

Many Healed After Sabbath Sunset

³²At evening, when the sun had set, they brought to Him all who were sick and those who were demon-possessed. ³³And the whole city was gathered together at the door. ³⁴Then He healed many who were sick with various diseases, and cast out many demons; and He did not allow the demons to speak, because they knew Him.

Preaching in Galilee

³⁵Now in the morning, having risen a long while before daylight, He went out and departed to a solitary place; and there He prayed. ³⁶And Simon and those who were with Him searched for Him. ³⁷When they found Him, they said to Him, "Everyone is looking for You."

³⁸But He said to them, "Let us go into the next towns, that I may preach there also, because for this purpose I have come forth."

³⁹And He was preaching in their synagogues throughout all Galilee, and casting out demons.

Jesus Cleanses a Leper

⁴⁰Now a leper came to Him, imploring Him, kneeling down to Him and saying to Him, "If You are willing, You can make me clean."

⁴¹Then Jesus, moved with compassion, stretched out His hand and touched him, and said to him, "I am willing; be cleansed." ⁴²As soon as He had spoken, immediately the leprosy left him, and he was cleansed. ⁴³And He strictly warned him and sent him away at once, ⁴⁴and said to him, "See that you say nothing to anyone; but go your way, show yourself to the priest, and offer for your cleansing those things which Moses commanded, as a testimony to them."

⁴⁵However, he went out and began to proclaim it freely, and to spread the matter, so that Jesus could no longer openly enter the city, but was outside in deserted places; and they came to Him from every direction.

Jesus Forgives and Heals a Paralytic

2 And again He entered Capernaum after some days, and it was heard that He was in the house. ²Immediatelyᵃ many gathered together, so that there was no longer room to receive them, not even near the door. And He preached the word to them. ³Then they came to Him, bringing a paralytic who was carried by four men. ⁴And when they could not come near Him because of the crowd, they uncovered the roof where He was. So when they had broken through, they let down the bed on which the paralytic was lying.

⁵When Jesus saw their faith, He said to the paralytic, "Son, your sins are forgiven you."

⁶And some of the scribes were sitting there and reasoning in their hearts, ⁷"Why does this Man speak blasphemies like this? Who can forgive sins but God alone?"

1:27 ᵃNU-Text reads What is this? A new doctrine with authority.
2:2 ᵃNU-Text omits Immediately.

1:21 The synagogues came into Jewish life during the Exile when the Jews did not have access to the temple. They were meeting places for prayer and study of the Torah. Capernaum was the home of Peter.

1:32–34 Jesus' miracles primarily called attention to the offering of the kingdom. With each account of His healings, His main mission became more difficult because the people were more interested in immediate solutions to physical problems than long-lasting solutions to spiritual needs.

1:35 Jesus' prayer life so fascinated the disciples that they asked Him to teach them to pray (Luke 11:1). It was not that they needed additional prayer formulas. Judaism provided prayers for almost every action of the day. As they observed Jesus, they realized that something in His prayer life went beyond mere ritual. Through prayer He was refreshed and invigorated; He consistently sought time to pray (Matt. 6:6; 14:13, 23; 26:39; Luke 4:42, 43).

1:40, 41 Leprosy included a variety of skin diseases (see Matt. 8:2, 3, note).

[8]But immediately, when Jesus perceived in His spirit that they reasoned thus within themselves, He said to them, "Why do you reason about these things in your hearts? [9]Which is easier, to say to the paralytic, '*Your* sins are forgiven you,' or to say, 'Arise, take up your bed and walk'? [10]But that you may know that the Son of Man has power on earth to forgive sins"— He said to the paralytic, [11]"I say to you, arise, take up your bed, and go to your house." [12]Immediately he arose, took up the bed, and went out in the presence of them all, so that all were amazed and glorified God, saying, "We never saw *anything* like this!"

Matthew the Tax Collector

[13]Then He went out again by the sea; and all the multitude came to Him, and He taught them. [14]As He passed by, He saw Levi the *son* of Alphaeus sitting at the tax office. And He said to him, "Follow Me." So he arose and followed Him.

[15]Now it happened, as He was dining in *Levi's* house, that many tax collectors and sinners also sat together with Jesus and His disciples; for there were many, and they followed Him. [16]And when the scribes and[a] Pharisees saw Him eating with the tax collectors and sinners, they said to His disciples, "How *is it* that He eats and drinks with tax collectors and sinners?"

[17]When Jesus heard *it,* He said to them, "Those who are well have no need of a physician, but those who are sick. I did not come to call *the* righteous, but sinners, to repentance."[a]

Jesus Is Questioned About Fasting

[18]The disciples of John and of the Pharisees were fasting. Then they came and said to Him, "Why do the disciples of John and of the Pharisees fast, but Your disciples do not fast?"

[19]And Jesus said to them, "Can the friends of the bridegroom fast while the bridegroom is with them? As long as they have the bridegroom with them they cannot fast. [20]But the days will come when the bridegroom will be taken away from them, and then they will fast in those days. [21]No one sews a piece of unshrunk cloth on an old garment; or else the new piece pulls away from the old, and the tear is made worse. [22]And no one puts new wine into old wineskins; or else the new wine bursts the wineskins, the wine is spilled, and the wineskins are ruined. But new wine must be put into new wineskins."

Jesus Is Lord of the Sabbath

[23]Now it happened that He went through the grainfields on the Sabbath; and as they went His disciples began to pluck the heads of grain. [24]And the Pharisees said to Him, "Look, why do they do what is not lawful on the Sabbath?"

[25]But He said to them, "Have you never read what David did when he was in need and hungry, he and those with him: [26]how he went into the house of God *in the days* of Abiathar the high priest, and ate the showbread, which is not lawful to eat except for the priests, and also gave some to those who were with him?"

[27]And He said to them, "The Sabbath was made for man, and not man for the Sabbath. [28]Therefore the Son of Man is also Lord of the Sabbath."

Healing on the Sabbath

3 And He entered the synagogue again, and a man was there who had a withered hand. [2]So they watched Him closely, whether He would heal him on the Sabbath, so that they might accuse Him. [3]And He said to the man who had the withered hand, "Step forward." [4]Then He said to them, "Is it lawful on the Sabbath to do good or to do evil, to save life or to kill?" But they kept silent. [5]And when He had looked around at them with anger, being grieved by the hardness of their hearts, He said to the man, "Stretch out your hand." And he stretched *it* out, and his hand was restored as whole as the other.[a] [6]Then the Pharisees went out and immediately plotted with the Herodians against Him, how they might destroy Him.

A Great Multitude Follows Jesus

[7]But Jesus withdrew with His disciples to the sea. And a great multitude from Galilee followed Him, and from Judea [8]and Jerusalem and Idumea and beyond the Jordan; and those from Tyre and

---

2:16 [a]NU-Text reads *of the.*   **2:17** [a]NU-Text omits *to repentance.*
3:5 [a]NU-Text omits *as whole as the other.*

2:8 Three miracles actually took place: Jesus knew their thoughts; He forgave their sins; and He physically healed the paralytic.

2:10 Jesus' claim is clear: He does the work only God can do; therefore, He is God.

2:14 Levi (or Matthew) was a tax collector for Herod Antipas (see Matt. 9:9). He received the same invitation Peter, Andrew, James, and John received (see Mark 1:16–20). Like the others, he followed Jesus immediately.

2:16 The Pharisees called everyone who did not follow their interpretation of the Torah "sinners." Unlike Jesus, they sepa-rated themselves from such people (see Mark 7:1–5, note; see chart, Jewish Sects). Jesus did not fit their concept of how the Messiah should act.

2:23–28 One of Jesus' greatest objections to the Pharisees was their determination to put their traditions before the needs of people (see Luke 11:46).

3:5 Few things caused anger in Jesus, but even justifiable anger at the evil He saw in the hearts of these men could not quench His compassion for them (see chart, The Emotions of Jesus).

Sidon, a great multitude, when they heard how many things He was doing, came to Him. [9]So He told His disciples that a small boat should be kept ready for Him because of the multitude, lest they should crush Him. [10]For He healed many, so that as many as had afflictions pressed about Him to touch Him. [11]And the unclean spirits, whenever they saw Him, fell down before Him and cried out, saying, "You are the Son of God." [12]But He sternly warned them that they should not make Him known.

The Twelve Apostles

[13]And He went up on the mountain and called to *Him* those He Himself wanted. And they came to Him. [14]Then He appointed twelve,[a] that they might be with Him and that He might send them out to preach, [15]and to have power to heal sicknesses and[a] to cast out demons: [16]Simon,[a] to whom He gave the name Peter; [17]James the *son* of Zebedee and John the brother of James, to whom He gave the name Boanerges, that is, "Sons of Thunder"; [18]Andrew, Philip, Bartholomew, Matthew, Thomas, James the *son* of Alphaeus, Thaddaeus, Simon the Cananite; [19]and Judas Iscariot, who also betrayed Him. And they went into a house.

A House Divided Cannot Stand

[20]Then the multitude came together again, so that they could not so much as eat bread. [21]But when His own people heard *about this*, they went out to lay hold of Him, for they said, "He is out of His mind."

[22]And the scribes who came down from Jerusalem said, "He has Beelzebub," and, "By the ruler of the demons He casts out demons."

[23]So He called them to *Himself* and said to them in parables: "How can Satan cast out Satan? [24]If a kingdom is divided against itself, that kingdom cannot stand. [25]And if a house is divided against itself, that house cannot stand. [26]And if Satan has risen up against himself, and is divided, he cannot stand, but has an end. [27]No one can enter a strong man's house and plunder his goods, unless he first binds the strong man. And then he will plunder his house.

The Unpardonable Sin

[28]"Assuredly, I say to you, all sins will be forgiven the sons of men, and whatever blasphemies they may utter; [29]but he who blasphemes against the Holy Spirit never has forgiveness, but is sub-

ject to eternal condemnation"— [30]because they said, "He has an unclean spirit."

Jesus' Mother and Brothers Send for Him

[31]Then His brothers and His mother came, and standing outside they sent to Him, calling Him. [32]And a multitude was sitting around Him; and they said to Him, "Look, Your mother and Your brothers[a] are outside seeking You."

[33]But He answered them, saying, "Who is My mother, or My brothers?" [34]And He looked around in a circle at those who sat about Him, and said, "Here are My mother and My brothers! [35]For whoever does the will of God is My brother and My sister and mother."

The Parable of the Sower

4 And again He began to teach by the sea. And a great multitude was gathered to Him, so that He got into a boat and sat *in it* on the sea; and the whole multitude was on the land facing the sea. [2]Then He taught them many things by parables, and said to them in His teaching:

[3]"Listen! Behold, a sower went out to sow. [4]And it happened, as he sowed, *that* some *seed* fell by the wayside; and the birds of the air[a] came and devoured it. [5]Some fell on stony ground, where it did not have much earth; and immediately it sprang up because it had no depth of earth. [6]But when the sun was up it was scorched, and because it had no root it withered away. [7]And some *seed* fell among thorns; and the thorns grew up and choked it, and it yielded no crop. [8]But other *seed* fell on good ground and yielded a crop that sprang up, increased and produced: some thirtyfold, some sixty, and some a hundred."

[9]And He said to them,[a] "He who has ears to hear, let him hear!"

The Purpose of Parables

[10]But when He was alone, those around Him with the twelve asked Him about the parable. [11]And He said to them, "To you it has been given to know the mystery of the kingdom of God; but to those who are outside, all things come in parables, [12]so that

---

3:14 [a]NU-Text adds *whom He also named apostles.*   **3:15** [a]NU-Text omits *to heal sicknesses and.*   **3:16** [a]NU-Text reads *and He appointed the twelve: Simon....*   **3:32** [a]NU-Text and M-Text add *and Your sisters.*   **4:4** [a]NU-Text and M-Text omit *of the air.*   **4:9** [a]NU-Text and M-Text omit *to them.*

3:13–19 Jesus called out men from diverse educational preparation and vocational backgrounds to be His disciples (see Matt. 10:1, 2).

3:28, 29 To commit the unpardonable sin, the perpetrator must know what he is doing (see Matt. 12:31, note).

3:31–35 Jesus never undermined the family unit. The first family unit was commissioned by the Creator in the Garden of Eden (see Matt. 12:46–50, note).

4:3–9 The sower and the seed are the same in each instance; only the soils differ (see Matt. 13:3–9, note).

Perspective by Emilie Barnes

A DEEPER WALK OF FAITH (Drawn from *More Faith in My Day*)

One of the conditions for safe, enjoyable boating is to make sure that the water is deep enough. If the water is too shallow, a person runs the risk of running aground and breaking out the bottom of their boat. Similarly, spiritual shallowness is not a good condition for any woman's personal life!

How can you develop a deep walk with the Lord—one that protects you from the shallowness of life? In Proverbs 2:1–9, we find these four provisions that help a person "walk with depth":

Saturate Your Life with the Word. Respond to the Word of God and know it inside and out. Have faith in God's inspiration of Scripture (2 Tim. 3:16). If you doubt inspiration, you will doubt verse after verse, and the Bible will hold no constants for you.

Desire God's Word. Be open to what God is saying to you, and begin to desire what He has for you: "turning your ear to wisdom and applying your heart to understanding" (vs. 2 NIV). Make reading God's Word a daily habit. Make it a priority.

People do what they want to do. All of us make choices and when we don't make time for God in our day, when we don't make time for the most important relationship in our life, when we don't make time to read His words to us, we are probably not making the best choices. Choose to do what is *important*, not only what is *urgent*.

The more you know of God's Word, the more you will fall in love with God's words and seek to live by them.

Develop a Prayer Life. Prayer is the way you really get to know who God is. It is a time when God can speak to your heart. Proverbs 2:3 challenges us to "call out for insight and cry aloud for understanding." As a part of your prayer time each day:

- PRAISE God for who He is, the Creator and Sustainer of the whole universe who is interested in each of us who are in His family (Ps. 150, Matt. 10:30).
- THANK God for all He has done for you . . . for all He is doing for you . . . and for all that He will do for you in the future (Phil. 4:6).
- CONFESS your sins. Tell God about the things you have done and said and thought for which you are sorry. He tells us in 1 John 1:9 that He is "faithful and righteous to forgive us our sins."
- PRAY for your family . . . and for friends or neighbors who have needs, physical or spiritual. Ask God to work in the heart of someone you hope will come to know Jesus as Savior. Pray for your government officials, for your minister and church officers, for missionaries and other Christian servants (Phil. 2:4).
- PRAY, too, for yourself. Ask for guidance for the day ahead. Ask God to help you do His will . . . and ask Him to arrange opportunities to serve Him throughout the day (Phil. 4:6).

Be Consistent in Your Walk. Prospectors often spend years searching for gold or silver. They are persistent and consistent. Make that your approach to God's Word. There are no overnight miracles when it comes to overcoming the shallowness of life. The race of life is not a sprint, but a marathon.

If a woman will abide by these four principles, she will learn "the fear and the knowledge of God" (vs. 5 NIV). That is a high-tide mark! Your boat will not run aground in shallow spiritual waters if you truly know and have a deep reverential awe of God.

'Seeing they may see and not perceive,
And hearing they may hear and not understand;
Lest they should turn,
And their sins be forgiven them.' "[a]

The Parable of the Sower Explained

[13]And He said to them, "Do you not understand this parable? How then will you understand all the parables? [14]The sower sows the word. [15]And these are the ones by the wayside where the word is sown. When they hear, Satan comes immediately and takes away the word that was sown in their hearts. [16]These likewise are the ones sown on stony ground who, when they hear the word, immediately receive it with gladness; [17]and they have no root in themselves, and so endure only for a time. Afterward, when tribulation or persecution arises for the word's sake, immediately they stumble. [18]Now these are the ones sown among thorns; *they are* the ones who hear the word, [19]and the cares of this world, the deceitfulness of riches, and the desires for other things entering in choke the word, and it becomes unfruitful. [20]But these are the ones sown on good ground, those who hear the word, accept *it*, and bear fruit: some thirtyfold, some sixty, and some a hundred."

Light Under a Basket

[21]Also He said to them, "Is a lamp brought to be put under a basket or under a bed? Is it not to

4:12 [a]Isaiah 6:9, 10

be set on a lampstand? [22]For there is nothing hidden which will not be revealed, nor has anything been kept secret but that it should come to light. [23]If anyone has ears to hear, let him hear."

[24]Then He said to them, "Take heed what you hear. With the same measure you use, it will be measured to you; and to you who hear, more will be given. [25]For whoever has, to him more will be given; but whoever does not have, even what he has will be taken away from him."

The Parable of the Growing Seed

[26]And He said, "The kingdom of God is as if a man should scatter seed on the ground, [27]and should sleep by night and rise by day, and the seed should sprout and grow, he himself does not know how. [28]For the earth yields crops by itself: first the blade, then the head, after that the full grain in the head. [29]But when the grain ripens, immediately he puts in the sickle, because the harvest has come."

The Parable of the Mustard Seed

[30]Then He said, "To what shall we liken the kingdom of God? Or with what parable shall we picture it? [31]It is like a mustard seed which, when it is sown on the ground, is smaller than all the seeds on earth; [32]but when it is sown, it grows up and becomes greater than all herbs, and shoots out large branches, so that the birds of the air may nest under its shade."

Jesus' Use of Parables

[33]And with many such parables He spoke the word to them as they were able to hear it. [34]But without a parable He did not speak to them. And when they were alone, He explained all things to His disciples.

Wind and Wave Obey Jesus

[35]On the same day, when evening had come, He said to them, "Let us cross over to the other side." [36]Now when they had left the multitude, they took Him along in the boat as He was. And other little boats were also with Him. [37]And a great windstorm arose, and the waves beat into the boat, so that it was already filling. [38]But He was in the stern, asleep on a pillow. And they awoke Him and said to Him, "Teacher, do You not care that we are perishing?" [39]Then He arose and rebuked the wind, and said to the sea, "Peace, be still!" And the wind ceased and there was a great calm. [40]But He said to them, "Why are you so fearful? How is it that you have no faith?"[a] [41]And they feared exceedingly, and said to one another, "Who can this be, that even the wind and the sea obey Him!"

A Demon-Possessed Man Healed

5 Then they came to the other side of the sea, to the country of the Gadarenes.[a] [2]And when He had come out of the boat, immediately there met Him out of the tombs a man with an unclean spirit, [3]who had his dwelling among the tombs; and no one could bind him,[a] not even with chains, [4]because he had often been bound with shackles and chains. And the chains had been pulled apart by him, and the shackles broken in pieces; neither could anyone tame him. [5]And always, night and day, he was in the mountains and in the tombs, crying out and cutting himself with stones.

[6]When he saw Jesus from afar, he ran and worshiped Him. [7]And he cried out with a loud voice

4:40 [a]NU-Text reads *Have you still no faith?* **5:1** [a]NU-Text reads *Gerasenes.* **5:3** [a]NU-Text adds *anymore.*

5:1–20 Jesus reached out to the Gentiles, even in seemingly hopeless situations (see Matt. 8:28–34, note).

5:2 Healing in cases of demon possession illustrates the victory of the supernatural over unusually powerful evil forces. Demons are wicked spirit beings that are personal and intelligent (Acts 16:16–18) and who may seek to express themselves through another living creature (Matt. 12:43–45). They can marshal supernatural strength (Luke 8:29; Acts 19:13–16) and are aware of God's destiny for them (Matt. 8:29; 2 Pet. 2:4). These are apparently fallen angels who took part in Satan's rebellion (Is. 14:12–15; Ezek. 28:14, 15; Jude 6). "Demon-possessed" (Gk. *daimonizomai;* see Matt. 8:28–33; 9:32, 33) is referenced in other NT descriptions, including "having" demons (Mark. 7:25; 9:17; Luke 4:33; 8:27; 13:11) and being "tormented" by them (Luke 6:18; Acts 5:16).

Scripture has no evidence that believers can be demon-possessed. The Christian's responsibility is not to look for demons but to be aware of their existence and possible influence and to stand against them in the authority of Jesus Christ (Eph. 6:10–12; 1 Pet. 5:8, 9).

Satan and his demons work through temptation, direct opposition to God's work, and varying levels of influence, oppression, and possession (Matt. 4:1–11; Acts 16:16–18; Mark

5:1–5; Luke 13:10–17). Demons can cause physical affliction (Matt. 12:22; 17:14–18) as well as emotional turmoil (1 Sam. 16:14; Mark 5:1–5). In addition, they work in the arena of the mind, causing people to believe lies (Acts 5:3), to embrace worldly wisdom (James 3:13–16), and to accept doctrinal error as truth (1 Tim. 4:1–5). When Jesus encountered the demonic, He did not engage in prolonged conversations with demons, frequently forbidding them to speak altogether. Based on His authority as God, He commanded them to depart from the individual they had possessed (Mark 1:23–25). The void that is left in a person's life after healing of demon possession needs to be filled (see Matt. 12:43–45). The only permanent defense against demon possession is the experience of the New Birth, which includes the permanent indwelling of the Holy Spirit. This presupposes renouncing sinful practices and cleansing one's life of anything that suggests demonic influence. The believer is then able to walk in the Spirit's fullness, to practice consistent prayer and Bible study, to experience healing in other areas of emotional and spiritual brokenness, and to be involved in healthy, godly relationships (see Ps. 13; 133; Eccl. 1; 2 Cor. 5; Gal. 6; James 5, Healing; Deut. 18, the Occult; 1 Sam. 15, Witchcraft).

JAIRUS'S RESURRECTED DAUGHTER

Jesus' claim to be the Messiah sent the hopes of the Jewish people soaring. They witnessed His healings of the physical body, His mastery over nature, and His power over demons. Jairus, an official in charge of the services and care of the synagogue, may have shared the skepticism of the Jewish leaders, but a personal dilemma sent him to the Teacher.

The twelve-year-old daughter of this distraught father was at the point of death. Hope for the future of her Jewish family lay in this young woman. In earnest supplication, Jairus pled with Jesus to come and lay His hands of healing upon her. He led the Master and His disciples through the curious and crushing throngs with an urgent pace. Suddenly Jesus stopped and asked, "Who touched me?" A desperately ill woman had simply touched the hem of His garment.

Jairus must have winced at the interruption; for him time was important. His anxious spirit must have gladdened when he saw the miracle of restoration for a woman who had suffered for as long as his little girl had been alive.

But at that moment of rejoicing, his own servants arrived with tragic news: His daughter had already died. It was too late.

At that instant of hopelessness Jesus spoke to him, "Do not be afraid; only believe, and she will be made well" (Luke 8:50). The Lord helped Jairus refocus on faith and hope. Slicing through the confusion, Jesus selected Peter, James, and John to accompany Him into the home of these grief-stricken parents. The wailing mourners were there, and He spoke to them, "Do not weep; she is not dead, but sleeping" (v. 52). At this they scoffed in disbelief. He ordered the mourners to leave, and in quiet privacy He took the lifeless girl's hand and said, "Little girl, arise." She stood and walked, and the Great Physician ordered that she be given food.

The Savior alone gives life to every young woman, and He cares deeply. Each of the three synoptic gospels records this miracle, not only verifying the deity of Jesus Christ but also reminding us that He is still our High Priest, sympathizing with us in our weaknesses. He invites us to "come boldly to the throne of grace, that we may obtain mercy and find grace to help in time of need" (Heb. 4:16).

See also Matt. 9:18–26; Luke 8:41–56; notes on Children (2 Sam. 21); Girlhood (Prov. 1)

and said, "What have I to do with You, Jesus, Son of the Most High God? I implore You by God that You do not torment me."

8For He said to him, "Come out of the man, unclean spirit!" 9Then He asked him, "What *is* your name?"

And he answered, saying, "My name *is* Legion; for we are many." 10Also he begged Him earnestly that He would not send them out of the country.

11Now a large herd of swine was feeding there near the mountains. 12So all the demons begged Him, saying, "Send us to the swine, that we may enter them." 13And at once Jesus[a] gave them permission. Then the unclean spirits went out and entered the swine (there were about two thousand); and the herd ran violently down the steep place into the sea, and drowned in the sea.

14So those who fed the swine fled, and they told *it* in the city and in the country. And they went out to see what it was that had happened. 15Then they came to Jesus, and saw the one *who had been* demon-possessed and had the legion, sitting and clothed and in his right mind. And they were afraid. 16And those who saw it told them how it happened to him *who had been* demon-possessed, and about the swine. 17Then they began to plead with Him to depart from their region.

18And when He got into the boat, he who had been demon-possessed begged Him that he might be with Him. 19However, Jesus did not permit him, but said to him, "Go home to your friends, and tell them what great things the Lord has done for you, and how He has had compassion on you." 20And he departed and began to proclaim in Decapolis all that Jesus had done for him; and all marveled.

A Girl Restored to Life and a Woman Healed

21Now when Jesus had crossed over again by boat to the other side, a great multitude gathered to Him; and He was by the sea. 22And behold, one of the rulers of the synagogue came, Jairus by name. And when he saw Him, he fell at His feet 23and begged Him earnestly, saying, "My little daughter lies at the point of death. Come and lay Your hands on her, that she may be healed, and she will live." 24So *Jesus* went with him, and a great multitude followed Him and thronged Him.

25Now a certain woman had a flow of blood for twelve years, 26and had suffered many things from many physicians. She had spent all that she had

5:13 aNU-Text reads *And He gave.*

and was no better, but rather grew worse. ²⁷When she heard about Jesus, she came behind *Him* in the crowd and touched His garment. ²⁸For she said, "If only I may touch His clothes, I shall be made well."

²⁹Immediately the fountain of her blood was dried up, and she felt in *her* body that she was healed of the affliction. ³⁰And Jesus, immediately knowing in Himself that power had gone out of Him, turned around in the crowd and said, "Who touched My clothes?"

³¹But His disciples said to Him, "You see the multitude thronging You, and You say, 'Who touched Me?'"

³²And He looked around to see her who had done this thing. ³³But the woman, fearing and trembling, knowing what had happened to her, came and fell down before Him and told Him the whole truth. ³⁴And He said to her, "Daughter, your faith has made you well. Go in peace, and be healed of your affliction."

³⁵While He was still speaking, *some* came from the ruler of the synagogue's *house* who said, "Your daughter is dead. Why trouble the Teacher any further?"

³⁶As soon as Jesus heard the word that was spoken, He said to the ruler of the synagogue, "Do not be afraid; only believe." ³⁷And He permitted no one to follow Him except Peter, James, and John the brother of James. ³⁸Then He came to the house of the ruler of the synagogue, and saw a tumult and those who wept and wailed loudly. ³⁹When He came in, He said to them, "Why make this commotion and weep? The child is not dead, but sleeping."

⁴⁰And they ridiculed Him. But when He had put them all outside, He took the father and the mother of the child, and those *who were* with Him, and entered where the child was lying. ⁴¹Then He took the child by the hand, and said to her, "Talitha, cumi," which is translated, "Little girl, I say to you, arise." ⁴²Immediately the girl arose and walked, for she was twelve years *of age*. And they were overcome with great amazement. ⁴³But He commanded them strictly that no one should know it, and said that *something* should be given her to eat.

Jesus Rejected at Nazareth

6 Then He went out from there and came to His own country, and His disciples followed Him. ²And when the Sabbath had come, He began to teach in the synagogue. And many hearing *Him* were astonished, saying, "Where *did* this Man *get* these things? And what wisdom *is* this which is given to Him, that such mighty works are performed by His hands! ³Is this not the carpenter, the Son of Mary, and brother of James, Joses, Judas, and Simon? And are not His sisters here with us?" So they were offended at Him.

⁴But Jesus said to them, "A prophet is not without honor except in his own country, among his own relatives, and in his own house." ⁵Now He could do no mighty work there, except that He laid His hands on a few sick people and healed *them*. ⁶And He marveled because of their unbelief. Then He went about the villages in a circuit, teaching.

Sending Out the Twelve

⁷And He called the twelve to *Himself,* and began to send them out two *by* two, and gave them power over unclean spirits. ⁸He commanded them to take nothing for the journey except a staff—no bag, no bread, no copper in *their* money belts— ⁹but to wear sandals, and not to put on two tunics.

¹⁰Also He said to them, "In whatever place you enter a house, stay there till you depart from that place. ¹¹And whoeverᵃ will not receive you nor hear you, when you depart from there, shake off the dust under your feet as a testimony against them.ᵇ Assuredly, I say to you, it will be more tolerable for Sodom and Gomorrah in the day of judgment than for that city!"

¹²So they went out and preached that *people* should repent. ¹³And they cast out many demons, and anointed with oil many who were sick, and healed *them*.

John the Baptist Beheaded

¹⁴Now King Herod heard *of Him,* for His name had become well known. And he said, "John the

6:11 ᵃNU-Text reads *whatever place*. ᵇNU-Text omits the rest of this verse.

5:27 Anyone touched by this woman who was bleeding would be made unclean. However, when she touched Jesus, He made her clean (see Matt. 9:20–22, note).

6:1 His own country would be Nazareth. Even though Bethlehem was the place of Jesus' birth, He was known as a Nazarene because He grew to manhood in this small village (Mark 1:9; see map, Events in Christ's Ministry).

6:3 Offended has the connotation of mistrust, scandal, and disapproval. Because they could not explain Him, they rejected Him.

6:4 Various proverbs were similar to this one in both Jewish and Gentile usage, but Jesus made a particular point by using the word "prophet," a reference to someone with God's message. Perhaps the familiarity of Jesus to His fellow villagers kept them from seeing Him as God's Son. They certainly had seen His miracles and heard His life-changing teaching. Many probably heard of the extraordinary circumstances surrounding His birth. If Jesus was rejected by those in His own hometown, believers should not be surprised when the world rejects them as well (John 17:14).

LEISURE · A TIME TO REST AND PLAY

The Bible speaks in a negative way about "idleness" (Prov. 6:6–11; 1 Tim. 5:13), referring to those who are lazy by such loathsome words as "slothful," "sluggard," and "slack hand"—and very positively about labor and work (Luke 10:7; 1 Cor. 3:8, 9; Eph. 4:28, 1 Thess. 4:11). Given the admonition that we are to work six days and rest one (Ex. 34:21), we might conclude that the Bible is about all work and no fun. That is far from the truth!

Jesus expected His disciples to "come aside" periodically for rest, and Scripture has repeated references to the benefits of "making merry" (Prov. 15:13, 15; 17:22; Luke 15:32).

The Bible speaks of more than seventy days a year in which "no customary work" is to be done (Lev. 23:7, 8): the seven-day feasts that mark Passover, Tabernacles, and Weeks, as well as the Feast of Trumpets, and every Sabbath day! In addition to rest and prayer, leisure days in the Bible are associated with food, gift-giving, singing, and great joy (Rev. 11:10).

A time of rest from work is advocated for those who are experiencing grief (Matt. 14:10–13), those who are seeking spiritual empowerment to do God's will (Matt. 4:1, 11), those who are entering into an intense period of prayer (Matt. 14:23), and those who are newly married (Deut. 24:5).

See also Eccl. 3:1–8; notes on Celebrations and Holidays (Ex. 12); Employment (Eccl. 9; Acts 18; 2 Cor. 2; Col. 3; 1 Pet. 2); Family (Gen. 32; 1 Sam. 3; Ps. 78; 127); Traditions (1 Sam. 7)

Baptist is risen from the dead, and therefore these powers are at work in him."

[15]Others said, "It is Elijah."

And others said, "It is the Prophet, or[a] like one of the prophets."

[16]But when Herod heard, he said, "This is John, whom I beheaded; he has been raised from the dead!" [17]For Herod himself had sent and laid hold of John, and bound him in prison for the sake of Herodias, his brother Philip's wife; for he had married her. [18]Because John had said to Herod, "It is not lawful for you to have your brother's wife."

[19]Therefore Herodias held it against him and wanted to kill him, but she could not; [20]for Herod feared John, knowing that he *was* a just and holy man, and he protected him. And when he heard him, he did many things, and heard him gladly.

[21]Then an opportune day came when Herod on his birthday gave a feast for his nobles, the high officers, and the chief *men* of Galilee. [22]And when Herodias' daughter herself came in and danced, and pleased Herod and those who sat with him, the king said to the girl, "Ask me whatever you want, and I will give *it* to you." [23]He also swore to her, "Whatever you ask me, I will give you, up to half my kingdom."

[24]So she went out and said to her mother, "What shall I ask?"

And she said, "The head of John the Baptist!"

[25]Immediately she came in with haste to the king and asked, saying, "I want you to give me at once the head of John the Baptist on a platter."

[26]And the king was exceedingly sorry; *yet,* because of the oaths and because of those who sat with him, he did not want to refuse her. [27]Immediately the king sent an executioner and commanded his head to be brought. And he went and beheaded him in prison, [28]brought his head on a platter, and gave it to the girl; and the girl gave it to her mother. [29]When his disciples heard *of it,* they came and took away his corpse and laid it in a tomb.

Feeding the Five Thousand

[30]Then the apostles gathered to Jesus and told Him all things, both what they had done and what they had taught. [31]And He said to them, "Come aside by yourselves to a deserted place and rest a while." For there were many coming and going, and they did not even have time to eat. [32]So they departed to a deserted place in the boat by themselves.

[33]But the multitudes[a] saw them departing, and many knew Him and ran there on foot from all the cities. They arrived before them and came together to Him. [34]And Jesus, when He came out, saw a great multitude and was moved with compassion for them, because they were like sheep not having a shepherd. So He began to teach them many things. [35]When the day was now far spent, His disciples came to Him and said, "This is a deserted place, and already the hour *is* late. [36]Send them away, that they may go into the surrounding country and villages and buy themselves bread;[a] for they have nothing to eat."

[37]But He answered and said to them, "You give them something to eat."

··················

6:15 [a]NU-Text and M-Text omit *or.*   6:33 [a]NU-Text and M-Text read *they.*   6:36 [a]NU-Text reads *something to eat* and omits the rest of this verse.

6:37–42 The feeding of the 5,000 is the only miracle recorded in all four gospels (Matt. 14:13–21; Luke 9:12–17; John 6:5–13).

This miracle, as well as other miracles Jesus performed, was to verify that the kingdom was being offered. Provision for

THE QUEENS OF THE NEW TESTAMENT

NAME	GENERAL INFORMATION
Bernice	Elder daughter of Herod Agrippa I; Married her uncle, the king of Chalcis; Consort to her brother Herod Agrippa II; Visited Festus with Agrippa and listened to Paul's defense (Acts 25:13, 23; 26:30); Mistress to Roman emperors Vespasian and Titus.
Candace	Title of the queens of Ethiopia; A member of her imperial staff accepted Christ as his Savior and was baptized by the evangelist Philip (Acts 8:27, 28); Tradition holds that this queen also became a Christian.
Drusilla	Younger daughter of Herod Agrippa I; Wife of Aziz of Emesa; Wife of Procurator Felix of Judea; Present for Paul's second appearance before Felix (Acts 24:24).
Herodias	Daughter of Aristobulus and Berenice (sister to Herod Agrippa I); Granddaughter of Herod the Great; Married her uncle, Herod Philip; Mother of Salome, according to the Jewish historian Josephus; Consort to Herod Antipas (her brother-in-law); Responsible for the death of John the Baptist (Matt. 14:1–12; Mark 6:17).
Queen of the South	Identified as Nikauli by the Jewish historian Josephus; Visitor to Solomon's court (1 Kin. 10:1–13); Historic visit to Solomon noted by Jesus (Matt. 12:42; Luke 11:31).
Unnamed queen in the Book of Revelation	Reference to the city of Babylon—its wickedness and destruction (Rev. 18:7–10).

See also Queen of Sheba (1 Kin. 10); Herodias and Salome (Matt. 14); Candace (Acts 8); Drusilla (Acts 24);
Bernice (Acts 25); charts, The Queens of the Old Testament; The Family Tree of Herod.

And they said to Him, "Shall we go and buy two hundred denarii worth of bread and give them *something* to eat?"

[38]But He said to them, "How many loaves do you have? Go and see."

And when they found out they said, "Five, and two fish."

[39]Then He commanded them to make them all sit down in groups on the green grass. [40]So they sat down in ranks, in hundreds and in fifties. [41]And when He had taken the five loaves and the two fish, He looked up to heaven, blessed and broke the loaves, and gave *them* to His disciples to set before them; and the two fish He divided among *them* all. [42]So they all ate and were filled. [43]And they took up twelve baskets full of fragments and of the fish.

feasts of the Messiah had been foretold (Is. 25:6–9); but Jesus was not only providing for the multitudes, He was also training the disciples. Their mission was not to send people away, but to "give them something to eat" (Mark 6:37). Jesus blessed, broke, multiplied, and gave the food to the disciples; then they served it. The disciples participated by bringing the little they had, sharing the abundance He gave, and gathering the leftovers. Jesus was the chief Shepherd who would supply all their needs (Jer. 23:4).

TOUCHING *AN EXPRESSION OF LOVE*

The woman appeared out of nowhere. "If only I may touch His garment," she whispered under her breath. She pushed her way through the crowd and touched the hem of Jesus' robe. And the woman, who had suffered a continuous blood flow for twelve years, was healed.

While touching and kissing were common in biblical days, Levitical Law forbade many forms of touching. A Hebrew could not touch an unclean animal (Lev. 11:8), a woman following childbirth (Lev. 12:2), a victim of leprosy (Lev. 13:11), or a woman in her menstrual cycle (Lev. 15:19).

Jesus, motivated by a love that transcended the Law, frequently touched others. He touched a leprous man (Mark 1:41), a blind man's eyes (John 9:6), the dead body of Jairus' daughter (Mark 5:41), and a deaf-mute's tongue (Mark 7:33). He gave no thought to Himself as He reached out to others. Jesus also allowed others to touch Him. A woman "who was a sinner" washed and kissed His feet (Luke 7:38). A bleeding woman touched His robe's hem (Matt. 9:20, 21). Jesus often healed and imparted His compassion through touch because touching communicates empathy, affection, healing, and affirmation. Those who have felt His touch must reach out in turn to touch others. There is no better way to feel a person's heartbeat than to embrace that one in a holy hug!

See also notes on Healing (James 5); Love (1 John 4); Romance (Song 2); Sexual Purity (1 Cor. 7)

---

⁴⁴Now those who had eaten the loaves were about[a] five thousand men.

Jesus Walks on the Sea

⁴⁵Immediately He made His disciples get into the boat and go before Him to the other side, to Bethsaida, while He sent the multitude away. ⁴⁶And when He had sent them away, He departed to the mountain to pray. ⁴⁷Now when evening came, the boat was in the middle of the sea; and He *was* alone on the land. ⁴⁸Then He saw them straining at rowing, for the wind was against them. Now about the fourth watch of the night He came to them, walking on the sea, and would have passed them by. ⁴⁹And when they saw Him walking on the sea, they supposed it was a ghost, and cried out; ⁵⁰for they all saw Him and were troubled. But immediately He talked with them and said to them, "Be of good cheer! It is I; do not be afraid." ⁵¹Then He went up into the boat to them, and the wind ceased. And they were greatly amazed in themselves beyond measure, and marveled. ⁵²For they had not understood about the loaves, because their heart was hardened.

Many Touch Him and Are Made Well

⁵³When they had crossed over, they came to the land of Gennesaret and anchored there. ⁵⁴And when they came out of the boat, immediately the people recognized Him, ⁵⁵ran through that whole surrounding region, and began to carry about on beds those who were sick to wherever they heard He was. ⁵⁶Wherever He entered, into villages, cities, or the country, they laid the sick in the marketplaces, and begged Him that they might just touch the hem of His garment. And as many as touched Him were made well.

Defilement Comes from Within

7 Then the Pharisees and some of the scribes came together to Him, having come from Jerusalem. ²Now when[a] they saw some of His disciples eat bread with defiled, that is, with unwashed hands, they found fault. ³For the Pharisees and all the Jews do not eat unless they wash *their* hands in a special way, holding the tradition of the elders. ⁴*When they come* from the marketplace, they do not eat unless they wash. And there are many other things which they have received and hold, *like* the washing of cups, pitchers, copper vessels, and couches.

⁵Then the Pharisees and scribes asked Him, "Why do Your disciples not walk according to the tradition of the elders, but eat bread with unwashed hands?"

⁶He answered and said to them, "Well did Isaiah prophesy of you hypocrites, as it is written:

'This people honors Me with their lips,
But their heart is far from Me.

········· ·········
6:44 ᵃNU-Text and M-Text omit *about.*   **7:2** ᵃNU-Text omits *when* and *they found fault.*

6:44 The crowds of people were counted by numbering the men. Had the women and children been counted, the number would have been much higher.

7:1–5 The Pharisees existed to preserve and demonstrate God's laws. In their zeal to do this, they built up a system of their own interpretation, which became a body of traditions that often superseded Scripture when the two sources did not agree. Ceremonial washing was one of these elevated traditions (see Mark 1:22; chart, Jewish Sects).

7:6–8 Jesus showed no mercy to the ones who were the supposed shepherds of the people. "Hypocrite" was a Greek theatrical term describing someone who acted the part of another (see Matt. 7:1–6, note).

7And in vain they worship Me,
Teaching as doctrines the commandments of men.'[a]

8For laying aside the commandment of God, you hold the tradition of men[a]—the washing of pitchers and cups, and many other such things you do."

9He said to them, "*All too* well you reject the commandment of God, that you may keep your tradition. 10For Moses said, *'Honor your father and your mother';*[a] and, *'He who curses father or mother, let him be put to death.'*[b] 11But you say, 'If a man says to his father or mother, "Whatever profit you might have received from me *is* Corban"—' (that is, a gift *to God*), 12then you no longer let him do anything for his father or his mother, 13making the word of God of no effect through your tradition which you have handed down. And many such things you do."

14When He had called all the multitude to *Himself,* He said to them, "Hear Me, everyone, and understand: 15There is nothing that enters a man from outside which can defile him; but the things which come out of him, those are the things that defile a man. 16If anyone has ears to hear, let him hear!"[a]

17When He had entered a house away from the crowd, His disciples asked Him concerning the parable. 18So He said to them, "Are you thus without understanding also? Do you not perceive that whatever enters a man from outside cannot defile him, 19because it does not enter his heart but his stomach, and is eliminated, *thus* purifying all foods?"[a] 20And He said, "What comes out of a man, that defiles a man. 21For from within, out of the heart of men, proceed evil thoughts, adulteries, fornications, murders, 22thefts, covetousness, wickedness, deceit, lewdness, an evil eye, blasphemy, pride, foolishness. 23All these evil things come from within and defile a man."

A Gentile Shows Her Faith

24From there He arose and went to the region of Tyre and Sidon.[a] And He entered a house and wanted no one to know *it,* but He could not be hidden. 25For a woman whose young daughter had an unclean spirit heard about Him, and she came and fell at His feet. 26The woman was a Greek, a Syro-Phoenician by birth, and she kept asking Him to cast the demon out of her daughter. 27But Jesus said to her, "Let the children be filled first, for it is not good to take the children's bread and throw *it* to the little dogs."

28And she answered and said to Him, "Yes, Lord, yet even the little dogs under the table eat from the children's crumbs."

29Then He said to her, "For this saying go your way; the demon has gone out of your daughter."

30And when she had come to her house, she found the demon gone out, and her daughter lying on the bed.

Jesus Heals a Deaf-Mute

31Again, departing from the region of Tyre and Sidon, He came through the midst of the region of Decapolis to the Sea of Galilee. 32Then they brought to Him one who was deaf and had an impediment in his speech, and they begged Him to put His hand on him. 33And He took him aside from the multitude, and put His fingers in his ears, and He spat and touched his tongue. 34Then, looking up to heaven, He sighed, and said to him, "Ephphatha," that is, "Be opened."

35Immediately his ears were opened, and the impediment of his tongue was loosed, and he spoke plainly. 36Then He commanded them that they should tell no one; but the more He commanded them, the more widely they proclaimed *it.* 37And they were astonished beyond measure, saying, "He has done all things well. He makes both the deaf to hear and the mute to speak."

Feeding the Four Thousand

8In those days, the multitude being very great and having nothing to eat, Jesus called His disciples *to Him* and said to them, 2"I have compassion

---

7:7 [a]Isaiah 29:13   7:8 [a]NU-Text omits the rest of this verse.   7:10 [a]Exodus 20:12; Deuteronomy 5:16 [b]Exodus 21:17   7:16 [a]NU-Text omits this verse.   7:19 [a]NU-Text ends quotation with *eliminated,* setting off the final clause as Mark's comment that Jesus has declared all foods clean.   7:24 [a]NU-Text omits *and Sidon.*

7:9–12 Corban was a practice in which an individual dedicated possessions to God but retained the use of those possessions (see Matt. 15:1–7, note).

7:13 Traditions can be dangerous because they are human inventions. When they clash with Scripture, the initial reaction sometimes is to preserve what people have created rather than to preserve God's Word (see 1 Sam. 7, Traditions).

7:14–23 Specific food regulations were given in the OT, but the religious leaders had developed many other regulations as part of their oral tradition. This process had progressed to the point that some religious leaders believed righteousness and unrighteousness could be determined by food eaten. Jesus condemned this belief because it obscured the real issue—that the heart, not food, is the source of uncleanness.

7:24–30 The Syro-Phoenician woman was a Gentile who reached out to the Savior (see Matt. 15:21–28; Matt. 15, Syro-Phoenician Woman).

7:32–37 This account of a unique healing is found only in the Gospel of Mark. The Lord's procedure is unlike any other recorded healings. In all likelihood Jesus had particular teaching objectives in mind. Without doubt His touch and His oneness with the Father accomplished the miracle.

8:1–9 This miraculous feeding of the 4,000 is similar to the account of the feeding of the 5,000 found elsewhere (see Matt. 15:32–39, note).

on the multitude, because they have now continued with Me three days and have nothing to eat. [3]And if I send them away hungry to their own houses, they will faint on the way; for some of them have come from afar."

[4]Then His disciples answered Him, "How can one satisfy these people with bread here in the wilderness?"

[5]He asked them, "How many loaves do you have?"

And they said, "Seven."

[6]So He commanded the multitude to sit down on the ground. And He took the seven loaves and gave thanks, broke *them* and gave *them* to His disciples to set before *them;* and they set *them* before the multitude. [7]They also had a few small fish; and having blessed them, He said to set them also before *them.* [8]So they ate and were filled, and they took up seven large baskets of leftover fragments. [9]Now those who had eaten were about four thousand. And He sent them away, [10]immediately got into the boat with His disciples, and came to the region of Dalmanutha.

The Pharisees Seek a Sign

[11]Then the Pharisees came out and began to dispute with Him, seeking from Him a sign from heaven, testing Him. [12]But He sighed deeply in His spirit, and said, "Why does this generation seek a sign? Assuredly, I say to you, no sign shall be given to this generation."

Beware of the Leaven of the Pharisees and Herod

[13]And He left them, and getting into the boat again, departed to the other side. [14]Now the disciples[a] had forgotten to take bread, and they did not have more than one loaf with them in the boat. [15]Then He charged them, saying, "Take heed, beware of the leaven of the Pharisees and the leaven of Herod."

[16]And they reasoned among themselves, saying, "*It is* because we have no bread."

[17]But Jesus, being aware of *it,* said to them, "Why do you reason because you have no bread? Do you not yet perceive nor understand? Is your heart still[a] hardened? [18]Having eyes, do you not see? And having ears, do you not hear? And do you not remember? [19]When I broke the five loaves for the five thousand, how many baskets full of fragments did you take up?"

They said to Him, "Twelve."

[20]"Also, when I broke the seven for the four thousand, how many large baskets full of fragments did you take up?"

And they said, "Seven."

[21]So He said to them, "How *is it* you do not understand?"

A Blind Man Healed at Bethsaida

[22]Then He came to Bethsaida; and they brought a blind man to Him, and begged Him to touch him. [23]So He took the blind man by the hand and led him out of the town. And when He had spit on his eyes and put His hands on him, He asked him if he saw anything.

[24]And he looked up and said, "I see men like trees, walking."

[25]Then He put *His* hands on his eyes again and made him look up. And he was restored and saw everyone clearly. [26]Then He sent him away to his house, saying, "Neither go into the town, nor tell anyone in the town."[a]

Peter Confesses Jesus as the Christ

[27]Now Jesus and His disciples went out to the towns of Caesarea Philippi; and on the road He asked His disciples, saying to them, "Who do men say that I am?"

[28]So they answered, "John the Baptist; but some *say,* Elijah; and others, one of the prophets."

[29]He said to them, "But who do you say that I am?"

Peter answered and said to Him, "You are the Christ."

[30]Then He strictly warned them that they should tell no one about Him.

·············· ··············

8:14 [a]NU-Text and M-Text read they.　8:17 [a]NU-Text omits still.
8:26 [a]NU-Text reads *"Do not even go into the town."*

8:11 The Pharisees had personally observed Jesus' miracles. They did not look at miracles as signs drawing them to belief but as a means of seeking to entrap Jesus (see Matt. 12:38–40, note).

8:12 Jesus sighed (Gk. *anastenazō*), denoting deep disappointment and grief. The word is found only here in the NT. Jesus could not help but be overwhelmed with grief that these religious leaders who had long immersed themselves in Scripture would be so indifferent to Him and His mission (see chart, The Emotions of Jesus).

8:13–15 Leaven here represents the evil of the Pharisees who refused to accept God's Son by faith, while they professed to uphold God and His Word (see Mark 7:1–5, note; see chart, Jewish Sects). The disciples' greater danger would not come from God-haters or atheists but from professing God-lovers who were determined to design their own religion (see Matt. 16:5–12).

8:30 Jesus forbade the disciples to share what they knew because they still did not understand His mission—the Cross. The ultimate work of salvation could be easily obscured by momentary desires for healings, provisions, and political power. The people (including the disciples) sought a mighty ruler who would make their present lives easier. Instead, they were faced with the mighty God whose mission was first of all to make their eternity secure.

WOMEN MINISTERING TO JESUS

WOMAN	HER MINISTRY	PRACTICAL APPLICATION
Mary (Luke 2:51, 52)	She nurtured Jesus as He grew into manhood.	Mothers are to rear their children by nurturing them in the Lord (Eph. 6:4).
Susanna (Luke 8:1–3)	She supported the ministry of Jesus with her energies and resources.	Women have opportunity to invest time, energy, and resources (1 Tim. 6:17–19).
Mary of Bethany (Luke 10:39)	She listened to Jesus as He shared spiritual truth.	Women must take time to study God's Word and to listen for His voice (2 Tim. 2:15; Heb. 4:12).
The Samaritan woman (John 4:28–30)	She heard Jesus share the gospel, accepted His grace, then began sharing her testimony with others.	Women, too, have the responsibility to share the Good News of the gospel (1 Pet. 3:15).
The mother-in-law of Peter (Mark 1:29–31)	She was hospitable to Jesus and His disciples.	In a sense, your hospitality is always offered ultimately to Jesus (Col. 3:17, 23, 24).
The widow with two mites (Mark 12:41–44)	She was generous in her support of the kingdom.	The Lord never expects you to give more than you have—only to be generous with that entrusted to you (Heb. 6:10).
Mary of Bethany (Matt. 26:6–13)	She prepared the body of Jesus for burial.	Even mundane tasks are important (Mark 14:8).
Mary Magdalene (Matt. 27:55; John 19:25; 20:16)	She did not desert Jesus when He was rejected. She was the first to proclaim the Resurrection.	Women must stand firm in the faith even in times of discouragement and persecution (Rom. 8:35–39). They must be ready to share the Good News of the Resurrection (1 Pet. 3:15).

Jesus praised women for their faith (Mark 7:24–30) and used women and their homes as well as their household tasks as examples in His parables (Matt. 13:33; 24:41; see chart, Women and the Parables of Jesus). Women played a vital role not only in the church and in kingdom ministries but also in personal ministries to Jesus.

Jesus Predicts His Death and Resurrection

31And He began to teach them that the Son of Man must suffer many things, and be rejected by the elders and chief priests and scribes, and be killed, and after three days rise again. 32He spoke this word openly. Then Peter took Him aside and began to rebuke Him. 33But when He had turned around and looked at His disciples, He rebuked

---

8:31 Jesus' favorite title for Himself appears to be "Son of Man." The disciples had referred to Him as the Christ and the Son of the living God (see Matt. 16:16). These titles were accurate. Yet Jesus used "Son of Man" to describe Himself more

Peter, saying, "Get behind Me, Satan! For you are not mindful of the things of God, but the things of men."

Take Up the Cross and Follow Him

³⁴When He had called the people to *Himself*, with His disciples also, He said to them, "Whoever desires to come after Me, let him deny himself, and take up his cross, and follow Me. ³⁵For whoever desires to save his life will lose it, but whoever loses his life for My sake and the gospel's will save it. ³⁶For what will it profit a man if he gains the whole world, and loses his own soul? ³⁷Or what will a man give in exchange for his soul? ³⁸For whoever is ashamed of Me and My words in this adulterous and sinful generation, of him the Son of Man also will be ashamed when He comes in the glory of His Father with the holy angels."

Jesus Transfigured on the Mount

9 And He said to them, "Assuredly, I say to you that there are some standing here who will not taste death till they see the kingdom of God present with power."

²Now after six days Jesus took Peter, James, and John, and led them up on a high mountain apart by themselves; and He was transfigured before them. ³His clothes became shining, exceedingly white, like snow, such as no launderer on earth can whiten them. ⁴And Elijah appeared to them with Moses, and they were talking with Jesus. ⁵Then Peter answered and said to Jesus, "Rabbi, it is good for us to be here; and let us make three tabernacles: one for You, one for Moses, and one for Elijah"— ⁶because he did not know what to say, for they were greatly afraid.

⁷And a cloud came and overshadowed them; and a voice came out of the cloud, saying, "This is My beloved Son. Hear Him!" ⁸Suddenly, when they had looked around, they saw no one anymore, but only Jesus with themselves.

⁹Now as they came down from the mountain, He commanded them that they should tell no one the things they had seen, till the Son of Man had risen from the dead. ¹⁰So they kept this word to themselves, questioning what the rising from the dead meant.

¹¹And they asked Him, saying, "Why do the scribes say that Elijah must come first?"

¹²Then He answered and told them, "Indeed, Elijah is coming first and restores all things. And how is it written concerning the Son of Man, that He must suffer many things and be treated with contempt? ¹³But I say to you that Elijah has also come, and they did to him whatever they wished, as it is written of him."

A Boy Is Healed

¹⁴And when He came to the disciples, He saw a great multitude around them, and scribes disputing with them. ¹⁵Immediately, when they saw Him, all the people were greatly amazed, and running to *Him,* greeted Him. ¹⁶And He asked the scribes, "What are you discussing with them?"

¹⁷Then one of the crowd answered and said, "Teacher, I brought You my son, who has a mute spirit. ¹⁸And wherever it seizes him, it throws him down; he foams at the mouth, gnashes his teeth, and becomes rigid. So I spoke to Your disciples, that they should cast it out, but they could not."

¹⁹He answered him and said, "O faithless generation, how long shall I be with you? How long shall I bear with you? Bring him to Me." ²⁰Then they brought him to Him. And when he saw Him, immediately the spirit convulsed him, and he fell on the ground and wallowed, foaming at the mouth.

²¹So He asked his father, "How long has this been happening to him?"

And he said, "From childhood. ²²And often he has thrown him both into the fire and into the water to destroy him. But if You can do anything, have compassion on us and help us."

²³Jesus said to him, "If you can believe,^a all things *are* possible to him who believes."

²⁴Immediately the father of the child cried out and said with tears, "Lord, I believe; help my unbelief!"

• • • • • • • • • • • • • • • •

9:23 ^aNU-Text reads *"'If You can!' All things. . . ."*

---

than 80 times. This designation is found in the OT as a reference to man (Ps. 8:4; 80:17) and as a means of addressing the prophet Ezekiel (Ezek. 2:1; 3:1). In the Gospel of Mark, the term seems to link eschatological glory with earthly suffering and death. Jesus described the mission of the "Son of Man" as serving others and giving His life as a ransom (Mark 10:45). The future of the "Son of Man" involved coming with great power and glory (Mark 8:38; 13:26) and sitting at the right hand of God the Father (Mark 14:62).

8:32, 33 Jesus' mission did not fit Peter's agenda for the Messiah. Peter, in effect, was doing the same thing Satan had tried to do with Jesus in the wilderness temptation. Yet Jesus again refused to act on His own apart from the Father. Peter received a stinging rebuke because He was in opposition to the Father's will. Nothing would dissuade Jesus from His mission (Phil. 2:8; Heb. 10:7).

9:14–23 The remaining disciples had been trying to cast a demon out of a boy. The Lord's rebuke (v. 19) indicated their faith in Him had wavered, and thus they were unable to cast out the demon. Whether Jesus' words, "If you can believe, all things are possible to him who believes," were directed to the boy's father or to the disciples is not clear (v. 23). They both needed the message.

9:24 The father's honest response of recognizing that he believed yet knowing his belief was imperfect, represented the first step in pleasing God. The second step was to cry out to God.

> *Whatever God asks you to be, He enables you to be!*
>
> Anne Ortlund

25When Jesus saw that the people came running together, He rebuked the unclean spirit, saying to it, "Deaf and dumb spirit, I command you, come out of him and enter him no more!" 26Then *the spirit* cried out, convulsed him greatly, and came out of him. And he became as one dead, so that many said, "He is dead." 27But Jesus took him by the hand and lifted him up, and he arose.

28And when He had come into the house, His disciples asked Him privately, "Why could we not cast it out?"

29So He said to them, "This kind can come out by nothing but prayer and fasting."a

Jesus Again Predicts His Death and Resurrection

30Then they departed from there and passed through Galilee, and He did not want anyone to know *it.* 31For He taught His disciples and said to them, "The Son of Man is being betrayed into the hands of men, and they will kill Him. And after He is killed, He will rise the third day." 32But they did not understand this saying, and were afraid to ask Him.

Who Is the Greatest?

33Then He came to Capernaum. And when He was in the house He asked them, "What was it you disputed among yourselves on the road?" 34But they kept silent, for on the road they had disputed among themselves who *would be the* greatest. 35And He sat down, called the twelve, and said to them, "If anyone desires to be first, he shall be last of all and servant of all." 36Then He took a little child and set him in the midst of them. And when He

had taken him in His arms, He said to them, 37"Whoever receives one of these little children in My name receives Me; and whoever receives Me, receives not Me but Him who sent Me."

Jesus Forbids Sectarianism

38Now John answered Him, saying, "Teacher, we saw someone who does not follow us casting out demons in Your name, and we forbade him because he does not follow us."

39But Jesus said, "Do not forbid him, for no one who works a miracle in My name can soon afterward speak evil of Me. 40For he who is not against us is on oura side. 41For whoever gives you a cup of water to drink in My name, because you belong to Christ, assuredly, I say to you, he will by no means lose his reward.

Jesus Warns of Offenses

42"But whoever causes one of these little ones who believe in Me to stumble, it would be better for him if a millstone were hung around his neck, and he were thrown into the sea. 43If your hand causes you to sin, cut it off. It is better for you to enter into life maimed, rather than having two hands, to go to hell, into the fire that shall never be quenched— 44where

> *Their worm does not die*
> *And the fire is not quenched.'*a

<hr />

9:29 aNU-Text omits *and fasting.*   9:40 aM-Text reads *against you is on your side.*   9:44 aNU-Text omits this verse.

<hr />

9:29 **Fasting** is a means of focusing one's entire attention on God (see Matt. 6:16–18, note).

9:33–35 **The argument over positions in the kingdom** presented an opportunity for Jesus to continue teaching the disciples about what would be involved in genuine discipleship. Possibly this episode came about because three disciples—Peter, James, and John—had been given special opportunities to be with Jesus (Mark 5:35–42; 9:2–13). Whatever the reason, they still did not understand Jesus. He had clearly taught self-denial as a prerequisite for following Him (Mark 8:34; see also Mark 10, Servanthood).

9:36, 37 **Jesus used a small child** to illustrate servanthood and the demeanor necessary for discipleship. Genuine greatness would mean caring for and treating with respect the most humble and seemingly insignificant among us. No one ever cared more about children than Jesus.

9:42 **Little ones** probably refers more to unprepared disciples

or babes in the faith than to children. Causing others to stumble was a major offense with serious consequences.

9:43–48 **Hell** derives from the Valley of Hinnom (Heb. *ge' hinnom*), a ravine south of the city of Jerusalem. Here, during the monarchy period, apostasizing Jews adopted the cultic practices of Palestine and cremated their children in honor of the gods Baal and Molech (2 Kin. 23:10; Jer. 7:31, 32; 32:35). As a result, the Valley of Hinnom became known in Jewish tradition as the dump heap, the place of destruction by fire (Jer. 31:40). Jesus used graphic language to warn His hearers that the torments of hell are real and eternal and that this eternal separation from God and all that is good should be avoided at all costs.

On the day of God's final judgment, there is no prerogative for changing one's mind. Salvation is God's gift to those who have put their faith and trust in Him (Eph. 2:8). Scripture teaches clearly that your earthly response to Jesus irrevocably determines your eternal destiny—heaven or hell (see 1 Cor. 15, Death; Eph. 2, Salvation; 2 Tim 4, Heaven).

ENABLING CODEPENDENCY IN ACTION

Enabling is codependency in action. An enabler is someone who responds to another's problem by attempting to "take care of" the situation by making things all right. Feeling that the other person's problem is most likely her fault, an enabler allows the behavior to determine her worth. Only when she is doing for others does she feel "I'm somebody, I'm appreciated, I have value." This over-developed sense of responsibility makes it hard to "let go" and allow others to take responsibility for their own behavior and problems.

The solution to the quicksand of enabling is found in a new understanding of what God says about your relationships with others and about who God is and who you are. Scripture makes it clear that no one is responsible for the actions of others (Rom. 14:12). When the rich young ruler came to Jesus (Mark 10:17–22), Jesus spoke truth to him, then let him make his own decision. He did not attempt to follow the young man or manipulate his actions—though He loved him dearly.

Letting go is hard. However, understanding that God alone is the Great Shepherd (John 10:11) and that He does His job well (Is. 40:11) makes it possible for you to release even one greatly loved to the Lord.

The enabler, most of all, needs to understand who she is in Christ (Eph. 1:17, 18). She is of great value because God loves her—not because of what she does but for who she is as His beloved daughter. The Lord loved her before she had a chance to accomplish or fail at anything; and as a new creation in Christ Jesus, she is holy and blameless in His eyes (Eph. 1:4). God's love and mercy toward her are rich and great (Eph. 2:4, 5), and she is His child because God wills for her to be so, not because she has earned favor on her own merit (Eph. 1:5).

See also Ezek. 33:20; 36:19; Rom. 14:12; 2 Cor. 10:12; notes on Codependency (Gen. 27); Identity in Christ (Col. 2); Self-esteem (2 Cor. 10)

---

⁴⁵And if your foot causes you to sin, cut it off. It is better for you to enter life lame, rather than having two feet, to be cast into hell, into the fire that shall never be quenched— ⁴⁶where

'Their worm does not die
And the fire is not quenched.'ᵃ

⁴⁷And if your eye causes you to sin, pluck it out. It is better for you to enter the kingdom of God with one eye, rather than having two eyes, to be cast into hell fire— ⁴⁸where

'Their worm does not die
And the fire is not quenched.'ᵃ

Tasteless Salt Is Worthless

⁴⁹"For everyone will be seasoned with fire,ᵃ and every sacrifice will be seasoned with salt. ⁵⁰Salt *is* good, but if the salt loses its flavor, how will you season it? Have salt in yourselves, and have peace with one another."

Marriage and Divorce

10 Then He arose from there and came to the region of Judea by the other side of the Jordan. And multitudes gathered to Him again, and as He was accustomed, He taught them again.

²The Pharisees came and asked Him, "Is it lawful for a man to divorce *his* wife?" testing Him. ³And He answered and said to them, "What did Moses command you?"

⁴They said, "Moses permitted *a man* to write a certificate of divorce, and to dismiss *her.*"

⁵And Jesus answered and said to them, "Because of the hardness of your heart he wrote you this precept. ⁶But from the beginning of the creation, God 'made them male and female.'ᵃ ⁷'For this reason a man shall leave his father and mother and be joined to his wife, ⁸and the two shall become one flesh';ᵃ so then they are no longer two, but one flesh. ⁹Therefore what God has joined together, let not man separate."

¹⁰In the house His disciples also asked Him again about the same *matter.* ¹¹So He said to them, "Whoever divorces his wife and marries another commits adultery against her. ¹²And if a woman divorces her husband and marries another, she commits adultery."

Jesus Blesses Little Children

¹³Then they brought little children to Him, that He might touch them; but the disciples rebuked

---

9:46 ᵃNU-Text omits the last clause of verse 45 and all of verse 46.
9:48 ᵃIsaiah 66:24   9:49 ᵃNU-Text omits the rest of this verse.
10:6 ᵃGenesis 1:27; 5:2   10:8 ᵃGenesis 2:24

10:2 The Pharisees were not interested in answers but in entrapment. Divorce was one of the challenging issues of the day (see Matt. 19, Divorce).

10:9–12 See Matthew 5, Remarriage.

10:13–16 Seeking the blessing of a great teacher for children was common (see Matt. 19:13, note; Ps. 128, Children).

those who brought *them.* ¹⁴But when Jesus saw *it,* He was greatly displeased and said to them, "Let the little children come to Me, and do not forbid them; for of such is the kingdom of God. ¹⁵Assuredly, I say to you, whoever does not receive the kingdom of God as a little child will by no means enter it." ¹⁶And He took them up in His arms, laid *His* hands on them, and blessed them.

Jesus Counsels the Rich Young Ruler

¹⁷Now as He was going out on the road, one came running, knelt before Him, and asked Him, "Good Teacher, what shall I do that I may inherit eternal life?"

¹⁸So Jesus said to him, "Why do you call Me good? No one *is* good but One, *that is,* God. ¹⁹You know the commandments: *'Do not commit adultery,' 'Do not murder,' 'Do not steal,' 'Do not bear false witness,' 'Do not defraud,' 'Honor your father and your mother.' "*ᵃ

²⁰And he answered and said to Him, "Teacher, all these things I have kept from my youth."

²¹Then Jesus, looking at him, loved him, and said to him, "One thing you lack: Go your way, sell whatever you have and give to the poor, and you will have treasure in heaven; and come, take up the cross, and follow Me."

²²But he was sad at this word, and went away sorrowful, for he had great possessions.

With God All Things Are Possible

²³Then Jesus looked around and said to His disciples, "How hard it is for those who have riches to enter the kingdom of God!" ²⁴And the disciples were astonished at His words. But Jesus answered again and said to them, "Children, how hard it is for those who trust in richesᵃ to enter the kingdom of God! ²⁵It is easier for a camel to go through the eye of a needle than for a rich man to enter the kingdom of God."

²⁶And they were greatly astonished, saying among themselves, "Who then can be saved?"

²⁷But Jesus looked at them and said, "With men *it is* impossible, but not with God; for with God all things are possible."

²⁸Then Peter began to say to Him, "See, we have left all and followed You."

²⁹So Jesus answered and said, "Assuredly, I say to you, there is no one who has left house or brothers or sisters or father or mother or wifeᵃ or children or lands, for My sake and the gospel's, ³⁰who shall not receive a hundredfold now in this time—houses and brothers and sisters and mothers and children and lands, with persecutions—and in the age to come, eternal life. ³¹But many *who are* first will be last, and the last first."

Jesus a Third Time Predicts His Death and Resurrection

³²Now they were on the road, going up to Jerusalem, and Jesus was going before them; and they were amazed. And as they followed they were afraid. Then He took the twelve aside again and began to tell them the things that would happen to Him: ³³"Behold, we are going up to Jerusalem, and the Son of Man will be betrayed to the chief priests and to the scribes; and they will condemn Him to death and deliver Him to the Gentiles; ³⁴and they will mock Him, and scourge Him, and spit on Him, and kill Him. And the third day He will rise again."

Greatness Is Serving

³⁵Then James and John, the sons of Zebedee, came to Him, saying, "Teacher, we want You to do for us whatever we ask."

³⁶And He said to them, "What do you want Me to do for you?"

³⁷They said to Him, "Grant us that we may sit, one on Your right hand and the other on Your left, in Your glory."

³⁸But Jesus said to them, "You do not know what you ask. Are you able to drink the cup that I drink, and be baptized with the baptism that I am baptized with?"

³⁹They said to Him, "We are able."

So Jesus said to them, "You will indeed drink

10:19 ªExodus 20:12–16; Deuteronomy 5:16–20   10:24 ªNU-Text omits *for those who trust in riches.*   10:29 ªNU-Text omits *or wife.*

10:17–22 Jesus loved the young man who approached Him and sought to reach the man by revealing the blind spots in his spiritual life (see Matt. 19:16–22, note).

10:24 The disciples were astonished because they believed that riches indicated the blessing of God and subsequently an assurance of heavenly reward. Riches themselves are neither good nor bad. But when they take the place of God by being the object of trust, that trust indicates money has become an idol.

10:28–31 See Matthew 19:28, 29, note.

10:32–34 All Jewish worship centered in Jerusalem. Earlier Jesus had begun telling the disciples what would happen there, but this time He added details. Though the events would seem tragic, Jesus concluded with the triumph of the Resurrection.

10:35–45 Jesus reversed human ideas of who and what is important (see Matt. 20:20–24, note). He illustrated genuine greatness and spiritual ranking in His own life as He served others rather than expecting others to wait upon Him. He covered His glory for a time and assumed the humble role of a lowly servant (Phil. 2:6–8). His self-sacrifice inspires believers to experience the same victory through denying self and obeying the Father. This theme verse of the Gospel of Mark presents the King of Glory, the One whom angels worship, honor, and serve, the One who came to the world with one goal—to serve, even to the point of laying down His life (Mark 10:45). "Ransom" suggests the idea of release, and "His life" is the ransom to be paid.

SERVANTHOOD BECOMING GREAT IN JESUS' WAY

To study biblical servanthood is to study Jesus. Jesus' only Master was the Father (Is. 53:4–6, 10–12; John 4:34). He served others because that was the Father's assignment (John 17:4–12). Jesus assumed the title of "servant," and this title is incorporated within the messianic prophecies in which He is described as the "servant of the Lord" (Is. 42:1–7; 49:1–7; 50:4–11; 52:13—53:12). In fact, Jesus understood Himself as the fulfillment of Isaiah's "suffering servant."

Even before He went to the Cross, Jesus made sure the disciples understood servanthood. They watched in amazement as He redefined leadership by taking a towel and washing their dirty feet. In His life, biblical leadership and servanthood were synonymous. Many divinely appointed leaders described themselves as "servants."

Normally servanthood is placed at the bottom rung of the ladder of success, with authority at the top. Jesus, in a revolutionary way, flipped the ladder right side up. In imitating Him, servants neither lose their identities nor become doormats; they become great (Mark 10:43).

Many women rendered service: Ruth served her mother-in-law Naomi (Ruth 1:16, 17); Esther served her people in one of their darkest hours (Esth. 4:16); the prophetess Anna served the Lord in the temple (Luke 2:37); Mary of Bethany anointed the Savior with costly oil (Matt. 26:6–10). Women followed Him faithfully even to the Cross in order to minister to His needs (Matt. 27:55).

There is no shame in biblical servanthood (Is. 49:23), which carries the imprimatur of the Lord's confidence (Is. 42:1). Such a servant works with a gentle, sensitive spirit (v. 2) and refuses to quit under suffering (v. 3). The God-honoring servant ultimately does not fail (v. 4), presents worthy goals (v. 4), is undergirded by the Lord (v. 6; Is. 49:5), and is rewarded with a fulfilling ministry (Is. 42:7; 49:4, 6) that glorifies the Lord (Is. 49:3).

The followers of Jesus should be easily recognized (Mark 10:43; John 13:13–16). They will be humbly ready for service in every way (Eph. 6:5–9; Phil. 2:6–8; Col. 3:17).

See also John 13:1–17; Heb. 5:8; 10:7; 1 Pet. 2:21–24; 1 John 2:6; notes on Commitment (Matt. 16); Obedience (Philem.); Sacrificial Living (Mic. 7); Spiritual Discipline (2 Pet. 3); Submission (1 Pet. 3); Surrender (James 4)

---

the cup that I drink, and with the baptism I am baptized with you will be baptized; ⁴⁰but to sit on My right hand and on My left is not Mine to give, but *it is for those* for whom it is prepared."

⁴¹And when the ten heard *it,* they began to be greatly displeased with James and John. ⁴²But Jesus called them to *Himself* and said to them, "You know that those who are considered rulers over the Gentiles lord it over them, and their great ones exercise authority over them. ⁴³Yet it shall not be so among you; but whoever desires to become great among you shall be your servant. ⁴⁴And whoever of you desires to be first shall be slave of all. ⁴⁵For even the Son of Man did not come to be served, but to serve, and to give His life a ransom for many."

Jesus Heals Blind Bartimaeus

⁴⁶Now they came to Jericho. As He went out of Jericho with His disciples and a great multitude, blind Bartimaeus, the son of Timaeus, sat by the road begging. ⁴⁷And when he heard that it was Jesus of Nazareth, he began to cry out and say, "Jesus, Son of David, have mercy on me!"

⁴⁸Then many warned him to be quiet; but he cried out all the more, "Son of David, have mercy on me!"

⁴⁹So Jesus stood still and commanded him to be called.

Then they called the blind man, saying to him, "Be of good cheer. Rise, He is calling you."

⁵⁰And throwing aside his garment, he rose and came to Jesus.

⁵¹So Jesus answered and said to him, "What do you want Me to do for you?"

The blind man said to Him, "Rabboni, that I may receive my sight."

⁵²Then Jesus said to him, "Go your way; your faith has made you well." And immediately he received his sight and followed Jesus on the road.

The Triumphal Entry

11 Now when they drew near Jerusalem, to Bethphageᵃ and Bethany, at the Mount of Olives, He sent two of His disciples; ²and He said to them, "Go into the village opposite you; and as

···················

11:1 ᵃM-Text reads *Bethsphage.*

11:1 The location of Bethphage (lit. "house of figs") is unknown, but it must have been close to Jerusalem. Bethany was about two miles east of Jerusalem. Jesus made this trip many times. He stayed in the home of Mary, Martha, and Lazarus

and was able to walk into Jerusalem to minister (Matt. 21:17; John 12:1).

11:2–8 The Triumphal Entry occurred the week before the Crucifixion, as the culmination of the offer of the kingdom.

soon as you have entered it you will find a colt tied, on which no one has sat. Loose it and bring *it.* [3]And if anyone says to you, 'Why are you doing this?' say, 'The Lord has need of it,' and immediately he will send it here."

[4]So they went their way, and found the[a] colt tied by the door outside on the street, and they loosed it. [5]But some of those who stood there said to them, "What are you doing, loosing the colt?"

[6]And they spoke to them just as Jesus had commanded. So they let them go. [7]Then they brought the colt to Jesus and threw their clothes on it, and He sat on it. [8]And many spread their clothes on the road, and others cut down leafy branches from the trees and spread *them* on the road. [9]Then those who went before and those who followed cried out, saying:

"Hosanna!
'Blessed is He who comes in the name of the LORD!'[a]
[10]Blessed *is* the kingdom of our father David
That comes in the name of the Lord![a]
Hosanna in the highest!"

[11]And Jesus went into Jerusalem and into the temple. So when He had looked around at all things, as the hour was already late, He went out to Bethany with the twelve.

The Fig Tree Withered

[12]Now the next day, when they had come out from Bethany, He was hungry. [13]And seeing from afar a fig tree having leaves, He went to see if perhaps He would find something on it. When He came to it, He found nothing but leaves, for it was not the season for figs. [14]In response Jesus said to it, "Let no one eat fruit from you ever again."
And His disciples heard *it.*

Jesus Cleanses the Temple

[15]So they came to Jerusalem. Then Jesus went into the temple and began to drive out those who bought and sold in the temple, and overturned the tables of the money changers and the seats of those who sold doves. [16]And He would not allow anyone to carry wares through the temple. [17]Then He taught, saying to them, "Is it not written, *'My house shall be called a house of prayer for all nations'?*[a] But you have made it a *'den of thieves.'*"[b]

[18]And the scribes and chief priests heard it and sought how they might destroy Him; for they feared Him, because all the people were astonished at His teaching. [19]When evening had come, He went out of the city.

The Lesson of the Withered Fig Tree

[20]Now in the morning, as they passed by, they saw the fig tree dried up from the roots. [21]And Peter, remembering, said to Him, "Rabbi, look! The fig tree which You cursed has withered away."

[22]So Jesus answered and said to them, "Have faith in God. [23]For assuredly, I say to you, whoever says to this mountain, 'Be removed and be cast into the sea,' and does not doubt in his heart, but believes that those things he says will be done, he will have whatever he says. [24]Therefore I say to you, whatever things you ask when you pray, believe that you receive *them,* and you will have *them.*

Forgiveness and Prayer

[25]"And whenever you stand praying, if you have anything against anyone, forgive him, that your Father in heaven may also forgive you your trespasses.

11:4 [a]NU-Text and M-Text read *a.*　11:9 [a]Psalm 118:26　11:10 [a]NU-Text omits *in the name of the Lord.*　11:17 [a]Isaiah 56:7　[b]Jeremiah 7:11

Zechariah prophesied Israel's king would come "lowly and riding on a donkey" (Zech. 9:9). Because of this reference, the donkey became the animal associated with the Messiah. When Christ returns in glory to establish His kingdom, He will make a royal military entrance, riding a white horse (Rev. 19:11).

11:9 Hosanna (Heb. lit. "save now") was originally a prayer by which God's power to save was invoked, but it evolved into a mere shout or greeting.

11:12–14 The significance of cursing the fig tree is difficult to discern. Its occurrence within the context of the cleansing of the temple may illustrate the barrenness of the religious system, which should have been a place where the people could be fed spiritually but in fact offered no such nourishment.

11:15–17 Many money changers in the temple had become merely money makers. Some profited from dishonest practices (see Matt. 21:12, 13, note).

11:18 The priesthood had deteriorated into a political system in which political power was needed both to gain an office and to serve in it. No longer were priests descendants of Zadok (1 Chr. 24), the line from which the chief priests had come

from the time of Solomon until Antiochus IV (see Matt. 24:15, note). The conquering ruler selected the high priests. Eventually, the office deteriorated into one that could be gained through bribing the ruling powers. Consequently, chief priests, along with the captains and treasurers of the temple, were members of wealthy and influential families who formed a small, powerful group within society (see chart, Jewish Sects).

11:25, 26 Though prayer is the most powerful resource known to man, it becomes impotent when the one praying harbors unforgiveness (Matt. 6:13, 14; 7:7; 17:20; 18:19; Luke 11:9; 17:6). Jesus was not suggesting the loss of salvation. Two aspects of forgiveness are presented: forgiveness that brings salvation (a once-and-for-all event accomplished solely by Jesus on the Cross), and the forgiveness among believers that preserves fellowship. The key words "your Father" established this latter aspect. A believer's position as a family member cannot be lost, but fellowship can be broken. The security of belonging to the family is wonderful, but the severity found in the absence of forgiveness cannot be taken lightly. A real understanding of God's forgiveness will produce the forgiveness of others (see Matt. 18:21, note).

[26]But if you do not forgive, neither will your Father in heaven forgive your trespasses."[a]

Jesus' Authority Questioned

[27]Then they came again to Jerusalem. And as He was walking in the temple, the chief priests, the scribes, and the elders came to Him. [28]And they said to Him, "By what authority are You doing these things? And who gave You this authority to do these things?"

[29]But Jesus answered and said to them, "I also will ask you one question; then answer Me, and I will tell you by what authority I do these things: [30]The baptism of John—was it from heaven or from men? Answer Me."

[31]And they reasoned among themselves, saying, "If we say, 'From heaven,' He will say, 'Why then did you not believe him?' [32]But if we say, 'From men' "—they feared the people, for all counted John to have been a prophet indeed. [33]So they answered and said to Jesus, "We do not know."

And Jesus answered and said to them, "Neither will I tell you by what authority I do these things."

The Parable of the Wicked Vinedressers

12 Then He began to speak to them in parables: "A man planted a vineyard and set a hedge around *it*, dug *a place for* the wine vat and built a tower. And he leased it to vinedressers and went into a far country. [2]Now at vintage-time he sent a servant to the vinedressers, that he might receive some of the fruit of the vineyard from the vinedressers. [3]And they took *him* and beat him and sent *him* away empty-handed. [4]Again he sent them another servant, and at him they threw stones,[a] wounded *him* in the head, and sent *him* away shamefully treated. [5]And again he sent another, and him they killed; and many others, beating some and killing some. [6]Therefore still having one son, his beloved, he also sent him to them last, saying, 'They will respect my son.' [7]But those vinedressers said among themselves, 'This is the heir. Come, let us kill him, and the inheritance will be ours.' [8]So they took him and killed *him* and cast *him* out of the vineyard.

[9]"Therefore what will the owner of the vineyard do? He will come and destroy the vinedressers, and give the vineyard to others. [10]Have you not even read this Scripture:

'The stone which the builders rejected
    Has become the chief cornerstone.
[11]This was the Lord's doing,
    And it is marvelous in our eyes'? "[a]

[12]And they sought to lay hands on Him, but feared the multitude, for they knew He had spoken the parable against them. So they left Him and went away.

The Pharisees: Is It Lawful to Pay Taxes to Caesar?

[13]Then they sent to Him some of the Pharisees and the Herodians, to catch Him in *His* words. [14]When they had come, they said to Him, "Teacher, we know that You are true, and care about no one; for You do not regard the person of men, but teach the way of God in truth. Is it lawful to pay taxes to Caesar, or not? [15]Shall we pay, or shall we not pay?"

But He, knowing their hypocrisy, said to them, "Why do you test Me? Bring Me a denarius that I may see *it*." [16]So they brought *it*.

And He said to them, "Whose image and inscription *is* this?" They said to Him, "Caesar's."

[17]And Jesus answered and said to them, "Render to Caesar the things that are Caesar's, and to God the things that are God's."

And they marveled at Him.

The Sadducees: What About the Resurrection?

[18]Then *some* Sadducees, who say there is no resurrection, came to Him; and they asked Him, saying: [19]"Teacher, Moses wrote to us that if a man's brother dies, and leaves *his* wife behind, and leaves no children, his brother should take his wife and raise up offspring for his brother. [20]Now there were seven brothers. The first took a wife; and dying, he left no offspring. [21]And the second took her, and he died; nor did he leave any offspring. And the third likewise. [22]So the seven had

---

11:26 [a]NU-Text omits this verse. **12:4** [a]NU-Text omits *and at him they threw stones.* **12:11** [a]Psalm 118:22, 23

12:1–8 Jesus knew of His impending death. In this parable, He presented His coming rejection and death (see Matt. 21:33–41, note).

12:14 The issue of paying taxes to Rome was a sensitive one. Many Zealots held that paying tribute to a Gentile monarch was equivalent to treason against the Lord (Israel's true King). The common people struggled with this issue. Refusing to pay taxes put their lives and properties at risk; yet they did not want to offend God. The Pharisees were sure that they had caught Jesus, since they thought His only options would be to advocate rebellion against Rome (which would lead to His arrest) or to rebel against God (which would undermine the support of the people). Jesus not only diffused their trap,

but He also gave the people the answer they were seeking concerning paying taxes.

12:18–27 The opposition of religious leaders to Jesus had been steadily growing because of His teachings and actions. Each group attempted to discredit Him with argumentative issues of the day. The Pharisees came with the issue of divorce (Mark 10:2); the chief priests, scribes, and elders raised the question of His authority (Mark 11:27, 28); the Pharisees and Herodians introduced the issue of taxes (Mark 12:13, 14); now the Sadducees addressed their favorite issue—the resurrection. The Sadducees did not believe in a resurrection nor the direct involvement of God in lives (see Matt. 22:23–33, note).

JEWISH SECTS

SECTS	ORIGIN	DESCRIPTION	BELIEFS
Essenes	Could have evolved from *Hasidim** or Zealots because of their reaction to a corrupt priesthood.	A group of ascetics who withdrew to settle in monastic, communal communities like Qumran on the Dead Sea.	• Held property and possessions in common. • Most were celibate (adopting male children to perpetuate the communities). • Pacifists. • Exclusive and introverted, caring for their own needs within the sect. • Simple in dress and lifestyle. • Rigidly kept the Law and observed ritual self-baptism. • Believed in immortality of soul but with no bodily resurrection.
Herodians	Named because of their support for Herod the Great and his dynasty.	Political group, probably having representation from varied religious perspectives and including many wealthy and politically influential Jews.	• Supported the Hellenization of culture and incorporation of Graeco-Roman policies in Palestine. • Favored autonomy on local level and resisted challenge to the status quo but accepted foreign rule. • Opposed Jesus (Matt. 22:15–22; Mark 3:6; 12:13–17).
Pharisees ("the separated ones")	Probably descendants of the *Hasidim*.	Largest of the Jewish sects; composed mostly of middle class, especially merchants and tradesmen (John 3:1–16); developers of the oral tradition and interpreters of the Law (Talmud and Mishnah); legalistic, self-righteous, and haughty (Matt. 5:20; 9:14; Luke 7:36–39; 18:9–14).	• Monotheistic. • Very concerned with Sabbath observance, tithing, and purification rituals (Matt. 23:2–36; Luke 11:37–44). • Believed in resurrection of the body, life after death, and the reality of demons and angels (Acts 23:6–10). • Opposed Jesus (Matt. 16:1–12; 22:15–22, 34–46; Mark 3:6).
Sadducees ("the righteous ones" or "judges" from Gk. *syndikoi*)	Claimed to be descendants of Zadok, the high priest under David and Solomon (see 2 Sam. 8:17; 1 Kin. 1:34, 35) and boasted of possible link to Aaron.	Possibly from Hasmonean priesthood but definitely from aristocracy; sect from which most high priests came during the days of Jesus (Acts 5:17, 18); in charge of temple and its services (Ezek. 40:44–46).	• Accepted only Torah as authoritative. • Held to literal interpretation of the written Law and rejected oral law as binding. • Believed in absolute freedom of human will. • Denied life after death, resurrection of body, divine providence, and existence of demons and angels (Mark 12:18–27; Luke 20:27–40). • Opposed Pharisees (Acts 23:6–10) and Jesus (Matt. 3:7–10; 16:1–12).
Zealots	Possibly came from those involved in Jewish revolt against Rome (A.D. 6).	Extremists among Pharisees, noted for religious zeal and nationalism.	• Patriotism and religion inseparable. • Fanatical in their Jewish faith and devotion to the Law. • Opposed Roman rule in Palestine; refused to pay taxes; engaged in terrorism against Rome. • Opposed Herodians and Sadducees. • From Zealots, Jesus recruited Judas Iscariot and Simon the Canaanite (Luke 6:15, 16; Acts 1:13).

*Hasidim–*Freedom fighters during the Maccabean period; later the most strict and orthodox Jews.*

THE WIDOW WITH TWO MITES

Jesus was teaching the people about the hypocrisy of the scribes. He described them as lusting for recognition, seeking the best positions, stealing from the helpless, yet making a pretense of being religious (Mark 12:38–40). Sitting in the women's court where the offering receptacles were located (see 2 Kin. 12:9), Jesus used one woman as an example. The comparison is spectacular.

Widowhood was one of the most vulnerable positions of the time (see Mark 12:40). A widow had less capacity for earning than slaves; and unless she had family or friends to protect and help her, she was most likely destitute and perhaps even homeless.

This particular widow was down to her last two mites (worth a fraction of a penny). Jesus drew the attention of the disciples to this woman, who brought delight to His heart. The sound of her tiny offering as it dropped into the metal receptacle must have been pitiful compared with the rattling of the many coins from the rich. They had apportioned a small percentage of their wealth; she had little, but all she had was given to God.

This was the last event of Jesus' public teaching. The act of this humble, needy widow seems to summarize all His teaching. She was not meeting a great need (ultimately God's resources are unlimited), but rather she was recognizing that everything belongs to God. Because she was in His hands, she could willingly and joyously offer all she had to Him.

See also Luke 21:1–4; notes on Commitment (Matt. 16); Influence (Esth. 4)

---

her and left no offspring. Last of all the woman died also. ²³Therefore, in the resurrection, when they rise, whose wife will she be? For all seven had her as wife."

²⁴Jesus answered and said to them, "Are you not therefore mistaken, because you do not know the Scriptures nor the power of God? ²⁵For when they rise from the dead, they neither marry nor are given in marriage, but are like angels in heaven. ²⁶But concerning the dead, that they rise, have you not read in the book of Moses, in the *burning bush passage,* how God spoke to him, saying, '*I am the God of Abraham, the God of Isaac, and the God of Jacob'*?ᵃ ²⁷He is not the God of the dead, but the God of the living. You are therefore greatly mistaken."

The Scribes: Which Is the First Commandment of All?

²⁸Then one of the scribes came, and having heard them reasoning together, perceivingᵃ that He had answered them well, asked Him, "Which is the first commandment of all?"

²⁹Jesus answered him, "The first of all the commandments *is:* '*Hear, O Israel, the Lᴏʀᴅ our God, the Lᴏʀᴅ is one.* ³⁰*And you shall love the Lᴏʀᴅ your God with all your heart, with all your soul, with all your mind, and with all your strength.'*ᵃ This *is* the first commandment.ᵇ ³¹And the second, like *it, is* this: '*You shall love your neighbor as yourself.'*ᵃ There is no other commandment greater than these."

³²So the scribe said to Him, "Well *said,* Teacher. You have spoken the truth, for there is one God, and there is no other but He. ³³And to love Him with all the heart, with all the understanding, with all the soul,ᵃ and with all the strength, and to love one's neighbor as oneself, is more than all the whole burnt offerings and sacrifices."

³⁴Now when Jesus saw that he answered wisely, He said to him, "You are not far from the kingdom of God."

But after that no one dared question Him.

Jesus: How Can David Call His Descendant Lord?

³⁵Then Jesus answered and said, while He taught in the temple, "How *is it* that the scribes say that the Christ is the Son of David? ³⁶For David himself said by the Holy Spirit:

'The Lᴏʀᴅ said to my Lord,
"Sit at My right hand,
Till I make Your enemies Your footstool." ' ᵃ

³⁷Therefore David himself calls Him '*Lord*'; how is He *then* his Son?"

And the common people heard Him gladly.

Beware of the Scribes

³⁸Then He said to them in His teaching, "Beware of the scribes, who desire to go around in

················

12:26 ᵃExodus 3:6, 15   12:28 ᵃNU-Text reads *seeing.*   12:30 ᵃDeuteronomy 6:4, 5 ᵇNU-Text omits this sentence.   12:31 ᵃLeviticus 19:18   12:33 ᵃNU-Text omits *with all the soul.*   12:36 ᵃPsalm 110:1

12:28 This scribe may have been sincere in seeking answers. Jesus made clear that a right relationship to God must precede all others (see Matt. 22:37–40).

12:35–37 The challenge was not to question Scripture but to determine its proper interpretation. David affirmed that the Messiah would be his Lord and thus greater than he (Ps. 110).

Jesus fulfilled all Scripture, including this promise to David. As the Son of David, He was also the exalted Lord and promised Messiah (see Matt. 22:41–46, note).

12:38–40 The danger of creating a clerical class apart from the laity would have been a threat to any generation. These teachers of the Law wore unique robes, expected special fa-

long robes, *love* greetings in the marketplaces, [39]the best seats in the synagogues, and the best places at feasts, [40]who devour widows' houses, and for a pretense make long prayers. These will receive greater condemnation."

The Widow's Two Mites

[41]Now Jesus sat opposite the treasury and saw how the people put money into the treasury. And many *who were* rich put in much. [42]Then one poor widow came and threw in two mites,[a] which make a quadrans. [43]So He called His disciples to *Himself* and said to them, "Assuredly, I say to you that this poor widow has put in more than all those who have given to the treasury; [44]for they all put in out of their abundance, but she out of her poverty put in all that she had, her whole livelihood."

Jesus Predicts the Destruction of the Temple

13 Then as He went out of the temple, one of His disciples said to Him, "Teacher, see what manner of stones and what buildings *are here!*"

[2]And Jesus answered and said to him, "Do you see these great buildings? Not *one* stone shall be left upon another, that shall not be thrown down."

The Signs of the Times and the End of the Age

[3]Now as He sat on the Mount of Olives opposite the temple, Peter, James, John, and Andrew asked Him privately, [4]"Tell us, when will these things be? And what *will be* the sign when all these things will be fulfilled?"

[5]And Jesus, answering them, began to say: "Take heed that no one deceives you. [6]For many will come in My name, saying, 'I am *He,*' and will deceive many. [7]But when you hear of wars and rumors of wars, do not be troubled; for *such things* must happen, but the end *is* not yet. [8]For nation will rise against nation, and kingdom against kingdom. And there will be earthquakes in various places, and there will be famines and troubles.[a] These *are* the beginnings of sorrows.

[9]"But watch out for yourselves, for they will deliver you up to councils, and you will be beaten in the synagogues. You will be brought[a] before rulers and kings for My sake, for a testimony to them. [10]And the gospel must first be preached to all the nations. [11]But when they arrest *you* and deliver you up, do not worry beforehand, or premeditate[a] what you will speak. But whatever is given you in that hour, speak that; for it is not you who speak, but the Holy Spirit. [12]Now brother will betray brother to death, and a father *his* child; and children will rise up against parents and cause them to be put to death. [13]And you will be hated by all for My name's sake. But he who endures to the end shall be saved.

The Great Tribulation

[14]"So when you see the '*abomination of desolation,'*[a] spoken of by Daniel the prophet,[b] standing where it ought not" (let the reader understand), "then let those who are in Judea flee to the mountains. [15]Let him who is on the housetop not go down into the house, nor enter to take anything out of his house. [16]And let him who is in the field not go back to get his clothes. [17]But woe to those who are pregnant and to those who are nursing babies in those days! [18]And pray that your flight may not be in winter. [19]For *in* those days there will be tribulation, such as has not been since the beginning of the creation which God created until this time, nor ever shall be. [20]And unless the Lord had shortened those days, no flesh would be saved; but for the elect's sake, whom He chose, He shortened the days.

[21]"Then if anyone says to you, 'Look, here *is* the Christ!' or, 'Look, *He is* there!' do not believe it. [22]For false christs and false prophets will rise and show signs and wonders to deceive, if possible, even the elect. [23]But take heed; see, I have told you all things beforehand.

The Coming of the Son of Man

[24]"But in those days, after that tribulation, the sun will be darkened, and the moon will not give its light; [25]the stars of heaven will fall, and the powers in the heavens will be shaken. [26]Then they will see the Son of Man coming in the clouds with great power and glory. [27]And then He will send His angels, and gather together His elect from the

---

12:42 [a]Greek *lepta,* very small copper coins worth a fraction of a penny **13:8** [a]NU-Text omits *and troubles.* **13:9** [a]NU-Text and M-Text read *will stand.* **13:11** [a]NU-Text omits *or premeditate.* **13:14** [a]Daniel 11:31; 12:11 [b]NU-Text omits *spoken of by Daniel the prophet.*

---

vors, received coveted honors, and were treated as prestigious guests at the social events of the day. They sought the honor belonging only to God.

12:41–44 This widow in her poverty stands in stark contrast to the scribes in their proud arrogance. The setting for this event is the Court of the Women (see chart, The Plan of Herod's Temple). The widow's wholehearted, sacrificial devotion won the Lord's praise and commendation. She put into the temple treasury the insignificant copper coins (Gk. *lepta;* see chart, Money and Measurements in the Bible).

13:1, 2 The Romans, led by Titus, destroyed Jerusalem in A.D. 70.

13:3–13 Some scholars interpret this passage to be Jesus' declaration that the end of the age would be forthcoming in His generation (see Matt. 24:3, note). Others suggest that Mark 13 contains traditional, apocalyptic (having to do with the future), and redactional sayings (collected from various sources). However, the more consistent view seems to be that the material be accepted as coming from Jesus since it represents His teaching and provides instruction for His disciples before His death.

four winds, from the farthest part of earth to the farthest part of heaven.

The Parable of the Fig Tree

28"Now learn this parable from the fig tree: When its branch has already become tender, and puts forth leaves, you know that summer is near. 29So you also, when you see these things happening, know that it[a] is near—at the doors! 30Assuredly, I say to you, this generation will by no means pass away till all these things take place. 31Heaven and earth will pass away, but My words will by no means pass away.

No One Knows the Day or Hour

32"But of that day and hour no one knows, not even the angels in heaven, nor the Son, but only the Father. 33Take heed, watch and pray; for you do not know when the time is. 34It is like a man going to a far country, who left his house and gave authority to his servants, and to each his work, and commanded the doorkeeper to watch. 35Watch therefore, for you do not know when the master of the house is coming—in the evening, at midnight, at the crowing of the rooster, or in the morning— 36lest, coming suddenly, he find you sleeping. 37And what I say to you, I say to all: Watch!"

The Plot to Kill Jesus

14 After two days it was the Passover and the Feast of Unleavened Bread. And the chief priests and the scribes sought how they might take Him by trickery and put Him to death. 2But they said, "Not during the feast, lest there be an uproar of the people."

The Anointing at Bethany

3And being in Bethany at the house of Simon the leper, as He sat at the table, a woman came having an alabaster flask of very costly oil of spikenard. Then she broke the flask and poured it on His head. 4But there were some who were indignant among themselves, and said, "Why was this fragrant oil wasted? 5For it might have been sold for more than three hundred denarii and given to the poor." And they criticized her sharply.

6But Jesus said, "Let her alone. Why do you trouble her? She has done a good work for Me. 7For you have the poor with you always, and whenever you wish you may do them good; but Me you do not have always. 8She has done what she could. She has come beforehand to anoint My body for burial. 9Assuredly, I say to you, wherever this gospel is preached in the whole world, what this woman has done will also be told as a memorial to her."

Judas Agrees to Betray Jesus

10Then Judas Iscariot, one of the twelve, went to the chief priests to betray Him to them. 11And when they heard it, they were glad, and promised to give him money. So he sought how he might conveniently betray Him.

Jesus Celebrates the Passover with His Disciples

12Now on the first day of Unleavened Bread, when they killed the Passover lamb, His disciples said to Him, "Where do You want us to go and prepare, that You may eat the Passover?"

13And He sent out two of His disciples and said to them, "Go into the city, and a man will meet you carrying a pitcher of water; follow him. 14Wherever he goes in, say to the master of the house, 'The Teacher says, "Where is the guest room in which I may eat the Passover with My disciples?" ' 15Then he will show you a large upper room, furnished and prepared; there make ready for us."

16So His disciples went out, and came into the city, and found it just as He had said to them; and they prepared the Passover.

17In the evening He came with the twelve. 18Now as they sat and ate, Jesus said, "Assuredly, I say to you, one of you who eats with Me will betray Me."

19And they began to be sorrowful, and to say to Him one by one, "Is it I?" And another said, "Is it I?"[a]

20He answered and said to them, "It is one of the twelve, who dips with Me in the dish. 21The Son of Man indeed goes just as it is written of Him, but woe to that man by whom the Son of Man is betrayed! It would have been good for that man if he had never been born."

·················

13:29 [a]Or He   14:19 [a]NU-Text omits this sentence.

13:30 This generation could have alluded to the generation who witnessed the things He described. For other options, see Matthew 24:34, note.

14:1, 2 The Passover and the subsequent Feast of Unleavened Bread were important celebrations to the Jews. The Passover commemorated the last night in Egypt when the angel passed over all who had the sacrificial blood displayed on their doorposts. The firstborn sons of those who did not have the blood on their doorposts (mostly Egyptians) were killed. The Feast of Unleavened Bread took place following the Passover and lasted seven days. It commemorated the Exodus from Egypt (see Ex. 11; 12; chart, The Feasts of Israel).

14:3–5 Mary of Bethany was identified as the woman who anointed Jesus. Judas was noted as the one who voiced an objection (see Matt. 26:6–13, note; John 11, Mary of Bethany).

14:20 Betrayal was an abominable act in the ancient Near East, and the betrayal of a friend after eating with him was the height of treachery.

When you return a blessing for an insult, you will inherit a blessing!

Linda Dillow

Jesus Institutes the Lord's Supper

²²And as they were eating, Jesus took bread, blessed and broke *it,* and gave *it* to them and said, "Take, eat;ᵃ this is My body."

²³Then He took the cup, and when He had given thanks He gave *it* to them, and they all drank from it. ²⁴And He said to them, "This is My blood of the newᵃ covenant, which is shed for many. ²⁵Assuredly, I say to you, I will no longer drink of the fruit of the vine until that day when I drink it new in the kingdom of God."

²⁶And when they had sung a hymn, they went out to the Mount of Olives.

Jesus Predicts Peter's Denial

²⁷Then Jesus said to them, "All of you will be made to stumble because of Me this night,ᵃ for it is written:

'I will strike the Shepherd,
*And the sheep will be scattered.'*ᵇ

²⁸"But after I have been raised, I will go before you to Galilee."

²⁹Peter said to Him, "Even if all are made to stumble, yet I *will* not *be."*

³⁰Jesus said to him, "Assuredly, I say to you that today, *even* this night, before the rooster crows twice, you will deny Me three times."

³¹But he spoke more vehemently, "If I have to die with You, I will not deny You!"

And they all said likewise.

The Prayer in the Garden

³²Then they came to a place which was named Gethsemane; and He said to His disciples, "Sit here while I pray." ³³And He took Peter, James, and John with Him, and He began to be troubled and deeply distressed. ³⁴Then He said to them, "My soul is exceedingly sorrowful, *even* to death. Stay here and watch."

³⁵He went a little farther, and fell on the ground, and prayed that if it were possible, the hour might pass from Him. ³⁶And He said, "Abba, Father, all things *are* possible for You. Take this cup away from Me; nevertheless, not what I will, but what You *will."*

³⁷Then He came and found them sleeping, and said to Peter, "Simon, are you sleeping? Could you not watch one hour? ³⁸Watch and pray, lest you enter into temptation. The spirit indeed *is* willing, but the flesh *is* weak."

³⁹Again He went away and prayed, and spoke the same words. ⁴⁰And when He returned, He found them asleep again, for their eyes were heavy; and they did not know what to answer Him.

⁴¹Then He came the third time and said to them, "Are you still sleeping and resting? It is enough! The hour has come; behold, the Son of Man is being betrayed into the hands of sinners. ⁴²Rise, let us be going. See, My betrayer is at hand."

Betrayal and Arrest in Gethsemane

⁴³And immediately, while He was still speaking, Judas, one of the twelve, with a great multitude with swords and clubs, came from the chief priests and the scribes and the elders. ⁴⁴Now His betrayer had given them a signal, saying, "Whomever I kiss, He is the One; seize Him and lead *Him* away safely."

⁴⁵As soon as he had come, immediately he went up to Him and said to Him, "Rabbi, Rabbi!" and kissed Him.

⁴⁶Then they laid their hands on Him and took Him. ⁴⁷And one of those who stood by drew his sword and struck the servant of the high priest, and cut off his ear.

⁴⁸Then Jesus answered and said to them, "Have you come out, as against a robber, with swords and clubs to take Me? ⁴⁹I was daily with you in the temple teaching, and you did not seize Me. But the Scriptures must be fulfilled."

⁵⁰Then they all forsook Him and fled.

A Young Man Flees Naked

⁵¹Now a certain young man followed Him, having a linen cloth thrown around *his* naked *body.* And the young men laid hold of him, ⁵²and he left the linen cloth and fled from them naked.

Jesus Faces the Sanhedrin

⁵³And they led Jesus away to the high priest; and with him were assembled all the chief priests,

---

14:22 ᵃNU-Text omits *eat.*   **14:24** ᵃNU-Text omits *new.*   **14:27** ᵃNU-Text omits *because of Me this night.* ᵇZechariah 13:7

14:32 Gethsemane (lit. "oil press") was a garden on the Mount of Olives where Jesus went often to pray (see Matt. 26:36–44, note).

14:51 This incident seems to be autobiographical since it would be unusual to include such trivia unless the naked young man was John Mark himself.

the elders, and the scribes. [54]But Peter followed Him at a distance, right into the courtyard of the high priest. And he sat with the servants and warmed himself at the fire.

[55]Now the chief priests and all the council sought testimony against Jesus to put Him to death, but found none. [56]For many bore false witness against Him, but their testimonies did not agree.

[57]Then some rose up and bore false witness against Him, saying, [58]"We heard Him say, 'I will destroy this temple made with hands, and within three days I will build another made without hands.' " [59]But not even then did their testimony agree.

[60]And the high priest stood up in the midst and asked Jesus, saying, "Do You answer nothing? What *is it* these men testify against You?" [61]But He kept silent and answered nothing.

Again the high priest asked Him, saying to Him, "Are You the Christ, the Son of the Blessed?"

[62]Jesus said, "I am. And you will see the Son of Man sitting at the right hand of the Power, and coming with the clouds of heaven."

[63]Then the high priest tore his clothes and said, "What further need do we have of witnesses? [64]You have heard the blasphemy! What do you think?"

And they all condemned Him to be deserving of death.

[65]Then some began to spit on Him, and to blindfold Him, and to beat Him, and to say to Him, "Prophesy!" And the officers struck Him with the palms of their hands.[a]

Peter Denies Jesus, and Weeps

[66]Now as Peter was below in the courtyard, one of the servant girls of the high priest came. [67]And when she saw Peter warming himself, she looked at him and said, "You also were with Jesus of Nazareth."

[68]But he denied it, saying, "I neither know nor understand what you are saying." And he went out on the porch, and a rooster crowed.

[69]And the servant girl saw him again, and be-

gan to say to those who stood by, "This is *one* of them." [70]But he denied it again.

And a little later those who stood by said to Peter again, "Surely you are *one* of them; for you are a Galilean, and your speech shows *it*."[a]

[71]Then he began to curse and swear, "I do not know this Man of whom you speak!"

[72]A second time *the* rooster crowed. Then Peter called to mind the word that Jesus had said to him, "Before the rooster crows twice, you will deny Me three times." And when he thought about it, he wept.

Jesus Faces Pilate

15 Immediately, in the morning, the chief priests held a consultation with the elders and scribes and the whole council; and they bound Jesus, led *Him* away, and delivered *Him* to Pilate. [2]Then Pilate asked Him, "Are You the King of the Jews?"

He answered and said to him, "*It is as* you say."

[3]And the chief priests accused Him of many things, but He answered nothing. [4]Then Pilate asked Him again, saying, "Do You answer nothing? See how many things they testify against You!"[a] [5]But Jesus still answered nothing, so that Pilate marveled.

Taking the Place of Barabbas

[6]Now at the feast he was accustomed to releasing one prisoner to them, whomever they requested. [7]And there was one named Barabbas, *who was* chained with his fellow rebels; they had committed murder in the rebellion. [8]Then the multitude, crying aloud,[a] began to ask *him to do* just as he had always done for them. [9]But Pilate answered them, saying, "Do you want me to release to you the King of the Jews?" [10]For he knew that the chief priests had handed Him over because of envy.

[11]But the chief priests stirred up the crowd, so that he should rather release Barabbas to them.

14:65 [a]NU-Text reads *received Him with slaps.*   14:70 [a]NU-Text omits *and your speech shows it.*   15:4 [a]NU-Text reads *of which they accuse You.*   15:8 [a]NU-Text reads *going up.*

14:53–64 Jesus had both religious and civil trials (see Matt. 26:59, 60, note; Mark 15:2–15; Luke 23:6–12). The religious trial occurred in three stages: before Annas, then twice before Caiaphas and the Sanhedrin (see chart, The Last Week in the Life of Jesus). Unable to find testimony that agreed on any charges, the Sanhedrin finally used Jesus' own confession to find Him guilty of blasphemy (Mark 14:62–64).

15:1–5 The Jewish trial resulted in a charge of blasphemy, which, for the Jews, but not for the Romans, was a capital offense. The Jews were restricted in carrying out a death penalty. Therefore, Jesus was brought before Pilate, then Herod (Luke 23:6–12), then Pilate again. Finally, He was accused of rebellion, which was a charge Rome took seriously.

15:10 The chief priests "had handed Him over because of envy." Pilate, who was politically astute, knew what was going on. The chief priests felt threatened because Jesus spoke the words and did the works that brought Him the affections of the people. The position and prestige of the religious leaders were at stake. From their perspective, Jesus had to be eliminated.

15:11–14 Pilate obviously thought Jesus was innocent. He suggested giving Jesus the benefit of the Passover amnesty (a custom of releasing a prisoner at Passover time), offering Jesus' accusers a way out without losing face. However, Pilate underestimated their hatred. Barabbas was evidently a notorious insurrectionist. He may have been already scheduled to die.

[12]Pilate answered and said to them again, "What then do you want me to do *with Him* whom you call the King of the Jews?"

[13]So they cried out again, "Crucify Him!"

[14]Then Pilate said to them, "Why, what evil has He done?"

But they cried out all the more, "Crucify Him!"

[15]So Pilate, wanting to gratify the crowd, released Barabbas to them; and he delivered Jesus, after he had scourged *Him,* to be crucified.

The Soldiers Mock Jesus

[16]Then the soldiers led Him away into the hall called Praetorium, and they called together the whole garrison. [17]And they clothed Him with purple; and they twisted a crown of thorns, put it on His *head,* [18]and began to salute Him, "Hail, King of the Jews!" [19]Then they struck Him on the head with a reed and spat on Him; and bowing the knee, they worshiped Him. [20]And when they had mocked Him, they took the purple off Him, put His own clothes on Him, and led Him out to crucify Him.

The King on a Cross

[21]Then they compelled a certain man, Simon a Cyrenian, the father of Alexander and Rufus, as he was coming out of the country and passing by, to bear His cross. [22]And they brought Him to the place Golgotha, which is translated, Place of a Skull. [23]Then they gave Him wine mingled with myrrh to drink, but He did not take *it.* [24]And when they crucified Him, they divided His garments, casting lots for them to determine what every man should take.

[25]Now it was the third hour, and they crucified Him. [26]And the inscription of His accusation was written above:

THE KING OF THE JEWS.

[27]With Him they also crucified two robbers, one on His right and the other on His left. [28]So the Scripture was fulfilled[a] which says, *"And He was numbered with the transgressors."*[b]

[29]And those who passed by blasphemed Him, wagging their heads and saying, "Aha! *You* who destroy the temple and build *it* in three days, [30]save Yourself, and come down from the cross!"

[31]Likewise the chief priests also, mocking

PROPHECIES FULFILLED AT THE CROSS

He was forsaken (Zech. 13:7; Matt. 26:56).

He was crucified (Ps. 22:16; Matt. 27:35; John 20:25).

His garments were divided (Ps. 22:18; Matt. 27:35).

He was crucified with two criminals (Is. 53:12; Matt. 27:38).

He was ridiculed and taunted (Ps. 22:7; 70:3; Matt. 27:39–43).

He was looked upon with sneering (Ps. 22:17; Luke 23:35).

He was given wine with gall (Ps. 69:21; Matt. 27:34, 48).

He cried from the Cross (Ps. 22:1; Mark 15:34).

He prayed for His enemies (Is. 53:12; Luke 23:34).

He had no bones broken (Ps. 34:20; John 19:33).

He had His side pierced (Zech. 12:10; John 19:34).

He was in darkness (Amos 8:9; Matt. 27:45).

He was buried in a rich man's tomb (Is. 53:9; Matt. 27:57–60).

These Old Testament prophecies concerning the Messiah were perfectly fulfilled in Jesus Christ.

among themselves with the scribes, said, "He saved others; Himself He cannot save. [32]Let the Christ, the King of Israel, descend now from the cross, that we may see and believe."[a]

Even those who were crucified with Him reviled Him.

Jesus Dies on the Cross

[33]Now when the sixth hour had come, there was darkness over the whole land until the ninth hour. [34]And at the ninth hour Jesus cried out with a loud voice, saying, "Eloi, Eloi, lama sabachthani?" which is translated, *"My God, My God, why have You forsaken Me?"*[a]

[35]Some of those who stood by, when they heard *that,* said, "Look, He is calling for Elijah!" [36]Then someone ran and filled a sponge full of sour wine, put *it* on a reed, and offered *it* to Him to drink, saying, "Let Him alone; let us see if Elijah will come to take Him down."

15:28 [a]Isaiah 53:12 [b]NU-Text omits this verse.   **15:32** [a]M-Text reads *believe Him.*   **15:34** [a]Psalm 22:1

15:15 The scourging (or flogging) itself often led to death. The prisoner was stripped and his hands tied to a post above his head. Two men on either side rhythmically laid the blows with full force using a whip made of strips of leather imbedded with sharp pieces of glass and lead. The whip was designed to flay the flesh and tissues down to the bone.

15:21 A condemned man customarily was required to carry his own cross through the city to the place of crucifixion. That

they had to get another to carry Jesus' Cross indicated the seriousness of the beatings He had endured.

15:22 The place of Crucifixion was called Golgotha (lit. "Place of a Skull"), possibly because its rock formation resembled a skull.

15:24, 25 Crucifixion created the environment for a long, slow death, usually from asphyxiation and/or shock (see Matt. 27:32–38, note).

When the Lord takes one partner to be with Him in the heavenly home,
He restores the one left on earth and gives to the one remaining a new
assignment to ministry and a fresh opportunity for spiritual growth.

Dorothy Kelley Patterson

[37]And Jesus cried out with a loud voice, and breathed His last.

[38]Then the veil of the temple was torn in two from top to bottom. [39]So when the centurion, who stood opposite Him, saw that He cried out like this and breathed His last,[a] he said, "Truly this Man was the Son of God!"

[40]There were also women looking on from afar, among whom were Mary Magdalene, Mary the mother of James the Less and of Joses, and Salome, [41]who also followed Him and ministered to Him when He was in Galilee, and many other women who came up with Him to Jerusalem.

Jesus Buried in Joseph's Tomb

[42]Now when evening had come, because it was the Preparation Day, that is, the day before the Sabbath, [43]Joseph of Arimathea, a prominent council member, who was himself waiting for the kingdom of God, coming and taking courage, went in to Pilate and asked for the body of Jesus. [44]Pilate marveled that He was already dead; and summoning the centurion, he asked him if He had been dead for some time. [45]So when he found out from the centurion, he granted the body to Joseph. [46]Then he bought fine linen, took Him down, and wrapped Him in the linen. And he laid Him in a tomb which had been hewn out of the rock, and rolled a stone against the door of the tomb. [47]And Mary Magdalene and Mary *the mother* of Joses observed where He was laid.

He Is Risen

16 Now when the Sabbath was past, Mary Magdalene, Mary *the mother* of James, and Salome bought spices, that they might come and anoint Him. [2]Very early in the morning, on the first *day* of the week, they came to the tomb when the sun had risen. [3]And they said among themselves, "Who will roll away the stone from the door of the tomb for us?" [4]But when they looked up, they saw that the stone had been rolled away—for it was very large. [5]And entering the tomb, they saw a young man clothed in a long white robe sitting on the right side; and they were alarmed.

[6]But he said to them, "Do not be alarmed. You seek Jesus of Nazareth, who was crucified. He is risen! He is not here. See the place where they laid Him. [7]But go, tell His disciples—and Peter—that He is going before you into Galilee; there you will see Him, as He said to you."

[8]So they went out quickly[a] and fled from the tomb, for they trembled and were amazed. And they said nothing to anyone, for they were afraid.

Mary Magdalene Sees the Risen Lord

[9]Now when *He* rose early on the first *day* of the week, He appeared first to Mary Magdalene, out of whom He had cast seven demons. [10]She went

····················

15:39 [a]NU-Text reads *that He thus breathed His last.*   **16:8** [a]NU-Text and M-Text omit *quickly.*

15:38 The veil of the temple was a carefully woven curtain hanging between the holy place and Most Holy Place (Heb. 9:3). It reminded the people of their separation from God (see Matt. 27:51; Luke 23:45, notes).

15:40 The women who were faithful were there during the Crucifixion as well as at the tomb (see chart, Women and Jesus in His Last Days).

15:43 A wealthy, secret follower of Jesus provided the tomb for His burial (see Matt. 27:57-60).

16:1–3 The women went to the tomb to anoint Jesus' body with the traditional spices. Though Mary may have understood that His death was imminent, no one understood that Jesus would be resurrected, even though He had said He would be.

16:4 Mark gave no explanation as to how the stone was moved. Matthew attributed its removal to the angel (Matt. 28:2).

16:6 The angel's mission was to make clear that the Resurrection had taken place—there was no room for any other explanation. The stone had been rolled away not to let Jesus out, but to let His followers in to see the empty tomb.

16:7 To affirm Peter in this unique way was a gracious act of lovingkindness on the part of the Lord. Peter likely felt he was disqualified as a disciple because of his previous denials of Jesus.

16:8 The Gospel of Mark, according to many, originally ended at verse 8. The following verses are considered a summary of post-Resurrection appearances that were added later. This conclusion is based on a change in style and vocabulary as well as manuscript evidence, since many manuscripts lack these verses. Nonetheless, the other gospels record basically the same happenings as verses 9–15. For the Great Commission, see Matthew 28:18, 19, 20, notes.

and told those who had been with Him, as they mourned and wept. [11]And when they heard that He was alive and had been seen by her, they did not believe.

Jesus Appears to Two Disciples

[12]After that, He appeared in another form to two of them as they walked and went into the country. [13]And they went and told *it* to the rest, *but* they did not believe them either.

The Great Commission

[14]Later He appeared to the eleven as they sat at the table; and He rebuked their unbelief and hardness of heart, because they did not believe those who had seen Him after He had risen. [15]And He said to them, "Go into all the world and preach the gospel to every creature. [16]He who believes and is baptized will be saved; but he who does not believe will be condemned. [17]And these signs will follow those who believe: In My name they will cast out demons; they will speak with new tongues; [18]they[a] will take up serpents; and if they drink anything deadly, it will by no means hurt them; they will lay hands on the sick, and they will recover."

Christ Ascends to God's Right Hand

[19]So then, after the Lord had spoken to them, He was received up into heaven, and sat down at the right hand of God. [20]And they went out and preached everywhere, the Lord working with *them* and confirming the word through the accompanying signs. Amen.[a]

· · · · · · · · · · · · · · · ·

16:18 [a]NU-Text reads *and in their hands they will.* **16:20** [a]Verses 9–20 are bracketed in NU-Text as not original. They are lacking in Codex Sinaiticus and Codex Vaticanus, although nearly all other manuscripts of Mark contain them.

AUTHOR

According to church tradition, the author of the third gospel is Luke, a medical doctor and traveling companion of Paul (Col. 4:14; 2 Tim. 4:11). Luke referred often to his journeys with Paul (Acts 16:10–17; 20:5–15; 21:1–18; 27:1—28:16). The apostle described Luke as "beloved" (Col. 4:14), indicating the closeness of their relationship. Early church fathers Jerome and Eusebius identified Luke as possibly from Antioch of Syria. Whether he was Jew or Gentile is uncertain, although he has been generally identified as a Gentile. Luke later adopted Philippi as his home, investing his life in the young ministry of the Philippian church.

DATE

Luke's gospel and the Book of Acts were probably written between A.D. 59 and 63. The fact that Luke recorded Jesus' prophecy of Jerusalem's destruction in A.D. 70 by the Romans (Luke 21:20–24) but failed to record the actual happening of this significant event, helps establish the date of the gospel. The years between A.D. 59 and 61 are most probable for dating the Gospel of Luke.

BACKGROUND

SETTING: Luke probably began writing the books of Luke and Acts in Rome during Paul's imprisonment there. Another possibility is that Luke may have begun these books during Paul's earlier imprisonment in Caesarea, then continued them later (Acts 24:23).

AUDIENCE: Luke addressed the gospel to Theophilus (Luke 1:1–4). Although Theophilus may not have been a believer, he had at least received some instruction in the faith and may have been struggling with his faith, especially its Jewish origins. Luke wrote to reassure Theophilus and to confirm God's working in history through Jesus the Messiah. It is also possible that "Theophilus" was a figurative way of addressing any Christian or group of Christians, since the name means "lover of God." Luke's wider audience probably included Gentile inquirers and Christians who needed encouragement in the faith.

PURPOSE: Luke wanted to write a historical work in chronological sequence. Another purpose for writing Luke/Acts might have been to confirm to Roman authorities that Christianity posed no political threat.

LITERARY CHARACTERISTICS: The Gospel of Luke is a selective history that conveys a theological message. Showing the stages of Jesus' ministry, Luke wrote with distinctive detail, being careful to note historical events. He presented Christ as the One through whom people of all socioeconomic classes could find redemption. Luke highlighted Christ's high esteem and appreciation for women. Mary and Elizabeth are key figures in Luke 1 and 2. Luke is the only gospel writer to mention Anna and Joanna (Luke 2:36–38; 8:3; 24:10).

The central theme in Luke is that Jesus is the Savior of all. Individuals from all ethnic and socioeconomic groups, both men and women, can find salvation in Him.

Dedication to Theophilus

1 Inasmuch as many have taken in hand to set in order a narrative of those things which have been fulfilled[a] among us, [2]just as those who from the beginning were eyewitnesses and ministers of the word delivered them to us, [3]it seemed good to me also, having had perfect understanding of all things from the very first, to write to you an orderly account, most excellent Theophilus, [4]that you may know the certainty of those things in which you were instructed.

John's Birth Announced to Zacharias

[5]There was in the days of Herod, the king of Judea, a certain priest named Zacharias, of the division of Abijah. His wife *was* of the daughters of Aaron, and her name *was* Elizabeth. [6]And they were both righteous before God, walking in all the commandments and ordinances of the Lord blameless. [7]But they had no child, because Elizabeth was barren, and they were both well advanced in years.

[8]So it was, that while he was serving as priest before God in the order of his division, [9]according to the custom of the priesthood, his lot fell to burn incense when he went into the temple of the Lord. [10]And the whole multitude of the people was praying outside at the hour of incense. [11]Then an angel of the Lord appeared to him, standing on the right side of the altar of incense. [12]And when Zacharias saw *him*, he was troubled, and fear fell upon him.

[13]But the angel said to him, "Do not be afraid, Zacharias, for your prayer is heard; and your wife Elizabeth will bear you a son, and you shall call his name John. [14]And you will have joy and gladness, and many will rejoice at his birth. [15]For he will be great in the sight of the Lord, and shall drink neither wine nor strong drink. He will also be filled with the Holy Spirit, even from his mother's womb. [16]And he will turn many of the children of Israel to the Lord their God. [17]He will also go before Him in the spirit and power of Elijah, *'to turn the hearts of the fathers to the children,'*[a] and the disobedient to the wisdom of the just, to make ready a people prepared for the Lord."

[18]And Zacharias said to the angel, "How shall I know this? For I am an old man, and my wife is well advanced in years."

[19]And the angel answered and said to him, "I am Gabriel, who stands in the presence of God, and was sent to speak to you and bring you these glad tidings. [20]But behold, you will be mute and not able to speak until the day these things take place, because you did not believe my words which will be fulfilled in their own time."

[21]And the people waited for Zacharias, and marveled that he lingered so long in the temple. [22]But when he came out, he could not speak to them; and they perceived that he had seen a vision in the temple, for he beckoned to them and remained speechless.

[23]So it was, as soon as the days of his service were completed, that he departed to his own house. [24]Now after those days his wife Elizabeth conceived; and she hid herself five months, saying, [25]"Thus the Lord has dealt with me, in the days when He looked on *me,* to take away my reproach among people."

Christ's Birth Announced to Mary

[26]Now in the sixth month the angel Gabriel was sent by God to a city of Galilee named Nazareth, [27]to a virgin betrothed to a man whose name was Joseph, of the house of David. The virgin's name *was* Mary. [28]And having come in, the angel said to her, "Rejoice, highly favored *one,* the Lord *is* with you; blessed *are* you among women!"[a]

[29]But when she saw *him,*[a] she was troubled at his saying, and considered what manner of greeting this was. [30]Then the angel said to her, "Do not be afraid, Mary, for you have found favor with God. [31]And behold, you will conceive in your womb and bring forth a Son, and shall call His name JESUS. [32]He will be great, and will be called the Son of the Highest; and the Lord God will give Him the throne of His father David. [33]And He

· · · · · · · · · · · · · · · · · · ·

1:1 [a]Or *are most surely believed*   **1:17** [a]Malachi 4:5, 6   **1:28** [a]NU-Text omits *blessed are you among women.*   **1:29** [a]NU-Text omits *when she saw him.*

1:1–4 Luke addressed his treatise to Theophilus (Gk., lit. "lover of God"). The exact identity of Theophilus is unknown. Some have suggested that he might have been a Roman official. "Theophilus" may also have been a literary device, a way of addressing all Christians—"lovers of God" or believers in a particular community.

1:5–25 The events describing the announcements and births of John the Baptist and Jesus are carefully paralleled. The same angel, Gabriel, appeared to Zacharias and to Mary. Both were told of a future birth; both births were to be unusual; both sons would be a fulfillment of God's plan and of OT prophecies.

1:27 Mary and Joseph were betrothed but did not live together

as husband and wife. According to Jewish custom, betrothal was a time of engagement that was as binding as marriage. The Law of Moses concerning breaking a betrothal by adultery, rape, fornication, or incest called for death by stoning (Deut. 22:23–30). When Mary became pregnant during her betrothal, Joseph decided to divorce her quietly. However, God explained to Joseph in a dream that Mary's conception was the miracle of the Holy Spirit (see Mary of Nazareth).

1:31–35 The angel Gabriel told Mary that her Son's name would be "Jesus" (lit. "*Yahweh* is salvation"). In Mary's womb, God became incarnate through the working of the Holy Spirit (see John 1:14, note).

will reign over the house of Jacob forever, and of His kingdom there will be no end."

³⁴Then Mary said to the angel, "How can this be, since I do not know a man?"

³⁵And the angel answered and said to her, "*The* Holy Spirit will come upon you, and the power of the Highest will overshadow you; therefore, also, that Holy One who is to be born will be called the Son of God. ³⁶Now indeed, Elizabeth your relative has also conceived a son in her old age; and this is now the sixth month for her who was called barren. ³⁷For with God nothing will be impossible."

³⁸Then Mary said, "Behold the maidservant of the Lord! Let it be to me according to your word." And the angel departed from her.

Mary Visits Elizabeth

³⁹Now Mary arose in those days and went into the hill country with haste, to a city of Judah, ⁴⁰and entered the house of Zacharias and greeted Elizabeth. ⁴¹And it happened, when Elizabeth heard the greeting of Mary, that the babe leaped in her womb; and Elizabeth was filled with the Holy Spirit. ⁴²Then she spoke out with a loud voice and said, "Blessed *are* you among women, and blessed *is* the fruit of your womb! ⁴³But why *is* this *granted* to me, that the mother of my Lord should come to me? ⁴⁴For indeed, as soon as the voice of your greeting sounded in my ears, the babe leaped in my womb for joy. ⁴⁵Blessed *is* she who believed, for there will be a fulfillment of those things which were told her from the Lord."

The Song of Mary

⁴⁶And Mary said:

"My soul magnifies the Lord,
⁴⁷And my spirit has rejoiced in God my Savior.
⁴⁸For He has regarded the lowly state of His
    maidservant;
  For behold, henceforth all generations will call
    me blessed.
⁴⁹For He who is mighty has done great things for
    me,
  And holy *is* His name.
⁵⁰And His mercy *is* on those who fear Him
  From generation to generation.
⁵¹He has shown strength with His arm;
  He has scattered *the* proud in the imagination
    of their hearts.

⁵²He has put down the mighty from *their*
    thrones,
  And exalted *the* lowly.
⁵³He has filled *the* hungry with good things,
  And *the* rich He has sent away empty.
⁵⁴He has helped His servant Israel,
  In remembrance of *His* mercy,
⁵⁵As He spoke to our fathers,
  To Abraham and to his seed forever."

⁵⁶And Mary remained with her about three months, and returned to her house.

Birth of John the Baptist

⁵⁷Now Elizabeth's full time came for her to be delivered, and she brought forth a son. ⁵⁸When her neighbors and relatives heard how the Lord had shown great mercy to her, they rejoiced with her.

Circumcision of John the Baptist

⁵⁹So it was, on the eighth day, that they came to circumcise the child; and they would have called him by the name of his father, Zacharias. ⁶⁰His mother answered and said, "No; he shall be called John."

⁶¹But they said to her, "There is no one among your relatives who is called by this name." ⁶²So they made signs to his father—what he would have him called.

⁶³And he asked for a writing tablet, and wrote, saying, "His name is John." So they all marveled. ⁶⁴Immediately his mouth was opened and his tongue *loosed,* and he spoke, praising God. ⁶⁵Then fear came on all who dwelt around them; and all these sayings were discussed throughout all the hill country of Judea. ⁶⁶And all those who heard *them* kept *them* in their hearts, saying, "What kind of child will this be?" And the hand of the Lord was with him.

Zacharias' Prophecy

⁶⁷Now his father Zacharias was filled with the Holy Spirit, and prophesied, saying:

⁶⁸"Blessed *is* the Lord God of Israel,
  For He has visited and redeemed His people,
⁶⁹And has raised up a horn of salvation for us
  In the house of His servant David,
⁷⁰As He spoke by the mouth of His holy
    prophets,
  Who *have been* since the world began,

1:46–55 Mary's song, commonly called the "Magnificat," (lit. "song of praise"), is similar to the psalm of Hannah upon the birth of her son Samuel (1 Sam. 2:1–10). Personal in tone, Mary's song praises the faithfulness of God to His promises. The song also praises Him for His blessings upon those who humble themselves before Him (see chart, Hymns and Songs Associated with Women).

1:59–63 Circumcision was an act performed on the eighth day after a male child's birth. The procedure was usually done by the father and involved cutting away the foreskin of the male genital (see Gen. 17, Circumcision). At John's circumcision, Elizabeth announced and Zacharias confirmed the child's name.

ELIZABETH — *A Spiritual Mentor*

Elizabeth is described by Luke as a woman of integrity and obedience (Luke 1:6). As both the daughter and wife of a priest (v. 5), she lived a righteous life, even though she carried a quiet sorrow because of her childlessness. Then a miracle occurred. Her husband Zacharias, who served in the temple at Jerusalem, was the first person in four hundred years to receive a direct word from God that is recorded in Scripture. While he was burning incense, an angel appeared to announce that his wife Elizabeth would have a child who would be named John (v. 13).

Elizabeth was the first to recognize Mary of Nazareth as the mother of the Messiah. When Mary came to visit during Elizabeth's sixth month of pregnancy, John leaped inside Elizabeth's womb when Mary spoke (v. 41). Elizabeth understood immediately the imminence of the Messiah's birth. What a joyful time the two expectant mothers must have had as the godly Elizabeth shared hospitality and wise advice with her young cousin. Her interaction with the young Mary clearly distinguishes Elizabeth as an outstanding mentor (see Titus 2:3-5).

Mary left after three months, but Elizabeth's joy continued with the birth of her own child (see Luke 1:14, 24, 25). Not only did Elizabeth miraculously conceive a child in her old age, but also God once again came to His people in fulfillment of centuries of eager anticipation. John the Baptist became a powerful preacher of the message of repentance and the forerunner who introduced the Messiah. Jesus said that no one was greater than this son of Elizabeth (Matt. 11:11).

Elizabeth could have faced her old age with a sense of failure and waning faith, but her vibrancy of spirit serves as a reminder that God watches over every woman with loving care. Elizabeth trusted and God rewarded her. She shared herself liberally with Mary, and undoubtedly she trained her son in the Lord while she lived out her faith before him.

See also Luke 1:5-25, 57-66; notes on Aging (Is. 46); Mentoring (2 Kin. 2)

71That we should be saved from our enemies
And from the hand of all who hate us,
72To perform the mercy *promised* to our fathers
And to remember His holy covenant,
73The oath which He swore to our father
Abraham:
74To grant us that we,
Being delivered from the hand of our enemies,
Might serve Him without fear,
75In holiness and righteousness before Him all
the days of our life.

76"And you, child, will be called the prophet of the
Highest;
For you will go before the face of the Lord to
prepare His ways,
77To give knowledge of salvation to His people
By the remission of their sins,
78Through the tender mercy of our God,
With which the Dayspring from on high has
visited[a] us;
79To give light to those who sit in darkness and
the shadow of death,
To guide our feet into the way of peace."

80So the child grew and became strong in spirit, and was in the deserts till the day of his manifestation to Israel.

Christ Born of Mary

2 And it came to pass in those days *that* a decree went out from Caesar Augustus that all the world should be registered. 2This census first took place while Quirinius was governing Syria. 3So all went to be registered, everyone to his own city.

4Joseph also went up from Galilee, out of the city of Nazareth, into Judea, to the city of David, which is called Bethlehem, because he was of the house and lineage of David, 5to be registered with Mary, his betrothed wife,[a] who was with child. 6So it was, that while they were there, the days were completed for her to be delivered. 7And she brought forth her firstborn Son, and wrapped Him in swaddling cloths, and laid Him in a manger, because there was no room for them in the inn.

1:78 [a]NU-Text reads *shall visit.*   2:5 [a]NU-Text omits *wife.*

1:76–80 John the Baptist was a prophet sent by God to announce the coming of the Messiah and to preach the message of repentance. John (lit. "*Yahweh* has been gracious") began his ministry near the Jordan River in A.D. 26 or 27 (see Matt. 3:1, note).

2:1–7 The reason for Mary's travel with Joseph to Bethlehem is uncertain, for women were not usually required to register

(see map, Mary's Travel). Jesus was Mary's firstborn. His birth in "David's city" fulfilled prophecy (Mic. 5:2) and drew attention to His messianic role. Mary wrapped the infant Jesus in long strips of cloth called "swaddling cloths" in order to keep His limbs straight. She placed Him in a manger or feeding trough for animals. His humble stable birth emphasizes the poverty and obscurity that surrounded His early years.

HYMNS AND SONGS ASSOCIATED WITH WOMEN

NAME	DESCRIPTION	REFERENCE
The children of Israel (led by Moses)	A song of deliverance.	Ex. 15:1–18
Miriam	A song of victory, accompanied by timbrels and dances.	Ex. 15:20, 21
Deborah (with Barak)	A song of victory after Israel's defeat of the Canaanites.	Judg. 5:1–31
Israelite women	A song to celebrate David's defeat of Goliath.	1 Sam. 18:6, 7
Women (and men) singers	Music in corporate worship.	2 Sam. 19:35; 2 Chr. 35:25; Neh. 7:67
Female (and male) singers	Music for personal pleasure.	Eccl. 2:8
Daughters of Zion	A song of praise.	Zeph. 3:14
Mary	A song of praise for the honor of being the mother of the Messiah.	Luke 1:46–55
All believers	Spiritual songs of thanksgiving and praise.	Eph. 5:19; Col. 3:16
144,000 saints	A song glorifying the Lamb.	Rev. 14:1–3

Glory in the Highest

⁸Now there were in the same country shepherds living out in the fields, keeping watch over their flock by night. ⁹And behold,ᵃ an angel of the Lord stood before them, and the glory of the Lord shone around them, and they were greatly afraid. ¹⁰Then the angel said to them, "Do not be afraid, for behold, I bring you good tidings of great joy which will be to all people. ¹¹For there is born to you this day in the city of David a Savior, who is Christ the Lord. ¹²And this *will be* the sign to you: You will find a Babe wrapped in swaddling cloths, lying in a manger."

¹³And suddenly there was with the angel a multitude of the heavenly host praising God and saying:

¹⁴"Glory to God in the highest,
And on earth peace, goodwill toward men!"ᵃ

¹⁵So it was, when the angels had gone away from them into heaven, that the shepherds said to one another, "Let us now go to Bethlehem and see this thing that has come to pass, which the Lord has made known to us." ¹⁶And they came with haste and found Mary and Joseph, and the Babe lying in a manger. ¹⁷Now when they had seen *Him,* they made widelyᵃ known the saying which was told them concerning this Child. ¹⁸And all those who heard *it* marveled at those things which were told them by the shepherds. ¹⁹But Mary kept all these things and pondered *them* in her heart. ²⁰Then the shepherds returned, glorifying and praising God for all the things that they had heard and seen, as it was told them.

Circumcision of Jesus

²¹And when eight days were completed for the circumcision of the Child,ᵃ His name was called

2:9 ᵃNU-Text omits *behold.* **2:14** ᵃNU-Text reads *toward men of goodwill.* **2:17** ᵃNU-Text omits *widely.* **2:21** ᵃNU-Text reads *for His circumcision.*

2:8–17 Shepherds of that day were often viewed as outcasts and as dishonest and unclean according to the Law. They were usually in the fields with their sheep from March to November.

MARY OF NAZARETH   *An Honored Mother*

No other human being was closer to Jesus Christ on earth than Mary, His mother. Each of the gospels and the Book of Acts includes her as a woman uniquely gifted to share her Son's earthly life. As a mother, she is one of us, but as the mother of our Lord, she is blessed above all women.

Matthew introduced Mary of Nazareth as the betrothed wife of Joseph, "a just man" (Matt. 1:19). When the angel Gabriel appeared to her with the birth announcement (Luke 1:26–28), Mary's response clearly revealed her keen understanding of Scripture and her ready willingness to obey God.

The awesome concept of yielding her virgin body to the Holy Spirit as His instrument was sure to be misunderstood, but Mary's spirit of total trust earned God's pleasure (Luke 1:38). Overwhelming as the news was, she submitted herself to the assignment with joy. Her song of praise (Luke 1:46–55) describes a perceptive heart of overflowing exaltation to her Lord.

Intertwined with spiritual insight, however, were Mary's anxieties. When at age twelve Jesus failed to join the family as they returned from Jerusalem (Luke 2:41–50), when the wine at the wedding feast was insufficient (John 2:1–12), when she was concerned during His ministry (Mark 6:2, 3; Luke 8:19) or horrified at His Crucifixion, her Son graciously responded to His mother's disquiet on each occasion. He tenderly placed her in the care of John before He died (John 19:25–27).

Mary and Joseph became the parents of other children. Mary probably experienced early widowhood, but she shines as a faithful wife and mother. When Mary appeared publicly, standing at the Cross (John 19:25) and praying after the Lord's ascension (Acts 1:12–14), she demonstrated her courage to the world. She was marked as "one of His," liable for persecution along with the disciples.

The unknown maiden from the despised Galilean town of Nazareth (see John 1:46) illuminates for all time the basic nature of womanhood: entrusting to the next generation the message of God's faithfulness, whether through the rearing of one's own child or through the task of spiritual nurturing that might extend beyond the family circle. Not only was Mary God's sovereign choice to bear the Christ Child, but she was also a devoted and humble follower of her Messiah.

See also Matt. 1:16–25; Mark 3:31; Luke 2:1–52; John 2:1–5; 19:25–27; Acts 1:14; notes on Femininity (Ps. 144); Motherhood (1 Sam. 1); The Virgin Birth (Is. 7)

JESUS, the name given by the angel before He was conceived in the womb.

Jesus Presented in the Temple

22Now when the days of her purification according to the law of Moses were completed, they brought Him to Jerusalem to present *Him* to the Lord 23(as it is written in the law of the Lord, "*Every male who opens the womb shall be called holy to the* LORD"),a 24and to offer a sacrifice according to what is said in the law of the Lord, "*A pair of turtledoves or two young pigeons.*"a

Simeon Sees God's Salvation

25And behold, there was a man in Jerusalem whose name *was* Simeon, and this man *was* just and devout, waiting for the Consolation of Israel, and the Holy Spirit was upon him. 26And it had been revealed to him by the Holy Spirit that he would not see death before he had seen the Lord's Christ. 27So he came by the Spirit into the temple. And when the parents brought in the Child Jesus,

to do for Him according to the custom of the law, 28he took Him up in his arms and blessed God and said:

29"Lord, now You are letting Your servant depart
    in peace,
  According to Your word;
30For my eyes have seen Your salvation
31Which You have prepared before the face of all
    peoples,
32A light to *bring* revelation to the Gentiles,
  And the glory of Your people Israel."

33And Joseph and His mothera marveled at those things which were spoken of Him. 34Then Simeon blessed them, and said to Mary His mother, "Behold, this *Child* is destined for the fall and rising of many in Israel, and for a sign which will be spoken against 35(yes, a sword will pierce

....

2:23 aExodus 13:2, 12, 15   2:24 aLeviticus 12:8   2:33 aNU-Text reads *And His father and mother.*

2:22–24 Childbirth was associated with ceremonial uncleanness (Lev. 12:1–8; see John 16, Childbirth), since the bodily discharges occurring at birth were considered impure. Mary had to undergo a ritual to restore her cleanness in order to attain her ceremonial purity before God. The purification period after the birth of a male child lasted 40 days. The ritual after childbirth for an impoverished family included the offering of turtledoves or pigeons.

THE PLAN OF HEROD'S TEMPLE

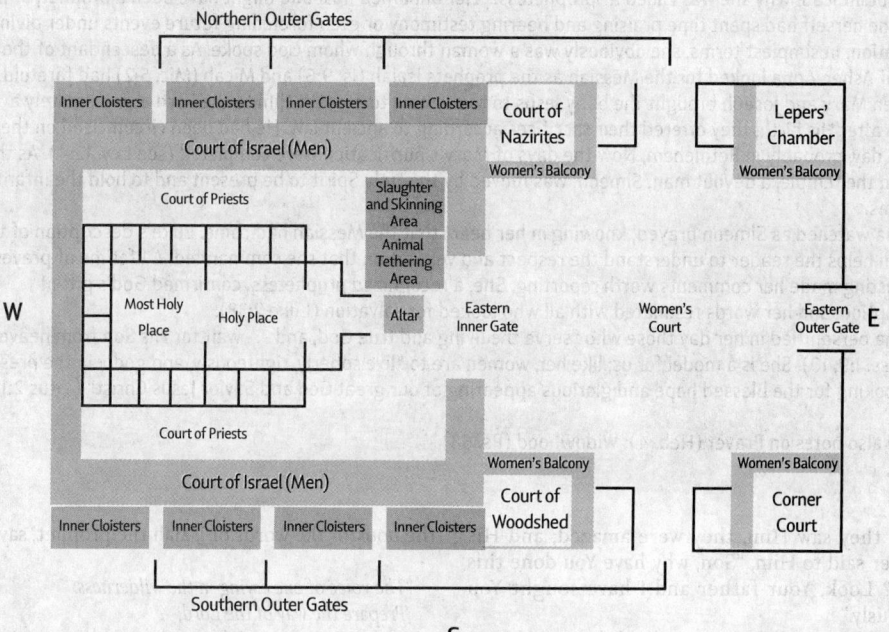

through your own soul also), that the thoughts of many hearts may be revealed."

Anna Bears Witness to the Redeemer

[36]Now there was one, Anna, a prophetess, the daughter of Phanuel, of the tribe of Asher. She was of a great age, and had lived with a husband seven years from her virginity; [37]and this woman *was* a widow of about eighty-four years,[a] who did not depart from the temple, but served *God* with fastings and prayers night and day. [38]And coming in that instant she gave thanks to the Lord,[a] and spoke of Him to all those who looked for redemption in Jerusalem.

The Family Returns to Nazareth

[39]So when they had performed all things according to the law of the Lord, they returned to Galilee, to their *own* city, Nazareth. [40]And the Child grew and became strong in spirit,[a] filled with wisdom; and the grace of God was upon Him.

The Boy Jesus Amazes the Scholars

[41]His parents went to Jerusalem every year at the Feast of the Passover. [42]And when He was twelve years old, they went up to Jerusalem according to the custom of the feast. [43]When they had finished the days, as they returned, the Boy Jesus lingered behind in Jerusalem. And Joseph and His mother[a] did not know *it;* [44]but supposing Him to have been in the company, they went a day's journey, and sought Him among *their* relatives and acquaintances. [45]So when they did not find Him, they returned to Jerusalem, seeking Him. [46]Now so it was *that* after three days they found Him in the temple, sitting in the midst of the teachers, both listening to them and asking them questions. [47]And all who heard Him were astonished at His understanding and answers. [48]So

2:37 [a]NU-Text reads *a widow until she was eighty-four.*   2:38 [a]NU-Text reads *to God.*   2:40 [a]NU-Text omits *in spirit.*   2:43 [a]NU-Text reads *And His parents.*

2:36–38 Anna (lit. "grace") was an 84-year-old prophetess who recognized Jesus as the promised Messiah when Joseph and Mary brought Him to the temple for His dedication. As an attendant of the temple, Anna was a widow whose life was devoted entirely to God (see Anna).

ANNA *A Faithful Prophetess*

Anna, the daughter of Phanuel, was eighty-four years of age and long widowed. Apparently she was a member of the resident staff at the temple in Jerusalem, devoting herself to continual service in the temple. The text does not indicate why she was called a "prophetess." Her unnamed husband might have been a prophet, or perhaps she herself had spent time praising and bearing testimony or even foretelling future events under divine inspiration. In simplest terms, she obviously was a woman through whom God spoke. As a descendant of the tribe of Asher, Anna looked for the Messiah as the prophets Isaiah (Is. 9:6) and Micah (Mic. 5:2) had foretold.

When Mary and Joseph brought the baby Jesus to the temple to present Him to the Lord approximately a month after His birth, they offered their sacrifices according to ancient law. He had been circumcised on the eighth day, probably in Bethlehem. Now the days of Mary's purification were completed (see Lev. 12:4). As they were in the temple, a devout man, Simeon, was moved by the Holy Spirit to be present and to hold the Infant in his arms.

Anna watched as Simeon prayed, knowing in her heart that the Messiah had come. Luke's description of this woman helps the reader to understand the respect and veneration that she commanded. A lifetime of prayer and fasting made her comments worth reporting. She, a recognized prophetess, confirmed God's gift of redemption, and her words resonated with all who looked for salvation (Luke 2:38).

Anna personified in her day those who "serve the living and true God, and . . . wait for His Son from heaven" (1 Thess. 1:9, 10). She is a model for us; like her, women are to "live soberly, righteously, and godly in the present age, looking for the blessed hope and glorious appearing of our great God and Savior Jesus Christ" (Titus 2:12, 13).

See also notes on Prayer (Heb. 4); Widowhood (Ps. 68)

---

when they saw Him, they were amazed; and His mother said to Him, "Son, why have You done this to us? Look, Your father and I have sought You anxiously."

49And He said to them, "Why did you seek Me? Did you not know that I must be about My Father's business?" 50But they did not understand the statement which He spoke to them.

Jesus Advances in Wisdom and Favor

51Then He went down with them and came to Nazareth, and was subject to them, but His mother kept all these things in her heart. 52And Jesus increased in wisdom and stature, and in favor with God and men.

John the Baptist Prepares the Way

3 Now in the fifteenth year of the reign of Tiberius Caesar, Pontius Pilate being governor of Judea, Herod being tetrarch of Galilee, his brother Philip tetrarch of Iturea and the region of Trachonitis, and Lysanias tetrarch of Abilene, 2while Annas and Caiaphas were high priests,a the word of God came to John the son of Zacharias in the wilderness. 3And he went into all the region around the Jordan, preaching a baptism of repentance for the remission of sins, 4as it is written in the book of the words of Isaiah the prophet, saying:

"The voice of one crying in the wilderness:
'Prepare the way of the Lord;
Make His paths straight.
5Every valley shall be filled
And every mountain and hill brought low;
The crooked places shall be made straight
And the rough ways smooth;
6And all flesh shall see the salvation of God.' "a

John Preaches to the People

7Then he said to the multitudes that came out to be baptized by him, "Brood of vipers! Who warned you to flee from the wrath to come? 8Therefore bear fruits worthy of repentance, and do not begin to say to yourselves, 'We have Abraham as *our* father.' For I say to you that God is able to raise up children to Abraham from these stones. 9And even now the ax is laid to the root of the trees. Therefore every tree which does not bear good fruit is cut down and thrown into the fire."

10So the people asked him, saying, "What shall we do then?"

3:2 aNU-Text and M-Text read *in the high priesthood of Annas and Caiaphas.* 3:6 aIsaiah 40:3–5

3:3–9 John traveled throughout the Jordan valley, and his ministry was characterized by a call to repentance for the forgiveness of sins. All four gospel writers described him as "the voice of one crying in the wilderness" (Is. 40:3). Only Luke added a further quotation from Isaiah 40:4, 5. Matthew stated that the Sadducees and Pharisees listened to John, but Luke noted that "the multitudes" were also present. In this way, Luke emphasized that John's message was for the whole nation of Israel and foreshadowed God's offer of grace for everyone.

THE FAMILY TREE OF JESUS*

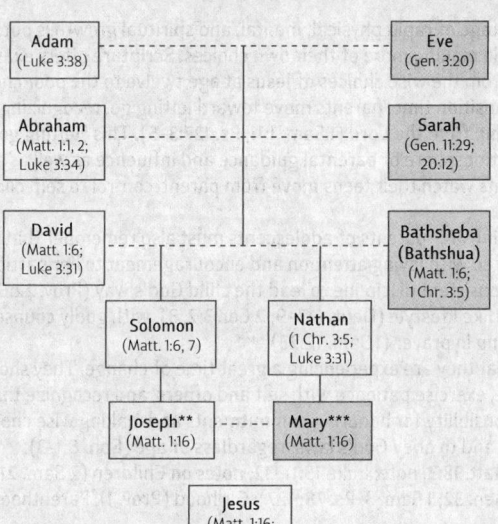

Adam
(Luke 3:38)

Eve
(Gen. 3:20)

Abraham
(Matt. 1:1, 2;
Luke 3:34)

Sarah
(Gen. 11:29;
20:12)

David
(Matt. 1:6;
Luke 3:31)

Bathsheba
(Bathshua)
(Matt. 1:6;
1 Chr. 3:5)

Solomon
(Matt. 1:6, 7)

Nathan
(1 Chr. 3:5;
Luke 3:31)

Joseph**
(Matt. 1:16)

Mary***
(Matt. 1:16)

Jesus
(Matt. 1:16;
Luke 3:23)

* This is not a complete genealogy; some
generations are skipped. Tamar, Rahab, and
Ruth are other women in the lineage
mentioned (Matt. 1:2, 5).
** Joseph has the legal, royal record in Matthew.
*** Mary has the natural, royal record in Luke
(see Luke 3:23).

Women
- - - - - Marital Relationships
Descendant

¹¹He answered and said to them, "He who has two tunics, let him give to him who has none; and he who has food, let him do likewise."

¹²Then tax collectors also came to be baptized, and said to him, "Teacher, what shall we do?"

¹³And he said to them, "Collect no more than what is appointed for you."

¹⁴Likewise the soldiers asked him, saying, "And what shall we do?"

So he said to them, "Do not intimidate anyone or accuse falsely, and be content with your wages."

¹⁵Now as the people were in expectation, and all reasoned in their hearts about John, whether he was the Christ *or* not, ¹⁶John answered, saying to all, "I indeed baptize you with water; but One mightier than I is coming, whose sandal strap I am not worthy to loose. He will baptize you with the Holy Spirit and fire. ¹⁷His winnowing fan *is* in His hand, and He will thoroughly clean out His threshing floor, and gather the wheat into His barn; but the chaff He will burn with unquenchable fire."

¹⁸And with many other exhortations he preached to the people. ¹⁹But Herod the tetrarch, being rebuked by him concerning Herodias, his brother Philip's wife,ª and for all the evils which Herod had done, ²⁰also added this, above all, that he shut John up in prison.

3:19 ªNU-Text reads *his brother's wife.*

3:17 Winnowing grain with wooden forks was the ancient way of separating the grain from the inedible parts. When the stalks were tossed into the air, the wind blew away the straw and chaff. The heavier grain fell to the ground (Is. 30:24). The chaff was then gathered to burn in the cooking oven. Luke used the example of winnowing to predict unbelieving Israel's exclusion from God's kingdom and the gathering of Gentile outcasts into the kingdom. "Unquenchable fire" fitted the description of the ever-burning fires of Jerusalem's garbage dump, "Gehenna."

3:19, 20 John the Baptist denounced Herod Antipas, who divorced his wife in order to win Herodias' hand in marriage (see Matt. 14, Herodias and Salome). The daughter of Aristobulus and Bernice, Herodias was first married to Philip and bore a daughter, Salome (see chart, The Family Tree of Herod the Great). John's rebuke of Herod for his marital infidelities would later cost John his life (Matt. 14:1, note; Mark 6:16–28).

ADOLESCENCE   THE IN-BETWEEN STAGE

This in-between stage of rapid physical, mental, and spiritual growth is potentially a time during which young people begin making more of their own choices. Scripture offers examples of teens making choices, ranging from the wise choices of Jesus at age twelve to the poor choices of the prodigal son.

During this transition time, parents move toward letting go, recognizing that the child has been given in stewardship from the Lord (1 Sam. 1:11; Ps. 127:3–5). This "letting go" gives adolescents room for growth in an atmosphere of parental guidance and influence as well as accountability (Rom. 14:12; 1 Cor. 10:13). Parents watch their teens move from parent-control to self-control and then hopefully to God-control.

In the midst of this "letting go," parents of adolescents must also remember that God created each child uniquely; each must be reared with loving attention and encouragement to her particular talents, gifts, and personality (Prov. 3:27), with consistent discipline to lead the child God's way (Prov. 22:6; 27:5), with the faithful example of a consistent Christlike lifestyle (Deut. 6:7–9; 2 Cor. 3:2, 3), with godly counsel and advice (Prov. 12:15; 19:20), and with undergirding in prayer (1 Sam. 12:23).

Teens need to realize that they are experiencing a great time of change. They should cling to the spiritual values they know to be true, exercise patience with self and others, and recognize that increased authority over their own lives means responsibility for honoring commitments and making wise choices. God commands children to honor their parents and to obey God's laws, regardless of age (Eph. 6:1–3).

See also Gen. 37:1–36; Matt. 18:3; note; Luke 15:11–32; notes on Children (2 Sam. 21; Ps. 128; Prov. 22; Luke 15); Dating (1 Tim. 4); Family (Gen. 32; 1 Sam. 3; Ps. 78; 127); Girlhood (Prov. 1); Parenthood (Prov. 10); Siblings (Gen. 37)

John Baptizes Jesus

²¹When all the people were baptized, it came to pass that Jesus also was baptized; and while He prayed, the heaven was opened. ²²And the Holy Spirit descended in bodily form like a dove upon Him, and a voice came from heaven which said, "You are My beloved Son; in You I am well pleased."

The Genealogy of Jesus Christ

²³Now Jesus Himself began *His ministry at* about thirty years of age, being (as was supposed) *the* son of Joseph, *the son* of Heli, ²⁴*the son* of Matthat,ᵃ *the son* of Levi, *the son* of Melchi, *the son* of Janna, *the son* of Joseph, ²⁵*the son* of Mattathiah, *the son* of Amos, *the son* of Nahum, *the son* of Esli, *the son* of Naggai, ²⁶*the son* of Maath, *the son* of Mattathiah, *the son* of Semei, *the son* of Joseph, *the son* of Judah, ²⁷*the son* of Joannas, *the son* of Rhesa, *the son* of Zerubbabel, *the son* of Shealtiel, *the son* of Neri, ²⁸*the son* of Melchi, *the son* of Addi, *the son* of Cosam, *the son* of Elmodam, *the son* of Er, ²⁹*the son* of Jose, *the son* of Eliezer, *the son* of Jorim, *the son* of Matthat, *the son* of Levi, ³⁰*the son* of Simeon, *the son* of Judah, *the son* of Joseph, *the son* of Jonan, *the son* of Eliakim, ³¹*the son* of Melea, *the son* of Menan, *the son* of Mattathah, *the son* of Nathan, *the son* of David, ³²*the son* of Jesse, *the son* of Obed, *the son* of Boaz, *the son* of Salmon, *the son* of Nahshon, ³³*the son* of Amminadab, *the son* of Ram, *the son* of Hezron, *the son* of Perez, *the son* of Judah, ³⁴*the son* of Jacob, *the son* of Isaac, *the son* of Abraham, *the son* of Terah, *the son* of Nahor, ³⁵*the son of* Serug, *the son* of Reu, *the son* of Peleg, *the son* of Eber, *the son* of Shelah, ³⁶*the son* of Cainan, *the son* of Arphaxad, *the son* of Shem, *the son* of Noah, *the son* of Lamech, ³⁷*the son* of Methuselah, *the son of* Enoch, *the son* of Jared, *the son* of Mahalalel, *the son* of Cainan, ³⁸*the son* of Enosh, *the son* of Seth, *the son* of Adam, *the son* of God.

Satan Tempts Jesus

4 Then Jesus, being filled with the Holy Spirit, returned from the Jordan and was led by the Spirit intoᵃ the wilderness, ²being tempted for forty days by the devil. And in those days He ate nothing, and afterward, when they had ended, He was hungry.

··

3:24 ᵃThis and several other names in the genealogy are spelled somewhat differently in the NU-Text. Since the New King James Version uses the Old Testament spelling for persons mentioned in the New Testament, these variations, which come from the Greek, have not been footnoted. **4:1** ᵃNU-Text reads *in.*

3:21–38 Jesus' baptism was viewed by Luke as the climax of John's ministry. A voice from heaven affirmed Jesus' divine sonship. The Spirit's descent upon Him at baptism established Jesus' role as the Anointed One. Luke traced Jesus' lineage back to Adam to emphasize the fact that Jesus was the Son of Adam as well as the divine Son of God (see chart, The Family Tree of Jesus).

4:1–15 After His baptism and before the beginning of His public ministry, Jesus was led by the Spirit to battle the devil in the Judean desert. Luke alone stated that Jesus was "filled with the Holy Spirit" (v. 1). The temptation was preceded by a fast that lasted 40 days and nights. By appealing to His hunger and by questioning His divine sonship, Satan attempted to divert Jesus from His mission. Jesus did not yield

³And the devil said to Him, "If You are the Son of God, command this stone to become bread."

⁴But Jesus answered him, saying,ᵃ "It is written, 'Man shall not live by bread alone, but by every word of God.' "ᵇ

⁵Then the devil, taking Him up on a high mountain, showed Himᵃ all the kingdoms of the world in a moment of time. ⁶And the devil said to Him, "All this authority I will give You, and their glory; for *this* has been delivered to me, and I give it to whomever I wish. ⁷Therefore, if You will worship before me, all will be Yours."

⁸And Jesus answered and said to him, "Get behind Me, Satan!ᵃ Forᵇ it is written, 'You shall worship the Lord your God, and Him only you shall serve.' "ᶜ

⁹Then he brought Him to Jerusalem, set Him on the pinnacle of the temple, and said to Him, "If You are the Son of God, throw Yourself down from here. ¹⁰For it is written:

'He shall give His angels charge over you,
To keep you,'

¹¹and,

'In their hands they shall bear you up,
Lest you dash your foot against a stone.' "ᵃ

¹²And Jesus answered and said to him, "It has been said, 'You shall not tempt the LORD your God.' "ᵃ

¹³Now when the devil had ended every temptation, he departed from Him until an opportune time.

Jesus Begins His Galilean Ministry

¹⁴Then Jesus returned in the power of the Spirit to Galilee, and news of Him went out through all the surrounding region. ¹⁵And He taught in their synagogues, being glorified by all.

Jesus Rejected at Nazareth

¹⁶So He came to Nazareth, where He had been brought up. And as His custom was, He went into the synagogue on the Sabbath day, and stood up to read. ¹⁷And He was handed the book of the prophet Isaiah. And when He had opened the book, He found the place where it was written:

¹⁸"The Spirit of the LORD is upon Me,
Because He has anointed Me
To preach the gospel to the poor;

He has sent Me to heal the brokenhearted,ᵃ
To proclaim liberty to the captives
And recovery of sight to the blind,
To set at liberty those who are oppressed;
¹⁹To proclaim the acceptable year of the LORD."ᵃ

²⁰Then He closed the book, and gave *it* back to the attendant and sat down. And the eyes of all who were in the synagogue were fixed on Him. ²¹And He began to say to them, "Today this Scripture is fulfilled in your hearing." ²²So all bore witness to Him, and marveled at the gracious words which proceeded out of His mouth. And they said, "Is this not Joseph's son?"

²³He said to them, "You will surely say this proverb to Me, 'Physician, heal yourself! Whatever we have heard done in Capernaum,ᵃ do also here in Your country.' " ²⁴Then He said, "Assuredly, I say to you, no prophet is accepted in his own country. ²⁵But I tell you truly, many widows were in Israel in the days of Elijah, when the heaven was shut up three years and six months, and there was a great famine throughout all the land; ²⁶but to none of them was Elijah sent except to Zarephath,ᵃ *in the region* of Sidon, to a woman *who was* a widow. ²⁷And many lepers were in Israel in the time of Elisha the prophet, and none of them was cleansed except Naaman the Syrian."

²⁸So all those in the synagogue, when they heard these things, were filled with wrath, ²⁹and rose up and thrust Him out of the city; and they led Him to the brow of the hill on which their city was built, that they might throw Him down over the cliff. ³⁰Then passing through the midst of them, He went His way.

Jesus Casts Out an Unclean Spirit

³¹Then He went down to Capernaum, a city of Galilee, and was teaching them on the Sabbaths. ³²And they were astonished at His teaching, for His word was with authority. ³³Now in the synagogue there was a man who had a spirit of an unclean demon. And he cried out with a loud voice, ³⁴saying, "Let *us* alone! What have we to do with

---

4:4 ᵃDeuteronomy 8:3 ᵇNU-Text omits *but by every word of God.* 4:5 ᵃNU-Text reads *And taking Him up, he showed Him.* 4:8 ᵃNU-Text omits *Get behind Me, Satan.* ᵇNU-Text and M-Text omit *For.* ᶜDeuteronomy 6:13 4:11 ᵃPsalm 91:11, 12 4:12 ᵃDeuteronomy 6:16 4:18 ᵃNU-Text omits *to heal the brokenhearted.* 4:19 ᵃIsaiah 61:1, 2 4:23 ᵃHere and elsewhere the NU-Text spelling is *Capharnaum.* 4:26 ᵃGreek *Sarepta*

---

to Satan, but three times He countered Satan's temptations by quoting Scripture (Deut. 6:13; 6:16; 8:3). Realizing his failure, Satan departed to wait for an "opportune time." Angels then came and ministered to Jesus. Afterward, Jesus returned to Galilee to begin His ministry.

4:16–30 Jesus' first sermon in the synagogue of His hometown Nazareth involved the fulfillment of Scripture. When the

Isaiah scroll was given to Jesus, He stood and read (Is. 61:1, 2; 58:6), omitting "the day of vengeance of our God." Then He began to preach. After this rejection, there is no record that Jesus ever returned to Nazareth to minister.

4:33–37, 41 Signs of affliction by demons in the NT included unusual strength, foaming at the mouth, speechlessness or an unnatural voice, blindness, unbridled fierceness, and

You, Jesus of Nazareth? Did You come to destroy us? I know who You are—the Holy One of God!"

[35]But Jesus rebuked him, saying, "Be quiet, and come out of him!" And when the demon had thrown him in *their* midst, it came out of him and did not hurt him. [36]Then they were all amazed and spoke among themselves, saying, "What a word this *is!* For with authority and power He commands the unclean spirits, and they come out." [37]And the report about Him went out into every place in the surrounding region.

Peter's Mother-in-Law Healed

[38]Now He arose from the synagogue and entered Simon's house. But Simon's wife's mother was sick with a high fever, and they made request of Him concerning her. [39]So He stood over her and rebuked the fever, and it left her. And immediately she arose and served them.

Many Healed After Sabbath Sunset

[40]When the sun was setting, all those who had any that were sick with various diseases brought them to Him; and He laid His hands on every one of them and healed them. [41]And demons also came out of many, crying out and saying, "You are the Christ,[a] the Son of God!"

And He, rebuking *them,* did not allow them to speak, for they knew that He was the Christ.

Jesus Preaches in Galilee

[42]Now when it was day, He departed and went into a deserted place. And the crowd sought Him and came to Him, and tried to keep Him from leaving them; [43]but He said to them, "I must preach the kingdom of God to the other cities also, because for this purpose I have been sent." [44]And He was preaching in the synagogues of Galilee.[a]

Four Fishermen Called as Disciples

5 So it was, as the multitude pressed about Him to hear the word of God, that He stood by the Lake of Gennesaret, [2]and saw two boats standing by the lake; but the fishermen had gone from them and were washing *their* nets. [3]Then He got into one of the boats, which was Simon's, and asked him to put out a little from the land. And He sat down and taught the multitudes from the boat.

[4]When He had stopped speaking, He said to Simon, "Launch out into the deep and let down your nets for a catch."

[5]But Simon answered and said to Him, "Master, we have toiled all night and caught nothing; nevertheless at Your word I will let down the net." [6]And when they had done this, they caught a great number of fish, and their net was breaking. [7]So they signaled to *their* partners in the other boat to come and help them. And they came and filled both the boats, so that they began to sink. [8]When Simon Peter saw *it,* he fell down at Jesus' knees, saying, "Depart from me, for I am a sinful man, O Lord!"

[9]For he and all who were with him were astonished at the catch of fish which they had taken; [10]and so also *were* James and John, the sons of Zebedee, who were partners with Simon. And Jesus said to Simon, "Do not be afraid. From now on you will catch men." [11]So when they had brought their boats to land, they forsook all and followed Him.

Jesus Cleanses a Leper

[12]And it happened when He was in a certain city, that behold, a man who was full of leprosy saw Jesus; and he fell on *his* face and implored Him, saying, "Lord, if You are willing, You can make me clean."

[13]Then He put out *His* hand and touched him, saying, "I am willing; be cleansed." Immediately the leprosy left him. [14]And He charged him to tell no one, "But go and show yourself to the priest, and make an offering for your cleansing, as a testimony to them, just as Moses commanded."

[15]However, the report went around concerning Him all the more; and great multitudes came together to hear, and to be healed by Him of their infirmities. [16]So He Himself *often* withdrew into the wilderness and prayed.

•••••••••••••••••••••••

4:41 [a]NU-Text omits *the Christ.*   4:44 [a]NU-Text reads *Judea.*

---

control of personality and actions by an evil spirit. NT writers were careful to distinguish demon possession from disease, although demons could cause disease (see Matt. 17:14–18). Here the demons recognized Jesus as "the Holy One of God," "the Christ, the Son of God," thus bearing witness to Jesus' authority and identity. In order not to arouse political misconceptions about His messianic mission, Jesus rebuked the demons and silenced them. Whenever Christ spoke to the demons, they had to obey Him (see Mark 5:2, note).

5:12–15 Leprosy described a variety of skin disorders from psoriasis to true leprosy. The symptoms could be mild, with white patches on the skin, or severe, with oozing sores and the loss of fingers and/or toes. For the Hebrews, the disease

left its victims ceremonially unclean, unfit for worship. Anyone who came into contact with a leper was also considered unclean. Therefore, lepers were kept isolated from the rest of the community. Since a leper was not allowed in the city, the healing probably took place on the city's outskirts. Lepers were forbidden to approach other people and were required to call out "unclean" to prevent accidental contact. Jesus, however, touched the leper and healed him.

5:16 Withdrawing to a place of solitude to pray was a regular practice for Jesus. He was pre-eminently a Person of prayer, maintaining close fellowship with His Father. Only Luke recorded the prayers of Jesus at His baptism (Luke 3:21), at the Transfiguration (Luke 9:29), before choosing the apostles (Luke 6:12, 13), at Caesarea-Philippi (Luke 9:18), and on the

EVENTS IN CHRIST'S MINISTRY

GREAT SEA
(MEDITERRANEAN)

MT.
HERMON

Syro-Phoenician
woman's daughter
healed (Mark 7).

Peter's Confession
(Matt. 16).

Tyre

Caesarea
Philippi

Peter's mother-in-law
healed (Luke 4).

Healing of Jairus'
daughter and
woman with
issue of blood
(Luke 8).

Chorazin

Bethsaida

Capernaum

Cana

Sea of
Chinnereth
(Galilee)

Water turned
to wine (John 2).

MT. TABOR

Infirm woman
healed (Luke 13).

Nazareth

Nain

Gadara

Mary's hometown;
boyhood home
to Jesus (Luke 2).

Widow's son
raised (Luke 7).

Sychar

Woman at the
well (John 4).

Ephraim

Jordan River

Mary Magdalene
and the other
Mary watched
over the tomb
(Matt. 27).

Jericho

Jesus appeared
after Resurrection
to Mary Magdalene
(Matt. 28).

Emmaus

Jerusalem

MT. OF OLIVES

Bethany

Home of Mary
and Martha;
place of Jesus'
anointing
(Matt. 26).

Bethlehem

Dead Sea

Birthplace of
Jesus (Luke 2).

| 0 | | 300 Mi. |

| 0 | | 300 Km. |

—N—

Jesus Forgives and Heals a Paralytic

[17]Now it happened on a certain day, as He was teaching, that there were Pharisees and teachers of the law sitting by, who had come out of every town of Galilee, Judea, and Jerusalem. And the power of the Lord was *present* to heal them.[a] [18]Then behold, men brought on a bed a man who was paralyzed, whom they sought to bring in and

5:17 [a]NU-Text reads *present with Him to heal.*

Cross (Luke 23:34). Jesus often prayed early in the mornings in a solitary place (Mark 1:35), and on other occasions He prayed all night (Luke 6:12). John 17 records the longest prayer of Jesus in the NT (see chart, Lessons from the Model Prayer).

5:17–19 **The house** probably had an external staircase leading to a flat roof. In the NT period, to escape the cramped interior of the house, women often did their daily chores on the roof. The paralytic was lowered through the roof into Jesus' pres-

lay before Him. [19]And when they could not find how they might bring him in, because of the crowd, they went up on the housetop and let him down with *his* bed through the tiling into the midst before Jesus.

[20]When He saw their faith, He said to him, "Man, your sins are forgiven you."

[21]And the scribes and the Pharisees began to reason, saying, "Who is this who speaks blasphemies? Who can forgive sins but God alone?"

[22]But when Jesus perceived their thoughts, He answered and said to them, "Why are you reasoning in your hearts? [23]Which is easier, to say, 'Your sins are forgiven you,' or to say, 'Rise up and walk'? [24]But that you may know that the Son of Man has power on earth to forgive sins"—He said to the man who was paralyzed, "I say to you, arise, take up your bed, and go to your house."

[25]Immediately he rose up before them, took up what he had been lying on, and departed to his own house, glorifying God. [26]And they were all amazed, and they glorified God and were filled with fear, saying, "We have seen strange things today!"

Matthew the Tax Collector

[27]After these things He went out and saw a tax collector named Levi, sitting at the tax office. And He said to him, "Follow Me." [28]So he left all, rose up, and followed Him.

[29]Then Levi gave Him a great feast in his own house. And there were a great number of tax collectors and others who sat down with them. [30]And their scribes and the Pharisees[a] complained against His disciples, saying, "Why do You eat and drink with tax collectors and sinners?"

[31]Jesus answered and said to them, "Those who are well have no need of a physician, but those who are sick. [32]I have not come to call *the* righteous, but sinners, to repentance."

Jesus Is Questioned About Fasting

[33]Then they said to Him, "Why do[a] the disciples of John fast often and make prayers, and likewise those of the Pharisees, but Yours eat and drink?"

[34]And He said to them, "Can you make the friends of the bridegroom fast while the bridegroom is with them? [35]But the days will come when the bridegroom will be taken away from them; then they will fast in those days."

[36]Then He spoke a parable to them: "No one puts a piece from a new garment on an old one;[a] otherwise the new makes a tear, and also the piece that was *taken* out of the new does not match the old. [37]And no one puts new wine into old wineskins; or else the new wine will burst the wineskins and be spilled, and the wineskins will be ruined. [38]But new wine must be put into new wineskins, and both are preserved.[a] [39]And no one, having drunk old *wine,* immediately[a] desires new; for he says, 'The old is better.' "[b]

Jesus Is Lord of the Sabbath

6 Now it happened on the second Sabbath after the first[a] that He went through the grainfields. And His disciples plucked the heads of grain and ate *them,* rubbing *them* in *their* hands. [2]And some of the Pharisees said to them, "Why are you doing what is not lawful to do on the Sabbath?"

[3]But Jesus answering them said, "Have you not even read this, what David did when he was hungry, he and those who were with him: [4]how he went into the house of God, took and ate the showbread, and also gave some to those with him, which is not lawful for any but the priests to eat?"

....

5:30 [a]NU-Text reads *But the Pharisees and their scribes.* **5:33** [a]NU-Text omits *Why do,* making the verse a statement. **5:36** [a]NU-Text reads *No one tears a piece from a new garment and puts it on an old one.* **5:38** [a]NU-Text omits *and both are preserved.* **5:39** [a]NU-Text omits *immediately.* [b]NU-Text reads *good.* **6:1** [a]NU-Text reads *on a Sabbath.*

---

ence. The roof described by Mark seemed to have been made of mud, grass, and branches that formed a supporting lattice for an outer covering of clay tiles (Mark 2:4).

5:21 Blasphemy (lit. "slander" or "defamation") referred to the act of insulting the character of God. This capital crime required the stoning to death of the offender (Lev. 24:14–16). NT Jewish leaders regarded Jesus as a blasphemer (Mark 2:7), for He claimed messianic status (Luke 22:69). Luke, as well as the scribes and Pharisees, believed that only God could forgive sins. Through this account Luke made Jesus' claim to deity clear to his readers.

5:34, 35 The bridal metaphor is used throughout the Bible in reference to God's people. In the OT, the prophets presented Israel as an unfaithful bride, guilty of adultery (see Hos. 3:1). In the NT, the bride often refers to the church and her relationship with Christ (see Rev. 21:2, 9). The bride belongs to the Bridegroom, who is Christ (John 3:29).

5:37–39 Liquid was kept in the cured skins of small animals (usually goats). The skins were carefully sewn together so as to be watertight. While new skins that retained their elasticity served as adequate containers for new wine that was still fermenting, old skins would have lost their elasticity and could easily burst. Jesus used the metaphor of wineskins to indicate that the radically "new" gospel He brought could not be contained within the "old" Judaism of the Pharisees.

6:1, 2 God's people in the OT celebrated every seventh day as holy, a day for worship and rest, since God rested on the seventh day after creation (see chart, The Principle of the Sabbath). They did not work on the Sabbath (Heb. *shabbat,* lit. "seventh day" from the verb meaning "to cease" or "to rest"), for its observance was part of their covenant with God. Plucking grain would have been considered work. The penalty for desecrating the Sabbath was death (Ex. 35:1–3). Jesus observed the Sabbath as a day of worship, but He would not conform to the trivial restrictions of oral tradition.

God has a way of using those the world calls "nobodies."

Sandy Smith

⁵And He said to them, "The Son of Man is also Lord of the Sabbath."

Healing on the Sabbath

⁶Now it happened on another Sabbath, also, that He entered the synagogue and taught. And a man was there whose right hand was withered. ⁷So the scribes and Pharisees watched Him closely, whether He would heal on the Sabbath, that they might find an accusation against Him. ⁸But He knew their thoughts, and said to the man who had the withered hand, "Arise and stand here." And he arose and stood. ⁹Then Jesus said to them, "I will ask you one thing: Is it lawful on the Sabbath to do good or to do evil, to save life or to destroy?"^a ¹⁰And when He had looked around at them all, He said to the man,^a "Stretch out your hand." And he did so, and his hand was restored as whole as the other.^b ¹¹But they were filled with rage, and discussed with one another what they might do to Jesus.

The Twelve Apostles

¹²Now it came to pass in those days that He went out to the mountain to pray, and continued all night in prayer to God. ¹³And when it was day, He called His disciples to *Himself;* and from them He chose twelve whom He also named apostles: ¹⁴Simon, whom He also named Peter, and Andrew his brother; James and John; Philip and Bartholomew; ¹⁵Matthew and Thomas; James the *son* of Alphaeus, and Simon called the Zealot; ¹⁶Judas *the son* of James, and Judas Iscariot who also became a traitor.

Jesus Heals a Great Multitude

¹⁷And He came down with them and stood on a level place with a crowd of His disciples and a great multitude of people from all Judea and Jerusalem, and from the seacoast of Tyre and Sidon, who came to hear Him and be healed of their diseases, ¹⁸as well as those who were tormented with unclean spirits. And they were healed. ¹⁹And the whole multitude sought to touch Him, for power went out from Him and healed *them* all.

The Beatitudes

²⁰Then He lifted up His eyes toward His disciples, and said:

"Blessed *are you* poor,
　For yours is the kingdom of God.
²¹Blessed *are you* who hunger now,
　For you shall be filled.
Blessed *are you* who weep now,
　For you shall laugh.
²²Blessed are you when men hate you,
　And when they exclude you,
　And revile *you,* and cast out your name as
　　evil,
　For the Son of Man's sake.
²³Rejoice in that day and leap for joy!
　For indeed your reward *is* great in heaven,
　For in like manner their fathers did to the
　　prophets.

Jesus Pronounces Woes

²⁴"But woe to you who are rich,
　For you have received your consolation.
²⁵Woe to you who are full,
　For you shall hunger.
Woe to you who laugh now,
　For you shall mourn and weep.
²⁶Woe to you^a when all^b men speak well of you,
　For so did their fathers to the false
　　prophets.

Love Your Enemies

²⁷"But I say to you who hear: Love your enemies, do good to those who hate you, ²⁸bless those who curse you, and pray for those who spitefully use you. ²⁹To him who strikes you on the *one* cheek, offer the other also. And from him who takes away your cloak, do not withhold *your* tunic either. ³⁰Give to everyone who asks of you. And from him who takes away your goods do not ask

····················

6:9 ^aM-Text reads *to kill.*   **6:10** ^aNU-Text and M-Text read *to him.* ^bNU-Text omits *as whole as the other.*   **6:26** ^aNU-Text and M-Text omit *to you.* ^bM-Text omits *all.*

6:45 The heart stood for the whole person in both Hebrew and Greek thought. The heart was the center of the body's essential functions: physical, intellectual, emotional, moral, and spiritual. The heart was seen as the dwelling place of the Spirit (2 Cor. 1:22; Eph. 3:17). Jesus' point here was that a person's actions flowed out of inner attitudes and choices, whether these were "good" or "evil."

6:48, 49 The preferred house foundation was bedrock or cut stone. The house "dug deep" may describe a house with a basement. Luke described a house hit by a torrent of water, an analogy of divine judgment. Like the house built "on the earth without a foundation," those who rejected Jesus would face destruction, while the house "founded on the rock" of Jesus' teaching would be saved from devastation.

THE WIDOW OF NAIN

This nameless woman surfaces uniquely in Luke's gospel in one of many biblical references to widows. Levitical law warned against taking advantage of widows (Ex. 22:22). Moses taught that God defends the cause of the fatherless and widows (Deut. 10:18). The early church cared for widows (Acts 6:1), and James defined pure religion as visiting (looking after) orphans and widows in their trouble (James 1:27).

As if to underscore this divine concern, Jesus interrupted a funeral procession just outside the Galilean town of Nain. There is a peculiar sadness in the description, "the only son of his mother" (Luke 7:12). No family accompanied the lone woman, who was in the process of burying her only child. With a crowd watching, Jesus approached the bier, ignoring circumstance and ceremony, and even contaminated himself by contact with a dead body.

The verb translated "had compassion" (v. 13) relates to the inner parts of the body, considered to be the seat of emotions. Jesus had an emotional response to the sight. However, He looked at the mother and spoke to her, "Do not weep." His words sound ludicrous under the circumstances. She had suffered a great loss, which had left her destitute. But the Lord of life demonstrated His power as well as His compassion.

"Young man, I say to you, arise" (v. 14). In full view of many witnesses, Jesus once again asserted His authority over sin and death. Fear and awe swept the crowd as the young man got up and began to talk. Jesus then presented him to his mother. Like Elijah, who had raised the widow's son and returned him to his mother (1 Kin. 17:23), the Lord confirmed His deep pity for a bereaved mother.

Although no response is recorded, the mother must certainly have joined her neighbors in praising God. She learned the validity of the Messiah's claim, "I am the resurrection and the life" (John 11:25). Her encounter with the Lord of life previews that when death comes, believers do not "sorrow as others who have no hope" (1 Thess. 4:13). Paul explained that the last enemy to be destroyed is death (1 Cor. 15:26); yet its terror is only temporary.

See also notes on Children (2 Sam. 21); Widowhood (Ps. 68; Jer. 29)

---

them back. ³¹And just as you want men to do to you, you also do to them likewise.

³²"But if you love those who love you, what credit is that to you? For even sinners love those who love them. ³³And if you do good to those who do good to you, what credit is that to you? For even sinners do the same. ³⁴And if you lend *to those* from whom you hope to receive back, what credit is that to you? For even sinners lend to sinners to receive as much back. ³⁵But love your enemies, do good, and lend, hoping for nothing in return; and your reward will be great, and you will be sons of the Most High. For He is kind to the unthankful and evil. ³⁶Therefore be merciful, just as your Father also is merciful.

Do Not Judge

³⁷"Judge not, and you shall not be judged. Condemn not, and you shall not be condemned. Forgive, and you will be forgiven. ³⁸Give, and it will be given to you: good measure, pressed down, shaken together, and running over will be put into your bosom. For with the same measure that you use, it will be measured back to you."

³⁹And He spoke a parable to them: "Can the blind lead the blind? Will they not both fall into the ditch? ⁴⁰A disciple is not above his teacher, but everyone who is perfectly trained will be like his teacher. ⁴¹And why do you look at the speck in your brother's eye, but do not perceive the plank in your own eye? ⁴²Or how can you say to your brother, 'Brother, let me remove the speck that *is* in your eye,' when you yourself do not see the plank that *is* in your own eye? Hypocrite! First remove the plank from your own eye, and then you will see clearly to remove the speck that is in your brother's eye.

A Tree Is Known by Its Fruit

⁴³"For a good tree does not bear bad fruit, nor does a bad tree bear good fruit. ⁴⁴For every tree is known by its own fruit. For *men* do not gather figs from thorns, nor do they gather grapes from a bramble bush. ⁴⁵A good man out of the good treasure of his heart brings forth good; and an evil man out of the evil treasure of his heart[a] brings forth evil. For out of the abundance of the heart his mouth speaks.

Build on the Rock

⁴⁶"But why do you call Me 'Lord, Lord,' and not do the things which I say? ⁴⁷Whoever comes to Me, and hears My sayings and does them, I will show you whom he is like: ⁴⁸He is like a man building a house, who dug deep and laid the foundation on the rock. And when the flood arose, the stream beat vehemently against that house, and could not

6:45 ᵃNU-Text omits *treasure of his heart.*

shake it, for it was founded on the rock.ª ⁴⁹But he who heard and did nothing is like a man who built a house on the earth without a foundation, against which the stream beat vehemently; and immediately it fell.ª And the ruin of that house was great."

Jesus Heals a Centurion's Servant

7 Now when He concluded all His sayings in the hearing of the people, He entered Capernaum. ²And a certain centurion's servant, who was dear to him, was sick and ready to die. ³So when he heard about Jesus, he sent elders of the Jews to Him, pleading with Him to come and heal his servant. ⁴And when they came to Jesus, they begged Him earnestly, saying that the one for whom He should do this was deserving, ⁵"for he loves our nation, and has built us a synagogue."

⁶Then Jesus went with them. And when He was already not far from the house, the centurion sent friends to Him, saying to Him, "Lord, do not trouble Yourself, for I am not worthy that You should enter under my roof. ⁷Therefore I did not even think myself worthy to come to You. But say the word, and my servant will be healed. ⁸For I also am a man placed under authority, having soldiers under me. And I say to one, 'Go,' and he goes; and to another, 'Come,' and he comes; and to my servant, 'Do this,' and he does it."

⁹When Jesus heard these things, He marveled at him, and turned around and said to the crowd that followed Him, "I say to you, I have not found such great faith, not even in Israel!" ¹⁰And those who were sent, returning to the house, found the servant well who had been sick.ª

Jesus Raises the Son of the Widow of Nain

¹¹Now it happened, the day after, that He went into a city called Nain; and many of His disciples went with Him, and a large crowd. ¹²And when He came near the gate of the city, behold, a dead man was being carried out, the only son of his mother; and she was a widow. And a large crowd from the city was with her. ¹³When the Lord saw her, He had compassion on her and said to her, "Do not weep." ¹⁴Then He came and touched the open coffin, and those who carried him stood still. And He said, "Young man, I say to you, arise." ¹⁵So he who was dead sat up and began to speak. And He presented him to his mother.

¹⁶Then fear came upon all, and they glorified God, saying, "A great prophet has risen up among us"; and, "God has visited His people." ¹⁷And this report about Him went throughout all Judea and all the surrounding region.

John the Baptist Sends Messengers to Jesus

¹⁸Then the disciples of John reported to him concerning all these things. ¹⁹And John, calling two of his disciples to him, sent them to Jesus,ª saying, "Are You the Coming One, or do we look for another?"

²⁰When the men had come to Him, they said, "John the Baptist has sent us to You, saying, 'Are You the Coming One, or do we look for another?' " ²¹And that very hour He cured many of infirmities, afflictions, and evil spirits; and to many blind He gave sight.

²²Jesus answered and said to them, "Go and tell John the things you have seen and heard: that the blind see, the lame walk, the lepers are cleansed, the deaf hear, the dead are raised, the poor have the gospel preached to them. ²³And blessed is he who is not offended because of Me."

²⁴When the messengers of John had departed, He began to speak to the multitudes concerning John: "What did you go out into the wilderness to see? A reed shaken by the wind? ²⁵But what did you go out to see? A man clothed in soft garments? Indeed those who are gorgeously appareled and live in luxury are in kings' courts. ²⁶But what did you go out to see? A prophet? Yes, I say to you, and more than a prophet. ²⁷This is he of whom it is written:

'Behold, I send My messenger before Your face,
Who will prepare Your way before You.'ª

²⁸For I say to you, among those born of women there is not a greater prophet than John the Baptist;ª but he who is least in the kingdom of God is greater than he."

²⁹And when all the people heard Him, even the tax collectors justified God, having been baptized with the baptism of John. ³⁰But the Pharisees and

---

6:48 ªNU-Text reads for it was well built. 6:49 ªNU-Text reads collapsed. 7:10 ªNU-Text omits who had been sick. 7:19 ªNU-Text reads the Lord. 7:27 ªMalachi 3:1 7:28 ªNU-Text reads there is none greater than John.

7:2 Centurions were career soldiers who kept the Roman military strong. They were usually put in charge of 100 soldiers. This centurion probably served with the forces of Herod Antipas. He had wealth, as well as character and integrity, and he had heard of Jesus. He was a compassionate man, expressing concern for his gravely ill servant. Jesus was impressed with his great faith. The NT highlights several centurions positively, including the centurion who witnessed Jesus' death and identified Him as God's Son (Mark 15:39); Cornelius, who was converted and thus opened the way for the church's outreach to Gentiles (Acts 10); and Julius, who treated Paul with kindness (Acts 27:3).

7:14 Jesus was moved with compassion for the widow whose son was awaiting burial (see The Widow of Nain). Coffins were not generally used in biblical times. The body was placed on an open bier, or bed, before burial. Often made of wooden boards, these biers were portable. Even though touching a dead body made one ceremonially unclean, Jesus disregarded this convention (Num. 19:11, 16).

SINNER AT SIMON'S HOUSE

Luke simply refers to this nameless woman as a "sinner," perhaps a prostitute who walked the streets of Nain in southwest Galilee. The self-righteous Pharisees despised this public woman. No proper woman would enter such a gathering in the house of a prominent Pharisee uninvited.

Her actions toward Jesus seemed even more crass. Standing beside Him, she knelt at His feet and began to cry. Her warm tears dropped one by one onto His feet. Then she undid her hair, a public act considered disgraceful for a woman of her day. With her long tresses, she wiped Jesus' dusty feet, washing them, and kissing them. Around her neck dangled an alabaster flask of perfume, no doubt representing the substance of her personal resources. She removed the flask and poured the costly, fragranced oil on His freshly cleansed feet. This was an act of worship.

Simon the host denounced Jesus and questioned the "Prophet's" integrity for allowing a woman of such notorious reputation to touch and disgrace Him. While the Pharisees looked only at the woman's outward actions, Jesus saw her heart, lonely and sad, penitent—a loving heart that honored Him as Lord and sought forgiveness for a sinful, wasted life.

To the men's astonishment, Jesus defended the woman. He reminded them that this woman had performed the common courtesies due any invited guest. Simon had neglected to wash Jesus' feet, to offer a welcoming kiss, or to anoint His head with oil, appropriate gestures of hospitality. The woman, humbly and graciously, offered to Him all these welcoming acts. The master Teacher used this occasion to teach love, forgiveness, and faith.

The nameless woman who came in disgrace departed Simon's house in peace. Jesus publicly forgave her sins, and she went her way with a freshly cleansed heart and a new life in Christ.

See also Luke 24:47, note; chart on Your Path to Freedom; notes on Forgiveness (Ps. 51; Luke 17).

---

lawyers rejected the will of God for themselves, not having been baptized by him.

31And the Lord said,a "To what then shall I liken the men of this generation, and what are they like? 32They are like children sitting in the marketplace and calling to one another, saying:

'We played the flute for you,
    And you did not dance;
We mourned to you,
    And you did not weep.'

33For John the Baptist came neither eating bread nor drinking wine, and you say, 'He has a demon.' 34The Son of Man has come eating and drinking, and you say, 'Look, a glutton and a winebibber, a friend of tax collectors and sinners!' 35But wisdom is justified by all her children."

A Sinful Woman Forgiven

36Then one of the Pharisees asked Him to eat with him. And He went to the Pharisee's house, and sat down to eat. 37And behold, a woman in the city who was a sinner, when she knew that Jesus sat at

the table in the Pharisee's house, brought an alabaster flask of fragrant oil, 38and stood at His feet behind Him weeping; and she began to wash His feet with her tears, and wiped them with the hair of her head; and she kissed His feet and anointed them with the fragrant oil. 39Now when the Pharisee who had invited Him saw this, he spoke to himself, saying, "This Man, if He were a prophet, would know who and what manner of woman this is who is touching Him, for she is a sinner."

40And Jesus answered and said to him, "Simon, I have something to say to you."

So he said, "Teacher, say it."

41"There was a certain creditor who had two debtors. One owed five hundred denarii, and the other fifty. 42And when they had nothing with which to repay, he freely forgave them both. Tell Me, therefore, which of them will love him more?"

43Simon answered and said, "I suppose the one whom he forgave more."

And He said to him, "You have rightly judged." 44Then He turned to the woman and said to Si-

••••••••••••••••••

7:31aNU-Text and M-Text omit And the Lord said.

7:37 The flask Luke described served as a container for perfume. Such flasks were made of carved stone, though they were not always made of alabaster as their name would indicate. Suspended from a cord, this flask without handles was worn around the neck of a Jewish woman. It was shaped with a long neck that was broken off when the expensive, perfumed oil was needed (see Ex. 30, Cosmetics). Mark and John

record the cost of the oil used here as 300 denarii (Mark 14:5; John 12:5; see chart, Money and Measurements in the Bible).

7:38 The sinful woman stood behind Jesus by His feet. Since people did not sit at the table when eating but instead reclined beside it, the woman could reach Jesus' feet easily (see Sinner at Simon's House).

mon, "Do you see this woman? I entered your house; you gave Me no water for My feet, but she has washed My feet with her tears and wiped *them* with the hair of her head. [45]You gave Me no kiss, but this woman has not ceased to kiss My feet since the time I came in. [46]You did not anoint My head with oil, but this woman has anointed My feet with fragrant oil. [47]Therefore I say to you, her sins, *which are* many, are forgiven, for she loved much. But to whom little is forgiven, *the same* loves little."

[48]Then He said to her, "Your sins are forgiven."

[49]And those who sat at the table with Him began to say to themselves, "Who is this who even forgives sins?"

[50]Then He said to the woman, "Your faith has saved you. Go in peace."

Many Women Minister to Jesus

8 Now it came to pass, afterward, that He went through every city and village, preaching and bringing the glad tidings of the kingdom of God. And the twelve *were* with Him, [2]and certain women who had been healed of evil spirits and infirmities—Mary called Magdalene, out of whom had come seven demons, [3]and Joanna the wife of Chuza, Herod's steward, and Susanna, and many others who provided for Him[a] from their substance.

The Parable of the Sower

[4]And when a great multitude had gathered, and they had come to Him from every city, He spoke by a parable: [5]"A sower went out to sow his seed. And as he sowed, some fell by the wayside; and it was trampled down, and the birds of the air devoured it. [6]Some fell on rock; and as soon as it sprang up, it withered away because it lacked moisture. [7]And some fell among thorns, and the thorns sprang up with it and choked it. [8]But others fell on good ground, sprang up, and yielded a crop a hundredfold." When He had said these things He cried, "He who has ears to hear, let him hear!"

The Purpose of Parables

[9]Then His disciples asked Him, saying, "What does this parable mean?"

[10]And He said, "To you it has been given to know the mysteries of the kingdom of God, but to the rest *it is given* in parables, that

'Seeing they may not see,
And hearing they may not understand.'[a]

The Parable of the Sower Explained

[11]"Now the parable is this: The seed is the word of God. [12]Those by the wayside are the ones who hear; then the devil comes and takes away the word out of their hearts, lest they should believe and be saved. [13]But the ones on the rock *are those* who, when they hear, receive the word with joy; and these have no root, who believe for a while and in time of temptation fall away. [14]Now the ones *that* fell among thorns are those who, when they have heard, go out and are choked with cares, riches, and pleasures of life, and bring no fruit to maturity. [15]But the ones *that* fell on the good ground are those who, having heard the word with a noble and good heart, keep *it* and bear fruit with patience.

The Parable of the Revealed Light

[16]"No one, when he has lit a lamp, covers it with a vessel or puts *it* under a bed, but sets *it* on a lampstand, that those who enter may see the light. [17]For nothing is secret that will not be revealed, nor *anything* hidden that will not be known and come to light. [18]Therefore take heed how you hear. For whoever has, to him *more* will be given; and whoever does not have, even what he seems to have will be taken from him."

Jesus' Mother and Brothers Come to Him

[19]Then His mother and brothers came to Him, and could not approach Him because of the crowd. [20]And it was told Him *by some*, who said, "Your mother and Your brothers are standing outside, desiring to see You."

[21]But He answered and said to them, "My mother and My brothers are these who hear the word of God and do it."

•••••••••••••••••••

8:3 [a]NU-Text and M-Text read *them*. **8:10** [a]Isaiah 6:9

8:5 See Matthew 13:3, note.

8:9, 10 To bring new understanding to God's truth, Jesus told stories or parables. Jesus' parables proclaimed the gospel, and He often used parables when put into situations of conflict. The central theme in Jesus' parables was the kingdom of God. Parables involved the use of metaphors, which could be understood only by those who would search for the meaning therein, thus separating the genuine seeker from the indifferent listener (see chart, Women and the Parables of Jesus).

8:14, 15 Fruit is used in various ways throughout the Bible. For instance, one's descendant is the "fruit of the womb" (Gen. 30:2). Fruit can refer to righteousness (Phil. 1:11), light (Eph.

5:9), moral purity, repentance (Matt. 3:8), or Christian converts. Here Jesus used "fruit" to describe the rewards given for living in obedience to God's Word.

8:16 Light overcomes darkness: Thus, a lamp should not be hidden but should be allowed to provide illumination. Archaeologists have unearthed lamps used in homes dating from before Abraham to after Christ. OT period lamps were open bowls of pottery, with wicks of flax, and using olive oil for fuel (see article, What They Left Behind). More ornate lamps were produced later. When used as a metaphor, light represented life. Lack of light, or darkness, portrayed death. Jesus, the Light of the World, overcame darkness, or death (John 1:4, 5).

JOANNA · *Wealthy but Humble*

Joanna, a name that means "Yahweh's Gift," was the wife of Chuza, the steward of Herod Antipas. Holding such an important position, Chuza would have earned a good salary. No doubt, he provided Joanna with a nice home and every available luxury of that day. Yet, when Joanna met Jesus, He healed her of an unrecorded illness or evil spirit that controlled her life (Luke 8:2), and Joanna made a self-sacrificing decision. She chose to risk her comfortable lifestyle in order to become a follower of Jesus Christ.

Life was difficult for the women who served Jesus and His disciples. Yet Joanna joined these women in giving unselfishly not only of her time and energies but also of whatever money she had to support the Lord's work.

Joanna went to Jesus' tomb on the early Sunday morning following the Crucifixion. She is listed as one of the women who reported the Resurrection of Jesus to the eleven disciples.

Joanna could have lived out her years focusing on the luxuries and privileges provided by her wealthy and influential husband. Instead she was willing to give up her mansion on earth for the mansion in Heaven she knew would be hers when she committed herself to Christ. Joanna was privileged to be among the last at the Cross as well as among the first to witness the empty tomb and proclaim the Lord's Resurrection. She stands in history as a woman with position and possessions whose devotion to her Lord is exemplified in humble service.

See also Luke 24:10; notes on Commitment (Matt. 16); Servanthood (Mark 10)

Wind and Wave Obey Jesus

²²Now it happened, on a certain day, that He got into a boat with His disciples. And He said to them, "Let us cross over to the other side of the lake." And they launched out. ²³But as they sailed He fell asleep. And a windstorm came down on the lake, and they were filling *with water,* and were in jeopardy. ²⁴And they came to Him and awoke Him, saying, "Master, Master, we are perishing!"

Then He arose and rebuked the wind and the raging of the water. And they ceased, and there was a calm. ²⁵But He said to them, "Where is your faith?"

And they were afraid, and marveled, saying to one another, "Who can this be? For He commands even the winds and water, and they obey Him!"

A Demon-Possessed Man Healed

²⁶Then they sailed to the country of the Gadarenes,[a] which is opposite Galilee. ²⁷And when He stepped out on the land, there met Him a certain man from the city who had demons for a long time. And he wore no clothes,[a] nor did he live in a house but in the tombs. ²⁸When he saw Jesus, he cried out, fell down before Him, and with a loud voice said, "What have I to do with You, Jesus, Son of the Most High God? I beg You, do not torment me!" ²⁹For He had commanded the unclean spirit to come out of the man. For it had often seized him, and he was kept under guard, bound with chains and shackles; and he broke the bonds and was driven by the demon into the wilderness.

³⁰Jesus asked him, saying, "What is your name?"

And he said, "Legion," because many demons had entered him. ³¹And they begged Him that He would not command them to go out into the abyss.

³²Now a herd of many swine was feeding there on the mountain. So they begged Him that He would permit them to enter them. And He permitted them. ³³Then the demons went out of the man and entered the swine, and the herd ran violently down the steep place into the lake and drowned.

³⁴When those who fed *them* saw what had happened, they fled and told *it* in the city and in the country. ³⁵Then they went out to see what had happened, and came to Jesus, and found the man from whom the demons had departed, sitting at the feet of Jesus, clothed and in his right mind. And they were afraid. ³⁶They also who had seen *it* told them by what means he who had been demon-possessed was healed. ³⁷Then the whole multitude of the surrounding region of the Gadarenes[a] asked Him to depart from them, for they were seized with great fear. And He got into the boat and returned.

³⁸Now the man from whom the demons had departed begged Him that he might be with Him. But Jesus sent him away, saying, ³⁹"Return to your own house, and tell what great things God has done for you." And he went his way and proclaimed throughout the whole city what great things Jesus had done for him.

8:26 [a]NU-Text reads *Gerasenes.* 8:27 [a]NU-Text reads *who had demons and for a long time wore no clothes.* 8:37 [a]NU-Text reads *Gerasenes.*

8:30–32 The abyss is a place of confinement for spirits, the place where Satan will be bound during the millennium (Rev. 20:1–3). The demons, who called themselves "Legion," recognized Jesus. They knew that Jesus would command them to come out of the man. They begged Jesus not to send them into the abyss, which referred to the "bottomless pit," the "dark abode of the dead."

SUSANNA   *A Faithful Servant*

Susanna's name means "lily," and she was one of the many women who followed Jesus in His city-to-city ministry. Like Mary Magdalene and Joanna, Susanna had been healed by Jesus of either a debilitating sickness or evil spirits. She then became a leader among the women who served Jesus and His disciples and supported them financially.

Jesus loved and respected the band of devoted women. He valued them and obviously appreciated their generous and selfless giving. His actions toward women repeatedly expressed appreciation for their God-given abilities. He taught the women just as He taught the men. Luke records the words of the two men who addressed the women at the empty tomb with a reminder of the words Jesus had taught them, while in Galilee, about His Crucifixion and Resurrection (Luke 24:8).

Jesus wanted women to be involved in God's work, and in His brief ministry, He laid the concrete foundation on which women have faithfully built for the past two millennia.

See also Mark 15:40, 41; notes on Feminine Leadership (1 Sam. 25); Servanthood (Mark 10)

A Girl Restored to Life and a Woman Healed

⁴⁰So it was, when Jesus returned, that the multitude welcomed Him, for they were all waiting for Him. ⁴¹And behold, there came a man named Jairus, and he was a ruler of the synagogue. And he fell down at Jesus' feet and begged Him to come to his house, ⁴²for he had an only daughter about twelve years of age, and she was dying.

But as He went, the multitudes thronged Him. ⁴³Now a woman, having a flow of blood for twelve years, who had spent all her livelihood on physicians and could not be healed by any, ⁴⁴came from behind and touched the border of His garment. And immediately her flow of blood stopped.

⁴⁵And Jesus said, "Who touched Me?"

When all denied it, Peter and those with him[a] said, "Master, the multitudes throng and press You, and You say, 'Who touched Me?' "[b]

⁴⁶But Jesus said, "Somebody touched Me, for I perceived power going out from Me." ⁴⁷Now when the woman saw that she was not hidden, she came trembling; and falling down before Him, she declared to Him in the presence of all the people the reason she had touched Him and how she was healed immediately.

⁴⁸And He said to her, "Daughter, be of good cheer;[a] your faith has made you well. Go in peace."

⁴⁹While He was still speaking, someone came from the ruler of the synagogue's *house,* saying to him, "Your daughter is dead. Do not trouble the Teacher."[a]

⁵⁰But when Jesus heard *it,* He answered him, saying, "Do not be afraid; only believe, and she will be made well." ⁵¹When He came into the house, He permitted no one to go in[a] except Peter, James, and John,[b] and the father and mother of the girl. ⁵²Now all wept and mourned for her; but He said, "Do not weep; she is not dead, but sleeping." ⁵³And they ridiculed Him, knowing that she was dead.

⁵⁴But He put them all outside,[a] took her by the hand and called, saying, "Little girl, arise." ⁵⁵Then her spirit returned, and she arose immediately. And He commanded that she be given *something* to eat. ⁵⁶And her parents were astonished, but He charged them to tell no one what had happened.

Sending Out the Twelve

9 Then He called His twelve disciples together and gave them power and authority over all demons, and to cure diseases. ²He sent them to preach the kingdom of God and to heal the sick. ³And He said to them, "Take nothing for the journey, neither staffs nor bag nor bread nor money; and do not have two tunics apiece.

⁴"Whatever house you enter, stay there, and from there depart. ⁵And whoever will not receive you, when you go out of that city, shake off the very dust from your feet as a testimony against them."

⁶So they departed and went through the towns, preaching the gospel and healing everywhere.

Herod Seeks to See Jesus

⁷Now Herod the tetrarch heard of all that was done by Him; and he was perplexed, because it was said by some that John had risen from the

8:45 [a]NU-Text omits *and those with him.* [b]NU-Text omits *and You say, 'Who touched Me?'* 8:48 [a]NU-Text omits *be of good cheer.* 8:49 [a]NU-Text adds *anymore.* 8:51 [a]NU-Text adds *with Him.* [b]NU-Text and M-Text read *Peter, John, and James.* 8:54 [a]NU-Text omits *put them all outside.*

9:5 Jews routinely removed the dust from their shoes whenever they visited Gentile lands since they considered the dust as defiled. Jesus instructed the apostles, who preached the kingdom of God and healed the sick, to "shake off the very dust" from their feet as a testimony against those who rejected them. Those who rejected the gospel also rejected Jesus and would face God's judgment.

THE HOMELESS *A LOWLY ESTATE*

The homeless, considered the most destitute of all the poor, are positioned to bring great honor to God. Their lowly state makes it possible for God to raise them up with great visibility before an unbelieving world. God's own son was "homeless" (Luke 2:7; 9:58) during periods of His life. Yet at His death, which appeared to be His lowest point, He was highly exalted above all men (Phil. 2:5–10).

Jesus used extreme cases to reveal to the world the extent of the Father's grace, mercy, power, and lovingkindness. His giving sight to the man born blind (John 9:6–7); His raising Lazarus, dead four days, from the grave (John 11:38–44); His forgiveness of well-known prostitutes and adulteresses (John 8:1–12); and His calling Saul, the murderer and persecutor of the church, to be an apostle all serve as examples of God's promise to lift up the down-trodden and to bring satisfaction to those in need (Ex. 3:7; Prov. 3:34).

In a spiritual sense, all are "homeless" on this earth. The believer's true home remains yet to be seen; it is not one made with human hands (Ps. 39:12; Heb. 11:13–16). You are always to be sensitive and responsive to those who are weaker (Ps. 82:3, 4; Prov. 31:8, 9; Rom. 15:1).

See also chart on Jesus' Pilgrimage; notes on Depression (1 Sam. 16); Evangelism (John 6; Col. 4; 1 Pet. 3); Poverty (Luke 14); Suffering (Ps. 33; 113; Is. 43; 1 Pet. 5)

dead, [8]and by some that Elijah had appeared, and by others that one of the old prophets had risen again. [9]Herod said, "John I have beheaded, but who is this of whom I hear such things?" So he sought to see Him.

Feeding the Five Thousand

[10]And the apostles, when they had returned, told Him all that they had done. Then He took them and went aside privately into a deserted place belonging to the city called Bethsaida. [11]But when the multitudes knew *it,* they followed Him; and He received them and spoke to them about the kingdom of God, and healed those who had need of healing. [12]When the day began to wear away, the twelve came and said to Him, "Send the multitude away, that they may go into the surrounding towns and country, and lodge and get provisions; for we are in a deserted place here."

[13]But He said to them, "You give them something to eat."

And they said, "We have no more than five loaves and two fish, unless we go and buy food for all these people." [14]For there were about five thousand men.

Then He said to His disciples, "Make them sit down in groups of fifty." [15]And they did so, and made them all sit down.

[16]Then He took the five loaves and the two fish, and looking up to heaven, He blessed and broke *them,* and gave *them* to the disciples to set before the multitude. [17]So they all ate and were filled, and twelve baskets of the leftover fragments were taken up by them.

Peter Confesses Jesus as the Christ

[18]And it happened, as He was alone praying, *that* His disciples joined Him, and He asked them, saying, "Who do the crowds say that I am?"

[19]So they answered and said, "John the Baptist, but some *say* Elijah; and others *say* that one of the old prophets has risen again."

[20]He said to them, "But who do you say that I am?"

Peter answered and said, "The Christ of God."

Jesus Predicts His Death and Resurrection

[21]And He strictly warned and commanded them to tell this to no one, [22]saying, "The Son of Man must suffer many things, and be rejected by the elders and chief priests and scribes, and be killed, and be raised the third day."

Take Up the Cross and Follow Him

[23]Then He said to *them* all, "If anyone desires to come after Me, let him deny himself, and take up his cross daily,[a] and follow Me. [24]For whoever desires to save his life will lose it, but whoever loses his life for My sake will save it. [25]For what profit is it to a man if he gains the whole world, and is himself destroyed or lost? [26]For whoever is ashamed of Me and My words, of him the Son of Man will be ashamed when He comes in His *own* glory, and *in His* Father's, and of the holy angels. [27]But I tell you truly, there are some standing here who shall not taste death till they see the kingdom of God."

•••••••••••••••••

9:23 [a]M-Text omits *daily.*

9:16, 17 The feeding of the 5,000 is a miracle recorded in all four gospels (Matt. 14:21, note).

9:27 Some believed that Jesus was referring to His return. However, since these first disciples died before He returned,

Jesus Transfigured on the Mount

28Now it came to pass, about eight days after these sayings, that He took Peter, John, and James and went up on the mountain to pray. 29As He prayed, the appearance of His face was altered, and His robe *became* white *and* glistening. 30And behold, two men talked with Him, who were Moses and Elijah, 31who appeared in glory and spoke of His decease which He was about to accomplish at Jerusalem. 32But Peter and those with him were heavy with sleep; and when they were fully awake, they saw His glory and the two men who stood with Him. 33Then it happened, as they were parting from Him, *that* Peter said to Jesus, "Master, it is good for us to be here; and let us make three tabernacles: one for You, one for Moses, and one for Elijah"—not knowing what he said.

34While he was saying this, a cloud came and overshadowed them; and they were fearful as they entered the cloud. 35And a voice came out of the cloud, saying, "This is My beloved Son.[a] Hear Him!" 36When the voice had ceased, Jesus was found alone. But they kept quiet, and told no one in those days any of the things they had seen.

A Boy Is Healed

37Now it happened on the next day, when they had come down from the mountain, that a great multitude met Him. 38Suddenly a man from the multitude cried out, saying, "Teacher, I implore You, look on my son, for he is my only child. 39And behold, a spirit seizes him, and he suddenly cries out; it convulses him so that he foams *at the mouth;* and it departs from him with great difficulty, bruising him. 40So I implored Your disciples to cast it out, but they could not."

41Then Jesus answered and said, "O faithless and perverse generation, how long shall I be with you and bear with you? Bring your son here." 42And as he was still coming, the demon threw him down and convulsed *him.* Then Jesus rebuked the unclean spirit, healed the child, and gave him back to his father.

Jesus Again Predicts His Death

43And they were all amazed at the majesty of God.

But while everyone marveled at all the things which Jesus did, He said to His disciples, 44"Let these words sink down into your ears, for the Son of Man is about to be betrayed into the hands of men." 45But they did not understand this saying, and it was hidden from them so that they did not perceive it; and they were afraid to ask Him about this saying.

Who Is the Greatest?

46Then a dispute arose among them as to which of them would be greatest. 47And Jesus, perceiving the thought of their heart, took a little child and set him by Him, 48and said to them, "Whoever receives this little child in My name receives Me; and whoever receives Me receives Him who sent Me. For he who is least among you all will be great."

Jesus Forbids Sectarianism

49Now John answered and said, "Master, we saw someone casting out demons in Your name, and we forbade him because he does not follow with us."

50But Jesus said to him, "Do not forbid *him,* for he who is not against us[a] is on our[b] side."

A Samaritan Village Rejects the Savior

51Now it came to pass, when the time had come for Him to be received up, that He steadfastly set His face to go to Jerusalem, 52and sent messengers before His face. And as they went, they entered a village of the Samaritans, to prepare for Him. 53But they did not receive Him, because His face was *set* for the journey to Jerusalem. 54And when His disciples James and John saw *this,* they said, "Lord, do You want us to command fire to come down from heaven and consume them, just as Elijah did?"[a]

55But He turned and rebuked them,[a] and said, "You do not know what manner of spirit you are of. 56For the Son of Man did not come to destroy men's lives but to save *them.*"[a] And they went to another village.

The Cost of Discipleship

57Now it happened as they journeyed on the road, *that* someone said to Him, "Lord, I will follow You wherever You go."

9:35 [a]NU-Text reads *This is My Son, the Chosen One.* 9:50 [a]NU-Text reads *you.* [b]NU-Text reads *your.* 9:54 [a]NU-Text omits *just as Elijah did.* 9:55 [a]NU-Text omits the rest of this verse. 9:56 [a]NU-Text omits the first sentence of this verse.

---

other interpretations have been offered. Suggestions include the destruction of Jerusalem, the beginning of missionary outreach at Pentecost, or the coming of the Holy Spirit at Pentecost. A probable explanation could be that He was referring to the Transfiguration (vv. 28–36).

9:30 Moses was the leader who delivered the Israelites from Egyptian slavery and delivered the Law. Elijah was a 9th century B.C. prophet from Tishbe of Gilead, remembered for his victory in the encounter with 450 prophets of Baal (see 1 Kin. 18:19–40). Elijah represented the prophets; he was expected to return before the end of the age (Mal. 4:5, 6).

EDUCATION   *STUDYING AT THE FEET OF JESUS*

Mary of Bethany is noted among the first women of the Christian era as one who pursued a "theological education" at the feet of Jesus. Luke thoughtfully records that Mary sat at Jesus' feet and heard His word in a time when it was highly untraditional for a woman to be taught, especially by an esteemed rabbi. When Mary was criticized, Jesus Himself commended her for choosing the better way (Luke 10:38–42).

A woman need not enroll in a Bible college or seminary to sit at Jesus' feet and hear His word; but a ministry could be enhanced and extended by formal theological education, which provides a systematic study of God and the way He relates to us.

When the Lord calls a woman to a Christian vocation, she should devote herself to the same high standards of training as she would to prepare for any other vocation. We dare not offer less to the Lord's work than we would to a "secular" profession. When intellectual integrity and academic excellence are pursued with a heart fully devoted to the Lord, God is glorified, and that is the ultimate goal of theological education.

See also notes on Education (Deut. 6; Prov. 12; 2 Tim. 3); Spiritual Gifts (Rom. 12); Women's Ministries (John 4; Acts 2; 1 Cor. 11; Eph. 2; 1 Tim. 3; Titus 2); portrait of Mary of Bethany (John 11)

[58]And Jesus said to him, "Foxes have holes and birds of the air *have* nests, but the Son of Man has nowhere to lay *His* head."

[59]Then He said to another, "Follow Me."

But he said, "Lord, let me first go and bury my father."

[60]Jesus said to him, "Let the dead bury their own dead, but you go and preach the kingdom of God."

[61]And another also said, "Lord, I will follow You, but let me first go *and* bid them farewell who are at my house."

[62]But Jesus said to him, "No one, having put his hand to the plow, and looking back, is fit for the kingdom of God."

The Seventy Sent Out

10 After these things the Lord appointed seventy others also,[a] and sent them two by two before His face into every city and place where He Himself was about to go. [2]Then He said to them, "The harvest truly *is* great, but the laborers *are* few; therefore pray the Lord of the harvest to send out laborers into His harvest. [3]Go your way; behold, I send you out as lambs among wolves. [4]Carry neither money bag, knapsack, nor sandals;

and greet no one along the road. [5]But whatever house you enter, first say, 'Peace to this house.' [6]And if a son of peace is there, your peace will rest on it; if not, it will return to you. [7]And remain in the same house, eating and drinking such things as they give, for the laborer is worthy of his wages. Do not go from house to house. [8]Whatever city you enter, and they receive you, eat such things as are set before you. [9]And heal the sick there, and say to them, 'The kingdom of God has come near to you.' [10]But whatever city you enter, and they do not receive you, go out into its streets and say, [11]'The very dust of your city which clings to us[a] we wipe off against you. Nevertheless know this, that the kingdom of God has come near you.' [12]But[a] I say to you that it will be more tolerable in that Day for Sodom than for that city.

Woe to the Impenitent Cities

[13]"Woe to you, Chorazin! Woe to you, Bethsaida! For if the mighty works which were done in you had been done in Tyre and Sidon, they would have repented long ago, sitting in sackcloth and ashes.

·····················
10:1 [a]NU-Text reads *seventy-two others.*   **10:11** [a]NU-Text reads *our feet.*   **10:12** [a]NU-Text and M-Text omit *But.*

10:1 After Jesus appointed the 70, He sent them out in pairs on this dangerous mission (v. 3). The two together would provide support for one another; two witnesses were needed for the mission described (vv. 11–15; see Num. 35:30).

10:5, 6 Peace referred to salvation and blessing. It held more meaning than just a friendly greeting. The "house" represented the people living there, not the dwelling structure. The "son of peace" referred to a believer. If faith was not present in the household, the blessing would be ineffective.

10:12 God judged Sodom and Gomorrah and destroyed the two cities with "brimstone and fire" (Gen. 19:24). Although their exact location is not known, Sodom and Gomorrah were two cities in Palestine during Abraham's time. Sodom was

known for its wickedness (Gen. 18:20). The word "sodomite," referring to a citizen of Sodom, came to denote the sin of homosexuality. Jesus' point was that God's judgment on these cities would be mild compared with what would befall those who rejected the gospel message.

10:13 Sackcloth, an article of clothing made from rough cloth (usually goat or camel hair), was worn by the ancients to show mourning, anguish, or repentance. Ashes were either placed on the head or piled into a heap. The mourner would sit upon the ashes and usually fast as well.

10:13–15 Capernaum was located on the western edge of the Sea of Galilee, and Chorazin and Bethsaida were to the north of the lake where Jesus had ministered and performed mira-

*Ultimate hatred and ultimate love met on those two crosspieces of wood.
Suffering and love were brought into harmony.*

Elisabeth Elliot

---

[14]But it will be more tolerable for Tyre and Sidon at the judgment than for you. [15]And you, Capernaum, who are exalted to heaven, will be brought down to Hades.[a] [16]He who hears you hears Me, he who rejects you rejects Me, and he who rejects Me rejects Him who sent Me."

The Seventy Return with Joy

[17]Then the seventy[a] returned with joy, saying, "Lord, even the demons are subject to us in Your name."

[18]And He said to them, "I saw Satan fall like lightning from heaven. [19]Behold, I give you the authority to trample on serpents and scorpions, and over all the power of the enemy, and nothing shall by any means hurt you. [20]Nevertheless do not rejoice in this, that the spirits are subject to you, but rather[a] rejoice because your names are written in heaven."

Jesus Rejoices in the Spirit

[21]In that hour Jesus rejoiced in the Spirit and said, "I thank You, Father, Lord of heaven and earth, that You have hidden these things from *the* wise and prudent and revealed them to babes. Even so, Father, for so it seemed good in Your sight. [22]All[a] things have been delivered to Me by My Father, and no one knows who the Son is except the Father, and who the Father is except the Son, and *the one* to whom the Son wills to reveal Him."

[23]Then He turned to *His* disciples and said privately, "Blessed *are* the eyes which see the things you see; [24]for I tell you that many prophets and kings have desired to see what you see, and have not seen *it*, and to hear what you hear, and have not heard *it*."

The Parable of the Good Samaritan

[25]And behold, a certain lawyer stood up and tested Him, saying, "Teacher, what shall I do to inherit eternal life?"

[26]He said to him, "What is written in the law? What is your reading *of it?*"

[27]So he answered and said, " 'You shall love the Lord your God with all your heart, with all your soul, with all your strength, and with all your mind,'[a] and 'your neighbor as yourself.' "[b]

[28]And He said to him, "You have answered rightly; do this and you will live."

[29]But he, wanting to justify himself, said to Jesus, "And who is my neighbor?"

[30]Then Jesus answered and said: "A certain *man* went down from Jerusalem to Jericho, and fell among thieves, who stripped him of his clothing, wounded *him*, and departed, leaving *him* half dead. [31]Now by chance a certain priest came down that road. And when he saw him, he passed by on the other side. [32]Likewise a Levite, when he arrived at the place, came and looked, and passed by on the other side. [33]But a certain Samaritan, as he journeyed, came where he was. And when he saw him, he had compassion. [34]So he went to *him* and bandaged his wounds, pouring on oil and wine; and he set him on his own animal, brought him to an inn, and took care of him. [35]On the next day, when he departed,[a] he took out two denarii, gave *them* to the innkeeper, and said to him, 'Take care of him; and whatever more you spend, when I come again, I will repay you.' [36]So which of these three do you think was neighbor to him who fell among the thieves?"

[37]And he said, "He who showed mercy on him."
Then Jesus said to him, "Go and do likewise."

Mary and Martha Worship and Serve

[38]Now it happened as they went that He entered a certain village; and a certain woman named Martha welcomed Him into her house. [39]And she had a sister called Mary, who also sat at Jesus'[a] feet and heard His word. [40]But Martha was distracted with much serving, and she approached

---

10:15 [a]NU-Text reads *will you be exalted to heaven? You will be thrust down to Hades!* 10:17 [a]NU-Text reads *seventy-two.* 10:20 [a]NU-Text and M-Text omit *rather.* 10:22 [a]M-Text reads *And turning to the disciples He said, "All . . .* 10:27 [a]Deuteronomy 6:5 [b]Leviticus 19:18 10:35 [a]NU-Text omits *when he departed.* 10:39 [a]NU-Text reads *the Lord's.*

---

cles. The people of these cities had been given ample opportunity to believe in Jesus as the Messiah. Their rejection of Him would lead to even greater judgment than that which God had poured on the sinful, pagan cities of Tyre and Sidon.

10:30–35 Although Jericho was only about 17 miles from Jerusalem, the road was steep and treacherous and involved a descent of about 3,000 feet. The priest would not relinquish his ceremonial cleanness to touch a man who might be dead. The Levite did not stop and help the injured man, probably for the same reason. Since Samaritans and Jews were bitter enemies, Jesus' listeners would have been astonished that Jesus chose to make a Samaritan the hero of the story, and this would serve to underscore His point: A true neighbor compassionately serves others in need.

Him and said, "Lord, do You not care that my sister has left me to serve alone? Therefore tell her to help me."

⁴¹And Jesusᵃ answered and said to her, "Martha, Martha, you are worried and troubled about many things. ⁴²But one thing is needed, and Mary has chosen that good part, which will not be taken away from her."

The Model Prayer

11 Now it came to pass, as He was praying in a certain place, when He ceased, *that* one of His disciples said to Him, "Lord, teach us to pray, as John also taught his disciples."

²So He said to them, "When you pray, say:

Our Father in heaven,ᵃ
Hallowed be Your name.
Your kingdom come.ᵇ
Your will be done
On earth as *it is* in heaven.
³Give us day by day our daily bread.
⁴And forgive us our sins,
For we also forgive everyone who is indebted
   to us.
And do not lead us into temptation,
But deliver us from the evil one."ᵃ

A Friend Comes at Midnight

⁵And He said to them, "Which of you shall have a friend, and go to him at midnight and say to him, 'Friend, lend me three loaves; ⁶for a friend of mine has come to me on his journey, and I have nothing to set before him'; ⁷and he will answer from within and say, 'Do not trouble me; the door is now shut, and my children are with me in bed; I cannot rise and give to you'? ⁸I say to you, though he will not rise and give to him because he is his friend, yet because of his persistence he will rise and give him as many as he needs.

Keep Asking, Seeking, Knocking

⁹"So I say to you, ask, and it will be given to you; seek, and you will find; knock, and it will be opened to you. ¹⁰For everyone who asks receives, and he who seeks finds, and to him who knocks it will be opened. ¹¹If a son asks for breadᵃ from any father among you, will he give him a stone? Or if *he asks* for a fish, will he give him a serpent instead of a fish? ¹²Or if he asks for an egg, will he offer him a scorpion? ¹³If you then, being evil, know how to give good gifts to your children, how

much more will *your* heavenly Father give the Holy Spirit to those who ask Him!"

A House Divided Cannot Stand

¹⁴And He was casting out a demon, and it was mute. So it was, when the demon had gone out, that the mute spoke; and the multitudes marveled. ¹⁵But some of them said, "He casts out demons by Beelzebub,ᵃ the ruler of the demons."

¹⁶Others, testing *Him,* sought from Him a sign from heaven. ¹⁷But He, knowing their thoughts, said to them: "Every kingdom divided against itself is brought to desolation, and a house *divided* against a house falls. ¹⁸If Satan also is divided against himself, how will his kingdom stand? Because you say I cast out demons by Beelzebub. ¹⁹And if I cast out demons by Beelzebub, by whom do your sons cast *them* out? Therefore they will be your judges. ²⁰But if I cast out demons with the finger of God, surely the kingdom of God has come upon you. ²¹When a strong man, fully armed, guards his own palace, his goods are in peace. ²²But when a stronger than he comes upon him and overcomes him, he takes from him all his armor in which he trusted, and divides his spoils. ²³He who is not with Me is against Me, and he who does not gather with Me scatters.

An Unclean Spirit Returns

²⁴"When an unclean spirit goes out of a man, he goes through dry places, seeking rest; and finding none, he says, 'I will return to my house from which I came.' ²⁵And when he comes, he finds *it* swept and put in order. ²⁶Then he goes and takes with *him* seven other spirits more wicked than himself, and they enter and dwell there; and the last *state* of that man is worse than the first."

Keeping the Word

²⁷And it happened, as He spoke these things, that a certain woman from the crowd raised her voice and said to Him, "Blessed *is* the womb that bore You, and *the* breasts which nursed You!"

²⁸But He said, "More than that, blessed *are* those who hear the word of God and keep it!"

10:41 ᵃNU-Text reads *the Lord.* **11:2** ᵃNU-Text omits *Our* and *in heaven.* ᵇNU-Text omits the rest of this verse. **11:4** ᵃNU-Text omits *But deliver us from the evil one.* **11:11** ᵃNU-Text omits the words from *bread* through *for* in the next sentence. **11:15** ᵃNU-Text and M-Text read *Beelzebul.*

11:1–4 After watching Jesus pray, one of His disciples asked Him to teach them how to pray. Jesus offered this model prayer, often called the "Lord's Prayer" or the "Disciple's Prayer." Believers from the days of the early church until the present generation have used this prayer in an endless variety of circumstances (see chart, Lessons from the Model Prayer).

11:15 Beelzebub (also "Beelzeboul" or "Beelzebul") is the name given to the prince of demons, Satan (see chart, The Names for Satan). The name probably originated from "Baalzebub" (lit. "lord of the flies" or "lord of dung"). When King Ahaziah fell through the lattice in an upper room in Samaria and injured himself, he inquired of this Philistine god (2 Kin. 1:2).

Seeking a Sign

29And while the crowds were thickly gathered together, He began to say, "This is an evil generation. It seeks a sign, and no sign will be given to it except the sign of Jonah the prophet.a 30For as Jonah became a sign to the Ninevites, so also the Son of Man will be to this generation. 31The queen of the South will rise up in the judgment with the men of this generation and condemn them, for she came from the ends of the earth to hear the wisdom of Solomon; and indeed a greater than Solomon *is* here. 32The men of Nineveh will rise up in the judgment with this generation and condemn it, for they repented at the preaching of Jonah; and indeed a greater than Jonah *is* here.

The Lamp of the Body

33"No one, when he has lit a lamp, puts *it* in a secret place or under a basket, but on a lampstand, that those who come in may see the light. 34The lamp of the body is the eye. Therefore, when your eye is good, your whole body also is full of light. But when *your eye* is bad, your body also *is* full of darkness. 35Therefore take heed that the light which is in you is not darkness. 36If then your whole body *is* full of light, having no part dark, *the* whole *body* will be full of light, as when the bright shining of a lamp gives you light."

Woe to the Pharisees and Lawyers

37And as He spoke, a certain Pharisee asked Him to dine with him. So He went in and sat down to eat. 38When the Pharisee saw *it,* he marveled that He had not first washed before dinner.

39Then the Lord said to him, "Now you Pharisees make the outside of the cup and dish clean, but your inward part is full of greed and wickedness. 40Foolish ones! Did not He who made the outside make the inside also? 41But rather give alms of such things as you have; then indeed all things are clean to you.

42"But woe to you Pharisees! For you tithe mint and rue and all manner of herbs, and pass by justice and the love of God. These you ought to have done, without leaving the others undone. 43Woe to you Pharisees! For you love the best seats in the synagogues and greetings in the marketplaces. 44Woe to you, scribes and Pharisees, hypocrites!a For you are like graves which are not seen, and the men who walk over *them* are not aware *of them."*

45Then one of the lawyers answered and said to Him, "Teacher, by saying these things You reproach us also."

46And He said, "Woe to you also, lawyers! For you load men with burdens hard to bear, and you yourselves do not touch the burdens with one of your fingers. 47Woe to you! For you build the tombs of the prophets, and your fathers killed them. 48In fact, you bear witness that you approve the deeds of your fathers; for they indeed killed them, and you build their tombs. 49Therefore the wisdom of God also said, 'I will send them prophets and apostles, and *some* of them they will kill and persecute,' 50that the blood of all the prophets which was shed from the foundation of the world may be required of this generation, 51from the blood of Abel to the blood of Zechariah who perished between the altar and the temple. Yes, I say to you, it shall be required of this generation.

52"Woe to you lawyers! For you have taken away the key of knowledge. You did not enter in yourselves, and those who were entering in you hindered."

53And as He said these things to them,a the scribes and the Pharisees began to assail *Him*

11:29 aNU-Text omits *the prophet.* 11:44 aNU-Text omits *scribes and Pharisees, hypocrites.* 11:53 aNU-Text reads *And when He left there.*

11:29, 30 Jonah was a prophet during the reign of Jeroboam II (see the Book of Jonah, Introduction: Author). Though God commanded Jonah to go to the wicked city of Nineveh, he fled to Tarshish (see Jon. 1—4). When the crowd wanted Jesus to give them a "sign," He gave them "the sign of Jonah." As Jonah had been a sign to Nineveh, Jesus would be a sign to His generation (see Luke 11:32). Jonah's three days and three nights in the belly of the fish and his sudden reappearance pictured the time Jesus would spend in the grave, followed by His Resurrection.

11:31 Solomon, David's son by Bathsheba, became the 3rd king of Israel and ruled for 40 years. Solomon is remembered for his God-given wisdom, administrative ability, great wealth, and prolific writing. Solomon was also responsible for building the temple at Jerusalem (see chart, The Plan of Solomon's Temple).

11:38 Pharisees were required to be diligent in washing their hands before eating. This necessity for ceremonial purity

symbolized removing the dirt of the sinful world from their hands. The principles of ceremonial cleanness affected every part of a Hebrew's life (see Lev. 10, Clean vs. Unclean).

11:42 Rue is a shrub with strong-smelling leaves that grows on hills in the Holy Land. Both mint and rue were tithed by the religious leaders (see chart, Herbs of the Bible).

11:46 The lawyers described by Jesus made the everyday lives of the Jews unbearably hard due to their many additions to the Mosaic Law. Although they told the people to obey these difficult rules, they did nothing to help them do so.

11:49–51 Jesus quoted from an unknown source. His point was that although these people claimed to honor the prophets, they were inwardly rejecting them. As a result, they would be held responsible for the deaths of the prophets. Jesus mentioned Abel (Gen. 4:8) and Zechariah the priest (2 Chr. 24:20, 21) as examples of innocent men killed while serving God. These examples were taken from the first and last books of the Hebrew OT.

vehemently, and to cross-examine Him about many things, [54]lying in wait for Him, and seeking to catch Him in something He might say, that they might accuse Him.[a]

Beware of Hypocrisy

12 In the meantime, when an innumerable multitude of people had gathered together, so that they trampled one another, He began to say to His disciples first *of all*, "Beware of the leaven of the Pharisees, which is hypocrisy. [2]For there is nothing covered that will not be revealed, nor hidden that will not be known. [3]Therefore whatever you have spoken in the dark will be heard in the light, and what you have spoken in the ear in inner rooms will be proclaimed on the housetops.

Jesus Teaches the Fear of God

[4]"And I say to you, My friends, do not be afraid of those who kill the body, and after that have no more that they can do. [5]But I will show you whom you should fear: Fear Him who, after He has killed, has power to cast into hell; yes, I say to you, fear Him!

[6]"Are not five sparrows sold for two copper coins?[a] And not one of them is forgotten before God. [7]But the very hairs of your head are all numbered. Do not fear therefore; you are of more value than many sparrows.

Confess Christ Before Men

[8]"Also I say to you, whoever confesses Me before men, him the Son of Man also will confess before the angels of God. [9]But he who denies Me before men will be denied before the angels of God.

[10]"And anyone who speaks a word against the Son of Man, it will be forgiven him; but to him who blasphemes against the Holy Spirit, it will not be forgiven.

[11]"Now when they bring you to the synagogues and magistrates and authorities, do not worry about how or what you should answer, or what you should say. [12]For the Holy Spirit will teach you in that very hour what you ought to say."

The Parable of the Rich Fool

[13]Then one from the crowd said to Him, "Teacher, tell my brother to divide the inheritance with me."

[14]But He said to him, "Man, who made Me a judge or an arbitrator over you?" [15]And He said to them, "Take heed and beware of covetousness,[a] for one's life does not consist in the abundance of the things he possesses."

[16]Then He spoke a parable to them, saying: "The ground of a certain rich man yielded plentifully. [17]And he thought within himself, saying, 'What shall I do, since I have no room to store my crops?' [18]So he said, 'I will do this: I will pull down my barns and build greater, and there I will store all my crops and my goods. [19]And I will say to my soul, "Soul, you have many goods laid up for many years; take your ease; eat, drink, *and* be merry." ' [20]But God said to him, 'Fool! This night your soul will be required of you; then whose will those things be which you have provided?'

[21]"So *is* he who lays up treasure for himself, and is not rich toward God."

Do Not Worry

[22]Then He said to His disciples, "Therefore I say to you, do not worry about your life, what you will eat; nor about the body, what you will put on. [23]Life is more than food, and the body *is more* than clothing. [24]Consider the ravens, for they neither sow nor reap, which have neither storehouse nor barn; and God feeds them. Of how much more value are you than the birds? [25]And which of you by worrying can add one cubit to his stature? [26]If you then are not able to do *the* least, why are you anxious for the rest? [27]Consider the lilies, how they grow: they neither toil nor spin; and yet I say to you, even Solomon in all his glory was not arrayed like one of these. [28]If then God so clothes the grass, which today is in the field and tomorrow is thrown into the oven, how much more *will He clothe* you, O *you* of little faith?

11:54 [a]NU-Text omits *and seeking* and *that they might accuse Him.*
12:6 [a]Greek *assarion,* a coin of very small value **12:15** [a]NU-Text reads *all covetousness.*

12:1 Bread was made with leaven (actually sourdough), a small piece of fermented dough that slowly caused all the bread dough to rise. During the Passover celebration, Jews made bread without leaven. In the NT, leaven is sometimes used as a word picture for evil influence. Jesus compared the Pharisees' hypocrisy and corrupt teachings to leaven.

12:6 The sparrow, often a source of food for the poor, was considered ceremonially clean and could be eaten by Jews. It was an inexpensive bird, with five sparrows selling for two copper coins (see chart, Money and Measurements in the Bible). Jesus emphasized that God remembers even the most insignificant of His creatures. Believers can know with certainty that God cares about and governs every facet of their lives.

12:12 Jesus presented the third Person of the Trinity, the Holy Spirit, in His role as Teacher. Throughout the OT and NT, the Holy Spirit empowered believers. At times He equipped them with extraordinary wisdom and strength. Jesus emphasized the Holy Spirit as the Helper, giving assistance and delivering power at the very hour it is needed.

12:15 Covetousness is the selfish desire to have what another person owns, usually material possessions (see Prov. 30, Covetousness). It indicates ruthless greed, the all-consuming lust to own more, and was a sin. In Ephesians, Paul compared the covetous man with the idolater (see Eph. 5:5).

²⁹"And do not seek what you should eat or what you should drink, nor have an anxious mind. ³⁰For all these things the nations of the world seek after, and your Father knows that you need these things. ³¹But seek the kingdom of God, and all these things^a shall be added to you.

³²"Do not fear, little flock, for it is your Father's good pleasure to give you the kingdom. ³³Sell what you have and give alms; provide yourselves money bags which do not grow old, a treasure in the heavens that does not fail, where no thief approaches nor moth destroys. ³⁴For where your treasure is, there your heart will be also.

The Faithful Servant and the Evil Servant

³⁵"Let your waist be girded and *your* lamps burning; ³⁶and you yourselves be like men who wait for their master, when he will return from the wedding, that when he comes and knocks they may open to him immediately. ³⁷Blessed *are* those servants whom the master, when he comes, will find watching. Assuredly, I say to you that he will gird himself and have them sit down *to eat,* and will come and serve them. ³⁸And if he should come in the second watch, or come in the third watch, and find *them* so, blessed are those servants. ³⁹But know this, that if the master of the house had known what hour the thief would come, he would have watched and^a not allowed his house to be broken into. ⁴⁰Therefore you also be ready, for the Son of Man is coming at an hour you do not expect."

⁴¹Then Peter said to Him, "Lord, do You speak this parable *only* to us, or to all *people?*"

⁴²And the Lord said, "Who then is that faithful and wise steward, whom *his* master will make ruler over his household, to give *them their* portion of food in due season? ⁴³Blessed *is* that servant whom his master will find so doing when he comes. ⁴⁴Truly, I say to you that he will make him ruler over all that he has. ⁴⁵But if that servant says in his heart, 'My master is delaying his coming,' and begins to beat the male and female servants, and to eat and drink and be drunk, ⁴⁶the master of

that servant will come on a day when he is not looking for *him,* and at an hour when he is not aware, and will cut him in two and appoint *him* his portion with the unbelievers. ⁴⁷And that servant who knew his master's will, and did not prepare *himself* or do according to his will, shall be beaten with many *stripes.* ⁴⁸But he who did not know, yet committed things deserving of stripes, shall be beaten with few. For everyone to whom much is given, from him much will be required; and to whom much has been committed, of him they will ask the more.

Christ Brings Division

⁴⁹"I came to send fire on the earth, and how I wish it were already kindled! ⁵⁰But I have a baptism to be baptized with, and how distressed I am till it is accomplished! ⁵¹Do *you* suppose that I came to give peace on earth? I tell you, not at all, but rather division. ⁵²For from now on five in one house will be divided: three against two, and two against three. ⁵³Father will be divided against son and son against father, mother against daughter and daughter against mother, mother-in-law against her daughter-in-law and daughter-in-law against her mother-in-law."

Discern the Time

⁵⁴Then He also said to the multitudes, "Whenever you *see* a cloud rising out of the west, immediately you say, 'A shower is coming'; and so it is. ⁵⁵And when you see the south wind blow, you say, 'There will be hot weather'; and there is. ⁵⁶Hypocrites! You can discern the face of the sky and of the earth, but how *is it* you do not discern this time?

Make Peace with Your Adversary

⁵⁷"Yes, and why, even of yourselves, do you not judge what is right? ⁵⁸When you go with your

12:31 ^aNU-Text reads *His kingdom, and these things.*   **12:39** ^aNU-Text reads *he would not have allowed.*

12:37–40 Jesus spoke of His return and the importance of watching, waiting, and being ready for Him. He compared this watchfulness to the attitude servants should have when the master is away. Servants were responsible to protect the master's house with three watches or guard duties. The OT lists these as: the "beginning of the watches" (Lam. 2:19); the "middle watch" (Judg. 7:19); and the "morning watch" (Ex. 14:24). Since the servants would not know the hour in which their master would return, they were to be faithful and consistent in their watching.

12:45–47 This parable addressed the delay of Jesus' return. He described a faithful, watching servant (on guard duty), who grew weary of waiting for the master to return. The servant became lax in his watching and allowed the influence of the world to sway him from his responsibility. This parable would have special meaning for believers in the early

church, readers who expected the imminent return of Jesus in their own lifetimes and who were in danger of growing weary in their expectations.

12:49–51 Fire refers to the coming judgment of God. Fire can destroy what can be consumed, but it will purify what cannot be consumed. Jesus referred to His "baptism" as His Crucifixion in Jerusalem, during which He would be wholly immersed in the suffering of the Cross. His death, however, would be a fulfillment of prophecy, the supreme act of reconciliation of women and men to God. "Division" is the opposite of peace. The Jewish nation believed their promised Messiah would overthrow their enemies and reign in victory and peace. Jesus confirmed to His disciples that His coming had not brought peace but would instead cause dissension among families and friends.

AN INFIRM WOMAN

Only Luke mentions this bent-over woman who had spent the previous eighteen years staring at the floor, unable to stand or sit, or even to straighten her crooked back. Jesus and His disciples had traveled through her city in Perea on their way from Galilee to Judea. They entered the synagogue on the Sabbath to teach.

Jesus had deep compassion for this tragic woman. He touched her and healed her. When the ruler of the synagogue rebuked Jesus for the unlawful Sabbath healing, Jesus firmly exposed the inconsistency of those who would lead an ox to water on the Sabbath, yet oppose the healing of an afflicted woman.

How odd that Jesus refers to her as "a daughter of Abraham," since such a description is usually reserved for the "sons" of Abraham. In front of all the upright religious folk, Jesus gave this humble woman a place of honor when He affirmed that she, too, belonged to the family of Abraham.

After Jesus' tender touch, for the first time in eighteen years, this "daughter of Abraham" straightened her back, stretched to her full height, and, among the sons of Abraham, who perhaps now hung their heads in shame, she held her head high to the glory of God. Nothing honors the Savior any more than a heart of gratitude and a spirit of praise.

See also notes on Touching (Mark 7)

---

adversary to the magistrate, make every effort along the way to settle with him, lest he drag you to the judge, the judge deliver you to the officer, and the officer throw you into prison. ⁵⁹I tell you, you shall not depart from there till you have paid the very last mite."

Repent or Perish

13 There were present at that season some who told Him about the Galileans whose blood Pilate had mingled with their sacrifices. ²And Jesus answered and said to them, "Do you suppose that these Galileans were worse sinners than all *other* Galileans, because they suffered such things? ³I tell you, no; but unless you repent you will all likewise perish. ⁴Or those eighteen on whom the tower in Siloam fell and killed them, do you think that they were worse sinners than all *other* men who dwelt in Jerusalem? ⁵I tell you, no; but unless you repent you will all likewise perish."

The Parable of the Barren Fig Tree

⁶He also spoke this parable: "A certain *man* had a fig tree planted in his vineyard, and he came seeking fruit on it and found none. ⁷Then he said to the keeper of his vineyard, 'Look, for three years I have come seeking fruit on this fig tree and find none. Cut it down; why does it use up the

ground?' ⁸But he answered and said to him, 'Sir, let it alone this year also, until I dig around it and fertilize *it*. ⁹And if it bears fruit, *well*. But if not, after that^a you can cut it down.' "

A Spirit of Infirmity

¹⁰Now He was teaching in one of the synagogues on the Sabbath. ¹¹And behold, there was a woman who had a spirit of infirmity eighteen years, and was bent over and could in no way raise *herself* up. ¹²But when Jesus saw her, He called *her* to *Him* and said to her, "Woman, you are loosed from your infirmity." ¹³And He laid *His* hands on her, and immediately she was made straight, and glorified God.

¹⁴But the ruler of the synagogue answered with indignation, because Jesus had healed on the Sabbath; and he said to the crowd, "There are six days on which men ought to work; therefore come and be healed on them, and not on the Sabbath day."

¹⁵The Lord then answered him and said, "Hypocrite!^a Does not each one of you on the Sabbath loose his ox or donkey from the stall, and lead *it* away to water it? ¹⁶So ought not this woman, be-

---

13:9 ^aNU-Text reads *And if it bears fruit after that, well. But if not, you can cut it down.* **13:15** ^aNU-Text and M-Text read *Hypocrites!*

13:4 Jesus spoke of a disaster in Jerusalem that killed 18 people. The location of the tower at Siloam is unknown, although it may have been part of Jerusalem's wall near the pool of Siloam. Jesus' point was that extreme sinfulness is not demonstrated by whether or not someone is tragically killed. Ultimate deliverance from destruction is accomplished when a person has truly repented and entered God's kingdom.

13:6 The fig tree yielded sweet fruit in the summer. Figs could be dried and stored for future use. Jesus used this well-known tree to make a point about God's eternal judgment ("cut it down," v. 9). In this passage, the fig tree represented Israel,

which was in danger of God's judgment if it continued to reject its Messiah (see Matt. 20:1–15; 21:28–32, 33–46; John 15:1–11).

13:10–14 This woman was "bound" by Satan. She suffered a spinal problem, possibly some sort of spinal fusion, which caused her body to be bent. Her "infirmity" of 18 years was caused by demonic activity initiated by Satan (vv. 11, 16). The woman did not ask for healing. The act of restoration was initiated by Jesus Himself due to His compassion for her. The woman's healing caused controversy because Jesus healed her on the Sabbath (see An Infirm Woman).

ing a daughter of Abraham, whom Satan has bound—think of it—for eighteen years, be loosed from this bond on the Sabbath?" [17]And when He said these things, all His adversaries were put to shame; and all the multitude rejoiced for all the glorious things that were done by Him.

The Parable of the Mustard Seed

[18]Then He said, "What is the kingdom of God like? And to what shall I compare it? [19]It is like a mustard seed, which a man took and put in his garden; and it grew and became a large[a] tree, and the birds of the air nested in its branches."

The Parable of the Leaven

[20]And again He said, "To what shall I liken the kingdom of God? [21]It is like leaven, which a woman took and hid in three measures[a] of meal till it was all leavened."

The Narrow Way

[22]And He went through the cities and villages, teaching, and journeying toward Jerusalem. [23]Then one said to Him, "Lord, are there few who are saved?"

And He said to them, [24]"Strive to enter through the narrow gate, for many, I say to you, will seek to enter and will not be able. [25]When once the Master of the house has risen up and shut the door, and you begin to stand outside and knock at the door, saying, 'Lord, Lord, open for us,' and He will answer and say to you, 'I do not know you, where you are from,' [26]then you will begin to say, 'We ate and drank in Your presence, and You taught in our streets.' [27]But He will say, 'I tell you I do not know you, where you are from. Depart from Me, all you workers of iniquity.' [28]There will be weeping and gnashing of teeth, when you see Abraham and Isaac and Jacob and all the prophets in the kingdom of God, and yourselves thrust out. [29]They will come from the east and the west, from the north and the south, and sit down in the kingdom of God. [30]And indeed there are last who will be first, and there are first who will be last."

[31]On that very day[a] some Pharisees came, say-

ing to Him, "Get out and depart from here, for Herod wants to kill You."

[32]And He said to them, "Go, tell that fox, 'Behold, I cast out demons and perform cures today and tomorrow, and the third *day* I shall be perfected.' [33]Nevertheless I must journey today, tomorrow, and the *day* following; for it cannot be that a prophet should perish outside of Jerusalem.

Jesus Laments over Jerusalem

[34]"O Jerusalem, Jerusalem, the one who kills the prophets and stones those who are sent to her! How often I wanted to gather your children together, as a hen *gathers* her brood under *her* wings, but you were not willing! [35]See! Your house is left to you desolate; and assuredly,[a] I say to you, you shall not see Me until *the time* comes when you say, *'Blessed is He who comes in the name of the LORD!' "*[b]

A Man with Dropsy Healed on the Sabbath

14 Now it happened, as He went into the house of one of the rulers of the Pharisees to eat bread on the Sabbath, that they watched Him closely. [2]And behold, there was a certain man before Him who had dropsy. [3]And Jesus, answering, spoke to the lawyers and Pharisees, saying, "Is it lawful to heal on the Sabbath?"[a]

[4]But they kept silent. And He took *him* and healed him, and let him go. [5]Then He answered them, saying, "Which of you, having a donkey[a] or an ox that has fallen into a pit, will not immediately pull him out on the Sabbath day?" [6]And they could not answer Him regarding these things.

Take the Lowly Place

[7]So He told a parable to those who were invited, when He noted how they chose the best places, saying to them: [8]"When you are invited by anyone to a wedding feast, do not sit down in the best place, lest one more honorable than you be invited by him; [9]and he who invited you and him

---

13:19 [a]NU-Text omits *large*.　**13:21** [a]Greek *sata*, approximately two pecks in all　**13:31** [a]NU-Text reads *In that very hour*.　**13:35** [a]NU-Text and M-Text omit *assuredly*.　[b]Psalm 118:26　**14:3** [a]NU-Text adds *or not*.　**14:5** [a]NU-Text and M-Text read *son*.

13:16, 17 By calling the woman a daughter of Abraham, Jesus included her as a covenant member of Abraham's family in a public setting. While "son of Abraham" was used frequently throughout Scripture, to associate a woman with Abraham was rare. Although the Sabbath healing humiliated Jesus' adversaries, it made the people rejoice (v. 17).

13:19 The mustard seed was often planted by farmers in Palestine. Matthew and Mark point to the seed's small size and contrast this with the size of the full-grown tree (a mustard seed can produce a tree 30 feet tall). Luke, however, said nothing about the size but emphasized that birds can nest in its branches. Birds roosting in branches can represent the nations of the earth, emphasizing a universal kingdom in which all people, both Jew and Gentile, can share. While the kingdom

of God started small like a mustard seed (with a baby's birth, a young preacher, and a handful of disciples), the result (or the consummation of the kingdom's growth) would be extraordinary.

13:32 Jesus addressed Herod Antipas, the Galilean tetrarch, who had already beheaded John the Baptist. Herod wanted also to kill Jesus. When Jesus called Herod a "fox," He insinuated that Herod was deceitful and crafty as well as insignificant. Even the sly Herod could not impede God's divine plan.

13:34 Jesus lamented over Jerusalem. These words reveal Jesus' heart. The image of a hen and chicks depicted the love, protection, shelter, and care of a mother toward her children. Jesus' care for His people Israel is pictured (see chart, Female Metaphors for God).

POVERTY *PROVIDING FOR THOSE IN NEED*

Those counted among the poor were the needy, the weak, and those who were dependent—the orphans and the widows who were usually in the lower social classes and in need of protection from abuse and neglect. Virtually every prophet of the Old Testament prophesied against those who wrongfully oppressed the poor (Jer. 22:13–16).

God provided for the poor through His principle of gleaning. Landowners were instructed to leave the remaining grain around the outer perimeters of the fields for the poor to gather (Lev. 19:10; Ruth 2:2, 15, 16). The courts, too, were admonished to deal justly with the poor (Ex. 23:6, 7).

Jesus Himself was born into a poor family and called the poor His brethren (Matt. 25:40). The early church recognized the importance of caring for widows (Acts 6:1–6) and took offerings to meet their needs (Rom. 15:26). We are admonished to be mindful of the poor (Gal. 2:10).

Every believer will be held accountable for how she has responded to those in need. One of the ways to judge our relationship to Christ is to observe how we respond to the hungry, the thirsty, the naked, the stranger, and the prisoner (Matt. 25:31–46). Compassion is regarded as evidence of the presence of Christ inside the heart (1 Pet. 3:8; 1 John 3:16, 17).

God often chooses to reveal Himself to the world through the poor (James 2:5); rarely do the rich, great, and noble hear His call or choose His path (Matt. 19:16–24). Paul concluded that if the Lord used only the wealthy to extend His cause, critics would credit those people and their resources instead of God with the good that was done through them (1 Cor. 1:26).

The first step to having your physical needs met is to become "poor in spirit," recognizing that every heart separated from God is in spiritual poverty, which is far more tragic than physical poverty (Matt. 5:3). The Lord has promised to provide freely for His children (Rom. 8:32).

See also notes on The Homeless (Luke 9); Prejudice (Acts 15); Suffering (Ps. 33; 113; Is. 43; 1 Pet. 5)

come and say to you, 'Give place to this man,' and then you begin with shame to take the lowest place. ¹⁰But when you are invited, go and sit down in the lowest place, so that when he who invited you comes he may say to you, 'Friend, go up higher.' Then you will have glory in the presence of those who sit at the table with you. ¹¹For whoever exalts himself will be humbled, and he who humbles himself will be exalted."

¹²Then He also said to him who invited Him, "When you give a dinner or a supper, do not ask your friends, your brothers, your relatives, nor rich neighbors, lest they also invite you back, and you be repaid. ¹³But when you give a feast, invite *the* poor, *the* maimed, *the* lame, *the* blind. ¹⁴And you will be blessed, because they cannot repay you; for you shall be repaid at the resurrection of the just."

The Parable of the Great Supper

¹⁵Now when one of those who sat at the table with Him heard these things, he said to Him, "Blessed *is* he who shall eat bread[a] in the kingdom of God!"

¹⁶Then He said to him, "A certain man gave a great supper and invited many, ¹⁷and sent his servant at supper time to say to those who were invited, 'Come, for all things are now ready.' ¹⁸But they all with one *accord* began to make excuses. The first said to him, 'I have bought a piece of ground, and I must go and see it. I ask you to have me excused.' ¹⁹And another said, 'I have bought five yoke of oxen, and I am going to test them. I ask you to have me excused.' ²⁰Still another said, 'I have married a wife, and therefore I cannot come.' ²¹So that servant came and reported these things to his master. Then the master of the house, being angry, said to his servant, 'Go out quickly into the streets and lanes of the city, and bring in here *the* poor and *the* maimed and *the* lame and *the* blind.' ²²And the servant said, 'Master, it is done as you commanded, and still there is room.' ²³Then the master said to the servant, 'Go out into the highways and hedges, and compel *them* to come in, that my house may be filled. ²⁴For I say to you that

14:15 ᵃM-Text reads *dinner*.

14:13, 14 To give a feast for the poor, maimed, lame, and blind would be an act of generosity, since these people could not repay the host. Jesus implied that when the host only invited his desirable friends, his giving came from selfish ambition, not love. These four groups of people represented the lower social classes whom the rich and powerful could (and often did) easily abuse. The repayment for this good deed would take place at the "resurrection of the just."

14:26, 27 The cost of discipleship is heavy. Therefore, before entering into discipleship, the cost should be carefully calculated, for Christ must come first in the disciple's life. "To hate" means that the disciple's other loyalties must be subordinate to devotion to the Lord. A true disciple must also be willing to face martyrdom.

none of those men who were invited shall taste my supper.'"

Leaving All to Follow Christ

25Now great multitudes went with Him. And He turned and said to them, 26"If anyone comes to Me and does not hate his father and mother, wife and children, brothers and sisters, yes, and his own life also, he cannot be My disciple. 27And whoever does not bear his cross and come after Me cannot be My disciple. 28For which of you, intending to build a tower, does not sit down first and count the cost, whether he has *enough* to finish it— 29lest, after he has laid the foundation, and is not able to finish, all who see *it* begin to mock him, 30saying, 'This man began to build and was not able to finish'? 31Or what king, going to make war against another king, does not sit down first and consider whether he is able with ten thousand to meet him who comes against him with twenty thousand? 32Or else, while the other is still a great way off, he sends a delegation and asks conditions of peace. 33So likewise, whoever of you does not forsake all that he has cannot be My disciple.

Tasteless Salt Is Worthless

34"Salt *is* good; but if the salt has lost its flavor, how shall it be seasoned? 35It is neither fit for the land nor for the dunghill, *but* men throw it out. He who has ears to hear, let him hear!"

The Parable of the Lost Sheep

15 Then all the tax collectors and the sinners drew near to Him to hear Him. 2And the Pharisees and scribes complained, saying, "This Man receives sinners and eats with them." 3So He spoke this parable to them, saying:

4"What man of you, having a hundred sheep, if he loses one of them, does not leave the ninety-nine in the wilderness, and go after the one which is lost until he finds it? 5And when he has found *it*, he lays *it* on his shoulders, rejoicing. 6And when he comes home, he calls together *his* friends and neighbors, saying to them, 'Rejoice with me, for I have found my sheep which was lost!' 7I say to you that likewise there will be more joy in heaven over one sinner who repents than over ninety-nine just persons who need no repentance.

The Parable of the Lost Coin

8"Or what woman, having ten silver coins,a if she loses one coin, does not light a lamp, sweep the house, and search carefully until she finds *it?* 9And when she has found *it*, she calls *her* friends and neighbors together, saying, 'Rejoice with me, for I have found the piece which I lost!' 10Likewise, I say to you, there is joy in the presence of the angels of God over one sinner who repents."

The Parable of the Lost Son

11Then He said: "A certain man had two sons. 12And the younger of them said to *his* father, 'Father, give me the portion of goods that falls *to me.'* So he divided to them *his* livelihood. 13And not many days after, the younger son gathered all together, journeyed to a far country, and there wasted his possessions with prodigal living. 14But when he had spent all, there arose a severe famine in that land, and he began to be in want. 15Then he went and joined himself to a citizen of that country, and he sent him into his fields to feed swine. 16And he would gladly have filled his stomach with the pods that the swine ate, and no one gave him *anything.*

17"But when he came to himself, he said, 'How

15:8 aGreek *drachma,* a valuable coin often worn in a ten-piece garland by married women

---

15:8 Married women often wore valuable coins in garlands (or wreaths) on their heads (see The Woman Who Lost a Coin). Garlands were part of the bride's wedding headdress, perhaps her dowry (see chart, Head Coverings for Women). These silver coins (*drachmai*) may have been her savings or merely an ornament. Either way, the loss of such a coin would be a serious matter.

15:12 Upon the death of the father, the firstborn son would receive two-thirds of the inheritance. The younger son, however, would receive only one-third. If the family included daughters, the younger son's inheritance would be less so that the family could provide a dowry for the daughters when they married. The father agreed and divided his "goods." It was highly unusual for the younger son to be allowed to spend the inheritance before his father's death.

15:13 The younger son probably converted the goods to money ("gathered all together"). The far country could represent the "world" or any place distant from home. The younger son engaged in a reckless lifestyle, including sexual promiscuity (vv. 13, 30), and squandered his entire inheritance.

15:14–16 To avoid starvation in the time of famine, the son went to work for a Gentile. The fact that a Jewish man would help raise and care for pigs reveals his utter degradation, since swine were "unclean" animals to Jews.

15:17–24 When he came to himself (v. 17), he took the first step in repentance—the realization of wrongdoing (v. 18). He then asked to become a "hired servant" (v. 19). While an ordinary slave was considered part of the family, a hired servant (or day laborer) could be dismissed at any time, for he was not a family member. Though it was highly unusual for a proper Oriental father to run, Jesus portrayed God as the Father who ran, so great was His excitement over the return of His son. The son was forgiven and accepted back into the home (v. 20). The "best robe" was a sign of position; the "ring" indicated authority; the "sandals" (a sign of freedom and luxury) put on his bare feet set him apart from the barefoot slaves. Since meat was not ordinarily eaten at meals, the "fatted calf" noted a special occasion (vv. 22, 23).

THE WOMAN WHO LOST A COIN

This is the second of three parables in which Jesus clearly pictured God's loving concern for each individual sinner. After first telling about a shepherd (Luke 15:3–7), He gave an example with which the women in His audience could readily identify. He described a woman who loses one of her ten silver coins, worth about a day's wage (Matt. 20:2). These coins, which she wore as a headdress, represented her savings and probably formed part of her dowry. At issue was not only the value of the coin but also the fact that losing part of her dowry would be a shameful thing.

Jesus pictured her living in a peasant's house, which would have a low doorway and few or no windows. To find the coin she lit a lamp and diligently swept every nook, listening for the coin's telltale clink and watching for its gleam in the lamplight. When at last she found it, her joy knew no bounds! She rushed to tell her friends the wonderful news and called them to rejoice with her.

Jesus then applied the parable by declaring the joy that the angels share together with God when sinners return in repentance to Him. The self-righteous scribes and Pharisees in His audience clearly lacked this joy (Luke 15:2), but God's gracious acceptance was wonderful news to the ordinary women and men who heard Him (v. 1).

See also Lam. 3:22, note; chart on Head Coverings for Women; notes on Dowry (1 Kin. 9); Perseverance (Rev. 14)

many of my father's hired servants have bread enough and to spare, and I perish with hunger! ¹⁸I will arise and go to my father, and will say to him, "Father, I have sinned against heaven and before you, ¹⁹and I am no longer worthy to be called your son. Make me like one of your hired servants." '

²⁰"And he arose and came to his father. But when he was still a great way off, his father saw him and had compassion, and ran and fell on his neck and kissed him. ²¹And the son said to him, 'Father, I have sinned against heaven and in your sight, and am no longer worthy to be called your son.'

²²"But the father said to his servants, 'Bring^a out the best robe and put *it* on him, and put a ring on his hand and sandals on *his* feet. ²³And bring the fatted calf here and kill *it*, and let us eat and be merry; ²⁴for this my son was dead and is alive again; he was lost and is found.' And they began to be merry.

²⁵"Now his older son was in the field. And as he came and drew near to the house, he heard music and dancing. ²⁶So he called one of the servants and asked what these things meant. ²⁷And he said to him, 'Your brother has come, and because he has received him safe and sound, your father has killed the fatted calf.'

²⁸"But he was angry and would not go in. Therefore his father came out and pleaded with him. ²⁹So he answered and said to *his* father, 'Lo, these many years I have been serving you; I never transgressed your commandment at any time; and yet you never gave me a young goat, that I might make merry with my friends. ³⁰But as soon as this son of yours came, who has devoured your livelihood with harlots, you killed the fatted calf for him.'

³¹"And he said to him, 'Son, you are always with me, and all that I have is yours. ³²It was right that we should make merry and be glad, for your brother was dead and is alive again, and was lost and is found.' "

The Parable of the Unjust Steward

16 He also said to His disciples: "There was a certain rich man who had a steward, and an accusation was brought to him that this man was wasting his goods. ²So he called him and said to him, 'What is this I hear about you? Give an account of your stewardship, for you can no longer be steward.'

³"Then the steward said within himself, 'What shall I do? For my master is taking the stewardship away from me. I cannot dig; I am ashamed to beg. ⁴I have resolved what to do, that when I am put out of the stewardship, they may receive me into their houses.'

⁵"So he called every one of his master's debtors to *him*, and said to the first, 'How much do you owe my master?' ⁶And he said, 'A hundred measures^a of oil.' So he said to him, 'Take your bill, and sit down quickly and write fifty.' ⁷Then he said to another, 'And how much do you owe?' So he said, 'A hundred measures^a of wheat.' And he said to him, 'Take your bill, and write eighty.' ⁸So the master commended the unjust steward because he had dealt shrewdly. For the sons of this world are more shrewd in their generation than the sons of light.

15:22 ^{a}NU-Text reads *Quickly bring.* **16:6** ^{a}Greek *batos*, eight or nine gallons each (Old Testament *bath*) **16:7** ^{a}Greek *koros*, ten or twelve bushels each (Old Testament *kor*)

CHILDREN PARENTING ADULT CHILDREN

In the parable of the prodigal, Jesus provided a pattern for a healthy relationship between adult children and their parents (Luke 15:11–32):

- The father acknowledged the independence of both sons—even against his better judgment in the case of the younger (vv. 12, 31).
- Rather than demanding childlike obedience from the elder son, who protested the generous welcome extended to his wayward brother, the father reasoned with him as one adult to another (vv. 31, 32).
- The father allowed both sons to make their own decisions and bear the consequences of their actions.
- The father extended to each son unconditional, forgiving love (vv. 21–24, 31).

While even Jesus felt compelled to assert His adult independence (Matt. 12:46–50), adulthood does not preclude loving interdependence between children and parents. Noah's adult sons benefited from his protection (Gen. 6:18–22). Judah attempted to spare his elderly father Jacob from heartbreak (Gen. 44:19–34). While enduring the Cross, Jesus made provision for the care of His mother (John 19:26, 27).

The loving bond between parent and child is not to be broken by aging, inevitable transfer of residence, and subsequent realignment of loyalties. Rather it remains as an enduring commitment between parent and offspring from birth to death to be available to each other and responsive to each other's needs (Prov. 4:3–6, 10–13).

See also Gen. 4:1–16; 37:1–36; Matt. 18:3, note; notes on Change Points in Life (Eccl. 3); Children (2 Sam. 21; Ps. 128; Prov. 22); Family (Gen. 32; 1 Sam. 3; Ps. 78; 127); Motherhood (1 Sam. 1; Is. 49; Ezek. 16)

9"And I say to you, make friends for yourselves by unrighteous mammon, that when you fail,[a] they may receive you into an everlasting home. 10He who is faithful in what is least is faithful also in much; and he who is unjust in what is least is unjust also in much. 11Therefore if you have not been faithful in the unrighteous mammon, who will commit to your trust the true riches? 12And if you have not been faithful in what is another man's, who will give you what is your own?

13"No servant can serve two masters; for either he will hate the one and love the other, or else he will be loyal to the one and despise the other. You cannot serve God and mammon."

The Law, the Prophets, and the Kingdom

14Now the Pharisees, who were lovers of money, also heard all these things, and they derided Him. 15And He said to them, "You are those who justify yourselves before men, but God knows your hearts. For what is highly esteemed among men is an abomination in the sight of God.

16"The law and the prophets were until John. Since that time the kingdom of God has been preached, and everyone is pressing into it. 17And it is easier for heaven and earth to pass away than for one tittle of the law to fail.

18"Whoever divorces his wife and marries another commits adultery; and whoever marries her who is divorced from her husband commits adultery.

The Rich Man and Lazarus

19"There was a certain rich man who was clothed in purple and fine linen and fared sumptuously every day. 20But there was a certain beggar named Lazarus, full of sores, who was laid at his gate, 21desiring to be fed with the crumbs which fell[a] from the rich man's table. Moreover the dogs

16:9 [a]NU-Text reads it fails.　16:21 [a]NU-Text reads with what fell.

16:13 Mammon represented money, riches, or worldly possessions. Jesus used the illustration to depict a divided heart, one devoted to both money and God. Jesus' point is that service to Mammon prohibits giving wholehearted devotion to God (Luke 9:23–26).

16:18 Jesus emphasized that marriage is a lifelong commitment. Mosaic Law required a "certificate of divorce" when a man wanted to divorce his wife (Deut. 24:1). Some teachers held that a man could divorce his wife for any reason, no matter how trivial. Only in rare cases could a wife divorce her husband. But God hates divorce (Mal. 2:16). Jesus taught that divorce was a provision made simply because of the hardness of the human heart. God's original intention, however, was that a husband and wife remain in permanent union (Gen. 2:24, note; Matt. 19, Divorce; Mark 10:8).

16:19 To be clothed in purple indicated great wealth. Purple was an expensive dye made from mollusks found in the Mediterranean Sea (see chart, Colors in the Bible). Lydia, a believer from Thyatira, was a seller of purple cloth (Acts 16:14). Purple was worn by royalty and represented luxury. The "fine linen" probably refers to expensive Egyptian linen undergarments.

16:21 Food was eaten with the hands, not utensils, in Jesus' time. In order to clean their hands during the meal, the

STEWARDSHIP ACCOUNTABLE TO GOD

Accountability is an integral part of daily living. It is the requirement of the giver and the responsibility of the recipient (1 Cor. 4:2). The employed are accountable to the employer, the married to spouse and family, the citizen to society, and all of us to God (Rom. 14:12).

Jesus tells the parable about a rich man whose steward was accused of wasting his master's goods (Luke 16:1, 2). The steward was summoned and told, "Give an account of your stewardship." While this steward was able to act quickly and wisely to set things in order (vv. 3–9), Jesus used this story to make an important point: "He who is faithful in what is least is faithful also in much; and he who is unjust in what is least is unjust also in much" (v. 10).

God is Creator and Owner of all things (Deut. 10:14; Ps. 24:1, 2). All that is possessed comes as a gift from His hand (Acts 17:25). Our master Jesus Christ will ultimately require an accounting of each person's stewardship (2 Cor. 5:10).

Christian stewards can be prepared for that day of accountability by taking seriously their stewardship responsibilities. Whether the managed resource is time, talent, or money, the steward should endeavor to avoid waste, maximize return, and, above all, assure that the investment is pleasing to God.

Time should be used wisely; talents should be shared to edify others and glorify God; money should be spent carefully and given responsibly. Our drive to execute these requirements faithfully comes from having an acute awareness of our personal accountability to God (1 Pet. 4:10).

See also notes on Debt (Ps. 37); Financial Planning (Luke 19); Giving (2 Cor. 9); Gratitude (Ps. 95); Prosperity (Ps. 1); Time Management (Ps. 31)

---

came and licked his sores. ²²So it was that the beggar died, and was carried by the angels to Abraham's bosom. The rich man also died and was buried. ²³And being in torments in Hades, he lifted up his eyes and saw Abraham afar off, and Lazarus in his bosom.

²⁴"Then he cried and said, 'Father Abraham, have mercy on me, and send Lazarus that he may dip the tip of his finger in water and cool my tongue; for I am tormented in this flame.' ²⁵But Abraham said, 'Son, remember that in your lifetime you received your good things, and likewise Lazarus evil things; but now he is comforted and you are tormented. ²⁶And besides all this, between us and you there is a great gulf fixed, so that those who want to pass from here to you cannot, nor can those from there pass to us.'

²⁷"Then he said, 'I beg you therefore, father, that you would send him to my father's house, ²⁸for I have five brothers, that he may testify to them, lest they also come to this place of torment.' ²⁹Abraham

said to him, 'They have Moses and the prophets; let them hear them.' ³⁰And he said, 'No, father Abraham; but if one goes to them from the dead, they will repent.' ³¹But he said to him, 'If they do not hear Moses and the prophets, neither will they be persuaded though one rise from the dead.' "

Jesus Warns of Offenses

17 Then He said to the disciples, "It is impossible that no offenses should come, but woe *to him* through whom they do come! ²It would be better for him if a millstone were hung around his neck, and he were thrown into the sea, than that he should offend one of these little ones. ³Take heed to yourselves. If your brother sins against you,ᵃ rebuke him; and if he repents, forgive him. ⁴And if he sins against you seven times in a day, and seven times in a day returns to you,ᵃ saying, 'I repent,' you shall forgive him."

···································
17:3 ᵃNU-Text omits *against you.*   17:4 ᵃM-Text omits *to you.*

---

wealthy used chunks of bread. The bread was then dropped on the floor, here described as "crumbs which fell." The beggar waited for the bread to fall so that he could eat.

16:22 Lazarus, the beggar, was God's faithful servant. When he died, he was not buried. When unknown or unclaimed beggars died, their bodies were not buried but thrown into the burning garbage heap ("Gehenna") outside the city. Lazarus is portrayed in the afterlife as leaning his head on Abraham's bosom (perhaps reclining against Abraham's chest at a great feast table), indicating close fellowship. Luke identified the poor man by name (Lazarus), but he left the rich man unnamed.

16:26 The rich man's fate was irreversible and eternal. The

chasm or "great gulf fixed" was unbridgeable. The rich man was kept in misery in Hades, and Lazarus could not cross over the chasm to help him. Upon death, the respective destinies of the rich man and the poor man had been sealed for eternity.

17:2 Millstones were circular stones used for grinding grain. Some were small enough for women to use; others were so large that they required an animal's strength to operate. "Little ones" may refer to young believers or (possibly) believers of any age.

17:3, 4 Jesus spoke here of one believer sinning against another believer. If the one who committed the wrong repented, the believer wronged was obligated to forgive him and not

Faith and Duty

[5]And the apostles said to the Lord, "Increase our faith."

[6]So the Lord said, "If you have faith as a mustard seed, you can say to this mulberry tree, 'Be pulled up by the roots and be planted in the sea,' and it would obey you. [7]And which of you, having a servant plowing or tending sheep, will say to him when he has come in from the field, 'Come at once and sit down to eat'? [8]But will he not rather say to him, 'Prepare something for my supper, and gird yourself and serve me till I have eaten and drunk, and afterward you will eat and drink'? [9]Does he thank that servant because he did the things that were commanded him? I think not.[a] [10]So likewise you, when you have done all those things which you are commanded, say, 'We are unprofitable servants. We have done what was our duty to do.'"

Ten Lepers Cleansed

[11]Now it happened as He went to Jerusalem that He passed through the midst of Samaria and Galilee. [12]Then as He entered a certain village, there met Him ten men who were lepers, who stood afar off. [13]And they lifted up *their* voices and said, "Jesus, Master, have mercy on us!"

[14]So when He saw *them*, He said to them, "Go, show yourselves to the priests." And so it was that as they went, they were cleansed.

[15]And one of them, when he saw that he was healed, returned, and with a loud voice glorified God, [16]and fell down on *his* face at His feet, giving Him thanks. And he was a Samaritan.

[17]So Jesus answered and said, "Were there not ten cleansed? But where *are* the nine? [18]Were there not any found who returned to give glory to God except this foreigner?" [19]And He said to him, "Arise, go your way. Your faith has made you well."

The Coming of the Kingdom

[20]Now when He was asked by the Pharisees when the kingdom of God would come, He an-swered them and said, "The kingdom of God does not come with observation; [21]nor will they say, 'See here!' or 'See there!'[a] For indeed, the kingdom of God is within you."

[22]Then He said to the disciples, "The days will come when you will desire to see one of the days of the Son of Man, and you will not see *it*. [23]And they will say to you, 'Look here!' or 'Look there!'[a] Do not go after *them* or follow *them*. [24]For as the lightning that flashes out of one *part* under heaven shines to the other *part* under heaven, so also the Son of Man will be in His day. [25]But first He must suffer many things and be rejected by this generation. [26]And as it was in the days of Noah, so it will be also in the days of the Son of Man: [27]They ate, they drank, they married wives, they were given in marriage, until the day that Noah entered the ark, and the flood came and de-stroyed them all. [28]Likewise as it was also in the days of Lot: They ate, they drank, they bought, they sold, they planted, they built; [29]but on the day that Lot went out of Sodom it rained fire and brimstone from heaven and destroyed *them* all. [30]Even so will it be in the day when the Son of Man is revealed.

[31]"In that day, he who is on the housetop, and his goods *are* in the house, let him not come down to take them away. And likewise the one who is in the field, let him not turn back. [32]Remember Lot's wife. [33]Whoever seeks to save his life will lose it, and whoever loses his life will preserve it. [34]I tell you, in that night there will be two *men* in one bed: the one will be taken and the other will be left. [35]Two *women* will be grinding together: the one will be taken and the other left. [36]Two *men* will be in the field: the one will be taken and the other left."[a]

[37]And they answered and said to Him, "Where, Lord?"

17:9 [a]NU-Text ends verse with *commanded;* M-Text omits *him.*   17:21 [a]NU-Text reverses *here* and *there.*   17:23 [a]NU-Text reverses *here* and *there.*   17:36 [a]NU-Text and M-Text omit verse 36.

---

bear a grudge. The number of times he was to forgive his brother was unlimited.

17:11 Samaria, in the first century A.D., was the region of Palestine between Galilee in the north and Judea in the south. Its inhabitants included Jews who, over the centuries, had inter-married with Gentiles. They had also brought in foreign gods to worship. The result was considerable hatred and prejudice between the Jews and Samaritans. When a Jew traveled be-tween Galilee and Judea, he typically went a greater distance and crossed into Perea on the east bank of the Jordan to avoid going through Samaria. Jesus, however, felt no animosity to-ward the Samaritans (see John 4:4–6, note).

17:14–19 Mosaic Law gave the priests the responsibility of de-claring a leper's healing valid (see Matt. 8:2, 3, note). The per-son would then be allowed to reenter society. Only one of the ten, a Samaritan, returned to thank Jesus, (see Ps. 95, Grati-tude). Jesus was, no doubt, grieved over the ingratitude of the other nine.

17:28, 29 Lot was the nephew of Abraham and the son of Ha-ran. When Abraham traveled to Canaan, Lot and his house-hold went with him. Lot chose to settle in the fertile Jordan valley, and he eventually moved into Sodom. Even though the people of Sodom and Gomorrah were intensely evil, Jesus placed the emphasis on their lack of preparation for God's coming judgment.

17:34–36 Jesus used this picture to describe the separation that will happen at His return. "Night" emphasizes the unex-pectedness of His coming. Believers will be taken; non believ-ers will be left to face the judgment. Although He did not ex-plain the meaning of "taken," the emphasis is that the believers will be taken to Himself, escaping judgment.

17:37 When the disciples asked Jesus "where" His return would take place, Jesus answered with a word picture. "Body" represented a dead body, and an eagle (vulture) was a bird of prey. Since vultures would feed upon dead bodies, they would know where the carcasses lay. Jesus' point is that much as a

THE PERSISTENT WIDOW

Jesus was discussing the coming of God's Kingdom on earth (Luke 17:20–37), declaring that His return would be sudden and without warning. In the meantime, He encouraged His disciples to continue praying persistently for God's justice to be manifested so that the wrongs of this present evil age would be righted with triumph for His people (Luke 18:1, 7, 8).

To make His point, Jesus gave the example of a widow (vv. 18:2–5). Widows were often among the most vulnerable people in Jewish society, and apparently this one had no other family member to help plead her case. The wicked, arrogant, unjust judge was probably a Gentile official. He despised the woman and her cause and clearly considered her a nuisance. Nevertheless, he finally granted her request, not because he cared about her or her just cause but because she disturbed him with her persistent pleas.

The parable's central teaching is not that believers need to badger a reluctant God to meet their needs. After all, God and the unjust judge are opposites! Rather, if even an unjust judge will occasionally give justice, how much more will the righteous, loving Judge of all the earth hear the persistent cries of His distressed people. When the proper time comes, He will suddenly and speedily avenge them. Thus, women and men should remain steadfast and persistent in prayer as they await His Coming.

See also Lam. 3:22, note; Matt. 7:7–12; notes on Widowhood (Ps. 68; Jer. 29; 1 Cor. 2)

So He said to them, "Wherever the body is, there the eagles will be gathered together."

The Parable of the Persistent Widow

18 Then He spoke a parable to them, that men always ought to pray and not lose heart, ²saying: "There was in a certain city a judge who did not fear God nor regard man. ³Now there was a widow in that city; and she came to him, saying, 'Get justice for me from my adversary.' ⁴And he would not for a while; but afterward he said within himself, 'Though I do not fear God nor regard man, ⁵yet because this widow troubles me I will avenge her, lest by her continual coming she weary me.' "

⁶Then the Lord said, "Hear what the unjust judge said. ⁷And shall God not avenge His own elect who cry out day and night to Him, though He bears long with them? ⁸I tell you that He will avenge them speedily. Nevertheless, when the Son of Man comes, will He really find faith on the earth?"

The Parable of the Pharisee and the Tax Collector

⁹Also He spoke this parable to some who trusted in themselves that they were righteous, and despised others: ¹⁰"Two men went up to the temple to pray, one a Pharisee and the other a tax collector. ¹¹The Pharisee stood and prayed thus with himself, 'God, I thank You that I am not like other men—extortioners, unjust, adulterers, or even as this tax collector. ¹²I fast twice a week; I give tithes of all that I possess.' ¹³And the tax collector, standing afar off, would not so much as raise *his* eyes to heaven, but beat his breast, saying, 'God, be merciful to me a sinner!' ¹⁴I tell you, this man went down to his house justified *rather* than the other; for everyone who exalts himself will be humbled, and he who humbles himself will be exalted."

Jesus Blesses Little Children

¹⁵Then they also brought infants to Him that He might touch them; but when the disciples saw *it,* they rebuked them. ¹⁶But Jesus called them to *Him* and said, "Let the little children come to Me, and do not forbid them; for of such is the kingdom of God. ¹⁷Assuredly, I say to you, whoever does not receive the kingdom of God as a little child will by no means enter it."

Jesus Counsels the Rich Young Ruler

¹⁸Now a certain ruler asked Him, saying, "Good Teacher, what shall I do to inherit eternal life?"

¹⁹So Jesus said to him, "Why do you call Me

---

dead body would draw vultures, so unrepentant people would draw God's judgment.

18:2, 3 This dishonest judge represented corrupted power, for he neither feared God nor sought justice for the people. The widow represented complete helplessness, for she had no money to bribe him and no one powerful enough to intervene on her behalf (see The Persistent Widow).

18:10–14 Both public and private prayers were allowed in the temple. Pharisees often stood and prayed publicly in order to be heard by others. The tax collector, on the other hand, ashamed of his sinfulness, humbly bowed his head, beat his breast (a sign of grief), and prayed for God's mercy. That God heard the prayer of the tax collector and not of the Pharisee surprised Jesus' listeners (see chart, Lessons from the Model Prayer).

18:18–23 The rich ruler was most likely a member of the Sanhedrin or a synagogue ruler. He sought to flatter Jesus (v. 18) since this title of distinction was not commonly used among the rabbis. Jesus listed only those commandments that dealt with one's relationship with a neighbor (see Deut. 5:16–20).

WOMEN AND ANGELS

WOMAN	MINISTRY OF THE ANGEL	REFERENCE
Hagar	The "Angel of the Lord" gave helpful instructions, announced her future descendants, and offered comfort.	Gen. 16:7–12
Lot's wife	Angels led Lot and his family away from Sodom.	Gen. 19:15–26
Wife for Isaac	Abraham sent Eliezer, his oldest servant, to find a wife for his son Isaac. He told the servant that an angel would guide him to the right woman.	Gen. 24:1–7
Samson's mother	The "Angel of the Lord" announced an end to her barrenness and described the special nature of her son's ministry.	Judg. 13:1–24
Mary's betrothed	An angel calmed Joseph's doubts about Mary's faithfulness and announced her role as mother of the Messiah.	Matt. 1:20–25
Women at the empty tomb	An angel appeared at the empty tomb to tell the women that Jesus was alive.	Matt. 28:2–6
Elizabeth's husband	Gabriel announced the birth of John the Baptist to Zacharias.	Luke 1:5–25
Mary	Gabriel told Mary that she would be mother of the Messiah.	Luke 1:26–38
Shepherds who came to visit Mary and Jesus	Angels announced the birth of Jesus to shepherds near Bethlehem.	Luke 2:8–15

good? No one *is* good but One, *that is,* God. ²⁰You know the commandments: *'Do not commit adultery,' 'Do not murder,' 'Do not steal,' 'Do not bear false witness,' 'Honor your father and your mother.' '*[a]

²¹And he said, "All these things I have kept from my youth."

²²So when Jesus heard these things, He said to him, "You still lack one thing. Sell all that you have and distribute to the poor, and you will have treasure in heaven; and come, follow Me."

²³But when he heard this, he became very sorrowful, for he was very rich.

With God All Things Are Possible

²⁴And when Jesus saw that he became very sorrowful, He said, "How hard it is for those who have riches to enter the kingdom of God! ²⁵For it is easier for a camel to go through the eye of a needle than for a rich man to enter the kingdom of God."

²⁶And those who heard it said, "Who then can be saved?"

²⁷But He said, "The things which are impossible with men are possible with God."

²⁸Then Peter said, "See, we have left all[a] and followed You."

²⁹So He said to them, "Assuredly, I say to you, there is no one who has left house or parents or brothers or wife or children, for the sake of the kingdom of God, ³⁰who shall not receive many times more in this present time, and in the age to come eternal life."

18:20 [a]Exodus 20:12–16; Deuteronomy 5:16–20 **18:28** [a]NU-Text reads *our own.*

18:24, 25 Those rich in material possessions could be tempted to depend on earthly wealth rather than on God. The intellectually blessed could be tempted to depend on self-effort rather than on God. Jesus used a well-known figure of speech about a camel going through the eye of a needle to emphasize the difficulty rich people have in turning from their riches to find salvation (see Matt. 6:24, note).

FORGIVENESS *EXTENDING MERCY TO OTHERS*

When someone comes seeking your forgiveness, you have an obligation to grant forgiveness and extend mercy—even if the person has sinned against you repeatedly and regardless of how severe the sin may have been (Matt. 18:21, 22; Luke 17:4; Eph. 4:32; Col 3:12, 13). Your forgiveness of others is a prerequisite for your receiving God's forgiveness (Matt. 6:14, 15; Luke 11:4; James 2:13).

God does indeed forgive us (Ps. 32:1–5; 103:12; 130:3, 4; Is. 43:25; Jer. 31:34; Eph. 1:7; Col. 1:14; 2:13). We forgive others, if we do not want to disobey God and break our fellowship with Him (Matt. 6:14, 15; Mark 11:25, 26; Luke 17:3, 4). No less important is the willingness for one who blames God for wrongs experienced to remember that the Lord does not direct evil against us, though He may choose to allow us to go through a trial resulting from our own sinful choices or from the sinfulness of the world in which we live (Gen. 50:20; Deut. 32:4; Rom. 8:28, 38, 39). Finally, we must be willing to forgive ourselves since we are finite beings and since our failures often open the door for His glory and provide the environment for our own growth (Phil. 3:12–14).

Love is the prime ingredient in forgiveness (Prov. 10:12). Often the one wounded must forgive with an act of the will, giving time for working through feelings and experiencing healing. Forgiveness comes with the removal of past offenses from the mind (Phil. 3:13), followed by meditation upon Scripture (Ps. 119:157–160), giving over to God our hurts (1 Pet. 2:21–23), praying for the offender (1 Sam. 12:23; Matt. 5:44), and serving as a willing channel for God's grace. God has promised that He will take care of all judgment so that revenge is not an option (Rom. 12:19–21).

Meaningful forgiveness demands thought and planning. Forgiveness is the willingness to search for new solutions. Forgiveness insists on a new way—neither yours nor theirs but one mutually acceptable. You must use words that do not cast blame or create questions (Prov. 15:23). You must be concerned with seeking forgiveness only for your wrong (Ps. 51:1–4). You must remember that a forgiving attitude does not excuse self (Gen. 3:12), defend self (Gen. 3:10), or accuse another (Gen. 3:13).

Seeking forgiveness frees you to receive God's mercy (Prov. 28:13). Showing mercy by a forgiving spirit brings blessing from God and gratitude from the one forgiven. A forgiving spirit brings good to yourself (Prov. 11:17) and to others (15:23).

See also Matt. 5:23, 24; 6:12; 2 Cor. 2:3–11; charts on Your Path to Freedom; Journey to Forgiveness; notes on Communication (Prov. 15); Conflict (Song 5; Matt. 18); Forgiveness (Ps. 51); Friendship (Luke 1)

Jesus a Third Time Predicts His Death and Resurrection

31Then He took the twelve aside and said to them, "Behold, we are going up to Jerusalem, and all things that are written by the prophets concerning the Son of Man will be accomplished. 32For He will be delivered to the Gentiles and will be mocked and insulted and spit upon. 33They will scourge *Him* and kill Him. And the third day He will rise again."

34But they understood none of these things; this saying was hidden from them, and they did not know the things which were spoken.

A Blind Man Receives His Sight

35Then it happened, as He was coming near Jericho, that a certain blind man sat by the road begging. 36And hearing a multitude passing by, he asked what it meant. 37So they told him that Jesus of Nazareth was passing by. 38And he cried out, saying, "Jesus, Son of David, have mercy on me!"

39Then those who went before warned him that he should be quiet; but he cried out all the more, "Son of David, have mercy on me!"

40So Jesus stood still and commanded him to be brought to Him. And when he had come near, He asked him, 41saying, "What do you want Me to do for you?"

He said, "Lord, that I may receive my sight."

42Then Jesus said to him, "Receive your sight; your faith has made you well." 43And immediately he received his sight, and followed Him, glorifying God. And all the people, when they saw *it*, gave praise to God.

Jesus Comes to Zacchaeus' House

19 Then *Jesus* entered and passed through Jericho. 2Now behold, *there was* a man named Zacchaeus who was a chief tax collector, and he was rich. 3And he sought to see who Jesus was, but could not because of the crowd, for he was of short stature. 4So he ran ahead and climbed up into a sycamore tree to see Him, for He was going to pass that *way.* 5And when Jesus came to the place, He looked up and saw him,a and said to him, "Zacchaeus, make haste and come down, for today I must stay at your house." 6So he made haste and came down, and received Him joyfully. 7But when they saw *it,* they all complained, saying, "He has gone to be a guest with a man who is a sinner."

19:5 aNU-Text omits *and saw him.*

⁸Then Zacchaeus stood and said to the Lord, "Look, Lord, I give half of my goods to the poor; and if I have taken anything from anyone by false accusation, I restore fourfold."

⁹And Jesus said to him, "Today salvation has come to this house, because he also is a son of Abraham; ¹⁰for the Son of Man has come to seek and to save that which was lost."

The Parable of the Minas

¹¹Now as they heard these things, He spoke another parable, because He was near Jerusalem and because they thought the kingdom of God would appear immediately. ¹²Therefore He said: "A certain nobleman went into a far country to receive for himself a kingdom and to return. ¹³So he called ten of his servants, delivered to them ten minas,ᵃ and said to them, 'Do business till I come.' ¹⁴But his citizens hated him, and sent a delegation after him, saying, 'We will not have this *man* to reign over us.'

¹⁵"And so it was that when he returned, having received the kingdom, he then commanded these servants, to whom he had given the money, to be called to him, that he might know how much every man had gained by trading. ¹⁶Then came the first, saying, 'Master, your mina has earned ten minas.' ¹⁷And he said to him, 'Well *done,* good servant; because you were faithful in a very little, have authority over ten cities.' ¹⁸And the second came, saying, 'Master, your mina has earned five minas.' ¹⁹Likewise he said to him, 'You also be over five cities.'

²⁰"Then another came, saying, 'Master, here is your mina, which I have kept put away in a handkerchief. ²¹For I feared you, because you are an austere man. You collect what you did not deposit, and reap what you did not sow.' ²²And he said to him, 'Out of your own mouth I will judge you, *you* wicked servant. You knew that I was an austere man, collecting what I did not deposit and reaping what I did not sow. ²³Why then did you not put my money in the bank, that at my coming I might have collected it with interest?'

²⁴"And he said to those who stood by, 'Take the mina from him, and give *it* to him who has ten minas.' ²⁵(But they said to him, 'Master, he has ten minas.') ²⁶For I say to you, that to everyone who has will be given; and from him who does not have, even what he has will be taken away from him. ²⁷But bring here those enemies of mine, who did not want me to reign over them, and slay *them* before me.'"

The Triumphal Entry

²⁸When He had said this, He went on ahead, going up to Jerusalem. ²⁹And it came to pass, when He drew near to Bethphageᵃ and Bethany, at the mountain called Olivet, *that* He sent two of His disciples, ³⁰saying, "Go into the village opposite *you,* where as you enter you will find a colt tied, on which no one has ever sat. Loose it and bring *it* here. ³¹And if anyone asks you, 'Why are you loosing *it?*' thus you shall say to him, 'Because the Lord has need of it.'"

³²So those who were sent went their way and found *it* just as He had said to them. ³³But as they were loosing the colt, the owners of it said to them, "Why are you loosing the colt?"

³⁴And they said, "The Lord has need of him." ³⁵Then they brought him to Jesus. And they threw their own clothes on the colt, and they set Jesus on him. ³⁶And as He went, *many* spread their clothes on the road.

³⁷Then, as He was now drawing near the descent of the Mount of Olives, the whole multitude of the disciples began to rejoice and praise God with a loud voice for all the mighty works they had seen, ³⁸saying:

" 'Blessed is the King who comes in the name of the
LORD!'ᵃ
Peace in heaven and glory in the highest!"

³⁹And some of the Pharisees called to Him from the crowd, "Teacher, rebuke Your disciples."

⁴⁰But He answered and said to them, "I tell you that if these should keep silent, the stones would immediately cry out."

Jesus Weeps over Jerusalem

⁴¹Now as He drew near, He saw the city and wept over it, ⁴²saying, "If you had known, even you,

---

19:13 ᵃThe *mina* (Greek *mna,* Hebrew *minah*) was worth about three months' salary.   19:29 ᵃM-Text reads *Bethsphage.*   19:38 ᵃPsalm 118:26

19:20, 21 The mina was worth about 100 drachmas, or three months' wages (Matt. 25:14–30, note; see chart, Money and Measurements in the Bible).

19:29 Bethphage was near Bethany, although the exact location is unknown. The village of Bethany, a suburb of Jerusalem, was two or three miles from Jerusalem near the Mount of Olives on Jerusalem's east side. To enter Jerusalem, Jesus had to go down the Mount of Olives, through the Kidron valley (a deep ravine), and through the Eastern Gate (later called the "Golden Gate").

19:30–36 The village opposite probably referred to Bethphage. The loan of the colt was seemingly prearranged with the phrase "because the Lord has need of it" as a password (v. 31). The donkey symbolized that Jesus came in peace. The colt had never been ridden; thus it could be used for a sacred purpose (see Zech. 9:9). The disciples' clothes made a saddle for Jesus (Luke 20:35). "Spreading their clothes on the road" was an act of honor and made a triumphal carpet (v. 36).

Good financial planning is a part of wise stewardship. To be a truly effective steward, you must believe unequivocally that the money being managed is someone else's money—God's money. Having this perspective gives a person the freedom to use finances as a tool to accomplish God's purposes, recognizing that no one comes into this world with any possessions, and no one will leave with anything (Eccl. 5:15).

God has entrusted each person with certain resources. Money is something that God uses to test your ability to handle properly the other gifts He desires to give you (Luke 16:11). One day He will ask for an accounting of how you managed the resources He has given you (Luke 19:11–26). A wife who manages resources wisely is a blessing to her husband and family (Prov. 31:28).

You are wise to remember:

- The earth and all its fullness is the Lord's (Ps. 24:1). Every resource, even money, is His, and you are simply stewards of His resources.
- Avoid an overly consumptive lifestyle. The Bible teaches moderation in all things (1 Cor. 9:25).
- Avoid debt (Prov. 22:7; Rom. 13:8).
- Maintain a savings program. (Prov. 12:11).
- Set long-term goals (Prov. 13:22).
  See also notes on Debt (Ps. 37); Goal Setting (Is. 58); Priorities (Matt. 6)

especially in this your day, the things *that make* for your peace! But now they are hidden from your eyes. [43]For days will come upon you when your enemies will build an embankment around you, surround you and close you in on every side, [44]and level you, and your children within you, to the ground; and they will not leave in you one stone upon another, because you did not know the time of your visitation."

Jesus Cleanses the Temple

[45]Then He went into the temple and began to drive out those who bought and sold in it,[a] [46]saying to them, "It is written, *'My house is*[a] *a house of prayer,'*[b] but you have made it a *'den of thieves.'*"[c]

[47]And He was teaching daily in the temple. But the chief priests, the scribes, and the leaders of the people sought to destroy Him, [48]and were unable to do anything; for all the people were very attentive to hear Him.

Jesus' Authority Questioned

20 Now it happened on one of those days, as He taught the people in the temple and preached the gospel, *that* the chief priests and the scribes, together with the elders, confronted *Him* [2]and spoke to Him, saying, "Tell us, by what authority are You doing these things? Or who is he who gave You this authority?"

[3]But He answered and said to them, "I also will ask you one thing, and answer Me: [4]The baptism of John—was it from heaven or from men?"

[5]And they reasoned among themselves, saying, "If we say, 'From heaven,' He will say, 'Why then[a] did you not believe him?' [6]But if we say, 'From men,' all the people will stone us, for they are persuaded that John was a prophet." [7]So they answered that they did not know where *it was* from.

[8]And Jesus said to them, "Neither will I tell you by what authority I do these things."

The Parable of the Wicked Vinedressers

[9]Then He began to tell the people this parable: "A certain man planted a vineyard, leased it to vinedressers, and went into a far country for a long time. [10]Now at vintage-time he sent a servant to the vinedressers, that they might give him some of the fruit of the vineyard. But the vinedressers beat him and sent *him* away empty-handed. [11]Again he sent another servant; and they beat him also, treated *him* shamefully, and sent *him* away empty-handed. [12]And again he sent a third; and they wounded him also and cast *him* out.

[13]"Then the owner of the vineyard said, 'What

·················

19:45 [a]NU-Text reads *those who were selling.*   19:46 [a]NU-Text reads *shall be.* [b]Isaiah 56:7 [c]Jeremiah 7:11   20:5 [a]NU-Text and M-Text omit *then.*

19:45, 46 Every Jewish man coming to Jerusalem for the Passover feast had to pay a temple tax equivalent to two days of a laborer's wage (see chart, Money and Measurements in the Bible). Many types of currencies were circulating, and, since only special temple coins were acceptable, money changers could charge a fee for the necessary exchange. Money changers could make handsome profits at the expense of the people. A temple visit usually involved a sacrifice. If a man brought his own animal, the temple authorities would inspect it for perfection. To make sure an animal passed inspection, many people bought their animal sacrifices at booths set up in the temple. However, these animal sellers often charged outrageous prices, thus making a high profit for themselves. Jesus forcefully drove out those who exploited the worshipers.

shall I do? I will send my beloved son. Probably they will respect *him* when they see him.' ¹⁴But when the vinedressers saw him, they reasoned among themselves, saying, 'This is the heir. Come, let us kill him, that the inheritance may be ours.' ¹⁵So they cast him out of the vineyard and killed *him.* Therefore what will the owner of the vineyard do to them? ¹⁶He will come and destroy those vinedressers and give the vineyard to others."

And when they heard *it* they said, "Certainly not!"

¹⁷Then He looked at them and said, "What then is this that is written:

'The stone which the builders rejected
Has become the chief cornerstone'?ᵃ

¹⁸Whoever falls on that stone will be broken; but on whomever it falls, it will grind him to powder."

¹⁹And the chief priests and the scribes that very hour sought to lay hands on Him, but they feared the peopleᵃ— for they knew He had spoken this parable against them.

The Pharisees: Is It Lawful to Pay Taxes to Caesar?

²⁰So they watched *Him,* and sent spies who pretended to be righteous, that they might seize on His words, in order to deliver Him to the power and the authority of the governor. ²¹Then they asked Him, saying, "Teacher, we know that You say and teach rightly, and You do not show personal favoritism, but teach the way of God in truth: ²²Is it lawful for us to pay taxes to Caesar or not?"

²³But He perceived their craftiness, and said to them, "Why do you test Me?ᵃ ²⁴Show Me a denarius. Whose image and inscription does it have?"

They answered and said, "Caesar's."

²⁵And He said to them, "Render therefore to Caesar the things that are Caesar's, and to God the things that are God's."

²⁶But they could not catch Him in His words in the presence of the people. And they marveled at His answer and kept silent.

The Sadducees: What About the Resurrection?

²⁷Then some of the Sadducees, who deny that there is a resurrection, came to *Him* and asked Him, ²⁸saying: "Teacher, Moses wrote to us *that* if a man's brother dies, having a wife, and he dies without children, his brother should take his wife and raise up offspring for his brother. ²⁹Now there were seven brothers. And the first took a wife, and died without children. ³⁰And the secondᵃ took her as wife, and he died childless. ³¹Then the third took her, and in like manner the seven also; and they left no children,ᵃ and died. ³²Last of all the woman died also. ³³Therefore, in the resurrection, whose wife does she become? For all seven had her as wife."

³⁴Jesus answered and said to them, "The sons of this age marry and are given in marriage. ³⁵But those who are counted worthy to attain that age, and the resurrection from the dead, neither marry nor are given in marriage; ³⁶nor can they die anymore, for they are equal to the angels and are sons of God, being sons of the resurrection. ³⁷But even Moses showed in the *burning* bush *passage* that the dead are raised, when he called the Lord *'the God of Abraham, the God of Isaac, and the God of Jacob.'*ᵃ ³⁸For He is not the God of the dead but of the living, for all live to Him."

³⁹Then some of the scribes answered and said, "Teacher, You have spoken well." ⁴⁰But after that they dared not question Him anymore.

Jesus: How Can David Call His Descendant Lord?

⁴¹And He said to them, "How can they say that the Christ is the Son of David? ⁴²Now David himself said in the Book of Psalms:

'The Lord said to my Lord,
"Sit at My right hand,
⁴³Till I make Your enemies Your footstool." 'ᵃ

⁴⁴Therefore David calls Him *'Lord';* how is He then his Son?"

Beware of the Scribes

⁴⁵Then, in the hearing of all the people, He said to His disciples, ⁴⁶"Beware of the scribes, who desire to go around in long robes, love greetings in the marketplaces, the best seats in the synagogues, and the best places at feasts, ⁴⁷who devour widows' houses, and for a pretense make long prayers. These will receive greater condemnation."

•••••••••••••••••••••
20:17 ᵃPsalm 118:22   20:19 ᵃM-Text reads *but they were afraid.*
20:23 ᵃNU-Text omits *Why do you test Me?*   20:30 ᵃNU-Text ends
verse 30 here.   20:31 ᵃNU-Text and M-Text read *the seven also left
no children.*   20:37 ᵃExodus 3:6, 15   20:43 ᵃPsalm 110:1

20:22 **Jews,** ages 14 to 65, were required to pay a tax to Caesar. Jews hated to pay this poll tax, which was one denarius (see chart, Money and Measurements in the Bible). Tiberius was the emperor at that time. Embossed on the front of the coin was the face of Caesar Tiberius, which demonstrated this right to impose the tax (v. 24).

20:27 **The Sadducees** (lit. "righteous ones") claimed to be descendants of Zadok, high priest under David (see chart, Jewish Sects). They organized shortly after the Maccabean revolt (167–160 B.C.). They disappeared in A.D. 70 when the Jerusalem temple was destroyed. They were a wealthy, politically active, materialistic group who opposed both the Pharisees and Jesus. They denied the existence of angels and demons, life after death, and bodily resurrection.

The Widow's Two Mites

21 And He looked up and saw the rich putting their gifts into the treasury, [2]and He saw also a certain poor widow putting in two mites. [3]So He said, "Truly I say to you that this poor widow has put in more than all; [4]for all these out of their abundance have put in offerings for God,[a] but she out of her poverty put in all the livelihood that she had."

Jesus Predicts the Destruction of the Temple

[5]Then, as some spoke of the temple, how it was adorned with beautiful stones and donations, He said, [6]"These things which you see— the days will come in which not *one* stone shall be left upon another that shall not be thrown down."

The Signs of the Times and the End of the Age

[7]So they asked Him, saying, "Teacher, but when will these things be? And what sign *will there be* when these things are about to take place?"

[8]And He said: "Take heed that you not be deceived. For many will come in My name, saying, 'I am *He*,' and, 'The time has drawn near.' Therefore[a] do not go after them. [9]But when you hear of wars and commotions, do not be terrified; for these things must come to pass first, but the end *will* not *come* immediately."

[10]Then He said to them, "Nation will rise against nation, and kingdom against kingdom. [11]And there will be great earthquakes in various places, and famines and pestilences; and there will be fearful sights and great signs from heaven. [12]But before all these things, they will lay their hands on you and persecute *you*, delivering *you* up to the synagogues and prisons. You will be brought before kings and rulers for My name's sake. [13]But it will turn out for you as an occasion for testimony. [14]Therefore settle *it* in your hearts not to meditate beforehand on what you will answer; [15]for I will give you a mouth and wisdom which all your adversaries will not be able to contradict or resist. [16]You will be betrayed even by parents and brothers, relatives and friends; and they will put *some* of you to death. [17]And you will be hated by all for My name's sake. [18]But not a hair of your head shall be lost. [19]By your patience possess your souls.

The Destruction of Jerusalem

[20]"But when you see Jerusalem surrounded by armies, then know that its desolation is near.

[21]Then let those who are in Judea flee to the mountains, let those who are in the midst of her depart, and let not those who are in the country enter her. [22]For these are the days of vengeance, that all things which are written may be fulfilled. [23]But woe to those who are pregnant and to those who are nursing babies in those days! For there will be great distress in the land and wrath upon this people. [24]And they will fall by the edge of the sword, and be led away captive into all nations. And Jerusalem will be trampled by Gentiles until the times of the Gentiles are fulfilled.

The Coming of the Son of Man

[25]"And there will be signs in the sun, in the moon, and in the stars; and on the earth distress of nations, with perplexity, the sea and the waves roaring; [26]men's hearts failing them from fear and the expectation of those things which are coming on the earth, for the powers of the heavens will be shaken. [27]Then they will see the Son of Man coming in a cloud with power and great glory. [28]Now when these things begin to happen, look up and lift up your heads, because your redemption draws near."

The Parable of the Fig Tree

[29]Then He spoke to them a parable: "Look at the fig tree, and all the trees. [30]When they are already budding, you see and know for yourselves that summer is now near. [31]So you also, when you see these things happening, know that the kingdom of God is near. [32]Assuredly, I say to you, this generation will by no means pass away till all things take place. [33]Heaven and earth will pass away, but My words will by no means pass away.

The Importance of Watching

[34]"But take heed to yourselves, lest your hearts be weighed down with carousing, drunkenness, and cares of this life, and that Day come on you unexpectedly. [35]For it will come as a snare on all those who dwell on the face of the whole earth. [36]Watch therefore, and pray always that you may be counted worthy[a] to escape all these things that will come to pass, and to stand before the Son of Man."

[37]And in the daytime He was teaching in the

21:4 [a]NU-Text omits *for God.* 21:8 [a]NU-Text omits *Therefore.* 21:36 [a]NU-Text reads *may have strength.*

21:1, 2 The treasury was the part of the Court of the Women that held 13 collection boxes known as "The Trumpets." Each box stated how its contents would be spent. The widow represented the poorest of the poor in 1st-century Judea (see Mark 12:41–44, note; Mark 12, Widow with Two Mites). A widow could find few ways to earn money. The mite was the least valuable coin in use (see chart, Money and Measurements in the Bible).

21:8 Jesus warned the people about false teachers who would come and claim to be the Messiah, giving a prediction about the end time. He forewarned His disciples about the coming persecution they would face from both the Gentiles and the Jews. The years between the Crucifixion and A.D. 70 proved a harsh period of persecution for believers.

THE LAST WEEK IN THE LIFE OF JESUS

A.D. 33 IN JERUSALEM

SUNDAY	• The triumphal entry into Jerusalem (Mark 11:1–11).
MONDAY	• Cleansing the temple in Jerusalem (Mark 11:15–19).
TUESDAY	• Challenge of Jesus' authority before the Sanhedrin (Luke 20:1–8). • Foretelling of the destruction of Jerusalem and Jesus' return (Matt. 24:15–28). • Anointing of Jesus at Bethany (John 12:2–8). • Judas' bargain with the Jewish rulers to betray Jesus (Luke 22:3–6).
WEDNESDAY	
THURSDAY	• The Passover meal with His disciples and institution of the Memorial Supper (Mark 14:22–26; John 13:1–30). • Prayer in Gethsemane for His disciples (John 17:1–26).
FRIDAY	• His betrayal and arrest in Gethsemane (Mark 14:43–50). • Questioning by Annas, the former high priest (John 18:12–24). • Condemnation by Caiaphas and the Sanhedrin (Mark 14:53–65). • Peter's denial (John 18:15–27). • Formal condemnation by the Sanhedrin (Luke 22:66–71). • Judas' suicide (Matt. 27:3–10). • The trial of Jesus before Pilate (Luke 23:1–5). • Jesus' appearance before Herod Antipas (Luke 23:6–12). • Formal sentence to death by Pilate (Luke 23:13–25). • Jesus' Crucifixion between two thieves (Mark 15:16–27). • The tearing of the temple's veil (Matt. 27:51–56). • Jesus' burial in the tomb of Joseph of Arimathea (John 19:31–42).
SATURDAY	
SUNDAY	• Jesus' Resurrection from the dead (Luke 24:1–9).

temple, but at night He went out and stayed on the mountain called Olivet. ³⁸Then early in the morning all the people came to Him in the temple to hear Him.

The Plot to Kill Jesus

22 Now the Feast of Unleavened Bread drew near, which is called Passover. ²And the chief priests and the scribes sought how they might kill Him, for they feared the people.

³Then Satan entered Judas, surnamed Iscariot, who was numbered among the twelve. ⁴So he went his way and conferred with the chief priests and captains, how he might betray Him to them. ⁵And they were glad, and agreed to give him money. ⁶So he promised and sought opportunity to betray Him to them in the absence of the multitude.

Jesus and His Disciples Prepare the Passover

⁷Then came the Day of Unleavened Bread, when the Passover must be killed. ⁸And He sent Peter and John, saying, "Go and prepare the Passover for us, that we may eat."

22:1 Jews celebrated Passover and the Feast of Unleavened Bread for seven days around the middle of March ("Nisan," see charts, The Jewish Sacred Calendar; The Feasts of Israel). It was the most important of Hebrew feasts. Large crowds attended the festival. To remember their deliverance from Egyptian slavery, they ate unleavened bread as their ancestors had done on the night of their hasty departure from Egypt (see Ex. 12).

[9]So they said to Him, "Where do You want us to prepare?"

[10]And He said to them, "Behold, when you have entered the city, a man will meet you carrying a pitcher of water; follow him into the house which he enters. [11]Then you shall say to the master of the house, 'The Teacher says to you, "Where is the guest room where I may eat the Passover with My disciples?" ' [12]Then he will show you a large, furnished upper room; there make ready."

[13]So they went and found it just as He had said to them, and they prepared the Passover.

Jesus Institutes the Lord's Supper

[14]When the hour had come, He sat down, and the twelve[a] apostles with Him. [15]Then He said to them, "With *fervent* desire I have desired to eat this Passover with you before I suffer; [16]for I say to you, I will no longer eat of it until it is fulfilled in the kingdom of God."

[17]Then He took the cup, and gave thanks, and said, "Take this and divide *it* among yourselves; [18]for I say to you,[a] I will not drink of the fruit of the vine until the kingdom of God comes."

[19]And He took bread, gave thanks and broke *it,* and gave *it* to them, saying, "This is My body which is given for you; do this in remembrance of Me."

[20]Likewise He also *took* the cup after supper, saying, "This cup *is* the new covenant in My blood, which is shed for you. [21]But behold, the hand of My betrayer *is* with Me on the table. [22]And truly the Son of Man goes as it has been determined, but woe to that man by whom He is betrayed!"

[23]Then they began to question among themselves, which of them it was who would do this thing.

The Disciples Argue About Greatness

[24]Now there was also a dispute among them, as to which of them should be considered the greatest. [25]And He said to them, "The kings of the Gentiles exercise lordship over them, and those who exercise authority over them are called 'benefactors.' [26]But not so *among* you; on the contrary, he who is greatest among you, let him be as the younger, and he who governs as he who serves. [27]For who *is* greater, he who sits at the table, or he who serves? *Is* it not he who sits at the table? Yet I am among you as the One who serves.

[28]"But you are those who have continued with Me in My trials. [29]And I bestow upon you a kingdom, just as My Father bestowed *one* upon Me, [30]that you may eat and drink at My table in My kingdom, and sit on thrones judging the twelve tribes of Israel."

Jesus Predicts Peter's Denial

[31]And the Lord said,[a] "Simon, Simon! Indeed, Satan has asked for you, that he may sift *you* as wheat. [32]But I have prayed for you, that your faith should not fail; and when you have returned to *Me,* strengthen your brethren."

[33]But he said to Him, "Lord, I am ready to go with You, both to prison and to death."

[34]Then He said, "I tell you, Peter, the rooster shall not crow this day before you will deny three times that you know Me."

Supplies for the Road

[35]And He said to them, "When I sent you without money bag, knapsack, and sandals, did you lack anything?"

So they said, "Nothing."

[36]Then He said to them, "But now, he who has a money bag, let him take *it,* and likewise a knapsack; and he who has no sword, let him sell his garment and buy one. [37]For I say to you that this which is written must still be accomplished in Me: 'And He was numbered with the transgressors.'[a] For the things concerning Me have an end."

[38]So they said, "Lord, look, here *are* two swords."

And He said to them, "It is enough."

The Prayer in the Garden

[39]Coming out, He went to the Mount of Olives, as He was accustomed, and His disciples also followed Him. [40]When He came to the place, He said to them, "Pray that you may not enter into temptation."

[41]And He was withdrawn from them about a stone's throw, and He knelt down and prayed, [42]saying, "Father, if it is Your will, take this cup away from Me; nevertheless not My will, but Yours, be done." [43]Then an angel appeared to Him from heaven, strengthening Him. [44]And being in agony, He prayed more earnestly. Then His sweat became like great drops of blood falling down to the ground.[a]

22:14 [a]NU-Text omits *twelve.*   22:18 [a]NU-Text adds *from now on.*
22:31 [a]NU-Text omits *And the Lord said.*   22:37 [a]Isaiah 53:12
22:44 [a]NU-Text brackets verses 43 and 44 as not in the original text.

22:10, 11 Jesus and His disciples needed a room in which to celebrate the Passover meal. To secure a room, Jesus told them to look for a man "carrying a pitcher of water," possibly by prearrangement (v. 10). To meet a man carrying such a heavy pitcher was highly unusual, since this was considered a woman's job.

22:39–43 The cup represents Jesus' suffering. Jesus struggled so intensely in prayer that an angel appeared to give Him additional strength. The Garden of Gethsemane was located on the Mount of Olives (v. 39; see Matt. 26:36–44, note).

45When He rose up from prayer, and had come to His disciples, He found them sleeping from sorrow. 46Then He said to them, "Why do you sleep? Rise and pray, lest you enter into temptation."

Betrayal and Arrest in Gethsemane

47And while He was still speaking, behold, a multitude; and he who was called Judas, one of the twelve, went before them and drew near to Jesus to kiss Him. 48But Jesus said to him, "Judas, are you betraying the Son of Man with a kiss?"

49When those around Him saw what was going to happen, they said to Him, "Lord, shall we strike with the sword?" 50And one of them struck the servant of the high priest and cut off his right ear.

51But Jesus answered and said, "Permit even this." And He touched his ear and healed him.

52Then Jesus said to the chief priests, captains of the temple, and the elders who had come to Him, "Have you come out, as against a robber, with swords and clubs? 53When I was with you daily in the temple, you did not try to seize Me. But this is your hour, and the power of darkness."

Peter Denies Jesus, and Weeps Bitterly

54Having arrested Him, they led *Him* and brought Him into the high priest's house. But Peter followed at a distance. 55Now when they had kindled a fire in the midst of the courtyard and sat down together, Peter sat among them. 56And a certain servant girl, seeing him as he sat by the fire, looked intently at him and said, "This man was also with Him."

57But he denied Him,a saying, "Woman, I do not know Him."

58And after a little while another saw him and said, "You also are of them."

But Peter said, "Man, I am not!"

59Then after about an hour had passed, another confidently affirmed, saying, "Surely this *fellow* also was with Him, for he is a Galilean."

60But Peter said, "Man, I do not know what you are saying!"

Immediately, while he was still speaking, the roostera crowed. 61And the Lord turned and looked at Peter. Then Peter remembered the word of the Lord, how He had said to him, "Before the rooster crows,a you will deny Me three times." 62So Peter went out and wept bitterly.

Jesus Mocked and Beaten

63Now the men who held Jesus mocked Him and beat Him. 64And having blindfolded Him, they struck Him on the face and asked Him,a saying, "Prophesy! Who is the one who struck You?" 65And many other things they blasphemously spoke against Him.

Jesus Faces the Sanhedrin

66As soon as it was day, the elders of the people, both chief priests and scribes, came together and led Him into their council, saying, 67"If You are the Christ, tell us."

But He said to them, "If I tell you, you will by no means believe. 68And if I also ask *you,* you will by no means answer Me or let *Me* go.a 69Hereafter the Son of Man will sit on the right hand of the power of God."

70Then they all said, "Are You then the Son of God?"

So He said to them, "You *rightly* say that I am."

71And they said, "What further testimony do we need? For we have heard it ourselves from His own mouth."

Jesus Handed Over to Pontius Pilate

23 Then the whole multitude of them arose and led Him to Pilate. 2And they began to accuse Him, saying, "We found this *fellow* perverting thea nation, and forbidding to pay taxes to Caesar, saying that He Himself is Christ, a King."

3Then Pilate asked Him, saying, "Are You the King of the Jews?"

He answered him and said, "*It is as* you say."

4So Pilate said to the chief priests and the crowd, "I find no fault in this Man."

5But they were the more fierce, saying, "He stirs up the people, teaching throughout all Judea, beginning from Galilee to this place."

Jesus Faces Herod

6When Pilate heard of Galilee,a he asked if the Man were a Galilean. 7And as soon as he knew that He belonged to Herod's jurisdiction, he sent Him to Herod, who was also in Jerusalem at that time.

••••••••••••••••

22:57 aNU-Text reads *denied it.* 22:60 aNU-Text and M-Text read *a rooster.* 22:61 aNU-Text adds *today.* 22:64 aNU-Text reads *And having blindfolded Him, they asked Him.* 22:68 aNU-Text omits *also* and *Me or let Me go.* 23:2 aNU-Text reads *our.* 23:6 aNU-Text omits *of Galilee.*

22:47, 48 A kiss from a student to his master was a sign of respect. The kiss also represented acceptance and reverence. In the early church, the "holy kiss" was a sign used to greet others, impart blessing, and express Christian unity (Rom. 16:16; 2 Cor. 13:12; 1 Thess. 5:26). The fact that Judas, a disciple, would betray his Master (Jesus) with a kiss heightened the atrocity.

23:1 Pontius Pilate was governor (actually "procurator") of Judea (see chart, New Testament Political Rulers). Coming to power in A.D. 26, Pilate unjustly provoked the Jews and made life difficult for them. Jesus was brought to Pilate because the Jews at that time had no authority to enforce capital punishment; only Pilate could authorize the death sentence. In the eyes of the Jews, Jesus was guilty of blasphemy. But He had not been found guilty of any crime warranting Roman intervention.

[8]Now when Herod saw Jesus, he was exceedingly glad; for he had desired for a long *time* to see Him, because he had heard many things about Him, and he hoped to see some miracle done by Him. [9]Then he questioned Him with many words, but He answered him nothing. [10]And the chief priests and scribes stood and vehemently accused Him. [11]Then Herod, with his men of war, treated Him with contempt and mocked *Him,* arrayed Him in a gorgeous robe, and sent Him back to Pilate. [12]That very day Pilate and Herod became friends with each other, for previously they had been at enmity with each other.

Taking the Place of Barabbas

[13]Then Pilate, when he had called together the chief priests, the rulers, and the people, [14]said to them, "You have brought this Man to me, as one who misleads the people. And indeed, having examined *Him* in your presence, I have found no fault in this Man concerning those things of which you accuse Him; [15]no, neither did Herod, for I sent you back to him;[a] and indeed nothing deserving of death has been done by Him. [16]I will therefore chastise Him and release *Him*" [17](for it was necessary for him to release one to them at the feast).[a]

[18]And they all cried out at once, saying, "Away with this *Man,* and release to us Barabbas"— [19]who had been thrown into prison for a certain rebellion made in the city, and for murder.

[20]Pilate, therefore, wishing to release Jesus, again called out to them. [21]But they shouted, saying, "Crucify *Him,* crucify Him!"

[22]Then he said to them the third time, "Why, what evil has He done? I have found no reason for death in Him. I will therefore chastise Him and let *Him* go."

[23]But they were insistent, demanding with loud voices that He be crucified. And the voices of these men and of the chief priests prevailed.[a] [24]So Pilate gave sentence that it should be as they requested. [25]And he released to them[a] the one they requested, who for rebellion and murder had been thrown into prison; but he delivered Jesus to their will.

The King on a Cross

[26]Now as they led Him away, they laid hold of a certain man, Simon a Cyrenian, who was coming from the country, and on him they laid the cross that he might bear *it* after Jesus.

[27]And a great multitude of the people followed Him, and women who also mourned and lamented Him. [28]But Jesus, turning to them, said, "Daughters of Jerusalem, do not weep for Me, but weep for yourselves and for your children. [29]For indeed the days are coming in which they will say, 'Blessed *are* the barren, wombs that never bore, and breasts which never nursed!' [30]Then they will begin '*to say to the mountains, "Fall on us!" and to the hills, "Cover us!"* '[a] [31]For if they do these things in the green wood, what will be done in the dry?"

[32]There were also two others, criminals, led with Him to be put to death. [33]And when they had come to the place called Calvary, there they crucified Him, and the criminals, one on the right hand and the other on the left. [34]Then Jesus said, "Father, forgive them, for they do not know what they do."[a]

And they divided His garments and cast lots. [35]And the people stood looking on. But even the rulers with them sneered, saying, "He saved others; let Him save Himself if He is the Christ, the chosen of God."

[36]The soldiers also mocked Him, coming and offering Him sour wine, [37]and saying, "If You are the King of the Jews, save Yourself."

[38]And an inscription also was written over Him in letters of Greek, Latin, and Hebrew:[a]

THIS IS THE KING OF THE JEWS.

[39]Then one of the criminals who were hanged blasphemed Him, saying, "If You are the Christ,[a] save Yourself and us."

[40]But the other, answering, rebuked him, saying, "Do you not even fear God, seeing you are under the same condemnation? [41]And we indeed justly, for we receive the due reward of our deeds; but this Man has done nothing wrong." [42]Then he said to Jesus, "Lord,[a] remember me when You come into Your kingdom."

[43]And Jesus said to him, "Assuredly, I say to you, today you will be with Me in Paradise."

••••••••••••••••••••

23:15 [a]NU-Text reads *for he sent Him back to us.* 23:17 [a]NU-Text omits verse 17. 23:23 [a]NU-Text omits *and of the chief priests.* 23:25 [a]NU-Text and M-Text omit *to them.* 23:30 [a]Hosea 10:8 23:34 [a]NU-Text brackets the first sentence as a later addition. 23:38 [a]NU-Text omits *written and in letters of Greek, Latin, and Hebrew.* 23:39 [a]NU-Text reads *Are You not the Christ?* 23:42 [a]NU-Text reads *And he said, "Jesus, remember me.*

23:21 Crucifixion, though once considered too brutal a penalty for anyone but slaves, had become a common form of capital punishment to execute any enemy of the state. In the ancient world, crucifixion proved a painful and humiliating way to die. The condemned criminal was made to carry his own cross to the place of execution. Too weak from the beating to carry His Cross all the way to the execution site, Jesus was helped by a passerby, Simon from Cyrene, a city in northern Africa (v. 26).

23:42, 43 Matthew and Mark noted that the thieves, crucified on each side of Jesus, abused Him (Matt. 27:44; Mark 15:32). Only Luke recorded that one of them repented and sought mercy as he suffered death on the cross. Jesus assured him of salvation and a place in "Paradise."

*In all dangers, troubles, and extremities, which fell to our Saviour,
when all men fled Him, living or dead, women never forsook Him.*

—Ester Sowerman, 1617

Jesus Dies on the Cross

[44]Now it was[a] about the sixth hour, and there was darkness over all the earth until the ninth hour. [45]Then the sun was darkened,[a] and the veil of the temple was torn in two. [46]And when Jesus had cried out with a loud voice, He said, "Father, *'into Your hands I commit My spirit.' "*[a] Having said this, He breathed His last.

[47]So when the centurion saw what had happened, he glorified God, saying, "Certainly this was a righteous Man!"

[48]And the whole crowd who came together to that sight, seeing what had been done, beat their breasts and returned. [49]But all His acquaintances, and the women who followed Him from Galilee, stood at a distance, watching these things.

Jesus Buried in Joseph's Tomb

[50]Now behold, *there was* a man named Joseph, a council member, a good and just man. [51]He had not consented to their decision and deed. *He was* from Arimathea, a city of the Jews, who himself was also waiting[a] for the kingdom of God. [52]This man went to Pilate and asked for the body of Jesus. [53]Then he took it down, wrapped it in linen, and laid it in a tomb *that was* hewn out of the rock, where no one had ever lain before. [54]That day was the Preparation, and the Sabbath drew near.

[55]And the women who had come with Him from Galilee followed after, and they observed the tomb and how His body was laid. [56]Then they returned and prepared spices and fragrant oils. And they rested on the Sabbath according to the commandment.

He Is Risen

24 Now on the first *day* of the week, very early in the morning, they, and certain *other*

women with them,[a] came to the tomb bringing the spices which they had prepared. [2]But they found the stone rolled away from the tomb. [3]Then they went in and did not find the body of the Lord Jesus. [4]And it happened, as they were greatly[a] perplexed about this, that behold, two men stood by them in shining garments. [5]Then, as they were afraid and bowed *their* faces to the earth, they said to them, "Why do you seek the living among the dead? [6]He is not here, but is risen! Remember how He spoke to you when He was still in Galilee, [7]saying, 'The Son of Man must be delivered into the hands of sinful men, and be crucified, and the third day rise again.' "

[8]And they remembered His words. [9]Then they returned from the tomb and told all these things to the eleven and to all the rest. [10]It was Mary Magdalene, Joanna, Mary *the mother* of James, and the other *women* with them, who told these things to the apostles. [11]And their words seemed to them like idle tales, and they did not believe them. [12]But Peter arose and ran to the tomb; and stooping down, he saw the linen cloths lying[a] by themselves; and he departed, marveling to himself at what had happened.

The Road to Emmaus

[13]Now behold, two of them were traveling that same day to a village called Emmaus, which was seven miles[a] from Jerusalem. [14]And they talked together of all these things which had happened. [15]So it was, while they conversed and reasoned, that Jesus Himself drew near and went with them.

23:44 [a]NU-Text adds *already*.   23:45 [a]NU-Text reads *obscured*. 23:46 [a]Psalm 31:5   23:51 [a]NU-Text reads *who was waiting*.   24:1 [a]NU-Text omits *and certain other women with them*.   24:4 [a]NU-Text omits *greatly*.   24:12 [a]NU-Text omits *lying*.   24:13 [a]Literally sixty stadia

23:45 The veil of the temple referred to the thick curtain used to separate the Most Holy Place (the innermost sanctuary where God's presence was uniquely found) from the rest of the temple (see chart, The Plan of Herod's Temple). Only on the Day of Atonement could the high priest enter the Most Holy Place to offer sacrifices to God on behalf of himself, his family, and the people of Israel (Lev. 16:2). The offerings restored fellowship with God. The ripping of the "veil" in two symbolized a great truth: Through Jesus' death as a sacrifice for sin, people no longer had to depend on a sacrificial system but could instead have direct access to God through Christ (see Rom. 5:2; Eph. 2:18; 3:12).

23:53 Joseph from Arimathea, a wealthy and important member of the Sanhedrin in Jerusalem, was evidently a secret fol-

lower of Jesus. Joseph personally removed Jesus' body from the Cross and, with the help of Nicodemus, another influential follower, prepared the body for burial. Jewish law forbade a crucified body to hang on the cross after sunset. Preparation would include wrapping the body in long strips of linen, with various spices placed within the linen shroud. Joseph placed the body in the tomb he had prepared for himself. Crucified criminals were usually buried in a common place. Tombs at that time were carved out of rock and thus expensive. Some had several compartments that could be used for a number of people. Joseph's tomb was new.

24:13–16 Emmaus seems to have been located about seven miles from Jerusalem. As two unnamed disciples traveled from Jerusalem to Emmaus on the day of Jesus' Resurrection,

¹⁶But their eyes were restrained, so that they did not know Him.

¹⁷And He said to them, "What kind of conversation *is* this that you have with one another as you walk and are sad?"ᵃ

¹⁸Then the one whose name was Cleopas answered and said to Him, "Are You the only stranger in Jerusalem, and have You not known the things which happened there in these days?"

¹⁹And He said to them, "What things?"

So they said to Him, "The things concerning Jesus of Nazareth, who was a Prophet mighty in deed and word before God and all the people, ²⁰and how the chief priests and our rulers delivered Him to be condemned to death, and crucified Him. ²¹But we were hoping that it was He who was going to redeem Israel. Indeed, besides all this, today is the third day since these things happened. ²²Yes, and certain women of our company, who arrived at the tomb early, astonished us. ²³When they did not find His body, they came saying that they had also seen a vision of angels who said He was alive. ²⁴And certain of those *who were* with us went to the tomb and found *it* just as the women had said; but Him they did not see."

²⁵Then He said to them, "O foolish ones, and slow of heart to believe in all that the prophets have spoken! ²⁶Ought not the Christ to have suffered these things and to enter into His glory?" ²⁷And beginning at Moses and all the Prophets, He expounded to them in all the Scriptures the things concerning Himself.

The Disciples' Eyes Opened

²⁸Then they drew near to the village where they were going, and He indicated that He would have gone farther. ²⁹But they constrained Him, saying, "Abide with us, for it is toward evening, and the day is far spent." And He went in to stay with them.

³⁰Now it came to pass, as He sat at the table with them, that He took bread, blessed and broke *it*, and gave it to them. ³¹Then their eyes were opened and they knew Him; and He vanished from their sight.

³²And they said to one another, "Did not our heart burn within us while He talked with us on the road, and while He opened the Scriptures to us?" ³³So they rose up that very hour and returned to Jerusalem, and found the eleven and those *who were* with them gathered together, ³⁴saying, "The Lord is risen indeed, and has appeared to Simon!" ³⁵And they told about the things *that had happened* on the road, and how He was known to them in the breaking of bread.

Jesus Appears to His Disciples

³⁶Now as they said these things, Jesus Himself stood in the midst of them, and said to them, "Peace to you." ³⁷But they were terrified and frightened, and supposed they had seen a spirit. ³⁸And He said to them, "Why are you troubled? And why do doubts arise in your hearts? ³⁹Behold My hands and My feet, that it is I Myself. Handle Me and see, for a spirit does not have flesh and bones as you see I have."

⁴⁰When He had said this, He showed them His hands and His feet.ᵃ ⁴¹But while they still did not believe for joy, and marveled, He said to them, "Have you any food here?" ⁴²So they gave Him a piece of a broiled fish and some honeycomb.ᵃ ⁴³And He took *it* and ate in their presence.

The Scriptures Opened

⁴⁴Then He said to them, "These *are* the words which I spoke to you while I was still with you, that all things must be fulfilled which were written in the Law of Moses and *the* Prophets and *the* Psalms concerning Me." ⁴⁵And He opened their understanding, that they might comprehend the Scriptures.

⁴⁶Then He said to them, "Thus it is written, and thus it was necessary for the Christ to suffer and to riseᵃ from the dead the third day, ⁴⁷and that repentance and remission of sins should be preached in His name to all nations, beginning at Jerusalem. ⁴⁸And you are witnesses of these things. ⁴⁹Behold, I send the Promise of My Father upon you; but tarry in the city of Jerusalemᵃ until you are endued with power from on high."

24:17 ᵃNU-Text reads *as you walk? And they stood still, looking sad.* 24:40 ᵃSome printed New Testaments omit this verse. It is found in nearly all Greek manuscripts. 24:42 ᵃNU-Text omits *and some honeycomb.* 24:46 ᵃNU-Text reads *written, that the Christ should suffer and rise.* 24:49 ᵃNU-Text omits *Jerusalem.*

---

the Lord joined them. At first they did not recognize Him (v. 16). Luke recorded three Resurrection appearances (see chart, The Appearances of the Risen Christ).

24:36–43 The Resurrection of Jesus Christ was a physical reality. When He "stood in the midst of them," the disciples were shocked, "terrified, and frightened" (v. 37). They thought Jesus was a ghost. Jesus read their hearts, and to prove Himself physically alive, He showed them His pierced hands and feet and invited them to "handle" and "see" Him (v. 39). Then He went one step further to dispel their unbelief by asking for and eating food—something no disembodied spirit could do.

24:47 Repentence in the NT distinguishes the changing of direction of life in order to be obedient (Luke 3:8, 9) from the observing of rituals in life with the hope of escaping penalty. "To repent" (Gk. *metamelomai*) expresses regret in the way things turned out (such as in the case of Judas, Matt. 27:3), while another word (Gk. *metanoeō*), means "to change your mind" or "to feel remorse" (Luke 13:3; 2 Cor. 7:10). This is the type of repentance exhibited by the woman of Samaria who

The Ascension

⁵⁰And He led them out as far as Bethany, and He lifted up His hands and blessed them. ⁵¹Now it came to pass, while He blessed them, that He was parted from them and carried up into heaven.

⁵²And they worshiped Him, and returned to Jerusalem with great joy, ⁵³and were continually in the temple praising andᵃ blessing God. Amen.ᵇ

··············

24:53 ᵃNU-Text omits *praising and.* ᵇNU-Text omits *Amen.*

---

bore testimony of what the Messiah had done in her life (John 4:28, 29, 42).

Repentance in the OT is expressed more in the corporate than in the individual sense. The people felt their guilt more as a nation than as individuals, and God's judgment tended to affect the entire nation just as repentance was expressed more as corporate ritual than individual confession (Ezek. 14:1–3). The ritual involved in this repentance was easily distorted so that a genuine change of the heart did not necessarily occur. The prophets warned about the dangers of insincere repentance (Hos. 5:6; 6:6). Ritual alone could not substitute for a heart's determination (2 Cor. 7:10). Turning from sin must be accompanied by turning to the Lord, which in turn manifests itself in a holy or "set apart" lifestyle (Mic. 6:8).

Individual repentance and contrition of heart precede the receiving of God's gifts, for only when we are willing to admit that we *are not* and *cannot* be sufficient in ourselves, can we receive Him who *is* and *can*. Repentance is a continuing action in the lives of believers as we grieve for sins committed against a holy God and daily turn from our sinful natures that are self-dependent to depend upon Christ and what He has done on the Cross. Genuine repentance brings abundant life in Christ (John 10:10).

Repentance, for the Creator God, is the willing of change ("relent" in Ps. 106:45; Jer. 18:8). God is not swayed, as we are, to change His mind based upon whim or reason. However, based upon our obedience, He can remember us in His mercies. On the other hand, as His creation, we repent by changing the will. This repentance, then, means to turn away from a sinful past with sorrow of heart and to embrace joyfully a future in Christ Jesus (Phil. 3:13, 14; see also Ps. 51, Forgiveness; 2 Cor. 7, Guilt; Eph. 2, Salvation).

John

AUTHOR

The apostle John was the son of Zebedee, a seemingly well-to-do man (Mark 1:20), and Salome, who was the sister of Jesus' mother Mary (John 19:25; see also Matt. 27:56, 61; Mark 15:40, 47). John wrote his gospel toward the end of his life. Scholars have long debated the authorship of the gospel since it claims only to have been written by the "beloved disciple" (John 21:20, 24). Clement of Alexandria called the Gospel of John the "spiritual Gospel."

DATE

John (lit. "*Yahweh* has been gracious") was joined by Peter and James in Jesus' inner circle (Mark 5:37; 9:2; 14:33). As fishermen, John and his brother James lived in Capernaum. Jesus labeled them *Boanerges* (lit. "sons of thunder," Mark 3:17). John and Peter were described as "uneducated and untrained men" (Acts 4:13). John referred to himself throughout this gospel as "the disciple whom Jesus loved" (John 21:20, 24). He was an eyewitness to the life and ministry of Jesus and ministered longer than any other disciple. John was present at the Last Supper (John 13:23–26), stood at the Cross with Jesus' mother (John 19:25–27), accompanied Peter to the empty tomb (John 20:2–10), and recognized Jesus after His Resurrection (John 21:7).

John is also credited with writing the epistles of First, Second, and Third John as well as the Book of Revelation. He played an active role in the Jerusalem church (Acts 3:1) and later served as pastor of the church at Ephesus. The Book of Revelation was written while he was in exile on the island of Patmos during the reign of Emperor Domitian (Rev. 1:9).

Most scholars believe that John's gospel was the last of the four gospels to be written. Although dates have been suggested from A.D. 60 to 90, church tradition narrows the date to sometime between A.D. 80 and 95.

BACKGROUND

SETTING: Irenaeus supports the theory that John wrote the gospel when he lived in Ephesus, a large and cosmopolitan city housing one of the largest Christian communities in the Gentile world of the first century.

PURPOSE: The Gospel of John presents Jesus as the divine Word, the *Logos* (Gk., lit. "Word"), the Christ, and the Son of God. Jesus is the Revealer and Redeemer. He is the sacrificial "Lamb" who came to take away "the sin of the world" (John 1:29). John's gospel is often seen as the most evangelistic of the four gospels.

AUDIENCE: John wrote this evangelistic gospel to fellow Jews, encouraging them to confess Jesus as the Christ. The Jews who accepted Christ were expelled from the synagogue and were persecuted by the Jewish community. John's gospel helped provide the Christian community with purpose and identity.

LITERARY CHARACTERISTICS: The Gospel of John is a theological retelling of history. It is written in narrative form. While it does not contain parables, as do Matthew, Mark, and Luke, the book does record allegories and extended discourses used by Jesus in His teaching ministry.

THEMES

More than any other book in the New Testament, John introduces Jesus as the unique Son of God (John 20:31). The gospel begins with an introduction (John 1:1–51), then proceeds into the ministry of Christ (John 2:1—4:54), the opposition He experienced (John 5:1—12:50), and finally His deeds and words (John 13:1—21:25).

OUTLINE

Perspective   by Dee Brestin and Kathy Troccoli

JESUS, GOD'S REFRESHING WORD (From *Forever in Love with Jesus*, 65-68)

When *The Word* spoke the world into being in Genesis, it was Jesus, in the mystery of the Trinity, speaking the world into existence. When "the Word of the Lord came to Hosea," it was Jesus, in the mystery of the Trinity, speaking to Hosea. When the law was given to Moses, it was Jesus communicating to the heart of His people. Not only does the Word include *memra*, or God's supportive presence among His people, but it contains the Law: the words, and the holy judgment of God as seen in the Torah. (The Torah is the first five books of Moses: Genesis through Deuteronomy.)

This communicative aspect of the Word has both a terrible and wonderful side. It can feel terrible when it convicts us of sin. It can seem harsh when you read of someone being cast out into the outer darkness where there is weeping and gnashing of teeth. It can be wonderful when we hear how wide and high His love is, when He tells us He will never leave us, and when He promises us that one day, we will no longer weep.

Because God is always good and just, what may seem terrible is not. It is a holy mystery. The picture of Jesus coming on a white horse one day with fire in His eyes and a sword in His mouth causes us to tremble. And yet, that day is when He is waging war against all the enemies of His bride, because He is holy and just. We have come to love this picture of Jesus because we see the sword being used on our behalf and in our defense. The sword, Paul told us in Ephesians 6, represents the Word of God, and we can use it, as well, to defeat our spiritual enemies. When the enemy comes, and he will, we can use the sword of the Spirit, the Word of God, against him.

Jesus, as the Word, is here with us and is filled with wisdom, power, and comfort. And as He, through His Spirit and His Word, falls upon hearts eager to receive, He cannot help but produce fruit. Hosea talked about the Lord coming to us "like the rain, like the latter and former rain to the earth" (6:3). Likewise, Isaiah extends the analogy, and in his picture is an exciting truth: *For as the rain comes down, and the snow from heaven, and do not return there, but water the earth, and make it bring forth and bud, that it may give seed to the sower and bread to the eater, so shall My word be that goes forth from My mouth; it shall not return to Me void, but it shall accomplish what I please, and it shall prosper in the thing for which I sent*" (55:10, 11).

Do you see? Once rain and snow have started falling, they never suddenly reverse their course. In the same way, once *The Word* has started speaking into our hearts, it doesn't all of a sudden, like a child say, "I take it back." Once He has started a new creative work in us, He will bring it to completion (Phil. 1:6).

The Eternal Word

1 In the beginning was the Word, and the Word was with God, and the Word was God. [2]He was in the beginning with God. [3]All things were made through Him, and without Him nothing was made that was made. [4]In Him was life, and the life was the light of men. [5]And the light shines in the darkness, and the darkness did not comprehend[a] it.

John's Witness: The True Light

[6]There was a man sent from God, whose name *was* John. [7]This man came for a witness, to bear witness of the Light, that all through him might believe. [8]He was not that Light, but *was sent* to bear witness of that Light. [9]That was the true Light which gives light to every man coming into the world.[a]

[10]He was in the world, and the world was made through Him, and the world did not know Him. [11]He came to His own,[a] and His own[b] did not receive Him. [12]But as many as received Him, to them He gave the right to become children of God, to those who believe in His name: [13]who were born, not of blood, nor of the will of the flesh, nor of the will of man, but of God.

1:5 [a]Or *overcome*   **1:9** [a]Or *That was the true Light which, coming into the world, gives light to every man.*   **1:11** [a]That is, His own things or domain   [b]That is, His own people

---

1:1, 2 Jesus Christ has always existed and will exist eternally. He is the living Word. Jesus and God the Father, along with the Holy Spirit, have always had an intimate relationship as the triune God. Jesus is God who took on a human body and nature in order to redeem mankind (see chart, The Definitive Christological Passages).

1:4 Gnosticism, a dualistic heresy that reached its full strength in the 2nd and 3rd centuries A.D., regarded the spiritual as being inherently good and the earthly (that is, the created world) as inherently evil. Asceticism is another response to this concept that the created order is inherently evil. John may have emphasized Christ's humanity in his gospel in order to combat the beginnings of the philosophical-spiritual ideology called Gnosticism. Gnostics believed that the spirit world contained many different levels of knowledge and that everyone must ascend through them to achieve *gnôsis* (Gk.), a secret inner knowledge resulting in salvation and available only to those who had their consciousness raised to such a level.

Gnostics argued that through Christ they had experienced a spiritual resurrection and had arrived at knowledge (Gk. *gnôsis*). Therefore, since the sins of the body were totally unconnected with the spiritual life, they were free on a spiritual

The Word Becomes Flesh

[14]And the Word became flesh and dwelt among us, and we beheld His glory, the glory as of the only begotten of the Father, full of grace and truth.

[15]John bore witness of Him and cried out, saying, "This was He of whom I said, 'He who comes after me is preferred before me, for He was before me.'"

[16]And[a] of His fullness we have all received, and grace for grace. [17]For the law was given through Moses, *but* grace and truth came through Jesus Christ. [18]No one has seen God at any time. The only begotten Son,[a] who is in the bosom of the Father, He has declared *Him*.

A Voice in the Wilderness

[19]Now this is the testimony of John, when the Jews sent priests and Levites from Jerusalem to ask him, "Who are you?"

[20]He confessed, and did not deny, but confessed, "I am not the Christ."

[21]And they asked him, "What then? Are you Elijah?"

He said, "I am not."

"Are you the Prophet?"

And he answered, "No."

[22]Then they said to him, "Who are you, that we may give an answer to those who sent us? What do you say about yourself?"

[23]He said: "I *am*

The voice of one crying in the wilderness:
"Make straight the way of the LORD," '[a]

as the prophet Isaiah said."

[24]Now those who were sent were from the Pharisees. [25]And they asked him, saying, "Why then do you baptize if you are not the Christ, nor Elijah, nor the Prophet?"

[26]John answered them, saying, "I baptize with water, but there stands One among you whom you do not know. [27]It is He who, coming after me, is preferred before me, whose sandal strap I am not worthy to loose."

[28]These things were done in Bethabara[a] beyond the Jordan, where John was baptizing.

The Lamb of God

[29]The next day John saw Jesus coming toward him, and said, "Behold! The Lamb of God who takes away the sin of the world! [30]This is He of whom I said, 'After me comes a Man who is preferred before me, for He was before me.' [31]I did not know Him; but that He should be revealed to Israel, therefore I came baptizing with water."

[32]And John bore witness, saying, "I saw the Spirit descending from heaven like a dove, and He remained upon Him. [33]I did not know Him, but He who sent me to baptize with water said to me, 'Upon whom you see the Spirit descending, and remaining on Him, this is He who baptizes with the Holy Spirit.' [34]And I have seen and testified that this is the Son of God."

The First Disciples

[35]Again, the next day, John stood with two of his disciples. [36]And looking at Jesus as He walked, he said, "Behold the Lamb of God!"

[37]The two disciples heard him speak, and they followed Jesus. [38]Then Jesus turned, and seeing them following, said to them, "What do you seek?"

1:16 [a]NU-Text reads *For.*   1:18 [a]NU-Text reads *only begotten God.*
1:23 [a]Isaiah 40:3   1:28 [a]NU-Text and M-Text read *Bethany.*

---

plane to worship God through Christ Jesus and on a physical plane to do as they pleased. Paul strongly taught against this viewpoint as did the early church fathers (2 Cor. 7:1; Eph. 4:17–24). First Timothy 1:3–7 and Jude 3–19 may also refer to teachers of incipient (or developing) Gnosticism.

Since Gnostics believed the flesh is always evil, they taught that a sinless Christ could not have become truly human. The Gnostics were divided over the Incarnation. The Docetic Gnostics claimed that Christ's human body was only an illusion, while Cerinthian Gnostics taught that God's divine spirit filled the human Jesus at His baptism but fled before His death. Like all other tenets of Gnostic belief, Scripture refutes both of these positions (Col. 1:15–18; Heb. 2:14; 1 John 4:2–6; see 1 Cor. 1, Heresies; Gal. 4, Christology; Eph. 2, Salvation).

1:14 Jesus Christ, the eternal Word of God and Second Person of the Trinity, "became flesh." To His divine nature He added a perfect human nature. As Paul later explained, this involved His "taking the form of a bondservant, and coming in the likeness of men" (Phil. 2:7). As the incarnate God, His wholly divine and perfectly human natures are forever united—without change, mixture, or separation—in one Person (John 10:30; Col. 2:9; 1 John 1:1–5). "Dwelt" (Gk. *skēnoō,* sharing its

root with *skēnē,* lit. "tent") refers to the fact that God dwelt temporarily among His people as the perfect God-Man, Jesus Christ, just as God manifested His presence to His people in the tabernacle in the wilderness (Ex. 24:16; 40:35; see chart, The Plan of the Tabernacle).

1:23 John the Baptist was thought by some to be the prophet Isaiah (see Is. 40:3), while others believed he was Elijah. The Jews believed that Elijah would appear on earth before the Messiah would come, and John resembled Elijah. He dressed like a prophet; he was rugged; he lived in the wilderness; and, like Elijah, he was a prophet. Jesus praised John as a great prophet, and he was popular among the Jews of his day. His ministry began near the Jordan River around A.D. 26. He was sent as a "voice" to prepare the people for the coming of the Messiah.

1:29 John called Jesus the Lamb of God. In this title, John pictured the Passover lamb slain at the time of deliverance of the children of Israel from Egyptian slavery (see Ex. 12:12, 13). To the Jews, the slaughtered lamb represented meekness, innocence, sacrifice, redemption, and the substitutionary forgiveness of sins (see chart, The Plan of the Tabernacle).

WEDDINGS A PUBLIC COMMITMENT

In Bible times, the period of engagement (or betrothal) was spent in preparation—the groom preparing a home for his bride and the bride preparing herself and her trousseau. When the time came for the marriage to be consummated, the groom went to the bride's home (often at an unannounced time) to accompany her to his home where they met friends of the two families, as arranged by the groom, not the bride (see Judg. 14:5–11; Matt. 25:1–13). Wedding celebrations generally lasted a week, during which time the bride and groom dressed and were treated as royalty amidst festivities and the presentation of gifts (Gen. 29:27; Judg. 14:12–18; John 2:1–11).

In the modern era, weddings range from formal, solemn ceremonies to informal, private gatherings. The type of ceremony is not necessarily important, but these biblical criteria are:

1) The marriage should be established in the name of the Lord Jesus (Mark 10:9), and
2) Thanks should be given to God (Col. 3:17). A wedding should be a time of worship and should celebrate each marriage partner's commitment grounded in the love of God.

Weddings are much more than beautiful gowns, crowds of people, and expensive decorating. A wedding is a time of COMMITMENT. It should include worship and giving thanks to God as well as the celebrating of the wonderful blessing God has given both the bride and groom.

The wedding ceremony is an appropriate time to reflect on the example of unconditional love, which God has demonstrated (Rom. 5:8). The couple should "commit" to follow the Lord in their home no matter what circumstances arise and "till death do us part" (see Matt. 19:6). The importance of this permanency of the union grows out of the fact that the vows are not merely between one man and one woman but include the heavenly Father Himself, and also because such commitment is modeled after Christ's commitment to the church (Eph. 5:21–33).

See also Gen. 2:15–25; notes on Celebrations and Holidays (Ex. 12); Engagement (Matt. 1); Marriage (Gen. 2; 2 Sam. 6; Prov. 5; Hos. 2; Amos 3; 2 Cor. 13; Heb. 12); Traditions (1 Sam. 7); Vows (Num. 30)

They said to Him, "Rabbi" (which is to say, when translated, Teacher), "where are You staying?"

[39] He said to them, "Come and see." They came and saw where He was staying, and remained with Him that day (now it was about the tenth hour).

[40] One of the two who heard John *speak,* and followed Him, was Andrew, Simon Peter's brother. [41] He first found his own brother Simon, and said to him, "We have found the Messiah" (which is translated, the Christ). [42] And he brought him to Jesus.

Now when Jesus looked at him, He said, "You are Simon the son of Jonah.[a] You shall be called Cephas" (which is translated, A Stone).

Philip and Nathanael

[43] The following day Jesus wanted to go to Galilee, and He found Philip and said to him, "Follow Me." [44] Now Philip was from Bethsaida, the city of Andrew and Peter. [45] Philip found Nathanael and said to him, "We have found Him of whom Moses in the law, and also the prophets, wrote—Jesus of Nazareth, the son of Joseph."

[46] And Nathanael said to him, "Can anything good come out of Nazareth?"

Philip said to him, "Come and see."

[47] Jesus saw Nathanael coming toward Him, and said of him, "Behold, an Israelite indeed, in whom is no deceit!"

[48] Nathanael said to Him, "How do You know me?"

Jesus answered and said to him, "Before Philip called you, when you were under the fig tree, I saw you."

[49] Nathanael answered and said to Him, "Rabbi, You are the Son of God! You are the King of Israel!"

[50] Jesus answered and said to him, "Because I said to you, 'I saw you under the fig tree,' do you believe? You will see greater things than these." [51] And He said to him, "Most assuredly, I say to you, hereafter[a] you shall see heaven open, and the angels of God ascending and descending upon the Son of Man."

1:42 [a]NU-Text reads *John.*   1:51 [a]NU-Text omits *hereafter.*

1:38 Rabbi (lit. "great one," "master," or "teacher") was a title of respect used by students of their wise teachers. The title later became especially identified with the teachers of the Law of Moses.

1:46 Jesus gave prominence to Nazareth, a city not mentioned in the OT. Located between the Sea of Galilee and the Mediterranean Sea, Nazareth was Jesus' hometown, where He grew from boyhood to manhood. With Nathanael's question, John revealed Nazareth's poor reputation. The people of Nazareth would later reject Jesus (see Mark 6:4, note).

THE DEFINITIVE CHRISTOLOGICAL PASSAGES

THE CHRIST	HIS DIVINE RELATIONSHIP	HIS DIVINE WORK	HIS DIVINE NAME	HIS DIVINE NATURE
The Gospel of John (John 1; 14)	The Word (John 1:1, 14) Radiant glory (John 1:14; 14:7) Only begotten (John 1:14, 18) Son (John 3:16)	Creation of all (John 1:1–3) Salvation (John 1:12, 13)	Theos (Gk., lit. God) (John 1:1, 18)	Fully God (John 1:18; 14:6) Fully man (John 1:14)
The Epistle to the Philippians (Phil. 2)	Form of God (Phil. 2:6) Equal with God (Phil. 2:6) Bondservant (Phil. 2:7)	Salvation (Phil. 2:6–8)	Theos (Gk., lit. God) (Phil. 2:6)	Fully God (Phil. 2:6) Fully man (Phil. 2:7, 8)
The Epistle to the Colossians (Col. 1; 2)	The image of the invisible God (Col. 1:15, 19) Firstborn (Col. 1:15, 18) The Son He [God] loves (Col. 1:13)	Creation of all (Col. 1:16–18) Salvation (Col. 1:4, 5, 19–22; 2:6, 13–15)	Theotétos (Gk., lit. Godhead) (Col. 2:9)	Fully God (Col. 1:19; 2:9) Fully man (Col. 2:9)
The Epistle to the Hebrews (Heb. 1; 2)	The revelation of God (Heb. 1:2) Firstborn (Heb. 1:6) Son (Heb. 1:2, 5, 8)	Creation of all (Heb. 1:2, 3, 10) Salvation (Heb. 1:3; 2:10, 11)	Theos (Gk., lit. God) (Heb. 1:8)	Fully God (Heb. 1:3) Fully man (Heb. 1:6; 2:14–18)

Water Turned to Wine

2 On the third day there was a wedding in Cana of Galilee, and the mother of Jesus was there. ²Now both Jesus and His disciples were invited to the wedding. ³And when they ran out of wine, the mother of Jesus said to Him, "They have no wine."

⁴Jesus said to her, "Woman, what does your concern have to do with Me? My hour has not yet come."

⁵His mother said to the servants, "Whatever He says to you, do *it.*"

⁶Now there were set there six waterpots of stone, according to the manner of purification of the Jews, containing twenty or thirty gallons apiece. ⁷Jesus said to them, "Fill the waterpots with water." And they filled them up to the brim. ⁸And He said to them, "Draw *some* out now, and take *it* to the master of the feast." And they took *it.* ⁹When the master of the feast had tasted the water that was made wine, and did not know where it came from (but the servants who had drawn the water knew), the master of the feast called the

2:1, 2 The wedding at Cana was attended by Jesus, His mother, and His disciples. The town was located in Galilee, although its exact location is unknown. A wedding in Jesus' day could last as long as a week (see Weddings). To run out of wine was an embarrassing and inhospitable offense for the wedding host. At the request of His mother Mary, Jesus performed the first miracle of His public ministry by turning water into wine (see chart, Jesus' Miracles Among Women).

2:4 Jesus showed no disrespect when He addressed His mother as "woman" instead of "mother." His public ministry had begun, and with the Cross before Him, He was possibly putting some distance between Himself and His mother to spare her added suffering. This polite form of address was used by Jesus in addressing other women (John 4:21; 20:13;

see Matt. 15:28; Luke 13:12). Mary acknowledged her own confidence in her Son and approval of His independent action as she instructed the servants to follow His instructions. Although Jesus was still her Son, He was now more than her Child: He was her Lord. Jesus was aware of God's timing regarding His mission on earth. A miracle or "sign" would help the people understand His identity and purpose.

2:6 The waterpots, often made of clay but sometimes of stone, were vessels used for storing water. Each waterpot contained about 17 to 25 gallons of water. Six waterpots would have held 100 to 150 gallons. The Jews used water for cleansing and purification rituals, and these large stone waterpots probably stored the water used for washing. Smaller waterpots were used by women to transport water from wells.

JESUS' MIRACLES AMONG WOMEN	
MIRACLE	**REFERENCES**
Healing Peter's mother-in-law	Matt. 8:14, 15 Mark 1:30, 31 Luke 4:38, 39
Raising Jairus' daughter	Matt. 9:18, 23–25 Mark 5:22, 24, 35–42 Luke 8:40–42, 49–55
Healing the hemorrhaging woman	Matt. 9:20–22 Mark 5:25–34 Luke 8:43–48
Healing the Canaanite woman's daughter	Matt. 15:21–28 Mark 7:24–30
Raising the widow of Nain's son	Luke 7:11–15
Healing the infirm woman	Luke 13:11–13
Turning water into wine at the wedding in Cana at request of Jesus' mother	John 2:1–11

bridegroom. ¹⁰And he said to him, "Every man at the beginning sets out the good wine, and when the *guests* have well drunk, then the inferior. You have kept the good wine until now!"

¹¹This beginning of signs Jesus did in Cana of Galilee, and manifested His glory; and His disciples believed in Him.

¹²After this He went down to Capernaum, He, His mother, His brothers, and His disciples; and they did not stay there many days.

Jesus Cleanses the Temple

¹³Now the Passover of the Jews was at hand, and Jesus went up to Jerusalem. ¹⁴And He found in the temple those who sold oxen and sheep and doves, and the money changers doing business. ¹⁵When He had made a whip of cords, He drove them all out of the temple, with the sheep and the oxen, and poured out the changers' money and overturned the tables. ¹⁶And He said to those who sold doves, "Take these things away! Do not make My Father's house a house of merchandise!" ¹⁷Then His disciples remembered that it was written, *"Zeal for Your house has eaten*ᵃ *Me up."*ᵇ

¹⁸So the Jews answered and said to Him, "What sign do You show to us, since You do these things?"

¹⁹Jesus answered and said to them, "Destroy this temple, and in three days I will raise it up."

²⁰Then the Jews said, "It has taken forty-six years to build this temple, and will You raise it up in three days?"

²¹But He was speaking of the temple of His body. ²²Therefore, when He had risen from the dead, His disciples remembered that He had said this to them;ᵃ and they believed the Scripture and the word which Jesus had said.

The Discerner of Hearts

²³Now when He was in Jerusalem at the Passover, during the feast, many believed in His name when they saw the signs which He did. ²⁴But Jesus did not commit Himself to them, because He knew all *men,* ²⁵and had no need that anyone should testify of man, for He knew what was in man.

The New Birth

3 There was a man of the Pharisees named Nicodemus, a ruler of the Jews. ²This man came to Jesus by night and said to Him, "Rabbi, we know that You are a teacher come from God; for no one can do these signs that You do unless God is with him."

³Jesus answered and said to him, "Most assuredly, I say to you, unless one is born again, he cannot see the kingdom of God."

•••••••••••••••••••••

2:17 ᵃNU-Text and M-Text read *will eat.* ᵇPsalm 69:9   2:22 ᵃNU-Text and M-Text omit *to them.*

2:19–22 The temple in Jerusalem was the central place for Jewish worship, the dwelling place of the presence of God. King David planned to build the temple, but his son Solomon actually built it. This building stood for almost 400 years, but it was finally plundered and burned by the Babylonians in 586 B.C. The Jews in Babylon were given permission to rebuild the temple, and the new governor, Zerubbabel, completed the structure in 516 B.C. Beginning in 19 B.C., Herod added to the temple and refurbished it so that it was much more magnificent than Zerubbabel's temple. Mary and Joseph brought the infant Jesus to be circumcised in this temple, and Jesus taught there at age 12. It was destroyed in A.D. 70 by the Romans under Titus. The Jews thought Jesus referred to Herod's temple in Jerusalem. Jesus, however, did not say He would destroy the actual temple building. Jesus was speaking of Himself as the temple and of His own death and Resurrection.

3:1 Nicodemus, a pious and knowledgeable teacher, was a Pharisee and a member of the Jewish Sanhedrin. This highest Jewish court had 70 distinguished members. Nicodemus came from an important aristocratic family in Jerusalem and was an authority on Scripture. His coming at night could have been for any of several reasons: He wanted to speak to Jesus in secret so as not to arouse suspicion or to evoke criticism among his Sanhedrin colleagues; he wanted the privacy that night afforded so as not to be competitive with, nor intimidated by, the daytime crowds that surrounded Jesus; because of the darkness of his own great sins, he may have wanted private counsel with Jesus, the Light (v. 2); or perhaps he simply could not wait until morning. Nicodemus later publicly participated in Jesus' burial by supplying abundant spices to be folded within the shroud wrapped around Jesus' body.

3:3–10 Nicodemus was confused by Jesus' emphasis on rebirth. The word "again" (Gk. *anothen*) has several meanings: "from conception" or "the very beginning," "anew" or "a sec-

Women can splash the world with the love of Christ . . . through kindness, caring, touching, meeting needs, and telling of their love for Christ.

Esther Burroughs

---

[4]Nicodemus said to Him, "How can a man be born when he is old? Can he enter a second time into his mother's womb and be born?"

[5]Jesus answered, "Most assuredly, I say to you, unless one is born of water and the Spirit, he cannot enter the kingdom of God. [6]That which is born of the flesh is flesh, and that which is born of the Spirit is spirit. [7]Do not marvel that I said to you, 'You must be born again.' [8]The wind blows where it wishes, and you hear the sound of it, but cannot tell where it comes from and where it goes. So is everyone who is born of the Spirit."

[9]Nicodemus answered and said to Him, "How can these things be?"

[10]Jesus answered and said to him, "Are you the teacher of Israel, and do not know these things? [11]Most assuredly, I say to you, We speak what We know and testify what We have seen, and you do not receive Our witness. [12]If I have told you earthly things and you do not believe, how will you believe if I tell you heavenly things? [13]No one has ascended to heaven but He who came down from heaven, *that is,* the Son of Man who is in heaven.[a] [14]And as Moses lifted up the serpent in the wilderness, even so must the Son of Man be lifted up, [15]that whoever believes in Him should not perish but[a] have eternal life. [16]For God so loved the world that He gave His only begotten Son, that whoever believes in Him should not perish but have everlasting life. [17]For God did not send His Son into the world to condemn the world, but that the world through Him might be saved.

[18]"He who believes in Him is not condemned; but he who does not believe is condemned already, because he has not believed in the name of the only begotten Son of God. [19]And this is the condemnation, that the light has come into the world, and men loved darkness rather than light, because their deeds were evil. [20]For everyone practicing evil hates the light and does not come to the light, lest his deeds should be exposed. [21]But he who does the truth comes to the light, that his deeds may be clearly seen, that they have been done in God."

John the Baptist Exalts Christ

[22]After these things Jesus and His disciples came into the land of Judea, and there He remained with them and baptized. [23]Now John also was baptizing in Aenon near Salim, because there was much water there. And they came and were baptized. [24]For John had not yet been thrown into prison.

[25]Then there arose a dispute between *some* of John's disciples and the Jews about purification. [26]And they came to John and said to him, "Rabbi, He who was with you beyond the Jordan, to whom you have testified— behold, He is baptizing, and all are coming to Him!"

[27]John answered and said, "A man can receive nothing unless it has been given to him from heaven. [28]You yourselves bear me witness, that I said, 'I am not the Christ,' but, 'I have been sent before Him.' [29]He who has the bride is the bridegroom; but the friend of the bridegroom, who stands and hears him, rejoices greatly because of the bridegroom's voice. Therefore this joy of mine is fulfilled. [30]He must increase, but I *must* decrease. [31]He who comes from above is above all; he who is of the earth is earthly and speaks of the earth. He who comes from heaven is above all. [32]And what He has seen and heard, that He testifies; and no one receives His testimony. [33]He who has received His testimony has certified that God is true. [34]For He whom God has sent speaks the words of God, for God does not give the Spirit by

---

3:13 [a]NU-Text omits *who is in heaven.*   3:15 [a]NU-Text omits *not perish but.*

---

ond time," "from above" or "from God." Nicodemus knew a physical rebirth was impossible. "Spirit" (Gk. *pneuma*) can also mean "wind," depending on the context. Jesus used the word to illustrate the Spirit's activity. Jesus made the point to Nicodemus that he must be born of the Spirit in order to understand the spiritual things of God.

3:13 Jesus described Himself as the One who descended from heaven, the Son of Man. The description "Son of Man" appears more than 80 times in the gospels, but only four times in the NT outside the gospels. "Son of Man" points to Jesus' special ministry and commission from God; His suffering, death, and Resurrection; and His return.

3:14, 15 John stressed both the shame of the Cross and the majesty of the Resurrection throughout his gospel. God punished the Israelites in the wilderness with deadly serpents after they had complained and spoken against God and Moses (see Num. 21:4–9). Many people were bitten and died. When the people repented and begged for mercy, God told Moses to lift a fiery serpent high upon a pole within the camp. God promised that anyone looking at the raised bronze serpent would be healed of the snake's venomous bite and saved from death. The OT incident pointed to Jesus, who would be lifted up on a Cross as the sacrifice necessary for salvation.

THE SAMARITAN WOMAN

Perhaps in order to avoid the respectable townswomen who filled their water jars at sunrise and sunset, "the Samaritan woman" came to the well at noon, the hottest hour of the day. This immoral woman, who had had five husbands, now lived with a man who was not her husband.

When Jesus purposely passed through Samaria on His way to Galilee, He met and spoke to the woman at Jacob's Well, near the city of Sychar, breaking three major social rules:

- First, women were considered greatly inferior to men; in public no Middle Eastern man ever spoke to a woman, not even to his wife, mother, or sister.
- Second, no Jew ever spoke to a Samaritan. Jews believed Samaritans had betrayed their faith because they had intermarried with foreigners. The Jews and Samaritans hated and avoided each other.
- Third, no self-respecting man, especially a teacher, would ever speak to a woman of such despicable reputation. This woman was a well-known social outcast.

Jesus disregarded these social barriers when He conversed with the Samaritan woman. He revealed Himself as the greatly anticipated Messiah, offering forgiveness, redemption, and new life. She drank from His cup of living water, ran back to town to the very ones who despised her, the people of Samaria. There she proclaimed with unembarrassed excitement the arrival of the promised Messiah.

The people of Samaria eagerly responded to Christ. They, too, yearned for His living water. Later, Jesus would challenge His disciples to witness in Samaria (Acts 1:8), and Philip, a deacon, would open a mission there (Acts 8:5). Yet the Good News of Jesus Christ was first proclaimed to the people of Samaria through the testimony of a sinful, immoral woman who drank the offered water and was forgiven, cleansed, and renewed, never again to thirst.

See also notes on Adultery (Hos. 3); Forgiveness (Ps. 51; Luke 17)

---

measure. ³⁵The Father loves the Son, and has given all things into His hand. ³⁶He who believes in the Son has everlasting life; and he who does not believe the Son shall not see life, but the wrath of God abides on him."

A Samaritan Woman Meets Her Messiah

4 Therefore, when the Lord knew that the Pharisees had heard that Jesus made and baptized more disciples than John ²(though Jesus Himself did not baptize, but His disciples), ³He left Judea and departed again to Galilee. ⁴But He needed to go through Samaria.

⁵So He came to a city of Samaria which is called Sychar, near the plot of ground that Jacob gave to his son Joseph. ⁶Now Jacob's well was there. Jesus therefore, being wearied from *His* journey, sat thus by the well. It was about the sixth hour.

⁷A woman of Samaria came to draw water. Jesus said to her, "Give Me a drink." ⁸For His disciples had gone away into the city to buy food.

⁹Then the woman of Samaria said to Him, "How is it that You, being a Jew, ask a drink from me, a Samaritan woman?" For Jews have no dealings with Samaritans.

¹⁰Jesus answered and said to her, "If you knew the gift of God, and who it is who says to you, 'Give Me a drink,' you would have asked Him, and He would have given you living water."

¹¹The woman said to Him, "Sir, You have nothing to draw with, and the well is deep. Where then do You get that living water? ¹²Are You greater than our father Jacob, who gave us the well, and drank from it himself, as well as his sons and his livestock?"

¹³Jesus answered and said to her, "Whoever drinks of this water will thirst again, ¹⁴but whoever drinks of the water that I shall give him will never thirst. But the water that I shall give him will become in him a fountain of water springing up into everlasting life."

¹⁵The woman said to Him, "Sir, give me this water, that I may not thirst, nor come here to draw."

4:4–6 Jesus did not follow the usual way for Jews to travel between Galilee and Judea, which was to avoid Samaritan territory by crossing to the east bank of the Jordan River (vv. 3, 4). At Sychar, Jacob bought a piece of land from the children of Hamor for 100 pieces of money and pitched his tent (v. 5; see Gen. 33:18–20). While Jesus was resting at Jacob's well, a site not mentioned in the OT, He met the Samaritan woman (see The Samaritan Woman).

4:7 For a woman to come to the well at noon, the hottest part of the day, was unusual. Middle Eastern women usually filled their water jars in the early morning and at sunset, when it was cooler. The Samaritan woman was a woman of bad reputation and may have filled her jars at noon in order to avoid meeting other women who would shun her.

4:9 Jesus simply disregarded the social rules of His day in order to talk with the Samaritan woman.

> *Jesus did not take volunteers as disciples. He put His finger on each one . . . because He saw potential in them.*
>
> Gail MacDonald

16Jesus said to her, "Go, call your husband, and come here."

17The woman answered and said, "I have no husband."

Jesus said to her, "You have well said, 'I have no husband,' 18for you have had five husbands, and the one whom you now have is not your husband; in that you spoke truly."

19The woman said to Him, "Sir, I perceive that You are a prophet. 20Our fathers worshiped on this mountain, and you Jews say that in Jerusalem is the place where one ought to worship."

21Jesus said to her, "Woman, believe Me, the hour is coming when you will neither on this mountain, nor in Jerusalem, worship the Father. 22You worship what you do not know; we know what we worship, for salvation is of the Jews. 23But the hour is coming, and now is, when the true worshipers will worship the Father in spirit and truth; for the Father is seeking such to worship Him. 24God *is* Spirit, and those who worship Him must worship in spirit and truth."

25The woman said to Him, "I know that Messiah is coming" (who is called Christ). "When He comes, He will tell us all things."

26Jesus said to her, "I who speak to you am *He*."

The Whitened Harvest

27And at this *point* His disciples came, and they marveled that He talked with a woman; yet no one said, "What do You seek?" or, "Why are You talking with her?"

28The woman then left her waterpot, went her way into the city, and said to the men, 29"Come, see a Man who told me all things that I ever did. Could this be the Christ?" 30Then they went out of the city and came to Him.

31In the meantime His disciples urged Him, saying, "Rabbi, eat."

32But He said to them, "I have food to eat of which you do not know."

33Therefore the disciples said to one another, "Has anyone brought Him *anything* to eat?"

34Jesus said to them, "My food is to do the will of Him who sent Me, and to finish His work. 35Do you not say, 'There are still four months and *then* comes the harvest'? Behold, I say to you, lift up your eyes and look at the fields, for they are already white for harvest! 36And he who reaps receives wages, and gathers fruit for eternal life, that both he who sows and he who reaps may rejoice together. 37For in this the saying is true: 'One sows and another reaps.' 38I sent you to reap that for which you have not labored; others have labored, and you have entered into their labors."

The Savior of the World

39And many of the Samaritans of that city believed in Him because of the word of the woman who testified, "He told me all that I *ever* did." 40So when the Samaritans had come to Him, they urged Him to stay with them; and He stayed there two days. 41And many more believed because of His own word.

42Then they said to the woman, "Now we believe, not because of what you said, for we ourselves have heard *Him* and we know that this is indeed the Christ,[a] the Savior of the world."

Welcome at Galilee

43Now after the two days He departed from there and went to Galilee. 44For Jesus Himself testified that a prophet has no honor in his own country. 45So when He came to Galilee, the Galileans received Him, having seen all the things He did in Jerusalem at the feast; for they also had gone to the feast.

A Nobleman's Son Healed

46So Jesus came again to Cana of Galilee where He had made the water wine. And there was a certain nobleman whose son was sick at Capernaum. 47When he heard that Jesus had come out of Judea into Galilee, he went to Him and implored Him to

4:42 [a]NU-Text omits *the Christ.*

4:20–24 The ancient city of Samaria was located about 40 miles north of Jerusalem. Years before, a remnant of Israel's Jews in Samaria had intermarried with Gentiles and had begun to worship foreign gods. The Samaritans worshiped at Mount Gerizim, where they had been given permission to build a temple. A small Samaritan community continues to worship there even now.

4:25, 26 The Jews of Samaria were also awaiting the arrival of

the promised Messiah (see Deut. 18:15, 18). Jesus told the Samaritan woman that He was the long-awaited Messiah. The woman believed Jesus' self-disclosure and told others the Good News.

4:46 The man was a royal official in the court of Herod Antipas, the tetrarch of Galilee. Whether he was a Jew or Gentile is not known. The fact that a nobleman would request the help of a "carpenter" is extraordinary.

WOMEN'S MINISTRIES WOMEN IN EVANGELISM

Jesus affirmed the ministry of women in evangelism. This was most evident in His interaction with the Samaritan woman at the well of Sychar (John 4:1–30). Culturally, Jews and Samaritans did not associate with each other. Moreover, for a rabbi to speak to a woman in public was considered improper. Christ's regard for this woman was therefore truly revolutionary. After their meeting, she returned to her city and presented her witness. Many believed in Him because of her testimony (vv. 28, 39). At that time, women were not considered reliable witnesses; yet Christ chose a woman as His witness.

God chose women as the first witnesses of Christ's Resurrection (Matt. 28:1–8), and they were en-trusted with Christ's first post-Resurrection message to His disciples (John 20:15–18). The coming of the Spirit reinforced the role of women in evangelism. Women, together with men, were empowered to be wit-nesses to the ends of the earth (Acts 1:8). The establishment of the Philippian church involved women (Acts 16:11–15), and women were involved in spreading the gospel in Berea (Acts 17:12). New Testament women, along with men, were commissioned to be the "light of the world" and were thus extensively involved in the min-istry of evangelism (Matt. 5:14–16).

See also chart on Spiritual Gifts of Women in the Bible; notes on Evangelism (John 6; Col. 4; 1 Pet. 3); Spiritual Gifts (Rom. 12); Women's Ministries (Acts 2; 1 Cor. 11; Eph. 2; 1 Tim. 3; Titus 2).

come down and heal his son, for he was at the point of death. [48]Then Jesus said to him, "Unless you *people* see signs and wonders, you will by no means believe."

[49]The nobleman said to Him, "Sir, come down before my child dies!"

[50]Jesus said to him, "Go your way; your son lives." So the man believed the word that Jesus spoke to him, and he went his way. [51]And as he was now going down, his servants met him and told *him,* saying, "Your son lives!"

[52]Then he inquired of them the hour when he got better. And they said to him, "Yesterday at the seventh hour the fever left him." [53]So the father knew that *it was* at the same hour in which Jesus said to him, "Your son lives." And he himself be-lieved, and his whole household.

[54]This again *is* the second sign Jesus did when He had come out of Judea into Galilee.

A Man Healed at the Pool of Bethesda

5 After this there was a feast of the Jews, and Jesus went up to Jerusalem. [2]Now there is in Je-rusalem by the Sheep *Gate* a pool, which is called in Hebrew, Bethesda,[a] having five porches. [3]In these lay a great multitude of sick people, blind, lame,

paralyzed, waiting for the moving of the water. [4]For an angel went down at a certain time into the pool and stirred up the water; then whoever stepped in first, after the stirring of the water, was made well of whatever disease he had.[a] [5]Now a cer-tain man was there who had an infirmity thirty-eight years. [6]When Jesus saw him lying there, and knew that he already had been *in that condition* a long time, He said to him, "Do you want to be made well?"

[7]The sick man answered Him, "Sir, I have no man to put me into the pool when the water is stirred up; but while I am coming, another steps down before me."

[8]Jesus said to him, "Rise, take up your bed and walk." [9]And immediately the man was made well, took up his bed, and walked.

And that day was the Sabbath. [10]The Jews therefore said to him who was cured, "It is the Sabbath; it is not lawful for you to carry your bed."

[11]He answered them, "He who made me well said to me, 'Take up your bed and walk.' "

[12]Then they asked him, "Who is the Man who

··················
5:2 [a]NU-Text reads *Bethzatha*. **5:4** [a]NU-Text omits *waiting for the moving of the water* at the end of verse 3, and all of verse 4.

4:53 An ordinary household with its variety of relationships was basic to society in ancient times. The word "household" could suggest an immediate family, the servants of that fam-ily, an extended family, and even the descendants of a partic-ular nation. The head of the household usually determined the faith of the household. Thus, it was that the nobleman's "whole household" followed him in believing in Jesus.

5:2 The Sheep Gate is one of the entrances carved into Jerusa-lem's city wall. Pools were reservoirs, often cut from stone, that collected rainwater for drinking and other purposes. Wa-ter was a valuable and precious resource in the arid Middle East. These pools were usually deep enough for swimming.

The pool at Bethesda was a famous place where the handi-capped and sick gathered because of its reputed healing properties.

5:10 The Sabbath was the seventh day of the week, the day God rested from creating the world (Gen. 2:2, 3). It was a holy day of rest for all Jews, as well as foreigners, slaves, and even animals (see chart, The Principle of the Sabbath). Desecra-tion of the Sabbath could be punished by death. The prohibi-tion against carrying one's bed on the Sabbath was just one of the numerous oral laws (a part of the tradition of the elders) that had grown from the Law of Moses.

said to you, 'Take up your bed and walk'?" [13]But the one who was healed did not know who it was, for Jesus had withdrawn, a multitude being in *that* place. [14]Afterward Jesus found him in the temple, and said to him, "See, you have been made well. Sin no more, lest a worse thing come upon you."

[15]The man departed and told the Jews that it was Jesus who had made him well.

Honor the Father and the Son

[16]For this reason the Jews persecuted Jesus, and sought to kill Him,[a] because He had done these things on the Sabbath. [17]But Jesus answered them, "My Father has been working until now, and I have been working."

[18]Therefore the Jews sought all the more to kill Him, because He not only broke the Sabbath, but also said that God was His Father, making Himself equal with God. [19]Then Jesus answered and said to them, "Most assuredly, I say to you, the Son can do nothing of Himself, but what He sees the Father do; for whatever He does, the Son also does in like manner. [20]For the Father loves the Son, and shows Him all things that He Himself does; and He will show Him greater works than these, that you may marvel. [21]For as the Father raises the dead and gives life to *them,* even so the Son gives life to whom He will. [22]For the Father judges no one, but has committed all judgment to the Son, [23]that all should honor the Son just as they honor the Father. He who does not honor the Son does not honor the Father who sent Him.

Life and Judgment Are Through the Son

[24]"Most assuredly, I say to you, he who hears My word and believes in Him who sent Me has everlasting life, and shall not come into judgment, but has passed from death into life. [25]Most assuredly, I say to you, the hour is coming, and now is, when the dead will hear the voice of the Son of God; and those who hear will live. [26]For as the Father has life in Himself, so He has granted the Son to have life in Himself, [27]and has given Him authority to execute judgment also, because He is the Son of Man. [28]Do not marvel at this; for the hour is coming in which all who are in the graves will hear His voice [29]and come forth—those who have done good, to the resurrection of life, and those who have done evil, to the resurrection of condemnation. [30]I can of Myself do nothing. As I hear, I judge; and My judgment is righteous, because I do not seek My own will but the will of the Father who sent Me.

The Fourfold Witness

[31]"If I bear witness of Myself, My witness is not true. [32]There is another who bears witness of Me, and I know that the witness which He witnesses of Me is true. [33]You have sent to John, and he has borne witness to the truth. [34]Yet I do not receive testimony from man, but I say these things that you may be saved. [35]He was the burning and shining lamp, and you were willing for a time to rejoice in his light. [36]But I have a greater witness than John's; for the works which the Father has given Me to finish—the very works that I do—bear witness of Me, that the Father has sent Me. [37]And the Father Himself, who sent Me, has testified of Me. You have neither heard His voice at any time, nor seen His form. [38]But you do not have His word abiding in you, because whom He sent, Him you do not believe. [39]You search the Scriptures, for in them you think you have eternal life; and these are they which testify of Me. [40]But you are not willing to come to Me that you may have life.

[41]"I do not receive honor from men. [42]But I know you, that you do not have the love of God in you. [43]I have come in My Father's name, and you do not receive Me; if another comes in his own name, him you will receive. [44]How can you believe, who receive honor from one another, and do not seek the honor that *comes* from the only God? [45]Do not think that I shall accuse you to the Father; there is *one* who accuses you—Moses, in whom you trust. [46]For if you believed Moses, you would believe Me; for he wrote about Me. [47]But if you do not believe his writings, how will you believe My words?"

Feeding the Five Thousand

6 After these things Jesus went over the Sea of Galilee, which is *the Sea* of Tiberias. [2]Then a great multitude followed Him, because they saw His signs which He performed on those who were diseased. [3]And Jesus went up on the mountain, and there He sat with His disciples.

[4]Now the Passover, a feast of the Jews, was near. [5]Then Jesus lifted up *His* eyes, and seeing a great multitude coming toward Him, He said to Philip, "Where shall we buy bread, that these may eat?" [6]But this He said to test him, for He Himself knew what He would do.

[7]Philip answered Him, "Two hundred denarii worth of bread is not sufficient for them, that every one of them may have a little."

[8]One of His disciples, Andrew, Simon Peter's brother, said to Him, [9]"There is a lad here who has five barley loaves and two small fish, but what are they among so many?"

[10]Then Jesus said, "Make the people sit down." Now there was much grass in the place. So the men sat down, in number about five thousand.

5:16 [a]NU-Text omits *and sought to kill Him.*

PROBLEM SOLVING SEEKING GOD'S SOLUTION

The first step in overcoming problems, whether they are physical, emotional, or spiritual, is to admit you are in need and desire a change. Jesus asked the man who had been lying by the Bethesda pool for thirty-eight years a very important question: "Do you want to be made well?" (John 5:1–15). In other words, Do you care enough about your problem to do something about it—even if it requires on your part some action, effort, sacrifice, or even suffering?

As is typical of so many in need, this man answered the Lord with self-pity. When Jesus sees you in need of help and sends a willing person to help, do you play the martyr role? "There's no hope for me. Nobody loves me." The person who clings to this attitude is unlikely to experience healing.

Because Jesus is gracious and knows your deepest desires, He often cuts through your weeping and self-martyrdom and puts you to the test. "Get up," He says. "Take your problem and move on. Do not wait for other people to pity you. Get up."

If you are in need of a touch from the Lord, ask yourself if you are so eager to be changed that you are willing to do something about your situation. When you let God know you are obedient to His will and eager to do whatever it takes for you to be whole, He will send Jesus in the form of a person, a verse from His Word, or a new thought in your mind. Act upon what God tells you to do. He made you, and He knows how to fix precisely what is broken within you.

Finally, when you feel God's power bring about positive changes in your life, do not let doubters convince you these changes are only coincidence. Walk firmly away as did the man with his mat under his arm and say simply "Jesus healed me."

See also Matt. 6:1–4; Mark 5:2, note; John 9:1–41; Phil. 2:13; notes on Counseling (Prov. 8); Decision Making (1 Cor. 8); Healing (Ps. 13; 133; Eccl. 1; 2 Cor. 5; Gal. 6; James 5); Obedience (Philem.); Surrender (James 4)

11And Jesus took the loaves, and when He had given thanks He distributed *them* to the disciples, and the disciples[a] to those sitting down; and likewise of the fish, as much as they wanted. 12So when they were filled, He said to His disciples, "Gather up the fragments that remain, so that nothing is lost." 13Therefore they gathered *them* up, and filled twelve baskets with the fragments of the five barley loaves which were left over by those who had eaten. 14Then those men, when they had seen the sign that Jesus did, said, "This is truly the Prophet who is to come into the world."

Jesus Walks on the Sea

15Therefore when Jesus perceived that they were about to come and take Him by force to make Him king, He departed again to the mountain by Himself alone.

16Now when evening came, His disciples went down to the sea, 17got into the boat, and went over the sea toward Capernaum. And it was already dark, and Jesus had not come to them. 18Then the sea arose because a great wind was blowing. 19So when they had rowed about three or four miles,[a] they saw Jesus walking on the sea and drawing near the boat; and they were afraid. 20But He said to them, "It is I; do not be afraid." 21Then they willingly received Him into the boat, and immediately the boat was at the land where they were going.

The Bread from Heaven

22On the following day, when the people who were standing on the other side of the sea saw that there was no other boat there, except that one which His disciples had entered,[a] and that Jesus had not entered the boat with His disciples, but His disciples had gone away alone— 23however, other boats came from Tiberias, near the place where they ate bread after the Lord had given thanks— 24when the people therefore saw that Jesus was not there, nor His disciples, they also got into boats and came to Capernaum, seek-

---

6:11 [a]NU-Text omits *to the disciples, and the disciples.* 6:19 [a]Literally *twenty-five or thirty stadia* 6:22 [a]NU-Text omits *that* and *which His disciples had entered.*

6:15 The Jews awaited the Prophet (the Messiah) that Moses had promised to them (Deut. 18:15). After the feeding of the 5,000, the crowd believed that Jesus was that Prophet, the Promised One. Jesus, like Moses, had miraculously fed the large crowds. They thought, however, that their Messiah would become a conqueror. Therefore, the crowd reacted strongly, even violently, and sought to capture or kidnap Jesus to take Him to Jerusalem and make Him their king. They wanted Jesus to assume political leadership, to set up a kingdom, and to release them from the yoke of Roman authority. Jesus understood the situation and slipped away into the mountains to escape them.

ing Jesus. 25And when they found Him on the other side of the sea, they said to Him, "Rabbi, when did You come here?"

26Jesus answered them and said, "Most assuredly, I say to you, you seek Me, not because you saw the signs, but because you ate of the loaves and were filled. 27Do not labor for the food which perishes, but for the food which endures to everlasting life, which the Son of Man will give you, because God the Father has set His seal on Him."

28Then they said to Him, "What shall we do, that we may work the works of God?"

29Jesus answered and said to them, "This is the work of God, that you believe in Him whom He sent."

30Therefore they said to Him, "What sign will You perform then, that we may see it and believe You? What work will You do? 31Our fathers ate the manna in the desert; as it is written, 'He gave them bread from heaven to eat.' "a

32Then Jesus said to them, "Most assuredly, I say to you, Moses did not give you the bread from heaven, but My Father gives you the true bread from heaven. 33For the bread of God is He who comes down from heaven and gives life to the world."

34Then they said to Him, "Lord, give us this bread always."

35And Jesus said to them, "I am the bread of life. He who comes to Me shall never hunger, and he who believes in Me shall never thirst. 36But I said to you that you have seen Me and yet do not believe. 37All that the Father gives Me will come to Me, and the one who comes to Me I will by no means cast out. 38For I have come down from heaven, not to do My own will, but the will of Him who sent Me. 39This is the will of the Father who sent Me, that of all He has given Me I should lose nothing, but should raise it up at the last day. 40And this is the will of Him who sent Me, that everyone who sees the Son and believes in Him may have everlasting life; and I will raise him up at the last day."

Rejected by His Own

41The Jews then complained about Him, because He said, "I am the bread which came down from heaven." 42And they said, "Is not this Jesus, the son of Joseph, whose father and mother we know? How is it then that He says, 'I have come down from heaven'?"

43Jesus therefore answered and said to them, "Do not murmur among yourselves. 44No one can come to Me unless the Father who sent Me draws him; and I will raise him up at the last day. 45It is written in the prophets, 'And they shall all be taught by God.'a Therefore everyone who has heard and learnedb from the Father comes to Me. 46Not that anyone has seen the Father, except He who is from God; He has seen the Father. 47Most assuredly, I say to you, he who believes in Mea has everlasting life. 48I am the bread of life. 49Your fathers ate the manna in the wilderness, and are dead. 50This is the bread which comes down from heaven, that one may eat of it and not die. 51I am the living bread which came down from heaven. If anyone eats of this bread, he will live forever; and the bread that I shall give is My flesh, which I shall give for the life of the world."

52The Jews therefore quarreled among themselves, saying, "How can this Man give us His flesh to eat?"

53Then Jesus said to them, "Most assuredly, I say to you, unless you eat the flesh of the Son of Man and drink His blood, you have no life in you. 54Whoever eats My flesh and drinks My blood has eternal life, and I will raise him up at the last day. 55For My flesh is food indeed,a and My blood is drink indeed. 56He who eats My flesh and drinks My blood abides in Me, and I in him. 57As the living Father sent Me, and I live because of the Father, so he who feeds on Me will live because of Me. 58This is the bread which came down from

6:31 aExodus 16:4; Nehemiah 9:15; Psalm 78:24   6:45 aIsaiah 54:13 bM-Text reads hears and has learned.   6:47 aNU-Text omits in Me. 6:55 aNU-Text reads true food and true drink.

6:31–33 God supplied manna to feed the Israelites as they fled Egyptian slavery and as they traveled, with Moses as their leader, for 40 years throughout the wilderness. Manna, a small, round substance, appeared each morning with the dew. This "bread from heaven" was then gathered, made into cakes, and either baked or boiled (see Ex. 16:13–36). The people believed that when the Messiah came, He would bring them "manna." The OT "manna" pointed to the true Bread of Heaven, Jesus.

6:52–57 Flesh and blood represented life, in particular Christ's self-sacrificed life fueled by His self-sacrificing love. "My flesh" referred to Jesus' body, which He gave up in death (v. 54). "My blood" referred to the shedding of His

blood on the cross at Calvary (v. 54). This imagery would sound familiar to those from pagan backgrounds in ancient times. They routinely offered sacrifices to their gods and actually ate part of the cooked flesh of the sacrifice. They would have considered eating the sacrificed flesh as becoming one with a god, in the sense of sharing an identity with that deity. The Jew of Jesus' day would have understood blood to stand for life. Thus, to drink Jesus' blood would suggest bringing His life into their lives. This paradox then explains both the essence of the gospel (Christ's sacrifice of His life) and the essence of personal holiness (our unique partaking of His life into our own). Christ came from the Father to offer the gift of Himself to all who would receive Him (vv. 51, 54, 56).

EVANGELISM DIVINE APPOINTMENTS

Jesus took every opportunity to make the message of God's love and forgiveness known. Although He was weary as He sat by the well of Sychar, He accepted the arrival of a woman from Samaria as a "divine appointment." Asking for a drink of water, He got her attention and engaged her in conversation, then proceeded to make His message relevant to her life and situation. What a great example of how believers can share their faith!

Just as women are increasingly choosing the "good life" without regard for biblical standards, this woman had chosen to live in a way that was not pleasing to God. Many are looking for what they perceive to be the best quality of life without regard for the relevancy of Christ's message to their daily lives.

Without an application of biblical standards, individuals as well as an entire nation tend to sink into moral decadence and disintegrate. The Bible alone is God's textbook about how to relate to God and to one another—husbands to wives, parents to children, employer to employee, friend to friend. Your view of God will determine much of your lifestyle. God has given His timeless blueprint, which when followed humbly and with obedience, gives the greatest quality of life the human heart can know.

Christian women have the "fresh water" for which the thirsty hearts of all people yearn. They must learn to make His message relevant, to anticipate divine appointments, and to be ready to show that the life Jesus offers is desirable and attractive.

Jesus always met with those who had honest questions or needs on their terms regarding place, method of access, or style of communication. He never, however, changed His message or altered the way in which He loved.

See also John 4:5–42; 10:10; 17:2, 3; notes on Access to God (Rom. 10); Evangelism (Col. 4; 1 Pet. 3); Salvation (Eph. 2)

---

heaven—not as your fathers ate the manna, and are dead. He who eats this bread will live forever."

59These things He said in the synagogue as He taught in Capernaum.

Many Disciples Turn Away

60Therefore many of His disciples, when they heard *this*, said, "This is a hard saying; who can understand it?"

61When Jesus knew in Himself that His disciples complained about this, He said to them, "Does this offend you? 62*What* then if you should see the Son of Man ascend where He was before? 63It is the Spirit who gives life; the flesh profits nothing. The words that I speak to you are spirit, and *they* are life. 64But there are some of you who do not believe." For Jesus knew from the beginning who they were who did not believe, and who would betray Him. 65And He said, "Therefore I have said to you that no one can come to Me unless it has been granted to him by My Father."

66From that *time* many of His disciples went back and walked with Him no more. 67Then Jesus said to the twelve, "Do you also want to go away?"

68But Simon Peter answered Him, "Lord, to whom shall we go? You have the words of eternal life. 69Also we have come to believe and know that You are the Christ, the Son of the living God."a

70Jesus answered them, "Did I not choose you, the twelve, and one of you is a devil?" 71He spoke of Judas Iscariot, *the son* of Simon, for it was he who would betray Him, being one of the twelve.

Jesus' Brothers Disbelieve

7After these things Jesus walked in Galilee; for He did not want to walk in Judea, because the Jewsa sought to kill Him. 2Now the Jews' Feast of Tabernacles was at hand. 3His brothers therefore said to Him, "Depart from here and go into Judea, that Your disciples also may see the works that You

6:69 aNU-Text reads *You are the Holy One of God.*   7:1 aThat is, the ruling authorities

---

6:66–69 The crowd that followed Jesus was very large, but they began to discover that His teachings were difficult to put into practice. In fact, following Him pointed to the possibility of sharing in His suffering and violent death. Slowly His disciples began to fall away. Perhaps those who left Jesus could foresee or anticipate the "tragedy" that would befall Jesus at the hands of the Roman government. Others, perhaps, lost interest or hope in Jesus. Their action prompted Jesus to ask the 12 disciples if they, too, would "go away." Jesus was not surprised by the many who turned away from Him. He knew of their discontentment, for He could read their hearts.

7:2 The Feast of Tabernacles (or Feast of Ingathering) lasted seven days (see chart, The Feasts of Israel). The celebrations

When you seek truth you seek God whether you know it or not.

Blessed Theresia Benedicta (Edith Stein)

---

are doing. [4]For no one does anything in secret while he himself seeks to be known openly. If You do these things, show Yourself to the world." [5]For even His brothers did not believe in Him.

[6]Then Jesus said to them, "My time has not yet come, but your time is always ready. [7]The world cannot hate you, but it hates Me because I testify of it that its works are evil. [8]You go up to this feast. I am not yet[a] going up to this feast, for My time has not yet fully come." [9]When He had said these things to them, He remained in Galilee.

The Heavenly Scholar

[10]But when His brothers had gone up, then He also went up to the feast, not openly, but as it were in secret. [11]Then the Jews sought Him at the feast, and said, "Where is He?" [12]And there was much complaining among the people concerning Him. Some said, "He is good"; others said, "No, on the contrary, He deceives the people." [13]However, no one spoke openly of Him for fear of the Jews.

[14]Now about the middle of the feast Jesus went up into the temple and taught. [15]And the Jews marveled, saying, "How does this Man know letters, having never studied?"

[16]Jesus[a] answered them and said, "My doctrine is not Mine, but His who sent Me. [17]If anyone wills to do His will, he shall know concerning the doctrine, whether it is from God or *whether* I speak on My own *authority*. [18]He who speaks from himself seeks his own glory; but He who seeks the glory of the One who sent Him is true, and no unrighteousness is in Him. [19]Did not Moses give you the law, yet none of you keeps the law? Why do you seek to kill Me?"

[20]The people answered and said, "You have a demon. Who is seeking to kill You?"

[21]Jesus answered and said to them, "I did one work, and you all marvel. [22]Moses therefore gave you circumcision (not that it is from Moses, but from the fathers), and you circumcise a man on the Sabbath. [23]If a man receives circumcision on the Sabbath, so that the law of Moses should not be broken, are you angry with Me because I made a man completely well on the Sabbath? [24]Do not judge according to appearance, but judge with righteous judgment."

Could This Be the Christ?

[25]Now some of them from Jerusalem said, "Is this not He whom they seek to kill? [26]But look! He speaks boldly, and they say nothing to Him. Do the rulers know indeed that this is truly[a] the Christ? [27]However, we know where this Man is from; but when the Christ comes, no one knows where He is from."

[28]Then Jesus cried out, as He taught in the temple, saying, "You both know Me, and you know where I am from; and I have not come of Myself, but He who sent Me is true, whom you do not know. [29]But[a] I know Him, for I am from Him, and He sent Me."

[30]Therefore they sought to take Him; but no one laid a hand on Him, because His hour had not yet come. [31]And many of the people believed in Him, and said, "When the Christ comes, will He do more signs than these which this *Man* has done?"

Jesus and the Religious Leaders

[32]The Pharisees heard the crowd murmuring these things concerning Him, and the Pharisees and the chief priests sent officers to take Him. [33]Then Jesus said to them,[a] "I shall be with you a little while longer, and *then* I go to Him who sent Me. [34]You will seek Me and not find *Me,* and where I am you cannot come."

[35]Then the Jews said among themselves,

7:8 [a]NU-Text omits *yet.*   7:16 [a]NU-Text and M-Text read *So Jesus.*
7:26 [a]NU-Text omits *truly.*   7:29 [a]NU-Text and M-Text omit *But.*
7:33 [a]NU-Text and M-Text omit *to them.*

---

included the ingathering of crops. Participants made booths or "tabernacles" of tree branches. These booths represented shelter and protection. The Israelites lived in these booths throughout the festival period in order to remember their fathers who, when they left Egypt and journeyed in the wilderness, had lived in similar structures.

7:34 Jesus spoke to nominal disciples, those who were not willing to invest their lives in a personal commitment to Him. Jesus referred to His death, telling them that He would go to the Father and they would not be able to find Him. These Jews

had put their trust in belonging to the family of Abraham. They had not put their trust in God's plan of salvation through Jesus. Jesus told them, in effect, that when they did come to an understanding of God and the Good News and wanted to place their faith in Him, it would then be too late.

7:35 God had given the Jews the land of Palestine, the Promised Land, for an inheritance. The Dispersion or Diaspora, which took place over several centuries, was responsible for forcing the Jews out of Palestine. This scattering of the Jews throughout the world was due to the Assyrians' capture

FORGIVEN ADULTERESS

The woman caught in the very act of sexual immorality is simply known as the adulteress. Israel's covenant law prohibited adultery (Ex. 20:14). The punishment of death was dictated for both the adulterous man and woman (Lev. 20:10). Yet while this woman faced death, the man with whom she had been involved went free.

The accusing scribes and Pharisees threw the woman at Jesus' feet. They sought to trap Jesus between His allegiance to the Law and His merciful love for all, even those who violated the Law.

The adulteress was guilty of sin. The Mosaic Law stated that she deserved the sentence of death (Deut. 17:5, 6). The zealous religious leaders quoted the Law and waited impatiently for Jesus to respond.

Then Jesus answered, slowly and wisely. For the Messiah clarified the Law's intent and reminded each religious leader of his own sins and of his own guilt in breaking the Law of Moses. Each one knew, somewhere deep within his own sinful heart, that he, too, deserved the sentence of death.

Jesus also affirmed the sanctity of marriage, making it clear that men, as well as women, are expected to keep their vows. He did not condemn the woman caught in the act of adultery. Instead, He forgave her, as He would later forgive the very people who nailed Him to a Cross (see John 3:17). Jesus faced the sentence of death Himself, for the adulteress, for the sinful scribes and Pharisees, for everyone. His grace provides hope for every sinful soul (see John 8:12).

See also notes on Adultery (Hos. 3); Forgiveness (Ps. 51; Luke 17)

"Where does He intend to go that we shall not find Him? Does He intend to go to the Dispersion among the Greeks and teach the Greeks? 36What is this thing that He said, 'You will seek Me and not find Me, and where I am you cannot come'?"

The Promise of the Holy Spirit

37On the last day, that great *day* of the feast, Jesus stood and cried out, saying, "If anyone thirsts, let him come to Me and drink. 38He who believes in Me, as the Scripture has said, out of his heart will flow rivers of living water." 39But this He spoke concerning the Spirit, whom those believing[a] in Him would receive; for the Holy[b] Spirit was not yet *given*, because Jesus was not yet glorified.

Who Is He?

40Therefore many[a] from the crowd, when they heard this saying, said, "Truly this is the Prophet." 41Others said, "This is the Christ."

But some said, "Will the Christ come out of Galilee? 42Has not the Scripture said that the Christ comes from the seed of David and from the town of Bethlehem, where David was?" 43So there was a division among the people because of Him. 44Now some of them wanted to take Him, but no one laid hands on Him.

Rejected by the Authorities

45Then the officers came to the chief priests and Pharisees, who said to them, "Why have you not brought Him?"

46The officers answered, "No man ever spoke like this Man!"

47Then the Pharisees answered them, "Are you also deceived? 48Have any of the rulers or the Pharisees believed in Him? 49But this crowd that does not know the law is accursed."

50Nicodemus (he who came to Jesus by night,[a] being one of them) said to them, 51"Does our law judge a man before it hears him and knows what he is doing?"

52They answered and said to him, "Are you also from Galilee? Search and look, for no prophet has arisen[a] out of Galilee."

An Adulteress Faces the Light of the World

53And everyone went to his *own* house.[a]

8 But Jesus went to the Mount of Olives. 2Now early[a] in the morning He came again into the temple, and all the people came to Him;

···················

7:39 [a]NU-Text reads *who believed.* [b]NU-Text omits Holy. 7:40 [a]NU-Text reads *some.* 7:50 [a]NU-Text reads *before.* 7:52 [a]NU-Text reads *is to rise.* 7:53 [a]The words *And everyone* through *sin no more* (8:11) are bracketed by NU-Text as not original. They are present in over 900 manuscripts. 8:2 [a]M-Text reads *very early.*

---

of Israel (722 B.C.), the capture of Judah by the Babylonians (586 B.C.), and other wars fought in Palestine by the Romans and Greeks. Some simply came upon hard times and emigrated to other places to find work and resources. In Jesus' time, as many Jews lived outside of Palestine as lived in the Land.

7:38 The particular quotation from Scripture used by Jesus has never been identified with certainty. He probably had in mind Psalm 78:15, 16 and Zechariah 14:8 (see also Ezek. 47:1–11; Rev. 22:1, 2). The "heart" was believed to be the seat of the emotions, the innermost being of a person. In essence, Jesus said that the person would have a continual, life-giving source of satisfaction within.

The gate of Heaven is very low; only the humble can enter it.

St. Elizabeth Seton

and He sat down and taught them. [3]Then the scribes and Pharisees brought to Him a woman caught in adultery. And when they had set her in the midst, [4]they said to Him, "Teacher, this woman was caught[a] in adultery, in the very act. [5]Now Moses, in the law, commanded[a] us that such should be stoned.[b] But what do You say?"[c] [6]This they said, testing Him, that they might have *something* of which to accuse Him. But Jesus stooped down and wrote on the ground with *His* finger, as though He did not hear.[a]

[7]So when they continued asking Him, He raised Himself up[a] and said to them, "He who is without sin among you, let him throw a stone at her first." [8]And again He stooped down and wrote on the ground. [9]Then those who heard *it*, being convicted by *their* conscience,[a] went out one by one, beginning with the oldest *even* to the last. And Jesus was left alone, and the woman standing in the midst. [10]When Jesus had raised Himself up and saw no one but the woman, He said to her,[a] "Woman, where are those accusers of yours?[b] Has no one condemned you?"

[11]She said, "No one, Lord."

And Jesus said to her, "Neither do I condemn you; go and[a] sin no more."

[12]Then Jesus spoke to them again, saying, "I am the light of the world. He who follows Me shall not walk in darkness, but have the light of life."

Jesus Defends His Self-Witness

[13]The Pharisees therefore said to Him, "You bear witness of Yourself; Your witness is not true."

[14]Jesus answered and said to them, "Even if I bear witness of Myself, My witness is true, for I know where I came from and where I am going; but you do not know where I come from and where I am going. [15]You judge according to the flesh; I judge no one. [16]And yet if I do judge, My judgment is true; for I am not alone, but I *am* with the Father who sent Me. [17]It is also written in your law that the testimony of two men is true. [18]I am One who bears witness of Myself, and the Father who sent Me bears witness of Me."

[19]Then they said to Him, "Where is Your Father?"

Jesus answered, "You know neither Me nor My Father. If you had known Me, you would have known My Father also."

[20]These words Jesus spoke in the treasury, as He taught in the temple; and no one laid hands on Him, for His hour had not yet come.

Jesus Predicts His Departure

[21]Then Jesus said to them again, "I am going away, and you will seek Me, and will die in your sin. Where I go you cannot come."

[22]So the Jews said, "Will He kill Himself, because He says, 'Where I go you cannot come'?"

[23]And He said to them, "You are from beneath; I am from above. You are of this world; I am not of this world. [24]Therefore I said to you that you will die in your sins; for if you do not believe that I am *He,* you will die in your sins."

[25]Then they said to Him, "Who are You?"

And Jesus said to them, "Just what I have been saying to you from the beginning. [26]I have many things to say and to judge concerning you, but He who sent Me is true; and I speak to the world those things which I heard from Him."

[27]They did not understand that He spoke to them of the Father.

[28]Then Jesus said to them, "When you lift up the Son of Man, then you will know that I am *He,* and *that* I do nothing of Myself; but as My Father taught Me, I speak these things. [29]And He who sent Me is with Me. The Father has not left Me alone, for I always do those things that please Him." [30]As He spoke these words, many believed in Him.

The Truth Shall Make You Free

[31]Then Jesus said to those Jews who believed Him, "If you abide in My word, you are My disciples

8:4 [a]M-Text reads *we found this woman.* **8:5** [a]M-Text reads *in our law Moses commanded.* [b]NU-Text and M-Text read *to stone such.* [c]M-Text adds *about her.* **8:6** [a]NU-Text and M-Text omit *as though He did not hear.* **8:7** [a]M-Text reads *He looked up.* **8:9** [a]NU-Text and M-Text omit *being convicted by their conscience.* **8:10** [a]NU-Text omits *and saw no one but the woman;* M-Text reads *He saw her and said.* [b]NU-Text and M-Text omit *of yours.* **8:11** [a]NU-Text and M-Text add *from now on.*

8:4, 5 The Law of Moses had strict rules about sexuality (Ex. 20:14). The punishment for adultery was death by stoning for both the man and the woman (Lev. 20:10). If Jesus confirmed the death penalty, His compassion would be questioned; if He refused to confirm the penalty, He would be accused of con-

tradicting God's Law. He wisely referred the question to the woman's accusers, for Jewish law also called for the witness to cast the first stone in the case of capital punishment (see Forgiven Adulteress).

indeed. [32]And you shall know the truth, and the truth shall make you free."

[33]They answered Him, "We are Abraham's descendants, and have never been in bondage to anyone. How *can* You say, 'You will be made free'?"

[34]Jesus answered them, "Most assuredly, I say to you, whoever commits sin is a slave of sin. [35]And a slave does not abide in the house forever, *but* a son abides forever. [36]Therefore if the Son makes you free, you shall be free indeed.

Abraham's Seed and Satan's

[37]"I know that you are Abraham's descendants, but you seek to kill Me, because My word has no place in you. [38]I speak what I have seen with My Father, and you do what you have seen with[a] your father."

[39]They answered and said to Him, "Abraham is our father."

Jesus said to them, "If you were Abraham's children, you would do the works of Abraham. [40]But now you seek to kill Me, a Man who has told you the truth which I heard from God. Abraham did not do this. [41]You do the deeds of your father."

Then they said to Him, "We were not born of fornication; we have one Father—God."

[42]Jesus said to them, "If God were your Father, you would love Me, for I proceeded forth and came from God; nor have I come of Myself, but He sent Me. [43]Why do you not understand My speech? Because you are not able to listen to My word. [44]You are of *your* father the devil, and the desires of your father you want to do. He was a murderer from the beginning, and does not stand in the truth, because there is no truth in him. When he speaks a lie, he speaks from his own *resources,* for he is a liar and the father of it. [45]But because I tell the truth, you do not believe Me. [46]Which of you convicts Me of sin? And if I tell the truth, why do you not be-

lieve Me? [47]He who is of God hears God's words; therefore you do not hear, because you are not of God."

Before Abraham Was, I AM

[48]Then the Jews answered and said to Him, "Do we not say rightly that You are a Samaritan and have a demon?"

[49]Jesus answered, "I do not have a demon; but I honor My Father, and you dishonor Me. [50]And I do not seek My *own* glory; there is One who seeks and judges. [51]Most assuredly, I say to you, if anyone keeps My word he shall never see death."

[52]Then the Jews said to Him, "Now we know that You have a demon! Abraham is dead, and the prophets; and You say, 'If anyone keeps My word he shall never taste death.' [53]Are You greater than our father Abraham, who is dead? And the prophets are dead. Who do You make Yourself out to be?"

[54]Jesus answered, "If I honor Myself, My honor is nothing. It is My Father who honors Me, of whom you say that He is your[a] God. [55]Yet you have not known Him, but I know Him. And if I say, 'I do not know Him,' I shall be a liar like you; but I do know Him and keep His word. [56]Your father Abraham rejoiced to see My day, and he saw *it* and was glad."

[57]Then the Jews said to Him, "You are not yet fifty years old, and have You seen Abraham?"

[58]Jesus said to them, "Most assuredly, I say to you, before Abraham was, I AM."

[59]Then they took up stones to throw at Him; but Jesus hid Himself and went out of the temple,[a] going through the midst of them, and so passed by.

....

8:38 [a]NU-Text reads *heard from.*   **8:54** [a]NU-Text and M-Text read *our.*   **8:59** [a]NU-Text omits the rest of this verse.

8:32–36 The Jews put blind trust in religious tradition and ceremonies. They depended on ancestry and obedience to the Law of Moses and the oral tradition of the elders for their hope. Throughout the years, they had been in bondage to Egypt, Babylonia, Persia, Syria, and, at present, Rome. Regardless of their political slavery, they felt free spiritually because they were a holy nation, an elect race chosen by God. Jesus disagreed with them and thus angered them. He told them they were slaves of sin, not sons of God, and that only through Him could they find true spiritual freedom.

8:41 With much pride, the Jews assured Jesus that they were born from the seed of Abraham. They probably meant to insult Jesus directly. The common belief among the Jews was that Mary had been unfaithful to Joseph and that Jesus was the illegitimate son of Mary, the result of an adulterous union.

8:44 The devil (Satan) is mentioned only a few times in the

OT (see chart, The Names for Satan). The chief of the fallen angels, Satan is always an adversary to God (see chart, A Portrait of the Adversary). In the NT, the gospel writers taught that Satan is a personal being, the agent and originator of evil. John considered Satan the "ruler of this world" (John 12:31; 14:30; 16:11). The self-righteous Jews claimed God as their Father. Jesus, however, told them that they were indeed Abraham's descendants and physical progeny. But in spirit, their father was not God, but the devil. Their behavior confirmed their parentage.

8:58, 59 When asked His identity, Jesus responded, "I AM." This enraged the Jews. "I AM" is the name for God that He had revealed to Moses (Ex. 3:13, 14). Thus, Jesus identified Himself as One with God. The Jews considered this statement blasphemy (lit. "harmful speech" or "slander"). In the OT sense, blasphemy meant showing disrespect to the character and name of God. The penalty for blasphemy (for a Jew or foreigner) was death by stoning (Lev. 24:14–16).

A Man Born Blind Receives Sight

9 Now as *Jesus* passed by, He saw a man who was blind from birth. [2]And His disciples asked Him, saying, "Rabbi, who sinned, this man or his parents, that he was born blind?"

[3]Jesus answered, "Neither this man nor his parents sinned, but that the works of God should be revealed in him. [4]I[a] must work the works of Him who sent Me while it is day; *the* night is coming when no one can work. [5]As long as I am in the world, I am the light of the world."

[6]When He had said these things, He spat on the ground and made clay with the saliva; and He anointed the eyes of the blind man with the clay. [7]And He said to him, "Go, wash in the pool of Siloam" (which is translated, Sent). So he went and washed, and came back seeing.

[8]Therefore the neighbors and those who previously had seen that he was blind[a] said, "Is not this he who sat and begged?"

[9]Some said, "This is he." Others *said*, "He is like him."[a]

He said, "I am *he*."

[10]Therefore they said to him, "How were your eyes opened?"

[11]He answered and said, "A Man called Jesus made clay and anointed my eyes and said to me, 'Go to the pool of[a] Siloam and wash.' So I went and washed, and I received sight."

[12]Then they said to him, "Where is He?"

He said, "I do not know."

The Pharisees Excommunicate the Healed Man

[13]They brought him who formerly was blind to the Pharisees. [14]Now it was a Sabbath when Jesus made the clay and opened his eyes. [15]Then the Pharisees also asked him again how he had received his sight. He said to them, "He put clay on my eyes, and I washed, and I see."

[16]Therefore some of the Pharisees said, "This Man is not from God, because He does not keep the Sabbath."

Others said, "How can a man who is a sinner do such signs?" And there was a division among them.

THE NAMES FOR SATAN	
NAME	**REFERENCE**
Abaddon (Heb., lit. "destruction")	Rev. 9:11
The accuser of our brethren	Rev. 12:10
The adversary (Gk. *antidikos*, lit. "opponent")	1 Pet. 5:8
The angel of the bottomless pit	Rev. 9:11
Apollyon (Gk., lit. "destroyer")	Rev. 9:11
Beelzebub, the ruler of the demons	Matt. 12:24
Belial	2 Cor. 6:15
The devil (Gk. *diabalos*, lit. "one who casts through")	John 8:44
The dragon	Rev. 12:7; 20:2
The enemy	Matt. 13:39
The god of this age	2 Cor. 4:4
The king of Tyre	Ezek. 28:11–19
Liar	John 8:44
Lucifer (Heb., lit. "day star")	Is. 14:12–21
Murderer	John 8:44
The prince of the power of the air	Eph. 2:2
A roaring lion	1 Pet. 5:8
The ruler of the darkness	Eph. 6:12
The ruler of this world	John 12:31; 14:30
Satan (Heb., lit. "adversary")	Mark 1:12, 13
The serpent of old	Rev. 20:2
The tempter	1 Thess. 3:5
The wicked one	Matt. 13:19

9:4 [a]NU-Text reads *We*.   **9:8** [a]NU-Text reads *a beggar*.   **9:9** [a]NU-Text reads *"No, but he is like him."*   **9:11** [a]NU-Text omits *the pool of*.

9:2 Blindness was common in Jesus' day, often resulting from a birth defect, infection, leprosy, cataracts, or advanced age. The Jews associated blindness (and suffering in general) with sin:

- The man might have sinned while still in his mother's womb (some Jews believed in prenatal sin);
- The man, in his pre-existent state (an idea that emerged from the Greek philosopher Plato about 427–327 B.C.) might have sinned before his conception;
- The blind man's parents might have sinned and brought the affliction of blindness upon their son. Jews believed the sins of the parents could cause suffering for the child (see Ex. 20:5; 34:7; Num. 14:18).

9:6, 7 This healing was one of two healings in which Jesus

used saliva (see Mark 7:33). No medicinal value was associated with the pool of Siloam, a water supply located just inside the southeastern city wall. The pool was an engineering feat for that day created by the construction of Hezekiah's tunnel, which diverted waters from Siloam to the Gihon spring (a less vulnerable point to the Assyrian armies). Dug through solid rock, this 583-yard tunnel of Hezekiah provided water diverted into the city from the Kidron valley outside the city wall in the event of an enemy siege. The Siloam pool measured 20 by 30 feet and is still used as a source of water.

9:16 A debate occurred when the Pharisees accused Jesus of not keeping the Sabbath:

- Jesus had made clay, and they considered that work forbidden on the Sabbath;

O R G A N I Z A T I O N ORDERING OUR DAYS

The concept of organization in Scripture relates far more to our relationships with people than to the handling of things. Organization allows us to move through life with order and purpose. This discipline is not reserved only for organized people, for God delights in helping each person to turn weakness into strength and to bring order from chaos (1 Cor. 14:40). He redeems our time as well as our souls (Col. 4:5).

Smooth communication, effective problem solving, successful task management, and coordination of life's pursuits is just as necessary for meaningful interpersonal relationships as for juggling events and sorting activities. The Lord insisted, through the advice of Jethro, that Moses establish a multi-tiered judicial system, which effectively placed "men of truth" as rulers of thousands, hundreds, fifties, and tens (Ex. 18:13–26). Jesus created order so that the hungry crowds could be fed by seating the people on the grass, allowing the disciples to move freely among them with bread and fish (Matt. 15:35). Jesus, in sending out His disciples, organized them in teams of two and gave them well-ordered guidelines (Mark 6:7).

Decision making, assignment of space, accomplishment of tasks, and clear lines of communication are thus ordered with one goal in mind—that our lives and environment might be so ordered as to give maximum freedom for achieving His goals. In organizing home or office, priority should be given to policies and structures that benefit and bless people. People always matter more to the Lord than rules, a principle readily evident in the ministry of Jesus, who frequently overstepped the boundaries set by the "religious" leaders of His day in order to bring truth, comfort, and healing to those in need.

See also Eph. 5:15, 16; notes on Goal Setting (Is. 58); Priorities (Matt. 6); Time Management (Ps. 31)

17They said to the blind man again, "What do you say about Him because He opened your eyes?"

He said, "He is a prophet."

18But the Jews did not believe concerning him, that he had been blind and received his sight, until they called the parents of him who had received his sight. 19And they asked them, saying, "Is this your son, who you say was born blind? How then does he now see?"

20His parents answered them and said, "We know that this is our son, and that he was born blind; 21but by what means he now sees we do not know, or who opened his eyes we do not know. He is of age; ask him. He will speak for himself." 22His parents said these things because they feared the Jews, for the Jews had agreed already that if anyone confessed that He was Christ, he would be put out of the synagogue. 23Therefore his parents said, "He is of age; ask him."

24So they again called the man who was blind, and said to him, "Give God the glory! We know that this Man is a sinner."

25He answered and said, "Whether He is a sinner or not I do not know. One thing I know: that though I was blind, now I see."

26Then they said to him again, "What did He do to you? How did He open your eyes?"

27He answered them, "I told you already, and you did not listen. Why do you want to hear it again? Do you also want to become His disciples?"

28Then they reviled him and said, "You are His disciple, but we are Moses' disciples. 29We know that God spoke to Moses; as for this fellow, we do not know where He is from."

30The man answered and said to them, "Why, this is a marvelous thing, that you do not know where He is from; yet He has opened my eyes! 31Now we know that God does not hear sinners; but if anyone is a worshiper of God and does His will, He hears him. 32Since the world began it has been unheard of that anyone opened the eyes of one who was born blind. 33If this Man were not from God, He could do nothing."

34They answered and said to him, "You were completely born in sins, and are you teaching us?" And they cast him out.

True Vision and True Blindness

35Jesus heard that they had cast him out; and when He had found him, He said to him, "Do you believe in the Son of God?"a

36He answered and said, "Who is He, Lord, that I may believe in Him?"

37And Jesus said to him, "You have both seen Him and it is He who is talking with you."

··················
9:35 aNU-Text reads Son of Man.

- Jesus had healed the blind man (v. 14), and any non-life-threatening medical attention was not allowed on the Sabbath;
- Jesus had put saliva on the man's eyes, a practice not allowed on the Sabbath.

Therefore, the Pharisees thought Jesus could not have come from God. But others, astounded and impressed by Jesus' miracles ("signs"), could not consider Jesus a "sinner."

Love him totally who gave himself totally for your love.

St. Clare of Assisi

---

[38]Then he said, "Lord, I believe!" And he worshiped Him.

[39]And Jesus said, "For judgment I have come into this world, that those who do not see may see, and that those who see may be made blind."

[40]Then *some* of the Pharisees who were with Him heard these words, and said to Him, "Are we blind also?"

[41]Jesus said to them, "If you were blind, you would have no sin; but now you say, 'We see.' Therefore your sin remains.

Jesus the True Shepherd

10 "Most assuredly, I say to you, he who does not enter the sheepfold by the door, but climbs up some other way, the same is a thief and a robber. [2]But he who enters by the door is the shepherd of the sheep. [3]To him the doorkeeper opens, and the sheep hear his voice; and he calls his own sheep by name and leads them out. [4]And when he brings out his own sheep, he goes before them; and the sheep follow him, for they know his voice. [5]Yet they will by no means follow a stranger, but will flee from him, for they do not know the voice of strangers." [6]Jesus used this illustration, but they did not understand the things which He spoke to them.

Jesus the Good Shepherd

[7]Then Jesus said to them again, "Most assuredly, I say to you, I am the door of the sheep. [8]All who *ever* came before Me[a] are thieves and robbers, but the sheep did not hear them. [9]I am the door. If anyone enters by Me, he will be saved, and will go in and out and find pasture. [10]The thief does not come except to steal, and to kill, and to destroy. I have come that they may have life, and that they may have *it* more abundantly.

[11]"I am the good shepherd. The good shepherd gives His life for the sheep. [12]But a hireling, *he who is* not the shepherd, one who does not own the sheep, sees the wolf coming and leaves the sheep and flees; and the wolf catches the sheep and scatters them. [13]The hireling flees because he is a hireling and does not care about the sheep. [14]I am the good shepherd; and I know My *sheep,* and am known by My own. [15]As the Father knows Me, even so I know the Father; and I lay down My life for the sheep. [16]And other sheep I have which are not of this fold; them also I must bring, and they will hear My voice; and there will be one flock *and* one shepherd.

[17]"Therefore My Father loves Me, because I lay down My life that I may take it again. [18]No one takes it from Me, but I lay it down of Myself. I have power to lay it down, and I have power to take it again. This command I have received from My Father."

[19]Therefore there was a division again among the Jews because of these sayings. [20]And many of them said, "He has a demon and is mad. Why do you listen to Him?"

[21]Others said, "These are not the words of one who has a demon. Can a demon open the eyes of the blind?"

The Shepherd Knows His Sheep

[22]Now it was the Feast of Dedication in Jerusalem, and it was winter. [23]And Jesus walked in the temple, in Solomon's porch. [24]Then the Jews surrounded Him and said to Him, "How long do You keep us in doubt? If You are the Christ, tell us plainly."

[25]Jesus answered them, "I told you, and you do

10:8 [a]M-Text omits *before Me.*

9:39–41 Jesus used this situation in which individuals were responding to Him so differently to make a point about blindness and sight. On one side was the man born blind, now fully seeing and on his knees worshiping the Lord. On the other side were the religious leaders, stubborn and hard-hearted, rejecting Jesus and calling for His death. In Jesus' day, blindness was a metaphor for sin. Sight was a metaphor for righteousness. Jesus told the Pharisees that, even though they could see clearly physically, they were deliberately choosing to be blind spiritually.

10:2–5 Sheep provided food, milk, and clothing. A shepherd fed them, led them to water, guarded them lest they wander off and get lost, protected them from predators (usually wolves), carried them when they were sick or weak, and constantly cared for them. The job of shepherding was a tiring

and dangerous one. Often the shepherd spent years with a particular herd of sheep and called each sheep by its own descriptive name. The sheep knew and followed the voice of their shepherd, but they would not respond to a stranger's voice. The shepherd went "before them" to make sure the path was safe for the sheep (v. 4). The "door" referred to the entrance of the sheepfold (v. 2). Jesus described Himself as the Good Shepherd, a metaphor the people of His day would have understood clearly.

10:16 The other sheep was a reference to the Gentiles. "This fold" was a reference to Judaism. Jesus anticipated the mission to the Gentiles after His death and Resurrection. The Gentiles, as well as the believing Jews, would share an intimate relationship with Him.

MENTAL HEALTH   *A SOUND MIND*

When Jesus referred to the abundant life, He described a life in balance, all aspects of which are under the authority of God, and one in which an individual would grow in the image of Christ. Elements necessary for positive mental health include: reasonable independence (Prov. 31:12–16), trustworthiness (v. 11), the ability to take responsibility (v. 13), the ability to work under rules and authority (Heb. 13:7), tolerance of others (Eph. 4:32), the ability to show friendliness and love (Prov. 17:17), a sense of humor (v. 22), the capacity to give and take (Eccl. 3:5), and most of all a devotion beyond self (1 John 4:10, 11). Jesus not only provided salvation but also underscored the quality of life and set new standards for the abundant life.

Because a healthy life is intertwined with a healthy mind, Christians are warned by Paul to guard what the mind absorbs so that they do not become "blinded" to the truth (2 Cor. 3:14; 4:3, 4). Scripture strongly states that what goes into the mind comes out in actions, good or negative (Prov. 23:7; Mark 7:20–23). In healing the Gadarene demoniac, Jesus put him in his right mind (Luke 8:35). The restored man surely returned to a useful role in his home and community, and he did not forget to testify of God's goodness to him (Luke 8:39).

Paul encouraged Timothy by saying, "God has not given us a spirit of fear, but of power and of love and of a sound mind" (2 Tim. 1:7). We can be certain the Lord wants us to enjoy excellent mental health.

See also Josh. 1:8, 9; Ps. 1:2; 16:7–9; 119; Matt. 15:10–20; Mark 5:1–20; 5:2, note; Phil. 2:5–11; notes on Conscience (2 Cor. 1); Emotions (Ps. 42); Healing (Ps. 13; 133; Eccl. 1; 2 Cor. 5; Gal. 6; James 5)

not believe. The works that I do in My Father's name, they bear witness of Me. 26But you do not believe, because you are not of My sheep, as I said to you.ᵃ 27My sheep hear My voice, and I know them, and they follow Me. 28And I give them eternal life, and they shall never perish; neither shall anyone snatch them out of My hand. 29My Father, who has given *them* to Me, is greater than all; and no one is able to snatch *them* out of My Father's hand. 30I and *My* Father are one."

Renewed Efforts to Stone Jesus

31Then the Jews took up stones again to stone Him. 32Jesus answered them, "Many good works I have shown you from My Father. For which of those works do you stone Me?"

33The Jews answered Him, saying, "For a good work we do not stone You, but for blasphemy, and because You, being a Man, make Yourself God."

34Jesus answered them, "Is it not written in your law, *'I said, "You are gods" '?*ᵃ 35If He called them gods, to whom the word of God came (and the Scripture cannot be broken), 36do you say of Him

whom the Father sanctified and sent into the world, 'You are blaspheming,' because I said, 'I am the Son of God'? 37If I do not do the works of My Father, do not believe Me; 38but if I do, though you do not believe Me, believe the works, that you may know and believeᵃ that the Father *is* in Me, and I in Him." 39Therefore they sought again to seize Him, but He escaped out of their hand.

The Believers Beyond Jordan

40And He went away again beyond the Jordan to the place where John was baptizing at first, and there He stayed. 41Then many came to Him and said, "John performed no sign, but all the things that John spoke about this Man were true." 42And many believed in Him there.

The Death of Lazarus

11 Now a certain *man* was sick, Lazarus of Bethany, the town of Mary and her sister

10:26 ᵃNU-Text omits *as I said to you.*   10:34 ᵃPsalm 82:6   10:38 ᵃNU-Text reads *understand.*

10:22 The Feast of Dedication of the Temple of the Altar or the Feast of the Purification of the Temple (*Hanukkah*) occurs in December and lasts eight days. A candle is lit each day in observance of this celebration, often called the Feast of Lights.

The feast celebrates the victories of Judas Maccabaeus (165 B.C.). When Antiochus Epiphanes, the king of Syria (175–164 B.C.), tried to abolish the Jewish religion, he attacked Jerusalem. He killed 80,000 Jews, profaned the temple courts and chambers, and sacrificed swine to the pagan god Zeus on the temple altar. Judas Maccabaeus and his brothers fought Epiphanes and won. They cleansed and restored the temple and rebuilt the altar. This Feast of Hanukkah is still celebrated by the Jews. John referred to the various Jewish feasts more than the other gospel writers (see chart, The Feasts of Israel).

10:23 Jesus walked on Solomon's porch, a structure with a roof supported by rows of 40-foot-high pillars. This structure would have protected Jesus from the wintry weather. People often walked there to meditate, pray, and teach. It is also called "the portico of Solomon" or "Solomon's colonnade." While Solomon had built the oldest of the porches on the east side, Herod had built the porch on which Jesus walked.

10:30–33 Jesus referred to Himself as one with God, separate in Person but identical in nature. The godhead includes Father, Son, and Holy Spirit—a triunity of separate persons united in essence as one. The Jews regarded Jesus' claim to be one with God as blasphemy.

Martha. [2]It was *that* Mary who anointed the Lord with fragrant oil and wiped His feet with her hair, whose brother Lazarus was sick. [3]Therefore the sisters sent to Him, saying, "Lord, behold, he whom You love is sick."

[4]When Jesus heard *that*, He said, "This sickness is not unto death, but for the glory of God, that the Son of God may be glorified through it."

[5]Now Jesus loved Martha and her sister and Lazarus. [6]So, when He heard that he was sick, He stayed two more days in the place where He was. [7]Then after this He said to *the* disciples, "Let us go to Judea again."

[8]*The* disciples said to Him, "Rabbi, lately the Jews sought to stone You, and are You going there again?"

[9]Jesus answered, "Are there not twelve hours in the day? If anyone walks in the day, he does not stumble, because he sees the light of this world. [10]But if one walks in the night, he stumbles, because the light is not in him." [11]These things He said, and after that He said to them, "Our friend Lazarus sleeps, but I go that I may wake him up."

[12]Then His disciples said, "Lord, if he sleeps he will get well." [13]However, Jesus spoke of his death, but they thought that He was speaking about taking rest in sleep.

[14]Then Jesus said to them plainly, "Lazarus is dead. [15]And I am glad for your sakes that I was not there, that you may believe. Nevertheless let us go to him."

[16]Then Thomas, who is called the Twin, said to his fellow disciples, "Let us also go, that we may die with Him."

I Am the Resurrection and the Life

[17]So when Jesus came, He found that he had already been in the tomb four days. [18]Now Bethany was near Jerusalem, about two miles[a] away. [19]And many of the Jews had joined the women around Martha and Mary, to comfort them concerning their brother.

[20]Now Martha, as soon as she heard that Jesus was coming, went and met Him, but Mary was sitting in the house. [21]Now Martha said to Jesus, "Lord, if You had been here, my brother would not have died. [22]But even now I know that whatever You ask of God, God will give You."

[23]Jesus said to her, "Your brother will rise again."

[24]Martha said to Him, "I know that he will rise again in the resurrection at the last day."

[25]Jesus said to her, "I am the resurrection and the life. He who believes in Me, though he may die, he shall live. [26]And whoever lives and believes in Me shall never die. Do you believe this?"

[27]She said to Him, "Yes, Lord, I believe that You are the Christ, the Son of God, who is to come into the world."

Jesus and Death, the Last Enemy

[28]And when she had said these things, she went her way and secretly called Mary her sister, saying, "The Teacher has come and is calling for you." [29]As soon as she heard *that,* she arose quickly and came to Him. [30]Now Jesus had not yet come into the town, but was[a] in the place where Martha met Him. [31]Then the Jews who were with her in the house, and comforting her, when they saw that Mary rose up quickly and went out, followed her, saying, "She is going to the tomb to weep there."[a]

[32]Then, when Mary came where Jesus was, and saw Him, she fell down at His feet, saying to Him, "Lord, if You had been here, my brother would not have died."

[33]Therefore, when Jesus saw her weeping, and the Jews who came with her weeping, He groaned in the spirit and was troubled. [34]And He said, "Where have you laid him?"

They said to Him, "Lord, come and see."

[35]Jesus wept. [36]Then the Jews said, "See how He loved him!"

····················

11:18 [a]Literally *fifteen stadia*   11:30 [a]NU-Text adds *still.*   11:31 [a]NU-Text reads *supposing that she was going to the tomb to weep there.*

11:11–14 Lazarus from Bethany, along with his sisters Mary and Martha, was a personal friend of Jesus (see chart, Women and Their Families in the New Testament). Jesus told the disciples that Lazarus was asleep, using the term "sleep" as a euphemism for death (see Matt. 9:24; Acts 7:60; 1 Cor. 15:6; 1 Thess. 4:13).

11:17 Death and burial usually took place on the same day in Jesus' time, due to the hot climate. The body was carefully but hurriedly wrapped in strips of cloth with expensive spices and ointments. Jesus probably began His journey to Bethany the day of, or the day after, Lazarus' death and burial. The journey took two to three days. When Jesus arrived in Bethany, Lazarus would have been in the tomb four days, which John carefully noted. Jewish tradition taught that the deceased person's soul hovered over the body for three days after death in hopes of reunion. However untrue, this superstition was widely believed. The fact that Lazarus had been dead for four days instead of three left little doubt in Jewish minds that Lazarus' restoration to life by Jesus was, in fact, an unmistakable miracle.

11:33 Jesus groaned in the spirit and was troubled when He saw Mary and the others grieving and weeping (see chart, The Emotions of Jesus). The verb translated "groaned" may mean "deeply disturbed." "Troubled" (Gk. *tarassō*) has the connotation of being agitated or disturbed. Jesus could have been perplexed and grieved for several reasons:

- His heart was filled with indignation against sin, the cause of suffering and death.
- A large number of strangers had traveled from the Passover feast in Jerusalem to wail at Lazarus' funeral, and He might have been angered by their hypocrisy. Often funeral wailing was only an artificial display of emotion.

MARY OF BETHANY *A Committed Follower*

Mary of Bethany stands as a role model for every dedicated disciple of Christ. She was apparently unmarried, living with her older sister Martha and their brother Lazarus. Their home was a friendly retreat for the Lord, who may have been in their age group.

Mary, more than any other in the New Testament, is associated with sitting at Jesus' feet, a testimony to her hunger for spiritual truth and understanding (Luke 10:39; John 11:32; 12:3). Yet she not only sat at His feet; she also served Him by anointing Him with costly ointment to show her desire to meet practical needs as well as to seek spiritual blessing.

Mary's example demonstrates her strong decision-making capability. She chose, Jesus said, to listen to Him, and later her gift of ointment poured out in preparation for His burial was a premeditated act of worship. She was contemplative and sensitive, not given to verbal expression. When Lazarus died, tears and very few words expressed her heart's grief. Jesus understood and wept with her (John 11:35).

True to Jesus' prophecy, Mary has lived in history as one personifying commitment. Three gospels include her significant sacrificial gesture—ten and one-third ounces of pure spikenard ointment, worth a year's wages, lavished in humility upon her Savior (Matt. 26:6–13; Mark 14:1–9; John 12:1–8). Mary, a woman characterized by spiritual insight and readiness to act upon her faith, was thus commended by Christ (Matt. 26:13).

See also Matt. 26:6–13; Mark 14:1–9; Luke 10:38–42; John 11:28–36, 45; 12:3–8; chart on Women and Jesus; note on Heroines (Heb. 11)

37 And some of them said, "Could not this Man, who opened the eyes of the blind, also have kept this man from dying?"

Lazarus Raised from the Dead

38 Then Jesus, again groaning in Himself, came to the tomb. It was a cave, and a stone lay against it. 39 Jesus said, "Take away the stone."

Martha, the sister of him who was dead, said to Him, "Lord, by this time there is a stench, for he has been *dead* four days."

40 Jesus said to her, "Did I not say to you that if you would believe you would see the glory of God?" 41 Then they took away the stone *from the place* where the dead man was lying.[a] And Jesus lifted up *His* eyes and said, "Father, I thank You that You have heard Me. 42 And I know that You always hear Me, but because of the people who are standing by I said *this,* that they may believe that You sent Me." 43 Now when He had said these things, He cried with a loud voice, "Lazarus, come forth!" 44 And he who had died came out bound hand and foot with graveclothes, and his face was wrapped with a cloth. Jesus said to them, "Loose him, and let him go."

The Plot to Kill Jesus

45 Then many of the Jews who had come to Mary, and had seen the things Jesus did, believed in Him. 46 But some of them went away to the Pharisees and told them the things Jesus did. 47 Then the chief priests and the Pharisees gathered a council and said, "What shall we do? For this Man works many signs. 48 If we let Him alone like this, everyone will believe in Him, and the Romans will come and take away both our place and nation."

11:41 a NU-Text omits *from the place where the dead man was lying.*

- Tears might have come to Jesus because He entered so deeply into the agony of others.
- Jesus could have foreseen His own approaching Crucifixion and grieved in advance for those who would mourn His death.

11:35 John gave insight into the deep compassion of Jesus (see chart, The Emotions of Jesus). Even though Jesus knew He could restore Lazarus to physical life, He wept with sorrow and sympathy. Here, the word "wept" did not refer to the wailing that customarily accompanied funerals in that day. Funeral wailing ordinarily meant uninhibited loud crying, even screaming or shrieking. This open display of emotion was often done by people who did not know or care about the dead person. The more dramatic the wailing, the greater tribute the Jews believed they paid to the deceased. In Jesus' case, the word "wept" simply means "shedding tears" (see Ps. 56,

Tears). Obviously, Jesus suffered a deep agony of spirit and was genuinely moved by Lazarus's death. Jesus' tears provided remarkable insight into His true humanity.

11:48 Jesus' raising of Lazarus from the dead caused many of the Jews to believe in Him. Jewish authorities felt they could no longer allow Jesus to work miracles and convert the Jews. The Sadducees and Pharisees quickly called a meeting of the Sanhedrin (the Jewish supreme court) to discuss the problem (see chart, Jewish Sects). The Jewish nation held a privileged status within the Roman Empire, and the Sanhedrin feared that Jesus would gain a large following, cause a civil uproar, and anger the governing Roman Empire. If that happened, these religious leaders would lose their positions and political power. The high priest Caiaphas suggested that Jesus should be killed (v. 50).

[49]And one of them, Caiaphas, being high priest that year, said to them, "You know nothing at all, [50]nor do you consider that it is expedient for us[a] that one man should die for the people, and not that the whole nation should perish." [51]Now this he did not say on his own *authority;* but being high priest that year he prophesied that Jesus would die for the nation, [52]and not for that nation only, but also that He would gather together in one the children of God who were scattered abroad. [53]Then, from that day on, they plotted to put Him to death. [54]Therefore Jesus no longer walked openly among the Jews, but went from there into the country near the wilderness, to a city called Ephraim, and there remained with His disciples.

[55]And the Passover of the Jews was near, and many went from the country up to Jerusalem before the Passover, to purify themselves. [56]Then they sought Jesus, and spoke among themselves as they stood in the temple, "What do you think— that He will not come to the feast?" [57]Now both the chief priests and the Pharisees had given a command, that if anyone knew where He was, he should report *it,* that they might seize Him.

The Anointing at Bethany

12 Then, six days before the Passover, Jesus came to Bethany, where Lazarus was who had been dead,[a] whom He had raised from the dead. [2]There they made Him a supper; and Martha served, but Lazarus was one of those who sat at the table with Him. [3]Then Mary took a pound of very costly oil of spikenard, anointed the feet of Jesus, and wiped His feet with her hair. And the house was filled with the fragrance of the oil.

[4]But one of His disciples, Judas Iscariot, Simon's *son,* who would betray Him, said, [5]"Why was this fragrant oil not sold for three hundred denarii[a] and given to the poor?" [6]This he said, not that he cared for the poor, but because he was a

thief, and had the money box; and he used to take what was put in it. [7]But Jesus said, "Let her alone; she has kept[a] this for the day of My burial. [8]For the poor you have with you always, but Me you do not have always."

The Plot to Kill Lazarus

[9]Now a great many of the Jews knew that He was there; and they came, not for Jesus' sake only, but that they might also see Lazarus, whom He had raised from the dead. [10]But the chief priests plotted to put Lazarus to death also, [11]because on account of him many of the Jews went away and believed in Jesus.

The Triumphal Entry

[12]The next day a great multitude that had come to the feast, when they heard that Jesus was coming to Jerusalem, [13]took branches of palm trees and went out to meet Him, and cried out:

"Hosanna!
'Blessed is He who comes in the name of the Lord!'[a]
The King of Israel!"

[14]Then Jesus, when He had found a young donkey, sat on it; as it is written:

[15]"Fear not, daughter of Zion;
Behold, your King is coming,
Sitting on a donkey's colt."[a]

[16]His disciples did not understand these things at first; but when Jesus was glorified, then they remembered that these things were written about Him and *that* they had done these things to Him.

11:50 [a]NU-Text reads *you.*   **12:1** [a]NU-Text omits *who had been dead.*   **12:5** [a]About one year's wages for a worker   **12:7** [a]NU-Text reads *that she may keep.*   **12:13** [a]Psalm 118:26   **12:15** [a]Zechariah 9:9

12:3 The perfumed ointment with which Mary anointed the feet of Jesus was genuine spikenard, scarce and thus very expensive. Spikenard was a fragrant herb obtained from the roots of a plant grown in the Himalayas and transported to Palestine by camel. "Three hundred denarii" equals the annual wages of an average worker (v. 5; see chart, Money and Measurements in the Bible).

12:3–7 Jewish pilgrims were preparing for the Passover Feast, which was only six days away. Jesus visited His good friends Lazarus (whom He had raised from the dead), Martha, and Mary in Bethany. Martha cooked and served the supper (see Martha). Jesus would die during the Passover feast, and Mary seemed to sense Jesus' approaching death. With actions symbolic of preparing a body for burial, Mary took her most precious possession, "fragrant oil," and lovingly poured it over Jesus' feet (v. 5; see Mary of Bethany). Then, not caring what the others thought of her, she wiped His feet with her hair. A woman in Mary's day would never let her hair down in public but would keep it firmly bound or braided. The fact that Mary anointed His feet instead of His head demonstrated her hu-

mility. Only servants attended to the feet. When Judas (the money-keeper and betrayer) objected to Mary's extravagance, Jesus silenced Judas and praised Mary's actions.

12:10, 11 The chief priests wanted to kill not only Jesus but also Lazarus, who had become important evidence of Jesus' miracles (John 11:43–45). The Sadducees feared an insurrection by Jesus and His followers. Such disruption of peace might cost them their position of power and influence. The chief priests, who were all Sadducees, did not believe in the resurrection of the dead. Confronted with a clearly living Lazarus, they felt their foundation of power slipping away.

12:13, 14 Large crowds met Jesus coming into Jerusalem for the Passover feast. They spread palm branches in His entry path. Palm trees were among the earliest cultivated trees. They were a symbol of victory and success as well as of beauty. Images of the trees decorated the temple, and its branches were used as part of the Feast of Tabernacles' celebration. The people received Jesus into Jerusalem as the promised Messiah, shouting *Hosanna* (Heb., lit. "save now").

MARTHA *A Busy Hostess*

Jesus often went to the home of Martha, who was apparently single, whether by choice or circumstances, and living in Bethany with her sister Mary and their brother Lazarus. John's comment shows that Jesus and the family from Bethany were close friends (John 11:5). Martha seemed to enjoy her gift of hospitality and her probable position as the older of the two sisters.

Three scenes appear to reveal Martha's intensity, which the Lord faced with loving firmness, as recorded by Luke (Luke 10:41, 42). Martha's irritation with her sister led to a confrontation with Jesus as, in effect, she blamed Him for Mary's lack of assistance. His loving response was not a condemnation of Martha's servant's heart or a rejection of her zealous and gracious hospitality. He simply asked her to reconsider her priorities, to make her choices on the basis of eternal values instead of immediate pressures, and He suggested that she allow Mary to make her own choices.

Several months later, Lazarus became ill while Jesus was traveling many miles away. Although the sisters sent for Him, by the time the Lord arrived in Bethany, Lazarus was dead and had been buried for four days. Ignoring the custom of mourners to remain in their homes, Martha took the initiative to meet Jesus as He approached the town and to attribute her brother's untimely death to Jesus' delay in reaching Bethany (John 11:21). Again, with trusting faith, Martha acknowledged Jesus' power over death (v. 22). Jesus explained that He Himself was the Resurrection. She agreed and saw an immediate manifestation of that faith in her brother's resurrection (v. 44).

The third glimpse of Martha was reported by John (John 12:2). The simple fact that Martha assumed hostessing duties once more confirms the fact that her uncommon talents were being used. Undoubtedly she had become a disciple who experienced God's power in practical service. Jesus, as well as countless others, needed the physical refreshment of Martha's warm hospitality. She did not consider her homemaking responsibilities as worthless drudgery. She obviously loved her home and counted it joy to pour her energies into the efficient management of her household. Martha is a poignant reminder to every woman of the balance between fellowship with the family and the work necessary to meet their mundane needs.

See also Luke 10:38–42; John 12:1–3; notes on Envy (Prov. 14); Hospitality (1 Pet. 4)

---

[17]Therefore the people, who were with Him when He called Lazarus out of his tomb and raised him from the dead, bore witness. [18]For this reason the people also met Him, because they heard that He had done this sign. [19]The Pharisees therefore said among themselves, "You see that you are accomplishing nothing. Look, the world has gone after Him!"

The Fruitful Grain of Wheat

[20]Now there were certain Greeks among those who came up to worship at the feast. [21]Then they came to Philip, who was from Bethsaida of Galilee, and asked him, saying, "Sir, we wish to see Jesus."

[22]Philip came and told Andrew, and in turn Andrew and Philip told Jesus.

[23]But Jesus answered them, saying, "The hour has come that the Son of Man should be glorified. [24]Most assuredly, I say to you, unless a grain of wheat falls into the ground and dies, it remains alone; but if it dies, it produces much grain. [25]He who loves his life will lose it, and he who hates his life in this world will keep it for eternal life. [26]If anyone serves Me, let him follow Me; and where I am, there My servant will be also. If anyone serves Me, him *My* Father will honor.

Jesus Predicts His Death on the Cross

[27]"Now My soul is troubled, and what shall I say? 'Father, save Me from this hour'? But for this purpose I came to this hour. [28]Father, glorify Your name."

Then a voice came from heaven, *saying,* "I have both glorified *it* and will glorify *it* again."

[29]Therefore the people who stood by and heard *it* said that it had thundered. Others said, "An angel has spoken to Him."

[30]Jesus answered and said, "This voice did not come because of Me, but for your sake. [31]Now is the judgment of this world; now the ruler of this world will be cast out. [32]And I, if I am lifted up from the earth, will draw all *peoples* to Myself." [33]This He said, signifying by what death He would die.

[34]The people answered Him, "We have heard from the law that the Christ remains forever; and

---

12:31, 32 The ruler of this world was John's synonym for Satan (see chart, The Names for Satan). Through succumbing to Satan's temptation, the man and woman had been driven out of the Garden of Eden by God. Though Jesus' Crucifixion seemed to indicate that the ruler of this world had won, actually His death on the Cross would render Satan impotent and would forever break the power of this Evil One. "Lifted up" referred to the way Jesus would die by crucifixion (v. 32). "All peoples" was a reference to people from all nations, regardless of nationality, race, or status.

how *can* You say, 'The Son of Man must be lifted up'? Who is this Son of Man?"

³⁵Then Jesus said to them, "A little while longer the light is with you. Walk while you have the light, lest darkness overtake you; he who walks in darkness does not know where he is going. ³⁶While you have the light, believe in the light, that you may become sons of light." These things Jesus spoke, and departed, and was hidden from them.

Who Has Believed Our Report?

³⁷But although He had done so many signs before them, they did not believe in Him, ³⁸that the word of Isaiah the prophet might be fulfilled, which he spoke:

"Lord, who has believed our report?
And to whom has the arm of the LORD been revealed?"^a

³⁹Therefore they could not believe, because Isaiah said again:

⁴⁰"He has blinded their eyes and hardened their hearts,
Lest they should see with their eyes,
Lest they should understand with their hearts and
    turn,
So that I should heal them."^a

⁴¹These things Isaiah said when^a he saw His glory and spoke of Him.

Walk in the Light

⁴²Nevertheless even among the rulers many believed in Him, but because of the Pharisees they did not confess *Him*, lest they should be put out of the synagogue; ⁴³for they loved the praise of men more than the praise of God.

⁴⁴Then Jesus cried out and said, "He who believes in Me, believes not in Me but in Him who sent Me. ⁴⁵And he who sees Me sees Him who sent Me. ⁴⁶I have come *as* a light into the world, that whoever believes in Me should not abide in darkness. ⁴⁷And if anyone hears My words and does not believe,^a I do not judge him; for I did not come to judge the world but to save the world. ⁴⁸He who rejects Me, and does not receive My words, has that which judges him—the word that I have spoken will judge him in the last day. ⁴⁹For I have not spoken on My own *authority;* but the Father who sent Me gave Me a command, what I should say and what I should speak. ⁵⁰And I know that His command is everlasting life. Therefore, whatever I speak, just as the Father has told Me, so I speak."

Jesus Washes the Disciples' Feet

13 Now before the Feast of the Passover, when Jesus knew that His hour had come that He should depart from this world to the Father, having loved His own who were in the world, He loved them to the end.

²And supper being ended,^a the devil having already put it into the heart of Judas Iscariot, Simon's *son,* to betray Him, ³Jesus, knowing that the Father had given all things into His hands, and that He had come from God and was going to God, ⁴rose from supper and laid aside His garments, took a towel and girded Himself. ⁵After that, He poured water into a basin and began to wash the disciples' feet, and to wipe *them* with the towel with which He was girded. ⁶Then He came to Simon Peter. And *Peter* said to Him, "Lord, are You washing my feet?"

⁷Jesus answered and said to him, "What I am doing you do not understand now, but you will know after this."

⁸Peter said to Him, "You shall never wash my feet!"

Jesus answered him, "If I do not wash you, you have no part with Me."

⁹Simon Peter said to Him, "Lord, not my feet only, but also *my* hands and *my* head!"

¹⁰Jesus said to him, "He who is bathed needs only to wash *his* feet, but is completely clean; and you are clean, but not all of you." ¹¹For He knew who would betray Him; therefore He said, "You are not all clean."

¹²So when He had washed their feet, taken His garments, and sat down again, He said to them, "Do you know what I have done to you? ¹³You call Me Teacher and Lord, and you say well, for *so* I am. ¹⁴If I then, *your* Lord and Teacher, have washed your feet, you also ought to wash one another's feet. ¹⁵For I have given you an example, that you should do as I have done to you. ¹⁶Most assuredly, I say to you, a servant is not greater than his master; nor is he who is sent greater than he who sent him. ¹⁷If you know these things, blessed are you if you do them.

Jesus Identifies His Betrayer

¹⁸"I do not speak concerning all of you. I know whom I have chosen; but that the Scripture may be fulfilled, *'He who eats bread with Me^a has lifted up his heel against Me.'*^b ¹⁹Now I tell you before it

---

12:38 ^aIsaiah 53:1   12:40 ^aIsaiah 6:10   12:41 ^aNU-Text reads *because.*   12:47 ^aNU-Text reads *keep them.*   13:2 ^aNU-Text reads *And during supper.*   13:18 ^aNU-Text reads *My bread.*   ^bPsalm 41:9

13:4, 5 To wash the feet of others was a slave's job in NT times. People wore sandals and walked along the unpaved dusty roads of Palestine. A servant would wash the guests' feet as they came into the house. Jesus Himself took a towel, knelt, and washed His disciples' feet. In doing so, Jesus gave

His disciples a tremendous example to follow. They, too, must be willing to serve, to wash the feet of others. He showed them that love meant servanthood (see Mark 10, Servanthood). Through this passage, John gave keen insight into the character and love of Jesus.

comes, that when it does come to pass, you may believe that I am *He.* ²⁰Most assuredly, I say to you, he who receives whomever I send receives Me; and he who receives Me receives Him who sent Me."

²¹When Jesus had said these things, He was troubled in spirit, and testified and said, "Most assuredly, I say to you, one of you will betray Me." ²²Then the disciples looked at one another, perplexed about whom He spoke.

²³Now there was leaning on Jesus' bosom one of His disciples, whom Jesus loved. ²⁴Simon Peter therefore motioned to him to ask who it was of whom He spoke.

²⁵Then, leaning back^a on Jesus' breast, he said to Him, "Lord, who is it?"

²⁶Jesus answered, "It is he to whom I shall give a piece of bread when I have dipped *it.*" And having dipped the bread, He gave *it* to Judas Iscariot, *the son* of Simon. ²⁷Now after the piece of bread, Satan entered him. Then Jesus said to him, "What you do, do quickly." ²⁸But no one at the table knew for what reason He said this to him. ²⁹For some thought, because Judas had the money box, that Jesus had said to him, "Buy *those things* we need for the feast," or that he should give something to the poor.

³⁰Having received the piece of bread, he then went out immediately. And it was night.

The New Commandment

³¹So, when he had gone out, Jesus said, "Now the Son of Man is glorified, and God is glorified in Him. ³²If God is glorified in Him, God will also glorify Him in Himself, and glorify Him immediately. ³³Little children, I shall be with you a little while longer. You will seek Me; and as I said to the Jews, 'Where I am going, you cannot come,' so now I say to you. ³⁴A new commandment I give to you, that you love one another; as I have loved you, that you also love one another. ³⁵By this all will know that you are My disciples, if you have love for one another."

Jesus Predicts Peter's Denial

³⁶Simon Peter said to Him, "Lord, where are You going?"

Jesus answered him, "Where I am going you cannot follow Me now, but you shall follow Me afterward."

³⁷Peter said to Him, "Lord, why can I not follow You now? I will lay down my life for Your sake."

³⁸Jesus answered him, "Will you lay down your life for My sake? Most assuredly, I say to you, the rooster shall not crow till you have denied Me three times.

The Way, the Truth, and the Life

14 "Let not your heart be troubled; you believe in God, believe also in Me. ²In My Father's house are many mansions;^a if *it were* not *so,* I would have told you. I go to prepare a place for you.^b ³And if I go and prepare a place for you, I will come again and receive you to Myself; that where I am, *there* you may be also. ⁴And where I go you know, and the way you know."

⁵Thomas said to Him, "Lord, we do not know where You are going, and how can we know the way?" ⁶Jesus said to him, "I am the way, the truth, and the life. No one comes to the Father except through Me.

The Father Revealed

⁷"If you had known Me, you would have known My Father also; and from now on you know Him and have seen Him."

⁸Philip said to Him, "Lord, show us the Father, and it is sufficient for us."

⁹Jesus said to him, "Have I been with you so long, and yet you have not known Me, Philip? He who has seen Me has seen the Father; so how can you say, 'Show us the Father'? ¹⁰Do you not believe that I am in the Father, and the Father in Me? The words that I speak to you I do not speak on My own *authority;* but the Father who dwells in Me does the works. ¹¹Believe Me that I *am* in the Father and the Father in Me, or else believe Me for the sake of the works themselves.

The Answered Prayer

¹²"Most assuredly, I say to you, he who believes in Me, the works that I do he will do also; and greater

••••••••••••••••••••••••••••••••••

13:25 ^aNU-Text and M-Text add *thus.* **14:2** ^aLiterally *dwellings* ^bNU-Text adds a word which would cause the text to read either *if it were not so, would I have told you that I go to prepare a place for you?* or *if it were not so I would have told you; for I go to prepare a place for you.*

13:23 Some scholars believe that Lazarus, whom Jesus raised from the dead, was the disciple "whom Jesus loved." It is more plausible, however, that John, the author of the book, was speaking of himself. However, this disciple who sat next to Jesus in the place of honor is not specifically identified in the text. Reclining instead of sitting at the table for a meal was customary, although usually optional. "Leaning on Jesus' bosom" would be a natural position for a person reclining next to Jesus. Here, however, this position of honor also expressed an intimate fellowship.

13:26 Judas was a common name in Jesus' day. Iscariot (Aram., lit. "man of Kerioth") was the only disciple out of the 12 from Judea. He kept and managed the money for the disciples, often stealing portions for himself (John 12:5, 6). Judas Iscariot is remembered primarily as the one who betrayed Jesus for 30 pieces of silver. An unrepentant Judas later hung himself (see Luke 24:47, note).

13:38 Roosters served as time indicators. They typically crowed first at midnight, then a second time at three o'clock in the morning. So accurate was their crowing that the Roman guards relied on roosters to signal a changing of the guard. True to Jesus' prophecy, Peter had denied Jesus three times by a few hours before dawn.

WOMEN AND THEIR FAMILIES IN THE NEW TESTAMENT

WOMAN	HER FAMILY	COMMENTS
Elizabeth (Luke 1:5–25, 57–80)	Husband Zacharias—a priest; Son John the Baptist-forerunner of the Messiah	Homemaker; she had a pregnancy and bore a child late in life; her son was hated because of his prophetic ministry, and he was brutally murdered in the prime of life.
Mary of Nazareth (Luke 1:26–38; 2:1–21; John 19:25–27)	Husband Joseph—a carpenter; Son Jesus—the Messiah; Sons James, Joses, Judas, Simon; Daughter unnamed (Mark 6:3; Luke 4:22)	Homemaker; she endured gossip and rejection from family and friends because of her unique pregnancy before her marriage to Joseph; she watched the Crucifixion of her son Jesus; she showed an unwavering commitment to the Lord.
Unnamed mother-in-law (Mark 1:30, 31)	Son-in-law Peter—a fisherman; and one of the apostles	She had an illness that brought her close to death; Jesus healed her; she exhibited a servant's heart.
Wife of Zebedee (Matt. 20:20–28; 27:55, 56)	Husband Zebedee—a fisherman; Sons James and John	Homemaker; she was proud of her sons and encouraged their advancement; her unbridled ambition was unwise.
The woman of Canaan (Matt. 15:21–28)	Daughter possessed by demons	Member of minority race; single parent; her faith gained Jesus' attention and brought healing to her daughter.
Jairus' wife (Mark 5:22–24, 35–42)	Husband Jairus—synagogue leader; Daughter aged twelve	Homemaker; experienced death of only child; turned to and trusted in Christ; experienced joy of having daughter restored to life.
Anna (Luke 2:36–38)	None	Widow (84 years of age) who served in the temple; she made prophetic pronouncement concerning the Christ Child; alone most of her life but never bitter or self-centered.
Widow of Nain (Luke 7:11–16)	Son	Single parent; she lost her only son, but Jesus restored the boy to her; her faith was noteworthy for all.
Joanna (Luke 8:1–3)	Husband Chuza—Herod's steward	Affluent; Joanna gave generously of her time and resources to further the work of the kingdom.
Mary and Martha of Bethany (Luke 10:38–42; John 11:1–41)	Brother Lazarus	Unmarried sisters; Martha offered hospitality to Jesus and His followers; Mary sat at Jesus' feet to study and learn spiritual things; both sisters looked to the Lord in faith at the death of their brother, and Jesus raised him from the dead.
Woman of Samaria (John 4:7–42)	Live-in-lover who was not her husband	Divorced (five previous husbands); she listened to Jesus and accepted His offer of salvation.
Woman caught in adultery (John 8:3–11)	None stated	Lived in immorality; confronted about her sin, she was forgiven by Jesus.
Mother (John 9:1–41)	Husband; Son who was blind	Homemaker; reared disabled child to adulthood; Jesus restored the son's sight; perhaps the nurture of these parents helped the son to remain loyal to Jesus even under pressures.
Sapphira (Acts 5:1–11)	Husband Ananias	Wealthy; tried to deceive the church and died under judgment of the Lord.
Four sisters from Caesarea (Acts 21:9)	Father Philip—an evangelist	Unmarried sisters living with their father and helping him in his ministry; they were committed to serving the Lord.
Mary (Acts 12:12–17)	Son John Mark—traveled with missionary Barnabas (his kinsman); Rhoda—household servant	Homemaker; an affluent woman; seemingly a single parent; opened her home to believers for meetings; reared her son in the nurture of the Lord; her son also made a great contribution to the kingdom of Christ.
Eunice (Acts 16:1; 2 Tim. 1:3–7)	Husband (Gentile); Son Timothy; Mother Lois	Homemaker; interfaith marriage; both she and her mother (Lois) invested wisely in young Timothy's spiritual nurture.
Lydia of Philippi (Acts 16:13–40)	None mentioned	Businesswoman; hospitable; courageous in helping to begin a church in a hostile environment.
Priscilla (Acts 18:1–28; Rom. 16:3; 1 Cor. 16:19; 2 Tim. 4:19)	Husband Aquila	Without children; partner in tentmaking business and in ministry; gift for mentoring.
Drusilla (Acts 24:24)	Husband Felix	Jewish daughter of Herod Agrippa I; married Roman procurator of Judea; she was ambitious and without moral scruples.
Bernice (Acts 25:13–27)	Brother (and lover) Herod Agrippa II	Daughter of Herod Agrippa I and sister of Drusilla; lived in incest and immorality.
Apphia (Philem. 2)	Husband Philemon (possibly); Slave Onesimus	Opened her home to meetings of believers; committed supporter of the apostle Paul.

CHILD CARE PROTECTING OUR CHILDREN

In Bible times, children seemingly always had care within the context of family—often a large extended family. Children were rarely out of reach of familiar, loving arms and authoritative, life-shaping discipline. Seeking child care beyond the family circle necessitates that parents attempt to recreate the special nurturing a parent can best provide in the protection and peace of the family circle. To build self-confidence, trust, and contentment from afar can be a stressful challenge for all.

Nothing seems worse, in biblical terms, than for us to feel we have been left as orphans, isolated and alone. Jesus assured His disciples, when they began to fear the worst about their future with Him, "I will not leave you orphans: I will come to you" (John 14:18). Something in the nature of divine love finds its fullest realization when intimacy, nearness, and availability are there for the taking.

The story of divine love in the Bible reveals a "being there" quality from beginning to end. Child care outside the home may be expedient for some families, but such a decision should always be bathed in prayer and carefully weighed. If we, as parents, are God's representatives to our children in this world, we must make sure that a "being there" quality is built into all our dealings with our children and make our decisions about child care accordingly.

See also Deut. 6:1–9; Ps. 127; 128; 139; Ezek. 16:20, 21; Matt. 18:3, note; notes on Children (2 Sam. 21; Ps. 128; Prov. 22; Luke 15); Employment (Is. 26); Motherhood (1 Sam. 1; Is. 49; Ezek. 16)

---

works than these he will do, because I go to My Father. [13]And whatever you ask in My name, that I will do, that the Father may be glorified in the Son. [14]If you ask[a] anything in My name, I will do *it*.

Jesus Promises Another Helper

[15]"If you love Me, keep[a] My commandments. [16]And I will pray the Father, and He will give you another Helper, that He may abide with you forever— [17]the Spirit of truth, whom the world cannot receive, because it neither sees Him nor knows Him; but you know Him, for He dwells with you and will be in you. [18]I will not leave you orphans; I will come to you.

Indwelling of the Father and the Son

[19]"A little while longer and the world will see Me no more, but you will see Me. Because I live, you will live also. [20]At that day you will know that I *am* in My Father, and you in Me, and I in you. [21]He who has My commandments and keeps them, it is he who loves Me. And he who loves Me will be loved by My Father, and I will love him and manifest Myself to him."

[22]Judas (not Iscariot) said to Him, "Lord, how is it that You will manifest Yourself to us, and not to the world?"

[23]Jesus answered and said to him, "If anyone loves Me, he will keep My word; and My Father will love him, and We will come to him and make Our home with him. [24]He who does not love Me does not keep My words; and the word which you hear is not Mine but the Father's who sent Me.

The Gift of His Peace

[25]"These things I have spoken to you while being present with you. [26]But the Helper, the Holy Spirit, whom the Father will send in My name, He will teach you all things, and bring to your remembrance all things that I said to you. [27]Peace I leave with you, My peace I give to you; not as the world gives do I give to you. Let not your heart be troubled, neither let it be afraid. [28]You have heard Me say to you, 'I am going away and coming *back* to you.' If you loved Me, you would rejoice because I said,[a] 'I am going to the Father,' for My Father is greater than I.

········ ········

14:14 [a]NU-Text adds *Me*. 14:15 [a]NU-Text reads *you will keep*. 14:28 [a]NU-Text omits *I said*.

14:16, 17 Jesus referred to the Holy Spirit as "another Helper" He would send to the disciples after He returned to the Father (v. 16). Jesus requested the Holy Spirit, and the Father gave the Spirit in answer to His request. When speaking of the Holy Spirit, John used "Helper" (Gk., *paraklētos,* lit. "one who is called beside") and "Spirit of Truth" to designate the Holy Spirit, the third Person of the Trinity. The Holy Spirit as mediator or intercessor indwells the believer and serves as the revealer of God's will, the Teacher, the Agent of empowerment, the Comforter, and the Counselor (see chart, The Work of the Holy Spirit).

14:18 Jesus compared Himself to an earthly father who would

die and leave helpless children as orphans. No doubt, the disciples already sensed that tragedy would follow. Speaking here of the Resurrection, Jesus promised to return to the disciples.

14:26 The Holy Spirit is the third Person of the Trinity and thus should be referenced as "He," not "it" (John 14:17; 15:26; 16:7, 13). He possesses all God's attributes and is fully God. Throughout history God has acted, revealed His will, empowered individuals, and disclosed His personal presence through the Holy Spirit.

The Holy Spirit has specific functions. In the OT, the Holy Spirit was given to an individual at a specific time to aid in ac-

Right priorities and good time management demand an awareness that today is the only time with which we ever have to work. The past is irretrievably gone, and the future is only a possibility.

Dorothy Kelley Patterson

29"And now I have told you before it comes, that when it does come to pass, you may believe. 30I will no longer talk much with you, for the ruler of this world is coming, and he has nothing in Me. 31But that the world may know that I love the Father, and as the Father gave Me commandment, so I do. Arise, let us go from here.

The True Vine

15 "I am the true vine, and My Father is the vinedresser. 2Every branch in Me that does not bear fruit He takes away;[a] and every *branch* that bears fruit He prunes, that it may bear more fruit. 3You are already clean because of the word which I have spoken to you. 4Abide in Me, and I in you. As the branch cannot bear fruit of itself, unless it abides in the vine, neither can you, unless you abide in Me.

5"I am the vine, you *are* the branches. He who abides in Me, and I in him, bears much fruit; for without Me you can do nothing. 6If anyone does not abide in Me, he is cast out as a branch and is withered; and they gather them and throw *them* into the fire, and they are burned. 7If you abide in Me, and My words abide in you, you will[a] ask what you desire, and it shall be done for you. 8By this My Father is glorified, that you bear much fruit; so you will be My disciples.

Love and Joy Perfected

9"As the Father loved Me, I also have loved you; abide in My love. 10If you keep My commandments, you will abide in My love, just as I have kept My Father's commandments and abide in His love. 11"These things I have spoken to you, that My joy may remain in you, and *that* your joy may be full. 12This is My commandment, that you love one another as I have loved you. 13Greater love has no one than this, than to lay down one's life for his friends. 14You are My friends if you do whatever I command you. 15No longer do I call you servants, for a servant does not know what his master is doing; but I have called you friends, for all things that I heard from My Father I have made known to you. 16You did not choose Me, but I chose you and appointed you that you should go and bear fruit, and *that* your fruit should remain, that whatever you ask the Father in My name He may give you. 17These things I command you, that you love one another.

The World's Hatred

18"If the world hates you, you know that it hated Me before *it hated* you. 19If you were of the

- - - - - - - - - - - - - - - -

15:2 [a]Or *lifts up*   15:7 [a]NU-Text omits *you will.*

---

complishing a particular assignment or mission (Num. 11:26; Ezek. 2:2). He was not constantly present in the life of every follower of *Yahweh.* However, from the coming of the Spirit in the NT until the end of the age, the Holy Spirit indwells all believers from the moment they trust completely in the Lord and His saving power. When an individual accepts Jesus as Savior, the Holy Spirit comes to indwell, never to leave (Eph. 4:30).

The Holy Spirit is the believer's greatest asset and is essential for survival in this sinful world. The Holy Spirit is the believer's advocate (Gk. *parakletos,* lit. "one called alongside"; John 14:16). In other words, the Holy Spirit is "Comforter" and "Teacher" (John 16:7, 13). The Holy Spirit gives the believer help and advice for living the Christian life. As moment by moment believers surrender their lives to God and allow themselves to be used for God's service, the filling of the Holy Spirit occurs. Through the filling of the Holy Spirit believers are controlled by the Spirit and equipped for service (Eph. 5:18–21; Rom. 12, Spiritual Gifts; 2 Cor. 1, Conscience; Eph. 5, God's Will; 1 Pet. 2, Priesthood of the Believer; see chart, the Work of the Holy Spirit).

15:1–5 Vines grow all over Palestine. Every year, gardeners prune the branches in order to produce high-quality fruit. The branch is considered useless unless it produces fruit. Fruitless vines are drastically cut back. The pruned limbs are good for nothing and are destroyed. The OT pictured Israel as the vineyard of God. The vine became a symbol for the nation of Israel. Jesus called Himself the "true" Vine, using the vine and branches as an analogy to show how a believer must abide (live or remain) in Him (v. 1). His followers who believed in Him were the branches on God's vine. The branches had no source of life within themselves but received life from the Vine. Without the Vine, the branches could produce no fruit and were good for nothing.

15:15 While the disciples must be servants to others, as Jesus demonstrated when He washed their feet (John 13:4, 5), Jesus considered them His friends. Only to His friends would Jesus give such a revelation of God and His purposes on the earth. The disciples did not choose Jesus; rather Jesus chose them. Jesus no longer called them "servants" (Gk. *doulos,* lit. "slave"). He offered them something far better than this, a personal and intimate relationship with God, the sort of rare relationship that exists between confidants or close friends.

CHILDBIRTH: *THE MIRACLE OF BIRTH*

Although Scripture often uses childbirth and motherhood as a metaphor, the reality and importance of birth is also present. The womb is the natural incubator prepared by the Creator for the protection and growth of the child. If birth occurs prematurely (Ex. 21:22–25) the result could be tragic, such as the death of the mother (1 Sam. 4:19–22) or the death of the child (Ps. 58:8; Hos. 9:14).

Other allusions to the birth process in Scripture include personnel, such as the midwives (Gen. 35:17; Ex. 1:15); props, such as the birthstool (Ex. 1:16); procedures, such as the cutting of the navel cord that binds the child to the mother and the cleansing of the child (Ezek. 16:4); and penalties, such as the woman's ritual uncleanness for forty to eighty days after the birth (Lev. 12:1–8).

Pain contrasts with joy in the miracle of childbirth. The conception and birth of a child exemplify God's greatest creative masterpiece (Gen. 1:26–28). The bringing forth of young from the womb is an experience marked by extreme contrast. Most women who have borne a child will agree that carrying the child is very uncomfortable, and the birth of the baby is downright painful. But the indescribable joy of the new life created encourages every mother to rejoice. The pain is quickly forgotten, "for joy that a human being is born into the world" (John 16:21).

See also Gen. 3:16; Matt. 18:3, note; 1 Tim. 2:15; notes on Children (2 Sam. 21; Ps. 128; Prov. 22; Luke 15); Fall of Creation (Gen. 3); Motherhood (1 Sam. 1; Is. 49; Ezek. 16); Pregnancy (Judg. 13)

---

world, the world would love its own. Yet because you are not of the world, but I chose you out of the world, therefore the world hates you. [20]Remember the word that I said to you, 'A servant is not greater than his master.' If they persecuted Me, they will also persecute you. If they kept My word, they will keep yours also. [21]But all these things they will do to you for My name's sake, because they do not know Him who sent Me. [22]If I had not come and spoken to them, they would have no sin, but now they have no excuse for their sin. [23]He who hates Me hates My Father also. [24]If I had not done among them the works which no one else did, they would have no sin; but now they have seen and also hated both Me and My Father. [25]But *this happened* that the word might be fulfilled which is written in their law, 'They hated Me without a cause.'[a]

The Coming Rejection

[26]"But when the Helper comes, whom I shall send to you from the Father, the Spirit of truth who proceeds from the Father, He will testify of Me. [27]And you also will bear witness, because you have been with Me from the beginning.

16 "These things I have spoken to you, that you should not be made to stumble. [2]They will put you out of the synagogues; yes, the time is coming that whoever kills you will think that he offers God service. [3]And these things they will do to you[a] because they have not known the Father nor Me. [4]But these things I have told you, that when the[a] time comes, you may remember that I told you of them.

"And these things I did not say to you at the beginning, because I was with you.

The Work of the Holy Spirit

[5]"But now I go away to Him who sent Me, and none of you asks Me, 'Where are You going?' [6]But because I have said these things to you, sorrow has filled your heart. [7]Nevertheless I tell you the truth. It is to your advantage that I go away; for if I do not go away, the Helper will not come to you; but if I depart, I will send Him to you. [8]And when He has come, He will convict the world of sin, and of righteousness, and of judgment: [9]of sin, because they do not believe in Me; [10]of righteousness, because I go to My Father and you see Me no more; [11]of judgment, because the ruler of this world is judged.

[12]"I still have many things to say to you, but you cannot bear *them* now. [13]However, when He, the Spirit of truth, has come, He will guide you into all truth; for He will not speak on His own *authority*, but whatever He hears He will speak; and He will tell you things to come. [14]He will glorify Me, for He will take of what is Mine and declare *it* to you. [15]All things that the Father has are Mine. Therefore I said that He will take of Mine and declare *it* to you.[a]

Sorrow Will Turn to Joy

[16]"A little while, and you will not see Me; and again a little while, and you will see Me, because I go to the Father."

[17]Then *some* of His disciples said among themselves, "What is this that He says to us, 'A little while, and you will not see Me; and again a little while, and you will see Me'; and, 'because I go to

---

15:25 [a]Psalm 69:4   16:3 [a]NU-Text and M-Text omit *to you.*   16:4 [a]NU-Text reads *their.*   16:15 [a]NU-Text and M-Text read *He takes of Mine and will declare it to you.*

The soul to be rescued, washed, redeemed, saved, sanctified, and glorified–
He saw this glorious jewel and He gave Himself for it.

Catherine Booth

the Father'?" [18]They said therefore, "What is this that He says, 'A little while'? We do not know what He is saying."

[19]Now Jesus knew that they desired to ask Him, and He said to them, "Are you inquiring among yourselves about what I said, 'A little while, and you will not see Me; and again a little while, and you will see Me'? [20]Most assuredly, I say to you that you will weep and lament, but the world will rejoice; and you will be sorrowful, but your sorrow will be turned into joy. [21]A woman, when she is in labor, has sorrow because her hour has come; but as soon as she has given birth to the child, she no longer remembers the anguish, for joy that a human being has been born into the world. [22]Therefore you now have sorrow; but I will see you again and your heart will rejoice, and your joy no one will take from you.

[23]"And in that day you will ask Me nothing. Most assuredly, I say to you, whatever you ask the Father in My name He will give you. [24]Until now you have asked nothing in My name. Ask, and you will receive, that your joy may be full.

Jesus Christ Has Overcome the World

[25]"These things I have spoken to you in figurative language; but the time is coming when I will no longer speak to you in figurative language, but I will tell you plainly about the Father. [26]In that day you will ask in My name, and I do not say to you that I shall pray the Father for you; [27]for the Father Himself loves you, because you have loved Me, and have believed that I came forth from God. [28]I came forth from the Father and have come into the world. Again, I leave the world and go to the Father."

[29]His disciples said to Him, "See, now You are speaking plainly, and using no figure of speech! [30]Now we are sure that You know all things, and have no need that anyone should question You. By this we believe that You came forth from God."

[31]Jesus answered them, "Do you now believe? [32]Indeed the hour is coming, yes, has now come, that you will be scattered, each to his own, and will leave Me alone. And yet I am not alone, be-

cause the Father is with Me. [33]These things I have spoken to you, that in Me you may have peace. In the world you will[a] have tribulation; but be of good cheer, I have overcome the world."

Jesus Prays for Himself

17 Jesus spoke these words, lifted up His eyes to heaven, and said: "Father, the hour has come. Glorify Your Son, that Your Son also may glorify You, [2]as You have given Him authority over all flesh, that He should[a] give eternal life to as many as You have given Him. [3]And this is eternal life, that they may know You, the only true God, and Jesus Christ whom You have sent. [4]I have glorified You on the earth. I have finished the work which You have given Me to do. [5]And now, O Father, glorify Me together with Yourself, with the glory which I had with You before the world was.

Jesus Prays for His Disciples

[6]"I have manifested Your name to the men whom You have given Me out of the world. They were Yours, You gave them to Me, and they have kept Your word. [7]Now they have known that all things which You have given Me are from You. [8]For I have given to them the words which You have given Me; and they have received *them*, and have known surely that I came forth from You; and they have believed that You sent Me.

[9]"I pray for them. I do not pray for the world but for those whom You have given Me, for they are Yours. [10]And all Mine are Yours, and Yours are Mine, and I am glorified in them. [11]Now I am no longer in the world, but these are in the world, and I come to You. Holy Father, keep through Your name those whom You have given Me,[a] that they may be one as We *are.* [12]While I was with them in the world,[a] I kept them in Your name. Those whom You gave Me I have kept;[b] and none of them is lost except the son of perdition, that the Scripture might be fulfilled. [13]But now I come to You,

---

16:33 [a]NU-Text and M-Text omit *will.* 17:2 [a]M-Text reads *shall.* 17:11 [a]NU-Text and M-Text read *keep them through Your name which You have given Me.* 17:12 [a]NU-Text omits *in the world.* [b]NU-Text reads *in Your name which You gave Me. And I guarded them;* (or *it;*).

16:33 The world represented the earthly system that was opposed to Jesus. John pictured the world and Christ as direct opposites. Through Jesus' life, death, and Resurrection, He overcame the world. In His life, He overcame the temptation to sin directed at Him by the Evil One. In His death, He became sin for each person and thus overcame the power of sin.

In His Resurrection, He overcame death and arose victoriously from its stronghold. Jesus told the disciples that the world would bring them tribulation but that He would bring them peace. John ended his discourse with this encouraging statement of victory.

PERFECTIONISM *AN UNREACHABLE GOAL*

The compelling need to be more than what you are capable of ever becoming is the driving motivation behind perfectionism. It stems from deep insecurity, a gnawing fear that being the woman God made you to be is somehow not good enough.

The longing for absolute perfection is rooted in the lost recollection of Paradise. Within every believer is an internal barometer of how things ought to be, a deep yearning for the perfection that only heaven will bring. Something inside knows that no matter how good things are—they should be better. One day they will be, but not now. Knowing how it could be while living with how it actually is often causes an unhealthy tension.

Understanding the innate desire for perfection can lead to a deeper anticipation and hope in eternity. It also helps release the demand that life in the present must satisfy all longings.

At the same time, the Lord calls each believer to pursue wholeness and soundness of spirit—concepts that are frequently described as "perfect" in the New Testament (Matt. 5:48). The foremost trait you are called to perfect in your life is the ability to love (1 John 4:17–19). "Completion" or perfection as human beings is not possible, however, as the result of your own striving. It is the manifestation of God's work in you (Heb. 13:20, 21).

See also Is. 14:13; 2 Cor. 12:9; Gal. 6:1–5, 14, 15; notes on Contentment (1 Tim. 6); Employment (Eccl. 9; Acts 18; 2 Cor. 2; Col. 3; 1 Pet. 2); Humility (Phil. 2); Priorities (Matt. 6)

and these things I speak in the world, that they may have My joy fulfilled in themselves. ¹⁴I have given them Your word; and the world has hated them because they are not of the world, just as I am not of the world. ¹⁵I do not pray that You should take them out of the world, but that You should keep them from the evil one. ¹⁶They are not of the world, just as I am not of the world. ¹⁷Sanctify them by Your truth. Your word is truth. ¹⁸As You sent Me into the world, I also have sent them into the world. ¹⁹And for their sakes I sanctify Myself, that they also may be sanctified by the truth.

Jesus Prays for All Believers

²⁰"I do not pray for these alone, but also for those who will[a] believe in Me through their word; ²¹that they all may be one, as You, Father, *are* in Me, and I in You; that they also may be one in Us, that the world may believe that You sent Me. ²²And the glory which You gave Me I have given them, that they may be one just as We are one: ²³I in them, and You in Me; that they may be made perfect in one, and that the world may know that You have sent Me, and have loved them as You have loved Me.

²⁴"Father, I desire that they also whom You gave Me may be with Me where I am, that they may behold My glory which You have given Me; for You loved Me before the foundation of the

world. ²⁵O righteous Father! The world has not known You, but I have known You; and these have known that You sent Me. ²⁶And I have declared to them Your name, and will declare *it,* that the love with which You loved Me may be in them, and I in them."

Betrayal and Arrest in Gethsemane

18 When Jesus had spoken these words, He went out with His disciples over the Brook Kidron, where there was a garden, which He and His disciples entered. ²And Judas, who betrayed Him, also knew the place; for Jesus often met there with His disciples. ³Then Judas, having received a detachment *of troops,* and officers from the chief priests and Pharisees, came there with lanterns, torches, and weapons. ⁴Jesus therefore, knowing all things that would come upon Him, went forward and said to them, "Whom are you seeking?"

⁵They answered Him, "Jesus of Nazareth."

Jesus said to them, "I am *He.*" And Judas, who betrayed Him, also stood with them. ⁶Now when He said to them, "I am *He,*" they drew back and fell to the ground.

⁷Then He asked them again, "Whom are you seeking?"

And they said, "Jesus of Nazareth."

··

17:20 ªNU-Text and M-Text omit *will.*

17:14–16 In this beautiful prayer, which is actually the Lord's prayer, since Jesus prayed these words before His approaching death, He asked the Father not to take the disciples out of the world (see chart, Lessons from the Model Prayer). Instead He asked the Father to protect the disciples from the Evil One, who is Satan. Jesus commissioned the disciples and sent them into the world to spread the Good News of the gospel.

17:20 Jesus prayed to the Father in behalf of all believers, not just for His small band of disciples. These were the "other sheep" to whom Jesus referred (John 10:16). He prayed for the Jews as well as the Gentiles, for all the people who would come to believe in Jesus through the disciples' testimonies. His prayer embraced the distant future.

[8]Jesus answered, "I have told you that I am *He*. Therefore, if you seek Me, let these go their way," [9]that the saying might be fulfilled which He spoke, "Of those whom You gave Me I have lost none."

[10]Then Simon Peter, having a sword, drew it and struck the high priest's servant, and cut off his right ear. The servant's name was Malchus. [11]So Jesus said to Peter, "Put your sword into the sheath. Shall I not drink the cup which My Father has given Me?"

Before the High Priest

[12]Then the detachment *of troops* and the captain and the officers of the Jews arrested Jesus and bound Him. [13]And they led Him away to Annas first, for he was the father-in-law of Caiaphas who was high priest that year. [14]Now it was Caiaphas who advised the Jews that it was expedient that one man should die for the people.

Peter Denies Jesus

[15]And Simon Peter followed Jesus, and so *did* another[a] disciple. Now that disciple was known to the high priest, and went with Jesus into the courtyard of the high priest. [16]But Peter stood at the door outside. Then the other disciple, who was known to the high priest, went out and spoke to her who kept the door, and brought Peter in. [17]Then the servant girl who kept the door said to Peter, "You are not also *one* of this Man's disciples, are you?"

He said, "I am not."

[18]Now the servants and officers who had made a fire of coals stood there, for it was cold, and they warmed themselves. And Peter stood with them and warmed himself.

Jesus Questioned by the High Priest

[19]The high priest then asked Jesus about His disciples and His doctrine.

[20]Jesus answered him, "I spoke openly to the world. I always taught in synagogues and in the temple, where the Jews always meet,[a] and in secret I have said nothing. [21]Why do you ask Me? Ask those who have heard Me what I said to them. Indeed they know what I said."

[22]And when He had said these things, one of the officers who stood by struck Jesus with the palm of his hand, saying, "Do You answer the high priest like that?"

[23]Jesus answered him, "If I have spoken evil, bear witness of the evil; but if well, why do you strike Me?"

[24]Then Annas sent Him bound to Caiaphas the high priest.

Peter Denies Twice More

[25]Now Simon Peter stood and warmed himself. Therefore they said to him, "You are not also *one* of His disciples, are you?"

He denied *it* and said, "I am not!"

[26]One of the servants of the high priest, a relative *of him* whose ear Peter cut off, said, "Did I not see you in the garden with Him?" [27]Peter then denied again; and immediately a rooster crowed.

In Pilate's Court

[28]Then they led Jesus from Caiaphas to the Praetorium, and it was early morning. But they themselves did not go into the Praetorium, lest they should be defiled, but that they might eat the Passover. [29]Pilate then went out to them and said, "What accusation do you bring against this Man?"

[30]They answered and said to him, "If He were not an evildoer, we would not have delivered Him up to you."

[31]Then Pilate said to them, "You take Him and judge Him according to your law."

Therefore the Jews said to him, "It is not lawful for us to put anyone to death," [32]that the saying of Jesus might be fulfilled which He spoke, signifying by what death He would die.

[33]Then Pilate entered the Praetorium again, called Jesus, and said to Him, "Are You the King of the Jews?"

[34]Jesus answered him, "Are you speaking for yourself about this, or did others tell you this concerning Me?"

[35]Pilate answered, "Am I a Jew? Your own nation and the chief priests have delivered You to me. What have You done?"

[36]Jesus answered, "My kingdom is not of this world. If My kingdom were of this world, My servants would fight, so that I should not be delivered to the Jews; but now My kingdom is not from here."

[37]Pilate therefore said to Him, "Are You a king then?"

· · · · · · · · · · · · · · · · · · ·

18:15 [a]M-Text reads *the other*.   **18:20** [a]NU-Text reads *where all the Jews meet*.

18:15 Peter and another disciple stayed, but the others fled. The identity of the unnamed disciple is uncertain. He is often connected with Joseph of Arimathea (who gave his new, stone-cut tomb for Jesus' body). Nicodemus may have been the one, for he helped Joseph prepare Jesus' body for burial. Tradition holds that John himself was the disciple. Whoever this unnamed man might have been, he was well known to the high priest.

18:28 While the Sanhedrin could pronounce death, only the Romans could carry out the execution. Jesus was led from Caiaphas to the Praetorium, which was probably located next to Herod's palace. The members of the Sanhedrin, however, would not enter the Praetorium (the governor's residence), where Jesus was mocked by the soldiers before He was crucified, lest they be ceremonially defiled. If defiled, they could not eat the Passover.

A U T H O R I T Y   WHO'S IN CHARGE?

God Himself is the ultimate authority and the source of all human authority. Christians are commanded to recognize God's authority behind human governing institutions by being compliant and respectful citizens.

Even when human authority, corrupted by sin, is bent on evil purposes, God is working concurrently through that power to accomplish His perfect purposes. This paradox is never more strikingly revealed than when Jesus, standing before Pilate said, "You could have no power at all against Me unless it had been given you from above" (John 19:11). The purposes of the human authorities that led to Jesus' Crucifixion were stained with evil. At the same time, God's good, gracious, and loving purpose of redemption was being accomplished through those human powers, even though they did not acknowledge Him as the source of their authority.

All power and authority is God's alone and He uses it always for the ultimate good of His children. Even when we do not see the beginning or ending of God's plan, we have to trust Him to be the Alpha and Omega, Beginning and Ending of all things, including the events of our individual lives (Rev. 22:13).

See also Rom. 13:1; Heb. 13:7, 17; notes on Government and Citizenship (Rom. 13); Rebellion (Num. 16); Submission (1 Pet. 3)

Jesus answered, "You say *rightly* that I am a king. For this cause I was born, and for this cause I have come into the world, that I should bear witness to the truth. Everyone who is of the truth hears My voice."

38Pilate said to Him, "What is truth?" And when he had said this, he went out again to the Jews, and said to them, "I find no fault in Him at all.

Taking the Place of Barabbas

39"But you have a custom that I should release someone to you at the Passover. Do you therefore want me to release to you the King of the Jews?"

40Then they all cried again, saying, "Not this Man, but Barabbas!" Now Barabbas was a robber.

The Soldiers Mock Jesus

19 So then Pilate took Jesus and scourged *Him.* 2And the soldiers twisted a crown of thorns and put *it* on His head, and they put on Him a purple robe. 3Then they said,a "Hail, King of the Jews!" And they struck Him with their hands.

4Pilate then went out again, and said to them, "Behold, I am bringing Him out to you, that you may know that I find no fault in Him."

Pilate's Decision

5Then Jesus came out, wearing the crown of thorns and the purple robe. And *Pilate* said to them, "Behold the Man!"

6Therefore, when the chief priests and officers saw Him, they cried out, saying, "Crucify *Him,* crucify *Him!* "

Pilate said to them, "You take Him and crucify *Him,* for I find no fault in Him."

7The Jews answered him, "We have a law, and according to oura law He ought to die, because He made Himself the Son of God."

8Therefore, when Pilate heard that saying, he was the more afraid, 9and went again into the Praetorium, and said to Jesus, "Where are You from?" But Jesus gave him no answer.

10Then Pilate said to Him, "Are You not speaking to me? Do You not know that I have power to crucify You, and power to release You?"

11Jesus answered, "You could have no power at all against Me unless it had been given you from above. Therefore the one who delivered Me to you has the greater sin."

12From then on Pilate sought to release Him, but the Jews cried out, saying, "If you let this Man go, you are not Caesar's friend. Whoever makes himself a king speaks against Caesar."

13When Pilate therefore heard that saying, he brought Jesus out and sat down in the judgment seat in a place that is called *The* Pavement, but in Hebrew, Gabbatha. 14Now it was the Preparation

19:3 aNU-Text reads *And they came up to Him and said.* **19:7** aNU-Text reads *the law.*

19:1 Scourging was a severe form of punishment. The victim was tied to a post so that his back was fully exposed. Then he was whipped 39 times with a leather lash containing sharpened pieces of bone and lead. A servant or soldier administered the lashes, 13 to the victim's chest and 26 to his back. The beating literally tore away the flesh. The punishment was not only cruel, but it was also used before crucifixion to hasten the death of the condemned person. Often the victim died

before the 39th lash (see Deut. 25:3, note). Pilate ordered that Jesus be scourged.

19:12 Pontius Pilate, the anti-Semitic Roman governor/procurator of Judea, wanted to release Jesus after he had been scourged (see chart, New Testament Political Rulers). The crowd threatened Pilate by saying that he would no longer be a "friend" of Caesar unless he yielded to their demands and

Day of the Passover, and about the sixth hour. And he said to the Jews, "Behold your King!"

[15]But they cried out, "Away with *Him,* away with *Him!* Crucify Him!"

Pilate said to them, "Shall I crucify your King?"

The chief priests answered, "We have no king but Caesar!"

[16]Then he delivered Him to them to be crucified. Then they took Jesus and led *Him* away.[a]

The King on a Cross

[17]And He, bearing His cross, went out to a place called *the Place* of a Skull, which is called in Hebrew, Golgotha, [18]where they crucified Him, and two others with Him, one on either side, and Jesus in the center. [19]Now Pilate wrote a title and put *it* on the cross. And the writing was:

JESUS OF NAZARETH,
THE KING OF THE JEWS.

[20]Then many of the Jews read this title, for the place where Jesus was crucified was near the city; and it was written in Hebrew, Greek, *and* Latin.

[21]Therefore the chief priests of the Jews said to Pilate, "Do not write, 'The King of the Jews,' but, 'He said, "I am the King of the Jews." ' "

[22]Pilate answered, "What I have written, I have written."

[23]Then the soldiers, when they had crucified Jesus, took His garments and made four parts, to each soldier a part, and also the tunic. Now the tunic was without seam, woven from the top in one piece. [24]They said therefore among themselves, "Let us not tear it, but cast lots for it, whose it

shall be," that the Scripture might be fulfilled which says:

"They divided My garments among them,
And for My clothing they cast lots."[a]

Therefore the soldiers did these things.

Behold Your Mother

[25]Now there stood by the cross of Jesus His mother, and His mother's sister, Mary the *wife* of Clopas, and Mary Magdalene. [26]When Jesus therefore saw His mother, and the disciple whom He loved standing by, He said to His mother, "Woman, behold your son!" [27]Then He said to the disciple, "Behold your mother!" And from that hour that disciple took her to his own *home.*

It Is Finished

[28]After this, Jesus, knowing[a] that all things were now accomplished, that the Scripture might be fulfilled, said, "I thirst!" [29]Now a vessel full of sour wine was sitting there; and they filled a sponge with sour wine, put *it* on hyssop, and put *it* to His mouth. [30]So when Jesus had received the sour wine, He said, "It is finished!" And bowing His head, He gave up His spirit.

Jesus' Side Is Pierced

[31]Therefore, because it was the Preparation *Day,* that the bodies should not remain on the cross on the Sabbath (for that Sabbath was a high day), the Jews asked Pilate that their legs might be

---

19:16 [a]NU-Text omits *and led Him away.*   19:24 [a]Psalm 22:18   19:28 [a]M-Text reads *seeing.*

---

crucified Jesus. Pilate was directly responsible to the emperor, Tiberius Caesar, for the Roman judicial, military, and financial operations in Judea. He feared that the Jews would draft a formal complaint against him, arousing the wrath of Tiberius. Such action would most certainly cost his position and perhaps even his life. John carefully recorded Pilate's "not guilty" verdict of Jesus to prove that Jesus was innocent of any crime against the Roman government.

19:13 After questioning Him, Pilate brought Jesus out to the "Pavement" (Heb. *Gabbatha;* Gk. *lithostroton,* lit. "stone pavement"). On this elevated platform (whether natural or man-made) in front of the Praetorium, Pilate sat in the judgment seat to pronounce his official decisions.

19:14 The Friday of Passover week, or Preparation Day, was used to prepare for the Sabbath, including such tasks as cooking food to be eaten on the Sabbath and drawing extra water, since any type of work was prohibited on the Sabbath. Jesus was sentenced, executed, and buried on this Friday (see chart, The Last Week in the Life of Jesus).

19:19, 20 Pilate, the Roman procurator (A.D. 26–36), hated the Jewish people (see chart, New Testament Political Rulers). To ridicule them, he wrote a mocking title for Jesus and put it on the Cross for public view. Often a tablet naming the criminal's crimes was hung around the dying man's neck. The sign ironically declared the true title of Jesus. It was written in Hebrew,

Greek, and Latin, thus indicating, though unintentionally, that the death of Jesus Christ had universal implications.

19:23, 24 Roman soldiers nailed Jesus to the Cross. Tradition holds that Mary wove the robe worn by her Son Jesus. The robe was woven in one piece as was the robe worn by the high priest (see chart, The High Priest's Clothing). The symbolism here is rich, for the high priest served as a mediator between God and the people. Since the robe could not be torn without ruining it, the soldiers threw dice ("cast lots," v. 24) for the garment, thus fulfilling the OT prophecy (Ps. 22:18).

19:26, 27 Several women (Jesus' mother Mary and her sister Salome, Mary the wife of Clopas, and Mary Magdalene), as well as John, one of the 12 disciples, stood beneath the Cross as Jesus died (see chart, Women and Jesus). Jesus, even in His agony, was concerned about the future welfare of His mother. As the eldest Son, He took the responsibility of providing His mother with a protector and provider, the "disciple whom He loved," John.

19:31, 32 Crucifixion often would take days to kill its victim. Breaking the victim's legs caused the body to go into shock and hastened death. Roman law demanded that a criminal hang on the cross until he died, no matter how long that took. The body was then fed to the vultures. Jewish law, however, required that a body be removed the same day and buried before evening. The Jews could not allow a body to hang upon

CAREGIVERS   *A COMMITMENT TO ELDERLY PARENTS*

The Bible's plan for families is a fairly straightforward one. Parents care for children until they reach adulthood; then children have a responsibility for the care of their parents. This was considered an integral part of "honoring" mothers and fathers, as commanded by the Law (Ex. 20:12). In Old Testament times, parents and children generally lived together or in proximity all their lives. Jacob and his wives, their maids, his children and grandchildren were considered a family unit as they journeyed to Egypt for provision at the hand of Joseph (Gen. 46:5–27).

Jesus was critical of those Pharisees who refused to provide for the material needs of their parents under the guise of giving their all to the Lord (Mark 7:10–13). Paul wrote to Timothy concerning the responsibility of children to parents (1 Tim. 5:4). While on the Cross, Jesus made certain that His widowed mother had a means of provision (John 19:26, 27).

While obligated to provide materially for parents, an adult child is not obligated to meet all of a parent's emotional or spiritual needs, and she is never to follow in a parent's pattern of sin (Ezek. 18:19–22). Children are to follow the leading of the Lord for their own lives (Matt. 8:21, 22; Mark 10: 29, 30).

See also notes on Children (Luke 15); Family (Gen. 32; 1 Sam. 3; Ps. 78; 127); Parenthood (Prov. 10); Widowhood (Ps. 68; Jer. 29; 1 Cor. 2); portrait of Ruth (Ruth 2)

broken, and *that* they might be taken away. [32]Then the soldiers came and broke the legs of the first and of the other who was crucified with Him. [33]But when they came to Jesus and saw that He was already dead, they did not break His legs. [34]But one of the soldiers pierced His side with a spear, and immediately blood and water came out. [35]And he who has seen has testified, and his testimony is true; and he knows that he is telling the truth, so that you may believe. [36]For these things were done that the Scripture should be fulfilled, *"Not one of His bones shall be broken."*[a] [37]And again another Scripture says, *"They shall look on Him whom they pierced."*[a]

Jesus Buried in Joseph's Tomb

[38]After this, Joseph of Arimathea, being a disciple of Jesus, but secretly, for fear of the Jews, asked Pilate that he might take away the body of Jesus; and Pilate gave *him* permission. So he came and took the body of Jesus. [39]And Nicodemus, who at first came to Jesus by night, also came, bringing a mixture of myrrh and aloes, about a hundred pounds. [40]Then they took the body of Jesus, and bound it in strips of linen with the spices, as the custom of the Jews is to bury. [41]Now in the place where He was crucified there was a garden, and in the garden a new tomb in which no one had yet been laid. [42]So there they laid Jesus, because of

the Jews' Preparation *Day,* for the tomb was nearby.

The Empty Tomb

20 Now on the first *day* of the week Mary Magdalene went to the tomb early, while it was still dark, and saw *that* the stone had been taken away from the tomb. [2]Then she ran and came to Simon Peter, and to the other disciple, whom Jesus loved, and said to them, "They have taken away the Lord out of the tomb, and we do not know where they have laid Him."

[3]Peter therefore went out, and the other disciple, and were going to the tomb. [4]So they both ran together, and the other disciple outran Peter and came to the tomb first. [5]And he, stooping down and looking in, saw the linen cloths lying *there;* yet he did not go in. [6]Then Simon Peter came, following him, and went into the tomb; and he saw the linen cloths lying *there,* [7]and the handkerchief that had been around His head, not lying with the linen cloths, but folded together in a place by itself. [8]Then the other disciple, who came to the tomb first, went in also; and he saw and believed. [9]For as yet they did not know the Scripture, that

•••••••••••••••••••••••

19:36 [a]Exodus 12:46; Numbers 9:12; Psalm 34:20   **19:37** [a]Zechariah 12:10

the cross on the Sabbath, which was the next day. Jesus' legs were not broken, for He was already dead when the soldiers came and broke the legs of the criminals who were crucified on each side of Him. The fact that none of Jesus' bones were broken fulfilled another prophecy (v. 36; Ps. 34:20; chart, Prophecies Fulfilled on the Cross).

20:7 Upon hearing Mary's story, Peter and John ran to the tomb. They expected to find the grave clothes gone, for they suspected a thief had stolen the body. Instead, they found the

shroud resting exactly where the body had been placed. Instead of a disheveled mess, the clothes were still neatly folded as if around a body. Jesus was gone, but His grave clothes lay in the same folded fashion. A handkerchief (or towel or napkin) was used to cover the face of the dead for burial. The handkerchief that covered Jesus' head was still in place where His head had lain. The position of the grave clothes puzzled Peter, John, and Mary, for they had not yet understood that the Resurrection had occurred.

WOMEN AND JESUS

WOMAN	EVENT	WOMAN'S RESPONSE	CULTURE'S RESPONSE	JESUS' RESPONSE
MARY, THE MOTHER OF JESUS	The angel's announcement (Luke 1:26–28, 46–55)	Questioning how this could happen but praising in obedience	Putting away an unmarried, pregnant woman	Sending His messenger to bless her
	The Savior's birth (Luke 2:9–11, 19)	Pondering Jesus' nature as divine and human	Another illegitimate birth	Seeing the joyous event as part of His redemptive plan
	Jesus' circumcision (Luke 2:25–28)	Taking Jesus to the temple with Joseph	Curiosity over the prophecies and the rumors	Prophecies of His birth through Simeon and Anna
	Jesus' visit to the temple (Luke 2:41–52)	Keeping all Jesus said in her heart	Insistence on complete obedience to parents	Gently telling His mother that He was doing the Father's business
	The wedding at Cana (John 2:1–11)	Instructing servants to do what Jesus said	Enjoying the result of Jesus' miracle, while indifferent to His mission	Showing Mary that He was working within the Father's timing, though answering her request
	Jesus' speaking to the multitudes (Matt. 12:46–50; Mark 3:31–35; Luke 8:19–21)	Sending word for Jesus to come to her	Expecting Jesus' obedience to His parents	Affirming to Mary that she (and His brothers) did not have special privileges
	Jesus' death on the Cross (Luke 23:27; John 19:26)	Witnessing this heart-rending event	Observing curiously the events	Jesus' seeing to the care of His mother
	The events after the Resurrection (Acts 1:11, 14)	Continuing in prayer and supplication	Surprised but apathetic	Assuming His place with the Father in heaven
ANNA	Jesus' circumcision (Luke 2:25, 26, 36–38)	Giving thanks for Jesus and recognizing Him as Redeemer	Though occasionally acknowledging the contributions of women, rejecting their equality of personhood	The presence of the Holy Spirit
THE SAMARITAN WOMAN	The meeting at Jacob's well (John 4:3–34)	Surprised that Jesus would speak to her, suspecting that He is the Messiah, and sharing the Good News	Feelings of aversion from the rabbis about conversing with or imparting spiritual truths to women	Initiating the conversation, sharing the profound truths, and presenting Himself as Messiah
THE WOMAN TAKEN IN ADULTERY	Attempt to trap Jesus (John 8:1–11)	Silent during the entire encounter until Jesus directly addressed her	Believing men were seduced by women	Not denying her sin, not condemning her, but freeing her
MARY MAGDALENE	Her healing from demonic possession (Luke 8:2, 3)	Following and ministering to Jesus	Rejecting any ministries by women	Accepting support from those accompanying Him, valuing their commitment to Him as that of the men
	The visit to the tomb (John 20:11–18)	Coming with other women, remaining, and weeping	Rejection of a woman's testimony as valid	Letting her be the first to see and talk to Him, the first to tell others
MARY OF BETHANY	Jesus' visit in her home (Luke 10:38–42)	Sitting at Jesus' feet, waiting to be taught	Refusing to see the teaching of spiritual truths as appropriate for women	Teaching her, encouraging her to learn
	The death of Lazarus (John 11:28–36)	Weeping at Jesus' feet	The refusal of rabbis to talk to women in public	Weeping with Mary in her sorrow
MARTHA OF BETHANY	Jesus' visit in her home (Luke 10:38–42)	Being distracted with service	Not expecting women to learn	Encouraging her to learn, while enjoying her hospitality
	The death of Lazarus (John 11:17–27)	Questioning Jesus	Rejection on the part of religious leaders and others of any spiritual nurture for women	Answering her questions, discussing profound doctrines
THE HEMORRHAGING WOMAN	Her healing (Mark 5:25–34)	Touching Jesus' garment	Avoiding being touched by or touching any woman with an issue of blood	Stating that she touched Him but forgiving rather than condemning her; acknowledging her great faith
GENERAL OBSERVATIONS	Footwashing (John 13:1–5)		"A wife's duty was to wash her husband's feet"	Jesus, the footwasher
	Encounter with prejudice (John 4:7–29, 39–42)		"The woman is in all things inferior to man" (Josephus)	Jesus treating women equally
	Adultery in the heart (Matt. 5:27–30)		Women should be secluded because lust is inevitable	Men relating to women without lust

See also portraits of Anna (Luke 2); Forgiven Adulteress (John 8); the Hemorrhaging Woman (Matt. 9); Martha (John 11); Mary of Bethany (John 11); Mary Magdalene (John 20); Mary of Nazareth (Luke 1); the Samaritan Woman (John 4).

MARY MAGDALENE   *A Devoted Woman*

Mary lived in Magdala (now called El Mejdel, located south of the Plain of Gennesaret on the shores of the Sea of Galilee), an important agricultural, fishing, and trade center. Suffering from demon possession, Mary met Jesus face to face, an encounter that changed her life. Jesus cast from Mary the seven evil demonic spirits that had ruled and ruined her life (see Mark 16:9).

The gospel writers distinguished demon possession from other diseases. The New Testament clearly describes its symptoms—for example, speechlessness (Matt. 9:33), violence (Matt. 8:28), blindness (Matt. 12:22), convulsions (Mark 1:26), foaming at the mouth (Luke 9:39). Mary's demonic possession may have been physical, mental, or spiritual illness, or perhaps even immorality (though there is no textual evidence for prostitution on her part).

After her healing experience, Mary became a devoted follower of Christ. Unflappable in her faithfulness, she was counted among the small group of women who, at their own expense, served Jesus and His disciples as they preached and ministered to the masses.

Mary became an important leader among the ministering women. Scripture mentions her fourteen times. She proved to be a passionate follower who gave her time, energy, and wealth to the Lord's work. She faithfully followed Jesus throughout His ministry. Even when nearly everyone fled with fear after Christ's arrest, Mary lingered lovingly all the way to the Cross and witnessed His painful death. Mary remained faithful to Jesus long after the others had given up hope. Early one morning, after the Jewish Sabbath ended, she crept through the predawn darkness to the tomb. In her arms she carried the customary spices to prepare the Lord's body for burial.

The Lord richly rewarded Mary for her faithfulness to Him. For when she arrived at the tomb, the heavy stone slab that sealed the three-foot square entrance had been removed. To her horror, Mary discovered the tomb empty, but her grief turned to joy when she came face to face with Jesus, the risen Lord. In His incredible grace, God chose a faithful woman, Mary of Magdala, to proclaim to the disciples and to the world the glorious life-changing news of the Resurrection of Jesus Christ. Imagine her excitement! "I have seen the Lord!" she shouted with unequaled enthusiasm to the small band of bewildered and unbelieving disciples (Mark 16:11).

Mary Magdalene's devoted faithfulness to Jesus and her announcement of Christ's victory over death shouts to women everywhere how an encounter with Christ changes a life forever. Mary Magdalene personifies the many women for whom Christ has demonstrated His depth of mercy and forgiveness.

See also Matt. 27:56, 61; 28:1; Mark 15:40, 47; 16:9; Luke 8:2; 24:10; charts on Women and Jesus in His Last Days; Women and Jesus; note on Commitment (Matt. 16).

He must rise again from the dead. [10]Then the disciples went away again to their own homes.

Mary Magdalene Sees the Risen Lord

[11]But Mary stood outside by the tomb weeping, and as she wept she stooped down *and looked* into the tomb. [12]And she saw two angels in white sitting, one at the head and the other at the feet, where the body of Jesus had lain. [13]Then they said to her, "Woman, why are you weeping?"

She said to them, "Because they have taken away my Lord, and I do not know where they have laid Him."

[14]Now when she had said this, she turned around and saw Jesus standing *there*, and did not know that it was Jesus. [15]Jesus said to her, "Woman, why are you weeping? Whom are you seeking?"

She, supposing Him to be the gardener, said to Him, "Sir, if You have carried Him away, tell me where You have laid Him, and I will take Him away."

[16]Jesus said to her, "Mary!"

She turned and said to Him,[a] "Rabboni!" (which is to say, Teacher).

[17]Jesus said to her, "Do not cling to Me, for I have not yet ascended to My Father; but go to My brethren and say to them, 'I am ascending to My Father and your Father, and *to* My God and your God.'"

[18]Mary Magdalene came and told the disciples that she had seen the Lord,[a] and *that* He had spoken these things to her.

The Apostles Commissioned

[19]Then, the same day at evening, being the first *day* of the week, when the doors were shut where the disciples were assembled,[a] for fear of the Jews, Jesus came and stood in the midst, and said to them, "Peace *be* with you." [20]When He had said this, He showed them *His* hands and His side.

20:16 [a]NU-Text adds *in Hebrew.*   20:18 [a]NU-Text reads *disciples, "I have seen the Lord,"* . . .   20:19 [a]NU-Text omits *assembled.*

Then the disciples were glad when they saw the Lord.

²¹So Jesus said to them again, "Peace to you! As the Father has sent Me, I also send you." ²²And when He had said this, He breathed on *them,* and said to them, "Receive the Holy Spirit. ²³If you forgive the sins of any, they are forgiven them; if you retain the *sins* of any, they are retained."

Seeing and Believing

²⁴Now Thomas, called the Twin, one of the twelve, was not with them when Jesus came. ²⁵The other disciples therefore said to him, "We have seen the Lord."

So he said to them, "Unless I see in His hands the print of the nails, and put my finger into the print of the nails, and put my hand into His side, I will not believe."

²⁶And after eight days His disciples were again inside, and Thomas with them. Jesus came, the doors being shut, and stood in the midst, and said, "Peace to you!" ²⁷Then He said to Thomas, "Reach your finger here, and look at My hands; and reach your hand *here,* and put *it* into My side. Do not be unbelieving, but believing."

²⁸And Thomas answered and said to Him, "My Lord and my God!"

²⁹Jesus said to him, "Thomas,ᵃ because you have seen Me, you have believed. Blessed *are* those who have not seen and *yet* have believed."

That You May Believe

³⁰And truly Jesus did many other signs in the presence of His disciples, which are not written in this book; ³¹but these are written that you may believe that Jesus is the Christ, the Son of God, and that believing you may have life in His name.

Breakfast by the Sea

21 After these things Jesus showed Himself again to the disciples at the Sea of Tiberias, and in this way He showed *Himself:* ²Simon Peter, Thomas called the Twin, Nathanael of Cana in Galilee, the *sons* of Zebedee, and two others of His disciples were together. ³Simon Peter said to them, "I am going fishing."

They said to him, "We are going with you also." They went out and immediatelyᵃ got into the boat, and that night they caught nothing. ⁴But when the morning had now come, Jesus stood on the shore; yet the disciples did not know that it was Jesus. ⁵Then Jesus said to them, "Children, have you any food?"

They answered Him, "No."

⁶And He said to them, "Cast the net on the right side of the boat, and you will find *some.*" So they cast, and now they were not able to draw it in because of the multitude of fish.

⁷Therefore that disciple whom Jesus loved said to Peter, "It is the Lord!" Now when Simon Peter heard that it was the Lord, he put on *his* outer garment (for he had removed it), and plunged into the sea. ⁸But the other disciples came in the little boat (for they were not far from land, but about two hundred cubits), dragging the net with fish. ⁹Then, as soon as they had come to land, they saw a fire of coals there, and fish laid on it, and bread. ¹⁰Jesus said to them, "Bring some of the fish which you have just caught."

¹¹Simon Peter went up and dragged the net to land, full of large fish, one hundred and fifty-three; and although there were so many, the net was not broken. ¹²Jesus said to them, "Come *and* eat breakfast." Yet none of the disciples dared ask Him, "Who are You?"—knowing that it was the Lord. ¹³Jesus then came and took the bread and gave it to them, and likewise the fish.

¹⁴This *is* now the third time Jesus showed Himself to His disciples after He was raised from the dead.

Jesus Restores Peter

¹⁵So when they had eaten breakfast, Jesus said to Simon Peter, "Simon, *son* of Jonah,ᵃ do you love Me more than these?"

He said to Him, "Yes, Lord; You know that I love You."

He said to him, "Feed My lambs."

¹⁶He said to him again a second time, "Simon, *son* of Jonah,ᵃ do you love Me?"

He said to Him, "Yes, Lord; You know that I love You."

He said to him, "Tend My sheep."

¹⁷He said to him the third time, "Simon, *son* of Jonah,ᵃ do you love Me?" Peter was grieved because He said to him the third time, "Do you love Me?"

And he said to Him, "Lord, You know all things; You know that I love You."

Jesus said to him, "Feed My sheep. ¹⁸Most assuredly, I say to you, when you were younger, you girded yourself and walked where you wished; but when you are old, you will stretch out your hands, and another will gird you and carry *you* where you do not wish." ¹⁹This He spoke, signifying by what

---

20:29 ᵃNU-Text and M-Text omit *Thomas.* **21:3** ᵃNU-Text omits *immediately.* **21:15, 16, 17** ᵃNU-Text reads *John.*

21:18, 19 Jesus prophesied that Peter would die as a result of following Him. He made a comparison between Peter's life as a youth and as an old man. Jesus indicated that Peter would die a martyr's death. "Stretch out your hands" referred to crucifixion. Tradition holds that Peter was crucified upside down in Rome between A.D. 64 and 68.

death he would glorify God. And when He had spoken this, He said to him, "Follow Me."

The Beloved Disciple and His Book

²⁰Then Peter, turning around, saw the disciple whom Jesus loved following, who also had leaned on His breast at the supper, and said, "Lord, who is the one who betrays You?" ²¹Peter, seeing him, said to Jesus, "But Lord, what *about* this man?"

²²Jesus said to him, "If I will that he remain till I come, what *is that* to you? You follow Me."

²³Then this saying went out among the brethren that this disciple would not die. Yet Jesus did not say to him that he would not die, but, "If I will that he remain till I come, what *is that* to you?"

²⁴This is the disciple who testifies of these things, and wrote these things; and we know that his testimony is true.

²⁵And there are also many other things that Jesus did, which if they were written one by one, I suppose that even the world itself could not contain the books that would be written. Amen.

Acts

AUTHOR

Although not mentioned by name, Luke, the Gentile physician (Col. 4:14), is believed to be the author of the Book of Acts, the companion volume to the Gospel of Luke. The dear friend and traveling companion of Paul, Luke was an eyewitness to many of the events he recorded in Acts. His well-written books illustrate Luke's keen knowledge of Greek literature and language.

DATE

The Book of Acts ends abruptly with Paul in his second year of house imprisonment in Rome, which began around A.D. 60. Luke does not give information concerning Paul's trial or death (Paul died between A.D. 66 and 68). Nor does Acts record the Neronian persecution (A.D. 64–68) or the destruction of Jerusalem (A.D. 70). Scholars believe Luke would have included these important events if he had written Acts after A.D. 64. Thus, Acts was probably written sometime between A.D. 61 and 63.

BACKGROUND

SETTING: Luke wrote Luke and Acts while in Rome with Paul during the time of the apostle's first Roman imprisonment.

PURPOSE: The Book of Acts provides the history of the early Christian church. It tells how the gospel spread with miraculous and unhindered success from its Jewish roots in Jerusalem to Rome, the center of the Roman Empire. Acts especially follows the activities of the two apostles, Peter and Paul. As a historian, Luke had researched the events found in Luke and Acts so that he might provide a reliable written account for his readers. He also wanted his readers to know with certainty what they had been taught about the Christian faith. He desired to confirm them in their faith. He wanted his readers to live a strong and committed Christian life even in the midst of a pagan world.

AUDIENCE: Acts is addressed to a specific person, Theophilus. While Luke might have written to a specific man by the name of "Theophilus," many have suggested that Luke addressed all those who love God, since "Theophilus" means "lover of God." Either way, Luke wrote Acts to be read by many. These readers were evidently familiar with the Roman Empire and Asia Minor but perhaps not with Palestine, which would explain Luke's carefully researched information about places in Palestine.

LITERARY CHARACTERISTICS: Acts is written in narrative style with a precise beginning and ending, characters, and a plot. Luke clearly meant the books of Luke and Acts to be read as a unified composition.

THEMES

- An accounting of the spread of the gospel, universal in nature, unhindered in action, and unending in scope;

- The unique role of the Holy Spirit in equipping those who share the gospel and in energizing the church;
- The development of a theology in which early Jewish Christians became a more inclusive people of God, adding believing Gentiles to the church.

OUTLINE

Prologue

1 The former account I made, O Theophilus, of all that Jesus began both to do and teach, [2]until the day in which He was taken up, after He through the Holy Spirit had given commandments to the apostles whom He had chosen, [3]to whom He also presented Himself alive after His suffering by many infallible proofs, being seen by them during forty days and speaking of the things pertaining to the kingdom of God.

The Holy Spirit Promised

[4]And being assembled together with *them*, He commanded them not to depart from Jerusalem, but to wait for the Promise of the Father, "which," *He said*, "you have heard from Me; [5]for John truly baptized with water, but you shall be baptized with the Holy Spirit not many days from now." [6]Therefore, when they had come together, they asked Him, saying, "Lord, will You at this time restore the kingdom to Israel?" [7]And He said to them, "It is not for you to know times or seasons which the Father has put in His own authority. [8]But you shall receive power when the Holy Spirit has come upon you; and you shall be witnesses to Me[a] in Jerusalem, and in all Judea and Samaria, and to the end of the earth."

Jesus Ascends to Heaven

[9]Now when He had spoken these things, while they watched, He was taken up, and a cloud received Him out of their sight. [10]And while they looked steadfastly toward heaven as He went up, behold, two men stood by them in white apparel, [11]who also said, "Men of Galilee, why do you stand gazing up into heaven? This *same* Jesus, who was taken up from you into heaven, will so come in like manner as you saw Him go into heaven."

The Upper Room Prayer Meeting

[12]Then they returned to Jerusalem from the mount called Olivet, which is near Jerusalem, a Sabbath day's journey. [13]And when they had entered, they went up into the upper room where they were staying: Peter, James, John, and Andrew; Philip and Thomas; Bartholomew and Matthew; James *the son* of Alphaeus and Simon the Zealot; and Judas *the son* of James. [14]These all continued with one accord in prayer and supplication,[a] with the women and Mary the mother of Jesus, and with His brothers.

Matthias Chosen

[15]And in those days Peter stood up in the midst of the disciples[a] (altogether the number of names was about a hundred and twenty), and said, [16]"Men *and* brethren, this Scripture had to be fulfilled, which the Holy Spirit spoke before by the mouth of David concerning Judas, who became a guide to those who arrested Jesus; [17]for he was numbered with us and obtained a part in this ministry."

[18](Now this man purchased a field with the wages of iniquity; and falling headlong, he burst open in the middle and all his entrails gushed out. [19]And it became known to all those dwelling in Jerusalem; so that field is called in their own language, Akel Dama, that is, Field of Blood.)

[20]"For it is written in the Book of Psalms:

'Let his dwelling place be desolate,
  And let no one live in it';[a]

and,

'Let[b] another take his office.'[c]

[21]"Therefore, of these men who have accompanied us all the time that the Lord Jesus went in and out among us, [22]beginning from the baptism of John to that day when He was taken up from us, one of these must become a witness with us of His resurrection."

[23]And they proposed two: Joseph called Barsabas, who was surnamed Justus, and Matthias. [24]And they prayed and said, "You, O Lord, who know the hearts of all, show which of these two You have chosen [25]to take part in this ministry and

---

1:8 [a]NU-Text reads *My witnesses.*   **1:14** [a]NU-Text omits *and supplication.*   **1:15** [a]NU-Text reads *brethren.*   **1:20** [a]Psalm 69:25 [b]Psalm 109:8 [c]Greek *episkopen,* position of overseer

---

1:1 Luke may have been writing to a specific man named Theophilus (Gk., lit. "lover of God" or "dear to God"), or he may have been addressing all those who love God. The Gospel of Luke is also addressed to Theophilus.

1:8 To be a witness (Gk. *martus*) for Jesus was costly to men and women who faithfully shared the gospel and, according to history, suffered torture and even death. Because of this, *martus* eventually was transliterated as, and became synonymous with, "martyr." A witness is a person who has seen an event and, in a court of law, can tell her own experience based on personal observation. Here, Christ challenged believers to bear witness of Him in their lifestyle and speech.

1:9–11 Jesus' return to His glory is described in this passage.

Forty days had passed since the Resurrection. Luke recorded Christ's Ascension in both Luke and Acts. The Ascension followed Jesus' commission to the disciples to be His witnesses. From somewhere on the Mount of Olives, Jesus was taken up into heaven as the disciples watched. At the same time, two men wearing white clothes spoke to them of Christ's return, noting that He would return just as He had gone.

1:18–20 Akel Dama (Aram., lit. "field of blood") was the piece of land where Judas, the disciple who betrayed Jesus, killed himself. The land had been bought with the 30 pieces of silver paid to Judas for his betrayal of Jesus (Matt. 27:3–10).

1:23, 26 The disciples proposed two men to replace Judas Iscariot, who had committed suicide after he betrayed Jesus.

WOMEN'S MINISTRIES   COWORKERS IN THE KINGDOM

Women in the New Testament were not spectators. They played an active, vibrant, and vital role in the day-to-day function of the church. God poured out His Spirit upon both sons and daughters (Joel 2:28; Acts 2:17, 18), and Spirit-empowered women ministered using the full spectrum of gifts. Besides evangelism, prophecy, teaching, and discipleship, women were involved in countless other ministries, together with service to their families (1 Tim. 5:10), according to their respective spiritual gifts (Acts 1:14; 12:12; 1 Cor. 12:8–10; 1 Tim. 5:5; Philem. 2). Women were an active part of the assembly in Philippi (Acts 16:11–15) and were involved in the establishment of churches in Thessalonica (Acts 17:4) and Berea (Acts 17:12).

Paul often referred to women as his "fellow workers." He specifically acknowledged Mary (Rom. 16:6), Tryphena, Tryphosa, and Persis (Rom. 16:12), Euodia and Syntyche (Phil. 4:2), and Priscilla (Rom. 16:3) as women who had labored hard for the gospel. The coming of the kingdom revolutionized the involvement of ordinary people in the work of God. Whether Jew or Greek, slave or free, male or female—kingdom ministry became the responsibility of all.

See also chart on Spiritual Gifts of Women in the Bible; notes on Evangelism (John 6; Col. 4; 1 Pet. 3); Spiritual Gifts (Rom. 12); Women's Ministries (John 4; 1 Cor. 11; Eph. 2; 1 Tim. 3; Titus 2)

apostleship from which Judas by transgression fell, that he might go to his own place." ²⁶And they cast their lots, and the lot fell on Matthias. And he was numbered with the eleven apostles.

Coming of the Holy Spirit

2 When the Day of Pentecost had fully come, they were all with one accord^a in one place. ²And suddenly there came a sound from heaven, as of a rushing mighty wind, and it filled the whole house where they were sitting. ³Then there appeared to them divided tongues, as of fire, and *one* sat upon each of them. ⁴And they were all filled with the Holy Spirit and began to speak with other tongues, as the Spirit gave them utterance.

The Crowd's Response

⁵And there were dwelling in Jerusalem Jews, devout men, from every nation under heaven. ⁶And when this sound occurred, the multitude came together, and were confused, because everyone heard them speak in his own language. ⁷Then

they were all amazed and marveled, saying to one another, "Look, are not all these who speak Galileans? ⁸And how *is it that* we hear, each in our own language in which we were born? ⁹Parthians and Medes and Elamites, those dwelling in Mesopotamia, Judea and Cappadocia, Pontus and Asia, ¹⁰Phrygia and Pamphylia, Egypt and the parts of Libya adjoining Cyrene, visitors from Rome, both Jews and proselytes, ¹¹Cretans and Arabs—we hear them speaking in our own tongues the wonderful works of God." ¹²So they were all amazed and perplexed, saying to one another, "Whatever could this mean?"

¹³Others mocking said, "They are full of new wine."

Peter's Sermon

¹⁴But Peter, standing up with the eleven, raised his voice and said to them, "Men of Judea and all who dwell in Jerusalem, let this be known to you,

2:1 ^aNU-Text reads *together*.

These two men had a close association with Jesus when He began His ministry, and they had witnessed Jesus' Ascension. Joseph Barsabas (lit. "son of the elder") was also known as Justus (Lat.). He might have been the brother of Judas Barsabas (see Acts 15:22). Matthias (lit. "gift of *Yah*") has no other mention in Scripture. The disciples prayed over selecting the 12th disciple, then cast lots to determine God's choice for the position (see Prov. 6:33). This method of determining God's will was common enough at the time, but no record exists of its use after Pentecost (see Ex. 28:15; Deut. 33:8, notes). Matthias was chosen to replace Judas.

2:1 Fifty days after Jesus' Resurrection, the Holy Spirit came upon the believers during the Feast of Pentecost, also called the Feast of Weeks (see chart, The Feasts of Israel).

2:2–4 The Book of Acts has been called "the book of the Holy Spirit." Luke, among the four gospel writers, placed the heaviest emphasis on the Holy Spirit (see chart, The Work of the

Holy Spirit). The "wind" and "fire," both familiar signs of the presence of God, provided a visual representation of the Holy Spirit's ministry of filling and equipping each believer for a special role in Christ's ministry. Some have said that the wind symbolized power and the fire purity. The unusual speaking in "tongues" or diverse languages underscored the universal outreach of the church, a reversal of the Babel experience (Gen. 11). At Babel the language was confused so that people could no longer understand one another; at Pentecost the linguistic miracle ("other tongues") enabled people visiting from outside Judea, including Jews who no longer understood Hebrew or Aramaic, to understand the message of the gospel. So unusual was this occurrence that the believers were accused by others of being drunk with "new wine" (see Acts 2:13). This Spirit-gift was the fulfillment of the promise made by Jesus (John 14—16).

THE WORK OF THE HOLY SPIRIT

ATTRIBUTES: WHO HE IS	RECORD: WHAT HE HAS DONE	WORK: WHAT HE WILL DO
	IN THE OLD TESTAMENT:	
He possesses omniscience (1 Cor. 2:11, 12).	He was active at creation (Gen. 1:2).	He will guide the believer (Acts 8:29; Rom. 8:14).
He possesses omnipresence (Ps. 139:7).	He was the bestower of supernatural giftedness (Gen. 41:38).	He will give assurance of salvation (Rom. 8:14–17).
He possesses omnipotence (Job 33:4).	He was the giver of creativity (Ex. 31:2–5).	He will be the believer's teacher (1 John 2:27).
He is truth (1 John 5:6).	He was the source of power (Judg. 3:9, 10).	He will intercede (Rom. 8:26).
He gives life (Luke 11:13).	He inspired prophecy (1 Sam. 19:20, 23).	He will comfort (John 14:16).
He possesses creative wisdom (Is. 40:13).	He was the mediator of God's message (Mic. 3:8).	He will sanctify (2 Thess. 2:13).
He possesses all the attributes of deity; He is God (Acts 5:3, 4).	**IN THE NEW TESTAMENT:**	He will accomplish regeneration (John 3:6).
	He was part of the Incarnation (Luke 1:35).	He will make you aware of sin (John 16:8).
	He declared the truth about Christ (John 16:13, 14).	He will convince you of the truth of the gospel (John 16:8, 13, 14).
	He endowed believers with power for witnessing (Acts 1:8).	He will empower you to witness (Acts 1:8; 4:31).
	He poured out God's love (Rom. 5:5).	He will destroy the power of sin in your life (Rom. 8:2–6).
	He interceded (Rom. 8:26).	He will lead and even control your life (Rom. 8:14; Gal. 5:16, 25).
	He was the inspiration for the writing of Holy Scripture (2 Tim. 3:16; 2 Pet. 1:21).	He will distribute gifts to be used in the kingdom (1 Cor. 12:4–11).
	He distributed giftedness for ministry (1 Cor. 12:4–11).	
	He empowered believers with characteristics for godly living (Gal. 5:22, 23).	
	He strengthened believers within (Eph. 3:16).	

The Holy Spirit *was promised as a gift to believers* (Luke 24:49; John 14:16; Acts 1:5). *Part of His ministry is to seal believers at the moment they place saving faith in Christ. The term "seal" includes four truths: He is a provision of security, a mark of ownership, a certification of genuineness, and a sign of approval* (Eph. 4:30). *Indeed, the Holy Spirit's presence in the believing woman's life is the final evidence, both to herself and to others, of the truth of what she has believed. Further, He is the down payment, providing both a foretaste of the believer's spiritual inheritance and a legal claim to the fullness of that inheritance in the future* (see 2 Cor. 1:22).

and heed my words. [15]For these are not drunk, as you suppose, since it is *only* the third hour of the day. [16]But this is what was spoken by the prophet Joel:

[17]'*And it shall come to pass in the last days, says God,*
    That I will pour out of My Spirit on all flesh;
    Your sons and your daughters shall prophesy,
    Your young men shall see visions,
    Your old men shall dream dreams.
[18]*And on My menservants and on My maidservants*
    I will pour out My Spirit in those days;
    And they shall prophesy.
[19]*I will show wonders in heaven above*
    And signs in the earth beneath:
    Blood and fire and vapor of smoke.
[20]*The sun shall be turned into darkness,*
    And the moon into blood,
    Before the coming of the great and awesome day of the
    LORD.
[21]*And it shall come to pass*
    That whoever calls on the name of the LORD
    Shall be saved.'[a]

[22]"Men of Israel, hear these words: Jesus of Nazareth, a Man attested by God to you by miracles, wonders, and signs which God did through Him in your midst, as you yourselves also know— [23]Him, being delivered by the determined purpose and foreknowledge of God, you have taken[a] by lawless hands, have crucified, and put to death; [24]whom God raised up, having loosed the pains of death, because it was not possible that He should be held by it. [25]For David says concerning Him:

'*I foresaw the LORD always before my face,*
    For He is at my right hand, that I may not be shaken.
[26]*Therefore my heart rejoiced, and my tongue was glad;*
    Moreover my flesh also will rest in hope.
[27]*For You will not leave my soul in Hades,*
    Nor will You allow Your Holy One to see corruption.
[28]*You have made known to me the ways of life;*
    You will make me full of joy in Your presence.'[a]

[29]"Men *and* brethren, let *me* speak freely to you of the patriarch David, that he is both dead and buried, and his tomb is with us to this day. [30]Therefore, being a prophet, and knowing that

God had sworn with an oath to him that of the fruit of his body, according to the flesh, He would raise up the Christ to sit on his throne,[a] [31]he, foreseeing this, spoke concerning the resurrection of the Christ, that His soul was not left in Hades, nor did His flesh see corruption. [32]This Jesus God has raised up, of which we are all witnesses. [33]Therefore being exalted to the right hand of God, and having received from the Father the promise of the Holy Spirit, He poured out this which you now see and hear.

[34]"For David did not ascend into the heavens, but he says himself:

'*The LORD said to my Lord,*
    "*Sit at My right hand,*
[35]*Till I make Your enemies Your footstool.*" '[a]

[36]"Therefore let all the house of Israel know assuredly that God has made this Jesus, whom you crucified, both Lord and Christ."

[37]Now when they heard *this*, they were cut to the heart, and said to Peter and the rest of the apostles, "Men *and* brethren, what shall we do?"

[38]Then Peter said to them, "Repent, and let every one of you be baptized in the name of Jesus Christ for the remission of sins; and you shall receive the gift of the Holy Spirit. [39]For the promise is to you and to your children, and to all who are afar off, as many as the Lord our God will call."

A Vital Church Grows

[40]And with many other words he testified and exhorted them, saying, "Be saved from this perverse generation." [41]Then those who gladly[a] received his word were baptized; and that day about three thousand souls were added *to them.* [42]And they continued steadfastly in the apostles' doctrine and fellowship, in the breaking of bread, and in prayers. [43]Then fear came upon every soul, and many wonders and signs were done through the apostles. [44]Now all who believed were together, and had all things in common, [45]and sold their

·············· ····· ······

2:21 [a]Joel 2:28–32   **2:23** [a]NU-Text omits *have taken.*   **2:28** [a]Psalm 16:8–11   **2:30** [a]NU-Text omits *according to the flesh, He would raise up the Christ* and completes the verse with *He would seat one on his throne.*   **2:35** [a]Psalm 110:1   **2:41** [a]NU-Text omits *gladly.*

2:23, 24 The death of Jesus on the Cross was not accidental. Luke clearly informed his readers that the Cross was in the eternal plan of God for the salvation of the world. "Having loosed the pains of death" refers to the fact that death could not hold Jesus, a reference to His Resurrection (v. 24).

2:29 Peter referred to King David, who had requested escape from *Sheol* (Heb., lit. "the place of the dead," for both righteous and wicked; see Ps. 16:8–11). Peter told the Jews that David was not speaking of himself, for eventually David died and was buried in a tomb. Instead, David spoke prophetically

of one of his descendants, Jesus the promised Messiah, whom God would raise from the dead.

2:37–41 Peter's listeners were deeply convicted of their sin (v. 37). When they asked Peter what they should do, he urged them to repent (the changing of mind that would result in their turning from sin and placing their faith in Christ) and be baptized (a public testimony to their repentance and faith in Christ). Large numbers responded to Peter's words and repented, believed, and were baptized (see Luke 24:47, note). In doing so, they committed themselves to the community of believers.

My deafness forces me to depend on God more so that I can hear through Him. He brought me peace and taught me how to overcome my deafness.

Heather Whitestone
Miss America 1995

possessions and goods, and divided them among all, as anyone had need.

[46]So continuing daily with one accord in the temple, and breaking bread from house to house, they ate their food with gladness and simplicity of heart, [47]praising God and having favor with all the people. And the Lord added to the church[a] daily those who were being saved.

A Lame Man Healed

3 Now Peter and John went up together to the temple at the hour of prayer, the ninth *hour.* [2]And a certain man lame from his mother's womb was carried, whom they laid daily at the gate of the temple which is called Beautiful, to ask alms from those who entered the temple; [3]who, seeing Peter and John about to go into the temple, asked for alms. [4]And fixing his eyes on him, with John, Peter said, "Look at us." [5]So he gave them his attention, expecting to receive something from them. [6]Then Peter said, "Silver and gold I do not have, but what I do have I give you: In the name of Jesus Christ of Nazareth, rise up and walk." [7]And he took him by the right hand and lifted *him* up, and immediately his feet and ankle bones received strength. [8]So he, leaping up, stood and walked and entered the temple with them—walking, leaping, and praising God. [9]And all the people saw him walking and praising God. [10]Then they knew that it was he who sat begging alms at the Beautiful Gate of the temple; and they were filled with wonder and amazement at what had happened to him.

Preaching in Solomon's Portico

[11]Now as the lame man who was healed held on to Peter and John, all the people ran together to them in the porch which is called Solomon's, greatly amazed. [12]So when Peter saw *it,* he responded to the people: "Men of Israel, why do you marvel at this? Or why look so intently at us, as though by our own power or godliness we had made this man walk? [13]The God of Abraham, Isaac, and Jacob, the God of our fathers, glorified His Servant Jesus, whom you delivered up and denied in the presence of Pilate, when he was determined to let *Him* go. [14]But you denied the Holy One and the Just, and asked for a murderer to be granted to you, [15]and killed the Prince of life, whom God raised from the dead, of which we are witnesses. [16]And His name, through faith in His name, has made this man strong, whom you see and know. Yes, the faith which *comes* through Him has given him this perfect soundness in the presence of you all.

[17]"Yet now, brethren, I know that you did *it* in ignorance, as *did* also your rulers. [18]But those things which God foretold by the mouth of all His prophets, that the Christ would suffer, He has thus fulfilled. [19]Repent therefore and be converted, that your sins may be blotted out, so that times of refreshing may come from the presence of the Lord, [20]and that He may send Jesus Christ, who was preached to you before,[a] [21]whom heaven must receive until the times of restoration of all things, which God has spoken by the mouth of all His holy prophets since the world began. [22]For Moses truly said to the fathers, *'The Lord your God will raise up for you a Prophet like me from your brethren. Him you shall hear in all things, whatever He says to you.* [23]*And it shall be that every soul who will not hear that Prophet shall be utterly destroyed from among the people.'*[a] [24]Yes, and all the prophets, from Samuel and those who follow, as many as have spoken, have also foretold[a] these days. [25]You are sons of the

---

2:47 [a]NU-Text omits *to the church.* **3:20** [a]NU-Text and M-Text read *Christ Jesus, who was ordained for you before.* **3:23** [a]Deuteronomy 18:15, 18, 19 **3:24** [a]NU-Text and M-Text read *proclaimed.*

3:2, 3 Peter and John were going into the temple to pray. At the Beautiful Gate, which Christian tradition has identified as the Golden Gate on the eastern side of the temple, the apostles met a lame beggar. Beggars often gathered around temple entrances to ask for "alms" or gifts for the poor.

3:22, 23 Moses delivered the Israelites from Egyptian bondage and founded the nation of Israel. God gave Moses laws to provide religious and social structure for the nation and the personal authority to render judgment when those laws were violated. In this passage, Peter declared Jesus to be the "Prophet" about whom Moses spoke (Deut. 18:15–19; see also John 6:14). Christ is pictured as having a ministry similar to Moses because He brought both deliverance and judgment.

3:24 Samuel's mother Hannah was barren, but God answered her prayer for a son (1 Sam. 1:10). She dedicated Samuel to the Lord before his birth (see 1 Sam. 1, Hannah). After he was weaned, she sent the boy to the priest Eli at the Shiloh sanctuary to be reared as a servant of God. God gave Samuel his prophetic role in the days of his youth (1 Sam. 3).

ADVERSITY   A MOUNTAIN TO CLIMB

Adversity is not God's ultimate desire for His creation; yet, there is a clear message that God uses adversity. He is in control over the most adverse of circumstances. We are wrong to presume that God is necessarily in the business of removing our adverse circumstances or reversing the situation that led to adversity. Rather, the Bible points to the conclusion that instead of taking us *out* of adversity God is much more interested in taking us *through* it, using the adversity to effect something good in our lives (Is. 43:2; Rom. 5:3–5; James 1:2–4).

Naomi and Ruth provide a great example of triumph over adversity. Women in Bible times had few independent or autonomous rights. As a result, most women depended upon the patronage of father, family, or husband. To lack such a protecting relationship was to invite adversity in many guises. Naomi's family left Judah and went to Moab in search of food. There Naomi not only subsequently suffered the loss of her husband but later the loss of her two sons as well. Utterly unprotected in a foreign land, she determined to return to her native city Bethlehem for safety.

Naomi's story is significant because of the faithfulness of her daughter-in-law Ruth, who could have chosen the protection of her homeland, Moab, but rather gave up her own rights. Ruth did not choose the suffering of widowhood, but she did choose the vulnerability and possible suffering involved in following Naomi back to Judah, turning her back on the security and protection of her family in Moab (Ruth 1). Here God clearly emerges as the Protector of the unprotected who place their faith in Him. The womanly wisdom of Naomi foreshadows Jesus' character as revealed in the New Testament where He seeks those in need of being defended. Naomi was able to direct Ruth to Boaz, her kinsman redeemer, who, as Ruth's husband, became a guardian both for her and Naomi. In this story of faith were to be sown the seeds that would ultimately result in the birth not only of Israel's greatest king, David, but also of the Lord Jesus Christ Himself. This is one of the clearest examples of how God's ultimate purpose is worked out through human adversity.

On a completely different plane, Esther first experienced adversity in being an orphan. Yet God provided loving nurture for her through her cousin Mordecai. Her utter trust in the sovereign God helped her to place all her human resources in God's hands, and as a result the Jews, God's people, were ultimately preserved.

Adversity is something from which the human condition naturally recoils, but the higher message of the Bible exhorts believers to embrace every circumstance God sends or allows, even to go as far as to "count it all joy" in the hope that God's ultimate purposes will be fulfilled (James 1:20).

See also Matt. 5:11, 12; John 16:13; Rom. 8:28–39; 2 Cor. 12:9; notes on Depression (1 Sam. 16); Pain (Job 7; 2 Cor. 12); Persecution (2 Cor. 4); Spiritual Warfare (Eph. 6); Suffering (Ps. 33; 113; Is. 43; 1 Pet. 5); portrait of Naomi (Ruth 1)

---

prophets, and of the covenant which God made with our fathers, saying to Abraham, *'And in your seed all the families of the earth shall be blessed.'* [a] 26 To you first, God, having raised up His Servant Jesus, sent Him to bless you, in turning away every one *of you* from your iniquities."

Peter and John Arrested

4 Now as they spoke to the people, the priests, the captain of the temple, and the Sadducees came upon them, 2 being greatly disturbed that they taught the people and preached in Jesus the resurrection from the dead. 3 And they laid hands on them, and put *them* in custody until the next day, for it was already evening. 4 However, many of those who heard the word believed; and the number of the men came to be about five thousand.

Addressing the Sanhedrin

5 And it came to pass, on the next day, that their rulers, elders, and scribes, 6 as well as Annas the high priest, Caiaphas, John, and Alexander, and as many as were of the family of the high priest, were gathered together at Jerusalem. 7 And

3:25 a Genesis 22:18; 26:4; 28:14

4:3 The Sadducees did not believe in bodily resurrection; therefore, Peter's proclamation of Jesus' Resurrection greatly disturbed them (see chart, Jewish Sects). The temple authorities feared that Peter and John would cause a riot among the people because of their teachings about Jesus. If a riot ensued, the Romans could easily take away the priestly power and authority of the religious leaders. Thus they arrested Peter and John and placed them in jail until the next day.

4:6 Annas had been high priest from A.D. 6 to 15. He was replaced by Caiaphas but remained an elder statesman. Jesus, as well as Peter and other church leaders, was questioned by Annas, who had five sons who served as high priests (Eleazar, Jonathan, Theophilus, Matthias, and Annas II). Caiaphas was the high priest at the time of Jesus' Crucifixion. He was Annas' son-in-law and held the position of high priest longer than any other member of Annas' family (A.D. 18–36). Little is known of John and Alexander.

*The true test of walking in the Spirit will not be the way we act
but the way we react to the daily frustrations of life.*

Beverly LaHaye

when they had set them in the midst, they asked, "By what power or by what name have you done this?"

[8]Then Peter, filled with the Holy Spirit, said to them, "Rulers of the people and elders of Israel: [9]If we this day are judged for a good deed *done* to a helpless man, by what means he has been made well, [10]let it be known to you all, and to all the people of Israel, that by the name of Jesus Christ of Nazareth, whom you crucified, whom God raised from the dead, by Him this man stands here before you whole. [11]This is the *'stone which was rejected by you builders, which has become the chief cornerstone.'*[a] [12]Nor is there salvation in any other, for there is no other name under heaven given among men by which we must be saved."

The Name of Jesus Forbidden

[13]Now when they saw the boldness of Peter and John, and perceived that they were uneducated and untrained men, they marveled. And they realized that they had been with Jesus. [14]And seeing the man who had been healed standing with them, they could say nothing against it. [15]But when they had commanded them to go aside out of the council, they conferred among themselves, [16]saying, "What shall we do to these men? For, indeed, that a notable miracle has been done through them *is* evident to all who dwell in Jerusalem, and we cannot deny *it.* [17]But so that it spreads no further among the people, let us severely threaten them, that from now on they speak to no man in this name."

[18]So they called them and commanded them not to speak at all nor teach in the name of Jesus. [19]But Peter and John answered and said to them, "Whether it is right in the sight of God to listen to you more than to God, you judge. [20]For we cannot but speak the things which we have seen and heard." [21]So when they had further threatened

them, they let them go, finding no way of punishing them, because of the people, since they all glorified God for what had been done. [22]For the man was over forty years old on whom this miracle of healing had been performed.

Prayer for Boldness

[23]And being let go, they went to their own *companions* and reported all that the chief priests and elders had said to them. [24]So when they heard that, they raised their voice to God with one accord and said: "Lord, You *are* God, who made heaven and earth and the sea, and all that is in them, [25]who by the mouth of Your servant David[a] have said:

> 'Why did the nations rage,
> And the people plot vain things?
> [26]The kings of the earth took their stand,
> And the rulers were gathered together
> Against the LORD and against His Christ.'[a]

[27]"For truly against Your holy Servant Jesus, whom You anointed, both Herod and Pontius Pilate, with the Gentiles and the people of Israel, were gathered together [28]to do whatever Your hand and Your purpose determined before to be done. [29]Now, Lord, look on their threats, and grant to Your servants that with all boldness they may speak Your word, [30]by stretching out Your hand to heal, and that signs and wonders may be done through the name of Your holy Servant Jesus."

[31]And when they had prayed, the place where they were assembled together was shaken; and they were all filled with the Holy Spirit, and they spoke the word of God with boldness.

4:11 [a]Psalm 118:22   **4:25** [a]NU-Text reads *who through the Holy Spirit, by the mouth of our father, Your servant David.*   **4:26** [a]Psalm 2:1, 2

4:11 The cornerstone of the building, which symbolized strength, held two walls together. Here Peter quoted Psalm 118:22, naming Jesus Christ as the Chief Cornerstone, the very foundation of the Christian faith, which the "builders" (Jewish rulers) had rejected.

4:13, 14 Peter and John amazed the court, primarily because they were unschooled or uneducated in rabbinic theology and were ordinary nonprofessional men. As the court listened to Peter and John speak, they realized that Jesus, who Himself had sought neither formal theological education nor the status of rabbi, was the source of their teachings. Considering

this fact, they "marveled" at the healing of the lame man. They could neither deny the miracle, nor could they afford to acknowledge it.

4:21–23 The man's age suggested that he had passed the point when cures usually or naturally occurred. Fearing the excitement of the people who had witnessed this healing and had seen the man walk, the council could do nothing but threaten Peter and John and release them. After their release, Peter and John rejoined their friends and reported their experiences.

SAPPHIRA   *A Deceitful Beauty*

Married to Ananias, Sapphira, whose name means "beautiful" or "sapphire," was the first woman singled out for prominence in Acts. But Sapphira failed God and, in doing so, caused her own death. Throughout the ages, her name has been linked, not with "beauty," but with deliberate deceit.

Sapphira and Ananias apparently had an agreeable marriage and cooperated with each other. As members of the early Jerusalem church and devoted disciples of Jesus, they had allied themselves with the apostles.

But Sapphira and her husband made a fatal mistake in judgment. They mixed greed with generosity. The members of the church in Jerusalem sold their property and presented the proceeds as a gift to the apostles. Such selflessness earned admiration, and their gift of money was then used to help the poor.

Selfishness and deceit entered into the hearts of this couple, however. They sold their plot of ground but submitted only a portion of the profits. The couple then lied about the full price received for their land so that they could keep part of the money for themselves, while appearing to give all profit to the church. With perceptive insight, Peter challenged Ananias about his duplicity and sin against God. Ananias, caught in his own deliberate lie, fell down and died instantly.

Several hours later, Sapphira came to Peter. She, too, was questioned about the price of the land. Unaware of her husband's death, Sapphira confirmed his deceit. Peter also charged her with offense to the Spirit of God, informed her of Ananias' death, then predicted her own imminent death. Immediately, she fell down and died and was buried next to her husband.

The deaths of Sapphira and Ananias stunned and frightened the small congregation. God showed Sapphira and Ananias as well as the Jerusalem church that He allows no dishonesty in His relationship with His disciples. Through the tragic story of Sapphira, the "beautiful one," God continues to show women that one's relationship with the Lord must be based on more than outward beauty and empty promises—that is, upon the integrity of a heart commitment.

See also Acts 4:32–35; notes on Submission (1 Pet. 3); Testing (Ps. 11)

Sharing in All Things

32Now the multitude of those who believed were of one heart and one soul; neither did anyone say that any of the things he possessed was his own, but they had all things in common. 33And with great power the apostles gave witness to the resurrection of the Lord Jesus. And great grace was upon them all. 34Nor was there anyone among them who lacked; for all who were possessors of lands or houses sold them, and brought the proceeds of the things that were sold, 35and laid *them* at the apostles' feet; and they distributed to each as anyone had need.

36And Joses,a who was also named Barnabas by the apostles (which is translated Son of Encouragement), a Levite of the country of Cyprus, 37having land, sold *it,* and brought the money and laid *it* at the apostles' feet.

Lying to the Holy Spirit

5But a certain man named Ananias, with Sapphira his wife, sold a possession. 2And he kept back *part* of the proceeds, his wife also being aware *of it,* and brought a certain part and laid *it* at the apostles' feet. 3But Peter said, "Ananias, why has Satan filled your heart to lie to the Holy Spirit and keep back *part* of the price of the land for yourself? 4While it remained, was it not your own? And after it was sold, was it not in your own control? Why have you conceived this thing in your heart? You have not lied to men but to God."

5Then Ananias, hearing these words, fell down and breathed his last. So great fear came upon all those who heard these things. 6And the young

·························

4:36 aNU-Text reads *Joseph.*

4:36, 37 Joses (Joseph), a Levite, was a native of the island of Cyprus. The apostles added Barnabas (Aram., lit. "son of encouragement") to his name. Barnabas was also known for his generous monetary gifts to the early church. He was a Hellenistic Jew (one whose residence had been in the cities located within the Roman Empire), and he was the kinsman of John Mark. He formed a natural link between the Hellenistic world and the Jerusalem church.

5:1–11 The story of Ananias and Sapphira showed that the early church consisted of imperfect people (see Sapphira). Luke compared the generosity of Barnabas with the selfish-

ness and deceitfulness of Ananias (lit. "*Yahweh* has dealt graciously") and Sapphira, members of the early Jerusalem church. When this couple sold private property, they purposely did not give all the proceeds from the sale to the fellowship. They then lied by saying they had given the full amount. When asked about the proceeds held back, first Ananias and then Sapphira lied both to the Holy Spirit and to the church leaders. Both husband and wife, at different times, were struck dead. This experience brought great fear to the other church members.

> *So focus first on God himself;*
> *be practical in deed.*
> *And as you tell your world of Christ,*
> *you'll find he'll meet your need!*
>
> Jill Briscoe

---

men arose and wrapped him up, carried *him* out, and buried *him*.

⁷Now it was about three hours later when his wife came in, not knowing what had happened. ⁸And Peter answered her, "Tell me whether you sold the land for so much?"

She said, "Yes, for so much."

⁹Then Peter said to her, "How is it that you have agreed together to test the Spirit of the Lord? Look, the feet of those who have buried your husband *are* at the door, and they will carry you out." ¹⁰Then immediately she fell down at his feet and breathed her last. And the young men came in and found her dead, and carrying *her* out, buried *her* by her husband. ¹¹So great fear came upon all the church and upon all who heard these things.

Continuing Power in the Church

¹²And through the hands of the apostles many signs and wonders were done among the people. And they were all with one accord in Solomon's Porch. ¹³Yet none of the rest dared join them, but the people esteemed them highly. ¹⁴And believers were increasingly added to the Lord, multitudes of both men and women, ¹⁵so that they brought the sick out into the streets and laid *them* on beds and couches, that at least the shadow of Peter passing by might fall on some of them. ¹⁶Also a multitude gathered from the surrounding cities to Jerusalem, bringing sick people and those who were tormented by unclean spirits, and they were all healed.

Imprisoned Apostles Freed

¹⁷Then the high priest rose up, and all those who *were* with him (which is the sect of the Sadducees), and they were filled with indignation,

¹⁸and laid their hands on the apostles and put them in the common prison. ¹⁹But at night an angel of the Lord opened the prison doors and brought them out, and said, ²⁰"Go, stand in the temple and speak to the people all the words of this life."

²¹And when they heard *that,* they entered the temple early in the morning and taught. But the high priest and those with him came and called the council together, with all the elders of the children of Israel, and sent to the prison to have them brought.

Apostles on Trial Again

²²But when the officers came and did not find them in the prison, they returned and reported, ²³saying, "Indeed we found the prison shut securely, and the guards standing outsideᵃ before the doors; but when we opened them, we found no one inside!" ²⁴Now when the high priest,ᵃ the captain of the temple, and the chief priests heard these things, they wondered what the outcome would be. ²⁵So one came and told them, saying,ᵃ "Look, the men whom you put in prison are standing in the temple and teaching the people!"

²⁶Then the captain went with the officers and brought them without violence, for they feared the people, lest they should be stoned. ²⁷And when they had brought them, they set *them* before the council. And the high priest asked them, ²⁸saying, "Did we not strictly command you not to teach in this name? And look, you have filled Jerusalem with your doctrine, and intend to bring this Man's blood on us!"

²⁹But Peter and the *other* apostles answered and

5:23 ᵃNU-Text and M-Text omit *outside.* **5:24** ᵃNU-Text omits *the high priest.* **5:25** ᵃNU-Text and M-Text omit *saying.*

5:15 The Sanhedrin had warned the apostles not to teach about Jesus. Not only did the apostles continue to teach about Christ, but they taught boldly and openly from Solomon's Porch, the outermost, raised part of the temple surrounded with columns. Increasingly, both women and men became believers. They continued to bring large numbers of sick people to Peter for healing. People were so impressed with Peter's ability to heal that many believed even his "shadow" had healing powers.

5:17, 18 Peter's healing ministry in the temple attracted large numbers of people. The Sadducees were controlled by jealousy fueled both by the popularity of the apostles with the people and by fear of the ruling Romans. Thus they decided they must take action to stop the activities of the apostles. Not only Peter and John but all the apostles were arrested and imprisoned. Throughout his writings, Luke portrayed the Sadducees as the primary enemy of Christianity (see chart, Jewish Sects). Luke presented the Pharisees, however, in a kinder, more positive light.

said: "We ought to obey God rather than men. [30]The God of our fathers raised up Jesus whom you murdered by hanging on a tree. [31]Him God has exalted to His right hand *to be* Prince and Savior, to give repentance to Israel and forgiveness of sins. [32]And we are His witnesses to these things, and *so* also *is* the Holy Spirit whom God has given to those who obey Him."

Gamaliel's Advice

[33]When they heard *this,* they were furious and plotted to kill them. [34]Then one in the council stood up, a Pharisee named Gamaliel, a teacher of the law held in respect by all the people, and commanded them to put the apostles outside for a little while. [35]And he said to them: "Men of Israel, take heed to yourselves what you intend to do regarding these men. [36]For some time ago Theudas rose up, claiming to be somebody. A number of men, about four hundred, joined him. He was slain, and all who obeyed him were scattered and came to nothing. [37]After this man, Judas of Galilee rose up in the days of the census, and drew away many people after him. He also perished, and all who obeyed him were dispersed. [38]And now I say to you, keep away from these men and let them alone; for if this plan or this work is of men, it will come to nothing; [39]but if it is of God, you cannot overthrow it—lest you even be found to fight against God."

[40]And they agreed with him, and when they had called for the apostles and beaten *them,* they commanded that they should not speak in the name of Jesus, and let them go. [41]So they departed from the presence of the council, rejoicing that they were counted worthy to suffer shame for His[a] name. [42]And daily in the temple, and in every house, they did not cease teaching and preaching Jesus *as* the Christ.

Seven Chosen to Serve

6 Now in those days, when *the number of* the disciples was multiplying, there arose a complaint against the Hebrews by the Hellenists,[a] because their widows were neglected in the daily distribution. [2]Then the twelve summoned the multitude of the disciples and said, "It is not desirable that we should leave the word of God and serve tables. [3]Therefore, brethren, seek out from among you seven men of *good* reputation, full of the Holy Spirit and wisdom, whom we may appoint over this business; [4]but we will give ourselves continually to prayer and to the ministry of the word."

[5]And the saying pleased the whole multitude. And they chose Stephen, a man full of faith and the Holy Spirit, and Philip, Prochorus, Nicanor, Timon, Parmenas, and Nicolas, a proselyte from Antioch, [6]whom they set before the apostles; and when they had prayed, they laid hands on them.

[7]Then the word of God spread, and the number of the disciples multiplied greatly in Jerusalem, and a great many of the priests were obedient to the faith.

Stephen Accused of Blasphemy

[8]And Stephen, full of faith[a] and power, did great wonders and signs among the people. [9]Then there arose some from what is called the Synagogue of the Freedmen (Cyrenians, Alexandrians, and those from Cilicia and Asia), disputing with Stephen. [10]And they were not able to resist the wisdom and

---

5:41 [a]NU-Text reads *the name;* M-Text reads *the name of Jesus.* 6:1 [a]That is, Greek-speaking Jews 6:8 [a]NU-Text reads *grace.*

5:34 Gamaliel was a highly respected Pharisee, a teacher of the Law and a member of the Sanhedrin. The grandson of the great rabbi Hillel, Gamaliel was known for his wisdom. He was Paul's teacher in Jerusalem and intervened on behalf of the apostles when the Sanhedrin attempted to kill them.

5:36 Gamaliel referred to the rebellion of Theudas when he intervened in the Sanhedrin's plot to kill the apostles. He reminded the Sanhedrin that there had been other messianic rebellions that were unsuccessful. Theudas, the leader of a previous Jewish uprising of some 400 men, failed in his revolt. Later he was beheaded and his followers killed. This Theudas was not the same man who led a later rebellion, following the rebellion of Judas (v. 37). Rebellions of this type were common in the 1st century. Gamaliel suggested that the Sanhedrin watch and wait before they took violent action against the apostles.

6:1 The Hellenists were Greek-speaking Christian Jews. They were often viewed with suspicion by the Aramaic-speaking Jews of Palestine, and they generally neither spoke nor understood Aramaic, the native language of Palestine. Hellenistic widows, often destitute, were coming to Palestine in increasing numbers, and these women needed help. Conflict erupted over the equal distribution of food to the widows. Seemingly the Hellenistic widows were being neglected, since the giving of charity was controlled by the Palestinian Jews. This conflict was the first major division to confront the early church.

6:3–6 To ease the conflict over the distribution of food among Hellenistic widows, the apostles chose seven men with Greek names, which probably meant they themselves were Hellenists (v. 5). Certain qualities were expected of the men: a good reputation, wisdom, and the filling of the Holy Spirit. These seven were set before the apostles, who prayed over them and laid hands on them, symbolizing their administrative appointment in the church. With this benevolent work delegated to the seven men, the apostles were free to devote themselves fully to church worship and preaching the Word. This response to the conflict over the widows greatly pleased the congregation.

6:8 Stephen (Gk., lit. "crown"), one of the seven men chosen to minister to the widows (v. 5), became the first Christian martyr. His speech to the Sanhedrin and his subsequent stoning were witnessed by Saul of Tarsus, who later became Paul, the great missionary and martyr.

The key to gaining self-control is yielding control of the self to the control of the Holy Spirit.

Rhonda H. Kelley

---

the Spirit by which he spoke. [11]Then they secretly induced men to say, "We have heard him speak blasphemous words against Moses and God." [12]And they stirred up the people, the elders, and the scribes; and they came upon *him,* seized him, and brought *him* to the council. [13]They also set up false witnesses who said, "This man does not cease to speak blasphemous[a] words against this holy place and the law; [14]for we have heard him say that this Jesus of Nazareth will destroy this place and change the customs which Moses delivered to us." [15]And all who sat in the council, looking steadfastly at him, saw his face as the face of an angel.

Stephen's Address: The Call of Abraham

[7] Then the high priest said, "Are these things so?"

[2]And he said, "Brethren and fathers, listen: The God of glory appeared to our father Abraham when he was in Mesopotamia, before he dwelt in Haran, [3]and said to him, *'Get out of your country and from your relatives, and come to a land that I will show you.'*[a] [4]Then he came out of the land of the Chaldeans and dwelt in Haran. And from there, when his father was dead, He moved him to this land in which you now dwell. [5]And *God* gave him no inheritance in it, not even *enough* to set his foot on. But even when *Abraham* had no child, He promised to give it to him for a possession, and to his descendants after him. [6]But God spoke in this way: that his descendants would dwell in a foreign land, and that they would bring them into bondage and oppress *them* four hundred years. [7]*And the nation to whom they will be in bondage I will judge,'*[a] said God, *'and after that they shall come out and serve Me in this place.'*[b] [8]Then He gave him the covenant of circumcision; and so *Abraham* begot Isaac and circumcised him on the eighth day; and Isaac *begot* Jacob, and Jacob *begot* the twelve patriarchs.

The Patriarchs in Egypt

[9]"And the patriarchs, becoming envious, sold Joseph into Egypt. But God was with him [10]and delivered him out of all his troubles, and gave him favor and wisdom in the presence of Pharaoh, king of Egypt; and he made him governor over Egypt and all his house. [11]Now a famine and great trouble came over all the land of Egypt and Canaan, and our fathers found no sustenance. [12]But when Jacob heard that there was grain in Egypt, he sent out our fathers first. [13]And the second *time* Joseph was made known to his brothers, and Joseph's family became known to the Pharaoh. [14]Then Joseph sent and called his father Jacob and all his relatives to *him,* seventy-five[a] people. [15]So Jacob went down to Egypt; and he died, he and our fathers. [16]And they were carried back to Shechem and laid in the tomb that Abraham bought for a sum of money from the sons of Hamor, *the father* of Shechem.

God Delivers Israel by Moses

[17]"But when the time of the promise drew near which God had sworn to Abraham, the people

---

6:13 [a]NU-Text omits *blasphemous.* 7:3 [a]Genesis 12:1 7:7 [a]Genesis 15:14 [b]Exodus 3:12 7:14 [a]Or *seventy* (compare Exodus 1:5)

7:4 **The Chaldeans** lived in central and southeastern Mesopotamia (modern-day Iraq), the land between the Tigris and Euphrates rivers. God had revealed Himself to Abraham in Mesopotamia. The city of Haran became Abraham's home for some years before he moved on to Palestine. Stephen began his defense with Abraham, with whom Jewish history began. The supposed discrepancy as to where God issued His call to Abram is easily explained. God could have spoken to him twice—in Ur and in Haran. Also, the call could have come to Abram in Ur with the Haran incident as parenthetical background (see Gen. 11:27–32; 12:1–3; 15:7; Neh. 9:7).

7:6 **The length of time in bondage** is obviously here rounded off to 400 years. Elsewhere in the book it is rounded off to 450 years (Acts 13:9, 20). Both are appropriate since the precise number of years in Egyptian slavery, according to most evangelical scholars, was 430 years (Ex. 12:40). The allusion to "this place" is apparently to Canaan (Acts. 7:7; Gen. 15:13–15; Ex. 3:12).

7:8 **Beginning with Abraham,** the Israelites practiced circumcision as a sign of their covenant with God (see Gen. 17, Circumcision).

7:16 **Shechem,** located on the slope of Mount Ebal in north central Palestine, was the first capital of the northern kingdom of Israel and an important city long before the Israelites settled there. Jacob settled at Shechem and bought land from the sons of Hamor. Due to the famine predicted by Joseph, Jacob and all his sons traveled to Egypt and died there. The remains of Joseph and Jacob were returned to Canaan. Seventy people went down to Egypt (Gen. 46:27; Ex. 1:5). However, the Septuagint text, which evidently was used by Stephen, added two sons of Manasseh, two sons of Ephraim, and one grandson of Ephraim, making a total of 75 (see Gen. 46:20). Joseph was buried at Shechem. Again Stephen was bringing together two historical events: Abraham's purchase of Machpelah in Hebron (Gen. 23:17, 18) and Jacob's purchase of a field in Shechem (Gen. 33:19). Stephen's use of the plural "they" indicates the use of this acceptable method of streamlining the recounting of history.

grew and multiplied in Egypt [18]till another king arose who did not know Joseph. [19]This man dealt treacherously with our people, and oppressed our forefathers, making them expose their babies, so that they might not live. [20]At this time Moses was born, and was well pleasing to God; and he was brought up in his father's house for three months. [21]But when he was set out, Pharaoh's daughter took him away and brought him up as her own son. [22]And Moses was learned in all the wisdom of the Egyptians, and was mighty in words and deeds.

[23]"Now when he was forty years old, it came into his heart to visit his brethren, the children of Israel. [24]And seeing one of *them* suffer wrong, he defended and avenged him who was oppressed, and struck down the Egyptian. [25]For he supposed that his brethren would have understood that God would deliver them by his hand, but they did not understand. [26]And the next day he appeared to *two of* them as they were fighting, and *tried to* reconcile them, saying, 'Men, you are brethren; why do you wrong one another?' [27]But he who did his neighbor wrong pushed him away, saying, *'Who made you a ruler and a judge over us? [28]Do you want to kill me as you did the Egyptian yesterday?'*[a] [29]Then, at this saying, Moses fled and became a dweller in the land of Midian, where he had two sons.

[30]"And when forty years had passed, an Angel of the Lord[a] appeared to him in a flame of fire in a bush, in the wilderness of Mount Sinai. [31]When Moses saw *it,* he marveled at the sight; and as he drew near to observe, the voice of the Lord came to him, [32]saying, *'I am the God of your fathers—the God of Abraham, the God of Isaac, and the God of Jacob.'*[a] And Moses trembled and dared not look. [33]*'Then the* LORD *said to him, "Take your sandals off your feet, for the place where you stand is holy ground. [34]I have surely seen the oppression of My people who are in Egypt; I have heard their groaning and have come down to deliver them. And now come, I will send you to Egypt." '*[a]

[35]"This Moses whom they rejected, saying, *'Who made you a ruler and a judge?'*[a] is the one God sent to

be a ruler and a deliverer by the hand of the Angel who appeared to him in the bush. [36]He brought them out, after he had shown wonders and signs in the land of Egypt, and in the Red Sea, and in the wilderness forty years.

Israel Rebels Against God

[37]"This is that Moses who said to the children of Israel,[a] *'The* LORD *your God will raise up for you a Prophet like me from your brethren. Him you shall hear.'*[b] [38]"This is he who was in the congregation in the wilderness with the Angel who spoke to him on Mount Sinai, and *with* our fathers, the one who received the living oracles to give to us, [39]whom our fathers would not obey, but rejected. And in their hearts they turned back to Egypt, [40]saying to Aaron, *'Make us gods to go before us; as for this Moses who brought us out of the land of Egypt, we do not know what has become of him.'*[a] [41]And they made a calf in those days, offered sacrifices to the idol, and rejoiced in the works of their own hands. [42]Then God turned and gave them up to worship the host of heaven, as it is written in the book of the Prophets:

'Did you offer Me slaughtered animals and sacrifices during forty years in the wilderness, O house of Israel?
[43]*You also took up the tabernacle of Moloch, And the star of your god Remphan, Images which you made to worship; And I will carry you away beyond Babylon.'*[a]

God's True Tabernacle

[44]"Our fathers had the tabernacle of witness in the wilderness, as He appointed, instructing Moses to make it according to the pattern that he had seen, [45]which our fathers, having received it in turn, also brought with Joshua into the land

---

7:28, 35 [a]Exodus 2:14   **7:30** [a]NU-Text omits *of the Lord.*   **7:32** [a]Exodus 3:6, 15   **7:34** [a]Exodus 3:5, 7, 8, 10   **7:37** [a]Deuteronomy 18:15   [b]NU-Text and M-Text omit *Him you shall hear.*   **7:40** [a]Exodus 32:1, 23   **7:43** [a]Amos 5:25–27

7:20, 21 Since Stephen had been accused of speaking against Moses, he gave a fuller account of Moses than he did of the other biblical characters cited (Acts 6:11). That Moses took the side of one of the quarreling Israelites in no way suggests he was not trying to make peace between the two men (Acts 7:26; see Ex. 2:13). Stephen's description of Moses as "mighty in words" is an observation of what Moses became (Acts 7:22) and stands in contrast to Moses' self-evaluation (Ex. 4:10–16).

7:29 Midian was the land to which Moses fled from Pharaoh after he was charged with killing an Egyptian (Ex. 2:15). Some confusion exists about the exact location of Midian, but evidence points to northwestern Arabia east of the Gulf of Aqaba. There Moses met Jethro, the priest of Midian, and married his daughter. Moses fled Egypt because of his fear of the pharaoh (Ex. 2:15) and the rejection by his people (Acts 7:29).

7:30 In the wilderness of Mount Sinai, Moses came upon a bush that was burning but not consumed by the fire. Through the burning bush, God captured Moses' attention and instructed him to return to Egypt and deliver the Hebrew people out of slavery (see Ex. 3:2). Stephen reversed the chronological order of these events in suggesting that God revealed Himself to Moses before telling him to remove his sandals. However, Stephen could well have been merely emphasizing that the God appearing to Moses was the God of his ancestors Abraham, Isaac, and Jacob (Acts 7:32, 33; see Ex. 3:5, 6).

7:44 The tabernacle was a sacred sanctuary where God met with His people. The "tabernacle of witness" or tent of witness was an elaborate portable tent used by the children of Israel in the wilderness. After the sin of worshiping the golden calf at Mount Sinai, Moses set up the sacred tent outside the camp, for God refused to dwell in the midst of the Israelites.

I knew nothing; I was nothing. For this reason God picked me out.

St. Catherine Laboure

possessed by the Gentiles, whom God drove out before the face of our fathers until the days of David, ⁴⁶who found favor before God and asked to find a dwelling for the God of Jacob. ⁴⁷But Solomon built Him a house.

⁴⁸"However, the Most High does not dwell in temples made with hands, as the prophet says:

⁴⁹'Heaven is My throne,
  And earth is My footstool.
  What house will you build for Me? says the LORD,
  Or what is the place of My rest?
⁵⁰Has My hand not made all these things?'ᵃ

Israel Resists the Holy Spirit

⁵¹"*You* stiff-necked and uncircumcised in heart and ears! You always resist the Holy Spirit; as your fathers *did,* so *do* you. ⁵²Which of the prophets did your fathers not persecute? And they killed those who foretold the coming of the Just One, of whom you now have become the betrayers and murderers, ⁵³who have received the law by the direction of angels and have not kept *it.*"

Stephen the Martyr

⁵⁴When they heard these things they were cut to the heart, and they gnashed at him with *their* teeth. ⁵⁵But he, being full of the Holy Spirit, gazed into heaven and saw the glory of God, and Jesus standing at the right hand of God, ⁵⁶and said, "Look! I see the heavens opened and the Son of Man standing at the right hand of God!"

⁵⁷Then they cried out with a loud voice, stopped their ears, and ran at him with one ac-

cord; ⁵⁸and they cast *him* out of the city and stoned *him.* And the witnesses laid down their clothes at the feet of a young man named Saul. ⁵⁹And they stoned Stephen as he was calling on *God* and saying, "Lord Jesus, receive my spirit." ⁶⁰Then he knelt down and cried out with a loud voice, "Lord, do not charge them with this sin." And when he had said this, he fell asleep.

Saul Persecutes the Church

8 Now Saul was consenting to his death.
At that time a great persecution arose against the church which was at Jerusalem; and they were all scattered throughout the regions of Judea and Samaria, except the apostles. ²And devout men carried Stephen *to his burial,* and made great lamentation over him.

³As for Saul, he made havoc of the church, entering every house, and dragging off men and women, committing *them* to prison.

Christ Is Preached in Samaria

⁴Therefore those who were scattered went everywhere preaching the word. ⁵Then Philip went down to theᵃ city of Samaria and preached Christ to them. ⁶And the multitudes with one accord heeded the things spoken by Philip, hearing and seeing the miracles which he did. ⁷For unclean spirits, crying with a loud voice, came out of many who were possessed; and many who were paralyzed and lame were healed. ⁸And there was great joy in that city.

···················

7:50 ᵃIsaiah 66:1, 2 8:5 ᵃOr a

Only Moses actually entered the tent. Stephen rightly identified this period in Israel's history as one of apostasy (vv. 42, 43). Some have misunderstood the prophet Amos who described the period as *exemplary,* though with the obvious intent of denouncing Israel as well (Amos 5:25).

7:58, 59 Stephen had spoken boldly and with unusual courage. The devout Jews believed Stephen had committed blasphemy or spoken evil against God. The Sanhedrin was infuriated by Stephen's accusations. Although stoning was the penalty for blasphemy (see Deut. 13:6–11), the Romans had taken away the Jews' right to execute a person. Thus this act was a mob reaction to Stephen's statement, not a formal execution. Stephen was ready to become the first Christian martyr. Luke quietly introduced Saul of Tarsus here, stating that Saul watched in agreement as Stephen was being murdered.

8:3 Saul was the Jewish name of Paul, who is better known by

this official Roman name. Paul was born in the Roman city Tarsus and possessed Roman citizenship. He became a scholar in Jewish tradition and in the interpretation of Scripture, studying under the famous rabbi Gamaliel. Like all Jewish boys, Paul had to learn a trade. His trade was tentmaking. As a Pharisee, he committed himself to teaching and practicing OT laws and traditions. He zealously persecuted and imprisoned followers of Jesus Christ.

8:5 Jews and Samaritans hated each other for various religious and political reasons. They would go miles out of their way to avoid one another. After the stoning of Stephen, persecution increased, and Jewish believers were scattered. Philip, one of the seven chosen to do the work of deacons (Acts 6:5), took the gospel into Samaria, where God greatly blessed his ministry. He was the father of four unmarried daughters, who were prophetesses (see Acts 21, The Daughters of Philip).

CANDACE   *The Queen of the Ethiopians*

Almost nothing is known about this woman. Candace was the title used by the queens of Meroe, the capital of Ethiopia, a region of Nubia just south of Egypt.

This woman surfaced briefly, not because she was a prominent figure but because of the actions of her servant. Scripture records her servant as "a man of Ethiopia, a eunuch of great authority under Candace the queen of the Ethiopians" (Acts 8:27).

An angel of the Lord told the apostle Philip to travel from Jerusalem to Gaza. Philip obeyed and met the Ethiopian eunuch during his journey. The eunuch was reading from Isaiah the prophet when Philip encountered him. After a deep, but brief, theological conversation, the eunuch became a believer in Jesus Christ. When they came to some water, upon the eunuch's request, Philip baptized him. The new believer went on his way, rejoicing. He is not mentioned again.

When the eunuch returned home, did his newfound faith and vibrant testimony have an impact on his queen, Candace? The Bible does not say. Even with her royal status, the queen remains secondary as Scripture highlights her servant, the Ethiopian eunuch. For one day on the road from Jerusalem to Gaza, he made a decision that granted him royal status even greater than that of a queen. He became a son of the heavenly King.

See also notes on Evangelism (John 6); Government and Citizenship (Rom. 13)

The Sorcerer's Profession of Faith

⁹But there was a certain man called Simon, who previously practiced sorcery in the city and astonished the people of Samaria, claiming that he was someone great, ¹⁰to whom they all gave heed, from the least to the greatest, saying, "This man is the great power of God." ¹¹And they heeded him because he had astonished them with his sorceries for a long time. ¹²But when they believed Philip as he preached the things concerning the kingdom of God and the name of Jesus Christ, both men and women were baptized. ¹³Then Simon himself also believed; and when he was baptized he continued with Philip, and was amazed, seeing the miracles and signs which were done.

The Sorcerer's Sin

¹⁴Now when the apostles who were at Jerusalem heard that Samaria had received the word of God, they sent Peter and John to them, ¹⁵who, when they had come down, prayed for them that they might receive the Holy Spirit. ¹⁶For as yet He had fallen upon none of them. They had only been baptized in the name of the Lord Jesus. ¹⁷Then they laid hands on them, and they received the Holy Spirit.

¹⁸And when Simon saw that through the laying on of the apostles' hands the Holy Spirit was given, he offered them money, ¹⁹saying, "Give me this power also, that anyone on whom I lay hands may receive the Holy Spirit."

²⁰But Peter said to him, "Your money perish with you, because you thought that the gift of God could be purchased with money! ²¹You have neither part nor portion in this matter, for your heart is not right in the sight of God. ²²Repent therefore of this your wickedness, and pray God if perhaps the thought of your heart may be forgiven you. ²³For I see that you are poisoned by bitterness and bound by iniquity."

²⁴Then Simon answered and said, "Pray to the Lord for me, that none of the things which you have spoken may come upon me."

²⁵So when they had testified and preached the word of the Lord, they returned to Jerusalem, preaching the gospel in many villages of the Samaritans.

Christ Is Preached to an Ethiopian

²⁶Now an angel of the Lord spoke to Philip, saying, "Arise and go toward the south along the road which goes down from Jerusalem to Gaza." This is desert. ²⁷So he arose and went. And behold, a man

---

8:9 Simon, from Samaria, was a magician. Whether or not he believed the gospel Philip preached is not clear, but he was baptized. Later, however, anticipating increased personal power and prestige, Simon tried to buy for himself the gift of laying on of hands and the resulting power of the Holy Spirit (vv. 18, 19). To this day, the word "simony" refers to the unworthy buying and selling of ecclesiastical offices.

8:26 The road from Jerusalem to Gaza was a busy avenue of travel. Gaza (Old or Desert Gaza) had been destroyed in 93 B.C., and the new Gaza had been built just to the south of the

old site in 57 B.C. Positioned along a major coastal plain highway three miles inland from the Mediterranean Sea, this Philistine city connected Egypt with the rest of the ancient Near East. On this well-traveled road Philip met the eunuch from Ethiopia.

8:27 Eunuchs were men who were deprived of some or all of their sexual organs. In the ancient Near East, eunuchs generally were considered extremely trustworthy. Royalty often employed them, sometimes as keepers of harems. The unnamed eunuch was returning from worship in Jerusalem to his

OBSESSIONS   *INVADING THE MIND*

An obsession is an idea, usually charged with emotion, that repetitively and insistently invades the consciousness even if unwelcome. When these ideas are manifested in behavior patterns, they are called compulsions.

Obsessions often indicate serious underlying difficulties. They are pervasive and become problematic when they interfere substantially with the ability to think rationally. Obsessions are usually short-lived and can be minimized or negated by diverting your attention. They usually occur in one of the following ways:

1) impulsive obsessions—ideas that lead to actions which are repetitive and can be destructive (the persecution of Christians by Saul of Tarsus, Acts 8:3; Gal. 1:13);

2) inhibiting obsessions—doubts about actions (the actions and reactions of King David in his lust for Bathsheba, 2 Sam. 11:1–17); or

3) intellectual obsessions—questions about the purpose of life or ultimate destiny (the thought-provoking encounter of the rich young ruler with Jesus, Matt. 19:16–22).

Ultimately, only the Lord Jesus can remove the anxieties and worries that accompany obsessive behavior. He has challenged believers to trust Him with their cares (1 Pet. 5:7). Being free of obsessions is part of experiencing "the mind of Christ," which is available to all believers (1 Cor. 2:16).

See also 1 Sam. 18—20; Ps. 55:22; Matt. 6:25–34; Mark 5:22, note; notes on Codependency (Gen. 27); Conscience (2 Cor. 1); Healing (Ps. 13; 133; Eccl. 1; 2 Cor. 5; Gal. 6; James 5); Manipulation (Gen. 27); Worry (Rom. 8)

---

of Ethiopia, a eunuch of great authority under Candace the queen of the Ethiopians, who had charge of all her treasury, and had come to Jerusalem to worship, [28]was returning. And sitting in his chariot, he was reading Isaiah the prophet. [29]Then the Spirit said to Philip, "Go near and overtake this chariot."

[30]So Philip ran to him, and heard him reading the prophet Isaiah, and said, "Do you understand what you are reading?"

[31]And he said, "How can I, unless someone guides me?" And he asked Philip to come up and sit with him. [32]The place in the Scripture which he read was this:

"He was led as a sheep to the slaughter;
And as a lamb before its shearer is silent,
So He opened not His mouth.
[33]In His humiliation His justice was taken away,
And who will declare His generation?
For His life is taken from the earth."[a]

[34]So the eunuch answered Philip and said, "I ask you, of whom does the prophet say this, of himself or of some other man?" [35]Then Philip opened his mouth, and beginning at this Scripture, preached Jesus to him. [36]Now as they went down the road, they came to some water. And the eunuch said, "See, *here is* water. What hinders me from being baptized?"

[37]Then Philip said, "If you believe with all your heart, you may."

And he answered and said, "I believe that Jesus Christ is the Son of God."[a]

[38]So he commanded the chariot to stand still. And both Philip and the eunuch went down into the water, and he baptized him. [39]Now when they came up out of the water, the Spirit of the Lord caught Philip away, so that the eunuch saw him no more; and he went on his way rejoicing. [40]But Philip was found at Azotus. And passing through, he preached in all the cities till he came to Caesarea.

The Damascus Road: Saul Converted

9 Then Saul, still breathing threats and murder against the disciples of the Lord, went to the high priest [2]and asked letters from him to the synagogues of Damascus, so that if he found any who were of the Way, whether men or women, he might bring them bound to Jerusalem.

[3]As he journeyed he came near Damascus, and suddenly a light shone around him from heaven.

•••••••••••••••••

8:33 [a]Isaiah 53:7, 8   8:37 [a]NU-Text and M-Text omit this verse. It is found in Western texts, including the Latin tradition.

---

homeland of Ethiopia (the region of Nubia just south of Egypt). He was an important official in the court of Candace, a title for all the queens of Ethiopia (see Candace; chart, The Queens of the New Testament).

8:40 Azotus or Ashdod, recorded in history as early as the Late Bronze period, was one of five principal cities of the Philistines. It was located ten miles north of Ashkelon and two-and-a-half miles east of the Mediterranean Sea. In the 1st century, Ashdod was an important center for the production of purple wool.

9:3, 4 Through God's dramatic intervention and continuing transformation in his life, Paul became the greatest early

DORCAS *The Generous Disciple*

Dorcas is named for the gazelle, a small, graceful, and swift antelope known for its radiant, glowing eyes. Dorcas (Gk.) or Tabitha (Heb. or Aram.) was apparently well named. Dorcas, a Hellenist or Jewess who lived among the Greeks and spoke the Greek language, had become a Christian. Luke, the author of Acts calls her a Christian "disciple," the first and only time in the New Testament this title is used to describe a woman.

Dorcas lived in Joppa, a beautiful city situated on the Mediterranean coast, thirty-five miles northwest of Jerusalem. Being a seacoast city, Joppa saw numerous husbands and fathers depart into the dangers of perilous waters. Many men never returned from the sea, and they left behind them bereaved and destitute widows and orphans.

Dorcas had a heart for the Lord. She had loving eyes that saw another's most urgent need. With skilled fingers, this disciple put her faith into everyday action. She stitched beautiful garments (see Prov. 31:13, 20) and distributed them generously to the city's widows and children, the most pitiful victims of shipwrecks and storms.

Joppa's residents loved Dorcas for her continual humble but worthwhile deeds of kindness and charity. After Dorcas became sick and died, her grieving friends prepared her body for burial, then sent two men to nearby Lydda to fetch the apostle Peter.

Peter came quickly. When he entered the upper chamber where the lifeless body lay, he saw the many widows wearing the garments Dorcas had sewn. Asking them to leave, Peter knelt and prayed. He said, "Tabitha, arise." Taking her hand, Peter lifted her up and called her beloved friends to welcome her back to life. What a celebration that must have been!

The seacoast city of Joppa was no longer the same after Dorcas returned to life. Upon hearing and seeing the miracle of the living Dorcas, many turned to the Lord and believed. No doubt this generous disciple, gifted with skilled fingers and a heart for the Lord, picked up her needle and thread and continued her compassionate and benevolent ministry to all who lived around her. How often does a woman offer the most meaningful service to God by doing what seems to be the least important thing to the world?

See also notes on Needlework (Ex. 28); Servanthood (Mark 10)

---

[4]Then he fell to the ground, and heard a voice saying to him, "Saul, Saul, why are you persecuting Me?"

[5]And he said, "Who are You, Lord?"

Then the Lord said, "I am Jesus, whom you are persecuting.[a] It *is* hard for you to kick against the goads."

[6]So he, trembling and astonished, said, "Lord, what do You want me to do?"

Then the Lord *said* to him, "Arise and go into the city, and you will be told what you must do."

[7]And the men who journeyed with him stood speechless, hearing a voice but seeing no one. [8]Then Saul arose from the ground, and when his eyes were opened he saw no one. But they led him by the hand and brought *him* into Damascus. [9]And he was three days without sight, and neither ate nor drank.

Ananias Baptizes Saul

[10]Now there was a certain disciple at Damascus named Ananias; and to him the Lord said in a vision, "Ananias."

And he said, "Here I am, Lord."

[11]So the Lord *said* to him, "Arise and go to the street called Straight, and inquire at the house of Judas for *one* called Saul of Tarsus, for behold, he is praying. [12]And in a vision he has seen a man named Ananias coming in and putting *his* hand on him, so that he might receive his sight."

[13]Then Ananias answered, "Lord, I have heard from many about this man, how much harm he has done to Your saints in Jerusalem. [14]And here he has authority from the chief priests to bind all who call on Your name."

[15]But the Lord said to him, "Go, for he is a chosen vessel of Mine to bear My name before Gentiles, kings, and the children of Israel. [16]For I will show him how many things he must suffer for My name's sake."

[17]And Ananias went his way and entered the house; and laying his hands on him he said,

---

9:5 [a]NU-Text and M-Text omit the last sentence of verse 5 and begin verse 6 with *But arise and go.*

---

witness and missionary to the risen Lord, taking the gospel to the Gentiles.

9:12 Laying on of hands was an OT custom that was also practiced in rabbinic Judaism for the ordination of a student to serve as a rabbi (see Gen. 48:14, 20; Num. 27:15–17; Deut.

34:9). In the NT, hands were placed on a person for healing (see Mark 8:23–25; Acts 9:12, 17), for blessing (Matt. 19:13–15), for setting someone apart for a specific ministry (Acts 6:6; 13:3), and as a visible sign of God's promise to pour out His Spirit (Acts 8:17; 19:6).

*Living in the past is the only prison that will prevent you
from soaring into an abundant future.*

Claudine Boutros

"Brother Saul, the Lord Jesus,[a] who appeared to you on the road as you came, has sent me that you may receive your sight and be filled with the Holy Spirit." [18]Immediately there fell from his eyes *something* like scales, and he received his sight at once; and he arose and was baptized.

[19]So when he had received food, he was strengthened. Then Saul spent some days with the disciples at Damascus.

Saul Preaches Christ

[20]Immediately he preached the Christ[a] in the synagogues, that He is the Son of God. [21]Then all who heard were amazed, and said, "Is this not he who destroyed those who called on this name in Jerusalem, and has come here for that purpose, so that he might bring them bound to the chief priests?" [22]But Saul increased all the more in strength, and confounded the Jews who dwelt in Damascus, proving that this *Jesus* is the Christ.

Saul Escapes Death

[23]Now after many days were past, the Jews plotted to kill him. [24]But their plot became known to Saul. And they watched the gates day and night, to kill him. [25]Then the disciples took him by night and let *him* down through the wall in a large basket.

Saul at Jerusalem

[26]And when Saul had come to Jerusalem, he tried to join the disciples; but they were all afraid of him, and did not believe that he was a disciple. [27]But Barnabas took him and brought *him* to the apostles. And he declared to them how he had seen the Lord on the road, and that He had spoken to him, and how he had preached boldly at Damascus in the name of Jesus. [28]So he was with

them at Jerusalem, coming in and going out. [29]And he spoke boldly in the name of the Lord Jesus and disputed against the Hellenists, but they attempted to kill him. [30]When the brethren found out, they brought him down to Caesarea and sent him out to Tarsus.

The Church Prospers

[31]Then the churches[a] throughout all Judea, Galilee, and Samaria had peace and were edified. And walking in the fear of the Lord and in the comfort of the Holy Spirit, they were multiplied.

Aeneas Healed

[32]Now it came to pass, as Peter went through all *parts of the country*, that he also came down to the saints who dwelt in Lydda. [33]There he found a certain man named Aeneas, who had been bedridden eight years and was paralyzed. [34]And Peter said to him, "Aeneas, Jesus the Christ heals you. Arise and make your bed." Then he arose immediately. [35]So all who dwelt at Lydda and Sharon saw him and turned to the Lord.

Dorcas Restored to Life

[36]At Joppa there was a certain disciple named Tabitha, which is translated Dorcas. This woman was full of good works and charitable deeds which she did. [37]But it happened in those days that she became sick and died. When they had washed her, they laid *her* in an upper room. [38]And since Lydda was near Joppa, and the disciples had heard that Peter was there, they sent two men to him, imploring *him* not to delay in coming to them. [39]Then Peter arose and went with them. When he had come, they brought *him* to the upper room.

· · · · · · · · · · · · · · · · · ·

9:17 [a]M-Text omits *Jesus*.   **9:20** [a]NU-Text reads *Jesus*.   **9:31** [a]NU-Text reads *church . . . was edified*.

9:25 Paul worked and preached in Damascus for about three years. "The wall" refers to the wide wall that was built around the city to fortify and protect it from invaders. Some walls in biblical times were built wide enough for one to six chariots to be driven side-by-side atop them. Paul escaped over this city wall with the help of friends by means of a rope and large basket.

9:32 Lydda was located at the intersection of the route from Egypt to Babylon with the road from Joppa to Jerusalem. The district capital of Samaria, Lydda was evangelized through Peter's ministry, and by the 2nd century a strong Christian church existed there. Peter referred to the Christians at Lydda as "saints" (Gk. *hagios*, lit. "set apart" or "holy"). The term

became a synonym for Christians in the early church and stressed the fact that God had declared them holy and righteous in His eyes and had set them apart for His purposes.

9:36 Tabitha (Aram., lit. "gazelle") or Dorcas (Gk.) lived in Joppa and ministered constantly to the many widows who lived there. Joppa was a seacoast town, and women would often lose their seafaring husbands to accidents at sea. Dorcas was especially generous in her sewing of garments for the widows, who greatly loved and admired her. When Dorcas died, the widows gathered around her and showed off the many lovely articles of clothing she had made for them. Peter restored Dorcas to life and, in doing so, brought many to personal faith in Christ (see Dorcas).

RACIAL RELATIONS *NO RESPECTER OF PERSONS*

The task of each Christian woman is twofold—to proclaim the gospel and to love her neighbor. Jesus Christ demonstrates that racial relations must be based on love (Mark 2:15–17; 7:25–30) and that the gospel is intended for all races, tribes, and nations (Luke 2:32; Rev. 14:6).

The Bible does not contain any clear definition of race, referring instead to nations, tribes, tongues, and peoples. Yet racial prejudices appear to be intolerable. The Lord showed His displeasure by disciplining Miriam for her criticism of Moses' Ethiopian wife (Num. 12:1–15). Jonah was disciplined when he refused to take his ministry to those of another culture (Jon. 1:12). Peter, after opening the "door of faith to the Gentiles," was admonished when his behavior did not exemplify grace (Acts 10:15; Gal. 2:11–18). We must avoid the idea that God approves any mistreatment according to race.

The Bible contains no justification that the people of one race are superior to those of another. Eve is called the "mother of all living" (Gen. 3:20), and all are created in the image of God (Gen. 1:26, 27). All people are under the power of sin and are sinners, and everyone falls short of the glory of God and needs redemption (Rom. 3:23). Jesus Christ did not die on the Cross exclusively for one group but for all (John 1:29; Rom. 8:32). God does not respect persons according to their outward status or condition, and neither should His children (Luke 6:43–45; James 2:1).

The evaluative question must be, "Would God be pleased with the way I treat those of other races?" As ambassadors of Christ, believers must exemplify His standard of love for all people (2 Cor. 5:20; John 15:12).

See also Mal. 2:11; Acts 10:9–43; notes on Equality (Gal. 3); Evangelism (John 6; Col. 4; 1 Pet. 3); Missions (Acts 1; 1 Cor. 9); Prejudice (Acts 15)

And all the widows stood by him weeping, showing the tunics and garments which Dorcas had made while she was with them. ⁴⁰But Peter put them all out, and knelt down and prayed. And turning to the body he said, "Tabitha, arise." And she opened her eyes, and when she saw Peter she sat up. ⁴¹Then he gave her *his* hand and lifted her up; and when he had called the saints and widows, he presented her alive. ⁴²And it became known throughout all Joppa, and many believed on the Lord. ⁴³So it was that he stayed many days in Joppa with Simon, a tanner.

Cornelius Sends a Delegation

10 There was a certain man in Caesarea called Cornelius, a centurion of what was called the Italian Regiment, ²a devout *man* and one who feared God with all his household, who gave alms generously to the people, and prayed to God always. ³About the ninth hour of the day he saw clearly in a vision an angel of God coming in and saying to him, "Cornelius!"

⁴And when he observed him, he was afraid, and said, "What is it, lord?"

So he said to him, "Your prayers and your alms have come up for a memorial before God. ⁵Now send men to Joppa, and send for Simon whose surname is Peter. ⁶He is lodging with Simon, a tanner, whose house is by the sea.ᵃ He will tell you what you must do." ⁷And when the angel who spoke to him had departed, Cornelius called two of his household servants and a devout soldier from among those who waited on him continually. ⁸So when he had explained all *these* things to them, he sent them to Joppa.

Peter's Vision

⁹The next day, as they went on their journey and drew near the city, Peter went up on the housetop to pray, about the sixth hour. ¹⁰Then he became very hungry and wanted to eat; but while they made ready, he fell into a trance ¹¹and saw heaven opened and an object like a great sheet bound at the four corners, descending to him and let down to the earth. ¹²In it were all kinds of four-footed animals of the earth, wild beasts, creeping

···································

10:6 ᵃNU-Text and M-Text omit the last sentence of this verse.

9:43 Peter stayed in the seaport city of Joppa "many days" and discipled the new believers. During this time, he lived in the house of Simon, a tanner of animal skins. Peter's stay in the house of a tanner is interesting, since handling dead animals in order to tan their skin was considered by the Jews a profession ceremonially "unclean." For some reason, Peter disregarded these strict Jewish laws, perhaps as part of God's preparation for his Gentile mission at Caesarea. During his stay in Simon's house, Peter experienced a vision from God concerning clean and unclean food (see Acts 10:9–16).

10:1 Cornelius, a centurion, was stationed in Caesarea, a city named for Augustus Caesar. A centurion was a Roman army officer in charge of 100 soldiers. Cornelius was kind to the Jewish people; and although he was a Gentile, he worshiped God. Through Peter's gospel presentation, Cornelius became a follower of Jesus Christ. Peter baptized Cornelius, the first Gentile convert, and Cornelius's conversion marked the beginning of Gentile missionary activity.

10:10–16 While staying at the home of Simon the tanner in Joppa, Peter went up to the housetop to pray at midday.

I cannot be called anything else than what I am, a Christian.

St. Perpetua

things, and birds of the air. [13]And a voice came to him, "Rise, Peter; kill and eat."

[14]But Peter said, "Not so, Lord! For I have never eaten anything common or unclean."

[15]And a voice *spoke* to him again the second time, "What God has cleansed you must not call common." [16]This was done three times. And the object was taken up into heaven again.

Summoned to Caesarea

[17]Now while Peter wondered within himself what this vision which he had seen meant, behold, the men who had been sent from Cornelius had made inquiry for Simon's house, and stood before the gate. [18]And they called and asked whether Simon, whose surname was Peter, was lodging there. [19]While Peter thought about the vision, the Spirit said to him, "Behold, three men are seeking you. [20]Arise therefore, go down and go with them, doubting nothing; for I have sent them."

[21]Then Peter went down to the men who had been sent to him from Cornelius,[a] and said, "Yes, I am he whom you seek. For what reason have you come?"

[22]And they said, "Cornelius *the* centurion, a just man, one who fears God and has a good reputation among all the nation of the Jews, was divinely instructed by a holy angel to summon you to his house, and to hear words from you." [23]Then he invited them in and lodged *them.*

On the next day Peter went away with them, and some brethren from Joppa accompanied him.

Peter Meets Cornelius

[24]And the following day they entered Caesarea. Now Cornelius was waiting for them, and had called together his relatives and close friends. [25]As Peter was coming in, Cornelius met him and fell down at his feet and worshiped *him.* [26]But Peter lifted him up, saying, "Stand up; I myself am also a man." [27]And as he talked with him, he went in and found many who had come together. [28]Then he

said to them, "You know how unlawful it is for a Jewish man to keep company with or go to one of another nation. But God has shown me that I should not call any man common or unclean. [29]Therefore I came without objection as soon as I was sent for. I ask, then, for what reason have you sent for me?"

[30]So Cornelius said, "Four days ago I was fasting until this hour; and at the ninth hour[a] I prayed in my house, and behold, a man stood before me in bright clothing, [31]and said, 'Cornelius, your prayer has been heard, and your alms are remembered in the sight of God. [32]Send therefore to Joppa and call Simon here, whose surname is Peter. He is lodging in the house of Simon, a tanner, by the sea.[a] When he comes, he will speak to you.' [33]So I sent to you immediately, and you have done well to come. Now therefore, we are all present before God, to hear all the things commanded you by God."

Preaching to Cornelius' Household

[34]Then Peter opened *his* mouth and said: "In truth I perceive that God shows no partiality. [35]But in every nation whoever fears Him and works righteousness is accepted by Him. [36]The word which *God* sent to the children of Israel, preaching peace through Jesus Christ—He is Lord of all— [37]that word you know, which was proclaimed throughout all Judea, and began from Galilee after the baptism which John preached: [38]how God anointed Jesus of Nazareth with the Holy Spirit and with power, who went about doing good and healing all who were oppressed by the devil, for God was with Him. [39]And we are witnesses of all things which He did both in the land of the Jews and in Jerusalem, whom they[a] killed by hanging on a tree. [40]Him God raised up on the

10:21 [a]NU-Text and M-Text omit *who had been sent to him from Cornelius.* 10:30 [a]NU-Text reads *Four days ago to this hour, at the ninth hour.* 10:32 [a]NU-Text omits the last sentence of this verse. 10:39 [a]NU-Text and M-Text add *also.*

Houses typically had flat roofs, enabling a person to escape the heat of a small, crowded house and to enjoy cool breezes as well as privacy and quiet. Often daily work was done on the roofs. The Jews had strict regulations about what could and could not be eaten, and Peter had never eaten what a Jew considered an unclean animal (see Lev. 10, Clean vs. Unclean). The sheet, however, contained a variety of animals, both clean and unclean. By repeating the vision of the sheet three times, God underscored the importance of His message to Peter (Acts 10:16).

10:28 Extreme prejudice existed between Jews and Gentiles in biblical days. Jews referred to Gentiles as dogs, considered them unclean, and would have little to do with them. No orthodox Jew would enter the house of a Gentile, much less sit down at his table to eat. Peter's vision of the clean and unclean animals convinced him that, just as there is no clean or unclean animal flesh, so no human being should be considered clean or unclean. Through God's revelation, Peter recognized that Jesus Christ had died for all people.

MARY   *The Mother of John Mark*

Scripture mentions Mary, the mother of John Mark, only once. During the persecution of Herod Agrippa, this brave woman offered her house to the first group of Christians at Jerusalem as a place to worship God and to pray.

Mary was a woman of means, with servants and a house large enough to accommodate the entire Jerusalem congregation. Since Scripture records no husband, Mary was probably a widow.

Times proved difficult for Christ's followers during those early turbulent years. Herod Agrippa had imprisoned Peter after killing James, the brother of John, with the sword. Yet, in spite of the risks involved, Mary courageously opened her home regularly to Christians.

After an angel miraculously escorted him from prison, Peter went immediately to Mary's house, a familiar place of hospitality for the disciples. There he found the entire congregation praying for his release.

With the dauntless example of a mother like Mary, no wonder John Mark became a missionary, church leader, and the author of the second gospel.

See also notes on Feminine Leadership (1 Sam. 25); Motherhood (1 Sam. 1)

---

third day, and showed Him openly, ⁴¹not to all the people, but to witnesses chosen before by God, *even* to us who ate and drank with Him after He arose from the dead. ⁴²And He commanded us to preach to the people, and to testify that it is He who was ordained by God *to be* Judge of the living and the dead. ⁴³To Him all the prophets witness that, through His name, whoever believes in Him will receive remission of sins."

The Holy Spirit Falls on the Gentiles

⁴⁴While Peter was still speaking these words, the Holy Spirit fell upon all those who heard the word. ⁴⁵And those of the circumcision who believed were astonished, as many as came with Peter, because the gift of the Holy Spirit had been poured out on the Gentiles also. ⁴⁶For they heard them speak with tongues and magnify God.

Then Peter answered, ⁴⁷"Can anyone forbid water, that these should not be baptized who have received the Holy Spirit just as we *have?*" ⁴⁸And he commanded them to be baptized in the name of the Lord. Then they asked him to stay a few days.

Peter Defends God's Grace

11 Now the apostles and brethren who were in Judea heard that the Gentiles had also received the word of God. ²And when Peter came up to Jerusalem, those of the circumcision contended with him, ³saying, "You went in to uncircumcised men and ate with them!"

⁴But Peter explained *it* to them in order from the beginning, saying: ⁵"I was in the city of Joppa praying; and in a trance I saw a vision, an object descending like a great sheet, let down from heaven by four corners; and it came to me. ⁶When I observed it intently and considered, I saw four-footed animals of the earth, wild beasts, creeping things, and birds of the air. ⁷And I heard a voice saying to me, 'Rise, Peter; kill and eat.' ⁸But I said, 'Not so, Lord! For nothing common or unclean has at any time entered my mouth.' ⁹But the voice answered me again from heaven, 'What God has cleansed you must not call common.' ¹⁰Now this was done three times, and all were drawn up again into heaven. ¹¹At that very moment, three men stood before the house where I was, having been sent to me from Caesarea. ¹²Then the Spirit told me to go with them, doubting nothing. Moreover these six brethren accompanied me, and we entered the man's house. ¹³And he told us how he had seen an angel standing in his house, who said to him, 'Send men to Joppa, and call for Simon whose surname is Peter, ¹⁴who will tell you words by which you and all your household will be saved.' ¹⁵And as I began to speak, the Holy Spirit fell upon them, as upon us at the beginning. ¹⁶Then I remembered the word of the Lord, how He said, 'John indeed baptized with water, but you shall be baptized with the Holy Spirit.' ¹⁷If therefore God gave them the same gift as *He gave* us when we believed on the Lord Jesus Christ, who was I that I could withstand God?"

¹⁸When they heard these things they became silent; and they glorified God, saying, "Then God

---

10:45–48 Those of the circumcision were the orthodox Jews (v. 45). The Jews were "astonished" when the Gentiles received the Holy Spirit because they would not have expected God to bless these who were outside the covenant. With the outpouring of the Holy Spirit, the Gentiles began to "speak with tongues" (the ability to speak in languages never stud-

ied, see Acts 2:2–4, note) and to "magnify" God (Acts 10:46). Speaking in other languages offered proof to the Jews that the Gentiles had received the Holy Spirit, since this was the same sign that God had given to the Jews on Pentecost. Peter immediately baptized them and stayed in their household for "a few days" to nurture them in their new faith (v. 48).

Being a Christian is not doing certain things but doing everything a certain way.

Mary Crowley

---

has also granted to the Gentiles repentance to life."

Barnabas and Saul at Antioch

¹⁹Now those who were scattered after the persecution that arose over Stephen traveled as far as Phoenicia, Cyprus, and Antioch, preaching the word to no one but the Jews only. ²⁰But some of them were men from Cyprus and Cyrene, who, when they had come to Antioch, spoke to the Hellenists, preaching the Lord Jesus. ²¹And the hand of the Lord was with them, and a great number believed and turned to the Lord.

²²Then news of these things came to the ears of the church in Jerusalem, and they sent out Barnabas to go as far as Antioch. ²³When he came and had seen the grace of God, he was glad, and encouraged them all that with purpose of heart they should continue with the Lord. ²⁴For he was a good man, full of the Holy Spirit and of faith. And a great many people were added to the Lord. ²⁵Then Barnabas departed for Tarsus to seek Saul. ²⁶And when he had found him, he brought him to Antioch. So it was that for a whole year they assembled with the church and taught a great many people. And the disciples were first called Christians in Antioch.

Relief to Judea

²⁷And in these days prophets came from Jerusalem to Antioch. ²⁸Then one of them, named Agabus, stood up and showed by the Spirit that there was going to be a great famine throughout all the world, which also happened in the days of Claudius Caesar. ²⁹Then the disciples, each according to his ability, determined to send relief to the brethren dwelling in Judea. ³⁰This they also did, and sent it to the elders by the hands of Barnabas and Saul.

Herod's Violence to the Church

12 Now about that time Herod the king stretched out *his* hand to harass some from the church. ²Then he killed James the brother of John with the sword. ³And because he saw that it pleased the Jews, he proceeded further to seize Peter also. Now it was *during* the Days of Unleavened Bread. ⁴So when he had arrested him, he put *him* in prison, and delivered *him* to four squads of soldiers to keep him, intending to bring him before the people after Passover.

Peter Freed from Prison

⁵Peter was therefore kept in prison, but constant[a] prayer was offered to God for him by the church. ⁶And when Herod was about to bring him out, that night Peter was sleeping, bound with two chains between two soldiers; and the guards before the door were keeping the prison. ⁷Now behold, an angel of the Lord stood by *him,* and a light shone in the prison; and he struck Peter on the side and raised him up, saying, "Arise quickly!" And his chains fell off *his* hands. ⁸Then the angel said to him, "Gird yourself and tie on your sandals"; and so he did. And he said to him, "Put on your garment and follow me." ⁹So he went out and followed him, and did not know that what was done by the angel was real, but thought he was seeing a vision. ¹⁰When they were past the first and the second guard posts, they came to the iron

12:5 [a]NU-Text reads *constantly* (or *earnestly*).

11:22 Barnabas (lit. "son of encouragement") was sent to Antioch. He was a generous man who earlier sold his material possessions and gave the money to the Jerusalem church (Acts 4:36). He was sent by the Jerusalem church to verify and guide this radical church growth among the Gentiles. Barnabas was the man responsible for bringing Paul to Antioch, and he later accompanied Paul on his first missionary journey (Acts 13:1–3; see map, Paul's First Missionary Journey).

11:26 Many Jews who lived outside Palestine (known as Diaspora Jews) settled in Antioch, the first place where believers in Christ were called "Christians." What started as a nickname became a means of identifying those who lived and behaved like Christ.

11:28 Agabus was a prophet (Gk. *prophētēs*, lit. "proclaimer" or "interpreter" or "one who speaks for"). Prophets had an important ministry in the early church and were held in high esteem. They not only told the future, but they also revealed the will of God. Agabus visited the church at Antioch and predicted a universal famine, which happened a decade later. As a result, the church at Antioch began a famine relief program for the congregation in Jerusalem.

12:2 Herod Agrippa I, the grandson of Herod the Great, began to attack Christians and especially their leaders (see chart, The Family Tree of Herod the Great). This outbreak of persecution against Christians had both religious and political intent. Herod had been careful to observe Jewish customs and thus popularize himself with the Jews. In order to gain and keep their support, Herod beheaded James, the son of Zebedee and brother of John. Then Herod imprisoned Peter but postponed his execution until after the Passover Feast.

RHODA — *A Fragrant Life*

Rhoda's name means "rose." She lived about A.D. 43, during the first Christian persecution of Herod Agrippa, the grandson of the infamous Herod the Great (see Matt. 2). She was the maid of John Mark's mother Mary, in whose home the small congregation in Jerusalem often gathered to pray. One night, they had prayed long past midnight for the release of Peter from prison. Since James, the brother of John, had already been put to death, the infant church feared the same fate for Peter.

During the prayer session, Rhoda heard a knock at the gate and ran to the door. She immediately recognized Peter's voice when he spoke to her. But in her excitement, she failed to open the door. She left Peter standing outside the closed gate. Bolting into the room and interrupting those praying, Rhoda announced with great excitement that Peter himself stood at the door.

The Christians did not believe her. They even questioned her sanity. They concluded that the "visitor" was Peter's angel, as it was a common Jewish belief that every Israelite was given a special guardian angel who resembled him. They knew Peter was being held in a well-guarded prison. Rhoda never doubted whose voice she had heard. She was terribly excited but not surprised that God had heard the prayers of the young congregation. Unlike the others, who had to open the door and see Peter with their own eyes, Rhoda had faith great enough to know God would answer their prayers, even in the most unexpected way. The mundane tasks assigned to Rhoda as a household servant did not keep her from experiencing the joys of being a part of kingdom business through her genuine, believing faith.

See also notes on Boldness (Prov. 28); Prayer (Jer. 33)

---

gate that leads to the city, which opened to them of its own accord; and they went out and went down one street, and immediately the angel departed from him.

[11]And when Peter had come to himself, he said, "Now I know for certain that the Lord has sent His angel, and has delivered me from the hand of Herod and *from* all the expectation of the Jewish people."

[12]So, when he had considered *this,* he came to the house of Mary, the mother of John whose surname was Mark, where many were gathered together praying. [13]And as Peter knocked at the door of the gate, a girl named Rhoda came to answer. [14]When she recognized Peter's voice, because of *her* gladness she did not open the gate, but ran in and announced that Peter stood before the gate. [15]But they said to her, "You are beside yourself!" Yet she kept insisting that it was so. So they said, "It is his angel."

[16]Now Peter continued knocking; and when they opened *the door* and saw him, they were astonished. [17]But motioning to them with his hand to keep silent, he declared to them how the Lord had brought him out of the prison. And he said, "Go, tell these things to James and to the brethren." And he departed and went to another place.

[18]Then, as soon as it was day, there was no small stir among the soldiers about what had become of Peter. [19]But when Herod had searched for him and not found him, he examined the guards and commanded that *they* should be put to death.

And he went down from Judea to Caesarea, and stayed *there.*

Herod's Violent Death

[20]Now Herod had been very angry with the people of Tyre and Sidon; but they came to him with one accord, and having made Blastus the king's personal aide their friend, they asked for peace, because their country was supplied with food by the king's *country.*

[21]So on a set day Herod, arrayed in royal apparel, sat on his throne and gave an oration to them. [22]And the people kept shouting, "The voice of a god and not of a man!" [23]Then immediately an angel of the Lord struck him, because he did not give glory to God. And he was eaten by worms and died.

[24]But the word of God grew and multiplied.

Barnabas and Saul Appointed

[25]And Barnabas and Saul returned from[a] Jerusalem when they had fulfilled *their* ministry, and

··················
12:25 [a]NU-Text and M-Text read *to.*

12:23 Herod Agrippa, the son of Aristobulus and grandson of Herod the Great, ruled Palestine as king from A.D. 41–44 (see charts, The Family Tree of Herod the Great; New Testament Political Rulers). After Passover, Herod Agrippa returned to his residence at Caesarea to settle a quarrel with the people of Tyre and Sidon. On the second day of a festival honoring Emperor Claudius, Herod clad himself in a silver robe. When

the robe glistened in the sunlight, the dazzled crowd cried out to Herod, calling him a god. He did not rebuke their claim but instead enjoyed the adulation. Immediately Herod became ill and after several days of intense pain, he died. Luke considered the death of Herod as punishment from God.

12:25 Accompanying Paul and Barnabas as they returned from the Jerusalem church to Antioch was John Mark, the son

There is no better way to influence your children for godliness than to have in your home men and women who are Spirit-filled servants of God.

Joyce Rogers

they also took with them John whose surname was Mark.

13 Now in the church that was at Antioch there were certain prophets and teachers: Barnabas, Simeon who was called Niger, Lucius of Cyrene, Manaen who had been brought up with Herod the tetrarch, and Saul. [2]As they ministered to the Lord and fasted, the Holy Spirit said, "Now separate to Me Barnabas and Saul for the work to which I have called them." [3]Then, having fasted and prayed, and laid hands on them, they sent *them* away.

Preaching in Cyprus

[4]So, being sent out by the Holy Spirit, they went down to Seleucia, and from there they sailed to Cyprus. [5]And when they arrived in Salamis, they preached the word of God in the synagogues of the Jews. They also had John as *their* assistant.

[6]Now when they had gone through the island[a] to Paphos, they found a certain sorcerer, a false prophet, a Jew whose name *was* Bar-Jesus, [7]who was with the proconsul, Sergius Paulus, an intelli-

gent man. This man called for Barnabas and Saul and sought to hear the word of God. [8]But Elymas the sorcerer (for so his name is translated) withstood them, seeking to turn the proconsul away from the faith. [9]Then Saul, who also *is called* Paul, filled with the Holy Spirit, looked intently at him [10]and said, "O full of all deceit and all fraud, *you* son of the devil, *you* enemy of all righteousness, will you not cease perverting the straight ways of the Lord? [11]And now, indeed, the hand of the Lord *is* upon you, and you shall be blind, not seeing the sun for a time."

And immediately a dark mist fell on him, and he went around seeking someone to lead him by the hand. [12]Then the proconsul believed, when he saw what had been done, being astonished at the teaching of the Lord.

At Antioch in Pisidia

[13]Now when Paul and his party set sail from Paphos, they came to Perga in Pamphylia; and John, departing from them, returned to Jerusalem.

13:6 [a]NU-Text reads *the whole island.*

---

of Mary, in whose house the church worshiped. John Mark became an important helper to Paul and Barnabas. He, too, preached the gospel to the Gentiles. He later wrote the Gospel of Mark for Gentile Christians.

13:1 Luke listed five prophets and teachers residing at Antioch.

- Barnabas (lit. "son of encouragement") was a peacemaker; he often settled disputes between the Jewish and Gentile Christians; he was responsible for bringing Paul (or Saul) to Antioch.

- Simeon was also called "Niger" (lit. "black").

- Little is known about Lucius except that he was from Cyrene in northern Africa.

- Manaen, who grew up with Herod Antipas (4 B.C. to A.D. 37; see chart, New Testament Political Rulers), was probably a member of the court.

- Saul or Paul, a trained rabbi and Pharisee, became a great missionary and martyr of the early Christian church.

These men came from different traditions, backgrounds, and religions, but they were unified in their mission for Christ.

13:2 Fasting can be both a private and a community act, in which people put aside food (and/or drink) for a period of time (see Matt. 6:16–18, note). The early church fasted and prayed in order to understand and receive direction in their task of taking the gospel of Jesus Christ throughout the world.

13:4, 5 Seleucia, a Syrian city located about 15 miles from Antioch on the Mediterranean coast, was founded in 301 B.C. by

Seleucus Nicator, a general of Alexander the Great. The missionaries boarded a ship after leaving Seleucia and traveled some 130 miles to Cyprus, an island 138 miles long and 60 miles wide located in the eastern Mediterranean Sea. The Romans took control of Cyprus in 57 or 58 B.C. The mountainous island contained an abundance of trees and copper mines whose products were widely marketed. Cyprus was the birthplace of Barnabas, Paul's companion on his first missionary journey. Salamis was the most important city on the island. Most sailing in the Mediterranean had to be done from May to September due to severe weather, fog, and storms at sea.

13:6 Paphos, the capital of Cyprus, was located on the southwest side of the island. Paphos was an important center for the worship of Venus, the goddess of love (see chart, Graeco-Roman Goddesses).

13:7, 8 Sergius Paulus, an "intelligent man," was the governor of Cyprus. This Gentile was converted to Christianity after hearing the gospel. Bar-Jesus or Elymas, the magician, was his personal sorcerer (Gk. *magos*). Many important men had personal wizards or sorcerers because of the prevalence of superstition. He saw the faith of the missionaries as a real threat to his career and livelihood. Elymas was struck with temporary blindness when he tried to prevent the governor from hearing the gospel.

13:13 Perga was located eight miles from the Mediterranean Sea in the province of Pamphylia. Paul, Barnabas, and John Mark headed for Perga after leaving Paphos. At this point Paul evidently took leadership in the missionary endeavors. Barnabas, however, who had previously been in charge, did

EMPLOYMENT   CHOOSING A PROFESSION

The Bible provides numerous examples of professions and jobs. In most cases, professions in the Old Testament were "inherited"—passed down from father to son or mother to daughter in something of a mentoring manner or apprenticeship relationship. Occasionally, a person's special talents in a particular area or the call of God on the person's life were noted, and that person then was singled out for a unique position, such as when Deborah became a judge of Israel (Judg. 4:4, 5).

In the New Testament, women and men enjoyed much more autonomy in "choosing" a line of work or a profession. Lydia was a notable businesswoman in the textile industry (Acts 16:14); Dorcas was a well-respected seamstress (Acts 9:39); and Priscilla worked in the tentmaking trade (Acts 18:2, 3).

The understanding of the New Testament believers, however, was that their entire lives were subject to God's command and direction, including their choices of careers. The Holy Spirit was to be trusted both for direction and timing.

The idea of a "career path" was not regarded as something that a person must engineer on her own, but something that flowed naturally from a person's talents and abilities and in response to opportunities that arose. You are to be motivated in your work by a desire to use your abilities to their fullest for the glory of God rather than being motivated by positions on corporate ladders, work incentives, higher salaries, or cultural standards of prestige and status.

The Bible clearly warns against worshiping the work of your own hands or exalting that which you have created or earned to the place of supreme honor in your life (Ps. 115:1–8; Jer. 25:6, 7).

See also Employment (Eccl. 9; Acts 18; 2 Cor. 2; Col. 3; 1 Pet. 2); Priorities (Matt. 6); Time Management (Ps. 31)

---

¹⁴But when they departed from Perga, they came to Antioch in Pisidia, and went into the synagogue on the Sabbath day and sat down. ¹⁵And after the reading of the Law and the Prophets, the rulers of the synagogue sent to them, saying, "Men *and* brethren, if you have any word of exhortation for the people, say on."

¹⁶Then Paul stood up, and motioning with *his* hand said, "Men of Israel, and you who fear God, listen: ¹⁷The God of this people Israelᵃ chose our fathers, and exalted the people when they dwelt as strangers in the land of Egypt, and with an uplifted arm He brought them out of it. ¹⁸Now for a time of about forty years He put up with their ways in the wilderness. ¹⁹And when He had destroyed seven nations in the land of Canaan, He distributed their land to them by allotment.

²⁰"After that He gave *them* judges for about four hundred and fifty years, until Samuel the prophet. ²¹And afterward they asked for a king; so God gave them Saul the son of Kish, a man of the tribe of Benjamin, for forty years. ²²And when He had removed him, He raised up for them David as king, to whom also He gave testimony and said, '*I have found David*ᵃ the *son* of Jesse, *a man after My own heart, who will do all My will.*'ᵇ ²³From this man's seed, according to *the* promise, God raised up for Israel a Savior—Jesus—ᵃ ²⁴after John had first preached, before His coming, the baptism of repentance to all the people of Israel. ²⁵And as John was finishing his course, he said, 'Who do you think I am? I am not *He*. But behold, there comes One after me, the sandals of whose feet I am not worthy to loose.'

²⁶"Men *and* brethren, sons of the family of Abraham, and those among you who fear God, to you the word of this salvation has been sent. ²⁷For

---

13:17 ᵃM-Text omits *Israel*.   13:22 ᵃPsalm 89:20   ᵇ1 Samuel 13:14
13:23 ᵃM-Text reads *for Israel salvation*.

---

not seem to mind and worked diligently with Paul. Young John Mark, their helper, gave up at this stage in the journey and went home. Paul found it extremely hard to excuse John Mark for this action. Paul and Barnabas later split company over a dispute concerning whether John Mark should travel with them on the second missionary journey (see Acts 15:38, 39).

13:15 Exhortation, such as in the phrases "Listen" and "Beware therefore," occurs at the beginning and end of Paul's message to the Jews in Pisidia (vv. 16, 40). His words were not just one more discourse on a Sabbath day but an urgent message that demanded action from the hearers (vv. 38–41). Before Paul's ministry, Moses, the prophets, and Jesus called out to women and men throughout the ages to hear the truth from God and believe it (Ex. 24:3; John 3:23; 2 Pet. 1:19). In ex-

horting one another, be equally urgent and uncompromisingly clear in bringing the message of Christ to one another and to the unbeliever (see Ps. 149, Praise; Matt. 28; John 6; Col. 4; 1 Pet. 3, Evangelism; Rom. 12, Spiritual Gifts; Eph. 4, Encouragement).

13:21 Saul, whose father was Kish from the tribe of Benjamin, reigned as the first king of a united Israel. Once an effective king, Saul eventually became deranged. Due to fear and jealousy, he tried to kill David, the shepherd boy whom God had anointed to become king after him. He also ordered the slaughter of 85 priests at Nob (1 Sam. 22:17–19). The day before his tragic death, Saul disguised himself and consulted the witch of En Dor (1 Sam. 28:3–25).

PAUL'S FIRST MISSIONARY JOURNEY

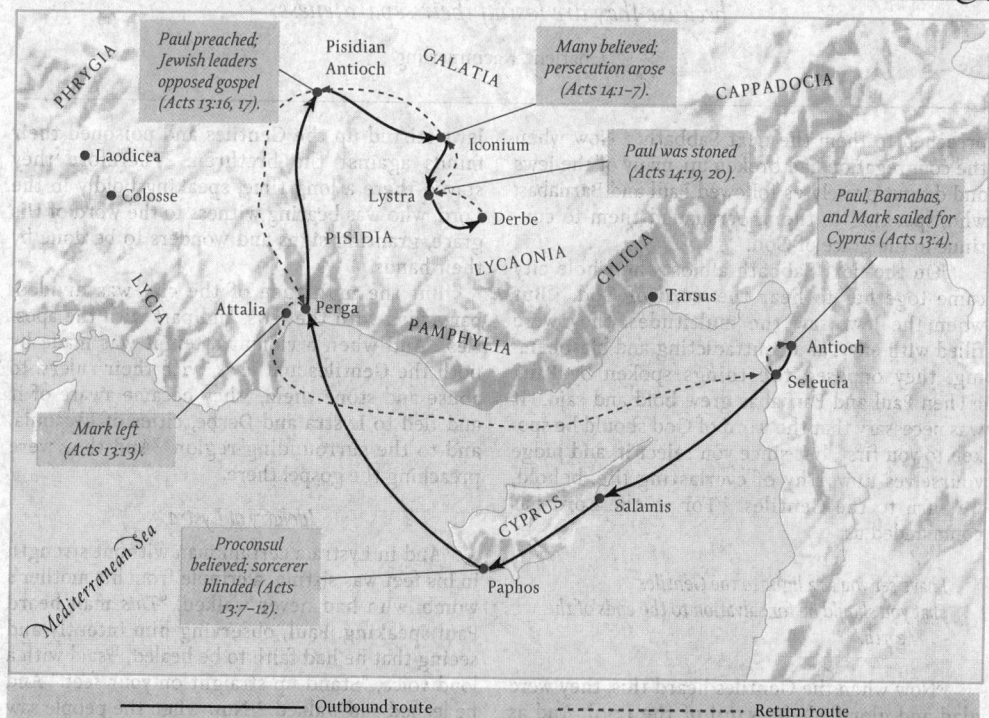

Paul preached;
Jewish leaders
opposed gospel
(Acts 13:16, 17).

Many believed;
persecution arose
(Acts 14:1–7).

Paul was stoned
(Acts 14:19, 20).

Paul, Barnabas,
and Mark sailed for
Cyprus (Acts 13:4).

Mark left
(Acts 13:13).

Proconsul
believed; sorcerer
blinded (Acts
13:7–12).

PHRYGIA · GALATIA · CAPPADOCIA · Pisidian Antioch · Iconium · Laodicea · Colosse · Lystra · Derbe · PISIDIA · LYCAONIA · CILICIA · LYCIA · Attalia · Perga · PAMPHYLIA · Tarsus · Antioch · Seleucia · Mediterranean Sea · CYPRUS · Salamis · Paphos

——————— Outbound route   - - - - - - - - - - - Return route

those who dwell in Jerusalem, and their rulers, because they did not know Him, nor even the voices of the Prophets which are read every Sabbath, have fulfilled *them* in condemning *Him.* 28And though they found no cause for death *in Him,* they asked Pilate that He should be put to death. 29Now when they had fulfilled all that was written concerning Him, they took *Him* down from the tree and laid *Him* in a tomb. 30But God raised Him from the dead. 31He was seen for many days by those who came up with Him from Galilee to Jerusalem, who are His witnesses to the people. 32And we declare to you glad tidings—that promise which was made to the fathers. 33God has fulfilled this for us their children, in that He has raised up Jesus. As it is also written in the second Psalm:

'You are My Son,
    Today I have begotten You.'a

34And that He raised Him from the dead, no more to return to corruption, He has spoken thus:

'I will give you the sure mercies of David.'a

35Therefore He also says in another *Psalm:*

'You will not allow Your Holy One to see
    corruption.'a

36"For David, after he had served his own generation by the will of God, fell asleep, was buried with his fathers, and saw corruption; 37but He whom God raised up saw no corruption. 38Therefore let it be known to you, brethren, that through this Man is preached to you the forgiveness of sins; 39and by Him everyone who believes is justified from all things from which you could not be justified by the law of Moses. 40Beware therefore, lest what has been spoken in the prophets come upon you:

41'Behold, you despisers,
    Marvel and perish!
For I work a work in your days,
    A work which you will by no means believe,
    Though one were to declare it to you.' "a

Blessing and Conflict at Antioch

42So when the Jews went out of the synagogue,a the Gentiles begged that these words might be

13:33 aPsalm 2:7   13:34 aIsaiah 55:3   13:35 aPsalm 16:10   13:41
aHabakkuk 1:5   13:42 aOr And when they went out of the synagogue
of the Jews; NU-Text reads And when they went out of the synagogue, they begged.

Christians are losing their power and influence . . .
because they are losing their separateness.

Charlene Kaemmerling

preached to them the next Sabbath. ⁴³Now when the congregation had broken up, many of the Jews and devout proselytes followed Paul and Barnabas, who, speaking to them, persuaded them to continue in the grace of God.

⁴⁴On the next Sabbath almost the whole city came together to hear the word of God. ⁴⁵But when the Jews saw the multitudes, they were filled with envy; and contradicting and blaspheming, they opposed the things spoken by Paul. ⁴⁶Then Paul and Barnabas grew bold and said, "It was necessary that the word of God should be spoken to you first; but since you reject it, and judge yourselves unworthy of everlasting life, behold, we turn to the Gentiles. ⁴⁷For so the Lord has commanded us:

'I have set you as a light to the Gentiles,
That you should be for salvation to the ends of the
earth.' "[a]

⁴⁸Now when the Gentiles heard this, they were glad and glorified the word of the Lord. And as many as had been appointed to eternal life believed.

⁴⁹And the word of the Lord was being spread throughout all the region. ⁵⁰But the Jews stirred up the devout and prominent women and the chief men of the city, raised up persecution against Paul and Barnabas, and expelled them from their region. ⁵¹But they shook off the dust from their feet against them, and came to Iconium. ⁵²And the disciples were filled with joy and with the Holy Spirit.

At Iconium

14 Now it happened in Iconium that they went together to the synagogue of the Jews, and so spoke that a great multitude both of the Jews and of the Greeks believed. ²But the unbelieving

Jews stirred up the Gentiles and poisoned their minds against the brethren. ³Therefore they stayed there a long time, speaking boldly in the Lord, who was bearing witness to the word of His grace, granting signs and wonders to be done by their hands.

⁴But the multitude of the city was divided: part sided with the Jews, and part with the apostles. ⁵And when a violent attempt was made by both the Gentiles and Jews, with their rulers, to abuse and stone them, ⁶they became aware of it and fled to Lystra and Derbe, cities of Lycaonia, and to the surrounding region. ⁷And they were preaching the gospel there.

Idolatry at Lystra

⁸And in Lystra a certain man without strength in his feet was sitting, a cripple from his mother's womb, who had never walked. ⁹*This* man heard Paul speaking. Paul, observing him intently and seeing that he had faith to be healed, ¹⁰said with a loud voice, "Stand up straight on your feet!" And he leaped and walked. ¹¹Now when the people saw what Paul had done, they raised their voices, saying in the Lycaonian *language,* "The gods have come down to us in the likeness of men!" ¹²And Barnabas they called Zeus, and Paul, Hermes, because he was the chief speaker. ¹³Then the priest of Zeus, whose temple was in front of their city, brought oxen and garlands to the gates, intending to sacrifice with the multitudes.

¹⁴But when the apostles Barnabas and Paul heard this, they tore their clothes and ran in among the multitude, crying out ¹⁵and saying, "Men, why are you doing these things? We also are men with the same nature as you, and preach to you that you should turn from these useless things to the living God, who made the heaven,

13:47 [a]Isaiah 49:6

13:51 Paul suffered much persecution in Iconium, a city in the province of Galatia. To shake the dust from one's feet was to declare Gentile territory to be unclean. The devout Jews rejected the gospel. Thus, the missionaries shook dust from their feet as they left the city to show that the Jews had become like Gentiles, whom the Jews considered unclean.

14:12–14 The people in Lystra were very superstitious. When Paul healed the lame man (v. 8), the people reacted as pagans toward Paul and Barnabas. They immediately began to worship Barnabas as Zeus, the king of the gods, and Paul as Hermes, the god of speech, believing that these missionaries

were the gods visiting in human flesh. Ancient legend had stated that Hermes and Zeus once came to earth incognito. The people did not recognize them as gods during that earthly visit and thus showed them no hospitality. As a result, the gods destroyed all but two of the city's inhabitants. Wanting to avoid such a possibility, the local priest of Zeus prepared to worship the missionaries with sacrificial animals. Because the people spoke in the Lycaonian language, Paul and Barnabas were slow to understand exactly what was happening. When finally they understood, the men tore their clothes as a sign of outrageous disgust and sought to stop the people.

THE TIMELINE OF PAUL

PAUL'S MISSIONARY JOURNEYS			
1st Missionary Journey A.D. 48–50 Galatia Cyprus (Acts 13—14)	2nd Missionary Journey A.D. 51–53 Macedonia Achaia Greece (Acts 15:39—18:22)	3rd Missionary Journey A.D. 54–57 Asia Greece (Acts 18:23—21:17)	4th Missionary Journey A.D. 59–60 Caesarea Crete Malta Rome (Acts 27; 28)

PAUL'S LIFE

Birth A.D. 1–5(?) (Acts 22:3)	Conversion A.D. 34—35 (Acts 9:1–19)		Philippi Imprisonment A.D. 58–60 (Acts 16:16–40)	Roman Imprisonment A.D. 60–63 (Acts 27—28)

A.D. 1   A.D. 20   A.D. 30   A.D. 40   A.D. 50   A.D. 60   A.D. 70

1st Trip to Jerusalem A.D. 37–38 (Acts 9:26–29)	2nd Trip to Jerusalem A.D. 48 (Acts 11:27–30)	Caesarean Imprisonment A.D. 58–60 (Acts 23:23—26:32)	Death Probably in Rome (Acts 28:30, 31)

PAUL'S WRITINGS

1 THESS. A.D. 50–52 2 THESS. A.D. 51–52	GALATIANS A.D. 55–57 1 COR. A.D. 56–57 2 COR. A.D. 56–57 ROMANS A.D. 55–59	EPHESIANS A.D. 60–63 PHILIPPIANS A.D. 60–63 COLOSSIANS A.D. 60–63 PHILEMON A.D. 60–63	1 TIMOTHY A.D. 62–64 TITUS A.D. 62–64 2 TIMOTHY A.D. 66–67

the earth, the sea, and all things that are in them, [16]who in bygone generations allowed all nations to walk in their own ways. [17]Nevertheless He did not leave Himself without witness, in that He did good, gave us rain from heaven and fruitful seasons, filling our hearts with food and gladness." [18]And with these sayings they could scarcely restrain the multitudes from sacrificing to them.

Stoning, Escape to Derbe

[19]Then Jews from Antioch and Iconium came there; and having persuaded the multitudes, they stoned Paul and dragged him out of the city, supposing him to be dead. [20]However, when the disciples gathered around him, he rose up and went into the city. And the next day he departed with Barnabas to Derbe.

Strengthening the Converts

[21]And when they had preached the gospel to that city and made many disciples, they returned to Lystra, Iconium, and Antioch, [22]strengthening the souls of the disciples, exhorting them to continue in the faith, and saying, "We must through many tribulations enter the kingdom of God." [23]So when they had appointed elders in every church, and prayed with fasting, they commended them

PREJUDICE · *IMPEDING THE KINGDOM'S GROWTH*

Prejudice denies believers free fellowship, thereby impeding access to the spiritual gifts God has placed throughout the body of Christ. The different gifts and their varied administrations are given so that all the people of God might be made stronger (1 Cor. 12:7).

Jews and Gentiles had been longtime adversaries when God directed Peter, a Jew, to go to the home of Cornelius, a Gentile. Though reluctant, Peter obeyed and went to the Gentile home and preached, and the entire family believed (Acts 10:28–35). Peter marveled at God's grace. Peter's visit initiated open access to the gospel of Jesus Christ for all.

Believers are wise to use caution when segregating themselves according to ethnic, gender, or socio-economic differences. All believers are one in Christ (Gal. 3:28). Communication and shared fellowship are perhaps the greatest weapons against prejudice because they weaken hasty, harsh judgments and clear the way for compassion.

See also Gal. 3:28; notes on Fruit of the Spirit (Ps. 86; Rom. 5; 15; 1 Cor. 10; 13; Gal. 5; Eph. 4; Col. 3; 2 Thess. 1; Rev. 2); The Homeless (Luke 9); Poverty (Luke 14); Prisoners (Is. 61); Racial Relations (Acts 10)

to the Lord in whom they had believed. ²⁴And after they had passed through Pisidia, they came to Pamphylia. ²⁵Now when they had preached the word in Perga, they went down to Attalia. ²⁶From there they sailed to Antioch, where they had been commended to the grace of God for the work which they had completed.

²⁷Now when they had come and gathered the church together, they reported all that God had done with them, and that He had opened the door of faith to the Gentiles. ²⁸So they stayed there a long time with the disciples.

Conflict over Circumcision

15 And certain *men* came down from Judea and taught the brethren, "Unless you are circumcised according to the custom of Moses, you cannot be saved." ²Therefore, when Paul and Barnabas had no small dissension and dispute with them, they determined that Paul and Barnabas and certain others of them should go up to Jerusalem, to the apostles and elders, about this question.

³So, being sent on their way by the church, they passed through Phoenicia and Samaria, describing the conversion of the Gentiles; and they caused great joy to all the brethren. ⁴And when they had come to Jerusalem, they were received by the church and the apostles and the elders; and they reported all things that God had done with them. ⁵But some of the sect of the Pharisees who believed rose up, saying, "It is necessary to circumcise them, and to command *them* to keep the law of Moses."

The Jerusalem Council

⁶Now the apostles and elders came together to consider this matter. ⁷And when there had been much dispute, Peter rose up *and* said to them: "Men *and* brethren, you know that a good while ago God chose among us, that by my mouth the Gentiles should hear the word of the gospel and believe. ⁸So God, who knows the heart, acknowledged them by giving them the Holy Spirit, just as *He did* to us, ⁹and made no distinction between us and them, purifying their hearts by faith. ¹⁰Now therefore, why do you test God by putting a yoke on the neck of the disciples which neither our fathers nor we were able to bear? ¹¹But we believe that through the grace of the Lord Jesus Christ[a] we shall be saved in the same manner as they."

¹²Then all the multitude kept silent and listened to Barnabas and Paul declaring how many miracles and wonders God had worked through them among the Gentiles. ¹³And after they had become silent, James answered, saying, "Men *and* brethren, listen to me: ¹⁴Simon has declared how God at the first visited the Gentiles to take out of them a people for His name. ¹⁵And with this the words of the prophets agree, just as it is written:

¹⁶'After this I will return
  And will rebuild the tabernacle of David, which has
    fallen down;

· · · · · · · · · · · · · · · ·

15:11 [a]NU-Text and M-Text omit *Christ.*

14:24, 25 Pamphylia was a small district located in Asia Minor, now southern Turkey. About 80 miles long and 20 miles wide, Pamphylia was inhabited by non-Hellenized people, making communication of the gospel difficult. Attalia in Asia Minor was located on the Mediterranean coast. After leaving Attalia, Paul and Barnabas sailed to Seleucia.

15:10 The yoke was a wooden instrument placed on the necks

or backs of working farm animals, enabling two animals to pull a plow together and thus doubling their strength. In this passage, Peter referred to the yoke as an instrument of bondage and hardship that improperly linked Jews and Gentiles together. He argued that Gentile believers should not be made to undergo circumcision nor forced to a strict keeping of the Law of Moses.

God has designed work as the common denominator
for the Christian and non-Christian, and the job is the place
where the Christian must meet the non-Christian world.

Mary Whelchel

I will rebuild its ruins,
And I will set it up;
[17] *So that the rest of mankind may seek the LORD,*
Even all the Gentiles who are called by My name,
Says the LORD who does all these things.'[a]

[18]"Known to God from eternity are all His works.[a] [19]Therefore I judge that we should not trouble those from among the Gentiles who are turning to God, [20]but that we write to them to abstain from things polluted by idols, *from* sexual immorality,[a] *from* things strangled, and *from* blood. [21]For Moses has had throughout many generations those who preach him in every city, being read in the synagogues every Sabbath."

The Jerusalem Decree

[22]Then it pleased the apostles and elders, with the whole church, to send chosen men of their own company to Antioch with Paul and Barnabas, *namely,* Judas who was also named Barsabas,[a] and Silas, leading men among the brethren. [23]They wrote this *letter* by them:

The apostles, the elders, and the brethren,

To the brethren who are of the Gentiles in Antioch, Syria, and Cilicia:

Greetings.

[24]Since we have heard that some who went out from us have troubled you with words, unsettling your souls, saying, "*You must* be circumcised and keep the law"[a]— to whom we gave no *such* commandment— [25]it seemed good to us, being assembled with one accord, to send chosen men to you with our beloved Barnabas and Paul, [26]men who have risked their lives for the name of our Lord Jesus Christ. [27]We have therefore sent Judas and Silas, who will also report the same things by word of

mouth. [28]For it seemed good to the Holy Spirit, and to us, to lay upon you no greater burden than these necessary things: [29]that you abstain from things offered to idols, from blood, from things strangled, and from sexual immorality.[a] If you keep yourselves from these, you will do well.

Farewell.

Continuing Ministry in Syria

[30]So when they were sent off, they came to Antioch; and when they had gathered the multitude together, they delivered the letter. [31]When they had read it, they rejoiced over its encouragement. [32]Now Judas and Silas, themselves being prophets also, exhorted and strengthened the brethren with many words. [33]And after they had stayed *there* for a time, they were sent back with greetings from the brethren to the apostles.[a] [34]However, it seemed good to Silas to remain there.[a] [35]Paul and Barnabas also remained in Antioch, teaching and preaching the word of the Lord, with many others also.

Division over John Mark

[36]Then after some days Paul said to Barnabas, "Let us now go back and visit our brethren in every city where we have preached the word of the Lord, *and see* how they are doing." [37]Now Barnabas was determined to take with them John called Mark. [38]But Paul insisted that they should not take with them the one who had departed from them in Pamphylia, and had not gone with them to the work. [39]Then the contention became so

15:17 [a]Amos 9:11, 12   **15:18** [a]NU-Text (combining with verse 17) reads *Says the Lord, who makes these things known from eternity (of old).* **15:20** [a]Or *fornication*   **15:22** [a]NU-Text and M-Text read *Barsabbas.* **15:24** [a]NU-Text omits *saying, "You must be circumcised and keep the law."*   **15:29** [a]Or *fornication*   **15:33** [a]NU-Text reads *to those who had sent them.*   **15:34** [a]NU-Text and M-Text omit this verse.

15:22 Barsabas and Silas were chosen by the Jerusalem church to travel with Barnabas and Paul to Antioch. Silas accompanied both Paul and Peter on their respective missionary journeys.

15:37–40 Paul decided that he and Barnabas should return to the Christian churches they had birthed to observe the work of the congregation and to strengthen them in the faith. Barnabas wanted to take John Mark with them, but Paul op-

posed this, since the young man had deserted them on the first journey. Paul and Barnabas argued sharply over the issue, then went their separate ways. Barnabas took John Mark and sailed to Cyprus. Paul took Silas and returned to Syria and Cilicia. No record exists of Paul and Barnabas working together again. Barnabas' faith in John Mark proved to be justified, and the young man became a valuable Christian worker (2 Tim. 4:11).

LYDIA   *An Influential Businesswoman*

Lydia came from Thyatira, a city in the western province of Lydia in Asia Minor. Her name originally might have been the designation of her home, "a woman of Lydia." At the time Lydia met Paul, she lived at Philippi, a leading city of Macedonia on the European continent.

As a wealthy and influential businesswoman, Lydia sold articles dyed purple, a prized color made from certain mollusks—a respectable and lucrative trade. She had a spacious home that could accommodate many guests and servants to meet their needs. This had to be a rare achievement in her day. She surely must have been a hard-working, bold, intelligent woman to achieve the success she enjoyed.

One Sabbath day, Lydia went to the river's shore that had been designated by the Roman authorities of Philippi as a place of prayer and worship for the Jews. There she met Paul and Silas, who had been in Philippi only a short time. While others along the river may have rejected Paul's words about Jesus, Lydia accepted them and became a believer. Once she believed, she made a confession of her faith to her whole world through baptism and then, she assembled her entire household, told them what had happened to her, and asked them to believe. After her entire household accepted Christ as Savior and were baptized, Lydia invited Paul and Silas to stay in her home. When Paul and Silas were thrown into a Philippian prison, Lydia visited them and attended to their needs. Her house became the meeting place of the first European church.

Lydia was quick to perceive that what had been hers before her conversion—home, business, and possessions—now belonged to the Lord. She had a new partner, the Lord Jesus; a new purpose, to serve Him; and a new satisfaction in seeking to be effective and successful in order to glorify the Lord. Her career aspirations did not hinder her sharing the gospel with family and friends. She was not too busy to take time for hospitality (Acts 16:15).

Lydia's name appears in Scripture only twice. She was seemingly the first Gentile convert in Europe, the first Christian businesswoman, and the first believer to open her home as a worship center for European Christians. Not only to Paul and the early church but also to the generations to come, Lydia proved the importance and influence of a woman of determination, foresight, and generosity.

See also Acts 16:40; notes on Employment (Eccl. 9); Feminine Leadership (1 Sam. 25)

---

sharp that they parted from one another. And so Barnabas took Mark and sailed to Cyprus; ⁴⁰but Paul chose Silas and departed, being commended by the brethren to the grace of God. ⁴¹And he went through Syria and Cilicia, strengthening the churches.

Timothy Joins Paul and Silas

16 Then he came to Derbe and Lystra. And behold, a certain disciple was there, named Timothy, *the* son of a certain Jewish woman who believed, but his father *was* Greek. ²He was well spoken of by the brethren who were at Lystra and Iconium. ³Paul wanted to have him go on with him. And he took *him* and circumcised him because of the Jews who were in that region, for they all knew that his father was Greek. ⁴And as they went through the cities, they delivered to them the decrees to keep, which were determined by

the apostles and elders at Jerusalem. ⁵So the churches were strengthened in the faith, and increased in number daily.

The Macedonian Call

⁶Now when they had gone through Phrygia and the region of Galatia, they were forbidden by the Holy Spirit to preach the word in Asia. ⁷After they had come to Mysia, they tried to go into Bithynia, but the Spiritᵃ did not permit them. ⁸So passing by Mysia, they came down to Troas. ⁹And a vision appeared to Paul in the night. A man of Macedonia stood and pleaded with him, saying, "Come over to Macedonia and help us." ¹⁰Now after he had seen the vision, immediately we sought to go to Macedonia, concluding that the Lord had called us to preach the gospel to them.

16:7 ªNU-Text adds *of Jesus.*

16:1–3 Timothy's father was Greek and his mother Jewish. Timothy became Paul's close friend and trusted fellow worker (Phil. 2:20). Paul probably witnessed young Timothy's conversion in Lystra, and he chose Timothy to replace John Mark as his traveling companion. Because of Timothy's mixed Greek and Jewish background, Paul had the young man circumcised. Timothy represented Paul when the latter was imprisoned and could not travel. When Paul faced death in

Rome, Timothy was the one called to be with him (see 1 Timothy, Introduction: Author).

16:8 Paul passed through the province of Mysia and came to Troas, a city in northwestern Asia Minor. Troas, which Paul visited during his second and third missionary journeys, was located ten miles from the city of Troy. Under the leadership of Emperor Augustus, Troas became a Roman colony and a highly valued seaport.

Christ does not force our will. He only takes what we give Him. But He does give Himself entirely until He sees that we yield ourselves entirely to Him.

St. Teresa of Avila

Lydia Baptized at Philippi

[11]Therefore, sailing from Troas, we ran a straight course to Samothrace, and the next *day* came to Neapolis, [12]and from there to Philippi, which is the foremost city of that part of Macedonia, a colony. And we were staying in that city for some days. [13]And on the Sabbath day we went out of the city to the riverside, where prayer was customarily made; and we sat down and spoke to the women who met *there.* [14]Now a certain woman named Lydia heard *us.* She was a seller of purple from the city of Thyatira, who worshiped God. The Lord opened her heart to heed the things spoken by Paul. [15]And when she and her household were baptized, she begged *us,* saying, "If you have judged me to be faithful to the Lord, come to my house and stay." So she persuaded us.

Paul and Silas Imprisoned

[16]Now it happened, as we went to prayer, that a certain slave girl possessed with a spirit of divination met us, who brought her masters much profit by fortune-telling. [17]This girl followed Paul and us, and cried out, saying, "These men are the servants of the Most High God, who proclaim to us the way of salvation." [18]And this she did for many days.

But Paul, greatly annoyed, turned and said to the spirit, "I command you in the name of Jesus Christ to come out of her." And he came out that very hour. [19]But when her masters saw that their hope of profit was gone, they seized Paul and Silas and dragged *them* into the marketplace to the authorities.

[20]And they brought them to the magistrates, and said, "These men, being Jews, exceedingly trouble our city; [21]and they teach customs which are not lawful for us, being Romans, to receive or observe." [22]Then the multitude rose up together against them; and the magistrates tore off their clothes and commanded *them* to be beaten with rods. [23]And when they had laid many stripes on them, they threw *them* into prison, commanding the jailer to keep them securely. [24]Having received such a charge, he put them into the inner prison and fastened their feet in the stocks.

The Philippian Jailer Saved

[25]But at midnight Paul and Silas were praying and singing hymns to God, and the prisoners were listening to them. [26]Suddenly there was a great earthquake, so that the foundations of the prison were shaken; and immediately all the doors were opened and everyone's chains were loosed. [27]And the keeper of the prison, awaking from sleep and seeing the prison doors open, supposing the prisoners had fled, drew his sword and was about to kill himself. [28]But Paul called with a loud voice, saying, "Do yourself no harm, for we are all here."

[29]Then he called for a light, ran in, and fell down trembling before Paul and Silas. [30]And he brought them out and said, "Sirs, what must I do to be saved?"

[31]So they said, "Believe on the Lord Jesus Christ, and you will be saved, you and your household." [32]Then they spoke the word of the Lord to him and to all who were in his house. [33]And he took them the same hour of the night and washed *their* stripes. And immediately he and all his *family* were baptized. [34]Now when he had brought them into his house, he set food before them; and he rejoiced, having believed in God with all his household.

Paul Refuses to Depart Secretly

[35]And when it was day, the magistrates sent the officers, saying, "Let those men go."

[36]So the keeper of the prison reported these words to Paul, saying, "The magistrates have sent to let you go. Now therefore depart, and go in peace."

[37]But Paul said to them, "They have beaten us openly, uncondemned Romans, *and* have thrown *us* into prison. And now do they put us out secretly? No indeed! Let them come themselves and get us out."

[38]And the officers told these words to the magistrates, and they were afraid when they heard that they were Romans. [39]Then they came and pleaded with them and brought *them* out, and asked *them* to depart from the city. [40]So they went out of the prison and entered *the house of* Lydia; and when they had seen the brethren, they encouraged them and departed.

Preaching Christ at Thessalonica

17 Now when they had passed through Amphipolis and Apollonia, they came to Thessalonica, where there was a synagogue of the Jews. [2]Then Paul, as his custom was, went in to them,

---

17:1 Paul and Silas passed through Amphipolis, a city near the Aegean Gulf, on their way to Thessalonica. Apollonia was about 30 miles beyond Amphipolis, and Thessalonica was still 38 miles farther. The cosmopolitan city of Thessalonica,

THE FORTUNE-TELLING SLAVE

Divination was widely practiced in the ancient Middle East. This attempt to contact supernatural powers sought unknown answers that usually foretold the future. The Old Testament strongly condemns such practices (see Lev. 19:26; Jer. 27:9).

Paul and Silas had come to preach in Philippi where they met a fortune teller. We know her only as a "certain slave girl possessed with a spirit of divination." Luke recognized her phenomena as being identical to those of the priestesses of Delphi. In other words, she was not seen as merely a lunatic or skillful ventriloquist but was indeed possessed of a demonic spirit, giving her extraordinary powers to predict the future, which was strictly forbidden (see Lev. 19:31). Her masters used and abused her, receiving much money from her fortune-telling, especially by making her answer those with problems and difficulties who were more vulnerable to such deception.

The girl followed Paul and Silas for days, crying out loudly and hindering their ministry. Annoyed, Paul exorcised the problem-causing demonic spirit from the girl's body. Deprived of their potential gain, her masters dragged Paul and Silas into the marketplace and had them beaten and imprisoned.

In prison, however, Paul and Silas witnessed the power of the living Christ. Not only were they miraculously delivered, but the keeper of the prison and his entire family were saved and baptized.

Acts mentions no more about the fortune-telling slave girl. However, her testimony stands forever to prove that God can bring glory even out of the most harsh and unfair situations.

See also notes on The Occult (Deut. 18); Witchcraft (1 Sam. 15)

and for three Sabbaths reasoned with them from the Scriptures, [3]explaining and demonstrating that the Christ had to suffer and rise again from the dead, and *saying*, "This Jesus whom I preach to you is the Christ." [4]And some of them were persuaded; and a great multitude of the devout Greeks, and not a few of the leading women, joined Paul and Silas.

Assault on Jason's House

[5]But the Jews who were not persuaded, becoming envious,[a] took some of the evil men from the marketplace, and gathering a mob, set all the city in an uproar and attacked the house of Jason, and sought to bring them out to the people. [6]But when they did not find them, they dragged Jason and some brethren to the rulers of the city, crying out, "These who have turned the world upside down have come here too. [7]Jason has harbored them, and these are all acting contrary to the decrees of Caesar, saying there is another king—Jesus." [8]And they troubled the crowd and the rulers of the city when they heard these things. [9]So when they had taken security from Jason and the rest, they let them go.

Ministering at Berea

[10]Then the brethren immediately sent Paul and Silas away by night to Berea. When they arrived,

they went into the synagogue of the Jews. [11]These were more fair-minded than those in Thessalonica, in that they received the word with all readiness, and searched the Scriptures daily *to find out* whether these things were so. [12]Therefore many of them believed, and also not a few of the Greeks, prominent women as well as men. [13]But when the Jews from Thessalonica learned that the word of God was preached by Paul at Berea, they came there also and stirred up the crowds. [14]Then immediately the brethren sent Paul away, to go to the sea; but both Silas and Timothy remained there. [15]So those who conducted Paul brought him to Athens; and receiving a command for Silas and Timothy to come to him with all speed, they departed.

The Philosophers at Athens

[16]Now while Paul waited for them at Athens, his spirit was provoked within him when he saw that the city was given over to idols. [17]Therefore he reasoned in the synagogue with the Jews and with the *Gentile* worshipers, and in the marketplace daily with those who happened to be there. [18]Then[a] certain Epicurean and Stoic philosophers encountered him. And some said, "What does this babbler want to say?"

··

17:5 [a]NU-Text omits *who were not persuaded;* M-Text omits *becoming envious.*   17:18 [a]NU-Text and M-Text add *also.*

founded by a general of Alexander the Great and located on the Thermaic Gulf, was one of the important commercial centers of Greece.

17:15, 16 Paul preached to the Greek philosophers in Athens. Few people were won to Christ, and no viable church seems to

have been established there at the time of Paul's visit. Named for Athena, the goddess of wisdom, this ancient city was originally settled before 3000 B.C. (see chart, Graeco-Roman Goddesses). Paul preached to the extremely religious Athenians from the Areopagus, a hill about 370 feet high near the Acropolis (v. 19).

PAUL'S SECOND MISSIONARY JOURNEY

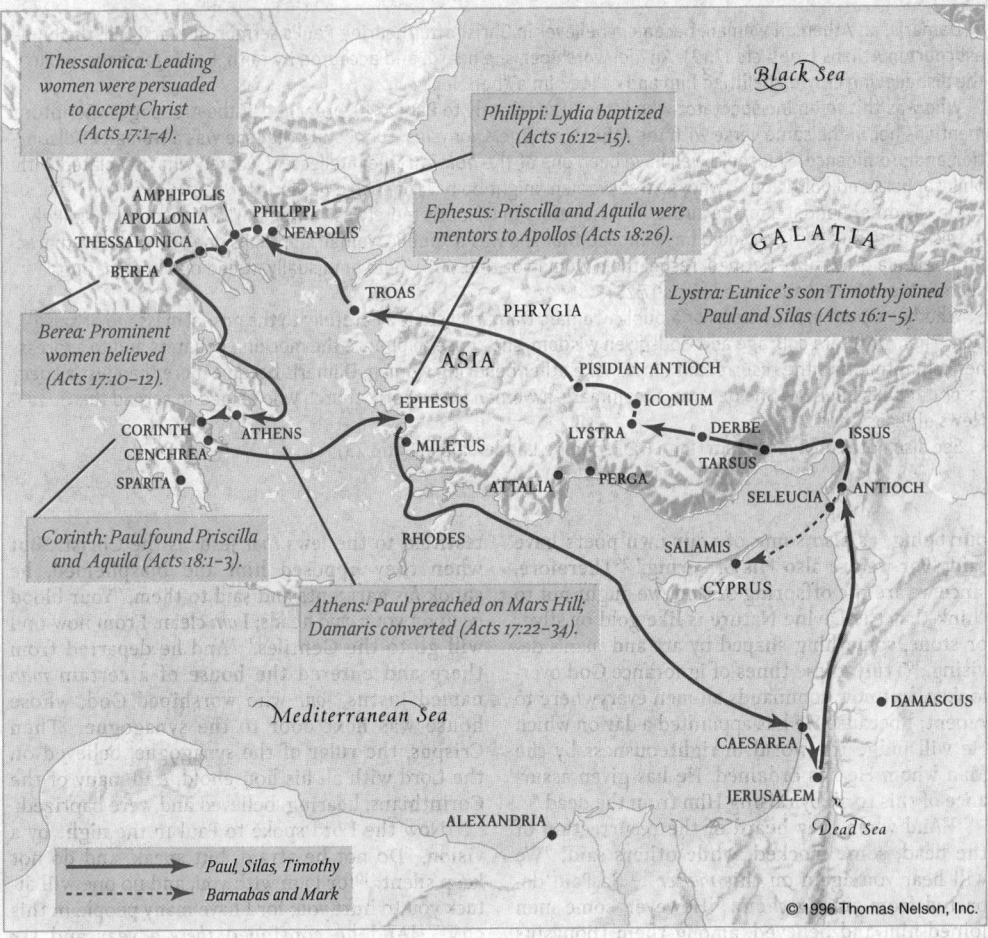

Thessalonica: Leading women were persuaded to accept Christ (Acts 17:1–4).

Philippi: Lydia baptized (Acts 16:12–15).

Ephesus: Priscilla and Aquila were mentors to Apollos (Acts 18:26).

Lystra: Eunice's son Timothy joined Paul and Silas (Acts 16:1–5).

Berea: Prominent women believed (Acts 17:10–12).

Corinth: Paul found Priscilla and Aquila (Acts 18:1–3).

Athens: Paul preached on Mars Hill; Damaris converted (Acts 17:22–34).

Black Sea

GALATIA

PHRYGIA

ASIA

Mediterranean Sea

Dead Sea

AMPHIPOLIS
APOLLONIA
THESSALONICA
BEREA
PHILIPPI
NEAPOLIS
TROAS
PISIDIAN ANTIOCH
EPHESUS
ICONIUM
CORINTH
ATHENS
LYSTRA
DERBE
ISSUS
CENCHREA
MILETUS
TARSUS
SPARTA
ATTALIA
PERGA
SELEUCIA
ANTIOCH
RHODES
SALAMIS
CYPRUS
DAMASCUS
CAESAREA
JERUSALEM
ALEXANDRIA

→ Paul, Silas, Timothy
⇢ Barnabas and Mark

© 1996 Thomas Nelson, Inc.

Others said, "He seems to be a proclaimer of foreign gods," because he preached to them Jesus and the resurrection.

[19]And they took him and brought him to the Areopagus, saying, "May we know what this new doctrine *is* of which you speak? [20]For you are bringing some strange things to our ears. Therefore we want to know what these things mean." [21]For all the Athenians and the foreigners who were there spent their time in nothing else but either to tell or to hear some new thing.

Addressing the Areopagus

[22]Then Paul stood in the midst of the Areopagus and said, "Men of Athens, I perceive that in all things you are very religious; [23]for as I was passing through and considering the objects of your worship, I even found an altar with this inscription:

TO THE UNKNOWN GOD.

Therefore, the One whom you worship without knowing, Him I proclaim to you: [24]God, who made the world and everything in it, since He is Lord of heaven and earth, does not dwell in temples made with hands. [25]Nor is He worshiped with men's hands, as though He needed anything, since He gives to all life, breath, and all things. [26]And He has made from one blood[a] every nation of men to dwell on all the face of the earth, and has determined their preappointed times and the boundaries of their dwellings, [27]so that they should seek the Lord, in the hope that they might grope for Him and find Him, though He is not far from each one of us; [28]for in Him we live and move and have

---

17:26 [a]NU-Text omits *blood.*

DAMARIS   *A Courageous Believer*

Damaris, an Athenian woman, became a believer in Christ after hearing Paul's sermon at Mars' Hill, the highest court in Athens (see Acts 17:19). An idol worshiper, she heard, and accepted by faith, Paul's message, while the disbelieving crowds belittled him and called him a "babbler."

Who was this feminine spectator who listened so intently to Paul as he preached at the Areopagus? Scripture mentions her in the same verse with the Athenian judge, Dionysius, suggesting that she was a woman of distinction and prominence. She could well have been one of the *hetairai* (the intellectual women who associated with philosophers and politicians), who, as free women, might be part of such a gathering.

On the other hand, Luke, the author of Acts refers to Damaris merely as "a woman," which, though unlikely in this setting and context, could have implied that she was a "public woman," perhaps one of low moral character or even a prostitute. Refined, respectable women of that day would not usually attend public gatherings such as the one Paul addressed (Acts 17:22).

Whether a prominent woman or a public woman, Damaris listened carefully to the gospel message of salvation. Then with rare courage and God-given wisdom, she chose to oppose the mocking debaters and to express her commitment to the resurrected Christ. Like other believing women, Damaris became more than just a spectator of Paul's ministry. She became a teammate, a woman in the early church who helped to spread the Good News of Jesus Christ.

See also notes on Evangelism (John 6); Feminine Leadership (1 Sam. 25)

---

our being, as also some of your own poets have said, 'For we are also His offspring.' [29]Therefore, since we are the offspring of God, we ought not to think that the Divine Nature is like gold or silver or stone, something shaped by art and man's devising. [30]Truly, these times of ignorance God overlooked, but now commands all men everywhere to repent, [31]because He has appointed a day on which He will judge the world in righteousness by the Man whom He has ordained. He has given assurance of this to all by raising Him from the dead."

[32]And when they heard of the resurrection of the dead, some mocked, while others said, "We will hear you again on this *matter*." [33]So Paul departed from among them. [34]However, some men joined him and believed, among them Dionysius the Areopagite, a woman named Damaris, and others with them.

Ministering at Corinth

18After these things Paul departed from Athens and went to Corinth. [2]And he found a certain Jew named Aquila, born in Pontus, who had recently come from Italy with his wife Priscilla (because Claudius had commanded all the Jews to depart from Rome); and he came to them. [3]So, because he was of the same trade, he stayed with them and worked; for by occupation they were tentmakers. [4]And he reasoned in the synagogue every Sabbath, and persuaded both Jews and Greeks.

[5]When Silas and Timothy had come from Macedonia, Paul was compelled by the Spirit, and testified to the Jews *that* Jesus *is* the Christ. [6]But when they opposed him and blasphemed, he shook *his* garments and said to them, "Your blood *be* upon your *own* heads; I *am* clean. From now on I will go to the Gentiles." [7]And he departed from there and entered the house of a certain *man* named Justus,[a] one who worshiped God, whose house was next door to the synagogue. [8]Then Crispus, the ruler of the synagogue, believed on the Lord with all his household. And many of the Corinthians, hearing, believed and were baptized.

[9]Now the Lord spoke to Paul in the night by a vision, "Do not be afraid, but speak, and do not keep silent; [10]for I am with you, and no one will attack you to hurt you; for I have many people in this city." [11]And he continued *there* a year and six months, teaching the word of God among them.

[12]When Gallio was proconsul of Achaia, the Jews with one accord rose up against Paul and brought him to the judgment seat, [13]saying, "This *fellow* persuades men to worship God contrary to the law."

[14]And when Paul was about to open *his* mouth, Gallio said to the Jews, "If it were a matter of wrongdoing or wicked crimes, O Jews, there would be reason why I should bear with you. [15]But if it is a question of words and names and your own law, look *to it* yourselves; for I do not want to be a judge of such *matters*." [16]And he drove them from the judgment seat. [17]Then all the Greeks[a] took

18:7 [a]NU-Text reads *Titius Justus*.   18:17 [a]NU-Text reads *they all*.

18:17 Sosthenes was ruler of the synagogue in Corinth. Crispus, who had become a Christian, was the former ruler. When the proconsul Gallio would not take sides and prosecute Paul,

the Jews incited a mob that angrily took revenge by beating Sosthenes.

PRISCILLA   *A Respected Christian Leader*

Priscilla, whom Paul usually called by her more formal name, Prisca, was his valued "fellow worker" (Rom. 16:3). As a Jewess who had come out of Rome, she and her husband Aquila were deeply involved in the spread of the gospel. Her name unexpectedly precedes her husband's in three of the six references to them (Acts 18:18; Rom. 16:3; 2 Tim. 4:19). This may have indicated that she belonged to a higher social class than Aquila, or it could have designated her as the more active of the two in Christian service. It could have merely been an expression of deference toward Priscilla as a woman.

When Paul arrived in Corinth in late A.D. 50, he worked with this dynamic couple in their tentmaking business (Acts 18:3). They had recently been forced to relocate from Rome, due to the emperor's edict expelling all Jews. Likely Priscilla and Aquila were already Christians since Paul described Stephanas and his household as the first converts in Corinth (1 Cor. 16:15). In any case, as they worked together in the shop and in evangelistic outreach, Priscilla and Aquila had the priceless opportunity to be taught and trained personally by the apostle Paul.

When Paul left Corinth a year and a half later (Acts 18:11), Priscilla and Aquila accompanied him as far as Ephesus (Acts 18:18, 19). For several years they were leaders in the Ephesian church. In addition to leading a house church (1 Cor. 16:19), they had a significant ministry to Apollos. Although an eloquent speaker, Apollos had some serious gaps in his understanding of the Christian message. Priscilla and Aquila wisely took Apollos aside privately and, with extraordinary wisdom, tact, and courage, lovingly gave him a thorough, step-by-step explanation of Christian doctrine (Acts 18:26).

Sometime after Paul's visit in A.D. 57, Priscilla and Aquila returned to Rome, for Paul later sends special greetings to them and to the members of the house church that they led (Rom. 16:3, 4). Interestingly, he also mentioned a time when they risked their lives to save his, possibly at the time of the Ephesian riot (Acts 19:23–41). From Rome they evidently returned to Ephesus, for the last mention of this dedicated Christian couple comes at the very end of Paul's life, when he greeted them in his last letter to Timothy (2 Tim. 4:19).

Priscilla presented a picture of a strong, competent woman who was actively involved in Christian ministry. Though she managed her household and pursued a trade, she found time to gain a thorough understanding of Scripture, and she was obviously adept in teaching. As a well-respected leader in the early church, she was also noted for her hospitality. She worked side-by-side with her husband, and together they made a significant contribution to the spread of the gospel in the early decades.

See also Acts 18:18, 26; Rom. 16:3–4; 1 Cor. 16:19; 2 Tim. 4:19; notes on Feminine Leadership (1 Sam. 25); Women's Ministries (1 Tim. 3)

Sosthenes, the ruler of the synagogue, and beat *him* before the judgment seat. But Gallio took no notice of these things.

Paul Returns to Antioch

¹⁸So Paul still remained a good while. Then he took leave of the brethren and sailed for Syria, and Priscilla and Aquila *were* with him. He had *his* hair cut off at Cenchrea, for he had taken a vow. ¹⁹And he came to Ephesus, and left them there; but he himself entered the synagogue and reasoned with the Jews. ²⁰When they asked *him* to stay a longer time with them, he did not consent, ²¹but took leave of them, saying, "I must by all means keep this coming feast in Jerusalem;ᵃ but I will return again to you, God willing." And he sailed from Ephesus.

²²And when he had landed at Caesarea, and gone up and greeted the church, he went down to Antioch. ²³After he had spent some time *there*, he departed and went over the region of Galatia and Phrygia in order, strengthening all the disciples.

Ministry of Apollos

²⁴Now a certain Jew named Apollos, born at Alexandria, an eloquent man *and* mighty in the Scriptures, came to Ephesus. ²⁵This man had been instructed in the way of the Lord; and being fervent in spirit, he spoke and taught accurately the things of the Lord, though he knew only the baptism of John. ²⁶So he began to speak boldly in the

18:21 ᵃNU-Text omits *I must* through *Jerusalem.*

18:19 Ephesus, an important city in Asia Minor, played a major part in the spread of early Christianity. Located at the mouth of the Cayster River, this commercial seaport flourished along the major overland trade route. The city was under Roman control at the time of Paul and was the fourth largest city in the known world.

18:24 Apollos was an Alexandrian Jew who became an influential minister and powerful preacher. Priscilla and Aquila taught him Christian doctrine in Ephesus. Paul stayed in Ephesus almost three years, longer than he stayed anywhere.

The longest foot in the world is the distance between the mind and the heart, unless bridged by the Holy Spirit.

Claudine Boutros

---

synagogue. When Aquila and Priscilla heard him, they took him aside and explained to him the way of God more accurately. [27]And when he desired to cross to Achaia, the brethren wrote, exhorting the disciples to receive him; and when he arrived, he greatly helped those who had believed through grace; [28]for he vigorously refuted the Jews publicly, showing from the Scriptures that Jesus is the Christ.

Paul at Ephesus

19 And it happened, while Apollos was at Corinth, that Paul, having passed through the upper regions, came to Ephesus. And finding some disciples [2]he said to them, "Did you receive the Holy Spirit when you believed?"

So they said to him, "We have not so much as heard whether there is a Holy Spirit."

[3]And he said to them, "Into what then were you baptized?"

So they said, "Into John's baptism."

[4]Then Paul said, "John indeed baptized with a baptism of repentance, saying to the people that they should believe on Him who would come after him, that is, on Christ Jesus."

[5]When they heard *this*, they were baptized in the name of the Lord Jesus. [6]And when Paul had laid hands on them, the Holy Spirit came upon them, and they spoke with tongues and prophesied. [7]Now the men were about twelve in all.

[8]And he went into the synagogue and spoke boldly for three months, reasoning and persuading concerning the things of the kingdom of God. [9]But when some were hardened and did not believe, but spoke evil of the Way before the multitude, he departed from them and withdrew the disciples, reasoning daily in the school of Tyrannus. [10]And this continued for two years, so that all who dwelt in Asia heard the word of the Lord Jesus, both Jews and Greeks.

Miracles Glorify Christ

[11]Now God worked unusual miracles by the hands of Paul, [12]so that even handkerchiefs or aprons were brought from his body to the sick, and the diseases left them and the evil spirits

went out of them. [13]Then some of the itinerant Jewish exorcists took it upon themselves to call the name of the Lord Jesus over those who had evil spirits, saying, "We[a] exorcise you by the Jesus whom Paul preaches." [14]Also there were seven sons of Sceva, a Jewish chief priest, who did so.

[15]And the evil spirit answered and said, "Jesus I know, and Paul I know; but who are you?"

[16]Then the man in whom the evil spirit was leaped on them, overpowered[a] them, and prevailed against them,[b] so that they fled out of that house naked and wounded. [17]This became known both to all Jews and Greeks dwelling in Ephesus; and fear fell on them all, and the name of the Lord Jesus was magnified. [18]And many who had believed came confessing and telling their deeds. [19]Also, many of those who had practiced magic brought their books together and burned *them* in the sight of all. And they counted up the value of them, and *it* totaled fifty thousand *pieces* of silver. [20]So the word of the Lord grew mightily and prevailed.

The Riot at Ephesus

[21]When these things were accomplished, Paul purposed in the Spirit, when he had passed through Macedonia and Achaia, to go to Jerusalem, saying, "After I have been there, I must also see Rome." [22]So he sent into Macedonia two of those who ministered to him, Timothy and Erastus, but he himself stayed in Asia for a time.

[23]And about that time there arose a great commotion about the Way. [24]For a certain man named Demetrius, a silversmith, who made silver shrines of Diana,[a] brought no small profit to the craftsmen. [25]He called them together with the workers of similar occupation, and said: "Men, you know that we have our prosperity by this trade. [26]Moreover you see and hear that not only at Ephesus, but throughout almost all Asia, this Paul has persuaded and turned away many people, saying that they are not gods which are made with hands. [27]So not only is this trade of ours in danger of falling

•••••••••••••••••••••••••••••

19:13 [a]NU-Text reads *I.* 19:16 [a]M-Text reads *and they overpowered.*
[b]NU-Text reads *both of them.* 19:24 [a]Greek *Artemis*

19:9 Although little is known about Tyrannus, his school in Ephesus was well-known in its day. Tyrannus was a philosopher, a man who had authority. When Jewish opposition forced Paul to stop preaching at the synagogue, Paul

preached for two years at the school or lecture hall of Tyrannus. While in Ephesus, Paul wrote the first Epistle to the Corinthians.

GRAECO-ROMAN GODDESSES

NAME	DESCRIPTION
Aphrodite (Greek) (see Venus)	Goddess of sexual love and beauty; identified with Semitic (Phoenician) goddess Ishtar/Astarte; temple in Corinth supposedly employed a thousand cultic prostitutes, contributing to city's immorality
Artemis (Greek) (see Diana)	Daughter of Leto and Zeus; sister of Apollo; goddess of fertility; mother goddess of Asia Minor; helper of women in childbirth; giver of gentle death to women; her temple was one of the seven wonders of the world and the object of pilgrimage; represented in sculpture as female figure with multiple breasts; Paul encountered her devotees in Ephesus ("Diana," Acts 19:21–40)
Athena (Greek) (see Minerva)	Guardian and namesake of Athens; goddess of wisdom, fertility, and war
Cybele (Roman)	Mother-earth; known as "the Great Mother"
Demeter (Greek) (see Ceres)	Goddess of grain and changing seasons; guardian of marriage
Diana (Roman) (see Artemis)	Goddess of fertility; goddess of the moon, hunting, wild animals, and virginity (see Acts 19:21–40); Paul encountered her devotees in Ephesus (Acts 19:21–40)
Hera (Greek) (see Juno)	Wife of Zeus; goddess of women, marriage, and motherhood
Hestia (Greek) (see Vesta)	Goddess of the hearth, the center of home and family
Juno (Roman) (see Hera)	Wife of Jupiter; goddess of women; goddess of the rainbow; queen of the gods
Minerva (Roman) (see Athena)	Goddess of wisdom, fertility, and war
Venus (Roman) (see Aphrodite)	Daughter of Jupiter; wife of Vulcan; mother of Cupid; goddess of love and beauty
Vesta (see Hestia)	Goddess of the hearth, the center of home and family
Ceres (Roman) (see Demeter)	Daughter of Saturn and Rhea; mother of Proserpine, who became the wife of Pluto; queen of the Dead; goddess of agriculture

Note: The Greeks and Romans had many comparable deities, though those related would not be considered exactly the same. Graeco-Roman gods mentioned in the New Testament include: Hermes (Acts 14:12), Mars (Acts 17:22), Zeus (Acts 14:12, 13). The name of Hades, the Greek god of the underworld, was assigned to the abode of the dead in the New Testament (Matt. 11:23; Luke 10:15).

You must give to the Bible attention with intention, and it is intention that will necessitate attention. . . . We must know what we are about.

Henrietta Mears

into disrepute, but also the temple of the great goddess Diana may be despised and her magnificence destroyed,ᵃ whom all Asia and the world worship."

²⁸Now when they heard *this*, they were full of wrath and cried out, saying, "Great *is* Diana of the Ephesians!" ²⁹So the whole city was filled with confusion, and rushed into the theater with one accord, having seized Gaius and Aristarchus, Macedonians, Paul's travel companions. ³⁰And when Paul wanted to go in to the people, the disciples would not allow him. ³¹Then some of the officials of Asia, who were his friends, sent to him pleading that he would not venture into the theater. ³²Some therefore cried one thing and some another, for the assembly was confused, and most of them did not know why they had come together. ³³And they drew Alexander out of the multitude, the Jews putting him forward. And Alexander motioned with his hand, and wanted to make his defense to the people. ³⁴But when they found out that he was a Jew, all with one voice cried out for about two hours, "Great *is* Diana of the Ephesians!"

³⁵And when the city clerk had quieted the crowd, he said: "Men of Ephesus, what man is there who does not know that the city of the Ephesians is temple guardian of the great goddess Diana, and of the *image* which fell down from Zeus? ³⁶Therefore, since these things cannot be denied, you ought to be quiet and do nothing rashly. ³⁷For you have brought these men here who are neither robbers of temples nor blasphemers of yourᵃ goddess. ³⁸Therefore, if Demetrius and his fellow craftsmen have a case against anyone, the courts are open and there are proconsuls. Let them bring charges against one another. ³⁹But if you have any other inquiry to make, it shall be determined in the lawful assembly. ⁴⁰For we are in danger of being called in question for today's uproar, there being no reason which we may give to account for this disorderly gathering." ⁴¹And when he had said these things, he dismissed the assembly.

Journeys in Greece

20 After the uproar had ceased, Paul called the disciples to *himself*, embraced *them*, and departed to go to Macedonia. ²Now when he had gone over that region and encouraged them with many words, he came to Greece ³and stayed three months. And when the Jews plotted against him as he was about to sail to Syria, he decided to return

through Macedonia. ⁴And Sopater of Berea accompanied him to Asia—also Aristarchus and Secundus of the Thessalonians, and Gaius of Derbe, and Timothy, and Tychicus and Trophimus of Asia. ⁵These men, going ahead, waited for us at Troas. ⁶But we sailed away from Philippi after the Days of Unleavened Bread, and in five days joined them at Troas, where we stayed seven days.

Ministering at Troas

⁷Now on the first *day* of the week, when the disciples came together to break bread, Paul, ready to depart the next day, spoke to them and continued his message until midnight. ⁸There were many lamps in the upper room where theyᵃ were gathered together. ⁹And in a window sat a certain young man named Eutychus, who was sinking into a deep sleep. He was overcome by sleep; and as Paul continued speaking, he fell down from the third story and was taken up dead. ¹⁰But Paul went down, fell on him, and embracing *him* said, "Do not trouble yourselves, for his life is in him." ¹¹Now when he had come up, had broken bread and eaten, and talked a long while, even till daybreak, he departed. ¹²And they brought the young man in alive, and they were not a little comforted.

From Troas to Miletus

¹³Then we went ahead to the ship and sailed to Assos, there intending to take Paul on board; for so he had given orders, intending himself to go on foot. ¹⁴And when he met us at Assos, we took him on board and came to Mitylene. ¹⁵We sailed from there, and the next *day* came opposite Chios. The following *day* we arrived at Samos and stayed at Trogyllium. The next *day* we came to Miletus. ¹⁶For Paul had decided to sail past Ephesus, so that he would not have to spend time in Asia; for he was hurrying to be at Jerusalem, if possible, on the Day of Pentecost.

The Ephesian Elders Exhorted

¹⁷From Miletus he sent to Ephesus and called for the elders of the church. ¹⁸And when they had come to him, he said to them: "You know, from the first day that I came to Asia, in what manner I always lived among you, ¹⁹serving the Lord with all humility, with many tears and trials which happened to me by the plotting of the Jews; ²⁰how I

19:27 ᵃNU-Text reads *she be deposed from her magnificence.* 19:37 ᵃNU-Text reads *our.* 20:8 ᵃNU-Text and M-Text read *we.*

*The fact that I am a woman does not make me a different kind of Christian,
but the fact that I am a Christian does make me a different kind of woman.*

Elisabeth Elliot

kept back nothing that was helpful, but proclaimed it to you, and taught you publicly and from house to house, 21testifying to Jews, and also to Greeks, repentance toward God and faith toward our Lord Jesus Christ. 22And see, now I go bound in the spirit to Jerusalem, not knowing the things that will happen to me there, 23except that the Holy Spirit testifies in every city, saying that chains and tribulations await me. 24But none of these things move me; nor do I count my life dear to myself,a so that I may finish my race with joy, and the ministry which I received from the Lord Jesus, to testify to the gospel of the grace of God.

25"And indeed, now I know that you all, among whom I have gone preaching the kingdom of God, will see my face no more. 26Therefore I testify to you this day that I *am* innocent of the blood of all *men.* 27For I have not shunned to declare to you the whole counsel of God. 28Therefore take heed to yourselves and to all the flock, among which the Holy Spirit has made you overseers, to shepherd the church of Goda which He purchased with His own blood. 29For I know this, that after my departure savage wolves will come in among you, not sparing the flock. 30Also from among yourselves men will rise up, speaking perverse things, to draw away the disciples after themselves. 31Therefore watch, and remember that for three years I did not cease to warn everyone night and day with tears.

32"So now, brethren, I commend you to God and to the word of His grace, which is able to build you up and give you an inheritance among all those who are sanctified. 33I have coveted no one's silver or gold or apparel. 34Yes,a you yourselves know that these hands have provided for my necessities, and for those who were with me. 35I have shown you in every way, by laboring like this, that you must support the weak. And remember the words of the Lord Jesus, that He said, 'It is more blessed to give than to receive.' "

36And when he had said these things, he knelt down and prayed with them all. 37Then they all wept freely, and fell on Paul's neck and kissed him, 38sorrowing most of all for the words which he spoke, that they would see his face no more. And they accompanied him to the ship.

Warnings on the Journey to Jerusalem

21 Now it came to pass, that when we had departed from them and set sail, running a straight course we came to Cos, the following *day* to Rhodes, and from there to Patara. 2And finding a ship sailing over to Phoenicia, we went aboard and set sail. 3When we had sighted Cyprus, we passed it on the left, sailed to Syria, and landed at Tyre; for there the ship was to unload her cargo. 4And finding disciples,a we stayed there seven days. They told Paul through the Spirit not to go up to Jerusalem. 5When we had come to the end of those days, we departed and went on our way; and they all accompanied us, with wives and children, till *we were* out of the city. And we knelt down on the shore and prayed. 6When we had taken our leave of one another, we boarded the ship, and they returned home.

7And when we had finished *our* voyage from Tyre, we came to Ptolemais, greeted the brethren, and stayed with them one day. 8On the next *day* we who were Paul's companionsa departed and came to Caesarea, and entered the house of Philip the evangelist, who was *one* of the seven, and stayed with him. 9Now this man had four virgin daughters who prophesied. 10And as we stayed many days, a certain prophet named Agabus came down from Judea. 11When he had come to us, he took Paul's belt, bound his *own* hands and feet, and said, "Thus says the Holy Spirit, 'So shall the Jews at Jerusalem bind the man who owns this belt, and deliver *him* into the hands of the Gentiles.' "

12Now when we heard these things, both we and those from that place pleaded with him not to go up to Jerusalem. 13Then Paul answered, "What do you mean by weeping and breaking my heart? For I am ready not only to be bound, but also to die at Jerusalem for the name of the Lord Jesus."

14So when he would not be persuaded, we ceased, saying, "The will of the Lord be done."

Paul Urged to Make Peace

15And after those days we packed and went up to Jerusalem. 16Also some of the disciples from Caesarea went with us and brought with them a certain Mnason of Cyprus, an early disciple, with whom we were to lodge.

17And when we had come to Jerusalem, the

20:24 aNU-Text reads *But I do not count my life of any value or dear to myself.* 20:28 aM-Text reads *of the Lord and God.* 20:34 aNU-Text and M-Text omit *Yes.* 21:4 aNU-Text reads *the disciples.* 21:8 aNU-Text omits *who were Paul's companions.*

THE DAUGHTERS OF PHILIP

These four extraordinary women were the daughters of the evangelist Philip, who had been one of the seven disciples set apart for special service in the early church (see Acts 6:1–7). Since no mention is made of the wife and mother in this home, Philip may have been a widower whose daughters presided over his home and cared for his needs. The text does not indicate the ages of the unnamed women, though their spiritual gifts would suggest a maturity of years and wealth of experience. At least for a time the women were unmarried, having chosen celibacy or the single life, possibly because of their sense of being especially devoted to God in using their special gift (see 1 Cor. 7:25–34). The idea of a life consecrated to God in virginity was not new and had received the sanction of the Lord Himself (see Matt. 19:12).

Concerning their actual sphere of service in the early church, there is no explicit information. Their gift for "prophecy" must be interpreted harmoniously with Paul's references to this gift (see 1 Cor. 11:5; 14:1). Their ministry could have been among women, as Miriam in the Old Testament (see Ex. 15:20). Whether or not they accompanied Philip on his evangelistic excursions is not noted, but they surely would have had opportunities to share the gospel and disciple women in whatever setting they found themselves, especially in the Greek society in which they lived.

In any case, these women certainly must have been well versed in Scripture, and they worked among the leaders of the early church, sharing in the privileges of the gospel with unusual opportunities both to grow in the Lord and to make a contribution to the Kingdom.

See also Joel 2:28; Acts 2:17; note on Women's Ministries (1 Cor. 11)

brethren received us gladly. [18]On the following *day* Paul went in with us to James, and all the elders were present. [19]When he had greeted them, he told in detail those things which God had done among the Gentiles through his ministry. [20]And when they heard *it*, they glorified the Lord. And they said to him, "You see, brother, how many myriads of Jews there are who have believed, and they are all zealous for the law; [21]but they have been informed about you that you teach all the Jews who are among the Gentiles to forsake Moses, saying that they ought not to circumcise *their* children nor to walk according to the customs. [22]What then? The assembly must certainly meet, for they will[a] hear that you have come. [23]Therefore do what we tell you: We have four men who have taken a vow. [24]Take them and be purified with them, and pay their expenses so that they may shave *their* heads, and that all may know that those things of which they were informed concerning you are nothing, but *that* you yourself also walk orderly and keep the law. [25]But concerning the Gentiles who believe, we have written *and* decided that they should observe no such thing, except[a] that they should keep themselves from *things* offered to idols, from blood, from things strangled, and from sexual immorality."

Arrested in the Temple

[26]Then Paul took the men, and the next day, having been purified with them, entered the tem-

ple to announce the expiration of the days of purification, at which time an offering should be made for each one of them.

[27]Now when the seven days were almost ended, the Jews from Asia, seeing him in the temple, stirred up the whole crowd and laid hands on him, [28]crying out, "Men of Israel, help! This is the man who teaches all *men* everywhere against the people, the law, and this place; and furthermore he also brought Greeks into the temple and has defiled this holy place." [29](For they had previously[a] seen Trophimus the Ephesian with him in the city, whom they supposed that Paul had brought into the temple.)

[30]And all the city was disturbed; and the people ran together, seized Paul, and dragged him out of the temple; and immediately the doors were shut. [31]Now as they were seeking to kill him, news came to the commander of the garrison that all Jerusalem was in an uproar. [32]He immediately took soldiers and centurions, and ran down to them. And when they saw the commander and the soldiers, they stopped beating Paul. [33]Then the commander came near and took him, and commanded *him* to be bound with two chains; and he asked who he was and what he had done. [34]And some

· · · · · · · · · · · · · · · · · · · ·

21:22 [a]NU-Text reads *What then is to be done? They will certainly.*
21:25 [a]NU-Text omits *that they should observe no such thing, except.*
21:29 [a]M-Text omits *previously.*

21:28, 29 Trophimus was a Gentile from Ephesus. Taking a Gentile into the temple would bring defilement, and the Asian Jews assumed Paul had taken Trophimus into the temple.

PAUL'S THIRD MISSIONARY JOURNEY

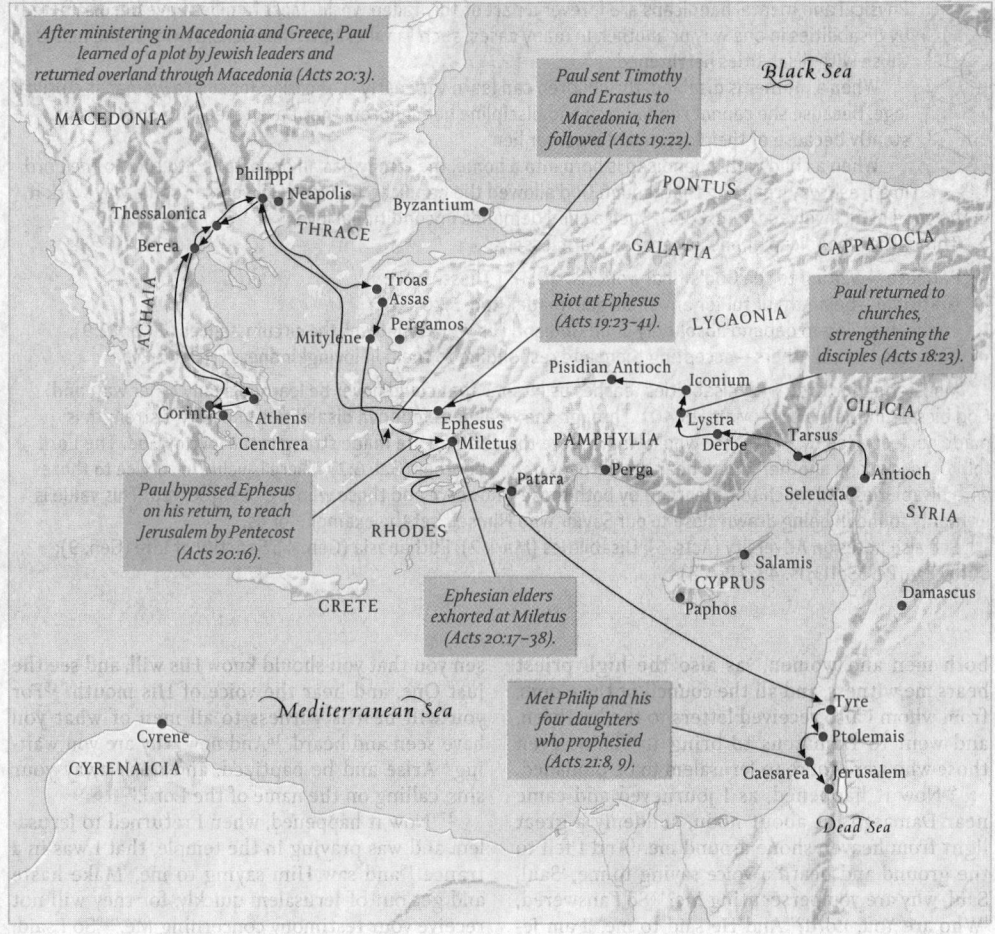

After ministering in Macedonia and Greece, Paul learned of a plot by Jewish leaders and returned overland through Macedonia (Acts 20:3).

Paul sent Timothy and Erastus to Macedonia, then followed (Acts 19:22).

Riot at Ephesus (Acts 19:23–41).

Paul returned to churches, strengthening the disciples (Acts 18:23).

Paul bypassed Ephesus on his return, to reach Jerusalem by Pentecost (Acts 20:16).

Ephesian elders exhorted at Miletus (Acts 20:17-38).

Met Philip and his four daughters who prophesied (Acts 21:8, 9).

among the multitude cried one thing and some another.

So when he could not ascertain the truth because of the tumult, he commanded him to be taken into the barracks. ³⁵When he reached the stairs, he had to be carried by the soldiers because of the violence of the mob. ³⁶For the multitude of the people followed after, crying out, "Away with him!"

Addressing the Jerusalem Mob

³⁷Then as Paul was about to be led into the barracks, he said to the commander, "May I speak to you?"

He replied, "Can you speak Greek? ³⁸Are you not the Egyptian who some time ago stirred up a rebellion and led the four thousand assassins out into the wilderness?"

³⁹But Paul said, "I am a Jew from Tarsus, in Cilicia, a citizen of no mean city; and I implore you, permit me to speak to the people."

⁴⁰So when he had given him permission, Paul stood on the stairs and motioned with his hand to the people. And when there was a great silence, he spoke to *them* in the Hebrew language, saying,

22 "Brethren and fathers, hear my defense before you now." ²And when they heard that he spoke to them in the Hebrew language, they kept all the more silent.

Then he said: ³"I am indeed a Jew, born in Tarsus of Cilicia, but brought up in this city at the feet of Gamaliel, taught according to the strictness of our fathers' law, and was zealous toward God as you all are today. ⁴I persecuted this Way to the death, binding and delivering into prisons

DISABILITIES · THE VALUE OF SPECIAL-NEEDS CHILDREN

Physical and mental handicaps are forever a part of this fallen world. Most families have been affected by disabilities in one way or another. In many cases, such families have their sensitivities to the needs of those with disabilities heightened.

When a mother is disabled, the children can learn very early that caring for such a woman is a privilege. Because she cannot run to catch and discipline her children, they have to learn to obey her instantly because of their love and respect for her.

When a child with a handicap is born into a home, the family has an opportunity to turn to the Lord in a fresh way, realizing that though God allowed the handicap to occur, He would in some way work it to the good of all involved (Rom. 8:28). Such a child demands unconditional love.

Through the handicap of one, others can learn lessons:

- Patience—waiting to see God's final work (Is. 40:31; 1 Thess. 5:14);
- Gratitude—being thankful for any small gain made (Eph. 5:20);
- Faith—learning to depend absolutely upon God and His Word whatever the circumstances (2 Cor. 12:9);
- Kindness toward others—accepting them and responding to them in lovingkindness (Heb. 12:2).

Ministering to those with disabilities teaches us lessons that could never be learned in any other way, and God blesses in the process (Matt. 25:40). Through the weakness found in disabilities, the Lord's strength is made perfect (Heb. 11:34). Those who lovingly serve the disabled are made strong in the love of God. The Lord told us to love one another and to bear the burdens of one another (Gal. 6:2). There is value in service to those with disabilities and much to be learned by both those who serve and those who are being served. This value is primarily found in being drawn close to our Savior who Himself set the example for us.

See also notes on Adversity (Acts. 5); Disabilities (Mark 2); Euthanasia (Gen. 4); Sanctity of Life (Gen. 9); Suffering (Ps. 33; 113; Is. 43; 1 Pet. 5)

both men and women, [5]as also the high priest bears me witness, and all the council of the elders, from whom I also received letters to the brethren, and went to Damascus to bring in chains even those who were there to Jerusalem to be punished.

[6]"Now it happened, as I journeyed and came near Damascus at about noon, suddenly a great light from heaven shone around me. [7]And I fell to the ground and heard a voice saying to me, 'Saul, Saul, why are you persecuting Me?' [8]So I answered, 'Who are You, Lord?' And He said to me, 'I am Jesus of Nazareth, whom you are persecuting.'

[9]"And those who were with me indeed saw the light and were afraid,[a] but they did not hear the voice of Him who spoke to me. [10]So I said, 'What shall I do, Lord?' And the Lord said to me, 'Arise and go into Damascus, and there you will be told all things which are appointed for you to do.' [11]And since I could not see for the glory of that light, being led by the hand of those who were with me, I came into Damascus.

[12]"Then a certain Ananias, a devout man according to the law, having a good testimony with all the Jews who dwelt there, [13]came to me; and he stood and said to me, 'Brother Saul, receive your sight.' And at that same hour I looked up at him. [14]Then he said, 'The God of our fathers has cho-

sen you that you should know His will, and see the Just One, and hear the voice of His mouth. [15]For you will be His witness to all men of what you have seen and heard. [16]And now why are you waiting? Arise and be baptized, and wash away your sins, calling on the name of the Lord.'

[17]"Now it happened, when I returned to Jerusalem and was praying in the temple, that I was in a trance [18]and saw Him saying to me, 'Make haste and get out of Jerusalem quickly, for they will not receive your testimony concerning Me.' [19]So I said, 'Lord, they know that in every synagogue I imprisoned and beat those who believe on You. [20]And when the blood of Your martyr Stephen was shed, I also was standing by consenting to his death,[a] and guarding the clothes of those who were killing him.' [21]Then He said to me, 'Depart, for I will send you far from here to the Gentiles.'"

Paul's Roman Citizenship

[22]And they listened to him until this word, and *then* they raised their voices and said, "Away with such a *fellow* from the earth, for he is not fit to live!" [23]Then, as they cried out and tore off *their*

22:9 [a]NU-Text omits *and were afraid.*   22:20 [a]NU-Text omits *to his death.*

22:23 **Throwing dust in the air** showed contempt or scorn, and here it might have been a demand for justice born out of intense anger. The mention of Gentiles stirred up the mob. The real point of contention was that Paul believed Jews and Gentiles were equal apart from the Law of Moses (see Eph. 2:11–22; 3:2–6).

> *Christianity does not offer escape from circumstances;*
> *it offers conquest of circumstances.*
>
> Jan Silvious

clothes and threw dust into the air, 24the commander ordered him to be brought into the barracks, and said that he should be examined under scourging, so that he might know why they shouted so against him. 25And as they bound him with thongs, Paul said to the centurion who stood by, "Is it lawful for you to scourge a man who is a Roman, and uncondemned?"

26When the centurion heard *that,* he went and told the commander, saying, "Take care what you do, for this man is a Roman."

27Then the commander came and said to him, "Tell me, are you a Roman?"

He said, "Yes."

28The commander answered, "With a large sum I obtained this citizenship."

And Paul said, "But I was born *a citizen.*"

29Then immediately those who were about to examine him withdrew from him; and the commander was also afraid after he found out that he was a Roman, and because he had bound him.

The Sanhedrin Divided

30The next day, because he wanted to know for certain why he was accused by the Jews, he released him from *his* bonds, and commanded the chief priests and all their council to appear, and brought Paul down and set him before them.

23 Then Paul, looking earnestly at the council, said, "Men *and* brethren, I have lived in all good conscience before God until this day." 2And the high priest Ananias commanded those who stood by him to strike him on the mouth. 3Then Paul said to him, "God will strike you, *you* whitewashed wall! For you sit to judge me according to the law, and do you command me to be struck contrary to the law?"

4And those who stood by said, "Do you revile God's high priest?"

5Then Paul said, "I did not know, brethren, that he was the high priest; for it is written, *'You shall not speak evil of a ruler of your people.'*"a

6But when Paul perceived that one part were Sadducees and the other Pharisees, he cried out in the council, "Men *and* brethren, I am a Pharisee, the son of a Pharisee; concerning the hope and resurrection of the dead I am being judged!"

7And when he had said this, a dissension arose between the Pharisees and the Sadducees; and the assembly was divided. 8For Sadducees say that there is no resurrection—and no angel or spirit; but the Pharisees confess both. 9Then there arose a loud outcry. And the scribes of the Pharisees' party arose and protested, saying, "We find no evil in this man; but if a spirit or an angel has spoken to him, let us not fight against God."a

10Now when there arose a great dissension, the commander, fearing lest Paul might be pulled to pieces by them, commanded the soldiers to go down and take him by force from among them, and bring *him* into the barracks.

The Plot Against Paul

11But the following night the Lord stood by him and said, "Be of good cheer, Paul; for as you have testified for Me in Jerusalem, so you must also bear witness at Rome."

12And when it was day, some of the Jews banded together and bound themselves under an oath, saying that they would neither eat nor drink till they had killed Paul. 13Now there were more than forty who had formed this conspiracy. 14They came to the chief priests and elders, and said, "We have bound ourselves under a great oath that we will eat nothing until we have killed Paul. 15Now

23:5 aExodus 22:28   23:9 aNU-Text omits last clause and reads *what if a spirit or an angel has spoken to him?*

24:1 The orator Tertullus opposed Paul as the prosecutor before the Roman governor of Judea, Felix (see chart, New Testament Political Rulers). He accused Paul of causing political unrest and defiling the temple. Whether he was a Jew or a Roman is uncertain, but he did possess distinctive gifts in judicial oratory. He began his speech to Felix with extreme but, no doubt, false flattery.

25:11 The new procurator, Festus, wanted to uphold Roman law, while at the same time keeping peace with the Jews who opposed Paul. Roman law provided that a citizen who believed he was not being treated justly could appeal to the emperor. Such an appeal could only be made if the person had

not already been sentenced by a lower tribunal. Except in the case of murder and other crimes, the "criminal" had to be sent to Rome for a personal audience with the emperor. Festus had no choice but to send Paul to Rome.

25:13 Herod Agrippa II, the son of Herod Agrippa I, and his sister Bernice came to Caesarea to visit Festus (see charts, The Family Tree of Herod the Great; New Testament Political Rulers). Their visit coincided with Paul's appeal to Caesar. It was rumored that the relationship between Agrippa II and Bernice was incestuous (see Bernice). Festus took this opportunity to engage Agrippa in helping him draft a written report of Paul's "crimes."

DRUSILLA   *A Shameful Beauty*

A daughter of Herod Agrippa and the younger sister of Bernice, Drusilla, a professing Jewess, may have been named for Emperor Caligula's sister. Her great-grandfather, Herod the Great, murdered Jewish baby boys in his effort to destroy the newborn Jesus, the promised Messiah.

Drusilla was a woman of rare beauty—beauty that corrupted her and led to her moral decadence. When only fourteen years old, she married King Azizus of Emessa. A year or so after her marriage, Felix, the Roman governor of Judea, persuaded Drusilla to leave Azizus and to marry him illegally.

Mentioned only once in Scripture, Drusilla was present when the imprisoned apostle Paul gave his defense of the gospel before Felix. From Paul's own lips, she heard firsthand the Good News of Jesus Christ. Drusilla, however, did not respond to Paul's message. The apostle's words so frightened Felix that, to please the Jews, the governor returned Paul to his confinement under house arrest.

Drusilla lived a shameful, wasted life. Before her forty-first birthday, she died a horrible, violent death. While she and her only child, Agrippa, were in Pompeii, Mount Vesuvius erupted, burying under burning lava Pompeii and Herculaneum, as well as Drusilla and her son.

See also notes on Adultery (Hos. 3); Sexual Immorality (Prov. 6)

you, therefore, together with the council, suggest to the commander that he be brought down to you tomorrow,[a] as though you were going to make further inquiries concerning him; but we are ready to kill him before he comes near."

16So when Paul's sister's son heard of their ambush, he went and entered the barracks and told Paul. 17Then Paul called one of the centurions to *him* and said, "Take this young man to the commander, for he has something to tell him." 18So he took him and brought *him* to the commander and said, "Paul the prisoner called me to *him* and asked *me* to bring this young man to you. He has something to say to you."

19Then the commander took him by the hand, went aside, and asked privately, "What is it that you have to tell me?"

20And he said, "The Jews have agreed to ask that you bring Paul down to the council tomorrow, as though they were going to inquire more fully about him. 21But do not yield to them, for more than forty of them lie in wait for him, men who have bound themselves by an oath that they will neither eat nor drink till they have killed him; and now they are ready, waiting for the promise from you."

22So the commander let the young man depart, and commanded *him*, "Tell no one that you have revealed these things to me."

Sent to Felix

23And he called for two centurions, saying, "Prepare two hundred soldiers, seventy horsemen, and two hundred spearmen to go to Caesarea at the third hour of the night; 24and provide mounts to set Paul on, and bring *him* safely to Felix the governor." 25He wrote a letter in the following manner:

26Claudius Lysias,

To the most excellent governor Felix:

Greetings.

27This man was seized by the Jews and was about to be killed by them. Coming with the troops I rescued him, having learned that he was a Roman. 28And when I wanted to know the reason they accused him, I brought him before their council. 29I found out that he was accused concerning questions of their law, but had nothing charged against him deserving of death or chains. 30And when it was told me that the Jews lay in wait for the man,[a] I sent him immediately to you, and also commanded his accusers to state before you the charges against him.

Farewell.

31Then the soldiers, as they were commanded, took Paul and brought *him* by night to Antipatris. 32The next day they left the horsemen to go on with him, and returned to the barracks. 33When they came to Caesarea and had delivered the letter to the governor, they also presented Paul to him. 34And when the governor had read *it*, he asked what province he was from. And when he understood that he *was* from Cilicia, 35he said, "I will hear you when your accusers also have come." And he commanded him to be kept in Herod's Praetorium.

·········· ·········· ··········

23:15 [a]NU-Text omits *tomorrow*.   23:30 [a]NU-Text reads *there would be a plot against the man*.

In the end God alone can save a nation. When God chooses to work in a nation,
He always does it through the individual choices of people.

Mary Farrar

Accused of Sedition

24 Now after five days Ananias the high priest came down with the elders and a certain orator *named* Tertullus. These gave evidence to the governor against Paul.

[2]And when he was called upon, Tertullus began his accusation, saying: "Seeing that through you we enjoy great peace, and prosperity is being brought to this nation by your foresight, [3]we accept *it* always and in all places, most noble Felix, with all thankfulness. [4]Nevertheless, not to be tedious to you any further, I beg you to hear, by your courtesy, a few words from us. [5]For we have found this man a plague, a creator of dissension among all the Jews throughout the world, and a ringleader of the sect of the Nazarenes. [6]He even tried to profane the temple, and we seized him,[a] and wanted to judge him according to our law. [7]But the commander Lysias came by and with great violence took *him* out of our hands, [8]commanding his accusers to come to you. By examining him yourself you may ascertain all these things of which we accuse him." [9]And the Jews also assented,[a] maintaining that these things were so.

The Defense Before Felix

[10]Then Paul, after the governor had nodded to him to speak, answered: "Inasmuch as I know that you have been for many years a judge of this nation, I do the more cheerfully answer for myself, [11]because you may ascertain that it is no more than twelve days since I went up to Jerusalem to worship. [12]And they neither found me in the temple disputing with anyone nor inciting the crowd, either in the synagogues or in the city. [13]Nor can they prove the things of which they now accuse me. [14]But this I confess to you, that according to the Way which they call a sect, so I worship the God of my fathers, believing all things which are written in the Law and in the Prophets. [15]I have hope in God, which they themselves also accept, that there will be a resurrection of *the* dead,[a] both of *the* just and *the* unjust. [16]This *being* so, I myself always strive to have a conscience without offense toward God and men.

[17]"Now after many years I came to bring alms and offerings to my nation, [18]in the midst of which some Jews from Asia found me purified in the temple, neither with a mob nor with tumult. [19]They ought to have been here before you to object if they had anything against me. [20]Or else let those who are *here* themselves say if they found any wrongdoing[a] in me while I stood before the council, [21]unless *it is* for this one statement which I cried out, standing among them, 'Concerning the resurrection of the dead I am being judged by you this day.' "

Felix Procrastinates

[22]But when Felix heard these things, having more accurate knowledge of *the* Way, he adjourned the proceedings and said, "When Lysias the commander comes down, I will make a decision on your case." [23]So he commanded the centurion to keep Paul and to let *him* have liberty, and told him not to forbid any of his friends to provide for or visit him.

[24]And after some days, when Felix came with his wife Drusilla, who was Jewish, he sent for Paul and heard him concerning the faith in Christ. [25]Now as he reasoned about righteousness, self-control, and the judgment to come, Felix was afraid and answered, "Go away for now; when I have a convenient time I will call for you." [26]Meanwhile he also hoped that money would be given him by Paul, that he might release him.[a] Therefore he sent for him more often and conversed with him.

[27]But after two years Porcius Festus succeeded Felix; and Felix, wanting to do the Jews a favor, left Paul bound.

Paul Appeals to Caesar

25 Now when Festus had come to the province, after three days he went up from Caesarea to Jerusalem. [2]Then the high priest[a] and the chief men of the Jews informed him against Paul; and they petitioned him, [3]asking a favor against him, that he would summon him to Jerusalem—while *they* lay in ambush along the road to kill him. [4]But Festus answered that Paul should be kept at Caesarea, and that he himself was going *there* shortly. [5]"Therefore," he said, "let those who have authority among you go down with *me* and accuse this man, to see if there is any fault in him."

[6]And when he had remained among them more

24:6 [a]NU-Text ends the sentence here and omits the rest of verse 6, all of verse 7, and the first clause of verse 8. **24:9** [a]NU-Text and M-Text read *joined the attack.* **24:15** [a]NU-Text omits *of the dead.* **24:20** [a]NU-Text and M-Text read *say what wrongdoing they found.* **24:26** [a]NU-Text omits *that he might release him.* **25:2** [a]NU-Text reads *chief priests.*

BERNICE   *An Unrepentant Sinner*

As the daughter of Herod Agrippa I and the older sister of Drusilla, Bernice was born about A.D. 28 into a racially mixed family. At age thirteen she was married to Marcus, the son of Tiberius Julius Alexander. Marcus died, and she next married her uncle, Herod of Chalcis. They had two sons, Berniceanus and Hyrancus. Widowed again about A.D. 48, Bernice was the subject of incestuous scandal when she became a consort to her own brother, Agrippa II. Years later, she married a third time to Ptolemy, king of Cicilia. The marriage, however, did not last, and she returned to her brother. She was later the mistress of the Roman emperors Vespasian and his son Titus.

Bernice, a woman of strong opinions, was once a dauntless defender of the Jewish people. Some sources report that she even risked her own life to intercede on behalf of the Jews. So strong was her faith that at one time she shaved her head and walked barefoot in keeping a vow to God. But her lifestyle pulled her away, and Bernice evidently abandoned her Jewish faith.

When Agrippa and Bernice went to Caesarea with Festus on state business, Agrippa agreed to hear the case of a prisoner, the apostle Paul. Bernice heard Paul argue his case for Christ; yet she ignored his message. Maintaining her wicked ways, Bernice died in Rome after the fall of Jerusalem. Bernice represents all those women throughout history who have heard the gospel, yet have chosen to reject Christ. She embraced a sinful life that caused the deterioration of her character—a character that could have been changed by Jesus Christ, making her useful in the Kingdom.

See also Acts 25:23; 26:30; notes on Adultery (Hos. 3); Sexual Purity (1 Cor. 7)

than ten days, he went down to Caesarea. And the next day, sitting on the judgment seat, he commanded Paul to be brought. [7]When he had come, the Jews who had come down from Jerusalem stood about and laid many serious complaints against Paul, which they could not prove, [8]while he answered for himself, "Neither against the law of the Jews, nor against the temple, nor against Caesar have I offended in anything at all."

[9]But Festus, wanting to do the Jews a favor, answered Paul and said, "Are you willing to go up to Jerusalem and there be judged before me concerning these things?"

[10]So Paul said, "I stand at Caesar's judgment seat, where I ought to be judged. To the Jews I have done no wrong, as you very well know. [11]For if I am an offender, or have committed anything deserving of death, I do not object to dying; but if there is nothing in these things of which these men accuse me, no one can deliver me to them. I appeal to Caesar."

[12]Then Festus, when he had conferred with the council, answered, "You have appealed to Caesar? To Caesar you shall go!"

Paul Before Agrippa

[13]And after some days King Agrippa and Bernice came to Caesarea to greet Festus. [14]When they had been there many days, Festus laid Paul's case before the king, saying: "There is a certain man left a prisoner by Felix, [15]about whom the chief priests and the elders of the Jews informed *me*, when I was in Jerusalem, asking for a judgment against him. [16]To them I answered, 'It is not

the custom of the Romans to deliver any man to destruction[a] before the accused meets the accusers face to face, and has opportunity to answer for himself concerning the charge against him.' [17]Therefore when they had come together, without any delay, the next day I sat on the judgment seat and commanded the man to be brought in. [18]When the accusers stood up, they brought no accusation against him of such things as I supposed, [19]but had some questions against him about their own religion and about a certain Jesus, who had died, whom Paul affirmed to be alive. [20]And because I was uncertain of such questions, I asked whether he was willing to go to Jerusalem and there be judged concerning these matters. [21]But when Paul appealed to be reserved for the decision of Augustus, I commanded him to be kept till I could send him to Caesar."

[22]Then Agrippa said to Festus, "I also would like to hear the man myself."

"Tomorrow," he said, "you shall hear him."

[23]So the next day, when Agrippa and Bernice had come with great pomp, and had entered the auditorium with the commanders and the prominent men of the city, at Festus' command Paul was brought in. [24]And Festus said: "King Agrippa and all the men who are here present with us, you see this man about whom the whole assembly of the Jews petitioned me, both at Jerusalem and here, crying out that he was not fit to live any longer. [25]But when I found that he had committed nothing deserving of death, and that he himself had

25:16 [a]NU-Text omits *to destruction*, although it is implied.

Perhaps we don't want to come face to face with the unsurrendered areas of our lives. We like our lives just as they are, even if it is less than God's best.

Sandy Smith

appealed to Augustus, I decided to send him. [26]I have nothing certain to write to my lord concerning him. Therefore I have brought him out before you, and especially before you, King Agrippa, so that after the examination has taken place I may have something to write. [27]For it seems to me unreasonable to send a prisoner and not to specify the charges against him."

Paul's Early Life

26 Then Agrippa said to Paul, "You are permitted to speak for yourself."

So Paul stretched out his hand and answered for himself: [2]"I think myself happy, King Agrippa, because today I shall answer for myself before you concerning all the things of which I am accused by the Jews, [3]especially because you are expert in all customs and questions which have to do with the Jews. Therefore I beg you to hear me patiently.

[4]"My manner of life from my youth, which was spent from the beginning among my own nation at Jerusalem, all the Jews know. [5]They knew me from the first, if they were willing to testify, that according to the strictest sect of our religion I lived a Pharisee. [6]And now I stand and am judged for the hope of the promise made by God to our fathers. [7]To this *promise* our twelve tribes, earnestly serving *God* night and day, hope to attain. For this hope's sake, King Agrippa, I am accused by the Jews. [8]Why should it be thought incredible by you that God raises the dead?

[9]"Indeed, I myself thought I must do many things contrary to the name of Jesus of Nazareth. [10]This I also did in Jerusalem, and many of the saints I shut up in prison, having received authority from the chief priests; and when they were put to death, I cast my vote against *them.* [11]And I punished them often in every synagogue and compelled *them* to blaspheme; and being exceedingly enraged against them, I persecuted *them* even to foreign cities.

Paul Recounts His Conversion

[12]"While thus occupied, as I journeyed to Damascus with authority and commission from the chief priests, [13]at midday, O king, along the road I saw a light from heaven, brighter than the sun, shining around me and those who journeyed with me. [14]And when we all had fallen to the ground, I heard a voice speaking to me and saying in the Hebrew language, 'Saul, Saul, why are you perse-

cuting Me? *It is* hard for you to kick against the goads.' [15]So I said, 'Who are You, Lord?' And He said, 'I am Jesus, whom you are persecuting. [16]But rise and stand on your feet; for I have appeared to you for this purpose, to make you a minister and a witness both of the things which you have seen and of the things which I will yet reveal to you. [17]I will deliver you from the *Jewish* people, as well as *from* the Gentiles, to whom I now[a] send you, [18]to open their eyes, *in order* to turn *them* from darkness to light, and *from* the power of Satan to God, that they may receive forgiveness of sins and an inheritance among those who are sanctified by faith in Me.'

Paul's Post-Conversion Life

[19]"Therefore, King Agrippa, I was not disobedient to the heavenly vision, [20]but declared first to those in Damascus and in Jerusalem, and throughout all the region of Judea, and *then* to the Gentiles, that they should repent, turn to God, and do works befitting repentance. [21]For these reasons the Jews seized me in the temple and tried to kill *me.* [22]Therefore, having obtained help from God, to this day I stand, witnessing both to small and great, saying no other things than those which the prophets and Moses said would come— [23]that the Christ would suffer, that He would be the first to rise from the dead, and would proclaim light to the *Jewish* people and to the Gentiles."

Agrippa Parries Paul's Challenge

[24]Now as he thus made his defense, Festus said with a loud voice, "Paul, you are beside yourself! Much learning is driving you mad!"

[25]But he said, "I am not mad, most noble Festus, but speak the words of truth and reason. [26]For the king, before whom I also speak freely, knows these things; for I am convinced that none of these things escapes his attention, since this thing was not done in a corner. [27]King Agrippa, do you believe the prophets? I know that you do believe."

[28]Then Agrippa said to Paul, "You almost persuade me to become a Christian."

[29]And Paul said, "I would to God that not only you, but also all who hear me today, might become both almost and altogether such as I am, except for these chains."

26:17 [a]NU-Text and M-Text omit *now.*

I need nothing but God, and to lose myself in the heart of God.

St. Margaret Mary Alacoque

30When he had said these things, the king stood up, as well as the governor and Bernice and those who sat with them; 31and when they had gone aside, they talked among themselves, saying, "This man is doing nothing deserving of death or chains."

32Then Agrippa said to Festus, "This man might have been set free if he had not appealed to Caesar."

The Voyage to Rome Begins

27 And when it was decided that we should sail to Italy, they delivered Paul and some other prisoners to *one* named Julius, a centurion of the Augustan Regiment. 2So, entering a ship of Adramyttium, we put to sea, meaning to sail along the coasts of Asia. Aristarchus, a Macedonian of Thessalonica, was with us. 3And the next *day* we landed at Sidon. And Julius treated Paul kindly and gave *him* liberty to go to his friends and receive care. 4When we had put to sea from there, we sailed under *the shelter of* Cyprus, because the winds were contrary. 5And when we had sailed over the sea which is off Cilicia and Pamphylia, we came to Myra, *a city* of Lycia. 6There the centurion found an Alexandrian ship sailing to Italy, and he put us on board.

7When we had sailed slowly many days, and arrived with difficulty off Cnidus, the wind not permitting us to proceed, we sailed under *the shelter of* Crete off Salmone. 8Passing it with difficulty, we came to a place called Fair Havens, near the city *of* Lasea.

Paul's Warning Ignored

9Now when much time had been spent, and sailing was now dangerous because the Fast was already over, Paul advised them, 10saying, "Men, I perceive that this voyage will end with disaster and much loss, not only of the cargo and ship, but also our lives." 11Nevertheless the centurion was more persuaded by the helmsman and the owner of the ship than by the things spoken by Paul. 12And because the harbor was not suitable to winter in, the majority advised to set sail from there also, if by any means they could reach Phoenix, a harbor of Crete opening toward the southwest and northwest, *and* winter *there.*

In the Tempest

13When the south wind blew softly, supposing that they had obtained *their* desire, putting out to sea, they sailed close by Crete. 14But not long after, a tempestuous head wind arose, called Euroclydon.[a] 15So when the ship was caught, and could not head into the wind, we let *her* drive. 16And running under *the shelter of* an island called Clauda,[a] we secured the skiff with difficulty. 17When they had taken it on board, they used cables to undergird the ship; and fearing lest they should run aground on the Syrtis[a] *Sands*, they struck sail and so were driven. 18And because we were exceedingly tempest-tossed, the next *day* they lightened the ship. 19On the third *day* we threw the ship's tackle overboard with our own hands. 20Now when neither sun nor stars appeared for many days, and no small tempest beat on *us*, all hope that we would be saved was finally given up.

21But after long abstinence from food, then Paul stood in the midst of them and said, "Men, you should have listened to me, and not have sailed from Crete and incurred this disaster and loss. 22And now I urge you to take heart, for there will be no loss of life among you, but only of the ship. 23For there stood by me this night an angel of the God to whom I belong and whom I serve, 24saying, 'Do not be afraid, Paul; you must be brought before Caesar; and indeed God has granted you all those who sail with you.' 25Therefore take heart, men, for I believe God that it will be just as it was told me. 26However, we must run aground on a certain island."

27Now when the fourteenth night had come, as we were driven up and down in the Adriatic *Sea*, about midnight the sailors sensed that they were drawing near some land. 28And they took soundings and found *it* to be twenty fathoms; and when they had gone a little farther, they took soundings again and found *it* to be fifteen fathoms. 29Then, fearing lest we should run aground on the rocks, they dropped four anchors from the stern, and prayed for day to come. 30And as the sailors were seeking to escape from the ship, when they had let down the skiff into the sea, under pretense of putting out an-

27:14 aNU-Text reads *Euraquilon.*   27:16 aNU-Text reads *Cauda.*
27:17 aM-Text reads *Syrtes.*

27:14 On the ship to Rome, Paul encountered Euroclydon, a northeast wind that produced mighty waves. So severe was the storm that Paul's ship was wrecked. Sailing was not usu-ally done after September due to difficult weather. Paul sailed during the first half of October.

PAUL'S FOURTH MISSIONARY JOURNEY

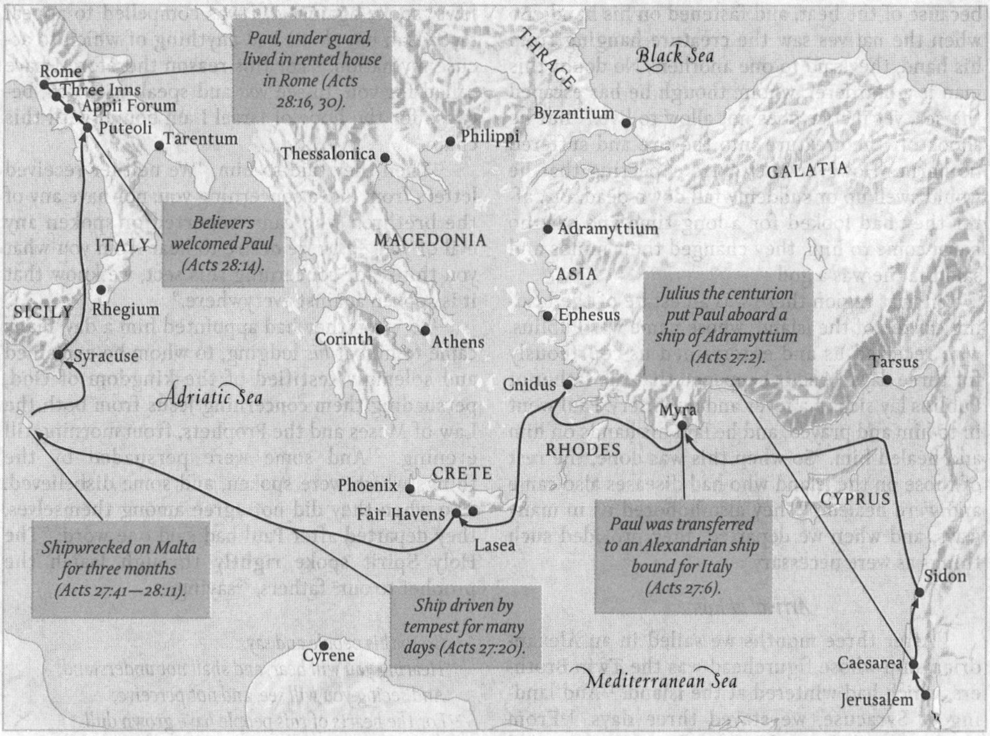

Paul, under guard, lived in rented house in Rome (Acts 28:16, 30).

Rome
Three Inns
Appii Forum
Puteoli
Tarentum

THRACE

Black Sea

Byzantium

Philippi

Thessalonica

GALATIA

ITALY

Believers welcomed Paul (Acts 28:14).

MACEDONIA

Adramyttium

ASIA

SICILY Rhegium

Ephesus

Julius the centurion put Paul aboard a ship of Adramyttium (Acts 27:2).

Tarsus

Syracuse

Corinth Athens

Cnidus

Adriatic Sea

Myra

RHODES

CYPRUS

Phoenix CRETE

Fair Havens

Lasea

Paul was transferred to an Alexandrian ship bound for Italy (Acts 27:6).

Sidon

Shipwrecked on Malta for three months (Acts 27:41—28:11).

Ship driven by tempest for many days (Acts 27:20).

Cyrene

Mediterranean Sea

Caesarea

Jerusalem

chors from the prow, [31]Paul said to the centurion and the soldiers, "Unless these men stay in the ship, you cannot be saved." [32]Then the soldiers cut away the ropes of the skiff and let it fall off.

[33]And as day was about to dawn, Paul implored *them* all to take food, saying, "Today is the fourteenth day you have waited and continued without food, and eaten nothing. [34]Therefore I urge you to take nourishment, for this is for your survival, since not a hair will fall from the head of any of you." [35]And when he had said these things, he took bread and gave thanks to God in the presence of them all; and when he had broken *it* he began to eat. [36]Then they were all encouraged, and also took food themselves. [37]And in all we were two hundred and seventy-six persons on the ship. [38]So when they had eaten enough, they lightened the ship and threw out the wheat into the sea.

Shipwrecked on Malta

[39]When it was day, they did not recognize the land; but they observed a bay with a beach, onto which they planned to run the ship if possible. [40]And they let go the anchors and left *them* in the sea, meanwhile loosing the rudder ropes; and they hoisted the mainsail to the wind and made for shore. [41]But striking a place where two seas met, they ran the ship aground; and the prow stuck fast and remained immovable, but the stern was being broken up by the violence of the waves.

[42]And the soldiers' plan was to kill the prisoners, lest any of them should swim away and escape. [43]But the centurion, wanting to save Paul, kept them from *their* purpose, and commanded that those who could swim should jump *overboard* first and get to land, [44]and the rest, some on boards and some on *parts* of the ship. And so it was that they all escaped safely to land.

Paul's Ministry on Malta

28 Now when they had escaped, they then found out that the island was called Malta. [2]And the natives showed us unusual kindness; for they kindled a fire and made us all welcome,

28:1 The island of Malta is located 50 miles southwest of Sicily, and here the apostle Paul was shipwrecked. In order to prevent the prisoners from escaping, the soldiers asked permission to kill them. Their request was denied, for to kill one prisoner meant that all the prisoners must be killed. Paul had been helpful during the trauma. The 276 persons aboard the wrecked ship swam for Malta, and all arrived there safely.

because of the rain that was falling and because of the cold. ³But when Paul had gathered a bundle of sticks and laid *them* on the fire, a viper came out because of the heat, and fastened on his hand. ⁴So when the natives saw the creature hanging from his hand, they said to one another, "No doubt this man is a murderer, whom, though he has escaped the sea, yet justice does not allow to live." ⁵But he shook off the creature into the fire and suffered no harm. ⁶However, they were expecting that he would swell up or suddenly fall down dead. But after they had looked for a long time and saw no harm come to him, they changed their minds and said that he was a god.

⁷In that region there was an estate of the leading citizen of the island, whose name was Publius, who received us and entertained us courteously for three days. ⁸And it happened that the father of Publius lay sick of a fever and dysentery. Paul went in to him and prayed, and he laid his hands on him and healed him. ⁹So when this was done, the rest of those on the island who had diseases also came and were healed. ¹⁰They also honored us in many ways; and when we departed, they provided such things as were necessary.

Arrival at Rome

¹¹After three months we sailed in an Alexandrian ship whose figurehead was the Twin Brothers, which had wintered at the island. ¹²And landing at Syracuse, we stayed three days. ¹³From there we circled round and reached Rhegium. And after one day the south wind blew; and the next day we came to Puteoli, ¹⁴where we found brethren, and were invited to stay with them seven days. And so we went toward Rome. ¹⁵And from there, when the brethren heard about us, they came to meet us as far as Appii Forum and Three Inns. When Paul saw them, he thanked God and took courage.

¹⁶Now when we came to Rome, the centurion delivered the prisoners to the captain of the guard; but Paul was permitted to dwell by himself with the soldier who guarded him.

Paul's Ministry at Rome

¹⁷And it came to pass after three days that Paul called the leaders of the Jews together. So when they had come together, he said to them: "Men *and* brethren, though I have done nothing against our people or the customs of our fathers, yet I was delivered as a prisoner from Jerusalem into the hands of the Romans, ¹⁸who, when they had examined me, wanted to let *me* go, because there was no cause for putting me to death. ¹⁹But when the Jewsᵃ spoke against *it*, I was compelled to appeal to Caesar, not that I had anything of which to accuse my nation. ²⁰For this reason therefore I have called for you, to see *you* and speak with *you*, because for the hope of Israel I am bound with this chain."

²¹Then they said to him, "We neither received letters from Judea concerning you, nor have any of the brethren who came reported or spoken any evil of you. ²²But we desire to hear from you what you think; for concerning this sect, we know that it is spoken against everywhere."

²³So when they had appointed him a day, many came to him at *his* lodging, to whom he explained and solemnly testified of the kingdom of God, persuading them concerning Jesus from both the Law of Moses and the Prophets, from morning till evening. ²⁴And some were persuaded by the things which were spoken, and some disbelieved. ²⁵So when they did not agree among themselves, they departed after Paul had said one word: "The Holy Spirit spoke rightly through Isaiah the prophet to ourᵃ fathers, ²⁶saying,

'Go to this people and say:
"Hearing you will hear, and shall not understand;
And seeing you will see, and not perceive;
²⁷For the hearts of this people have grown dull.
Their ears are hard of hearing,
And their eyes they have closed,
Lest they should see with their eyes and hear with
    their ears,
Lest they should understand with their hearts and
    turn,
So that I should heal them." 'ᵃ

²⁸"Therefore let it be known to you that the salvation of God has been sent to the Gentiles, and they will hear it!" ²⁹And when he had said these words, the Jews departed and had a great dispute among themselves.ᵃ

³⁰Then Paul dwelt two whole years in his own rented house, and received all who came to him, ³¹preaching the kingdom of God and teaching the things which concern the Lord Jesus Christ with all confidence, no one forbidding him.

••••••••••••••••••••••••

28:19 ᵃThat is, the ruling authorities   **28:25** ᵃNU-Text reads *your.*
28:27 ᵃIsaiah 6:9, 10   **28:29** ᵃNU-Text omits this verse.

SOME GREAT PREACHERS AND THEIR SERMONS

PREACHER	CONGREGATION	SERMON	TEXT
Peter	Crowds at Pentecost	The meaning of Pentecost	Acts 2:14–40
	Crowds at the temple	Call to repentance for crucifying the Messiah	Acts 3:12–26
	Sanhedrin	Testimony on healing	Acts 4:5–12
	Gentiles	Salvation for Gentiles as well as Jews	Acts 10:28–47
	Church at Jerusalem	Defense of ministry to the Gentiles	Acts 11:4–18
	Jerusalem Council	Salvation by grace for all	Acts 15:7–11
Stephen	Sanhedrin	Overview of Old Testament history	Acts 7:1–60
Paul	Synagogue at Antioch	Fulfillment of Old Testament prophecy in Jesus	Acts 13:16–41
	Ephesian elders	Call to faithfulness	Acts 20:17–35
	Crowd at Jerusalem	Testimony of conversion and calling	Acts 22:1–21
	Sanhedrin	Defense as a Pharisee and Roman citizen	Acts 23:1–6
	King Agrippa	Testimony of his conversion and sharing of the gospel	Acts 26:1–32
	Jewish leaders at Rome	Testimony of his Jewish heritage	Acts 28:17–20
James	Jerusalem Council	Absence of requirements for circumcision for Gentile converts	Acts 15:13–21

Romans

AUTHOR

The apostle Paul wrote the Epistle to the Romans. Paul, who at birth received the Jewish name Saul, was born in the city of Tarsus located in Cilicia (Acts 22:3). His birth occurred probably between A.D. 1 and 5. Although he grew up in Greek culture, Paul remained loyal to his Hebrew heritage (Phil. 3:5). As citizens of Rome, members of his family were probably wealthy and socially influential (Acts 22:28). A Pharisee, Saul received the finest available education from the renowned teacher Gamaliel (Acts 22:3; Gal. 1:14). Not only did Saul adhere to a life governed by the Law of Moses, but most likely he followed its strictest interpretations laid down by generations of Jewish teachers.

DATE

Saul launched vicious attacks on the followers of Christ (Acts 8:1–3). In the midst of his authorized and zealous pursuit of the followers of "the Way," he was blinded by a supernatural light and heard the voice of Jesus Christ (Acts 9:1–19). Confronted by Christ Himself, Paul's life was permanently redirected. His zeal as a messenger for Christ was as dedicated as had been his former role as persecutor. Changing his name to the Greek "Paul" (Acts 13:9), he proclaimed Christ's "Good News" to the Gentiles with an all-consuming passion.

In his lifetime, Paul launched at least four missionary journeys into previously unreached countries (3 recorded in Acts), survived tremendous opposition and hardship, and wrote letters to instruct and encourage those who had become believers (see maps, Paul's First, Second, Third, and Fourth Missionary Journeys). Imprisonment often resulted from Paul's contention with the religious legalism of the Jews. The Book of Acts ends with Paul under house arrest in his own rented house in Rome (Acts 28:30, 31). Events surrounding the end of Paul's life are uncertain. After a possible release and a later imprisonment in Rome, Paul may have been tried and executed for his continued proclamation of the gospel of Jesus Christ (see 2 Tim.), which he comprehensively articulated in his letter to the church at Rome.

Paul probably wrote this letter to the Christians in Rome from Corinth between A.D. 55 and 59 on his third missionary journey, perhaps in the winter of A.D. 57 (see map, Paul's Third Missionary Journey). At the time Paul wrote to the church at Rome, he had never visited that church. He was preparing to go to Jerusalem and personally deliver a significant offering the churches had collected for the needy Christians in Jerusalem. Paul was uncertain regarding what might happen to him in Jerusalem. He, therefore, wrote his theology and sent it to Rome because he could foresee the strategic importance of that church for the future.

BACKGROUND

SETTING: The Roman church may have been formed by believers who heard Peter's message during the celebration of Pentecost (Acts 2). Paul had never visited the church

at Rome, but he recognized the strategic significance of the church there. Thus Paul shared in detail the basic tenets of Christianity with these believers.

PURPOSE: Paul had several purposes in writing to the Roman church. He wrote the Book of Romans to explain why he had been delayed in visiting the Roman believers and to prepare the way for his anticipated visit (Rom. 1:10–13). Paul wanted the Romans to know that he had not abandoned his mission to the Gentiles. He wanted them to know he had not lost confidence in the gospel of Christ for all people (Rom. 1:16). Paul also desired to promote unity and to resolve a possible conflict between Jewish and Gentile Christians.

AUDIENCE: The letter is addressed to Christians in Rome. Paul had neither founded nor visited the church at Rome, which consisted of both Jews and Gentiles. The variety of backgrounds and interpretations within that church called for a clear, concise articulation of the work of Christ. Paul's focus was upon Christ's life, death, and Resurrection.

LITERARY CHARACTERISTICS: Paul's letter to the Romans has the literary framework of a lawyer establishing his case carefully and accurately. Of all Paul's letters, the Epistle to the Romans comes closest to being a systematic theological treatise. Through the literary form of a letter (with greeting, body of information, and closing signature) and the application of rhetorical skills of questioning argument, Paul presented a clear explanation of God's purposes throughout history, culminating in the sending of His Son for the salvation of all who would turn to Him in faith.

THEMES

The major theme of Romans is that of righteousness received as a gift from God, not achieved by works of the Law (Rom. 1:16, 17). Salvation comes by grace through faith (Rom. 3:21–31). Other themes include mankind's rejection of God's revelation, death to sin and life in Christ by the Holy Spirit's power, Christian freedom, God's sovereignty, God's plan of salvation as encompassing Gentiles as well as Jews, obedience to Christ involving sacrificial commitment, and practical Christian living.

OUTLINE

Greeting

1 Paul, a bondservant of Jesus Christ, called *to be* an apostle, separated to the gospel of God [2]which He promised before through His prophets in the Holy Scriptures, [3]concerning His Son Jesus Christ our Lord, who was born of the seed of David according to the flesh, [4]*and* declared *to be* the Son of God with power according to the Spirit of holiness, by the resurrection from the dead. [5]Through Him we have received grace and apostleship for obedience to the faith among all nations for His name, [6]among whom you also are the called of Jesus Christ;

[7]To all who are in Rome, beloved of God, called *to be* saints:

Grace to you and peace from God our Father and the Lord Jesus Christ.

Desire to Visit Rome

[8]First, I thank my God through Jesus Christ for you all, that your faith is spoken of throughout the whole world. [9]For God is my witness, whom I serve with my spirit in the gospel of His Son, that without ceasing I make mention of you always in my prayers, [10]making request if, by some means, now at last I may find a way in the will of God to come to you. [11]For I long to see you, that I may impart to you some spiritual gift, so that you may be established— [12]that is, that I may be encouraged together with you by the mutual faith both of you and me.

[13]Now I do not want you to be unaware, brethren, that I often planned to come to you (but was hindered until now), that I might have some fruit among you also, just as among the other Gentiles. [14]I am a debtor both to Greeks and to barbarians, both to wise and to unwise. [15]So, as much as is in me, *I am* ready to preach the gospel to you who are in Rome also.

The Just Live by Faith

[16]For I am not ashamed of the gospel of Christ,[a] for it is the power of God to salvation for everyone who believes, for the Jew first and also for the Greek. [17]For in it the righteousness of God is revealed from faith to faith; as it is written, *"The just shall live by faith."*[a]

God's Wrath on Unrighteousness

[18]For the wrath of God is revealed from heaven against all ungodliness and unrighteousness of men, who suppress the truth in unrighteousness, [19]because what may be known of God is manifest in them, for God has shown *it* to them. [20]For since the creation of the world His invisible *attributes* are clearly seen, being understood by the things that are made, *even* His eternal power and Godhead, so that they are without excuse, [21]because, although they knew God, they did not glorify *Him* as God, nor were thankful, but became futile in their thoughts, and their foolish hearts were darkened. [22]Professing to be wise, they became fools, [23]and changed the glory of the incorruptible God into an image made like corruptible man—and birds and four-footed animals and creeping things.

[24]Therefore God also gave them up to uncleanness, in the lusts of their hearts, to dishonor their bodies among themselves, [25]who exchanged the truth of God for the lie, and worshiped and served the creature rather than the Creator, who is blessed forever. Amen.

[26]For this reason God gave them up to vile

1:16 [a]NU-Text omits *of Christ.* 1:17 [a]Habakkuk 2:4

1:1–4 Paul introduced himself as a bondservant, a slave of his master Jesus Christ. Such a sense of utter devotion springs from the great love Christ had demonstrated. Paul (Gk. *paulos*, lit. "small" or "little") was called or set apart by God to be an apostle, one who is sent by authority with a mission.

1:7 Saints demonstrate their unique relationship to Christ by setting themselves apart from a worldly lifestyle and giving themselves wholly to the Lord. God calls believers to this set-apart lifestyle in which they increasingly demonstrate outwardly the inward transformation of the heart (Rom. 12:1, 2). Paul typically employed this greeting (Rom. 1:5; 1 Cor. 1:3; 2 Cor. 1:2; Gal. 1:3; Eph. 1:2). "Peace" refers to the sense of wholeness and well-being that comes through a right relationship with God. The Hebrews used "peace" (*shalom*) as a greeting. The Greeks often greeted one another with a word similar to "grace" but meaning "joy." Paul employed a distinctive combination of these familiar salutations.

1:11 A spiritual gift comes from and is given by the Holy Spirit and has the effect of edifying the body (see chart, The Work of the Holy Spirit). Paul listed seven of the spiritual gifts (Rom. 12:6–8; see chart, Spiritual Gifts of Women in the Bible).

1:14 The Greeks were those who accepted Hellenistic culture and spoke the Greek language. The barbarians were viewed as the uncultured.

1:16, 17 The righteousness of God is not simply a moral attribute. God's righteousness is revealed in His work of salvation. Paul stressed the importance of living by faith, the heart of Paul's theme in his letter to the Romans (see Hab. 2:4; Gal. 3:11; Heb. 10:38).

1:20 God has revealed Himself not only in history but also in the beauty and order of His created world (see Ps. 19:1–6) thereby removing any excuse for ignorance of Himself. Although sin distorts, it does not remove the possibility of perceiving God in nature (see Acts 14:15).

1:24, 25 God's wrath involves abandoning individuals to the consequences of their wrong choices. God's mercy is operating even in His wrath as He seeks to draw them back to Himself.

1:26, 27 Homosexuality was practiced commonly in the pagan world of Paul's day. Paul condemned this practice as contrary to God's design (see Lev. 18, Homosexuality).

A SURVEY OF PAUL'S EPISTLES

BOOK	DATE WRITTEN	PLACE WRITTEN	RECIPIENTS	THEME	PRIMARY WOMEN
ROMANS	A.D. 55–59	Corinth	Saints in Rome (Rom. 1:7)	God's gift of righteousness	Mary (Rom. 16:6) Persis (Rom. 16:12) Phoebe (Rom. 16:1, 2) Priscilla (Rom 16:3, 4) Rufus' mother (Rom. 16:13) Tryphena and Tryphosa (Rom. 16:12)
1 CORINTHIANS	A.D. 56–57	Ephesus	Church at Corinth (1 Cor. 1:2)	Love as the basis for Christian ethics	Chloe (1 Cor. 1:11) Priscilla (1 Cor. 16:19)
2 CORINTHIANS	A.D. 56–57	Macedonia	Church at Corinth (2 Cor. 1:1)	The ministry of reconciliation	
GALATIANS	A.D. 55–57	Antioch(?)	Churches of Galatia (Gal. 1:2)	Justification by faith	
EPHESIANS	A.D. 60–63	Rome	Saints of Ephesus (Eph. 1:1)	The church: the body of Christ	
PHILIPPIANS	A.D. 60–63	Rome	Saints in Philippi (Phil. 1:1)	Humility resulting in unity and joy	Euodia and Syntyche (Phil. 4:2, 3)
COLOSSIANS	A.D. 60–63	Rome	Saints at Colosse (Col. 1:2)	Combating false teachings	
1 THESSALONIANS	A.D. 50–52	Corinth	Church in Thessalonica (1 Thess. 1:1)	Christ's return	
2 THESSALONIANS	A.D. 51–52	Corinth	Church in Thessalonica (2 Thess. 1:1)	The faithfulness of the Lord	
1 TIMOTHY	A.D. 62–64	Macedonia(?)	Timothy (1 Tim. 1:2)	Pastoral advice	
2 TIMOTHY	A.D. 66–67	Rome	Timothy (2 Tim. 1:2)	A farewell word of encouragement	Claudia (2 Tim. 4:21) Lois and Eunice (2 Tim. 1:5)
TITUS	A.D. 62–64	Macedonia(?)	Titus (Titus 1:4)	Guidelines for Christian living	Apphia (Philem. 2)
PHILEMON	A.D. 60–63	Rome	Philemon (Philem. 1)	Christ's transforming love	

Paul touched the lives of other women not mentioned in the Epistles (see also Bernice, Acts 25; Drusilla, Acts 24; Lydia, Acts 16).

ATTRIBUTES OF GOD   HE IS LONGSUFFERING

God's judgment is sure (Rev. 19:2, 11). God is called "longsuffering" because He does not execute judgment immediately. He waits (Is. 42:14–16), not to see what will happen—He knows what will happen; not to see more clearly—He sees perfectly; not to gain more information—He knows everything. God waits because His priority is self-revelation, not judgment.

Longsuffering is not the absence of anger but being slow to anger (Ps. 145:8). God's longsuffering shows an infinite amount of power, mercy, patience, and love—all of which He has in abundance (Num. 14:18).

God, for a time, tolerates insults, rejection, and indifference in order to draw people to repentance (Rom. 2:4). His longsuffering is linked with His great compassion and becomes active in order to draw us to Himself (2 Pet. 3:9).

See also Ex. 34:6; Ps. 51:1; 86:15; 103:8; Jer. 3:12; Lam. 3:22, note; Nah. 1:3; Rom. 9:22, 23; 15:5, 6; notes on Attributes of God (Ex. 33; Deut. 4; 32; 2 Chr. 19; Job 23; 42; Ps. 25; 90; 102; 119; Is. 6; 65; Jer. 23; Eph. 1; 1 John 5); Commitment (Matt. 16); Forgiveness (Ps. 51; Luke 17); Fruit of the Spirit (Ps. 86; Rom. 5; 15; 1 Cor. 10; 13; Gal. 5; Eph. 4; Col. 3; 2 Thess. 1; Rev. 2)

passions. For even their women exchanged the natural use for what is against nature. [27]Likewise also the men, leaving the natural use of the woman, burned in their lust for one another, men with men committing what is shameful, and receiving in themselves the penalty of their error which was due.

[28]And even as they did not like to retain God in *their* knowledge, God gave them over to a debased mind, to do those things which are not fitting; [29]being filled with all unrighteousness, sexual immorality,[a] wickedness, covetousness, maliciousness; full of envy, murder, strife, deceit, evil-mindedness; *they are* whisperers, [30]backbiters, haters of God, violent, proud, boasters, inventors of evil things, disobedient to parents, [31]undiscerning, untrustworthy, unloving, unforgiving,[a] unmerciful; [32]who, knowing the righteous judgment of God, that those who practice such things are deserving of death, not only do the same but also approve of those who practice them.

God's Righteous Judgment

2 Therefore you are inexcusable, O man, whoever you are who judge, for in whatever you judge another you condemn yourself; for you who judge practice the same things. [2]But we know that the judgment of God is according to truth against those who practice such things. [3]And do you think this, O man, you who judge those practicing such things, and doing the same, that you will escape the judgment of God? [4]Or do you despise the riches of His goodness, forbearance, and longsuffering, not knowing that the goodness of God leads you to repentance? [5]But in accordance with your hardness and your impenitent heart you are treasuring up for yourself wrath in the day of wrath and revelation of the righteous judgment of God, [6]who *"will render to each one according to his deeds"*:[a] [7]eternal life to those who by patient continuance in doing good seek for glory, honor, and immortality; [8]but to those who are self-seeking and do not obey the truth, but obey unrighteousness— indignation and wrath, [9]tribulation and anguish, on every soul of man who does evil, of the Jew first and also of the Greek; [10]but glory, honor, and peace to everyone who works what is good, to the Jew first and also to the Greek. [11]For there is no partiality with God.

[12]For as many as have sinned without law will

· · · · · · · · · · · · · ·

1:29 [a]NU-Text omits *sexual immorality*.   **1:31** [a]NU-Text omits *unforgiving*.   **2:6** [a]Psalm 62:12; Proverbs 24:12

1:28 The individual with a debased or degenerate mind no longer can perceive God and ultimately will reap spiritual death as the consequence of his sin (v. 32; see Rom. 6:23). "Fitting" as employed by Stoic philosophers described appropriate or proper conduct.

2:4 The contemptible attitude of the Jews stood in stark contrast to the goodness of God (v. 5). God had shown abundant kindness and patience despite the nation's persistent rebellion and rejection of His will. Judgment had only been postponed, not overlooked (Amos 3:1, 2). God's kindness gives opportunity for repentance, but the Jews interpreted it as a sign of immunity from judgment (Acts 3:19; 2 Pet. 3:9).

2:5–10 Without the exercise of wrath against evil, God would be an unrighteous and immoral God (see 2 Chr. 19, Attributes of God). Those who continually sin make themselves the object of God's "wrath" (Gk. *orgē*, meaning "the eternal divine disposition of settled anger"). Paul anticipated a future day when God would righteously judge the world. God's judgment includes everyone; yet it is individually assigned (Rom. 2:6; 2 Cor. 5:10). The judgment described here, based on deeds, is applied to two groups: the righteous (Rom. 2:7, 10) and the wicked (vv. 8, 9). For Paul, as well as for James, faith must issue in deeds (see Rom. 1:17; James 2:17).

2:12–15 God's justice demands from both Jew and Gentile absolute righteousness, which can never be obtained through

also perish without law, and as many as have sinned in the law will be judged by the law [13](for not the hearers of the law *are* just in the sight of God, but the doers of the law will be justified; [14]for when Gentiles, who do not have the law, by nature do the things in the law, these, although not having the law, are a law to themselves, [15]who show the work of the law written in their hearts, their conscience also bearing witness, and between themselves *their* thoughts accusing or else excusing *them*) [16]in the day when God will judge the secrets of men by Jesus Christ, according to my gospel.

The Jews Guilty as the Gentiles

[17]Indeed[a] you are called a Jew, and rest on the law, and make your boast in God, [18]and know *His* will, and approve the things that are excellent, being instructed out of the law, [19]and are confident that you yourself are a guide to the blind, a light to those who are in darkness, [20]an instructor of the foolish, a teacher of babes, having the form of knowledge and truth in the law. [21]You, therefore, who teach another, do you not teach yourself? You who preach that a man should not steal, do you steal? [22]You who say, "Do not commit adultery," do you commit adultery? You who abhor idols, do you rob temples? [23]You who make your boast in the law, do you dishonor God through breaking the law? [24]For *"the name of God is blasphemed among the Gentiles because of you,"*[a] as it is written.

Circumcision of No Avail

[25]For circumcision is indeed profitable if you keep the law; but if you are a breaker of the law, your circumcision has become uncircumcision. [26]Therefore, if an uncircumcised man keeps the righteous requirements of the law, will not his uncircumcision be counted as circumcision? [27]And will not the physically uncircumcised, if he fulfills the law, judge you who, *even* with *your* written *code* and circumcision, *are* a transgressor of the law? [28]For he is not a Jew who *is one* outwardly, nor *is* circumcision that which *is* outward in the flesh; [29]but *he is* a Jew who *is one* inwardly; and circumcision *is that* of the heart, in the Spirit, not in the letter; whose praise *is* not from men but from God.

God's Judgment Defended

3 What advantage then has the Jew, or what *is* the profit of circumcision? [2]Much in every way! Chiefly because to them were committed the oracles of God. [3]For what if some did not believe? Will their unbelief make the faithfulness of God without effect? [4]Certainly not! Indeed, let God be true but every man a liar. As it is written:

"That You may be justified in Your words,
And may overcome when You are judged."[a]

[5]But if our unrighteousness demonstrates the righteousness of God, what shall we say? *Is* God unjust who inflicts wrath? (I speak as a man.) [6]Certainly not! For then how will God judge the world?

[7]For if the truth of God has increased through my lie to His glory, why am I also still judged as a sinner? [8]And *why* not *say,* "Let us do evil that good may come"?—as we are slanderously reported and as some affirm that we say. Their condemnation is just.

All Have Sinned

[9]What then? Are we better *than they?* Not at all. For we have previously charged both Jews and Greeks that they are all under sin. [10]As it is written:

"There is none righteous, no, not one;
[11]*There is none who understands;*
There is none who seeks after God.
[12]*They have all turned aside;*

2:17 [a]NU-Text reads *But if.*   **2:24** [a]Isaiah 52:5; Ezekiel 36:22   **3:4** [a]Psalm 51:4

---

inadequate human efforts to keep the Law. Good works do not bring salvation; salvation brings good works. All have received some degree of God's revelation and thus stand responsible (Rom. 1:20, 21).

2:17–24 The Jews regarded themselves as better than the Gentiles because they possessed the Law; yet they did not keep the Law. The hypocrisy and contradiction between Jewish belief and behavior caused the Gentiles to blaspheme God's name. The Gentiles concluded that the God of a people who behaved in such fashion could not be a worthy God (see Is. 52:5).

2:25–29 Circumcision, regarded as the sign of the covenant, had marked the Jewish male since the time of Abram (see Gen. 17, Circumcision). Many Jews in Paul's time believed the physical circumcision of the body insured membership in God's family (see Acts 15:1–29).

2:29 The designation Jew is derived from Judah (Heb., lit. "praise"; see Gen. 29:35), one of Jacob's sons and one of the 12 tribes of Israel. Paul utilized a wordplay in this verse to emphasize that the true Jew is one who inwardly depends on God and submits to Him, not one who relies on external appearance and the approval of men.

3:1, 2 Paul acknowledged the benefits of belonging to the Jewish nation—possession of the oracles of God, through which God revealed Himself. This privilege carried with it a heavy responsibility.

3:10–18 Paul linked together a number of OT passages to emphasize that all have sinned (see Ps. 5:9, 10; 14:1-3; 36:1-4; Is. 59:7, 8). The various references to parts of the human body (throat, tongue, lips, mouth, feet, eyes) reveal that sin corrupts throughout. "Fear of God" refers to reverent respect (Rom. 3:18).

WORRY   THE PARALYSIS OF FAITH

Depending on context, words translated as "cares" and "concerns" or "fear" and "anxiety" can be either right or wrong attitudes in a Christian's life. Fear is right when it is reverence toward God because of His holiness (Is. 8:13); and care is good when showing concern for others (1 Cor. 12:25; 2 Cor. 11:28).

But worry is always wrong, for it paralyzes active faith in your life. When you worry, you assume responsibility for things you were never intended to handle. Jesus repeatedly taught: "Do not worry" (Gk. *merimneō*, lit. "to divide the mind"), even about the basic essentials of life (Matt. 6:25–34). Worry divides your mind between useful and hurtful thinking. Worrying does not change anything (Matt. 6:27) except to draw your focus away from God and His faithfulness and righteousness to concerns about the things of life, such as possessions and material goods (Matt. 6:31). Worry is a choking, harmful emotion that saps your energy and elevates human strength and ingenuity above God's strength and His purposeful plan.

Sources of worry include change, lack of understanding, and lack of control over your life. Worry opens the door to worldliness, that is, preoccupation with the things of this life. Though the children of Israel had watched God split open the Red Sea to deliver them from Egypt, they could not believe He would provide water in the desert to meet their needs. Worry is the opposite of faith, suggesting that God cannot be trusted to take care of you or to provide what you need (Phil. 4:19). Worry causes fear to crowd out faith. Thus, in the final reckoning, "the cowardly" are listed alongside the "unbelieving" (Rev. 21:8).

Linking worry with unbelief, Scripture gives direction for a return to full faith. The road from worry to faith begins with recognition that worry is sin and confession of lack of faith (Ps. 139:23), continues with deliverance (Ps. 34:4), and finally ends with the assurance that absolutely nothing can separate you from the love of God who is the great I AM (Rom. 8:35; Ex. 3:14, 15). In place of anxious thoughts, you then freely offer thanksgiving from a heart established with trust in God as all sufficient (Ps. 112:7, 8; Phil. 4:6, 7).

See also Ps. 23:1–6; 94:19; Luke 10:40–42; notes on Attributes of God (Job 23); Blessings (Gen. 12); Contentment (1 Tim. 6); Fear (Ps. 27); Gratitude (Ps. 95); Promises of God (2 Pet. 1); Providence (Eccl. 7)

They have together become unprofitable;
There is none who does good, no, not
one."[a]
[13] "Their throat is an open tomb;
With their tongues they have practiced
deceit";[a]
"The poison of asps is under their lips";[b]
[14] "Whose mouth is full of cursing and bitterness."[a]
[15] "Their feet are swift to shed blood;
[16] Destruction and misery are in their ways;
[17] And the way of peace they have not
known."[a]
[18] "There is no fear of God before their eyes."[a]

[19] Now we know that whatever the law says, it says to those who are under the law, that every mouth may be stopped, and all the world may become guilty before God. [20] Therefore by the deeds of the law no flesh will be justified in His sight, for by the law *is* the knowledge of sin.

God's Righteousness Through Faith

[21] But now the righteousness of God apart from the law is revealed, being witnessed by the Law and the Prophets, [22] even the righteousness of God, through faith in Jesus Christ, to all and on all[a] who believe. For there is no difference; [23] for all have sinned and fall short of the glory of God, [24] being justified freely by His grace through the redemption that is in Christ Jesus, [25] whom God set forth *as* a propitiation by His blood, through faith, to demonstrate His righteousness, because

•••••••••••••••••••••
3:12 [a]Psalms 14:1–3; 53:1–3; Ecclesiastes 7:20   3:13 [a]Psalm 5:9 [b]Psalm 140:3   3:14 [a]Psalm 10:7   3:17 [a]Isaiah 59:7, 8   3:18 [a]Psalm 36:1   3:22 [a]NU-Text omits *and on all.*

3:23 Sin (Gk. *hamartia*, lit. "to miss the mark") falls short of attaining God's standard. Sin is often identified as deeds, such as stealing, murder, adultery, or lying (Ex. 20:1–17; Deut. 5:1–21). However, a more fundamental attitude deep within the human heart underlies all "sins" and is expressed as "I know better than God in this matter." This attitude led Eve to that first, fatal, disobedient act in the Garden of Eden. Adam had told her that God had forbidden the eating of the fruit, but when the fruit was presented to her as good, pleasant, and desirable, she allowed her own judgment to take precedence over the Word directly from God, and she ate the forbidden fruit (Gen. 3:3, 6). God has not given us His Word so we

can make a reasoned evaluation of His judgment and decide whether or not we want to obey. He has given us His Word because that Word is truth and life, and we are to obey it without question and with unhesitating confidence. To follow our own judgments in disobedience of God's Word is to put self in the place of God (Prov. 3:5, 7; 14:12), no matter how innocent or noble the deed may seem (see Luke 24:47, note; Num. 16, Rebellion; Ps. 51, Forgiveness; 2 Cor. 7, Guilt; Philem., Obedience).

3:24 Justification is a legal term referring to a right standing before God (see chart, Theological Terms). That standing can

in His forbearance God had passed over the sins that were previously committed, [26]to demonstrate at the present time His righteousness, that He might be just and the justifier of the one who has faith in Jesus.

Boasting Excluded

[27]Where *is* boasting then? It is excluded. By what law? Of works? No, but by the law of faith. [28]Therefore we conclude that a man is justified by faith apart from the deeds of the law. [29]Or *is He* the God of the Jews only? *Is He* not also the God of the Gentiles? Yes, of the Gentiles also, [30]since *there is* one God who will justify the circumcised by faith and the uncircumcised through faith. [31]Do we then make void the law through faith? Certainly not! On the contrary, we establish the law.

Abraham Justified by Faith

4 What then shall we say that Abraham our father has found according to the flesh? [2]For if Abraham was justified by works, he has *something* to boast about, but not before God. [3]For what does the Scripture say? *"Abraham believed God, and it was accounted to him for righteousness."*[a] [4]Now to him who works, the wages are not counted as grace but as debt.

David Celebrates the Same Truth

[5]But to him who does not work but believes on Him who justifies the ungodly, his faith is accounted for righteousness, [6]just as David also describes the blessedness of the man to whom God imputes righteousness apart from works:

[7]*"Blessed are those whose lawless deeds are forgiven,*

And whose sins are covered;
[8]*Blessed is the man to whom the* LORD *shall not impute sin."*[a]

Abraham Justified Before Circumcision

[9]*Does* this blessedness then *come* upon the circumcised *only,* or upon the uncircumcised also? For we say that faith was accounted to Abraham for righteousness. [10]How then was it accounted? While he was circumcised, or uncircumcised? Not while circumcised, but while uncircumcised. [11]And he received the sign of circumcision, a seal of the righteousness of the faith which *he had while still* uncircumcised, that he might be the father of all those who believe, though they are uncircumcised, that righteousness might be imputed to them also, [12]and the father of circumcision to those who not only *are* of the circumcision, but who also walk in the steps of the faith which our father Abraham *had while still* uncircumcised.

The Promise Granted Through Faith

[13]For the promise that he would be the heir of the world *was* not to Abraham or to his seed through the law, but through the righteousness of faith. [14]For if those who are of the law *are* heirs, faith is made void and the promise made of no effect, [15]because the law brings about wrath; for where there is no law *there is* no transgression.

[16]Therefore *it is* of faith that *it might be* according to grace, so that the promise might be sure to all the seed, not only to those who are of the law, but also to those who are of the faith of

4:1 [a]Or *Abraham our (fore)father according to the flesh has found?*
4:3 [a]Genesis 15:6   4:8 [a]Psalm 32:1, 2

never be earned. "Redemption" refers to the act by which a slave is given freedom. Through faith in Christ, sinners are delivered from slavery to sin.

3:25 Propitiation (Gk. *hilastērion*) has the idea of appeasing or satisfying. Thus propitiation refers to the work of Christ on the Cross, by which He both satisfied the demands of God's justice and canceled the sinner's guilt. In other texts, the same Greek word is translated "mercy seat."Christ's death on the Cross is interpreted in terms of the Day of Atonement, on which the blood of the sacrificial animals was sprinkled on the mercy seat in the Most Holy Place to atone for the sins of the people (see Lev. 16:14–16). In either case, through the death of Christ on the Cross, God took the initiative to bring mankind into right relationship with Himself.

4:1–4 Paul used the example of Abraham to emphasize the significance of faith. Abraham responded in faith to God's call (Gen. 12:1–3). "Accounted" (Gk. *logizomai*) is a bookkeeping term. Abraham's faith resulted in "balanced books" with God (Rom. 4:3). Paul had encountered Jews who claimed they did not need to have faith in Christ for salvation because they were descendants of Abraham. Paul countered that argument by showing that Abraham himself was made right with God by faith.

4:5–8 Paul next turned to David, Israel's celebrated king, as another example of an individual who received God's free pardon (vv. 7, 8; see 2 Sam. 11:1—12:23; Ps. 32:1, 2). No sacrifice for such grave offenses as David had committed was prescribed in the Law. David could only cast himself on the mercy of God (see Heb. 11:6).

4:9–12 Circumcision was a physical sign or seal of the covenant between God and His chosen nation (see Gen. 17, Circumcision). But God did not give Abraham this sign of the covenant until Abraham was 99 years old (see Gen. 17:1–14). Many years prior to that time Abraham had responded to God in faith and received right standing before God. He was justified before he was circumcised (see Gen. 15:6).

4:13–15 Right standing with God comes only through faith. Abraham received God's promise by faith long before the Law of Moses was given. Salvation does not come by keeping the Law. Legalism shifts the focus from the power of God to the ability of individuals to keep the Law. With the Law came increased awareness of sin and of God's wrath. With faith came the realization of God's promise (2 Cor. 4:6).

4:16–25 The true heirs of Abraham are those who receive the promises of God by faith as Abraham did. All who place faith

FRUIT OF THE SPIRIT   PEACE

In both the Old and New Testaments, peace is described as the result of having a right relationship to God and with others (see Rom. 5:1, 2). The Greek word *eirēnē* has a meaning similar to the Hebrew word *shalom*. Spiritual peace describes a sense of well-being and fulfillment that comes from God and is dependent on His presence alone (Gal. 5:22).

Inner spiritual peace is experienced by any believer who walks in the Spirit despite surrounding turmoil. The true "peace of God" protects the hearts and minds of believers from worry, fear, and anxiety. It transcends all logic or rationale (Phil. 4:7). The God of Peace who offers salvation also promises His presence and power in the lives of His children. His presence creates in us a quiet confidence, regardless of circumstances, people, or things.

Though impossible to comprehend fully, true peace is a fruit of the Holy Spirit (Gal. 5:22) and a part of the "whole armor of God" (Eph. 6:11, 13). According to the apostle Paul, our understanding and experiencing of the gospel produces peace that allows us to walk boldly into spiritual battle (Eph. 6:11, 13) and to survive all manner of difficulty and danger. The believer receives peace from God as a virtue of holy living and a protection from evil forces. Where the peace of God is present, there is no room for worry.

See also Rom. 15:13; Col. 3:15; notes on Confidence (Is. 30); Distress (Ps. 18); Fruit of the Spirit (Ps. 86; Rom. 15; 1 Cor. 10; 13; Gal. 5; Eph. 4; Col. 3; 2 Thess. 1; Rev. 2); Heaven (2 Tim. 4)

Abraham, who is the father of us all [17](as it is written, *"I have made you a father of many nations"*[a]) in the presence of Him whom he believed— God, who gives life to the dead and calls those things which do not exist as though they did; [18]who, contrary to hope, in hope believed, so that he became the father of many nations, according to what was spoken, *"So shall your descendants be."*[a] [19]And not being weak in faith, he did not consider his own body, already dead (since he was about a hundred years old), and the deadness of Sarah's womb. [20]He did not waver at the promise of God through unbelief, but was strengthened in faith, giving glory to God, [21]and being fully convinced that what He had promised He was also able to perform. [22]And therefore *"it was accounted to him for righteousness."*[a]

[23]Now it was not written for his sake alone that it was imputed to him, [24]but also for us. It shall be imputed to us who believe in Him who raised up Jesus our Lord from the dead, [25]who was delivered up because of our offenses, and was raised because of our justification.

Faith Triumphs in Trouble

5 Therefore, having been justified by faith, we have[a] peace with God through our Lord Jesus Christ, [2]through whom also we have access by faith into this grace in which we stand, and rejoice in hope of the glory of God. [3]And not only *that,* but we also glory in tribulations, knowing that tribulation produces perseverance; [4]and perseverance, character; and character, hope. [5]Now hope does not disappoint, because the love of God has been poured out in our hearts by the Holy Spirit who was given to us.

••••••••••••••••••••••••••••••••••

4:17 [a]Genesis 17:5   **4:18** [a]Genesis 15:5   **4:22** [a]Genesis 15:6   **5:1** [a]Another ancient reading is, *let us have peace.*

---

in Jesus Christ are heirs of God's promise. The genuine descendants of Abraham are not those who have Abraham's blood but those who possess Abraham's faith.

4:19 Abraham and Sarah were unable to conceive a child in their old age. Abraham's body and Sarah's womb were considered dead, since both were past childbearing age. The word "dead" in this verse provides a link with the assertion that God "gives life to the dead" (v. 17). Abraham's faith in the promises of God did not waver or falter.

5:1–11 The believer receives: a new relationship with God (vv. 1, 2), a new perspective on difficulty (vv. 3–5), and a new assurance of security (vv. 6–11).

5:1 Peace here is much more than the absence of conflict; it is an objective reality that brings harmony to life. Those who have not experienced the new relationship with God are subject to His wrath (Rom. 1:18; 8:7, 8). The relationship between

God and His creation is restored through faith in Christ, dissolving all enmity. The result is peace.

5:2 Every believer has free, abundant, and immediate access to God. The term "access" also can refer to a harbor or haven where ships come to anchor, conveying the idea of shelter from the stormy seas of life.

5:3–5 Christian women can enjoy the new perspective of glorying or rejoicing in tribulations because of the benefits gained by the proper response to suffering. The Greek word translated "tribulation" can mean "pressure" (v. 3). Paul encouraged Christians to rejoice in these pressures because they produce "perseverance" or endurance, the spirit that actively meets and overcomes life's difficulties. Next, endurance produces character. The Greek term Paul used for "character" can refer to metal purified of dross. Finally, the woman whose character has met the tests of life and emerged victorious possesses "hope" based on the eternal love and power of God.

Self-sacrifice through self-control is necessary for self-fulfillment.

Rhonda H. Kelley

Christ in Our Place

[6]For when we were still without strength, in due time Christ died for the ungodly. [7]For scarcely for a righteous man will one die; yet perhaps for a good man someone would even dare to die. [8]But God demonstrates His own love toward us, in that while we were still sinners, Christ died for us. [9]Much more then, having now been justified by His blood, we shall be saved from wrath through Him. [10]For if when we were enemies we were reconciled to God through the death of His Son, much more, having been reconciled, we shall be saved by His life. [11]And not only *that*, but we also rejoice in God through our Lord Jesus Christ, through whom we have now received the reconciliation.

Death in Adam, Life in Christ

[12]Therefore, just as through one man sin entered the world, and death through sin, and thus death spread to all men, because all sinned— [13](For until the law sin was in the world, but sin is not imputed when there is no law. [14]Nevertheless death reigned from Adam to Moses, even over those who had not sinned according to the likeness of the transgression of Adam, who is a type of Him who was to come. [15]But the free gift *is* not like the offense. For if by the one man's offense many died, much more the grace of God and the gift by the grace of the one Man, Jesus Christ, abounded to many. [16]And the gift *is* not like *that which came* through the one who sinned. For the judgment *which came* from one *offense resulted* in condemnation, but the free gift *which*

came from many offenses *resulted* in justification. [17]For if by the one man's offense death reigned through the one, much more those who receive abundance of grace and of the gift of righteousness will reign in life through the One, Jesus Christ.) [18]Therefore, as through one man's offense *judgment came* to all men, resulting in condemnation, even so through one Man's righteous act *the free gift came* to all men, resulting in justification of life. [19]For as by one man's disobedience many were made sinners, so also by one Man's obedience many will be made righteous. [20]Moreover the law entered that the offense might abound. But where sin abounded, grace abounded much more, [21]so that as sin reigned in death, even so grace might reign through righteousness to eternal life through Jesus Christ our Lord.

Dead to Sin, Alive to God

6 What shall we say then? Shall we continue in sin that grace may abound? [2]Certainly not! How shall we who died to sin live any longer in it? [3]Or do you not know that as many of us as were baptized into Christ Jesus were baptized into His death? [4]Therefore we were buried with Him through baptism into death, that just as Christ was raised from the dead by the glory of the Father, even so we also should walk in newness of life. [5]For if we have been united together in the likeness of His death, certainly we also shall be *in the likeness* of His resurrection, [6]knowing this, that our old man was crucified with *Him*, that the body of sin might be done away with, that we should no

---

5:6–11 Jesus' unique love (Gk. *agapē*) focuses on the nature of the one loving rather than on the merit of the one being loved. God's nature is self-giving love, which always acts in the best interest of His creation, even of His enemies (v. 8). "Reconciliation" describes the new relationship with Christ (vv. 10, 11).

5:12–14 Death comes to all because all have sinned (see Rom. 3:23). Condemned in Adam we can be redeemed in Christ. We remain profoundly affected by Adam's sin, having inherited a sinful nature from him.

6:1, 2 The proper response to God's grace is gratitude. Those with a distorted perspective argued that since grace would be more abundant where sin was greater, they should go on sinning in order to experience more of God's grace (Rom. 5:20). Such an attitude trifled with God's grace and reflected a total lack of understanding of the New Birth. When an individual accepts Christ in faith, the sinful desires of the old nature are put to death and the believer receives a new nature through

Christ's resurrected life (Rom. 6:2; see also 2 Cor. 5:17). God does not need more sins to reveal His grace; He desires more lives to reflect His righteousness and goodness.

6:3, 4 Paul utilized the imagery of baptism to support his argument. Death to sin and resurrection to life eternal are the focus here. The woman who has accepted Christ by faith has committed herself to a new kind of life. Baptism is a sign of this wonderful reality.

6:5–14 The old man and the body of sin refer to the old self or sinful human nature (v. 6). The "body of sin" also could designate all of unredeemed humanity in bondage to sin and death in opposition to the "body of Christ" or the church. The believer has died to sin (vv. 5–8). The ethical demands of the Christian life are based on the new relationship Christians have with Christ (vv. 11–13). Failure in Christian living results from failure to appropriate Christ's power in daily living (v. 14).

FREEDOM *NO MORE BONDAGE*

In both Old and New Testaments, freedom refers to liberation from slavery, whether in a socio-political sense (see Joseph's imprisonment, Gen. 39:20–23), a spiritual sense (Gal. 4:21—5:15), or with regard to our mortality (Heb. 2:15).

Given this context, our freedom—whether political or spiritual—depends on God's initiative (Mic. 6:4; Rom. 8:2). When Adam and Eve sinned, God came to them (Gen. 3:8) with the promise of freedom from sin's curse (Gen. 3:15).

This promise was fulfilled when God sent His Son to be the Way to eternal freedom (Luke 4:18, 19). We do not have to be slaves of sin (John 8:34), for the Truth (that is, Christ) can make us free if we will accept the price of deliverance (John 8:31, 32). Paradoxically we are freed from sin's bondage for a purpose: to become "slaves of God" (Rom. 6:22). We are free *from* the judgment of ourselves and others (Rom. 5:9) and, at the same time, free *for* service to Him and others (Gal. 5:13, 14). Ultimate freedom, that is, being ransomed from the slavery of sin, is vital to any understanding of redemption through the blood of Christ (Rom. 6:15–23).

See also Is. 61:1; 2 Cor. 3:17; notes on Access to God (Rom. 10); Government and Citizenship (Rom. 13); Priesthood of the Believer (1 Pet. 2).

longer be slaves of sin. 7For he who has died has been freed from sin. 8Now if we died with Christ, we believe that we shall also live with Him, 9knowing that Christ, having been raised from the dead, dies no more. Death no longer has dominion over Him. 10For *the death* that He died, He died to sin once for all; but *the life* that He lives, He lives to God. 11Likewise you also, reckon yourselves to be dead indeed to sin, but alive to God in Christ Jesus our Lord.

12Therefore do not let sin reign in your mortal body, that you should obey it in its lusts. 13And do not present your members *as* instruments of unrighteousness to sin, but present yourselves to God as being alive from the dead, and your members *as* instruments of righteousness to God. 14For sin shall not have dominion over you, for you are not under law but under grace.

From Slaves of Sin to Slaves of God

15What then? Shall we sin because we are not under law but under grace? Certainly not! 16Do you not know that to whom you present yourselves slaves to obey, you are that one's slaves whom you obey, whether of sin *leading* to death, or of obedience *leading* to righteousness? 17But God be thanked that *though* you were slaves of sin, yet you obeyed from the heart that form of doctrine to which you were delivered. 18And having been set free from sin, you became slaves of righteousness. 19I speak in human *terms* because of the weakness of your flesh. For just as you presented your members *as* slaves of uncleanness, and of lawlessness *leading* to *more* lawlessness, so now present your members *as* slaves *of* righteousness for holiness.

20For when you were slaves of sin, you were free in regard to righteousness. 21What fruit did you have then in the things of which you are now ashamed? For the end of those things *is* death. 22But now having been set free from sin, and having become slaves of God, you have your fruit to holiness, and the end, everlasting life. 23For the wages of sin *is* death, but the gift of God *is* eternal life in Christ Jesus our Lord.

Freed from the Law

7Or do you not know, brethren (for I speak to those who know the law), that the law has dominion over a man as long as he lives? 2For the woman who has a husband is bound by the law to *her* husband as long as he lives. But if the husband dies, she is released from the law of *her* husband. 3So then if, while *her* husband lives, she marries another man, she will be called an adulteress; but if her husband dies, she is free from that law, so that she is no adulteress, though she has married another man. 4Therefore, my brethren, you also

6:15–22 Some viewed salvation as a deliverance only from the consequences of sin and its *penalty* rather than deliverance from its *power* as well. Paul utilized an analogy from the slave market to deal with this casual attitude toward sin. One is either a slave of sin or a slave of righteousness (vv. 16–18). The Greek word translated "slaves" is the same word Paul used to describe himself as a "bond-servant" of Christ (v. 16; Rom. 1:1). Obedience to God is the measure of devotion to Him.

7:1–6 Paul denounced a religion that consists of trying to earn merit with God by keeping the Law. He employed the analogy of marriage. A married woman is bound to her husband as long as he lives. When her husband dies, however, she is free to remarry (see 1 Cor. 7:39). Christians, having died to the Law, are free to be joined to Christ (see Gal. 2:19, 20). The Christian woman has been delivered from slavery to the Law as her old master and experiences a life of freedom in Christ, her new Lord. The motive for her new life of fruitfulness comes not from the Law's demands but from a desire to respond to God's love (Rom. 7:4). The Holy Spirit provides the power to live in newness of life with Christ (v. 6).

FLESH VS. SPIRIT

SINFUL NATURE	SPIRITUAL NATURE
Focuses on things of the flesh (Rom. 8:5)	Focuses on things of the Spirit (Rom. 8:5)
Is death (Rom. 8:6)	Is life and peace (Rom. 8:6)
Is enmity against God (Rom. 8:7)	Meets the requirement of the Law (Rom. 8:4)
Means you do not have the Spirit of Christ and are not His (Rom. 8:9)	Means that Christ lives in you and you are in the Spirit (Rom. 8:9)
Is not subject to the Law of God (Rom. 8:7)	Is life (Rom. 8:10)
Cannot please God (Rom. 8:8)	Will give life to your mortal bodies (Rom. 8:11)

A heart set on worldly, carnal things lacks the power to resist sin. Such a mind-set leads to death and eternal separation from God (see Ps. 1:1–6; Gal. 5:19–24).

have become dead to the law through the body of Christ, that you may be married to another—to Him who was raised from the dead, that we should bear fruit to God. ⁵For when we were in the flesh, the sinful passions which were aroused by the law were at work in our members to bear fruit to death. ⁶But now we have been delivered from the law, having died to what we were held by, so that we should serve in the newness of the Spirit and not *in* the oldness of the letter.

Sin's Advantage in the Law

⁷What shall we say then? *Is* the law sin? Certainly not! On the contrary, I would not have known sin except through the law. For I would not have known covetousness unless the law had said, *"You shall not covet."*ª ⁸But sin, taking opportunity by the commandment, produced in me all *manner of evil* desire. For apart from the law sin *was* dead. ⁹I was alive once without the law, but when the commandment came, sin revived and I died. ¹⁰And the commandment, which *was* to *bring* life, I found to *bring* death. ¹¹For sin, taking occasion by the commandment, deceived me, and by it killed *me.* ¹²Therefore the law *is* holy, and the commandment holy and just and good.

Law Cannot Save from Sin

¹³Has then what is good become death to me? Certainly not! But sin, that it might appear sin, was producing death in me through what is good, so that sin through the commandment might become exceedingly sinful. ¹⁴For we know that the law is spiritual, but I am carnal, sold under sin. ¹⁵For what I am doing, I do not understand. For what I will to do, that I do not practice; but what I hate, that I do. ¹⁶If, then, I do what I will not to do, I agree with the law that *it is* good. ¹⁷But now, *it is* no longer I who do it, but sin that dwells in me. ¹⁸For I know that in me (that is, in my flesh) nothing good dwells; for to will is present with me, but *how* to perform what is good I do not find. ¹⁹For the good that I will *to do,* I do not do; but the evil I will not *to do,* that I practice. ²⁰Now if I do what I will not *to do,* it is no longer I who do it, but sin that dwells in me.

²¹I find then a law, that evil is present with me, the one who wills to do good. ²²For I delight in the law of God according to the inward man. ²³But I see another law in my members, warring against

7:7 ªExodus 20:17; Deuteronomy 5:21

7:14–25 Several interpretations have been suggested for these verses:

- A reflection of life before conversion;
- The experience of the saved or unsaved who seek merely to obey the Law;
- A picture of the carnal Christian's internal struggle between the spiritual nature's desire to obey God and the fleshly nature's desire to go one's own way;
- The process of growing sanctification after conversion.

The latter seems more probable. Though the believing woman would be delivered from the guilt and penalty of sin, she would not be free from the presence of sin until Christ returned. The struggle against sin continues throughout life on earth. The difference for the Christian woman, who has the mind of Christ, is that there is the hope of being rescued from her sins and the power to achieve victory over the sinful nature. Even though the struggle with sin remains while on earth, the Christian is no longer condemned before God but stands righteous before Him.

FATHERHOOD OF GOD   *MY HEAVENLY FATHER*

In recent years, much discussion has been given to the practice of referring to God as "Father." While clearly God transcends sexuality, being neither male nor female, the writers of the Bible were inspired to address Him with male pronouns. The Spirit of God enables believers to call God "Abba, Father" (lit. "Daddy," Rom. 8:15).

God revealed Himself throughout the Old Testament as "Father" (Jer. 3:19), and this was the term Jesus used in addressing Him (John 17). The Fatherhood of God is not merely one of many suitable "God metaphors." It is in a class of its own, what scholars would label as an analogy *sui generis.* The title "Father" not only tells us what God does—or what some aspect of His character is like; rather, it identifies more of who He actually is. The same cannot be said of biblical God metaphors such as "tree," "door," "rock," "mother hen," or "mistress of the house."

True Fatherhood is grounded in the basis of God's being—in the basis of God the Father relating to the Son and the Spirit. Human fatherhood is but an imperfect symbol of this transcendent reality. The Fatherhood of God is not inconsequential or alterable, for it is the primary basis by which God has determined that believers will relate to Him: "I will be a Father to you, And you shall be My sons and daughters, Says the Lord Almighty" (2 Cor. 6:18).

See also Deut. 32:6,18; Is. 63:16; Jer. 3:19; Lam. 3:22, note; Mal. 2:10; John 10:38; notes on Attributes of God (Ex. 33; Deut. 4; 32; 2 Chr. 19; Job 23; 42; Ps. 25; 90; 102; 119; Is. 6; 65; Jer. 23; Rom. 2; Eph. 1; 1 John 5); Female Metaphors for God (Num. 11); Goddess Religion (Ex. 20); Patriarchy (Gen. 28)

the law of my mind, and bringing me into captivity to the law of sin which is in my members. ²⁴O wretched man that I am! Who will deliver me from this body of death? ²⁵I thank God—through Jesus Christ our Lord!

So then, with the mind I myself serve the law of God, but with the flesh the law of sin.

Free from Indwelling Sin

8 *There* is therefore now no condemnation to those who are in Christ Jesus,ᵃ who do not walk according to the flesh, but according to the Spirit. ²For the law of the Spirit of life in Christ Jesus has made me free from the law of sin and death. ³For what the law could not do in that it was weak through the flesh, God *did* by sending His own Son in the likeness of sinful flesh, on account of sin: He condemned sin in the flesh, ⁴that the righteous requirement of the law might be fulfilled in us who do not walk according to the flesh but according to the Spirit. ⁵For those who live according to the flesh set their minds on the things of the flesh, but those *who live* according to the Spirit, the things of the Spirit. ⁶For to be carnally minded *is*

death, but to be spiritually minded *is* life and peace. ⁷Because the carnal mind *is* enmity against God; for it is not subject to the law of God, nor indeed can be. ⁸So then, those who are in the flesh cannot please God.

⁹But you are not in the flesh but in the Spirit, if indeed the Spirit of God dwells in you. Now if anyone does not have the Spirit of Christ, he is not His. ¹⁰And if Christ *is* in you, the body *is* dead because of sin, but the Spirit *is* life because of righteousness. ¹¹But if the Spirit of Him who raised Jesus from the dead dwells in you, He who raised Christ from the dead will also give life to your mortal bodies through His Spirit who dwells in you.

Sonship Through the Spirit

¹²Therefore, brethren, we are debtors—not to the flesh, to live according to the flesh. ¹³For if you live according to the flesh you will die; but if by the Spirit you put to death the deeds of the body, you will live. ¹⁴For as many as are led by the Spirit of God, these are sons of God. ¹⁵For you did

8:1 ᵃNU-Text omits the rest of this verse.

8:1 Paul contrasted walking in the flesh with walking in the Spirit. "Walk" refers to lifestyle, and walking in the flesh is living according to the sinful, selfish dictates of one's desires (see Gal. 5:19–21). Walking in the Spirit describes a life yielded to the control of God's Spirit (see Gal. 5:22, 23).

8:9–11 The Spirit of God permanently indwells every believer at the moment that individual believes in Jesus Christ. The presence or absence of the Holy Spirit within determines whether or not one has experienced salvation (Gal. 2:20).

8:12–17 As children of God, Christians are debtors (v. 12). They are obligated not to live according to the sinful, selfish desires

of the flesh. "The deeds of the body" is another designation for fleshly or carnal desires (v. 13). Those who are led by God's Spirit are indeed God's children (v. 14). Obedience is the test of personal relationship with the Lord.

Believers are God's children and his heirs by adoption (vv. 15, 17; see Esth. 2, Adoption). The adopted individual was regarded as a new person beginning a new life. Legally, the adopted one gained all the rights of one born into the family as the legitimate heir to the father's estate. God's children enjoy security in their relationship with Him. They also enjoy intimacy. "Abba" (Aram., lit. "Daddy") was the familiar expression of intimacy used by Jewish children to address their fathers (Rom. 8:15).

not receive the spirit of bondage again to fear, but you received the Spirit of adoption by whom we cry out, "Abba, Father." [16]The Spirit Himself bears witness with our spirit that we are children of God, [17]and if children, then heirs—heirs of God and joint heirs with Christ, if indeed we suffer with *Him,* that we may also be glorified together.

From Suffering to Glory

[18]For I consider that the sufferings of this present time are not worthy *to be compared* with the glory which shall be revealed in us. [19]For the earnest expectation of the creation eagerly waits for the revealing of the sons of God. [20]For the creation was subjected to futility, not willingly, but because of Him who subjected *it* in hope; [21]because the creation itself also will be delivered from the bondage of corruption into the glorious liberty of the children of God. [22]For we know that the whole creation groans and labors with birth pangs together until now. [23]Not only *that,* but we also who have the firstfruits of the Spirit, even we ourselves groan within ourselves, eagerly waiting for the adoption, the redemption of our body. [24]For we were saved in this hope, but hope that is seen is not hope; for why does one still hope for what he sees? [25]But if we hope for what we do not see, we eagerly wait for *it* with perseverance.

[26]Likewise the Spirit also helps in our weaknesses. For we do not know what we should pray for as we ought, but the Spirit Himself makes intercession for us[a] with groanings which cannot be uttered. [27]Now He who searches the hearts knows what the mind of the Spirit *is,* because He makes intercession for the saints according to *the will of God.*

[28]And we know that all things work together for good to those who love God, to those who are the called according to *His* purpose. [29]For whom He foreknew, He also predestined *to be* conformed to the image of His Son, that He might be the firstborn among many brethren. [30]Moreover whom He predestined, these He also called; whom He called, these He also justified; and whom He justified, these He also glorified.

God's Everlasting Love

[31]What then shall we say to these things? If God *is* for us, who *can be* against us? [32]He who did not spare His own Son, but delivered Him up for us all, how shall He not with Him also freely give us all things? [33]Who shall bring a charge against God's elect? *It is* God who justifies. [34]Who *is* he who condemns? *It is* Christ who died, and furthermore is also risen, who is even at the right hand of God, who also makes intercession for us. [35]Who shall separate us from the love of Christ? *Shall* tribulation, or distress, or persecution, or famine, or nakedness, or peril, or sword? [36]As it is written:

"For Your sake we are killed all day long;
We are accounted as sheep for the slaughter."[a]

[37]Yet in all these things we are more than conquerors through Him who loved us. [38]For I am persuaded that neither death nor life, nor angels nor principalities nor powers, nor things present nor things to come, [39]nor height nor depth, nor any other created thing, shall be able to separate us from the love of God which is in Christ Jesus our Lord.

Israel's Rejection of Christ

9 I tell the truth in Christ, I am not lying, my conscience also bearing me witness in the Holy Spirit, [2]that I have great sorrow and continual grief in my heart. [3]For I could wish that I myself were accursed from Christ for my brethren, my countrymen[a] according to the flesh, [4]who are Israelites, to whom *pertain* the adoption, the glory, the covenants, the giving of the law, the service *of God,* and the promises; [5]of whom *are* the fathers

---

8:26 [a]NU-Text omits *for us.*   **8:36** [a]Psalm 44:22   **9:3** [a]Or *relatives*

8:18–25 Paul contrasted the sufferings of the present with the glorious hope for the future. Paul had suffered greatly for the sake of the gospel (see 2 Cor. 1:8–11; 4:7–12, 16–18; 11:23–30). Yet he affirmed that those sufferings were nothing compared to the future glory he anticipated (see 2 Cor. 4:17). God's children will participate in the glory of Christ; they will experience complete conformity to Christ (see Col. 1:27). The Feast of Weeks or Pentecost involved the dedication of the firstfruits of the wheat harvest to the Lord (Lev. 23:15–21). Believers have received the firstfruits of the Holy Spirit as God's down payment or guarantee of ultimate victory (Rom. 8:24, 25).

8:26, 27 The Spirit helps believers know how to pray (v. 26). Paul prayed for the removal of a hindrance in his life, but God did not take away that burden (2 Cor. 12:7–10). The Spirit articulates those prayer burdens that God's people cannot even express. The Spirit's intercession can be trusted because He intercedes according to God's will (Rom. 8:27).

8:28 God works for good in all things. This verse does not affirm that all things are good or that all things work together for good for all people. Rather the great promise is that God will overrule and work even through the tragedies caused by sin's presence in the world to accomplish His purposes in the lives of those who love Him and who have responded to His call.

8:29, 30 God alone has complete knowledge, for certainly nothing can be hidden from Him (Prov. 15:11; Is. 29:15, 16; Matt. 10:29–31; Heb. 4:13). Foreknowledge must be understood as a part of God's relationship to His creation (Jer. 1:5). Reconciling God's foreknowledge with the moral responsibility of mankind is a wonderful mystery in the tension of theology. In any case, God's salvation is born out of His eternal purposes and is not dependent upon human initiative or the world's changing circumstances (Rom. 8:21, 22; 1 Pet. 1:20).

9:1–5 Paul expressed his grief over the fact that most of the Jews were alienated from God (vv. 1–5). Paul wished himself

ACCESS TO GOD — A PERSONAL ENCOUNTER

Under the old covenant, human access to God was limited. Only the high priest once a year could enter the Most Holy Place to meet directly with the Lord.

New Covenant believers, however, regarded the tearing of the veil, the thick curtain that separated the holy place from the Most Holy Place, at the time of the Crucifixion as a sign that all could freely come to God through Christ Jesus (Matt. 27:51–54; Eph. 2:13).

PRIOR to the death of Jesus on the Cross . . .

- Only priests (of the Levite tribe) could offer gifts and sacrifices;
- Only Hebrews could be called the sons and daughters of the Lord;
- Only those who kept the Day of Atonement were considered in right relationship with God;
- Only those who fully knew and followed the Law could be called righteous.

AFTER the death of Jesus on the Cross . . .

- Whoever calls on the name of the Lord shall be saved (Rom. 10:12–13);
- A person can be called a child of God regardless of race, sex, or social status (Gal. 3:26–29; 4:1–7; Col. 3:9–11);
- Whoever believes in Christ shall be counted as righteous (1 John 2:29) and shall inherit everlasting life (John 3:16);
- All who believe can make the ultimate sacrifice to God, which is to do His will with all of your heart, mind, and soul (Rom. 12:1; Heb. 10:7).

See also Dan. 2:23, note; notes on Forgiveness (Ps. 51; Luke 17); God's Will (Eph. 5); Priesthood of the Believer (1 Pet. 2); Salvation (Eph. 2)

---

and from whom, according to the flesh, Christ came, who is over all, *the* eternally blessed God. Amen.

Israel's Rejection and God's Purpose

[6]But it is not that the word of God has taken no effect. For they *are* not all Israel who *are* of Israel, [7]nor *are they* all children because they are the seed of Abraham; but, *"In Isaac your seed shall be called."*[a] [8]That is, those who *are* the children of the flesh, these *are* not the children of God; but the children of the promise are counted as the seed. [9]For this *is* the word of promise: *"At this time I will come and Sarah shall have a son."*[a]

[10]And not only *this,* but when Rebecca also had conceived by one man, *even* by our father Isaac [11](for *the children* not yet being born, nor having done any good or evil, that the purpose of God according to election might stand, not of works but of Him who calls), [12]it was said to her, *"The older*

shall serve the younger."[a] [13]As it is written, *"Jacob I have loved, but Esau I have hated."*[a]

Israel's Rejection and God's Justice

[14]What shall we say then? Is there unrighteousness with God? Certainly not! [15]For He says to Moses, *"I will have mercy on whomever I will have mercy, and I will have compassion on whomever I will have compassion."*[a] [16]So then *it is* not of him who wills, nor of him who runs, but of God who shows mercy. [17]For the Scripture says to the Pharaoh, *"For this very purpose I have raised you up, that I may show My power in you, and that My name may be declared in all the earth."*[a] [18]Therefore He has mercy on whom He wills, and whom He wills He hardens.

[19]You will say to me then, "Why does He still find fault? For who has resisted His will?" [20]But

········
9:7 [a]Genesis 21:12   **9:9** [a]Genesis 18:10, 14   **9:12** [a]Genesis 25:23   **9:13** [a]Malachi 1:2, 3   **9:15** [a]Exodus 33:19   **9:17** [a]Exodus 9:16

"accursed" (Gk. *anathema*) and devoted to destruction in place of his countrymen (Rom. 9:3). Although Paul's mission was primarily to the Gentiles, he never ceased to show deep concern for his brothers "according to the flesh," that is, his fellow Jews (v. 3). Paul mentioned some advantages enjoyed by the Jews in their relationship with God that made their rejection of Christ even more tragic (vv. 4, 5): The glory of God's presence, the covenants, the Law, and the promises. Even Jesus the Messiah was born a Jew.

9:14–18 Israel's rejection must be understood in light of Israel's responsibility (see Rom. 9—11). God rejected Israel be-

cause Israel rejected God. Likewise God raised up Pharaoh and hardened his heart (Rom. 9:17, 18) even as Pharaoh first decided to reject God (Ex. 4:21; 5:2; see Ex. 14, Justice; chart, The Ten Plagues on Egypt). God raised up Pharaoh to demonstrate His power; yet Pharaoh rejected God in his own heart (Ex. 8:15). God let Pharaoh have his own way, hardening Pharaoh's heart in his disbelief (Ex. 7:3, 4, note).

9:19–26 God is not required to answer to mankind. Just as the clay lacks power and authority to question the work of the potter, so no one has authority to question the ways of God. In all things, God, as the potter, prepared vessels both

indeed, O man, who are you to reply against God? Will the thing formed say to him who formed *it*, "Why have you made me like this?" [21]Does not the potter have power over the clay, from the same lump to make one vessel for honor and another for dishonor?

[22]*What* if God, wanting to show *His* wrath and to make His power known, endured with much longsuffering the vessels of wrath prepared for destruction, [23]and that He might make known the riches of His glory on the vessels of mercy, which He had prepared beforehand for glory, [24]even us whom He called, not of the Jews only, but also of the Gentiles?

[25]As He says also in Hosea:

"I will call them My people, who were not My people,
   And her beloved, who was not beloved."[a]
[26]"And it shall come to pass in the place where it was said to them,
   'You are not My people,'
   There they shall be called sons of the living God."[a]

[27]Isaiah also cries out concerning Israel:[a]

"Though the number of the children of Israel be as the sand of the sea,
   The remnant will be saved.
[28]For He will finish the work and cut it short in righteousness,
   Because the LORD will make a short work upon the earth."[a]

[29]And as Isaiah said before:

"Unless the LORD of Sabaoth[a] had left us a seed,
   We would have become like Sodom,
   And we would have been made like Gomorrah."[b]

Present Condition of Israel

[30]What shall we say then? That Gentiles, who did not pursue righteousness, have attained to righteousness, even the righteousness of faith; [31]but Israel, pursuing the law of righteousness, has not attained to the law of righteousness.[a] [32]Why? Because *they did* not *seek it* by faith, but as it were, by the works of the law.[a] For they stumbled at that stumbling stone. [33]As it is written:

"Behold, I lay in Zion a stumbling stone and rock of offense,
   And whoever believes on Him will not be put to shame."[a]

Israel Needs the Gospel

10 Brethren, my heart's desire and prayer to God for Israel[a] is that they may be saved. [2]For I bear them witness that they have a zeal for God, but not according to knowledge. [3]For they being ignorant of God's righteousness, and seeking to establish their own righteousness, have not submitted to the righteousness of God. [4]For Christ *is* the end of the law for righteousness to everyone who believes.

[5]For Moses writes about the righteousness which is of the law, "The man who does those things shall live by them."[a] [6]But the righteousness of faith speaks in this way, "Do not say in your heart, 'Who will ascend into heaven?' "[a] (that is, to bring Christ down *from above*) [7]or, " 'Who will descend into the abyss?' "[a] (that is, to bring Christ up from the dead). [8]But what does it say? "The word is near you, in your mouth and in your heart"[a] (that is, the word of faith which we preach): [9]that if you confess with your mouth the Lord Jesus and believe in your heart that God has raised Him from the dead, you will be saved. [10]For with the heart one

· ·

9:25 [a]Hosea 2:23   **9:26** [a]Hosea 1:10   **9:27** [a]Isaiah 10:22, 23   **9:28** [a]NU-Text reads *For the LORD will finish the work and cut it short upon the earth.*   **9:29** [a]Literally, in Hebrew, *Hosts* [b]Isaiah 1:9   **9:31** [a]NU-Text omits *of righteousness.*   **9:32** [a]NU-Text reads *by works.*   **9:33** [a]Isaiah 8:14; 28:16   **10:1** [a]NU-Text reads *them.*   **10:5** [a]Leviticus 18:5   **10:6** [a]Deuteronomy 30:12   **10:7** [a]Deuteronomy 30:13   **10:8** [a]Deuteronomy 30:14

for destruction in order to reveal His wrath and power and for mercy to reveal His glory and love. God acts consistently with His character as He has revealed Himself in Christ. Gentiles as well as Jews were included in God's redemptive plan (vv. 25, 26; see Hos. 1:10; 2:23). "My people" is covenant language indicating the restoration of the covenant relationship (Rom. 9:25, 26; see Jer. 32:38). The designation "vessels of wrath" refers to the unbelieving to whom God has unceasingly extended pleading hands (Rom. 9:22; see 10:21).

9:27–29 Paul emphasized that only a remnant of Israel or the Jews would experience salvation (Is. 1:9; 10:22, 23). The title "Lord of Sabaoth" or Lord of Hosts is a reminder of God's sovereignty (Rom. 9:29).

9:30–33 Paul contrasted Jews and Gentiles. The apostle's greater concern was the failure of Israel. For the Jews, Christ was a "stumbling stone" because they persisted in trying to attain righteousness by keeping the Law (vv. 32, 33). The

Gentiles, in contrast, accepted by faith the righteousness of God. This does not imply that all Gentiles will be saved. Only those who avoid the mistake of Israel—that is, dependence upon the Law for salvation—will experience redemption (v. 24). Nowhere is it any clearer that works are futile as a means of justification. Those who place their faith in God need never fear that He might prove unreliable (v. 33; see Is. 8:14; 28:16).

10:1–13 All people, both Jew and Gentile, experience right standing with God in the same way (v. 12). The Jews failed in their search to obtain a right relationship with God by keeping the Law (vv. 1–3). Paul declared that Christ is the end or goal of the Law (v. 4). The Law was fulfilled in Christ. Both Jews and Gentiles receive right standing with God by faith in Christ (vv. 8–13; compare v. 13 with Joel 2:32). God in Christ has done everything necessary for salvation (Rom. 10:6, 7). No human effort or accomplishment can save and make a person right with God (Eph 2:8, 9).

believes unto righteousness, and with the mouth confession is made unto salvation. [11]For the Scripture says, *"Whoever believes on Him will not be put to shame."*[a] [12]For there is no distinction between Jew and Greek, for the same Lord over all is rich to all who call upon Him. [13]For *"whoever calls on the name of the LORD shall be saved."*[a]

Israel Rejects the Gospel

[14]How then shall they call on Him in whom they have not believed? And how shall they believe in Him of whom they have not heard? And how shall they hear without a preacher? [15]And how shall they preach unless they are sent? As it is written:

"How beautiful are the feet of those who preach the
gospel of peace,[a]
Who bring glad tidings of good things!"[b]

[16]But they have not all obeyed the gospel. For Isaiah says, *"LORD, who has believed our report?"*[a] [17]So then faith *comes* by hearing, and hearing by the word of God.

[18]But I say, have they not heard? Yes indeed:

"Their sound has gone out to all the earth,
And their words to the ends of the world."[a]

[19]But I say, did Israel not know? First Moses says:

"I will provoke you to jealousy by those who are not a
nation,
I will move you to anger by a foolish nation."[a]

[20]But Isaiah is very bold and says:

"I was found by those who did not seek Me;
I was made manifest to those who did not ask for
Me."[a]

[21]But to Israel he says:

"All day long I have stretched out My hands
To a disobedient and contrary people."[a]

Israel's Rejection Not Total

11 I say then, has God cast away His people? Certainly not! For I also am an Israelite, of the seed of Abraham, *of* the tribe of Benjamin. [2]God has not cast away His people whom He foreknew. Or do you not know what the Scripture says of Elijah, how he pleads with God against Israel, saying, [3]*"LORD, they have killed Your prophets and torn down Your altars, and I alone am left, and they seek my life"*?[a] [4]But what does the divine response say to him? *"I have reserved for Myself seven thousand men who have not bowed the knee to Baal."*[a] [5]Even so then, at this present time there is a remnant according to the election of grace. [6]And if by grace, then *it is* no longer of works-; otherwise grace is no longer grace.[a] But if *it is* of works, it is no longer grace; otherwise work is no longer work.

[7]What then? Israel has not obtained what it seeks; but the elect have obtained it, and the rest were blinded. [8]Just as it is written:

"God has given them a spirit of stupor,
Eyes that they should not see
And ears that they should not hear,
To this very day."[a]

[9]And David says:

"Let their table become a snare and a trap,
A stumbling block and a recompense to them.
[10]*Let their eyes be darkened, so that they do not see,*
And bow down their back always."[a]

Israel's Rejection Not Final

[11]I say then, have they stumbled that they should fall? Certainly not! But through their fall, to provoke them to jealousy, salvation *has come* to the Gentiles. [12]Now if their fall *is* riches for the

---

10:11 [a]Isaiah 28:16   10:13 [a]Joel 2:32   10:15 [a]NU-Text omits *preach the gospel of peace, Who.*   [b]Isaiah 52:7; Nahum 1:15   10:16 [a]Isaiah 53:1   10:18 [a]Psalm 19:4   10:19 [a]Deuteronomy 32:21   10:20 [a]Isaiah 65:1   10:21 [a]Isaiah 65:2   11:3 [a]1 Kings 19:10, 14   11:4 [a]1 Kings 19:18   11:6 [a]NU-Text omits the rest of this verse.   11:8 [a]Deuteronomy 29:4; Isaiah 29:10   11:10 [a]Psalm 69:22, 23

10:14–21 God's own people, the Jews, rejected His message. Paul clearly stated that Israel was responsible for rejecting the gospel. Paul refuted any potential arguments the Jews might raise, such as claiming that they lacked messengers from God (vv. 14–17), an opportunity to hear (v. 18), or a clear understanding of the message (vv. 19–21). Paul clearly assigned responsibility to the Jews for rejecting the gospel. Israel's failure stemmed not from a lack of hearing or understanding but from disobedience and rebellion (v. 21).

11:1–10 God preserved a faithful remnant. Paul identified himself as belonging to this remnant of Jewish believers (v. 1). The remnant provided evidence that God had not totally abandoned His people. Good works do not merit God's grace; they are evidence of His grace (vv. 5, 6; see Eph. 2:8–10). Paul

quoted Isaiah 29:10 to illustrate the blindness of disobedience (Rom. 11:8). Some understand that this verse does not describe God's intended result for His people but the inevitable result when people close their hearts and minds to God. Others believe God's grace is extended to the elect who constitute the remnant (vv. 5–9), while those remaining are blinded in their sins (vv. 7, 8).

11:11–24 The Jews' rejection of the gospel amazingly resulted in its being extended more quickly to the Gentiles. The 1st-century missionaries proclaimed the gospel to the Jews first as recorded in the Book of Acts. When the Jews rejected the message, the Christians turned to the Gentile audience (see Acts 13:46). Nevertheless, Paul had not given up on the Jews. Paul employed the imagery of an olive tree to warn the

*Essential to hospitality is the open heart which results in an open home . . .
be it a small room, a modest apartment, or a mansion–
in which we can practice hospitality.*

Karen Mains

---

world, and their failure riches for the Gentiles, how much more their fullness!

[13]For I speak to you Gentiles; inasmuch as I am an apostle to the Gentiles, I magnify my ministry, [14]if by any means I may provoke to jealousy *those who are* my flesh and save some of them. [15]For if their being cast away *is* the reconciling of the world, what *will* their acceptance *be* but life from the dead?

[16]For if the firstfruit *is* holy, the lump *is* also *holy;* and if the root *is* holy, so *are* the branches. [17]And if some of the branches were broken off, and you, being a wild olive tree, were grafted in among them, and with them became a partaker of the root and fatness of the olive tree, [18]do not boast against the branches. But if you do boast, *remember that* you do not support the root, but the root *supports* you.

[19]You will say then, "Branches were broken off that I might be grafted in." [20]Well *said.* Because of unbelief they were broken off, and you stand by faith. Do not be haughty, but fear. [21]For if God did not spare the natural branches, He may not spare you either. [22]Therefore consider the goodness and severity of God: on those who fell, severity; but toward you, goodness,[a] if you continue in *His* goodness. Otherwise you also will be cut off. [23]And they also, if they do not continue in unbelief, will be grafted in, for God is able to graft them in again. [24]For if you were cut out of the olive tree which is wild by nature, and were grafted contrary to nature into a cultivated olive tree, how much more will these, who *are* natural *branches,* be grafted into their own olive tree?

[25]For I do not desire, brethren, that you should be ignorant of this mystery, lest you should be wise in your own opinion, that blindness in part has happened to Israel until the fullness of the Gentiles has come in. [26]And so all Israel will be saved,[a] as it is written:

"The Deliverer will come out of Zion,
    And He will turn away ungodliness from Jacob;
[27]For this is My covenant with them,
    When I take away their sins."[a]

[28]Concerning the gospel *they are* enemies for your sake, but concerning the election *they are* beloved for the sake of the fathers. [29]For the gifts and the calling of God *are* irrevocable. [30]For as you were once disobedient to God, yet have now obtained mercy through their disobedience, [31]even so these also have now been disobedient, that through the mercy shown you they also may obtain mercy. [32]For God has committed them all to disobedience, that He might have mercy on all.

[33]Oh, the depth of the riches both of the wisdom and knowledge of God! How unsearchable *are* His judgments and His ways past finding out!

[34]"For who has known the mind of the LORD?
    Or who has become His counselor?"[a]
[35]"Or who has first given to Him
    And it shall be repaid to him?"[a]

[36]For of Him and through Him and to Him *are* all things, to whom *be* glory forever. Amen.

Living Sacrifices to God

12 I beseech you therefore, brethren, by the mercies of God, that you present your bodies a living sacrifice, holy, acceptable to God, *which is* your reasonable service. [2]And do not be conformed

---

11:22 [a]NU-Text adds *of God.*   11:26 [a]Or *delivered*   11:27 [a]Isaiah 59:20, 21   11:34 [a]Isaiah 40:13; Jeremiah 23:18   11:35 [a]Job 41:11

Gentiles against boasting about their new status (Rom. 11:17–24). The unbelieving Jews are the natural branches that have been cut from God's olive tree. The Gentile believers are only wild olive branches that have been grafted in. How much more easily can the natural branches again be grafted into the tree when Jews respond in faith (vv. 23, 24)!

11:25–36 Israel will never experience utter rejection or abandonment. Always a remnant of believers will exist. Paul affirmed that "all Israel will be saved," not suggesting every individual Jew, but a great number of Jews would turn to Christ in the end times (v. 26). The phrase "all Israel" includes "the

fullness of the Gentiles" (v. 25). A few critical scholars interpret "all Israel" to include the idea that all people ultimately will experience salvation, which is universalism. Still others believe that "all Israel" is a spiritual designation for the church. The eschatological understanding seems the better interpretation. Paul ended this passage on a note of praise celebrating God's wisdom and grace toward mankind (vv. 33–36).

12:1, 2 Paul turned to practical matters concerning the application of salvation (see Rom. 12—15). These verses constitute a call ("beseech," Gk. *parakalō* , lit. "call alongside") to

SPIRITUAL GIFTS *EQUIPPED FOR SERVICE*

Spiritual gifts are special abilities given to believers for ministry and service. God is the divine source of all gifts (1 Pet. 4:10), and His gifts are very diverse (1 Cor. 12:4, 5). These spiritual gifts are not given only to the elite, however. Each believer receives at least one spiritual gift (1 Cor. 12:7–11). All spiritual gifts are to be used for Christian service, not for personal edification (Eph. 4:11–16).

The "gifts of the Spirit" are unique manifestations of the Holy Spirit. While natural or inherited talents are also God-given, spiritual gifts are not dependent upon genetic codes and are specifically intended to serve others. Whereas the "fruit of the Holy Spirit" refers to the character of a believer, the "gifts of the Spirit" describe the service of a believer. At the time of salvation, a believer receives the gift of the Holy Spirit's presence; then throughout life she uses specific spiritual gifts given by the Spirit for the benefit of others.

The New Testament identifies a variety of spiritual gifts. Paul's listing of about twenty different spiritual gifts is not to be considered comprehensive but rather presents examples of the diversity of potential gifts available for service.

Two New Testament words describe these gifts: "Spirit gifts" (Gk. *pneumatikōn*, 1 Cor. 12:1), designed for the edification of the church, and "grace gifts" (Gk. *charismatōn*, 1 Cor. 12:4), not given according to our personal desires or productivity but sovereignly dispensed by God. The words are obviously synonymous, though emphasizing different aspects.

Some of the gifts are employed in serving, others in teaching, and all for edifying the church. Most important in the eyes of the Lord is not the particular gift but rather an individual's faithfulness to use the gift bestowed unselfishly and for the edification of the church.

One of the greatest challenges a Christian woman faces is that of discovering and using her specific spiritual gifts. Personal Bible study and prayer can help a Christian unwrap unique gifts of the Spirit. Various inventories are also available to assess spiritual gifts. Since God has carefully selected specific spiritual gifts for each of His children, each Christian is responsible for discovering, developing, and using her personal gifts for God's service.

See also 1 Cor. 12:28–31; chart on Spiritual Gifts of Women in the Bible; notes on Feminine Leadership (1 Sam. 25); Fruit of the Spirit (Ps. 86; Rom. 5; 15; 1 Cor. 10; 13; Gal. 5; Eph. 4; Col. 3; 2 Thess. 1; Rev. 2); Women's Ministries (John 4; Acts 2; 1 Cor. 11; Eph. 2; 1 Tim. 3; Titus 2)

to this world, but be transformed by the renewing of your mind, that you may prove what *is* that good and acceptable and perfect will of God.

Serve God with Spiritual Gifts

³For I say, through the grace given to me, to everyone who is among you, not to think *of himself* more highly than he ought to think, but to think soberly, as God has dealt to each one a measure of faith. ⁴For as we have many members in one body, but all the members do not have the same function, ⁵so we, *being* many, are one body in Christ, and individually members of one another. ⁶Having

then gifts differing according to the grace that is given to us, *let us use them:* if prophecy, *let us prophesy* in proportion to our faith; ⁷or ministry, *let us use it* in *our* ministering; he who teaches, in teaching; ⁸he who exhorts, in exhortation; he who gives, with liberality; he who leads, with diligence; he who shows mercy, with cheerfulness.

Behave Like a Christian

⁹*Let* love *be* without hypocrisy. Abhor what is evil. Cling to what is good. ¹⁰*Be* kindly affectionate to one another with brotherly love, in honor giving preference to one another; ¹¹not lagging in

committed living. In light of "the mercies of God," all that God has done for believers as presented in the earlier chapters of Romans, God's people should in gratitude offer a consecrated lifestyle to Him (Rom. 12:1). The verb "present" (Gk. *parastesai*, "receive challenge") can carry the connotation of "to place at the disposal of" or "to yield." The Christian woman's sacrifice to God is to live her life as holy or set apart to God and to please Him. Her lifestyle is to express complete devotion to the Lord. The believer is not to be molded by the pressures of the sinful world ("conformed," Gk. *skematizō*, v. 2). The believer is to experience a transformation (Gk. *metamorphoō*, lit. "to change"), a new way of thinking made possible through the power of the Holy Spirit. The verb is used sparingly elsewhere in the NT—only twice concerning the Trans-

figuration of Jesus and once concerning the change in believers who are contemplating Jesus (Matt. 17:2; Mark 9:2; 2 Cor. 3:18).

12:9–21 Paul's letters always include a practical section instructing believers how to live daily as a Christian. Paul began by an appeal to love—the primary motivating factor in Christian living. Christlike behavior or character includes showing genuine love (without hypocrisy); avoiding evil and holding to good; respecting others; being diligent in service; demonstrating hope, joy, patience, and steadfastness; meeting the needs of others; showing hospitality; living humbly and peaceably; and repaying evil with good. Parts of this passage are reminiscent of Jesus' teachings in the Sermon on the

GOVERNMENT AND CITIZENSHIP LAW AND ORDER

Contrary to the thinking of most people, government is not limited to state and federal rule or even to secular jurisdiction. Government—which is management, oversight, policy-making, and administration—exists on many levels and in virtually all areas of life.

First and foremost, God's people are called to obey God as Judge, Lawgiver, and King (Is. 33:22). Second, people are called to govern themselves—to rule their spirits (Prov. 25:28). This stands in sharp contrast to the self-indulgent spirit of the present age.

The family is the primary arena for governance within a God-fearing society. Husbands are to be the spiritual leaders of their wives and children (Eph. 5:23, 6:1), and parents are to govern their children (Eph. 6:1–4). Schools govern children, and employers govern workers (Col. 3:22). Society provides numerous examples of "cultural government," including friendships and associations (Prov. 13:20; 1 Cor. 15:33). Finally, civil government exists to enforce good conduct among its citizenry (Rom. 13:1–7).

God, the King of kings (Rev. 19:16), commissioned government in its multiple forms to promote order and godliness. Our duty as citizens is to obey and pray for all our leaders (1 Tim. 2:1, 2).

See also Micah 6:8; notes on Authority (John 19); Feminine Leadership (1 Sam. 25); Obedience (Philem.); Submission (1 Pet. 3)

---

diligence, fervent in spirit, serving the Lord; [12]rejoicing in hope, patient in tribulation, continuing steadfastly in prayer; [13]distributing to the needs of the saints, given to hospitality.

[14]Bless those who persecute you; bless and do not curse. [15]Rejoice with those who rejoice, and weep with those who weep. [16]Be of the same mind toward one another. Do not set your mind on high things, but associate with the humble. Do not be wise in your own opinion.

[17]Repay no one evil for evil. Have regard for good things in the sight of all men. [18]If it is possible, as much as depends on you, live peaceably with all men. [19]Beloved, do not avenge yourselves, but *rather* give place to wrath; for it is written, "Vengeance is Mine, I will repay,"[a] says the Lord. [20]Therefore

"If your enemy is hungry, feed him;
  If he is thirsty, give him a drink;
  For in so doing you will heap coals of fire on his
    head."[a]

[21]Do not be overcome by evil, but overcome evil with good.

Submit to Government

13 Let every soul be subject to the governing authorities. For there is no authority except from God, and the authorities that exist are ap-pointed by God. [2]Therefore whoever resists the authority resists the ordinance of God, and those who resist will bring judgment on themselves. [3]For rulers are not a terror to good works, but to evil. Do you want to be unafraid of the authority? Do what is good, and you will have praise from the same. [4]For he is God's minister to you for good. But if you do evil, be afraid; for he does not bear the sword in vain; for he is God's minister, an avenger to *execute* wrath on him who practices evil. [5]Therefore *you* must be subject, not only because of wrath but also for conscience' sake. [6]For because of this you also pay taxes, for they are God's ministers attending continually to this very thing. [7]Render therefore to all their due: taxes to whom taxes *are due,* customs to whom customs, fear to whom fear, honor to whom honor.

Love Your Neighbor

[8]Owe no one anything except to love one another, for he who loves another has fulfilled the law. [9]For the commandments, "You shall not commit adultery," "You shall not murder," "You shall not steal," "You shall not bear false witness,"[a] "You shall not covet,"[b] and if *there is* any other commandment, are *all* summed up in this saying, namely, "You shall love

13:19 [a]Deuteronomy 32:35 12:20 [a]Proverbs 25:21, 22 13:9 [a]NU-Text omits "You shall not bear false witness." [b]Exodus 20:13–15, 17; Deuteronomy 5:17–19, 21

Mount (Matt. 5—7). A genuine relationship with Christ will be evident in personal relationships with others.

13:1–7 Paul recognized that government is ordained by God. Thus Christians should obey the law and pay their taxes out of a sense of service to God (vv. 1, 2). Paul viewed the government as God's instrument to prevent chaos in the world. Paul may have emphasized the need for civil obedience on the part of Christians to disassociate them completely from cer-tain rebellious Jews. The Jews, particularly the Zealots, were noted for their insurrections. The government provided to individuals certain protections and services that they could not enjoy otherwise.

13:8–10 Paul summarized a Christian's obligations to others in the commandment to love one's neighbor, identified as anyone in need. A believer who demonstrates love by acting in the best interest of another person has fulfilled the Law

PORNOGRAPHY *A DEGRADING IMAGE*

Pornography assaults the senses and sensibilities of the Christian. Scripture admonishes us to live holy and moral lives (Lev. 18; 19; 1 Cor. 6:9) and to respect every God-created individual (Rom. 14:19).

Pornography depicts not only sexually explicit material but drug abuse and violence. Its most devastating aspect is the false presentation of women and children as sexual objects who supposedly enjoy brutality and violence. Pornography encourages images that are antithetical to the biblical concept of sexuality and features a degrading and unrealistic portrayal of sexual intimacy. It condones antisocial, destructive behavior, and its use has a subtle, drugging effect on morality.

Pornography becomes a moral problem in that it subordinates and exploits God's plan for sexuality and encourages sadistic and violent practices. To assume that pornography has no influence on behavior is naive at best and irresponsible at worst. Our entire educational system has proven that what we read or view does shape beliefs and behaviors. Children, because of their impressionability and underdeveloped skills of discernment, need particular protection from pornography in all forms.

Whatever its form, pornography denigrates God's ideal (Eph. 4:17–19). Christians are encouraged to seek— even to "meditate" on—all that is true, noble, just, pure, lovely, and of a good report (Phil. 4:8).

See also Prov. 20:9; Lam. 5:11, 12; Matt. 5:8; 18:3, note; Mark 7:21–23; 1 Pet. 4:1–3; notes on Children (2 Sam. 21; Ps. 128; Prov. 22; Luke 15); Date Rape (2 Sam. 13); Purity (1 John 3); Rape (Gen. 34); Sexual Immorality (Prov. 6); Temptation (Heb. 2)

---

your neighbor as yourself."c 10Love does no harm to a neighbor; therefore love *is* the fulfillment of the law.

Put on Christ

11And *do* this, knowing the time, that now *it is* high time to awake out of sleep; for now our salvation *is* nearer than when we *first* believed. 12The night is far spent, the day is at hand. Therefore let us cast off the works of darkness, and let us put on the armor of light. 13Let us walk properly, as in the day, not in revelry and drunkenness, not in lewdness and lust, not in strife and envy. 14But put on the Lord Jesus Christ, and make no provision for the flesh, to *fulfill its* lusts.

The Law of Liberty

14 Receive one who is weak in the faith, *but* not to disputes over doubtful things. 2For one believes he may eat all things, but he who is weak eats *only* vegetables. 3Let not him who eats despise him who does not eat, and let not him who does not eat judge him who eats; for God has received him. 4Who are you to judge another's servant? To his own master he stands or falls. Indeed, he will be made to stand, for God is able to make him stand.

5One person esteems *one* day above another; another esteems every day *alike.* Let each be fully convinced in his own mind. 6He who observes the day, observes *it* to the Lord;a and he who does not observe the day, to the Lord he does not observe *it.* He who eats, eats to the Lord, for he gives God thanks; and he who does not eat, to the Lord he does not eat, and gives God thanks. 7For none of us lives to himself, and no one dies to himself. 8For if we live, we live to the Lord; and if we die, we die to the Lord. Therefore, whether we live or die, we are

·····················
13:9 cLeviticus 19:18   **14:6** aNU-Text omits the rest of this sentence.

(see Matt. 22:35–40). The debt of love can never be fully paid (Rom. 13:8).

13:11–14 The early Christians anticipated the return of Christ in the near future. "Knowing the time" (Gk. *kairos*), meaning "right time," is a reference to the time when Christians have an opportunity to take a stand for God (v. 11). Thus Paul exhorted Christians to awaken from sleep. The present age of darkness was passing; the new day of Christ's return was dawning. The Christian woman's hope in the Lord's return should motivate her to consistent, daily, Christlike living. Anticipation of Christ's return should encourage rather than discourage ethical living.

14:1–13 Paul's understanding of freedom in Christ was characterized by a deep respect for others. Although Paul identified those who felt bound by external matters like dietary regulations as weak in the faith, he indicated that their convictions were not to be taken lightly. These persons were not to be ridiculed or treated with contempt. Neither were the weaker believers to condemn the stronger ones. Freedom in Christ means that a believing woman is free to follow her own convictions. It also means that each Christian must allow other believers that same freedom. Therefore no basis exists for judging one another. Christ alone qualifies as Judge (vv. 10–12). Furthermore, one should focus not primarily on herself but rather on others, seeking not to present a stumbling block to their faith. "Stumbling block" refers to any attitude or action that causes another believer to sin or to become confused about God's character and purposes (v. 13). The kind of attitude Paul encouraged would promote unity and harmony in the church. Liberty is to be regulated by love. Elsewhere Paul viewed unity as vital to the life of God's people (see 1 Cor. 12:12–27; Phil., Introduction: Outline on Unity).

the Lord's. [9]For to this end Christ died and rose[a] and lived again, that He might be Lord of both the dead and the living. [10]But why do you judge your brother? Or why do you show contempt for your brother? For we shall all stand before the judgment seat of Christ.[a] [11]For it is written:

> "As I live, says the LORD,
> Every knee shall bow to Me,
> And every tongue shall confess to God."[a]

[12]So then each of us shall give account of himself to God. [13]Therefore let us not judge one another anymore, but rather resolve this, not to put a stumbling block or a cause to fall in *our* brother's way.

The Law of Love

[14]I know and am convinced by the Lord Jesus that *there is* nothing unclean of itself; but to him who considers anything to be unclean, to him *it is* unclean. [15]Yet if your brother is grieved because of *your* food, you are no longer walking in love. Do not destroy with your food the one for whom Christ died. [16]Therefore do not let your good be spoken of as evil; [17]for the kingdom of God is not eating and drinking, but righteousness and peace and joy in the Holy Spirit. [18]For he who serves Christ in these things[a] *is* acceptable to God and approved by men.

[19]Therefore let us pursue the things *which* make for peace and the things by which one may edify another. [20]Do not destroy the work of God for the sake of food. All things indeed *are* pure, but *it is* evil for the man who eats with offense. [21]*It is* good neither to eat meat nor drink wine nor *do anything* by which your brother stumbles or is offended or is made weak.[a] [22]Do you have faith?[a] Have *it* to yourself before God. Happy *is* he who does not condemn himself in what he approves. [23]But he who doubts is condemned if he eats, be-cause *he does* not *eat* from faith; for whatever *is* not from faith is sin.[a]

Bearing Others' Burdens

15We then who are strong ought to bear with the scruples of the weak, and not to please ourselves. [2]Let each of us please *his* neighbor for *his* good, leading to edification. [3]For even Christ did not please Himself; but as it is written, *"The reproaches of those who reproached You fell on Me."*[a] [4]For whatever things were written before were written for our learning, that we through the patience and comfort of the Scriptures might have hope. [5]Now may the God of patience and comfort grant you to be like-minded toward one another, according to Christ Jesus, [6]that you may with one mind *and* one mouth glorify the God and Father of our Lord Jesus Christ.

Glorify God Together

[7]Therefore receive one another, just as Christ also received us,[a] to the glory of God. [8]Now I say that Jesus Christ has become a servant to the circumcision for the truth of God, to confirm the promises *made* to the fathers, [9]and that the Gentiles might glorify God for *His* mercy, as it is written:

> "For this reason I will confess to You among the
> Gentiles,
> And sing to Your name."[a]

[10]And again he says:

> "Rejoice, O Gentiles, with His people!"[a]

14:9 [a]NU-Text omits *and rose.* 14:10 [a]NU-Text reads *of God.* 14:11 [a]Isaiah 45:23 14:18 [a]NU-Text reads *this.* 14:21 [a]NU-Text omits *or is offended or is made weak.* 14:22 [a]NU-Text reads *The faith which you have—have.* 14:23 [a]M-Text puts Romans 16:25–27 here. 15:3 [a]Psalm 69:9 15:7 [a]NU-Text and M-Text read *you.* 15:9 [a]2 Samuel 22:50; Psalm 18:49 15:10 [a]Deuteronomy 32:43

14:14–23 Paul asserted that in Christ the dietary laws of the OT are no longer in effect (see Mark 7:19; Acts 10). However, a more mature believer should do nothing that might hinder the faith of a weaker believer. In the kingdom of God, love is more important than liberty; relationships are more important than observing regulations. One aspect of the kingdom of God is God's reign in the hearts of believers (Luke 17:21; John 3:3). The kingdom of God is the realm where God's sovereignty is recognized and His will is supreme. The believer is to live in a manner that promotes harmony and edifies or builds up others. Paul asserted that all failure to live by faith is sin, that is, missing God's aim for life (Rom. 14:23).

15:1–6 Paul encouraged a life of self-denial and consideration for others within the fellowship of believers. He specifically referred to the duty of the stronger toward the weaker members of the body of Christ (see Gal. 6:1, 2). He set before the Roman Christians the example of Christ. The Greek word translated "bear" (Rom. 15:1) is the same word used of Christ

bearing His Cross (John 19:17). Paul realized that people change more quickly in an atmosphere of love than in an atmosphere of criticism. A genuine consideration for the concerns and needs of others promotes harmony and unity within the church. Such unity (Rom. 15:6) brings glory to God (Rom. 3:23, note; see Ps. 19:1, note). Strength in a woman of God is evident by her willingness to focus on the needs of others and her desire to foster a spirit of genuine harmony among God's people.

15:7–13 The fellowship of believers is to be inclusive rather than exclusive. Paul emphasized the unity of Jew and Gentile within the body of Christ. Christ came to His own people, to the "circumcision" or the Jews, but they did not receive Him (v. 8; John 1:11). Christ also came for the Gentiles. Paul quoted the OT to show the place of the Gentiles in God's plan (Deut. 32:43; 2 Sam. 22:50; Ps. 18:49; 117:1; Is. 11:1, 10). Because Christ has freely welcomed all into His family, His family members should welcome one another with full acceptance.

A number of Hebrew and Greek words are used in the Bible to convey the concept of joy. In fact, the word "joy" is found more than 150 times in the Bible.

Joy comes from God as a result of faith and obedience (John 15:10, 11; Rom. 15:13). The abundance of joy is in direct proportion to the intimacy and steadfastness of a believer's walk with the Lord. Sin in a believer's life can rob her of joy (Ps. 51:8, 12). True joy is evident regardless of circumstances. The Spirit-filled believer continues to rejoice even amidst troubles (James 1:2, 3). Biblical joy is clearly different from earthly, temporal pleasures that are bound to circumstances.

The purpose of joy is to provide blessing for the believer. Joy enables you to enjoy all that God has given—health, family, friends, opportunities, and salvation. As you experience true joy, your joy can then be shared with others (Rom. 12:15). Abundant joy is a fruit of the Holy Spirit for those who walk in faith.

See also notes on Contentment (1 Tim. 6); Fruit of the Spirit (Ps. 86; Rom. 5; 1 Cor. 10; 13; Gal. 5; Eph. 4; Col. 3; 2 Thess. 1; Rev. 2); Humor (Prov. 17); Praise (Ps. 149)

[11]And again:

"Praise the LORD, all you Gentiles!
    Laud Him, all you peoples!"[a]

[12]And again, Isaiah says:

"There shall be a root of Jesse;
    And He who shall rise to reign over the
        Gentiles,
    In Him the Gentiles shall hope."[a]

[13]Now may the God of hope fill you with all joy and peace in believing, that you may abound in hope by the power of the Holy Spirit.

From Jerusalem to Illyricum

[14]Now I myself am confident concerning you, my brethren, that you also are full of goodness, filled with all knowledge, able also to admonish one another.[a] [15]Nevertheless, brethren, I have written more boldly to you on *some* points, as reminding you, because of the grace given to me by God, [16]that I might be a minister of Jesus Christ to the Gentiles, ministering the gospel of God,

that the offering of the Gentiles might be acceptable, sanctified by the Holy Spirit. [17]Therefore I have reason to glory in Christ Jesus in the things *which pertain* to God. [18]For I will not dare to speak of any of those things which Christ has not accomplished through me, in word and deed, to make the Gentiles obedient— [19]in mighty signs and wonders, by the power of the Spirit of God, so that from Jerusalem and round about to Illyricum I have fully preached the gospel of Christ. [20]And so I have made it my aim to preach the gospel, not where Christ was named, lest I should build on another man's foundation, [21]but as it is written:

"To whom He was not announced, they shall see;
    And those who have not heard shall
        understand."[a]

Plan to Visit Rome

[22]For this reason I also have been much hindered from coming to you. [23]But now no longer

• •
15:11 [a]Psalm 117:1   **15:12** [a]Isaiah 11:10   **15:14** [a]M-Text reads *others.*
15:21 [a]Isaiah 52:15

15:14–21 Paul was a pioneer missionary. His goal was to preach the gospel in areas where it had never been heard (vv. 20, 21). He identified himself as a minister of Christ to the Gentiles. Paul had shared the gospel on journeys from Jerusalem to the frontier area of Illyricum, a Roman province bordering the eastern side of the Adriatic Sea (v. 19). Again Paul commended the virtues of his readers (v. 14; see Rom. 1:8, 12). Paul boldly instructed the Romans because God had commissioned him to minister (Rom. 15:15, 16). He expressed faith in the triune God, referring to God, Jesus Christ, and the Holy Spirit (vv. 16–19). He claimed glory not on his own merits but only as a servant or minister of Christ (vv. 17, 18). Any woman who genuinely desires to serve Christ focuses not on what she is able to achieve by her own efforts but rather on Christ who is at work in her life.

15:22–33 Paul had long desired to visit the Romans, but each

time he had been delayed (Rom. 1:10–15). He did not want them to think that he had abandoned his mission to the Gentiles. He was preparing to go to Jerusalem because the Gentile churches had collected a significant offering for the Jewish church in Jerusalem (Rom. 15:25, 26). The church in Jerusalem had great financial needs. Paul wanted to deliver the offering in person to make sure Christians understood the significance of the offering for the unity of Jews and Gentiles in the church. Though he wanted to visit Rome and then journey to Spain, Paul was apprehensive about his visit to Jerusalem to deliver the offering (vv. 24, 28). Paul requested the Roman Christians to pray for him (vv. 30–32). This doxology may have formed an intended ending of the letter to the Roman Christians (v. 33; see Rom. 16:3, 4, note). However, Paul was moved further by the Holy Spirit to pen chapter 16.

PHOEBE · *A Significant Servant*

Phoebe was a Gentile Christian from the port city of Cenchrea. Her name, derived from Greek mythology, means "pure" or "radiant as the moon." Paul described Phoebe as a "servant" (Gk. *diakonon*) and "helper" (Gk. *prostatis*). She may have been a patron of some sort.

In Greek cities, rulers routinely appointed patrons to look after the interests of foreigners. Therefore, Phoebe may have functioned in an official capacity to protect the rights and meet the needs of Cenchrea's numerous foreign visitors and resident Jews. She was obviously a person of significance who used her wealth and influence in the service of the Christians there.

On this occasion, Phoebe had traveled to Rome, possibly on a business trip. Paul, knowing that she would pass through Corinth, took the opportunity to write to the Roman Christians. This letter commended Phoebe, its bearer, to the church in Rome. Paul knew that the Roman Christians would be able to provide Phoebe with hospitality and fellowship, as well as with advice on the state of Roman politics and law.

Paul spoke highly of Phoebe. He introduced her to the Roman Christians as "sister," "servant," "saint," and "helper." Though the word here translated "servant" is also transliterated as "deacon," note both generic and technical usages of the word. The Greek root means literally "one who ministers or serves." Of course, taken in that sense, the word describes not only Phoebe and other "deaconesses" in the early church but also countless women who have given and do give themselves untiringly to the work of the Kingdom through ministries within the local church. However, the word is also used by some in a technical sense to describe a functional ecclesiastical office such as assigned to Stephen (Acts 6:1–7). This office was created to equip a corps of godly saints to meet physical and social needs so that the apostles would not be pulled away from the primary ministry of the Word (Acts 6:4).

Certainly in the New Testament sense of deacon or deaconess, women can find ample opportunity for service with or without an official title. On the other hand, if deacon or deaconess is considered a position of official spiritual leadership, there are other passages for consideration (see 1 Tim. 2:11–15; 3:8–13). In any case, Paul noted that Phoebe was a highly capable Greek woman of significant social status, and apparently through the gospel, she had also overcome the pagan origins of her name to gain status—in Paul's eyes—as a pure and radiant light for Jesus.

See also notes on Feminine Leadership (1 Sam. 25); Women's Ministries (Acts 2; Titus 2)

---

having a place in these parts, and having a great desire these many years to come to you, [24]whenever I journey to Spain, I shall come to you.[a] For I hope to see you on my journey, and to be helped on my way there by you, if first I may enjoy your *company* for a while. [25]But now I am going to Jerusalem to minister to the saints. [26]For it pleased those from Macedonia and Achaia to make a certain contribution for the poor among the saints who are in Jerusalem. [27]It pleased them indeed, and they are their debtors. For if the Gentiles have been partakers of their spiritual things, their duty is also to minister to them in material things. [28]Therefore, when I have performed this and have sealed to them this fruit, I shall go by way of you to Spain. [29]But I know that when I come to you, I shall come in the fullness of the blessing of the gospel[a] of Christ.

[30]Now I beg you, brethren, through the Lord Jesus Christ, and through the love of the Spirit, that you strive together with me in prayers to God for me, [31]that I may be delivered from those in Judea who do not believe, and that my service for Jerusalem may be acceptable to the saints, [32]that I may come to you with joy by the will of God, and may be refreshed together with you. [33]Now the God of peace *be* with you all. Amen.

Sister Phoebe Commended

16 I commend to you Phoebe our sister, who is a servant of the church in Cenchrea, [2]that you may receive her in the Lord in a manner worthy of the saints, and assist her in whatever business she has need of you; for indeed she has been a helper of many and of myself also.

Greeting Roman Saints

[3]Greet Priscilla and Aquila, my fellow workers in Christ Jesus, [4]who risked their own necks for my life, to whom not only I give thanks, but also

· · · · · · · · · · · · · · · · · · ·

15:24 [a]NU-Text omits *I shall come to you* (and joins *Spain* with the next sentence).   15:29 [a]NU-Text omits *of the gospel*.

16:1, 2 Phoebe (lit. "radiant" or "bright") is identified as a "sister" and "servant" in the church at Cenchrea, a seaport for Corinth. Women played a significant role in the life of the early church (see Phoebe; see also chart, Spiritual Gifts of Women in the Bible; Women Using Their Gifts in the Early Church).

JUNIA   *A Respected and Diligent Co-Laborer*

In Romans, Paul greeted a number of believers—including many women—by name (Rom. 16:3–15). One of his friends was Junia. "Junia" may have been a contraction of the male name "Junianus," but some believe Junia was a woman. For Junia, John Chrysostom so identified Junia and spoke in glowing terms of her service for the Kingdom. The coupling of her name with Andronicus could suggest that the two were married.

Andronicus and Junia were Paul's Jewish "countrymen" who had, at some time, been in prison with him. Their conversions were before Paul's, which indicates that they were among the earliest Palestinian Christians in Jerusalem. Paul stated that Andronicus and Junia were of note among the apostles. Whether referring to a man or woman, the exact nature of this apostleship is certainly not clear in the text.

"Apostle" means "sent one," and the term most often refers to the twelve disciples called and sent out by Jesus, to Matthias (who succeeded Judas), and to Paul himself. In this case, however, Paul seemingly used the word in a broader sense, not implying official status but suggesting that the ones so designated were commissioned to spread the gospel and in that sense had been sent by the Lord. Also, Barnabas was named an apostle without fulfilling the usual requirements.

In any case, Junia was respected and recognized for unique commissioning as well as for outstanding contribution to the Kingdom. If indeed a woman, this believer would further exemplify the already established fact that Christ commissioned both women and men to proclaim the gospel.

See also notes on Feminine Leadership (1 Sam. 25); Women's Ministries (Acts 2; Titus 2)

---

all the churches of the Gentiles. [5]Likewise *greet* the church that is in their house.

Greet my beloved Epaenetus, who is the first-fruits of Achaia[a] to Christ. [6]Greet Mary, who labored much for us. [7]Greet Andronicus and Junia, my countrymen and my fellow prisoners, who are of note among the apostles, who also were in Christ before me.

[8]Greet Amplias, my beloved in the Lord. [9]Greet Urbanus, our fellow worker in Christ, and Stachys, my beloved. [10]Greet Apelles, approved in Christ. Greet those who are of the *household* of Aristobulus. [11]Greet Herodion, my countryman.[a] Greet those who are of the *household* of Narcissus who are in the Lord.

[12]Greet Tryphena and Tryphosa, who have labored in the Lord. Greet the beloved Persis, who labored much in the Lord. [13]Greet Rufus, chosen in the Lord, and his mother and mine. [14]Greet Asyncritus, Phlegon, Hermas, Patrobas, Hermes, and the brethren who are with them. [15]Greet Philologus and Julia, Nereus and his sister, and Olympas, and all the saints who are with them.

[16]Greet one another with a holy kiss. The[a] churches of Christ greet you.

Avoid Divisive Persons

[17]Now I urge you, brethren, note those who cause divisions and offenses, contrary to the doctrine which you learned, and avoid them. [18]For those who are such do not serve our Lord Jesus[a] Christ, but their own belly, and by smooth words and flattering speech deceive the hearts of the simple. [19]For your obedience has become known to all. Therefore I am glad on your behalf; but I want you to be wise in what is good, and simple concerning evil. [20]And the God of peace will crush Satan under your feet shortly.

The grace of our Lord Jesus Christ *be* with you. Amen.

Greetings from Paul's Friends

[21]Timothy, my fellow worker, and Lucius, Jason, and Sosipater, my countrymen, greet you.

•••

16:5 [a]NU-Text reads *Asia*.   **16:11** [a]Or *relative*   **16:16** [a]NU-Text reads *All the churches*.   **16:18** [a]NU-Text and M-Text omit *Jesus*.

16:3, 4 Priscilla and Aquila were Paul's close friends, who, like him, were tentmakers. Paul met them in Corinth (Acts 18:1–3). When Paul left Corinth for Ephesus, he took this noteworthy couple with him (see Acts 18:18, 19). A church met in the house of Aquila and Priscilla (1 Cor. 16:19), who courageously risked their lives for Paul (Rom. 16:4).

16:5–16 Paul extended greetings to a number of lesser known individuals. Epaenetus is identified as Paul's first convert in Achaia or Asia (v. 5). A number of women appear in this group Paul greeted. Mary, one of six women called Mary in the NT, is characterized as a hard worker for the sake of the gospel (v. 6). The names listed in verse 12 are women's

names. Tryphena and Tryphosa mean "dainty" and "delicate." Persis was a slave name. Paul referred to the mother of Rufus as a dear mother to him also (v. 13). Julia may be the wife of Philologus (v. 15). Rabbis practiced the custom of greeting one another with a kiss. Jesus' disciples followed the practice, and this method of greeting was used in the early church (v. 16).

16:17–20 Paul described those who caused division as selfish and smooth-talking (v. 18). He referred to God as "the God of peace" (v. 20; see Rom. 15:33). God desired not division but peace and harmony among His people. The crushing of Satan calls to mind an earlier reference (Rom. 16:20; see Gen. 3:15).

PAUL'S COMMENDATION OF WOMEN

WOMAN	SERVICE RENDERED
Apphia	Hosted the church in her home (Philem. 2)
Euodia and Syntyche	Labored with Paul in the gospel (Phil. 4:2, 3)
Lydia	Heard Paul and opened her home to him and fellow believers (Acts 16:11–15, 40; see also Phil. 1:1, 3–6)
Mary	Labored much for the gospel (Rom. 16:6)
Persis	Labored much in the Lord (Rom. 16:12)
Phoebe	Helped many (Rom. 16:1, 2)
Priscilla	Risked her life for Paul's life (Rom. 16:3, 4)
Rufus' mother	Fulfilled the role of a mother to Paul (Rom. 16:13)
Tryphena and Tryphosa	Labored in the Lord (Rom. 16:12)

²²I, Tertius, who wrote *this* epistle, greet you in the Lord.

²³Gaius, my host and *the host* of the whole church, greets you. Erastus, the treasurer of the city, greets you, and Quartus, a brother. ²⁴The grace of our Lord Jesus Christ *be* with you all. Amen.ᵃ

Benediction

²⁵Now to Him who is able to establish you according to my gospel and the preaching of Je-

sus Christ, according to the revelation of the mystery kept secret since the world began ²⁶but now made manifest, and by the prophetic Scriptures made known to all nations, according to the commandment of the everlasting God, for obedience to the faith— ²⁷to God, alone wise, *be* glory through Jesus Christ forever. Amen.ᵃ

· · · · · · · · · · · · · · · · ·

16:24 ᵃNU-Text omits this verse.   **16:27** ᵃM-Text puts Romans 16:25–27 after Romans 14:23.

16:21–27 Paul sent greetings from those working with him. Timothy, the best known of this group of workers, was a native of Lystra (see Acts 16:1–3). Gaius is identified as Paul's host. Tertius functioned as Paul's secretary or amanuensis. A final benediction or doxology is included (Rom. 16:25–27). The "mystery" now revealed is God's gift of salvation for all

through Jesus Christ (vv. 25, 26). The purpose of preaching the gospel is identified as "for obedience to the faith" (v. 26). Paul ended this chapter on a note of praise, the only appropriate response to God who graciously has done so much for all through His Son Jesus Christ.

1 Corinthians

The language, style, and theology of 1 Corinthians are all typically Pauline. Paul identified himself as the author, and the authenticity of this claim has never been seriously challenged.

The church at Corinth was established by Paul about A.D. 50 during an eighteen-month stay on his second missionary journey (Acts 18:1–17; see map, Paul's Second Missionary Journey). Later, while in Ephesus on his third journey (Acts 19), Paul received disturbing reports of sexual immorality among the Corinthian believers. In response, he wrote them a letter, which has not been found (1 Cor. 5:9–11). Some from the household of Chloe, who may have been a member of the church in Corinth, went to Paul, informing him of divisive factions within the church (see 1 Cor. 1, Chloe). Before Paul could reply, another delegation from Corinth arrived with a letter containing questions (1 Cor. 7:1; 16:17). Paul immediately sent Timothy to Corinth to help correct the problems (1 Cor. 4:17). He also wrote them a letter (1 Cor.), anticipating that it would arrive before Timothy did (1 Cor. 16:10). Paul wrote 1 Corinthians near the end of his time in Ephesus (1 Cor. 16:8) about A.D. 56.

SETTING: Corinth, located on a narrow isthmus of land, was the political capital of Greece and the seat of its commercial and intellectual life. As the land route between northern Greece and the Peloponnese and the funnel controlling shipping between the East and the West, Corinth was the emporium of Mediterranean trade.

The city had a reputation not only for luxury but also for sexual vice and sacred prostitution. Ancient Corinth had been the site of a temple of Aphrodite, the goddess of love, where hundreds of temple prostitutes had plied their trade (see chart, Graeco-Roman Goddesses). Corinth was totally destroyed in 146 B.C., but the Greeks quickly reinstituted goddess worship when the city was rebuilt by the Romans a hundred years later. Roman deities, as well as the eastern mystery cults of Asia and Egypt, were introduced to Corinth at that time. At least twenty-six temples and sacred places were built to honor the various gods and goddesses. Furthermore, along with the massive influx of people came a significant Jewish population who built a synagogue to worship God. Corinth attracted tradesmen, businessmen, philosophers, and artists from all corners of the known world. It was a bustling cosmopolitan center with a broad plethora of peoples, cultures, and religions.

PURPOSE: First Corinthians was written to resolve ethical, doctrinal, and practical problems that had arisen in the recently established church in Corinth.

AUDIENCE: Corinth was a Roman colony, and many of its citizens immigrated from Italy. The population was augmented by Greeks, Levantines (including Jews), Egyptians,

and Asians. Both culturally and socio-economically the church mirrored this diversity. Among the people Paul named in his letter were Jews, Romans, Greeks, aristocrats, and slaves.

THEMES

The Corinthians were proud of their knowledge. They considered themselves spiritually mature. Throughout this letter, Paul contrasted worldly and spiritual wisdom. His primary theme was that love, and not knowledge, provides the basis for Christian ethics.

OUTLINE

CHLOE *A Founding Mother of the Faith*

Paul's letter to the Corinthian church addresses the influences of their pagan culture. The apostle is disturbed that members of Chloe's household have reported among believers disputes which threaten to divide the local body at Corinth. Regardless of whether or not Chloe was from Corinth, she was certainly well known by the Corinthians.

The term "household" could mean immediate members of her family, fellow-worshipers of the church meeting in her house, or servants belonging to her. Whether those in Chloe's household were involved in the disputes or merely relating details about the group is uncertain. They did report the matter to the apostle Paul.

Little is known about Chloe, but Paul called her by name. This passage supports the fact that Paul had many women as friends and that he esteemed them as co-heirs in the gospel. In contrast to their places in secular society, women were considered to be valuable and influential participants in the building up of the Christian church.

See also notes on Influence (Esth. 4); Feminine Leadership (1 Sam. 25)

Greeting

1 Paul, called *to be* an apostle of Jesus Christ through the will of God, and Sosthenes *our* brother,

[2] To the church of God which is at Corinth, to those who are sanctified in Christ Jesus, called *to be* saints, with all who in every place call on the name of Jesus Christ our Lord, both theirs and ours:

[3] Grace to you and peace from God our Father and the Lord Jesus Christ.

Spiritual Gifts at Corinth

[4] I thank my God always concerning you for the grace of God which was given to you by Christ Jesus, [5] that you were enriched in everything by Him in all utterance and all knowledge, [6] even as the testimony of Christ was confirmed in you, [7] so that you come short in no gift, eagerly waiting for the revelation of our Lord Jesus Christ, [8] who will also confirm you to the end, *that you may be* blameless in the day of our Lord Jesus Christ. [9] God *is* faithful, by whom you were called into the fellowship of His Son, Jesus Christ our Lord.

Sectarianism Is Sin

[10] Now I plead with you, brethren, by the name of our Lord Jesus Christ, that you all speak the same thing, and *that* there be no divisions among you, but *that* you be perfectly joined together in the same mind and in the same judgment. [11] For it

has been declared to me concerning you, my brethren, by those of Chloe's *household,* that there are contentions among you. [12] Now I say this, that each of you says, "I am of Paul," or "I am of Apollos," or "I am of Cephas," or "I am of Christ." [13] Is Christ divided? Was Paul crucified for you? Or were you baptized in the name of Paul?

[14] I thank God that I baptized none of you except Crispus and Gaius, [15] lest anyone should say that I had baptized in my own name. [16] Yes, I also baptized the household of Stephanas. Besides, I do not know whether I baptized any other. [17] For Christ did not send me to baptize, but to preach the gospel, not with wisdom of words, lest the cross of Christ should be made of no effect.

Christ the Power and Wisdom of God

[18] For the message of the cross is foolishness to those who are perishing, but to us who are being saved it is the power of God. [19] For it is written:

"I will destroy the wisdom of the wise,
And bring to nothing the understanding of the
  prudent."[a]

[20] Where *is* the wise? Where *is* the scribe? Where *is* the disputer of this age? Has not God made foolish the wisdom of this world? [21] For since, in the wisdom of God, the world through wisdom did not know God, it pleased God through the foolishness of the message preached

•••••••••••••••••••

1:19 [a]Isaiah 29:14

1:2 **Paul addressed the Corinthian believers as saints** (Gk. *hagiois,* lit. "set apart" or "holy" ones), a favorite description for Christians in this corrective epistle. He used the word more than 60 times in his letters. Through Jesus, believers have been forgiven and set apart from sin. Paul reminded the Corinthians of this fact. They were saints—God's holy, sanctified people—and they ought to be acting as such.

1:11 **Contentions** (Gk. *eris*) suggests a "sharp challenge," "quarreling," or "strife." Paul received information about these "contentions" from members of Chloe's household (see Chloe).

1:21 **Quarreling and divisiveness** had erupted among the Corinthians in the name of "wisdom." The people within the

to save those who believe. ²²For Jews request a sign, and Greeks seek after wisdom; ²³but we preach Christ crucified, to the Jews a stumbling block and to the Greeks[a] foolishness, ²⁴but to those who are called, both Jews and Greeks, Christ the power of God and the wisdom of God. ²⁵Because the foolishness of God is wiser than men, and the weakness of God is stronger than men.

Glory Only in the Lord

²⁶For you see your calling, brethren, that not many wise according to the flesh, not many mighty, not many noble, *are called.* ²⁷But God has chosen the foolish things of the world to put to shame the wise, and God has chosen the weak things of the world to put to shame the things which are mighty; ²⁸and the base things of the world and the things which are despised God has chosen, and the things which are not, to bring to nothing the things that are, ²⁹that no flesh should glory in His presence. ³⁰But of Him you are in Christ Jesus, who became for us wisdom from God—and righteousness and sanctification and redemption— ³¹that, as it is written, *"He who glories, let him glory in the LORD."*[a]

Christ Crucified

2 And I, brethren, when I came to you, did not come with excellence of speech or of wisdom declaring to you the testimony[a] of God. ²For I determined not to know anything among you except Jesus Christ and Him crucified. ³I was with you in weakness, in fear, and in much trembling. ⁴And my speech and my preaching *were* not with persuasive words of human[a] wisdom, but in demonstration of the Spirit and of power, ⁵that

your faith should not be in the wisdom of men but in the power of God.

Spiritual Wisdom

⁶However, we speak wisdom among those who are mature, yet not the wisdom of this age, nor of the rulers of this age, who are coming to nothing. ⁷But we speak the wisdom of God in a mystery, the hidden *wisdom* which God ordained before the ages for our glory, ⁸which none of the rulers of this age knew; for had they known, they would not have crucified the Lord of glory.

⁹But as it is written:

"Eye has not seen, nor ear heard,
Nor have entered into the heart of man
The things which God has prepared for those who love Him."[a]

¹⁰But God has revealed *them* to us through His Spirit. For the Spirit searches all things, yes, the deep things of God. ¹¹For what man knows the things of a man except the spirit of the man which is in him? Even so no one knows the things of God except the Spirit of God. ¹²Now we have received, not the spirit of the world, but the Spirit who is from God, that we might know the things that have been freely given to us by God. ¹³These things we also speak, not in words which man's wisdom teaches but which the Holy[a] Spirit teaches, comparing spiritual things with spiritual. ¹⁴But the natural man does not receive the things of the Spirit of God, for they are

---

1:23 ªNU-Text reads *Gentiles.* 1:31 ªJeremiah 9:24 2:1 ªNU-Text reads *mystery.* 2:4 ªNU-Text omits *human.* 2:9 ªIsaiah 64:4 2:13 ªNU-Text omits *Holy.*

---

church had aligned themselves with various Christian leaders, boasting in the wisdom of one over the other. The theme of wisdom dominated Paul's discussion (1 Cor. 1—3). Paul argued that God's wisdom is foolishness to humanly-conceived wisdom. On their own, people fail to know God. They can only gain a true knowledge of God through the Spirit, whom they receive upon believing the "foolishness" of the gospel. Paul asserted that it pleased God to arrange things in this manner. If God were to be found through human wisdom, He would only be accessible to the elite. But by extending salvation through His "foolishness" (which is wiser than men, 1 Cor. 1:25), God forces His creation to trust and glory in Him, and not in the wisdom of sinful flesh (v. 29).

1:26–28 Paul explained that the gospel of Christ appears foolish to human reason. To further his point, he encouraged the Corinthians to remember their own humble origins. According to human standards, most of them were not intelligent, influential, or rich. On the contrary, they were members of the common lower class and would have been considered weak, lowly, and even despised. Nevertheless, God called them. A "call" (Gk. *klēsis*) is an invitation or an official summons by God to enter into a personal relationship with Him. A call is not based on human wisdom or status but on the grace of

God who, in His "foolishness," has chosen the unworthy things of the world to shame those of high human worth. This was done so that His chosen people would glory in *Him* and not in their own status or accomplishments.

2:6–8 God's wisdom is a "mystery" that was formerly hidden from human eyes but was revealed through Christ and made understandable to believers through the Spirit. The Corinthians had the wisdom of God, yet were living by the wisdom of men (1 Cor. 3:1).

2:11 The key to understanding God's wisdom lies with the Spirit. No individual possesses the ability to know God or God's wisdom; only God can know God. The thrust of Paul's argument was easily understood by the Corinthians, who were familiar with the Greek philosophic principle of "like is known only by like." The Spirit knows the things of God because the Spirit *is* God. The Spirit is therefore the link between God and humanity that makes knowing God possible.

2:14–16 The natural woman cannot receive the things of God, for they are foolishness to her. "Foolish" means dull, insipid, or tasteless, and this is precisely how spiritual things are perceived by those who do not have the Spirit. Such individuals lack the capacity to discern the truth, excellence, or beauty of

HERESIES *FALSE DOCTRINES IN THE CHURCH*

Heresy (Gk. *hairesis*) is properly defined as "the taking" of a choice, option, way, plan, or philosophic set of principles. The basic idea is "choice." The word most often denotes the existence within a parent body of a group of self-willed individuals who have a sectarian spirit. However, the term was also used in the New Testament to refer to Christians who were considered separatists or sectarians by some of the Jewish religious leaders (Acts 24:14; 28:22).

Paul refers to heretic parties appearing within the church and implies that these divisions demonstrate the falsity or genuineness of our faith (1 Cor. 11:18, 19). Heretic divisions occur when God's people are not walking in the Spirit (Gal. 5:20), and heretics are to be admonished twice, then disciplined or rejected (Titus 3:10).

"Heresy" in the sense of doctrinal error occurs when the person and work of Jesus Christ is denied (2 Pet. 2:1). Gnosticism (Col. 2:8–23; 1 Tim. 6:20) and Docetism (1 John 4:2, 3; 2 John 7) are among the doctrinal heresies challenged in the New Testament.

Modern heresies show a startling resemblance to the ancient ones. The New Age movement tends to regard everything as a part of God rather than acknowledging God as transcendent. Heresies often reject the full deity or full humanity of Christ and typically add some form of human works to the finished work of Christ on the Cross.

See also John 1:4, note; Acts 5:17; 15:5; notes on Cults (2 Cor. 11); Goddess Religion (Ex. 20); Idolatry (Is. 42)

---

foolishness to him; nor can he know *them*, because they are spiritually discerned. [15]But he who is spiritual judges all things, yet he himself is *rightly* judged by no one. [16]For *"who has known the mind of the LORD that he may instruct Him?"*[a] But we have the mind of Christ.

Sectarianism Is Carnal

3 And I, brethren, could not speak to you as to spiritual *people* but as to carnal, as to babes in Christ. [2]I fed you with milk and not with solid food; for until now you were not able *to receive it,* and even now you are still not able; [3]for you are still carnal. For where *there are* envy, strife, and divisions among you, are you not carnal and behaving like *mere* men? [4]For when one says, "I am of Paul," and another, "I *am* of Apollos," are you not carnal?

Watering, Working, Warning

[5]Who then is Paul, and who *is* Apollos, but ministers through whom you believed, as the Lord

gave to each one? [6]I planted, Apollos watered, but God gave the increase. [7]So then neither he who plants is anything, nor he who waters, but God who gives the increase. [8]Now he who plants and he who waters are one, and each one will receive his own reward according to his own labor.

[9]For we are God's fellow workers; you are God's field, *you are* God's building. [10]According to the grace of God which was given to me, as a wise master builder I have laid the foundation, and another builds on it. But let each one take heed how he builds on it. [11]For no other foundation can anyone lay than that which is laid, which is Jesus Christ. [12]Now if anyone builds on this foundation *with* gold, silver, precious stones, wood, hay, straw, [13]each one's work will become clear; for the Day will declare it, because it will be revealed by fire; and the fire will test each one's work, of what sort it is. [14]If anyone's work which he has built on *it* en-

2:16 [a]Isaiah 40:13

---

divine things, judging them to be absurd and distasteful. Paul valued self-judgment (1 Cor. 11:31), constructive criticism (1 Cor. 11:17), and church discipline (1 Cor. 5:3–5), but he argued that believers are ultimately accountable to God alone and cannot be judged by those who are operating out of a carnal mind-set. Because the Corinthians were not demonstrating "the mind of Christ," they were not in a position to judge Paul.

3:2, 3 The Corinthians were preoccupied with attaining wisdom and in wisdom's name had aligned themselves with their favorite leader. Their divisiveness revealed human pride at the root of their desire. According to Paul, true spirituality does not lead to an elitist attitude but rather to a deeper understanding of the profound mystery of God—Christ crucified (1 Cor. 3:2).

3:10–15 The judgment seat of Christ (Gk. *bēma*) is not the

place for assigning eternal destiny but rather for determining rewards for believers (see Rom. 14:10; 2 Cor. 5:10; chart, Judgments in the New Testament). This judgment is marked by these characteristics:

• Only those whose foundation is laid in Jesus Christ will appear (1 Cor. 3:11);

• Every believer has a choice to build with the valuable and lasting or with the worthless and fleeting (vv. 12, 13);

• These works will be judged by the discerning gaze of Christ Himself (v. 13; see Rev. 1:14; 2:18);

• Rewards will be given for those works of permanent value (1 Cor. 3:14);

• Worthless and insincere works will be destroyed, but the believer will be saved, even without reward (v. 15).

Religious commitment to a monogamous relationship, seeing your spouse's needs as equal or even more important than our own, give the Christian marriage an edge in marital and sexual satisfaction.

Mary Ann Mayo

---

dures, he will receive a reward. [15]If anyone's work is burned, he will suffer loss; but he himself will be saved, yet so as through fire.

[16]Do you not know that you are the temple of God and *that* the Spirit of God dwells in you? [17]If anyone defiles the temple of God, God will destroy him. For the temple of God is holy, which *temple* you are.

Avoid Worldly Wisdom

[18]Let no one deceive himself. If anyone among you seems to be wise in this age, let him become a fool that he may become wise. [19]For the wisdom of this world is foolishness with God. For it is written, *"He catches the wise in their own craftiness";*[a] [20]and again, *"The LORD knows the thoughts of the wise, that they are futile."*[a] [21]Therefore let no one boast in men. For all things are yours: [22]whether Paul or Apollos or Cephas, or the world or life or death, or things present or things to come—all are yours. [23]And you *are* Christ's, and Christ *is* God's.

Stewards of the Mysteries of God

4 Let a man so consider us, as servants of Christ and stewards of the mysteries of God. [2]Moreover it is required in stewards that one be found faithful. [3]But with me it is a very small thing that I should be judged by you or by a human court.[a] In fact, I do not even judge myself. [4]For I know of nothing against myself, yet I am not justified by this; but He who

judges me is the Lord. [5]Therefore judge nothing before the time, until the Lord comes, who will both bring to light the hidden things of darkness and reveal the counsels of the hearts. Then each one's praise will come from God.

Fools for Christ's Sake

[6]Now these things, brethren, I have figuratively transferred to myself and Apollos for your sakes, that you may learn in us not to think beyond what is written, that none of you may be puffed up on behalf of one against the other. [7]For who makes you differ *from another?* And what do you have that you did not receive? Now if you did indeed receive *it,* why do you boast as if you had not received *it?*

[8]You are already full! You are already rich! You have reigned as kings without us—and indeed I could wish you did reign, that we also might reign with you! [9]For I think that God has displayed us, the apostles, last, as men condemned to death; for we have been made a spectacle to the world, both to angels and to men. [10]We *are* fools for Christ's sake, but you *are* wise in Christ! We *are* weak, but you *are* strong! You *are* distinguished, but we *are* dishonored! [11]To the present hour we both hunger and thirst, and we are poorly clothed, and beaten, and homeless. [12]And we labor, working with our

•••••••••••••••••••••
3:19 [a]Job 5:13   **3:20** [a]Psalm 94:11   **4:3** [a]Literally *day*

3:16, 17 Paul described the Corinthians as God's temple (Gk. *naos*), referring to the innermost dwelling place of God, the Most Holy Place, in contrast to the entire temple complex (Gk. *hiera*). Because of the indwelling Holy Spirit, the Corinthians were God's Most Holy Place. The words "defile" and "destroy" are the same in the Greek text, meaning "spoil" or "ruin" instead of "annihilate." The idea then is that when an individual spoils God's temple, God will then spoil him. Paul pointed out that God had only one temple in Corinth, and the Corinthians were that temple.

4:1 Many Corinthian believers were rejecting both Paul's teaching and his authority. Paul reasserted his authority, while emphasizing his role as "servant" and "steward" of the mysteries of God—the truths of the gospel. A "steward" (Gk. *oikonomos*) is the servant who is entrusted with the administration of his master's business or property.

4:3–5 Paul left the judgment of motives and thoughts of others completely in God's domain. He affirmed his own indifference to the Corinthians' judgment of him; he lacked fear for

any judgment of himself by others; and he refused to judge himself (v. 3). Nevertheless, Paul did not consider his thoughts and actions automatically justified, and he continued to declare that ultimately God was his judge (v. 4; chart, The Judgments in the New Testament). This "time" (Gk. *kairos*) is the Lord's chosen time rather than "time" (Gk. *chronos*) in the sense of merely a sequence of chronological events. "The counsels of the hearts" suggests the motives behind actions.

4:7–9 The Corinthians viewed their gifts as personal accomplishments, and they were critical of others, particularly Paul. Conquering Roman generals staged parades to display their armies as well as the booty of their conquest. At the end of the procession, positioned as a "spectacle," were the prisoners condemned to die in the arena. Paul used this imagery to convey the utter humiliation and degradation with which he was being treated by the Corinthians. The Corinthians were puffed up with their own self-worth. Figuratively, they had positioned themselves at the front of the parade as the victors and Paul at the end as a condemned prisoner.

COMPETITION   *WHEN SISTERS FIGHT*

Competition in the sense of a common struggle for the same objective can be a healthy thing. It can inspire us to study harder and run faster. To be challenged and pushed to reach a goal is not wrong in itself. However, when sin starts to edge its way into the competition, the goal of personal achievement is distorted into an obsession to "show up" someone else. Such competition can move our eyes from focus on the intended goal and instead make us dwell upon comparing ourselves to another. This makes competition wrong (2 Cor. 10:12).

Competition has become so commonplace in our culture that we assume it is acceptable to God in any form. Scripture does not support that position. The ideal advocated in the Bible is cooperation, agreement, and unity among believers. Several metaphors are used to describe such cooperation among believers: we are a "building" with parts jointly fitted together, a "body of Christ," a "chosen generation," and a "royal priesthood" (1 Cor. 12:27; Eph. 2:20–22; 1 Pet. 2:9). The bestowal of the Holy Spirit upon the early church came as those gathered reached "one accord in one place" (Acts 2:1). The apostle Paul spoke on numerous occasions of the need for unity of spirit (Eph. 4:3).

When Jesus came to visit, Mary and Martha started using their gifts of service. Mary sat at Jesus' feet, loving and being loved by Him. Martha, a practical "doer," started preparing food and a place to rest. However, Martha looked away from her goal of serving Christ and began to evaluate Mary's performance. Both women were serving in meaningful ways. The problem came when Martha, in her anxiety, overlooked the fact that she and her sister were both on the same team and began to sit in judgment of her sister (Luke 10:41, 42).

The gifts of the Spirit are to work in harmony with one another as the Holy Spirit directs, so that the entire body of believers is built up (1 Cor. 12:7, 11, 12). We are responsible for one another's welfare; we are to pray for one another; we are called to be one-minded and to live in peace (2 Cor. 13:11). Indeed, when arguments arise, we are to give "preference" to one another—or to defer for the sake of achieving harmony (Rom. 12:10).

See also notes on Conflict (Song 5; Matt. 18); Forgiveness (Ps. 51; Luke 17); Friendship (Luke 1); Fruit of the Spirit (Col. 3); portraits of Euodia and Syntyche (Phil. 4); Martha (John 11); Mary of Bethany (John 11)

own hands. Being reviled, we bless; being persecuted, we endure; [13]being defamed, we entreat. We have been made as the filth of the world, the offscouring of all things until now.

Paul's Paternal Care

[14]I do not write these things to shame you, but as my beloved children I warn *you.* [15]For though you might have ten thousand instructors in Christ, yet *you do* not *have* many fathers; for in Christ Jesus I have begotten you through the gospel. [16]Therefore I urge you, imitate me. [17]For this reason I have sent Timothy to you, who is my beloved and faithful son in the Lord, who will remind you of my ways in Christ, as I teach everywhere in every church.

[18]Now some are puffed up, as though I were not coming to you. [19]But I will come to you shortly, if the Lord wills, and I will know, not the word of those who are puffed up, but the power. [20]For the kingdom of God *is* not in word but in power. [21]What do you want? Shall I come to you with a rod, or in love and a spirit of gentleness?

Immorality Defiles the Church

5 It is actually reported *that there is* sexual immorality among you, and such sexual immorality as is not even named[a] among the Gentiles—that a man has his father's wife! [2]And you are puffed up, and have not rather mourned, that he who has done this deed might be taken away from among you. [3]For I indeed, as absent in body but present in spirit, have already judged (as though I were present) him who has so done this deed. [4]In the name of our Lord Jesus Christ, when you are gathered together, along with my spirit, with the power of our Lord Jesus Christ, [5]deliver such a one to Satan for the destruction of the flesh, that his spirit may be saved in the day of the Lord Jesus.[a]

[6]Your glorying *is* not good. Do you not know that

•••••••••••••••••
5:1 [a]NU-Text omits *named.*   5:5 [a]NU-Text omits *Jesus.*

4:18–20 Some Corinthians had become puffed up in their own wisdom. They claimed to be spiritual, but Paul reminded them that true religion does not consist in the professions of the mouth, but in the reality of the Spirit's control of one's life.

5:1 Jewish law forbade a son to marry his stepmother (Lev. 18:8; Deut. 22:30). This incest was also taboo in Greek

culture. Nevertheless, a man in the church at Corinth was sexually involved with his father's wife or perhaps even married to her. Paul was incredulous that in the name of "wisdom" they could bring the gospel into disrepute and condone a kind of sexual immorality even disallowed by pagans.

5:6–8 Israelite women used the sourdough process for making their bread. Every week they would withhold a small

JUDGMENTS IN THE NEW TESTAMENT

NAME	SCRIPTURE	DESCRIPTION
1. The judgment of the Cross itself	All who have accepted Christ as Savior have passed from death to life, and sin is thus judged.	Rom. 8:34
2. The judgment of angels	According to Peter, this judgment is in the future; according to Paul, believers will be judges.	1 Cor. 6:3; 2 Pet. 2:4
3. The judgment of the church	The church must exercise judgment within its own fellowship.	1 Cor. 5:13
4. The judgment seat of Christ	Believers face this judgment immediately upon their translation into heaven. This becomes the reward seat of Christ.	Rom. 14:10; 2 Cor. 5:10
5. The Sheep and Goat Judgment	This judgment determines who will enter the millennial kingdom at the end of the Great Tribulation.	Matt. 25:32–46
6. The Great White Throne Judgment	This judgment apparently takes place at the end of earth's history after the millennium. It is God's ultimate judgment against the lost.	Rev. 20:11–15

a little leaven leavens the whole lump? ⁷Therefore purge out the old leaven, that you may be a new lump, since you truly are unleavened. For indeed Christ, our Passover, was sacrificed for us.ᵃ ⁸Therefore let us keep the feast, not with old leaven, nor with the leaven of malice and wickedness, but with the unleavened *bread* of sincerity and truth.

Immorality Must Be Judged

⁹I wrote to you in my epistle not to keep company with sexually immoral people. ¹⁰Yet *I* certainly *did* not *mean* with the sexually immoral people of this world, or with the covetous, or extortioners, or idolaters, since then you would need to go out of the world. ¹¹But now I have written to you not to keep company with anyone named a brother, who is sexually immoral, or covetous, or an idolater, or a reviler, or a drunkard, or an extortioner— not even to eat with such a person.

¹²For what *have* I *to do* with judging those also who are outside? Do you not judge those who are inside? ¹³But those who are outside God judges. Therefore *"put away from yourselves the evil person."*ᵃ

Do Not Sue the Brethren

6 Dare any of you, having a matter against another, go to law before the unrighteous, and not before the saints? ²Do you not know that the saints will judge the world? And if the world will be judged by you, are you unworthy to judge the smallest matters? ³Do you not know that we shall judge angels? How much more, things that pertain to this life? ⁴If then you have judgments concerning things pertaining to this life, do you appoint those who are least esteemed by the church to

5:7 ᵃNU-Text omits *for us.*   5:13 ᵃDeuteronomy 17:7; 19:19; 22:21, 24; 24:7

portion of bread dough and allow it to ferment as a "starter" for the following week's batch. When added to new ingredients, the leaven "starter" would ferment the whole lump. This process continued for an entire year until the Feast of Unleavened Bread (Ex. 12:15; 13:6) when all the old leaven from the house was cleared so that a completely fresh start might be made. Leaven is symbolic of the process by which evil spreads to affect an entire community. The Corinthians failed to realize that the incestuous man's sin was like leaven.

5:13 While believers are to associate freely with all people outside the church, their fellowship within the church is to be

limited to those who are committed to holiness. Those who persist in sinning—not those who are struggling to *overcome* sin—do not belong to the community.

6:1-8 Two members of the church in Corinth had taken a grievance before the civil magistrates at the judgment seat (Gk. *bēma*), publicly located in the midst of the city marketplace. Paul was appalled that Spirit-filled believers should submit their disagreements to the judgment of non-believers, who were totally lacking in spiritual insight (vv. 5, 6). Pagan courts were not the proper arena for the administration of justice between Christians. The ethics of Christian behavior

SEXUAL PURITY *PRINCIPLE MUST RULE PASSION*

The love life of a Christian is a crucial battleground. Each Christian woman must consider the authority of Christ over human passions, then set her heart on purity. Chastity means abstention from sexual activity outside of marriage and is a Christian obligation. For the Christian there is one rule and one rule only: total abstention from sexual activity prior to marriage and total faithfulness within marriage (1 Cor. 7:1–9).

Christians are to prize the sanctity of sex. This means learning the disciplines of longing, loneliness, uncertainty, hope, trust, and unconditional commitment to Christ—a commitment requiring that regardless of what passion we may feel, we must be pure.

Chastity presupposes not taking lightly any act or thought that is not appropriate to the kind of commitment you have to God. To equate any and every personal sexual desire as natural, healthy, and God-given is a powerful lie. God does not give desires that cannot be fulfilled according to His standards of holiness, wholeness, and purity. Sexual purity is one of the foremost means of safeguarding a marriage from behaviors that pollute, corrupt, infect, or destroy it—physically, emotionally, or spiritually.

Purity means freedom from contamination, from anything that would spoil the taste or the pleasure, reduce the power, or in any way adulterate what a thing is meant to be. Within marriage, sexual union is natural, healthy, and pleasurable not only for the moment—but for all of life together. Sexual intimacy is natural, in the sense in which the original Designer created it to be. When virginity and purity are no longer protected and prized, there is dullness, monotony, and sheer boredom. By trying to grab fulfillment everywhere, you find it nowhere.

Purity before marriage consists of giving ourselves to and for each other in obedience to God. Passion must be held by principle. The principle is love—not merely erotic, sentimental, or sexual feeling. There is no other way to control passion and no other route to purity and joy. If you choose to avoid the sin of sexual immorality, that is God's ideal; but if you have already given away your virginity, the message of the gospel proclaims New Birth, a new beginning, and a new creation (2 Cor. 5:17).

The Scriptures have strong admonitions about abstaining from both adultery and fornication. Paul made special mention of sins related to the body. He clearly stated that the body of the believer belongs to the Lord (1 Cor. 6:19). It is His temple (1 Cor. 3:16). A believing woman is to use both her body and spirit to bring glory and praise to God (1 Cor. 6:20).

Fornication—engaging in sexual activity with a person outside the commitment of marriage—is a sin against your own body. Physically, this sin can reap diseases from which those who keep themselves sexually pure are protected. This sin also can reap emotional distress that those who practice purity do not experience. Spiritually, those who habitually practice this sin will miss the fullness of His blessings. Fornication (Gk. *Porneia)* can describe harlotry and prostitution (Rev. 2:14, 20) and various other forms of unchastity (John 8:41; Acts 15:20; 1 Cor. 5:1).

Masturbation is defined as the self-stimulation or manipulation of the genital organs, often to the point of sexual climax or orgasm. Some consider it a means of reducing excessive sexual tension when the normal sexual activity of married life is unavailable or as an alternative for promiscuity or fornication. On the other hand, such self-gratification may originate in lustful fantasies for selfish pleasure. Women should be aware of the danger of masturbating while fantasizing about a desired but inappropriate sexual partner, which Jesus equates with actual commission of sexual intercourse (Matt. 5:27, 28).

Scripture neither explicitly condones nor condemns masturbation. Jesus does not mention it, nor does Paul include it in his list of vile passions (Rom. 1:26–31). Nevertheless, the moral and psychological ramifications of masturbation can prove disruptive to a relationship with God as well as others, particularly in a marriage. Certainly masturbation does not fulfill God's plan for sexual intimacy between husband and wife (Gen. 2:24).

Overall, Scripture advocates an ever-present awareness that human beings are more than sexual or physical. God is interested in our wholeness, which encompasses every area of life.

See also 1 Cor. 6:13–18; 1 Thess. 4:3–6; notes on Dating (1 Tim. 4); Marriage (Gen. 2; 2 Sam. 6; Prov. 5; Hos. 2; Amos 3; 2 Cor. 13; Heb. 12); Sexual Immorality (Prov. 6); Sexuality (Song 4), and annotations on Rom. 3:23, Gal. 5:19–21; Eph. 5:5; note on Self-Centeredness (James 3)

---

judge? ⁵I say this to your shame. Is it so, that there is not a wise man among you, not even one, who will be able to judge between his brethren? ⁶But brother goes to law against brother, and that before unbelievers!

⁷Now therefore, it is already an utter failure

---

demanded that either the dispute be resolved within the church (v. 4) or that the wronged party choose the more excellent way and endure the injustice without seeking redress (vv. 7, 8).

for you that you go to law against one another. Why do you not rather accept wrong? Why do you not rather *let yourselves* be cheated? [8]No, you yourselves do wrong and cheat, and *you do* these things *to your* brethren! [9]Do you not know that the unrighteous will not inherit the kingdom of God? Do not be deceived. Neither fornicators, nor idolaters, nor adulterers, nor homosexuals,[a] nor sodomites, [10]nor thieves, nor covetous, nor drunkards, nor revilers, nor extortioners will inherit the kingdom of God. [11]And such were some of you. But you were washed, but you were sanctified, but you were justified in the name of the Lord Jesus and by the Spirit of our God.

Glorify God in Body and Spirit

[12]All things are lawful for me, but all things are not helpful. All things are lawful for me, but I will not be brought under the power of any. [13]Foods for the stomach and the stomach for foods, but God will destroy both it and them. Now the body *is* not for sexual immorality but for the Lord, and the Lord for the body. [14]And God both raised up the Lord and will also raise us up by His power.

[15]Do you not know that your bodies are members of Christ? Shall I then take the members of Christ and make *them* members of a harlot? Certainly not! [16]Or do you not know that he who is joined to a harlot is one body *with her?* For *"the two,"* He says, *"shall become one flesh."*[a] [17]But he who is joined to the Lord is one spirit *with Him.*

[18]Flee sexual immorality. Every sin that a man does is outside the body, but he who commits sexual immorality sins against his own body. [19]Or do you not know that your body is the temple of the Holy Spirit *who is* in you, whom you have from God, and you are not your own? [20]For you were bought at a price; therefore glorify God in your body[a] and in your spirit, which are God's.

Principles of Marriage

7 Now concerning the things of which you wrote to me:

It is good for a man not to touch a woman. [2]Nevertheless, because of sexual immorality, let each man have his own wife, and let each woman have her own husband. [3]Let the husband render to his wife the affection due her, and likewise also the wife to her husband. [4]The wife does not have authority over her own body, but the husband *does.* And likewise the husband does not have authority over his own body, but the wife *does.* [5]Do not deprive one another except with consent for a time, that you may give yourselves to fasting and prayer; and come together again so that Satan does not tempt you because of your lack of self-control. [6]But I say this as a concession, not as a commandment. [7]For I wish that all men were even as I myself. But each one has his own gift from God, one in this manner and another in that.

[8]But I say to the unmarried and to the widows: It is good for them if they remain even as I am; [9]but if they cannot exercise self-control, let them marry. For it is better to marry than to burn *with passion.*

···············

6:9 [a]That is, catamites   **6:16** [a]Genesis 2:24   **6:20** [a]NU-Text ends the verse at *body.*

6:9 Sodomites is a reference to men who engage in sexual acts with other men (see Lev. 18, Homosexuality).

6:12 All things are lawful for me was the theological slogan the Corinthians had adopted to justify their behavior. Paul affirmed his own doctrine of Christian liberty. But the Corinthians needed to understand that the "lawfulness" of any given behavior was qualified by its "helpfulness." Freedom to act as one pleases is not really freedom at all. It is the most insidious form of bondage. Paul provided guidelines for decision making (see 1 Cor. 8, Decision Making).

6:18, 19 Some within the Christian community had continued to visit prostitutes, arguing that they were unaffected by behavior that merely involved the body. Paul sternly pointed out that what Christians intimately do with their bodies affects the spiritual state of their souls. This is particularly the case with sexual sin. The "one flesh" union of marital sex reflects realities about God. Sexual activity outside of this context violates the image that God has stamped into our psyches and even into our bodies as male and female.

7:4 Normal sexual behavior is summarized by the apostle as an intimacy in which the bodies of husband and wife belong to one another. The phrase "authority over" (Gk. *exousiazō*, lit. "has rights over") applies equally to both and connotes exclusivity (see 1 Cor. 6:16). Furthermore, neither is to withhold marital rights from the other except for a spiritual pursuit, and that only with consent and limitation (1 Cor. 7:5; see 1 Cor. 6:17). Paul may have been addressing some who were trying to practice celibacy within marriage under the guise of spiritual superiority (1 Cor. 7:5). Nevertheless, Paul is also making clear the importance of physical intimacy in marriage by speaking in the strongest terms ("deprive," meaning "defraud") of sexual abstinence within marriage.

7:8 Marriage is a temporary institution and thus will not continue throughout eternity (Matt. 22:30). Being married is of no greater value than being single but is simply a picture of the greater relationship that exists between Christ and the believer. Those who are called to singleness for the sake of the gospel are in a unique position, not "distracted" by the day-to-day realities of the human marital relationship, to concentrate more fully on the eternal relationship to which marriage points and to which all are ultimately called (1 Cor. 7:35; see Ps. 62; Celibacy;1 Cor. 12, Singleness; John 2).

7:9 To burn has been interpreted primarily in two ways: as a reference to the fires of judgment, which might ensue as a result of sexual sin, or as a metaphor for unbridled passions. The latter seems more likely since the emphasis is on self-control and since Paul is here addressing believers.

CELIBACY · A VOW OF ABSTINENCE

To be celibate is to refrain from sexual intercourse. In Scripture, sexual behavior is always considered subject to the will. For a believer to live in purity is a personal obligation to obey fully the commandments of the Lord.

For some, celibacy becomes a lifelong vow so that they might more fully and completely give themselves to the Lord and His church (1 Cor. 7:32–34). It can be a call to love Christ wholeheartedly just as Christ loves the church (Eph. 5:29), to be "holy both in body and in spirit" (1 Cor. 7:34).

Celibate Christians have the opportunity to imitate Christ in a unique way during their earthly pilgrimage. Dying to self, they can focus their love on God for the sake of His kingdom (Matt. 19:12). For those who make such a commitment by faith, the Lord gives the grace to withstand sexual temptation and to live a sexually pure life (1 Cor. 7:17; 2 Cor. 12:9).

The Bible does not advocate celibacy within marriage (1 Cor. 7:3–5), and Paul advises those who have strong sexual desires to marry rather than "to burn with passion" (v. 9).

See also notes on Commitment (Matt. 16); Sexual Purity (1 Cor. 7); Singleness (Ps. 62; 1 Cor. 7)

Keep Your Marriage Vows

[10]Now to the married I command, *yet* not I but the Lord: A wife is not to depart from *her* husband. [11]But even if she does depart, let her remain unmarried or be reconciled to *her* husband. And a husband is not to divorce *his* wife.

[12]But to the rest I, not the Lord, say: If any brother has a wife who does not believe, and she is willing to live with him, let him not divorce her. [13]And a woman who has a husband who does not believe, if he is willing to live with her, let her not divorce him. [14]For the unbelieving husband is sanctified by the wife, and the unbelieving wife is sanctified by the husband; otherwise your children would be unclean, but now they are holy. [15]But if the unbeliever departs, let him depart; a brother or a sister is not under bondage in such *cases.* But God has called us to peace. [16]For how do you know, O wife, whether you will save *your* husband? Or how do you know, O husband, whether you will save *your* wife?

Live as You Are Called

[17]But as God has distributed to each one, as the Lord has called each one, so let him walk. And so I ordain in all the churches. [18]Was anyone called while circumcised? Let him not become uncircumcised. Was anyone called while uncircumcised? Let him not be circumcised. [19]Circumcision is nothing and uncircumcision is nothing, but keeping the commandments of God *is what matters.* [20]Let each one remain in the same calling in which he was called. [21]Were you called *while* a slave? Do not be concerned about it; but if you can be made free, rather use *it.* [22]For he who is called in the Lord *while* a slave is the Lord's freedman. Likewise he who is called *while* free is Christ's slave. [23]You were bought at a price; do not become slaves of men. [24]Brethren, let each one remain with God in that *state* in which he was called.

To the Unmarried and Widows

[25]Now concerning virgins: I have no commandment from the Lord; yet I give judgment as one whom the Lord in His mercy has made trustworthy. [26]I suppose therefore that this is good because of the present distress—that *it is* good for a man to remain as he is: [27]Are you bound to a wife? Do not seek to be loosed. Are you loosed from a wife? Do not seek a wife. [28]But even if you do marry, you have not sinned; and if a virgin marries, she has not sinned. Nevertheless such will have trouble in the flesh, but I would spare you.

[29]But this I say, brethren, the time *is* short, so that from now on even those who have wives should be as though they had none, [30]those who weep as though they did not weep, those who rejoice as though they did not rejoice, those who

---

7:14–16 In this example, two non-Christians married, and one was converted. The emphasis is redemptive, though the passage itself is difficult to interpret. Some consider "sanctified" to be a reference to the legitimacy of the marriage (v. 14). Others consider the apostle's concern to be the believer's moral and spiritual impact on the unbelieving partner and the couple's children. The latter seems more accurate—not suggesting that salvation comes to all through the believer but suggesting that the sanctified life of a believer can channel the blessings of God to all in the household. The redemptive theme is that eventually the unbelieving partner would be won to Christ (1 Cor. 7:16; see 2 Cor. 6, Husbands; 1 Pet. 3:1, 2, note).

7:17–19 Celibacy, circumcision, and freedom were no more or less spiritual than marriage, uncircumcision, and slavery. Paul was concerned that the Corinthians not seek change as though it had spiritual significance, which it did not.

7:29–31 Paul reminded the Corinthians of the impermanence of the world and the shortness of their lives. To describe the shortness of time, Paul used a word (Gk. *sustellō,* lit. "to send together") that suggested "short" in the sense of all events

buy as though they did not possess, ³¹and those who use this world as not misusing *it*. For the form of this world is passing away.

³²But I want you to be without care. He who is unmarried cares for the things of the Lord—how he may please the Lord. ³³But he who is married cares about the things of the world—how he may please *his* wife. ³⁴There is ᵃ a difference between a wife and a virgin. The unmarried woman cares about the things of the Lord, that she may be holy both in body and in spirit. But she who is married cares about the things of the world—how she may please *her* husband. ³⁵And this I say for your own profit, not that I may put a leash on you, but for what is proper, and that you may serve the Lord without distraction.

³⁶But if any man thinks he is behaving improperly toward his virgin, if she is past the flower of youth, and thus it must be, let him do what he wishes. He does not sin; let them marry. ³⁷Nevertheless he who stands steadfast in his heart, having no necessity, but has power over his own will, and has so determined in his heart that he will keep his virgin,ᵃ does well. ³⁸So then he who gives *her* ᵃ in marriage does well, but he who does not give *her* in marriage does better.

³⁹A wife is bound by law as long as her husband lives; but if her husband dies, she is at liberty to be married to whom she wishes, only in the Lord. ⁴⁰But she is happier if she remains as she is, according to my judgment—and I think I also have the Spirit of God.

Be Sensitive to Conscience

8 Now concerning things offered to idols: We know that we all have knowledge. Knowledge puffs up, but love edifies. ²And if anyone thinks that he knows anything, he knows nothing yet as he ought to know. ³But if anyone loves God, this one is known by Him.

⁴Therefore concerning the eating of things offered to idols, we know that an idol *is* nothing in the world, and that *there is* no other God but one. ⁵For even if there are so-called gods, whether in heaven or on earth (as there are many gods and many lords), ⁶yet for us *there is* one God, the Father, of whom *are* all things, and we for Him; and one Lord Jesus Christ, through whom *are* all things, and through whom we *live*.

⁷However, *there is* not in everyone that knowledge; for some, with consciousness of the idol, until now eat *it* as a thing offered to an idol; and their conscience, being weak, is defiled. ⁸But food does not commend us to God; for neither if we eat are we the better, nor if we do not eat are we the worse.

⁹But beware lest somehow this liberty of yours become a stumbling block to those who are weak. ¹⁰For if anyone sees you who have knowledge eating in an idol's temple, will not the conscience of him who is weak be emboldened to eat those things offered to idols? ¹¹And because of your knowledge shall the weak brother perish, for whom Christ died? ¹²But when you thus sin against the brethren, and wound their weak conscience, you sin against Christ. ¹³Therefore, if food makes my brother stumble, I will never again eat meat, lest I make my brother stumble.

A Pattern of Self-Denial

9 Am I not an apostle? Am I not free? Have I not seen Jesus Christ our Lord? Are you not my work in the Lord? ²If I am not an apostle to others, yet doubtless I am to you. For you are the seal of my apostleship in the Lord.

³My defense to those who examine me is this: ⁴Do we have no right to eat and drink? ⁵Do we have no right to take along a believing wife, as *do* also the other apostles, the brothers of the Lord, and Cephas? ⁶Or *is it* only Barnabas and I *who* have no right to refrain from working? ⁷Who ever goes to war at his own expense? Who plants a vineyard

---

7:34 ᵃM-Text adds *also*.   **7:37** ᵃOr *virgin daughter*   **7:38** ᵃNU-Text reads *his own virgin*.

---

were drawing together toward the time of the Lord's return. Therefore, the Corinthians were to keep themselves as free as possible from the ordinary pressures and distractions of life. Marriage, the processes of birth and death, material possessions, and all the other things that belong to this age are of a temporary nature. These are legitimate, but Christians are to view them from the perspective of eternity. Their lives are to focus on the eternal and not on the temporal.

7:36, 37 The action of a father toward his daughter seems to be in view, or perhaps a man and his fiancée, though this passage cannot be interpreted with certainty. Paul continued to be clear in upholding the sanctity of marriage, while indicating the beauty of a celibate life committed unto God.

8:1, 2 Things offered to idols could allude to meat sold in the markets or to meat served at such banquets. The feasts were attended by some converts to Christianity who argued that since idols were "nothing," they were free to eat the meat.

Furthermore, they looked down upon those whose consciences prohibited their participation. Paul argued that love and not knowledge was the basis of Christian conduct. Although idols were indeed "nothing," this little bit of knowledge had puffed them up and had prevented their correct behavior toward their Christian friends.

8:10–12 Real idolatry, not just the eating of meat, was the issue at hand. Paul denied that any true "gods" were involved in paganism but pointed out what the Corinthians failed to note: Pagan religion was often the locus of demonic activity. The issue was not that of merely "offending" someone in the church but of weakening someone's commitment to Christ. The Corinthians had arrogantly insisted on their own rights and freedoms and had jeopardized the spiritual well-being of others.

8:13 See 1 Corinthians 6:12, note.

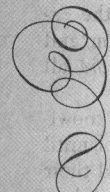

DECISION MAKING *TOUGH CHOICES*

Every person faces decisions with immediate and long-term consequences. For the Christian woman, wise decisions can be made with the confidence that God directs her every step as she seeks His will in prayer, Bible study, and listening to the Holy Spirit, the divine Counselor (John 14:26; 15:26). While Scripture offers precise guidance for many issues in our daily lives, the Bible appears silent on others.

In all cases, you can benefit from the principles Paul offered to the first-century Corinthian believers who were facing the moral dilemma of eating meat sacrificed to idols:

1) Will the course considered lead a fellow Christian to sin by your example? (1 Cor 8:13)
2) Will the action provide strength and encouragement to your own life? (1 Cor. 6:12; 10:23)
3) Will the action ultimately glorify God? (1 Cor. 10:31)

These same questions are appropriate for your prayerful consideration in every decision you make.

See also notes on Access to God (Rom. 10); Authority (John 19); Change Points in Life (Eccl. 3); God's Will (Eph. 5); Intuition (Heb. 5); Priorities (Matt. 6)

and does not eat of its fruit? Or who tends a flock and does not drink of the milk of the flock?

⁸Do I say these things as a *mere* man? Or does not the law say the same also? ⁹For it is written in the law of Moses, *"You shall not muzzle an ox while it treads out the grain."*[a] Is it oxen God is concerned about? ¹⁰Or does He say *it* altogether for our sakes? For our sakes, no doubt, *this* is written, that he who plows should plow in hope, and he who threshes in hope should be partaker of his hope. ¹¹If we have sown spiritual things for you, *is it* a great thing if we reap your material things? ¹²If others are partakers of *this* right over you, *are we* not even more?

Nevertheless we have not used this right, but endure all things lest we hinder the gospel of Christ. ¹³Do you not know that those who minister the holy things eat *of the things* of the temple, and those who serve at the altar partake of *the offerings of* the altar? ¹⁴Even so the Lord has commanded that those who preach the gospel should live from the gospel.

¹⁵But I have used none of these things, nor have I written these things that it should be done so to me; for it *would be* better for me to die than that anyone should make my boasting void. ¹⁶For if I preach the gospel, I have nothing to boast of, for necessity is laid upon me; yes, woe is me if I do not preach the gospel! ¹⁷For if I do this willingly, I have a reward; but if against my will, I have been entrusted with a stewardship. ¹⁸What is my reward then? That when I preach the gospel, I may present the gospel of Christ[a] without charge, that I may not abuse my authority in the gospel.

Serving All Men

¹⁹For though I am free from all *men,* I have made myself a servant to all, that I might win the more; ²⁰and to the Jews I became as a Jew, that I might win Jews; to those *who are* under the law, as under the law,[a] that I might win those *who are* under the law; ²¹to those *who are* without law, as without law (not being without law toward God,[a] but under law toward Christ[b]), that I might win those *who are* without law; ²²to the weak I became as[a] weak, that I might win the weak. I have become all things to all *men,* that I might by all means save some. ²³Now this I do for the gospel's sake, that I may be partaker of it with *you.*

Striving for a Crown

²⁴Do you not know that those who run in a race all run, but one receives the prize? Run in such a

············

9:9 [a]Deuteronomy 25:4   9:18 [a]NU-Text omits *of Christ.*   9:20 [a]NU-Text adds *though not being myself under the law.*   9:21 [a]NU-Text reads *God's law.* [b]NU-Text reads *Christ's law.*   9:22 [a]NU-Text omits *as.*

9:10, 11 Though Paul may have been supported financially in some way by patrons like Lydia (see Acts 16:15), he seemed to favor supporting himself through tentmaking. Problems arose when the Corinthians observed other teachers (perhaps Apollos and Peter) accepting patronage. Because of Paul's refusal to do the same, they began to question the authenticity of his apostleship. Paul argued that although he had the *right* to be supported by them, he also had the right to *refuse* support. He had chosen to preach the gospel without pay so that he could not be accused of benefiting financially from what he taught. By presenting the gospel "free of charge," he himself was "free from all men," constrained to preach only by obedience to Christ (1 Cor. 9:19).

9:19 Paul conformed to the culture and practices of those with whom he worked. When with Jews, he observed Jewish custom; when with Gentiles, Gentile custom. With the "weak," those who were over-scrupulous in their observances, he was particularly careful to regulate his conduct to their standards. Paul's adaptability appeared as "inconsistency" to his critics. They had failed to note that his "inconsistency" was governed by a greater principle to which he consistently yielded. "I have become all things to all men, that I might by all means save some" (1 Cor. 9:22). Paul was uncompromising on beliefs and behaviors that were governed by the gospel but flexible and adaptable on those matters that were not.

THE TWO TYPES OF WISDOM

WORLDLY WISDOM	SPIRITUAL WISDOM
Sees the message of the Cross as foolishness (1 Cor. 1:18)	Realizes the message of the Cross is the power of God (1 Cor. 1:18)
Does not know God (1 Cor. 1:21)	Demonstrates the power of God (1 Cor. 2:5)
Boasts in men (1 Cor. 3:21)	Glories in the Lord (1 Cor. 1:31)
Takes pride in human knowledge (1 Cor. 8:2)	Knows the mind of Christ (1 Cor. 2:16)
Is puffed up (1 Cor. 4:6)	Seeks meekness and humility (1 Cor. 2:3)
Criticizes leadership (1 Cor. 4:8)	Submits to spiritual leadership (1 Cor. 14:37; 16:16)
Relies on the power of words (1 Cor. 4:20)	Relies on the power of God (1 Cor. 4:20)
Takes pride in personal accomplishments (1 Cor. 4:7)	Recognizes God as source of everything (1 Cor. 6:19, 20)
Scoffs at differences (1 Cor. 12:21)	Respects diversity (1 Cor. 12:11)
Insists on personal rights (1 Cor. 8:9)	Becomes servant of all (1 Cor. 9:19)
Is insensitive to others (1 Cor. 8:11)	Edifies others (1 Cor. 8:1)
Arrogantly wounds others (1 Cor. 8:12)	Seeks another's well-being (1 Cor. 10:24)
Leads to envy, strife, and division (1 Cor.1:10; 3:3)	Pursues unity (1 Cor. 12:13)
Is full of malice (1 Cor. 14:20)	Walks in the way of love (1 Cor. 13:1)
Is subject to "fall" (1 Cor. 10:12)	Stands up under temptation (1 Cor. 10:13)
Will be caught in its own craftiness (1 Cor. 3:19)	Maintains self-control and discipline (1 Cor. 6:12; 9:27)
Has immature understanding (1 Cor. 3:1; 14:20)	Develops maturity (1 Cor. 2:6)
Will not last (1 Cor. 3:15)	Will last (1 Cor. 3:10–14)

way that you may obtain *it*. ²⁵And everyone who competes *for the prize* is temperate in all things. Now they *do it* to obtain a perishable crown, but we *for* an imperishable *crown*. ²⁶Therefore I run thus: not with uncertainty. Thus I fight: not as *one who* beats the air. ²⁷But I discipline my body and bring *it* into subjection, lest, when I have preached to others, I myself should become disqualified.

Old Testament Examples

10 Moreover, brethren, I do not want you to be unaware that all our fathers were under the cloud, all passed through the sea, ²all were baptized into Moses in the cloud and in the sea, ³all ate the same spiritual food, ⁴and all drank the same spiritual drink. For they drank of that spiritual Rock that followed them, and that Rock was

9:27 The Greeks hosted the great athletic festivals of the Olympic and Isthmian games. The latter were held at Corinth and were therefore familiar to the recipients of Paul's letter. Contestants in the games participated in ten months of mandatory training. If they failed to complete this training, they were barred from competition. The major attraction at the games was the lengthy race, and that was the illustration Paul used to depict the faithful Christian life. Paul contended that his actions had not been those of an aimless competitor but were comparable to those of the

MISSIONS   PREPARED TO SERVE

Anyone with a mission to win someone to Christ becomes a missionary. You become a missionary because you have a mission to share the message of salvation. There are ways to equip yourself for the greatest effectiveness:

- Become acquainted with the customs of those to whom you minister (1 Cor. 9:22).
- Learn to speak the language of those with whom you work.
- Make an effort to eat their foods (1 Cor. 10:27).
- Be willing to wear their ethnic clothing, especially for festive occasions.
- Listen to their problems (Gal. 6:2).
- Pray for individuals and specific needs (James 5:16).
- Avoid local politics (Acts 5:29).
- Treat others as you yourself wish to be treated (Matt. 7:12).
- Never compromise your faith (Rom. 1:16).

See also notes on Evangelism (John 6; Col. 4; 1 Pet. 3); Missions (Acts 1); Prejudice (Acts 15); Racial Relations (Acts 10); Salvation (Eph. 2)

Christ. ⁵But with most of them God was not well pleased, for *their bodies* were scattered in the wilderness.

⁶Now these things became our examples, to the intent that we should not lust after evil things as they also lusted. ⁷And do not become idolaters as *were* some of them. As it is written, *"The people sat down to eat and drink, and rose up to play."*ᵃ ⁸Nor let us commit sexual immorality, as some of them did, and in one day twenty-three thousand fell; ⁹nor let us tempt Christ, as some of them also tempted, and were destroyed by serpents; ¹⁰nor complain, as some of them also complained, and were destroyed by the destroyer. ¹¹Now allᵃ these things happened to them as examples, and they were written for our admonition, upon whom the ends of the ages have come.

¹²Therefore let him who thinks he stands take heed lest he fall. ¹³No temptation has overtaken you except such as is common to man; but God *is* faithful, who will not allow you to be tempted beyond what you are able, but with the temptation will also make the way of escape, that you may be able to bear *it*.

Flee from Idolatry

¹⁴Therefore, my beloved, flee from idolatry. ¹⁵I speak as to wise men; judge for yourselves what I say. ¹⁶The cup of blessing which we bless, is it not the communion of the blood of Christ? The bread which we break, is it not the communion of the body of Christ? ¹⁷For we, *though* many, are one bread *and* one body; for we all partake of that one bread.

¹⁸Observe Israel after the flesh: Are not those who eat of the sacrifices partakers of the altar? ¹⁹What am I saying then? That an idol is anything, or what is offered to idols is anything? ²⁰Rather, that the things which the Gentiles sacrifice they sacrifice to demons and not to God, and I do not want you to have fellowship with demons. ²¹You cannot drink the cup of the Lord and the cup of demons; you cannot partake of the Lord's table and of the table of demons. ²²Or do we provoke the Lord to jealousy? Are we stronger than He?

· ·

10:7 ᵃExodus 32:6   **10:11** ᵃNU-Text omits *all*.

---

athlete who had trained with the goal of winning. Paul had disciplined himself—curtailing his own rights for exercising his freedoms—all for the sake of the gospel. He admonished the Corinthians to do the same so that they, too, might attain the eternal prize.

10:4 The Israelites were supplied with water from the rock of Meribah both at the beginning (Ex. 17:1–7) and toward the end of their desert wanderings in the Pentateuch narrative (Num. 20:2–13). Jewish legend referred to a water-supplying "rock" which traveled alongside the people throughout their 40-year journey. Paul did not endorse this account as literal history but affirmed that a supernatural "Rock" had indeed accompanied them, and that "Rock" was Jesus.

10:11, 12 The Corinthians had become overconfident in their spirituality; so Paul directed their attention to the example of

the Israelite people. He pointed out that although the Israelites had consumed the same spiritual food and drink as the Corinthians, they had failed to please God (vv. 3, 4). They had fallen into sins of idolatry and sexual immorality, complaining against God and tempting Him. To "tempt" (Gk. *ekpeirazō*, lit. "to put to the test") God is to try or test His patience thoroughly (v. 10). The Israelites had pushed God to the limit by constantly compromising His commands. Paul admonished the Corinthians to exercise caution, for they were beginning to place confidence in their own spiritual state and were thus susceptible to falling into sin just as the Israelites had done.

10:21, 22 The cup of libation poured at the end of pagan feasts in honor of the sponsoring deity was incompatible with drinking the cup of the Lord. The Lord's cup, symbolic of the

FRUIT OF THE SPIRIT *SELF-CONTROL*

Self-discipline is essential to personal development, spiritual growth, and Christian service. However, self-discipline does not "just happen" or appear as a natural trait. People must practice self-control in order to lead disciplined lives. For the Christian woman, God's unlimited power can be added to limited human willpower to develop divine discipline. Divine discipline requires a personal action to receive the Holy Spirit's power.

Christians must learn to discipline both outward behaviors and inward feelings in order to be godly. Words and actions as well as thoughts and passions must be acceptable to God (Ps. 19:14). A disciplined life involves a genuine, personal commitment to obey God's statutes, and frequently it requires lifestyle changes. God's supernatural power is added to personal willpower as believers practice His presence, receive His power, and seek His joy.

The acceptance by, affirmation from, and accountability to other people also help a believer develop self-control. Divine discipline should be a part of every believer's spiritual growth. A personal choice to become disciplined can effect change in others as well.

Scripture teaches that self-control is the crowning fruit of the Holy Spirit (Gal. 5:22). Without self-control, the believer has little opportunity to experience fully the blessings of God.

See also 1 Tim. 4:7, 8; Titus 2:4, 5; Heb. 12:11; 2 Pet. 1:5–7; notes on Fruit of the Spirit (Ps. 86; Rom. 5; 15; 1 Cor. 13; Gal. 5; Eph. 4; Col. 3; 2 Thess. 1; Rev. 2); Perseverance (Rev. 14); Spiritual Discipline (2 Pet. 3)

All to the Glory of God

23 All things are lawful for me,[a] but not all things are helpful; all things are lawful for me,[b] but not all things edify. 24 Let no one seek his own, but each one the other's *well-being.*

25 Eat whatever is sold in the meat market, asking no questions for conscience' sake; 26 for *"the earth is the LORD's, and all its fullness."*[a]

27 If any of those who do not believe invites you *to dinner,* and you desire to go, eat whatever is set before you, asking no question for conscience' sake. 28 But if anyone says to you, "This was offered to idols," do not eat it for the sake of the one who told you, and for conscience' sake;[a] for *"the earth is the LORD's, and all its fullness."*[b] 29 "Conscience," I say, not your own, but that of the other. For why is my liberty judged by another *man's* conscience? 30 But if I partake with thanks, why am I evil spoken of for *the food* over which I give thanks?

31 Therefore, whether you eat or drink, or whatever you do, do all to the glory of God. 32 Give no offense, either to the Jews or to the Greeks or to the church of God, 33 just as I also please all *men* in all *things,* not seeking my own profit, but the *profit* of many, that they may be saved.

11 Imitate me, just as I also *imitate* Christ.

Head Coverings

2 Now I praise you, brethren, that you remember me in all things and keep the traditions just as I delivered *them* to you. 3 But I want you to know that the head of every man is Christ, the head of woman *is* man, and the head of Christ *is* God. 4 Every man praying or prophesying, having *his* head covered, dishonors his head. 5 But every woman who prays or prophesies with *her* head

10:23 [a]NU-Text omits *for me.* [b]NU-Text omits *for me.*   10:26 [a]Psalm 24:1   10:28 [a]NU-Text omits the rest of this verse. [b]Psalm 24:1

believer's relationship to God, excluded the possibility of any relationship to demons. Furthermore, sharing the bread of the Lord, which was symbolic of the believer's communion with Christ's body—the church—barred them from communing (and therefore being bound) with people who communed with demons (v. 17). Attendance at pagan feasts therefore violated both the vertical dimension of their relationship to God and the horizontal dimension of their relationship to each other.

10:23 See 1 Cor. 6:12, note; 8, Decision Making.

10:31 See 1 Cor. 6:12, note; 8, Decision Making.

11:3 Paul presented headship as divinely ordered: God-Christ, Christ-man, man-woman (see chart, Theological Foundation for Headship). A Christian perspective on authority radically differs from that of the world. To begin, Christian authority is for the purpose of service. Jesus commanded those in author-

ity to exercise their roles with love, humility, and justice (Luke 22:24–27). Husbands, for example, were instructed to imitate Christ's servant leadership in their relationships to their wives (Eph. 5:25–29; see chart, Role Relationships Between Men and Women). Also, the husband's headship is not based upon any inherent virtue of the male. Rather, the relationship between redeemed man and woman is a model that is to reflect to the world the nature of the relationships within the Godhead as well as God's relationship to His church. Finally, the relationship between God and Christ helps us understand what headship means. The Father and Son are always equal in essence, including the time of Jesus' subordination during His Incarnation; yet they have different roles (Phil. 2:6, 7). Likewise, the different roles of man and woman do not imply the superiority of one, or the inferiority of the other. Paul was careful to point out that they are interdependent and equal—"all things are from God" (1 Cor. 11:8–12).

WEIGHT CONTROL *A DISCIPLINED BODY*

If you struggle with weight control, God's Word has both encouragement and admonishment:

1. Be accepting. God designed your physical make-up. Refrain from criticizing His creation (Ps. 139:13–16).
2. Be grateful. God has given you a triumphal new nature at your conversion. You are admonished to give thanks to God who gives you victory in the Lord Jesus Christ (1 Cor. 15:57).
3. Be careful. The Bible, speaking for moderation and against gluttony, condemns over-indulgence (Prov. 23:20–21). Resist extra helpings and rich foods that add additional inches.
4. Be disciplined. Achieving temperance in eating will strengthen other areas in your life. Paul proclaimed that although all things were lawful for him, he refused to be brought under the power of any (1 Cor. 10:23) because all things were not helpful to him (1 Cor. 6:12).
5. Be active. Regular exercise will help you to reach and maintain your ideal weight. Activity also improves productivity, cardiovascular stamina, and mental alertness. The writer of Hebrews encourages believers to run with endurance (Heb. 12:1; see also 1 Tim. 4:8).
6. Be persistent. Just as Paul finished the race (2 Tim. 4:7), you, too, can persevere if you set a goal and move forward victoriously to achieve it!

See also 1 Cor. 10:23—11:1; Phil. 4:13; notes on Fitness (Phil. 1); Fruit of the Spirit (1 Cor. 10); Nutrition (Lev. 11)

---

uncovered dishonors her head, for that is one and the same as if her head were shaved. [6]For if a woman is not covered, let her also be shorn. But if it is shameful for a woman to be shorn or shaved, let her be covered. [7]For a man indeed ought not to cover *his* head, since he is the image and glory of God; but woman is the glory of man. [8]For man is not from woman, but woman from man. [9]Nor was man created for the woman, but woman for the man. [10]For this reason the woman ought to have *a symbol of* authority on *her* head, because of the angels. [11]Nevertheless, neither *is* man independent of woman, nor woman independent of man, in the Lord. [12]For as woman *came* from man, even so man also *comes* through woman; but all things are from God.

[13]Judge among yourselves. Is it proper for a woman to pray to God with her head uncovered? [14]Does not even nature itself teach you that if a man has long hair, it is a dishonor to him? [15]But if a woman has long hair, it is a glory to her; for *her* hair is given to her[a] for a covering. [16]But if anyone seems to be contentious, we have no such custom, nor *do* the churches of God.

Conduct at the Lord's Supper

[17]Now in giving these instructions I do not praise *you*, since you come together not for the better but for the worse. [18]For first of all, when you come together as a church, I hear that there are divisions among you, and in part I believe it. [19]For

there must also be factions among you, that those who are approved may be recognized among you. [20]Therefore when you come together in one place, it is not to eat the Lord's Supper. [21]For in eating, each one takes his own supper ahead of *others;* and one is hungry and another is drunk. [22]What! Do you not have houses to eat and drink in? Or do you despise the church of God and shame those who have nothing? What shall I say to you? Shall I praise you in this? I do not praise *you.*

Institution of the Lord's Supper

[23]For I received from the Lord that which I also delivered to you: that the Lord Jesus on the *same* night in which He was betrayed took bread; [24]and when He had given thanks, He broke *it* and said, "Take, eat;[a] this is My body which is broken[b] for you; do this in remembrance of Me." [25]In the same manner *He* also *took* the cup after supper, saying, "This cup is the new covenant in My blood. This do, as often as you drink *it,* in remembrance of Me."

[26]For as often as you eat this bread and drink this cup, you proclaim the Lord's death till He comes.

Examine Yourself

[27]Therefore whoever eats this bread or drinks *this* cup of the Lord in an unworthy manner will be

---

11:15 [a]M-Text omits *to her.* **11:24** [a]NU-Text omits *Take, eat.* [b]NU-Text omits *broken.*

11:23–34 The observance of the Lord's Supper begins with giving "thanks" (Gk. *eucharisteō*, lit. "give thanks," transliterated "eucharist," (v. 24). This experience is also a memorial of Christ's atonement on the Cross (vv. 24, 25), an experience of fellowship among believers (v. 18); a testimony of Christ's

death in their behalf (v. 26), and a means by which believers are challenged to examine their spiritual lives (v. 28). The sharing of a common loaf indicated the unity of the body of Christ. Eating the bread and drinking the cup are also a reminder of the Lord's sacrificial death on the Cross.

HEAD COVERINGS FOR WOMEN

TYPE OF COVERING	DESCRIPTION
Headband (Heb. *shabis*)	Probably a head ornament or front-band of gold or silver (Is. 3:18, 20; v. 18, "scarves" in NKJV).
Headdress (Heb. *pe'er*)	Ornamental head covering worn by wealthy women, probably wound about the head (Is. 3:20; Ezek. 24:17). Also used to describe the garland of the bridegroom or turban worn by men as well as the cap worn by priests (Is. 61:10; Ezek. 24:17, 23; 44:18).
Head covering (Gk. *peribolaios*, lit. "covering")	First Corinthians probably refers to some kind of hair covering—perhaps even a shawl. The wearing of long, loose hair by an adulteress confirms that such would be considered shameful (Num. 5:18). The importance of the covering seems to be twofold: to show clear distinction between the sexes and to affirm publicly a wife's commitment to her husband's leadership (1 Cor. 11:2–16). This custom may have been especially important to the Corinthians because of the pagan and immoral influence around them.
Veil (Heb. *tsaciph*)	Rebekah put on a veil when she approached Isaac before her marriage, perhaps as a sign of her betrothal. The veil was to be removed at the time of marriage (Gen. 24:65). Tamar used the veil to trick Judah (Gen. 38:14, 19).
(Heb. *redid*)	The veil-like, thin garment was probably for summer (Song 5:7; Is. 3:23).
(Heb. *tsamah*)	This face veil (lit. "locks") was probably ornamental, perhaps a long train of adornment for women of high social standing (Song 4:1, 3; 6:7; Is. 47:2).
(Heb. *mispachoth*)	This covering (probably a cap fitting close to the head) is associated with the activities of false prophetesses (Ezek. 13:18, 21).

Full veiling does not seem to be part of the Old Testament culture. However, head coverings were important to women in biblical days. They not only offered protection from the elements but also served as symbols of modesty and, for a married woman, as a token of her commitment to her husband.

The theological principle of divine order remains unchanged even though its specific manifestations, such as a woman's covering her head in Corinth, may differ from place to place and culture to culture (see chart, Theological Foundations for Headship). This order was evident in the chronological sequence of creation (1 Cor. 11:8, 9). Furthermore, woman was man's "glory" (v. 7). This concept refers to the act of "manifesting or pointing to the role of another." The woman, who pointed to the man, was to be covered in the presence of God; while man, who pointed to God, was not. The practice was also followed "because of the angels" (v. 10). Paul reasoned that angels, the most submissive of all creatures, would be offended by non-compliance. Furthermore, God had provided a natural analogy that emphasized the appropriateness of the head covering: "Nature" favors women over men in the provision of hair on the head (vv. 13–15). Finally, Paul appealed to the universality of Christian practice (v. 16). The principle of headship was important, and its symbol was to be observed in all the churches.

WOMEN'S MINISTRIES   THE GIFT OF PROPHECY

The Bible abounds with many examples of women who ministered prophetically. The prophetess Miriam led the women to celebrate the Lord's triumph over Egypt (Ex. 15:20, 21). Deborah was a prophetess who functioned as a judge (Judg. 4:4, 5), and the prophetess Huldah was consulted on behalf of the king (2 Kin. 22:14–20). Other Old Testament women had prophetic ministries as well (Is. 8:3).

In the New Testament, we encounter Anna (Luke 2:36–38) and the four daughters of the evangelist Philip (Acts 21:9). Joel foretold that both sons and daughters would prophesy after God poured His Spirit out on all flesh (Joel 2:28)—a promise that was cited by Peter at the time of Pentecost (Acts 2:17, 18). Paul encouraged women to exercise the gift of prophecy and instructed them how to do so in the public assembly of the church (1 Cor. 11:5).

The nature of prophecy changed with the outpouring of God's Spirit. Old Testament prophets, individually commissioned by God, were to be put to death if they misrepresented God's message to the people (Deut. 13:1–5; 18:20–22). New Testament prophecy, on the other hand, was a gift given to many believers, and its transmission was not guaranteed as infallible. It needed to be sifted, weighed, and evaluated by the leadership of the church (1 Cor. 14:29; 1 Thess. 5:20, 21). Nevertheless, it was regarded as a valuable and necessary gift for the church and an area of effective ministry for women.

See also chart on Spiritual Gifts of Women in the Bible (1 Cor. 12); notes on Spiritual Gifts (Rom. 12); Women's Ministries (John 4; Acts 2; Eph. 2; 1 Tim. 3; Titus 2)

---

guilty of the body and blood[a] of the Lord. 28But let a man examine himself, and so let him eat of the bread and drink of the cup. 29For he who eats and drinks in an unworthy manner[a] eats and drinks judgment to himself, not discerning the Lord's[b] body. 30For this reason many *are* weak and sick among you, and many sleep. 31For if we would judge ourselves, we would not be judged. 32But when we are judged, we are chastened by the Lord, that we may not be condemned with the world.

33Therefore, my brethren, when you come together to eat, wait for one another. 34But if anyone is hungry, let him eat at home, lest you come together for judgment. And the rest I will set in order when I come.

Spiritual Gifts: Unity in Diversity

12 Now concerning spiritual *gifts*, brethren, I do not want you to be ignorant: 2You know that[a] you were Gentiles, carried away to these dumb idols, however you were led. 3Therefore I make known to you that no one speaking by the Spirit of God calls Jesus accursed, and no one can say that Jesus is Lord except by the Holy Spirit.

4There are diversities of gifts, but the same Spirit. 5There are differences of ministries, but the same Lord. 6And there are diversities of activities, but it is the same God who works all in all. 7But the manifestation of the Spirit is given to each one for the profit *of all:* 8for to one is given the word of wisdom through the Spirit, to another the word of knowledge through the same Spirit, 9to another faith by the same[a] Spirit, to another gifts of healings by the same[a] Spirit, 10to another the working of miracles, to another prophecy, to another discerning of spirits, to another *different* kinds of tongues, to another the interpretation of tongues. 11But one and the same Spirit works all these things, distributing to each one individually as He wills.

Unity and Diversity in One Body

12For as the body is one and has many members, but all the members of that one body, being many, are one body, so also *is* Christ. 13For by one Spirit we were all baptized into one body—whether Jews

---

11:27 [a]NU-Text and M-Text read *the blood.*   11:29 [a]NU-Text omits *in an unworthy manner.* [b]NU-Text omits *Lord's.*   12:2 [a]NU-Text and M-Text add *when.*   12:9 [a]NU-Text reads *one.*

11:29 As an alternative to the cultic feasts of the pagans, the Corinthians had begun to sponsor their own "love feasts," celebrated in conjunction with the Lord's Supper. Apparently, the rich Christians were feasting and drinking in isolated cliques, while the poor remained hungry. Emphasizing social divisions among themselves was an offense against the body of Christ, for it contradicted both the purpose of Christ's self-sacrifice and the spirit in which it was made. The reality of the Corinthians' common standing in the Lord was not to be compromised by prejudice and divisive, judgmental spirits (v. 30).

12:3 The title Lord (Gk. *kurios*), a term of respect for people of high rank or distinction, was also used in a unique way to refer to God. Confessing Jesus as Lord was understood as confessing Jesus as God. Whether or not the Spirit of God was guiding someone was determined by whether or not that person would confess "Jesus is Lord."

12:13 All Christians, regardless of race, social standing, or gender, are baptized into Christ's body and receive Christ's Spirit (Gal. 3:28). The implication is not that social, cultural, or gender differences be obliterated but rather that these differ-

SINGLENESS · MANY OPPORTUNITIES

Singleness is a permanent state in life for some people and a temporary state in life for most. Adam was created by God and knew an experience of solitude in the garden before God created Eve. Most teenagers and young adults today experience a similar period of aloneness. The response of faith is to see singleness as a call to a committed life, not a lonely life. Made in the image of God (Gen. 1:26), the single woman ideally lives in a covenant relationship with God and is called to develop her gifts—human and spiritual—to contribute to the building up of the church (1 Cor. 12:7).

St. Francis deSales observed that the single person who later marries faces the challenge of preserving a heart capable of love—as opposed to a heart "quite worn out, spoiled, and weary with love instead of a whole and sincere heart."

The single woman is called to develop a deep love relationship with the Lord and to channel her love in pure, productive, and generous ways to the benefit of others. A vital spiritual life can be her anchor for chastity and a source of stability in an evil and perverse generation (Luke 9:41; 11:29).

The single person can experience great freedom to devote herself to work, friendship, and service—all of which can contribute greatly to the church and the extension of God's kingdom on the earth. The single person has an opportunity to give a unique level of service to those in need—a level of service that is unfettered and "without distraction" (1 Cor. 7:35).

A generous willingness to assist others can lead to happiness and fulfillment for the single woman. A spirit of generous service, which can be a tremendous witness to the power of God, is a gift to be sought from God.

See also Dan. 2:23, Gal. 5:16–26, 1 Cor. 7:32–35; notes on Celibacy (1 Cor. 7); Sacrificial Living (Mic. 7); Servanthood (Mark 10); Singleness (Ps. 62; 1 Cor. 7)

---

or Greeks, whether slaves or free—and have all been made to drink into[a] one Spirit. [14]For in fact the body is not one member but many.

[15]If the foot should say, "Because I am not a hand, I am not of the body," is it therefore not of the body? [16]And if the ear should say, "Because I am not an eye, I am not of the body," is it therefore not of the body? [17]If the whole body *were* an eye, where *would be* the hearing? If the whole *were* hearing, where *would be* the smelling? [18]But now God has set the members, each one of them, in the body just as He pleased. [19]And if they were all one member, where *would* the body *be?*

[20]But now indeed *there are* many members, yet one body. [21]And the eye cannot say to the hand, "I have no need of you"; nor again the head to the feet, "I have no need of you." [22]No, much rather, those members of the body which seem to be weaker are necessary. [23]And those *members* of the body which we think to be less honorable, on these we bestow greater honor; and our unpresentable *parts* have greater modesty, [24]but our presentable *parts* have no need. But God composed the body, having given greater honor to that *part* which lacks

it, [25]that there should be no schism in the body, but *that* the members should have the same care for one another. [26]And if one member suffers, all the members suffer with *it;* or if one member is honored, all the members rejoice with *it.*

[27]Now you are the body of Christ, and members individually. [28]And God has appointed these in the church: first apostles, second prophets, third teachers, after that miracles, then gifts of healings, helps, administrations, varieties of tongues. [29]*Are* all apostles? *Are* all prophets? *Are* all teachers? *Are* all workers of miracles? [30]Do all have gifts of healings? Do all speak with tongues? Do all interpret? [31]But earnestly desire the best[a] gifts. And yet I show you a more excellent way.

The Greatest Gift

13 Though I speak with the tongues of men and of angels, but have not love, I have become sounding brass or a clanging cymbal. [2]And though I have *the gift of* prophecy, and understand all mysteries and all knowledge, and though

---

12:13 [a]NU-Text omits *into.*   12:31 [a]NU-Text reads *greater.*

---

ences are of no consequence with regard to one's access to God.

12:20–24 The Corinthians regarded some spiritual gifts as superior to others. Paul argued that just as the physical body is comprised of parts with different roles and functions, so the body of the church exhibits variety in the giftedness of its members. Furthermore, he argued that the appearance of bodily parts is deceptive. Their apparent "weakness" has no direct relationship to their value or necessity. The hidden in-

ternal organs are not attractive, yet are much more essential to one's health than the visible, external ones. Also, the "unpresentable" sexual organs are given higher honor by being carefully clothed (v. 23). The members of the church body that appear to be weak and less worthy are accorded greater honor either by the importance of their function or by the special attention they require.

12:31 The Corinthians were preoccupied with who was wiser, more spiritual, more liberated, or more important. Therefore,

FRUIT OF THE SPIRIT LOVE

In both Hebrew (*ahab*) and Greek (*agapē*), words translated "love" are action words, indicating conscious acts on behalf of a beloved. However, biblical love seems to demand going beyond merely a particular behavior to include a certain inner attitude, that is, a positive inner response (1 John 3:17).

While several Greek words describe specific forms of love, the Greek word *agapē* most expresses Christlike, selfless love. Unselfish, loyal, benevolent concern for the well-being of another is called by Paul "the greatest" gift of all (1 Cor. 13:13). Christian love is a fruit of the Holy Spirit, a virtue of godly living (Gal. 5:22).

The attributes of love reflect both feelings and loving acts (1 Cor. 13:4–8). True love is characterized as

- patient and slow to anger (v. 4)
- kind and gentle to all (v. 4)
- unselfish and giving (v. 5)
- truthful and honest (v. 6)
- hopeful and encouraging (v. 7)
- enduring, without end (v. 7)

Biblical love is not envious, proud, self-centered, rude, or provoking (vv. 4, 5).

Without love, the gifts of the Spirit are deemed worthless and the fruit of the Spirit incomplete (v. 8). Christian love is eternal. While all else fails, love never fails. It is a permanent, unconditional concern for others that results from the indwelling power of the Holy Spirit, rather than from human effort or desire.

See also Lam. 3:22, note; John 15:13; 1 John 3:11–18; notes on Attributes of God (Ex. 33; Deut. 4; 32; 2 Chr. 19; Job 23; 42; Ps. 25; 90; 102; 119; Is. 6; 65; Jer. 23; Rom. 2; Eph. 1; 1 John 5); Fruit of the Spirit (Ps. 86; Rom. 5; 15; 1 Cor. 9; Gal. 5; Eph. 4; Col. 3; 2 Thess. 1; Rev. 2); Love (1 John 4); Marriage (Gen. 2; 2 Sam. 6; Prov. 5; Hos. 2; Amos 3; 2 Cor. 13; Heb. 12); Romance (Song 2)

I have all faith, so that I could remove mountains, but have not love, I am nothing. ³And though I bestow all my goods to feed *the poor,* and though I give my body to be burned,ᵃ but have not love, it profits me nothing.

⁴Love suffers long *and* is kind; love does not envy; love does not parade itself, is not puffed up; ⁵does not behave rudely, does not seek its own, is not provoked, thinks no evil; ⁶does not rejoice in iniquity, but rejoices in the truth; ⁷bears all things, believes all things, hopes all things, endures all things.

⁸Love never fails. But whether *there are* prophecies, they will fail; whether *there are* tongues, they will cease; whether *there is* knowledge, it will vanish away. ⁹For we know in part and we prophesy in part. ¹⁰But when that which

is perfect has come, then that which is in part will be done away.

¹¹When I was a child, I spoke as a child, I understood as a child, I thought as a child; but when I became a man, I put away childish things. ¹²For now we see in a mirror, dimly, but then face to face. Now I know in part, but then I shall know just as I also am known.

¹³And now abide faith, hope, love, these three; but the greatest of these *is* love.

Prophecy and Tongues

14 Pursue love, and desire spiritual *gifts,* but especially that you may prophesy. ²For he who speaks in a tongue does not speak to men but to

•••••••••••••••••••••••
13:3 ᵃNU-Text reads *so I may boast.*

---

they desired to have what they viewed as the "best" spiritual gift—speaking in tongues. Paul did not rebuke them for seeking "the best" but pointed out that their assessment of the value of tongues was erroneous. The "best" gift, he argued, was not the flashy outward one but rather a gift such as prophecy, which edified the whole church (1 Cor. 14:12). Paul wanted them to use their gifts in "a more excellent way"—the way of love.

13:2 Paul considered the gift of prophecy to be of primary significance for the Christian community (1 Thess. 5:19, 20; 1 Cor. 14:1–25). The Corinthians, on the other hand, favored "knowledge" (1 Cor. 1:5; 8:1). Love is the essential undergirding for the proper management of any spiritual gift.

13:12, 13 The city of Corinth was famous for producing some of the finest bronze mirrors in antiquity. Paul used the analogy of looking in a mirror to explain the indirect nature of one's view of God and His ways. One "sees" God and His "mysteries" only indirectly and partially. Although good, the image is limited (v. 12) and falls short of the real thing. Spiritual gifts were undoubtedly good but were only necessary for the present age of partial seeing and knowledge. Christian love, on the other hand, was eternal. Paul wanted the Corinthians to correct their perspective and focus on the greatness of the eternal rather than that of the temporal.

14:1 The verb to prophesy (Gk. *prophēteuō*, lit. "to speak forth") is found more than 25 times in the NT. Paul used it

SPIRITUAL GIFTS OF WOMEN IN THE BIBLE

SPIRITUAL GIFT	SCRIPTURE REFERENCE	FUNCTION	HOW TO RECOGNIZE	GIFTED WOMAN
Prophecy	Luke 2:36–38	Proclamation in order to edify	• Ability to address audiences with inspired message	Anna
Serving (Ministry, Helps)	Luke 4:38, 39	Service	• Joy in doing for others and meeting needs	Peter's Mother-in-Law
Teaching	Acts 18:24–28	Instruction that is understood	• Understanding difficult matters; • Ability to deliver instruction effectively	Priscilla
Exhortation	John 4:28–30	Persuasion and encouragement	• Ability to inspire and persuade	Samaritan Woman
Giving	Luke 21:2–4	Undergirding and supporting	• Joy in giving, expecting nothing in return	Widow with Two Mites
Leading (Administration)	Judg. 4:4–14	Administration	• Organized; inspires cooperation and teamwork	Deborah
Mercy	Acts 9:36–42	Tender sensitivity	• Concern for those who are hurting	Dorcas
Wisdom	Luke 1:46–56	Application of truth	• Ability to apply knowledge and understanding to life situations	Mary of Nazareth
Knowledge	1 Sam. 2:1–10	Insight and perception	• Understanding of facts and situations	Hannah
Faith	Matt. 15:21–28	Optimism and confidence	• Confidence in the Lord and ability to inspire others	Syro-Phoenician Woman
Discernment	1 Sam. 25:2–42	Ability to make judgments	• Ability to determine good or evil and see beyond surface	Abigail
Evangelism	Acts 21:9	Ability to witness in any situation	• Loves people; talks easily; rejoices to share Christ	Daughters of Philip
Hospitality	John 12:1, 2	Assistance and service	• Unselfish desire to meet the needs of others	Martha
Speaking	Ex. 15:20, 21	Talks easily and inspires others	• Likes to talk; interested in others	Miriam
Celibacy	Acts 16:11–15	Devotion	• Content to remain single	Lydia (possibly single)

God's Spirit is present from the beginning and is the giver of life (Gen. 1:2; Job 33:4). The coming of the Holy Spirit to dwell permanently in the hearts of believers is specifically recorded in the New Testament to coincide with the Day of Pentecost (Acts 2:17, 18) and is a direct partial fulfillment of the prophecy of Joel 2:28, 29. Thus, the attributing of gifts to Old Testament women or New Testament women ministering before the coming of the Spirit at Pentecost would be considered inappropriate by some and difficult to define by all. Even after Pentecost, the possible reference to a gift is so brief as to make it impossible to identify the assignment with certainty. Nevertheless, we can be inspired by gifted women who have gone before.

Spiritual gifts cannot be sought or grasped; rather, they are divinely bestowed, not to magnify the individual possessing the gift but to enhance her efforts for ministry. The gifts were poured out upon women and men, but without requirement that every gift be found in either sex. For example, there is little evidence that the gift of apostleship was given to a woman, nor do we see clear examples in the text of the gifts of healings and miracles given to women. Though everyone has some gift(s), no one has all the gifts. Never does God give a gift to be used in contradiction to His written Word just as His Spirit never leads anyone to exercise a gift that contradicts Scripture. The sovereignly bestowed gifts are to be used according to the purposes of the Holy Spirit for the edification of the church.

WIDOWHOOD *FILLING THE EMPTINESS*

During intense grief, widows need intimate times with family. In quietness and seclusion anxious hearts express heartache, fears, loss, and pain (Phil. 4:6). Communication flows; prayer times increase; God's plans are seen more clearly as He is allowed to fill our emptiness with Himself (Eph. 5:17, 18).

Often without realizing it, an outpouring of God's grace comes through obedience (2 Kin. 4:5). No one is exempt from its overflow. Family and friends are touched by its reality. And hope is renewed through faithfulness in doing God's implicit will (Jer. 29:11–14).

Offering empty vessels to God involves hands, bodies, brains, emotions, thoughts, dreams (Rom. 12:1, 2). It is giving Him all we are, have, or hope to be. Behind shut doors we can immerse ourselves in His presence (Ps. 139:23, 24).

God could go on filling cleansed, empty vessels, but He knows just how much is needed (Phil. 4:6, 19). His ending of the flow is as deliberate as the beginning. His oil will always be in sufficient supply (2 Kin. 4:6).

God's intentions for women emerging from the life-changing experience of widowhood and child rearing are unlimited. He has provided material needs (2 Kin. 4:7). And He sent His Son that we might have life, and that we might have it more abundantly (John 10:10). With the presence of God's Spirit within, widows can find new relationships and responsibilities, which should be accepted by them with great joy, realizing that each is a gift from God's heart (Eph. 3:16–21).

See also Matt. 18:3, note; notes on Brokenheartedness (Ps. 34); Children (2 Sam. 21; Ps. 128; Prov. 22; Luke 15); Death (1 Cor. 15); Family (Gen. 32; 1 Sam. 3; Ps. 78; 127); Grief (Is. 53); Loneliness (Eccl. 4); Sorrow (Rev. 21); Widowhood (Ps. 68; Jer. 29); portraits of The Prophet's Widow (2 Kin. 4); Widow with Two Mites (Mark 12)

God, for no one understands *him;* however, in the spirit he speaks mysteries. ³But he who prophesies speaks edification and exhortation and comfort to men. ⁴He who speaks in a tongue edifies himself, but he who prophesies edifies the church. ⁵I wish you all spoke with tongues, but even more that you prophesied; for[a] he who prophesies *is* greater than he who speaks with tongues, unless indeed he interprets, that the church may receive edification.

Tongues Must Be Interpreted

⁶But now, brethren, if I come to you speaking with tongues, what shall I profit you unless I speak to you either by revelation, by knowledge, by prophesying, or by teaching? ⁷Even things without life, whether flute or harp, when they make a sound, unless they make a distinction in the sounds, how will it be known what is piped or played? ⁸For if the trumpet makes an uncertain sound, who will prepare for battle? ⁹So likewise you, unless you utter by the tongue words easy to understand, how will it be known what is spoken? For you will be speaking into the air. ¹⁰There are, it may be, so many kinds of languages in the world, and none of them *is* without significance. ¹¹Therefore, if I do not know the meaning of the language, I shall be a foreigner to him who speaks, and he who speaks *will be* a foreigner to me. ¹²Even so you, since you are zealous for spiritual *gifts, let it be* for the edification of the church *that* you seek to excel.

¹³Therefore let him who speaks in a tongue pray that he may interpret. ¹⁴For if I pray in a tongue, my spirit prays, but my understanding is unfruitful. ¹⁵What is *the conclusion* then? I will pray with the spirit, and I will also pray with the understanding. I will sing with the spirit, and I will also sing with the understanding. ¹⁶Otherwise, if you bless with the spirit, how will he who occupies the place of the uninformed say "Amen" at your giving of thanks, since he does not understand what you

····················

14:5 [a]NU-Text reads *and.*

11 times, all in 1 Corinthians. To prophesy is to speak a divine message as directed by the Spirit of God. The message may be ethical, that is, to comfort, exhort, teach (1 Cor. 14:3); revelatory or revealing supernatural knowledge of a particular situation (Matt. 26:68); or it may point to the future or foretell (Matt. 15:7). Prophecy is Spirit-inspired speech from God to His creation (1 Cor. 14:2, 3). All prophetic messages were to be "tested" for their prophetic character (1 Cor. 14:29; 1 Thess. 5:19–21) and for their agreement with the teachings of Scripture (Deut. 13:1–5; Matt. 7:15; 24:11; 2 Pet. 2:1).

14:5 The Corinthians had a tendency to exaggerate the importance of the gift of speaking in tongues. This gift, they reasoned, constituted the highest and greatest form of spirituality. Paul disagreed. He compared the gift of tongues with that of prophecy. He pointed out that the benefit of tongues was limited by the ability of the congregation to understand what was said. Prophecy, on the other hand, was intelligible; thus, it was "greater" because it served the *whole* body: In order to be "great" in the kingdom, one must become the servant of all (Mark 10:43). Since the Corinthians were intent on seeking the greatest gifts, Paul argued that they should seek those that served the whole body rather than those that merely benefited themselves.

WHAT IS LOVE?

WORD	MEANING	COMMENTS	BIBLICAL USAGE
Agapē (Gk.)	Indicates a choice to serve God, to love neighbor, to accept self without expecting something in return (Matt. 22:34–40).	Appears rarely in secular Greek writings; Coined by New Testament writers to describe God's love (John 3:16); Christian love is based on the deliberate choice of the lover rather than the worthiness of the one loved (1 Cor. 13:1–13).	Love: is longsuffering is kind is not jealous is not boastful is not arrogant is not rude is not selfish is not resentful does not think evil rejoices in truth bears all things believes all things hopes all things endures all things (1 Cor. 13:1–13).
Philia (Gk.)	Refers to esteem and affection reflected in the loving concern friends have for one another.	Used in the New Testament (John 21:15–17; Titus 2:4); Sometimes used interchangeably or synonymously with *agapē*.	The nature of Peter's love is the question. Jesus uses *agapē* (unselfish commitment) in His questions; Peter uses *philia* (esteem or high regard) in his response. Perhaps his caution comes from his bitter experience of denying the Lord (John 21:15–17). The love of a woman for her husband and children must be marked with *philia* or esteem and respect, not just *agape* or unselfish commitment (Titus 2:4; see also Eph. 5:33).
Eros (Gk.)	Describes appetitive, self-centered love, including sexual desire and physical craving.	Does not appear in the New Testament.	
Storgē (Gk.)	Alludes to affection, especially among family members.	Does not appear in the New Testament.	

say? [17]For you indeed give thanks well, but the other is not edified.

[18]I thank my God I speak with tongues more than you all; [19]yet in the church I would rather speak five words with my understanding, that I may teach others also, than ten thousand words in a tongue.

Tongues a Sign to Unbelievers

[20]Brethren, do not be children in understanding; however, in malice be babes, but in understanding be mature.

[21]In the law it is written:

"With men of other tongues and other lips

I will speak to this people;
And yet, for all that, they will not hear Me,"[a]

says the Lord.

[22]Therefore tongues are for a sign, not to those who believe but to unbelievers; but prophesying is not for unbelievers but for those who believe. [23]Therefore if the whole church comes together in one place, and all speak with tongues, and there come in *those who are* uninformed or unbelievers, will they not say that you are out of your mind? [24]But if all prophesy, and an unbeliever or an uninformed person comes in, he is convinced by all, he is convicted by all. [25]And thus[a] the secrets of his heart are revealed; and so, falling down on *his* face, he will worship God and report that God is truly among you.

Order in Church Meetings

[26]How is it then, brethren? Whenever you come together, each of you has a psalm, has a teaching, has a tongue, has a revelation, has an interpretation. Let all things be done for edification. [27]If anyone speaks in a tongue, *let there be* two or at the most three, *each* in turn, and let one interpret. [28]But if there is no interpreter, let him keep silent in church, and let him speak to himself and to God. [29]Let two or three prophets speak, and let the others judge. [30]But if *anything* is revealed to another who sits by, let the first keep silent. [31]For you can all prophesy one by one, that all may learn and all may be encouraged. [32]And the spirits of the prophets are subject to the prophets. [33]For God is not *the author* of confusion but of peace, as in all the churches of the saints.

[34]Let your[a] women keep silent in the churches, for they are not permitted to speak; but *they are* to be submissive, as the law also says. [35]And if they want to learn something, let them ask their own husbands at home; for it is shameful for women to speak in church.

[36]Or did the word of God come *originally* from you? Or *was it* you only that it reached? [37]If anyone thinks himself to be a prophet or spiritual, let him acknowledge that the things which I write to you are the commandments of the Lord. [38]But if anyone is ignorant, let him be ignorant.[a]

[39]Therefore, brethren, desire earnestly to prophesy, and do not forbid to speak with tongues. [40]Let all things be done decently and in order.

The Risen Christ, Faith's Reality

15 Moreover, brethren, I declare to you the gospel which I preached to you, which also you received and in which you stand, [2]by which also you are saved, if you hold fast that word which I preached to you—unless you believed in vain.

[3]For I delivered to you first of all that which I also received: that Christ died for our sins according to the Scriptures, [4]and that He was buried, and that He rose again the third day according to the Scriptures, [5]and that He was seen by Cephas, then by the twelve. [6]After that He was seen by over five hundred brethren at once, of whom the greater part remain to the present, but some have fallen asleep. [7]After that He was seen by James, then by all the apostles. [8]Then last of all He was seen by me also, as by one born out of due time.

[9]For I am the least of the apostles, who am not

14:21 [a]Isaiah 28:11, 12   **14:25** [a]NU-Text omits *And thus.*   **14:34** [a]NU-Text omits *your.*   **14:38** [a]NU-Text reads *if anyone does not recognize this, he is not recognized.*

14:26 Everyone had opportunity to participate in the corporate ministry of the church in NT times. During worship, various members offered psalms, teachings, tongues, revelations, and interpretations. Paul encouraged this practice, but stressed that all aspects of corporate worship were to edify the church. "Edification" (Gk. *oikodome*, lit. "house building") was used figuratively as growing, improving, or maturing. Paul was concerned that spiritual gifts not be exercised in the interest of self-development or self-display, but rather according to the law of love that served and built others up.

14:34, 35 Paul recognized that women were praying and prophesying in public worship and did not condemn them for doing so (1 Cor. 11:5). Yet here he commanded that women "keep silent in the churches" (1 Cor. 14:34). One way of resolving what some consider a discrepancy is by considering the particular type of speech that Paul disallowed. In this passage, he was probably discussing the gift of prophecy, and more specifically, the evaluation or judgment of prophecy (1 Cor. 14:29–39). Paul allowed women to participate in worship and, indeed, expected that they would do so (v. 26), but here he may have been forbidding them from giving spoken criticisms of the prophecies that were made because he was concerned that the principle of headship be evidenced in the public assembly of believers. Women's silence during the evaluation of prophecy was one of the ways in which this was to be accomplished. Another way to understand this command for women to be silent is in relationship to Paul's command to the believers to do all things "decently and in order" (v. 40). God "is not the author of confusion" (v. 33). The women could have been displaying some kind of disorderly conduct (v. 35). Others suggest, since the subject of major discussion in chapter 14 is tongues, that the prohibition to women is to refrain from ecstatic utterance. Clearly this cannot mean that women are forbidden altogether to speak in the assembly (1 Cor. 11:5).

15:2 To hold fast means to keep in memory and to hold firmly. It implies continued holding and lasting possession. Paul wanted the Corinthians to hold fast to the essence of the gospel—Jesus' death and Resurrection—lest their faith be "in vain," that is, without cause or purpose.

15:4 The Resurrection body of Christ had these characteristics: He could pass through shut doors (John 20:19, 26); He could vanish from view (Luke 24:31); His body was real and could be touched (Luke 24:39; John 20:17, 27); He was able to eat (Luke 24:42, 43).

THE APPEARANCES OF THE RISEN CHRIST

The Resurrection has been interpreted as
    false information
    fictitious story
    *factual event

By recording the appearance of Christ after His Resurrection, the New Testament removes all doubt.
He has risen!

LOCATION	REFERENCE	PEOPLE
In or around Jerusalem	To Mary Magdalene	John 20:11–18
	To the other women	Matt. 28:8–10
	To Peter	Luke 24:34
	To ten disciples	Luke 24:36–43; John 20:19–25
	To eleven disciples, including Thomas	John 20:26–29
	To those who observed His Ascension	Luke 24:50–53; Acts 1:4–12
On the Emmaus Road	To two disciples	Luke 24:13–35
In Galilee	To the disciples	Matt. 28:16–20; John 21:1–24
Unknown	To 500 people	1 Cor. 15:6
Unknown	To James and the apostles	1 Cor. 15:7
On the road to Damascus	To Paul	Acts 9:1–6; 18:9, 10; 22:1–8; 23:11; 26:12–18; 1 Cor. 15:8

worthy to be called an apostle, because I persecuted the church of God. ¹⁰But by the grace of God I am what I am, and His grace toward me was not in vain; but I labored more abundantly than they all, yet not I, but the grace of God *which was* with me. ¹¹Therefore, whether *it was* I or they, so we preach and so you believed.

The Risen Christ, Our Hope

¹²Now if Christ is preached that He has been raised from the dead, how do some among you say that there is no resurrection of the dead? ¹³But if there is no resurrection of the dead, then Christ is not risen. ¹⁴And if Christ is not risen, then our preaching *is* empty and your faith *is* also empty. ¹⁵Yes, and we are found false witnesses of God, because we have testified of God that He raised up

Christ, whom He did not raise up—if in fact the dead do not rise. ¹⁶For if *the* dead do not rise, then Christ is not risen. ¹⁷And if Christ is not risen, your faith *is* futile; you are still in your sins! ¹⁸Then also those who have fallen asleep in Christ have perished. ¹⁹If in this life only we have hope in Christ, we are of all men the most pitiable.

The Last Enemy Destroyed

²⁰But now Christ is risen from the dead, *and* has become the firstfruits of those who have fallen asleep. ²¹For since by man *came* death, by Man also *came* the resurrection of the dead. ²²For as in Adam all die, even so in Christ all shall be made alive. ²³But each one in his own order: Christ the firstfruits, afterward those *who are* Christ's at His coming. ²⁴Then *comes* the end, when He

15:17 Some Ancient Greek philosophy viewed everything spiritual as intrinsically good and everything physical as intrinsically evil. To those holding this view, the idea of a resurrected body would have been repugnant. The Corinthians were affected by contemporary philosophy. Although they had faith in the Resurrection of Christ, some had begun to question the resurrection of believers. Paul demonstrated that the two go hand in hand (vv. 13-19). Resurrection is not only possible but

is essential to the Christian faith. In order to vindicate the work of His Son, God raised Christ from the dead. Therefore, a denial of the resurrection of the dead is a denial of the gospel. Paul argued that if Christ were not risen from the dead, all believers throughout history would have believed for nothing, lived for nothing, and died for nothing.

15:23 Prior to reaping their fields, Israelites were to bring a representative sample of their crop to the priests as an

DEATH — THE END OR THE BEGINNING?

Jesus Christ repeatedly overturned the enemy, Death, and robbed Death of its sting (1 Cor. 15:26; 2 Tim. 1:8–10). After Lazarus' dead body had been in its grave for four days, Jesus prayed, then called Lazarus back to life (John 11:1–44). When Jesus arrived at the house of Jairus, He found the ruler's twelve-year-old daughter dead. He took the child by the hand and told her to arise. To her parents' astonishment, she came back to life (Mark 5:38–42). Jesus stopped a funeral procession in Nain. He touched the open coffin of a widow's only son and commanded him back to life. Then Jesus presented the living son to his mother (Luke 7:11–15).

In Scripture, death is often connected with sin (Rom. 6:23; 5:12–21). Death was considered a curse when it occurred to someone in the prime of life or to a childless person.

Death has two stages: 1) The permanent cessation of all bodily vital functions and the separation of the spirit and soul from the body (James 2:26); and finally 2) Resurrection in Christ (Is. 26:19). Through His death and resurrection, Jesus gives to all hope for everlasting life (John 5:24).

See also Mark 9:43–48, note; Luke 8:41–56; notes on Euthanasia (Gen. 4); Grief (Is. 53); Heaven (2 Tim. 4)

---

delivers the kingdom to God the Father, when He puts an end to all rule and all authority and power. 25For He must reign till He has put all enemies under His feet. 26The last enemy *that* will be destroyed *is* death. 27For *"He has put all things under His feet."*ᵃ But when He says "all things are put under *Him,"* *it is* evident that He who put all things under Him is excepted. 28Now when all things are made subject to Him, then the Son Himself will also be subject to Him who put all things under Him, that God may be all in all.

Effects of Denying the Resurrection

29Otherwise, what will they do who are baptized for the dead, if the dead do not rise at all? Why then are they baptized for the dead? 30And why do we stand in jeopardy every hour? 31I affirm, by the boasting in you which I have in Christ Jesus our Lord, I die daily. 32If, in the manner of men, I have fought with beasts at Ephesus, what advantage *is it* to me? If *the* dead do not rise, *"Let us eat and drink, for tomorrow we die!"*ᵃ

33Do not be deceived: "Evil company corrupts good habits." 34Awake to righteousness, and do not sin; for some do not have the knowledge of God. I speak *this* to your shame.

A Glorious Body

35But someone will say, "How are the dead raised up? And with what body do they come?"

36Foolish one, what you sow is not made alive unless it dies. 37And what you sow, you do not sow that body that shall be, but mere grain—perhaps wheat or some other *grain.* 38But God gives it a body as He pleases, and to each seed its own body.

39All flesh *is* not the same flesh, but *there is* one *kind of* fleshᵃ of men, another flesh of animals, another of fish, *and* another of birds.

40*There are* also celestial bodies and terrestrial bodies; but the glory of the celestial *is* one, and the *glory* of the terrestrial *is* another. 41*There is* one glory of the sun, another glory of the moon, and another glory of the stars; for *one* star differs from *another* star in glory.

42So also *is* the resurrection of the dead. *The body* is sown in corruption, it is raised in incorruption. 43It is sown in dishonor, it is raised in glory. It is sown in weakness, it is raised in power. 44It is sown a natural body, it is raised a spiritual body. There is a natural body, and there is a spiritual body. 45And so it is written, *"The first man Adam became a living being."*ᵃ The last Adam *became* a life-giving spirit.

46However, the spiritual is not first, but the natural, and afterward the spiritual. 47The first man *was* of the earth, *made* of dust; the second Man *is* the Lordᵃ from heaven. 48As *was* the man of

---

15:27 ᵃPsalm 8:6 15:32 ᵃIsaiah 22:13 15:39 ᵃNU-Text and M-Text omit *of flesh.* 15:45 ᵃGenesis 2:7 15:47 ᵃNU-Text omits *the Lord.*

---

offering to the Lord (Lev. 23:10). Full harvest was not allowed until this sample, called the "firstfruits," was offered. This practice was behind Paul's imagery of Christ as the "firstfruits." Christ's Resurrection was the first sample of the coming harvest of the resurrection of the believing dead. He Himself was the offering made to the Father on their behalf. In referring to Christ as "firstfruits," Paul furthered his resurrection argument. The "firstfruits" were only the initial installment; the rest of the crop would follow. Therefore, in order to complete the Father's harvest, it

was necessary that all those who believed in Christ also be resurrected.

15:29 A difficult and obscure text cannot structure biblical doctrine. Though there is no easy explanation, the sense seems to be that the preposition "for" (Gk. *huper*) is better translated "concerning" so that Christian baptism "concerning" death as it relates to the Resurrection is meaningless unless the Resurrection is, in fact, true.

15:45 Paul concluded his presentation on the doctrine of the Resurrection by explaining that there were two types of bod-

Love begins at home, and it is not how much we do . . .
but how much love we put in that action.

Mother Teresa

dust, so also *are* those *who are made* of dust; and as *is* the heavenly *Man,* so also *are* those *who are* heavenly. [49]And as we have borne the image of the *man* of dust, we shall also bear[a] the image of the heavenly *Man.*

Our Final Victory

[50]Now this I say, brethren, that flesh and blood cannot inherit the kingdom of God; nor does corruption inherit incorruption. [51]Behold, I tell you a mystery: We shall not all sleep, but we shall all be changed— [52]in a moment, in the twinkling of an eye, at the last trumpet. For the trumpet will sound, and the dead will be raised incorruptible, and we shall be changed. [53]For this corruptible must put on incorruption, and this mortal *must* put on immortality. [54]So when this corruptible has put on incorruption, and this mortal has put on immortality, then shall be brought to pass the saying that is written: *"Death is swallowed up in victory."*[a]

[55]*"O Death, where is your sting?*[a]
O Hades, where is your victory?"[b]

[56]The sting of death *is* sin, and the strength of sin *is* the law. [57]But thanks *be* to God, who gives us the victory through our Lord Jesus Christ.

[58]Therefore, my beloved brethren, be steadfast, immovable, always abounding in the work of the Lord, knowing that your labor is not in vain in the Lord.

Collection for the Saints

16 Now concerning the collection for the saints, as I have given orders to the

churches of Galatia, so you must do also: [2]On the first *day* of the week let each one of you lay something aside, storing up as he may prosper, that there be no collections when I come. [3]And when I come, whomever you approve by *your* letters I will send to bear your gift to Jerusalem. [4]But if it is fitting that I go also, they will go with me.

Personal Plans

[5]Now I will come to you when I pass through Macedonia (for I am passing through Macedonia). [6]And it may be that I will remain, or even spend the winter with you, that you may send me on my journey, wherever I go. [7]For I do not wish to see you now on the way; but I hope to stay a while with you, if the Lord permits.

[8]But I will tarry in Ephesus until Pentecost. [9]For a great and effective door has opened to me, and *there are* many adversaries.

[10]And if Timothy comes, see that he may be with you without fear; for he does the work of the Lord, as I also *do.* [11]Therefore let no one despise him. But send him on his journey in peace, that he may come to me; for I am waiting for him with the brethren.

[12]Now concerning *our* brother Apollos, I strongly urged him to come to you with the brethren, but he was quite unwilling to come at this time; however, he will come when he has a convenient time.

···············

15:49 [a]M-Text reads *let us also bear.* **15:54** [a]Isaiah 25:8 **15:55** [a]Hosea 13:14 [b]NU-Text reads *O Death, where is your victory? O Death, where is your sting?*

---

ies, "natural" and "spiritual" (v. 46). The first man, Adam, was created with a natural, physical body, which became subject to decay and death. Jesus Christ, "the last Adam," overcame death and was given a "spiritual" (glorified), immortal body. Therefore, by virtue of creation, Adam was "of the earth," and by virtue of the Resurrection, Christ was "from heaven" (v. 47). Paul said that these two were prototypes: the first bearers of the two kinds of bodies. The first man Adam represents all those who share in having a physical body. The last Adam represents all those who bear His spiritual likeness. The first Adam was human, the last, infinitely more. Believers have borne the image of the former, and they shall someday also bear the image of the latter (v. 49).

15:50–52 Paul affirmed that some Christians would not face death. When Christ returns, the dead in Christ will be raised first (v. 52), but then those believers who are alive will be

caught up to meet Him (vv. 51, 52; see 1 Thess. 4:17, note; chart, Glossary Terms in Eschatology).

16:2 Paul had solicited various churches for contributions for the needy Christians in Jerusalem (Rom. 15:26; 2 Cor. 8:1–5). In NT times, Jerusalem was a poor city. The area had experienced a severe famine some years earlier, and many residents remained financially stressed (Acts 11:28). Paul instructed the Corinthians to set aside some money each week according to how much they had prospered. This amount was not to be a certain percentage of their income. It was, rather, to be based upon the believer's personal examination of his own heart. The Corinthian contributions not only brought relief to the poor but also brought unity between Gentile and Jewish Christians. Paul reasoned that since the Gentiles had shared in the Jew's spiritual blessings, they ought to reciprocate by giving some of their material blessings to the Jews (Rom. 15:27; 2 Cor. 9:12–14).

Final Exhortations

[13]Watch, stand fast in the faith, be brave, be strong. [14]Let all *that* you *do* be done with love.

[15]I urge you, brethren—you know the household of Stephanas, that it is the firstfruits of Achaia, and *that* they have devoted themselves to the ministry of the saints— [16]that you also submit to such, and to everyone who works and labors with *us*.

[17]I am glad about the coming of Stephanas, Fortunatus, and Achaicus, for what was lacking on your part they supplied. [18]For they refreshed my spirit and yours. Therefore acknowledge such men.

Greetings and a Solemn Farewell

[19]The churches of Asia greet you. Aquila and Priscilla greet you heartily in the Lord, with the church that is in their house. [20]All the brethren greet you.

Greet one another with a holy kiss.

[21]The salutation with my own hand— Paul's.

[22]If anyone does not love the Lord Jesus Christ, let him be accursed.[a] O Lord, come![b]

[23]The grace of our Lord Jesus Christ *be* with you. [24]My love *be* with you all in Christ Jesus. Amen.

••••••••••••••••••

16:22 [a]Greek *anathema* [b]Aramaic *Maranatha*

16:14 Paul did not use the word *love* frequently in this letter, but two crucial passages (1 Cor. 8:1–3; 13), as well as this closing imperative, indicate that he regarded love as the essential girder for all of his ethical instructions. "Let all that you do" would have included the divisive quarrels (1 Cor. 1–3), their attitude toward him (1 Cor. 4; 9), church discipline (1 Cor. 5), the lawsuits (1 Cor. 6), marital relationships (1 Cor. 7), the abuse of the "weak" (1 Cor. 8—10), the abuse of the poor at the Lord's

Supper, and the failure to edify the church in worship (1 Cor. 11—14). Had they followed the way of love, they would not have encountered many of these problems. The Corinthians had all the gifts, but love is what they needed most.

16:19 Aquila and Priscilla were a unique husband-wife team who were viewed as capable teachers in the early church. Both had a significant influence on the learned Apollos (see Acts 18, Priscilla).

2 Corinthians

AUTHOR

In style and content, no other letter is more characteristic of the apostle Paul than 2 Corinthians. This letter contains much autobiographical information as well as references to people, situations, and events with which Paul and his readers were obviously familiar. The conclusion that Paul is the author of 2 Corinthians is indisputable.

DATE

Second Corinthians was written from somewhere in Macedonia (2 Cor. 2:13; 7:5–7) during Paul's third missionary journey (see map, Paul's Third Missionary Journey). Paul was revisiting the churches that he had founded during his second journey; so he may have composed the letter in Philippi or Thessalonica (see map, Paul's Second Missionary Journey). Second Corinthians is closely related to 1 Corinthians; only a few months had elapsed between the writing of the two letters. Therefore, this epistle was written during the late summer or autumn of the year 56 A.D. After writing, Paul continued to travel in Macedonia as far as the borders of Illyricum (Rom. 15:19). Then, as promised in the letter, he journeyed to Corinth to spend the winter months of 56–57 A.D.

BACKGROUND

SETTING: For information on the city of Corinth, see the Introduction to 1 Corinthians. Paul wrote 1 Corinthians to resolve doctrinal and ethical problems in the church at Corinth. He also sent Timothy to help the Corinthians correct the problems in their congregation (1 Cor. 4:17). Apparently, these measures did not have the desired effect. Therefore, Paul sailed directly from Ephesus to Corinth, seeking personally to resolve the matters. This second visit was painful for him (2 Cor. 2:1). One man in particular took the lead in defying Paul's authority.

Paul returned to Ephesus disheartened, full of sorrow, and humiliated (2 Cor. 2:5; 7:12; 12:21). He sent the Corinthians a third letter, scathingly disciplinary in nature (2 Cor. 7:8, 9). It was borne by Titus, but this third letter is not extant today (2 Cor. 2:3, 4). Paul left Ephesus in the spring of A.D. 56, bound for Macedonia (Acts 20:1; see map, Paul's Third Missionary Journey). He planned to rendezvous with Titus on a stopover in Troas in order to receive news about the situation in Corinth (2 Cor. 2:13).

Paul waited anxiously for Titus until the opportunity for navigation across the Aegean had ceased for the winter. Then, knowing Titus would need to take the land route through Macedonia, Paul departed. He finally met Titus in Macedonia and received good news about the general condition of the Corinthian church as well as bad news about a small faction that continued to oppose him. Paul wrote a fourth letter—the epistle identified as 2 Corinthians—to prepare the Corinthian church for his third visit (Acts 20:2, 3). The first letter (1 Cor. 5:9) and third letter (2 Cor. 2:3, 4) have been lost. The second letter is 1 Corinthians, and the fourth, 2 Corinthians.

PURPOSE: Paul was overjoyed to hear from Titus that the Corinthians had accepted the reproofs of his disciplinary letter and had dealt with the offender. To vindicate himself in their eyes, Paul explained his conduct in the matter and defended his integrity. He reinforced the authenticity of both his apostleship and his message. The dominating purpose of this epistle was to prepare the Corinthian church for Paul's impending third visit.

AUDIENCE: The church in Corinth consisted mainly of converted Gentiles, some Romans, and a few Jews. Most of these had little education and were low in social status. According to 1 Corinthians, immorality was rife in the church, and the believers had become proud and divisive. Second Corinthians was written after most of these problems had been resolved. However, a small faction of anti-Paul activists remained.

LITERARY CHARACTERISTICS: Second Corinthians is the most personal and intimate of all Paul's letters as well as the one containing the majority of autobiographical references. The tone of the first seven chapters is loving and gentle, but after that point the tone becomes quite severe. Some scholars have suggested that the latter portion of 2 Corinthians was part of the "tearful letter," but little evidence exists to support this theory. The transition in tone from chapter seven to eight is substantial. However, transitions to difficult subjects are always awkward. Paul needed to confront the Corinthians directly in order to win their affections for a singular devotion to Christ and to himself as Christ's apostle. That he put off his severe remarks until the end of his letter is not surprising.

THEMES

In 2 Corinthians, Paul was seeking to vindicate himself and expose the false apostles who were disrupting the Corinthian church. He discussed the correct motives for serving Christ and pointed out that he, as an apostle, had served both diligently and faithfully. The primary theme of the letter is that obedience to Christ means respect and submission to the authority of Christ's messenger—in this case, Paul. A second, underlying theme is that of selfless giving—both in Christian service and in the sharing of personal possessions and resources.

OUTLINE

Greeting

1 Paul, an apostle of Jesus Christ by the will of God, and Timothy *our* brother,

To the church of God which is at Corinth, with all the saints who are in all Achaia:

[2]Grace to you and peace from God our Father and the Lord Jesus Christ.

Comfort in Suffering

[3]Blessed *be* the God and Father of our Lord Jesus Christ, the Father of mercies and God of all comfort, [4]who comforts us in all our tribulation, that we may be able to comfort those who are in any trouble, with the comfort with which we ourselves are comforted by God. [5]For as the sufferings of Christ abound in us, so our consolation also abounds through Christ. [6]Now if we are afflicted, *it is* for your consolation and salvation, which is effective for enduring the same sufferings which we also suffer. Or if we are comforted, *it is* for your consolation and salvation. [7]And our hope for you *is* steadfast, because we know that as you are partakers of the sufferings, so also *you will partake* of the consolation.

Delivered from Suffering

[8]For we do not want you to be ignorant, brethren, of our trouble which came to us in Asia: that we were burdened beyond measure, above strength, so that we despaired even of life. [9]Yes, we had the sentence of death in ourselves, that we should not trust in ourselves but in God who raises the dead, [10]who delivered us from so great a death, and does[a] deliver us; in whom we trust that He will still deliver *us,* [11]you also helping together in prayer for us, that thanks may be given by many persons on our[a] behalf for the gift *granted* to us through many.

Paul's Sincerity

[12]For our boasting is this: the testimony of our conscience that we conducted ourselves in the

· · · · · · · · · · · · · · · · · · ·

1:10 [a]NU-Text reads *shall.*   1:11 [a]M-Text reads *your behalf.*

1:4 Paul mentioned tribulations (Gk. *thlipsis,* lit. "burdens," "afflictions," or "troubles") nine times in this letter (twice in v. 4; see also v. 8; 2 Cor. 2:4; 4:17; 6:4; 7:4; 8:2, 13) and the corresponding verb three times: "afflicted" (2 Cor. 1:6); "hard pressed" (2 Cor. 4:8); "troubled" (2 Cor. 7:5). Paul experienced numerous troubles as did many because of their allegiance to the gospel. These believers not only endured trials, but they were actually able to derive benefit from them. Difficult experiences forced them to focus on the internal rather than the external, and the eternal rather than the temporal (2 Cor. 4:17, 18). They received the comfort of God in time of trial. This consolation enabled them, in turn, to help others through difficult experiences.

1:12 In a previous letter, Paul expressed the hope of visiting Corinth for an extended stay after visiting Macedonia (1 Cor. 16:5–7). However, he modified his original plan and passed quickly through Corinth en route to Macedonia, intending to return for a lengthy visit later. Paul encountered strong opposition and public insult in Corinth and therefore canceled his return visit (2 Cor. 2:5; 7:12; 12:21). The Corinthians did not understand the rationale behind Paul's twice-changed travel plans and accused him of duplicity and fickleness. Paul defended his integrity and explained that his recent conduct was sincere and true to a higher power—being guided not by earthly wisdom but by the grace of God. "Sincerity" connotes the idea of being found unstained when examined in sunlight. Paul was not fickle, but reliable. His character would be found pure beneath the searching gaze of God (1 Cor. 4:4, 5).

CONSCIENCE RIGHT OR WRONG?

Conscience is a universal, innate, God-given capacity to distinguish between right and wrong (Rom. 2:14, 15). It has two functions: to urge an individual to do what is perceived to be right; and subsequently to commend or condemn, depending on whether the individual did what was perceived as right. A person who has a "good" and "pure" conscience consistently and genuinely acts in conformity with an inner set of godly standards (2 Cor. 1:12; 1 Tim. 1:5, 19; 3:9).

Conscience can be distorted, however. While this inner set of standards will be accurate if it is based on biblical truth, the conscience will be unreliable if faulty standards have been consistently presented to it as being true. The old saying, "Let your conscience be your guide," will only be true if the individual's conscience has been infused with godly principles. Thus, Christian parents have the important responsibility of communicating accurate standards of right and wrong to their children.

Conscience can also be disabled. For example, it can become insensitive and calloused if the person consistently acts contrary to its standards (Eph. 4:19). Even more seriously, the conscience can become "seared" and of no value through deliberately choosing to believe the lies of deceiving spirits rather than God's truth (1 Tim. 4:2).

See also 2 Tim. 1:3; Titus 1:15; notes on Decision Making (1 Cor. 8); Problem Solving (John 5); Wisdom (James 1).

world in simplicity and godly sincerity, not with fleshly wisdom but by the grace of God, and more abundantly toward you. ¹³For we are not writing any other things to you than what you read or understand. Now I trust you will understand, even to the end ¹⁴(as also you have understood us in part), that we are your boast as you also *are* ours, in the day of the Lord Jesus.

Sparing the Church

¹⁵And in this confidence I intended to come to you before, that you might have a second benefit— ¹⁶to pass by way of you to Macedonia, to come again from Macedonia to you, and be helped by you on my way to Judea. ¹⁷Therefore, when I was planning this, did I do it lightly? Or the things I plan, do I plan according to the flesh, that with me there should be Yes, Yes, and No, No? ¹⁸But *as God is* faithful, our word to you was not Yes and No. ¹⁹For the Son of God, Jesus Christ, who was preached among you by us— by me, Silvanus, and Timothy— was not Yes and No, but in Him was Yes. ²⁰For all the promises of God in Him *are* Yes, and in Him Amen, to the glory of God through us. ²¹Now He who establishes us with you in Christ and has anointed us *is* God, ²²who also has sealed us and given us the Spirit in our hearts as a guarantee.

²³Moreover I call God as witness against my soul, that to spare you I came no more to Corinth. ²⁴Not that we have dominion over your faith, but are fellow workers for your joy; for by faith you stand.

2 But I determined this within myself, that I would not come again to you in sorrow. ²For if I make you sorrowful, then who is he who makes me glad but the one who is made sorrowful by me?

Forgive the Offender

³And I wrote this very thing to you, lest, when I came, I should have sorrow over those from whom I ought to have joy, having confidence in you all that my joy is *the joy* of you all. ⁴For out of much affliction and anguish of heart I wrote to you, with many tears, not that you should be grieved, but that you might know the love which I have so abundantly for you.

⁵But if anyone has caused grief, he has not grieved me, but all of you to some extent— not to be too severe. ⁶This punishment which *was inflicted* by the majority *is* sufficient for such a man, ⁷so that, on the contrary, you *ought* rather to forgive and comfort *him,* lest perhaps such a one be swallowed up with too much sorrow. ⁸Therefore I urge

---

1:18–20 The Corinthians had accused Paul of being shifty, of saying "yes" and "no" in the same breath. Paul explained that his twice-changed travel plans were associated with the well-being of the Corinthians and not suggestive of a lack of reliability (v. 23). God is faithful, and the message preached by Paul was based on the Person of Jesus Christ, who completely affirms all of God's promises to His people. "Amen" (v. 20; Heb. and Gk., lit. "let it be so") was the response of those who accepted the gospel, experiencing security in Christ. Paul's actions were prompted by God, who was and is completely and totally faithful.

2:7 Paul's authority as an apostle had been publicly challenged during his last visit to Corinth. Paul apparently later wrote the Corinthians a letter (which has since been lost) that helped them understand the connection between a challenge to his authority and their own spiritual well-being as a body of believers (2 Cor. 2:3, 4). In wronging Paul, the offender had wronged the church (2 Cor. 2:5). In response to Paul's letter, the Corinthians disciplined the offender, who was apparently penitent. Therefore, Paul urged the church to forgive and comfort him (2 Cor. 2:11).

EMPLOYMENT   *WITNESS IN THE MARKETPLACE*

God intended for believers to be people with a distinctive fragrance that can be identified. This fragrance should be recognized everywhere, including jobs, homes, communities, social engagements.

Scripture teaches that the aroma of Jesus Christ has different effects on different people (2 Cor. 2:14–16). To those who know Christ or are searching to know the truth, it is the aroma of life. But to those who are perishing and who have no desire to live any other way, it is the aroma of death. The fragrance of Jesus Christ will attract some people, and it will repel others. God has purposely placed you with this distinctive fragrance among different kinds of people.

The fact that not all with whom you come in contact are impressed with your Christian aroma should not be surprising. Jesus warned that in this world believers will suffer persecution (Matt. 5:11, 12). However you need to be certain that the aroma of Jesus and not an aroma that comes from your lack of compassion and love for others causes the adverse reaction.

Being a witness on the job is much tougher than most can imagine. Often ears are deaf and hearts are cold to even the most effective witness (Acts 26:28). If you are not spreading the fragrance of the Lord Jesus Christ, then you are failing those around you who are searching for truth. The most effective sharing of your faith begins with a heart of love and caring, seeing people though His eyes, the way God sees them. God has given you the opportunity in the marketplace to be His fragrance to a lost world.

See also 2 Kin. 5:1–15; Acts 16:11–15; notes on Employment (Eccl. 9; Acts 18; Col. 3; 1 Pet. 2); Evangelism (John 6; Col. 4; 1 Pet. 3); Friendship (Luke 1); Salvation (Eph. 2)

---

you to reaffirm *your* love to him. [9]For to this end I also wrote, that I might put you to the test, whether you are obedient in all things. [10]Now whom you forgive anything, I also *forgive.* For if indeed I have forgiven anything, I have forgiven that one[a] for your sakes in the presence of Christ, [11]lest Satan should take advantage of us; for we are not ignorant of his devices.

Triumph in Christ

[12]Furthermore, when I came to Troas to *preach* Christ's gospel, and a door was opened to me by the Lord, [13]I had no rest in my spirit, because I did not find Titus my brother; but taking my leave of them, I departed for Macedonia.

[14]Now thanks *be* to God who always leads us in triumph in Christ, and through us diffuses the fragrance of His knowledge in every place. [15]For we are to God the fragrance of Christ among those who are being saved and among those who are perishing. [16]To the one *we are* the aroma of death *leading* to death, and to the other the aroma

of life *leading* to life. And who *is* sufficient for these things? [17]For we are not, as so many,[a] peddling the word of God; but as of sincerity, but as from God, we speak in the sight of God in Christ.

Christ's Epistle

3 Do we begin again to commend ourselves? Or do we need, as some *others,* epistles of commendation to you or *letters* of commendation from you? [2]You are our epistle written in our hearts, known and read by all men; [3]clearly you are an epistle of Christ, ministered by us, written not with ink but by the Spirit of the living God, not on tablets of stone but on tablets of flesh, *that is,* of the heart.

The Spirit, Not the Letter

[4]And we have such trust through Christ toward God. [5]Not that we are sufficient of ourselves to think of anything as *being* from ourselves, but

2:10 [a]NU-Text reads *For indeed, what I have forgiven, if I have forgiven anything, I did it.*   2:17 [a]M-Text reads *the rest.*

2:14 Paul's image of a triumphal parade was based on the Roman victory procession in which enemy prisoners were forced to march to reward a conquering general. God through Christ, has vanquished His enemies (Rom. 5:10; Col. 2:15). Paul, who had formerly been an enemy of God, was now taken captive by Christ and led in triumph. In the Roman parade, incense was burned. Paul compared this aroma to the knowledge of Christ, diffused like a fragrance through those whom Christ had captured.

2:16 OT animal sacrifices were a sweet aroma to God (Gen. 8:21; Ex. 29:18). However, after Christ offered Himself as the ultimate sacrifice for sin (Heb. 9:12), animal sacrifices became unnecessary. God now desires that an aroma be offered up to Him through the holy lives of Christians (Rom. 12:1). To God,

this aroma is sweet; and to those who are being saved, it is the aroma of life. But to those who reject God, the aroma of Christ is a repugnant death stench.

3:3 Emissaries to NT churches often bore letters of recommendation, establishing the bearer's identity and credentials. The Corinthians themselves were the epistle or letter establishing Paul's credibility. The conversion of the Corinthians was a supernatural work, confirming that Paul, whom God used for the work, was a minister of Christ. The old covenant was inscribed on stone tablets (Ex. 24:12), but the New Covenant was written on human hearts (Ezek. 11:19).

3:5, 6 Who was sufficient for the overwhelming responsibility of being the aroma of Christ in the world (2 Cor. 2:16)? No one

APPEARANCE   UNFADING BEAUTY

A Christian should be a complement to the kingdom of God in every aspect of life (2 Cor. 3:2, 3). Maintaining a clean, neat, modest, and appropriate appearance is a responsibility. To neglect how you look can diminish your total effectiveness since Scripture describes your body as the dwelling place of the Holy Spirit (1 Cor. 3:16, 17; 6:19, 20)! What is nurtured internally is ultimately manifested externally (Prov. 23:7).

Appropriate attire is essential for women who represent Christ. Women are admonished not merely to have outward adornment but to use such adornment to emphasize what is within (1 Pet. 3:3, 4). A Christlike spirit is preferred over excessive make-up, gaudy jewelry, or revealing clothes. Style and beauty, however, need not be compromised. We can be stylish with modesty and flair!

Good manners also blend into your total image. Consideration of another's feelings and opinions is an opportunity to reflect the character traits described in Scripture as the fruit of the Spirit (Gal. 5:22, 23). Having appropriate social skills can relax and free you to impart energy and concentration in other areas, such as sharing a witness for Christ or extending hospitality. Christians are watched, and their lives are scrutinized (Matt. 5:16). How others interpret your words and actions will be, to a great extent, how they regard Christ. Christ's love ought to shine! Unfading beauty is not dependent upon the outer frame but is achieved with the balance of personifying Christ's love and taking care of God's handiwork (1 Pet. 3:3, 4).

See also Prov. 31:22, 30; notes on Beauty (Prov. 4); Femininity (Ps. 144); Modesty (Is. 3); Self-esteem (2 Cor. 10)

our sufficiency *is* from God, [6]who also made us sufficient as ministers of the new covenant, not of the letter but of the Spirit;[a] for the letter kills, but the Spirit gives life.

Glory of the New Covenant

[7]But if the ministry of death, written *and* engraved on stones, was glorious, so that the children of Israel could not look steadily at the face of Moses because of the glory of his countenance, which *glory* was passing away, [8]how will the ministry of the Spirit not be more glorious? [9]For if the ministry of condemnation *had* glory, the ministry of righteousness exceeds much more in glory. [10]For even what was made glorious had no glory in this respect, because of the glory that excels. [11]For if what is passing away *was* glorious, what remains *is* much more glorious.

[12]Therefore, since we have such hope, we use great boldness of speech— [13]unlike Moses, *who* put a veil over his face so that the children of Israel could not look steadily at the end of what was passing away. [14]But their minds were blinded. For

until this day the same veil remains unlifted in the reading of the Old Testament, because the *veil* is taken away in Christ. [15]But even to this day, when Moses is read, a veil lies on their heart. [16]Nevertheless when one turns to the Lord, the veil is taken away. [17]Now the Lord is the Spirit; and where the Spirit of the Lord *is*, there *is* liberty. [18]But we all, with unveiled face, beholding as in a mirror the glory of the Lord, are being transformed into the same image from glory to glory, just as by the Spirit of the Lord.

The Light of Christ's Gospel

4 Therefore, since we have this ministry, as we have received mercy, we do not lose heart. [2]But we have renounced the hidden things of shame, not walking in craftiness nor handling the word of God deceitfully, but by manifestation of the truth commending ourselves to every man's conscience in the sight of God. [3]But even if our gospel is veiled, it is veiled to those who are perishing,

3:6 [a]Or *spirit*

could possibly be adequate for such a task. Human resources are pitifully insufficient. However, Paul argued that Christ equips believers with divine resources and thus makes them sufficient as ministers of the New Covenant. Therefore, reliance on human rather than divine authority with regard to letters of commendation was short-sighted (2 Cor. 3:1–3).

3:18 When Moses came down from Sinai with the tablets of the Law, his face physically reflected the fact that he had been speaking directly to God (Ex. 34:33–35). Paul maintained that as glorious as Moses' face was, it was a fading, temporal glory. It is outshone by the glory of the gospel, which, through the Spirit, transforms believers into the image

of God from glory to ever increasing glory. The New Covenant is superior to the old covenant, for the Spirit removes the veil that obscures one's view of God. With unveiled faces, believers behold God's glory and are being transformed into His image.

4:3, 4 Some of Paul's critics maintained that Paul's message was obscure. Paul argued the problem was not with his message but rather with the veil that covered people's minds and prevented them from seeing truth (2 Cor. 3:15). Unbelievers, "those who are perishing," have had their minds blinded by the "god of this age," Satan (2 Cor. 4:3, 4; see Eph. 2:2), who, though defeated by Christ (Heb. 2:14), temporarily continues

THE GLORY OF THE NEW COVENANT

OLD COVENANT	NEW COVENANT
The Law was written on stone tablets (2 Cor. 3:3).	The New Covenant is written on human hearts (2 Cor. 3:3).
The letter of the Law kills (2 Cor. 3:6).	The Spirit of the Lord gives liberty and life (2 Cor. 3:6, 17).
The Law brings condemnation (2 Cor. 3:9).	The New Covenant brings righteousness (2 Cor. 3:9).
The old covenant was passing away (2 Cor. 3:11).	The New Covenant remains forever (2 Cor. 3:11).
The Israelites could not look on God without a veil (2 Cor. 3:13).	All can look upon the glory of the Lord (2 Cor. 3:16, 18).
The glory of the old covenant was passing (2 Cor. 3:11).	The glory of the New Covenant is ever increasing (2 Cor. 3:18).

[4]whose minds the god of this age has blinded, who do not believe, lest the light of the gospel of the glory of Christ, who is the image of God, should shine on them. [5]For we do not preach ourselves, but Christ Jesus the Lord, and ourselves your bondservants for Jesus' sake. [6]For it is the God who commanded light to shine out of darkness, who has shone in our hearts to *give* the light of the knowledge of the glory of God in the face of Jesus Christ.

Cast Down but Unconquered

[7]But we have this treasure in earthen vessels, that the excellence of the power may be of God and not of us. [8]*We are* hard-pressed on every side, yet not crushed; *we are* perplexed, but not in despair; [9]persecuted, but not forsaken; struck down, but not destroyed— [10]always carrying about in the body the dying of the Lord Jesus, that the life of Jesus also may be manifested in our body. [11]For we who live are always delivered to death for Jesus' sake, that the life of Jesus also may be manifested in our mortal flesh. [12]So then death is working in us, but life in you.

[13]And since we have the same spirit of faith, according to what is written, *"I believed and therefore I spoke,"*[a] we also believe and therefore speak, [14]knowing that He who raised up the Lord Jesus will also raise us up with Jesus, and will present *us* with you. [15]For all things *are* for your sakes, that grace, having spread through the many, may cause thanksgiving to abound to the glory of God.

Seeing the Invisible

[16]Therefore we do not lose heart. Even though our outward man is perishing, yet the inward *man* is being renewed day by day. [17]For our light affliction, which is but for a moment, is working for us a far more exceeding *and* eternal weight of glory, [18]while we do not look at the things which are seen, but at the things which are not seen. For the things which are seen *are* temporary, but the things which are not seen *are* eternal.

4:13 [a]Psalm 116:10

his hold over the world to prevent people from seeing the light of the gospel (1 John 5:19).

4:7 Pottery, bought for one or two copper coins in the Corinthian marketplace, was often used as a receptacle for wick lamps. Though cheap and fragile they fulfilled their job as a holder for the lamp wicks. Paul used the imagery of these jars of clay to illustrate the sharp contrast between himself and the grandeur of the message he bore. He was ordinary and unimpressive, but he preached a gospel of light and power. God intended this so that the true source of the message be recognized as divine and not human.

4:17, 18 Paul suffered severely for the sake of the gospel. But when he reflected on his struggles in light of eternity, he saw them as being light and momentary. Only by comparing the *weight* of these sufferings to the *weight* of eternal glory would these sufferings pale into insignificance. Even though afflictions may cause the outer person to waste away, the life-giving Spirit renews the inner person day by day in preparation for the glory to come. Paul encouraged the Corinthians to shift their focus away from the heaviness of temporary, external circumstances toward the internal and eternal weight of glory that is the inheritance of those who believe.

PERSECUTION *HOPE UNDER FIRE*

The Bible records examples of persecution for the faith in both Old and New Testaments. Accounts of persecution in the Old Testament involved nations as a whole and individuals in particular. The prophets were persecuted because of their faith in God and their obedience to His will (Acts 7:52). In the New Testament, the church body, the twelve disciples, and individual Christians were persecuted for taking a stand for the Lord (Matt. 5:11, 12; 1 Cor. 15:9). Jesus suffered great persecution from the religious leaders of His day (John 5:16).

Persecution typically involves harassment and oppression for religious convictions, which results in physical or emotional suffering and affliction. Tribulation is to be an expected aspect of the Christian's life, in part because Christians are to live according to standards and principles that are more righteous than those advocated by unbelievers (2 Tim. 3:12). However, persecution for the faith is neither unbearable nor useless (John 16:33).

Although persecution may be an inevitable part of a Christian woman's life, she is neither to seek out persecution nor to bring persecution on herself. Much of what is perceived as persecution may actually be a consequence of abuse, a matter of poor self-esteem, or the result of an error in judgment. Believers must be wise in discerning the true source of persecution and the motives that evoke it.

Persecution is also inevitable for these reasons: (1) The sinful world hates God (John 15:18); (2) the things of the flesh battle the things of the Spirit (Gal. 4:29); (3) tribulation is inevitable in the midst of righteous living (Matt. 5:10); yet (4) believers are undergirded with help, strength, and power from God to face their tribulations (Rom. 8:35–39).

Christians are to face persecution with patience, endurance, and steadfastness (Rom. 12:12; James 5:7–11). They are to endure persecution and, in the process, receive strength and power to be "more than conquerors" (Rom. 8:35–39). Blessing can actually be experienced in the midst of persecution (1 Pet. 3:14; 4:12–14) because the Christian facing persecution for the kingdom's sake is not forsaken by God (2 Cor. 4:7–10).

See also notes on Adversity (Acts 5); Fruit of the Spirit (Ps. 86; Rom. 5; 15; 1 Cor. 10; 13; Gal. 5; Eph. 4; Col. 3; 2 Thess. 1; Rev. 2); Perseverance (Rev. 14); Suffering (Ps. 33; 113; Is. 43; 1 Pet. 5); Testing (Ps. 11)

Assurance of the Resurrection

5 For we know that if our earthly house, *this* tent, is destroyed, we have a building from God, a house not made with hands, eternal in the heavens. ²For in this we groan, earnestly desiring to be clothed with our habitation which is from heaven, ³if indeed, having been clothed, we shall not be found naked. ⁴For we who are in *this* tent groan, being burdened, not because we want to be unclothed, but further clothed, that mortality may be swallowed up by life. ⁵Now He who has prepared us for this very thing *is* God, who also has given us the Spirit as a guarantee.

⁶So *we are* always confident, knowing that while we are at home in the body we are absent from the Lord. ⁷For we walk by faith, not by sight. ⁸We are confident, yes, well pleased rather to be absent from the body and to be present with the Lord.

The Judgment Seat of Christ

⁹Therefore we make it our aim, whether present or absent, to be well pleasing to Him. ¹⁰For we must all appear before the judgment seat of Christ, that each one may receive the things *done* in the body, according to what he has done, whether good or bad. ¹¹Knowing, therefore, the terror of the Lord, we persuade men; but we are well known to God, and I also trust are well known in your consciences.

Be Reconciled to God

¹²For we do not commend ourselves again to you, but give you opportunity to boast on our be-

5:1–4 The body is sometimes compared to a "house" in which the soul dwells and sometimes to a garment with which it is clothed (v. 1). Paul combined these two figures here. He spoke of putting on a "house" as though it were a garment. Paul longed for the day when his mortal, temporal body would be replaced by an immortal, imperishable, spiritual one (Phil. 3:21). He certainly had experienced burdens of sorrow and suffering in his life. However, Paul groaned for heaven because his deepest desire was to be fully "present" with the Lord (2 Cor. 5:6, 8).

5:9 The ultimate goal of Paul's life was to be "well pleasing"

to the Lord (Gal 1:10; Col. 1:10). This aim was in effect during his time on earth ("present" in the body), and it would remain undiminished in heaven ("absent" from the body). The certainty of judgment and the prospect of eternal glory enabled Paul to persevere through hardship and motivated him to handle the ministry of the gospel with utmost integrity (2 Cor. 6:3).

5:10 Only believers will appear before Christ's "judgment seat" (Gk. *bēma*). Salvation is not the subject of judgment but rather works (see Rom 14:10; 1 Cor. 3:13; chart, Judgments in the New Testament).

HEALING OF SHAME   *A RIGHT UNDERSTANDING OF SELF*

Guilt is a God-given emotion that occurs when a woman's mistakes and faults are brought to her own mind or publicly exposed. This may be a personal reminder of her own limitations and sinfulness. Shame, however, says that the person herself is bad, of no value, or unworthy to exist—that she is hopelessly defective, unlovable, inferior, and worthless. Shame begins externally with a subtle implication through silence and neglect or with verbal denunciation through words of abuse. When such messages are repeated often enough, whether through words or actions, they become internalized into a false belief: I must be bad to deserve such terrible treatment. This becomes the core identity and the basis of thousands of future, flawed choices for the one suffering from shame.

Healing of shame begins when a woman identifies and confesses the lies she has believed about herself. She then must begin to replace those lies with biblical truth about who God is and who she is as His beloved child—a person of immeasurable worth, righteous and uncondemned (Rom. 8:1, 31–39; 2 Cor. 5:17, 21).

Sometimes the victimizing acts done to a person may be so shame-producing that she is still emotionally bound by that shame, even though she mentally understands her worth in God's eyes. Or, if she herself has actually committed shameful acts, a deep sense of shame may remain even after confession and repentance. In these situations, those acts must be brought into the presence of Jesus. Ultimately, only He brings full emotional cleansing and freedom.

See also Ps. 31:1, 2; Mark 5:2, note; Luke 7:36–50; 15:11–24; 19:1–10; notes on Family (1 Sam. 3); Guilt (2 Cor. 7); Healing (Ps. 13; 133; Eccl. 1; Gal. 6; James 5); Identity in Christ (Col. 2); Self-esteem (2 Cor. 10)

---

half, that you may have *an answer* for those who boast in appearance and not in heart. [13]For if we are beside ourselves, *it is* for God; or if we are of sound mind, *it is* for you. [14]For the love of Christ compels us, because we judge thus: that if One died for all, then all died; [15]and He died for all, that those who live should live no longer for themselves, but for Him who died for them and rose again.

[16]Therefore, from now on, we regard no one according to the flesh. Even though we have known Christ according to the flesh, yet now we know *Him* thus no longer. [17]Therefore, if anyone *is* in Christ, *he is* a new creation; old things have passed away; behold, all things have become new. [18]Now all things *are* of God, who has reconciled us to Himself through Jesus Christ, and has given us the ministry of reconciliation, [19]that is, that God was in Christ reconciling the world to Himself, not imputing their trespasses to them, and has committed to us the word of reconciliation.

[20]Now then, we are ambassadors for Christ, as though God were pleading through us: we implore *you* on Christ's behalf, be reconciled to God. [21]For He made Him who knew no sin *to be* sin for us, that we might become the righteousness of God in Him.

Marks of the Ministry

6We then, *as* workers together *with Him* also plead with *you* not to receive the grace of God in vain. [2]For He says:

"In an acceptable time I have heard you,
   And in the day of salvation I have helped you."[a]

Behold, now *is* the accepted time; behold, now *is* the day of salvation.

[3]We give no offense in anything, that our ministry may not be blamed. [4]But in all *things* we commend ourselves as ministers of God: in much patience, in tribulations, in needs, in distresses, [5]in stripes, in imprisonments, in tumults, in labors, in sleeplessness, in fastings; [6]by purity, by knowledge, by longsuffering, by kindness, by the Holy Spirit, by sincere love, [7]by the word of truth, by the power of God, by the armor of righteousness on the right hand and on the left, [8]by honor and dishonor, by evil report and good report; as deceivers, and *yet* true; [9]as unknown, and *yet* well known; as dying, and behold we live; as chastened, and *yet* not killed; [10]as sorrowful, yet always rejoicing; as poor, yet making many rich; as having nothing, and *yet* possessing all things.

6:2 [a]Isaiah 49:8

5:16 Prior to Paul's conversion, he had decided that Jesus could not possibly be the Messiah. However, his conception of Christ was based on fleshly knowledge. His view radically changed when he encountered Christ face to face on the road to Damascus (Acts 9:4). In Christ, the new way of knowing is spiritual in nature. Paul argued that spiritual wisdom does not

evaluate people on the basis of external appearances, as the Corinthians were in the habit of doing. Therefore, he urged them to discard their old, carnal ways of assessment so that they could evaluate others according to the new nature that had been given them through Christ (2 Cor. 1:12).

HUSBANDS *MARRIAGE TO AN UNBELIEVER*

While knowingly marrying an unbeliever violates God's Word (2 Cor. 6:14), Scripture provides very practical encouragement to those who find themselves the wives of unsaved husbands.

- *Win without a word.* Do not preach to an unsaved husband. He cannot comprehend spiritual truths (2 Cor. 4:4; 1 Pet. 3:1–4). Regeneration is the work of the Holy Spirit. God desires repentance for all (2 Pet. 3:9).
- *Cultivate a quiet and gentle spirit.* A wife who is saved will at times disagree with her unsaved husband. You may disagree but do not be disagreeable. Avoid agitation and harshness. Concentrate on being the best wife possible. Relax and enjoy your husband. Do not condemn him. Mirror God's love through your pure character and generosity toward him.
- *Be submissive in your love.* Demonstrate loving respect for your husband. However, submission does not require agreeing to engage in sinful activities or living in fear (2 Tim. 1:7). If your husband dangerously mistreats you or your children, seek protection from civil authorities.
- *Pray for your husband's salvation.* While his salvation is not guaranteed, your faith and prayers act as a catalyst, binding Satan and opening your husband's heart to the Holy Spirit (Acts 16:31).

See also 1 Sam. 25:2–39; notes on Evangelism (John 6; Col. 4; 1 Pet. 3); Husbands (Job 31); Marriage (Gen. 2; 2 Sam. 6; Prov. 5; Hos. 2; Amos 3; 2 Cor. 13; Heb. 12); Masculinity (Gen. 2); Wives (Prov. 31); portrait of Abigail (1 Sam. 25)

Be Holy

¹¹O Corinthians! We have spoken openly to you, our heart is wide open. ¹²You are not restricted by us, but you are restricted by your *own* affections. ¹³Now in return for the same (I speak as to children), you also be open.

¹⁴Do not be unequally yoked together with unbelievers. For what fellowship has righteousness with lawlessness? And what communion has light with darkness? ¹⁵And what accord has Christ with Belial? Or what part has a believer with an unbeliever? ¹⁶And what agreement has the temple of God with idols? For you[a] are the temple of the living God. As God has said:

*"I will dwell in them
And walk among them.*

*I will be their God,
And they shall be My people."*[b]

¹⁷Therefore

*"Come out from among them
And be separate, says the Lord.
Do not touch what is unclean,
And I will receive you."*[a]
¹⁸*"I will be a Father to you,
And you shall be My sons and daughters,
Says the LORD Almighty."*[a]

7 Therefore, having these promises, beloved, let us cleanse ourselves from all filthiness of the

6:16 [a]NU-Text reads *we.* [b]Leviticus 26:12; Jeremiah 32:38; Ezekiel 37:27 6:17 [a]Isaiah 52:11; Ezekiel 20:34, 41 6:18 [a]2 Samuel 7:14

6:12 Paul's defense of his changed travel plans and description of his apostolic ministry were to influence the Corinthians to reciprocate the love that he had selflessly poured out upon them.

6:14 Opposites cannot be harmoniously joined (vv. 14–16). The alliances Paul had in mind may have been mixed marriages, improper business associations, or relationships with pagan idolaters (1 Cor. 10:14; see Neh. 10, Interfaith Marriage; 2 Cor. 6, Husbands). However, he most likely was referring to associations with false apostles. He considered these false prophets responsible for the recent schism in his relationship with the Corinthian church (2 Cor. 11:13–15).

6:17 To buffer his argument against alliances with pagans, Paul cited portions of Isaiah and Ezekiel referring to Israel's redemption from bondage. God delivered the Israelites so they could be holy and free from pagan influences for fellowship with Him. Paul argued that in order to attain personal holiness and enjoy God's presence, the Corinthians needed likewise to sever ties with pagan idolaters and false apostles.

He was *not* saying that believers should avoid contact with unbelievers. On the contrary, he encouraged Christians to associate with the unsaved of the world (1 Cor. 5:9, 10). However, Paul was concerned that the Corinthians avoid fellowship or communion with pagans within the church ("religious" unbelievers). He did not want them thus to be led astray from sincere and pure devotion to Christ (2 Cor. 11:3).

7:1 God promised His presence (2 Cor. 6:16) and a special relationship to those who would obey Him (2 Cor. 6:17, 18). Because the promises are from *God*, Christians must be meticulous to fulfill their responsibilities in satisfying the conditions. First, believers are expected to cleanse themselves by turning from everything that contaminates the body or spirit—including every person who bends the truth (2 Cor. 2:17; 4:2). Second, they are to work toward "perfecting" holiness (2 Cor. 7:1). The use of the present participle in "perfecting" signifies a continual process by which their holiness is brought to completion (v. 1).

Many of us don't need a facelift; we need a heart transplant.

Rhonda H. Kelley

flesh and spirit, perfecting holiness in the fear of God.

The Corinthians' Repentance

²Open *your hearts* to us. We have wronged no one, we have corrupted no one, we have cheated no one. ³I do not say *this* to condemn; for I have said before that you are in our hearts, to die together and to live together. ⁴Great *is* my boldness of speech toward you, great *is* my boasting on your behalf. I am filled with comfort. I am exceedingly joyful in all our tribulation.

⁵For indeed, when we came to Macedonia, our bodies had no rest, but we were troubled on every side. Outside *were* conflicts, inside *were* fears. ⁶Nevertheless God, who comforts the downcast, comforted us by the coming of Titus, ⁷and not only by his coming, but also by the consolation with which he was comforted in you, when he told us of your earnest desire, your mourning, your zeal for me, so that I rejoiced even more.

⁸For even if I made you sorry with my letter, I do not regret it; though I did regret it. For I perceive that the same epistle made you sorry, though only for a while. ⁹Now I rejoice, not that you were made sorry, but that your sorrow led to repentance. For you were made sorry in a godly manner, that you might suffer loss from us in nothing. ¹⁰For godly sorrow produces repentance *leading* to salvation, not to be regretted; but the sorrow of the world produces death. ¹¹For observe this very thing, that you sorrowed in a godly manner: What diligence it produced in you, *what* clearing *of yourselves*, *what* indignation, *what* fear, *what* vehement desire, *what* zeal, *what* vindication! In all *things* you proved yourselves to be clear in this matter. ¹²Therefore, although I wrote to you, *I did* not *do it* for the sake of him who had done the wrong, nor for the sake of him who suffered wrong, but that

our care for you in the sight of God might appear to you.

The Joy of Titus

¹³Therefore we have been comforted in your comfort. And we rejoiced exceedingly more for the joy of Titus, because his spirit has been refreshed by you all. ¹⁴For if in anything I have boasted to him about you, I am not ashamed. But as we spoke all things to you in truth, even so our boasting to Titus was found true. ¹⁵And his affections are greater for you as he remembers the obedience of you all, how with fear and trembling you received him. ¹⁶Therefore I rejoice that I have confidence in you in everything.

Excel in Giving

8 Moreover, brethren, we make known to you the grace of God bestowed on the churches of Macedonia: ²that in a great trial of affliction the abundance of their joy and their deep poverty abounded in the riches of their liberality. ³For I bear witness that according to *their* ability, yes, and beyond *their* ability, *they were* freely willing, ⁴imploring us with much urgency that we would receiveᵃ the gift and the fellowship of the ministering to the saints. ⁵And not *only* as we had hoped, but they first gave themselves to the Lord, and *then* to us by the will of God. ⁶So we urged Titus, that as he had begun, so he would also complete this grace in you as well. ⁷But as you abound in everything—in faith, in speech, in knowledge, in all diligence, and in your love for us—*see* that you abound in this grace also.

Christ Our Pattern

⁸I speak not by commandment, but I am testing the sincerity of your love by the diligence of

8:4 ᵃNU-Text and M-Text omit *that we would receive,* thus changing text to *urgency for the favor and fellowship....*

7:8 Following his painful visit, Paul wrote a harsh disciplinary letter to the Corinthians (see Introduction: Setting). He regretted doing this, but the Corinthians did respond to his correction with godly sorrow (v. 11). Such sorrow produced in them a concerted effort to make amends ("diligence"), a desire to vindicate themselves ("clearing of yourselves"), "indignation" against the person who had opposed Paul, alarm at their own passivity ("fear"), a deep longing and concern for Paul ("vehement desire and zeal"; see 2 Cor. 7:7), and a readiness to see justice done ("vindication"; see v. 11). They demonstrated that they did not, in fact, support the man who had

publicly opposed Paul. Therefore, their sin was not so much that they had done wrong but that by their indifference they had failed to do what was right.

8:1, 2 Paul had organized a collection for the poor in Jerusalem (Gal. 2:10; Rom. 15:25–28). The Corinthians volunteered to contribute, but their good intentions did not translate into practical aid. Paul made another appeal to them, citing the example of the Macedonian churches, who had become involved entirely on their own initiative, though deeply poor and greatly afflicted (2 Cor. 8:2).

GUILT A SPIRITUAL WEIGHT

Guilt is the emotional and spiritual weight we bear as the result of sin against others and against God. Christ taught that the acknowledgement of our true guilt is the door through which we can experience the cleansing and renewal of being forgiven (1 John 1:9, 10).

There are two kinds of guilt: false guilt and true guilt. False guilt is what the apostle Paul refers to as "the sorrow of the world" (2 Cor. 7:9, 10). He describes a nebulous sense of free-floating regret and guilt which seem to have no clear source and leave only a deep feeling of condemnation. True guilt, on the other hand, is "godly sorrow [that] produces repentance leading to salvation."

True guilt is the gentle, persistent prodding of the Holy Spirit, which leads us to acknowledge that we have indeed failed or fallen short of God's law (Rom. 3:23). That recognition of failure compels us to repent and seek God's forgiveness and to experience once again the freedom and restoration made possible by Christ's all-sufficient sacrifice (Rom. 5:10). Guilt that leads to repentance liberates the soul.

See also Gen. 3:1–7; 4:1–8; Mark 5:2, note; Luke 24:47, note; Rom. 3:23, note; 1 John 1:5–10; notes on Forgiveness (Ps. 51; Luke 17); Healing (Ps. 13; 133; Eccl. 1; 2 Cor. 5; Gal. 6; James 5); Shame (Ps. 119)

others. 9For you know the grace of our Lord Jesus Christ, that though He was rich, yet for your sakes He became poor, that you through His poverty might become rich.

10And in this I give advice: It is to your advantage not only to be doing what you began and were desiring to do a year ago; 11but now you also must complete the doing *of it;* that as *there was* a readiness to desire *it,* so *there* also *may be* a completion out of what *you* have. 12For if there is first a willing mind, *it is* accepted according to what one has, *and* not according to what he does not have.

13For *I do* not *mean* that others should be eased and you burdened; 14but by an equality, *that* now at this time your abundance *may supply* their lack, that their abundance also may *supply* your lack— that there may be equality. 15As it is written, *"He who gathered much had nothing left over, and he who gathered little had no lack."*a

Collection for the Judean Saints

16But thanks *be* to God who putsa the same earnest care for you into the heart of Titus. 17For he not only accepted the exhortation, but being

more diligent, he went to you of his own accord. 18And we have sent with him the brother whose praise *is* in the gospel throughout all the churches, 19and not only *that,* but who was also chosen by the churches to travel with us with this gift, which is administered by us to the glory of the Lord Himself and *to show* your ready mind, 20avoiding this: that anyone should blame us in this lavish gift which is administered by us— 21providing honorable things, not only in the sight of the Lord, but also in the sight of men.

22And we have sent with them our brother whom we have often proved diligent in many things, but now much more diligent, because of the great confidence which *we have* in you. 23If *anyone inquires* about Titus, *he is* my partner and fellow worker concerning you. Or if our brethren *are inquired about, they are* messengers of the churches, the glory of Christ. 24Therefore show to them, anda before the churches, the proof of your love and of our boasting on your behalf.

• • • • • • • • • • • • • • • • •

8:15 aExodus 16:18   **8:16** aNU-Text reads *has put.*   **8:24** aNU-Text and M-Text omit *and.*

8:9 The supreme reason for Christian generosity is the self-giving and self-impoverishment of Christ, who gave up His glory and His rightful position in heaven on our behalf. Christ became what the Corinthians were (poor) so that they could become what He is (rich). Self-sacrifice is the proper test of love. The example of Christ and the debt Christians owe Him should lead them to be generous toward others.

8:15 Paul did not intend that the financial relief of the saints at Jerusalem should impoverish those in Corinth. He was not advocating an artificial equalization of property but rather the relief of need. Paul stressed that all believers had a duty to contribute out of their own abundance to the needs of the poor, but he also stressed that the poor were to work and support themselves to the best of their ability (2 Thess. 3:10). The give and take "equality" (translated "fair" in Col. 4:1) he had in mind could be illustrated by God's provision of manna for

the Israelites in the wilderness (Ex. 16:18). All the Israelites gathered manna to eat; but when they measured the amounts, the ones who had gathered more only had as much as they required, even as did the ones who had gathered less. There was neither excess nor insufficiency but equality of provision according to each one's needs.

8:20, 21 Paul was aware that his critics would seize any opportunity to accuse him. It was not enough that honesty be practiced in the Lord's sight; Paul also felt it imperative to be open and honest in the sight of people (Prov. 3:4). Therefore, Paul did not take the gift of money to the church in Jerusalem but sent it with Titus, whom the Corinthians loved and trusted. Furthermore, he had the churches (perhaps those of Judea, Asia Minor, and/or Macedonia) choose two other men to accompany Titus.

Living by faith is not easy, but it is essential.
It is the only weapon for adversity that cannot fail.

— Dorothy Kelley Patterson

Administering the Gift

9 Now concerning the ministering to the saints, it is superfluous for me to write to you; ²for I know your willingness, about which I boast of you to the Macedonians, that Achaia was ready a year ago; and your zeal has stirred up the majority. ³Yet I have sent the brethren, lest our boasting of you should be in vain in this respect, that, as I said, you may be ready; ⁴lest if *some* Macedonians come with me and find you unprepared, we (not to mention you!) should be ashamed of this confident boasting.[a] ⁵Therefore I thought it necessary to exhort the brethren to go to you ahead of time, and prepare your generous gift beforehand, which *you had* previously promised, that it may be ready as *a matter of* generosity and not as a grudging obligation.

The Cheerful Giver

⁶But this *I say:* He who sows sparingly will also reap sparingly, and he who sows bountifully will also reap bountifully. ⁷So let each one *give* as he purposes in his heart, not grudgingly or of necessity; for God loves a cheerful giver. ⁸And God *is* able to make all grace abound toward you, that you, always having all sufficiency in all *things,* may have an abundance for every good work. ⁹As it is written:

"He has dispersed abroad,
 He has given to the poor;
 His righteousness endures forever."[a]

¹⁰Now may[a] He who supplies seed to the sower, and bread for food, supply and multiply the seed you have *sown* and increase the fruits of your righteousness, ¹¹while *you are* enriched in everything for all liberality, which causes thanksgiving through us to God. ¹²For the administration of this service not only supplies the needs of the saints, but also is abounding through many thanksgivings to God, ¹³while, through the proof of this ministry, they glorify God for the obedience of your confession to the gospel of Christ, and for *your* liberal sharing with them and all *men,* ¹⁴and by their prayer for you, who long for you because of the exceeding grace of God in you. ¹⁵Thanks *be* to God for His indescribable gift!

The Spiritual War

10 Now I, Paul, myself am pleading with you by the meekness and gentleness of Christ— who in presence *am* lowly among you, but being absent am bold toward you. ²But I beg *you* that when I am present I may not be bold with that confidence by which I intend to be bold against some, who think of us as if we walked according to the flesh. ³For though we walk in the flesh, we do not war according to the flesh. ⁴For the weapons of our warfare *are* not carnal but mighty in God for pulling down strongholds, ⁵casting down arguments and every high thing that exalts itself against the knowledge of God, bringing every thought into captivity to the obedience of Christ, ⁶and being ready to punish all disobedience when your obedience is fulfilled.

9:4 [a]NU-Text reads *this confidence.* **9:9** [a]Psalm 112:9 **9:10** [a]NU-Text reads *Now He who supplies . . . will supply. . . .*

9:6 Paul associated the act of giving with the principle of sowing and reaping. Farmers can keep and eat all of their grain, or they can "lose" it by throwing it over the ground. Naturally, the more generous the sowing, the more bountiful the rewards. This principle holds true in the spiritual sphere as well. The liberal giver need not fear destitution, for this giver would receive in return gifts out of all proportion to what had been given (Prov. 11:24, 25; 19:17; Luke 6:38). Christ loves givers who are sincere (not reluctant), spontaneous (not under compulsion), and joyful (not begrudging). He does not look at the amount but at the heart (Mark 12:41–44).

9:10 Generous giving seems hazardous to those who have little; however, the risk dims in light of the greatness of God's power. All resources ultimately come from God, and Paul insisted that God is able to increase these resources for the purpose of giving. God supplies the seed and also multiplies the harvest. The Macedonians had given out of extreme poverty. But such seed as God had supplied, they had sown in liberal-

ity. The results of their generosity would be—for both themselves and the recipients of their gift—of a magnitude out of all proportion to the original quantity given.

9:14, 15 This section concludes in the same way it began—by focusing on the grace of God (2 Cor. 8:1). "Thanks" (Gk. *charis*) is the same word translated "grace" or "favor" (2 Cor. 9:15). The indescribable gift is God's grace or favor, which rests upon those who believe (v.15). Gratitude for God's gift brings to an end all debate on the question of giving. It is only proper that those who have benefited from such a vast, incomparable spiritual gift should generously and freely give material gifts to relieve the needs of others.

10:4–6 Paul knew that the Corinthians were in grave danger of being led astray from the gospel. The Corinthian church needed to express loyalty to Christ by demonstrating loyalty to Paul, Christ's representative (2 Cor. 5:20; 7:15). Paul urged the Corinthians to use spiritual weapons to war against the

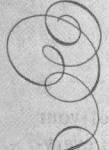

GIVING *A GENEROUS HEART*

A generous heart is one marked by evidence of the Holy Spirit's work in your life. God's love is demonstrated in the giving of His Son (John 3:16). Giving time, energies, and financial resources is the expression of a grateful heart, the natural response of a woman who realizes she has been lavished with God's grace (Eph. 1:7, 8).

In the Old Testament, the Jewish tithe (the first one tenth) was a prescribed percentage of a person's income. It belonged to the Lord and was used to provide for the priests, the temple, and the needy. Offerings were made on special occasions (see Ex. 35:21—36:7) and as an obligatory part of public sacrifices of thanksgiving, blessing, or sorrow.

In the New Testament, emphasis is placed upon the believer's heart and attitude. Paul declared that a Christian's giving should be the overflow of a worshipful heart and a matter of conviction before God (2 Cor. 9:7). Giving to others in a spirit of forgiveness—without judgment or condemnation—brings joyful, abundant rewards (Luke 6:37, 38).

See also Gal. 6:6–10; Phil. 4:10–20; 1 Tim. 6:3–10; chart on The Offerings of the Lord; notes on Debt (Ps. 37); Financial Planning (Luke 19); Gratitude (Ps. 95); Stewardship (Luke 16); portrait of Widow with Two Mites (Mark 12)

Reality of Paul's Authority

⁷Do you look at things according to the outward appearance? If anyone is convinced in himself that he is Christ's, let him again consider this in himself, that just as he *is* Christ's, even so we *are* Christ's.ᵃ ⁸For even if I should boast somewhat more about our authority, which the Lord gave usᵃ for edification and not for your destruction, I shall not be ashamed— ⁹lest I seem to terrify you by letters. ¹⁰"For *his* letters," they say, "*are* weighty and powerful, but *his* bodily presence *is* weak, and *his* speech contemptible." ¹¹Let such a person consider this, that what we are in word by letters when we are absent, such *we will* also *be* in deed when we are present.

Limits of Paul's Authority

¹²For we dare not class ourselves or compare ourselves with those who commend themselves. But they, measuring themselves by themselves, and comparing themselves among themselves, are not wise. ¹³We, however, will not boast beyond measure, but within the limits of the sphere which God appointed us—a sphere which especially includes you. ¹⁴For we are not overextending ourselves (as though *our authority* did not extend to you), for it was to you that we came with the gospel of Christ; ¹⁵not boasting of things beyond measure, *that is,* in other men's labors, but having hope, *that* as your faith is increased, we shall be greatly enlarged by you in our sphere, ¹⁶to preach the gospel in the *regions* beyond you, *and* not to boast in another man's sphere of accomplishment.

¹⁷But *"he who glories, let him glory in the* LORD.*"*ᵃ ¹⁸For not he who commends himself is approved, but whom the Lord commends.

Concern for Their Faithfulness

11 Oh, that you would bear with me in a little folly— and indeed you do bear with me. ²For I am jealous for you with godly jealousy. For I have betrothed you to one husband, that I may present

---

10:7 ᵃNU-Text reads *even as we are.*   10:8 ᵃNU-Text omits *us.*   10:17 ᵃJeremiah 9:24

"strong man," Satan (Luke 11:21). Paul urged them to pull down the strongholds that had been established in their minds by making every thought obedient to Christ. When they had "fulfilled" obedience, Paul could, with their support, punish the false apostles and those who continued to follow these deceivers (2 Cor. 10:6).

10:7 Certain religious leaders had presented themselves to the Corinthian church as ministers of Christ (2 Cor. 11:23). They brought letters of recommendation (2 Cor. 3:1), commended themselves (2 Cor. 10:12), and identified themselves with so called "super apostles" (2 Cor. 11:5). These men had credentials, social status, education, and persuasive rhetoric (1 Cor 1:26; 2:1). However, despite outward appearances, they were not genuine apostles (2 Cor. 11:13). They opposed Paul (2 Cor. 10:10), sought monetary gain (2 Cor. 2:17), and indulged in

sensuality (2 Cor. 12:21). Paul urged the Corinthians to evaluate these men by spiritual rather than carnal standards.

10:18 The apostles who were seeking to turn the Corinthian church against Paul were frauds. They evaluated and commended themselves by human standards (v. 12). They claimed authority over the Corinthian church and by their own virtue had thus transgressed the proper limits of an apostle (vv. 13,16). Paul had limits of authority that he did not breach (v. 15). These leaders exalted themselves, claimed ownership of the ministry in Corinth, and took personal credit for the growth there. Paul argued that such self-commendation was not of Christ (Jer. 9:23, 24).

11:2 Paul used a wedding metaphor to present himself as the father of the bride, offering the Corinthians as pure and undefiled to Christ, the Bridegroom.

SELF-ESTEEM A HEALTHY YOU

Self-esteem is how each individual values herself. Poor self-esteem (bad, condemning feelings about yourself) are weights that keep believers under condemnation and cause them to be less than what God intends. Believers are to combat such feelings of inferiority (Heb. 12:1).

Proper self-esteem in a follower of Christ is a matter of recognizing and confronting yourself in your humanity, including the tendency to sin, "going astray" (1 Pet. 2:25). It is also a matter of embracing Jesus' work on the Cross—His grace that covers a multitude of sins. The process of comprehending God's infinite care for the individual—each with unique strengths and weaknesses—puts a perspective on self-esteem. Psalm 139 expresses the wonder of being uniquely created by God and the intimate care of His presence at all times. Jesus tenderly described His love for His children (Matt. 6:25–34).

Prerequisites to healthy self-esteem include these:

- Recognize the need of a Savior (Is. 53:6).
- Accept being "in the beloved" (Eph. 1:6; Rom. 8:1).
- Move forward in God's plan for your life (Phil. 3:13, 14).
- Have a realistic view of yourself (Rom. 12:3).
- Avoid comparisons to others (2 Cor. 10:12).

A person with healthy self-esteem is marked by these characteristics:

- Resting in "ownership" by God (1 Cor. 3:16).
- Submitting to being the "workmanship" of God (Eph. 2:10).
- Appreciating the differences of others (1 Cor. 12:1–31).
- Willingness to take risks, steps of faith (Esth. 4:13–16).
- Forging good relationships with others (Ruth 1:16, 17).

God does not evaluate human worth as we do. He looks to the heart within, while we tend to look only at the outer frame (1 Sam. 16:7; 1 Pet. 3:3, 4). The heart of a healthy self-esteem is recognizing that "self" must be seen as created for God's glory. We might more accurately say that within every believer there must be "God-esteem," which accepts whatever lot in life is ours.

We must be willing to change weaknesses into strengths when possible—and when that is not possible, we are to look for opportunities for God to be glorified even in our failures and suffering. God does not make mistakes, and He is never finished working in us as He continues to refine and edify, helping each woman reach her maximum potential (1 Pet. 5:10). Negatives can be changed into positives and tragedies into triumphs with the Savior's touch.

See also notes on Appearance (2 Cor. 3); Beauty (Prov. 4); Identity in Christ (Col. 2); Image of God (Ps. 8)

you as a chaste virgin to Christ. ³But I fear, lest somehow, as the serpent deceived Eve by his craftiness, so your minds may be corrupted from the simplicity[a] that is in Christ. ⁴For if he who comes preaches another Jesus whom we have not preached, or *if* you receive a different spirit which you have not received, or a different gospel which you have not accepted—you may well put up with it!

Paul and False Apostles

⁵For I consider that I am not at all inferior to the most eminent apostles. ⁶Even though *I am* un-trained in speech, yet *I am* not in knowledge. But we have been thoroughly manifested[a] among you in all things.

⁷Did I commit sin in humbling myself that you might be exalted, because I preached the gospel of God to you free of charge? ⁸I robbed other churches, taking wages *from them* to minister to you. ⁹And when I was present with you, and in need, I was a burden to no one, for what I lacked the brethren who came from Macedonia supplied. And in everything I kept myself from being

11:3 [a]NU-Text adds *and purity.*   11:6 [a]NU-Text omits *been.*

11:3 Paul cautioned the Corinthians that Satan, the father of all lies (John 8:44), would seek to distract them from the simplicity of the gospel. Satan would attempt to deceive them with complicated and persuasive arguments, just as he had once deceived Eve (Gen. 3:13; see 1 Tim. 2:14). The teachings of the false apostles sounded good, but in actuality they "corrupted" the Christian message (2 Cor. 11:3). The false apostles

promoted a spirit of human wisdom and *gnōsis* (2 Cor. 10:5; see 1 Cor. 2:12; 2 Cor. 1:12), a spirit of bondage to legalistic requirements (2 Cor. 3:6), and a spirit of compromise (2 Cor. 6:14—7:1; 12:21). This spirit was different than the spirit of liberty (2 Cor. 3:17; Gal. 2:4; 5:1), the spirit of love, joy, and peace (Rom. 14:17; Gal. 5:22), and the spirit of power (Eph. 3:20; Col. 1:11; 2 Tim. 1:7) that Paul preached.

CULTS *FRAUDULENT FAITH*

A "cult" is a religious group that has been established upon a special message not found in the Bible. Most cultic leaders testify of visions, revelations, spirit guides, or audible voices from heaven that have revealed truth to them alone. Their messages are characteristically apocalyptic and are often presented as "inspired."

Cultic leaders are nearly always authoritarian. They typically encourage their followers to adopt a legalistic lifestyle and persecution mentality, adopting an outlook of "exclusivity" for the group.

Many people have suffered from the brainwashing and other fraudulent tactics of cults. Grievances include the lack of full disclosure when luring potential members into the cult through extortion, poor nutrition, sleep deprivation, auditory bombardment, as well as far more severe instances of slavery, physical abuse, and sexual exploitation. Cults tend to entice followers with what appear to be generous expressions of concern and a desire to meet the deep needs of people who are confused, suffering, dejected, or searching for meaning in life. In the minds of many Christian leaders, the increase in cult membership worldwide is a direct indicator of the church's failure to meet these needs genuinely and fully.

See also John 1:4, note; Gal. 1:6–9; notes on Heresies (1 Cor. 1); Paganism (Jer. 7)

burdensome to you, and so I will keep *myself.* ¹⁰As the truth of Christ is in me, no one shall stop me from this boasting in the regions of Achaia. ¹¹Why? Because I do not love you? God knows!

¹²But what I do, I will also continue to do, that I may cut off the opportunity from those who desire an opportunity to be regarded just as we are in the things of which they boast. ¹³For such *are* false apostles, deceitful workers, transforming themselves into apostles of Christ. ¹⁴And no wonder! For Satan himself transforms himself into an angel of light. ¹⁵Therefore *it is* no great thing if his ministers also transform themselves into ministers of righteousness, whose end will be according to their works.

Reluctant Boasting

¹⁶I say again, let no one think me a fool. If otherwise, at least receive me as a fool, that I also may boast a little. ¹⁷What I speak, I speak not according to the Lord, but as it were, foolishly, in this confidence of boasting. ¹⁸Seeing that many boast according to the flesh, I also will boast. ¹⁹For you put up with fools gladly, since you *yourselves* are

wise! ²⁰For you put up with it if one brings you into bondage, if one devours *you,* if one takes *from you,* if one exalts himself, if one strikes you on the face. ²¹To *our* shame I say that we were too weak for that! But in whatever anyone is bold—I speak foolishly—I am bold also.

Suffering for Christ

²²Are they Hebrews? So *am* I. Are they Israelites? So *am* I. Are they the seed of Abraham? So *am* I. ²³Are they ministers of Christ?—I speak as a fool—I *am* more: in labors more abundant, in stripes above measure, in prisons more frequently, in deaths often. ²⁴From the Jews five times I received forty *stripes* minus one. ²⁵Three times I was beaten with rods; once I was stoned; three times I was shipwrecked; a night and a day I have been in the deep; ²⁶*in* journeys often, *in* perils of waters, *in* perils of robbers, *in* perils of *my own* countrymen, *in* perils of the Gentiles, *in* perils in the city, *in* perils in the wilderness, *in* perils in the sea, *in* perils among false brethren; ²⁷in weariness and toil, in sleeplessness often, in hunger and thirst, in fastings often, in cold and nakedness— ²⁸besides

---

11:14, 15 Satan is the father of all lying, and there is no truth in him (John 8:44). His proper sphere is darkness (Eph. 6:12; Col. 1:13). However, he has the ability to transform himself or masquerade as an angel of light. He can change his outward form to appear to be what he is not. Christ has His ministers, and so has Satan. If Satan is able to present himself in a guise so foreign to his real nature, it is no surprise that those who serve him would be able to do the same. The false apostles in the church in Corinth were perverting the truth. Outwardly they appeared to be religious (ministers of righteousness), but neither their character nor their doctrine conformed to the Word of God. They were simply masquerading as messengers of light.

11:17 The Corinthians evaluated others according to external appearances; so Paul used their standard for evaluating him-

self. Although he regarded this to be an exercise in foolishness, he maintained that he could match and even outdo all the boastful claims of the false apostles. Paul compared his own ministry with theirs and demonstrated that even on the basis of externals, their apostleship was deficient. They had not known the fellowship of Christ's sufferings as he had. They had not been beaten, stoned, shipwrecked, imprisoned, nor had they hungered, thirsted, or gone sleepless for the sake of the kingdom. Although they had some claim to Jewish nationality and lineage; as far as ministry was concerned, they were completely lacking. Paul could boast more than they. However, he recognized that this was foolish, for it was not his own but Christ's power he used for all he had experienced and accomplished (2 Cor. 12:9).

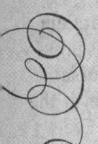

PAIN | *TURNING PHYSICAL AFFLICTION INTO JOY*

Pain was part of the God-given consequence to mankind for believing Satan and disobeying God in the Garden of Eden. Women were to experience pain in childbirth and men, the pain of labor as they worked the ground (Gen. 3:16, 17). As a result the "whole creation groans and labors with birth pangs" (Rom. 8:22). Everyone is subject to pain until God brings "a new heaven and a new earth" and "there shall be no more pain" (Rev. 21:1, 4).

Job, "a blameless and upright man" (Job 2:3), experienced pain as a result of Satan's direct attack (vv. 1–10). Job illustrates what often happens when a person experiences unrelieved pain. He isolated himself (v. 8). His wife became impatient and lacked understanding (v. 9). Job's focus was on himself, even to the point of desiring death as a release (Job 3:20, 21).

The New Testament emphasizes pain's partnership with joy. The woman, through labor, experiences the joy of new life (John 16:21). Paul and Silas sang and prayed while in pain, and the result was their deliverance and the salvation of their jailer's household (Acts 16:23–25, 34). Perhaps Paul knew of the medicinal value of a "merry heart" (Prov. 17:22). Christ, who endured the Cross for the joy that was set before Him (Heb. 12:2), understands pain. He walks with Christians through their painful hours (Ps. 9:9, 10; Is. 41:10).

See also Mark 5:2, note; notes on Adversity (Acts 5); Contentment (1 Tim. 6); Healing (Ps. 13; 133; Eccl. 1; 2 Cor. 5; Gal. 6; James 5); Suffering (Ps. 33; 113; Is. 43; 1 Pet. 5)

---

the other things, what comes upon me daily: my deep concern for all the churches. [29]Who is weak, and I am not weak? Who is made to stumble, and I do not burn *with indignation?*

[30]If I must boast, I will boast in the things which concern my infirmity. [31]The God and Father of our Lord Jesus Christ, who is blessed forever, knows that I am not lying. [32]In Damascus the governor, under Aretas the king, was guarding the city of the Damascenes with a garrison, desiring to arrest me; [33]but I was let down in a basket through a window in the wall, and escaped from his hands.

The Vision of Paradise

12 It is doubtless[a] not profitable for me to boast. I will come to visions and revelations of the Lord: [2]I know a man in Christ who fourteen years ago—whether in the body I do not know, or whether out of the body I do not know, God knows—such a one was caught up to the third heaven. [3]And I know such a man—whether in the body or out of the body I do not know, God knows— [4]how he was caught up into Paradise and heard inexpressible words, which it is not lawful for a man to utter. [5]Of such a one I will boast; yet of myself I will not boast, except in my infirmities. [6]For though I might desire to boast, I will not be a

fool; for I will speak the truth. But I refrain, lest anyone should think of me above what he sees me *to be* or hears from me.

The Thorn in the Flesh

[7]And lest I should be exalted above measure by the abundance of the revelations, a thorn in the flesh was given to me, a messenger of Satan to buffet me, lest I be exalted above measure. [8]Concerning this thing I pleaded with the Lord three times that it might depart from me. [9]And He said to me, "My grace is sufficient for you, for My strength is made perfect in weakness." Therefore most gladly I will rather boast in my infirmities, that the power of Christ may rest upon me. [10]Therefore I take pleasure in infirmities, in reproaches, in needs, in persecutions, in distresses, for Christ's sake. For when I am weak, then I am strong.

Signs of an Apostle

[11]I have become a fool in boasting;[a] you have compelled me. For I ought to have been commended by you; for in nothing was I behind the most eminent apostles, though I am nothing. [12]Truly the signs of an apostle were accomplished

12:1 [a]NU-Text reads *necessary, though not profitable, to boast.*
12:11 [a]NU-Text omits *in boasting.*

12:7 Paul knew there was a danger that others would think more highly of him than they ought because of the visions and revelations he had experienced. However, he himself was protected from self-exaltation by a persistent "thorn in the flesh." No one knows with certainty the nature of Paul's "thorn in the flesh." It may have been a physical malady such as defective eyesight, a lisp, epilepsy, or recurrent malaria. Or, perhaps it was spiritual in nature—temptation or satanic persecution. It may have even been an individual or group who continually ha-

rassed Paul. In any case, it was bothersome to him. But instead of removing the "thorn," God assured Paul that His grace and strength would be sufficient for Paul to bear it. Paul's "thorn in the flesh" destroyed his pride and kept him dependent on divine power. Therefore, although unpleasant, Paul regarded the "thorn" as an aid rather than a handicap.

12:12 The false apostles in Corinth had many external credentials. However, Paul pointed out that they had twisted the

MARRIAGE — GOD'S PROVISION

After the Fall of man, Adam and Eve had continued contact with God, evidenced by the fact that Cain and Abel were taught that they were to bring an offering to God. The Lord did not withdraw His presence, even though He allowed the consequences of the sin of Adam and Eve to follow in due course.

Scripture reveals that God was available to women to aid them in their difficulties. God is never the enemy of His children but their most dependable and faithful friend (John 15:14). He assuaged Eve's sorrow at Abel's death by giving her another son (Gen. 4:25). He encouraged Sarah in the time of her barrenness (Gen. 18:10, 14). He answered Rebekah when she inquired of Him (Gen. 25:22, 23). God spoke to Deborah (Judg. 4:6), instructed Samson's mother (Judg. 13:3–5), gave Ruth direction (the Book of Ruth), comforted Hannah and healed her barrenness (1 Sam. 1:26, 27), and used Esther to save her people (Esth. 8).

When Jesus was to be born, an angel of God visited Mary to describe her role in the Incarnation (Luke 1:28–33). God filled Mary with His presence, both literally (through the life planted in her womb) and spiritually (through the presence of the Holy Spirit).

Jesus, in all of His teaching, pointed to the Father's original plan for Christian marriage in which the wife was to be an equal partner to be loved and protected (Matt. 19:4–6). Paul gave instruction to husbands and wives as to how they are to relate in the home (Eph. 5:22–33). God never gives a command to His children unless He makes provision for them to obey. He has given the power of the Holy Spirit to help believers withstand temptation (2 Pet. 2:9) and the presence of Christ that becomes their spiritual armor in withstanding the enemy's fiery darts (Eph. 6:10–18). He also extends His presence through loving and supportive fellow believers in the church (2 Cor. 13:11). He prepares for protection from abuses through establishing civil authorities (Rom. 13:1).

When both husband and wife know the Lord as personal Savior, the Holy Spirit lives in their hearts. As they submit to His Lordship, they are enabled to follow His directions. The husband will be empowered to love his wife as Christ loved the church (Eph. 5:25), and the wife will be inspired to submit as unto the Lord (Eph. 5:22, 24). The atmosphere of the home will become one of joy (Eph. 5:19–21) as hurtful attitudes are laid aside (Eph. 4:25–31). Forgiveness and kindness will become house rules (v. 32).

Couples are enabled to overcome temptation with faithfulness to each other (see 1 John 5:4, 5). When husband and wife give their expectations to God and focus on the good, then peace will rule in their hearts and in their home (Phil. 4:6–8).

See also notes on Biblical Equality (Eph. 5); Family (Gen. 32; 1 Sam. 3; Ps. 78; 127); Husbands (Job 31; 2 Cor. 6); Marriage (Gen. 2; 2 Sam. 6; Prov. 5; Hos. 2; Amos 3; Heb. 13); Providence (Eccl. 7); Wives (Prov. 31)

---

among you with all perseverance, in signs and wonders and mighty deeds. [13]For what is it in which you were inferior to other churches, except that I myself was not burdensome to you? Forgive me this wrong!

Love for the Church

[14]Now *for* the third time I am ready to come to you. And I will not be burdensome to you; for I do not seek yours, but you. For the children ought not to lay up for the parents, but the parents for the children. [15]And I will very gladly spend and be spent for your souls; though the more abundantly I love you, the less I am loved.

[16]But be that *as it may,* I did not burden you. Nevertheless, being crafty, I caught you by cunning! [17]Did I take advantage of you by any of those whom I sent to you? [18]I urged Titus, and sent our brother with *him.* Did Titus take advantage of you? Did we not walk in the same spirit? Did *we* not *walk* in the same steps?

[19]Again, do you think[a] that we excuse ourselves to you? We speak before God in Christ. But *we do* all things, beloved, for your edification. [20]For I fear lest, when I come, I shall not find you such as I wish, and *that* I shall be found by you such as you

12:19 [a]NU-Text reads *You have been thinking for a long time. . . .*

---

truth of the gospel and were lacking in godly character. In contrast, Paul's character and message were above reproach. According to Paul, a genuine apostle preaches the gospel of Christ, shows the character of Christ, and ministers in the power of Christ.

12:15 Paul had determined not to accept financial support from the Corinthians while working among them. He explained that it was not their property but their hearts that he was eager to win. Furthermore, they were his spiritual chil-

dren (1 Cor. 4:15). Just as earthly parents provide for their offspring, so Paul was more than glad to spend his own resources and to be "spent" personally on their behalf. To be "spent" means to be consumed, used up, or spent entirely. Despite the Corinthians' rejection of him, there was no limit to Paul's love for them.

12:20 Paul was pondering his impending visit to Corinth. He was concerned that the Corinthians deal with the contents of his letter and repent before he arrived. He explained that his

do not wish; lest *there be* contentions, jealousies, outbursts of wrath, selfish ambitions, backbitings, whisperings, conceits, tumults; [21]lest, when I come again, my God will humble me among you, and I shall mourn for many who have sinned before and have not repented of the uncleanness, fornication, and lewdness which they have practiced.

Coming with Authority

13 This *will be* the third *time* I am coming to you. *"By the mouth of two or three witnesses every word shall be established."*[a] [2]I have told you before, and foretell as if I were present the second time, and now being absent I write[a] to those who have sinned before, and to all the rest, that if I come again I will not spare— [3]since you seek a proof of Christ speaking in me, who is not weak toward you, but mighty in you. [4]For though He was crucified in weakness, yet He lives by the power of God. For we also are weak in Him, but we shall live with Him by the power of God toward you.

[5]Examine yourselves *as to* whether you are in the faith. Test yourselves. Do you not know yourselves, that Jesus Christ is in you?— unless indeed you are disqualified. [6]But I trust that you will know that we are not disqualified.

Paul Prefers Gentleness

[7]Now I[a] pray to God that you do no evil, not that we should appear approved, but that you should do what is honorable, though we may seem disqualified. [8]For we can do nothing against the truth, but for the truth. [9]For we are glad when we are weak and you are strong. And this also we pray, that you may be made complete. [10]Therefore I write these things being absent, lest being present I should use sharpness, according to the authority which the Lord has given me for edification and not for destruction.

Greetings and Benediction

[11]Finally, brethren, farewell. Become complete. Be of good comfort, be of one mind, live in peace; and the God of love and peace will be with you.

[12]Greet one another with a holy kiss.

[13]All the saints greet you.

[14]The grace of the Lord Jesus Christ, and the love of God, and the communion of the Holy Spirit *be* with you all. Amen.

13:1 [a]Deuteronomy 19:15 **13:2** [a]NU-Text omits *I write.* **13:7** [a]NU-Text reads *we.*

boasting was not for the purpose of outdoing his opponents but for the purpose of purifying and building up the church (vv. 1–18). Paul's awareness of their sins caused him to fear lest he not find the Corinthians as he wished (repentant) and lest they find him as they did not wish (forceful and disciplinary).

13:1 Paul wrote 2 Corinthians in anticipation of his third visit. In this, more than any other letter, the apostle Paul poured out his heart. Paul deeply loved the Corinthians and endured many affronts and indignities for their sake. But he dared not endure the charge against the genuineness of his apostleship, for such was no less than a challenge to the authority of Christ. Paul pleaded with the Corinthians to repent so that he would not need to discipline them. He much preferred for them to be strong and himself to be regarded as weak (2 Cor.

13:9). Judgment would be secured "by the mouth of two or three witnesses" (Deut. 19:15). This process was laid down in Mosaic Law and was approved by Christ as applicable to settling disputes within the church (Matt. 18:16).

13:11 Paul urged the Corinthians to become complete (Gk. *katartisis*, vv. 9, 11). The related verb (Gk. *katartizō*) is used to describe the disciples' mending of their nets (Matt. 4:21). Paul wanted the Corinthians to repair the problems in their midst in order that they, as a body, might be whole. A list of eight sins are characteristic of a divided church, followed by sins of immorality (2 Cor. 12:20, 21), which had earlier caused Paul to write 1 Corinthians. Paul was glad for the repentance that had already taken place (2 Cor. 7:9) but was keenly aware that the Corinthians needed more in order to become complete.

Galatians

AUTHOR

Paul, a Jewish apostle of Christ, established many New Testament churches and wrote twelve epistles or letters, including this one, which he autographed (Gal. 1:1; 5:2).

DATE

The exact date for Galatians is uncertain and is dependent on the location of the actual recipients of the letter as being in North or South Galatia. If written to churches founded on Paul's first missionary journey to South Galatia, then the date would be A.D. 48 to 50 (see map, Paul's First Missionary Journey). If written to churches founded on the second missionary journey to North Galatia, then A.D. 55 to 57 would be more accurate (see map, Paul's Second Missionary Journey).

BACKGROUND

SETTING: The influence of Greek and Roman culture was confusing to new converts in young churches. Many members of a legalistic Jewish party (Judaizers) taught that salvation for Gentiles must include Jewish circumcision and adherence to the Mosaic Law.

PURPOSE: Paul presented a strong defense of his apostolic mission, emphasizing justification by faith alone, and setting forth his instructions for Christian living.

AUDIENCE: The churches in the region of Galatia are the initial recipients of this letter, but its message is also for churches in every generation.

LITERARY CHARACTERISTICS: This Pauline epistle follows the typical format of a first-century, Graeco-Roman letter. It is in the form of personal correspondence.

THEMES

Within the epistle are found these themes:
- Justification is by faith, not by keeping the Law;
- Christian freedom, which is freedom *from* the Law and freedom *for* service to God, is declared; and
- Guidelines for Christian living are given.

OUTLINE

Introduction (1:1–24)
    The greeting (1:1–5)
    The message (1:6–9)
    The testimony (1:10–17)
    The followers (1:18–24)
  I. The Presentation of the Gospel (2:1–21)
    A. A defense of the gospel (2:1–10)

    B. The rejection of justification by works (2:11–21)
  II. The Reconciliation of Law and Grace (3:1–29)
    A. The gift of grace (3:1–9)
    B. The curse of the Law (3:10–14)
    C. The promises of God (3:15–18)

Greeting

1 Paul, an apostle (not from men nor through man, but through Jesus Christ and God the Father who raised Him from the dead), [2]and all the brethren who are with me,

To the churches of Galatia:

[3]Grace to you and peace from God the Father and our Lord Jesus Christ, [4]who gave Himself for our sins, that He might deliver us from this present evil age, according to the will of our God and Father, [5]to whom *be* glory forever and ever. Amen.

Only One Gospel

[6]I marvel that you are turning away so soon from Him who called you in the grace of Christ, to a different gospel, [7]which is not another; but there are some who trouble you and want to pervert the gospel of Christ. [8]But even if we, or an angel from heaven, preach any other gospel to you than what we have preached to you, let him be accursed. [9]As we have said before, so now I say again, if anyone preaches any other gospel to you than what you have received, let him be accursed.

[10]For do I now persuade men, or God? Or do I seek to please men? For if I still pleased men, I would not be a bondservant of Christ.

Call to Apostleship

[11]But I make known to you, brethren, that the gospel which was preached by me is not according to man. [12]For I neither received it from man, nor was I taught *it,* but *it came* through the revelation of Jesus Christ.

[13]For you have heard of my former conduct in Judaism, how I persecuted the church of God beyond measure and *tried to* destroy it. [14]And I advanced in Judaism beyond many of my contemporaries in my own nation, being more exceedingly zealous for the traditions of my fathers.

[15]But when it pleased God, who separated me from my mother's womb and called *me* through His grace, [16]to reveal His Son in me, that I might preach Him among the Gentiles, I did not immediately confer with flesh and blood, [17]nor did I go up to Jerusalem to those *who were* apostles before me; but I went to Arabia, and returned again to Damascus.

Contacts at Jerusalem

[18]Then after three years I went up to Jerusalem to see Peter,[a] and remained with him fifteen days. [19]But I saw none of the other apostles except James, the Lord's brother. [20](Now *concerning* the things which I write to you, indeed, before God, I do not lie.)

1:18 [a]NU-Text reads *Cephas.*

1:3 Paul's introductory greeting is a prayer for "grace" (Gk. *charis*), meaning "unmerited favor," and "peace" (Gk. *eirēnē*), a sense of well-being resulting from a personal relationship with God unaffected by the circumstances of life. Paul wanted his fellow believers in Galatia to experience God's presence in their daily lives.

1:4 The atonement of Christ triumphs over Satan's powers and frees the Christian from the penalty of sin, which is death (Rom. 6:23). Ultimate deliverance for the believer comes with physical death or with the return of Christ Jesus.

1:6–10 Paul was disappointed that many new converts were following false teachers who taught a "different" (Gk. *heteros*) gospel, meaning "another of a different kind." The Judaizers, who were a legalistic Jewish party within the early church, tried to combine Christ's message of salvation with the context of the Mosaic Law (Deut. 4:2). Immature Christians believed their distorted teachings, which demanded more than justification by faith alone. False teachings continue to be very persuasive. Paul warned the Galatians that those who preach the gospel must preach "another" (Gk. *allos*) gospel, meaning "another of the same kind," the true gospel that comes from God, lest they be "accursed" (Gk. *anathema*, lit. "set aside for destruction").

1:14–17 Paul firmly answered the accusing question of the Judaizers: Whose gospel do you preach? His personal testimony explained the divine source of his message (vv. 15, 16) and confirmed his pride in his Jewish heritage (v. 14). God's hand guided Paul from birth through life and into ministry. Paul's reference to his separation from his "mother's womb" suggests his familiarity with Jeremiah 1:5.

Perspective by Kimberly Daniels

WALKING IN THE LIGHT OF THE WORD (Drawn from *Clean House, Strong House*)

The Word of God challenges us to walk in the "light." Jesus said, *Walk while you have the light, lest darkness overtake you; he who walks in darkness does not know where he is going. While you have the light, believe in the light, that you may become sons of light (John 12:35–36).* The Bible says of God's Word: *Your word is a lamp to my feet and a light to my path (Ps. 119:105).* To walk in the light means that we make a conscious decision *not* to walk in darkness. We make decisions with our will that we *will* develop spiritual eyes to see, and then walk in light.

There are three Greek words that address the concept of darkness:

- *Skoteinos*—opaque and full of darkness; to be a blockhead that cannot see the truth. We find this word in Luke 11:34, which tells us that when the eye is evil, the body is full of darkness.
- *Skotos*—a shady, obscure darkness (producing swindlers, liars, and deceivers). This word is in Luke 11:35, which says that we, as believers, must be careful that the light in us be not darkness.
- *Skotia*—obscure, not clear, shady, lukewarm, dim, insipid, unable to distinguish. This word is in John 1:5, which tells us that sometimes even when the light shines in the darkness, the darkness still does not comprehend it.

These words for darkness paint a picture of what we must NOT do if we are to walk in light! These are the manifestations of a person who is in darkness:

- Operating in shady or obscure ways in ministry, even in dealing with people on an everyday basis (Luke 11:35)
- Walking in a spirit of lukewarmness. The lukewarm church was the only one that God did not have a good thing to say about when He addressed the seven churches in the Book of Revelation (Rev. 3:16).
- Exhibiting or showing stubbornness in doctrine or an ungodly drive to be *religiously right* coupled with an "unteachable spirit." This promotes darkness and hinders new truths. It leads to a shipwreck of faith and a warfare that is not good (1 Tim. 1:19–20; 2 Tim. 2:17–18).
- Being a breeding ground for carnality with no spiritual discipline in the areas of what is holy and what is common (Lev. 10:10).

The Word of God will challenge you again and again to give up darkness! It will challenge you to be open, honest, straightforward . . . to be "hot" in your faith . . . to be teachable . . . to give up pride and self-righteousness . . . and to become pure, holy, and separate from the world.

The world must be able to distinguish the difference between us and all others who claim to come in the name of God. We must allow the Word of God to change us and guide us, and truly to *enlighten* us.

---

²¹Afterward I went into the regions of Syria and Cilicia. ²²And I was unknown by face to the churches of Judea which *were* in Christ. ²³But they were hearing only, "He who formerly persecuted us now preaches the faith which he once *tried to* destroy." ²⁴And they glorified God in me.

Defending the Gospel

2 Then after fourteen years I went up again to Jerusalem with Barnabas, and also took Titus with *me.* ²And I went up by revelation, and communicated to them that gospel which I preach among the Gentiles, but privately to those who were of reputation, lest by any means I might run, or had run, in vain. ³Yet not even Titus who *was* with me, being a Greek, was compelled to be circumcised.

⁴And *this occurred* because of false brethren secretly brought in (who came in by stealth to spy out our liberty which we have in Christ Jesus, that they might bring us into bondage), ⁵to whom we did not yield submission even for an hour, that the truth of the gospel might continue with you.

⁶But from those who seemed to be something—whatever they were, it makes no difference to me; God shows personal favoritism to no man—for those who seemed *to be something* added nothing to me. ⁷But on the contrary, when they saw that the gospel for the uncircumcised had been committed to me, as *the gospel* for the circumcised *was* to Peter ⁸(for He who worked effectively in Peter for the apostleship to the circumcised also worked effectively in me toward the

---

1:23, 24 Many observers marveled at the change in Paul's life (compare Acts 8:3 with 9:20, 21). Saul, who had persecuted Christians, became Paul who preached the gospel message. Though his actions did not save him, the changes in Paul's lifestyle brought glory to God. The power of God can transform any sinner into a new creation (2 Cor. 5:17).

2:6 Christian leaders who are highly respected may disappoint us. God does not show favoritism based on position or performance (Rom. 2:11). Leaders are to be respected, but ultimate allegiance must be to Christ. It is possible to respect *office* without reverencing *person.*

LAW AND GRACE

THE FUNCTION		THE EFFECT	
OF LAW	OF GRACE	OF LAW	OF GRACE
The Law is based on works (Gal. 3:10).	Grace is based on faith (Gal. 3:11, 12).	The Law puts us under a curse (Gal. 3:10).	Grace justifies us by faith (Gal. 3:3, 24).
The Law guards us (Gal. 3:23; 4:2).	Grace centers us in Christ (Gal. 3:24).	The Law keeps us for faith (Gal. 3:23).	Grace lives in us (Gal. 2:20).
The Law tutors us (Gal. 3:24).	Grace certifies our freedom (Gal. 4:30, 31).	The Law shows us the way to Christ (Gal. 3:24).	Grace adopts us as heirs (Gal. 4:7).

Gentiles), [9]and when James, Cephas, and John, who seemed to be pillars, perceived the grace that had been given to me, they gave me and Barnabas the right hand of fellowship, that we *should* go to the Gentiles and they to the circumcised. [10]*They desired* only that we should remember the poor, the very thing which I also was eager to do.

No Return to the Law

[11]Now when Peter[a] had come to Antioch, I withstood him to his face, because he was to be blamed; [12]for before certain men came from James, he would eat with the Gentiles; but when they came, he withdrew and separated himself, fearing those who were of the circumcision. [13]And the rest of the Jews also played the hypocrite with him, so that even Barnabas was carried away with their hypocrisy.

[14]But when I saw that they were not straightforward about the truth of the gospel, I said to Peter before *them* all, "If you, being a Jew, live in the manner of Gentiles and not as the Jews, why do you[a] compel Gentiles to live as Jews?[b] [15]We *who are* Jews by nature, and not sinners of the Gentiles, [16]knowing that a man is not justified by the works

of the law but by faith in Jesus Christ, even we have believed in Christ Jesus, that we might be justified by faith in Christ and not by the works of the law; for by the works of the law no flesh shall be justified.

[17]"But if, while we seek to be justified by Christ, we ourselves also are found sinners, *is* Christ therefore a minister of sin? Certainly not! [18]For if I build again those things which I destroyed, I make myself a transgressor. [19]For I through the law died to the law that I might live to God. [20]I have been crucified with Christ; it is no longer I who live, but Christ lives in me; and the *life* which I now live in the flesh I live by faith in the Son of God, who loved me and gave Himself for me. [21]I do not set aside the grace of God; for if righteousness *comes* through the law, then Christ died in vain."

Justification by Faith

3 O foolish Galatians! Who has bewitched you that you should not obey the truth,[a] before

2:11 [a]NU-Text reads *Cephas*. 2:14 [a]NU-Text reads *how can you.* [b]Some interpreters stop the quotation here. 3:1 [a]NU-Text omits *that you should not obey the truth.* [b]NU-Text omits *among you.*

2:9 James, Cephas (or Peter), and John preached the gospel to the Jews, while Paul and Barnabas worked among the Gentiles. Instead of criticizing others for their differences, the challenge to believers is to work together to spread the gospel to all people.

2:15, 16 Paul did not reject the Law. Instead, he said, the Law was "holy and just and good" (Rom. 7:12). The Law protects from sin, convicts of sin, and brings to Christ. While the Law does not justify, it does guide in daily Christian living (Rom. 3:20). Paul stated generally that an individual is not justified by the Law but by faith in Jesus; he stated personally that one is justified through faith in Jesus; he stated universally that no one will ever be justified by works. Justification is an act of God through Christ, freely making righteous anyone who believes by faith (see chart, Theological Terms).

2:20, 21 Paul described the justified believer as being "crucified with Christ" (v. 20), as spiritually alive (Rom. 7:4, 6), as possessing life through Christ within (Gal. 2:20; see John 14:20; Col. 1:27), as living a life of faith (Gal. 2:20; Rom. 1:17); and as knowing who made that life possible. Then Paul noted that justification by works ("the law") is diametrically opposite to justification by grace through faith. He also noted that faith plus works is ultimately works (Gal. 4:19–31). If salvation can be earned, then God is merely giving what is earned or deserved, which declares grace null and void and in which case, Christ would have died in vain. While godly living is still essential to the spread of the gospel, obedience to the Law is the fruit of salvation and not a prerequisite for salvation. No one was ever saved by keeping the Law. We do good works not in order to be saved but because we have been saved. Paul, like all believers, had to die to self (Rom. 7:6).

CHRISTOLOGY *THE PERSON OF CHRIST*

Because God's plan of salvation depends on His being the God-Man, the study of Christ's nature and person (known as Christology) is central to Christianity. If a Christological position is in error, other doctrines will also suffer.

As God, Christ is Creator (Col. 1:15), Head of the church (Col. 1:18), highest authority (Matt. 28:18), upholder of all things (Heb. 1:3), and King of kings (Rev. 17:14). As Man, He is the Son of a woman (Gal. 4:4), Mediator (1 Tim. 2:5), bondservant (Phil. 2:7), and High Priest (Heb. 7:11–22).

Three important standards are part of an evangelical Christology:

- The reality of His two natures: He is both God and man;
- The integrity of His two natures: they are not contradictory; and
- The unmingled union of these two natures in one. Each nature is independent of the other.

Because the Incarnation is a mystery (1 Tim. 3:16), much controversy was generated in the early church as to how God and man could be one. The Ebionites, Jews who held to a belief in one God, claimed that Christ was not divine, believing that God chose the man Jesus to be Messiah because Jesus had fulfilled the Mosaic law. Arianism, a fourth-century heresy, declared that Christ was a creature, less than God but more than man. The Gnostics denied that Christ was fully human. All of these heresies were refuted by the Council of Chalcedon in A.D. 451, which declared that Jesus is truly God with undiminished deity and truly man with full humanity (John 1:14; Acts 17:3; Heb. 2:14). He is Prophet (John 6:14; 7:40), Priest (Heb. 3:1; 4:14), and King (Ps. 2:6; Mic. 5:2).

See also John 1:4, note; chart on The Definitive Christological Passages; note on Heresies (1 Cor. 1)

whose eyes Jesus Christ was clearly portrayed among you[b] as crucified? [2]This only I want to learn from you: Did you receive the Spirit by the works of the law, or by the hearing of faith? [3]Are you so foolish? Having begun in the Spirit, are you now being made perfect by the flesh? [4]Have you suffered so many things in vain—if indeed *it was* in vain?

[5]Therefore He who supplies the Spirit to you and works miracles among you, *does He do it* by the works of the law, or by the hearing of faith?— [6]just as Abraham *"believed God, and it was accounted to him for righteousness."*[a] [7]Therefore know that *only* those who are of faith are sons of Abraham. [8]And the Scripture, foreseeing that God would justify the Gentiles by faith, preached the gospel to Abraham beforehand, saying, *"In you all the nations shall be blessed."*[a] [9]So then those who *are* of faith are blessed with believing Abraham.

The Law Brings a Curse

[10]For as many as are of the works of the law are under the curse; for it is written, *"Cursed is everyone who does not continue in all things which are written in the book of the law, to do them."*[a] [11]But that no one is justified by the law in the sight of God *is* evident,

for *"the just shall live by faith."*[a] [12]Yet the law is not of faith, but *"the man who does them shall live by them."*[a]

[13]Christ has redeemed us from the curse of the law, having become a curse for us (for it is written, *"Cursed is everyone who hangs on a tree"*[a]), [14]that the blessing of Abraham might come upon the Gentiles in Christ Jesus, that we might receive the promise of the Spirit through faith.

The Changeless Promise

[15]Brethren, I speak in the manner of men: Though *it is* only a man's covenant, yet *if it is* confirmed, no one annuls or adds to it. [16]Now to Abraham and his Seed were the promises made. He does not say, "And to seeds," as of many, but as of one, *"And to your Seed,"*[a] who is Christ. [17]And this I say, *that* the law, which was four hundred and thirty years later, cannot annul the covenant that was confirmed before by God in Christ,[a] that it should make the promise of no effect. [18]For if the inheritance *is* of the law, *it is* no longer of promise; but God gave *it* to Abraham by promise.

• • • • • • • • • • • • • • • • •

3:6 [a]Genesis 15:6 3:8 [a]Genesis 12:3; 18:18; 22:18; 26:4; 28:14 3:10 [a]Deuteronomy 27:26 3:11 [a]Habakkuk 2:4 3:12 [a]Leviticus 18:5 3:13 [a]Deuteronomy 21:23 3:16 [a]Genesis 12:7; 13:15; 24:7 3:17 [a]NU-Text omits *in Christ.*

3:7–9 Abraham believed by faith and became a son of God. (Gen. 12:1-3). Gentiles, like Abraham, receive salvation through personal faith (see Gen. 15:6).

3:10 All who look only to their own works as commendation to God are truly under a curse. These who trust in works foolishly believe they have the ability within themselves to do whatever God commands. Yet there is no way humanly possible to obey the Law in all ways at all times. The Law cannot

justify or save; it can only condemn (Deut. 27:26). It is not human works but Christ's work that justifies.

3:16 God gave the promise of justification by faith to Abraham and the Law for righteous living to Moses. The Greek word *epangelia* (lit. "an unchangeable promise") is used nine times in chapter 3. The same covenant promises made to Abraham for his justification are made to all who believe by faith in each succeeding generation (see Prov. 13, Inheritance).

HAGAR AND SARAH: A CONTRAST IN WOMEN

HAGAR	SARAH
Mother of Ishmael (Gen. 16:15)	Mother of Isaac (Gen. 21:2, 3)
Bondwoman (Gal. 4:22, 23)	Freewoman (Gal. 4:22, 23)
Covenant of the flesh (Gal. 4:23)	Covenant of promise (Gal. 4:23)
Based on Law given on Mt. Sinai (Gal. 4:24)	Based on New Covenant in Christ (Gal. 4:4–7)
Born according to the flesh (Gal. 4:29)	Born by the Spirit (Gal. 4:29, 30)
Under the Law (Gal. 4:21–23)	Under grace (Gal. 3:13, 14)
Justification by works (Gal. 3:12–14)	Justification by faith alone (Gal. 3:11)
The Jerusalem enslaved to legalism (Gal. 4:25)	The heavenly Jerusalem of the future for all believers (Gal. 4:26)
Slaves in bondage (Gal. 4:24)	Sons in freedom (Gal. 4:26)

See also Sarah (Gen. 11); Hagar (Gen. 16); chart, Law and Grace

Purpose of the Law

[19]What purpose then *does* the law *serve?* It was added because of transgressions, till the Seed should come to whom the promise was made; *and it was* appointed through angels by the hand of a mediator. [20]Now a mediator does not *mediate* for one *only,* but God is one.

[21]*Is* the law then against the promises of God? Certainly not! For if there had been a law given which could have given life, truly righteousness would have been by the law. [22]But the Scripture has confined all under sin, that the promise by faith in Jesus Christ might be given to those who believe. [23]But before faith came, we were kept under guard by the law, kept for the faith which would afterward be revealed. [24]Therefore the law was our tutor *to bring us* to Christ, that we might be justified by faith. [25]But after faith has come, we are no longer under a tutor.

Sons and Heirs

[26]For you are all sons of God through faith in Christ Jesus. [27]For as many of you as were baptized into Christ have put on Christ. [28]There is neither Jew nor Greek, there is neither slave nor free, there is neither male nor female; for you are all one in Christ Jesus. [29]And if you *are* Christ's, then you are Abraham's seed, and heirs according to the promise.

4 Now I say *that* the heir, as long as he is a child, does not differ at all from a slave, though he is master of all, [2]but is under guardians and stewards until the time appointed by the father. [3]Even so we, when we were children, were in bondage under the elements of the world. [4]But when the fullness of the time had come, God sent forth His Son, born[a] of a woman, born under the law, [5]to redeem those

4:4 [a]Or made

3:24 God's Law was never intended to justify sinners. As a "tutor" (Gk. *paidagogos*), the Law was given as a standard to reveal human sinfulness and inadequacy. The role of a teacher is to instruct, protect, and correct. The "tutor" played a unique role in ancient Greek and Roman households. Wealthy parents began with a wet-nurse who cared for newborn babies. Then a nanny-figure appeared to nurture young children. About age six, the children were placed under the care of a household servant or slave (Gk. *paidagogos*) who was in charge of rearing his master's offspring until late adolescence, including education and discipline. Though some were kind and loving, the dominant image seems to be one of

harshness (see ch.3). The Law is still a teacher, though Christ alone is the Savior. The Law defines the righteous requirements of God and exposes all people as guilty of being unable to meet every requirement of the Law perfectly. Those who believe in Him are no longer considered guilty but counted as righteous or justified before God (Rom. 10:4; see chart, Law and Grace).

3:28 In Christ, all are one (John 17:11). There is no distinction of race, rank, or sex at the foot of the Cross. God is impartial. The only ultimate dividing line among people is the condition of the individual soul (see Equality).

HEALING — OVERCOMING ADDICTIONS IN HIS POWER

Simply stopping an addictive behavior is rarely sufficient for true wholeness in the addict's life. The underlying cause—for which the addiction provides protection by covering up painful, shame-filled feelings and unmet needs—must also be healed. Without healing the underlying pain, taking away its mask only increases pain and anxiety and often leads to either the return of that addiction or the substitution of another one.

Healing begins with a recognition that an addiction exists and that the person is unable to overcome that addiction in her own power. With this must come a willingness to allow God to touch and meet the underlying need. As God begins to meet the deeper need, the addict then finds herself able to make the Spirit-empowered choice both to lay down the addictive behavior that has served as pseudo-protection and to follow and obey Jesus as He renews her mind (Luke 9:23–25; Rom. 12:1, 2).

The importance of support and accountability by caring believers cannot be overstated. They are frequently used by God both to mirror the seriousness of the problem to the addict and to provide the consistent encouragement and strength needed to overcome the addiction (Gal. 6:2, 3).

See also Mark 5:2, note; 1 Cor. 6:12; Gal. 5:19–21; Col. 3:8; 2 Tim. 3:2–5; notes on Addictions (2 Pet. 2); Healing (Ps. 13; 133; Eccl. 1; 2 Cor. 5; James 5); Substance Abuse (Prov. 23)

In Christ, there is freedom from bondage. Believers are no longer slaves; they are free–not through their own merit but through God's redeeming grace.

Rhonda H. Kelley

who were under the law, that we might receive the adoption as sons.

6And because you are sons, God has sent forth the Spirit of His Son into your hearts, crying out, "Abba, Father!" 7Therefore you are no longer a slave but a son, and if a son, then an heir of[a] God through Christ.

Fears for the Church

8But then, indeed, when you did not know God, you served those which by nature are not gods. 9But now after you have known God, or rather are known by God, how *is it that* you turn again to the weak and beggarly elements, to which you desire again to be in bondage? 10You observe days and months and seasons and years. 11I am afraid for you, lest I have labored for you in vain.

12Brethren, I urge you to become like me, for I *became* like you. You have not injured me at all. 13You know that because of physical infirmity I preached the gospel to you at the first. 14And my trial which was in my flesh you did not despise or reject, but you received me as an angel of God, *even* as Christ Jesus. 15What[a] then was the blessing you *enjoyed?* For I bear you witness that, if possible, you would have plucked out your own eyes and given them to me. 16Have I therefore become your enemy because I tell you the truth?

17They zealously court you, *but* for no good; yes, they want to exclude you, that you may be zealous for them. 18But it is good to be zealous in a good thing always, and not only when I am present with you. 19My little children, for whom I labor in birth again until Christ is formed in you, 20I would like to be present with you now and to change my tone; for I have doubts about you.

••••••••••••••••••

4:7 [a]NU-Text reads *through God* and omits *through Christ.* 4:15 [a]NU-Text reads *Where.*

4:5–7 Paul reminded his readers that the Christian was once under Law but is now under grace. In redemption, individuals become children of God, adopted into His family—heirs to His riches on earth and in heaven (Rom. 8:16, 17).

4:8–10 The believers in Galatia were being drawn into the ritualism of the Judaizers. "Days" would refer to the Sabbath as well as to specific feast days. "Months" is a reference to the celebrations such as those addressed with sarcasm by Isaiah (Is. 1:14). "Seasons" indicates the feast celebrations, and "years" is probably a reference to the Jubilee years. Paul placed this ritualistic observance in the same category as pagan festivals when the observance of these events was distorted into legalistic ritual.

4:19, 20 Many new Christians in Galatia had returned to false teachings and lost the joy of their salvation. Deeply troubled, Paul called the Galatian believers his "little children," and he compared his relationship to them as to a mother in labor who longs for her child to be born—an intensely painful, but intimate experience. Paul labored for his "little children" to be born into the fullness of Christ. "Spiritual parents" love those whom they led to Christ as a mother loves her child.

A CHOICE IN LIFESTYLES

THE WORKS OF THE FLESH (GAL. 5:19–21)	THE FRUIT OF THE SPIRIT (GAL. 5:22, 23)
Adultery	Love
Fornication	Joy
Uncleanness	Peace
Lewdness	Longsuffering
Idolatry	Kindness
Sorcery	Goodness
Hatred	Faithfulness
Contentions	Gentleness
Jealousies	Self-control
Outbursts of wrath	
Selfish ambitions	
Dissensions	
Heresies	
Envy	
Murders	
Drunkenness	
Revelries	

Two Covenants

²¹Tell me, you who desire to be under the law, do you not hear the law? ²²For it is written that Abraham had two sons: the one by a bondwoman, the other by a freewoman. ²³But he *who was* of the bondwoman was born according to the flesh, and he of the freewoman through promise, ²⁴which things are symbolic. For these are theᵃ two covenants: the one from Mount Sinai which gives birth to bondage, which is Hagar— ²⁵for this Hagar is Mount Sinai in Arabia, and corresponds to Jerusalem which now is, and is in bondage with her children— ²⁶but the Jerusalem above is free, which is the mother of us all. ²⁷For it is written:

"Rejoice, O barren,
You who do not bear!
Break forth and shout,
You who are not in labor!

For the desolate has many more children
Than she who has a husband."ᵃ

²⁸Now we, brethren, as Isaac *was*, are children of promise. ²⁹But, as he who was born according to the flesh then persecuted him *who was born* according to the Spirit, even so *it is* now. ³⁰Nevertheless what does the Scripture say? *"Cast out the bondwoman and her son, for the son of the bondwoman shall not be heir with the son of the freewoman."*ᵃ ³¹So then, brethren, we are not children of the bondwoman but of the free.

Christian Liberty

5 Stand fast therefore in the liberty by which Christ has made us free,ᵃ and do not be entan-

---

4:24 ᵃNU-Text and M-Text omit *the*. 4:27 ᵃIsaiah 54:1 4:30 ᵃGenesis 21:10 5:1 ᵃNU-Text reads *For freedom Christ has made us free; stand fast therefore.*

4:27 Jerusalem is likened to a childless widow sitting in the gates in her sackcloth and ashes (Is. 54:1). She was bereft of her husband, who had been taken into captivity, and she had no children to care for her. Yet God admonished her to be joyful and happy. Whatever the precise interpretation, the underlying admonition of moving from a barren condition to a fruitful one and from sorrow to joy would come only through this intervention of *Yahweh* Himself (Is. 54:5). God's grace is the foundation for justification and faith as well as eternal hope.

4:28, 29 Abraham had two sons—Ishmael of the flesh by Hagar and Isaac of the Spirit by Sarah. Ishmael represents the

covenant of bondage given to Moses through the Law; Isaac, the covenant of promise given to Abraham through Christ. Christians are children of the covenant promise. They can expect an inheritance of freedom from bondage. Christians must expect persecution, receive their inheritance, and experience God's grace. The two mothers represent two doctrines of salvation. Hagar represents works or human effort; Sarah, grace or divine initiation (see chart, Hagar and Sarah: A Contrast in Women). Both covenants continue to be upheld.

5:1, 2 Again Paul challenged his friends in Galatia to stand firm in their faith and not to return to the bondage of the Law. Christ died to set free, while the Law continues to en-

FRUIT OF THE SPIRIT — A REFLECTION OF THE CHARACTER OF GOD

The "fruit" of the Holy Spirit refers to the godly attributes of those who "walk in the Spirit" (Gal. 5:16). The true manifestation of the Holy Spirit at work in a believer's life is that the believer becomes increasingly more like Christ in character and actions. The fruit of the Spirit should characterize the life of every believer, not just the spiritually mature.

The fruit of the Holy Spirit affects the believer's relationship with God, others, and self. As Christians grow in their relationship with the Lord, they develop unselfish love, true joy, and lasting peace. As they build relationships with others, they are challenged to reflect His patience, kindness, and goodness. As they mature spiritually, Christians discover an inner strength which results in faithfulness, gentleness, and self-control.

While the fruit of the Holy Spirit is not necessary for salvation, these godly virtues are evidence of salvation and the genuine work of the Holy Spirit (Matt. 7:17). The life of Christ is manifested by the fruit of the Spirit; the ministry of Christ is accomplished by the gifts of the Spirit. Followers of Christ not only receive the blessings of God but also reflect His character to all whom they encounter.

See also Lam. 3:22, note; Dan. 2:23, note; Eph. 5:8–10; Heb. 12:11; James 3:18; notes on Attributes of God (Ex. 33; Deut. 4; 32; 2 Chr. 19; Job 23; 42; Ps. 25; 90; 102; 119; Is. 6; 65; Jer. 23; Rom. 2; Eph. 1; 1 John 5); Fruit of the Spirit (Ps. 86; Rom. 5; 15; 1 Cor. 10; 13; Eph. 4; Col. 3; 2 Thess. 1; Rev. 2); Spiritual Discipline (2 Pet. 3); Spiritual Gifts (Rom. 12)

gled again with a yoke of bondage. ²Indeed I, Paul, say to you that if you become circumcised, Christ will profit you nothing. ³And I testify again to every man who becomes circumcised that he is a debtor to keep the whole law. ⁴You have become estranged from Christ, you who *attempt to* be justified by law; you have fallen from grace. ⁵For we through the Spirit eagerly wait for the hope of righteousness by faith. ⁶For in Christ Jesus neither circumcision nor uncircumcision avails anything, but faith working through love.

Love Fulfills the Law

⁷You ran well. Who hindered you from obeying the truth? ⁸This persuasion does not *come* from Him who calls you. ⁹A little leaven leavens the whole lump. ¹⁰I have confidence in you, in the Lord, that you will have no other mind; but he who troubles you shall bear his judgment, whoever he is.

¹¹And I, brethren, if I still preach circumcision, why do I still suffer persecution? Then the offense of the cross has ceased. ¹²I could wish that those who trouble you would even cut themselves off!

¹³For you, brethren, have been called to liberty; only do not *use* liberty as an opportunity for the flesh, but through love serve one another. ¹⁴For all the law is fulfilled in one word, *even* in this: "*You shall love your neighbor as yourself.*"ᵃ ¹⁵But if you bite and devour one another, beware lest you be consumed by one another!

Walking in the Spirit

¹⁶I say then: Walk in the Spirit, and you shall not fulfill the lust of the flesh. ¹⁷For the flesh lusts against the Spirit, and the Spirit against the flesh; and these are contrary to one another, so that you do not do the things that you wish. ¹⁸But if you are led by the Spirit, you are not under the law.

¹⁹Now the works of the flesh are evident, which are: adultery,ᵃ fornication, uncleanness, lewdness, ²⁰idolatry, sorcery, hatred, contentions, jealousies, outbursts of wrath, selfish ambitions, dissensions, heresies, ²¹envy, murders,ᵃ drunkenness, revelries, and the like; of which I tell you beforehand, just as I also told *you* in time past, that those who practice such things will not inherit the kingdom of God.

²²But the fruit of the Spirit is love, joy, peace, longsuffering, kindness, goodness, faithfulness, ²³gentleness, self-control. Against such there is no law. ²⁴And those *who are* Christ's have crucified the

....
5:14 ᵃLeviticus 19:18   **5:19** ᵃNU-Text omits *adultery*.   **5:21** ᵃNU-Text omits *murders*.

---

slave (2 Cor. 3:17). The Law is a heavy yoke—a daily burden for those in bondage. However, for the believer, Christ's "yoke is easy" and His "burden is light" (Matt. 11:30). There is great freedom in Christ!

5:13 Justification by faith does not require works, but it does result in godly living. Paul also believed that "faith without works is dead" (James 2:20). However, he saw examples of extremism in the Galatian Christians. On the one hand, some Galatians were too legalistic. On the other hand, some were totally lawless. The freedom in Christ is freedom to choose what is right. Paul states that the right thing to do is to love and serve one another (1 Cor. 9:19).

While Christians are not spared suffering, they are promised deliverance from sin and the inner resources through the indwelling Holy Spirit to live a righteous life in Christ.

Rhonda H. Kelley

flesh with its passions and desires. [25]If we live in the Spirit, let us also walk in the Spirit. [26]Let us not become conceited, provoking one another, envying one another.

Bear and Share the Burdens

[6]Brethren, if a man is overtaken in any trespass, you who *are* spiritual restore such a one in a spirit of gentleness, considering yourself lest you also be tempted. [2]Bear one another's burdens, and so fulfill the law of Christ. [3]For if anyone thinks himself to be something, when he is nothing, he deceives himself. [4]But let each one examine his own work, and then he will have rejoicing in himself alone, and not in another. [5]For each one shall bear his own load.

Be Generous and Do Good

[6]Let him who is taught the word share in all good things with him who teaches.

[7]Do not be deceived, God is not mocked; for whatever a man sows, that he will also reap. [8]For he who sows to his flesh will of the flesh reap corruption, but he who sows to the Spirit will of the Spirit reap everlasting life. [9]And let us not grow weary while doing good, for in due season we shall reap if we do not lose heart. [10]Therefore, as we have opportunity, let us do good to all, especially to those who are of the household of faith.

Glory Only in the Cross

[11]See with what large letters I have written to you with my own hand! [12]As many as desire to make a good showing in the flesh, these *would* compel you to be circumcised, only that they may not suffer persecution for the cross of Christ. [13]For not even those who are circumcised keep the law, but they desire to have you circumcised that they may boast in your flesh. [14]But God forbid that I should boast except in the cross of our Lord Jesus Christ, by whom[a] the world has been crucified to me, and I to the world. [15]For in Christ Jesus neither circumcision nor uncircumcision avails anything, but a new creation.

Blessing and a Plea

[16]And as many as walk according to this rule, peace and mercy *be* upon them, and upon the Israel of God.

[17]From now on let no one trouble me, for I bear in my body the marks of the Lord Jesus.

[18]Brethren, the grace of our Lord Jesus Christ *be* with your spirit. Amen.

6:14 [a]Or *by which* (the cross)

5:25 The Christian faith is not a list of "don'ts" but of "dos." When believers "walk in the Spirit," they avoid the deeds of the flesh and "do" the things of the Spirit (Rom. 8:4, 5). The fruit of the Spirit refers to the virtues of godly living that result naturally from a walk in the Spirit. The focus is not to keep the letter of the Law but to follow in the love of Jesus Christ. The fruit of the Spirit is evident in all believers who live out their faith (see Ps. 86; Rom. 5; 15; 1 Cor. 9; 13; Gal. 5; Eph. 4; Col. 3; 2 Thess. 1; Rev. 2, Fruit of the Spirit; chart, A Choice of Lifestyles).

6:2 A responsibility of salvation is personal accountability. Another Christian responsibility is helping others when they become burdened down by sin or problems (Acts 20:35).

6:8 Paul used an example of farming to explain the results of sin and righteousness. Sowing to the flesh leads to a life of sin and corruption. Sowing to the Spirit leads to a life of righteousness and holiness. The believer who sows to her own flesh does not lose the Spirit, but she loses the fruit of the Spirit (Gal. 5:22, 23). However, the believer who sows to the Spirit experiences a harvest of righteousness and peace.

6:9, 10 Busy Christians often grow tired, but they should not become weary. "Tired" describes a physical condition, while "weary" describes a spiritual attitude (see Is. 40, Fatigue). There is much work to be done. Paul encouraged the Christians to persevere. They were not to relax (Gk. *ekluō*) their standards or give up doing the good they had learned. This mandate is not an invitation to become a workaholic but rather a pep talk to continue walking by faith without becoming discouraged or losing heart (see Luke 18:1; 2 Cor. 4:1; 2 Thess. 3:13). Trust God for a harvest of eternal blessings and the strength to do His will.

6:14 God's gift of grace through faith is a guarantee that one cannot depend on works for salvation. If good works were the way to be justified, we would boast of personal righteousness as did the Judaizers. However, Christ removed that tendency when He died on the Cross to provide our justification. Now believers must boast about Christ who died to justify all those who believe in Him.

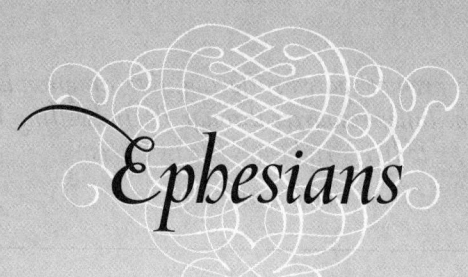

Ephesians

AUTHOR

Although Paul's authorship has been questioned by critical scholars in recent years, several factors support the position that the apostle wrote the Book of Ephesians.

- Paul specifically states that he is the author (Eph. 1:1; 3:1).
- The early church fathers were unanimous in ascribing the letter to Paul, some (Clement of Rome and Ignatius) quoting almost verbatim from it.
- The theology expressed in Ephesians is entirely consistent with that of other unquestioned Pauline letters.
- The letter's similarity in content with Colossians (more than 75 of its 155 verses) probably indicates that these letters were penned during the same imprisonment.
- Paul's wider range of style and vocabulary in Ephesians is compatible with his high level of education and the particular subject matter discussed in the letter.

DATE

The letter was written during Paul's first Roman imprisonment (Acts 28:16–31), about A.D. 60–63. Since no hint of his release from prison is given in the letter, it was probably written nearer the beginning of the imprisonment, perhaps about A.D. 60.

BACKGROUND

SETTING: Ephesus was the most important commercial center in Asia Minor (present-day Turkey). Regional trade routes intersected there, and the city possessed a fine natural harbor. Its magnificent temple to the Greek goddess Artemis (Diana to the Romans) was known throughout the Hellenistic world as a center for pagan worship and the magical arts (Acts 19:35; see chart, Graeco-Roman Goddesses).

Paul visited Ephesus at the end of his second missionary journey and left behind Priscilla and Aquila to minister (Acts 18:18–21; see map, Paul's Second Missionary Journey). On his third journey, he spent about three years there, and Ephesus became a center for evangelistic outreach to the rest of the province (Acts 19:8, 10). Paul's Spirit-empowered ministry was marked by mighty miracles, and great numbers were won to Christ (Acts 19:18–20). At one point, a riot was instigated by pagan craftsmen, whose idol-making business had been hurt by so many people turning to Christ and renouncing their pagan ways (Acts 19:21–41).

PURPOSE: Ephesians, unlike other Pauline Epistles, was not written to handle specific problems in the church or to correct particular errors of false teaching. Instead, Paul first proclaimed the spiritual resources believers have received so that they might fulfill God's overall purpose for the church: to bring praise and glory to Himself (Eph. 1). Next, he explained how God had reconciled believers both to Himself and to one another as members of Christ's body, the church (Eph. 2; 3). He then exhorted them to draw on these resources in order to live in loving, maturing unity with one another in the church fellowship, in the family, and in the arena of spiritual battle (Eph. 4–6).

AUDIENCE: This letter was written primarily to Gentile believers living in Asia Minor (Eph. 2:11–13). Since some ancient manuscripts omit the phrase "in Ephesus" (Eph. 1:1), scholars have suggested that this was a circular letter meant to be read to several churches in the area. In this case, the appropriate church's name would have been inserted in the opening line. In view of the strategic importance of the Ephesian church, it seems most likely that the letter was originally addressed to that church; then copies were made to be circulated. Similarly, Paul intended his letters to the churches in Colosse and Laodicea to be read to one another (Col. 4:16). The letter to the Laodiceans may be Ephesians, or it may be a lost epistle that has not been preserved.

THEMES

The apostle Paul presented his most exhaustive case for the authenticity of his apostleship (Eph. 3:1–13). He also expounded upon the unity of Jew and Gentile wrought by the work of Christ on the Cross (Eph. 2:11–18). He developed the glorious theme of the believer's position in Christ and God's purpose for the world as accomplished through the church, using these metaphors: the building (Eph. 2:21), the body (Eph. 4:16), and the bride (Eph. 5:22–33). Paul also presented the believer's corresponding responsibilities in living the Christian life with his clearest statement on the importance of relationships within the family (Eph. 5:21—6:4).

OUTLINE

Introduction: Salutation (1:1, 2)

I. The Provisions for a Unified Walk (1:3—3:21)
  A. The blessedness of God's provision (1:3–14)
    1. The provision of an inheritance for believers (1:3)
    2. A description of the inheritance (1:4–14)
  B. A prayer for the believers' enlightenment (1:15–23)
    1. God's gift of spiritual insight (1:15–18)
    2. An explanation of the rich inheritance (1:19–23)
  C. Salvation by grace (2:1–10)
    1. Death apart from Christ (2:1–3)
    2. Life in Christ (2:4–10)
  D. God's corporate dwelling place (2:11–22)
    1. A possibility because of Christ's blood (2:11–13)
    2. The unity of Jews and Gentiles in Christ (2:14–22)
  E. The revelation of God's mystery (3:1–13)
    1. The mystery of the equality of Jew and Gentile (3:1–7)
    2. The purpose of Paul's ministry (3:8–13)
  F. A prayer for strength (3:14–21)
    1. Spiritual strengthening (3:14–17)
    2. Understanding Christ's love (3:18, 19)
    3. A doxology (3:20, 21)

II. The Practice of a Unified Walk (4:1—6:20)
  A. A unified walk (4:1–16)
    1. Unity because of God's unity (4:1–6)
    2. Unity through exercising spiritual gifts (4:7–16)
  B. A transformed walk (4:17–32)
    1. Renewed minds (4:17–24)
    2. Constructive behavior (4:25–32)
  C. A loving walk (5:1–6)
    1. Positive aspect: loving others (5:1, 2)
    2. Negative aspect: abstaining from evil (5:3–6)
  D. A luminous walk (5:7–14)
    1. Walking in the light (5:7–10)
    2. Exposing unrighteousness (5:11–14)
  E. A Spirit-filled walk (5:15–21)
    1. Redeeming God's opportunities (5:15–17)
    2. Walking in the Spirit (5:18–21)
  F. A walk with redeemed relationships (5:22—6:9)
    1. Wives and husbands (5:22–33)
    2. Children and parents (6:1–4)
    3. Slaves and masters (6:5–9)
  G. A victorious walk (6:10–20)
    1. Standing empowered in God's armor (6:10–13)
    2. A description of God's armor (6:14–17)
    3. Prayer throughout the battle (6:18–20)

Conclusion: Benediction (6:21–24)

ATTRIBUTES OF GOD   HE IS THE ESSENCE OF GRACE

Grace and mercy are fraternal twins. They are initiated by the same Person, spring from the same source, and appear simultaneously; but they are not identical. Mercy does not give us what we do deserve; grace gives us what we do not deserve.

"Grace" (Gk. *charis*) denotes goodwill, kindness, and benefit. It evokes images of a superior granting favors to an undeserving inferior. The Lord's grace includes undeserved favor, unexpected acceptance, and unconditional love.

Jesus is the giver of grace (John 1:14, 17). A sampling of "grace gifts" includes: salvation (Eph. 2:8), adoption (Eph. 1:5), inheritance (Eph. 1:11), heavenly citizenship (Phil. 3:20), holiness (Eph. 1:4), access to God (Eph. 2:18), forgiveness (Eph. 1:7), preparation for service (1 Pet. 2:5–9), the indwelling of the Holy Spirit (Eph. 1:13), the armor of God (Eph. 6:10–18), and much more. No wonder His grace is called "manifold" (1 Pet. 4:10).

Sin is no match for God's grace. Whatever sin's impact may be, His grace is more potent (Rom. 5:20). God is a giving God. He gives out of His love and loves to give—grace is one of His greatest pleasures (Eph. 1:5, 9).

See also Lam. 3:22, note; Luke 24:47, note; Rom. 5:17; 2 Cor. 12:9; Titus 2:11; notes on Access to God (Rom. 10); Attributes of God (Ex. 33; Deut. 4; 32; 2 Chr. 19; Job 23; 42; Ps. 25; 90; 102; 119; Is. 6; 65; Jer. 23; Rom. 2; 1 John 5); Forgiveness (Ps. 51; Luke 17); Promises of God (2 Pet. 1); Salvation (Eph. 2)

Greeting

1 Paul, an apostle of Jesus Christ by the will of God,

To the saints who are in Ephesus, and faithful in Christ Jesus:

[2]Grace to you and peace from God our Father and the Lord Jesus Christ.

Redemption in Christ

[3]Blessed *be* the God and Father of our Lord Jesus Christ, who has blessed us with every spiritual blessing in the heavenly *places* in Christ, [4]just as He chose us in Him before the foundation of the world, that we should be holy and without blame before Him in love, [5]having predestined us to adoption as sons by Jesus Christ to Himself, according to the good pleasure of His will, [6]to the praise of the glory of His grace, by which He made us accepted in the Beloved.

[7]In Him we have redemption through His blood, the forgiveness of sins, according to the riches of His grace [8]which He made to abound toward us in all wisdom and prudence, [9]having made known to us the mystery of His will, according to His good pleasure which He purposed in Himself, [10]that in the dispensation of the fullness of the times He might gather together in one all things in Christ, both[a] which are in heaven and which are on earth—in Him. [11]In Him also we have obtained an inheritance, being predestined according to the purpose of Him who works all things according to the counsel of His will, [12]that we who first trusted in Christ should be to the praise of His glory.

[13]In Him you also *trusted,* after you heard the word of truth, the gospel of your salvation; in whom also, having believed, you were sealed with the Holy Spirit of promise, [14]who[a] is the guarantee of our inheritance until the redemption of the purchased possession, to the praise of His glory.

1:10 [a]NU-Text and M-Text omit *both.*   1:14 [a]NU-Text reads *which.*

1:1 Paul had not appointed himself to the apostolic ministry, nor had the early church. Rather, he had been chosen and commissioned by God Himself (Acts 9:3–6, 10–16; see Gal. 1:1). Thus he was not merely offering private opinions, as a gifted but fallible human teacher might do; rather, he was God's apostle, writing under the inspiration of the Holy Spirit, and his words carried God's authority.

1:4–6 In eternity past, when only God existed, He chose those who would believe in Christ (v. 11; Rom. 8:30; 2 Thess. 2:13). God's past choice has present consequences: Those He chose have been set apart to walk in holiness of life (Rom. 8:29; Eph. 2:10). A further consequence of the believers' election is that they were "predestined" or "marked out beforehand" to be adopted as children into God's family with all the rights, privi-

leges, and inheritance of natural-born children (Rom. 8:15–17, 23; Gal. 4:4–7).

1:7 In redemption, believers have been released from bondage to sin (Heb. 9:15) through the priceless payment of the blood of Christ (Col. 1:20). Christ's substitutionary death fully satisfied God's justice (Rom. 3:23, 24; Eph. 2:13). Through "the forgiveness of sins," a woman's relationship with God is restored since sins no longer form a barrier between her and God. Redemption and forgiveness are not identical, but a central feature of redemption is the forgiveness of sins (Col. 1:14).

1:11, 12 Paul focused on Jewish believers ("we"). The Jews had been the first to hear the gospel message and to trust in Christ as Messiah (v. 12). Of course, many Gentiles also believed once the gospel was presented to them (v. 13), and they shared equally with Jews in God's inheritance (vv. 13, 14).

SALVATION *GOD'S DELIVERANCE*

Salvation can be described as "snatching" someone from serious danger. Just as you would "snatch" your child from before an oncoming automobile to save his life, the Lord Jesus saves or "snatches" every individual who trusts in Him from the pathway that leads to eternal death in Hell (Rom. 6:23). Salvation thus can best be understood as God's deliverance. In the Old Testament, God delivered Israel from their enemies many times (Judg. 3:9, 15, 28). In the New Testament, God delivered sinners from eternity in Hell (Acts. 16:31).

Salvation requires not only God's initial action but also your response. There are basically three aspects of God's salvation or deliverance: justification, sanctification, and glorification. Justification is God's deliverance from sin's penalty. When a person accepts Christ into her life, she becomes totally free from the penalty of sin and spiritual death (Rom. 3:23–25). The penalty for sins that have been committed in the past or sins that will be committed in the future has been paid through the death of Jesus Christ on the Cross.

Sanctification is God's progressive deliverance of a believer from sin's power (Eph. 5:26; 1 Thess. 5:23). God's desire is that a believer mature and become more Christlike, that she become free from sin's control in her life. But if the believer sins because of her fallen nature, God has made provision (1 John 1:9). God has given the Holy Spirit to aid believers in the process of sanctification.

Glorification is God's ultimate deliverance of the believer from sin's presence. Glorification will not be actualized until the Lord returns for His children (1 Cor. 15:51–57). While you are living on this earth, you will always be in the presence of sin. However, those who have trusted in Christ will one day be free from sin completely.

Your personal response to God's action is also of utmost importance in salvation:

- You must know who Christ is, what He has done, and what He is able to do.
- You must have a conviction that this knowledge about Christ is true.
- You must act upon that knowledge and conviction, trusting in Christ daily.

You must have a personal encounter with Christ, surrendering your life to the Lord. At this point salvation or "deliverance" occurs. From that point throughout eternity, the power of Christ in the believer is greater than the power of sin over that believer (2 Tim. 1:12), and Christ, in turn, covers your sins by having paid the penalty for those sins through His death on the Cross. You then are challenged to live for Him and grow in His grace.

See also Rom. 6:1–4; Eph. 4:22–24; 2 Pet. 1:2–9; chart on Theological Terms; notes on Access to God (Rom. 10); Freedom (Rom. 6); Heaven (2 Tim. 4); Identity In Christ (Col. 2); Obedience (Philem.); Surrender (James 4)

Prayer for Spiritual Wisdom

[15]Therefore I also, after I heard of your faith in the Lord Jesus and your love for all the saints, [16]do not cease to give thanks for you, making mention of you in my prayers: [17]that the God of our Lord Jesus Christ, the Father of glory, may give to you the spirit of wisdom and revelation in the knowledge of Him, [18]the eyes of your understanding[a] being enlightened; that you may know what is the hope of His calling, what are the riches of the glory of His inheritance in the saints, [19]and what *is* the exceeding greatness of His power toward us who believe, according to the working of His mighty power [20]which He worked in Christ when He raised Him from the dead and seated *Him* at His right hand in the heavenly *places,* [21]far above all principality and power and might and dominion, and every name

that is named, not only in this age but also in that which is to come. [22]And He put all *things* under His feet, and gave Him *to be* head over all *things* to the church, [23]which is His body, the fullness of Him who fills all in all.

By Grace Through Faith

2 And you *He made alive,* who were dead in trespasses and sins, [2]in which you once walked according to the course of this world, according to the prince of the power of the air, the spirit who now works in the sons of disobedience, [3]among whom also we all once conducted ourselves in the lusts of our flesh, fulfilling the desires of the flesh and of the mind, and were by nature children of wrath, just as the others.

··
1:18 [a]NU-Text and M-Text read *hearts.*

1:17 The term spirit here may be understood either as an attitude or, most probably, as a reference to the Holy Spirit (see Is. 11:2; chart, The Work of the Holy Spirit). The Spirit already fully indwells all believers (Rom. 8:9), but Paul wants them to be fully endowed with His insight and discernment as they grow in their experiential knowledge of God.

2:3 Paul's change in pronouns ("we," v. 3) signals that his reference was not only to those of Gentile background ("you," v. 1) but also to those like himself who came from Jewish stock. Every human being, apart from a saving relationship with Christ, is subject to divine wrath (John 3:36).

WOMEN'S MINISTRIES
SERVING IN THE LOCAL CHURCH

Judge, prophetess, handmaiden, missionary, queen, and businesswoman—these are a few of the ministries God has given women throughout biblical history. As "heirs of God and joint heirs with Christ" (Rom. 8:17) and members of "the body of Christ" (1 Cor. 12:27), every woman receives God's gifts to be used for His glory. The possibilities are as limitless as the needs of the world.

Jesus speaks each woman's name as He did that of Mary in the garden following His Resurrection (see John 20:11–18). When a woman's response is as loving as Mary's, Jesus answers as he did to Mary with a mission and message: "Go to My brethren and say to them, 'I am ascending to My Father and your Father, and to My God and your God'" (John 20:17).

Jesus' desire is that each woman yield herself to Him in utter dependence, recognizing that "without Me you can do nothing" (John 15:5), and relying on His Spirit to fulfill the special ministry He selects for her—a ministry appropriate to her talents and effective in her generation. God challenges each of us as He did Queen Esther, "Yet who knows whether you have come to the kingdom for such a time as this?" (Esth. 4:14).

Each woman is hand-picked by God, situated in Christ's body just as He desires, and is indispensable in reaching her particular sphere of influence for Christ. If a woman feels inadequate for the ministry task the Lord reveals to her, she need only remember Jesus' words, "My grace is sufficient for you, for My strength is made perfect in weakness" (2 Cor. 12:9).

See also Rom. 8:12–17; 1 Cor. 12:12–31; notes on Commitment (Matt. 16); God's Will (Eph. 5); Spiritual Gifts (Rom. 12); Surrender (James 4); Women's Ministries (John 4; Acts 2; 1 Cor. 11; 1 Tim. 3; Titus 2)

---

⁴But God, who is rich in mercy, because of His great love with which He loved us, ⁵even when we were dead in trespasses, made us alive together with Christ (by grace you have been saved), ⁶and raised *us* up together, and made *us* sit together in the heavenly *places* in Christ Jesus, ⁷that in the ages to come He might show the exceeding riches of His grace in *His* kindness toward us in Christ Jesus. ⁸For by grace you have been saved through faith, and that not of yourselves; *it is* the gift of God, ⁹not of works, lest anyone should boast. ¹⁰For we are His workmanship, created in Christ Jesus for good works, which God prepared beforehand that we should walk in them.

Brought Near by His Blood

¹¹Therefore remember that you, once Gentiles in the flesh—who are called Uncircumcision by what is called the Circumcision made in the flesh by hands— ¹²that at that time you were without Christ, being aliens from the commonwealth of Israel and strangers from the covenants of promise, having no hope and without God in the world.

¹³But now in Christ Jesus you who once were far off have been brought near by the blood of Christ.

Christ Our Peace

¹⁴For He Himself is our peace, who has made both one, and has broken down the middle wall of separation, ¹⁵having abolished in His flesh the enmity, *that is,* the law of commandments *contained* in ordinances, so as to create in Himself one new man *from* the two, *thus* making peace, ¹⁶and that He might reconcile them both to God in one body through the cross, thereby putting to death the enmity. ¹⁷And He came and preached peace to you who were afar off and to those who were near. ¹⁸For through Him we both have access by one Spirit to the Father.

Christ Our Cornerstone

¹⁹Now, therefore, you are no longer strangers and foreigners, but fellow citizens with the saints and members of the household of God, ²⁰having been built on the foundation of the apostles and prophets, Jesus Christ Himself being the chief cor-

---

2:4, 5 "Mercy" withholds from a person what is deserved (in this case, judgment); "grace" gives what is not deserved—salvation (v. 5).

2:8, 9 Faith is not itself a work that somehow merits salvation; rather it is a response of trust stimulated by the Holy Spirit and leading to salvation. God's purpose in making salvation a free gift is to eliminate any possibility of people boasting in their own self-efforts (Rom. 3:27).

2:10 Those who have been saved by God's grace are His "workmanship" (lit. "masterpiece" or "work of art"), specially created by Him for the purpose of doing "good works." In eternity past God prepared these good works that He will ac-

complish in and through each believer by the power of His indwelling Spirit.

2:14–19 God has established peace between Jews and Gentiles by destroying the hostile barrier of spiritual enmity between them. Christ fulfilled the Law (Matt. 5:17; Rom. 10:4), rendering it "abolished" or complete. Through Christ the Law is fulfilled not by human effort of Jews or Gentiles but by faith in Christ, who satisfies the Law.

2:20 Paul described the church by using the metaphor of a building. The NT apostles and prophets had a unique and indispensable part in establishing the church. Jesus Christ is Himself the "chief cornerstone." This is literally the "cap-

FRUIT OF THE SPIRIT *GENTLENESS*

Those who walk in the Spirit possess a quality of gentleness that is one of the hallmarks necessary for Christian unity. Paul challenges believers to a life worthy of their calling in Christ Jesus that is characterized by lowliness, gentleness, longsuffering, mutual forbearance, and peace (Eph. 4:1–3).

"Gentleness" or "meekness" (Gk. *prautēs*) refers to a humble, submissive attitude that is the opposite of pride. Not to be confused with weakness, gentleness is strength that is submitted to God and channeled into service to others. The Old Testament characterizes God as gentle (2 Sam. 22:36; Ps. 18:35). The New Testament describes Jesus as "gentle and lowly [humble] in heart" (Matt. 11:29; 2 Cor. 10:1). Believers, like their Lord, should pursue gentleness (1 Tim. 6:11) and wear it like a garment (Col. 3:12).

The godly virtue of gentleness, which is a quality of the heart, is counted as being more influential than outward beauty in winning an unbelieving husband to Christ (1 Pet. 3:1–4). A gentle spirit is precious to God. Gentleness is a fruit of the Holy Spirit necessary for godliness (holy, Christlike living), goodness (kindness toward others), and giftedness (service in the name of Jesus).

See also notes on Encouragement (Eph. 4); Fruit of the Spirit (Ps. 86; Rom. 5; 15; 1 Cor. 10; 13; Gal. 5; Col. 3; 2 Thess. 1; Rev. 2); Humility (Phil. 2); Submission (1 Pet. 3); Wives (Prov. 31)

---

ner*stone,* ²¹in whom the whole building, being fitted together, grows into a holy temple in the Lord, ²²in whom you also are being built together for a dwelling place of God in the Spirit.

The Mystery Revealed

3 For this reason I, Paul, the prisoner of Christ Jesus for you Gentiles— ²if indeed you have heard of the dispensation of the grace of God which was given to me for you, ³how that by revelation He made known to me the mystery (as I have briefly written already, ⁴by which, when you read, you may understand my knowledge in the mystery of Christ), ⁵which in other ages was not made known to the sons of men, as it has now been revealed by the Spirit to His holy apostles and prophets: ⁶that the Gentiles should be fellow heirs, of the same body, and partakers of His promise in Christ through the gospel, ⁷of which I became a minister according to the gift of the grace of God given to me by the effective working of His power.

Purpose of the Mystery

⁸To me, who am less than the least of all the saints, this grace was given, that I should preach among the Gentiles the unsearchable riches of Christ, ⁹and to make all see what *is* the fellowshipᵃ of the mystery, which from the beginning of the ages has been hidden in God who created all things through Jesus Christ;ᵇ ¹⁰to the intent that now the manifold wisdom of God might be made known by the church to the principalities and powers in the heavenly *places,* ¹¹according to the eternal purpose which He accomplished in Christ Jesus our Lord, ¹²in whom we have boldness and access with confidence through faith in Him. ¹³Therefore I ask that you do not lose heart at my tribulations for you, which is your glory.

3:9 ᵃNU-Text and M-Text read *stewardship (dispensation).* ᵇNU-Text omits *through Jesus Christ.*

We never cry out to God and receive a returned check stamped "Insufficient Grace."

Sandy Smith

---

stone," the binding stone that holds the entire building together. This building is described as a temple (Gk. *naos*), the inner sanctuary in which God dwells by His Spirit.

3:1 Paul had already discussed the union of Jewish and Gentile believers into a new entity—the church. He began to pray that they might experience the power and the love of Christ that they would need to live in practical unity with one another in this life.

3:2–7 Paul reminded the Ephesians that by revelation God

gave him a special stewardship (lit., "dispensation") that was for their benefit. This stewardship, which he had written about earlier, is a "mystery" (Gk. *musterion*), referring to God's wise plan that was previously hidden (v. 9; see Eph. 2:11–22). The focus here is on the union of Jew and Gentile as equal partners in the church—the body of Christ (Eph. 3:6).

3:10 Paul's reference is to the new relationship between believing Jews and Gentiles in one body.

ENCOURAGEMENT *WORDS THAT BUILD UP*

Paul's words admonish us to speak only good, not corrupt, words—ones that build up, encourage, and edify. Our words are to constitute a gift to the hearer (Eph. 4:29).

Jesus and Paul are examples for us in their use of uplifting words to encourage. Even when his ship started to sink, Paul gave words of encouragement (Acts 27:22). When Jesus' disciples were sinking, He spoke encouragement to them (Matt. 14:27). When Paul was being persecuted, the Lord appeared beside him and encouraged him (Acts 23:11).

Many people are bowed down under heavy emotional loads and are weary of life's struggles. How eager they are to hear a word of encouragement (1 Thess. 5:11)! Often we turn the other way, but the Lord wants to give us kind words to say if we are willing to make ourselves available (Is. 50:4).

In Proverbs, the book of wisdom, much is written about the value of encouraging words (Prov. 16:24; 25:11). Not only do pleasant words taste sweet, but their use can lift us up to high places (Prov. 22:11). Whether we want to be encouragers because Jesus said "be of good cheer," because Paul urged us to "take heart," or because we are simply called to lift up the weary, edify the saints, and evangelize the lost—whatever our reason for wishing to bring sweetness to the soul, now is the time to start (James 4:17).

See also Deut. 1:21, 29, 30; Ezra 10:4; Ps. 145:14; Mic. 2:7; Luke 22:32; Acts 13:15, note; Heb. 3:13; notes on Communication (Prov. 15); Love (1 John 4); Spiritual Gifts (Rom. 12)

Appreciation of the Mystery

14For this reason I bow my knees to the Father of our Lord Jesus Christ,[a] 15from whom the whole family in heaven and earth is named, 16that He would grant you, according to the riches of His glory, to be strengthened with might through His Spirit in the inner man, 17that Christ may dwell in your hearts through faith; that you, being rooted and grounded in love, 18may be able to comprehend with all the saints what *is* the width and length and depth and height— 19to know the love of Christ which passes knowledge; that you may be filled with all the fullness of God.

20Now to Him who is able to do exceedingly abundantly above all that we ask or think, according to the power that works in us, 21to Him *be* glory in the church by Christ Jesus to all generations, forever and ever. Amen.

Walk in Unity

4I, therefore, the prisoner of the Lord, beseech you to walk worthy of the calling with which you were called, 2with all lowliness and gentleness, with longsuffering, bearing with one another in love, 3endeavoring to keep the unity of the Spirit in the bond of peace. 4*There is* one body and one Spirit, just as you were called in one hope of your calling; 5one Lord, one faith, one baptism; 6one God and Father of all, who *is* above all, and through all, and in you[a] all.

Spiritual Gifts

7But to each one of us grace was given according to the measure of Christ's gift. 8Therefore He says:

"When He ascended on high,
He led captivity captive,
And gave gifts to men."[a]

9(Now this, *"He ascended"*— what does it mean but that He also first[a] descended into the lower parts of the earth? 10He who descended is also the One who ascended far above all the heavens, that He might fill all things.)

11And He Himself gave some *to be* apostles, some prophets, some evangelists, and some pastors and teachers, 12for the equipping of the saints for the work of ministry, for the edifying of the body of Christ, 13till we all come to the unity of the faith and of the knowledge of the Son of God, to a perfect man, to the measure of the stature of

••••••••••••••••••••
3:14 [a]NU-Text omits *of our Lord Jesus Christ.* 4:6 [a]NU-Text omits *you*; M-Text reads *us.* 4:8 [a]Psalm 68:18 4:9 [a]NU-Text omits *first.*

3:14, 15 **Although God is the Creator** of all human beings and angels, only those who have placed personal faith in Jesus Christ are His children and may call Him Father (John 1:12; Rom. 8:15, 16). The idea of a "father" is derived from God and not from human beings. He is the first Father, and none existed before Him.

3:16–19 **Paul's prayer** has two parts. First, he prayed that God, whose resources are limitless, would grant believers inner strengthening in their present experience (Eph. 3:16). As a result of this empowering, Christ would become fully at home in

their lives (v. 17) with access to each area of their lives and as the governing factor in their attitudes and conduct. Paul's second petition was based on the fact that believers have already been placed in the body of Christ, being rooted and grounded in love (v. 17). He prayed that they might be empowered to grasp the immensity of Christ's love and to know that love in their personal experience (vv. 18, 19).

4:12–16 **These gifted individuals** seek to equip other believers to do the work of the ministry by leading them into doctrinal

GOD'S WILL CONFORMING TO HIS PURPOSE

A mature Christian seeks God's will and asks for God's wisdom when she is facing a major decision. Believers must pray about decisions—especially life decisions such as "Where shall I go to college?" "Should I marry this man?" "Should I bring my ailing parent to live in my home?" Such decisions have serious consequences, and they deserve the prayerful seeking of God's perfect wisdom. But knowing God's will does not happen solely in prayer. It also requires a commitment to knowing His Word.

The Bible teaches that realizing (or proving) God's will is the result of habitually conforming your thinking and behavior to God's Word over a lifetime. As a Christian woman reads the Bible day by day, her mind is renewed with a new way of thinking about life. Worldly ideas, attitudes, and prejudices are replaced by thoughts that conform to God's ways. This process takes time, and there are no shortcuts. The transformation is never complete until death.

The Christian who has ongoing fellowship with the Lord through His Word comes to decisions equipped with a biblically informed way of thinking. Knowing God's will at major decision points is much easier if you are seeking God's will every day in Bible reading and prayer.

See also Dan. 2:23, note; Rom. 12:1, 2; Eph. 1:9; Col. 1:9; notes on Access to God (Rom. 10); Change Points in Life (Eccl. 3); Decision Making (1 Cor. 8)

---

the fullness of Christ; [14]that we should no longer be children, tossed to and fro and carried about with every wind of doctrine, by the trickery of men, in the cunning craftiness of deceitful plotting, [15]but, speaking the truth in love, may grow up in all things into Him who is the head— Christ— [16]from whom the whole body, joined and knit together by what every joint supplies, according to the effective working by which every part does its share, causes growth of the body for the edifying of itself in love.

The New Man

[17]This I say, therefore, and testify in the Lord, that you should no longer walk as the rest of[a] the Gentiles walk, in the futility of their mind, [18]having their understanding darkened, being alienated from the life of God, because of the ignorance that is in them, because of the blindness of their heart; [19]who, being past feeling, have given themselves over to lewdness, to work all uncleanness with greediness.

[20]But you have not so learned Christ, [21]if indeed you have heard Him and have been taught by Him, as the truth is in Jesus: [22]that you put off, concerning your former conduct, the old man which grows corrupt according to the deceitful lusts, [23]and be renewed in the spirit of your mind, [24]and that you put on the new man which was created according to God, in true righteousness and holiness.

Do Not Grieve the Spirit

[25]Therefore, putting away lying, "Let each one of you speak truth with his neighbor,"[a] for we are members of one another. [26]"Be angry, and do not sin":[a] do not let the sun go down on your wrath, [27]nor give place to the devil. [28]Let him who stole steal no longer, but rather let him labor, working with his hands what is good, that he may have something to give him who has need. [29]Let no corrupt word

4:17 [a]NU-Text omits the rest of.   4:25 [a]Zechariah 8:16   4:26 [a]Psalm 4:4

---

and practical stability. This mutual edification (v. 12) will continue until the church reaches maturity and unity (v. 13). The mature church will no longer be led astray doctrinally (v. 14) and will exhibit the character qualities of Christ by mutually edifying itself (vv. 15, 16).

4:17–19 The Ephesians were admonished to avoid the lifestyle typical of unbelieving Gentiles all around them. This lifestyle was characterized by "futility," being empty and without purpose. The understanding of unbelievers had been darkened because they had chosen not to receive God's revelation (Rom. 1:21; 2 Cor. 4:4); they were "alienated" or separated from the life of God and so were unable to hear His voice; they were willfully ignorant of God and His truth (see 2 Tim. 3:7; 1 Pet. 1:4); and their hearts had become blinded and calloused so that they were insensitive to God and had no fear of the consequences of their actions (see John 12:37–40). They

had given themselves over to self-indulgent immorality characterized by an insatiable desire for more.

4:22–24 Unlike the unbelievers described, the Ephesians had learned life-changing new truth in Christ: Believers are to put off "the old man," a phrase referring to the sinful lifestyle driven by desires that deceptively promised joy but did not give it; they are to allow the Holy Spirit to renew their thought patterns, changing them from impurity to holiness (Rom. 12:2; Phil. 4:8); they are to put on "the new man," a phrase referring to a new lifestyle of holiness and righteous living. This new lifestyle is put on positionally when a person receives Christ and needs to be lived out experientially through the Spirit's empowering (Col. 3:9, 10).

4:26, 27 God has a plan for dealing with anger (see Ps. 13, Healing; Eccl. 7, Anger; chart, How Can You Prevent Inappropriate Anger).

ROLE RELATIONSHIPS BETWEEN MEN AND WOMEN

ORIGINAL RELATIONSHIP: CREATION	DISTORTION OF THE RELATIONSHIP: THE FALL	RESTORATION OF THE RELATIONSHIP: REDEMPTION
Man and woman are perfectly related to one another and to God (Gen. 2:25).	The relationship between the man and the woman and their relationship to God are distorted by the presence of sin (Gen. 3:7, 8).	Jesus Christ as Redeemer models both servant leadership for the man and selfless submission for the woman (Eph. 5:23–27; Phil. 2:5–8).

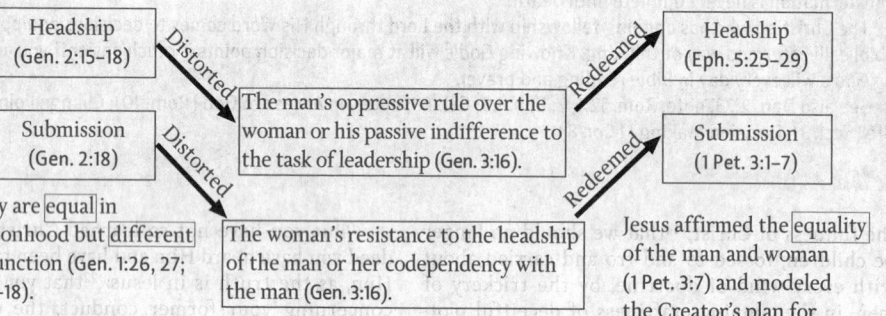

Headship (Gen. 2:15–18)

Distorted

The man's oppressive rule over the woman or his passive indifference to the task of leadership (Gen. 3:16).

Redeemed

Headship (Eph. 5:25–29)

Submission (Gen. 2:18)

Distorted

Submission (1 Pet. 3:1–7)

They are equal in personhood but different in function (Gen. 1:26, 27; 2:15–18).

The woman's resistance to the headship of the man or her codependency with the man (Gen. 3:16).

Redeemed

Jesus affirmed the equality of the man and woman (1 Pet. 3:7) and modeled the Creator's plan for different roles. He also gave directives to counteract abuses.

According to the egalitarian position, no difference existed between the man and the woman prior to the Fall. They were equal in personhood (as is also true in the complementarian position) and the same in role and function (while the complementarian position maintains a difference in role assignment for the man and for the woman).

See also Gen. 1:26; 2:24; Gal. 3:28; Eph. 5:22–24, 25–31, notes; notes on Headship (Gen. 1); The Creation of the Woman (Gen. 2); Complementarity (Eph. 5); Egalitarianism (Rom. 9); Submission (1 Pet. 3)

---

proceed out of your mouth, but what is good for necessary edification, that it may impart grace to the hearers. [30]And do not grieve the Holy Spirit of God, by whom you were sealed for the day of redemption. [31]Let all bitterness, wrath, anger, clamor, and evil speaking be put away from you, with all malice. [32]And be kind to one another, tenderhearted, forgiving one another, even as God in Christ forgave you.

Walk in Love

5 Therefore be imitators of God as dear children. [2]And walk in love, as Christ also has loved us and given Himself for us, an offering and a sacrifice to God for a sweet-smelling aroma.

[3]But fornication and all uncleanness or covetousness, let it not even be named among you, as is fitting for saints; [4]neither filthiness, nor foolish talking, nor coarse jesting, which are not fitting, but rather giving of thanks. [5]For this you know,[a] that no fornicator, unclean person, nor covetous man, who is an idolater, has any inheritance in the kingdom of Christ and God. [6]Let no one deceive you with empty words, for because of these things the wrath of God comes upon the sons of disobedience. [7]Therefore do not be partakers with them.

Walk in Light

[8]For you were once darkness, but now *you are*

....

5:5 [a]NU-Text reads *For know this.*

4:30 Believers should not grieve the Holy Spirit through sins such as unwholesome speech (v. 29) and the outpouring of repressed anger (v. 31). Since only persons can be grieved, this verse affirms the fact that the Holy Spirit is a Person.

4:32 The basis for believers forgiving others is the fact that they themselves have been graciously forgiven by God (Gk. *charizomai*), and released from any *obligation* to make restitution (see Ps. 133, Healing).

BIBLICAL EQUALITY — DISTINCT BUT COMPLEMENTARY ROLES

Male and female were created as equal and complementary expressions of the image of God. Both bear His image fully, though in different ways. Their distinct roles in relationship to each other provide a picture of who God is and how He relates to His people.

Christ Jesus is equal with God the Father, yet submissive and responsive to Him (Phil. 2:6–8). God the Father loves the Son and exalts Him. The pattern is repeated in the relationship between Christ and the church. Christ provides loving, servant leadership; the church responds with respect and submission as Christ's "Bride" (Eph. 5:22–33). Another counterpart to the picture is the relationship between church leaders and local bodies of believers (Heb. 13:7, 17).

Sin has distorted the relationship between man and woman at every level, but believers are called to relate according to the Creator's plan instituted in the Garden of Eden before sin entered the world (Gen. 2:15–25). This plan is marked by a holy reciprocity in which the husband's love awakens a responsive submission from the wife just as a wife's respect and appreciation draws from her husband leadership and love.

In Christ, distinctions of rank or sex are removed; yet throughout the New Testament, social and sexual distinctions are clearly seen in the family, the state, and the church. The equality of believers Christ reflects a oneness of relationship, not a sameness of function.

Each individual stands before God created in His image, yet, at the same time, a sinner in need of salvation (Gen. 1:27; Rom. 3:23). Therefore, each person has at the same time both an infinite equality of worth before God and in the midst of others and a total equality of need for Jesus Christ as Savior. Yet out of this same "lump of clay" called humanity, the Creator has chosen to make vessels of various kinds and for various purposes according to His will (Is. 29:16; Rom. 9:19-21). Therefore, in contrast to the world's view, biblical equality recognizes the equality of all people before God but also recognize God's right to assign people different functions and roles (Ezek. 33:17).

A woman's rewards are not based upon her role in the kingdom but upon her faithfulness in fulfilling the assignment God gives. Fully equal before God, women and men enjoy the same free grace, are called to the same obedience, and are capable of receiving the same spiritual gifts and blessings. Yet woman is not man, and man is not woman. They are equal in worth and personhood as the creation of God but remain functionally different in the role assignments each is to fulfill.

See also Gen. 1:27; Col. 3:18, 19; 1 Pet. 3:7; notes on Freedom (Rom. 6); Patriarchy (Gen. 28); Submission (1 Pet. 3), charts on Role Relationships Between Men and Women; Submission; Marriage (Gen. 2; 2 Sam. 6; Prov. 5; Hos. 2; Amos 3; 2 Cor. 13; Heb. 13)

---

light in the Lord. Walk as children of light [9](for the fruit of the Spirit[a] *is* in all goodness, righteousness, and truth), [10]finding out what is acceptable to the Lord. [11]And have no fellowship with the unfruitful works of darkness, but rather expose *them.* [12]For it is shameful even to speak of those things which are done by them in secret. [13]But all things that are exposed are made manifest by the light, for whatever makes manifest is light. [14]Therefore He says:

"Awake, you who sleep,
Arise from the dead,
And Christ will give you
light."

Walk in Wisdom

[15]See then that you walk circumspectly, not as fools but as wise, [16]redeeming the time, because the days are evil.

[17]Therefore do not be unwise, but understand what the will of the Lord *is.* [18]And do not be drunk with wine, in which is dissipation; but be filled with the Spirit, [19]speaking to one another in psalms and hymns and spiritual songs, singing and making melody in your heart to the Lord, [20]giving thanks always for all things to God the Father in the name of our Lord Jesus Christ, [21]submitting to one another in the fear of God.[a]

••••••••••••••••••••••••

5:9 [a]NU-Text reads *light.* **5:21** [a]NU-Text reads *Christ.*

5:18 The command to be filled applies to all believers. The passive voice of the verb indicates that this is not a manufactured experience; the Holy Spirit fills and controls them. Further, the present tense of the command indicates that there can be many, successive fillings. This filling is not to be confused with the "baptism of the Spirit" (1 Cor. 12:13), which occurs at the point of conversion.

5:19–21 As a result of the Spirit's filling, believers will communicate with one another in an edifying manner. The Greek verb used includes all sorts of speech—singing of "psalms" (OT psalms), "hymns" (praises composed by Christians), and "spiritual songs" (spontaneous, Spirit–inspired praise). Second, they will sing praises to the Lord (see chart, Hymns and Songs Associated with Women). Third, they will continually give thanks to the Father (Col. 3:17; 1 Thess. 5:18). Fourth, they will mutually submit to one another.

CHILDREN *A REQUIREMENT TO OBEY*

Children are to obey both their parents. This relationship exists "in the Lord," and the implication is that children and parents live under the authority of Jesus Christ (Eph. 6:1). Children cannot be subject to their parents in a way that is contrary to the obedience they owe to Jesus Christ. They should obey their parents because this is "right" in God's eyes, as illustrated by the fourth Commandment (vv. 1, 2). A child's education would typically include the Ten Commandments; so Paul is drawing attention to truth children would already know. The word "honor" includes the ideas of respect and esteem (v. 2). Life lived in submission to legitimate authority would benefit the child with a better and longer life (v. 3; see Deut. 5:16). The term "father" can be used to represent both parents (see similar usage in Heb. 11:23). Unreasonable demands by parents will provoke children to anger and can push them to perpetual bitterness with the result that children lose hope of ever performing well enough to please (Col. 3:21). Parents should instead rear their children in an atmosphere of nurturing: godly training in what is right, correction of what is wrong, and encouragement at every turn.

See also chart on The Ten Commandments Throughout Scripture; notes on Children (Ps. 128); Parenthood (Prov. 10)

Marriage—Christ and the Church

²²Wives, submit to your own husbands, as to the Lord. ²³For the husband is head of the wife, as also Christ is head of the church; and He is the Savior of the body. ²⁴Therefore, just as the church is subject to Christ, so *let* the wives *be* to their own husbands in everything.

²⁵Husbands, love your wives, just as Christ also loved the church and gave Himself for her, ²⁶that He might sanctify and cleanse her with the washing of water by the word, ²⁷that He might present her to Himself a glorious church, not having spot or wrinkle or any such thing, but that she should be holy and without blemish. ²⁸So husbands ought to love their own wives as their own bodies; he who loves his wife loves himself. ²⁹For no one ever hated his own flesh, but nourishes and cherishes it, just as the Lord *does* the church. ³⁰For we are members of His body,ᵃ of His flesh and of His bones. ³¹*"For this reason a man shall leave his father and mother and be joined to his wife, and the two shall become one flesh."*ᵃ ³²This is a great mystery, but I speak concerning Christ and the church. ³³Nevertheless let each one of you in particular so love his own wife as himself, and let the wife *see* that she respects *her* husband.

Children and Parents

6 Children, obey your parents in the Lord, for this is right. ²*"Honor your father and mother,"* which is the first commandment with promise: ³*"that it may be well with you and you may live long on the earth."*ᵃ

⁴And you, fathers, do not provoke your children to wrath, but bring them up in the training and admonition of the Lord.

···················
5:30 ᵃNU-Text omits the rest of this verse. **5:31** ᵃGenesis 2:24 **6:3** ᵃDeuteronomy 5:16

5:22—6:9 As Paul elaborated on the subject of submission, he showed what would happen in specific relationships within the family (see 1 Pet. 3, Submission; charts, Role Relationships Between Men and Women; Submission).

5:22-24 The exhortation specifies that wives are to submit themselves to their "own" husbands (v. 22). Paul in no way suggests that wives are inferior to their husbands or that they, as women, must submit to all other men. The wife's submission is voluntary rather than forced (v. 22). God does not ask a wife to submit herself to her husband in violation of her Christian responsibility to walk in holiness and righteousness before Him. The marriage relationship is raised to lofty heights as Paul compared it to the relationship of Christ and His church (v. 23). The husband is not the Savior of the wife's body. Nevertheless, the analogy holds that the husband is to be the protector of his wife (see Gen. 2:15–17, note). In voluntary submission, the wife can serve her husband, just as the church serves Christ, with freedom and dignity.

5:25–31 Paul's exhortation is equally clear to husbands: They are to love their wives (an admonition expressed six times in vv. 25–33) in the same manner in which Christ sacrificially loved the church (v. 25). Husbands must not be "bitter" or harsh with their wives (Col. 3:19). Christ's love for His church is presently manifested in His work of atonement (Eph. 5:25) and sanctification (v. 26) so that He might in the end times present her as a pure and spotless bride (v. 27). Returning to the marriage relationship, Paul explained that the husband should love his wife as his own body because the two are actually one (v. 28; see Gen. 2:24). "Body" is used here, as elsewhere, to refer to the whole person (Rom. 12:1; Phil. 1:20). God prescribed that marriage provide a picture of the ultimate and eternal love between Christ and His church.

5:33 Paul summarized by reminding each husband to love his own wife sacrificially as himself and by reminding each wife to show respect to her husband as the God-ordained leader of the family "as to the Lord" (v. 22; see charts, Role Relationships Between Men and Women; Theological Foundations for Headship).

FATHERHOOD   PROTECTOR AND PROVIDER

The earliest concept of God for a child is greatly impacted by the relationship she has with her own father. Fathers in the Bible were the supreme authoritative figures in their families. With but a word they could determine the fate of their offspring. In contrast to this autocratic image of fatherhood, Paul's advice to fathers emphasizes patience (Eph. 6:4). The father Jesus describes, just as the heavenly Father, loves unconditionally, forgives without strings attached, and gives abundantly (Luke 15:11–32).

Still, Scripture presents a tender side to fatherhood. A temple official came to Jesus frantic for his daughter's healing (Matt. 9:18–26); Jacob and David displayed deep sorrow at the loss of their sons (Gen. 37:33–35; 2 Sam. 13:35–39); both Noah and Joseph (the father of Jesus) followed God's direction and provided escapes from danger for their children (Gen. 7:5; Matt. 2:13–23). Biblical fathers are not perfect; they made mistakes. Eli did not set limits for his sons (1 Sam. 2:12; 3:13); David did not spend much time with his sons, nor did he live an exemplary life before them (2 Sam. 12:13, 14; 24:10). The best earthly father is one who has a vibrant fellowship with the heavenly Father and thus has access to the Lord's unlimited wisdom and vast resources (Eph. 5:15, 16).

A mother helps to fashion a good father. She makes him feel loved and accepted, treating him with respect. She shows respect for his position of leadership. She does not undermine his authority. She offers encouragement, reflective interaction, and supportive interest.

Fathers certainly are reminded of the importance of making their children feel wanted (Ps. 127:3–5). Fathers are to instruct their children (Deut. 6:1–9; Prov. 4:1; 6:20), train them (Ps. 78:5–7; Prov. 22:6), and correct them (Prov. 13:24). The shelter and security provided by a godly father should give freedom for growth without overprotection from challenges or tasks that teach responsibility (1 Sam. 3:1–10).

See also notes on Family (Gen. 32; 1 Sam. 3; Ps. 78; 127); Fatherhood of God (Rom. 8); Husbands (Job 31; 2 Cor. 6); Motherhood (1 Sam. 1; Is. 49; Ezek. 16); Parenthood (Prov. 10); Patriarchy (Gen. 28)

Bondservants and Masters

[5]Bondservants, be obedient to those who are your masters according to the flesh, with fear and trembling, in sincerity of heart, as to Christ; [6]not with eyeservice, as men-pleasers, but as bondservants of Christ, doing the will of God from the heart, [7]with goodwill doing service, as to the Lord, and not to men, [8]knowing that whatever good anyone does, he will receive the same from the Lord, whether *he is* a slave or free.

[9]And you, masters, do the same things to them, giving up threatening, knowing that your own Master also[a] is in heaven, and there is no partiality with Him.

The Whole Armor of God

[10]Finally, my brethren, be strong in the Lord and in the power of His might. [11]Put on the whole armor of God, that you may be able to stand against the wiles of the devil. [12]For we do not wrestle against flesh and blood, but against principalities, against powers, against the rulers of the darkness of this age,[a] against spiritual *hosts* of wickedness in the heavenly *places*. [13]Therefore take up the whole armor of God, that you may be able to withstand in the evil day, and having done all, to stand.

[14]Stand therefore, having girded your waist with

• • • • • • • • • • • • • • • •

6:9 [a]NU-Text reads *He who is both their Master and yours.*   **6:12** [a]NU-Text reads *rulers of this darkness.*

6:5–8 Slaves had no option about obedience, except when to obey their masters would violate their obedience to Christ. Paul understood that slaves were considered the legal property of their masters. However, he addressed them on an equal level and with the same courtesy extended to their masters. Nowhere in Scripture is slavery presented as a divinely established institution. The service of slaves should be characterized by a deep desire to avoid poor workmanship, as in any other vocation, and by sincerity of heart (lit. "singleness"), meaning the absence of duplicity. They should serve eagerly, as if they were serving Christ Himself, knowing that this is only an "earthly" (Gk. *kata sarkon,* "according to the flesh") relationship and that God will fully reward their faithfulness (Col. 3:24). Such rewards are never dependent upon social status. Thus these principles are also appropriate in employment relationships (see Prov. 24, Employment; chart, Women in the Workplace).

6:11 Satan's wiles or schemings are directed against the church corporately (Eph. 4:2, 21, 31–32; 5:5) and believers personally (Acts 5:3; 10:38; 1 Tim. 4:1–5). The devil lives up to his name through falsely accusing believers before God (1 John 2:1, 2; Rev. 12:9) and maligning God before believers (Gen. 3:1), as well as through stirring up turmoil in the world by his accusations (James 3;13–16; chart, The Names for Satan; A Portrait of the Adversary).

6:14 The picture of God's armor is of a Roman soldier's tunic, pulled up and tucked into his belt so that he could fight or work unhindered. Living a life of honesty and integrity enables the Christian to be one in purpose with Jesus Christ, who is the Truth, and to be unhindered in the battle against Satan, who is a deceiver and liar (see chart, A Portrait of the Adversary). The breastplate covered the body from neck to thigh and was usually made of bronze. Believers do not need to

SPIRITUAL WARFARE *THE ARMOR OF GOD*

When a woman becomes a child of God, she not only inherits God's blessings but God's enemies as well. The Lord's foremost enemy is Satan, whose purpose is to destroy His work (John 8:44), but Jesus came in order to "destroy the works of the devil" (1 John 3:8).

Satan is a fallen angel (Is. 14:12–15) and as such is only a created being. He is in no way equal to God, the Creator. While Satan is superior in intellect and strength to mankind, he is inferior to God in every way. Believers have the power of the indwelling resurrected Christ over them and protecting them (1 John 4:4).

In addition, believers have been given the whole armor of God "to stand against the wiles of the devil" (Eph. 6:11). Each piece of the armor is to be "put on" to help believers overcome the temptations and attacks of the Evil One.

1) *Having Girded Your Waist With Truth* (v. 14): The waist or abdomen area was generally thought to be the seat of emotions. To gird this area with truth is to commit your emotions to believe the truth. Often a person knowingly allows herself to believe a lie because of fear or self-pity. Believers must hold a commitment to truth regardless of the repercussions (John 8:32, 36).

2) *Having Put On the Breastplate of Righteousness* (Eph. 6:14): The breast is generally thought of as the place of the soul. The heart must be kept pure and righteous because sin gives a foothold to the enemy. Confession and forgiveness on the basis of the blood of Christ cleanse the heart (1 John 1:9).

3) *Having Shod Your Feet With the Preparation of the Gospel of Peace* (Eph. 6:15): Proper shoes enable the feet to go from place to place. The believer is to be about her Father's business, which is to spread the gospel of peace and reconciliation. An undaunted sense of this mission keeps the believer headed in the right direction (Matt. 28:19, 20).

4) *Taking the Shield of Faith* (Eph. 6:16): The Wicked One is "the accuser of our brethren" (Rev. 12:10) and will send his fiery darts to instill doubt, fear, and guilt. Faith acts as an invisible shield that deflects such false accusations (Heb. 11:6).

5) *Take the Helmet of Salvation* (Eph. 6:17): A helmet protects the head, that is, the brain and thoughts. Assurance of salvation is a mighty defense against doubt and insecurity and the kinds of works bred by them (1 John 5:11–13).

6) *Take the Sword of the Spirit* (Eph. 6:17): The Word of God, the only offensive weapon in this armor, was used by the Lord Jesus against Satan (Luke 4:1–13). The living Word is powerful, effective, and instructive (Heb. 4:12; 2 Tim. 3:16, 17).

7) *Praying Always* (Eph. 6:18): Prayer opens the channels between us and God. In the midst of battle, we as believers must keep in constant communication with our Leader for directions and encouragement. Our prayers for one another are important and effectual (James 5:16).

See also Neh. 4—7; Mark 5:2, note; Luke 11:14–26; Rom. 3:23, note; 2 Cor. 10:3–5; 1 Pet. 5:8, 9; chart on Strategies in Spiritual Warfare; note on Temptation (Heb. 2)

---

truth, having put on the breastplate of righteousness, [15]and having shod your feet with the preparation of the gospel of peace; [16]above all, taking the shield of faith with which you will be able to quench all the fiery darts of the wicked one. [17]And take the helmet of salvation, and the sword of the Spirit, which is the word of God; [18]praying always with all prayer and supplication in the Spirit, being watchful to this end with all perseverance and supplication for all the saints— [19]and for me, that utterance may be given to me, that I may open my mouth boldly to make known the mystery of the gospel,

---

seek protection or right standing with God through works of their own; they can confidently stand in what Christ has done in their behalf (2 Cor. 5:21).

6:15 The soldier wore sandals with cleats made of sharp nails designed to give firm footing on even the most rugged terrain. "Preparation" may have the sense of readiness to share the gospel to others at a moment's notice. "Preparation" may also refer to a prepared foundation that consists of the gospel of peace with God (Eph. 2:17).

6:16 This long, oblong, or oval shield was crafted from two layers of wood covered with linen or animal hides, bound together with iron. When fighting side by side, soldiers could hold these shields together to form a long wall. Soaked in water, they served as adequate defense against the enemy's "fiery darts"—arrows that had been dipped in pitch and ignited. The shield of faith offers God's unlimited resources of power and wisdom (Eph. 3:16–21) to resist the fiery darts of distressing circumstances and temptation to evil (1 Cor. 10:13).

6:17 The soldier's bronze helmet had leather attachments to hold it in place. Christians can experience protection from Satan's attacks as they rest confidently in their position as members of God's family (John 1:12, 13), set apart for His pur-

Miss no single opportunity of making some small sacrifice, here by a smiling look, there by a kindly word; always doing it all for love.

St. Therese of Lisieux

---

[20] for which I am an ambassador in chains; that in it I may speak boldly, as I ought to speak.

A Gracious Greeting

[21] But that you also may know my affairs *and* how I am doing, Tychicus, a beloved brother and faithful minister in the Lord, will make all things known to you; [22] whom I have sent to you for this very purpose, that you may know our affairs, and *that* he may comfort your hearts.

[23] Peace to the brethren, and love with faith, from God the Father and the Lord Jesus Christ. [24] Grace *be* with all those who love our Lord Jesus Christ in sincerity. Amen.

---

poses (Rom. 15:16; 1 Cor. 1:2; 2 Thess. 2:13). Further, they can know God's present work of sanctification in their lives, experiencing deliverance from sin (Gal. 5:16; Phil. 2:12, 13; Col. 1:10) and having the guarantee of future, eternal deliverance from every kind of evil (1 Thess. 5:8). The short, two-edged sword enabled the heavily-armed soldier to attack deftly and defeat his enemy at close range. The believer's sword may be understood to be either "supplied by the Spirit" or "used by the Spirit." Paul further identified this sword as "the word of God" (see Heb. 4:12). "Word" (Gk. *rhēma*) most probably refers to specific sections of Scripture the Holy Spirit brings to mind to meet a particular need. Jesus' use of specific sections of Deuteronomy in His encounter with Satan in the wilderness exemplifies this (Matt. 4:4, 7, 10).

6:18 Prayer is not listed as a separate weapon of warfare but is rather given an all-encompassing status. Prayer is to be constant (1 Thess. 5:17) as the Christian prepares for battle, engages in it, and rests from it. All kinds of prayer are to be offered through the power of the Holy Spirit.

Philippians

AUTHOR

The apostle Paul, in a night vision a decade before the writing of this letter, received a call to preach in the region of Macedonia (Phil. 1:1; see Acts 16:6–10). Paul had never before been to Europe, but, obedient to the vision, he sailed to Macedonia's coastal port Neapolis, then walked nine miles inland to Philippi, the area's "foremost city" (Acts 16:12). Timothy, his young disciple and traveling companion on that trip, may have served as an amanuensis or secretary for this letter (Phil. 1:1; Acts 16:1–5; 1 Tim. 1:1, 2; 2 Tim. 1:1, 2). Philippians is categorized as one of Paul's four prison epistles (see chart, The Timeline of Paul).

DATE

After several subsequent visits to Philippi and the receiving of occasional financial support, Paul, now imprisoned in Rome, wrote this letter to the Philippians around A.D. 60–63.

BACKGROUND

SETTING: Philippi's original name was Krenides (lit. "Little Fountains"), a delightful town set on a hill with an abundance of springs for water supply. Philippi's river bank was mentioned as a gathering place for prayer for Lydia and other women (Acts 16:13).

In 356 B.C., when Philip of Macedon began his reign over the surrounding province of Macedonia, he gave his own name to these springs (lit. "the Philips"). In 42 B.C., Philippi became famous as a battlesite. Julius Caesar had been assassinated, and four of his generals vied to replace him: Cassius and Brutus fought Octavius and Mark Antony at Philippi. Octavius and Mark Antony were victorious, then fought each other for the top position. Octavius won, pronounced himself emperor, and changed his name to Augustus (even naming a month of the year after himself). With that, Rome was no longer a republic but an empirical dictatorship. About thirty years later, "a decree went out from Caesar Augustus that all the world should be registered" (Luke 2:1). Under God, this caesar determined the birthplace of Jesus.

Meanwhile, Augustus retreated often to his Philippi resort, the site of his great triumph, and designated it a Roman colony (Acts 16:12). For the Philippians, this designation made a tremendous social and psychological difference: The surrounding province of Macedonia, physically lower in elevation, now had no authority over them. And like all other Roman citizens, they were exempt from taxes, could buy and sell as they pleased, could file legal suits, and could assume privileges appropriate to being part of empirical Rome (Acts 16:20, 21, 37–39). This situation might explain their tendency to arrogance and the need for Paul to stress humility in his letter to them.

AUDIENCE: These Philippians are our cultural forebears—progressive westerners. When Paul crossed the water westward from Troas to Philippi—from Asia to Europe, culturally he took a giant step. The women of Philippi had great independence. They gath-

ered for meetings (Acts 16:13); they ran their own businesses (Acts 16:14); and they even feuded in the church (Phil. 4:2, 3).

Women played a prominent part in the Book of Philippians—perhaps as much or more than any other single book. The Philippian story began with women meeting on "the riverside, where prayer was customarily made" (Acts 16:12, 13). Since Philippi became the first European city in which Paul preached, his first European convert may have been a woman, Lydia of Philippi and her household (Acts 16:14); later came a Philippian jailer and his family (Acts 16:27–34). Paul's persecution began over his compassion for a young woman—a Philippian girl abused by the occult (Acts 16:16–19). And a decade later, trouble within the church focused on two feuding women, Euodia and Syntyche (Phil. 4:2, 3).

In the ten intervening years since his first visit, Paul, coming and going from Philippi several times, had been arrested, tried, and sent to Rome to a higher court, where he was soon to be on trial for his life before Nero (see chart, Political Rulers in the New Testament). Normally prisoners would have been held in some isolated dungeon and then executed; but because Paul was a Roman citizen, he had appealed to Caesar himself. Therefore, he was under house arrest and could write letters as well as receive visitors and gifts (Acts 28:30, 31). We have no biblical record of his death; tradition says he was later convicted and executed, following a second Roman imprisonment (see 2 Tim. 1:16, 17).

PURPOSE: The Philippians had occasionally sent Paul money, the latest support being delivered by young Epaphroditus, a member of their church. When Epaphroditus got deathly sick and then recovered, Paul wrote to the Philippians for two reasons: to thank them for their gift (Phil. 4:10–20) and to return Epaphroditus with the letter, so they could see for themselves that he was well again (Phil. 2:25, 27–30). He may also have used this letter to announce Timothy's coming visit (Phil. 2:19), to express his own desire to come again to Philippi (Phil. 2:24), to address the problem between the two women in the Philippian church (Phil. 4:2), or perhaps some combination of these.

LITERARY CHARACTERISTICS: As in Paul's other epistles, Philippians unfolds in the style of personal correspondence, opening with the mention of the author (which in subsequent generations has been moved to the closing of a letter), followed by the salutation or names of the addressees. There follows the formal greeting, then the body of the letter with final words of greeting as the conclusion. One unique feature of this letter is what some have described as a Christological hymn (Phil. 2:5–11). This beautiful, rhythmical passage presents a brief lesson in Christology, beginning with Jesus' pre-incarnate state, followed by His Incarnation, Crucifixion, and ultimately His heavenly exaltation.

THEMES

The letter is not primarily a doctrinal dissertation but a personal note: a flower as much to be enjoyed in a garden or vase as to be studied under a microscope. Its major themes, rather than being sequentially laid out, are mentioned and then interrupted many times.

The primary emphasis is joy (an idea occurring more than fifteen times) with resultant unity and humility as secondary emphases. The book from beginning to end lends itself to a rich study of these wonderful themes, around which the following outlines were built.

OUTLINE ON JOY

I. Paul, the Model (3:17; 4:9)
  A. Paul's rejoicing at the time of writing
    1. When he prayed for the Philippians (1:4)

2. When he heard Christ had been preached (1:16–18)
3. When the Philippians sent him money (4:10, 17)

B. Paul's anticipation for more rejoicing in the future
   1. When the Philippians became truly unified (2:2)
   2. When the Philippians were completed at the day of Christ (2:16)

II. The Philippians, the Followers
   A. In specific situations

1. "Rejoice with me," even if I am executed (2:17, 18).
2. "Rejoice" with Epaphroditus over his recovery (2:28).

B. Always, because it is right
   1. I minister to you for the purpose of your "progress and joy" (1:25, 26).
   2. It is a Christian characteristic (3:3).
   3. You must (3:1; 4:4)!

OUTLINE ON UNITY

I. Exhortations to Church Unity
   A. By Paul's delicate inclusiveness "You," "All [of you]," "you all," (1:1, 4, 7, 8, and others)
   B. By Paul's straightforward commands
      1. Urgings, implicit or explicit, to "one spirit," "one accord," "one mind" (1:27; 2:2, and others)
      2. Warnings, implicit or explicit, against "conceit," "disputing," disagreements (2:3, 14, and others)

II. Threats to Church Unity
   A. Doctrinal danger: legalism in the church (3:2–16)
      1. A warning against those who press for strict observance of laws (3:2, 3)
      2. The testimony of Paul as a former legalist (3:4–6)
      3. Paul's antidote: focus on Christ and His future (3:7–14)

B. Doctrinal danger: license in the church (3:18–21)
   1. Warning against those who opt for self-indulgence (3:18, 19)
   2. Paul's antidote: focus on Christ and His future (3:20, 21)

C. Relational danger: pride among church members
   1. Warnings against and examples of the "self-first" mentality (2:3, 21; 3:18, 19)
   2. Paul's antidotes: lowliness of mind (2:3, 5); not "self-esteem" but "others' esteem" (2:3, 4, 19, 20, 30; 3:15; 4:15–18).

D. Relational danger: a personal "dispute" in the church (4:2, 3)
   1. Warning to two women by name (4:2)
   2. Paul's antidote: enlist a third party to help reconcile (4:3)

OUTLINE ON HUMILITY

I. Three Models of Self-emptying
   A. Paul, writer of the letter (1:1), emptying himself of the desire for:
      1. Recognition (1:12–18)
      2. Personal profit (3:8; 4:16, 17)
      3. Life itself (1:21–24)
   B. Christ, subject of the letter (2:5–8), emptying Himself of the desire for:
      1. Recognition (2:7)
      2. Personal profit (2:7, 8)
      3. Life itself (2:8)
   C. Epaphroditus, bearer of the letter (2:25–30), emptying himself of the desire for:
      1. Recognition (2:26)

2. Personal profit (2:25, 27)
3. Life itself (2:30)

II. God's Way "Up" Is "Down" (see charts, Jesus' Pilgrimage; Paul's Pilgrimage)
   A. Christ's life (2:6–11)
      1. His voluntary descent into self-emptying (2:6–8)
      2. The Father's determination to lift Him up (2:9–11)
   B. Paul's life (3:4–10)
      1. His climb toward self-exaltation (3:4–6)
      2. His voluntary descent into self-emptying (3:8–10)

PRAYERS FOR YOUR CHILDREN

PRAYER REQUEST	SCRIPTURE PROMISE
Personal salvation and a committed life	1 Cor. 1:4–9; Gal. 1:3–5; Eph. 1:3–14; 3:14–21; Phil. 1:3–11; 2 Tim. 1:3–7
Sense of security and love	Ps. 91:10–12; John 17:14–17; Rom. 8:35–39
Presentation of a good example and worthy testimony	Eph. 6:1–4; 1 Thess. 1:2–10; 2 Thess. 1:3–8; Philem. 4–7
Development of the mind of Christ	Phil. 2:5–11; Col. 1:3–12
Knowledge of right and wrong	Prov. 20:11; 28:13; Phil. 1:9, 10
Protection from evil	Prov. 4:14, 15; Gal. 5:16; Eph. 6:11; James 4:7–9
Resistance to false teachings	Matt. 7:15; Col 2:8
Godly decision making	Prov. 3:5, 6; Rom. 12:1, 2; 1 Cor. 10:13, 31; Phil. 3:12–14
Establishment of realistic goals for life	Ps. 32:8; 138:8; 143:8–10; Prov. 4:20–27
Wise friendships	Prov. 13:20; 22:24, 25
A godly husband or wife and a happy marriage	2 Cor. 6:14; Eph. 5:22, 23
Management of time and stress	Prov. 16:9; Phil. 4:6
Development of good work habits	Col. 3:23; 2 Tim. 2:15
Discipline in financial planning	Mark 12:41–44; 2 Thess. 3:7–10

Greeting

1 Paul and Timothy, bondservants of Jesus Christ,

To all the saints in Christ Jesus who are in Philippi, with the bishops[a] and deacons:

²Grace to you and peace from God our Father and the Lord Jesus Christ.

Thankfulness and Prayer

³I thank my God upon every remembrance of you, ⁴always in every prayer of mine making request for you all with joy, ⁵for your fellowship in the gospel from the first day until now, ⁶being confident of this very thing, that He who has begun a good work in you will complete *it* until the day of Jesus Christ; ⁷just as it is right for me to think this of you all, because I have you in my heart, inasmuch as both in my chains and in the defense and confirmation of the gospel, you all

1:1 ªLiterally *overseers*

1:1 Paul omitted his usual title of "apostle." He was writing to the Philippians, not so much as an authority as a friend. "We are servants, you are saints" suggests the appealing humility that will become one of the letter's key themes.

1:2 Paul combined two languages and cultures in this unique greeting: "Grace" (Gk. *charis*) and "peace" (Gk. *eirēnē*; Heb. *shalom*). Both are typical greetings, and they are linked in a special greeting for a racially blended church. The church at Philippi had been blended from the start: Jewish women met for prayer (Acts 16:13); they were joined by Lydia, a Gentile

who became a Jewish proselyte (Acts 16:14, 15); then a Gentile jailer and his family were added (Acts 16:30–33). But beyond the simple greeting, Paul is linking two important Christian concepts, God's gifts to His children of "grace" or unmerited favor and "peace." Ultimately, there can be no peace without first receiving His grace.

1:5 Your fellowship in the gospel is Paul's way of acknowledging their financial support. At this time, he only alluded to receiving the gift; later he would thank them specifically (Phil. 4:10–19).

1:6 The day of Jesus Christ is a reference to the return of

FITNESS · A LIFESTYLE OF TOTAL HEALTH

Taking care of your physical body, also known as the Lord's temple, is a balancing act: We must attempt to achieve physical wellness and fitness without becoming narcisstic and self-consumed. Practicing healthy living and self-control can glorify God and make a person more effective in her daily walk with Him and her relationships with others. If a woman feels good, she usually has energy and enthusiasm that not only benefit herself, but others.

Stress control, exercise, and dietary moderation are key elements of total fitness (Phil. 4:6, 7). We are to work toward self-control in everything (1 Cor. 9:25), especially consumption of food (Matt. 6:25) and the use of alcoholic beverages (Eph. 5:18). We are to avoid gluttony (Prov. 23:20).

Also consider that Jesus and the apostles walked everywhere. Most people now get much less physical activity than God intended for the human body. Consistent daily activity can help people to remain happy and fit.

Though Paul minimized its importance, he recognized the value of exercise (1 Tim. 4:8). Solomon well knew the wisdom of the Lord is "health to your flesh, And strength to your bones" (Prov. 3:8).

Mental and emotional fitness, as well as physical fitness, are of major concern in our stressful world. As science and technology advance, we learn more about the complex interaction among the mental, emotional, spiritual, and physical aspects of life. We can be comforted to see that the Lord spoke about these interactions thousands of years ago (Prov. 17:22). Scripture was the first to record that a merry heart and courage can foster the healing of even very serious and life-threatening illnesses. James wrote that prayer and the anointing of oil in the name of the Lord was helpful in healing (James 5:14), and Daniel followed certain dietary principles and emerged healthier than his colleagues (Dan. 1:11–14). The Lord even said that His dietary and health statutes were designed as preventive medicine—so that His people might contract none of the Egyptian diseases (Ex. 15:26).

See also notes on Appearance (2 Cor. 3); Gluttony (Prov. 23); Nutrition (Lev. 11); Weight Control (1 Cor. 11)

---

are partakers with me of grace. [8]For God is my witness, how greatly I long for you all with the affection of Jesus Christ.

[9]And this I pray, that your love may abound still more and more in knowledge and all discernment, [10]that you may approve the things that are excellent, that you may be sincere and without offense till the day of Christ, [11]being filled with the fruits of righteousness which *are* by Jesus Christ, to the glory and praise of God.

Christ Is Preached

[12]But I want you to know, brethren, that the things *which happened* to me have actually turned out for the furtherance of the gospel, [13]so that it has become evident to the whole palace guard, and to all the rest, that my chains are in Christ; [14]and most of the brethren in the Lord, having become confident by my chains, are much more bold to speak the word without fear.

[15]Some indeed preach Christ even from envy and strife, and some also from goodwill: [16]The former[a] preach Christ from selfish ambition, not sincerely, supposing to add affliction to my chains;

[17]but the latter out of love, knowing that I am appointed for the defense of the gospel. [18]What then? Only *that* in every way, whether in pretense or in truth, Christ is preached; and in this I rejoice, yes, and will rejoice.

To Live Is Christ

[19]For I know that this will turn out for my deliverance through your prayer and the supply of the Spirit of Jesus Christ, [20]according to my earnest expectation and hope that in nothing I shall be ashamed, but with all boldness, as always, so now also Christ will be magnified in my body, whether by life or by death. [21]For to me, to live *is* Christ, and to die *is* gain. [22]But if *I* live on in the flesh, this *will mean* fruit from *my* labor; yet what I shall choose I cannot tell. [23]For[a] I am hard-pressed between the two, having a desire to depart and be with Christ, *which is* far better. [24]Nevertheless to remain in the flesh *is* more needful for you. [25]And being confident of this, I know that I shall remain

---

1:16 [a]NU-Text reverses the contents of verses 16 and 17. 1:23 [a]NU-Text and M-Text read *But.*

Christ. It is mentioned six times in the NT, three of them in this letter (vv. 6, 10; Phil. 2:16). This reference is not to be confused with the day of the Lord or Judgment Day. Paul here emphasized the keeping power of God in salvation. The Philippians were secure in their salvation, not only for the present but for the future as well.

1:7 Paul expressed an interesting progression: "Both in my chains" or while he was awaiting trial under house arrest, "in the defense and confirmation of the gospel" or when the time for his trial would come, and finally, "my deliverance" (v. 19) or specifically his acquittal.

JESUS' PILGRIMAGE

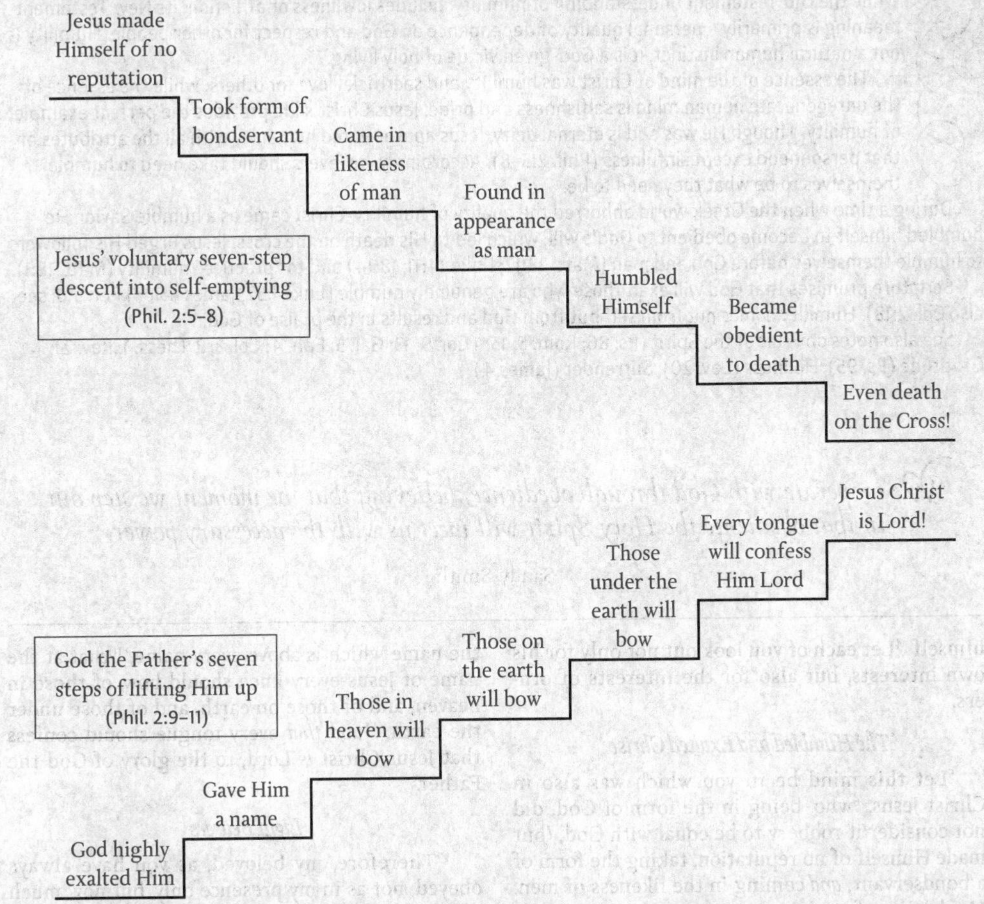

Jesus made Himself of no reputation

Took form of bondservant

Came in likeness of man

Found in appearance as man

Humbled Himself

Became obedient to death

Even death on the Cross!

Jesus' voluntary seven-step descent into self-emptying (Phil. 2:5–8)

Jesus Christ is Lord!

Every tongue will confess Him Lord

Those under the earth will bow

Those on the earth will bow

God the Father's seven steps of lifting Him up (Phil. 2:9–11)

Those in heaven will bow

Gave Him a name

God highly exalted Him

and continue with you all for your progress and joy of faith, ²⁶that your rejoicing for me may be more abundant in Jesus Christ by my coming to you again.

Striving and Suffering for Christ

²⁷Only let your conduct be worthy of the gospel of Christ, so that whether I come and see you or am absent, I may hear of your affairs, that you stand fast in one spirit, with one mind striving together for the faith of the gospel, ²⁸and not in any way terrified by your adversaries, which is to them a proof of perdition, but to you of salvation,ᵃ and that from God. ²⁹For to you it has been granted on behalf of

Christ, not only to believe in Him, but also to suffer for His sake, ³⁰having the same conflict which you saw in me and now hear *is* in me.

Unity Through Humility

2 Therefore if *there is* any consolation in Christ, if any comfort of love, if any fellowship of the Spirit, if any affection and mercy, ²fulfill my joy by being like-minded, having the same love, *being* of one accord, of one mind. ³*Let* nothing *be done* through selfish ambition or conceit, but in lowliness of mind let each esteem others better than

1:28 ᵃNU-Text reads *of your salvation*.

2:1 Paul's exhortation concerns unity within the church (see Introduction: Outline on Unity). He presents four arguments for unity: their position in Christ and the responsibilities in that relationship; their resources of comfort and encourage-

ment (Gk. *paraklēsis*, from *parakaleō*, lit. "to call alongside") prompted by love from Christ; their reward of fellowship within the body of Christ; their opportunity for compassion. Paul did not call for unity at the expense of commitment to

HUMILITY A YIELDING OF THE HEART

While the Old Testament understanding of humility includes lowliness or affliction, its New Testament meaning is primarily a personal quality of dependence on God and respect for other people. Humility is not a natural human instinct; it is a God-given virtue of holy living.

The essence of the mind of Christ was humility and sacrificial love for others, while the essence of the unregenerate human mind is selfishness and pride. Jesus Christ's life provides the perfect example of humility. Though He was and is eternal deity, Jesus appropriated humanity with all the attributes of that personhood except sinfulness (Phil. 2:5–8). Accordingly, believers should take heed to humble themselves to be what they need to be.

During a time when the Greek world abhorred the quality of humility, Christ came as a humble Savior. He humbled himself to become obedient to God's will, which led to His death on the cross. Jesus urged His followers to humble themselves before God and man (Matt. 23:12; Luke 14:11; 18:14) and to "practice" humility (Matt. 18:1).

Scripture promises that God will exalt those who are genuinely humble (Luke 1:52; James 4:10; 1 Pet. 5:6; see also Col. 2:18). Humility comes not from self but from God and results in the praise of God.

See also notes on Fruit of the Spirit (Ps. 86; Rom. 5; 15; 1 Cor. 9; 13; Gal. 5; Eph. 4; Col. 3; 2 Thess. 1; Rev. 2); Gratitude (Ps. 95); Holiness (Lev. 20); Surrender (James 4)

> *We cooperate with God through obedience, believing that the moment we step out in that obedience the Holy Spirit will meet us with the necessary power.*
>
> Sandy Smith

himself. ⁴Let each of you look out not only for his own interests, but also for the interests of others.

The Humbled and Exalted Christ

⁵Let this mind be in you which was also in Christ Jesus, ⁶who, being in the form of God, did not consider it robbery to be equal with God, ⁷but made Himself of no reputation, taking the form of a bondservant, *and* coming in the likeness of men. ⁸And being found in appearance as a man, He humbled Himself and became obedient to *the point of* death, even the death of the cross. ⁹Therefore God also has highly exalted Him and given Him the name which is above every name, ¹⁰that at the name of Jesus every knee should bow, of those in heaven, and of those on earth, and of those under the earth, ¹¹and *that* every tongue should confess that Jesus Christ *is* Lord, to the glory of God the Father.

Light Bearers

¹²Therefore, my beloved, as you have always obeyed, not as in my presence only, but now much more in my absence, work out your own salvation with fear and trembling; ¹³for it is God who works in you both to will and to do for *His* good pleasure.

---

truth, but he made clear that his own joy could not be complete until the believers at Philippi were "like-minded" (v. 2; see Phil. 4:2).

2:6 This great Christological section is known as the *kenōsis* passage (vv. 6–11; see John 1:1–18; Col. 1:15–23; 2:9, 10; Heb. 1:1–4; chart, The Definitive Christological Passages) The "form" (Gk. *morphē*) of God indicated the essential inward reality that would manifest the outward, visible glory of God in heaven. Satan had grasped for equality with God (Is. 14:12–14); Adam and Eve had grasped for it (Gen. 3:5, 6); but Christ had no need to grasp for that which He already had (Phil. 2:6).

2:7 The phrase made Himself of no reputation (Gk. *kenōsis*, lit. "empty") expressed the idea that He set aside, not His deity, but the glory of His deity—His privileges (v. 7; see John 13:3, 4; 1 Pet. 3, Submission). "Coming in the likeness of men" was a new phenomenon (Phil. 2:7). God had made man in His

likeness (Gen. 1:26); now He voluntarily made Himself in man's likeness. In so doing "He humbled Himself" (Phil. 2:8; the same word translated "lowliness" in v. 3).

2:8 The death of the Cross was His final humiliation (v. 8). No Roman citizen could be crucified: Paul the writer was exempt; the Philippian readers, unless they were slaves, were exempt. This form of death carried an OT curse (Deut. 21:23).

2:10, 11 The bowing of every knee will be no mere genuflection but an expression of total submission (v. 10) from more beings than we can now envision (v. 10; see Rev. 5:13). "Jesus Christ is Lord" includes three names (Phil. 2:11): Jesus, His earthly name (Acts 2:22); Christ, His messianic title or intercessory name (Acts 2:31); and Lord, His glorious eternal title (Acts 2:36; Rev. 17:14).

2:12, 13 Work out your own salvation has no thought of "work for . . ." in the sense of personal work for gain. Justification

PAUL'S PILGRIMAGE

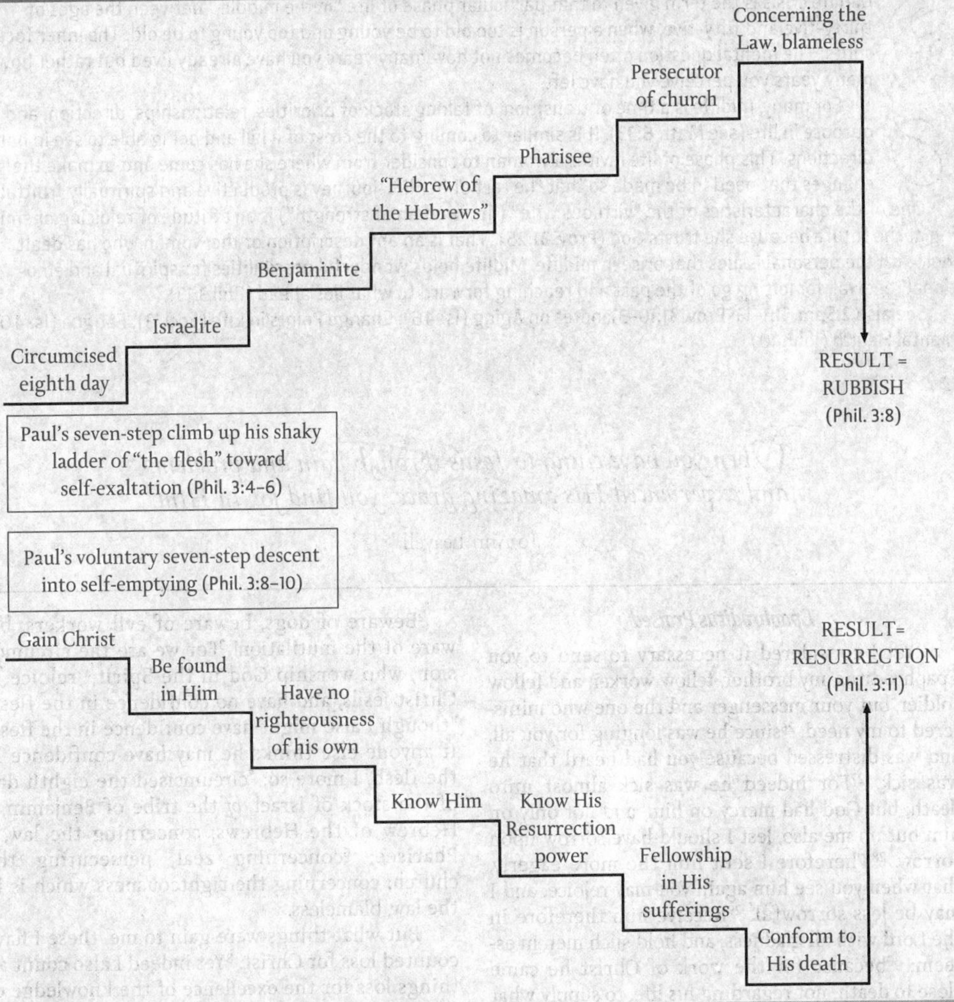

Concerning the
Law, blameless

Persecutor
of church

Pharisee

"Hebrew of
the Hebrews"

Benjaminite

Israelite

Circumcised
eighth day

RESULT =
RUBBISH
(Phil. 3:8)

Paul's seven-step climb up his shaky
ladder of "the flesh" toward
self-exaltation (Phil. 3:4–6)

Paul's voluntary seven-step descent
into self-emptying (Phil. 3:8–10)

Gain Christ

RESULT=
RESURRECTION
(Phil. 3:11)

Be found
in Him

Have no
righteousness
of his own

Know Him

Know His
Resurrection
power

Fellowship
in His
sufferings

Conform to
His death

Timothy Commended

¹⁴Do all things without complaining and disputing, ¹⁵that you may become blameless and harmless, children of God without fault in the midst of a crooked and perverse generation, among whom you shine as lights in the world, ¹⁶holding fast the word of life, so that I may rejoice in the day of Christ that I have not run in vain or labored in vain.

¹⁷Yes, and if I am being poured out *as a drink offering* on the sacrifice and service of your faith, I am glad and rejoice with you all. ¹⁸For the same reason you also be glad and rejoice with me.

¹⁹But I trust in the Lord Jesus to send Timothy to you shortly, that I also may be encouraged when I know your state. ²⁰For I have no one like-minded, who will sincerely care for your state. ²¹For all seek their own, not the things which are of Christ Jesus. ²²But you know his proven character, that as a son with *his* father he served with me in the gospel. ²³Therefore I hope to send him at once, as soon as I see how it goes with me. ²⁴But I trust in the Lord that I myself shall also come shortly.

---

must be followed by sanctification (see chart, Theological Terms). Believers are to "work" out their faith in their exter-

nal, daily lives in the sure knowledge that "it is God who works in" them to guide and empower.

MIDLIFE CRISIS *IN THE MIDDLE OF LIFE*

Midlife crisis is the term given to that particular phase of life "in the middle," between the ages of thirty-five and fifty-five, when a person is too old to be young and too young to be old. The inner focus shifts. The mental question often becomes not how many years you have already lived but rather how many years you perceive you have left.

For many, midlife is a time of transition, of taking stock of priorities, relationships, direction, and purpose in life (see Matt. 6:33). It is similar to coming to the crest of a hill and being able to see in both directions. This phase of life invites a woman to consider from where she has come and to make the changes that need to be made so that the rest of her life-journey is productive and spiritually fruitful.

One of the characteristics of the "virtuous wife" (lit. "woman of strength") is an attitude of rejoicing or smiling at the future because she trusts God (Prov. 31:25). That is an apt description of the woman who has dealt well with the personal issues that arise in midlife. Midlife holds wonderful possibilities for spiritual and emotional renewal, for letting go of the past and reaching forward to what lies ahead (Phil 3:13).

See also 2 Sam. 11:1–13; Prov. 31:10–31; notes on Aging (Is. 46); Change Points in Life (Eccl. 3); Fatigue (Is. 40); Mental Health (John 10)

When you have clung to Jesus through pain and problems and experienced His amazing grace, you find joy in Him.

Jo Ann Leavell

Epaphroditus Praised

[25]Yet I considered it necessary to send to you Epaphroditus, my brother, fellow worker, and fellow soldier, but your messenger and the one who ministered to my need; [26]since he was longing for you all, and was distressed because you had heard that he was sick. [27]For indeed he was sick almost unto death; but God had mercy on him, and not only on him but on me also, lest I should have sorrow upon sorrow. [28]Therefore I sent him the more eagerly, that when you see him again you may rejoice, and I may be less sorrowful. [29]Receive him therefore in the Lord with all gladness, and hold such men in esteem; [30]because for the work of Christ he came close to death, not regarding his life, to supply what was lacking in your service toward me.

All for Christ

3 Finally, my brethren, rejoice in the Lord. For me to write the same things to you *is* not tedious, but for you *it is* safe.

[2]Beware of dogs, beware of evil workers, beware of the mutilation! [3]For we are the circumcision, who worship God in the Spirit,[a] rejoice in Christ Jesus, and have no confidence in the flesh, [4]though I also might have confidence in the flesh. If anyone else thinks he may have confidence in the flesh, I more so: [5]circumcised the eighth day, of the stock of Israel, *of* the tribe of Benjamin, a Hebrew of the Hebrews; concerning the law, a Pharisee; [6]concerning zeal, persecuting the church; concerning the righteousness which is in the law, blameless.

[7]But what things were gain to me, these I have counted loss for Christ. [8]Yet indeed I also count all things loss for the excellence of the knowledge of Christ Jesus my Lord, for whom I have suffered the loss of all things, and count them as rubbish, that I may gain Christ [9]and be found in Him, not having my own righteousness, which *is* from the

·······························

3:3 [a]NU-Text and M-Text read *who worship in the Spirit of God.*

3:2 Dogs in the ancient Near East were mostly street roamers, scavengers (v. 2). Jews frequently called Gentiles "dogs." By "dogs" Paul meant Jewish legalists who insisted on the rite of circumcision for all believers. Paul's implications were emotional and strong: Circumcision was neat, planned surgery; yet the Judaizers would rip, tear, and mutilate tender, new believers! But those who had voluntarily "cut away" all confidence in the flesh, were the true circumcision (v. 3).

3:5 Converts to Judaism were circumcised as adults; Ishmaelites, when they were 13; genuine Jews, on the eighth day (Luke 2:21). Paul's ancestry traced back to Jacob (Israel)

through Rachel, Jacob's favorite wife, and their especially adored Benjamin, the youngest and only son born in the Land of Promise. The tribe of Benjamin produced Israel's first king, Saul, for whom Paul, at his birth, was named. The phrase "a Hebrew of the Hebrews" may have been an allusion to his pure Jewish ancestry since both parents were Jews, or the phrase may also have suggested Jewish upbringing. Despite his birth and rearing in the midst of the Diaspora or scattering of the Jews, his primary roots were Jewish (Acts 6:1; 22:2, 3). Paul was not only a Pharisee but also the son of a Pharisee (Acts 23:6; see chart, Jewish Sects).

EUODIA AND SYNTYCHE   *Women in Dispute*

Euodia and Syntyche were involved in the building of the church in Philippi around 61 A.D. Their diligent leadership in the church was recognized by the apostle Paul himself as well as other believers (Phil. 4:3). Therefore, their dispute threatened to affect the harmony and well-being of the entire congregation.

Paul's solution was twofold. First, he called the women to "be of the same mind." They were to avoid foolish disputes and those things which were "unprofitable." They were rather to build up the body by letting each esteem others better than herself and to look out not only for her own interest but for the interest of others (Phil. 2:3, 4). Even though their issues may have been important from a human perspective, they were not "profitable" from a spiritual one.

The second action Paul took was to make an urgent plea to the other leaders in the church to help Euodia and Syntyche reconcile and return to the "same mind" in the Lord. The body is to work together to help one another function lovingly and harmoniously in Christ.

Right relationships are essential for the health of the church. When Christian women have the mind of Christ, they do not demand their own ways. Instead, they choose what is most loving and edifying for the building up of the whole congregation—that is, what is "profitable." This is not easy, especially when doctrinal issues are involved. Therefore, much prayer, humility, and counsel from the Word of God is needed to help reconcile differences.

See also Phil. 2:2, 14; 3:16; 1 Cor. 1:11; notes on Conflict (Matt. 18); Leadership (1 Sam. 25)

---

law, but that which *is* through faith in Christ, the righteousness which is from God by faith; [10]that I may know Him and the power of His resurrection, and the fellowship of His sufferings, being conformed to His death, [11]if, by any means, I may attain to the resurrection from the dead.

Pressing Toward the Goal

[12]Not that I have already attained, or am already perfected; but I press on, that I may lay hold of that for which Christ Jesus has also laid hold of me. [13]Brethren, I do not count myself to have apprehended; but one thing *I do,* forgetting those things which are behind and reaching forward to those things which are ahead, [14]I press toward the goal for the prize of the upward call of God in Christ Jesus.

[15]Therefore let us, as many as are mature, have this mind; and if in anything you think otherwise, God will reveal even this to you. [16]Nevertheless, to *the degree* that we have already attained, let us walk by the same rule,[a] let us be of the same mind.

Our Citizenship in Heaven

[17]Brethren, join in following my example, and note those who so walk, as you have us for a pattern. [18]For many walk, of whom I have told you often, and now tell you even weeping, *that they are* the enemies of the cross of Christ: [19]whose end *is* destruction, whose god *is their* belly, and *whose* glory *is* in their shame—who set their mind on earthly things. [20]For our citizenship is in heaven, from which we also eagerly wait for the Savior, the Lord Jesus Christ, [21]who will transform our lowly body that it may be conformed to His glorious body, according to the working by which He is able even to subdue all things to Himself.

4 Therefore, my beloved and longed-for brethren, my joy and crown, so stand fast in the Lord, beloved.

Be United, Joyful, and in Prayer

[2]I implore Euodia and I implore Syntyche to be of the same mind in the Lord. [3]And[a] I urge you also, true companion, help these women who labored with me in the gospel, with Clement also, and the rest of my fellow workers, whose names *are* in the Book of Life.

3:16 [a]NU-Text omits *rule* and the rest of the verse.   4:3 [a]NU-Text and M-Text read *Yes.*

3:10 Resurrection . . . sufferings . . . death—for Christ, this order would be wrong; but for believers, it is right. Only when believers come to know His Resurrection power are they able to fellowship with Him in sufferings and die to sin and self.

3:21 Christ will transform the earthly "lowly form," a term pointing to the weakness or humble status of the mortal body rather than its sinfulness. Then this glorified body of the believer will conform or become similar in form to Christ's Resurrection body (see 1 John 3:2). This new spiritual body will be a wedding garment suitable for heaven.

4:3 True companion (Gk. *suzuge,* lit. "yokefellow") is interpreted by some as the proper name of a leader in the church and by others as a reference to the task of arbitration. In any case, the method for resolving this quarrel between the two women is somewhat different from what is suggested in Matthew 18:15–17. A peacemaker is appointed (Matt. 5:19). Paul's use of "yokefellow" suggests a field plow with a yoke or wooden crossbar, holding two loops or collars. Oxen had to bow their heads to unite to do a task in harmony. Euodia and Syntyche were true believers who worked with Paul in the

STRESS MANAGEMENT — *PEACE THAT PASSES UNDERSTANDING*

Through prayer, supplication, and thanksgiving, you can realize a "peace . . . which surpasses all understanding" and know that this peace "will guard your hearts and minds" (Phil 4:6, 7).

Your natural human desire for acceptance, status, and possessions can create tension within. If you perceive that your needs or desires are not going to be met, you may experience anxiety and stress. How can you "be anxious for nothing" in the face of such situations?

Managing stress for a Christian begins with understanding yourself and knowing what Scripture teaches about the nature of God. To understand yourself means to know your basic nature, the potential of your strengths, and the limits of your weaknesses. This is no small task, for self-deception can prevent clear discernment (Jer. 17:9). Pride and independence can block self-awareness. God Himself must give the self-awareness needed (Jer. 17:10). Only He can show clearly where change is needed and bring about that change in basic human nature (Ps. 139:23, 24).

An understanding of the nature of God comes from His self-revelation in Scripture and in Christ (John 1:14, 18). Knowing and accepting the unchanging nature of God produces stability and peace (Mal. 3:6; Heb. 13:8). Understanding the quality of His character inspires trust (1 John 1:5).

Much of stress dissipates when you acknowledge your dependence upon God and submit to His leadership (Ps. 73:26; 1 Pet. 5:6, 7), recognizing that you are locked into time and space as finite creatures, while He is infinite, eternal, and omnipresent.

See also 2 Cor. 5:17; notes on Confidence (Is. 30); Depression (1 Sam. 16); Distress (Ps. 18); Emotions (Ps. 42); Fatigue (Is. 40); Health (Prov. 3); Priorities (Matt. 6); Worry (Rom. 8)

---

⁴Rejoice in the Lord always. Again I will say, rejoice!

⁵Let your gentleness be known to all men. The Lord *is* at hand.

⁶Be anxious for nothing, but in everything by prayer and supplication, with thanksgiving, let your requests be made known to God; ⁷and the peace of God, which surpasses all understanding, will guard your hearts and minds through Christ Jesus.

Meditate on These Things

⁸Finally, brethren, whatever things are true, whatever things *are* noble, whatever things *are* just, whatever things *are* pure, whatever things *are* lovely, whatever things *are* of good report, if *there is* any virtue and if *there is* anything praiseworthy—meditate on these things. ⁹The things which you learned and received and heard and saw in me, these do, and the God of peace will be with you.

Philippian Generosity

¹⁰But I rejoiced in the Lord greatly that now at last your care for me has flourished again; though you surely did care, but you lacked opportunity. ¹¹Not that I speak in regard to need, for I have learned in whatever state I am, to be content: ¹²I know how to be abased, and I know how to abound. Everywhere and in all things I have learned both to be full and to be hungry, both to abound and to suffer need. ¹³I can do all things through Christᵃ who strengthens me.

¹⁴Nevertheless you have done well that you shared in my distress. ¹⁵Now you Philippians know also that in the beginning of the gospel, when I departed from Macedonia, no church shared with me concerning giving and receiving but you only. ¹⁶For even in Thessalonica you sent *aid* once and again for my necessities. ¹⁷Not that I seek the gift, but I seek the fruit that abounds to your account. ¹⁸Indeed I have all and abound. I am full, having received from Epaphroditus the things *sent* from you, a sweet-smelling aroma, an acceptable sacrifice, well pleasing to God. ¹⁹And my God shall supply all your need according to His riches in glory by Christ Jesus. ²⁰Now to our God and Father *be* glory forever and ever. Amen.

····················

4:13 ᵃNU-Text reads *Him who.*

---

gospel ministry. But they were divided in their thinking and needed to be reconciled in order to benefit the whole church. Perhaps Paul had these two women in mind throughout his letter, with its heavy emphasis on humility and unity.

4:10–19 Paul modeled Christian courtesy, delicacy, tact. He expressed deep gratitude (vv. 10, 14). Yet he also used this as an opportunity to teach the Philippians more about the providence and provision of God and the expectancy and contentment of the believer who would wait on the Lord (vv. 11, 14).

Believers are to be "content," not *with* circumstances but *in* circumstances (v. 11). This godly contentment does not preclude drive, ambition, or righting wrongs in life (see 1 Tim. 6, Contentment). Such faith was not his at birth but was painfully and tediously developed by walking with the Lord so that he learned to be content with anything, to live above things, to be unaffected by circumstance.

4:19 My God shall supply all your need is to be seen in its context. Such amazing generosity does not allow for foolish and

To learn humility is to learn contentment in all circumstances. Humility is not in what we own or achieve, but in maintaining a teachable attitude, a willingness to bend to the will of the Father.

Jan Silvious

Greeting and Blessing

²¹Greet every saint in Christ Jesus. The brethren who are with me greet you. ²²All the saints greet you, but especially those who are of Caesar's household.

²³The grace of our Lord Jesus Christ be with you all.[a] Amen.

4:23 [a]NU-Text reads *your spirit.*

frivolous spending on our part while God is considered responsible for necessities. Rather, because the Philippians had been so generous in their Christian giving, God would meet their needs as well (vv. 8–10; see 2 Cor. 9:7, 8).

Colossians

Paul undoubtedly wrote this Epistle to the Colossians, although he did not visit the congregation personally. Bound in chains in Rome, Paul wrote this letter of encouragement, admonition, and warning to the Colossians, probably at the same time he wrote Philemon (Col. 4:10).

Paul's Epistle to the Colossians is dated during his house arrest in Rome, probably A.D. 60–63 (Acts 28:16–31). Some recent scholars have questioned this time frame and have even postulated that this epistle was written well into the second century to refute a well-developed Gnosticism. Others suggest the letter was written during an imprisonment in Ephesus. However, both theories lack strong evidence. This prison letter was most likely written within the same year as Philemon and Ephesians.

SETTING: The church at Colosse was predominantly a Gentile church along with a few Jewish cultural elites. The faith of these new converts was being distorted by Greek mystery religions and mysticism as well as threatened by some Jewish laws and customs. Epaphras had evidently brought word to Paul of this heresy that had infiltrated the church (Col. 1:7). This heresy must be defined from the text itself, for it is diverse and somewhat complicated. Basically Paul refuted several deviations:

- A strict obligation to certain foods and drinks;
- A digression from the supremacy of Christ and His sufficiency for all;
- A denial of the humanity of Christ;
- A "super-knowledge" of Christ, which boasted of added wisdom and insight.

PURPOSE: Paul urged the Colossians to preserve true doctrine in the church regarding the sufficiency and supremacy of Christ. Also, he provided Christian readers with a practical theology for day-to-day living and growth in the faith.

AUDIENCE: The new converts in the city of Colosse in the Lychus Valley were the recipients of this letter. Epaphras and Timothy had evangelized this city, along with the cities of Hierapolis and Laodicea (Col. 4:13).

LITERARY CHARACTERISTICS: Although Paul's style differs in this letter from some of his other epistles, he follows a typical Graeco-Roman correspondence form, identifying himself as the author at the beginning of the letter.

- Christ is God's only "Son" and a principal participant in creation;
- False asceticism and ritualistic observances are denounced;
- A new freedom "in Christ" is expounded, along with practical guidelines for Christian living.

Greeting

1 Paul, an apostle of Jesus Christ by the will of God, and Timothy our brother,

[2]To the saints and faithful brethren in Christ *who are* in Colosse:

Grace to you and peace from God our Father and the Lord Jesus Christ.[a]

Their Faith in Christ

[3]We give thanks to the God and Father of our Lord Jesus Christ, praying always for you, [4]since we heard of your faith in Christ Jesus and of your love for all the saints; [5]because of the hope which is laid up for you in heaven, of which you heard before in the word of the truth of the gospel, [6]which has come to you, as *it has* also in all the world, and is bringing forth fruit,[a] as *it is* also among you since the day you heard and knew the grace of God in truth; [7]as you also learned from Epaphras, our dear fellow servant, who is a faithful minister of Christ on your behalf, [8]who also declared to us your love in the Spirit.

Preeminence of Christ

[9]For this reason we also, since the day we heard it, do not cease to pray for you, and to ask that you may be filled with the knowledge of His

---

1:2 [a]NU-Text omits *and the Lord Jesus Christ.* 1:6 [a]NU-Text and M-Text add *and growing.*

1:1 Paul's authority for writing this letter is found in his identity as an "apostle" (Gk. *apostolos*, lit. "one sent") of Jesus Christ.

1:2 Saints (lit. "ones set apart") includes all believers and not just certain ones with unique virtues. The virtues, in fact, stem from the fact that these believers are now "in Christ," a phrase used by Paul more than 160 times in his writings, here in Colossians more than 10 times.

1:7 Epaphras, probably the "minister" of the Colossian fellowship and the man most responsible for bringing the gospel message to the Lychus Valley, is with Paul as this letter is written and most likely will deliver it to the believers in Colosse. He was converted under Paul's preaching in Ephesus (Col. 4:12).

1:9 Paul began his defense against the Colossian heresy by first explaining that full "knowledge" (Gk. *epignōsis*) of God is not reserved for a select few, as the Gnostics claimed in referring to their own supposedly superior knowledge (Gk. *gnōsis*). Rather, this full knowledge, once a mystery hidden, is now available to anyone who would sincerely seek God.

IDENTITY IN CHRIST *A MEMBER OF HIS FAMILY*

Believers are secured by the supernatural glue of the Trinity. To be separated from Christ would require prying open the hand of the Father (John 10:29) and being snatched from the Son (v. 28) after breaking the seal of the Holy Spirit (Eph. 1:13, 14).

Jesus became one of us so that we could be one of His. In securing our salvation, God did more than forgive us; He made us members of His family (Eph. 2:19). Just as a newborn baby girl arrives with a genetic code that is permanently hers, each spiritually born-again person receives a spiritual genetic code (2 Cor. 5:17, 18). In accepting Christ and bonding ourselves to Him through faith, each one of us becomes a new creation with forgiveness for sins in the past, guidance and nurture for the present, and security and hope in the future (2 Cor. 5:17).

We have access to all that Jesus is; we, as joint heirs, potentially have all He has (Rom. 8:17). God hears us because He hears Christ (Heb. 4:14–16) and loves us the way He loves Christ (Rom. 8:39). In a nutshell, identity in Christ means every child of God can point to Jesus and before the Father's throne testify: "I'm with Him."

See also Matt. 12:47–50; Rom. 8:9–11; Eph. 2:10; notes on Access to God (Rom. 10); Inheritance (Prov. 13); Priesthood of the Believer (1 Pet. 2); Promises of God (2 Pet. 1); Self-esteem (2 Cor. 10)

---

will in all wisdom and spiritual understanding; [10]that you may walk worthy of the Lord, fully pleasing *Him,* being fruitful in every good work and increasing in the knowledge of God; [11]strengthened with all might, according to His glorious power, for all patience and longsuffering with joy; [12]giving thanks to the Father who has qualified us to be partakers of the inheritance of the saints in the light. [13]He has delivered us from the power of darkness and conveyed *us* into the kingdom of the Son of His love, [14]in whom we have redemption through His blood,[a] the forgiveness of sins.

[15]He is the image of the invisible God, the firstborn over all creation. [16]For by Him all things were created that are in heaven and that are on earth, visible and invisible, whether thrones or dominions or principalities or powers. All things were created through Him and for Him. [17]And He is before all things, and in Him all things consist. [18]And He is the head of the body, the church, who is the beginning, the firstborn

from the dead, that in all things He may have the preeminence.

Reconciled in Christ

[19]For it pleased *the Father that* in Him all the fullness should dwell, [20]and by Him to reconcile all things to Himself, by Him, whether things on earth or things in heaven, having made peace through the blood of His cross.

[21]And you, who once were alienated and enemies in your mind by wicked works, yet now He has reconciled [22]in the body of His flesh through death, to present you holy, and blameless, and above reproach in His sight— [23]if indeed you continue in the faith, grounded and steadfast, and are not moved away from the hope of the gospel which you heard, which was preached to every creature under heaven, of which I, Paul, became a minister.

1:14 [a]NU-Text and M-Text omit *through His blood.*

Your husband will never truly be yours until you have first given him back to God. He is yours only when you are willing to let him go wherever God calls him and do what God wants him to do.

Lila Trotman

1:15–20 The description of Christ is written in the form of an early Christian hymn. Paul detailed the supremacy and sufficiency of Christ by describing Him as the "image" or exact replica of God Himself (see chart, The Definitive Christological Passages). Paul disputed the Colossian heresy by proclaiming Christ *is* God Himself, not simply an emanation or angelic being. Because of this, all creation is under His power and authority. Christ has always been pre-eminent or in "first place."

1:20–22 The term reconciliation is important to Paul's theology of restoring mankind to a proper relationship with God. But this reconciliation can only come through "the blood of His cross," reflecting the atoning significance of Christ's penal, substitutionary death. Paul taught the necessity of a blood sacrifice, fulfilling the OT covenant between God and His people in order that they might be restored to a relationship with Him (Lev. 17:11; see Heb. 9:22).

CREATIVITY   EXPRESSING YOUR GIFTS

Human creativity differs from that of the Lord God in two ways: He is capable of creating out of nothing, and His creativity is unlimited (Gen. 1:1—2:3). Human creativity is locked into the natural world and is limited to that which can be experienced and thought, and in many respects, to that which can be articulated or framed in language, art, or music.

Because humans are created in the image of a creative God, they have the potential for creativity, which may surface in a myriad of ways: resolving a problem, hatching an idea, adapting a recipe, stretching a budget, or many other expressions of self. Creativity is not limited to the artistic but adds to all of life a personal imprimatur with zest and joy. Creativity is not necessarily originality but rather a determination to bring about change (2 Cor. 5:17). This ultimately means losing both self and limitations in Christ.

Creativity demands focus, commitment, and discipline. Believers are to create only that which is for good (1 Pet. 4:19), and they must never worship that which was created (Rom. 1:25). They must look within for God-given gifts, believe in divinely appointed abilities, maximize circumstances and situations, wait with patience for guidance from the Holy Spirit, and proceed with perseverance to accomplish the tasks God has given. Failure is a useful tool for creativity because it may become a stepping-stone to something better. Sometimes creativity calls forth a new course of action (Phil. 3:12-14); always it presupposes a heart turned toward God (Ps. 51:10). More often than not creativity means new discoveries and possibilities (2 Cor. 5:17).

See also notes on Celebrations and Holidays (Ex. 12); Flexibility (Deut. 10); Homemaking (Prov. 24); Hospitality (1 Pet. 4); Spiritual Gifts (Rom. 12)

Sacrificial Service for Christ

24I now rejoice in my sufferings for you, and fill up in my flesh what is lacking in the afflictions of Christ, for the sake of His body, which is the church, 25of which I became a minister according to the stewardship from God which was given to me for you, to fulfill the word of God, 26the mystery which has been hidden from ages and from generations, but now has been revealed to His saints. 27To them God willed to make known what are the riches of the glory of this mystery among the Gentiles: whicha is Christ in you, the hope of glory. 28Him we preach, warning every man and teaching every man in all wisdom, that we may present every man perfect in Christ Jesus. 29To this *end* I also labor, striving according to His working which works in me mightily.

Not Philosophy but Christ

2 For I want you to know what a great conflict I have for you and those in Laodicea, and *for* as many as have not seen my face in the flesh, 2that their hearts may be encouraged, being knit together in love, and *attaining* to all riches of the full assurance of understanding, to the knowledge of the mystery of God, both of the Father anda of Christ, 3in whom are hidden all the treasures of wisdom and knowledge.

4Now this I say lest anyone should deceive you with persuasive words. 5For though I am absent in the flesh, yet I am with you in spirit, rejoicing to see your *good* order and the steadfastness of your faith in Christ.

6As you therefore have received Christ Jesus the Lord, so walk in Him, 7rooted and built up in Him and established in the faith, as you have been taught, abounding in ita with thanksgiving.

8Beware lest anyone cheat you through philosophy and empty deceit, according to the tradition

1:27 aM-Text reads *who*.   2:2 aNU-Text omits *both of the Father and*.
2:7 aNU-Text omits *in it*.

1:24 Paul did not see his sufferings as qualifying him for a higher plane of reward. Rather, Paul viewed his sufferings as part of his commission to proclaim the "mystery" of God's riches to all people and to describe the new life of Christ indwelling all those whom He has redeemed. Christ then would reign within the hearts of all believers.

1:27 This mystery revealed is "Christ in you, the hope of glory." God willed to make this mystery known, not only to the Jew but also to the Gentiles to whom Paul was sent.

1:28 Faithful Christian preaching will warn against heresy and teach the truths of Christ. Then all believers may be presented to God perfect, not in themselves, but in Christ. This is the mystery hidden and now revealed!

2:8 Paul warned these new believers not to confuse true doctrine with the heresies that abounded in the Colossian church. The phrase "basic principles of the world" (Gk. *stoicheia*) refers to demonic powers or evil angelic beings who would "cheat" (or "plunder" or "take captive"). The heresy that would pull the believer away was undoubtedly an early form of Gnosticism (see John 1:4, note). The heresy described is very persuasive (Col. 2:4); it is based on human tradition instead of divine revelation (v. 8); it is legalistic (v. 16); it involves worship of angels (v. 18); it is mystical with visions and revelations (v. 18); it calls for asceticism (v. 23). This elitist, intellectual group possessing unusual intelligence, knowledge, and wisdom (vv. 4–23) relates to a worldly philosophy that

EMPLOYMENT   THE REWARDS OF WORK

One basis of good management is to recognize and reward employees for outstanding performance. Still, many employees feel that they never receive the recognition or rewards they deserve from their earthly employers.

Believers are in an ideal situation when it comes to the question of rewards because God has a recognition and incentive program better than any employer could ever devise. He promises that as they perform everyday duties as unto Him, He will recognize and reward them, whether employers ever appreciate them or not (Matt. 6:19–21; Heb. 6:10).

Jesus taught that if believers rely solely on rewards from others, they will miss God's reward. He shows that if the motivation is to be recognized and rewarded here on earth, that will be the full extent of the reward. He advises us to work for recognition from God, not others—for rewards that are eternal not temporal (Matt. 6:1–4).

Earthly recognition is rarely given fairly. Some receive recognition they do not deserve, and others who deserve recognition never get it. Furthermore, earthly recognition is fickle; the winds of fame can shift suddenly. God's recognition, by comparison, lasts through eternity, is fairly distributed, and will be there always.

What a difference when believers understand that people's rewards and recognition are not what is needed. When they are working for the Lord's approval, they are freed from being a slave to people (Heb. 11:5; 13:21; 1 John 3:22). When they know they are going to get their reward from the Lord, whether or not people recognize their contribution matters less and less. They are free from that need to please others in order to be accepted (Eph. 6:6; 1 Thess. 2:4).

See also Eccl. 3:1–15; Col. 3:17; notes on Blessings (Gen. 12); Change Points in Life (Eccl. 3); Contentment (1 Tim. 6); Employment (Eccl. 9; Acts 18; 2 Cor. 2; 1 Pet. 2); Friendship (Luke 1)

---

of men, according to the basic principles of the world, and not according to Christ. ⁹For in Him dwells all the fullness of the Godhead bodily; ¹⁰and you are complete in Him, who is the head of all principality and power.

Not Legalism but Christ

¹¹In Him you were also circumcised with the circumcision made without hands, by putting off the body of the sins[a] of the flesh, by the circumcision of Christ, ¹²buried with Him in baptism, in which you also were raised with *Him* through faith in the working of God, who raised Him from the dead. ¹³And you, being dead in your trespasses and the uncircumcision of your flesh, He has made alive together with Him, having forgiven you all trespasses, ¹⁴having wiped out the hand-writing of requirements that was against us, which was contrary to us. And He has taken it out of the way, having nailed it to the cross. ¹⁵Having disarmed principalities and powers, He made a public spectacle of them, triumphing over them in it.

¹⁶So let no one judge you in food or in drink, or regarding a festival or a new moon or sabbaths, ¹⁷which are a shadow of things to come, but the substance is of Christ. ¹⁸Let no one cheat you of your reward, taking delight in *false* humility and worship of angels, intruding into those things which he has not[a] seen, vainly puffed up by his fleshly mind, ¹⁹and not holding fast to the Head, from whom all the body, nourished and knit

2:11 ᵃNU-Text omits *of the sins*.   2:18 ᵃNU-Text omits *not*.

---

combines a man-made religion purporting to sanctify the believer through her own knowledge and philosophy with the practice of ceremonial rituals. Paul explicitly stated that genuine faith rests on Christ and Christ alone.

2:9 The Gnostic idea that Jesus never existed as a genuine human being but rather had a phantom or angelic form contradicts the reality of Jesus as both divine and human.

2:11 Paul spoke of a new circumcision—not a physical act, but a spiritual circumcision that sets believers free from the sins of the flesh. The Colossians were mainly Gentiles and probably had never been physically circumcised. Paul emphasized three main points:

1) Spiritual circumcision with Christ helps free us from the power of the flesh and emphasizes a believer's completeness in Christ (vv. 11, 12).

2) The symbol of baptism is used to signify that through Christ's death on the Cross believers died to their old sinful natures and were freed from the penalty of their sins (vv. 13, 14). This symbolism affirms that NT baptism does not correspond to OT circumcision.

3) The Resurrection of Christ pictures how believers can now have victory over the forces of evil and walk in newness of life (v. 15).

2:16–23 Paul warned the Colossians even further against false Gnostic regulations and practices (see John 1:4, note). Believers have been freed from such requirements and demands. The new life and power of a believer comes from being "in Christ" and not from any outside observances.

MY IDENTITY IN CHRIST

WHO AM I IN CHRIST?

AS A CHRISTIAN . . .	SCRIPTURE REFERENCE
I am chosen by God.	Eph. 1:4
I am adopted by God.	Eph. 1:5
I am a child of God in His family.	1 John 3:1
I am forgiven by God for all my sins.	1 John 1:9
I am reconciled to God, in harmony with Him.	Rom. 5:10
I am seen by God as holy, blameless, above reproach.	Col. 1:21, 22
I am sealed with God's Holy Spirit.	Eph. 1:13
I am called to accomplish God's purpose.	Rom. 8:28, 30
I am a full citizen among God's people.	Eph. 2:19
I am justified—declared right in God's sight.	Rom. 5:1
I am sanctified—set apart by God's spirit.	1 Cor. 6:11
I am redeemed—bought with Christ's blood.	Eph. 1:7
I am cleansed by Christ's blood for all my sin.	1 John 1:7
I am an heir of God and a joint-heir with Christ.	Rom. 8:16, 17
I am complete in Christ.	Col. 2:10
I am an ambassador for Christ.	2 Cor. 5:20
I am being conformed to the character of Christ.	Rom. 8:29

Thank you, Lord, for giving me worth and letting me see I have purpose.

---

together by joints and ligaments, grows with the increase *that is* from God.

20Therefore,ᵃ if you died with Christ from the basic principles of the world, why, as *though* living in the world, do you subject yourselves to regulations— 21"Do not touch, do not taste, do not handle," 22which all concern things which perish with the using—according to the commandments and doctrines of men? 23These things indeed have an appearance of wisdom in self-imposed religion, *false* humility, and neglect of the body, *but are* of no value against the indulgence of the flesh.

Not Carnality but Christ

3 If then you were raised with Christ, seek those things which are above, where Christ is, sitting at the right hand of God. 2Set your mind on things above, not on things on the earth. 3For you died, and your life is hidden with Christ in God. 4When

· · · · · · · · · · · · · · · · · · · ·
2:20 ᵃNU-Text and M-Text omit *Therefore.*

EVANGELISM *THE ROLE OF PRAYER*

History confirms that evangelism alone rarely produces spiritual awakening. Rather, prayer produces spiritual awakening, and spiritual awakening inevitably produces evangelism (Col. 4:2–6). Thus, two important elements that are often neglected are appropriately linked by Paul in a bonding that makes one ineffective without the other *evangelism* and *prayer*. To be more devoted to the activities of evangelism with little more than a token commitment to prayer will not bring the fruit God wants to give.

Women have traditionally been a great resource in prayer. Paul admonished both women and men to "continue earnestly" and be vigilant as they pray "with thanksgiving"; to pray for "open" doors; and to pray for the ability to "speak" with an understood message and "open hearts" (Col. 4:2–6). Paul also asks that "utterance may be given to me, that I may open my mouth boldly to make known the mystery of the gospel" (Eph. 6:18–20).

Taking initiative and being bold is not natural for all women. Perhaps we are not "bold" or able to speak well because we have not asked God for these qualities. The disciples prayed for boldness (Acts 4:29). Not only are we to pray for others to be effective in evangelism, but we are also to ask God to make us personally effective in seizing every opportunity for the advancement of the gospel.

United, specific, and strategic prayer has been answered by God to change history. Not only in biblical times, but also in recent history, dramatic results have come when God's people prayed "in one accord."

Following their release from prison, Peter and John met with other believers to pray. As they gave their report to their companions, they all "raised their voice to God with one accord" (Acts 4:24). Scripture affirms that when believers unite "with one accord," God hears and answers, and lives are changed (2 Chr. 7:14). People will act when they are concerned enough to pray. As women unite to pray in one accord, God enables them to be used to introduce others to Christ and help change the world.

See also Acts 4:23–32; 1 Cor. 16:9; notes on Boldness (Prov. 28); Evangelism (John 6; 1 Pet. 3); Prayer (Jer. 33; Heb. 4; 1 John 5; 3 John); Renewal (Hab. 3); Salvation (Eph. 2)

Christ *who is* our life appears, then you also will appear with Him in glory.

⁵Therefore put to death your members which are on the earth: fornication, uncleanness, passion, evil desire, and covetousness, which is idolatry. ⁶Because of these things the wrath of God is coming upon the sons of disobedience, ⁷in which you yourselves once walked when you lived in them.

⁸But now you yourselves are to put off all these: anger, wrath, malice, blasphemy, filthy language out of your mouth. ⁹Do not lie to one another, since you have put off the old man with his deeds, ¹⁰and have put on the new *man* who is renewed in knowledge according to the image of Him who created him, ¹¹where there is neither Greek nor Jew, circumcised nor uncircumcised, barbarian, Scythian, slave *nor* free, but Christ *is* all and in all.

Character of the New Man

¹²Therefore, as *the* elect of God, holy and beloved, put on tender mercies, kindness, humility, meekness, longsuffering; ¹³bearing with one another, and forgiving one another, if anyone has a complaint against another; even as Christ forgave you, so you also *must do.* ¹⁴But above all these things put on love, which is the bond of perfection. ¹⁵And let the peace of God rule in your hearts, to which also you were called in one body; and be thankful. ¹⁶Let the word of Christ dwell in you richly in all wisdom, teaching and admonishing one another in psalms and hymns and spiritual songs, singing with grace in your hearts to the Lord. ¹⁷And whatever you do in word or deed, *do* all in the name of the Lord Jesus, giving thanks to God the Father through Him.

3:5 Put to death (Gk. *nekron*) denotes to "reckon as dead." Paul, too, calls Christians not to kill themselves literally but to be continually in the process of extinguishing evil desires or lusts.

3:12 In contrast with putting to death their old sinful natures, Christians are admonished to "put on" (Gk. *enduō*) qualities of mercy, kindness, humility, and finally love (Gk. *agapē*). This love is available to those who are "in Christ." It binds them together in an unbreakable fellowship (see chart, What is Love).

3:18 To submit (Gk. *hupotassō*, lit. "to line up under") suggests a voluntary relinquishment of one's rights to another.

Paul always used this term to describe the role assignment of a wife to her husband (1 Cor. 14:34; Eph. 5:21, 22; Titus 2:5; 1 Pet. 3:1). The concept suggests mutual submission and intimacy, promoting a union ordained by God with love as the binding agent. Love characterizes the servant leadership of the husband and awakens the submissive cooperation of the wife (see chart, Role Relationships Between Men and Women). Only through the power of the Holy Spirit can a woman truly relinquish her desires and line up under her husband's leadership (see 1 Pet. 3, Submission; chart, Submission).

FRUIT OF THE SPIRIT *KINDNESS*

Kindness, in both Old and New Testaments, refers to steadfast love expressed in actions. The Hebrew word *chesed* and the Greek word *chrestotes* involve both emotions and actions. In summary, steadfast love expressed in actions is kindness.

"Marvelous kindness" is an attribute of the Lord (Ps. 31:21). God shows kindness abundantly to His children (2 Sam. 2:6; Neh. 9:17; Ps. 117:2). His lovingkindness is everlasting (Is. 54:10).

God wants His children to be kind to one another (Eph. 4:32) and expects them to express brotherly kindness even in the midst of trials (2 Cor. 6:6). As a fruit of the Holy Spirit (Gal. 5:22), kindness is a virtue to be added to faith (2 Pet. 1:5–7). Kindness, not a natural human reaction, must be developed in the believer in order for her to minister to others in the name of a loving God.

See also Ps. 31:21; notes on Attributes of God (Rom. 2); Friendship (Luke 1); Fruit of the Spirit (Ps. 86; Rom. 5; 15; 1 Cor. 9; 13; Gal. 5; Eph. 4; 2 Thess. 1; Rev. 2); Love (1 John 3); Romance (Song 2)

The Christian Home

18Wives, submit to your own husbands, as is fitting in the Lord.

19Husbands, love your wives and do not be bitter toward them.

20Children, obey your parents in all things, for this is well pleasing to the Lord.

21Fathers, do not provoke your children, lest they become discouraged.

22Bondservants, obey in all things your masters according to the flesh, not with eyeservice, as men-pleasers, but in sincerity of heart, fearing God. 23And whatever you do, do it heartily, as to the Lord and not to men, 24knowing that from the Lord you will receive the reward of the inheritance; for[a] you serve the Lord Christ. 25But he who does wrong will be repaid for what he has done, and there is no partiality.

4 Masters, give your bondservants what is just and fair, knowing that you also have a Master in heaven.

Christian Graces

2Continue earnestly in prayer, being vigilant in it with thanksgiving; 3meanwhile praying also for us, that God would open to us a door for the word, to speak the mystery of Christ, for which I am also in chains, 4that I may make it manifest, as I ought to speak.

5Walk in wisdom toward those *who are* outside, redeeming the time. 6*Let* your speech always *be* with grace, seasoned with salt, that you may know how you ought to answer each one.

Final Greetings

7Tychicus, a beloved brother, faithful minister, and fellow servant in the Lord, will tell you all the news about me. 8I am sending him to you for this very purpose, that he[a] may know your circumstances and comfort your hearts, 9with Onesimus, a faithful and beloved brother, who is *one* of you. They will make known to you all things which *are* happening here.

10Aristarchus my fellow prisoner greets you, with Mark the cousin of Barnabas (about whom you received instructions: if he comes to you, welcome him), 11and Jesus who is called Justus. These

. . . .

3:24 [a]NU-Text omits *for.*   **4:8** [a]NU-Text reads *you may know our circumstances and he may.*

3:20, 21 For the husband to have an obligation to his wife and his children was a radical concept for the 1st-century world. In a Christian family, reciprocal relationships and responsibilities were not only planned by the Creator but also are clearly expected from believers (see chart, Role Relationships Between Men and Women).

Fathers were commanded not to provoke or irritate (Gk. *erethizō*) their children so as to dishearten or discourage them (see Eph. 6:4). They are expected to exercise godly leadership in discerning individual guidance for each child.

3:23 A Spirit-filled Christian will find in his labor the promise of reward from his true Master, the Lord Jesus Christ, and should thus consider that work as a service to the Lord (see Eccl. 9:10).

4:2, 3 Prayer calls for appropriate action as well as a proper attitude. Paul used the imperative verb to admonish all believ-

ers to pray-pray-pray! Only through prayer can believers keep alert to all trials and opportunities.

4:5 Paul asked believers to interact with those in the world with wisdom, tempering their speech and seasoning it with salt. Salty language could mean that believers are not to be dull and predictable in their speech but gracious and interesting in order to draw others to life in Christ. Or, it could be a reference to salt as stinging the conscience and awakening a lost world to an awareness of the choice between sin and righteousness (see Matt. 5:13). Therefore, believers redeem or use their time wisely by taking every opportunity to influence others for Christ.

4:7–17 Tychius (v. 7), Onesimus (v. 9), Aristarchus (v. 10), Mark (v. 10), Justus (v. 11), Epaphras (v. 12), Luke (v. 14), Demas (v. 14), and Archippus (v. 17) are all mentioned as Paul's

I know Christ dwells within me all the time, guiding me and inspiring me whenever I do or say anything. A light, of which I caught no glimmer before, comes to me at the very moment when it is needed.

St. Therese of Lisieux

---

are my only fellow workers for the kingdom of God who are of the circumcision; they have proved to be a comfort to me.

¹²Epaphras, who is *one* of you, a bondservant of Christ, greets you, always laboring fervently for you in prayers, that you may stand perfect and complete[a] in all the will of God. ¹³For I bear him witness that he has a great zeal[a] for you, and those who are in Laodicea, and those in Hierapolis. ¹⁴Luke the beloved physician and Demas greet you. ¹⁵Greet the brethren who are in Laodicea, and Nymphas and the church that *is* in his[a] house.

Closing Exhortations and Blessing

¹⁶Now when this epistle is read among you, see that it is read also in the church of the Laodiceans, and that you likewise read the *epistle* from Laodicea. ¹⁷And say to Archippus, "Take heed to the ministry which you have received in the Lord, that you may fulfill it."

¹⁸This salutation by my own hand— Paul. Remember my chains. Grace *be* with you. Amen.

····················

4:12 ªNU-Text reads *fully assured.*   4:13 ªNU-Text reads *concern.*
4:15 ªNU-Text reads *Nympha . . . her house.*

---

co-laborers, who brought comfort to one another in the ministry of the gospel (vv. 8, 11).

4:15 The early church usually met in the homes of Christians. Paul mentioned the church meeting in Nymphas' house. Women, no doubt, had an important opportunity to show graciousness, hospitality, and even leadership in these early house churches. Other examples of families opening their homes for worship and instruction include Priscilla and Aquila (Rom. 16:5; 1 Cor. 16:19), Archippus (Philem.), and Mary, the mother of John Mark (Acts 12:12).

1 Thessalonians

Internal and external evidence supports the authorship of Paul for this epistle. Internally, Paul claims authorship (1 Thess. 1:1; 2:18). Externally, the vast majority of scholars from the days of the early church fathers to the present support Pauline authorship. Furthermore, the epistle is typically Pauline in form and consistent with Paul's teachings and character.

DATE

Shortly after arriving Thessalonica, Paul was forced to move on to Berea, then to Athens, and finally to Corinth (Acts 17:1–10). It was from Corinth, on Paul's second missionary journey (A.D. 50–52), that he wrote to the Thessalonian believers. First Thessalonians was at least one of and may have been the earliest of Paul's epistles.

BACKGROUND

SETTING: Thessalonica was the capital of Macedonia and its largest city. It was located on the main Roman highway (Via Egnatia) to the east. Paul realized the global ramifications of reaching these influential people. The city was basically Greek but had a strong Jewish community as well.

PURPOSE: Paul wrote this epistle after he received a report from Timothy, who had just returned from visiting these new believers (1 Thess. 3:6). Paul determined:

1) To express his thanksgiving and general satisfaction over their growth and witness as new believers;
2) To answer the charges that had been brought against him by some Jewish opponents;
3) To encourage the believers to continue their hard work, perseverance, and growth until Jesus returned; and finally
4) To correct certain misunderstandings they had in regard to future eschatological (end time) events.

AUDIENCE: Primarily, this letter was directed to the new converts of Thessalonica. These converts consisted of pagan idolaters (1 Thess. 1:10), "God-fearing" Greeks (1 Thess. 1:8), along with some Jews. Also, quite a few of the "leading women" of Thessalonica had been converted (Acts 17:1–4). Paul instructed that this epistle should be read to "all" the people (1 Thess. 5:27), which includes believers throughout the centuries.

LITERARY CHARACTERISTICS: This epistle is Pauline in structure and characteristics. The vocabulary used is much like that of Paul in his other writings. Silvanus (Silas) and Timothy were with him (1 Thess. 1:1), and Paul did not feel the need to use the title of "apostle." His spiritual authority and leadership were never questioned at Thessalonica.

The theme of 1 Thessalonians is eschatological. Interestingly, every chapter ends with a reference to Christ's coming again (1 Thess. 1:10; 2:19; 3:13; 4:13–18; 5:24). Christ's return and the events leading to His return are discussed. Paul gives the Thessalonians a future hope. He desired that this hope would encourage the Thessalonians to endure suffering, become more Christ-like each day, walk closer to God, and spread His gospel to all without delay. Paul's encouragements and exhortations are meant to enhance the believer's spiritual growth.

OUTLINE

Introduction (1:1)
I. Remembrances of the Thessalonians (1:2—3:13)
  A. Thessalonian believers (1:2–10)
    1. Thanksgiving for the faith of the Thessalonians (1:2–7)
    2. The outpouring of the faith of the Thessalonians (1:8–10)
  B. Paul's ministry (2:1–16)
    1. Paul's defense of his character and message (2:1–12)
    2. The acceptance of Paul's character and message (2:13–16)
  C. Timothy's ministry (2:17—3:13)
    1. Timothy's return to encourage and strengthen (2:17—3:5)
    2. Timothy's report (3:6–13)

II. The Application for Thessalonian Believers (4:1—5:24)
  A. Living to please the Lord (4:1–12)
    1. A lifestyle of holiness (4:1–8)
    2. A lifestyle of love (4:9, 10)
    3. A lifestyle of steadfastness (4:11, 12)
  B. Waiting for the Lord's return (4:13—5:11)
    1. A comforting promise (4:13–18)
    2. A challenging command (5:1–11)
  C. Growing in the Lord (5:12–24)
    1. A respect for godly leadership (5:12, 13)
    2. A respect for fellow believers (5:14, 15)
    3. A respect for Christ's headship (5:16–24)
Conclusion (5:25–28)

Greeting

1 Paul, Silvanus, and Timothy,

To the church of the Thessalonians in God the Father and the Lord Jesus Christ:

Grace to you and peace from God our Father and the Lord Jesus Christ.[a]

Their Good Example

[2]We give thanks to God always for you all, making mention of you in our prayers, [3]remembering without ceasing your work of faith, labor of love, and patience of hope in our Lord Jesus Christ in the sight of our God and Father, [4]knowing, beloved brethren, your election by God. [5]For our gospel did not come to you in word only, but also in power, and in the Holy Spirit and in much assurance, as you know what kind of men we were among you for your sake.

[6]And you became followers of us and of the Lord, having received the word in much affliction, with joy of the Holy Spirit, [7]so that you became examples to all in Macedonia and Achaia who believe. [8]For from you the word of the Lord has

1:1 [a]NU-Text omits *from God our Father and the Lord Jesus Christ.*

1:1 Paul's use of grace to you and peace revealed that he was speaking directly to believers that they would receive "grace" (Gk. *charis*) in light of Christ's sacrificial love for His children (see chart, Theological Terms). Paul included both the Greek and Jewish converts by using the usual greeting of each ("grace" for the Greeks; "peace" for the Jews).

1:2, 3 Labor suggests working to the point of exhaustion. Christ demonstrated this costly love in His humiliating and sacrificial death on the Cross. Also, the Thessalonians displayed a "patience" with an active constancy during difficult circumstances.

1:8 Sounded forth gives the picture of a trumpet blast that has sounded and is still ringing in the ears of all those who heard it. The Thessalonians' strong faith and firm testimony were echoing throughout the surrounding areas.

He who suffers most, has the most to give.

Jo Ann Leavell

sounded forth, not only in Macedonia and Achaia, but also in every place. Your faith toward God has gone out, so that we do not need to say anything. ⁹For they themselves declare concerning us what manner of entry we had to you, and how you turned to God from idols to serve the living and true God, ¹⁰and to wait for His Son from heaven, whom He raised from the dead, *even* Jesus who delivers us from the wrath to come.

Paul's Conduct

2For you yourselves know, brethren, that our coming to you was not in vain. ²But evenᵃ after we had suffered before and were spitefully treated at Philippi, as you know, we were bold in our God to speak to you the gospel of God in much conflict. ³For our exhortation *did* not *come* from error or uncleanness, nor *was it* in deceit.

⁴But as we have been approved by God to be entrusted with the gospel, even so we speak, not as pleasing men, but God who tests our hearts. ⁵For neither at any time did we use flattering words, as you know, nor a cloak for covetousness—God *is* witness. ⁶Nor did we seek glory from men, either from you or from others, when we might have made demands as apostles of Christ. ⁷But we were gentle among you, just as a nursing *mother* cherishes her own children. ⁸So, affectionately longing for you, we were well pleased to impart to you not only the gospel of God, but also our own lives, because you had become dear to us. ⁹For you remember, brethren, our labor and toil; for laboring night and day, that we might not be a burden to any of you, we preached to you the gospel of God.

¹⁰You *are* witnesses, and God *also*, how devoutly and justly and blamelessly we behaved ourselves among you who believe; ¹¹as you know how we exhorted, and comforted, and chargedᵃ every one of you, as a father *does* his own children, ¹²that you would walk worthy of God who calls you into His own kingdom and glory.

Their Conversion

¹³For this reason we also thank God without ceasing, because when you received the word of God which you heard from us, you welcomed *it* not *as* the word of men, but as it is in truth, the word of God, which also effectively works in you who believe. ¹⁴For you, brethren, became imitators of the churches of God which are in Judea in Christ Jesus. For you also suffered the same things from your own countrymen, just as they *did* from the Judeans, ¹⁵who killed both the Lord Jesus and their own prophets, and have persecuted us; and they do not please God and are contrary to all men, ¹⁶forbidding us to speak to the Gentiles that they may be saved, so as always to fill up *the measure of* their sins; but wrath has come upon them to the uttermost.

Longing to See Them

¹⁷But we, brethren, having been taken away from you for a short time in presence, not in heart, endeavored more eagerly to see your face with great desire. ¹⁸Therefore we wanted to come to you—even I, Paul, time and again—but Satan hindered us. ¹⁹For what *is* our hope, or joy, or crown of rejoicing? *Is it* not even you in the presence of our

2:2 ᵃNU-Text and M-Text omit *even*.   2:11 ᵃNU-Text and M-Text read *implored*.

2:7 Paul compared his love for the Thessalonians with that of a mother for her child. He used the example of a "nursing mother." In other words, Paul fed these baby believers with the gospel and the truth (1 Pet. 2:2). He taught them how to survive just as a mother imparts food and wisdom to her children. Paul wanted the Thessalonians to realize his love and sacrificial contribution so that his influence on them could be even greater. Paul chose the word "cherishes" carefully because it demonstrates an attitude as well as an activity of love.

2:11, 12 Paul presented a plan for discipling new believers. He compared this behavior to a father's treatment of his children. First, a believer needs to be "exhorted" (Gk. *parakaleō*), a colorful word combining exhortation and encouragement. A believer must be given advice and counsel, combined with encouragement. These two principles work together to bring a

believer to maturity. Second, a believer needs to be "comforted" during those difficult trials and temptations of life. Third, a believer must be "charged" or challenged to follow the Lord's teachings.

2:13 The Word of God is an energizing force. The term "works" (Gk. *energeitai*) has the idea of "energy," which demonstrates the power of God's Word in a believer's life.

2:18 Paul reminded these believers of the power of Satan, and he claimed that his return to Thessalonica had been "hindered" by Satan. This term often describes a military battle that suggests sabotaging possible routes of travel in order to interrupt and delay the enemy's invasion. Paul used this reference also to remind the Thessalonians of Satan's power in their lives. They must guard against Satan controlling their lives and bringing discouragement to them.

Lord Jesus Christ at His coming? [20]For you are our glory and joy.

Concern for Their Faith

3 Therefore, when we could no longer endure it, we thought it good to be left in Athens alone, [2]and sent Timothy, our brother and minister of God, and our fellow laborer in the gospel of Christ, to establish you and encourage you concerning your faith, [3]that no one should be shaken by these afflictions; for you yourselves know that we are appointed to this. [4]For, in fact, we told you before when we were with you that we would suffer tribulation, just as it happened, and you know. [5]For this reason, when I could no longer endure it, I sent to know your faith, lest by some means the tempter had tempted you, and our labor might be in vain.

Encouraged by Timothy

[6]But now that Timothy has come to us from you, and brought us good news of your faith and love, and that you always have good remembrance of us, greatly desiring to see us, as we also *to see* you— [7]therefore, brethren, in all our affliction and distress we were comforted concerning you by your faith. [8]For now we live, if you stand fast in the Lord.

[9]For what thanks can we render to God for you, for all the joy with which we rejoice for your sake before our God, [10]night and day praying exceedingly that we may see your face and perfect what is lacking in your faith?

Prayer for the Church

[11]Now may our God and Father Himself, and our Lord Jesus Christ, direct our way to you. [12]And may the Lord make you increase and abound in love to one another and to all, just as we *do* to you, [13]so that He may establish your hearts blameless in holiness before our God and Father at the coming of our Lord Jesus Christ with all His saints.

Plea for Purity

4 Finally then, brethren, we urge and exhort in the Lord Jesus that you should abound more and more, just as you received from us how you ought to walk and to please God; [2]for you know what commandments we gave you through the Lord Jesus.

[3]For this is the will of God, your sanctification: that you should abstain from sexual immorality; [4]that each of you should know how to possess his own vessel in sanctification and honor, [5]not in passion of lust, like the Gentiles who do not know God; [6]that no one should take advantage of and defraud his brother in this matter, because the Lord *is* the avenger of all such, as we also forewarned you and testified. [7]For God did not call us to uncleanness, but in holiness. [8]Therefore he who rejects *this* does not reject man, but God, who has also given[a] us His Holy Spirit.

A Brotherly and Orderly Life

[9]But concerning brotherly love you have no need that I should write to you, for you yourselves are taught by God to love one another; [10]and indeed you do so toward all the brethren who are in all Macedonia. But we urge you, brethren, that you increase more and more; [11]that you also aspire to lead a quiet life, to mind your own busi-

·····················
4:8 [a]NU-Text reads *who also gives.*

3:2, 3 Although Paul could not return to Thessalonica himself, he sent Timothy, bearing authority as a brother, minister, and fellow laborer. Paul wanted the believers to be renewed and established in their faith so that the outward pressures they were facing would not shake their faith, love, and determination. He saw and met their need for encouragement, even when he could not be present himself. Paul realized that encouragement often saves a person from being "shaken" in faith.

3:6–10 Timothy returned to Paul with a positive report of how the Thessalonians' faith was strong even amidst "affliction" (external pressure) and "distress" (internal pressure). This brought Paul much joy and encouragement (v. 9). Seeing the faith of other believers is always challenging and uplifting. The evidence of the Thessalonians' perseverance under trial gave Paul great joy as he struggled through his own trials.

3:10 Paul assured the Thessalonians of his consistent and earnest prayers for them "night and day . . . exceedingly." His desire was to repair any damage they had experienced from persecutions and false teachers. "Perfect" is also used as a reference to mending torn fishing nets or setting broken bones (Mark 1:19). Paul desired to strengthen the church doctrinally and morally in order to develop faith to its fullest.

4:1–8 The Thessalonians had a reputation for being sexually promiscuous. Paul gave three motivations for a lifestyle of holiness:

1) It is the will of God (v. 3);
2) It is honoring the gift of one's spouse (v. 4); and
3) It avoids sin against one's brother (v. 6).

4:3 Sexual immorality or "fornication" (Gk. *porneia*) refers to all sexual indulgence: premarital sex, extramarital sex, homosexuality, lesbianism, sodomy, rape, and incest. Holiness requires abstaining from such practices.

4:4, 5 Vessel could refer to the believer's body but most likely refers to one's spouse. In a similar passage, the wife is called the "weaker vessel" (1 Pet. 3:7). The same terms for "honor" (Gk. *timēn*) and "vessel" (Gk. *skeuei*) are used in each passage. A marriage should be sanctified (set apart) and honored (reverenced). "Passion of lust" (Gk. *pathei epithumias*, lit. "hot-after passion") is a strong expression describing the strength and danger of uncontrolled desire.

4:11, 12 The term aspire came to mean "to be industrious." Working hard, staying out of everyone else's business and concentrating on the many tasks the Lord has given her to do (Titus 2:3–5) is a lifestyle that will enable a believing woman

GLOSSARY OF TERMS IN ESCHATOLOGY

Allegorical interpretation—a method that looks for a sense deemed higher than the literal sense in an otherwise apparently historical statement.

Apocalypse (Gk. *apokalupsis*, lit. "the unveiling")—the English transliteration of the Greek title for the Book of Revelation.

Bēma—the judgment seat or reward seat before which each Christian must appear (2 Cor. 5:10).

Eschatology—the study of last things or the events that are awaiting future fulfillment.

Harpazō (Gk., lit. "to catch up or snatch away")—This word is used to describe the translation of believers at the Lord's return (Matt. 24:30, 31; 24:32–44; John 14:2, 3; 1 Cor. 15:51–57; Col. 3:4; 1 Thess. 4:13–18; Rev. 20:6).

Kingdom—may refer to (1) the reign of Christ in the hearts of believers, (2) the heavenly kingdom, or (3) the earthly kingdom of Christ.

Israel—except in rare instances, a reference to the literal national group designated Israel.

Millennium—Latin word for one thousand (1,000) years (Is. 11:1–9; Jer. 31:31–34; Joel 3:17–21; Amos 9:11–15; Mic. 4:1–5; Luke 1:31–33; 1 Cor. 15:24–28).

Rapture (Lat. *ratio*, meaning "to snatch or seize")—This non-biblical word is used to describe the removal of Christians from the world at the return of Christ (see *Harpazō*).

Tribulation—seven-year period of unparalleled distress on earth (Is. 2:19; 24:1, 3, 6, 19–21; Jer. 30:7; Dan. 12:1; Joel 2:1, 2; Amos 5:18, 20; Zeph. 1:14–18; Matt. 24:21, 22; Luke 21:25, 26; 1 Thess. 5:3; Rev. 6:1–17).

---

ness, and to work with your own hands, as we commanded you, [12]that you may walk properly toward those who are outside, and *that* you may lack nothing.

The Comfort of Christ's Coming

[13]But I do not want you to be ignorant, brethren, concerning those who have fallen asleep, lest you sorrow as others who have no hope. [14]For if we believe that Jesus died and rose again, even so God will bring with Him those who sleep in Jesus.[a]

[15]For this we say to you by the word of the Lord, that we who are alive *and* remain until the coming of the Lord will by no means precede those who are asleep. [16]For the Lord Himself will descend from heaven with a shout, with the voice of an archangel, and with the trumpet of God. And the dead in Christ will rise first. [17]Then we who are alive *and* remain shall be caught up together with them in the clouds to meet the Lord in the air. And thus we shall always be with the Lord. [18]Therefore comfort one another with these words.

4:14 [a]Or *those who through Jesus sleep*

---

to have a flawless testimony before believers as well as unbelievers (1 Thess. 4:12).

4:13, 14 Those who have fallen asleep are believers who have died. This phrase focuses on the status of the body at death and suggests a temporary state of rest, from which one will awaken. At the moment of death, the believer is immediately in the presence of the Lord (2 Cor. 5:8), a truth affirmed when Jesus brings with Him those who sleep in Him (1 Thess. 4:14). Believers who are still living are caught up (Gk. *harpazō*, v. 17). The Lord will change their bodies into a glorified state (see "rapture" or chart, Glossary Terms for Eschatology).

The Day of the Lord

5 But concerning the times and the seasons, brethren, you have no need that I should write to you. [2]For you yourselves know perfectly that the day of the Lord so comes as a thief in the night. [3]For when they say, "Peace and safety!" then sudden destruction comes upon them, as labor pains upon a pregnant woman. And they shall not escape. [4]But you, brethren, are not in darkness, so that this Day should overtake you as a thief. [5]You are all sons of light and sons of the day. We are not of the night nor of darkness. [6]Therefore let us not sleep, as others *do*, but let us watch and be sober. [7]For those who sleep, sleep at night, and those who get drunk are drunk at night. [8]But let us who are of the day be sober, putting on the breastplate of faith and love, and *as* a helmet the hope of salvation. [9]For God did not appoint us to wrath, but to obtain salvation through our Lord Jesus Christ, [10]who died for us, that whether we wake or sleep, we should live together with Him.

[11]Therefore comfort each other and edify one another, just as you also are doing.

Various Exhortations

[12]And we urge you, brethren, to recognize those who labor among you, and are over you in the Lord and admonish you, [13]and to esteem them very highly in love for their work's sake. Be at peace among yourselves.

[14]Now we exhort you, brethren, warn those who are unruly, comfort the fainthearted, uphold the weak, be patient with all. [15]See that no one renders evil for evil to anyone, but always pursue what is good both for yourselves and for all.

[16]Rejoice always, [17]pray without ceasing, [18]in everything give thanks; for this is the will of God in Christ Jesus for you.

[19]Do not quench the Spirit. [20]Do not despise prophecies. [21]Test all things; hold fast what is good. [22]Abstain from every form of evil.

Blessing and Admonition

[23]Now may the God of peace Himself sanctify you completely; and may your whole spirit, soul, and body be preserved blameless at the coming of our Lord Jesus Christ. [24]He who calls you *is* faithful, who also will do *it.*

[25]Brethren, pray for us.

[26]Greet all the brethren with a holy kiss.

[27]I charge you by the Lord that this epistle be read to all the holy[a] brethren.

[28]The grace of our Lord Jesus Christ *be* with you. Amen.

·················

5:27 [a]NU-Text omits *holy.*

5:6 The term sleep refers to the spiritual indifference that characterized those who were living without Christ. Believers were to be alert and active, not docile and passive.

5:11 Paul reiterated his concept of the church. Paul knew that in order for believers to grow in their faith, they must have love and encouragement. He sent Timothy back to the Thessalonians to provide this support (1 Thess. 3:2, 3). Throughout the NT, believers are encouraged to serve and minister to one another, following the example of Christ (Rom. 12:10, 16; Gal. 6:2; James 5:16).

5:12, 13 The leaders whom God places over His people are described by the phrase "those who labor among you," which is also rendered "those who work even when weary." These leaders possess the Lord's authority ("in the Lord"). God places them in a position to "admonish" or instruct believers. Paul commanded believers to love and honor their pastors ("those who labor among you, and are over you in the Lord"). This support was not due to the pastor's personality but to his divinely assigned position and ministry (Heb. 13:7, 17).

5:16–18 These exhortations refer to a believer's inner life, her personal relationship to the Lord. These three attitudes or activities should be present in every believer's life: joy (v. 16), prayer (v. 17), and thanksgiving (v. 18). The Thessalonians were apparently under tremendous persecutions by the Judaizers (see Acts 17:5–9). In the midst of their persecution in Thessalonica, these requests seem absurd. Yet, these requested actions are not in response to their present circumstances but to their future hope in Christ and will be accomplished through the power of the Holy Spirit in them. Two things should enable the believer to give thanks in all circumstances: seeing a beneficial purpose to every trial and having an inward sense of joy and peace from the Father.

5:21, 22 Paul commanded the Thessalonians to "test all things," with the idea of testing to prove genuine. As a result of this testing, Paul left them with two options. If something is found to be true and good, they are to "hold fast" to it; if found to be evil, they are to "abstain" from every form of it.

2 Thessalonians

AUTHOR

The evidence clearly supports Pauline authorship for this epistle, though there has been more discussion on 2 Thessalonians than on his previous Thessalonian letter. However, once again strong internal and external evidence supports Pauline authorship. Paul himself claimed authorship (2 Thess. 1:1; 3:17). Furthermore, the testimony of the early church strongly favors Pauline authorship. A careful reading of the two epistles reveals similarity of style, language, and theology.

DATE

This epistle was probably written a few months after Paul's first epistle to the Thessalonians (A.D. 51–52). Paul was anxious to continue his communication with the Thessalonian believers. He was still in Corinth when he wrote. Though some question which epistle was penned first, that 1 Thessalonians preceded this second epistle can be affirmed with confidence (2 Thess. 2:15).

BACKGROUND

SETTING: Thessalonica, the capital city of Macedonia, was a major trade city connecting Macedonia to the Roman Empire in the east. The geographical location of Thessalonica was significant for evangelizing the east.

PURPOSE: Paul wrote to clarify his teachings on the return of Christ. Ostensibly, Paul had received word that his previous teachings had been misunderstood by some. He also continued to encourage the Thessalonians in their faith.

AUDIENCE: Paul again wrote to the believers in Thessalonica. These included the "God-fearing" Greeks, prominent women, and those Jews who had believed in Christ.

THEMES

God's faithfulness is prevalent in this epistle. Paul attempted to encourage the Thessalonians once again in regard to their persecutions and trials (2 Thess. 1). Paul also explained some aspects of the Lord's return, which apparently had caused confusion for the Thessalonians. He also warned them about the dangers of idleness and encouraged a life of self-control (2 Thess. 3:6–15).

OUTLINE

Introduction (1:1, 2)
I. Paul's Acknowledgment of God's
   Faithfulness (1:3–12)
   A. A thankful heart (1:3, 4)
   B. A just God (1:5–10)
   C. A personal prayer (1:11, 12)

II. Paul's Discussion of Christ's Return
    (2:1–17)
    A. The coming day of the Lord (2:1, 2)
    B. The discussion of the man of sin
       (2:3–12)
    C. The believer's responsibility (2:13–15)

Greeting

1 Paul, Silvanus, and Timothy,

To the church of the Thessalonians in God our Father and the Lord Jesus Christ:

²Grace to you and peace from God our Father and the Lord Jesus Christ.

God's Final Judgment and Glory

³We are bound to thank God always for you, brethren, as it is fitting, because your faith grows exceedingly, and the love of every one of you all abounds toward each other, ⁴so that we ourselves boast of you among the churches of God for your patience and faith in all your persecutions and tribulations that you endure, ⁵*which is* manifest evidence of the righteous judgment of God, that you may be counted worthy of the kingdom of God, for which you also suffer; ⁶since *it is* a righteous thing with God to repay with tribulation those who trouble you, ⁷and to *give* you who are troubled rest with us when the Lord Jesus is revealed from heaven with His mighty angels, ⁸in flaming fire taking vengeance on those who do not know God, and on those who do not obey the gospel of our Lord Jesus Christ. ⁹These shall be punished with everlasting destruction from the presence of the Lord and from the glory of His power, ¹⁰when He comes, in that Day, to be glorified in His saints and to be admired among all those who believe,ᵃ because our testimony among you was believed.

¹¹Therefore we also pray always for you that our God would count you worthy of *this* calling, and fulfill all the good pleasure of *His* goodness and the work of faith with power, ¹²that the name of our Lord Jesus Christ may be glorified in you, and you in Him, according to the grace of our God and the Lord Jesus Christ.

The Great Apostasy

2 Now, brethren, concerning the coming of our Lord Jesus Christ and our gathering together to Him, we ask you, ²not to be soon shaken in mind or troubled, either by spirit or by word or by letter, as if from us, as though the day of Christᵃ had come. ³Let no one deceive you by any means; for *that Day will not come* unless the falling away comes first, and the man of sinᵃ is revealed, the son of perdition, ⁴who opposes and exalts himself above all that is called God or that is worshiped, so that he sits as Godᵃ in the temple of God, showing himself that he is God.

⁵Do you not remember that when I was still with you I told you these things? ⁶And now you know what is restraining, that he may be revealed in his own time. ⁷For the mystery of lawlessness is already at work; only Heᵃ who now restrains *will do*

. . . .

1:10 ᵃNU-Text and M-Text read *have believed.* **2:2** ᵃNU-Text reads *the Lord.* **2:3** ᵃNU-Text reads *lawlessness.* **2:4** ᵃNU-Text omits *as God.* **2:7** ᵃOr *he*

1:2 In both of Paul's epistles to the Thessalonians, he offered them grace before peace. "Grace" (unmerited favor) or salvation must precede a true "peace" (see 1 Thess. 1:1, note).

1:6, 7 God's righteousness has two functions: God "repays" or "gives in return" affliction to those who afflict believers (v. 6), God would grant the afflicted believers "rest" or "gracious relief" from the many difficulties they would face because of their stand for God's truth (2 Cor. 2:13; 7:5; 8:13).

1:8, 9 Paul used the word obey to mean saving faith (v. 8). Anyone who has not accepted the gospel will suffer "everlasting destruction" or be cut off from the presence of the Lord forever (v. 9).

1:10 In that Day refers to the time in the Last Days when God would show His power and demonstrate His glory over all His opponents. Many have called this the "day of the Lord" (1 Thess. 5:2; see charts, Millennial Views; Questions from the Book of Revelation).

2:3 Paul described two events that will take place prior to or just after the Day of the Lord begins (see Matt. 12:29; Mark 3:27; John 7:5). Paul did not say the Thessalonians would see this phenomenon—only that the events had not yet transpired. First, the "falling away" (Gk. *apostasia*, lit. "a standing away from"). "Apostasy" is a transliteration of this word. This time will be one of open rebellion against God—not a passive rebellion but an active and fervent one. Second, "the man of sin" will be revealed. This "man of sin" seems to be a human being and, therefore, should not be identified as Satan or any other superhuman figure. He is also known as the "beast" (Rev. 13:1–10) and the Antichrist (1 John 2:18). As a person who embodies the evil of the world, he will actively resist the power and the Person of Christ and will be destroyed at the return of Christ to the earth (2 Thess. 2:8; see charts, Millennial Views; Questions from the Book of Revelation).

2:6 Paul referred to the Holy Spirit as one who would restrain evil in the world (see chart, The Work of the Holy Spirit).

FRUIT OF THE SPIRIT *GOODNESS*

God's goodness is expressed in creation (Gen. 1:31) and experienced in salvation (Phil. 1:6). The psalmist proclaims the goodness of God as great (Ps. 31:19) and as eternal (Ps. 23:6; 52:1). God is the true essence of goodness, the Author of unlimited, undeserved generosity.

Though God alone is truly good, Scripture encourages believers to seek goodness by modeling their lives after Christ Jesus. For the Christian, goodness is not simply the absence of evil; it is righteousness accompanied by acts of kindness. As a fruit of the Holy Spirit, goodness is a natural result of love, joy, peace, longsuffering, and kindness at work in a person's life (Gal. 5:22, 23). It is the outward expression of inward change in a believer's heart—the invisible power of a holy God overcoming the sinful nature that is in all people.

True goodness is difficult to attain. It manifests itself only in a life totally committed to the Lord and is a requirement for effective ministry. Service to others is counted as evidence of the goodness of God at work in the life of a believer (2 Thess. 1:11, 12).

See also Rom. 15:14; notes on Attributes of God (Ps. 25); Fruit of the Spirit (Ps. 86; Rom. 5; 15; 1 Cor. 10; 13; Gal. 5; Eph. 4; Col. 3; Rev. 2); Purity (1 John 3); Sacrificial Living (Mic. 7)

so until He[b] is taken out of the way. [8]And then the lawless one will be revealed, whom the Lord will consume with the breath of His mouth and destroy with the brightness of His coming. [9]The coming of the *lawless one* is according to the working of Satan, with all power, signs, and lying wonders, [10]and with all unrighteous deception among those who perish, because they did not receive the love of the truth, that they might be saved. [11]And for this reason God will send them strong delusion, that they should believe the lie, [12]that they all may be condemned who did not believe the truth but had pleasure in unrighteousness.

Stand Fast

[13]But we are bound to give thanks to God always for you, brethren beloved by the Lord, because God from the beginning chose you for salvation through sanctification by the Spirit and belief in the truth, [14]to which He called you by our gospel, for the obtaining of the glory of our Lord Jesus Christ. [15]Therefore, brethren, stand fast and hold the traditions which you were taught, whether by word or our epistle.

[16]Now may our Lord Jesus Christ Himself, and our God and Father, who has loved us and given *us* everlasting consolation and good hope by grace,

[17]comfort your hearts and establish you in every good word and work.

Pray for Us

3 Finally, brethren, pray for us, that the word of the Lord may run *swiftly* and be glorified, just as *it is* with you, [2]and that we may be delivered from unreasonable and wicked men; for not all have faith.

[3]But the Lord is faithful, who will establish you and guard *you* from the evil one. [4]And we have confidence in the Lord concerning you, both that you do and will do the things we command you.

[5]Now may the Lord direct your hearts into the love of God and into the patience of Christ.

Warning Against Idleness

[6]But we command you, brethren, in the name of our Lord Jesus Christ, that you withdraw from every brother who walks disorderly and not according to the tradition which he[a] received from us. [7]For you yourselves know how you ought to follow us, for we were not disorderly among you; [8]nor did we eat anyone's bread free of charge, but worked with labor and toil night and day, that we

··················
2:7 [b]Or *he*   3:6 [a]NU-Text and M-Text read *they*.

2:7 The evil in the world is a "mystery of lawlessness." A mystery (Gk. *musterion*) is something which God has chosen not to reveal at this time. Although sin is already active and prevalent, the full manifestation of that sin has not yet been revealed.

2:13 The Thessalonian believers were "beloved" ("constantly being loved personally by God"). Paul identified "sanctification" (Gk. *hagios*, lit. "set apart") as part of the salvation process (see chart, Theological Terms).

2:15 Even though believers are called by God to salvation through His grace, they clearly have a responsibility to stand firmly in the faith and keep themselves from being misled by false teachings.

3:3–5 The Christian life depends upon who God is and what He does for us and in us. Paul explained to the Thessalonians that God is faithful. Therefore, He can be depended upon to bring about the accomplishment of good works and to guard them from evil. Paul did not put his confidence in the Thessalonian believers but in their God (Phil. 2:13).

3:7 The term ought is a strong word in the Greek language; it is often translated "must." Paul was reminding the Thessalonians that their idleness was against the example that had

THEOLOGICAL TERMS

TERM	DESCRIPTION
Salvation	Deliverance from the penalty and power of sin (Eph. 2:8)
Faith	Complete trust in and commitment to God (Phil. 3:2–9)
Grace	Undeserved acceptance and love from God (Eph. 2:8)
Justification	Initial act of salvation in which a person is brought into right relationship with Jesus Christ (Rom. 3:21–26)
Sanctification	Work of the Holy Spirit in the life of the believer, resulting in increasing personal holiness (2 Thess. 2:13)
Glorification	Final act of salvation in which the believer is transformed into the likeness of Christ (Rom. 8:30)

might not be a burden to any of you, ⁹not because we do not have authority, but to make ourselves an example of how you should follow us.

¹⁰For even when we were with you, we commanded you this: If anyone will not work, neither shall he eat. ¹¹For we hear that there are some who walk among you in a disorderly manner, not working at all, but are busybodies. ¹²Now those who are such we command and exhort through our Lord Jesus Christ that they work in quietness and eat their own bread.

¹³But *as for* you, brethren, do not grow weary *in* doing good. ¹⁴And if anyone does not obey our word in this epistle, note that person and do not keep company with him, that he may be ashamed. ¹⁵Yet do not count *him* as an enemy, but admonish *him* as a brother.

Benediction

¹⁶Now may the Lord of peace Himself give you peace always in every way. The Lord *be* with you all.

¹⁷The salutation of Paul with my own hand, which is a sign in every epistle; so I write.

¹⁸The grace of our Lord Jesus Christ *be* with you all. Amen.

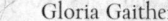

For influencing an unbelieving spouse, it's important that we wives not major on "churchianity," but major on the things that Jesus taught —attitudes, reactions.

Gloria Gaither

---

been set before them. Once again, Paul used the word "follow" (Gk. *mimeomai*, lit. "imitate") as believers are exhorted to mimic the example that Paul set before them.

3:11 Paul made it clear that every believer is to be a hard worker. Idleness, whether in the workplace or at home, produces gossip and laziness. Paul warned against the danger of not working (v. 10). A believer must be busy preparing her heart and mind for the return of the Lord. Believers must be examples to the world. Every believer should demonstrate hope by diligently working as the final day approaches.

3:16 Paul wanted the Thessalonians to turn to the Lord for their peace, no matter what the circumstances.

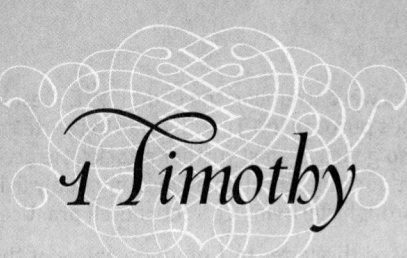

1 Timothy

THE PASTORAL EPISTLES

First Timothy, Titus, and Second Timothy are called the Pastoral Epistles. They were probably written in this order. They are generally viewed as Paul's last letters and share some common characteristics. First, they were addressed to individuals, although they were also intended to be read before the churches for which Timothy and Titus were responsible. Second, Paul was especially concerned to deal with the pressing problem of false teachers who were leading believers astray. Third, they were written toward the end of Paul's life when the need for greater ecclesiastical structure was becoming more apparent.

AUTHOR

The apostle Paul traditionally has been considered the author of the Pastoral Epistles, and all three letters explicitly state that he is the author (1 Tim. 1:1; 2 Tim. 1:1; Tit. 1:1). Some scholars began to question Pauline authorship in the early nineteenth century; however, these arguments can be sufficiently answered, and there is no compelling reason to doubt that Paul wrote these letters. First, while it is impossible to fit the events mentioned in the Pastorals into Paul's career as recorded in Acts, nothing in the NT precludes his release from the Roman imprisonment of A.D. 60–63 (Acts 28:16–31; see Introduction: Date). Second, a church structure involving elders (also called bishops or pastors) and deacons is entirely in keeping with the situation that must have existed in Paul's day. Third, the heresy Paul attacked is hardly the complex system of second-century Gnosticism. While the heresy in the Pastorals has Gnostic elements, these elements were already present in the first century, and the heretics Paul encountered seem to be Judaizers who had linked pagan speculations with Jewish legalism (see 1 Tim. 1:4, 7; Tit. 1:14). Fourth, while it is true that Paul used a wider vocabulary and range of style in the Pastorals than he did elsewhere, this was in keeping with his high level of education, his exposure to various people groups in the Mediterranean world, and the subject matter he discussed in these letters. Further, he might have dictated these letters to an amanuensis or secretary, who, under the direction of the Holy Spirit, had some freedom in the precise wording of the letters.

DATE

The Pastoral Epistles are generally considered to have been written between A.D. 62 and 67. Paul's first Roman imprisonment was approximately A.D. 60–63 (Acts 28:16–31). After this he was evidently set free, for both 1 Timothy and Titus picture Paul as traveling freely in the eastern Mediterranean region, to Ephesus (1 Tim. 1:3; 3:14), to Crete (Titus 1:5), and to Nicopolis in the eastern Adriatic Sea (Titus 3:12). He wrote 1 Timothy and Titus sometime during this period of freedom, probably A.D. 62–65. He later was imprisoned again and during this time wrote 2 Timothy. Early church tradition agrees that Paul was executed by the Roman emperor Nero in late A.D. 67 or early 68. The most probable date for 1 Timothy is between A.D. 62 and 64.

PURPOSE: False teachers were troubling the church at Ephesus (1 Tim. 1:3–11; 4:1–5). Paul's purpose in 1 Timothy was to refute their heretical doctrines and practices as well as to guard against further attacks. He accomplished this purpose through teaching correct doctrine, through advocating godly living by both elders and church members, and through clarifying correct church practice.

AUDIENCE: Paul addressed this letter to Timothy, a native of the city of Lystra in Asia Minor. Although his father was a Gentile, Timothy's mother and grandmother were Jewish, and he was taught the Scripture from an early age (Acts 16:1; 2 Tim. 1:5; 3:15). He probably first heard the gospel through Paul. Since Paul referred to Timothy as his spiritual child (1 Cor. 4:17; 2 Tim. 2:1), he was at least Timothy's primary mentor and quite possibly the one who led him to personal faith in Christ.

Timothy later traveled extensively with Paul and at times served as the apostle's representative to churches, especially at Thessalonica, Corinth, and Philippi (1 Cor. 4:17; 16:10; Phil. 2:19–24; 1 Thess. 3:2, 6). At Ephesus, too, Timothy, though not the long-term pastor, brought doctrinal and organizational stability and provided the loving, firm direction Paul himself would have given. Thus this letter was also intended to be read aloud to the Ephesian church so that it would serve as Paul's written authorization for Timothy to make the changes specified.

Salutation (1:1, 2)

I. Sound Doctrine (1:3–20)
   A. The nature of the false doctrine (1:3–11)
   B. Paul's transformation through sound doctrine (1:12–17)
   C. Timothy's responsibility to sound doctrine (1:18–20)

II. The Worship Assembly (2:1–15)
   A. Prayer for all individuals (2:1–7)
   B. Men and women in the worship assembly (2:8–15)

III. Church Leaders (3:1–16)
   A. The character qualities of elders (3:1–7)
   B. The character qualities of deacons (3:8–13)
   C. The reason for writing (3:14–16)

IV. False Teachers (4:1–16)
   A. The appearance of false teachers (4:1–5)
   B. Timothy's response to false teachers (4:6–11)
   C. A personal encouragement for ministry (4:12–16)

V. Church Members (5:1—6:10)
   A. Older and younger members (5:1, 2)
   B. Widows (5:3–16)
   C. Elders (5:17–25)
   D. Slaves (6:1, 2)
   E. Heretical church members (6:3–10)

VI. The Christian Servant (6:11–21)

Women in silence are the "listening church, which the teaching church must again and again become."

Charlotte von Kirschbaum

Greeting

1 Paul, an apostle of Jesus Christ, by the commandment of God our Savior and the Lord Jesus Christ, our hope,

[2]To Timothy, a true son in the faith:

Grace, mercy, *and* peace from God our Father and Jesus Christ our Lord.

No Other Doctrine

[3]As I urged you when I went into Macedonia—remain in Ephesus that you may charge some that they teach no other doctrine, [4]nor give heed to fables and endless genealogies, which cause disputes rather than godly edification which is in faith. [5]Now the purpose of the commandment is love from a pure heart, *from* a good conscience, and *from* sincere faith, [6]from which some, having strayed, have turned aside to idle talk, [7]desiring to be teachers of the law, understanding neither what they say nor the things which they affirm.

[8]But we know that the law *is* good if one uses it lawfully, [9]knowing this: that the law is not made for a righteous person, but for *the* lawless and insubordinate, for *the* ungodly and for sinners, for *the* unholy and profane, for murderers of fathers and murderers of mothers, for manslayers, [10]for fornicators, for sodomites, for kidnappers, for liars, for perjurers, and if there is any other thing that is contrary to sound doctrine, [11]according to the glorious gospel of the blessed God which was committed to my trust.

Glory to God for His Grace

[12]And I thank Christ Jesus our Lord who has enabled me, because He counted me faithful, put-ting *me* into the ministry, [13]although I was formerly a blasphemer, a persecutor, and an insolent man; but I obtained mercy because I did *it* ignorantly in unbelief. [14]And the grace of our Lord was exceedingly abundant, with faith and love which are in Christ Jesus. [15]This *is* a faithful saying and worthy of all acceptance, that Christ Jesus came into the world to save sinners, of whom I am chief. [16]However, for this reason I obtained mercy, that in me first Jesus Christ might show all long-suffering, as a pattern to those who are going to believe on Him for everlasting life. [17]Now to the King eternal, immortal, invisible, to God who alone is wise,[a] *be* honor and glory forever and ever. Amen.

Fight the Good Fight

[18]This charge I commit to you, son Timothy, according to the prophecies previously made concerning you, that by them you may wage the good warfare, [19]having faith and a good conscience, which some having rejected, concerning the faith have suffered shipwreck, [20]of whom are Hymenaeus and Alexander, whom I delivered to Satan that they may learn not to blaspheme.

Pray for All Men

2 Therefore I exhort first of all that supplications, prayers, intercessions, *and* giving of thanks be made for all men, [2]for kings and all who are in authority, that we may lead a quiet and peaceable life in all godliness and reverence. [3]For this *is* good and acceptable in the sight of God our Savior, [4]who desires all men to be saved and to come to the knowledge of the truth. [5]For *there is*

1:17 [a]NU-Text reads *to the only God.*

1:3–7 False teachers, whose doctrine was a mixture of Christian teaching, regulations from the Mosaic Law of Judaism, and pagan Gnostic speculations, had come to Ephesus bringing discord rather than growth in grace.

1:8 The Law of Moses was good, but these false teachers used it incorrectly by making obedience to the Law mandatory for Christians. The Law should pinpoint sin for the unbeliever. Paul demonstrated this through giving a sin list that followed the Ten Commandments in exact sequence (vv. 1:9, 10; see chart, The Ten Commandments Throughout Scripture).

1:18 NT prophecy involves reporting something that God has revealed for edification, exhortation, and comfort (1 Cor. 14:3). Significant prophecies had previously been made about Timothy (1 Tim. 4:14). Paul often used figures of speech re-lated to warfare when the context involved struggle against evil spiritual forces or opponents of the gospel (2 Cor. 10:1–6; Eph. 6:10–17; 2 Tim. 2:3, 4; Philem. 1).

1:20 Hymenaeus and Alexander taught that the Resurrection was already past (see 2 Tim. 2:17, 18, note). Although evidence is lacking to identify Alexander with other men by that name in Scripture, both he and Hymenaeus were certainly leaders in the Ephesian church. Both had rejected "the faith" (the gospel) and were in the process of bringing "the faith" to ruin ("shipwreck") among believers (1 Tim. 1:19). These men had been excommunicated by Paul, who had placed them back into Satan's domain, the world (1 John 5:19). This discipline was corrective and redemptive in intent, for Paul wanted them to recognize their sin and repent (see 1 Cor. 5:1–5).

Teaching is a gift (1 Cor. 12:28, 29; Eph. 4:11; Rom. 12:7) that God's Spirit gives to both women and men. All believers are to teach one another (Col. 3:16) and to share with the community what they have learned (1 Cor. 14:26).

Priscilla, together with her husband Aquila, instructed a Christian brother, Apollos, in matters of theology (Acts 18:26). The apostle Paul recognized Priscilla's ministry and obviously loved and respected her as well as other female co-laborers (Rom. 16:3, 6, 12; Phil 4:3). Paul also encouraged older women to teach the younger women (Titus 2:3–5) and admonished Timothy to respect Lois and Eunice, his mother and grandmother, for instructing him in the faith (2 Tim. 1:3–5).

Although Paul was a great advocate for women to exercise spiritual gifts, he taught that gifts needed to be exercised in a manner that honors the Word of God (1 Tim. 2:12). New Testament women were encouraged to exercise teaching ministries but were to do so within the God-ordained pattern of male-female complementarity.

See also chart on Spiritual Gifts of Women in the Bible; notes on Biblical Equality (Eph. 5); Education (Deut. 6; Prov. 12; 2 Tim. 3); Spiritual Gifts (Rom. 12); Women's Ministries (John 4; Acts 2; 1 Cor. 11; Eph. 2; Titus 2)

one God and one Mediator between God and men, *the* Man Christ Jesus, ⁶who gave Himself a ransom for all, to be testified in due time, ⁷for which I was appointed a preacher and an apostle—I am speaking the truth in Christ[a] *and* not lying—a teacher of the Gentiles in faith and truth.

Men and Women in the Church

⁸I desire therefore that the men pray everywhere, lifting up holy hands, without wrath and doubting; ⁹in like manner also, that the women adorn themselves in modest apparel, with propriety and moderation, not with braided hair or gold or pearls or costly clothing, ¹⁰but, which is proper for women professing godliness, with good works. ¹¹Let a woman learn in silence with all submission. ¹²And I do not permit a woman to teach or to have authority over a man, but to be in silence. ¹³For Adam was formed first, then Eve. ¹⁴And Adam was not deceived, but the woman being deceived, fell

· · · · · · · · · · · · · · · · · · · ·

2:7 ªNU-Text omits *in Christ.*

2:9, 10 Women should preserve modesty in both dress and attitude. By contrast, they should avoid dressing ostentatiously and focus their attention on good works appropriate for godliness. Some women might have been dressing in a flashy, even sensual, manner acceptable in their former pagan lifestyle but out of place in the church. Others might have been dressing to reflect their higher social status. For the great majority, who were from the lower classes, this ostentatious attire could have proven a barrier to their sharing in the life of the church (see 1 Cor. 11:20, 21).

2:11 Women should learn with an attitude of quiet submissiveness. Paul seemingly wanted to be certain the women were well-grounded in the Word of God (2 Tim. 3:6, 7). This should be:

• "In silence" (Gk. *hēsuchia*), meaning "quietness," a more appropriate meaning since women did normally speak in the worship assembly (1 Tim. 2:11, 12; see 1 Cor. 11:5; 14:26);

• "With all submission," suggesting that instruction was to be received respectfully.

Women were to receive instruction in the worship assembly with a heart of quiet receptivity to the Word.

2:12 Paul clarified his directive: Women were not "to teach or to have authority over a man." Paul spoke of a consistent practice of teaching or exercising authority, which would not preclude an occasional teaching situation to be done by a woman for men. In the NT the verb "teach" (Gk. *didaskō*) nearly always refers to teaching in group settings. The teacher expounded the OT Scripture and the apostles' teachings (1 Cor. 4:17; 2 Tim. 2:2) and presented the implications of that truth for daily living (see Matt. 28:19, 20). The verb

translated "to have authority" (Gk. *authenteō*) occurs only here in the NT and is rarely used in ancient literature. Although it can possibly mean "to domineer" or "to usurp authority," the meaning "to have authority" seems preferable. Third, although the grammar allows for this phrase to refer to a single activity (as "to teach authoritatively"), the word "or" makes it preferable to view these as two separate activities. Since authority and submission are important issues, teaching seems to be a subset of holding authority. That is, some women were violating God's pattern of authority and submission through their teaching in the assembly (1 Tim 2:13, 14).

2:13, 14 Paul gave theological reasons for his directive that women in the worship assembly learn in a quiet and submissive manner rather than having a position of teaching or exercising authority over men. Through the rabbinic method of summary citation, Paul used a summary statement (v. 13 and Gen. 2:4–24; 1 Tim. 2:14 and Gen. 3:1–25). In both cases, Paul was making an implied application by analogy based on the Genesis account. Adam was created before Eve, implying that Adam's prior creation carried with it some degree of responsibility and authority. This authority is possibly based on the OT concept of primogeniture, through which the eldest son became the family head, a leader of family worship, and the recipient of a double portion of the inheritance (Deut. 21:15–17). Paul may have been asserting that Adam's status as the eldest carried with it the leadership fitting a firstborn son. He was in no way teaching an essential superiority of the man over the woman; instead, he was showing how man's leadership in the church harmonized with the Creator's design for the home and community. Thus Paul's unstated application was that just as in creation the final responsibility rested with the man, so it

POLYGAMY *MORE THAN ONE WIFE*

Polygamy, though practiced by some Old Testament saints, was in no way God's ideal for marriage. As ordained of God, marriage was bonding between two people—one male and one female (Gen. 2:24). Adam and Eve were monogamists. After the Fall, the institution of marriage suffered from sin's entry into the world just as did all other aspects of creation.

The predominant effects of bigamy and polygamy are negative:

- Abraham's relationship with Sarah's maid, Hagar, resulted in much jealousy and discord (Gen. 16:5).
- David's sons by various wives fought among themselves for the throne (2 Sam. 5:13; 13:22–30).
- Solomon's 700 wives and 300 concubines turned his heart from the Lord (1 Kin. 11:1–8).

No examples of polygamy are cited in the New Testament. Jesus reiterated God's original design that "the two shall become one flesh" as the ideal of marriage (Mark 10:2–12). Early church leaders were explicitly told to be the husband of only one wife (1 Tim. 3:2, 12; Titus 1:6). At the same time, the New Testament teaching on marriage repudiates adultery, divorce, and marrying and divorcing several wives in succession (Matt. 5:27–32; Rom. 7:2, 3; 1 Cor. 7:2–16).

See also notes on Divorce (Matt. 19); Husbands (Job 31; 2 Cor. 6); Marriage (Gen. 2; 2 Sam. 6; Prov. 5; Hos. 2; Amos 3; 2 Cor. 13; Heb. 13); Remarriage (Matt. 5); Wives (Prov. 31); portrait of Hannah (1 Sam. 1)

---

into transgression. ¹⁵Nevertheless she will be saved in childbearing if they continue in faith, love, and holiness, with self-control.

Qualifications of Overseers

3 This *is* a faithful saying: If a man desires the position of a bishop,ᵃ he desires a good work. ²A

bishop then must be blameless, the husband of one wife, temperate, sober-minded, of good behavior, hospitable, able to teach; ³not given to wine, not violent, not greedy for money,ᵃ but gentle, not quarrelsome, not covetous; ⁴one who rules his own

3:1 ᵃLiterally *overseer* **3:3** ᵃNU-Text omits *not greedy for money*.

---

also should in the church. Paul again was not suggesting that women were less intelligent or were more easily deceived than men. Instead, he used the account of the Fall to point out the role reversal that occurred when Adam knowingly allowed himself to be led into sin by his wife. God had originally instructed Adam concerning the forbidden fruit (Gen. 2:17), and the Lord clearly placed the ultimate responsibility with Adam (Rom. 5:12; see Gen. 3:17, where "heeded" has the sense of "obeyed"). Thus Paul's application by analogy was that this role reversal that caused so much trouble in the beginning should not be repeated in the worship assembly through the consistent practice of the teaching of men by women.

2:15 Paul closed with an awesome challenge and worthy reward. Of many interpretations, the one that most adequately handles the textual data is that women will be saved (with the focus on salvation's future rewards) through faithfulness to their appointed role, summed up in the example of motherhood. Four key grammatical issues are involved in this verse. "Nevertheless" (Gk. *de*) both provides a contrast with verse 14 and introduces a conclusion about the results of women fulfilling their God-given roles. The phrase "she will be saved" (Gk. *sōzō*), most commonly refers to some aspect of spiritual salvation. In this case, however, Paul's focus seems to be on the future aspect of salvation, when believers' works will be judged and rewards given (Rom. 14:10; 1 Cor. 3:10–15; 2 Cor. 5:10). His use of the future tense of the verb as well as his stress on the need for women to keep living lives that are characterized by holiness and obedience and worthy of future rewards makes this clear. "Childbearing" is one of the good works that is to be part of the godly woman's lifestyle (see 1 Tim. 2:10). While the term can have the literal meaning of bearing or rearing children, its use here is figurative (a synec-

doche, in which a part of something represents the whole). Thus Paul used child-rearing as a representative example of the activities in which Christian women of his day would likely be involved. This was especially appropriate since, with shortened age spans, marriage and child-rearing typically encompassed much if not all of a woman's life and were activities highly valued by a 1st-century woman.

Paul closed his instructions to women by stressing the inner qualities that were to accompany this lifestyle: "faith," "love," "holiness," and "self-control." This last quality, actually the same Greek term earlier translated "moderation," served as a closing bracket for Paul's remarks to women (v. 9). In summary, Paul stated the expected result of women fulfilling their God-appointed role in life, with accompanying inner attitudes of godliness: They would experience the fullness of future salvation, including the judging of their works and the receiving of rewards (v. 15). Altogether these activities and attitudes comprised the "good works" with which she was to clothe herself (v. 10).

3:1 Three terms were used interchangeably in the NT to refer to this office: "bishop" or "overseer" (Acts 20:28; Phil. 1:1; Titus 1:7; 1 Pet. 5:2), "elder" or "presbyter" (Acts 20:17; 1 Tim. 5:17, 19; Titus 1:5; 1 Pet. 5:1, 5), and "pastor" (Eph. 4:11). Paul began with a general characteristic which summarized all the rest: "blameless" (1 Tim. 3:2; Titus 1:7). He then listed six personal characteristics (1 Tim. 3:2), faults to be avoided (v. 3), and the quality of relationships appropriate in the home, the church, and non-Christian society (vv. 4–7).

3:2 An overseer must be faithful to his wife—a "one-woman man." Paul was not requiring that elders be married, though most were in his day. An elder could be a widower or single (1 Cor. 7:25–28; 9:5, 6), as Timothy probably was (see also 1 Tim. 3:1).

DATING RELATING TO ONE ANOTHER

Dating relationships are not described in Scripture. You can assume, however, that dating is subject to God's general principles pertaining to relationships. God is very clear about how you are to relate to one another.

1) Dating teens must honor their parents and respect their counsel (Eph. 6:2).
2) The dating partner must be considered. God's Word is very clear when it says, "Do not be un-equally yoked together with unbelievers" (2 Cor. 6:14). You are wise to ask whether or not your date has a personal and growing relationship with the Lord. Also you should consider whether that relationship is evident in your date's lifestyle.
3) You must examine yourself. Are you spending time with the Lord daily (Matt. 6:33)? Are you de-pending on the Lord to meet your needs of love and security? Are you an example for Christ to all those with whom you have contact (1 Tim. 4:12)? The Lord calls for you to have a loving relationship with and a commitment to Him that supersedes any dating relationship.

See also Prov. 31:30; 1 Cor. 6:19, 20; 13:4–8; Gal. 5:13; Eph. 4:1–3; 2 Tim. 2:22; notes on Commitment (Matt. 16); Engagement (Matt. 1); Friendship (Luke 1); Identity in Christ (Col. 2); Love (1 John 3); Marriage (Gen. 2; 2 Sam. 6; Prov. 5; Hos. 2; Amos 3; 2 Cor. 13; Heb. 12)

house well, having *his* children in submission with all reverence ⁵(for if a man does not know how to rule his own house, how will he take care of the church of God?); ⁶not a novice, lest being puffed up with pride he fall into the *same* condemnation as the devil. ⁷Moreover he must have a good testimony among those who are outside, lest he fall into reproach and the snare of the devil.

Qualifications of Deacons

⁸Likewise deacons *must be* reverent, not dou-ble-tongued, not given to much wine, not greedy for money, ⁹holding the mystery of the faith with a pure conscience. ¹⁰But let these also first be tested; then let them serve as deacons, being *found* blameless. ¹¹Likewise, *their* wives *must be* reverent, not slanderers, temperate, faithful in all things. ¹²Let deacons be the husbands of one wife, ruling *their* children and their own houses well. ¹³For those who have served well as deacons obtain for themselves a good standing and great boldness in the faith which is in Christ Jesus.

The Great Mystery

¹⁴These things I write to you, though I hope to come to you shortly; ¹⁵but if I am delayed, *I write*

so that you may know how you ought to conduct yourself in the house of God, which is the church of the living God, the pillar and ground of the truth. ¹⁶And without controversy great is the mystery of godliness:

God[a] was manifested in the flesh,
Justified in the Spirit,
Seen by angels,
Preached among the Gentiles,
Believed on in the world,
Received up in glory.

The Great Apostasy

4 Now the Spirit expressly says that in latter times some will depart from the faith, giving heed to deceiving spirits and doctrines of demons, ²speaking lies in hypocrisy, having their own conscience seared with a hot iron, ³forbid-ding to marry, *and commanding* to abstain from foods which God created to be received with thanksgiving by those who believe and know the truth. ⁴For every creature of God *is* good, and nothing is to be refused if it is received with

····················
3:16 ᵃNU-Text reads *Who.*

3:8–11 Deacon (Gk. *diakonos*) was used to refer to a "servant," whether male or female. Paul gave deacon qualifications paralleling those of the elders, for the deacons. The qualifica-tions of a group of women—deacons' wives or women who were deaconesses are given. Phoebe, who was a faithful ser-vant in the church, was called a *diakonos* (Rom. 16:1).

"Wives" (Gk. *gunaikas*) can be translated "women," in which case this would be a discussion of women who were dea-conesses. The text remains clear that their ministry was one of service, as is implied by the word itself and other examples in Scripture (Acts 6:1–7; see Acts 2; Rom. 16, Phoebe; Eph. 2, Women's Ministries). The NKJV translators have added "their,"

indicating a preference for "wives." It is reasonable that the wives of deacons would have been expected to help their hus-bands in service. Their exemplary function would demand cor-responding character qualities. No such qualifications are listed separately for the wives of bishops (1 Tim. 3:1–7).

4:1 Paul explicitly identified the source of the false teachers' doctrines as demonic. Part of the work of evil spirits is to cause people to believe lies (Acts 5:3), to embrace worldly wisdom (James 3:13–16), and to accept doctrinal error as truth (2 Cor. 11:14; 1 Tim. 4:1–5).

4:2 The false teachers are pictured as lacking the ability to

HOMEMAKING IN THE BIBLE

Household Tasks

Women have traditionally invested much of their time in the daily tasks that are necessary for maintaining the family household. Such is commended in Proverbs 31:10–31 and the admonition instructing women to be "homemakers" (Gk. *oikourgos*, lit. "home workers") in Titus 2:5.
These tasks were routine:

- Drawing water (Gen. 24:19, 20, 43, 44)
- Grinding grain (Is. 47:2; Matt. 24:41; Luke 17:35).
- Spinning wool, weaving fabric, making clothing, laundering garments (Prov. 31:13; Acts 9:36–42)
- Preparing food (Prov. 31:15)
- Caring for children (Prov. 31:21)

Social Tasks

- Offering welcome, food, and rest (Gen. 18:6; 1 Tim. 5:10)

Spiritual Tasks

Women have always played a vital part in the spiritual nurture of their children. They, by nature of time invested and their own natural nurturing skills, have a unique role of influence and responsibility for instruction.

- Shaping the spiritual values of children* (Deut. 6:7–9; Prov. 31:21; 2 Tim. 1:3–5).
- Preparing for the Sabbath—filling the oil lamps, cooking special foods in advance of the Sabbath, drawing extra water
- For many generations in Judaism, the wife and mother has prayed for her family after lighting the candles on the Sabbath
- Someone in the family would then recite Proverbs 31:10–31 in her honor.

*Interestingly, a child's Jewish heritage is determined through the maternal link.

thanksgiving; ⁵for it is sanctified by the word of God and prayer.

A Good Servant of Jesus Christ

⁶If you instruct the brethren in these things, you will be a good minister of Jesus Christ, nourished in the words of faith and of the good doctrine which you have carefully followed. ⁷But reject profane and old wives' fables, and exercise yourself toward godliness. ⁸For bodily exercise profits a little, but godliness is profitable for all things, having promise of the life that now is and of that which is to come. ⁹This *is* a faithful saying and worthy of all acceptance. ¹⁰For to this *end* we both labor and suffer reproach,ᵃ because we trust in the living God, who is *the* Savior of all men, es-

pecially of those who believe. ¹¹These things command and teach.

Take Heed to Your Ministry

¹²Let no one despise your youth, but be an example to the believers in word, in conduct, in love, in spirit,ᵃ in faith, in purity. ¹³Till I come, give attention to reading, to exhortation, to doctrine. ¹⁴Do not neglect the gift that is in you, which was given to you by prophecy with the laying on of the hands of the eldership. ¹⁵Meditate on these things; give yourself entirely to them, that your progress may be evident to all. ¹⁶Take heed to

4:10 ᵃNU-Text reads *we labor and strive.*   4:12 ᵃNU-Text omits *in spirit.*

distinguish right from wrong. Because Paul used such a strong term (Gk. *kausteriazō*, "seared"), the focus was probably on a more radical act of perversion—perhaps the time when the individuals consciously turned from the truth of God's Word and made themselves vulnerable to the deceiving spirits behind the false doctrine (see 2 Cor. 1, Conscience).

4:14 This gracious endowment was a Spirit-given ability to teach and preach the gospel, the very resource needed to refute the false teachers and win people to Christ (1 Tim. 1:18;

2 Tim. 1:6, 7, 14). It was confirmed to Timothy through prophetic utterances accompanied by the laying on of hands by the elders (see 1 Tim. 1:18, note). The situation in 1 Timothy 4:14 seems to be similar to that described in Acts 13:1–3 where the Holy Spirit revealed His will, apparently through those with prophetic gifting (Acts 13:1), and the gathered teachers and prophets laid their hands on Paul and Barnabas to release them for their missionary ministry (Acts 13:3).

CONTENTMENT   *THE ULTIMATE ACCEPTANCE*

Contentment is the ultimate acceptance of yourself, your surroundings, your past, and your future. For a believer, finding contentment should be effortless. Jesus has paid the price for your sin and has given you a secure future of eternity in His presence, free of all pain and sorrow (Eph. 2:8, 9; Rev. 21:4). The suffering you experience now should be viewed in light of an eternity to be spent with the Savior (Rev. 21:7). God provided a way for you to be rescued from an eternity in hell—He is sufficient to meet your needs in this world that He created (Phil. 4:13, 19).

Yet reaching this blessed state of contentment is not an easy task. Satisfaction when you have very real unmet needs, freedom from worry when you have overwhelming concerns, patience in letting God work when pressures abound—these seem like impossible dreams. Happiness—despite heartaches caused by the past, in the midst of tragedies experienced in the present, based on promises trusted for the future—is not merely a human pursuit but demands spiritual resources only found in the indwelling Holy Spirit.

God chose not to give you contentment as a gift. He chose rather to teach you to be content as you allow Him to be ruler in your life. Contentment is learned (Phil. 4:11). As you trust God's gifts to be sufficient and His assignments to be appropriate, you can accept the way you look, the means you have been given, the family in which you are living, the struggles through which you have gone, the job you have, being content and fulfilled in all (2 Cor. 3:5, 6; 12:9).

On the other hand, acceptance does not mean stagnation. Dissatisfaction with areas in your life that can be changed, within divine guidelines, may help you to see that something is missing. When this happens, you dare not adopt the "Canaan" syndrome of complaining. Remember that God's people were not allowed to enter the Promised Land because of their murmuring (Josh. 5:6). Rather, take that dissatisfaction to the Lord and see what He would challenge you to do, being willing in the meantime to be "content" as you work toward ultimate goals. This is the balance between "I have learned to be content," and "I can do all things through Christ" (Phil. 4:11, 13).

You must trust that God has given you everything needed for this moment in time. You should be content with yourself, your family, your surroundings, your job, or your past. As you depend on the Lord, you are content as you pursue His goals for your life.

See also 1 Cor. 7:17–24; 2 Cor. 4:18; notes on Bitterness (Heb. 12); Fruit of the Spirit (Ps. 86; Rom. 5; 15; 1 Cor. 9; 13; Gal. 5; Eph. 4; Col. 3; 2 Thess. 1; Rev. 2); God's Will (Eph. 5); Happiness (Prov. 16); Worry (Rom. 8)

---

yourself and to the doctrine. Continue in them, for in doing this you will save both yourself and those who hear you.

Treatment of Church Members

5 Do not rebuke an older man, but exhort *him* as a father, younger men as brothers, ²older women as mothers, younger women as sisters, with all purity.

Honor True Widows

³Honor widows who are really widows. ⁴But if any widow has children or grandchildren, let them first learn to show piety at home and to repay their parents; for this is good andᵃ acceptable before God. ⁵Now she who is really a widow, and

left alone, trusts in God and continues in supplications and prayers night and day. ⁶But she who lives in pleasure is dead while she lives. ⁷And these things command, that they may be blameless. ⁸But if anyone does not provide for his own, and especially for those of his household, he has denied the faith and is worse than an unbeliever.

⁹Do not let a widow under sixty years old be taken into the number, *and not unless* she has been the wife of one man, ¹⁰well reported for good works: if she has brought up children, if she has lodged strangers, if she has washed the saints' feet, if she has relieved the afflicted, if she has diligently followed every good work.

·······················

5:4 ᵃNU-Text and M-Text omit *good and.*

5:3–16 The care of widows had always been a priority among God's people (see Ex. 22:22; Ps. 68:5; Is. 1:17; Acts 6:1–6; 9:36–41; James 1:27). The proper and equitable care of widows caused the first major disagreement in the Jerusalem church (Acts 6:1). Guidelines were needed for the Ephesian church. Paul wanted to deal with the younger widows, who may well have been among those drawn away by the false teachers (2 Tim. 3:6). He contrasted them with other—

usually older—widows, whom he classified as "really widows" (1 Tim. 5:3). Guidelines for receiving assistance from the church were specific: widows genuinely in need (1 Tim. 5:3, 5, 16), without family and friends to care for them (vv. 4, 5, 8, 16), and godly, praying widows (vv. 5, 9, 10). He advised the "younger widows" to remarry and to become godly wives and mothers (vv. 11–15).

WEALTH — *BLESSING OR CURSE?*

The Bible teaches that wealth comes from God and will be returned to Him. Wealth should bring praise to God. At times, God chooses to bless His children with wealth. Abraham, Isaac, Solomon, and even Job received wealth as a blessing from God (Gen. 13:2; 26:12–14; 1 Kin. 3:13; Job 42:12).

Material wealth is given to mankind as a stewardship. God, the owner of all things, expects His children to care for His possessions and return them to Him (Luke 12:42). Wealth is also intended to bring praise to God. Believers who give money to help others bless the Lord (2 Cor. 8:1–5).

Sixteen of the thirty-nine parables of Jesus deal with wealth. In Scripture, more references are made to money than salvation. Jesus dealt with money because money matters to people. Material wealth can be a blessing or a curse. The power of wealth is subtle (1 Tim. 6:10). The source of wealth is secure (Matt. 6:25, 26). The temptation of wealth is spending (James 4:3). The strategy of wealth is saving (Matt. 25:27). The purpose of wealth is sharing (Acts 20:35).

God expects His children to use the wealth they receive from Him to bless others and to bring glory to Him. In the parable of the talents, Jesus promised an abundance to all who possess His kingdom and eternal life to all who trust in Him (Matt. 25:14–30).

See also Mark 10:17–22; notes on Blessings (Gen. 12); Financial Planning (Luke 19); Giving (2 Cor. 9); Prosperity (Ps. 2); Stewardship (Luke 16)

---

¹¹But refuse *the* younger widows; for when they have begun to grow wanton against Christ, they desire to marry, ¹²having condemnation because they have cast off their first faith. ¹³And besides they learn *to be* idle, wandering about from house to house, and not only idle but also gossips and busybodies, saying things which they ought not. ¹⁴Therefore I desire that *the* younger *widows* marry, bear children, manage the house, give no opportunity to the adversary to speak reproachfully. ¹⁵For some have already turned aside after Satan. ¹⁶If any believing man or[a] woman has widows, let them relieve them, and do not let the church be burdened, that it may relieve those who are really widows.

Honor the Elders

¹⁷Let the elders who rule well be counted worthy of double honor, especially those who labor in the word and doctrine. ¹⁸For the Scripture says, *"You shall not muzzle an ox while it treads out the grain,"*[a] and, *"The laborer is worthy of his wages."*[b] ¹⁹Do not receive an accusation against an elder except from two or three witnesses. ²⁰Those who are sinning rebuke in the presence of all, that the rest also may fear.

²¹I charge *you* before God and the Lord Jesus Christ and the elect angels that you observe these things without prejudice, doing nothing with partiality. ²²Do not lay hands on anyone hastily, nor share in other people's sins; keep yourself pure.

²³No longer drink only water, but use a little wine for your stomach's sake and your frequent infirmities.

5:16 [a]NU-Text omits *man or.*   5:18 [a]Deuteronomy 25:4   [b]Luke 10:7

Whatever the degree of involvement and however the relationship works itself out, the command is clear. Older women are to encourage and equip younger women to live for God's glory.

Susan Hunt

5:19–21 Accusations against elders were to be substantiated (v. 19), following the Mosaic practice (Deut. 17:6) reaffirmed by Jesus (Matt. 18:16). Those found guilty should be disciplined publicly (1 Tim. 5:20) as a warning to other believers—whether or not they were elders—who were involved in the same sins. All such discipline should be administered impartially and without prejudice (v. 21).

5:22–25 The setting apart of an elder for service (see 1 Tim. 4:14, note) should be done thoughtfully and after carefully observing the person's lifestyle.

5:23 In Paul's exhortation on personal purity, he pointed out that an ascetic practice that adversely affected health would not keep a person pure (v. 22). Impure water supplies often made wine a common beverage. Timothy may have been totally abstaining from this beverage, possibly as an ascetic practice. Paul encouraged Timothy to use some wine medicinally to alleviate his stomach ailments.

Compiling our traditions and oral or written histories will give our children an identity with their Christian heritage.

Charlene Kaemmerling

---

[24]Some men's sins are clearly evident, preceding *them* to judgment, but those of some *men* follow later. [25]Likewise, the good works *of some* are clearly evident, and those that are otherwise cannot be hidden.

Honor Masters

6 Let as many bondservants as are under the yoke count their own masters worthy of all honor, so that the name of God and *His* doctrine may not be blasphemed. [2]And those who have believing masters, let them not despise *them* because they are brethren, but rather serve *them* because those who are benefited are believers and beloved. Teach and exhort these things.

Error and Greed

[3]If anyone teaches otherwise and does not consent to wholesome words, *even* the words of our Lord Jesus Christ, and to the doctrine which accords with godliness, [4]he is proud, knowing nothing, but is obsessed with disputes and arguments over words, from which come envy, strife, reviling, evil suspicions, [5]useless wranglings[a] of men of corrupt minds and destitute of the truth, who suppose that godliness is a *means of* gain. From such withdraw yourself.[b]

[6]Now godliness with contentment is great gain. [7]For we brought nothing into *this* world, *and it is* certain[a] we can carry nothing out. [8]And having food and clothing, with these we shall be content. [9]But those who desire to be rich fall into temptation and a snare, and *into* many foolish and harmful lusts which drown men in destruction and perdition. [10]For the love of money is a root of all *kinds of* evil, for which some have strayed from the faith in their greediness, and pierced themselves through with many sorrows.

The Good Confession

[11]But you, O man of God, flee these things and pursue righteousness, godliness, faith, love, patience, gentleness. [12]Fight the good fight of faith, lay hold on eternal life, to which you were also called and have confessed the good confession in the presence of many witnesses. [13]I urge you in the sight of God who gives life to all things, and *before* Christ Jesus who witnessed the good confession before Pontius Pilate, [14]that you keep *this* commandment without spot, blameless until our Lord Jesus Christ's appearing, [15]which He will manifest in His own time, *He who is* the blessed and only Potentate, the King of kings and Lord of lords, [16]who alone has immortality, dwelling in unapproachable light, whom no man has seen or can see, to whom *be* honor and everlasting power. Amen.

Instructions to the Rich

[17]Command those who are rich in this present age not to be haughty, nor to trust in uncertain riches but in the living God, who gives us richly all things to enjoy. [18]*Let them* do good, that they be rich in good works, ready to give, willing to share, [19]storing up for themselves a good foundation for the time to come, that they may lay hold on eternal life.

Guard the Faith

[20]O Timothy! Guard what was committed to your trust, avoiding the profane *and* idle babblings and contradictions of what is falsely called knowledge— [21]by professing it some have strayed concerning the faith.

Grace *be* with you. Amen.

···················

6:5 [a]NU-Text and M-Text read *constant friction.* [b]NU-Text omits this sentence.   **6:7** [a]NU-Text omits *and it is certain.*

6:9, 10 Paul warned against the greedy pursuit of riches, and he cited several results of such greed:

- it made a person vulnerable to yield consistently to temptation;
- it created a snare for the person;
- this sin gave birth to other evil desires;
- this sin could pull a person to the depths of depravity as a lead weight pulled down a fish net;
- it became a root cause of many other kinds of evil that would cause a person to wander from a pure faith in Christ;
- it became a source of great grief to the person.

6:17–19 Paul never condemned those who were wealthy, for he knew God loved to provide abundantly for His children's needs (1 Tim. 4:3, 4; see Eccl. 5:19, 20). Instead, he was concerned that they not arrogantly make riches an idol in which they trusted for security. Further, he wanted them to share with those in need and thereby lay up eternal rewards for themselves.

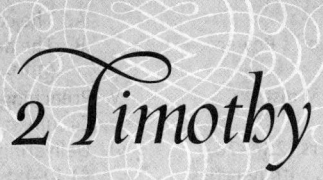

2 Timothy

AUTHOR

The apostle Paul traditionally has been considered the author of 2 Timothy, and the letter explicitly states that he is the author (2 Tim. 1:1; see 1 Tim., Introduction: Author).

DATE

After being freed from the Roman captivity described in Acts 28, Paul apparently traveled in the eastern Mediterranean region (1 Tim. 1:3; 3:14; Titus 1:5; 3:12). During this time, Paul wrote 1 Timothy and Titus, probably between A.D. 62 and 65. After this he was imprisoned again, and during this time he wrote 2 Timothy. Early church tradition agrees that Paul was executed by the Roman emperor Nero. Since Nero committed suicide in June A.D. 68 and since Paul asked Timothy to come to him "before winter," this last letter must have been written before the autumn of A.D. 67 (2 Tim. 4:21). The most likely date is A.D. 66–67.

BACKGROUND

SETTING: Paul wrote 2 Timothy from prison, probably shortly before his death. Timothy was seemingly still in Ephesus when Paul sent him this second epistle.

PURPOSE: Paul's primary purpose of the letter was to ask Timothy to join him in Rome (2 Tim. 4:9, 11, 13, 21). Paul was in prison and knew he would not live much longer (2 Tim. 4:6–8). Others who had previously ministered to him, with the exception of Luke, were no longer there, and he longed for Timothy's company (2 Tim. 4:11). Paul also wrote the letter to strengthen Timothy's loyalty to the Lord Jesus Christ in the face of the suffering his young disciple would certainly face (see 2 Tim. 1:8; 2:3; 3:12; 4:5).

AUDIENCE: This warmly personal letter was addressed to Timothy and included specific instructions for him. However, like 1 Timothy and Titus, the letter was intended to be read to the church at Ephesus since it would serve as a written authorization for Timothy to carry out Paul's directives included therein (2 Tim. 2:2; 3:1; see 1 Tim., Introduction: Audience).

THEMES

Paul used this letter to encourage consistent Christian living even in the midst of difficulties and trials (2 Tim. 1:8, 13; 2:1, 3, 5, 15; 3: 1, 10–14; 4:1–5). The apostle sent a clear message that this Christian lifestyle was only possible in the strength of Christ.

Greeting

1 Paul, an apostle of Jesus Christ[a] by the will of God, according to the promise of life which is in Christ Jesus,

[2] To Timothy, a beloved son:

Grace, mercy, *and* peace from God the Father and Christ Jesus our Lord.

Timothy's Faith and Heritage

[3] I thank God, whom I serve with a pure conscience, as *my* forefathers *did,* as without ceasing I remember you in my prayers night and day, [4] greatly desiring to see you, being mindful of your tears, that I may be filled with joy, [5] when I call to remembrance the genuine faith that is in you, which dwelt first in your grandmother Lois and your mother Eunice, and I am persuaded is in you also. [6] Therefore I remind you to stir up the gift of God which is in you through the laying on of my hands. [7] For God has not given us a spirit of fear, but of power and of love and of a sound mind.

Not Ashamed of the Gospel

[8] Therefore do not be ashamed of the testimony of our Lord, nor of me His prisoner, but share with me in the sufferings for the gospel according to the power of God, [9] who has saved us and called *us* with a holy calling, not according to our works, but according to His own purpose and grace which was given to us in Christ Jesus before time began, [10] but has now been revealed by the appearing of our Savior Jesus Christ, *who* has abolished death and brought life and immortality to light through the gospel, [11] to which I was appointed a preacher, an apostle, and a teacher of the Gentiles.[a] [12] For this reason I also suffer these things; nevertheless I am not ashamed, for I know whom I have believed and am persuaded that He is able to keep what I have committed to Him until that Day.

Be Loyal to the Faith

[13] Hold fast the pattern of sound words which you have heard from me, in faith and love which are in Christ Jesus. [14] That good thing which was committed to you, keep by the Holy Spirit who dwells in us.

[15] This you know, that all those in Asia have turned away from me, among whom are Phygellus and Hermogenes. [16] The Lord grant mercy to the household of Onesiphorus, for he often refreshed me, and was not ashamed of my chain; [17] but when he arrived in Rome, he sought me out very zealously and found *me.* [18] The Lord grant to him that he may find mercy from the Lord in that Day— and you know very well how many ways he ministered *to me*[a] at Ephesus.

- - - - - - - - - - - - - - - - - -

1:1 [a]NU-Text and M-Text read *Christ Jesus.*   1:11 [a]NU-Text omits *of the Gentiles.*   1:18 [a] *To me* is from the Vulgate and a few Greek manuscripts.

1:6, 7 Paul had just expressed his confidence in Timothy's genuine faith (v. 5). He then exhorted the young man to continue fanning into flame the gift for ministry that the Spirit had imparted to him at the time Paul and other elders had prayed for Timothy and had publicly recognized his giftedness through the laying on of hands (see 1 Tim. 4:14, note). The word "spirit," though sometimes understood as "an attitude," is much more likely a reference here to the Spirit of God (2 Tim. 1:7; see Is. 11:2).The Holy Spirit imparted to Timothy love, power, and level-headed wisdom, interacting with his basic ministry giftedness. These qualities were exactly what Timothy would need to carry out Paul's exhortation to stand unashamed and stead-fast in the face of persecution (2 Tim. 1:8–14).

LOIS AND EUNICE *Nurturers of Faith*

Eunice was a Jewess who took the responsibility of teaching her son Timothy the Holy Scriptures, making him "wise for salvation through faith" (2 Tim. 3:15). Her husband was a Greek Gentile. He may have died during Timothy's early years. In any case, there is no evidence that her husband ever cared to walk with a perfect heart before God.

Two factors molded Timothy's life. From early childhood his godly mother Eunice and his faithful grandmother Lois touched his life. Unknowingly, they prepared him for God's call to salvation and then for ministry by teaching him the Word of God (2 Tim. 3:15). Later, as an adult, he heard reaffirmed the gospel message, which was believed first by his mother Eunice and his grandmother Lois (2 Tim. 1:5).

During the apostle Paul's first missionary journey around A.D. 46, Eunice and Lois were converted to Christ in Lystra. Reflecting a true faith (v. 5), they lived out what they believed. Paul affirmed that the same faith of Timothy's mother and grandmother was, subsequently, in Timothy himself, bringing joy to Paul. The faithfulness of this mother and grandmother to true doctrine, grounded in God's Word and kept by the Holy Spirit, was not easily swayed.

Eunice and Lois are valuable models. Women can know God's Word, and they can faithfully teach it to their children. Like Eunice and Lois, they can carefully nurture a true faith and be diligent to possess right doctrine. They can model for their children godliness rather than worldliness and Christlikeness as opposed to self-centeredness. Eunice and Lois are living testimonies that nothing in a mother's life is more important than a personal and vibrant faith modeled before her children.

See also Acts 16:1; notes on Grandparenting (Ps. 71); Motherhood (1 Sam. 1)

Be Strong in Grace

2 You therefore, my son, be strong in the grace that is in Christ Jesus. ²And the things that you have heard from me among many witnesses, commit these to faithful men who will be able to teach others also. ³You therefore must endure[a] hardship as a good soldier of Jesus Christ. ⁴No one engaged in warfare entangles himself with the affairs of *this* life, that he may please him who enlisted him as a soldier. ⁵And also if anyone competes in athletics, he is not crowned unless he competes according to the rules. ⁶The hardworking farmer must be first to partake of the crops. ⁷Consider what I say, and may[a] the Lord give you understanding in all things.

⁸Remember that Jesus Christ, of the seed of David, was raised from the dead according to my gospel, ⁹for which I suffer trouble as an evildoer, *even* to the point of chains; but the word of God is not chained. ¹⁰Therefore I endure all things for the sake of the elect, that they also may obtain the salvation which is in Christ Jesus with eternal glory.

¹¹*This is* a faithful saying:

For if we died with *Him,*
    We shall also live with *Him.*
¹²If we endure,
    We shall also reign with *Him.*
If we deny *Him,*
    He also will deny us.
¹³If we are faithless,
    He remains faithful;
    He cannot deny Himself.

Approved and Disapproved Workers

¹⁴Remind *them* of these things, charging *them* before the Lord not to strive about words to no profit, to the ruin of the hearers. ¹⁵Be diligent to present yourself approved to God, a worker who

2:3 [a]NU-Text reads *You must share.* 2:7 [a]NU-Text reads *the Lord will give you.*

2:2 Paul outlined a pattern of spiritual multiplication here with four generations of disciples in view. Paul had committed the gospel message to Timothy, who would commit it to faithful disciples. In turn, they would teach other disciples.

2:3–7 Paul used three analogies to exhort Timothy to stand strong in the midst of persecution and difficulty in the ministry. First, like the soldier who avoided entangling himself in civilian affairs in order to please his commanding officer, Timothy was instructed to focus his attention on pleasing the Lord Jesus rather than "looking back" for an easier path, as others had done (see 2 Tim. 1:15; Luke 9:61, 62). Second, like an athlete who competed according to the game's regulations

in order to win the prize, Timothy would have to comply with the ministry's "rules," which included the possibility of suffering, while promising great reward (2 Tim. 4:8; see 1 Cor. 9:24–27). Third, like the farmer who labored hard so that he could partake of his crops, Timothy was challenged to work with future rewards in view.

2:11–13 Paul emphasized both the necessity of present suffering and the promise of future reward (2 Tim. 1; 2). God would override a person's faithlessness in the face of persecution through His abundant grace and faithfulness (Luke 22:21, 22; Phil. 1:6). Failure to do so would be a denial of His own gracious nature.

EDUCATION *TAUGHT IN ORDER TO TEACH*

The Lord instructs us through His Word and the inspiration of the Holy Spirit—for a purpose:

- that we might gain a heart of wisdom (Ps. 90:12), knowing how to live in right relationship with God and other people;
- that we might experience peace and rest from adversity (Ps. 94:12, 13);
- that we might know *how* to apply God's Word to everyday experiences (Luke 12:12);
- and, above all, that we might make "disciples" of others (Matt. 28:19; Col. 1:28).

We are to teach others primarily that Jesus is the Christ (Acts 5:42) and that Scripture is truth—as opposed to fables, false doctrines, and genealogies (1 Tim. 1:3). In teaching Christ, our methods are to be *convincing* (arguing persuasively), *rebuking* (speaking against evil), and *exhorting* (advocating the good). We are to use the Scriptures to

- establish doctrine—declaring what is right;
- provide reproof—defining what is wrong;
- make corrections—telling how to change wrong to right;
- and to instruct in righteousness—applying truth to life's circumstances.

The ultimate goal for a teacher is to see her students engage in good works (2 Tim. 3:16–17; 4:1–5).

Jesus is the prime example of what a teacher is to be. Teachers are not to commercialize the teaching of the Law as merely an economic venture (Mic. 3:11), and they must recognize that they are subject to a greater accountability than their students (James 3:1).

See also Matt. 18:3, note; notes on Children (2 Sam. 21; Ps. 128; Prov. 22; Luke 15); Education (Deut. 6; Prov. 12); Spiritual Discipline (2 Pet. 3); Wisdom (James 1)

---

does not need to be ashamed, rightly dividing the word of truth. 16But shun profane *and* idle babblings, for they will increase to more ungodliness. 17And their message will spread like cancer. Hymenaeus and Philetus are of this sort, 18who have strayed concerning the truth, saying that the resurrection is already past; and they overthrow the faith of some. 19Nevertheless the solid foundation of God stands, having this seal: "The Lord knows those who are His," and, "Let everyone who names the name of Christ[a] depart from iniquity."

20But in a great house there are not only vessels of gold and silver, but also of wood and clay, some for honor and some for dishonor. 21Therefore if anyone cleanses himself from the latter, he will be a vessel for honor, sanctified and useful for the Master, prepared for every good work. 22Flee also youthful lusts; but pursue righteousness, faith, love, peace with those who call on the Lord out of a pure heart. 23But avoid foolish and igno-

rant disputes, knowing that they generate strife. 24And a servant of the Lord must not quarrel but be gentle to all, able to teach, patient, 25in humility correcting those who are in opposition, if God perhaps will grant them repentance, so that they may know the truth, 26and *that* they may come to their senses *and escape* the snare of the devil, having been taken captive by him to *do* his will.

Perilous Times and Perilous Men

3 But know this, that in the last days perilous times will come: 2For men will be lovers of themselves, lovers of money, boasters, proud, blasphemers, disobedient to parents, unthankful, unholy, 3unloving, unforgiving, slanderers, without self-control, brutal, despisers of good, 4traitors, headstrong, haughty, lovers of pleasure rather than lovers of God, 5having a form of godliness but denying its power. And from such people

···················

2:19 [a]NU-Text and M-Text read *the Lord.*

2:15 **God's laborer has the responsibility** of skillfully handling the Word of God so that when the workmanship is inspected, it will be approved with no reason for shame. Whether Paul's metaphor refers to cutting stones, wood, or perhaps a straight highway is uncertain, but the emphasis is clear: God's Word should be handled correctly and accurately.

2:17, 18 **Hymenaeus and Philetus** were two of the false teachers troubling the Ephesian church (see 1 Tim. 1:20, note). They denied the believer's future bodily resurrection and instead taught that the believer could have only a spiritual death and

resurrection in union with Christ at the time of conversion. This doctrine was especially dangerous because it could ultimately lead to a denial of Christ's bodily Resurrection, as had happened at Corinth (1 Cor. 15:12–19).

3:1 **The last days** began with Christ's Incarnation, included Timothy's day (2 Tim. 3:5), and would continue until Christ's return. This period would be characterized by sinful attitudes and deeds that would continually permeate society (vv. 1–5; see 1 Tim. 4:1–3).

Perspective   by Nancy Leigh DeMoss

GETTING THE WORD INTO YOU (Drawn from *A Place of Quiet Rest*, 181-195)

Have you ever had the experience of reading a portion of Scripture—perhaps even several pages or chapters—only to stop and realize that you have absolutely no idea what you just read? That has happened to me more times than I care to admit.

I want to suggest a practical step that will help make the Word come alive within you. This practice will help you concentrate on what you are reading and can keep your devotions from becoming boring and dry. Keep in mind that it is not enough that we should just *read* the Word. The object is that the words that are printed on the page would become indelibly written on our hearts. God never intended that we should merely get into His Word—His intent is that the Word should get into us. So how do we go about getting the Word grafted into our hearts and lives? Here is one key.

Without question, next to the Holy Spirit, the single greatest help in my personal devotional life has been to read the Scripture with paper and pen in hand, so I can record insights from the Word. As I write down what God is saying to my heart through His Word, the words are lifted off the page and become full of meaning and life to me. There are several types of writing that can be helpful in studying the Word; most of these are illustrated in the Scripture itself.

Write out portions of the Word

In Deuteronomy 17:18-19, God gave these instructions to the kings of Israel: *When he sits on the throne of his kingdom, that he shall write for himself a copy of this law in a book...And it shall be with him, and he shall read it all the days of his life.*

What was the point of this exercise? God knew how prone His people were to forget what He had told them. Over and over, He challenged them to "remember" Him, to remember His law, to remember what He had done for them. Writing out the Word of God was one practical way to help them remember.

And it can help us remember. Taking time to write out specific passages from the Word forces us to think about what we are reading and to observe the details of the text more carefully.

Write in your Bible

This suggestion is not specifically found in the Scripture (remember that hardly anyone owned a copy of the Bible before the sixteenth century), but it has been a practical help and blessing in my growing love affair with the Word. When I was a child, my parents encouraged us to underline verses that we found especially meaningful. Over the years, I have read and "marked up" many different copies of the Bible.

In addition to underlining phrases or verses for emphasis, I frequently circle or bracket repeated words or phrases. I also write cross references in the margin, as well as jot down notes about the meaning of specific words or phrases in the passage. When the Lord uses a verse or passage to address a specific need in my life or to encourage or convict my heart in an unusual way, I often indicate the date on which that personal encounter with the living God took place. The space in the margins is sometimes used to write brief, personal responses to the truth, such as, "Yes, Lord," "I agree," "Change my heart, O God," or "Make this true in my life, Lord."

Record insights into the Word of God

When the apostle John was in exile on the isle of Patmos, he was given a vision of heaven. The Lord Jesus appeared to him and said, "Write on a scroll what you see . . . Write, therefore, what you have seen" (Rev. 1:11, 19).

Over the years, I have recorded in my personal journals hundreds and hundreds of pages of observations and insights that the Holy Spirit has shown me while reading and meditating on the Word. Capturing these insights helps us to clarify, understand and remember the ways of God. The process of writing them down deepens our love and appreciation for the truth of God's Word. You say, How do I know what to write? Many Bible teachers suggest asking three basic questions each time you read the Bible:

What does it say? (Make observations about the text.)

1. *Summarize.* After reading the passage, try to come up with a title for the entire book, the chapter, and the individual paragraphs. Look for a key verse that captures the heart of the passage. Write a brief summary of the passage, including the major points.
2. *Paraphrase.* Try to write the passage in your own words.
3. *Ask questions.* Use the same questions you ask if you were writing a newspaper account: *Who? What? When? Where? Why? How?*
4. *Look for patterns.* Look for repeated words or phrases to help you understand what the author intends to emphasize.
5. *Look for cross-references.* The Holy Spirit may bring to mind other verses that relate to, confirm, or shed further light on what you are reading.

What does it mean? (Look for the implications or the interpretations of the text.)
  1. What does this passage teach me about God?
  2. What does this passage teach me about Jesus?
  3. What does this passage teach me about man?
  4. Are there any promises to claim?
  5. Are there any commands to obey?
  6. Are there any examples to follow?
  7. Are there any sins to avoid?

What should I do? (Make practical application of the text.)
  1. How does this truth apply to my life? To my situation?
  2. In view of this truth, what changes need to be made in my life?
  3. What practical steps can I take to apply this truth to my life?

Record milestones in your spiritual pilgrimage
  Over the years I have kept a record of many significant markers in my walk with God. While most of these experiences center around specific circumstances in my life, invariably they are birthed out of the Word of God, as the Spirit uses whatever I may be reading at that time to shed light on my path.

---

turn away! 6For of this sort are those who creep into households and make captives of gullible women loaded down with sins, led away by various lusts, 7always learning and never able to come to the knowledge of the truth. 8Now as Jannes and Jambres resisted Moses, so do these also resist the truth: men of corrupt minds, disapproved concerning the faith; 9but they will progress no further, for their folly will be manifest to all, as theirs also was.

The Man of God and the Word of God

10But you have carefully followed my doctrine, manner of life, purpose, faith, longsuffering, love, perseverance, 11persecutions, afflictions, which happened to me at Antioch, at Iconium, at Lystra—what persecutions I endured. And out of them all the Lord delivered me. 12Yes, and all who desire to live godly in Christ Jesus will suffer persecution. 13But evil men and impostors will grow worse and worse, deceiving and being deceived. 14But you must continue in the things which you have learned and been assured of, knowing from whom you have learned them, 15and that from childhood you have known the Holy Scriptures,

which are able to make you wise for salvation through faith which is in Christ Jesus.

16All Scripture *is* given by inspiration of God, and *is* profitable for doctrine, for reproof, for correction, for instruction in righteousness, 17that the man of God may be complete, thoroughly equipped for every good work.

Preach the Word

4 I charge *you* therefore before God and the Lord Jesus Christ, who will judge the living and the dead ata His appearing and His kingdom: 2Preach the word! Be ready in season *and* out of season. Convince, rebuke, exhort, with all longsuffering and teaching. 3For the time will come when they will not endure sound doctrine, but according to their own desires, *because* they have itching ears, they will heap up for themselves teachers; 4and they will turn *their* ears away from the truth, and be turned aside to fables. 5But you be watchful in all things, endure afflictions, do the work of an evangelist, fulfill your ministry.

· · · · · · · · · · · · · · · · · · ·

4:1 aNU-Text omits *therefore* and reads *and by* for *at.*

3:6 Gullible women (Gk. *gunaikaria*, lit. "little women") is used only here in the NT. In extra-biblical literature, the term is often a contemptuous diminutive. The women are also described as "loaded down with sins" (lit. "heaped on") and "led away" (lit. "swayed") by "various lusts," indicating their vulnerability to the false teachers. These women continually sought greater knowledge, but the very falseness of their teaching left them in ignorance of the truth (v. 7).

3:8, 9 Jannes and Jambres, according to a Jewish tradition, were religious impostors who would be publicly exposed in their folly (Ex. 7:11, 12, 22; 8:7).

3:16 Scripture was God-breathed (Gk. *theopneustos*). God communicated to individuals the specific truths. The Holy Spirit superintended this process so that there were no errors in the original writings (2 Pet. 1:21). This written Word is both infallible (it cannot be broken; John 10:35) and, because it is God's Word, authoritative. God's Word is not only inspired; it is also "profitable." Its usefulness is seen in four areas: teaching people God's truth; reproving or rebuking those who are sinning (see 1 Tim. 5:20; 2 Tim. 4:2); correcting those who are in error (see 2 Tim. 2:25); training people to walk in God's righteous ways.

HEAVEN *LIVING FOREVER IN HIS PRESENCE*

Scripture alludes to heaven in three different ways: the vast expanse of space surrounding the earth or firmament or atmosphere (Gen. 1:8), the matchless celestial universe (Ps. 19:1), and the longed-for dwelling place of God (Heb. 4:14). The reality that Christians will one day live forever in the presence of the Lord is a fundamental doctrine of the faith.

The Bible only gives a few glimpses of this heavenly abode. Heaven is a place prepared for believers (John 14:1–3), one without sorrow, darkness, or any kind of sin (Rev. 21:1–7). In heaven, we will be like Christ; yet we will be able to recognize one another (1 John 3:2). The most important thing about heaven, however, is the presence of God. We will be forever with Him.

Heaven is not meant to be an ethereal concept stored in some mental safe-deposit box until we feel the need of it. We are to live now in the light of eternity. The values and perspective of eternity should guide our lives in the present (2 Pet. 3:11).

See also Mark 9:43–48, note; Acts 1:1–11; Rom. 8:18–30; Rev. 22; notes on Promises of God (2 Pet. 1); Salvation (Eph. 2)

Paul's Valedictory

⁶For I am already being poured out as a drink offering, and the time of my departure is at hand. ⁷I have fought the good fight, I have finished the race, I have kept the faith. ⁸Finally, there is laid up for me the crown of righteousness, which the Lord, the righteous Judge, will give to me on that Day, and not to me only but also to all who have loved His appearing.

The Abandoned Apostle

⁹Be diligent to come to me quickly; ¹⁰for Demas has forsaken me, having loved this present world, and has departed for Thessalonica—Crescens for Galatia, Titus for Dalmatia. ¹¹Only Luke is with me. Get Mark and bring him with you, for he is useful to me for ministry. ¹²And Tychicus I have sent to Ephesus. ¹³Bring the cloak that I left with Carpus at Troas when you come—and the books, especially the parchments.

¹⁴Alexander the coppersmith did me much harm. May the Lord repay him according to his works. ¹⁵You also must beware of him, for he has greatly resisted our words.

¹⁶At my first defense no one stood with me, but all forsook me. May it not be charged against them.

The Lord Is Faithful

¹⁷But the Lord stood with me and strengthened me, so that the message might be preached fully through me, and *that* all the Gentiles might hear. Also I was delivered out of the mouth of the lion. ¹⁸And the Lord will deliver me from every evil work and preserve *me* for His heavenly kingdom. To Him *be* glory forever and ever. Amen!

Come Before Winter

¹⁹Greet Prisca and Aquila, and the household

4:6 Paul knew that the time of his death ("my departure") was near. He vividly portrayed this through a word picture from Jewish liturgy. The last part of a sacrificial offering was the "drink offering," an offering of wine poured over the sacrifice (see Num. 5:1–10). Paul saw his ministry as an offering to the Lord (Rom. 15:16; Phil. 2:17), and his death would be the final act of that sacrifice.

4:7 Paul's statement that he had "kept the faith" may mean that either he had guarded and preserved the doctrine God had entrusted to him, or, more probably, he had been loyal to the ministry responsibility that God had given him to the end.

4:8 Paul joyfully looked forward to receiving the victor's crown, probably a reference to the reward given for living a righteous life. It would be given by the righteous Lord Himself.

4:14, 15 Alexander was a common name, and not enough evidence exists to identify him with other men by this name in Scripture. "The coppersmith" seems to have been a description given to distinguish him from others by that

name. The harm he had done, whatever its nature, was serious enough for Paul to warn Timothy strongly to beware of him.

4:16–18 This preliminary hearing was evidently a time when charges were read against Paul, and he had opportunity both to make a defense and to have others speak in his behalf. Although everyone else abandoned him, the Lord Himself stood with Paul and strengthened him. The fruit of the Lord's intervention was twofold: He enabled Paul to proclaim the gospel boldly; He delivered Paul from the immediate threat of death. Even though Paul had no doubt that death was not far away (v. 6), he had full confidence that God would provide protection and deliverance through the maze of men's evil works into "His heavenly kingdom."

4:20 Though God often heals the sick, He does not heal every illness. The situation of Trophimus is a sober reminder that healing ultimately rests in the sovereign will of an all-wise, all-powerful God. Often through trials of illness we learn our most valuable lessons about both God and ourselves (2 Cor. 12:7–10).

CLAUDIA   *A Sincere Supporter*

Claudia is mentioned only in this short second letter to Timothy, in which Paul exudes fatherly tenderness and good will. She is included in a list of presumed members of the Roman church who send greetings to the young pastor. She should certainly be included among the most respected and influential women of Gentile background who heard and accepted the gospel. Probably these four people mentioned were leaders in the church or simply believers who had met Timothy personally when he was with Paul in Rome. Some commentators suggest Linus as Claudia's son and Pudens as her husband. In any case, women and men joined together in greeting and in ministry without distinction.

The family of faith is also emphasized in this personalized greeting, undoubtedly in response to Jesus' prayer for unity and love among His brethren (see John 17:20–23). Claudia was a faithful encourager of Paul and a committed supporter of the congregation of believers.

See also notes on Influence (Esth. 4); Feminine Leadership (1 Sam. 25)

of Onesiphorus. [20]Erastus stayed in Corinth, but Trophimus I have left in Miletus sick.

[21]Do your utmost to come before winter.

Eubulus greets you, as well as Pudens, Linus, Claudia, and all the brethren.

Farewell

[22]The Lord Jesus Christ[a] be with your spirit. Grace be with you. Amen.

....

4:22 [a]NU-Text omits *Jesus Christ.*

Titus

The apostle Paul is the author of the Book of Titus. His authorship is supported by internal evidence, including his autograph in the salutation as well as the consistency of his theology and language in the text (Titus 1:1). The vast majority of the early church fathers supported this position as well.

This letter was written about the same time as Paul's first letter to Timothy, between A.D. 62 and 64. During this time he was free from prison in Rome and traveling to Nicopolis where he planned to spend the winter.

SETTING: After Paul's first Roman imprisonment, he may have planted a church on the Mediterranean island of Crete. He left Titus there to organize and instruct the new converts. This fact indicates Paul's confidence in Titus. The moral decadence in Crete was well known, and Titus faced almost immediate opposition.

AUDIENCE: This letter was sent to Titus, Paul's Greek convert, who was one of his first Gentile co-laborers. Titus played a significant role in the development of the church. He was an uncircumcised Gentile who accompanied Paul to Jerusalem. Titus exemplified believing Gentiles and appropriately pleaded the case for salvation by grace alone, without the requirement of circumcision (Gal. 2:1–5). When Paul was delayed in going to Corinth because of his work in Ephesus, he sent Titus to handle the difficult situation (strife, fornication; see 1 Cor. 1:11; 5:1). His accomplishments in Corinth were a great encouragement to Paul (2 Cor. 7:6, 13, 14; 8:6, 16, 23; 12:18). Based on Paul's assignments to Titus, the young protégé apparently was a resourceful leader with organizational skills.

PURPOSE: Paul wrote this letter to give Titus authorization and guidance regarding the doctrine, government, and piety of the church. The apostle told Titus what he should teach and how he should apply it to the various groups within the congregation.

These are classic Pauline themes:

- Sovereign grace indicates the fact that God is in control of all things. This fact gives assurance and confidence to believers. In the Old Testament, "grace" (Heb. *chen*) means "favor," "kindness," as in the "graciousness" of a superior toward an inferior with no obligation of the superior to show such "kindness." In the New Testament, "grace" (Gk. *charis*) refers to God's undeserved, redemptive love demonstrated in Christ. God's faithfulness to His covenant promise to save His people is established and maintained by "grace."

- Sound doctrine refers to absolute truth as taught in Holy Scripture. What God says, He will not change.
- Servant living or the placing of oneself under the authority and Lordship of Jesus Christ is a lifestyle of obedience to His Word.

Paul's theological and pedagogical logic are interwoven in these themes. Understanding that salvation is by grace alone is foundational for correct doctrine. Right doctrine rightly applied results in right living. To begin with instruction in servant living apart from instruction about God, will produce only outward, temporary change. True, lasting change in lifestyle is only possible when the heart is changed by God's grace.

OUTLINE

Greeting

1 Paul, a bondservant of God and an apostle of Jesus Christ, according to the faith of God's elect and the acknowledgment of the truth which accords with godliness, ²in hope of eternal life which God, who cannot lie, promised before time began, ³but has in due time manifested His word through preaching, which was committed to me according to the commandment of God our Savior;

⁴To Titus, a true son in *our* common faith:

Grace, mercy, *and* peace from God the Father and the Lord Jesus Christ[a] our Savior.

Qualified Elders

⁵For this reason I left you in Crete, that you should set in order the things that are lacking, and appoint elders in every city as I commanded you— ⁶if a man is blameless, the husband of one wife, having faithful children not accused of dissipation or insubordination. ⁷For a bishop[a] must be blameless, as a steward of God, not self-willed, not quick-tempered, not given to wine, not violent, not greedy for money, ⁸but hospitable, a lover of what is good, sober-minded, just, holy, self-controlled, ⁹holding fast the faithful word as he has been taught, that he may be able, by sound

1:4 ᵃNU-Text reads *and Christ Jesus.*   1:7 ᵃLiterally *overseer*

1:4 **Paul's spiritual relationship to Titus and Timothy** does not devalue the physical family but shows that the spiritual family is a "true" family bonding (v. 2), offering great comfort to those whose families are dysfunctional (see 1 Sam. 3, Family).

1:5 **Elders** (Gk., *presbuteroi*, also "pastors" or "bishops") are those appointed in the NT church to have spiritual care and oversight; the designation indicates maturity of spiritual experience (see Acts 11:30; Phil. 1:1; see 1 Pet. 5:1–3, note).

1:6–9 **Men and women are equal** in their position in Christ but have different roles or functions in the family and church (Gal. 3, Equality; see chart, Role Relationships Between Men and Women).

1:6 **The ability to manage his own family** is a prerequisite for the elder (or bishop or pastor) who would manage the spiritual family in the church (see 1 Tim. 3:4). This particular requirement would be difficult to meet without the help of a supportive wife (see Lev. 21, The Pastor's Wife).

1:8 **Being hospitable** (Gk. *philoxenos*, lit. "loving strangers" or "friendly") is very difficult without the help of a supportive wife (see 1 Pet. 4, Hospitality; chart, Hospitality or Entertainment).

GODPARENTS SPIRITUAL PARENTING

Paul refers to Titus as "a true son in our common faith" (Titus 1:4), and Timothy "a true son in the faith" and a "beloved son" (1 Tim. 1:2; 2 Tim. 1:2). Titus and Timothy, of course, were not Paul's flesh-and-blood sons but rather young men he considered to be his "spiritual children."

The early Christians very often were ostracized from their communities or disowned by their families. Thus, the bonding together of the "family of Christ" included the creation of a new order of parents and children. Jesus alluded to this when He said to Peter that those who give up family for His sake and the gospel's will receive in return "brothers and sisters and mothers and children" (Mark 10:30).

Spiritual parents in the early church had the opportunity to help rear followers of Christ who would experience the presence and power of God at work in their lives. This role involved active (and often daily) participation in a child's life and an ongoing mentoring of the child in how to live out the Christian life in the church and community. Over the centuries, the role of spiritual parents has varied. Foremost, they certainly should seek to impart to the child a love for Scripture, a commitment to a personal relationship with the Lord Jesus, and a link to an organized body of believers in which the child can serve the Lord and be edified in the faith. In addition, they have the opportunity to pray for and with the child, encouraging an ongoing, personal communication by the child with God.

See also Matt. 18:3, note; notes on Children (2 Sam. 21; Ps. 128; Prov. 22; Luke 15); Family (Gen. 32; 1 Sam. 3; Ps. 78; 127); Grandparenthood (Ps. 71); Inheritance (Prov. 13); Mentoring (2 Kin. 2)

---

doctrine, both to exhort and convict those who contradict.

The Elders' Task

10For there are many insubordinate, both idle talkers and deceivers, especially those of the circumcision, 11whose mouths must be stopped, who subvert whole households, teaching things which they ought not, for the sake of dishonest gain. 12One of them, a prophet of their own, said, "Cretans *are* always liars, evil beasts, lazy gluttons." 13This testimony is true. Therefore rebuke them sharply, that they may be sound in the faith, 14not giving heed to Jewish fables and commandments of men who turn from the truth. 15To the pure all things are pure, but to those who are defiled and unbelieving nothing is pure; but even their mind and conscience are defiled. 16They profess to know God, but in works they deny *Him,* being abominable, disobedient, and disqualified for every good work.

Qualities of a Sound Church

2 But as for you, speak the things which are proper for sound doctrine: 2that the older men be sober, reverent, temperate, sound in faith, in love, in patience; 3the older women likewise, that they be reverent in behavior, not slanderers, not given to much wine, teachers of good things— 4that they admonish the young women to love their husbands, to love their children, 5*to be* discreet, chaste, homemakers, good, obedient to their own husbands, that the word of God may not be blasphemed.

6Likewise, exhort the young men to be sober-minded, 7in all things showing yourself *to be* a pattern of good works; in doctrine *showing* integrity, reverence, incorruptibility,[a] 8sound speech that cannot be condemned, that one who is an opponent may be ashamed, having nothing evil to say of you.[a]

2:7 [a]NU-Text omits *incorruptibility*. 2:8 [a]NU-Text and M-Text read *us*.

1:10–12 Jewish believers in Crete insisted that circumcision was necessary in order to be saved, adding works to salvation. These false teachers were motivated by dishonest gain (v. 11). Paul used the description of Epimenides, a Cretan poet, to substantiate his point regarding the character of the Cretans (v. 12).

2:2, 3 The value of the faith and life of older members of the congregation is recognized (see Is. 46, Aging) as a combination of spiritual maturity and life experiences (see Lev. 19:32; Job 12:12; Prov. 16:31; 17:6). Paul is often wrongly accused of devaluing women. Paul neither wanted nor expected shallow thinking or careless living from the female members of the congregation (see chart, Spiritual Mothering).

2:3–5 Women equipping women is not an exhaustive statement about the role of women in the church, but training younger women is an important part of the responsibility of spiritually mature women. Whereas truth is truth, gender does determine how some aspects of truth are lived out in daily life. Training women to live as godly women is best done by older, spiritually mature women. The responsibility to see that this is done is given to the pastor of the church (v. 1). Certainly this lays the foundation for women's ministries in the local church (see John 4; Acts 2; 1 Cor. 11; Eph. 2; 1 Tim. 2, Women's Ministries). "Admonish" (Gk. *sophronizō*, lit. "to cause to be of sound mind") suggests training that would develop sound judgment and wisdom. The relationship between the women is not formal and structured but a nurturing, spiritual mothering. The goal of the older woman/younger woman relationship is compelling—that God's Word would not be dishonored. God's Word is honorable regardless of the behavior of women, but seemingly the behavior of Christian women plays an important part in the honor that the world gives to God's Word.

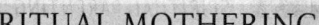

SPIRITUAL MOTHERING

THE MENTOR AND NOVICE	THE CURRICULUM	THE REWARDS	THE BIBLICAL EXAMPLE
• "Aged Women" (Gk. presbutidas) could be understood as spiritually mature women. The criterion is not limited to age (Titus 2:3).	Lifestyle Example (Titus 2:3) "reverent" behavior—godly conduct, dress, and conversation	To prevent blasphemy of the Word of God (Titus 2:5).	Naomi → Ruth • Naomi won Ruth to faith in Yahweh (Ruth 1:16, 17). • She gave Ruth wise counsel to win the heart of Boaz (Ruth 2:20, 22; 3:3–6). • She helped nurture Ruth's son Obed (Ruth 4:15, 16).
• To teach the "younger women" (Gk. neas) again is not only a reference to youth but connotes freshness or what is new. New converts and those who have not been discipled are in view (v. 3).	Warnings (v. 3) • slander (fault-finding, gossip, false accusation) • drunkenness	To give young women the opportunity for spiritual ministry (vv. 12–15).	Deborah → Barak • Deborah guided him into battle (Judg. 4:6, 14). • She accepted Barak's call for help (Judg. 4:9, 10). • She celebrated the victory in song (Judg. 5:1–31).
	Admonitions (vv. 4, 5) • lovers of their husbands (v. 4, Gk. philandrous, connoting "esteem" or "respect") • lovers of their children (v. 4, Gk. philoteknous) • sensible (v. 5, Gk. sophron) • chaste or sexually pure (v. 5, Gk. agnas) • homeworkers (v. 5, Gk. oikourgous) • good (v. 5, Gk. agathas) • submissive to their husbands (v. 5, Gk. hupotasso; also used in Eph. 5:21; Col. 3:18; 1 Pet. 3:1).	To guard the sanctity of the home.	Elizabeth → Mary • Elizabeth encouraged Mary (Luke 1:41–45). • She offered Mary hospitality and refuge (Luke 1:56). Priscilla → Apollos • Priscilla, with her husband Aquila, received spiritual preparation from the apostle Paul (Acts 18:1–4). • They patiently shared their understanding of Scripture (Acts 18:24–28). • Priscilla kept her home open to believers (Rom. 16:3–5).

[9]*Exhort* bondservants to be obedient to their own masters, to be well pleasing in all *things*, not answering back, [10]not pilfering, but showing all good fidelity, that they may adorn the doctrine of God our Savior in all things.

Trained by Saving Grace

[11]For the grace of God that brings salvation has appeared to all men, [12]teaching us that, deny-ing ungodliness and worldly lusts, we should live soberly, righteously, and godly in the present age, [13]looking for the blessed hope and glorious appearing of our great God and Savior Jesus Christ, [14]who gave Himself for us, that He might redeem us from every lawless deed and purify for Himself *His* own special people, zealous for good works.

[15]Speak these things, exhort, and rebuke with all authority. Let no one despise you.

WOMEN'S MINISTRIES · DISCIPLING THE BELIEVER

One of the largest and most vital areas of ministry for New Testament women was that of discipleship. In the Great Commission, Jesus Christ commanded that His disciples "make" disciples of others (Matt. 28:19, 20). This process involved two principles, as illustrated in the lives of Jesus and His apostles: association and instruction.

To begin, a disciple associated or interacted with a protégé on a personal basis. Jesus, for example, had chosen His disciples so that they might "be with Him" (Mark 3:14). The apostle Paul also recognized that discipleship occurred in the context of close relationships or in the "sharing" of life (1 Thess. 1:7, 8).

The second aspect of discipleship was instruction. Disciples were to be taught how to be obedient (Matt. 28:20) in order that they might be firmly rooted, built up in Christ, and established in the faith (Col. 2:6, 7). Paul instructed that all spiritually mature women had the responsibility to mentor those women who were less mature (Titus 2:3–5). Through discipling other women and bringing them to maturity in Christ, New Testament women glorified God and were integrally involved in kingdom ministry (John 15:7, 8).

See also chart on Spiritual Gifts of Women in the Bible; notes on Evangelism (John 6; Col. 4; 1 Pet. 3); Mentoring (2 Kin. 2); Spiritual Discipline (2 Pet. 3); Women's Ministries (John 4; Acts 2; 1 Cor. 11; Eph. 2; 1 Tim. 3)

Graces of the Heirs of Grace

3 Remind them to be subject to rulers and authorities, to obey, to be ready for every good work, ²to speak evil of no one, to be peaceable, gentle, showing all humility to all men. ³For we ourselves were also once foolish, disobedient, deceived, serving various lusts and pleasures, living in malice and envy, hateful and hating one another. ⁴But when the kindness and the love of God our Savior toward man appeared, ⁵not by works of righteousness which we have done, but according to His mercy He saved us, through the washing of regeneration and renewing of the Holy Spirit, ⁶whom He poured out on us abundantly through Jesus Christ our Savior, ⁷that having been justified by His grace we should become heirs according to the hope of eternal life.

⁸This is a faithful saying, and these things I want you to affirm constantly, that those who have believed in God should be careful to maintain good works. These things are good and profitable to men.

Avoid Dissension

⁹But avoid foolish disputes, genealogies, contentions, and strivings about the law; for they are unprofitable and useless. ¹⁰Reject a divisive man after the first and second admonition, ¹¹knowing that such a person is warped and sinning, being self-condemned.

Final Messages

¹²When I send Artemas to you, or Tychicus, be diligent to come to me at Nicopolis, for I have decided to spend the winter there. ¹³Send Zenas the lawyer and Apollos on their journey with haste, that they may lack nothing. ¹⁴And let our *people* also learn to maintain good works, to *meet* urgent needs, that they may not be unfruitful.

Farewell

¹⁵All who *are* with me greet you. Greet those who love us in the faith.

Grace *be* with you all. Amen.

3:1 Though their citizenship is in heaven (Phil. 3:20), believers are to live in this world in such a way as to be salt and light (Matt. 5:13–16). Civil authorities are appointed by God to maintain law and order, whether they recognize their divine appointment or not, so that believers can fulfill the good works God has given them to do (see Rom. 13, Government and Citizenship). However, if the civil law contradicts the Law of God, the believer is to "obey God rather than men" (Acts 5:29).

3:2–4 Paul gave examples of good works and reminded believers of the works that characterized their former lifestyle. Believers must never attribute their good works to self-effort. Calling to mind former disobedience reminds believers that good works are the result of the kindness and love of God (see Deut. 15:15; Rev. 2:5).

3:4–7 With the emphasis on godly living, Paul wanted to be sure that no one misunderstood and thought that good works could contribute to salvation (see chart, Law and Grace).

3:5 Regeneration (Gk. *palinge nēsia*, lit. "becoming again" or "being born again") is produced by "the word of truth" (James 1:18; 1 Pet. 1:23) and the Holy Spirit (John 3:5, 6). Regeneration and renewal describe the work of God in changing a heart from one that has a propensity to evil to one that is capable of faith and good works (Ezek. 36:26, 27).

3:7 Justified (Gk. *dikaioō*, "declared righteous") is always passive in reference to mankind because it is the work of God. Justification is the legal acquittal of guilt and the pronouncement of the sinner as righteous on the basis of the finished work of Christ (see chart, Theological Terms).

WOMEN IN THE WORKPLACE

Characteristics of Godly Businesswomen
Conscientious—"well pleasing in all things" (Titus 2:9)
Diligent—"whatever your hand finds to do, do it with your might" (Eccl. 9:10)
Integrity—"not pilfering" (Titus 2:10)
Loyal—"showing all good fidelity" (Titus 2:10)
Peaceful—"not answering back" (Titus 2:9)
Respectful of authority—"to be subject to... authorities" (Titus 3:1)
Seasoned speech—"know how you ought to answer each one" (Col. 4:6)

Examples of Godly Businesswomen
Lydia (Acts 16:13–15, 40)
    Hosted a group of believers in her home and used her resources to support the work of the kingdom.
Priscilla (Acts 18:1–3)
    Ministered with her husband to the apostle Paul.
    Participated in evangelism, discipling, teaching, and mentoring.

Types of Businesses in Biblical Days
Construction (Shallum's daughters—Neh. 3:12)
Garment industry (Dorcas—Acts 9:36–42)
Government (Deborah—Judg. 4:4, 5)
Maid or Household Worker (Rhoda—Acts 12:13)
Manufacturing (Priscilla—Acts 18:3)
Midwives (Shiphrah and Puah—Ex. 1:15, 16)
Musicians (Singers—Eccl. 2:8)
Nurse/Nanny/Companion (Deborah—Gen. 24:59; 35:8)
Retail (Lydia—Acts 16:14)
Wet Nurse (Jochebed—Ex. 2:7, 9)

It is interesting that of all the ways Paul could have told the women to combat the decadence of their culture, he told them to invest their energies in training the younger women to live Christianly in their society.

Susan Hunt

Philemon

AUTHOR

Paul is the author of this short epistle. His authorship is rarely questioned due to the similarity of the book's style with other Pauline books and the circumstances related within the book itself and in the Book of Colossians.

DATE

As one of the books written during Paul's first imprisonment, Philemon would have been composed at some time between A.D. 60 and 63.

BACKGROUND

SETTING: Tychicus is believed to have carried this personal letter to Philemon in his hometown of Colosse, as he accompanied the returning slave Onesimus (Col. 4:7–9).

PURPOSE: Through this glimpse into the life of Paul and the relationships he maintained and nurtured, future generations are encouraged to express Christian charity in practical terms.

AUDIENCE: When faced with the task of restoring a broken relationship, Paul appealed to his friend Philemon to forgive a fellow believer and accept him as a brother in Christ. Though he could have chosen to fight against the institution of slavery common to that day, Paul appealed to the transforming power of God's love to bring about needed change in individual lives and social structure. Just as Christ pleads the cases of believers before the Father and offers His own life to pay the price for their sins, Paul appealed to the master of this runaway slave, offering to pay from his own resources any debt incurred, in the hope of achieving reconciliation.

LITERARY CHARACTERISTICS: The Book of Philemon is written in correspondence format. Though brief, the letter is quite personal and specific as to its intent. Paul's method is a marvelous example of mitigating or moderating exhortation (see Philem. 17–21, note).

THEMES

In his other epistles, Paul explained how the love of Christ would transform a believer to live in accordance with God's will. In this uniquely personal letter, the reader has the opportunity to observe that in action.

OUTLINE

OBEDIENCE *DOING GOD'S WILL*

The Bible clearly commands us always to obey the Lord (Deut. 4:30; 11:1–32; Dan. 7:27; Acts 5:29). Specifically, we are required to hear His Word and do His will (James 1:22).

Our obedience is to flow out of our love for God (1 John 2:3, 4). If we love the Lord, we will want to serve Him; and in serving Him, we will want to obey His commandments. Acts of obedience, therefore, are to be reflective of an inner reality that we love the Lord deeply and are committed to Him completely.

We are also to obey the human authorities that the Lord has placed in our lives, recognizing that all authority flows from God and is ultimately part of His plan (Heb. 13:7, 17; 1 Pet. 2:13, 14). Scripture advocates clearly that wives submit to husbands (Eph. 5:22), children obey parents (Eph. 6:1), slaves obey masters (Col. 3:22), Christians obey church leaders (1 Thess. 5:12, 13; Heb. 13:7), and citizens obey government officials (Heb. 13:17).

Obedience is not an automatic response. It must be learned, and conversely, we must teach it to our children (see Deut. 6:7–9). Obedience to those in the line of authority is part of God's plan for establishing peace and security so that we might not only fulfill our own potential but effectively extend the gospel to others.

In obeying those God has placed over us in authority, we must recognize that we are never to break the commandments of God (see Jochebed as well as Daniel, Shadrach, Meshach, and Abednego as examples of those who disobeyed civil authorities in their ultimate obedience to the Lord—Ex. 1:17; 2:3–10; Dan. 3:9–26; 6:13–22). We are to obey the requests of authorities that are within the bounds of righteousness, regardless of our personal desires, preferences, opinions, or perceptions—trusting the Lord to honor our obedience, to guide those in authority over us, and to deal with those authorities as He wills. The consequences of our obedience lie in His domain.

The Lord promises deliverance from our enemies (Ex. 23:22), strength, and blessings as we obey. Disobedience, on the other hand, results in disaster—materially, psychologically, and spiritually. Even so, disobedience is a part of the sinful nature and is inevitable in all our lives. Israel frequently failed to hear and do God's will (Jer. 7:13; Hos. 9:17). When we disobey, we can take heart that disobedience is forgivable. The Lord offers undeserved mercy and complete forgiveness to those who confess their disobedience (Rom. 11:30–32) and make a new choice to obey.

See also Matt. 18:3, note; notes on Authority (John 19); Children (2 Sam. 21; Ps. 128; Prov. 22; Luke 15); Commitment (Matt. 16); Decision Making (1 Cor. 8); Forgiveness (Ps. 51; Luke 17); Submission (1 Pet. 3)

Greeting

Paul, a prisoner of Christ Jesus, and Timothy *our* brother,

To Philemon our beloved *friend* and fellow laborer, [2]to the beloved[a] Apphia, Archippus our fellow soldier, and to the church in your house:

[3]Grace to you and peace from God our Father and the Lord Jesus Christ.

Philemon's Love and Faith

[4]I thank my God, making mention of you always in my prayers, [5]hearing of your love and faith which you have toward the Lord Jesus and toward all the saints, [6]that the sharing of your faith may become effective by the acknowledgment of every good thing which is in you[a] in Christ Jesus. [7]For we have[a] great joy[b] and consolation in your love, because the hearts of the saints have been refreshed by you, brother.

The Plea for Onesimus

[8]Therefore, though I might be very bold in Christ to command you what is fitting, [9]*yet* for

- - - - - - - - - - - - - - - - - - - -
2 [a]NU-Text reads *to our sister Apphia.* 6 [a]NU-Text and M-Text read *us.* 7 [a]NU-Text reads *had.* [b]M-Text reads *thanksgiving.*

---

2 Apphia is believed to be Philemon's wife. Archippus apparently was a leader in the church that met in Philemon's home and may have been the son of Philemon and Apphia. In the context of this book, Philemon's wife played a crucial role in carrying out the desires that Paul expressed because household slaves such as Onesimus would have fallen under her supervision. Archippus would be instrumental in leading the church to accept Paul's instructions regarding Onesimus as a new believer.

4–7 Paul took the time to commend his friend Philemon for

spiritual maturity, while expressing the potential he sees for further growth in a specific area (vv. 7, 20). Paul frequently cited this quality as a source for his encouragement (see Rom. 15:32; 1 Cor. 16:18; 2 Cor. 7:13; 2 Tim. 1:16). God often calls upon women to provide refreshing acts of kindness to others. In contrast to the weariness that takes its toll as stress comes into a life, the spiritual and physical refreshment offered by a Christian brings rest and renewal.

9 Paul appealed to Philemon to let love be the primary motive

WOMEN USING THEIR GIFTS IN THE EARLY CHURCH

WOMAN	WHAT SHE DID
Apphia	She hosted believers in her home (Philem. 2).
Damaris	She responded to the gospel (Acts 17:34).
Dorcas	She reached out to the poor and needy (Acts 9:36–42; see also Prov. 31:20).
Elizabeth	She served as a mentor or spiritual mother to Mary of Nazareth and undoubtedly to many others (Luke 1:39–56).
Lydia	She supported Paul in his ministries (Acts 16:11–15).
Mary Magdalene	She proclaimed the gospel (Mark 16:9, 10; see also 1 Pet. 3:15).
Mary of Nazareth	She prayed (Luke 2:19; Acts 1:14).
Older women	They were to teach women about godly character and home responsibilities (Titus 2:3–5).
Phoebe	She was a courier for transporting one of Paul's letters (Rom. 16:1).
Priscilla	She, with her husband, traveled throughout the country doing evangelism and missions. They also taught the learned Apollos (Acts 18:18, 26). They suffered for their faith (Rom. 16:4).
Women of wealth	They supported Jesus' work; their generosity was a blessing to the kingdom work (Mark 15:40; 16:1; Luke 8:3; 23:55—24:10; Heb. 6:10).

love's sake I rather appeal *to you*— being such a one as Paul, the aged, and now also a prisoner of Jesus Christ— [10]I appeal to you for my son Onesimus, whom I have begotten *while* in my chains, [11]who once was unprofitable to you, but now is profitable to you and to me.

[12]I am sending him back.[a] You therefore receive him, that is, my own heart, [13]whom I wished to keep with me, that on your behalf he might minister to me in my chains for the gospel. [14]But without your consent I wanted to do nothing, that your good deed might not be by compulsion, as it were, but voluntary.

[15]For perhaps he departed for a while for this *purpose*, that you might receive him forever, [16]no longer as a slave but more than a slave—a beloved brother, especially to me but how much more to you, both in the flesh and in the Lord.

Philemon's Obedience Encouraged

[17]If then you count me as a partner, receive him as *you would* me. [18]But if he has wronged you or owes anything, put that on my account. [19]I, Paul, am writing with my own hand. I will repay— not to mention to you that you owe me even your own self besides. [20]Yes, brother, let me have joy from you in the Lord; refresh my heart in the Lord.

- - - - - - - - - - - - - - - - -

12 [a]NU-Text reads *back to you in person, that is, my own heart.*

---

for responding positively to his request to accept Onesimus. Love often compels us to do that which cannot be explained by any other motive.

10, 11 Onesimus means "profitable." Thus, Paul employed a play on words to reiterate that the once profitable slave, Onesimus, had proven himself unprofitable by leaving his master, Philemon. Now he may once again be viewed as profitable in ministering to Paul on behalf of Philemon.

14 Paul might have used compulsion to admonish Philemon to follow his instructions. But such a response would not have been made out of conviction. Instead, the "voluntary" act of love carries a commitment to the renewed relationship that only Christ can provide.

17–21 Paul used four imperatives: "receive him" (v. 17), "put" (v. 18), "refresh" (v. 20), and "prepare" (v. 22). Philemon's obedience, coupled with his love (v. 9), would bring Paul joy and a refreshed heart.

A servant is one who gets excited about making somebody else successful.

— Beverly LaHaye

---

[21]Having confidence in your obedience, I write to you, knowing that you will do even more than I say. [22]But, meanwhile, also prepare a guest room for me, for I trust that through your prayers I shall be granted to you.

Farewell

[23]Epaphras, my fellow prisoner in Christ Jesus, greets you, [24]*as do* Mark, Aristarchus, Demas, Luke, my fellow laborers.

[25]The grace of our Lord Jesus Christ *be* with your spirit. Amen.

Hebrews

AUTHOR

The Book of Hebrews is completely anonymous. Scholars have proposed Paul, Luke, Barnabas, Apollos, Priscilla, and others as its author. The book itself suggests that the writer's extensive education included both Hellenistic and Jewish influences. A gift for teaching and a heart for ministry and discipleship is also evident.

DATE

The description of the Jewish sacrificial system and its priestly service (Heb. 8—10) suggests that Hebrews was written before the destruction of the temple in A.D. 70. The religious sacrifices referenced, however, relate to the Old Testament tabernacle, not those of the temple. Other evidence, such as the description of the persecution endured (Heb. 10:32–34) and predicted (Heb. 12:4), indicates a time of writing before A.D. 70. The latter implies the intensity of persecution during the reign of Nero, beginning in A.D. 64. The author probably wrote the epistle sometime during or just after A.D. 64.

BACKGROUND

SETTING: Jewish Christians addressed were experiencing social and physical persecution (Heb. 10:32–34) from both Jews and Gentiles. Their sufferings threatened their commitment to Christ. They needed a renewal of confidence and an exhortation to persevere.

PURPOSE: The writer purposed to prevent some kind of reversion to Judaism by presenting the sufficiency and superiority of Christ. He tried to help struggling Christians understand that Jesus Christ fulfilled the Law and the prophecy of the Old Testament. He exhorted believers of every age to fulfill their part in God's redemptive mission and to mature in their faith.

AUDIENCE: The author wrote to Jewish Christians who had been exposed to persecution, although none had yet died for the faith (Heb. 12:4). They hesitated to separate themselves decisively from Judaism in order to press ahead in the Christian faith. Their reluctance to sever their last ties with a religion that enjoyed the protection of Roman law stemmed perhaps from an understanding of the consequences that total commitment to Christ would bring.

LITERARY CHARACTERISTICS:

- Hebrews ends like a letter, but it lacks the usual opening salutation. The book represents a carefully composed, formal writing, such as a tract or sermon. Since the author clearly addressed a particular group, his work may be called an epistle.
- The author quoted the Old Testament extensively, especially the Book of Psalms. He used almost exclusively the major Greek translation of the Hebrew Old Testament or Septuagint (LXX).

- Hebrews provides a clearer discussion of the Christian understanding of the Old Testament than any other New Testament book. The Law and the prophecies of the Old Testament point undeniably to Christ and find their fulfillment in Him.

THEMES

- Christ is supreme and completely sufficient for salvation.
- Christianity is superior to Judaism.
- The New Covenant is superior to the old covenant.
- Living by faith is superior to living by legalism.
- Christians must persevere and mature in their spiritual lives.

OUTLINE

God's Supreme Revelation

1 God, who at various times and in various ways spoke in time past to the fathers by the prophets, [2]has in these last days spoken to us by *His* Son, whom He has appointed heir of all things, through whom also He made the worlds; [3]who being the brightness of *His* glory and the express image of His person, and upholding all things by the word of His power, when He had by Himself[a] purged our[b] sins, sat down at the right hand of the Majesty on high, [4]having become so much better than the angels, as He has by inheritance obtained a more excellent name than they.

1:3 [a]NU-Text omits *by Himself.* [b]NU-Text omits *our.*

1:1–3 This prologue represents one of the great Christological passages of the New Testament (see John 1:1–18; Phil. 2:6–11; Col. 1:15–20; see chart, The Definitive Christological Passages). It establishes the theme of the epistle's doctrinal division: the superiority of Christ (Heb. 1:4—10:18). God has spoken in a variety of ways in the past, such as in a burning bush to Moses (Ex. 3:2) and in a temple vision to Isaiah (Is. 6:1–9). He has spoken through "the prophets" (Heb. 1:1)—all those in pre-Christian times who spoke for or represented God. Yet, Christ is superior to all others. The revelation God gave through Christ, therefore, is superior to earlier revelations. Not only that, it is final. "In these last days" (v. 2) means that in Jesus the messianic age has appeared. Jesus is more than simply the last in a long line of prophets. Although He has in-augurated a completely new age, continuity exists between the old and new revelations.

1:2, 3 The author stressed that Jesus, as God's Son, has a divine nature. "Heir of all things" is a title of dignity, showing that Christ has the supreme place in all the universe (v. 2). "Glory" and "image" reveal that the Son is an exact representation of God (v. 3). When one sees Jesus, he sees God's being and essence. By "upholding all things," Christ carries creation toward its goal (v. 3). The Son of God came to deal with the problem of the sins of mankind. He "purged" or removed those sins, producing a complete cleansing. Sitting at God's "right hand" indicates that Christ has finished His saving work (v. 3). Now He is in the place of highest honor (see Phil. 2:6–11).

The Son Exalted Above Angels

[5]For to which of the angels did He ever say:

"You are My Son,
Today I have begotten You"?[a]

And again:

"I will be to Him a Father,
And He shall be to Me a Son"?[b]

[6]But when He again brings the firstborn into the world, He says:

"Let all the angels of God worship Him."[a]

[7]And of the angels He says:

"Who makes His angels spirits
And His ministers a flame of fire."[a]

[8]But to the Son *He says:*

"Your throne, O God, is forever and ever;
A scepter of righteousness is the scepter of Your
kingdom.
[9]*You have loved righteousness and hated*
lawlessness;
Therefore God, Your God, has anointed You
With the oil of gladness more than Your
companions."[a]

[10]And:

"You, LORD, in the beginning laid the foundation of the
earth,
And the heavens are the work of Your hands.
[11]*They will perish, but You remain;*
And they will all grow old like a garment;
[12]*Like a cloak You will fold them up,*
And they will be changed.
But You are the same,
And Your years will not fail."[a]

WARNINGS FOR BELIEVERS	
WARNING	**REFERENCE**
Do not reject Christ's superiority!	Heb. 1:1–4
Do not neglect your salvation!	Heb. 2:1–4
Do not reject Christ!	Heb. 3:7–15
Do not fail to enter Christ's rest!	Heb. 4:11–13
Do not sin willfully!	Heb. 10:26–31
Do not reject God's grace!	Heb. 12:14–17
Do not reject the heavenly voice!	Heb. 12:25–29

[13]But to which of the angels has He ever said:

"Sit at My right hand,
Till I make Your enemies Your footstool"?[a]

[14]Are they not all ministering spirits sent forth to minister for those who will inherit salvation?

Do Not Neglect Salvation

2 Therefore we must give the more earnest heed to the things we have heard, lest we drift away. [2]For if the word spoken through angels proved steadfast, and every transgression and disobedience received a just reward, [3]how shall we escape if we neglect so great a salvation, which at the first began to be spoken by the Lord, and was confirmed to us by those who heard *Him,* [4]God also bearing witness both with signs and wonders, with various miracles, and gifts of the Holy Spirit, according to His own will?

The Son Made Lower than Angels

[5]For He has not put the world to come, of which we speak, in subjection to angels. [6]But one testified in a certain place, saying:

1:5 [a]Psalm 2:7 [b]2 Samuel 7:14   **1:6** [a]Deuteronomy 32:43 (Septuagint, Dead Sea Scrolls); Psalm 97:7   **1:7** [a]Psalm 104:4   **1:9** [a]Psalm 45:6, 7   **1:12** [a]Psalm 102:25–27   **1:13** [a]Psalm 110:1

1:5–14 The author used seven quotations from the OT to prove to his Jewish-Christian readers the superiority of Christ to the angels. The Jews highly regarded angels as God's intermediaries in conveying the Law to Moses (see Heb. 2:2). The writer interpreted these OT quotes christologically or messianically; that is, he took passages originally referring to God or to Israel's king and applied them to Christ.

1:14 In contrast to Jesus, who sits in royal state at God's right hand (v. 13), all angels are no more than "ministering spirits" or servants. They minister to saved persons. The word "spirits" preserves their place of dignity, but their function remains that of service.

2:1–4 The writer warned against drifting away from the superior gospel of Christ and neglecting the "great salvation" offered by Him (v. 3). With these words, the problem addressed by the author begins to emerge. He was writing to Jewish converts to Christianity who were confronting the temptation to renounce their new faith and return to Judaism.

2:1 The author called his readers to pay attention and act on "the things we have heard" or the whole gospel message. "Give the more earnest heed" suggests both "to focus the mind or attention on a thing" and "to act upon what one perceives." Inattentiveness leads to regression and susceptibility to the temptation to sin.

2:2 The word spoken through angels refers to the Mosaic Law. The OT does not refer to angels specifically in connection with the giving of the Law, but the NT mentions their presence (Acts 7:38, 53; Gal. 3:19). Intertestamental and rabbinic Judaism do as well. If the revered and "steadfast" Law came through angels, how much more should one respect the message that came through the Son of God!

TEMPTATION   AN ENTICEMENT TO SIN

Every person is tempted by someone or something, at some point in life! Even Jesus was tempted (Heb. 2:18). His example, however, provides us with an assurance that we are capable of resisting temptation; and in overcoming temptation, we emerge strengthened in spirit. Even when attracted by what is wrong, we can choose to do what is right.

Temptation is an "enticement to sin" that arises from human desires and passions (James 1:14; 1 John 2:16). Enticement may also be from the devil, who is called "the tempter" (Matt. 4:3).

The Bible states explicitly that God does not tempt us (James 1:13–15), but He does allow us to be tested by circumstances and by the enemy of our souls in order that we might grow in our obedience to Him (see example of Jesus, Heb. 5:7–10), in our reliance on Him for strength, and in our commitment to His commandments (Gen. 22:1–18). Furthermore, the Lord promises to provide a "way of escape" so that we are not tempted beyond what we are able to bear (1 Cor. 10:13; 2 Pet. 2:9). When the tempter's influence is resisted, he must flee from us (James 4:7).

Satan's strategy for temptation is clearly evident in his dealings with Eve:

- He questions God's Word (Gen. 3:1);
- He contradicts God by not telling the whole truth (Gen. 3:4); and
- He attempts to substitute a seemingly "good" or "worthy" goal for disobedience, distorting and misquoting God's Word (Gen. 3:5).

These same strategies were at work in Satan's temptation of Jesus in the wilderness (Matt. 4:1–11).

The Bible promises that those who withstand life's temptations will receive "the crown of life which the Lord has promised to those who love Him" (James 1:12). We can be led on a daily basis by the Holy Spirit into God's paths (Matt. 6:13), to the point where we resist the tempter's voice calling us to stray.

See also Rom. 3:23, note; notes on Conscience (2 Cor. 1); Seduction (Judg. 16); Sexual Immorality (Prov. 6); portrait of Delilah (Judg. 16)

"What is man that You are mindful of him,
  Or the son of man that You take care of him?
[7] You have made him a little lower than the angels;
  You have crowned him with glory and honor,[a]
  And set him over the works of Your hands.
[8] You have put all things in subjection under his
  feet."[a]

For in that He put all in subjection under him, He left nothing *that is* not put under him. But now we do not yet see all things put under him. [9] But we see Jesus, who was made a little lower than the angels, for the suffering of death crowned with glory and honor, that He, by the grace of God, might taste death for everyone.

Bringing Many Sons to Glory

[10] For it was fitting for Him, for whom *are* all things and by whom *are* all things, in bringing many sons to glory, to make the captain of their salvation perfect through sufferings. [11] For both He who sanctifies and those who are being sanctified *are* all of one, for which reason He is not ashamed to call them brethren, [12] saying:

"I will declare Your name to My brethren;
  In the midst of the assembly I will sing praise to You."[a]

[13] And again:

"I will put My trust in Him."[a]

And again:

"Here am I and the children whom God has given Me."[b]

[14] Inasmuch then as the children have partaken of flesh and blood, He Himself likewise shared in the same, that through death He might destroy him who had the power of death, that is, the devil, [15] and release those who through fear of death were all their lifetime subject to bondage. [16] For indeed He does not give aid to angels, but He does give aid to the seed of Abraham. [17] Therefore, in all things He had to be made like *His* brethren, that He might be a merciful and faithful High

---

2:7 [a]NU-Text and M-Text omit the rest of verse 7.   2:8 [a]Psalm 8:4–6
2:12 [a]Psalm 22:22   2:13 [a]2 Samuel 22:3; Isaiah 8:17 [b]Isaiah 8:18

2:6 Testified shows the seriousness of the quote that follows (Ps. 8:4–6). The author did not give the OT reference, though he undoubtedly knew the source because he quoted the passage accurately. The entire letter shows the author's familiarity with the Psalms, as well as the Pentateuch.

2:17 As the High Priest, Jesus has made "propitiation" (Gk. *hilaskesthai*) for "sins." Propitiation refers to a sacrifice that satisfies God's justice and turns away His wrath. A previously broken relationship between God and man caused by the latter's sin will be restored. The Christian use of "propitiation"

Priest in things *pertaining* to God, to make propitiation for the sins of the people. [18]For in that He Himself has suffered, being tempted, He is able to aid those who are tempted.

The Son Was Faithful

3 Therefore, holy brethren, partakers of the heavenly calling, consider the Apostle and High Priest of our confession, Christ Jesus, [2]who was faithful to Him who appointed Him, as Moses also *was faithful* in all His house. [3]For this One has been counted worthy of more glory than Moses, inasmuch as He who built the house has more honor than the house. [4]For every house is built by someone, but He who built all things *is* God. [5]And Moses indeed *was* faithful in all His house as a servant, for a testimony of those things which would be spoken *afterward*, [6]but Christ as a Son over His own house, whose house we are if we hold fast the confidence and the rejoicing of the hope firm to the end.[a]

Be Faithful

[7]Therefore, as the Holy Spirit says:

"Today, if you will hear His voice,
[8]Do not harden your hearts as in the rebellion,
In the day of trial in the wilderness,
[9]Where your fathers tested Me, tried Me,
And saw My works forty years.
[10]Therefore I was angry with that generation,
And said, 'They always go astray in their heart,
And they have not known My ways.'
[11]So I swore in My wrath,
'They shall not enter My rest.' "[a]

[12]Beware, brethren, lest there be in any of you an evil heart of unbelief in departing from the living God; [13]but exhort one another daily, while it is called "Today," lest any of you be hardened through the deceitfulness of sin. [14]For we have become partakers of Christ if we hold the beginning of our confidence steadfast to the end, [15]while it is said:

"Today, if you will hear His voice,
Do not harden your hearts as in the rebellion."[a]

Failure of the Wilderness Wanderers

[16]For who, having heard, rebelled? Indeed, *was it* not all who came out of Egypt, *led* by Moses? [17]Now with whom was He angry forty years? *Was it* not with those who sinned, whose corpses fell in the wilderness? [18]And to whom did He swear that they would not enter His rest, but to those who did not obey? [19]So we see that they could not enter in because of unbelief.

The Promise of Rest

4 Therefore, since a promise remains of entering His rest, let us fear lest any of you seem to have come short of it. [2]For indeed the gospel was preached to us as well as to them; but the word which they heard did not profit them,[a] not being mixed with faith in those who heard *it.* [3]For we who have believed do enter that rest, as He has said:

"So I swore in My wrath,
'They shall not enter My rest,' "[a]

- - - - - - - - - - - - - - - -

3:6 [a]NU-Text omits *firm to the end.* **3:11** [a]Psalm 95:7-11 **3:15** [a]Psalm 95:7, 8 **4:2** [a]NU-Text and M-Text read *profit them,* since they were not united by faith with those who heeded it. **4:3** [a]Psalm 95:11

does not include the pagan idea of bribing a deity to appease his wrath. Although propitiation is necessary to God's holiness in opposition to evil, out of His love (Rom. 5:8) He provides the means of propitiation, through His Son, Jesus Christ (Rom. 3:25).

3:1 The NT refers to Jesus as "Apostle" only in this verse. The idea that God sent Him, however, occurs frequently, especially in John's Gospel. The basic idea of "apostle" centers on that of mission. The Father sent Jesus to accomplish His purpose, to be the Savior of the world (1 John 2:2; 4:14). "High Priest" stresses the sacrificial nature of that mission, drawing attention to the humanity of Jesus. He accomplished His work as Apostle and High Priest as a man.

3:7-19 The author warned his readers not to make the same mistake the Israelites did (vv. 7-11, 15). Despite God's miraculous deliverance from Egypt, they grumbled against Him. They rejected the Law and participated in immorality and idolatry. Later they refused to enter the Promised Land. The writer cautioned his readers that if they also "harden" their hearts (v. 8), refuse to believe (v. 12), depart "from the living God" (v. 12), sin (vv. 13, 17), fail to persevere "to the end" (v. 14), rebel (v. 16), and disobey (v. 18), they, too, would not

enter God's "rest." To "harden" the heart means to disobey the voice of God and act in accordance with one's own desires.

3:12 An evil heart of unbelief stands in marked contrast to the faithfulness attributed to both Jesus and Moses. "Drift away" (Gk. *pararreō*, Heb. 2:1) and "departing" (Gk. *aposterai*, Heb. 3:12) indicate that the readers face the temptation of apostasy or willful rejection of the Christian faith. Jews might contend that they served the same God as the Christians; so they would not be departing from God if they returned to Judaism. But to reject Christ is to reject God.

3:19 The Israelites "could not enter" God's rest because their "unbelief" prevented them from enjoying the Promised Land of Canaan. Sin is self-defeating, and unbelief prevents one from entering God's rest. The writer used the example of the Israelites as a warning to his readers (see vv. 7-18).

4:1 If the ancient Israelites failed to enter the rest, all must beware lest they, too, fail to enter the blessing. The exhortation "let us fear" emphatically warns the readers not to be complacent. A generation of Israelites to whom the rest was promised missed it. The readers should take heed lest they make the same mistake and forfeit an eternal reward.

Perspective by Stormie Omartian

TEN GOOD REASONS TO READ GOD'S WORD (From *The Power of Praying*)

1. *To know where you are going.* You can't foresee the future or exactly where you are heading, but God's Word will guide you (Ps. 119:133).
2. *To have wisdom.* Knowledge of God's Word is where wisdom begins to grow in you (Ps. 19:7).
3. *To find success.* When you live according to the teachings of the Bible, life works (Josh. 1:8).
4. *To live in purity.* You must live a life of holiness and purity in order to enjoy more of the Lord's presence, but you can't be made pure without being cleansed through God's Word (Ps. 119:9).
5. *To obey God.* If you don't understand what God's laws are, how can you obey them? (Ps. 119:33–35).
6. *To have joy.* You cannot be free of anxiety and unrest without the Word of God in your heart (Ps. 19:8).
7. *To grow in faith.* You can't grow in faith without reading and hearing the Word of God (Rom. 10:17).
8. *To find deliverance.* You won't know what you need to be free of unless you study God's Word to find out (John 8:31–32).
9. *To have peace.* God will give you a peace that the world can't give, but you must find it first in His Word (Ps. 119:165).
10. *To distinguish good from evil.* Everything has become so relative today, how can you know for sure what is right and wrong without God's Word? (Ps. 119:11).

although the works were finished from the foundation of the world. [4]For He has spoken in a certain place of the seventh *day* in this way: *"And God rested on the seventh day from all His works"*;[a] [5]and again in this *place: "They shall not enter My rest."*[a]

[6]Since therefore it remains that some *must* enter it, and those to whom it was first preached did not enter because of disobedience, [7]again He designates a certain day, saying in David, *"Today,"* after such a long time, as it has been said:

"Today, if you will hear His voice,
Do not harden your hearts."[a]

[8]For if Joshua had given them rest, then He would not afterward have spoken of another day. [9]There remains therefore a rest for the people of God. [10]For he who has entered His rest has himself also ceased from his works as God *did* from His.

The Word Discovers Our Condition

[11]Let us therefore be diligent to enter that rest, lest anyone fall according to the same example of disobedience. [12]For the word of God *is* living and powerful, and sharper than any twoedged sword, piercing even to the division of soul and spirit, and of joints and marrow, and is a discerner of the thoughts and intents of the heart. [13]And there is no creature hidden from His sight, but all things *are* naked and open to the eyes of Him to whom we *must give* account.

Our Compassionate High Priest

[14]Seeing then that we have a great High Priest who has passed through the heavens, Jesus the Son of God, let us hold fast *our* confession. [15]For we do not have a High Priest who cannot sympathize with our weaknesses, but was in all *points* tempted as *we are, yet* without sin. [16]Let us therefore come boldly to the throne of grace, that we may obtain mercy and find grace to help in time of need.

Qualifications for High Priesthood

5 For every high priest taken from among men is appointed for men in things *pertaining* to God, that he may offer both gifts and sacrifices for sins. [2]He can have compassion on those who are ignorant and going astray, since he himself is also subject to weakness. [3]Because of this he is required as for the people, so also for himself, to offer *sacrifices* for sins. [4]And no man takes this honor to himself, but he who is called by God, just as Aaron *was.*

A Priest Forever

[5]So also Christ did not glorify Himself to become High Priest, but *it was* He who said to Him:

4:4 [a]Genesis 2:2   **4:5** [a]Psalm 95:11   **4:7** [a]Psalm 95:7, 8

4:10 The author defined entering God's rest for the believer as "ceasing from his works," just as God ceased from His. In one sense, to receive salvation means to stop relying on one's works and rest securely on what Christ has done (see Eph. 2:8, 9). Also, in another sense, the works of the believer done in the Lord embody the completeness and fulfillment that come only from entering God's rest.

4:13–16 Nothing is hidden from God, for everything is "naked" (lit. "uncovered" or "laid bare") before Him (v. 13). Yet believers are encouraged to approach God boldly because of their confidence in their High Priest—Jesus. As High Priest, Jesus can sympathize with the weaknesses of His people. He knows by experience all their trials and temptations. Yet, He never failed or sinned.

PRAYER A GOD-GIVEN PRIORITY

While many believers sincerely desire to spend time with God in prayer, few actually do. Spiritual discipline is necessary to make prayer a priority in our lives. God, however, has made prayer a priority—directing His children to pray first, often, and always. Therefore, prayer should become a priority for us!

Scripture speaks repeatedly of the importance of prayer. Paul says to pray about everything (Phil. 4:6). Believers should make all requests known to God. In addition, believers are admonished to pray regularly and frequently. David promised the Lord, "Evening and morning and at noon I will pray" (Ps. 55:17). Jesus prayed for extended periods of time, especially when making important decisions (Luke 6:12). Certainly when facing challenges or trials, a believer should pray (James 5:13). Paul exhorted the Christians in Thessalonica to pray without ceasing (1 Thess. 5:17). Prayer becomes not only an attitude of the heart but also a continual dialogue with the Lord.

When praying, take time to be still and hear a word from God (Ps. 46:10). The Bible dictates no specific time or place for prayer. However, a believer may find it easier to maintain the priority of prayer when she establishes a definite time and place to pray as part of her daily schedule (Luke 18:1).

Prayer should occupy a place in the heart; it also needs a place in the home. While every believer does not need a prayer closet (Matt. 6:6), all believers should have a place of solitude free from distraction in order to pray in private.

To help make prayer a priority, you may want to use a prayer journal or devotional book or write out a prayer list and revise it often. Share your commitment to prayer with others, both to encourage them and to hold yourself accountable for praying regularly.

See also Dan. 2:23, note; notes on Prayer (Jer. 33; 1 John 5; 3 John); Priorities (Matt. 6)

"You are My Son,
    Today I have begotten You."[a]

[6]As He also says in another *place:*

"You are a priest forever
    According to the order of Melchizedek";[a]

[7]who, in the days of His flesh, when He had offered up prayers and supplications, with vehement cries and tears to Him who was able to save Him from death, and was heard because of His godly fear, [8]though He was a Son, *yet* He learned obedience by the things which He suffered. [9]And having been perfected, He became the author of eternal salvation to all who obey Him, [10]called by God as High Priest *"according to the order of Melchizedek,"* [11]of whom we have much to say, and hard to explain, since you have become dull of hearing.

Spiritual Immaturity

[12]For though by this time you ought to be teachers, you need *someone* to teach you again the first principles of the oracles of God; and you have come to need milk and not solid food. [13]For everyone who partakes *only* of milk *is* unskilled in the word of righteousness, for he is a babe. [14]But solid food belongs to those who are of full age, *that is,* those who by reason of use have their senses exercised to discern both good and evil.

The Peril of Not Progressing

6 Therefore, leaving the discussion of the elementary *principles* of Christ, let us go on to perfection, not laying again the foundation of repentance from dead works and of faith toward God, [2]of the doctrine of baptisms, of laying on of hands,

5:5 [a]Psalm 2:7   5:6 [a]Psalm 110:4

5:5–10 Jesus Christ had unique qualifications to serve as High Priest.
- He was appointed in a different way than others—by God speaking through Scripture (see Ps. 110:4). The Son of God is High Priest after the order of Melchizedek, not that of Aaron (see Heb. 7:1–10, note).
- Christ prevailed in prayer to God (Heb. 5:7), in Gethsemane.
- Christ was an obedient Son, even in His suffering.
- His suffering "perfected" Him (v. 9). This does not suggest that Jesus was imperfect and that out of His imperfection He became perfect. His perfection was experienced from having actually suffered. He always had the perfection of being ready to suffer. He added to that the perfection of having actually suffered (v. 9).

5:9 Jesus became the author of eternal salvation through the perfection of suffering. "Eternal salvation" occurs only here in the NT, although it also appears in Isaiah 45:17. Christian salvation is eternal because it is based on the sacrifice of Christ Himself, accomplished once-for-all, never to be repeated, and forever valid. "To all who obey Him" does not mean that believers earn their salvation by their obedience. Rather, they responded in obedience to trust Christ for salvation. The outworking of their Christian faith is in their being obedient in daily life. Once again, the author encouraged his readers to persevere in their commitment to Christ.

5:10 See Hebrews 7:1–10, note.

6:1 Repentance (Gk. *metanoias*) refers to a spiritual and moral change of attitude toward God that results in a change

of resurrection of the dead, and of eternal judgment. ³And this we will[a] do if God permits.

⁴For *it is* impossible for those who were once enlightened, and have tasted the heavenly gift, and have become partakers of the Holy Spirit, ⁵and have tasted the good word of God and the powers of the age to come, ⁶if they fall away,[a] to renew them again to repentance, since they crucify again for themselves the Son of God, and put *Him* to an open shame.

⁷For the earth which drinks in the rain that often comes upon it, and bears herbs useful for those by whom it is cultivated, receives blessing from God; ⁸but if it bears thorns and briers, *it is* rejected and near to being cursed, whose end *is* to be burned.

A Better Estimate

⁹But, beloved, we are confident of better things concerning you, yes, things that accompany salvation, though we speak in this manner. ¹⁰For God *is* not unjust to forget your work and labor of[a] love which you have shown toward His name, *in that* you have ministered to the saints, and do minister. ¹¹And we desire that each one of you show the same diligence to the full assurance of hope until the end, ¹²that you do not become sluggish, but imitate those who through faith and patience inherit the promises.

God's Infallible Purpose in Christ

¹³For when God made a promise to Abraham, because He could swear by no one greater, He swore by Himself, ¹⁴saying, *"Surely blessing I will bless you, and multiplying I will multiply you."*[a] ¹⁵And so, after he had patiently endured, he obtained the promise. ¹⁶For men indeed swear by the greater, and an oath for confirmation *is* for them an end of all dispute. ¹⁷Thus God, determining to show more abundantly to the heirs of promise the immutability of His counsel, confirmed *it* by an oath, ¹⁸that by two immutable things, in which it *is* impossible for God to lie, we might[a] have strong consolation, who have fled for refuge to lay hold of the hope set before *us*.

¹⁹This *hope* we have as an anchor of the soul, both sure and steadfast, and which enters the *Presence* behind the veil, ²⁰where the forerunner has entered for us, *even* Jesus, having become High Priest forever according to the order of Melchizedek.

The King of Righteousness

7 For this Melchizedek, king of Salem, priest of the Most High God, who met Abraham returning from the slaughter of the kings and blessed him, ²to whom also Abraham gave a tenth part of all, first being translated "king of righteousness," and then also king of Salem, meaning "king of peace," ³without father, without mother, without genealogy, having neither beginning of days nor end of life, but made like the Son of God, remains a priest continually.

⁴Now consider how great this man *was*, to whom even the patriarch Abraham gave a tenth of the spoils. ⁵And indeed those who are of the sons

---

6:3 ªM-Text reads *let us do.* **6:6** ªOr *and have fallen away* **6:10** ªNU-Text omits *labor of.* **6:14** ªGenesis 22:17 **6:18** ªM-Text omits *might.*

---

of direction away from sin and toward Him (see Luke 24:47, note). "Repentance from dead works" may allude to the Jewish idea of attaining justification by works. Such efforts would be dead because they are ineffective—they cannot provide salvation.

6:4–6 Can a genuine Christian lose salvation? Other NT passages indicate that true believers possess eternal security (see John 6:39, 40; 10:27–29; 1 John 2:1). The four verbal actions—"enlightened, tasted the heavenly gift, become partakers of the Holy Spirit, tasted the good word of God"—do seem to express authentic Christian conversion experience (Heb. 6:4, 5). Some interpret this passage as providing the strongest argument against reinstatement *if* it were possible to lose salvation. If the hypothetical case clearly describes a genuine believer, the verses would then assure believers of salvation. Other verses confirm the writer's belief that salvation cannot be lost (see v. 19; Heb. 10:14).

6:6 Interpretations include the following:

1) A true Christian can revert to a lost condition.

2) The author poses a hypothetical rather than a realistic possibility: *If* a Christian could lose his salvation, *then* it would be impossible for him to be resaved. But salvation cannot be lost; a genuine believer cannot go back and must press on.

3) The threatened judgment refers to loss of *reward* not loss of salvation (see 1 Cor. 3:12–15).

4) The writer was addressing individuals seeking salvation rather than genuine Christians.

5) Professing Christians must outwardly demonstrate that their commitment is real by perseverance against opposition and temptation.

From God's perspective, it is not *really* possible to be saved and then lost, but it may *appear* possible from a human perspective. Perseverance is the test of the reality of faith.

7:1–10 The first mention of Melchizedek records his meeting with Abraham, at which time Melchizedek blessed Abraham and Abraham paid tithes to Melchizedek. Superiors bless inferiors; inferiors pay tithes to superiors. Melchizedek's superiority to Abraham, the father of the Hebrew people, also makes him superior to the latter's descendants, including Levi, the father of the priestly tribe (Gen. 14:18–20). There are also allusions to him elsewhere (Ps. 110:4; Heb. 5:6–11; 7:1–28). The author of Hebrews offers the most extensive discussion of Melchizedek and his priesthood. The author affirmed that true righteousness comes through the priesthood of Melchizedek (Heb., lit. "king of righteousness"). He was also identified as "king of Salem" (Heb., "peace"), probably an ancient name for Jerusalem (Ps. 76:2; see Heb. 7:2). The name also implies that peace with God comes through a priesthood like that of Melchizedek.

7:3 Without father or mother is a phrase used in Greek literature to describe orphans or illegitimate children or people

Remember that nothing is small in the eyes of God. Do all that you do with love.

St. Therese of Lisieux

of Levi, who receive the priesthood, have a commandment to receive tithes from the people according to the law, that is, from their brethren, though they have come from the loins of Abraham; [6]but he whose genealogy is not derived from them received tithes from Abraham and blessed him who had the promises. [7]Now beyond all contradiction the lesser is blessed by the better. [8]Here mortal men receive tithes, but there he *receives them,* of whom it is witnessed that he lives. [9]Even Levi, who receives tithes, paid tithes through Abraham, so to speak, [10]for he was still in the loins of his father when Melchizedek met him.

Need for a New Priesthood

[11]Therefore, if perfection were through the Levitical priesthood (for under it the people received the law), what further need *was there* that another priest should rise according to the order of Melchizedek, and not be called according to the order of Aaron? [12]For the priesthood being changed, of necessity there is also a change of the law. [13]For He of whom these things are spoken belongs to another tribe, from which no man has officiated at the altar.

[14]For *it is* evident that our Lord arose from Judah, of which tribe Moses spoke nothing concerning priesthood.[a] [15]And it is yet far more evident if, in the likeness of Melchizedek, there arises another priest [16]who has come, not according to the law of a fleshly commandment, but according to the power of an endless life. [17]For He testifies:[a]

"You are a priest forever
According to the order of Melchizedek."[b]

[18]For on the one hand there is an annulling of the former commandment because of its weakness and unprofitableness, [19]for the law made nothing perfect; on the other hand, *there is the* bringing in of a better hope, through which we draw near to God.

Greatness of the New Priest

[20]And inasmuch as *He was* not *made priest* without an oath [21](for they have become priests without an oath, but He with an oath by Him who said to Him:

"The LORD has sworn
And will not relent,
'You are a priest forever[a]
According to the order of Melchizedek' "),[b]

[22]by so much more Jesus has become a surety of a better covenant.

[23]Also there were many priests, because they were prevented by death from continuing. [24]But He, because He continues forever, has an unchangeable priesthood. [25]Therefore He is also able to save to the uttermost those who come to God through Him, since He always lives to make intercession for them.

[26]For such a High Priest was fitting for us, *who is* holy, harmless, undefiled, separate from sinners, and has become higher than the heavens; [27]who does not need daily, as those high priests, to offer up sacrifices, first for His own sins and then for the people's, for this He did once for all when He offered up Himself. [28]For the law appoints as high priests men who have weakness, but the word of the oath, which came after the law, *appoints* the Son who has been perfected forever.

7:14 [a]NU-Text reads *priests.*   7:17 [a]NU-Text reads *it is testified.* [b]Psalm 110:4   7:21 [a]NU-Text ends the quotation here. [b]Psalm 110:4

whose parentage was not noteworthy. In connection with the phrase "without genealogy" and the explanation "neither beginning of days nor end of life," however, the description becomes unique and extraordinary. The description of Melchizedek seems to fit Jesus better than anyone else. In conclusion, there are two possible interpretations for this extraordinary figure: He is a person in history whom Abraham recognized as having superior spiritual authority, or he represents a theophany or Christophany (a visible appearance of God in bodily form).

7:26 The writer summarized the qualities that make Jesus the ideal High Priest foreshadowed in Melchizedek:

• He meets the demands required by His own sacrificial work.

• Jesus perfectly fulfills all that God is and all that He requires. He is righteous, possessing a character that can never be charged with error or impurity.

• "Harmless" means innocent or blameless in the sense of being without guile.

• "Undefiled" means unstained or uncontaminated. This quality contrasts with the ritual cleanliness that constantly preoccupied the Levitical high priesthood. Jesus possesses complete moral purity.

• "Separate from sinners" recognizes that Jesus' sinlessness sets Him apart from others. No one can compare with Him who is now exalted "higher than the heavens" to share the throne of God, making Him the perfect intercessor (see vv. 1–10, 3, notes).

INTUITION *WISE SENSITIVITIES*

Intuition is the ability to sense something that is not readily evident—to "know" something without deducing that knowledge through reasoning. In the Bible, this ability is called discernment:

- of spirits—including discerning the purposes and truth of God and the operation of beings in the spiritual realm (1 Cor. 12:10; 1 John 4:1);
- of the human will (Heb. 4:12).

Jesus was intuitive. We are told repeatedly that in His dealings with unrighteous men, He knew "their thoughts," even though Jesus personally had no guile and no experience with sin (Matt. 12:25; John 6:6, 64). Abigail showed discerning intuition in her evaluation of the danger to her household from David and his men and in her wise intervention to protect her husband and his property (1 Sam. 25:2–35).

Intuition frequently operates at the level of "motive"—recognizing the "plans" of a person's heart (Prov. 16:9). It is closely aligned with dreams, visions, and the interpretation of natural signs (Matt. 16:2–4). Discernment is regarded as a spiritual gift and, as such, is subject to verification by the Word of God through multiple witnesses (1 Cor. 12:10).

See also 1 Cor. 2:14; notes on Decision Making (1 Cor. 8); God's Will (Eph. 5); Influence (Esth. 4); Wives (Prov. 31)

The New Priestly Service

8 Now *this is* the main point of the things we are saying: We have such a High Priest, who is seated at the right hand of the throne of the Majesty in the heavens, ²a Minister of the sanctuary and of the true tabernacle which the Lord erected, and not man.

³For every high priest is appointed to offer both gifts and sacrifices. Therefore *it is* necessary that this One also have something to offer. ⁴For if He were on earth, He would not be a priest, since there are priests who offer the gifts according to the law; ⁵who serve the copy and shadow of the heavenly things, as Moses was divinely instructed when he was about to make the tabernacle. For He said, *"See that you make all things according to the pattern shown you on the mountain."*ᵃ ⁶But now He has obtained a more excellent ministry, inasmuch as He is also Mediator of a better covenant, which was established on better promises.

A New Covenant

⁷For if that first *covenant* had been faultless, then no place would have been sought for a second. ⁸Because finding fault with them, He says:

"Behold, the days are coming, says the LORD, when I will make a new covenant with the house of Israel and with the house of Judah— ⁹*not according to the covenant that I made with their fathers in the day when I took them by the hand to lead them out of the land of Egypt; because they did not continue in My covenant, and I disregarded them, says the LORD.* ¹⁰*For this is the covenant that I will make with the house of Israel after those days, says the LORD: I will put My laws in their mind and write them on their hearts; and I will be their God, and they shall be My people.* ¹¹*None of them shall teach his neighbor, and none his brother, saying, 'Know the LORD,' for all shall know Me, from the least of them to the greatest of them.* ¹²*For I will be merciful to their unrighteousness, and their sins and their lawless deeds*ᵃ *I will remember no more."*ᵇ

¹³In that He says, *"A new covenant,"* He has made the first obsolete. Now what is becoming obsolete and growing old is ready to vanish away.

The Earthly Sanctuary

9 Then indeed, even the first *covenant* had ordinances of divine service and the earthly sanctu-

•••••••••••••••

8:5 ᵃExodus 25:40   **8:12** ᵃNU-Text omits *and their lawless deeds.* ᵇJeremiah 31:31–34

8:1–5 The author contrasted the true tabernacle in heaven (v. 2) with the mere "copy and shadow" on earth (v. 5), which God commanded Moses to construct (Ex. 25—27). The sacrifices which took place in the Mosaic tabernacle and later temples represented only pictures or symbols of the sacrifice of Christ. Only Christ's sacrifice has eternal significance. Christ continues to serve as "Minister" in the true tabernacle through intercession for believers (Heb. 8:2).

8:6–13 The idea of a better covenant is now expanded (see Heb. 7:22). Christ Himself is the "Mediator" (Heb. 8:6), a legal term for one who arbitrates between two parties. Christ me-

diates between God and mankind. He established the "new covenant" (v. 8). This introduction of the "new" suggests that the "old" must be replaced. Its establishment on "better promises" (v. 6) makes the New Covenant better than the old. The New Covenant provides forgiveness of sins (v. 12). It involves an inward and personal relationship with God (v. 10). Consequently, there is no longer any place for the old covenant, which was faulty, "obsolete," "growing old," and "ready to vanish away" (vv. 7, 13).

9:1–10 The superiority of the New Covenant is developed by pointing to the significance of the way of worship in the old

ary. [2]For a tabernacle was prepared: the first *part,* in which *was* the lampstand, the table, and the showbread, which is called the sanctuary; [3]and behind the second veil, the part of the tabernacle which is called the Holiest of All, [4]which had the golden censer and the ark of the covenant overlaid on all sides with gold, in which *were* the golden pot that had the manna, Aaron's rod that budded, and the tablets of the covenant; [5]and above it were the cherubim of glory overshadowing the mercy seat. Of these things we cannot now speak in detail.

Limitations of the Earthly Service

[6]Now when these things had been thus prepared, the priests always went into the first part of the tabernacle, performing the services. [7]But into the second part the high priest *went* alone once a year, not without blood, which he offered for himself and *for* the people's sins *committed* in ignorance; [8]the Holy Spirit indicating this, that the way into the Holiest of All was not yet made manifest while the first tabernacle was still standing. [9]It *was* symbolic for the present time in which both gifts and sacrifices are offered which cannot make him who performed the service perfect in regard to the conscience— [10]*concerned* only with foods and drinks, various washings, and fleshly ordinances imposed until the time of reformation.

The Heavenly Sanctuary

[11]But Christ came *as* High Priest of the good things to come,[a] with the greater and more perfect tabernacle not made with hands, that is, not of this creation. [12]Not with the blood of goats and calves, but with His own blood He entered the Most Holy Place once for all, having obtained eternal redemption. [13]For if the blood of bulls and goats and the ashes of a heifer, sprinkling the unclean, sanctifies for the purifying of the flesh, [14]how much more shall the blood of Christ, who through the eternal Spirit offered Himself without spot to God, cleanse your conscience from dead works to serve the living God? [15]And for this reason He is the Mediator of the new covenant, by means of death, for the redemption of the transgressions under the first covenant, that those who are called may receive the promise of the eternal inheritance.

The Mediator's Death Necessary

[16]For where there *is* a testament, there must also of necessity be the death of the testator. [17]For a testament *is* in force after men are dead, since it has no power at all while the testator lives. [18]Therefore not even the first *covenant* was dedicated without blood. [19]For when Moses had spoken every precept to all the people according to the law, he took the blood of calves and goats, with water, scarlet wool, and hyssop, and sprinkled both the book itself and all the people, [20]saying, *"This is the blood of the covenant which God has commanded you."*[a] [21]Then likewise he sprinkled with blood both the tabernacle and all the vessels of the ministry. [22]And according to the law almost all things are purified with blood, and without shedding of blood there is no remission.

Greatness of Christ's Sacrifice

[23]Therefore *it was* necessary that the copies of the things in the heavens should be purified with these, but the heavenly things themselves with better sacrifices than these. [24]For Christ has not entered the holy places made with hands, *which are* copies of the true, but into heaven itself, now to appear in the presence of God for us; [25]not that He should offer Himself often, as the high priest enters the Most Holy Place every year with blood of another— [26]He then would have had to suffer

9:11 [a]NU-Text reads *that have come.*   9:20 [a]Exodus 24:8

---

one. The tabernacle is described (see vv. 2–5; Ex. 25–27); the sacrifices made in it are noted (Heb. 9:6–20, see Lev. 16). The focus is not on the temple but on the long-vanished tabernacle. Only Jews in or near Jerusalem had access to the temple, but all Jews knew about the tabernacle from Scripture. The way the tabernacle was set up and used reflected the ineffectiveness of the old covenant. The old way centered on external matters like foods, drinks, and various ceremonial washings. These had a place until the "time of reformation," that is, the time of the New Covenant that Christ inaugurated (Heb. 9:10). This covenant replaced all the old outward regulations. The Holy Spirit used the pattern of the tabernacle to teach important truths (v. 8; see chart, The Plan of the Tabernacle).

9:11–14 Christ, as High Priest of the good things to come, has entered "the greater and more perfect tabernacle" that is in heaven. In the presence of God, the Most Holy Place, He offered His own blood (v. 11). Jesus accomplished by this act:

• "eternal redemption" (v. 12);

• the cleansing of the "conscience" of those saved "from dead works" or useless rituals (v. 14).

In contrast, the Levitical sacrifices could only cleanse "the flesh" (v. 13).

9:15–24 The death of Christ was necessary:

• It put the New Covenant into effect (vv. 16, 17);

• It made possible "redemption of the transgressions" (v. 15), "eternal inheritance" (v. 15), and the forgiveness of sins (v. 22);

• It purified the "heavenly things" (vv. 23, 24).

9:26–28 Clearly Christ accomplished all that to which the Levitical priesthood and OT sacrificial system had pointed (vv. 24–26). Believers are now living in the end times (v. 26). The return of Christ is presented as imminent (v. 28). Salvation in this context refers to its consummation and perfection at the return of Christ. "Apart from sin" indicates that sin needs no further atonement. Christ dealt with sin at His first coming.

often since the foundation of the world; but now, once at the end of the ages, He has appeared to put away sin by the sacrifice of Himself. 27And as it is appointed for men to die once, but after this the judgment, 28so Christ was offered once to bear the sins of many. To those who eagerly wait for Him He will appear a second time, apart from sin, for salvation.

Animal Sacrifices Insufficient

10For the law, having a shadow of the good things to come, *and* not the very image of the things, can never with these same sacrifices, which they offer continually year by year, make those who approach perfect. 2For then would they not have ceased to be offered? For the worshipers, once purified, would have had no more consciousness of sins. 3But in those *sacrifices there is* a reminder of sins every year. 4For *it is* not possible that the blood of bulls and goats could take away sins.

Christ's Death Fulfills God's Will

5Therefore, when He came into the world, He said:

"Sacrifice and offering You did not desire,
  But a body You have prepared for Me.
6In burnt offerings and sacrifices for sin
  You had no pleasure.
7Then I said, 'Behold, I have come—
  In the volume of the book it is written of Me—
  To do Your will, O God.' "a

8Previously saying, *"Sacrifice and offering, burnt offerings, and offerings for sin You did not desire, nor had pleasure in them"* (which are offered according to the law), 9then He said, *"Behold, I have come to do Your will, O God."*a He takes away the first that He may establish the second. 10By that will we have been sancti-

fied through the offering of the body of Jesus Christ once *for all.*

Christ's Death Perfects the Sanctified

11And every priest stands ministering daily and offering repeatedly the same sacrifices, which can never take away sins. 12But this Man, after He had offered one sacrifice for sins forever, sat down at the right hand of God, 13from that time waiting till His enemies are made His footstool. 14For by one offering He has perfected forever those who are being sanctified.

15But the Holy Spirit also witnesses to us; for after He had said before,

16*"This is the covenant that I will make with them after those days, says the* LORD: *I will put My laws into their hearts, and in their minds I will write them,"*a 17*then He adds, "Their sins and their lawless deeds I will remember no more."*a 18Now where there is remission of these, *there is* no longer an offering for sin.

Hold Fast Your Confession

19Therefore, brethren, having boldness to enter the Holiest by the blood of Jesus, 20by a new and living way which He consecrated for us, through the veil, that is, His flesh, 21and *having* a High Priest over the house of God, 22let us draw near with a true heart in full assurance of faith, having our hearts sprinkled from an evil conscience and our bodies washed with pure water. 23Let us hold fast the confession of *our* hope without wavering, for He who promised *is* faithful. 24And let us consider one another in order to stir up love and good works, 25not forsaking the assembling of ourselves together, as *is* the manner of some, but exhorting *one another*, and so much the more as you see the Day approaching.

•••••••••••••••••••••••••••••••••••
10:7 aPsalm 40:6–8   10:9 aNU-Text and M-Text omit *O God.*   10:16 aJeremiah 31:33   10:17 aJeremiah 31:34

10:1–18 The failure of the Law (vv. 1–5), Christ's final sacrifice, and the forgiveness of sins (vv. 5–18) are summarized and emphasized. The Law, as "a shadow," anticipates "the good things to come" in Christ (v. 1). Its sacrifices were unable to provide forgiveness, the meaning of "perfect" (v. 1). Even after making such sacrifices, the worshiper still had a painful consciousness of sin (v. 2). The author interpreted Psalm 40:6–8 christologically (Heb.10:5–7). He saw the words of the psalm as being spoken by Christ to God at the time of the Incarnation. God had no desire for any further sacrifices. Jesus, therefore, committed Himself to obey God in His human body and to offer that body as a once-for-all sacrifice that actually sanctifies (v. 10). His active obedience abolished the need for Levitical sacrifices.

10:19–25 The beginning of the ethical or practical division of Hebrews is marked by verse 19. The contemplation of what Christ has done (Heb. 1:1—10:18) should stir His people to action:

• Believers are to draw near to God with a true heart (Heb.

10:22). They can do this because Christ's work has opened the way to God for all believers (vv. 19–21).

• Believers are to "hold fast the confession of our hope" in Christ (v. 23).

• Believers should consider how to "stir up" or stimulate others to "love and good works" (v. 24). This includes meeting together for worship and exhorting one another to be faithful (v. 25).

  Persecution had caused some readers to neglect Christian fellowship; others were being drawn toward the Jewish synagogue for the same reason.

10:20 This verse refers to the tearing of the curtain between the holy place and the Most Holy Place in the Jerusalem temple the moment Jesus died, symbolizing the opening of access to God. An analogy exists between the tearing of Christ's "flesh" and the tearing of the "veil" of the temple.

10:22 The washing of our bodies with pure water refers to baptism. Believer's baptism is not an outward rite cleansing

*Joy is a net of love by which you can catch souls. . . . We can
do no great things—only small things with great love.*

Mother Teresa

The Just Live by Faith

²⁶For if we sin willfully after we have received the knowledge of the truth, there no longer remains a sacrifice for sins, ²⁷but a certain fearful expectation of judgment, and fiery indignation which will devour the adversaries. ²⁸Anyone who has rejected Moses' law dies without mercy on *the testimony of* two or three witnesses. ²⁹Of how much worse punishment, do you suppose, will he be thought worthy who has trampled the Son of God underfoot, counted the blood of the covenant by which he was sanctified a common thing, and insulted the Spirit of grace? ³⁰For we know Him who said, *"Vengeance is Mine, I will repay,"*ª says the Lord.ᵇ And again, *"The LORD will judge His people."*ᶜ ³¹It is a fearful thing to fall into the hands of the living God.

³²But recall the former days in which, after you were illuminated, you endured a great struggle with sufferings: ³³partly while you were made a spectacle both by reproaches and tribulations, and partly while you became companions of those who were so treated; ³⁴for you had compassion on meª in my chains, and joyfully accepted the plundering of your goods, knowing that you have a better and an enduring possession for yourselves in heaven.ᵇ

³⁵Therefore do not cast away your confidence, which has great reward. ³⁶For you have need of endurance, so that after you have done the will of God, you may receive the promise:

³⁷*"For yet a little while,*
And Heª who is coming will come and will not tarry.
³⁸*Now theª just shall live by faith;*
But if anyone draws back,
*My soul has no pleasure in him."*ᵇ

³⁹But we are not of those who draw back to perdition, but of those who believe to the saving of the soul.

By Faith We Understand

11 Now faith is the substance of things hoped for, the evidence of things not seen. ²For by it the elders obtained a *good* testimony.

³By faith we understand that the worlds were framed by the word of God, so that the things which are seen were not made of things which are visible.

10:30 ªDeuteronomy 32:35   ᵇNU-Text omits *says the Lord.* ᶜDeuteronomy 32:36   **10:34** ªNU-Text reads *the prisoners* instead of *me in my chains.*   ᵇNU-Text omits *in heaven.*   **10:37** ªOr *that which* **10:38** ªNU-Text reads *My just one.*   ᵇHabakkuk 2:3, 4

the body from ritual defilement. Baptism represents the outward sign of an inward cleansing from sin. The sprinkling of the "hearts" signifies the effect of the blood of Christ on the inmost being.

10:26–31 Do these verses describe a genuine Christian or one who only appears to be professing Christ (see Heb. 6:4–6, note)? "If we sin willfully" places the emphasis on responsible sin, transgression into which people knowingly enter (Heb. 10:26). Apostasy was evidently in mind. If an individual rejects the "sacrifice" of Christ, there is no other who can provide forgiveness for sins (v. 26). The result can only be "judgment" (vv. 27, 30), "punishment" (v. 29), and death (v. 28).

10:29 The sin of apostasy is further defined with three indictments:

1) Trampling "the Son of God underfoot," implying not only rejecting Christ but also despising Him;

2) Profaning Christ's blood, which ratified the New Covenant;

3) Insulting "the Spirit," who applies the "grace" of God, insolent self-assertion that disregards the respect due the Holy Spirit Himself.

10:32–34 The recipients of this book have already endured the sufferings of persecution. The writer implied they would face more such adversity. These verses provide insight into the nature of most persecutions prior to the executions of

Nero in A.D. 64–65. They involved mob action, public ridicule, and plundering of property, all of which the authorities ignored.

11:1–40 In this chapter on the champions of faith, the subjective aspect of the term "faith" (Gk. *pistis*) is sometimes emphasized; other times the objective aspect of "faithfulness" is the emphasis. Only the context determines which concept is stressed. The majority of the more than 24 uses of the term in this chapter, however, focus on the idea of faithfulness—active obedience rather than trust. The letter's recipients already believed in God and had accepted Christ. The author did not need to lead his readers to conversion. He desired instead to encourage faithfulness in the Christian life. He intended this passage to inspire its readers to follow the example of the faithful OT heroes and heroines.

11:1 A partial definition of faith or faithfulness (Gk. *pistis*) is provided (v. 1). This term is defined by two words: "substance" (Gk. *hupostasis*, lit. "that which stands under") and "evidence" (Gk. *elenchos*, lit. "proof"). Faith then is the foundation for the Christian life and the means by which all unseen things are tested. "Faith" is the nominal form of the verb "to believe" (Gk. *pisteuein*). Faith, therefore, means trust or confidence in what God has promised, resulting in a life of faithfulness and perseverance. Faith is the only essential response to the grace of God (v. 6). Justification is the result of that faith.

HEROINES ROLE MODELS FOR WOMEN

Nearly all human behavior is the result of imitating others. A woman's role models or "heroines" are a good indication of the character traits that she desires in her own life and is likely to emulate. Fortunately, in Scripture Christian women have examples of many women who exhibited great courage, faithfulness, and achievement—women we might take as personal role models and women we might lift up to our daughters.

Above all, we are to choose for ourselves and our daughters role models who are righteous—those who are in right standing with God and who are seeking to live pure, godly lives. We are created in the image of God (Gen. 1:26, 27), and we are expected to reflect the image of Christ (Rom. 8:29). While the Bible records some examples of unrighteous lives (Heb. 4:11; 2 Pet. 2:6), it has many more examples of those who lived righteous lives of faith (Phil. 3:17; 2 Thess. 3:9). We must make certain always that our role models—and those our children seek to follow—are women and men who give a godly example in word, conduct, love, spirit, faith, and purity (1 Tim. 4:12).

Hebrews 11 records the lives of a number of women and men of faith and gives instruction for modeling godly behavior. These women and men were not always famous or highly exalted by the masses of people in their day (Heb. 11:35–38), but all had a "good testimony" and played a vital role in God's unfolding plan. As a whole, they displayed a good testimony, a righteous witness, useful gifts, godly fear, absolute obedience, unfailing hope, and patient endurance.

See also Titus 2:3–5; notes on Feminine Leadership (1 Sam. 25); Influence (Esth. 4); Motherhood (1 Sam. 1; Is. 49; Ezek. 16)

Faith at the Dawn of History

4By faith Abel offered to God a more excellent sacrifice than Cain, through which he obtained witness that he was righteous, God testifying of his gifts; and through it he being dead still speaks.

5By faith Enoch was taken away so that he did not see death, *"and was not found, because God had taken him"*;[a] for before he was taken he had this testimony, that he pleased God. 6But without faith *it is* impossible to please *Him*, for he who comes to God must believe that He is, and *that* He is a rewarder of those who diligently seek Him.

7By faith Noah, being divinely warned of things not yet seen, moved with godly fear, prepared an ark for the saving of his household, by which he condemned the world and became heir of the righteousness which is according to faith.

Faithful Abraham

8By faith Abraham obeyed when he was called to go out to the place which he would receive as an inheritance. And he went out, not knowing where he was going. 9By faith he dwelt in the land of promise as *in* a foreign country, dwelling in tents with Isaac and Jacob, the heirs with him of the same promise; 10for he waited for the city which has foundations, whose builder and maker *is* God.

11By faith Sarah herself also received strength to conceive seed, and she bore a child[a] when she was past the age, because she judged Him faithful who had promised. 12Therefore from one man, and him as good as dead, were born *as many* as the stars of the sky in multitude—innumerable as the sand which is by the seashore.

The Heavenly Hope

13These all died in faith, not having received the promises, but having seen them afar off were assured of them,[a] embraced *them* and confessed that they were strangers and pilgrims on the earth. 14For those who say such things declare plainly that they seek a homeland. 15And truly if they had called to mind that *country* from which they had come out, they would have had opportunity to return. 16But now they desire a better, that is, a heavenly *country.* Therefore God is not ashamed to be called their God, for He has prepared a city for them.

The Faith of the Patriarchs

17By faith Abraham, when he was tested, offered up Isaac, and he who had received the promises offered up his only begotten *son,* 18of whom it

11:5 [a]Genesis 5:24   **11:11** [a]NU-Text omits *she bore a child.*   **11:13** [a]NU-Text and M-Text omit *were assured of them.*

11:11 Although Sarah laughed when first hearing that she was to have a child, her disbelief evidently turned to faith long before the birth of her son, Isaac (Gen. 18:12). God gave the outstanding patriarch, Abraham, a woman of faith as his wife. She, too, had to believe that the God who made promises would honor His Word, despite how impossible it must have seemed to her as a woman long past childbearing years. Sarah was willing to have her attitude changed. Her faith grew as a result (see Gen. 11, Sarah).

THE NAMES OF JESUS

NAME	DESCRIPTION	REFERENCE
Alpha and Omega	The Beginning and End of all things.	Rev. 21:6
Bread of Life	The one essential food.	John 6:35
Chief Cornerstone	A sure foundation of life.	Eph. 2:20
Christ (Gk. *Christos*, lit. "the Anointed One")	This title makes clear Jesus' redemptive mission and affirms Him as the fulfillment of Old Testament prophecy.	Matt. 16:16; Heb. 5:5; 13:8
God	The Father of all.	Heb. 1:8
High Priest	The Perfect Mediator.	Heb. 3:1; 4:14
Immanuel (Heb., lit. "God with us")	The One who always stands with us.	Matt. 1:23
Jesus (Gk. *Iēsous*, lit. "Yahweh saves")	His personal name.	Matt. 1:21; Heb. 2:9; 13:8
King of Kings, Lord of Lords	The Sovereign Almighty.	Rev. 19:16
Lamb of God	Offered His life as a sacrifice for sins.	John 1:29
Light of the World	One who brings hope and gives guidance.	John 9:5
Lord	Sovereign Creator and Redeemer.	Rom. 10:9; Heb. 7:14; 1 Cor. 2:8
Mediator	Redeemer who brings forgiven sinners into the presence of God.	1 Tim. 2:5; Heb. 8:6; 9:15
Messiah (Heb., lit. "the Anointed One")	The title connecting Christ with the Old Testament prophecy of a coming Prophet, Priest, and King.	John 1:41
Prophet	Faithful Proclaimer of God's Word.	Luke 13:33
Rabbi/Teacher	A title of respect for one who teaches the Scripture.	John 3:2
Savior (Gk. *sōtēr*)	One who delivers from sin and death.	John 4:42
Shepherd	One who gives guidance and protection.	John 10:11; 1 Pet. 5:4; Heb. 13:20
Son of David	A title connecting Jesus with the Davidic throne, affirming God's covenant with David.	Matt. 9:27
Son of God	A title of deity, signifying Jesus' unique intimacy with the Father.	Matt. 27:54; John 20:31
Son of Man	A title identifying Jesus with us.	Matt. 20:28
Word (Gk. *logos*)	A unique communication of God to man from creation until now.	John 1:1

See also chart, Names of God.

BITTERNESS CHOOSING RESENTMENT

Suffering does not automatically make a person stronger or better. The way you respond to suffering determines whether that hurt makes you better or bitter.

God has provided His grace to soothe in times of hurting. Refusing that grace creates an inner environment where bitterness can grow. Every woman at some point in her life experiences being wronged by another. She then chooses either to forgive or to dwell upon the wrongdoing until she becomes bitter. To be bitter is a choice to be faced by every woman. When a root of bitterness springs up, it not only destroys her inner peace but also can cause physical illness. Bitterness defiles all those it touches, starting with the one who is bitter, but extending to other relationships (see Heb. 12:15). Furthermore, the one embittered becomes enslaved to the person toward whom that bitterness is directed.

Ruth is a prime example of one who refused bitterness. She lost her familiar homeland, her language, the religion in which she had been reared, the freedoms of citizenship, and the familial network in which she had lived all her life. She made new commitments, assumed new responsibilities, and that within a land in which she was considered an alien and enemy. Yet her faith enabled her to move forward against overwhelming adversity and thus to experience the amazing providence of *Yahweh*, the God of Israel. Ruth paid a great price. She did indeed suffer hurt and hardship, but she was rewarded for her faithfulness by being part of the lineage of the Messiah. Naomi, on the other hand, returned to a familiar land and people and once again found herself under the protection of *Yahweh*. She did lose a husband and two sons, but she gained an incomparable daughter-in-law (Ruth 4:15) whose loving devotion became a model unto the generations (Ruth 1:16, 17). She went through a cycle of bitterness (Ruth 1:20, 21), but through her faith Naomi was cleansed from bitterness and restored to a right relationship with the Lord and others. She, too, experienced again joy and usefulness as she looked beyond her circumstances and said "no" to bitterness and "yes" to God's sovereign grace and plan for her life (Ruth 4:13-17).

Bitterness can have far-reaching, long-lasting, and self-destructive effects. A bitter woman must first turn to Christ (Rom. 5:8-10). Once she has accepted His forgiveness, then she is not only able but also commanded to forgive others (Matt. 6:12). One very practical way to do that is to replace bitterness with love (1 Cor. 13:4-7; Gal. 5:22), especially by showing love to the one who has wronged her.

See also Mark 5:2, note; Eph. 4:31; James 3:14; notes on Blessings (Gen. 12); Covetousness (Prov. 30); Envy (Prov. 14); Forgiveness (Ps. 51; Luke 17); Gratitude (Ps. 95); Healing (Ps. 13; 133; Eccl. 1; 2 Cor. 5; Gal. 6; James 5); Suffering (Ps. 33; 113; Is. 43; 1 Pet. 5).

---

was said, *"In Isaac your seed shall be called,"*[a] [19]concluding that God *was* able to raise *him* up, even from the dead, from which he also received him in a figurative sense.

[20]By faith Isaac blessed Jacob and Esau concerning things to come.

[21]By faith Jacob, when he was dying, blessed each of the sons of Joseph, and worshiped, *leaning* on the top of his staff.

[22]By faith Joseph, when he was dying, made mention of the departure of the children of Israel, and gave instructions concerning his bones.

The Faith of Moses

[23]By faith Moses, when he was born, was hidden three months by his parents, because they saw *he was* a beautiful child; and they were not afraid of the king's command.

[24]By faith Moses, when he became of age, refused to be called the son of Pharaoh's daughter, [25]choosing rather to suffer affliction with the people of God than to enjoy the passing pleasures of sin, [26]esteeming the reproach of Christ greater riches than the treasures in[a] Egypt; for he looked to the reward.

[27]By faith he forsook Egypt, not fearing the wrath of the king; for he endured as seeing Him who is invisible. [28]By faith he kept the Passover and the sprinkling of blood, lest he who destroyed the firstborn should touch them.

[29]By faith they passed through the Red Sea as by dry *land, whereas* the Egyptians, attempting to do so, were drowned.

By Faith They Overcame

[30]By faith the walls of Jericho fell down after they were encircled for seven days. [31]By faith the harlot Rahab did not perish with those who did not believe, when she had received the spies with peace.

••••••••••••••••••

11:18 [a]Genesis 21:12 **11:26** [a]NU-Text and M-Text read *of.*

11:31 The last specifically named champion of faith is Rahab— a woman, a Gentile, and an outcast because of her chosen livelihood. A prostitute initially seems an unlikely example of faith; yet both Jews and Christians highly regarded Rahab

³²And what more shall I say? For the time would fail me to tell of Gideon and Barak and Samson and Jephthah, also *of* David and Samuel and the prophets: ³³who through faith subdued kingdoms, worked righteousness, obtained promises, stopped the mouths of lions, ³⁴quenched the violence of fire, escaped the edge of the sword, out of weakness were made strong, became valiant in battle, turned to flight the armies of the aliens. ³⁵Women received their dead raised to life again.

Others were tortured, not accepting deliverance, that they might obtain a better resurrection. ³⁶Still others had trial of mockings and scourgings, yes, and of chains and imprisonment. ³⁷They were stoned, they were sawn in two, were tempted,ᵃ were slain with the sword. They wandered about in sheepskins and goatskins, being destitute, afflicted, tormented— ³⁸of whom the world was not worthy. They wandered in deserts and mountains, *in* dens and caves of the earth.

³⁹And all these, having obtained a good testimony through faith, did not receive the promise, ⁴⁰God having provided something better for us, that they should not be made perfect apart from us.

The Race of Faith

12Therefore we also, since we are surrounded by so great a cloud of witnesses, let us lay aside every weight, and the sin which so easily en-

snares *us,* and let us run with endurance the race that is set before us, ²looking unto Jesus, the author and finisher of *our* faith, who for the joy that was set before Him endured the cross, despising the shame, and has sat down at the right hand of the throne of God.

The Discipline of God

³For consider Him who endured such hostility from sinners against Himself, lest you become weary and discouraged in your souls. ⁴You have not yet resisted to bloodshed, striving against sin. ⁵And you have forgotten the exhortation which speaks to you as to sons:

"My son, do not despise the chastening of the LORD,
Nor be discouraged when you are rebuked by Him;
⁶*For whom the* LORD *loves He chastens,*
*And scourges every son whom He receives."*ᵃ

⁷Ifᵃ you endure chastening, God deals with you as with sons; for what son is there whom a father does not chasten? ⁸But if you are without chastening, of which all have become partakers, then you are illegitimate and not sons. ⁹Furthermore, we have had human fathers who corrected *us,* and we

························

11:37 ᵃNU-Text omits *were tempted.* **12:6** ᵃProverbs 3:11, 12 **12:7** ᵃNU-Text and M-Text read *It is for discipline that you endure; God....*

(see Josh. 2, Rahab). She is mentioned favorably as an example to follow because her faith was not without works (James 2:25). She is also listed in the genealogy of the Lord as the wife of Salmon (Matt. 1:5). Although she came from a pagan people, she acted decisively out of her deep convictions about *Yahweh,* about whom she must have heard from the Hebrew spies. She risked her life for God's people. Rahab exercised her faith.

11:32–38 Six more champions of faith are named—four judges (Gideon, Barak, Samson, and Jephthah), one king (David), and the last of the judges and first of the prophets (Samuel). Then a long list of what they and others accomplished through their faith is compiled. Some of these descriptions are general, making them difficult to associate with a specific person. Others can be linked to definite individuals. For instance, Daniel "stopped the mouths of lions" (v. 33; Dan. 6:22). Shadrach, Meshach, and Abednego "quenched the violence of fire" (Heb. 11:34; Dan. 3). The victory of Gideon and his small force of 300 men (Judg. 7:7) illustrates the principle that the army of men "out of weakness were made strong" (Heb. 11:34). The widow of Zarephath and the Shunammite woman "received their dead raised to life again" (Heb. 11:35; 1 Kin. 17, The Widow of Zarephath; 2 Kin. 4, The Shunammite Woman). The priest Zechariah was "stoned" (Heb. 11:37; 2 Chr. 24:20–22).

11:37, 38 Many of God's people lived simply, wearing apparel of sheepskins or goatskins—Elijah (2 Kin. 1:8) and John the Baptist (Mark 1:6). This summary concerns people whose circumstances of poverty and persecution singled them out as undesirable from the viewpoint of the world (Heb. 11:32–38).

The writer of Hebrews, however, exclaimed that "the world was not worthy" of them (v. 38). They were, after all, the people of God and recipients of His blessings.

12:1 The writer compared the Christian life to a long-distance race. The runners—believers—find themselves surrounded by a great "cloud of witnesses," or the heroes of faithfulness. These witnesses are not heavenly spectators who observe the conduct of Christians, but those who have given testimony by their examples (see Heb. 11). Christians can run the race of life well only by laying aside any impediment that hinders one from putting forward his best effort. "Sin," especially that of "unbelief," also forms a crippling hindrance to good running. A distance race requires endurance, persistence, and sustained effort—not a short sprint.

12:2, 3 Jesus Christ, the supreme example of endurance, is the finisher or perfecter in the sense that apart from Him we can do nothing (John 15:5). He was even crucified in the most shameful way. Still He remained faithful because of "the joy that was set before Him" (Heb. 12:2). As a result of His faithful obedience, Jesus Christ is now seated at the "right hand of the throne of God" (v. 2; see Ps. 110:1). Believers who follow His example, will also have a reward.

12:4–13 Difficulties come to everybody, but they are easier to bear when one accepts them as meaningful. The author pointed out that Christ's suffering accomplished salvation for all who believe (v. 2). The Savior, who suffered, will not lead His followers into meaningless trials. Suffering forms part of God's "chastening" or discipline of His children (v. 5). Such correction shows God's love and is for the good of the child, producing the character of "righteousness" (v. 11).

MARRIAGE PHYSICAL INTIMACY

Man and woman are radically different physically, emotionally, and spiritually; yet they are designed by God to complement each other. "Become one flesh" combines all aspects of life. It is presented first in the Old Testament (Gen. 2:24) and repeated four times in the New Testament, with the idea not only of procreation but of mutuality in meeting needs and as an illustration of the relationship between Christ and His Bride, the church (Matt. 19:5; Mark 10:8; 1 Cor. 6:16; Eph. 5:31).

Only in monogamy does the idea of becoming one flesh have any significance. From this broader perspective of union, intercourse includes the exchange of thoughts and feelings. The act of marriage is the highest form of the communication of love for one another and the ultimate expression of intimacy. It provides a language that can express love without words. Indeed, there are no words to express all that is felt. Faith in God is the bond of the marriage covenant; sexual intimacy is the Holy Spirit's seal.

The quality of the celebration of sexual intimacy depends on the quality of the total marriage relationship. There can be very little fulfillment in the realm of physical intimacy if there is little closeness in the overall union. Since God designed male and female to fit together and instilled within each a desire for the other, no problems are exclusively sexual in nature. Difficulties in physical intimacy are nearly always a symptom of problems in other areas of the relationship.

The attitude of the wife about herself, her husband, and about lovemaking will determine her response in physical intimacy. If expectations are unmet or if negative emotions of jealousy, rejection, or bitterness exist, physical intimacy will be hampered. Sexual union is not to be used as a weapon or a reward but is nonetheless a rightful need and expectation of each marriage partner (1 Cor. 7:3–5).

See also 1 Thess. 4:1–8; notes on Husbands (Job 31; 2 Cor. 6); Marriage (Gen. 2; 2 Sam. 6; Prov. 5; Hos. 2; Amos 3; 2 Cor. 13); Sexuality (Song 4); Sexual Purity (1 Cor. 7); Wives (Prov. 31)

---

paid *them* respect. Shall we not much more readily be in subjection to the Father of spirits and live? [10]For they indeed for a few days chastened *us* as seemed *best* to them, but He for *our* profit, that *we* may be partakers of His holiness. [11]Now no chastening seems to be joyful for the present, but painful; nevertheless, afterward it yields the peaceable fruit of righteousness to those who have been trained by it.

Renew Your Spiritual Vitality

[12]Therefore strengthen the hands which hang down, and the feeble knees, [13]and make straight paths for your feet, so that what is lame may not be dislocated, but rather be healed.

[14]Pursue peace with all *people,* and holiness, without which no one will see the Lord: [15]looking carefully lest anyone fall short of the grace of God; lest any root of bitterness springing up cause trouble, and by this many become defiled; [16]lest there *be* any fornicator or profane person like Esau, who for one morsel of food sold his birthright. [17]For you know that afterward, when he wanted to inherit the blessing, he was rejected, for he found no place for repentance, though he sought it diligently with tears.

The Glorious Company

[18]For you have not come to the mountain that[a] may be touched and that burned with fire, and to blackness and darkness[b] and tempest, [19]and the sound of a trumpet and the voice of words, so that those who heard *it* begged that the word should not be spoken to them anymore. [20](For they could

•••••••••••••••••
12:18 [a]NU-Text reads *to that which.* [b]NU-Text reads *gloom.*

12:15 Believers are cautioned to avoid any root of bitterness (see Deut. 29:18; Bitterness). Bitterness results from intense animosity and resentment. This bitter "root" bears bitter fruit, such as ill-will, unresolved anger, jealousy, dissension, and immorality. A plant grows slowly, but what is in the root will definitely surface in time. Bitterness may spring up in the heart of one individual, but if it is allowed to develop, it can have wide-ranging effects. The solution to bitterness and its consequences is forgiveness (see Eph. 4:31, 32).

12:15–17 Esau was not spiritually minded but rather a man concerned with material things. "Profane" suggests "godless" or "unhallowed" (v. 16). Esau exemplified an immoral, godless person who had contempt for his spiritual privileges (see Gen. 25:29–34).

12:18–24 The mountain refers to Mt. Sinai (v. 18). It symbolizes the Law, the sacrificial system, and the Aaronic priesthood—everything associated with Judaism. By contrast, believers "have come to Mount Zion and to the city of the living God, the heavenly Jerusalem" (v. 22). The "church" is that city or homeland the patriarchs sought (v. 23; Heb. 11:10, 14–16). The church is the "general assembly" of the firstborn (Heb. 12:23). The church consists of "the spirits" of righteous persons "made perfect" in Christ. Christians can come to God, "the Judge of all," without fear because of "Jesus the Mediator of the new covenant" (vv. 23, 24).

not endure what was commanded: *"And if so much as a beast touches the mountain, it shall be stoned*[a] *or shot with an arrow."*[b] [21]And so terrifying was the sight *that* Moses said, *"I am exceedingly afraid and trembling."*[a]

[22]But you have come to Mount Zion and to the city of the living God, the heavenly Jerusalem, to an innumerable company of angels, [23]to the general assembly and church of the firstborn *who are* registered in heaven, to God the Judge of all, to the spirits of just men made perfect, [24]to Jesus the Mediator of the new covenant, and to the blood of sprinkling that speaks better things than *that of* Abel.

Hear the Heavenly Voice

[25]See that you do not refuse Him who speaks. For if they did not escape who refused Him who spoke on earth, much more *shall we not escape* if we turn away from Him who *speaks* from heaven, [26]whose voice then shook the earth; but now He has promised, saying, *"Yet once more I shake*[a] *not only the earth, but also heaven."*[b] [27]Now this, *"Yet once more,"* indicates the removal of those things that are being shaken, as of things that are made, that the things which cannot be shaken may remain.

[28]Therefore, since we are receiving a kingdom which cannot be shaken, let us have grace, by which we may[a] serve God acceptably with reverence and godly fear. [29]For our God *is* a consuming fire.

Concluding Moral Directions

13Let brotherly love continue. [2]Do not forget to entertain strangers, for by so *doing* some have unwittingly entertained angels. [3]Remember the prisoners as if chained with them— those who are mistreated— since you yourselves are in the body also.

[4]Marriage *is* honorable among all, and the bed undefiled; but fornicators and adulterers God will judge.

[5]*Let your* conduct *be* without covetousness; *be* content with such things as you have. For He Himself has said, *"I will never leave you nor forsake you."*[a] [6]So we may boldly say:

> *"The LORD is my helper;*
> *I will not fear.*
> *What can man do to me?"*[a]

Concluding Religious Directions

[7]Remember those who rule over you, who have spoken the word of God to you, whose faith follow, considering the outcome of *their* conduct. [8]Jesus Christ *is* the same yesterday, today, and forever. [9]Do not be carried about[a] with various and strange doctrines. For *it is* good that the heart be established by grace, not with foods which have not profited those who have been occupied with them.

[10]We have an altar from which those who serve the tabernacle have no right to eat. [11]For the bodies of those animals, whose blood is brought into the sanctuary by the high priest for sin, are burned outside the camp. [12]Therefore Jesus also, that He might sanctify the people with His own blood, suffered outside the gate. [13]Therefore let us go forth to Him, outside the camp, bearing His reproach. [14]For here we have no continuing city, but we seek the one to come. [15]Therefore by Him let us continually offer the sacrifice of praise to God, that is, the fruit of *our* lips, giving thanks to His name. [16]But do not forget to do good and to share, for with such sacrifices God is well pleased.

[17]Obey those who rule over you, and be submissive, for they watch out for your souls, as those

- - - - - - - - - - - - - - - -

12:20 [a]NU-Text and M-Text omit the rest of this verse. [b]Exodus 19:12, 13 **12:21** [a]Deuteronomy 9:19 **12:26** [a]NU-Text reads *will shake.* [b]Haggai 2:6 **12:28** [a]M-Text omits *may.* **13:5** [a]Deuteronomy 31:6, 8; Joshua 1:5 **13:6** [a]Psalm 118:6 **13:9** [a]NU-Text and M-Text read *away.*

13:1–19 This chapter exhorts believers to social (vv. 1–3), personal (vv. 4–6), and religious (vv. 7–19) duties. "Brotherly love" is the most important (v. 1). Hospitality (v. 2) alludes to such passages as Genesis 18:1–8; 19:1–22; and Judges 6:11–24. There were many itinerant missionaries in the 1st century. Filth and immorality characterized the public inns. Without hospitality in Christian homes, the spread of the faith would have been more difficult. The marriage bed is a euphemism for sexual intercourse in marriage, which is affirmed as important and exclusive (see Gen. 2:24, note). An "adulterer" (Gk. *moichous*, Heb. 13:4) is one who violates the sanctity of marriage. A "fornicator" (Gk. *pornous*) covers a wider spectrum of immorality. The foods refer probably to Jewish sacrificial meals (v. 9).

13:7 Believers should treat their spiritual leaders with respect. These leaders spoke "the word of God" through preaching or teaching. The author exhorted his readers to follow their examples of faith. The reference may be to leaders who had died. However, believers are urged to have a responsible attitude toward those currently in places of authority as well. Believers should "obey" and "be submissive" to these spiritual leaders because they carry a weighty responsibility (v. 17). "Watch out" literally means "keep oneself awake" (v. 17). "Must give account" reminds those who exercise authority that they must also accept responsibility for their actions (v. 17). Christians' readiness to obey and submit will encourage leaders to do their tasks "with joy and not with grief" (v. 17). Performing any leadership ministry joyfully excludes a dictatorial approach.

13:8 Earthly leaders will come and go, but Jesus always remains the same (vv. 7, 17). The followers of Jesus Christ can rely on Him. They can base their conduct on the certainty of His unchanging nature. The first readers of Hebrews and those who follow should never lose heart. They can trust His help, His grace, His power, and His guidance forever.

who must give account. Let them do so with joy and not with grief, for that would be unprofitable for you.

Prayer Requested

[18]Pray for us; for we are confident that we have a good conscience, in all things desiring to live honorably. [19]But I especially urge *you* to do this, that I may be restored to you the sooner.

Benediction, Final Exhortation, Farewell

[20]Now may the God of peace who brought up our Lord Jesus from the dead, that great Shepherd of the sheep, through the blood of the ever-lasting covenant, [21]make you complete in every good work to do His will, working in you[a] what is well pleasing in His sight, through Jesus Christ, to whom *be* glory forever and ever. Amen.

[22]And I appeal to you, brethren, bear with the word of exhortation, for I have written to you in few words. [23]Know that *our* brother Timothy has been set free, with whom I shall see you if he comes shortly.

[24]Greet all those who rule over you, and all the saints. Those from Italy greet you.

[25]Grace *be* with you all. Amen.

••••••••••••••••••••••••

13:21 [a]NU-Text and M-Text read *us.*

13:20 Jesus is described as the great Shepherd of the sheep (Is. 63:11; John 10; 1 Pet. 2:25). The metaphor stresses the care of the Lord for His own, for sheep are helpless without their shepherd. The shepherd also has absolute sovereignty over His flock. "Great" signifies that Christ is not to be ranked with other shepherds. He is unique.

James

The author of this book was most likely James, one of the sons of Joseph and Mary and thus the half-brother of Jesus. Like other family members, James did not accept the claims of Christ until after the Resurrection (see 1 Cor. 15:7). However, he eventually became an elder of the church in Jerusalem and was respected as a leader throughout the network of early churches (see Acts 15:6–21 concerning his role in the Jerusalem Council).

DATE

According to the Jewish historian Josephus, James was martyred in A.D. 62. Thus, the book had to be written prior to that date. Within the letter, James referred to a simple church order of teachers and elders who met in assemblies or synagogues (James 2:2). Such conditions were prominent among the Jerusalem believers between A.D. 45 and 60. The contents of the letter also indicate that the epistle may have been written as early as A.D. 48, shortly before the meeting of the Jerusalem Council described in Acts 15. While the exact date is uncertain, that James was written sometime between A.D. 48 and 62 is a reasonable conclusion. Possibly it was the first New Testament book to be written.

BACKGROUND

SETTING: The Book of James was probably written from Jerusalem, where James served as pastor.

PURPOSE: James wrote this letter to offer practical, pastoral advice to those Jewish believers who had been dispersed by persecution.

AUDIENCE: James' reference to the "twelve tribes which are scattered abroad" may have been a figurative description of the body of Christians dispersed among the unbelieving nations (James 1:1). But the reference to a distinctively Jewish body of believers seems to indicate that James was writing to Jewish Christians. Historical events forced the Jews to flee their homeland of Judea and settle in areas where the gospel had not yet been carried. James wanted these believers—some of whom were former members of the congregation in Jerusalem—to stay on course with their mission. He offered them instruction as to how they could continue to mature as Christians and urged them to take responsibility for their own spiritual progress.

THEMES

James was aware of the struggle his readers would face as they attempted to uphold their Christian faith under persecution. He offered words of encouragement and urged them to focus on the victory that would ultimately belong to them. Furthermore, he provided practical advice to unify the believers whose fellowship was threatened by a lack of love, unchristian speech, and bitter attitudes.

To attain the spiritual maturity described in this letter, James urged these believers to develop their faith by seeking wisdom from God (James 3:17, 18). He reminded them that they had a choice: They could either give in to sin and suffer its tragic consequences, or they could stand firm and experience the maturing of their faith by accepting the trials that would inevitably come. James maintained that the latter would produce patience and would ultimately perfect and complete them as Christians (James 1:2–4). The prevalent theme of the Book of James is how to develop an enduring faith.

Greeting to the Twelve Tribes

1 James, a bondservant of God and of the Lord Jesus Christ,

To the twelve tribes which are scattered abroad:

Greetings.

Profiting from Trials

²My brethren, count it all joy when you fall into various trials, ³knowing that the testing of your faith produces patience. ⁴But let patience have *its* perfect work, that you may be perfect and complete, lacking nothing. ⁵If any of you lacks wisdom, let him ask of God, who gives to all liberally and without reproach, and it will be given to him. ⁶But let him ask in faith, with no doubting, for he who doubts is like a wave of the sea driven and tossed by the wind. ⁷For let not that man suppose that he will receive anything from the Lord; ⁸*he is* a double-minded man, unstable in all his ways.

The Perspective of Rich and Poor

⁹Let the lowly brother glory in his exaltation, ¹⁰but the rich in his humiliation, because as a flower of the field he will pass away. ¹¹For no sooner has the sun risen with a burning heat than it withers the grass; its flower falls, and its beautiful appearance perishes. So the rich man also will fade away in his pursuits.

Loving God Under Trials

¹²Blessed *is* the man who endures temptation; for when he has been approved, he will receive the crown of life which the Lord has promised to those who love Him. ¹³Let no one say when he is tempted, "I am tempted by God"; for God cannot be tempted by evil, nor does He Himself tempt anyone. ¹⁴But each one is tempted when he is

1:1 While James could have identified himself as Jesus' brother or even as a leader of the prestigious Jerusalem church, he proudly called himself a "bondservant of God and of the Lord Jesus Christ." Bondservants were slaves who had been released from their obligation but who willingly remained in a condition of servitude out of respect for their masters. Likewise, James gladly offered his life in bondservice to God—the Master who gave him freedom. Thus, James expressed his willingness to obey, laid aside his own rights to follow God's will, and pledged loyalty to the Lord regardless of personal loss, humiliation, or danger.

1:4 The potential a Christian woman has for maturity relates to the realization of her God-given destiny. She is striving to reach a goal that only God can enable her to achieve.

WISDOM FEAR OF THE LORD

Wisdom is the process of discernment in which choices are weighed and alternatives judged. For the godly person, choices are always to be made in keeping with God's purposes and desires.

In the Old Testament, wisdom was used in a variety of ways. Its usage ranged from describing artistic skill (Ex. 36:1–3) and financial savvy (Prov. 8:18–21) to the ability to discern truth. Wisdom is regarded as being very practical in application. It flows from a reverential awe of God and a deep respect for God's Word (Prov. 1:7; 2:6). The wise person is repeatedly described as one who acknowledges, relies upon, and trusts God's superior understanding. Wise decisions are those that keep a person from all that is wicked and perverse (Prov. 2:7–9, 12).

The wisdom literature of the Bible—Job, Proverbs, Ecclesiastes, and selected Psalms—contains passages that offer very practical advice and give observations about the results of wise and foolish choices. Throughout the Book of Proverbs, wisdom is portrayed as a woman (for example, Prov. 1; 8; 9). Wisdom begs and pleads for women and men to choose the way that leads to health and life, the way of fearing the Lord that brings purpose and meaning to life and the development of a living relationship with God. The wisdom of Proverbs is applied in a special way to the many relationships that women have: wife-husband; mother-child; daughter-parent; friend-friend; employer-employee; and neighbor-neighbor.

Wisdom for the believer is a knowledge of God's will that allows her to live a life that is pleasing to the Lord (Col. 1: 9, 10). Wisdom is evident when a person leads a life that is marked by purity, peace, gentleness, a yielding spirit, mercy, and "good fruits, without partiality and without hypocrisy" (James 3:17).

The Good News throughout Scripture is that the Lord gives wisdom liberally and without reproach to all who ask Him (James 1:5, 6). In other words, if we ask the Lord in faith to show us what to do, what to say, and how to live, we can count on Him to reveal to us His answer.

See also notes on Attributes of God (Is. 65); Counseling (Prov. 8); Decision Making (1 Cor. 8); God's Will (Eph. 5); Problem Solving (John 5); Portrait of Wisdom Personified (Prov. 9)

---

drawn away by his own desires and enticed. [15]Then, when desire has conceived, it gives birth to sin; and sin, when it is full-grown, brings forth death.

[16]Do not be deceived, my beloved brethren. [17]Every good gift and every perfect gift is from above, and comes down from the Father of lights, with whom there is no variation or shadow of turning. [18]Of His own will He brought us forth by the word of truth, that we might be a kind of firstfruits of His creatures.

Qualities Needed in Trials

[19]So then,[a] my beloved brethren, let every man be swift to hear, slow to speak, slow to wrath; [20]for the wrath of man does not produce the righteousness of God.

Doers—Not Hearers Only

[21]Therefore lay aside all filthiness and overflow of wickedness, and receive with meekness the implanted word, which is able to save your souls.

[22]But be doers of the word, and not hearers only, deceiving yourselves. [23]For if anyone is a hearer of the word and not a doer, he is like a man observing his natural face in a mirror; [24]for he observes himself, goes away, and immediately forgets what kind of man he was. [25]But he who looks into the perfect law of liberty and continues *in it,* and is not a forgetful hearer but a doer of the work, this one will be blessed in what he does.

[26]If anyone among you[a] thinks he is religious, and does not bridle his tongue but deceives his own heart, this one's religion *is* useless. [27]Pure and undefiled religion before God and the Father is this: to visit orphans and widows in their trouble, *and* to keep oneself unspotted from the world.

Beware of Personal Favoritism

2 My brethren, do not hold the faith of our Lord Jesus Christ, *the Lord* of glory, with partiality.

1:19 [a]NU-Text reads *Know this* or *This you know.*   1:26 [a]NU-Text omits *among you.*

1:18 In Israel, the first sheaf of harvested grain was always offered to God (Ex. 34:22; Lev. 23:9–14). These "firstfruits" were a foretaste of what was yet to be gathered. James explained that he and other Jewish Christians were a "kind of firstfruits." They were the first yield of a much greater harvest that was yet to be gathered as a result of the spread of the gospel.

1:25 Christians follow a new law—the law of liberty. Unlike

the Mosaic Law that required the observance of external rules and regulations, the law of liberty guides the Christian internally through the Spirit of God. It motivates believers to submit to the truth found in God's Word and guides them into right living. Through the law of liberty, they are empowered to overcome their own selfish desires in order to practice the discipline that will produce maturity in their lives.

2:1–9 In the 1st century, society was characterized by distinctive

Perspective by Roberta Hromas and Jan Dargatz

SIMPLE WAYS TO KNOW YOUR BIBLE BETTER (From 52 *Ways to Know Your Bible Better*)

The Bible is like no other book you have ever read. It is actually a series of books written over several centuries by many authors writing primarily in two ancient languages. It is written in a number of literary styles, with books of varying length and emphasis on different subjects. Still, that isn't what makes the Bible different.

What sets the Bible apart is its one continuous theme—a thread that runs from cover to cover: God is, God creates, and God desires a relationship with His highest creation, the human race. All of the books of the Bible point toward that central theme. Many lesser themes and principles run parallel. There is unity in the thought of the Bible, even though the voices and stories are diverse. The symbols run true from cover to cover. The New Testament fulfills the Old in countless ways. The words of the prophets come to pass. The Bible's teachings fit together layer upon layer upon layer—each passage showing us another facet of the same brilliant gemstone.

Get Acquainted with the Whole of the Bible. Thumb through the Bible from cover to cover. See how the Bible is put together. The Bible has sixty-six books, thirty-nine in the Old Testament (Hebrew Scriptures) and twenty-seven in the New Testament (Christian Scriptures). Within each book, the content has been divided into numbered chapters and then into numbered passages called verses. When the Bible was written originally, the chapter and verse designations were not part of the manuscript. They were added later to make it easier for us to locate and refer to specific passages.

New Insights into Familiar Passages. How can you find living meaning in a passage that you may have read many times? Here are three ways:

- *Take a look at each word in a verse or short passage.* Ask, "What does this mean and why is THIS word chosen for precisely THIS verse?"
- *Read the passage aloud very slowly.* Listen to yourself read each word.
- *Read aloud an entire passage "on your feet."* Walk and read—your mind will be less likely to wander to other things. Read aloud the teachings of Jesus in the "Sermon on the Mount" (Matt. 5–7), the sermons of Peter (Acts 2:14–36; Acts 4:8–20; and Acts 10:23–43), the sermon of Stephen (Acts 7), the discourses of Paul before Felix and Agrippa (Acts 24–25), the message of King David (2 Sam. 22), and the sermon of King Solomon (2 Chr. 6). You may want to read aloud the letters of Paul, Peter, James and John. (The books of Romans; 1 and 2 Corinthians; Galatians; Ephesians; Philippians; Colossians; 1 and 2 Peter; 1, 2, and 3 John; James; and Hebrews. These books were originally letters read aloud in the churches). Also read aloud the Psalms.

Mark Up Your Bible. Underline passages that hold particular meaning for you. Circle words that prick your interest. Write in the margins. Put dates by certain passages that seem to give you specific direction in your life.

---

[2]For if there should come into your assembly a man with gold rings, in fine apparel, and there should also come in a poor man in filthy clothes, [3]and you pay attention to the one wearing the fine clothes and say to him, "You sit here in a good place," and say to the poor man, "You stand there," or, "Sit here at my footstool," [4]have you not shown partiality among yourselves, and become judges with evil thoughts?

[5]Listen, my beloved brethren: Has God not chosen the poor of this world *to be* rich in faith and heirs of the kingdom which He promised to those who love Him? [6]But you have dishonored the poor man. Do not the rich oppress you and drag you into the courts? [7]Do they not blaspheme that noble name by which you are called?

[8]If you really fulfill *the* royal law according to the Scripture, *"You shall love your neighbor as yourself,"*[a] you do well; [9]but if you show partiality, you commit sin, and are convicted by the law as transgressors. [10]For whoever shall keep the whole law, and yet stumble in one *point,* he is guilty of all. [11]For He who said, *"Do not commit adultery,"*[a] also

2:8 [a]Leviticus 19:18   2:11 [a]Exodus 20:14; Deuteronomy 5:18

---

upper and lower classes. James called on Christians to rid their fellowship of such external social distinctions. James reminded his readers that the kingdom of heaven belongs to those who are poor in spirit, and not necessarily those rich in possessions (Matt. 5:3). He referred to the divine judgment awaiting those who showed favoritism and, in this context, misused their wealth (James 2:9–11; 5:1–5). James pointed out that God is pleased to use the poor of the world to spread and reveal His message, for although the poor are lacking in material resources, they are often rich in faith. Material possessions can hinder faith, for the rich are tempted to place their security in their wealth rather than in God.

2:8 The command to Israelites to love their neighbors as themselves (Lev. 19:18) was restated by Jesus Christ in His

Guard your tongue when your husband is angry.

St. Monica

---

said, *"Do not murder."*[b] Now if you do not commit adultery, but you do murder, you have become a transgressor of the law. [12]So speak and so do as those who will be judged by the law of liberty. [13]For judgment is without mercy to the one who has shown no mercy. Mercy triumphs over judgment.

Faith Without Works Is Dead

[14]What *does it* profit, my brethren, if someone says he has faith but does not have works? Can faith save him? [15]If a brother or sister is naked and destitute of daily food, [16]and one of you says to them, "Depart in peace, be warmed and filled," but you do not give them the things which are needed for the body, what *does it* profit? [17]Thus also faith by itself, if it does not have works, is dead.

[18]But someone will say, "You have faith, and I have works." Show me your faith without your[a] works, and I will show you my faith by my[b] works. [19]You believe that there is one God. You do well. Even the demons believe—and tremble! [20]But do you want to know, O foolish man, that faith without works is dead?[a] [21]Was not Abraham our father justified by works when he offered Isaac his son on the altar? [22]Do you see that faith was working together with his works, and by works faith was made perfect? [23]And the Scripture was fulfilled which says, *"Abraham believed God, and it was accounted to him for righteousness."*[a] And he was called the friend of God. [24]You see then that a man is justified by works, and not by faith only.

[25]Likewise, was not Rahab the harlot also justified by works when she received the messengers and sent *them* out another way?

[26]For as the body without the spirit is dead, so faith without works is dead also.

The Untamable Tongue

3 My brethren, let not many of you become teachers, knowing that we shall receive a stricter judgment. [2]For we all stumble in many things. If anyone does not stumble in word, he *is* a perfect man, able also to bridle the whole body. [3]Indeed,[a] we put bits in horses' mouths that they may obey us, and we turn their whole body. [4]Look also at ships: although they are so large and are driven by fierce winds, they are turned by a very small rudder wherever the pilot desires. [5]Even so the tongue is a little member and boasts great things.

See how great a forest a little fire kindles! [6]And the tongue *is* a fire, a world of iniquity. The tongue is so set among our members that it defiles the whole body, and sets on fire the course of nature; and it is set on fire by hell. [7]For every kind of beast and bird, of reptile and creature of the sea, is tamed and has been tamed by mankind. [8]But no man can tame the tongue. *It is* an unruly evil, full of deadly poison. [9]With it we bless our God and Father, and with it we curse men, who have been made in the similitude of God. [10]Out of the same mouth proceed blessing and cursing. My brethren, these things ought not to be so. [11]Does a spring send forth fresh *water* and bitter from the same opening? [12]Can a fig tree, my brethren, bear olives, or a grapevine bear figs? Thus no spring yields both salt water and fresh.[a]

2:11 [b]Exodus 20:13; Deuteronomy 5:17　2:18 [a]NU-Text omits *your.* [b]NU-Text omits *my.*　2:20 [a]NU-Text reads *useless.*　2:23 [a]Genesis 15:6　3:3 [a]NU-Text reads *Now if.*　3:12 [a]NU-Text reads *Neither can a salty spring produce fresh water.*

Sermon on the Mount and extended in its proper interpretation to include even one's enemies (Matt. 5:43–45). James referred to this all-encompassing principle by which Christians are to live as the "royal law."

2:13 God is the ultimate judge. He alone is in a position to offer "mercy" (Gk. *eleos*). God's gift of mercy is extended when an individual places her faith in Christ. It cancels and therefore "triumphs over" the judgment sinners deserve. God expects the same response from believers toward others.

2:22 A salvation based on faith does not exclude good works, which are the natural byproduct of faith. Therefore, James is not in conflict with Paul, who insisted that a person was justified by faith alone (Eph. 2:9). Paul was dealing with the danger of legalism and criticized the notion that salvation could be earned through works. James was concerned with believ-

ers who had an immature faith devoid of good works. A genuine faith stirs the heart to glorify God through practical actions (see Eph. 2:10).

3:11, 12 Speech is a barometer of spirituality, for it reveals what is in the heart (Matt. 12:36, 37). Though small, the tongue is capable of causing great damage. The reference is not merely to profanity but also to slander. A woman who is deceitful and inconsistent toward God in her heart will also be deceitful and inconsistent in her speech. James pointed out that just as it is unnatural for a spring to send fresh and bitter water from the same opening, so it is unnatural for Christians to praise God and yet have a propensity to speak evil against others (James 3:10). The tongue can be an instrument of evil or a conduit of blessing, depending on whether or not it is harnessed by the Spirit of God.

SELF-CENTEREDNESS *LOOKING OUT FOR NUMBER ONE*

Sin cannot be understood or described without reference to self-centeredness. "The flesh" (Gal. 5:24; 1 John 2:16) is self-focused. Carnality is self-expression in behalf of your own interests.

The self is the unique gift of God to each person, the basis of individuality, the bearer of the divine image. But turned in upon itself, self becomes the source of temptation, the evidence of sin, and the obstacle to holiness (Rom. 1:28–31; 7:14, 15; Eph. 4:17–24; James 1:14, 15).

"Every evil thing" can be traced back to the desire to gratify self, whether envy, boasting, lying, wisdom that is "earthly, sensual, demonic" (James 3:14–16), or the many other descriptions of ungodliness in human behavior. This mind-set ultimately leads to destruction (Phil. 3:19).

Self-centeredness is a product of the will: We choose whether the center of our affections will be self or God (Matt. 6:24). When we trust God with our innermost being, then our wills also belong to Him, and His will becomes our motivation. Jesus describes self-denial as that state in which God has center stage (Matt. 16:24).

See also Rom. 2:5–11; 3:23, note; 1 Cor. 3:1–3; notes on Bitterness (Heb. 12); Fruit of the Spirit (Ps. 86; Rom. 5; 15; 1 Cor. 10; 13; Gal. 5; Eph. 4; Col. 3; 2 Thess. 1; Rev. 2); Image of God (Ps. 8); Obsessions (Acts 9); Self-esteem (2 Cor. 10)

Heavenly Versus Demonic Wisdom

13 Who *is* wise and understanding among you? Let him show by good conduct *that* his works *are done* in the meekness of wisdom. 14 But if you have bitter envy and self-seeking in your hearts, do not boast and lie against the truth. 15 This wisdom does not descend from above, but *is* earthly, sensual, demonic. 16 For where envy and self-seeking *exist,* confusion and every evil thing *are* there. 17 But the wisdom that is from above is first pure, then peaceable, gentle, willing to yield, full of mercy and good fruits, without partiality and without hypocrisy. 18 Now the fruit of righteousness is sown in peace by those who make peace.

Pride Promotes Strife

4 Where do wars and fights *come* from among you? Do *they* not *come* from your *desires for* pleasure that war in your members? 2 You lust and do not have. You murder and covet and cannot obtain. You fight and war. Yet[a] you do not have because you do not ask. 3 You ask and do not receive, because you ask amiss, that you may spend *it* on your pleasures. 4 Adulterers and[a] adulteresses! Do you not know that friendship with the world is enmity with God? Whoever therefore wants to be a friend of

the world makes himself an enemy of God. 5 Or do you think that the Scripture says in vain, "The Spirit who dwells in us yearns jealously"?

6 But He gives more grace. Therefore He says:

*"God resists the proud,
But gives grace to the humble."*[a]

Humility Cures Worldliness

7 Therefore submit to God. Resist the devil and he will flee from you. 8 Draw near to God and He will draw near to you. Cleanse *your* hands, *you* sinners; and purify *your* hearts, *you* double-minded. 9 Lament and mourn and weep! Let your laughter be turned to mourning and *your* joy to gloom. 10 Humble yourselves in the sight of the Lord, and He will lift you up.

Do Not Judge a Brother

11 Do not speak evil of one another, brethren. He who speaks evil of a brother and judges his brother, speaks evil of the law and judges the law. But if you judge the law, you are not a doer of the law but a judge. 12 There is one Lawgiver,[a] who is

···············

4:2 [a]NU-Text and M-Text omit *Yet.*   4:4 [a]NU-Text omits *Adulterers and.*   4:6 [a]Proverbs 3:34   4:12 [a]NU-Text adds *and Judge.*

3:13–18 James pointed out that earthly wisdom differs from heavenly wisdom in a number of ways. First, the source is different. While the "wisdom" (Gk. *sophia*) from above originates in the heart and mind of God, earthly wisdom originates with the devil. Godly wisdom communicates concern for others through a gentle, yielding, merciful spirit; earthly wisdom is selfish and reveals a bitter jealousy toward detractors. Godly wisdom is productive; earthly wisdom confuses and tears down through evil intent. By analyzing the source, intent, and result of wisdom one can discern whether or not it is worthy of acceptance (see chart, The Two Types of Wisdom).

4:4, 5 In the OT Israel is pictured as the bride of Yahweh (Is.

54:1–6; Jer. 2:2; Hos. 2:5). This imagery would have been familiar to James' Jewish readers. James argued that through their selfish, quarrelsome behavior, his readers were seeking "friendship with the world." They were breaking their covenant with God and committing spiritual adultery. God would not tolerate a rival. He requires total, unwavering allegiance from the people with whom He has joined Himself. By calling his readers "adulterers and adulteresses," James wanted to prick their consciences, encourage their repentance, and renew their commitment to love and obey God alone.

4:11 Do not speak evil (Gk. *katalalon*) covers more than slander, extending to any form of speaking against someone, in-

SURRENDER   SUBMITTING IN LOVE

The Bible clearly commands believers to surrender to God—to obey His Word and submit to His will. While surrender is not natural or easy, a believing woman truly experiences freedom to live only through her surrender to God. On the Cross, Jesus exemplified total surrender to the will of God. By His Resurrection from the grave and exaltation in heaven, He illustrates the blessings that inevitably follow obedient surrender (Phil. 2:5–11).

Surrender means to yield voluntarily to the authority of another. For the Christian, ultimate author-ity lies with God. Scripture teaches believers to surrender to God's way. The Word of God should super-sede all other authorities in the believer's life.

God's Word reveals His nature, His work, and His plans. Mary, the mother of Jesus, expressed her obedience to God's Word when she accepted her role in the birth of the Savior (Luke 1:38). Total sur-render to God requires both a knowledge and understanding of what the Bible teaches and a commitment to obey its directives.

Surrender to the authority of the Word of God leads the believer to the challenge of submitting her own will to God. Complete trust in God demands that a woman relinquish all rights to direct the course of her own life. By surrendering to God's will, she affirms that her heavenly Father knows best. Personal aspirations become sec-ondary to God's divine plan. James pointed out the practical value of submission: Those who submit to God's will come under God's care (James 4:7–10).

Furthermore, all who submit become involved in some form of ministry to others (1 Cor. 16:15, 16). Believers are cautioned that surrender is not genuine until it is total. Scripture exhorts believers to surrender *all* to the Lord (Luke 9:23).

God calls the believer to surrender self and submit to His Word and His will. He promises to lead, strengthen, and bless those who answer His call to obedience.

See also notes on Commitment (Matt. 16); Fruit of the Spirit (Ps. 86; Rom. 5; 15; 1 Cor. 10; 13; Gal. 5; Eph. 4; Col. 3; 2 Thess. 1; Rev. 2); Obedience (Philem.); Submission (1 Pet. 3)

---

able to save and to destroy. Who[b] are you to judge another?[c]

Do Not Boast About Tomorrow

[13]Come now, you who say, "Today or tomorrow we will[a] go to such and such a city, spend a year there, buy and sell, and make a profit"; [14]whereas you do not know what *will happen* tomorrow. For what *is* your life? It is even a vapor that appears for a little time and then vanishes away. [15]Instead you *ought* to say, "If the Lord wills, we shall live and do this or that." [16]But now you boast in your arrogance. All such boasting is evil.

[17]Therefore, to him who knows to do good and does not do *it,* to him it is sin.

Rich Oppressors Will Be Judged

5 Come now, *you* rich, weep and howl for your miseries that are coming upon *you!* [2]Your riches are corrupted, and your garments are moth-eaten. [3]Your gold and silver are corroded, and their corro-sion will be a witness against you and will eat your flesh like fire. You have heaped up treasure in the last days. [4]Indeed the wages of the laborers who mowed your fields, which you kept back by fraud, cry out; and the cries of the reapers have reached the ears of the Lord of Sabaoth.[a] [5]You have lived on the earth in pleasure and luxury; you have fattened

4:12 [b]NU-Text and M-Text read *But who.* [c]NU-Text reads *a neighbor.* **4:13** [a]M-Text reads *let us.*   **5:4** [a]Literally, in Hebrew, *Hosts*

---

cluding truth, if it is delivered in a harsh and unkind way. Speech is evil when it is motivated by the desire to harm oth-ers or to exalt oneself. Such speech questions legitimate au-thority (Num. 21:5; 2 Cor. 10:7–13), slanders others (Ps. 101:5), or brings incorrect accusations (1 Pet. 2:12; 3:16). The form of James' rebuke suggests that his readers were speaking against each other in one or more of these ways. They were breaking the commandment to love their neighbors as them-selves. When love is present, abusive speech is not (Eph. 4:15).

4:17 James reminded his readers that sins of omission are just as real and serious as sins of commission. In His parable, Jesus condemned one servant for failing to use the money with which he was entrusted (Luke 19:11–27) and another who knew his master's will and failed to do it (Luke 12:47). Failure

to do what is known to be right is sin. The greater the knowl-edge, the greater is our accountability.

5:4 James accused the rich of defrauding their workers of pay. Employers were warned against oppressing a hired servant (Deut. 24:14, 15). In an image reminiscent of Cain's blood cry-ing out to God, James pictured wages themselves "crying out" and making God aware of the injustice (Gen. 4:10). The term "Sabaoth" is a transliteration of a Hebrew word meaning "army." The title "Lord of Sabaoth" thus pictures God as the powerful leader of a great army. James emphasized that God is not unaware of those who oppress the poor; he makes it clear that God is holy, powerful, and determined to judge those who oppress the poor.

HEALING PRAYING FOR SICKNESS

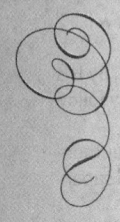

Physical illness and death are a result of the Fall. Throughout the Old and New Testaments individuals prayed for healing. God sometimes gave it directly (Gen. 20:17; 2 Kin. 5:1–14) and sometimes mediated it through an individual such as a prophet (Num. 12:1–15), an apostle (Acts 3:1–8; 9:32–35; 14:8–10), or an ordinary believer (Acts 8:5–8). Jesus healed as an integral part of His ministry (Matt. 8:14, 15; 9:2–7; 12:15, 16). The gospels record forty-one distinct healings as well as others that are mentioned generally. Medicinal agents were sometimes used (2 Kin. 20:1–7; Mark. 6:13; 7:33; 8:23).

Since a person's body, soul, and spirit interrelate (1 Thess. 5:23), physical imbalance, sickness, or injury can affect spiritual or emotional areas of a person's life, and emotional and spiritual issues can have physical ramifications. In praying for healing of body, be aware of this interrelation and pray as God directs in any of these areas (James 5:14–16).

Although not everyone is healed physically (2 Cor. 12:7–10; Gal. 4:13), believers nevertheless have the privilege of praying for the sick. James directs the elders of the church to pray for the sick (James 5:14–18), and gifts of healing are made available to believers for this purpose (1 Cor. 12:9, 28–30).

See also 1 Kin. 17:17–24; Matt. 8:14, 15; Mark 5:2, note; Luke 13:11–13; notes on Fitness (Phil. 1); Healing (Ps. 13; 133; Eccl. 1; 2 Cor. 5; Gal. 6); Nutrition (Lev. 11)

your hearts as[a] in a day of slaughter. [6]You have condemned, you have murdered the just; he does not resist you.

Be Patient and Persevering

[7]Therefore be patient, brethren, until the coming of the Lord. See *how* the farmer waits for the precious fruit of the earth, waiting patiently for it until it receives the early and latter rain. [8]You also be patient. Establish your hearts, for the coming of the Lord is at hand.

[9]Do not grumble against one another, brethren, lest you be condemned.[a] Behold, the Judge is standing at the door! [10]My brethren, take the prophets, who spoke in the name of the Lord, as an example of suffering and patience. [11]Indeed we count them blessed who endure. You have heard of the perseverance of Job and seen the end *intended by* the Lord—that the Lord is very compassionate and merciful.

[12]But above all, my brethren, do not swear, either by heaven or by earth or with any other oath. But let your "Yes" be "Yes," and *your* "No," "No," lest you fall into judgment.[a]

Meeting Specific Needs

[13]Is anyone among you suffering? Let him pray. Is anyone cheerful? Let him sing psalms. [14]Is anyone among you sick? Let him call for the elders of the church, and let them pray over him, anointing him with oil in the name of the Lord. [15]And the prayer of faith will save the sick, and the Lord will raise him up. And if he has committed sins, he will be forgiven. [16]Confess *your* trespasses[a] to one another, and pray for one another, that you may be healed. The effective, fervent prayer of a righteous man avails much. [17]Elijah was a man with a nature like ours, and he prayed earnestly that it would not rain; and it did not rain on the land for three years and six months. [18]And he prayed again, and the heaven gave rain, and the earth produced its fruit.

Bring Back the Erring One

[19]Brethren, if anyone among you wanders from the truth, and someone turns him back, [20]let him know that he who turns a sinner from the error of his way will save a soul[a] from death and cover a multitude of sins.

······················

5:5 [a]NU-Text omits *as.*   5:9 [a]NU-Text and M-Text read *judged.*
5:12 [a]M-Text reads *hypocrisy.*   5:16 [a]NU-Text reads *Therefore confess your sins.*   5:20 [a]NU-Text reads *his soul.*

5:6 Accumulating wealth at the expense of the poor often had legal sanction. Rich employers regularly perverted the legal system through bribery or other forms of injustice (Amos 2:6; 5:12; Mic. 2:2; 6:9–16). The poor did not have the resources or the influence to avenge mistreatment. Therefore, they simply did not "resist." When James said that the rich had "murdered the just," perhaps he was referring to the practical outcome of the failure of the rich to pay the wages of their workers: To take away someone's living is to murder him; to deprive an employee of wages is to shed blood. Believers, on the other hand, must recognize God as the ultimate avenger of justice, and they must put their trust in the Lord (Matt. 5:39; Rom. 12:19).

5:7–11 James encouraged those who were oppressed to be "patient" (Gk. *makrothumon,* vv. 7, 8, 10; *hupomon,* v. 11). The former indicates a longsuffering, loving attitude toward others, while the latter generally denotes inner strength and determination. James encouraged Christians to "establish" their hearts, meaning to strengthen the heart with the hope of Christ's coming. Focusing on that hope guards against a vindictive spirit and produces patience under oppression. The Lord is slow to anger; yet He *will* come, and He will not leave the guilty unpunished (Ex. 34:6, 7).

1 Peter

The author of this epistle clearly identifies himself as "Peter, an apostle of Jesus Christ" (1 Pet. 1:1). Although this claim has been accepted throughout church history, some scholars have questioned Peter's authorship, suggesting that the book's excellent literary style seems too advanced for a Galilean fisherman. However, Luke states that Peter's impact on the religious leaders was impressive (Acts 4:13). After his thirty years of ministry, Peter's usage of the language certainly should have improved and his presentations could well have become more polished. Some suggest that Silvanus acted as Peter's amanuensis or secretary, recording his message (1 Pet. 5:12). The early church fathers maintained that the epistle was composed by the apostle himself. There is no compelling reason to deny Petrine authorship.

In this letter, Peter referred to serious persecution as imminent (1 Pet. 1:6, 7). Therefore, many scholars feel that the book was written just prior to the persecutions of Nero, which began in A.D. 64. Evidently, persecutions had already begun in some parts of the Roman Empire and in Rome in particular, if "Babylon" is used symbolically for the Roman capital (1 Pet. 5:13, note). First Peter was probably written in A.D. 63–64.

SETTING: Trials were common to first-century Christians. The Book of Acts testifies that Christians were slandered, defamed, boycotted, mobbed, imprisoned, and even killed because of their faith. Public suspicion and antagonism escalated with time. Christians believed in a Messiah, Jesus the King, who would someday return to establish His kingdom on earth. This idea made rulers nervous. They viewed Christians as a potential menace to the security of the empire. The first official persecution was instigated by Nero, who blamed the Christians for the burning of Rome in A.D. 64. The government forthwith instituted regular proceedings against Christians so that it became a criminal offense to bear the name of Christ in many quarters of the empire. One historian records that Christians were slaughtered, with public approval, for the alleged crime of promoting hatred of the human race. Peter wrote this epistle just prior to the outbreak of the Neronian persecution. He was acutely aware of the ever increasing antagonism toward Christians and anticipated that the situation would worsen. His foresight was correct. Both Peter and the apostle Paul were subsequently tortured and killed for their faith in Jesus, according to early church tradition. Peter is said to have been crucified upside down.

PURPOSE: In view of the start of government-sanctioned persecution, the rising opposition from the surrounding pagan world, and the everyday hostility from unsaved neighbors and family, Peter wrote to give Christians counsel on how to live in difficult times (see chart, Suffering in Divine Perspective). He desired that they follow Christ's

example (1 Pet. 2:21) and that the life of Christ might become evident in their godly response to opposition and trial (1 Pet. 4:16). He encouraged them to focus on the eternal (1 Pet. 1:3–9). Peter wanted Christians to be prepared to give an answer when their faith was attacked and when they faced trials as a result of trying to live out their Christian faith in the everyday world (1 Pet. 3:15).

AUDIENCE: The letter is addressed to the "pilgrims of the Dispersion" (1 Pet. 1:1). This common designation was applied to Christian Jews scattered by persecution throughout the Roman Empire. Peter applied it to converted Gentiles who had similarly been scattered (1 Pet. 2:9, 10). The letter was to be circulated through Pontus, Galatia, Cappadocia, Asia, and Bithynia—the region now known as Turkey.

THEMES

The theme of 1 Peter is summarized: "I have written to you briefly, exhorting and testifying that this is the true grace of God in which you stand" (1 Pet. 5:12). "Grace" (Gk. *charis,* lit. "favor") is a common theme in Peter's letter (1 Pet. 1:2, 10, 13; 3:7; 4:10; 5:5, 10, 12). Some have defined "grace" through the acrostic:

God's
Riches
At
Christ's
Expense.

Interwoven with the theme of grace is a second theme of encouragement in suffering. God gives grace to believers, particularly in the midst of suffering and difficulty (see chart, Suffering in Divine Perspective).

OUTLINE

Introduction: Greeting (1:1, 2)
I. An Abundant Inheritance (1:3—2:10)
  A. The living hope (1:3–21)
    1. Its foundation (1:3–12)
    2. Its outworking in conduct (1:13–21)
  B. The living Word (1:22—2:3)
    1. The enduring Word (1:22–25)
    2. The growing believer (2:1–3)
  C. The living stone (2:4–10)
    1. The spiritual house (2:4, 5)
    2. The chief cornerstone (2:6–8)
    3. The priesthood of believers (2:9, 10)
II. The Pilgrim Life (2:11—4:11)
  A. Our obligation (2:11, 12)
  B. Our conduct (2:13—3:12)
    1. In civil affairs (2:13–17)
    2. In domestic affairs (2:18—3:7)
    3. In a response of blessing (3:8–12)
  C. Our conscience (3:13–22)
    1. Expectation of suffering (3:13, 14)

    2. Encouragement in suffering (3:15–17)
    3. The example of Christ (3:18–22)
  D. Our obedience (4:1–6)
    1. The concept (4:1, 2)
    2. The past life (4:3, 4)
    3. The future (4:5, 6)
  E. Our accountability (4:7–11)
    1. A people of prayer (4:7)
    2. A people of love (4:8, 9)
    3. A people who minister (4:10)
    4. A people who seek God's glory (4:11)
III. The Fiery Trial (4:12—5:9)
  A. The coming King (4:12–19)
  B. The reward for elders (5:1–4)
  C. The vigilant congregation (5:5–9)
    1. In submission with humility (5:5, 6)
    2. Full of faith (5:7)
    3. Watchful for danger (5:8, 9)
Conclusion (5:10–14)

SUFFERING IN DIVINE PERSPECTIVE

HUMAN SUFFERING	DIVINE PERSPECTIVE
Various trials (1 Pet. 1:6).	Rejoice; they are temporary (1 Pet. 1:6).
Unjust authority (1 Pet. 2:18).	Silence evil men by doing good. Follow the example of Christ (1 Pet. 2:21).
Suffering for doing what is right (1 Pet. 3:14).	Be ready to give testimony of your faith (1 Pet. 3:15).
Suffering because of a determination to resist carnal desires (1 Pet. 4:1).	Give up carnal pursuits (1 Pet. 4:2).
Religious persecution (1 Pet. 4:12–14).	Be partakers in Christ's sufferings (1 Pet. 4:13, 14).
Suffering as part of God's refining fire for spiritual growth (1 Pet. 4:19).	Commit your life to Him; He is faithful (1 Pet. 4:19).
Suffering from the attack of Satan (1 Pet. 5:8).	Resist Satan; be steadfast in faith (1 Pet. 5:9).

Greeting to the Elect Pilgrims

1 Peter, an apostle of Jesus Christ,

To the pilgrims of the Dispersion in Pontus, Galatia, Cappadocia, Asia, and Bithynia, [2]elect according to the foreknowledge of God the Father, in sanctification of the Spirit, for obedience and sprinkling of the blood of Jesus Christ:

Grace to you and peace be multiplied.

A Heavenly Inheritance

[3]Blessed *be* the God and Father of our Lord Jesus Christ, who according to His abundant mercy has begotten us again to a living hope through the resurrection of Jesus Christ from the dead, [4]to an inheritance incorruptible and undefiled and that does not fade away, reserved in heaven for you, [5]who are kept by the power of God through faith for salvation ready to be revealed in the last time.

[6]In this you greatly rejoice, though now for a little while, if need be, you have been grieved by various trials, [7]that the genuineness of your faith, *being* much more precious than gold that perishes, though it is tested by fire, may be found to praise, honor, and glory at the revelation of Jesus Christ, [8]whom having not seen[a] you love. Though now you do not see *Him,* yet believing, you rejoice with joy inexpressible and full of glory, [9]receiving the end of your faith—the salvation of *your* souls.

1:8 [a]M-Text reads *known.*

1:2 God's election of believers is according to His "foreknowledge" (Gk. *prognōsin,* lit. "before knowledge"). The idea suggests "prior choice with loving involvement." Christ was "foreordained" (Gk. *proeginōskō,* v. 20), and Israel was also "known" (Amos 3:2). In each case, more than mere knowledge is involved. In a similar way, God chooses believers (Rom. 8:29). Reconciling the sovereignty of God and freedom of mankind is a formidable challenge. However, there are some general reasons for the importance of election, and this doctrine clearly is found in Scripture. Election establishes salvation as God's work from start to finish; salvation cannot be earned (Eph. 2:8, 9). Election provides assurance of salvation (Rom. 8:35). Election bears testimony to God's providential care for His children (Rom. 8:38, 39). Finally, election is another sign of God's hand on history (Rom. 8:20–22). God's choice is "in sanctification of the Spirit" (1 Pet. 1:2). In other words, the Holy Spirit draws and motivates Christians to believe. God elects believers so that they might be obedient.

Obedience and purification through the redemptive work of Christ ("sprinkling of the blood of Jesus Christ") is His ultimate goal.

1:3, 4 The Bible describes two inheritances for the believer. All believers have God as their inheritance and as a result will go to heaven when they die (see Gal. 4:7). This inheritance is received on the grounds of faith alone. However, another inheritance is offered on the basis of works as a reward or payment for faithful service (Col. 3:24; 1 Pet. 1:4, 6, 7).

1:5 When the word salvation is used, most people assume that it refers to final deliverance from hell. Salvation also includes victorious endurance (2 Cor. 1:6; Phil. 2:12, 13), deliverance from spiritual impoverishment (James 1:21; 2:14), and personal sanctification (1 Tim. 4:16). In 1 Peter 1:5, salvation is a future event associated with the establishment of the coming messianic kingdom.

Perspective by Linda Dillow

THE LINK BETWEEN FAITH AND GOD'S WORD (Drawn from *Calm My Anxious Heart*)

Faith raises us above our circumstances. It enables us to be content even when life doesn't make sense. Faith is the bulwark that keeps us strong even when we're assailed by agonizing thoughts about what might happen or by what has happened. Faith is a vital component in our relationship with God and in our ability to be content. But what is faith, really?

To begin to answer that question, we must first understand the meaning of the word *assurance* as it relates to faith. In the early 1900s, scholars uncovered thousands of letters, receipts, and other documents from a two-thousand-year-old Greek colony. This word *assurance* appeared many times. Literally translated it means "title deed." A title deed is something we own. Likewise, faith is something we own; it is ours. But we must do more than possess faith intellectually—we must own it in our hearts. Faith is not something to be reasoned from afar, but something we throw ourselves into—heart, mind, and soul.

God does not demand that you and I have *blind* faith, but *abandoned* faith, a faith that trusts Him fully. Through His Word, God willingly reveals much about who He is, what His plans are, and what He requires of us. As we come to see Him and know Him, He urges, "Trust Me." Hundreds of times in the Bible God implores us to trust Him. We tend to make trust a gray area, but with God the issue is often black and white. We either trust Him or we don't. We're for Him or we're against Him.

Faith is linked to God's Word in two vital life-giving ways:

Based on God's Word, Not Feelings. First, faith is based on God's Word, not our feelings. Many women have strong feelings, but:

- God's Word is truer than anything we feel.
- God's Word is truer than anything we experience.
- God's Word is truer than any circumstance we will ever face.
- God says of His Word, *Heaven and earth will pass away, but my words will never pass away (Matt. 24:35)* and, *The word of the Lord stands forever (1 Pet. 1:25).*

You can trust God's word *always* to tell you Who God is and what God has promised to you.

Rooted in God's Character. Second, faith is rooted in God's character, which is revealed by God's Word. God gave us His Word to reveal to us what He desires for us. He sent us His Son Jesus, the "Word made flesh" to show us what He is like. God's Word tells us repeatedly, through countless verses and true stories that

- *God is Sovereign*. He controls all things. He is in control of all the uncontrollables in our lives—what we can't see, what doesn't make sense to us, and what we don't understand. What God decrees for us is for our good. That means that there is no difficulty, pain, or trial that happens to us by chance. There are no accidents, no mistakes, no miscalculations. And what He has decreed is intended for our eternal good and for His glory. His absolute sovereignty means that I can trust Him with my tiniest doubt or with my most heart-wrenching fear.
- *God is Wise*. The word *wisdom* in the Bible is the translation of a Hebrew word that means "skill." Applied to God, it means that He has the skill necessary to direct us in any and every situation. He is the Great Physician, the Healer, the skillful Creator. He knows everything about you and has the skill necessary to conceptualize the best possible plan not only for the entire world but also for *your* life. This being so, we can trust God, knowing that everything that happens to us was thought out by an infinitely wise Person, and all that happens will ultimately be for our good and His glory.
- *God is Love*. God's Word tells us that He loves us with an everlasting love (Jer. 31:3). God promises that He will go before you, that He will always be with you, that He will never, never, never leave you nor forsake you (Heb. 13:5). Nothing—not death, nor life, angels nor demons, the present nor the future—*nothing* in all of creation is able to separate you from the love of God that is in Christ Jesus. Faith in God is so much easier when we have the confident assurance that He loves us!

Walking by faith is difficult, but our faith pleases our Holy God (Heb. 11:6), and we do not walk the path alone. Our wise, sovereign, loving Lord walks with us . . . always.

[10]Of this salvation the prophets have inquired and searched carefully, who prophesied of the grace *that would come* to you, [11]searching what, or what manner of time, the Spirit of Christ who was in them was indicating when He testified beforehand the sufferings of Christ and the glories that would follow. [12]To them it was revealed that, not to themselves, but to us[a] they were ministering the things which now have been reported to you through those who have preached the gospel to you by the Holy Spirit sent from heaven—things which angels desire to look into.

Living Before God Our Father

[13]Therefore gird up the loins of your mind, be sober, and rest *your* hope fully upon the grace that is to be brought to you at the revelation of Jesus Christ; [14]as obedient children, not conforming yourselves to the former lusts, *as* in your ignorance; [15]but as He who called you *is* holy, you also be holy in all *your* conduct, [16]because it is written, "Be holy, for I am holy."[a]

[17]And if you call on the Father, who without partiality judges according to each one's work, conduct yourselves throughout the time of your stay *here* in fear; [18]knowing that you were not redeemed with corruptible things, *like* silver or gold, from your aimless conduct *received* by tradition from your fathers, [19]but with the precious blood of Christ, as of a lamb without blemish and without spot. [20]He indeed was foreordained before the foundation of the world, but was manifest in these last times for you [21]who through Him believe in God, who raised Him from the dead and gave Him glory, so that your faith and hope are in God.

The Enduring Word

[22]Since you have purified your souls in obeying the truth through the Spirit[a] in sincere love of the brethren, love one another fervently with a pure heart, [23]having been born again, not of corruptible seed but incorruptible, through the word of God which lives and abides forever,[a] [24]because

"All flesh is as grass,
And all the glory of man[a] *as the flower of the grass.*
The grass withers,

· · · · · · · · · · · · · · · ·

1:12 [a]NU-Text and M-Text read *you*. 1:16 [a]Leviticus 11:44, 45; 19:2; 20:7 1:22 [a]NU-Text omits *through the Spirit*. 1:23 [a]NU-Text omits *forever*. 1:24 [a]NU-Text reads *all its glory*.

God will never assign you an overload.

Jo Ann Leavell

1:13 The image reflected in the phrase "gird up the loins of your mind" is reminiscent of the ancient Near Eastern custom of pulling up long robes and tucking them into belts when running or participating in strenuous activity. This action left the legs unencumbered. The "loins" (the lower back muscles) were regarded as the center of physical strength and power. Peter challenged believers to maximize all their intellectual and moral faculties. They are to discipline their minds by binding up all loosely flowing thoughts and speculations that might distract them from the gospel and hamper their obedience (2 Pet. 3:1). Peter used the same word to encourage spiritual alertness in prayer and in resisting the attacks of Satan (1 Pet. 4:7; 5:8).

EMPLOYMENT
RELATING TO AUTHORITY

Authority is necessary in order to operate a business of any kind. Therefore, people in positions of authority are part of God's plan for orderliness in the world. We are directed to submit ourselves to the people who have risen to those positions of directing work to be done. To rebel against that authority is to rebel against God's order, which, according to Paul, will bring God's judgment on us (Judg. 21:25). The authority over us may even be incompetent or inadequate in some way, but that authority is to be respected. Obviously there have been and are people in positions of authority who should never be there. But that was true when Paul wrote his letter to the Romans. The principle still holds true: we may not respect the people themselves, but we must respect their authority. Only when that authority would lead us to compromise Christian principles should we refuse to submit (Matt. 22:17–21).

Submission is yielding to the authority of another. Respecting someone means, in part, to treat with consideration. Both can be done contrary to feelings, by an act of the will, especially when empowered by the Holy Spirit. Peter teaches that the servant—the employee—should perform job-related tasks with excellence, even in the face of unfair treatment. Peter goes on to say that it is commendable to bear up under unfair treatment, for that kind of suffering finds favor with God (v. 20).

Unjust suffering is precious to God because that is how Christ suffered, and when believers endure unjust treatment with patience and tolerance, they are sharing in His suffering. No one in the flesh wants to suffer unjustly. But when they desire to follow in the steps of Christ and find favor with God, they can endure and discover in the process a closer relationship to our Savior.

When this principle is applied to difficult management relationships, God changes our thinking and our attitudes so that much of the stress and frustration of the relationship is relieved. God has told us that His yoke is easy and His burden is light. Accepting it from God's hands and letting Him guide our reactions—even to the point of suffering unjustly—is easier than the normal human reactions of anger, bitterness, and vengeance.

See also Prov. 25:15; Eccl. 9:10; Rom. 13:1, 2; notes on Authority (John 19); Conflict (Matt. 18); Employment (Eccl. 9; Acts 18; 2 Cor. 2; Col. 3); Stress Management (Phil. 4); Submission (1 Pet. 3)

And its flower falls away,
²⁵But the word of the LORD endures forever."ᵃ

Now this is the word which by the gospel was preached to you.

2 Therefore, laying aside all malice, all deceit, hypocrisy, envy, and all evil speaking, ²as newborn babes, desire the pure milk of the word, that you may grow thereby,ᵃ ³if indeed you have tasted that the Lord *is* gracious.

The Chosen Stone and His Chosen People

⁴Coming to Him *as to* a living stone, rejected indeed by men, but chosen by God *and* precious, ⁵you also, as living stones, are being built up a spiritual house, a holy priesthood, to offer up spiritual sacrifices acceptable to God through Jesus Christ. ⁶Therefore it is also contained in the Scripture,

"Behold, I lay in Zion
A chief cornerstone, elect, precious,

And he who believes on Him will by no means be put to shame."ᵃ

⁷Therefore, to you who believe, *He is* precious; but to those who are disobedient,ᵃ

"The stone which the builders rejected
Has become the chief cornerstone,"ᵇ

⁸and

"A stone of stumbling
And a rock of offense."ᵃ

They stumble, being disobedient to the word, to which they also were appointed.

⁹But you *are* a chosen generation, a royal priesthood, a holy nation, His own special people, that you may proclaim the praises of Him who called you out of darkness into His marvelous

1:25 ᵃIsaiah 40:6–8 **2:2** ᵃNU-Text adds *up to salvation.* **2:6** ᵃIsaiah 28:16 **2:7** ᵃNU-Text reads *to those who disbelieve.* ᵇPsalm 118:22 **2:8** ᵃIsaiah 8:14

2:1–3 Christians require proper spiritual nourishment if they are to grow in spiritual maturity. This nourishment is to be sought with the same intense eagerness exhibited in very young infants who yearn for feeding (v. 2). Spiritual milk is pure when it is unmixed—not contaminated with evil such as "malice," "deceit," "hypocrisy," "envy," and "all evil speaking"

(v. 1). In order for their nourishment to be "pure," believers must remove all these hindrances to growth. The verb "laying aside" commonly refers to washing off defilement or to taking off filthy clothes. Repentance is thus a prerequisite for receiving nourishment from the Word and for growing in maturity as a Christian.

SUBMISSION

DEFINITION	METHOD	EXAMPLE	REWARDS
• An attitude of the will	"As to the Lord" (Eph. 5:22)	Jesus: He had no other purpose (Heb. 10:7).	A vibrant witness (1 Pet. 3:1)
• More than obedience	"To your own husbands" (Eph. 5:22; 1 Pet. 3:1)	To submit was joy (Ps. 40:7, 8).	A means of glorifying God (1 Pet. 3:5, 6)
• Resting, leaning, trusting, abandoning yourself to the Lord	An act of the will (1 Pet. 3:1, 2)	He did not consider His will (John 5:30).	A means for teaching spiritual truths (Eph. 5:25–32)
• Void of stubbornness	Extends to "everything" (Eph. 5:24)	Mary: "Let it be to me" (Luke 1:38).	A way to train children (Titus 2:3–5)
	Patterned after the relationship between Christ and the church (Eph. 5:25–32)	Esther: "I will go . . . if I perish, I perish" (Esth. 4:16).	The object of human love and divine protection (Eph. 5:25; 1 Pet. 3:7)
	A response to love (Eph. 5:24, 25)		A way to increase worth (1 Pet. 3:4)
	Extends to everyone: • The church to Christ (Eph. 5:24);		A means for liberating creativity (1 Pet. 3:7)
	• All believers to God (Heb. 12:9; James 4:7), to spiritual leaders (Heb. 13:17), to governing authorities (Rom. 13:1, 5; Titus 3:1; 1 Pet. 2:13), to one another (Eph. 5:21);		
	• Wives to husbands (Eph. 5:22, 24; Col. 3:18; Titus 2:5; 1 Pet. 3:1, 5);		
	• Children to parents (Eph. 6:1–3);		
	• Slaves to masters (Titus 2:9; 1 Pet. 2:18)		

SUBMISSION *AS UNTO THE LORD*

Submission means to put all of yourself—understandings, knowledge, opinions, feelings, energies—at the disposal of a person in authority over you. This never means subjecting yourself to abusive tyranny, nor does it suggest mindless acquiescence to the whims of another. It is the yielding of humble and intelligent obedience—without suggestion of inferiority or worthlessness. A wife's deference to her husband is a duty owed to the Lord. A wife's submission is not as much to her husband, a mere man, as it is to God and His plan for marriage.

Relationships in life are merely the classroom for teaching submission to the will of God. The word translated "submissive" (Gk. *hupotassō*) means literally "to place under,"—for example, husbands (Eph. 5:22; Col. 3:18; Titus 2:5; 1 Pet. 3:1, 5), parents (Luke 2:51), masters (Titus 2:9; 1 Pet. 2:18), secular authorities (Rom. 13:1; Titus 3:1; 1 Pet. 2:13), and church officials (1 Pet. 5:5). The word is also used with respect to God (1 Cor. 15:28; Heb. 12:9; James 4:7) and to Christ (Eph. 5:24).

The Book of Esther provides a possible study in submission. Queen Vashti—self-ruled, greedy, selfish, cowardly—was unwise in disobeying Ahasuerus, who was not only her husband but also her king. She sought to cover her disobedience with the pretense of propriety and attempted to hide her pride with a show of modesty. The text gives no evidence that Ahasuerus did any more than give a ridiculous and distasteful command. Obedience only to "reasonable requests" is selfish license, not good judgment.

On the other hand, Esther was obedient, grateful, selfless, and courageous. She was a member of a minority race, an orphan child bereft of family and friends and saddled with awesome and fearful responsibility. Yet Esther rose to the occasion with an inner beauty of spirit and unshaking commitment to God's providence. She was obedient to her foster father (Esth. 2:20), cooperative with authorities over her (Esth. 2:8, 9, 15), and submissive to her husband (Esth. 2:17; 5:2–4; 8:3).

See also Esth. 1:15–22; Heb. 13:17; notes on Biblical Equality (Eph. 5); Marriage (Gen. 2; 2 Sam. 6; Prov. 5; Hos. 2; Amos 3; 2 Cor. 13; Heb. 12); Obedience (Philem.); Wives (Prov. 31); portraits of Esther (Esth. 2); Sarai (Gen. 11); Vashti (Esth. 1)

---

light; [10]who once *were* not a people but *are* now the people of God, who had not obtained mercy but now have obtained mercy.

Living Before the World

[11]Beloved, I beg *you* as sojourners and pilgrims, abstain from fleshly lusts which war against the soul, [12]having your conduct honorable among the Gentiles, that when they speak against you as evildoers, they may, by *your* good works which they observe, glorify God in the day of visitation.

Submission to Government

[13]Therefore submit yourselves to every ordinance of man for the Lord's sake, whether to the king as supreme, [14]or to governors, as to those who are sent by him for the punishment of evil-

doers and *for the* praise of those who do good. [15]For this is the will of God, that by doing good you may put to silence the ignorance of foolish men— [16]as free, yet not using liberty as a cloak for vice, but as bondservants of God. [17]Honor all *people.* Love the brotherhood. Fear God. Honor the king.

Submission to Masters

[18]Servants, *be* submissive to *your* masters with all fear, not only to the good and gentle, but also to the harsh. [19]For this *is* commendable, if because of conscience toward God one endures grief, suffering wrongfully. [20]For what credit *is it* if, when you are beaten for your faults, you take it patiently? But when you do good and suffer, if you take it patiently, this *is* commendable before God.

2:13 Submission is the theme of this section (1 Pet. 2:13—3:7). The natural response is to demand rights and refuse to yield to another person; it is a supernatural response to give up rights and yield. True submission involves refusing to seek self-interest and instead assuming voluntary commitment of service to others (Phil. 2:3, 4). This volitional submission is seen in several spheres of relationships: citizens to government (1 Pet. 2:13–17); slaves to masters (vv. 18–25); and wives to husbands (1 Pet. 3:1–7).

2:18–25 The institution of slavery was deeply rooted in the economic and social structure of the ancient Near East and

the Graeco-Roman world. Conditions and treatment of slaves varied, but their social status was unquestionably low and their lives often difficult. Nowhere in Scripture is slavery condoned. Peter's aim in this epistle was not to argue against slavery but to give comfort and guidance to those who were suffering in it. He reminded believers to follow the example of Jesus, who suffered greatly on their behalf. Suffering is part of the Christian calling (v. 21; 1 Pet. 3:9), for it serves the purpose of making the believer more Christlike (1 Pet. 1:7). Suffering is a useful tool for convicting others of sin (1 Pet. 3:15, 16) and attracting them to the gospel (1 Pet. 2:12).

EVANGELISM *PERSONAL TESTIMONY*

Nothing is any more effective in drawing someone to Jesus Christ than the sharing of personal testimony (John 4:39; 11:32). Believers should always be ready to share. A personal testimony catches the attention of those listening and holds the interest of the unbeliever (John 4:28-30).

By its very nature, a personal testimony is unique. It should describe your life before receiving Christ, how you realized your need for Christ, what steps you took to become a Christian, how Christ helps you and makes a difference in your daily life, and any unique ways Christ has dealt with you in drawing you to Himself. A personal testimony is difficult to refute because an individual is sharing truth that has come to her firsthand through her own personal experience with God (John 4:29).

A personal testimony is an opportunity for you to identify with the unbeliever and to show how Christ makes the difference in a person's life (John 4:42). Preparing a thoughtful and logical defense of the faith enables the believer to present the gospel in a persuasive manner, answering with clear and precise reasons for her hope in Jesus Christ (1 Pet. 3:15).

See also 2 Chr. 7:11-16; 15:1-19; 20:1-25; Neh. 8:1-18; Acts 13:15, note; notes on Evangelism (John 6; Col. 4); Salvation (Eph. 2); Women's Ministries (John 4; Acts 2; 1 Cor. 11; Eph. 2; 1 Tim. 3; Titus 2)

---

[21]For to this you were called, because Christ also suffered for us,[a] leaving us[b] an example, that you should follow His steps:

[22]"Who committed no sin,
   Nor was deceit found in His mouth";[a]

[23]who, when He was reviled, did not revile in return; when He suffered, He did not threaten, but committed *Himself* to Him who judges righteously; [24]who Himself bore our sins in His own body on the tree, that we, having died to sins, might live for righteousness— by whose stripes you were healed. [25]For you were like sheep going astray, but have now returned to the Shepherd and Overseer[a] of your souls.

Submission to Husbands

3 Wives, likewise, *be* submissive to your own husbands, that even if some do not obey the word, they, without a word, may be won by the conduct of their wives, [2]when they observe your chaste conduct *accompanied* by fear. [3]Do not let your adorn-

· · · · · · · · · · · · · · · ·

2:21 [a]NU-Text reads *you*. [b]NU-Text and M-Text read *you*.   **2:22** [a]Isaiah 53:9   **2:25** [a]Greek *Episkopos*

Life is intricately and intimately linked with Jesus. In fact, Jesus is life–He said so Himself. So when we look for life worth living, we must look for it not in happy or heartbreaking circumstances, health, or even relationships. Life is in Christ.

Joni Eareckson Tada

2:23 The only way Christ could silently endure suffering was to entrust Himself to His Father, who would judge righteously and right all wrongs. Following His example is the only way believers can endure suffering. To retaliate is to assume a right they do not have (Rom. 12:19). God takes responsibility for dealing with the offending party. Believers also are responsible for making the right response, then trusting the offender to God.

3:1 The distinctive behavior of the Christian wife is signaled at once by the key expression "likewise," which applies to the wife and also to the husband (vv. 1, 7). Both follow Jesus, the Suffering Servant, whose suffering ultimately led to healing. Both are servants, seeking to serve one another and others for Christ's sake.

3:1, 2 Words come easy; yet a wife's "gentle and quiet spirit" is the healing agent her husband needs (vv. 3, 4). She is allowed the same incredible privilege given to the Lord Jesus, to suffer in order to bring healing to another. Although the reference

given is specifically concerning a non-believing husband, the application is also for the Christian husband who is being disobedient to the Lord in a certain area of his life. The wife's "conduct" or lifestyle is to be accompanied by "fear" or reverence in the sense of respect.

3:3, 4 The idea is not that outward appearance is unimportant but rather that the inward qualities are more important. Outward beauty is corruptible; inward beauty, incorruptible. This hidden beauty of the heart is displayed by a "gentle and quiet spirit" (v. 4). This quality is not a reference to genetically acquired personality traits, such as being a person of few words, but rather to an inner attitude marked by the absence of anxiety, coupled with a trust in God as the blessed controller of all things. "Precious" (Gk. *timē*, lit. "value" or "price") is used elsewhere in 1 Peter: the shed blood of Jesus Christ is "precious" (1 Pet. 1:19), and He is the "precious" cornerstone of our faith (1 Pet. 2:6). A woman characterized by a "gentle and quiet spirit" is not only precious to God and a glory to her husband but also a joy to all who are around her!

HOSPITALITY
THE GIFT OF WELCOME

Hospitality is the practice of welcoming, sheltering, and feeding—with no thought of personal gain—those who come to your door. Much more than elegant menus, elaborate table settings, or lavish entertainment—hospitality is sharing what we have and who we are with whomever God sends. Hospitality includes setting aside time for fellowship and being flexible in order to accommodate impromptu gatherings.

For the people of the Bible, hospitality was not merely a matter of good manners but a necessity in the harsh desert regions. Hospitality was openly rewarded, as when Rahab was given protection at Jericho's fall for having extended hospitality to Joshua's spies (Josh. 2:12–14). Lack of hospitality was punished, as when Nabal died after refusing to offer hospitality to David's men (1 Sam. 25:2–39).

In the New Testament, Jesus modeled perfect hospitality as He moved beyond mundane physical needs to meet deeper needs of those who came to Him (Matt. 15:32–39). The New Testament writers also tell Christians to extend hospitality to other believers (Rom. 12:13; 1 Pet. 4:9; 3 John 8). Elders and deacons, in particular, were to be hospitable (1 Tim 3:2, Titus 1:8). The only time believers were exhorted not to show hospitality was in the case of false teachers, who might draw them away from the faith (2 John 10, 11). Those who received hospitality but did not work to support themselves and assist the host family were also to be expelled (2 Thess. 3:10–13).

You can share your heart and life with others, even if the meal is simple and the setting is humble. The most important gift of welcome simply says I care, I love you, and I have prepared a place for you.

Hospitality must begin at home. Believers are "through love [to] serve one another" (Gal. 5:13), "without grumbling" (1 Pet. 4:8–10), maintaining calmness and self-control (1 Pet. 3:4), working energetically and heartily (Col. 3:23), and presenting hospitality "as to the Lord" (Matt. 25:40; Col. 3:23, 24). The resources available for hospitality include time, the offering of food "in due season" (Ps. 104:27), money (see Matt. 25:34–40), energy, creativity, and love (Titus 2:4; 1 John 4:11).

Rewards accompany hospitality. Sharing with and serving others demands sacrifices, and you are promised that your sacrifices do not go unnoticed (Heb. 6:10). Anything done for Christ not only lasts but also is multiplied (see Matt. 25:14–30). Spiritual rewards are also forthcoming (Acts 20:35). For example, the men traveling to Emmaus invited a stranger to eat with them and found themselves breaking bread with Jesus Himself (Luke 24:13–32).

Just as the sunshine reveals the beauty of a stained glass window, hospitality allows the light of God's Son to shine from your heart. This love is readily and effectively transferred as you open your home to others and share Christian hospitality.

See also Matt. 23:11; 1 Tim. 5:10; Heb. 13:2; notes on Creativity (Col. 1); Flexibility (Deut. 10); Homemaking (Prov. 24); Mealtime (Ps. 104); portrait on Martha (John 11)

---

ment be *merely* outward— arranging the hair, wearing gold, or putting on *fine* apparel— ⁴rather *let it be* the hidden person of the heart, with the incorruptible *beauty* of a gentle and quiet spirit, which is very precious in the sight of God. ⁵For in this manner, in former times, the holy women who trusted in God also adorned themselves, being submissive to their own husbands, ⁶as Sarah obeyed Abraham, calling him lord, whose daughters you are if you do good and are not afraid with any terror.

A Word to Husbands

⁷Husbands, likewise, dwell with *them* with understanding, giving honor to the wife, as to the weaker vessel, and as *being* heirs together of the grace of life, that your prayers may not be hindered.

3:5, 6 Sarah is an example of a woman who trusted God and obeyed her husband. Abraham lied in identifying Sarah as his sister and not his wife (Gen. 20:1–18), and Sarah was immediately taken into the king's harem! Sarah was not trusting Abraham; he had been deceptive and more concerned with saving himself than protecting his wife. Sarah trusted God by giving Him time to work in Abraham's life and in this difficult situation. God intervened and told Abimelech in a dream that Sarah was Abraham's wife. Obviously, if Abimelech had attempted to force Sarah into a sexual liasion, she would have had to tell him the truth and say a definite "no" to intimacy. Sarah is our example because she trusted her sovereign God by giving Him time to work.

3:7 Husbands, as wives, are obliged to follow Christ's example. The first stated duty for husbands is to dwell with their wives with "understanding" (Gk. *kata gnōsin,* lit. "according to knowledge"). The considerate attitude described for husbands likely includes knowledge of God's plan for marriage as well as a personalized understanding of the needs, desires, and goals of their own respective wives. Second, husbands are to give "honor" (Gk. *timē,* lit. "precious") to their wives—respecting and esteeming them (see vv. 3, 4, note). According to Peter, wives are "weaker," possibly an allusion to the fact that a woman's physical strength is not usually equal to her husband's. Both have the dignity of being "heirs together of the grace of life." This realization is the key to mutuality in

HOSPITALITY OR ENTERTAINMENT

CHRISTIAN HOSPITALITY	WORLDLY ENTERTAINING
Provides a safe place (Prov. 31:21)	Opens a show place
Seeks to serve others (1 Pet. 4:8–10)	Wants to impress others
Puts people before things (Matt. 10:42)	Elevates things above people
Makes what is mine yours (Acts 2:44)	Claims all as mine and admires it
Takes no thought for whatever reward or compensation is in it for me (Matt. 6:1–4)	Expects something in return (praise and reciprocation)
Frames itself according to God's Word (Matt. 5:43–48)	Models itself after the world (television, magazines, neighbors, etc.)
Offers freedom that liberates, enabling you to exercise your gifts and creativity to the fullest (Rom. 8:2)	Becomes a taskmaster that enslaves, requiring you to meet the expectations of others

Called to Blessing

[8]Finally, all *of you be* of one mind, having compassion for one another; love as brothers, *be* tenderhearted, *be* courteous;[a] [9]not returning evil for evil or reviling for reviling, but on the contrary blessing, knowing that you were called to this, that you may inherit a blessing. [10]For

"He who would love life
  And see good days,
  Let him refrain his tongue from evil,
  And his lips from speaking deceit.
[11]Let him turn away from evil and do good;
  Let him seek peace and pursue it.
[12]For the eyes of the LORD are on the righteous,
  And His ears are open to their prayers;
  But the face of the LORD is against those who do evil."[a]

Suffering for Right and Wrong

[13]And who *is* he who will harm you if you become followers of what is good? [14]But even if you

should suffer for righteousness' sake, *you are* blessed. *"And do not be afraid of their threats, nor be troubled."*[a] [15]But sanctify the Lord God[a] in your hearts, and always *be* ready to *give* a defense to everyone who asks you a reason for the hope that is in you, with meekness and fear; [16]having a good conscience, that when they defame you as evildoers, those who revile your good conduct in Christ may be ashamed. [17]For *it is* better, if it is the will of God, to suffer for doing good than for doing evil.

Christ's Suffering and Ours

[18]For Christ also suffered once for sins, the just for the unjust, that He might bring us[a] to God, being put to death in the flesh but made alive by the Spirit, [19]by whom also He went and preached to the spirits in prison, [20]who formerly

3:8 [a]NU-Text reads *humble.*   3:12 [a]Psalm 34:12–16   3:14 [a]Isaiah 8:12   3:15 [a]NU-Text reads *Christ as Lord.*   3:18 [a]NU-Text and M-Text read *you.*

marriage (see also Eph. 5:21). A husband's failure to treat his wife with dignity and love would hinder his relationship not only with her but also with God.

3:9 Many relationships develop an "evil for evil" or insult for insult pattern of interaction. Peter noted that to achieve intimacy, both parties must cultivate Christ's pattern of rendering a blessing when experiencing hurt or unjust treatment (1 Pet. 2:21–24). This response is a distinctive characteristic of the Christian ethic (see Matt. 5:43–46; Rom. 12:17–21). Peter gave three reasons for this unusual response to hurt (1 Pet. 3:9–12). First, the one who gives a blessing to others will re-

ceive a blessing in return (v. 9). Second, positive responses produce an attitude of enjoyment and love for life (v. 10). Third, God hears the prayers of those who follow this pattern and turns His face against those who do not (v. 12). Seeking peace and pursuing it by disciplining one's tongue has practical rewards and is wise in all relationships (v. 11).

3:18–22 The spirits in prison could refer to evil angels, to individuals who have died, or to the people who were alive at the time of Noah (v. 19). The passage is difficult to interpret. Christ apparently preached to these "spirits" after His death and before His Resurrection, or perhaps He preached through

CROWNS · WORTHY REWARDS

Two Greek words for crown include *diadema*, referring to the crown worn by a king, and *stephanos*, referring to the crown bestowed in the athletic games or on the field of battle (v. 4). The former is conferred by birthright; the latter, by personal victory.

At the judgment seat (Gk. *bēma*) of Christ, believers will be rewarded, and one aspect of those rewards is a series of crowns (2 Cor. 5:10). These crowns include the crown of rejoicing, given as a reward for winning others to Christ (1 Thess. 2:19); the crown of righteousness awarded to those who have lived life in view of His return (2 Tim. 4:6–8); the crown of life awarded to those who have suffered persecution or martyrdom for their faith (James 1:12; Rev. 2:10); a crown of mastery awarded to those who have disciplined the body and been victorious over it (1 Cor. 9:24–27); and a crown of glory awarded to those church leaders who have faithfully cared for the sheep (1 Pet. 5:4). God richly rewards those who have persevered and lived in obedience (Matt. 5:5, 12; 19:27–30; 25:14–30; Luke 19:12–27).

See also chart on Judgments in the New Testament

God points to the peaceful attitude of suffering people to teach others about Himself.

Joni Eareckson Tada

were disobedient, when once the Divine longsuffering waited[a] in the days of Noah, while *the* ark was being prepared, in which a few, that is, eight souls, were saved through water. [21]There is also an antitype which now saves us—baptism (not the removal of the filth of the flesh, but the answer of a good conscience toward God), through the resurrection of Jesus Christ, [22]who has gone into heaven and is at the right hand of God, angels and authorities and powers having been made subject to Him.

[4]Therefore, since Christ suffered for us[a] in the flesh, arm yourselves also with the same mind, for he who has suffered in the flesh has ceased from sin, [2]that he no longer should live the rest of *his* time in the flesh for the lusts of men, but for the will of God. [3]For we *have spent* enough of our past lifetime[a] in doing the will of the Gentiles—when we walked in lewdness, lusts, drunkenness, revelries, drinking parties, and abominable idolatries. [4]In regard to these, they think it strange that you do not run with *them* in the same flood of dissipation, speaking evil of *you*. [5]They will give an account to Him who is ready to judge the living and the dead. [6]For this reason the gospel was preached also to those who are dead, that they might be judged according to men in the flesh, but live according to God in the spirit.

Serving for God's Glory

[7]But the end of all things is at hand; therefore be serious and watchful in your prayers. [8]And above all things have fervent love for one another, for *"love will cover a multitude of sins."*[a] [9]*Be* hospitable to one another without grumbling. [10]As each one has received a gift, minister it to one another, as good stewards of the manifold grace of God. [11]If anyone speaks, *let him speak* as the oracles of God. If anyone ministers, *let him do it* as with the ability which God supplies, that in all things God may be glorified through Jesus Christ, to whom belong

3:20 [a]NU-Text and M-Text read *when the longsuffering of God waited patiently.* 4:1 [a]NU-Text omits *for us.* 4:3 [a]NU-Text reads *time.* 4:8 [a]Proverbs 10:12

Noah to the antediluvians prior to the flood (v. 22). The content of Christ's message was likely a victorious proclamation of the defeat of the enemies of God. Peter mentioned this because he wanted the suffering Christians to know that one day their persecutors would face this condemning proclamation just like the evil spirits of the days of Noah.

3:21 Baptism is an "antitype" or picture of salvation, showing Christ's death, burial, and Resurrection as well as portraying the believer's death to sin and resurrection to walk in a new life.

4:6 Some presume that those who are dead have physically died without accepting Christ. They advocate praying for the dead, presuming that the dead are offered a second chance of salvation. However, Scripture says that judgment comes after death (Heb. 9:27). "Those who are dead" refers to Christians who have died. They heard and believed the gospel when they were alive; and they died, possibly due to persecution. Although these departed believers were condemned on earth, they now reign with God in heaven.

4:11 Spiritual gifts mentioned by Peter are: speaking gifts ("if anyone speaks") and serving gifts ("if anyone ministers"). To this a third category might be added, sometimes called the "sign gifts" based upon the title ascribed to them (Heb. 2:3,

SUFFERING   A PATH TO VICTORY

Suffering covers a wide range of human experiences. While not giving rise to a sense of ultimate despair, the Bible is neither idyllic nor escapist and does not give any easy answers to the question of suffering. Suffering is assured; yet, even in suffering the sovereignty of God prevails. God is able to bring meaning into even the worst situations of suffering.

People can suffer affliction from being mentally or physically tormented by others or from within. Others suffer due to hardship, circumstances, or human actions (1 Thess. 3:4; 2 Cor. 1:6). For many women there is suffering in the process of childbirth (John 16:21); for others, suffering seems to follow obedience to God, as in the ill-treatment of the Israelites (Acts 7:34), quite clearly displayed in the passion of our Lord Jesus Christ as well as in the lives of those who followed him (Acts 11:19).

The Bible speaks forcefully about these different facets of suffering that women can encounter: the emptiness of barrenness, the frustration of relationships, the uncertainty of circumstances, and the dilemma of helplessness.

See also Judg. 11:29–48; 2 Sam. 13:1–22; 2 Kin. 4:8–37; notes on Adversity (Acts 5); Pain (Job 7; 2 Cor. 12); Providence (Eccl. 7); Suffering (Ps. 33; 113; Is. 43)

---

the glory and the dominion forever and ever. Amen.

Suffering for God's Glory

¹²Beloved, do not think it strange concerning the fiery trial which is to try you, as though some strange thing happened to you; ¹³but rejoice to the extent that you partake of Christ's sufferings, that when His glory is revealed, you may also be glad with exceeding joy. ¹⁴If you are reproached for the name of Christ, blessed *are you,* for the Spirit of glory and of God rests upon you.ᵃ On their part He is blasphemed, but on your part He is glorified. ¹⁵But let none of you suffer as a murderer, a thief, an evildoer, or as a busybody in other people's matters. ¹⁶Yet if *anyone suffers* as a Christian, let him not be ashamed, but let him glorify God in this matter.ᵃ

¹⁷For the time *has come* for judgment to begin at the house of God; and if *it begins* with us first, what will *be* the end of those who do not obey the gospel of God? ¹⁸Now

"If the righteous one is scarcely saved,
*Where will the ungodly and the sinner appear?"*ᵃ

¹⁹Therefore let those who suffer according to the will of God commit their souls *to Him* in doing good, as to a faithful Creator.

Shepherd the Flock

5 The elders who are among you I exhort, I who am a fellow elder and a witness of the sufferings of Christ, and also a partaker of the glory that will be revealed: ²Shepherd the flock of God which is among you, serving as overseers, not by compulsion but willingly,ᵃ not for dishonest gain but eagerly; ³nor as being lords over those entrusted to you, but being examples to the flock; ⁴and when the Chief Shepherd appears, you will receive the crown of glory that does not fade away.

Submit to God, Resist the Devil

⁵Likewise you younger people, submit yourselves to *your* elders. Yes, all of *you* be submissive to one another, and be clothed with humility, for

---

4:14 ᵃNU-Text omits the rest of this verse.   **4:16** ᵃNU-Text reads *name.*   **4:18** ᵃProverbs 11:31   **5:2** ᵃNU-Text adds *according to God.*

---

4). Several listings of spiritual gifts are found in the NT (Rom. 12:3–8; 1 Cor. 7:7; 12:8–10, 28–30; Eph. 4:11, 12; Heb. 2:3, 4; 1 Pet. 4:10, 11; see chart, Spiritual Gifts of Women in the Bible). Of these, the sign gifts are specifically miraculous in nature and are used to confirm the validity of the apostolic ministry (see 2 Cor. 12:12). The serving gifts consist of leadership, faith, administration, helps, and celibacy. The sign gifts include miracles, healing, tongues, interpretation of tongues, the word of wisdom, and the word of knowledge. Speaking gifts include apostleship, prophecy, discernment of spirits, teaching, evangelism, and exhortation. Each believer has a spiritual gift to serve others, to edify the church, and to glorify the Lord (1 Pet. 4:10, 11; 1 Cor. 12:7).

4:17 Judgment (Gk. *krisis*) does not necessarily mean "condemnation" but rather suggests a testing or evaluation that

results in approval or disapproval. This "fiery trial" purifies, strengthens, and edifies believers, making them holy (v. 12).

5:1–3 The role of the pastor is described with three words:

- Elders (Gk. *presbuteros*) is a term that suggests the respect and esteem due a pastor by virtue of his divinely appointed office (v. 1);
- Shepherd (Gk. *poimainō*), used as a verb in the text, describes a pastor's spiritual ministries—to feed, protect, guide, and pray for the flock of God (v. 2);
- Overseers (Gk. *episkopos*) emphasizes administrative responsibilities (v. 2).

These terms are synonymous; yet each has a distinctive nuance of meaning in describing the pastoral office.

Iron till it be thoroughly heated is incapable to be wrought; so God sees good to cast some men into the furnace of affliction, and then beats them on His anvil into what frame He pleases.

Anne Bradstreet

"God resists the proud,
  But gives grace to the humble."[a]

[6]Therefore humble yourselves under the mighty hand of God, that He may exalt you in due time, [7]casting all your care upon Him, for He cares for you.

[8]Be sober, be vigilant; because[a] your adversary the devil walks about like a roaring lion, seeking whom he may devour. [9]Resist him, steadfast in the faith, knowing that the same sufferings are experienced by your brotherhood in the world. [10]But may[a] the God of all grace, who called us[b] to His eternal glory by Christ Jesus, after you have suffered a while, perfect, establish, strengthen, and

settle *you.* [11]To Him *be* the glory and the dominion forever and ever. Amen.

Farewell and Peace

[12]By Silvanus, our faithful brother as I consider him, I have written to you briefly, exhorting and testifying that this is the true grace of God in which you stand.

[13]She who is in Babylon, elect together with *you,* greets you; and *so does* Mark my son. [14]Greet one another with a kiss of love.

Peace to you all who are in Christ Jesus. Amen.

···················
5:5 [a]Proverbs 3:34   5:8 [a]NU-Text and M-Text omit *because.*   5:10 [a]NU-Text reads *But the God of all grace . . . will perfect, establish, strengthen, and settle you.* [b]NU-Text and M-Text read *you.*

5:8 The activity of Satan against believers is mentioned in various ways throughout the NT (see chart, A Portrait of the Adversary). Satan tempts believers to lie (Acts 5:3); he accuses and slanders them (Rev. 12:10); he entices them toward sexual sin (1 Cor. 7:5); he places obstacles in their path (1 Thess. 2:18); he causes persecution (Rev. 2:10); and he causes pseudo-Christians to infiltrate among true Christians to promote confusion and division in the church (Matt. 13:38,

39). The Christian's defense involves being on guard, sober, vigilant (1 Pet. 5:8), taking a stand against the devil and resisting him (v. 9; James 4:7; Eph. 6:11–18).

5:13 Babylon on the Euphrates is probably in view. However, some suggest that "Babylon" is an anachronym for Rome because of its comparable luxury and increasing decadence. Mark is likely a reference to John Mark (Acts 12:12; 13:5; 15:36–39).

2 Peter

TITLE

The letter is identified as coming from Simon Peter (2 Pet. 1:1), a claim supported by several features in the text, particularly the author's reference to being an eyewitness of Jesus' Transfiguration (2 Pet. 1:18) and his labeling of this letter as being his second to these readers (2 Pet. 3:1). However, some in the early church doubted that this letter actually came from Peter. Eusebius (A.D. 265–340) referred to the book as one of the "disputed writings." The reservation to accept it as Petrine came from the fact that it was not quoted by any of the ancient presbyters in their writings. In fact, the book was not cited by name until Origen, who wrote at the beginning of the third century. It is notable, however, that Origen quoted from it as Scripture six times.

DATE

Another reason some in the ancient church were skeptical was the frequent use of Peter's name by some writers to gain acceptance for unorthodox literature. Furthermore, the style of 1 and 2 Peter is significantly different. The Greek used in 1 Peter is polished and sophisticated, among the finest examples of linguistic style in the New Testament. Second Peter is different in style and vocabulary. Jerome, an ancient church father, suggested that the differences could be explained by the fact that Peter acknowledged Silvanus as his amanuensis or secretary in his first letter (1 Pet. 5:12). If Peter penned the second letter without Silvanus' help, that, together with a change in time and circumstances, could account for the obvious variations.

Modern critical scholars have had similar reservations about the authorship of 2 Peter. However, as further studies of the epistle have been made, the findings serve to reaffirm rather than refute Petrine authorship. In particular, though differences in style are apparent in the two letters, there are also striking similarities. Both use common Hebraisms; both exhibit verbal repetition; both employ words used nowhere else in the New Testament. Especially interesting is a study that compares word usage. First and 2 Peter score as close on word comparison studies as 1 Timothy and Titus, in which case both letters coming from the same source is not questioned. Therefore, concluding that Peter is the author of the second as well as the first letter is based on solid and sound evidence.

Second Peter was written shortly before Peter's death (2 Pet. 1:13, 14). We have no knowledge of the exact date of his death, but the early church historian Eusebius proposed that Peter was martyred during the Neronian persecutions (A.D. 64–68). Accordingly, scholars have assigned A.D. 65–66 as the most probable date.

BACKGROUND

SETTING: The setting of 2 Peter is difficult to determine. However, given that the letter was written by Peter near the end of his life, it would have originated in Rome. The recipients were probably Christians living in Asia Minor. This area was one of the main seedbeds of Gnostic thought (see John 1:4, note).

AUDIENCE: We are unable to identify who received the epistle with certainty because Peter refrained from naming his audience. In his first letter, Peter said that his readers were "the pilgrims of the Dispersion in Pontus, Galatia, Cappadocia, Asia, and Bithynia" (1 Pet. 1:1). His second epistle is not addressed to any particular group. However, in his greeting Peter said, "Beloved, I now write to you this second epistle" (2 Pet. 3:l). If 1 Peter was the first letter he wrote them, then we can conclude that the recipients of 2 Peter are the same Jewish and Gentile Christians living in Asia Minor.

PURPOSE: This letter has the tone of a last will and testament. Peter acknowledged that he was near the end of his life, and communicated the truths dearest to his heart. In this letter, Peter resolutely urged believers to make fruitful progress in their Christian faith. He also wanted them to be aware of the dangers of false doctrines and heretical teachers, who, even this early in the life of the Christian church, were distorting the gospel of Christ. Finally, he gave the believers solid teaching to help them understand and prepare for the day of the Lord, which will include both judgment and the establishing of the "new heavens and a new earth in which righteousness dwells" (2 Pet. 3:13).

THEMES

The prevalent theme of 2 Peter is the presentation of a means for discerning false doctrine and identifying heretical teachers. Secondary themes include the authority of apostolic teaching and the certainty of Christ's return.

OUTLINE

Greeting the Faithful

1 Simon Peter, a bondservant and apostle of Jesus Christ,

To those who have obtained like precious faith with us by the righteousness of our God and Savior Jesus Christ:

[2] Grace and peace be multiplied to you in the knowledge of God and of Jesus our Lord, [3] as His divine power has given to us all things that *pertain* to life and godliness, through the knowledge of Him who called us by glory and virtue, [4] by which have been given to us exceedingly great and precious promises, that through these you may be partakers of the divine nature, having escaped the corruption *that is* in the world through lust.

Fruitful Growth in the Faith

[5] But also for this very reason, giving all diligence, add to your faith virtue, to virtue knowledge, [6] to knowledge self-control, to self-control perseverance, to perseverance godliness, [7] to godliness brotherly kindness, and to brotherly kind-

---

1:4 Jesus made many glorious promises to those who believe in Him (see John 6:35; 8:12; 11:25). Believers are promised a share in His moral goodness during this life and in His glory in the afterlife. Believers can claim God's "precious promises." The phrase "partakers of the divine nature" does not suggest that people become "gods." Rather, Peter is teaching that to repent and believe is to enter into a family relationship with God in which the children are to show forth the characteristics of their heavenly Father (see Rom. 8:9; Gal. 2:20; 1 John 5:1).

PROMISES OF GOD *THE SEED OF HOPE*

The Bible is filled with the precious promises of God to His children. As many as 30,000 different promises are recorded in Scripture. These promises of God are simple and sure. Because of who God is, His Word can be trusted.

A promise is the pledge to another to fulfill a specified act. Scripture records promises by God to His children (John 14:13), by God to Jesus (John 13:3–5), by one individual to another (Neh. 5:12), and by a believer to God (Eccl. 5:4–10). Christians are invited to claim God's promises related to forgiveness, heaven, the Holy Spirit, answered prayer, guidance, comfort, and protection.

While the promises of God are afforded to all believers, they do carry a few stipulations. God's children must humble themselves, pray, seek God's will, and turn from evil in order to receive God's promises (2 Chr. 7:14). The fulfillment of God's promises is directly related to the obedient responses of God's children. There is great hope in the promises of God!

See also Lam. 3:22, note; 2 Cor. 1:20; Gal. 3:16; 2 Pet. 3:9; notes on Attributes of God (Ex. 33; Deut. 4; 32; 2 Chr. 19; Job 23; 42; Ps. 25; 90; 102; 119; Is. 6; 65; Jer. 23; Rom. 2; Eph. 1; 1 John 5); Blessings (Gen. 12); Gratitude (Ps. 95); Providence (Eccl. 7)

---

ness love. [8]For if these things are yours and abound, *you* will be neither barren nor unfruitful in the knowledge of our Lord Jesus Christ. [9]For he who lacks these things is shortsighted, even to blindness, and has forgotten that he was cleansed from his old sins.

[10]Therefore, brethren, be even more diligent to make your call and election sure, for if you do these things you will never stumble; [11]for so an entrance will be supplied to you abundantly into the everlasting kingdom of our Lord and Savior Jesus Christ.

Peter's Approaching Death

[12]For this reason I will not be negligent to remind you always of these things, though you know and are established in the present truth. [13]Yes, I think it is right, as long as I am in this tent, to stir you up by reminding *you*, [14]knowing that shortly I *must* put off my tent, just as our Lord Jesus Christ showed me. [15]Moreover I will be careful to ensure that you always have a reminder of these things after my decease.

The Trustworthy Prophetic Word

[16]For we did not follow cunningly devised fables when we made known to you the power and coming of our Lord Jesus Christ, but were eyewitnesses of His majesty. [17]For He received from God the Father honor and glory when such a voice came to Him from the Excellent Glory: "This is My beloved Son, in whom I am well pleased." [18]And we heard this voice which came from heaven when we were with Him on the holy mountain.

[19]And so we have the prophetic word confirmed,[a] which you do well to heed as a light that shines in a dark place, until the day dawns and the morning star rises in your hearts; [20]knowing this first, that no prophecy of Scripture is of any private interpretation,[a] [21]for prophecy never came by the will of man, but holy men of God[a] spoke *as they were* moved by the Holy Spirit.

Destructive Doctrines

2 But there were also false prophets among the people, even as there will be false teachers among you, who will secretly bring in destructive heresies, even denying the Lord who bought them, *and* bring on themselves swift destruction. [2]And many will follow their destructive ways, because of whom the way of truth will be

---

1:19 [a]Or *We also have the more sure prophetic word.*   1:20 [a]Or *origin*
1:21 [a]NU-Text reads *but men spoke from God.*

1:11 Peter encouraged believers to be diligent in Christian living by reminding them at their journey's end of the lavish reward—a place in the "everlasting kingdom" of Jesus. His metaphor concerning entry into the kingdom recalls the honor paid to a victor in the Olympic games of ancient Greece. The athlete's home city, because of its pride, would welcome the victor back through a newly opened gate in the city wall rather than through the usual gate. Peter referred to the tension between what believers already had and what they still lacked (v. 4). Believers are already "partakers of the divine nature," but they still must press on to enter the everlasting kingdom. This tension was meant to promote steadfastness in Christian living.

1:20, 21 In this part of Peter's letter, he is likely replying to charges made by false teachers about the reliability of the Christian message. To their suggestion that the apostles were concocting myths about Jesus, Peter countered that his is an eyewitness verification of the power and glory of Jesus (vv. 16, 17). Peter argued that the Transfiguration of Jesus was a fulfillment of OT prophecy. And lest the false teachers suggest rejecting Peter's authority by questioning its divine origin, implying that the prophets simply produced their own fantasies, Peter strongly reasserted that the OT was written by men who were moved by the Holy Spirit to speak God's words. The Holy Spirit "moved" (Gk. *pherō*, lit. "carried along") the writers of Holy Scripture to record the words of the Bible.

ADDICTIONS CONTROLLING BEHAVIORS

In contrast to some in the Corinthian church, the apostle Paul emphasized to Christians the importance of refusing to develop controlling, addictive behaviors (1 Cor. 6:12). An addiction is not simply a bad habit. It is a felt need for an external substance (drugs, alcohol, food), activity (work, shopping), unhealthy relationship (that is, with an abusive person), or certain feelings or circumstances (being in control, ecstatic feelings). An addiction is an excessive, overpowering need that is repetitive and insistent. The first phase of an addiction is usually a mental preoccupation with the feeling, substance, or act. The second phase is doing whatever is necessary to have it.

Relief or pleasure is always involved in an addiction, even though unpleasant consequences may follow. Although its power may be denied, the addiction controls the addicted woman to such an extent that reason or logic alone cannot free her. The thing to which she is addicted becomes a priority in her life and will ultimately prove destructive.

Addictions mask emotional pain by offering an escape from reality. The Lord's desire for the addicted woman is not only that she will embrace reality and face honestly herself, others, and God (Is. 59:12) but also that she might be healed of the pain driving her to seek an escape (Is. 58:6).

See also Gal. 5:19–21; Col. 3:8; 2 Tim. 3:2–5; notes on Alcoholism (Prov. 20); Codependency (Gen. 27); Eating Disorders (Lev. 26); Enabling (Mark 10); Healing (Gal. 6); Substance Abuse (Prov. 23)

---

blasphemed. ³By covetousness they will exploit you with deceptive words; for a long time their judgment has not been idle, and their destruction doesᵃ not slumber.

Doom of False Teachers

⁴For if God did not spare the angels who sinned, but cast *them* down to hell and delivered *them* into chains of darkness, to be reserved for judgment; ⁵and did not spare the ancient world, but saved Noah, *one of* eight *people,* a preacher of righteousness, bringing in the flood on the world of the ungodly; ⁶and turning the cities of Sodom and Gomorrah into ashes, condemned *them* to destruction, making *them* an example to those who afterward would live ungodly; ⁷and delivered righteous Lot, *who was* oppressed by the filthy conduct of the wicked ⁸(for that righteous man, dwelling among them, tormented *his* righteous soul from day to day by seeing and hearing *their* lawless deeds)— ⁹then the Lord knows how to deliver the godly out of temptations and to reserve the unjust under punishment for the day of judgment, ¹⁰and especially those who walk according to the flesh in the lust of uncleanness and despise authority. *They are* presumptuous, self-willed. They

are not afraid to speak evil of dignitaries, ¹¹whereas angels, who are greater in power and might, do not bring a reviling accusation against them before the Lord.

Depravity of False Teachers

¹²But these, like natural brute beasts made to be caught and destroyed, speak evil of the things they do not understand, and will utterly perish in their own corruption, ¹³and will receive the wages of unrighteousness, *as* those who count it pleasure to carouse in the daytime. *They are* spots and blemishes, carousing in their own deceptions while they feast with you, ¹⁴having eyes full of adultery and that cannot cease from sin, enticing unstable souls. They have a heart trained in covetous practices, *and are* accursed children. ¹⁵They have forsaken the right way and gone astray, following the way of Balaam the *son* of Beor, who loved the wages of unrighteousness; ¹⁶but he was rebuked for his iniquity: a dumb donkey speaking with a man's voice restrained the madness of the prophet.

2:3 ᵃM-Text reads *will not.*

2:4–6 God would judge the guilty and save the righteous. He used graphic illustrations to remind his readers of judgment God had executed in the past but assured them that the godly would be spared (v. 10). Peter alluded to a well-known apocryphal text, the Book of Enoch, which referred to God's punishment of disobedient angels (v. 4). Apparently, some rebellious angels were put into "chains of darkness" to await judgment, while others were left free to afflict mankind. God sent the sinning angels to "Tartarus," which, according to Greek mythology, is the precinct in hell reserved for the worst offenders. Peter borrowed this image from the Greek poet

Homer to make a point to his Greek readers. He took pains to show that even though there were only eight people left who lived righteous lives, God did not overlook them when He sent His judgment of the flood on an otherwise rebellious creation (v. 5; see 1 Pet. 3:19, 20). Peter referred to the well-known example of the destruction of corrupt cities in the ancient world by fire (2 Pet. 2:6). The point in all these examples was to remind readers that those who rise up against the authority of God, as the false teachers in Peter's day were doing, would experience punishment for their offenses.

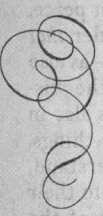

SPIRITUAL DISCIPLINE *GROWING IN CHRIST*

Spiritual discipline is essential for Christian growth and development. Though at first painful, spiritual discipline resulting from obedience and faith produces abundant blessings (Heb. 12:11). Every believer should seek to become disciplined in order to grow spiritually.

Spiritual discipline is a continual process that helps the believer mature in Christ and know God's will. It is as much an attitude of commitment as it is an activity in holiness. Specific spiritual disciplines may include personal training in Bible study, prayer, worship, fellowship, service, or witnessing, among other godly practices. A conscientious, creative pursuit of these spiritual disciplines should continue throughout a believer's life (Heb. 6:11, 12).

Spiritual discipline is essential to deliverance from the power of sin and obedience to God's will. Without spiritual discipline, believers cannot walk with Christ, grow in faith, or receive the heavenly rewards awaiting those who diligently practice spiritual discipline.

See also Dan. 2:23, note; 1 Cor. 9:27; 1 Tim. 4:12; 2 Tim. 2:15; 2 Pet. 1:10, 11; notes on Commitment (Matt. 16); Fruit of the Spirit (Ps. 86; Rom. 5; 15; 1 Cor. 10; 13; Gal. 5; Eph. 4; Col. 3; 2 Thess. 1; Rev. 2); Holiness (Lev. 20); Obedience (Philem.); Surrender (James 4)

---

[17]These are wells without water, clouds[a] carried by a tempest, for whom is reserved the blackness of darkness forever.[b]

Deceptions of False Teachers

[18]For when they speak great swelling *words* of emptiness, they allure through the lusts of the flesh, through lewdness, the ones who have actually escaped[a] from those who live in error. [19]While they promise them liberty, they themselves are slaves of corruption; for by whom a person is overcome, by him also he is brought into bondage. [20]For if, after they have escaped the pollutions of the world through the knowledge of the Lord and Savior Jesus Christ, they are again entangled in them and overcome, the latter end is worse for them than the beginning. [21]For it would have been better for them not to have known the way of righteousness, than having known *it*, to turn from the holy commandment delivered to them. [22]But it has happened to them according to the true proverb: *"A dog returns to his own vomit,"*[a] and, "a sow, having washed, to her wallowing in the mire."

God's Promise Is Not Slack

3 Beloved, I now write to you this second epistle (in *both of* which I stir up your pure minds by way of reminder), [2]that you may be mindful of the words which were spoken before by the holy prophets, and of the commandment of us,[a] the apostles of the Lord and Savior, [3]knowing this first: that scoffers will come in the last days, walking according to their own lusts, [4]and saying, "Where is the promise of His coming? For since the fathers fell asleep, all things continue as *they were* from the beginning of creation." [5]For this they willfully forget: that by the word of God the heavens were of old, and the earth standing out of water and in the water, [6]by which the world *that* then existed perished, being flooded with water. [7]But the heavens and the earth *which* are now preserved by the same word, are reserved for fire until the day of judgment and perdition of ungodly men.

....

2:17 [a]NU-Text reads *and mists.* [b]NU-Text omits *forever.* **2:18** [a]NU-Text reads *are barely escaping.* **2:22** [a]Proverbs 26:11 **3:2** [a]NU-Text and M-Text read *commandment of the apostles of your Lord and Savior* or *commandment of your apostles of the Lord and Savior.*

2:17–19 Peter described the characteristics of false teachers. First, false teachers make empty promises (v. 17). Peter described them as "wells without water" and "clouds carried by a tempest"—rain clouds that promise to end an agonizing drought but are driven away by sharp gusts of wind. False teachers raise expectations but dash them in the end. The second hallmark of false teachers is moral laxity (v. 18). These teachers maintained that spiritual salvation was all that mattered and that what Christians did with their bodies was of no consequence. Paul had to face a similar heresy in his letter to the Corinthians (1 Cor. 6:19). False teachers promise "liberty," but in reality their ways keep people in bondage to sin (2 Pet. 2:19).

2:22 To the Jews, both dogs and pigs were unclean animals (see Matt. 7:6). Dogs purge themselves of internal impurities by vomiting; washing removes external impurities from a pig. Yet both dogs and pigs, by nature, return to the source of their contamination. Peter used these metaphors to emphasize the inclination of false teachers to return to a life of immorality and pretense, even though they have a knowledge of the truth. Mere intellectual knowledge of truth cannot liberate from the bondage of sinful human nature.

3:5–7 Nature provides no assurance that things will continue as they always have. God Himself is in charge of nature. God would judge ungodliness and destroy the present heavens and earth through fire (v. 7; see Deut. 32:22; Is. 30:30; Mal. 4:1; 2 Thess. 1:8; Heb. 12:9; 1 Pet. 1:7).

[8]But, beloved, do not forget this one thing, that with the Lord one day *is* as a thousand years, and a thousand years as one day. [9]The Lord is not slack concerning *His* promise, as some count slackness, but is longsuffering toward us,[a] not willing that any should perish but that all should come to repentance.

The Day of the Lord

[10]But the day of the Lord will come as a thief in the night, in which the heavens will pass away with a great noise, and the elements will melt with fervent heat; both the earth and the works that are in it will be burned up.[a] [11]Therefore, since all these things will be dissolved, what manner *of persons* ought you to be in holy conduct and godliness, [12]looking for and hastening the coming of the day of God, because of which the heavens will be dissolved, being on fire, and the elements will melt with fervent heat? [13]Nevertheless we, according to His promise, look for new heavens and a new earth in which righteousness dwells.

Be Steadfast

[14]Therefore, beloved, looking forward to these things, be diligent to be found by Him in peace, without spot and blameless; [15]and consider *that* the longsuffering of our Lord *is* salvation—as also our beloved brother Paul, according to the wisdom given to him, has written to you, [16]as also in all his epistles, speaking in them of these things, in which are some things hard to understand, which untaught and unstable *people* twist to their own destruction, as *they do* also the rest of the Scriptures.

[17]You therefore, beloved, since you know *this* beforehand, beware lest you also fall from your own steadfastness, being led away with the error of the wicked; [18]but grow in the grace and knowledge of our Lord and Savior Jesus Christ.

To Him *be* the glory both now and forever. Amen.

··················

3:9 [a]NU-Text reads *you.*   **3:10** [a]NU-Text reads *laid bare* (literally *found*).

3:8, 9 Scoffers were questioning the certainty of God's judgment (v. 4). God sees time in a way not possible for us: A long time to us may be short in God's eternal perspective, and a day that might seem inconsequential to us could be like a thousand years to the Lord. Peter's first line of defense against the scoffers was to teach the Christians to regard time in a different way. His second was to assure them that the delay in the fulfillment of the Lord's promise was not due to His indifference or impotence but rather because of His mercy. God wants to save as many people as will respond to His call (see Ezek. 18:23; Rom. 11:32; 1 Tim. 2:4).

3:13 The final Day of Judgment will not result in annihilation of the present order but rather a complete renewal of that order. What will be annihilated is sin; thus the new creation will be the dwelling place of righteousness, a truly blissful home

for the children of God. This promise gives the Christian hope and encouragement to remain steadfast in righteousness until the day of the Lord.

3:16 Peter feared that the false teachers might take advantage of ignorant, unstable people by distorting the teachings of Paul so that God's truth was turned into a lie. For example, some teachers reasoned that since Paul taught justification by faith, Christians could do whatever they liked. They argued that the more an individual sinned, the more God had the opportunity to demonstrate His grace (see Rom. 3:5–8; 6:1). This interpretation was clearly a distortion of Paul's intent. Peter understood Paul's writings to speak the word of the Lord just as did the prophets of old (see 1 Thess. 2:13). Distorting the words of the apostles led not simply to error, but to destruction.

1 John

Although the writer did not identify himself, early church fathers, such as Clement of Alexandria, Origen, and Tertullian, named John as the author. Irenaeus (A.D. 130–200), who heard the eyewitness of Polycarp, bishop of Smyrna and a disciple of John the apostle, also specified that the epistle was penned by John, the Lord's disciple. Thus, there is strong evidence that John, the son of Zebedee and the apostle of Jesus, composed this letter.

The three letters of John were probably written from Ephesus to the churches in the surrounding area of Asia Minor (modern Turkey). Tradition assigns the writing of these letters to the latter years of John's life, dating them between A.D. 80 and 95. The exact date, however, is not certain.

SETTING: The recipients of the letter had been exposed to the heretical teachings of a group of people who had left their church (1 John 2:19). This group believed that spiritual things were good and physical things were evil. For them, the divine Christ, the Son of God, was not the same human Jesus who came to suffer and die for the sins of the world. They claimed to have a direct knowledge of God and to be morally perfect. However, their sinful behavior, lack of love, and prideful claims betrayed their heretical belief (see John 1:4, note; 1 Cor. 1, Heresies).

PURPOSE: John wrote to strengthen the faith of the believers (1 John 1:4). He encouraged them to hold to the apostolic teaching and to express that gospel through love and righteous living (1 John 2:1, 26). As a remedy against the onslaught of heretical views, he also assured believers of forgiveness, victory, and eternal life through Jesus Christ (1 John 5:13).

AUDIENCE: Historically, the heresy closest in character to that described in the epistle was the Gnostic heresy taught in Asia Minor by Cerinthus. Therefore, it is probable that the letter was addressed to the churches in Asia Minor.

LITERARY CHARACTERISTICS: The literary character of the epistle evades classification. In its greeting and conclusion, it lacks the features typical of a first-century letter. Nevertheless, the author is apparently addressing a specific situation with which he is familiar. First John could be a circular letter containing a written sermon or address.

• A true claim of the knowledge of God entails the acknowledgment that Jesus is both fully divine and fully human.

- Right belief goes hand-in-hand with right conduct; love and righteous living cannot be separated from right belief.
- Right faith produces confidence in forgiveness, in prayer, in victory against the Evil One, and in the possession of eternal life.

What Was Heard, Seen, and Touched

1 That which was from the beginning, which we have heard, which we have seen with our eyes, which we have looked upon, and our hands have handled, concerning the Word of life— ²the life was manifested, and we have seen, and bear witness, and declare to you that eternal life which was with the Father and was manifested to us— ³that which we have seen and heard we declare to you, that you also may have fellowship with us; and truly our fellowship *is* with the Father and with His Son Jesus Christ. ⁴And these things we write to you that your[a] joy may be full.

Fellowship with Him and One Another

⁵This is the message which we have heard from Him and declare to you, that God is light and in Him is no darkness at all. ⁶If we say that we have fellowship with Him, and walk in darkness, we lie and do not practice the truth. ⁷But if we walk in

1:4 [a]NU-Text and M-Text read *our.*

1:3, 4 Fellowship (Gk. *koinōnia*, lit. "common," "communion," "partnership") expresses the most intimate kind of relationship. Joy would increase as believers became more intimate in their fellowship with God (John 3:29; 15:11; 16:24; 17:13; 2 John 12). Fullness of joy on earth would point toward perfect joy in heaven when fellowship with God would be consummated (1 Cor. 13:12).

1:6–10 John exposed and contradicted three false claims of heretical teachers. They claimed to have partnership with God (v. 6), but they practiced and promoted immorality. They denied that they possessed a sinful nature (v. 8), but everyone sins and needs to be cleansed from unrighteousness (v. 9). They denied that their conduct was displeasing to God (v. 10), thus accusing God of lying (v. 6).

WHAT IS OF GOD AND WHAT IS NOT OF GOD

WHAT IS OF GOD	WHAT IS NOT OF GOD
Light (1 John 1:5, 7; 2:9, 10)	Darkness (1 John 1:5, 6; 2:9, 11)
Truth (1 John 1:6; 2:4)	Lies (1 John 1:6; 2:4)
Life and eternal life (1 John 1:2; 3:14)	Death (1 John 3:14)
Love (1 John 2:10; 3:11)	Hate and fear (1 John 2:11; 4:18)
Love with action (1 John 3:18)	Lack of compassion (1 John 3:17)
That which remains forever (1 John 2:17)	That which is temporal (1 John 2:17)
Having no sin (1 John 3:5, 6)	Sin (1 John 3:4)
Righteousness (1 John 2:29; 3:7, 12)	Evil acts (1 John 3:8, 12)
Acknowledgment of the humanity of Christ (1 John 4:2)	Denial of the humanity of Christ (1 John 4:3)
Acknowledgment of the divinity of Jesus (1 John 4:15)	Denial of the divinity of Jesus (1 John 2:22)
The Spirit of God (1 John 4:2)	The spirit of the Antichrist (1 John 4:3)
The Spirit of Truth (1 John 4:6)	The spirit of falsehood (1 John 4:6)
Faith (1 John 5:4, 10)	Unbelief (1 John 5:10)

the light as He is in the light, we have fellowship with one another, and the blood of Jesus Christ His Son cleanses us from all sin.

⁸If we say that we have no sin, we deceive ourselves, and the truth is not in us. ⁹If we confess our sins, He is faithful and just to forgive us *our* sins and to cleanse us from all unrighteousness. ¹⁰If we say that we have not sinned, we make Him a liar, and His word is not in us.

2My little children, these things I write to you, so that you may not sin. And if anyone sins, we have an Advocate with the Father, Jesus Christ the righteous. ²And He Himself is the propitiation for our sins, and not for ours only but also for the whole world.

The Test of Knowing Him

³Now by this we know that we know Him, if we keep His commandments. ⁴He who says, "I know Him," and does not keep His commandments, is a liar, and the truth is not in him. ⁵But whoever keeps His word, truly the love of God is perfected in him. By this we know that we are in Him. ⁶He

1:7 The symbolism of light is used metaphorically. Intellectually, light is truth, and darkness is ignorance or error. Morally, light is purity; darkness, impurity. Light also symbolizes righteousness and holiness; light is the agent that reveals and guides in truth (Ps. 119:105). Right living—and not merely right thinking—is the hallmark of the person who has "fellowship" with God (1 John 1:6).

2:1, 2 Advocate (Gk. *paraklētos,* lit. "one called alongside") is a courtroom term for a person who defends and pleads the cause of someone on trial. Used in this context, Jesus is the one who intercedes before God on behalf of the sinner. This same

word is used elsewhere in the NT to describe the work of the Holy Spirit. Jesus is also the "propitiation" (Gk. *hilasmos,* v. 2), which suggests appeasement and satisfaction. In the OT, this word presents the idea of placating the anger or judgment of an injured party. A cognate form designates the mercy seat (Heb. 9:5). Jesus' blood covers the sinner, who then stands in favor with God (1 John 1:7). Jesus does not ask God to declare sinners innocent, but rather He asks the Father to grant them pardon because of what He did on their behalf.

2:3–6 John recorded two tests of true Christianity, introduced by the formula "by this we know." The first test is moral

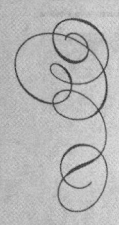

CONFESSION AGREEING WITH GOD

Confession is a significant element in the worship of God in both Old and New Testaments. Declaration and acknowledgment are a part of the believer's confession of faith. Scripture convicts the individual to acknowledge sin and receive forgiveness (Ps. 32:5; Prov. 28:13; 1 John 1:9). James admonished believers to confess sin to others and restore fellowship (James 5:16). Jesus offered confession of faith and commitment to God (Matt. 10:32, 33; Luke 12:8). Confession is a necessary part of reconciliation and restoration; its opposite is denial of wrongdoing, which leads to alienation within a relationship.

The word confession is a combination of two Greek words, *homos*, meaning "same," and *legō* meaning "to say." In its truest form, confession is "to say the same" or "to agree." Believers are called to say the same thing about sin God says—to see sin as God sees it. A theological understanding of confession includes both an acknowledgment of specific sins and a recognition that sin needs to be forgiven.

When the believer confesses personal sin and professes faith in Christ, then God will faithfully and justly forgive sin and cleanse unrighteousness (1 John 1:9). Confession is essential to the believer's relationship with God and to a fellowship with other people.

See also Luke 24:47, note; Rom. 3:23, note; 10:9, 10; notes on Forgiveness (Ps. 51; Luke 17); Salvation (Eph. 2)

who says he abides in Him ought himself also to walk just as He walked.

7Brethren,[a] I write no new commandment to you, but an old commandment which you have had from the beginning. The old commandment is the word which you heard from the beginning.[b] 8Again, a new commandment I write to you, which thing is true in Him and in you, because the darkness is passing away, and the true light is already shining. 9He who says he is in the light, and hates his brother, is in darkness until now. 10He who loves his brother abides in the light, and there is no cause for stumbling in him. 11But he who hates his brother is in darkness and walks in darkness, and does not know where he is going, because the darkness has blinded his eyes.

Their Spiritual State

12I write to you, little children,
Because your sins are forgiven you for His name's sake.
13I write to you, fathers,
Because you have known Him *who is* from the beginning.

I write to you, young men,
Because you have overcome the wicked one.
I write to you, little children,
Because you have known the Father.
14I have written to you, fathers,
Because you have known Him *who is* from the beginning.
I have written to you, young men,
Because you are strong, and the word of God abides in you,
And you have overcome the wicked one.

Do Not Love the World

15Do not love the world or the things in the world. If anyone loves the world, the love of the Father is not in him. 16For all that *is* in the world—the lust of the flesh, the lust of the eyes, and the pride of life—is not of the Father but is of the world. 17And the world is passing away, and the lust of it; but he who does the will of God abides forever.

·················

2:7 [a]NU-Text reads *Beloved*. [b]NU-Text omits *from the beginning*.

obedience (v. 3). Only those who obey God can rightly claim to know Him. The second test is love for others. If believers are keeping God's Word, the love of God is being "perfected" in their lives (v. 5). The knowledge of God or Christ is not a mystical experience, an intellectual grasp, or a vision of the divine. It is obedience to God's command to believe in Jesus as the Son of God and to love God and others (v. 5; 1 John 3:23; 4:7, 8, 11).

2:5 **Genuine Christians** are "in Him," meaning that they literally "live in God." It is synonymous with abiding in Him (v. 6), knowing Him (v. 3), loving Him (v. 5; 1 John 3:24), and obeying Him. Elsewhere, John referred to Christians abiding in Jesus (John 15:4–10) and Jesus abiding in them (John 14:20–23; 17:21, 23, 26; 1 John 4:4), describing the close fellowship between believers and God. The test of this fellowship is again expressed in terms of practical living (1 John 2:6).

2:16 **John explained why love for the world is incompatible with love for God** by listing three typical features of worldly desires: "the lust of the flesh"—sensuality or unbridled desire for food, drink, or sexual gratification; "the lust of the eyes"—superficiality and materialism, depicting the greed that is aroused by what one sees; "the pride of life" or arrogance. The word for "life" denotes possessions—the things that support life. "Pride" refers to boasting. Certainly, the flesh, the eyes, and possessions are given by God and are not evil in themselves. However, John's point is that everything is tainted by sin and that sin has twisted natural human desires to stand in opposition to true knowledge of God (see Gen. 3:6; Matt. 4:1–11).

TRUE KNOWLEDGE OF GOD

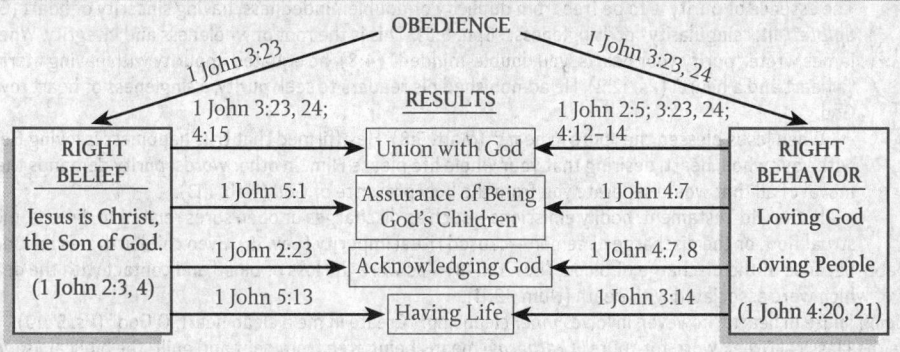

OBEDIENCE

1 John 3:23

1 John 3:23, 24

RESULTS

RIGHT BELIEF		RIGHT BEHAVIOR

1 John 3:23, 24; 4:15 → Union with God ← 1 John 2:5; 3:23, 24; 4:12–14

RIGHT BELIEF

Jesus is Christ, the Son of God.

(1 John 2:3, 4)

1 John 5:1 → Assurance of Being God's Children ← 1 John 4:7

1 John 2:23 → Acknowledging God ← 1 John 4:7, 8

1 John 5:13 → Having Life ← 1 John 3:14

RIGHT BEHAVIOR

Loving God

Loving People

(1 John 4:20, 21)

Deeper love . . . down to our very soul.
It's there we have an anchor who will not let us go;
The Lord who calmed the sea is the One who sees us through;
He's given us . . . a deeper love.

Diane Machen

Deceptions of the Last Hour

18Little children, it is the last hour; and as you have heard that thea Antichrist is coming, even now many antichrists have come, by which we know that it is the last hour. 19They went out from us, but they were not of us; for if they had been of us, they would have continued with us; but *they went out* that they might be made manifest, that none of them were of us.

20But you have an anointing from the Holy One, and you know all things.a 21I have not written to you because you do not know the truth, but because you know it, and that no lie is of the truth.

22Who is a liar but he who denies that Jesus is the Christ? He is antichrist who denies the Father and the Son. 23Whoever denies the Son does not have the Father either; he who acknowledges the Son has the Father also.

Let Truth Abide in You

24Therefore let that abide in you which you heard from the beginning. If what you heard from the beginning abides in you, you also will abide in

the Son and in the Father. 25And this is the promise that He has promised us— eternal life.

26These things I have written to you concerning those who *try to* deceive you. 27But the anointing which you have received from Him abides in you, and you do not need that anyone teach you; but as the same anointing teaches you concerning all things, and is true, and is not a lie, and just as it has taught you, you willa abide in Him.

The Children of God

28And now, little children, abide in Him, that whena He appears, we may have confidence and not be ashamed before Him at His coming. 29If you know that He is righteous, you know that everyone who practices righteousness is born of Him.

3 Behold what manner of love the Father has bestowed on us, that we should be called

············

2:18 aNU-Text omits *the.*   **2:20** aNU-Text reads *you all know.*   **2:27** aNU-Text reads *you abide.*   **2:28** aNU-Text reads *if.*

2:18, 22 Believers are living in the last hour, the last days before Christ's return and the final judgment. These last days will be characterized by an influx of "antichrists," the false prophets who teach that Jesus is not the Christ, the Son of God (v. 22), who have no relationship with the Father (v. 23), who are liars (v. 22) and deceivers (2 John 7; see 2 Thess. 2:3, note).

2:27 Anointing (Gk. *chrisma*) refers to the role of the indwelling Holy Spirit in teaching God's Word to the believer (v. 20). John was not arguing against careful Bible exposition and the ministry of teaching; he was merely emphasizing the Holy Spirit's role in confirming truth to the believer's heart. Both the Word and the Spirit are necessary to safeguard against doctrinal error (1 John 1:10).

PURITY SINCERITY OF HEART

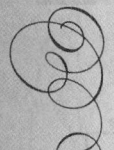

The essence of purity is to be free from duplicity or doublemindedness, having sincerity of heart (Gk. *aploteti*, lit. "singularity" or "singleness," Eph. 6:5). This is the root of wholeness and integrity. When James wrote "purify your hearts, you double-minded" (4:8), he equated impurity with having literally "a heart and a heart" (Ps. 12:2). He admonished his readers to seek purity, a singleness of heart toward God.

When Jesus blessed the "pure in heart" (Matt. 5:8), He affirmed that true happiness is loving God with your whole heart, desiring that your whole life please Him. In other words, purity demands the removal of all that would separate you from the holy presence of God (Hab. 1:13).

In the Old Testament, bodily emissions—such as discharges or open sores related to disease, menstrual flow, or the discharge of semen—caused ritual impurity (Lev. 15). Even childbirth was included—probably because of the discharge of blood, (Lev. 12:1–8)—as were the loss of blood and contact with the dead, both of which were associated with death (Num. 19:11).

Being "pure in heart," however, involves *inner* cleansing: "Create in me a clean heart, O God" (Ps. 51:10). While the classical Greek word for "pure" (*katharos*) means being free from debt and guilt, the biblical usage includes more than forgiveness. To be pure means to be single-minded—free from the civil war of a divided self. It is being free from falsehood, hypocrisy, or pretense. The woman who is rightly related to Jesus Christ will be pure in heart and life (2 Tim. 2:21, 22).

Everyone who has the hope of seeing God "purifies himself, just as He is pure" (1 John 3:3). Such a person begins and maintains a love relationship with God based on integrity and singularity of purpose. A pure life cannot exist without a pure heart set upon the Lord.

See also Ezek. 36:25; John 17:17–23; 1 John 1:9; notes on Attributes of God (Is. 6); Holiness (Lev. 20); Integrity (Ps. 27); Self-centeredness (James 3); Sexual Purity (1 Cor. 7)

---

children of God!^a Therefore the world does not know us,^b because it did not know Him. ²Beloved, now we are children of God; and it has not yet been revealed what we shall be, but we know that when He is revealed, we shall be like Him, for we shall see Him as He is. ³And everyone who has this hope in Him purifies himself, just as He is pure.

Sin and the Child of God

⁴Whoever commits sin also commits lawlessness, and sin is lawlessness. ⁵And you know that He was manifested to take away our sins, and in Him there is no sin. ⁶Whoever abides in Him does not sin. Whoever sins has neither seen Him nor known Him.

⁷Little children, let no one deceive you. He who practices righteousness is righteous, just as He is righteous. ⁸He who sins is of the devil, for the devil has sinned from the beginning. For this purpose the Son of God was manifested, that He might destroy the works of the devil. ⁹Whoever has been born of God does not sin, for His seed remains in him; and he cannot sin, because he has been born of God.

The Imperative of Love

¹⁰In this the children of God and the children of the devil are manifest: Whoever does not practice righteousness is not of God, nor *is* he who does not love his brother. ¹¹For this is the message that you heard from the beginning, that we should love one another, ¹²not as Cain *who* was of the wicked one and murdered his brother. And why did he murder him? Because his works were evil and his brother's righteous.

¹³Do not marvel, my brethren, if the world hates you. ¹⁴We know that we have passed from

•••••••••••••••••••••••••••

3:1 ^aNU-Text adds *And we are.* ^bM-Text reads *you.*

3:6–9 Some false teachers believed that knowledge had made them perfect and sinless. Others maintained that sin did not matter because it did not affect their spiritual souls. John earlier refuted the former error (1 John 1:8, 10). He argued that everyone (including the Christian) sins and that God graciously extends forgiveness to those who sin. In this section, John refuted the latter error (1 John 3:6, 9). Both statements use expressions that indicate a settled character, habitual practice, an engrained propensity toward sin. Therefore, John is not denying the possibility of sin in the Christian; he is merely arguing that habitual sinning is incompatible with the

Christian life. It is the *incongruity* rather than the *impossibility* of sin in the Christian that John had in mind.

3:9 Habitual sin is not consistent with the Christian life because the Christian has been "born of God" and implanted with the seed of God, which may refer to the Word of God, the Holy Spirit, the divine nature, or some combination of these three. Everyone born of God has received the abiding influence of the seed of God and is constantly compelled to become more and more like Jesus. Believers cannot *continue* to live in sin (see 2 Cor. 5:17; 2 Pet. 1:4).

3:14 God's essential nature is love (1 John 4:7, 8, 19), and love

LOVE — *MORE THAN A GOOD FEELING*

Throughout Scripture we are assured of God's love and reminded that the proof of God's boundless love is that Christ died for us (Rom. 5:8; 1 John 4:9, 10). But love is not simply meant to make us feel good—rather to motivate us to respond in ways that make us emulate His goodness. Love sometimes demands that we act in very practical and even uncomfortable ways.

- Love is not optional (1 John 3:11, 23; 4:11). We are commanded to love one another.
- Love is demonstrative (1 John 3:14; 4:7, 20). Our love for God is shown to the degree we show love to others.
- Love is active, an act of the will (1 John 3:17). We are commanded to do the acts of love. If we shut our eyes to the needs of others, our love for God is called into question.
- Love is responsive (1 John 4:19). We are able to love because we have been and are loved by God. This love causes us to respond lovingly to others (1 John 4:21).

See also Rom. 5:8; 1 Cor. 13:13; notes on Attributes of God (1 John 5); Fruit of the Spirit (1 Cor. 13); Marriage (Gen. 2; 2 Sam. 6; Prov. 5; Hos. 2; Amos 3; 2 Cor. 13; Heb. 12); Romance (Song 2)

---

death to life, because we love the brethren. He who does not love *his* brother[a] abides in death. 15Whoever hates his brother is a murderer, and you know that no murderer has eternal life abiding in him.

The Outworking of Love

16By this we know love, because He laid down His life for us. And we also ought to lay down *our* lives for the brethren. 17But whoever has this world's goods, and sees his brother in need, and shuts up his heart from him, how does the love of God abide in him?

18My little children, let us not love in word or in tongue, but in deed and in truth. 19And by this we know[a] that we are of the truth, and shall assure our hearts before Him. 20For if our heart condemns us, God is greater than our heart, and knows all things. 21Beloved, if our heart does not condemn us, we have confidence toward God. 22And whatever we ask we receive from Him, because we keep His commandments and do those things that are pleasing in His sight. 23And this is His commandment: that we should believe on the name of His Son Jesus Christ and love one another, as He gave us[a] commandment.

The Spirit of Truth and the Spirit of Error

24Now he who keeps His commandments abides in Him, and He in him. And by this we know that He abides in us, by the Spirit whom He has given us.

4 Beloved, do not believe every spirit, but test the spirits, whether they are of God; because many false prophets have gone out into the world. 2By this you know the Spirit of God: Every spirit that confesses that Jesus Christ has come in the flesh is of God, 3and every spirit that does not confess that[a] Jesus Christ has come in the flesh is not of God. And this is the *spirit* of the Antichrist, which you have heard was coming, and is now already in the world.

4You are of God, little children, and have overcome them, because He who is in you is greater than he who is in the world. 5They are of the world. Therefore they speak *as* of the world, and the world hears them. 6We are of God. He who knows God hears us; he who is not of God does not hear us. By this we know the spirit of truth and the spirit of error.

3:14 [a]NU-Text omits *his brother.* 3:19 [a]NU-Text reads *we shall know.* 3:23 [a]M-Text omits *us.* 4:3 [a]NU-Text omits *that* and *Christ has come in the flesh.*

---

is His will for His people (1 John 2:7–11; 3:11). True children of God not only renounce sin but also demonstrate their new birth by taking on the very nature of God (see 1 John 4, Attributes of God). Love is the pre-eminent Christian virtue (1 Cor. 13:2; see Love; chart, What Is Love?) It is the firstfruit of the Spirit (Gal. 5:22; see 1 Cor. 13, Love), and the test of true faith (Gal. 5:6; 1 John 3:19). Love is the most striking evidence of whether or not someone is "in" Christ (1 John 2:5). The love we have for others provides the assurance that we have moved from the way of darkness and death to the way of light and life (1 John 2:9, 11).

4:1 John warned his readers not to be naive in their acceptance of doctrinal teachings. He explained that all such teachings must be tested to determine whether they are of divine or evil origin. The surest test of their being inspired by God is christological, that they acknowledge and accept both the human and divine nature of Jesus (vv. 2, 3). This acceptance goes beyond a recognition of Christ's identity. Even evil spirits recognized the deity of Jesus during His ministry (Mark 1:24; 3:11; 5:7, 8). John was saying that the Spirit of God can be discerned because that Spirit always honors the Son of God (John 15:26; 1 Cor. 12:3). To confess Jesus involves a recognition of His true identity, an open proclamation of faith in Him, and the practical dimension of obedience to His Word (1 John 5:2).

ALL ABOUT LOVE

QUESTION	ANSWER	REFERENCE
The source of love	God	1 John 4:7–10, 16
The model of love	Christ	1 John 3:16
The manifestation of love by believers	Love for others	1 John 4:21
The extent of love	Sacrifice of life	1 John 3:16
The results of love	Abiding presence of God and life	1 John 4:12, 16; 1 John 3:14

*Lord, You are the beginning, the end, and the very essence of love in me.
Open my eyes to see as You see and love others through me.*

Sandy Smith

Knowing God Through Love

⁷Beloved, let us love one another, for love is of God; and everyone who loves is born of God and knows God. ⁸He who does not love does not know God, for God is love. ⁹In this the love of God was manifested toward us, that God has sent His only begotten Son into the world, that we might live through Him. ¹⁰In this is love, not that we loved God, but that He loved us and sent His Son *to be* the propitiation for our sins. ¹¹Beloved, if God so loved us, we also ought to love one another.

Seeing God Through Love

¹²No one has seen God at any time. If we love one another, God abides in us, and His love has been perfected in us. ¹³By this we know that we abide in Him, and He in us, because He has given us of His Spirit. ¹⁴And we have seen and testify that the Father has sent the Son *as* Savior of the world. ¹⁵Whoever confesses that Jesus is the Son of God, God abides in him, and he in God. ¹⁶And we have known and believed the love that God has for us. God is love, and he who abides in love abides in God, and God in him.

The Consummation of Love

¹⁷Love has been perfected among us in this: that we may have boldness in the day of judgment; because as He is, so are we in this world. ¹⁸There is no fear in love; but perfect love casts out fear, because fear involves torment. But he who fears has not been made perfect in love. ¹⁹We love Himᵃ because He first loved us.

Obedience by Faith

²⁰If someone says, "I love God," and hates his brother, he is a liar; for he who does not love his brother whom he has seen, how canᵃ he love God whom he has not seen? ²¹And this commandment we have from Him: that he who loves God *must* love his brother also.

5 Whoever believes that Jesus is the Christ is born of God, and everyone who loves Him who begot also loves him who is begotten of Him. ²By this we know that we love the children of God, when we love God and keep His commandments. ³For this is the love of God, that we keep His commandments. And His commandments are not burdensome. ⁴For whatever is born of God overcomes the world. And this is the victory that has overcome the world— ourᵃ faith. ⁵Who is he who overcomes the world, but he who believes that Jesus is the Son of God?

4:19 ᵃNU-Text omits *Him.* 4:20 ᵃNU-Text reads *he cannot.* 5:4 ᵃM-Text reads *your.*

4:18 Fear (Gk. *phobeomai*) means "to be frightened," "alarmed," or "terrified." John pointed out that people fear because they anticipate pain, torture, or punishment. Yet he argued that the person who stands in a relationship of love with God need not be afraid of God. If a person is afraid of God, she does not yet have a mature relationship with Him. As love for God increases, fear is "cast out." The phrase is emphatic: Fear is "driven away." John concluded his thought with a profound statement regarding the believer's relationship to God: "We love Him because He first loved us" (v. 19). God's love is primary; our love is merely a response to His eternal love for us.

ATTRIBUTES OF GOD *HE IS LOVE*

Love is not a definition of God—God is infinitely more—but God is the definition of love. Without Him, love does not exist (John 3:16; 1 John 4:8–10). Biblical love (Gk. *agape*) is active, yet selfless. Though most graphically and fully illustrated in God's love for us, *agape* love is also God's pattern for our love for Him (1 John 4:19) and for our love for one another (Eph. 5:25; 1 Pet. 1:22). Its basis is God's deliberate, active, sacrificial giving of His Son for our redemption. To be loved by God means that He has set His sights on us and is actively wooing us toward Himself at all times.

God's love is self-starting (1 John 4:10), indestructible (Rom. 8:38, 39), undeserved (Rom. 3:23), compassionate (Is. 49:15), constant (Jer. 31:3), immeasurable (Eph. 3:18, 19), voluntary (Rom. 5:8), and a gift (John 3:16). He did not begin loving at the Cross, nor will He love us more tomorrow than He does today. There is nothing we can do, think, or say that will change His love because there are no surprises for God—He knows us totally and loves us anyway (Ps. 139:1–5).

The goal of God's love is to have us with Him throughout eternity (1 John 4:16). He presented and made possible the accomplishment of this goal through Jesus and His sacrifice on the Cross (John 1:14–18).

See also Lam. 3:22, note; Eph. 2:4; notes on Attributes of God (Ex. 33; Deut. 4; 32; 2 Chr. 19; Job 23; 42; Ps. 25; 90; 102; 119; Is. 6; 65; Jer. 23; Rom. 2; Eph. 1); Forgiveness (Ps. 51; Luke 17); Fruit of the Spirit (1 Cor. 13); Promises of God (2 Pet. 1); Salvation (Eph. 2)

The Certainty of God's Witness

⁶This is He who came by water and blood—Jesus Christ; not only by water, but by water and blood. And it is the Spirit who bears witness, because the Spirit is truth. ⁷For there are three that bear witness in heaven: the Father, the Word, and the Holy Spirit; and these three are one. ⁸And there are three that bear witness on earth:ᵃ the Spirit, the water, and the blood; and these three agree as one.

⁹If we receive the witness of men, the witness of God is greater; for this is the witness of God whichᵃ He has testified of His Son. ¹⁰He who believes in the Son of God has the witness in himself; he who does not believe God has made Him a liar, because he has not believed the testimony that God has given of His Son. ¹¹And this is the testimony: that God has given us eternal life, and this life is in His Son. ¹²He who has the Son has life; he who does not have the Son of God does not have life. ¹³These things I have written to you who

believe in the name of the Son of God, that you may know that you have eternal life,ᵃ and that you may *continue to* believe in the name of the Son of God.

Confidence and Compassion in Prayer

¹⁴Now this is the confidence that we have in Him, that if we ask anything according to His will, He hears us. ¹⁵And if we know that He hears us, whatever we ask, we know that we have the petitions that we have asked of Him.

¹⁶If anyone sees his brother sinning a sin *which does not lead* to death, he will ask, and He will give him life for those who commit sin not *leading* to death. There is sin *leading* to death. I do not say that he should pray about that. ¹⁷All unrighteousness is sin, and there is sin not *leading* to death.

• • • • • • • • • • • • • • • • •

5:8 ᵃNU-Text and M-Text omit the words from *in heaven* (verse 7) through *on earth* (verse 8). Only four or five very late manuscripts contain these words in Greek.   **5:9** ᵃNU-Text reads *God, that.*   **5:13** ᵃNU-Text omits the rest of this verse.

5:6–8 Some heretics suggested that the Spirit of God came upon Jesus at the time of His baptism but left Him just before His Crucifixion. Therefore, they maintained that Jesus was not really God when He died. John insisted that Jesus possessed the Holy Spirit throughout His entire earthly life. His divinity was verified by a number of witnesses. On the earth, water, blood, and the Spirit bear testimony. "Water" likely refers to the baptism of Jesus; whereas "blood" refers to His Crucifixion. The Holy Spirit verified the deity of Christ because He foretold Christ's coming, (1 Pet. 1:10–12), revealed His identity to John the Baptist (John 1:32–34; see Mark 1:11) and to the apostles (1 John 1:2; see Matt. 16:17), and indwells those who believe in Him (1 John 5:10). John argued that Jesus was truly God—before His birth, at birth, during His death, when He rose again, and throughout eternity.

5:13 The recipients of John's letter had been unsettled by false

teachers and were unsure of their spiritual status. Throughout this letter, John gave them doctrinal, moral, and social tests by which to examine themselves and others. His ultimate aim, as expressed in this verse, is that they might "know" that they have eternal life and that they might "continue" to believe in Jesus. The word "know" indicates a present certainty and assurance. John affirmed that believers can be certain of a number of things. They can know with certainty that the Son of God has come and has given them an understanding. They can know Him who is true and be in Him who is true. Finally, they can be assured that they have fellowship with the true God and that they possess eternal life (1 John 3:20).

5:16, 17 The sin leading to death has been explained in numerous ways. Some suggest that the reference is to sin resulting in physical death. Others explain spiritual death as that which

PRAYER   GOD-AUTHORIZED PURPOSES

Prayer is the opportunity God gives His children to become intimately acquainted with Him. As a conversation with God, prayer enables the believer to build a personal relationship with the Lord. Prayer is an expression of a believer's dependence on God and, at the same time, an affirmation of God's promise to the redeemed for spiritual power.

The primary purpose of prayer is to seek God's will (1 John 5:14). Jesus in His model prayer told His disciples to ask according to the will of God (Matt. 6:10). When a believer talks to the Father, each request for help and every desire for guidance should be asked in the name of Jesus. All of the conditions related to prayer are bound up in this phrase—"according to His will."

Prayer provides an opportunity for adoration, praise, thanksgiving, confession of sin, and requests for self and for others. Numerous formats for prayer are possible—in fact, prayer is as unique as each person—but all prayer has as a central purpose the opportunity to express yourself fully and honestly to the Lord, to listen for His reply (very often in the form of insight, assurance, and joy), and to participate in the "mystery" of seeing God's purposes on this earth accomplished.

Prayer also offers an opportunity for Christian fellowship and guidance for the church. Prayer is not intended as a means of impressing others or manipulating God (Matt. 6:5, 6) but as a way of genuinely seeking God's strength and direction.

See also Dan. 2:23, note; notes on Confession (1 John 1); Gratitude (Ps. 95); Praise (Ps. 149); Prayer (Jer. 33; Heb. 4; 3 John)

Knowing the True—Rejecting the False

18We know that whoever is born of God does not sin; but he who has been born of God keeps himself,[a] and the wicked one does not touch him.

19We know that we are of God, and the whole world lies *under the sway of* the wicked one.

20And we know that the Son of God has come and has given us an understanding, that we may know Him who is true; and we are in Him who is true, in His Son Jesus Christ. This is the true God and eternal life.

21Little children, keep yourselves from idols. Amen.

·················

5:18 [a]NU-Text reads *him*.

---

would come to the false teachers who heard the gospel but openly rejected it. The effectiveness of prayers offered for believers is affirmed (vv. 14–17), but no such assurance accompanies intercession for unbelievers.

2 John

AUTHOR

Technically this epistle is anonymous, but the early church strongly affirmed John the apostle as its author. As was common in a Greek letter, the author identified himself at the beginning—in the case of this epistle, as the "elder" (Gk. *presbuteros,* lit. "older one"), denoting a position of authority. Furthermore, the author obviously had a personal knowledge and relationship with the recipients (2 John 1; 3 John 1) These observations correspond both with the fact that John wrote his books during his later years and that he likely held a position of great influence within the church (1 Tim. 5:17, 19). In either case, the writer knew and loved the recipients (2 John 1), who respected his teachings (2 John 4–6). An apostle of Jesus, John, the son of Zebedee and brother of James (Mark 1:19, 20), wrote with obvious similarities in style and content as are found in all the works incorporated within the Johannine literature (the Gospel of John; 1, 2, 3 John; Rev.).

DATE

The actual date, place, and order of the letters of John are unknown, but most scholars believe he wrote the epistles after he wrote his Gospel. This would date the letter about A.D. 90.

BACKGROUND

SETTING: This epistle and the other books written by John are believed to have been written from Ephesus while he was ministering to the churches in Asia Minor.

AUDIENCE: John used the expression "the elect lady" (Gk. *eklēktē kuria*) and "her children" in identifying the recipients of his letter. This designation could refer to a particular woman or to a church body and the individual members of the church, respectively. The personification of the church is not unusual for John (see Rev. 21:9).

PURPOSE: First and 2 John are set in the midst of a similar situation: the teachings of false teachers. Second John, in particular, warns believers about receiving itinerant heretics into their homes (2 John 10). This letter may have been written in anticipation of an upcoming visit (2 John 12).

THEMES

Speaking with authority and assurance, John developed his main themes of "love" (Gk. *agapē,* occurring four times) and "truth" (Gk. *alētheia,* occurring five times). "Love" is an outgrowth of maintaining the truth and is a common command of John (see 1 John 5:3; 2 John 6). The "truth" is the revelation that Jesus Christ was both perfectly divine and yet fully human (1 John 4:3; 2 John 7). Heretical theology concerning the Incarnation presented a departure from this "truth." Most scholars agree that the denial of an incarnate Jesus stemmed from the Platonic, pre-Gnostic belief that all matter was evil and thus suggesting that Jesus could never have been both God and man. Such

denials were in their beginning stages; however, because of these, John implored "his children" to use spiritual discernment in their contact and support of itinerant teachers (2 John 10, 11).

John exhorted his readers to maintain their strong stance of "walking in truth" and expressing this truth through practical love toward one another. He also warned Christians to be wary of those who do not adhere to the message of Jesus' Incarnation (2 John 7). Christian love does not include offering shelter to false itinerant teachers (2 John 10). Finally, John commended their faithfulness (2 John 4) and expressed his desire to see them again (2 John 12).

Greeting the Elect Lady

The Elder,

To the elect lady and her children, whom I love in truth, and not only I, but also all those who have known the truth, [2]because of the truth which abides in us and will be with us forever:

[3]Grace, mercy, *and* peace will be with you[a] from God the Father and from the Lord Jesus Christ, the Son of the Father, in truth and love.

Walk in Christ's Commandments

[4]I rejoiced greatly that I have found *some* of your children walking in truth, as we received commandment from the Father. [5]And now I plead with you, lady, not as though I wrote a new commandment to you, but that which we have had from the beginning: that we love one another.

[6]This is love, that we walk according to His commandments. This is the commandment, that as you have heard from the beginning, you should walk in it.

Beware of Antichrist Deceivers

[7]For many deceivers have gone out into the world who do not confess Jesus Christ *as* coming in the flesh. This is a deceiver and an antichrist. [8]Look to yourselves, that we[a] do not lose those things we worked for, but *that* we[b] may receive a full reward.

[9]Whoever transgresses[a] and does not abide in the doctrine of Christ does not have God. He who abides in the doctrine of Christ has both the Father and the Son. [10]If anyone comes to you and does not bring this doctrine, do not receive him

3 [a]NU-Text and M-Text read *us.*   8 [a]NU-Text reads *you.*   [b]NU-Text reads *you.*   9 [a]NU-Text reads *goes ahead.*

---

1 Elect lady (Gk. *eklēktē kuria,* lit. "chosen lady") may refer to John's personification of a local congregation. If this is true, then John's references to the "lady" (v. 5) and "elect sister" (v. 13) would designate churches that know each other. However, it is just as likely that the designation may refer to an esteemed friend (see The Elect Lady).

4–6 John had apparently received news that his readers were following his admonitions. "Walking in truth" requires a heart that believes in the truth of the message of the incarnate Christ and a lifestyle that reveals this message by showing love to others (vv. 5, 6). Belief and action go hand-in-hand (1 John 3:23). Indeed truth is something to believe and live.

9, 10 Transgresses (Gk. *parabainō,* lit. "run ahead of" or "go before") was used by John sarcastically to criticize the teachers who claimed they had advanced knowledge of Jesus Christ and thus appeared to "run ahead" of the truth spiritually (see Introduction: Themes). John used some of his most intense language to warn his friends not to extend hospitality to such false teachers. Hospitality often included shelter and lodging as well as a formal greeting. To "greet" (Gk. *charein*) suggests the extension of joy or prosperity. Greeting the false teachers granted a special blessing to them and, in essence, would indicate approval of their wrong deeds and heretical teachings. John argued that Christian hospitality does not extend to include those teachers who twist and malign the Word of God.

THE ELECT LADY

John's second epistle is addressed to "the elect lady and her children." The church, as the bride of Christ, is often referenced in feminine terms. Thus, John was possibly writing to an established group of believers. However, correspondence with an esteemed friend and her family is equally possible. Interestingly, the Greek word *kuria*, translated "lady," could have been a proper name. If so, John may have been instructing a particular lady regarding a situation she had encountered in her home. Certainly, if that be the case, she is a woman of excellent character whose godly influence touched the lives of those around her, including her own children.

The Roman Empire had an extensive network of roads, allowing its citizens to travel freely and extensively. Inns were located at twenty-two-mile intervals, but the average inn was unsanitary, noisy, and frequented by thieves. People therefore tried to stay with acquaintances or acquaintances of friends when they traveled. Because the gospel was being spread by traveling missionaries, hospitality was considered one of the chief expressions of Christian love (Rom. 12:13; Heb. 13:16). Unfortunately, when it became known that Christians would feed and house those who claimed to be spreading the gospel, many pseudo-missionaries began to take advantage of them. The elect lady may have found herself in this situation.

John exhorted her to continue to offer hospitality but cautioned her to be alert to spot deceivers. He encouraged her to balance the Christian imperative to love with safeguards against the abuse of Christian fellowship. Even in the midst of hospitality and other ministries, a woman must walk in truth and lovingly admonish her children in the ways of the Lord.

See also notes on Evangelism (John 6); Hospitality (1 Pet. 4)

According to the Bible, truth must be married to love,
honesty must be intertwined with kindness.

Gigi Tchividjian

---

into your house nor greet him; [11]for he who greets him shares in his evil deeds.

John's Farewell Greeting

[12]Having many things to write to you, I did not wish *to do so* with paper and ink; but I hope to come to you and speak face to face, that our joy may be full.

[13]The children of your elect sister greet you. Amen.

3 John

TITLE

John, the apostle of Jesus Christ, is also known as the "beloved disciple." He probably wrote this letter from the city of Ephesus. John referred to himself as "THE ELDER," meaning he was in a position of influence and authority in the church.

DATE

John wrote this letter near the end of his life between A.D. 80 and 95, probably about A.D. 90 or about the same time he wrote 2 John.

BACKGROUND

SETTING: In 2 John, the apostle's specific concern was truth; in 3 John, his concern is love. Three key concepts are skillfully interwoven in this brief epistle: love, truth, and witness. Six times John used a form of "love" or "beloved" (Gk. *agapē*). John also mentioned "truth" seven times in this letter (3 John 1, 3, 4, 8, 12). He encouraged believers to know the truth and to continue to "walk" in it, giving testimony of their being of God (3 John 3, 4, 11).

PURPOSE: The apostle John wrote to encourage his friend Gaius to hold to the "truth." He also encouraged Gaius to continue in the ministry of hospitality. Included in John's letter is a rebuke directed towards Diotrephes, a domineering man in one of the Asian churches. Diotrephes was rebuked for spurning John's authority and for refusing hospitality to traveling missionaries. Also included is a commendation of Demetrius, whose life exemplified true Christian faith and conduct.

AUDIENCE: This letter was sent to Gaius, a man in a church in Asia Minor. Gaius was a common Roman name (see Acts 19:29; 20:4; Rom. 16:23). Nothing is known about this Gaius, except that John loved Gaius as his spiritual child (3 John 4).

THEMES

In this brief epistle, several themes appear:

- The truth of the gospel;
- The love of the truth;
- The ministry of hospitality;
- The unfolding of a good testimony.

OUTLINE

Introduction (v. 1)
   I. John's Appreciation for Gaius (vv. 2–4)
  II. The Duty of Hospitality (vv. 5–8)
 III. A Warning Against Diotrephes (vv. 9, 10)
 IV. A Commendation of Demetrius (vv. 11, 12)
Conclusion (vv. 13, 14)

PRAYER　ASKING FOR GOD'S PROVISION

Many Christians have needs that are not met simply because they do not pray (James 4:2). While God does not promise to provide all we want, He does provide all we need (Phil. 4:19). He is our all-sufficient Provider.

Prayer for provision is generally expressed in one of two ways: personal petitions or intercession. Personal petitions are the requests a believing woman makes for her own needs. Intercessions are prayers for the needs of others. Even when the believer does not know fully how to pray, the Holy Spirit intercedes on the believer's behalf (Rom. 8:26, 27).

While the model prayer Jesus gave includes only a request for daily bread (Matt. 6:11), Jesus introduced that prayer to His followers by telling them to ask the Father for whatever they needed (Matt. 6:8). God promises to provide for the needs of His children. He provides for their physical needs of food, clothing, and shelter. He provides for their spiritual needs through prayer, Bible study, and ministries in His name. He provides for their personal needs through intimate relationships with God and other believers. God will provide for His children as they seek His help through prayer. God desires to provide for our total well-being—spiritually, physically, and materially (3 John 2). His source of supply is unlimited!

See also Dan. 2:23, note; notes on Prayer (Jer. 33; Heb. 4; 1 John 5); Providence (Eccl. 7)

Greeting to Gaius

The Elder,

To the beloved Gaius, whom I love in truth:

[2] Beloved, I pray that you may prosper in all things and be in health, just as your soul prospers. [3] For I rejoiced greatly when brethren came and testified of the truth *that is* in you, just as you walk in the truth. [4] I have no greater joy than to hear that my children walk in truth.[a]

Gaius Commended for Generosity

[5] Beloved, you do faithfully whatever you do for the brethren and[a] for strangers, [6] who have borne witness of your love before the church. *If* you send them forward on their journey in a manner worthy of God, you will do well, [7] because they went forth for His name's sake, taking nothing from the Gentiles. [8] We therefore ought to receive[a] such, that we may become fellow workers for the truth.

Diotrephes and Demetrius

[9] I wrote to the church, but Diotrephes, who loves to have the preeminence among them, does not receive us. [10] Therefore, if I come, I will call to mind his deeds which he does, prating against us with malicious words. And not content with that, he himself does not receive the brethren, and forbids those who wish to, putting *them* out of the church.

[11] Beloved, do not imitate what is evil, but what is good. He who does good is of God, but[a] he who does evil has not seen God.

[12] Demetrius has a *good* testimony from all, and from the truth itself. And we also bear witness, and you know that our testimony is true.

Farewell Greeting

[13] I had many things to write, but I do not wish to write to you with pen and ink; [14] but I hope to see you shortly, and we shall speak face to face.

Peace to you. Our friends greet you. Greet the friends by name.

· · · · · · · · · · · · · · · · · ·

4 [a]NU-Text reads the truth.　5 [a]NU-Text adds especially.　8 [a]NU-Text reads support.　11 [a]NU-Text and M-Text omit but.

3, 4 The theme of truth stands out (vv. 1, 3, 4, 8, 12). Gaius may have withstood false teaching. He was habitually conducting himself in the "sphere of the truth." This included his moral, intellectual, and spiritual life, and his total devotion to the true gospel. John rejoiced that his spiritual child was habitually abiding and walking in the truth of the gospel (see 1 John 2:6, 28).

6 Christian missionaries rightly took nothing from the pagans; so they were dependent on help from the Christians on their journeys. As God's representatives, they were to be treated as one would treat God (see Matt. 25:35–40). Hospitality is a Christian duty that pleases God (see 1 Pet. 4, Hospitality; chart, Hospitality or Entertainment).

9 John described three men in his letter. Gaius actively demonstrated his faith through love and hospitality toward others (v. 5). He entertained traveling missionaries, even though others disapproved of this practice (v. 10). Diotrephes was another prominent member of an Asian church. Whether he and Gaius were members of the same church or different churches is not known. He arrogantly refused to associate with traveling missionaries and tried to excommunicate those who did. In pride and arrogance, Diotrephes spurned the authority of John and caused division in the church (vv. 9, 10). Demetrius had a good reputation among believers (v. 12). Gaius and Demetrius had accepted truth and were walking in it. Diotrephes trusted in his own knowledge and rejected rightful authority. Throughout this letter, John emphasized the necessity to know the truth, to submit to the truth, and to act on the truth.

Jude

AUTHOR

The writer of this epistle identified himself as Jude, "a bondservant of Jesus Christ, and brother of James" (Jude 1). From very early in the history of the church, Jude was recognized as not only the brother of James, the well-known leader of the church in Jerusalem, but, like James, as the half-brother of the Lord. He did not refer to himself as an apostle but rested his authority first on his servanthood to Jesus and then on his relationship to James.

Matthew 13:55 and Mark 6:3 refer to the brothers of Jesus. Among the names given are James and Judas (or Jude). If this writer is actually a brother of Jesus, why doesn't he clearly say so? The answer, given from as far back in church history as Clement of Alexandria (second century), is his humility. Jude's brother James was commonly understood to be the brother of the Lord, and Jude found it sufficient to use his relationship to James to make his introduction. Both James and Jude preferred to think of themselves as servants of Jesus. Perhaps they did so out of humble acknowledgment that during their family life with Him they did not believe in Him (see John 7:5).

DATE

Any attempt to establish the date of this letter immediately faces the questions raised by the relationship between 2 Peter and Jude. Even a casual reading reveals striking similarities between the two books. Scholars have wondered whether one author used the other's work. Some believe that Jude used Peter's letter. These date the writing of Jude after Peter's death, which occurred about A.D. 66 or 67. Others say that Jude's letter has priority, dating it before Peter's martyrdom. A third possibility is that both Peter and Jude made use of a common source, a catechetical tract used in the early church to instruct believers about false teachers. If that was the case, an early date is indicated. Assigning the epistle an exact date is impossible; however, probably Jude was written sometime between A.D. 65–80.

BACKGROUND

SETTING: The place from which the Book of Jude was written has never been identified with certainty, although Palestine and Egypt have been suggested.

AUDIENCE: The epistle does not give any information about its original recipients. Nevertheless, the content of the letter indicates that Jude's intended audience was well versed in Old Testament Scripture. The author commended them for their knowledge of the Exodus (Jude 5), angels (Jude 6), and the destruction of Sodom and Gomorrah (Jude 7). They are also acquainted with Jewish literature current in the first century (Jude 9, 14). Furthermore, there are no references to Gentiles. It appears, therefore, that the recipients of Jude's letter were Jewish converts to Christianity who had been dispersed throughout Asia Minor.

PURPOSE: Jude's purpose was to discuss salvation. The false teachers made it necessary for him to add a warning about the mixture of truth and error.

THEMES

Apparently Jude intended to write about the salvation he and his readers had in common (Jude 3), but news of a dangerous heresy caused him to change direction. He devoted the major part of his epistle to instructing believers concerning false teachers who were infiltrating the Christian community. He gave graphic descriptions of the corruptions they taught and the destruction for which they were headed. Near the end of the epistle, he reminded the believers to be devoted to edifying themselves with their "most holy faith" (Jude 20). Jude concluded his letter with what has become one of the most beloved benedictions in the Christian church (Jude 24, 25).

OUTLINE

Introduction: Greeting (vv. 1, 2)
   I. An Altered Purpose (v. 3)
  II. Dangers from Ungodly Men (v. 4)
 III. Historical Examples of False Teachers (vv. 5–9)
 IV. A Description of False Teachers (vv. 10–19)
  V. The Aim of Achieving Holiness (vv. 20–23)
Conclusion: Benediction (vv. 24, 25)

Greeting to the Called

Jude, a bondservant of Jesus Christ, and brother of James,

To those who are called, sanctified[a] by God the Father, and preserved in Jesus Christ:

[2]Mercy, peace, and love be multiplied to you.

Contend for the Faith

[3]Beloved, while I was very diligent to write to you concerning our common salvation, I found it necessary to write to you exhorting you to contend earnestly for the faith which was once for all delivered to the saints. [4]For certain men have crept in unnoticed, who long ago were marked out for this condemnation, ungodly men, who turn the grace of our God into lewdness and deny the only Lord God[a] and our Lord Jesus Christ.

Old and New Apostates

[5]But I want to remind you, though you once knew this, that the Lord, having saved the people out of the land of Egypt, afterward destroyed those who did not believe. [6]And the angels who did not keep their proper domain, but left their own abode, He has reserved in everlasting chains under darkness for the judgment of the great day; [7]as Sodom and Gomorrah, and the cities around them in a similar manner to these, having given themselves over to sexual immorality and gone after strange flesh, are set forth as an example, suffering the vengeance of eternal fire.

[8]Likewise also these dreamers defile the flesh, reject authority, and speak evil of dignitaries. [9]Yet Michael the archangel, in contending with the devil, when he disputed about the body of Moses,

---

1 [a]NU-Text reads *beloved.*   4 [a]NU-Text omits *God.*

---

6 Jude reviewed examples of how disobedience against God in the past brought about divine judgment (vv. 5–7). He pointed out that God did not even spare the angels who rebelled but imprisoned them (v. 6). Jude cited a reference from *I Enoch,* an apocryphal book with which he was sure his audience was familiar. According to this account, some angels who participated in Satan's rebellion were immediately imprisoned with chains, where they still await their final judgment. Others remain active agents of Satan. If even the angels do not escape punishment for their pride, then certainly those who "deny the only Lord God and our Lord Jesus Christ" will not escape (v. 4).

POSITIVE THINKING | GOD'S THOUGHTS, OUR THOUGHTS

An entire branch of popular psychology is based on this proverb: "As he thinks in his heart, so is he" (Prov. 23:7). Psychologists teach that the way people think affects their emotions, their ability to relate to others, and their ability to cope in difficult circumstances. They maintain that positive thinking increases happiness and success in life.

Christians are to be positive thinkers (Phil. 4:11, 13). However, the Bible teaches that this trait is not gained through mere personal effort. Rather, it is a byproduct of the indwelling presence of the Holy Spirit. Believers are to meditate on things that are true, noble, just, pure, lovely, and of good report (Phil. 4:8). Their minds are to be filled with virtuous and praiseworthy thoughts. Those whose hearts have not been changed by God's Spirit will find that ultimately they are powerless to combat the evil in their minds, for the condition of their hearts determines the condition of their thoughts (Matt. 15:19), and ungodly thoughts will inevitably manifest themselves in ungodly speech and action (Jude 15, 16). The power of the Holy Spirit enables the Christian to make every thought obedient to Christ (2 Cor. 10:5) and truly to think, speak, and act positively.

See also notes on Contentment (1 Tim. 6); Fruit of the Spirit (Rom. 15); Problem Solving (John 5)

---

dared not bring against him a reviling accusation, but said, "The Lord rebuke you!" [10]But these speak evil of whatever they do not know; and whatever they know naturally, like brute beasts, in these things they corrupt themselves. [11]Woe to them! For they have gone in the way of Cain, have run greedily in the error of Balaam for profit, and perished in the rebellion of Korah.

Apostates Depraved and Doomed

[12]These are spots in your love feasts, while they feast with you without fear, serving *only* themselves. *They are* clouds without water, carried about[a] by the winds; late autumn trees without fruit, twice dead, pulled up by the roots; [13]raging waves of the sea, foaming up their own shame; wandering stars for whom is reserved the blackness of darkness forever.

[14]Now Enoch, the seventh from Adam, prophesied about these men also, saying, "Behold, the Lord comes with ten thousands of His saints, [15]to execute judgment on all, to convict all who are ungodly among them of all their ungodly deeds which they have committed in an ungodly way,

and of all the harsh things which ungodly sinners have spoken against Him."

Apostates Predicted

[16]These are grumblers, complainers, walking according to their own lusts; and they mouth great swelling *words,* flattering people to gain advantage. [17]But you, beloved, remember the words which were spoken before by the apostles of our Lord Jesus Christ: [18]how they told you that there would be mockers in the last time who would walk according to their own ungodly lusts. [19]These are sensual persons, who cause divisions, not having the Spirit.

Maintain Your Life with God

[20]But you, beloved, building yourselves up on your most holy faith, praying in the Holy Spirit, [21]keep yourselves in the love of God, looking for the mercy of our Lord Jesus Christ unto eternal life.

[22]And on some have compassion, making a distinction;[a] [23]but others save with fear, pulling *them*

···················

12 [a]NU-Text and M-Text read *along.* 22 [a]NU-Text reads *who are doubting* (or *making distinctions*).

---

11 **Jude pronounced a woe on corrupt teachers** in much the same way that Jesus did in His public teaching. To make his point as specific as possible, Jude used three examples of individuals in Israel's history to depict the characteristics of the false teachers. Cain was unloving toward even his brother Abel. He envied the good deeds that Abel did (see Gen. 4:1–15). Balaam, in his greed for money, led Israel into immorality and idolatry at Baal Peor (see Num. 22—24; 31:16). Korah rebelled against God's appointed leaders of Israel (see Num. 16:1–40) and suffered a dramatic fate. The evil teachers who threatened the Christian believers of Jude's day were likewise characterized by selfishness, envy, hatred, greed, immorality, idolatry, and rebellion.

14, 15 **Jude ended his dramatic description** of the false teachers by predicting an inescapable judgment for them (v. 13). He

again quoted a passage from the apocryphal book of *I Enoch,* a volume of religious writing widely known and respected in the two centuries before and after the birth of Christ. The author of *I Enoch* prophesied concerning a future judgment by the Lord. He pictured the Lord coming with "ten thousands of His saints" to execute judgment. Jesus affirmed that "when the Son of Man comes in His glory, and all the holy angels with Him, then He will sit on the throne of His glory" (Matt. 25:31). Although Jude did not regard as Scripture the apocryphal quote he used, he recognized that it accurately portrayed what would happen at the end of time. God will execute judgment, and the ungodly will not escape punishment.

22, 23 **Although Jude deplored and condemned false teachers,** he recommended an attitude of compassion toward those who were swayed by their message. Some required gentle

Wounds do heal, but there are times to allow the Great Physician to perform surgery so they heal right.

Nancie Carmichael

out of the fire,[a] hating even the garment defiled by the flesh.

Glory to God

[24]Now to Him who is able to keep you[a] from
   stumbling,
And to present *you* faultless
Before the presence of His glory with
   exceeding joy,
[25]To God our Savior,[a]

Who alone is wise,[b]
Be glory and majesty,
Dominion and power,[c]
Both now and forever.
Amen.

•••••••••••••••••

23 [a]NU-Text adds *and on some have mercy with fear* and omits *with fear* in first clause.   24 [a]M-Text reads *them.*   25 [a]NU-Text reads *To the only God our Savior.* [b]NU-Text omits *Who . . . is wise* and adds *Through Jesus Christ our Lord.* [c]NU-Text adds *Before all time.*

correction; others, however, would need to be pulled "out of the fire" forcefully (v. 23). Jude used the image of soiled clothes as a metaphor for sin (see Zech. 3:3, 4; Rev. 3:4). He said that Christians ought to hate "even the garment defiled by the flesh" (Jude 23). Jude wanted his readers to avoid all contamination by sin, hating sin as much as they would loathe

soiled undergarments. To treat sin as normal and common-place is a temptation. However, Jude identified this attitude as a betrayal of the gospel. Christians have been "clothed" in righteousness. Therefore, they ought to be repulsed by their old, filthy "garment" of sin.

Revelation

AUTHOR

Some early church fathers ascribed the authorship of Revelation to John the apostle. Beginning with this early tradition, the John who wrote the Book of Revelation has been identified as John the apostle (Rev. 1:1, 4, 9; 21:2; 22:8). No solid evidence refutes this view. The language and style of Revelation differ from that of the Gospel and Epistles of John. However, these differences could be due to the literary nature of the Book of Revelation as apocalyptic writing (see Introduction: Literary Characteristics). Revelation's description of Jesus as the "Word" and the "Lamb of God" mirrors those within the fourth gospel, adding weight to the argument that the apostle John was the author. He identified himself as a servant of Jesus (Rev. 1:1) and as a brother and companion to the recipients of his letter (Rev. 1:9). Some scholars maintain that Revelation 1:2 is not only a reference to the visions of the book but also an apostolic claim.

The John of Revelation witnessed "the word of God" and "the testimony of Jesus Christ, to all things that he saw," suggesting that the author was the apostle (Rev. 1:2). A primary criterion for apostolic authority was to be an eyewitness to the message, ministry, and Resurrection of Jesus Christ (see Acts 1:21, 22).

DATE

Revelation was written during a period of impending persecution for Christians. The Roman emperor Nero officially sanctioned the torture and extermination of Christians, whom he blamed for the great fire in Rome in A.D. 64. Following his suicide in A.D. 68, emperor worship grew, reaching its peak during the reign of Domitian (A.D. 81–96). During this time, the persecution of Christians intensified. Early church tradition strongly favors the latter part of Domitian's reign (A.D. 90–96) as the date for Revelation.

BACKGROUND

SETTING: Augustus, who succeeded Julius Caesar as emperor of Rome, encouraged his subjects to regard emperors as "gods." Caligula reinforced this concept, and from the time of Nero to Domitian "the cult of the emperor" gained greater and greater influence. Citizens and subjects of the empire who refused to confess that the emperor was divine and to worship him were tortured, executed, or exiled as traitors.

John was exiled to the island of Patmos, a prison island that may have been used to quarry rock. He wrote the Book of Revelation during his exile there.

PURPOSE: John received his revelation about the victory of God in the face of terror and evil during a period of great persecution for the church. In the Book of Revelation, God's impending judgment of the wicked Roman Empire is a prelude to His judgment at the end of time. John's message is that God has already triumphed over evil and that He will totally destroy all evil at the end of time. John wanted the Christians in the churches of Asia to let the knowledge of God's ultimate victory encourage them to perseverance and faith in the midst of persecution.

AUDIENCE: Revelation is addressed to seven churches located in seven cities of the Roman province of Asia, an area now known as Turkey (Rev. 1:4). The cities were situated in a circular pattern (see map, The Seven Churches of Asia Minor). They may have served as centralized postal centers for surrounding geographical regions. Likely the entire Book of Revelation was circulated to all the churches in the province.

LITERARY CHARACTERISTICS: Revelation is an example of apocalyptic literature, which flourished during the last two centuries B.C. and the first century A.D. An apocalypse is a revelation or unveiling made by an angel or other celestial being. The message is expressed in vivid, and sometimes picturesque, symbols. The apocalyptists were pessimistic about human efforts to overcome evil. They expressed the conviction that God would intervene and forcibly destroy the evil forces that oppressed His people. Often, this deliverance was associated with the coming of the Messiah, who would inaugurate the kingdom of God.

Revelation differs from traditional apocalyptic literature in several ways. Apocalypses were usually pseudonymous, written in the name of some illustrious figure of the past. But John emphasized that *he* was writing what had been personally revealed to him (Rev. 1:1, 4, 9; 21:2; 22:8).

John's apocalypse was optimistic. Although it portrayed the massive struggle between good and evil, John was confident that a decisive victory was at hand: God's Messiah, Jesus, had *already* come, had *already* conquered, and would come again to complete His work. Finally, John repeatedly called his writing a *prophecy* (Rev. 1:3; 22:7, 10, 18, 19). Apocalypses were traditionally written to recount past historical events. John, on the other hand, took the stance of a prophet, looking resolutely to the future and the return of Christ.

THEMES

The primary emphasis of the Book of Revelation or the Apocalypse (Gk. *apokalupsis,* lit. "unveiling") is the triumphant Christ who is unveiled in His glory. Many refer to the book as eschatology (Gk., lit. "study of the last"). Eschatology is not merely a study of the end times but the historic completion of the revealed purposes of God. The book unfolds into natural divisions (Rev. 1:19): "the things which you have seen" or John's vision of the resurrected and glorified Christ (Rev. 1); "the things which are" or a description of the churches (Rev. 2; 3); and "the things which will take place after this" or a prophetic unfolding of future events (Rev. 4—22). The central event is the return of Jesus Christ (Rev. 1:7).

OUTLINE

Introduction and Benediction

1 The Revelation of Jesus Christ, which God gave Him to show His servants— things which must shortly take place. And He sent and signified *it* by His angel to His servant John, [2]who bore witness to the word of God, and to the testimony of Jesus Christ, to all things that he saw. [3]Blessed *is* he who reads and those who hear the words of this prophecy, and keep those things which are written in it; for the time *is* near.

Greeting the Seven Churches

[4]John, to the seven churches which are in Asia:

Grace to you and peace from Him who is and who was and who is to come, and from the seven Spirits who are before His throne, [5]and from Jesus Christ, the faithful witness, the firstborn from the dead, and the ruler over the kings of the earth.

1:1–3 Time in the framework of eternity is beyond human understanding. (see v. 3; Rev. 22:6, 7, 10, 20). A better translation of "shortly" (Gk. *en tachei*) is "certainly." Though some of the book had reference to events at hand, much also looks forward to the future consummation of history in Christ. From an eternal perspective, end-time events are just around the corner, and believers must order their lives accordingly.

1:4–8 Him who is and who was and who is to come is an adaptation of the name God made known to Moses in the revelation of the burning bush (v. 4; see Ex. 3:14). The "seven Spirits" sym-

bolize the Holy Spirit (Rev. 1:4; see v. 20; Zech. 4:1–6; chart, The Significance of Numbers in Scripture). That the "seven Spirits" are before the throne (Rev. 1:4; 4:5) and are the seven eyes of the Lamb (Rev. 5:6) reinforces that the Spirit is also God. The description of Jesus Christ emphasizes His victory over death, His role of Redeemer, and His rule over the nations of the world (Rev. 1:7, see also Dan. 7:13; Zech. 12:10). Alpha and Omega are the first and last letters of the Greek alphabet (Rev. 1:8), underscoring that God is sovereign and eternal. Several times John applied titles used of the Father to Christ (Rev. 22:13).

Perspective   by Stormie Omartian

THE BIBLE IS GOD'S LOVE LETTER (Drawn from *Just Enough Light for the Step I'm On*)

People who say the Bible isn't relevant today obviously don't know the Author. They read it like a storybook or a history lesson, having no idea of the power behind it. They don't hear the Shepherd's voice because they have not become one of His sheep. But those of us who immerse ourselves in it, who press in deeper and deeper, know its power. We love His Word like a love letter that we read over and over because we desire to be close to the one who wrote it. We long to connect with and remember everything about that person. We want to understand how he thinks. We yearn to hear his voice again in our mind. We crave his touch. When we hunger for those same things from God, we learn to appreciate His love letter—the Bible—in that exact way.

Of course, if we don't love the person who sent us the love letter, it is meaningless. It holds no life for us. The key to receiving the full message in God's love letter is to love God. Because I love Him, I hear His voice speaking to me when I read His Word. If I read it often, the words find residence in my heart and bring me life.

God's Love Letters Guide Us. In the theater, lights at the front of the stage that are level with the performer's feet are called footlights. They act as a guide to help the actors know where to go and keep them from falling into the orchestra pit. God has provided footlights for us, too—to guide us as we walk and to keep us from falling into the pit.

Those of us who have read the Bible many times from cover to cover have to be careful not to fall into the trap of thinking that the light we had last year, last month, last week, or even yesterday is enough to keep us safely on the path today. Neither can we read God's Word just once and then be finished like we can with any other book. The light we receive from God's Word must be renewed, revitalized, and solidly reestablished daily.

God's Love Letters Defend Us. When Satan came to tempt Jesus in the wilderness, Jesus spoke the Word of God to refute everything Satan said. Jesus told him that we live "by every word that proceeds from the mouth of God" (Matt. 4:4). If God's own Son refuted the devil in that way, shouldn't we do the same? Only God's Word in our mind, on our heart, and out of our lips will burn away the darkness of untruth and arm us with a double-edged sword more powerful than any weapon the opposition can use against us. Who does not need that?

God's Love Letters Give Us Hope. There are no times so hopeless in our lives that God's Word will not shed light on the situation and bring us comfort. If you find yourself struggling with hopelessness, loss, sickness, or temptation, make God's Word an ongoing presence in your life. Hook up to it like an IV and let it flow continuously through your spiritual veins. Its light will burn hopelessness out of your life.

Hunger for God's Word like food. Thirst for it like water. Soak in it like a Jacuzzi. Put it on like a garment. Weave it into your soul so that it becomes part of the fabric of your life. When you do, you won't just be trudging up the trail. You will be dancing in the footlights.

To Him who loved us and washed[a] us from our sins in His own blood, [6]and has made us kings[a] and priests to His God and Father, to Him *be* glory and dominion forever and ever. Amen.

[7]Behold, He is coming with clouds, and every eye will see Him, even they who pierced Him. And all the tribes of the earth will mourn because of Him. Even so, Amen.

[8]"I am the Alpha and the Omega, *the* Beginning and *the* End,"[a] says the Lord,[b] "who is and who was and who is to come, the Almighty."

Vision of the Son of Man

[9]I, John, both[a] your brother and companion in the tribulation and kingdom and patience of Jesus Christ, was on the island that is called Patmos for the word of God and for the testimony of Jesus Christ. [10]I was in the Spirit on the Lord's Day, and I heard behind me a loud voice, as of a trumpet, [11]saying, "I am the Alpha and the Omega, the First and the Last,"[a] and, "What you see, write in a book and send *it* to the seven churches which are in Asia:[b] to Ephesus, to Smyrna, to Pergamos, to Thyatira, to Sardis, to Philadelphia, and to Laodicea."

[12]Then I turned to see the voice that spoke with me. And having turned I saw seven golden lampstands, [13]and in the midst of the seven lampstands *One* like the Son of Man, clothed with a garment

1:5 [a]NU-Text reads *loves us and freed;* M-Text reads *loves us and washed.* **1:6** [a]NU-Text and M-Text read *a kingdom.* **1:8** [a]NU-Text and M-Text omit *the Beginning and the End.* [b]NU-Text and M-Text add *God.* **1:9** [a]NU-Text and M-Text omit *both.* **1:11** [a]NU-Text and M-Text omit *I am* through third *and.* [b]NU-Text and M-Text omit *which are in Asia.*

1:11–18 John described Christ as "One like the Son of Man" (v. 13; see Dan. 7:13). Jesus favored this title to describe Himself and His mission (Matt. 16:13; Mark 8:31; Luke 19:10; John 13:31).

1:19 This key verse suggests the structure of the book (see Introduction: Themes).

FRUIT OF THE SPIRIT — *FAITHFULNESS*

Faithfulness is the quality descriptive of God's ongoing relationship to the world and a believer's desired relationship to God and to others. The Old and New Testaments praise God for His faithfulness and challenge God's people to develop faithfulness in their lives. Steadfast loyalty and unwavering trust are considered essential virtues for personal and spiritual growth.

"Faithfulness" (Gk. *pistis*) is a manifestation of the fruit of the Spirit that pertains to loyalty and trustworthiness. Scripture teaches that God is faithful (Lam. 3:22, 23). Jesus was praised by the Father for His faithfulness even unto death on the Cross (Phil. 2:7–10). Many of those who followed the Lord were called faithful. Moses was faithful in the face of oppression (Heb. 11:23–25), and Ruth was faithful as she experienced great loss (Ruth 1:16). The early church was faithful when facing persecution (Acts 8:4), and Paul was faithful in his ministry (2 Tim. 4:6–8).

Believers today are called to faithfulness to God, to self, and to others. A believer is challenged to maintain steadfast trust in God, even amidst trials and suffering. Faithfulness to self results from faith in God and precedes faithfulness to others. Dependability and commitment to others is an essential expression of faithfulness in love and service.

The Lord said, "Be faithful until death, and I will give you the crown of life" (Rev. 2:10). The unfailing faith of a follower of Christ will be rewarded for all eternity.

See also Lam. 3:22, note; notes on Commitment (Matt. 16); Fruit of the Spirit (Ps. 86; Rom. 5; 15; 1 Cor. 10; 13; Gal. 5; Eph. 4; Col. 3; 2 Thess. 1); Perseverance (Rev. 14)

---

down to the feet and girded about the chest with a golden band. ¹⁴His head and hair *were* white like wool, as white as snow, and His eyes like a flame of fire; ¹⁵His feet *were* like fine brass, as if refined in a furnace, and His voice as the sound of many waters; ¹⁶He had in His right hand seven stars, out of His mouth went a sharp two-edged sword, and His countenance *was* like the sun shining in its strength. ¹⁷And when I saw Him, I fell at His feet as dead. But He laid His right hand on me, saying to me,[a] "Do not be afraid; I am the First and the Last. ¹⁸I *am* He who lives, and was dead, and behold, I am alive forevermore. Amen. And I have the keys of Hades and of Death. ¹⁹Write[a] the things which you have seen, and the things which are, and the things which will take place after this. ²⁰The mystery of the seven stars which you saw in My right hand, and the seven golden lampstands: The seven stars are the angels of the seven churches, and the seven lampstands which you saw[a] are the seven churches.

The Loveless Church

2 "To the angel of the church of Ephesus write, 'These things says He who holds the seven stars in His right hand, who walks in the midst of the seven golden lampstands: ²"I know your works, your labor, your patience, and that you cannot bear those who are evil. And you have tested those who say they are apostles and are not, and have found them liars; ³and you have persevered and have patience, and have labored for My name's sake and have not become weary. ⁴Nevertheless I have *this* against you, that you have left your first love. ⁵Remember therefore from where you have fallen; repent and do the first works, or else I will come to you quickly and remove your lampstand from its place—unless you repent. ⁶But this you have, that you hate the deeds of the Nicolaitans, which I also hate.

⁷"He who has an ear, let him hear what the Spirit says to the churches. To him who overcomes I will give to eat from the tree of life, which is in the midst of the Paradise of God." '

The Persecuted Church

⁸"And to the angel of the church in Smyrna write,

1:17 [a]NU-Text and M-Text omit *to me.* **1:19** [a]NU-Text and M-Text read *Therefore, write.* **1:20** [a]NU-Text and M-Text omit *which you saw.*

1:20 Each of the seven letters in Revelation is addressed to the "angel" (Gk. *angelos*, lit. "messenger") of the respective church. Though not identified with certainty, this "angel" may be the pastor or shepherd of the congregation addressed. The churches themselves are symbolized by the lampstand (Zech. 4:1–6).

The letters follow a common pattern: Christ began with a statement about Himself, continued with a description of the church, and concluded with a promise. He commended the church; He presented the complaints (if any) against them; He corrected their error (see chart, The Seven Churches of Revelation).

2:1–7 Ephesus, the most important seaport and the major cultural, commercial, and religious center in Asia Minor, was famous for its temple to Artemis, its superstitious practices, and magical arts (Acts 19:19, 35; see chart, Graeco-Roman Goddesses).The identity of the Nicolaitans, as well as the nature of their practices, is unclear. "Nicolaitan" may also be a play on two Greek words (*nikaō* and *laos*), meaning "people conquerors" or "overcomers of the people," and perhaps stressing the authoritarian nature of the group.

2:8–11 The church in Smyrna, modern-day Izmir, is addressed in the second letter (see chart, The Seven Churches of Revela-

*The prophetic messages of Revelation are not given to satisfy
curiosity, but to proclaim God's will directly to His people so that
they might be encouraged to live godly lives.*

Shari Lee Witt Hofstetter

'These things says the First and the Last, who was dead, and came to life: ⁹"I know your works, tribulation, and poverty (but you are rich); and *I know* the blasphemy of those who say they are Jews and are not, but *are* a synagogue of Satan. ¹⁰Do not fear any of those things which you are about to suffer. Indeed, the devil is about to throw *some* of you into prison, that you may be tested, and you will have tribulation ten days. Be faithful until death, and I will give you the crown of life.

¹¹"He who has an ear, let him hear what the Spirit says to the churches. He who overcomes shall not be hurt by the second death." '

The Compromising Church

¹²"And to the angel of the church in Pergamos write,

'These things says He who has the sharp two-edged sword: ¹³"I know your works, and where you dwell, where Satan's throne *is.* And you hold fast to My name, and did not deny My faith even in the days in which Antipas *was* My faithful martyr, who was killed among you, where Satan dwells. ¹⁴But I have a few things against you, because you have there those who hold the doctrine of Balaam, who taught Balak to put a stumbling block before the children of Israel, to eat things sacrificed to idols, and to commit sexual immorality. ¹⁵Thus you also have those who hold the doctrine of the Nicolaitans, which thing I hate.ª ¹⁶Repent, or else I will come to you quickly and will fight against them with the sword of My mouth.

¹⁷"He who has an ear, let him hear what the Spirit says to the churches. To him who overcomes I will give some of the hidden manna to eat. And I will give him a white stone, and on the stone a new name written which no one knows except him who receives *it*." '

The Corrupt Church

¹⁸"And to the angel of the church in Thyatira write,

'These things says the Son of God, who has

2:15 ªNU-Text and M-Text read *likewise* for *which thing I hate.*

---

tion). This beautiful coastal city was situated at the end of the eastern Asian trade route and was a center for Roman emperor worship. Polycarp, the most famous of the early church's martyrs, was the bishop of Smyrna. This church is one of two for whom the Lord has no criticism. Two words for the devil are used in Revelation: *diabolos* (Gk., lit. "slanderer" or "accuser," v. 10) and "Satan" (Heb., lit. "adversary," vv. 9, 13, 24). The devil is the one who opposes and accuses the people of God (see Zech. 3:1; Job 1:6–12; 1 Pet. 5:8; see charts, Names for Satan; A Portrait of the Adversary).

2:12–17 Pergamos, modern-day Bergama, was the ancient capital of Asia. On the cone-shaped hill towering 800 feet above the surrounding valley many temples were built, the most famous of which was dedicated to Asklepius, the Greek god of healing. This center for the cultic worship of the emperor, was also a prominent center for pagan cults, including the cult of *Zeus Soter* (Gk., lit. "Zeus, the Savior") and the healing cult of Asklepius. "Satan's throne" almost certainly referred to these Satanic cults. Antipas, a member of the Pergamite church, demonstrated his firm commitment to Jesus Christ as the first Christian martyr of Asia. According to tradition, he was slowly roasted to death in a bronze kettle during the reign of Domitian. The prophet Balaam had been asked by Balak, king of Moab, to curse Israel. But Balaam was restrained by God and admonished three times to bless the nation instead (Num. 22—24). Afterwards, Balaam apparently advised Balak that Israel would forfeit God's blessing and protection if the Moabites could seduce the Israelites by

using women, probably temple prostitutes. The Israelites did succumb to sexual immorality and pagan sexual rituals and were judged by God for this transgression (Num. 25:1–3; 31:15, 16). Christ warned the church in Pergamos that if they would not repent of this sensuality and antinomianism (meaning "against the law"), He would fight against them with the sword of His mouth (Rev. 2:16).

2:17 God miraculously fed the children of Israel with manna in the wilderness. Afterwards, a pot of manna was put into the ark in the tabernacle (Ex. 16:32–34; Heb. 9:4). White stones were used to signify acquittal by a jury; they were also used as tokens of admission to public festivals or banquets.

2:18–29 Although not a strong seat of emperor worship, Thyatira, known today as Akhisar, was founded as a military outpost and known for its many trade guilds. To participate in the trade industry, a citizen needed to be a member of the appropriate guild. Guild members often participated in common meals dedicated to pagan deities—meals that often ended in unbridled sexual orgies. The Thyatiran church tolerated Jezebel (almost certainly a name used by John to refer to the woman's character), who taught sexual immorality and who, like the Balaamites, was associated with idolatry (v. 20; see Jezebel; see also 1 Kin. 16:29–33; 18, Jezebel; chart, Women in the Book of Revelation). Judgment on God's people is discipline, meant for correction, but judgment on the truly wicked (those who have ultimately rejected the gospel) is for eternity.

JEZEBEL *A False Prophetess*

Jezebel, the wicked queen of Israel during the ninth century B.C., led the covenant people into the worship of pagan gods. She constantly clamored for her gods to have the same rights as the Lord God of Israel. She was a strong, self-willed character who manipulated and controlled others in order to get her way (1 Kin. 21:25, 26).

The name "Jezebel" means "without cohabitation." Jezebel refused to "live together" or "co-habit" with anyone; she yielded to no authority except her own. She encouraged God's people to commit both physical and spiritual fornication in the idolatrous worship of other gods. This "harlotry" was intolerable to *Yahweh,* and He condemned Jezebel, her husband Ahab, and all their offspring, to death (1 Kin. 21:23–25).

In Revelation 2:20, the church of Thyatira is rebuked for tolerating "that woman Jezebel" in their midst. The historic Jezebel had been dead for nearly a thousand years, but a false prophetess with the same spirit had appeared in this first-century church. Like the first Jezebel, she was fiercely independent and unsubmissive in character. Also like Jezebel, she led the people of God into idolatry and immorality under the guise of religion. This woman promoted a proto-Gnostic heresy that claimed to tap into the secret mysteries and "the depths" of God—a phrase which she undoubtedly borrowed from Paul's letters (Rom. 11:33; 1 Cor. 2:10). Her doctrines bore enough semblance to orthodox Christianity to "seduce" Christ's servants, but in essence, her degenerate mysticism promoted "the depths of Satan" by encouraging believers to accept idolatry and pagan state-worship (Rev. 2:24). Even though the majority of the church in Thyatira were increasing in love and faith, they were tolerant of this woman and her evil teaching. Christ was not so tolerant. He responds with a grim humor: Do Jezebel and her followers want to get into bed? Do they, as His Bride, want to commit physical and spiritual adultery? If so, then Christ would personally provide a bed in which they could lay—a "bed" of sickness, tribulation, and death.

Jezebel typifies a spirit of independence and rebellion against God. This spirit, which arrogantly accommodates Christianity to the religious mind-set of the world, is a spirit which God does not tolerate (see Rom. 12:2). The Lord says, "On this one will I look: On him who is humble and of a contrite spirit, and who trembles at My word" (Is. 66:2).

See also 1 Kin. 16:31; 18:4, 13; 19:1, 2; 21:1–16, 23–26; 22:52–53; 2 Kin. 9:7, 22, 30–37; John 1:4, note; note on Goddess Religion (Ex. 20)

---

eyes like a flame of fire, and His feet like fine brass: [19]"I know your works, love, service, faith,[a] and your patience; and *as* for your works, the last *are* more than the first. [20]Nevertheless I have a few things against you, because you allow[a] that woman[b] Jezebel, who calls herself a prophetess, to teach and seduce[c] My servants to commit sexual immorality and eat things sacrificed to idols. [21]And I gave her time to repent of her sexual immorality, and she did not repent.[a] [22]Indeed I will cast her into a sickbed, and those who commit adultery with her into great tribulation, unless they repent of their[a] deeds. [23]I will kill her children with death, and all the churches shall know that I am He who searches the minds and hearts. And I will give to each one of you according to your works.

[24]"Now to you I say, and[a] to the rest in Thyatira, as many as do not have this doctrine, who have not known the depths of Satan, as they say, I will[b] put on you no other burden. [25]But hold fast what you have till I come. [26]And he who overcomes, and keeps My works until the end, to him I will give power over the nations—

[27]'He shall rule them with a rod of iron;
They shall be dashed to pieces like the potter's vessels'[a]—

as I also have received from My Father; [28]and I will give him the morning star.

[29]"He who has an ear, let him hear what the Spirit says to the churches." '

The Dead Church

3 "And to the angel of the church in Sardis write, 'These things says He who has the seven Spirits of God and the seven stars: "I know your works, that you have a name that you are alive, but you are dead. [2]Be watchful, and strengthen the things which remain, that are ready to die, for I

• • • • • • • • • • • • • • • •

2:19 [a]NU-Text and M-Text read *faith, service.*   2:20 [a]NU-Text and M-Text read *I have against you that you tolerate.* [b]M-Text reads *your wife Jezebel.* [c]NU-Text and M-Text read *and teaches and seduces.* 2:21 [a]NU-Text and M-Text read *time to repent, and she does not want to repent of her sexual immorality.* 2:22 [a]NU-Text and M-Text read *her.* 2:24 [a]NU-Text and M-Text omit *and.* [b]NU-Text and M-Text omit *will.* 2:27 [a]Psalm 2:9

3:1–6 Sardis, formerly the capital city of the kingdom of Lydia, was located at the junction of several major Roman roads. Its citizens zealously promoted emperor worship and were known for their luxurious, indulgent lifestyles.

THE SEVEN CHURCHES OF REVELATION

CHURCH	COMMENDATION	COMPLAINT	CORRECTION	JUDGMENT	PROMISE
Ephesus (Rev. 2:1–7)	• rejecting evil • patience • labor • testing false apostles • perseverance	• lost their love for Jesus	• remember • repent • do the first works	• removal of lampstand	• access to the Tree of Life
Smyrna (Rev. 2:8–11)	• enduring suffering and poverty	none	none	none	• the crown of life
Pergamos (Rev. 2:12–17)	• faithfulness to Christ—even in the face of martyrdom	• tolerated immorality, idolatry, and heresies	• repent	• the sword of Christ's mouth	• hidden manna • a white stone • a new name
Thyatira (Rev. 2:18–29)	• love • service • faith • patience	• tolerance of Jezebel and her wickedness	• repent	• casting of Jezebel's consorts into the Great Tribulation and killing her children	• rule over nations • possession of the morning star
Sardis (Rev. 3:1–6)	• few who have remained faithful	• deadness despite reputation for life	• repent • strengthen what remains	• approach of Christ Himself	• clothed in white garments • permanent listing in Book of Life • confession of name before the Father
Philadelphia (Rev. 3:7–13)	• faithfulness	none	none	none	• an open door • deliverance from Great Tribulation • permanent place in temple of God • a new name
Laodicea (Rev. 3:14–22)	none	• indifference • over-estimate of status before God	• repent • seek genuine spiritual riches	• expulsion from the mouth of the Lord	• sharing Christ's throne

have not found your works perfect before God.[a] ³Remember therefore how you have received and heard; hold fast and repent. Therefore if you will not watch, I will come upon you as a thief, and you will not know what hour I will come upon you.

Sardis was built on a steep hill and considered impregnable to attack. Twice, however, enemy troops captured the city due to their failure to watch.

⁴You[a] have a few names even in Sardis who have not defiled their garments; and they shall walk with

. . . .

3:2 ªNU-Text and M-Text read *My God.* 3:4 ªNU-Text and M-Text read *Nevertheless you have a few names in Sardis.*

3:7 The key of David is an adaptation of a promise given to Eliakim that he would be appointed chief steward of the king and given the key to the king's house—the house of David (Is.

THE SEVEN CHURCHES OF ASIA MINOR

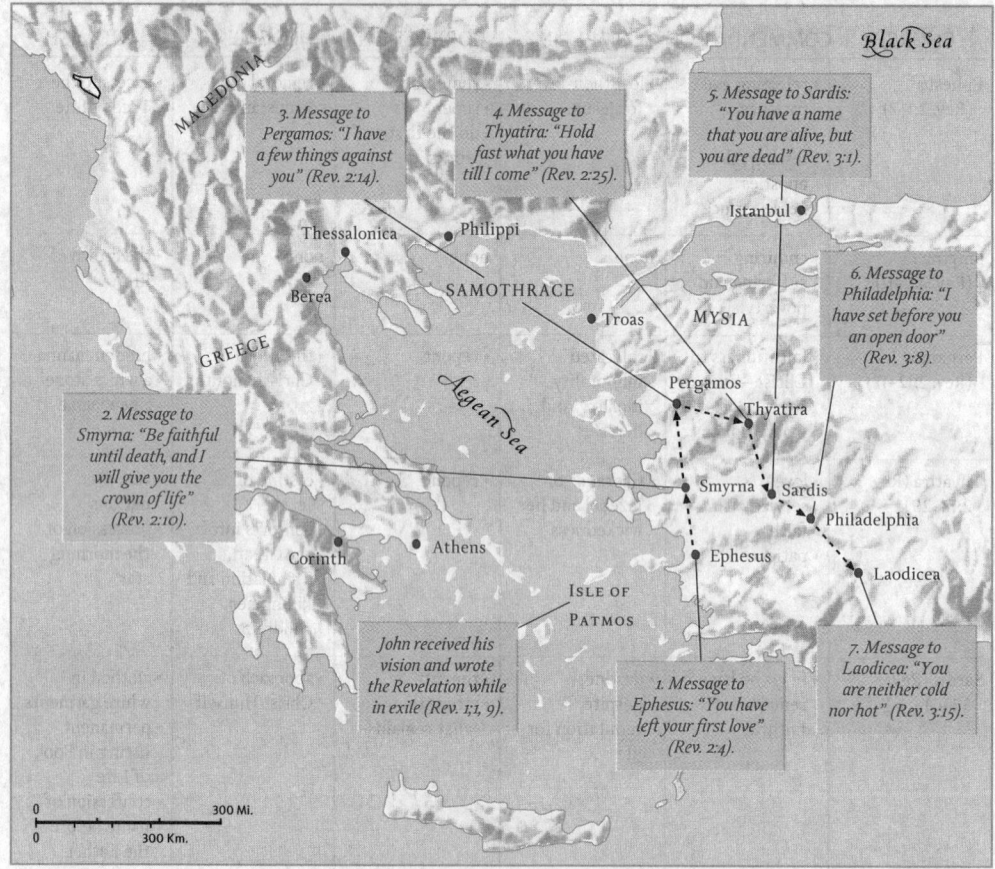

Black Sea

MACEDONIA

3. *Message to Pergamos: "I have a few things against you" (Rev. 2:14).*

4. *Message to Thyatira: "Hold fast what you have till I come" (Rev. 2:25).*

5. *Message to Sardis: "You have a name that you are alive, but you are dead" (Rev. 3:1).*

Thessalonica • Philippi

Istanbul •

Berea

SAMOTHRACE

MYSIA

6. *Message to Philadelphia: "I have set before you an open door" (Rev. 3:8).*

GREECE

• Troas

Pergamos

Thyatira

Aegean Sea

2. *Message to Smyrna: "Be faithful until death, and I will give you the crown of life" (Rev. 2:10).*

Smyrna • Sardis •

Philadelphia

Corinth • • Athens

Ephesus •

Laodicea

ISLE OF PATMOS

John received his vision and wrote the Revelation while in exile (Rev. 1:1, 9).

1. *Message to Ephesus: "You have left your first love" (Rev. 2:4).*

7. *Message to Laodicea: "You are neither cold nor hot" (Rev. 3:15).*

0 _____ 300 Mi.
0 _____ 300 Km.

The seven churches named actually existed in seven cities of Asia Minor during John's time (Rev. 2:3). Some believe that these churches represent seven periods of church history from the time of Christ until the time of His return. Others believe they depict various types of Christian congregations that have existed throughout history.

Me in white, for they are worthy. ⁵He who overcomes shall be clothed in white garments, and I will not blot out his name from the Book of Life; but I will confess his name before My Father and before His angels.

⁶"He who has an ear, let him hear what the Spirit says to the churches." ʼ

The Faithful Church

⁷"And to the angel of the church in Philadelphia write,

'These things says He who is holy, He who is true, *"He who has the key of David, He who opens and no one shuts, and shuts and no one opens"*;ᵃ ⁸"I know your works. See, I have set before you an open door, and no one can shut it;ᵃ for you have a little strength, have kept My word, and have not denied My name. ⁹Indeed I will make *those* of the synagogue of Satan, who say they are Jews and are not, but lie—indeed I will make them come and worship before

••••••••••••••••••••••
3:7 ᵃIsaiah 22:22   **3:8** ᵃNU-Text and M-Text read *which no one can shut.*

22:22). As the king's representative, Eliakim was authorized to exercise full authority in administering the affairs of the palace. The people of Israel, and the Jews living in Philadelphia, symbolically claimed this promise for themselves. They denied that Gentiles, or anyone who did not practice Judaism,

could gain entrance into the kingdom of God. Christ assured the Philadelphian believers that He alone held the power to grant or deny entrance into God's kingdom (Rev. 3:8, 10).

3:7–13 Philadelphia, modern-day Alasehir, was located at the gateway to the high central plateau of the province of Asia

Jesus, I am resting, resting
In the joy of what Thou art;
I am finding out the greatness
Of Thy loving heart.

Jean Sophie Pigott, 1876

your feet, and to know that I have loved you. ¹⁰Because you have kept My command to persevere, I also will keep you from the hour of trial which shall come upon the whole world, to test those who dwell on the earth. ¹¹Behold,ᵃ I am coming quickly! Hold fast what you have, that no one may take your crown. ¹²He who overcomes, I will make him a pillar in the temple of My God, and he shall go out no more. I will write on him the name of My God and the name of the city of My God, the New Jerusalem, which comes down out of heaven from My God. And *I will write on him* My new name.

¹³"He who has an ear, let him hear what the Spirit says to the churches." '

The Lukewarm Church

¹⁴"And to the angel of the church of the Laodiceansᵃ write,

'These things says the Amen, the Faithful and True Witness, the Beginning of the creation of God: ¹⁵"I know your works, that you are neither cold nor hot. I could wish you were cold or hot. ¹⁶So then, because you are lukewarm, and neither cold nor hot,ᵃ I will vomit you out of My mouth. ¹⁷Because you say, 'I am rich, have become wealthy, and have need of nothing'—and do not know that you are wretched, miserable, poor, blind, and naked— ¹⁸I counsel you to buy from Me gold refined in the fire, that you may be rich; and white garments, that you may be clothed, *that* the shame of your nakedness may not be revealed; and anoint

your eyes with eye salve, that you may see. ¹⁹As many as I love, I rebuke and chasten. Therefore be zealous and repent. ²⁰Behold, I stand at the door and knock. If anyone hears My voice and opens the door, I will come in to him and dine with him, and he with Me. ²¹To him who overcomes I will grant to sit with Me on My throne, as I also overcame and sat down with My Father on His throne.

²²"He who has an ear, let him hear what the Spirit says to the churches." ' "

The Throne Room of Heaven

4 After these things I looked, and behold, a door *standing* open in heaven. And the first voice which I heard *was* like a trumpet speaking with me, saying, "Come up here, and I will show you things which must take place after this."

²Immediately I was in the Spirit; and behold, a throne set in heaven, and *One* sat on the throne. ³And He who sat there wasᵃ like a jasper and a sardius stone in appearance; and *there was* a rainbow around the throne, in appearance like an emerald. ⁴Around the throne *were* twenty-four thrones, and on the thrones I saw twenty-four elders sitting, clothed in white robes; and they had crownsᵃ of gold on their heads. ⁵And from the

---

3:11 ᵃNU-Text and M-Text omit *Behold.* 3:14 ᵃNU-Text and M-Text read *in Laodicea.* 3:16 ᵃNU-Text and M-Text read *hot nor cold.* 4:3 ᵃM-Text omits *And He who sat there was* (which makes the description in verse 3 modify the throne rather than God). 4:4 ᵃNU-Text and M-Text read *robes, with crowns.*

---

and had great commercial importance. Its name, meaning "brother love," commemorated the love and loyalty of Emperor Attalus II to his brother Eumenes II.

3:14–22 Laodicea, known in modern times as Pamukkale, was the wealthiest city in Phrygia during Roman times. Famous for its banking, medical school, and textile industry, its only major weakness was an inadequate water supply.

3:15–18 A metaphor drawn from cooking described the Laodicean church. "Hot" may be a reference to the medicinal waters of Hierapolis, near Laodicea. The Laodicean church did not provide the heat of healing for the spiritually sick, nor cool refreshment for the spiritually weary.

3:19–22 Christ summoned believers who were complacent, lax, lifeless, indifferent, and tolerant of evil (v. 20). He rebukes and chastens those whom He loves (Heb. 12:6). Christ offers gold for our poverty, white garments for our nakedness, and salve for our blind eyes (Rev. 3:17, 18). He promises that

He will dine with those who open the door to Him. In the ancient Jewish world, sharing a meal with someone was a symbol of trust, affection, intimacy, and loyalty. The promise of intimacy with Christ is expressed in the invitation to open the door, so He can come in to dine (Rev. 3:20).

4:1–11 John's description of the heavenly throne provides a small glimpse of God's glory and majesty. John did not (or could not) describe the throne or the One sitting upon it. He merely conveyed his vision in terms of precious stones (see Ex. 28, Jewelry). In John's time, glass was usually dark and opaque. Clear glass was enormously expensive. The sea of glass before the throne of God could represent the awesome approach to God or simply His majesty (Ex. 24:10; Ezek. 1:22, 26).

4:4, 5 The twenty-four, white-robed elders seated upon thrones around the throne of God represent redeemed humanity (see chart, Questions from the Book of Revelation).

MILLENNIAL VIEWS

Premillennial/Pretribulation View
Christ will literally reign on earth 1,000 years. The church is taken out before the Tribulation.

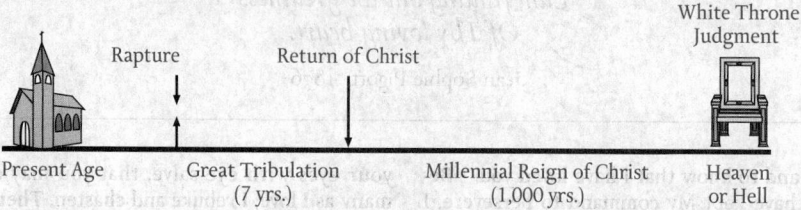

Premillennial/Midtribulation View
Christ will literally reign on earth 1,000 years. Church remains in Tribulation 3 1/2 years, then is taken out.

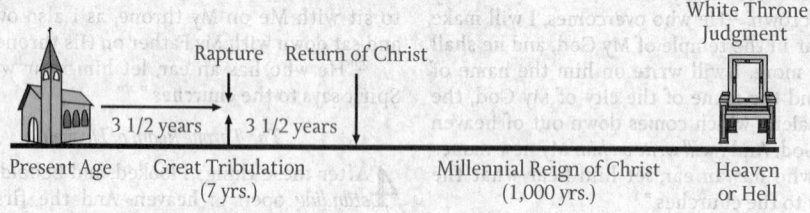

Premillennial/Posttribulation View
Christ will literally reign on earth 1,000 years. The church goes through the Tribulation.

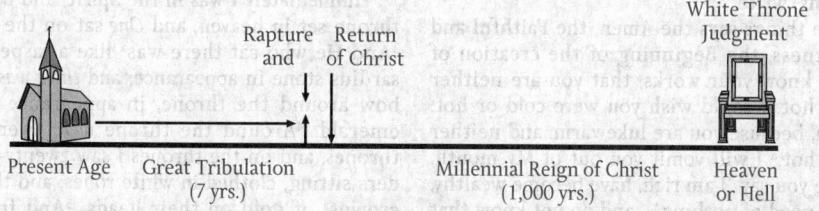

Amillennial View
Treats Christ's millennial reign as symbolic, rejecting literal 1,000 years reign on earth.

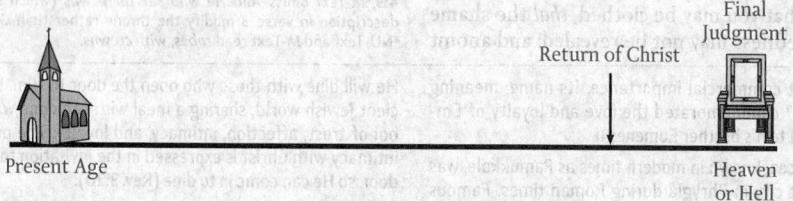

Postmillennial View
Suggests Christ will return at conclusion of millennial age.

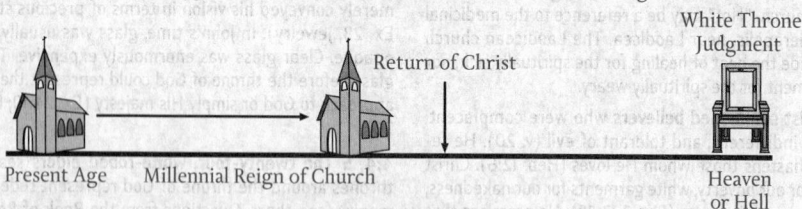

The cause of Christ can be painful and costly. It is about sacrifice. But the sacrifice is motivated by love, not fear. And the love is what sets us free.

Jeanette Thomason

---

throne proceeded lightnings, thunderings, and voices.[a] Seven lamps of fire *were* burning before the throne, which are the[b] seven Spirits of God.

[6]Before the throne *there was*[a] a sea of glass, like crystal. And in the midst of the throne, and around the throne, *were* four living creatures full of eyes in front and in back. [7]The first living creature *was* like a lion, the second living creature like a calf, the third living creature had a face like a man, and the fourth living creature *was* like a flying eagle. [8]*The* four living creatures, each having six wings, were full of eyes around and within. And they do not rest day or night, saying:

> "Holy, holy, holy,[a]
> Lord God Almighty,
> Who was and is and is to come!"

[9]Whenever the living creatures give glory and honor and thanks to Him who sits on the throne, who lives forever and ever, [10]the twenty-four elders fall down before Him who sits on the throne and worship Him who lives forever and ever, and cast their crowns before the throne, saying:

> [11]"You are worthy, O Lord,[a]
> To receive glory and honor and power;
> For You created all things,
> And by Your will they exist[b] and were created."

The Lamb Takes the Scroll

5 And I saw in the right *hand* of Him who sat on the throne a scroll written inside and on the back, sealed with seven seals. [2]Then I saw a strong angel proclaiming with a loud voice, "Who is worthy to open the scroll and to loose its seals?" [3]And no one in heaven or on the earth or under the earth was able to open the scroll, or to look at it.

[4]So I wept much, because no one was found worthy to open and read[a] the scroll, or to look at it. [5]But one of the elders said to me, "Do not weep. Behold, the Lion of the tribe of Judah, the Root of David, has prevailed to open the scroll and to loose[a] its seven seals."

[6]And I looked, and behold,[a] in the midst of the throne and of the four living creatures, and in the midst of the elders, stood a Lamb as though it had been slain, having seven horns and seven eyes, which are the seven Spirits of God sent out into all the earth. [7]Then He came and took the scroll out of the right hand of Him who sat on the throne.

Worthy Is the Lamb

[8]Now when He had taken the scroll, the four living creatures and the twenty-four elders fell down before the Lamb, each having a harp, and golden bowls full of incense, which are the prayers of the saints. [9]And they sang a new song, saying:

4:5 [a]NU-Text and M-Text read *voices, and thunderings.* [b]M-Text omits *the.* **4:6** [a]NU-Text and M-Text add *something like.* **4:8** [a]M-Text has *holy* nine times. **4:11** [a]NU-Text and M-Text read *our Lord and God.* [b]NU-Text and M-Text read *existed.* **5:4** [a]NU-Text and M-Text omit *and read.* **5:5** [a]NU-Text and M-Text omit *to loose.* **5:6** [a]NU-Text and M-Text read *I saw in the midst . . . a Lamb standing.*

The number "24" may be the sum of the 12 patriarchs in the OT and the 12 apostles of the NT who sing the song of Moses and the song of the Lamb (Rev. 15:3). The white robes depict their purity (see Rev. 3:18); the crowns, their victory (Rev. 2:10). The seven lamps of fire burning in front of the throne are the seven Spirits of God, symbolizing the presence of the Holy Spirit (see Rev. 1:4).

4:7–11 Their many eyes could represent unceasing watchfulness, while their wings suggest swiftness. The four heads may represent the various aspects of nature: wild beast, domesticated animals, human beings, and flying creatures. The creatures could therefore represent praise and adoration flowing from all of God's creation, and/or they could represent angels, who are God's agents in overseeing the created order.

5:1 Seals were used in ancient times to prevent the unauthorized reading of a letter. A seal would often consist of wax and have the writer's sign, usually made with a signet ring. Here, the seals function as symbols of the hidden plan of God to be removed in order to view God's complete plan (see chart, The Significance of Numbers in Scripture).

5:5 Jesus' position as the second Person of the Trinity is not the emphasis here but rather the fact that He has suffered and triumphed as the Messiah. The "Lion of the tribe of Judah" is a messianic title (Gen. 49:8–10). The title "Root of David" indicates that the messianic King would be a descendant of King David (Is. 11:1–10; Rom. 15:12). Christ claims both these titles for Himself.

5:6 Lambs held special significance in the OT. At one time, the Lord passed through Egypt and killed the firstborn son in every household except those who had sprinkled their doorposts with the blood of an unblemished lamb (Ex. 12:13). This event was remembered in Israel by the annual sacrifice of the Passover lamb (see chart, The Feasts of Israel). John identified Jesus as the "Lamb of God" (John 1:29), and Peter taught that the spotless Lamb, Jesus, had secured salvation for all who believe in Him (1 Pet. 1:19).

5:8–14 The Lamb in John's vision had seven horns and seven eyes. In the OT, a horn is a common symbol of strength (Deut. 33:17; Ps. 18:2; 112:9). The seven horns represent the fullness of power the Lamb possesses (Rev. 5:6). The Lamb's seven

"You are worthy to take the scroll,
And to open its seals;
For You were slain,
And have redeemed us to God by Your blood
Out of every tribe and tongue and people and
nation,
[10]And have made us[a] kings[b] and priests to our
God;
And we[c] shall reign on the earth."

[11]Then I looked, and I heard the voice of many
angels around the throne, the living creatures,
and the elders; and the number of them was ten
thousand times ten thousand, and thousands of
thousands, [12]saying with a loud voice:

"Worthy is the Lamb who was slain
To receive power and riches and wisdom,
And strength and honor and glory and
blessing!"

[13]And every creature which is in heaven and on
the earth and under the earth and such as are in
the sea, and all that are in them, I heard saying:

"Blessing and honor and glory and power
Be to Him who sits on the throne,
And to the Lamb, forever and ever!"[a]

[14]Then the four living creatures said, "Amen!"
And the twenty-four[a] elders fell down and worshiped Him who lives forever and ever.[b]

First Seal: The Conqueror

6 Now I saw when the Lamb opened one of the
seals;[a] and I heard one of the four living creatures saying with a voice like thunder, "Come and
see." [2]And I looked, and behold, a white horse. He
who sat on it had a bow; and a crown was given to
him, and he went out conquering and to conquer.

Second Seal: Conflict on Earth

[3]When He opened the second seal, I heard the
second living creature saying, "Come and see."[a]
[4]Another horse, fiery red, went out. And it was
granted to the one who sat on it to take peace
from the earth, and that *people* should kill one another; and there was given to him a great sword.

Third Seal: Scarcity on Earth

[5]When He opened the third seal, I heard the
third living creature say, "Come and see." So I
looked, and behold, a black horse, and he who sat
on it had a pair of scales in his hand. [6]And I heard
a voice in the midst of the four living creatures
saying, "A quart[a] of wheat for a denarius,[b] and
three quarts of barley for a denarius; and do not
harm the oil and the wine."

Fourth Seal: Widespread Death on Earth

[7]When He opened the fourth seal, I heard the
voice of the fourth living creature saying, "Come
and see." [8]So I looked, and behold, a pale horse.
And the name of him who sat on it was Death, and
Hades followed with him. And power was given to
them over a fourth of the earth, to kill with
sword, with hunger, with death, and by the beasts
of the earth.

Fifth Seal: The Cry of the Martyrs

[9]When He opened the fifth seal, I saw under
the altar the souls of those who had been slain for
the word of God and for the testimony which they
held. [10]And they cried with a loud voice, saying,

·················
5:10 [a]NU-Text and M-Text read *them.* [b]NU-Text reads *a kingdom.*
[c]NU-Text and M-Text read *they.*   **5:13** [a]M-Text adds *Amen.*   **5:14**
[a]NU-Text and M-Text omit *twenty-four.* [b]NU-Text and M-Text omit
Him who lives forever and ever.   **6:1** [a]NU-Text and M-Text read
seven seals.   **6:3** [a]NU-Text and M-Text omit *and see.*   **6:6** [a]Greek
choinix; that is, approximately one quart [b]This was approximately
one day's wage for a worker.

---

eyes depict His complete and perfect knowledge and insight
(v. 6; Zech. 4:10). The eyes of the Lamb are also identified as
the seven Spirits of God (Rev. 6:6; see Rev. 2:1). In this imagery, John symbolized the relationship between Christ and
the Holy Spirit (John 15:26). When the Lamb took the scroll,
the four creatures and 24 elders fell down and worshiped
Him, and the entire heavenly court joined in singing His praise
(Rev. 6:9, 10). "Ten thousand" is a rhetorical phrase for an infinitely large number (Rev. 5:11; see Dan. 7:10; Heb. 12:22).

6:1–8 The seven seals, the seven trumpets (Rev. 8; 9), the
seven thunders (Rev. 10:2–4), and the seven bowls (Rev. 16)
are four series of judgments in multiples of seven. These
events are part of the tragic period called the Great Tribulation, during which judgment is poured out on a world that has
rejected the Lord. This period is characterized by the wrath
and judgment of God, the awakening of Israel's longing for
the Messiah, and preparation for Christ's return (see chart,
Questions from the Book of Revelation). Four horses, whose
colors are symbolic of the events they initiate, are sent to the

earth (see Zech. 1:8, 9; 6:1–8; chart, Colors in the Bible). The
white horse represents conquest (see "man of sin," 1 Thess.
2:3, 4, note; Rev. 13; chart, The Prophecy of Seventy Weeks).
The second rider sits upon a red horse (symbolizing bloodshed and war) and is given a great sword. The rider of the
black horse carries a pair of scales, which were used to measure grain. Each person consumed an average of one quart of
this main dietary staple daily. Barley was cheaper than wheat
and was considered the food of the poor. All a man's daily
earnings, a denarius, would be needed to buy food (see chart,
Money and Measurements in the Bible). Though food would
be scarce, other staples of an ordinary diet, such as oil and
wine, would not. Thus, the black horse represents a condition
of severe scarcity but not of worldwide starvation. The fourth
horse, pale in color, represents death, which will strike more
than a quarter of the earth's population through war, famine,
pestilence, and wild beasts.

6:9–11 The fifth seal revealed an altar (v. 9). In the OT, the
blood of the sacrificial animal was poured out at the base of

QUESTIONS FROM THE BOOK OF REVELATION

POINT OF DISCUSSION	AMILLENNIAL VIEWPOINT	PREMILLENNIAL VIEWPOINT	POSTMILLENNIAL VIEWPOINT
Millennial view	Christ has no literal reign on earth. Revelation does not present actual events—past or future. Its message is symbolic of the great struggle between good and evil.	Christ will return, usher in millennial age, and rule on earth. Beginning with Revelation 4, the events described belong to the future age. They present through prophecy God's plan for the consummation of the age.	Christ will return at the end of the millennial age. Meantime the world progresses under the missionary success of the church.
Twenty-four elders (Rev. 4:4, 10; 5:8, 14)	Represent all the redeemed.	Represent the saints gathered together in heaven as the family of God.	Represent all the redeemed.
144,000 (Rev. 7:4–8)	The redeemed on earth who are protected from God's wrath.	Jews who will be converted during the Tribulation after the church has been raptured.	The redeemed people of God.
Great Tribulation (Rev. 7:14)	Persecution of Christians in John's time representative of tribulation throughout history.	The exhibition of the wrath and judgment of God in final preparation for the return of the Lord.	Symbolic of tribulation suffered throughout history.
Forty-two months or 1,260 days (Rev. 11:2, 3)	Indefinite time of evil influence.	Half of seven-year Tribulation period.	Indefinite time of pagan desolation.
Woman (Rev. 12:1–6)	True people of God under old and new covenants.	Israel, not the church.	True people of God under old and new covenants.
1,260 days (Rev. 12:6)	Indefinite time period.	First half of Tribulation after church is raptured.	Indefinite time period.
Seven heads (Rev. 13:1)	Roman emperors.	A revival of the ancient Roman Empire greatly expanded.	Roman emperors.
Ten horns (Rev. 13:1)	Symbol of power.	Ten powers that will combine to make the federation of nations of new Rome.	Symbol of power.
Babylon—woman (Rev. 17:5)	Historic Rome.	Resurgence of the apostate church.	Representing evil.
Wife (Rev. 19:7)	All the redeemed.	The church (except Old Testament or Tribulation saints).	All the redeemed.
Armageddon (Rev. 19:19–21)	Not literally at end of time but symbolizing power of God's Word in overcoming evil.	Literal bloody battle at Armageddon (valley of Megiddo) at end of Great Tribulation between kings of the East and federation of nations of new Rome; they are all defeated by Christ. The millennium begins.	Representing power of God's Word overcoming evil forces.
Millennium (Rev. 20:2–6)	Symbolic reference to period from Christ's Incarnation to His return.	A literal 1,000-year period during which Christ rules with His people.	A lengthy period of expansion and spiritual prosperity brought about by preaching the gospel.

"How long, O Lord, holy and true, until You judge and avenge our blood on those who dwell on the earth?" [11]Then a white robe was given to each of them; and it was said to them that they should rest a little while longer, until both *the number of* their fellow servants and their brethren, who would be killed as they *were,* was completed.

Sixth Seal: Cosmic Disturbances

[12]I looked when He opened the sixth seal, and behold,[a] there was a great earthquake; and the sun became black as sackcloth of hair, and the moon[b] became like blood. [13]And the stars of heaven fell to the earth, as a fig tree drops its late figs when it is shaken by a mighty wind. [14]Then the sky receded as a scroll when it is rolled up, and every mountain and island was moved out of its place. [15]And the kings of the earth, the great men, the rich men, the commanders,[a] the mighty men, every slave and every free man, hid themselves in the caves and in the rocks of the mountains, [16]and said to the mountains and rocks, "Fall on us and hide us from the face of Him who sits on the throne and from the wrath of the Lamb! [17]For the great day of His wrath has come, and who is able to stand?"

The Sealed of Israel

7 After these things I saw four angels standing at the four corners of the earth, holding the four winds of the earth, that the wind should not blow on the earth, on the sea, or on any tree. [2]Then I saw another angel ascending from the east, having the seal of the living God. And he cried with a loud voice to the four angels to whom it was granted to harm the earth and the sea, [3]saying, "Do not harm the earth, the sea, or the trees till we have sealed the servants of our God on their foreheads." [4]And I heard the number of those who were sealed. One hundred *and* forty-four thousand of all the tribes of the children of Israel *were* sealed:

[5]of the tribe of Judah twelve thousand *were* sealed;[a]
of the tribe of Reuben twelve thousand *were* sealed;
of the tribe of Gad twelve thousand *were* sealed;
[6]of the tribe of Asher twelve thousand *were* sealed;
of the tribe of Naphtali twelve thousand *were* sealed;
of the tribe of Manasseh twelve thousand *were* sealed;
[7]of the tribe of Simeon twelve thousand *were* sealed;
of the tribe of Levi twelve thousand *were* sealed;
of the tribe of Issachar twelve thousand *were* sealed;
[8]of the tribe of Zebulun twelve thousand *were* sealed;
of the tribe of Joseph twelve thousand *were* sealed;
of the tribe of Benjamin twelve thousand *were* sealed.

A Multitude from the Great Tribulation

[9]After these things I looked, and behold, a great multitude which no one could number, of all nations, tribes, peoples, and tongues, standing before the throne and before the Lamb, clothed with white robes, with palm branches in their hands, [10]and crying out with a loud voice, saying, "Salvation *belongs* to our God who sits on the throne, and to the Lamb!" [11]All the angels stood around the throne and the elders and the four living crea-

························

6:12 [a]NU-Text and M-Text omit *behold.* [b]NU-Text and M-Text read *the whole moon.*   6:15 [a]NU-Text and M-Text read *the commanders, the rich men.*   7:5 [a]In NU-Text and M-Text *were sealed* is stated only in verses 5a and 8c; the words are understood in the remainder of the passage.

---

the altar (Ex. 29:12; Lev. 4:7). Here, the martyrs cry out that God in His righteous judgment will condemn the enemies of God's people. This passage is similar to the OT imprecatory psalms, in which the psalmist pleaded with God to destroy his enemies (see chart, The Types of Psalms). The church had already faced persecution and would experience more to come.

6:12–17 Cataclysmic upheaval is a usual part of last-days' imagery in Scripture (see Is. 13:9, 10; Joel 2:30, 31; 2 Pet. 3:10). Here the extent of the disturbance is cosmic in scope and breaks forth at the opening of the sixth seal. Catastrophic language is also found in Christ's teaching that tribulation and cosmic upheaval will precede the coming of the Lord (Matt. 24:29, 30).

7:1, 2 The angels represent God's personal control of the world He has created. The four winds are destructive agents of God (see chart, The Significance of Numbers in Scripture). "The seal of the living God" is placed on the foreheads of the righteous so that the agents of destruction would spare them

(v. 2). This symbolism goes back to Ezekiel's vision (Ezek. 9:4). Seals were important symbols in an era when many people were illiterate. Both in Revelation and Ezekiel God seals His people to preserve them from the destruction that will befall others.

7:4–8 A seal indicates God's declaration of ownership and His protection. Scholars have proposed a number of interpretations as to the identity of the 144,000 who were sealed, but two views predominate. Premillennialists believe that the number refers to actual members of the Jewish nation, affirming God's continued faithfulness to His promises to Israel, and perhaps a harbinger of the great revival envisioned by Paul (see Rom. 9; 10). The careful listing of each tribe also supports this interpretation. Postmillennialists and amillennialists do not believe that the 144,000 are limited to Jews but that they represent the church as a whole (see chart, Questions from the Book of Revelation).

WOMEN IN THE BOOK OF REVELATION

WOMAN	DESCRIPTION
Jezebel (Rev. 2:20–23)	Taught people in the church at Thyatira to worship false gods and encouraged immorality;
	Christ promised to judge Jezebel and her children.
The Woman Giving Birth (Rev. 12:1–6, 13–17)	A contrast to Jezebel;
	God gives her protection when she is attacked by the dragon;
	She is identified as Israel.
Babylon, the Great Harlot (Rev. 14:8; 17:1–6, 15, 18; 18:1–24)	Babylon is judged and destroyed for persecuting God's people and corrupting others.
The Bride of the Lamb (Rev. 19:7, 8)	Represents the church;
	The Bride readies herself for the marriage feast.

tures, and fell on their faces before the throne and worshiped God, [12]saying:

"Amen! Blessing and glory and wisdom,
Thanksgiving and honor and power and might,
Be to our God forever and ever.
Amen."

[13]Then one of the elders answered, saying to me, "Who are these arrayed in white robes, and where did they come from?"

[14]And I said to him, "Sir,[a] you know."

So he said to me, "These are the ones who come out of the great tribulation, and washed their robes and made them white in the blood of the Lamb. [15]Therefore they are before the throne of God, and serve Him day and night in His temple. And He who sits on the throne will dwell among them. [16]They shall neither hunger anymore nor thirst anymore; the sun shall not strike them, nor any heat; [17]for the Lamb who is

in the midst of the throne will shepherd them and lead them to living fountains of waters.[a] And God will wipe away every tear from their eyes."

Seventh Seal: Prelude to the Seven Trumpets

8 When He opened the seventh seal, there was silence in heaven for about half an hour. [2]And I saw the seven angels who stand before God, and to them were given seven trumpets. [3]Then another angel, having a golden censer, came and stood at the altar. He was given much incense, that he should offer *it* with the prayers of all the saints upon the golden altar which was before the throne. [4]And the smoke of the incense, with the prayers of the saints, ascended before God from the angel's hand. [5]Then the angel took the censer, filled it with fire from the altar, and threw *it* to the

7:14 [a]NU-Text and M-Text read *My lord*.   7:17 [a]NU-Text and M-Text read *to fountains of the waters of life*.

7:14, 15 The Great Tribulation refers to the seven-year period of unparalleled trouble on earth, concluding with the return of Christ (Dan. 12:1; Mark 13:19; see chart Questions from the Book of Revelation). The believers who came through the Tribulation are pictured as wearing white robes before the throne of God and serving Him day and night in the temple. Each of the 16 references to the temple in Revelation designates the inner shrine of the temple or the place of the intimate dwelling of God's presence with His people. For John's readers, the imagery would invoke memories of the tabernacle in the desert (Lev. 26:11–13). The term would

have been understood to mean the immediate presence of God. The whole of heaven is likened to the sanctuary in which all believers are priests enjoying fellowship with God forever (Rev. 1:6; 5:10).

8:1–3 Prior to the sounding of the trumpets, an angel with a golden censer stands before the altar to offer up the prayers of the saints. The censer is a firepan used to hold live coals for burning incense (Ex. 27:3; 1 Kin. 7:50). Incense both represents and purifies the prayers of the saints (Ps. 141:2; Rev. 5:8).

earth. And there were noises, thunderings, lightnings, and an earthquake.

[6]So the seven angels who had the seven trumpets prepared themselves to sound.

First Trumpet: Vegetation Struck

[7]The first angel sounded: And hail and fire followed, mingled with blood, and they were thrown to the earth.[a] And a third of the trees were burned up, and all green grass was burned up.

Second Trumpet: The Seas Struck

[8]Then the second angel sounded: And *something* like a great mountain burning with fire was thrown into the sea, and a third of the sea became blood. [9]And a third of the living creatures in the sea died, and a third of the ships were destroyed.

Third Trumpet: The Waters Struck

[10]Then the third angel sounded: And a great star fell from heaven, burning like a torch, and it fell on a third of the rivers and on the springs of water. [11]The name of the star is Wormwood. A third of the waters became wormwood, and many men died from the water, because it was made bitter.

Fourth Trumpet: The Heavens Struck

[12]Then the fourth angel sounded: And a third of the sun was struck, a third of the moon, and a third of the stars, so that a third of them were darkened. A third of the day did not shine, and likewise the night.

[13]And I looked, and I heard an angel[a] flying through the midst of heaven, saying with a loud voice, "Woe, woe, woe to the inhabitants of the earth, because of the remaining blasts of the trumpet of the three angels who are about to sound!"

Fifth Trumpet: The Locusts from the Bottomless Pit

9 Then the fifth angel sounded: And I saw a star fallen from heaven to the earth. To him was given the key to the bottomless pit. [2]And he opened the bottomless pit, and smoke arose out of the pit like the smoke of a great furnace. So the sun and the air were darkened because of the smoke of the pit. [3]Then out of the smoke locusts came upon the earth. And to them was given power, as the scorpions of the earth have power. [4]They were commanded not to harm the grass of the earth, or any green thing, or any tree, but only those men who do not have the seal of God on their foreheads. [5]And they were not given *authority* to kill them, but to torment them *for* five months. Their torment *was* like the torment of a scorpion when it strikes a man. [6]In those days men will seek death and will not find it; they will desire to die, and death will flee from them.

[7]The shape of the locusts was like horses prepared for battle. On their heads were crowns of something like gold, and their faces *were* like the faces of men. [8]They had hair like women's hair, and their teeth were like lions' *teeth.* [9]And they had breastplates like breastplates of iron, and the sound of their wings *was* like the sound of chariots with many horses running into battle. [10]They had tails like scorpions, and there were stings in their tails. Their power *was* to hurt men five months. [11]And they had as king over them the angel of the bottomless pit, whose name in Hebrew *is* Abaddon, but in Greek he has the name Apollyon.

[12]One woe is past. Behold, still two more woes are coming after these things.

Sixth Trumpet: The Angels from the Euphrates

[13]Then the sixth angel sounded: And I heard a voice from the four horns of the golden altar which is before God, [14]saying to the sixth angel who had the trumpet, "Release the four angels who are bound at the great river Euphrates." [15]So the four angels, who had been prepared for the

---

8:7 [a]NU-Text and M-Text add *and a third of the earth was burned up.*
8:13 [a]NU-Text and M-Text read *eagle.*

8:7–12 The precise nature of the disturbances is difficult to determine (vv. 8–10). But clearly the trumpets bring about earthly disasters of immense proportions with destructive consequences. The consequences of the first four trumpets seem restricted to the realm of nature as God's judgment on a planet in rebellion against Him. Wormwood is a non-poisonous plant with a strong bitter taste. It is often used as a metaphor for calamity and sorrow (vv. 10, 11; see Prov. 5:3, 4; Jer. 9:15; see chart, The Herbs of the Bible). The judgment of the fourth trumpet is reminiscent of the Egyptian plague of darkness (Rev. 8:12; see Ex. 10:21–23). These references to the plagues of Egypt suggest that the final exodus (deliverance) of God's people from bondage will occur at that time (see chart, The Ten Plagues on Egypt).

9:1–12 When the fifth trumpet sounded, John saw "a star fallen from heaven to earth" (v. 1). This star refers to an unidentified demonic being, perhaps even Satan. Jesus spoke of a fall of Satan (Luke 10:18), as did Isaiah (Is. 14:12; see chart, A Portrait of the Adversary). The "bottomless pit" (Gk. *abyssos,* lit. "abyss") is the residence of the Antichrist before he appears on earth (Rev. 9:1; 11:7) and the place where Satan is bound during the millennium (Rev. 20:3). It appears to be a place for the imprisonment of demons (Luke 8:31). The locusts represent demonic forces that are released and allowed to torment and bring judgment upon unrepentant humanity (see also Joel 2:1–12, 25). The king of the locusts is the "angel of the bottomless pit" (Rev. 9:11). *Abaddon* (Heb.) and *Apollyon* (Gk.) mean "the destroyer" (see chart, The Names for Satan).

9:13–21 At the sounding of the sixth trumpet, God releases four angels who were bound on the banks of the Euphrates River, the ideal eastern limit of the Promised Land (v. 14; Gen.

THE SIGNIFICANCE OF NUMBERS IN SCRIPTURE

THE NUMBER	BIBLICAL SIGNIFICANCE
1	Unity (Gen. 2:24); independent existence (Deut. 6:4)
2	An addition—strength, help (Eccl. 4:9–12)
3	Simplest compound unity; the number for God (Matt. 28:19)
4	The world with its four seasons and directions (Rev. 7:1)
5	Mankind with the various five-membered parts of the body (Lev. 14:14–16)
6	Evil, failure; it falls short of the number seven, which represents perfection (Rev. 13:18)
7	Perfection or completeness; a number representing earth crowned with heaven (Rev. 1:4)
10	Five doubled and thus human completeness (Rev. 2:10)
12	God's perfect manifestation of Himself to the created order (Rev. 21:12)

Note: Throughout Scripture numbers often have symbolic as well as literal meanings. In the Book of Revelation the number seven is especially prevalent, appearing more than fifty times.

hour and day and month and year, were released to kill a third of mankind. ¹⁶Now the number of the army of the horsemen *was* two hundred million; I heard the number of them. ¹⁷And thus I saw the horses in the vision: those who sat on them had breastplates of fiery red, hyacinth blue, and sulfur yellow; and the heads of the horses *were* like the heads of lions; and out of their mouths came fire, smoke, and brimstone. ¹⁸By these three *plagues* a third of mankind was killed—by the fire and the smoke and the brimstone which came out of their mouths. ¹⁹For their power^a is in their mouth and in their tails; for their tails *are* like serpents, having heads; and with them they do harm.

²⁰But the rest of mankind, who were not killed by these plagues, did not repent of the works of their hands, that they should not worship demons,

and idols of gold, silver, brass, stone, and wood, which can neither see nor hear nor walk. ²¹And they did not repent of their murders or their sorceries^a or their sexual immorality or their thefts.

The Mighty Angel with the Little Book

10 I saw still another mighty angel coming down from heaven, clothed with a cloud. And a rainbow *was* on his head, his face *was* like the sun, and his feet like pillars of fire. ²He had a little book open in his hand. And he set his right foot on the sea and *his* left *foot* on the land, ³and cried with a loud voice, as *when* a lion roars. When he cried out, seven thunders uttered their voices.

<hr>

9:19 ^aNU-Text and M-Text read *the power of the horses.* **9:21** ^aNU-Text and M-Text read *drugs.*

15:18). Hordes of Gentile kingdoms were situated beyond the river. An invasion from across the Euphrates would constitute an invasion of the enemies of Israel and of God (Is. 7:20; 8:7; Jer. 46:10). The fifth trumpet brought torture; this trumpet brings death. An army of two hundred million is described as killing a third of mankind (Rev. 9:16, 18). This inconceivably large force—more than the entire population of the earth at the time Revelation was written—is beyond human comprehension. Many see this as an actual army, while some identify this language as symbolic of a demonic host. In any case, the outpouring of suffering and death at the sounding of the fifth

and sixth trumpets seems terrible; yet its purpose is merciful. It is designed to encourage people to repent before it is too late to do so (vv. 20, 21).

10:1–3 The angel was clothed in a cloud. Clouds are depicted as the chariot of God by which heavenly beings ascend and descend (Ps. 104:13; Dan. 7:13; Acts 1:9). The description of this angel is similar to descriptions of the Son of Man in His glory and is interpreted by many as a reference to Christ. Others identify this angel as a messenger reflecting a measure of heavenly glory.

[4]Now when the seven thunders uttered their voices,[a] I was about to write; but I heard a voice from heaven saying to me,[b] "Seal up the things which the seven thunders uttered, and do not write them."

[5]The angel whom I saw standing on the sea and on the land raised up his hand[a] to heaven [6]and swore by Him who lives forever and ever, who created heaven and the things that are in it, the earth and the things that are in it, and the sea and the things that are in it, that there should be delay no longer, [7]but in the days of the sounding of the seventh angel, when he is about to sound, the mystery of God would be finished, as He declared to His servants the prophets.

John Eats the Little Book

[8]Then the voice which I heard from heaven spoke to me again and said, "Go, take the little book which is open in the hand of the angel who stands on the sea and on the earth."

[9]So I went to the angel and said to him, "Give me the little book."

And he said to me, "Take and eat it; and it will make your stomach bitter, but it will be as sweet as honey in your mouth."

[10]Then I took the little book out of the angel's hand and ate it, and it was as sweet as honey in my mouth. But when I had eaten it, my stomach became bitter. [11]And he[a] said to me, "You must prophesy again about many peoples, nations, tongues, and kings."

The Two Witnesses

11 Then I was given a reed like a measuring rod. And the angel stood,[a] saying, "Rise and measure the temple of God, the altar, and those who worship there. [2]But leave out the court which

is outside the temple, and do not measure it, for it has been given to the Gentiles. And they will tread the holy city underfoot for forty-two months. [3]And I will give power to my two witnesses, and they will prophesy one thousand two hundred and sixty days, clothed in sackcloth."

[4]These are the two olive trees and the two lampstands standing before the God[a] of the earth. [5]And if anyone wants to harm them, fire proceeds from their mouth and devours their enemies. And if anyone wants to harm them, he must be killed in this manner. [6]These have power to shut heaven, so that no rain falls in the days of their prophecy; and they have power over waters to turn them to blood, and to strike the earth with all plagues, as often as they desire.

The Witnesses Killed

[7]When they finish their testimony, the beast that ascends out of the bottomless pit will make war against them, overcome them, and kill them. [8]And their dead bodies will lie in the street of the great city which spiritually is called Sodom and Egypt, where also our[a] Lord was crucified. [9]Then those from the peoples, tribes, tongues, and nations will see their dead bodies three-and-a-half days, and not allow[a] their dead bodies to be put into graves. [10]And those who dwell on the earth will rejoice over them, make merry, and send gifts to one another, because these two prophets tormented those who dwell on the earth.

•••••••••••••••••••••

10:4 [a]NU-Text and M-Text read sounded. [b]NU-Text and M-Text omit to me. **10:5** [a]NU-Text and M-Text read right hand. **10:11** [a]NU-Text and M-Text read they. **11:1** [a]NU-Text and M-Text omit And the angel stood. **11:4** [a]NU-Text and M-Text read Lord. **11:8** [a]NU-Text and M-Text read their. **11:9** [a]NU-Text and M-Text read nations see . . . and will not allow.

10:4 John was instructed not to record what he had just heard. The Book of Revelation gives hope for the future and inspires godly living in the present; it is not meant to provide a total blueprint for the end times. Believers ought to live as if these events could begin at any time; they should be cautious in accepting any teaching which claims to give full particulars of future events.

10:8–11 The first book was intended to be opened (Rev. 5); this one was to be eaten, indicating full assimilation of its contents (see Ezek. 3:1–3; Jer. 15:16). God's words are sweet as honey in his mouth (Rev. 10:10; see Ps. 19:10; 119:103); but as the implications of the words were pondered, they became bitter in his stomach. The judgments of God are sweet in bringing evil to a proper end, but the wrath of God is bitter as it falls on the unrepentant.

11:1, 2 The reed, a bamboo-like cane, often reached 20 feet in height and grew readily along the shores of the Jordan River. Being straight and light, it was a convenient measuring tool. The court of the Gentiles is excluded because the Gentiles symbolize those who have utterly rejected God. Many believe that the 42 months (3½ years or 1,260 days) correspond to

one half of Daniel's seventieth week (see charts, The Prophecy of Seventy Weeks; Questions from the Book of Revelation). After the Antichrist breaks his covenant with Israel, the nation will undergo incredible suffering, including the occupation of Jerusalem by Gentiles. Others interpret the period as a symbolic length of time in which God deals with humanity.

11:3–10 The two witnesses are also identified as olive trees and lampstands (Zech. 4:12–14). Some see this imagery as a reference to Moses and Elijah, or to the OT and NT, or even to God's people as a whole. Yet there seems no compelling reason to identify these as more than individuals in history who will be raised up as God's witnesses in Jerusalem in the last days, to have a powerful ministry similar to that of Moses and Elijah. The witnesses will stand in opposition to the False Prophet (see Rev. 13:11–18). People will be condemned and destroyed because of the prophetic words they utter (Jer. 5:14), but these prophets are not to be harmed until their mission is complete (Rev. 11:7–10). The Beast, the primary opponent of God's people in the final days, is mentioned here for the first time (see Rev. 13; 17). That he comes out of the bottomless pit emphasizes his demonic nature.

BEATITUDES IN THE BOOK OF REVELATION

BEATITUDE	EMPHASIS	REFERENCE
1. The blessedness of those reading, hearing, and keeping this prophecy.	1. The importance of the Word of God.	Rev. 1:3
2. The happiness of the dead who die in the Lord.	2. The blessings of eternal life.	Rev. 14:13
3. The respect of those watching and keeping their garments.	3. The anticipation of the Lord's return.	Rev. 16:15
4. The delight of those invited to the marriage supper of the Lamb.	4. The joy of God's presence.	Rev. 19:9
5. The blessedness of those who participate in the first resurrection.	5. The freedom of deliverance from death.	Rev. 20:6
6. The joy of keeping the words of this prophecy.	6. The necessity of obedience to the Word.	Rev. 22:7
7. The happy result of washing one's robe and accessing the Tree of Life.	7. The guarantee of eternal sustenance.	Rev. 22:14

The Witnesses Resurrected

[11]Now after the three-and-a-half days the breath of life from God entered them, and they stood on their feet, and great fear fell on those who saw them. [12]And they[a] heard a loud voice from heaven saying to them, "Come up here." And they ascended to heaven in a cloud, and their enemies saw them. [13]In the same hour there was a great earthquake, and a tenth of the city fell. In the earthquake seven thousand people were killed, and the rest were afraid and gave glory to the God of heaven.

[14]The second woe is past. Behold, the third woe is coming quickly.

Seventh Trumpet: The Kingdom Proclaimed

[15]Then the seventh angel sounded: And there were loud voices in heaven, saying, "The kingdoms[a] of this world have become the kingdoms of our Lord and of His Christ, and He shall reign forever and ever!" [16]And the twenty-four elders who sat before God on their thrones fell on their faces and worshiped God, [17]saying:

"We give You thanks, O Lord God Almighty,
The One who is and who was and who is to come,[a]
Because You have taken Your great power and reigned.
[18]The nations were angry, and Your wrath has come,
And the time of the dead, that they should be judged,
And that You should reward Your servants the prophets and the saints,
And those who fear Your name, small and great,
And should destroy those who destroy the earth."

[19]Then the temple of God was opened in heaven, and the ark of His covenant[a] was seen in

11:12 [a]M-Text reads I.　11:15 [a]NU-Text and M-Text read kingdom . . . has become.　11:17 [a]NU-Text and M-Text omit and who is to come.　11:19 [a]M-Text reads the covenant of the Lord.

11:11–13 God's elect are not defeated by death. The resurrection of the two witnesses indicates God's power and triumph. John's message is that God's people should never lose hope, even amidst overwhelming odds, for the outcome has already been made sure. Christ's Resurrection and work of redemption have secured the victory (1 Cor. 10:20).

11:19 The ark of His covenant, a chest made of acacia wood, symbolized the throne or presence of God among His people (Deut. 10:1, 2). In OT times, the ark stood in the inner part of the tabernacle or temple—the Most Holy Place—to which only the high priest had access. John reminded his readers that they would see the ark. They would be in the presence of God. All that God promised would be fulfilled.

His temple. And there were lightnings, noises, thunderings, an earthquake, and great hail.

The Woman, the Child, and the Dragon

12 Now a great sign appeared in heaven: a woman clothed with the sun, with the moon under her feet, and on her head a garland of twelve stars. [2] Then being with child, she cried out in labor and in pain to give birth.

[3] And another sign appeared in heaven: behold, a great, fiery red dragon having seven heads and ten horns, and seven diadems on his heads. [4] His tail drew a third of the stars of heaven and threw them to the earth. And the dragon stood before the woman who was ready to give birth, to devour her Child as soon as it was born. [5] She bore a male Child who was to rule all nations with a rod of iron. And her Child was caught up to God and His throne. [6] Then the woman fled into the wilderness, where she has a place prepared by God, that they should feed her there one thousand two hundred and sixty days.

Satan Thrown Out of Heaven

[7] And war broke out in heaven: Michael and his angels fought with the dragon; and the dragon and his angels fought, [8] but they did not prevail, nor was a place found for them[a] in heaven any longer. [9] So the great dragon was cast out, that serpent of old, called the Devil and Satan, who deceives the whole world; he was cast to the earth, and his angels were cast out with him.

[10] Then I heard a loud voice saying in heaven, "Now salvation, and strength, and the kingdom of our God, and the power of His Christ have come, for the accuser of our brethren, who accused them before our God day and night, has been cast down.

[11] And they overcame him by the blood of the Lamb and by the word of their testimony, and they did not love their lives to the death. [12] Therefore rejoice, O heavens, and you who dwell in them! Woe to the inhabitants of the earth and the sea! For the devil has come down to you, having great wrath, because he knows that he has a short time."

The Woman Persecuted

[13] Now when the dragon saw that he had been cast to the earth, he persecuted the woman who gave birth to the male *Child.* [14] But the woman was given two wings of a great eagle, that she might fly into the wilderness to her place, where she is nourished for a time and times and half a time, from the presence of the serpent. [15] So the serpent spewed water out of his mouth like a flood after the woman, that he might cause her to be carried away by the flood. [16] But the earth helped the woman, and the earth opened its mouth and swallowed up the flood which the dragon had spewed out of his mouth. [17] And the dragon was enraged with the woman, and he went to make war with the rest of her offspring, who keep the commandments of God and have the testimony of Jesus Christ.[a]

The Beast from the Sea

13 Then I[a] stood on the sand of the sea. And I saw a beast rising up out of the sea, having seven heads and ten horns,[b] and on his horns ten crowns, and on his heads a blasphemous name. [2] Now the beast which I saw was like a leopard, his

---

12:8 [a]M-Text reads *him.* 12:17 [a]NU-Text and M-Text omit *Christ.* 13:1 [a]NU-Text reads *he.* [b]NU-Text and M-Text read *ten horns and seven heads.*

12:1–12 John related a series of visions: the birth of the Messiah, Satan's continuous attempts to destroy Him, Christ's exaltation, God's casting down of Satan, and Satan's retaliation against God's people. Although believers face evil and persecution on earth, Christ has already conquered Satan, and believers, too, are able to overcome Satan by the blood of the Lamb (v. 11).

12:3–5 The Dragon (Gk. *drakon*, is a synonym for the word translated "serpent" (Gk. *ophis*; Gen. 3:1)), represents Satan (Rev. 12:9). Multiple heads, horns, and diadems refer to his power, splendor, and wealth (v. 3; Dan. 8:10; 2 Cor. 4:4). He is massive and fearful in appearance and is intent on devouring the Child (Rev. 12:4). The woman represents Israel—the people of God (v. 1; Gal. 4:26). The metaphor of Israel as a woman in labor is also used elsewhere (Is. 26:17; 66:7, 8; Mic. 4:10; 5:3). The woman's Child refers to Christ. (Ps. 2:9; 1 Cor. 15:25; Rev. 2:27; 19:15).

12:7–9 Angels (lit. "messengers") were considered ambassadors who spoke and acted in human affairs on behalf of their sender. Michael is the chief guardian angel of Israel (Dan. 10:13, 21; 12:1; Jude 9). He will lead God's angelic forces in battle against the "dragon and his angels" (Rev. 12:7). The victory

ultimately is won because of the faithfulness of the Saints and their reliance on the "blood of the Lamb" (v. 11). Victory over Satan is not always evident in the physical realm. Yet believers can stand fast and have power over the Evil One (Matt. 24:13; Rev. 12:11).

12:13–17 The woman fled (v. 6; Dan. 7:25; chart, Women in the Book of Revelation). Israel is assured of God's ultimate protection. The flood of water is symbolic of Satan's massive effort to destroy God's plan. Most commentators believe that the first part of this vision depicts the overthrow of Satan in heaven, while the latter depicts his persecution of the saints on earth, "the rest of her offspring." Regardless, the message is the same: Satan had already been defeated, and his efforts to overcome God's people are in vain.

13:1, 2 An intensification of evil will accompany the appearance of "the Antichrist" (1 John 2:18), "the man of sin," or "the son of perdition" (2 Thess. 2:3). The sea is a symbol of chaos, on which must be imposed the order of creation (Gen. 1:2). The Beast rises up out of the sea, which indicates that the Antichrist may emerge from a situation of political chaos (Is. 7:20). John's description of the Beast is similar to his description of Satan (Rev. 12:3), indicating a close relationship be-

feet were like *the feet of* a bear, and his mouth like the mouth of a lion. The dragon gave him his power, his throne, and great authority. ³And I saw one of his heads as if it had been mortally wounded, and his deadly wound was healed. And all the world marveled and followed the beast. ⁴So they worshiped the dragon who gave authority to the beast; and they worshiped the beast, saying, "Who *is* like the beast? Who is able to make war with him?"

⁵And he was given a mouth speaking great things and blasphemies, and he was given authority to continueª for forty-two months. ⁶Then he opened his mouth in blasphemy against God, to blaspheme His name, His tabernacle, and those who dwell in heaven. ⁷It was granted to him to make war with the saints and to overcome them. And authority was given him over every tribe,ª tongue, and nation. ⁸All who dwell on the earth will worship him, whose names have not been written in the Book of Life of the Lamb slain from the foundation of the world.

⁹If anyone has an ear, let him hear. ¹⁰He who leads into captivity shall go into captivity; he who kills with the sword must be killed with the sword. Here is the patience and the faith of the saints.

The Beast from the Earth

¹¹Then I saw another beast coming up out of the earth, and he had two horns like a lamb and spoke like a dragon. ¹²And he exercises all the authority of the first beast in his presence, and causes the earth and those who dwell in it to worship the first beast, whose deadly wound was healed. ¹³He performs great signs, so that he even makes fire come down from heaven on the earth in the sight of men. ¹⁴And he deceives thoseª who dwell on the earth by those signs which he was granted to do in the sight of the beast, telling those who dwell on the earth to make an image to the beast who was wounded by the sword and lived. ¹⁵He was granted *power* to give breath to the image of the beast, that the image of the beast should both speak and cause as many as would not worship the image of the beast to be killed. ¹⁶He causes all, both small and great, rich and poor, free and slave, to receive a mark on their right hand or on their foreheads, ¹⁷and that no one may buy or sell except one who has the mark orª the name of the beast, or the number of his name.

¹⁸Here is wisdom. Let him who has understanding calculate the number of the beast, for it is the number of a man: His number *is* 666.

The Lamb and the 144,000

14 Then I looked, and behold, aª Lamb standing on Mount Zion, and with Him one hundred *and* forty-four thousand, havingᵇ His Father's name written on their foreheads. ²And I heard a voice from heaven, like the voice of many waters, and like the voice of loud thunder. And I heard the sound of harpists playing their harps. ³They sang as it were a new song before the throne, before the four living creatures, and the elders; and no one could learn that song except the hundred *and* forty-four thousand who were redeemed from the earth. ⁴These are the ones who were not defiled with women, for they are virgins. These are the ones who follow the Lamb wherever He goes. These were redeemedª from *among* men, *being* firstfruits to God and to the Lamb. ⁵And in their mouth was found no deceit,ª for they are without fault before the throne of God.ᵇ

The Proclamations of Three Angels

⁶Then I saw another angel flying in the midst of heaven, having the everlasting gospel to preach

---

13:5 ªM-Text reads *make war.*   13:7 ªNU-Text and M-Text add *and people.*   13:14 ªM-Text reads *my own people.*   13:17 ªNU-Text and M-Text omit *or.*   14:1 ªNU-Text and M-Text read *the.* ᵇNU-Text and M-Text add *His name and.*   14:4 ªM-Text adds *by Jesus.*   14:5 ªNU-Text and M-Text read *falsehood.* ᵇNU-Text and M-Text omit *before the throne of God.*

---

tween the two. The Beast derives his power, rule, and authority directly from Satan (Rev. 13:2). He may represent a final ruler in whom will be concentrated the terror and glory of empires of the past (see chart, Questions from the Book of Revelation).

13:3–8 Blasphemy is an act by which the honor of God is insulted. The haughty Beast will blaspheme God's name and God's people (v. 6). The Beast's power will be solidified by the appearance of a second beast (see vv. 11–15). Although the power of the Beast will be great, it is limited. He can only do what God allows him to do (v. 5). The Antichrist cannot ultimately destroy those upon whom God has set His seal.

13:11–15 A second beast, representing a false religion and accompanied by miracles, will be highly persuasive and credible. These miracles will be copies of those in Scripture: healings, fire from heaven (1 Kin. 18:38), and resurrection (Rev. 13:12).

13:16–18 God marks His people and sets them apart as His own (Rev. 7:3). The Beast has a countermark by which he brands those who worship him. The "mark" referred to brands on animals and symbolized ownership. It was also a technical term for the imperial stamp on trade documents and for the impression on Roman coins. John gave the name of the Beast in symbolic form "666" (see chart, The Significance of Numbers in Scripture).

14:1–5 The 144,000 sealed with the name of the Father stand in direct opposition to those fixed with the mark of the Beast (vv. 1–5). The reference to those who were "not defiled with women . . . virgins" probably alludes to those who had abstained from the overwhelming corruption of sin in the world (v. 4). Marriage is occasionally represented in Scripture as a form of chastity (Heb. 13:4). Therefore, the phrase may refer to a state of spiritual purity instead of to a state of physical virginity.

PERSEVERANCE *ENDURING WITH PATIENCE*

"Perseverance" is the biblical term used to describe Christians who faithfully endure and remain steadfast in the face of opposition, attack, and discouragement. Those who focus on Jesus can bear up under any load. Perseverance involves *patience*—the ability to endure without complaint and with calmness (James 1:2–4). Perseverance also includes *persistence* in accomplishing goals and *permanence* for a lifetime of commitment (2 Pet. 1:5–7).

Christians are to persevere in prayer (Eph. 6:18), in faith (Heb. 12:1, 2), in obedience (Rev. 14:12), and in service (1 Cor. 15:58). As believers commit themselves daily to godly living, they are abundantly rewarded by the Lord with the fruit of His Spirit for all eternity. Daily recommitment leads to lasting discipline.

The world is not comfortable with commitment. Promises are easily broken and contracts are frequently altered. The children of God are called to a life of commitment to God and each other. To faith, virtue, and knowledge, the believer is required to add self-control and perseverance (2 Pet. 1:5–7). The promise is that those who endure and persevere in overcoming evil will be greatly rewarded with God's blessings both now and in eternity (Matt. 24:13; Heb. 11:6; Rev. 21:7).

See also Rom. 5:3–5; 2 Tim. 3:10–14; James 5:11; 2 Pet. 1:5–7; notes on Commitment (Matt. 16); Fruit of the Spirit (Ps. 86; Rom. 5; 15; 1 Cor. 10; 13; Gal. 5; Eph. 4; Col. 3; 2 Thess. 1; Rev. 2); Persecution (2 Cor. 4); Spiritual Discipline (2 Pet. 3)

to those who dwell on the earth—to every nation, tribe, tongue, and people— [7]saying with a loud voice, "Fear God and give glory to Him, for the hour of His judgment has come; and worship Him who made heaven and earth, the sea and springs of water."

[8]And another angel followed, saying, "Babylon[a] is fallen, is fallen, that great city, because she has made all nations drink of the wine of the wrath of her fornication."

[9]Then a third angel followed them, saying with a loud voice, "If anyone worships the beast and his image, and receives *his* mark on his forehead or on his hand, [10]he himself shall also drink of the wine of the wrath of God, which is poured out full strength into the cup of His indignation. He shall be tormented with fire and brimstone in the presence of the holy angels and in the presence of the Lamb. [11]And the smoke of their torment ascends forever and ever; and they have no rest day or night, who worship the beast and his image, and whoever receives the mark of his name."

[12]Here is the patience of the saints; here *are* those[a] who keep the commandments of God and the faith of Jesus.

[13]Then I heard a voice from heaven saying to me,[a] "Write: 'Blessed *are* the dead who die in the Lord from now on.'"

"Yes," says the Spirit, "that they may rest from their labors, and their works follow them."

Reaping the Earth's Harvest

[14]Then I looked, and behold, a white cloud, and on the cloud sat *One* like the Son of Man, having on His head a golden crown, and in His hand a sharp sickle. [15]And another angel came out of the temple, crying with a loud voice to Him who sat on the cloud, "Thrust in Your sickle and reap, for the time has come for You[a] to reap, for the harvest of the earth is ripe." [16]So He who sat on the cloud thrust in His sickle on the earth, and the earth was reaped.

•••••••••••••••••••

14:8 [a]NU-Text reads *Babylon the great is fallen,* is fallen, which has made; M-Text reads *Babylon the great is fallen. She has made.* **14:12** [a]NU-Text and M-Text omit *here are those.* **14:13** [a]NU-Text and M-Text omit *to me.* **14:15** [a]NU-Text and M-Text omit *for You.*

14:8 Babylon was a code name for Rome to the 1st-century Christians (see chart, Women in the Book of Revelation). Babylon was the great enemy of Israel in OT times, and the Jews had suffered greatly under its idolatry and corruption (Is. 21:9; Jer. 50:2; 51:8). This memory had been passed down in a variety of writings and oral traditions, the books of Daniel and Esther chief among them. Christians viewed the Roman Empire as equaling or excelling the spiritual corruption of Babylon. Babylon had deceived and seduced the nations into drinking the wine of her cup—wealth, luxury, and moral laxity. But John warned that Babylon's cup of sensual delight will turn out to be the cup of "the wrath of God" (Rev. 14:10). In

the OT, God's wrath was commonly pictured as a cup of wine to be drunk (Ps. 75:8; Is. 51:17; Jer. 25:15).

14:11–13 The Beast and his followers are tortured forever. This verse refutes the concept of annihilationism—the philosophy that the condemned are destroyed by God and have no continued conscious existence. The fate of the saints, as contrasted with the fate of the wicked, is "rest from their labors" instead of everlasting torment (v. 13). "Rest" suggests a cessation; "labors" are difficult trials. The phrase thus describes a cessation of toil, a refreshment (see chart, Beatitudes in the Book of Revelation).

COLORS IN THE BIBLE

COLOR	EXAMPLES IN SCRIPTURE
BLACK Commonly used to depict famine and death	• marble (Esth. 1:6) • diseased skin (Job 30:30) • darkest night (Prov. 7:9) • healthy hair (Song 5:11; Matt. 5:36) • the sky (Jer. 4:28) • faces of those under siege (Lam. 4:8) • darkening of the sun (Rev. 6:12) • horses (Zech. 6:2, 6; Rev. 6:5)
BLUE Derived from a species of shellfish	• fabric in the tabernacle and temple (Ex. 26:1; 2 Chr. 2:7) • curtains in the palace (Esth. 1:6) • clothing (Jer. 10:9; Ezek. 23:6)
BROWN Dark, blackish hue	• sheep (Gen. 30:32, 33, 35, 40)
GRAY	• hair of older people (Gen. 42:38; Deut. 32:25; Prov. 20:29)
GREEN Typically used to describe vegetation	• leprous plague spots (Lev. 13:49; 14:37) • green trees and grass (Deut. 12:2; 2 Kin. 17:10; Mark 6:39; Luke 23:31; Rev. 8:7) • pastures (Ps. 23:2) • marriage bed (Song 1:16)
PURPLE Made from most precious of ancient dyes. Lydia was a seller of purple (Acts 16:14).	• in the tabernacle and temple (Ex. 26:1; 27:16; 2 Chr. 2:14) • royal robes (Judg. 8:26) • garments of the virtuous woman (Prov. 31:22) • clothing of rulers (Ezek. 23:6) • Jesus' robe (Mark 15:17, 20; John 19:2) • garment of a harlot (Rev. 17:4)
RED Used to describe blood, life, and war; synonyms like "scarlet" and "crimson" also used; dye extracted from the tola worm (see Ps. 22:6 in which this figure is used to describe Jesus' passion)	• Esau's hair (Gen. 25:25) • Jacob's stew (Gen. 25:30) • thread placed on newborn's wrist by midwife (Gen. 38:28) • sacrificial heifer (Num. 19:2) • Rahab's window cord (Josh. 2:18) • fabric in the temple (2 Chr. 2:7, 14; 3:14) • metaphor for sin (Is. 1:18) • Jesus' robe (Matt. 27:28) • the Dragon and the harlot's beast (Rev. 12:3; 17:3)
WHITE Portrays purity, righteousness, and joy	• animals (Gen. 30:35; Zech. 1:8; Rev. 6:2; 19:11) • manna (Ex. 16:31) • garments and robes (Eccl. 9:8; Dan. 7:9) • metaphor for cleansing of sins (Ps. 51:7; Is. 1:18) • the Shulamite's beloved (Song 5:10) • the clothes of the transfigured Christ (Matt. 17:2)
YELLOW	• hair in a leprous spot (Lev. 13:30, 32) • the metal gold (Ps. 69:13)

Passages of Scripture referring to women are shaded.

Reaping the Grapes of Wrath

17Then another angel came out of the temple which is in heaven, he also having a sharp sickle. 18And another angel came out from the altar, who had power over fire, and he cried with a loud cry to him who had the sharp sickle, saying, "Thrust in your sharp sickle and gather the clusters of the vine of the earth, for her grapes are fully ripe." 19So the angel thrust his sickle into the earth and gathered the vine of the earth, and threw *it* into the great winepress of the wrath of God. 20And the winepress was trampled outside the city, and blood came out of the winepress, up to the horses' bridles, for one thousand six hundred furlongs.

Prelude to the Bowl Judgments

15 Then I saw another sign in heaven, great and marvelous: seven angels having the seven last plagues, for in them the wrath of God is complete.

2And I saw *something* like a sea of glass mingled with fire, and those who have the victory over the beast, over his image and over his mark[a] *and* over the number of his name, standing on the sea of glass, having harps of God. 3They sing the song of Moses, the servant of God, and the song of the Lamb, saying:

"Great and marvelous *are* Your works,
  Lord God Almighty!
  Just and true *are* Your ways,
  O King of the saints![a]
4Who shall not fear You, O Lord, and glorify
    Your name?
  For *You* alone *are* holy.
  For all nations shall come and worship before
    You,
  For Your judgments have been manifested."

5After these things I looked, and behold,[a] the temple of the tabernacle of the testimony in heaven was opened. 6And out of the temple came the seven angels having the seven plagues, clothed in pure bright linen, and having their chests girded with golden bands. 7Then one of the four living creatures gave to the seven angels seven golden bowls full of the wrath of God who lives forever and ever. 8The temple was filled with smoke from the glory of God and from His power, and no one was able to enter the temple till the seven plagues of the seven angels were completed.

16 Then I heard a loud voice from the temple saying to the seven angels, "Go and pour out the bowls[a] of the wrath of God on the earth."

First Bowl: Loathsome Sores

2So the first went and poured out his bowl upon the earth, and a foul and loathsome sore

••••••••••••••••

15:2 [a]NU-Text and M-Text omit *over his mark.*   **15:3** [a]NU-Text and M-Text read *nations.*   **15:5** [a]NU-Text and M-Text omit *behold.*   **16:1** [a]NU-Text and M-Text read *seven bowls.*

14:20 The imagery is that of the harvest. John saw an angel gather the vine of the earth and throw it into the "great winepress of the wrath of God" (v. 19). This harvest represents judgment and not salvation. The same idea of a harvest of grapes occurs elsewhere in Scripture (Is. 63:3; Joel 3:13). The grapes are trampled "outside the city," suggesting that these people are banished from the presence of God (Rev. 14:20). The blood of those trampled by the feet of God will be deep—"up to the horses' bridles"—and will flow far (1,600 furlongs is approximately 200 miles). This description of bloodshed vividly depicts the extent of God's judgment. All who oppose the reign of God will be crushed.

15:2–4 The sea of glass indicates the presence of God (Rev. 4:6; see Ex. 24:9, 10). John saw those who had triumphed standing on the sea of glass, carrying harps of God. These victors will sing a triumph song celebrating their victory and the victory of those who preceded them. The "song of Moses" was sung on Sabbath evenings to commemorate Israel's great deliverance from Egypt (Ex. 15; Deut. 32). The "song of the Lamb" commemorates the resurrected Lord's triumph over evil and the final exodus of His people from slavery to sin (Rev. 15:3). This song praises the great and marvelous works of God.

15:5–7 John saw seven angels come out of the temple to carry seven golden bowls full of the wrath of God to earth. These judgments come from the Most Holy Place in heaven. They are passed to the angels by one of the four living creatures from before God's throne. The "tabernacle of the testimony" was the dwelling place of God among His people Israel during their 40 years of wandering in the wilderness (Rev. 15:5). The seven golden bowls filled with plagues are perhaps reminiscent of the plagues on Egypt during the Exodus.

16:1–14 The plagues of the seven bowls are similar to those of the seven trumpets and to the plagues of Egypt (see chart, The Ten Plagues on Egypt). However, a significant difference exists between the trumpet plagues and the bowl plagues. The former are limited to a portion of the earth (one-third), while the latter appear to be universally destructive. The bowl plagues are God's response to Satan's final and greatest effort to overthrow God's kingdom. The first plague directly affects people, similar to the plague of boils inflicted on the Egyptians (v. 2; see Ex. 9:10; Deut. 28:35).

The second plague turns the sea to blood (Rev. 16:3; see Ex. 7:17–21), and every living creature in the sea dies. The third bowl poisons the rivers and springs (Rev. 16:4). The fourth produces excessive heat from the sun (vv. 8, 9). The fifth angel pours out his bowl "on the throne of the beast," causing darkness and pain (vv. 10, 11; see Ex. 10:21–23). The sixth bowl does not inflict a plague directly upon the people but prepares the way for the "kings from the east" (Rev. 16:12). This plague is similar to the sixth trumpet, when an invasion of innumerable hosts kills a third of mankind (Rev. 9:13–19). In the case of the sixth bowl, the barrier that holds back pagan kingdoms will likely be removed as these kingdoms will then join forces with the Beast (see Rev. 17:12–14, note).

*God allows pain that we might learn to trust His faithfulness,
sufficiency, and tender love for us.*

Sandy Smith

---

came upon the men who had the mark of the beast and those who worshiped his image.

Second Bowl: The Sea Turns to Blood

³Then the second angel poured out his bowl on the sea, and it became blood as of a dead *man;* and every living creature in the sea died.

Third Bowl: The Waters Turn to Blood

⁴Then the third angel poured out his bowl on the rivers and springs of water, and they became blood. ⁵And I heard the angel of the waters saying:

"You are righteous, O Lord,ᵃ
The One who is and who was and who is to be,ᵇ
Because You have judged these things.
⁶For they have shed the blood of saints and prophets,
And You have given them blood to drink.
Forᵃ it is their just due."

⁷And I heard another fromᵃ the altar saying, "Even so, Lord God Almighty, true and righteous *are* Your judgments."

Fourth Bowl: Men Are Scorched

⁸Then the fourth angel poured out his bowl on the sun, and power was given to him to scorch men with fire. ⁹And men were scorched with great heat, and they blasphemed the name of God who has power over these plagues; and they did not repent and give Him glory.

Fifth Bowl: Darkness and Pain

¹⁰Then the fifth angel poured out his bowl on the throne of the beast, and his kingdom became full of darkness; and they gnawed their tongues because of the pain. ¹¹They blasphemed the God of heaven because of their pains and their sores, and did not repent of their deeds.

Sixth Bowl: Euphrates Dried Up

¹²Then the sixth angel poured out his bowl on the great river Euphrates, and its water was dried up, so that the way of the kings from the east might be prepared. ¹³And I saw three unclean spirits like frogs *coming* out of the mouth of the dragon, out of the mouth of the beast, and out of the mouth of the false prophet. ¹⁴For they are spirits of demons, performing signs, *which* go out to the kings of the earth andᵃ of the whole world, to gather them to the battle of that great day of God Almighty.

¹⁵"Behold, I am coming as a thief. Blessed *is* he who watches, and keeps his garments, lest he walk naked and they see his shame."

¹⁶And they gathered them together to the place called in Hebrew, Armageddon.ᵃ

Seventh Bowl: The Earth Utterly Shaken

¹⁷Then the seventh angel poured out his bowl into the air, and a loud voice came out of the temple of heaven, from the throne, saying, "It is done!" ¹⁸And there were noises and thunderings and lightnings; and there was a great earthquake, such a mighty and great earthquake as had not occurred since men were on the earth. ¹⁹Now the great city was divided into three parts,

• • • • • • • • • • • • • • • • •

16:5 ᵃNU-Text and M-Text omit *O Lord.* ᵇNU-Text and M-Text read *who was, the Holy One.* 16:6 ᵃNU-Text and M-Text omit *For.* 16:7 ᵃNU-Text and M-Text omit *another from.* 16:14 ᵃNU-Text and M-Text omit *of the earth and.* 16:16 ᵃM-Text reads *Megiddo.*

16:13–15 Unclean spirits are seen coming out of the mouths of the Dragon, the Beast, and the False Prophet (v. 13), demonstrating the demonic inspiration of the enemies of God. They go out to enlist people on earth to gather in order to fight "the battle of that great day of God Almighty" (v. 14). John often referred to "the last day" (John 6:39; 11:24; 12:48). The battle of that great day is the last grand finale when all the forces of evil will join to fight against God. Jesus interjected a word to the church, exhorting them to watch or awaken and to "keep" their garments, an obvious reference to spiritual diligence (Rev. 16:15; Matt. 24:42–44). The church in Laodicea had been advised to buy garments from Christ in order to guard against spiritual poverty and nakedness (Rev. 3:18).

16:16 The Dragon, Beast, and False Prophet are successful in gathering the world together in the place called Armageddon

(Heb., lit. "mountain of Megiddo"). Megiddo, historically a well-known battlesite, is located between the Galilean and Mediterranean seas about 15 miles southeast of modern Haifa. Barak and Deborah overthrew the Canaanites at Megiddo (Judg. 5:19), and Pharoah Necho killed King Josiah there (2 Kin. 23:29; 2 Chr. 35:22).

16:17–21 The seventh bowl brings judgment on Babylon, the capital of the Beast's empire. The pronouncement "it is done" indicates completed action and is followed by phenomena that manifest the power and glory of God (v. 17; see Rev. 4:5; 8:5; 11:19). Babylon is devastated by a great earthquake. The city collapses and is split into three parts, symbolic of its complete ruin (see Rev. 11:13). The exact weight of a "talent" seems to have been more than a hundred pounds (Rev. 16:21; see chart, Money and Measurements in the Bible).

and the cities of the nations fell. And great Babylon was remembered before God, to give her the cup of the wine of the fierceness of His wrath. [20]Then every island fled away, and the mountains were not found. [21]And great hail from heaven fell upon men, *each hailstone* about the weight of a talent. Men blasphemed God because of the plague of the hail, since that plague was exceedingly great.

The Scarlet Woman and the Scarlet Beast

17 Then one of the seven angels who had the seven bowls came and talked with me, saying to me,[a] "Come, I will show you the judgment of the great harlot who sits on many waters, [2]with whom the kings of the earth committed fornication, and the inhabitants of the earth were made drunk with the wine of her fornication."

[3]So he carried me away in the Spirit into the wilderness. And I saw a woman sitting on a scarlet beast *which was* full of names of blasphemy, having seven heads and ten horns. [4]The woman was arrayed in purple and scarlet, and adorned with gold and precious stones and pearls, having in her hand a golden cup full of abominations and the filthiness of her fornication.[a] [5]And on her forehead a name *was* written:

MYSTERY, BABYLON THE GREAT,
THE MOTHER OF HARLOTS AND
OF THE ABOMINATIONS
OF THE EARTH.

[6]I saw the woman, drunk with the blood of the saints and with the blood of the martyrs of Jesus. And when I saw her, I marveled with great amazement.

The Meaning of the Woman and the Beast

[7]But the angel said to me, "Why did you marvel? I will tell you the mystery of the woman and of the beast that carries her, which has the seven heads and the ten horns. [8]The beast that you saw was, and is not, and will ascend out of the bottomless pit and go to perdition. And those who dwell on the earth will marvel, whose names are not written in the Book of Life from the foundation of the world, when they see the beast that was, and is not, and yet is.[a]

[9]"Here *is* the mind which has wisdom: The seven heads are seven mountains on which the woman sits. [10]There are also seven kings. Five have fallen, one is, *and* the other has not yet come. And when he comes, he must continue a short time. [11]The beast that was, and is not, is himself also the eighth, and is of the seven, and is going to perdition.

[12]"The ten horns which you saw are ten kings who have received no kingdom as yet, but they receive authority for one hour as kings with the beast. [13]These are of one mind, and they will give their power and authority to the beast. [14]These will make war with the Lamb, and the Lamb will overcome them, for He is Lord of lords and King of kings; and those *who are* with Him *are* called, chosen, and faithful."

[15]Then he said to me, "The waters which you saw, where the harlot sits, are peoples, multitudes, nations, and tongues. [16]And the ten horns which you saw on[a] the beast, these will hate the harlot, make her desolate and naked, eat her flesh and burn her with fire. [17]For God has put it into their hearts to fulfill His purpose, to be of one mind, and to give their kingdom to the beast, until the words of God are fulfilled. [18]And the woman whom you saw is that great city which reigns over the kings of the earth."

• • • • • • • • • • • • • • • • • •

17:1 [a]NU-Text and M-Text omit *to me.*   17:4 [a]M-Text reads *the filthiness of the fornication of the earth.*   17:8 [a]NU-Text and M-Text read *and shall be present.*   17:16 [a]NU-Text and M-Text read *saw, and the beast.*

17:1–18 The metaphor of harlotry was often used to depict Israel's infidelity to God (Is. 1:21; Jer. 2:20; 3:1; Ezek. 16:15; Hos. 2:5; 3:3; 4:15). The harlot Babylon here is a personification of wickedness and spiritual corruption. Her clothing of purple and scarlet reflects splendor and luxury (see chart, Colors in the Bible). The term "abominations" is associated with idolatry. The glittering appearance of the harlot masks her utter moral and religious corruption. The harlot is obviously responsible for the persecution and death of a great number of believers (v. 6). She has a name written on her forehead (see charts, Questions from the Book of Revelation; Women in the Book of Revelation). The saints of God were sealed on their foreheads (Rev. 7:3; 9:4; 13:12; 14:1) as were the followers of the Beast (Rev. 13:17). In Rome prostitutes customarily wore headbands embroidered with their names. This harlot is the source of all false religions that ensnare. Her significance is not obvious to everyone and must be revealed (Rev. 17:5). "The seven heads" may be an allusion to the city of Rome, which was built on seven hills (v. 9). But the hills are also

"seven kings." The historical succession of Roman emperors does not correspond with the description of the kings provided (v. 10). Perhaps the vision indicates that the great harlot sits upon a succession of empires.

17:12–14 The Beast's ten horns are "ten kings" who may be independent earthly rulers (v. 12; see chart, Questions from the Book of Revelation). The number "ten" could be exact or merely symbolic of completeness. These kings have short reigns ("one hour"), are associated with the Beast, receive authority "with" him (v. 12), collaborate together and lend their support to the Beast's rule, and will be involved in the great war against the Lamb (v. 14).

17:16–18 The harlot appears to represent the capital city of the Beast's empire (v. 18). The "ten horns" will begin to hate her. They will make her desolate and naked, stripping her of every resource (v. 16). The metaphor used is taken from the actions of wild beasts (Ps. 27:2; Jer. 10:25; Mic. 3:3; Zeph. 3:3). Finally, she will be completely destroyed (Rev. 17:16).

The Fall of Babylon the Great

18After these things I saw another angel coming down from heaven, having great authority, and the earth was illuminated with his glory. [2]And he cried mightily[a] with a loud voice, saying, "Babylon the great is fallen, is fallen, and has become a dwelling place of demons, a prison for every foul spirit, and a cage for every unclean and hated bird! [3]For all the nations have drunk of the wine of the wrath of her fornication, the kings of the earth have committed fornication with her, and the merchants of the earth have become rich through the abundance of her luxury."

[4]And I heard another voice from heaven saying, "Come out of her, my people, lest you share in her sins, and lest you receive of her plagues. [5]For her sins have reached[a] to heaven, and God has remembered her iniquities. [6]Render to her just as she rendered to you,[a] and repay her double according to her works; in the cup which she has mixed, mix double for her. [7]In the measure that she glorified herself and lived luxuriously, in the same measure give her torment and sorrow; for she says in her heart, 'I sit as queen, and am no widow, and will not see sorrow.' [8]Therefore her plagues will come in one day—death and mourning and famine. And she will be utterly burned with fire, for strong is the Lord God who judges[a] her.

The World Mourns Babylon's Fall

[9]"The kings of the earth who committed fornication and lived luxuriously with her will weep and lament for her, when they see the smoke of her burning, [10]standing at a distance for fear of her torment, saying, 'Alas, alas, that great city Babylon, that mighty city! For in one hour your judgment has come.'

[11]"And the merchants of the earth will weep and mourn over her, for no one buys their merchandise anymore: [12]merchandise of gold and silver, precious stones and pearls, fine linen and purple, silk and scarlet, every kind of citron wood, every kind of object of ivory, every kind of object of most precious wood, bronze, iron, and marble; [13]and cinnamon and incense, fragrant oil and frankincense, wine and oil, fine flour and wheat, cattle and sheep, horses and chariots, and bodies and souls of men. [14]The fruit that your soul longed for has gone from you, and all the things which are rich and splendid have gone from you,[a] and you shall find them no more at all. [15]The merchants of these things, who became rich by her, will stand at a distance for fear of her torment, weeping and wailing, [16]and saying, 'Alas, alas, that great city that was clothed in fine linen, purple, and scarlet, and adorned with gold and precious stones and pearls! [17]For in one hour such great riches came to nothing.' Every shipmaster, all who travel by ship, sailors, and as many as trade on the sea, stood at a distance [18]and cried out when they saw the smoke of her burning, saying, 'What is like this great city?'

[19]"They threw dust on their heads and cried out, weeping and wailing, and saying, 'Alas, alas, that great city, in which all who had ships on the sea became rich by her wealth! For in one hour she is made desolate.'

[20]"Rejoice over her, O heaven, and you holy apostles[a] and prophets, for God has avenged you on her!"

Finality of Babylon's Fall

[21]Then a mighty angel took up a stone like a great millstone and threw it into the sea, saying, "Thus with violence the great city Babylon shall be

· · · · · · · · · · · · · · · ·

18:2 [a]NU-Text and M-Text omit *mightily.*   18:5 [a]NU-Text and M-Text read *have been heaped up.*   18:6 [a]NU-Text and M-Text omit *to you.*   18:8 [a]NU-Text and M-Text read *has judged.*   18:14 [a]NU-Text and M-Text read *been lost to you.*   18:20 [a]NU-Text and M-Text read *saints and apostles.*

18:1–6 A series of announcements and visions detail the fall of the harlot Babylon. This section mirrors the prophetic doom songs sung over the fall of Tyre (Ezek. 26—28) and the historic city Babylon (Is. 13, 14; 21; Jer. 50; 51). A voice from heaven warns God's people to flee the city. A similar summons was issued by the prophet Jeremiah (Jer. 51:6, 45). Therefore, although Babylon persecuted and martyred Christians, obviously some believers still lived there. They are warned to flee the city to avoid the temptation to compromise their faith and to escape the coming judgment.

18:7 Babylon was guilty of pride and self-glorification, echoing that of historic Babylon (Is. 47:7–9; Ezek. 28:2; Zeph. 2:15). Babylon, a city of self-indulgence, luxury, and wealth, seduced people into the sins of complacency, self-sufficiency, and rejection of God. "Repay her double" is an OT phrase indicating the full measure of punishment (Rev. 18:6; see Jer. 16:18; 17:18). Babylon mixed a bitter drink for the inhabitants of the world; therefore, the angels will pour out plagues that "mix double for her" (Rev. 18:6).

18:9–19 Political rulers (v. 9), economic leaders ("merchants of the earth," v. 11), and those in the transport industry ("shipmaster," "sailors," sea traders, v. 17)—all join together to lament Babylon's fall. Their grief is not for the city herself but rather for their personal economic ruin. Their mourning is pictured as intense (Rev. 18:19; see Ezek. 27:30).

18:20—19:4 In contrast to the grief of the kings and merchants of earth, the desolation of Babylon is a cause of rejoicing in heaven. God has answered the prayers of the martyrs who cried day and night for Him to avenge their blood (Rev. 6:10). They sing a song of thanksgiving and praise to God for his "true and righteous" judgments (Rev. 19:2). "Alleluia" (Gk., lit. "praise *Yahweh*") is a word used extensively in the psalms and in Hebrew liturgy (Ps. 106:48; 111:1; 112:1). The word "amen" (lit. "so be it") indicates the 24 elders' assent to the praise of the great multitude (Rev. 19:4).

thrown down, and shall not be found anymore. [22]The sound of harpists, musicians, flutists, and trumpeters shall not be heard in you anymore. No craftsman of any craft shall be found in you anymore, and the sound of a millstone shall not be heard in you anymore. [23]The light of a lamp shall not shine in you anymore, and the voice of bridegroom and bride shall not be heard in you anymore. For your merchants were the great men of the earth, for by your sorcery all the nations were deceived. [24]And in her was found the blood of prophets and saints, and of all who were slain on the earth."

Heaven Exults over Babylon

19 After these things I heard[a] a loud voice of a great multitude in heaven, saying, "Alleluia! Salvation and glory and honor and power *belong* to the Lord[b] our God! [2]For true and righteous *are* His judgments, because He has judged the great harlot who corrupted the earth with her fornication; and He has avenged on her the blood of His servants *shed* by her." [3]Again they said, "Alleluia! Her smoke rises up forever and ever!" [4]And the twenty-four elders and the four living creatures fell down and worshiped God who sat on the throne, saying, "Amen! Alleluia!" [5]Then a voice came from the throne, saying, "Praise our God, all you His servants and those who fear Him, both[a] small and great!"

[6]And I heard, as it were, the voice of a great multitude, as the sound of many waters and as the sound of mighty thunderings, saying, "Alleluia! For the[a] Lord God Omnipotent reigns! [7]Let us be glad and rejoice and give Him glory, for the marriage of the Lamb has come, and His wife has made herself ready." [8]And to her it was granted to be arrayed in fine linen, clean and bright, for the fine linen is the righteous acts of the saints.

[9]Then he said to me, "Write: 'Blessed *are* those who are called to the marriage supper of the Lamb!' " And he said to me, "These are the true sayings of God." [10]And I fell at his feet to worship him. But he said to me, "See *that you do* not *do that!*

I am your fellow servant, and of your brethren who have the testimony of Jesus. Worship God! For the testimony of Jesus is the spirit of prophecy."

Christ on a White Horse

[11]Now I saw heaven opened, and behold, a white horse. And He who sat on him *was* called Faithful and True, and in righteousness He judges and makes war. [12]His eyes *were* like a flame of fire, and on His head *were* many crowns. He had[a] a name written that no one knew except Himself. [13]He *was* clothed with a robe dipped in blood, and His name is called The Word of God. [14]And the armies in heaven, clothed in fine linen, white and clean,[a] followed Him on white horses. [15]Now out of His mouth goes a sharp[a] sword, that with it He should strike the nations. And He Himself will rule them with a rod of iron. He Himself treads the winepress of the fierceness and wrath of Almighty God. [16]And He has on *His* robe and on His thigh a name written:

KING OF KINGS AND
LORD OF LORDS.

The Beast and His Armies Defeated

[17]Then I saw an angel standing in the sun; and he cried with a loud voice, saying to all the birds that fly in the midst of heaven, "Come and gather together for the supper of the great God,[a] [18]that you may eat the flesh of kings, the flesh of captains, the flesh of mighty men, the flesh of horses and of those who sit on them, and the flesh of all *people,* free[a] and slave, both small and great."

[19]And I saw the beast, the kings of the earth, and their armies, gathered together to make war

•••••••••••••••••••

19:1 [a]NU-Text and M-Text add *something like.* [b]NU-Text and M-Text omit *the Lord.* 19:5 [a]NU-Text and M-Text omit *both.* 19:6 [a]NU-Text and M-Text read *our.* 19:12 [a]M-Text adds *names written, and.* 19:14 [a]NU-Text and M-Text read *pure white linen.* 19:15 [a]M-Text adds *two-edged.* 19:17 [a]NU-Text and M-Text read *the great supper of God.* 19:18 [a]NU-Text and M-Text read *both free.*

19:6–10 The marriage of the Lamb occurs at the return of Christ when He is reunited with His earthly church. The voice of a great multitude announces this event. Jesus used the wedding imagery to depict His present and future relationship to the church. He called Himself the Bridegroom (Mark 2:19) and likened the coming of His kingdom to a wedding feast (Matt. 22:1–14; 25:1–13). Believers are "married" to the Lord (1 Cor. 6:17; 2 Cor. 11:2). Paul compared the relationship of Christ and the church to that of a husband and wife (Eph. 5:25–27). Believers are the holy Jerusalem, the bride, the Lamb's wife (Rev. 19:7, 8; 21:9, 10; see charts, Questions from the Book of Revelation; Women in the Book of Revelation).

19:11–16 The white horse signifies victory and implies that the rider would ride toward final triumph. His unknown name indicates that no person can fully comprehend the depths of His being (v. 12). This rider goes forth to judge and make war

but does so in righteousness (v. 11; see Is. 11:4). His robe is dipped in blood. On His robe and on His thigh a fourth name is written: Christ knows Himself by His hidden name; the churches know Him as the "Faithful and True" and "The Word of God" (Rev. 19:11, 13). Now He reveals Himself to the world as "KING OF KINGS AND LORD OF LORDS" (v. 16), a name indicative of His absolute and complete sovereignty. He is riding toward the time when every knee will bow and acknowledge Him as Lord (Phil. 2:9–11).

19:17–21 The Antichrist and all who have aligned themselves with him are gathered to make war against the Lord (v. 17; see Ezek. 39:17–20; chart, Questions from the Book of Revelation). The battle itself is not described; John merely recorded the final result: the Beast and the False Prophet are cast alive into the lake of fire, and the Beast's followers are killed (Rev. 19:20, 21).

against Him who sat on the horse and against His army. ²⁰Then the beast was captured, and with him the false prophet who worked signs in his presence, by which he deceived those who received the mark of the beast and those who worshiped his image. These two were cast alive into the lake of fire burning with brimstone. ²¹And the rest were killed with the sword which proceeded from the mouth of Him who sat on the horse. And all the birds were filled with their flesh.

Satan Bound 1,000 Years

20 Then I saw an angel coming down from heaven, having the key to the bottomless pit and a great chain in his hand. ²He laid hold of the dragon, that serpent of old, who is *the* Devil and Satan, and bound him for a thousand years; ³and he cast him into the bottomless pit, and shut him up, and set a seal on him, so that he should deceive the nations no more till the thousand years were finished. But after these things he must be released for a little while.

The Saints Reign with Christ 1,000 Years

⁴And I saw thrones, and they sat on them, and judgment was committed to them. Then *I saw* the souls of those who had been beheaded for their witness to Jesus and for the word of God, who had not worshiped the beast or his image, and had not received *his* mark on their foreheads or on their hands. And they lived and reigned with Christ for a[a] thousand years. ⁵But the rest of the dead did not live again until the thousand years were finished. This *is* the first resurrection. ⁶Blessed and holy *is* he who has part in the first resurrection. Over such the second death has no power, but they shall be priests of God and of Christ, and shall reign with Him a thousand years.

Satanic Rebellion Crushed

⁷Now when the thousand years have expired, Satan will be released from his prison ⁸and will go out to deceive the nations which are in the four corners of the earth, Gog and Magog, to gather them together to battle, whose number *is* as the sand of the sea. ⁹They went up on the breadth of the earth and surrounded the camp of the saints and the beloved city. And fire came down from God out of heaven and devoured them. ¹⁰The devil, who deceived them, was cast into the lake of fire and brimstone where[a] the beast and the false prophet *are.* And they will be tormented day and night forever and ever.

The Great White Throne Judgment

¹¹Then I saw a great white throne and Him who sat on it, from whose face the earth and the heaven fled away. And there was found no place for them. ¹²And I saw the dead, small and great, standing before God,[a] and books were opened. And another book was opened, which is *the Book* of Life. And the dead were judged according to their works, by the things which were written in the books. ¹³The sea gave up the dead who were in it, and Death and Hades delivered up the dead who were in them. And they were judged, each one according to his works. ¹⁴Then Death and Hades were cast into the lake of fire. This is the second death.[a] ¹⁵And anyone not found written in the Book of Life was cast into the lake of fire.

All Things Made New

21 Now I saw a new heaven and a new earth, for the first heaven and the first earth had passed away. Also there was no more sea. ²Then I, John,[a] saw the holy city, New Jerusalem, coming down out of heaven from God, prepared as a bride adorned for her husband. ³And I heard a loud voice from heaven saying, "Behold, the tabernacle of God *is* with men, and He will dwell with them, and they

---

20:4 [a]M-Text reads *the.*   20:10 [a]NU-Text and M-Text add *also.*   20:12 [a]NU-Text and M-Text read *the throne.*   20:14 [a]NU-Text and M-Text add *the lake of fire.*   21:2 [a]NU-Text and M-Text omit *John.*

20:1–15 The millennium (Lat. *mille,* lit. "thousand;" *annum,* lit "year") has been greatly debated (see charts, Millennial Views); Questions from the Book of Revelation).

In the premillennial view, after the victory of Armageddon, Christ will rule with the resurrected saints for 1,000 years, after which Satan will break forth in a final rebellion and again be crushed. Then God will permanently establish the new heaven and new earth.

According to the postmillennial view, after 1,000 literal or figurative years of theocratic rule, Christ will return to raise the dead, judge the world, and institute the new heaven and new earth. The triumph of a godly world view and political structure over an ungodly one is in view.

The amillennial view regards the 1,000-year period as wholly symbolic, arguing that Christ already rules from heaven over the church and in the hearts of His people. The rule of the saints is spiritual and not political.

20:4–6 Those who will rule with Christ as priests are not restricted to those coming out of the Tribulation period but will include all the faithful in Christ from every age (Heb. 7; 1 Pet. 2:5, 9; see chart, Beatitudes in the Book of Revelation).

20:7–10 So great is the depravity of man that even in the clear triumph of the gospel, Satan leads many into a hopeless rebellion. In Ezekiel 38, Gog is the prince of the land of Magog and comes from the north to invade the nation of Israel. In Revelation, Gog and Magog likely represent nations who side with Satan in rebellion against God.

20:11–15 The final rebellion of Satan prepares the way for the Great White Throne Judgment (see chart, Judgments in the New Testament). The issue of this judgment is the eternal destiny of all humanity—eternal life or eternal punishment (Matt. 25:46; Rom. 14:10). "Works" reveal the condition of the heart, and they are the evidence of (not the grounds for) eternal reward or condemnation (Rev. 20:12; see Rom. 2:6).

SORROW *NO MORE TEARS*

Everyone has experienced sorrow. It is a fact of life. The Bible has numerous accounts of people who experienced sorrow at some point in their lives. Jacob was sorrowful over the loss of his wife Rachel (Gen. 48:7) and over his helplessness to save his son Joseph (Gen. 42:38). Hannah was full of sorrow because of her barrenness (1 Sam. 1:15), and Tamar wept bitterly over the tragedy of being raped by her own half-brother (2 Sam. 13:19). Queen Esther was heavyhearted and shed tears of sorrow because of the proposed destruction of her people (Esth. 8:3). The psalmist experienced sorrow during oppression and times of trouble (Ps. 13:2; 90:10). Even wisdom brings the sorrow of knowing that all of life is not joyous (Eccl. 1:18). Finally, perhaps the ultimate sorrow for a woman was that endured by Mary, the mother of the Lord, as she watched the cruel torture and execution of her Son (Luke 2:34, 35).

Scripture speaks of a godly sorrow that leads to repentance and to life (2 Cor. 7:9) as opposed to a worldly sorrow that leads to death (2 Cor. 7:10). Yet God spares His children sorrow upon sorrow (Phil. 2:27)—in other words, sorrow with no hope of joy.

A time is coming when sorrow will end (Is. 60:20). You can look forward to a new heaven and a new earth where mourning will turn to gladness and comfort into joy (Is. 61:1–3).

See also Luke 24:47, note; notes on Death (1 Cor. 15); Fruit of the Spirit (Rom. 15); Grief (Is. 53); Tears (Ps. 56)

---

shall be His people. God Himself will be with them *and be* their God. ⁴And God will wipe away every tear from their eyes; there shall be no more death, nor sorrow, nor crying. There shall be no more pain, for the former things have passed away."

⁵Then He who sat on the throne said, "Behold, I make all things new." And He said to me,ᵃ "Write, for these words are true and faithful."

⁶And He said to me, "It is done!ᵃ I am the Alpha and the Omega, the Beginning and the End. I will give of the fountain of the water of life freely to him who thirsts. ⁷He who overcomes shall inherit all things,ᵃ and I will be his God and he shall be My son. ⁸But the cowardly, unbelieving,ᵃ abominable, murderers, sexually immoral, sorcerers, idolaters, and all liars shall have their part in the lake which burns with fire and brimstone, which is the second death."

The New Jerusalem

⁹Then one of the seven angels who had the seven bowls filled with the seven last plagues came to meᵃ and talked with me, saying, "Come, I will show you the bride, the Lamb's wife."ᵇ ¹⁰And he carried me away in the Spirit to a great and high mountain, and showed me the great city, the holyᵃ Jerusalem, descending out of heaven from God, ¹¹having the glory of God. Her light *was* like a most precious stone, like a jasper stone, clear as crystal. ¹²Also she had a great and high wall with twelve gates, and twelve angels at the gates, and names written on them, which are *the names* of the twelve tribes of the children of Israel: ¹³three gates on the east, three gates on the north, three gates on the south, and three gates on the west.

•••••••••••••••••••

21:5 ᵃNU-Text and M-Text omit *to me*.   21:6 ᵃM-Text omits *It is done*.   21:7 ᵃM-Text reads *overcomes, I shall give him these things*.   21:8 ᵃM-Text adds *and sinners*.   21:9 ᵃNU-Text and M-Text omit *to me*.   ᵇM-Text reads *I will show you the woman, the Lamb's bride*.   21:10 ᵃNU-Text and M-Text omit *the great* and read *the holy city, Jerusalem*.

21:9–21 John was summoned by one of the seven angels who had the seven bowls to come and see the Lamb's wife—"the holy Jerusalem" (v. 10). From a vantage point of a high mountain, perhaps a reference to the actual site of Jerusalem, John saw the great city descending out of heaven from God (Ps. 48:1, 2; Is. 2:2; Ezek. 40:2; 43:12–16; Zech. 8:22; 14:16). The most striking feature of this city is that she bears the "glory of God" (Rev. 21:11). John's description of the city mirrored the language he used when trying to describe the glory of the heavenly throne (Rev. 4), as he used the metaphor of precious stones to speak of its indescribable radiance.

The city had a "great and high wall," indicating that she was secure and inviolable (Rev. 21:12). The walls have 12 gates over which 12 angels stand guard (Is. 62:6; Ezek. 48:31; see chart, the Significance of Numbers in Scripture). Angels as gatekeepers may be a mark of dignity or an indication that the angels are in control of who enters. The gates are marked with the names of the twelve tribes of Israel, and twelve

foundations are inscribed with the names of the twelve apostles (Ezek. 48:31; Eph. 2:20), indicating that the city includes the nation Israel of the OT as well as the universal church of the NT.

The angel measures the city with a "gold reed" (Rev. 21:15). The measurements reveal a perfectly symmetrical quadrangle, "twelve thousand furlongs" (about 1,500 miles; see chart, Money and Measurements in the Bible) in length and breadth and height (v. 16). This cubic shape may represent the perfection and vastness of the New Jerusalem, or it may be reminiscent of the shape of the Most Holy Place (1 Kin. 6:20). The building materials are spectacular: jasper (Is. 54:11; see Rev. 4:1–11, note), gold, pearls, and all kinds of precious stones (see Ex. 28, Jewelry). The splendor of this city is unsurpassed. She stands in glorious radiance "as a bride adorned for her husband" (Rev. 21:2), ready for her marriage to the Lamb (Rev. 19:6–10).

[14]Now the wall of the city had twelve foundations, and on them were the names[a] of the twelve apostles of the Lamb. [15]And he who talked with me had a gold reed to measure the city, its gates, and its wall. [16]The city is laid out as a square; its length is as great as its breadth. And he measured the city with the reed: twelve thousand furlongs. Its length, breadth, and height are equal. [17]Then he measured its wall: one hundred *and* forty-four cubits, *according* to the measure of a man, that is, of an angel. [18]The construction of its wall was *of* jasper; and the city *was* pure gold, like clear glass. [19]The foundations of the wall of the city *were* adorned with all kinds of precious stones: the first foundation *was* jasper, the second sapphire, the third chalcedony, the fourth emerald, [20]the fifth sardonyx, the sixth sardius, the seventh chrysolite, the eighth beryl, the ninth topaz, the tenth chrysoprase, the eleventh jacinth, and the twelfth amethyst. [21]The twelve gates *were* twelve pearls: each individual gate was of one pearl. And the street of the city *was* pure gold, like transparent glass.

The Glory of the New Jerusalem

[22]But I saw no temple in it, for the Lord God Almighty and the Lamb are its temple. [23]The city had no need of the sun or of the moon to shine in it,[a] for the glory[b] of God illuminated it. The Lamb *is* its light. [24]And the nations of those who are saved[a] shall walk in its light, and the kings of the earth bring their glory and honor into it.[b] [25]Its gates shall not be shut at all by day (there shall be no night there). [26]And they shall bring the glory and the honor of the nations into it.[a] [27]But there shall by no means enter it anything that defiles, or causes[a] an abomination or a lie, but only those who are written in the Lamb's Book of Life.

The River of Life

22 And he showed me a pure[a] river of water of life, clear as crystal, proceeding from the throne of God and of the Lamb. [2]In the middle of its street, and on either side of the river, *was* the tree of life, which bore twelve fruits, each *tree* yielding its fruit every month. The leaves of the tree *were* for the healing of the nations. [3]And there shall be no more curse, but the throne of God and of the Lamb shall be in it, and His servants shall serve Him. [4]They shall see His face, and His name *shall be* on their foreheads. [5]There shall be no night there: They need no lamp nor light of the sun, for the Lord God gives them light. And they shall reign forever and ever.

The Time Is Near

[6]Then he said to me, "These words *are* faithful and true." And the Lord God of the holy[a] prophets sent His angel to show His servants the things which must shortly take place.

[7]"Behold, I am coming quickly! Blessed *is* he who keeps the words of the prophecy of this book."

[8]Now I, John, saw and heard[a] these things. And when I heard and saw, I fell down to worship before the feet of the angel who showed me these things.

[9]Then he said to me, "See *that you do* not *do that.* For[a] I am your fellow servant, and of your brethren the prophets, and of those who keep the words of this book. Worship God." [10]And he said to me, "Do not seal the words of the prophecy of this book, for the time is at hand. [11]He who is unjust, let him be unjust still; he who is filthy, let him be filthy still; he who is righteous, let him be righteous[a] still; he who is holy, let him be holy still."

Jesus Testifies to the Churches

[12]"And behold, I am coming quickly, and My reward *is* with Me, to give to every one according to

---

21:14 [a]NU-Text and M-Text read *twelve names.*   21:23 [a]NU-Text and M-Text omit *in it.* [b]M-Text reads *the very glory.*   21:24 [a]NU-Text and M-Text omit *of those who are saved.* [b]M-Text reads *the glory and honor of the nations to Him.*   21:26 [a]NU-Text adds *that they may enter in.*   21:27 [a]NU-Text and M-Text read *anything profane, nor one who causes.*   22:1 [a]NU-Text and M-Text omit *pure.*   22:6 [a]NU-Text and M-Text read *spirits of the prophets.*   22:8 [a]NU-Text and M-Text read *am the one who heard and saw.*   22:9 [a]NU-Text and M-Text omit *For.*   22:11 [a]NU-Text and M-Text read *do right.*

21:22–27 There is no temple in the New Jerusalem. In OT times, the temple was viewed as the dwelling place of God. After Christ's Resurrection, the people of God took over the function of the historic temple, for the Spirit of God came to dwell in them (1 Cor. 3:16; Eph. 2:21; see chart, The Temples of the Bible). In the age to come, no temple is needed, for God will live among His people in face-to-face communion.

22:1, 2 The symbolism of a river is common in biblical thought (Ps. 46:4; John 4:10, 14). In Ezekiel's vision, the river brought life everywhere it flowed (Ezek. 47:1–12). The river contains the water of life; and the tree growing beside the river is the tree of life (Gen. 3:24). The tree bears fruit constantly, and the leaves of the tree are for the "healing of the nations" (Rev. 22:2). John noted the contrast between the future and the present age. The present age is characterized by dark-

ness, sin, evil, destruction, and affliction. Conditions in the New Jerusalem will not be so. There will be no night, no death, no sorrow, no crying, and no pain, for "the former things have passed away" (Rev. 21:4; Sorrow). God Himself will be with His people and will wipe away every tear from their eyes (Rev. 21:3, 4).

22:10 Prophets who received visions regarding future events were often told to seal their prophecy (Is. 8:16; Dan. 8:26; 12:4, 9), meaning that the contents were inaccessible to others. The angel instructed John *not* to seal the words of this revelation, for "the time is at hand" (Rev. 22:10). The return of Christ is imminent, and believers must watch and be ready (Rev. 16:15; see also Matt. 24:42–44; Luke 19:11). The words of this prophecy are to remain unsealed so that anyone can read, ponder, and learn from them.

his work. [13]I am the Alpha and the Omega, *the* Beginning and *the* End, the First and the Last."[a]

[14]Blessed *are* those who do His commandments,[a] that they may have the right to the tree of life, and may enter through the gates into the city. [15]But[a] outside *are* dogs and sorcerers and sexually immoral and murderers and idolaters, and whoever loves and practices a lie.

[16]"I, Jesus, have sent My angel to testify to you these things in the churches. I am the Root and the Offspring of David, the Bright and Morning Star."

[17]And the Spirit and the bride say, "Come!" And let him who hears say, "Come!" And let him who thirsts come. Whoever desires, let him take the water of life freely.

A Warning

[18]For[a] I testify to everyone who hears the words of the prophecy of this book: If anyone adds to these things, God will add[b] to him the plagues that are written in this book; [19]and if anyone takes away from the words of the book of this prophecy, God shall take away[a] his part from the Book[b] of Life, from the holy city, and *from* the things which are written in this book.

I Am Coming Quickly

[20]He who testifies to these things says, "Surely I am coming quickly."

Amen. Even so, come, Lord Jesus!

[21]The grace of our Lord Jesus Christ *be* with you all.[a] Amen.

· · · · · · · · · · · · · · · · ·

22:13 [a]NU-Text and M-Text read *the First and the Last, the Beginning and the End.*   **22:14** [a]NU-Text reads *wash their robes.*   **22:15** [a]NU-Text and M-Text omit *But.*   **22:18** [a]NU-Text and M-Text omit *For.* [b]M-Text reads *may God add.*   **22:19** [a]M-Text reads *may God take away.* [b]NU-Text and M-Text read *tree of life.*   **22:21** [a]NU-Text reads *with all;* M-Text reads *with all the saints.*

22:17–21 The final verses of Revelation contain an open invitation to "come." The Spirit of God and the church extend the invitation to anyone who "thirsts" and "desires" (v. 17). Both words express a deep inner longing. In this case, the objective is the water of life that flows from the throne of God. Anyone who longs for this water is beckoned to come and take freely, as a gift and without charge. The plea is urgent, for Christ promises that He is coming quickly (v. 20), and His people and all creation groan for that great day (Rom. 8:22, 23).

APPENDIX

 WEIGHTS AND MEASURES

 WHAT THEY LEFT BEHIND: WOMEN, ARCHAEOLOGY, AND THE BIBLE

 WOMEN AND CHILDREN IN BIBLICAL NARRATIVE

 ACKNOWLEDGMENTS

 INDEX

 MAPS AND CHARTS IN *THE WOMAN'S STUDY BIBLE*

 CONCORDANCE

 MAPS

MONEY AND MEASUREMENTS IN THE BIBLE

MONETARY UNITS

Translations	Equivalents
talent	3,000 shekels; 6,000 bekas
shekel	4 days' wages; 2 bekas; 20 gerahs
bekah	1/2 shekel; 10 gerahs
gerah	1/20 shekel
drachma	2 days' wages; 1/2 Jewish silver shekel
piece of money	4 drachmas
tribute	2 drachmas
piece of silver	1 day's wage
mite	1/2 of a Roman kodrantes
denarius	25 denarii; 1 day's wage
copper coin	1/16 of a denarius
penny, quadrans	1/4 of an assarius

WEIGHTS

Translations	Equivalents	Weights
talent	60 minas; 3,000 shekels	about 75 pounds for common talent, about 150 pounds for royal talent
mina	50 shekels	1.25 pounds
shekel	2 bekas; 20 gerahs	about 0.4 ounce (11.4 grams) for common shekel
half a shekel	1/2 shekel; 10 gerahs	about 0.8 ounce for royal shekel about 0.2 ounce (5.7 grams)
gerah	1/20 shekel	about .02 ounce (.57 grams)
pound		12 ounces

MEASURES OF LENGTH

Translations	Equivalents	Length
day's journey		about 20 miles
mile	8 stadia	4,854 feet
Sabbath day's journey	6 stadia	3,637 feet
furlong	1/8 Roman mile	606 feet
measuring rod, reed	3 paces; 6 cubits	9 feet (10.5 feet in Ezekiel)
fathom	4 cubits	6 feet
pace	1/3 rod; 2 cubits	3 feet
cubit	1/2 pace; 2 spans	18 inches
span	1/2 cubit; 3 handbreadths	9 inches
handbreadth	1/3 span; 4 fingers	3 inches
finger	1/4 handbreadth	.75 inches

MONEY AND MEASUREMENTS IN THE BIBLE

LIQUID MEASURES

Translations	Equivalents	Measure
kor	10 baths	60 gallons
gallons		10.2 gallons
measure, bath	6 hins	6 gallons
hin	2 kabs	1 gallon
kab	4 logs	2 quarts
log	1/4 kab	1 pint

DRY MEASURES

Translations	Equivalents	Measure
homer	10 ephahs	6.52 bushels
kor, measure	1 homer; 10 ephahs	6.52 bushels
half homer	1/2 kor	3.26 bushels
ephah	1/10 homer	.65 bushel, 20.8 quarts
basket		7.68 quarts
measure	1/3 ephah	7 quarts
omer	1/10 ephah; 1 4/5 kag	2.08 quarts
kab	4 logs	1.16 quarts
measure		1 quart
pot		1 1/16 pints
log	1/4 kab	.58 pint

What They Left Behind:
Women, Archaeology, and the Bible

MARSHA A. ELLIS SMITH

Many of the topical notes and annotations in this Bible have information that deals with women's lives during Bible times. What kind of clothes did women wear? Did they wear makeup? What kind of foods did they cook? Did they have perfume? Many questions such as these have been answered. The purpose of this article is to give some idea of how the answers to these questions about women in Bible times are derived.

At one level, archaeology is a bit like the search for a missing person, which is a very difficult, time-consuming, and painstaking process. The search would begin in the home of the missing person with what the person had left behind. The likes, dislikes, and everyday activities of the person would be important as would each material object and how it was used. However, in archaeology, the difficulty of being removed by thousands of years from the "missing person" and her belongings is added to that process. You now have an accurate analogy for understanding the enormous task of biblical archaeology.

What is the purpose of biblical archaeology? Its purpose is *not* to "prove" the Bible is true. That is unnecessary. Archaeology, however, can provide invaluable information on the customs and background of the biblical time period and, therefore, can be a tremendous help in understanding and interpreting the biblical material.

Women Archaeologists

Archaeology as a science began in the 1800s. The archaeological expeditions prior to that time were mostly treasure hunts. Although most of the names found among the more famous biblical archaeologists are male, some women have reached a high-ranking status in the world of archaeology.

Possibly the first person to excavate an artifact in the Middle East was Lady Hester Lucy Stanhope, an English noblewoman. In 1815, Lady Stanhope traveled to Ashkelon, a site near the Mediterranean Coast in Palestine, to search for gold. Instead of finding gold, she found a colossal marble statue, which she ordered smashed into pieces before she left Palestine so that the Ottomans would not think she was trying to smuggle it back to England.

Dame Kathleen Kenyon is probably the most familiar name among female biblical archaeologists. She conducted extensive excavations at Jericho from 1952 through 1958 and has made many other contributions to the world of archaeology. Among other women appearing in the history of biblical archaeology are Dorothy Garrod, noted for the work she began on Palestinian caves in the area of Mt. Carmel in 1929, and Hetty Goldman, who began excavating at ancient Tarsus (hometown of Paul) in 1934. Recent biblical archaeology has produced several significant women contributors: Ruth Amiram, whose *Ancient Pottery of the Holy Land* provides an invaluable tool for the study of pottery types in Israel; Crystal M. Bennett, who has worked extensively at many Edomite sites; and Carol L. Meyers, as well as many others who have also made notable contributions.

Women in Archaeology

Just as women have made significant contributions to the study of ancient life, the study of women in ancient life has produced several categories of finds that yield information—art, artifacts, inscriptions and extrabiblical writings, and similar cultural heritages.

Art. The manner in which women were depicted in ancient art reveals much about their daily lives and their status in society.

Tomb paintings from Egypt, bas-reliefs from Mesopotamia, mosaics from Israel and other Mediterranean countries, sculptures from Greece and Rome, and figurines from many of these countries give glimpses of women within these ancient cultures.

Artifacts. Thousands upon thousands of artifacts have been found in the Middle East, dating from ancient times. Although the biblical era ranges from the beginning of time through around A.D. 100, most of the artifacts that would be of interest to students of the Bible come from the time of Abraham, or around 2000 B.C., through the Bronze and Iron Ages, the Babylonian and Persian periods, and up through the Hellenistic and the Early Roman periods (ending about A.D. 70). However, sometimes an artifact from the second or third centuries A.D. yields information about the biblical period.

Women's Activities in the Home. The daily domestic duties of biblical women are the source of many material remains at excavation sites (see Luke 17:2; 22:10, 11 notes). Oil lamps of varying sizes were used for lighting in the home. Kitchens were filled with clay pots and "frying pans" of assorted sizes and shapes (both metal and pottery; see John 2:6; 4:7, notes). Grinding stones were used in the preparation of meal to be used in bread recipes. Clay ovens dating from the Iron Age have been unearthed at Megiddo and others from the New Testament period at Pompeii (see Luke 12:1, note). Olive presses provided the means to squeeze from the fruit of the olive the oil necessary for cooking.

Women's Clothing and Cosmetics. Bronze fibulae (or brooches), early precursors of the modern safety pin and a means for fastening clothing, have been unearthed at several sites in the Mediterranean area. Items thought to be buttons were later determined to be toys for children.

Jewelry, dating from both Old and New Testament times, is abundant at Middle Eastern excavations (see Ex. 28, Jewelry). Beads, bracelets, necklaces, pins, and ear-rings in a variety of materials, including silver, gold, and bronze, and sometimes inset with various gemstones, have been discovered at many sites. Hairpins from the Persian era (538–332 B.C.), carved from bone (usually cattle, camel, or donkey bone), have been found at Ashkelon in Israel and at many Roman sites.

Delicate bottles for ointments and perfumes from the Roman period were made from a variety of materials—bronze, glass, silver, alabaster—with the larger ones often containing oils used in the bathing process. The smaller, slender-necked perfume bottles (sometimes referred to as "tear bottles") enabled the perfume to be dispensed in drops (see Luke 7:37, note).

Cosmetic paraphernalia seems to have been very important to ancient women, particularly those of the Graeco-Roman world. Cosmetic boxes and dishes, mirrors made from both bronze and silver (see Ex. 38:8, note), bronze tweezers, spatulas used in the makeup application process, and numerous other toilet articles, many of which date from the New Testament period, have been discovered at sites throughout the Mediterranean world (see Ex. 30, Cosmetics; Esth. 2, Beauty Preparations).

At the site of Old Testament Jerusalem, ancient bathrooms have been unearthed including two toilet seats. These differ from toilet seats discovered at other locations in Israel in that each is a large block of limestone with one central hole extending from top to bottom and another smaller hole off to the side. Those at other locations are thin slabs of stone with round openings placed above shallow pits. The second smaller openings are conjectured to have been utilized as men's urinals. These date from 600–500 B.C. with probably at least one in use at the beginning of the Babylonian Captivity in 586 B.C.

Women's Activities Outside the Home. Music played an important role in the life of ancient Israel, as is evidenced in both biblical and extra-biblical references, and women evidently were integrally involved in this

role (see Luke 1:46-55, note; charts, Hymns and Songs Associated With Women; Musical Instruments of the Old Testament). On Cyprus many terracotta figurines of women hand-drum players have been excavated. Israelite terracottas may have served as models for the Cypriot ones, though fewer such objects have been discovered in Israel. In the 1940s, few musical instruments were among the finds at archaeological excavations in Israel. However, by 1982, more than three hundred pieces of musical instruments and artistic representations of instruments had been found. These range in date from early Bronze times to the Byzantine period (just past New Testament times). Women's involvement in musical activity is indicated in many of these finds.

Evidence does show that some women were involved in business enterprises outside the home, although the extent to which this occurred is undetermined. One such businesswoman was Lydia, seller of purple (see Acts 16, Lydia). Archaeological finds in the last ten years have shed new light upon the purple dye industry in the Mediterranean world. The purple material was the most desirable and expensive (partially due to its colorfastness). This "Tyrian purple" was wool colored with a dye made from tiny Mediterranean mollusks. The process and the structures involved in this industry have been thoroughly studied and excavated. Additional methods of purple dyeing utilizing plants and other materials were developed. Thyatira was a center for this purple dye industry. Thus, Lydia may have been a dealer in the Thyatira purple cloth, or she may have been an importer of the royal "Tyrian purple." Either way, she was a smart, and probably wealthy, businesswoman.

Human Remains. Bone fragments are not as abundant in Middle Eastern excavations as are other artifacts. Therefore, the discovery of bones is considered a major find. One such find occurred in Jerusalem in 1970 at the site known as "the Burnt House." As the house was excavated, it became apparent that the destruction of the house was due to fire and that the date of that burning was around A.D. 70—the time of the Roman devastation of Jerusalem. Many finds in that burned layer caused an emotional response in the archaeologists involved in the excavation. The most moving moment, however, came when the bones of a young woman in her twenties were found in a doorway of the home. She was crouched at the kitchen door and looked as if she had collapsed as she was trying to exit the house. Seemingly, while trying to escape the burning of her home by the invading army, she was overtaken by the flames or smoke before she could reach safety.

Inscriptions and Extrabiblical Writings. Inscriptions and ancient writings are a significant source of data regarding women in biblical times. A few examples are a lengthy version of the Exodus 15:21 "Song of Miriam" found in a Dead Sea Scroll fragment, episodes in the lives of biblical women from Josephus' writings, another Dead Sea Scroll fragment reflecting the Essenes' negative view of women, cuneiform tablets describing cultural practices (possible background for the "wife as sister" accounts in the lives of Abraham and Isaac), and an Akkadian tablet from the Ras Shamra texts (coming from ancient Ugarit in Syria) describing the removal of clothes as a symbol of giving up both power and position (possible background for Old Testament passages involving women and the removal of clothes; see Is. 47:1, 2; Ezek. 16:37; Hos. 2:3, 10).

Sexuality and Gynecology. Although woman's sexuality is often depicted in a suggestive manner in ancient art (as in Pompeiian art and in much of the finds at Ashkelon), examples do exist in which the nurturing aspect of woman's sexuality is displayed (as in many paintings, figurines, and sculptures of mothers nursing their infants). Artifacts also offer data related to a woman's sexuality, as is evidenced by the interpretation of certain ancient Egyptian, open-ended figure-vases as objects used in the practice of midwifery. While some tend to think of sexuality only in reference to visual art and artifacts, inscriptions and an-

cient writings present data in this realm also. In Ephesus, an inscription on an ancient sidewalk gives directions to a nearby brothel, leaving little to the imagination. Restrictive purity regulations associated with menstruation can be read not only in the biblical material (see Lev. 15:19, 20; Mark 5:25–34) but also in Josephus, the Dead Sea Scrolls, and other ancient Jewish writings.

Women's Clothing and Cosmetics. Some inscriptions are found and translated, yet their meanings remain a mystery. An inscription dating around 1400–1200 B.C. was discovered in 1920 at Ugarit in Syria, and finally, in 1977, clarified by rabbinic writings from the fourth century A.D. The phrase in question—"the city of gold"—had not been seen in any other material from the Old Testament time period. Rabbinic literature has now revealed that the phrase refers to a golden, turreted crown that was worn as decoration by women. Such a crown has been identified in several pieces of ancient art in Syria.

Similar Cultures. Although the study of similar cultures does not fit within the strict definition of biblical archaeology, sometimes in the context of hunting for the meaning of an artifact or a situation, other cultures offer helpful information. This cross-cultural study can be illustrated by many examples from Bedouin culture. Bedouins continue to live in much the same way they lived centuries, even millennia, ago. Bedouin shepherdesses today carry the same kind of goat skin water container as is mentioned in Genesis 21:14 because the porous skin helps keep the water cool. Modern Bedouin girls wear nose rings like the one Eliezer placed on Rebecca's nose (Gen. 24:47). A more serious example of Bedouin culture explaining biblical material is the Bedouin dependence upon its own clan for vengeance. This provides vital background information about the response of Dinah's brothers to her rape by Shechem (Gen. 34).

An object that previously was thought to be a religious incense burner is another example of the use of similar cultural practices to assist in the interpretation of the use of an artifact. When W. F. Albright retranslated the inscription on the object, he discovered that its use had been secular, not religious. Then in a 1868 publication, he found a passage dealing with semi-nomadic women of Sudan, which not only explained the way that type of "cosmetic" incense burner was still being used in the 1800s but also explained a passage regarding the use of ointments and perfumes in Esther 2:12 and in Psalm 45:8.

Biblical archaeology has contributed invaluable information to the study of Scripture and will certainly be of help in the future as excavations continue. Much that helps in understanding the women of the Bible has already been found. As more women archaeologists become involved in the excavations and writings about the interpretations of the artifacts, more emphasis will be given to data relating to women in biblical times.

Women and Children in Biblical Narrative

ELEONORE STUMP

In the history of the Christian tradition, biblical commentators have mostly been men. Often these commentators have been interested in finding, as directly as possible, theological lessons in the biblical texts. Generally, that theological interest prompted a deep and sensitive interpretation of the texts, but sometimes insufficient attention has been given to the *details* of biblical stories. Stories that involve some human conflict or drama, well worth reflecting on, from time to time have been treated as if the human details were disposable wrapping on some far more interesting theological lesson. In particular, commentators on biblical stories involving women or children sometimes have seemed uninterested in the roles of the women and children in those stories. If we do not pay attention to all the details in the biblical stories, however, we may well miss important parts of what the Bible has to teach us in those passages.

This point is best illustrated with an example. We can see the importance of noticing the women and children in biblical stories by thinking about one of the most famous biblical stories—Abraham's offering up of Isaac. Many well-known commentators, including Origen, Augustine, Jerome, Aquinas, Nicholas of Lyra, Luther, Calvin, and Kierkegaard, have made interesting and insightful interpretations of this story. Nonetheless, for all their excellence, none of the commentators has satisfactorily answered basic questions raised by the story. Why did God put Abraham to the test as He did? That is, why would God ask Abraham to sacrifice his son? What is praiseworthy about Abraham's willingness to kill his own child? Why should Abraham's consent to destroy his son make him the father of faith? Part of the reason commentators have difficulty answering these questions is that they do not pay sufficient attention in the stories

about Abraham to the roles of the women and children (except for Isaac, of course).

Perhaps some think of Abraham as married to one woman, Sarah, and having one son, Isaac. But, in fact, the Bible names for Abraham three women as wives or concubines and eight sons (see chart, The Family Tree of Abraham). The stories about these other wives and children are all useful for understanding the offering of Isaac, but the focus of this article is on just one other story, the expulsion of Hagar and Ishmael.

When it looked as if Sarah might never have children, Sarah gave her maid Hagar to Abraham to be his concubine, and in the course of time Hagar gave birth to a son, Ishmael. Then when Sarah was ninety years old, she did give birth to Isaac. Ishmael was fourteen years old at the time of Isaac's birth, and suddenly he had a brother. When Isaac was weaned—no doubt when he was between two and four years old—Abraham made a great feast. Ishmael was probably around sixteen or seventeen years old at the time. During the feast Ishmael mocked Isaac or gave him some other sort of trouble, and Sarah caught him doing so. Sarah had been jealous and violent toward Hagar in the past. At this point she blew up. She demanded that Abraham expel not only Ishmael but also Hagar, and she wanted them thrown out into the desert, where they were likely either to die of thirst or to be captured and sold for slaves.

What Sarah wanted was terrible. Ishmael had been Abraham's only child for more than fourteen years, and Hagar had been part of this complicated family for even longer. Throwing them out was a terrible betrayal of the love and trust that must have existed between Abraham and his teenaged boy and between Abraham and Hagar. Both Abraham and Sarah must have known that what Sarah demanded would likely prove to be the death of Hagar and Ishmael.

That Abraham was willing even to consider doing what Sarah wanted shows how ferocious her wrath must have been. But even so, Abraham could not bring himself to agree to her demands. At this point, God intervened in the struggle between Abraham and Sarah—very surprisingly by siding with murderously angry Sarah. Although Sarah's intentions were bad, the result she wanted, that only Isaac should count as Abraham's heir, was the result God had foreordained all along. So God sided with Sarah, but He went contrary to Sarah's bad intentions because He again promised to make Ishmael a great nation. So what Sarah saw as a way of ruining Ishmael and getting rid of him, God promised to turn into a way of making Ishmael something glorious.

God's promise, then, relieved Abraham of the burden of betraying the trust between him and his son and between him and his concubine. Abraham could send them out into the desert without thinking that he was furthering Sarah's plan to destroy them. He could also explain God's promise to Hagar and Ishmael. He could make clear to them that by giving in to Sarah, he was not acting in a way to bring about their deaths or even their ruin because God was guaranteeing His protection of and blessing upon their lives.

God's promise let Abraham give in to Sarah without being guilty of a moral wrong. Abraham *trusted* God's promise to make of Ishmael a great nation. If Abraham had not believed God's promise when the lives of Ishmael and Hagar were at stake, then Abraham would have been guilty of betraying their trust and harming them. As a result of God's promise, Abraham stopped struggling within himself over whether to do what Sarah wanted, and he assented to her demands. He rose up early in the morning and sent Hagar and Ishmael out into the desert with only a loaf of bread and a bottle of water. That would be a terrible way to treat your son and his mother—unless you believed God's promise to make them into something glorious in the desert.

On the other hand, contrast Abraham's reaction to this promise of God with other occasions on which Abraham talked to God. When God promised Abraham a biological offspring, Abraham asked for a sign to confirm the truth of the promise. On that occasion, when the issue was abandoning Hagar and Ishmael in the desert, Abraham did not ask for any sign to reassure him of their safety. When what was at stake was the lives of total strangers in Sodom and Gomorrah, Abraham bargained with God. Where the lives of his son and concubine were at risk, Abraham did not bargain in any of the ways he might have done. He did not ask God whether he might accompany Hagar and Ishmael to some oasis or whether he might send a convoy of servants to set up Hagar and Ishmael to be self-supporting by giving them herds and flocks. He just sent Ishmael and Hagar to walk off into the desert with less than a full day's provision of food and water. Even given the reassurance of God's promise, there was something distressing about the readiness with which Abraham acquiesced to Sarah's demands that he throw out his concubine and his son.

The next and last recorded episode during which God came to talk to Abraham was the offering of Isaac. The age of Isaac is not clear at this point, but he was old enough to carry a substantial load of wood up a mountain, while still being young enough to be quite diffident toward his father. To suppose that he was teenaged, maybe sixteen or seventeen, around the age of Ishmael at the time when Abraham abandoned Ishmael and Hagar in the desert, is not unreasonable.

At the outset of God's message to Abraham on this occasion was an elaborate identification of Isaac, "your son, your only son Isaac, whom you love" (Gen. 22:2). The phrase "your only son" is striking. If you had abandoned one of your two boys in the desert, would you be able to hear that phrase "your only son" without wincing and immediately thinking of Ishmael? And if the person who guaranteed the safety of the son you abandoned then used the expression "your only son" to refer to Isaac, wouldn't you

immediately think of the boy you had abandoned and wonder in what sense Isaac was an only son?

The content of God's message is enough to turn a father's heart to stone: Take your only son—that is, the only son you have left—and offer him up as a burnt offering. But think of the expulsion of Ishmael again. God had told Abraham to act in a way that seemed likely to bring about Ishmael's death, except for God's promise to make Ishmael a great nation. Because Abraham believed the promise about Ishmael, he could abandon Ishmael in the desert without fear of harm to his son, however reasonable it would otherwise seem to believe that Ishmael would die out in the desert with only a little food and water. Now God was requiring the sacrifice of Isaac. But Abraham also had a promise from God about Isaac: God had also promised to make Isaac a great nation.

If God is good and His promises are trustworthy, then Isaac would have children who would count as Abraham's descendants, inherit the land of Canaan, and increase greatly in number. But when God told Abraham to sacrifice Isaac, Isaac was still a boy without children of his own. If Isaac died, God's promises about him would not have been true. Put another way, if God's promises are trustworthy, then Isaac would not die in his youth, however reasonable it seemed to think that he would.

In the case of Ishmael, family life was made much easier for Abraham if he believed that God's promises are true; trusting God's promises gave him a good reason to give in to his furious wife Sarah. Now things were different. Doing what looked certain to bring about the death of Isaac was as strongly opposed to Abraham's self-interest as it could be. But if Abraham had not trusted God's promise about Isaac, what will we think, looking back on Abraham's behavior toward Ishmael? Won't we think that his apparent trust in God's promises then was just an excuse, a rationalization, for taking the easy way out where Sarah was concerned? If he refused to entrust Isaac to God's promises,

although he was willing to abandon Ishmael on the strength of God's promise, won't we think that, after all, there was something terrible about his willingness to expel Ishmael?

In asking Abraham to sacrifice Isaac, God was, in effect, asking Abraham what he would have done on that earlier occasion if it had been Isaac instead of Ishmael. Abraham had to trust God's promises and acknowledge His goodness, or he had to make clear that in the expulsion of Ishmael he was just using God's promise as a convenient excuse for doing a wrong action. This trial, then, would refine Abraham. Whichever way he acted, this time he would have to act out of unmixed motives. Abraham's options were to refuse to do what looked likely to bring about the death of Isaac—because he did not after all trust in God's promises—or to be willing to sacrifice Isaac, believing that in doing so he would not bring about Isaac's death—because he believed in God's promise to make of Isaac a great nation.

Abraham passed the test. He treated Isaac as he treated Ishmael. In this case, too, he rose up early in the morning and obeyed God's command. Treating the two cases in the same way required believing that even if he sacrificed Isaac, Isaac would live and flourish and be the source of a great nation. Is there anything too hard for God? So Abraham passed the test just by virtue of believing that in sacrificing Isaac he would not be bringing Isaac's life to an end because God is good, and His promises are trustworthy.

In this way of seeing the story, Abraham's line to the servants is not a polite fib. "Stay here with the donkey," he told them; "the lad and I will go yonder and worship, and we will come back to you" (Gen. 22:5). Similarly, when he told Isaac, "God will provide for Himself the lamb for a burnt offering" (Gen. 22:8), he was not engaging in tender deception or unconsciously cruel irony, as he would be doing if he thought he were going off to kill Isaac. Here, too, Abraham believed what he said.

Nonetheless, although he believed,

Abraham might still have been in anguish as he said these lines. Think about a man who discovers, while mountain climbing with his son, that the only way to safety lies across a large crevice. If he did not believe his son could make it, he would not ask him to leap. But the father may be bathed in sweat, with years taken off his life, by the time the boy makes it over. The test God set for Abraham was a hard and painful one. But Abraham's ready acquiescence to Sarah's demand to abandon Hagar and Ishmael in the desert made this test a good and right one for Abraham.

What Hebrews 11 says about Abraham presupposes this way of reading the story, too. Abraham acted on faith in offering up Isaac because he believed that the offering of Isaac did not invalidate the promises of God, since God could even raise Isaac from the dead (Heb. 11:17–19).

God's verdict on Abraham is that Abraham had passed the test. As he raised the knife over Isaac, God told Abraham, "Do not lay your hand on the lad, or do anything to him; for now I know that you fear God, since you have not withheld your son, your only son, from Me" (Gen. 22:12). What God said is just right. If Abraham had refused to trust Isaac to God after having been willing to expel Ishmael on God's promise, he would have been mocking rather than fearing God, acting as if God did not matter or did not mind much about the death of innocent children. But until Abraham had to choose whether or not to trust Isaac to God, perhaps no one could have known whether Abraham feared God because Abraham's motives in the case of Ishmael were confused and mixed together. God knew: The trial over Isaac refined Abraham's character. Because Abraham believed in God's goodness and the trustworthiness of God's promises, Abraham was willing to trust his son, his only son, to God. That is why Abraham is the father of faith.

If we remember Hagar and Ishmael when we read the story of the offering of Isaac, we can answer the questions that often arise in connection with that story. The expulsion of Ishmael makes it clear why God should try Abraham and why the test should take the form it did. What is at issue in the test was whether Abraham would believe in God's goodness in Isaac's case as well as in Ishmael's. What is praiseworthy about Abraham, what makes him the father of faith, is not his readiness to kill his child to please God. It is his willingness to trust in God's goodness and to believe God's promises, even when apparently those promises would surely turn out to be false. What makes Abraham the father of faith, then, is not just that he believed in God's existence or that he was obedient to God. He did believe in God's existence, and he was obedient. What makes him the father of faith, however, was his belief that God is good and thus would never break His promises to His people.

If we focus only on Abraham (or Abraham and Isaac), as many interpreters do, and if we are not willing to pay serious and careful attention to the various women and children in the narrative, we will miss all this side of the story about the offering of Isaac. As a result, we could have a much harder time understanding why God would have asked Abraham to sacrifice his son, and it would be more difficult to grasp the sort of faith the Bible is recommending to us here. The same point applies to many other passages in the Bible as well. If we think carefully about the women and the children in those stories, we will see a side of the story, important for our understanding of the Bible's message, which we would have missed otherwise.

See also Gen. 21:1–21; 22:1–19; Heb. 11:17–19; notes on Children (2 Sam. 21; Ps. 128; Prov. 22; Luke 15); Obedience (Philem.); Patriarchy (Gen. 28); Promises of God (2 Pet. 1)

BIBLIOGRAPHY FOR "WHAT THEY LEFT BEHIND: WOMEN, ARCHAEOLOGY AND THE BIBLE"

Pauline Albenda, "Western Asiatic Women in the Iron Age: Their Image Revealed," *Biblical Archaeologist* 46 (Spring 1983).

"Albright the Beautician Reveals Secrets of Queen Esther's Cosmetic Aids," *Biblical Archaeology Review* 2 (March 1976).

Betsy Halpern Amaru, "Portraits of Biblical Women in Josephus' Antiquities," *Journal of Jewish Studies* 39 (Autumn 1988).

Ruth Amiram, *Ancient Pottery of the Holy Land* (Jerusalem: Masada Press, 1969).

Nachman Avigad, "How the Wealthy Lived in Herodian Jerusalem," *Biblical Archaeology Review* 2 (December 1976).

Nahman Avigad, "Jerusalem in Flames—The Burnt House Captures a Moment in Time," *Biblical Archaeology Review* 9 (November/December 1983).

Clinton Bailey, "How Desert Culture Helps Us Understand the Bible: Bedouin Law Explains Reaction to Rape of Dinah," *Bible Review* 7 (August 1991).

Gabriel Barkay, "The Divine Name Found in Jerusalem," *Biblical Archaeology Review* 9 (March/April 1983).

Bathja Bayer, "The Finds That Could Not Be," *Biblical Archaeology Review* 8 (January/February 1982).

E. M. Blaiklock, "A Chronological Table of Archeologists and Their Work," *Zondervan Pictorial Encyclopedia of the Bible* (Grand Rapids, Michigan: Zondervan, 1975) vol. 1, pp. 266–277.

E. M. Blaiklock and R. K. Harrison, eds., *The New International Dictionary of Biblical Archaeology* (Grand Rapids, Michigan: Zondervan, 1983).

George J. Brooke, "Power to the Powerless—A Long-Lost Song of Miriam, *Biblical Archaeology Review* 20 (May/June 1994).

Magen Broshi, "Beware the Wiles of the Wanton Woman," *Biblical Archaeology Review* 9 (July/August 1983).

Trent C. Butler, ed., *The Holman Bible Dictionary* (Nashville, Tennessee: Holman Bible Publishers, 1991).

"Buzz or Button," *Biblical Archaeology Review* 17 (May/June 1991).

Jane Cahill, Karl Reinhard, David Tarler, and Peter Warnock, "Scientists Examine Remains of Ancient Bathroom," *Biblical Archaeology Review* 17 (May/June 1991).

"Glossary: How to Date a Cooking Pot," *Biblical Archaeology Review* 18 (September/October 1992).

"Is the Cultic Installation at Dan Really an Olive Press?" *Biblical Archaeology Review* 10 (November/December 1984).

Kathleen Kenyon, *Digging Up Jericho* (1957), *Excavations at Jericho*, 2 vols. (1960, 1965), *Archaeology in the Holy Land* (1960), *The Bible and Recent Archaeology* (1978).

Ann Killebrew and Steven Fine, "Qatzrin: Reconstructing Village Life in Talmudic Times," *Biblical Archaeology Review* 17 (May/June 1991).

Barbara S. Lesko, "Women's Monumental Mark on Ancient Egypt," *Biblical Archaeologist* 54 (March 1991): 4–15

Herbert Lockyer, Sr., ed., *Nelson's Illustrated Bible Dictionary* (Nashville, Tennessee: Thomas Nelson Publishers, 1986).

Carol L. Meyers, "Of Drums and Damsels," *Biblical Archaeologist* 54 (March 1991).

Peter Roger Stuart Moorey, "British Women in Near Eastern Archaeology: Kathleen Kenyon and the Pioneers," *Palestine Exploration Quarterly* 124 (July-December 1992).

Kjeld Nielsen, "Ancient Aromas Good and Bad," *Bible Review* 7 (June 1991).

"The Patriarchs' Wives as Sisters—Is the Anchor Bible Wrong?" *Biblical Archaeology Review* 1 (September 1975).

Shalom M. Paul, "Jerusalem of Gold—A Song and an Ancient Crown," *Biblical Archaeology Review* 3 (December 1977).

Charles R. Pfeiffer, ed., *The Biblical World: A Dictionary of Biblical Archaeology* (Grand Rapids, Michigan: Baker Book House, 1966).

John B. Polhill, *Acts*, The New American Commentary, vol. 26 (Nashville, Tennessee: Broadman Press, 1992), p. 349, footnote 24.

H. Rand, "Figure-Vases in Ancient Egypt and Hebrew Midwives," *Israel Exploration Quarterly* 20:3–4 (1970).

Stan Rummel, "Clothes Maketh the Man—An Insight from Ancient Ugarit," *Biblical Archaeology Review* 2 (June 1976).

Marla J. Selvidge, "Mark 5:25–34 and Leviticus 15:19–20: A Reaction to Restrictive Purity Regulations," *Journal of Biblical Literature* 103 (December 1984).

Neil Asher Silberman, "Restoring the Reputation of

Lady Hester Lucy Stanhope: A Little-known Episode in the Beginnings of Archaeology in the Holy Land," *Biblical Archaeology Review* 10 (July/August 1984).

Brunilde Sismondo Ridgway, "Ancient Greek Women and Art: The Material Evidence," *American Journal of Archaeology* 91 (July 1987).

Michael T. Shoemaker, "Herod's Lady's Earring?" *Biblical Archaeology Review* 17 (July/August 1991).

Lawrence E. Stager, "Eroticism & Infanticide at Ashkelon," *Biblical Archaeology Review* 17 (July/August 1991).

William H. Stephens, *The New Testament World in Pictures* (Nashville, Tennessee: Broadman Press, 1987).

Robert R. Stieglitz, "The Minoan Origin of Tyrian Purple," *Biblical Archaeologist* 54 (March 1994).

Varda Sussman, "Lighting the Way Through History: The Evolution of Ancient Oil Lamps," *Biblical Archaeology Review* 11 (March/April 1985).

Danny Syon, "Gamla—Portrait of a Rebellion," *Biblical Archaeology Review* 18 (January/February 1992).

Merrill C. Tenney, *The Zondervan Pictorial Encyclopedia of the Bible*, 5 vols. (Grand Rapids, Michigan: Zondervan, 1975).

Paula Wapnish, "Beauty and Utility in Bone—New Light on Bone Crafting," *Biblical Archaeology Review* 17 (July/August 1991).

Elizabeth Lyding Will, "Women in Pompeii," *Archaeology* 32 (September/October 1979).

"You Can Never Find One When You Need One," *Biblical Archaeology Review* 18 (November/December 1992).

Sybil Zimmerman, "Housewares and Recipes from 2000 Years Ago," *Biblical Archaeology Review* 7 (September/October 1981).

Selected Sources for Inspirational Quotations

Catherine Booth. *Aggressive Christianity* copyright © by Worldwide Publications.

Jill Briscoe. *De-Baiting the Woman Trap* copyright © 1994 by Jill Briscoe. Published by Baker Books. Used by permission.

Nancie Carmichael. *Virtue* March/April 1995. Used by permission.

Ronda De Sola Chervin, comp. *Quotable Saints* copyright © 1992 by Ronda De Sola Chervin, published by Servant Publications.

Mary C. Crowley. *Think Mink!* copyright © 1976 by Fleming H. Revell Company.

Linda Dillow. *Creative Counterpart* copyright © 1977, 1986 by Linda Dillow. Published by Thomas Nelson, Inc.

Cindy Lewis Dake. *Contempo* May 1992. Published by the Women's Missionary Union, Southern Baptist Convention.

Elisabeth Elliot. *Let Me Be a Woman* copyright © 1976 by Tyndale House Publishers, Inc. *A Slow and*

Certain Light copyright © 1973 by Elisabeth Elliot Leitch. Published by Word, Inc. *A Path Through Suffering* copyright © 1990 by Elisabeth Elliot Gren. Published by Servant Publications.

Mary Farrar. *Christian Book Review* May/June 1995.

Joy P. Gage. *Every Woman's Privilege* copyright © 1986 by Joy Gage, published by Multnomah Press. Also, Mrs. Gage as quoted in *Heart to Heart with Pastors' Wives*, compiled by Lynne Dugan. Copyright © 1994 by Lynne Dugan. Published by Regal Books, a division of Gospel Light.

Gloria Gaither, Gigi Graham Tchividjian, Susan Alexander Yates. *Marriage: Questions Women Ask* copyright © 1992 by Christianity Today, Inc. Published by Multnomah Press.

Ruth Bell Graham. Quoted in *Today's Christian Woman* January/February 1991.

Catherine Hickem. Quoted in *Heart to Heart with Pastors' Wives*, compiled by Lynne Dugan. Copyright © 1994 by Lynne Dugan. Published by Regal Books, a division of Gospel Light.

Susan Hunt. *Spiritual Mothering* copyright © 1992 by Susan Hunt. Published by Legacy Communications.

Helen Keller. Quoted in *Great Quotes from Great Women* copyright © 1991 by Celebrating Excellence, Inc.

Rhonda Harrington Kelley. *Divine Discipline* copyright © 1992 by Rhonda Harrington Kelley, published by Pelican Publishing Company, Inc.

Carol Kent. *Today's Christian Woman*. Interview by Jan L. Senn. 1995.

Beverly LaHaye. *The Spirit-Controlled Woman* copyright © 1976 by Harvest House Publishers.

Jo Ann Paris Leavell. *Joy in the Journey* copyright © 1994 by Jo Ann Paris Leavell, published by Pelican Publishing Company, Inc.

Gail MacDonald. Quoted in *Heart to Heart with Pastors' Wives*, compiled by Lynne Dugan. Copyright © 1994 by Lynne Dugan. Published by Regal Books, a division of Gospel Light.

Karen Mains. *Open Heart, Open Home* copyright © 1976 by David C. Cook Publishers. *Making Sunday Special* copyright © 1984 by Karen Mains. Published by Word Books.

Mary Ann Mayo. *Virtue* May/June 1995. Used by permission.

Henrietta Mears. *What the Bible Is All About* copyright © 1953, 1954, 1960, 1966 by Gospel Light Publications. Revised edition copyright © 1983. Published by Regal Books.

Mother Teresa of Calcutta. Quoted in *Journey Magazine* November 1994. Published by the Baptist Sunday School Board.

Anne Ortlund. *Disciplines of the Beautiful Woman* copyright © 1977, 1984 by Word, Inc. Used by permission. *Disciplines of the Heart* copyright © 1987 by Word, Inc. Used by permission.

Dorothy Kelley Patterson. *A Woman Seeking God*

(Nashville: Broadman Press, 1992). All rights reserved. Used by permission.

Joyce Rogers. *The Secret to a Woman's Influence* (Nashville: Broadman Press, 1988). All rights reserved. Used by permission.

Amy Roth. Quoted in *Journey Magazine* November 1994. Published by the Baptist Sunday School Board.

Jan Silvious. *Meditations for the Busy Woman* copyright © 1993 by Jan Silvious.

Jeanette Thomason. *Virtue* March/April 1995. Used by permission.

Lila Trotman. Quoted in *The Spirit-Controlled Woman* by Beverly LaHaye. Copyright © 1976 by Harvest House Publishers.

Bertha Von Suttner. Quoted in *Great Quotes from Great Women* copyright © 1991 by Celebrating Excellence, Inc.

Mary Welchel. *The Christian Working Woman* copyright © 1989, 1994. Published by Revell.

Sheila West. Quoted in *Journey Magazine*, published 1995 by the Baptist Sunday School Board.

Heather Whitestone. *Christian Single* January 1995. Interview by Amy Adams. Published by the Baptist Sunday School Board.

Mary Lou Whitlock. Quoted in *Heart to Heart with Pastors' Wives*, compiled by Lynne Dugan. Copyright © 1994 by Lynne Dugan. Published by Regal Books, a division of Gospel Light.

PERSPECTIVE ARTICLES

Permission is gratefully acknowledged for use of the following materials:

"Getting to Know the Author" by Anne Graham Lotz, excerpted from *God's Story* (Nashville, TN: W Publishing Group, 1999), pp. viii–xl (prologue), copyright 1999 by AGL.

"A Balanced Spiritual Diet" by Nancy Leigh DeMoss, excerpted from *A Place of Quiet Rest* (Chicago: Moody Publishers, 2000), pp. 168–172, copyright 2000 by Nancy Leigh DeMoss.

"Beginning to Read and Study the Bible" by Roberta Hromas, excerpted from *Passport to the Bible* (Wheaton, IL: Tyndale House, 1980), copyright by Roberta Hromas.

"The Word of God: A Precious Treasure" by Nancy Leigh DeMoss, excerpted from *A Place of Quiet Rest*, pp. 146–149.

"A Deeper Walk of Faith" by Emilie Barnes, adapted from *More Faith in My Day* (Eugene, OR: Harvest House Publishers, 2005), pp. 7–8, copyright 2005 by Bob and Emilie Barnes; and from *15 Minutes Alone with God* (Eugene, OR: Harvest House Publishers, 1994), pp. 7 and 9, copyright 1994 by Harvest House.

"Jesus, God's Refreshing Word" by Dee Brestin and Kathy Troccoli, excerpted from *Forever in Love with Jesus* (Nashville, TN: W Publishing Group 2004), pp. 65–68, copyright 2004 by Dee Brestin and Kathy Troccoli.

"Walking in the Light of the Word" by Kimberly Daniels, adapted from *Clean House Strong House* (Lake Mary, FL: Charisma House, 2003), pp. viii–x (preface), copyright 2003 by Kimberly Daniels.

"Getting the Word Into You" by Nancy Leigh DeMoss, excerpted from *A Place of Quiet Rest*, pp. 181–195.

"Ten Good Reasons to Read God's Word" by Stormie Omartian, excerpted from *The Power of Praying* (Eugene, OR: Harvest House Publishers, 2004), p. 104, copyright 2004 by Stormie Omartian.

"Getting to Know Your Bible" by Roberta Hromas, excerpted from *52 Ways to Know Your Bible Better*, (Nashville, TN: Thomas Nelson, 1992), Copyright by American Christian Trust.

"The Link Between Faith and God's Word" by Linda Dillow, adapted from *Calm My Anxious Heart* (Colorado Springs, CO: NavPress, 1998), pp. 134–145, copyright by Linda Dillow.

"The Bible is God's Love Letter" by Stormie Omartian, adapted from *Just Enough Light for the Step I'm On* (Eugene, OR: Harvest House Publishers, 1999), pp. 47–51, copyright 1999 by Stormie Omartian.

INDEX

A Reference Guide to the Special Features

The special features of **The Woman's Study Bible** include **Annotations** *(N)* identifying people and places, commenting on significant verses, and explaining difficult passages; **Articles** *(A)* on subjects of interest to women; **Charts** *(C)* with an overview of biblical themes and life situations; **Maps** *(M)* designed to help your understanding of the geographical situations with a special focus on biblical women and important events in their lives; **Portraits** *(P)* sketching the lives of biblical women; and **Topical Notes** *(T)* with practical application of the principles of Scripture to everyday living. All of these elements have been extensively cross-referenced throughout **The Woman's Study Bible**. This guide will aid you in finding additional material on subjects of interest to you.

MAPS AND CHARTS IN *THE WOMAN'S STUDY BIBLE*

CONCORDANCE

A

ABASED
I know how to be *a* .....Phil 4:12

ABBA
And He said, "A ..... Mark 14:36
whom we cry out, "A ... Rom 8:15

ABHOR
Therefore I *a* myself .....Job 42:6

ABHORRED
a His own inheritance ..Ps 106:40

ABIDE
the Most High Shall *a* ....Ps 91:1
Him, "If you *a* ....John 8:31
"If you *a* in Me ....John 15:7
a in My love ....John 15:9

ABIDES
He who *a* in Me ....John 15:5
will of God *a* forever .1 John 2:17

ABIDING
not have His word *a* ....John 5:38

ABILITY
to his own *a* ....Matt 25:15
a which God supplies ..1 Pet 4:11

ABLE
shall give as he is *a* ...Deut 16:17
whom we serve is *a* .....Dan 3:17
God is *a* to raise up .....Matt 3:9
fear Him who is *a* .....Matt 10:28
you *a* to drink the .....Matt 20:22
that He is *a* ....2 Tim 1:12
learning and never *a* ...2 Tim 3:7
that God was *a* to .....Heb 11:19

ABOLISHED
having *a* in His flesh ....Eph 2:15
Christ, who has *a* .....2 Tim 1:10

ABOMINABLE
deny Him, being *a* .....Titus 1:16
unbelieving, and *a* ....Rev 21:8

ABOMINATION
Yes, seven are an *a* ....Prov 6:16
the scoffer is an *a* ......Prov 24:9
prayer is an *a* ....Prov 28:9
and place there the *a* ...Dan 11:31
the *a* of desolation .....Dan 12:11
the '*a* of desolation,' ...Matt 24:15

ABOMINATIONS
delights in their *a* ....Is 66:3
a golden cup full of *a* ....Rev 17:4

ABOUND
the offense might *a* .....Rom 5:20
sin that grace may *a* .....Rom 6:1
to make all grace *a* .....2 Cor 9:8
and I know how to *a* ....Phil 4:12

ABOUNDED
But where sin *a* ....Rom 5:20

ABOUNDING
immovable, always *a* .1 Cor 15:58

ABOVE
that is in heaven *a* ....Ex 20:4
A it stood seraphim ....Is 6:2
"He who comes from *a* . John 3:31
I am from *a* ....John 8:23
given you from *a* .....John 19:11
things which are *a* ....Col 3:1
perfect gift is from *a* .. James 1:17

ABSENT
in the body we are *a* ....2 Cor 5:6

ABSTAIN
we write to them to *a* ..Acts 15:20
A from every form ..1 Thess 5:22

ABUNDANCE
put in out of their *a* ...Mark 12:44
not consist in the *a* ...Luke 12:15

ABUNDANT
in labors more *a* ......2 Cor 11:23

ABUNDANTLY
a satisfied with the ....Ps 36:8
may have it more *a* ...John 10:10
to do exceedingly *a* .....Eph 3:20

ACCEPT
offering, I will not *a* ....Jer 14:12
Should I *a* this from .....Mal 1:13

ACCEPTABLE
a time I have heard ....Is 49:8
proclaim the *a* year ....Is 61:2
proclaim the a year ....Luke 4:19
is that good and *a* ....Rom 12:2

ACCEPTABLY
we may serve God *a* ...Heb 12:28

ACCEPTED
Behold, now is the *a* ....2 Cor 6:2
which He made us *a* .....Eph 1:6

ACCESS
whom also we have *a* ....Rom 5:2

ACCOMPLISHED
all things were now *a* .John 19:28

ACCORD
continued with one *a* ...Acts 1:14

ACCOUNT
they will give *a* ....Matt 12:36
put that on my *a* ....Philem 18

ACCOUNTED
in the LORD, and He *a* ...Gen 15:6
his faith is *a* ....Rom 4:5
God, and it was a ....Gal 3:6
God, and it was a .....James 2:23

ACCURSED
not know the law is *a* ..John 7:49
of God calls Jesus *a* ...1 Cor 12:3
to you, let him be *a* ....Gal 1:8

ACCUSATION
over His head the *a* ....Matt 27:37
they might find an *a* ....Luke 6:7

ACCUSE
they began to *a* Him ...Luke 23:2

ACCUSED
while He was being *a* ..Matt 27:12

ACCUSER
a of our brethren ....Rev 12:10

ACCUSING
their thoughts *a* ....Rom 2:15

ACKNOWLEDGE
a my transgressions ......Ps 51:3
In all your ways *a* ....Prov 3:6

ACKNOWLEDGES
a the Son has the .....1 John 2:23

ACQUAINT
a yourself with Him ....Job 22:21

ACQUAINTED
A Man of sorrows and *a* ...Is 53:3

ACQUIT
at all *a* the wicked ....Nah 1:3

ACT
in the very *a* ....John 8:4

ACTIONS
by Him *a* are weighed ..1 Sam 2:3

ACTS
of Your awesome *a* ......Ps 145:6

ADD
Do not *a* to His words ..Prov 30:6

ADDED
And the Lord *a* to the ...Acts 2:47
It was *a* because of ......Gal 3:19

ADMONISH
a him as a ....2 Thess 3:15

ADMONITION
written for our *a* .....1 Cor 10:11
in the training and *a* .....Eph 6:4

ADOPTION
the Spirit of *a* ....Rom 8:15
waiting for the *a* ....Rom 8:23
to whom pertain the *a* ...Rom 9:4

ADORN
also, that the women *a* ..1 Tim 2:9

ADORNED
God also *a* themselves ...1 Pet 3:5
prepared as a bride *a* ....Rev 21:2

ADRIFT
A among the dead ....Ps 88:5

ADULTERER
The eye of the *a* ....Job 24:15

ADULTERERS
nor idolaters, nor *a* .....1 Cor 6:9
a God will judge ....Heb 13:4

ADULTEROUS
a generation ....Matt 12:39

ADULTERY
You shall not commit *a* ..Ex 20:14
already committed *a* .....Matt 5:28

ADVANTAGE

is divorced commits *a* . . Matt 5:32
another commits *a* . . . . Mark 10:11
those who commit *a* . . . . . Rev 2:22

ADVANTAGE

a that I go away . . . . John 16:7
Satan should take *a* . . . 2 Cor 2:11

ADVERSARIES

and there are many *a* . . 1 Cor 16:9
terrified by your *a* . . . . . . Phil 1:28

ADVERSARY

"Agree with your *a* . . . . . Matt 5:25
opportunity to the *a* . . . 1 Tim 5:14
a the devil walks . . . . 1 Pet 5:8

ADVERSITY

I shall never be in *a* . . . . . . Ps 10:6
the day of *a* consider . . . . Eccl 7:14

ADVICE

in this I give my *a* . . . . . 2 Cor 8:10

ADVOCATE

sins, we have an A . . . . 1 John 2:1

AFAR

and not a God *a* . . . . Jer 23:23
to you who were *a* . . . . . . Eph 2:17
having seen them *a* . . . . Heb 11:13

AFFAIRS

himself with the *a* . . . . . . 2 Tim 2:4

AFFECTION

to his wife the *a* . . . . 1 Cor 7:3

AFFECTIONATE

Be kindly *a* to one . . . . . Rom 12:10

AFFIRM

you to *a* constantly . . . . . . Titus 3:8

AFFLICT

a Your heritage . . . . Ps 94:5
For He does not *a* . . . . . . Lam 3:33

AFFLICTED

To him who is *a* . . . . Job 6:14
hears the cry of the *a* . . . Job 34:28
days of the *a* are evil . . Prov 15:15
Smitten by God, and *a* . . . . Is 53:4
"O you *a* one . . . . Is 54:11
being destitute, *a* . . . . . . Heb 11:37

AFFLICTING

A the just and taking . . Amos 5:12

AFFLICTION

is, the bread of *a* . . . . Deut 16:3
a take hold of me . . . . . . Job 30:16
and it is an evil *a* . . . . Eccl 6:2
For our light *a* . . . . 2 Cor 4:17
supposing to add *a* . . . . . . Phil 1:16

AFRAID

garden, and I was *a* . . . . . Gen 3:10
saying, "Do not be *a* . . . Gen 15:1
none will make you *a* . . . . Lev 26:6
ungodliness made me *a* . . Ps 18:4
Whenever I am *a* . . . . Ps 56:3
one will make them *a* . . . . . Is 17:2
do not be *a* . . . . Matt 14:27
if you do evil, be *a* . . . . Rom 13:4
do good and are not *a* . . . 1 Pet 3:6

AFTERWARD

a receive me to glory . . . . Ps 73:24
you shall follow Me *a* . John 13:36

AGAIN

'You must be born *a* . . . . John 3:7
having been born *a* . . . . 1 Pet 1:23

AGAINST

come to 'set a man *a* . . Matt 10:35
or house divided *a* . . . . Matt 12:25
Me is *a* Me . . . . Matt 12:30
a the Spirit will not . . . . Matt 12:31
lifted up his heel a . . . . John 13:18
LORD and *a* His Christ . . Acts 4:26
to kick *a* the goads . . . . . . Acts 9:5
a the promises of God . . . Gal 3:21
we do not wrestle *a* . . . . . Eph 6:12
I have a few things *a* . . . . Rev 2:20

AGE

the grave at a full *a* . . . . . Job 5:26
and in the *a* to come . . Mark 10:30

AGED

a one as Paul, the *a* . . . . . Philem 9

AGES

ordained before the *a* . . . 1 Cor 2:7

AGONY

And being in *a* . . . . Luke 22:44

AGREE

that if two of you *a* . . . . Matt 18:19

AGREED

unless they are *a* . . . . Amos 3:3

AGREEMENT

what *a* has the temple . 2 Cor 6:16

AIR

the birds of the *a* . . . . . . Gen 1:26
of the *a* have nests . . . . . Luke 9:58
of the power of the *a* . . . . . Eph 2:2
the Lord in the *a* . . . . 1 Thess 4:17

ALIENATED

darkened, being *a* . . . . Eph 4:18
you, who once were *a* . . . . Col 1:21

ALIENS

A have devoured his . . . . . Hos 7:9
Christ, being *a* . . . . Eph 2:12

ALIKE

esteems every day *a* . . . Rom 14:5

ALIVE

I kill and I make *a* . . . . Deut 32:39
was dead and is *a* . . . . Luke 15:24
presented Himself *a* . . . . . Acts 1:3
indeed to sin, but *a* . . . . . Rom 6:11
all shall be made *a* . . . 1 Cor 15:22
that we who are *a* . . . 1 Thess 4:15
and behold, I am *a* . . . . . . Rev 1:18
These two were cast *a* . . Rev 19:20

ALLELUIA

Again they said, "A . . . . Rev 19:3

ALLOW

a Your Holy One . . . . Ps 16:10
a My faithfulness . . . . Ps 89:33
a Your Holy One . . . . . . Acts 2:27

ALLURE

of emptiness, they *a* . . . . 2 Pet 2:18

ALMOND

a tree blossoms . . . . Eccl 12:5

ALMOST

a persuade me to . . . . . . Acts 26:28

ALOES

of myrrh and *a* . . . . John 19:39

ALPHA

"I am the A and the . . . . . . Rev 1:8
"I am the A and the . . . . Rev 22:13

ALTAR

Then Noah built an *a* . . . Gen 8:20
'An *a* of earth you . . . . . . Ex 20:24
it to you upon the *a* . . . . Lev 17:11
your gift to the *a* . . . . Matt 5:23
swears by the *a* . . . . . . Matt 23:18
I even found an *a* . . . . . Acts 17:23
We have an *a* from . . . . Heb 13:10

ALTARS

Even Your *a*, O LORD . . . . . Ps 84:3
and torn down Your a . . Rom 11:3

ALTERED

of His face was *a* . . . . . . Luke 9:29

ALWAYS

delight, Rejoicing *a* . . . . . Prov 8:30
the poor with you *a* . . . . Matt 26:11
lo, I am with you *a* . . . . Matt 28:20
to them, that men *a* . . . . Luke 18:1
immovable, *a* . . . . 1 Cor 15:58
Rejoice in the Lord *a* . . . . Phil 4:4
thus we shall *a* . . . . . . 1 Thess 4:17
a be ready to give a . . . . 1 Pet 3:15

AM

to Moses, "I A WHO I . . . . Ex 3:14
First and I *a* the Last . . . . . . Is 44:6
in My name, I *a* . . . . Matt 18:20
a the bread of life . . . . . . John 6:35
a the light of the . . . . John 8:12
I *a* from above . . . . John 8:23
Abraham was, I A . . . . John 8:58
"I *a* the door . . . . John 10:9
a the good shepherd . . . John 10:11
a the resurrection . . . . . John 11:25
to him, "I *a* the way . . . . John 14:6
of God I *a* what I *a* . . . 1 Cor 15:10

AMBASSADOR

for which I am an *a* . . . . . Eph 6:20

AMBASSADORS

we are *a* for Christ . . . . 2 Cor 5:20

AMBITION

Christ from selfish *a* . . . . Phil 1:16

AMEN

are Yes, and in Him A . 2 Cor 1:20
creatures said, "A . . . . Rev 5:14

ANCHOR

hope we have as an *a* . . . Heb 6:19

ANCIENT

Do not remove the *a* . . . Prov 23:10
"until the A of Days . . . . Dan 7:22

ANGEL

"Behold, I send an A . . . . Ex 23:20
Manoah said to the A . . Judg 13:17
the A of His Presence . . . . . Is 63:9
things, behold, an *a* . . . . Matt 1:20
for an *a* of the Lord . . . . Matt 28:2
Then an *a* of the Lord . . Luke 1:11
And behold, an *a* . . . . Luke 2:9
a appeared to Him . . . . Luke 22:43
For an *a* went down at . . John 5:4
a has spoken to Him . . John 12:29
But at night an *a* . . . . Acts 5:19
A who appeared to him . Acts 7:35
immediately an *a* . . . . . . Acts 12:23
himself into an *a* . . . . . 2 Cor 11:14
even if we, or an *a* . . . . . . Gal 1:8
Then I saw a strong *a* . . . . Rev 5:2
Jesus, have sent My *a* . . Rev 22:16

ANGELS

If He charges His *a* . . . . . Job 4:18
lower than the *a* . . . . Ps 8:5
He shall give His *a* . . . . . Ps 91:11
He shall give His a . . . . . Matt 4:6
not even the *a* . . . . Matt 24:36

and all the holy *a* . . . . Matt 25:31
twelve legions of *a* . . . . Matt 26:53
And she saw two *a* . . . . John 20:12
and worship of *a* . . . . Col 2:18
much better than the *a* . . . Heb 1:4
entertained *a* . . . . Heb 13:2
things which *a* desire . . 1 Pet 1:12
did not spare the *a* . . . . . . 2 Pet 2:4
a who did not keep . . . . Jude 6

ANGER

For His *a* is but for a . . . . . Ps 30:5
gracious, Slow to *a* . . . . . . Ps 103:8
Nor will He keep His *a* . . Ps 103:9
around at them with *a* . . Mark 3:5
bitterness, wrath, *a* . . . . . Eph 4:31

ANGRY

Cain, "Why are you *a* . . . . Gen 4:6
"Let not the Lord be *a* . Gen 18:30
the Son, lest He be *a* . . . . . Ps 2:12
a man stirs up strife . . . Prov 29:22
right for you to be *a* . . . . . Jon 4:4
you that whoever is *a* . . . Matt 5:22
"Be a, and do not . . . . Eph 4:26

ANGUISH

remembers the *a* . . . . . . John 16:21
tribulation and *a* . . . . Rom 2:9

ANIMAL

of every clean *a* . . . . Gen 7:2
set him on his own *a* . . Luke 10:34

ANIMALS

of *a* after their kind . . . . . Gen 6:20
of four-footed *a* . . . . Acts 10:12

ANNUL

years later, cannot *a* . . . . . Gal 3:17

ANNULS

is confirmed, no one *a* . . . Gal 3:15

ANOINT

a my head with oil . . . . Ps 23:5
when you fast, *a* . . . . Matt 6:17
a My body for burial . . . Mark 14:8
a your eyes with eye . . . . Rev 3:18

ANOINTED

"Surely the LORD's *a* . . 1 Sam 16:6
destroy the LORD's *a* . . 2 Sam 1:14
"Do not touch My *a* . . 1 Chr 16:22
Because He has a . . . . . . Luke 4:18
but this woman has *a* . . Luke 7:46
a the eyes of the . . . . John 9:6
that Mary who *a* . . . . . . John 11:2
Jesus, whom You *a* . . . . . Acts 4:27
and has *a* us is God . . . 2 Cor 1:21

ANOINTING

But you have an *a* . . . . 1 John 2:20

ANOTHER

that you love one *a* . . . . John 13:34

ANSWER

Call, and I will *a* . . . . Job 13:22
How shall I *a* Him . . . . . . Job 31:14
the day that I call, *a* . . . . . Ps 102:2
In Your faithfulness *a* . . Ps 143:1
a turns away wrath . . . . Prov 15:1
a a fool according . . . . . . Prov 26:4
or what you should *a* . Luke 12:11
you may have an *a* . . . . 2 Cor 5:12

ANT

Go to the *a* . . . . Prov 6:6

ANTICHRIST

heard that the *A* . . . . . . 1 John 2:18
a who denies the . . . . . 1 John 2:22
is a deceiver and an *a* . . . 2 John 7

ANTITYPE

a which now saves us . . 1 Pet 3:21

ANXIETIES

the multitude of my *a* . . . . Ps 94:19

ANXIETY

A in the heart of man . . Prov 12:25

ANXIOUS

Be *a* for nothing . . . . Phil 4:6

APART

justified by faith *a* . . . . . Rom 3:28

APOSTLE

called to be an *a* . . . . Rom 1:1
consider the *A* . . . . Heb 3:1

APOSTLES

of the twelve *a* . . . . Matt 10:2
He also named . . . . Luke 6:13
am the least of the *a* . . 1 Cor 15:9
none of the other *a* . . . . . Gal 1:19
gave some to be *a* . . . . . Eph 4:11

APOSTLESHIP

in this ministry and *a* . . Acts 1:25
are the seal of my *a* . . . . 1 Cor 9:2

APPAREL

gold rings, in fine *a* . . . . James 2:2
or putting on fine *a* . . . . . 1 Pet 3:3

APPEAL

love's sake I rather *a* . . . Philem 9

APPEAR

and let the dry land *a* . . . . Gen 1:9
also outwardly *a* . . . . . . Matt 23:28
God would *a* . . . . Luke 19:11
For we must all *a* . . . . . 2 Cor 5:10

APPEARANCE

Do not look at his *a* . . 1 Sam 16:7
judge according to *a* . . . . John 7:24
those who boast in *a* . . 2 Cor 5:12
found in *a* as a man . . . . . . Phil 2:8

APPEARED

an angel of the Lord *a* . Luke 1:11
who *a* in glory and . . . . . Luke 9:31
brings salvation has *a* . . Titus 2:11
of the ages, He has *a* . . . . Heb 9:26

APPEARING

Lord Jesus Christ's *a* . . 1 Tim 6:14
and the dead at His *a* . . . 2 Tim 4:1
who have loved His *a* . . . 2 Tim 4:8

APPEARS

can stand when He *a* . . . . Mal 3:2
who is our life *a* . . . . Col 3:4
the Chief Shepherd *a* . . . 1 Pet 5:4
that when He *a* . . . . . . 1 John 2:28

APPETITE

are a man given to *a* . . . Prov 23:2

APPLE

And my law as the *a* . . . . Prov 7:2

APPLES

fitly spoken is like *a* . . . Prov 25:11

APPLIED

a my heart to know . . . . Eccl 7:25

APPOINT

For God did not *a* . . . . 1 Thess 5:9

APPOINTED

And as it is *a* for men . . . Heb 9:27

APPROACH

year, make those who *a* . Heb 10:1

APPROACHING

as you see the Day *a* . . . Heb 10:25

APPROVE

do the same but also *a* . . Rom 1:32

APPROVED

to God and *a* by men . . Rom 14:18
to present yourself *a* . . . 2 Tim 2:15

ARBITRATOR

Me a judge or an *a* . . . . Luke 12:14

ARCHANGEL

the voice of an *a* . . . . 1 Thess 4:16

ARGUMENTS

casting down *a* and . . . . 2 Cor 10:5

ARISE

A, shine . . . . Is 60:1
But the LORD will *a* . . . . Is 60:2
you who sleep, *A* . . . . . . Eph 5:14

ARK

"Make yourself an *a* . . . . Gen 6:14
him, she took an *a* . . . . Ex 2:3
Bezalel made the *a* . . . . . . Ex 37:1
in heaven, and the *a* . . . Rev 11:19

ARM

with an outstretched *a* . . . . Ex 6:6
Have you an *a* like God . . Job 40:9
strength with His *a* . . . . Luke 1:51
a yourselves also with . . . 1 Pet 4:1

ARMED

a strong man, fully *a* . . Luke 11:21

ARMIES

And he sent out his *a* . . . Matt 22:7
surrounded by *a* . . . . . . Luke 21:20
And the *a* in heaven . . . . Rev 19:14
the earth, and their *a* . . . Rev 19:19

ARMOR

Put on the whole *a* . . . . . . Eph 6:11

ARMS

are the everlasting *a* . . Deut 33:27
took Him up in his *a* . . . Luke 2:28

AROMA

the one we are the *a* . . . 2 Cor 2:16
for a sweet-smelling *a* . . . Eph 5:2

AROUSED

LORD was greatly *a* . . . . Num 11:10
Then Joseph, being *a* . . . Matt 1:24

ARRAYED

his glory was not *a* . . . . . Matt 6:29
"Who are these *a* . . . . Rev 7:13

ARROGANCE

Pride and *a* and the . . . . Prov 8:13

ARROW

a that flies by day . . . . Ps 91:5

ARROWS

a pierce me deeply . . . . . . Ps 38:2
Like *a* in the hand of . . . . Ps 127:4

ASCEND

Who may *a* into the . . . . . . Ps 24:3
If I *a* into heaven . . . . Ps 139:8
'I will *a* into heaven . . . . . . Is 14:13
see the Son of Man *a* . . . John 6:62

ASCENDED

You have *a* on high .....Ps 68:18
"No one has *a* ....John 3:13
"*When He a* on high .....Eph 4:8

ASCENDING

the angels of God *a* ....John 1:51

ASCRIBE

A strength to God ....Ps 68:34

ASHAMED

Let me not be *a* ....Ps 25:2
And Israel shall be *a* ....Hos 10:6
For whoever is *a* ....Mark 8:38
am not *a* of the gospel . Rom 1:16
Therefore God is not *a* . Heb 11:16

ASHES

become like dust and *a* . Job 30:19
in sackcloth and *a* ....Luke 10:13

ASIDE

lay something *a* ....1 Cor 16:2
lay *a* all filthiness ....James 1:21
Therefore, laying *a* .....1 Pet 2:1

ASK

when your children *a* ....Josh 4:6
"*A* a sign for yourself .....Is 7:11
whatever things you *a* . Matt 21:22
a, and it will be ....Luke 11:9
that whatever You *a* ..John 11:22
a anything in My .....John 14:14
in that day you will *a* . John 16:23
above all that we *a* .....Eph 3:20
wisdom, let him *a* ....James 1:5
But let him *a* in faith ...James 1:6
because you do not *a* ...James 4:2

ASKS

For everyone who *a* .....Matt 7:8
you who, if his son *a* ...Matt 7:9
Or if he *a* for a fish ...Luke 11:11

ASLEEP

But He was *a* ....Matt 8:24
some have fallen *a* ....1 Cor 15:6
those who are *a* .....1 Thess 4:15

ASSEMBLING

not forsaking the *a* ....Heb 10:25

ASSEMBLY

a I will praise You ....Ps 22:22
fast, Call a sacred *a* .....Joel 1:14
a I will sing praise ......Heb 2:12
to the general *a* ....Heb 12:23

ASSURANCE

riches of the full *a* ....Col 2:2
Spirit and in much *a* . 1 Thess 1:5
to the full *a* of hope .....Heb 6:11

ASSURE

a our hearts before ...1 John 3:19

ASSURED

learned and been *a* ....2 Tim 3:14

ASTONISHED

Just as many were *a* .....Is 52:14
who heard Him were *a* . Luke 2:47

ASTRAY

one of them goes *a* ....Matt 18:12
like sheep going *a* .....1 Pet 2:25

ATONEMENT

the blood that makes *a* . Lev 17:11
for it is the Day of *A* ..Lev 23:28
there will be no *a* ......Is 22:14

ATTAIN

It is high, I cannot *a* .....Ps 139:6

worthy to *a* that age .. Luke 20:35
by any means, I may *a* .. Phil 3:11

ATTENTION

My son, give *a* to my ...Prov 4:20

ATTENTIVE

Let Your ears be *a* ......Ps 130:2

ATTESTED

a Man *a* by God to you . Acts 2:22

AUSTERE

because you are an *a* . Luke 19:21

AUTHOR

For God is not the *a* ..1 Cor 14:33
unto Jesus, the *a* ....Heb 12:2

AUTHORITIES

a that exist are ....Rom 13:1

AUTHORITY

them as one having *a* ..Matt 7:29
"All *a* has been given .. Matt 28:18
a I will give You ....Luke 4:6
and has given Him *a* ...John 5:27
You have given Him *a* ..John 17:2
the flesh, reject *a* ....Jude 8

AUTUMN

a trees without fruit ......Jude 12

AVAILS

of a righteous man *a* .. James 5:16

AVENGE

Beloved, do not *a* .....Rom 12:19
a our blood on those ....Rev 6:10

AVENGER

the Lord is the *a* ......1 Thess 4:6

AWAKE

be satisfied when I *a* ....Ps 17:15
it is high time to *a* .....Rom 13:11
A to righteousness ....1 Cor 15:34

AWAY

the wind drives *a* ....Ps 1:4
Do not cast me *a* ....Ps 51:11
A time to cast *a* ....Eccl 3:5
fair one, And come *a* ...Song 2:10
minded to put her *a* ....Matt 1:19
and earth will pass *a* .. Matt 24:35
"I am going *a* ....John 8:21
they cried out, "*A* .....John 19:15
unless the falling *a* ...2 Thess 2:3
in Asia have turned *a* ..2 Tim 1:15
heard, lest we drift *a* .....Heb 2:1
if they fall *a* ....Heb 6:6
can never take *a* ....Heb 10:11
world is passing *a* ....1 John 2:17
if anyone takes *a* ....Rev 22:19

AWESOME

a is this place ....Gen 28:17
God, the great and *a* ....Deut 7:21
By *a* deeds in ....Ps 65:5
O God, You are more *a* .. Ps 68:35
Your great and *a* name ...Ps 99:3

AWL

his ear with an *a* ....Ex 21:6

AX

If the *a* is dull ....Eccl 10:10
And even now the *a* ....Matt 3:10

B

BABBLER

"What does this *b* .....Acts 17:18

BABBLINGS

the profane and idle *b* . 1 Tim 6:20

BABE

the *b* leaped in my .....Luke 1:44
You will find a *B* ......Luke 2:12
for he is a *b* ....Heb 5:13

BABES

Out of the mouth of *b* ......Ps 8:2
revealed them to *b* ....Matt 11:25
of the mouth of b .....Matt 21:16
as to carnal, as to *b* .....1 Cor 3:1
as newborn *b* ....1 Pet 2:2

BACK

for the fool's *b* ....Prov 26:3
I gave My *b* to those ......Is 50:6
plow, and looking *b* ....Luke 9:62
of those who draw *b* ...Heb 10:39
someone turns him *b* . James 5:19

BACKBITERS

b, haters of God ....Rom 1:30

BACKBITING

b tongue an angry .....Prov 25:23

BACKSLIDER

The *b* in heart will be .. Prov 14:14

BACKSLIDINGS

And I will heal your *b* ....Jer 3:22

BACKWARD

ten degrees *b* ....2 Kin 20:11

BAD

b trees bears *b* fruit ....Matt 7:17

BAG

"nor *b* for your ....Matt 10:10

BAKED

b unleavened cakes .....Ex 12:39

BAKER

the butler and the *b* .....Gen 40:1

BALANCES

Falsifying the *b* ....Amos 8:5

BALD

every head shall be *b* ...Jer 48:37

BALDHEAD

Go up, you *b* ....2 Kin 2:23

BALM

no *b* in Gilead ....Jer 8:22

BANDAGED

and *b* his wounds .....Luke 10:34

BANKERS

my money with the *b* .. Matt 25:27

BANNERS

we will set up our *b* ......Ps 20:5
as an army with *b* ....Song 6:4

BANQUET

b that I have prepared ...Esth 5:4

BANQUETING

He brought me to the *b* .. Song 2:4

BAPTISM

coming to his *b* ....Matt 3:7
b that I am baptized ...Matt 20:22
"But I have a *b* ......Luke 12:50
said, "Into John's *b* .....Acts 19:3
Lord, one faith, one *b* ....Eph 4:5
buried with Him in *b* ....Col 2:12

BAPTISMS
of the doctrine of *b* . . . . Heb 6:2

BAPTIZE
"I indeed *b* you with . . . . Matt 3:11
Himself did not *b* . . . . John 4:2

BAPTIZED
b will be saved . . . . Mark 16:16
every one of you be *b* . . . Acts 2:38
all his family were *b* . . . Acts 16:33
Arise and be *b* . . . . Acts 22:16
were *b* into Christ . . . . Rom 6:3
I thank God that I *b* . . . 1 Cor 1:14
Spirit we were all *b* . . . 1 Cor 12:13

BAPTIZING
b them in the name of . Matt 28:19

BARBARIAN
nor uncircumcised, *b* . . . . Col 3:11

BARLEY
here who has five *b* . . . . . John 6:9

BARN
the wheat into my *b* . . . Matt 13:30

BARNS
reap nor gather into *b* . . Matt 6:26
I will pull down my *b* . Luke 12:18

BARREN
But Sarai was *b* . . . . Gen 11:30
"Sing, O *b* . . . . Is 54:1

BASE
and the *b* things of . . . . 1 Cor 1:28

BASIN
poured water into a *b* . . John 13:5

BASKET
and put it under a *b* . . . . Matt 5:15
I was let down in a *b* . 2 Cor 11:33

BASKETS
they took up twelve *b* . Matt 14:20

BATHED
to him, "He who is *b* . . John 13:10

BATS
To the moles and *b* . . . . Is 2:20

BATTLE
b is the LORD's . . . . 1 Sam 17:47
the *b* to the strong . . . . . . Eccl 9:11
became valiant in *b* . . . . Heb 11:34

BEAR
greater than I can *b* . . . . . Gen 4:13
whom Sarah shall *b* . . . . Gen 17:21
not *b* false witness . . . . . . Ex 20:16
b their iniquities . . . . Is 53:11
child, and *b* a Son . . . . . . Matt 1:23
A good tree cannot *b* . . . Matt 7:18
how long shall I *b* . . . . . Matt 17:17
by, to *b* His cross . . . . . Mark 15:21
whoever does not *b* . . . Luke 14:27
are strong ought to *b* . . . Rom 15:1
B one another's . . . . Gal 6:2
b the sins of many . . . . . . Heb 9:28

BEARD
the edges of your *b* . . . . Lev 19:27
Running down on the *b* . . Ps 133:2

BEARING
goes forth weeping, *B* . . Ps 126:6
And He, *b* His cross . . . John 19:17
b His reproach . . . . Heb 13:13

BEARS
Every branch that *b* . . . . John 15:2

BEAST
You preserve man and *b* . . Ps 36:6
And I saw a *b* rising . . . . Rev 13:1
the mark of the *b* . . . . . . Rev 19:20

BEASTS
like brute *b* . . . . Jude 10

BEAT
b their swords into . . . . Is 2:4
spat in His face and *b* . Matt 26:67

BEATEN
Three times I was *b* . . 2 Cor 11:25

BEAUTIFUL
B in elevation . . . . Ps 48:2
has made everything *b* . . Eccl 3:11
my love, you are as *b* . . . Song 6:4
How *b* upon the . . . . Is 52:7
indeed appear *b* . . . . Matt 23:27

BEAUTIFY
b the place of My . . . . Is 60:13

BEAUTY
"The *b* of Israel is . . . . 2 Sam 1:19
To behold the *b* . . . . Ps 27:4
see the King in His *b* . . . . . Is 33:17
no *b* that we should . . . . Is 53:2

BECAME
b a living being . . . . Gen 2:7
to the Jews I *b* . . . . 1 Cor 9:20

BED
I remember You on my *b* . Ps 63:6
if I make my *b* in hell . . Ps 139:8
"Arise, take up your *b* . . . Matt 9:6
be two men in one *b* . Luke 17:34
and the *b* undefiled . . . . . Heb 13:4

BEDS
sing aloud on their *b* . . . . Ps 149:5

BEFOREHAND
up, do not worry *b* . . . . Mark 13:11
told you all things *b* . . Mark 13:23
when He testified *b* . . . . 1 Pet 1:11

BEG
b you as sojourners . . . . 1 Pet 2:11

BEGAN
since the world *b* . . . . . . Luke 1:70

BEGGAR
there was a certain *b* . . Luke 16:20

BEGGARLY
weak and *b* elements . . . . . Gal 4:9

BEGINNING
b God created the . . . . Gen 1:1
In the *b* was the Word . . . John 1:1
a murderer from the *b* . . John 8:44
True Witness, the *B* . . . . . Rev 3:14
and the Omega, the *B* . . . Rev 21:6

BEGOTTEN
I have *b* You . . . . Ps 2:7
glory as of the only *b* . . . John 1:14
loves him who is *b* . . . . 1 John 5:1

BEGUILING
b unstable souls . . . . 2 Pet 2:14

BEGUN
Having *b* in the Spirit . . . . Gal 3:3

BEHALF
you on Christ's *b* . . . . . . 2 Cor 5:20

BEHAVE
does not *b* rudely . . . . . . 1 Cor 13:5

BEHAVED
blamelessly we *b* . . . . 1 Thess 2:10

BEHAVIOR
of good *b*, hospitable . . . 1 Tim 3:2

BEHEADED
and had John *b* . . . . Matt 14:10

BEHOLD
B, the virgin shall . . . . Is 7:14
Judah, "*B* your God . . . . . . Is 40:9
"*B* the Lamb of God . . . . John 1:36
to them, "*B* the Man . . . . John 19:5
B what manner of . . . . . 1 John 3:1

BEHOLDING
with unveiled face, *b* . . 2 Cor 3:18

BEING
move and have our *b* . . Acts 17:28
who, *b* in the form of . . . . . Phil 2:6

BELIEVE
tears, "Lord, I *b* . . . . Mark 9:24
have no root, who *b* . . . . Luke 8:13
slow of heart to *b* . . . . . Luke 24:25
to those who *b* . . . . John 1:12
this, that they may *b* . . John 11:42
that you may *b* . . . . John 20:31
the Lord Jesus and *b* . . . Rom 10:9
Christ, not only to *b* . . . . . Phil 1:29
comes to God must *b* . . . . Heb 11:6
b that there is one . . . . James 2:19
Even the demons *b* . . . James 2:19

BELIEVED
And he *b* in the LORD . . . Gen 15:6
Who has *b* our report . . . . . Is 53:1
seen Me, you have *b* . . John 20:29
"Abraham *b* God . . . . Rom 4:3
whom I have *b* . . . . 2 Tim 1:12

BELIEVERS
example to the *b* . . . . . . 1 Tim 4:12

BELIEVES
The simple *b* every . . . . Prov 14:15
that whoever *b* in Him . John 3:16
"He who *b* in the Son . . John 3:36
with the heart one *b* . . . Rom 10:10

BELIEVING
you ask in prayer, *b* . . . Matt 21:22

BELLY
On your *b* you shall go . . Gen 3:14
and Jonah was in the *b* . . Jon 1:17
whose god is their *b* . . . . . Phil 3:19

BELOVED
so He gives His *b* . . . . . . Ps 127:2
My *b* is mine . . . . Song 2:16
"This is My *b* . . . . Matt 3:17
us accepted in the *B* . . . . . . Eph 1:6
Luke the *b* physician . . . . Col 4:14
"This is My *b* . . . . 2 Pet 1:17

BELT
with a leather *b* . . . . Matt 3:4

BEND
The wicked *b* their bow . . . Ps 11:2

BENEATH
"You are from *b* . . . . John 8:23

BENEFACTORS
them are called '*b* . . . . Luke 22:25

BENEFIT
have a second *b* . . . . 2 Cor 1:15

BESEECH

b you therefore . . . . Rom 12:1

BESIDE

He leads me *b* the . . . . Ps 23:2
"Paul, you are *b* . . . . Acts 26:24

BEST

desire the *b* . . . . 1 Cor 12:31

BESTOWED

love the Father has *b* . . 1 John 3:1

BETRAY

you, one of you will *b* . Matt 26:21

BETRAYED

Man is about to be *b* . . Matt 17:22

BETRAYER

See, My *b* is at . . . . Matt 26:46

BETRAYING

"Judas, are you . . . . . Luke 22:48

BETRAYS

who is the one who *b* . John 21:20

BETROTH

"I will *b* you to Me . . . . . . Hos 2:19

BETROTHED

to a virgin *b* to a man . . Luke 1:27

BETTER

b than sacrifice . . . . . . 1 Sam 15:22
It is *b* to trust in . . . . Ps 118:8
For it is *b* to marry . . . . . 1 Cor 7:9
Christ, which is far *b* . . . . Phil 1:23
b than the angels . . . . Heb 1:4
b things concerning . . . . . . Heb 9:9

BEWARE

"*B* of false prophets . . . . Matt 7:15

BEWITCHED

b you that you should . . . . Gal 3:1

BEYOND

advanced in Judaism *b* . . Gal 1:14

BILLOWS

b have gone over me . . . . . Ps 42:7

BIND

and whatever you *b* . . . Matt 16:19
'*B* him hand and foot . . Matt 22:13

BIRD

soul, "Flee as a *b* . . . . Ps 11:1

BIRDS

b make their nests . . . . . . Ps 104:17
"Look at the *b* . . . . Matt 6:26
have holes and *b* . . . . Matt 8:20

BIRTH

the day of one's *b* . . . . . Eccl 7:1
Now the *b* of Jesus . . . . . Matt 1:18
will rejoice at his *b* . . . . Luke 1:14
conceived, it gives *b* . . James 1:15

BIRTHDAY

was Pharaoh's *b* . . . . Gen 40:20

BIRTHRIGHT

Esau despised his *b* . . . . Gen 25:34

BISHOP

the position of a *b* . . . . . . 1 Tim 3:1
b must be blameless . . . . . Titus 1:7

BIT

and they *b* the people . . Num 21:6

BITE

A serpent may *b* . . . . Eccl 10:11
But if you *b* and . . . . Gal 5:15

BITTER

b herbs they . . . . Ex 12:8
and do not be *b* . . . . Col 3:19
But if you have *b* . . . . . James 3:14

BITTERLY

And Hezekiah wept *b* . . 2 Kin 20:3
went out and wept *b* . . . Matt 26:75

BITTERNESS

you are poisoned by *b* . . Acts 8:23
b springing up cause . . . Heb 12:15

BLACK

one hair white or *b* . . . . . Matt 5:36
a *b* horse . . . . Rev 6:5
and the sun became *b* . . . Rev 6:12

BLACKNESS

whom is reserved the *b* . . . Jude 13

BLACKSMITH

I have created the *b* . . . . . . Is 54:16

BLADE

first the *b* . . . . Mark 4:28

BLAME

be holy and without *b* . . . . Eph 1:4

BLAMELESS

and that man was *b* . . . . . . Job 1:1
body be preserved *b* . 1 Thess 5:23

BLAMELESSLY

b we behaved . . . . . . 1 Thess 2:10

BLASPHEME

b Your name forever . . . . Ps 74:10
compelled them to *b* . . . Acts 26:11
b that noble name . . . . . James 2:7

BLASPHEMED

who passed by *b* Him . Matt 27:39
great heat, and they *b* . . . Rev 16:9

BLASPHEMER

I was formerly a *b* . . . . 1 Tim 1:13

BLASPHEMES

b the name of the . . . . . . Lev 24:16
"This Man *b* . . . . Matt 9:3

BLASPHEMIES

is this who speaks *b* . . . . Luke 5:21

BLASPHEMY

but the *b* against . . . . . . Matt 12:31
was full of names of *b* . . . Rev 17:3

BLEATING

"What then is this *b* . 1 Sam 15:14

BLEMISH

be holy and without *b* . . . Eph 5:27
as of a lamb without *b* . 1 Pet 1:19

BLEMISHED

to the Lord what is *b* . . . . Mal 1:14

BLESS

b those who *b* you . . . . . . Gen 12:3
You go unless You *b* . . . Gen 32:26
"The LORD *b* you and . . Num 6:24
b the LORD at all . . . . Ps 34:1
b You while I live . . . . Ps 63:4
b His holy name . . . . Ps 103:1
b those who curse . . . . . Luke 6:28
B those who . . . . Rom 12:14
Being reviled, we *b* . . . . 1 Cor 4:12

BLESSED

B is the man who walks . . . . Ps 1:1
B is the man to whom . . . . Ps 32:2
B is the nation whose . . . . Ps 33:12
B is he who comes . . . . . Ps 118:26
rise up and call her *b* . . Prov 31:28
"*B* are the poor in . . . . Matt 5:3
B are those who mourn . . Matt 5:4
B are the meek . . . . Matt 5:5
B are those who hunger . Matt 5:6
B are the merciful . . . . Matt 5:7
B are the pure in . . . . Matt 5:8
B are the peacemakers . . Matt 5:9
B are those who are . . . . Matt 5:10
B is He who comes . . . . Matt 21:9
'It is more *b* to give . . . . Acts 20:35
B be the God and . . . . Eph 1:3
"*B* are the dead who . . . . Rev 14:13

BLESSING

And you shall be a *b* . . . . Gen 12:2
before you today a *b* . . Deut 11:26
shall be showers of *b* . Ezek 34:26
and you shall be a *b* . . Zech 8:13
that the *b* of Abraham . . . Gal 3:14
with every spiritual *b* . . . . Eph 1:3

BLIND

To open *b* eyes . . . . Is 42:7
His watchmen are *b* . . . . . Is 56:10
b leads the *b* . . . . Matt 15:14
to Him, "Are we *b* . . . . . John 9:40
miserable, poor, *b* . . . . . . Rev 3:17

BLINDED

and the rest were *b* . . . . . Rom 11:7

BLINDS

a bribe, for a bribe *b* . . Deut 16:19

BLOOD

of your brother's *b* . . . . . Gen 4:10
b shall be shed . . . . Gen 9:6
b that makes . . . . Lev 17:11
hands are full of *b* . . . . Is 1:15
And the moon into *b* . . . . Joel 2:31
For this is My *b* . . . . Matt 26:28
"His *b* be on us and . . Matt 27:25
covenant in My *b* . . . . . Luke 22:20
were born, not of *b* . . . . . John 1:13
b has eternal life . . . . . . John 6:54
with His own *b* . . . . Acts 20:28
propitiation by His *b* . . . Rom 3:25
justified by His *b* . . . . Rom 5:9
through His *b* . . . . Eph 1:7
brought near by the *b* . . Eph 2:13
against flesh and *b* . . . . . Eph 6:12
peace through the *b* . . . . . Col 1:20
with the precious *b* . . . . 1 Pet 1:19
b of Jesus Christ His . . . 1 John 1:7
our sins in His own *b* . . . . Rev 1:5
us to God by Your *b* . . . . . Rev 5:9
them white in the *b* . . . . Rev 7:14
overcame him by the *b* . Rev 12:11
a robe dipped in *b* . . . . . Rev 19:13

BLOODSHED

me from the guilt of *b* . . . Ps 51:14

BLOODTHIRSTY

The LORD abhors the *b* . . . . . Ps 5:6

BLOSSOM

and *b* as the rose . . . . Is 35:1

BLOT

from my sins, and *b* . . . . . Ps 51:9
and I will not *b* . . . . Rev 3:5

BLOTTED

your sins may be *b* . . . . Acts 3:19

BLOW

with a very severe *b* . . . . Jer 14:17

BLOWS
"The wind b where it .... John 3:8

BOAST
puts on his armor b ... 1 Kin 20:11
and make your b .... Rom 2:17
lest anyone should b ..... Eph 2:9

BOASTERS
God, violent, proud, b .. Rom 1:30

BOASTING
Where is b then .... Rom 3:27

BODIES
b a living sacrifice ...... Rom 12:1
not know that your b .. 1 Cor 6:15
wives as their own b .... Eph 5:28

BODILY
b form like a dove ..... Luke 3:22
of the Godhead b .... Col 2:9

BODY
of the b is the eye ...... Matt 6:22
those who kill the b ... Matt 10:28
this is My b .... Matt 26:26
of the temple of His b .. John 2:21
deliver me from this b .. Rom 7:24
redemption of our b .... Rom 8:23
members in one b ...... Rom 12:4
But I discipline my b .. 1 Cor 9:27
b which is broken .... 1 Cor 11:24
baptized into one b .... 1 Cor 12:13
are the b of Christ .... 1 Cor 12:27
though I give my b .. 1 Cor 13:3
It is sown a natural b . 1 Cor 15:44
in the b of His flesh ...... Col 1:22
our sins in His own b .. 1 Pet 2:24

BOILS
Job with painful b .... Job 2:7

BOLDLY
therefore come b .... Heb 4:16

BOLDNESS
in whom we have b ..... Eph 3:12
that we may have b ... 1 John 4:17

BOND
love, which is the b ...... Col 3:14

BONDAGE
out of the house of b .... Ex 13:14
again with a yoke of b .... Gal 5:1

BONDS
"Let us break Their b ...... Ps 2:3

BONDSERVANTS
B, be obedient to .... Eph 6:5
Masters, give your b ...... Col 4:1

BONDWOMAN
the one by a b .... Gal 4:22

BONE
b clings to my skin ..... Job 19:20

BONES
I can count all My b ..... Ps 22:17
and my b waste away ... Ps 31:10
I kept silent, my b .... Ps 32:3
the wind, Or how the b . Eccl 11:5
say to them, 'O dry b .. Ezek 37:4
of dead men's b .... Matt 23:27
b shall be broken ..... John 19:36

BOOK
are written in the b ...... Gal 3:10
in the Lamb's B .... Rev 21:27
the prophecy of this b .. Rev 22:18

BOOKS
b there is no end ...... Eccl 12:12
not contain the b ...... John 21:25
and b were opened ..... Rev 20:12

BOOTH
of Zion is left as a b .... Is 1:8

BORDERS
and enlarge the b ...... Matt 23:5

BORE
And to Sarah who b .... Is 51:2
b the sin of many .... Is 53:12
b our sicknesses .... Matt 8:17
Himself b our sins ..... 1 Pet 2:24
b a male Child who was . Rev 12:5

BORN
A time to be b .... Eccl 3:2
unto us a Child is b .... Is 9:6
b Jesus who is called ... Matt 1:16
unless one is b again .... John 3:3
"That which is b .... John 3:6
having been b again .... 1 Pet 1:23
who loves is b of God . . 1 John 4:7

BORROWER
b is servant to the ...... Prov 22:7

BORROWS
The wicked b and does .. Ps 37:21

BOSOM
to Abraham's b .... Luke 16:22
Son, who is in the b .... John 1:18

BOTTOMLESS
ascend out of the b ...... Rev 17:8
the key to the b .... Rev 20:1

BOUGHT
b the threshing floor . 2 Sam 24:24
all that he had and b .. Matt 13:46
For you were b at a ..... 1 Cor 6:20
denying the Lord who b . 2 Pet 2:1

BOUND
on earth will be b ..... Matt 16:19
And see, now I go b ... Acts 20:22
who has a husband is b .. Rom 7:2
Are you b to a wife .... 1 Cor 7:27
Devil and Satan, and b .. Rev 20:2

BOUNTIFULLY
and he who sows b ..... 2 Cor 9:6

BOW
"You shall not b .... Ex 23:24
let us worship and b ...... Ps 95:6
who sat on it had a b ..... Rev 6:2

BOWED
stood all around and b .. Gen 37:7
And they b the knee ... Matt 27:29

BOWL
and poured out his b .... Rev 16:2

BOWLS
Go and pour out the b ... Rev 16:1

BOX
had the money b ...... John 13:29

BOYS
Shall be full of b .... Zech 8:5

BRAIDED
not with b hair or ...... 1 Tim 2:9

BRANCH
raise to David a B .... Jer 23:5

forth My Servant the B .. Zech 3:8
b that bears fruit He .... John 15:2

BRANCHES
vine, you are the b ..... John 15:5

BRASS
become sounding b .... 1 Cor 13:1

BRAVE
in the faith, be b ...... 1 Cor 16:13

BREAD
brought out b .... Gen 14:18
shall eat unleavened b ... Ex 23:15
not live by b alone ..... Deut 8:3
b eaten in secret is ..... Prov 9:17
B gained by deceit is .. Prov 20:17
Cast your b upon the .... Eccl 11:1
for what is not b .... Is 55:2
these stones become b ... Matt 4:3
not live by b alone ..... Matt 4:4
this day our daily b ... Matt 6:11
eating, Jesus took b ... Matt 26:26
"I am the b of life ...... John 6:48
betrayed took b ...... 1 Cor 11:23

BREADTH
is as great as its b ...... Rev 21:16

BREAK
covenant I will not b .... Ps 89:34
together to b bread ..... Acts 20:7

BREAKING
in the b of bread .... Acts 2:42
b bread from house to .. Acts 2:46

BREAKS
Until the day b .... Song 2:17

BREAST
back on Jesus' b ...... John 13:25

BREASTPLATE
righteousness as a b ..... Is 59:17
having put on the b ..... Eph 6:14

BREASTS
Your two b are like .... Song 4:5
b which nursed You .. Luke 11:27

BREATH
nostrils the b of life ...... Gen 2:7
that there was no b .. 1 Kin 17:17
Man is like a b .... Ps 144:4
everything that has b .... Ps 150:6
"Surely I will cause b .. Ezek 37:5
gives to all life, b ...... Acts 17:25
power to give b .... Rev 13:15

BREATHES
indeed he b his last .... Job 14:10

BRETHREN
and you are all b .... Matt 23:8
least of these My b ... Matt 25:40
among many b .... Rom 8:29
thus sin against the b .. 1 Cor 8:12
over five hundred b .... 1 Cor 15:6
perils among false b .. 2 Cor 11:26
sincere love of the b .... 1 Pet 1:22
we love the b .... 1 John 3:14
our lives for the b ... 1 John 3:16

BRIBE
you shall take no b .... Ex 23:8
b blinds the eyes ...... Deut 16:19

BRIBES
hand is full of b .... Ps 26:10

BRICK
people straw to make b .... Ex 5:7

BRICKS
"Come, let us make b ...Gen 11:3

BRIDE
I will show you the b ....Rev 21:9
the Spirit and the b ....Rev 22:17

BRIDEGROOM
And as the b rejoices ......Is 62:5
mourn as long as the b .Matt 9:15
went out to meet the b ..Matt 25:1
the friend of the b ......John 3:29

BRIDLE
b the whole body ......James 3:2

BRIER
b shall come up the ......Is 55:13

BRIERS
there shall come up b ......Is 5:6

BRIGHTER
a light from heaven, b .Acts 26:13

BRIGHTNESS
And kings to the b ....Is 60:3
who being the b ....Heb 1:3

BRIMSTONE
the lake of fire and b ...Rev 20:10

BRING
b back his soul ....Job 33:30
b My righteousness ......Is 46:13
Who shall b a charge ...Rom 8:33
b Christ down from ....Rom 10:6
even so God will b ...1 Thess 4:14

BROAD
b is the way that ......Matt 7:13

BROKE
b them at the foot of ....Ex 32:19
He blessed and b ......Matt 14:19
b the legs of the ......John 19:32

BROKEN
this stone will be b ....Matt 21:44
Scripture cannot be b .John 10:35
body which is b ......1 Cor 11:24

BROKENHEARTED
He heals the b And ......Ps 147:3

BRONZE
So Moses made a b ....Num 21:9
b walls against the ......Jer 1:18
a third kingdom of b ....Dan 2:39

BROOD
"B of vipers ....Matt 12:34
hen gathers her b ......Luke 13:34

BROOK
disciples over the B ....John 18:1

BROOKS
for the water b ....Ps 42:1

BROTHER
"Where is Abel your b ...Gen 4:9
b offended is harder ...Prov 18:19
b will deliver up ......Matt 10:21
how often shall my b ..Matt 18:21
b will rise again ......John 11:23
b goes to law against ...1 Cor 6:6
Whoever hates his b ..1 John 3:15

BROTHERHOOD
Love the b ....1 Pet 2:17

BROTHERLY
b love continue ....Heb 13:1

BROTHER'S
Am I my b keeper ....Gen 4:9
at the speck in your b ...Matt 7:3

BROTHERS
is My mother, or My b .Mark 3:33
b are these who hear ..Luke 8:21

BRUISE
He shall b your head ....Gen 3:15
the LORD to b Him ....Is 53:10

BRUISED
He was b for our ....Is 53:5
b reed He will not .....Matt 12:20

BUCKLER
be your shield and b ......Ps 91:4

BUFFET
of Satan to b me ......2 Cor 12:7

BUILD
b ourselves a city ......Gen 11:4
"Would you b a house .2 Sam 7:5
labor in vain who b ....Ps 127:1
down, And a time to b ...Eccl 3:3
'This man began to b .Luke 14:30
What house will you b ..Acts 7:49
"For if I b again ....Gal 2:18

BUILDER
foundations, whose b ..Heb 11:10

BUILDING
in whom the whole b ....Eph 2:21

BUILDS
take heed how he b ....1 Cor 3:10

BUILT
has b her house ....Prov 9:1
to a wise man who b ...Matt 7:24
having been b on the ....Eph 2:20

BULLS
For if the blood of b .....Heb 9:13

BULWARKS
Mark well her b ....Ps 48:13

BUNDLE
man's b of money ......Gen 42:35

BURDEN
Cast your b on the ......Ps 55:22
easy and My b is light .Matt 11:30
we might not be a b ..1 Thess 2:9
on you no other b ....Rev 2:24

BURDENS
"For they bind heavy b .Matt 23:4
Bear one another's b .....Gal 6:2

BURDENSOME
I myself was not b ....2 Cor 12:13
are not b ....1 John 5:3

BURIAL
she did it for My b ....Matt 26:12
for the day of My b ....John 12:7

BURIED
Therefore we were b ....Rom 6:4
and that He was b .....1 Cor 15:4
b with Him in baptism ...Col 2:12

BURN
the bush does not b ....Ex 3:3
"Did not our heart b ..Luke 24:32

BURNED
If anyone's work is b ..1 Cor 3:15
my body to be b ......1 Cor 13:3

BURNING
b torch that passed ....Gen 15:17
b fire shut up in my ......Jer 20:9
plucked from the b ....Amos 4:11

BURNT
lamb for a b offering ....Gen 22:7
delight in b offering .....Ps 51:16

BURST
the new wine will b ....Luke 5:37

BURY
and let the dead b ......Matt 8:22

BUSH
from the midst of a b ......Ex 3:2

BUSINESS
about My Father's b ....Luke 2:49

BUSYBODIES
at all, but are b ......2 Thess 3:11

BUTLER
b did not remember ....Gen 40:23

BUTTER
were smoother than b ...Ps 55:21

BUY
Yes, come, b wine and ...Is 55:1
"I counsel you to b ......Rev 3:18
and that no one may b .Rev 13:17

BUYS
has and b that field ....Matt 13:44

BYWORD
has made me a b ....Job 17:6

C

CAGE
foul spirit, and a c ......Rev 18:2

CAKE
Ephraim is a c ....Hos 7:8

CAKES
and love the raisin c .....Hos 3:1

CALAMITY
will laugh at your c ....Prov 1:26

CALCULATED
c the dust of the ....Is 40:12

CALDRON
this city is the c ....Ezek 11:3

CALF
and made a molded c ....Ex 32:4
bring the fatted c .....Luke 15:23

CALL
C upon Him while He .....Is 55:6
c His name JESUS ......Matt 1:21
c the righteous ....Matt 9:13
Lord our God will c ....Acts 2:39
c them My people .....Rom 9:25
c and election sure .....2 Pet 1:10

CALLED
c the light Day ....Gen 1:5
c his wife's name Eve ...Gen 3:20
I have c you by your ....Is 43:1
"Out of Egypt I c ......Matt 2:15
city c Nazareth ....Matt 2:23
For many are c ......Matt 20:16
to those who are the c ..Rom 8:28
these He also c ....Rom 8:30
c children of God ......1 John 3:1

CALLING

the gifts and the c .... Rom 11:29
For you see your c .... 1 Cor 1:26
remain in the same c .. 1 Cor 7:20

CALLS

c them all by name ...... Ps 147:4
David himself c ...... Mark 12:37
c his own sheep .... John 10:3

CALM

there was a great c .... Matt 8:26

CAMEL

it is easier for a c .... Matt 19:24

CAMP

to Him, outside the c ... Heb 13:13

CAN

I c do all things .... Phil 4:13

CANCER

will spread like c ...... 2 Tim 2:17

CANOPY

His c around Him was ... Ps 18:11

CAPSTONE

bring forth the c .... Zech 4:7

CAPTAIN

Which, having no c ...... Prov 6:7

CAPTIVE

and be led away c .... Luke 21:24
He led captivity c .... Eph 4:8

CAPTIVES

and make c .... 2 Tim 3:6

CAPTIVITY

every thought into c ... 2 Cor 10:5

CARCASS

"For wherever the c ... Matt 24:28

CARE

"Lord, do You not c ... Luke 10:40
how will he take c ...... 1 Tim 3:5

CARED

he said, not that he c ... John 12:6

CAREFULLY

I shall walk c all my ..... Is 38:15

CARELESS

But he who is c .... Prov 19:16

CARES

No one c for my soul .... Ps 142:4
for He c for you .... 1 Pet 5:7

CARNAL

c mind is enmity .... Rom 8:7

CARNALLY

c minded is death .... Rom 8:6

CAROUSE

count it pleasure to c ... 2 Pet 2:13

CARPENTER

"Is this not the c .... Mark 6:3

CARRIED

And c our sorrows .... Is 53:4

CARRY

for you to c your bed ... John 5:10
it is certain we can c .... 1 Tim 6:7

CARRYING

will meet you c .... Mark 14:13

CASE

Festus laid Paul's c .... Acts 25:14

CASSIA

myrrh and aloes and c .... Ps 45:8

CAST

Why are you c down ..... Ps 42:5
whole body to be c ..... Matt 5:29
My name they will c .. Mark 16:17
by no means c out ..... John 6:37
c their crowns before .... Rev 4:10
the great dragon was c .. Rev 12:9

CASTING

c down arguments ..... 2 Cor 10:5
c all your care .... 1 Pet 5:7

CASTS

perfect love c out ..... 1 John 4:18

CATCH

c Him in His words ... Mark 12:13
now on you will c ...... Luke 5:10

CATCHES

and the wolf c the ..... John 10:12
c the wise in their ..... 1 Cor 3:19

CAUGHT

him was a ram c .... Gen 22:13
her Child was c up ...... Rev 12:5

CAUSE

hated Me without a c .. John 15:25
For this c I was born .. John 18:37

CAVES

in dens and c of the .... Heb 11:38

CEASE

and night Shall not c .... Gen 8:22
He makes wars c .... Ps 46:9
tongues, they will c .... 1 Cor 13:8

CEASING

pray without c ...... 1 Thess 5:17

CEDAR

dwell in a house of c ... 2 Sam 7:2

CEDARS

the LORD breaks the c ..... Ps 29:5

CELESTIAL

but the glory of the c .1 Cor 15:40

CENSER

Aaron, each took his c ... Lev 10:1

CERTAINTY

you may know the c .... Luke 1:4

CERTIFICATE

a man to write a c ..... Mark 10:4

CHAFF

be chased like the c ...... Is 17:13
He will burn up the c ... Matt 3:12

CHAIN

pit and a great c .... Rev 20:1

CHAINED

of God is not c .... 2 Tim 2:9

CHAINS

And his c fell off ...... Acts 12:7
am, except for these c . Acts 26:29

CHAMBERS

brought me into his c .... Song 1:4

CHAMPION

And a c went out ..... 1 Sam 17:4

CHANGE

now and to c my tone ... Gal 4:20
there is also a c .... Heb 7:12

CHANGED

c the glory of the .... Rom 1:23
but we shall all be c .. 1 Cor 15:51

CHANGERS'

and poured out the c ... John 2:15

CHANGES

c the times and the ..... Dan 2:21

CHANNELS

c of the sea were seen ... Ps 18:15

CHARIOT

that suddenly a c ...... 2 Kin 2:11

CHARIOTS

Some trust in c .... Ps 20:7

CHARITABLE

you do not do your c .... Matt 6:1
c deeds which she ...... Acts 9:36

CHARM

C is deceitful and ..... Prov 31:30

CHARMS

who sew magic c ..... Ezek 13:18

CHASE

Five of you shall c ...... Lev 26:8

CHASTE

present you as a c ..... 2 Cor 11:2

CHASTEN

a father does not c ...... Heb 12:7
I love, I rebuke and c .... Rev 3:19

CHASTENED

c us as seemed best .... Heb 12:10

CHASTENING

do not despise the c ..... Job 5:17
Now no c seems to be .. Heb 12:11

CHASTENS

the LORD loves He c ..... Heb 12:6

CHASTISEMENT

The c for our peace .... Is 53:5

CHATTER

c leads only to .... Prov 14:23

CHEAT

Beware lest anyone c ..... Col 2:8

CHEATED

let yourselves be c ...... 1 Cor 6:7

CHEEK

on your right c .... Matt 5:39

CHEEKBONE

my enemies on the c .... Ps 3:7

CHEEKS

His c are like a bed .... Song 5:13

CHEER

"Son, be of good c ...... Matt 9:2

CHEERFUL

for God loves a c .... 2 Cor 9:7

CHEERFULNESS
shows mercy, with c .... Rom 12:8

CHEESE
And curdle me like c ... Job 10:10

CHERISHES
but nourishes and c ..... Eph 5:29

CHERUBIM
above it were the c .... Heb 9:5

CHIEF
of whom I am c .... 1 Tim 1:15
Zion a c cornerstone .... 1 Pet 2:6

CHILD
Train up a c in the ..... Prov 22:6
For unto us a C .... Is 9:6
virgin shall be with c ... Matt 1:23
of God as a little c .... Mark 10:15
So the c grew and ..... Luke 1:80
When I was a c ...... 1 Cor 13:11
She bore a male C ...... Rev 12:5

CHILDBEARING
she will be saved in c .. 1 Tim 2:15

CHILDBIRTH
pain as a woman in c ..... Is 13:8

CHILDHOOD
c you have known ..... 2 Tim 3:15

CHILDLESS
give me, seeing I go c ... Gen 15:2
this man down as c ..... Jer 22:30

CHILDREN
c are a heritage .... Ps 127:3
c rise up and call her .. Prov 31:28
and become as little c .. Matt 18:3
"Let the little c .... Matt 19:14
the right to become c ... John 1:12
now we are c of God .. 1 John 3:2

CHOOSE
therefore c life .... Deut 30:19
"You did not c .... John 15:16

CHOSE
just as He c us in Him .... Eph 1:4

CHOSEN
servant whom I have c ... Is 43:10
whom I have c .... John 13:18
c the foolish things .... 1 Cor 1:27
Has God not c the ..... James 2:5

CHRIST
Jesus who is called C ... Matt 1:16
"You are the C .... Matt 16:16
a Savior, who is C ..... Luke 2:11
It is C who died .... Rom 8:34
to be justified by C ...... Gal 2:17
been crucified with C .... Gal 2:20
C is head of the .... Eph 5:23
to me, to live is C ...... Phil 1:21
which is C in you .... Col 1:27
C who is our .... Col 3:4
Jesus C is the same ..... Heb 13:8
C His Son cleanses us .. 1 John 1:7
that Jesus is the C ..... 1 John 5:1

CHRISTIAN
anyone suffers as a C .. 1 Pet 4:16

CHRISTIANS
were first called C ..... Acts 11:26

CHRISTS
"For false c and ...... Matt 24:24

CHURCH
rock I will build My c . Matt 16:18

c daily those who were . Acts 2:47
Himself a glorious c .... Eph 5:27
as the Lord does the c ... Eph 5:29
body, which is the c ..... Col 1:24
assembly and c .... Heb 12:23

CHURCHES
these things in the c .... Rev 22:16

CIRCLE
who sits above the c .... Is 40:22

CIRCUMCISE
is necessary to c them .. Acts 15:5

CIRCUMCISED
among you shall be c .. Gen 17:10
who will justify the c ... Rom 3:30
if you become c .... Gal 5:2

CIRCUMCISION
c is that of the heart .... Rom 2:29
C is nothing and ...... 1 Cor 7:19
Christ Jesus neither c ..... Gal 5:6

CIRCUMSPECTLY
then that you walk c .... Eph 5:15

CISTERN
from your own c .... Prov 5:15

CITIES
He overthrew those c .. Gen 19:25
three parts, and the c ... Rev 16:19

CITIZEN
But I was born a c ..... Acts 22:28

CITIZENS
but fellow c with the .... Eph 2:19

CITIZENSHIP
For our c is in heaven ... Phil 3:20

CITY
shall make glad the c ... Ps 46:4
c has become a harlot ..... Is 1:21
How lonely sits the c .... Lam 1:1
c that is set on a ...... Matt 5:14
He has prepared a c ... Heb 11:16
have no continuing c ... Heb 13:14
John, saw the holy c .... Rev 21:2

CLAP
of the field shall c .... Is 55:12

CLAY
pit, out of the miry c ...... Ps 40:2
We are the c .... Is 64:8
blind man with the c .... John 9:6
have power over the c .. Rom 9:21

CLEAN
He who has c hands and .. Ps 24:4
make yourselves c .... Is 1:16
c out His threshing ..... Matt 3:12
You can make me c ..... Matt 8:2
"You are not all c ..... John 13:11
"You are already c ..... John 15:3

CLEANSE
C me from secret ...... Ps 19:12
And c me from my sin .... Ps 51:2
How can a young man c . Ps 119:9
might sanctify and c ..... Eph 5:26
us our sins and to c .... 1 John 1:9

CLEANSED
"Were there not ten c . Luke 17:17

CLEANSES
Christ His Son c .... 1 John 1:7

CLEAR
of life, c as crystal ...... Rev 22:1

CLIFF
secret places of the c ... Song 2:14

CLIMBS
c up some other way ... John 10:1

CLING
C to what is good ...... Rom 12:9

CLINGS
And My tongue c .... Ps 22:15

CLOAK
let him have your c ..... Matt 5:40
using liberty as a c ..... 1 Pet 2:16

CLODS
The c of the valley ..... Job 21:33

CLOSE
c friends abhor me ..... Job 19:19

CLOSED
The deep c around me .... Jon 2:5

CLOTH
a piece of unshrunk c ... Matt 9:16

CLOTHE
He not much more c .... Matt 6:30

CLOTHED
of skin, and c them ..... Gen 3:21
A man c in soft .... Matt 11:8
naked and you c ...... Matt 25:36
legion, sitting and c .... Mark 5:15
desiring to be c .... 2 Cor 5:2
that you may be c ...... Rev 3:18

CLOTHES
c became shining .... Mark 9:3
many spread their c ... Luke 19:36
a poor man in filthy c .. James 2:2

CLOTHING
c they cast lots .... Ps 22:18
do you worry about c ... Matt 6:28
to you in sheep's c .... Matt 7:15
c they cast lots .... John 19:24

CLOTHS
in swaddling c .... Luke 2:12

CLOUD
My rainbow in the c .... Gen 9:13
day in a pillar of c ..... Ex 13:21
He led them with the c ... Ps 78:14
behold, a bright c ..... Matt 17:5
of Man coming in a c . Luke 21:27
c received Him out of ... Acts 1:9
by so great a c .... Heb 12:1

CLOUDS
Man coming on the c .. Matt 24:30
with them in the c .... 1 Thess 4:17
are c without water .... Jude 12
He is coming with c ...... Rev 1:7

CLOUDY
them by day with a c .... Neh 9:12

CLOVEN
chew the cud or have c . Deut 14:7

CLUSTER
beloved is to me a c .... Song 1:14

COAL
in his hand a live c .... Is 6:6

COALS
doing you will heap c .. Rom 12:20

COBRA
the lion and the c . . . . Ps 91:13

COBRA'S
shall play by the c . . . . Is 11:8

COFFIN
and he was put in a c . . Gen 50:26
touched the open c . . . . . Luke 7:14

COIN
if she loses one c . . . . . . Luke 15:8

COLD
and harvest, C and . . . . . . Gen 8:22
of many will grow c . . . Matt 24:12
that you are neither c . . . Rev 3:15

COLLECTION
concerning the c . . . . . . 1 Cor 16:1

COLT
on a donkey, A c . . . . Zech 9:9
on a donkey, A c . . . . Matt 21:5

COME
He will c and save you . . . . Is 35:4
who have no money, C . . . . Is 55:1
Your kingdom c . . . . Matt 6:10
"C to Me . . . . Matt 11:28
I have c in My . . . . John 5:43
thirsts, let him c . . . . . . John 7:37
c as a light into the . . . . John 12:46
O Lord, c . . . . 1 Cor 16:22
the door, I will c . . . . Rev 3:20

COMELINESS
He has no form or c . . . . . . Is 53:2

COMES
Lord's death till He c . 1 Cor 11:26

COMFORT
and Your staff, they c . . . . Ps 23:4
yes, c My people . . . . Is 40:1
c each other . . . . 1 Thess 5:11

COMFORTED
So Isaac was c after . . . Gen 24:67
Refusing to be c . . . . Jer 31:15

COMFORTER
She had no c . . . . Lam 1:9

COMFORTS
I, even I, am He who c . . . Is 51:12

COMING
see the Son of Man c . Mark 13:26
mightier than I is c . . . . Luke 3:16
are Christ's at His c . . 1 Cor 15:23
Behold, I am c . . . . Rev 3:11
"Surely I am c . . . . Rev 22:20

COMMAND
c I have received . . . . . . John 10:18
and I know that His c . John 12:50
if you do whatever I c . John 15:14

COMMANDED
not endure what was c . Heb 12:20

COMMANDMENT
c of the LORD is pure . . . . . Ps 19:8
which is the great c . . . Matt 22:36
"A new c I give to . . . . John 13:34
which is the first c . . . . . . Eph 6:2
And this is His c . . . . . 1 John 3:23

COMMANDMENTS
covenant, the Ten C . . . . . Ex 34:28
as doctrines the c . . . . . . Matt 15:9
c hang all the Law . . . . Matt 22:40
"He who has My c . . . . John 14:21

COMMANDS
with authority He c . . . . Mark 1:27

COMMEND
But food does not c . . . . . 1 Cor 8:8

COMMENDABLE
patiently, this is c . . . . . . 1 Pet 2:20

COMMENDED
c the unjust steward . . . . Luke 16:8

COMMENDS
but whom the Lord c . 2 Cor 10:18

COMMIT
"You shall not c . . . . Ex 20:14
into Your hands I c . . . Luke 23:46

COMMITS
sin also c lawlessness . . 1 John 3:4

COMMITTED
c Himself to Him who . . . 1 Pet 2:23

COMMON
c people heard Him . . . Mark 12:37
had all things in c . . . . . . Acts 2:44
concerning our c . . . . Jude 3

COMMOTION
there arose a great c . . . Acts 19:23

COMMUNED
I c with my heart . . . . Eccl 1:16

COMMUNION
c of the Holy Spirit . . . 2 Cor 13:14

COMPANION
a man my equal, My c . . . Ps 55:13

COMPANIONS
while you became c . . . . Heb 10:33

COMPANY
Great was the c . . . . Ps 68:11
to an innumerable c . . . . Heb 12:22

COMPARE
c ourselves with . . . . . . 2 Cor 10:12

COMPARED
are not worthy to be c . . Rom 8:18

COMPASSION
are a God full of c . . . . . . Ps 86:15
He was moved with c . . . Matt 9:36
whomever I will have c . Rom 9:15
He can have c on those . . . Heb 5:2

COMPASSIONATE
the Lord is very c . . . . . James 5:11

COMPASSIONS
because His c fail not . . . Lam 3:22

COMPEL
c them to come in . . . . Luke 14:23

COMPELS
the love of Christ c . . . . 2 Cor 5:14

COMPLAINED
some of them also c . . 1 Cor 10:10

COMPLAINERS
These are grumblers, c . . . Jude 16

COMPLAINING
all things without c . . . . . . Phil 2:14

COMPLAINT
For the LORD has a c . . . . . Mic 6:2

COMPLETE
work in you will c . . . . . . Phil 1:6
and you are c in Him . . . . Col 2:10
of God may be c . . . . . . 2 Tim 3:17

COMPLETELY
sanctify you c . . . . 1 Thess 5:23

COMPOSED
But God c the body . . . 1 Cor 12:24

COMPREHEND
which we cannot c . . . . . . Job 37:5
the darkness did not c . . . John 1:5

CONCEAL
of God to c a matter . . . . Prov 25:2

CONCEALED
Than love carefully c . . . Prov 27:5

CONCEIT
selfish ambition or c . . . . . Phil 2:3

CONCEITED
Let us not become c . . . . . Gal 5:26

CONCEIVE
the virgin shall c . . . . Is 7:14
And behold, you will c . Luke 1:31

CONCEIVED
in sin my mother c . . . . Ps 51:5

CONCERN
Neither do I c myself . . . . Ps 131:1

CONCERNED
Is it oxen God is c . . . . . . 1 Cor 9:9

CONCESSION
But I say this as a c . . . . . 1 Cor 7:6

CONCLUSION
Let us hear the c . . . . . . Eccl 12:13

CONDEMN
world to c the world . . . . John 3:17

CONDEMNATION
can you escape the c . . Matt 23:33
"And this is the c . . . . . . John 3:19
Their c is just . . . . Rom 3:8
therefore now no c . . . . . . Rom 8:1

CONDEMNED
does not believe is c . . . . John 3:18
c sin in the flesh . . . . Rom 8:3

CONDEMNS
Who is he who c . . . . Rom 8:34

CONDUCT
from your aimless c . . . . . 1 Pet 1:8
may be won by the c . . . . 1 Pet 3:1

CONFESS
c my transgressions . . . . . Ps 32:5
that if you c with . . . . . . Rom 10:9
every tongue shall c . . . Rom 14:11
If we c our sins . . . . 1 John 1:9

CONFESSED
c that He was Christ . . . John 9:22

CONFESSES
c that Jesus is the . . . . 1 John 4:15

CONFESSION
with the mouth c . . . . . . Rom 10:10
High Priest of our c . . . . . . Heb 3:1
let us hold fast our c . . . . Heb 4:14

CONFIDENCE
c shall be your ....Is 30:15
Jesus, and have no c ....Phil 3:3

CONFINED
the Scripture has c ......Gal 3:22

CONFIRM
who will also c ....1 Cor 1:8

CONFIRMED
covenant that was c ......Gal 3:17
c it by an oath ....Heb 6:17

CONFIRMING
c the word through ... Mark 16:20

CONFLICT
to know what a great c ...Col 2:1

CONFLICTS
Outside were c ....2 Cor 7:5

CONFORMED
predestined to be c .....Rom 8:29
And do not be c ....Rom 12:2

CONFUSE
c their language ....Gen 11:7

CONFUSED
the assembly was c ....Acts 19:32

CONGREGATION
Nor sinners in the c........Ps 1:5
God stands in the c ......Ps 82:1

CONQUER
conquering and to c ......Rev 6:2

CONQUERORS
we are more than c ....Rom 8:37

CONSCIENCE
convicted by their c ....John 8:9
strive to have a c ......Acts 24:16

CONSECRATED
c this house which you ..1 Kin 9:3

CONSENT
and does not c to ....1 Tim 6:3

CONSENTED
He had not c to their ..Luke 23:51

CONSENTING
Now Saul was c to his ...Acts 8:1

CONSIDER
When I c Your heavens ....Ps 8:3
My people do not c.........Is 1:3
C the lilies of the ......Matt 6:28
"C the ravens ....Luke 12:24
c Him who endured .....Heb 12:3

CONSIST
in Him all things c ....Col 1:17

CONSOLATION
if there is any c ....Phil 2:1
us everlasting c .....2 Thess 2:16

CONSOLE
c those who mourn........Is 61:3

CONSTANT
c prayer was ....Acts 12:5

CONSUME
whom the Lord will c .2 Thess 2:8

CONSUMED
but the bush was not c ....Ex 3:2

mercies we are not c....Lam 3:22
beware lest you be c .....Gal 5:15

CONSUMING
our God is a c fire .....Heb 12:29

CONTAIN
of heavens cannot c ....2 Chr 2:6
c the books that ....John 21:25

CONTEMPT
and be treated with c ..Mark 9:12

CONTEMPTIBLE
and his speech c .....2 Cor 10:10

CONTEND
c earnestly for the ....Jude 3

CONTENT
state I am, to be c ....Phil 4:11
covetousness; be c ......Heb 13:5

CONTENTIONS
sorcery, hatred, c........Gal 5:20

CONTENTIOUS
anyone seems to be c .1 Cor 11:16

CONTENTMENT
c is great gain ....1 Tim 6:6

CONTINUAL
a merry heart has a c ..Prov 15:15
c coming she weary ....Luke 18:5

CONTINUALLY
heart was only evil c .....Gen 6:5
will give ourselves c .....Acts 6:4
remains a priest c ....Heb 7:3

CONTINUE
Shall we c in sin that ....Rom 6:1
C earnestly in prayer .....Col 4:2
Let brotherly love c .....Heb 13:1

CONTINUED
c steadfastly in the .....Acts 2:42

CONTRADICTIONS
idle babble and c ......1 Tim 6:20

CONTRARY
to worship God c ......Acts 18:13

CONTRIBUTION
to make a certain c ....Rom 15:26

CONTRITE
A broken and a c ....Ps 51:17
poor and of a c spirit ......Is 66:2

CONTROVERSY
For the Lord has a c ....Jer 25:31

CONVERSION
describing the c ....Acts 15:3

CONVERTED
unless you are c ....Matt 18:3

CONVICT
He has come, He will c .John 16:8

CONVICTS
"Which of you c ....John 8:46

CONVINCED
Let each be fully c .....Rom 14:5

COOKED
c their own children ....Lam 4:10

COOL
and c my tongue ......Luke 16:24

COPIES
necessary that the c .....Heb 9:23

COPPER
sold for two c coins ....Luke 12:6

COPPERSMITH
c did me much harm ..2 Tim 4:14

COPY
who serve the c ....Heb 8:5

CORD
this line of scarlet c ....Josh 2:18

CORDS
had made a whip of c ..John 2:15

CORNER
was not done in a c ....Acts 26:26

CORNERSTONE
become the chief c ....Matt 21:42
in Zion A chief c ....1 Pet 2:6

CORRECT
C your son ....Prov 29:17

CORRECTED
human fathers who c ....Heb 12:9

CORRECTION
Do not withhold c .....Prov 23:13
for reproof, for c ......2 Tim 3:16

CORRECTS
the Lord loves He c ....Prov 3:12

CORRODED
and silver are c ....James 5:3

CORRUPT
in these things they c ....Jude 10

CORRUPTED
for all flesh had c ....Gen 6:12
Your riches are c ......James 5:2

CORRUPTIBLE
redeemed with c ....1 Pet 1:18

CORRUPTION
Your Holy One to see c ..Ps 16:10
c inherit incorruption .1 Cor 15:50
having escaped the c ....2 Pet 1:4

COST
and count the c ....Luke 14:28

COULD
c remove mountains ...1 Cor 13:2
which no one c number ...Rev 7:9

COUNCILS
deliver you up to c ....Mark 13:9

COUNSEL
Who walks not in the c ....Ps 1:1
We took sweet c ....Ps 55:14
guide me with Your c ....Ps 73:24
according to the c ....Eph 1:11
immutability of His c ....Heb 6:17
"I c you to buy from ....Rev 3:18

COUNSELOR
be called Wonderful, C .....Is 9:6

COUNSELORS
c there is safety ....Prov 11:14

COUNT
c my life dear to ....Acts 20:24
His promise, as some c ..2 Pet 3:9

COUNTED

Even a fool is c ....Prov 17:28
who rule well be c ....1 Tim 5:17

COUNTENANCE

The LORD lift up His c ..Num 6:26
with a sad c ....Matt 6:16
His c was like ....Matt 28:3
of the glory of his c .....2 Cor 3:7

COUNTRY

"Get out of your c ......Gen 12:1
that is, a heavenly c ....Heb 11:16

COUNTRYMEN

for my brethren, my c ...Rom 9:3

COURAGE

strong and of good c ...Deut 31:6

COURT

They zealously c ....Gal 4:17

COURTEOUS

be tenderhearted, be c ...1 Pet 3:8

COURTS

and into His c ....Ps 100:4

COVENANT

I will establish My c ....Gen 6:18
the LORD made a c .....Gen 15:18
will show them His c ....Ps 25:14
sons will keep My c ....Ps 132:12
I will make a new c .....Jer 31:31
the Messenger of the c ...Mal 3:1
cup is the new c ....Luke 22:20
He says, "A new c ......Heb 8:13
Mediator of the new c ..Heb 12:24
of the everlasting c ....Heb 13:20

COVENANTS

the glory, the c ....Rom 9:4

COVER

He shall c you with ....Ps 91:4
c a multitude of sins ..James 5:20

COVERED

Whose sin is c ....Ps 32:1
c all their sin ....Ps 85:2
For there is nothing c ..Matt 10:26

COVERING

spread a cloud for a c ..Ps 105:39

COVERINGS

and made themselves c ...Gen 3:7

COVET

"You shall not c ....Ex 20:17

COVETED

c no one's silver ....Acts 20:33

COVETOUS

nor thieves, nor c ......1 Cor 6:10

COVETOUSNESS

heed and beware of c .Luke 12:15

COWARDLY

the c, unbelieving ....Rev 21:8

CRAFTILY

His people, to deal c ....Ps 105:25

CRAFTINESS

deceived Eve by his c ..2 Cor 11:3
in the cunning c ....Eph 4:14

CRAFTSMAN

instructor of every c ....Gen 4:22

CRAFTY

the devices of the c ......Job 5:12
Nevertheless, being c .2 Cor 12:16

CREAM

were bathed with c ......Job 29:6

CREATE

peace and c calamity ......Is 45:7

CREATED

So God c man in His ....Gen 1:27
Has not one God c ......Mal 2:10
c in Christ Jesus ....Eph 2:10
new man which was c ...Eph 4:24

CREATION

know that the whole c ...Rom 8:22
Christ, he is a new c ...2 Cor 5:17
anything, but a new c ....Gal 6:15

CREATOR

Remember now your C .Eccl 12:1
God, the LORD, The C ....Is 40:28
rather than the C ....Rom 1:25

CREATURE

the gospel to every c ..Mark 16:15

CREATURES

firstfruits of His c .....James 1:18

CREDIT

For what c is it if ......1 Pet 2:20

CREDITOR

There was a certain c ..Luke 7:41

CREEP

sort are those who c ....2 Tim 3:6

CREEPING

c thing and beast of .....Gen 1:24

CREPT

For certain men have c ....Jude 4

CRIB

donkey its master's c ....Is 1:3

CRIED

the poor who c out .....Job 29:12
of the depths I have c ....Ps 130:1

CRIES

your brother's blood c ...Gen 4:10

CRIMES

land is filled with c .....Ezek 7:23

CRIMINALS

also two others, c .....Luke 23:32

CROOKED

c places shall be made ....Is 40:4
in the midst of a c ....Phil 2:15

CROSS

does not take his c ....Matt 10:38
to bear His c ....Matt 27:32
down from the c ......Matt 27:40
lest the c of Christ .....1 Cor 1:17
boast except in the c ....Gal 6:14
the enemies of the c .....Phil 3:18
Him endured the c ......Heb 12:2
shall not follow a c ....Ex 23:2

CROWN

c the year with Your ....Ps 65:11
they had twisted a c ...Matt 27:29
obtain a perishable c ..1 Cor 9:25
laid up for me the c ....2 Tim 4:8
on His head a golden c .Rev 14:14

CROWNED

angels, And You have c ...Ps 8:5
athletics, he is not c ....2 Tim 2:5

CROWNS

His head were many c ..Rev 19:12

CRUCIFIED

"Let Him be c ....Matt 27:22
Calvary, there they c ..Luke 23:33
lawless hands, have c ...Acts 2:23
that our old man was c ..Rom 6:6
Jesus Christ and Him c .1 Cor 2:2
"I have been c ....Gal 2:20

CRUCIFY

out again, "C Him ....Mark 15:13

CRUEL

hate me with c hatred ...Ps 25:19

CRUELTY

the haunts of c ....Ps 74:20

CRUSH

of peace will c ....Rom 16:20

CRUSHED

every side, yet not c ....2 Cor 4:8

CRUST

man is reduced to a c ...Prov 6:26

CRY

and their c came up to ....Ex 2:23
Does not wisdom c ......Prov 8:1
at midnight a c ....Matt 25:6
His own elect who c ....Luke 18:7

CRYING

nor sorrow, nor c ....Rev 21:4

CRYSTAL

a sea of glass, like c ......Rev 4:6

CUBIT

can add one c ....Matt 6:27

CUNNING

the serpent was more c ...Gen 3:1
c craftiness of deceitful ..Eph 4:14

CUP

My c runs over ....Ps 23:5
Then He took the c ....Matt 26:27
possible, let this c .....Matt 26:39
c is the new covenant .Luke 22:20
cannot drink the c ....1 Cor 10:21
c is the new ....1 Cor 11:25

CURE

and to c diseases ....Luke 9:1

CURES

and perform c ....Luke 13:32

CURSE

c the ground for man's ..Gen 8:21
C God and die ....Job 2:9
"I will send a c ....Mal 2:2
law are under the c ......Gal 3:10

CURSED

c more than all cattle ....Gen 3:14
from Me, you c ....Matt 25:41

CURSES

I will curse him who c ...Gen 12:3

CURTAIN

the heavens like a c .....Ps 104:2

CUSTOM

according to the c ......Acts 15:1

CUT

CUT

evildoers shall be c . . . . Ps 37:9
the wicked will be c . . . . Prov 2:22

CYMBAL

or a clanging c . . . . 1 Cor 13:1

D

DAILY

Give us this day our d . . Matt 6:11
take up his cross d . . . . . Luke 9:23
the Scriptures d . . . . Acts 17:11

DANCE

mourn, And a time to d . . Eccl 3:4
And you did not d . . . . . Matt 11:17

DANCED

Then David d before . . 2 Sam 6:14

DANCING

saw the calf and the d . . Ex 32:19
he heard music and d . Luke 15:25

DARE

someone would even d . . . Rom 5:7

DARK

I tell you in the d . . . . . . Matt 10:27
shines in a d place . . . . . 2 Pet 1:19

DARKENED

their understanding d . . . Eph 4:18

DARKNESS

d He called Night . . . . Gen 1:5
Those who sat in d . . . . . Ps 107:10
d Have seen a . . . . Is 9:2
And deep d the people . . . . Is 60:2
body will be full of d . . . Matt 6:23
cast out into outer d . . . . Matt 8:12
d rather than light . . . . . John 3:19
For you were once d . . . . . Eph 5:8
called you out of d . . . . . 1 Pet 2:9
d is reserved . . . . 2 Pet 2:17
and in Him is no d . . 1 John 1:5
d is passing away . . . . . 1 John 2:8

DARTS

quench all the fiery d . . . Eph 6:16

DASH

You shall d them to . . . . Ps 2:9
Lest you d your foot . . . . . Matt 4:6

DASHED

infants shall be d . . . . . . Hos 13:16

DAUGHTER

"Rejoice greatly, O d . . . . Zech 9:9
"Fear not, d of Zion . . . John 12:15
the son of Pharaoh's d . Heb 11:24

DAUGHTERS

of God saw the d . . . . Gen 6:2
d shall prophesy . . . . Acts 2:17

DAY

God called the light D . . . Gen 1:5
And d and night . . . . Gen 8:22
the Sabbath d . . . . Ex 20:8
For a d in Your courts . . . Ps 84:10
d the LORD has . . . . Ps 118:24
not strike you by d . . . . . . Ps 121:6
For the d of the LORD . . . . Joel 2:11
who can endure the d . . . Mal 3:2
d our daily bread . . . . . . Matt 6:11
sent Me while it is d . . . . John 9:4
person esteems one d . . . Rom 14:5
D will declare it . . . . 1 Cor 3:13
again the third d . . . . . . 1 Cor 15:4
with the Lord one d . . . . 2 Pet 3:8

DAYS

d are swifter than a . . . . . . Job 7:6
of woman Is of few d . . . . Job 14:1
The d of our lives are . . . . Ps 90:10
Before the difficult d . . . . Eccl 12:1
shortened those d . . . . Mark 13:20
raise it up in three d . . . . John 2:20

DAYSPRING

With which the D . . . . . . Luke 1:78

DEACONS

with the bishops and d . . . Phil 1:1
d must be reverent . . . . . 1 Tim 3:8
d be the husbands . . . . . 1 Tim 3:12

DEAD

But the d know nothing . . Eccl 9:5
d bury their own d . . . . . Matt 8:22
not the God of the d . . . Matt 22:32
this my son was d . . . . . . Luke 15:24
d will hear the voice . . . . John 5:25
was raised from the d . . . . Rom 6:4
yourselves to be d . . . . . . Rom 6:11
be Lord of both the d . . . Rom 14:9
resurrection of the d . . 1 Cor 15:12
And the d in Christ . 1 Thess 4:16
without works is d . . . . James 2:26
And the d were judged . Rev 20:12

DEADLY

drink anything d . . . . . Mark 16:18
evil, full of d poison . . . . James 3:8

DEADNESS

the d of Sarah's womb . . Rom 4:19

DEAF

d shall be unstopped . . . . . . Is 35:5
are cleansed and the d . . Matt 11:5

DEAL

My Servant shall d . . . . Is 52:13

DEATH

d parts you and me . . . . Ruth 1:17
and the shadow of d . . . . Job 10:21
I sleep the sleep of d . . . . . Ps 13:3
of the shadow of d . . . . Ps 23:4
house leads down to d . . Prov 2:18
who hate me love d . . . . Prov 8:36
swallow up d forever . . . . . . Is 25:8
no pleasure in the d . . . Ezek 18:32
who shall not taste d . . Matt 16:28
but has passed from d . . John 5:24
Nevertheless d reigned . Rom 5:14
D no longer has . . . . Rom 6:9
the wages of sin is d . . . . Rom 6:23
the Lord's d . . . . 1 Cor 11:26
since by man came d . 1 Cor 15:21
D is swallowed up in . 1 Cor 15:54
The sting of d is sin . . 1 Cor 15:56
is sin leading to d . . . . . 1 John 5:16
Be faithful until d . . . . . . Rev 2:10
shall be no more d . . . . . . Rev 21:4
which is the second d . . . Rev 21:8

DEBTOR

I am a d both to . . . . Rom 1:14
that he is a d to keep . . . . . Gal 5:3

DEBTORS

as we forgive our d . . . . . Matt 6:12
of his master's d . . . . Luke 16:5
brethren, we are d . . . . . . Rom 8:12

DECEIT

Nor was any d in His . . . . . Is 53:9
philosophy and empty d . . Col 2:8
no sin, nor was d . . . . . . 1 Pet 2:22
mouth was found no d . . Rev 14:5

DECEITFUL

deliver me from the d . . . . Ps 43:1

"The heart is d . . . . Jer 17:9
are false apostles, d . . 2 Cor 11:13

DECEITFULLY

an idol, Nor sworn d . . . . . Ps 24:4
the word of God d . . . . . 2 Cor 4:2

DECEITFULNESS

this world and the d . . . Matt 13:22

DECEIVE

rise up and d many . . . . Matt 24:11
Let no one d you with . . . . Eph 5:6
we have no sin, we d . . 1 John 1:8

DECEIVED

"The serpent d . . . . Gen 3:13
the commandment, d . . . Rom 7:11
deceiving and being d . 2 Tim 3:13

DECEIVER

how that d said . . . . . . Matt 27:63
This is a d and an . . . . 2 John 7

DECEIVES

heed that no one d . . . . . Matt 24:4

DECENTLY

all things be done d . . . 1 Cor 14:40

DECEPTIVE

you with d words . . . . 2 Pet 2:3

DECISION

in the valley of d . . . . Joel 3:14

DECLARE

The heavens d the . . . . Ps 19:1
d Your name to My . . . . . Ps 22:22
seen and heard we d . . . 1 John 1:3

DECLARED

and d to be the Son of . . . Rom 1:4

DECREE

"I will declare the d . . . . Ps 2:7
in those days that a d . . . Luke 2:1

DEDICATION

it was the Feast of D . . John 10:22

DEED

you do in word or d . . . . . Col 3:17

DEEDS

because their d . . . . John 3:19
"You do the d . . . . John 8:41
one according to his d . . . Rom 2:6
you put to death the d . . Rom 8:13

DEEP

LORD God caused a d . . . . Gen 2:21
d uttered its voice . . . . Hab 3:10
"Launch out into the d . . Luke 5:4
I have been in the d . . 2 Cor 11:25

DEEPER

D than Sheol . . . . Job 11:8

DEEPLY

But He sighed d . . . . Mark 8:12

DEER

As the d pants for the . . . . . Ps 42:1
shall leap like a d . . . . Is 35:6

DEFEATED

and Israel was d . . . . . . 1 Sam 4:10

DEFEND

D the fatherless . . . . Is 1:17

DEFENSE

For wisdom is a d . . . . . . Eccl 7:12

DEFILE

am appointed for the *d* . . Phil 1:17
be ready to give a *d* . . . . 1 Pet 3:15

DEFILE

also these dreamers *d* . . . . . Jude 8

DEFILED

lest they should be *d* . . John 18:28
and conscience are *d* . . . Titus 1:15

DEFILES

mouth, this *d* a man . . . Matt 15:11
it anything that *d* . . . . . . Rev 21:27

DEFRAUD

d his brother in this . . . 1 Thess 4:6

DEGREES

go forward ten *d* . . . . . 2 Kin 20:9

DELICACIES

of the king's *d* . . . . Dan 1:5

DELICATE

a lovely and *d* woman . . . . . Jer 6:2

DELIGHT

But his *d* is in the . . . . Ps 1:2
I *d* to do Your will . . . . Ps 40:8
And I was daily His *d* . . Prov 8:30
And let your soul *d* . . . . . . Is 55:2
call the Sabbath a *d* . . . . . Is 58:13
For I *d* in the law of . . . . Rom 7:22

DELIGHTS

For the LORD *d* in you . . . . . Is 62:4

DELIVER

Let Him *d* Him . . . . Ps 22:8
I will *d* him and honor . . . Ps 91:15
into temptation, But *d* . . Matt 6:13
let Him *d* Him now if . . Matt 27:43
And the Lord will *d* . . . 2 Tim 4:18
d the godly out of . . . . 2 Pet 2:9

DELIVERANCE

not accepting *d* . . . . Heb 11:35

DELIVERED

who was *d* up because . . Rom 4:25
was once for all *d* . . . . Jude 3

DELIVERER

D will come out of . . . . Rom 11:26

DELIVERS

even Jesus who *d* . . . . 1 Thess 1:10

DELUSION

send them strong *d* . . 2 Thess 2:11

DEMON

Jesus rebuked the *d* . . . Matt 17:18
and have a *d* . . . . John 8:48

DEMONIC

is earthly, sensual, *d* . . James 3:15

DEMONS

authority over all *d* . . . . . . Luke 9:1
the *d* are subject . . . . . . Luke 10:17
Even the *d* believe . . . . James 2:19

DEMONSTRATE

faith, to *d* His . . . . Rom 3:25

DEMONSTRATES

d His own love toward . . . Rom 5:8

DEN

cast him into the *d* . . . . . Dan 6:16
it a '*d* of thieves . . . . Matt 21:13

DENARIUS

the laborers for a *d* . . . . . Matt 20:2

DENIED

before men will be *d* . . . Luke 12:9
Peter then *d* again . . . . John 18:27
d the Holy One and the . Acts 3:14
things cannot be *d* . . . . Acts 19:36
household, he has *d* . . . . 1 Tim 5:8

DENIES

But whoever *d* . . . . Matt 10:33
d that Jesus is the . . . . 1 John 2:22

DENY

let him *d* himself . . . . . . Matt 16:24
He cannot *d* Himself . . . 2 Tim 2:13

DENYING

but *d* its power . . . . 2 Tim 3:5
d the Lord who bought . . 2 Pet 2:1

DEPART

scepter shall not *d* . . . . . Gen 49:10
on the left hand, '*D* . . . . Matt 25:41
will *d* from the faith . . . . 1 Tim 4:1

DEPARTING

heart of unbelief in *d* . . . . Heb 3:12

DEPARTURE

d savage wolves will . . . Acts 20:29
and the time of my *d* . . . 2 Tim 4:6

DEPRESSION

of man causes *d* . . . . . . Prov 12:25

DEPTH

nor height nor *d* . . . . Rom 8:39
Oh, the *d* of the . . . . Rom 11:33

DEPTHS

our sins Into the *d* . . . . . . Mic 7:19

DERISION

shall hold them in *d* . . . . . . Ps 2:4

DESCEND

d now from the cross . Mark 15:32
Lord Himself will *d* . . 1 Thess 4:16

DESCENDANTS

"We are Abraham's *d* . . John 8:33

DESCENDED

He who *d* is also the . . . . Eph 4:10

DESCENDING

God ascending and *d* . . . John 1:51
the holy Jerusalem, *d* . . . Rev 21:10

DESERT

d shall rejoice . . . . Is 35:1
'Look, He is in the *d* . . . Matt 24:26

DESERTED

d place by Himself . . . . Matt 14:13

DESERTS

They wandered in *d* . . . . Heb 11:38

DESIGN

with an artistic *d* . . . . Ex 26:31

DESIRABLE

the eyes, and a tree *d* . . . . Gen 3:6

DESIRE

d shall be for your . . . . . . Gen 3:16
Behold, You *d* truth in . . . . Ps 51:6
"Father, I *d* that . . . . . . John 17:24
all manner of evil *d* . . . . . Rom 7:8
Brethren, my heart's *d* . . Rom 10:1

DESIRE

d the best gifts . . . . 1 Cor 12:31
the two, having a *d* . . . . . . Phil 1:23

DESIRED

d are they than gold . . . . . Ps 19:10
One thing I have *d* . . . . Ps 27:4

DESIRES

shall give you the *d* . . . . . . Ps 37:4
the devil, and the *d* . . . . John 8:44
not come from your *d* . . James 4:1

DESOLATE

any more be termed *D* . . . . Is 62:4
house is left to you *d* . . Matt 23:38

DESOLATION

the '*abomination of d* . . Matt 24:15

DESPAIRED

strength, so that we *d* . . . 2 Cor 1:8

DESPISE

one and *d* the other . . . . . Matt 6:24
d the riches of His . . . . Rom 2:4

DESPISED

He is *d* and rejected . . . . Is 53:3
the things which are *d* . 1 Cor 1:28

DESPISES

d his neighbor sins . . . . Prov 14:21

DESPISING

the cross, *d* the shame . . . Heb 12:2

DESTITUTE

of corrupt minds and *d* . 1 Tim 6:5

DESTROY

Why should you *d* . . . . . . Eccl 7:16
shall not hurt nor *d* . . . . Is 11:9
I did not come to *d* . . . . . Matt 5:17
Him who is able to *d* . . Matt 10:28
Barabbas and *d* Jesus . Matt 27:20
to save life or to *d* . . . . . . Luke 6:9
d men's lives but to . . . . Luke 9:56
d the wisdom of the . . . 1 Cor 1:19
able to save and to *d* . . James 4:12

DESTROYED

d all living things . . . . Gen 7:23
house, this tent, is *d* . . . . 2 Cor 5:1

DESTRUCTION

You turn man to *d* . . . . Ps 90:3
d that lays waste . . . . Ps 91:6
your life from *d* . . . . Ps 103:4
Pride goes before *d* . . . Prov 16:18
whose end is *d* . . . . Phil 3:19
with everlasting *d* . . . 2 Thess 1:9

DESTRUCTIVE

bring in *d* heresies . . . . . . 2 Pet 2:1

DETERMINED

d their preappointed . . . Acts 17:26
For I *d* not to know . . . . . 1 Cor 2:2

DEVICE

there is no work or *d* . . . Eccl 9:10

DEVICES

not ignorant of his *d* . . . 2 Cor 2:11

DEVIL

to be tempted by the *d* . . . Matt 4:1
prepared for the *d* . . . . Matt 25:41
of your father the *d* . . . . John 8:44
give place to the *d* . . . . . . Eph 4:27
the snare of the *d* . . . . . . 2 Tim 2:26
the works of the *d* . . . . . 1 John 3:8

DEVIOUS

And who are *d* . . . . Prov 2:15

DEVISES
d wickedness on his ......Ps 36:4
But a generous man *d* .....Is 32:8

DEVOID
who is *d* of wisdom ....Prov 11:12

DEVOTED
Your servant, who is *d* ..Ps 119:38

DEVOUR
For you *d* widows' ....Matt 23:14
bite and *d* one another ...Gal 5:15
whom he may *d* ....1 Pet 5:8
d her Child as ....Rev 12:4

DEVOURED
wild beast has *d* ......Gen 37:20
birds came and *d* them . Matt 13:4
of heaven and *d* them ...Rev 20:9

DEVOUT
man was just and *d* ....Luke 2:25
d soldier from among ...Acts 10:7

DEW
God give you Of the *d* ..Gen 27:28

DIADEMS
ten horns, and seven *d* ..Rev 12:3

DIAMOND
d it is engraved ....Jer 17:1

DICTATES
according to the *d* ......Jer 23:17

DIE
it you shall surely *d* .....Gen 2:17
but a person shall *d* ...2 Chr 25:4
I shall not *d* ....Ps 118:17
born, And a time to *d* ....Eccl 3:2
eat of it and not *d* ......John 6:50
to you that you will *d* ...John 8:24
though he may *d* ......John 11:25
one man should *d* ....John 11:50
the flesh you will *d* .....Rom 8:13
For as in Adam all *d* ..1 Cor 15:22
and to *d* is gain ....Phil 1:21
for men to *d* once ......Heb 9:27
are the dead who *d* .....Rev 14:13

DIED
And all flesh *d* ....Gen 7:21
in due time Christ *d* .....Rom 5:6
Christ *d* for us ....Rom 5:8
Now if we *d* with ....Rom 6:8
and He *d* for all ....2 Cor 5:15
for if we *d* with Him ...2 Tim 2:11

DIES
alive unless it *d* ......1 Cor 15:36

DIFFERS
for one star *d* from ...1 Cor 15:41

DILIGENCE
d it produced in you ...2 Cor 7:11

DILIGENT
d makes rich ....Prov 10:4

DILIGENTLY
d lest anyone fall ......Heb 12:15

DIM
His eyes were not *d* ....Deut 34:7

DIMLY
we see in a mirror, *d* .1 Cor 13:12

DINE
come in to him and *d* ....Rev 3:20

DINNER
invites you to *d* ......1 Cor 10:27

DIP
d your piece of bread ...Ruth 2:14

DIPPED
clothed with a robe *d* ...Rev 19:13

DIRECT
Now may the Lord *d* ..2 Thess 3:5

DIRT
cast up mire and *d* ....Is 57:20

DISARMED
d principalities ....Col 2:15

DISASTER
will end with *d* ....Acts 27:10

DISCERN
d the face of the sky ....Matt 16:3
senses exercised to *d* ....Heb 5:14

DISCERNED
they are spiritually *d* ..1 Cor 2:14

DISCERNER
d of the thoughts ....Heb 4:12

DISCERNS
a wise man's heart *d* .....Eccl 8:5

DISCIPLE
he cannot be My *d* ....Luke 14:26
d whom Jesus loved ....John 21:7

DISCIPLES
word, you are My *d* ....John 8:31
but we are Moses' *d* ....John 9:28

DISCIPLINES
he who loves him *d* ....Prov 13:24

DISCORD
And one who sows *d* ...Prov 6:19

DISCOURAGED
lest they become *d* ....Col 3:21
become weary and *d* ....Heb 12:3

DISCRETION
D will preserve you ....Prov 2:11

DISFIGURE
d their faces that ....Matt 6:16

DISGUISES
And he *d* his face ......Job 24:15

DISHONOR
Father, and you *d* Me ...John 8:49
d their bodies among ...Rom 1:24
It is sown in *d* ....1 Cor 15:43

DISHONORED
But you have *d* the .....James 2:6

DISHONORS
For son *d* father ....Mic 7:6

DISOBEDIENT
out My hands To a *d* ...Rom 10:21

DISORDERLY
for this *d* gathering ....Acts 19:40

DISPENSATION
d of the fullness of ......Eph 1:10

DISPERSION
the pilgrims of the *D* ...1 Pet 1:1

DISPLEASE
LORD see it, and it *d* ...Prov 24:18

DISPLEASED
they were greatly *d* ....Matt 20:24
it, He was greatly *d* ...Mark 10:14

DISPUTE
there was also a *d* ....Luke 22:24

DISPUTER
Where is the *d* of this ..1 Cor 1:20

DISPUTES
But avoid foolish *d* ......Titus 3:9

DISQUALIFIED
should become *d* ......1 Cor 9:27

DISQUIETED
And why are you *d* ....Ps 42:5

DISSENSION
had no small *d* and .....Acts 15:2

DISSIPATION
not accused of *d* ....Titus 1:6

DISSOLVED
the heavens will be *d* ...2 Pet 3:12

DISTINCTION
compassion, making a *d* ..Jude 22

DISTRESS
d them in His deep ....Ps 2:5
tribulation, or *d* ....Rom 8:35

DISTRESSED
and deeply *d* ....Mark 14:33

DISTRESSES
Bring me out of my *d* ....Ps 25:17

DISTRIBUTED
and they *d* to each as ...Acts 4:35

DISTRIBUTING
d to the needs of the ...Rom 12:13

DITCH
will fall into a *d* ....Matt 15:14

DIVERSITIES
There are *d* ....1 Cor 12:4

DIVIDE
d the spoil with the ....Prov 16:19
"Take this and *d* .....Luke 22:17

DIVIDED
and the waters were *d* ...Ex 14:21
they were not *d* ....2 Sam 1:23
"Every kingdom *d* .....Matt 12:25
Is Christ *d* ....1 Cor 1:13

DIVIDES
at home *d* the spoil ......Ps 68:12

DIVIDING
rightly *d* the word of ..2 Tim 2:15

DIVINATION
shall you practice *d* ....Lev 19:26
a spirit of *d* met us ....Acts 16:16

DIVINE
d service and the ....Heb 9:1

DIVISION
So there was a *d* ....John 7:43

DIVISIONS
those who cause *d* .....Rom 16:17
persons, who cause *d* ....Jude 19

DIVISIVE

Reject a *d* man after ... Titus 3:10

DIVORCE

her a certificate of *d* .... Deut 24:1
a certificate of *d* ...... Mark 10:4

DO

men to *d* to you, *d* ..... Matt 7:12
He sees the Father *d* .... John 5:19
without Me you can *d* .. John 15:5
"Sirs, what must I *d* ... Acts 16:30
d evil that good may ..... Rom 3:8
or whatever you *d, d* .. 1 Cor 10:31

DOCTRINE

What new *d* is this .... Mark 1:27
"My *d* is not Mine ...... John 7:16
with every wind of *d* .... Eph 4:14
is contrary to sound *d* . 1 Tim 1:10
is profitable for *d* ..... 2 Tim 3:16
not endure sound *d* ..... 2 Tim 4:3

DOCTRINES

commandments and *d* .... Col 2:22
various and strange *d* ... Heb 13:9

DOERS

But be *d* of the word .. James 1:22

DOG

d is better than a .... Eccl 9:4
d returns to his own .... 2 Pet 2:22

DOGS

what is holy to the *d* ..... Matt 7:6
d eat the crumbs ...... Matt 15:27
But outside are *d* ...... Rev 22:15

DOMINION

let them have *d* .... Gen 1:26
d is an everlasting ...... Dan 4:34
sin shall not have *d* .... Rom 6:14
glory and majesty, *D* ..... Jude 25

DONKEY

d its master's crib .... Is 1:3
and riding on a *d* .... Zech 9:9
colt, the foal of a *d* .... Matt 21:5
d speaking with a ...... 2 Pet 2:16

DOOM

for the day of *d* .... Prov 16:4

DOOR

stone against the *d* .... Matt 27:60
to you, I am the *d* ...... John 10:7
before you an open *d* .... Rev 3:8
I stand at the *d* .... Rev 3:20

DOORKEEPER

I would rather be a *d* .... Ps 84:10

DOORPOSTS

write them on the *d* ..... Deut 6:9

DOORS

up, you everlasting *d* ..... Ps 24:7

DOUBLE

from the LORD's hand *D* .. Is 40:2
worthy of *d* honor ..... 1 Tim 5:17

DOUBLE-MINDED

he is a *d* man .... James 1:8

DOUBT

faith, why did you *d* .. Matt 14:31

DOUBTING

in faith, with no *d* ..... James 1:6

DOUBTS

why do *d* arise in ..... Luke 24:38
for I have *d* about you ... Gal 4:20

DOVE

d found no resting .... Gen 8:9
descending like a *d* ..... Matt 3:16

DOVES

and harmless as *d* ..... Matt 10:16

DOWNCAST

who comforts the *d* ..... 2 Cor 7:6

DRAGNET

d that was cast .... Matt 13:47

DRAGON

they worshiped the *d* .... Rev 13:4
He laid hold of the *d* .... Rev 20:2

DRAINED

All faces are *d* .... Joel 2:6

DRANK

them, and they all *d* .. Mark 14:23

DRAW

d honey from the .... Deut 32:13
me to *d* near to God ..... Ps 73:28
And the years *d* .... Eccl 12:1
will *d* all peoples ...... John 12:32
D near to God and He .. James 4:8

DRAWS

your redemption *d* .... Luke 21:28

DREAM

Now Joseph had a *d* .... Gen 37:5
Your old men shall *d* .... Joel 2:28
to Joseph in a *d* .... Matt 2:13
things today in a *d* .... Matt 27:19

DREAMERS

d defile the flesh .... Jude 8

DREAMS

Nebuchadnezzar had *d* ... Dan 2:1

DRIED

of her blood was *d* .... Mark 5:29
saw the fig tree *d* ..... Mark 11:20

DRIFT

have heard, lest we *d* ..... Heb 2:1

DRINK

gave me vinegar to *d* .... Ps 69:21
Lest they *d* and forget .. Prov 31:5
follow intoxicating *d* ...... Is 5:11
d the milk of the .... Is 60:16
bosom, That you may *d* .. Is 66:11
"Bring wine, let us *d* .... Amos 4:1
that day when I *d* ..... Matt 26:29
mingled with gall to *d* . Matt 27:34
with myrrh to *d* ...... Mark 15:23
to her, "Give Me a *d* ..... John 4:7
him come to Me and *d* .. John 7:37
do, as often as you *d* .. 1 Cor 11:25
No longer *d* only ...... 1 Tim 5:23

DRINKS

to her, "Whoever *d* ..... John 4:13
d My blood has .... John 6:54
he who eats and *d* .... 1 Cor 11:29

DRIPPING

His lips are lilies, *D* .... Song 5:13

DROSS

purge away your *d* .... Is 1:25

DROUGHT

in the year of *d* .... Jer 17:8
"For I called for a *d* ..... Hag 1:11

DROVE

So He *d* out the man .... Gen 3:24
temple of God and *d* ... Matt 21:12

DROWN

Nor can the floods *d* .... Song 8:7
harmful lusts which *d* ... 1 Tim 6:9

DROWSINESS

d will clothe a .... Prov 23:21

DRUNK

of the wine and was *d* ... Gen 9:21
the guests have well *d* .. John 2:10
"For these are not *d* .... Acts 2:15
and another is *d* ...... 1 Cor 11:21
I saw the woman, *d* ..... Rev 17:6

DRUNKARD

to and fro like a *d* .... Is 24:20
or a reviler, or a *d* ..... 1 Cor 5:11

DRUNKEN

I am like a *d* man .... Jer 23:9

DRUNKENNESS

will be filled with *d* ... Ezek 23:33
not in revelry and *d* ... Rom 13:13
envy, murders, *d* .... Gal 5:21

DRY

place, and let the *d* ..... Gen 1:9
made the sea into *d* ..... Ex 14:21
It was *d* on the fleece ... Judg 6:40
will be done in the *d* .. Luke 23:31

DUE

pay all that was *d* ..... Matt 18:34
d time Christ died .... Rom 5:6
d season we shall .... Gal 6:9
exalt you in *d* time ...... 1 Pet 5:6

DULL

heart of this people *d* ...... Is 6:10
people have grown *d* .. Matt 13:15

DUMB

the tongue of the *d* .... Is 35:6

DUST

formed man of the *d* ..... Gen 2:7
d you shall return .... Gen 3:19
And repent in *d* .... Job 42:6
that we are *d* .... Ps 103:14
counted as the small *d* ... Is 40:15
city, shake off the *d* ... Matt 10:14
of the man of *d* .... 1 Cor 15:49

DUTY

done what was our *d* .. Luke 17:10

DWELL

Who may *d* in Your holy .. Ps 15:1
"I *d* in the high and ...... Is 57:15
"I will *d* in them .... 2 Cor 6:16
that Christ may *d* .... Eph 3:17
men, and He will *d* ..... Rev 21:3

DWELLING

built together for a *d* .... Eph 2:22
a foreign country, *d* ..... Heb 11:9

DWELLS

He who *d* in the secret .... Ps 91:1
but the Father who *d* .. John 14:10
d all the fullness .... Col 2:9
which righteousness *d* .. 2 Pet 3:13
you, where Satan *d* ..... Rev 2:13

DWELT

became flesh and *d* .... John 1:14
By faith he *d* in the ..... Heb 11:9

DYING

in the body the *d* ...... 2 Cor 4:10

E

EAGLE

fly away like an *e* ...... Prov 23:5

EAGLES

The way of an *e* . . . . Prov 30:19
like a flying *e* . . . . Rev 4:7

EAGLES

up with wings like *e* . . . . . . Is 40:31
e will be gathered . . . . . Matt 24:28

EAGLES'

how I bore you on *e* . . . . . . Ex 19:4

EAR

shall pierce his *e* . . . . Ex 21:6
And the *e* of the wise . . Prov 18:15
e is uncircumcised . . . . Jer 6:10
you hear in the *e* . . . . . . Matt 10:27
cut off his right *e* . . . . . . John 18:10
not seen, nor e heard . . . 1 Cor 2:9
"He who has an *e* . . . . Rev 2:7

EARLY

Very *e* in the morning . Mark 16:2
arrived at the tomb *e* . . Luke 24:22

EARNESTLY

He prayed more *e* . . . . Luke 22:44
e that it would not . . . . James 5:17
you to contend *e* . . . . Jude 3

EARS

And hear with their *e* . . . . . Is 6:10
"He who has *e* . . . . . . Matt 11:15
they have itching *e* . . . . . 2 Tim 4:3

EARTH

to judge the *e* . . . . 1 Chr 16:33
foundations of the *e* . . . . . Job 38:4
e is the LORD's . . . . Ps 24:1
You had formed the *e* . . . . Ps 90:2
there was ever an *e* . . . . Prov 8:23
e abides forever . . . . Eccl 1:4
for the meek of the *e* . . . . . . Is 11:4
e is My footstool . . . . Is 66:1
I will darken the *e* . . . . . . Amos 8:9
shall inherit the *e* . . . . Matt 5:5
heaven and *e* pass . . . . . Matt 5:18
e as it is in heaven . . . . Matt 6:10
treasures on *e* . . . . Matt 6:19
then shook the *e* . . . . . . Heb 12:26
heaven and a new *e* . . . . . Rev 21:1

EARTHLY

"If I have told you *e* . . . . John 3:12
that if our *e* house . . . . . . 2 Cor 5:1
their mind on *e* things . . . Phil 3:19
from above, but is *e* . . . James 3:15

EARTHQUAKE

after the wind an *e* . . . 1 Kin 19:11
there was a great *e* . . . . . Matt 28:2

EARTHQUAKES

And there will be *e* . . . . Mark 13:8

EASIER

"Which is *e*, to say . . . . . Mark 2:9
"It is *e* for a camel . . . . Mark 10:25

EAST

goes toward the *e* . . . . . . Gen 2:14
wise men from the *E* . . . . Matt 2:1
many will come from *e* . Matt 8:11
will come from the *e* . . Luke 13:29

EAT

you may freely *e* . . . . Gen 2:16
'You shall not *e* . . . . Gen 3:17
e this scroll . . . . Ezek 3:1
life, what you will *e* . . . . Matt 6:25
give us His flesh to *e* . . . John 6:52
one believes he may *e* . . Rom 14:2
e meat nor drink wine . Rom 14:21
I will never again *e* . . . . 1 Cor 8:13
neither shall he *e* . . . . 2 Thess 3:10

EATEN

Have you *e* from the . . . . Gen 3:11
he was *e* by worms . . . . Acts 12:23

EATS

receives sinners and *e* . . Luke 15:2
"Whoever *e* My flesh . . . John 6:54
e this bread will live . . . . John 6:58
He who *e*, *e* to the . . . . . Rom 14:6
unworthy manner *e* . . . 1 Cor 11:29

EDIFICATION

has given me for *e* . . . . 2 Cor 13:10
rather than godly *e* . . . . . 1 Tim 1:4

EDIFIES

puffs up, but love *e* . . . . . 1 Cor 8:1

EDIFY

but not all things *e* . . . 1 Cor 10:23

EDIFYING

of the body for the *e* . . . . Eph 4:16

ELDER

against an *e* except . . . . 1 Tim 5:19

ELDERS

the tradition of the *e* . . . . Matt 15:2
be rejected by the *e* . . . . Luke 9:22
they had appointed *e* . . Acts 14:23
e who rule well be . . . . 1 Tim 5:17
lacking, and appoint *e* . . Titus 1:5
e obtained a good . . . . Heb 11:2
e who are among you I . . 1 Pet 5:1
I saw twenty-four *e* . . . . . . Rev 4:4

ELDERSHIP

of the hands of the *e* . . 1 Tim 4:14

ELECT

gather together His *e* . . Matt 24:31
e have obtained it . . . . . . Rom 11:7
e according to the . . . . 1 Pet 1:2
A chief cornerstone, *e* . . 1 Pet 2:6

ELECTION

call and *e* sure . . . . 2 Pet 1:10

ELEMENTS

weak and beggarly *e* . . . . . Gal 4:9
e will melt with . . . . 2 Pet 3:10

ELEVEN

numbered with the *e* . . . . Acts 1:26

ELOQUENT

an *e* man and mighty . . Acts 18:24

EMBALM

to *e* his father . . . . Gen 50:2

ENCOURAGED

is, that I may be *e* . . . . . . Rom 1:12
and all may be *e* . . . . . 1 Cor 14:31

END

make me to know my *e* . . Ps 39:4
shall keep it to the *e* . . . Ps 119:33
e is the way of death . . Prov 14:12
Declaring the *e* . . . . Is 46:10
what shall be the *e* . . . . . Dan 12:8
the harvest is the *e* . . . . Matt 13:39
always, even to the *e* . . Matt 28:20
He loved them to the *e* . John 13:1
For Christ is the *e* . . . . . Rom 10:4
But the *e* of all . . . . 1 Pet 4:7
the latter *e* is worse . . . 2 Pet 2:20
My works until the *e* . . . . Rev 2:26
Beginning and the *E* . . . Rev 22:13

ENDLESS

and *e* genealogies . . . . . . 1 Tim 1:4
to the power of an *e* . . . . Heb 7:16

ENDURANCE

e the race that . . . . Heb 12:1

ENDURE

as the sun and moon *e* . . . . Ps 72:5
His name shall *e* . . . . Ps 72:17
persecuted, we *e* . . . . . . 1 Cor 4:12

ENDURED

he had patiently *e* . . . . Heb 6:15
e as seeing Him who . . . Heb 11:27
consider Him who *e* . . . . . Heb 12:3

ENDURES

And His truth *e* . . . . Ps 100:5
For His mercy *e* . . . . Ps 136:1
But he who *e* to the . . . Matt 10:22
e only for a while . . . . . Matt 13:21
for the food which *e* . . . . John 6:27
he has built on it *e* . . . . 1 Cor 3:14
hopes all things, *e* . . . . 1 Cor 13:7
word of the LORD e . . . . . 1 Pet 1:25

ENDURING

the LORD is clean, *e* . . . . . . Ps 19:9

ENEMIES

the presence of my *e* . . . . . Ps 23:5
e will lick the dust . . . . Ps 72:9
to you, love your *e* . . . . Matt 5:44
e will be those . . . . Matt 10:36
e we were reconciled . . . Rom 5:10
till He has put all *e* . . . 1 Cor 15:25
were alienated and *e* . . . . Col 1:21
His *e* are made His . . . . Heb 10:13

ENEMY

If your *e* is hungry . . . . Prov 25:21
rejoice over me, my *e* . . . . . Mic 7:8
and hate your *e* . . . . Matt 5:43
last *e* that will be . . . . . 1 Cor 15:26
become your *e* because . . Gal 4:16
count him as an *e* . . . 2 Thess 3:15
makes himself an *e* . . . . James 4:4

ENJOY

richly all things to *e* . . . 1 Tim 6:17
than to *e* the passing . . . Heb 11:25

ENJOYMENT

So I commended *e* . . . . . . Eccl 8:15

ENLIGHTEN

E my eyes . . . . Ps 13:3

ENLIGHTENED

those who were once *e* . . . Heb 6:4

ENMITY

And I will put *e* . . . . Gen 3:15
the carnal mind is *e* . . . . . Rom 8:7
in His flesh the *e* . . . . Eph 2:15

ENRAPTURED

And always be *e* . . . . Prov 5:19

ENRICHED

while you are *e* . . . . 2 Cor 9:11

ENSNARED

The wicked is *e* . . . . Prov 12:13

ENSNARES

sin which so easily *e* . . . . Heb 12:1

ENTER

E into His gates . . . . Ps 100:4
you will by no means *e* . Matt 5:20
"*E* by the narrow . . . . . . Matt 7:13
e the kingdom of God . Matt 19:24
E into the joy of your . . Matt 25:21
and pray, lest you *e* . . . Matt 26:41
"Strive to *e* through . . . Luke 13:24
who have believed do *e* . . Heb 4:3
e the temple till the . . . . . Rev 15:8

ENTERED

Then Satan *e* Judas ....Luke 22:3
through one man sin *e* ..Rom 5:12
ear heard, Nor have e ..1 Cor 2:9
the forerunner has *e* ....Heb 6:20
e the Most Holy Place ...Heb 9:12

ENTERS

If anyone *e* by Me ......John 10:9

ENTHRONED

You are holy, *E* in ....Ps 22:3

ENTIRELY

give yourself *e* ....1 Tim 4:15

ENTREAT

being defamed, we *e* ...1 Cor 4:13

ENTREATED

e our God for this ......Ezra 8:23

ENVIOUS

patriarchs, becoming *e* ...Acts 7:9

ENVY

e slays a simple ....Job 5:2
e is rottenness ....Prov 14:30
not let your heart *e* ....Prov 23:17
full of *e* ....Rom 1:29
not in strife and *e* .....Rom 13:13
love does not *e* ....1 Cor 13:4
e, murders ....Gal 5:21
living in malice and *e* ...Titus 3:3

EPISTLE

You are our *e* written ...2 Cor 3:2

EPISTLES

as also in all his *e* ......2 Pet 3:16

ERR

My people Israel to *e* ....Jer 23:13

ERROR

a sinner from the *e* ...James 5:20
led away with the *e* ....2 Pet 3:17
run greedily in the *e* .....Jude 11

ERRORS

can understand his *e* ....Ps 19:12

ESCAPE

e all these things .....Luke 21:36
same, that you will *e* ....Rom 2:3
make the way of *e* ....1 Cor 10:13
how shall we *e* if we .....Heb 2:3

ESCAPED

after they have *e* ......2 Pet 2:20

ESTABLISH

seeking to *e* their own ..Rom 10:3
faithful, who will *e* ....2 Thess 3:3
E your hearts ....James 5:8
a while, perfect, *e* ......1 Pet 5:10

ESTABLISHED

Your throne is *e* ....Ps 93:2
built up in Him and *e* .....Col 2:7
covenant, which was *e* ....Heb 8:6

ESTEEM

and we did not *e* ....Is 53:3
e others better than ......Phil 2:3

ESTEEMED

For what is highly *e* ...Luke 16:15

ESTEEMS

One person *e* one day ..Rom 14:5

ETERNAL

e God is your refuge ..Deut 33:27

For man goes to his *e* ...Eccl 12:5
and inherit *e* life ......Matt 19:29
in the age to come, *e* .Mark 10:30
not perish but have *e* ...John 3:15
you think you have *e* ...John 5:39
I give them *e* life ......John 10:28
"And this is *e* life ......John 17:3
the gift of God is *e* .....Rom 6:23
are not seen are *e* .....2 Cor 4:18
lay hold on *e* life ......1 Tim 6:12
e life which was ....1 John 1:2

ETERNITY

Also He has put *e* ......Eccl 3:11
One who inhabits *e* ......Is 57:15

EUNUCH

of Ethiopia, a *e* ....Acts 8:27

EUNUCHS

made themselves *e* ....Matt 19:12

EVANGELIST

of Philip the *e* ....Acts 21:8
do the work of an *e* ....2 Tim 4:5

EVANGELISTS

some prophets, some *e* ..Eph 4:11

EVERLASTING

from *E* is Your name .....Is 63:16
awake, Some to *e* life ...Dan 12:2
not perish but have *e* ...John 3:16
who sent Me has *e* .....John 5:24
endures to *e* life ....John 6:27
in Him may have *e* .....John 6:40
believes in Me has *e* ....John 6:47
e destruction from ....2 Thess 1:9

EVIDENCE

e of things not seen .....Heb 11:1

EVIDENT

e that our Lord arose ....Heb 7:14

EVIL

of good and *e* ....Gen 2:9
knowing good and *e* .....Gen 3:5
his heart was only *e* ......Gen 6:5
I will fear no *e* ....Ps 23:4
e more than good ....Ps 52:3
To do *e* is like sport ...Prov 10:23
e will bow before the ..Prov 14:19
Keeping watch on the *e* .Prov 15:3
e All the days of her ...Prov 31:12
to those who call *e* ....Is 5:20
of peace and not of *e* ...Jer 29:11
Seek good and not *e* ...Amos 5:14
deliver us from the *e* ...Matt 6:13
"If you then, being *e* ....Matt 7:11
e treasure brings ......Matt 12:35
everyone practicing *e* ...John 3:20
done any good or *e* .....Rom 9:11
Repay no one *e* for .....Rom 12:17
provoked, thinks no *e* ..1 Cor 13:5

EVILDOER

"If He were not an *e* ...John 18:30
suffer trouble as an *e* ...2 Tim 2:9

EVILDOERS

e shall be cut off ....Ps 37:9
from me, you *e* ....Ps 119:115
iniquity, A brood of *e* ......Is 1:4
against you as *e* ....1 Pet 2:12

EXALT

e His name together ......Ps 34:3
E the humble ....Ezek 21:26
And he shall *e* himself ..Dan 8:25

EXALTATION

who rejoice in My *e* ......Is 13:3
brother glory in his *e* ...James 1:9

EXALTED

Let God be *e* ....2 Sam 22:47
I will be *e* among the ....Ps 46:10
You are *e* far above ......Ps 97:9
His name alone is *e* ....Ps 148:13
valley shall be *e* ....Is 40:4
"Him God has *e* ....Acts 5:31
And lest I should be *e* .2 Cor 12:7
also has highly *e* ....Phil 2:9

EXALTS

Righteousness *e* ....Prov 14:34
high thing that *e* ......2 Cor 10:5
e himself above all ....2 Thess 2:4

EXAMINE

But let a man *e* ....1 Cor 11:28
But let each one *e* ....Gal 6:4

EXAMPLE

to make her a public *e* ..Matt 1:19
I have given you an *e* .John 13:15
youth, but be an *e* .....1 Tim 4:12
us, leaving us an *e* .....1 Pet 2:21
are set forth as an *e* ....Jude 7

EXAMPLES

to them as *e* ....1 Cor 10:11
to you, but being *e* ......1 Pet 5:3

EXCHANGE

give in *e* for his soul ...Matt 16:26

EXCHANGED

Nor can it be *e* ....Job 28:17
e the truth of God for ...Rom 1:25

EXCUSE

now they have no *e* ...John 15:22
they are without *e* ......Rom 1:20

EXCUSES

began to make *e* ......Luke 14:18

EXECUTE

e judgment also ....John 5:27
e wrath on him who ....Rom 13:4

EXECUTES

e justice for me ....Mic 7:9

EXERCISE

e yourself toward ....1 Tim 4:7

EXHORT

e him as a father ....1 Tim 5:1
Speak these things, *e* ...Titus 2:15
e one another ....Heb 3:13

EXHORTATION

he who exhorts, in *e* ....Rom 12:8
to reading, to *e* ....1 Tim 4:13

EXHORTED

know how we *e* .....1 Thess 2:11

EXIST

by Your will they *e* .....Rev 4:11

EXPECT

an hour you do not *e* ..Luke 12:40

EXPECTATION

the people were in *e* ....Luke 3:15
a certain fearful *e* ......Heb 10:27

EXPLAIN

no one who could *e* ....Gen 41:24
"*E* this parable to us ...Matt 15:15
to say, and hard to *e* ....Heb 5:11

EXPLAINED

He *e* all things to His ..Mark 4:34

EXPOSED

his deeds should be *e* . . . John 3:20

EXPOUNDED

He *e* to them in all . . . . Luke 24:27

EXPRESS

of His glory and the *e* . . . . Heb 1:3

EXTORTION

they are full of *e* . . . . . . Matt 23:25

EXTORTIONERS

e will inherit . . . . 1 Cor 6:10

EYE

the ear, But now my *e* . . . Job 42:5
guide you with My *e* . . . . . . Ps 32:8
e is not satisfied . . . . Eccl 1:8
the apple of His *e* . . . . . . Zech 2:8
if your right *e* . . . . Matt 5:29
it was said, 'An *e* . . . . Matt 5:38
plank in your own *e* . . . . Matt 7:3
e causes you to sin . . . Matt 18:9
Or is your *e* evil . . . . . . Matt 20:15
the *e* of a needle . . . . Luke 18:25
the twinkling of an *e* . 1 Cor 15:52
every *e* will see Him . . . . . . Rev 1:7
your eyes with *e* salve . . . Rev 3:18

EYES

e will be opened . . . . Gen 3:5
And my *e* shall behold . . Job 19:27
e are ever toward the . . . . Ps 25:15
The *e* of the LORD are . . Ps 34:15
I will lift up my *e* . . . . . . Ps 121:1
but the *e* of a fool . . . . . Prov 17:24
be wise in his own *e* . . . Prov 26:5
You have dove's *e* . . . . Song 1:15
e have seen the King . . . . . . Is 6:5
Who have *e* and see . . . . Jer 5:21
rims were full of *e* . . . . Ezek 1:18
You are of purer *e* . . . . . . Hab 1:13
blessed are your *e* . . . . . Matt 13:16
"He put clay on my *e* . . . John 9:15
e they have closed . . . . . Acts 28:27
E that they should not . . Rom 11:8
have seen with our *e* . . 1 John 1:1
the lust of the *e* . . . . . . 1 John 2:16
as snow, and His *e* . . . . . . Rev 1:14
creatures full of *e* . . . . . . Rev 4:6
horns and seven *e* . . . . . . Rev 5:6

EYESERVICE

not with *e* . . . . Eph 6:6

EYEWITNESSES

the beginning were *e* . . . . Luke 1:2
e of His majesty . . . . 2 Pet 1:16

F

FABLES

nor give heed to *f* . . . . . . 1 Tim 1:4
cunningly devised *f* . . . . 2 Pet 1:16

FACE

"For I have seen God *f* . Gen 32:30
f shone while he . . . . Ex 34:29
sins have hidden His *f* . . . . . Is 59:2
f shone like the sun . . . . . Matt 17:2
dimly, but then *f* . . . . 1 Cor 13:12
with unveiled *f* . . . . 2 Cor 3:18
withstood him to his *f* . . . . Gal 2:11
They shall see His *f* . . . . . Rev 22:4

FADE

We all *f* as a leaf . . . . Is 64:6
rich man also will *f* . . . James 1:11
and that does not *f* . . . . . . 1 Pet 1:4

FADES

withers, the flower *f* . . . . . . Is 40:7

FAIL

tittle of the law to *f* . . . Luke 16:17
faith should not *f* . . . . . Luke 22:32
they will *f* . . . . 1 Cor 13:8
Your years will not f . . . . Heb 1:12

FAILING

"men's hearts *f* . . . . Luke 21:26

FAILS

Love never *f* . . . . 1 Cor 13:8

FAINT

shall walk and not *f* . . . . . . Is 40:31

FAINTS

My soul *f* for Your . . . . Ps 119:81
And the whole heart *f* . . . . . Is 1:5
the earth, Neither *f* . . . . . . Is 40:28

FAITH

shall live by his *f* . . . . Hab 2:4
you, O you of little *f* . . . . Matt 6:30
not found such great *f* . . Matt 8:10
that you have no *f* . . . . . Mark 4:40
"Increase our *f* . . . . Luke 17:5
will He really find *f* . . . . Luke 18:8
are sanctified by *f* . . . . . Acts 26:18
God is revealed from *f* . . Rom 1:17
f apart from the deeds . . Rom 3:28
his *f* is accounted for . . . . Rom 4:5
those who are of the *f* . . Rom 4:16
f which we preach . . . . . Rom 10:8
f comes by hearing . . . . Rom 10:17
and you stand by *f* . . . . Rom 11:20
in proportion to our *f* . . . Rom 12:6
Do you have *f* . . . . Rom 14:22
though I have all *f* . . . . . 1 Cor 13:2
And now abide *f* . . . . . 1 Cor 13:13
For we walk by *f* . . . . . . 2 Cor 5:7
the flesh I live by *f* . . . . . Gal 2:20
f are sons of Abraham . . . . Gal 3:7
But after *f* has come . . . . Gal 3:25
of the household of *f* . . . . Gal 6:10
been saved through *f* . . . . Eph 2:8
one Lord, one *f* . . . . Eph 4:5
taking the shield of *f* . . . . Eph 6:16
your work of *f* . . . . 1 Thess 1:3
for not all have *f* . . . . . . 2 Thess 3:2
the mystery of the *f* . . . . 1 Tim 3:9
I have kept the *f* . . . . 2 Tim 4:7
in our common *f* . . . . Titus 1:4
not being mixed with *f* . . . Heb 4:2
f is the substance . . . . . . Heb 11:1
without *f* it is . . . . Heb 11:6
says he has *f* . . . . James 2:14
Show me your *f* . . . . . . James 2:18
and not by *f* only . . . . . James 2:24
f will save the sick . . . . James 5:15
add to your *f* virtue . . . . . 2 Pet 1:5
the patience and the *f* . . Rev 13:10

FAITHFUL

God, He is God, the *f* . . . . Deut 7:9
LORD preserves the *f* . . . . . Ps 31:23
eyes shall be on the *f* . . . . Ps 101:6
But who can find a *f* . . . Prov 20:6
the Holy One who is *f* . . Hos 11:12
"Who then is a *f* . . . . . . Matt 24:45
good and *f* servant . . . . Matt 25:23
"He who is *f* in what . . Luke 16:10
judged me to be *f* . . . . . Acts 16:15
God is *f* . . . . 1 Cor 1:9
is my beloved and *f* . . . . 1 Cor 4:17
But as God is *f* . . . . 2 Cor 1:18
f brethren in Christ . . . . . Col 1:2
who calls you is *f* . . . . 1 Thess 5:24
This is a *f* saying and . . 1 Tim 1:15
f High Priest in . . . . Heb 2:17
He who promised is *f* . . Heb 10:23
He is *f* and just to . . . . . 1 John 1:9
Be *f* until death . . . . Rev 2:10
words are true and *f* . . . Rev 21:5

FAITHFULNESS

I have declared Your *f* . . . Ps 40:10
Your *f* also surrounds . . . . . Ps 89:8
f endures to all . . . . Ps 119:90
Great is Your *f* . . . . Lam 3:23
unbelief make the *f* . . . . . . Rom 3:3

FAITHLESS

"O *f* generation . . . . Mark 9:19
If we are *f* . . . . 2 Tim 2:13

FALL

a deep sleep to *f* . . . . Gen 2:21
Let them *f* by their . . . . . . Ps 5:10
righteous man may *f* . . Prov 24:16
But the wicked shall *f* . Prov 24:16
the blind, both will *f* . . Matt 15:14
the stars will *f* . . . . Matt 24:29
"I saw Satan *f* . . . . Luke 10:18
take heed lest he *f* . . . . 1 Cor 10:12
if they *f* away . . . . Heb 6:6
lest anyone *f* short of . . Heb 12:15
and rocks, "F on us . . . . . Rev 6:16

FALLEN

"Babylon is *f* . . . . Is 21:9
you have *f* from grace . . . . Gal 5:4
"Babylon is *f* . . . . Rev 14:8

FALLING

great drops of blood *f* . Luke 22:44
f away comes first . . . . 2 Thess 2:3

FALSE

"You shall not bear *f* . . . . Ex 20:16
I hate every *f* way . . . . . Ps 119:104
f witness shall perish . . Prov 21:28
"Beware of *f* prophets . . Matt 7:15
f christs and *f* . . . . Matt 24:24
and we are found *f* . . . 1 Cor 15:15
of *f* brethren . . . . Gal 2:4
f prophets have gone . . 1 John 4:1
mouth of the *f* prophet . Rev 16:13

FALSEHOOD

For their deceit is *f* . . . . Ps 119:118
Offspring of *f* . . . . Is 57:4

FALSELY

of evil against you *f* . . . . Matt 5:11
f called knowledge . . . . 1 Tim 6:20

FAMILIES

in you all the *f* . . . . Gen 12:3
the God of all the *f* . . . . . . Jer 31:1
in your seed all the f . . . . Acts 3:25

FAMILY

shall mourn, every *f* . . . Zech 12:12
f were baptized . . . . Acts 16:33

FAMINES

And there will be *f* . . . . . Matt 24:7

FAMISH

righteous soul to *f* . . . . . . Prov 10:3

FAMISHED

honorable men are *f* . . . . Is 5:13

FAR

Your judgments are *f* . . . . . Ps 10:5
Be not *f* from Me . . . . Ps 22:11
The LORD is *f* from . . . . Prov 15:29
their heart is *f* from . . . . Matt 15:8
going to a *f* country . . . Mark 13:34
though He is not *f* . . . . . Acts 17:27
you who once were *f* . . . . Eph 2:13

FARMER

The hard-working *f* . . . . . 2 Tim 2:6
See how the *f* waits . . . James 5:7

FASHIONED

have made me and *f* . . . . Job 10:8

FASHIONS

He *f* their hearts . . . . Ps 33:15

FAST

f as you do this day . . . . Is 58:4
f that I have chosen . . . . Is 58:5
"Moreover, when you *f* . Matt 6:16
disciples do not *f* . . . . . . Matt 9:14
'I *f* twice a week . . . . . Luke 18:12

FASTED

'When you *f* and . . . . Zech 7:5
And when He had *f* . . . . . Matt 4:2

FASTING

by prayer and *f* . . . . Matt 17:21
give yourselves to *f* . . . . . 1 Cor 7:5

FASTINGS

in sleeplessness, in *f* . . . . 2 Cor 6:5

FAT

and you will eat the *f* . . Gen 45:18
f is the LORD's . . . . Lev 3:16

FATHER

man shall leave his *f* . . . . Gen 2:24
and you shall be a *f* . . . . Gen 17:4
I was a *f* to the poor . . . . Job 29:16
A *f* of the fatherless . . . . . Ps 68:5
f pities his children . . . . . Ps 103:13
God, Everlasting *F* . . . . Is 9:6
You, O LORD, are our *F* . . Is 63:16
time cry to Me, 'My *F* . . . . Jer 3:4
For I am a *F* to Israel . . . . Jer 31:9
"A son honors his *f* . . . . . . Mal 1:6
Have we not all one *F* . . . Mal 2:10
Our *F* in heaven . . . . Matt 6:9
"He who loves *f* . . . . Matt 10:37
know the *F* . . . . Matt 11:27
'He who curses *f* . . . . . . Matt 15:4
for One is your *F* . . . . . . Matt 23:9
"*F* will be divided . . . . . Luke 12:53
F loves the Son . . . . John 3:35
F raises the dead . . . . John 5:21
F judges no one . . . . John 5:22
He has seen the *F* . . . . . . John 6:46
F who sent Me bears . . . John 8:18
we have one *F* . . . . John 8:41
of your *f* the devil . . . . . John 8:44
"I and My *F* are one . . . John 10:30
'I am going to the *F* . . . . John 14:28
came forth from the *F* . John 16:28
that he might be the *f* . . Rom 4:11
one God and *F* of all . . . . . Eph 4:6
"I will be to Him a *F* . . . . Heb 1:5
down from the *F* . . . . . . James 1:17
if you call on the *F* . . . . . 1 Pet 1:17
and testify that the *F* . 1 John 4:14

FATHERLESS

the helper of the *f* . . . . Ps 10:14
He relieves the *f* . . . . Ps 146:9
do not defend the *f* . . . . Is 1:23
they may rob the *f* . . . . Is 10:2
You the *f* finds mercy . . Hos 14:3

FATHER'S

you in My *F* kingdom . Matt 26:29
I must be about My *F* . . Luke 2:49
F house are many . . . . . John 14:2
that a man has his *f* . . . . 1 Cor 5:1

FATHERS

the LORD God of our *f* . . . Ezra 7:27
f trusted in You . . . . Ps 22:4
our ears, O God, our *f* . . . . Ps 44:1
f ate the manna . . . . John 6:31
of whom are the *f* . . . . . . Rom 9:5
unaware that all our *f* . . 1 Cor 10:1

FATNESS

of the root and *f* . . . . . . Rom 11:17

FAULT

I have found no *f* . . . . . Luke 23:14
does He still find *f* . . . . . Rom 9:19
of God without *f* . . . . Phil 2:15

FAULTLESS

covenant had been *f* . . . . . . Heb 8:7
to present you *f* . . . . Jude 24

FAULTS

"I remember my *f* . . . . . . Gen 41:9
me from secret *f* . . . . Ps 19:12

FAVOR

granted me life and *f* . . . Job 10:12
His *f* is for life . . . . Ps 30:5
A good man obtains *f* . . Prov 12:2
and stature, and in *f* . . . Luke 2:52
God and having *f* . . . . . . Acts 2:47

FAVORED

"Rejoice, highly *f* . . . . . . Luke 1:28

FAVORITISM

not show personal *f* . . . Luke 20:21
God shows personal *f* . . . . . Gal 2:6

FEAR

live, for I *f* God . . . . Gen 42:18
to put the dread and *f* . Deut 2:25
said, "Does Job *f* . . . . Job 1:9
Yes, you cast off *f* . . . . . . Job 15:4
The *f* of the LORD is . . . . . Ps 19:9
of death, I will *f* . . . . Ps 23:4
Whom shall I *f* . . . . Ps 27:1
Oh, *f* the LORD . . . . Ps 34:9
There is no *f* of God . . . . . Ps 36:1
The *f* of the LORD is . . . Ps 111:10
The *f* of man brings a . Prov 29:25
F God and keep His . . . Eccl 12:13
Let Him be your *f* . . . . Is 8:13
"Be strong, do not *f* . . . . . . Is 35:4
who would not *f* . . . . Jer 10:7
f Him who is able . . . . . Matt 10:28
"Do not *f* . . . . Luke 12:32
"Do you not even *f* . . . Luke 23:40
And walking in the *f* . . . . Acts 9:31
given us a spirit of *f* . . . 2 Tim 1:7
those who through *f* . . . . Heb 2:15
because of His godly *f* . . . . Heb 5:7
F God . . . . 1 Pet 2:17
love casts out *f* . . . . 1 John 4:18

FEARED

He is also to be *f* . . . . . 1 Chr 16:25
f God more than . . . . Neh 7:2
Yourself, are to be *f* . . . . . Ps 76:7
Then those who *f* . . . . Mal 3:16

FEARFUL

It is a *f* thing to . . . . Heb 10:31

FEARFULLY

f and wonderfully . . . . . . Ps 139:14

FEARING

sincerity of heart, *f* . . . . . Col 3:22
forsook Egypt, not *f* . . . . Heb 11:27

FEARS

upright man, one who *f* . . . Job 1:8
me from all my *f* . . . . Ps 34:4
nation whoever *f* . . . . . Acts 10:35
f has not been made . . 1 John 4:18

FEAST

and you shall keep a *f* . Num 29:12
hate, I despise your *f* . . Amos 5:21
every year at the *F* . . . . . Luke 2:41
when you give a *f* . . . . . Luke 14:13
Now the Passover, a *f* . . . John 6:4
great day of the *f* . . . . . . John 7:37

FEASTING

go to the house of *f* . . . . . . Eccl 7:2

FEASTS

the best places at *f* . . . Luke 20:46
spots in your love *f* . . . . . . Jude 12

FED

and *f* you with manna . . . Deut 8:3
f you with milk and . . . . . 1 Cor 3:2

FEEBLE

strengthened the *f* . . . . Job 4:4
And there was none *f* . . Ps 105:37
And my flesh is *f* . . . . . . Ps 109:24
hang down, and the *f* . . Heb 12:12

FEED

ravens to *f* you there . . . 1 Kin 17:4
and *f* your flocks . . . . Is 61:5
to him, "*F* My lambs . . John 21:15
your enemy hungers, *f* . Rom 12:20
goods to *f* the poor . . . . 1 Cor 13:3

FEEDS

your heavenly Father *f* . . Matt 6:26

FEET

all things under his *f* . . . . . . Ps 8:6
He makes my *f* like the . . Ps 18:33
You have set my *f* . . . . Ps 31:8
For their *f* run to . . . . Prov 1:16
Her *f* go down to death . . Prov 5:5
mountains Are the *f* . . . . . . Is 52:7
place of My *f* glorious . . . . Is 60:13
in that day His *f* . . . . . . Zech 14:4
two hands or two *f* . . . . Matt 18:8
began to wash His *f* . . . Luke 7:38
wash the disciples' *f* . . . John 13:5
f are swift to shed . . . . . Rom 3:15
beautiful are the *f* . . . . Rom 10:15
things under His *f* . . . . 1 Cor 15:27
and having shod your *f* . Eph 6:15
fell at His *f* as dead . . . . . Rev 1:17

FELLOW

begins to beat his *f* . . . Matt 24:49
f citizens with the . . . . . . Eph 2:19
Gentiles should be *f* . . . . . Eph 3:6
I am your *f* servant . . . Rev 19:10

FELLOWSHIP

doctrine and *f* . . . . Acts 2:42
were called into the *f* . . 1 Cor 1:9
f has righteousness . . . . 2 Cor 6:14
the right hand of *f* . . . . Gal 2:9
And have no *f* with the . . Eph 5:11
of love, if any *f* . . . . Phil 2:1
and the *f* of His . . . . Phil 3:10
we say that we have *f* . . 1 John 1:6
the light, we have *f* . . . 1 John 1:7

FERVENT

f prayer of a . . . . James 5:16
will melt with *f* . . . . 2 Pet 3:10

FERVENTLY

love one another *f* . . . . . 1 Pet 1:22

FEW

let your words be *f* . . . . . . Eccl 5:2
and there are *f* . . . . Matt 7:14
but the laborers are *f* . . . Matt 9:37
called, but *f* chosen . . . . Matt 20:16
"Lord, are there *f* . . . . . Luke 13:23

FIDELITY

but showing all good *f* . Titus 2:10

FIELD

Let the *f* be joyful . . . . . . Ps 96:12
"The *f* is the world . . . . Matt 13:38
and buys that *f* . . . . Matt 13:44
you are God's *f* . . . . 1 Cor 3:9

FIERY

LORD sent *f* serpents . . . . Num 21:6
shall make them as a *f* . . . . Ps 21:9
burning *f* furnace . . . . Dan 3:6
concerning the *f* . . . . 1 Pet 4:12

FIG

f leaves together . . . . Gen 3:7
"Look at the *f* . . . . Luke 21:29
'I saw you under the *f* . . John 1:50

FIGHT

"The LORD will *f* . . . . Ex 14:14
Our God will *f* for us . . . . Neh 4:20
My servants would *f* . . . John 18:36
to him, let us not *f* . . . . . . Acts 23:9
F the good *f* . . . . 1 Tim 6:12
have fought the good *f* . . 2 Tim 4:7

FIGHTS

your God is He who *f* . . Josh 23:10
because my lord *f* . . . . 1 Sam 25:28
f come from among . . . . James 4:1

FIGS

thornbushes or *f* . . . . Matt 7:16
or a grapevine bear *f* . . James 3:12

FILL

f the earth and subdue . . Gen 1:28
"Do I not *f* heaven . . . . . Jer 23:24
f this temple with . . . . Hag 2:7
"*F* the waterpots . . . . John 2:7
that He might *f* . . . . Eph 4:10

FILLED

the whole earth be *f* . . . . . Ps 72:19
For they shall be *f* . . . . . . Matt 5:6
"Let the children be *f* . . Mark 7:27
would gladly have *f* . . . Luke 15:16
being *f* with all . . . . Rom 1:29
but be *f* with the . . . . Eph 5:18
be warmed and *f* . . . . . James 2:16

FILTHY

with *f* garments . . . . Zech 3:3
poor man in *f* clothes . . . James 2:2
oppressed by the *f* . . . . . 2 Pet 2:7
let him be *f* . . . . Rev 22:11

FIND

sure your sin will *f* . . . . Num 32:23
waters, For you will *f* . . . Eccl 11:1
seek, and you will *f* . . . . . Matt 7:7
f a Babe wrapped . . . . . . Luke 2:12
f no fault in this Man . . . Luke 23:4
f grace to help in . . . . Heb 4:16

FINDS

f me *f* life . . . . Prov 8:35
f a wife *f* a good . . . . Prov 18:22
and he who seeks *f* . . . . . Matt 7:8
f his life will lose . . . . . . Matt 10:39
and he who seeks *f* . . . . Luke 11:10

FINGER

written with the *f* . . . . . . Ex 31:18
dip the tip of his *f* . . . . . Luke 16:24
"Reach your *f* . . . . John 20:27

FINISH

he has enough to *f* . . . . Luke 14:28
has given Me to *f* . . . . . . John 5:36

FINISHED

f the work which You . . John 17:4
He said, "It is *f* . . . . John 19:30
I have *f* the race . . . . 2 Tim 4:7

FIRE

rained brimstone and *f* . Gen 19:24
to him in a flame of *f* . . . . . Ex 3:2
who answers by *f* . . . . 1 Kin 18:24
LORD was not in the *f* . 1 Kin 19:12

We went through *f* . . . . . . Ps 66:12
f goes before Him . . . . Ps 97:3
burns as the *f* . . . . Is 9:18
you walk through the *f* . . . . Is 43:2
f that burns all the . . . . Is 65:5
He break out like *f* . . . . . Amos 5:6
for conflict by *f* . . . . Amos 7:4
like a refiner's *f* . . . . Mal 3:2
the Holy Spirit and *f* . . . Matt 3:11
f is not quenched . . . . . . Mark 9:44
"I came to send *f* . . . . . Luke 12:49
tongues, as of *f* . . . . Acts 2:3
f taking vengeance . . 2 Thess 1:8
and that burned with *f* . Heb 12:18
And the tongue is a *f* . . . James 3:6
vengeance of eternal *f* . . . . Jude 7
into the lake of *f* . . . . Rev 20:14

FIRM

of the hope *f* to the . . . . . . Heb 3:6

FIRMAMENT

Thus God made the *f* . . . . . Gen 1:7
f shows His handiwork . . . Ps 19:1

FIRST

f father sinned . . . . Is 43:27
desires to be *f* . . . . Matt 20:27
f shall be slave . . . . Mark 10:44
the gospel must *f* . . . . . Mark 13:10
evil, of the Jew *f* . . . . Rom 2:9
f man Adam became . . 1 Cor 15:45
that we who *f* trusted . . . Eph 1:12
Him because He *f* . . . . 1 John 4:19
I am the *F* and the . . . . . Rev 1:17
you have left your *f* . . . . . Rev 2:4
is the *f* resurrection . . . . . Rev 20:5

FIRSTBORN

LORD struck all the *f* . . . . Ex 12:29
brought forth her *f* . . . . . Matt 1:25
that He might be the *f* . . Rom 8:29
invisible God, the *f* . . . . . Col 1:15
the beginning, the *f* . . . . . Col 1:18
witness, the *f* from . . . . . . Rev 1:5

FIRSTFRUITS

also who have the *f* . . . . Rom 8:23
and has become the *f* . 1 Cor 15:20
Christ the *f* . . . . 1 Cor 15:23

FISH

had prepared a great *f* . . . Jon 1:17
belly of the great *f* . . . . Matt 12:40
five loaves and two *f* . . Matt 14:17
and likewise the *f* . . . . . John 21:13

FISHERS

and I will make you *f* . . . Matt 4:19

FIVE

f smooth stones . . . . . . 1 Sam 17:40
about *f* thousand men . Matt 14:21
and *f* were foolish . . . . . Matt 25:2

FIXED

is a great gulf *f* . . . . Luke 16:26

FLAME

appeared to him in a *f* . . . . Ex 3:2
tormented in this *f* . . . . Luke 16:24
and His ministers a f . . . . . Heb 1:7
and His eyes like a *f* . . . . Rev 1:14

FLAMES

the LORD divides the *f* . . . Ps 29:7

FLAMING

f sword which turned . . . Gen 3:24
in *f* fire taking . . . . 2 Thess 1:8

FLATTER

They *f* with their . . . . Ps 5:9

FLATTERED

Nevertheless they *f* . . . . . Ps 78:36

FLATTERING

f speech deceive . . . . . . Rom 16:18
swelling words, *f* . . . . Jude 16

FLATTERS

f his neighbor Spreads . . Prov 29:5

FLATTERY

shall corrupt with *f* . . . . Dan 11:32

FLAVOR

the salt loses its *f* . . . . . . Matt 5:13

FLAX

f He will not quench . . . Matt 12:20

FLEE

Or where can I *f* . . . . Ps 139:7
And the shadows *f* . . . . . Song 2:17
who are in Judea *f* . . . . Matt 24:16
F sexual immorality . . 1 Cor 6:18
f these things and . . . . . 1 Tim 6:11
devil and he will *f* . . . . . James 4:7

FLESH

bone of my bones And *f* . Gen 2:23
shall become one *f* . . . . . . Gen 2:24
f had corrupted their . . . . Gen 6:12
f I shall see God . . . . Job 19:26
My *f* also will rest in . . . . . Ps 16:9
is wearisome to the *f* . . . Eccl 12:12
And all *f* shall see it . . . . . Is 40:5
"All *f* is grass . . . . Is 40:6
out My Spirit on all *f* . . . Joel 2:28
two shall become one f . Matt 19:5
were shortened, no *f* . . . Matt 24:22
shall become one f . . . . Mark 10:8
the Word became *f* . . . . John 1:14
I shall give is My *f* . . . . John 6:51
f profits nothing . . . . John 6:63
of God, but with the *f* . . Rom 7:25
on the things of the *f* . . . Rom 8:5
to the *f* you will die . . . . Rom 8:13
f should glory in His . . . 1 Cor 1:29
"shall become one *f* . . . 1 Cor 6:16
For the *f* lusts . . . . Gal 5:17
have crucified the *f* . . . . Gal 5:24
may boast in your *f* . . . . Gal 6:13
the lust of the *f* . . . . . . 1 John 2:16
has come in the *f* . . . . . 1 John 4:2

FLESHLY

f wisdom but by the . . . 2 Cor 1:12
f lusts which . . . . 1 Pet 2:11

FLIES

Dead *f* putrefy the . . . . . Eccl 10:1

FLOAT

and he made the iron *f* . . 2 Kin 6:6

FLOCK

lead Joseph like a *f* . . . . . . Ps 80:1
He will feed His *f* . . . . Is 40:11
you do not feed the *f* . . . Ezek 34:3
my God, "Feed the *f* . . . . Zech 11:4
sheep of the f . . . . Matt 26:31
"Do not fear, little *f* . . . Luke 12:32
there will be one *f* . . . . . John 10:16
Shepherd the *f* of God . . 1 Pet 5:2
examples to the *f* . . . . 1 Pet 5:3

FLOOD

the waters of the *f* . . . . . Gen 7:10
them away like a *f* . . . . . . Ps 90:5
the days before the *f* . . . Matt 24:38
bringing in the *f* . . . . 2 Pet 2:5
of his mouth like a *f* . . . Rev 12:15

FLOODS

me, And the *f* of . . . . Ps 18:4

FLOURISH
f on the dry ground . . . . Is 44:3
rain descended, the *f* . . . Matt 7:25

FLOURISH
the righteous shall *f* . . . . . Ps 72:7

FLOW
of his heart will *f* . . . . . . John 7:38

FLOWER
As a *f* of the field . . . . . . Ps 103:15
beauty is a fading *f* . . . . . . Is 28:4
grass withers, the *f* . . . . . . Is 40:7
of man as the f . . . . 1 Pet 1:24

FLOWERS
f appear on the earth . . . Song 2:12

FLOWING
'a land *f* with milk . . . . . . Deut 6:3
the Gentiles like a *f* . . . . . Is 66:12

FLUTE
play the harp and *f* . . . . . Gen 4:21

FLUTES
instruments and *f* . . . . Ps 150:4

FLUTISTS
harpists, musicians, *f* . . . Rev 18:22

FLY
soon cut off, and we *f* . . . . Ps 90:10

FOLLOW
f You wherever You go . Matt 8:19
He said to him, "F" . . . . . . Matt 9:9
up his cross, and *f* . . . . . Mark 8:34
will by no means *f* . . . . . John 10:5
serves Me, let him *f* . . . John 12:26
that you should *f* . . . . . . 1 Pet 2:21
f the Lamb wherever . . . . Rev 14:4
and their works *f* . . . . . . Rev 14:13

FOLLOWED
f the LORD my God . . . . . Josh 14:8
we have left all and *f* . Mark 10:28

FOLLOWS
f Me shall not walk . . . . John 8:12

FOLLY
taken much notice of *f* . . Job 35:15
not turn back to *f* . . . . Ps 85:8
F is joy to him who is . Prov 15:21
F is set in great . . . . Eccl 10:6

FOOD
you it shall be for *f* . . . . . Gen 1:29
that lives shall be *f* . . . . . . Gen 9:3
f which you eat shall . . . Ezek 4:10
the fields yield no *f* . . . . . Hab 3:17
That there may be *f* . . . . Mal 3:10
to give them *f* . . . . Matt 24:45
and you gave Me *f* . . . . Matt 25:35
and he who has *f* . . . . . . Luke 3:11
have you any *f* . . . . John 21:5
they ate their *f* . . . . Acts 2:46
our hearts with *f* . . . . . . Acts 14:17
destroy with your *f* . . . . Rom 14:15
f makes my brother . . . . 1 Cor 8:13
the same spiritual *f* . . . 1 Cor 10:3
sower, and bread for *f* . 2 Cor 9:10
And having *f* and . . . . 1 Tim 6:8
and not solid *f* . . . . Heb 5:12
But solid *f* belongs to . . . . Heb 5:14
of *f* sold his . . . . Heb 12:16
destitute of daily *f* . . . . James 2:15

FOODS
f which God . . . . 1 Tim 4:3

FOOL
f has said in his . . . . Ps 14:1
is like sport to a *f* . . . . . Prov 10:23

---

f is right in his own . . . . Prov 12:15
is too lofty for a *f* . . . . . . Prov 24:7
whoever says, 'You *f* . . . Matt 5:22
I have become a *f* . . . . 2 Cor 12:11

FOOLISH
I was so *f* and . . . . Ps 73:22
f pulls it down with . . . . Prov 14:1
f man squanders it . . . . Prov 21:20
Has not God made *f* . . . . 1 Cor 1:20
O *f* Galatians . . . . Gal 3:1
were also once *f* . . . . Titus 3:3
But avoid *f* disputes . . . . . Titus 3:9

FOOLISHLY
I speak *f* . . . . 2 Cor 11:21

FOOLISHNESS
F is bound up in the . . . Prov 22:15
devising of *f* is sin . . . . . Prov 24:9
of the cross is *f* . . . . 1 Cor 1:18
Because the *f* of God . . . 1 Cor 1:25

FOOLS
f despise wisdom . . . . Prov 1:7
folly of *f* is deceit . . . . . . Prov 14:8
F mock at sin . . . . Prov 14:9
We are *f* for Christ's . . . 1 Cor 4:10

FOOT
will not allow your *f* . . . . . Ps 121:3
f will not stumble . . . . . . Prov 3:23
From the sole of the *f* . . . . . Is 1:6
f causes you to sin . . . . . . Matt 18:8
you dash your f . . . . Luke 4:11
If the *f* should say . . . . 1 Cor 12:15

FOOTSTOOL
Your enemies Your *f* . . . . Ps 110:1
Your enemies Your f . . . Matt 22:44

FORBID
said, "Do not *f* . . . . Mark 9:39
"Can anyone *f* . . . . Acts 10:47
f that I should boast . . . . . Gal 6:14

FORBIDDING
f to marry . . . . 1 Tim 4:3

FOREFATHERS
conscience, as my *f* . . . . 2 Tim 1:3

FOREHEADS
put a mark on the *f* . . . . . Ezek 9:4
seal of God on their *f* . . . . Rev 9:4
his mark on their *f* . . . . . Rev 20:4

FOREIGNER
"I am a *f* and a . . . . Gen 23:4
of me, since I am a *f* . . . . Ruth 2:10
to God except this *f* . . . Luke 17:18

FOREIGNERS
f who were there . . . . . . Acts 17:21
longer strangers and *f* . . . Eph 2:19

FOREKNEW
For whom He *f* . . . . Rom 8:29
His people whom He *f* . . Rom 11:2

FOREKNOWLEDGE
purpose and *f* of God . . . Acts 2:23

FOREORDAINED
He indeed was *f* . . . . 1 Pet 1:20

FORESAW
'*I f the LORD* . . . . Acts 2:25

FORESEEING
f that God would . . . . Gal 3:8

FORESEES
A prudent man *f* . . . . . . Prov 22:3

FORETOLD
have also *f* these days . . . Acts 3:24
killed those who *f* . . . . . . Acts 7:52

FOREVER
and eat, and live *f* . . . . . . Gen 3:22
to our children *f* . . . . . . Deut 29:29
LORD sits as King *f* . . . . . Ps 29:10
Do not cast us off *f* . . . . . . Ps 44:23
throne, O God, is *f* . . . . Ps 45:6
"You are a priest *f* . . . . . Ps 110:4
His mercy endures *f* . . . . Ps 136:1
of our God stands *f* . . . . . . Is 40:8
My salvation will be *f* . . . . . Is 51:6
will not cast off *f* . . . . . . Lam 3:31
Like the stars *f* . . . . Dan 12:3
and the glory *f* . . . . Matt 6:13
the Christ remains *f* . . . John 12:34
who is blessed *f* . . . . . . 2 Cor 11:31
to whom be glory *f* . . . . Gal 1:5
generation, *f* and ever . . . Eph 3:21
and Father be glory *f* . . . Phil 4:20
throne, O God, is f . . . . . . Heb 1:8
lives and abides *f* . . . . . . 1 Pet 1:23
of darkness *f* . . . . Jude 13
power, Both now and *f* . . Jude 25
And they shall reign *f* . . Rev 22:5

FOREVERMORE
Blessed be the LORD *f* . . . Ps 89:52
this time forth and *f* . . . . . Ps 113:2
behold, I am alive *f* . . . . . Rev 1:18

FORGAVE
to repay, he freely *f* . . . . Luke 7:42
God in Christ *f* . . . . Eph 4:32
even as Christ *f* . . . . Col 3:13

FORGET
f the LORD who . . . . Deut 6:12
I will not *f* Your word . . Ps 119:16
If I *f* you . . . . Ps 137:5
My son, do not *f* . . . . Prov 3:1
f the LORD your Maker . . . Is 51:13
f your work and labor . . . Heb 6:10

FORGETFULNESS
in the land of *f* . . . . Ps 88:12

FORGETS
and immediately *f* . . . . James 1:24

FORGETTING
f those things which . . . . . Phil 3:13

FORGIVE
f their sin and heal . . . . 2 Chr 7:14
good, and ready to *f* . . . . . Ps 86:5
And *f* us our debts . . . . . . Matt 6:12
Father will also *f* . . . . . . Matt 6:14
his heart, does not *f* . . . Matt 18:35
Who can *f* sins but God . Mark 2:7
f the sins of any . . . . . . John 20:23
you ought rather to *f* . . . 2 Cor 2:7
F me this wrong . . . . . . 2 Cor 12:13
f us our sins and to . . . . 1 John 1:9

FORGIVEN
sins be f them . . . . Mark 4:12
to whom little is *f* . . . . . . Luke 7:47
f you all trespasses . . . . . Col 2:13
your sins are *f* . . . . 1 John 2:12

FORGIVENESS
But there is *f* with . . . . . . Ps 130:4
preached to you the *f* . . . Acts 13:38
they may receive *f* . . . . . Acts 26:18
His blood, the *f* . . . . Eph 1:7

FORGIVES
f all your iniquities . . . . . . Ps 103:3
is this who even *f* . . . . . . Luke 7:49

FORGIVING

tenderhearted, f . . . . Eph 4:32
and f one another . . . . Col 3:13

FORGOT

Joseph, but f . . . . Gen 40:23
They soon f His works . . Ps 106:13

FORGOTTEN

f the God who . . . . Deut 32:18
not one of them is f . . . . Luke 12:6
f the exhortation . . . . Heb 12:5
f that he was . . . . 2 Pet 1:9

FORM

earth was without f . . . . . . Gen 1:2
Who would f a god or . . . Is 44:10
f the light and create . . . . . . Is 45:7
descended in bodily f . . . Luke 3:22
time, nor seen His f . . . . John 5:37
For the f of this . . . . 1 Cor 7:31
who, being in the f . . . . . . Phil 2:6
having a f of . . . . 2 Tim 3:5

FORMED

And the LORD God f . . . . . . Gen 2:7
f my inward parts . . . . . . Ps 139:13
say of him who f . . . . Is 29:16
"Before I f you in . . . . Jer 1:5
Will the thing f . . . . Rom 9:20
until Christ is f . . . . Gal 4:19

FORMER

f days better than . . . . . . Eccl 7:10
f rain to the earth . . . . Hos 6:3
f prophets preached . . . . . Zech 1:4
your f conduct . . . . Eph 4:22
f things have passed . . . . Rev 21:4

FORMS

clay say to him who f . . . . . Is 45:9
f the spirit of man . . . . . . Zech 12:1

FORNICATION

"We were not born of f . John 8:41
of the wrath of her f . . . . . Rev 14:8

FORNICATOR

you know, that no f . . . . . . Eph 5:5
lest there be any f . . . . . Heb 12:16

FORNICATORS

but f and adulterers . . . . . Heb 13:4

FORSAKE

But I did not f . . . . Ps 119:87
father, And do not f . . . . . Prov 1:8
of you does not f . . . . . . Luke 14:33
never leave you nor f . . . . Heb 13:5

FORSAKEN

My God, why have You f . Ps 22:1
seen the righteous f . . . . . Ps 37:25
a mere moment I have f . . . Is 54:7
God, why have You f . . Matt 27:46
persecuted, but not f . . . . 2 Cor 4:9
for Demas has f . . . . 2 Tim 4:10

FORSAKING

f the assembling . . . . Heb 10:25

FORSOOK

f God who made him . . Deut 32:15
all the disciples f . . . . . . Matt 26:56
with me, but all f . . . . . . 2 Tim 4:16

FORTRESS

is my rock, my f . . . . . . 2 Sam 22:2
my rock of refuge, a f . . . . Ps 31:2

FOUND

f a helper comparable . . . Gen 2:20
a thousand I have f . . . . . Eccl 7:28
LORD while He may be f . . Is 55:6
fruit on it and f none . . . Luke 13:6

he was lost and is f . . . Luke 15:24
f the Messiah" (which . . John 1:41
and be f in Him . . . . Phil 3:9

FOUNDATION

Of old You laid the f . . . . Ps 102:25
the earth without a f . . . Luke 6:49
loved Me before the f . . John 17:24
I have laid the f . . . . 1 Cor 3:10
f can anyone lay than . . 1 Cor 3:11
us in Him before the f . . . Eph 1:4
not laying again the f . . . . Heb 6:1
Lamb slain from the f . . . Rev 13:8

FOUNDATIONS

when I laid the f . . . . Job 38:4
And the f of the wall . . . Rev 21:19

FOUNTAIN

will become in him a f . . John 4:14

FOUNTAINS

on that day all the f . . . . . Gen 7:11
lead them to living f . . . . . Rev 7:17

FRAGRANCE

was filled with the f . . . . John 12:3
we are to God the f . . . . 2 Cor 2:15

FREE

'You will be made f . . . . John 8:33
And having been set f . . Rom 6:18
Jesus has made me f . . . . Rom 8:2
is neither slave nor f . . . . Gal 3:28
Christ has made us f . . . . . Gal 5:1
he is a slave or f . . . . Eph 6:8

FREED

has died has been f . . . . . . Rom 6:7

FREEDMAN

slave is the Lord's f . . . . 1 Cor 7:22

FREELY

the garden you may f . . . Gen 2:16
F you have received . . . . Matt 10:8
f give us all . . . . Rom 8:32
the water of life f . . . . . . Rev 22:17

FRIEND

of Abraham Your f . . . . 2 Chr 20:7
f who sticks closer . . . . Prov 18:24
a f of tax collectors . . . . Matt 11:19
of you shall have a f . . . Luke 11:5
f Lazarus sleeps . . . . . . John 11:11
he was called the f . . . . James 2:23
wants to be a f . . . . James 4:4

FRIENDS

My f scorn me . . . . Job 16:20
the rich has many f . . . . Prov 14:20
one's life for his f . . . . . John 15:13
I have called you f . . . . . John 15:15
to forbid any of his f . . . Acts 24:23

FROGS

your territory with f . . . . . . Ex 8:2
f coming out of the . . . . . Rev 16:13

FRUIT

showed them the f . . . . Num 13:26
brings forth its f . . . . Ps 1:3
f is better than gold . . . . Prov 8:19
with good by the f . . . . . Prov 12:14
like the first f . . . . Is 28:4
does not bear good f . . . . Matt 3:10
good tree bears good f . . Matt 7:17
not drink of this f . . . . Matt 26:29
and blessed is the f . . . . Luke 1:42
life, and bring no f . . . . . Luke 8:14
and he came seeking f . Luke 13:6
'And if it bears f . . . . . . Luke 13:9
branch that bears f . . . . John 15:2
that you bear much f . . . John 15:8
should go and bear f . . John 15:16

God, you have your f . . . Rom 6:22
that we should bear f . . . . Rom 7:4
But the f of the . . . . Gal 5:22
yields the peaceable f . . Heb 12:11
Now the f of . . . . James 3:18
autumn trees without f . . . Jude 12
tree yielding its f . . . . Rev 22:2

FRUITFUL

them, saying, "Be f . . . . . Gen 1:22
wife shall be like a f . . . . Ps 128:3
pleasing Him, being f . . . Col 1:10

FRUITS

Therefore bear f . . . . Matt 3:8
know them by their f . . . Matt 7:16
of mercy and good f . . . James 3:17
which bore twelve f . . . . Rev 22:2

FULFILL

for us to f all . . . . Matt 3:15
f the law of Christ . . . . Gal 6:2
f my joy by being . . . . Phil 2:2
and f all the good . . . . 2 Thess 1:11
If you really f . . . . James 2:8

FULFILLED

the law till all is f . . . . . . Matt 5:18
of the Gentiles are f . . . Luke 21:24
all things must be f . . . Luke 24:44
of the law might be f . . . . Rom 8:4
loves another has f . . . . . Rom 13:8
For all the law is f . . . . . . Gal 5:14

FULFILLMENT

love is the f of the . . . . . Rom 13:10

FULL

and it was f of bones . . . Ezek 37:1
whole body will be f . . . . Matt 6:22
your joy may be f . . . . . John 15:11
You are already f . . . . . . 1 Cor 4:8
learned both to be f . . . . Phil 4:12

FULLNESS

f we have all received . . John 1:16
But when the f of the . . . . Gal 4:4
filled with all the f . . . . . . Eph 3:19
Him dwells all the f . . . . . . Col 2:9

FURNACE

you out of the iron f . . . Deut 4:20
of a burning fiery f . . . . . Dan 3:6
cast them into the f . . . Matt 13:42
the smoke of a great f . . . Rev 9:2

FURY

Thus will I spend My f . Ezek 6:12
in anger and f On the . . . Mic 5:15

G

GAIN

and to die is g . . . . Phil 1:21
rubbish, that I may g . . . . Phil 3:8
is a means of g . . . . 1 Tim 6:5
contentment is great g . . 1 Tim 6:6
for dishonest g . . . . 1 Pet 5:2

GAINED

g five more talents . . . . Matt 25:20

GAINS

g the whole world . . . . Matt 16:26

GALL

They also gave me g . . . . Ps 69:21
wine mingled with g . . . Matt 27:34

GAP

and stand in the g . . . . Ezek 22:30

GARDEN

LORD God planted a g . . . . Gen 2:8

GARMENT

g enclosed Is my .... Song 4:12
Eden, the g of God .... Ezek 28:13
where there was a g .... John 18:1
g a new tomb in ...... John 19:41

GARMENT

the hem of His g ...... Matt 9:20
on a wedding g ...... Matt 22:11
cloth on an old g ..... Mark 2:21
all grow old like a g .... Heb 1:11
hating even the g .... Jude 23

GARMENTS

g did not wear out on .... Deut 8:4
They divide My g .... Ps 22:18
from Edom, With dyed g .. Is 63:1
"Take away the filthy g . Zech 3:4
man clothed in soft g ... Matt 11:8
spread their g on the ... Matt 21:8
and divided His g ..... Matt 27:35
by them in shining g ... Luke 24:4
g are moth-eaten .... James 5:2
be clothed in white g ..... Rev 3:5

GATE

by the narrow g .... Matt 7:13
by the Sheep G a pool ... John 5:2
laid daily at the g .... Acts 3:2
suffered outside the g .. Heb 13:12

GATES

up your heads, O you g ... Ps 24:7
The LORD loves the g ..... Ps 87:2
is known in the g ..... Prov 31:23
Go through the g .... Is 62:10
and the g of Hades .... Matt 16:18
wall with twelve g ..... Rev 21:12
g were twelve pearls .... Rev 21:21
g shall not be shut .... Rev 21:25

GATHER

And a time to g stones ... Eccl 3:5
g the lambs with His ..... Is 40:11
g His wheat into the .... Matt 3:12
sow nor reap nor g ..... Matt 6:26
Do men g grapes from .. Matt 7:16
g where I have not .... Matt 25:26
g together His .... Mark 13:27

GATHERED

g some of every kind .. Matt 13:47
the nations will be g ... Matt 25:32

GATHERING

g together of the .... Gen 1:10
g together to Him ..... 2 Thess 2:1

GATHERS

The Lord GOD, who g ..... Is 56:8
together, as a hen g ... Matt 23:37

GAVE

to be with me, she g .... Gen 3:12
g You this authority ... Matt 21:23
that He g His only ..... John 3:16
Those whom You g ... John 17:12
but God g the increase .. 1 Cor 3:6
g Himself for our sins .... Gal 1:4
g Himself for me .... Gal 2:20
g Himself for it .... Eph 5:25

GENERATION

One g passes away ...... Eccl 1:4
who will declare His g ... Is 53:8
and adulterous g ...... Matt 12:39
this g will by no ...... Matt 24:34
from this perverse g .... Acts 2:40
But you are a chosen g .. 1 Pet 2:9

GENERATIONS

be remembered in all g .. Ps 45:17
g will call me blessed .. Luke 1:48

GENEROUS

no longer be called g ...... Is 32:5

GENTILES

G were separated .... Gen 10:5
As a light to the G .... Is 42:6
G shall come to your ...... Is 60:3
all these things the G ... Matt 6:32
into the way of the G ... Matt 10:5
revelation to the G .... Luke 2:32
G are fulfilled ...... Luke 21:24
My name before G ..... Acts 9:15
poured out on the G ... Acts 10:45
a light to the G .... Acts 13:47
also the God of the G ... Rom 3:29
mystery among the G ... Col 1:27
a teacher of the G ...... 1 Tim 2:7

GENTLE

from Me, for I am g ... Matt 11:29
we were g among ... 1 Thess 2:7
to be peaceable, g .... Titus 3:2
only to the good and g . 1 Pet 2:18
ornament of a g .... 1 Pet 3:4

GENTLENESS

love and a spirit of g .. 1 Cor 4:21
g, self-control .... Gal 5:23
all lowliness and g ...... Eph 4:2
Let your g be known to .. Phil 4:5
love, patience, g .... 1 Tim 6:11

GHOST

supposed it was a g .... Mark 6:49

GIFT

it is the g of God ...... Eccl 3:13
"If you knew the g ...... John 4:10
but the g of God is ..... Rom 6:23
each one has his own g . 1 Cor 7:7
though I have the g .... 1 Cor 13:2
it is the g of God .... Eph 2:8
Do not neglect the g ... 1 Tim 4:14
you to stir up the g ..... 2 Tim 1:6
tasted the heavenly g .... Heb 6:4
Every good g and ..... James 1:17

GIFTS

You have received g ..... Ps 68:18
and Seba Will offer g ... Ps 72:10
how to give good g ..... Matt 7:11
rich putting their g ..... Luke 21:1
g differing .... Rom 12:6
are diversities of g ..... 1 Cor 12:4
and desire spiritual g . 1 Cor 14:1
captive, And gave g ..... Eph 4:8

GIRD

G Your sword upon Your . Ps 45:3
and another will g ..... John 21:18
Therefore g up the ..... 1 Pet 1:13

GIRDED

a towel and g Himself .. John 13:4

GIVE

g you the desires .... Ps 37:4
Yes, the LORD will g ..... Ps 85:12
G me understanding .... Ps 119:34
"G to him who asks .... Matt 5:42
G us this day our .... Matt 6:11
what you have and g .. Matt 19:21
authority I will g .... Luke 4:6
g them eternal life .... John 10:28
commandment I g ..... John 13:34
but what I do have I g .... Acts 3:6
g us all things .... Rom 8:32
G no offense .... 1 Cor 10:32
g him who has need .... Eph 4:28
g thanks to God ..... 2 Thess 2:13
g yourself entirely ..... 1 Tim 4:15

GIVEN

to him more will be g .. Matt 13:12
has, more will be g .... Matt 25:29
to whom much is g ... Luke 12:48

g Me I should lose ..... John 6:39
Spirit was not yet g .... John 7:39

GIVES

g life to the world ...... John 6:33
"All that the Father g .. John 6:37
The good shepherd g .. John 10:11
not as the world g ..... John 14:27
g us richly all things ... 1 Tim 6:17
who g to all liberally .. James 1:5
g grace to the humble . James 4:6

GLAD

streams shall make g ..... Ps 46:4
I was g when they said .. Ps 122:1
make merry and be g . Luke 15:32
he saw it and was g .... John 8:56

GLADNESS

me hear joy and g .... Ps 51:8
Serve the LORD with g ... Ps 100:2

GLORIFIED

and they g the God of . Matt 15:31
Jesus was not yet g ..... John 7:39
when Jesus was g ..... John 12:16
this My Father is g ..... John 15:8
"I have g You on the .... John 17:4
g His Servant Jesus ..... Acts 3:13
these He also g .... Rom 8:30
things God may be g ... 1 Pet 4:11

GLORIFY

g your Father in .... Matt 5:16
"Father, g Your name . John 12:28
"He will g Me .... John 16:14
"And now, O Father, g . John 17:5
death he would g ..... John 21:19
therefore g God in ..... 1 Cor 6:20
also Christ did not g .... Heb 5:5
ashamed, but let him g . 1 Pet 4:16

GLORIOUS

G things are spoken ...... Ps 87:3
g splendor of Your ...... Ps 145:5
habitation, holy and g .... Is 63:15
it to Himself a g .... Eph 5:27
be conformed to His g ... Phil 3:21
g appearing of our ..... Titus 2:13

GLORY

show me Your g .... Ex 33:18
g has departed from .. 1 Sam 4:21
Who is this King of g ..... Ps 24:8
Your power and Your g ... Ps 63:2
wise shall inherit g ..... Prov 3:35
It is the g of God to .... Prov 25:2
g I will not give .... Is 42:8
that they may have g .... Matt 6:2
the power and the g .... Matt 6:13
g was not arrayed ...... Matt 6:29
will come in the g ..... Matt 16:27
power and great g .... Matt 24:30
"G to God in the .... Luke 2:14
and we beheld His g ... John 1:14
and manifested His g ... John 2:11
not seek My own g ..... John 8:50
"Give God the g ...... John 9:24
g which I had with ...... John 17:5
g which You gave Me . John 17:22
he did not give g ...... Acts 12:23
doing good seek for g .... Rom 2:7
fall short of the g .... Rom 3:23
in faith, giving g ...... Rom 4:20
the adoption, the g ..... Rom 9:4
the riches of His g ..... Rom 9:23
God, alone wise, be g .. Rom 16:27
who glories, let him g .. 1 Cor 1:31
to His riches in g .... Phil 4:19
appear with Him in g ... Col 3:4
For you are our g .... 1 Thess 2:20
many sons to g .... Heb 2:10
grass, And all the g .... 1 Pet 1:24
to whom belong the g .. 1 Pet 4:11
for the Spirit of g ...... 1 Pet 4:14

GLORYING

the presence of His g .....Jude 24
O Lord, to receive g .....Rev 4:11
g of God illuminated ...Rev 21:23

GLORYING

Your g is not good ......1 Cor 5:6

GLUTTON

you say, 'Look, a g .....Luke 7:34

GLUTTONS

g shames his ....Prov 28:7
evil beasts, lazy g ......Titus 1:12

GNASHING

will be weeping and g ..Matt 8:12

GO

'Let My people g ....Ex 5:1
For wherever you g ....Ruth 1:16
Those who g down to ...Ps 107:23
Where can I g from .....Ps 139:7
to whom shall we g ....John 6:68
g you cannot come .....John 8:21
I g to prepare a place ...John 14:2
shall g out no more .....Rev 3:12

GOADS

to kick against the g .....Acts 9:5

GOAL

I press toward the g .....Phil 3:14

GOATS

his sheep from the g ...Matt 25:32
with the blood of g .....Heb 9:12
g could take away ......Heb 10:4

GOD

G created the heavens ....Gen 1:1
Abram of G Most ......Gen 14:19
and I will be their G ...Gen 17:8
"I am the LORD your G ...Ex 20:2
G is a consuming fire ...Deut 4:24
If the LORD is G ......1 Kin 18:21
G is greater than all ....2 Chr 2:5
You have been My G ...Ps 22:10
G is our refuge ....Ps 46:1
G is in the midst of ...Ps 46:5
me a clean heart, O G ...Ps 51:10
Our G is the G ....Ps 68:20
Who is so great a G ....Ps 77:13
Restore us, O G ....Ps 80:7
You alone are G ....Ps 86:10
Exalt the LORD our G .....Ps 99:9
Yes, our G is merciful ...Ps 116:5
For G is in heaven ....Eccl 5:2
Counselor, Mighty G ....Is 9:6
G is my salvation ....Is 12:2
stricken, Smitten by G ...Is 53:4
"G with us ....Matt 1:23
in G my Savior ....Luke 1:47
the Word was with G ...John 1:1
"For G so loved the ....John 3:16
"G is Spirit ....John 4:24
"My Lord and my G ...John 20:28
Christ is the Son of G ...Acts 8:37
Indeed, let G be true .....Rom 3:4
If G is for us ....Rom 8:31
G is faithful ....1 Cor 1:9
G shall supply all ......Phil 4:19
and I will be their G ...Heb 8:10
G is a consuming fire ...Heb 12:29
for G is love ....1 John 4:8
No one has seen G ....1 John 4:12
G Himself will be ......Rev 21:3
and I will be his G ......Rev 21:7

GODDESS

after Ashtoreth the g ...1 Kin 11:5
of the great g Diana ...Acts 19:35

GODHEAD

eternal power and G ....Rom 1:20
the fullness of the G ......Col 2:9

GODLINESS

is the mystery of g ....1 Tim 3:16
g with contentment .....1 Tim 6:6
having a form of g .....2 Tim 3:5
to perseverance g ....2 Pet 1:6

GODLY

who desire to live g ...2 Tim 3:12
reverence and g fear ...Heb 12:28
to deliver the g ....2 Pet 2:9

GODS

God is God of g ....Deut 10:17
I said, "You are g ....Ps 82:6
yourselves with g ....Is 57:5
If He called them g ....John 10:35
g have come down to ..Acts 14:11

GOLD

g I do not have ....Acts 3:6
with braided hair or g ..1 Tim 2:9
a man with g rings .....James 2:2
Your g and silver are ...James 5:3
more precious than g ....1 Pet 1:7
like silver or g ....1 Pet 1:18
of the city was pure g ..Rev 21:21

GONE

like sheep have g ....Is 53:6

GOOD

God saw that it was g ...Gen 1:10
but God meant it for g .Gen 50:20
indeed accept g ....Job 2:10
is none who does g ....Ps 14:1
Truly God is g to ....Ps 73:1
g word makes it glad ..Prov 12:25
on the evil and the g ...Prov 15:3
A merry heart does g ..Prov 17:22
Learn to do g ....Is 1:17
talked to me, with g ....Zech 1:13
they may see your g ....Matt 5:16
"A g man out of the ...Matt 12:35
No one is but One .....Matt 19:17
For she has done a g ...Matt 26:10
g works I have shown .John 10:32
went about doing g ....Acts 10:38
g man someone would ...Rom 5:7
in my flesh) nothing ...Rom 7:18
overcome evil with g ...Rom 12:21
Jesus for g works ....Eph 2:10
fruitful in every g ....Col 1:10
know that the law is g ..1 Tim 1:8
For this is g and ....1 Tim 2:3
bishop, he desires a g ...1 Tim 3:1
for this is g and ....1 Tim 5:4
prepared for every g ...2 Tim 2:21
Every g gift and ......James 1:17

GOODNESS

"I will make all My g ...Ex 33:19
and abounding in g .....Ex 34:6
"You are my Lord, My g ..Ps 16:2
Surely g and mercy ......Ps 23:6
That I would see the g ...Ps 27:13
the riches of His g ......Rom 2:4
consider the g and ....Rom 11:22
kindness, g ....Gal 5:22

GOSPEL

The beginning of the g ..Mark 1:1
and believe in the g ....Mark 1:15
g must first be ....Mark 13:10
separated to the g ....Rom 1:1
not ashamed of the g ....Rom 1:16
to a different g ....Gal 1:6
the everlasting g ....Rev 14:6

GOVERNMENT

And the g will be upon .....Is 9:6

GRACE

But Noah found g ....Gen 6:8
G is poured upon Your ....Ps 45:2

The LORD will give g .....Ps 84:11
the Spirit of g ....Zech 12:10
and the g of God was ...Luke 2:40
g and truth came ....John 1:17
And great g was upon ...Acts 4:33
receive abundance of g ..Rom 5:17
g is no longer g ....Rom 11:6
For you know the g .....2 Cor 8:9
g is sufficient ....2 Cor 12:9
The g of the Lord ....2 Cor 13:14
you have fallen from g ....Gal 5:4
to the riches of His g .....Eph 1:7
g you have been ....Eph 2:8
g was given according ....Eph 4:7
G be with all those .....Eph 6:24
shaken, let us have g ...Heb 12:28
But He gives more g ....James 4:6
but grow in the g ......2 Pet 3:18

GRACIOUS

he said, "God be g .....Gen 43:29
I will be g to whom I ....Ex 33:19
at the g words which ...Luke 4:22
that the Lord is g ....1 Pet 2:3

GRAFTED

in unbelief, will be g ...Rom 11:23

GRAIN

it treads out the g ......Deut 25:4
be revived like g ....Hos 14:7
to pluck heads of g .....Matt 12:1
unless a g of wheat ....John 12:24

GRAPES

brought forth wild g ....Is 5:2
have eaten sour g .....Ezek 18:2
Do men gather g ....Matt 7:16
g are fully ripe ....Rev 14:18

GRASS

The g withers ....Is 40:7
so clothes the g ....Matt 6:30
"All flesh is as g ....1 Pet 1:24

GRAVE

my soul up from the g ....Ps 30:3
And they made His g ......Is 53:9
the power of the g .....Hos 13:14

GRAVES

g were opened ....Matt 27:52
g which are not ....Luke 11:44
g will hear His voice ...John 5:28

GRAY

the man of g hairs ....Deut 32:25

GREAT

and make your name g ..Gen 12:2
For the LORD is g .....1 Chr 16:25
Who does g things ....Job 5:9
g is the Holy One ....Is 12:6
G is Your faithfulness ..Lam 3:23
he shall be called g .....Matt 5:19
one pearl of g price ...Matt 13:46
desires to become g ...Matt 20:26
g drops of blood .....Luke 22:44
appearing of our g .....Titus 2:13
g men, the rich men ....Rev 6:15
Mystery, Babylon the G .Rev 17:5
the dead, small and g ...Rev 20:12

GREATER

of heaven is g ....Matt 11:11
place there is One g ....Matt 12:6
g than Jonah is here ...Matt 12:41
g than Solomon is .....Matt 12:42
a servant is not g .....John 13:16
"G love has no one ...John 15:13
'A servant is not g ....John 15:20
who prophesies is g ...1 Cor 14:5
God is g ....1 John 3:20
witness of God is g ....1 John 5:9

GREATEST

little child is the *g* .... Matt 18:4
but the *g* of these is ... 1 Cor 13:13

GREATNESS

is the exceeding *g* .... Eph 1:19

GREED

part is full of *g* ..... Luke 11:39

GREEDINESS

all uncleanness with *g* .. Eph 4:19

GREEDY

of everyone who is *g* ... Prov 1:19
not violent, not *g* ..... 1 Tim 3:3

GREEK

written in Hebrew, *G* ... John 19:20
and also for the *G* ...... Rom 1:16
is neither Jew not *G* .... Gal 3:28

GREEN

lie down in *g* pastures .... Ps 23:2

GRIEF

and acquainted with *g* ..... Is 53:3
joy and not with *g* ..... Heb 13:17

GRIEVE

g the Holy Spirit .... Eph 4:30

GRIEVED

earth, and He was *g* ..... Gen 6:6
g His Holy Spirit .... Is 63:10
with anger, being *g* ..... Mark 3:5

GROAN

even we ourselves *g* .... Rom 8:23
who are in this tent *g* ... 2 Cor 5:4

GROANING

I am weary with my *g* ..... Ps 6:6
Then Jesus, again *g* ... John 11:38

GROANINGS

g which cannot .... Rom 8:26

GROUND

"Cursed is the *g* .... Gen 3:17
you stand is holy *g* .... Ex 3:5
up your fallow *g* .... Jer 4:3
others fell on good *g* .... Matt 13:8
bought a piece of *g* ... Luke 14:18
God, the pillar and *g* .. 1 Tim 3:15

GROUNDED

being rooted and *g* ...... Eph 3:17

GROW

truth in love, may *g* ..... Eph 4:15
but *g* in the grace and .. 2 Pet 3:18

GRUDGINGLY

in his heart, not *g* ..... 2 Cor 9:7

GUARANTEE

in our hearts as a *g* .... 2 Cor 1:22
us the Spirit as a *g* .... 2 Cor 5:5
who is the *g* of our ..... Eph 1:14

GUIDE

He will be our *g* .... Ps 48:14
g our feet into the ..... Luke 1:79
has come, He will *g* ... John 16:13

GUIDES

to you, blind *g* .... Matt 23:16

GUILT

of your fathers' *g* ..... Matt 23:32

GUILTLESS

g who takes His name .... Ex 20:7
have condemned the *g* .. Matt 12:7

GUILTY

"We are truly *g* .... Gen 42:21
world may become *g* ... Rom 3:19
in one point, he is *g* ... James 2:10

GULF

you there is a great *g* . Luke 16:26

H

HABITATION

Is God in His holy *h* ...... Ps 68:5
but He blesses the *h* .... Prov 3:33
Jerusalem, a quiet *h* ..... Is 33:20
from His holy *h* .... Zech 2:13
be clothed with our *h* .. 2 Cor 5:2

HADES

be brought down to *H* . Matt 11:23
H shall not .... Matt 16:18
in torments in *H* ...... Luke 16:23
not leave my soul in H .. Acts 2:27
I have the keys of *H* ..... Rev 1:18
H were cast into the .... Rev 20:14

HAIL

of the plague of the *h* ... Rev 16:21

HAIR

you cannot make one *h* . Matt 5:36
"But not a *h* of your .. Luke 21:18
not with braided *h* ...... 1 Tim 2:9
h like women's *h* .... Rev 9:8

HAIRS

"But the very *h* ...... Matt 10:30

HALLOWED

the Sabbath day and *h* .. Ex 20:11
who is holy shall be *h* ..... Is 5:16
heaven, *H* be Your name . Matt 6:9

HAND

the *h* of God was ..... 1 Sam 5:11
My times are in Your *h* . Ps 31:15
"Sit at My right *h* .... Ps 110:1
heart is in the *h* .... Prov 21:1
Whatever your *h* ...... Eccl 9:10
is at his right *h* .... Eccl 10:2
do not withhold your *h* .. Eccl 11:6
My *h* has laid the .... Is 48:13
Behold, the LORD's *h* ..... Is 59:1
are the work of Your *h* .... Is 64:8
"Am I a God near at *h* .. Jer 23:23
of heaven is at *h* .... Matt 3:2
if your right *h* .... Matt 5:30
do not let your left *h* ..... Matt 6:3
h causes you to sin ... Mark 9:43
sitting at the right *h* .. Mark 14:62
at the right *h* of God .... Acts 7:55
The Lord is at *h* .... Phil 4:5
"Sit at My right *h* .... Heb 1:13
down at the right *h* .... Heb 10:12

HANDIWORK

firmament shows His *h* ... Ps 19:1

HANDLE

H Me and see .... Luke 24:39
do not taste, do not *h* .... Col 2:21

HANDLED

and our hands have *h* .. 1 John 1:1

HANDS

took his life in his *h* .... 1 Sam 19:5
but His *h* make whole ... Job 5:18
They pierced My *h* .... Ps 22:16
h formed the dry land .... Ps 95:5
than having two *h* ...... Matt 18:8
"Behold My *h* and .... Luke 24:39
h the print of the ...... John 20:25

his *h* what is good ...... Eph 4:28
the laying on of the *h* .. 1 Tim 4:14
to fall into the *h* .... Heb 10:31

HANDWRITING

having wiped out the *h* .. Col 2:14

HANGED

went and *h* himself ..... Matt 27:5

HANGS

h the earth on nothing ... Job 26:7
is everyone who h .... Gal 3:13

HAPPY

H is the man who has ... Ps 127:5

HARD

I knew you to be a *h* .. Matt 25:24
"This is a *h* saying .... John 6:60
are some things *h* ...... 2 Pet 3:16

HARDEN

But I will *h* his heart ..... Ex 4:21
h your hearts as* .... Heb 3:8

HARDENED

But Pharaoh *h* his .... Ex 8:32
their heart was *h* .... Mark 6:52
and h their hearts ..... John 12:40
lest any of you be *h* ..... Heb 3:13

HARDENS

whom He wills He *h* .... Rom 9:18

HARDSHIP

h as a good soldier ..... 2 Tim 2:3

HARLOT

of a *h* named Rahab ..... Josh 2:1
h is one body with ... 1 Cor 6:16
of the great *h* who ...... Rev 17:1

HARLOTRIES

Let her put away her *h* ... Hos 2:2

HARLOTRY

are the children of *h* ..... Hos 2:4
For the spirit of *h* .... Hos 5:4

HARLOTS

h enter the .... Matt 21:31
Great, The Mother of *H* . Rev 17:5

HARP

Lamb, each having a *h* ... Rev 5:8

HARPS

We hung our *h* Upon the . Ps 137:2

HARVEST

Seedtime and *h* .... Gen 8:22
"The *h* is past .... Jer 8:20
h truly is plentiful ..... Matt 9:37
sickle, because the *h* .. Mark 4:29
already white for *h* ..... John 4:35

HASTENS

and he sins who *h* ...... Prov 19:2

HASTILY

utter anything *h* .... Eccl 5:2

HASTY

Do you see a man *h* ... Prov 29:20

HATE

love the LORD, *h* evil ..... Ps 97:10
h every false way ..... Ps 119:104
h the double-minded ... Ps 119:113
I *h* and abhor lying .... Ps 119:163
love, And a time to *h* .... Eccl 3:8
You who *h* good and ..... Mic 3:2
either he will *h* .... Matt 6:24

HATED

But Esau I have h . . . . .Mal 1:3
"And you will be h . . . .Matt 10:22
have seen and also h . .John 15:24
but Esau I have h . . . . . .Rom 9:13
For no one ever h . . . . . .Eph 5:29

HATEFUL

h woman when she is . Prov 30:23
in malice and envy, h . . .Titus 3:3

HATERS

backbiters, h of God . . . .Rom 1:30

HATES

six things the LORD h . . . Prov 6:16
lose it, and he who h . .John 12:25
"If the world h . . . . . . .John 15:18
h his brother is . . . . . . .1 John 2:11

HAUGHTY

bring down h looks . . . . . .Ps 18:27
my heart is not h . . . . .Ps 131:1
h spirit before a fall . . .Prov 16:18

HEAD

He shall bruise your h . . .Gen 3:15
and gave Him to be h . . .Eph 1:22
For the husband is h . . . .Eph 5:23

HEAL

O LORD, h me . . . . .Ps 6:2
h your backslidings . . . .Jer 3:22
torn, but He will h . . . . . . .Hos 6:1
"H the sick . . . . .Matt 10:8
So that I should h . . . . .Matt 13:15
sent Me to h the . . . . . .Luke 4:18
Physician, h yourself . . .Luke 4:23

HEALED

And return and be h . . . . . .Is 6:10
His stripes we are h . . . . .Is 53:5
"When I would have h . . .Hos 7:1
and He h them . . . . .Matt 4:24
that you may be h . . . .James 5:16
his deadly wound was h .Rev 13:3

HEALING

shall arise With h . . . . .Mal 4:2
and h all kinds of . . . . . .Matt 4:23
tree were for the h . . . . . .Rev 22:2

HEALINGS

to another gifts of h . . .1 Cor 12:9

HEALS

h all your diseases . . . . . . .Ps 103:3
Jesus the Christ h . . . . . .Acts 9:34

HEALTH

all things and be in h . . . .3 John 2

HEAR

"H, O Israel . . . . .Deut 6:4
Him you shall h . . . . . . .Deut 18:15
H me when I call . . . . .Ps 4:1
O You who h prayer . . . . .Ps 65:2
ear, shall He not h . . . . . . .Ps 94:9
h rather than to give . . . . .Eccl 5:1
'Hearing you will h . . . .Matt 13:14
heed what you h . . . . . . .Mark 4:24
that God does not h . . . .John 9:31
And how shall they h . .Rom 10:14
man be swift to h . . . . .James 1:19
h what the Spirit says . . . .Rev 2:7

HEARD

h their cry because of . . . . .Ex 3:7
that they will be h . . . .Matt 6:7
h the word believed . . . . .Acts 4:4
not seen, nor ear h . . .1 Cor 2:9
things that you have h . .2 Tim 2:2
the word which they h . . .Heb 4:2

which we have h . . . . . .1 John 1:1
Lord's Day, and I h . . . . .Rev 1:10

HEARER

if anyone is a h . . . . . . .James 1:23

HEARERS

for not the h of the . . . .Rom 2:13
the word, and not h . . .James 1:22

HEARING

'Keep on h . . . . .Is 6:9
h they do not . . . . .Matt 13:13
h they may hear . . . . . .Mark 4:12
or by the h of faith . . . . . . .Gal 3:2

HEARS

out, and the LORD h . . . . . .Ps 34:17
of God h God's words . .John 8:47
"And if anyone h . . . . . .John 12:47
who is of the truth h . .John 18:37
He who knows God h . .1 John 4:6
And let him who h . . . . .Rev 22:17

HEART

h was only evil . . . . .Gen 6:5
h rejoices in the LORD . .1 Sam 2:1
gave him another h . . . .1 Sam 10:9
LORD looks at the h . . . .1 Sam 16:7
his wives turned his h . .1 Kin 11:4
He pierces my h . . . . . . .Job 16:13
My h also instructs me . . . .Ps 16:7
h is overflowing . . . . .Ps 45:1
h shall depart from me . .Ps 101:4
look and a proud h . . . . . .Ps 101:5
with my whole h . . . . . . .Ps 111:1
as he thinks in his h . . . .Prov 23:7
h reveals the man . . . . .Prov 27:19
trusts in his own h . . . .Prov 28:26
The h of the wise is . . . . .Eccl 7:4
And a wise man's h . . . . .Eccl 8:5
h yearned for him . . . . . .Song 5:4
And the whole h . . . . .Is 1:5
The yearning of Your h . .Is 63:15
h is deceitful above . . . . .Jer 17:9
I will give them a h . . . .Jer 24:7
and take the stony h . .Ezek 11:19
yourselves a new h . . . .Ezek 18:31
are the pure in h . . . . . . .Matt 5:8
is, there your h . . . . . . .Matt 6:21
of the h proceed evil . .Matt 15:19
h will flow rivers . . . . . .John 7:38
"Let not your h . . . . . . .John 14:1
Satan filled your h . . . . .Acts 5:3
h that God has raised . . .Rom 10:9
refresh my h in the . . . .Philem 20
and shuts up his h . . . .1 John 3:17

HEARTILY

you do, do it h . . . . .Col 3:23

HEARTS

God tests the h . . . . .Ps 7:9
And he will turn The h . . .Mal 4:6
h failing them from . . .Luke 21:26
will guard your h . . . . .Phil 4:7
of God rule in your h . . . .Col 3:15

HEATHEN

repetitions as the h . . . . . .Matt 6:7

HEAVEN

called the firmament H . . .Gen 1:8
LORD looks down from h . .Ps 14:2
word is settled in h . . . . .Ps 119:89
For God is in h . . . . .Eccl 5:2
"H is My throne . . . . .Is 66:1
for the kingdom of h . . . .Matt 3:2
your Father in h . . . . . . .Matt 5:16
On earth as it is in h . . . .Matt 6:10
"H and earth will . . . . . .Matt 24:35
Him a sign from h . . . . .Mark 8:11
have sinned against h . .Luke 15:18
you shall see h . . . . .John 1:51
one has ascended to h . .John 3:13

the true bread from h . . .John 6:32
a voice came from h . . .Luke 12:28
sheet, let down from h . .Acts 11:5
laid up for you in h . . . . . . .Col 1:5
there was silence in h . . .Rev 8:1
Now I saw a new h . . . . .Rev 21:1

HEAVENLY

your h Father will . . . . . .Matt 6:14
h host praising God . . . .Luke 2:13
if I tell you h things . . . .John 3:12
blessing in the h . . . . .Eph 1:3
a better, that is, a h . . . .Heb 11:16
the living God, the h . . .Heb 12:22

HEAVENS

and the highest h . . . . .Deut 10:14
h cannot contain . . . . . .1 Kin 8:27
h declare the glory . . . . . . .Ps 19:1
For as the h are high . . .Ps 103:11
behold, I create new h . . . .Is 65:17
and behold, the h . . . . . .Matt 3:16
h will be shaken . . . . . .Matt 24:29
h are the work of Your . .Heb 1:10
h will pass away . . . . . . .2 Pet 3:10

HEEDS

h counsel is wise . . . . . .Prov 12:15

HEEL

you shall bruise His h . . .Gen 3:15
has lifted up his h . . . . . . .Ps 41:9
Me has lifted up his h .John 13:18

HEIGHT

nor h nor depth . . . . .Rom 8:39
length and depth and h . .Eph 3:18

HEIR

He has appointed h . . . . . .Heb 1:2
world and became h . . . .Heb 11:7

HEIRS

if children, then h . . . . . .Rom 8:17
should be fellow h . . . . . . .Eph 3:6

HELL

shall be turned into h . . . . .Ps 9:17
go down alive into h . . . . .Ps 55:15
H and Destruction are . .Prov 27:20
be in danger of h fire . . .Matt 5:22
to be cast into h . . . . .Matt 18:9
condemnation of h . . . . .Matt 23:33
power to cast into h . . . .Luke 12:5

HELMET

And take the h of . . . . . . .Eph 6:17
and love, and as a h . . .1 Thess 5:8

HELP

May He send you h . . . . . . .Ps 20:2
A very present h . . . . .Ps 46:1
He is their h and . . . . .Ps 115:9
Our h is in the name . . . . .Ps 124:8
h my unbelief . . . . .Mark 9:24
and find grace to h . . . . . .Heb 4:16

HELPED

fall, but the LORD h . . . . .Ps 118:13
of salvation I have h . . . . .Is 49:8
h His servant Israel . . . .Luke 1:54

HELPER

I will make him a h . . . . .Gen 2:18
Behold, God is my h . . . . .Ps 54:4
give you another H . . . .John 14:16
"But when the H . . . . . .John 15:26
"The LORD is my h . . . . .Heb 13:6

HELPFUL

all things are not h . . . .1 Cor 6:12

HELPS

the Spirit also h . . . . .Rom 8:26

HEM

and touched the *h* . . . . . . Matt 9:20

HERE

Then I said, "*H* am I . . . . Is 6:8

HERESIES

dissensions, *h* . . . . Gal 5:20

HERITAGE

for that is his *h* . . . . Eccl 3:22
This is the *h* of the . . . . . . Is 54:17
of My people, My *h* . . . . . . Joel 3:2
The flock of Your *h* . . . . . Mic 7:14

HIDDEN

And my sins are not *h* . . . . Ps 69:5
Your word I have *h* . . . . . Ps 119:11
h that will not . . . . Matt 10:26
the *h* wisdom which . . . . 1 Cor 2:7
bring to light the *h* . . . . 1 Cor 4:5
have renounced the *h* . . 2 Cor 4:2
rather let it be the *h* . . . . 1 Pet 3:4
give some of the *h* . . . . . . Rev 2:17

HIDE

H me under the shadow . . Ps 17:8
You shall *h* them in . . . . . Ps 31:20
You *h* Your face . . . . Ps 104:29
darkness shall not *h* . . . . Ps 139:12
You are God, who *h* . . . . . Is 45:15
"Fall on us and *h* . . . . Rev 6:16

HIDES

He *h* His face . . . . Ps 10:11

HIDING

You are my *h* place . . . . Ps 32:7

HIGH

priest of God Most *H* . . Gen 14:18
For the LORD Most *H* . . . . . Ps 47:2
"I dwell in the *h* . . . . Is 57:15
know That the Most *H* . . Dan 4:17
up on a *h* mountain by . . Matt 17:1
your mind on *h* things . . Rom 12:16
h thing that exalts . . . . . 2 Cor 10:5
and faithful *H* Priest . . . . Heb 2:17

HIGHER

you, 'Friend, go up *h* . . Luke 14:10

HIGHWAY

in the desert A *h* . . . . Is 40:3

HIGHWAYS

h shall be elevated . . . . Is 49:11
go into the *h* . . . . Matt 22:9

HILL

My King on My holy *h* . . . . . Ps 2:6
h cannot be hidden . . . . . Matt 5:14
and h brought low . . . . . . Luke 3:5

HILLS

of the everlasting *h* . . . . Gen 49:26
of the *h* are His also . . . . . . Ps 95:4
up my eyes to the *h* . . . . . Ps 121:1

HINDER

all things lest we *h* . . . . 1 Cor 9:12

HINDERED

Who *h* you from obeying . Gal 5:7
prayers may not be *h* . . . . 1 Pet 3:7

HOLD

right hand shall *h* . . . . . . Ps 139:10
h fast that word . . . . 1 Cor 15:2
h fast and repent . . . . Rev 3:3

HOLIER

near me, For I am *h* . . . . . . Is 65:5

HOLIEST

the way into the *H* . . . . . . Heb 9:8

HOLINESS

You, glorious in *h* . . . . . . Ex 15:11
I have sworn by My *h* . . . Ps 89:35
the Highway of *H* . . . . Is 35:8
to the Spirit of *h* . . . . Rom 1:4
spirit, perfecting *h* . . . . . . 2 Cor 7:1
uncleanness, but in *h* . 1 Thess 4:7
be partakers of His *h* . . Heb 12:10

HOLY

where you stand is *h* . . . . . Ex 3:5
day, to keep it *h* . . . . Ex 20:8
LORD your God am *h* . . . Lev 19:2
h seed is mixed . . . . Ezra 9:2
God sits on His *h* . . . . Ps 47:8
God, in His *h* mountain . . Ps 48:1
"*H, h, h* . . . . Is 6:3
child of the *H* Spirit . . . . Matt 1:18
baptize you with the *H* . . Mark 1:8
who speak, but the *H* . Mark 13:11
H Spirit will come . . . . . Luke 1:35
H Spirit descended . . . . Luke 3:22
Father give the *H* . . . . Luke 11:13
H Spirit will teach . . . . Luke 12:12
H Spirit was not . . . . John 7:39
H Spirit has come . . . . . . Acts 1:8
all filled with the *H* . . . . . Acts 2:4
receive the *H* Spirit . . . . Acts 19:2
joy in the *H* . . . . Rom 14:17
H Spirit teaches . . . . . . 1 Cor 2:13
that we should be *h* . . . . . Eph 1:4
were sealed with the *H* . . Eph 1:13
partakers of the *H* . . . . . . Heb 6:4
H Spirit sent from . . . . . 1 Pet 1:12
it is written, "*Be h* . . . . . 1 Pet 1:16
moved by the *H* Spirit . 2 Pet 1:21
anointing from the *H* . 1 John 2:20
says He who is *h* . . . . Rev 3:7
For You alone are *h* . . . . Rev 15:4
is *h*, let him be *h* . . . . . . Rev 22:11

HOME

sparrow has found a *h* . . Ps 84:3
to his eternal *h* . . . . Eccl 12:5
that while we are at *h* . . 2 Cor 5:6
to show piety at *h* . . . . . . 1 Tim 5:4

HOMEMAKERS

be discreet, chaste, *h* . . . . Titus 2:5

HONEY

and with *h* from the . . . . . Ps 81:16
was locusts and wild *h* . . . Matt 3:4

HONEYCOMB

than honey and the *h* . . . . Ps 19:10
fish and some *h* . . . . Luke 24:42

HONOR

"*H* your father and your . Ex 20:12
will deliver him and *h* . . . Ps 91:15
H and majesty are . . . . Ps 96:6
H the LORD with your . . . . Prov 3:9
before is *h* humility . . . . Prov 15:33
spirit will retain *h* . . . . . Prov 29:23
Father, where is My *h* . . . . Mal 1:6
is not without *h* . . . . Matt 13:57
'*H* your father and . . . . . . Matt 15:4
h the Son just as they . . John 5:23
"I do not receive *h* . . . . . John 5:41
but I *h* My Father . . . . . . John 8:49
"If I *h* Myself . . . . John 8:54
him My Father will *h* . . John 12:26
to whom fear, *h* . . . . Rom 13:7
sanctification and *h* . . 1 Thess 4:4
alone is wise, be *h* . . . . . 1 Tim 1:17
and clay, some for *h* . . . 2 Tim 2:20
no man takes this *h* . . . . . Heb 5:4
from God the Father *h* . 2 Pet 1:17
give glory and *h* . . . . Rev 4:9

HONORABLE

His work is *h* and . . . . Ps 111:3
holy day of the LORD *h* . . Is 58:13
providing *h* things . . . . . 2 Cor 8:21
Marriage is *h* among . . . . Heb 13:4
having your conduct *h* . 1 Pet 2:12

HONORS

'This people *h* Me . . . . . . Mark 7:6
It is My Father who *h* . . John 8:54

HOPE

h He has uprooted . . . . . Job 19:10
also will rest in *h* . . . . Ps 16:9
My *h* is in You . . . . Ps 39:7
For You are my *h* . . . . Ps 71:5
I *h* in Your word . . . . . . Ps 119:147
good that one should *h* . Lam 3:26
to *h*, in *h* believed . . . . . Rom 4:18
h does not disappoint . . . Rom 5:5
were saved in this *h* . . . . Rom 8:24
now abide faith, *h* . . . . 1 Cor 13:13
life only we have *h* . . . . 1 Cor 15:19
may know what is the *h* . Eph 1:18
were called in one *h* . . . . . Eph 4:4
Christ in you, the *h* . . . . . Col 1:27
Jesus Christ, our *h* . . . . . 1 Tim 1:1
for the blessed *h* . . . . . . Titus 2:13
to lay hold of the *h* . . . . . Heb 6:18
in of a better *h* . . . . Heb 7:19
who has this *h* in Him . 1 John 3:3

HOPED

substance of things *h* . . . . Heb 11:1

HORSE

and behold, a white *h* . . . . Rev 6:2
and behold, a white *h* . . Rev 19:11

HOSANNA

H in the highest . . . . Matt 21:9

HOSPITABLE

Be *h* to one another . . . . . 1 Pet 4:9

HOSTS

The LORD of *h* is with . . . . . Ps 46:7
Praise Him, all His *h* . . . . Ps 148:2
against spiritual *h* . . . . . . Eph 6:12

HOUR

is coming at an *h* . . . . . . Matt 24:44
"But the *h* is coming . . . John 4:23
save Me from this *h* . . . John 12:27
keep you from the *h* . . . . . Rev 3:10

HOUSE

as for me and my *h* . . . . Josh 24:15
Through wisdom a *h* . . . Prov 24:3
better to go to the *h* . . . . . Eccl 7:2
h was filled with . . . . Is 6:4
h divided against . . . . . Matt 12:25
h shall be called a . . . . . Matt 21:13
make My Father's *h* . . . . John 2:16
h are many mansions . . . John 14:2
publicly and from *h* . . . . Acts 20:20
who rules his own *h* . . . . 1 Tim 3:4
the church in your *h* . . . . Philem 2
For every *h* is built . . . . . . Heb 3:4
His own *h*, whose *h* . . . . . Heb 3:6

HOUSEHOLD

the ways of her *h* . . . . . Prov 31:27
be those of his own h . . Matt 10:36
h were baptized . . . . Acts 16:15
saved, you and your *h* . Acts 16:31
who are of Caesar's *h* . . Phil 4:22

HOUSEHOLDER

h who brings out of . . . Matt 13:52

HOUSES

H and riches are an . . . Prov 19:14
who has left *h* or . . . . . Matt 19:29
you devour widows' *h* . Matt 23:14

HOVERING

Spirit of God was *h* ......Gen 1:2

HUMBLE

man Moses was very *h* . Num 12:3
the cry of the *h* ....Ps 9:12
h shall hear of it and .....Ps 34:2
contrite and *h* spirit ......Is 57:15
A meek and *h* people ...Zeph 3:12
associate with the *h* ...Rom 12:16
gives grace to the *h* ....James 4:6
H yourselves in the ....James 4:10
gives grace to the *h* .....1 Pet 5:5
h yourselves under the ..1 Pet 5:6

HUMBLED

as a man, He *h* Himself ...Phil 2:8

HUMBLES

h Himself to behold .....Ps 113:6

HUMILITY

the Lord with all *h* ....Acts 20:19
delight in false *h* ....Col 2:18
mercies, kindness, *h* .....Col 3:12
h correcting those .....2 Tim 2:25
gentle, showing all *h* ....Titus 3:2
and be clothed with *h* ...1 Pet 5:5

HUNGER

They shall neither *h* ......Is 49:10
are those who *h* ....Matt 5:6
for you shall *h* ....Luke 6:25
to Me shall never *h* ....John 6:35
hour we both *h* ....1 Cor 4:11
"They shall neither *h* ....Rev 7:16

HUNGRY

and fills the *h* ....Ps 107:9
gives food to the *h* ......Ps 146:7
'for I was *h* and you ...Matt 25:35
did we see You *h* ......Matt 25:37
to be full and to be *h* ....Phil 4:12

HUNTER

Nimrod the mighty *h* ....Gen 10:9
Esau was a skillful *h* ...Gen 25:27

HURT

h a woman with child ...Ex 21:22
but I was not *h* ....Prov 23:35
another to his own *h* .....Eccl 8:9
They shall not *h* ....Is 11:9
it will by no means *h* . Mark 16:18
shall not be *h* by the ....Rev 2:11

HUSBAND

She also gave to her *h* ....Gen 3:6
h safely trusts her ....Prov 31:11
your Maker is your *h* .....Is 54:5
now have is not your *h* . John 4:18
you will save your *h* ...1 Cor 7:16
the *h* of one wife ......1 Tim 3:2

HUSBANDS

H, love your wives ......Eph 5:25
Let deacons be the *h* ..1 Tim 3:12

HYMN

they had sung a *h* .....Matt 26:30

HYMNS

praying and singing *h* .Acts 16:25
in psalms and *h* ....Eph 5:19

HYPOCRISY

you are full of *h* ......Matt 23:28
Pharisees, which is *h* ..Luke 12:1
Let love be without *h* ..Rom 12:9
away with their *h* ......Gal 2:13
and without *h* ....James 3:17
malice, all deceit, *h* .....1 Pet 2:1

HYPOCRITE

and the joy of the *h* .....Job 20:5
For everyone is a *h* ....Is 9:17
also played the *h* ....Gal 2:13

HYPOCRITES

not be like the *h* ....Matt 6:5
do you test Me, you *h* . Matt 22:18
and Pharisees, *h* ......Matt 23:13

I

IDLE

i person will suffer ....Prov 19:15
i word men may ......Matt 12:36
saw others standing *i* ...Matt 20:3
they learn to be *i* ......1 Tim 5:13

IDOL

thing offered to an *i* ....1 Cor 8:7
That an *i* is anything . 1 Cor 10:19

IDOLATER

or covetous, or an *i* ....1 Cor 5:11

IDOLATERS

fornicators, nor *i* ....1 Cor 6:9
and murderers and *i* ....Rev 22:15

IDOLATRIES

and abominable *i* ....1 Pet 4:3

IDOLATRY

beloved, flee from *i* ...1 Cor 10:14
i, sorcery ....Gal 5:20

IDOLS

land is also full of *i* ....Is 2:8
in the room of his *i* ....Ezek 8:12
who regard worthless *i* ...Jon 2:8
You who abhor *i* ......Rom 2:22
yourselves from *i* .....1 John 5:21
worship demons, and *i* ..Rev 9:20

IGNORANCE

that you did it in *i* ......Acts 3:17
i God overlooked ......Acts 17:30
sins committed in *i* ......Heb 9:7

IGNORANTLY

because I did it *i* ......1 Tim 1:13

ILLUMINATED

after you were *i* ....Heb 10:32
and the earth was *i* ......Rev 18:1
for the glory of God *i* ...Rev 21:23

IMAGE

Us make man in Our *i* ...Gen 1:26
since he is the *i* ....1 Cor 11:7
He is the *i* of the ....Col 1:15
and not the very *i* ....Heb 10:1
the beast and his *i* ......Rev 14:9

IMAGINATION

the proud in the *i* .....Luke 1:51

IMITATE

as I also *i* Christ ....1 Cor 11:1

IMMANUEL

shall call His name I ......Is 7:14
shall call His name I ....Matt 1:23

IMMORAL

murderers, sexually *i* ...Rev 21:8

IMMORALITY

except sexual *i* ....Matt 5:32
abstain from sexual *i* . 1 Thess 4:3

IMMORTAL

to the King eternal, *i* ...1 Tim 1:17

IMMORTALITY

mortal must put on *i* ..1 Cor 15:53
who alone has *i* ....1 Tim 6:16

IMMOVABLE

be steadfast, *i* ....1 Cor 15:58

IMMUTABLE

that by two *i* things .....Heb 6:18

IMPART

that it may *i* grace ......Eph 4:29

IMPENITENT

i heart you are ....Rom 2:5

IMPOSSIBLE

God nothing will be *i* ...Luke 1:37
without faith it is *i* ......Heb 11:6

IMPUTE

the LORD does not *i* ....Ps 32:2

IMPUTED

might be *i* to them .....Rom 4:11
but sin is not *i* ....Rom 5:13

IMPUTES

i righteousness apart ....Rom 4:6

INCORRUPTIBLE

the glory of the *i* ......Rom 1:23
dead will be raised *i* . 1 Cor 15:52
to an inheritance *i* ......1 Pet 1:4

INCORRUPTION

corruption inherit *i* ...1 Cor 15:50

INCREASE

Of the *i* of His ....Is 9:7
Lord, "I our faith ......Luke 17:5
"He must *i* ....John 3:30
but God gave the *i* ......1 Cor 3:6

INCREASES

who have no might He *i* ..Is 40:29

INCURABLE

Your sorrow is *i* ....Jer 30:15

INDIGNATION

i which will devour ....Heb 10:27
into the cup of His *i* ....Rev 14:10

INEXCUSABLE

Therefore you are *i* ......Rom 2:1

INEXPRESSIBLE

Paradise and heard *i* ...2 Cor 12:4
you rejoice with joy *i* ....1 Pet 1:8

INFALLIBLE

suffering by many *i* .....Acts 1:3

INFIRMITIES

"He Himself took our *i* ..Matt 8:17

INHERIT

love me to *i* wealth .....Prov 8:21
i the kingdom ....Matt 25:34
unrighteous will not *i* ...1 Cor 6:9
who overcomes shall *i* ...Rev 21:7

INHERITANCE

"You shall have no *i* ..Num 18:20
is the place of His *i* .....Deut 32:9
the portion of my *i* ......Ps 16:5
i shall be forever ....Ps 37:18
He will choose our *i* .....Ps 47:4
will arise to your *i* ....Dan 12:13
God gave him no *i* ......Acts 7:5
and give you an *i* ......Acts 20:32
For if the *i* is of the ......Gal 3:18
we have obtained an *i* ...Eph 1:11

INIQUITIES
be partakers of the *i* .....Col 1:12
receive as an *i* ....Heb 11:8
i incorruptible ....1 Pet 1:4

INIQUITIES
i have overtaken me .....Ps 40:12
forgives all your *i* ....Ps 103:3
LORD, should mark *i* .....Ps 130:3
was bruised for our *i* ......Is 53:5
He shall bear their *i* ......Is 53:11
i have separated you ....Is 59:2

INIQUITY
God, visiting the *i* of the ..Ex 20:5
was brought forth in *i* ....Ps 51:5
If I regard *i* in my .....Ps 66:18
i have dominion ....Ps 119:133
i will reap sorrow ......Prov 22:8
A people laden with *i* ....Is 1:4
i is taken away.............Is 6:7
has laid on Him the *i* ......Is 53:6
will remember their *i* .....Hos 9:9
to those who devise *i* ....Mic 2:1
like You, Pardoning *i* ....Mic 7:18
all you workers of *i* ...Luke 13:27
a fire, a world of *i* ......James 3:6

INJUSTICE
i have your fathers ....Jer 2:5

INN
room for them in the *i* ...Luke 2:7
brought him to an *i* ...Luke 10:34

INNOCENCE
washed my hands in *i* ..Ps 73:13

INNOCENT
because I was found *i* ...Dan 6:22
saying, "I am *i* ....Matt 27:24
this day that I am *i* ....Acts 20:26

INQUIRED
Therefore David *i* .....1 Sam 23:2
the prophets have *i* ....1 Pet 1:10

INQUIRY
shall make careful *i* ...Deut 19:18

INSANE
images, And they are *i* ..Jer 50:38

INSPIRATION
is given by *i* of God ...2 Tim 3:16

INSTRUCT
I will *i* you and teach .....Ps 32:8
LORD that he may *i* ....1 Cor 2:16

INSTRUCTED
This man had been *i* ...Acts 18:25
are excellent, being *i* ...Rom 2:18
Moses was divinely *i* .....Heb 8:5

INSTRUCTION
seeing you hate *i* ....Ps 50:17
Hear *i* and be wise ....Prov 8:33
Give *i* to a wise man .....Prov 9:9
for correction, for *i* ....2 Tim 3:16

INSTRUCTS
My heart also *i* ....Ps 16:7

INSTRUMENTS
your members as *i* .....Rom 6:13

INSUBORDINATE
for the lawless and *i* ....1 Tim 1:9

INSUBORDINATION
of dissipation or *i* ....Titus 1:6

INSULTED
will be mocked and *i* ..Luke 18:32
i the Spirit of grace ....Heb 10:29

INSULTS
nor be afraid of their *i* .....Is 51:7

INTEGRITY
In the *i* of my heart .....Gen 20:5
in doctrine showing *i* ....Titus 2:7

INTERCEDE
the LORD, who will *i* ...1 Sam 2:25

INTERCESSION
of many, And made *i* .....Is 53:12
Spirit Himself makes *i* ..Rom 8:26
always lives to make *i* ...Heb 7:25

INTERCESSOR
that there was no *i* ....Is 59:16

INTEREST
collected it with *i* .....Luke 19:23

INTERPRET
Do all *i*? ....1 Cor 12:30
pray that he may *i* ....1 Cor 14:13

INTERPRETATION
to another the *i* ....1 Cor 12:10
of any private *i* ....2 Pet 1:20

INTERPRETATIONS
"Do not *i* belong to .....Gen 40:8

INVISIBLE
of the world His *i* ....Rom 1:20
is the image of the *i* .....Col 1:15
eternal, immortal, *i* ....1 Tim 1:17
as seeing Him who is *i* ..Heb 11:27

INWARD
You have formed my *i* ..Ps 139:13
God according to the *i* ..Rom 7:22
i man is being ....2 Cor 4:16

INWARDLY
i they are ....Matt 7:15
is a Jew who is one *i* ...Rom 2:29

IRON
i sharpens *i* ....Prov 27:17
its feet partly of *i* ......Dan 2:33

ISRAEL
"Hear, O *I* ....Deut 6:4
For they are not all *I* ....Rom 9:6
and upon the *I* of God ...Gal 6:16

ITCHING
they have *i* ears ....2 Tim 4:3

J

JEALOUS
God, am a *j* God ....Ex 20:5
a consuming fire, a *j* ....Deut 4:24
For I am *j* for you .....2 Cor 11:2

JEALOUSY
provoked Him to *j* ....Deut 32:16
as strong as death, *j* .....Song 8:6
for you with godly *j* ...2 Cor 11:2

JEOPARDY
stand in *j* every hour .1 Cor 15:30

JESTING
talking, nor coarse *j* ......Eph 5:4

JESUS
J Christ was as ....Matt 1:18
shall call His name *J* ....Matt 1:21
J was led up by the .....Matt 4:1
and laid hands on *J* .....Matt 26:50

and destroy *J* ....Matt 27:20
J withdrew with His ....Mark 3:7
J went into ....Mark 11:11
they were eating, *J* ...Mark 14:22
and he delivered *J* ...Mark 15:15
truth came through *J* ...John 1:17
J lifted up His eyes .....John 6:5
J wept ....John 11:35
J was crucified ....John 19:20
"This *J* God has raised ..Acts 2:32
of Your holy Servant *J* .Acts 4:30
believed on the Lord *J* .Acts 11:17
your mouth the Lord *J* ..Rom 10:9
among you except *J* ....1 Cor 2:2
perfect in Christ *J* ....Col 1:28
But we see *J* ....Heb 2:9
looking unto *J* ....Heb 12:2
Revelation of *J* Christ ....Rev 1:1
so, come, Lord *J* ......Rev 22:20

JOIN
of the rest dared *j* ......Acts 5:13

JOINED
and mother and be *j* ....Gen 2:24
what God has *j* ....Matt 19:6
the whole body, *j* ....Eph 4:16

JOINT
j as He wrestled ....Gen 32:25
My bones are out of *j* ....Ps 22:14
j heirs with Christ ......Rom 8:17

JOINTS
and knit together by *j* ....Col 2:19
and spirit, and of *j* ......Heb 4:12

JOT
one *j* or one tittle ....Matt 5:18

JOY
is fullness of *j* ....Ps 16:11
j comes in the morning ...Ps 30:5
j you will draw ....Is 12:3
ashes, The oil of *j* ....Is 61:3
shall sing for *j* ....Is 65:14
receives it with *j* ......Matt 13:20
Enter into the *j* ......Matt 25:21
in my womb for *j* ......Luke 1:44
there will be more *j* ....Luke 15:7
did not believe for *j* ...Luke 24:41
My *j* may remain in ...John 15:11
they may have My *j* ...John 17:13
the Spirit is love, *j* ......Gal 5:22
are our glory and *j* ..1 Thess 2:20
j that was set before ....Heb 12:2
count it all *j* ....James 1:2
with exceeding *j* ....1 Pet 4:13

JOYFUL
Make a *j* shout to the ....Ps 100:1
And make them *j* ....Is 56:7

JUDGE
The LORD *j* between .....Gen 16:5
coming to *j* the earth .1 Chr 16:33
sword The LORD will *j* ...Is 66:16
deliver you to the *j* ......Matt 5:25
"*J* not ....Matt 7:1
who made Me a *j* .....Luke 12:14
j who did not fear God .Luke 18:2
As I hear, I *j* ....John 5:30
"Do not *j* according ...John 7:24
I *j* no one ....John 8:15
j the world but to .....John 12:47
this, O man, who *j* ...Rom 2:3
Therefore let us not *j* ..Rom 14:13
Christ, who will *j* ....2 Tim 4:1
But if you *j* the law ...James 4:11

JUDGES
He makes the *j* of the ....Is 40:23
For the Father *j* ....John 5:22
he who is spiritual *j* ...1 Cor 2:15
j me is the Lord ....1 Cor 4:4
Him who *j* righteously ..1 Pet 2:23

JUDGMENT

Teach me good *j* . . . . Ps 119:66
from prison and from *j* . . . . Is 53:8
be in danger of the *j* . . . . Matt 5:21
shall not come into *j* . . . . John 5:24
and My *j* is righteous . . . John 5:30
if I do judge, My *j* . . . . . John 8:16
"Now is the *j* . . . . John 12:31
the righteous *j* . . . . Rom 1:32
j which came from one . Rom 5:16
appear before the *j* . . 2 Cor 5:10
after this the *j* . . . . Heb 9:27
time has come for *j* . . . . 1 Pet 4:17
a long time their *j* . . . . 2 Pet 2:3
darkness for the *j* . . . . Jude 6

JUDGMENTS

The *j* of the LORD are . . Ps 19:9
unsearchable are His *j* . Rom 11:33

JUST

Noah was a *j* man . . . . Gen 6:9
j man who perishes . . . . . Eccl 7:15
j shall live by his . . . . Hab 2:4
her husband, being a *j* . . Matt 1:19
resurrection of the *j* . . . Luke 14:14
j persons who need no . Luke 15:7
the Holy One and the *J* . Acts 3:14
dead, both of the *j* . . . . . Acts 24:15
j shall live by faith . . . . . Rom 1:17
that He might be *j* . . . . . Rom 3:26
j men made perfect . . . . Heb 12:23
have murdered the *j* . . . . James 5:6
He is faithful and *j* . . . . 1 John 1:9

JUSTICE

j as the noonday . . . . Ps 37:6
And Your poor with *j* . . . . . Ps 72:2
j the measuring line . . . . . Is 28:17
the LORD is a God of *j* . . Is 30:18
He will bring forth *j* . . . . . . Is 42:1
J is turned back . . . . Is 59:14
I, the LORD, love *j* . . . . . . Is 61:8
truth, and His ways *j* . . . . Dan 4:37
'Execute true *j* . . . . Zech 7:9
"Where is the God of *j* . . Mal 2:17
And He will declare j . . Matt 12:18
His humiliation His j . . . . Acts 8:33

JUSTIFICATION

because of our *j* . . . . Rom 4:25
offenses resulted in *j* . . . Rom 5:16

JUSTIFIED

Me that you may be *j* . . . . Job 40:8
words you will be *j* . . . . Matt 12:37
"But wisdom is *j* . . . . . . Luke 7:35
j rather than the . . . . . . Luke 18:14
who believes is *j* . . . . . . Acts 13:39
"That You may be j . . . . . . Rom 3:4
law no flesh will be *j* . . . Rom 3:20
j freely by His grace . . . . Rom 3:24
having been *j* by . . . . Rom 5:1
these He also *j* . . . . Rom 8:30
that we might be *j* . . . . . . Gal 2:16
no flesh shall be *j* . . . . . . Gal 2:16
the harlot also *j* . . . . . . James 2:25

JUSTIFIES

He who *j* the wicked . . . Prov 17:15
It is God who *j* . . . . Rom 8:33

JUSTIFY

wanting to *j* himself . . . Luke 10:29
"You are those who *j* . Luke 16:15
is one God who will *j* . . . Rom 3:30

K

KEEP

k you wherever you . . . . Gen 28:15
day, to *k* it holy . . . . Ex 20:8

Let all the earth *k* . . . . . . Hab 2:20
k the commandments . . Matt 19:17
"If you love Me, *k* . . . . John 14:15
k through Your name . . John 17:11
orderly and *k* the law . . Acts 21:24
k the unity of the . . . . Eph 4:3
k His commandments . . 1 John 2:3

KEEPER

Am I my brother's *k* . . . . . Gen 4:9
The LORD is your *k* . . . . . Ps 121:5

KEEPS

k truth forever . . . . Ps 146:6
k the commandment . . . Prov 19:16
none of you *k* the law . . John 7:19
born of God *k* . . . . 1 John 5:18
and *k* his garments . . . . Rev 16:15

KEPT

For I have *k* the . . . . . 2 Sam 22:22
these things I have *k* . . Matt 19:20
love, just as I have *k* . . John 15:10
k back part of the . . . . . . Acts 5:2
I have *k* the faith . . . . . . 2 Tim 4:7
who are *k* by the power . 1 Pet 1:5

KEY

taken away the *k* . . . . Luke 11:52
"He who has the k . . . . Rev 3:7

KEYS

I will give you the *k* . . . Matt 16:19
And I have the *k* . . . . Rev 1:18

KILL

k the Passover . . . . Ex 12:21
I *k* and I make alive . . Deut 32:39
"Am I God, to *k* . . . . . . 2 Kin 5:7
A time to *k* . . . . Eccl 3:3
of them they will *k* . . . . Luke 11:49
afraid of those who *k* . . Luke 12:4
Why do you seek to *k* . . John 7:19
k and eat . . . . Acts 10:13

KILLED

Abel his brother and *k* . . Gen 4:8
for Your sake we are *k* . . Ps 44:22
and scribes, and be *k* . . Matt 16:21
Siloam fell and *k* them . Luke 13:4
k the Prince of life . . . . . Acts 3:15
Your sake we are k . . . . Rom 8:36
k both the Lord . . . . . 1 Thess 2:15

KILLS

the one who *k* the . . . . Matt 23:37
for the letter *k* . . . . 2 Cor 3:6

KIND

animals after their *k* . . . . Gen 6:20
k can come out by . . . . . . Mark 9:29
suffers long and is *k* . . . 1 Cor 13:4
And be *k* to one . . . . Eph 4:32

KINDLY

Julius treated Paul *k* . . . Acts 27:3
k affectionate to one . . . Rom 12:10

KINDNESS

For His merciful *k* . . . . . . Ps 117:2
k shall not depart . . . . Is 54:10
I remember you, The *k* . . . Jer 2:2
by longsuffering, by *k* . . 2 Cor 6:6
longsuffering, *k* . . . . Gal 5:22
and to brotherly *k* . . . . . 2 Pet 1:7

KING

"Yet I have set My *K* . . . . Ps 2:6
The LORD is *K* forever . . . . Ps 10:16
And the *K* of glory . . . . . . Ps 24:7
For God is my *K* . . . . . . Ps 74:12
when your *k* is a child . Eccl 10:16
and the everlasting *K* . . Jer 10:10
the LORD shall be *K* . . . . Zech 14:9
who has been born *K* . . . . Matt 2:2

This Is Jesus The *K* . . . . Matt 27:37
"Behold your *K* . . . . John 19:14
Now to the *K* eternal . . 1 Tim 1:17
only Potentate, the *K* . . 1 Tim 6:15
this Melchizedek, *k* . . . . . . Heb 7:1
K of Kings and Lord . . . Rev 19:16

KINGDOM

Yours is the *k* . . . . 1 Chr 29:11
k is the LORD's . . . . Ps 22:28
the scepter of Your *k* . . . . . Ps 45:6
is an everlasting *k* . . . . . Ps 145:13
k which shall never be . . Dan 2:44
High rules in the *k* . . . . . . Dan 4:17
"Repent, for the *k* . . . . . . Matt 3:2
for Yours is the *k* . . . . . . Matt 6:13
"But seek first the *k* . . . Matt 6:33
the mysteries of the *k* . Matt 13:11
are the sons of the *k* . . . Matt 13:38
of such is the *k* . . . . Matt 19:14
back, is fit for the *k* . . . Luke 9:62
against nation, and *k* . . Luke 21:10
he cannot see the *k* . . . . . John 3:3
he cannot enter the *k* . . . John 3:5
If My *k* were of this . . . John 18:36
for the *k* of God is . . . . Rom 14:17
will not inherit the *k* . . . Gal 5:21
the scepter of Your k . . . . Heb 1:8
we are receiving a *k* . . . Heb 12:28

KINGDOMS

the *k* were moved . . . . Ps 46:6
showed Him all the *k* . . . . Matt 4:8
have become the *k* . . . . . Rev 11:15

KINGS

The *k* of the earth set . . . . . . Ps 2:2
By me *k* reign . . . . Prov 8:15
governors and *k* . . . . . . Matt 10:18
k have desired to see . . Luke 10:24
You have reigned as *k* . . 1 Cor 4:8
and has made us *k* . . . . . . Rev 1:6
that the way of the *k* . . . Rev 16:12

KISS

K the Son . . . . Ps 2:12
"You gave Me no *k* . . . . Luke 7:45
one another with a *k* . . . 1 Pet 5:14

KISSED

they *k* one another . . . 1 Sam 20:41
and *k* Him . . . . Matt 26:49
and she *k* His feet and . Luke 7:38

KNEE

That to Me every *k* . . . . Is 45:23
have not bowed the k . . . Rom 11:4
of Jesus every *k* . . . . Phil 2:10

KNEES

make firm the feeble *k* . . . . Is 35:3
this reason I bow my *k* . . Eph 3:14
and the feeble *k* . . . . . . Heb 12:12

KNEW

in the womb I *k* . . . . Jer 1:5
to them, 'I never *k* . . . . . . Matt 7:23
k what was in man . . . . . John 2:25
He made Him who *k* . . . 2 Cor 5:21

KNIT

be encouraged, being *k* . . . Col 2:2

KNOCK

k, and it will be . . . . Matt 7:7
at the door and *k* . . . . . . Rev 3:20

KNOW

k good and evil . . . . Gen 3:22
k that I am the LORD . . . . . . Ex 6:7
k that my Redeemer . . . . Job 19:25
make me to *k* wisdom . . . . Ps 51:6
Who can *k* it . . . . Jer 17:9
saying, 'K the LORD . . . Jer 31:34
k what hour your . . . . . Matt 24:42

KNOWLEDGE

an oath, "I do not *k* ...Matt 26:72
the world did not *k* ...John 1:10
We speak what We *k* ...John 3:11
k that You are ....John 6:69
My voice, and I *k* .....John 10:27
If you *k* these things ..John 13:17
k whom I have ....John 13:18
are sure that You *k* ....John 16:30
k that I love You ...John 21:15
k times or seasons ....Acts 1:7
and said, "Jesus I *k* ...Acts 19:15
wisdom did not *k* ......1 Cor 1:21
nor can he *k* them .....1 Cor 2:14
For we *k* in part and ...1 Cor 13:9
k the love of Christ .....Eph 3:19
k whom I have ....2 Tim 1:12
we *k* that we *k* Him ..1 John 2:3
and you *k* all things ..1 John 2:20
By this we *k* love .....1 John 3:16
k that He abides .....1 John 3:24
k that we are of God ..1 John 5:19
"I *k* your works ....Rev 2:2

KNOWLEDGE

and the tree of the *k* .....Gen 2:9
unto night reveals *k* .....Ps 19:2
k is too wonderful ....Ps 139:6
people store up *k* ......Prov 10:14
k spares his words .....Prov 17:27
and he who increases *k* .Eccl 1:18
k is that wisdom ....Eccl 7:12
k shall increase ....Dan 12:4
more accurate *k* ....Acts 24:22
having the form of *k* ...Rom 2:20
law is the *k* of sin .....Rom 3:20
whether there is *k* .....1 Cor 13:8
Christ which passes *k* ...Eph 3:19
is falsely called *k* .....1 Tim 6:20
in the grace and *k* .....2 Pet 3:18

KNOWN

If you had *k* Me ....John 8:19
My sheep, and am *k* ...John 10:14
The world has not *k* ...John 17:25
peace they have not k ..Rom 3:17
"For who has *k* ....Rom 11:34
after you have *k* ....Gal 4:9
requests be made *k* .....Phil 4:6
k the Holy Scriptures ..2 Tim 3:15

KNOWS

"For God *k* that in ....Gen 3:5
k what is in the ....Dan 2:22
k the things you have ....Matt 6:8
and hour no one *k* ....Matt 24:36
God *k* your hearts ....Luke 16:15
searches the hearts *k* ...Rom 8:27
k the things of God ....1 Cor 2:11
k those who are His ....2 Tim 2:19
to him who *k* to do ....James 4:17
and *k* all things ......1 John 3:20

L

LABOR

Six days you shall *l* ......Ex 20:9
things are full of *l* ....Eccl 1:8
has man for all his *l* ....Eccl 2:22
He shall see the *l* ....Is 53:11
to Me, all you who *l* ...Matt 11:28
"Do not *l* for the .....John 6:27
knowing that your *l* ..1 Cor 15:58
but rather let him *l* .....Eph 4:28
mean fruit from my *l* ...Phil 1:22
your work of faith, *l* ..1 Thess 1:3
forget your work and *l* ..Heb 6:10
your works, your *l* ....Rev 2:2

LABORED

l more abundantly ....1 Cor 15:10
for you, lest I have *l* .....Gal 4:11

LABORERS

but the *l* are few ....Matt 9:37

LABORING

l night and day ....1 Thess 2:9

LABORS

entered into their *l* .....John 4:38
creation groans and *l* ...Rom 8:22
l more abundant ......2 Cor 11:23
may rest from their *l* ...Rev 14:13

LACK

What do I still *l* ....Matt 19:20
"One thing you *l* .....Mark 10:21

LADDER

and behold, a *l* ....Gen 28:12

LAID

the place where they *l* ..Mark 16:6
"Where have you *l* ...John 11:34

LAKE

cast alive into the *l* .....Rev 19:20

LAMB

but where is the *l* ....Gen 22:7
He was led as a *l* ....Is 53:7
The *L* of God who .....John 1:29
the elders, stood a *L* ....Rev 5:6
"Worthy is the *L* ......Rev 5:12
by the blood of the *L* ...Rev 12:11

LAME

l shall leap like a ....Is 35:6
blind see and the *l* ....Matt 11:5
And a certain man *l* ....Acts 3:2

LAMENTATION

was heard in Ramah, l ..Matt 2:18
and made great *l* ....Acts 8:2

LAMP

Your word is a *l* ....Ps 119:105
the *l* of the wicked .....Prov 13:9
his *l* will be put out ....Prov 20:20
"Nor do they light a *l* ...Matt 5:15
"The *l* of the body ......Matt 6:22
when he has lit a *l* .....Luke 8:16
l gives you light ......Luke 11:36
does not light a *l* ......Luke 15:8
burning and shining *l* ..John 5:35

LAMPS

he made its seven *l* ......Ex 37:23
and trimmed their *l* .....Matt 25:7

LAMPSTAND

branches of the *l* ....Ex 25:32
a basket, but on a *l* .....Matt 5:15
and remove your *l* ....Rev 2:5

LAND

l that I will show you ....Gen 12:1
l flowing with milk ....Ex 3:8
They will see the *l* .....Is 33:17
Bethlehem, in the l ......Matt 2:6

LANGUAGE

whole earth had one *l* ...Gen 11:1
speak in his own *l* ....Acts 2:6
blasphemy, filthy *l* ....Col 3:8

LANGUAGES

according to their *l* ...,.Gen 10:20

LAST

He shall stand at *l* ......Job 19:25
First and I am the *L* ......Is 44:6
l will be first ....Matt 20:16
the First and the *L* .....Rev 1:11

LATTER

l times some will ....1 Tim 4:1

LAUGH

"Why did Sarah *l* ......Gen 18:13
Woe to you who *l* .....Luke 6:25

LAUGHS

The Lord *l* at him ....Ps 37:13

LAUGHTER

your *l* be turned to .....James 4:9

LAW

stones a copy of the *l* ...Josh 8:32
The *l* of the LORD is ....Ps 19:7
I delight in Your *l* ......Ps 119:70
Oh, how I love Your *l* ...Ps 119:97
And Your *l* is truth ....Ps 119:142
l will proceed from Me ....Is 51:4
in whose heart is My *l* ....Is 51:7
The *L* is no more ....Lam 2:9
The *l* of truth was in ....Mal 2:6
to destroy the *L* ....Matt 5:17
for this is the *L* ....Matt 7:12
hang all the *L* and the .Matt 22:40
"The *l* and the ....Luke 16:16
l was given through ....John 1:17
"Does our *l* judge a ....John 7:51
l is the knowledge ......Rom 3:20
because the *l* brings ....Rom 4:15
when there is no *l* ......Rom 5:13
you are not under *l* .....Rom 6:14
For what the *l* could ....Rom 8:3
l that I might live ......Gal 2:19
under guard by the *l* ....Gal 3:23
born under the *l* ....Gal 4:4
l is fulfilled in one .....Gal 5:14
into the perfect *l* ......James 1:25
fulfill the royal *l* ....James 2:8

LAWFUL

Is it *l* to pay taxes .....Matt 22:17
All things are *l* ....1 Cor 6:12

LAWGIVER

There is one *L* ....James 4:12

LAWLESS

l one will be revealed .2 Thess 2:8

LAWLESSNESS

Me, you who practice *l* .Matt 7:23
l is already at work ...2 Thess 2:7

LAWYERS

"Woe to you also, *l* ...Luke 11:46

LAY

nowhere to *l* His head ..Matt 8:20
l hands may receive .....Acts 8:19

LAZINESS

l the building decays ...Eccl 10:18

LAZY

l man will be put to ....Prov 12:24
wicked and *l* servant ..Matt 25:26
liars, evil beasts, *l* ......Titus 1:12

LEAD

L me in Your truth and ...Ps 25:5
And do not *l* us into ....Matt 6:13
"Can the blind *l* ....Luke 6:39

LEADS

He *l* me in the paths ......Ps 23:3
And if the blind *l* ......Matt 15:14

LEAF

plucked olive *l* ....Gen 8:11

LEAN

all your heart, And *l* .....Prov 3:5

LEAP

Then the lame shall *l* ......Is 35:6

LEARN

L to do good .... Is 1:17
yoke upon you and *l* ... Matt 11:29

LEARNED

Me The tongue of the *l* .... Is 50:4
have not so *l* Christ ..... Eph 4:20
in all things I have *l* .... Phil 4:12

LEARNING

l is driving you mad ... Acts 26:24

LEAST

so, shall be called *l* .... Matt 5:19

LEAVE

a man shall *l* his .... Gen 2:24
For You will not *l* .... Ps 16:10
"*I* will never *l* .... Heb 13:5

LEAVEN

of heaven is like *l* ..... Matt 13:33
l leavens the whole .... Gal 5:9

LEAVES

and they sewed fig *l* ..... Gen 3:7
The *l* of the tree .... Rev 22:2

LED

l them forth by the ..... Ps 107:7
For as many as are *l* .... Rom 8:14

LEFT

l hand know what your .. Matt 6:3

LEND

"And if you *l* .... Luke 6:34

LENDER

is servant to the *l* ...... Prov 22:7

LENDS

ever merciful, and *l* ..... Ps 37:26

LENGTH

is your life and the *l* ... Deut 30:20

LEOPARD

or the *l* its spots .... Jer 13:23

LEPERS

"And many *l* were in ... Luke 4:27

LET

"*L* there be light .... Gen 1:3

LETTER

for the *l* kills .... 2 Cor 3:6
or by word or by *l* .... 2 Thess 2:2

LETTERS

does this Man know *l* .. John 7:15

LEVIATHAN

"Can you draw out *L* .... Job 41:1

LEVITE

"Likewise a *L* .... Luke 10:32

LEWDNESS

wickedness, deceit, *l* ... Mark 7:22

LIAR

for he is a *l* and the .... John 8:44
but every man a *l* ...... Rom 3:4
we make Him a *l* .... 1 John 1:10
his brother, he is a *l* .. 1 John 4:20

LIARS

"All men are *l* .... Ps 116:11
l shall have their .... Rev 21:8

LIBERALITY

he who gives, with *l* .... Rom 12:8

LIBERALLY

who gives to all *l* ...... James 1:5

LIBERTY

year, and proclaim *l* .... Lev 25:10
'To proclaim *l* to the ... Luke 4:18
into the glorious *l* ..... Rom 8:21
Lord is, there is *l* ...... 2 Cor 3:17
therefore in the *l* .... Gal 5:1

LIE

Do not *l* to one .... Col 3:9
God, who cannot *l* ...... Titus 1:2
an abomination or a *l* .. Rev 21:27

LIED

You have not *l* to men ... Acts 5:4

LIES

sin *l* at the door .... Gen 4:7
speaking *l* in .... 1 Tim 4:2

LIFE

the breath of *l* .... Gen 2:7
'For the *l* of the .... Lev 17:11
before you today *l* ..... Deut 30:15
He will redeem their *l* ... Ps 72:14
word has given me *l* ... Ps 119:50
She is a tree of *l* .... Prov 3:18
finds me finds *l* .... Prov 8:35
L is more than .... Luke 12:23
l was the light .... John 1:4
so the Son gives *l* ...... John 5:21
spirit, and they are *l* .... John 6:63
have the light of *l* .... John 8:12
and I lay down My *l* .... John 10:15
resurrection and the *l* . John 11:25
you lay down your *l* ... John 13:38
l which I now live ...... Gal 2:20
l is hidden with .... Col 3:3
For what is your *l* ...... James 4:14
l was manifested ...... 1 John 1:2
and the pride of *l* .... 1 John 2:16
has given us eternal *l* . 1 John 5:11
the Lamb's Book of *L* .. Rev 21:27
right to the tree of *l* .... Rev 22:14
the water of *l* freely .... Rev 22:17
from the Book of *L* ..... Rev 22:19

LIFT

I will *l* up my eyes to .... Ps 121:1
Lord, and He will *l* .... James 4:10

LIFTED

your heart is *l* .... Ezek 28:2
in Hades, he *l* up his ... Luke 16:23
the Son of Man be *l* ..... John 3:14
"And I, if I am *l* .... John 12:32

LIGHT

"Let there be *l* .... Gen 1:3
The Lord is my *l* .... Ps 27:1
and a *l* to my path ..... Ps 119:105
The *l* of the righteous .. Prov 13:9
The Lord gives *l* ...... Prov 29:13
Truly the *l* is sweet .... Eccl 11:7
let us walk in the *l* .... Is 2:5
l shall break forth .... Is 58:8
"You are the *l* .... Matt 5:14
"Let your *l* so shine .... Matt 5:16
than the sons of *l* ...... Luke 16:8
and the life was the *l* .... John 1:4
darkness rather than *l* .. John 3:19
saying, "I am the *l* .... John 8:12
God who commanded .. 2 Cor 4:6
Walk as children of *l* ..... Eph 5:8
You are all sons of *l* .. 1 Thess 5:5
into His marvelous *l* .. 1 Pet 2:9
to you, that God is *l* ... 1 John 1:5
l as He is in the .... 1 John 1:7
says he is in the *l* ...... 1 John 2:9
The Lamb is its *l* .... Rev 21:23

LIGHTNING

"For as the *l* .... Matt 24:27
countenance was like *l* .. Matt 28:3

LIGHTNINGS

the throne proceeded *l* .... Rev 4:5

LIGHTS

"Let there be *l* .... Gen 1:14
whom you shine as *l* .... Phil 2:15

LIKENESS

according to Our *l* ...... Gen 1:26
carved image—any *l* ..... Ex 20:4
when I awake in Your *l* .. Ps 17:15
and coming in the *l* ...... Phil 2:7

LILY

the *l* of the valleys ...... Song 2:1

LIMIT

to the sea its *l* .... Prov 8:29

LINE

upon precept, *L* upon .... Is 28:10
I am setting a plumb *l* .. Amos 7:8

LINEN

wrapped Him in the *l* . Mark 15:46

LINGER

salvation shall not *l* ...... Is 46:13

LION

l shall eat straw .... Is 11:7

LIONS

the mouths of *l* .... Heb 11:33

LIPS

off all flattering *l* .... Ps 12:3
The *l* of the righteous .. Prov 10:21
But the *l* of .... Prov 20:15
am a man of unclean *l* ...... Is 6:5
other I *I* will speak ... 1 Cor 14:21
from evil, And his *l* .... 1 Pet 3:10

LISTEN

you are not able to *l* .... John 8:43
you who fear God, *l* ... Acts 13:16

LISTENS

But whoever *l* to me .... Prov 1:33

LITTLE

Though you are *l* .... Mic 5:2
l ones only a cup ...... Matt 10:42
"O you of *l* faith ...... Matt 14:31
to whom *l* is forgiven .. Luke 7:47
faithful in a very *l* .... Luke 19:17

LIVE

eat, and *l* forever .... Gen 3:22
a man does, he shall *l* ... Lev 18:5
"Seek Me and *l* .... Amos 5:4
But the just shall *l* ...... Hab 2:4
l by bread alone .... Matt 4:4
"for in Him we *l* ...... Acts 17:28
l peaceably with all .... Rom 12:18
the life which I now *l* ... Gal 2:20
If we *l* in the Spirit ..... Gal 5:25
to me, to *l* is Christ ...... Phil 1:21

LIVED

died and rose and *l* ..... Rom 14:9
And they *l* and reigned .. Rev 20:4

LIVES

but man *l* by every ..... Deut 8:3
but Christ *l* in me .... Gal 2:20
to lay down our *l* ..... 1 John 3:16
"I am He who *l* .... Rev 1:18

LIVING

and man became a *l* ..... Gen 2:7
in the light of the *l* ...... Ps 56:13

LOATHSOME

the dead, but of the *l* .. Matt 22:32
do you seek the *l* ....Luke 24:5
the word of God is *l* .....Heb 4:12
l creature was like a ......Rev 4:7

LOATHSOME

But a wicked man is *l* .. Prov 13:5

LOAVES

have here only five *l* ... Matt 14:17
you are of the *l* ....John 6:26

LOCUST

What the chewing *l* ......Joel 1:4

LOCUSTS

and his food was *l* ....Matt 3:4

LOFTY

Wisdom is too *l* ....Prov 24:7

LONG

your days may be *l* .....Deut 5:16
Who *l* for death ....Job 3:21
I *l* for Your salvation .. Ps 119:174
go around in *l* robes .. Mark 12:38

LONGSUFFERING

is love, joy, peace, *l* ......Gal 5:22
and gentleness, with *l* ....Eph 4:2
for all patience and *l* .....Col 1:11
might show all *l* ....1 Tim 1:16
once the Divine *l* ....1 Pet 3:20
and consider that the *l* . 2 Pet 3:15

LOOK

A proud *l* ....Prov 6:17
"*L* to Me ....Is 45:22
l on Me whom they ...Zech 12:10
say to you, '*L* here .....Luke 17:23
while we do not *l* ......2 Cor 4:18

LOOKED

For He *l* down from ....Ps 102:19
He *l* for justice ....Is 5:7
the Lord turned and *l* . Luke 22:61
for he *l* to the reward .. Heb 11:26

LOOKING

the plow, and *l* back ...Luke 9:62
l for the blessed hope .. Titus 2:13
l unto Jesus ....Heb 12:2
l carefully lest ....Heb 12:15
l for the mercy of ....Jude 21

LOOKS

The lofty *l* of man ....Is 2:11
to you that whoever *l* ...Matt 5:28

LOOSE

and whatever you *l* ....Matt 16:19
said to them, "*L* him ..John 11:44

LOOSED

the silver cord is *l* ......Eccl 12:6

LORD

L is my strength ....Ex 15:2
L our God, the *L* ......Deut 6:4
You alone are the *L* .....Neh 9:6
The *L* of hosts ....Ps 24:10
Gracious is the *L* ......Ps 116:5
L surrounds His people .. Ps 125:2
The *L* is righteous ....Ps 129:4
L is near to all who ....Ps 145:18
L is a God of justice ......Is 30:18
L Our Righteousness .....Jer 23:6
"The *L* is one ....Zech 14:9
shall not tempt the L ....Matt 4:7
shall worship the L .....Matt 4:10
Son of Man is also *L* .. Mark 2:28
who is Christ the *L* ....Luke 2:11
L is risen indeed ......Luke 24:34
Me Teacher and *L* ....John 13:13
He is *L* of all ....Acts 10:36

with your mouth the *L* .. Rom 10:9
say that Jesus is *L* .....1 Cor 12:3
second Man is the *L* .. 1 Cor 15:47
the Spirit of the *L* .....2 Cor 3:17
that Jesus Christ is *L* ...Phil 2:11
and deny the only *L* ....Jude 4
L God Omnipotent ......Rev 19:6

LORDS

for He is Lord of *l* .....Rev 17:14

LOSE

save his life will *l* ....Matt 16:25

LOSES

but if the salt *l* ....Matt 5:13
and *l* his own soul .....Matt 16:26

LOSS

count all things *l* ....Phil 3:8

LOST

save that which was *l* .. Matt 18:11
and none of them is *l* .. John 17:12
You gave Me I have *l* ...John 18:9

LOTS

garments, casting *l* ... Mark 15:24
And they cast their *l* ....Acts 1:26

LOUD

cried out with a *l* .....Matt 27:46
I heard behind me a *l* ...Rev 1:10

LOVE

l your neighbor as .....Lev 19:18
l the LORD your God .....Deut 6:5
Oh, *l* the LORD ....Ps 31:23
he has set his *l* ....Ps 91:14
Oh, how I *l* Your law ...Ps 119:97
l covers all sins ....Prov 10:12
A time to *l* ....Eccl 3:8
banner over me was *l* ...Song 2:4
l is as strong as ....Song 8:6
do justly, To *l* mercy ......Mic 6:8
to you, *l* your enemies ..Matt 5:44
which of them will *l* ....Luke 7:42
you do not have the *l* ...John 5:42
if you have *l* for one ...John 13:35
"If you *l* Me ....John 14:15
and My Father will *l* ...John 14:23
l one another as I .....John 15:12
l has no one than this .John 15:13
because the *l* of God .....Rom 5:5
to *l* one another ....Rom 13:8
L suffers long and is ... 1 Cor 13:4
L never fails .... 1 Cor 13:8
greatest of these is *l* .. 1 Cor 13:13
For the *l* of Christ .....2 Cor 5:14
of the Spirit is *l* ....Gal 5:22
Husbands, *l* your wives .. Eph 5:25
the commandment is *l* .. 1 Tim 1:5
For the *l* of money is .. 1 Tim 6:10
Let brotherly *l* ....Heb 13:1
having not seen you *l* ...1 Pet 1:8
for "*l* will cover a ......1 Pet 4:8
brotherly kindness *l* .....2 Pet 1:7
By this we know *l* ....1 John 3:16
Beloved, let us *l* ......1 John 4:7
for God is *l* ....1 John 4:8
There is no fear in *l* ..1 John 4:18
l Him because He ....1 John 4:19
loves God must *l* ....1 John 4:21
For this is the *l* ....1 John 5:3
have left your first *l* ......Rev 2:4

LOVED

L one and friend You ....Ps 88:18
Yet Jacob I have *l* ....Mal 1:2
forgiven, for she *l* .....Luke 7:47
so *l* the world that .....John 3:16
whom Jesus *l* ....John 13:23
"As the Father *l* ....John 15:9
l them as You have ....John 17:23
the Son of God, who *l* ...Gal 2:20

l the church and gave ...Eph 5:25
Beloved, if God so *l* ...1 John 4:11
To Him who *l* us and ....Rev 1:5

LOVELY

he is altogether *l* ....Song 5:16
whatever things are *l* .....Phil 4:8

LOVES

"He who *l* father or ....Matt 10:37
l his life will lose ......John 12:25
l Me will be loved .....John 14:21
l a cheerful giver ....2 Cor 9:7
If anyone *l* the world . 1 John 2:15
l God must love his .. 1 John 4:21

LOVINGKINDNESS

To declare Your *l* ....Ps 92:2

LOWER

made him a little l ....Heb 2:7

LOWLINESS

with all *l* and ....Eph 4:2

LOWLY

for I am gentle and *l* ... Matt 11:29
in presence am *l* ....2 Cor 10:1
l brother glory ....James 1:9

LUKEWARM

because you are *l* ....Rev 3:16

LUST

looks at a woman to *l* .. Matt 5:28
not fulfill the *l* ....Gal 5:16
You *l* and do not have .. James 4:2
the *l* of the flesh ......1 John 2:16

LUSTS

to fulfill its *l* ....Rom 13:14
also youthful *l* ....2 Tim 2:22
and worldly *l* ....Titus 2:12
to the former *l* ....1 Pet 1:14
abstain from fleshly *l* .. 1 Pet 2:11
to their own ungodly *l* ....Jude 18

LUTE

Praise Him with the *l* ....Ps 150:3

LUXURY

in pleasure and *l* ....James 5:5
the abundance of her *l* .. Rev 18:3

LYING

I hate and abhor *l* .....Ps 119:163
righteous man hates *l* ...Prov 13:5
not trust in these *l* ....Jer 7:4
signs, and *l* wonders .. 2 Thess 2:9

M

MADE

m the stars also ....Gen 1:16
things My hand has *m* ....Is 66:2
All things were *m* ....John 1:3

MADNESS

m is in their hearts ....Eccl 9:3

MAGIC

m brought their books . Acts 19:19

MAGNIFIED

let Your name be *m* ...2 Sam 7:26
the Lord Jesus was *m* .. Acts 19:17
also Christ will be *m* ....Phil 1:20

MAGNIFIES

"My soul *m* the Lord ...Luke 1:46

MAGNIFY

m the LORD with me ......Ps 34:3

MAIDSERVANT
"Behold the m ....Luke 1:38

MAIDSERVANTS
m I will pour out My ....Acts 2:18

MAJESTY
right hand of the M ......Heb 1:3
eyewitnesses of His m ..2 Pet 1:16
wise, Be glory and m .....Jude 25

MAKE
"Let Us m man in Our ..Gen 1:26
m you a great nation ....Gen 12:2
"You shall not m ....Ex 20:4
m Our home with .....John 14:23

MAKER
M is your husband ....Is 54:5
has forgotten his M .....Hos 8:14
builder and m is God ..Heb 11:10

MALICE
in m be babes ....1 Cor 14:20
laying aside all m ....1 Pet 2:1

MAN
"Let Us make m ....Gen 1:26
m that You are mindful ....Ps 8:4
of the Son of M ......Matt 24:27
"Behold the M ....John 19:5
by m came death .....1 Cor 15:21
our outward m ......2 Cor 4:16
the m of God may .....2 Tim 3:17
is the number of a m ...Rev 13:18

MANGER
and laid Him in a m .....Luke 2:7

MANIFEST
m Myself to him ......John 14:21

MANIFESTATION
But the m of the ....1 Cor 12:7

MANIFESTED
"I have m Your name ..John 17:6
God was m in the .....1 Tim 3:16
the life was m ....1 John 1:2

MANIFOLD
the m wisdom of God ...Eph 3:10

MANNA
of Israel ate m ....Ex 16:35
"Our fathers ate the m .John 6:31

MANNER
Is this the m of man ..2 Sam 7:19
in an unworthy m ....1 Cor 11:27
what m of love ....1 John 3:1

MANSIONS
house are many m .....John 14:2

MANTLE
Then he took the m ....2 Kin 2:14

MARK
And the LORD set a m ...Gen 4:15
receives the m ....Rev 14:11

MARRED
So His visage was m .....Is 52:14

MARRIAGE
M is honorable among ..Heb 13:4

MARRIED
But he who is m ....1 Cor 7:33

MARRY
they neither m nor ....Matt 22:30
forbidding to m ....1 Tim 4:3

MARRYING
and drinking, m ....Matt 24:38

MARTYRS
the blood of the m ......Rev 17:6

MARVELED
Jesus heard it, He m ....Matt 8:10
so that Pilate m ....Mark 15:5

MARVELOUS
It is m in our eyes ......Ps 118:23
of darkness into His m ..1 Pet 2:9

MASTER
a servant like his m ...Matt 10:25
greater than his m ....John 15:20
and useful for the M ...2 Tim 2:21

MASTERS
can serve two m ......Luke 16:13
who have believing m ..1 Tim 6:2

MATTERS
the weightier m ....Matt 23:23

MATURE
understanding be m ..1 Cor 14:20
us, as many as are m ....Phil 3:15

MEANT
but God m it for good ..Gen 50:20

MEASURE
a perfect and just m ...Deut 25:15
give the Spirit by m ....John 3:34
to each one a m ....Rom 12:3

MEASURED
m the waters in the ......Is 40:12
you use, it will be m .....Matt 7:2

MEASURES
house differing m .....Deut 25:14

MEASURING
behold, a man with a m ..Zech 2:1
m themselves by .....2 Cor 10:12

MEAT
will never again eat m .1 Cor 8:13

MEDIATOR
by the hand of a m ......Gal 3:19
is one God and one M ..1 Tim 2:5
to Jesus the M of the ...Heb 12:24

MEDICINE
does good, like m .....Prov 17:22

MEDICINES
you will use many m ....Jer 46:11

MEDITATE
but you shall m ....Josh 1:8
M within your heart on ....Ps 4:4
I will m on Your ....Ps 119:15
m beforehand on .....Luke 21:14
m on these things ....Phil 4:8

MEDITATES
in His law he m ....Ps 1:2

MEDITATION
of my mouth and the m ..Ps 19:14
It is my m all the day ...Ps 119:97

MEDIUM
a woman who is a m ...Lev 20:27

MEDIUM'S
shall be like a m ....Is 29:4

MEDIUMS
"Seek those who are m ....Is 8:19

MEEK
with equity for the m ......Is 11:4
Blessed are the m ....Matt 5:5

MEEKNESS
are done in the m .....James 3:13

MEET
prepare to m your .....Amos 4:12
m the Lord in the ....1 Thess 4:17

MELODY
singing and making m ..Eph 5:19

MELT
the elements will m ....2 Pet 3:10

MEMBER
body is not one m ....1 Cor 12:14

MEMBERS
you that one of your m .Matt 5:29
do not present your m ..Rom 6:13
neighbor, for we are m ..Eph 4:25

MEMORIAL
and this is My m ....Ex 3:15
also be told as a m ....Matt 26:13

MEMORY
The m of the righteous ..Prov 10:7

MEN
m began to call on the ..Gen 4:26
make you fishers of m ..Matt 4:19
goodwill toward m .....Luke 2:14
heaven or from m .....Luke 20:4
Likewise also the m ....Rom 1:27
the Lord, and not to m ...Eph 6:7
between God and m ....1 Tim 2:5

MENSERVANTS
And also on My m ......Joel 2:29
And on My m and on ...Acts 2:18

MERCHANDISE
house a house of m ....John 2:16

MERCIES
give you the sure m ...Acts 13:34

MERCIFUL
LORD, the LORD God, m ...Ex 34:6
He is ever m ....Ps 37:26
Blessed are the m ....Matt 5:7
saying, 'God be m ....Luke 18:13
"For I will be m ....Heb 8:12

MERCY
but showing m to ....Ex 20:6
and abundant in m ....Num 14:18
m endures forever ....1 Chr 16:34
M and truth have met ....Ps 85:10
m is everlasting ....Ps 100:5
Let not m and truth .....Prov 3:3
For I desire m and not ....Hos 6:6
do justly, To love m ....Mic 6:8
'I desire m and not .....Matt 9:13
And His m is on those ..Luke 1:50
"I will have m ....Rom 9:15
that He might have m .Rom 11:32
m has made ....1 Cor 7:25
as we have received m ..2 Cor 4:1
God, who is rich in m ....Eph 2:4
but I obtained m ....1 Tim 1:13
that he may find m ....2 Tim 1:18
to His m He saved us ....Titus 3:5
that we may obtain m ..Heb 4:16

MERRY
m heart makes a ......Prov 15:13
we should make m ....Luke 15:32

MESSENGER

"Behold, I send My *m* . . . . Mal 3:1
'Behold, I send My *m* . . Matt 11:10

MESSIAH

Until *M* the Prince . . . . . . Dan 9:25
"We have found the *M* . John 1:41

MIDST

God is in the *m* . . . . Ps 46:5
I am there in the *m* . . . . Matt 18:20

MIGHT

'My power and the *m* . . . Deut 8:17
'Not by *m* nor by . . . . Zech 4:6
in the power of His *m* . . Eph 6:10
honor and power and *m* . Rev 7:12

MIGHTIER

coming after me is *m* . . . Matt 3:11

MIGHTY

He was a *m* hunter . . . . . . Gen 10:9
m have fallen . . . . 2 Sam 1:19
The LORD *m* in battle . . . . . Ps 24:8
their Redeemer is *m* . . Prov 23:11
m has done great . . . . . Luke 1:49
the flesh, not many *m* . 1 Cor 1:26
the working of His *m* . . Eph 1:19

MILK

come, buy wine and *m* . . . . Is 55:1
shall flow with *m* . . . . Joel 3:18
have come to need *m* . . . . Heb 5:12
desire the pure *m* . . . . . . 1 Pet 2:2

MILLSTONE

m were hung around . . . Matt 18:6
a stone like a great *m* . . Rev 18:21

MIND

put wisdom in the *m* . . . . Job 38:36
perfect peace, Whose *m* . . . Is 26:3
I myself serve the . . . . Rom 7:25
who has known the *m* . . Rom 11:34
Be of the same *m* . . . . . Rom 12:16
in his own *m* . . . . Rom 14:5
has known the *m* . . . . . 1 Cor 2:16
are out of your *m* . . . . . 1 Cor 14:23
Let this *m* be in you . . . . . . Phil 2:5
love and of a sound *m* . . 2 Tim 1:7

MINDFUL

is man that You are *m* . . . . . Ps 8:4
for you are not *m* . . . . . Matt 16:23
is man that You are *m* . . . . Heb 2:6

MINDS

put My law in their *m* . . . Jer 31:33
I stir up your pure *m* . . . . 2 Pet 3:1

MINISTER

For he is God's *m* . . . . . . Rom 13:4
you will be a good *m* . . . 1 Tim 4:6

MINISTERS

for they are God's *m* . . . Rom 13:6
If anyone *m* . . . . 1 Pet 4:11

MINISTRIES

are differences of *m* . . 1 Cor 12:5

MINISTRY

But if the *m* of death . . . . 2 Cor 3:7
since we have this *m* . . . . 2 Cor 4:1
has given us the *m* . . . . 2 Cor 5:18
for the work of *m* . . . . . . Eph 4:12
fulfill your *m* . . . . 2 Tim 4:5
a more excellent *m* . . . . . . Heb 8:6

MIRACLE

one who works a *m* . . . . Mark 9:39

MIRACLES

worked unusual *m* . . . . Acts 19:11
the working of *m* . . . . . 1 Cor 12:10

MISERY

And remember his *m* . . . Prov 31:7

MITES

putting in two *m* . . . . Luke 21:2

MOCK

Fools *m* at sin . . . . Prov 14:9
to the Gentiles to *m* . . . Matt 20:19

MOCKED

noon, that Elijah *m* . . . 1 Kin 18:27
deceived, God is not *m* . . . . Gal 6:7

MOCKER

Wine is a *m* . . . . Prov 20:1

MOCKS

He who *m* the poor . . . . . Prov 17:5

MODERATION

with propriety and *m* . . . 1 Tim 2:9

MOMENT

In a *m* they die . . . . Job 34:20
in a *m*, in the . . . . 1 Cor 15:52

MONEY

be redeemed without *m* . . . Is 52:3
And you who have no *m* . . Is 55:1
and hid his lord's *m* . . Matt 25:18
to give him *m* . . . . Mark 14:11
"Carry neither *m* . . . . . . Luke 10:4
I sent you without *m* . . Luke 22:35
be purchased with *m* . . . . Acts 8:20
not greedy for *m* . . . . . . 1 Tim 3:3
m is a root of all . . . . . . 1 Tim 6:10

MONEYCHANGERS

the tables of the *m* . . . . Matt 21:12

MOON

until the *m* is no more . . . . Ps 72:7
m will not give its . . . . Mark 13:24

MORNING

Evening and *m* and at . . . Ps 55:17
Lucifer, son of the *m* . . . . . Is 14:12
very early in the *m* . . . . Luke 24:1
the Bright and *M* Star . . Rev 22:16

MORTAL

sin reign in your *m* . . . . . Rom 6:12
and this *m* must put . . 1 Cor 15:53

MORTALITY

m may be swallowed . . . 2 Cor 5:4

MOTH

where *m* and rust . . . . . . Matt 6:19

MOTHER

because she was the *m* . . Gen 3:20
leave his father and *m* . . Matt 19:5
"Behold your *m* . . . . John 19:27
The *M* of Harlots . . . . . . Rev 17:5

MOUNT

come up to *M* Sinai . . . . Ex 19:23
They shall *m* up with . . . . Is 40:31

MOUNTAIN

to Horeb, the *m* . . . . Ex 3:1
let us go up to the *m* . . . . . . Is 2:3
became a great *m* . . . . . Dan 2:35
are you, O great *m* . . . . . Zech 4:7
you will say to this *m* . . Matt 17:20
Him on the holy *m* . . . . . 2 Pet 1:18

MOUNTAINS

m were brought forth . . . . . Ps 90:2
m shall depart And the . . . Is 54:10
in Judea flee to the *m* . Matt 24:16
that I could remove *m* . 1 Cor 13:2

MOURN

A time to *m* . . . . Eccl 3:4
are those who *m* . . . . Matt 5:4
of the earth will *m* . . . . . . Rev 1:7

MOURNED

and have not rather *m* . . 1 Cor 5:2

MOURNING

shall be a great *m* . . . . . Zech 12:11
be turned to *m* and . . . . James 4:9

MOUTH

"Who has made man's *m* . . Ex 4:11
Out of the *m* of babes . . . . Ps 8:2
knowledge, But the *m* . Prov 10:14
The *m* of an immoral . . Prov 22:14
And a flattering *m* . . . . Prov 26:28
m speaking pompous . . . Dan 7:8
m defiles a man . . . . Matt 15:11
m I will judge you . . . . Luke 19:22
I will give you a *m* . . . . Luke 21:15
m confession is made . . Rom 10:10
m great swelling words . . . Jude 16
vomit you out of My *m* . . Rev 3:16

MOVED

she shall not be *m* . . . . Ps 46:5
spoke as they were *m* . . 2 Pet 1:21

MUCH

m study is . . . . Eccl 12:12
to whom *m* is given . . . Luke 12:48

MULTIPLIED

of the disciples *m* . . . . Acts 6:7
of God grew and *m* . . . . Acts 12:24

MULTIPLY

"Be fruitful and *m* . . . . . . Gen 1:22
m the descendants . . . . . . Jer 33:22

MULTITUDE

stars of heaven in *m* . . . . Deut 1:10
In the *m* of words sin . . Prov 10:19
compassion on the *m* . . Matt 15:32
with the angel a *m* . . . . . Luke 2:13
"love will cover a *m* . . . . . 1 Pet 4:8
and behold, a great *m* . . . . Rev 7:9

MURDER

"You shall not *m* . . . . Ex 20:13
'You shall not *m* . . . . . . Matt 5:21
You *m* and covet and . . James 4:2

MURDERED

up Jesus whom you *m* . . Acts 5:30

MURDERER

He was a *m* from the . . . John 8:44
his brother is a *m* . . . . . 1 John 3:15

MURDERERS

and profane, for *m* . . . . . 1 Tim 1:9
abominable, *m* . . . . Rev 21:8

MURDERS

evil thoughts, *m* . . . . Matt 15:19

MUSING

while I was *m* . . . . Ps 39:3

MUTILATION

beware of the *m* . . . . Phil 3:2

MUZZLE

"You shall not *m* . . . . . . 1 Tim 5:18

MYSTERIES

to you to know the *m* .. Matt 13:11
and understand all *m* .. 1 Cor 13:2

MYSTERY

given to know the *m* ... Mark 4:11
wisdom of God in a *m* .. 1 Cor 2:7
I tell you a *m* .... 1 Cor 15:51
made known to us the *m* . Eph 1:9
the *m* of godliness ..... 1 Tim 3:16

N

NAILED

n it to the cross .... Col 2:14

NAKED

And they were both *n* ... Gen 2:25
knew that they were *n* .... Gen 3:7
"*N* I came from my ...... Job 1:21
'I was *n* and you ...... Matt 25:36
but all things are *n* ..... Heb 4:13
brother or sister is *n* .. James 2:15
poor, blind, and *n* ..... Rev 3:17

NAKEDNESS

or famine, or *n* .... Rom 8:35
n may not be revealed ... Rev 3:18

NAME

Abram called on the *n* .. Gen 13:4
Israel shall be your *n* .. Gen 35:10
This is My *n* forever ..... Ex 3:15
shall not take the *n* ..... Ex 20:7
and awesome is .... Deut 28:58
excellent is Your *n* .... Ps 8:1
n will put their trust ..... Ps 9:10
be His glorious *n* ..... Ps 72:19
do not call on Your *n* ..... Ps 79:6
to Your *n* give glory ..... Ps 115:1
above all Your *n* .... Ps 138:2
A good *n* is to be ...... Prov 22:1
what is His Son's *n* .... Prov 30:4
be called by a new *n* .... Is 62:2
Everlasting is Your *n* ..... Is 63:16
They will call on My *n* . Zech 13:9
to you who fear My *n* .... Mal 4:2
Hallowed be Your *n* ..... Matt 6:9
prophesied in Your *n* ... Matt 7:22
n Gentiles will trust ... Matt 12:21
together in My *n* ...... Matt 18:20
will come in My *n* ..... Matt 24:5
who believe in His *n* ... John 1:12
comes in his own *n* .... John 5:43
his own sheep by *n* .... John 10:3
through faith in His *n* .. Acts 3:16
there is no other *n* ..... Acts 4:12
which is above every *n* .. Phil 2:9
deed, do all in the *n* .... Col 3:17
a more excellent *n* ...... Heb 1:4
you hold fast to My *n* ... Rev 2:13
n that you are alive ...... Rev 3:1
having His Father's *n* ... Rev 14:1
and glorify Your *n* ...... Rev 15:4
n written that no one ... Rev 19:12

NAMED

I have *n* you .... Is 45:4

NAME'S

saved them for His *n* .... Ps 106:8

NARROW

"Enter by the *n* gate .... Matt 7:13

NATION

make you a great *n* ..... Gen 12:2
exalts a *n* .... Prov 14:34
n that was not called ...... Is 65:1
make them one *n* .... Ezek 37:22
since there was a *n* .... Dan 12:1
n will rise against ...... Matt 24:7
"for he loves our *n* ...... Luke 7:5

those who are *not* a *n* . Rom 10:19
tribe, tongue, and *n* ..... Rev 13:7

NATIONS

Why do the *n* rage .... Ps 2:1
I will give You the *n* ..... Ps 2:8
n shall serve Him .... Ps 72:11
disciples of all the *n* .. Matt 28:19
who was to rule all *n* ... Rev 12:5
the healing of the *n* ... Rev 22:2

NATURAL

exchanged the *n* ...... Rom 1:26
the men, leaving the *n* .. Rom 1:27
did not spare the *n* .... Rom 11:21
n man does not .... 1 Cor 2:14
It is sown a *n* body ... 1 Cor 15:44

NATURE

"We who are Jews by *n* . Gal 2:15
by *n* children of wrath .... Eph 2:3
of the divine *n* .... 2 Pet 1:4

NEAR

the word is very *n* ..... Deut 30:14
upon Him while He is *n* ... Is 55:6
know that it is *n* ...... Matt 24:33
kingdom of God is *n* .. Luke 21:31
"The word is *n* .... Rom 10:8
to those who were *n* ... Eph 2:17
for the time is *n* .... Rev 1:3

NEARER

now our salvation is *n* . Rom 13:11

NEED

the things you have *n* .... Matt 6:8
supply all your *n* .... Phil 4:19
to help in time of *n* ..... Heb 4:16

NEGLECT

if we *n* so great a .... Heb 2:3

NEGLECTED

n the weightier .... Matt 23:23

NEIGHBOR

'you shall love your *n* .. Lev 19:18
"You shall love your *n* .. Matt 5:43
"And who is my *n* .... Luke 10:29
"You shall love your *n* .. Rom 13:9

NEVER

in Me shall *n* thirst ..... John 6:35
in Me shall *n* die ...... John 11:26
Love *n* fails .... 1 Cor 13:8
n take away sins ...... Heb 10:11
"I will *n* leave you ...... Heb 13:5
prophecy *n* came by .... 2 Pet 1:21

NEW

And there is nothing *n* ... Eccl 1:9
"For behold, I create *n* ... Is 65:17
n every morning .... Lam 3:23
wine into *n* wineskins .. Matt 9:17
of the *n* covenant ..... Matt 26:28
n commandment I ... John 13:34
he is a *n* creation ...... 2 Cor 5:17
when I will make a *n* .... Heb 8:8
n heavens and a *n* ..... 2 Pet 3:13
n name written which ... Rev 2:17
And they sang a *n* .... Rev 5:9
And I saw a *n* heaven ... Rev 21:1
I make all things *n* ...... Rev 21:5

NEWNESS

also should walk in *n* .... Rom 6:4

NIGHT

darkness He called *N* .... Gen 1:5
It is a *n* of solemn ...... Ex 12:42
pillar of fire by *n* .... Ex 13:22
gives songs in the *n* .... Job 35:10
and continued all *n* .... Luke 6:12
man came to Jesus by *n* . John 3:2

n is coming when no .... John 9:4
came to Jesus by *n* .... John 19:39
as a thief in the *n* ..... 1 Thess 5:2
there shall be no *n* ..... Rev 21:25

NINETY-NINE

he not leave the *n* ..... Matt 18:12

NOTHING

"I can of Myself do *n* ... John 5:30
Me you can do *n* .... John 15:5
men, it will come to *n* .. Acts 5:38
have not love, I am *n* .. 1 Cor 13:2
Be anxious for *n* .... Phil 4:6
For we brought *n* .... 1 Tim 6:7

NOURISHED

"I have *n* and .... Is 1:2

NOURISHES

n and cherishes it .... Eph 5:29

NUMBER

if a man could *n* .... Gen 13:16
teach us to *n* our days ... Ps 90:12
which no one could *n* .... Rev 7:9
His *n* is 666 .... Rev 13:18

O

OATH

for the sake of your *o* .... Eccl 8:2
he denied with an *o* ... Matt 26:72
o which He swore ..... Luke 1:73

OATHS

shall perform your *o* .... Matt 5:33

OBEDIENCE

o many will be made ... Rom 5:19
captivity to the *o* ...... 2 Cor 10:5
yet He learned *o* .... Heb 5:8

OBEDIENT

you are willing and *o* ...... Is 1:19
of the priests were *o* ..... Acts 6:7
make the Gentiles *o* ... Rom 15:18
Himself and became *o* .... Phil 2:8
as *o* children .... 1 Pet 1:14

OBEY

God and *o* His voice .... Deut 4:30
His voice we will *o* .... Josh 24:24
o is better than ...... 1 Sam 15:22
o God rather than men .. Acts 5:29
and do not *o* the truth ... Rom 2:8
yourselves slaves to *o* .. Rom 6:16
o your parents in all ..... Col 3:20
Bondservants, *o* in all .... Col 3:22
those who do not *o* ... 2 Thess 1:8
O those who rule ...... Heb 13:17

OBEYED

of sin, yet you *o* .... Rom 6:17
they have not all *o* .... Rom 10:16
By faith Abraham *o* ..... Heb 11:8

OBSERVATION

does not come with *o* . Luke 17:20

OBSERVE

teaching them to *o* all . Matt 28:20

OBTAIN

also may *o* mercy ..... Rom 11:31
o salvation through ... 1 Thess 5:9

OBTAINED

o a part in this .... Acts 1:17
yet have now *o* mercy . Rom 11:30
endured, he *o* the .... Heb 6:15

OBTAINS

o favor from the Lord .. Prov 8:35

OFFEND

lest we o them . . . . Matt 17:27
than that he should o . . . Luke 17:2
them, "Does this o . . . . . John 6:61

OFFENDED

they were o at Him . . . . Matt 13:57

OFFENSE

and a rock of o . . . . Is 8:14
You are an o to Me . . . . Matt 16:23
by the one man's o . . . . . Rom 5:17
the o of the cross . . . . Gal 5:11
sincere and without o . . . Phil 1:10
And a rock of o . . . . 1 Pet 2:8

OFFENSES

For o must come . . . . . . Matt 18:7
impossible that no o . . . . Luke 17:1

OFFER

come and o your gift . . . Matt 5:24
let us continually o . . . . Heb 13:15

OFFERED

to eat those things o . . . 1 Cor 8:10
so Christ was o . . . . Heb 9:28
o one sacrifice . . . . Heb 10:12

OFFERING

o You did not require . . . . . Ps 40:6
You make His soul an o . . Is 53:10
Himself for us, an o . . . . . . Eph 5:2
o You did not . . . . Heb 10:5
o He has perfected . . . . . Heb 10:14

OFFERINGS

and offered burnt o . . . . . Gen 8:20
In burnt o . . . . Heb 10:6

OFFICE

sitting at the tax o . . . . Matt 9:9

OFFSPRING

wife and raise up o . . . . Matt 22:24
we are also His o . . . . . . Acts 17:28
am the Root and the O . Rev 22:16

OFTEN

o I wanted to gather . . Luke 13:34
as o as you eat this . . . 1 Cor 11:26

OIL

a bin, and a little o . . . 1 Kin 17:12
very costly fragrant o . . . Matt 26:7
anointing him with o . . James 5:14
and do not harm the o . . . . Rev 6:6

OLD

young, and now am o . . . . Ps 37:25
was said to those of o . . . Matt 5:21
but when you are o . . . . John 21:18
Your o men shall dream Acts 2:17
o man was crucified . . . . . Rom 6:6
o things have passed . . 2 Cor 5:17
have put off the o man . . . . Col 3:9
that serpent of o . . . . Rev 20:2

OLDER

o shall serve the . . . . Gen 25:23
not rebuke an o man . . . 1 Tim 5:1

OLDEST

beginning with the o . . . . John 8:9

OLIVE

a freshly plucked o . . . . . Gen 8:11
o tree which is wild . . . Rom 11:24

OMNIPOTENT

For the Lord God O . . . . . Rev 19:6

ONCE

died, He died to sin o . . . Rom 6:10

ONE

"O thing you lack . . . . Mark 10:21
o thing is needed . . . . . Luke 10:42
I and My Father are o . John 10:30
that they may be o . . . . John 17:11
o accord in the temple . . Acts 2:46
for you are all o . . . . Gal 3:28
to create in Himself o . . Eph 2:15
o Lord . . . . Eph 4:5
o faith . . . . Eph 4:5
o baptism . . . . Eph 4:5
o God and Father of . . . . . Eph 4:6
For there is o God and . . 1 Tim 2:5
o Mediator between . . . . 1 Tim 2:5
a thousand years as o . . . 2 Pet 3:8

OPENED

o not His mouth . . . . Is 53:7
o the Scriptures . . . . . . Luke 24:32
o their understanding . Luke 24:45
Now I saw heaven . . . . Rev 19:11

OPENS

him the doorkeeper o . . John 10:3
and shuts and no one o . . . Rev 3:7

OPINION

be wise in your own o . Rom 11:25

OPINIONS

falter between two o . . 1 Kin 18:21

OPPORTUNITY

But sin, taking o . . . . Rom 7:8
as we have o . . . . Gal 6:10
but you lacked o . . . . Phil 4:10

OPPRESS

he loves to o . . . . Hos 12:7
o the widow or the . . . . . Zech 7:10
Do not the rich o . . . . . . James 2:6

OPPRESSED

for all who are o . . . . Ps 103:6
The tears of the o . . . . Eccl 4:1
He was o and He was . . . . . Is 53:7
all who were o . . . . Acts 10:38

OPPRESSES

o the poor reproaches . Prov 14:31

OPPRESSION

have surely seen the o . . . . . Ex 3:7
their life from o . . . . Ps 72:14
brought low through o . . Ps 107:39
me from the o . . . . Ps 119:134
considered all the o . . . . . . Eccl 4:1
o destroys a wise . . . . Eccl 7:7
justice, but behold, o . . . . . . Is 5:7
surely seen the o . . . . Acts 7:34

ORACLES

received the living o . . . . Acts 7:38
were committed the o . . . . Rom 3:2
principles of the o . . . . . . Heb 5:12

ORDAINED

o you a prophet . . . . Jer 1:5
whom He has o . . . . Acts 17:31

ORDER

decently and in o . . . . . 1 Cor 14:40

ORDERS

o his conduct aright I . . . . Ps 50:23

ORDINANCE

resists the o of God . . . Rom 13:2

ORDINANCES

and fleshly o imposed . . . Heb 9:10

ORPHANS

will not leave you o . . . John 14:18
to visit o and widows . James 1:27

OUGHT

These you o to have . . . Matt 23:23
pray for as we o . . . . Rom 8:26
persons o you to be . . . 2 Pet 3:11

OUTCAST

they called you an o . . . . Jer 30:17

OUTCASTS

will assemble the o . . . . Is 11:12

OUTRAN

the other disciple o . . . . John 20:4

OUTSIDE

and dish, that the o . . . . Matt 23:26
Pharisees make the o . Luke 11:39
toward those who are o . . . Col 4:5
to Him, o the camp . . . Heb 13:13
But o are dogs and . . . . Rev 22:15

OUTSTRETCHED

and with an o arm . . . . . Deut 26:8

OUTWARD

at the o appearance . . . 1 Sam 16:7
adornment be merely o . . 1 Pet 3:3

OUTWARDLY

not a Jew who is one o . Rom 2:28

OVERCAME

My throne, as I also o . . . Rev 3:21
"And they o him by . . . . Rev 12:11

OVERCOME

good cheer, I have o . . . John 16:33
and the Lamb will o . . . Rev 17:14

OVERCOMES

of God o the world . . . . 1 John 5:4
o I will give to eat . . . . Rev 2:7
o shall not be hurt . . . . . . Rev 2:11
o shall inherit all . . . . Rev 21:7

OVERSEER

to the Shepherd and O . 1 Pet 2:25

OVERSEERS

you, serving as o . . . . 1 Pet 5:2

OVERSHADOW

of the Highest will o . . . Luke 1:35

OVERTHREW

As God o Sodom and . . . Jer 50:40

OVERTHROW

o the faith of some . . . . 2 Tim 2:18

OVERTHROWN

and Nineveh shall be o . . . Jon 3:4

OVERTHROWS

And o the mighty . . . . . . Job 12:19
o them in the night . . . . Job 34:25
o the words of the . . . . . Prov 22:12

OVERWHELM

o the fatherless . . . . Job 6:27

OVERWHELMED

and my spirit was o . . . . . . Ps 77:3
my spirit is o within . . . . . Ps 143:4

OVERWORK

Do not o to be rich . . . . . Prov 23:4

OWE

O no one anything . . . . . Rom 13:8

OWED

o him ten thousand . . . . Matt 18:24

OWN

He came to His o . . . . . . John 1:11
having loved His o . . . . . John 13:1
would love its o . . . . . . John 15:19
you are not your o . . . . 1 Cor 6:19
But each one has his o . . 1 Cor 7:7
For all seek their o . . . . . Phil 2:21
from our sins in His o . . . . Rev 1:5

OX

shall not muzzle an o . . . Deut 25:4
o knows its owner . . . . Is 1:3
Sabbath loose his o . . . Luke 13:15
shall not muzzle an o . . . 1 Cor 9:9

P

PACIFIES

A gift in secret p . . . . . . Prov 21:14

PAIN

p you shall bring . . . . Gen 3:16
p as a woman in . . . . Is 13:8
Why is my p perpetual . . Jer 15:18
shall be no more p . . . . . . Rev 21:4

PAINED

My heart is severely p . . . . Ps 55:4
I am p in my very . . . . Jer 4:19

PAINFUL

for the present, but p . . . Heb 12:11

PAINS

The p of death . . . . Ps 116:3
having loosed the p . . . . . Acts 2:24

PAINT

your eyes with p . . . . Jer 4:30

PALACE

enter the King's p . . . . . . Ps 45:15
guards his own p . . . . . Luke 11:21
evident to the whole p . . . Phil 1:13

PALACES

Out of the ivory p . . . . Ps 45:8

PALE

behold, a p horse . . . . Rev 6:8

PALM

p branches in their . . . . Rev 7:9

PALMS

struck Him with the p . Matt 26:67

PAMPERS

p his servant from . . . . . Prov 29:21

PANGS

The p of death . . . . Ps 18:4
labors with birth p . . . . . Rom 8:22

PARABLE

do You speak this p . . . Luke 12:41

PARABLES

rest it is given in p . . . . . Luke 8:10

PARADISE

will be with Me in P . . Luke 23:43
in the midst of the P . . . . . . Rev 2:7

PARDON

He will abundantly p . . . . . Is 55:7
p all their iniquities . . . . . . Jer 33:8

PARDONING

is a God like You, p . . . . . Mic 7:18

PARENTS

will rise up against p . . Matt 10:21
has left house or p . . . . Luke 18:29
disobedient to p . . . . Rom 1:30

PART

chosen that good p . . . . Luke 10:42
you, you have no p . . . . . John 13:8
For we know in p . . . . . 1 Cor 13:9
shall take away his p . . . Rev 22:19

PARTAKE

for we all p of that . . . . 1 Cor 10:17

PARTAKER

in hope should be p . . . 1 Cor 9:10
Christ, and also a p . . . . . 1 Pet 5:1

PARTAKERS

Gentiles have been p . . Rom 15:27
know that as you are p . 2 Cor 1:7
qualified us to be p . . . . . . Col 1:12

PARTIAL

You shall not be p . . . . . Lev 19:15

PARTIALITY

that God shows no p . . . Acts 10:34
doing nothing with p . . 1 Tim 5:21
good fruits, without p . James 3:17

PASS

I will p over you . . . . Ex 12:13
When you p through the . . Is 43:2
and earth will p . . . . Matt 24:35

PASSED

forbearance God had p . Rom 3:25
High Priest who has p . . . Heb 4:14
know that we have p . 1 John 3:14

PASSES

of Christ which p . . . . Eph 3:19

PASSION

uncleanness, p . . . . Col 3:5

PASSIONS

gave them up to vile p . . Rom 1:26

PASSOVER

It is the LORD's P . . . . Ex 12:11
I will keep the P . . . . . Matt 26:18
indeed Christ, our P . . . . 1 Cor 5:7
By faith he kept the P . . Heb 11:28

PASTORS

and some p and . . . . Eph 4:11

PASTURE

the sheep of Your p . . . . . . Ps 74:1
in and out and find p . . . John 10:9

PASTURES

to lie down in green p . . . . Ps 23:2

PATH

You will show me the p . . Ps 16:11

PATHS

He leads me in the p . . . . . Ps 23:3
Make His p straight . . . . Matt 3:3
and make straight p . . . Heb 12:13

PATIENCE

'Master, have p . . . . . . Matt 18:26
and bear fruit with p . . . Luke 8:15
labor of love, and p . . 1 Thess 1:3
faith, love, p . . . . 1 Tim 6:11
your faith produces p . . James 1:3
p have its perfect . . . . . . James 1:4
in the kingdom and p . . . . Rev 1:9

PATIENT

rejoicing in hope, p . . . . Rom 12:12
the weak, be p . . . . . . 1 Thess 5:14

PATIENTLY

if you take it p . . . . 1 Pet 2:20

PATRIARCHS

begot the twelve p . . . . . . Acts 7:8

PATTERN

p which you were . . . . Ex 26:30
as you have us for a p . . . Phil 3:17
p shown you on the . . . . . . Heb 8:5

PEACE

you, And give you p . . . . Num 6:26
both lie down in p . . . . Ps 4:8
p have those who . . . . . Ps 119:165
I am for p . . . . Ps 120:7
war, And a time of p . . . . Eccl 3:8
Father, Prince of P . . . . Is 9:6
keep him in perfect p . . . . Is 26:3
p they have not . . . . Is 59:8
slightly, Saying, 'P . . . . . . Jer 6:14
place I will give p . . . . . . Hag 2:9
is worthy, let your p . . . Matt 10:13
that I came to bring p . Matt 10:34
And on earth p . . . . Luke 2:14
if a son of p is there . . . Luke 10:6
that make for your p . . Luke 19:42
leave with you, My p . . John 14:27
Me you may have p . . . John 16:33
Grace to you and p . . . . . Rom 1:7
by faith, we have p . . . . . . Rom 5:1
God has called us to p 1 Cor 7:15
p will be with you . . . . 2 Cor 13:11
Spirit is love, joy, p . . . . . Gal 5:22
He Himself is our p . . . . Eph 2:14
and the p of God . . . . Phil 4:7
And let the p of God . . . . Col 3:15
faith, love, p . . . . 2 Tim 2:22
meaning "king of p," . . . . . Heb 7:2

PEACEABLE

is first pure, then p . . . . James 3:17

PEACEABLY

on you, live p . . . . Rom 12:18

PEACEFUL

in a p habitation . . . . Is 32:18

PEACEMAKERS

Blessed are the p . . . . Matt 5:9

PEARL

had found one p . . . . . . Matt 13:46

PEARLS

nor cast your p . . . . Matt 7:6
gates were twelve p . . . . Rev 21:21

PENTECOST

P had fully come . . . . Acts 2:1

PEOPLE

will take you as My p . . . . Ex 6:7
p shall be my p . . . . Ruth 1:16
p who know the joyful . . . Ps 89:15
We are His p and the . . . . Ps 100:3
"Blessed is Egypt My p . . Is 19:25
to make ready a p . . . . . Luke 1:17
take out of them a p . . Acts 15:14
who were not My p . . . . Rom 9:25
they shall be My p . . . . 2 Cor 6:16
LORD will judge His p . . Heb 10:30
but are now the p . . . . . . 1 Pet 2:10
tribe and tongue and p . . . Rev 5:9
they shall be His p . . . . . Rev 21:3

PERCEIVE

seeing, but do not p . . . . . . Is 6:9
may see and not p . . . . . Mark 4:12

PERDITION
except the son of p . .John 17:12
revealed, the son of p . 2 Thess 2:3
who draw back to p . . . . Heb 10:39

PERFECT
Noah was a just man, p . .Gen 6:9
Father in heaven is p . . . Matt 5:48
they may be made p . .John 17:23
and p will of God . . . . . . Rom 12:2
when that which is p . 1 Cor 13:10
present every man p . .Col 1:28
good gift and every p . James 1:17
in word, he is a p . . . . . James 3:2
p love casts out fear . . 1 John 4:18

PERFECTED
third day I shall be p . Luke 13:32
or am already p . . . . .Phil 3:12
Son who has been p . . . . Heb 7:28

PERFECTION
let us go on to p . . . . Heb 6:1

PERISH
so that we may not p . . . .Jon 1:6
little ones should p . . . .Matt 18:14
in Him should not p . . . .John 3:16
they shall never p . . . John 10:28
among those who p . . . 2 Thess 2:10
that any should p . . . . . . .2 Pet 3:9

PERISHABLE
do it to obtain a p . . . . . 1 Cor 9:25

PERISHED
Truth has p and has . . . . .Jer 7:28

PERISHING
We are p . . . . .Matt 8:25

PERMIT
do not p a woman . . . . . 1 Tim 2:12

PERMITS
we will do if God p . . . . . . .Heb 6:3

PERMITTED
p no one to do them . . . .Ps 105:14
we are p . . . . .2 Cor 4:8

PERSECUTE
when they revile and p . Matt 5:11

PERSECUTED
If they p Me . . . . .John 15:20
p, but not forsaken . . . . .2 Cor 4:9

PERSECUTES
wicked in his pride p . . . . .Ps 10:2

PERSECUTION
p arises because of . . . .Matt 13:21
At that time a great p . . . .Acts 8:1
do I still suffer p . . . . .Gal 5:11

PERSECUTOR
a blasphemer, a p . . . . . 1 Tim 1:13

PERSEVERANCE
tribulation produces p . . . Rom 5:3

PERSEVERE
kept My command to p . . Rev 3:10

PERSISTENCE
p he will rise and . . . . . . Luke 11:8

PERSON
do not regard the p . . . .Matt 22:16
express image of His p . . .Heb 1:3

PERSUADE
"You almost p me . . . . .Acts 26:28

PERSUADED
neither will they be p . Luke 16:31
p that He is able . . . . . .2 Tim 1:12

PERSUASIVE
p words of human . . . . . .1 Cor 2:4

PERVERSE
your way is p . . . . .Num 22:32
p man sows strife . . . . .Prov 16:28
from this p generation . .Acts 2:40

PERVERT
"You shall not p . . . . . .Deut 16:19
p the gospel of Christ . . . . .Gal 1:7

PERVERTING
will you not cease p . . . .Acts 13:10

PERVERTS
p his ways will become . Prov 10:9

PESTILENCE
from the perilous p . . . . . .Ps 91:3
Before Him went p . . . . . .Hab 3:5

PESTILENCES
will be famines, p . . . . . .Matt 24:7

PETITIONS
p that we have asked . 1 John 5:15

PHARISEE
to pray, one a P . . . . . .Luke 18:10

PHILOSOPHERS
p encountered him . . . .Acts 17:18

PHILOSOPHY
cheat you through p . . . . . .Col 2:8

PHYSICIAN
have no need of a p . . . .Matt 9:12

PHYSICIANS
her livelihood on p . . . .Luke 8:43

PIECES
they took the thirty p . . .Matt 27:9

PIERCE
a sword will p . . . . .Luke 2:35

PIERCED
p My hands and My feet . Ps 22:16
whom they have p . . . .Zech 12:10
of the soldiers p . . . . . .John 19:34
p themselves through . . 1 Tim 6:10
and they also who p . . . . . .Rev 1:7

PIERCING
p even to the division . . .Heb 4:12

PILGRIMAGE
heart is set on p . . . . .Ps 84:5
In the house of my p . . .Ps 119:54

PILGRIMS
we are aliens and p . . 1 Chr 29:15
were strangers and p . .Heb 11:13

PILLAR
and she became a p . . . .Gen 19:26
and by night in a p . . . . .Ex 13:21
the living God, the p . . 1 Tim 3:15

PILLARS
break their sacred p . . . .Ex 34:13
Blood and fire and p . . . .Joel 2:30
and his feet like p . . . . . .Rev 10:1

PIT
who go down to the p . . . .Ps 28:1
a harlot is a deep p . . . .Prov 23:27
my life in the p . . . . .Lam 3:53

up my life from the p . . . . .Jon 2:6
into the bottomless p . . . .Rev 20:3

PITIABLE
of all men the most p . 1 Cor 15:19

PITS
The proud have dug p . .Ps 119:85

PITY
for someone to take p . . .Ps 69:20
p He redeemed them . . . . . .Is 63:9
just as I had p . . . . .Matt 18:33

PLACE
Come, see the p . . . . . . .Matt 28:6
My word has no p . . . . .John 8:37
I go to prepare a p . . . . .John 14:2
might go to his own p . . .Acts 1:25

PLACES
And the rough p . . . . .Is 40:4
They love the best p . . . .Matt 23:6
in the heavenly p . . . . . . .Eph 1:3

PLAGUE
bring yet one more p . . . . .Ex 11:1

PLAGUES
p that are written . . . . . .Rev 22:18

PLANK
First remove the p . . . . . .Matt 7:5

PLANS
He makes the p of the . . .Ps 33:10
that devises wicked p . . .Prov 6:18

PLANT
A time to p . . . . .Eccl 3:2
Him as a tender p . . . . .Is 53:2
p of an alien vine . . . . . . .Jer 2:21
p which My heavenly . Matt 15:13

PLANTED
shall be like a tree p . . . . . .Ps 1:3
by the roots and be p . .Luke 17:6
I p, Apollos watered . . . .1 Cor 3:6

PLANTS
neither he who p . . . . . . .1 Cor 3:7

PLATTER
head here on a p . . . . . .Matt 14:8

PLEASANT
food, that it was p . . . . . . .Gen 3:6
how good and how p . . .Ps 133:1

PLEASANTNESS
ways are ways of p . . . . .Prov 3:17

PLEASE
in the flesh cannot p . . . .Rom 8:8
p his neighbor for his . . .Rom 15:2
he may p the Lord . . . . .1 Cor 7:32
is impossible to p Him . . .Heb 11:6

PLEASED
Then You shall be p . . . . .Ps 51:19
in whom I am well p . . . .Matt 3:17
God was not well p . . . .1 Cor 10:5
testimony, that he p . . . . .Heb 11:5

PLEASES
Whatever the Lord p . . . .Ps 135:6

PLEASING
sacrifice, well p . . . . .Phil 4:18
for this is well p . . . . .Col 3:20
in you what is well p . . .Heb 13:21

PLEASURE
Do good in Your good p . Ps 51:18
p will be a poor man . .Prov 21:17

shall perform all My *p* . . . . Is 44:28
your Father's good *p* . . Luke 12:32
to the good *p* of His . . . . . . Eph 1:5
for sin You had no p . . . . Heb 10:6
My soul has no p . . . . . . Heb 10:38
p that war in your . . . . . James 4:1

PLEASURES

Your right hand are *p* . . Ps 16:11
cares, riches, and *p* . . . . Luke 8:14
to enjoy the passing *p* . . Heb 11:25

PLOW

put his hand to the *p* . . . Luke 9:62

PLOWED

You have *p* . . . . Hos 10:13

PLOWMAN

p shall overtake the . . . Amos 9:13

PLUCK

p the heads of grain . . . Mark 2:23

PLUCKED

cheeks to those who *p* . . . . . Is 50:6
And His disciples *p* . . . . . Luke 6:1
you would have *p* . . . . Gal 4:15

PLUNDER

p the Egyptians . . . . Ex 3:22
The *p* of the poor is . . . . Is 3:14
house and *p* his goods . Matt 12:29

PLUNDERED

a people robbed and *p* . . . Is 42:22
"And when you are *p* . . . . Jer 4:30

PLUNDERING

me Because of the *p* . . . . Is 22:4
accepted the *p* of your . Heb 10:34

POETS

some of your own *p* . . . Acts 17:28

POISON

"The p of asps is . . . . Rom 3:13

POISONED

p by bitterness . . . . Acts 8:23

POLLUTIONS

have escaped the *p* . . . . . 2 Pet 2:20

POMP

had come with great *p* . Acts 25:23

POMPOUS

and a mouth speaking *p* . . Dan 7:8

PONDER

P the path of your . . . . . . Prov 4:26

PONDERED

p them in her heart . . . . Luke 2:19

PONDERS

p all his paths . . . . Prov 5:21

POOR

p will never cease . . . . . Deut 15:11
So the *p* have hope . . . . . . Job 5:16
I delivered the *p* . . . . Job 29:12
p shall eat and be . . . . Ps 22:26
But I am *p* and needy . . . . Ps 40:17
Let the *p* and needy . . . . . Ps 74:21
He raises the *p* . . . . Ps 113:7
slack hand becomes *p* . . . Prov 10:4
p man is hated even . . . . Prov 14:20
has mercy on the *p* . . . . Prov 14:21
who oppresses the *p* . . . Prov 14:31
p reproaches his . . . . Prov 17:5
Do not rob the *p* . . . . . . Prov 22:22
that same *p* man . . . . Eccl 9:15
The alien or the *p* . . . . . . Zech 7:10

"Blessed are the *p* . . . . Matt 5:3
p have the gospel . . . . Matt 11:5
"For you have the *p* . . . Matt 26:11
sakes He became *p* . . . . . 2 Cor 8:9
should remember the *p* . . Gal 2:10
God not chosen the *p* . . James 2:5
wretched, miserable, *p* . . Rev 3:17

PORTION

O LORD, You, are the *p* . . . . Ps 16:5
heart and my *p* forever . . Ps 73:26
You are my *p* . . . . Ps 119:57
I will divide Him a *p* . . . . . Is 53:12
rejoice in their *p* . . . . Is 61:7
The *P* of Jacob is not . . . Jer 10:16
"The LORD is my *p* . . . . . Lam 3:24
and appoint him his *p* . Matt 24:51
to give them their *p* . . . Luke 12:42
give me the *p* . . . . Luke 15:12

POSSESS

descendants shall *p* . . . . Gen 22:17
p the land which . . . . Josh 1:11
"By your patience *p* . . . Luke 21:19
p his own vessel . . . . . . 1 Thess 4:4

POSSESSED

"The LORD *p* me at . . . . . Prov 8:22

POSSESSING

and yet *p* all things . . . . 2 Cor 6:10

POSSESSION

as an everlasting *p* . . . . . . Gen 17:8
and an enduring *p* . . . . . Heb 10:34

POSSESSIONS

and sold their *p* . . . . Acts 2:45

POSSIBLE

God all things are *p* . . . Matt 19:26
p that the blood . . . . Heb 10:4

POUR

p My Spirit on your . . . . . . Is 44:3
P out Your fury . . . . Jer 10:25
That I will *p* out My . . . . Joel 2:28
"And I will *p* . . . . Zech 12:10
angels, "Go and *p* . . . . . . Rev 16:1

POURED

I am *p* out like water . . . . Ps 22:14
grace is *p* upon Your . . . . . Ps 45:2
strong, Because He *p* . . . . Is 53:12
and My fury will be *p* . . . Jer 7:20
broke the flask and *p* . . Mark 14:3
I am already being *p* . . . . 2 Tim 4:6
whom He *p* out on us . . . Titus 3:6

POVERTY

leads only to *p* . . . . Prov 14:23
p put in all the . . . . Luke 21:4
and their deep *p* . . . . 2 Cor 8:2
p might become rich . . . . 2 Cor 8:9
tribulation, and *p* . . . . Rev 2:9

POWER

that I may show My *p* . . . . Ex 9:16
him who is without *p* . . . . Job 26:2
p who can understand . . Job 26:14
p belongs to God . . . . Ps 62:11
p Your enemies shall . . . . . Ps 66:3
gives strength and *p* . . . . Ps 68:35
a king is, there is *p* . . . . . . Eccl 8:4
No one has *p* over the . . . . Eccl 8:8
'Not by might nor by *p* . . Zech 4:6
the kingdom and the *p* . . Matt 6:13
the Son of Man has *p* . . . Matt 9:6
Scriptures nor the *p* . . . Matt 22:29
p went out from Him . . Luke 6:19
are endued with *p* . . . . Luke 24:49
I have *p* to lay it . . . . John 10:18
"You could have no *p* . John 19:11
you shall receive *p* . . . . . . Acts 1:8
though by our own *p* . . . Acts 3:12

man is the great *p* . . . . . . Acts 8:10
"Give me this *p* . . . . Acts 8:19
for it is the *p* . . . . Rom 1:16
saved it is the *p* . . . . 1 Cor 1:18
Greeks, Christ the *p* . . . 1 Cor 1:24
that the *p* of Christ . . . . 2 Cor 12:9
greatness of His *p* . . . . . . Eph 1:19
the Lord and in the *p* . . . . Eph 6:10
to His glorious *p* . . . . Col 1:11
the glory of His *p* . . . . . 2 Thess 1:9
of fear, but of *p* . . . . 2 Tim 1:7
by the word of His *p* . . . . Heb 1:3
p of death, that . . . . Heb 2:14
as His divine *p* . . . . 2 Pet 1:3
Dominion and *p* . . . . Jude 25
to him I will give *p* . . . . . . Rev 2:26
honor and glory and *p* . . Rev 5:13

POWERFUL

of the LORD is *p* . . . . Ps 29:4
of God is living and *p* . . . Heb 4:12

POWERS

principalities and *p* . . . . . Col 2:15
word of God and the *p* . . . Heb 6:5

PRAISE

p shall be of You in . . . . . Ps 22:25
the people shall *p* . . . . Ps 45:17
P is awaiting You . . . . Ps 65:1
Let all the peoples *p* . . . . . Ps 67:3
p shall be continually . . . . Ps 71:6
And the heavens will *p* . . . Ps 89:5
Seven times a day I *p* . . Ps 119:164
that has breath *p* . . . . Ps 150:6
Let another man *p* . . . . . Prov 27:2
let her own works *p* . . . Prov 31:31
And your gates *P* . . . . Is 60:18
He makes Jerusalem a *p* . . Is 62:7
For You are my *p* . . . . . . Jer 17:14
Me a name of joy, a *p* . . . Jer 33:9
give you fame and *p* . . . Zeph 3:20
You have perfected p . . Matt 21:16
men more than the *p* . . John 12:43
p is not from men but . . Rom 2:29
Then each one's *p* . . . . . . 1 Cor 4:5
should be to the *p* . . . . . . Eph 1:12
to the glory and *p* . . . . . . Phil 1:11
I will sing p to You . . . . . Heb 2:12
the sacrifice of *p* . . . . . . Heb 13:15
and for the *p* of those . . 1 Pet 2:14
saying, "P our God . . . . . Rev 19:5

PRAISED

daily He shall be *p* . . . . . . Ps 72:15
LORD's name is to be *p* . . . Ps 113:3
and greatly to be *p* . . . . . Ps 145:3
the Most High and *p* . . . . Dan 4:34

PRAISES

it is good to sing *p* . . . . . . Ps 147:1
and he *p* . . . . Prov 31:28

PRAISEWORTHY

if there is anything *p* . . . . . Phil 4:8

PRAISING

They will still be *p* . . . . . . Ps 84:4
of the heavenly host *p* . . Luke 2:13
in the temple *p* . . . . . . Luke 24:53

PRAY

at noon I will *p* . . . . Ps 55:17
who hate you, and *p* . . . Matt 5:44
"And when you *p* . . . . . . Matt 6:5
manner, therefore, *p* . . . . Matt 6:9
"Watch and *p* . . . . Matt 26:41
"Lord, teach us to *p* . . . . Luke 11:1
"And I will *p* . . . . John 14:16
I do not *p* for the . . . . John 17:9
"I do not *p* for . . . . John 17:20
p without ceasing . . . . 1 Thess 5:17
Brethren, *p* for us . . . 1 Thess 5:25
Let him *p* . . . . James 5:13

PRAYED

to one another, and *p* . James 5:16
say that he should *p* . . 1 John 5:16

PRAYED

p more earnestly . . . . . . Luke 22:44
p earnestly that it . . . . . James 5:17

PRAYER

p made in this place . . . 2 Chr 7:15
And my *p* is pure . . . . Job 16:17
A *p* to the God of my . . . . . Ps 42:8
P also will be made . . . . . . Ps 72:15
He shall regard the *p* . . . Ps 102:17
to the LORD, But the *p* . . Prov 15:8
go out except by *p* . . . . Matt 17:21
all night in *p* to God . . . . Luke 6:12
continually to *p* . . . . Acts 6:4
where *p* was . . . . Acts 16:13
steadfastly in *p* . . . . Rom 12:12
to fasting and *p* . . . . 1 Cor 7:5
always with all *p* . . . . . . Eph 6:18
but in everything by *p* . . . Phil 4:6
the word of God and *p* . . 1 Tim 4:5
And the *p* of faith . . . . James 5:15

PRAYERS

though You make many *p* . Is 1:15
pretense make long *p* . . Matt 23:14
fervently for you in *p* . . . Col 4:12
p may not be hindered . . 1 Pet 3:7
which are the *p* . . . . Rev 5:8

PREACH

time Jesus began to *p* . . . Matt 4:17
you hear in the ear, *p* . . Matt 10:27
P the gospel to the . . . . . Luke 4:18
And how shall they *p* . . Rom 10:15
p Christ crucified . . . . . 1 Cor 1:23
I or they, so we *p* . . . . 1 Cor 15:11
P the word . . . . 2 Tim 4:2

PREACHED

p that people . . . . Mark 6:12
out and *p* . . . . Mark 16:20
of sins should be *p* . . . . Luke 24:47
p Christ to them . . . . Acts 8:5
lest, when I have *p* . . . . 1 Cor 9:27
than what we have *p* . . . . . Gal 1:8
the gospel was *p* . . . . Heb 4:2
also He went and *p* . . . . 1 Pet 3:19

PREACHER

they hear without a *p* . . Rom 10:14
I was appointed a *p* . . . . 1 Tim 2:7

PREACHES

the Jesus whom Paul *p* Acts 19:13
p another Jesus . . . . 2 Cor 11:4
p any other gospel . . . . Gal 1:9
p the faith which he . . . . . Gal 1:23

PREACHING

p Jesus as the . . . . Acts 5:42
not risen, then our *p* . . 1 Cor 15:14

PRECEPTS

all His *p* are sure . . . . Ps 111:7
how I love Your *p* . . . . . Ps 119:159

PRECIOUS

P in the sight of the . . . . Ps 116:15
She is more *p* than . . . . Prov 3:15
p things shall not . . . . Is 44:9
if you take out the *p* . . . Jer 15:19
farmer waits for the *p* . . James 5:7
more *p* than gold . . . . . . 1 Pet 1:7
who believe, He is *p* . . . 1 Pet 2:7
p in the sight of . . . . 1 Pet 3:4

PREDESTINED

foreknew, He also *p* . . . Rom 8:29
having *p* us to . . . . Eph 1:5
inheritance, being *p* . . . . . Eph 1:11

PREEMINENCE

He may have the *p* . . . . . . Col 1:18
loves to have the *p* . . . . . 3 John 9

PREFERENCE

in honor giving *p* . . . . . . Rom 12:10

PREJUDICE

these things without *p* . 1 Tim 5:21

PREMEDITATE

p what you will . . . . . . Mark 13:11

PREPARATION

Now it was the P . . . . . . John 19:14
your feet with the *p* . . . . . Eph 6:15

PREPARE

p a table before me in . . . Ps 23:5
P the way of the LORD . . Mark 1:3
p a place for you . . . . . . John 14:2

PREPARED

for whom it is *p* . . . . . . Matt 20:23
Which You have *p* . . . . . Luke 2:31
mercy, which He had *p* . Rom 9:23
things which God has *p* . 1 Cor 2:9
Now He who has *p* . . . . 2 Cor 5:5
p beforehand that we . . . Eph 2:10
God, for He has *p* . . . . . Heb 11:16

PRESENCE

themselves from the *p* . . . Gen 3:8
went out from the *p* . . . . Gen 4:16
P will go with you . . . . . . Ex 33:14
afraid in any man's *p* . . . Deut 1:17
p is fullness of joy . . . . . . Ps 16:11
shall dwell in Your *p* . . . Ps 140:13
not tremble at My *p* . . . . . Jer 5:22
shall shake at My *p* . . . Ezek 38:20
and drank in Your *p* . . Luke 13:26
full of joy in Your *p* . . . . Acts 2:28
but his bodily *p* . . . . . . 2 Cor 10:10
obeyed, not as in my *p* . . Phil 2:12

PRESENT

we are all *p* before . . . . Acts 10:33
evil is *p* with me . . . . Rom 7:21
p your bodies a living . . . Rom 12:1
or death, or things *p* . . . 1 Cor 3:22
absent in body but *p* . . . 1 Cor 5:3
that He might *p* . . . . Eph 5:27
p you faultless . . . . Jude 24

PRESERVE

He shall *p* your soul . . . . . Ps 121:7
The LORD shall *p* . . . . Ps 121:8
loses his life will *p* . . . . Luke 17:33
every evil work and *p* . 2 Tim 4:18

PRESERVED

soul, and body be *p* . . 1 Thess 5:23

PRESERVES

For the LORD *p* the . . . . . . Ps 31:23
p the souls of His . . . . Ps 97:10
who keeps his way *p* . . Prov 16:17

PRETENSE

p make long prayers . . Matt 23:14

PRICE

one pearl of great *p* . . Matt 13:46
were bought at a *p* . . . . 1 Cor 6:20

PRIDE

p serves as . . . . Ps 73:6
By *p* comes nothing . . . Prov 13:10
P goes before . . . . Prov 16:18
her daughter had *p* . . . . Ezek 16:49
was hardened in *p* . . . . . Dan 5:20
For the *p* of the . . . . Zech 11:3
evil eye, blasphemy, *p* . Mark 7:22
p he fall into the . . . . 1 Tim 3:6
eyes, and the *p* . . . . . . 1 John 2:16

PRIEST

he was the *p* of God . . . Gen 14:18

PROFANING

p forever According . . . . . Ps 110:4
So He shall be a *p* . . . . . Zech 6:13
and faithful High P . . . . . Heb 2:17
we have a great High P . Heb 4:14
p forever according . . . . . . Heb 5:6
Christ came as High P . . Heb 9:11

PRIESTHOOD

p being changed . . . . Heb 7:12
has an unchangeable *p* . . Heb 7:24
generation, a royal *p* . . . 1 Pet 2:9

PRIESTS

to Me a kingdom of *p* . . . . Ex 19:6
Her *p* teach for pay . . . . . Mic 3:11
made us kings and *p* . . . . Rev 1:6

PRINCE

is the house of the *p* . . . Job 21:28
Everlasting Father, P . . . . . . Is 9:6
Until Messiah the P . . . . Dan 9:25
days without king or *p* . . Hos 3:4
p asks for gifts . . . . Mic 7:3
"and killed the P . . . . . . Acts 3:15
His right hand to be P . . Acts 5:31
the *p* of the power . . . . . . Eph 2:2

PRINCES

to put confidence in *p* . . . Ps 118:9
He brings the *p* . . . . Is 40:23

PRISON

and put him into the *p* . Gen 39:20
Bring my soul out of *p* . . Ps 142:7
in darkness from the *p* . . . Is 42:7
the opening of the *p* . . . . . Is 61:1
John had heard in *p* . . . Matt 11:2
I was in *p* and you . . . Matt 25:36

PRIZE

the goal for the *p* . . . . . . Phil 3:14

PROCEED

of the same mouth *p* . . James 3:10

PROCEEDED

for I *p* forth . . . . John 8:42

PROCEEDS

by every word that *p* . . . Deut 8:3
by every word that *p* . . . Matt 4:4
Spirit of truth who *p* . . John 15:26

PROCLAIM

began to *p* it freely . . . . Mark 1:45
knowing, Him I *p* . . . . . . Acts 17:23
drink this cup, you *p* . 1 Cor 11:26

PROCLAIMED

p the good news . . . . Ps 40:9
he went his way and *p* . Luke 8:39

PROCLAIMER

"He seems to be a *p* . . . Acts 17:18

PROCLAIMS

good news, Who *p* . . . . Is 52:7

PRODIGAL

with *p* living . . . . Luke 15:13

PROFANE

and priest are *p* . . . . Jer 23:11
tried to *p* the temple . . . . Acts 24:6
But reject *p* and old . . . 1 Tim 4:7

PROFANED

and *p* My Sabbaths . . . . Ezek 22:8

PROFANENESS

of Jerusalem *p* has . . . . . . Jer 23:15

PROFANING

p the covenant of the . . . . Mal 2:10

PROFESS

They p to know God ... Titus 1:16

PROFIT

For what p is it to ..... Matt 16:26
"For what will it p ..... Mark 8:36
"For what p is it to .....Luke 9:25
her masters much p ... Acts 16:16
brought no small p .... Acts 19:24
what is the p of .... Rom 3:1
seeking my own p .... 1 Cor 10:33
Christ will p you .... Gal 5:2
about words to no p ... 2 Tim 2:14
them, but He for our p . Heb 12:10
What does it p ....James 2:14
sell, and make a p ... James 4:13

PROFITABLE

It is doubtless not p .... 2 Cor 12:1
of God, and is p .... 2 Tim 3:16

PROFITS

have not love, it p ..... 1 Cor 13:3

PROMISE

"Behold, I send the P . Luke 24:49
but to wait for the P .... Acts 1:4
"For the p is to you ..... Acts 2:39
for the hope of the p ... Acts 26:6
p might be sure ...... Rom 4:16
Therefore, since a p ...... Heb 4:1
to the heirs of p .... Heb 6:17
did not receive the p ... Heb 11:39

PROMISED

faithful who had p ..... Heb 11:11

PROMISES

For all the p of God ... 2 Cor 1:20
his Seed were the p ..... Gal 3:16
having received the p .. Heb 11:13
great and precious p .... 2 Pet 1:4

PROPER

you, but for what is p .. 1 Cor 7:35
but, which is p .... 1 Tim 2:10

PROPERLY

Let us walk p .... Rom 13:13

PROPHECY

to another p .... 1 Cor 12:10
for p never came by ... 2 Pet 1:21
is the spirit of p ...... Rev 19:10
of the book of this p .... Rev 22:19

PROPHESIED

Lord, have we not p .... Matt 7:22
and the law p .... Matt 11:13

PROPHESIES

p edifies the church .... 1 Cor 14:4

PROPHESY

prophets, "Do not p ...... Is 30:10
The prophets p falsely ... Jer 5:31
your daughters shall p .. Joel 2:28
Who can but p .... Amos 3:8
saying, "P to us .... Matt 26:68
your daughters shall p .. Acts 2:17
in part and we p .... 1 Cor 13:9

PROPHET

raise up for you a P ... Deut 18:15
"I alone am left a p .. 1 Kin 18:22
I ordained you a p .... Jer 1:5
The p is a fool .... Hos 9:7
Nor was I a son of a p . Amos 7:14
send you Elijah the p ..... Mal 4:5
p shall receive a ...... Matt 10:41
p is not without honor . Matt 13:57
by Daniel the p ...... Mark 13:14
is not a greater p ...... Luke 7:28
it cannot be that a p ... Luke 13:33

who was a P ....Luke 24:19
"Are you the P .... John 1:21
"This is truly the P .... John 6:14
with him the false p .... Rev 19:20

PROPHETIC

p word confirmed ...... 2 Pet 1:19

PROPHETS

the Law or the P ...... Matt 5:17
is the Law and the P .... Matt 7:12
or one of the p ...... Matt 16:14
the tombs of the p ..... Matt 23:29
indeed, I send you a .. Matt 23:34
one who kills the p ... Matt 23:37
Then many false p .... Matt 24:11
Moses and the p ...... Luke 16:29
are sons of the p .... Acts 3:25
p did your fathers not ... Acts 7:52
"To Him all the p ...... Acts 10:43
do you believe the p ... Acts 26:27
by the Law and the P ... Rom 3:21
have killed Your p ...... Rom 11:3
to be apostles, some p .. Eph 4:11
this salvation the p ..... 1 Pet 1:10
because many false p .. 1 John 4:1
found the blood of p .... Rev 18:24

PROPITIATION

set forth as a p .... Rom 3:25
to God, to make p ...... Heb 2:17
He Himself is the p .... 1 John 2:2
His Son to be the p .... 1 John 4:10

PROPRIETY

modest apparel, with p . 1 Tim 2:9

PROSPER

they p who love you ..... Ps 122:6
of the LORD shall p .... Is 53:10
against you shall p .... Is 54:17
up as he may p .... 1 Cor 16:2
I pray that you may p ... 3 John 2

PROSPERED

since the LORD has p ... Gen 24:56

PROSPERING

His ways are always p .... Ps 10:5

PROSPERITY

p all your days .... Deut 23:6
p the destroyer .... Job 15:21
Now in my p I said .... Ps 30:6
has pleasure in the p .... Ps 35:27
When I saw the p .... Ps 73:3
I pray, send now p ..... Ps 118:25
that we have our p .... Acts 19:25

PROSPEROUS

will make your way p .... Josh 1:8

PROSPERS

just as your soul p ...... 3 John 2

PROUD

tongue that speaks p ...... Ps 12:3
And fully repays the p ... Ps 31:23
does not respect the p ... Ps 40:4
a haughty look and a p .. Ps 101:5
p He knows from afar ... Ps 138:6
Everyone p .... Prov 16:5
by wine, He is a p ...... Hab 2:5
He has scattered the p . Luke 1:51
"God resists the p .... 1 Pet 5:5

PROVERB

of a drunkard Is a p .... Prov 26:9
one shall take up a p .... Mic 2:4
to the true p .... 2 Pet 2:22

PROVERBS

three thousand p ...... 1 Kin 4:32
in order many p .... Eccl 12:9

PROVIDE

"My son, God will p .... Gen 22:8
"P neither gold nor ..... Matt 10:9
if anyone does not p .... 1 Tim 5:8

PROVIDED

these hands have p .... Acts 20:34
p something better ..... Heb 11:40

PROVISION

no p for the flesh ...... Rom 13:14

PROVOKE

"Do they p Me to .... Jer 7:19
you, fathers, do not p .... Eph 6:4

PROVOKED

p the Most High .... Ps 78:56
his spirit was p .... Acts 17:16
seek its own, is not p . 1 Cor 13:5

PRUDENCE

To give p to the .... Prov 1:4
wisdom, dwell with p ... Prov 8:12
us in all wisdom and p ... Eph 1:8

PRUDENT

p man covers shame ... Prov 12:16
A p man conceals ..... Prov 12:23
The wisdom of the p .... Prov 14:8
p considers well ...... Prov 14:15
heart will be called p .. Prov 16:21
p man foresees evil ..... Prov 22:3
Therefore the p .... Amos 5:13
from the wise and p ... Matt 11:25

PRUDENTLY

Servant shall deal p ...... Is 52:13

PRUNES

that bears fruit He p .... John 15:2

PSALM

each of you has a p ... 1 Cor 14:26

PSALMIST

And the sweet p ...... 2 Sam 23:1

PSALMS

to one another in p ..... Eph 5:19
Let him sing p .... James 5:13

PUNISH

p the righteous is ...... Prov 17:26
Shall I not p them for ..... Jer 5:9

PUNISHED

p them often in every .. Acts 26:11
These shall be p ...... 2 Thess 1:9

PUNISHES

will you say when He p . Jer 13:21

PUNISHMENT

p is greater than I ...... Gen 4:13
you do in the day of p ..... Is 10:3
p they shall perish ...... Jer 10:15
not turn away its p ..... Amos 1:3
into everlasting p .... Matt 25:46
p which was inflicted ... 2 Cor 2:6
Of how much worse p .. Heb 10:29
sent by him for the p .. 1 Pet 2:14
the unjust under p ...... 2 Pet 2:9

PURE

a mercy seat of p gold ... Ex 25:17
'My doctrine is p .... Job 11:4
that he could be p ..... Job 15:14
of the LORD are p .... Ps 12:6
ways of a man are p .... Prov 16:2
a generation that is p ... Prov 30:12
things indeed are p .... Rom 14:20
whatever things are p .... Phil 4:8
keep yourself p .... 1 Tim 5:22

PURER

p all things are *p* . . . . Titus 1:15
above is first *p* . . . . James 3:17
babes, desire the *p* . . . . . . 1 Pet 2:2
just as He is *p* . . . . 1 John 3:3

PURER

p eyes than to behold . . . Hab 1:13

PURGE

P me with hyssop . . . . Ps 51:7

PURGED

away, And your sin *p* . . . . . . Is 6:7

PURIFICATION

with the water of *p* . . . . Num 31:23

PURIFIED

all things are *p* . . . . Heb 9:22
Since you have *p* . . . . . . 1 Pet 1:22

PURIFIES

hope in Him *p* himself . 1 John 3:3

PURIFY

and *p* your hearts . . . . . . James 4:8

PURIFYING

p their hearts by . . . . Acts 15:9
sanctifies for the *p* . . . . . . Heb 9:13

PURIM

called these days *P* . . . . . Esth 9:26

PURITY

spirit, in faith, in *p* . . . . 1 Tim 4:12

PURPOSE

A time for every *p* . . . . Eccl 3:1
But for this *p* I came . . John 12:27
by the determined *p* . . . . Acts 2:23
to fulfill His *p* . . . . Rev 17:17

PURSUE

p righteousness . . . . Rom 9:30
P love . . . . 1 Cor 14:1

PURSUES

flee when no one *p* . . . . Prov 28:1

Q

QUAIL

and it brought *q* . . . . . . Num 11:31

QUARREL

He will not q nor cry . . Matt 12:19
the Lord must not *q* . . . 2 Tim 2:24

QUARRELSOME

but gentle, not *q* . . . . 1 Tim 3:3

QUEEN

heart, 'I sit as *q* . . . . Rev 18:7

QUENCH

Many waters cannot *q* . . . Song 8:7
flax He will not *q* . . . . . Matt 12:20
q all the fiery . . . . Eph 6:16
Do not *q* the Spirit . . 1 Thess 5:19

QUENCHED

that shall never be *q* . . . Mark 9:43

QUESTIONS

and asking them *q* . . . . . Luke 2:46

QUICKLY

with your adversary *q* . . Matt 5:25
"Surely I am coming *q* . Rev 22:20

QUIET

aspire to lead a *q* . . . 1 Thess 4:11
a gentle and *q* spirit . . . . 1 Pet 3:4

QUIETNESS

a handful with *q* . . . . Eccl 4:6
In *q* and confidence . . . . . . Is 30:15
of righteousness, *q* . . . . . . Is 32:17
that they work in *q* . . 2 Thess 3:12

R

RABBI

be called by men, '*R* . . . Matt 23:7

RACA

to his brother, '*R* . . . . . . Matt 5:22

RACE

man to run its *r* . . . . Ps 19:5
r is not to the swift . . . . . Eccl 9:11
I have finished the *r* . . . . 2 Tim 4:7
with endurance the *r* . . . Heb 12:1

RAGE

Why do the nations *r* . . . . . . Ps 2:1
'Why did the nations r . . Acts 4:25

RAIN

had not caused it to *r* . . . . Gen 2:5
And the *r* was on the . . . . Gen 7:12
I will *r* down on him . . Ezek 38:22
given you the former *r* . . Joel 2:23
the good, and sends *r* . . . Matt 5:45
"and the *r* descended . . . Matt 7:25
r that often comes . . . . Heb 6:7
that it would not *r* . . . . James 5:17

RAINBOW

"I set My *r* in the . . . . Gen 9:13
and there was a *r* . . . . Rev 4:3

RAINED

r fire and brimstone . . . Luke 17:29

RAINS

r righteousness . . . . Hos 10:12

RAISE

third day He will *r* . . . . . . Hos 6:2
in three days I will *r* . . . . John 2:19
and I will *r* him up at . . . John 6:40
and the Lord will *r* . . . . James 5:15

RAISED

be killed, and be *r* . . . . Matt 16:21
just as Christ was *r* . . . . . . Rom 6:4
Spirit of Him who *r* . . . . Rom 8:11
"How are the dead *r* . . 1 Cor 15:35
the dead will be *r* . . . . . 1 Cor 15:52
and *r* us up together . . . . . Eph 2:6

RAISES

"For as the Father *r* . . . . John 5:21
but in God who *r* . . . . 2 Cor 1:9

RAN

You *r* well . . . . Gal 5:7

RANSOM

to give His life a *r* . . . . Mark 10:45
who gave Himself a *r* . . . 1 Tim 2:6

RANSOMED

And the *r* of the LORD . . . . Is 35:10
redeemed Jacob, And *r* . . Jer 31:11

RASH

Do not be *r* with your . . . . Eccl 5:2

RASHLY

and do nothing *r* . . . . . . Acts 19:36

RAVENOUS

inwardly they are *r* . . . . Matt 7:15

RAVENS

"Consider the *r* . . . . Luke 12:24

REACHING

r forward to those . . . . Phil 3:13

READ

day, and stood up to *r* . . Luke 4:16
hearts, known and *r* . . . . 2 Cor 3:2

READER

the *r* understand . . . . . Mark 13:14

READINESS

the word with all *r* . . . . Acts 17:11

READING

r the prophet Isaiah . . . . Acts 8:30

READS

Blessed is he who *r* . . . . . . Rev 1:3

READY

and those who were *r* . Matt 25:10
"Lord, I am *r* . . . . Luke 22:33
Be *r* in season and out . . 2 Tim 4:2
and always be *r* . . . . 1 Pet 3:15

REAP

they neither sow nor *r* . . Matt 6:26
you knew that I *r* . . . . . Matt 25:26

REAPED

You have *r* iniquity . . . . Hos 10:13

REAPERS

r are the angels . . . . Matt 13:39

REAPING

r what I did not . . . . Luke 19:22

REAPS

sows and another *r* . . . . . John 4:37

REASON

"Come now, and let us *r* . . . Is 1:18
who asks you a *r* . . . . . . 1 Pet 3:15

REASONED

for three Sabbaths *r* . . . . Acts 17:2

REBEL

if you refuse and *r* . . . . Is 1:20

REBELLING

more against Him By *r* . . Ps 78:17

REBELLION

hearts as in the *r* . . . . Heb 3:8

REBELLIOUS

day long to a *r* people . . . . Is 65:2

REBUILD

God, to *r* its ruins . . . . . . Ezra 9:9
r it as in the days of . . . Amos 9:11

REBUKE

Turn at my *r* . . . . Prov 1:23
R a wise man . . . . Prov 9:8
r is better Than love . . . Prov 27:5
R the oppressor . . . . Is 1:17
sins against you, *r* . . . . Luke 17:3
Do not *r* an older man . . 1 Tim 5:1
who are sinning *r* . . . . . 1 Tim 5:20
"The Lord *r* you . . . . Jude 9
"As many as I love, I *r* . . Rev 3:19

REBUKED

r the winds and the . . . . Matt 8:26
r their unbelief . . . . . . Mark 16:14
but he was *r* for his . . . 2 Pet 2:16

REBUKES

ear that hears the *r* . . . Prov 15:31

RECEIVE

believing, you will *r* ... Matt 21:22
and His own did not *r* .. John 1:11
will come again and *r* .. John 14:3
the world cannot *r* .... John 14:17
Ask, and you will *r* .... John 16:24
"R the Holy Spirit .... John 20:22
"Lord Jesus, *r* .... Acts 7:59
r the Holy Spirit .... Acts 19:2
R one who is weak ..... Rom 14:1
r the Spirit by the .... Gal 3:2
suppose that he will *r* .. James 1:7

RECEIVED

But as many as *r* .... John 1:12
for God has *r* him ..... Rom 14:3
For I *r* from the Lord . 1 Cor 11:23
r Christ .... Col 2:6
R up in glory .... 1 Tim 3:16

RECEIVES

r you *r* Me .... Matt 10:40
and whoever *r* Me ..... Mark 9:37

RECONCILE

and that He might *r* ..... Eph 2:16

RECONCILED

First be *r* to your .... Matt 5:24
we were *r* .... Rom 5:10
Christ's behalf, be *r* .. 2 Cor 5:20

RECONCILIATION

now received the *r* ..... Rom 5:11
to us the word of *r* .... 2 Cor 5:19

RECONCILING

cast away is the *r* ..... Rom 11:15
God was in Christ *r* .... 2 Cor 5:19

REDEEM

But God will *r* my soul ... Ps 49:15
r their life from .... Ps 72:14
was going to *r* Israel .. Luke 24:21
r those who were .... Gal 4:5
us, that He might *r* ..... Titus 2:14

REDEEMED

Let the *r* of the LORD ... Ps 107:2
r shall walk there .... Is 35:9
sea a road For the *r* ... Is 51:10
And you shall be *r* ...... Is 52:3
and *r* His people ...... Luke 1:68
Christ has *r* us from ..... Gal 3:13
that you were not *r* .... 1 Pet 1:18
were slain, And have *r* ... Rev 5:9

REDEEMER

For I know that my *R* ... Job 19:25
Our *R* from Everlasting ... Is 63:16

REDEEMING

r the time .... Eph 5:16

REDEMPTION

those who looked for *r* . Luke 2:38
your *r* draws near .... Luke 21:28
grace through the *r* .... Rom 3:24
the adoption, the *r* ..... Rom 8:23
sanctification and *r* .... 1 Cor 1:30
In Him we have *r* .... Eph 1:7
for the day of *r* .... Eph 4:30
obtained eternal *r* .... Heb 9:12

REED

r He will not break .... Is 42:3
r shaken by the wind ... Matt 11:7

REFINED

us as silver is *r* .... Ps 66:10

REFINER

He will sit as a *r* .... Mal 3:3

REFORMATION

until the time of *r* .... Heb 9:10

REFRESH

r my heart in the Lord . Philem 20

REFRESHED

his spirit has been *r* ... 2 Cor 7:13
for he often *r* .... 2 Tim 1:16

REFRESHES

r the soul of his .... Prov 25:13

REFRESHING

r may come from the ... Acts 3:19

REFUGE

eternal God is your *r* .. Deut 33:27
God is our *r* and .... Ps 46:1
who have fled for *r* ..... Heb 6:18

REGARD

r iniquity in my heart .... Ps 66:18
did not fear God nor *r* .. Luke 18:2

REGARDED

my hand and no one *r* .. Prov 1:24
r the lowly state .... Luke 1:48

REGARDS

r a rebuke will be ..... Prov 13:18

REGENERATION

to you, that in the *r* .... Matt 19:28
the washing of *r* .... Titus 3:5

REGISTERED

So all went to be *r* ...... Luke 2:3

REGRETTED

but afterward he *r* ..... Matt 21:29

REGULATIONS

yourselves to *r* .... Col 2:20

REIGN

"And He will *r* ...... Luke 1:33
righteousness will *r* .... Rom 5:17
so grace might *r* .... Rom 5:21
do not let sin *r* .... Rom 6:12
For He must *r* till He .. 1 Cor 15:25
of Christ, and shall *r* .... Rev 20:6

REIGNED

so that as sin *r* .... Rom 5:21
You have *r* as kings .... 1 Cor 4:8
And they lived and *r* .... Rev 20:4

REIGNS

to Zion, "Your God *r* ..... Is 52:7
Lord God Omnipotent *r* . Rev 19:6

REJECT

"All too well you *r* ..... Mark 7:9
R a divisive man .... Titus 3:10

REJECTED

He is despised and *r* ...... Is 53:3
r Has become the ..... Matt 21:42
many things and be *r* . Luke 17:25
Moses whom they *r* .... Acts 7:35
to a living stone, *r* ...... 1 Pet 2:4

REJECTION

you shall know My *r* .. Num 14:34

REJECTS

he who *r* Me *r* .... Luke 10:16

REJOICE

R in the LORD .... Ps 33:1
of Your wings I will *r* ..... Ps 63:7
Let them *r* before God .... Ps 68:3
Let the heavens *r* .... Ps 96:11

Let the earth *r* .... Ps 97:1
We will *r* and be glad .. Ps 118:24
She shall *r* in time to .. Prov 31:25
R, O young man .... Eccl 11:9
your heart shall *r* .... Is 66:14
Do not *r* over me .... Mic 7:8
do not *r* .... Luke 10:20
you would *r* .... John 14:28
but the world will *r* .... John 16:20
and your heart will *r* . John 16:22
R with those who ..... Rom 12:15
and in this I *r* .... Phil 1:18
faith, I am glad and *r* .... Phil 2:17
R in the Lord always ..... Phil 4:4
R always .... 1 Thess 5:16
yet believing, you *r* ...... 1 Pet 1:8

REJOICED

And my spirit has *r* ..... Luke 1:47
In that hour Jesus *r* ... Luke 10:21
Abraham *r* .... John 8:56

REJOICES

glad, and my glory *r* ..... Ps 16:9
but *r* in the truth ...... 1 Cor 13:6

REJOICING

come again with *r* ...... Ps 126:6
he went on his way *r* ... Acts 8:39
confidence and the *r* ..... Heb 3:6

RELENT

sworn And will not *r* ... Ps 110:4
sworn And will not r .... Heb 7:21

RELENTED

and God *r* from the ...... Jon 3:10

RELENTING

I am weary of *r* .... Jer 15:6

RELIGION

in self-imposed *r* .... Col 2:23
and undefiled *r* .... James 1:27

RELIGIOUS

things you are very *r* .. Acts 17:22

REMAIN

that My joy may *r* ..... John 15:11
your fruit should *r* .... John 15:16
"If I will that he *r* ..... John 21:22
the greater part *r* ...... 1 Cor 15:6
are alive and *r* ...... 1 Thess 4:15
the things which *r* .... Rev 3:2

REMAINS

"While the earth *r* ...... Gen 8:22
Therefore your sin *r* .... John 9:41
There *r* therefore a .... Heb 4:9

REMEMBER

"*R* the Sabbath day ...... Ex 20:8
But we will *r* the name .... Ps 20:7
r Your name in the ..... Ps 119:55
R now your Creator .... Eccl 12:1
r the former things ...... Is 43:18
and their sin I will *r* .... Jer 31:34
In wrath *r* mercy .... Hab 3:2
And to *r* His holy ...... Luke 1:72
"*R* Lot's wife .... Luke 17:32
r the words of the ..... Acts 20:35
R that Jesus Christ .... 2 Tim 2:8
R those who rule .... Heb 13:7

REMEMBERED

Then God *r* Noah .... Gen 8:1
r His covenant with ...... Ex 2:24
r His covenant forever .... Ps 105:8
yea, we wept When we *r* . Ps 137:1
And Peter *r* the word .. Matt 26:75
r the word of the Lord . Acts 11:16

REMEMBRANCE

r my song in the night .... Ps 77:6
Put Me in *r* .... Is 43:26

REMISSION (col-bridge continued)

do this in r of Me .....Luke 22:19
do this in r of Me .....1 Cor 11:24

REMISSION

for the r ....Mark 1:4
Jesus Christ for the r ...Acts 2:38
where there is r........Heb 10:18

REMNANT

The r will return ....Is 10:21
time there is a r ....Rom 11:5

REMORSEFUL

condemned, was r ....Matt 27:3

REMOVE

r this cup from Me ....Luke 22:42
r your lampstand ....Rev 2:5

REMOVED

Though the earth be r ....Ps 46:2
And the hills be r ....Is 54:10
this mountain, 'Be r ...Matt 21:21

REND

So r your heart ....Joel 2:13

RENDER

What shall I r to the ....Ps 116:12
"R therefore to Caesar .Matt 22:21

RENEW

r a steadfast ....Ps 51:10
on the LORD Shall r .....Is 40:31

RENEWED

that your youth is r......Ps 103:5
inward man is being r .2 Cor 4:16
and be r in the spirit ....Eph 4:23

RENEWING

transformed by the r ...Rom 12:2

RENOWN

were of old, men of r .....Gen 6:4

REPAID

Shall evil by r ....Jer 18:20

REPAY

again, I will r ....Luke 10:35
they cannot r ....Luke 14:14
R no one evil for evil ..Rom 12:17
is Mine, I will r ....Rom 12:19
r their parents ....1 Tim 5:4

REPAYS

the LORD, Who fully r .....Is 66:6

REPENT

I abhor myself, And r ....Job 42:6
"R, for the kingdom .....Matt 3:2
you r you will all .....Luke 13:3
said to them, "R ....Acts 2:38
men everywhere to r ....Acts 17:30
be zealous and r ......Rev 3:19

REPENTANCE

you with water unto r ...Matt 3:11
a baptism of r for the ...Mark 1:4
persons who need no r .Luke 15:7
renew them again to r ....Heb 6:6
found no place for r ....Heb 12:17
all should come to r .....2 Pet 3:9

REPENTED

it, because they r ......Matt 12:41

REPETITIONS

r as the heathen do ......Matt 6:7

REPORT

Who has believed our r ....Is 53:1
things are of good r ......Phil 4:8

REPROACH

R has broken my heart ..Ps 69:20
with dishonor comes r ..Prov 18:3
not remember the r ....Is 54:4
Because I bore the r ....Jer 31:19
these things You r ....Luke 11:45
lest he fall into r........1 Tim 3:7
esteeming the r ....Heb 11:26
and without r ....James 1:5

REPROACHED

If you are r for the .....1 Pet 4:14

REPROACHES

is not an enemy who r ..Ps 55:12
in infirmities, in r.....2 Cor 12:10

REPROOF

for doctrine, for r .....2 Tim 3:16

REPROOFS

R of instruction are ....Prov 6:23

REPUTATION

seven men of good r .....Acts 6:3
made Himself of no r .....Phil 2:7

REQUEST

He gave them their r ....Ps 106:15
For Jews r a sign ......1 Cor 1:22

REQUESTS

r be made known ....Phil 4:6

REQUIRE

offering You did not r ....Ps 40:6
what does the LORD r .....Mic 6:8

REQUIRED

your soul will be r ....Luke 12:20
him much will be r ....Luke 12:48

REQUIREMENTS

keeps the righteous r ...Rom 2:26
r that was against us ....Col 2:14

RESERVED

"I have r for Myself ....Rom 11:4
r in heaven for you ......1 Pet 1:4
habitation, He has r ....Jude 6

RESIST

r an evil person ....Matt 5:39
r the Holy Spirit ....Acts 7:51
R the devil and he .....James 4:7

RESISTED

For who has r His will ..Rom 9:19
for he has greatly r ....2 Tim 4:15
You have not yet r ......Heb 12:4

RESISTS

"God r the proud ......James 4:6
for "God r the proud ....1 Pet 5:5

RESPECT

of the law held in r .....Acts 5:34
and we paid them r .....Heb 12:9

RESPECTED

And the LORD r Abel .....Gen 4:4

REST

is the Sabbath of r ......Ex 31:15
to build a house of r ...1 Chr 28:2
R in the LORD ....Ps 37:7
fly away and be at r ......Ps 55:6
"This is the r ....Is 28:12
is the place of My r ....Is 66:1
and I will give you r ...Matt 11:28
shall not enter My r .....Heb 3:11
remains therefore a r .....Heb 4:9

(continued col 3)

that they should r ....Rev 6:11
"that they may r ....Rev 14:13
But the r of the dead ....Rev 20:5

RESTED

He had done, and He r ...Gen 2:2
"And God r on the ....Heb 4:4

RESTORATION

until the times of r ......Acts 3:21

RESTORE

R to me the joy ....Ps 51:12
"So I will r to you ....Joel 2:25
and will r all things ....Matt 17:11
You at this time r ....Acts 1:6
who are spiritual r ....Gal 6:1

RESTORES

He r my soul ....Ps 23:3

RESTRAINS

only He who now r ...2 Thess 2:7

RESTRAINT

They break all r ....Hos 4:2

RESTS

r quietly in the heart ..Prov 14:33

RESURRECTION

to her, "I am the r .....John 11:25
them Jesus and the r ..Acts 17:18
the likeness of His r ....Rom 6:5
say that there is no r .1 Cor 15:12
and the power of His r ..Phil 3:10
obtain a better r ....Heb 11:35
This is the first r ....Rev 20:5

RETAIN

r the sins of any ......John 20:23

RETURN

womb, naked shall he r .Eccl 5:15
Let him r to the LORD .....Is 55:7
me, and I will r ....Jer 31:18
"R to Me ....Zech 1:3
he says, 'I will r ......Matt 12:44

RETURNED

astray, but have now r .1 Pet 2:25

RETURNING

r evil for evil or ....1 Pet 3:9

RETURNS

As a dog r to his own ..Prov 26:11
"A dog r to his own ....2 Pet 2:22

REVEAL

the Son wills to r Him .Matt 11:27
r His Son in me ....Gal 1:16

REVEALED

things which are r ....Deut 29:29
righteousness to be r ......Is 56:1
the Son of Man is r ...Luke 17:30
the wrath of God is r ....Rom 1:18
glory which shall be r ..Rom 8:18
the Lord Jesus is r ....2 Thess 1:7
lawless one will be r ..2 Thess 2:8
ready to be r in the ......1 Pet 1:5
when His glory is r ....1 Pet 4:13
r what we shall be .....1 John 3:2

REVEALER

Lord of kings, and a r ...Dan 2:47

REVEALING

waits for the r ....Rom 8:19

REVEALS

as a talebearer r.......Prov 20:19
r His secret to His ......Amos 3:7

REVELATION

Where there is no r ... . Prov 29:18
it came through the r ... . Gal 1:12
spirit of wisdom and r ... Eph 1:17
r He made known to ..... Eph 3:3
and glory at the r .... 1 Pet 1:7

REVERENCE

and r My sanctuary .... Lev 19:30
God acceptably with r .. Heb 12:28

REVERENT

man who is always r .. Prov 28:14
their wives must be r .. 1 Tim 3:11

REVILE

are you when they r .... Matt 5:11
r God's high priest ..... Acts 23:4

REVILED

crucified with Him r .. Mark 15:32
who, when He was r ... 1 Pet 2:23

REVIVAL

give us a measure of r ... Ezra 9:8

REVIVE

Will You not r us .... Ps 85:6
two days He will r .... Hos 6:2

REVIVED

came, sin r and I died .... Rom 7:9

REWARD

exceedingly great r ..... Gen 15:1
look, And see the r ...... Ps 91:8
Behold, His r is with ..... Is 40:10
for great is your r ...... Matt 5:12
you, they have their r .... Matt 6:2
no means lose his r .... Matt 10:42
we receive the due r .. Luke 23:41
will receive his own r ... 1 Cor 3:8
cheat you of your r ..... Col 2:18
for he looked to the r .. Heb 11:26
quickly, and My r ..... Rev 22:12

REWARDS

Whoever r evil for ..... Prov 17:13
And follows after r .... Is 1:23

RICH

Abram was very r ..... Gen 13:2
The r and the poor ..... Prov 22:2
r rules over the poor .... Prov 22:7
r man is wise in his .. Prov 28:11
Do not curse the r .... Eccl 10:20
it is hard for a r .... Matt 19:23
to you who are r ...... Luke 6:24
the r man's table ...... Luke 16:21
for he was very r ..... Luke 18:23
You are already r .... 1 Cor 4:8
though He was r .... 2 Cor 8:9
who desire to be r ..... 1 Tim 6:9
of this world to be r ... James 2:5
you say, 'I am r .... Rev 3:17

RICHES

R and honor are .... Prov 8:18
R do not profit .... Prov 11:4
in his r will fall .... Prov 11:28
of the wise is their r ... Prov 14:24
and r are an .... Prov 19:14
of the LORD Are r ..... Prov 22:4
r are not forever ...... Prov 27:24
do you despise the r ..... Rom 2:4
make known the r ..... Rom 9:23
what are the r .... Eph 1:18
show the exceeding r ..... Eph 2:7
the unsearchable r ..... Eph 3:8
r than the treasures .. Heb 11:26
To receive power and r .. Rev 5:12

RICHLY

Christ dwell in you r ..... Col 3:16
God, who gives us r ... 1 Tim 6:17

RIGHT

the r of the firstborn ... Deut 21:17
"Is your heart r ...... 2 Kin 10:15
Lord, "Sit at My r .... Ps 110:1
a way which seems r .. Prov 14:12
clothed and in his r .. Mark 5:15
to them He gave the r .. John 1:12
your heart is not r ...... Acts 8:21
seven stars in His r ...... Rev 2:1

RIGHTEOUS

also destroy the r ...... Gen 18:23
and they justify the r ... Deut 25:1
that he could be r ...... Job 15:14
"The r see it and .... Job 22:19
r shows mercy and ...... Ps 37:21
I have not seen the r ..... Ps 37:25
The LORD loves the r ... Ps 146:8
r is a well of life ...... Prov 10:11
r will be gladness ..... Prov 10:28
r will be delivered ..... Prov 11:21
r will be recompensed . Prov 11:31
the prayer of the r ..... Prov 15:29
r are bold as a lion ... Prov 28:1
r considers the cause ... Prov 29:7
Do not be overly r ..... Eccl 7:16
event happens to the r ... Eccl 9:2
with My r right hand ..... Is 41:10
By His knowledge My r .. Is 53:11
The r perishes .... Is 57:1
they sell the r .... Amos 2:6
not come to call the r ... Matt 9:13
r men desired to see ... Matt 13:17
r will shine forth as ... Matt 13:43
that they were r .... Luke 18:9
this was a r .... Luke 23:47
"There is none r ...... Rom 3:10
r man will one die ... Rom 5:7
Jesus Christ the r ...... 1 John 2:1

RIGHTEOUSLY

should live soberly, r ... Titus 2:12
to Him who judges r ... 1 Pet 2:23

RIGHTEOUSNESS

it to him for r .... Gen 15:6
I put on r .... Job 29:14
I call, O God of my r ...... Ps 4:1
from the LORD, And r ..... Ps 24:5
shall speak of Your r ... Ps 35:28
the good news of r ..... Ps 40:9
heavens declare His r ..... Ps 50:6
R and peace have .... Ps 85:10
R will go before Him .... Ps 85:13
r endures forever .... Ps 111:3
r delivers from death ... Prov 10:2
The r of the blameless .. Prov 11:5
the way of r is life ..... Prov 12:28
R exalts a nation ..... Prov 14:34
He who follows r ..... Prov 21:21
R lodged in it .... Is 1:21
in the LORD I have r ...... Is 45:24
r will be forever .... Is 51:8
I will declare your r ..... Is 57:12
r as a breastplate ...... Is 59:17
r goes forth as .... Is 62:1
The Lord Our R .... Jer 23:6
to David A Branch of r ... Jer 33:15
The r of the righteous .. Ezek 18:20
who turn many to r ..... Dan 12:3
to fulfill all r .... Matt 3:15
exceeds the r of the .... Matt 5:20
to you in the way of r . Matt 21:32
For in it the r .... Rom 1:17
even the r of God ..... Rom 3:22
accounted to him for r ... Rom 4:22
r will reign in life ..... Rom 5:17
might reign through r ... Rom 5:21
ignorant of God's r ..... Rom 10:3
might become the r ..... 2 Cor 5:21
the breastplate of r ...... Eph 6:14
not having my own r .... Phil 3:9
r which we have .... Titus 3:5
not produce the r ..... James 1:20

a preacher of r .... 2 Pet 2:5
a new earth in which r . 2 Pet 3:13
who practices r .... 1 John 2:29
He who practices r .... 1 John 3:7

RIGHTLY

wise uses knowledge r .. Prov 15:2
r dividing the word .... 2 Tim 2:15

RISE

for He makes His sun r . Matt 5:45
third day He will r .... Matt 20:19
third day He will r .... Luke 18:33
be the first to r ...... Acts 26:23
in Christ will r ...... 1 Thess 4:16

RISEN

there has not r .... Matt 11:11
disciples that He is r .... Matt 28:7
"The Lord is r ...... Luke 24:34
then Christ is not r ... 1 Cor 15:13
if Christ is not r ...... 1 Cor 15:17
But now Christ is r ... 1 Cor 15:20

RIVER

peace to her like a r ...... Is 66:12
he showed me a pure r .. Rev 22:1

RIVERS

By the r of Babylon ..... Ps 137:1
All the r run into the .... Eccl 1:7
his heart will flow r .... John 7:38

ROAR

The LORD also will r .... Joel 3:16

ROARING

and the waves r ...... Luke 21:25
walks about like a r ..... 1 Pet 5:8

ROARS

"The LORD r from ...... Amos 1:2
as when a lion r .... Rev 10:3

ROB

"Will a man r God .... Mal 3:8

ROBBED

r other churches .... 2 Cor 11:8

ROBBER

is a thief and a r ...... John 10:1
Barabbas was a r ..... John 18:40

ROBBERS

also crucified two r ... Mark 15:27
Me are thieves and r ... John 10:8

ROBBERY

did not consider it r ...... Phil 2:6

ROBE

'Bring out the best r ... Luke 15:22
on Him a purple r ...... John 19:2
Then a white r was .... Rev 6:11

ROBES

have stained all My r ...... Is 63:3
go around in long r ... Luke 20:46
clothed with white r ...... Rev 7:9

ROCK

you shall strike the r ..... Ex 17:6
and struck the r ...... Num 20:11
For their r is not ... Deut 32:31
"The LORD is my r ... 2 Sam 22:2
And who is a r ..... 2 Sam 22:32
Blessed be my R ..... 2 Sam 22:47
For You are my r ...... Ps 31:3
r that is higher than ..... Ps 61:2
been mindful of the R .... Is 17:10
shadow of a great r .... Is 32:2
his house on the r ..... Matt 7:24
r I will build My .... Matt 16:18

stumbling stone and r ..Rom 9:33
R that followed them .. 1 Cor 10:4

ROD

Your *r* and Your staff .....Ps 23:4
shall come forth a *R* ......Is 11:1
rule them with a r ....Rev 2:27

ROOM

you a large upper *r* ...Mark 14:15
no *r* for them in the .....Luke 2:7
into the upper *r* ....Acts 1:13

ROOT

day there shall be a *R* ....Is 11:10
because they had no *r* ..Matt 13:6
of money is a *r* ....1 Tim 6:10
lest any *r* of ....Heb 12:15
I am the *R* and the .....Rev 22:16

ROOTED

r and built up in Him .....Col 2:7

ROSE

end Christ died and *r* ...Rom 14:9
buried, and that He *r* .. 1 Cor 15:4
Jesus died and *r* .....1 Thess 4:14

RULE

And he shall *r* ....Gen 3:16
puts an end to all *r* ...1 Cor 15:24
let the peace of God *r* ....Col 3:15
Let the elders who *r* ...1 Tim 5:17
Remember those who *r* ..Heb 13:7

RULER

to Me The One to be *r* ....Mic 5:2
by Beelzebub, the *r* ....Matt 12:24
the *r* of this world ....John 12:31
'Who made you a *r* .....Acts 7:27

RULERS

And the *r* take counsel .....Ps 2:2
"You know that the *r* ..Matt 20:25
which none of the *r* ...1 Cor 2:8
powers, against the *r* ....Eph 6:12

RULES

That the Most High *r* ....Dan 4:17
that the Most High *r* ....Dan 4:32
r his own house well ....1 Tim 3:4

RULING

r their children ....1 Tim 3:12

RUMORS

hear of wars and *r* ......Matt 24:6

RUN

r and not be weary ....Is 40:31
us, and let us *r* ....Heb 12:1

S

SABAOTH

S had left us a ....Rom 9:29
ears of the Lord of *S* ...James 5:4

SABBATH

"Remember the *S* ....Ex 20:8
S was made for man ...Mark 2:27

SABBATHS

S you shall keep ....Ex 31:13

SACRIFICE

to the Lord than *s* ......Prov 21:3
For the Lord has a *s* .....Is 34:6
of My offerings they *s* ...Hos 8:13
Lord has prepared a *s* ...Zeph 1:7
desire mercy and not s ..Matt 9:13
an offering and a *s* ....Eph 5:2
put away sin by the *s* ...Heb 9:26

no longer remains a *s* ..Heb 10:26
offer the *s* of praise ....Heb 13:15

SACRIFICED

s their sons And their ...Ps 106:37

SACRIFICES

The *s* of God are a ......Ps 51:17
multiple of your *s* ....Is 1:11
priests, to offer up *s* .....Heb 7:27
s God is well pleased ...Heb 13:16

SAFE

he has received him *s* . Luke 15:27

SAFELY

make them lie down *s* ...Hos 2:18

SAFETY

say, "Peace and *s* .....1 Thess 5:3

SAINTS

s who are on the earth ....Ps 16:3
does not forsake His *s* ...Ps 37:28
Is the death of His *s* ....Ps 116:15
war against the *s* ....Dan 7:21
Jesus, called to be *s* ....1 Cor 1:2
the least of all the *s* ....Eph 3:8
be glorified in His *s* ..2 Thess 1:10
all delivered to the *s* ......Jude 3
shed the blood of *s* ......Rev 16:6

SALT

shall season with *s* .....Lev 2:13
"You are the *s* ....Matt 5:13
s loses its flavor ....Mark 9:50

SALVATION

still, and see the *s* ....Ex 14:13
S belongs to the Lord ......Ps 3:8
is my light and my *s* .....Ps 27:1
God is the God of *s* .....Ps 68:20
joy in the God of my *s* ...Hab 3:18
raised up a horn of *s* ...Luke 1:69
"Nor is there *s* ....Acts 4:12
the power of God to *s* ..Rom 1:16
now is the day of *s* ....2 Cor 6:2
work out your own *s* ....Phil 2:12
chose you for *s* ......2 Thess 2:13
neglect so great a *s* ......Heb 2:3

SAMARITAN

a drink from me, a *S* ....John 4:9

SANCTIFICATION

will of God, your *s* ....1 Thess 4:3

SANCTIFIED

they also may be *s* ....John 17:19
but you were *s* ....1 Cor 6:11
for it is *s* by the ....1 Tim 4:5

SANCTIFIES

For both He who *s* ......Heb 2:11

SANCTIFY

s My great name ......Ezek 36:23
"*S* them by Your ......John 17:17
that He might *s* ....Eph 5:26

SANCTUARY

let them make Me a *s* ....Ex 25:8
and the earthly *s* ....Heb 9:1

SAND

descendants as the *s* ...Gen 32:12
innumerable as the *s* ...Heb 11:12

SAT

into heaven, and *S* ....Mark 16:19
And He who *s* there was ..Rev 4:3

SATAN

before the Lord, and *S* ....Job 1:6
"Away with you, *S* ......Matt 4:10

"Get behind Me, *S* ....Matt 16:23
"How can *S* cast out ...Mark 3:23
S has asked for you ...Luke 22:31
to the working of *S* ...2 Thess 2:9
known the depths of *S* ..Rev 2:24
years have expired, *S* ...Rev 20:7

SATIATED

s the weary soul ....Jer 31:25

SATISFIED

I shall be *s* when I ....Ps 17:15
that are never *s* ......Prov 30:15
of His soul, and be *s* ....Is 53:11

SATISFIES

s the longing soul ....Ps 107:9

SATISFY

s us early with Your .....Ps 90:14
long life I will *s* ....Ps 91:16
for what does not *s* ....Is 55:2

SAVE

Oh, *s* me for Your ....Ps 6:4
s the children of the ......Ps 72:4
s the souls of the ....Ps 72:13
That it cannot *s* ....Is 59:1
s you And deliver you ...Jer 15:20
other, That he may *s* ...Hos 13:10
Jesus, for He will *s* .....Matt 1:21
s his life will ....Matt 16:25
s that which was ......Matt 18:11
let Him *s* Himself if ...Luke 23:35
but to *s* the world ....John 12:47
the world to *s* sinners . 1 Tim 1:15

SAVED

"He *s* others ....Matt 27:42
That we should be *s* ....Luke 1:71
"Your faith has *s* ......Luke 7:50
might be *s* ....John 3:17
them, saying, "Be *s* .....Acts 2:40
what must I do to be *s* ..Acts 16:30
which also you are *s* ...1 Cor 15:2
grace you have been *s* ....Eph 2:8
to His mercy He *s* ....Titus 3:5
of those who are *s* ....Rev 21:24

SAVES

antitype which now *s* ..1 Pet 3:21

SAVIOR

I, the Lord, am your *S* ...Is 60:16
rejoiced in God my *S* ...Luke 1:47
the city of David a *S* ...Luke 2:11
up for Israel a *S* ....Acts 13:23
God, who is the *S* .....1 Tim 4:10
and *S* Jesus Christ .....Titus 2:13

SAWN

stoned, they were *s* ....Heb 11:37

SAY

"But I *s* to you that .....Matt 5:22
"But who do you *s* ....Matt 16:15

SAYING

This is a faithful *s* .....1 Tim 1:15

SAYINGS

whoever hears these *s* ..Matt 7:24

SCALES

on it had a pair of *s* ......Rev 6:5

SCARLET

your sins are like *s* ....Is 1:18

SCATTER

I will *s* you among the ..Lev 26:33

SCATTERED

"Israel is like *s* sheep ...Jer 50:17
the sheep will be s ....Mark 14:27

SCATTERS
not gather with Me s ..Matt 12:30

SCEPTER
s shall not depart ......Gen 49:10

SCHEMER
Will be called a s ....Prov 24:8

SCHEMES
sought out many s ......Eccl 7:29

SCHISM
there should be no s ..1 Cor 12:25

SCHOOL
daily in the s of ....Acts 19:9

SCOFF
They s at kings ....Hab 1:10

SCOFFER
"He who corrects a s ....Prov 9:7
s is an abomination ....Prov 24:9

SCOFFERS
s will come in the ....2 Pet 3:3

SCORCHED
And men were s with ....Rev 16:9

SCORN
My friends s me ....Job 16:20

SCORNS
He s the scornful ....Prov 3:34

SCORPIONS
on serpents and s .....Luke 10:19
They had tails like s .....Rev 9:10

SCOURGE
will mock Him, and s .Mark 10:34

SCOURGES
s every son whom ......Heb 12:6

SCRIBES
"Beware of the s .....Mark 12:38

SCRIPTURE
S cannot be broken ...John 10:35
All S is given by ......2 Tim 3:16

SCRIPTURES
S must be fulfilled ....Mark 14:49

SCROLL
eat this s ....Ezek 3:1
the sky receded as a s ...Rev 6:14

SEA
drowned in the Red S ...Ex 15:4
who go down to the s ...Ps 107:23
and the s obey Him .....Matt 8:27
throne there was a s ......Rev 4:6
there was no more s ....Rev 21:1

SEAL
stands, having this s ...2 Tim 2:19

SEALED
by whom you were s ....Eph 4:30

SEAM
tunic was without s ...John 19:23

SÉANCE
"Please conduct a s ...1 Sam 28:8

SEARCH
glory of kings is to s ....Prov 25:2
s the Scriptures ....John 5:39

SEARCHED
s the Scriptures ....Acts 17:11

SEARCHES
For the Spirit s ....1 Cor 2:10

SEASON
Be ready in s and out ...2 Tim 4:2

SEASONED
how shall it be s ....Matt 5:13

SEASONS
the times and the s ...1 Thess 5:1

SEAT
shall make a mercy s ....Ex 25:17
before the judgment s .2 Cor 5:10

SEATS
at feasts, the best s .....Matt 23:6

SECRET
s things belong ....Deut 29:29
In the s place of His ......Ps 27:5
Father who is in the s ....Matt 6:6

SECRETLY
He lies in wait s ....Ps 10:9

SECRETS
For He knows the s ......Ps 44:21
God will judge the s ....Rom 2:16

SECT
to the strictest s ....Acts 26:5

SECURELY
nation that dwells s .....Jer 49:31

SEDUCED
flattering lips she s .....Prov 7:21

SEE
in my flesh I shall s ....Job 19:26
For they shall s God .....Matt 5:8
seeing they do not s ...Matt 13:13
rejoiced to s My day ....John 8:56
They shall s His face ....Rev 22:4

SEED
He shall see His s ....Is 53:10
S were the promises .....Gal 3:16
you are Abraham's s ....Gal 3:29

SEEDS
the good s are the .....Matt 13:38

SEEK
pray and s My face ....2 Chr 7:14
S the LORD while He ......Is 55:6
s, and you will find ......Matt 7:7
of Man has come to s .Luke 19:10
"You will s Me and ....John 7:34
For all s their own ......Phil 2:21
s those things which ......Col 3:1

SEEKING
like a roaring lion, s .....1 Pet 5:8

SEEKS
There is none who s ....Rom 3:11

SEEMS
is a way which s ....Prov 14:12

SEEN
s God face to face .....Gen 32:30
No one has s God at ....John 1:18
s Me has s the ....John 14:9
things which are not s .2 Cor 4:18

SEES
s his brother in need ..1 John 3:17

SELF-CONFIDENT
a fool rages and is s ...Prov 14:16

SELF-CONTROL
gentleness, s ....Gal 5:23
to knowledge s ....2 Pet 1:6

SELF-CONTROLLED
just, holy, s ....Titus 1:8

SELF-SEEKING
envy and s exist ......James 3:16

SELL
s whatever you have ..Mark 10:21

SEND
"Behold, I s you out ...Matt 10:16
has sent Me, I also s ...John 20:21

SENSES
of use have their s ......Heb 5:14

SENSIBLY
who can answer s .....Prov 26:16

SENSUAL
but is earthly, s ....James 3:15

SENT
unless they are s ......Rom 10:15

SEPARATED
it pleased God, who s ....Gal 1:15

SEPARATES
who repeats a matter s .Prov 17:9

SEPARATION
the middle wall of s .....Eph 2:14

SERAPHIM
Above it stood s ....Is 6:2

SERIOUS
therefore be s and ....1 Pet 4:7

SERPENT
s was more cunning ......Gen 3:1
"Make a fiery s ....Num 21:8
Moses lifted up the s ...John 3:14

SERPENTS
be wise as s ....Matt 10:16

SERVANT
s will rule over a son ...Prov 17:2
good and faithful s ....Matt 25:21

SERVANTS
are unprofitable s .....Luke 17:10

SERVE
to be served, but to s ..Matt 20:28
but through love s ....Gal 5:13

SERVES
"If anyone s Me ....John 12:26

SERVICE
is your reasonable s ....Rom 12:1
with good will doing s ....Eph 6:7

SERVING
fervent in spirit, s .....Rom 12:11

SET
"See, I have s ....Deut 30:15
s aside the grace ....Gal 2:21

SETTLE
"Therefore s it in .....Luke 21:14

SETTLED
O LORD, Your word is s .Ps 119:89

SEVEN
s churches which are ..... Rev 1:4

SEVENTY
"*S* weeks are .... Dan 9:24

SEVERE
not to be too *s* .... 2 Cor 2:5

SEVERITY
the goodness and *s* .... Rom 11:22

SHADE
may nest under its *s* ... Mark 4:32

SHADOW
In the *s* of His hand .... Is 49:2
the law, having a *s* ..... Heb 10:1

SHAKE
s the earth .... Is 2:19
I will *s* all nations .... Hag 2:7

SHAKEN
not to be soon *s* ...... 2 Thess 2:2

SHAKES
s the Wilderness .... Ps 29:8

SHAME
never be put to *s* ...... Joel 2:26
to put to *s* the wise .... 1 Cor 1:27
glory is in their *s* .... Phil 3:19

SHAMEFUL
For it is *s* even to .... Eph 5:12

SHARE
to do good and to *s* .... Heb 13:16

SHARING
for your liberal *s* ...... 2 Cor 9:13

SHARP
S as a two-edged sword .. Prov 5:4

SHARPEN
s their tongue like a ...... Ps 64:3

SHARPENS
My adversary *s* His ..... Job 16:9

SHARPNESS
I should use *s* .... 2 Cor 13:10

SHEATH
your sword into the *s* .. John 18:11

SHEAVES
Bringing his *s* .... Ps 126:6
gather them like *s* .... Mic 4:12

SHED
which is *s* for many ... Matt 26:28

SHEDDING
blood, and without *s* .... Heb 9:22

SHEEP
s will be scattered ...... Zech 13:7
having a hundred *s* .... Luke 15:4
and I know My *s* ..... John 10:14
"*He was led as a s* ...... Acts 8:32

SHEEPFOLDS
lie down among the *s* .... Ps 68:13

SHEET
object like a great *s* .... Acts 10:11

SHELTER
the Lord will be a *s* ..... Joel 3:16

SHELTERS
s him all the day long . Deut 33:12

SHEOL
not leave my soul in *S* .. Ps 16:10
the belly of *S* I cried ...... Jon 2:2

SHEPHERD
The Lord is my *s* .... Ps 23:1
His flock like a *s* .... Is 40:11
'I will strike the *S* ..... Matt 26:31
"I am the good *s* ...... John 10:11
the dead, that great *S* .. Heb 13:20
S the flock of God .... 1 Pet 5:2
when the Chief *S* .... 1 Pet 5:4

SHEPHERDS
"And I will give you *s* .... Jer 3:15
s have led them astray ... Jer 50:6

SHIELD
I am your *s* .... Gen 15:1
truth shall be your *s* ..... Ps 91:4
all, taking the *s* .... Eph 6:16

SHINE
Lord make His face *s* .. Num 6:25
among whom you *s* ..... Phil 2:15

SHINED
them a light has *s* .... Is 9:2

SHINES
heed as a light that *s* ... 2 Pet 1:19

SHINING
light is already *s* ...... 1 John 2:8

SHIPS
down to the sea in *s* .... Ps 107:23

SHIPWRECK
faith have suffered *s* .. 1 Tim 1:19

SHOOT
They *s* out the lip .... Ps 22:7

SHORT
have sinned and fall *s* .. Rom 3:23

SHORTENED
those days were *s* ..... Matt 24:22

SHOUT
heaven with a *s* ..... 1 Thess 4:16

SHOW
a land that I will *s* ...... Gen 12:1
s Him greater works ... John 5:20

SHOWBREAD
s which was not lawful . Matt 12:4

SHOWERS
make it soft with *s* ...... Ps 65:10

SHREWDLY
because he had dealt *s* . Luke 16:8

SHRINES
who made silver *s* ..... Acts 19:24

SHRIVELED
You have *s* me up .... Job 16:8

SHUFFLES
with his eyes, He *s* .... Prov 6:13

SHUNNED
feared God and *s* evil ..... Job 1:1

SHUT
For you *s* up the ...... Matt 23:13

SHUTS
s his eyes from seeing .... Is 33:15
who opens and no one s .. Rev 3:7

SICK
I was *s* and you .... Matt 25:36
faith will save the *s* ... James 5:15

SICKLE
"Thrust in Your *s* ..... Rev 14:15

SICKNESS
will sustain him in *s* ... Prov 18:14
"This *s* is not unto ..... John 11:4

SICKNESSES
And bore our s .... Matt 8:17

SIDE
The Lord is on my *s* ..... Ps 118:6

SIFT
s the nations with the .... Is 30:28

SIGH
our years like a *s* .... Ps 90:9

SIGHING
For my *s* comes before ... Job 3:24

SIGHT
and see this great *s* .... Ex 3:3
by faith, not by *s* .... 2 Cor 5:7

SIGN
will give you a *s* .... Is 7:14
seeks after a *s* .... Matt 12:39
For Jews request a *s* ... 1 Cor 1:22

SIGNS
and let them be for *s* .... Gen 1:14
cannot discern the *s* .... Matt 16:3
did many other *s* ...... John 20:30

SILENCE
That You may *s* .... Ps 8:2
seal, there was *s* .... Rev 8:1

SILENT
season, and am not *s* ..... Ps 22:2

SILK
covered you with *s* .... Ezek 16:10

SILLY
They are *s* children ...... Jer 4:22

SILVER
may buy the poor for *s* . Amos 8:6
him thirty pieces of *s* .. Matt 26:15

SIMILITUDE
been made in the *s* ..... James 3:9

SIMPLE
making wise the *s* .... Ps 19:7

SIMPLICITY
corrupted from the *s* ... 2 Cor 11:3

SIN
and be sure your *s* .... Num 32:23
Be angry, and do not *s* ..... Ps 4:4
s is always before me ..... Ps 51:3
soul an offering for *s* ... Is 53:10
And He bore the *s* ...... Is 53:12
who takes away the *s* .. John 1:29
"He who is without *s* ... John 8:7
convict the world of *s* .. John 16:8
s entered the world ..... Rom 5:12
s is not imputed .... Rom 5:13
s shall not have .... Rom 6:14
Shall we *s* because we .. Rom 6:15
Him who knew no *s* ... 2 Cor 5:21

SINCERE
man of s is revealed .. 2 Thess 2:3
we are, yet without s .... Heb 4:15
do it, to him it is s .... James 4:17
say that we have no s .. 1 John 1:8
and he cannot s .... 1 John 3:9

SINCERE
and from s faith .... 1 Tim 1:5

SINCERITY
simplicity and godly s . 2 Cor 1:12

SINFUL
from me, for I am a s .... Luke 5:8
become exceedingly s .. Rom 7:13

SING
Let him s psalms ..... James 5:13

SINGERS
The s went before .... Ps 68:25

SINGING
His presence with s ...... Ps 100:2
and spiritual songs, s .... Eph 5:19

SINISTER
Who understands s ..... Dan 8:23

SINK
I s in deep mire .... Ps 69:2
to s he cried out .... Matt 14:30

SINNED
You only, have I s .... Ps 51:4
"Father, I have s ...... Luke 15:18
for all have s and ...... Rom 3:23
that we have not s .... 1 John 1:10

SINNER
s who repents than .... Luke 15:7
the ungodly and the s .. 1 Pet 4:18

SINNERS
in the path of s .... Ps 1:1
the righteous, but s .... Matt 9:13
while we were still s .... Rom 5:8
many were made s .... Rom 5:19
the world to save s .... 1 Tim 1:15
such hostility from s .... Heb 12:3

SINS
from presumptuous s .... Ps 19:13
You, Our secret s .... Ps 90:8
The soul who s shall ... Ezek 18:4
if your brother s ...... Matt 18:15
s according to the ..... 1 Cor 15:3
the forgiveness of s ...... Eph 1:7
If we confess our s .... 1 John 1:9
propitiation for our s .. 1 John 2:2

SISTER
is My brother and s ... Matt 12:50

SIT
but to s on My right ... Matt 20:23
"S at My right hand ..... Heb 1:13
I will grant to s .... Rev 3:21

SITS
It is He who s above ..... Is 40:22
so that he s as God ... 2 Thess 2:4

SITTING
where Christ is, s .... Col 3:1

SKILL
hand forget its s .... Ps 137:5

SKILLFULNESS
guided them by the s .... Ps 78:72

SKIN
God made tunics of s .... Gen 3:21

LORD and said, "S .... Job 2:4
Ethiopian change his s .. Jer 13:23

SKIP
He makes them also s .... Ps 29:6

SKIPPING
upon the mountains, S .. Song 2:8

SKULL
to say, Place of a S .... Matt 27:33

SKY
s receded as a scroll .... Rev 6:14

SLACK
The Lord is not s .... 2 Pet 3:9

SLAIN
is the Lamb who was s .. Rev 5:12

SLANDER
whoever spreads s .... Prov 10:18

SLANDERERS
be reverent, not s ..... 1 Tim 3:11

SLANDEROUSLY
as we are s reported ..... Rom 3:8

SLAUGHTER
led as a lamb to the s ..... Is 53:7
as sheep for the s ...... Rom 8:36

SLAVE
commits sin is a s ...... John 8:34

SLAVES
should no longer be s .... Rom 6:6

SLAY
s the righteous .... Gen 18:25

SLEEP
God caused a deep s .... Gen 2:21
neither slumber nor s .... Ps 121:4
He gives His beloved s ... Ps 127:2
and many s .... 1 Cor 11:30
We shall not all s ..... 1 Cor 15:51

SLEEPERS
gently the lips of s ...... Song 7:9

SLEEPING
"Are you still s .... Matt 26:45

SLEEPLESSNESS
in labors, in s .... 2 Cor 6:5

SLEEPS
"Our friend Lazarus s . John 11:11

SLEPT
I lay down and s .... Ps 3:5

SLIGHTED
is the one who is s ..... Prov 12:9

SLING
he had, and his s .... 1 Sam 17:40

SLIP
Their foot shall s ...... Deut 32:35

SLIPPERY
set them in s places ..... Ps 73:18

SLOOPS
all the beautiful s .... Is 2:16

SLOW
hear, s to speak, s .... James 1:19

SLUGGARD
will you slumber, O s .... Prov 6:9

SLUMBERING
upon men, While s ..... Job 33:15

SMALL
And I saw the dead, s .. Rev 20:12

SMELL
and he smelled the s ... Gen 27:27

SMELLS
s the battle from afar ... Job 39:25

SMITTEN
Him stricken, S .... Is 53:4

SMOKE
was filled with s .... Rev 15:8

SMOOTH
And the rough places s .... Is 40:4

SMOOTH-SKINNED
man, and I am a s ..... Gen 27:11

SNAIL
s which melts away as .... Ps 58:8

SNARE
is a fowler's s .... Hos 9:8
it will come as a s .... Luke 21:35
and escape the s ...... 2 Tim 2:26

SNARED
All of them are s .... Is 42:22

SNARES
who seek my life lay s ... Ps 38:12

SNATCH
neither shall anyone s . John 10:28

SNATCHES
s away what was ...... Matt 13:19

SNEER
And you s at it .... Mal 1:13

SNIFFED
They s at the wind .... Jer 14:6

SNORTING
s strikes terror .... Job 39:20

SNOW
shall be whiter than s .... Ps 51:7
shall be as white as s ...... Is 1:18

SOAKED
Their land shall be s ...... Is 34:7

SOAP
lye, and use much s ..... Jer 2:22

SOBER
the older men be s ...... Titus 2:2

SOBERLY
think, but to think s .... Rom 12:3

SODA
And like vinegar on s .. Prov 25:20

SODOMITES
nor homosexuals, nor s . 1 Cor 6:9

SOJOURNER
no s had to lodge .... Job 31:32

SOJOURNERS
are strangers and s .... Lev 25:23

SOLD
s his birthright .... Gen 25:33

SOLDIER
s all that he had .... Matt 13:46
but I am carnal, *s* ...... Rom 7:14

SOLDIER
hardship as a good *s* .... 2 Tim 2:3

SOLDIERS
s twisted a crown ...... John 19:2

SOLITARILY
heritage, Who dwell *s* ... Mic 7:14

SOLITARY
God sets the *s* in .... Ps 68:6

SOMEBODY
up, claiming to be *s* ..... Acts 5:36

SOMETHING
thinks himself to be *s* ..... Gal 6:3

SON
Me, 'You are My *S* .... Ps 2:7
is born, Unto us a *S* .... Is 9:6
fourth is like the *S* ...... Dan 3:25
will bring forth a *S* ...... Matt 1:21
"This is My beloved *S* .... Matt 3:17
Jesus, You *S* of God .... Matt 8:29
are the Christ, the *S* ... Matt 16:16
Whose *S* is He .... Matt 22:42
of the *S* of Man ...... Matt 24:37
'I am the *S* of God ... Matt 27:43
of Jesus Christ, the *S* ... Mark 1:1
out, the only *s* .... Luke 7:12
The only begotten *S* .... John 1:18
that this is the *S* ...... John 1:34
of the only begotten *S* .. John 3:18
S can do nothing ...... John 5:19
s abides forever .... John 8:35
you believe in the *S* .... John 9:35
I said, 'I am the *S* ..... John 10:36
behold your *s* .... John 19:26
Jesus Christ is the *S* .... Acts 8:37
by sending His own *S* ... Rom 8:3
not spare His own *S* .... Rom 8:32
live by faith in the *S* ..... Gal 2:20
God sent forth His *S* .... Gal 4:4
the knowledge of the *S* .. Eph 4:13
"You are My *S* .... Heb 1:5
though He was a *S* ...... Heb 5:8
but made like the *S* ..... Heb 7:3
"This is My beloved *S* .. 2 Pet 1:17
denies the *S* .... 1 John 2:23
One like the *S* of Man ... Rev 1:13

SONG
Sing to Him a new *s* ...... Ps 33:3
He has put a new *s* ...... Ps 40:3
I will sing a new *s* ...... Ps 144:9
they sang a new *s* .... Rev 5:9

SONGS
my Maker, Who gives *s* .. Job 35:10
and spiritual *s* .... Eph 5:19

SONS
s shall come from afar .... Is 60:4
He will purify the *s* ...... Mal 3:3
you may become a .... John 12:36
who are of faith are *s* ..... Gal 3:7
the adoption as *s* .... Gal 4:5
in bringing many *s* ...... Heb 2:10
speaks to you as to *s* .... Heb 12:5

SOON
For it is *s* cut off .... Ps 90:10

SOOTHED
or bound up, Or *s* .... Is 1:6

SORCERER
But Elymas the *s* .... Acts 13:8

SORCERERS
outside are dogs and *s* .. Rev 22:15

SORCERESS
shall not permit a *s* ..... Ex 22:18

SORCERY
idolatry, *s* .... Gal 5:20

SORES
and putrefying *s* .... Is 1:6

SORROW
multiply your *s* .... Gen 3:16
s is continually .... Ps 38:17
And He adds no *s* ..... Prov 10:22
Your *s* is incurable ..... Jer 30:15
them sleeping from *s* .. Luke 22:45
s will be turned ...... John 16:20
s produces repentance . 2 Cor 7:10
s as others who ...... 1 Thess 4:13
no more death, nor *s* ... Rev 21:4

SORROWFUL
But I am poor and *s* .... Ps 69:29
he went away *s* ...... Matt 19:22
soul is exceedingly *s* ... Matt 26:38
and I may be less *s* ..... Phil 2:28

SORROWS
s shall be multiplied ...... Ps 16:4
by men, A Man of *s* .... Is 53:3
are the beginning of *s* . Matt 24:8

SORRY
s that He had made man . Gen 6:6
For you were made *s* ... 2 Cor 7:9

SOUGHT
I *s* the LORD .... Ps 34:4
s what was lost .... Ezek 34:4

SOUL
with all your *s* .... Deut 6:5
"My *s* loathes my life ..... Job 10:1
s draws near the Pit .... Job 33:22
will not leave my *s* ...... Ps 16:10
converting the *s* .... Ps 19:7
He restores my *s* .... Ps 23:3
you cast down, O my *s* ... Ps 42:5
Let my *s* live .... Ps 119:175
No one cares for my *s* ... Ps 142:4
me wrongs his own *s* ... Prov 8:36
When You make His *s* ... Is 53:10
s delight itself .... Is 55:2
The *s* of the father As .. Ezek 18:4
able to destroy both *s* . Matt 10:28
and loses his own *s* .... Matt 16:26
with all your s .... Matt 22:37
your whole spirit, *s* .. 1 Thess 5:23
to the saving of the *s* ... Heb 10:39
his way will save a *s* .. James 5:20
health, just as your *s* .... 3 John 2

SOULS
And will save the *s* ..... Ps 72:13
And he who wins *s* .... Prov 11:30
unsettling your *s* ...... Acts 15:24
is able to save your *s* . James 1:21

SOUND
voice was like the *s* .... Ezek 43:2
do not *s* a trumpet ...... Matt 6:2
s words which you .... 2 Tim 1:13

SOUNDNESS
him this perfect *s* .... Acts 3:16

SOUNDS
a distinction in the *s* ... 1 Cor 14:7

SOW
s trouble reap .... Job 4:8
Those who *s* in tears .... Ps 126:5
Blessed are you who *s* ... Is 32:20
"They *s* the wind .... Hos 8:7
s is not made alive .... 1 Cor 15:36

SOWER
"Behold, a *s* went ...... Matt 13:3

SOWN
s spiritual things ...... 1 Cor 9:11
of righteousness is *s* .. James 3:18

SOWS
s the good seed is the .. Matt 13:37
'One *s* and another ..... John 4:37
for whatever a man *s* ..... Gal 6:7

SPARE
He who did not *s* .... Rom 8:32
if God did not *s* .... 2 Pet 2:4

SPARES
s his rod hates his ..... Prov 13:24

SPARK
the work of it as a *s* .... Is 1:31

SPARKLES
it is red, When it *s* .... Prov 23:31

SPARKS
to trouble, As the *s* ...... Job 5:7

SPARROW
s has found a home .... Ps 84:3

SPARROWS
than many *s* .... Matt 10:31

SPAT
Then they *s* on Him ... Matt 27:30

SPEAK
only the word that I *s* . Num 22:35
oh, that God would *s* .... Job 11:5
And a time to *s* .... Eccl 3:7
s anymore in His name ... Jer 20:9
or what you should *s* .. Matt 10:19
to you when all men *s* .. Luke 6:26
s what I have seen ..... John 8:38
He hears He will *s* .... John 16:13
Spirit and began to *s* ... Acts 2:4

SPEAKING
envy, and all evil *s* ..... 1 Pet 2:1

SPEAKS
to face, as a man *s* ...... Ex 33:11
God has sent *s* .... John 3:34
When he *s* a lie .... John 8:44
he being dead still *s* ..... Heb 11:4
of sprinkling that *s* .... Heb 12:24

SPEAR
His side with a *s* ...... John 19:34

SPEARS
And their *s* into .... Is 2:4

SPECK
do you look at the *s* ..... Matt 7:3

SPECTACLE
you were made a *s* ..... Heb 10:33

SPEECH
one language and one *s* . Gen 11:1
his *s* contemptible .... 2 Cor 10:10
s always be with grace .... Col 4:6

SPEECHLESS
your mouth for the *s* ... Prov 31:8

SPEED
they shall come with *s* .... Is 5:26

SPEEDILY
I call, answer me *s* ...... Ps 102:2

SPEND
you *s* money for ....Is 55:2
amiss, that you may *s* ..James 4:3

SPENT
"But when he had *s* ...Luke 15:14

SPEW
nor hot, I will *s* ....Rev 3:16

SPIDER
s skillfully grasps .....Prov 30:28

SPIES
men who had been *s* ....Josh 6:23

SPIN
neither toil nor *s* ......Matt 6:28

SPINDLE
her hand holds the *s* ...Prov 31:19

SPIRIT
And the *S* of God was ....Gen 1:2
S shall not strive ....Gen 6:3
S that is upon you ....Num 11:17
portion of your *s* ....2 Kin 2:9
Then a *s* passed ....Job 4:15
hand I commit my *s* ......Ps 31:5
The *s* of a man is the ..Prov 20:27
s will return to God .....Eccl 12:7
S has gathered them .....Is 34:16
I have put My *S* ....Is 42:1
"The *S* of the Lord ....Is 61:1
S entered me when He ..Ezek 2:2
and a new *S* ....Ezek 18:31
"I will put My *S* .....Ezek 36:27
walk in a false *s* ....Mic 2:11
and He saw the *S* ......Matt 3:16
I will put My S ....Matt 12:18
S descending upon ....Mark 1:10
s indeed is willing ....Mark 14:38
go before Him in the *s* .Luke 1:17
manner of *s* you are of .Luke 9:55
hands I commit My s ..Luke 23:46
they had seen a *s* .....Luke 24:37
"God is *S* ....John 4:24
I speak to you are *s* ....John 6:63
"the *S* of truth ....John 14:17
but if a *s* or an angel ....Acts 23:9
the flesh but in the *S* ....Rom 8:9
does not have the *S* .....Rom 8:9
s that we are children ..Rom 8:16
what the mind of the *S* .Rom 8:27
to us through His *S* ...1 Cor 2:10
gifts, but the same *S* ...1 Cor 12:4
but the *S* gives life ......2 Cor 3:6
Now the Lord is the *S* .2 Cor 3:17
Having begun in the *S* ....Gal 3:3
has sent forth the *S* ....Gal 4:6
with the Holy *S* ....Eph 1:13
the unity of the *S* ....Eph 4:3
stand fast in one *s* ......Phil 1:27
S expressly says that ...1 Tim 4:1
S who dwells in us ......James 4:5
made alive by the *S* ....1 Pet 3:18
do not believe every *s* .1 John 4:1
you know the *S* ....1 John 4:2
has given us of His *S* .1 John 4:13
S who bears witness ...1 John 5:6
not having the *S* ....Jude 19
I was in the *S* on the ....Rev 1:10
him hear what the *S* ......Rev 2:7
And the *S* and the ......Rev 22:17

SPIRITS
Who makes His angels *s* .Ps 104:4
heed to deceiving *s* .....1 Tim 4:1

SPIRITUAL
s judges all things .....1 Cor 2:15
However, the *s* is not .1 Cor 15:46
s restore such a one ......Gal 6:1

SPIRITUALLY
s minded is life ....Rom 8:6

SPITEFULLY
for those who *s* ....Matt 5:44

SPITTING
face from shame and *s* ....Is 50:6

SPLENDOR
on the glorious *s* ....Ps 145:5

SPOIL
He shall divide the *s* .....Is 53:12

SPOILER
I have created the *s* ......Is 54:16

SPOKE
"No man ever *s* ....John 7:46
I was a child, I *s* ......1 Cor 13:11
in various ways *s* ....Heb 1:1
s as they were moved ..2 Pet 1:21

SPOKEN
I have not *s* in secret .....Is 45:19
why am I evil *s* ....1 Cor 10:30

SPOKESMAN
"So he shall be your *s* ....Ex 4:16

SPONGE
them ran and took a *s* .Matt 27:48

SPOT
church, not having *s* ....Eph 5:27
Himself without *s* ......Heb 9:14

SPOTS
These are *s* in your ......Jude 12

SPREAD
Then the word of God *s* ..Acts 6:7

SPREADS
s them out like a tent .....Is 40:22

SPRING
Truth shall *s* out of ......Ps 85:11
s send forth fresh .....James 3:11

SPRINGING
a fountain of water *s* ...John 4:14

SPRINGS
And the thirsty land *s* .....Is 35:7

SPRINKLE
"Then I will *s* ....Ezek 36:25

SPRINKLED
having our hearts *s* ....Heb 10:22

SPRINKLING
s that speaks ....Heb 12:24

SPROUT
and the seed should *s* ..Mark 4:27

SQUARES
voice in the open *s* .....Prov 1:20

STAFF
this Jordan with my *s* ..Gen 32:10
Your rod and Your *s* .....Ps 23:4
on the top of his *s* ....Heb 11:21

STAGGER
they will drink and *s* ....Jer 25:16

STAGGERS
As a drunken man *s* ......Is 19:14

STAKES
s will ever be removed ...Is 33:20

STALLS
be no herd in the *s* ......Hab 3:17

STAMMERERS
s will be ready ....Is 32:4

STAMMERING
s tongue that you ....Is 33:19

STAMPING
At the noise of the *s* .....Jer 47:3

STAND
one shall be able to *s* ...Deut 7:24
lives, And He shall *s* ....Job 19:25
ungodly shall not *s* ......Ps 1:5
not lack a man to *s* .....Jer 35:19
And who can *s* when He ..Mal 3:2
that kingdom cannot *s* .Mark 3:24
he will be made to *s* ....Rom 14:4
Watch, *s* fast in the ...1 Cor 16:13
for by faith you *s* .....2 Cor 1:24
having done all, to *s* ....Eph 6:13
S therefore ....Eph 6:14
of God in which you *s* .1 Pet 5:12
"Behold, I *s* at the ......Rev 3:20

STANDARD
Lord will lift up a *s* ......Is 59:19

STANDING
they love to pray *s* ......Matt 6:5
and the Son of Man *s* ...Acts 7:56

STANDS
him who thinks he *s* ..1 Cor 10:12

STAR
For we have seen His *s* ..Matt 2:2
Bright and Morning *S* ..Rev 22:16

STARS
He made the *s* also ......Gen 1:16
born as many as the *s* ..Heb 11:12

STATE
learned in whatever *s* ...Phil 4:11

STATURE
in wisdom and *s* ....Luke 2:52

STATUTE
shall be a perpetual *s* ....Lev 3:17

STATUTES
the *s* of the Lord are .....Ps 19:8
Teach me Your *s* ....Ps 119:12

STAY
S here and watch .....Matt 26:38

STEADFAST
brethren, be *s* ....1 Cor 15:58
soul, both sure and *s* ....Heb 6:19
Resist him, *s* in the ......1 Pet 5:9

STEADFASTLY
s set His face to go .....Luke 9:51
And they continued *s* ...Acts 2:42

STEADFASTNESS
good order and the *s* .....Col 2:5

STEADILY
could not look *s* ....2 Cor 3:13

STEADY
and his hands were *s* ....Ex 17:12

STEAL
"You shall not *s* ....Ex 20:15

STEM (cont.)

thieves break in and *s* .. Matt 6:19
night and *s* Him away . Matt 27:64

STEM

forth a Rod from the *s* .... Is 11:1

STENCH

there will be a *s* .... Is 3:24
this time there is a *s* ... John 11:39

STEP

s has turned from the .... Job 31:7

STEPS

The *s* of a good man ..... Ps 37:23
And established my *s* .... Ps 40:2
the LORD directs his *s* ... Prov 16:9
should follow His *s* .... 1 Pet 2:21

STEWARD

be blameless, as a *s* ..... Titus 1:7

STEWARDS

of Christ and *s* .... 1 Cor 4:1

STEWARDSHIP

entrusted with a *s* ..... 1 Cor 9:17

STICK

'For Joseph, the *s* ..... Ezek 37:16

STICKS

a man gathering *s* ..... Num 15:32

STIFF

rebellion and your *s* ... Deut 31:27

STIFF-NECKED

"You *s* and .... Acts 7:51

STILL

When I awake, I am *s* .. Ps 139:18
sea, "Peace, be *s* ...... Mark 4:39

STILLBORN

burial, I say that a *s* ..... Eccl 6:3

STINGS

like a serpent, And *s* .. Prov 23:32

STIR

I remind you to *s* .... 2 Tim 1:6

STIRRED

So the LORD *s* up the .... Hag 1:14

STIRS

It *s* up the dead for .... Is 14:9

STOCKS

s that were in the .... Jer 20:2

STOIC

and *S* philosophers ..... Acts 17:18

STOMACH

Foods for the *s* .... 1 Cor 6:13

STOMACH'S

little wine for your *s* ... 1 Tim 5:23

STONE

him, a pillar of *s* .... Gen 35:14
s shall be a witness .... Josh 24:27
s which the builders .... Ps 118:22
I lay in Zion a *s* .... Is 28:16
take the heart of *s* ... Ezek 36:26
will give him a *s* .... Matt 7:9
s will be broken ...... Matt 21:44
s which the builders .. Luke 20:17
those works do you *s* .. John 10:32
Him as to a living *s* ..... 1 Pet 2:4

STONED

s Stephen as he was .... Acts 7:59
They were *s* .... Heb 11:37

STONES

Abraham from these *s* ... Matt 3:9
command that these *s* ... Matt 4:3

STONY

fell on *s* ground .... Mark 4:5

STOOPED

And again He *s* down ... John 8:8

STOPPED

her flow of blood *s* ..... Luke 8:44

STORE

exist are kept in *s* .... 2 Pet 3:7

STORK

s has her home in the ... Ps 104:17

STORM

He calms the *s* .... Ps 107:29
for a shelter from *s* .... Is 4:6

STRAIGHT

Make *s* in the desert A .... Is 40:3
and make *s* paths for .. Heb 12:13

STRAIGHTFORWARD

that they were not *s* ..... Gal 2:14

STRAIN

"Blind guides, who *s* .. Matt 23:24

STRAITS

and desperate *s* .... Deut 28:53

STRANGE

s thing happened ...... 1 Pet 4:12

STRANGER

and loves the *s* .... Deut 10:18
I was a *s* and you ..... Matt 25:35

STRANGERS

know the voice of *s* ..... John 10:5
you are no longer *s* ..... Eph 2:19

STRANGLING

that my soul chooses *s* ... Job 7:15

STRAP

than I, whose sandal *s* .. Mark 1:7

STRAW

stones, wood, hay, *s* ... 1 Cor 3:12

STRAY

Who make my people *s* ... Mic 3:5

STRAYED

Yet I have not *s* .... Ps 119:110
some have *s* .... 1 Tim 6:10

STREAM

like a flowing *s* .... Is 66:12

STREAMS

He also brought *s* .... Ps 78:16

STREET

In the middle of its *s* .... Rev 22:2

STREETS

You taught in our *s* ... Luke 13:26

STRENGTH

s no man shall .... 1 Sam 2:9
The LORD is the *s* .... Ps 27:1
is our refuge and *s* ...... Ps 46:1
They go from *s* to .... Ps 84:7
S and honor are her ... Prov 31:25
might He increases *s* ..... Is 40:29
O LORD, my *s* and my ... Jer 16:19

were still without *s* ...... Rom 5:6
s is made perfect ...... 2 Cor 12:9

STRENGTHEN

And He shall *s* .... Ps 27:14
S the weak hands .... Is 35:3
s your brethren ...... Luke 22:32
s the things .... Rev 3:2

STRENGTHENED

unbelief, but was *s* ..... Rom 4:20
stood with me and *s* ... 2 Tim 4:17

STRENGTHENING

s the souls of the ...... Acts 14:22

STRENGTHENS

through Christ who *s* .... Phil 4:13

STRETCH

are old, you will *s* ..... John 21:18

STRETCHED

I have *s* out my hands .... Ps 88:9
"All day long I have *s* . Rom 10:21

STRETCHES

For he *s* out his hand ... Job 15:25

STRICKEN

of My people He was *s* .... Is 53:8

STRIFE

man stirs up *s* .... Prov 15:18
even from envy and *s* ... Phil 1:15
which come envy, *s* .... 1 Tim 6:4

STRIKE

The sun shall not *s* ...... Ps 121:6
"*S* the Shepherd .... Zech 13:7
'I will *s* the Shepherd .. Matt 26:31

STRINGED

of your *s* instruments .. Amos 5:23

STRIP

S yourselves .... Is 32:11

STRIPES

s we are healed .... Is 53:5
s you were healed ..... 1 Pet 2:24

STRIVE

"My Spirit shall not *s* .... Gen 6:3
"*S* to enter through ... Luke 13:24
the Lord not to *s* ...... 2 Tim 2:14

STRIVING

for a man to stop *s* ..... Prov 20:3

STROKE

with a mighty *s* .... Jer 14:17

STRONG

The LORD *s* and mighty ... Ps 24:8
S is Your hand .... Ps 89:13
"When a *s* man ..... Luke 11:21
We then who are *s* ..... Rom 15:1
weak, then I am *s* ... 2 Cor 12:10
my brethren, be *s* ...... Eph 6:10
were made *s* .... Heb 11:34

STRONGHOLD

of my salvation, my *s* ..... Ps 18:2

STRUCK

s the rock twice .... Num 20:11
the hand of God has *s* .. Job 19:21
Behold, He *s* the rock .... Ps 78:20
in My wrath I *s* .... Is 60:10
s the head from the ..... Hab 3:13
took the reed and *s* .... Matt 27:30

STUBBLE

do wickedly will be *s* ..... Mal 4:1

STUBBORN
"If a man has a *s* . . . . . . Deut 21:18

STUBBORN-HEARTED
"Listen to Me, you *s* . . . . . . Is 46:12

STUBBORNNESS
do not look on the *s* . . . . Deut 9:27

STUDIED
having never *s* . . . . John 7:15

STUMBLE
have caused many to *s* . . . Mal 2:8
you will be made to *s* . . Matt 26:31
immediately they *s* . . . . Mark 4:17
who believe in Me to *s* . Mark 9:42
For we all *s* in many . . . James 3:2

STUMBLED
s that they should . . . . . Rom 11:11

STUMBLES
immediately he *s* . . . . . . Matt 13:21

STUMBLING
the deaf, nor put a *s* . . . . Lev 19:14
But a stone of *s* . . . . Is 8:14
Behold, I will lay *s* . . . . . . Jer 6:21
I lay in Zion a s . . . . Rom 9:33
this, not to put a *s* . . . . . Rom 14:13
of yours become a *s* . . . 1 Cor 8:9
and "*A stone of s* . . . . . . 1 Pet 2:8
to keep you from *s* . . . . . Jude 24

STUPID
hates correction is *s* . . . . Prov 12:1

SUBDUE
s all things to . . . . Phil 3:21

SUBJECT
for it is not *s* . . . . Rom 8:7
Let every soul be *s* . . . . . Rom 13:1
all their lifetime *s* . . . . . . Heb 2:15

SUBJECTED
because of Him who *s* . . Rom 8:20

SUBJECTION
put all things in s . . . . Heb 2:8

SUBMISSION
his children in *s* . . . . 1 Tim 3:4

SUBMISSIVE
Yes, all of you be *s* . . . . . . 1 Pet 5:5

SUBMIT
Therefore *s* to God . . . . . James 4:7
s yourselves to every . . . 1 Pet 2:13

SUBSIDED
and the waters *s* . . . . Gen 8:1

SUBSTANCE
Bless his *s* . . . . Deut 33:11

SUCCESS
please give me *s* . . . . . . Gen 24:12
But wisdom brings *s* . . . Eccl 10:10

SUCCESSFUL
Joseph, and he was a *s* . . Gen 39:2

SUDDENLY
s there was with the . . . . Luke 2:13

SUE
s you and take away . . . . Matt 5:40

SUFFER
for the Christ to *s* . . . . . Luke 24:46
Christ, if indeed we *s* . . . Rom 8:17
in Him, but also to *s* . . . . Phil 1:29

SUFFERED
s these things and to . . Luke 24:26
for whom I have *s* . . . . Phil 3:8
after you have *s* . . . . . . 1 Pet 5:10

SUFFERING
anyone among you *s* . . James 5:13

SUFFERINGS
I consider that the *s* . . . . Rom 8:18
perfect through *s* . . . . Heb 2:10

SUFFERS
Love *s* long and is . . . . . 1 Cor 13:4

SUFFICIENCY
but our *s* is from God . . . 2 Cor 3:5

SUFFICIENT
S for the day is its . . . . . . Matt 6:34

SUM
How great is the *s* . . . . . . Ps 139:17

SUMMER
and heat, Winter and *s* . . Gen 8:22

SUMPTUOUSLY
fine linen and fared *s* . Luke 16:19

SUN
So the *s* stood still . . . . Josh 10:13
s shall not strike you . . . . Ps 121:6
s returned ten degrees . . . . . Is 38:8
The *s* and moon grow . . . Joel 2:10
s shall go down on the . . . . Mic 3:6
for He makes His *s* . . . . . Matt 5:45
the *s* was darkened . . Luke 23:45
do not let the *s* . . . . Eph 4:26
s became black as . . . . Rev 6:12
had no need of the *s* . . . . Rev 21:23

SUPPER
to eat the Lord's *S* . . . . 1 Cor 11:20
took the cup after *s* . . . 1 Cor 11:25
together for the *s* . . . . . . Rev 19:17

SUPPLICATION
by prayer and *s* . . . . Phil 4:6

SUPPLIES
by what every joint *s* . . . . Eph 4:16

SUPPLY
And my God shall *s* . . . . . Phil 4:19

SUPPORT
this, that you must *s* . . . Acts 20:35

SUPREME
to the king as *s* . . . . 1 Pet 2:13

SURE
s your sin will find . . . . Num 32:23
call and election *s* . . . . . . 2 Pet 1:10

SURETY
Be *s* for Your servant . . Ps 119:122
Jesus has become a *s* . . . Heb 7:22

SURROUND
LORD, mercy shall *s* . . . . . . Ps 32:10

SURROUNDED
also, since we are *s* . . . . . Heb 12:1

SURVIVOR
was no refugee or *s* . . . . Lam 2:22

SUSPICIONS
reviling, evil *s* . . . . 1 Tim 6:4

SUSTAIN
S me with cakes of . . . . . . Song 2:5

SWADDLING
Him in *s* cloths . . . . Luke 2:7

SWALLOW
a gnat and *s* a camel . . Matt 23:24

SWEAR
'You shall not *s* . . . . Matt 5:33
began to curse and *s* . . Matt 26:74

SWEARING
By *s* and lying . . . . Hos 4:2

SWEARS
but whoever *s* by the . . Matt 23:18

SWEAT
His *s* became like . . . . . Luke 22:44

SWEET
s are Your words . . . . . . Ps 119:103
but it will be as *s* . . . . Rev 10:9

SWEETNESS
mouth like honey in *s* . . Ezek 3:3

SWELLING
they speak great *s* . . . . . 2 Pet 2:18

SWIFT
let every man be *s* . . . . James 1:19

SWIM
night I make my bed *s* . . . . Ps 6:6

SWOON
As they *s* like the . . . . Lam 2:12

SWORD
s which turned every . . . . Gen 3:24
The *s* of the LORD is . . . . . . Is 34:6
'A *s* is sharpened . . . . . . Ezek 21:9
Bow and *s* of battle I . . . . Hos 2:18
to bring peace but a *s* . Matt 10:34
for all who take the *s* . . Matt 26:52
the *s* of the Spirit . . . . Eph 6:17
than any two-edged *s* . . . Heb 4:12
mouth goes a sharp *s* . . . Rev 19:15

SWORDS
shall beat their *s* . . . . Is 2:4

SWORE
So I s in My wrath* . . . . . . Heb 3:11

SWORN
"By Myself I have *s* . . . . Gen 22:16
"The LORD has *s* . . . . Heb 7:21

SYMBOLIC
which things are *s* . . . . . . Gal 4:24

SYMPATHIZE
Priest who cannot *s* . . . . . Heb 4:15

SYMPATHY
My *s* is stirred . . . . Hos 11:8

SYNAGOGUE
but are a *s* of Satan . . . . . . Rev 2:9

T

TABERNACLE
t He shall hide me . . . . Ps 27:5
I will abide in Your *t* . . . . . Ps 61:4
And we'll rebuild the t . . Acts 15:16
and more perfect *t* . . . . . . Heb 9:11

TABERNACLES
Feast of *T* was at hand . . John 7:2

TABLE
prepare a *t* before me . . . . Ps 23:5

dogs under the *t* . . . . Mark 7:28
of the Lord's *t* . . . . 1 Cor 10:21

TABLES

and overturned the *t* . . Matt 21:12

TABLET

is engraved On the *t* . . . . . Jer 17:1

TAIL

t drew a third of the . . . . Rev 12:4

TAKE

t Your Holy Spirit . . . . Ps 51:11
"*T* My yoke upon . . . . . Matt 11:29
and *t* up his cross . . . . . Mark 8:34
My life that I may *t* . . . John 10:17

TAKEN

He was *t* from prison . . . . . Is 53:8
one will be *t* and the . . Matt 24:40
until He is *t* out of . . . . 2 Thess 2:7

TALEBEARER

t reveals secrets . . . . Prov 11:13

TALENT

went and hid your *t* . . . Matt 25:25

TALK

shall *t* of them when . . . . Deut 6:7

TALKED

within us while He *t* . . Luke 24:32

TALKERS

both idle *t* and . . . . Titus 1:10

TAMBOURINE

The mirth of the *t* . . . . Is 24:8

TARES

the *t* also appeared . . . . Matt 13:26

TARGET

You set me as Your *t* . . . . Job 7:20

TARRY

come and will not t . . . . Heb 10:37

TASK

this burdensome *t* . . . . . . Eccl 1:13

TASTE

Oh, *t* and see that the . . . . . Ps 34:8
might *t* death for . . . . Heb 2:9

TASTED

t the heavenly gift . . . . Heb 6:4

TAUGHT

as His counselor has *t* . . . . Is 40:13
from man, nor was I *t* . . . Gal 1:12

TAUNT

and a byword, a *t* . . . . Jer 24:9

TAX

t collectors do the . . . . . . Matt 5:46

TAXES

t to whom *t* . . . . Rom 13:7

TEACH

"Can anyone *t* . . . . Job 21:22
T me Your paths . . . . Ps 25:4
t you the fear of the . . . . . Ps 34:11
t transgressors Your . . . . Ps 51:13
So *t* us to number our . . . Ps 90:12
t you again the first . . . . . Heb 5:12

TEACHER

for One is your *T* . . . . Matt 23:8

know that You are a *t* . . . John 3:2
named Gamaliel, a *t* . . . . Acts 5:34
a *t* of the Gentiles in . . . . 1 Tim 2:7

TEACHERS

than all my *t* . . . . Ps 119:99
prophets, third *t* . . . . . . 1 Cor 12:28
and some pastors and *t* . . Eph 4:11
desiring to be *t* . . . . 1 Tim 1:7
there will be false *t* . . . . . 2 Pet 2:1

TEACHES

the Holy Spirit *t* . . . . 1 Cor 2:13
the same anointing *t* . . 1 John 2:27

TEACHING

"*t* them to observe all . Matt 28:20
t every man in all . . . . Col 1:28

TEAR

I, even I, will *t* . . . . Hos 5:14
will wipe away every *t* . . Rev 21:4

TEARS

my couch with my *t* . . . . Ps 6:6
mindful of your *t* . . . . . . 2 Tim 1:4
it diligently with *t* . . . . . Heb 12:17

TEETH

You have broken the *t* . . . . . Ps 3:7

TELL

"Who can *t* if God . . . . Jon 3:9
t him his fault . . . . Matt 18:15
whatever they *t* . . . . Matt 23:3
He comes, He will *t* . . . . John 4:25

TEMPERATE

prize is *t* in all . . . . 1 Cor 9:25
husband of one wife, *t* . . 1 Tim 3:2

TEMPEST

And suddenly a great *t* . Matt 8:24

TEMPLE

So Solomon built the *t* . 1 Kin 6:14
LORD is in His holy *t* . . . . . . Ps 11:4
One greater than the *t* . . Matt 12:6
"Destroy this *t* . . . . John 2:19
your body is the *t* . . . . 1 Cor 6:19
grows into a holy *t* . . . . . Eph 2:21
sits as God in the *t* . . . 2 Thess 2:4
and the Lamb are its *t* . . Rev 21:22

TEMPLES

t made with hands . . . . . Acts 7:48

TEMPORARY

which are seen are *t* . . . 2 Cor 4:18

TEMPT

t the LORD your God . . . . . Matt 4:7
does He Himself *t* . . . . James 1:13

TEMPTATION

do not lead us into *t* . . . . Matt 6:13
man who endures *t* . . . James 1:12

TEMPTED

forty days, *t* by Satan . . Mark 1:13
lest you also be *t* . . . . Gal 6:1
in all points *t* . . . . Heb 4:15

TEMPTER

Now when the *t* came . . . Matt 4:3

TENDER

your heart was *t* . . . . . 2 Kin 22:19

TENDERHEARTED

to one another, *t* . . . . Eph 4:32

TENDS

t a flock and does not . . . 1 Cor 9:7

TENT

earthly house, this *t* . . . . 2 Cor 5:1

TENTMAKERS

occupation they were *t* . . Acts 18:3

TENTS

Than dwell in the *t* . . . . . . Ps 84:10

TERRESTRIAL

bodies and *t* bodies . . . 1 Cor 15:40

TERRIBLE

is great and very *t* . . . . . . Joel 2:11

TERRIFIED

and not in any way *t* . . . . Phil 1:28

TERRIFY

me with dreams And *t* . . . Job 7:14

TERRIFYING

t was the sight . . . . Heb 12:21

TERROR

are nothing, You see *t* . . . Job 6:21
not be afraid of the *t* . . . . . Ps 91:5

TERRORS

consumed with *t* . . . . Ps 73:19

TEST

said, "Why do you *t* . . . Matt 22:18
T all things . . . . 1 Thess 5:21
but *t* the spirits . . . . 1 John 4:1

TESTAMENT

where there is a *t* . . . . Heb 9:16

TESTED

God *t* Abraham . . . . Gen 22:1
Where your fathers t . . . . . Heb 3:9
though it is *t* by fire . . . . . 1 Pet 1:7

TESTIFIED

who has seen has *t* . . . . John 19:35
which He has *t* . . . . 1 John 5:9

TESTIFIES

that the Holy Spirit *t* . . Acts 20:23

TESTIFY

t what We have . . . . John 3:11
t that the Father . . . . . . 1 John 4:14

TESTIFYING

was righteous, God *t* . . . . Heb 11:4

TESTIMONIES

those who keep His *t* . . . . Ps 119:2
t are my meditation . . . . Ps 119:99

TESTIMONY

two tablets of the *T* . . . . . Ex 31:18
under your feet as a *t* . . Mark 6:11
no one receives His *t* . . . John 3:32
not believed the *t* . . . . . 1 John 5:10
For the *t* of Jesus is . . . . Rev 19:10

TESTING

came to Him, *t* Him . . . . Matt 19:3

TESTS

men, but God who *t* . . 1 Thess 2:4

THANK

"I *t* You, Father . . . . Matt 11:25
t You that I am not . . . Luke 18:11

THANKFUL

as God, nor were *t* . . . . . . Rom 1:21

THANKFULNESS

Felix, with all *t* . . . . Acts 24:3

THANKS

the cup, and gave t .... Matt 26:27
T be to God for His .... 2 Cor 9:15

THANKSGIVING

His presence with t ...... Ps 95:2
into His gates with t ..... Ps 100:4
supplication, with t ...... Phil 4:6

THEATER

and rushed into the t .. Acts 19:29

THIEF

do not despise a t ...... Prov 6:30
because he was a t ..... John 12:6
Lord will come as a t .. 2 Pet 3:10

THIEVES

And companions of t ...... Is 1:23

THINGS

in heaven give good t ... Matt 7:11
kept all these t .... Luke 2:51
share in all good t .... Gal 6:6

THINK

t you have eternal ..... John 5:39
not to t of himself ...... Rom 12:3

THINKS

Yet the LORD t upon me . Ps 40:17
For as he t in his .... Prov 23:7
t he stands take heed . 1 Cor 10:12

THIRST

those who hunger and t . Matt 5:6
in Me shall never t .... John 6:35
anymore nor t anymore . Rev 7:16

THIRSTS

My soul t for God .... Ps 42:2
saying, "If anyone t .... John 7:37
freely to him who t ..... Rev 21:6

THIRSTY

I was t and you gave .. Matt 25:35

THISTLES

or figs from t .... Matt 7:16

THORN

a t in the flesh was .... 2 Cor 12:7

THORNBUSHES

gather grapes from t .... Matt 7:16

THORNS

Both t and thistles it .... Gen 3:18
some fell among t ...... Matt 13:7
wearing the crown of t . John 19:5

THOUGHT

You understand my t ..... Ps 139:2
I t as a child .... 1 Cor 13:11

THOUGHTS

The LORD knows the t ... Ps 94:11
unrighteous man his t ..... Is 55:7
"For My t are not your .... Is 55:8
Jesus, knowing their t ... Matt 9:4
heart proceed evil t .... Matt 15:19
The LORD knows the t . 1 Cor 3:20

THREAT

shall flee at the t .... Is 30:17

THREATEN

suffered, He did not t .. 1 Pet 2:23

THREATENING

to them, giving up t ...... Eph 6:9

THREATS

still breathing t .... Acts 9:1

THREE

hope, love, these t .... 1 Cor 13:13

THRESH

it is time to t her .... Jer 51:33

THRESHING

t shall last till the ...... Lev 26:5

THROAT

t is an open tomb ..... Rom 3:13

THRONE

Your t, O God, is .... Ps 45:6
Lord sitting on a t .... Is 6:1
"Heaven is My t .... Is 66:1
for it is God's t .... Matt 5:34
will give Him the t .... Luke 1:32
"Your t, O God, is ...... Heb 1:8
come boldly to the t .... Heb 4:16
My Father on His t ...... Rev 3:21
I saw a great white t ... Rev 20:11

THRONES

invisible, whether t ...... Col 1:16

THRONG

house of God in the t .... Ps 55:14

THROW

t Yourself down .... Matt 4:6

THROWN

neck, and he were t .... Mark 9:42

THRUST

and rose up and t ...... Luke 4:29

THUNDER

The voice of Your t ...... Ps 77:18
the voice of loud t ...... Rev 14:2

THUNDERED

"The LORD t from .... 2 Sam 22:14

THUNDERINGS

the sound of mighty t ... Rev 19:6

THUNDERS

The God of glory t .... Ps 29:3

TIDINGS

I bring you good t ..... Luke 2:10

TILL

no man to t the ground ... Gen 2:5

TILLER

but Cain was a t .... Gen 4:2

TILLS

t his land will have .... Prov 28:19

TIME

pray to You In a t .... Ps 32:6
for the t is near .... Rev 1:3

TIMES

the signs of the t ...... Matt 16:3
not for you to know t .... Acts 1:7
last days perilous t ..... 2 Tim 3:1

TITHE

And he gave him a t ... Gen 14:20
For you pay t of mint .. Matt 23:23

TITHES

and to bring the t ...... Neh 10:37
Bring all the t .... Mal 3:10

TITHING

the year of t .... Deut 26:12

TITLE

Now Pilate wrote a t .. John 19:19

TITTLE

away, one jot or one t .. Matt 5:18

TODAY

T I have begotten You ..... Ps 2:7
t you will be with Me . Luke 23:43
"T, if you will hear .... Heb 3:7
the same yesterday, t ... Heb 13:8

TOIL

t you shall eat of .... Gen 3:17

TOILED

"Master, we have t ...... Luke 5:5

TOLD

Behold, I have t ...... Matt 28:7
so, I would have t ...... John 14:2

TOLERABLE

you, it will be more t .. Matt 10:15

TOMB

in the garden a new t . John 19:41

TOMBS

like whitewashed t .... Matt 23:27

TOMORROW

drink, for t we die .... Is 22:13
do not worry about t ... Matt 6:34
what will happen t .... James 4:14

TONGUE

remember you, Let my t . Ps 137:6
forever, But a lying t .. Prov 12:19
t breaks a bone .... Prov 25:15
t should confess that ... Phil 2:11
does not bridle his t .. James 1:26
no man can tame the t . James 3:8
every nation, tribe, t .... Rev 14:6

TONGUES

From the strife of t ...... Ps 31:20
speak with new t ..... Mark 16:17
divided t, as of fire ...... Acts 2:3
I speak with the t ..... 1 Cor 13:1

TOOTH

eye for an eye and a t .. Matt 5:38

TOPHET

the high places of T ...... Jer 7:31

TORCH

and like a fiery t .... Zech 12:6

TORCHES

When he had set the t .. Judg 15:5
come with flaming t ..... Nah 2:3

TORMENT

You come here to t ..... Matt 8:29
t ascends forever ...... Rev 14:11

TORMENTED

And they will be t ...... Rev 20:10

TORMENTS

"And being in t .... Luke 16:23

TORN

of the temple was t .... Matt 27:51

TORTURED

Others were t .... Heb 11:35

TOSSED

t to and fro and .... Eph 4:14

TOTTER

drunkard, And shall t .... Is 24:20

TOUCH
"If only I may *t* ....Matt 9:21

TOUCHED
t my mouth with it ....Is 6:7

TOUCHES
He *t* the hills ....Ps 104:32

TOWER
t whose top is in the ....Gen 11:4
a watchman in the *t* ....Is 21:5

TRACKED
t our steps So that we ..Lam 4:18

TRADERS
are princes, Whose *t* ......Is 23:8

TRADITION
transgress the *t* ....Matt 15:2
according to the *t* ....Col 2:8

TRAIN
T up a child in the .....Prov 22:6

TRAINED
those who have been *t* .Heb 12:11

TRAINING
bring them up in the *t* ....Eph 6:4

TRAITOR
also became a *t* ....Luke 6:16

TRAITORS
t, headstrong ....2 Tim 3:4

TRAMPLE
serpent you shall *t* ......Ps 91:13
swine, lest they *t* ....Matt 7:6

TRAMPLED
t the Son of God ....Heb 10:29
the winepress was *t* ....Rev 14:20

TRANCE
t I saw a vision ....Acts 11:5

TRANSFIGURED
and was *t* before them ..Matt 17:2

TRANSFORMED
this world, but be *t* .....Rom 12:2

TRANSGRESS
do Your disciples *t* .....Matt 15:2

TRANSGRESSED
"Yes, all Israel has *t* ....Dan 9:11
t your commandment .Luke 15:29

TRANSGRESSES
Whoever *t* and does not .2 John 9

TRANSGRESSION
no law there is no *t* .....Rom 4:15
deceived, fell into *t* ....1 Tim 2:14

TRANSGRESSIONS
mercies, Blot out my *t* ....Ps 51:1
For I acknowledge my *t* ..Ps 51:3
was wounded for our *t* ....Is 53:5
For the *t* of My people ....Is 53:8

TRANSGRESSOR
I make myself a *t* ....Gal 2:18

TRANSGRESSORS
Then I will teach *t* ......Ps 51:13
numbered with the *t* .....Is 53:12

TRAP
of Israel, As a *t* ....Is 8:14

TRAPS
for me, And from the *t* ..Ps 141:9

TRAVEL
you *t* land and sea ....Matt 23:15

TRAVELER
t who turns aside ....Jer 14:8

TRAVELING
lie waste, The *t* ....Is 33:8

TREACHEROUS
are insolent, *t* ....Zeph 3:4

TREACHEROUSLY
"This man dealt *t* ....Acts 7:19

TREAD
You shall *t* upon the .....Ps 91:13

TREADS
an ox while it t ....1 Tim 5:18
t the winepress ....Rev 19:15

TREASURE
and you will have *t* ....Matt 19:21
he who lays up *t* ......Luke 12:21
But we have this *t* .....2 Cor 4:7

TREASURED
t the words of His ......Job 23:12

TREASURER
Erastus, the *t* of the ...Rom 16:23

TREASURES
it more than hidden *t* ....Job 3:21
I will give you the *t* ......Is 45:3
for yourselves *t* ....Matt 6:19
are hidden all the *t* ......Col 2:3
riches than the *t* ....Heb 11:26

TREATY
Now Solomon made a *t* .1 Kin 3:1

TREE
you eaten from the *t* ....Gen 3:11
t Planted by the ....Ps 1:3
like a native green *t* .....Ps 37:35
t bears good fruit ....Matt 7:17
His own body on the *t* .1 Pet 2:24
the river, was the *t* .....Rev 22:2

TREES
late autumn *t* without ....Jude 12
the sea, or the *t* ....Rev 7:3

TREMBLE
That the nations may *t* ....Is 64:2
they shall fear and *t* .....Jer 33:9

TREMBLED
Then everyone who *t* ....Ezra 9:4
the earth shook and *t* .....Ps 18:7
and indeed they *t* ....Jer 4:24

TREMBLING
in fear, and in much *t* ...1 Cor 2:3
t you received ....2 Cor 7:15
flesh, with fear and *t* .....Eph 6:5

TRENCH
and he made a *t* ......1 Kin 18:32

TRESPASSES
forgive men their *t* .....Matt 6:14
not imputing their *t* ....2 Cor 5:19
who were dead in *t* ......Eph 2:1

TRIAL
concerning the fiery *t* ..1 Pet 4:12

TRIBE
the Lion of the *t* ....Rev 5:5
blood Out of every *t* ....Rev 5:9

TRIBES
t which are scattered ....James 1:1

TRIBULATION
there will be great *t* ...Matt 24:21
world you will have *t* .John 16:33
with her into great *t* ....Rev 2:22
out of the great *t* ....Rev 7:14

TRIBULATIONS
t enter the kingdom ...Acts 14:22
but we also glory in *t* ...Rom 5:3
t that you endure .....2 Thess 1:4

TRIED
A *t* stone, a precious .....Is 28:16

TRIMMED
and *t* their lamps ....Matt 25:7

TRIUMPH
always leads us in *t* ...2 Cor 2:14

TRIUMPHED
the Lᴏʀᴅ, For He has *t* ....Ex 15:1

TRODDEN
t the winepress alone .....Is 63:3

TROUBLE
few days and full of *t* ....Job 14:1
t He shall hide me ....Ps 27:5
not in *t* as other men ....Ps 73:5
will be with him in *t* .....Ps 91:15
Savior in time of *t* ....Jer 14:8
there are some who *t* .....Gal 1:7

TROUBLED
worried and *t* ....Luke 10:41
shaken in mind or *t* ...2 Thess 2:2

TROUBLES
Out of all their *t* ....Ps 25:22
will be famines and *t* ..Mark 13:8
him out of all his *t* ......Acts 7:10

TROUBLING
wicked cease from *t* .....Job 3:17

TRUE
He who sent Me is *t* ....John 7:28
Indeed, let God be *t* .....Rom 3:4
whatever things are *t* ....Phil 4:8
Him who is *t* ....1 John 5:20
for these words are *t* ....Rev 21:5

TRUMPET
deed, do not sound a *t* ...Matt 6:2
t makes an uncertain ..1 Cor 14:8
For the *t* will sound ..1 Cor 15:52

TRUST
T in the Lᴏʀᴅ ....Ps 37:3
T in the Lᴏʀᴅ with all ....Prov 3:5
Do not *t* in a friend ....Mic 7:5
who *t* in riches ....Mark 10:24

TRUSTED
"He *t* in the Lᴏʀᴅ ....Ps 22:8
"He *t* in God ....Matt 27:43

TRUSTS
But he who *t* in the ......Ps 32:10

TRUTH
led me in the way of *t* ..Gen 24:48
Behold, You desire *t* ......Ps 51:6
t shall be your shield .....Ps 91:4
And Your law is *t* .....Ps 119:142

t is fallen in the .... Is 59:14
called the City of *T* ...... Zech 8:3
you shall know the *t* ..... John 8:32
"I am the way, the *t* .... John 14:6
He, the Spirit of *t* .... John 16:13
to Him, "What is *t* .... John 18:38
who suppress the *t* ..... Rom 1:18
but, speaking the *t* ...... Eph 4:15
your waist with *t* .... Eph 6:14
I am speaking the *t* ..... 1 Tim 2:7
they may know the *t* .. 2 Tim 2:25
the knowledge of the *t* .. 2 Tim 3:7
that we are of the *t* ... 1 John 3:19
the Spirit is *t* .... 1 John 5:6

TRY
which is to *t* you .... 1 Pet 4:12

TUMULT
Your enemies make a *t* ... Ps 83:2

TUNIC
Also he made him a *t* ... Gen 37:3

TUNICS
the LORD God made *t* ... Gen 3:21

TURBAN
"Remove the *t* .... Ezek 21:26

TURN
you shall not *t* .... Deut 17:11
"Repent, *t* away from .. Ezek 14:6
on your right cheek, *t* .. Matt 5:39
t them from darkness .. Acts 26:18

TURNED
The wicked shall be *t* ..... Ps 9:17
of Israel, They have *t* ...... Is 1:4
and how you *t* .... 1 Thess 1:9

TURNING
marvel that you are *t* ..... Gal 1:6
or shadow of *t* .... James 1:17

TURNS
A soft answer *t* .... Prov 15:1
that he who *t* .... James 5:20

TURTLEDOVE
t Is heard in our land .. Song 2:12

TUTOR
the law was our *t* .... Gal 3:24

TWIST
unstable people *t* to .... 2 Pet 3:16

TWO
T are better than one .... Eccl 4:9
t shall become one ..... Matt 19:5
new man from the *t* ..... Eph 2:15

TYPE
of Adam, who is a *t* .... Rom 5:14

U

UNAFRAID
Do you want to be *u* .... Rom 13:3

UNBELIEF
because of their *u* ..... Matt 13:58
help my *u* .... Mark 9:24
did it ignorantly in *u* .. 1 Tim 1:13
enter in because of *u* .... Heb 3:19

UNBELIEVERS
yoked together with *u* .2 Cor 6:14

UNBELIEVING
Do not be *u* .... John 20:27

u nothing is pure ...... Titus 1:15
"But the cowardly, *u* .... Rev 21:8

UNCIRCUMCISED
not the physically *u* .... Rom 2:27

UNCLEAN
I am a man of *u* lips .... Is 6:5
man common or *u* ..... Acts 10:28
there is nothing *u* ..... Rom 14:14
that no fornicator, *u* ...... Eph 5:5

UNCLEANNESS
men's bones and all *u* .. Matt 23:27
flesh in the lust of *u* .... 2 Pet 2:10

UNCLOTHED
we want to be *u* .... 2 Cor 5:4

UNCOVERS
u deep things out of .... Job 12:22

UNDEFILED
incorruptible and *u* ...... 1 Pet 1:4

UNDERMINE
And you *u* your friend ... Job 6:27

UNDERSTAND
if there are any who *u* .... Ps 14:2
hearing, but do not *u* .... Is 6:9
"Why do you not *u* .... John 8:43
lest they should u ..... Acts 28:27
some things hard to *u* .. 2 Pet 3:16

UNDERSTANDING
His *u* is infinite .... Ps 147:5
lean not on your own *u* .. Prov 3:5
u will find good .... Prov 19:8
His *u* is unsearchable .... Is 40:28
also still without *u* .... Matt 15:16
also pray with the *u* .. 1 Cor 14:15
the Lord give you *u* .... 2 Tim 2:7
Who is wise and *u* .... James 3:13

UNDERSTANDS
There is none who u .... Rom 3:11

UNDERSTOOD
Then I *u* their end .... Ps 73:17
clearly seen, being *u* .... Rom 1:20

UNDESIRABLE
gather together, O *u* .... Zeph 2:1

UNDIGNIFIED
I will be even more *u* .2 Sam 6:22

UNDISCERNING
u, untrustworthy .... Rom 1:31

UNDONE
"Woe is me, for I am *u* ..... Is 6:5

UNEDUCATED
that they were *u* .... Acts 4:13

UNFAITHFUL
way of the *u* is hard ... Prov 13:15

UNFAITHFULLY
back and acted *u* .... Ps 78:57

UNFORGIVING
unloving, *u* .... Rom 1:31

UNFORMED
substance, being yet *u* .. Ps 139:16

UNFRUITFUL
and it becomes *u* ...... Mark 4:19

UNGODLINESS
heaven against all *u* .... Rom 1:18

UNGODLY
u shall not stand .... Ps 1:5
Christ died for the *u* ..... Rom 5:6

UNHOLY
the holy and *u* .... Ezek 22:26

UNINFORMED
the place of the *u* ..... 1 Cor 14:16

UNINTENTIONALLY
kills his neighbor *u* .... Deut 4:42

UNITE
U my heart to fear ...... Ps 86:11

UNITY
to dwell together in *u* .... Ps 133:1
to keep the *u* of the ...... Eph 4:3

UNJUST
commended the *u* ...... Luke 16:8
of the just and the *u* ... Acts 24:15
For God is not *u* .... Heb 6:10

UNJUSTLY
long will you judge *u* ..... Ps 82:2

UNKNOWN
To The *U* God .... Acts 17:23

UNLEAVENED
the Feast of *U* Bread .... Ex 12:17

UNLOVING
untrustworthy, *u* .... Rom 1:31

UNMERCIFUL
unforgiving, *u* .... Rom 1:31

UNPREPARED
with me and find you *u* .2 Cor 9:4

UNPRESENTABLE
u parts have greater .. 1 Cor 12:23

UNPROFITABLE
'We are *u* servants .... Luke 17:10
for that would be *u* .... Heb 13:17

UNPUNISHED
wicked will not go *u* ... Prov 11:21

UNQUENCHABLE
up the chaff with *u* ..... Matt 3:12

UNRESTRAINED
that the people were *u* ... Ex 32:25

UNRIGHTEOUS
u man his thoughts .... Is 55:7
u will not inherit the .... 1 Cor 6:9

UNRIGHTEOUSNESS
all ungodliness and *u* .... Rom 1:18
cleanse us from all *u* .. 1 John 1:9
All *u* is sin .... 1 John 5:17

UNRULY
those who are *u* ...... 1 Thess 5:14

UNSEARCHABLE
u are His judgments ... Rom 11:33

UNSKILLED
only of milk is *u* .... Heb 5:13

UNSPOTTED
to keep oneself *u* ...... James 1:27

UNSTABLE
U as water .... Gen 49:4

UNSTOPPED
of the deaf shall be *u* . . . . . . Is 35:5

UNTAUGHT
which *u* and unstable . . 2 Pet 3:16

UNTRUSTWORTHY
undiscerning, *u* . . . . Rom 1:31

UNWASHED
eat bread with *u* hands . . Mark 7:5

UNWISE
Therefore do not be *u* . . . Eph 5:17

UNWORTHY
u manner will be . . . . . 1 Cor 11:27

UPHOLD
U me according to . . . . Ps 119:116

UPHOLDING
u all things by the . . . . Heb 1:3

UPHOLDS
LORD *u* all who fall . . . . . Ps 145:14

UPPER
show you a large *u* . . . Mark 14:15

UPRIGHT
u is His delight . . . . Prov 15:8

UPRIGHTNESS
princes for their *u* . . . . . Prov 17:26

UPROOT
u the wheat with . . . . . . Matt 13:29

URIM
Thummim and Your *U* . Deut 33:8

US
"God with *u* . . . . Matt 1:23
If God is for *u* . . . . Rom 8:31
of them were of *u* . . . . 1 John 2:19

USE
who spitefully *u* you . . . . Matt 5:44
u liberty as an . . . . Gal 5:13

USELESS
one's religion is *u* . . . . . James 1:26

USES
if one *u* it lawfully . . . . . . 1 Tim 1:8

USING
u liberty as a . . . . 1 Pet 2:16

USURY
'Take no *u* or . . . . Lev 25:36

UTTER
u dark sayings of old . . . . . Ps 78:2

UTTERANCE
the Spirit gave them *u* . . . Acts 2:4

UTTERED
which cannot be *u* . . . . . Rom 8:26

UTTERMOST
u those who come . . . . . . Heb 7:25

UTTERS
Day unto day *u* speech . . . . Ps 19:2

V

VAGABOND
v you shall be on the . . . . Gen 4:12

VAIN
the people plot a *v* . . . . Ps 2:1
you believed in *v* . . . . . . 1 Cor 15:2

VALIANT
They are not *v* for the . . . . . Jer 9:3

VALIANTLY
God we will do *v* . . . . Ps 60:12

VALLEY
v shall be exalted . . . . Is 40:4

VALOR
a mighty man of *v* . . . 1 Sam 16:18

VALUE
of more *v* than they . . . . Matt 6:26

VALUED
It cannot be *v* in the . . . . Job 28:16

VANISH
knowledge, it will *v* . . . . 1 Cor 13:8

VANISHED
and He *v* from their . . . Luke 24:31

VANITY
of vanities, all is *v* . . . . Eccl 1:2

VAPOR
best state is but *v* . . . . Ps 39:5
It is even a *v* that . . . . . James 4:14

VARIATION
whom there is no *v* . . . James 1:17

VEGETABLES
and let them give us *v* . . . Dan 1:12
is weak eats only *v* . . . . . Rom 14:2

VEHEMENT
of fire, A most *v* . . . . Song 8:6

VEIL
v of the temple was . . . . Matt 27:51
Presence behind the *v* . . . Heb 6:19

VENGEANCE
V is Mine . . . . Deut 32:35

VENOM
It becomes cobra *v* . . . . . Job 20:14

VESSEL
like a potter's *v* . . . . Ps 2:9
for he is a chosen *v* . . . . . Acts 9:15

VESSELS
treasure in earthen *v* . . . . 2 Cor 4:7

VEXED
grieved, and I was *v* . . . . . Ps 73:21

VICE
as a cloak for *v* . . . . 1 Pet 2:16

VICTIM
And plucked the *v* . . . . . . Job 29:17

VICTORY
v that has overcome . . . 1 John 5:4

VIEW
"Go, *v* the land . . . . Josh 2:1

VIGILANT
Be sober, be *v* . . . . 1 Pet 5:8

VIGOR
nor his natural *v* . . . . Deut 34:7

VILE
them up to *v* passions . . Rom 1:26

VINDICATED
know that I shall be *v* . . Job 13:18

VINDICATION
Let my *v* come from . . . . . . Ps 17:2

VINE
"I am the true *v* . . . . John 15:1

VINEDRESSER
and My Father is the *v* . John 15:1

VINEGAR
As *v* to the teeth and . . Prov 10:26

VINES
foxes that spoil the *v* . . . Song 2:15

VINEYARD
Who plants a *v* and . . . . . 1 Cor 9:7

VIOLENCE
was filled with *v* . . . . Gen 6:11
of heaven suffers *v* . . . . Matt 11:12

VIOLENT
haters of God, *v* . . . . Rom 1:30

VIPER
And stings like a *v* . . . . Prov 23:32

VIPERS
to them, "Brood of *v* . . . . . Matt 3:7

VIRGIN
v shall conceive . . . . Is 7:14
"Behold, the *v* shall . . . . Matt 1:23

VIRGINS
v who took their lamps . Matt 25:1

VIRTUE
to your faith *v* . . . . 2 Pet 1:5

VISAGE
v was marred more than . Is 52:14

VISIBLE
that are on earth, *v* . . . . . . Col 1:16

VISION
in a trance I saw a *v* . . . . Acts 11:5
to the heavenly *v* . . . . . . Acts 26:19

VISIONS
young men shall see *v* . . . Joel 2:28

VISIT
v orphans and . . . . James 1:27

VISITATION
God in the day of *v* . . . . 1 Pet 2:12

VISITED
Israel, for He has *v* . . . . Luke 1:68

VISITING
v the iniquity of the . . . . . Ex 20:5

VISITOR
am a foreigner and a *v* . . Gen 23:4

VITALITY
v was turned into the . . . . . Ps 32:4

VOICE
fire a still small *v* . . . . 1 Kin 19:12
if you will hear His *v* . . . . . Ps 95:7
"The *v* of one crying . . . . Matt 3:3
And suddenly a *v* . . . . . . Matt 3:17
for they know his *v* . . . . John 10:4

VOICES
the truth hears My *v* ..John 18:37
If anyone hears My *v* ....Rev 3:20

VOICES
And there were loud *v* ..Rev 11:15

VOID
they are a nation *v* ....Deut 32:28
heirs, faith is made *v* ...Rom 4:14

VOLUME
in the v of the book .....Heb 10:7

VOLUNTEERS
Your people shall be *v* ..Ps 110:3

VOMIT
returns to his own v ....2 Pet 2:22

VOW
for he had taken a *v* ...Acts 18:18

VOWS
to reconsider his *v* ....Prov 20:25

W

WAGE
w the good warfare ....1 Tim 1:18

WAGES
For the *w* of sin is ......Rom 6:23
Indeed the *w* of the ....James 5:4

WAIL
"Son of man, *w* ....Ezek 32:18

WAILING
There will be *w* ....Matt 13:42

WAIT
w patiently for Him ....Ps 37:7
those who *w* on the ......Is 40:31
To those who eagerly *w* .Heb 9:28

WAITED
w patiently for the ....Ps 40:1
Divine longsuffering *w* .1 Pet 3:20

WAITING
ourselves, eagerly *w* ....Rom 8:23
from that time *w* ....Heb 10:13

WAITS
the creation eagerly *w* ..Rom 8:19

WAKE
that whether we *w* ...1 Thess 5:10

WALK
w before Me and be .....Gen 17:1
Yea, though I *w* ....Ps 23:4
W prudently when you ...Eccl 5:1
"This is the way, *w* ......Is 30:21
be weary, they shall *w* ..Is 40:31
w humbly with your God .Mic 6:8
W while you have the .John 12:35
so we also should *w* ....Rom 6:4
For we *w* by faith ......2 Cor 5:7
W in the Spirit ....Gal 5:16
And *w* in love ....Eph 5:2
that you may *w* worthy ..Col 1:10
and they shall *w* ....Rev 3:4

WALKED
Methuselah, Enoch *w* ...Gen 5:22
The people who *w* ....Is 9:2
in which you once *w* .....Eph 2:2

WALKING
not *w* in craftiness ......2 Cor 4:2

WALKS
the LORD your God *w* ..Deut 23:14
is the man Who *w* ....Ps 1:1
he who *w* in darkness .John 12:35
adversary the devil *w* ...1 Pet 5:8

WALL
then the *w* of the city ....Josh 6:5
you whitewashed *w* ....Acts 23:3
a window in the *w* ....2 Cor 11:33
Now the *w* of the city ..Rev 21:14

WALLS
By faith the *w* of ....Heb 11:30

WANDER
they have loved to *w* ....Jer 14:10

WANDERED
They *w* in deserts and .Heb 11:38

WANDERERS
And they shall be *w* .....Hos 9:17

WANDERING
w stars for whom is ......Jude 13

WANDERS
among you *w* ....James 5:19

WANT
I shall not *w* ....Ps 23:1

WANTING
balances, and found *w* ..Dan 5:27

WANTON
have begun to grow *w* .1 Tim 5:11

WAR
"There is a noise of *w* ...Ex 32:17
w may rise against ....Ps 27:3
shall they learn *w* ....Is 2:4
going to make *w* .....Luke 14:31
You fight and *w* ....James 4:2
fleshly lusts which *w* ...1 Pet 2:11
judges and makes *w* ....Rev 19:11

WARFARE
to her, That her *w* ....Is 40:2
w entangles ....2 Tim 2:4

WARMED
in peace, be *w* ....James 2:16

WARMING
she saw Peter *w* .....Mark 14:67

WARMS
w them in the dust .....Job 39:14

WARN
w those who are .....1 Thess 5:14

WARNED
Then, being divinely *w* .Matt 2:12
Who *w* you to flee ....Matt 3:7

WARNING
w every man and ....Col 1:28

WARPED
such a person is *w* .....Titus 3:11

WARRING
w against the law of ....Rom 7:23

WARRIOR
He runs at me like a *w* .Job 16:14

WARS
you will hear of *w* ......Matt 24:6
Where do *w* and fights .James 4:1

WASH
w myself with snow .....Job 9:30
W me thoroughly ....Ps 51:2
w His feet with her ....Luke 7:38
said to him, "Go, *w* .....John 9:7
w the disciples' ....John 13:5
w away your sins .....Acts 22:16

WASHED
w his hands before ....Matt 27:24
But you were *w* ....1 Cor 6:11
Him who loved us and *w* .Rev 1:5

WASHING
us, through the *w* ....Titus 3:5

WASHINGS
and drinks, various *w* ...Heb 9:10

WASTE
the cities are laid *w* ....Is 6:11
"Why this *w* ....Matt 26:8

WASTED
this fragrant oil *w* .....Mark 14:4

WASTELAND
w shall be glad ....Is 35:1

WASTING
that this man was *w* ....Luke 16:1

WATCH
is past, And like a *w* ......Ps 90:4
"*W* therefore ....Matt 24:42

WATCHED
he would have *w* ....Matt 24:43

WATCHES
Blessed is he who *w* ....Rev 16:15

WATCHFUL
But you be *w* in all .....2 Tim 4:5

WATCHING
he comes, will find *w* .Luke 12:37

WATCHMAN
I have made you a *w* ...Ezek 3:17

WATCHMEN
I have set *w* on your .....Is 62:6

WATER
Eden to *w* the garden ...Gen 2:10
I am poured out like *w* ...Ps 22:14
For I will pour *w* ....Is 44:3
given you living *w* .....John 4:10
rivers of living *w* ......John 7:38
can yield both salt *w* ..James 3:12
the Spirit, the *w* ......1 John 5:8
are clouds without *w* ...Jude 12
let him take the *w* ......Rev 22:17

WATERED
I planted, Apollos *w* ....1 Cor 3:6

WATERS
me beside the still *w* .....Ps 23:2
Though its *w* roar and ...Ps 46:3
your bread upon the *w* ..Eccl 11:1
thirsts, Come to the *w* ....Is 55:1
fountain of living *w* .....Jer 2:13
living fountains of *w* ....Rev 7:17

WAVE
Its fruit shall *w* ....Ps 72:16

WAVER
He did not *w* at the .....Rom 4:20

WAVERING
of our hope without *w* .Heb 10:23

WAVES
sea, tossed by the *w* . . . Matt 14:24

WAX
My heart is like *w* . . . . Ps 22:14

WAY
As for God, His *w* . . . 2 Sam 22:31
the LORD knows the *w* . . . . . Ps 1:6
Teach me Your *w* . . . . Ps 27:11
in the *w* everlasting . . . . Ps 139:24
w that seems right . . . Prov 14:12
The *w* of the just is . . . . Is 26:7
wicked forsake his *w* . . . . . . Is 55:7
And pervert the *w* . . . . . . Amos 2:7
he will prepare the *w* . . . . . Mal 3:1
and broad is the *w* . . . . . Matt 7:13
will prepare Your w . . . Matt 11:10
to him, "I am the *w* . . . . John 14:6
to him the *w* . . . . Acts 18:26
to have known the *w* . . 2 Pet 2:21

WAYS
For all His *w* are . . . . Deut 32:4
transgressors Your *w* . . . . Ps 51:13
w please the LORD . . . . . . Prov 16:7
"Stand in the *w* . . . . Jer 6:16
and owns all your *w* . . . . Dan 5:23
w are everlasting . . . . Hab 3:6
unstable in all his *w* . . . James 1:8
and true are Your *w* . . . . Rev 15:3

WEAK
gives power to the *w* . . . . . Is 40:29
knee will be as *w* . . . . . . Ezek 7:17
but the flesh is *w* . . . . . . Matt 26:41
Receive one who is *w* . . Rom 14:1
God has chosen the *w* . . 1 Cor 1:27
We are *w* . . . . 1 Cor 4:10
w I became as *w* . . . . . . 1 Cor 9:22
For when I am *w* . . . . . 2 Cor 12:10

WEAKENED
w my strength in the . . . Ps 102:23

WEAKENS
w the hands of the men . . Jer 38:4

WEAKER
the wife, as to the *w* . . . . . 1 Pet 3:7

WEAKNESS
w were made strong . . . Heb 11:34

WEAKNESSES
also helps in our *w* . . . . . Rom 8:26

WEALTH
W gained by . . . . Prov 13:11

WEALTHY
rich, have become *w* . . . . Rev 3:17

WEANED
w child shall put his . . . . Is 11:8

WEAPON
w formed against you . . . . Is 54:17

WEAPONS
For the *w* of our . . . . 2 Cor 10:4

WEAR
'What shall we *w* . . . . Matt 6:31

WEARIED
You have *w* Me with . . . . . Is 43:24
therefore, being *w* . . . . . . John 4:6

WEARINESS
say, 'Oh, what a *w* . . . . . . Mal 1:13

WEARISOME
and much study is *w* . . . Eccl 12:12

WEARY
shall run and not be *w* . . . Is 40:31
And let us not grow *w* . . . . Gal 6:9
do not grow *w* in . . . . 2 Thess 3:13

WEATHER
'It will be fair *w* . . . . Matt 16:2

WEDDING
day there was a *w* . . . . . . John 2:1

WEEK
the first day of the *w* . . . Matt 28:1

WEEKS
w are determined . . . . . . Dan 9:24

WEEP
A time to *w* . . . . Eccl 3:4
You shall *w* no more . . . . . Is 30:19
are you who *w* . . . . Luke 6:21
do not *w* . . . . Luke 23:28
w with those who *w* . . . Rom 12:15

WEEPING
the noise of the *w* . . . . . . Ezra 3:13
They shall come with *w* . . Jer 31:9
There will be *w* . . . . Matt 8:12
by the tomb *w* . . . . John 20:11

WEIGH
O Most Upright, You *w* . . . . Is 26:7

WEIGHED
You have been *w* . . . . Dan 5:27

WEIGHS
eyes, But the LORD *w* . . . Prov 16:2

WEIGHT
us lay aside every *w* . . . . Heb 12:1

WEIGHTIER
have neglected the *w* . . Matt 23:23

WELFARE
does not seek the *w* . . . . . Jer 38:4

WELL
have done *w* . . . . Prov 31:29
wheel broken at the *w* . . Eccl 12:6
"Those who are *w* . . . . . . Matt 9:12
said to him, 'W done . . Matt 25:21

WELLS
These are *w* without . . . 2 Pet 2:17

WENT
They *w* out from us . . . 1 John 2:19

WEPT
out and *w* bitterly . . . . . Matt 26:75
saw the city and *w* . . . . Luke 19:41
Jesus *w* . . . . John 11:35

WET
his body was *w* with . . . . Dan 4:33

WHEAT
w falls into the . . . . John 12:24

WHEEL
in the middle of a *w* . . . . Ezek 1:16

WHEELS
noise of rattling *w* . . . . Nah 3:2

WHERE
not knowing *w* he was . . Heb 11:8

WHIP
A *w* for the horse . . . . . . Prov 26:3

WHIRLWIND
Job out of the *w* . . . . Job 38:1
has His way In the *w* . . . . Nah 1:3

WHISPER
my ear received a *w* . . . . . Job 4:12

WHISPERER
w separates the best . . . Prov 16:28

WHISPERERS
they are *w* . . . . Rom 1:29

WHISPERINGS
backbitings, *w* . . . . 2 Cor 12:20

WHITE
clothed in *w* garments . . . . Rev 3:5
behold, a *w* horse . . . . Rev 6:2
and made them *w* . . . . . . Rev 7:14

WHOLE
w body were an eye . . 1 Cor 12:17

WHOLESOME
not consent to *w* words . 1 Tim 6:3

WHOLLY
w followed the LORD . . . . Deut 1:36

WICKED
w shall be silent . . . . 1 Sam 2:9
w shall be no more . . . . . . Ps 37:10
if there is any *w* . . . . Ps 139:24
w forsake his way . . . . Is 55:7
And desperately *w* . . . . . . Jer 17:9
the sway of the *w* . . . . 1 John 5:19

WICKEDLY
God will never do *w* . . . . Job 34:12

WICKEDNESS
LORD saw that the *w* . . . . . Gen 6:5
in the tents of *w* . . . . Ps 84:10
man repented of his *w* . . . Jer 8:6
is full of greed and *w* . Luke 11:39
sexual immorality, *w* . . . Rom 1:29
and overflow of *w* . . . . James 1:21

WIDE
open your hand *w* . . . . . . Deut 15:8
w is the gate and . . . . Matt 7:13
to you, our heart is *w* . . 2 Cor 6:11

WIDOW
the fatherless and *w* . . . . Ps 146:9
How like a *w* is she . . . . . . Lam 1:1
Then one poor *w* . . . . . Mark 12:42
w has children or . . . . 1 Tim 5:4

WIDOW'S
And I caused the *w* . . . . . Job 29:13

WIDOWS
w were neglected . . . . Acts 6:1
visit orphans and *w* . . . James 1:27

WIFE
and be joined to his *w* . . . Gen 2:24
w finds a good thing . . . Prov 18:22
But a prudent *w* . . . . . . Prov 19:14
"Go, take yourself a *w* . . . Hos 1:2
divorces his *w* . . . . Mark 10:11
'I have married a *w* . . . Luke 14:20
"Remember Lot's *w* . . . Luke 17:32
so love his own *w* . . . . . . Eph 5:33
the husband of one *w* . . . Titus 1:6
bride, the Lamb's *w* . . . . Rev 21:9

WILD
olive tree which is *w* . . Rom 11:24

WILDERNESS
I will make the *w* . . . . Is 41:18

of one crying in the w ...Matt 3:3
the serpent in the *w* ....John 3:14

WILES
to stand against the *w* ...Eph 6:11

WILL
w be done On earth as ..Matt 6:10
but he who does the *w* ..Matt 7:21
not My *w* ....Luke 22:42
flesh, nor of the *w* ....John 1:13
not to do My own *w* ....John 6:38
w is present with me ...Rom 7:18
and perfect *w* of God ...Rom 12:2
works in you both to *w* ..Phil 2:13
according to His own *w* ..Heb 2:4
work to do His *w* ......Heb 13:21

WILLFULLY
For if we sin *w* ....Heb 10:26
For this they *w* ....2 Pet 3:5

WILLING
If you are *w* and ....Is 1:19
The spirit indeed is *w* .Matt 26:41
w that any should ....2 Pet 3:9

WILLINGLY
by compulsion but *w* ....1 Pet 5:2

WILLOWS
our harps Upon the *w* ...Ps 137:2

WILLS
to whom the Son *w* ....Matt 11:27
it is not of him who *w* ..Rom 9:16
say, "If the Lord *w* ....James 4:15

WIN
to all, that I might *w* ...1 Cor 9:19

WIND
the chaff which the *w* ......Ps 1:4
reed shaken by the *w* ...Matt 11:7
"The *w* blows where ....John 3:8
of a rushing mighty *w* ...Acts 2:2

WINDOWS
not open for you the *w* ..Mal 3:10

WINDS
be, that even the *w* .....Matt 8:27

WINDSTORM
And a great *w* arose ...Mark 4:37

WINE
W is a mocker ....Prov 20:1
love is better than *w* ....Song 1:2
Yes, come, buy *w* ....Is 55:1
they gave Him sour *w* .Matt 27:34
do not be drunk with *w* .Eph 5:18
not given to much *w* ....Titus 2:3

WINEBIBBERS
Do not mix with *w* ....Prov 23:20

WINEPRESS
"I have trodden the *w* .....Is 63:3
into the great *w* ....Rev 14:19
Himself treads the *w* ...Rev 19:15

WINESKINS
new wine into old *w* ....Matt 9:17

WING
One *w* of the cherub ...1 Kin 6:24

WINGS
the shadow of Your *w* ....Ps 36:7
With healing in His *w* ....Mal 4:2

WINNOW
You shall *w* them ....Is 41:16

WINS
w souls is wise ....Prov 11:30

WINTER
For lo, the *w* is past ....Song 2:11
flight may not be in *w* .Matt 24:20

WIPE
w away every tear ......Rev 21:4

WISDOM
for this is your *w* ....Deut 4:6
man who finds *w* ......Prov 3:13
Get *w* ....Prov 4:5
is the beginning of *w* ...Prov 9:10
w is justified by her ...Matt 11:19
Jesus increased in *w* ...Luke 2:52
riches both of the *w* ...Rom 11:33
the gospel, not with *w* .1 Cor 1:17
w of this world ....1 Cor 3:19
not with fleshly *w* .....2 Cor 1:12
all the treasures of *w* .....Col 2:3
If any of you lacks *w* ...James 1:5
power and riches and *w* .Rev 5:12

WISE
Do not be *w* in your .....Prov 3:7
who wins souls is *w* ...Prov 11:30
Therefore be *w* as .....Matt 10:16
five of them were *w* ....Matt 25:2
to God, alone *w* ......Rom 16:27
Where is the *w* ....1 Cor 1:20
not as fools but as *w* ...Eph 5:15
able to make you *w* ...2 Tim 3:15

WISELY
you do not inquire *w* ....Eccl 7:10

WISER
he was *w* than all men .1 Kin 4:31
of God is *w* than men ..1 Cor 1:25

WISH
w it were already .....Luke 12:49

WISHED
Then he *w* death for ......Jon 4:8

WITCHCRAFT
is as the sin of *w* ....1 Sam 15:23

WITHDRAW
From such *w* yourself ...1 Tim 6:5

WITHER
also shall not *w* ....Ps 1:3

WITHERS
The grass *w* ....Is 40:7
The grass w ....1 Pet 1:24

WITHHELD
And your sins have *w* ....Jer 5:25

WITHHOLD
good thing will He *w* ....Ps 84:11

WITHOUT
pray *w* ceasing ......1 Thess 5:17
w works is dead ......James 2:26

WITHSTAND
you may be able to *w* ...Eph 6:13

WITHSTOOD
I *w* him to his face ......Gal 2:11

WITNESS
all the world as a *w* ..Matt 24:14
This man came for a *w* ..John 1:7
do not receive Our *w* ...John 3:11
Christ, the faithful *w* .....Rev 1:5
beheaded for their *w* ....Rev 20:4

WITNESSED
is revealed, being *w* ....Rom 3:21

WITNESSES
"You are My *w* ....Is 43:10
presence of many *w* ...1 Tim 6:12
so great a cloud of *w* ....Heb 12:1

WIVES
Husbands, love your *w* ..Eph 5:25
w must be reverent ....1 Tim 3:11

WOLF
The *w* and the lamb ......Is 65:25

WOLVES
out as lambs among *w* .Luke 10:3
savage *w* ....Acts 20:29

WOMAN
She shall be called *W* ...Gen 2:23
whoever looks at a *w* ...Matt 5:28
Then the *w* of Samaria ..John 4:9
"*W*, behold your .....John 19:26
natural use of the *w* ....Rom 1:27
His Son, born of a *w* .....Gal 4:4
w being deceived ......1 Tim 2:14
w clothed with the sun ..Rev 12:1

WOMB
nations are in your *w* ..Gen 25:23
in the *w* I knew you ....Jer 1:5
is the fruit of your *w* ...Luke 1:42

WOMEN
O fairest among *w* ......Song 1:8
w will be grinding .....Matt 24:41
are you among *w* ......Luke 1:28
admonish the young *w* ..Titus 2:4
times, the holy *w* ....1 Pet 3:5

WONDER
marvelous work and a *w* .Is 29:14

WONDERFUL
Things too *w* for me .....Job 42:3
name will be called *W* ......Is 9:6

WONDERFULLY
fearfully and *w* made ...Ps 139:14

WONDERS
"And I will show *w* .....Joel 2:30
signs, and lying *w* ....2 Thess 2:9

WONDROUS
w works declare that .....Ps 75:1

WONDROUSLY
God, Who has dealt *w* ...Joel 2:26

WOOD
precious stones, *w* .....1 Cor 3:12

WOODCUTTERS
but let them be *w* ....Josh 9:21

WOOL
They shall be as *w* ....Is 1:18
hair were white like *w* ..Rev 1:14

WORD
w is very near you ....Deut 30:14
w I have hidden ....Ps 119:11
w is a lamp to my feet .Ps 119:105
Every *w* of God is pure .Prov 30:5
the *w* of our God ....Is 40:8
for every idle *w* ......Matt 12:36
The seed is the *w* ......Luke 8:11
beginning was the *W* ....John 1:1
W became flesh and ...John 1:14
Your *w* is truth ....John 17:17
Let the *w* of Christ ......Col 3:16
to you in *w* only ......1 Thess 1:5

WORDS

by the *w* of His power . . . . Heb 1:3
For the *w* of God is . . . . . Heb 4:12
does not stumble in *w* . . . James 3:2
through the *w* of God . . 1 Pet 1:23
let us not love in *w* . . . 1 John 3:18
name is called The *W* . . Rev 19:13

WORDS

Let the *w* of my mouth . . Ps 19:14
The *w* of the wise are . . Eccl 12:11
pass away, but My *w* . . Matt 24:35
You have the *w* of . . . . . John 6:68
not with wisdom of *w* . . 1 Cor 1:17
those who hear the *w* . . . . Rev 1:3

WORK

day God ended His *w* . . . . Gen 2:2
people had a mind to *w* . . Neh 4:6
the *w* of Your fingers . . . . . Ps 8:3
Man goes out to his *w* . . Ps 104:23
w is honorable and . . . . . Ps 111:3
will bring every *w* . . . . Eccl 12:14
For I will *w* a *w* . . . . Hab 1:5
could do no mighty *w* . . . Mark 6:5
"This is the *w* of God . . . John 6:29
"I must *w* the works . . . . John 9:4
w which You have . . . . . John 17:4
know that all things *w* . . Rom 8:28
w is no longer *w* . . . . . . Rom 11:6
Do not destroy the *w* . . Rom 14:20
abounding in the *w* . . 1 Cor 15:58
If anyone will not *w* . 2 Thess 3:10
but a doer of the *w* . . . James 1:25

WORKED

which He *w* in Christ . . . Eph 1:20

WORKER

w is worthy of his . . . . . Matt 10:10
w who does not need . . 2 Tim 2:15

WORKERS

we are God's fellow *w* . . 1 Cor 3:9

WORKING

Father has been *w* . . . . . John 5:17
through faith in the *w* . . . . Col 2:12

WORKMANSHIP

For we are His *w* . . . . Eph 2:10

WORKS

are Your wonderful *w* . . . . Ps 40:5
And let her own *w* . . . . Prov 31:31
"For I know their *w* . . . . . Is 66:18
show Him greater *w* . . . . John 5:20
w that I do he will do . John 14:12
might stand, not of *w* . . . Rom 9:11
same God who *w* . . . . . . 1 Cor 12:6
not justified by the *w* . . . . Gal 2:16
Now the *w* of the flesh . . . Gal 5:19
not of *w*, lest anyone . . . . Eph 2:9
for it is God who *w* . . . . . Phil 2:13
but does not have *w* . . James 2:14
also justified by *w* . . . . James 2:25
"I know your *w* . . . . Rev 2:2
their *w* follow them . . . . Rev 14:13
according to their *w* . . . . Rev 20:12

WORLD

"The field is the *w* . . . . Matt 13:38
He was in the *w* . . . . . . John 1:10
God so loved the *w* . . . . John 3:16
His Son into the *w* . . . . John 3:17
w cannot hate you . . . . . John 7:7
You are of this *w* . . . . . John 8:23
overcome the *w* . . . . . . John 16:33
w may become guilty . . . Rom 3:19
be conformed to this *w* . . Rom 12:2
loved this present *w* . . 2 Tim 4:10
Do not love the *w* . . . 1 John 2:15
w is passing away . . . . 1 John 2:17

WORLDS

also He made the *w* . . . . . . Heb 1:2

WORM

But I am a *w* . . . . Ps 22:6
w does not die . . . . Mark 9:44

WORMS

he was eaten by *w* . . . . Acts 12:23

WORMWOOD

of the star is *W* . . . . Rev 8:11

WORRY

to you, do not *w* . . . . Matt 6:25

WORRYING

w can add one . . . . Matt 6:27

WORSE

w than their fathers . . . . . . Jer 7:26

WORSHIP

come to *w* Him . . . . Matt 2:2
w what you do not . . . . . John 4:22
the angels of God *w* . . . . . Heb 1:6

WORSHIPED

on their faces and *w* . . . . Rev 11:16

WORSHIPER

if anyone is a *w* . . . . John 9:31

WORTH

make my speech *w* . . . . . Job 24:25

WORTHLESS

Indeed they are all *w* . . . . . Is 41:29

WORTHLESSNESS

long will you love *w* . . . . Ps 4:2

WORTHY

present time are not *w* . . Rom 8:18
to walk *w* . . . . Eph 4:1
the world was not *w* . . . Heb 11:38
"*W* is the Lamb who . . . . Rev 5:12

WOUND

And my *w* incurable . . . . Jer 15:18
and his deadly *w* . . . . Rev 13:3

WOUNDED

But He was *w* for our . . . . . Is 53:5

WOUNDING

killed a man for *w* . . . . . . Gen 4:23

WOUNDS

Faithful are the *w* . . . . . . Prov 27:6

WRANGLINGS

useless *w* of men of . . . . 1 Tim 6:5

WRATH

speak to them in His *w* . . . . Ps 2:5
Surely the *w* of man . . . . . Ps 76:10
So I swore in My *w* . . . . . . Ps 95:11
W is cruel and anger a . Prov 27:4
in My *w* I struck you . . . . . Is 60:10
w remember mercy . . . . . . Hab 3:2
For the *w* of God is . . . . Rom 1:18
up for yourself *w* . . . . Rom 2:5
nature children of *w* . . . . . Eph 2:3
sun go down on your *w* . Eph 4:26
Let all bitterness, *w* . . . Eph 4:31
holy hands, without *w* . . 1 Tim 2:8
So I swore in My *w* . . . . . Heb 3:11
not fearing the *w* . . . . . . Heb 11:27
for the *w* of man . . . . . James 1:20
of the wine of the *w* . . . . Rev 14:8

for in them the *w* . . . . . . Rev 15:1
fierceness of His *w* . . . . . Rev 16:19

WRATHFUL

w man stirs up strife . . Prov 15:18

WRESTLE

For we do not *w* . . . . Eph 6:12

WRETCHED

w man that I am . . . . Rom 7:24
know that you are *w* . . . . Rev 3:17

WRETCHEDNESS

let me see my *w* . . . . . Num 11:15

WRINGING

w the nose produces . . . Prov 30:33

WRINKLE

not having spot or *w* . . . . Eph 5:27

WRITE

w them on their hearts . . Heb 8:10

WRITING

the *w* was the *w* . . . . Ex 32:16

WRITINGS

do not believe his *w* . . . . John 5:47

WRITTEN

tablets of stone, *w* . . . . . . Ex 31:18
your names are *w* . . . . Luke 10:20
"What I have *w* . . . . . . John 19:22

WRONG

done nothing *w* . . . . . . Luke 23:41
But he who does *w* . . . . . . Col 3:25

WRONGED

We have *w* no one . . . . . 2 Cor 7:2

WRONGS

me *w* his own soul . . . . . Prov 8:36

WROTE

stooped down and *w* . . . . John 8:6

WROUGHT

And skillfully *w* . . . . Ps 139:15

Y

YEAR

the acceptable *y* . . . . Is 61:2
of sins every *y* . . . . Heb 10:3

YEARS

and for days and *y* . . . . . . Gen 1:14
lives are seventy *y* . . . . Ps 90:10
when He was twelve *y* . Luke 2:42
with Him a thousand *y* . . Rev 20:6

YES

let your 'Y' be 'Y,' . . . . . . Matt 5:37

YESTERDAY

For we were born *y* . . . . Job 8:9

YOKE

"Take My *y* upon you . Matt 11:29

YOKED

Do not be unequally *y* . 2 Cor 6:14

YOUNG

I have been *y* . . . . Ps 37:25
she may lay her *y* . . . . Ps 84:3
I write to you, *y* . . . . . 1 John 2:13

YOUNGER

Likewise you *y* people . . . 1 Pet 5:5

YOURS

the battle is not y . . . . 2 Chr 20:15
Y is the kingdom . . . . Matt 6:13
all Mine are Y . . . . John 17:10
for I do not seek y . . . . 2 Cor 12:14

YOUTH

the sins of my y . . . . Ps 25:7

and y are vanity . . . . Eccl 11:10
I have kept from my y . Matt 19:20

YOUTHFUL

Flee also y lusts . . . . 2 Tim 2:22

YOUTHS

y shall faint and be . . . . Is 40:30

Z

ZEAL

The z of the LORD of . . 2 Kin 19:31
"Z for Your house has . John 2:17
that they have a z . . . . . . Rom 10:2

ZEALOUS

z for good works . . . . . . Titus 2:14

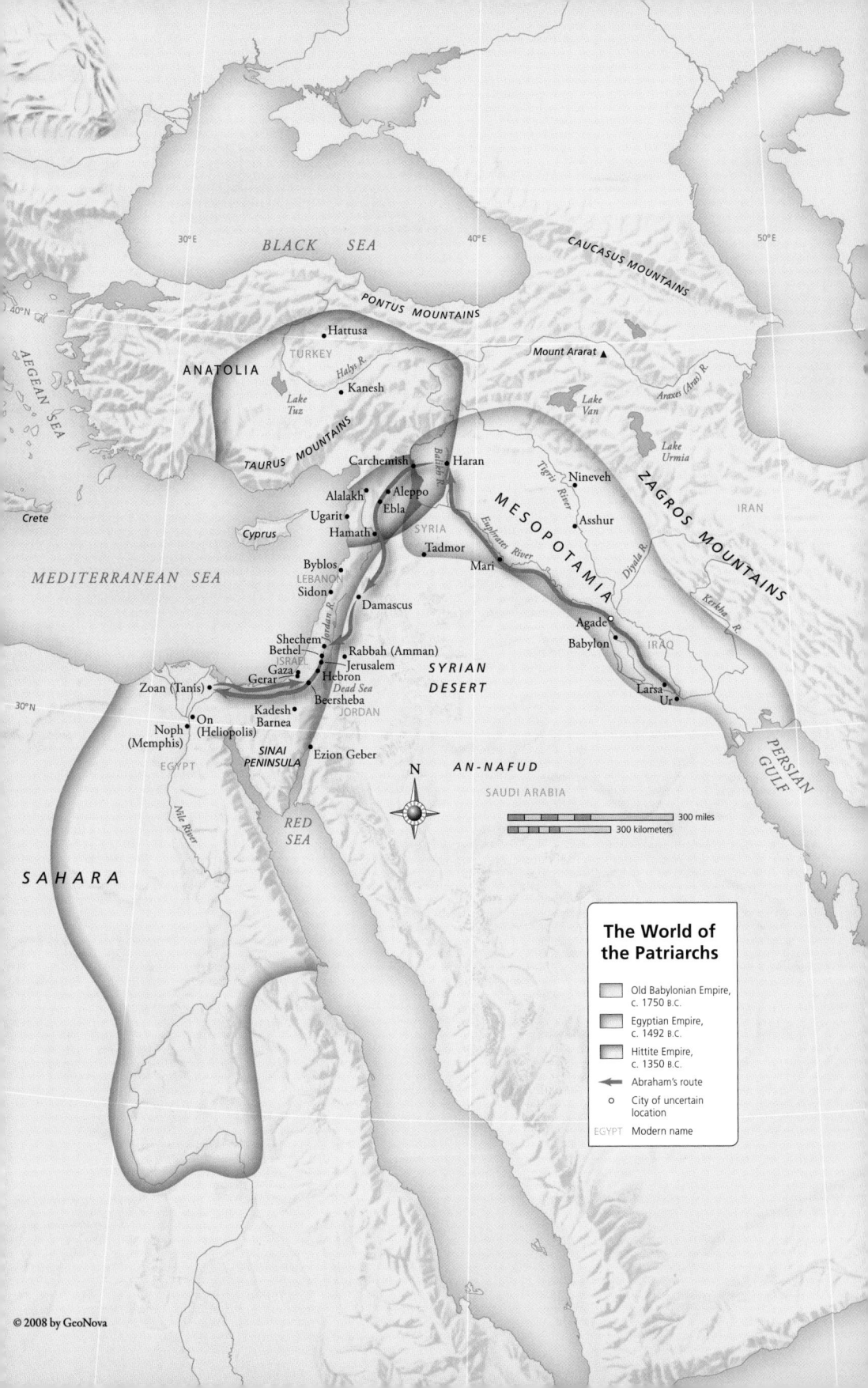

BLACK SEA

CAUCASUS MOUNTAINS

30°E

40°E

50°E

PONTUS MOUNTAINS

ANATOLIA

TURKEY

Mount Ararat ▲

40°N

Hattusa

Halys R.

Araxes (Aras) R.

Lake Van

Lake Urmia

AEGEAN SEA

Kanesh

Lake Tuz

ZAGROS MOUNTAINS

TAURUS MOUNTAINS

Carchemish

Haran

Nineveh

IRAN

Crete

Alalakh

Aleppo

Ebla

Balikh R.

MESOPOTAMIA

Tigris River

Asshur

Ugarit

SYRIA

Hamath

Cyprus

Euphrates River

Diyala R.

Kerkha R.

MEDITERRANEAN SEA

Byblos

LEBANON

Tadmor

Mari

Sidon

Damascus

Jordan R.

Agade

Shechem

Babylon

Bethel

Rabbah (Amman)

IRAQ

ISRAEL

Jerusalem

SYRIAN

Gaza

Hebron

Larsa

Zoan (Tanis)

Gerar

Dead Sea

DESERT

Ur

30°N

Beersheba

JORDAN

Kadesh

Barnea

Noph

On

(Memphis)

(Heliopolis)

SINAI

Ezion Geber

PERSIAN GULF

EGYPT

PENINSULA

AN-NAFUD

N

SAUDI ARABIA

Nile River

RED SEA

SAHARA

300 miles

300 kilometers

The World of the Patriarchs

Old Babylonian Empire, c. 1750 B.C.

Egyptian Empire, c. 1492 B.C.

Hittite Empire, c. 1350 B.C.

← Abraham's route

○ City of uncertain location

EGYPT Modern name

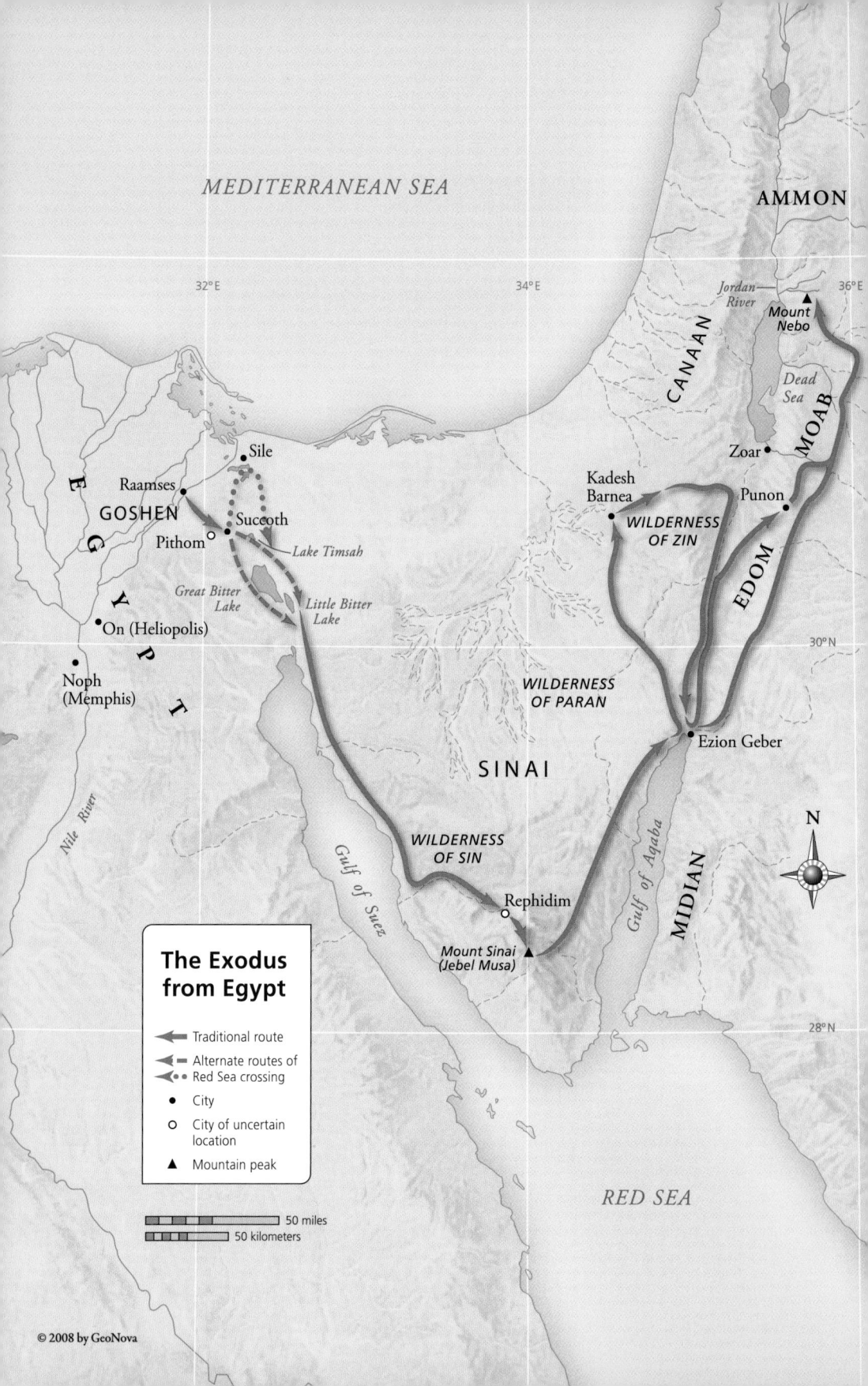

The Exodus
from Egypt

→ Traditional route
◄- Alternate routes of
◄·· Red Sea crossing
● City
○ City of uncertain location
▲ Mountain peak

50 miles
50 kilometers

MEDITERRANEAN SEA

AMMON

32°E   34°E   36°E

Jordan River

Mount Nebo ▲

CANAAN

Dead Sea

MOAB

Zoar ●

Kadesh Barnea ●   Punon ●

WILDERNESS OF ZIN

EDOM

Sile ●

Raamses ●

GOSHEN

Suceoth ●

Pithom ○

Lake Timsah

Great Bitter Lake   *Little Bitter Lake*

E G Y P T

On (Heliopolis) ●

Noph (Memphis) ●

Nile River

WILDERNESS OF PARAN

30°N

SINAI

Ezion Geber ●

Gulf of Suez

WILDERNESS OF SIN

Gulf of Aqaba

MIDIAN

Rephidim ○

Mount Sinai (Jebel Musa) ▲

N

28°N

RED SEA

© 2008 by GeoNova

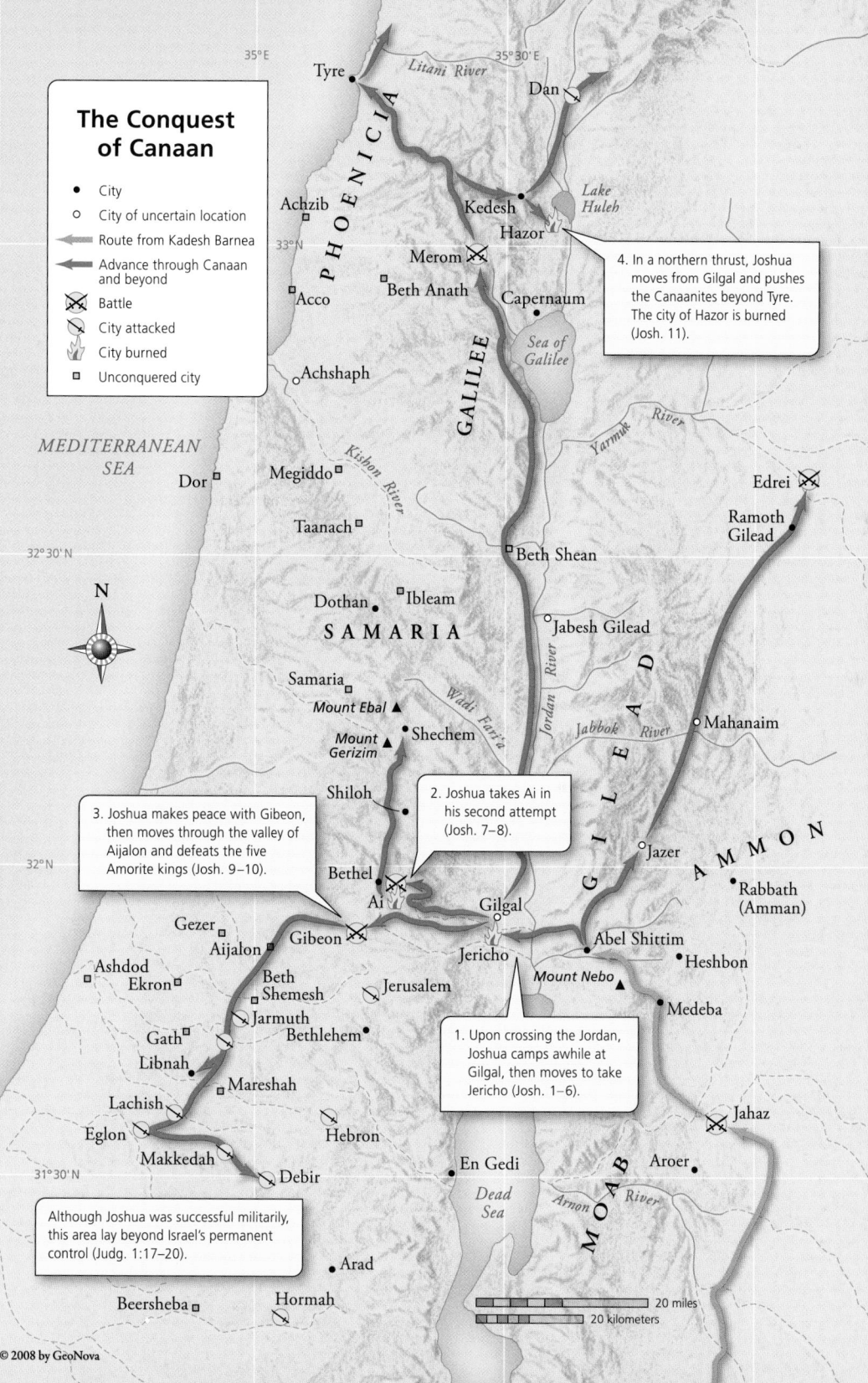

The Conquest of Canaan

- • City
- ○ City of uncertain location
- ← Route from Kadesh Barnea
- ← Advance through Canaan and beyond
- ⊠ Battle
- City attacked
- City burned
- ▫ Unconquered city

4. In a northern thrust, Joshua moves from Gilgal and pushes the Canaanites beyond Tyre. The city of Hazor is burned (Josh. 11).

2. Joshua takes Ai in his second attempt (Josh. 7–8).

3. Joshua makes peace with Gibeon, then moves through the valley of Aijalon and defeats the five Amorite kings (Josh. 9–10).

1. Upon crossing the Jordan, Joshua camps awhile at Gilgal, then moves to take Jericho (Josh. 1–6).

Although Joshua was successful militarily, this area lay beyond Israel's permanent control (Judg. 1:17–20).

20 miles

20 kilometers

© 2008 by GeoNova

MEDITERRANEAN SEA

PHOENICIA

GALILEE

SAMARIA

GILEAD

AMMON

MOAB

Litani River

Yarmuk River

Jordan River

Jabbok River

Kishon River

Wadi Far'a

Arnon River

Sea of Galilee

Lake Huleh

Dead Sea

Tyre
Dan
Achzib
Kedesh
Hazor
Merom
Beth Anath
Capernaum
Acco
Achshaph
Dor
Megiddo
Taanach
Beth Shean
Edrei
Ramoth Gilead
Dothan
Ibleam
Jabesh Gilead
Samaria
Mount Ebal ▲
Mount Gerizim ▲
Shechem
Mahanaim
Shiloh
Jazer
Bethel
Rabbath (Amman)
Ai
Gilgal
Gezer
Gibeon
Aijalon
Abel Shittim
Jericho
Heshbon
Ashdod
Ekron
Beth Shemesh
Jerusalem
Mount Nebo ▲
Medeba
Jarmuth
Gath
Bethlehem
Libnah
Mareshah
Lachish
Hebron
Eglon
Makkedah
Debir
En Gedi
Aroer
Jahaz
Arad
Beersheba
Hormah

N

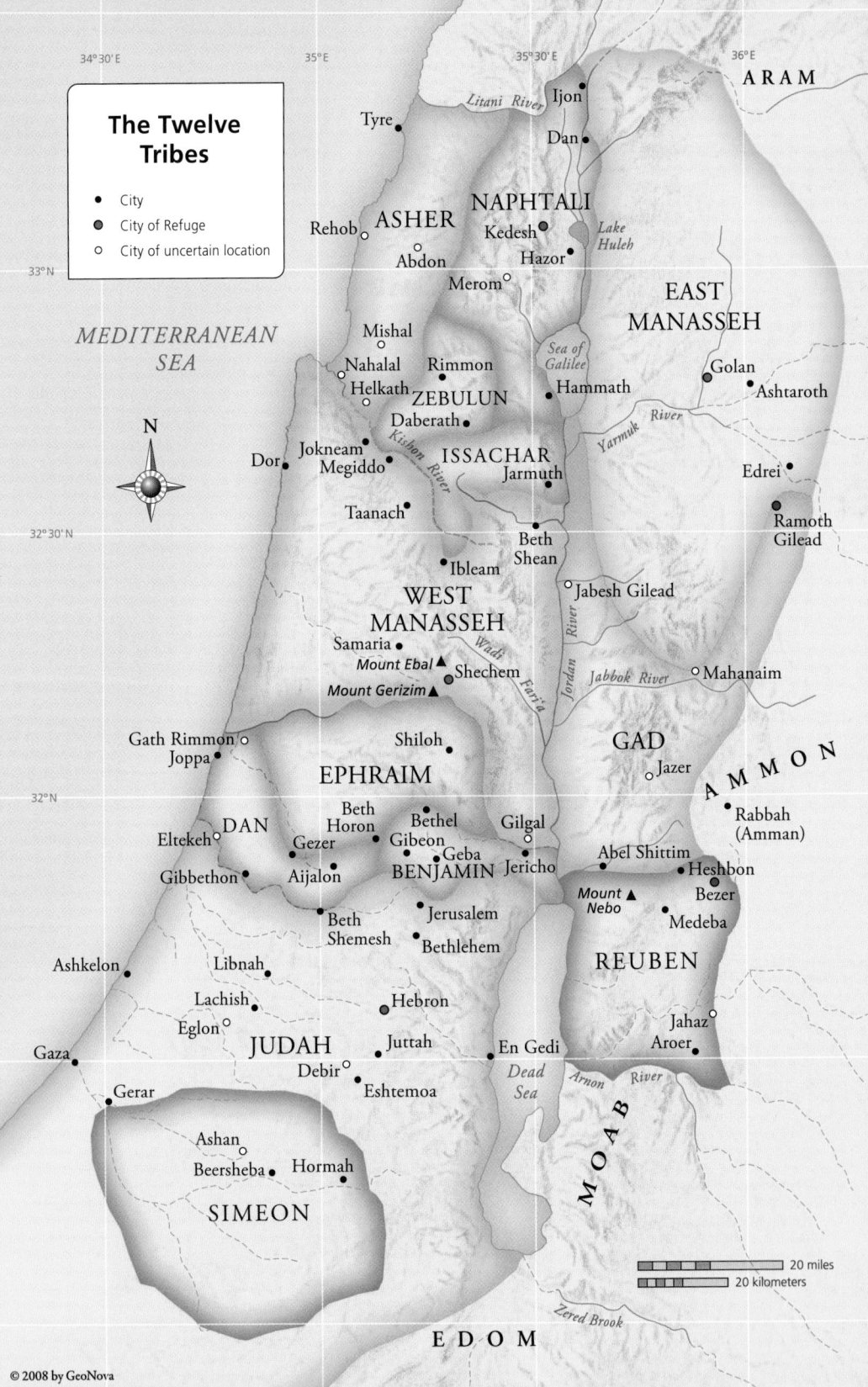

The Twelve Tribes

- • City
- • City of Refuge
- ○ City of uncertain location

34°30'E • 35°E • 35°30'E • 36°E

ARAM

Litani River

Tyre
Ijon
Dan

ASHER • NAPHTALI

Rehob • Kedesh • *Lake Huleh*

Abdon

Merom

33°N

EAST MANASSEH

MEDITERRANEAN SEA

Mishal

Nahalal • Rimmon
Helkath

ZEBULUN

Daberath

Sea of Galilee

Hammath

Golan • Ashtaroth

River

Yarmuk

Dor • Jokneam
Megiddo

ISSACHAR

Jarmuth

Edrei

32°30'N

Taanach

Beth Shean

Ramoth Gilead

N

Ibleam

WEST MANASSEH

Jabesh Gilead

Samaria

Mount Ebal ▲ Shechem

Mount Gerizim ▲

Wadi

Farah

Jabbok River • Mahanaim

Gath Rimmon

Joppa

Shiloh

EPHRAIM

GAD

Jazer

32°N

DAN

Beth Horon • Bethel
Gezer • Gibeon
Aijalon • Geba

BENJAMIN

Gilgal

Jericho

AMMON

Rabbah (Amman)

Eltekeh

Gibbethon

Abel Shittim

Heshbon
Bezer

Mount Nebo ▲

Medeba

Beth Shemesh

Jerusalem

Bethlehem

REUBEN

Ashkelon

Libnah

Lachish • Hebron

Eglon • Juttah

Jahaz
Aroer

Gaza

JUDAH

Debir • Eshtemoa

En Gedi

Dead Sea

Arnon River

MOAB

Gerar

Ashan

Beersheba • Hormah

SIMEON

20 miles
20 kilometers

EDOM

Zered Brook

© 2008 by GeoNova

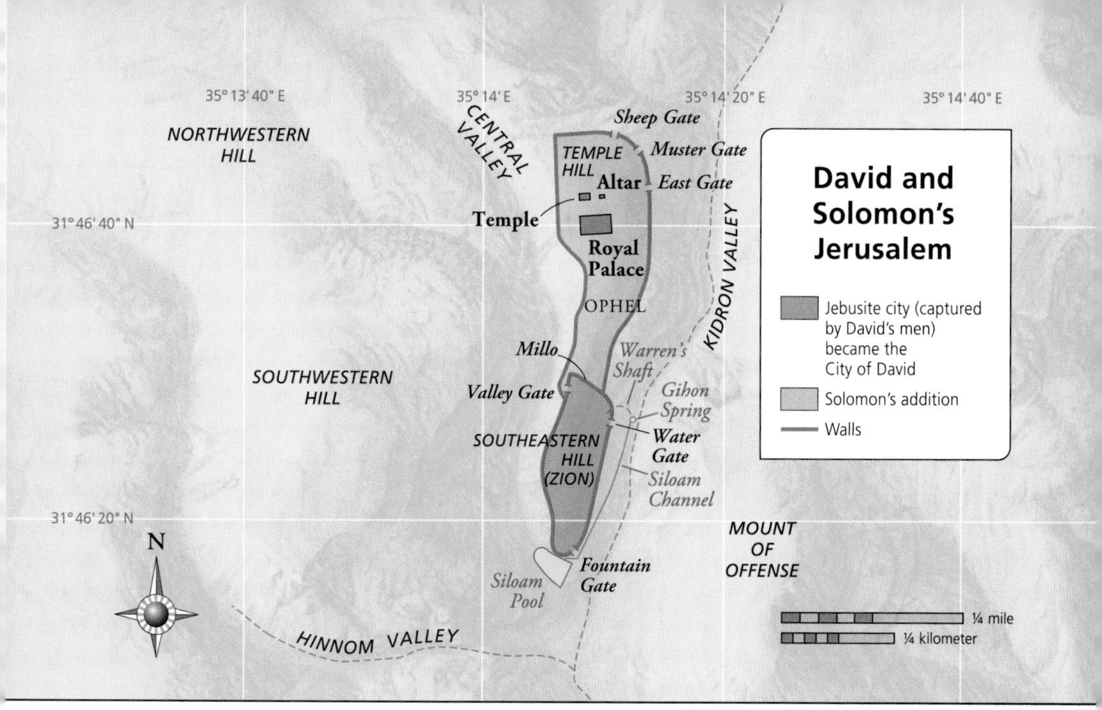

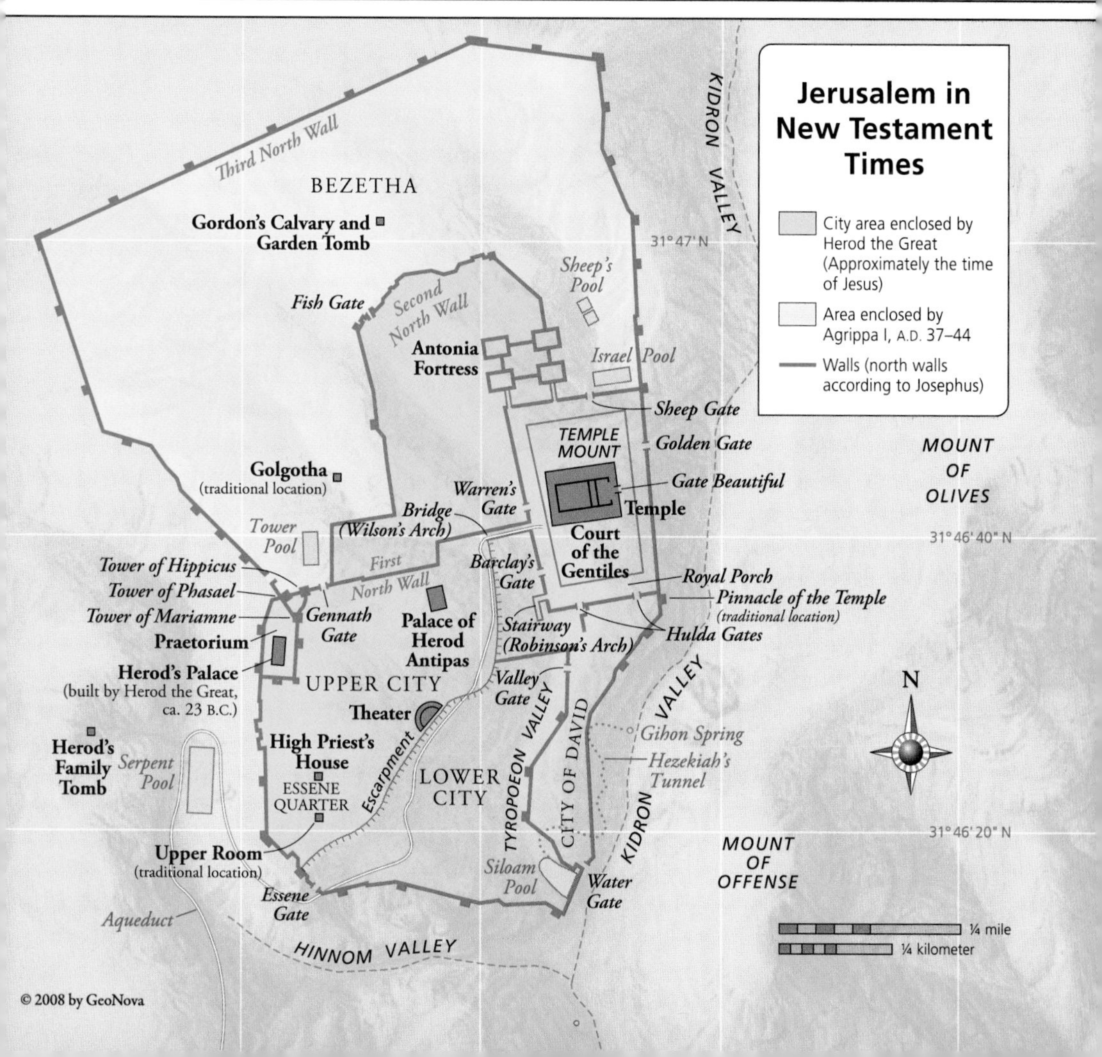

David and Solomon's Jerusalem

NORTHWESTERN HILL

35° 13' 40" E

35° 14' E

35° 14' 20" E

35° 14' 40" E

31° 46' 40" N

CENTRAL VALLEY

Sheep Gate

TEMPLE HILL

Muster Gate

Altar

East Gate

Temple

Royal Palace

OPHEL

KIDRON VALLEY

SOUTHWESTERN HILL

Millo

Warren's Shaft

Valley Gate

Gihon Spring

SOUTHEASTERN HILL (ZION)

Water Gate

Siloam Channel

31° 46' 20" N

Siloam Pool

Fountain Gate

MOUNT OF OFFENSE

N

HINNOM VALLEY

¼ mile

¼ kilometer

Legend

Jebusite city (captured by David's men) became the City of David

Solomon's addition

Walls

Jerusalem in New Testament Times

Third North Wall

BEZETHA

Gordon's Calvary and Garden Tomb

KIDRON VALLEY

31° 47' N

Fish Gate

Second North Wall

Sheep's Pool

Antonia Fortress

Israel Pool

Golgotha
(traditional location)

Sheep Gate

TEMPLE MOUNT

Golden Gate

Warren's Gate

Temple

Gate Beautiful

Tower Pool

Bridge (Wilson's Arch)

Court of the Gentiles

MOUNT OF OLIVES

31° 46' 40" N

Tower of Hippicus

First North Wall

Barclay's Gate

Tower of Phasael

Royal Porch

Tower of Mariamne

Gennath Gate

Palace of Herod Antipas

Stairway (Robinson's Arch)

Pinnacle of the Temple
(traditional location)

Hulda Gates

Praetorium

Herod's Palace
(built by Herod the Great, ca. 23 B.C.)

UPPER CITY

Valley Gate

TYROPOEON VALLEY

CITY OF DAVID

Theater

Gihon Spring

Herod's Family Tomb

Serpent Pool

High Priest's House

Hezekiah's Tunnel

ESSENE QUARTER

LOWER CITY

Escarpment

KIDRON VALLEY

N

31° 46' 20" N

Upper Room
(traditional location)

Siloam Pool

Water Gate

Essene Gate

MOUNT OF OFFENSE

Aqueduct

HINNOM VALLEY

¼ mile

¼ kilometer

Legend

City area enclosed by Herod the Great (Approximately the time of Jesus)

Area enclosed by Agrippa I, A.D. 37–44

Walls (north walls according to Josephus)

© 2008 by GeoNova

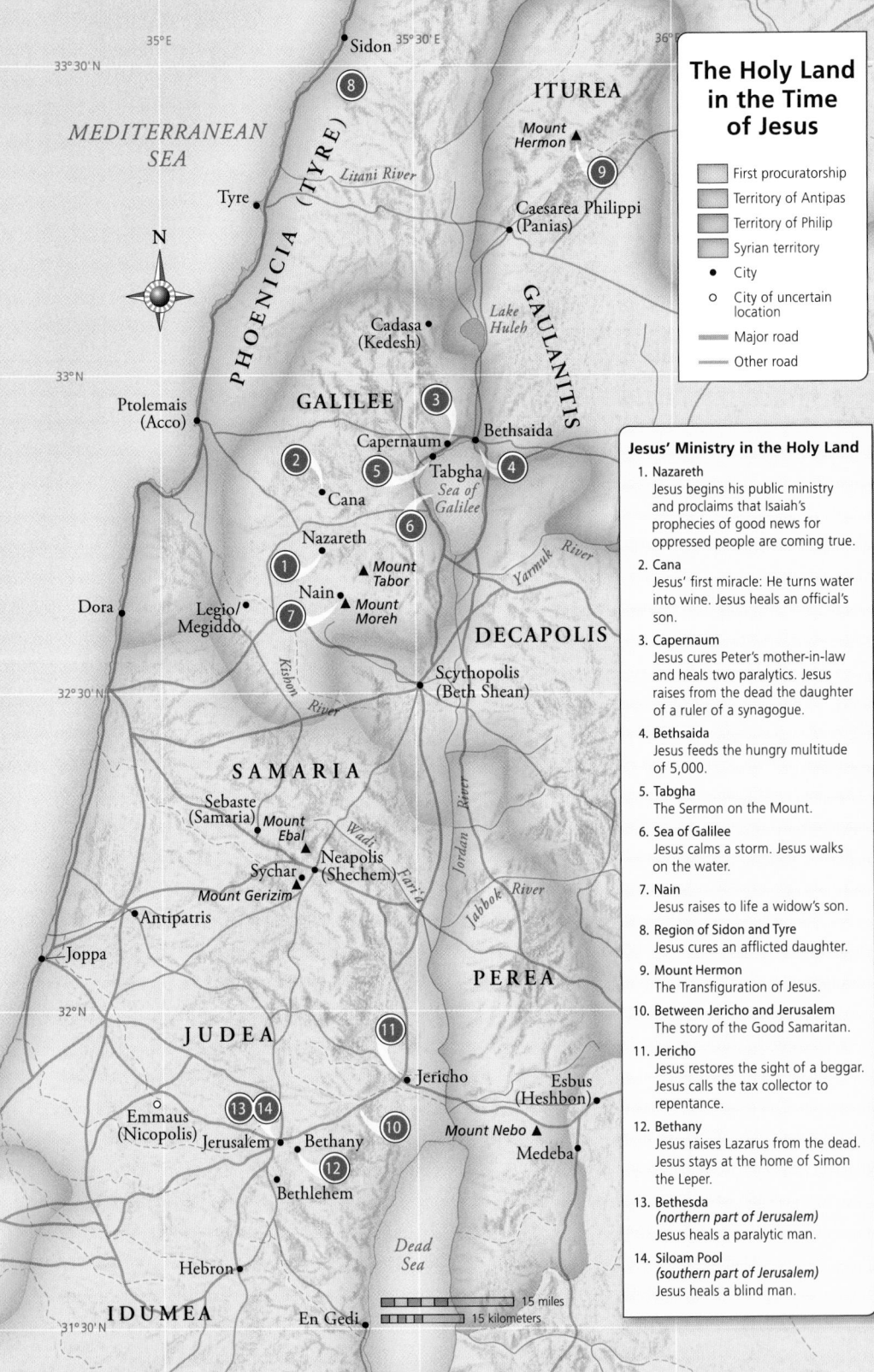

The Holy Land in the Time of Jesus

Legend:
- First procuratorship
- Territory of Antipas
- Territory of Philip
- Syrian territory
- • City
- ○ City of uncertain location
- ▬ Major road
- ▬ Other road

Jesus' Ministry in the Holy Land

1. **Nazareth**
Jesus begins his public ministry and proclaims that Isaiah's prophecies of good news for oppressed people are coming true.

2. **Cana**
Jesus' first miracle: He turns water into wine. Jesus heals an official's son.

3. **Capernaum**
Jesus cures Peter's mother-in-law and heals two paralytics. Jesus raises from the dead the daughter of a ruler of a synagogue.

4. **Bethsaida**
Jesus feeds the hungry multitude of 5,000.

5. **Tabgha**
The Sermon on the Mount.

6. **Sea of Galilee**
Jesus calms a storm. Jesus walks on the water.

7. **Nain**
Jesus raises to life a widow's son.

8. **Region of Sidon and Tyre**
Jesus cures an afflicted daughter.

9. **Mount Hermon**
The Transfiguration of Jesus.

10. **Between Jericho and Jerusalem**
The story of the Good Samaritan.

11. **Jericho**
Jesus restores the sight of a beggar. Jesus calls the tax collector to repentance.

12. **Bethany**
Jesus raises Lazarus from the dead. Jesus stays at the home of Simon the Leper.

13. **Bethesda**
(northern part of Jerusalem)
Jesus heals a paralytic man.

14. **Siloam Pool**
(southern part of Jerusalem)
Jesus heals a blind man.

Map labels: MEDITERRANEAN SEA, Sidon, ITUREA, Mount Hermon, Caesarea Philippi (Panias), GAULANITIS, Tyre, PHOENICIA (TYRE), Litani River, Lake Huleh, Cadasa (Kedesh), GALILEE, Ptolemais (Acco), Capernaum, Bethsaida, Cana, Tabgha, Sea of Galilee, Nazareth, Yarmuk River, DECAPOLIS, Dora, Mount Tabor, Nain, Mount Moreh, Legio/Megiddo, Kishon River, Scythopolis (Beth Shean), SAMARIA, Sebaste (Samaria), Mount Ebal, Wadi Fari'a, Jordan River, Jabbok River, Sychar, Neapolis (Shechem), Mount Gerizim, Antipatris, PEREA, Joppa, JUDEA, Jericho, Esbus (Heshbon), Emmaus (Nicopolis), Jerusalem, Bethany, Mount Nebo, Medeba, Bethlehem, Hebron, Dead Sea, IDUMEA, En Gedi

15 miles / 15 kilometers

© 2008 by GeoNova

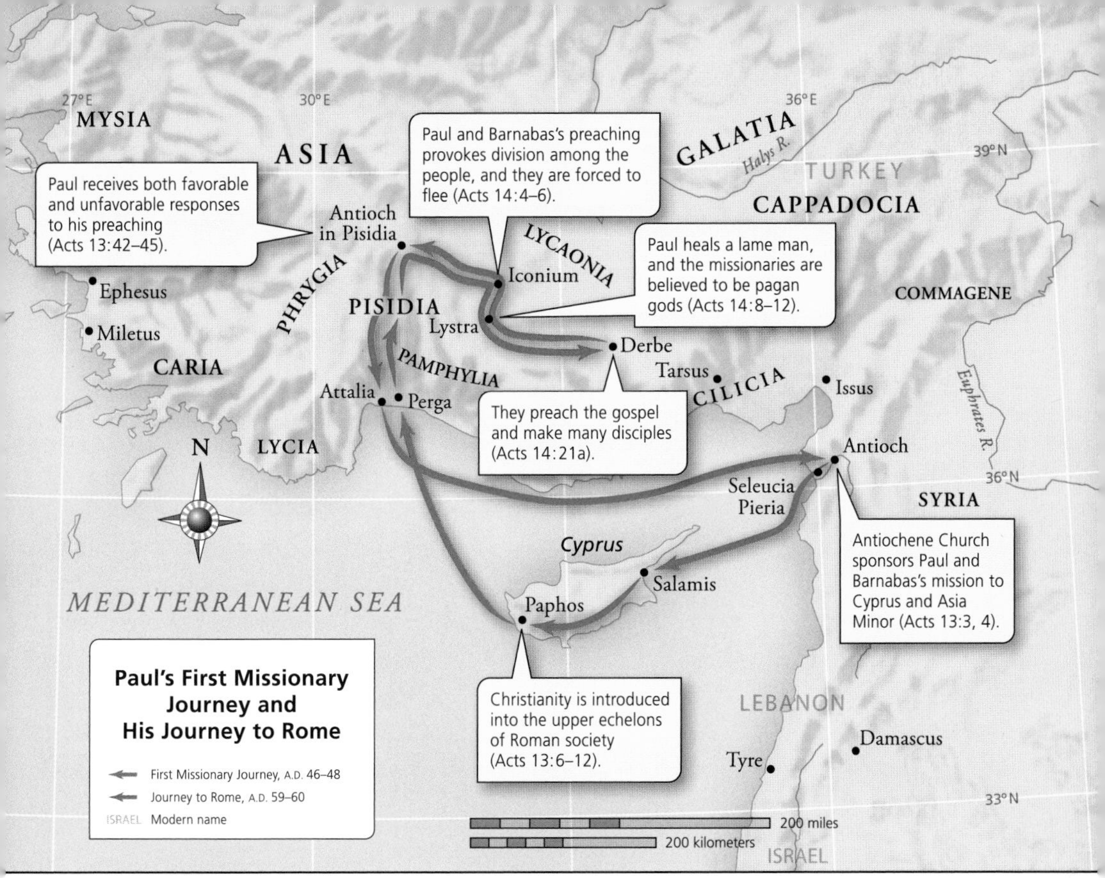

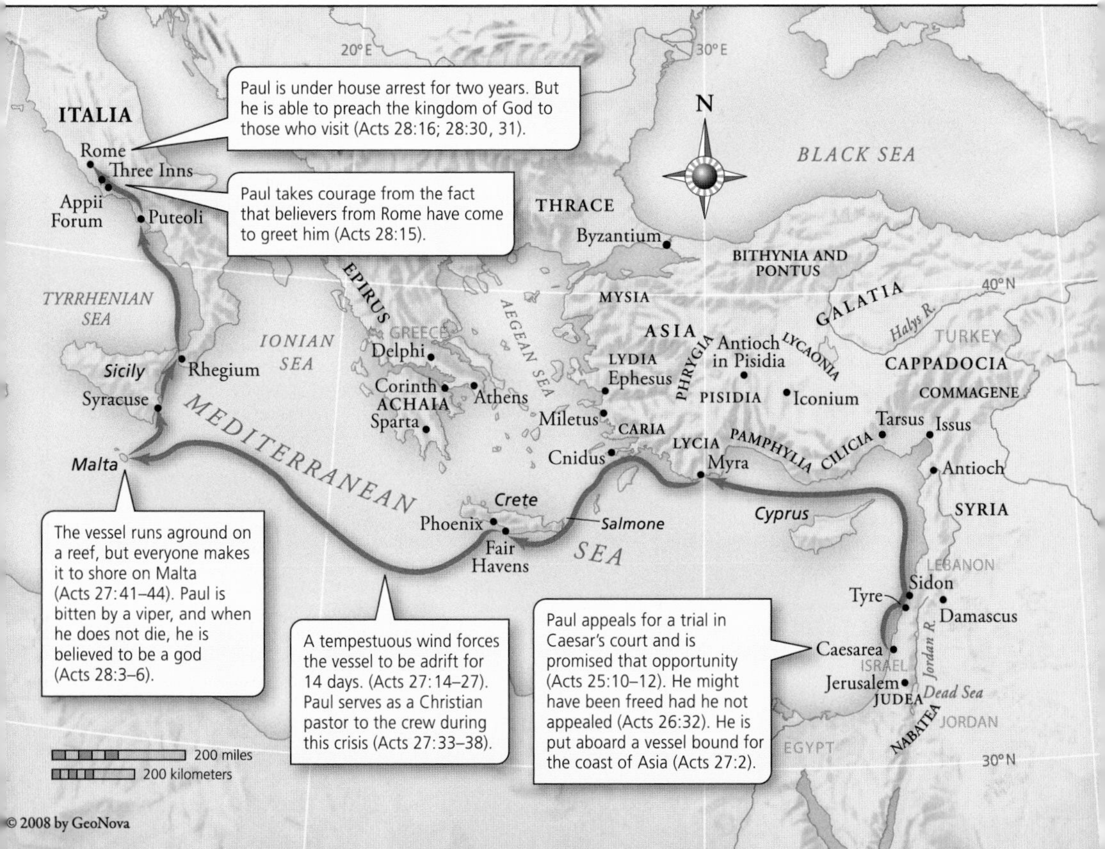

Paul's First Missionary Journey and His Journey to Rome

Paul receives both favorable and unfavorable responses to his preaching (Acts 13:42–45).

Paul and Barnabas's preaching provokes division among the people, and they are forced to flee (Acts 14:4–6).

Paul heals a lame man, and the missionaries are believed to be pagan gods (Acts 14:8–12).

They preach the gospel and make many disciples (Acts 14:21a).

Antiochene Church sponsors Paul and Barnabas's mission to Cyprus and Asia Minor (Acts 13:3, 4).

Christianity is introduced into the upper echelons of Roman society (Acts 13:6–12).

Paul's First Missionary Journey and His Journey to Rome

→ First Missionary Journey, A.D. 46–48
→ Journey to Rome, A.D. 59–60
ISRAEL Modern name

200 miles
200 kilometers

MYSIA · ASIA · GALATIA · TURKEY · CAPPADOCIA · COMMAGENE · Halys R. · Antioch in Pisidia · PHRYGIA · Ephesus · Miletus · CARIA · PISIDIA · LYCAONIA · Iconium · Lystra · Derbe · Tarsus · Issus · CILICIA · Euphrates R. · Antioch · PAMPHYLIA · Attalia · Perga · LYCIA · SYRIA · Seleucia Pieria · N · Cyprus · Salamis · Paphos · MEDITERRANEAN SEA · LEBANON · Damascus · Tyre · ISRAEL · 27°E · 30°E · 36°E · 39°N · 36°N · 33°N

Paul is under house arrest for two years. But he is able to preach the kingdom of God to those who visit (Acts 28:16; 28:30, 31).

Paul takes courage from the fact that believers from Rome have come to greet him (Acts 28:15).

The vessel runs aground on a reef, but everyone makes it to shore on Malta (Acts 27:41–44). Paul is bitten by a viper, and when he does not die, he is believed to be a god (Acts 28:3–6).

A tempestuous wind forces the vessel to be adrift for 14 days. (Acts 27:14–27). Paul serves as a Christian pastor to the crew during this crisis (Acts 27:33–38).

Paul appeals for a trial in Caesar's court and is promised that opportunity (Acts 25:10–12). He might have been freed had he not appealed (Acts 26:32). He is put aboard a vessel bound for the coast of Asia (Acts 27:2).

ITALIA · Rome · Three Inns · Appii Forum · Puteoli · TYRRHENIAN SEA · EPIRUS · GREECE · Delphi · IONIAN SEA · Sicily · Rhegium · Corinth · ACHAIA · Athens · Sparta · Syracuse · MEDITERRANEAN SEA · Malta · Phoenix · Crete · Fair Havens · Salmone · THRACE · Byzantium · BITHYNIA AND PONTUS · MYSIA · ASIA · LYDIA · Antioch in Pisidia · PHRYGIA · Ephesus · PISIDIA · LYCAONIA · Iconium · GALATIA · Halys R. · TURKEY · CAPPADOCIA · COMMAGENE · Tarsus · Issus · Miletus · CARIA · LYCIA · PAMPHYLIA · CILICIA · Cnidus · Myra · Antioch · SYRIA · Cyprus · LEBANON · Tyre · Sidon · Damascus · Caesarea · Jordan R. · Jerusalem · ISRAEL · JUDEA · Dead Sea · NABATEA · JORDAN · EGYPT · AEGEAN SEA · BLACK SEA · N · 20°E · 30°E · 40°N · 30°N

200 miles
200 kilometers

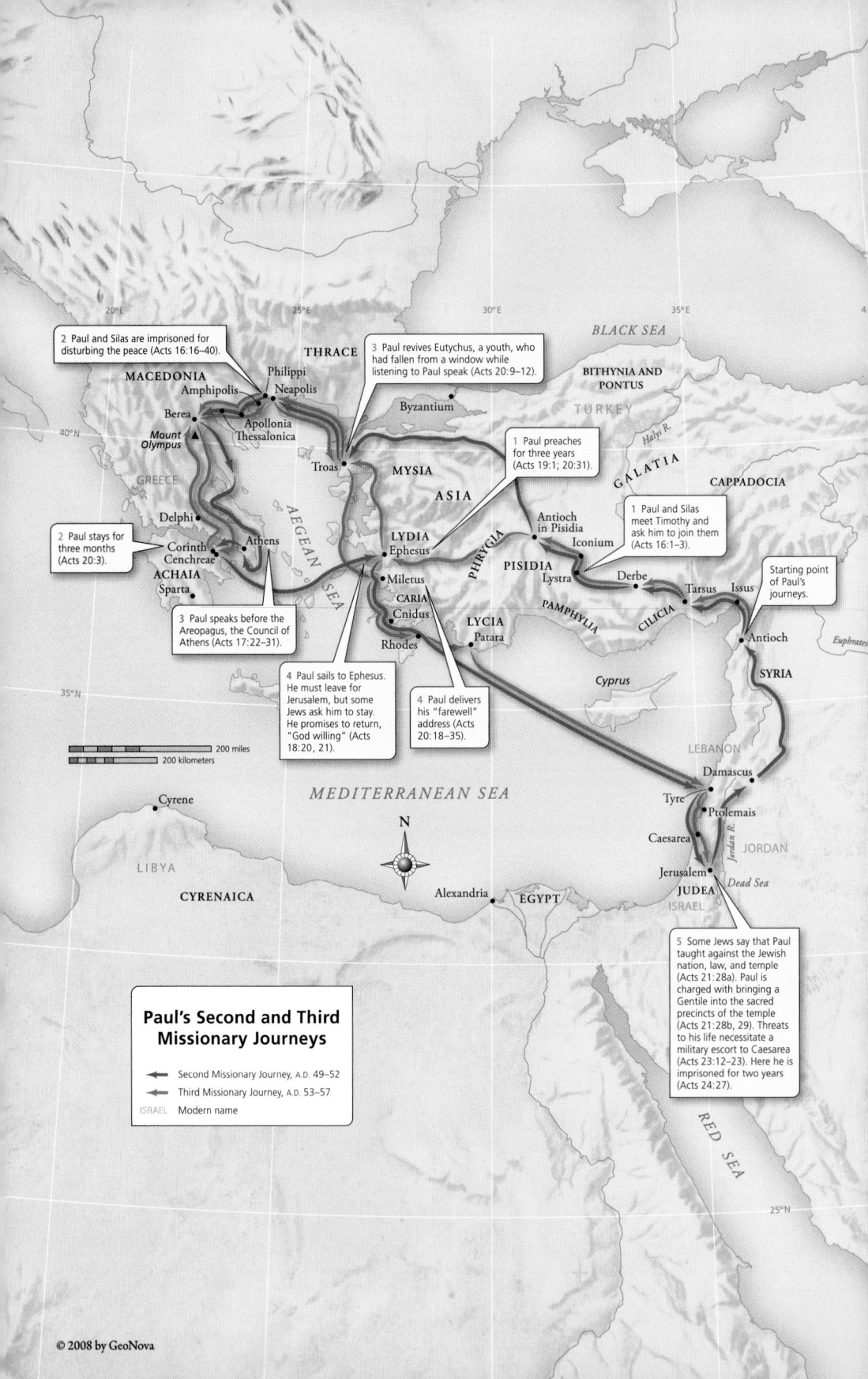

BLACK SEA

THRACE

2 Paul and Silas are imprisoned for disturbing the peace (Acts 16:16–40).

3 Paul revives Eutychus, a youth, who had fallen from a window while listening to Paul speak (Acts 20:9–12).

BITHYNIA AND PONTUS

MACEDONIA

Philippi
Neapolis

Amphipolis

TURKEY

Berea

Byzantium

Apollonia
Thessalonica

Mount
Olympus

Troas

MYSIA

Halys R.

1 Paul preaches for three years (Acts 19:1; 20:31).

GALATIA

CAPPADOCIA

GREECE

ASIA

Delphi

AEGEAN SEA

LYDIA
Ephesus

PHRYGIA

Antioch
in Pisidia
Iconium

1 Paul and Silas meet Timothy and ask him to join them (Acts 16:1–3).

2 Paul stays for three months (Acts 20:3).

Corinth
Cenchreae

Athens

PISIDIA

Lystra

Derbe

Starting point of Paul's journeys.

ACHAIA

Sparta

Miletus

CARIA
Cnidus

Tarsus

Issus

CILICIA

3 Paul speaks before the Areopagus, the Council of Athens (Acts 17:22–31).

Rhodes

LYCIA
Patara

PAMPHYLIA

Antioch

Euphrates

SYRIA

4 Paul sails to Ephesus. He must leave for Jerusalem, but some Jews ask him to stay. He promises to return, "God willing" (Acts 18:20, 21).

4 Paul delivers his "farewell" address (Acts 20:18–35).

Cyprus

MEDITERRANEAN SEA

LEBANON

Damascus

Tyre

Ptolemais

N

Cyrene

Caesarea

Jordan R.

JORDAN

LIBYA

Alexandria

EGYPT

Jerusalem

Dead Sea

CYRENAICA

JUDEA

ISRAEL

5 Some Jews say that Paul taught against the Jewish nation, law, and temple (Acts 21:28a). Paul is charged with bringing a Gentile into the sacred precincts of the temple (Acts 21:28b, 29). Threats to his life necessitate a military escort to Caesarea (Acts 23:12–23). Here he is imprisoned for two years (Acts 24:27).

RED SEA

Paul's Second and Third Missionary Journeys

◄─── Second Missionary Journey, A.D. 49–52

◄─── Third Missionary Journey, A.D. 53–57

ISRAEL   Modern name

200 miles

200 kilometers

© 2008 by GeoNova